The Concise Oxford–Duden German Dictionary

The Concise Oxford–Duden German Dictionary

Second Edition

German–English / English–German

Edited by
the Dudenredaktion
and the German Section of
the Oxford University Press
Dictionary Department

Chief Editors
M. Clark
O. Thyen

Oxford   New York

OXFORD UNIVERSITY PRESS

OXFORD
UNIVERSITY PRESS

Great Clarendon Street, Oxford OX2 6DP

Oxford University Press is a department of the University of Oxford.
It furthers the University's objective of excellence in research, scholarship,
and education by publishing worldwide in

Oxford New York

Auckland Bangkok Buenos Aires Cape Town Chennai
Dar es Salaam Delhi Hong Kong Istanbul Karachi Kolkata
Kuala Lumpur Madrid Melbourne Mexico City Mumbai Nairobi
São Paulo Shanghai Singapore Taipei Tokyo Toronto

and an associated company in Berlin

Published in the United States
by Oxford University Press Inc., New York

© Oxford University Press and Bibliographisches Institut
& F. A. Brockhaus AG 1991, 1997, 1998

First edition published 1991
This second edition published 1998

British Library Cataloguing in Publication Data

Data available

Library of Congress Cataloging in Publication Data

Data available

ISBN 0-19-864230-X

10 9 8 7 6 5 4

Typeset by Latimer Trend & Co. Ltd.
Printed in Great Britain by Clays Ltd.
Bungay, Suffolk

Preface

For this new edition the Concise Oxford-Duden German Dictionary has been enlarged and extensively updated to take account of new vocabulary and recent developments in English and German. Thousands of additional words and phrases, selected using the unparalleled databases maintained and continually expanded by Oxford University Press and the Dudenverlag, reflect scientific and technological innovations as well as changes in politics, culture, and society. Reforms to the spelling of German ratified by the governments of Germany, Austria, and Switzerland in 1996 have been fully incorporated and are clearly signposted.

This new edition includes as a special feature detailed usage boxes to help with important areas of grammar and vocabulary. They highlight differences between German and English which may create difficulty for the learner and translator, explaining them in detail, and provide clear illustrative examples. Other boxes give the user key facts about types of word that behave alike, for example, names of countries, languages, numbers, and days of the week. They provide ways of discussing topics such as age, dates, time, and measurements and offer essential practical information on asking the way, formulating greetings, apologizing, and letter-writing. Cross-references to the boxes are given at all the relevant entries, making them easily accessible points of reference for students and valuable aids to teaching.

Also new to this edition are a guide to exploring the Internet and a thematic word-finder providing quick and easy access to key expressions and constructions in a broad range of subject areas, including the environment, society, business and industry, communications, media, and the arts.

The editors believe that these new features and expanded, up-to-date coverage will enhance the reputation of the Concise Oxford-Duden German Dictionary as an easy-to-use and authoritative reference tool for school, college, and university students, business people, and all those who require the fullest possible information on German and English in a concise format.

Michael Clark
Oxford University Press

Editors and Contributors

Oxford University Press
Michael Clark
Bernadette Mohan
John Pheby
Robin Sawers
Gunhild Prowe

Data input
Susan Wilkin
Melissa Abbots
Philip Gerrish

Dudenverlag
Olaf Thyen
Werner Scholze-Stubenrecht
Magdalena Seubel
Brigitte Alsleben

Inhalt / Contents

Als Markenzeichen geschützte Wörter / Note on Proprietary Status

Erläuterungen zum deutsch-englischen Text / Key to German-English Entries

1. Stichwort und Aussprache / Headword and pronunciation

Stichwort. Alle Einträge sind streng alphabetisch angeordnet
Headword. All entries are listed in strict alphabetical order

> **bindend** *Adj.* binding (**für** on); definite ⟨*answer*⟩
> **Binder** *der;* ~s, ~ (**a**) (Krawatte) tie; (**b**) (Bindemittel) binder
> **Binde-:** ~**strich** *der* hyphen; ~**wort** *das* (Sprachw.) conjunction
> **Bind·faden** *der* string; **ein [Stück]** ~: a piece of string; **es regnet Bindfäden** (ugs.) it's raining cats and dogs (coll.)

Kompositablock. Eine Tilde ersetzt jeweils den gemeinsamen ersten Bestandteil der Komposita
Compound block with a swung dash representing the first element of each compound

Die Ausspracheangaben (in IPA-Lautschrift) stehen unmittelbar hinter dem Stichwort (s.S.xiv). Die Aussprache eines Kompositums ohne Ausspracheangabe lässt sich von derjenigen seiner Bestandteile herleiten
Pronunciation is shown in IPA immediately after the headword (see p. xiv). The pronunciation of a compound where none is given can be derived from the pronunciations of its elements

> **Bischof** /'bɪʃɔf/ *der;* ~s, **Bischöfe** /'bɪʃœfə/ bishop

> **Bremse¹** /'brɛmzə/ *die;* ~, ~**n** brake; **auf die** ~ **treten** put on the brakes
> **Bremse²** *die;* ~, ~**n** (Insekt) horsefly

Mehrere gleichgeschriebene, aber nicht bedeutungsgleiche Wörter erscheinen als separate Stichwörter und sind mit hochgestellten Ziffern nummeriert
Headwords spelt the same but with different meanings are entered separately with a raised number

Ein senkrechter Strich nach dem ersten Bestandteil eines zusammengesetzten Verbs zeigt an, dass es sich um eine unfeste Zusammensetzung handelt
A vertical bar indicates that a compound verb is separable

> **dar|bieten** (geh.) **1** *unr. tr. V.* perform. **2** *unr. refl. V.* **sich jmds. Blicken** ~: expose oneself to sb.'s gaze

> **dar|legen** *tr. V.* explain (*Dat.* to); set forth ⟨*reasons, facts*⟩; expound ⟨*theory*⟩

Ein unter einen Vokal gesetzter waagerechter Strich zeigt die Länge des Vokals und in mehrsilbigen Wörtern zugleich die Betonung der betreffenden Silbe an
An underline indicates a long vowel, stressed in words of more than one syllable

Ein hochgestellter Stern vor einem Stichwort zeigt an, dass es sich um eine alte, künftig nicht mehr gültige Schreibung handelt
An asterisk indicates an old spelling

> **dass, *daß** /das/ *Konj.* (**a**) that; **entschuldigen Sie bitte,** ~ **ich mich verspätet habe** please forgive me for...

Ein in mittlerer Höhe auf der Zeile stehender Punkt im Stichwort markiert die Kompositionsfuge eines Kompositums A dot marks the juncture of the elements of a compound	**Dattel·palme** *die* date palm
Ein unter einen Vokal gesetzter Punkt zeigt die Kürze des Vokals und in mehrsilbigen Wörtern zugleich die Betonung der betreffenden Silbe an An underdot indicates a short vowel, stressed in words of more than one syllable	**ẹggen** *tr. V.* (Landw.) harrow

2. Grammatische Angaben / Grammatical information

Grammatische Gliederungspunkte und Wortartangaben Grammatical categories and parts of speech	**ehrenhaft 1** *Adj.* honourable ⟨*intentions, person*⟩. **2** *adv.* ⟨*act*⟩ honourably	
Die Formen des Genitivs und des Plurals eines Substantivs Genitive and plural forms of a noun	**Entwịckler** *der;* ∼**s**, ∼ (Fot.) developer	
	gefrieren 1 *unr. itr. V.; mit sein* freeze. **2** *unr. tr. V.* [deep-] freeze ⟨*food*⟩	Der Hinweis *mit sein* zeigt an, dass das betreffende Verb die Perfekttempora mit dem Hilfsverb *sein* bildet *mit sein* indicates that a verb is conjugated with the auxiliary verb *sein* in its perfect tenses
Unregelmäßige Steigerungsformen eines Adjektivs Irregular comparative and superlative forms of an adjective	**fromm** /frɔm/; ∼**er** *od.* **frömmer** /ˈfrœmɐ/, ∼**st**… *od.* **frömmst**… **1** *Adj.* **(a)** pious, devout ⟨*person*⟩; devout…	

3. Semantische Gliederungspunkte und Angaben zu Stil, Sachbereich, räumlicher Zuordnung / Sense categories and labels

Semantische Gliederungspunkte Sense categories	**Geheim·nummer** *die* **(a)** (Bankw.) personal identification number; PIN; **(b)** (Telefonnummer) ex-directory number; unlisted number (Amer.)	
	gehören 1 *itr. V.* **(a)** (Eigentum sein) jmdm. ∼: belong to sb.; **das Haus gehört uns nicht** the house doesn't belong to us; we don't own the house; **wem gehört das Buch?** whose book is it?; who does the book belong to?; **(b)** (Teil eines Ganzen sein) **zu jmds. Freunden** ∼: be one of sb.'s…	Bedeutungsindikatoren Sense indicators

Stilistische Kennzeichnungen Style labels	**Geier** /ˈgaiɐ/ *der;* ~s, ~: vulture; **hols der** ~ (ugs.) to hell with it (coll.); **weiß der** ~ (salopp) God only knows (sl.); Christ knows (sl.)

	Genom /geˈnoːm/ *das;* ~s, ~e (Biol.) genome **Gurtstraffer** *der;* ~s, ~ (Kfz.-W.) [seat]belt tensioner	**Bereichsangaben** Subject labels

Angaben zur räumlichen Zuordnung Regional labels	**Holler** /ˈhɔlɐ/ *der;* ~s, ~ (bes. südd., österr.) ⇒ **Holunder** **Karre** /ˈkarə/ *die;* ~, ~n (bes. nordd.) (a) ⇒ **Karren;** (b) (abwertend: Fahrzeug) [old] heap (coll.)

4. Übersetzungen / Translations

Übersetzungen Translations	**Kleb·pflaster** *das* adhesive plaster; sticking plaster

	klein /klain/ **1** *Adj.* (a) ▶ 277 little; small ⟨*format, letter*⟩; little ⟨*finger, toe*⟩; small, short ⟨*steps*⟩; **das Kleid…**	**Durch Adjektive attribuierte Substantive** Nouns modified by an adjective
Kollokatoren (Wörter, mit denen zusammen das Stichwort häufig vorkommt) als Hilfe zur Auswahl der für den jeweiligen Kontext passenden Übersetzung Collocators—words often used with the headword, shown to help select the correct translation for each context	**klirren** /ˈklɪrən/ *itr. V.* ⟨*glasses, ice cubes*⟩ clink; ⟨*weapons in fight*⟩ clash; ⟨*window pane*⟩ rattle; ⟨*chains, spurs*⟩ clank, rattle; ⟨*harness*⟩ jingle; ~**der Frost** (fig.) sharp frost	**Als Subjekte zu Verben auftretende Wörter** Subjects of a verb
	kollegial /kɔleˈgiaːl/ **1** *Adj.* helpful and considerate. **2** *adv.* ⟨*act etc.*⟩ like a good colleague/good colleagues **komplett** /kɔmˈplɛt/ **1** *Adj.*… **2** *adv.* (a) fully ⟨*furnished, equipped*⟩; (b) (ugs.: ganz und gar) completely; totally	**Durch Adverbien attribuierte Verben oder Adjektive** Verbs or adjectives modified by an adverb
	konzipieren /kɔntsiˈpiːrən/ *tr. V.* draft ⟨*speech, essay*⟩; draw up, draft ⟨*plan, policy, etc.*⟩; design ⟨*device, car, etc.*⟩	**Als Objekte zu Verben auftretende Wörter** Objects of a verb

Das Zeichen ≈ signalisiert eine nur annähernde Entsprechung The sign ≈ is used to indicate approximate equivalence	**Malteser-** /malˈteːzɐ-/: ~**hilfsdienst** *der* ≈ St John Ambulance Brigade; ~**kreuz** *das* (auch Technik) Maltese…

5. Anwendungsbeispiele / Phrases

Beispiele (jeweils mit einer Tilde an Stelle des Stichworts) Examples (with a swung dash representing the headword)	**ragen** /ˈraːgn/ *itr. V.* (a) (vertikal) rise [up]; ⟨*mountains*⟩ tower up; **aus dem Wasser** ~: stick *or* jut right out of the water; **in den Himmel** ~: tower *or* soar into the sky; (b) (horizontal) project, stick out (**in** + *Akk.* into; **über** + *Akk.* over)

Teile von Anwendungsbeispielen, zwischen denen ein kursiv gesetztes *od.* steht, sind synonym und gegeneinander austauschbar
Parts of a phrase separated by *od.* are synonymous and interchangeable

Regierung *die;* ∼, ∼en (**a**) *o. Pl.* (Herrschaft) rule; (eines Monarchen) reign; **die** ∼ **übernehmen** *od.* **antreten** take over; come to power; (**b**) (Kabinett) government

Ruf /ruːf/ *der;* ∼[e]s, ∼e (**a**) call; (Schrei) shout; cry; (Tierlaut) call; (**b**) *o. Pl.* (fig.: Aufforderung, Forderung) call (**nach** for); (**c**) (Leumund) reputation; **ein Mann von gutem/schlechtem** ∼: a man with a good/bad reputation; **jmdn./etw. in schlechten** ∼ **bringen** give sb./sth. a bad name; **er/ es ist besser als sein** ∼: he/it is not as bad as he/it is made out to be

Teile von Anwendungbeispielen, zwischen denen ein Schrägstrich steht, sind syntaktisch gegeneinander austauschbar, aber nicht bedeutungsgleich
Parts of a phrase separated by a slash are syntactically interchangeable but have different meanings

6. Verweise / Cross-references

Ein Pfeil verweist auf ein bedeutungsgleiches anderes Stichwort
An arrow directs the user to another headword with the same meaning

Strampler *der;* ∼s, ∼: ⇒ **Strampelhöschen**

Mit *s. auch* wird auf ein Stichwort verwiesen, unter dem noch zusätzliche Informationen zu finden sind
s. auch directs the user to another headword where additional information can be found

töten /ˈtøːtn̩/ *tr., itr. V.* kill; *s. auch* **Nerv a**

tschechisch ▶ 388⌋, ▶ 487⌋ **1** *Adj.* Czech. **2** *adv.* ∼ **sprechend** Czech-speaking; *s. auch* **deutsch; Deutsch; Deutsche²**

Das Zeichen ▶ mit einer Zahl verweist auf eine Buchseite, auf der sich in einem Informationskasten zusätzliche Informationen finden
An arrow ▶ and a page-number cross-reference direct the user to a usage box containing additional information

Key to English-German Entries / Erläuterungen zum englisch-deutschen Text

1. Headword and pronunciation / Stichwort und Aussprache

Headword. All entries are listed in strict alphabetical order, except for *phrasal verbs*
Stichwort. Alle Einträge – mit Ausnahme *der Phrasal Verbs* – sind streng alphabetisch angeordnet

batch /bætʃ/ *n.* (**a**) (of loaves) Schub, *der;* (**b**) (of people) Gruppe, *die;* (of books, papers, etc.) Stapel, *der;* (of rules, regulations) Bündel, *das*
batch: ∼ **file** *n.* (Computing) Stapeldatei, *die;* ∼ '**processing** *n.* (Computing) Stapelverarbeitung, *die;* ∼ **production** *n.* Stapelfertigung, *die*
bate¹ /beɪt/ *v.t.* **with** ∼**d breath** mit angehaltenem Atem
bate² *n.* (Brit. coll.) Rage, *die* (ugs.); **be in a [terrible]** ∼: [schrecklich] in Rage sein; **get/fly into a** ∼: in Rage geraten
bath /bɑːθ/ **1** *n., pl.* ∼**s** /bɑːðz/ (**a**) Bad, *das;* **have** *or* **take a** ∼: ein Bad nehmen; (**b**) (vessel) ∼[**tub**] Badewanne, *die;* **room with** ∼: Zimmer mit Bad; (**c**) *usu. in pl.*

Compound block with a swung dash representing the first element of each compound
Kompositablock. Eine Tilde ersetzt jeweils den gemeinsamen ersten Bestandteil der Komposita

Each phrasal verb is entered on a new line immediately following the entry for the first element Die *Phrasal Verbs* folgen, jedes auf einer neuen Zeile, direkt auf den Eintrag zu ihrem Grundverb	**bear** [2] 1 *v.t.*, **bore** /bɔː(r)/, **borne...** ~ **a'way** *v.t.* wegtragen; davontragen ⟨*Preis usw.*⟩; **be borne away** fort- *od.* davongetragen werden ~ **'down** *v.i.* ~ **down on sb./sth.** auf jmdn./etw. zusteuern; ⟨*Wagen*⟩ auf jmdn./etw. zufahren *od.* -steuern ~ **'off** ⇨ ~ **away** ~ **on** ⇨ ~ **upon** ~ **'out** *v.t.* (fig.) bestätigen ⟨*Bericht, Erklärung*⟩; ~ **sb. out** jmdm. Recht geben	
	beastly /'biːstlɪ/ *adj.*, *adv.* (coll.) scheußlich	Pronunciation is shown in IPA immediately after the headword (see p. xiv). Die Ausspracheangaben (in IPA-Lautschrift) stehen unmittelbar hinter dem Stichwort (s. S. xiv)
Stress mark, showing stress on the following syllable. If no stress is shown in a compound block, it falls on the first element Betonungszeichen vor der betonten Silbe. Wo in Kompositablöcken keine Betonung angegeben ist, liegt der Ton auf dem ersten Bestandteil	**'beat-up** *adj.* (coll.) ramponiert (ugs.)	
	bluff [1] /blʌf/ 1 *n.* (act) Täuschungsmanöver, *das;* Bluff, *der* (ugs.); *see also* **call** 2 c. 2 *v.i. & t.* bluffen (ugs.) **bluff** [2] 1 *n.* (headland) Kliff, *das;* Steilküste, *die;* (inland) Steilhang, *der.* 2 *adj.* (abrupt, blunt, frank, hearty) raubeinig (ugs.)	Headwords spelt the same but with different meanings are entered separately with a raised number Mehrere gleich geschriebene, aber nicht bedeutungsgleiche Wörter erscheinen als separate Stichwörter und sind mit hochgestellten Ziffern nummeriert.

2. Grammatical information / Grammatische Angaben

Grammatical categories and parts of speech Grammatische Gliederungspunkte und Wortartangaben	**cannon** /'kænən/ 1 *n.* Kanone, *die.* 2 *v.i.* (Brit.) ~ **against sth.** gegen etw. prallen; ~ **into sb./sth.** mit etw./jmdm. zusammenprallen	
	consortium /kən'sɔːtɪəm/ *n., pl.* **consortia** /kən'sɔːtɪə/ Konsortium, *das*	Irregular plural of a noun Unregelmäßige Pluralform eines Substantivs
Irregular tenses of a verb (see also table on pp. 1224–26) Unregelmäßige Verbformen (siehe auch die Liste auf S. 1224–26)	**choose** /tʃuːz/ 1 *v.t.*, **chose** /tʃəʊz/, **chosen** /'tʃəʊzn/ (a) (select) wählen; (from a group) auswählen; ~ **sb. as** *or* **to...**	
	dub [1] /dʌb/ *v.t.*, **-bb-** (Cinemat.) synchronisieren **dub** [2] *v.t.*, **-bb-:** (a) ~ **sb. [a] knight** jmdn. zum Ritter...	Doubling of a final consonant of a verb before **-ed** *or* **-ing** Verdoppelung des Endkonsonanten eines Verbs vor -ed *oder* -ing
Irregular comparative and superlative forms of an adjective Unregelmäßige Steigerungsformen eines Adjektivs	**dry** /draɪ/ 1 *adj.*, **drier** /'draɪə(r)/, **driest** /'draɪɪst/ (a) trocken; trocken, (very ~) herb ⟨*Wein*⟩; ausgetrocknet	

3. Sense categories and labels / Semantische Gliederungspunkte und Angaben zu Stil, Sachbereich, räumlicher Zuordnung

Sense categories
Semantische
Gliederungspunkte

extremity /ɪk'strɛmɪtɪ/ *n.* (**a**) (of branch, road) äußerstes Ende; (of region) Rand, *der;* (**b**) *in pl.* (hands and feet) Extremitäten *Pl.*

facet /'fæsɪt/ *n.* (**a**) (of cut stone etc.) Facette, *die;* (**b**) (aspect) Seite, *die;* **every ∼:** alle Seiten

Sense indicators
Bedeutungsindikatoren

Subject labels
Bereichsangaben

fax: **∼ machine** *n.* Faxgerät, *das;* Fernkopierer, *der;* **∼ modem** *n.* (Computing) Faxmodem, *das;* **∼ number** *n.* Faxnummer, *die*
genome /'dʒiːnəʊm/ *n.* (Biol.) Genom, *das*

goalie /'gəʊlɪ/ *n.* (coll.) Tormann, *der;* Schlussmann, *der* (ugs.)
gob /gɒb/ *n.* (sl.) Schnauze, *die* (derb abwertend)

Style labels
Stilistische Kennzeichnungen

Regional labels
Angaben zur räumlichen
Zuordnung

hobo /'həʊbəʊ/ *n.,* *pl.* **∼es** (Amer.) Landstreicher, *der/* -streicherin, *die*
Hogmanay /'hɒgməneɪ/ *n.* (Scot., N. Engl.) Silvester, *der* *od. das*

4. Translations / Übersetzungen

Translations
Übersetzungen

ignore /ɪg'nɔː(r)/ *v.t.* ignorieren; nicht beachten; nicht befolgen ⟨*Befehl, Rat*⟩; übergehen, überhören ⟨*Frage, Bemerkung*⟩; **I shall ∼ that remark!** ich habe das nicht gehört!

insert 1 /ɪn'sɜːt/ *v.t.* (**a**) einlegen ⟨*Film*⟩; einwerfen ⟨*Münze*⟩; einsetzen ⟨*Herzschrittmacher*⟩; einstechen ⟨*Nadel*⟩; **∼ a piece of paper into the typewriter** ein Blatt Papier in die Schreibmaschine einspannen; (**b**)...

Objects of a verb
Als Objekte zu Verben
auftretende Wörter

**Collocators—words often
used with the headword,
shown to help select the
correct translation for each
context.**
Kollokatoren (Wörter, mit
denen zusammen das
Stichwort häufig vorkommt)
als Hilfe zur Auswahl der für
den jeweiligen Kontext
passenden Übersetzung

intense /ɪn'tens/ *adj.,* **∼r** /ɪn'tensə(r)/, **∼st** /ɪn'tensɪst/ (**a**) intensiv; stark ⟨*Hitze, Belastung*⟩; stark, heftig ⟨*Schmerzen*⟩; kräftig, intensiv ⟨*Farbe*⟩; äußerst groß ⟨*Aufregung*⟩; ungeheuer ⟨*Kälte, Helligkeit*⟩; (**b**) (eager, ardent) eifrig, lebhaft ⟨*Diskussion*⟩; stark, ausgeprägt...

**Nouns modified
by an adjective**
Durch Adjektive attribuierte
Substantive

intensify /ɪn'tensɪfaɪ/ 1 *v.t.* intensivieren. 2 *v.i.* zunehmen; ⟨*Hitze, Schmerzen:*⟩ stärker werden; ⟨*Kampf:*⟩ sich verschärfen

Subjects of a verb
Als Subjekte zu Verben
auftretende Wörter

keenly /'kiːnlɪ/ *adv.* (**a**) (sharply) scharf ⟨*geschliffen*⟩; (**b**) (eagerly) eifrig ⟨*arbeiten*⟩; brennend ⟨*interessiert sein*⟩; (**c**) (piercingly) scharf ⟨*ansehen*⟩; (**d**) (acutely) **be ∼ aware of sth.** sich (*Dat.*) einer Sache (*Gen.*) voll bewusst sein; **feel sth. ∼:** etw. deutlich fühlen

**Verbs or adjectives
modified by an adverb**
Durch Adverbien attribuierte
Verben oder Adjektive

The sign ≈ is used to indicate approximate equivalence Das Zeichen ≈ (signalisiert eine nur annähernde Entsprechung	**keg** /keg/ *n.* **(a)** (barrel) [kleines] Fass; Fässchen, *das;* **(b)** *attrib.* ~ **beer** *aus luftdichten Metallbehältern gezapftes, mit Kohlensäure versetztes Bier;* ≈ Fassbier, *das*

5. Phrases / Anwendungsbeispiele

Examples (with a swung dash representing the headword) Beispiele (jeweils mit einer Tilde an Stelle des Stichworts)	**quandary** /'kwɒndərɪ/ *n.* Dilemma, *das;* **this demand put him in a** ~: diese Forderung brachte ihn in eine verzwickte Lage; **he was in a** ~ **about what to do next** er wusste nicht, was er als Nächstes tun sollte	
	relapse /rɪ'læps/ **1** *v.i.* ⟨*Kranker:*⟩ einen Rückfall bekommen; ~ **into** zurückfallen in (+ *Akk.*) ⟨*Götzendienst, Barbarei*⟩; ~ **into silence/lethargy** wieder in Schweigen/Lethargie verfallen. **2** *n.* Rückfall, *der* (**into** in + *Akk.*)	**Parts of a phrase separated by a slash are syntactically interchangeable but have different meanings** Teile von Anwendungsbeispielen, zwischen denen ein Schrägstrich steht, sind syntaktisch gegeneinander austauschbar, aber nicht bedeutungsgleich
Parts of a phrase separated by *or* are synonymous and interchangeable Teile von Anwendungsbeispielen, zwischen denen ein kursiv gesetztes *or* steht, sind synonym und gegeneinander austauschbar	**queue** /kju:/ **1** *n.* Schlange, *die;* **a** ~ **of people/cars** eine Menschen-/Autoschlange; **stand** *or* **wait in a** ~: Schlange stehen; anstehen; **join the** ~: sich anstellen.	

6. Cross-references / Verweise

An arrow directs the user to another headword with the same meaning Ein Pfeil verweist auf ein bedeutungsgleiches anderes Stichwort	**satiate** /'seɪʃɪeɪt/ ⇨ **sate**	
	silver /'sɪlvə(r)/ **1** *n.* **(a)** *no pl., no indef. art.* Silber, *das;* **(b)** (colour, medal, vessels, cutlery) Silber, *das;* (cutlery of other material) Besteck, *das;* **(c)** *no pl., no indef. art.* (coins) Silbermünzen *Pl.;* Silber, *das* (ugs.). **2** *attrib. adj.* silbern; Silber⟨*pokal, -münze*⟩; *see also* **spoon. 3** *v.t.* ...	***see also* directs the user to another headword where additional information can be found** Mit *see also* wird auf ein Stichwort verwiesen, unter dem noch zusätzliche Informationen zu finden sind
An arrow ▶ and a page-number cross-reference direct the user to a usage box containing additional information Das Zeichen ▶ mit einer Zahl verweist auf eine Buchseite, auf der sich in einem Informationskasten zusätzliche Informationen finden	**solicitor** /sə'lɪsɪtə(r)/ *n.* ▶ **887** (Brit.: lawyer) Rechtsanwalt, *der/*-anwältin, *die (der/die nicht vor höheren Gerichten auftritt)*	

Die für das Deutsche verwendeten Zeichen der Lautschrift / Phonetic symbols used in transcriptions of German words

a	hat	hat	ŋ	lang	laŋ
aː	Bahn	baːn	o	Moral	moˈraːl
ɐ	Ober	ˈoːbɐ	oː	Boot	boːt
ɐ̯	Uhr	uːɐ̯	o̜	loyal	lo̜aˈjaːl
ã	Grand Prix	grãˈpriː	õ	Fondue	fõˈdyː
ãː	Abonnement	abɔnəˈmãː	õː	Fond	fõː
ai̯	weit	vai̯t	ɔ	Post	pɔst
au̯	Haut	hau̯t	ø	Ökonom	økoˈnoːm
b	Ball	bal	øː	Öl	øːl
ç	ich	ɪç	œ	göttlich	ˈɡœtlɪç
d	dann	dan	œ̃ː	Parfum	parˈfœ̃ː
dʒ	Gin	dʒɪn	ɔy̯	Heu	hɔy̯
e	Methan	meˈtaːn	p	Pakt	pakt
eː	Beet	beːt	pf	Pfahl	pfaːl
ɛ	mästen	ˈmɛstn̩	r	Rast	rast
ɛː	wählen	ˈvɛːlən	s	Hast	hast
ɛ̃	Ragoût fin	raguˈfɛ̃	ʃ	schal	ʃaːl
ɛ̃ː	Timbre	ˈtɛ̃ːbr(ə)	t	Tal	taːl
ə	Nase	ˈnaːzə	ts	Zahl	tsaːl
f	Fass	fas	tʃ	Matsch	matʃ
g	Gast	gast	u	kulant	kuˈlant
h	hat	hat	uː	Hut	huːt
i	vital	viˈtaːl	u̯	aktuell	akˈtu̯ɛl
iː	viel	fiːl	ʊ	Pult	pʊlt
i̯	Studie	ˈʃtuːdi̯ə	v	was	vas
ɪ	Birke	ˈbɪrkə	x	Bach	bax
j	ja	jaː	y	Physik	fyˈziːk
k	kalt	kalt	yː	Rübe	ˈryːbə
l	Last	last	y̯	Nuance	ˈny̯ãːsə
l̩	Nabel	ˈnaːbl̩	ʏ	Fülle	ˈfʏlə
m	Mast	mast	z	Hase	ˈhaːzə
n	Naht	naːt	ʒ	Genie	ʒeˈniː
n̩	baden	ˈbaːdn̩			

	Glottal stop, e.g. Aa [aˈǀa].	Stimmritzenverschlusslaut („Knacklaut"), z. B. Aa [aˈǀa].
ː	Length sign, indicating that the preceding vowel is long, e.g. Chrom [kroːm].	Längezeichen, bezeichnet Länge des unmittelbar davor stehenden Vokals, z. B. Chrom [kroːm].
˜	Indicates a nasal vowel, e.g. Fond [fõː].	Zeichen für nasale Vokale, z. B. Fond [fõː].
ˈ	Stress mark, immediately preceding a stressed syllable, e.g. Ballon [baˈlɔŋ].	Betonung, steht unmittelbar vor einer betonten Silbe, z. B. Ballon [baˈlɔŋ].
ˌ	Sign placed below a syllabic consonant, e.g. Büschel [ˈbyʃl̩].	Zeichen für silbischen Konsonanten, steht unmittelbar unter dem Konsonanten, z. B. Büschel [ˈbyʃl̩].
ˆ	Placed above or below a symbol indicates a non-syllabic vowel, e.g. Milieu [miˈli̯øː].	Halbkreis, untergesetzt oder übergesetzt, bezeichnet unsilbischen Vokal, z. B. Milieu [miˈli̯øː].

Die für das Englische verwendeten Zeichen der Lautschrift / Phonetic symbols used in transcriptions of English words

ɑː	bah	bɑː	m	mat	mæt
ɑ̃	ensemble	ɑ̃'sɑ̃mbl	n	not	nɒt
æ	fat	fæt	ŋ	sing	sɪŋ
æ̃	lingerie	'læ̃ʒərɪ	ɒ	got	gɒt
aɪ	fine	faɪn	ɔː	paw	pɔː
aʊ	now	naʊ	ɔ̃	fait accompli	feɪt æ'kɔ̃pliː
b	bat	bæt	ɔɪ	boil	bɔɪl
d	dog	dɒg	p	pet	pet
dʒ	jam	dʒæm	r	rat	ræt
e	met	met	s	sip	sɪp
eɪ	fate	feɪt	ʃ	ship	ʃɪp
eə	fairy	'feərɪ	t	tip	tɪp
əʊ	goat	gəʊt	tʃ	chin	tʃɪn
ə	ago	ə'gəʊ	θ	thin	θɪn
ɜː	fur	fɜː(r)	ð	the	ðə
f	fat	fæt	uː	boot	buːt
g	good	gʊd	ʊ	book	bʊk
h	hat	hæt	ʊə	tourist	'tʊərɪst
ɪ	bit, lately	bɪt, 'leɪtlɪ	ʌ	dug	dʌg
ɪə	nearly	'nɪəlɪ	v	van	væn
iː	meet	miːt	w	win	wɪn
j	yet	jet	x	loch	lɒx
k	kit	kɪt	z	zip	zɪp
l	lot	lɒt	ʒ	vision	'vɪʒn

: Length sign, indicating that the preceding vowel is long, e.g. boot [buːt].

Längezeichen, bezeichnet Länge des unmittelbar davor stehenden Vokals, z. B. boot [buːt].

' Stress mark, immediately preceding a stressed syllable, e.g. ago [ə'gəʊ].

Betonung, steht unmittelbar vor einer betonten Silbe, z. B. ago [ə'gəʊ].

(r) An 'r' in parentheses is pronounced only when immediately followed by a vowel sound, e.g. pare [peə(r)]; pare away [peər ə'weɪ].

Ein „r" in runden Klammern wird nur gesprochen, wenn im Textzusammenhang ein Vokal unmittelbar folgt, z. B. pare [peə(r)]; pare away [peər ə'weɪ].

German spellings in this dictionary

German spellings in this dictionary are in accordance with the reforms ratified by the governments of Germany, Austria, and Switzerland in July 1996 and in force since August 1998. Key points of the reforms are summarized below. In cases of doubt the editors have followed *Duden—Rechtschreibung der deutschen Sprache*, twenty-first edition, 1996.

To help the user who may not yet be familiar with the reforms, the German-English section of the dictionary gives both the new spellings and the old versions which will become 'invalid' in 2005 after a transition period during which both spellings are 'valid'. The old spellings are marked with an asterisk and are cross-referred where necessary to the new. For example, the translations of the compound verb *wiedererkennen* will no longer be found at this headword, since under the new spelling rules the word will vanish from the language. Instead they are covered by two phrases at the entry for *wieder: jemanden/etwas wieder erkennen* (in the form *jmdn./etw. ~ erkennen*) and *er war kaum wieder zu erkennen* (in the form *er war kaum ~ zu erkennen*). Similarly, the translations of the adjective previously written *belemmert* will be found at the new entry for the headword *belämmert*.

In a number of cases, however, implementing the new spelling rules has meant that just some, but not all, uses of a word have had to be transferred from one entry to another. In these cases the headword is not marked with an asterisk, but the entry is provided with a cross-reference to where the transferred information is now to be found. So, for example, the user who consults the entry for *leid* looking for a translation of the phrase previously written *jemandem leid tun* will find a cross-reference to the entry for the noun *Leid*, since according to the new spelling rules the word is written with a capital L in this expression. The headword *leid* itself is not marked with an asterisk, since it continues to exist in its own right as an adjective.

The following summary lists the most important changes:

1. The ß character
The ß character, which is generally replaced in Switzerland by a double s, will be retained in Germany and Austria, but will only be written after a long vowel (as in Fuß, Füße) and after a diphthong (as in Strauß, Sträuße).
> *Fluß, Baß, keß, läßt, Nußknacker* become in future: *Fluss, Bass, kess, lässt, Nussknacker*

2. Nominalized adjectives
Nominalized adjectives will be written with a capital even in set phrases.
> *sein Schäfchen ins trockene bringen, im trüben fischen, im allgemeinen* become in future: *sein Schäfchen ins Trockene bringen, im Trüben fischen, im Allgemeinen*

3. Words from the same word family
In certain cases the spelling of words belonging to the same family will be made uniform.
> *numerieren, überschwenglich* become in future: *nummerieren* (like Nummer), *überschwänglich* (being related to Überschwang)

4. The same consonant repeated three times
When the same consonant repeated three times occurs in compounds, all three will be written even when a vowel follows.
> *Brennessel, Schiffahrt* become in future: *Brennnessel, Schifffahrt* (exceptions are dennoch, Drittel, Mittag)

5. Verb, adjective and participle compounds

Verb, adjective and participle compounds will be written more frequently than previously in two words.

spazierengehen, radfahren, ernstgemeint, erdölexportierend become in future: *spazieren gehen, Rad fahren, ernst gemeint, Erdöl exportierend*

6. Compounds containing numbers in figures

Compounds containing numbers in figures will in future be written with a hyphen.

24karätig, 8pfünder become in future: *24-karätig, 8-Pfünder*

7. The division of words containing *st*

st will be treated like a normal combination of consonants and no longer be indivisible.

Ha-stig, Ki-ste become in future: *has-tig, Kis-te*

8. The division of words containing *ck*

The combination *ck* will not be divided and will go on to the next line.

Bäk-ker, schik-ken become in future: *Bä-cker, schi-cken*

9. The division of foreign words

Compound foreign words which are hardly recognized as such today may be divided by syllables, without regard to their original components.

He-li-ko-pter (from the Greek helix and pteron) may also become in future: *He-li-kop-ter*

10. The comma before *und*

Where two complete clauses are connected by *und* a comma will not be obligatory.

Karl war in Schwierigkeiten, und niemand konnte ihm helfen. may also in future be written: *Karl war in Schwierigkeiten und niemand konnte ihm helfen.*

11. The comma with infinitives and participles

Even longer clauses containing an infinitive or participle will not have to be divided off with a comma.

Er begann sofort, das neue Buch zu lesen. Ungläubig den Kopf schüttelnd, verließ er das Zimmer. may also in future be written: *Er begann sofort das neue Buch zu lesen. Ungläubig den Kopf schüttelnd verließ er das Zimmer.*

Im Wörterverzeichnis verwendete deutsche Abkürzungen / German abbreviations used in this Dictionary

a.	anderes; andere	Druckerspr.	Druckersprache
ä.	ähnliches; ähnliche	Druckw.	Druckwesen
Abk.	Abkürzung	dt.	deutsch
adj.	adjektivisch	DV	Datenverarbeitung
Adj.	Adjektiv	ehem.	ehemals, ehemalig
adv.	adverbial	Eisenb.	Eisenbahn
Adv.	Adverb	elektr.	elektrisch
Akk.	Akkusativ	Elektrot.	Elektrotechnik
amerik.	amerikanisch	Energievers.	Energieversorgung
Amtsspr.	Amtssprache	Energiewirtsch.	Energiewirtschaft
Anat.	Anatomie	engl.	englisch
Anthrop.	Anthropologie	etw.	etwas
Archäol.	Archäologie	ev.	evangelisch
Archit.	Architektur	fachspr.	fachsprachlich
Art.	Artikel	fam.	familiär
Astrol.	Astrologie	Fem.	Femininum
Astron.	Astronomie	Ferns.	Fernsehen
A.T.	Altes Testament	Fernspr.	Fernsprechwesen
attr.	attributiv	fig.	figurativ
Ausspr.	Aussprache	Finanzw.	Finanzwesen
Bauw.	Bauwesen	Fischereiw.	Fischereiwesen
Bergmannsspr.	Bergmannssprache	Fliegerspr.	Fliegersprache
berlin.	berlinisch	Flugw.	Flugwesen
bes.	besonders	Forstw.	Forstwesen
Bez.	Bezeichnung	Fot.	Fotografie
bibl.	biblisch	Frachtw.	Frachtwesen
bild. Kunst	bildende Kunst	Funkw.	Funkwesen
Biol.	Biologie	Gastr.	Gastronomie
Bodenk.	Bodenkunde	Gattungsz.	Gattungszahl
Börsenw.	Börsenwesen	Gaunerspr.	Gaunersprache
Bot.	Botanik	geh.	gehoben
BRD	Bundesrepublik Deutschland	Gen.	Genitiv
		Geneal.	Genealogie
brit.	britisch	Geogr.	Geographie
Bruchz.	Bruchzahl	Geol.	Geologie
Buchf.	Buchführung	Geom.	Geometrie
Buchw.	Buchwesen	Handarb.	Handarbeit
Bürow.	Bürowesen	Handw.	Handwerk
chem.	chemisch	Hausw.	Hauswirtschaft
christl.	christlich	Her.	Heraldik
Dat.	Dativ	hess.	hessisch
DDR	Deutsche Demokratische Republik	Hilfsv.	Hilfsverb
		hist.	historisch
Dekl.	Deklination	Hochschulw.	Hochschulwesen
Demonstrativ pron.	Demonstrativpronomen	Holzverarb.	Holzverarbeitung
		Indefinitpron.	Indefinitpronomen
d.h.	das heißt	indekl.	indeklinabel
dichter.	dichterisch		

Indik.	Indikativ	nordwestd.	nordwestdeutsch
Inf.	Infinitiv	ns.	nationalsozialistisch
Informationst.	Informationstechnik	N.T.	Neues Testament
Interj.	Interjektion	o.	ohne; oben
iron.	ironisch	o.Ä.	oder Ähnliches;
intr.	intransitiv		oder Ähnliche
Jagdw.	Jagdwesen	od.	oder
Jägerspr.	Jägersprache	Ordinalz.	Ordinalzahl
jmd.	jemand	orth.	orthodox
jmdm.	jemandem	ostd.	ostdeutsch
jmdn.	jemanden	österr.	österreichisch
jmds.	jemandes	Päd.	Pädagogik
Jugendspr.	Jugendsprache	Paläont.	Paläontologie
jur.	juristisch	Papierdt.	Papierdeutsch
Kardinalz.	Kardinalzahl	Parapsych.	Parapsychologie
kath.	katholisch	Parl.	Parlament
Kaufmannsspr.	Kaufmannssprache	Part.	Partizip
Kfz.-W.	Kraftfahrzeugwesen	Perf.	Perfekt
Kinderspr.	Kindersprache	Pers.	Person
Kochk.	Kochkunst	pfälz.	pfälzisch
Konj.	Konjunktion	Pharm.	Pharmazie
Kosew.	Kosewort	Philat.	Philatelie
Kunstwiss.	Kunstwissenschaft	Philos.	Philosophie
Kurzf.	Kurzform	Physiol.	Physiologie
Kurzw.	Kurzwort	Pl.	Plural
landsch.	landschaftlich	Plusq.	Plusquamperfekt
Landw.	Landwirtschaft	Polizeiw.	Polizeiwesen
Literaturw.	Literaturwissenschaft	Postw.	Postwesen
Luftf.	Luftfahrt	präd.	prädikativ
ma.	mittelalterlich	Prähist.	Prähistorie
MA.	Mittelalter	Präp.	Präposition
marx.	marxistisch	Präs.	Präsens
Mask.	Maskulinum	Prät.	Präteritum
Math.	Mathematik	Pron.	Pronomen
Mech.	Mechanik	Psych.	Psychologie
Med.	Medizin	Raumf.	Raumfahrt
Meeresk.	Meereskunde	Rechtsspr.	Rechtssprache
Met.	Meteorologie	Rechtsw.	Rechtswesen
Metall.	Metallurgie	refl.	reflexiv
Metallbearb.	Metallbearbeitung	regelm.	regelmäßig
Milit.	Militär	Rel.	Religion
Mineral.	Mineralogie	Relativpron.	Relativpronomen
mod.	modifizierend	rhein.	rheinisch
Modalv.	Modalverb	Rhet.	Rhetorik
Münzk.	Münzkunde	röm.	römisch
Mus.	Musik	röm.-kath.	römisch-katholisch
Mythol.	Mythologie	Rundf.	Rundfunk
Naturw.	Naturwissenschaft	s.	siehe
Neutr.	Neutrum	S.	Seite
niederdt.	niederdeutsch	scherzh.	scherzhaft
Nom.	Nominativ	schles.	schlesisch
nordamerik.	nordamerikanisch	schott.	schottisch
nordd.	norddeutsch	Schülerspr.	Schülersprache
nordostd.	nordostdeutsch	Schulw.	Schulwesen

schwäb.	schwäbisch	unbest.	unbestimmt
schweiz.	schweizerisch	unpers.	unpersönlich
Seemannsspr.	Seemannssprache	unr.	unregelmäßig
Seew.	Seewesen	usw.	und so weiter
Sexualk.	Sexualkunde	v.	von
Sg.	Singular	V.	Verb
s. o.	siehe oben	verächtl.	verächtlich
Soldatenspr.	Soldatensprache	veralt.	veraltet; veraltend
Sozialpsych.	Sozialpsychologie	Verhaltensf.	Verhaltensforschung
Sozialvers.	Sozialversicherung	verhüll.	verhüllend
Soziol.	Soziologie	Verkehrsw.	Verkehrswesen
spött.	spöttisch	Vermessungsw.	Vermessungswesen
Spr.	Sprichwort	Versicherungsw.	Versicherungswesen
Sprachw.	Sprachwissenschaft	vgl.	vergleiche
Steuerw.	Steuerwesen	Vkl.	Verkleinerungsform
Stilk.	Stilkunde	Völkerk.	Völkerkunde
Studentenspr.	Studentensprache	Völkerr.	Völkerrecht
s.u.	siehe unten	Volksk.	Volkskunde
Subj.	Subjekt	volkst.	volkstümlich
subst.	substantivisch; substantiviert	vulg.	vulgär
		Werbespr.	Werbesprache
Subst.	Substantiv	westd.	westdeutsch
südd.	süddeutsch	westfäl.	westfälisch
südwestd.	südwestdeutsch	Wiederholungsz.	Wiederholungszahlwort
Suff.	Suffix	wiener.	wienerisch
Sup.	Superlativ	Winzerspr.	Winzersprache
Textilw.	Textilwesen	Wirtsch.	Wirtschaft
Theol.	Theologie	Wissensch.	Wissenschaft
thüring.	thüringisch	Wz.	Warenzeichen
Tiermed.	Tiermedizin	Zahnmed.	Zahnmedizin
tirol.	tirolisch	z. B.	zum Beispiel
tr.	transitiv	Zeitungsw.	Zeitungswesen
Trenn.	Trennung	Zollw.	Zollwesen
u.	und	Zool.	Zoologie
u. a.	und andere[s]	Zus.	Zusammensetzung
u. Ä.	und Ähnliches	Zusschr.	Zusammenschreibung
ugs.	umgangssprachlich		

Im Wörterverzeichnis verwendete englische Abkürzungen / English abbreviations used in this Dictionary

abbr(s).	abbreviation(s)	def.	definite
abs.	absolute	Dent.	Dentistry
adj(s).	adjective(s)	derog.	derogatory
Admin.	Administration, Administrative	dial.	dialect
		Diplom.	Diplomacy
adv.	adverb	Dressm.	Dressmaking
Aeronaut.	Aeronautics	Eccl.	Ecclesiastical
Agric.	Agriculture	Ecol.	Ecology
Alch.	Alchemy	Econ.	Economics
Amer.	American, America	Educ.	Education
Anat.	Anatomy	Electr.	Electricity
Anglican Ch.	Anglican Church	ellipt.	elliptical
Anglo-Ind.	Anglo-Indian	emphat.	emphatic
Ant.	Antiquity	esp.	especially
Anthrop.	Anthropology	Ethnol.	Ethnology
arch.	archaic	Ethol.	Ethology
Archaeol.	Archaeology	euphem.	euphemistic
Archit.	Architecture	excl.	exclamation, exclamatory
art.	article	expr.	expressing
Astrol.	Astrology	fem.	feminine
Astron.	Astronomy	fig.	figurative
Astronaut.	Astronautics	Footb.	Football
attrib.	attributive	Gastr.	Gastronomy
Austral.	Australian, Australia	Geneal.	Genealogy
Bacteriol.	Bacteriology	Geog.	Geography
Bibl.	Biblical	Geol.	Geology
Bibliog.	Bibliography	Geom.	Geometry
Biochem.	Biochemistry	Graph. Arts	Graphic Arts
Biol.	Biology	Her.	Heraldry
Bookk.	Bookkeeping	Hist.	History, Historical
Bot.	Botany	Horol.	Horology
Brit.	British, Britain	Hort.	Horticulture
Can.	Canadian, Canada	Hydraulic Engin.	Hydraulic Engineering
Chem.	Chemistry	imper.	imperative
Cinemat.	Cinematography	impers.	impersonal
coll.	colloquial	incl.	including
collect.	collective	Ind.	Indian, India
comb.	combination	indef.	indefinite
Commerc.	Commerce, Commercial	Information Sci.	Information Science
Communication Res.	Communication Research	int.	interjection
		interrog.	interrogative
compar.	comparative	Int. Law	International Law
condit.	conditional	Ir.	Irish, Ireland
conj.	conjunction	iron.	ironical
Constr.	Construction	joc.	jocular
constr.	construed	Journ.	Journalism
contr.	contracted form	lang.	language

Ling.	Linguistics	**Prehist.**	Prehistory
Lit.	Literature	**prep.**	preposition
lit.	literal	**pres.**	present
Magn.	Magnetism	**pres. p.**	present participle
Managem.	Management	**pr. n.**	proper noun
masc.	masculine	**pron.**	pronoun
Math.	Mathematics	**Pros.**	Prosody
Mech.	Mechanics	**prov.**	proverbial
Mech. Engin.	Mechanical Engineering	**Psych.**	Psychology
Med.	Medicine	**p.t.**	past tense
Metalw.	Metalwork	**Railw.**	Railways
Metaph.	Metaphysics	**RC Ch.**	Roman Catholic Church
Meteorol.	Meteorology	**refl.**	reflexive
Mil.	Military	**rel.**	relative
Min.	Mineralogy	**Relig.**	Religion
Motor Veh.	Motor Vehicles	**Res.**	Research
Mount.	Mountaineering	**Rhet.**	Rhetoric
Mus.	Music	**rhet.**	rhetorical
Mythol.	Mythology	**S. Afr.**	South African, South Africa
n.	noun	**sb.**	somebody
Nat. Sci.	Natural Science	**Sch.**	School
Naut.	Nautical	**Sci.**	Science
neg.	negative	**Scot.**	Scottish, Scotland
N. Engl.	Northern English	**Shipb.**	Shipbuilding
ns.	nouns	**sing.**	singular
Nucl. Engin.	Nuclear Engineering	**sl.**	slang
Nucl. Phys.	Nuclear Physics	**Sociol.**	Sociology
Num.	Numismatics	**Soc. Serv.**	Social Services
N.Z.	New Zealand	**Soil Sci.**	Soil Science
obj.	object	**St. Exch.**	Stock Exchange
Oceanog.	Oceanography	**sth.**	something
Ornith.	Ornithology	**subord.**	subordinate
P	Proprietary name	**suf.**	suffix
Palaeont.	Palaeontology	**superl.**	superlative
Parapsych.	Parapsychology	**Surv.**	Surveying
Parl.	Parliament	**symb.**	symbol
pass.	passive	**tech.**	technical
Pharm.	Pharmacy	**Teleph.**	Telephony
Philat.	Philately	**Telev.**	Television
Philos.	Philosophy	**Theol.**	Theology
Phonet.	Phonetics	**Univ.**	University
Photog.	Photography	**usu.**	usually
phr(s).	phrase(s)	**v. aux.**	auxiliary verb
Phys.	Physics	**Vet. Med.**	Veterinary Medicine
Physiol.	Physiology	**v. i.**	intransitive verb
pl.	plural	**voc.**	vocative
poet.	poetical	**v. refl.**	reflexive verb
Polit.	Politics	**v. t.**	transitive verb
poss.	possessive	**v. t. & i.**	transitive and intransitive verb
postpos.	postpositive		
p.p.	past participle	**W. Ind.**	West Indian, West Indies
pred.	predicative	**Woodw.**	Woodwork
pref.	prefix	**Zool.**	Zoology

Aa

a, A /a:/ *das;* ~, ~ **(a)** (Buchstabe) a/A; **kleines a** small a; **großes A** capital A; **das A und O** (fig.) the essential thing/things (*Gen.* for); **von A bis Z** (fig. ugs.) from beginning to end; **wer A sagt, muss auch B sagen** (fig.) if one starts a thing, one must go through with it; **(b)** (Musik) [key of] A

ä, Ä /ɛ:/ *das;* ~, ~: a umlaut

à /a/ *Präp. mit Nom., Akk.* (Kaufmannsspr.) **zehn Marken à 50 Pfennig** ten stamps at 50 pfennigs each; **zehn Kisten à zwölf Flaschen** ten cases of twelve bottles each

A *Abk.* **(a) Autobahn; (b) Ampere** A

Aa /a'|a/ *das;* ~s (Kinderspr.) poo[-poo] (child lang.); **Aa machen** do poo-poo *or* big jobs (child lang.); do a big job (Amer. child lang.)

AA¹ *Abk.* **Anonyme Alkoholiker** AA

AA² /a:'|a:/ *das;* ~ *Abk.* **Auswärtiges Amt**

Aal /a:l/ *der;* ~[e]s, ~e eel; **glatt wie ein ~ sein** be as slippery as an eel; **sich [drehen und] winden** *od.* **krümmen wie ein ~:** twist and turn like an eel

aalen *refl. V.* (ugs.) **sich am Strand/in der Sonne ~:** lie stretched out on the beach/in the sun; **er ging an den Strand, um sich in der Sonne zu ~:** he went to the beach to stretch out in the sun

aal·glatt (abwertend) **1** *Adj.* slippery; ~ **sein** be as slippery as an eel. **2** *adv.* smoothly

Aas /a:s/ *das;* ~es, ~e *od.* **Äser** /'ɛ:zɐ/ **(a)** *Pl.* ~e carrion *no art.;* (kadaver) [rotting] carcass; **(b)** *Pl.* **Äser** (salopp) (abwertend) swine; (anerkennend) devil; **kein ~:** not one damned person

aasen *itr. V.* (ugs., bes. nordd.) **mit etw. ~:** be wasteful with sth.

Aas-: ~**fliege** *die* (Zool.) blowfly; ~**fresser** *der* (Zool.) carrion-eater; scavenger; ~**geier** *der* vulture; **wie [die]** ~**geier** (abwertend) like vultures

aasig *Adv.* (ugs.) ~ **kalt** damned cold; **es tut ~ weh** it hurts like mad (coll.)

ab /ap/ **1** *Präp. mit Dat.* **(a)** (zeitlich) from; **ab 1980** as from 1980; **Jugendliche ab 16 Jahren** young people over the age of 16; **ab [dem] 3. April** from the 3rd of April; **(b)** (bes. Kaufmannsspr.: räumlich) ex; **ab Werk** ex works; **ab Frankfurt fliegen** fly from Frankfurt; **(c)** ([Rang]folge) from … on[wards]; **ab 20 DM** from 20 DM [upwards]. **2** *Adv.* **(a)** (weg) off; away; **nicht weit ab vom Weg** not far [away] from the path; **an der Kreuzung links ab** turn off left at the junction; **[an etw. (***Dat.***)] ab sein** (ugs.: von etw. abgegangen sein) have come off [sth.]; **(b)** (ugs.: Aufforderung) off; away; **ab nach Hause** get off home; **ab die Post** (fig.) off you/we *etc.* go; **ab nach Kassel** (fig.) it's off and away; **(c)** (milit. Kommando) **Gewehr ab!** order arms!; **(d) ab und zu** *od.* (norddt.) **an** now and then; from time to time; *s. auch* **auf 3 e, f; von 1 a, b**

Abakus /'a(:)bakʊs/ *der;* ~, ~: abacus

ab|ändern *tr. V.* alter; change; amend (*text*)

Ab·änderung *die* alteration; (eines Paragraphen) amendment

ab|arbeiten 1 *tr. V.* **(a)** (abgelten) work for (*meal*); work off (*debt, amount*); **(b)** (abnutzen) wear out [with work]; *s. auch* **abgearbeitet. 2** *refl. V.* slave [away]; work like a slave

Ab·art *die* variety

ab·artig *Adj.* deviant; abnormal

Ab·artigkeit *die* abnormality; deviancy

ab|asten *refl. V.* (ugs.) slave [away]; **sich mit etw. ~:** heave sth. around

Abb. *Abk.* **Abbildung** Fig.

Ab·bau *der* **(a)** dismantling; (von Zelten, Lagern) striking; **(b)** (Senkung) reduction; **(c)** ⇨ **abbauen 1 d:** cutback (*Gen.* in); pruning; **der ~ von Vorurteilen** the breaking down of prejudices; **(d)** (Chemie, Biol.) breakdown; **(e)** (Bergbau) ⇨ **abbauen 1 f:** mining; quarrying; working

ab|bauen 1 *tr. V.* **(a)** dismantle; strike (*tent, camp*); dismantle, take down (*scaffolding*); **(b)** (senken) reduce (*wages*); **(c)** (beseitigen) gradually remove; break down (*prejudices, inhibitions*); **(d)** (verringern) cut back (*staff*); prune (*jobs*); **(e)** (Chemie, Biol.) break down (*carbohydrates, alcohol*); **(f)** (Bergbau) mine (*coal, gold*); quarry (*stone*); work (*seam*). **2** *itr. V.* fade; slow down; **körperlich ~:** decay physically

ab|beißen 1 *unr. tr. V.* bite off. **2** *unr. itr. V.* have a bite

ab|beizen *tr. V.* (Handw.) strip (*wooden object*)

ab|bekommen *unr. tr. V.* **(a)** get; **sie hat keinen Mann ~** (ugs.) she didn't catch herself a husband; **(b)** (hinnehmen müssen) **einen Schlag/ein paar Kratzer ~:** get hit/get a few scratches; **etwas ~** (getroffen werden) get *or* be hit; (verletzt werden) get *or* be hurt; **der Wagen hat nichts ~:** the car wasn't damaged; **(c)** (entfernen können) get (*paint, lid, chain*) off

ab|berufen *unr. tr. V.* recall (*ambassador, envoy*) (**aus, von** from)

Ab·berufung *die* recall

ab|bestellen *tr. V.* cancel

Ab·bestellung *die* cancellation

ab|betteln *tr. V.* (ugs.) **jmdm. etw. ~:** beg sth. from sb.

ab|bezahlen *tr. V.* pay off

ab|biegen 1 *unr. itr. V.; mit sein* ▶ 583 turn off; **links ~:** turn [off] left. **2** *unr. tr. V.* **(a)** bend (*rod, metal sheet, etc.*); **(b)** (ugs.: abwenden) get out of (coll.) (*obligation*); head off (coll.) (*row*)

Abbiege·spur *die* turning lane

Ab·bild *das* (eines Menschen) likeness; (eines Gegenstandes) copy; (fig.) portrayal

ab|bilden *tr. V.* copy; reproduce (*object, picture*); portray; depict (*person*); depict (*landscape*); (fig.) portray; depict

Ab·bildung *die* **(a)** (Bild) illustration; (Schaubild) diagram; **die ~ einer Frau** a/the picture of a woman; **~ 5** (in einem Buch) figure *or* fig. 5; **(b)** *o. Pl.* (das Abbilden) reproduction; (fig.) portrayal

ab|binden *unr. tr. V.* **(a)** (losbinden) untie; undo; **eine Schnur ~:** untie a piece of string; **(b)** (abschnüren) put a tourniquet on (*artery, arm, leg, etc.*); tie (*umbilical cord*)

Ab·bitte *die* (geh.) **jmdm. ~ leisten** *od.* **tun** ask sb.'s pardon

ab|blasen *unr. tr. V.* (ugs.: absagen) call off (*enterprise, party*)

ab|blättern *itr. V.; mit sein* flake off

ab|bleiben *unr. itr. V.; mit sein* (ugs., bes. nordd.) **wo ist er/es nur abgeblieben?** where has he/it got to (Brit.) *or* (Amer.) gone?; where can he/it be?

ab|blenden 1 *tr. V.* dip (Brit.), dim (Amer.) (*headlights*). **2** *itr. V.* dip (Brit.) *or* (Amer.) dim one's headlights

Abblend·licht *das; o. Pl.* dipped (Brit.) *or* (Amer.) dimmed beam; **mit ~ fahren** drive on dipped *or* dimmed headlights

ab|blitzen *itr. V.; mit sein* (ugs.) **sie ließ alle Verehrer ~:** she gave all her admirers the brush-off; **bei jmdm. [mit etw.] ~:** fail to get anywhere [with sth.] with sb. (coll.)

ab|blocken tr. V. (Sport, fig.) block

ab|brausen 1 tr. V. ⇒ **abduschen. 2** itr. V.; mit sein (ugs.) roar off

ab|brechen 1 unr. tr. V. **(a)** break off; (durchbrechen) break ‹needle, pencil›; **sich** (Dat.) **einen Fingernagel/Zahn** ~: break a fingernail/a tooth; **(b)** (abbauen) strike ‹tent, camp›; **(c)** (abreißen) demolish, pull down ‹building, tower›; **(d)** (beenden) break off ‹negotiations, [diplomatic] relations, discussion, connection, activity›; (vorzeitig, wider Erwarten) cut short ‹conversation, studies, holiday, activity›; **den Kampf** ~ (Boxen) stop the fight. **2** unr. itr. V. **(a)** mit sein (entzweigehen) break [off]; **(b)** (aufhören) break off; **(c)** mit sein (beendet werden) **die Verbindung brach ab** the connection was cut off. **3** unr. refl. V. **sich** (Dat.) **einen/keinen** ~ (salopp) put/not put oneself out

ab|bremsen 1 tr. V. **(a)** brake; **den Wagen** ~: slow the car down; **(b)** (retard ‹motion›; break ‹fall›. **2** itr. V. brake; apply the brakes

ab|brennen 1 unr. itr. V.; mit sein **(a)** be burned down; ‹farm› be burned out; **das Haus ist abgebrannt** the house has burned down; **wir sind schon zweimal abgebrannt** we've been burned out twice already; s. auch **Grundmauer; (b)** (sich aufbrauchen) ‹fuse› burn away; ‹candle› burn down; **abgebrannte Streichhölzer** used or burnt matches. **2** unr. tr. V. **(a)** let off ‹firework›; **(b)** burn down ‹building›

ab|bringen unr. tr. V. **jmdn. von etw.** ~: make sb. give up sth.; **jmdn. vom Kurs** ~: make sb. change course; **jmdn. von der Fährte** ~: throw sb. off the scent; **jmdn. davon** ~, **etw. zu tun** stop sb. doing sth.; (durch Worte) dissuade sb. from doing sth.; **jmdn. vom Thema** ~: get sb. away from the subject

ab|bröckeln itr. V.; mit sein (auch fig.) crumble away; ‹price, exchange rate› decline gradually

Ab·bruch der **(a)** o. Pl. (Abriss) demolition; pulling down; **(b)** (Beendigung) breaking-off; (Boxen) stopping; **(c) einer Sache** (Dat.) **[keinen]** ~ **tun** do [no] harm to sth.

abbruch-, Abbruch-: ~**firma** die demolition firm; ~**haus** das condemned house; ~**reif** Adj. ripe for demolition postpos.

ab|brummen tr. V. (ugs.) do (sl.) ‹prison sentence, time in prison›

ab|buchen tr. V. ‹bank› debit **(von** to); ‹creditor› claim by direct debit **(von** to); **etw.** ~ **lassen** (durch die Bank) pay sth. by standing order; (durch Gläubiger) pay sth. by direct debit

Ab·buchung die debiting

ab|bürsten tr. V. **(a)** brush off; **etw. von etw.** ~: brush sth. off sth.; **jmdm. die Haare/den Schmutz** ~: brush the hairs/the dirt off sb.; **(b)** (säubern) brush ‹garment›

ab|büßen tr. V. serve [out] ‹prison sentence›

Abc /a(:)be(:)'ts:e:/ das; ~ **(a)** ABC; **(b)** (fig.: Grundlagen) ABC; fundamentals pl.

ab|checken tr. V. check

Abc-Schütze der child just starting school

ABC-Waffen Pl. ABC weapons

ab|dampfen itr. V.; mit sein (ugs.: abfahren) set off

ab|danken itr. V. ‹monarch, ruler› abdicate; ‹government, minister› resign

Abdankung die; ~, ~**en** (eines Herrschers) abdication; (eines Ministers, einer Regierung) resignation

ab|decken tr. V. **(a)** open up; uncover ‹container›; ‹gale› take the roof/roofs off ‹house›, take the tiles off ‹roof›; **(b)** (herunternehmen, -reißen) take off; remove; **(c)** (abräumen) clear ‹table›; clear away ‹dishes›; **(d)** (schützen) cover ‹person›; (Schach) defend; **(e)** (Sport) mark ‹player›; **(f)** (bezahlen, ausgleichen) cover; meet ‹need, demand›

Abdecker der; ~**s**, ~ ▶ 85 | (veralt.) knacker (Brit.)

Abdeckerei die; ~, ~**en** (veralt.) knacker's yard (Brit.)

Ab·deckung die covering

ab|dichten tr. V. seal; seal, stop up ‹hole, crack, gap, etc.›; plug ‹leak›; (gegen Zugluft) draughtproof ‹door, window›

ab|drängen tr. V. push away; force away; drive ‹animal› away; **jmdn. von etw.** ~: push sb. away from sth.; **einen Spieler vom Ball** ~ (Fußball) force a player off the ball

ab|drehen 1 tr. V. **(a)** (ausschalten) turn off; turn or switch off ‹light, lamp, electricity, fire, radio›; **den Hahn** ~ (fig.) turn off the supply; **(b)** (abtrennen) twist off; s. auch **Gurgel; (c)** (abschrauben) screw off ‹lid, top›. **2** itr. V.; meist mit sein (die Richtung ändern) turn off

ab|driften itr. V.; mit sein (Seew.) be blown; make leeway (Naut.)

Ab·druck¹ der; Pl. **Abdrücke** mark; imprint; (Finger~) fingermark; (Fuß~) footprint; footmark; (Wachs~) impression; (Gips~) cast

Ab·druck² der; Pl. ~**e (a)** o. Pl. (Vorgang) printing; **(b)** (Ergebnis) (einer Grafik) print

ab|drucken tr. V. print; (veröffentlichen) publish

ab|drücken 1 itr. V. pull the trigger; shoot; **auf jmdn./etw.** ~: shoot or fire at sb./sth. **2** tr. V. **(a)** (abfeuern) fire ‹revolver, gun›; **(b)** (zudrücken) constrict; **(c) jmdm. die Luft** ~: stop sb. breathing. **3** refl. V. **(a) sich [in etw.** (Dat.)] ~: make marks [in sth.]; ‹track› be imprinted [in sth.]; **(b) sich [mit dem Fuß]** ~: push oneself away with one's foot

ab|dunkeln tr. V. darken ‹room›; dim ‹light›

ab|duschen tr. V. **sich/jmdn. [kalt/warm]** ~: take/give sb. a [cold/hot] shower; **sich/jmdm. den Rücken** ~: shower one's/sb.'s back

ab|ebben itr. V.; mit sein recede; abate

***abend** ⇒ **Abend** a

Abend /'a:bn̩t/ der; ~**s**, ~**e (a)** ▶ 240 | evening; **es wird** ~: evening is drawing in; **guten** ~! good evening; **eines [schönen]** ~**s** one evening; **am [frühen/späten]** ~: [early/late] in the evening; **am** ~ **vorher** od. **zuvor** the evening or night before; the previous evening; **bis zum [späten]** ~: until [late in the] evening; (als Frist) by [late] evening; **am selben/nächsten** ~: the same/following evening or night; **gegen** ~: towards evening; **zu** ~ **essen** have dinner; (allgemeiner) have one's evening meal; **heute/morgen/gestern** ~: this/tomorrow/yesterday evening; tonight/tomorrow night/last night; **Sonntag** ~: [on] Sunday evening or night; **was gibt es heute** ~ **[zu essen]?** what's for dinner/supper? s. auch **heilig** b; **Tag** a; **(b)** (Geselligkeit) evening; (Kultur~) soirée; **ein bunter** ~: a social [evening or night]

abend-, Abend-: ~**abitur** das 'Abitur' through evening classes; ~**an·zug** der dinner dress; evening suit; ~**blatt** das evening [news]paper; ~**brot** das evening meal; supper; **wann gibt es** ~**brot?** when's supper?; ~**dämmerung** die [evening] twilight; ~**essen** das dinner; ~**füllend** Adj. occupying a whole evening postpos., not pred.; **ein** ~**füllendes Programm** a full evening's programme; ~**gebet** das evening prayers pl.; (von Kindern) bedtime prayers pl.; ~**kasse** die box office (open on the evening of the performance); ~**kleid** das evening dress or gown; ~**kurs[us]** der evening class or course; ~**land** das; o. Pl. West; Occident (literary); ~**ländisch** /-lɛndɪʃ/ Adj. Western; Occidental (literary)

abendlich Adj.; nicht präd. evening; ‹quiet, coolness› of the evening; **die** ~**en Straßen der Stadt** the streets of the town at evening

Abend·mahl das; o. Pl. **(a)** (christl. Rel.) Communion; **das** ~ **nehmen** receive Communion; **(b)** (N. T.) Last Supper

Abend-: ~**mahl·zeit** die evening meal; ~**nach·richten** Pl. evening news sing.; ~**programm** das evening programmes pl.; ~**rot** das red glow of the sunset sky

abends Adv. ▶ 530 | in the evenings; **sechs Uhr** ~: six o'clock in the evening; **Montag** od. **montags** ~: [on] Monday evenings; **von morgens bis** ~: from morning to night; **spät** ~: late in the evening

Abend-: ~**schule** die night school; evening classes pl.; ~**schüler** der student at evening classes; ~**sonne** die evening sun; ~**stern** der evening star; ~**stunde** die evening hour; **in den frühen/späten** ~**stunden** early/late in the evening; ~**vorstellung** die evening performance; ~**zeitung** die ⇒ ~**blatt**

Abenteuer /'a:bntɔyɐ/ *das;* ~s, ~ **(a)** (auch fig.) adventure; **(b)** (Unternehmen) venture; **(c)** (Liebesaffäre) affair

abenteuerlich *Adj.* **(a)** (riskant) risky; hazardous; **(b)** (bizarr) bizarre

Abenteuer-: ~**roman** *der* adventure novel; ~**spielplatz** *der* adventure playground; ~**urlaub** *der* adventure holiday; **sie bieten** ~**urlaub an** they organize adventure holidays

Abenteurer /'a:bntɔyrɐ/ *der;* ~s, ~: adventurer

Abenteurerin *die;* ~, ~**nen** adventuress

aber /'a:bɐ/ **1** *Konj.* but; **wir** ~ ...: we, however, ...; ~ **trotzdem** but in spite of that; **oder** ~: or else; ~ **warum denn?** but why?; **das stimmt** ~ **nicht** but that's not right. **2** *Adv.* (veralt.: wieder); ~ **und abermals** again and again; time and again; **tausend und** ~ **tausend** thousands upon thousands. **3** *Partikel* **das ist** ~ **schön!** why, isn't that nice!; ~ **ja/nein!** why, yes/no! ~ **natürlich!** but *or* why of course!; **das ist** ~ **auch zu dumm** it's just 'too stupid *or* (Amer.) dumb; **du bist** ~ **groß!** aren't you tall!; ~, ~! now, now!

Aber·glaube[n] *der* **(a)** superstition; **(b)** (Vorurteil) myth

aber·gläubisch /-glɔybɪʃ/ *Adj.* superstitious

Aber·hunderte *Pl.* (geh.) hundreds [upon hundreds]

ab|erkennen *unr. tr. V.* jmdm. **ein Recht** ~: revoke sb.'s right; (Sport) **jmdm. den Sieg/Titel** ~: disallow sb.'s victory/strip sb. of his/her title

Ab·erkennung *die;* ~, ~**en** revocation; (Sport) **die** ~ **ihres Sieges/Titels** disallowing her victory/stripping her of her title

abermalig *Adj.; nicht präd.* renewed

abermals /'a:bɐma:ls/ *Adv.* once again; once more

ab|ernten *tr. V.* finish the harvesting of; finish harvesting *or* picking 〈fruit〉

Aber·tausende *Pl.* (geh.) thousands [upon thousands]

aber·witzig *Adj.* crazy

ab|essen *unr. tr. V.* **(a)** etw. **[von etw.]** ~: eat sth. off [sth.]; **(b)** (leer essen) clear 〈plate, table〉; **abgegessene Teller** empty plates

Abf. *Abk.* **Abfahrt** dep.

ab|fackeln *tr. V.* (Technik) flare off

ab|fahren 1 *unr. itr. V.; mit sein* **(a)** (wegfahren) leave; depart; **wo fährt der Zug nach Paris ab?** where does the Paris train leave from?; **(b)** (hinunterfahren) drive down; (Skisport) ski *or* go down; **(c)** (salopp) **auf jmdn./etw. [voll]** ~: be mad about sb./sth.; **(d)** (salopp) **jmdn.** ~ **lassen** tell sb. where he/she can go (sl.); **bei jmdm. ganz schön** ~: get absolutely nowhere with sb. (coll.). **2** *unr. tr. V.* **(a)** take away; **(b)** (abnutzen) wear out; **abgefahrene Reifen** worn tyres; **(c)** *auch mit sein* (entlangfahren) drive the whole length of 〈street, route〉; drive through 〈district〉

Ab·fahrt *die* **(a)** departure; **(b)** (Skisport) descent; (Strecke) run; **(c)** (Autobahn~) exit

abfahrt·bereit *Adj.* ready to go *or* leave

Abfahrts-: ~**lauf** *der* (Skisport) downhill [racing]; ~**läufer** *der* (Skisport) downhill racer

Abfahrt[s]·zeit *die* time of departure; departure time

Ab·fall *der* **(a)** rubbish, (Amer.) garbage *or* trash *no indef. art., no pl.;* (Fleisch~) offal *no indef. art., no pl.;* (Industrie~) waste *no indef. art.;* (auf der Straße) litter *no indef. art., no pl.;* **(b)** *o. Pl.* (Rückgang) drop 〈Gen., in + Dat. in〉

Abfall-: ~**beseitigung** *die* refuse disposal; (industriell) waste disposal; ~**eimer** *der* rubbish *or* waste bin; trash *or* garbage can (Amer.); (auf der Straße) litter bin; trash *or* litter basket *or* can (Amer.)

ab|fallen *unr. itr. V.; mit sein* **(a)** (ugs.) **wieviel fällt für jeden ab?** what will each person's share be?; **für dich wird auch eine Kleinigkeit** ~: you'll get something out of it too; **(b)** (herunterfallen) fall off; **von jmdm.** ~ (fig.) leave sb. **(c)** (sich lossagen) 〈country〉 secede; **vom Glauben/von jmdm.** ~: desert the faith/sb.; **(d)** (nachlassen) drop; **(e)** (bes. Sport: zurückfallen) drop *or* fall back; **(f)** (sich senken) 〈land, hillside, road〉 drop away; slope; **(g)** (im Vergleich) **gegenüber jmdm./etw.** *od.* **gegen jmdn./etw. stark** ~: be markedly inferior to sb./sth.

ab·fällig 1 *Adj.* disparaging; derogatory. **2** *adv.* **sich** ~ **über jmdn. äußern** make disparaging *or* derogatory remarks about sb.

Abfall-: ~**produkt** *das* (auch fig.) by-product; ~**verwertung** *die* recycling of waste

ab|fangen *unr. tr. V.* **(a)** intercept 〈agent, message, aircraft〉; **(b)** (auf-, anhalten) catch; **(c)** (abwehren) repel 〈charge, assault〉; ward off 〈blow, attack〉; (fig.) stop 〈development〉; cushion 〈impact〉; (unter Kontrolle bringen) get 〈vehicle, aircraft〉 under control

ab|färben *itr. V.* 〈colour, garment, etc.〉 run; **auf jmdn./etw.** ~ (fig.) rub off on sb./sth.

ab|fassen *tr. V.* write 〈report, letter, etc.〉; draw up 〈will〉

ab|fegen *tr. V.* **(a)** brush off; **etw. von etw.** ~: brush sth. off sth.; **(b)** (säubern) etw. ~: brush sth. clean

ab|feilen *tr. V.* **(a)** (entfernen) file off; **(b)** (verkürzen, glätten) file down

ab|fertigen *tr. V.* **(a)** handle, dispatch 〈mail〉; deal with 〈applicant, application〉; deal with, handle 〈passengers〉; serve 〈customer〉; clear 〈ship〉 for sailing; clear 〈aircraft〉 for take-off; clear 〈lorry〉 for departure; (kontrollieren) clear; check; **(b)** (ugs.: unfreundlich behandeln) **jmdn. [grob/ barsch]** ~: [roughly/rudely] turn sb. away

Ab·fertigung *die* ⇒ **abfertigen a:** handling; dispatching; serving; clearing for sailing/take-off/departure; (Kontrolle) clearance; checking

ab|feuern *tr. V.* fire; **Schüsse/eine Kanone [auf jmdn./etw.]** ~: fire shots/a cannon [at sb./sth.]

ab|finden 1 *unr. tr. V.* **jmdn. mit etw.** ~: compensate sb. with sth.; **seine Gläubiger** ~: settle with one's creditors; **er wurde großzügig abgefunden** he received a generous settlement. **2** *unr. refl. V.* **sich** ~: resign oneself; **sich mit etw.** ~: come to terms with sth.

Abfindung *die;* ~, ~**en (a)** (Summe) settlement; **eine** ~ **zahlen** make a settlement; **(b)** (Vorgang) (Entschädigung) compensation; (von Gläubigern) paying-off

Abfindungs·summe *die* ⇒ **Abfindung a**

ab|flachen *tr. V.* flatten [out]

ab|flauen *itr. V.; mit sein* die down; subside; 〈interest, conversation〉 flag; 〈business〉 become slack; **die Konjunktur flaut ab** the economy is running down

ab|fliegen 1 *unr. itr. V.; mit sein* 〈person〉 leave [by aeroplane]; 〈aircraft〉 take off; 〈bird〉 fly off *or* away; **die Maschine nach Brüssel fliegt um** 13^{30} **Uhr ab** the plane for Brussels leaves at 13.30. **2** *unr. tr. V.* fly over 〈district〉; fly along 〈road〉

ab|fließen *unr. itr. V.; mit sein* **(a)** flow off; (wegfließen) flow away; **aus etw.** ~: drain away from sth.; ~ **run off sth.; (b)** (sich leeren) empty

Ab·flug *der* departure

Abflug·zeit *die* departure time

Ab·fluss, ***Ab·fluß *der* **(a)** drain; (von Gewässern) outlet; (Rohr) drainpipe; (für Abwasser) waste-pipe; **(b)** *o. Pl.* (das Abfließen) draining away; **der** ~ **von Kapital ins Ausland** (fig.) the flow of capital abroad

Abfluss·rohr, ***Abfluß·rohr *das* outlet pipe

Ab·folge *die* sequence

ab|fragen *tr. V.* **(a)** test; **jmdn.** *od.* **jmdm. die Vokabeln** ~: test sb. on his/her vocabulary; **(b)** (DV) retrieve, read out 〈data〉; interrogate 〈measuring-instrument, store〉

ab|fressen *unr. tr. V.* **(a)** etw. **[von etw.]** ~: eat sth. off [sth.]; **(b)** (leer fressen) strip 〈tree, stem, etc.〉 bare

ab|frieren 1 *unr. itr. V.; mit sein* **die Ohren froren ihm ab** he lost his ears through frostbite. **2** *unr. refl. V.* **sich** (Dat.) **etw.** ~: lose sth. by frostbite; **sich** (Dat.) **einen** ~ (ugs.) freeze to death (coll.)

ab|frottieren *tr. V.* rub down [thoroughly]

ab|fühlen *tr. V.* feel

Abfuhr *die;* ~, ~**en (a)** removal; **(b)** jmdm. **eine** ~ **erteilen** rebuff sb.; turn sb. down; **sich eine** ~ **holen** be rebuffed *or* turned down

ab|führen 1 *tr. V.* **(a)** (nach Festnahme) take away; **(b)** (zahlen) pay out; pay 〈taxes〉; **(c)** *auch itr.* (abbringen) take away. **2** *itr. V.* (für Stuhlgang sorgen) be a laxative; have a laxative effect; **ein** ~**des Mittel** a laxative

Abführ·mittel *das* laxative; (stärker) purgative

Abfüll-: ~**anlage** *die* bottling/canning plant; ~**datum** *das* bottling/canning date

ab|füllen *tr. V.* fill ‹*sack, bottle, barrel*›; **Wein in Flaschen** ~: bottle wine; **Bier in Dosen** ~: can beer

ab|füttern *tr. V.* line ‹*jacket, coat*›

Ab·gabe *die* (a) handing in; (eines Briefes, Pakets, Telegramms) delivery; (eines Gesuchs, Antrags) submission; (b) (Steuer, Gebühr) tax; (auf Produkte) duty; (Gemeinde~) rate; (Beitrag) contribution; (c) (Ausstrahlung) release; emission; (d) (Sport: Abspiel) pass; (e) *o. Pl.* (das Abfeuern) firing; (f) (von Erklärungen) giving; (von Urteilen, Aussagen) making; (Stimm~) casting; (g) (Verkauf) selling; „~ **nur in Kisten**" 'sold only by the crate'

abgaben·frei 1 *Adj.* ‹*business, trade, product*› free from tax; (zollfrei) duty-free. **2** *adv.* without paying taxes

abgabe·pflichtig *Adj.* ‹*person, business, trade*› liable to tax; ‹*product*› subject to duty

Ab·gang *der* (a) leaving; departure; (Abfahrt) departure; (Theater) exit; (fig.) departure; **sich einen guten** ~ **verschaffen** (fig.) make a good exit; (b) (jmd., der ausscheidet) departure; (Schule) leaver; (c) (bes. Amtsspr.: Todesfall) death; (d) (Turnen) dismount; (e) *o. Pl.* (Ausscheidung) passing; (von Eiter, Würmern) discharge; (f) (Med.: Fehlgeburt) miscarriage; (g) *o. Pl.* (Absendung) dispatch; (h) *o. Pl.* (Kaufmannsspr.) **die Ware findet reißenden** ~: the product is a best seller

Abgangs·zeugnis *das* (Schulw.) ≈ leaving certificate

Ab·gas *das* exhaust; ~**e** exhaust fumes

abgas-, Abgas-: ~**entgiftung** *die* (Kfz-W.) emission control; ~**frei 1** *Adj.* exhaust-free ‹*engine*›; **2** *adv.* **das Auto fährt** ~**frei** the car produces no exhaust fumes; ~**katalysator** *der* (Kfz-W.) catalytic converter; ~**untersuchung** *die* (Kfz-W.) exhaust emission test

abgearbeitet *Adj.* work-worn ‹*hands*›

ab|geben 1 *unr. tr. V.* (a) (aushändigen) hand over; deliver ‹*letter, parcel, telegram*›; hand in, submit ‹*application*›; hand in ‹*school work*›; **etw. bei jmdm.** ~: deliver sth. *or* hand sth. over to sb.; **den Mantel an der Garderobe** ~: leave one's coat in the cloakroom; (b) *auch itr.* (abtreten) **jmdm. [etwas] von etw.** ~: let sb. have some of sth.; **den Vorsitz/die Spitze** ~: give up the chair/the leadership; **einen Punkt/Satz/eine Runde** ~ (Sport) drop a point/set/round; (c) (abfeuern) fire; (d) (ausstrahlen) emit ‹*radiation*›; radiate ‹*heat*›; give off ‹*gas*›; transmit ‹*radio message*›; (e) make ‹*judgement, statement*›; cast ‹*vote*›; **seine Stimme für jmdn.** ~: cast one's vote in favour of sb.; vote for sb.; (f) (fungieren als) make; **eine traurige Figur** ~: cut a sorry figure; (g) (verkaufen) sell; (zu niedrigem Preis) sell off; **gebrauchte Skier billig abzugeben** second-hand skis for sale cheap; (h) *auch itr.* (Sport: abspielen) pass. **2** *unr. refl. V.* (sich befassen) **sich mit jmdm./etw.** ~: spend time on sb./sth.; (geringschätzig) waste one's time on sb./sth.

ab·gebrannt *Adj.; nicht attr.* (ugs.) broke (coll.)

abgebrüht *Adj.* (ugs.) hardened

ab·gedroschen *Adj.* (ugs.) hackneyed; well-worn; trite

abgefeimt /ˈapgəfaimt/ *Adj.* infernally cunning ‹*villain, rogue*›; villainous ‹*scheme*›

ab·gegriffen *Adj.* (a) (abgenutzt) battered; (b) (fig.: abgedroschen) hackneyed; well-worn

abgehackt 1 *Adj.* clipped ‹*speech*›. **2** *adv.* ‹*speak*› in short bursts

ab·gehangen *Adj.* hung; **gut** ~**es Fleisch** well-hung meat

abgehärmt *Adj.* careworn; haggard

abgehärtet *Adj.* (körperlich) tough; (seelisch) callous

ab|gehen *unr. itr. V.; mit sein* (a) (sich entfernen) leave; go away *or* off; (Theater) exit; go off; (b) (ausscheiden) leave; **von der Schule** ~: leave school; (c) (abfahren) ‹*train, ship, bus*› leave, depart; (d) (abgeschickt werden) ‹*message, letter*› be sent [off]; (e) (abzweigen) branch off; (in andere Richtung) turn off; (f) (sich lösen) come off; ‹*spot, stain*› come out; ‹*avalanche*› come down; (g) (Turnen) dismount; (h) (abgerechnet werden) **von etw.** ~: have to be deducted from

*alte Schreibung (vgl. Hinweise auf S. xvi–xvii)

sth.; (i) (fehlen) **jmdm. geht etw. [völlig] ab** sb. is [totally] lacking in sth.; (j) **ihm ging einer ab** (derb) he shot his load (coarse)

abgehetzt *Adj.* exhausted; (außer Atem) breathless

abgekämpft *Adj.* worn out; exhausted

abgekartet *Adj.* (ugs.) pre-arranged; **von vornherein** ~: set up in advance; **eine** ~**e Sache** *od.* **ein** ~**es Spiel sein** be rigged in advance

abgeklärt *Adj.* serene

abgelagert *Adj.* mature ‹*wine*›; seasoned ‹*timber, tobacco*›; **gut** ~**es Holz** well-seasoned timber

ab·gelegen *Adj.* remote; (einsam) isolated; out-of-the-way ‹*district*›; (abgeschieden) secluded

ab|gelten *unr. tr. V.* satisfy, settle ‹*claim*›

abgemagert *Adj.* emaciated; wasted

ab·geneigt *Adj.* **einer Sache** (*Dat.*) ~ **sein** be averse to sth.; **[nicht]** ~ **sein, etw. zu tun** [not] be averse to doing sth.

abgenutzt *Adj.* worn ‹*tyre, chair, handle*›; well-used ‹*implement*›

Abgeordnete *der/die; adj. Dekl.* member [of parliament]; (z. B. in Frankreich) deputy

ab·gerissen *Adj.* ragged

Ab·gesandte *der/die* emissary

Ab·gesang *der* (a) (Abschied) **ein** ~ **auf etw.** (*Akk.*) a farewell to sth.; (b) (geh.: letztes Werk) swan-song

abgeschabt *Adj.* shabby; worn

ab·geschieden *Adj.* secluded; (abgelegen) isolated

ab·geschlagen *Adj.* (Sport) [well] beaten; ~ **auf dem neunten Tabellenplatz** in lowly ninth place

ab·geschlossen *Adj.* (a) (abgesondert) secluded; solitary; (b) (in sich geschlossen) enclosed; self-contained ‹*flat*›

abgeschmackt /ˈapgəʃmakt/ *Adj.* tasteless

ab·geschnitten *Adj.* isolated; **von der Außenwelt** ~: cut off from the outside world

ab·gesehen *Adv.:* ~ **von jmdm./etw.** apart from sb./sth.; ~ **davon, dass …:** apart from the fact that …

ab·gespannt *Adj.* weary; exhausted

ab·gestanden *Adj.* (a) (schal) flat; (b) (verbraucht) stale

ab·gestorben *Adj.* dead ‹*branch, tree*›; numb ‹*fingers, legs, etc.*›

abgestumpft *Adj.* apathetic and insensitive ‹*person*›; deadened ‹*conscience, perception*›

abgetakelt *Adj.* (salopp) faded

ab·getragen *Adj.* well-worn

ab·getreten *Adj.* worn down

abgewetzt *Adj.* well-worn; battered ‹*suitcase etc.*›

ab|gewinnen *unr. tr. V.* (a) **jmdm. etw.** ~: get sth. out of sb.; win sth. from sb.; **einer Sache** (*Dat.*) **etw.** ~: win *or* gain sth. from sth.; (b) (fig.) **ich kann ihm/dem nichts** ~: he/it does not do anything for me (coll.); *s. auch* **Geschmack a**

ab·gewogen *Adj.* carefully weighed; balanced ‹*judgement*›; carefully considered ‹*account*›

ab|gewöhnen 1 *tr. V.* **jmdm. etw.** ~: make sb. give up *or* stop sth. **2** *refl. V.* **sich** (*Dat.*) **etw.** ~: give up *or* stop sth.; **zum Abgewöhnen [sein]** (ugs.) [be] awful

abgezehrt *Adj.* emaciated

abgezirkelt *Adj.* measured out

ab|gießen *unr. tr. V.* pour away ‹*liquid*›; drain ‹*potatoes*›

Ab·glanz *der* distant echo; pale reflection

Ab·gott *der* idol

abgöttisch /ˈapgœtɪʃ/ **1** *Adj.* idolatrous. **2** *adv.* **jmdn.** ~ **verehren/lieben** idolize sb.

ab|graben *unr. tr. V.* dig out; *s. auch* **Wasser a**

ab|grasen *tr. V.* (a) graze away ‹*pasture*›; (b) (ugs.: absuchen) **etw. nach etw.** ~: comb *or* scour sth. for sth.

ab|grenzen *tr. V.* (a) bound; **etw. gegen** *od.* **von etw.** ~: separate sth. from sth.; (b) (unterscheiden) differentiate; distinguish; **sich von jmdm.** ~: differentiate oneself from sb.

Abgrenzung *die;* ~, ~**en** (a) boundary; (b) (Unterscheidung) differentiation

Ab·grund der (a) (Schlucht) abyss; chasm; (Abhang) precipice; (b) (fig. geh.) dark abyss; **die Abgründe der menschlichen Seele** the depths of the human soul

abgründig /'apɡrʏndɪç/ Adj. (geh.) inscrutable ‹smile›; hidden ‹meaning›; dark ‹secret›

abgrund·tief Adj. out and out

Ab·gruppierung die salary downgrading

ab|gucken (ugs.) **1** tr., auch itr. V. **[bei** od. **von] jmdm. etw.** ~: learn sth. by watching sb. **2** itr., auch tr. V. (abschreiben) **[bei jmdm.]** ~: copy [from sb.]; copy [sb. else's] work

Ab·guss, *Ab·guß der cast

ab|haben unr. tr. V. (ugs.) **etwas/ein Stück** usw. **[von etw.]** ~: have some/a piece etc. [of sth.]

ab|hacken tr. V. chop off

ab|haken tr. V. tick off; check off (Amer.)

ab|halten unr. tr. V. (a) **jmdn. etw. [von jmdm./etw.]** ~: keep sb./sth. off [sb./sth.]; (b) **jmdn. davon** ~, **etw. zu tun** stop sb. doing sth.; prevent sb. from doing sth.; (c) (durchführen) hold ‹elections, meeting, referendum›

ab|handeln tr. V. (a) **jmdm. etw.** ~: do a deal with sb. for sth.; (b) (darstellen) treat; deal with

abhanden /ap'handn̩/ in ~ **kommen** get lost; go astray; **etw. kommt jmdm.** ~: sb. loses sth.

Ab·handlung die treatise

Ab·hang der slope; incline

ab|hängen¹ unr. itr. V. **von jmdm./etw.** ~: depend on sb./sth.; **davon hängt sehr viel für mich ab** a lot depends on it for me

ab|hängen² **1** tr. V. (a) (abnehmen) take down; **ein Bild von der Wand** ~: take a picture [down] off the wall; (b) (abkuppeln) uncouple; (c) (ugs.: abschütteln) shake off ‹pursuer, competitor›. **2** itr. V. (den Hörer auflegen) hang up

abhängig /'aphɛŋɪç/ Adj. (a) **von jmdm./etw.** ~ **sein** (bedingt) depend on sb./sth.; (angewiesen) be dependent on sb./sth.; (b) (süchtig) addicted **(von** to); (c) (Sprachw.) indirect or reported ‹speech›; subordinate ‹clause›

Abhängigkeit die; ~, ~en (a) dependence; **in** ~ **von jmdm./etw. geraten** become dependent on sb./sth.; (b) (Sucht) addiction **(von** to)

Abhängigkeits·verhältnis das relationship of dependence **(zu** on)

ab|härten tr. V. harden

ab|hauen 1 unr. tr. V. (a) (abtrennen) chop off; (b) Prät. nur haute ab (abschlagen) knock off. **2** unr. itr. V.; mit sein; Prät. nur haute ab (salopp: verschwinden) beat it (sl.); **hau ab!** get lost! (sl.)

ab|heben 1 unr. tr., auch itr. V. (a) (abnehmen) lift off ‹lid, cover, etc.›; **[den Hörer]** ~: answer [the telephone]; (b) (Kartenspiel) (teilen) cut [the pack]; (nehmen) draw ‹card›; (c) (von einem Konto) withdraw ‹money›. **2** unr. itr. V. (a) ‹balloon› rise; ‹aircraft, bird› take off; ‹rocket› lift off. **3** unr. refl. V. stand out; contrast; **sich von** od. **gegen etw./von jmdm.** ~: stand out against or contrast with sth./sb.

ab|heften tr. V. file

ab|helfen unr. itr. V. **einem Missstand** ~: put an end to an abuse; **dem ist leicht abzuhelfen** that is easily remedied

ab|hetzen 1 tr. V. ride ‹horse etc.› to exhaustion. **2** refl. V. rush or dash [around]

Ab·hilfe die; o. Pl. action to improve matters; ~ **schaffen** find a remedy; put things right

ab|hobeln tr. V. plane down

ab|holen tr. V. collect, pick up ‹thing›; pick up, fetch ‹person›; **ich hole Sie am Bahnhof ab** I'll pick you up at the station

Abholer der; ~s, ~ (Postw.) addressee who collects mail from the post office instead of having it delivered

ab|holzen tr. V. fell ‹trees›; clear ‹area› [of trees]

ab|horchen tr. V. sound ‹chest, lungs›; **jmdn.** ~: sound sb.'s chest/lungs

ab|hören tr. V. (a) (abfragen) **jmdn.** od. **jmdn. Vokabeln** ~: test sb.'s vocabulary [orally]; (b) (heimlich anhören) listen to; (c) (überwachen) tap ‹telephone, telephone

conversation›; bug (coll.) ‹conversation, premises›; **jmdn.** ~: tap sb.'s telephone; (d) ⇒ **abhorchen**

Abhör·gerät das listening device; bug (coll.)

abhör·sicher Adj. bug-proof (coll.); tap-proof ‹telephone›

ab|hungern tr. V. take off, lose ‹weight›

Abi /'abi/ das; ~s, ~s (Schülerspr.) ⇒ **Abitur**

Abitur /abi'tuːɐ̯/ das; ~s, ~e Abitur (school-leaving examination at grammar school needed for entry to higher education); ≈ A levels (Brit.); **sein** od. **das** ~ **machen** do or take one's Abitur

Abiturient /abituˈri̯ɛnt/ der; ~en, ~en, **Abiturientin** die; ~, ~nen sb. who is taking/has passed the 'Abitur'

Abitur·zeugnis das Abitur certificate

ab|jagen tr. V. **jmdm. etw.** ~: finally get sth. away from sb.

Abk. Abk. Abkürzung abbr.

ab|kämmen tr. V. (absuchen) comb, scour **(nach** for)

ab|kanzeln tr. V. (ugs.) **jmdn.** ~: give sb. a dressing down; reprimand sb.

ab|kapseln tr. V. encapsulate; **sich gegen die Umwelt** ~ (fig.) isolate oneself from one's surroundings

ab|kassieren (ugs. abwertend) **1** itr. V. rake it in (coll.); **bei jmdm.** ~: fleece sb. **2** tr. V. fleece ‹person›; rake in (coll.) ‹money›

ab|kaufen tr. V. (a) **jmdm. etw.** ~: buy sth. from sb.; (b) (ugs.: glauben) **das kaufe ich dir nicht ab** I'm not buying that story (coll.)

ab|kehren¹ tr. V. turn away; **sich [von jmdm./etw.]** ~: turn away [from sb./sth.]; **die uns abgekehrte Seite des Mondes/des Schiffes** the far side of the moon/the ship

ab|kehren² tr. V. ⇒ **abfegen**

ab|kippen 1 tr., auch itr. V. (abladen) tip out; dump ‹refuse›. **2** itr. V.; mit sein (herunterfallen) tip over

ab|klappern tr. V. (ugs.) trudge round ‹town, district›; **alle Läden nach etw.** ~: do the rounds of all the shops looking for sth.

ab|klären tr. V. clear up; sort out (coll.); s. auch **abgeklärt 2**

Ab·klatsch der (abwertend) pale imitation; poor copy

ab|klemmen tr. V. (a) (zusammenpressen) clamp; (b) (lösen) disconnect

ab|klingen unr. itr. V.; mit sein (a) (leiser werden) grow fainter; (b) (nachlassen) subside; die away

ab|klopfen tr. V. (a) knock or tap off; **jmdm. etw. [von der Jacke]** ~: tap sth. off sb.['s jacket]; (b) (säubern) knock/tap the dirt/snow/crumbs etc. off; **sich** (Dat.) **die Hände** ~: clap one's hands together to knock the flour/powder etc. off; (c) (untersuchen) tap

ab|knallen tr. V. (salopp) shoot down; gun down

ab|knicken 1 tr. V. (a) (abbrechen) snap or break off; (b) (knicken) bend. **2** itr. V.; mit sein (a) (abbrechen) snap; break; (b) (einknicken) bend over

ab|knöpfen tr. V. (a) unbutton; (b) (salopp) **jmdm. Geld** ~: get money out of sb.

ab|knutschen tr. V. (ugs.) (a) kiss and fondle; (b) (sexuell) **jmdn.** ~/sich mit jmdm. ~: smooch (coll.) or (sl.) neck with sb.; **sich** ~: smooch (coll.); neck (coll.)

ab|kochen 1 tr. V. boil. **2** itr. V. (im Freien kochen) cook in the open air

ab|kommandieren tr. V. detail; (fig.) detail; send; **jmdn. zum Dienst/zu einer Einheit** ~: detail sb. for duty/to a unit; **jmdn. an die Front** ~: send sb. to the front

ab|kommen unr. itr. V.; mit sein (a) **vom Weg** ~: lose one's way; **vom Kurs** ~: go off course; **von der Fahrbahn** ~: leave the road; (b) (abschweifen) digress; **vom Thema** ~: stray from the topic; digress; (c) **von etw.** ~ (etw. aufgeben) give sth. up; **von einem Plan** ~: abandon or give up a plan; (d) (aus der Mode, außer Gebrauch kommen) ‹method, clothes› go out of fashion; ‹tradition› disappear

Ab·kommen das; ~s, ~: agreement; **ein** ~ **[über etw.** (Akk.)**] schließen** come to an agreement [on sth.]

abkömmlich /'apkœmlɪç/ Adj. free; available
ab|können unr. tr. V. (nordd.: mögen) stand; (vertragen) take
ab|koppeln tr. V. uncouple
ab|kratzen 1 tr. V. (a) (entfernen) (mit den Fingern) scratch off; (mit einem Werkzeug) scrape off; (b) (säubern) scrape [clean]. 2 itr. V.; mit sein (derb) croak (sl.); snuff it (sl.)
ab|kriegen tr. V. (ugs.) ⇒ **abbekommen**
ab|kühlen 1 tr. V. cool down; jmds. Eifer ~ (fig.) dampen sb.'s ardour; jmdn. ~ (fig.) cool sb. off. 2 itr. V.; meist mit sein cool down; get cooler; es hat stark abgekühlt (Met.) it has become a lot cooler. 3 refl. V. cool down; get cooler
Ab·kühlung die cooling
ab|kuppeln tr. V. ⇒ **abkoppeln**
ab|kürzen tr., itr. V. (a) (räumlich) shorten; den Weg ~: take a shorter route; (b) (zeitlich) cut short; (c) (kürzer schreiben) abbreviate (mit to)
Ab·kürzung die (a) (Weg) short cut; (b) (Wort) abbreviation; (c) (das Abkürzen) cutting short; zur ~ des Verfahrens to shorten the procedure
Abkürzungs·verzeichnis das list of abbreviations
ab|küssen tr. V. cover with kisses
ab|lachen itr. V. (salopp) laugh
ab|laden unr. tr., itr. V. (a) unload, offload ⟨case, sack, barrel, goods, vehicle⟩; dump, unload ⟨gravel, sand, rubble⟩; seine Sorgen bei jmdm. ~ (fig.) unburden oneself to sb.
Ab·lage die (a) (Vorrichtung) storage place; (b) (Bürow.) filing; (c) (schweiz.) ⇒ **Annahmestelle, Zweigstelle**
ab|lagern 1 tr. V. (a) (absetzen) deposit; (b) (deponieren) dump. 2 refl. V. be deposited
Ab·lagerung die (a) deposit; (b) (das Absetzen) deposition; (c) (das Deponieren) dumping
Ablass, *Ablaß /'aplas/ der; Ablasses, Ablässe (kath. Rel.) indulgence
ab|lassen 1 unr. tr. V. (a) (ablaufen lassen) let out (aus of); (b) (ausströmen lassen) let off ⟨steam⟩; let out ⟨air⟩; (c) (leeren) empty. 2 unr. itr. V. (a) (aufgeben) von etw. ~: give sth. up; (b) von jmdm./etw. ~: leave sb./sth. alone
Ablativ /'ablati:f/ der; ~s, ~e (Sprachw.) ablative
Ab·lauf der (a) (Verlauf) course; der ~ der Ereignisse the course of events; (b) (einer Veranstaltung) passing or going off; (c) o. Pl. (Ende) nach ~ eines Jahres after a year; nach ~ einer Frist at the end of a period of time
ab|laufen 1 unr. itr. V.; mit sein (a) (abfließen) flow away; (herausfließen) run or flow out; (b) (herabfließen) run down; von/an etw. (Dat.) ~: run off sth.; (c) (verlaufen) pass or go off; gut abgelaufen sein have gone or passed off well; (d) ⟨alarm clock⟩ run down; ⟨parking meter⟩ expire; (e) ⟨period, contract, passport⟩ expire; (f) ~ lassen play ⟨tape⟩; run ⟨film⟩ through. 2 unr. tr. V. (a) auch mit sein (entlanglaufen) walk all along; go over ⟨area⟩ on foot; (schnell) run all along; (b) (abnutzen) wear down
Ab·leben das; o. Pl. (geh.) decease; demise
ab|lecken tr. V. (a) lick off; (b) (säubern) lick clean; sich (Dat.) die Finger ~: lick one's fingers
ab|legen 1 tr. V. (a) (niederlegen) lay or put down; lay ⟨egg⟩; (b) (Bürow.) file; (c) (nicht mehr tragen) stop wearing; abgelegte Kleidung old clothes pl.; cast-offs pl.; (d) (aufgeben) give up ⟨habit⟩; lose ⟨shyness⟩; put aside ⟨arrogance⟩; (e) (machen, leisten) swear ⟨oath⟩; sit ⟨examination⟩; make ⟨confession⟩; s. auch **Bekenntnis a; Rechenschaft.** 2 tr., itr. V. (a) (ausziehen) take off; möchten Sie ~? would you like to take your coat off?; (b) (Kartenspiel) (abwerfen) discard; (auflegen) put down. 3 itr. V. (Seemannsspr.: losfahren) [vom Kai] ~: cast off
Ableger der; ~s, ~ (a) (Bot.) layer; (b) (Steckling) cutting; (fig.: Filiale) offshoot
ab|lehnen 1 tr. V. (a) (zurückweisen) decline; decline, turn down ⟨money, invitation, position⟩; reject ⟨suggestion, applicant⟩; (b) (nicht genehmigen) turn down; reject; reject, throw out ⟨bill⟩; (c) (verweigern) es ~, etw. zu tun refuse to do sth.; (d) (missbilligen) disapprove of; reject. 2 itr. V.

decline; sie haben ohne Begründung abgelehnt (nicht genehmigt) they rejected it/them without giving any reason
ablehnend 1 Adj. negative ⟨reply, attitude⟩; ein ~er Bescheid a rejection. 2 adv. einer Sache (Dat.) ~ gegenüberstehen take a negative view of sth.; sich ~ zu etw. äußern voice one's opposition to sth.
Ablehnung die; ~, ~en (a) (Zurückweisung) rejection; auf ~ stoßen meet with opposition; (b) (Missbilligung) disapproval; auf ~ stoßen meet with disapproval
ab|leiten 1 tr. V. (a) divert; (b) (herleiten; auch Sprachw., Math.) etw. aus/von etw. ~: derive sth. from sth.; (c) (Math.: differenzieren) differentiate ⟨function⟩. 2 refl. V. (sich herleiten) sich aus/von etw. ~: derive or be derived from sth.
Ab·leitung die (a) (das Ableiten; auch Math., Sprachw.) derivation; (b) (Sprachw.: Wort; Math.: Ergebnis des Differenzierens) derivative
ab|lenken 1 tr. V. (a) (weglenken) deflect; den Verdacht von sich ~ (fig.) divert suspicion from oneself; (b) auch itr. (abbringen) jmdn. von etw. ~: distract sb. from sth.; alles, was ablenkt everything that is distracting; (c) auch itr. (zerstreuen) divert; das lenkt dich davon ab that'll take your mind off it. 2 itr. V. [vom Thema] ~: change the subject
Ab·lenkung die (a) (Richtungsänderung) deflection; (b) (Störung) distraction; (c) (Zerstreuung) diversion
Ablenkungs·manöver das diversion[ary tactic]
ab|lesen¹ unr. tr. V. (a) pick off; (b) (säubern) pick clean; groom ⟨coat⟩
ab|lesen² 1 unr. tr., itr. V. (a) read ⟨speech, lecture⟩; werden Sie frei sprechen oder ~? will you be talking from notes or reading your speech?; (b) (feststellen, prüfen) check ⟨time, speed, temperature⟩; [das Gas/den Strom] ~: read the gas/electricity meter; die Temperatur auf dem od. am Thermometer ~: read off the temperature on the thermometer; das Thermometer/den Tacho ~: read the thermometer/speedo. 2 unr. tr. V. (erkennen) see; etw. an etw. (Dat.) ~: see sth. from sth.; jmdm. jeden Wunsch von den Augen ~: read sb.'s every wish in his/her eyes
ab|leugnen tr. V. deny
ab|lichten tr. V. (a) (fotokopieren) photocopy; (b) (fotografieren) take a photograph of
Ab·lichtung die (a) o. Pl. (das Fotografieren) photographing; (das Fotokopieren) photocopying; er ist mit der ~ der Beweisstücke fertig he has finished photographing/photocopying the evidence; (b) (Fotokopie) photocopy
ab|liefern tr. V. deliver ⟨goods⟩; hand in ⟨manuscript, examination paper, weapon, etc.⟩; (fig. ugs.) take/bring ⟨person⟩ (in/auf + Dat., bei to)
ab|löschen tr. V. (a) (trocknen) blot ⟨ink, letter, etc.⟩; (b) (abwischen) wipe ⟨blackboard⟩; wipe out ⟨writing⟩
ab|lösen 1 tr. V. (a) relieve; take over from; (ersetzen) replace; sich od. einander ~: take turns; (b) (lösen) etw. [von etw.] ~: get sth. off [sth.]; remove sth. [from sth.]; (c) (verhüll.: entlassen) remove from office. 2 refl. V. (sich lösen) ⟨retina⟩ become detached; sich von etw. ~: come off sth.
Ablöse·summe die (Sport) transfer fee
Ab·lösung die (a) (eines Postens) changing; (Ersetzung) replacement; ich schicke Ihnen jemanden zur ~: I'll send someone to relieve you; (b) (Ersatz) relief; (c) (der Netzhaut) detachment; (d) (verhüll.: Entlassung) removal
ab|luchsen /'aploksn/ tr. V. (salopp) jmdm. etw. ~: get or (sl.) wangle sth. out of sb.
Ab·luft die vitiated air
ab|lutschen tr. V. (a) etw. [von etw.] ~: suck sth. off [sth.]; (b) (säubern) suck clean; ein abgelutschter Bonbon a half-sucked sweet
ab|machen tr. V. (a) (ugs.) take off; take down ⟨sign, rope⟩; etw. von etw. ~: take sth. off sth.; (b) (vereinbaren) agree; arrange; abgemacht, wir kommen mit! all right, we'll come; (c) (klären) sort out; das muss er mit sich selbst ~: that's something he'll have to sort out by himself

---

*alte Schreibung (vgl. Hinweise auf S. xvi–xvii)

Abmachung *die;* ~, ~**en** agreement; arrangement; **eine** ~ [**mit jmdm.**] **treffen** come to an agreement *or* arrangement [with sb.]

ab|magern *itr. V.; mit sein* become thin; (absichtlich) slim; **bis auf die Knochen** ~: become a mere skeleton

Abmagerungs·kur *die* reducing diet; **eine** ~ **machen** go on a diet

ab|mähen *tr. V.* mow

ab|mahnen *tr. V.* ⇒ **verwarnen**

Ab·mahnung *die* ⇒ **Verwarnung**

ab|malen *tr. V.* paint a picture of (**aus, von** from)

Ab·marsch *der* departure

abmarsch·bereit *Adj.* ready to depart; (Milit.) ready to march

ab|marschieren *itr. V.; mit sein* depart; (Milit.) march off

ab|melden *tr. V.* (**a**) **sich/jmdn.** ~: report that one/sb. is leaving; (bei Wegzug) *notify the authorities that one/sb. is moving from an address;* **sich** [**bei jmdm.**] **vom Dienst** ~: report absent from duty [to sb.]; (**b**) **ein Auto** ~: cancel a car's registration; (**c**) (ugs.) [**bei jmdm.**] **abgemeldet sein** no longer be of interest [to sb.]; **der ist jetzt bei mir abgemeldet** I want nothing more to do with him

Ab·meldung *die* (**a**) (beim Weggehen) report that one is leaving; (**b**) (beim Wegzug) *registration of a move with the authorities at one's old address;* (**c**) **die** ~ **eines Autos** the cancellation of a car's registration

ab|messen *unr. tr. V.* measure; (fig.) measure; assess

Ab·messung *die meist Pl.* (Dimension) dimension; measurement

ab|mildern *tr. V.* (**a**) break, cushion ‹*fall, impact*›; (**b**) (fig.: abschwächen) tone down; take the edge off

Ab·moderation *die* (**a**) *o. Pl.* (das Abmoderieren) signing-off; **sie ist gerade bei der** ~: she is just signing off; (**b**) (Text, Wortlaut) sign-off; **sie hat sich** (*Dat.*) **eine witzige** ~ **einfallen lassen** she found something witty to sign off with

ab|moderieren *tr. V.* sign off at the end of ‹*programme, show*›

ab|montieren *tr. V.* take off, remove ‹*part, wheel*›; dismantle ‹*machine, equipment*›

ab|mühen *refl. V.* **sich** [**mit jmdm./etw.**] ~: toil [for sb.'s benefit/with sth.]; **sie mühte sich mit dem schweren Koffer ab** she struggled with the heavy suitcase

ab|murksen /-mʊrksn̩/ *tr. V.* (salopp) do in (sl.)

ab·mustern (Seemannsspr.) **1** *tr. V.* (entlassen) discharge. **2** *itr. V.* sign off; **von einem Schiff** ~: leave a ship

ab|nagen *tr. V.* **etw.** [**von etw.**] ~: gnaw sth. off [sth.]; **einen Knochen** ~: gnaw a bone

Abnahme /ˈapnɑːmə/ *die;* ~, ~**n** (**a**) (das Entfernen) removal; (**b**) (Verminderung) decrease; decline; (**c**) (Kauf) purchasing; **bei** ~ **größerer Mengen** when large quantities are purchased; (**d**) (Prüfung) (einer Strecke, eines Gebäudes) inspection and approval; (eines Fahrzeugs) testing and passing; (Freigabe) passing

Abnahme·garantie *die* guaranteed purchase; firm order

ab|nehmen 1 *unr. tr. V.* (**a**) (entfernen) take off; remove; take down ‹*picture, curtain, lamp*›; **jmdm. das Bein** ~: take sb.'s leg off; (**b**) (übernehmen) take; **jmdm. den Koffer** ~: take sb.'s suitcase [from him/her]; **kann/darf ich Ihnen etwas** ~? can/may I carry something for you?; **jmdm. seine Sorgen** ~: relieve sb. of his/her worries; (**c**) (entgegennehmen) **jmdm. ein Versprechen/einen Eid** ~: make sb. give a promise/swear an oath; **jmdm. die Beichte** ~: hear sb.'s confession; **eine Prüfung** ~: conduct an examination; (**d**) (prüfen) inspect and approve; test and pass ‹*vehicle*›; (**e**) (wegnehmen) take away ‹*driving licence, passport*›; **jmdm. etw.** ~: take sth. off sb.; (**f**) (abverlangen) **jmdm. etw.** ~: charge sb. sth.; (**g**) (abkaufen) **jmdm. etw.** ~: buy sth. from sb.; (**h**) (ugs.: glauben) **das nehme ich dir/ihm** *usw.* **nicht ab** I won't buy that (coll.); (**i**) (beim Telefon) pick up ‹*receiver*›; answer ‹*telephone*›; (**j**) *auch itr.* (Handarb.) decrease. **2** *unr. itr. V.* (**a**) (ans Telefon gehen) answer the telephone; **es nimmt niemand ab**

there is no answer; (**b**) ▶ **228**] (Gewicht verlieren) lose weight; **sechs Kilo** ~: lose six kilos; (**c**) (sich verringern) decrease; drop; ‹*attention, interest*› flag; ‹*brightness*› diminish; ‹*moon*› wane; **wir haben** ~**den Mond** there is a waning moon

Abnehmer *der;* ~**s**, ~: (**a**) (einer Ware) buyer; (**b**) (eines Geschenks) **wir haben dafür einen** ~ **gefunden** we found somebody willing to take it; **unser alter Kühlschrank hat einen dankbaren** ~ **gefunden** we found somebody who was glad to have our old fridge; **das wird sicher einen dankbaren** ~ **finden** somebody will be glad of it

Ab·neigung *die* dislike, aversion (**gegen** for)

ab|nicken *tr. V.* (ugs.) **etw.** ~: nod sth. through; let sth. through on the nod

abnorm /apˈnɔrm/ **1** *Adj.* abnormal. **2** *adv.* abnormally

ab|nutzen, (landsch.:) **ab|nützen 1** *tr. V.* wear out. **2** *refl. V.* wear out; become worn; **das Material nutzt sich rasch ab** the material wears very quickly

Ab·nutzung, (landsch.:) **Abnützung** *die;* ~: wear [and tear] *no indef. art.*

Abonnement /abɔnəˈmãː/ *das;* ~**s**, ~**s** subscription (*Gen.* to); (Theater) subscription ticket

Abonnent /abɔˈnɛnt/ *der;* ~**en**, ~**en** subscriber (*Gen.* to); (Theater) season ticket holder

abonnieren /abɔˈniːrən/ **1** *tr. V.* subscribe to; (Theater) get a season ticket for. **2** *itr. V.* (bes. schweiz.) **abonniert sein auf** (+ *Akk.*) have a subscription to ‹*newspaper, magazine, concerts*›; (Theater) have a season ticket for; (fig.) get as a matter of course

ab|ordnen *tr. V.* send; **jmdn. als Delegierten** ~: delegate sb.; **jmdn. zu einer Konferenz** ~: delegate sb. to a conference

Ab·ordnung *die* delegation

Aboriginal /ɛbəˈrɪdʒɪnəl/ *der;* ~**s**, ~**s** Aboriginal

Aborigine /ɛbəˈrɪdʒiniː/ *der;* ~**s**, ~**s** Aborigine

Abort[1] /aˈbɔrt/ *der;* ~[**e**]**s**, ~**e** (veralt., noch fachspr.) lavatory

Abort[2] *der;* ~**s**, ~**e** (Med.) (**a**) (Fehlgeburt) miscarriage; (**b**) (Abtreibung) abortion

ab|packen *tr. V.* pack; wrap ‹*bread*›; **abgepacktes Obst** packaged fruit

ab|passen *tr. V.* (**a**) (abwarten) wait for; (**b**) (aufhalten) catch

ab|pausen *tr. V.* trace

ab|perlen *itr. V.; mit sein* **von etw.** ~: roll off sth.

ab|pfeifen (Sport) **1** *unr. itr. V.* blow the whistle. **2** *unr. tr. V.* (**a**) (unterbrechen) [blow the whistle to] stop; (**b**) (beenden) blow the whistle for the end of ‹*match, game, half*›

Ab·pfiff *der* (Sport) final whistle; (Halbzeit~) half-time whistle

ab|pflücken *tr. V.* pick

ab|placken (ugs.), **ab|plagen** *refl. V.* slave away; flog oneself to death (coll.); **sich mit etw./jmdm.** ~: slave away at sth./for sb.'s benefit

ab|platzen *itr. V.; mit sein* ‹*lacquer, enamel, plaster*› flake off; ‹*button*› fly off

ab|prallen *itr. V.; mit sein* rebound; bounce off; ‹*missile*› ricochet; **an** *od.* **von etw.** (*Dat.*) ~: rebound/ricochet off sth.; **an jmdm.** ~ (fig.) bounce off sb.

Ab·produkt *das* waste product

ab|pumpen *tr. V.* pump out; extract ‹*milk*› by breast-pump

ab|putzen *tr. V.* (ugs.) (**a**) wipe; **jmdm./sich das Gesicht** *usw.* ~: clean sb.'s/one's face *etc.*; (**b**) (entfernen) **etw. von jmdm./etw.** ~: wipe sth. off sb./sth.

ab|quälen *refl. V.* **sich** [**mit etw.**] ~: struggle [with sth.]; **sich** (*Dat.*) **einen Brief** ~ (ugs.) force oneself to write a letter

ab|quetschen *tr. V.* **jmdm. einen Arm/ein Bein** ~: crush sb.'s arm/leg

ab|rackern *refl. V.* (ugs.) slave [away]; flog oneself to death (coll.); **sich mit etw.** ~: slave away at sth.

Abrakadabra /aːbrakaˈdaːbra/ *das;* ~s abracadabra

ab|rasieren *tr. V.* shave off; **jmdm./sich den Bart** ~: shave off sb.'s/one's beard

ab|raten *unr. itr., tr. V.* **jmdm. von etw.** ~: advise sb. against sth.; **jmdm. [davon]** ~, **etw. zu tun** advise sb. not to do sth. *or* against doing sth.

Ab·raum *der; o. Pl.* (Bergbau) overburden

ab|räumen *tr. V.* (a) clear away; (b) (leer machen) clear ⟨*table*⟩

ab|rauschen *itr. V.; mit sein* (ugs.) (schnell) rush off; (auffällig) sweep off

ab|reagieren 1 *tr. V.* work off; **seine Wut an jmdm.** ~: take one's anger out on sb. 2 *refl. V.* work off one's feelings

ab|rechnen 1 *itr. V.* (a) cash up; (b) **mit jmdm.** ~ (fig.) call sb. to account. 2 *tr. V.* (a) **die Kasse** ~: reckon up the till; total the cash *or* register (Amer.); **seine Spesen** ~: claim one's expenses; (b) (abziehen) deduct

Ab·rechnung *die* (a) (Schlussrechnung) cashing up *no art.;* **die Kellnerin machte die** ~: the waitress was cashing up; (b) (Aufstellung) statement; (Bilanz) balance; (Dokument) balance sheet; (c) (Vergeltung) reckoning; (d) (Abzug) deduction; **nach** ~ **der Unkosten** after deducting expenses

Ab·rede *die* (a) arrangement; agreement; (b) **etw. in** ~ **stellen** deny sth.

ab|regen *refl. V.* (ugs.) calm down; **reg dich ab!** cool it! (coll.); calm down!

ab|reiben *unr. tr. V.* (a) rub off; **etw. von etw.** ~: rub sth. off sth.; (b) (säubern) rub; **[sich** *(Dat.)*] **die Hände an der Hose** ~: rub one's hands on one's trousers; (c) (frottieren) rub down

Ab·reibung *die* (ugs.: Prügel) hiding (coll.); licking (Amer. coll.)

Ab·reise *die* departure (**nach** for); **bei meiner** ~ **when I left/leave**

ab|reisen *itr. V.; mit sein* leave (**nach** for)

ab|reißen 1 *unr. tr. V.* (a) (entfernen) tear off; tear down ⟨*poster, notice*⟩; pull off ⟨*button*⟩; break off ⟨*thread*⟩; *s. auch* **Kopf a**; (b) (niederreißen) demolish, pull down ⟨*building*⟩. 2 *unr. itr. V.; mit sein* (a) (sich lösen) fly off; ⟨*shoelace*⟩ break off; (b) (aufhören) come to an end; ⟨*connection, contact*⟩ be broken off

Abreiß·kalender *der* tear-off calendar

ab|richten *tr. V.* train

ab|riegeln *tr., itr. V.* (a) (zusperren) **[die Tür]** ~: bolt the door; (b) (absperren) seal *or* cordon off ⟨*area*⟩

ab|ringen *unr. tr. V.* **jmdm. etw.** ~: extract sth. from sb.; **sich** *(Dat.)* **ein Lächeln** ~: force a smile

Ab·riss, *Ab·riß *der* (a) *o. Pl.:* ⇒ **abreißen 1 b**: demolition; pulling down; (b) (knappe Darstellung) outline

Abriss·birne, *Abriß·birne *die* demolition ball; wrecker's ball; **die** ~ **kommt im Herbst** they're going to start demolition in autumn; **das Haus ist längst der** ~ **zum Opfer gefallen** they pulled the building down ages ago

ab|rollen 1 *tr. V.* unwind; **sich** ~: unwind [itself]. 2 *itr. V.; mit sein* (a) unwind [itself]; (b) (vonstatten gehen) go off; ⟨*events*⟩ unfold

ab|rücken 1 *tr. V.* (wegschieben) move away. 2 *itr. V.; mit sein* (a) move away; **von jmdm./etw.** ~: move away from sb./sth.; (b) (Milit.) move out; (c) (ugs.: sich entfernen) clear out (coll.)

Ab·ruf *der* (a) **auf** ~: on call; **sich auf** ~ **bereithalten** be on call; (b) (Kaufmannsspr.) request for delivery; **etw. auf** ~ **kaufen** buy sth. on call purchase

abrufbar *Adj.* (a) (DV) retrievable; (b) (Finanzw.) withdrawable

abruf·bereit *Adj.* (a) on call *postpos.;* (b) (Kaufmannsspr.) ready for delivery on demand *postpos.*

ab|rufen *unr. tr. V.* (a) summon, call ⟨*person*⟩; **er wurde ins Jenseits/aus diesem Leben abgerufen** (geh. verhüll.) he was taken from us; (b) (DV) retrieve; (c) (Kaufmannsspr.)

etw. ~: ask for sth. to be delivered; (d) (Finanzw.) withdraw

ab|runden *tr. V.* (a) round off; **abgerundete Ecken** rounded corners; (b) (auf eine runde Zahl bringen) round up/down (**auf** + *Akk.* to); **etw. nach oben/unten** ~: round sth. up/down; **ein Betrag von abgerundet 27,50 Mark** a rounded [up/down] sum of 27.50 marks; (c) (vervollkommnen) round off; complete

Ab·rundung *die* (a) rounding off; (b) (von Zahlen) rounding up/down; (c) (Vervollkommnung) rounding off

ab|rupfen *tr. V.* pull off

abrupt /apˈrʊpt/ 1 *Adj.* abrupt. 2 *adv.* abruptly

ab|rüsten *itr., tr. V.* disarm

Ab·rüstung *die;* ~: disarmament

ab|rutschen *itr. V.; mit sein* (a) (abgleiten) slip; **von etw.** ~: slip off sth.; **sie ist mit dem Messer abgerutscht** her knife slipped; (b) (nach unten rutschen) slide down; ⟨*earth*⟩ subside; ⟨*snow*⟩ give way; (fig.) ⟨*pupil, competitor, etc.*⟩ slip (**auf** + *Akk.* to)

Abs. *Abk.* (a) **Absatz c** para; (b) **Absender**

ABS *Abk.* **Antiblockiersystem**

ab|säbeln *tr. V.* (ugs.) hack off

ab·sacken *itr. V.; mit sein* (ugs.) (a) fall; ⟨*ground*⟩ subside; ⟨*aircraft*⟩ lose altitude; (b) (fig.) go downhill

Ab·sage *die* (a) (auf eine Einladung) refusal; (auf eine Bewerbung) rejection; **jmdm. eine** ~ **erteilen** reject sb.; (b) (Rundf.) closing announcement

ab|sagen 1 *tr. V.* cancel; withdraw ⟨*participation, cooperation*⟩. 2 *itr. V.* (a) **jmdm.** ~: tell sb. one cannot come; put sb. off (coll.); **telefonisch** ~: ring to say one cannot come (b) **dem Bewerber wurde abgesagt** the applicant was rejected

ab|sägen *tr. V.* (a) saw off; (b) (ugs.) **jmdn.** ~: get rid of sb.

ab|sahnen (ugs.) 1 *itr. V.* make a killing (coll.). 2 *tr. V.* **100 000 Mark** ~: pocket 100,000 marks

Ab·satz *der* (a) (am Schuh) heel; (b) (Textunterbrechung) break; **einen** ~ **machen** make a break; start a new line; (c) (Abschnitt) paragraph; (d) (Kaufmannsspr.) sales *pl.;* ~ **finden** sell; *s. auch* **reißend**; (e) (einer Innentreppe) landing; (zwischen Geschossen) half-landing; (f) (Mauer~) ledge

absatz-, Absatz-: ~**chance** *die* (Kaufmannsspr.) sales prospect; ~**flaute** *die* (Kaufmannsspr.) drop in sales; ~**förderung** *die* (Kaufmannsspr.) sales promotion; ~**gebiet** *das* (Kaufmannsspr.) sales territory; (von Produkten) market area; ~**markt** *der* (Kaufmannsspr.) market; ~**trick** *der* (Fußball) clever back-heel; ~**steigerung** *die* (Kaufmannsspr.) increase in sales; ~**weise** *Adv.* paragraph by paragraph

ab|saufen *unr. itr. V.; mit sein* (a) (salopp: untergehen) go to the bottom; (b) (derb: ertrinken) drown; (c) (ugs.) ⟨*engine, car*⟩ flood; (d) (salopp: sich mit Wasser füllen) flood; **abgesoffen sein** be under water; be flooded

ab|saugen *tr. V.* (a) suck away; **etw. aus/von etw.** ~: suck sth. out of/off sth.; (b) (säubern) hoover (Brit. coll.); vacuum

ab|schaben *tr. V.* (a) scrape off; (b) (säubern) scrape [clean]; *s. auch* **abgeschabt**

ab|schaffen 1 *tr. V.* (a) (beseitigen) abolish ⟨*regulation, institution*⟩; repeal ⟨*law*⟩; put an end to ⟨*injustice, abuse*⟩; **er möchte alle Flugzeuge** ~: he'd like to do away with aeroplanes completely; (b) (sich trennen von) get rid of. 2 *refl. V.* (südd., schweiz.) slave away; work oneself hard

Ab·schaffung *die* abolition; (von Gesetzen) repeal; (von Unrecht, Missstand) ending

ab|schälen 1 *tr. V.* (a) (lösen) peel off; **etw. von etw.** ~: peel sth. off sth.; (b) (befreien von) bark ⟨*tree*⟩. 2 *refl. V.* (sich lösen) peel off; **die Haut schält sich ab** the skin is peeling

ab|schalten 1 *tr., itr. V.* (ausschalten) switch off; turn off; shut down ⟨*power station*⟩. 2 *itr. V.* (fig. ugs.) switch off

ab|schätzen *tr. V.* estimate; size up ⟨*person, possibilities*⟩

abschätzig /ˈapʃɛtsɪç/ 1 *Adj.* derogatory; disparaging. 2 *adv.* derogatorily; disparagingly

Ab·schaum *der; o. Pl.* (abwertend) scum; dregs *pl.*

ab|scheiden *unr. tr. V.* (Chemie) precipitate; (Physiol.) secrete

Ab·scheu *der;* ~**s,** (selten:) *die;* ~**:** detestation; abhorrence; **einen** ~ **vor jmdm./etw. haben** detest *or* abhor sb./sth.

ab|scheuern *tr. V.* (a) scrub off; (b) (säubern) scrub; (c) (beschädigen) graze ‹*skin*›; wear away ‹*cloth*›

abscheulich /apˈʃɔylɪç/ **1** *Adj.* (a) (widerwärtig) disgusting, awful ‹*smell, taste*›; repulsive, awful ‹*sight*›; (b) (verwerflich, schändlich) disgraceful ‹*behaviour*›; abominable ‹*crime*›. **2** *adv.* (a) disgracefully; abominably; (b) (ugs.: sehr) ~ **frieren** freeze [half] to death (coll.); **das tut** ~ **weh** it hurts like hell (coll.); ~ **kalt/scharf** terribly cold/sharp (coll.)

Abscheulichkeit *die;* ~**:** ⇒ **abscheulich 1:** disgustingness; awfulness; repulsiveness; disgracefulness; abominableness

ab|schicken *tr. V.* send [off], post ‹*letter, parcel*›; dispatch, send [off], post ‹*goods, money*›

ab|schieben 1 *unr. tr. V.* (a) push *or* shove away; **das Bett von der Wand** ~**:** push *or* shove the bed away from the wall; (b) (abwälzen) shift; **die Verantwortung/Schuld auf jmdn.** ~**:** shift [the] responsibility/the blame on to sb.; (c) (Rechtsw.: ausweisen) deport; **jmdn. über die Grenze** ~**:** put sb. over the border; (d) (ugs.: entfernen) get rid of; **jmdn. in ein Heim** ~**:** shove sb. into a home (coll.). **2** *unr. itr. V.; mit sein* (salopp: weggehen) push off (coll.); shove off (coll.)

Ab·schiebung *die* (Rechtsw.) deportation

Abschied /ˈapʃiːt/ *der;* ~**[e]s,** ~**e** (a) (Trennung) parting (**von** from); farewell (**von** to); **[von jmdm./etw.]** ~ **nehmen** say goodbye [to sb./sth.]; take one's leave [of sb./sth.]; **beim** ~**:** at parting; when saying goodbye; **sich zum** ~ **die Hände schütteln** shake hands on parting; **jmdm. zum** ~ **zuwinken** wave goodbye to sb.; (b) (geh.: Entlassung) resignation; **seinen** ~ **nehmen** (geh.) resign; ‹*officer*› resign one's commission

Abschieds-: ~**besuch** *der* farewell visit; ~**brief** *der* farewell letter; ~**feier** *die* farewell ceremony; (Party) farewell *or* leaving party; ~**geschenk** *das* farewell *or* parting gift; ~**gruß** *der* goodbye; farewell; ~**kuss,** ***~**kuß** *der* goodbye *or* parting kiss; ~**rede** *die* farewell speech; ~**schmerz** *der; o. Pl.* sorrow at parting

ab|schießen *unr. tr. V.* (a) loose, fire ‹*arrow*›; fire ‹*rifle, pistol, cannon, missile*›; launch ‹*spacecraft*›; (b) (töten) take; (c) (ugs.: entfernen) kick *or* throw ‹*person*› out; (d) (von sich geben) fire off ‹*question*›; shoot ‹*glance*›; (e) (zerstören) shoot down ‹*aeroplane*›; put ‹*tank*› out of action; (f) (wegreißen) shoot off ‹*arm, leg, etc.*›

ab|schinden *unr. refl. V.* **sich** ~**:** work *or* (Brit. coll.) flog oneself to death

ab|schirmen *tr. V.* (a) (schutzen) shield; **jmdn./sich von der od. gegen die Umwelt** ~**:** screen sb./oneself off from the outside world; (b) (abhalten) screen off ‹*light, radiation*›

ab|schlachten *tr. V.* slaughter

ab|schlaffen /ˈapʃlafn̩/ *itr. V.; mit sein* (ugs.) wilt; sag; **ein abgeschlaffter Typ** a lackadaisical fellow; **er saß abgeschlafft im Sessel** he sat limply in his chair; **geistig** ~**:** lose one's intellectual vigour

Ab·schlag *der* (a) (Kaufmannsspr.) reduction; discount; (b) (Teilzahlung) interim payment; (Vorschuss) advance; (c) (Fußball) goalkeeper's kick out

ab|schlagen *unr. tr. V.* (a) knock off; (mit dem Beil, Schwert usw.) chop off; (b) (ablehnen) refuse; **jmdm. etw.** ~**:** refuse *or* deny sb. sth.; (c) (abwehren) beat *or* fend off; (d) (zerlegen) dismantle; strike ‹*tent*›; (e) *auch itr.* (Fußball) **[den Ball]** ~**:** kick the ball out

abschlägig /ˈapʃlɛːgɪç/ (Amtsspr.) **1** *Adj.* negative; **ein** ~**er Bescheid** a refusal *or* rejection. **2** *adv.* **jmdn.** ~ **bescheiden** refuse sb.

Abschlag[s]·zahlung *die* ⇒ **Abschlag b**

ab|schlecken *tr. V.* (österr., südd.) ⇒ **ablecken**

ab|schleifen 1 *unr. tr. V.* (a) (entfernen) (von Holz) sand off; (von Metall, Glas usw.) grind off; (b) (glätten) sand down ‹*wood*›; grind down ‹*metal, glass, etc.*›; smooth down ‹*broken tooth*›. **2** *unr. refl. V.* (sich abnutzen) wear away; **das schleift sich noch ab** (fig.) that will wear off in time

Abschlepp·dienst *der* (Kfz-W.) breakdown recovery service; tow[ing] service (Amer.)

ab|schleppen 1 *tr. V.* (a) tow away; (schleppen) tow; (b) (salopp: mitnehmen) **jmdn.** ~**:** drag sb. off. **2** *refl. V.* (ugs.: schwer tragen) **sich mit etw.** ~**:** break one's back carrying sth. (fig.)

Abschlepp-: ~**seil** *das* tow rope; (aus Draht) towing cable; ~**stange** *die* tow-bar; ~**wagen** *der* breakdown vehicle; tow truck (Amer.)

ab|schließen 1 *unr. tr. V.* (a) *auch itr.* (zuschließen) lock ‹*door, gate, cupboard*›; lock [up] ‹*house, flat, room, park*›; (b) (verschließen) seal; **etw. luftdicht** ~**:** seal sth. hermetically; (c) (begrenzen) border; (d) (zum Abschluss bringen) bring to an end; conclude; **sein Studium** ~**:** finish one's studies; (e) (vereinbaren) strike ‹*bargain, deal*›; make ‹*purchase*›; enter into ‹*agreement*›; **Geschäfte** ~**:** conclude deals; (im Handel) do business; *s. auch* **Versicherung b; Wette 2** *unr. itr. V.* (a) (begrenzt sein) be bordered (**mit** by); (b) (aufhören, enden) end; ~**d sagte er …:** in conclusion he said …; **mit einem Gewinn/Verlust** ~ (Kaufmannsspr.) show a profit/deficit; (c) **mit jmdm./etw. abgeschlossen haben** have finished with sb./sth.

Ab·schluss, *****Ab·schluß** *der* (a) (Verschluss) seal; (b) (abschließender Teil) edge; (c) (Beendigung) conclusion; end; **vor** ~ **der Arbeiten** before the completion of the work; **etw. zum** ~ **bringen** finish sth.; bring sth. to an end *or* a conclusion; **zum** ~ **unseres Programms** to end our programme; (d) (ugs.) ~**zeugnis) einen/keinen** ~ **haben** (Hochschulw.) ≈ have a/have no degree *or* (Amer.) diploma; (Schulw.) ≈ have some/no GCSE passes (Brit.); (Lehre) have/ not have finished one's apprenticeship; (e) (Kaufmannsspr.: Schlussrechnung) balancing; (f) (Kaufmannsspr.: geschäftliche Vereinbarung) business deal; (g) (eines Geschäfts, Vertrags) conclusion

Abschluss-, *****Abschluß-:** ~**prüfung** *die* (Hochschulw.) final examination; finals *pl.*; (Schulw.) leaving *or* (Amer.) final examination; ~**zeugnis** *das* (Schulw.) ≈ leaving certificate (Brit.); ≈ diploma (Amer.)

ab|schmecken *tr. V.* (a) (kosten) taste; try; (b) (würzen) season

ab|schmieren 1 *tr. V.* (a) (Technik) grease; (b) (ugs. abwertend: abschreiben) copy; ‹*child in school*› crib (**von, bei** from). **2** *itr. V.* (a) (ugs. abwertend) crib (**von, bei** from); (b) (Fliegerspr.) side-slip

ab|schminken *tr. V.* (a) **jmdn./sich** ~**:** remove sb.'s/ one's make-up; (b) **sich** (*Dat.*) **etw.** ~ (salopp) get sth. out of one's head

ab|schmirgeln *tr. V.;* (a) (polieren) rub down with emery; (mit Sandpapier) sand down; (b) (entfernen) rub off with emery; (mit Sandpapier) sand off

ab|schnallen *tr. V.* unfasten; **[sich** (*Dat.*)**] den Tornister** ~**:** take off one's knapsack; **sich** ~**:** unfasten one's seat belt

ab|schneiden 1 *unr. tr. V.* (a) (abtrennen) cut off; cut down ‹*sth. hanging*›; **etw. von etw.** ~**:** cut sth. off sth.; **sich** (*Dat.*) **den Finger** ~**:** cut one's finger off; **sich** (*Dat.*) **eine Scheibe Brot** ~**:** cut oneself a slice of bread; *s. auch* **Scheibe b;** (b) (kürzer schneiden) cut; **jmdm./sich die Haare** ~**:** cut sb.'s/one's hair; **ein Kleid [ein Stück]** ~**:** cut [a piece] off a dress; (c) **jmdm. den Weg** ~**:** take a short cut to get ahead of sb.; (d) (trennen, isolieren) cut off. **2** *unr. itr. V.* **bei etw. gut/schlecht** ~**:** do well/badly in sth.

Ab·schnitt *der* (a) (Kapitel) section; (b) (Milit.: Gebiet, Gelände) sector; (c) (Zeitspanne) phase; (d) (eines Formulars) [detachable] portion

ab|schnüren *tr. V.* constrict; (als medizinische Maßnahme) apply a tourniquet to; **jmdm. die Luft/das Blut** ~**:** stop sb. from breathing/restrict sb.'s circulation

ab|schöpfen *tr. V.* skim off; (fig.) siphon off ‹*profits*›; **den Rahm** ~ (fig.) cream off the best; **überschüssige Kaufkraft** ~**:** absorb excess spending power

ab|schrauben *tr. V.* unscrew [and remove]

ab|schrecken 1 *tr. V.* (a) (abhalten) deter; (b) (fernhalten) scare off; (c) (Kochk.) pour cold water over; put ⟨*boiled eggs*⟩ into cold water. **2** *itr. V.* act as a deterrent

abschreckend 1 *Adj.* (a) (warnend) deterrent; **ein ~es Beispiel für alle Raucher** a warning to all smokers; (b) (abstoßend) repulsive. **2** *adv.* **~ wirken** have a deterrent effect; **~ hässlich** repulsively ugly

Abschreckung *die;* ~: deterrence

ab|schreiben 1 *unr. tr. V.* (a) (kopieren) copy out; **sich** (*Dat.*) **etw.** ~: copy sth. down; (aus einem Buch, einer Zeitung usw.) copy sth. out; (b) **etw. von** *od.* **bei jmdm.** ~ (in der Schule) copy sth. from *or* off sb.; (als Plagiator) plagiarize sth. from sb.; (c) (Wirtsch.) amortize, write down (**mit** by); (d) (ugs.: verloren geben) write off; **jmdn. abgeschrieben haben** have written sb. off. **2** *unr. itr. V.* **bei** *od.* **von jmdm.** ~ (in der Schule) copy off sb.; (als Plagiator) copy from sb.

Ab·schreibung *die* (Wirtsch.) amortization

Abschreibungs·gesellschaft *die* (Wirtsch.) tax-loss company

Ab·schrift *die* copy

ab|schrubben *tr. V.* (ugs.) (a) scrub away *or* off; **sich/jmdm. den Schmutz** ~: scrub the dirt off oneself/sb.; (b) (säubern) scrub; **sich/jmdm. den Rücken** ~: scrub one's/sb.'s back [down]; **sich/jmdn.** ~: scrub oneself/sb. [down]

ab|schürfen *tr. V.* **sich** (*Dat.*) **die Knie/die Ellenbogen** ~: graze one's knees/one's elbows; **sich** (*Dat.*) **die Haut** ~: chafe the skin

Ab·schuss, **Ab·schuß der* (a) (eines Flugzeugs) shooting down; (eines Panzers) putting out of action; (b) (von Wild) shooting; (c) (das Abfeuern) (von Geschossen, Torpedos) firing; (in den Weltraum) launching

abschüssig /'ap-ʃʏsɪç/ *Adj.* downward sloping ⟨*land*⟩; **die Straße ist sehr** ~: the road goes steeply downhill

Abschuss·rampe, **Abschuß·rampe die* launch pad; launching pad

ab|schütteln *tr. V.* (a) shake down ⟨*fruit*⟩; [**sich** (*Dat.*)] **den Staub/den Schnee [vom Mantel]** ~: shake off the dust/the snow [from one's coat]; (b) (fig.) shake off ⟨*pursuer, marker, yoke of tyranny etc.*⟩

ab|schwächen 1 *tr. V.* (a) tone down, moderate ⟨*statement, criticism*⟩; (b) (verringern) lessen ⟨*effect, impression*⟩; cushion ⟨*blow, impact*⟩. **2** *refl. V.* ⟨*interest, demand*⟩ wane; **der Preisauftrieb schwächt sich ab** price increases are slowing down

Ab·schwächung *die;* ~, ~en (a) (Milderung) toning down, moderation; (abgemilderte Form) attenuation; (b) (eines Aufpralls, Stoßes usw.) cushioning; (c) (das Nachlassen) waning; (eines Hochs, Tiefs) weakening; (zahlenmäßig) drop (*Gen.* in)

ab|schwatzen *tr. V.* **jmdm. etw.** ~: talk sb. into giving one sth.

ab|schweifen *itr. V.; mit sein* digress

Abschweifung *die;* ~, ~en digression

ab|schwellen *unr. itr. V.; mit sein* go down

ab|schwenken *itr. V.; mit sein* turn aside; **links/rechts** ~ (abbiegen) turn left/right; (die Richtung allmählich ändern) bear to the left/right

ab|schwören *unr. itr. V.* **dem Teufel/seinem Glauben** ~: renounce the Devil/one's faith; **dem Alkohol/Laster** ~: forswear *or* swear off alcohol/vice

Ab·schwung *der* (a) (Turnen) dismount; **beim** ~: when dismounting; (b) (Wirtsch.) downward trend

ab|segeln *itr. V.; mit sein* sail away; **von Kiel** ~: sail from Kiel

ab|segnen *tr. V.* (ugs. scherzh.) sanction

absehbar *Adj.* foreseeable; **in** ~**er Zeit** within the foreseeable future; **etw. ist noch gar nicht** ~: sth. cannot yet be predicted; **auf** *od.* **für** ~**e Zeit** for the foreseeable future; **nicht** ~: unforeseeable

ab|sehen 1 *unr. tr. V.* (a) (voraussehen) predict; foresee ⟨*event*⟩; (b) **es auf etw.** (*Akk.*) **abgesehen haben** be

---

after sth.; **er hat es auf sie abgesehen** he's got his eye on her; **er hat es darauf abgesehen, uns zu ärgern** he's out to annoy us; **der Chef hat es auf ihn abgesehen** the boss has got it in for him. **2** *unr. itr. V.* (a) (nicht beachten) **von etw.** ~: leave aside *or* ignore sth.; *s. auch* **abgesehen**; (b) (verzichten) **von etw.** ~: refrain from sth.; **von einer Anzeige/Klage** ~: not report sth./not press charges

ab|seifen *tr. V.* **jmdn./sich** ~: soap sb./oneself down

ab|seilen 1 *tr. V.* lower [with a rope]. **2** *refl. V.* (Bergsteigen) abseil

*ab|sein ⇒ **ab 2a**

abseits /'apzaɪts/ **1** *Präp. mit Gen.* away from. **2** *Adv.* (a) (entfernt) far away; **etwas** ~: a little way away; (b) (Ballspiele) ~ **sein** *od.* **stehen** be offside

Abseits *das;* ~, ~ (a) (Ballspiele) **das war ein klares** ~: that was clearly offside; **im** ~ **stehen** be offside; **der Spieler lief ins** ~: the player put himself offside; (b) (fig.) **im** ~ **stehen** have been pushed out into the cold; **ins** ~ **geraten** be pushed out into the cold

ab|senden *unr. od. regelm. tr. V.* dispatch

Ab·sender *der* ▶ 107┃ sender; (Anschrift) sender's address

ab|senken 1 *refl. V.* **sich [zum See/Fluss hin]** ~: slope [down to the lake/river]. **2** *tr. V.* lower

Absenz /ap'zɛnts/ *die;* ~, ~en (a) absence [of mind]; (b) (bes. österr., schweiz.) absence (*from school*)

ab|servieren 1 *itr. V.* clear away. **2** *tr. V.* (a) **ein Gedeck/den Tisch** ~: clear away a cover/clear the table; (b) (salopp: absetzen, kaltstellen) throw out

absetzbar *Adj.* (a) (Steuerw.) [**steuerlich**] ~: [tax-]deductible; (b) (verkäuflich) saleable; (c) ⇒ **absetzen 1 d**: **er ist nicht** ~: he cannot be dismissed/be removed from office

ab|setzen 1 *tr. V.* (a) (abnehmen) take off; (b) (hinstellen) put down ⟨*glass, bag, suitcase*⟩; (c) (aussteigen lassen) **jmdn.** ~ (im öffentlichen Verkehr) put sb. down; let sb. out (Amer.); (im privaten Verkehr) drop sb. [off]; (d) (entlassen) dismiss ⟨*minister, official*⟩; remove ⟨*chancellor, judge*⟩ from office; depose ⟨*king, emperor*⟩; (e) (ablagern) deposit; (f) (absagen) drop; call off ⟨*strike, football match*⟩; (g) (nicht mehr anwenden) discontinue ⟨*treatment, therapy*⟩; stop taking ⟨*medicine, drug*⟩; (h) (von den Lippen nehmen) take ⟨*glass, trumpet*⟩ from one's lips; (i) (verkaufen) sell; (j) (Steuerw.) **etw. [von der Steuer]** ~: deduct sth. [from tax]. **2** *refl. V.* (a) (sich ablagern) be deposited; ⟨*dust*⟩ settle; ⟨*particles in suspension*⟩ settle out; (b) (sich distanzieren) **sich von etw.** ~: distance oneself from sth.; (c) (sich unterscheiden) ⇒ **abheben 3**; (d) (ugs.: sich davonmachen) get away

Absetzung *die;* ~, ~en ⇒ **absetzen 1 d**: dismissal; removal; deposition

ab|sichern 1 *tr. V.* (a) make safe; (b) (fig.) substantiate ⟨*argument, conclusions*⟩; validate ⟨*result*⟩; **tariflich abgesichert** protected by agreement *postpos*. **2** *refl. V.* safeguard oneself

Ab·sicht *die;* ~, ~en intention; **die** ~ **haben, etw. zu tun** plan *or* intend to do sth.; **etw. mit** ~ **tun** do sth. intentionally *or* deliberately; **etw. ohne** *od.* **nicht mit** ~ **tun** do sth. unintentionally; **in der besten** ~: with the best of intentions; **in betrügerischer** ~: with intent to deceive

ab·sichtlich 1 *Adj.* intentional; deliberate. **2** *adv.* intentionally; deliberately

ab|singen *unr. tr. V.* (a) etw. **vom Blatt** ~: sing sth. at sight; (b) **unter Absingen** (*Dat.*) **der Nationalhymne** singing the national anthem

ab|sinken *unr. itr. V.; mit sein* sink; (fig.) decline; ⟨*temperature, blood pressure*⟩ drop

Absinth /ap'zɪnt/ *der;* ~[e]s, ~e absinth[e]

ab|sitzen 1 *unr. tr. V.* (hinter sich bringen) sit through; sit out ⟨*hours of duty etc.*⟩; (im Gefängnis) serve; **zehn Jahre** ~: serve *or* ⟨coll.⟩ do ten years. **2** *unr. itr. V. mit sein* dismount (**von** from)

absolut /apzo'luːt/ **1** *Adj.* absolute. **2** *adv.* absolutely

Absolution /apzolu'tsi̯oːn/ *die;* ~, ~en (kath. Rel.) absolution; **jmdm. die** ~ **erteilen** give sb. absolution

---

Absolutismus *der;* ~ (hist.) absolutism *no art.*

absolutistisch 1 *Adj.* absolutist. 2 *adv.* in an absolutist manner

Absolvent /apzɔl'vɛnt/ *der;* ~**en**, ~**en**, **Absolventin** *die;* ~, ~**nen** (einer Schule) one who has taken the leaving *or* (Amer.) final examination; (einer Akademie, Hochschule) graduate

absolvieren /apzɔl'viːrən/ *tr. V.* (a) complete; **das Gymnasium** ~: complete a grammar-school education; (b) (erledigen, verrichten) put in ⟨*hours*⟩; do ⟨*performance, route, task*⟩; make ⟨*visit*⟩

Absolvierung *die;* ~: completion

ab·sonderlich *Adj.* strange; odd

ab|sondern 1 *tr. V.* (a) isolate ⟨*patient*⟩; separate ⟨*prisoner*⟩; (b) (Physiol.) secrete. 2 *refl. V.* isolate oneself

Absonderung *die;* ~, ~**en** (a) isolation; (b) (Physiol.) secretion

absorbieren *tr. V.* (fachspr., fig. geh.) absorb

Absorption /apzɔrp'tsi̯oːn/ *die;* ~ (fachspr., fig. geh.) absorption

ab|spalten *unr. od. regelm. refl. V.* split off *or* away

Ab·spann *der* (Ferns.) final credits *pl.*

ab|spannen *tr. V.* unharness ⟨*horse*⟩; unhitch ⟨*wagon*⟩; unyoke ⟨*oxen*⟩

Abspannung *die;* ~, ~**en** (Ermüdung) weariness; fatigue

ab|sparen *refl. V.* **sich** (*Dat.*) **etw. vom Munde** ~: scrimp and save for sth.

ab|speisen *tr. V.* **jmdn. mit etw.** ~: fob sb. off with sth.

abspenstig /'ap-ʃpɛnstɪç/ *Adj.; nicht attr.* **jmdm. etw.** ~ **machen** get sb. to part with sth.; **jmdm. den Freund/die Freundin** ~ **machen** steal sb.'s boy/girlfriend

ab|sperren 1 *tr. V.* (a) seal off; close off; (b) **jmdm. das Gas/das Wasser/den Strom** ~: cut off sb.'s gas/water/electricity; (c) (österr., südd.: abschließen) lock ⟨*door*⟩. 2 *itr. V.* (österr., südd.) lock up

Ab·sperrung *die* (a) sealing off; closing off; (b) (Sperre) barrier

Ab·spiel *das* (Ballspiele) (a) (das Abspielen) passing; (Schuss) pass

ab|spielen 1 *tr. V.* (a) play ⟨*record, tape*⟩; (b) **vom Blatt** ~: play ⟨*piece of music*⟩ at sight; (c) (Ballspiele) pass. 2 *refl. V.* take place. 3 *itr. V.* (Ballspiele) pass; **an jmdn.** ~: pass [the ball] to sb.

ab|splittern *itr. V.; mit sein* ⟨*wood*⟩ splinter off; ⟨*lacquer, paint*⟩ flake off

Ab·sprache *die* agreement; arrangement; **eine** ~ **treffen** come to an agreement *or* make an arrangement; **nach** ~ **mit** by arrangement with

ab|sprechen 1 *unr. tr. V.* (a) (aberkennen) **jmdm. etw.** ~: deprive sb. of sth.; (b) (ableugnen) **jmdm. etw.** ~: deny that sb. has sth.; **jmdm. das Recht auf etw.** (*Akk.*) ~: deny sb.'s right to sth.; **jmdm. das Recht** ~, **etw. zu tun** deny sb. the right to do sth.; (c) (vereinbaren) arrange. 2 *unr. refl. V.* come to *or* reach an agreement

ab|spreizen *tr. V.* stretch out ⟨*arm, leg*⟩ sideways; splay out ⟨*finger, toe*⟩

ab|sprengen *tr. V.* split off

ab|springen *unr. itr. V.; mit sein* (a) jump off; [**mit dem rechten/linken Bein**] ~: take off [on the right/ left leg]; (b) (herunterspringen) jump down; **vom Fahrrad/Pferd** ~: jump off one's bicycle/horse; **aus dem Flugzeug** ~: jump out of the aeroplane; (c) (abplatzen) come off; ⟨*paint*⟩ flake off

ab|spritzen *tr. V.* (a) spray off; (b) (reinigen) spray [down]

Ab·sprung *der* (a) (das Losspringen) take-off; (b) (das Herunterspringen) jump; (c) (fig.) break; **den** ~ **wagen** risk making the break

ab|spulen *tr. V.* unwind; **sich** ~: come unwound

ab|spülen 1 *tr. V.* (a) wash off ⟨*dirt, dust*⟩; (b) (reinigen) rinse off; **sich** (*Dat.*) **die Hände** *usw.* ~: rinse one's hands *etc.*; (c) (bes. südd.) **das Geschirr** ~: wash the dishes. 2 *itr. V.* (bes. südd.) ⇒ **abwaschen 2**

ab|stammen *itr. V.* be descended (**von** from)

Abstammung *die;* ~, ~**en** ▶ 388 ⌡ descent

Abstammungs·lehre *die* theory of evolution

Ab·stand *der* (a) (Zwischenraum) distance; **in 20 Meter** ~: at a distance of 20 metres; **im** ~ **von 10 Metern** 10 metres apart; ~ **halten** (auch fig.) keep one's distance; (b) (Unterschied) gap; difference; **mit** ~: by far; far and away; (c) (Zeitspanne) interval; (kürzer) gap; **in Abständen von 20 Minuten** at 20-minute intervals; (d) (geh.: Verzicht) **von etw.** ~ **nehmen** refrain from sth.; (e) (Entschädigung) compensation; (bei Übernahme einer Wohnung) *payment for furniture and fittings left by previous tenant*

ab|statten /'ap-ʃtatn̩/ *tr. V.* (geh.) **jmdm. einen Besuch** ~: pay sb. a visit

ab|stauben *tr., itr. V.* (a) dust; (b) (ugs.: stehlen) lift (sl.); pinch (ugs. Brit. coll.); nick (Brit. coll.)

ab|stechen 1 *unr. tr. V.* (a) slaughter ⟨*animal*⟩ (*by cutting its throat*); (b) (ablaufen lassen) tap ⟨*beer, wine*⟩. 2 *unr. itr. V.* **von etw./jmdm.** ~: contrast with sth./sb.

Abstecher *der;* ~**s**, ~: side-trip; (fig.: Abschweifung) digression

ab|stecken *tr. V.* (a) (abgrenzen) mark out; (fig.) define; (b) (Schneiderei) pin up ⟨*hem*⟩

ab|stehen *unr. itr. V.* (a) (nicht anliegen) stick out; ~**de Ohren** protruding ears; (b) (entfernt stehen) **40 cm/zu weit von etw.** ~: be 40 cm. away/too far away from sth.

Ab·steige *die;* ~, ~**n** (ugs. abwertend) cheap and crummy hotel (sl.)

ab|steigen *unr. itr. V.; mit sein* (a) [**vom Pferd/ Fahrrad**] ~: get off [one's horse/bicycle]; (b) (abwärts gehen) go down; descend; **gesellschaftlich** ~ (fig.) decline in social status; (c) (Sport) be relegated; (d) (sich einquartieren) **in einem Hotel** ~: put up at a hotel

Ab·steiger *der;* ~**s**, ~ (Sport) (vor dem Abstieg stehend) team threatened with *or* facing relegation; (abgestiegen) relegated team

ab|stellen *tr. V.* (a) (absetzen) put down; (b) (unterbringen, hinstellen) put; (parken) park; (c) (ausschalten, abdrehen) turn *or* switch off; turn off ⟨*gas, water*⟩; **jmdm. das Gas/den Strom** ~: cut sb.'s gas/electricity off; **jmdm. das Telefon** ~: disconnect sb.'s telephone; (d) (unterbinden) put a stop to; (e) (sein lassen) stop; (f) (beordern) assign; detail [off] ⟨*soldiers*⟩

Abstell-: ~**gleis** *das* siding; **jmdn. aufs** ~ **schieben** (fig. ugs.) put sb. out of harm's way; ~**kammer** *die* lumber-room; ~**raum** *der* storeroom

ab|stempeln *tr. V.* (a) frank ⟨*letter*⟩; cancel ⟨*stamp*⟩; (b) (fig.) **jmdn. als od. zum Verbrecher/als geisteskrank** ~: label *or* brand sb. as a criminal/as insane

ab|steppen *tr. V.* back stitch

ab|sterben *unr. itr. V.; mit sein* (a) (eingehen, verfallen) [gradually] die; (b) (gefühllos werden) go numb; **mir sind die Finger abgestorben** my fingers have gone numb

Ab·stich *der; o. Pl.* (a) (das Abstechen) cutting; (b) (Metall.) tapping

Ab·stieg *der;* ~**[e]s**, ~**e** (a) descent; (b) (Niedergang) decline; [**sozialer** *od.* **gesellschaftlicher**] ~: fall *or* drop in [social] status; (c) (Sport) relegation

ab|stillen 1 *tr. V.* wean. 2 *itr. V.* stop breastfeeding

ab|stimmen 1 *itr. V.* vote (**über** + *Akk.* on); **über etw.** (*Akk.*) ~ **lassen** put sth. to the vote. 2 *tr. V.* **etw. mit jmdm.** ~: discuss and agree sth. with sb.; (b) (harmonisieren) **etw. auf etw.** (*Akk.*) ~: suit sth. to sth.; **Zeitpläne/ Programme aufeinander** ~: coordinate timetables/ programmes

Ab·stimmung *die* (a) vote; ballot; **eine geheime** ~: a secret ballot; **bei der** ~: in the vote; (während der ~) during the voting; (b) (Absprache) agreement; (c) (Harmonisierung) coordination

Abstimmungs-: ~**ergebnis** *das* result of a/the vote; ~**niederlage** *die* defeat [in a/the vote]; ~**sieg** *der* victory [in a/the vote]

abstinent /apsti'nɛnt/ *Adj.* (a) teetotal; ~ **sein** be a non-drinker *or* a teetotaller; (b) **sexuell** ~: sexually abstinent; continent

Abstinenz /apstiˈnɛnts/ *die;* ~ (a) teetotalism; ~ **üben** be teetotal; (b) **sexuelle** ~: sexual abstinence; continence

Abstinenzler *der;* ~s, ~: teetotaller; non-drinker

ab|stoppen 1 *tr. V.* (a) halt; stop; check ‹*advance*›; stop ‹*machine*›; (b) (mit der Stoppuhr) **die Zeit** ~: measure the time with a stopwatch. **2** *itr. V.* come to a halt; ‹*person*› stop

Ab·stoß *der* (Fußball) goal-kick

ab|stoßen 1 *unr. tr. V.* (a) (wegstoßen) push off *or* away; **das Boot [vom Ufer]** ~: push the boat out [from the bank]; (b) (beschädigen) chip ‹*crockery, paintwork, stucco, plaster*›; batter ‹*furniture*›; *s. auch* **Horn;** (c) (verkaufen) sell off; (d) (Physik) repel; (e) (anwidern) repel; put off; **sich von jmdm./etw. abgestoßen fühlen** find sb./sth. repulsive. **2** *unr. itr. V.* (a) **mit sein** *od.* **haben** (sich entfernen) be pushed off; (b) (anwidern) be repulsive. **3** *refl. V.* **sich [vom Boden]** ~: push oneself off

abstoßend *Adj.* repulsive

Abstoßung *die;* ~, ~en (a) (Physik, auch fig.) repulsion; (b) (Verkauf) sale; (c) (Med., Physiol.) rejection

ab|stottern *tr. V.* (ugs.) pay for in instalments; pay off ‹*debt*› by instalments

ab|strafen *tr. V.* punish

Abstrafung *die* ~, ~en punishment

abstrahieren /apstraˈhiːrən/ *tr., itr. V.* (geh.) abstract (**aus** from)

ab|strahlen 1 *tr. V.* (Physik) radiate; (Funkw., Elektrot.) emit ‹*wave, frequency*›. **2** *itr. V.* (fig.) **auf jmdn./etw.** ~: influence *or* affect sb./sth.

Ab·strahlung *die;* ~ (Physik) radiation; (Funkw., Elektrot.) emission

abstrakt /apˈstrakt/ **1** *Adj.* abstract. **2** *adv.* abstractly; ~ **denken** think in the abstract

Abstraktion /apstrakˈtsi̯oːn/ *die;* ~, ~en (geh.) abstraction

ab|streichen *unr. tr. V.* (a) (abstreifen) wipe; (entfernen) wipe off; (b) (abziehen) knock off; **davon muss man die Hälfte** ~ (fig.) you have to take it with a pinch of salt

ab|streifen *tr. V.* (a) pull off; strip off ‹*berries*›; **sich/ jmdn. die Kleidung** ~: take off one's/sb.'s clothes; **die Asche [von der Zigarre]** ~: remove the ash [from one's cigar]; (b) wipe off; (säubern) wipe

Abstreifer *der;* ~s, ~ ⇒ **Fußabstreifer**

ab|streiten *unr. tr. V.* deny; **das kann ihm keiner** ~: you cannot deny him that

Ab·strich *der* (a) (Med.) swab; **einen** ~ **machen** take a swab; (b) (Streichung, Kürzung) cut; ~**e [an etw. (***Dat.***)] machen** make cuts [in sth.]; (Einschränkungen machen) make concessions [as regards sth.]

ab|stufen *tr. V.* (a) (staffeln) grade; (b) (nuancieren) differentiate

Ab·stufung *die;* ~, ~en (a) (Staffelung) gradation; (b) (Nuance) shade

ab|stumpfen (fig.) **1** *tr. V.* deaden. **2** *itr. V.; mit sein* **man stumpft ab** one's mind becomes deadened; **gegen etw.** ~: become dead to sth.

Ab·sturz *der* fall; (eines Flugzeugs) crash

ab|stürzen *itr. V.; mit sein* (a) fall; ‹*aircraft, pilot, passenger*› crash; (b) (geh.: abfallen) ‹*cliff*› plunge

Absturz·ursache *die* cause of the crash

ab|stützen 1 *refl. V.* support oneself (**mit** on, **an** + *Dat.* against). **2** *tr. V.* support

ab|suchen *tr. V.* search (**nach** for); (durchkämmen) comb (**nach** for); drag ‹*pond, river, etc.*› (**nach** for); **den Himmel/Horizont** ~ scan the sky/horizon (**nach** for)

absurd /apˈzʊrt/ *Adj.* absurd

Absurdität /apzʊrdiˈtɛːt/ *die;* ~, ~en absurdity

Abszess, *Abszeß /apsˈtsɛs/ *der* (österr. auch: *das*); **Abszesses, Abszesse** (a) (Med.) abscess; (b) (Geschwür) ulcer

*alte Schreibung (vgl. Hinweise auf S. xvi–xvii)

Abszisse /apsˈtsɪsə/ *die;* ~, ~en (Math.) abscissa

Abt /apt/ *der;* ~**[e]s, Äbte** /ˈɛptə/ abbot

Abt. *Abk.* **Abteilung**

ab|tanzen *itr. V.* (salopp) dance

ab|tasten *tr. V. etw.* ~: feel sth. all over

ab|tauen 1 *itr. V.; mit sein* (wegschmelzen) melt away; (eis-/schneefrei werden) become clear of ice/snow; ‹*refrigerator*› defrost. **2** *tr. V.* (schnee-/eisfrei machen) melt; thaw; de-ice ‹*vehicle windows*›; defrost ‹*refrigerator*›

Abtei /apˈtai̯/ *die;* ~, ~en abbey

Abteil *das;* ~**[e]s, ~e** compartment

ab|teilen *tr. V.* (a) (aufteilen) divide [up]; (b) (abtrennen) divide off

Ab·teilung *die* (a) department; (einer Behörde) department; section; (b) (Bot.) division; (c) (Milit.) unit

Abteilungs·leiter *der* head of department/section; departmental manager

ab|telefonieren *itr. V.* **[jmdm.]** ~: phone [sb.] to say one cannot come

ab|teufen *tr. V.* (Bergbau) sink

ab|tippen *tr. V.* (ugs.) type out

Äbtissin /ɛpˈtɪsɪn/ *die;* ~, ~**nen** abbess

ab|tönen *tr. V.* tint

ab|töten *tr. V.* destroy ‹*parasites, germs*›; deaden ‹*nerve, feeling*›; mortify ‹*desire*›

ab|tragen *unr. tr. V.* (a) (abnutzen) wear out; (b) (geh.: abräumen) clear away; (c) (einebnen) level; (Geol.) erode; (d) (abbauen) demolish

abträglich /ˈaptrɛːklɪç/ *Adj.* (geh.) **einer Sache** (*Dat.*) ~ **sein** be detrimental *or* harmful to sth.

ab|trainieren *tr. V.* **[sich (***Dat.***)] Fett/Pfunde** ~: get rid of fat/pounds

Ab·transport *der* ⇒ **abtransportieren:** taking away; removal; dispatch

ab|transportieren *tr. V.* take away; remove ‹*dead, injured*›; (befördern) dispatch ‹*goods*›

ab|treiben 1 *unr. tr. V.* (a) (wegtreiben) carry away; **jmdn./ein Schiff vom Kurs** ~: drive *or* carry sb./a ship off course; (b) abort ‹*foetus*›; **ein Kind** ~ **lassen** have an abortion. **2** *unr. itr. V.* (a) **mit sein** (weggetrieben werden) be carried away; ‹*ship*› be carried off course; (b) (einen Abort vornehmen lassen) have an abortion

Abtreibung *die;* ~, ~en abortion

ab|trennen *tr. V.* (a) detach; sever ‹*arm, leg, etc.*›; cut off ‹*button, collar, etc.*›; detach ‹*paper, voucher*›; (b) (abteilen) divide off

ab|treten 1 *unr. tr. V.* (a) **sich** (*Dat.*) **die Füße/ Schuhe** ~: wipe one's feet; (b) **jmdm. etw.** ~: let sb. have sth.; (c) (Rechtsw.) transfer; cede ‹*territory*›; (d) (abnutzen) wear down. **2** *unr. itr. V.; mit sein* (a) (Milit.) dismiss; (b) (Theater, auch fig.) exit; make one's exit; **von der Bühne** ~ (fig.) step down; leave the arena; (c) (zurücktreten) step down; ‹*monarch*› abdicate. **3** *unr. refl. V.* (sich abnutzen) become worn; **sich leicht/schnell** ~: wear [out] easily/ quickly

Abtreter *der;* ~s, ~ ⇒ **Fußabtreter**

Ab·tritt *der* (a) (Theater) exit; (b) (Rücktritt) resignation; (c) (veralt.: Toilette) privy (arch.)

ab|trocknen 1 *tr. V.* dry; **sich** (*Dat.*) **die Hände/das Gesicht/die Tränen** ~: dry one's hands/face/tears. **2** *itr. V.; mit sein* dry off

ab|tropfen *itr. V.; mit sein* drip off; ‹*lettuce, dishes*› drain; ‹*clothing*› drip-dry; **von etw.** ~: drip off sth.

abtrünnig *Adj.* (einer Partei) renegade; (einer Religion, Sekte) apostate; **der Kirche/dem Glauben** ~ **werden** desert the Church/the faith

Abtrünnige *der/die; adj. Dekl.* (einer Partei) renegade; deserter; (einer Religion, Sekte) apostate; turncoat

ab|tun *unr. tr. V.* dismiss; **etw. mit einer Handbewegung** ~: wave sth. aside

ab|tupfen *tr. V.* dab away; **sich** (*Dat.*) **die Stirn** ~: dab one's brow

ab|verlangen tr. V. jmdm. etw. ~: demand sth. of sb.

ab|wägen unr. od. regelm. tr. V. weigh up; **die Vor- und Nachteile gegeneinander ~:** weigh the advantages and disadvantages; s. auch **abgewogen**

ab|wählen tr. V. vote out; drop ‹school subject›

ab|wälzen tr. V. pass on (**auf** + Akk. to); shift ‹blame, responsibility› (**auf** + Akk. on to)

ab|wandeln tr. V. adapt; modify

ab|wandern itr. V.; mit sein (a) migrate (**aus** from, **in** + Akk. to); (in ein anderes Land) emigrate (**aus** from, **in** + Akk. to); (b) (fig.) move over

Ab·wanderung die (a) migration (**aus** from, **in** + Akk. to); (in ein anderes Land) emigration (**aus** from, **in** + Akk. to); (b) (fig.) moving over

Ab·wandlung die adaptation; modification

ab|warten 1 itr. V. wait; **sie warteten ab** they awaited events; **warten wir [erst mal] ab** let's wait and see; **sich ~d verhalten** adopt an attitude of 'wait and see'. 2 tr. V. wait for; **etw. ~** (das Ende von etw. ~) wait for sth. to end

abwärts /'apvɛrts/ Adv. downwards; (bergab) downhill; **den Fluss ~:** downstream; **der Fahrstuhl fährt ~:** the lift is going down; **seit damals ging es eigentlich immer nur ~** (fig.) from that time on things really only got worse

-abwärts adv. ▶ 193 | **rhein~/fluss~:** down the Rhine/down river or downstream

***abwärts|gehen** ⇒ **abwärts**

Abwasch¹ /'apvaʃ/ der; ~[e]s washing-up (Brit.); washing dishes (Amer.); **den ~ machen** do the washing-up/wash the dishes

Abwasch² die; ~, ~en (österr.) sink

abwaschbar Adj. washable

ab|waschen 1 unr. tr. V. (a) wash off; **etw. von etw. ~:** wash sth. off sth.; (b) (reinigen) wash [up] ‹dishes›; wash down ‹surface›. 2 unr. itr. V. wash up, do the washing-up (Brit.); wash the dishes (Amer.)

Ab·wasser das; Pl. **-wässer** sewage

ab|wechseln refl., itr. V. alternate; **wir wechselten uns ab** we took turns; **ich wechsle mich mit ihr beim Geschirrspülen ab** she and I take it in turns to do the dishes; **Regen und Sonne wechselten miteinander ab** it rained and was sunny by turns

abwechselnd Adv. alternately

Abwechslung die; ~, ~en variety; (Wechsel) change; **etwas/wenig ~:** some/not much variety; **zur ~:** for a change

abwechslungs·reich 1 Adj. varied. 2 adv. **der Urlaub verlief sehr ~reich** the holiday or (Amer.) vacation was full of variety; **sich ~reich ernähren** eat a varied diet

Ab·weg der: **auf ~e kommen** od. **geraten** go astray; **jmdn. auf ~e führen** lead sb. astray

abwegig Adj. (irrig) erroneous; false ‹suspicion›; (falsch) mistaken; wrong

Ab·wehr die; ~ (a) (Ablehnung) hostility; (b) (Zurückweisung) repulsion; (von Schlägen) fending off; (c) (Widerstand) resistance; (d) (Milit.: Geheimdienst) counter-intelligence; (e) (Sport) (Hintermannschaft) defence; (~aktion) clearance; clearing (Amer.)

ab|wehren 1 tr. V. (a) repulse; fend off, parry ‹blow›; (Sport) clear ‹ball, shot›; save ‹match point›; (b) (abwenden) avert ‹danger, consequences›; (c) (von sich weisen) avert ‹suspicion›; deny ‹rumour›; decline ‹thanks›; (d) (fernhalten) deter. 2 itr. V. (a) (Sport) clear; **zur Ecke ~:** clear the ball and give away or concede a corner; (b) (ablehnend reagieren) demur

Abwehr-: **~kraft** die power of resistance; **~spieler** der (Sport) defender

ab|weichen unr. itr. V.; mit sein (a) deviate; (b) (sich unterscheiden) differ

Abweichler /'apvaiçlɐ/ der; ~s, ~ (Politik) deviationist

Abweichung die; ~, ~en (a) deviation; (b) (Unterschied) difference

ab|weisen unr. tr. V. (a) turn away; turn down ‹suitor, applicant›; (b) (ablehnen) reject; dismiss ‹action, case, complaint›; disallow ‹claim›

abweisend 1 Adj. cold ‹tone of voice; look›; **in ~em Ton** coldly. 2 adv. coldly

Ab·weisung die; ~, ~en ⇒ **abweisen:** turning away; turning down; rejection; dismissal; disallowance

ab|wenden 1 unr. od. regelm. tr. V. (a) (wegwenden) turn away; **den Blick ~:** look away; avert one's gaze; (b) nur regelm. (verhindern) avert. 2 unr. od. regelm. refl. V. (a) turn away; (b) (fig.) **sich von jmdm. ~:** turn one's back on sb.

Ab·wendung die (Verhinderung) **zur ~ einer Sache** (Gen.) in order to avert sth.

ab|werben unr. tr. V. lure away, entice away (Dat. from)

ab|werfen 1 unr. tr. V. (a) drop; ‹tree› shed ‹leaves, needles›; ‹stag› shed ‹antlers›; throw off ‹clothing›; jettison ‹ballast›; throw ‹rider›; (Kartenspiel) discard; (fig.) cast or throw off ‹yoke of tyranny etc.›; (b) (herunterstoßen) knock down; (c) (ins Spielfeld werfen) throw out ‹ball›; (d) (einbringen) bring in; **viel ~:** show a big profit. 2 unr. itr. V. (Sport) throw the ball out

ab|werten 1 tr., itr. V. devalue. 2 tr. V. (fig.: herabwürdigen) run down; belittle

abwertend 1 Adj. derogatory. 2 adv. derogatorily; in a derogatory way

Ab·wertung die (a) devaluation; (b) (fig.: Herabwürdigung) reduction in status

abwesend 1 Adj. (a) absent; (b) (zerstreut) absent-minded. 2 adv. absent-mindedly

Abwesende der/die; adj. Dekl. absentee

Abwesenheit die; ~ (a) absence; **durch ~ glänzen** (iron.) be conspicuous by one's absence; (b) (fig.: Zerstreutheit) absent-mindedness

ab|wetzen tr., refl. V. wear away

ab|wickeln tr. V. (a) unwind; (b) (erledigen) deal with ‹case›; do ‹business›; (im Auftrag) handle ‹correspondence›; conduct, handle ‹transaction, negotiations›; (c) (Wirtsch.) wind up

Abwicklung die; ~, ~en (a) ⇒ **abwickeln b:** dealing (Gen. with); doing; handling; conducting; (b) (Kaufmannsspr., Rechtsw.: Liquidation) liquidation

ab|wiegeln 1 tr. V. pacify; calm down ‹crowd›. 2 itr. V. (abwertend) appease

ab|wiegen unr. tr. V. weigh out; weigh ‹single item›

Abwieglung die; ~, ~en (a) conciliation; (b) (abwertend) appeasement

ab|wimmeln tr. V. (ugs.) get rid of ‹person›; get out of ‹duty, responsibility, etc.›

ab|winken 1 itr. V. uninteressiert ~: wave it/them aside uninterestedly. 2 tr. V. (Motorsport) **ein Rennen ~:** wave the chequered flag; (bei einer Unterbrechung) stop a race

ab|wischen tr. V. (a) (wegwischen) wipe away; **sich/jmdm. etw. ~:** wipe sth. off oneself/sb.; **sich/jmdm. die Tränen ~:** dry one's/sb.'s tears; (b) (säubern) wipe; **sich/jmdm. die Nase/die Hände** usw. **~:** wipe one's/sb.'s nose/hands etc. (**an** + Dat. on)

ab|wracken /'apvrakn/ tr. V. scrap

Ab·wurf der (a) dropping; (von Ballast) jettisoning; (b) (Fußball) **beim ~ stolperte der Torwart** the goalkeeper stumbled as he threw the ball out; (c) (Handball, Wasserball) goal throw

ab|würgen tr. V. (ugs.) stifle; choke off; squash ‹proposal›; stall ‹car, engine›

ab|zahlen tr. V. pay off ‹debt, loan›

ab|zählen 1 tr. V. count; **„bitte das Fahrgeld abgezählt bereithalten!"** 'please tender exact fare'. 2 itr. V. (a) (Sport, Milit.) number off; **zu zweien/vieren ~:** number off in twos/fours; (b) (mit Abzählreim) count out

Abzähl·reim der counting-out rhyme

Ab·zahlung die; ~, ~en paying off; repayment; **etw. auf ~ kaufen/verkaufen** buy/sell sth. on easy terms or (Brit.) on HP

ab|zapfen tr. V. tap ‹beer, wine›; let, draw off ‹blood›; draw off ‹petrol›; **Strom ~:** tap the electricity supply

Ab·zeichen *das* (a) (Kennzeichen) emblem; (fig.) badge; (b) (Anstecknadel, Plakette) badge

ab|zeichnen 1 *tr. V.* (a) (nachzeichnen, kopieren) copy; (b) (signieren) initial. 2 *refl. V.* stand out; (fig.) begin to emerge; (drohend) loom

Abzieh·bild *das* transfer

ab|ziehen 1 *unr. tr. V.* (a) pull off; peel off ‹*skin*›; strip ‹*bed*›; (b) (Fot.) make a print/prints of; (c) (Druckw.) run off; etw. 50mal ∼: run off 50 copies of sth.; (d) (Milit., auch fig.) withdraw; (e) (subtrahieren) subtract; take away; (abrechnen) deduct; (f) (schälen) peel ‹*peach, almond, tomato*›; string ‹*runner bean*›; (g) (häuten) skin; (h) **eine Handgranate** ∼: pull the pin of a hand grenade; (i) (herausziehen) take out ‹*key*›. 2 *unr. itr. V., mit sein* (a) (sich verflüchtigen) escape; (b) (Milit.) withdraw; (c) (ugs.: weggehen) push off (coll.)

ab|zielen *itr. V.* **auf etw.** (*Akk.*) ∼: be aimed at *or* directed towards sth.

ab|zocken (salopp abwertend) 1 *itr. V.* rake it in (coll.). 2 *tr. V.* fleece ‹*person*›; rake in (coll.) ‹*money*›; **jmdm. 20.000 DM** ∼: fleece sb. of 20,000 DM

Ab·zug *der* (a) (an einer Schusswaffe) trigger; (b) (Fot.) print; (c) (Druckw.) proof; (d) (Verminderung) deduction; (e) *o. Pl.* (Abmarsch, auch fig.) withdrawal; (f) (Öffnung für Rauch usw.) vent

abzüglich /'aptsy:klıç/ *Präp. mit Gen.* (Kaufmannsspr.) less; ∼ **3 % Rabatt** less 3 % discount

abzugs-: ∼**fähig** *Adj.* (Steuerw.) [tax-]deductible; ∼**frei** *Adj.* (Steuerw.) tax-free

ab|zweigen 1 *itr. V.; mit sein* branch off. 2 *tr. V.* (a) (bereitstellen) set *or* put aside; **Geld für einen Plattenspieler** ∼: put aside *or* put by money to buy a record player; (b) (verhüll.: sich heimlich aneignen) appropriate

Abzweigung *die;* ∼, ∼**en** turn-off; (Gabelung) fork

Accessoire /aksɛ'soa:ɐ̯/ *das;* ∼**s**, ∼**s** (geh.) accessory

Aceton /atse'to:n/ *das;* ∼**s** (Chemie) acetone

ach /ax/ *Interj.* (a) (betroffen, mitleidig) oh [dear]; ∼ **Gott** o dear; (b) (bedauernd, unwirsch) oh; (c) (klagend) ah; alas (dated); (d) (erstaunt) oh; ∼ **wirklich?** no, really?; ∼, **der!** oh, him!; (e) ∼ **so!** oh, I see; ∼ **nein** no, no; ∼ **was** *od.* **wo!** of course not

Ach *in* **mit** ∼ **und Krach** (ugs.) by the skin of one's teeth

Achat /a'xa:t/ *der;* ∼**[e]s**, ∼**e** (Min.) agate

Ach-Laut *der* velar fricative; ach-laut

Achse /'aksə/ *die;* ∼, ∼**n** (a) (Rad∼) axle; **auf** ∼ **sein** (ugs.) be on the road *or* move; (b) (Dreh∼, Math., Astron.) axis; **sich um die** *od.* **seine eigene** ∼ **drehen** turn on one's/ its own axis

Achsel /'aksl̩/ *die;* ∼, ∼**n** (Schulter) shoulder; (∼höhle) armpit; **jmdn. über die** ∼ **ansehen** look down on sb.; look down one's nose at sb.; **die** *od.* **mit den** ∼**n zucken** shrug one's shoulders; **jmdn. unter den** ∼**n packen** seize sb. under the arms

achsel-, Achsel-: ∼**haare** *Pl.* hair *sing.* under one's arms; armpit hair *sing.;* ∼**höhle** *die* armpit; ∼**zucken** *das* shrug [of the shoulders]; ∼**zuckend** *Adj.* shrugging; **er ging** ∼**zuckend hinaus** he went out with a shrug [of the shoulders]

-achsig *Adj.* **drei-/sechs**∼: three-/six-axle

acht /axt/ *Kardinalz.* ▶22⟨, ▶530⟨, ▶600⟨ eight; **er ist** ∼ **[Jahre]** he is eight [years old]; **um** ∼ **[Uhr]** [o'clock]; **in** ∼ **Tagen** in a week's time; a week from now; **Freitag/morgen in** ∼ **Tagen** a week on Friday/a week tomorrow; **die Linie** ∼ **[der Straßenbahn]** the number eight [tram]; **es steht** ∼ **zu** ∼/∼ **zu zwei** (Sport) the score is eight all/eight [to] two

acht²: **wir waren zu** ∼: there were eight of us; **wir rückten ihm zu** ∼ **auf die Bude** (ugs.) eight of us dropped in on him

*acht³ ⇨ **Acht²**

acht … *Ordinalz.* ▶119⟨, ▶600⟨ eighth; **der** ∼**e** *od.* **8. September** the eighth of September; (*im Brief auch*) 8 September; **am** ∼**en** *od.* **8. September** on the eighth of

September; (*im Brief auch*) 8 September; **München**, **[den] 8. Mai 1984** Munich, 8 May 1984

Acht¹ *die;* ∼, ∼**en** (a) (Zahl) eight; **eine arabische/römische** ∼: an arabic/Roman eight; (b) (Figur) figure eight; (c) (ugs.: Verbiegung) buckle; **das Rad hat eine** ∼: the wheel is buckled; (d) (Spielkarte) eight; (e) (ugs.: Bus-, Bahnlinie) [number] eight

Acht² *in* **etw. außer** ∼ **lassen** disregard *or* ignore sth.; **sich in** ∼ **nehmen** take care; be careful; **sich vor jmdn./etw. in** ∼ **nehmen** be wary of sb./sth.; **auf jmdn./etw.** ∼ **geben** take care of *or* mind sb./sth.; **[auf jmds. Worte]** ∼ **geben** pay attention [to what sb. says]; ∼ **geben müssen, dass** … have to be careful that …; (vorsichtig sein) be careful; watch out; **gib** ∼**!** look out!; watch out!; **auf sich** (*Akk.*) ∼ **geben** be careful

Acht³ *die;* ∼ (hist.) outlawry; **jmdn. in** ∼ **und Bann tun** (kirchlich) anathematize sb.; put the ban on sb.; (fig.) ostracize sb.

-acht *die* (Kartenspiel) eight of …

achtbar *Adj.* (geh.) respectable; upright ‹*principles*›; **eine** ∼**e Leistung** a creditable performance

Achte *der/die; adj. Dekl.* eighth; **er war [in der Leistung] der** ∼: he came eighth; **der** ∼ **[des Monats]** the eighth [of the month]

acht-, Acht-: ∼**eck** *das;* ∼**s**, ∼**e** octagon; ∼**eckig** *Adj.* octagonal; ∼**einhalb** *Bruchz.* ▶600⟨ eight and a half

achtel /'axtl̩/ *Bruchz.* ▶600⟨ eighth; **ein** ∼ **Kilo** an eighth of a kilo

Achtel *das* (schweiz. meist der) ▶600⟨; ∼**s**, ∼ (a) eighth; (b) (ugs.: ∼pfund) eighth of a pound; ≈ two ounces; (c) (ugs.: ∼liter) eighth of a litre (*of wine*)

Achtel-: ∼**liter** *der, auch: das* eighth of a litre; ∼**note** *die* (Musik) quaver; ∼**pause** *die* (Musik) quaver rest; ∼**pfund** *das* eighth of a pound

*achte·mal ⇨ **Mal¹**

achten 1 *tr. V.* respect. 2 *itr. V.* **auf etw.** (*Akk.*) **[nicht]** ∼ ([nicht] acht auf etw. aufpassen) [not] mind *or* look after sth.; (von etw. [keine] Notiz nehmen) pay [no] attention *or* heed to sth.; **auf jmdn.** ∼: look out for sb.; (aufpassen) look after sb.

ächten /'ɛçtn̩/ *tr. V.* (a) (hist.) outlaw; (b) (gesellschaftlich) ostracize; **sich geächtet fühlen** feel like an outcast; (c) (verdammen) ban ‹*war, torture, etc.*›

Acht·ender *der;* ∼**s**, ∼ (Jägerspr.) eight-pointer

*achten·mal ⇨ **Mal¹**

achtens /'axtn̩s/ *Adv.* eighthly

Achter /'axtɐ/ *der;* ∼**s**, ∼ (a) (Rudern) eight; (b) ⇨ **Acht¹** a, b, c

Achter·bahn *die* roller coaster; ∼**bahn fahren** go *or* ride on the roller coaster

achterlei *Gattungsz.; indekl.* (a) *attr.* eight kinds *or* sorts of; eight different ‹*sorts, kinds, sizes*›; (b) *allein stehend* eight [different] things

achtern *Adv.* (Seemannsspr.) astern; aft

acht·fach *Vervielfältigungsz.* eightfold; **die** ∼**e Menge** eight times the quantity; **etw. in** ∼**er Ausfertigung schicken** send eight copies of sth.; ∼ **vergrößert/verkleinert, in** ∼**er Vergrößerung/Verkleinerung** magnified *or* enlarged/reduced eight times

Acht·fache *das; adj. Dekl.* **das** ∼**e von 4 ist 32** eight fours are *or* eight times four makes 32; **um das** ∼**e steigen** increase ninefold *or* nine times

*acht|geben ⇨ **Acht²**

acht-, Acht-: ∼**hundert** *Kardinalz.* ▶600⟨ eight hundred; ∼**jährig** *Adj.* (8 Jahre alt) eight-year-old *attrib.;* eight years old *pred.;* (8 Jahre dauernd) eight-year *attrib.;* ∼**jährige** *der/die; adj. Dekl.* eight-year-old; ∼**kampf** *der* (Turnen) eight-exercise gymnastic competition; ∼**kantig** 1 *Adj.* (Technik) eight-sided; 2 *adv.* (salopp) ∼**kantig rausfliegen** get kicked *or* (sl.) booted out; ∼**köpfig** *Adj.* eight-headed ‹*monster*›; ‹*family, committee*› of eight

acht·los 1 *Adj.; nicht präd.* heedless. 2 *adv.* heedlessly

acht-, Acht-: ∼**mal** *Adv.* eight times; ∼**mal so groß/soviel/so viele** eight times as big/as much/as many; ∼**malig** *Adj.; nicht präd.* **nach** ∼**maliger Aufforderung** at the eighth request; after being asked eight times; **~monatig** *Adj.* (8 Monate alt) eight-month-old *attrib.*; eight months old *pred.*; (8 Monate dauernd) eight-month *attrib.*; **~monatlich** 1 *Adj.* eight-monthly; im **~monatlichen** Turnus rotating every eight months; 2 *adv.* every eight months; **~prozentig** *Adj.* eight per cent

achtsam 1 *Adj.* (geh.) attentive. 2 *adv.* (sorgsam) carefully; with care; mit etw. [äußerst] **~** umgehen handle sth. with [extreme] care

acht-, Acht-: **~seitig** *Adj.* eight-page *attrib.* ‹*letter, article*›; **~spaltig** (Druckw.) 1 *Adj.* eight-column *attrib.*; **~spaltig sein** have eight columns; 2 *adv.* in eight columns; **~spänner** *der*; **~s**, **~:** eight-in-hand; **~spurig** *Adj.* eight-lane ‹*road*›; eight-track ‹*tape*›; **~spurig sein** have eight lanes/tracks; **~stellig** *Adj.* eight-figure *attrib.*; **~stellig sein** have eight figures *or* digits; **~stimmig** 1 *Adj.* eight-part *attrib.*; 2 *adv.* in eight parts; **~stöckig** *Adj.* eight-storey *attrib.*; **~stöckig sein** have eight storeys *or* floors; **~strophig** /~ʃtroːfɪç/ *Adj.* with eight verses *postpos., not pred.*; **~strophig sein** have eight verses; **~stunden·tag** /ˈ---/ *der* eight-hour day; **~stündig** *Adj.* eight-hour *attrib.*; mit **~stündiger** Verspätung eight hours late; nach **~stündigem** Warten after waiting for eight hours; **~tägig** *Adj.* (8 Tage alt) eight-day *attrib.*; (8 Tage dauernd) eight-day[-long] *attrib.*; mit **~tägiger** Verspätung eight days late; **~tausend** *Kardinalz.* ▶ 600 eight thousand; **~tausender** *der mountain over eight thousand metres high*; **~teilig** *Adj.* eight-piece ‹*tea service, tool-set, etc.*›; eight-part ‹*series, serial*›

Acht·uhr-: eight o'clock ‹*news, train, performance, etc.*›

Achtung *die*; **~** (a) (Wertschätzung) respect (*Gen.*, vor + *Dat.* for); **alle ~!** well done!; (b) (Aufmerksamkeit) attention; **~!** watch out!; **~!** Stillgestanden! (Milit.) attention!; **~**, **~!** your attention, please!; „**~**, Stufe!" 'mind the step'; **~**, fertig, los! on your marks, get set, go!

Ächtung *die*; **~**, **~en** (a) (hist.) outlawing; (b) (gesellschaftliche **~**) ostracism; (c) (Verdammung) banning

acht·zehn *Kardinalz.* ▶ 22 , ▶ 530 , ▶ 600 eighteen; mit **~** [Jahren] wird man volljährig one reaches the age of majority at eighteen; 18 Uhr 6 p.m.; (auf der 24-Stunden-Uhr) eighteen hundred hours; 1800; 18 Uhr 33 6.33 p.m.; (auf der 24-Stunden-Uhr) 1833

achtzehn-, Achtzehn-: **~hundert** *Kardinalz.* ▶ 600 eighteen hundred; **~jährig** *Adj.* (18 Jahre alt) eighteen-year-old *attrib.*; eighteen years old *pred.*; (18 Jahre dauernd) eighteen-year *attrib.*; **~jährige** *der/die; adj. Dekl.* eighteen-year-old

achtzehnt... *Ordinalz.* ▶ 119 , ▶ 600 eighteenth; *s. auch* acht...

achtzig /ˈaxtsɪç/ *Kardinalz.* ▶ 22 , ▶ 600 eighty; mit **~** [km/h] fahren drive at *or* (coll.) do eighty [k.p.h.]; über/etwa **~** [Jahre alt] sein be over/about eighty [years old]; mit **~** [Jahren] at eighty [years of age]; Mitte [der] **~** sein be in one's mid-eighties; auf **~** sein (fig. ugs.) be hopping mad (coll.)

achtzig *indekl. Adj.; nicht präd.* ein **~** Jahrgang an '80 vintage; die **~** Jahre the eighties

Achtziger[1] *der*; **~s**, **~** (80jähriger) eighty-year-old [man]; octogenarian

Achtziger[2] *die*; **~**, **~** (ugs.) (Briefmarke) eighty-pfennig/schilling *etc.* stamp

Achtzigerin *die*; **~**, **~nen** eighty-year-old [woman]; octogenarian

Achtziger·jahre *Pl.* ▶ 119 eighties *pl.*

achtzig·jährig *Adj.* (80 Jahre alt) eighty-year-old *attrib.*; eighty years old *pred.*; (80 Jahre dauernd) eighty-year *attrib.*

achtzigst... /ˈaxtsɪçst/ *Ordinalz.* ▶ 600 eightieth

Achtzigstel *das*; **~s**, **~:** ▶ 600 eightieth

Acht-: **~zimmer·wohnung** *die* eight-roomed flat; **~zylinder** *der* (ugs.) eight-cylinder [engine/car]; **~zylinder·motor** *der* eight-cylinder engine

ächzen /ˈɛçtsn̩/ *itr. V.* (a) (schwer stöhnen) groan; (b) (knarren) creak

Acker /ˈakɐ/ *der*; **~s**, **Äcker** /ˈɛkɐ/ field; auf dem **~:** in the field

Acker-: **~bau** *der; o. Pl.* agriculture *no indef. art.*; farming *no indef. art.*; **~bau** treiben farm; **~bau** und Viehzucht farming and stock-breeding; **~furche** *die* furrow; **~land** *das; o. Pl.* farmland

ackern *itr. V.* (salopp) slog one's guts out (coll.)

Acryl- /aˈkryːl.../**:** **~farbe** *die* acrylic; **~faser** *die* acrylic fibre; **~glas** *das* acrylic glass; **~lack** *der* acrylic varnish

a. D. /aːˈdeː/ *Abk.* außer Dienst retd.

A. D. *Abk.* Anno Domini AD

ad absurdum /at apˈzʊrdʊm/ in etw. **~** **~** führen demonstrate the absurdity of sth.

ADAC /aːdeːaːˈtseː/ *der*; **~** *Abk.* Allgemeiner Deutscher Automobilclub

ad acta /at ˈakta/ in etw. **~** **~** legen shelve sth.

Adagio /aˈdaːdʒo/ *das*; **~s**, **~s** (Musik) adagio

Adam /ˈaːdam/ (*der*) Adam; seit **~s** Zeiten since the beginning of time; bei **~** und Eva anfangen (ugs.) begin from the beginning

Adam Riese: das macht nach **~** **~** 4,50 Mark (ugs. scherzh.) my arithmetic makes it 4.50 marks (coll. joc.)

Adams-: **~apfel** *der* (ugs.) Adam's apple; **~kostüm** *das* (scherzh.) im **~kostüm** in one's birthday suit

Adaptation /adaptaˈtsi̯oːn/ *die*; **~**, **~en** adaptation

adaptieren /adapˈtiːrən/ *tr. V.* (a) adapt; für den Bildschirm/Film **~:** adapt for television/the screen; (b) (österr.: herrichten) fit out

Adaptierung *die*; **~**, **~en** (a) ⇒ **Adaptation**; (b) (österr.: Herrichtung) fitting-out

Adaption /adapˈtsi̯oːn/ *die*; **~**, **~en** ⇒ **Adaptation**

adäquat /atɛˈkvaːt/ 1 *Adj.* (passend) appropriate (*Dat.* to); suitable (*Dat.* for); (angemessen) adequate ‹*reward, payment*›; appropriate, suitable ‹*measures, means*›. 2 *adv.* (passend) suitably; appropriately; (angemessen) adequately

addieren /aˈdiːrən/ 1 *tr. V.* add [up]. 2 *itr. V.* add

Addition /adiˈtsi̯oːn/ *die*; **~**, **~en** addition

ade /aˈdeː/ *Interj.* (veralt., landsch.) farewell; jmdm. **~** sagen bid farewell to sb.; take one's leave of sb.

Adel /ˈaːdl̩/ *der*; **~s** nobility; von **~** sein be of noble blood; **~** verpflichtet noblesse oblige

adelig ⇒ **adlig**

Adelige ⇒ **Adlige**

adeln *tr. V.* jmdn. **~:** give sb. a title; (in den hohen Adel erheben) raise sb. to the peerage; (fig.) ennoble sb.

Adels-: **~familie** *die*, **~geschlecht** *das* noble family; **~prädikat** *das* title of nobility; **~stand** *der* nobility; (hoher Adel) nobility; peerage; jmdn. in den **~stand** erheben give sb. a title/raise sb. to the peerage; **~titel** *der* title

Ader /ˈaːdɐ/ *die*; **~**, **~n** ▶ 326 (a) (Anat., Zool.) blood vessel; vein; (b) *o. Pl.* (Anlage, Begabung) streak; (c) (Bot., Geol.) vein; (d) (Elektrot.) core

Aderlass, **·Aderlaß** /ˈaːdɐlas/ *der*; **Aderlasses**, **Aderlässe** /-lɛsə/ (Med.) bleeding

adieu /aˈdi̯øː/ *Interj.* (veralt.) adieu; farewell; jmdm. **~** sagen bid sb. adieu *or* farewell

Adjektiv /ˈatjɛktiːf/ *das*; **~s**, **~e** (Sprachw.) adjective

Adjutant /atjuˈtant/ *der*; **~en**, **~en** adjutant; aide-de-camp

Adlatus /atˈlaːtʊs/ *der*; **~**, **Adlaten** *od.* **Adlati** (scherzh.) loyal assistant

Adler /ˈaːdlɐ/ *der*; **~s**, **~:** eagle

Adler-: **~auge** *das* (fig.) eagle eye; **~horst** *der* eyrie; **~nase** *die* aquiline nose

adlig /ˈaːdlɪç/ *Adj.* noble; **~** sein be a noble [man/woman]

Adlige *der/die adj. Dekl.* noble [man/woman]

Administration /atminɪstraˈtsi̯oːn/ *die*; **~**, **~en** administration

administrativ /atminɪstraˈtiːf/ 1 *Adj.* administrative. 2 *adv.* administratively

Admiral /atmiˈraːl/ *der*; **~s**, **~e** *od.* **Admiräle** /atmiˈrɛːlə/ (a) ▶ 34 admiral; (b) (Schmetterling) red admiral

Admiralität /atmirali'tɛ:t/ *die;* ~, ~en admiralty

ADN /a:de:'|ɛn/ *Abk.* (DDR) **Allgemeiner Deutscher Nachrichtendienst** *GDR press agency*

adoptieren /adɔp'ti:rən/ *tr. V.* adopt

Adoption /adɔp'tsi̯o:n/ *die;* ~, ~en adoption

Adoptiv- /adɔp'ti:f-/: ~**eltern** *Pl.* adoptive parents; ~**kind** *das* adoptive *or* adopted child

Adrenalin /adrena'li:n/ *das;* ~s (Physiol., Med.) adrenalin

Adressat /adrɛ'sa:t/ *der;* ~en, ~en, **Adressatin** *die;* ~, ~nen addressee

Adreß·buch, ***Adreß·buch** *das* directory

Adresse /a'drɛsə/ *die;* ~, ~n (a) ▶ 107] address; **unter folgender** ~: at the following address; **bei jmdm. an die falsche** ~ **kommen** *od.* **geraten** (fig. ugs.) come to the wrong address (fig.); **bei jmdm. an der falschen** ~ **sein** (fig. ugs.) have come to the wrong place (fig.); **(b)** (geh.: Botschaft) message

Adressen-: ~**büro** *das* mailing-list broker; ~**liste** *die* address list; ~**verzeichnis** *das* directory of addresses

adressieren *tr. V.* address

adrett /a'drɛt/ **1** *Adj.* smart. **2** *adv.* smartly

Adria /'a:dri̯a/ *die;* ~: Adriatic

adriatisch /adri'a:tɪʃ/ *Adj.* Adriatic; **das Adriatische Meer** the Adriatic Sea

A-Dur *das;* ~ (Musik) A major

Advent /at'vɛnt/ *der;* ~s **(a)** Advent; **(b)** (Adventssonntag) Sunday in Advent

Advents-: ~**kalender** *der* Advent calendar; ~**kranz** *der; garland of evergreens with four candles for the Sundays in Advent;* ~**sonntag** *der* Sunday in Advent

Adverb /at'vɛrp/ *das;* ~s, ~ien (Sprachw.) adverb

adverbial /atvɛr'bi̯a:l/ (Sprachw.) **1** *Adj.* adverbial. **2** *adv.* adverbially; as an adverb

Advokat /atvo'ka:t/ *der;* ▶ 85] ~en, ~en (österr., schweiz., sonst veralt.) lawyer; advocate (arch.); (fig.: Fürsprecher) advocate

aero-, Aero- /aero- *od.* ɛ:ro-/: ~**dynamik** *die* aerodynamics *sing.;* ~**dynamisch** *Adj.* aerodynamic; ~**gramm** *das* air[-mail] letter; ~**sol** /~'zo:l/ *das;* ~s, ~e aerosol

Affäre *die;* ~, ~n affair; **sich aus der** ~ **ziehen** (ugs.) get out of it

Affe /'afə/ *der;* ~n, ~n **(a)** monkey; (Menschen~) ape; **(b)** (dummer Kerl) oaf; clot (Brit. coll.); **(c)** (Geck) dandy; **ein eingebildeter** ~: a conceited so-and-so (coll.); **(d)** (Milit. ugs.) knapsack

Affekt /a'fɛkt/ *der;* ~[e]s, ~e feeling; emotion; affect (Psych.); **im** ~: in the heat of the moment

Affekt·handlung *die* emotive act

affektiert /afɛk'ti:ɐt/ (abwertend) **1** *Adj.* affected. **2** *adv.* affectedly

affen-, Affen-: ~**artig** *Adj.* apelike; **mit** ~**artiger Geschwindigkeit** (ugs.) like a bat out of hell (coll.); ~**hitze** *die* (salopp) blazing heat; **gestern war eine** ~**hitze** yesterday was a real scorcher; ~**mensch** *der* ape-man; ~**schande** *die* (salopp) **es ist eine** ~**schande** it's monstrous; ~**tempo** *das* (salopp) **mit einem** ~**tempo** like mad (coll.); like the clappers (Brit. sl.); **ein** ~**tempo anschlagen** move like hell (coll.); ~**theater** *das* (salopp) farce; ~**zahn** *der* (salopp) ⇨ ~**tempo**

affig (ugs. abwertend) **1** *Adj.* dandyish; (lächerlich) ludicrous; (affektiert) affected. **2** *adv.* in a dandyish/a ludicrous/an affected way

Äffin /'ɛfɪn/ *die;* ~, ~nen female ape

affirmativ /afɪrma'i:f/ *Adj.* affirmative

Affront /a'frõ:/ *der;* ~s, ~s affront

Afghane /af'ga:nə/ *der;* ~n, ~n ▶ 388] **(a)** Afghan; **(b)** (Hund) Afghan hound

---

*alte Schreibung (vgl. Hinweise auf S. xvi–xvii)

Afghanin *die;* ~, ~nen Afghan

afghanisch *Adj.* ▶ 388] Afghan

Afghanistan /af'ga:nɪsta:n/ *(das);* ~s Afghanistan

Afrika /'a:frika/ *(das);* ~s Africa

Afrikaner /afri'ka:nɐ/ *der;* ~s, ~, **Afrikanerin** *die;* ~, ~nen African

afrikanisch *Adj.* African

Afro·amerikaner *der* Afro-American

After /'aftɐ/ *der;* ~s, ~: ▶ 326] anus

AG /a:'ge:/ *Abk. die;* ~, ~s **(a) Aktiengesellschaft** PLC (Brit.); Ltd. (private company) (Brit.); Inc. (Amer.); **(b) Arbeitsgemeinschaft**

Ägäis /ɛ'gɛ:ɪs/ *die;* ~: Aegean

ägäisch *Adj.* Aegean

Agave /a'ga:və/ *die;* ~, ~n (Bot.) agave

Agent /a'gɛnt/ *der;* ~en, ~en agent

Agenten-: ~**netz** *das* network of agents; ~**ring** *der* spy ring

Agentin *die;* ~, ~nen [female] agent

Agentur /agɛn'tu:ɐ/ *die;* ~, ~en agency

Aggregat /agre'ga:t/ *das;* ~[e]s, ~e (Technik) unit; (Elektrot.) set

Aggregat·zustand *der* (Chemie, Physik) state

Aggression /agrɛ'sio:n/ *die;* ~, ~en aggression

Aggressions·trieb *der* aggressive drive

aggressiv /agrɛ'si:f/ **1** *Adj.* aggressive. **2** *adv.* aggressively

Aggressivität *die;* ~: aggressiveness

Aggressor /a'grɛsɔr/ *der;* ~s, ~en /-'so:rən/ aggressor

agieren /a'gi:rən/ *itr. V.* act

agil /a'gi:l/ *Adj.* (beweglich) agile; (geistig rege) mentally alert

Agitation /agita'tsi̯o:n/ *die;* ~ (Politik) agitation; ~ **betreiben** agitate

Agitator /agi'ta:tor/ *der;* ~s, ~en /-ta'to:rən/ agitator

agitieren 1 *itr. V.* agitate. **2** *tr. V.* stir up

Agonie /ago'ni:/ *die;* ~, ~n: **in** ~ **liegen** be in the throes of death

Agrar·erzeugnis *das* agricultural *or* farm product; ~**se** agricultural *or* farm produce *or* products

agrarisch *Adj.* agrarian; agricultural

Agrar-: ~**land** *das; Pl.* ~**länder** agrarian country; ~**markt** *der* agrarian *or* agricultural products market; ~**politik** *die* agricultural policy; ~**produkt** ⇨ ~**erzeugnis**

Agronom /agro'no:m/ *der;* ~en, ~en agronomist

Agronomie /agrono'mi:/ *die;* ~: agronomy *no art.*

Ägypten /ɛ'gyptn/ *(das);* ~s Egypt

Ägypter *der;* ~s, ~: ▶ 388] Egyptian

ägyptisch *Adj.* ▶ 388], ▶ 487] Egyptian

ah /a:/ *Interj.* (verwundert) oh; (freudig, genießerisch) ah; (verstehend) oh; ah

äh /ɛ(:)/ *Interj.* **(a)** (angeekelt) ugh; **(b)** (stotternd) er; hum

aha /a'ha(:)/ *Interj.* (verstehend) oh[, I see]; (triumphierend) aha

Ahn /a:n/ *der;* ~[e]s *od.* ~en, ~en (geh.) forebear; ancestor; (fig.) father

ahnden /'a:ndn̩/ *tr. V.* (geh.) punish

Ahndung *die;* ~: punishment

Ahne *der;* ~n, ~n ⇨ **Ahn**

ähneln /'ɛ:nln̩/ *itr. V.* jmdm. ~: resemble *or* be like sb.; bear a resemblance to sb.; **jmdm. sehr/wenig** ~: strongly resemble *or* be very like sb./bear little resemblance to sb.; **einer Sache** (*Dat.*) ~: be similar to sth.; be like sth.; **sich sehr/wenig** ~: resemble each other very strongly *or* be very much alike/bear little resemblance to each other

ahnen /'a:nən/ **1** *tr. V.* **(a)** have a presentiment *or* premonition of; **(b)** (vermuten) suspect; (erraten) guess; **wer soll denn** ~, **dass** ...: who would know that ...; **das konnte ich doch nicht** ~**!** I had no way of knowing that; **du ahnst es nicht!** (ugs.) oh heck *or* Lord! (coll.); **(c)** (vage erkennen) just make out; **die Wagen waren in der Dunkelheit mehr zu** ~ **als zu sehen** one could sense the cars in the darkness, rather than see them. **2** *itr. V.* (geh.) **mir ahnt nichts Gutes** I fear the worst; **es ahnte mir, dass** ...: I suspected that ...

Ahnen-: ~**forschung** *die* genealogy; ~**galerie** *die* gallery of ancestral portraits; ~**tafel** *die* genealogical table; ~**verehrung** *die* ancestor-worship

ähnlich /'ɛːnlɪç/ **1** *Adj.* similar; **jmdm.** ~ **sein** be similar to *or* be like sb.; **jmdm.** ~ **sehen** resemble sb.; be like sb.; **das Kind ist seinem Vater** ~: the child takes after his father; **[so]** ~ **wie etw. aussehen/klingen** look/ sound like sth.; **das sieht dir/ihm** ~! (ugs.) that's you/ him all over; that's just like you/him. **2** *adv.* similarly; ⟨*answer, react*⟩ in a similar way *or* manner; ~ **dumm**/ **naiv** *usw.* **argumentieren** argue in a similarly stupid/ naïve *etc.* way *or* manner; **uns geht es** ~: it is/will be much the same for us; (wir denken, fühlen ~) we feel much the same. **3** *Präp. mit Dat.* like

Ähnlichkeit *die;* ~, ~**en** similarity; (ähnliches Aussehen) similarity; resemblance; **mit jmdm.** ~ **haben** be similar to *or* be like sb.; (im Aussehen) bear a resemblance to *or* be like sb.; **mit etw.** ~ **haben** bear a similarity to sth.

Ahnung *die;* ~, ~**en** **(a)** presentiment; premonition; **eine** ~ **haben, dass** ...: have a feeling *or* hunch that ...; **(b)** (Befürchtung) foreboding; **(c)** (ugs.: Kenntnisse) knowledge; **von etw. [viel]** ~ **haben** know [a lot] about sth.; **keine** ~! [I've] no idea; [I] haven't a clue; **haben Sie eine** ~, **wer/wie** ...? have you any idea who/how ...?

ahnungs·los 1 *Adj.* unsuspecting; (naiv, unwissend) naïve; **sich** ~ **stellen** play the innocent. **2** *adv.* unsuspectingly; (naiv, unwissend) naïvely

ahoi /a'hɔy/ *Interj.* (Seemannsspr.) **Boot/Schiff** *usw.* ~! boat/ship *etc.* ahoy!

Ahorn /'aːhɔrn/ *der;* ~**s**, ~**e** maple

Ähre /'ɛːrə/ *die;* ~, ~**n** (von Getreide) ear; head; (von Gräsern) head

Aids /eːts/ *das;* ~: ▶ 329 | AIDS

Aids-: ~**kranke** *der/die* person suffering from AIDS; ~**test** *der* AIDS test

Airbag /'ɛːɐbɛk/ *der;* ~**s**, ~**s** (Kfz.-W.) air bag

Akademie /akade'miː/ *die;* ~, ~**n** **(a)** academy; **(b)** (Bergbau, Forst~, Bau~) school; college

Akademiker /aka'deːmikɐ/ *der;* ~**s**, ~, **Akademikerin** *die;* ~, ~**nen** [university/college] graduate

akademisch *Adj.* academic. **2** *adv.* academically

Akazie /a'kaːtsjə/ *die;* ~, ~**n** acacia

Akklamation /aklama'tsjoːn/ *die;* ~, ~**en** acclamation

akklimatisieren *refl. V.* become *or* get acclimatized

Akkord /a'kɔrt/ *der;* ~**[e]s**, ~**e** **(a)** (Musik) chord; **(b)** (Wirtsch.) (~arbeit) piecework; (~lohn) piecework pay *no indef. art., no pl.;* (~satz) piece-rate; **im** ~ **sein** *od.* **arbeiten** be on piecework

Akkord-: ~**arbeit** *die* piecework; ~**arbeiter** *der* pieceworker

Akkordeon /a'kɔrdeɔn/ *das;* ~**s**, ~**s** accordion

Akkord·lohn *der* (Wirtsch.) piecework pay *no indef. art., no pl.*

akkreditieren /akredi'tiːrən/ *tr. V.* (bes. Dipl.) accredit **(bei** to)

Akkreditierung *die;* ~, ~**en** (bes. Dipl.) accreditation **(bei** to)

Akku /'aku/ *der;* ~**s**, ~**s** (ugs.) ⇒ **Akkumulator**

Akkumulator /akumu'laːtor/ *der;* ~**s**, ~**en** /-la'toːrən/ (Technik) accumulator (Brit.); storage battery *or* cell

akkurat /aku'raːt/ **1** *Adj.* **(a)** (sorgfältig) meticulous; (sauber) neat; **(b)** (exakt, genau) precise; exact. **2** *adv.* (sorgfältig) meticulously; (sauber) neatly

Akkusativ /'akuzatiːf/ *der;* ~**s**, ~**e** (Sprachw.) accusative [case]; **im/mit dem** ~ **stehen** be in/take the accusative [case]

Akkusativ·objekt *das* (Sprachw.) accusative *or* direct object

Akne /'aknə/ *die;* ~, ~**n** ▶ 329 | (Med.) acne

Akonto /a'kɔnto/ *das;* ~**s**, ~**s** *od.* **Akonten** (österr.), **Akonto·zahlung** *die* ⇒ **Anzahlung**

akquirieren /akvi'riːrən/ *itr. V.* (Wirtsch.) canvass [new] business

Akquisiteur /akvizi'tøːɐ/ *der;* ~**s**, ~**e** (Wirtsch.) canvasser

Akquisition /akvizitsjoːn/ *die;* ~, ~**en** (Wirtsch.) canvassing *no art.* for [new] business

Akquisitor /akvi'zitor/der;* ~**s**, ~**en** /-zi'toːrən/ (österr.) canvasser

Akribie /akri'biː/ *die;* ~ (geh.) meticulousness; meticulous precision

Akrobat /akro'baːt/ *der;* ~**en**, ~**en** ▶ 85 | acrobat

Akrobatik *die;* ~ **(a)** acrobatic skill; **(b)** (Übungen) acrobatics *pl.*

Akrobatin *die;* ~, ~**nen** ▶ 85 | acrobat

akrobatisch 1 *Adj.* acrobatic. **2** *adv.* acrobatically

Akt¹ /akt/ *der;* ~**[e]s**, ~**e** **(a)** act; **(b)** (Zeremonie) ceremony; ceremonial act; **(c)** (Geschlechtsakt) sexual act; **(d)** (Aktbild) nude

Akt² *der;* ~**[e]s**, ~**en** (bes. südd., österr.) ⇒ **Akte**

Akt·bild *das* nude [picture]

Akte *die;* ~, ~**en** file; **die** ~ **Schulze** the Schulze file; **das kommt in die** ~**n** it goes on file

Akten-: ~**deckel** *der* folder; ~**koffer** *der,* (iron.); ~**mappe** *die* **(a)** (~tasche) briefcase; **(b)** (~deckel) folder; ~**notiz** *die* note [for the files]; ~**ordner** *der* file; ~**schrank** *der* filing cabinet; ~**tasche** *die* briefcase; ~**zeichen** *das* reference

Akteur /ak'tøːɐ/ *der;* ~**s**, ~**e** person involved; (Theater) member of the cast; (Varietee) performer

Akt·foto *das* nude photo

Aktie /'aktsjə/ *die;* ~, ~**n** (Wirtsch.) share; ~**n** shares (Brit.); stock (Amer.); **die** ~**n fallen/steigen** share *or* stock prices are falling/rising

Aktien-: ~**gesellschaft** *die* joint-stock company; ~**index** *der* share index; ~**kapital** *das* share capital; ~**kurs** *der* share price; ~**mehrheit** *die* majority shareholding (Gen. in); ~**paket** *das* block of shares

Aktion /ak'tsjoːn/ *die;* ~, ~**en** **(a)** action *no indef. art.;* (militärisch) operation; **politische** ~**en** political action *sing.;* **(b)** (Kampagne) campaign; ~ **saubere Umwelt** campaign to clean up the environment; **(c)** *o. Pl.* (das Handeln) action; **in** ~ **treten** go into action; **(d)** (Kaufmannsspr.: Verkauf zu Sonderpreisen) sale

Aktionär /aktsjo'nɛːɐ/ *der;* ~**s**, ~**e** shareholder

aktions-, Aktions-: ~**einheit** *die* united action *no art.* (Gen. by); ~**fähig** *Adj.* capable of action *postpos.;* ~**preis** *der* (Kaufmannsspr.) sale price; ~**radius** *der* radius of action

aktiv /ak'tiːf/ **1** *Adj.* **(a)** active; **(b)** (Milit.) serving *attrib.* ⟨*officer, soldier*⟩; **er ist Soldat im** ~**en Dienst** he is a serving soldier. **2** *adv.* actively; **sich** ~ **verhalten** be active

Aktiv¹ /'aktiːf/ *das;* ~**s**, ~**e** (Sprachw.) active

Aktiv² /ak'tiːf/ *das;* ~**s**, ~**e** *od.* ~**s** (bes. ehem. DDR) committee

Aktiva /ak'tiːva/ *Pl.* (Wirtsch.) assets

Aktiv·bürger *der* (schweiz.) *citizen with full political and civil rights*

Aktive /ak'tiːvə/ *der/die; adj. Dekl.* (Sport) participant; (aktives Mitglied) active member

Aktiv·geschäft *das* (Finanzw.) lending and investment business

aktivieren *tr. V.* mobilize ⟨*party members, group, etc.*⟩; **den Kreislauf** ~: stimulate the circulation

Aktivierung *die;* ~, ~**en** (von Parteimitgliedern, einer Gruppe usw.) mobilization

aktivisch *Adj.* (Sprachw.) active

Aktivismus *der;* ~: activism *no art.*

Aktivist *der;* ~**en**, ~**en**, **Aktivistin** *die;* ~, ~**nen** activist

aktivistisch *Adj.* activist

Aktivität /aktiviˈtɛːt/ *die;* ~, ~**en** activity

Aktiv-: ~**posten** *der* (Kaufmannsspr., fig.) asset; ~**seite** *die* (Kaufmannsspr.) assets side; ~**urlaub** *der* (Werbespr.)

activity holiday; ~**vermögen** *das* (Kaufmannsspr.) realizable assets *pl.*; ~**zinsen** *Pl.* (Kaufmannsspr.) interest *sing.* receivable

Akt-: ~**malerei** *die* nude painting *no art.*; ~**modell** *das* nude model

aktualisieren /aktuali'tsi:rən/ *tr. V.* update.

Aktualisierung *die;* ~, ~**en** updating

Aktualität /aktuali'tɛ:t/ *die;* ~, ~**en** (a) (Gegenwartsbezug) relevance [to the present]; (b) (von Nachrichten usw.) topicality

aktuell /ak'tuɛl/ *Adj.* (a) (gegenwartsbezogen) topical; (gegenwärtig) current; (Mode: modisch) fashionable; **von** ~**er Bedeutung** of relevance to the present or current situation; **dieses Problem ist nicht mehr** ~: this is no longer a problem; (b) (neu) up-to-the-minute; **das Aktuellste von den Olympischen Spielen** the latest from the Olympics; **eine** ~**e Sendung** (Ferns., Rundf.) a [news and] current affairs programme

Akt-: ~**zeichnen** *das* nude drawing *no art.;* ~**zeichnung** *die* nude drawing

Akupressur /akuprɛ'su:ɐ̯/ *die;* ~, ~**en** (Med.) acupressure

akupunktieren (Med.) **1** *tr. V.* perform acupuncture on; **sich** ~ **lassen** have acupuncture. **2** *itr. V.* perform acupuncture

Akupunktur /akupʊŋk'tu:ɐ̯/ *die;* ~, ~**en** (Med.) acupuncture

Akustik /a'kʊstɪk/ *die;* ~ (a) (Lehre vom Schall) acoustics *sing., no art.;* (b) (Schallverhältnisse) acoustics *pl.*

akustisch 1 *Adj.* acoustic. **2** *adv.* acoustically; **ich habe Sie** ~ **nicht verstanden** I didn't hear or catch what you said

akut /a'ku:t/ **1** *Adj.* (a) (vordringlich) acute; pressing, urgent ‹question, issue›; (b) (Med.) acute. **2** *adv.* (Med.) in an acute form

AKW /a:ka:'ve:/ *das;* ~[s], ~s *Abk.* **Atomkraftwerk**

Akzeleration /aktselera'tsio:n/ *die;* ~, ~ (Anthrop., Astron.) acceleration

Akzelerator /aktsele'ra:tɔr/ *der;* ~, ~**en** /-ra'to:rən/ (Kerntechnik) accelerator

Akzent /ak'tsɛnt/ *der;* ~[e]s, ~**e** (a) (Sprachw.) accent; (Betonung) accent; stress; (b) (Sprachmelodie, Aussprache) accent; **mit starkem koreanischem** ~: with a strong Korean accent; (c) (Nachdruck, Gewicht) emphasis; stress; **den** ~ **[besonders] auf etw.** (*Akk.*) **legen** lay or put [particular] emphasis or stress on sth.; **neue** ~**e setzen** set new directions

akzent·frei 1 *Adj.* without an or any accent *postpos.* **2** *adv.* without an or any accent

akzentuieren /aktsɛntu'i:rən/ *tr. V.* (a) (deutlich aussprechen) enunciate; articulate; (betonen) accentuate; stress; (b) (fig.: hervorheben, auch Mode) accentuate

akzeptabel /aktsɛp'ta:bl̩/ **1** *Adj.* acceptable. **2** *adv.* acceptably

akzeptieren *tr. V.* accept

à la /a la/ (Gastr., ugs.) à la

Alabaster /ala'bastɐ/ *der;* ~**s**, ~: alabaster

à la carte /ala'kart/ (Gastr.) à la carte

Alarm /a'larm/ *der;* ~[e]s, ~**e** (a) alarm; (Flieger~) air-raid warning; ~ **geben** raise or sound or give the alarm; **blinder** ~: false alarm; ~ **schlagen** (ugs.) raise or sound the alarm; (b) (~zustand) alert

alarm-, Alarm-: ~**anlage** *die* alarm system; ~**bereit** *Adj.* on alert *postpos.;* ‹fire crew, police› on standby *postpos.,* standing by *pred.;* ~**bereitschaft** *die* ⇒ ~**bereit:** alert; **in [ständiger]** ~**bereitschaft** on [permanent] alert/standby; ~**glocke** *die* alarm bell

alarmieren *tr. V.* (a) alarm; ~**d** alarming; (b) (zu Hilfe rufen) call [out] ‹doctor, police, fire brigade, etc.›

Alarmierung *die;* ~: **bei rechtzeitiger** ~ **der Bergwacht** *usw.* if the mountain rescue service *etc.* is/had been called [out] in time

---

*alte Schreibung (vgl. Hinweise auf S. xvi–xvii)

Alarm-: ~**klingel** *die* alarm bell; ~**signal** *das* (auch fig.) warning signal; ~**sirene** *die* alarm or warning siren; ~**stufe** *die* alert stage; ~**stufe eins/zwei/drei** stage one/two/three alert; ~**übung** *die* practice drill; (Milit.) practice alert; ~**zeichen** *das* (fig.) warning signal; ~**zustand** *der* state of alert; **sich im** ~**zustand befinden** ‹troops› be on alert; ‹fire service, police› be on standby; ‹country, province› be on a state of alert

Alaska /a'laska/ (*das*); ~**s** Alaska

Alaun /a'laun/ *der;* ~**s**, ~**e** alum

Alaun·stift *der* styptic pencil

Albaner /al'ba:nɐ/ *der;* ~**s**, ~: ▶ 388 | Albanian

Albanien /al'ba:niən/ (*das*); ~**s** Albania

albanisch *Adj.* ▶ 388 |, ▶ 487 | Albanian; *s. auch* **deutsch; Deutsch; Deutsche²**

Albatros /'albatrɔs/ *der;* ~, ~**se** (Zool.) albatross

Alb-: ~**druck** *der; o. Pl.* nightmare; ~**drücken** *das;* ~**s** nightmares *pl.*

Alben ⇒ **Album**

albern¹ *itr. V.* fool about or around

albern² *Adj.* (a) silly; foolish; **sich** ~ **benehmen** act silly; **sich** (*Dat.*) ~ **vorkommen** feel silly; feel a fool; (b) (ugs.: nebensächlich) silly; stupid

Albernheit *die;* ~, ~**en** (a) *o. Pl.* silliness; foolishness; (b) (alberne Handlung) silliness; (alberne Bemerkung) silly remark

Albino /al'bi:no/ *der;* ~**s**, ~**s** albino

Alb·traum *der* nightmare

Album /'albʊm/ *das;* ~**s**, **Alben** album

Alchemie /alçe'mi:/ *usw.* (bes. österr.) ⇒ **Alchimie** *usw.*

Alchimie /alçi'mi:/ *die;* ~: alchemy *no art.*

Alchimist *der;* ~**en**, ~**en** alchemist

alchimistisch *Adj.* alchemical

Aldehyd /alde'hy:t/ *der;* ~**s**, ~**e** (Chem.) aldehyde

Alemanne /alə'manə/ *der;* ~**n**, ~**n**, **Alemannin** *die;* ~, ~**nen** Alemannian

alemannisch *Adj.* Alemannic

Alge /'algə/ *die;* ~, ~**n** alga

Algebra /'algebra, österr.: al'ge:bra/ *die;* ~, (fachspr.) **Algebren** algebra

algebraisch 1 *Adj.* algebraic. **2** *adv.* algebraically

Algerien /al'ge:riən/ (*das*); ~**s** Algeria

Algerier *der;* ~**s**, ~, ▶ 388 | Algerian

algerisch *Adj.* ▶ 388 | Algerian

Algier /'alʒi:ɐ̯/ (*das*); ~**s** ▶ 490 | Algiers

Algorithmus /algo'rɪtmʊs/ *der;* ~, **Algorithmen** (Math., DV) algorithm

alias /'a:lias/ *Adv.* alias

Alibi /'a:libi/ *das;* ~**s**, ~**s** (a) (Rechtsw.) alibi; (b) (Ausrede) alibi (coll.); excuse

Alimente /ali'mɛntə/ *Pl.* (veralt., noch ugs.) maintenance *sing.* (esp. for illegitimate child)

Alkali /al'ka:li/ *das;* ~**s**, **Alkalien** alkali

alkalisch *Adj.* (Chemie) alkaline

Alkohol /'alkoho:l/ *der;* ~**s**, ~**e** alcohol; **unter** ~ **stehen** (ugs.) be under the influence (coll.)

alkohol-, Alkohol-: ~**arm** *Adj.* low-alcohol *attr.;* low in alcohol *pred.;* ~**ausschank** *der* sale of alcohol[ic drinks]; ~**einfluss**, *** ~einfluß** *der* influence of alcohol or drink; **unter** ~**einfluss [stehen]** [be] under the influence of alcohol or drink; ~**fahne** *die* smell of alcohol [on one's breath]; **eine** ~**fahne haben** smell of alcohol; ~**frei** *Adj.* (a) non-alcoholic; ~**freie Getränke** soft or non-alcoholic drinks; (b) (ohne ~ausschank) dry ‹country, state, etc.›; ~**gehalt** *der* alcohol content; ~**genuss**, *** ~genuß** *der; o. Pl.* consumption of alcohol; ~**haltig** *Adj.* containing alcohol *postpos., not pred.*

Alkoholika /alko'ho:lika/ *Pl.* alcoholic drinks

Alkoholiker *der;* ~**s**, ~, **Alkoholikerin** *die;* ~, ~**nen** alcoholic

alkoholisch *Adj.* alcoholic

alkoholisiert *Adj.* inebriated; **in** ~**em Zustand** in a state of inebriation

Alkoholismus *der;* ~: alcoholism *no art.*

alkohol-, Alkohol-: ~**konsum** *der* consumption of alcohol; ~**krank** *Adj.* (Med.) alcoholic; ~**missbrauch**, ***~**mißbrauch** *der* alcohol abuse; ~**spiegel** *der* level of alcohol in one's blood; ~**süchtig** *Adj.* addicted to alcohol *postpos.;* alcoholic; ~**verbot** *das* ban on alcohol; ~**vergiftung** *die* alcohol[ic] poisoning

Alkoven /al'ko:vn̩/ *der;* ~**s**, ~: alcove; (Bettnische) bedrecess

all /al/ *Indefinitpron. u. unbest. Zahlw.* **1** *attr.* (ganz, gesamt…) all; **in** ~**er Deutlichkeit** in all clarity; ~**e Freude, die sie empfunden hat** all the joy she felt; ~**es Geld, das ich noch habe** all the money I have left; **ich kann diese Leute** ~**e nicht leiden** I can't stand any of these people; ~ **unser/mein** *usw.* …**:** all our/my *etc.* …; ~**es andere/Weitere/Übrige** everything else; ~**es Schöne/Neue/ Fremde** everything *or* all that is beautiful/new/strange; ~**e Fenster schließen** close all the windows; **wir/ihr/sie** ~**e** all of us/you/them; we/you/they all; ~**e Beteiligten/Anwesenden** all those involved/present; ~**e beide/**~**e zehn** both of them/all ten of them; ~**e Männer/Frauen/Kinder** all men/women/children; ~**e Bewohner der Stadt** all the inhabitants of the town; **ohne** ~**en Anlass** for no reason [at all]; without any reason [at all]; ~**e Jahre wieder** every year; ~**e fünf Minuten/Meter** every five minutes/metres; **Bücher** ~**er Art** books of all kinds; all kinds of books; **in** ~**er Eile** with all haste; **in** ~**er Ruhe** in peace and quiet; **trotz** ~**er Versuche/Anstrengungen** despite all [his/her/their/*etc.*] attempts/efforts. **2** *allein stehend* **(a)** ~**e** everyone; ~**e miteinander/auf einmal** all together/at once; ~**e, die** … all those who …; **(b)** ~**es** (auf Sachen bezogen) everything; (auf Personen bezogen) everybody; **das** ~**es** all that; **das ist** ~**es Unsinn** that is all nonsense; **was gab es** ~**es zu sehen?** what was there to see?; **was es nicht** ~**es gibt!** well, would you believe it!; well, I never!; **zu** ~**em fähig sein** (fig.) be capable of anything; ~**es in** ~**em** all in all; **vor** ~**em** above all; **das ist** ~**es** that's all *or* (coll.) it; **das sind** ~**es Gauner** (ugs.) they're all scoundrels; **wer** ~**es war** *od.* **wer war** ~**es da?** who was there?; ~**es mal herhören!** (ugs.) listen everybody!; (stärker befehlend) everybody listen!; ~**es aussteigen!** (ugs.) everyone *or* all out!; (vom Schaffner gesagt) all change!

All *das;* ~**s** space *no art.;* (Universum) universe

all·abendlich 1 *Adj.; nicht präd.* regular evening; **2** *adv.* every evening

alle *Adj.; nicht attr.* **(a)** (ugs.: verbraucht, verkauft usw.) ~ **sein** be all gone; ~ **werden** run out; **etw.** ~ **machen** finish sth. off; **(b)** (salopp: erschöpft) all in *pred.*

alle·dem *Pron.* **trotz** ~**:** in spite of *or* despite all that; **von** ~ **wusste er nichts** he knew nothing about all that; **bei** ~**:** for all that

Allee /a'le:/ *die;* ~, ~**n** avenue

Allee·baum *der* avenue tree

Allegorie /alego'ri:/ *die;* ~, ~**n** allegory

allegorisch *Adj.* allegorical

allein /a'lain/ **1** *Adj.; nicht attr.* **(a)** (ohne andere, für sich) alone; on one's/its own; by oneself/itself; **sie waren** ~ **im Zimmer** they were alone in the room; **ganz** ~**:** all on one's/its own; **jmdn.** ~ **lassen** leave sb. alone *or* on his/her own; **etw.** ~ **tun** do sth. oneself; **(b)** (einsam) alone. **2** *adv.* (ohne Hilfe) by oneself/itself; on one's/its own; **sie kann** ~ **schwimmen** she can swim by herself *or* on her own; **etw.** ~ **tun** do sth. oneself; **eine** ~ **erziehende Mutter** a single mother; **eine** ~ **stehende Frau** a woman living on her own *or* alone; (ledige Frau) a single woman; **ich bin** ~ **stehend** I live on my own *or* alone; (bin ledig) I am single; **von** ~**[e]** (ugs.) by oneself/itself. **3** *Adv.* **(a)** (geh.: ausschließlich) alone; **er** ~ **trägt die Verantwortung** he alone bears responsibility; **sie denkt** ~ **an sich** she thinks solely *or* only of herself; **nicht** ~ …, **sondern auch** …: not only …, but also …; **(b)** (von allem anderen abgesehen) **[schon]** ~ **der Gedanke/ [schon] der Gedanke** ~**:** the mere *or* very thought [of it]; ~ **die Nebenkosten** the additional costs alone

alleine (ugs.) ⇨ **allein**

allein-, Allein-: ~**erbe** *der* sole heir; ***~**erziehend** ⇨ allein 2; ~**erziehende** *der/die;* adj. Dekl. single parent; ~**gang** *der* (fig.) independent initiative; **etw. im** ~**gang tun** do sth. off one's own bat; ~**herrschaft** *die; o. Pl.* autocratic rule; (Diktatur) dictatorship; ~**herrscher** *der* (auch fig.) autocrat; (Diktator, auch fig.) dictator

alleinig *Adj.; nicht präd.* sole; sole, exclusive ⟨distribution rights⟩

allein-, Allein-: ~**inhaber** *der* (Wirtsch.) sole owner; ~**schuld** *die; o. Pl.* sole blame *or* responsibility *no indef. art.;* ~**sein** *das* **(a)** (das Verlassensein) loneliness; **(b)** (das Ungestörtsein) privacy; ***~**stehend** ⇨ allein 2; ~**stehende** *der/die; adj. Dekl.* person living on his/her own *or* alone; (Ledige[r]) single person; **ich als** ~**stehender** …: living on my own I …/as a single person I …; ~**unter·halter** *der* solo entertainer; ~**verdiener** *der* sole earner

alle·mal *Adv.* (ugs.) any time (coll.); **was der kann, das kann ich doch** ~**:** anything he can do, I can do too

allen·falls *Adv.* **(a)** (höchstens) at [the] most; at the outside; ~ **40 Leute** 40 people at most *or* at the outside; at most 40 people; **(b)** (bestenfalls) at best

allenthalben /'alənt'halbn̩/ *Adv.* (geh.) everywhere

aller-: ~**äußerst**… *Adj.; nicht präd.* **(a)** farthest; **(b)** (schlimmst…) worst; **im** ~**äußersten Fall** if the worst comes/came to the worst; ~**best**… **1** *Adj.* very best; **der/die/das Allerbeste sein** be the best of all; **es wäre das Allerbeste, wenn du ihn selbst fragst** the best thing [of all] would be for you to ask him yourself; **am** ~**besten wäre es, wenn** …: the best thing [of all] would be if …; **2** *adv.* **am** ~**besten** best of all; ~**dings 1** *Adv.* **(a)** (einschränkend) though; **es stimmt** ~**dings, dass** …: it's true though that …; **(b)** (zustimmend) [yes,] certainly; **Habe ich dich geweckt? — Allerdings!** Did I wake you up? — You certainly did!; **das war** ~**dings Pech** that was bad luck, to be sure; ~**erst**… *Adj.; nicht präd.* **(a)** very first; **als** ~**erste[r] etw. tun** be the very first to do sth.; **(b)** (allerbest…) very best; ~**frühestens** *Adv.* at the very earliest

Allergie /aler'gi:/ *die;* ~, ~**n** ▶ 329 (Med.) allergy; **eine** ~ **gegen etw. haben** have an allergy to sth.

allergisch 1 *Adj.* (Med., fig.) allergic (**gegen** to). **2** *adv.* **auf etw. (Akk.)** ~ **reagieren** (Med.) have an allergic reaction to sth.; **auf jmdn./etw.** ~ **reagieren** (fig.) be allergic to sb./sth.

aller-, Aller-: ~**größt**… *Adj.* utmost ⟨trouble, care, etc.⟩; biggest *or* largest ⟨car, house, town, etc.⟩ of all; tallest ⟨person⟩ of all; **am** ~**größten sein** be [the] biggest *or* largest/tallest of all; ~**hand** *indekl. unbest. Gattungsz.* (ugs.) **(a)** *attr.* all kinds *or* sorts of; **(b)** *allein stehend* all kinds *or* sorts of things; **das ist** ~**hand!** (viel) that's a lot; (sehr gut) that's quite something; **das ist ja** *od.* **doch** ~**hand!** that's just not on (Brit. coll.); that really is the limit (coll.); ~**heiligen** *das;* ~ (bes. kath. Kirche) All Saints' Day; All Hallows; ~**herzlichst**… *Adj.* warmest ⟨thanks, greetings, congratulations⟩; most cordial ⟨reception, welcome, invitation⟩; ~**höchst**… **1** *Adj.* highest … of all; **der** ~**höchste Gipfel** the highest peak of all; **es ist** ~**höchste Zeit, dass** …: it really is high time that …; **die** ~**höchsten Kreise** the very highest circles; **2** *adv.* **am** ~**höchsten** ⟨fly, jump, etc.⟩ the highest of all; ~**höchstens** *Adv.* at the very most

allerlei *indekl. unbest. Gattungsz.:* *attr.* all kinds *or* sorts of; *allein stehend* all kinds *or* sorts of things

Allerlei *das;* ~**s**, ~**s** (Gemisch) potpourri; (Durcheinander) jumble

aller-, Aller-: ~**letzt**… *Adj.; nicht präd.* **(a)** very last; **der/die Allerletzte sein** be the very last; **(b)** (ugs.: ~schlechtest…) most dreadful *or* awful (coll.); **das ist [ja** *od.* **wirklich] das Allerletzte** (ugs.) that [really] is the absolute limit; **(c)** (~neuest…) very latest; ~**liebst 1** *Adj.* **(a)** most favourite; **es wäre mir das Allerliebste** *od.* **am** ~**liebsten, wenn** …: I should like it best of all if …; **ihr Allerliebster/seine Allerliebste** her/his beloved; **(b)** (reizend) enchanting; delightful; **2** *adv.* **(a)** **etw. am**

~**liebsten tun** like doing sth. best of all; **am** ~**liebsten trinkt/mag er Wein** he likes wine best of all; **(b)** (reizend) delightfully; ~**meist**... 1 *Indefinitpron. u. unbest. Zahlw.* by far the most *attrib.;* **das** ~**meiste/am** ~**meisten** most of all/by far the most; **die** ~**meiste Zeit** by far the greatest part of the time; **die** ~**meisten [der Arbeiter** *usw.***]** the vast majority [of the workers *etc.*]; 2 *Adv.* **am** ~**meisten** most of all; **die am** ~**meisten befahrene Straße** by far the most travelled road; ~**min-dest**... *Adj.; nicht präd.* slightest; least; **das** ~**mindeste** the very least; **nicht das** ~**mindeste** absolutely nothing; **nicht im** ~**mindesten** not in the least or slightest; ~**nächst**... 1 *Adj.* very nearest *attrib.;* (räumliche od. zeitliche Reihenfolge ausdrückend) very next *attrib.;* very closest ‹*relatives*›; 2 *adv.* **am** ~**nächsten** nearest of all; ~**neu[e]st**... *Adj.* very latest *attrib.;* **das Allerneu[e]-ste** the very latest; ~**nötigst**..., ~**notwendigst**... 1 *Adj.* absolutely necessary; **es am** ~**nötigsten** od. ~**notwendigsten haben, etw. zu tun** be most in need of doing sth.; **das Allernötigste** what is/was absolutely necessary; 2 *adv.* **am** ~**nötigsten** ‹*need etc.*› most badly; ~**schlimmst**... 1 *Adj.* very worst *attrib.;* **am** ~**schlimmsten sein** be the worst of all; **der/die/das Allerschlimmste** the worst of all; 2 *adv.* **am** ~**schlimmsten** worst of all; ~**schönst**... 1 *Adj.* most beautiful *attrib.;* loveliest *attrib.;* (angenehmst...) very nicest *attrib.;* **das Allerschönste, was ich je gesehen habe** the loveliest thing I have ever seen; **das wäre ja noch das Allerschönste** that would beat everything; **am** ~**schönsten war, dass** ...: the best thing of all was that ...; 2 *adv.* **er schreibt/singt** *usw.* **am** ~**schönsten** his writing/singing *etc.* is the most beautiful of all; ~**seelen** *das;* ~ (kath. Kirche) All Souls' Day; ~**seits** *Adv.* **(a)** (alle zusammen) **guten Morgen** ~**seits!** good morning everyone or everybody; **(b)** (überall) on all sides; on every side; ~**seits sehr geschätzt sein** be highly regarded by everyone; ~**spätestens** *Adv.* at the very latest
Allerwelts-: ~**gesicht** *das* nondescript face; ~**kerl** *der* Jack of all trades; ~**mittel** *das* cure-all; ~**wort** *das* hackneyed word
aller-: ~**wenigst**... 1 *Adj.* least ... of all; *Pl.* fewest ... of all; **die** ~**wenigsten [Menschen] wissen das** very few [people] know that; **das Allerwenigste, was er hätte tun können** the very least he could have done; **am** ~**wenigsten abbekommen** get [the] least of all; 2 *adv.* **das am** ~**wenigsten!** anything but that!; ~**wenig-stens** *Adv.* at the very least
alle·samt *indekl. Indefinitpron. u. unbest. Zahlw.* (ugs.) all [of you/us/them]; **wir** ~: all of us; we all
Alles-: ~**fresser** *der* omnivore; ~**kleber** *der* all-purpose adhesive or glue; ~**könner** *der* all-rounder
all·gemein 1 *Adj.* general; universal ‹*conscription, suffrage*›; universally applicable ‹*law, rule*›; **auf** ~**en Wunsch** by popular or general request; **das** ~**e Wohl** the common good; **im** ~**en Interesse** in the common interest; in everybody's interest; **im Allgemeinen** in general; generally. 2 *adv.* **(a)** generally; **es ist** ~ **bekannt, dass** ...: it is common knowledge that ...; ~ **zugänglich** open to all or everybody; ~ **bildend** ‹*school, course, etc.*› providing a general or an all-round (*Amer.*) all-around education; ~ **gültig** universally or generally applicable ‹*law, rule*›; universally or generally valid ‹*law of nature, definition, thesis*›; ~ **verbindlich** universally binding; ~ **verständlich** comprehensible or intelligible to all *postpos.;* **etw.** ~ **verständlich erklären** explain sth. in a way comprehensible or intelligible to all; **(b)** (oft abwertend: unverbindlich) ‹*write, talk, discuss, examine, be worded*› in general terms; **eine** ~ **gehaltene Einführung** a general introduction
allgemein-, Allgemein-: ~**befinden** *das* (Med.) general state of health; general condition; ~**begriff** *der* (Philos., Sprachw.) general concept; ~**besitz** *der* (auch fig.) common property
*****allgemein·bildend** ⇨ allgemein 2 a
Allgemein·bildung *die; o. Pl.* general or all-round or (*Amer.*) all-around education;

*****allgemein·gültig** ⇨ allgemein 2 a
Allgemein-: ~**gültigkeit** *die* (eines Gesetzes) universal or general applicability; (eines Naturgesetzes, einer Definition, einer These) universal or general validity; ~**gut** *das* (fig.) common knowledge
Allgemeinheit *die;* ~ **(a)** generality; **(b)** (Öffentlichkeit) general public
Allgemein-: ~**medizin** *die; o. Pl.* general medicine; ~**mediziner** *der* general practitioner; GP; ~**platz** *der* platitude; commonplace
*****allgemein·verbindlich** *usw.:* ⇨ allgemein 2 a
Allgemein-: ~**wissen** *das* general knowledge; ~**wohl** *das* public welfare or good
All·heil·mittel *das* (auch fig.) cure-all; panacea
Alligator /ali'ga:tɔr/ *der;* ~**s,** ~**en** /...ga'to:rən/ alligator
alliiert *Adj.; nicht präd.* allied
Alliierte *der; adj. Dekl.* ally; **die** ~**n** the Allies
all-, All-: ~**jährlich** 1 *Adj.* annual; yearly; 2 *adv.* annually; every year; ~**mächtig** *Adj.* omnipotent; all-powerful; **der** ~**mächtige Gott** Almighty God; ~**mächtiger Gott!** (ugs.) good God!; heavens above!; ~**mäch-tige** *der; adj. Dekl.* **der** ~**mächtige** the Almighty; ~**mächtiger!** good God!; heavens above!
all·mählich 1 *Adj., nicht präd.* gradual. 2 *adv.* gradually. 3 *Adv.* **es wird** ~ **Zeit** it's about time; **ich werde** ~ **müde** I'm beginning to get tired; **wir sollten** ~ **gehen** it's time we got going
all-, All-: ~**monatlich** 1 *Adj.* monthly; 2 *adv.* monthly; every month; ~**morgendlich** 1 *Adj.; nicht präd.* regular morning; 2 *adv.* every morning; ~**partei-en·regierung** *die* all-party government; ~**rad·an-trieb** *der* (Kfz-W.) all-wheel drive
Allround·man /'ɔːl'raʊndmən/ *der;* ~**s, Allroundmen** all-rounder
all-: ~**seitig** 1 *Adj.* general; all-round, (*Amer.*) all-around *attrib.;* **zur** ~**seitigen Zufriedenheit** to the satisfaction of all or everyone; 2 *adv.* generally; **man war** ~**seitig einverstanden** there was agreement on all sides or general agreement; ~**seitig geachtet** highly regarded by everyone; ~**seits** *Adv.* everywhere; on all sides; (in jeder Hinsicht) in all respects; ~**seits geschätzt** highly regarded by everyone
All·tag *der* **(a)** (Werktag) weekday; **ein Mantel für den** ~: a coat for everyday wear; **zum** ~ **gehören** (fig.) be part of everyday life; **(b)** *o. Pl.* (Einerlei) daily routine; **der graue** ~: the dull routine of everyday life; **der** ~ **der Ehe** the day-to-day realities of married life
all·täglich *Adj.* ordinary ‹*face, person, appearance, etc.*›; everyday ‹*topic, event, sight*›; **ein nicht** ~**er Anblick** a sight one doesn't see every day; **etw. Alltägliches sein** be an everyday occurrence
Alltäglichkeit *die;* ~**,** ~**en (a)** *o. Pl.* ordinariness; **(b)** (alltäglicher Vorgang) everyday occurrence
all·tags *Adv.* [on] weekdays
Alltags- everyday *attrib.;* of everyday life *postpos., not pred.;* ~**pflicht** daily duty
Alltags-: ~**kleidung** *die* everyday or workaday clothes *pl.;* ~**trott** *der* (abwertend) daily round or grind
all-, All-: ~**wissend** *Adj.* omniscient; ~**wissenheit** *die;* ~: omniscience; ~**wöchentlich** 1 *Adj.* weekly; 2 *adv.* weekly; every week; ~**zeit** *Adv.* (veralt.) always; ~**zeit bereit!** be prepared!
all·zu *Adv.* all too; ~ **viele** far too many; **er war nicht** ~ **begeistert** he was not too or not all that enthusiastic; **nicht** ~ **viele** not all that many (coll.); not too many; ~ **bald** all too soon; **nicht** ~ **früh** not too early; **etw.** ~ **gern mögen** like sth. only too much; **etw.** ~ **gern tun** do sth. all too willingly; **ich esse zwar Fisch, aber nicht** ~ **gern** I'll eat fish, but I'm not all that fond or not overfond of it; ~ **lang[e]/oft** too long/often; ~ **sehr/viel** too much; **nicht** ~ **oft** not too often; not all that often (coll.)
*****allzu·bald** *usw.:* ⇨ allzu

All·zweck- all-purpose

Alm /alm/ *die;* ~, ~**en** mountain pasture; Alpine pasture

Almosen /'almo:zn̩/ *das;* ~**s**, ~ (a) (veralt.: Spende) alms *pl.;* **von** ~ **leben** live on charity; (b) (abwertend: dürftiges Entgelt) pittance

Alm·rausch *der;* ~[**e**]**s** (österr., südd.) Alpine rose; alpenrose

Aloe /'a:loe/ *die;* ~, ~**n** aloe

Alp /alp/ *die;* ~, ~**en** (bes. schweiz.) ⇒ **Alm**

Alpaka /al'paka/ *das;* ~**s**, ~**s** alpaca

Alpaka·wolle *die* alpaca wool

Alp-: ~**druck** ⇒ **Albdruck**; ~**drücken** ⇒ **Albdrücken**

Alpen *Pl. die* ~: the Alps

Alpen- Alpine

Alpen-: ~**glühen** *das;* ~**s** alpenglow; ~**land** *das; o. Pl.* Alpine country *or* region; ~**rose** *die* rhododendron; Alpine rose; ~**veilchen** *das* cyclamen

Alpha /'alfa/ *das;* ~[**s**], ~[**s**] alpha

Alphabet /alfa'be:t/ *das;* ~[**e**]**s**, ~**e** alphabet

alphabetisch 1 *Adj.* alphabetical. 2 *adv.* alphabetically

alphabetisieren *tr. V.* (a) (ordnen) arrange in alphabetical order *or* alphabetically; alphabetize; (b) (lesen u. schreiben lehren) *jmdn.* ~: teach sb. to read and write

Alphabetisierung *die;* ~: teaching literacy skills

alpha·numerisch (DV) 1 *Adj.* alphanumeric. 2 *adv.* alphanumerically

Alp·horn *das* alpenhorn

alpin /al'pi:n/ *Adj.* Alpine

Alpinist *der;* ~**en**, ~**en** Alpinist

Alp·traum ⇒ **Albtraum**

Alraune /al'raune/ *die;* ~, ~**n** mandrake

als /als/ *Konj.* (a) *Temporalsatz einleitend:* when; (während, indem) as; **gerade** ~: just as; **gleich** ~: as soon as; **damals,** ~: [in the days] when; (b) *Kausalsatz einleitend:* **um so mehr,** ~: all the more since *or* in that; *s. auch* **insofern; insoweit;** (c) ..., ~ **da sind** ... to wit; namely; **die [drei] Grundfarben,** ~ **da sind Rot, Blau und Gelb** the [three] primary colours, to wit *or* namely red, blue, and yellow; (d) *Vergleichspartikel* **größer/älter/ mehr** *usw.* ~ ... bigger/older/more *etc.* than ...; **kein anderer** *od.* **niemand anderes** ~ ... none other than; **niemand** *od.* **keiner** ~ ... nobody but ...; **nirgends anders** ~ ... nowhere but ...; **er ist alles andere** ~ **schüchtern** he is anything but shy; **du brauchst nichts [anderes] zu tun,** ~ **abzuwarten** all you need to do is just wait and see; **anders** ~ ... different/differently from ...; **lieber hänge ich mich auf,** ~ **dass ich ins Gefängnis gehe** I'd rather hang myself than go to prison, **die Kinder sind noch zu klein,** ~ **dass wir sie allein lassen könnten** the children are still too small for us to be able to leave them on their own; ~ [**wenn** *od.* **ob**] (+ *Konjunktiv II*) as if *or* though; **er tut so,** ~ **ob** *od.* **wenn er nichts wüsste, er tut so,** ~ **wüsste er nichts** he pretends not to know anything; ~ **wenn** *od.* **ob ich das nicht wüsste!** as if I didn't know!; **so viel/so weit** ~ **möglich** as much/as far as possible; *s. auch* **sowohl;** (e) ~ **Rentner/Arzt** *usw.* as a pensioner/doctor *etc.;* **du** ~ **Lehrer** ... as a teacher you ...; *jmdn.* ~ **faul/ Dummkopf bezeichnen** call sb. lazy/a fool; **sich** ~ **wahr/Lüge erweisen** prove to be true/a lie

als·baldig *Adj.; nicht präd.* (Papierdt.) immediate

also /'alzo/ 1 *Adv.* (folglich) so; therefore; ~ **kommst du mit?** so you're coming too? 2 *Partikel* (a) (das heißt) that is; (b) (nach Unterbrechung) well [then]; ~, **wie ich schon sagte** well [then], as I was saying; (c) (verstärkend) ~, **kommst du jetzt oder nicht?** well, are you coming now or not?; **na** ~! there you are[, you see]; ~ **schön** well all right then; ~ **so was/nein!** well, I don't know; well, really; ~ **gute Nacht** goodnight then; ~ **dann** right then

alt /alt/, **älter** /'ɛltɐ/, **ältest...** /'ɛltəst.../ *Adj.* (a) ▶ **22** old; **Alt und Jung** old and young; **seine** ~**en Eltern** his aged parents; **mein älterer/ältester Bruder** my elder/

eldest brother; **Cato der Ältere** Cato the Elder; **hier werde ich nicht** ~ (fig. ugs.) I won't be staying here long; ~ **aussehen** (fig. salopp) be in the cart (sl.); **eine sieben Jahre** ~**e Tochter** a seven-year-old daughter; **wie** ~ **bist du?** how old are you?; *s. auch* **Herr a;** (b) (nicht mehr frisch) old; ~**es Brot** stale bread; (c) (vom letzten Jahr) old; ~**e Äpfel/Kartoffeln** last year's apples/potatoes; **im** ~**en Jahr** (dieses Jahr) this year; (letztes Jahr) last year; (d) (seit langem bestehend) ancient; old; long-standing ⟨*acquaintance*⟩; long-serving ⟨*employee*⟩; **ein** ~**es Volk/ ein** ~**er Brauch** an ancient people/an ancient *or* old custom; **in** ~**er Freundschaft, dein** ... yours, as ever, ...; **am Alten hängen** cling to the past; (e) (antik, klassisch) ancient; (f) (vertraut) old familiar ⟨*streets, sights, etc.*⟩; **ganz der/die Alte sein** be just the same; **es bleibt alles beim Alten** things will stay as they were; (g) (ugs.) (vertraulich) ~**er Freund/**~**es Haus!** old friend/pal (coll.); (bewundernd) **ein** ~**er Fuchs/Gauner** an old fox/rascal; (verstärkend) **die** ~**e Hexe/der** ~**e Geizkragen** the old witch/skinflint; *s. auch* **Alte**

Alt¹ *der;* ~**s**, ~**e** (Musik) alto; (Frauenstimme) contralto; alto; (im Chor) altos *pl.;* contraltos *pl.*

Alt² *das;* ~**s**, ~: top fermented, dark beer

Altar /al'ta:ɐ̯/ *der;* ~[**e**]**s**, **Altäre** /al'tɛ:rə/ altar

Altar-: ~**bild** *das* altar-piece; ~**gerät** *das* altar furniture; ~**raum** *der* chancel

alt-, Alt-: ~**backen** *Adj.* (a) stale ⟨*bread, roll, etc.*⟩; (b) (abwertend: altmodisch) outdated ⟨*ideas, views, policies*⟩; ~**bau** *der; Pl.* ~**bauten** old building; ~**bau·wohnung** *die* flat (Brit.) *or* (Amer.) apartment in an old building; old flat (Brit.) *or* (Amer.) apartment; ~**bekannt** *Adj.* well-known; ~**bewährt** *Adj.* well-tried; long-standing ⟨*tradition, friendship*⟩; ~**bier** *das* ⇒ **Alt²;** ~**bundeskanzler** *der* former Federal Chancellor; ~**bundespräsident** *der* former Federal President

Alte *der/die; adj. Dekl.* (a) (alter Mensch) old man/woman; *Pl.* (alte Menschen) old people; (b) (salopp) (Vater, Ehemann) old man (coll.); (Mutter) old woman (coll.); (Ehefrau) missis (sl.); old woman (coll.); (Chef) boss (coll.); governor (sl.); (Chefin) boss (coll.); **die** ~**n** (Eltern) my/his *etc.* old man and old woman (coll.); (c) *Pl.* (Tiereltern) parents; (d) *Pl.* **die** ~**n** (geh.: Menschen der Antike) the ancients

alt-: ~**ehrwürdig** *Adj.* (geh.) venerable; time-honoured ⟨*customs*⟩; ~**eingeführt** *Adj.* old-established; ~**englisch** *Adj.* Old English

Alten-: ~**heim** *das* old people's home; ~**tages·stätte** *die* old people's day centre; ~**teil** *das in* **sich aufs** ~**teil zurückziehen** (fig.) retire; ~**wohn·heim** *das* old people's home

Alter *das;* ~**s**, ~: **▶ 22** age; (hohes ~) old age; **im** ~: in one's old age; **mit dem** ~: with age; **er ist in meinem** ~: he is my age; **im** ~ **von** at the age of; **eine Frau mittleren** ~**s** a middle-aged woman; **Kinder in diesem** ~: children of this age

älter /'ɛltɐ/ 1 ⇒ **alt.** 2 *Adj.* (nicht mehr jung) elderly; **eine Melodie für unsere** ~**en Hörer** a tune for our older listeners; **Ältere** (ältere Menschen) the elderly; *s. auch* **Mit·bürger**

Alterchen *das;* ~**s**, ~ (ugs.) grandad (coll.)

altern 1 *itr. V.; mit sein* (a) age; (b) (reifen) mature. 2 *tr. V.* age, mature ⟨*wine, spirits*⟩

alternativ /altɛrna'ti:f/ 1 *Adj.* alternative. 2 *adv.* alternatively; ⟨*work, farm*⟩ using alternative methods

Alternativ·bewegung *die* alternative movement

Alternative *die;* ~, ~**n** alternative

alt·erprobt *Adj.* well-tried

alters *in* **seit** ~, **von** ~ **her** (geh.) from time immemorial

alters-, Alters-: ~**erscheinung** *die* sign of old age; ~**gemäß** 1 *Adj.* ⟨*behaviour, education, etc.*⟩ appropriate to one's/its age; 2 *adv.* in a manner appropriate to one's/its age ~**genosse** *der,* ~**genossin** *die* contemporary; person/child of the same age; ~**grenze** *die* age limit; (für Rente) retirement age; ~**gründe** *Pl.* reasons of age; ~**gruppe** *die* age group; ~**heim** *das* old people's home; old-age home (Amer.); ~**rente** *die* old-age pension; ~**ruhe·geld** *das* retirement pension; ~**schwach** *Adj.* old and infirm ⟨*person*⟩; old and weak

Altersangaben

Wie alt?

Wie alt ist sie?	= How old is she?, What age is she?
Sie ist vierzig [Jahre alt]	= She is forty [years old] *od. (formeller)* forty years of age
Er ist gerade sechzig geworden	= He has just turned sixty
im Alter von zwanzig Jahren, mit zwanzig	= at the age of twenty, at twenty
ein Fünfzigjähriger	= a fifty-year-old [man], a man of fifty
eine Fünfzigjährige	= a fifty-year-old [woman], a woman of fifty
ein zehnjähriges Mädchen	= a ten-year-old girl
ein achtzigjähriger Rentner	= an eighty-year-old pensioner

Älter oder jünger?

Ich bin älter als du	= I'm older than you [are]
Sie ist viel jünger als er	= She's much younger than him *od.* than he is
Er ist vier Jahre älter als ich	= He's four years older than me *od. (formeller)* four years my senior
Du bist zwanzig Jahre jünger als sie	= You're twenty years younger than her *od. (formeller)* twenty years her junior
Sie sind gleich alt od. gleichaltrig	= They are the same age
Sie ist [genau] so alt wie Martin	= She is [just] the same age as Martin

Ungefähres Alter

Er ist um die fünfzig	= He's about fifty
Sie ist etwas über sechzig	= She's just over *od.* a little over sixty
Er wird bald vierzig	= He'll soon be forty, He's nearly forty
Sie geht auf die siebzig zu	= She's getting on for seventy
Sie sind in den Sechzigern	= They're in their sixties
Er ist Ende/Anfang/ Mitte dreißig	= He's in his late thirties/ early thirties/mid-thirties
Er ist noch ein Teenager	= He is still a teenager *od.* in his teens
Er ist gerade zehn geworden	= He's just ten
Das Kind ist noch keine zehn Jahre alt	= The child is barely ten years old
für Kinder unter zwölf [Jahren]	= for the under-twelves *od.* under-12s
für alle über sechzig	= for the over-sixties *od.* over-60s
Sie fühlt sich/sieht aus wie zwanzig	= She feels/looks like twenty

---

‹*animal*›; [old and] decrepit ‹*object*›; **eine ~schwache Frau** an infirm *or* frail old woman; **~schwäche** *die;* o. Pl. (bei Menschen) [old] age and infirmity; (bei Tieren) [old] age and weakness; (von Dingen) [age and] decrepitude; **~sichtig** *Adj.* presbyopic (Med.); **~stufe** *die* age; **~unterschied** *der* age difference; **~versorgung** *die* provision for one's old age; (System) pension scheme

Altertum *das;* **~s, Altertümer** /-ty:mɐ/ **(a)** o. Pl. antiquity *no art.;* **(b)** Pl. antiquities

altertümlich 1 *Adj.* old-fashioned. **2** in an old-fashioned style

Altertümlichkeit *die;* **~:** old-fashionedness

Altertums·forschung *die;* o. Pl. archaeology

Alterung *die;* **~, ~en (a)** (das Altwerden) ageing; **(b)** (von Werkstoffen) ageing; **(c)** (von Wein usw.) ageing; maturing

Älteste /'ɛltəstə/ *der/die; adj. Dekl.* **(a)** (Dorf~, Vereins~, Kirchen~ usw.) elder; **(b)** (Sohn, Tochter) eldest

alt-, Alt-: **~flöte** *die* (Querflöte) alto *or* bass flute; (Blockflöte) alto *or* treble recorder; (ugs. scherzh.) **1** *Adj.* old-fashioned. **2** *adv.* in an old-fashioned way; **~gedient** *Adj.* long-serving; **~glas·behälter** *der* bottle bank; **~griechisch** *Adj.* ancient Greek; (Ling.) classical *or* ancient Greek; **~griechisch** *das* classical *or* ancient Greek; **~her·gebracht** *Adj.* traditional; **~hochdeutsch** *Adj.* Old High German; **~hochdeutsch** *das* Old High German

Altistin *die;* **~, ~nen** (Musik) alto; contralto

alt-, Alt-: **~klug**; **~kluger**, **~klugst...** **1** *Adj.* precocious; **2** *adv.* precociously; **~klugheit** *die* precociousness; **~last** *die* **(a)** (Ökologie) old, improperly disposed of harmful waste *no indef. art.;* **(b)** (fig.) inherited problem

ältlich /'ɛltlɪç/ *Adj.* rather elderly; oldish

alt-, Alt-: **~material** *das* scrap; **~meister** *der* **(a)** (Vorbild) doyen; **(b)** (Sport) ex-champion; former champion;

~meisterin *die* **(a)** (Vorbild) doyenne; **(b)** ⇒ **~meister b**; **~metall** *das* scrap metal; **~modisch 1** *Adj.* old-fashioned; **2** *adv.* in an old-fashioned way; **~öl** *das* used oil; **~papier** *das* waste paper; **~philologe** *der* classical scholar; **~philologie** *die* classical studies *pl., no art.;* **~philologisch** *Adj.* classical; **~rosa** *indekl. Adj.* old rose

altruistisch (geh.) **1** *Adj.* altruistic. **2** *adv.* altruistically

alt-, Alt-: **~sänger** *der* alto; **~sängerin** *die* alto; contralto; **~schnee** *der* old snow; **~stadt** *die* old [part of the] town; **die Düsseldorfer ~stadt** the old part of Düsseldorf; **~stimme** *die* alto voice; (von Frau) alto *or* contralto voice; **~überliefert** *Adj.* traditional; **~väterisch** /-fɛːtərɪʃ/ **1** *Adj.* old-fashioned; **2** *adv.* in an old-fashioned way; **~vertraut** *Adj.* old familiar *attrib.;* **~waren·händler** *der* second-hand dealer

Alu¹ /'aːlu/ *das;* **~s** (ugs.) aluminium

Alu² *die;* **~** *Abk.:* (ugs.) **Arbeitslosenunterstützung** dole [money] (Brit.); unemployment pay

Alu·folie *die* aluminium foil

Aluminium /alu'miːni̯ʊm/ *das;* **~s** aluminium

Aluminium·folie *die* aluminium foil

am /am/ *Präp. + Art.* **(a)** = **an dem**; **(b)** (räumlich) **am Boden** on the floor; **Frankfurt am Main** Frankfurt on [the] Main; **am Rande** on the edge; **am Marktplatz** on the market square *or* place; **am Meer/Fluss** by the sea/ on *or* by the river; **am Anfang/Ende** at the beginning/ end; **sich am Kopf stoßen** bang one's head; **(c)** (österr.: auf dem) on the; **(d)** ▶24╎ (zeitlich) on; **am Freitag** on Friday; **am 19. November** on 19 November; **am Anfang/ Ende** at the beginning/end; **am letzten Freitag** last Friday; **(e)** (zur Bildung des Superlativs) **am gescheitesten/ schönsten sein** be the cleverest/most beautiful; **am schnellsten laufen** run [the] fastest; **das machen wir am besten nachher** it's best if we do it afterwards; **(f)** (nach bestimmten Verben) **am Gelingen eines Planes** *usw.*

---

*alte Schreibung (vgl. Hinweise auf S. xvi–xvii)

zweifeln have doubts about *or* doubt the success of a plan *etc.;* **am Wettbewerb teilnehmen** take part in the contest; **(g)** (zur Bildung der Verlaufsform) **am Verwelken/Verfallen sein** be wilting/decaying

Amalgam /amal'ga:m/ *das;* ~s, ~e (Chemie, auch fig.) amalgam

Amalgam·füllung *die* (Zahnmed.) amalgam filling

Amaryllis /ama'rylɪs/ *die;* ~, **Amaryllen** amaryllis

Amateur /ama'tø:ɐ̯/ *der;* ~s, ~e amateur

Amateur- amateur

amateurhaft **1** *Adj.* amateurish. **2** *adv.* amateurishly

Amazonas /ama'tso:nas/ *der;* ~: Amazon

Amazone /ama'tso:nə/ *die;* ~, ~n (Myth.) Amazon

Amazonien /ama'tso:niən/ *(das);* ~s Amazonia

Amboss, *Amboß /'ambɔs/ *der;* **Ambosses, Ambosse** anvil

ambulant /ambu'lant/ **1** *Adj.* **(a)** (Med.) outpatient *attrib.* ‹*treatment, therapy, etc.*›; **ein** ~**er Patient** an outpatient; **(b)** (umherziehend) itinerant. **2** *adv.* (Med.) **jmdn.** ~ **behandeln** treat sb. as an outpatient *or* give sb. outpatient treatment

Ambulanz /ambu'lants/ *die;* ~, ~en **(a)** (in Kliniken) outpatient[s'] department; **(b)** (Krankenwagen) ambulance

Ameise /'a:maizə/ *die;* ~, ~n ant

Ameisen-: ~**haufen** *der* anthill; ~**säure** *die; o. Pl.* formic acid; ~**staat** *der* ant colony

amen /'a:mɛn/ *Interj.* (christl. Rel.) amen; **zu allem ja und** ~ **sagen** (ugs.) agree to anything

Amen *das;* ~s, ~: Amen; **das ist so sicher wie das** ~ **in der Kirche** (ugs.) you can bet your bottom dollar on it

Amerika /a'me:rika/ *(das);* ~s America

Amerikaner /ameri'ka:nɐ/ *der;* ~s, ~ ▶ 388⌉ **(a)** American; **(b)** (Gebäck) *small, flat iced cake*

Amerikanerin *die;* ~, ~nen American

amerikanisch *Adj.* ▶ 388⌉ American *s. auch* **deutsch; Deutsch; Deutsche²**

amerikanisieren *tr. V.* Americanize

Amethyst /ame'tyst/ *der;* ~[e]s, ~e amethyst

Ami /'ami/ *der;* ~s, ~s (ugs.) Yank (coll.)

Amigo /a'mi:go/ *der;* ~s, ~s (ugs.) buddy (coll.)

Amino·säure /a'mi:no-/ *die* (Chemie) aminoacid

Ammann /'aman/ *der;* ~[e]s, **Ammänner** (schweiz.) (Gemeinde~, Bezirks~) ≈ mayor; (Land~) cantonal president

Amme /'amə/ *die;* ~, ~n wet-nurse; (Tier) foster-mother

Ammen·märchen *das* fairy tale *or* story

Ammer /'amɐ/ *die;* ~, ~n bunting

Ammoniak /amo'niak/ *das;* ~s (Chemie) ammonia

Amnestie /amnɛs'ti:/ *die;* ~, ~n amnesty

amnestieren *tr. V.* grant an amnesty to; amnesty

Amöbe /a'mø:bə/ *die;* ~, ~n (Biol.) amoeba

Amok /'a:mɔk/ *der;* ~ **laufen** run amok; (ugs.: wütend werden) go wild (coll.); ~ **fahren** go berserk at the wheel

Amok-: ~**fahrer** *der* berserk driver; ~**lauf** *der* crazed rampage; ~**läufer** *der* madman; **der** ~**läufer, der mehrere Menschen erschossen hatte** the man who had gone berserk and shot several people; ~**schütze** *der* crazed gunman

a-Moll *das;* ~: A minor

Amor /'a:mɔr/ *(der)* Cupid

amortisieren (Wirtsch.) **1** *tr. V.* repay ‹*investment, acquisition costs*›. **2** *refl. V.* pay for itself

Ampel /'ampl/ *die;* ~, ~n **(a)** (Verkehrs~) traffic lights *pl.;* **die** ~ **sprang auf Rot** the traffic lights turned to red; **an der nächsten** ~: at the next set of traffic lights; **(b)** (Hängelampe) hanging lamp; **(c)** (für Pflanzen) hanging flowerpot

Ampel-: ~**anlage** *die* set of traffic lights; ~**koalition** *die* (ugs.) *coalition between the SPD, FDP, and the Green Party*

Ampere /am'pɛːɐ̯/ *das;* ~[s], ~: ampere; amp (coll.)

Ampere·meter *das* ammeter

Amphibie /am'fi:biə/ *die;* ~, ~n (Zool.) amphibian

Amphibien·fahrzeug *das* amphibious vehicle

amphibisch *Adj.* amphibious

Amphi·theater /am'fi:-/ *das* amphitheatre

Ampulle /am'pʊlə/ *die;* ~, ~n (Med.) ampoule

Amputation /amputa'tsio:n/ *die;* ~, ~en (Med.) amputation

amputieren *tr.* *(auch itr.)* *V.* amputate; **jmdm. das Bein/den Arm** ~: amputate sb.'s leg/arm

Amsel /'amzl/ *die;* ~, ~n blackbird

Amt /amt/ *das;* ~[e]s, **Ämter** /'ɛmtɐ/ **(a)** (Stellung) post; position; (hohes politisches od. kirchliches ~) office; **sein** ~ **antreten** take up one's post/take up office; **im** ~ **sein** be in office; **für ein** ~ **kandidieren** be a candidate for a post *or* position/an office; **von** ~s **wegen** because of one's profession *or* job; **(b)** (Aufgabe) task; job; (Obliegenheit) duty; **seines** ~es **walten** (geh.) discharge the duties of one's office; **(c)** (Behörde) (Pass~, Finanz~, ~ für Statistik) office; (Sozial~, Fürsorge~, ~ für Denkmalpflege, Vermessungswesen) department; **von** ~s **wegen** by order of the authorities; *s. auch* **auswärtig c; (d)** (Gebäude usw.) office; **(e)** (Fernspr.) exchange; **das Fräulein vom** ~ (veralt.) the operator; **vom** ~ **vermittelt werden** be put through by the operator; **(f)** (kath. Rel.) [sung] mass

Amt·frau *die* ⇒ **Amtmännin**

amtieren *itr. V.* hold office; **der** ~**de Generalsekretär** the incumbent Secretary-General

amtlich **1** *Adj.* **(a)** *nicht präd.* official; ~**es Kennzeichen** (Kfz-W.) registration number; **(b)** *nicht attr.* (ugs.: sicher) definite; certain. **2** *adv.* officially

Amt·mann *der;* *Pl.* **Amtmänner** *od.* **Amtleute, Amt·männin** /-mɛnɪn/ *die;* ~, ~**nen** senior civil servant

amts-, Amts-: ~**anmaßung** *die* (Rechtsw.) unauthorized assumption of authority; ~**antritt** *der* assumption of office; ~**arzt** *der* medical officer; ~**ärztlich** **1** *Adj.; nicht präd.* ‹*examination*› by the medical officer; **2** *adv.* **sich** ~**ärztlich untersuchen lassen** have an official medical examination; ~**blatt** *das* official gazette; ~**deutsch** *das* (abwertend) officialese; ~**eid** *der* oath of office; ~**enthebung** *die* removal *or* dismissal from office; ~**führung** *die o. Pl.* discharge of one's office; ~**gericht** *das* **(a)** (Instanz) local *or* district court; **(b)** (Gebäude) local *or* district court building; ~**geschäfte** *Pl.* official duties; ~**handlung** *die* official act *or* duty; ~**hilfe** *die* official assistance (given by one authority to another); ~**kette** *die* chain of office; ~**leitung** *die* exchange line; ~**miene** *die* (meist iron.) official air; ~**müde** *Adj.* tired of office *postpos.;* ~**nachfolger** *der* successor in office; ~**person** *die* official; ~**schimmel** *der; o. Pl.* (scherzh.) officialism; bureaucracy; **der** ~**schimmel wiehert** that's bureaucracy for you; ~**sprache** *die* **(a)** *o. Pl.* (~deutsch) official language; officialese (derog.); **in der** ~**sprache** in official language/officialese; **(b)** (eines Landes, einer Organisation) official language; ~**stube** *die* (veralt.) office; ~**tracht** *die* robes *pl.* of office; official dress; ~**vorsteher** *der* head *or* chief [of a/the department]; ~**zeit** *die* period *or* term of office; ~**zimmer** *das* office

Amulett /amu'lɛt/ *das;* ~[e]s, ~e amulet; charm

amüsant /amy'zant/ **1** *Adj.* amusing; entertaining. **2** *adv.* in an amusing *or* entertaining way

amüsieren **1** *refl. V.* **(a)** (sich vergnügen) enjoy oneself; have a good time; **amüsier dich gut!** enjoy yourself!; have a good time!; **sich mit jmdm.** ~: have fun *or* a good time with sb.; **(b)** (belustigt sein) be amused; **sich über jmdn./etw.** ~: find sb./sth. funny; (über jmdn./etw. lachen) laugh at sb./sth.; (jmdn. verspotten) make fun of sb./sth. **2** *tr. V.* amuse; **amüsiert zusehen** look on with amusement

an /an/ ▶ 24⌉ **1** *Präp. mit Dat.* **(a)** (räumlich) at; (auf) on; **an einem Ort** at a place; **an der Wand hängen** be hanging on the wall; **an der Wand stehen** stand by *or* against the wall; **an der Mosel/Donau liegen** be [situated] on the Moselle/Danube; **Frankfurt an der Oder** Frankfurt on [the] Oder; **an etw. lehnen** lean against sth.; **Tür an Tür**

an

Räumlich: Wo?

Zur Beschreibung der Lage verwendet man meist **on**:

eine Verletzung am Knie	= a wound on the knee
die Bilder an der Wand	= the pictures on the wall
eine Stadt an der Mosel	= a town on the Moselle
ein Haus am Fluss	= a house on *od.* by the river

Hier wird **by** verwendet, um die Nähe zum Fluss auszudrücken. Ebenso:

Er stand am Fenster	= He stood by *od.* at the window

Wenn es um die Lage an einem Ort oder Gebäude geht, heißt es **at**:

am Tatort	= at the scene of the crime
am Haupteingang	= at the main entrance
an der Vorderseite	= at the front
am Ende der Straße	= at the end of the road
am Theater/Kino/ Bahnhof	= at the theatre/cinema/ station

Räumlich: Wohin?

Wenn *an* sich auf eine Bewegung in eine bestimmte Richtung bezieht, wird es meist mit **on** übersetzt:

Lehne es an den Baum	= Lean it on *od.* against the tree
Hänge es an die Wand	= Hang it on the wall
Schreibe es an die Tafel	= Write it on the blackboard
Sie legte ihren Kopf an seine Schulter	= She laid her head on his shoulder

Beim Wechsel von einer Person zur anderen bzw. von einem Ort zum anderen heißt es **to**:

Schicke es an deinen Bruder	= Send it to your brother
die Übergabe an den neuen Besitzer	= the transfer to the new owner
Sie wurde an eine andere Schule versetzt	= She was moved to another school

Zeitlich: Wann?

In Verbindung mit einem bestimmten Tag, Datum oder Wochentag wird *an* bzw. *am* mit **on** (ohne *the*) übersetzt:

am 6. Juli	= on July 6th · (*gesprochen:* on July the sixth, *in den USA auch:* July sixth)
am Mittwoch	= on Wednesday

an seinem Geburtstag	= on his birthday
an einem schönen Frühlingstag	= on a fine spring day

Ausnahmen (mit *the*) sind Daten ohne Angabe des Monats oder bestimmte Tage im Monat:

am 6.	= on the sixth
am ersten/letzten Sonntag im Monat	= on the first/last Sunday in the month

Bei vorangehenden oder folgenden Tagen steht meist nur *the*, d.h. *an* wird nicht übersetzt:

Am Tag/Mittwoch davor waren wir in London gewesen	= The day before/The previous Wednesday we had been in London
Am nächsten Tag fuhr er zurück	= The next day he went back
Am übernächsten Dienstag sind wir in Rom	= The Tuesday after next we'll be in Rome

In Verbindung mit Tageszeiten heißt es **in**, oder, wenn sie näher beschrieben werden, **on**:

am Morgen/ Nachmittag/Abend	= in the morning/ afternoon/evening
am ersten Morgen seines Besuchs	= on the first morning of his visit
an einem kalten Winterabend	= on a cold winter evening

Eine Ausnahme ist wieder:

am nächsten Morgen	= the next morning

In Verbindung mit Festen (süddeutscher Wortgebrauch) heißt es **at**:

an Ostern/Weihnachten	= at Easter/Christmas

Im Gegensatz zu *aus*

In der Bedeutung 'in Betrieb' wird *an* mit **on** übersetzt:

Das Licht/Die Spülmaschine ist an	= The light/The dishwasher is on

Im Gegensatz zu *ab*

Auf Fahrplänen (zur Angabe der Ankunftszeit) heißt es im Englischen **arriving** (Abkürzung **arr.**):

Köln an 17.30	= arriving *od.* arr. Cologne 17.30
an 12.30 – ab 12.35	= arr. 12.30 – dep. 1.35

next door to one another; **(b)** (zeitlich) on; **an jedem Sonntag** every Sunday; **an dem Abend, als er …:** [on] the evening he …; **an Ostern** (bes. südd.) at Easter; **(c)** (bei bestimmten Substantiven, Adjektiven und Verben) **arm/reich an Vitaminen** low/rich in vitamins; **jmdn. an etw. erkennen** recognize sb. by sth.; **ein Mangel an etw.** a shortage of sth.; **an etw. leiden** suffer from sth.; **es an der Leber haben** have liver trouble; **an einer Krankheit sterben** die of a disease; **es ist an ihm, das zu tun** it is up to him to do it; **er hat etwas an sich** there is sth. about him; **(d) an [und für] sich** (eigentlich) actually. **2** *Präp. mit Akk.* **(a)** to; (auf, gegen) on; **etw. an jmdn. schicken** send sth. to sb.; **etw. an etw. hängen** hang sth. on sth.; **(b)** (bei bestimmten Substantiven, Adjektiven und Verben) **an etw./jmdn.** believe in sth./sb.; **an etw. denken** think of sth.; **sich an etw. erinnern** remember *or* recall sth.; **an die Arbeit gehen** get down to work; **einen Gruß an jmdn. ausrichten lassen** send

greetings to sb.; **ich konnte kaum an mich halten vor Lachen/Ärger** I could hardly contain myself for laughing/hardly contain my anger. **3** *Adv.* **(a)** (Verkehrsw.) **Köln an:** 9.15 arriving Cologne 09.15; **(b)** (ugs.: in Betrieb) on; **die Waschmaschine/der Fernseher/das Licht/das Gas ist an** the washing machine/television/light/gas is on; **Scheinwerfer an!** spotlights on!; **(c)** (ugs.: ungefähr) around; about; **an [die] 20 000 DM** around *or* about 20, 000 DM; *s. auch* **ab 2 d; von 1 a, b**

Anabolikum /anaˈboːlikʊm/ *das;* ∼s, **Anabolika** (Med.) anabolic steroid

Anakonda /anaˈkɔnda/ *die;* ∼, ∼s anaconda

Analgetikum /analˈgeːtikʊm/ *das;* ∼s, **Analgetika** (Med.) analgesic

analog /anaˈloːk/ **1** *Adj.* **(a)** analogous (*Dat.,* **zu** to); **(b)** (Technik, DV) analogue. **2** *adv.* **(a)** analogously; **(b)** (Technik, DV) ⟨*display, reproduce*⟩ in analogue form

Analogie *die;* ~, ~n (geh., fachspr.) analogy; **in** ~ **zu etw.** in analogy to sth.

Analog-: ~**rechner** *der* (DV) analogue computer; ~**uhr** *die* analogue clock/watch

An·alphabet *der;* ~en, ~en illiterate [person]; ~ **sein** be illiterate

Analyse /ana'ly:zə/ *die;* ~, ~n (auch: Psycho~) analysis

analysieren *tr. V.* analyse

Analyst /ana'lʏst/ *der;* ~en, ~en (Börsenw.) analyst

analytisch 1 *Adj.* analytical. 2 *adv.* analytically

Anämie /anɛ'mi:/ *die;* ~, ~n ▶ 329 | (Med.) anaemia

Ananas /'ananas/ *die;* ~, ~ *od.* ~se pineapple

Anarchie /anar'çi:/ *die;* ~, ~n anarchy

anarchisch *Adj.* anarchic

Anarchismus *der;* ~: anarchism

Anarchist *der;* ~en, ~en anarchist

anarchistisch *Adj.* anarchistic

Anästhesie /an|ɛste'zi:/ *die;* ~, ~n (Med.) anaesthesia

Anästhesist *der;* ~en, ~en, **Anästhesistin** *die;* ~, ~nen (Med.) anaesthetist

Anatolien /ana'to:liən/ *(das);* ~s Anatolia

Anatomie /anato'mi:/ *die;* ~, ~n (a) anatomy; (b) (Institut) anatomical institute

anatomisch /ana'to:mɪʃ/ 1 *Adj.* anatomical. 2 *adv.* anatomically

an|bahnen 1 *tr. V.* initiate ‹negotiations, talks, process, etc.›; develop ‹relationship, connection›. 2 *refl. V.* ‹development› be in the offing; ‹friendship, relationship› start to develop

an|bandeln /'anbandln/ (südd., österr.), **an|bändeln** /'anbɛndln/ *itr. V.* (ugs.) **mit jmdm.** ~: get off with sb. (Brit. coll.); pick sb. up

An·bau *der; Pl.* ~**ten** (a) *o. Pl.* building; **die Genehmigung für den** ~ **einer Garage an ein Haus bekommen** receive permission to build a garage on to a house; (b) (Gebäude) extension; (c) *o. Pl.* (das Anpflanzen) cultivation; growing

an|bauen 1 *tr. V.* (a) build on; add; **eine Garage ans Haus** ~: build a garage on to the house; (b) (anpflanzen) cultivate; grow. 2 *itr. V.* (das Haus vergrößern) build an extension; (~ lassen) have an extension built

Anbau-: ~**gebiet** *das;* ~gebiete **für Getreide** cereal-growing *or* grain-growing areas; ~**gebiete für Rotwein** red-wine-growing areas *or* areas for red wine; ~**möbel** *das* unit furniture; ~**schrank** *der* cupboard unit

An·beginn *der* (geh.) beginning; **von** ~ **[an]** right from the beginning

an|behalten *unr. tr. V.* (ugs.) **etw.** ~: keep sth. on

an·bei *Adv.* (Amtsspr.) herewith; **Rückporto** ~: return postage enclosed

an|beißen 1 *unr. tr. V.* bite into; take a bite of; **er hat die Banane nur angebissen** he only took one bite of the banana. 2 *unr. itr. V.* (auch fig. ugs.) bite; **bei ihr hat noch keiner angebissen** (fig. ugs.) she hasn't managed to hook anybody yet

an|bekommen *unr. tr. V.* (ugs.) (a) (anziehen können) **etw.** ~: manage to get sth. on; (b) (anzünden *od.* starten können) **ein Feuer/Streichholz** ~: manage to get a fire going/a match to light; **den Motor** ~: manage to get the engine going *or* to start

an|belangen *tr. V.* **was mich/diese Sache** *usw.* **anbelangt** as far as I am/this matter is *etc.* concerned

an|bellen *tr. V.* bark at

an|beraumen /-bəʀaumən/ *tr. V.* (Amtsspr.) arrange, fix

an|beten *tr. V.* (auch fig.) worship

An·betracht *der:* **in** ~ **einer Sache** *(Gen.)* in consideration *or* view of sth.

an|betreffen *unr. tr. V.* **in was mich/diese Sache** *usw.* **anbetrifft** as far as I am/this matter is *etc.* concerned

an|betteln *tr. V.* **jmdn.** ~: beg from sb.; **jmdn. um etw.** ~: beg sb. for sth.

Anbetung *die;* ~, ~en (auch fig.) worship; (fig.: Verehrung) adoration

an|bezahlen *tr. V.* make a down payment on; pay a deposit on

an|biedern /-bi:dɐn/ *refl. V.* (abwertend) curry favour (**bei** with)

Anbiederung *die;* ~, ~en (abwertend) currying favour (**bei** with)

an|bieten 1 *unr. tr. V.* offer; **jmdm. etw.** ~: offer sb. sth.; **jmdm.** ~, **etw. zu tun** offer to do sth. for sb.; **Verhandlungen** ~: offer to negotiate. 2 *unr. refl. V.* (a) offer one's services (**als** as); **sich** ~, **etw. zu tun** offer to do sth.; (b) (nahe liegen) ‹opportunity› present itself; ‹possibility, solution› suggest *or* present itself; **es bietet sich an, das zu tun** it would seem to be the thing to do; (c) (geeignet sein) **sich für etw.** ~: be suitable for sth.

An·bieter *der* (Wirtsch.) supplier

an|binden *unr. tr. V.* (a) tie [up] (**an** + *Dat. od. Akk.* to); tie up, moor ‹boat› (**an** + *Dat. od. Akk.* to); tether ‹animal› (**an** + *Dat. od. Akk.* to); **er lässt sich nicht** ~ (fig.) he won't be tied down; *s. auch* **angebunden 2;** (b) (verbinden, anschließen) link (**an** + *Akk.* to)

an|blasen *unr. tr. V.* blow at

an|blecken *tr. V.* bare its/their teeth at

an|bleiben *unr. itr. V.; mit sein* (ugs.) stay on

an|blenden *tr. V.* flash [at]

An·blick *der* sight; **einen erfreulichen/traurigen** ~ **bieten** be a welcome/sad sight; **beim** ~ **der Pyramiden** at the sight of the Pyramids

an|blicken *tr. V.* look at

an|blinken *tr. V.* flash [at]

an|blinzeln *tr. V.* (a) blink at; (b) (zuzwinkern) wink at

an|bohren *tr. V.* (a) bore into; (mit der Bohrmaschine) bore *or* drill into; (b) (erschließen) tap [by drilling]

an|brechen 1 *unr. tr. V.* (a) crack; (b) (öffnen) open; start; **eine angebrochene Flasche** an opened bottle; (c) (zu verbrauchen beginnen) break into ‹supplies, reserves›; **einen Hundertmarkschein** ~: break into *or* (Amer.) break a hundred mark note. 2 *unr. itr. V.; mit sein* (geh.: beginnen) ‹dawn› break; ‹day› dawn, break; ‹darkness, night› come down, fall; ‹age, epoch› dawn

an|brennen 1 *unr. tr. V.* (anzünden) light. 2 *unr. itr. V.; mit sein* (a) burn; **ihm ist das Essen angebrannt** he has burnt the food; **nichts** ~ **lassen** (fig. ugs.) not miss out on anything; (b) (zu brennen beginnen) ‹wood, coal, etc.› catch

an|bringen *unr. tr. V.* (a) (befestigen) put up ‹sign, aerial, curtain, plaque› (**an** + *Dat.* on); fix ‹lamp, camera› (**an** + *Dat.* [on] to); **an etw.** *(Dat.)* **angebracht sein** be fixed [on] to sth.; (b) (äußern) make ‹request, complaint, comment, reference›; (c) (zeigen) display, demonstrate ‹knowledge, experience›; (d) (ugs.: herbeibringen) bring; (e) (ugs.: verkaufen) sell; move

An·bruch *der o. Pl.* (geh.) dawn[ing]; **der** ~ **des Tages** dawn; daybreak; **vor/nach/bei** *od.* **mit** ~ **der Nacht** before/after/at nightfall

an|brüllen *tr. V.* (a) ‹tiger, lion, etc.› roar at; ‹cow, bull, etc.› bellow at; (b) (ugs.: anschreien) bellow *or* bawl at

an|brummen *tr. V.* (auch ugs.: unfreundlich anreden) growl at

Andacht /'andaxt/ *die;* ~, ~en (a) *o. Pl.* (Sammlung im Gebet) silent prayer *or* worship; **in tiefer** ~: in deep devotion; **in** ~ **versunken** sunk in silent prayer *or* worship; sunk in one's devotions; (b) *o. Pl.* (innere Sammlung) rapt attention; (c) (Gottesdienst) prayers *pl.;* **eine** ~ **halten** hold a [short] service; **zur** ~**gehen** go to prayers *or* to the service

andächtig /'andɛçtɪç/ 1 *Adj.* (a) (ins Gebet versunken) devout; reverent; (b) (innerlich gesammelt) rapt; (c) *nicht präd.* (feierlich) reverent. 2 *adv.* (a) (ins Gebet versunken) devoutly; reverently; (b) (innerlich gesammelt) raptly

Andalusien /anda'lu:ziən/ *(das);* ~s Andalusia

Andante /an'dantə/ *das;* ~[s], ~s (Musik) andante

an|dauern *itr. V.* ‹negotiations› continue, go on; ‹weather, rain› last, continue

andauernd 1 *Adj.; nicht präd.* continual; constant. 2 *adv.* continually; constantly; **warum fragst du denn** ~ **dasselbe?** why do you keep on asking the same thing?

Anden /'andn̩/ *Pl. die* ∼: the Andes

an|denken *unr. tr. V.* start thinking about

An·denken *das;* ∼s, (a) *o. Pl.* memory; jmds. ∼ bewahren/in Ehren halten keep/ honour sb.'s memory; zum ∼ an jmdn./etw. to remind you/us *etc.* of sb./sth.; das schenke ich dir zum ∼: I'll give you that to remember me/us by; (b) (Erinnerungsstück) memento, souvenir; (Reise∼) souvenir

ander... /'andɐ.../ *Indefinitpron.* **1** *attr.* (a) other; ein ∼er Mann/eine ∼e Frau/ein ∼es Haus another man/woman/house; das Kleid gefällt mir nicht, haben Sie noch ∼e/ein ∼es? I don't like that dress, do you have any others/another?; der/die/das eine oder ∼e ... one or two ...; (b) (nächst...) next; am/bis zum ∼[e]n Tag [on] the/by the next *or* following day; (c) (verschieden) different; ∼er Meinung sein be of a different opinion; take a different view; das ∼e Geschlecht the opposite sex; bei ∼er Gelegenheit another time; (d) (neu) einen ∼en Job finden find another job; er ist ein ∼er Mensch geworden he is a changed man. **2** *allein stehend* (a) (Person) jemand ∼er *or* ∼es someone else; (in Fragen) anyone else; ein ∼r/eine ∼e: another [one]; die ∼n the others; alle ∼n all the others; everyone else; jeder/jede ∼e anyone *or* anybody else; kein ∼er/keine ∼e nobody *or* no one else; was ist mit den ∼n? what about the others *or* the rest?; niemand ∼er *od.* ∼es nobody *or* no one else; niemand ∼er *od.* ∼es als ...: nobody *or* no one but ...; einen ∼[e]n/eine ∼e haben (fig. ugs.) have found somebody *or* someone else; auf ∼e hören listen to others; nicht drängeln, einer nach dem ∼n don't push, one after the other; der eine oder [der] ∼e one or two *or* a few people; *s. auch* recht c; (b) (Sache) etwas ∼es something else; (in Fragen) anything else; nichts ∼es nothing else; not anything else; alles ∼e everything else; ein[e]s nach dem ∼[e]n first things first; ich will weder das eine noch das ∼e I don't want either; und ∼es/vieles ∼e mehr and more/much more besides; unter ∼[e]m among[st] other things; so kam eins zum ∼[e]n what with one thing on top of the other; das ist etwas [ganz] ∼es that's [something quite] different; von etwas ∼em sprechen talk about something else; alles ∼e als ...: anything but ...; ∼es zu tun haben have other things to do

anderen·falls *Adv.* otherwise

anderen·orts *Adv.* (geh.) elsewhere

anderer·seits *Adv.* on the other hand

Ander·konto *das* (Finanzw.) trust account; client account

ander·mal *Adv. in* ein ∼: another time

andern- ⇨ **anderen-**

ändern /'ɛndɐn/ **1** *tr. V.* change; alter; alter ⟨garment⟩; change ⟨person⟩; amend ⟨motion⟩; daran kann man nichts ∼: nothing can be done *or* there's nothing you/we *etc.* can do about it **2** *refl. V.* change; alter; ⟨person, weather⟩ change

anders /'andɐs/ *Adv.* (a) ⟨think, act, feel, do⟩ differently (als from *or esp. Brit.* to); ⟨be, look, sound, taste⟩ different (als from *or esp. Brit.* to); ∼ geartet different; of a different nature *postpos.;* ∼ lautend to the contrary *postpos.;* es war alles ganz ∼: it was all quite different; wie könnte es ∼ sein! (iron.) surprise, surprise! (iron.); mir wird ganz ∼ (ugs.) I feel weak at the knees; es kam ∼, als wir dachten things didn't turn out the way we expected; ich habe es mir ∼ überlegt I've changed my mind; ich kann auch ∼ (ugs.) you'd/he'd *etc.* better watch it (coll.); so und nicht ∼: this way and no other; exactly like that; wie nicht ∼ zu erwarten [war] as [was to be] expected; wenn es nicht ∼ geht if there is no other way; (b) (sonst) else; irgendwo/nirgendwo ∼: somewhere/nowhere else; niemand ∼: nobody else; jemand ∼: someone else; (verneint, in Fragen) anyone else; (c) (ugs.: andernfalls) otherwise; or else

anders·artig *Adj.* different

Anders·denkende *der/die; adj. Dekl.* dissident; dissenter

---

anderseits *Adv.* ⇨ **andererseits**

anders-, Anders-: ∼**farbig 1** *Adj.* different-coloured *attrib.;* of a different colour *postpos.;* **2** *adv.* ⟨decorated⟩ in a different colour;*∼**geartet** ⇨ **anders** a; ∼**gläubig** *Adj.* of a different faith *or* religion *postpos.;* ∼**gläubige** *der/die* person of a different faith *or* religion; die ∼**gläubigen** those of different faiths *or* religions; ∼**herum** *Adv.* the other way round *or* (Amer.) around; etw. ∼**herum** drehen turn sth. the other way; ∼**herum gehen/fahren** go/drive round *or* (Amer.) around the other way;*∼**lautend** ⇨ **anders** a; ∼**rum** (ugs.) **1** *Adv.* ⇨ ∼**herum;** **2** *Adj.; nicht attr.* ∼**rum** sein be a poof (Brit. coll.) *or* a fairy (sl.); be queer (sl. derog.); ∼**wo** *Adv.* (ugs.) elsewhere; (verneint, in Fragen) anywhere else; ∼**woher** *Adv.* (ugs.) from elsewhere; from somewhere else; (verneint, in Fragen) from anywhere else; ∼**wohin** *Adv.* (ugs.) elsewhere; somewhere else; (verneint, in Fragen) anywhere else

anderthalb /'andɐt'halp/ *Bruchz.* ▶ 600 one and a half; ∼ Pfund Mehl a pound and a half of flour; ∼ Stunden an hour and a half

anderthalb·fach *Vervielfältigungsz.* one and a half times; die ∼e Anzahl/Menge one and a half times the number/amount

anderthalb·mal *Adv.* one and a half times; ∼ so groß wie ...: half as big again as ...

Änderung *die;* ∼, ∼en ⇨ **ändern 1:** change (Gen. in); alteration (Gen. to); amendment (Gen. to)

Änderungs-: ∼**kündigung** *die* (Arbeitswelt) notice of intention to terminate agreement on terms and conditions of employment if changes to the agreement are not accepted; ∼**schneiderei** *die* tailor's [that does alterations]; ∼**vor·schlag** *der* suggestion for a change; (für Gesetz, Antrag usw.) suggestion for an amendment; ∼**wunsch** *der* request for a change

anderweitig /-vaitɪç/ **1** *Adj.; nicht präd.* other. **2** *adv.* (a) (auf andere Weise) in another way; ∼ beschäftigt sein be otherwise engaged; (b) (an jmd. anderen) to somebody else

an|deuten 1 *tr. V.* (a) (zu verstehen geben) intimate; hint; jmdm. etw. ∼: intimate *or* hint sth. to sb.; (b) (nicht ausführen) outline; (kurz erwähnen) indicate. **2** *refl. V.* (sich abzeichnen) be indicated

An·deutung *die* (a) (Anspielung) hint; eine ∼ machen give *or* drop a hint (über + *Akk.* about); (b) (schwaches Anzeichen) suggestion; hint

andeutungs·weise *Adv.* in the form of a hint *or* suggestion/hints *or* suggestions; davon war nur ∼ die Rede it was only hinted at

an|dichten *tr. V.* jmdm. etw. ∼: impute sth. to sb.

an|dienen 1 *tr. V.* jmdm. etw. ∼: offer sth. to sb.; (aufdringlich) press sth. on sb. **2** *refl. V.* sich jmdm. ∼: offer oneself *or* one's services to sb.; (aufdringlich) press oneself *or* one's services on sb.

an·diskutieren *tr. V.* [begin to] discuss briefly

an|docken *tr., itr. V.* (Raumf.) dock (an + *Dat.* with)

An·drang *der; o. Pl.* crowd; (Gedränge) crush; es herrschte großer ∼: there was a large crowd/great crush

an|drängen *itr. V.; mit sein* surge (gegen against); ⟨crowd⟩ surge forward; ⟨army⟩ push forward

andr... *usw.* ⇨ **ander...** *usw.*

Andreas /an'dre:as/ (der) Andrew

Andreas·kreuz *das* (a) St Andrew's cross; (b) (Verkehrsw.) diagonal cross

an|drehen *tr. V.* (a) (einschalten) turn on; (b) (ugs.: verkaufen) jmdm. etw. ∼: palm sb. off with sth.; palm sth. off on sb.; (c) (anziehen) screw ⟨nut⟩ on; screw ⟨screw⟩ in

andrerseits ⇨ **andererseits**

an|drohen *tr. V.* jmdm. etw. ∼: threaten sb. with sth.

An·drohung *die* threat; unter ∼ von Gewalt with the *or* under threat of violence

Android /andro'i:t/ *der;* ∼en, ∼en, **Androide** /andro'i:da/ *der;* ∼n, ∼n android

an|drücken *tr. V.* press down

an|ecken /-ɛkn̩/ *itr. V.; mit sein* (fig. ugs.) bei jmdm. ∼: rub sb. [up (Brit.)] the wrong way

an|eignen *refl. V.* (**a**) appropriate; **sich** (*Dat.*) **etw. widerrechtlich** ∼: misappropriate sth.; (**b**) (lernen) acquire; learn

An·eignung *die* (**a**) appropriation; **widerrechtliche** ∼: misappropriation; (**b**) (Lernen) acquisition; learning

an·einander *Adv.* ⟨*tie, hitch, push, press*⟩ together; ⟨*put, hold*⟩ next to each other *or* one another; ∼ **liegen** lie next to each other; ⟨*properties*⟩ adjoin [each other *or* one another; ∼ **grenzen** ⟨*properties, rooms, etc.*⟩ adjoin each other *or* one another; ⟨*countries*⟩ border on each other *or* one another; ∼ **geraten** (fig.: sich prügeln) come to blows (**mit** with); (fig.: sich streiten) quarrel (**mit** with); ∼ **denken** think of each other *or* one another; ∼ **vorbeigehen** pass each other *or* one another; go past each other *or* one another; **sich** ∼ **gewöhnen** get used to each other *or* one another; ∼ **vorbeireden** talk at cross purposes; **sich** ∼ **festhalten** hold each other *or* one another

*aneinander|geraten *usw.:* ⇒ **aneinander**

Anekdote /anek'do:tə/ *die;* ∼, ∼**n** anecdote

an|ekeln *tr. V.* disgust; nauseate; **du ekelst mich an** you make me sick; **sich angeekelt abwenden** turn away in disgust

Anemone /ane'mo:nə/ *die;* ∼, ∼**n** anemone

anerkannt *Adj.* recognized; recognized, acknowledged ⟨*authority, expert*⟩

an|erkennen *unr. tr. V.* (**a**) recognize ⟨*country, record, verdict, qualification, document*⟩; acknowledge ⟨*debt*⟩; accept ⟨*demand, bill, conditions, rules*⟩; allow ⟨*claim, goal*⟩; **jmdn. als gleichberechtigten Partner** ∼: accept sb. as an equal partner; (**b**) (nicht leugnen) acknowledge; (**c**) (würdigen) acknowledge, appreciate ⟨*achievement, efforts*⟩; appreciate ⟨*person*⟩; respect ⟨*viewpoint, opinion*⟩; **ein** ∼**der Blick** an appreciative look; ∼**d nicken** nod appreciatively

anerkennens·wert *Adj.* commendable

Anerkennung *die;* ∼, ∼**en** ⇒ **anerkennen:** (**a**) recognition; acknowledgement; acceptance; allowance; (**b**) acknowledgement; (**c**) acknowledgement; appreciation; respect (*Gen.* for)

an|fachen /-faxŋ/ *tr. V.* fan; (fig.) arouse ⟨*anger, enthusiasm*⟩; arouse, inflame ⟨*passion*⟩; inspire, stir up ⟨*hatred*⟩; inspire ⟨*hope*⟩; ferment ⟨*discord, war*⟩

an|fahren 1 *unr. tr. V.* (**a**) run into; hit; (**b**) (herbeifahren) deliver; (**c**) (ansteuern) stop *or* call at ⟨*village etc.*⟩; ⟨*ship*⟩ put in at ⟨*port*⟩; (**d**) (zurechtweisen) shout at; (**e**) (in Betrieb nehmen) commission ⟨*power station, blast furnace*⟩. **2** *unr. itr. V.; mit sein* (**a**) (starten) start off; (**b**) **angefahren kommen** come driving/riding along; (auf einen zu) come driving/ riding up

An·fahrt *die* (**a**) (das Anfahren) journey; (**b**) (Weg) approach

Anfahrts-: ∼**weg** *der* journey; ∼**zeit** *die* travelling time

An·fall *der* (**a**) (Attacke) attack; (epileptischer ∼, fig.) fit; **einen** ∼ **bekommen** have an attack/a fit; **in einem** ∼ **von …** (fig.) in a fit of …; (**b**) *o. Pl.* (Anfallendes) amount (**an** + *Dat.* of); (Ertrag) yield (**an** + *Dat.* of)

an|fallen 1 *unr. tr. V.* (**a**) (angreifen) attack; (**b**) (geh.: befallen) **Zweifel/Angst fiel mich an** I was assailed by doubt/fear. **2** *unr. itr V.; mit sein* ⟨*costs*⟩ arise, be incurred; ⟨*interest*⟩ accrue; ⟨*work*⟩ come up; ⟨*parcels etc.*⟩ accumulate

an·fällig *Adj.* ⟨*person*⟩ with a delicate constitution; ⟨*machine*⟩ susceptible to faults; **er ist sehr** ∼: he has a very delicate constitution; **gegen** *od.* **für etw.** ∼ **sein** be susceptible to sth.; **für eine Krankheit** ∼ **sein** be prone to an illness

Anfälligkeit *die* (einer Person) delicate constitution; (einer Maschine) susceptibility to faults

An·fang *der* beginning; start; (erster Abschnitt) beginning; [ganz] **am** ∼ **der Straße** [right] at the start of the street; **am** *od.* **zu** ∼: at first; to begin with; **von** ∼ **an** from the beginning *or* outset; ∼ **1984/der achtziger Jahre/Mai/ der Woche** *usw.* at the beginning of 1984/the eighties/ May/the week *etc.;* **von** ∼ **bis Ende** from beginning to end *or* start to finish; **der** ∼ **vom Ende** the beginning of the end; **im** ∼ **war das Wort** (bibl.) in the beginning was

the Word; **einen** ∼ **machen** make a start; **den** ∼ **machen** make a start; start; (als erster handeln) make the first move; **einen neuen** ∼ **machen** make a new *or* fresh start; **aller** ∼ **ist schwer** (Spr.) it's always difficult at the beginning; **in den** *od.* **seinen Anfängen stecken** be in its infancy

an|fangen 1 *unr. itr. V.* (**a**) begin; start; **das fängt ja gut an!** (ugs. iron.) that's a good start! (iron.); **er hat ganz klein/als ganz kleiner Angestellter angefangen** he started small/started [out] as a minor employee; **mit etw.** ∼: start [on] sth.; **fang nicht wieder damit an!** don't start [all] that again!; ∼, **etw. zu tun** start to do sth.; **es fängt an zu schneien** it's starting *or* beginning to snow; **fang doch nicht gleich an zu weinen** don't start crying; **angefangen bei** *od.* **mit** *od.* **von …:** starting *or* beginning with …; **Weiß fängt an** white starts; **er hat angefangen** (mit dem Streit o. ä.) he started it; (**b**) (zu sprechen ∼) begin; **von etw.** ∼: start on about sth.; (**c**) (eine Stelle antreten) start. **2** *unr. tr. V.* (**a**) begin; start; (anbrechen) start; **das Rauchen** ∼: start smoking; (**b**) (machen) do; **damit kann ich nichts/nicht viel** ∼: that's no/not much good to me; (das verstehe ich nicht/kaum) that doesn't mean anything/much to me; **kannst du noch etwas damit** ∼? is it any good *or* use to you?; **nichts mit sich anzufangen wissen** not know what to do with oneself

An·fänger *der;* ∼**s**, ∼, **An·fängerin** *die;* ∼, ∼**nen** beginner; (abwertend: Stümper) amateur

Anfänger·kurs *der* beginners' course; course for beginners

anfänglich /'anfɛŋlɪç/ *Adj.* initial

anfangs *Adv.* at first; initially

Anfangs-: ∼**buchstabe** *der* initial [letter]; first letter; ∼**gehalt** *das* starting salary; ∼**gründe** *Pl.* rudiments; ∼**schwierigkeit** *die; meist Pl.* initial difficulty; ∼**stadium** *das* initial stage; **im** ∼**stadium sein** be in its/their initial stages *pl.;* ∼**zeit** *die* starting time

an|fassen 1 *tr. V.* (**a**) (fassen, halten) take hold of; (**b**) (berühren) touch; (**c**) (bei der Hand nehmen) **jmdn.** ∼: take sb.'s hand; **fasst euch an** take each other's hand; (**d**) (angehen) approach, tackle ⟨*problem, task, etc.*⟩; (**e**) (behandeln) treat ⟨*person*⟩. **2** *itr. V.* (mithelfen) **[mit]** ∼: lend a hand

an|fauchen *tr. V.* (**a**) ⟨*cat*⟩ spit at; (**b**) (fig.) snap at

anfechtbar *Adj.* (**a**) (bes. Rechtsw.) contestable; (**b**) (kritisierbar, bestreitbar) disputable ⟨*statement, decision*⟩; ⟨*book*⟩ open to criticism

an|fechten *unr. tr. V.* (**a**) (bes. Rechtsw.) challenge, dispute ⟨*validity, authenticity, statement*⟩; contest ⟨*will*⟩; contest, challenge ⟨*decision*⟩; dispute ⟨*contract*⟩; challenge ⟨*law, opinion*⟩; (**b**) (beunruhigen) trouble; bother

Anfechtung *die;* ∼, ∼**en** (bes. Rechtsw.) ⇒ **anfechten a:** challenging; disputing; contesting

an|feinden /-faɪndn̩/ *tr. V.* treat with hostility

an|fertigen *tr. V.* make; make up ⟨*medicament, preparation*⟩; do ⟨*homework, translation*⟩; prepare, draw up ⟨*report*⟩; cut, make ⟨*key*⟩

An·fertigung *die* ⇒ **anfertigen:** making; doing; making up; preparing; drawing up; cutting

an|feuchten /-fɔɪçtn̩/ *tr. V.* moisten ⟨*lips, stamp*⟩; dampen ⟨*ironing, cloth, etc.*⟩

an|feuern *tr. V.* spur on; ∼**de Rufe/Gesten** shouts of encouragement/rousing gestures

An·feuerung *die* spurring on

an|flehen *tr. V.* beseech; implore; **jmdn. um etw.** ∼: beg sb. for sth.

an|fliegen 1 *unr. itr. V.; mit sein* ⟨*aircraft*⟩ fly in; (beim Landen) approach; come in to land; ⟨*bird etc.*⟩ fly in; **angeflogen kommen** come flying in; (auf einen zu) ⟨*bird*⟩ come flying up; **gegen den Wind** ∼: fly into the wind. **2** *unr. tr. V.* (**a**) fly to ⟨*city, country, airport*⟩; (beim Landen) approach ⟨*airport*⟩; (**b**) (ansteuern) ⟨*aircraft*⟩ approach; ⟨*bird*⟩ fly towards approach

An·flug *der* (**a**) approach; **die Maschine befindet sich im** ∼ **auf Berlin** the plane is now approaching Berlin; (**b**) (Hauch) hint; trace; (**c**) (Anwandlung) fit; **in einem** ∼ **von Großzügigkeit** in a fit of generosity

an|flunkern *tr. V.* (ugs.) tell fibs to

an|fordern *tr. V.* request, ask for ‹*help*›; ask for ‹*catalogue*›; order ‹*goods, materials*›; send for ‹*ambulance*›

An·forderung *die* (a) *o. Pl.* (das Anfordern) request (*Gen.* for); (b) (Anspruch) demand; **große/hohe ~en an jmdn./ etw. stellen** make great demands on sb./sth.; **den ~en nicht gewachsen sein/nicht genügen** not be up to the demands

An·frage *die* inquiry; (Parl.) question; **große/kleine ~** (Parl.) oral/written question

an|fragen *itr. V.* inquire; ask

an|fressen 1 *unr. tr. V.* (a) nibble [at]; ‹*bird*› peck [at]; (b) (zersetzen) eat away [at]. 2 *unr. refl. V.* **sich** (*Dat.*) **einen Bauch ~** (salopp) develop a paunch

an|freunden *refl. V.* make *or* become friends (**mit** with); **sich mit etw. ~** (fig.) get to like sth.

an|frieren *unr. itr. V.; mit sein* **an etw.** (*Dat.*) **~:** freeze to sth.

an|fügen *tr. V.* add

an|fühlen *refl. V.* feel

an|führen *tr. V.* (a) lead; lead, head ‹*procession*›; (b) (zitieren) quote; (c) (nennen) quote, give, offer ‹*example*›; give, offer ‹*details, reason, proof*›; (d) (ugs.: hereinlegen) have on (Brit. coll.); dupe

An·führer *der* (a) (Führer) leader; (b) (Rädelsführer) ringleader

An·führung *die* (a) leadership; (b) (das Zitieren, Zitat) quotation; (c) (Nennung) ⇒ **anführen c:** quotation; giving; offering

Anführungs·zeichen *das* quotation mark; inverted comma (Brit.)

an|füllen *tr. V.* fill [up]; **mit etw. angefüllt sein** be filled *or* full with sth.

An·gabe *die* (a) (das Mitteilen) giving; **ohne ~ von Gründen** without giving [any] reasons; (b) (Information) piece of information; **~n** information *sing.*; (c) (Anweisung) instruction; (d) *o. Pl.* (Prahlerei) boasting; bragging; (angeberisches Benehmen) showing-off; (e) (Ballspiele) service; serve; **[eine] ~ machen** serve; **ich habe [die] ~:** it's my serve

an|gaffen *tr. V.* (abwertend) gape at

an|geben 1 *unr. tr. V.* (a) give ‹*reason*›; declare ‹*income, dutiable goods*›; name, cite ‹*witness*›; **zur angegebenen Zeit** at the stated time; **wie oben angegeben** as stated *or* mentioned above; (b) (bestimmen) set ‹*course, direction*›; **den Takt ~:** keep time; (c) (veralt.: anzeigen, melden) report ‹*theft etc.*›; give away ‹*accomplice etc.*›. 2 *unr. itr. V.* (a) (prahlen) boast; brag; (sich angeberisch benehmen) show off; (b) (Ballspiele) serve

Angeber *der; ~s, ~:* boaster; braggart

Angeberei *die; ~:* boasting; bragging; (angeberisches Benehmen) showing-off

angeberisch (ugs.) 1 *Adj.* boastful ‹*person*›; pretentious, showy ‹*glasses, car, jacket*›. 2 *adv.* boastfully

Angebetete *der/die; adj. Dekl.* (meist scherzh.) beloved; (Idol) idol

angeblich 1 *Adj.* alleged. 2 *adv.* supposedly; allegedly; **er ist ~ krank** he is supposed to be ill; (er sagt, er sei krank) he says he's ill

an·geboren *Adj.* innate ‹*characteristic*›; congenital ‹*disease*›

An·gebot *das* (a) offer; (b) (Wirtsch.) (angebotene Menge) supply; (Sortiment) range; (c) (Kaufmannsspr.: Sonder~) special offer; **im ~:** on [special] offer; **~ der Woche** bargain of the week

an·gebracht *Adj.* appropriate

an·gebunden *Adj.* (a) tied down; (b) **kurz ~** (ugs.) short; abrupt

an·gegossen *Adj.* **wie ~ sitzen/passen** (ugs.) fit like a glove

angegraut /'angəgraut/ *Adj.* greying

an·gegriffen *Adj.* weakened ‹*health, stomach*›; strained ‹*nerves, voice*›; (erschöpft) exhausted; (nervlich) strained

---

an·geheiratet *Adj.* by marriage *postpos.*; **~ sein** be related by marriage

angeheitert /'angəhaitət/ *Adj.* tipsy; merry (coll.)

an|gehen 1 *unr. itr. V.; mit sein* (a) (sich einschalten, entzünden) ‹*radio, light, heating*› come on; ‹*fire*› catch, start burning; (b) (sich einschalten, entzünden lassen) ‹*radio, light*› go on; ‹*fire*› light, catch; (c) (ugs.: beginnen) start; (d) (anwachsen, wachsen) ‹*plant*› take root; (e) (geschehen dürfen) **es mag noch ~:** it's [just about] acceptable; **es geht nicht an, dass radikale Elemente die Partei unterwandern** radical elements must not be allowed to infiltrate the party; (f) (bes. nordd.: wahr sein) **das kann doch wohl nicht ~!** that can't be true!; (g) **gegen etw./jmdn. ~:** fight sth./sb. 2 *unr. tr. V.* (a) (angreifen) attack; (Sport) tackle; challenge; (b) (in Angriff nehmen) tackle ‹*problem, difficulty*›; take ‹*fence, bend*›; (c) (bitten) ask; **jmdn. um etw. ~:** ask sb. for sth.; (d) (betreffen) concern; **was geht dich das an?** what's it got to do with you?; **das geht dich nichts an** it's none of your business; **was das/mich angeht, [so] ...:** as far as that is/I am concerned ...

angehend *Adj.* budding; (zukünftig) prospective

an|gehören *itr. V.* **jmdm./einer Sache ~:** belong to sb./sth.; **der Regierung/einer Familie ~:** be a member of the government/a family

an·gehörig *Adj.* belonging (*Dat.* to)

Angehörige *der/die; adj. Dekl.* (a) (Verwandte) relative; relation; **der nächste ~:** the next of kin; (b) (Mitglied) member

Angeklagte /'angəkla:ktə/ *der/die; adj. Dekl.* accused; defendant

angeknackst *Adj.* (fig. ugs.) weakened

Angel /'aŋl/ *die; ~, ~n* (a) fishing rod; rod and line; **die ~ auswerfen** cast the line; (b) (Tür~, Fenster~ usw.) hinge; **etw. aus den ~n heben** lift sth. off its hinges; (fig.) turn sth. upside down

An·gelegenheit *die* matter; (Aufgabe, Problem) affair; concern; **öffentliche/kulturelle ~en** public/cultural affairs; **das ist meine/nicht meine ~:** that is my affair *or* business/not my concern *or* business; **kümmere dich um deine eigenen ~en!** mind your own business; **sich in jmds. ~en mischen** meddle in sb.'s affairs

Angel-: **~gerät** *das o. Pl.* fishing tackle; **~haken** *der* fish-hook

angeln 1 *tr. V.* (zu fangen suchen) fish for; (fangen) catch; **sie hat sich** (*Dat.*) **einen reichen Mann geangelt** (fig.) she has hooked a rich husband. 2 *itr. V.* angle; fish; **nach etw. ~** (fig.) fish for sth.

Angel-: **~rute** *die* fishing rod; **~sachse** *der* Anglo-Saxon; **~sächsisch** *Adj.* Anglo-Saxon; **~schein** *der* fishing permit *or* licence; **~schnur** *die* fishing line

an·gemessen 1 *Adj.* appropriate; reasonable, fair ‹*price, fee*›; adequate ‹*reward*›. 2 *adv.* ‹*behave*› appropriately; ‹*reward*› adequately; ‹*recompense*› reasonably, fairly

an·genehm 1 *Adj.* pleasant; agreeable; **ist Ihnen die Temperatur/ist es so ~?** is the temperature all right for you/is it all right like that?; **es ist mir gar nicht ~, dass ...:** I don't at all like it that ...; **~e Reise/Ruhe!** [have a] pleasant journey/have a good rest; **[sehr] ~!** delighted to meet you; **das Angenehme mit dem Nützlichen verbinden** combine business with pleasure. 2 *adv.* pleasantly; agreeably

angepasst, *angepaßt *Adj.* well adjusted

angeregt 1 *Adj.* lively; animated. 2 *adv.* **sich ~ unterhalten/~ diskutieren** have a lively *or* an animated conversation/discussion

an·geschlagen *Adj.* groggy; poor, weakened ‹*health*›

angeschmutzt /'angəʃmutst/ *Adj.* slightly soiled

angesehen *Adj.* respected

An·gesicht *das;* **~[e]s, ~er,** *österr. auch* **~e** (geh.) (a) (Gesicht) face; **von ~ zu ~:** face to face; (b) *in* **im ~** (+ *Gen.*) ⇒ **angesichts a**

angesichts *Präp. mit Gen.* (geh.) (a) **~ des Feindes/ der Gefahr/des Todes** in the face of the enemy/of danger/of death; **~ der Stadt/der Küste** in sight of the town/coast; (b) (fig.: in Anbetracht) in view of

---

*alte Schreibung (vgl. Hinweise auf S. xvi–xvii)

an·gespannt 1 *Adj.* **(a)** (angestrengt) close ‹*attention*›; taut ‹*nerves*›; **(b)** (kritisch) tense ‹*situation*›; tight ‹*market, economic situation*›. **2** *adv.* ‹*work*› concentratedly; ‹*listen*› with concentrated attention

angestellt *Adj.* **bei jmdm.** ~ **sein** be employed by sb.; work for sb.; **fest** ~ **sein** have a permanent position

Angestellte *der/die; adj. Dekl.* [salaried] employee; **Arbeiter und** ~: workers and salaried staff; blue- and white-collar workers; **sie ist** ~ **bei der Stadt** she works for the town council; (im Gegensatz zur Beamtin/Beamtin) she has a salaried position with the town council

Angestellten·versicherung *die* [salaried] employees' insurance

angestrengt 1 *Adj.* close ‹*attention*›; concentrated ‹*work, study, thought*›. **2** *adv.* ‹*work, think, search*› concentratedly

an·getan *Adj.* **von jmdm./etw.** ~ **sein** be taken with sb./sth.; **dazu** *od.* **danach** ~ **sein, etw. zu tun** (geh.) be suitable for doing sth.

an·getrunken *Adj.* [slightly] drunk

an·gewandt *Adj.; nicht präd.* applied

an·gewiesen *Adj.* **auf etw.** (*Akk.*) ~ **sein** have to rely on sth.; **auf jmdn./jmds. Unterstützung** ~ **sein** be dependent on *or* have to rely on sb./sb.'s support; **auf sich selbst** ~ **sein** be thrown back upon one's own resources

an|gewöhnen 1 *tr. V.* **jmdm. etw.** ~: get sb. used to sth.; accustom sb. to sth.; **jmdm.** ~, **etw. zu tun** get sb. used to *or* accustom sb. to doing sth. **2** *refl. V.* **sich** (*Dat.*) **etw.** ~: get into the habit of sth.; **sich** (*Dat.*) **schlechte Manieren** ~: become ill-mannered; **[es] sich** (*Dat.*) ~, **etw. zu tun** get into the habit of doing sth.; **sich** (*Dat.*) **das Rauchen** ~: take up smoking

An·gewohnheit *die* habit

Angina /aŋˈgiːna/ *die;* ~, **Anginen** ▶ 329 | angina

an|gleichen 1 *tr. V.* **etw.** ~ *tr. V.* **etw. einer Sache** (*Dat.*) *od.* **an etw.** (*Akk.*) ~: bring sth. into line with sth. **2** *unr. refl. V.* **sich jmdm./einer Sache** *od.* **an jmdn./etw.** ~: become like sb./sth.

Angler *der;* ~**s,** ~: angler

Anglikaner /aŋliˈkaːnɐ/ *der;* ~**s,** ~: Anglican

anglikanisch *Adj.* Anglican

Anglikanismus *der;* ~: Anglicanism *no art.*

anglisieren *tr. V.* Anglicize

Anglist *der;* ~**en,** ~**en** English specialist *or* scholar; Anglicist; (Student) English student

Anglistik *die;* ~: Anglistics *sing.;* English [language and literature]; English studies *pl., no art.*

Anglistin *die;* ~, ~**nen** ⇒ **Anglist**

Anglizismen *der;* ~, **Anglizismen** Anglicism

Anglo-: ~**amerikaner** *der* Anglo-American; ~**Amerikaner** *der* Anglo-Saxon; **die** ~: the British and the Americans; ~**amerikanerin** *die* Anglo-American

an|glotzen *tr. V.* (ugs.) gawp at (coll.)

Angola /aŋˈgoːla/ (*das*) ~**s** Angola

Angolaner *der;* ~**s,** ~: Angolan

Angora- /aŋˈgoːra/**:** ~**kaninchen** *das* angora rabbit; ~**katze** *die* angora cat; ~**wolle** *die* angora [wool]

angreifbar *Adj.* contestable

an|greifen 1 *unr. tr. V.* **(a)** (auch fig.) attack; **(b)** (schwächen) weaken, affect ‹*health, heart*›; affect ‹*stomach, intestine, voice*›; weaken ‹*person*›; **(c)** ([be]schädigen) attack ‹*metal*›; harm ‹*hands*›; **(d)** (anbrechen) break into ‹*supplies, savings, etc.*›. **2** *unr. itr. V.* (auch fig.) attack

An·greifer *der,* **Angreiferin** *die;* ~, ~**nen** (auch fig.) attacker

an|grenzen *itr. V.* **an etw.** (*Akk.*) ~: border on *or* adjoin sth.

An·griff *der* attack; **zum** ~ **übergehen** go over to the attack; take the offensive; **zum** ~ **blasen** (auch fig.) sound the charge *or* attack; **etw. in** ~ **nehmen** (fig.) set about *or* tackle sth.

angriffs-, Angriffs-: ~**krieg** *der* war of aggression; ~**lust** *die* aggression; aggressiveness; ~**lustig 1** *Adj.* aggressive; **2** *adv.* aggressively; ~**punkt** *der* (fig.) target

an|grinsen *tr. V.* grin at

angst /aŋst/ *Adj.* **jmdm. ist/wird [es]** ~ **[und bange]** sb. is/becomes afraid *or* frightened; (jmd. ist/wird unruhig) sb. is/becomes very worried *or* anxious

Angst *die;* ~, **Ängste** /ˈɛŋstə/ **(a)** (Furcht) fear (**vor** + *Dat.* of); (Psych.) anxiety; ~ **[vor jmdm./etw.] haben** be afraid *or* frightened [of sb./sth.]; **jmdn. in** ~ **und Schrecken versetzen** worry and frighten sb.; ~ **bekommen** *od.* (ugs.) kriegen, es mit der ~ [zu tun] bekommen *od.* (ugs.) kriegen become *or* get frightened *or* scared; **jmdm.** ~ **einflößen/einjagen/machen** frighten *or* scare sb.; **keine** ~! don't be afraid; **sich aus** ~ **verstecken** hide in fear; **aus** ~, **sich zu verraten, sagte er kein einziges Wort** he didn't say a word for fear of betraying himself; **(b)** (Sorge) worry; anxiety; ~ **[um jmdn./etw.] haben** be worried *or* anxious [about sb./ sth.]; **sie hat** ~, **ihn zu verletzen** she is worried about hurting him; **keine** ~! don't worry!

Angst-: ~**gefühl** *das* feeling of anxiety; ~**hase** *der* (ugs. abwertend) scaredy-cat (coll.)

ängstigen /ˈɛŋstɪɡŋ/ **1** *tr. V.* frighten; scare; (beunruhigen) worry. **2** *refl. V.* be frightened *or* afraid; (sich sorgen) worry; **sich vor etw.** (*Dat.*) /**um jmdn.** ~: be frightened *or* afraid of sth./worried about sb.

ängstlich /ˈɛŋstlɪç/ **1** *Adj.* **(a)** (verängstigt) anxious; apprehensive; **(b)** (furchtsam, schüchtern) timorous; timid; **(c)** (besorgt) worried; anxious. **2** *adv.* **(a)** (verängstigt) anxiously; apprehensively; **(b)** (besorgt) anxiously; **(c)** (übermäßig genau) meticulously; ~ **bemüht** *od.* **darauf bedacht sein, etw. zu tun** be at great pains to do sth.

Ängstlichkeit *die;* ~ **(a)** (Furchtsamkeit) timorousness; timidity; **(b)** (Schüchternheit) timidity; **(c)** (Besorgnis) anxiety

angst-, Angst-: ~**neurose** *die* anxiety neurosis; ~**psychose** *die* anxiety psychosis; ~**röhre** *die* (ugs. scherzh.) topper (coll.); top hat; ~**schweiß** *der* cold sweat; **der** ~**schweiß brach ihm aus** he broke out in a cold sweat; ~**verzerrt** *Adj.* ‹*face*› twisted in fear

an|gucken *tr. V.* (ugs.) look at; **sich** (*Dat.*) **etw./jmdn.** ~: look *or* have a look at sth./ sb.; **guck dir das/den an!** [just] look at that/him!

an|gurten *tr. V.* strap in; **sich** ~: put on one's seat belt; (im Flugzeug) fasten one's seat belt

an|haben *unr. tr. V.* **(a)** (ugs.: am Körper tragen) have on; **(b) jmdm./einer Sache etwas** ~ **können** be able to harm sb./harm *or* damage sth.; **(c)** (ugs.: in Betrieb haben) have on

An·halt *der* ⇒ **Anhaltspunkt**

an|halten 1 *unr. tr. V.* **(a)** stop; **den Atem** ~: hold one's breath; **(b)** (auffordern) urge; **(c) sich** (*Dat.*) **eine Hose/einen Rock** *usw.* ~: hold a pair of trousers/a skirt *etc.* up against oneself. **2** *unr. itr. V.* **(a)** stop; **(b)** (andauern) go on; last; **(c) [bei jmdm.] um jmdn.** *od.* **jmds. Hand** ~ (veralt.) ask [sb.] for sb.'s hand [in marriage]

anhaltend 1 *Adj.* constant; continuous. **2** *adv.* constantly; continuously

An·halter *der* hitch-hiker; **per** ~ **fahren** hitch[-hike]

An·halterin *die* hitch-hiker

Anhalts·punkt *der* clue (**für** to); (für eine Vermutung) grounds *pl.* (**für** for)

an·hand 1 *Präp. mit Gen.* with the help of. **2** *Adv.* ~ **von** with the help of

An·hang *der* **(a)** (eines Buches) appendix; **(b)** (Anhängerschaft) following; **(c)** (Verwandtschaft) family

an|hängen[1] *unr. itr. V.* (geh.) **(a)** (verbunden sein mit) be attached (*Dat.* to); **(b)** (glauben an) subscribe (*Dat.* to) ‹*belief, idea, theory, etc.*›

an|hängen[2] 1 *tr. V.* **(a)** hang up (**an** + *Akk.* on); **(b)** (ankuppeln) couple on (**an** + *Akk.* to); hitch up ‹*trailer*› (**an** + *Akk.* to); **(c)** (anfügen) add (**an** + *Akk.* to); **(d)** (ugs.: zuschreiben, anlasten) **jmdm. etw.** ~: blame sth. on sb.; **(e)** (ugs.: geben) **jmdm. etw.** ~: give sb. sth.. **2** *refl. V.* **(a)** hang on (**an** + *Akk.* to); **(b)** (ugs.: sich anschließen) **sich [an jmdn.** *od.* **bei jmdm.]** ~: tag along [with sb.] (coll.)

An·hänger *der* **(a)** (Mensch) supporter; (einer Sekte) adherent; follower; **(b)** (Wagen) trailer; **(c)** (Schmuckstück) pendant; **(d)** (Schildchen) label; tag

Anhänger·kupplung *die* tow bar

Anhängerschaft *die;* ∼, ∼**en** supporters *pl.;* (einer Sekte) followers *pl.;* adherents *pl.*

anhängig *Adj.* (Rechtsw.) pending ‹*action*›; **etw.** ∼ **machen** start legal proceedings over sth.

anhänglich *Adj.* devoted ‹*dog, friend*›

Anhänglichkeit *die;* ∼**:** devotion (**an** + *Akk.* to); **aus** [**alter**] ∼ (Nostalgie) out of old affection

Anhängsel /'anhɛŋzl/ *das;* ∼**s**, ∼**:** appendage (*Gen.* to)

an|hauchen *tr. V.* breathe on ‹*mirror, glasses*›; blow on ‹*fingers, hands*›

an|hauen *unr. tr. V.* (salopp) accost; **jmdn. um 50 Mark** ∼**:** touch (sl.) *or* tap sb. for 50 marks

an|häufen 1 *tr. V.* accumulate; amass. **2** *refl. V.* accumulate; pile up

An·häufung *die* (a) accumulation; amassing; (b) (Haufen) accumulation

an|heben *unr. tr. V.* (a) lift [up]; (b) (erhöhen) raise ‹*prices, wages, etc.*›

An·hebung *die* (Erhöhung) increase (*Gen.* in); raising (*Gen.* of)

an|heften *tr. V.* tack [on] ‹*hem, sleeve, etc.*›; attach ‹*label, list*›; put up ‹*sign, notice*›

anheim *in* jmdm. ∼ **fallen** (geh.) pass to sb.; **der Vergessenheit/der Zerstörung** ∼ **fallen** (geh.) sink into oblivion/fall prey to destruction; [**es**] **jmdm.** ∼ **stellen, etw. zu tun** (geh.) leave it to sb. to do sth.

anheimelnd *Adj.* homely; cosy

an|heizen 1 *tr. V.* (a) fire up ‹*stove, boiler, etc.*›; (b) (fig. ugs.) stimulate ‹*interest*›. **2** *itr. V.* put the heating on

an|heuern /'anhɔʏɐn/ **1** *tr. V.* (a) (Seemannsspr.) sign on; (b) (fig. ugs.: einstellen) sign on *or* up. **2** *itr. V.* (Seemannsspr.) sign on

An·hieb *der in* **auf** [**den ersten**] ∼ (ugs.) straight off; first go

an|himmeln /-hɪmln/ *tr. V.* (ugs.) (a) (verehren) idolize; worship; (b) (ansehen) gaze adoringly at

An·höhe *die* rise; elevation

an|hören 1 *tr. V.* listen to; **etw.** [**zufällig**] **mit** ∼**:** overhear sth.; **sich** (*Dat.*) **jmdn./etw.** ∼**:** listen to sb./sth.; **ich kann das nicht mehr mit** ∼**!** I can't listen to that any longer. **2** *refl. V.* sound

Anhörung *die;* ∼, ∼**en** hearing

Anilin /ani'liːn/ *das;* ∼**s** (Chemie) aniline

Anilin·leder *das* aniline leather

animalisch /ani'maːlɪʃ/ *Adj.* (a) animal *attrib.;* (b) (abwertend: triebhaft) animal *attrib.;* bestial

Animateur /anima'tøːɐ̯/ *der;* ∼**s**, ∼**e** host

Animation /anima'tsi̯oːn/ *die;* ∼, ∼**en** animation

Animier·dame *die* hostess

animieren /ani'miːrən/ *tr.* (*auch itr.*) *V.* encourage; **das soll zum Kaufen** ∼**:** that's to encourage people to buy

An·ion *das* (Chemie) anion

Anis /a'niːs/ *der;* ∼[**es**], ∼**e** (a) (Pflanze) anise; (b) (Gewürz) aniseed; (c) (Branntwein) aniseed brandy

Ank. *Abk.* **Ankunft** arr.

an|kämpfen *itr. V.* **gegen jmdn./etw.** ∼**:** fight [against] sb./sth.; **gegen den Strom/Wind** ∼**:** battle against the current/the wind

an|karren *tr. V.* (ugs.) cart along; bring along ‹*supporters, followers*›

An·kauf *der* purchase; „**Heinrich Meyer, An- und Verkauf**" 'Heinrich Meyer, second-hand dealer'

an|kaufen *tr. V.* purchase; buy

Anker /'aŋkɐ/ *der;* ∼**s**, ∼ (a) anchor; **vor** ∼ **gehen/liegen** drop anchor/lie at anchor; ∼ **werfen** drop anchor; (b) (Elektrot.) armature

ankern *itr. V.* (a) (vor Anker gehen) anchor; drop anchor; (b) (vor Anker liegen) be anchored; lie at anchor

Anker-: ∼**platz** *der* anchorage; ∼**wicklung** *die* (Elektrot.) armature winding; ∼**winde** *die* windlass

*alte Schreibung (vgl. Hinweise auf S. xvi–xvii)

an|ketten *tr. V.* chain up (**an** + *Akk. od. Dat.* to)

An·klage *die* (a) charge; **der Staatsanwalt hat** ∼ [**wegen Mordes gegen ihn**] **erhoben** the public prosecutor brought a charge [of murder against him]; **unter** ∼ **stehen** have been charged (**wegen** with); (b) (∼vertretung) prosecution

Anklage·bank *die; Pl.* ∼**bänke** dock; **auf der** ∼ **sitzen** (auch fig.) be in the dock

an|klagen 1 *tr. V.* (a) (Rechtsw.) charge; accuse; **jmdn. einer Sache** (*Gen.*) *od.* **wegen etw.** ∼**:** charge sb. with *or* accuse sb. of sth.; (b) (geh.: beschuldigen) accuse **2** *itr. V.* cry out in accusation; **jmdn.** ∼**d ansehen** look at sb. accusingly

An·kläger *der* prosecutor

Anklage-: ∼**schrift** *die* indictment; ∼**vertreter** *der* prosecuting counsel; counsel for the prosecution

an|klammern 1 *tr. V.* peg (Brit.) *or* (Amer.) pin ‹*clothes, washing*› up (**an** + *Akk.* to); clip ‹*copy, sheet, etc.*› (**an** + *Akk.* to); (mit Heftklammern) staple ‹*copy, sheet, etc.*› (**an** + *Akk.* on). **2** *refl. V.* **sich an jmdn./etw.** ∼**:** cling to *or* hang on to sb./sth.

An·klang *der in* [**bei jmdm.**] ∼ **finden** meet with [sb.'s] approval; find favour [with sb.]; **wenig/keinen/großen** ∼ **finden** be poorly/badly/well received (**bei** by)

an|kleben 1 *tr.* (*auch itr.*) *V.* stick up ‹*poster, etc.*› (**an** + *Akk.* on). **2** *itr. V.; mit sein* stick (**an** + *Dat.* to)

Ankleide·kabine *die* changing cubicle

an|kleiden *tr. V.* (geh.) dress; **sich** ∼**:** get dressed; dress [oneself]

Ankleide·raum *der* dressing room

an|klicken *tr. V.* (DV) click on

an|klingen *unr. itr. V.; auch mit sein* be discernible; **ein Thema** ∼ **lassen** touch on a theme

an|klopfen *itr. V.* knock (**an** + *Akk. od. Dat.* at *or* on)

an|knabbern *tr. V.* (ugs.) nibble [at]

an|knipsen *tr. V.* (ugs.) switch *or* put on

an|knüpfen 1 *tr. V.* (a) tie on (**an** + *Akk.* to); (b) (beginnen) start up ‹*conversation*›; establish ‹*relations, business links*›; form ‹*relationship*›; strike up ‹*acquaintance*›. **2** *itr. V.* **an etw.** (*Akk.*) ∼**:** take sth. up; **ich knüpfe dort an, wo wir vorige Woche aufgehört haben** I'll pick up where we left off last week

an|kommen *unr. itr. V.; mit sein* (a) (eintreffen) arrive; ‹*letter, parcel*› come, arrive; ‹*bus, train, plane*› arrive, get in; **seid ihr gut angekommen?** did you arrive safely *or* get there all right?; (b) (herankommen) come along; (c) (ugs.: Anklang finden) [**bei jmdm.**] [**gut**] ∼**:** go down [very] well [with sb.]; **er ist ein Typ, der bei den Frauen ankommt** he is the sort who is a success with women; (d) **gegen jmdn./etw.** ∼**:** be able to cope *or* deal with sb./ fight sth.; (e) *unpers.* **es kommt auf jmdn./etw. an** (jmd./etw. ist ausschlaggebend) it depends on sb./sth.; **es kommt auf etw.** (*Akk.*) **an** (etw. ist wichtig) sth. matters (*Dat.* to); **es kommt** [**ganz**] **darauf an, ob …: it** [all] depends whether …; **es kommt** [**ganz**] **darauf** *od.* **drauf an** (ugs.) it [all] depends; **es käme auf einen Versuch an** it's *or* it would be worth a try; **darauf kommt es mir nicht so sehr an** that doesn't matter so much to me; (f) **es auf etw.** (*Akk.*) ∼ **lassen** (etw. riskieren) [be prepared to] risk sth.; **es d[a]rauf** ∼ **lassen** (ugs.) take a chance; chance it

Ankömmling /'ankœmlɪŋ/ *der;* ∼**s**, ∼**e** newcomer

an|koppeln 1 *tr. V.* couple ‹*carriage*› up (**an** + *Akk.* to); hitch ‹*trailer*› up (**an** + *Akk.* to); dock ‹*spacecraft*› (**an** + *Akk.* with). **2** *itr. V.* ‹*spacecraft*› dock (**an** + *Akk.* with)

an|kotzen *tr. V.* (salopp) (a) throw up over; puke over (coarse); (b) (fig.: anwidern) **jmdn.** ∼**:** make sb. sick

an|kreiden *tr. V.* (ugs.) **jmdm. etw.** ∼**:** hold sth. against sb.

an|kreuzen *tr. V.* mark with a cross; put a cross beside

an|kündigen 1 *tr. V.* announce; **ein Gewitter** ∼**:** herald a storm; **eine angekündigte/nicht angekündigte Klassenarbeit** a class test announced in advance/

a surprise test. **2** *refl. V.* ‹*spring, storm*› announce itself; ‹*illness*› show itself

An·kündigung *die* announcement

Ankunft /'ankʊnft/ *die;* ~, **Ankünfte** arrival; „~" 'arrivals'

Ankunfts-: ~**halle** *die* (Flugw.) arrival[s] hall; ~**tafel** *die* arrivals board

an|kuppeln *tr. V.* ⇨ ankoppeln 1

an|kurbeln *tr. V.* (**a**) crank [up]; (**b**) (fig.) boost ‹*economy, production, etc.*›

Ankurb[e]lung *die;* ~, ~**en** (fig.) boosting; **Maßnahmen zur** ~ **der Wirtschaft** measures to boost the economy

Anl. *Abk.* Anlage encl.

an|lächeln *tr. V.* smile at; **jmdn. freundlich** ~: give a friendly smile to sb.

an|lachen 1 *tr. V.* smile at. **2** *refl. V.* **sich** (*Dat.*) **jmdn.** ~ (ugs.) get off with sb. (Brit. coll.); pick sb. up

An·lage *die* (**a**) *o. Pl.* (das Anlegen) (einer Kartei) establishment; (eines Parks, Gartens usw.) laying out; construction; (eines Parkplatzes, Stausees) construction; (**b**) (Grün~) park; (um ein Schloss, einen Palast usw. herum) grounds *pl.;* **öffentliche/städtische** ~**n** public/municipal parks and gardens; (**c**) (Angelegtes, Komplex) complex; (**d**) (Einrichtung) facilities *pl.;* **sanitäre/militärische** ~**n** sanitary facilities/military installations; **die elektrische** ~: the electrical equipment; (**e**) (Werk) plant; (**f**) (Musik~, Lautsprecher~ usw.) equipment; system; (**g**) (Geld~) investment; (**h**) (Konzeption) conception; (Struktur) structure; (**i**) (Veranlagung) aptitude, gift, talent (**zu** for); (Neigung) tendency, predisposition (**zu** to); (**j**) (Beilage zu einem Brief) enclosure; **als** ~ **sende ich Ihnen/erhalten Sie ein ärztliches Attest** please find enclosed/I enclose a medical certificate

Anlage-: ~**berater** *der* ▶ 85 | investment adviser; ~**kapital** *das* investment capital

Anlage·vermögen *das* fixed assets *pl.* or capital

an|landen *tr. V.* land

an|langen 1 *itr. V.; mit sein* arrive; **bei/auf/an etw.** (*Dat.*) ~: arrive at or reach sth. **2** *tr. V.* (**a**) (südd.: anfassen) touch; (**b**) ⇨ anbelangen

Anlass, *Anlaß /'anlas/ *der;* **Anlasses, Anlässe** /'anlɛsə/ (**a**) (Ausgangspunkt, Grund) cause (**zu** for); **der** ~ **des Streites** the cause of the dispute; **etw. zum** ~ **nehmen, etw. zu tun** use or take sth. as an opportunity to do sth.; **jmdm.** ~ **zu Beschwerden geben** give sb. cause for complaint; ~ **zur Sorge/Beunruhigung/Klage geben** give cause for concern/unease/complaint; **beim geringsten/kleinsten** ~: for the slightest reason; **aus aktuellem** ~: because of current events; (**b**) (Gelegenheit) occasion; **bei festlichen Anlässen** on festive occasions

an|lassen 1 *unr. tr. V.* (**a**) leave ‹*light, radio, heating, engine, tap, etc.*› on; leave ‹*candle*› burning; (**b**) keep ‹*coat, gloves, etc.*› on; (**c**) (in Gang setzen) start [up]. **2** *unr. refl. V.* **sich gut/schlecht** ~: make a or get off to a good/ bad or poor start

Anlasser *der;* ~**s,** ~ (Kfz-W.) starter

an·lässlich, *an·läßlich *Präp. mit Gen.* on the occasion of

an|lasten *tr. V.* **jmdm. ein Verbrechen** ~: accuse sb. of a crime; **jmdm. die Schuld an etw.** (*Dat.*) ~: blame sb. for sth.

An·lauf *der* (**a**) run-up; [**mehr**] ~ **nehmen** take [more of] a run-up; **mit/ohne** ~: with/without a run-up; **er sprang mit/ohne** ~: he did a running/standing jump; (**b**) (Versuch) attempt; **beim** od. **im ersten/dritten** ~: at the first/third attempt or (coll.) go

an|laufen 1 *unr. itr. V.; mit sein* (**a**) **angelaufen kommen** come running along; (auf einen zu) come running up; (**b**) **gegen jmdn./etw.** ~: run at sb./sth.; (**c**) (Anlauf nehmen) take a run-up; (**d**) (zu laufen beginnen) ‹*engine*› start [up]; (fig.) ‹*film*› open; ‹*production, search, campaign*› start; (**e**) (sich färben) turn; go; (**f**) (beschlagen) mist or steam up. **2** *unr. tr. V.* put in at ‹*port*›

Anlauf·stelle *die* place to go

An·laut *der* (Sprachw.) initial sound; **im** ~: in initial position

---

an|legen 1 *tr. V.* (**a**) (an etw. legen) put or lay ‹*domino, card*› [down] (**an** + *Akk.* next to); place, position ‹*ruler, protractor*› (**an** + *Akk.* on); put ‹*ladder*› up (**an** + *Akk.* against); **einen strengen Maßstab [an etw.** (*Akk.*)] ~: apply strict standards [to sth.]; (**b**) (an den Körper legen) **die Flügel/Ohren** ~: close its wings/lay its ears back; **die Arme** ~: put one's arms to one's sides; (**c**) (geh.: anziehen, umlegen) don; put on; (**d**) (schaffen) lay out ‹*town, garden, plantation, street*›; start ‹*file, album*›; compile ‹*statistics, index*›; (**e**) (gestalten, entwerfen) structure ‹*story, novel*›; (**f**) (investieren) invest; (**g**) (ausgeben) spend (**für** on); (**h**) **es darauf** ~, **etw. zu tun** be determined to do sth.; **er legt es auf einen Streit an** he is determined to have a fight. **2** *itr. V.* (**a**) (landen) moor; (**b**) (Kartenspiel) lay a card/cards; **bei jmdm.** ~: lay a card/cards on sb.'s hand; (**c**) (Domino) play [a domino/dominoes]; (**d**) (zielen) aim (**auf** + *Akk.* at). **3** *refl. V.* **sich mit jmdm.** ~: pick an argument or quarrel with sb.

Anleger *der;* ~**s,** ~ (**a**) (Schifffahrt) jetty; (**b**) (Investor) investor

Anlege-: ~**steg** *der* landing stage; jetty; ~**stelle** *die* mooring

an|lehnen 1 *tr. V.* (**a**) (an etw. lehnen) lean (**an** + *Akk.* od. *Dat.* against); (**b**) leave ‹*door*› slightly open or ajar; leave ‹*window*› slightly open; **die Tür war angelehnt** the door was [left] slightly open or ajar. **2** *refl. V.* **sich [an jmdn.** od. **jmdm./etw.]** ~: lean [on sb./against sth.]; **sich an ein Vorbild** ~ (fig.) follow an example

Anlehnung *die;* ~, ~**en: in** ~ **an jmdn./etw.** in imitation of or following sb./sth.

Anleihe *die;* ~, ~**n** (**a**) (Darlehen) loan; (**b**) (fig.) borrowing; **eine** ~ **bei Goethe/Picasso machen** borrow from Goethe/Picasso

an|leimen *tr. V.* stick or glue on (**an** + *Akk.* od. *Dat.* to)

an|leinen /-lainən/ *tr. V.* put ‹*dog*› on the lead; **Hunde sind anzuleinen** dogs must be kept on a lead

an|leiten *tr. V.* (**a**) instruct; teach; **jmdn. zur Selbstständigkeit** ~: teach sb. to be independent

An·leitung *die* instructions *pl.*

an|lernen *tr. V.* train; **ein angelernter Arbeiter** a semi-skilled worker

an|lesen 1 *unr. tr. V.* begin or start reading or to read. **2** *unr. refl. V.* **sich** (*Dat.*) **etw.** ~: learn sth. by reading or from books

an|liegen *unr. itr. V.* (**a**) (an etw. liegen) ‹*pullover etc.*› fit tightly or closely; ‹*hair, ears*› lie flat; **ein eng** ~**der Pullover** a tight- or close-fitting pullover; (**b**) (ugs.: vorliegen) be on; (zu erledigen sein) to be done

An·liegen *das;* ~**s,** ~ (Bitte) request; (Angelegenheit) matter; **etw. zu seinem persönlichen** ~ **machen** take a personal interest in sth.

anliegend *Adj.* (**a**) *nicht präd.* (angrenzend) adjacent; (**b**) (beiliegend) enclosed

Anlieger *der;* ~**s,** ~: resident; „~ **frei**" 'residents only'

an|locken *tr. V.* attract ‹*customers, tourists, etc.*›; lure ‹*bird, animal*›

an|löten *tr. V.* solder on (**an** + *Akk.* od. *Dat.* to)

an|lügen *tr. V.* lie to

Anm. *Abk.* Anmerkung

an|machen *tr. V.* (**a**) (anschalten, -zünden usw.) put or turn ‹*light, radio, heating*› on; light ‹*fire*›; (**b**) (bereiten) mix ‹*cement, plaster, paint, etc.*›; dress ‹*salad*›; (**c**) (ugs.: anbringen) put ‹*curtain, sign*› up; (**d**) (ugs.: ansprechen) chat up (Brit. coll.); (**e**) (ugs.: begeistern, erregen) get ‹*audience etc.*› going; **das macht mich ungeheuer/nicht an** it really turns me on (coll.) /does nothing for me (coll.)

an|mahnen *tr. V.* send a reminder about

an|malen *tr. V.* (**a**) (ugs.: bemalen) paint; **etw. rot** ~: paint sth. red; (**b**) (ugs.: schminken) paint; **sich** ~: paint one's face; (**c**) (hinmalen) paint (**an** + *Akk.* on); (ugs.: hinzeichnen) draw (**an** + *Akk.* on); **jmdm./sich einen Bart** ~: paint or draw a beard on sb.'s/one's face or on sb./oneself

An·marsch *der* advance; **im** ~ **sein** be advancing; (ugs. scherzh.: unterwegs sein) be on one's way

an|marschieren itr. V.; mit sein advance; **anmarschiert kommen** (ugs.) come marching along; (auf einen zu) come marching up

an|maßen /-maːsn̩/ refl. V. **sich** (Dat.) etw. ~: claim sth. [for oneself]; arrogate sth. to oneself; **darüber kannst du dir gar kein Urteil ~:** you have no right or it's not your place to pass judgement on that

an·maßend 1 Adj. presumptuous; (arrogant) arrogant. 2 adv. presumptuously; (arrogant) arrogantly

Anmaßung die; ~, ~en presumptuousness; presumption; (Arroganz) arrogance; **es ist eine ~ zu behaupten, dass …:** it is presumptuous to assert that …

an|melden tr. V. (a) (als Teilnehmer) enrol; **jmdn./sich zu einem Kursus/in** od. **bei einer Schule ~:** enrol sb./enrol for a course/at a school; **sich schriftlich ~:** register [in writing]; (b) (melden, anzeigen) license, get a licence for ‹television, radio›; apply for ‹patent›; register ‹domicile, car, trade mark›; **sich/seinen neuen Wohnsitz ~:** register one's new address; s. auch **Konkurs;** (c) (ankündigen) announce; **sind Sie angemeldet?** do you have an appointment?; **sich beim Arzt ~:** make an appointment to see the doctor; (d) (geltend machen) express, make known ‹reservation, doubt, wish›; put forward ‹demand›; (e) (Kartenspiele: ansagen) bid; (f) (Fernspr.) book

An·meldung die (a) (zur Teilnahme) enrolment; (b) ⇒ **anmelden** b: licensing; registration; **die ~ eines Patents** the application for a patent; (c) (Ankündigung) announcement; (beim Arzt, Anwalt usw.) making an appointment

an|merken tr. V. (a) jmdm. seinen Ärger/seine Verlegenheit usw. ~: notice that sb. is annoyed/embarrassed etc.; notice sb.'s annoyance/embarrassment etc.; **man merkt ihm [nicht] an, dass er krank ist** you can[not] tell that he is ill; **sich nichts ~ lassen** not let it show; (b) (geh.: bemerken) note

Anmerkung die; ~, ~en (a) (Fußnote) note; (b) (geh.: Bemerkung) comment; remark

An·moderation die (a) o. Pl. (das Anmoderieren) introducing; **sie ist noch bei der ~ der Sendung** she is still introducing the programme; (b) (Text, Wortlaut) introduction; **sie hat sich eine witzige ~ einfallen lassen** she thought of a witty way to introduce the programme

an·moderieren tr. V. introduce

An·mut die; ~ (geh.) grace; **mit ~:** gracefully

an|muten /-muːtn̩/ tr., auch itr. V. (geh.) **[jmdn.] fremd** usw. ~: seem strange etc. [to sb.]

an·mutig (geh.) 1 Adj. graceful ‹girl, gesture, movement, dance›; charming, delightful ‹girl, smile, picture, landscape›. 2 adv. ‹move, dance› gracefully; ‹smile, greet› charmingly, delightfully

an|nähen tr. V. sew on (**an** + Akk. to)

an|nähern refl. V. (a) approach; **sich einem Grenzwert ~** (Math.) converge towards a limit; (b) (fig.: [menschlich] näherkommen) **sich jmdm. ~:** come or get closer to sb.; (c) (sich angleichen) **sich einer Sache** (Dat.) **~:** come or get closer to sth. 2 tr. V. (angleichen) bring closer (Dat. to); **verschiedene Standpunkte einander ~:** bring differing points of view closer together

annähernd 1 Adv. almost; nearly; (ungefähr) approximately; **nicht ~ so teuer** not nearly as or nowhere near as expensive. 2 adj.; nicht präd. approximate; rough

Annäherung die; ~, ~en (a) approach (**an** + Akk. to); (b) (fig.) **es kam zu einer ~ der beiden Parteien** the two parties came or moved closer together; (c) (Angleichung) **eine ~ der gegenseitigen Standpunkte** bringing the points of view on each side closer together

Annäherungs·versuch der advance

Annahme /'anaːmə/ die; ~, ~n (a) acceptance; **die ~ eines Pakets verweigern** refuse to accept [delivery of] a parcel; (b) (Vermutung) assumption; **in der ~, dass …:** on the assumption that …; (c) ⇒ **Annahmestelle**

Annahme-: ~**schluss,** *~**schluß** der deadline [for acceptance]; **wann ist ~schluss?** when is the deadline [for acceptance]?; ~**stelle** die (für Lotto/Wetten usw.) place where coupons/bets are accepted; (für Reparaturen) repairs counter/department; (für Lieferungen) delivery point

---

*alte Schreibung (vgl. Hinweise auf S. xvi–xvii)

Annalen /a'naːlən/ Pl. annals; **in die ~ der Firma eingehen** go down in the annals of the firm

annehmbar 1 Adj. (a) acceptable; (b) (recht gut) reasonable. 2 adv. reasonably [well]

an|nehmen 1 unr. tr. V. (a) accept; take; accept ‹alms, invitation, condition, help, fate verdict, punishment›; take ‹food, telephone call›; accept, take [on] ‹task, job, repairs›; accept, take up ‹offer, invitation, challenge›; (b) (Sport) take; (c) (billigen) approve; approve, adopt ‹resolution›; (d) (aufnehmen) take on ‹worker, patient, pupil›; (e) (adoptieren) adopt; **jmdn. an Kindesstatt ~** (veralt.) adopt sb.; (f) (haften lassen) take ‹dye, ink›; **kein Wasser ~:** repel water; be water-repellent; (g) (sich aneignen) adopt ‹habit, mannerism›; adopt, assume ‹name, attitude›; (h) (bekommen) take on ‹look, appearance, form, tone, dimension›; (i) (vermuten) assume; presume; **ich nehme es an/nicht an** I assume or presume so/not; **das ist/ist nicht anzunehmen** that can/cannot be assumed; (j) (voraussetzen) assume; **etw. als gegeben** od. **Tatsache ~:** take sth. for granted or as read; **angenommen, [dass] …:** assuming [that] …; **das kannst du ~!** (ugs.) you bet! (coll.). 2 unr. refl. V. (geh.) **sich jmds./einer Sache ~:** look after sb./sth.

Annehmlichkeit die; ~, ~en comfort; (Vorteil) advantage

annektieren /anɛk'tiːrən/ tr. V. annex

Annektierung die; ~, ~en, **Annexion** /anɛ'ksi̯oːn/ die; ~, ~en annexation

anno /'ano/, *Anno in ~ 1910/68 usw. (veralt.) in [the year] 1910/'68 etc.; **seit ~ 1910** since [the year] 1910; ~ **dazumal** od. **dunnemals** od. **Tobak** (ugs. scherzh.) the year dot (Brit. coll.); long ago

Annonce /a'nõːsə/ die; ~, ~n advertisement; ad (coll.); advert (Brit. coll.)

annoncieren tr., itr. V. advertise

annullieren /anʊ'liːrən/ tr. V. annul

Annullierung die; ~, ~en annulment

Anode /a'noːdə/ die; ~, ~n (Physik) anode

an|öden /-øːdn̩/ tr. V. (ugs.) bore stiff (coll.) or to death (coll.)

anomal /'anomaːl/ 1 Adj. anomalous; abnormal. 2 adv. anomalously; abnormally

Anomalie die; ~, ~n anomaly; abnormality

anonym /ano'nyːm/ 1 Adj. anonymous. 2 adv. anonymously

Anonymität /anonymi'tɛːt/ die; ~: anonymity

Anorak /'anorak/ der; ~s, ~s anorak

an|ordnen tr. V. (a) (arrangieren) arrange; (b) (befehlen) order

An·ordnung die (a) (Ordnung) arrangement; (b) (Weisung) order; **auf meine ~/auf ~ des Arztes** on my/doctor's orders pl.

an·organisch Adj. inorganic

anormal 1 Adj. abnormal. 2 adv. abnormally

an|packen 1 tr. V. (a) (ugs.: anfassen) grab hold of; (b) (angehen) tackle; **packen wirs an!** let's get down to it; (c) (ugs.: behandeln) treat ‹person›. 2 itr. V. (ugs.: mithelfen) [mit] ~: lend a hand

an|passen 1 tr. V. (a) (passend machen) fit; (b) (abstimmen) suit (Dat. to). 2 refl. V. adapt [oneself] (Dat. to); ‹animal› adapt; (gesellschaftlich) conform

Anpassung die; ~, ~en adaptation (**an** + Akk. to); (der Renten, Löhne usw.) adjustment (**an** + Akk. to); (an die Gesellschaft) conformity

anpassungs·fähig Adj. adaptable

Anpassungs·fähigkeit die; o. Pl. adaptability (**an** + Akk. to)

an|peilen tr. V. (a) (Funkw.) take a bearing on; (b) (fig. ugs.) aim at; (c) (anvisieren) take a sight on

an|pfeifen (Sport) 1 unr. tr. V. blow the whistle to start ‹game, half›. 2 unr. itr. V. blow the whistle

An·pfiff der (a) (Sport) whistle for the start of play; **der ~ zur zweiten Halbzeit** the whistle for the start of the second half; (b) (salopp: Zurechtweisung) bawling-out (coll.)

an|pflanzen tr. V. (a) plant; (b) (anbauen) grow; cultivate

an|pflaumen /-pflaumən/ tr. V. (ugs.) tease; take the mickey out of (Brit. coll.)

an|pflocken /-pflɔkn̩/ *tr. V.* tether ‹*animal*›

an|pirschen *refl. V.* creep up (**an** + *Akk.* on)

an|pöbeln *tr. V.* (ugs.) abuse

An·prall *der;* ~[e]s impact (**auf, an** + *Akk.* with, **gegen** against)

an|prallen *itr. V.; mit sein* crash; **gegen** *od.* **an etw.** ~: crash into sb./against sth.

an|prangern /-praŋɐn/ *tr. V.* denounce

an|preisen *unr. tr. V.* extol; **jmdn./etw. jmdm.** ~: extol the virtues of sb./sth. to sb.; recommend sb./sth. highly to sb.

An·probe *die* fitting

an|probieren *tr. V.* try on

an|pumpen *tr. V.* (ugs.) borrow money from; **jmdn. um 20 Mark** ~: touch (sl.) *or* tap sb. for 20 marks

Anrainer /ˈanraɪnɐ/ *der;* ~s, ~ (**a**) (Nachbar) neighbour; (**b**) (bes. österr.: Anlieger) resident

Anrainer·staat *der:* **die** ~**en des Bodensees** the countries bordering on Lake Constance

an|rasen *itr. V.; mit sein* (ugs.) **angerast kommen** come racing along; (auf einen zu) come racing up

an|raten *unr. tr. V.* **jmdm. etw.** ~: recommend sth. to sb.; **auf Anraten des Arztes** on the *or* one's doctor's advice

anrechenbar *Adj.* [**auf etw.** (*Akk.*)] ~ **sein** count [towards sth.]

an|rechnen *tr. V.* (**a**) (gutschreiben, verbuchen) count; take into account; **er bekam einen Pluspunkt angerechnet** he was given an extra mark; **jmdm. etw. als Verdienst/Fehler** ~: count sth. to sb.'s credit/as sb.'s mistake; **jmdm. etw. hoch** ~: think highly of sb. for sth.; (**b**) (in Rechnung stellen) **jmdm. etw.** ~: charge sb. for sth.

anrechnungs·fähig *Adj.* (Papierdt.) ⇒ **anrechenbar**

An·recht *das* right; **ein** ~ **auf etw.** (*Akk.*) **haben** have a right to *or* be entitled to sth.

An·rede *die* ▶ 34 |, ▶ 107 | form of address

an|reden *tr. V.* address; **jmdn. mit dem Vornamen** ~: address *or* call sb. by his/her Christian name

an|regen 1 *tr. V.* (**a**) (ermuntern) prompt; **jmdn. zum Nachdenken** ~: make sb. think; (**b**) (vorschlagen) propose; suggest; ~, **etw. zu tun** propose *or* suggest doing sth. 2 *tr.* (*auch itr.*) *V.* stimulate ‹*imagination, digestion*›; sharpen, whet, stimulate ‹*appetite*›

anregend *Adj.* stimulating; ~ **wirken** act as a stimulant

An·regung *die* (**a**) ⇒ **anregen** 2: stimulation; sharpening; whetting; **zur** ~ **der Verdauung/des Appetits** to stimulate the digestion/whet *etc.* the appetite; (**b**) (Denkanstoß) stimulus; (**c**) (Vorschlag) proposal; suggestion

Anregungs·mittel *das* stimulant

an|reichern /-raɪçɐn/ 1 *tr. V.* (**a**) (auch Kerntechnik) enrich; **Trinkwasser mit Fluor** ~: add fluoride to drinking water; (**b**) (akkumulieren) accumulate. 2 *refl. V.* accumulate

Anreicherung *die;* ~, ~**en** (**a**) (auch Kerntechnik) enrichment; (**b**) (Akkumulation) accumulation

An·reise *die* journey [there/here]; **die** ~ **dauert 10 Stunden** the journey there/here takes ten hours; it takes 10 hours to get there/here

an|reisen *itr. V.; mit sein* travel there/here; **mit der Bahn** ~: go/come by train; travel there/here by train; **angereist kommen** come

an|reißen *unr. tr. V.* (**a**) partly tear; (**b**) (in Gang setzen) start [up]; (**c**) (anzünden) strike ‹*match*›; (**d**) (Technik) mark [out]; (**e**) (kurz ansprechen) touch on

An·reiz *der* incentive

an|reizen *tr. V.* (*auch itr.*) *V.* (**a**) (anspornen) stimulate; encourage; **das soll zum Sparen** ~: that is supposed to stimulate *or* act as an incentive to saving; (**b**) (anregen, erregen) stimulate

an|rempeln *tr. V.* barge into; (absichtlich) jostle

an|rennen 1 *unr. itr. V.; mit sein* (**a**) **angerannt kommen** come running along; (auf einen zu) come running up; (**b**) **gegen den Sturm/feindliche Stellungen** ~: run into *or* against the storm/storm enemy positions; **gegen**

jmdn./etw. ~ (fig.) fight against sb./sth. 2 *unr. refl. V.* (ugs.) **sich** (*Dat.*) **das Knie/den Kopf** [**an etw.** (*Dat.*)] ~: bump one's knee/head [on sth.]

Anrichte *die;* ~, ~**n** sideboard

an|richten *tr. V.* (**a**) (auch itr.) arrange ‹*food*›; (servieren) serve; **es ist angerichtet** (geh.) dinner is served; (**b**) cause ‹*disaster, confusion, devastation, etc.*›

an|ritzen *tr. V.* scratch

an|rollen *itr. V.; mit sein* (**a**) (zu rollen beginnen) ‹*vehicle, column, etc.*› start moving; (fig.) ‹*campaign, search operation*› start; (**b**) (heranrollen) roll up; ‹*aircraft*› taxi up; **angerollt kommen** come rolling along; (auf einen zu) come rolling up

anrüchig /ˈanrʏçɪç/ *Adj.* (**a**) (verrufen) disreputable; (**b**) (unanständig) indecent; (obszön) offensive

Anrüchigkeit *die;* ~ ⇒ **anrüchig:** disreputableness; indecency

an|rücken *itr. V.; mit sein* ‹*troops*› advance; move forward; ‹*firemen, police*› move in

An·ruf *der* (**a**) (telefonischer ~) call; (**b**) (Zuruf) call; (eines Wachtpostens) challenge

Anruf·beantworter *der;* ~s, ~: [telephone-]answering machine

an|rufen 1 *unr. tr. V.* (**a**) call *or* shout to; call ‹*sleeping person*›; hail ‹*ship*›; ‹*sentry*› challenge; (**b**) (geh.: anrufen, bitten) appeal to ‹*person, court*› (**um** for); call upon ‹*God*›; (**c**) (telefonisch ~) ring (Brit.); call. 2 *unr. itr. V.* ring (Brit.); call; **bei jmdm.** ~: ring (Brit.) *or* call sb.

Anrufer *der;* ~s, ~: caller

Anrufung *die;* ~, ~**en** (**a**) (einer Gottheit o. ä.) invocation; (**b**) (eines Gerichts) appeal (*Gen.* to)

an|rühren *tr. V.* (**a**) touch; (**b**) (bereiten) mix

ans /ans/ *Präp.* + *Art.* (**a**) = **an das**; (**b**) *mit subst. Inf.* **sich** ~ **Arbeiten machen** set to work

An·sage *die* (**a**) announcement; (**b**) (Kartenspiel) bid

an|sagen 1 *tr. V.* (**a**) (ankündigen) announce; *s. auch* **Kampf** d; (**b**) (Kartenspiel) bid. 2 *refl. V.* **sich** [**bei jmdm.**] ~: say that one is coming [to see sb.]

an|sägen *tr. V.* make a saw-cut in; start to saw through

Ansager *der;* ~s, ~, **Ansagerin** *die;* ~, ~**nen** (**a**) (Radio, Fernsehen) announcer; (**b**) (im Kabarett usw.) master of ceremonies; (Brit.) compère

an|sammeln 1 *tr. V.* accumulate; amass ‹*riches, treasure*›. 2 *refl. V.* (**a**) (zusammenströmen) gather; (**b**) (sich anhäufen) accumulate; (fig.) ‹*anger, excitement*› build up

An·sammlung *die* (**a**) (von Gegenständen) collection; (Haufen) pile, heap; (**b**) (von Menschen) crowd

ansässig /ˈanzɛsɪç/ *Adj.* resident

An·satz *der* (**a**) (Beginn) beginnings *pl.;* **die ersten Ansätze** the initial stages; **im** ~ (ansatzweise) to some extent; (**b**) (eines Körperteils) base; (**c**) (Math.) statement

Ansatz·punkt *der* starting point

ansatz·weise *Adv.* to some extent

an|saufen *unr. refl. V.* (salopp) **sich** (*Dat.*) **einen** [**Rausch**] ~: get plastered (sl.)

an|saugen *tr. V.* (geh. auch unr.) suck in *or* up

an|schaffen *tr. V.* [**sich** (*Dat.*)] **etw.** ~ (auch fig. ugs.) get [oneself] sth.; **sich** (*Dat.*) **Kinder** ~ (fig. ugs.) have children *or* (coll.) kids

An·schaffung *die* purchase; **sich zur** ~ **eines Autos entschließen** decide to get *or* buy a car

Anschaffungs-: ~**kosten** *Pl.* original *or* initial cost *sing.;* acquisition cost *sing.;* ~**wert** *der* value at the time of purchase

an|schalten *tr. V.* switch on

an|schauen *tr. V.* (bes. südd., österr., schweiz.) ⇒ **ansehen**

anschaulich 1 *Adj.* (deutlich) clear; (bildhaft, lebendig) vivid, graphic ‹*style, description*›; **etw.** ~ **machen** make sth. vivid; bring sth. to life. 2 *adv.* (deutlich) clearly; (bildhaft, lebendig) vividly; ‹*describe*› vividly, graphically

Anschaulichkeit *die;* ~ ⇒ **anschaulich** 1: clarity; vividness; graphicness

Anreden und Titel

Die vier grundlegenden Anreden im Englischen sind:

Mr (= Herr) für Männer

Mrs (= Frau) für verheiratete Frauen

Miss (= Fräulein bzw. Frau) für Mädchen und (auch ältere) unverheiratete Frauen

Ms (= Frau) für (meist jüngere) Frauen

Im modernen Sprachgebrauch wird **Ms** oft statt **Miss** oder **Mrs** verwendet, es hat sich allerdings nicht so durchgesetzt wie im Deutschen die Anrede **Frau** für alle Frauen. Alle vier Anreden können entweder mit oder ohne den Vornamen stehen. Die nachgestellte Bezeichnung **Esq** (*Esquire* = Herr) wird meist in höheren britischen gesellschaftlichen Kreisen auf Briefen statt **Mr** verwendet, gilt aber heute als etwas altmodisch. Ebenfalls nachgestellt wird in den USA die Abkürzung **Jr** (= Junior) für den Sohn eines gleichnamigen Vaters. Weitere Hinweise hinsichtlich der Form der Anschrift finden Sie unter **Briefe-schreiben**.

Wie man jemanden anredet

Im Allgemeinen ist der Gebrauch im englischen Sprachraum weniger formell als in Deutschland, Österreich und der Schweiz. Für die Anrede mit "Sie" gibt es im Englischen keine Entsprechung, es wird immer **you** verwendet. Unter Kollegen, Nachbarn, in Gruppen und Vereinen spricht man sich generell mit Vornamen an. Vor allem in den USA redet man praktisch jeden, den man kennenlernt, sofort mit Vornamen an.

Beachten Sie, dass die Anreden **Mr**, **Mrs**, **Miss** und **Ms** nicht allein stehen dürfen (Ausnahme: Lehrerinnen werden noch von Schulkindern mit "miss" angeredet) und auch nicht in Kombination mit Titeln verwendet werden können:

Guten Morgen, Herr Professor	= Good morning, professor
Guten Abend, Frau Doktor	= Good evening, doctor
Auf Wiedersehen, Herr Oberst	= Goodbye, colonel
Jawohl, Herr Minister	= Yes, minister

In solchen Fällen wird oft der Name des bzw. der Angesprochenen hinzugefügt: "Good morning, Professor Evans" usw. Generell wird im englischen Sprachraum weniger Gebrauch von Titeln gemacht, sodass es etwa für "Herr Direktor" keine Ent-sprechung gibt, man sagt also einfach **Mr** und den Namen.

Vorgesetzte beim Militär werden nicht mit dem Namen, sondern meist einfach mit **sir** oder der Rangbezeichnung angeredet, während in der Schule Lehrer und Lehrerinnen meist von den jüngeren Schülern mit **sir** bzw. **miss** angeredet werden.

Kunden in Geschäften, Restaurants usw. werden oft noch mit **sir** bzw. **madam** (im Plural **gentlemen** bzw. **ladies**) angeredet:

Was darf es sein?	= Can I help you, sir/madam?
Was wünscht der Herr/ die gnädige Frau zum Trinken?	= What would you like to drink, sir/madam?
Was wünschen die Damen/Herren?	= What would you like, ladies/gentlemen?

Anreden bei Würdenträgern und Adeligen

Ihre Majestät	= Your Majesty
Eure Hoheit	= Your Highness
Euer Gnaden	= Your Grace
Eure Eminenz	= Your Eminence
Eure Heiligkeit	= Your Holiness

Wenn man von jemandem spricht

Beachten Sie auch hier, dass im englischen Sprachraum weniger Gebrauch von Titeln gemacht wird. Die Bezeichnung *Herr* bzw. *Frau* wird in Kombinationen wie "Herr Doktor Reiter", "Frau Professor Elisabeth Meinhardt" nicht übersetzt, da **Mr, Mrs, Ms** und **Miss** nicht mit Titeln kombiniert werden dürfen:

Herr Doktor Dietrich Reiter	= Dr Dietrich Reiter
Frau Professor Elisabeth Meinhardt	= Professor Elisabeth Meinhardt
Herr Kapitän Richard Müller	= Captain Richard Müller
Herr Minister Baumann	= [the minister] Mr Baumann
Frau Direktorin Dr Stahlmeyer	= [the director/head teacher] Dr Stahlmeyer
Herr Kammersänger Eberhard Wächter	= Kammersänger Eberhard Wächter

Im letzten Beispiel gibt es keine Übersetzung, am besten lässt man den Titel also in der deutschen Originalform.

Adelstitel und Kirchentitel werden im Englischen ähnlich wie im Deutschen behandelt:

König Ludwig XIV. von Frankreich	= King Louis XIV of France (gesprochen Louis the Fourteenth)
Papst Johannes Paul II.	= Pope John Paul II (gesprochen John Paul the Second)
Prinzessin Ingeborg zu Schleswig-Holstein	= Princess Ingeborg of Schleswig-Holstein

---

Anschauung *die;* ~, ~**en** (a) (Auffassung) view; (Meinung) opinion; (b) (Wahrnehmung) experience; **aus eigener** ~: from personal *or* one's own experience

Anschauungs-: ~**material** *das* illustrative ma-terial; (für den Unterricht) visual aids *pl.;* ~**unterricht** *der* visual instruction; (fig.) object lesson

An·schein *der* appearance; **allem** *od.* **dem** ~ **nach** to all appearances; **es hat den** ~, **als ob** ...: it appears *or* looks as if ...; **sich** (*Dat.*) **den** ~ **geben**, **als ob man etw. glaubt** pretend to believe sth.

an·scheinend *Adv.* apparently; seemingly

an|scheißen *unr. tr. V.* (derb) (a) (betrügen) con (sl.); (b) (zurechtweisen) **jmdn.** ~: give sb. a bollocking (Brit. coarse); bawl sb. out (coll.)

an|schicken *refl. V.* (geh.) **sich** ~, **etw. zu tun** (sich bereit machen) get ready *or* prepare to do sth.; (anfangen, im Begriff sein) be about to do sth.; be on the point of doing sth.

an|schieben *unr. tr. V.* push

an|schießen *unr. tr. V.* (a) (durch Schuss verletzen) shoot and wound; **angeschossen** wounded; (b) (bes. Fußball) kick the ball against ‹*player*›; shoot straight at ‹*goalkeeper*›

An·schiss, *****An·schiß** *der* (salopp) bollocking (Brit. coarse); bawling-out (coll.); **einen** ~ **kriegen** get a bollock-ing (Brit. coarse); get bawled out (coll.)

An·schlag *der* (a) (Bekanntmachung) notice; (Plakat) poster; **einen** ~ **machen** put up a notice/poster; (b) (Attentat) as-sassination attempt; (auf ein Gebäude, einen Zug o. ä.) attack; **einen** ~ **auf jmdn. verüben** make an attempt on sb.'s life; (c) (Texterfassung) keystroke; **50 Anschläge pro Zeile** 50 characters and spaces per line; (d) (Musik) touch; (e)

---

*alte Schreibung (vgl. Hinweise auf S. xvi–xvii)

(Technik) stop; **(f) mit dem Gewehr im** ∼: with rifle/ rifles levelled **(g)** (Kaufmannsspr.) estimate; **etw. in** ∼ **bringen** take sth. into account or consideration

Anschlag·brett das noticeboard (Brit.); bulletin board (Amer.)

an|schlagen 1 unr. tr. V. **(a)** (aushängen) put up, post ⟨notice, announcement, message⟩ **(an** + Akk. on); **(b)** (beschädigen) chip. **2** unr. itr. V. mit sein **an etw.** (Akk.) ∼: knock against sth.; **mit dem Knie/Kopf an etw.** (Akk.) ∼: knock one's knee/head on sth. **3** unr. refl. V. **sich** (Dat.) **das Knie** usw. ∼: knock one's knee etc. **(an** + Dat. on)

an|schleichen 1 unr. refl. V. creep up **(an** + Akk. on). **2** unr. itr. V.; mit sein **angeschlichen kommen** come creeping along; (auf einen zu) come creeping up

an|schleppen tr. V. **(a)** (herbeibringen) drag along; **(b)** (zum Starten) tow-start ⟨car etc.⟩

an|schließen 1 unr. tr. V. **(a)** (mit Schloss) lock, secure **(an** + Akk. od. Dat. to); **(b)** (verbinden) connect **(an** + Akk. od. Dat. to); connect up ⟨electrical device⟩; (mit Stecker) plug in; **(c)** (anfügen) add. **2** unr. refl. V. **(a) sich jmdm.** ∼: join sb. **(b)** auch itr. **[sich] an etw.** (Akk.) ∼ (zeitlich) follow sth.; (räumlich) adjoin sth.

anschließend 1 Adv. afterwards; ∼ **an etw.** (Akk.) after sth. **2** adj. subsequent; **ein Vortrag mit** ∼**er Diskussion** a lecture followed by a discussion

An·schluss, ***An·schluß** der **(a)** connection; (Kabel) cable; ∼ **an etw.** (Akk.) **erhalten/haben** be connected [up] to sth.; **(b)** (telefonische Verbindung) connection; **[keinen]** ∼ **bekommen** [not] get through; **(c)** (Verkehrsw.) connection; **Sie haben** ∼ **nach …**: there is a connection to …; **(d)** (Fernsprecher) telephone; **kein** ∼ **unter dieser Nummer** number unobtainable; **(e)** o. Pl. (Kontakt) ∼ **finden** make friends; ∼ **suchen** want to meet and get to know people; **(f) im** ∼ **an etw.** (Akk.) following or after sth.

Anschluss·zug, ***Anschluß·zug** der connecting train

an|schmiegen 1 tr. V. nestle **(an** + Akk. against). **2** refl. V. nestle up, snuggle up **(an** + Akk. to, against)

an·schmiegsam Adj. affectionate ⟨child⟩; soft and smooth ⟨material⟩

an|schmieren tr. V. (ugs.: täuschen) con (sl.); diddle (coll.)

an|schnallen tr. V. strap on ⟨rucksack⟩; put on ⟨skis, skates⟩; **sich** ∼ (im Auto) put on one's seat belt; (im Flugzeug) fasten one's seat belt; „**bitte** ∼!" 'fasten your seat belts, please'

Anschnall·pflicht die; o. Pl. compulsory wearing of seat belts

an|schnauzen tr. V. (ugs.) shout at

an|schneiden unr. tr. V. **(a)** cut [the first slice of]; **(b)** (ansprechen) raise; broach

an|schrauben unr. tr. V. screw on **(an** + Akk. od. Dat. to)

an|schreiben 1 unr. tr. V. **(a)** (hinschreiben) write up **(an** + Akk. on); **(b)** (ugs.: stunden) [jmdm.] **etw.** ∼: chalk sth. up [to sb.'s account]; **bei jmdm. gut/schlecht angeschrieben sein** (ugs.) be in sb.'s good/bad books; be on sb.'s good/black list (Amer.); **(c)** (brieflich ansprechen) write to. **2** unr. itr. V. (ugs.: Kredit geben) give credit; ∼ **lassen** buy on tick (coll.)

An·schreiben das covering letter

an|schreien unr. tr. V. shout at

An·schrift die ▶ 107 | address

an|schuldigen /-ʃʊldɪgn̩/ tr. V. (geh.) accuse (Gen., wegen of)

Anschuldigung die; ∼, ∼**en** accusation

an|schwärzen tr. V. (ugs.) jmdn. ∼ (in Misskredit bringen) blacken sb.'s name; (schlecht machen) run sb. down **(bei** to); (denunzieren) inform or (Brit. coll.) grass on sb. **(bei** to)

an|schwellen unr. itr. V.; mit sein **(a)** (dicker werden) swell [up]; **stark angeschwollen** very swollen; **(b)** (lauter werden) grow louder; ⟨noise⟩ rise; **(c)** (zunehmen, auch fig.) swell, grow; ⟨water, river⟩ rise

an|schwemmen tr. V. wash up or ashore

an|schwimmen unr. itr. V.; mit sein **angeschwommen kommen** come swimming along; (auf einen zu) come swimming up

an|schwindeln tr. V. (ugs.) jmdn. ∼: tell sb. fibs

an|sehen unr. tr. V. **(a)** look at; **jmdn. groß/böse** ∼: stare at sb./give sb. an angry look; **hübsch** usw. **anzusehen sein** be pretty etc. to look at; **sich** (Dat.) **etw.** ∼: look at sth.; **sich** (Dat.) **ein Haus** ∼: look at or view a house; **sich** (Dat.) **ein Fernsehprogramm** ∼: watch a television programme; **sich** (Dat.) **ein Stück/einen Film** ∼: see a play/a film; **sieh [mal] [einer] an!** (ugs.) well, I never! (coll.); **das sehe sich einer an!** (ugs.) just look at that!; **(b)** (anmerken) **man sieht ihm sein Alter nicht an** he does not look his age; **man sieht ihr die Strapazen an** she's showing the strain; **man sieht ihr nicht an, dass sie krank ist** there is nothing to show that she is ill; **(c)** (zusehen bei) **etw. [mit]** ∼: watch sth.; **das kann man doch nicht [mit]** ∼: I/you can't just stand by and watch that; **ich kann das nicht länger [mit]** ∼: I can't stand this any longer; **(d)** (einschätzen) see; **(e)** (halten für) regard; consider; **jmdn. als seinen Freund/als Betrüger** ∼: regard sb. as a friend/a cheat; consider sb. [to be] a friend/a cheat; **etw. als/für seine Pflicht** ∼: consider sth. one's duty

Ansehen das; ∼**s** (Wertschätzung) [high] standing or reputation; **hohes** ∼ **genießen** enjoy high standing or a good reputation; **(b)** (geh.: Aussehen) appearance; **(c) ohne** ∼ **der Person** (Rechtsw.) without respect of persons

an·sehnlich Adj. **(a)** (beträchtlich) considerable; **(b)** (gut aussehend, stattlich) handsome

***an|sein** ⇒ **an 3 b**

an|setzen 1 tr. V. **(a)** position ⟨ladder, jack, drill, saw⟩; put ⟨pen⟩ to paper; put or place ⟨violin bow⟩ in the bowing position; put ⟨glass, trumpet⟩ to one's lips; **(b)** (anfügen) attach, put on **(an** + Akk. od. Dat. to); fit **(an** + Akk. od. Dat. on to); **(c)** (festlegen) fix ⟨meeting etc.⟩; fix, set ⟨deadline, date, price⟩; **(d)** (veranschlagen) estimate; **die Kosten mit drei Millionen** ∼: estimate the cost at three million; **(e)** (anrühren) mix; prepare; **(f)** (ausbilden) **Rost/Grünspan** ∼: go rusty/become covered with verdigris; **Fett** ∼: put on weight; **Knospen/Früchte** ∼: form buds/set fruit. **2** itr. V. **(a) zum Sprechen** ∼: open one's mouth to speak; **zur Landung** ∼: come in to land; **zum Sprung/Überholen** ∼: get ready or prepare to jump/ overtake; **(b) hier muss die Diskussion/Kritik** ∼: this is where the discussion/criticism must start

An·sicht die **(a)** opinion; view; **meiner** ∼ **nach** in my opinion or view; **anderer/der gleichen** ∼ **sein** be of a different/the same opinion; **der** ∼ **sein, dass …**: be of the opinion that …; **ich bin ganz Ihrer** ∼: I entirely agree with you; **da bin ich anderer** ∼: I disagree with you there; **die** ∼**en sind geteilt** opinion is divided; **(b)** (Bild) view; **(c) zur** ∼ (Kaufmannsspr.) on approval

Ansichts-: ∼**karte** die picture postcard; ∼**sache** die in ∼**sache sein** be a matter of opinion

an|siedeln 1 refl. V. settle; ⟨industry, bacteria⟩ become established. **2** tr. V. settle ⟨immigrant, refugee, etc.⟩; establish ⟨industry, species, variety, bacteria⟩

An·siedlung die **(a)** ⇒ **ansiedeln 2:** settlement; establishment; **(b)** (Siedlung) settlement

An·sinnen das; ∼**s**, ∼: [unreasonable] request; **ein freches/seltsames** usw. ∼: an impudent/a strange etc. request

ansonsten Adv. (ugs.) **(a)** (davon abgesehen) apart from that; otherwise; **(b)** (andernfalls) otherwise

an|spannen 1 tr. V. **(a)** harness, hitch up ⟨horse etc.⟩ **(an** + Akk. to); hitch up, yoke up ⟨oxen⟩ **(an** + Akk. to); hitch up ⟨carriage, cart, etc.⟩ **(an** + Akk. to); **(b)** (anstrengen) strain. **2** itr. V. hitch up; ∼ **lassen** have the carriage made ready

An·spannung die strain

an|spielen 1 itr. V. **(a) auf jmdn./etw.** ∼: allude to sb./sth.; **(b)** (Spiel beginnen) start; (Fußball) kick off; (Kartenspiele) lead. **2** tr. V. **(a)** (Sport) **jmdn.** ∼: pass to sb.; **(b)** (Kartenspiele: ins Spiel bringen) lead

Anspielung die; ∼, ∼**en** allusion **(auf** + Akk. to); (verächtlich, böse) insinuation **(auf** + Akk. about)

An·sporn *der* incentive

an|spornen /-ʃpɔrnən/ *tr. V.* (fig.) spur on; encourage

An·sprache *die* (a) speech; address; **eine ~ halten** make a speech; give an address; (b) (Kontakt) **~ suchen/ haben** look for/have sb. to talk to

ansprechbar *Adj.* **er ist jetzt nicht ~:** you can't talk to him now

an|sprechen 1 *unr. tr. V.* (a) speak to; (zudringlich) accost; **jmdn. mit „Herr Doktor" ~:** address sb. as 'doctor'; **jmdn. mit seinem Vornamen ~:** use sb.'s first name; **jmdn. auf etw./jmdn. ~:** speak to sb. about sth./sb.; (b) (gefallen) appeal to; (c) (zur Sprache bringen) mention; (kurz, oberflächlich) touch on. **2** *unr. itr. V.* (a) (reagieren) ⟨*patient, brake, clutch, etc.*⟩ respond (**auf** + *Akk.* to); (b) (wirken) work; **bei jmdm. gut/nicht ~:** have/not have the desired effect on sb.

ansprechend 1 *Adj.* attractive; attractive, appealing ⟨*personality*⟩. **2** *adv.* attractively

Ansprech·partner *der* contact

an|springen 1 *unr. itr. V.; mit sein* (a) ⟨*engine, car*⟩ start; (b) **angesprungen kommen** come bounding along; (auf einen zu) come bounding up; (c) (ugs.) **auf ein Angebot/Geschäft ~:** take up an offer/agree to a deal. **2** *unr. tr. V.* jump up at

An·spruch *der* (a) claim; (Forderung) demand; **hohe Ansprüche [an jmdn.] haben** *od.* **stellen** demand a great deal [of sb.]; **~ auf etw.** (*Akk.*) **erheben** lay claim to sth.; **[keine] Ansprüche stellen** make [no] demands; **in ~ nehmen** take up, take advantage of ⟨*offer*⟩; exercise ⟨*right*⟩; take up ⟨*time*⟩; **jmds. Zeit/Hilfe in ~ nehmen** make demands on sb.'s time/enlist sb.'s aid; **jmdn. [stark] in ~ nehmen** make [heavy] demands on sb.; **jmdn. völlig in ~ nehmen** take up all [of] sb.'s time; (b) (bes. Rechtsspr.: Anrecht) claim; **[einen] ~/keinen ~ auf etw.** (*Akk.*) **haben** be/not be entitled to sth.; **auf etw.** (*Akk.*) **~ erheben** assert one's entitlement to sth.

an·spruchs-: **~los 1** *Adj.* (a) undemanding; (b) (schlicht) unpretentious; simple; **2** *adv.* (a) undemandingly; ⟨*live*⟩ modestly, simply; (b) (schlicht) unpretentiously; simply; **~voll** *Adj.* (wählerisch) demanding, discriminating ⟨*gourmet, reader, audience*⟩; (schwierig) demanding; ambitious ⟨*subject*⟩

an|spucken *tr. V.* spit at

an|spülen *tr. V.* wash up *or* ashore

an|stacheln /-ʃtaxln/ *tr. V.* spur on (**zu** to)

Anstalt /'anʃtalt/ *die;* **~, ~en** (a) institution; (b) *Pl.* preparations; **[keine] ~ machen** *od.* (geh.) treffen make [no] preparations (**für** for); **~ machen/keine ~ machen, etw. zu tun** make a move/make no move to do sth.

An·stand *der o. Pl.* (a) decency; **keinen ~ haben** have no sense of decency; (b) (veralt.: Benehmen) good manners *pl.*

an·ständig 1 *Adj.* (a) (sittlich einwandfrei, rücksichtsvoll) decent; decent, clean ⟨*joke*⟩; (ehrbar) respectable; (gut angesehen) decent, respectable ⟨*job*⟩; (b) (ugs.: zufrieden stellend) decent; respectable ⟨*result, marks*⟩; (c) (ugs.: beträchtlich) sizeable ⟨*sum, amount, debts*⟩; **eine ~e Tracht Prügel** a good hiding (coll.). **2** *adv.* (a) (sittlich einwandfrei) decently; (ordentlich) properly; (b) (ugs.: zufrieden stellend) decent; **~ bezahlen** pay sb. pretty well; **ganz ~ abschneiden** do quite well; **~ arbeiten** do good work; (c) (ugs.: ziemlich) **~ ausschlafen** have a decent sleep; **jmdn. ~ eine knallen** really belt sb. one (coll.)

anstands·los *Adv.* without [any] objection

an|starren *tr. V.* stare at

an·statt *Konj.* **~ zu arbeiten/~, dass er arbeitet** instead of working

an|stauen 1 *tr. V.* dam up; (fig.) bottle up ⟨*feelings*⟩. **2** *refl. V.* ⟨*water*⟩ accumulate; (fig.) ⟨*feelings*⟩ build up

an|staunen *tr. V.* gaze *or* stare in wonder at; **jmdn./ etw. mit offenem Mund ~:** gape at sb./sth. in wonder

an|stechen *unr. tr. V.* (a) prick; puncture ⟨*tyre*⟩; (b) (anzapfen) tap ⟨*barrel*⟩

an|stecken 1 *tr. V.* (a) pin on ⟨*badge, brooch*⟩; **jmdm. eine Brosche/einen Ring ~:** pin a brooch on sb./put *or*

slip a ring on sb.'s finger; (b) (infizieren, auch fig.) infect (c) (bes. nordd., mitteld.) ⇒ **anzünden. 2** *itr. V.* be infectious *or* catching; (durch Berührung) be contagious; (fig.) be infectious *or* contagious

ansteckend *Adj.* infectious; (durch Berührung) contagious; (fig.) infectious; contagious

Ansteckung *die;* **~, ~en** infection; (durch Berührung) contagion

an|stehen *unr. itr. V.* (a) (warten) queue [up], (Amer.) stand in line (**nach** for); (b) (geh.: sich ziemen) **jmdm. [wohl/ übel] ~:** [well/ill] become sb.

an|steigen *unr. itr. V.; mit sein* (a) ⟨*hill*⟩ rise; ⟨*road, path*⟩ climb, ascend; ⟨*garden, ground*⟩ slope up, rise; (b) (höher werden) ⟨*water level, temperature, etc.*⟩ rise; ⟨*price, cost, rent, etc.*⟩ rise, go up, increase

an·stelle 1 *Präp. mit Gen.* instead of. **2** *Adv.* **~ von** instead of; *s. auch* **Stelle a**

an|stellen 1 *refl. V.* (a) (warten) queue [up], (Amer.) stand in line (**nach** for); (b) (ugs.: sich verhalten) act; behave; **sich dumm/ungeschickt ~:** act *or* behave stupidly/be clumsy; **sich dumm/ungeschickt bei etw. ~:** go about sth. stupidly/clumsily; **sich geschickt ~:** go about it well; **stell dich nicht [so] an!** don't make [such] a fuss! **2** *tr. V.* (a) (aufdrehen) turn on; (b) (einschalten) switch on; turn on, switch on ⟨*radio, television*⟩; start ⟨*engine*⟩; (c) (einstellen) employ (**als** as); **bei jmdm. angestellt sein** be employed by sb.; (d) (ugs.: beschäftigen) **jmdn. zum Kartoffelschälen** *usw.* **~:** get sb. to peel the potatoes *etc.;* (e) (anlehnen) **etw. an etw.** (*Akk.*) **~:** put *or* place sth. against sth.; (f) (anrichten) **etwas/Unfug ~:** get up to something/ to mischief; (g) (bewerkstelligen) manage; (h) (vornehmen) do ⟨*calculation*⟩; make ⟨*comparison, assumption*⟩

anstellig *Adj.* clever; skilful

An·stellung *die* (a) *o. Pl.* employment; (b) (Stellung) job; **ohne ~:** without a job; unemployed

Anstellungs·vertrag *der* contract of employment

Anstieg *der;* **~[e]s** rise, increase (*Gen.* in)

an|stiften *tr. V.* (a) (ins Werk setzen) instigate; (b) (verleiten) **jmdn. [dazu] ~, etw. zu tun** incite sb. to do sth.; **jmdn. zum Betrug/Mord/zu einem Verbrechen ~:** incite sb. to deception/to murder/to commit a crime

An·stifter *der,* **An·stifterin** *die* instigator

An·stiftung *die* incitement (**zu** to)

an|stimmen *tr. V.* start singing ⟨*song*⟩; start playing ⟨*piece of music*⟩; **ein Geschrei ~:** start shouting; **ein Freudengeheul ~:** burst into shouts of joy

An·stoß *der* (a) (Impuls) stimulus (**zu** for); **den [ersten] ~ zu etw. geben** initiate sth.; (b) **~ erregen** cause *or* give offence (**bei** to); **[keinen] ~ an etw.** (*Dat.*) **nehmen** [not] object to sth.; (sich [nicht] beleidigt fühlen) [not] take offence at sth.; *s. auch* **Stein b**; (c) (Fußball) kick-off; **den ~ ausführen** kick off

an|stoßen 1 *unr. itr. V.* (a) *mit sein* **an etw.** (*Akk.*) **~:** bump into sth.; **mit dem Kopf ~:** knock *or* bump one's head; (b) (auf etw. trinken) **[mit den Gläsern] ~:** clink glasses; **auf jmdn./etw. ~:** drink to sb./sth.; (c) (Fußball) kick off. **2** *unr. tr. V.* **jmdn./etw. ~:** give sb./sth. a push; **jmdn. aus Versehen ~:** knock into sb. inadvertently; **jmdn. mit dem Ellenbogen/Fuß ~** (als Zeichen) nudge/ kick sb.; **sich** (*Dat.*) **den Kopf/die Zehe ~:** knock *or* bang one's head/stub one's toe

anstößig /'anʃtøːsɪç/ **1** *Adj.* offensive. **2** *adv.* offensively

an|strahlen *tr. V.* (a) illuminate; (mit Scheinwerfer) floodlight; (im Theater) spotlight; (b) (anblicken) beam at

an|streben *tr. V.* (geh.) aspire to; (mit großer Anstrengung) strive for

an|streichen *unr. tr. V.* (a) (mit Farbe) paint; (mit Tünche) whitewash; (b) (markieren) mark

An·streicher *der* (ugs.) house-painter; painter

an|strengen /-ʃtrɛŋən/ **1** *refl. V.* (sich einsetzen) make an effort; exert oneself; (körperlich) exert oneself; **sich ~, etw. zu tun** make an effort to do sth.; **sich mehr/sehr ~:** make more of an effort/a great effort. **2** *tr. V.* (a) (anspannen) strain ⟨*eyes, ears, voice*⟩; **alle seine Kräfte ~:** make every effort; (körperlich) use all one's strength; **seine Fantasie ~:** exercise one's imagination; (b) (strapazieren) strain, put a strain on ⟨*eyes*⟩; **jmdn. [zu sehr]** ∼: be [too much of] a strain on sb.

anstrengend *Adj.* (körperlich) strenuous; (geistig) demanding; ∼ **für die Augen sein** be a strain on the eyes; **es war** ∼, **dem Vortrag zu folgen** following the lecture was a strain

Anstrengung *die;* ∼, ∼**en** (a) (Einsatz) effort; ∼**en machen** make an effort; **große** ∼**en machen, etw. zu tun** make every effort to do sth.; (b) (Strapaze) strain

An·strich *der* (Farbe) paint; (Tünche) whitewash; **der erste/zweite** ∼: the first/second coat

An·sturm *der* (a) (das Anstürmen) onslaught; (b) (Andrang) (auf Kaufhäuser, Schwimmbäder) rush (**auf** + *Akk.* to); (auf Banken, Waren) run (**auf** + *Akk.* on)

an|stürmen *itr. V.; mit sein* (a) **gegen etw.** ∼ ⟨*waves, wind*⟩ pound sth.; (Milit.) storm sth.; (b) **angestürmt kommen** come charging *or* rushing along; (auf einen zu) come charging *or* rushing up

an|suchen *itr. V.* (österr., sonst veralt.) **[bei jmdm.] um etw.** ∼ (beantragen) apply [to sb.] for sth.; (bitten) ask [sb.] for sth.

Ansuchen *das;* ∼**s**, ∼ (österr., sonst veralt.) (Gesuch) application (**auf** + *Akk.* for); (Bitte) request (**auf** + *Akk.* for); **auf jmds.** ∼ (*Akk.*) at sb.'s request

an|tanzen *itr. V.; mit sein* (ugs.) show up (coll.); **angetanzt kommen** turn up

Antarktika /ant'|arktika/ *(das);* ∼**s** Antarctica

Antarktis /ant'|arktıs/ *die;* ∼: **die** ∼: the Antarctic

antarktisch *Adj.* Antarctic

an|tasten *tr. V.* (a) (verbrauchen) break into ⟨*savings, provisions*⟩; (b) (beeinträchtigen) infringe, encroach on ⟨*right, freedom, privilege*⟩; encroach on ⟨*property, private life*⟩

An·teil *der* (a) (jmdm. zustehender Teil) share (**an** + *Dat.* of); ∼ **an etw.** (*Dat.*) **haben** share in sth.; (zu etw. beitragen) play *or* have a part in sth.; (b) (Wirtsch.) share; (c) *o. Pl.* (Interesse) interest (**an** + *Dat.* in); ∼ **an etw.** (*Dat.*) **nehmen** take an interest in sth.

anteilig 1 *Adj.* proportional; proportionate. **2** *adv.* proportionally; proportionately

An·teilnahme *die* (a) (Beteiligung) participation; **unter reger** ∼ **der Bevölkerung** with the active participation of the public; (b) (Interesse) interest (**an** + *Dat.* in); (c) (Mitgefühl) sympathy (**an** + *Dat.* with); **mit** ∼ **zuhören** listen sympathetically

Anteils·eigner *der* (Wirtsch.) shareholder

an|telefonieren *tr. V.* (ugs.) phone (coll.); call; ring (Brit.)

Antenne *die;* ∼, ∼**n** (Technik) aerial; antenna (Amer.); **eine/keine** ∼ **für etw. haben** (fig.) have a/no feeling for sth.

anthrazit /antra'tsi:t/ *Adj.; nicht attr.* anthracite[-grey]

Anthrazit¹ *der;* ∼**s**, ∼**e** anthracite

Anthrazit² *das;* ∼**s** anthracite grey

anthrazit-: ∼**farben**, ∼**farbig** *Adj.* anthracite[-coloured]; ∼**grau** *Adj.* anthracite-grey

Anthroposoph /antropo'zo:f/ *der;* ∼**en**, ∼**en** anthroposophist

Anthroposophie *die;* ∼: anthroposophy *no art.*

anthroposophisch *Adj.* anthroposophical

anti-, Anti- /anti-/: anti[-]

Anti·alkoholiker *der* (Abstinenzler) teetotaller

anti·autoritär 1 *Adj.* anti-authoritarian; **2** *adv.* in an anti-authoritarian manner

Antibiotikum /anti'bịo:tikʊm/ *das;* ∼**s**, **Antibiotika** (Med.) antibiotic

Anti·blockier·system *das* (Kfz-W.) anti-lock braking system

antik /an'ti:k/ *Adj.* (a) classical; (b) (aus vergangenen Zeiten) antique ⟨*furniture, fittings, etc.*⟩

Antike /an'ti:kə/ *die;* ∼, ∼**n** (a) classical antiquity *no art.;* (b) ([Kunst]gegenstand) classical work of art

Anti·körper *der* (Med.) antibody

Antillen /an'tılən/ *Pl.* **die [Großen/Kleinen]** ∼: the [Greater/Lesser] Antilles

Antilope /anti'lo:pə/ *die;* ∼, ∼**n** antelope

Antipathie /antipa'ti:/ *die;* ∼, ∼**n** antipathy (**gegen** to)

an|tippen *tr. V.* give ⟨*person, thing*⟩ a [light] tap; touch ⟨*accelerator, brake, etc.*⟩; (fig.) touch on ⟨*point, question*⟩

Antiquar /anti'kva:ɐ̯/ *der;* ∼**s**, ∼**e** antiquarian bookseller; (mit neueren gebrauchten Büchern) second-hand bookseller

Antiquariat /antikva'rịa:t/ *das;* ∼**s**, ∼**e** (Laden/Abteilung) antiquarian bookshop/department; (mit neueren gebrauchten Büchern) second-hand bookshop/department; **modernes** ∼: shop/department selling remainders, defective copies, cheap editions, reprints, etc.

antiquarisch 1 *Adj.* (Buchw.) antiquarian; (von neueren gebrauchten Büchern) second-hand. **2** *adv.* ⟨*buy*⟩ second-hand

antiquiert /anti'kvi:ɐ̯t/ (abwertend) **1** *Adj.* antiquated. **2** *adv.* in an antiquated way

Antiquität /antikvi'tɛ:t/ *die;* ∼, ∼**en** antique

Antiquitäten-: ∼**laden** *der* antique shop; ∼**sammler** *der* collector of antiques; ∼**sammlung** *die* collection of antiques

anti-, Anti-: ∼**semit** *der* anti-Semite; ∼**semitisch** *Adj.* anti-Semitic; anti-Semite; ∼**semitismus** *der* anti-Semitism; ∼**statisch** *Adj.* (Physik) antistatic; ∼**these** /'----/ *die* antithesis

antizipieren /antitsi'pi:rən/ *tr. V.* (geh.) anticipate

Antlitz /'antlıts/ *das;* ∼**es**, ∼**e** (dichter., geh.) countenance (literary); face

an|törnen /-tœrnən/ *tr. V.* (ugs.) **jmdn.** ∼ ⟨*drugs, music, etc.*⟩ turn sb. on (coll.)

Antrag /'antra:k/ *der;* ∼**[e]s**, **Anträge** (a) application, request (**auf** + *Akk.* for); (Rechtsw.: schriftlich) petition (**auf** + *Akk.* for); **einen** ∼ **stellen** make an application; (Rechtsw.: schriftlich) enter a petition; (b) (Formular) application form; (c) (Heirats∼) proposal of marriage; **jmdm. einen** ∼ **machen** propose to sb.

an|tragen *unr. tr. V.* (geh.) offer

Antrags·formular *das* application form

an|treffen *unr. tr. V.* find; (zufällig) come across

an|treiben *unr. tr. V.* (a) (vorwärts treiben) drive ⟨*animals, column of prisoners*⟩ on *or* along; (fig.) urge; **jmdn. zur Eile/zu immer besseren Leistungen** ∼ (fig.) urge sb. to hurry up/urge *or* drive sb. on to better and better performances; (b) (in Bewegung setzen) drive; (mit Energie versorgen) power; (c) (veranlassen) drive; **jmdn. [dazu]** ∼, **etw. zu tun** drive sb. to do sth.

an|treten 1 *unr. itr. V.; mit sein* (a) (sich aufstellen) form up; (in Linie) line up; (Milit.) fall in; (b) (sich stellen) meet one's opponent; (als Mannschaft) line up; ∼ **gegen** meet; (als Mannschaft) line up against; (c) (sich einfinden) report (**bei** to). **2** *unr. tr. V.* start ⟨*job, apprenticeship*⟩; take up ⟨*position, appointment*⟩; start, set out on ⟨*journey*⟩; begin ⟨*prison sentence*⟩; come into ⟨*inheritance*⟩

An·trieb *der* (a) drive; **ein Fahrzeug mit elektrischem** ∼: an electrically powered *or* driven vehicle; (b) (Anreiz) impulse; (Psych.) drive; impulse; **jmdn. neuen** ∼ **geben** give sb. fresh impetus; **aus eigenem** ∼: of one's own accord; on one's own initiative

Antriebs-: ∼**kraft** *die* (Technik) motive *or* driving power; ∼**rad** *das* (Technik) drive wheel; ∼**welle** *die* (Technik) drive shaft

an|trinken *unr. refl. V.* **sich** (*Dat.*) **einen Rausch/Schwips** ∼: get drunk/tipsy; **sich** (*Dat.*) **einen** ∼ (ugs.) get sloshed (coll.); **sich** (*Dat.*) **Mut** ∼: give oneself Dutch courage

An·tritt *der* beginning; **vor** ∼ **Ihres Urlaubs** before you go *or* before going on holiday (Brit.) *or* (Amer.) vacation; **vor** ∼ **der Reise** before setting out on the journey; **bei** ∼ **des Erbes/Amtes** on coming into the inheritance/taking up office

Antritts-: ∼**besuch** *der* [formal] first visit; **seinen** ∼**besuch bei jmdm. machen** pay one's [formal] first visit to sb.; ∼**rede** *die* inaugural speech; ∼**vorlesung** *die* inaugural lecture

an|tuckern *itr. V.; mit sein* (ugs.) **angetuckert kommen** come chugging along; (auf einen zu) come chugging up

an|tun *unr. tr. V.* **(a)** do (*Dat.* to); **sich** (*Dat.*) **etw. Gutes ~:** give oneself a treat; treat oneself; **jmdm. ein Leid ~:** hurt sb.; **jmdm. etwas Böses/ein Unrecht ~:** do sb. harm/an injustice; **sich** (*Dat.*) **etw. ~** (ugs. verhüll.) do away with oneself; **(b) das/er** *usw.* **hat es ihr angetan** she was taken with it/him *etc.; s. auch* **angetan**

Antwerpen /ant'vɛrpn/ (*das*); **~s ▶ 490 |** Antwerp

Antwort /'antvɔrt/ *die;* **~, ~en (a)** answer; reply; **er gab mir keine ~:** he didn't answer [me] *or* reply; he made no answer *or* reply; **er gab mir keine ~ auf meine Frage** he did not reply to *or* answer my question; **keine ~ ist auch eine ~:** your/her *etc.* silence speaks for itself; **(b)** (Reaktion) response; **als ~ auf etw.** (*Akk.*) in response to sth.

antworten 1 *itr. V.* **(a)** answer; reply; **auf etw.** (*Akk.*) **~:** answer sth.; reply to sth.; **jmdm. ~:** answer sb.; reply to sb.; **jmdm. auf seine Frage ~:** reply to *or* answer sb.'s question; **wie soll ich ihm ~?** what answer shall I give him?/what shall I tell him?; **(b)** (reagieren) respond (**auf** + *Akk.* to). **2** *tr. V.* answer; **was hat er geantwortet?** what was his answer?

Antwort-: **~schein** *der:* internationaler **~schein** (Postw.) international reply coupon; **~schreiben** *das* reply

an|vertrauen 1 *tr. V.* **(a) jmdm. etw. ~:** entrust sth. to sb.; entrust sb. with sth.; **(b)** (fig.) **jmdm./seinem Tagebuch etw. ~:** confide sth. to sb./one's diary. **2** *refl. V.* **(a) sich jmdm./einer Sache ~:** put one's trust in sb./sth.; **(b) sich jmdm. ~** (fig.: sich jmdm. mitteilen) confide in sb.

an|visieren /-vizi:rən/ *tr. V.* align the *or* one's sights on; aim at

an|wachsen *unr. itr. V.; mit sein* **(a)** (festwachsen) grow on; **wieder ~** ⟨*finger, toe*⟩ grow back on; **(b)** (Wurzeln schlagen) take root; **(c)** (zunehmen) increase; grow

an|wackeln *itr. V.; mit sein* (ugs.) **angewackelt kommen** come waddling along; (auf einen zu) come waddling up

an|wählen *tr. V.* dial; **jmdn. ~:** dial sb.'s number

Anwalt /'anvalt/ *der;* **~[e]s, Anwälte** /'anvɛltə/, **Anwältin** *die;* **~, ~nen ▶ 85 | (a)** (Rechts~) lawyer; solicitor (Brit.); attorney (Amer.); (vor Gericht) barrister (Brit.); attorney[-at-law] (Amer.); advocate (Scot.); **einen ~ nehmen** get a lawyer *or* (Amer.) an attorney; **(b)** (Fürsprecher) advocate; champion

Anwalts·büro *das* **(a)** (Räume) lawyer's office; solicitor's office (Brit.); **(b)** (Sozietät) firm of solicitors (Brit.); law firm (Amer.)

An·wandlung *die* mood; **in einer ~ von Großzügigkeit** *usw.* in a fit of generosity *etc.*

an|wärmen *tr. V.* warm up; warm ⟨*hands, feet*⟩

An·wärter *der* **(a)** candidate (**auf** + *Akk.* for); (Sport) contender (**auf** + *Akk.* for); **(b)** (auf den Thron) claimant; (Thronerbe) heir (**auf** + *Akk.* to)

An·wärterin *die* **(a)** ⇒ **Anwärter a; (b)** (auf den Thron) claimant; (Thronerbin) heiress (**auf** + *Akk.* to)

an|weisen *unr. tr. V.* **(a)** (beauftragen) **jmdn. ~:** give sb. instructions; **jmdn. ~, etw. zu tun** instruct *or* direct sb. to do sth.; **(b)** (zuweisen) **jmdm. etw. ~:** allocate sth. to sb.

An·weisung *die* instruction; **~ haben, etw. zu tun** have instructions to do sth.

anwendbar *Adj.* applicable (**auf** + *Akk.* to); **schwer ~:** difficult to apply

an|wenden *unr.* (*auch regelm.*) *tr. V.* use, employ ⟨*process, trick, method, violence, force*⟩; use ⟨*medicine, money, time*⟩; apply ⟨*rule, paragraph, proverb, etc.*⟩ (**auf** + *Akk.* to)

Anwender *der;* **~s, ~** (DV) user

An·wendung *die* **(a)** ⇒ **anwenden:** use; employment; application; **(b)** (DV) application

an|werben *unr. tr. V.* recruit (**für** to); (Milit.) enlist, recruit; **sich ~ lassen** be recruited; (Milit.) enlist (**für** in)

An·werbung *die* recruitment (**für** to)

an|werfen *unr. tr. V.* (ugs.: in Gang bringen) start [up] ⟨*machine, engine, vehicle*⟩

An·wesen *das* property

anwesend *Adj.* present (**bei** at)

Anwesende *der/die; adj. Dekl.* **die ~n** those present

Anwesenheit *die;* **~:** presence; **in ~ von** in the presence of

Anwesenheits·liste *die* attendance list

an|wetzen *itr. V.; mit sein* (ugs.) **angewetzt kommen** come rushing *or* tearing along; (auf einen zu) come rushing *or* tearing up

an|widern /-vi:dən/ *tr. V.* nauseate

an|winkeln /-vɪŋkln/ *tr. V.* bend

an|winseln *tr. V.* whimper at

Anwohner /'anvo:nɐ/ *der;* **~s, ~:** resident; **Parken nur für ~:** residents-only parking

An·wurf *der* [unjustified] reproach; (Beschuldigung) [false] accusation

an|wurzeln *itr. V.; mit sein* take root; **wie angewurzelt** [da]**stehen/stehenbleiben** stand rooted to the spot

An·zahl *die; o. Pl.* number; **eine ganze ~:** a whole lot

an|zahlen *tr. V.* put down ⟨*sum*⟩ as a deposit (**auf** + *Akk.* on); pay a deposit on ⟨*goods*⟩; (bei Ratenzahlung) make a down payment on ⟨*goods*⟩; **50 DM ~:** put down 50 marks as a deposit/make a down payment of 50 marks

An·zahlung *die* deposit; (bei Ratenzahlung) down payment; **eine ~ auf etw.** (*Akk.*) **machen** *od.* **leisten** put down *or* pay a deposit on sth./make a down payment on sth.

an|zapfen *tr. V.* tap

An·zeichen *das* sign; indication; (Med.) symptom; **alle ~ deuten darauf hin, dass …:** all the signs *or* indications are that …

Anzeige /'antsaigə/ *die;* **~, ~n (a)** (Straf~) report; **gegen jmdn. [eine] ~ [wegen etw.] erstatten** report sb. to the police/the authorities [for sth.]; **(b)** (Inserat) advertisement; **eine ~ aufgeben** place an advertisement; **(c)** (eines Instruments) display

an|zeigen *tr. V.* **(a)** (Strafanzeige erstatten) **jmdn./etw. ~:** report sb./sth. to the police/the authorities; **(b)** (zeigen) show; indicate; show ⟨*time, date*⟩

Anzeigen-: **~blatt** *das* advertiser; **~teil** *der* advertisement section *or* pages *pl.*

An·zeiger *der* indicator

Anzeige·tafel *die* (Sport) scoreboard

an|zetteln /-tsɛtln/ *tr. V.* (abwertend) hatch ⟨*plot, intrigue*⟩; instigate ⟨*revolt*⟩; foment ⟨*war*⟩

an|ziehen 1 *unr. tr. V.* **(a)** (an sich ziehen) draw up ⟨*knees, feet, etc.*⟩; **(b)** (anlocken) attract; draw; **sich von jmdm. angezogen fühlen** feel attracted to sb.; **(c)** (anspannen) tighten, pull tight ⟨*rope, wire, chain*⟩; **(d)** (festziehen) tighten ⟨*screw, knot, belt, etc.*⟩; put on, pull on ⟨*handbrake*⟩; **(e)** (ankleiden) dress; **sich ~:** get dressed; **(f)** put on ⟨*clothes*⟩; **sich** (*Dat.*) **etw. ~:** put sth. on; **was soll ich bloß ~?** what shall I wear? **2** *unr. itr. V.* **(a)** ⟨*price, article, share, etc.*⟩ go up; **(b)** *unpers.* **es zieht an** (ugs.) it's getting colder

anziehend *Adj.* attractive; engaging ⟨*manner, smile*⟩

Anziehungs·kraft *die* attractive force; (fig.) attraction

an|zischen *tr. V.* hiss at

An·zug *der* **(a)** suit; **(b) in im ~ sein** ⟨*danger*⟩ be imminent; ⟨*storm*⟩ be approaching; ⟨*fever, illness*⟩ be coming on; ⟨*enemy*⟩ be advancing

anzüglich /'antsy:klɪç/ **1** *Adj.* **(a)** insinuating ⟨*remark, question*⟩; **(b)** (anstößig) offensive ⟨*joke, remark*⟩. **2** *adv.* **(a)** in an insinuating way; **(b)** (anstößig) offensively

Anzüglichkeit *die;* **~, ~en** ⇒ **anzüglich 1: (a)** *o. Pl.* insinuating nature; offensiveness; **(b)** (Bemerkung) insinuating remark; offensive remark/joke

an|zünden *tr. V.* light; **ein Gebäude** *usw.* **~:** set fire to a building *etc.*; set a building *etc.* on fire

An·zünder *der* (Gas~) gas lighter; (Feuer~) firelighter (Brit.)

an|zweifeln *tr. V.* doubt; question

an|zwinkern *tr. V.* wink at

AOK /a:|o:'ka:/ *die;* **~** *Abk.* **Allgemeine Ortskrankenkasse**

Aorta /a'ɔrta/ *die;* ~, **Aorten** (Med.) aorta
apart /a'part/ **1** *Adj.* individual *attrib.;* ~ **sein** be individual in style. **2** *adv.* in an individual style
Apartheid /a'pa:ɐthait/ *die;* ~: apartheid *no art.*
Apartheid·politik *die* policy of apartheid
Apartment /a'partmənt/ *das;* ~s, ~s studio flat (Brit.); flatlet (Brit.); small flat (Brit.); studio apartment (Amer.)
Apathie /apa'ti:/ *die;* ~, ~n apathy
apathisch /a'pa:tıʃ/ **1** *Adj.* apathetic. **2** *adv.* apathetically
Aperitif /aperi'ti:f/ *der;* ~s, ~s aperitif
Apfel /'apfl/ *der;* ~s, **Äpfel** /'ɛpfl/ apple; **[etw.] für einen** ~ **und ein Ei [kaufen]** [buy sth.] for a song; **in den sauren** ~ **beißen [und etw. tun]** (ugs.) grasp the nettle [and do sth.]
Apfel-: ~**baum** *der* apple tree; ~**blüte** *die* **(a)** apple blossom; **(b)** (das Blühen) blossoming of the apple trees; **während der** ~**blüte** while the apple trees are/were in blossom; ~**kuchen** *der* apple-cake; (mit Äpfeln belegt) apple flan; **gedeckter** ~**kuchen** apple pie; ~**mus** *das* apple purée; ~**saft** *der* apple-juice
Apfelsine /apfl'zi:nə/ *die;* ~, ~n orange
Apfel-: ~**strudel** *der* apfelstrudel; ~**wein** *der* cider
Aphorismus /afo'rısmʊs/ *der;* ~, **Aphorismen** (geh.) aphorism
Aphrodisiakum /afrodi'zi:akʊm/ *das;* ~, **Aphrodisiaka** (Med.) aphrodisiac
apolitisch **1** *Adj.* apolitical. **2** *adv.* apolitically
Apostel /a'pɔstl/ *der;* ~s, ~: apostle; **die zwölf** ~: the twelve Apostles
Apotheke /apo'te:kə/ *die;* ~, ~n **(a)** chemist's [shop] (Brit.); drugstore (Amer.); **(b)** (Haus~) medicine cabinet; (Reise~, Bord~) first-aid kit
apotheken·pflichtig *Adj.* obtainable only at a chemist's [shop] (Brit.) *or* (Amer.) drugstore *postpos.*
Apotheker *der;* ~s, ~, **Apothekerin** *die;* ~, ~**nen** ▶85│ [dispensing] chemist (Brit.); druggist
App. *Abk.* (Fernspr.) **Apparat** ext.
Apparat /apa'ra:t/ *der;* ~[e]s, ~e **(a)** (Technik) apparatus *no pl.;* (Haushaltsgerät) appliance; (kleiner) gadget; **(b)** (Radio~) radio; (Fernseh~) television; (Rasier~) razor; (elektrisch) shaver; (Foto~) camera; **(c)** (Telefon) telephone; (Nebenstelle) extension; **am** ~**!** speaking!; **bleiben Sie am** ~**!** hold the line; **(d)** (Personen und Hilfsmittel) organization; (Verwaltungs~) system; **(e)** (ugs.: etwas Ausgefallenes, Riesiges) whopper (sl.)
Apparate·medizin *die; o. Pl.* (oft abwertend) high-technology medicine
Apparatur /apara'tu:ɐ/ *die;* ~, ~**en** apparatus *no pl.;* **komplizierte** ~**en** complicated equipment
Appartement /apartə'mã:/ *schweiz. auch:* -'mɛnt/ *das;* ~s, ~s (schweiz. auch: ~e) **(a)** ⇒ **Apartment; (b)** (Hotelsuite) suite
Appell /a'pɛl/ *der;* ~s, ~e **(a)** appeal (**zu** for, **an** + *Akk.* to); **einen** ~ **an jmdn. richten** make an appeal to sb.; appeal to sb.; **(b)** (Milit.) muster; (Anwesenheits~) roll-call; (Besichtigung) inspection; **zum** ~ **antreten** fall in for roll-call/inspection
appellieren *itr. V.* appeal (**an** + *Akk.* to)
Appetit /ape'ti:t/ *der;* ~[e]s, ~e (auch fig.) appetite (**auf** + *Akk.* for); ~ **auf etw. haben/bekommen** fancy sth.; **guten** ~**!** enjoy your meal!; **jmdm. den** ~ **verderben** spoil sb.'s appetite
appetit·anregend *Adj.* **(a)** (appetitlich) appetizing; **(b)** ⟨ *medicine etc.* ⟩ that stimulates the appetite
Appetit·happen *der* canapé
appetitlich **1** *Adj.* **(a)** appetizing; **(b)** (sauber, ansprechend) attractive and hygienic. **2** *adv.* **(a)** appetizingly; **(b)** (sauber, ansprechend) attractively and hygienically ⟨ *packed* ⟩
appetit·los **1** *Adj.* without any appetite *postpos.;* ~**los sein** have lost one's appetite. **2** *adv.* without any appetite
Appetit·losigkeit *die;* ~: lack of appetite
applaudieren /aplau'di:rən/ *itr. V.* applaud; **jmdm./ einer Sache** ~: applaud sb./sth.

Applaus /a'plaus/ *der;* ~es, ~e applause
Applikation /aplika'tsio:n/ *die;* ~, ~**en** (DV) application
Apposition *die;* ~, ~**en** (Sprachw.) apposition
Appretur /apre'tu:ɐ/ *die;* ~, ~**en** (Textilind.) dressing; finishing
Approbation /aproba'tsio:n/ *die;* ~, ~**en** licence to practise (as a doctor, dentist, chemist)
Aprikose /apri'ko:zə/ *die;* ~, ~**n** apricot
April /a'prıl/ *der;* ~[s], ~**e** ▶119│ April; **der** ~: April; ~, ~**!** April fool!; **der 1.** ~: the first of April; (in Bezug auf Aprilscherze) April Fool's *or* All Fools' Day; **jmdn. in den** ~ **schicken** make an April fool of sb.
April-: ~**scherz** *der* April-fool trick; **das ist doch wohl ein** ~**scherz!** (fig.) you/they *etc.* can't be serious!; ~**wetter** *das; o. Pl.* April weather
apropos /apro'po:/ *Adv.* apropos; by the way; incidentally
Aquädukt /akvɛ'dʊkt/ *der od. das;* ~[e]s, ~**e** aqueduct
Aquamarin *der;* ~s, ~**e** aquamarine
aquamarin·blau *Adj.* aquamarine
Aquaplaning /akva'pla:nıŋ/ *das;* ~[s] aquaplaning
Aquarell /akva'rɛl/ *das;* ~s, ~**e** watercolour [painting]
Aquarell-: ~**farbe** *die* watercolour; ~**maler** *der* watercolour painter; watercolourist; ~**malerei** *die* **(a)** *o. Pl.* watercolour painting; **(b)** (Bild) watercolour
Aquarium /a'kva:riʊm/ *das;* ~s, **Aquarien** aquarium
Äquator /ɛ'kva:tor/ *der;* ~s, ~**en** equator
Äquator·taufe *die* crossing-the-line ceremony
Aquavit /akva'vi:t/ *der;* ~s, ~**e** aquavit
äquivalent /ɛkviva'lɛnt/ *Adj.* equivalent
Äquivalent *das;* ~[e]s, ~**e** equivalent
Äquivalenz /ɛkviva'lɛnts/ *die;* ~, ~**en** equivalence
Ar /a:ɐ/ *das od. der;* ~s, ~**e** ▶189│ are
Ära /'ɛ:ra/ *die;* ~, **Ären** era; **die** ~ **Kreisky** the Kreisky era
Araber /'a:rabɐ/ *der;* ~s, ~, **Araberin** *die;* ~, ~**nen** ▶388│ Arab
Arabien /a'ra:biən/ *(das)* ~s Arabia
arabisch *Adj.* ▶388│, ▶487│ Arabian; Arab; Arabic ⟨ *language, numeral, alphabet, literature* ⟩; **die Arabische Halbinsel** the Arabian Peninsula; *s. auch* **deutsch; Deutsche²**
Arabisch *das;* ~[s] ▶487│ Arabic *s. auch* **Deutsch**
Aralie /a'ra:liə/ *die;* ~, ~**n** (Bot.) aralia
Arbeit /'arbait/ *die;* ~, ~**en (a)** work *no indef. art.;* **die** ~**[en] am Staudamm** [the] work on the dam; **an die** ~ **gehen, an die** ~ **machen** get down to work; **bei der** ~ **mit Chemikalien** when working with chemicals; **viel** ~ **haben** have a lot of work [to do]; **[wieder] an die** ~**!** [back] to work!; **etw. in** ~ **haben** be working on sth.; **erst die** ~**, dann das Vergnügen** business before pleasure; **(b)** *o. Pl.* (Mühe) trouble; ~ **machen** cause bother *or* trouble; **jmdm.** ~ **machen** make work for sb.; **sich** *(Dat.)* ~ **machen** take trouble [over sth.]; **(c)** *o. Pl.* (Arbeitsplatz) work *no indef. art.;* (Stellung) job; **eine** ~ **suchen/finden** look for/find work *or* a job; **die** ~ **Suchenden** those looking for work; **eine** ~ **als** ...: work *or* a job as ...; **zur** ~ (ugs.) **auf** ~ **gehen** go to work; **auf** ~ **sein** (ugs.) be at work; **vor/nach der** ~**:** before/after work; **(d)** (Aufgabe) job; **(e)** (Produkt) work; (handwerkliche ~) piece of work; (kurze schriftliche ~) article; **(f)** (Schulw.: Klassen~) test; **eine** ~ **schreiben/schreiben lassen** do/set a test
arbeiten **1** *itr. V.* **(a)** work; **zu** ~ **haben** have work to do; **an etw.** (*Dat.*) ~**:** work on sth.; **bei jmdm./einer Firma** *usw.* ~**:** work for sb./a company *etc.;* **seine Frau arbeitet** (ist berufstätig) his wife has a job *or* works; **die Zeit arbeitet für/gegen uns** time is on our side/against us; **(b)** (funktionieren) ⟨ *heart, lungs, etc.* ⟩ work, function; ⟨ *machine* ⟩ work, operate; **(c)** (sich verändern) ⟨ *wood* ⟩ warp; ⟨ *must* ⟩ ferment; ⟨ *dough* ⟩ rise. **2** *tr. V.* **(a)** (herstellen) make; (in Ton, Silber, usw.) work; make; fashion; **(b)** (tun) do; **was** ~ **Sie?** what are you doing?; (beruflich) what do you do for a living?; what's your job? **3** *refl. V.* **(a)** **sich müde/krank** ~**:** tire oneself out/make oneself ill with work; **sich zu**

Tode ~: work oneself to death; **sich** (*Dat.*) **die Hände wund** ~: work one's fingers to the bone; (**b**) (Strecke zurücklegen); **sich durch etw./in etw.** (*Akk.*) ~: work one's way through/into sth.; **sich nach oben** ~ (fig.) work one's way up; (**c**) *unpers.* **hier arbeitet es sich gut** this is a good place to work

Arbeiter *der;* ~**s**, ~: worker; (Bau~, Land~) labourer; (beim Straßenbau) workman

Arbeiter-: ~**bewegung** *die* (Politik) labour movement; ~**familie** *die* working-class family; ~**führer** *der* workers' leader

Arbeiterin *die;* ~, ~**nen** (auch Zool.) worker

Arbeiter-: ~**kind** *das* working-class child; ~**klasse** *die; o. Pl.* working class[es *pl.*]; ~**partei** *die* workers' party

Arbeiterschaft *die;* ~: workers *pl.*

Arbeiter-: ~**unruhen** *Pl.* unrest *sing.* among the workers; ~**viertel** *das* working-class district *or* area; ~**wohl·fahrt** *die; o. Pl.* workers' welfare association

Arbeit·geber *der* employer

Arbeitgeberin *die;* ~, ~**nen** [female] employer

Arbeitnehmer *der;* ~**s**, ~: employee

Arbeitnehmer·anteil *der* employee's contribution

Arbeitnehmerin *die;* ~, ~**nen** [female] employee

arbeitsam *Adj.* (geh. veralt.) industrious; hard-working

arbeits-, Arbeits-: ~**amt** *das* job centre (Brit.); employment exchange; labour exchange (Brit. dated); ~**anfang** *der* starting-time [at work]; ~**anfang ist um 6 Uhr** work starts at 6 a.m.; ~**anzug** *der* (**a**) (Overall) overalls *pl.;* (**b**) (Uniform) fatigue uniform; ~**aufwand** *der:* **mit großem** ~**aufwand** with a great deal of work; ~**auf·wendig 1** *Adj.* requiring a great deal of work *postpos., not pred.;* [**sehr**] ~**aufwendig sein** require a great deal of work; **2** *adv.* in a way that requires/required a great deal of work; ~**ausfall** *der* loss of working hours; ~**bedingungen** *Pl.* working conditions; ~**beginn** *der* ⇒ ~**anfang**; ~**belastung** *die* workload; ~**bereich** *der* area of work; (~gebiet) field of work; ~**beschaffung** *die* job creation; creation of employment; ~**beschaffungs·maßnahme** *die* job-creation measure; ~**beschaffungs·programm** *das* job-creation programme; ~**biene** *die* (**a**) (Zool.) worker bee; (**b**) (ugs.: emsige Frau) busy bee; ~**dienst** *der* (**a**) (Arbeit) (low-paid) community-service work; (**b**) (Organisation) community service agency; ~**eifer** *der* enthusiasm for one's work; ~**ende** *das* finishing-time [at work]; **nach/bei** ~**ende** after work/when it's time to go; **um fünf Uhr haben wir** *od.* **ist bei uns** ~**ende** we finish work at five o'clock; ~**erlaubnis** *die* work permit; ~**essen** *das* (bes. Politik) working lunch/dinner; ~**fähig** *Adj.* fit for work *postpos.;* (grundsätzlich) able to work *postpos.;* viable ‹*government*›; ~**fähigkeit** *die; o. Pl.* fitness for work; (grundsätzlich) ability to work; ~**frei** *Adj.* **zwei** ~**freie Tage pro Woche** two days off a week; **ein paar Tage/ eine Woche** ~**frei** a few days/a week off; **Montag ist/ haben wir** ~**frei** we've got Monday off; ~**gang** *der* (**a**) (einzelne Operation) operation; (**b**) (Ablauf) process; ~**gebiet** *das* field of work; ~**gemeinschaft** *die* team; (Hochschulw.) study group; ~**gerät** *das* (**a**) (Gegenstand) tool; (**b**) *o. Pl.* (Gesamtheit) tools *pl.;* equipment *no indef. art., no pl.;* ~**gericht** *das* industrial tribunal; ~**gruppe** *die* study group; ~**hypothese** *die* working hypothesis; ~**intensiv 1** *Adj.* labour-intensive; **2** *adv.* labour-intensively; ~**kampf** *der* industrial action; ~**kleidung** *die* work clothes *pl.;* ~**klima** *das; o. Pl.* working atmosphere; ~**kollege** *der* (bei Arbeitern) workmate (Brit.); fellow worker; (bei Angestellten, Beamten) colleague; ~**kraft** *die* (**a**) capacity for work; **die menschliche** ~**kraft wird durch Roboter ersetzt** human labour is being replaced by robots; (**b**) (Mensch) worker; ~**kreis** *der* study group; ~**lager** *das* labour camp; ~**leben** *das* (**a**) (Berufstätigkeit) working life; (**b**) (Arbeitswelt) world of work; working life *no art.;* ~**leistung** *die* rate of output; ~**lohn** *der* wage; wages *pl.;* (auf einer Rechnung) labour [costs *pl.*]; ~**los**

(**a**) *Adj.* unemployed; out of work *postpos.;* (**b**) *in* ~**loses Einkommen** unearned income

Arbeitslose *der/die; adj. Dekl.* unemployed person/ man/woman *etc.;* **die** ~**n** the unemployed *or* jobless

Arbeitslosen-: ~**geld** *das; o. Pl.* earnings-related unemployment benefit; ~**hilfe** *die; o. Pl.* (reduced-rate) unemployment benefit; ~**unterstützung** *die* (volkst.) unemployment benefit *or* pay; ~**versicherung** *die; o. Pl.* unemployment insurance

arbeits-, Arbeits-: ~**losigkeit** *die;* ~: unemployment *no indef. art.;* **eine** ~**losigkeit von 0,5 %** a level of unemployment of 0.5 %; ~**markt** *der* labour market; ~**material** *das* materials *pl.;* (einschließlich Werkzeugen) materials [and equipment *or* tools]; (für den Unterricht) teaching aids *pl.;* ~**mittel** *das* tool; ~**moral** *die* morale; ~**niederlegung** *die* walkout; **mit** ~**niederlegungen drohen** threaten walkouts

Arbeits-: ~**pause** *die* break; ~**pensum** *das* work quota; ~**pferd** *das* (auch fig.) workhorse; ~**platz** *der* (**a**) workplace; **am** ~**platz** at one's workplace; (**b**) (Stelle, Job) job; ~**platz·sicherung** *die* safeguarding of jobs; **zur** ~**platzsicherung** to safeguard jobs; ~**prozess**, ***~**prozeß** *der* work process; ~**raum** *der* (**a**) workroom; (**b**) ⇒ **Arbeitszimmer**; ~**recht** *das; o. Pl.* labour law; ~**rechtlich** *Adj.* ~**rechtliche Fragen/ Literatur** issues relating to/literature on labour law; ~**reich** *Adj.* ‹*life, week, etc.*› full of hard work; ~**richter** *der* judge on an industrial tribunal; ~**scheu** *Adj.* work-shy; ~**schluss**, ***~**schluß** *der* ⇒ ~**ende**; ~**schutz** *der* protection of health and safety standards at work; ~**sklave** *der* slave labourer; ~**speicher** *der* (DV) main memory; ~**stelle** *die* ⇒ **Stelle g**; ~**stil** *der* style of working; ~**stunde** *die* hour of work; **2** ~**stunden** (bei Reparaturen usw.) two hours' labour; **die Herstellung erfordert 2 000** ~**stunden** manufacture takes 2,000 man-hours; ~**suche** *die* search for a job *or* for work; **auf** ~**suche sein** be looking for a job; ~**tag** *der* working day; **mein erster** ~**tag nach dem Urlaub** my first day back at work after the holiday (Brit.) *or* (Amer.) vacation; ~**team** *das* team; ~**teilig 1** *Adj.* ‹*society, mode of production, etc.*› based on the division of labour; **2** *adv.* **die Produktion** ~**teilig organisieren** base production on the principle of the division of labour; ~**teilung** *die* division of labour; ~**tempo** *das* rate of work; work rate; ~**tier** *das* (**a**) work animal; (**b**) (Arbeitssüchtiger) compulsive worker; workaholic (coll.); ~**tisch** *der* work table; (für Schreibarbeiten) desk; (für technische Arbeiten) [work]- bench; ~**überlastung** *die* overwork

Arbeit·suchende *der/die; adj. Dekl.* person/man/ woman looking for work

arbeits-, Arbeits-: ~**unfähig** *Adj.* unable to work *postpos.;* (krankheitsbedingt) unfit for work *postpos.;* ~**unfall** *der* industrial accident; ~**un·willig** *Adj.* unwilling to work *postpos.;* ~**verhältnis** *das contractual relationship between employer and employee;* **ein** ~**verhältnis eingehen** enter employment; ~**vermittlung** *die* (**a**) (Tätigkeit) arranging employment; (**b**) (Stelle) employment exchange; job centre (Brit.); (Firma) employment agency; ~**vertrag** *der* contract of employment; ~**verweigerung** *die* refusal to work; ~**vor·gang** *der* work process; ~**vor·lage** *die:* **etw. als** ~**vorlage benutzen** work from sth.; **etw. dient jmdm. als** ~**vorlage** sb. works from sth.; ~**weise** *die* (**a**) way *or* method of working; (**b**) (Funktionsweise) mode of operation; ~**welt** *die* world of work; ~**willig** *Adj.* willing to work *postpos.;* ~**woche** *die* (**a**) week's work; **während seiner ersten** ~**woche** during his first week at work; (**b**) (wöchentliche** ~**zeit) working week; ~**wut** *die* mania for work; ~**zeit** *die* (**a**) working time; **die tägliche/wöchentliche** ~**zeit** the working day/week; (**b**) (der [beruflichen] Arbeit vorbehaltene Zeit) working hours *pl.;* **während der** ~**zeit** during working hours; (**c**) (als Ware) labour time; **2 Stunden** ~**zeit** two hours' labour; ~**zeit·ver·kürzung** *die* reduction in working hours; ~**zeug** *das; o. Pl.* (**a**) work things *pl.;* (**b**) (Kleidung) work[ing] things *pl. or* clothes *pl.;* ~**zimmer** *das* study

Archäologe /arçɛoˈloːgə/ *der;* ~**n**, ~**n** ▸**85**| archaeologist

Archäologie *die;* ~: archaeology *no art.*
Archäologin *die;* ~, ~**nen** ▶ 85 ⏋ archaeologist
archäologisch 1 *Adj.* archaeological. 2 *adv.* archaeologically
Arche /'arçə/ *die;* ~, ~**n** ark; **die** ~ **Noah** Noah's Ark
Archipel /arçi'pe:l/ *der;* ~**s**, ~**e** archipelago
Architekt /arçi'tɛkt/ *der;* ~**en**, ~**en**, **Architektin** *die;* ~, ~**nen** ▶ 85 ⏋ architect
Architektur /arçitɛk'tu:ɐ̯/ *die;* ~: architecture
Archiv /ar'çi:f/ *das;* ~**s**, ~**e** archives *pl.;* archive
archivieren *tr. V.* etw. ~: archive sth.; put sth. in the archives
ARD /a:|ɛr'de:/ *die;* ~ *Abk.* **Arbeitsgemeinschaft der öffentlich-rechtlichen Rundfunkanstalten der Bundesrepublik Deutschland** *national radio and television network in the FRG*
Areal /are'a:l/ *das;* ~**s**, ~**e** (a) (Fläche) area; (b) (Grundstück) grounds *pl.*
Ären ⇒ **Ära**
Arena /a're:na/ *die;* ~, **Arenen** (a) (hist., Sport, fig.) arena; (b) (für Stierkämpfe, Manege) ring
arg /ark/; **ärger** /'ɛrgɐ/, **ärgst…** /'ɛrgst…/ 1 *Adj.* (a) (geh., landsch.: schlimm) bad ‹*weather, condition, state*›; serious ‹*situation, wound*›; hard ‹*times*›; **an nichts Arges denken** be completely unsuspecting; **im Argen liegen** be in a sorry state; (b) (geh. veralt.: böse) wicked; evil; (c) (geh., landsch.: unangenehm groß, stark) severe ‹*pain, hunger, shock*›; severe, bitter ‹*disappointment*›; serious ‹*dilemma, error*›; extreme, (coll.) terrible ‹*embarrassment*›; gross ‹*exaggeration, injustice*›; **in** ~**er Bedrängnis/Not sein** be in desperate straits; **mein ärgster Feind** my worst enemy *or* arch-enemy; **unser ärgster Konkurrent** our most dangerous competitor. 2 *adv.* (geh., landsch.) extremely, (coll.) awfully, (coll.) terribly ‹*painful, cold, steep, expensive, heavy, etc.*›; severely, bitterly ‹*disappointed*›; extremely, (coll.) terribly ‹*embarrassed*›; ‹*suffer, weaken*› severely; ‹*offend*› deeply; ‹*deceive*› badly; ‹*rain, pull, punch*› hard; ‹*hurt*› a great deal; **ihr treibt es gar zu** ~! you're going too far!; **etwas** ~ **laut** a bit too loud; **es geht ihm** ~ **schlecht/gut** things are going really badly/well for him
ärger ⇒ **arg**
Ärger /'ɛrgɐ/ *der;* ~**s** (a) annoyance; (Zorn) anger; **jmds.** ~ **erregen** annoy sb.; **seinem** ~ **Luft machen** vent one's anger; **seinen** ~ **an jmdm. auslassen** vent one's anger on sb.; (b) (Unannehmlichkeiten) trouble; **häuslicher/beruflicher** ~: domestic problems *pl.*/problems *pl.* at work; **[jmdm.]** ~ **machen** cause [sb.] trouble; make trouble [for sb.]; **so ein** ~! how annoying!; ~ **bekommen** get into trouble
ärgerlich 1 *Adj.* (a) annoyed; (zornig) angry; **ein** ~**es Gesicht machen** look annoyed/angry; ~ **über etw.** (*Akk.*) **sein** be annoyed/angry about sth.; ~ **werden** get angry/annoyed; **wie** ~! how annoying! 2 *adv.* (a) with annoyance; (zornig) angrily; (b) (Ärger erregend) annoyingly; irritatingly
ärgern 1 *tr. V.* (a) **jmdn.** ~: annoy sb.; (zornig machen) make sb. angry; (b) (reizen, necken) tease. 2 *refl. V.* be annoyed; (zornig sein) be angry; (ärgerlich/zornig werden) get annoyed/angry; **sich über jmdn./etw.** ~: get annoyed/angry at sb./about sth.; **sich schwarz** *od.* **grün und blau** ~: fret and fume
Ärgernis *das;* ~**ses**, ~**se** (a) *o. Pl.* offence; **Erregung öffentlichen** ~**ses** (Rechtsspr.) creating a public nuisance; (b) (etw. Ärgerliches) annoyance; irritation; (c) (etw. Anstößiges) nuisance; (etw. Skandalöses) scandal; outrage
arg-, Arg-: ~**list** *das; o. Pl.* (Hinterlist) guile; deceit; (Heimtücke, Rechtsw.) malice; ~**listig** 1 *Adj.* (hinterlistig) guileful; deceitful; deceitful ‹*plan*›; (heimtückisch) malicious; ~**listige Täuschung** (Rechtsspr.) malicious deception; 2 *adv.* (hinterlistig) guilefully; (heimtückisch) maliciously; ~**listigkeit** *die;* ~ ⇒ ~**listig** 1: guilefulness; deceitfulness; malice; ~**los** 1 *Adj.* (a) guileless ‹*person*›; guileless, innocent ‹*question, remark*›; (b) (ohne Argwohn) unsuspecting; **wie kannst du nur so** ~**los sein?** how can you be so naïve?; 2 *adv.* (a) guilelessly; innocently; (b) (ohne Argwohn) unsuspectingly; ~**losigkeit** *die;* ~

(a) (eines Menschen) guilelessness; (einer Äußerung, Absicht) innocence; (b) (Vertrauensseligkeit) unsuspecting nature
ärgst… ⇒ **arg**
Argument /argu'mɛnt/ *das;* ~[**e**]**s**, ~**e** argument
Argumentation /argumɛnta'tsi̯o:n/ *die;* ~, ~**en** argumentation
argumentieren *itr. V.* argue; **mit etw.** ~: use sth. as an argument
Argwohn /'arkvo:n/ *der;* ~[**e**]**s** suspicion; ~ **gegen jmdn. hegen** be suspicious of sb.
argwöhnen /'arkvø:nən/ *tr. V.* (geh.) suspect
argwöhnisch (geh.) 1 *Adj.* suspicious. 2 *adv.* suspiciously
Arie /'a:ri̯ə/ *die;* ~, ~**n** aria
Aristokrat /arɪsto'kra:t/ *der;* ~**en**, ~**en** aristocrat
Aristokratie /arɪstokra'ti:/ *die;* ~, ~**n** aristocracy
Aristokratin *die;* ~, ~**nen** aristocrat
aristokratisch 1 *Adj.* aristocratic. 2 *adv.* aristocratically
Aristoteles /arɪs'to:telɛs/ (*der*) Aristotle
Arithmetik /arɪt'me:tɪk/ *die;* ~: arithmetic *no art.*
arithmetisch 1 *Adj.* arithmetical. 2 *adv.* arithmetically
Arkade /ar'ka:də/ *die;* ~, ~**n** arcade
Arktis /'arktɪs/ *die;* ~: **die** ~: the Arctic
arktisch 1 *Adj.* (auch fig.) arctic. 2 *adv.* **das Klima ist** ~ **beeinflusst** the climate is influenced by the Arctic
Arkus /'arkʊs/ *der;* ~, ~ /'arku:s/ (Geom.) arc
arm /arm/; **ärmer** /'ɛrmɐ/, **ärmst…** /'ɛrmst…/ *Adj.* (auch fig.) poor; **um etw. ärmer sein/werden** have lost/lose sth.; ~ **an Bodenschätzen/Nährstoffen** poor in mineral resources/nutrients; **das Gebiet ist** ~ **an Wasser** the area is short of water; ~ **an Vitaminen sein** ‹*food*› be lacking in *or* low in vitamins; **der/die Ärmste** *od.* **Arme** the poor man/boy/woman/girl; **ach, du Armer** *od.* **Ärmster!** (meist iron.) oh, you poor thing!; *s. auch* **dran b**
Arm *der;* ~[**e**]**s**, ~**e** (a) ▶ 326 ⏋ arm; **jmdn. am** ~ **führen** lead sb. by the arm; **jmdn.** ~ **nehmen** take sb.'s arm; take sb. by the arm; **jmdn. im** ~ **halten** embrace sb.; **sich** (*Dat.*) **in den** ~**en liegen** lie in each other's *or* one another's arms; **jmdn. am längeren** ~ **haben** (fig. ugs.) have more clout (coll.); **jmds. verlängerter** ~ **sein** (fig.) be sb.'s tool *or* instrument; **jmdn. auf den** ~ **nehmen** (fig. ugs.) have sb. on (Brit. coll.); pull sb.'s leg; **jmdm. in die** ~**e laufen** bump *or* run into sb.; **jmdm. [mit etw.] unter die** ~**e greifen** help sb. out [with sth.]; *s. auch* **Bein a**; (b) (armartiger Teil) arm; (c) (Ärmel) arm; sleeve; **ein Hemd/eine Bluse mit halbem** ~: a short-sleeved shirt/blouse
Armada /ar'ma:da/ *die;* ~, **Armaden** *u.* ~**s** (auch fig.) armada
Armatur /arma'tu:ɐ̯/ *die;* ~, ~**en** (Technik) (a) fitting; (b) *meist Pl.* (im Kfz) instrument
Armaturen·brett *das* instrument panel; (im Kfz) dashboard
Arm-: ~**band** *das* bracelet; (Uhr~) strap; ~**band·uhr** *die* wrist-watch; ~**binde** *die* armband; ~**brust** *die* crossbow
Ärmchen /'ɛrmçən/ *das;* ~**s**, ~: [little] arm
Arme *der/die; adj. Dekl.* poor man/woman;. pauper; **die** ~**n** the poor *pl; s. auch* **arm**
Armee /ar'me:/ *die;* ~, ~**n** (a) (auch fig.) army; (b) **die** ~ (die Streitkräfte) the armed forces *pl.*
Armee·fahrzeug *das* army vehicle
Ärmel /'ɛrməl/ *der;* ~**s**, ~: sleeve; **die** ~ **hochkrempeln** (fig. ugs.) roll up one's sleeves; **[sich** (*Dat.*)**] etw. aus dem** ~ **schütteln** (ugs.) produce sth. just like that
Armeleute·essen *das* poor man's food
Ärmel·kanal· *der:* **der** ~: the [English] Channel
Armen·haus *das* (hist., fig.) poorhouse
Armenien /ar'me:ni̯ən/ (*das*) ~**s** Armenia
Armenier *der;* ~**s**, ~, **Armenierin**, *die;* ~, ~**nen** ▶ 388 ⏋ Armenian

armenisch *Adj.* ▶388|, ▶487| Armenian; *s. auch* **deutsch; Deutsch; Deutsche²**

ärmer ⇨ **arm**

armieren *tr. V.* (a) (Milit. veralt.) arm; (b) (Technik) reinforce ‹*concrete*›; armour, sheathe ‹*cable*›

-armig *adj.* -armed

Arm-: ~**länge** *die* arm length; (als Maß) arm's length; ~**lehne** *die* armrest; ~**leuchter** *der* (a) candelabra; (b) (ugs.) berk (Brit. sl.); jerk (Amer. sl.)

ärmlich /'ɛrmlɪç/ **1** *Adj.* cheap ‹*clothing*›; shabby ‹*flat, office*›; meagre ‹*meal*›; **aus** ~**en Verhältnissen** from a poor family. **2** *adv.* cheaply ‹*dressed, furnished*›; ~ **leben/ wohnen** live in impoverished circumstances

Arm·reif *der* armlet

arm·selig 1 *Adj.* (a) (sehr arm, dürftig, unbefriedigend) miserable; miserable, wretched ‹*dwelling*›; pathetic ‹*result, figure*›; meagre ‹*meal, food*›; paltry ‹*return, salary, sum, fee*›; ~**e 10 Mark** a paltry 10 marks; (b) (abwertend: erbärmlich) miserable, wretched ‹*swindler, quack*›; pathetic, miserable, wretched ‹*coward*›; pathetic, miserable ‹*amateur, bungler*›. **2** *adv.* ~ **leben** lead *or* live a miserable life; ~ **eingerichtet** miserably *or* wretchedly furnished

Armseligkeit *die;* ~ ⇨ **armselig 1:** miserableness; wretchedness; patheticness; meagreness; paltriness

Arm·sessel *der* armchair

ärmst… ⇨ **arm**

Arm·stuhl *der* armchair

Armsünder·miene *die* (scherzh.) expression of misery and remorse

Armut /'armuːt/ *die;* ~ (auch fig.) poverty; **die** ~ **des Landes an Rohstoffen** (fig.) the country's lack of raw materials

Armuts-: ~**grenze** *die* poverty line; **an/unter[halb] der** ~**:** on/below the poverty line; ~**zeugnis** *das in* **ein** ~ **sein** be a sign of inadequacy

Arnika /'arnika/ *die;* ~, ~**s** arnica

Aroma /a'roːma/ *das;* ~**s, Aromen** (Duft) aroma; (Geschmack) flavour; taste

aromatisch /aro'maːtɪʃ/ *Adj.* (a) (duftend) aromatic; ~ **duften** give off an aromatic fragrance; (b) (wohlschmeckend) distinctive ‹*taste*›; **sehr** ~ **schmecken** have a very distinctive taste

Arrangement /arãʒə'mãː/ *das;* ~**s, ~s** (geh., Mus.) arrangement

arrangieren /arã'ziːrən/ **1** *tr. V.* (auch Musik) arrange. **2** *itr. V.* (auch Musik) **er kann gut** ~**:** he's a good arranger. **3** *refl. V.* **sich** ~**:** adapt, adjust; **sich mit jmdm.** ~**:** come to an accommodation with sb.; **sich mit etw.** ~**:** come to terms with sth.

Arrest /a'rɛst/ *der;* ~**[e]s, ~e** (Milit., Rechtsw., Schule) detention; **einen Schüler mit** ~ **bestrafen** (veralt.) punish a pupil by putting him in detention

Arrest·zelle *die* detention cell

arretieren /are'tiːrən/ *tr. V.* (a) *auch itr.* lock; (b) (veralt.: festnehmen) detain; arrest

arrivieren /ari'viːrən/ *itr. V.; mit sein* (geh.) arrive; **zum Superstar/zum Staatsfeind Nummer eins** ~**:** achieve superstar status/become public enemy number one

Arrivierte *der/die; adj. Dekl.* (geh.) man/woman who has/ had arrived; (abwertend) parvenu

arrogant /aro'gant/ (abwertend) **1** *Adj.* arrogant. **2** *adv.* arrogantly

Arroganz /aro'gants/ *die;* ~ (abwertend) arrogance

arrondieren /arõ'diːrən/ *tr. V.* (geh.) round off ‹*property, territory, etc.*›

Arsch /arʃ/ *der;* ~**[e]s, Ärsche** /'ɛrʃə/ (derb) (a) arse (Brit. coarse); bum (Brit. sl.); ass (Amer. sl.); **den** ~ **voll kriegen** get a bloody good hiding (Brit. sl.); **der** ~ **der Welt** (fig.) the back of beyond; **leck mich am** ~**!** (fig.) piss off (coarse); get stuffed (Brit. sl.); (verflucht noch mal!; na, so was!) bugger me! (Brit. coarse); **er kann mich [mal] am** ~ **lecken** (fig.) he can piss off (coarse); he can kiss my arse (Brit. coarse) *or* ass (Amer. sl.); **sich auf den** ~ **setzen** (fig.) (fleißig arbeiten) get *or* pull one's finger out (fig. sl.); (perplex sein) freak (sl.);

jmdm. in den ~ **kriechen** (fig.) kiss sb.'s arse (Brit. coarse) *or* ass (Amer. sl.); **jmdm. in den** ~ **treten** kick sb. *or* give sb. a kick up the arse (Brit. coarse) *or* kick in the ass (Amer. sl.); (fig.) give sb. a kick up the backside; **im** ~ **sein** (fig.) be buggered (coarse); (b) (widerlicher Mensch) arsehole (Brit. coarse); ass-hole (Amer. sl.); ~ **mit Ohren** arsehole (Brit. coarse); ass-hole (Amer. sl.); (c) (nichts geltender Mensch) piece of dirt

Arsch-: ~**backe** *die* (derb) cheek (sl.) [of the/one's arse (Brit. coarse) *or* bum (Brit. sl.) *or* ass (Amer. sl.)]; ~**kriecher** *der* (derb abwertend) arse-licker (Brit. coarse); ass-licker (Amer. sl.); ~**kriecherei** *die* (derb abwertend) arse-licking (Brit. coarse); ass-licking Brit.; ~**loch** *das* (fig. derb) arsehole (Brit. coarse); asshole (Amer. sl.)

Arsenal /arze'naːl/ *das;* ~**s, ~e** arsenal

Art /aːrt/ *die;* ~, ~**en** (a) (Sorte) kind; sort; (Biol.: Spezies) species; **Tische/Bücher aller** ~**:** tables/books of all kinds *or* sorts; all kinds *or* sorts of tables/books; **einzig in seiner** ~**:** unique of its kind; **jede** ~ **von Gewalt ablehnen** reject all forms of violence; **diese** ~ **[von] Menschen** that kind *or* sort of person; people like that; **[so] eine** ~ **…:** a sort *or* kind of …; **aus der** ~ **schlagen** not be true to type; (in einer Familie) be different from all the rest of the family; (b) *o. Pl.* (Wesen) nature; (Verhaltensweise) manner; way; **das entspricht nicht seiner** ~**:** it's not [in] his nature; that's not his way; (c) *o. Pl.* (gutes Benehmen) behaviour; **das ist doch keine** ~**!** that's no way to behave!; **die feine englische** ~ (ugs.) the proper way to behave; (d) (Weise) way; **auf diese** ~**:** in this way; **auf grausamste** ~**:** in the cruellest way; **in einer** ~**:** in a way; ~ **und Weise** way; **nach** ~ **des Hauses** (Kochk.) à la maison; **nach Schweizer** *od.* **auf schweizerische** ~ (Kochk.) Swiss style

arten·reich *Adj.* (Biol.) species-rich

Arten·schutz *der* protection of species; species protection

Arterie /ar'teːriə/ *die;* ~, ~**n** ▶326| artery

Arterien·verkalkung *die* ▶329| hardening of the arteries; arteriosclerosis (Med.)

Arterio·sklerose /arteriːo-/ *die* ▶329| (Med.) arteriosclerosis

artgerecht 1 *Adj.* appropriate for *or* to the species postpos. **2** *adv.* in a way appropriate for *or* to the species

Arthrose /ar'troːzə/ *die;* ~, ~**n** ▶329| (Med.) arthrosis

artig 1 *Adj.* (a) well-behaved; good; **sei** ~**:** be good; be a good boy/girl/dog *etc.;* (b) (geh. veralt.: höflich) courteous. **2** *adv.* (a) **sich** ~ **benehmen** be good; behave well; (b) (geh. veralt.: höflich) courteously

Artikel /ar'tiːkl/ *der;* ~**s, ~** (a) article; (b) (Ware) article; item

Artikulation /artikula'tsi̯oːn/ *die;* ~, ~**en** articulation

artikulieren 1 *tr., itr. V.* articulate. **2** *refl. V.* (geh.) (a) express oneself; (b) (zum Ausdruck kommen) express itself; be expressed

Artillerie /artɪlə'riː/ *die;* ~, ~**n** artillery

Artischocke /artɪ'ʃɔkə/ *die;* ~, ~**n** artichoke

Artist /ar'tɪst/ *der;* ~**en, ~en** ▶388| [variety/circus] artiste *or* performer

Artistik *die;* ~ (a) circus/variety performance *no art.;* (b) (Geschicklichkeit) skill

Artistin *die;* ~, ~**nen** ▶388| ⇨ **Artist**

artistisch 1 *Adj.* (a) **eine** ~**e Glanzleistung** a superb circus/variety performance; **sein** ~**es Können** his skill as a [circus/variety] artiste; (b) (geschickt) masterly. **2** *adv.* (a) **eine** ~ **anspruchsvolle Nummer** a circus/variety act of great virtuosity; (b) (geschickt) in a masterly way *or* fashion

Arznei /aːrts'nai̯/ *die;* ~, ~**en** (veralt.), **Arznei·mittel** *das* medicine; medicament; (zur äußeren Anwendung) medicament

Arzt /aːrtst/ *der;* ~**es, Ärzte** /'ɛːrtstə/ ▶85| doctor; physician (arch./formal); **zum** ~ **gehen** go to the doctor['s]; **Sie sollten mal zum** ~ **gehen** you ought to see a/the doctor; **praktischer** ~**:** general practitioner; GP

Ärzteschaft *die;* ~**:** medical professional

Arzt·helferin *die* ▶85| doctor's receptionist

Ärztin /'ɛːrtstɪn/ *die;* ~, ~**nen** ▶85| doctor; physician (formal)

ärztlich /'ɛːɐ̯tstlɪç/ **1** *Adj.* medical; **auf ~e Verordnung** on doctor's orders. **2** *adv.* **sich ~ behandeln lassen** have medical treatment

Arzt-: **~praxis** *die* doctor's surgery (Brit.) *or* practice; **~rechnung** *die* doctor's bill

as, As[1] /as/ *das; ~, ~* (Musik) [kɛy ʊf] A flat

As[2] ⇨ **Ass**

Asbest /as'bɛst/ *der; ~[e]s, ~e* asbestos

Asche /'aʃə/ *die; ~, ~n* ash[es *pl.*]; (sterbliche Reste) ashes *pl.;* **in ~ liegen/legen** (fig. geh.) lie/lay in ashes; *s. auch* **Friede; Schutt a**

Aschen-: **~bahn** *die* (Sport) cinder-track; **~becher** *der* ashtray; **~brödel** /-brøːdl̩/ *das; ~s, ~* (auch fig.) Cinderella; **~platz** *der* (Tennis) cinder-court

Ascher *der; ~s, ~* (ugs.) ashtray

Ascher·mittwoch *der* Ash Wednesday

Ascorbin·säure /askɔr'biːn-/ *die* ascorbic acid

Äser ⇨ **Aas**

asexuell *Adj.* asexual

Asiat /a'zi̯aːt/ *der; ~en, ~en,* **Asiatin** *die; ~, ~nen* Asian

asiatisch *Adj.* Asian

Asien /'aːzi̯ən/ *(das); ~s* Asia

Askese /as'keːzə/ *die; ~:* asceticism

Asket /as'keːt/ *der; ~en, ~en* ascetic

asketisch 1 *Adj.* ascetic. **2** *adv.* ascetically

asozial 1 *Adj.* asocial; (gegen die Gesellschaft gerichtet) antisocial; **ein ~er Mensch** a social misfit. **2** *adv.* asocially; antisocially

Asoziale *der/die; adj. Dekl.* social misfit

Aspekt /as'pɛkt/ *der; ~[e]s, ~e* aspect

Asphalt /as'falt/ *der; ~[e]s, ~e* asphalt

asphaltieren *tr. V.* asphalt

Asphalt·straße *die* asphalt road

Aspik /as'piːk/ *der* (österr. auch das); *~s, ~e* aspic

Aspirant /aspi'rant/ *der; ~en, ~en,* **Aspirantin** *die; ~, ~nen* candidate

aß /aːs/ *1. u. 3. Pers. Sg. Prät. v.* **essen**

Ass /as/ *das; ~es, ~:* ace

Assekuranz /aseku'rants/ *die; ~, ~en* (Wirtsch.) assurance (Brit.); insurance

Assel /'asl̩/ *die; ~, ~n* (Keller~, Mauer~) woodlouse

Assessor /a'sɛsɔr/ *der; ~s, ~en* /asɛ'soːrən/, **Assessorin** *die; ~, ~nen holder of a higher civil service post, e.g. teacher or lawyer, who has passed the necessary examinations but has not yet completed his/her probationary period*

Assimilation /asimila'tsi̯oːn/ *die; ~, ~en* assimilation **(an + Akk. to)**

Assistent /asɪs'tɛnt/ *der; ~en, ~en,* **Assistentin** *die; ~, ~nen* assistant; *s. auch* **wissenschaftlich**

Assistenz·arzt *der* junior doctor

assistieren *itr. V.* **[jmdm.]** *~:* assist [sb.] **(bei at)**

Assoziation /asotsi̯a'tsi̯oːn/ *die; ~, ~en* association

assoziieren 1 *tr. V.* (bes. Psych., geh.) associate; **bei einem Namen** *usw.* **etw.** *~:* associate sth. with a name etc. **2** *itr. V.* make associations; **frei** *~:* free-associate

Ast /ast/ *der; ~[e]s,* **Äste** /'ɛstə/ **(a)** branch; bough; **den ~ absägen, auf dem man sitzt** (fig. ugs.) saw off the branch one is sitting on; **auf dem absteigenden ~ sein** (fig. ugs.) be going downhill; **(b)** (in Holz) knot; **(c) sich** *(Dat.)* **einen ~ lachen** (ugs.) split one's sides [with laughter]

Aster /'astɐ/ *die; ~, ~n* aster; (Herbst~) Michaelmas daisy

Ast·gabel *die* (zwischen Stamm und Ast) fork of a/the tree; (zwischen Ast und Zweig) fork of a/the branch

Ästhet /ɛs'teːt/ *der; ~en, ~en* aesthete

Ästhetik /ɛs'teːtɪk/ *die; ~, ~en* **(a)** aesthetics *sing.;* **(b)** (das Ästhetische) aesthetics *pl.*

ästhetisch 1 *Adj.* aesthetic. **2** *adv.* aesthetically

ästhetisieren *tr. (auch itr.) V.* (geh.) aestheticize

Asthma /'astma/ *das; ~s* ▶ 329 ⌋ asthma

Asthmatiker /ast'maːtikɐ/ *der; ~s, ~:* asthmatic

asthmatisch 1 *Adj.* asthmatic. **2** *adv.* asthmatically

Ast·loch *das* knot-hole

ast·rein 1 *Adj.* **(a)** (ugs.) on the level (coll.); **(b)** (salopp: prima) fantastic (coll.); great (coll.). **2** *adv.* (salopp) fantastically (coll.)

Astrologe /astro'loːgə/ *der; ~n, ~n* astrologer; (fig.) forecaster; pundit

Astrologie *die; ~:* astrology *no art.*

Astrologin *die; ~, ~nen* ⇨ **Astrologe**

astrologisch 1 *Adj.* astrological. **2** *adv.* astrologically

Astronaut /astro'naut/ *der; ~en, ~en,* **Astronautin** *die; ~, ~nen* astronaut

Astronom /astro'noːm/ *der; ~en, ~en* astronomer

Astronomie *die; ~:* astronomy *no art.*

astronomisch *Adj.* astronomical

astro-, Astro- /astro…/**:** **~physik** *die* astrophysics *sing., no art.;* **~physikalisch 1** *Adj.* astrophysical; **2** *adv.* astrophysically; **~physiker** *der* astrophysicist

Ast·werk *das; ~[e]s* branches *pl.*

Asyl /a'zyːl/ *das; ~s, ~e* **(a)** [political] asylum; **jmdm. ~ gewähren** grant sb. asylum; **(b)** (Obdachlosen~) hostel [for the homeless]

Asylant /azy'lant/ *der; ~en, ~en,* **Asylantin** *die; ~, ~nen* person seeking/granted [political] asylum

Asyl-: **~bewerber** *der* person seeking [political] asylum; **~recht** *das* (Rechtsw.) **(a)** right of [political] asylum; **(b)** (eines Staates) right to grant [political] asylum; **~werber** *der; ~s, ~* (österr.) ⇨ **~bewerber**

asymmetrisch 1 *Adj.* asymmetrical. **2** *adv.* asymmetrically

asynchron 1 *Adj.* asynchronous. **2** *adv.* asynchronously

A. T. *Abk.* **Altes Testament** OT

Atelier /atə'li̯eː/ *das; ~s, ~s* studio

Atem /'aːtəm/ *der; ~s* breath; **sein ~ wurde schneller** his breathing became faster; **einen langen/den längeren ~ haben** (fig.) have great/the greater staying power; **jmdn. in ~ halten** keep sb. in suspense; **den ~ anhalten** hold one's breath; **~ holen** *od.* (geh.) schöpfen (fig.) get one's breath back; **außer ~ sein/geraten** *od.* **kommen** be/get out of breath; **[wieder] zu ~ kommen** get one's breath back; *s. auch* **ausgehen 1 b**

atem-, Atem-: **~beraubend 1** *Adj.* breathtaking; **2** *adv.* breath-takingly; **~beschwerden** *Pl.* trouble *sing.* with one's breathing; **~los 1** *Adj.* breathless; **2** *adv.* breathlessly; **~losigkeit** *die; ~:* breathlessness; **~not** *die; o. Pl.* difficulty in breathing; **~pause** *die* breathing space; **~übung** *die* breathing exercise; **~wege** *Pl.* respiratory tract *sing.* or passages; **~zug** *der* breath; **in einem** *od.* **im selben ~zug** in the same breath

Atheismus /ate'ɪsmʊs/ *der; ~:* atheism *no art.*

Atheist *der; ~en, ~en* atheist

atheistisch 1 *Adj.* atheistic. **2** *adv.* atheistically

Athen /a'teːn/ *(das); ~s* ▶ 490 ⌋ Athens

Athener **1** *indekl. Adj.; nicht präd.* Athens attrib.; of Athens postpos. **2** *der; ~s, ~:* ▶ 490 ⌋ Athenian

Äther /'ɛːtɐ/ *der; ~s, ~* (Chemie, Physik, geh.) ether

ätherisch /ɛ'teːrɪʃ/ *Adj.* (Chemie, dichter.) ethereal

Äthiopien /ɛ'ti̯oːpi̯ən/ *(das); ~s* Ethiopia

Athlet /at'leːt/ *der; ~en, ~en* **(a)** (Sportler) athlete; **(b)** (ugs.: kräftiger Mann) muscleman

Athletik /at'leːtɪk/ *die; ~:* athletics *sing., no art.*

athletisch *Adj.* athletic

Atlanten ⇨ **Atlas**

Atlantik /at'lantɪk/ *der; ~s* Atlantic

atlantisch *Adj.* (Geogr.) Atlantic; **der Atlantische Ozean** the Atlantic Ocean

Atlas /'atlas/ *der;* ~ *od.* ~**ses, Atlanten** *od.* ~**se** atlas

atmen /'a:tman/ *itr., tr. V.* breathe

Atmosphäre /atmo'sfɛ:rə/ *die;* ~, ~**n** (auch fig.) atmosphere

atmosphärisch 1 *Adj.* atmospheric. 2 *adv.* atmospherically

Atmung *die;* ~: breathing; respiration (as tech. term)

Atom /a'to:m/ *das;* ~**s,** ~**e** atom

atomar /ato'ma:ɐ̯/ 1 *Adj.* atomic; (Atomwaffen betreffend) nuclear; nuclear, atomic ‹*age, weapons*›. 2 *adv.* ~ **angetrieben** nuclear-powered; atomic-powered; ~ **aufrüsten** build up nuclear arms

Atom-: ~**bombe** *die* nuclear bomb; atom bomb; ~**bombenversuch** *der* nuclear [weapons] test; ~**bunker** *der* fallout shelter; ~**energie** *die; o. Pl.* nuclear *or* atomic energy *no indef. art.;* ~**explosion** *die* nuclear *or* atomic explosion

atomisieren *tr. V.* (a) (zerstören) **etw.** ~: smash sth. to atoms; (b) (zerstäuben) atomize ‹*liquid*›

atom-, Atom-: ~**kern** *der* atomic nucleus; ~**kraft** *die; o. Pl.* nuclear *or* atomic power *no indef. art.;* ~**kraftwerk** *das* nuclear *or* atomic power station; ~**krieg** *der* nuclear war; ~**macht** *die* nuclear power; ~**müll** *der* nuclear *or* atomic waste; ~**physik** *die* nuclear *or* atomic physics *sing., no art.;* ~**physiker** *der* nuclear *or* atomic physicist; ~**pilz** *der* mushroom cloud; ~**rakete** *die* (Waffe) nuclear *or* atomic missile; ~**reaktor** *der* nuclear reactor; ~**sprengkopf** *der* nuclear warhead; ~**strom** *der* (ugs.) electricity generated by nuclear power; ~**U-Boot** *das* nuclear[-powered] submarine; ~**waffe** *die* nuclear *or* atomic weapon; ~**waffen·frei** *Adj.* nuclear-free; ~**waffensperrvertrag** *der* Nuclear Non-proliferation Treaty; ~**zeit··alter** *das; o. Pl.* nuclear *or* atomic age

atonal *Adj.* (Musik) atonal

Atrium /'a:triʊm/ *das;* ~**s, Atrien** atrium

ätsch /ɛ:tʃ/ *Interj.* (Kinderspr.) ha ha

Attacke /a'takə/ *die;* ~, ~**n** (a) (auch Med.) attack (**auf** + *Akk.* on); (b) (Reiter~) [cavalry] charge; **eine** ~ **[gegen jmdn./etw.] reiten** charge [sb./sth.]; (fig.) make an attack [on sb./sth.]

attackieren *tr. V.* (a) attack; (b) (Milit.: zu Pferde) charge

Attentat /'atn̩ta:t/ *das;* ~**[e]s,** ~**e** assassination attempt; (erfolgreiches) assassination; **ein** ~ **auf jmdn. verüben** make an attempt on sb.'s life/assassinate sb.

Attentäter /'atn̩tɛ:tɐ/ *der;* ~**s,** ~, **Attentäterin** *die;* ~, ~**nen** would-be assassin; (bei erfolgreichem Attentat) assassin

Attest /a'tɛst/ *das;* ~**[e]s,** ~**e** medical certificate; doctor's certificate

attestieren *tr. V.* certify

Attitüde /ati'ty:də/ *die;* ~, ~**n** (geh.) posture

Attraktion /atrak'tsi̯o:n/ *die;* ~, ~**en** attraction

attraktiv /atrak'ti:f/ 1 *Adj.* attractive. 2 *adv.* attractively

Attraktivität /atraktivi'tɛ:t/ *die;* ~: attractiveness

Attrappe /a'trapə/ *die;* ~, ~**n** dummy

Attribut /atri'bu:t/ *das;* ~**[e]s,** ~**e** attribute

attributiv /atribu'ti:f/ (Sprachw.) 1 *Adj.* attributive. 2 *adv.* attributively

atypisch (geh.) 1 *Adj.* atypical. 2 *adv.* atypically

ätzen /'ɛtsn̩/ 1 *tr. V.* (a) etch; (b) (Med.) cauterize ‹*wound*›. 2 *itr. V.* corrode

ätzend 1 *Adj.* (a) corrosive; (fig.) caustic ‹*wit, remark, criticism*›; pungent ‹*smell*›; acrid ‹*smoke*›; (b) (Jugendspr.) grotty (Brit. coll.); grot (Brit. sl.). 2 *adv.* caustically ‹*ironic, critical*›

Ätzung *die;* ~, ~**en** (a) etching; (b) (Med.) cauterization

au /au/ *Interj.* (a) (bei Schmerz) ow; ouch; (b) (bei Überraschung, Begeisterung) oh

Aubergine /obɛr'ʒi:nə/ *die;* ~, ~**n** aubergine (Brit.); eggplant

auch /aux/ 1 *Adv.* (a) (ebenso, ebenfalls) as well; too; also; **Klaus war** ~ **dabei** Klaus was there as well *or* too; Klaus was also there; **Ich gehe jetzt. — Ich** ~: I'm going now — So am I; **Mir ist warm. — Mir** ~: I feel warm — So

do I; ... — **Ja, das** ~: ... — Yes, that too; ~ **gut!** that's all right too; **das kann ich** ~! I can do that too; **was er verspricht, tut er** ~: what he promises to do, he does; **nicht nur ..., sondern** ~ ...: not only ..., but also ...; **grüß deine Frau und** ~ **die Kinder** give my regards to your wife and the children too; **sehr gut, aber** ~ **teuer** very good but expensive too; ~ **das noch!** that's all I/we *etc.* need!; **oder** ~: or; **oder** ~ **nicht** or not, as the case may be; **das weiß ich** ~ **nicht** I don't know either; **ich habe** ~ **keine Lust/kein Geld** I don't feel like it either/don't have any money either; **das hat** ~ **nichts genützt** that did not help either; *s. auch* **sowohl**; (b) (sogar, selbst) even; ~ **wenn** even if; **wenn** ~: even if *or* though; **ohne** ~ **nur zu fragen/eine Sekunde zu zögern** without even asking/hesitating for a second; (c) (außerdem, im Übrigen) besides 2 *Partikel* (a) *not translated* **etwas anderes habe ich** ~ **nicht erwartet** I never expected anything else; **so schlimm ist es** ~ **[wieder] nicht** it's not as bad as all that; **nun hör aber** ~ **zu!** now listen!; **wozu [denn]** ~? what's the point? why should I/you *etc.*?; (b) (zweifelnd) **bist du dir** ~ **im klaren, was das bedeutet?** are you sure you understand what that means?; **bist du** ~ **glücklich?** are you truly happy?; **lügst du** ~ **nicht?** you're not lying, are you?; (c) (mit Interrogativpron.) **wo .../wer .../wann .../was ...** *usw.* ~ **[immer]** wherever/whoever/whenever/whatever *etc.* ...; **wie dem** ~ **sei** however that may be; (d) (konzessiv) **mag er** ~ **noch so klug sein** however clever he may be; **so oft ich** ~ **anrief** however often I rang; no matter how often I rang; **so sehr er sich** ~ **bemühte** much as he tried; **wenn** ~! never mind

Audienz /au'di̯ɛnts/ *die;* ~, ~**en** audience

Auditorium /audi'to:ri̯ʊm/ *das;* ~**s, Auditorien** (a) (Hörsaal) auditorium; (b) (Zuhörerschaft) audience

Auer·hahn /'auɐ-/ *der* [cock] capercaillie

auf /auf/ 1 *Präp. mit Dat.* (a) on; ~ **See** at sea; ~ **dem Baum** in the tree; ~ **der Erde** on earth; ~ **der Welt** in the world; ~ **der Straße** in the street; ~ **dem Platz** in the square; ~ **meinem Konto** in my account; ~ **beiden Augen blind** blind in both eyes; **das Thermometer steht** ~ 15° the thermometer stands at *or* reads 15°; (b) (in) at ‹*post office, town hall, police station*›; ~ **seinem Zimmer** (ugs.) in his room; ~ **der Schule/Uni** at school/university; (c) (bei) at ‹*party, wedding*›; on ‹*course, trip, walk, holiday, tour*›; (d) **was hat es damit** ~ **sich?** what's it all about? 2 *Präp. mit Akk.* (a) on; on to; **sich** ~ **einen Stuhl setzen** sit down on a chair; **sich** ~ **das Bett legen** lie down on the bed; **er nahm den Rucksack** ~ **den Rücken** he lifted the rucksack up on to his back; ~ **einen Berg steigen** climb up a mountain; **sich** (*Dat.*) **einen Hut** ~ **den Kopf setzen** put a hat on [one's head]; ~ **den Mond fliegen** fly to the moon; **jmdm.** ~ **den Fuß treten** step on sb.'s foot; ~ **die Straße gehen** go [out] into the street; **jmdn.** ~ **den Rücken legen** lay sb. on his/her back; **jmdn.** ~ **den Rücken drehen** turn sb. on to his/her back; **etw.** ~ **ein Konto überweisen** transfer sth. to an account; **das Thermometer ist** ~ 0° **gefallen** the thermometer has fallen to 0°; ~ **ihn!** (ugs.) get him!; (b) (zu) to; ~ **die Schule/Uni gehen** go to school/university; ~ **einen Lehrgang gehen** go on a course; (c) (bei Entfernungen) ~ 10 km **[Entfernung]** for [a distance of] 10 km; **wir näherten uns der Hütte [bis]** ~ 30 m we approached to within 30 m of the hut; (d) (zeitlich) for; ~ **Jahre [hinaus]** for years [to come]; **etw.** ~ **nächsten Mittwoch festlegen/verschieben** arrange sth. for/postpone sth. until next Wednesday; **die Nacht von Sonntag** ~ **Montag** Sunday night; **das fällt** ~ **einen Montag** it falls on a Monday; **wir verschieben es** ~ **den 3. Mai** we'll postpone it to 3 May; (e) (zur Angabe der Art und Weise) ~ **diese Art und Weise** in this way; ~ **die Tour erreichst du bei mir nichts** (ugs.) you won't get anywhere with me like that; ~ **deutsch** in German; ~ **das sorgfältigste/herzlichste** (geh.) most carefully/warmly; ~ **a enden** end in a; (f) (aufgrund) ~ **Wunsch** on request; ~ **vielfachen Wunsch [hin]** in response to numerous requests; ~ **meine Bitte** at my request; ~ **seine Initiative** on his initiative; ~ **Befehl** on command; ~ **meinen Vorschlag [hin]** at my suggestion; (g) (sonstige Verwendungen) **ein Teelöffel ∼ einen Liter Wasser** one teaspoon to one litre of water; **das Bier geht ∼ mich** (ugs.) the beer's on 'me (coll.); **∼ wen geht die Cola?** who's paying for the Coke?; **Welle ∼ Welle brandete ans Ufer** wave upon wave broke on the shore; **jmdn. ∼ Tb untersuchen** examine sb. for TB; **jmdn. ∼ seine Eignung prüfen** test sb.'s suitability; **∼ die Sekunde [genau]** [precise] to the second; **∼ ein gutes Gelingen** to our/your success; **∼ deine Gesundheit** your health; **∼ bald/morgen!** (bes. südd.) see you soon/tomorrow; **∼ 10 zählen** (bes. südd.) count [up] to 10; *s. auch* **einmal 1 a; machen 3 f. 3** *Adv.* (a) (Aufforderung, sich zu erheben) **∼!** up you get!; (zu einem Hund) up!; (b) **sie waren längst ∼ und davon** they had made off long before; (c) (bes. südd.: Aufforderung, zu handeln) **∼!** come on; (d) (Aufforderung, sich aufzumachen) **∼ ins Schwimmbad!** come on, off to the swimming pool!; (e) **∼ und ab** up and down; (hin und her) up and down; to and fro; (f) (Aufforderung, sich etw. aufzusetzen) **Helm/Hut/Brille ∼!** helmet/hat/glasses on!; (g) (ugs.: offen) open; **Fenster/Türen/Mund ∼!** open the window/doors/your mouth!; (h) (nicht im Bett) up. **4 ∼ dass** *Konj.* (veralt.) so that

auf|arbeiten *tr. V.* (a) (erledigen) catch up with ‹*correspondence etc.*›; (b) (studieren, analysieren) review ‹*literature, material*›; look back on and reappraise ‹*one's past, childhood*›; (c) (restaurieren, überholen) refurbish

auf|atmen *itr. V.* breathe a sigh of relief

auf|backen *regelm.* (*auch unr.*) *tr. V.* crisp up ‹*bread, rolls, etc.*›

auf|bahren *tr. V.* lay out ‹*body, corpse*›; **jmdn. ∼:** lay out sb.'s body; **aufgebahrt sein** ‹*king, president, etc.*› lie in state

Auf·bau *der; Pl.* ∼ten (a) *o. Pl.* construction; building; (fig.) building; **den wirtschaftlichen ∼ beschleunigen** speed up economic development; (b) *o. Pl.* (Biol.) synthesis; (c) *o. Pl.* (Struktur) structure; (d) *Pl.* (Schiffbau) superstructure *sing.*

auf|bauen 1 *tr. V.* (a) *auch itr.* (errichten, aufstellen) erect ‹*hut, kiosk, podium*›; set up ‹*equipment, train set*›; build ‹*house, bridge*›; put up ‹*tent*›; **ein Haus neu ∼:** rebuild a house; (b) (hinstellen, arrangieren) lay *or* set out ‹*food, presents, etc.*›; (c) (fig.: schaffen) build ‹*state, economy, social order, life, political party, etc.*›; build up ‹*business, organization, army, spy network*›; (d) (fig.: strukturieren) structure; (e) (fig.: fördern) **jmdn./etw. zu etw. ∼:** build sb./sth. up into sth.; **jmdn. als etw. ∼:** build sb. up as sth.; (f) (gründen) **etw. auf etw.** (*Dat.*) **∼:** base sth. upon sth.; (g) (Biol.) synthesize. **2** *itr. V.* **auf etw.** (*Dat.*) **∼:** be based on sth. **3** *refl. V.* (a) (ugs.: sich hinstellen) plant oneself; (b) (sich zusammensetzen) be composed (**aus** of)

aufbauend *Adj.* constructive ‹*criticism, geological process*›; restorative ‹*medicine*›; nutrient ‹*substance*›

auf|bäumen /ˈaʊfbɔʏmən/ *refl. V.* rear up; **sich gegen jmdn./etw. ∼** (fig.) rise up against sb./sth.

auf|bauschen *tr. V.* (a) billow; billow, belly [out] ‹*sail*›; (b) (fig.) blow up (coll.); exaggerate

auf|begehren *itr. V.* (geh.) rebel

auf|behalten *unr. tr. V.* **etw. ∼:** keep sth. on

auf|beißen *unr. tr. V.* **etw. ∼:** bite sth. open; **sich** (*Dat.*) **die Lippe ∼:** bite one's lip [and make it bleed]

auf|bekommen *unr. tr. V.* (a) (öffnen können) **etw. ∼:** get sth. open; (b) (aufessen können) manage to eat; (c) (aufgegeben bekommen) be given ‹*homework*›

auf|bereiten *tr. V.* (a) (Hüttenw., Bergbau) dress, prepare ‹*ore, coal*›; (b) (Wasserwirtsch.) purify; treat; (c) (Kerntechnik) reprocess

Auf·bereitung *die* ⇒ **aufbereiten a-c:** dressing ; preparation; purification; treatment; reprocesing

auf|bessern *tr. V.* improve; increase ‹*pension, wages, etc.*›

Auf·besserung *die* improvement (*Gen.* in); (von Renten, Löhnen, Gehältern) increase (*Gen.* in)

auf|bewahren *tr. V.* keep; store, keep ‹*medicines, food, provisions*›; **etw. kühl ∼:** store sth. in a cool place

Auf·bewahrung *die* ⇒ **aufbewahren:** keeping; storage; **jmdm. etw. zur ∼ geben/anvertrauen** give sth. to sb. for safe keeping/entrust sb. with the care of sth.

auf|biegen 1 *unr. tr. V.* **etw. ∼:** bend sth. open. **2** *unr. refl. V.* bend open

auf|bieten *unr. tr. V.* (a) (aufwenden) exert ‹*strength, energy, will-power, authority*›; call on ‹*skill, wit, powers of persuasion*›; (b) (einsetzen) call in ‹*police, troops*›

Aufbietung *die;* ∼**: unter ∼ aller Kräfte/seiner ganzen Überredungskunst** summoning up all one's strength/calling on all one's persuasive skills

auf|binden *unr. tr. V.* (a) (öffnen, lösen) untie; undo; (b) (hochbinden) tie *or* put up ‹*hair*›; (c) (auf den Rücken binden) **jmdn./einem Tier etw. ∼:** tie sth. on to sb.'s/an animal's back; (d) (ugs.: weismachen) **wer hat dir das aufgebunden?** who spun you that yarn?; **jmdm. ein Märchen/eine Fabel/etwas ∼:** spin sb. a yarn; ⇒ **auch Bär**

auf|blähen 1 *tr. V.* distend ‹*body, stomach*›; puff out ‹*cheeks, feathers*›; flare ‹*nostrils*›; billow, fill, belly [out] ‹*sail*›; (fig.: vergrößern) over-inflate. **2** *refl. V.* (a) ‹*sail*› billow *or* belly out; ‹*balloon, lungs, chest*› expand; ‹*stomach*› swell up, become swollen *or* distended; (b) (abwertend: sich aufspielen) puff oneself up

aufblasbar *Adj.* inflatable

auf|blasen *unr. tr. V.* blow up; inflate

auf|bleiben *unr. itr. V.; mit sein* (a) (geöffnet bleiben) stay open; (b) (nicht zu Bett gehen) stay up

auf|blenden 1 *tr. V.* **die Scheinwerfer ∼:** switch one's headlights to full beam; **mit aufgeblendeten Scheinwerfern fahren** drive with headlights on full beam. **2** *itr. V.* switch to full beam

auf|blicken *itr. V.* (a) look up; (kurz) glance up; **von etw. ∼:** look/glance up from sth.; (b) (verehrend) **zu jmdn. ∼:** look up to sb.

auf|blinken *itr. V.* (a) ‹*light*› flash; ‹*metal*› glint; (b) (ugs.: kurz aufblenden) flash one's headlights

auf|blitzen *itr. V.* flash; ‹*wave, white-caps*› sparkle

auf|blühen *itr. V.; mit sein* (a) bloom; come into bloom; ‹*bud*› open; (b) (fig.: aufleben) blossom [out]; (c) (fig.: einen Aufschwung nehmen) ‹*trade, business, town, industry*› flourish and expand; ‹*cultural life, science*› blossom and flourish

auf|bocken *tr. V.* jack up

auf|brauchen *tr. V.* use up

auf|brausen *itr. V.; mit sein* (fig.) flare up; **schnell/leicht ∼:** be quick-tempered *or* hot-tempered; have a quick temper

aufbrausend *Adj.* quick-tempered; hot-tempered

auf|brechen 1 *unr. tr. V.* (öffnen) break open ‹*lock, safe, box, crate, etc.*›; break into ‹*car*›; force [open] ‹*door*›. **2** *unr. itr. V.; mit sein* (a) (sich öffnen) ‹*bud*› open [up], burst [open]; ‹*ice [sheet], surface, ground*› break up; ‹*wound*› open; (b) (losgehen, -fahren) set off; start out

auf|bringen *unr. tr. V.* (a) (beschaffen) find; raise, find ‹*money*›; (fig.) find, summon [up] ‹*strength, energy, courage*›; find ‹*patience*›; (b) (kreieren) introduce, start ‹*fashion, custom*›; introduce ‹*slogan, theory*›; start, put about ‹*rumour*›; (c) (in Wut bringen) **jmdn. ∼:** make sb. angry; infuriate sb.; (d) (aufwiegeln) **jmdn. gegen jmdn./etw. ∼:** set sb. against sb./sth.; (e) (Seew.) seize

Auf·bruch *der* departure; (fig. geh.) awakening; **das Zeichen zum ∼ geben** give the signal to set off *or* leave

Aufbruchs·stimmung *die; o. Pl.* **es herrschte allgemeine ∼:** everybody was getting ready to go; **bist du schon in ∼?** are you all ready to go?

auf|brühen *tr. V.* brew [up]

auf|brüllen *itr. V.* let out *or* give a roar; ‹*animal*› bellow

auf|brummen *tr. V.* (ugs.) **jmdm. etw. ∼:** slap sth. on sb. (coll.)

auf|bürden *tr. V.* (geh.) **jmdm./einem Tier etw. ∼:** load sth. on to sb./an animal; **jmdm./sich etw. ∼** (fig.) burden sb./oneself with sth.

auf|decken 1 *tr. V.* (a) uncover; **das Bett ∼:** pull back the covers; **sich im Schlaf ∼:** throw off one's covers; (b) (Kartenspiele) show; **die od. seine Karten ∼** (fig.) lay one's cards on the table (fig.); (**c**) (enthüllen) expose ⟨*corruption, error, weakness, crime, plot, abuse, etc.*⟩; (erkennen und bewusst machen) reveal, uncover ⟨*connections, motive, cause, error, weakness, contradiction, etc.*⟩; (**d**) (für eine Mahlzeit) **etw. ~:** put sth. on the table. **2** *itr. V.* lay the table

Auf·deckung *die* ⇒ **aufdecken 1 c:** exposure; revelation; uncovering

auf|donnern *refl. V.* (ugs. abwertend) tart (Brit.) *or* doll oneself up (coll.); get tarted (Brit.) *or* dolled up (coll.)

auf|drängen 1 *tr. V.* **jmdm. etw. ~:** force sth. on sb. **2** *refl. V.* (**a**) **sich jmdm. ~:** force one's company *or* oneself on sb.; **ich will mich aber nicht ~:** I don't want to impose; (**b**) (fig.: in den Sinn kommen) **mir drängte sich der Verdacht auf, dass ...:** I couldn't help suspecting that ...; **dieser Gedanke drängt sich [einem] förmlich auf** one simply can't help but think so; the thought is unavoidable

auf|drehen 1 *tr. V.* (**a**) (öffnen) unscrew ⟨*bottle-cap, nut*⟩; undo ⟨*screw*⟩; turn on ⟨*tap, gas, water*⟩; open ⟨*valve, bottle, vice*⟩; (**b**) (ugs.: laut stellen) turn up ⟨*radio, record player, etc.*⟩; (**c**) (ugs.: aufziehen) wind up ⟨*musical box, watch, toy, etc.*⟩; **sich/jmdm. die Haare ~:** put one's/sb.'s hair in curlers. **2** *itr. V.* (ugs.) (**a**) (das Tempo steigern) open up; (**b**) (in Schwung kommen) get into the mood; get going

auf·dringlich 1 *Adj.* importunate, (coll.) pushy ⟨*person*⟩; insistent ⟨*music, advertisement, questioning*⟩; pestering *attrib.* ⟨*journalist*⟩; pungent ⟨*perfume, smell*⟩; loud, gaudy ⟨*colour, wallpaper*⟩; **sei nicht so ~!** don't pester so! **2** *adv.* ⟨*behave*⟩ importunately, (coll.) pushily; ⟨*ask*⟩ insistently

Aufdringlichkeit *die*; **~, ~en** (**a**) *o. Pl.* ⇒ **aufdringlich:** insistent manner; insistence; importunity; pushiness (coll.); pungency; (**b**) **die ~en der Männer** the over-familiarity *sing.* of the men

auf|dröseln /ˈaʊfdrøːzl̩n/ *tr. V.* (ugs., auch fig.) unravel

Auf·druck *der;* **~[e]s, ~e** imprint

auf|drucken *tr. V.* **etw. auf etw. (*Akk.*) ~:** print sth. on sth.

auf|drücken *tr. V.* (**a**) press (**auf** + *Akk.* on to); (**b**) (aufprägen, -stempeln) stamp (**auf** + *Akk.* on); **jmdm. einen Kuss ~:** plant a kiss on sb.; *s. auch* **Stempel a;** (**c**) (öffnen) push ⟨*door, window, etc.*⟩ open; squeeze ⟨*pimple, boil*⟩

auf·einander *Adv.* (**a**) on top of one another *or* each other; **die Zähne ~ beißen** clench one's teeth; **etw. ~ pressen/drücken** press sth. together; **~ prallen** crash into each other *or* one another; collide; ⟨*armies*⟩ clash; (fig.) ⟨*opinions*⟩ clash; **etw. ~ schichten** stack sth. up; **~ stoßen** bump together; ⟨*lines, streets*⟩ meet; (fig.) ⟨*opinions*⟩ clash; **~ treffen** hit each other *or* one another; (fig.) meet; (**b**) **~ folgen** follow each other *or* one another; **~ folgend** successive; **~ warten** wait for each other *or* one another; **~ zufliegen** fly towards one another *or* each other

*aufeinander|beißen *usw.:* ⇒ **aufeinander a**

Aufenthalt /ˈaʊfʔɛnthalt/ *der;* **~[e]s, ~e** (**a**) stay; **der ~ im Depot ist verboten** personnel/the public *etc.* are not permitted to remain within the depot; (**b**) (Fahrtunterbrechung) stop; (beim Umsteigen) wait; **[20 Minuten] ~ haben** stop [for 20 minutes]; (beim Umsteigen) have to wait [20 minutes]; (**c**) (geh.: Ort) residence

Aufenthalts-: **~dauer** *die* length of stay; **~erlaubnis** *die*, **~genehmigung** *die* residence permit; **~ort** *der* [place of] residence; **~raum** *der* (einer Schule o. ä.) common room (Brit.); (einer Jugendherberge) dayroom; (eines Betriebs o. ä.) recreation-room

auf|erlegen *tr. V.* (geh.) **jmdm. etw. ~:** impose sth. on sb.; **du solltest dir etwas Zurückhaltung ~:** you should exercise some restraint

auf|erstehen *unr. itr. V.; mit sein* rise [again]

Auferstehung *die;* **~, ~en** resurrection

auf|essen *unr. tr. (auch itr.) V.* eat up

auf|fädeln *tr. V.* **etw. [auf etw. (*Akk.*)] ~:** thread sth. on to sth.

auf|fahren 1 *unr. itr. V.; mit sein* (**a**) (aufprallen) **auf ein anderes Fahrzeug ~:** drive *or* run into the back of another vehicle; **auf etw./jmdn. ~:** drive *or* run into sth./sb.; (**b**) (aufschließen) [**dem Vordermann**] **zu dicht ~:** drive too close to the car in front; (**c**) (in Stellung gehen) move up [into position]; (**d**) (gen Himmel fahren) ascend; (**e**) (aufschrecken) start; **aus dem Schlaf ~:** awake with a start; (**f**) (aufbrausen) flare up. **2** *unr. tr. V.* (**a**) (in Stellung bringen) bring *or* move up; (**b**) (ugs.: auftischen) serve up

Auf·fahrt *die* (**a**) (das Hinauffahren) climb; drive up; **die ~ zum Gipfel** the drive up to the summit; (**b**) (eines Gebäudes) drive; (**c**) (zur Autobahn) slip road (Brit.); access road (Amer.); (**d**) (schweiz.: Himmelfahrt) Ascension [Day]

Auffahr·unfall *der* rear-end collision

auf|fallen *unr. itr. V.; mit sein* (**a**) stand out; **diese Fettflecken fallen kaum auf** these grease-marks are hardly noticeable; **mach es so, dass es nicht auffällt** do it so that it doesn't attract attention *or* so that nobody notices; **seine Abwesenheit fiel nicht auf** his absence was not noticed, **um [nicht] aufzufallen** so as [not] to attract attention; **jmdm. fällt etw. auf** sb. notices sth.; sth. strikes sb.; **er ist mir angenehm/unangenehm aufgefallen** he made a good/bad impression on me; (**b**) (auftreffen) fall (**auf** + *Akk.* on [to]); strike (**auf** + *Akk.* sth.)

auffallend 1 *Adj.* (auffällig) conspicuous; (eindrucksvoll, bemerkenswert) striking ⟨*contrast, figure, appearance, beauty, similarity*⟩. **2** *adv.* (auffällig) conspicuously; (eindrucksvoll, bemerkenswert) ⟨*contrast, differ*⟩ strikingly; **stimmt ~!** (scherzh.) you're so right!

auf·fällig 1 *Adj.* conspicuous; garish, loud ⟨*colour*⟩; **eine recht ~e Erscheinung sein** have a most striking appearance. **2** *adv.* conspicuously; **sich ~ kleiden** dress showily

auf|falten *tr. V.* fold open; unfold

auf|fangen *unr. tr. V.* (**a**) catch; (**b**) (aufnehmen, sammeln) collect; collect, catch ⟨*liquid*⟩

Auffang·lager *das* reception camp

auf|fassen *tr. V.* (**a**) (ansehen als) **etw. als etw. ~:** see *or* regard sth. as sth.; **etw. als Scherz/Kompliment** *usw.* **~:** take sth. as a joke/compliment *etc.;* **etw. persönlich/falsch ~:** take sth. personally/misunderstand sth.; (**b**) (begreifen) grasp; comprehend

Auf·fassung *die* view; (Begriff) conception; **nach meiner ~:** in my view; **der ~ sein, dass ...:** take the view that ...; be of the opinion that ...

Auffassungs-: **~gabe** *die*, **~vermögen** *das* powers *pl.* of comprehension

auffindbar *Adj.* findable; **es ist nirgends/nicht ~:** it's nowhere to be found/it can't be *or* isn't to be found; **schwer/leicht ~ sein** be hard/easy to find

auf|finden *unr. tr. V.* find

auf|fischen *tr. V.* (ugs.) fish out (coll.)

auf|flackern *itr. V.; mit sein* flicker up; (fig.) flare up; ⟨*hope*⟩ flicker up

auf|flammen *itr. V.; mit sein* (auch fig.) flare up

auf|fliegen *unr. itr. V.; mit sein* (**a**) (hochfliegen) fly up; (**b**) (ugs.: scheitern) ⟨*illegal organization, drug ring*⟩ be *or* get busted (coll.); **einen Schmugglerring ~ lassen** bust a smuggling ring (coll.)

auf|fordern *tr. V.* (**a**) **jmdn. ~, etw. zu tun** call upon *or* ask sb. to do sth.; **jmdn. zur Teilnahme/Zahlung ~:** call upon *or* ask sb. to take part/ask sb. for payment; **ich fordere Sie zum letzten Mal auf, ...:** I am asking you for the last time ...; (**b**) (einladen, ermuntern) **jmdn. ~, etw. zu tun** invite *or* ask sb. to do sth.; **jmdn. zu einem Spaziergang/zum Mitspielen ~:** invite sb. for a walk/invite *or* ask sb. to join in; **jmdn. [zum Tanz] ~:** ask sb. to dance

auffordernd 1 *Adj.* **mit einer ~en Geste** with a gesture of invitation. **2** *adv.* encouragingly

Auf·forderung *die* (**a**) request; (nachdrücklicher) demand; **nach dreimaliger/mehrmaliger ~:** after three/repeated requests; (**b**) (Einladung, Ermunterung) invitation

---

auf|forsten *tr. V.* afforest; **etw. wieder** ~: reforest sth.

auf|fressen 1 *unr. tr. V.* eat up; (fig.) swallow up ⟨*small business*⟩; eat up ⟨*savings, money, etc.*⟩; **er wird dich [deswegen] nicht [gleich]** ~ (ugs.) he won't *or* isn't going to bite your head off [for that]. **2** *unr. itr. V.* ⟨*animal*⟩ eat [all] its food up; (salopp) ⟨*person*⟩ eat [everything] up

auf|frischen *tr. V.* freshen up; brighten up ⟨*colour, paintwork*⟩; renovate ⟨*polish, furniture*⟩; (restaurieren) restore ⟨*tapestry, fresco, etc.*⟩; (fig.) revive ⟨*old memories*⟩; renew ⟨*acquaintance, friendship*⟩; **sein Englisch** ~: brush up one's English

auf|führen 1 *tr. V.* (a) put on, stage ⟨*play, ballet, opera*⟩; screen, put on ⟨*film*⟩; perform ⟨*piece of music*⟩; (b) (nennen) cite; quote; adduce; (in Liste) list. **2** *refl. V.* behave

Auf·führung *die* (a) performance; (b) ⇒ **aufführen 1 b**: citation; quotation; listing

auf|füllen *tr. V.* (a) fill up; (b) (fig.: ergänzen) replenish ⟨*stocks*⟩; (c) (ugs.: nachfüllen) **Wasser/Öl** ~: top up (Brit.) *or* (Amer.) fill up with water/oil

Auf·gabe *die* (a) (zu Bewältigendes) task; **es sich** (*Dat.*) **zur** ~ **machen, etw. zu tun** make it one's task *or* job to do sth.; (b) (Pflicht) task; responsibility; duty; (c) (fig.: Zweck, Funktion) function; (d) (Schulw.) (Übung) exercise; (Prüfungs~) question; (e) (Schulw.: Haus~) piece of homework; ~**n** homework *sing.*; (f) (Rechen~, Mathematik~) problem; (g) (Beendigung) abandonment; (h) (Kapitulation) retirement; (im Schach) resignation; **jmdn. zur** ~ **zwingen** force sb. to retire/resign; (i) ⇒ **aufgeben 1 b**: giving up; abandonment; dropping; (j) ⇒ **aufgeben 1 e**: posting (Brit.); mailing (Amer.); handing in; phoning in; placing; checking in

auf|gabeln *tr. V.* (salopp) pick up

Aufgaben·bereich *der* area of responsibility

Auf·gang *der* (a) (Mond~, Sonnen~ usw.) rising; (b) (Treppe) stairs *pl.;* staircase; stairway; (in einem Bahnhof, zu einer Galerie, einer Tribüne) steps *pl.;* (c) (Weg) **der** ~ **zur Burg** the path up to the castle

auf|geben 1 *unr. tr. V.* (a) give up; give up, stop ⟨*smoking, drinking*⟩; **gib's auf!** (ugs.) you might as well give up!; why don't you give up!; (b) (sich trennen von) give up ⟨*habit, job, flat, business, practice, etc.*⟩; give up, abandon, drop ⟨*plans, demand*⟩; give up, abandon ⟨*profession, attempt*⟩; (c) (verloren geben) give up ⟨*patient*⟩; give up hope on or with ⟨*wayward son, daughter, etc.*⟩; give up, abandon ⟨*chessman*⟩; **sich selbst** ~: give oneself up for lost; (d) (nicht länger zu gewinnen versuchen) give up ⟨*struggle*⟩; retire from ⟨*race, competition*⟩; **eine Partie** ~: concede a game; (e) (übergeben, übermitteln) post (Brit.), mail ⟨*letter, parcel*⟩; hand in, (telefonisch) phone in ⟨*telegram*⟩; place ⟨*advertisement, order*⟩; check ⟨*luggage, baggage*⟩ in; (f) (Schulw.: als Hausaufgabe) set (Brit.); assign (Amer.); (g) (zur Lösung vorlegen) **jmdm. ein Rätsel/eine Frage** ~: set (Brit.) *or* (Amer.) assign sb. a puzzle/pose sb. a question. **2** *unr. itr. V.* give up; (im Sport) retire; (Schach) resign

auf·geblasen *Adj.* puffed up

Auf·gebot *das* (a) (aufgebotene Menge) contingent; (Sport: Mannschaft) contingent; squad; (an Arbeitern) squad; **ein gewaltiges** ~ **an Polizisten/Fahrzeugen** a huge force of police/array of vehicles; (b) (zur Heirat) notice of an/the intended marriage; (kirchlich) banns *pl.;* **das** ~ **bestellen** give notice· of an/the intended marriage; (kirchlich) put up the banns

auf·gedreht *Adj.* (ugs.) in high spirits *pred.*

auf·gedunsen *Adj.* bloated

auf|gehen *unr. itr. V.; mit sein* (a) ⟨*sun, moon, etc.*⟩ rise; (b) (sich öffnen [lassen]) ⟨*door, parachute, wound*⟩ open; ⟨*stage curtain*⟩ go up, rise; ⟨*knot, button, zip, bandage, shoelace, stitching*⟩ come undone; ⟨*boil, pimple, blister*⟩ burst; ⟨*flower, bud*⟩ open [up]; (c) (keimen) come up; (d) (aufgetrieben werden) ⟨*dough, cake*⟩ rise; (e) (Math.) ⟨*calculation*⟩ work out, come out; ⟨*equation*⟩ come out; 7 **durch 3 geht nicht auf** threes into seven won't go; **seine Rechnung ging nicht auf** (fig.) he had miscalculated; (f) **etw. geht jmdm. auf** (etw. wird jmdm. klar) sb. realizes sth.; (g) **in etw.** (*Dat.*) ~: become absorbed into sth.; ⟨*person*⟩ be completely absorbed in sth.; *s. auch* **Flamme a**

auf|geilen *tr. V.* (salopp) **jmdn.** [**mit/durch etw.**] ~: get sb. randy [with sth.]; **sich** [**an etw.** (*Dat.*)] ~: get randy [with sth.]; (fig.) get worked up [about sth.]

aufgeklärt *Adj.* enlightened

aufgekratzt *Adj.* (ugs.) in high spirits *pred.*

auf·gelegt *Adj.* **gut/schlecht/heiter** *usw.* ~ **sein** be in a good/bad/cheerful *etc.* mood; **zu etw.** ~ **sein** be in the mood for sth.; **dazu** ~ **sein, etw. zu tun** be in the mood to do sth.

auf·gelöst *Adj.* distraught; *s. auch* **Träne**

aufgeräumt *Adj.* jovial

aufgeregt 1 *Adj.* excited; (beunruhigt) agitated. **2** *adv.* excitedly; (beunruhigt) agitatedly

Aufgeregtheit *die;* ~: excitement; agitation; (Nervosität) agitation

auf·geschlossen *Adj.* open-minded (**gegenüber** as regards, about); (interessiert, empfänglich) receptive, open (*Dat.*, **für** to); (mitteilsam) communicative; (zugänglich) approachable

Auf·geschlossenheit *die* ⇒ **aufgeschlossen**: openmindedness; receptiveness; openness; communicativeness; approachableness

auf·geschmissen *Adj.* (ugs.) **in** [**ganz schön**] ~ **sein** be [right] up the creek (sl.); be in a [real] fix

aufgeweckt *Adj.* bright; sharp

Aufgewecktheit *die;* ~: brightness; sharpness

auf|gießen *unr. tr. V.* make, brew [up] ⟨*tea*⟩; make ⟨*coffee*⟩

auf|gliedern *tr. V.* subdivide, break down, split up (**in** + *Akk.* into)

Auf·gliederung *die* subdivision; breakdown

auf|greifen *unr. tr. V.* (a) (festnehmen) pick up; (b) (sich befassen mit) take *or* pick up ⟨*subject, suggestion*⟩

auf·grund 1 *Präp. mit Gen.* on the basis *or* strength of. **2** *Adv.* ~ **von** on the basis *or* strength of

Auf·guss, *Auf·guß *der* infusion; (fig.) rehash

auf|haben (ugs.) **1** *unr. tr. V.* (a) (aufgesetzt haben) have on; wear; (b) (geöffnet haben) have ⟨*zip*⟩ undone; have ⟨*door, window, jacket, blouse*⟩ open; **die Augen** ~: have one's eyes open; (c) (aufbekommen haben) have got ⟨*cupboard, case, safe, etc.*⟩ open; have got ⟨*knot, zip*⟩ undone; (d) (für die Schule) **etw.** ~: have sth. as homework; **viel/wenig** ~: have a lot of/not have much homework; (e) (aufgegessen haben) have eaten up *or* finished. **2** *unr. itr. V.* ⟨*shop, office*⟩ be open; **wir haben bis 17.30 auf** we are open until 5.30 p.m.

auf|halsen /'aufhalzn/ *tr. V.* (ugs.) **jmdm./sich etw.** ~: saddle sb./oneself with sth.

auf|halten 1 *unr. tr. V.* (a) (anhalten) halt; halt, check ⟨*inflation, advance, rise in unemployment*⟩; **jmdn. an der Grenze** ~: hold sb. up at the border; (b) (stören) hold up; (c) (geöffnet halten) hold ⟨*sack, door, etc.*⟩ open; **die Augen** [**und Ohren**] ~: keep one's eyes [and ears] open; **die Hand** ~ (auch fig.) hold out one's hand. **2** *unr. refl. V.* (a) (sich befassen) **sich mit jmdm./etw.** ~: spend [a long] time on sb./sth.; **sich bei etw.** ~: linger over sth.; (b) (sich befinden) be; (verweilen) stay; **tagsüber hielt er sich im Museum auf** he spent the day in the museum

auf|hängen 1 *tr. V.* (a) hang up; hang ⟨*picture, curtains*⟩; (b) (erhängen) hang (**an** + *Dat.* from). **2** *refl. V.* hang oneself

Aufhänger *der;* ~**s**, ~ (a) (Schlaufe) loop; (b) (fig.: äußerer Anlass) peg

auf|häufen 1 *tr. V.* pile up; (fig.) amass ⟨*treasure, riches*⟩. **2** *refl. V.* (auch fig.) pile up; accumulate

auf|heben *unr. tr. V.* (a) pick up; (b) (aufbewahren) keep; preserve; **gut/schlecht aufgehoben sein** be/not be in good hands (**bei** with); (c) (abschaffen) abolish; repeal ⟨*law*⟩; rescind, revoke ⟨*order, instruction*⟩; cancel ⟨*contract*⟩; lift ⟨*ban, prohibition, blockade, siege, martial law*⟩; (d) (ausgleichen) cancel out; neutralize, cancel ⟨*effect*⟩; **sich** [**gegenseitig**] ~: cancel each other out

Aufheben *das;* ~**s** **in viel** ~[**s**]/**kein** ~ **von jmdm./ etw. machen** make a great fuss/not make any fuss about sb./sth.

Auf·hebung *die* (a) ⇒ **aufheben c**: abolition; repeal; rescindment; revocation; cancellation; lifting; (b) ⇒ **aufheben e**: closure; lifting

Aufhebungs·vertrag *der* agreement to terminate a/ the contract

auf|heitern 1 *tr. V.* cheer up. 2 *refl. V.* (a) ⟨*mood, face, expression*⟩ brighten; (b) ⟨*weather*⟩ clear *or* brighten up; ⟨*sky*⟩ brighten

Aufheiterung *die;* ~, ~**en** (a) cheering up; (b) (des Wetters) bright period

auf|heizen 1 *tr. V.* heat [up]; (fig.) inflame ⟨*tensions, conflict*⟩; fuel ⟨*mistrust*⟩. 2 *refl. V.* heat up

auf|hellen 1 *tr. V.* (a) brighten; lighten ⟨*hair, shadow, darkness*⟩; (b) (klären) shed *or* cast *or* throw light on. 2 *refl. V.* ⟨*sky, face, expression*⟩ brighten; ⟨*hair*⟩ turn *or* go lighter; ⟨*day, weather*⟩ brighten [up]

auf|hetzen *tr. V.* incite; **jmdn. zur Meuterei/zu Gewalttaten** ~: incite to mutiny/violence

auf|holen 1 *tr. V.* make up ⟨*time, delay*⟩. 2 *itr. V.* catch up; ⟨*train*⟩ make up time; ⟨*athlete, competitor*⟩ make up ground; (Zeit ~) make up time

auf|horchen *itr. V.* prick up one's ears; **jmdn.** ~ **lassen** (fig.) make sb. [sit up and] take notice

auf|hören *itr. V.* stop; ⟨*friendship*⟩ end; (ugs.: das Arbeitsverhältnis aufgeben) finish; **das muss** ~! this has got to stop!; **da hört [sich] doch alles auf!** (ugs.) that really is the limit! (coll.); **es hat aufgehört zu schneien** it's stopped snowing; **[damit]** ~, **etw. zu tun** stop doing sth.; **nicht [damit]** ~, **etw. zu tun** keep on doing sth.; **hört mit dem Lärm/Unsinn auf** stop that noise/nonsense

auf|kaufen *tr. V.* buy up

auf|keimen *itr. V.; mit sein* sprout; (fig.) ⟨*suspicion, doubt, fear, longing, reluctance*⟩ begin to grow; ⟨*hope, passion, love, sympathy*⟩ burgeon

auf|klappen *tr. V.* open [up] ⟨*suitcase, trunk*⟩; fold back ⟨*car hood*⟩; open ⟨*window, door, book, knife*⟩

auf|klären 1 *tr. V.* (a) (klären) clear up ⟨*matter, mystery, question, misunderstanding, error, confusion*⟩; solve ⟨*crime, problem*⟩; elucidate, explain ⟨*event, incident, cause*⟩; resolve ⟨*contradiction, disagreement*⟩; (b) *auch itr.* (auch scherzh.: informieren) enlighten; **jmdn. über jmdn./etw.** ~: enlighten sb. about sb./sth.; **jmdn. [darüber]** ~, **wie .../ was ...**: enlighten sb. how .../what ...; (c) (sexualkundlich) **ein Kind** ~: tell a child the facts of life; **aufgeklärt sein** know the facts of life. 2 *refl. V.* (a) (sich klären) ⟨*misunderstanding, mystery*⟩ be cleared up; (b) (sich aufhellen) ⟨*weather*⟩ clear up; brighten [up]; ⟨*sky*⟩ clear, brighten

aufklärerisch 1 *Adj.* ⟨*mission, intention*⟩ to instruct and inform. 2 *adv.* ~ **wirken** instruct and inform

Auf·klärung *die o. Pl.* (a) ⇒ **aufklären 1 a**: clearing up; solution; elucidation; explanation; resolution; (b) (auch scherzh.: Information) enlightenment; (c) **die** ~ **der Kinder** (über Sexualität); telling the children the facts of life; (d) **die** ~ (hist.) the Enlightenment

auf|kleben *tr. V.* stick on; (mit Kleister) paste on; (mit Klebstoff, Leim) stick *or* glue on

Auf·kleber *der* sticker

auf|knacken *tr. V.* crack [open]

auf|knöpfen *tr. V.* unbutton; undo

auf|knoten *tr. V.* untie, undo

auf|knüpfen (ugs.) 1 *tr. V.* string up (coll.). 2 *refl. V.* hang oneself

auf|kochen 1 *tr. V.* bring to the boil. 2 *itr. V. mit sein* come to the boil; **etw.** ~ **lassen** bring sth. to the boil

auf|kommen *unr. itr. V.; mit sein* (a) (entstehen) ⟨*wind*⟩ spring up; ⟨*storm, gale*⟩ blow up; ⟨*fog*⟩ come down; ⟨*rumour*⟩ start; ⟨*suspicion, doubt, feeling*⟩ arise; ⟨*fashion, style, invention*⟩ come in; ⟨*boredom*⟩ set in; ⟨*mood, atmosphere*⟩ develop; **etw.** ~ **lassen** give rise to sth.; (b) ~ **für** (bezahlen) bear, pay ⟨*costs*⟩; pay for ⟨*damage*⟩; pay, defray ⟨*expenses*⟩; be liable for ⟨*debts*⟩; stand ⟨*loss*⟩; **für jmdn.** ~: pay for sb.'s upkeep; (c) ~ **für** (verantwortlich sein für) be responsible for; (d) (auftreffen) land

Aufkommen *das;* ~**s**, ~ (Wirtsch.) revenue (**aus** from)

auf|kratzen *tr. V.* (a) (öffnen) scratch open ⟨*wound, sore*⟩; (b) (verletzen) scratch

auf|krempeln *tr. V.* roll up ⟨*sleeves, trousers*⟩; **jmdm./ sich die Ärmel** ~: roll up sb.'s/one's sleeves

auf|kreuzen *itr. V.; mit sein* (ugs.: erscheinen) turn up

auf|kriegen (ugs.) ⇒ **aufbekommen**

auf|kündigen *tr. V.* terminate ⟨*lease, contract*⟩; cancel ⟨*subscription, membership*⟩; foreclose ⟨*mortgage*⟩; **jmdm. die Freundschaft/den Gehorsam** ~ (geh.) break off one's friendship with sb./refuse sb. further obedience

Aufl. *Abk.* **Auflage** ed.

auf|lachen *itr. V.* give a laugh; laugh; (schallend) burst out laughing

auf|laden 1 *unr. tr.* (*auch itr.*) *V.* (a) load (**auf** + *Akk.* on [to]); **jmdm. etw.** ~ (ugs., fig.) load sb. with sth.; (b) charge [up] ⟨*battery*⟩; put ⟨*battery*⟩ on charge; **etw. wieder** ~: recharge sth. 2 *unr. refl.* ⟨*battery*⟩ charge, become charged; **sich wieder** ~: recharge; become recharged

Auf·lage *die* (a) (Buchw.) edition; (gedruckte ~ einer Zeitung) print run; (verkaufte ~ einer Zeitung) circulation; (b) (bes. Rechtsw.: Verpflichtung) condition; **mit der** ~, **etw. zu tun** with the condition that *or* on condition that one does sth.; **[es] jmdm. zur** ~ **machen, dass ...**: impose on sb. the condition that ...

Auflagen·höhe *die* (Buchw.) number of copies printed; (einer Zeitung) circulation

auf|lassen *unr. tr. V.* (ugs.) (a) (offenlassen) leave open; (b) (aufbehalten) keep on ⟨*hat etc.*⟩

auf|lauern *itr. V.* **jmdm.** ~: lie in wait for sb.; (um ihn zu überfallen) waylay sb.

Auf·lauf *der* (a) (Menschen~) crowd; (b) (Speise) soufflé

auf|laufen *unr. itr. V.; mit sein* (a) (Seemannsspr.) run aground (**auf** + *Akk.* on); (b) (Sport) **auf jmdn.** ~: run into sb.; **jmdn.** ~ **lassen** bodycheck sb.; (fig. ugs.) put paid to sb.'s [little] plans; (c) (sich ansammeln) accumulate

Auflauf·form *die* baking dish; (für Eierspeisen) soufflé dish

auf|leben *itr. V.; mit sein* revive; (fig.: wieder munter werden) come to life; liven up; **etw.** ~ **lassen** revive sth.

auf|lecken *tr. V.* lap up

auf|legen 1 *tr. V.* (a) put on; **noch ein Gedeck** ~: set another place; **den Hörer** ~: put down the receiver; (b) (Buchw.) publish; **ein Buch neu** *od.* **wieder** ~: bring out a new edition of a book; (nachdrucken) reprint a book. 2 *itr. V.* (den Hörer ~) hang up; ring off (Brit.); (b) (salopp) deejay (coll.)

auf|lehnen *refl. V.* **sich gegen jmdn./etw.** ~: rebel *or* revolt against sb./sth.

Auflehnung *die;* ~, ~**en** rebellion; revolt

auf|lesen *unr. tr. V.* pick up; gather [up]; (fig. ugs.) pick up, catch ⟨*germ, disease, illness*⟩

auf|leuchten *itr. V.; auch mit sein* light up; (für kurze Zeit) flash; ⟨*brake light*⟩ come on; (fig.) ⟨*eyes, face*⟩ light up

auf|liegen *unr. itr. V.* lie; rest

auf|listen *tr. V.* list

auf|lockern 1 *tr. V.* break up, loosen ⟨*soil*⟩; loosen ⟨*stuffing, hair*⟩; (fig.) introduce some variety into ⟨*landscape, lesson, lecture*⟩; relieve, break up ⟨*pattern, façade*⟩; make ⟨*mood, atmosphere, evening*⟩ more relaxed. 2 *refl. V.* ⟨*cloud*⟩ break

Auf·lockerung *die* ⇒ **auflockern 1**: breaking up; loosening; relieving; breaking up; **zur** ~ **des Vortrags** to introduce some variety into the lecture; **zur** ~ **der Stimmung/des Abends** to make the mood/evening more relaxed

auf|lodern *itr. V.; mit sein* (geh.) ⟨*fire*⟩ blaze *or* flare up; ⟨*flames*⟩ leap up; (fig.) ⟨*jealousy, hatred, anger, passion*⟩ flare up

auflösbar *Adj.* soluble; solvable, solvable ⟨*equation, problem*⟩

auf|lösen 1 *tr. V.* dissolve; resolve ⟨*difficulty, contradiction*⟩; solve ⟨*puzzle, equation*⟩; break off ⟨*engagement*⟩; terminate, cancel ⟨*arrangement, contract,* *agreement*〉; dissolve, disband 〈*organization*〉; break up 〈*household*〉. **2** *refl. V.* **(a)** dissolve **(in** + *Akk.* into); 〈*parliament*〉 dissolve itself; 〈*crowd, demonstration*〉 break up; 〈*fog, mist*〉 disperse, lift; 〈*cloud*〉 break up; 〈*empire, kingdom, social order*〉 disintegrate; **(b)** (sich aufklären) 〈*misunderstanding, difficulty, contradiction*〉 be resolved; 〈*puzzle, equation*〉 be solved

Auf·lösung *die* **(a)** ⇒ **auflösen 1:** dissolving; resolution; solution; breaking off; termination; cancellation; dissolution; disbandment; removal; **(b)** ⇒ **auflösen 2 a:** dissolving; dispersing; lifting; breaking up; disintegration; **(c)** (Verstörtheit) distraction

auf|machen 1 *tr. V.* **(a)** (öffnen) open; undo 〈*button, knot*〉; open, undo 〈*parcel, packet*〉; **(b)** (ugs.: eröffnen) open [up] 〈*shop, theatre, business, etc.*〉; **(c)** (gestalten) get up; present. **2** *itr. V.* **(a)** (geöffnet werden) 〈*shop, office, etc.*〉 open; **(b)** (ugs.: die Tür öffnen) open up; open the door; **jmdm. ~:** open the door to sb.; **mach auf!** open up!; **(c)** (ugs.: eröffnet werden) 〈*shop, business*〉 open [up]. **3** *refl. V.* (aufbrechen) set out; start [out]

Auf·macher *der* (Zeitungsw.) (Schlagzeile) lead headline; (Bild) main front-page photograph

Aufmachung *die;* ~, ~**en** presentation; (Kleidung) get-up; **ein Buch in ansprechender ~:** an attractively presented book

auf|malen *tr. V.* **etw. [auf etw. (*Akk.*)] ~:** paint sth. on [sth.]

auf|marschieren *itr. V.; mit sein* draw up; assemble; (heranmarschieren) march up; **Truppen sind an der Grenze aufmarschiert** troops were deployed along the border

aufmerksam 1 *Adj.* **(a)** attentive 〈*pupil, reader, observer*〉; keen, sharp 〈*eyes*〉; **jmdn. auf jmdn./etw. ~ machen** draw sb.'s attention to sb./sth.; bring sb./sth. to sb.'s notice; **jmdn. darauf ~ machen, dass ...:** draw sb.'s attention to or bring to sb.'s notice the fact that ...; **auf jmdn./etw. ~ werden** become aware of or notice sb./sth.; ~ **werden** notice; **(b)** (höflich) attentive; **danke, sehr ~:** thank you, that's very or most kind of you. **2** *adv.* attentively

Aufmerksamkeit *die;* ~, ~**en** **(a)** *o. Pl.* attention; **(b)** (Höflichkeit) attentiveness; **(c)** (Geschenk) **eine [kleine] ~:** a small gift

aufmischen *tr. V.* **(a)** liven up 〈*disco, meeting, city etc.*〉; shake up 〈*organization, political party, etc.*〉; **etw. richtig ~:** give sth. a good shake-up; **(b)** (ugs.: verprügeln) beat up

auf|möbeln *tr. V.* (ugs.) **(a)** (verbessern) do up; **(b)** (beleben) pep or buck up (coll.); (aufmuntern) buck (coll.) or cheer up

auf|motzen *tr. V.* (ugs.) tart up (Brit. coll.); doll up (coll.); soup up (coll.) 〈*car, engine*〉

auf|mucken, auf|mucksen *itr. V.* (ugs.) kick up or make a fuss; **gegen etw. ~:** balk at sth.

auf|muntern *tr. V.* cheer up; (beleben) liven up; pep up (coll.)

Aufmunterung *die;* ~, ~**en** ⇒ **aufmuntern:** cheering up; livening up; pepping up (coll.)

aufmüpfig /ˈaufmʏpfɪç/ (ugs.) **1** *Adj.* rebellious. **2** *adv.* rebelliously

Aufmüpfigkeit *die;* ~: rebelliousness

auf|nähen *tr. V.* sew on; **etw. auf etw. (*Akk.*) ~:** sew sth. on [to] sth.

Aufnahme *die;* ~, ~**n** **(a)** ⇒ **aufnehmen b:** opening; starting; establishment; taking up; **(b)** (Empfang) reception; (Beherbergung) accommodation; (ins Krankenhaus) admission; **bei jmdm. ~ finden** be taken in [and looked after] by sth.; **(c)** (in einen Verein, eine Schule, Organisation) admission **(in** + *Akk.* into); **(d)** (Finanzw.: von Geld) raising; **(e)** (Aufzeichnung) taking down; (von Personalien, eines Diktats) taking [down]; **(f)** (das Fotografieren) photographing; (eines Bildes) taking; (das Filmen) shooting; filming; **(g)** (Bild) picture; shot; photo[graph]; **eine ~ machen** take a picture or shot of photo[graph]; **(h)** (auf Tonträger) recording; **(i)** (Anklang) reception; response (*Gen.* to); **(j)** *o. Pl.* (Absorption) absorption; **(k)** (das Einschließen) inclusion

aufnahme-, Aufnahme-: ~**fähig** *Adj.* receptive (**für** to); ~**fähigkeit** *die; o. Pl.* receptivity (**für** to);

~**gebühr** *die* enrolment fee; ~**prüfung** *die* entrance examination; ~**studio** *das* (Tonstudio) recording studio; (Filmstudio) film studio

auf|nehmen *unr. tr. V.* **(a)** (hochheben) pick up; lift up; (aufsammeln) pick up; **(b)** (beginnen mit) open, start 〈*negotiations, talks*〉; establish 〈*relations, contacts*〉; take up 〈*studies, activity, fight, idea, occupation*〉; start 〈*production, investigation*〉; **(c)** **es mit jmdm. ~:** take sb. on; **es mit jmdm. ~/nicht ~ können** be a/no match for sb.; **(d)** (empfangen) receive; (beherbergen) take in; **in ein Krankenhaus aufgenommen werden** be admitted to a hospital; **(e)** (beitreten lassen) admit **(in** + *Akk.* to); **jmdn. als Mitglied in einen Verein ~:** admit sb. as a member of a club; **(f)** (einschließen) include; **(g)** (fassen) take; hold; **(h)** (erfassen) take in, absorb 〈*impressions, information, etc.*〉; **(i)** (absorbieren) absorb; **(j)** (Finanzw.) raise 〈*mortgage, money, loan*〉; **(k)** (reagieren auf) receive; **etw. positiv/mit Begeisterung ~:** give sth. a positive/an enthusiastic reception; **(l)** (aufschreiben) take down; take [down] 〈*dictation, particulars*〉; **(m)** (fotografieren) take a photograph of; photograph; take 〈*picture*〉; (filmen) film; **(n)** (auf Tonträger) record; **(o)** (Handarbeit) increase 〈*stitch*〉

auf|nötigen *tr. V.* **jmdm. etw. ~:** force sth. on sb.

auf|oktroyieren /ˈauf|ɔktroaiˌrən/ *tr. V.* **jmdm. etw. ~:** impose or force sth. on sb.

auf|opfern *refl. V.* devote oneself sacrificingly (**für** to)

aufopfernd 1 *Adj.* self-sacrificing. **2** *adv.* self-sacrificingly

Auf·opferung *die* self-sacrifice

aufopferungs·voll *Adj., adv.* ⇒ **aufopfernd**

auf|päppeln *tr. V.* feed up

auf|passen *itr. V.* **(a)** look or watch out; (konzentriert sein) pay attention; **paß mal auf!** (ugs.) (du wirst sehen) you just watch!; (hör mal zu!) now listen; **aufgepasst!** (ugs.) look or watch out!; **kannst du denn nicht ~?** can't you be more careful?; **(b)** **auf jmdn./etw. ~** (jmdn./etw. beaufsichtigen) keep an eye on sb./sth.

Aufpasser *der;* ~**s,** ~, **Aufpasserin** *die;* ~, ~**en** **(a)** (abwertend) spy; **(b)** (Wärter[in], Bewacher[in]) guard

auf|peitschen *tr. V.* whip up 〈*sea, waves*〉; inflame 〈*passions, emotions, senses*〉; inflame, stir up 〈*populace, crowd*〉

auf|pflanzen 1 *tr. V.* **(a)** (aufstellen) set up; **(b)** fix 〈*bayonet*〉. **2** *refl. V.* (ugs.) plant oneself

auf|picken *tr. V.* **(a)** (aufnehmen) 〈*bird*〉 peck up; (fig. ugs.) pick up 〈*expression, idea, piece of information*〉; **(b)** (öffnen) peck open

auf|platzen *itr. V.; mit sein* burst open; 〈*seam, cushion*〉 split open; 〈*wound*〉 open up

auf|plustern /ˈaufpluːstərn/ **1** *tr. V.* ruffle [up] 〈*feathers*〉; puff up 〈*cheeks*〉. **2** *refl. V.* 〈*bird*〉 ruffle [up] its feathers

auf|polieren *tr. V.* (auch fig.) polish up

Auf·prall *der;* ~**[e]s,** ~**e** impact

auf|prallen *itr. V.; mit sein* **auf etw. (*Akk.*) ~:** strike or hit sth.; (auffahren) collide with or run into sth.

Auf·preis *der* extra or additional charge; **gegen ~:** for an extra or additional charge

auf|pumpen *tr. V.* inflate; pump up, inflate 〈*tyre*〉; pump up or inflate the tyres of or on 〈*bicycle*〉

auf|putschen *tr. V.* (abwertend) stimulate; arouse 〈*passions, urge*〉; ~**de Mittel** stimulants; **sich mit Kaffee ~:** drink coffee as a stimulant

Aufputsch·mittel *das* stimulant

auf|quellen *unr. itr. V.; mit sein* swell up

auf|raffen *refl. V.* **(a)** pull oneself up [on to one's feet]; **(b)** (sich überwinden) pull oneself together; **sich dazu ~, etw. zu tun** bring oneself to do sth.; **sich zu einer Arbeit/Entscheidung ~:** bring oneself to do a piece of work/come to a decision

auf|rappeln *refl. V.* (ugs.) **(a)** struggle to one's/its feet; **(b)** (fig.) recover

auf|rauen, *auf|rauhen *tr. V.* roughen [up]; nap 〈*cloth*〉

auf|räumen 1 *tr. V.* **(a)** tidy or clear up; (fig.) sort out; **(b)** (wegräumen) clear or put away. **2** *itr. V.* **(a)** tidy or clear up; (fig.) sort things out; **(b) mit jmdm./etw.** ~ (jmdn./etw. beseitigen) eliminate sb./sth.

Aufräumungs·arbeiten *Pl.* clearance work *sing.*

auf|rechnen *tr. V.* etw. **gegen etw.** ~: set sth. off against sth.

auf·recht 1 *Adj.* **(a)** upright ‹*position*›; upright, erect ‹*posture, bearing*›; etw. ~ **hinstellen** place sth. upright *or* in an upright position; **(b)** (redlich) upright. **2** *adv.* ‹*walk, sit, hold oneself*› straight, erect; **sich kaum noch** ~ **halten können** be hardly able to stand

aufrecht|erhalten *unr. tr. V.* maintain; maintain, keep up ‹*deception, fiction, contact, custom*›

auf|regen 1 *tr. V.* excite; (ärgerlich machen) annoy; irritate; (beunruhigen) agitate; **du regst mich auf** you're getting on my nerves. **2** *refl. V.* get worked up (**über** + *Akk.* about); **nur keine** ~! don't get excited!

Auf·regung *die* excitement *no pl.;* (Beunruhigung) agitation *no pl.;* jmdn. **in** ~ **versetzen** make sb. excited/agitated; **nur keine** ~! don't get excited!

auf|reiben 1 *unr. tr. V.* **(a)** (zermürben) wear down; **(b)** (vernichten) wipe out; **(c)** (wund reiben) **sich** (*Dat.*) **die Hände/Fersen** *usw.* ~: rub one's hands/heels *etc.* sore. **2** *unr. refl. V.* wear oneself out

aufreibend 1 *Adj.* wearing; trying ‹*day, time*›; (stärker) gruelling. **2** *adv.* tryingly; exasperatingly

auf|reißen 1 *unr. tr. V.* **(a)** (öffnen) tear *or* rip open; tear open ‹*collar, shirt, etc.*›; wrench open ‹*drawer*›; fling open ‹*window, door*›; **die Augen/den Mund** ~: open one's eyes/mouth wide; **(b)** (beschädigen) tear *or* rip open; rip, tear ‹*clothes*›; break up ‹*road, soil*›; **sich** (*Dat.*) **die Haut/den Ellbogen** ~: gash one's skin/elbow. **2** *itr. V.; mit sein* ‹*clothes*› tear, rip; ‹*seam*› split; ‹*wound*› open; ‹*clouds*› break up

auf|reizen *tr. V.* excite ‹*senses, imagination*›; rouse ‹*passions*›; (provozieren) provoke

auf·reizend 1 *Adj.* provocative. **2** *adv.* provocatively

auf|richten 1 *tr. V.* **(a)** erect; **den Kopf/Oberkörper** ~: raise one's head/upper body; **jmdn.** ~ (auf die Beine stellen) help sb. up; **jmdn. im Bett** ~: sit sb. up in bed; **(b)** (trösten) **jmdn. [wieder]** ~: give fresh heart to sb. **2** *refl. V.* **(a)** stand up [straight]; (aus gebückter Haltung) straighten up; (nach einem Sturz) get to one's feet; **sich im Bett** ~: sit up in bed; **(b)** (Mut schöpfen) take heart; **sich an jmdm./etw. [wieder]** ~: take heart from sb./sth.

auf·richtig 1 *Adj.* sincere; honest, sincere ‹*person, efforts*›. **2** *adv.* sincerely

Auf·richtigkeit *die* sincerity

Auf·riss, *Auf·riß *der* **(a)** (Bautechnik) elevation; **(b)** (Darstellung) outline

auf|ritzen *tr. V.* **(a)** (öffnen) slit [open]; **(b)** (verletzen) scratch; **sich** (*Dat.*) **die Haut/den Arm** ~: scratch oneself/one's arm

auf|rollen *tr. V.* **(a)** roll up; **(b)** (auseinander rollen) unroll; unfurl ‹*flag*›

auf|rücken *itr. V.; mit sein* (auch fig.: befördert werden) move up

Auf·ruf *der* **(a)** call; **(b)** (Appell) appeal (**an** + *Akk.* to)

auf|rufen *unr. tr. V.* **(a)** jmdn. ~: call sb.; call sb.'s name; **einen Schüler** ~: call upon a pupil to answer; **(b)** *auch itr.* (auffordern) **jmdn.** ~, **etw. zu tun** call upon sb. to do sth.; **jmdn. zum Widerstand/zum Spenden** ~: call on sb. to resist/for donations; **zum Streik** ~: call a strike

Aufruhr *der;* ~s, ~e **(a)** (Rebellion) revolt; rebellion; **(b)** *o. Pl.* (Erregung) turmoil; **jmdn./etw. in** ~ **versetzen** plunge *or* throw sb./sth. into [a state of] turmoil

auf|rühren *tr. V.* stir up

aufrührerisch 1 *Adj.* **(a)** seditious; inflammatory; **(b)** rebellious. **2** *adv.* (rebellierend) seditiously

auf|runden *tr. V.* round off (**auf** + *Akk.* to)

auf|rüsten *tr., itr. V.* arm; **wieder** ~: rearm

Auf·rüstung *die* armament

auf|rütteln *tr. V.* (fig.) **jmdn.** ~: shake sb. up; **jmds. Gewissen** ~: stir sb.'s conscience; **jmdn. aus seiner**

---

*alte Schreibung (vgl. Hinweise auf S. xvi–xvii)

Apathie/Lethargie ~: shake sb. out of his/her apathy/lethargy

aufs *Präp.* + *Art.* **(a)** = **auf das; (b)** ~ **Klo gehen** (ugs.) go to the loo (Brit. coll.) *or* (Amer. coll.) john; **sich** ~ **Bitten verlegen** resort to appeals

auf|sagen *tr. V.* recite

auf|sammeln *tr. V.* **(a)** (aufheben) pick *or* gather up; **(b)** (ugs.: aufgreifen) pick up

aufsässig /'aʊfzɛsɪç/ **1** *Adj.* **(a)** recalcitrant; **(b)** (veralt.: rebellisch) rebellious. **2** *adv.* **(a)** recalcitrantly; **(b)** (veralt.: rebellisch) rebelliously

Auf·satz *der* **(a)** essay; (in einer Zeitschrift) article; **(b)** (aufgesetzter Teil) top *or* upper part

auf|saugen *unr.* (*auch regelm.*) *tr. V.* soak up; (fig.) absorb

auf|schauen (südd., österr., schweiz.) ⇒ **aufblicken**

auf|scheuchen *tr. V.* **(a)** put up ‹*birds, animals*›; **(b)** (ugs.: in Unruhe versetzen) startle

auf|scheuern *tr. V.* chafe; **sich** (*Dat.*) **die Haut/die Fersen** ~: chafe one's skin/heels

auf|schichten *tr. V.* stack up; build [up] ‹*wall, mound, stack, pile*›; pile up ‹*straw*› [in layers]

auf|schieben *unr. tr. V.* **(a)** (verschieben) postpone; put off; **aufgeschoben ist nicht aufgehoben** there'll be another opportunity; there is always another time; **(b)** slide open ‹*door, window*›; slide *or* draw back ‹*bolt*›

auf|schießen *unr. itr. V.; mit sein* **(a)** shoot up; ‹*flames*› shoot *or* leap up; **(b)** (schnell wachsen) shoot up; **ein lang aufgeschossener Junge** a tall gangling *or* gangly youth

Auf·schlag *der* **(a)** (Aufprall) impact; **(b)** (Preis~) extra charge; surcharge; **(c)** (Ärmel~) cuff; (Hosen~) turn-up; (Revers) lapel; **(d)** (Tennis usw.) serve; service; **ich habe** ~: it's my serve

auf|schlagen 1 *unr. itr. V.* **(a)** *mit sein* **auf etw.** (*Dat. od. Akk.*) ~: hit *or* strike sth.; **mit dem Kopf** ~: hit one's head on the ground/pavement *etc.;* **(b)** ‹*price, rent, article*› go up; **(c)** (Tennis usw.) serve; **Sie schlagen auf!** it's your serve. **2** *unr. tr. V.* **(a)** (öffnen) crack ‹*nut, egg*› [open]; knock a hole in ‹*ice*›; **sich** (*Dat.*) **das Knie/den Kopf** ~: fall and cut one's knee/head; **(b)** (aufblättern) open ‹*book, newspaper*›; (zurückschlagen) turn back ‹*bedclothes, blanket*›; **schlagt Seite 15 auf!** turn to page 15; **(c)** **die Augen** ~: open one's eyes; **(d)** (hoch-, umschlagen) turn up ‹*collar, trouser leg, sleeve*›; **(e)** (aufbauen) set up ‹*camp*›; pitch, put up ‹*tent*›; put up ‹*bed, hut, scaffolding*›; **(f)** etw. **auf einen Betrag/Preis** *usw.* ~: put sth. on an amount/a price *etc.*

auf|schlecken *tr. V.* lap up

auf|schließen 1 *unr. tr. V.* unlock; **jmdm. die Tür** ~: unlock the door for sb. **2** *unr. itr. V.* **(a)** **[jmdm.]** ~: unlock the door/gate *etc.* [for sb.]; **(b)** (aufrücken) close up; (Milit.) close ranks

auf|schlitzen *tr. V.* slit open; slash open ‹*stomach, dress*›

auf|schluchzen *tr. V.* give a sob

Auf·schluss, *Auf·schluß *der* information *no pl.;* **über etw.** (*Akk.*) ~ **geben** give *or* provide information about sth.; **jmdm. über etw.** (*Akk.*) ~ **geben** inform sb. about sth.

auf|schlüsseln *tr. V.* break down (**nach** according to)

aufschluss·reich, *aufschlußreich *Adj.* informative; (enthüllend) revealing

auf|schnappen *tr. V.* (ugs.) pick up

auf|schneiden 1 *unr. tr. V.* **(a)** cut open; cut ‹*knot*›; lance ‹*abscess, boil*›; **(b)** (zerteilen) cut; slice. **2** *unr. itr. V.* (ugs. abwertend) boast, brag (**mit** about)

Auf·schneider *der* (ugs. abwertend) boaster; braggart

auf|schnellen *itr. V.; mit sein* leap up

Auf·schnitt *der; o. Pl.* [assorted] cold meats *pl.;* (Käse) [assorted] cheeses *pl.*

auf|schnüren *tr. V.* undo, untie ‹*knot, parcel, string*›; unlace, undo ‹*shoe, boot, corset*›

auf|schrauben *tr. V.* **(a)** unscrew; unscrew the top of ‹*bottle, jar, etc.*›; **(b)** (auf etw. schrauben) screw on (**auf** + *Akk.* to)

auf|schrecken 1 *tr. V.* startle; make ⟨*person*⟩ jump; **jmdn. aus dem Schlaf** ∼: startle sb. from his/her sleep. **2** *regelm., auch unr. itr. V.; mit sein* start [up]; **aus dem Schlaf** ∼: awake with a start; start from one's sleep

Auf·schrei *der* cry; (stärker) yell; (schriller) scream; **ein** ∼ **[der Empörung** *od.* **Entrüstung]** (fig.) an outcry

auf|schreiben *unr. tr. V.* **(a)** write down; **[sich (***Dat.***)] etw.** ∼ (etw. notieren) make a note of sth.; **jmdn.** ∼ ⟨*policeman*⟩ book sb.; **(b)** (ugs.: verordnen) prescribe ⟨*medicine*⟩

auf|schreien *unr. itr. V.* cry out; (stärker) yell out; (schrill) scream

Auf·schrift *die* inscription

Auf·schub *der* delay; (Verschiebung) postponement; **die Sache duldet keinen** ∼: the matter brooks no delay; **jmdm.** ∼ **gewähren** (Zahlungs∼) allow *or* grant sb. a period of grace

auf|schürfen *tr. V.* **sich (***Dat.***) das Knie/die Haut** ∼: graze one's knee/oneself

auf|schwatzen, (bes. südd.) **auf|schwätzen** *tr. V.* **jmdm. etw.** ∼: talk sb. into having sth.; **sich (***Dat.***) etw.** ∼ **lassen** be talked into having sth.

auf|schwingen *unr. refl. V.* **sich dazu** ∼, **etw. zu tun** bring oneself to do sth.; **sich zu einem Entschluss** ∼: bring oneself to make a decision

Auf·schwung *der* **(a)** (Auftrieb) uplift; **das gab mir neuen** ∼: that gave me a lift; **(b)** (gute Entwicklung) upswing; upturn (*Gen.* in); **(c)** (Turnen) swing up

auf|sehen *unr. itr. V.* ⇒ **aufblicken**

Aufsehen *das;* ∼**s** stir; sensation; ∼ **erregen** cause *or* create a stir *or* sensation; **sich ohne großes** ∼ **davonmachen** make off without causing a lot of fuss

aufsehen·erregend *Adj.* sensational

Auf·seher *der,* **Auf·seherin** *die* (im Gefängnis) warder (Brit.); [prison] guard (Amer.); (im Park) park-keeper; (im Museum, auf dem Parkplatz) attendant; (bei Prüfungen) invigilator (Brit.); proctor (Amer.); (auf einem Gut, Sklaven∼) overseer

***auf|sein** ⇒ **auf g, h**

auf·seiten *Präp mit Gen.* ∼ **der Direktion** on the management side

auf|setzen 1 *tr. V.* **(a)** put on ⟨*hat, glasses, mask, smile, expression, etc.*⟩; **etw. [auf etw. (***Akk.***)]** ∼: put sth. on [sth.]; **sich (***Dat.***) etw.** ∼: put sth. on; *s. auch* **Horn a; (b)** (aufs Feuer setzen) put on; **Wasser [zum Kochen]** ∼: put water on [to boil]; **(c)** (verfassen) draw up ⟨*minutes, contract, will*⟩; **(d) jmdn.** ∼: sit sb. up; **(e)** (auf eine Unterlage) set down; put down ⟨*aircraft*⟩; **den Fuß** ∼: put one's foot on the ground *or* down. **2** *itr. V.* ⟨*aircraft*⟩ touch down, land. **3** *refl. V.* sit up

Auf·sicht *die* **(a)** *o Pl.* supervision; (bei Prüfungen) invigilation (Brit.); proctoring (Amer.); **[die]** ∼ **haben** *od.* **führen** be in charge (**über** + *Akk.* of); (bei Prüfungen) invigilate (Brit.); proctor (Amer.); ∼ **führend** in charge *postpos.;* supervising ⟨*authority*⟩; ⟨*teacher*⟩ in charge *or* on duty; **unter [jmds.]** ∼ **(***Dat.***)** under [sb.'s] supervision; **(b)** (Person) person in charge; (Lehrer) teacher in charge *or* on duty; (im Museum) attendant

aufsicht·führend ⇒ **Aufsicht a**

Aufsichts·rat *der* (Wirtsch.) **(a)** (Gremium) board of directors; supervisory board; **(b)** (Mitglied) member of the board [of directors] *or* supervisory board

auf|sitzen *unr. itr. V.; mit sein* **(a)** (auf ein Reittier) mount; (auf ein Fahrzeug) get on; **auf ein Pferd** ∼: mount a horse; **(b) jmdm./einer Sache** ∼: be taken in by sb./sth.

auf|spalten 1 *unr. (auch regelm.) tr. V.* split; (fig.) split [up]. **2** *unr. refl. V.* split

Auf·spaltung *die* splitting; (fig.) splitting [up]

auf|spannen *tr. V.* **(a)** open, put up ⟨*umbrella, parasol*⟩; stretch out ⟨*net, jumping-sheet*⟩; put up ⟨*tennis-net, badminton-net, etc.*⟩; **(b)** (befestigen) stretch, mount ⟨*canvas*⟩ (**auf** + *Akk.* on)

auf|sparen *tr. V.* (auch fig.) save [up]; keep

auf|spielen 1 *refl. V.* **(a)** (ugs. abwertend) put on airs; **(b) sich als Held/Märtyrer** ∼: act the hero/martyr. **2** *itr. V.* (musizieren) play; **zum Tanz** ∼: play dance music

auf|spießen *tr. V.* **(a)** run ⟨*animal, person*⟩ through; skewer ⟨*piece of meat*⟩; (mit der Gabel) take ⟨*piece of food*⟩ on one's fork; (auf die Hörner nehmen) gore; **(b)** (befestigen) pin ⟨*butterfly, insect*⟩

auf|splittern 1 *tr. V.* split up ⟨*party, group, country, etc.*⟩. **2** *refl. V.* ⟨*party, group, country, etc.*⟩ split up

auf|springen *unr. itr. V.; mit sein* **(a)** (hochspringen) jump *or* leap up; **(b)** (auf ein Fahrzeug) jump on; **auf etw. (***Akk.***)** ∼: jump on [to] sth.; **(c)** (rissig werden) crack; ⟨*skin, lips*⟩ crack, chap

auf|sprühen *tr. V.* spray on; **etw. auf etw. (***Akk.***)** ∼: spray sth. on [to] sth.

auf|spulen *tr. V.* wind ⟨*cotton, ribbon, fishing-line*⟩ on to a/the reel *or* spool

auf|spüren *tr. V.* (auch fig.) track down

auf|stacheln *tr. V.* incite; **jmdn. zur Revolte/zum Widerstand** ∼: incite sb. to revolt/offer resistance

Auf·stand *der* rebellion; revolt

auf·ständisch *Adj.* rebellious

Aufständische *der/die; adj. Dekl.* rebel

auf|stapeln *tr. V.* stack up

auf|stauen *refl. V.* ⟨*water*⟩ pile up; (fig.) ⟨*anger, aggression, bitterness, etc.*⟩ build up

auf|stechen *unr. tr. V.* lance, prick ⟨*boil*⟩; prick ⟨*blister*⟩; lance ⟨*abscess*⟩

auf|stecken 1 *tr. V.* **(a) sich (***Dat.***) das Haar/die Zöpfe** ∼: pin *or* put one's hair/plaits up; **(b)** (ugs.: aufgeben) **etw.** ∼: give sth. up; pack sth. in (sl.). **2** *itr. V.* (ugs.: aufgeben) retire

auf|stehen *unr. itr. V.* **(a)** *mit sein* stand up; (aus dem Liegen, aus einem Sessel) get up; **vom Tisch** ∼: rise from the table; **(b)** (offen stehen) ⟨*door, window, etc.*⟩ be open

auf|steigen *unr. itr. V.; mit sein* **(a)** (auf ein Fahrzeug) get *or* climb on; **auf etw. (***Akk.***)** ∼: get *or* climb on [to] sth.; **(b)** (bergan steigen) climb; **(c)** (hochsteigen) ⟨*air, smoke, mist, sap, bubble, moon, sun*⟩ rise; **eine** ∼**de Linie** (fig.) an ascending line; **(d)** (beruflich, gesellschaftlich) rise (**zu** to); **zum Direktor** ∼: rise to the post of *or* to be manager; **(c)** (hochfliegen) go up; ⟨*bird*⟩ soar up; **(f) in jmdm.** ∼ (geh.) ⟨*hatred, revulsion, fear, etc.*⟩ rise [up] in sb.; ⟨*memory, thought*⟩ come into sb.'s mind; ⟨*doubt*⟩ arise in sb.'s mind; **(g)** (Sport) be promoted, go up (**in** + *Akk.* to)

Auf·steiger *der* **(a)** a social climber; **(b)** (Sport) promotion side; (aufgestiegen) newly promoted side

auf|stellen 1 *tr. V.* **(a)** (hinstellen) put up (**auf** + *Akk.* on); set up ⟨*skittles*⟩; (aufrecht stellen) stand up; **(b)** (postieren) post; station; **(c)** (bilden) put together ⟨*team*⟩; raise ⟨*army*⟩; (Sport) select, pick ⟨*team*⟩; **(d)** (nominieren) nominate; put up; (Sport: auswählen) select, pick ⟨*player*⟩; **(e)** (errichten) put up, erect ⟨*scaffolding, monument*⟩; put in, install ⟨*machine*⟩; **(f)** (hochstellen) erect ⟨*spines*⟩; turn up ⟨*collar*⟩; prick up ⟨*ears*⟩; **(g)** (ausarbeiten) work out ⟨*programme, budget, plan*⟩; draw up ⟨*statute, balance sheet*⟩; make [out], draw up ⟨*list*⟩; set up ⟨*hypothesis*⟩; establish ⟨*norm*⟩; prepare ⟨*statistics*⟩; devise ⟨*formula*⟩; **(h)** (erzielen) set up, establish ⟨*record*⟩; **(i)** (formulieren) put forward ⟨*theory, conjecture, demand*⟩. **2** *refl. V.* position *or* place oneself; take up position; (in einer Reihe, zum Tanz) line up; **sich im Kreis** ∼: form a circle

Auf·stellung *die* **(a)** ⇒ **aufstellen 1 a:** putting up; setting up; standing up; **(b)** ⇒ **aufstellen 1 e:** putting up; erection; installation; **(c)** ⇒ **aufstellen 1 c:** putting together; raising; selection; picking; **(d)** ⇒ **aufstellen 1 d:** nomination; putting up; selection; picking; **(e)** (Milit.) ∼ **nehmen** *od.* **beziehen** line up; **(f)** ⇒ **aufstellen 1 g:** working out; drawing up; making out; setting up; establishment; preparation; **(g)** (das Erzielen) setting up; establishment; **(h)** (das Formulieren) putting forward; **(i)** (Liste) list; (Tabelle) table

Aufstieg *der;* ∼**[e]s,** ∼**e (a)** climb; ascent; **(b)** (fig.) rise; **den** ∼ **zum Geschäftsleiter/in den Vorstand schaffen** succeed in rising to the position of manager/rising to become a member of the board of directors; **(c)** (Sport) promotion

Aufstiegs·chance *die* prospect of promotion
auf|stöbern *tr. V.* (a) put up ⟨*birds, animals*⟩; (b) (entdecken) track down; run to earth
auf|stocken *tr. V.* (a) (auch itr.) **ein Gebäude ~:** add a storey to a building; **wir haben aufgestockt** we've added another storey; (b) (fig.) increase ⟨*capital, budget, funds, pensions*⟩; build up ⟨*supplies*⟩
auf|stöhnen *itr. V.* groan; **laut/erleichtert ~:** give *or* utter a loud groan/a sigh of relief
auf|stoßen 1 *unr. tr. V.* (a) (öffnen) push open; (mit einem Fußtritt) kick open; (b) (heftig aufsetzen) **etw. auf etw.** (*Akk.*) **~:** bang sth. down on sth. **2** *unr. itr. V.* (a) belch; burp (coll.); ⟨*baby*⟩ bring up wind, (coll.) burp; (b) *auch mit sein* **jmdm. ~:** repeat on sb.; **das könnte dir übel ~** (fig. ugs.) you could live to regret that
aufstrebend *Adj.* rising ⟨*talent, bourgeoisie, industry*⟩; ⟨*nation, people*⟩ striving for progress; **ein ~er junger Mann** an ambitious and up-and-coming young man
Auf·strich *der* (Brot~) spread
auf|stützen 1 *tr. V.* **die Ellbogen/Arme auf etw.** (*Akk. od. Dat.*) **~:** rest one's elbows/arms on sth.; **mit aufgestütztem Kopf** with one's head resting on one's hands. **2** *refl. V.* support oneself
auf|suchen *tr. V.* call on, go and see ⟨*friends, relatives*⟩; go to, go and see ⟨*doctor*⟩; **die Toilette ~:** go to the toilet
auf|summen, auf|summieren 1 *tr. V.* (DV) sum. **2** *refl. V.* add *or* mount up
auf|takeln /ˈaʊftaːkl̩n/ *refl. V.* (ugs. abwertend) tart (Brit.) *or* doll oneself up (coll.)
Auf·takt *der* (a) (Beginn) start; (b) (Musik) upbeat; anacrusis
auf|tanken 1 *tr. V.* fill up; refuel ⟨*aircraft*⟩. **2** *itr. V.* fill up; ⟨*aircraft*⟩ refuel
auf|tauchen *itr. V.; mit sein* (a) (aus dem Wasser) surface; ⟨*frogman, diver*⟩ surface, come up; (b) (sichtbar werden) appear; (aus dem Dunkel, dem Nebel) emerge; appear; (c) (kommen, gefunden werden) turn up; (d) (sich ergeben) ⟨*problem, question, difficulties*⟩ crop up, arise
auf|tauen 1 *tr. V.* thaw ⟨*ice, frozen food*⟩; thaw [out] ⟨*earth, ground*⟩. **2** *itr. V.; mit sein* (auch fig.) thaw; ⟨*earth, ground*⟩ thaw [out]
auf|teilen *tr. V.* (a) (verteilen) share out (**unter** + *Akk. od. Dat.* among); (b) (aufgliedern) divide [up] (**in** + *Akk.* into)
Auf·teilung *die* ⇒ **aufteilen a, b**: sharing out (**unter** + *Akk. od. Dat.* among); dividing [up] (**in** + *Akk.* into)
auf|tischen *tr. V.* (a) serve [up]; **jmdm. etw. ~:** serve sb. with sth.; (b) (ugs. abwertend: erzählen) serve up ⟨*excuses, lies, etc.*⟩; **jmdm. etw. ~:** serve sb. up with sth.
Auftrag *der; ~[e]s,* **Aufträge** (a) (Anweisung) instructions *pl.;* (Aufgabe) task; job; **in jmds. ~** (*Dat.*) (für jmdn.) on sb.'s behalf; (auf jmds. Anweisung) on sb.'s instructions; **jmdm. den ~ geben** *od.* **erteilen, etw. zu tun** instruct sb. to do sth.; give sb. the job of doing sth.; **einen ~ ausführen** carry out an instruction *or* order; **den ~ haben, etw. zu tun** have been instructed to do sth.; (b) (Bestellung) order; (bei Künstlern, Architekten usw.) commission; **ein ~ über etw.** (*Akk.*) an order/a commission for sth.; **etw. in ~ geben** (Kaufmannsspr.) order/commission sth. (**bei** from); (c) (Mission) task; mission
auf|tragen 1 *unr. tr. V.* (a) **jmdm. ~, etw. zu tun** instruct sb. to do sth.; **er hat mir aufgetragen, dich zu grüßen, er hat mir Grüße aufgetragen** he asked me to pass on his regards; (b) (aufstreichen) apply, put on ⟨*paint, make-up, ointment, etc.*⟩; **etw. auf etw.** (*Akk.*) **~:** apply sth. to sth.; put sth. on sth.; (c) (verschleißen) wear out ⟨*clothes*⟩. **2** *unr. itr. V.* (a) ⟨*clothes*⟩ be too bulky; (b) (ugs.: übertreiben) **dick ~:** lay it on with a trowel (coll.)
Auftrag-: **~geber** *der* client; customer; (eines Künstlers, Architekten, Schriftstellers usw.) client; **~nehmer** *der* contractor
auftrags-, Auftrags-: **~buch** *das* (Kaufmannsspr.) order book; **~gemäß 1** *Adj.* in accordance with instructions *postpos.;* **2** *adv.* as instructed; as ordered; as per instructions; **~lage** *die* (Kaufmannsspr.) situation as regards

---

orders; **~rückgang** *der* (Kaufmannsspr.) falling-off of orders
auf|treiben *unr. tr. V.* (a) (aufblähen) bloat; swell; make ⟨*dough*⟩ rise; (b) (ugs.: ausfindig machen) get hold of; **ein Quartier ~:** find somewhere to stay
auf|trennen *tr. V.* unpick; undo; unpick ⟨*garment*⟩
auf|treten 1 *unr. itr. V.; mit sein* (a) tread; **er kann mit dem verletzten Bein nicht ~:** he can't walk on *or* put his weight on his injured leg; (b) (sich benehmen) behave; **forsch/schüchtern ~:** have a forceful/shy manner; (c) (fungieren) appear; **als Zeuge/Kläger ~:** appear as a witness/a plaintiff; **als Vermittler ~:** act as mediator; (d) (als Künstler, Sänger usw.) appear; **sie ist seit Jahren nicht mehr aufgetreten** she hasn't given any public performances for years; **zum ersten Mal ~:** make one's first appearance; (e) (die Bühne betreten) enter; (f) (auftauchen) ⟨*problem, question, difficulty*⟩ crop up, arise; ⟨*difference of opinion*⟩ arise; (g) (vorkommen) occur; ⟨*pest, symptom, danger*⟩ appear. **2** *unr. tr. V.* kick open ⟨*door, gate*⟩
Auftreten *das;* **~s** (a) (Benehmen) manner; (b) ⇒ **auftreten 1 g:** occurrence; appearance
Auf·trieb *der o. Pl.* (a) (Physik) buoyancy; (in der Luft) lift; (b) (Elan, Aufschwung) impetus; **das hat ihm ~/neuen ~ gegeben** that has given him a lift/given him new impetus
Auf·tritt *der* (a) ⇒ **auftreten 1 d:** appearance; (b) ⇒ **auftreten 1 e:** entrance; (c) (Szene) scene
auf|trumpfen *itr. V.* show one's superiority; show how good one is; **„Na siehst du", trumpfte sie auf** there you are, she crowed
auf|tun 1 *unr. refl. V.* (geh.: sich öffnen) open; (fig.) open up (*Dat.* before). **2** *unr. tr. V.* (ugs.) (a) (entdecken) find; (b) (servieren) **jmdm./sich etw. ~:** help sb./oneself to sth. **3** *unr. itr. V.* **jmdm./sich ~** (ugs.) help sb./oneself (**von** to)
auf|türmen 1 *tr. V.* pile up (**zu** into). **2** *refl. V.* ⟨*mountain range*⟩ tower up; (fig.) ⟨*work, problems, difficulties*⟩ pile up
auf|wachen *itr. V.; mit sein* (auch fig.) wake up, awaken (**aus** from); **aus der Narkose/Ohnmacht ~:** come round from the anaesthetic/faint
auf|wachsen *unr. itr. V.; mit sein* grow up
auf|wallen *itr. V.; mit sein* boil up; **etw. ~ lassen** bring sth. to the boil; **in jmdm. ~** (fig. geh.) ⟨*joy, tenderness, hatred, passion, etc.*⟩ surge [up] within sb.
Auf·wand *der;* **~[e]s** (a) expenditure (**an** + *Dat.* of); (das Aufgewendete) cost; expense; **mit einem ~ von 1,5 Mio. Mark** at a cost of 1.5 million marks; **der dazu nötige ~ an Zeit/Kraft** the time/energy needed; (b) (Luxus) extravagance; **[großen] ~ treiben** be [very] extravagant
aufwändig ⇒ **aufwendig**
Aufwands·entschädigung *die* expense allowance
auf|wärmen 1 *tr. V.* heat *or* warm up ⟨*food*⟩; (fig. ugs.: wieder erwähnen) rake *or* drag up. **2** *refl. V.* warm oneself up
auf|warten *itr. V.* (a) (geh.) **jmdm. mit etw. ~** (anbieten) offer sb. sth.; (vorsetzen) serve sb. [with] sth.; (b) (fig.) **mit etw. ~:** come up with sth.
aufwärts *Adv.* upwards; (bergauf) upwards; uphill; **den Fluss ~:** upstream; **der Fahrstuhl fährt ~:** the lift is going up; **vom Major [an] ~:** from major up; **mit seiner Gesundheit/dem Geschäft geht es ~:** his health is improving/the firm is doing better; **mit ihm geht es ~:** he's doing better; (gesundheitlich) he's getting better
-aufwärts *adv.* ▶193 | **rhein~/fluss~:** up the Rhine/up river *or* upstream
Aufwärts·entwicklung *die* upward trend
***aufwärts|gehen** ⇒ **aufwärts**
Auf·wartung *die:* **jmdm. seine ~ machen** (geh.) make *or* pay a courtesy call on sb.
auf|wecken *tr. V.* wake [up]; waken; (fig.) waken
auf|weichen 1 *tr. V.* soften; **den Boden ~:** make the ground soft *or* sodden. **2** *itr. V.; mit sein* become soft; soften up
auf|weisen *unr. tr. V.* show; exhibit
auf|wenden *unr.* (auch regelm.) *tr. V.* use ⟨*skill, influence*⟩; expend ⟨*energy, resources*⟩; spend ⟨*money, time*⟩

auf·wendig 1 *Adj.* lavish; (kostspielig) costly; expensive. **2** *adv.* lavishly; (kostspielig) expensively

auf|werfen *unr. tr. V.* **(a)** (aufhäufen) pile *or* heap up ‹*earth, snow, etc.*›; build, raise ‹*embankment, dam, etc.*›; **(b)** (öffnen) fling open ‹*door, window*›; **(c)** (ansprechen) raise ‹*problem, question*›

auf|werten *tr. V.* **(a)** *auch itr.* revalue; **(b)** (fig.) enhance the status of; enhance ‹*standing, reputation, status*›

auf|wickeln *tr. V.* wind up; (ohne Rolle, Spule) roll *or* coil up; **jmdm./sich die Haare ~:** put sb.'s/one's hair in curlers

auf|wiegeln /ˈaʊfviːgl̩n/ *tr. V.* (abwertend) incite; stir up (**gegen** against); **jmdn. zum Aufstand/Streik ~:** incite sb. to rebel/strike

auf|wiegen *unr. tr. V.* make up for; **die Vorteile wiegen die Nachteile auf** the advantages offset the disadvantages

Auf·wind *der:* **im ~ sein** (fig.) be on the up and up

auf|wirbeln 1 *tr. V.* swirl up; swirl up, raise ‹*dust*›; *s. auch* **Staub. 2** *itr. V.; mit sein* swirl up

auf|wischen *tr. V.* **(a)** wipe *or* mopp up; **(b)** *auch itr.* (säubern) wipe, (mit Wasser) wash ‹*floor*›; *die od.* **in der Küche ~:** wipe/wash the kitchen floor

auf|wühlen *tr. V.* churn up ‹*water, sea, mud, soil*›; (fig.) stir ‹*person, emotions, passions*› deeply; **ein ~des Erlebnis** (fig.) a deeply moving experience

auf|zählen *tr. V.* enumerate; list

Auf·zählung *die* **(a)** enumeration; listing; **(b)** (Liste) list

auf|zeichnen *tr. V.* **(a)** (notieren) record; **(b)** (zeichnen) draw

Auf·zeichnung *die* record; (Magnetband~) recording; **~en** (Notizen) notes

auf|zeigen *tr. V.* (nachweisen) demonstrate; show; (darlegen) expound; (hinweisen auf) point out; highlight

auf|ziehen 1 *unr. tr. V.* **(a)** wind up ‹*clock, toy, etc.*›; **(b)** (öffnen) pull open ‹*drawer*›; open, draw [back] ‹*curtains*›; undo ‹*zip*›; **(c)** (befestigen) mount ‹*photograph, print, etc.*› (**auf** + *Akk.* on); stretch ‹*canvas*›; put on ‹*guitar string, violin string, etc.*›, *s. auch* **Saite; (d)** (großziehen) bring up, raise ‹*children*›; raise, rear ‹*animals*›; raise ‹*plants, vegetables*›; **(e)** (ugs.: gründen) set up ‹*company, department, business, political party, organization, system*›; **(f)** (ugs.: durchführen) organize, stage ‹*festival, event, campaign, rally*›; **(g)** (ugs.: necken) rib (coll.), tease (**mit, wegen** about). **2** *unr. itr. V.; mit sein* ‹*storm*› gather, come up; ‹*clouds*› gather; ‹*mist, haze*› come up

Auf·zucht *die* raising; rearing

Auf·zug *der* **(a)** (Lift) lift (Brit.); elevator (Amer.); (Lasten~, Bau~) hoist; **(b)** (abwertend: Aufmachung) get-up; **(c)** (Theater: Akt) act

auf|zwingen *unr. tr. V.* **jmdm. etw. ~:** force sth. [up]on sb.; **jmdm. seinen Willen ~:** impose one's will [up]on sb.

Aug·apfel *der* eyeball; **er hütet es wie seinen ~:** it's his most treasured possession

Auge /ˈaʊgə/ *das;* **~s, ~n (a)** ▶ 326 ɪ eye; **gute/schlechte ~n haben** have good/poor eyesight; **auf einem ~ blind sein** be blind in one eye; (fig.) have a one-sided view; **mit bloßem ~:** with the naked eye; **ihm fallen die ~n zu** his eyelids are drooping; **ganz kleine ~n haben** (fig.) be all sleepy; **mit verbundenen ~n** blindfold[ed]; **etw. im ~ haben** have sth. in one's eye; (fig.: haben wollen) have one's eye on sth.; **das ~ des Gesetzes** (fig.: Polizist) the law (coll.); **ihm/ihr** *usw.* **werden die ~n noch aufgehen** (fig.) he/she *etc.* is in for a rude awakening; **[große] ~n machen** (fig. ugs.) be wide-eyed; **da wird er ~n machen** (fig. ugs.) his eyes will pop out of his head; **ihnen fielen fast die ~n aus dem Kopf** their eyes nearly popped out of their heads; **da blieb kein ~ trocken** (fig. ugs.) everyone laughed till they cried; (es blieb niemand verschont) no one was safe; **ich traute meinen ~n nicht** (ugs.) I couldn't believe my eyes; **ich habe doch hinten keine ~n** (ugs.) I haven't got eyes in the back of my head; **ich kann doch meine ~n nicht überall haben!** I can't be looking everywhere at once; **sie hat ihre ~n überall** she doesn't miss a thing; **ein ~ od. beide ~n zudrücken** (fig.) turn a blind eye; **ein ~ auf jmdn./etw. geworfen haben** (fig.) have taken a liking to sb./have one's eye on sth.; **ein ~ auf jmdn./etw. haben** (Acht geben) keep an eye on sb./sth.; **ein ~/ein sicheres ~ für etw. haben** have an eye/a sure eye for sth.; **ich habe ja schließlich ~n im Kopf** (ugs.) I'm not blind, you know; **jmdm. die ~n öffnen** (fig.) open sb.'s eyes; **jmdm./etw. nicht aus den ~n lassen** not take one's eyes off sb./sth.; not let sb./sth. out of one's sight; **jmdn./etw. aus dem ~ od. den ~n verlieren** lose sight of sb./sth.; (fig.) lose contact *or* touch with sb./lose touch with sth.; **aus den ~n, aus dem Sinn!** (Spr.) out of sight, out of mind; **jmdn./etw. im ~ behalten** (fig.) keep an eye on sb./bear *or* keep sth. in mind; **in jmds. ~n** (*Dat.*) (fig.) to sb.'s mind; in sb.'s opinion; **jmdm. ins ~ od. in die ~n fallen** od. **springen** (fig.) hit sb. in the eye; **etw. ins ~ fassen** (fig.) consider sth.; **think about sth.; einer Sache** (*Dat.*) **ins ~ sehen** (fig.) face sth.; **der Wahrheit/Gefahr ins ~ sehen** (fig.) face up to the truth/danger; **ins ~ gehen** (fig. ugs.) end in disaster; end in failure; **~ um ~, Zahn um Zahn** an eye for an eye, a tooth for a tooth; **unter vier ~n** (fig.) in private; **unter jmds. ~n** (*Dat.*) right in front of sb.; right under sb.'s nose; **vor aller ~n** in front of everybody; **jmdm. etw. vor ~n führen** od. **halten** (fig.) bring sth. home to sb.; **wenn man sich** (*Dat.*) **das mal vor ~n führt** (fig.) when you stop and think about it; **(b)** (auf Würfeln, Dominosteinen usw.) pip; **drei ~n werfen** throw a three; **wie viele ~n hat er geworfen?** how many has he thrown?

äugen /ˈɔʏgn̩/ *itr. V.* peer

Augen-: **~arzt** *der* ▶ 85 ɪ eye specialist; **~aufschlag** *der* [upward] glance; **~binde** *die* blindfold

Augen·blick /*auch:* --ʹ-/ *der* ⇒ **Moment¹**

augenblicklich /*auch:* --ʹ--/ **1** *Adj.; nicht präd.* **(a)** (unverzüglich) immediate; **(b)** (gegenwärtig) present; (vorübergehend) temporary. **2** *adv.* **(a)** (sofort) immediately; at once; **(b)** (zur Zeit) at the moment

Augen-: **~braue** *die* ▶ 326 ɪ eyebrow; **~deckel** *der* (ugs.) eyelid; **~farbe** *die* colour of one's eyes; **~höhe** *die* eye level; **in/auf ~höhe** at/to eye level; **~klappe** *die* eye-patch; **~lid** *das* ▶ 326 ɪ eyelid; **~maß** *das; o. Pl.* **ein gutes/schlechtes ~maß haben** have a good eye/no eye for distances; **jegliches ~maß verlieren** (fig.) lose all sense of proportion; **~merk** *das:* **sein ~merk auf jmdn./etw. richten** od. **lenken** give one's attention to sb./sth.

Augen·schein *der; o. Pl.* (geh.) **(a)** (Eindruck) appearance; **dem ~ nach** by all appearances; **dem ersten ~ nach** at first sight; **(b)** (Betrachtung) inspection; **jmdn./etw. in ~ nehmen** have a close look at sb./sth.; give sb./sth. a close inspection

augen·scheinlich (geh.) **1** *Adj.* evident. **2** *adv.* evidently

augen-, Augen-: **~weide** *die; o. Pl.* feast for the eyes; **~wimper** *die* eyelash; **~winkel** *der* corner of one's eye; **~wischerei** *die* eyewash; **~zeuge** *der* eyewitness; **~zwinkern** *das;* **~s** wink; **~zwinkernd 1** *Adj.; nicht präd.* tacit ‹*agreement*›; **2** *adv.* with a wink

-äugig /-ˌɔʏgɪç/ *Adj.* -eyed

August¹ /aʊˈgʊst/ *der;* **~[e]s** od. **~, ~e** ▶ 119 ɪ August; *s. auch* **April**

August² /ˈaʊgʊst/ *in* **dummer ~:** clown

Auktion /aʊkˈtsi̯oːn/ *die;* **~, ~en** auction

Auktionator /aʊktsi̯oˈnaːtɐ/ *der;* **~s, ~en** /-naˈtoːrən/ auctioneer

Aula /ˈaʊla/ *die;* **~, Aulen** od. **~s** (einer Universität) [great] hall; (einer Schule) [assembly] hall

Aupair·mädchen /oˈpɛːr-/ *das* au pair [girl]

aus /aʊs/ **1** *Präp. mit Dat.* **(a)** (räumlich) out of; **~ dem Bett steigen** get out of bed; **~ der Flasche trinken** drink out of the bottle *or* from the bottle; **(b)** (Herkunft angebend, auch zeitlich) from; **~ Spanien** from Spain; **er kommt** od. **stammt ~ Hamburg** he comes from Hamburg; **jmdm. etw. ~ dem Urlaub mitbringen** bring sth. back from holiday *or* (Amer.) one's vacation for sb.; **~ dem Deutschen ins Englische** from German into English; **(c)** (Veränderung eines Zustandes angebend) **~ der Mode/**

Übung sein be out of fashion/training; ∼ **tiefem Schlaf erwachen** awake from a deep sleep; **(d)** (Grund, Ursache angebend) out of; **etw.** ∼ **Erfahrung wissen** know sth. from experience; ∼ **folgendem Grund** for the following reason; ∼ **Versehen** inadvertently; by mistake; ∼ **Furcht vor** for fear of; ∼ **Spaß/Jux** (ugs.) for fun/a laugh; **(e)** (bestehend ∼) of; (hergestellt ∼) made of; **eine Bank** ∼ **Holz/Stein** a bench made of wood/stone; a wooden/stone bench; **etw.** ∼ **Fertigteilen bauen** build sth. out of prefabricated components; **(f)** (Entwicklung angebend) ∼ **ihm ist ein guter Arzt geworden** he made a good doctor; ∼ **der Sache wird nichts** nothing will come of it; **etwas** ∼ **sich machen** make something of oneself; ∼ **ihm ist nichts geworden** he never made anything of his life. **2** *Adv.* **(a)** (ugs.: vorbei, zu Ende) ∼ **sein** ⟨*play, film, war*⟩ be over, have ended; **wann ist die Vorstellung** ∼**?** what time does the performance end?; **die Schule ist** ∼: school is out *or* has finished; **mit ihm ist es** ∼: he's had it (coll.); he's finished; **zwischen uns ist es** ∼: it's [all] over between us; ∼ **jetzt!** that's enough; ∼ **und vorbei** over and done with; **(b)** (ausgeschaltet, außer Betrieb) ∼ **sein** ⟨*radio, light, etc.*⟩ be off; „∼" (an Lichtschaltern) 'out'; (an Geräten) 'off'; **Licht/Radio** ∼**!** lights *pl.* out!/turn the radio off; **(c)** (nicht brennend) ∼ **sein** ⟨*fire, candle, etc.*⟩ be out; **(d)** **von ...** ∼: from ...; (fig.) **von mir** ∼ (ugs.) if you like *or* want; **von sich** ∼: of one's own accord; **(e)** (außer Haus, Sport: im Aus) ∼ **sein** be out; **(f) auf etw.** (*Akk.*) ∼ **sein** be after *or* interested in sth; *s. auch* **ein²**

Aus *das;* ∼ **(a) der Ball ging ins** ∼ (Tennis) the ball was out; (Fußball) the ball went out of play; **(b)** (fig.) end

aus|arbeiten *tr. V.* **(a)** (erstellen) work out, develop ⟨*guidelines, system, method*⟩; prepare, draw up ⟨*agenda, draft, regulations, contract*⟩; prepare ⟨*leaflet*⟩; **(b)** (vollenden) work out the details of ⟨*plan, proposal, list, lecture, etc.*⟩; elaborate the details of ⟨*picture, drawing*⟩

Ausarbeitung *die;* ∼, ∼**en** **(a)** ⇒ **ausarbeiten a:** working out; developing; preparation; drawing up; **(b)** ⇒ **ausarbeiten b:** working out the details; elaboration of the details

aus|arten *itr. V.; mit sein* degenerate **(in** + *Akk.,* **zu** into)

aus|atmen *itr., tr. V.* breathe out; exhale

aus|baden *tr. V.* (ugs.) carry (fig. coll.) *or* (Brit. sl.) take the can for; take the rap for (coll.)

aus|baggern *tr. V.* **(a)** excavate ⟨*hole, ditch, etc.*⟩; **(b)** (säubern) dredge ⟨*channel, river bed, etc.*⟩

aus|balancieren **1** *tr. V.* (auch fig.) balance. **2** *refl. V.* balance; (fig.) balance out

Aus·bau *der;* ∼**[e]s** **(a)** (Entfernung) removal **(aus** from); **(b)** (Erweiterung) extension; (einer Straße) improvement; **ein** ∼ **des Hauses** an extension to the house; **der** ∼ **der Beziehungen zwischen zwei Staaten** the building of closer relations between two states

aus|bauen *tr. V.* **(a)** (entfernen) remove **(aus** from); **(b)** (erweitern) extend; improve ⟨*road*⟩; (fig.) build up, cultivate ⟨*friendship, relationship*⟩; expand ⟨*theory, knowledge, market*⟩; extend ⟨*one's lead*⟩

aus|bedingen *unr. refl. V.* **sich** (*Dat.*) **etw.** ∼ (etw. verlangen) insist on sth.; (etw. zur Bedingung machen) make sth. a condition

aus|bessern *tr. V.* repair; fix (Amer.); mend ⟨*clothes*⟩; touch up ⟨*paintwork*⟩; **einen Schaden an etw.** (*Dat.*) ∼: repair damage to sth.

Aus·besserung *die* repair

aus|beulen **1** *tr. V.* **(a)** make baggy; **ausgebeulte Knie** baggy knees; **(b)** (von Beulen befreien) remove a dent/the dent/the dents in. **2** *refl. V.* ⟨*trousers*⟩ go baggy; ⟨*pocket*⟩ bulge

Aus·beute *die* yield

aus|beuten *tr. V.* exploit

Ausbeuter *der;* ∼**s**, ∼, **Ausbeuterin** *die;* ∼, ∼**nen** (abwertend) exploiter

Ausbeutung *die;* ∼, ∼**en** exploitation

aus|bezahlen *tr. V.* pay [out] ⟨*sum, wages, etc.*⟩; pay off ⟨*employee, worker*⟩; buy out ⟨*partner*⟩; **er bekommt 2 000 DM ausbezahlt** his take-home pay is 2,000 marks

aus|bilden **1** *tr. V.* **(a)** train; **sich in etw.** (*Dat.*) ∼ **lassen** take a training in sth.; (studieren) study sth.; **sich als** *od.* **zu etw.** ∼ **lassen** train to be sth.; (studieren) study to be sth.; **(b)** (fördern) cultivate, develop ⟨*talent, skill, feeling, etc.*⟩; **(c)** (entwickeln) develop. **2** *refl. V.* develop

Ausbilder *der;* ∼**s**, ∼, **Ausbilderin** *die;* ∼, ∼**nen** instructor

Aus·bildung *die* **(a)** training; **in der** ∼ **sein** be training; (an einer Lehranstalt) be at college; **(b)** (Entwicklung) development

Ausbildungs-: ∼**förderung** *die* provision of [education] grants; (für Berufsschüler, Lehrlinge) provision of training grants; ∼**platz** *der* trainee post; (für Lehrlinge) apprenticeship

aus|bitten *unr. refl. V.* **sich** (*Dat.*) **etw.** ∼: demand sth.; **ich bitte mir Ruhe/mehr Sorgfalt aus** I must insist on silence/that you take more care

aus|blasen *unr. tr. V.* blow out

aus|bleiben *unr. itr. V.; mit sein* **(a)** ⟨*guests, visitors, customers*⟩ stay away, fail to appear; ⟨*order, commission, help, offer, support, rain*⟩ fail to arrive; ⟨*effect, disaster, success, reward*⟩ fail to materialize; (nicht nach Hause kommen) stay out; **es konnte nicht** ∼**, dass ...:** it was inevitable that ...; **beim Ausbleiben der Regelblutung** if a period is missed; **wenn jahrelang der Regen ausbleibt** if the rains fail year after year; **(b)** (ugs.: ausgeschaltet bleiben) stay off

aus|blenden **1** *tr. V.* (Rundf., Ferns., Film) fade out. **2** *refl. V.* (Rundf., Ferns.) **sich [aus einer Übertragung]** ∼: fade oneself out [of a transmission]

Aus·blick *der* **(a)** view **(auf** + *Akk.* of); **(b)** (Vorausschau) preview **(auf** + *Akk.* of)

aus|bomben *tr. V.* bomb out

aus|booten *tr. V.* (ugs.) get rid of

aus|borgen *tr. V.* (ugs.) ⇒ **ausleihen**

aus|brechen **1** *unr. itr. V.; mit sein* **(a)** (entkommen, auch Milit.) break out **(aus** of); (fig.) break free **(aus** from); **(b)** (austreten) **jmdm. bricht der [kalte] Schweiß aus** sb. breaks into a [cold] sweat; **(c)** ⟨*volcano*⟩ erupt; **(d)** (beginnen) break out; ⟨*crisis*⟩ break; ⟨*misery, despair*⟩ set in; **(e) in Gelächter/Weinen** ∼: burst out laughing/crying; **in Beifall/Tränen** ∼: burst into applause/tears; **in den Ruf** ∼ „...." break into the cry, '...'; **in Schweiß** ∼: break out into a sweat; **in Zorn/Wut** ∼: explode with anger/rage; **(f)** (sich lösen) ⟨*hook, dowel, etc.*⟩ come out. **2** *unr. tr. V.* **sich** (*Dat.*) **einen Zahn** ∼: break a tooth

aus|breiten **1** *tr. V.* **(a)** (entfalten) spread [out] ⟨*map, cloth, sheet, etc.*⟩; open out ⟨*fan, newspaper*⟩; (nebeneinander legen) spread out; **ein Tuch über etw.** (*Akk. od. Dat.*) ∼: spread *or* put a cloth over sth.; **seine Ansichten/sein Leben** *usw.* **vor jmdm.** ∼ (fig.) unfold one's views/life story etc. to sb.; **(b)** (ausstrecken) **die Arme/Flügel** ∼: spread one's arms/its wings. **2** *refl. V.* **(a)** spread; **(b)** (ugs.: sich breit machen) spread oneself out

aus|brennen **1** *unr. itr. V.; mit sein* **(a)** (zu Ende brennen) burn out; **ausgebrannte Kernbrennstäbe** (fig.) spent nuclear fuel rods; **(b)** (zerstört werden) ⟨*building, room*⟩ be gutted, be burnt out; ⟨*ship, aircraft, vehicle*⟩ be burnt out. **2** *unr. tr. V.* cauterize ⟨*wound*⟩

Aus·bruch *der* **(a)** (Flucht) escape; (lit. or fig.), breakout (also Mil.) **(aus** from); **(b)** (Beginn) outbreak; **zum** ∼ **kommen** break out; ⟨*crisis, storm*⟩ break; **(c)** (Gefühls∼) outburst; (stärker) explosion; (von Wut, Zorn) eruption; explosion; **(d)** (eines Vulkans) eruption

aus|brüten *tr. V.* **(a)** hatch out; (im Brutkasten) incubate; **(b)** (fig. ugs.) hatch [up] ⟨*plot, scheme*⟩

aus|buchen *tr. V.* (Kaufmannsspr., Bankw.) **etw.** ∼ (streichen) delete sth. from the accounts; (abschreiben) write sth. off; *s. auch* **ausgebucht**

Ausbuchtung *die;* ~, ~**en** bulge

aus|buddeln *tr. V.* (ugs.) dig up

aus|bügeln *tr. V.* (fig. ugs.) iron out ‹*differences, defect*›; make good ‹*mistake*›

aus|buhen *tr. V.* (ugs.) boo

Aus·bund *der:* **ein** ~ **an** *od.* **von Tugend** a paragon *or* model of virtue; **ein** ~ **an** *od.* **von Bosheit** malice itself *or* personified

Aus·dauer *die* staying power; stamina; (Beharrlichkeit) perseverance; [**beim Lernen**] ~/**keine** ~ **haben** have/lack perseverance [when it comes to learning]

aus·dauernd 1 *Adj.* ‹*runner, swimmer, etc.*› with stamina *or* staying power; (beharrlich) persevering; tenacious. **2** *adv.* perseveringly; tenaciously

aus|dehnen 1 *tr. V.* (**a**) stretch ‹*clothes, piece of elastic*›; (fig.) extend ‹*power, borders, trading links*›; expand, increase ‹*capacity*›; (**b**) **etw. auf etw.** (**Akk.**) ~: extend sth. to sth.; (**c**) (zeitlich) prolong; **ausgedehnte Ausflüge/Spaziergänge** extended trips/walks. **2** *refl. V.* (**a**) (räumlich, fig.) ‹*metal, water, gas, etc.*› expand; ‹*fog, mist, fire, epidemic*› spread; (**b**) (zeitlich) go on (**bis** until)

Aus·dehnung *die* (**a**) expansion; (fig.: der Macht, von Beziehungen, Grenzen) extension; (**b**) (zeitlich) prolongation; (**c**) (Ausmaß, Größe) extent

aus|denken *unr. tr. V.* **sich** (*Dat.*) **etw.** ~: think of sth.; (erfinden) think sth. up; (sich vorstellen) imagine sth.; [**das ist**] **nicht auszudenken** it does not bear thinking about

aus|diskutieren *tr. V.* **etw.** ~: discuss sth. fully *or* thoroughly

aus|dörren *tr. V.* dry up; dry up, parch ‹*land, soil*›; parch ‹*throat*›

aus|drehen *tr. V.* turn off

Aus·druck¹ *der;* ~[**e**]**s, Ausdrücke** (**a**) expression; **zum** ~ **kommen** be expressed; find expression; **etw. zum** ~ **bringen** express sth.; give expression to sth.; **einer Sache** (*Dat.*) ~ **geben** *od.* **verleihen** (geh.) express sth.; (**b**) (Wort) expression; (Terminus) term; **du hast dich im** ~ **vergriffen** your choice of words is most unfortunate; **dumm/ärgerlich** *usw.* **ist gar kein** ~: stupid/angry *etc.* isn't the word for it

Aus·druck² *der;* ~[**e**]**s,** ~**e** (Nachrichtenw., DV) print out

aus|drucken *tr. V.* (**a**) (Nachrichtenw., DV) print out; (**b**) (angeben, aufführen) **im Katalog** [**mit 400 DM**] **ausgedruckt** listed in the catalogue [at 400 marks]; **in Abänderung unseres ausgedruckten Programms** in a change to our advertised programme

aus|drücken 1 *tr. V.* (**a**) squeeze ‹*juice*› out (**aus** of, from); squeeze [out] ‹*lemon, orange, grape, etc.*›; squeeze out ‹*sponge*›; squeeze ‹*boil, pimple*›; (**b**) stub out ‹*cigarette*›; pinch out ‹*candle*›; (**c**) (sagen, zum Ausdruck bringen) express; **anders ausgedrückt** to put it another way; **jmdm. seinen Dank** ~: express one's thanks to sb. **2** *refl. V.* (**a**) (sich äußern) express oneself; (**b**) (offenbar werden) be expressed

ausdrücklich /*od.* ˈ--/ **1** *Adj.; nicht präd.* express *attrib.* ‹*command, wish, etc.*›; explicit ‹*reservation*›. **2** *adv.* expressly; ‹*mention*› explicitly

ausdrucks-, Ausdrucks-: ~**los 1** *Adj.* expressionless ‹*face, eyes, etc.*›; unexpressive ‹*style, delivery, etc.*›; **2** *adv.* ‹*look*› expressionlessly; ‹*write, play*› unexpressively; ~**voll 1** *Adj.* expressive; **2** *adv.* expressively; ~**weise** *die* way of expressing oneself

aus|dünsten 1 *tr. V.* give off. **2** *itr. V.* transpire

Aus·dünstung *die* vapour; (Geruch) odour

aus·einander *Adv.* (**a**) (voneinander getrennt) apart; **weit** ~ **stehende Zähne** widely spaced teeth; **etw.** ~ **schreiben** write sth. as separate words; ~! get away from each other!; break it up!; ~ **sein** (ugs.) ‹*couple*› have separated; have split up; ‹*engagement*› have been broken off, be off; ‹*marriage, relationship, friendship*› have broken up; **etw.** ~ **bekommen** be able to get sth. apart; ~ **brechen** break up; **etw.** ~ **brechen** break sth. up; ~ **falten** unfold sth.; **eine Zeitung** ~ **falten** open a newspaper; ~ **gehen** (sich trennen) part; ‹*crowd*› disperse; (fig.) ‹*opinions, views*› differ, diverge; (ugs.) ‹*relationship, marriage*› break up; (ugs.: dick werden) get round and podgy; **zwei Dinge** ~ **halten** keep two things apart; (unterscheiden) distinguish between two things; **ich kann die beiden Brüder nicht** ~ **halten** I cannot tell the two brothers apart; ~ **laufen** run off in different directions; ‹*crowd*› scatter; ‹*paths, roads, etc.*› diverge; ~ **leben** grow apart (**mit** from); **etw.** ~ **nehmen** take sth. apart; dismantle sth.; **jmdm. etw.** ~ **setzen** explain sth. to sb.; **sich mit etw.** ~ **setzen** concern oneself with sth.; **sich mit jmdm.** ~ **setzen** have it out with sb.; **die Vögel/Tiere** ~ **treiben** scatter the birds/animals; **die Menge/Demonstranten/Wolken** ~ **treiben** disperse the crowd/demonstrators/clouds; (**b**) (eines aus dem anderen) **Behauptungen/Formeln** *usw.* ~ **ableiten** deduce propositions/formulae *etc.* one from another

*auseinander|bekommen *usw.:* ⇒ **auseinander a**

Auseinandersetzung *die;* ~, ~**en** (**a**) (Beschäftigung) examination (**mit** of); (**b**) (Streit) argument; (zwischen Arbeitgeber und Arbeitnehmer) dispute; **es kam zu einer** ~ **an** argument/a dispute developed (**wegen** over); (**c**) (Kampfhandlungen, Tätlichkeiten) clash;

*auseinander|treiben ⇒ **auseinander a**

aus|erkiesen *unr. tr. V.* (geh., Präsensformen dicht. veralt.) choose; **zu etw. auserkoren sein** be chosen for sth.

aus·erlesen *Adj.* (geh.) ⇒ **erlesen**

aus|fahren 1 *unr. tr. V.* (**a**) **jmdn.** ~ (im Kinderwagen, Rollstuhl) take sb. out for a walk; (im Auto o. Ä.) take sb. out for a drive *or* ride; (**b**) (ausliefern) deliver ‹*newspapers, parcels, laundry*›; (**c**) (Technik: nach außen bringen) extend ‹*aerial, crane, landing-flaps, telescope, etc.*›; lower ‹*undercarriage*›; raise ‹*periscope*›; (**d**) (abnutzen) damage; **ausgefahrene Straßen** rutted and damaged roads; (**e**) (maximal beschleunigen) drive ‹*car*› flat out. **2** *unr. itr. V.; mit sein* (**a**) (spazieren fahren) go out for a drive; (**b**) (hinausfahren) ‹*boat, ship*› put to sea; ‹*train*› leave, pull out; ‹*car, lorry*› leave; **aus dem Hafen** ~: leave harbour

Aus·fahrt *die* (**a**) (Weg, Straße, Stelle zum Hinausfahren) exit; (Autobahn~) slip road; (**b**) (das Hinausfahren) departure; **bei der** ~ **aus dem Hafen tutete das Schiff** as it left [the] harbour, the ship hooted

Aus·fall *der* (**a**) **zum** ~ **der Zähne führen** cause teeth to fall out; (**b**) (das Nichtstattfinden) cancellation; (**c**) *o. Pl.* (das Ausscheiden) retirement; (vor einem Rennen) withdrawal; (Abwesenheit) absence; (**d**) (einer Maschine, eines Autos) breakdown; (fig.: eines Organs) failure; loss of function; (**e**) (Ergebnis) outcome; result; (**f**) (Einbuße, Verlust) loss; (an Einnahmen, Lohn) drop (*Gen.* in); (**g**) (beleidigende Äußerungen) attack (**gegen** on)

aus|fallen *unr. itr. V.; mit sein* (**a**) (herausfallen) fall out; (**b**) (nicht stattfinden) be cancelled; **etw.** ~ **lassen** cancel sth.; (**c**) (ausscheiden) drop out; (während eines Rennens) retire; drop out; (fehlen) be absent; (**d**) (nicht mehr funktionieren) ‹*engine, brakes, signal*› fail; ‹*machine, car*› break down; **der Strom fiel aus** there was a power failure; (**e**) (geraten) turn out; **gut/schlecht** *usw.* ~: turn out well/badly *etc.*; **die Niederlage fiel sehr deutlich aus** the defeat turned out to be *or* was most decisive

ausfallend *Adj.* [**gegen jmdn.**] ~ **sein/werden** be/become abusive [towards sb.]

Ausfall·straße *die* (Verkehrsw.) main road [leading] out of the/a town/city

Ausfall·zeit *die* (Versicherungsw.) credited service period

aus|fechten *unr. tr. V.* fight out

aus|fegen 1 *tr. V.* (bes. nordd.) sweep out ‹*room etc.*›. **2** *itr. V.* sweep up

aus|feilen *tr. V.* file down ‹*key, cogwheel, etc.*›; file [out] ‹*hole*›; (fig.) polish ‹*speech, essay, etc.*›

aus|fertigen *tr. V.* (Amtsspr.) draw up ‹*document, agreement, will, etc.*›; issue ‹*passport, certificate*›; make out ‹*bill, receipt*›

Aus·fertigung *die* (Amtsspr.) (**a**) ⇒ **ausfertigen:** drawing up; issuing; making out; (**b**) (Exemplar) copy; **in doppelter/dreifacher** ~: in duplicate/triplicate; **etw. in vier** ~**en einreichen** submit four copies of sth.

aus·findig Adv. in jmdn./etw. ~ machen find sb./sth.

aus|fliegen 1 unr. itr. V.; mit sein fly out; **die ganze Familie ist ausgeflogen** (fig. ugs.) the whole family has gone out [for a walk/drive etc.]. **2** unr. tr. V. jmdn./etw. ~: fly sb./sth. out

aus|flippen itr. V.; mit sein (salopp) freak out (sl.)

Aus·flucht die; ~, **Ausflüchte** /-flʏçtə/ excuse; **Ausflüchte machen** make excuses

Aus·flug der outing; (vom Reisebüro o. Ä. organisiert, fig.) excursion; (Wanderung) ramble; walk; **einen ~ machen** go on an outing/on an excursion/for a ramble or walk

Ausflügler /ˈausflyːklɐ/ der; ~s, ~: tripper (Brit.); daytripper; excursionist (Amer.)

Ausflugs-: ~**dampfer** der pleasure steamer; ~**lokal** das restaurant/café catering for [day-]trippers; ~**ziel** das destination for [day-]trippers

Aus·fluss, **Aus·fluß* der (a) o. Pl. outflow; (b) (Med.: Absonderung) discharge; (c) (fig. geh.) product

aus|formen tr. V. shape (zu into); give [final] shape to ⟨text, work of art⟩

aus|formulieren tr. V. formulate ⟨ideas, questions⟩; flesh out ⟨paper⟩ [from notes]

aus|fragen tr. V. jmdn. ~: question sb., ask sb. questions; (verhören) interrogate sb.

aus|fransen itr. V.; mit sein fray

aus|fressen unr. tr. V. [et]was ausgefressen haben (ugs.) have been up to something (coll.)

Aus·fuhr die; ~, ~en ⇒ Export a, b

ausführbar Adj. practicable; workable ⟨plan⟩

aus|führen tr. V. (a) (ausgehen mit) jmdn. ~: take sb. out; (b) (spazieren führen) take ⟨person, animal⟩ for a walk; (c) (exportieren) export; (d) (durchführen) carry out ⟨work, repairs, plan, threat⟩; execute, carry out ⟨command, order, commission⟩; execute, perform ⟨movement, dance-step⟩; put ⟨idea, suggestion⟩ into practice; perform ⟨operation⟩; perform, carry out ⟨experiment, analysis⟩; **die ~de Gewalt** (Politik) the executive power; (e) (Fußball, Eishockey usw.) take ⟨penalty, free kick, corner⟩; (f) (ausarbeiten) **etw. ~:** work sth. out in detail or fully; (g) (erläutern, darlegen) explain

Ausfuhr·land das; Pl. **Ausfuhrländer** (Wirtsch.) (a) (Land, das ausführt) exporting country; (b) (Land, in das ausgeführt wird) export market

ausführlich /auch: ˈ--ˈ/ **1** Adj. detailed, full ⟨account, description, report, discussion⟩; thorough, detailed, full ⟨investigation, debate⟩; detailed ⟨introduction, instruction, letter⟩. **2** adv. in detail; ⟨investigate⟩ thoroughly, fully; **etw. ~er/sehr ~ beschreiben** describe sth. in more or greater/in great detail

Ausführlichkeit /auch: ˈ--ˈ/ die; ~ ⇒ **ausführlich l:** fullness; thoroughness; **mit großer ~:** in great detail

Ausfuhr·sperre die (Wirtsch.) ⇒ **Ausfuhrverbot**

Aus·führung die (a) o. Pl.: ⇒ **ausführen d:** carrying out; execution; performing; **zur ~ gelangen od. kommen** (Papierdt.) ⟨plan⟩ be carried out or put into effect; (b) (Fußball, Eishockey) taking; (c) (Art der Herstellung) (Version) version; (Finish) finish; (Modell) model; (Stil) style; (d) (Darlegung) explanation; (Bemerkung) remark; observation; (e) o. Pl. (Ausarbeitung) **der Entwurf war fertig, jetzt ging es an die ~ des Romans/der Einzelheiten** the draft was ready, and the next task was to work the novel out in detail/to work out the details

Ausfuhr·verbot das (Wirtsch.) export embargo

aus|füllen tr. V. (a) (füllen) fill in ⟨trench, excavation, gravel pit⟩; (zustopfen) fill in ⟨hole, joint⟩; (b) (beanspruchen, einnehmen) take up ⟨space, time⟩; ⟨person⟩ fill ⟨chair, doorway, etc.⟩; (c) (die erforderlichen Angaben eintragen in) fill in ⟨form, crossword puzzle⟩; (d) (verbringen) fill ⟨pause⟩; **seine freie Zeit mit etw. ~:** fill [up] one's free time with sth.; (e) (innerlich befriedigen) jmdn. ~: fulfil sb.; give sb. fulfilment; **ihr Beruf füllt sie ganz aus** she finds complete fulfilment in her work

Aus·gabe die (a) o. Pl.: ⇒ **ausgeben a:** distribution; giving out; serving; **die ~ des Essens erfolgt ab ...:**

lunch/dinner etc. is [served] from ...; (b) o. Pl. (das Aushändigen) issuing; (von Meldungen, Nachrichten) release; (c) (Geld~) item of expenditure; expense; ~**n** expenditure sing. (**für** on); **seine ~n überstiegen seine Einnahmen** his outgoings exceeded his income; (d) (Edition, Auflage) edition

Ausgabe·kurs der (Finanzw.) issue price

Ausgabe·stelle die (Schalter) issuing counter; (Büro) issuing office

Aus·gang der (a) o. Pl. (Erlaubnis zum Ausgehen) time off; (von Soldaten) leave; **zwei Tage ~ haben** ⟨servant⟩ have two days off; ⟨soldier⟩ have a two-day pass; **bis sechs Uhr ~ haben** ⟨servant⟩ be free till six; ⟨soldier⟩ have a pass until six; (b) (Tür, Tor) exit (Gen. from); (c) (Anat.: Öffnung eines Organs) outlet; (d) (Ende) end; (eines Romans, Films usw.) ending; (e) (Ergebnis) outcome; (eines Wettbewerbs) result; **ein Unfall mit tödlichem ~:** an accident with fatal consequences; a fatal accident; (f) (Ausgangspunkt) starting point; **seinen ~ von etw. nehmen** originate with sth.; (g) (Elektrot.) output

Ausgangs-: ~**lage** die initial position or situation; ~**position** die initial position; starting position; ~**punkt** der starting point; ~**sperre** die curfew; (für Soldaten) confinement to barracks; **[eine] ~sperre verhängen** impose a curfew/confine the soldiers/regiment etc. to barracks; ~**stellung** die starting position

aus|geben unr. tr. V. (a) (austeilen) distribute; give out; serve ⟨food, drinks⟩; (b) (aushändigen, bekannt geben; Finanzw., Postw.: herausgeben) issue; (c) (verbrauchen) spend ⟨money⟩ (**für** on); (d) (ugs.: spendieren) **einen ~:** treat everybody; (eine Runde geben) stand a round of drinks (coll.); **ich gebe [dir] einen aus** I'll treat you; (e) (fälschlich bezeichnen) **jmdn./etw. als od. für jmdn./etw. ~:** pretend sb./sth. is sb./sth.; **sich als jmd. od. für jmdn./etw. ~:** pretend to be sb./sth.; (f) (DV) output

ausgebucht Adj. booked up

ausgebufft /ˈausgəbʊft/ Adj. (salopp) (clever) canny; (durchtrieben) crafty

Aus·geburt die (geh. abwertend) (a) (übles Erzeugnis) evil product; **eine ~ der Hölle** the spawn of hell; (b) (Inbegriff) epitome

aus·gedient Adj. (ugs.) worn out, (Brit. coll.) clapped out, (Amer. sl.) beat up ⟨vehicle, engine, etc.⟩

aus·gefallen Adj. unusual

Ausgeflippte der/die; adj. Dekl. ~ (salopp) drop-out (coll.)

aus·geglichen Adj. (a) (harmonisch) balanced, harmonious ⟨structure, façade, etc.⟩; well-balanced ⟨person⟩; **ein ~es Wesen haben** have an even or well-balanced temperament; (b) (stabil) stable; equable ⟨climate⟩; (c) (Sport) even

Ausgeglichenheit die; ~ balance; harmony; **die ~ ihres Wesens/ihre ~:** the evenness of her temperament

aus|gehen unr. itr. V.; mit sein (a) go out; (b) (fast aufgebraucht sein; auch fig.) run out; **jmdm. geht etw. aus** sb. is running out of sth.; **ihm geht der Atem od. die Luft od.** (ugs.) **die Puste aus** he is getting short or out of breath; he is running out of puff (Brit. coll.); (fig.: er hat keine Kraft mehr) he is running out of steam; (fig.: er ist finanziell am Ende) he is going broke (coll.); (c) (ausfallen) ⟨hair⟩ fall out; (d) (aufhören zu brennen) go out; (e) (enden) end; **gut/schlecht ~:** turn out well/badly; ⟨story, film⟩ end happily/unhappily; (f) (herrühren) **von jmdm./etw. ~:** come from sb./sth.; (g) **von etw. ~** (etw. zugrunde legen) take sth. as one's starting point; **du gehst von falschen Voraussetzungen aus** you're starting from false assumptions; (h) **auf Abenteuer ~:** look for adventure; **auf Eroberungen ~** (scherzh.) set out or be aiming to make a few conquests; s. auch **leer a**; **straffrei**

ausgehend Adj.; nicht präd. **im ~en Mittelalter** towards the end of the Middle Ages; **das ~e 19. Jahrhundert** the end or closing years of the 19th century

ausgehungert Adj. starving; (abgezehrt) emaciated

aus·gelassen 1 Adj. exuberant ⟨mood, person⟩; lively ⟨party, celebration⟩; (wild) boisterous. **2** adv. exuberantly; (wild) boisterously; **es wurde ~ gefeiert** there was a lively party going on

Aus·gelassenheit *die* exuberance; (Wildheit) boisterousness

aus·gemacht 1 *Adj.* **(a)** (beschlossen) agreed; **(b)** *nicht präd.* (vollkommen) complete; complete, utter ‹*nonsense*›. **2** *adv.* (überaus) extremely; (ausgesprochen) decidedly

aus·genommen *Konj.* except [for]; apart from; **alle sind anwesend, ~ er** *od.* **er ~:** everyone is present apart from *or* except [for] him; **er kommt bestimmt, ~ es regnet** he's sure to come, unless it rains

ausgeprägt *Adj.* distinctive ‹*personality, character*›; marked ‹*inclination, tendency, disinclination*›; pronounced ‹*feature, tendency*›

ausgerechnet *Adv.* (ugs.) **~ heute/morgen** today/tomorrow of all days; **~ hier** here of all places; **~ du/das** you of all people/that of all things; **~ jetzt kommt er/muss er kommen** he would have to come [just] now [of all times]

aus·geschlafen *Adj.* (ugs.: gewitzt) wide-awake

aus·geschlossen *Adj.; nicht attr.* **das ist ~:** that is out of the question

aus·geschnitten *Adj.* low-cut ‹*dress, blouse, etc.*›; **ein tief/weit ~es Kleid** a dress with a plunging neckline; a very low-cut dress

aus·gesprochen 1 *Adj.* definite, marked ‹*preference, inclination, resemblance*›; pronounced ‹*dislike*›; marked ‹*contrast*›; **~es Pech/Glück haben** be decidedly unlucky/lucky; **ein ~es Talent für etw.** a definite talent for sth. **2** *adv.* decidedly; downright ‹*stupid, ridiculous, ugly*›

aus|gestalten *tr. V.* arrange; (formulieren) formulate

aus·gestorben *Adj.* **[wie] ~:** deserted

aus·gewachsen *Adj.* **(a)** fully-grown; **(b)** (fig. ugs.) real ‹*storm, gale*›; full-blown ‹*scandal*›; utter, complete ‹*nonsense, idiot*›

aus·gewogen *Adj.* balanced; [well-]balanced ‹*personality*›

Aus·gewogenheit *die;* **~:** balance

ausgezeichnet /od. '--'--/ **1** *Adj.* excellent; outstanding ‹*expert*›. **2** *adv.* excellently; **~ Tennis spielen können** be an excellent tennis player; **sie passt ~ zu ihm** she suits him very well indeed

ausgiebig /ˈaʊsɡiːbɪç/ **1** *Adj.* substantial, large ‹*meal*›. **2** *adv.* ‹*profit*› handsomely; ‹*read*› extensively; **von etw. ~ Gebrauch machen** make full use of sth.; **~ frühstücken** eat a substantial breakfast; **etw. ~ betrachten** have a long close look at sth.

aus|gießen *unr. tr. V.* **(a)** pour out **(aus** of); **(b)** (leeren) empty

Ausgleich *der;* **~[e]s, ~e (a)** (von Unregelmäßigkeiten) evening out; (von Spannungen) easing; (von Differenzen, Gegensätzen) reconciliation; (eines Konflikts) settlement; (Schadensersatz) compensation; **einen ~ der verschiedenen Interessen anstreben** strive to reconcile differing interests; **um ~ bemüht sein** be at pains to promote compromise; **als** *od.* **zum ~ für etw.** to make up *or* compensate for sth.; **zum ~ Ihrer Rechnung/Ihres Kontos** in settlement of your invoice/to balance your account; **(b)** *o. Pl.* (Sport) equalizer; **den ~ erzielen, zum ~ kommen** equalize; score the equalizer

aus|gleichen 1 *unr. tr. V.* even out ‹*irregularities*›; ease ‹*tensions*›; reconcile ‹*differences of opinion, contradictions*›; settle ‹*conflict*›; redress ‹*injustice*›; compensate for ‹*damage*›; equalize, balance ‹*forces, values*›; make up for, compensate for ‹*misfortune, lack*›; **~de Gerechtigkeit** poetic justice. **2** *unr. refl. V.* (sich nivellieren) balance out; (sich aufheben) cancel each other out; **das gleicht sich wieder aus** one thing makes up for the other. **3** *unr. itr. V.* (Sport) equalize; **zum 3:3 ~:** level the score[s] at three all

Ausgleichs·tor *das,* **Ausgleichs·treffer** *der* (Ballspiele) equalizer

aus|graben *unr. tr. V.* dig up; (Archäol.) excavate; dig out ‹*trapped person, avalanche victim, etc.*›; disinter, exhume ‹*body, corpse*›; (fig. ugs.) dig up; dig up, unearth ‹*old manuscripts, maps, etc.*›; **eine alte Geschichte wieder ~** (fig.) dig *or* rake up an old story

Aus·grabung *die* (Archäol.) excavation

Ausguck *der;* **~[e]s, ~e (a)** (ugs., Seemannsspr.) lookout post; **(b)** (Seemannsspr.: Matrose) lookout

Aus·guss, *Aus·guß *der* sink

aus|haben (ugs.) **1** *unr. tr. V.* (ausgezogen, abgelegt haben) have taken off. **2** *unr. itr. V.* (Schulschluss haben) have finished school; **wir haben um 12 aus** we finish school at 12

aus|haken 1 *tr. V.* unhook. **2** *itr. V.* (*unpers.*) **es hakte bei ihr aus** (ugs.) (sie begriff es nicht) she just didn't get it; (ihre Geduld war zu Ende) she lost her patience

aus|halten 1 *unr. tr. V.* **(a)** stand, bear, endure ‹*pain, suffering, hunger, blow, noise, misery, heat, etc.*›; withstand ‹*attack, pressure, load, test, wear and tear*›; stand up to ‹*strain, operation*›; **er konnte es zu Hause nicht mehr ~:** he couldn't stand it at home any more; **den Vergleich mit jmdm./etw. ~:** stand comparison with sb./sth.; **es lässt sich ~:** it's bearable; I can put up with it; **es ist nicht/nicht mehr zum Aushalten** it is/has become unbearable *or* more than anyone can bear; **(b)** (ugs. abwertend: jmds. Unterhalt bezahlen) keep; **er lässt sich von seiner Freundin ~:** he gets his girlfriend to keep him. **2** *unr. itr. V.* (durchhalten) hold out

aus|handeln *tr. V.* negotiate

aus|händigen *tr. V.* **jmdm. etw. ~:** hand sth. over to sb.

Aus·hang *der* notice; **einen ~ machen** put up a notice

aus|hängen¹ *unr. itr. V.* ‹*notice, timetable, etc.*› have been put up; **am schwarzen Brett ~:** be up on the noticeboard (Brit.) *or* (Amer.) bulletin board

aus|hängen² 1 *tr. V.* **(a)** put up ‹*notice, timetable, etc.*›; **(b)** take ‹*door*› off its hinges; take ‹*window*› out; unhitch ‹*coupling*›. **2** *refl. V.* ‹*chain*› come undone *or* unfastened; ‹*shutter, door, etc.*› come off its hinges

Aushänge·schild *das; Pl.* **~er** [advertising] sign; advertisement (lit. *or* fig.)

aus|harren *itr. V.* (geh.) hold out; **an jmds. Seite** (*Dat.*) **~:** remain at sb.'s side

aus|heben *unr. tr. V.* **(a)** dig out ‹*earth, sand, etc.*›; dig ‹*channel, trench, grave*›; **(b)** ⇒ **aushängen² 1 b; (c)** (aus dem Nest nehmen) steal ‹*eggs, birds*›; (leeren) rob ‹*nest*›; (fig.) break up ‹*gang, ring, etc.*›; raid ‹*club, casino, hiding place*›

aus|hecken *tr. V.* (ugs.) hatch ‹*plan, intrigue*›; plan ‹*attack*›

aus|heilen *itr. V.; mit sein* ‹*injury, organ*› heal [up]; ‹*patient, illness*› be cured

aus|helfen *unr. itr. V.* help out; **jmdm. ~:** help sb. out

Aus·hilfe *die* **(a)** *o. Pl.* help; **sie arbeitet in der Kantine zur ~:** she helps out in the canteen; **(b)** ⇒ **Aushilfskraft**

aushilfs-, Aushilfs-: **~arbeit** *die* temporary work *no pl.;* **~arbeiten** *Pl.* temporary work *sing.;* temporary jobs; **~kraft** *die* temporary worker; (in Läden, Gaststätten) temporary helper *or* assistant; (Sekretärin) temporary secretary; temp (coll.); **~weise** *adv.* on a temporary basis

aus|höhlen *tr. V.* hollow out; erode ‹*rock, cliff, etc.*›; (fig.: untergraben) undermine

aus|holen *itr. V.* **(a)** [mit dem Arm] **~:** draw back one's arm; (zum Schlag) raise one's arm; **er holte zum Schlag aus** he raised his fist/sword *etc.* to strike; **er holte zum Wurf aus** he drew back his arm ready to throw; **zum Gegenschlag ~** (fig.) prepare to counter-attack; **(b)** (fig.: beim Erzählen, Erklären usw.) go back a long way

aus|horchen *tr. V.* **jmdn. ~:** sound sb. out

aus|kehren *tr., itr. V.* (bes. südd.) ⇒ **ausfegen**

aus|kennen *unr. refl. V.* know one's way around *or* about; (in einer Sache) know what's what; **sie kennt sich in dieser Stadt aus** she knows her way around the town; **sich [gut] mit/in etw.** (*Dat.*) **~:** know [a lot] about sth.

aus|kippen *tr. V.* **(a)** tipp out; **(b)** (leeren) empty

aus|klammern *tr. V.* **(a)** (Math.) place outside the brackets; **(b)** (beiseite lassen) leave aside; (ausschließen) exclude

Aus·klang *der* (geh.) end; **zum ~ der Saison/des Festes** to end *or* close the season/festival

aus|kleiden 1 *tr. V.* (a) (geh.: entkleiden) undress; (b) (innen verkleiden) line. 2 *refl. V.* (geh.) undress; disrobe (formal)

aus|klingen *unr. itr. V.; mit sein* (a) ‹song› finish; ‹music, final notes› die away; (b) (fig.) end

aus|klinken 1 *tr. V.* release. 2 *refl. V.* release itself/themselves

aus|klopfen *tr. V.* (a) beat out (aus + *Dat.* of); (b) (säubern) beat ‹carpet›; knock *or* tap ‹pipe› out

aus|klügeln *tr. V.* think out; work out; **ein ausgeklügeltes System** a cleverly devised system

aus|knipsen *tr. V.* (ugs.) switch *or* turn off

aus|knobeln *tr. V.* (ugs.) (a) ⇒ **auswürfeln**; (b) (austüfteln) work out

aus|kochen *tr. V.* boil; (keimfrei machen) sterilize ‹instruments etc.› [in boiling water]

aus|kommen *unr. itr. V.; mit sein* (a) manage, (coll.) get by (**mit** on, **ohne** without); (b) (sich verstehen) **mit jmdm. [gut] ~:** get along *or* on [well] with sb.

Auskommen *das; ~s* livelihood; **sein ~ haben** make a living

aus|kosten *tr. V.* (geh.) **etw. ~:** enjoy sth. to the full

aus|kratzen *tr. V.* scrape out ‹dirt, remains, etc.› (**aus** from); scrape [out] ‹bowl, pan, etc.›

aus|kugeln *tr. V.* **sich** (*Dat.*) **den Arm** *usw.* **~:** put one's arm *etc.* out [of joint]; dislocate one's arm *etc.;* **jmdm. den Arm ~:** dislocate sb.'s arm

aus|kühlen 1 *tr. V.* chill ‹person, body› through. 2 *itr. V.; mit sein* cool down

aus|kundschaften *tr. V.* find out; find ‹opportunity›; track down ‹refuge, criminal, enemy, etc.›; spy out ‹place›

Auskunft *die; ~,* **Auskünfte** (a) piece of information; **Auskünfte** information *sing.;* [jmdm. über etw. (*Akk.*)] **~ geben** give [sb.] information [about sth.]; **sie gab auf alle Fragen ~:** she answered all the questions; **Auskünfte über jmdn./etw. einholen** obtain information about sb./sth.; (b) *o. Pl.* (Stelle) information desk/counter/office/centre *etc.;* „~" 'Information'; 'Enquiries' (Brit.); (c) (Fernspr.) directory enquiries *no art.* (Brit.); directory information *no art.* (Amer.)

Auskunftei *die; ~, ~en* private detective agency; (Kredit~) credit reference agency

Auskunfts-: **~beamte** *der* enquiry office clerk (Brit.); information office clerk (Amer.); **~schalter** *der* information counter

aus|kuppeln *itr. V.* disengage the clutch; declutch

aus|kurieren *tr. V.* **etw. ~:** heal sth. [completely]

aus|lachen *tr. V.* laugh at

aus|laden[1] *unr. tr. V.* unload

aus|laden[2] *unr. tr. V.* **jmdn. ~:** cancel one's invitation to sb.

Aus·lage *die* (a) *Pl.* (Unkosten) expenses; **unsere ~n für Strom/Heizung** *usw.* our outlay *sing.* on electricity/heating *etc.;* (b) (Schaufenster~) window display; **in der ~:** in the window

Aus·land *das; o. Pl.* foreign countries *pl.;* **im/ins ~:** abroad; **aus dem ~:** from abroad; **die Literatur/Intervention/Hilfe des ~s** foreign literature/intervention/aid; **die Meinung des ~s** opinion abroad; **das ~ hat zurückhaltend reagiert** foreign reaction *or* the reaction of other countries *pl.* was guarded

Ausländer *der; ~s, ~:* foreigner; alien (Admin. lang., Law)

ausländer·feindlich *Adj.* hostile to foreigners *postpos.*

Ausländerin *die; ~, ~nen* ⇒ **Ausländer**

ausländisch *Adj.; nicht präd.* foreign

Auslands-: **~aufenthalt** *der* stay abroad; **~gespräch** *das* (Fernspr.) international call; **~korrespondent** *der* foreign correspondent; **~reise** *die* trip abroad

aus|lassen 1 *unr. tr. V.* (a) (weglassen) leave out; leave out, omit ‹detail, passage, word, etc.›; (b) (versäumen) miss ‹chance, opportunity, etc.›; (c) (abreagieren) vent (**an** + *Dat.* on); (d) (ugs.: nicht anziehen, nicht einschalten) **etw. ~:** leave sth. off. 2 *unr. refl. V.* (abwertend) talk, speak; (schriftlich) write; (sich verbreiten) hold forth; **sich im Detail/näher ~:** go into detail/more detail

Auslassung *die; ~, ~en* (a) (Weglassung) omission; (b) *meist Pl.* (oft abwertend: Äußerung) remark

Auslassungs-: **~punkte** *Pl.* omission marks; ellipsis *sing.;* **~zeichen** *das* (Sprachw.) apostrophe

aus|lasten *tr. V.* (a) (voll ausnutzen) **etw. ~:** use sth. to full capacity; **ausgelastet sein** ‹mine, factory, etc.› be working to full capacity; (b) (voll beanspruchen) fully occupy

aus|latschen *tr. V.* (ugs.) wear ‹shoes etc.› out of shape

Auslauf *der* (a) *o. Pl.* **keinen/zu wenig ~ haben** have no/too little chance to run around outside; **der Hund braucht viel ~:** the dog needs plenty of exercise; (b) (Raum) space to run around in; (für Hühner, Enten usw.) run; (für Pferde) paddock

aus|laufen *unr. itr. V.; mit sein* (a) run out (**aus** of); ‹pus› drain; (b) (leer laufen) empty; ‹egg› run out; (c) (in See stechen) sail, set sail (**nach** for); (d) (erlöschen) ‹contract, agreement, etc.› run out; (e) (nicht fortgesetzt werden) ‹model, line› be dropped *or* discontinued; **etw. ~ lassen** drop *or* discontinue sth.; (f) (zum Stillstand kommen) come *or* roll to a stop

Aus·läufer *der* (a) (Geogr.) foothill *usu. in pl.;* (b) (Met.) (eines Hochs) ridge; (eines Tiefs) trough

aus|laugen *tr. V.* leach ‹soil›; (fig.) drain, exhaust, wear out ‹person›

aus|leben *tr. V.* give full expression to

aus|lecken *tr. V.* lick out

aus|leeren *tr. V.* empty [out]; empty ‹ashtray, dustbin, etc.›

aus|legen *tr. V.* (a) (hinlegen) lay out; display ‹goods, exhibits›; lay ‹bait›; put down ‹poison›; set ‹trap, net›; (b) (bedecken mit) **etw. mit Fliesen/Teppichboden ~:** tile/carpet sth.; **einen Schrank [mit Papier] ~:** line a cupboard [with paper]; (c) (leihen) lend; **jmdm. etw. od. etw. für jmdn. ~:** lend sb. sth.; lend sth. to sb.; (d) (interpretieren) interpret; **etw. falsch ~:** misinterpret sth.; **etw. als Furcht ~:** take sth. to be fear

Auslegung *die; ~, ~en* interpretation

aus|leiern (ugs.) 1 *itr. V.; mit sein* wear out; ‹clothes› go baggy; **ausgeleiert** worn out; baggy ‹pullover, trousers, etc.›. 2 *tr. V.* wear out; make ‹pullover, trousers, etc.› go baggy; make ‹rubber band› lose its stretch

Ausleihe *die; ~, ~n* (a) *o. Pl.* (das Ausleihen) lending; (b) (Stelle) issue desk

aus|leihen *unr. tr. V.* (a) **jmdm. od. an jmdn. etw. ~:** lend sb. sth.; lend sth. to sb.; (b) ⇒ **leihen b**

aus|lernen *itr. V.* finish one's apprenticeship; **man lernt nie aus** (Spr.) you learn something new every day

Aus·lese *die o. Pl.* selection

aus|lesen[1] *unr. tr. V.* pick out (**aus** from)

aus|lesen[2] *unr. tr. V.* (ugs.) finish [reading]

aus|liefern *tr. V.* (a) (übergeben) **jmdm. etw. od. etw. an jmdn. ~:** hand sth. over to sb.; **jmdn. an ein Land ~:** extradite sb. to a country; **jmdm./einer Sache ausgeliefert sein** (fig.) be at the mercy of sb./sth.; (b) *auch itr.* (Kaufmannsspr.: liefern) deliver

Aus·lieferung *die* (a) (Übergabe) handing over; (an ein Land) extradition; **jmds. ~ fordern** demand that sb. be handed over/extradited; (b) (Kaufmannsspr.: Lieferung) delivery

aus|liegen *unr. itr. V.* be displayed; ‹newspapers, plans, etc.› be laid out, be available

aus|löffeln *tr. V.* (a) spoon up [all of] ‹soup etc.›; **jetzt muss er die Suppe ~[, die er sich eingebrockt hat]** (fig.) he's made his [own] bed and now he must lie in it; (b) spoon up everything out of ‹plate, bowl, etc.›

aus|loggen *refl. V.* (DV) log off *or* out

aus|löschen *tr. V.* (a) extinguish, put out ‹fire, lamp›; snuff, put out, extinguish ‹candle›; (fig.) extinguish ‹life›; (b) (beseitigen) rub out, erase ‹drawing, writing›; ‹wind, rain› obliterate ‹tracks, writing›; (fig.) obliterate, wipe out ‹memory›; wipe out ‹people, population›

aus|losen *tr. V.* **etw. ~:** draw lots for sth.; **es wurde ausgelost, wer beginnt** lots were drawn to decide who would start; **den Gewinner ~:** draw lots to decide the winner

aus|lösen tr. V. (a) trigger ‹mechanism, device, etc.›; set off, trigger ‹alarm›; release ‹camera shutter›; (b) provoke ‹discussion, anger, laughter, reaction, outrage, heart attack, sympathy›; cause ‹sorrow, horror, surprise, disappointment, panic, war›; excite, arouse ‹interest, enthusiasm›; trigger [off] ‹crisis, chain of events, rebellion, strike›

Auslöser der; ~s, ~ (a) (Fot.) shutter release; (b) (fig.) trigger

Aus·losung die draw

Aus·lösung die (a) (eines Mechanismus) triggering; (eines Alarms) setting off; triggering; (b) ⇒ auslösen b: provocation; causing; exciting; arousal; triggering [off]

aus|loten tr. V. (Seew.) sound the depth of; sound, plumb ‹depth›; (fig.) sound out ‹intentions›; **ein Problem** ~ (fig.) try to get to the bottom of a problem

aus|lutschen tr. V. (ugs.) suck out ‹juice›; suck the juice from ‹orange, lemon, etc.›

aus|machen tr. V. (a) (ugs.) put out ‹light, fire, cigarette, candle›; turn or switch off ‹television, radio, hi-fi›; turn off ‹gas›; (b) (vereinbaren) agree; (c) (auszeichnen, kennzeichnen) make up; constitute; (d) (ins Gewicht fallen) make a difference; **wenig/nichts/viel** ~: make little/no/a great or big difference; (e) (stören) **das macht mir nichts aus** I don't mind [that]; **macht es Ihnen etwas aus, wenn …?** would you mind if …?; (f) (klären) settle; **etw. mit sich allein/mit seinem Gewissen** ~: sort sth. out for oneself/with one's conscience; (g) (erkennen) make out; (h) (betragen) come to; **der Zeitunterschied/die Entfernung macht …** the time difference/distance is …

aus|malen 1 tr. V. (a) (mit Farbe ausfüllen) colour in; (b) (mit Malereien ausschmücken) **das Innere einer Kirche** ~: decorate the interior of a church with murals/frescoes etc.; (c) (schildern) describe. **2** refl. V. **sich** (Dat.) **etw.** ~: picture sth. to oneself; imagine sth.

Aus·maß das size; dimensions pl.; **gewaltige** ~**e haben** be of huge or vast dimensions; **eine Katastrophe unvorstellbaren** ~**es** a disaster on an unimaginable scale

aus|mergeln /'aυsmεrgln/ tr. V. emaciate; **ausgemergelt** gaunt, emaciated ‹face, body›

aus|merzen /'aυsmεrtsn̩/ tr. V. eradicate ‹pests, insects, weeds, etc.›; eliminate ‹errors, slips, offensive passages›

aus|messen unr. tr. V. measure up

aus|misten tr. (auch itr.) V. (a) muck out; (b) (fig. ugs.) clear out

aus|mustern tr. V. (a) (Milit.) **jmdn.** ~: reject sb. as unfit [for service]; (b) (fig.) take ‹vehicle, machine› out of service

Aus·nahme die; ~, ~**n** exception; **mit** ~ **von Peter/des Pfarrers** with the exception of Peter/of the priest; **ohne** ~: without exception; **bei jmdm. eine** ~ **machen** make an exception in sb.'s case; ~**n bestätigen die Regel** the exception proves the rule

Ausnahme·fall der exceptional case

ausnahms-: ~**los** Adv. without exception; ~**weise** Adv. by way of or as an exception; **Dürfen wir mitkommen? — Ausnahmsweise ja** May we come too? — Yes, just this once; **kann ich heute** ~**weise mal früher weggehen?** can I go earlier today, as a special exception?

aus|nehmen 1 unr. tr. V. (a) gut ‹fish, rabbit, chicken›; (b) (ausschließen) exclude; (gesondert behandeln) make an exception of; **jeder irrt sich einmal, ich nehme mich nicht aus** everyone makes mistakes once in a while, and I'm no exception; (c) (die Eier herausnehmen aus) rob ‹nest›; (d) (ugs. abwertend: neppen) **jmdn.** ~: fleece sb. **2** unr. refl. V. (geh.) look; (sich anhören) sound

ausnehmend adv. (geh.) exceptionally

aus|nüchtern tr., itr., refl. V. sober up

Ausnüchterung die; ~, ~**en** sobering up; **jmdn. zur** ~ **auf die Wache bringen** take sb. to the [police] station to sober up

aus|nutzen, (bes. südd., österr.) **aus|nützen** tr. V. (a) (nutzen) **etw.** [**voll**] ~: take [full] advantage of it.; make [full] use of sth.; (b) (Vorteil ziehen aus) take advantage of; (ausbeuten) exploit

aus|packen 1 tr., itr. V. unpack (**aus** from); unwrap ‹present›. **2** itr. V. (ugs.) talk (coll.); squeal (sl.)

aus|peitschen tr. V. whip; (aufgrund eines Gerichtsurteils) flog

aus|pendeln itr. V.; mit sein commute; **die über die Grenze** ~**den Arbeitnehmer** those commuting to work over the border

Aus|pendler der commuter; **die Stadt hat mehr Einpendler als** ~: more people commute to the city than from it

aus|pfeifen unr. tr. V. **jmdn./etw.** ~: give sb./sth. the bird

aus|pflanzen tr. V. plant out

aus|plaudern tr. V. let out; blab

aus|plündern tr. V. (a) (ausrauben) **jmdn./etw.** ~: rob sb./sth. [of everything]; (b) (völlig plündern, auch fig.) plunder

aus|powern /-po:vɐn/ tr. V. (ugs. abwertend) bleed ‹country, nation› dry or white; exploit ‹workers, masses›; (fig.) impoverish ‹soil›

aus|prägen refl. V. develop; ‹peculiarity› become more pronounced

aus|pressen tr. V. press or squeeze out ‹juice›; squeeze ‹orange, lemon›; (mit einer Presse) press the juice from ‹grapes etc.›; press out ‹juice, oil›; (fig.: ausbeuten) squeeze ‹country, population, etc.› [dry]; s. auch **Zitrone**

aus|probieren tr. V. try out

Aus·puff der exhaust

aus|pumpen tr. V. pump out

aus|pusten tr. V. (ugs.) blow out; blow ‹egg›

Aus·putzer der; ~s, ~ (Fußball) sweeper

aus|quartieren tr. V. move out; billet out ‹troops›

aus|quatschen (salopp) **1** tr. V. let out; blab. **2** refl. V. **sich mit jmdm.** ~: have a really or (Amer.) real good chat with sb.; **sich bei jmdm.** ~: have a heart-to-heart with sb. (coll.)

aus|quetschen tr. V. (a) squeeze out ‹juice›; squeeze ‹orange, lemon, etc.›; (b) (ugs.: ausfragen) grill; (aus Neugier) pump; s. auch **Zitrone**

aus|radieren tr. V. rub out; erase; (fig.) annihilate, wipe out ‹village, city, etc.›; liquidate ‹person›

aus|rangieren tr. V. (ugs.) throw out; discard; scrap ‹vehicle, machine›

aus|rasieren tr. V. shave

aus|rasten itr. V.; mit sein (Technik) disengage; **er rastete aus, es rastete bei ihm aus** (fig. salopp) something snapped in him

aus|rauben tr. V. rob

aus|räuchern tr. V. (auch fig.) smoke out; fumigate ‹room›

aus|räumen 1 tr. V. (a) clear out; (b) (fig.) clear up; dispel ‹prejudice, suspicion, misgivings›. **2** itr. V. clear everything out

aus|rechnen tr. V. work out; (errechnen) work out; calculate; **das kannst du dir leicht** ~ (fig. ugs.) you can easily work that out [for yourself]; **sich** (Dat.) **Vorteile/gute Chancen** ~: reckon that one has advantages/good prospects

Aus·rede die excuse

aus|reden 1 itr. V. finish [speaking]. **2** tr. V. **jmdm. etw.** ~: talk sb. out of sth.

aus|reichen itr. V. be enough or sufficient (**zu** for); **die Zeit/der Platz reicht [nicht] aus** there's [not] enough or sufficient time/space

ausreichend 1 Adj. sufficient; enough; (als Note) fair. **2** adv. sufficiently

aus|reifen itr. V.; mit sein ‹fruit, cereal, etc.› ripen fully; ‹cheese, wine, etc.› mature fully

Aus·reise die: **vor/bei der** ~: before/when leaving the country; **jmdm. die** ~ **verweigern** refuse sb. permission to leave [the/a country]

aus|reisen itr. V.; mit sein leave [the country]; **nach/aus Italien** ~: go to/leave Italy

aus|reißen 1 unr. tr. V. tear out; pull out ‹plants, weeds›. **2** unr. itr. V.; mit sein (a) ‹[button] hole etc.› tear; (b) (ugs.: weglaufen) run away (**von,** Dat. from)

Aus·reißer *der*, **Ausreißerin** *die;* ~, ~**nen** (ugs.) runaway

aus|reiten *unr. itr. V.; mit sein* go for a ride; go riding

aus|renken *tr. V.* dislocate; **jmdm./sich den Arm** ~: dislocate sb.'s/one's arm; **sich [nach jmdm.] den Hals** ~ (ugs.) crane one's neck [to look for sb.]

aus|richten 1 *tr. V.* (a) (übermitteln) **jmdm. etw.** ~: tell sb. sth.; **ich werde es** ~: I'll pass the message on; **kann ich ihm etwas** ~? can I give him a message?; **richte ihr einen Gruß [von mir] aus** give her my regards; (b) (einheitlich anordnen) line up; (c) (fig.) **etw. auf jmdn./etw.** ~: orientate sth. towards sb./sth.; **etw. nach** *od.* **an jmdm./etw.** ~: gear sth. to sb./sth.; (d) (erreichen) accomplish; achieve; **bei jmdm. wenig/nichts** ~ **können** not be able to get very far/anywhere with sb.; **gegen jmdn./ etw. etwas** ~ **können** be able to do something against sb./sth. **2** *refl. V.* (a) (Milit.) dress ranks; **sich nach jmdm.** ~: line [oneself] up with sb.; (b) **sich an einem Vorbild** ~: follow an example

Aus·ritt *der* ride [out]

aus|rollen *tr. V.* roll out

aus|rotten *tr. V.* eradicate ⟨*weeds, vermin, etc.*⟩; (fig.) wipe out ⟨*family, enemy, species, etc.*⟩; eradicate, stamp out ⟨*superstition, idea, evil, etc.*⟩

aus|rücken *itr. V.; mit sein* (a) (bes. Milit.) move out; ⟨*fire brigade, police*⟩ turn out; (b) (ugs.: weglaufen) make off; **von zu Hause** ~: run away from home

Aus·ruf *der* cry

aus|rufen *unr. tr. V.* (a) call out; „**Schön!**" **rief er aus** 'Lovely', he exclaimed; **jmdn.** ~ **lassen** have a call put out for sb.; (im Hotel) have sb. paged; **die Haltestellen** ~: call out [the names of] the stops; **seine Waren** ~: cry one's wares; (b) (offiziell verkünden) proclaim; declare ⟨*state of emergency*⟩; call ⟨*strike*⟩; **jmdn. zum König/als Präsidenten** ~: proclaim sb. king/president

Ausrufe-: ~**satz** *der* (Sprachw.) exclamation; exclamatory clause; ~**zeichen** *das* exclamation mark

aus|ruhen 1 *refl., itr. V.* have a rest; **[sich] ein wenig/ richtig** ~: rest a little/have a proper *or* good rest; **ausgeruht sein** be rested; *s. auch* **Lorbeer c. 2** *tr. V.* (ruhen lassen) rest

aus|rüsten *tr. V.* equip; equip, fit out ⟨*ship*⟩; **ein Auto mit Sicherheitsgurten** ~: fit safety belts to a car; fit a car with safety belts

Aus·rüstung *die* (a) *o. Pl.* (das Ausrüsten) equipping; (von Schiffen) equipping; fitting out; **die** ~ **des Autos mit Gurten** *usw.* the fitting of belts *etc.* to the car; (b) (Ausrüstungsgegenstände) equipment *no pl.;* **eine neue** ~: a new set of equipment

aus|rutschen *itr. V.; mit sein* slip; (fig.) put one's foot in it

Ausrutscher *der;* ~**s**, ~ (ugs., auch fig.) slip

Aus·sage *die* (a) statement; stated view; **nach** ~ **der Experten** according to what the experts say; (b) (vor Gericht, bei der Polizei) statement; **eine** ~ **machen** make a statement; give evidence; **die** ~ **verweigern** refuse to make a statement; (vor Gericht) refuse to give evidence; (c) (geistiger Gehalt) message

aussage·kräftig *Adj.* meaningful

aus|sagen 1 *tr. V.* (a) say; **damit wird ausgesagt, dass** …: this expresses the idea that …; (b) (fig.) ⟨*picture, novel, etc.*⟩ express; (c) (vor Gericht, vor der Polizei) ~, **dass** …: state that …; (unter Eid) testify that … **2** *itr. V.* make a statement; (unter Eid) testify

aus|sägen *tr. V.* saw out

Aussage·satz *der* (Sprachw.) affirmative clause

Aus·satz *der; o. Pl.* (veralt.) leprosy

Aussätzige *der/die; adj. Dekl.* (veralt., fig.) leper

aus|saufen *unr. tr. (auch itr.) V.* (a) ⟨*animal*⟩ drink [up] ⟨*water etc.*⟩; empty ⟨*trough etc.*⟩; (b) (derb) drink

aus|saugen *regelm.* (geh. auch unr.) *tr. V.* suck out (aus of); (leer saugen) suck dry; **eine Apfelsine** ~: suck the juice from an orange; **eine Wunde** ~: suck the poison/ dirt *etc.* out of a wound

---

aus|schaben *tr. V.* (a) ⇒ **auskratzen;** (b) (Med.) curette

Ausschabung *die;* ~, ~**en** (Med.) curettage

aus|schalten *tr. V.* (a) (abstellen) switch *or* turn off; (b) (ausschließen) eliminate; exclude ⟨*emotion, influence*⟩; dismiss ⟨*doubt, objection*⟩; shut out ⟨*feeling, thought*⟩

Aus·schank *der;* ~[e]s, **Ausschänke** /ˈausʃɛŋkə/ (a) *o. Pl.* serving: „**Kein** ~ **an Jugendliche unter 16 Jahren**" 'persons under sixteen will not be served with alcoholic drinks'; (b) (Schanktisch) bar; counter

Aus·schau *in* nach jmdm./etw. ~ **halten** look out for *or* keep a lookout for sb./sth.

aus|schauen *itr. V.* **nach jmdm./ etw.** ~: look out for *or* keep a lookout for sb./sth.

aus|scheiden 1 *unr. itr. V.; mit sein* (a) aus etw. ~: leave sth.; **aus dem Amt** ~: leave office; (b) (Sport) be eliminated; (aufgeben) retire; (c) (nicht in Betracht kommen) **diese Möglichkeit/dieser Kandidat scheidet aus** this possibility/candidate has to be ruled out. **2** *unr. tr. V.* (Physiol.) excrete ⟨*waste*⟩; eliminate, expel ⟨*poison*⟩; exude ⟨*sweat*⟩; (Chem.) precipitate

Aus·scheidung *die* (a) *o. Pl.* ⇒ **ausscheiden 2:** excretion; elimination; expulsion; exudation; precipitation; (b) *Pl.* (Physiol.) excreta; (c) (Sport) qualifier

Ausscheidungs-: ~**organ** *das* (Physiol.) excretory organ; ~**spiel** *das* (Sport) qualifying game *or* match

aus|schenken *tr. V.* serve

aus|scheren *itr. V.; mit sein* ⟨*car, driver*⟩ pull out; ⟨*ship*⟩ break out of [the] line; ⟨*aircraft*⟩ peel off, break formation; (fig.) pull out

aus|schiffen *tr. V.* disembark ⟨*passengers*⟩; unload ⟨*cargo*⟩

aus|schildern *tr. V.* signpost

aus|schimpfen *tr. V.* **jmdn.** ~: give sb. a telling-off; tell sb. off

aus|schlachten *tr. V.* (a) (ugs.) cannibalize ⟨*machine, vehicle*⟩; break ⟨*vehicle*⟩ for spares; (b) (fig. ugs. abwertend) exploit; **etw. politisch** ~: make political capital out of sth.

aus|schlafen 1 *unr. itr., refl. V.* have a good *or* proper sleep; **ich war nicht ausgeschlafen** I hadn't had enough sleep. **2** *unr. tr. V.* **seinen Rausch** ~: sleep off the effects of alcohol

Aus·schlag *der* (a) (Haut~) rash; **[einen]** ~ **bekommen** break out *or* come out in a rash; (b) (eines Zeigers) deflection; (eines Pendels) swing; **den** ~ **geben** (fig.) turn *or* tipp the scales (fig.); **das gab den** ~ **für seine Entscheidung** that was the crucial factor in his decision; that decided him

aus|schlagen 1 *unr. tr. V.* (a) knock out; **jmdm. einen Zahn** ~: knock one of sb.'s teeth out; (b) (ablehnen) turn down; reject; refuse ⟨*inheritance*⟩. **2** *unr. itr. V.* (a) ⟨*horse*⟩ kick; (b) *auch mit sein* ⟨*needle, pointer*⟩ be deflected, swing; ⟨*divining-rod*⟩ dip; ⟨*scales*⟩ turn; ⟨*pendulum*⟩ swing; (c) *auch mit sein* (sprießen) come out [in bud]

ausschlag·gebend *Adj.* decisive; **das war** ~ **für seine Entscheidung** that was the crucial factor in his decision; that decided him

aus|schließen *unr. tr. V.* (a) exclude (aus from); **er schließt sich von allem aus** he won't join in anything; (b) (ausstoßen) expel (aus from); (c) (als nicht möglich, nicht gegeben annehmen, unmöglich machen) rule out; **einander** ~: be mutually exclusive; (d) (aussperren) lock out; *s. auch* **ausgeschlossen**

aus·schließlich /*od.* '-'--, -'--/ **1** *Adj.; nicht präd.* exclusive; exclusive, sole ⟨*concern, right*⟩. **2** *Adv.* (nur) exclusively; **das ist** ~ **sein Verdienst** the credit is his alone. **3** *Präp. mit Gen.* excluding; exclusive of

Ausschließlichkeit /*od.* '-'---/ *die;* ~: exclusiveness

aus|schlüpfen *itr. V.; mit sein* hatch [out]; ⟨*butterfly*⟩ emerge

aus|schlürfen *tr. V.* sip ⟨*drink*⟩ noisily; suck ⟨*oyster, egg*⟩; **sein Glas/seine Tasse** ~: empty one's glass/cup noisily

Aus·schluss, *****Aus·schluß** *der* (**a**) exclusion (**von** from); **unter ~ der Öffentlichkeit** with the public excluded; (Rechtsw.) in camera; (**b**) (Ausstoßung) expulsion (**aus** from)

aus|schmücken *tr. V.* decorate; deck out; (fig.) embellish ‹*story, incident, report, etc.*›

Ausschmückung *die;* ~, ~**en** ⇒ **ausschmücken**: decoration; decking out; embellishment

aus|schneiden *unr. tr. V.* cut out

Aus·schnitt *der* (**a**) (Zeitungs~) cutting, clipping; (**b**) (Hals~) neck; **ein tiefer ~:** a plunging neck-line; (**c**) (Teil, Auszug) part; (eines Textes) excerpt; (eines Films) clip; excerpt; (Bild~) detail; (**d**) (Kreis~) sector; (**e**) (Loch) [cut-out] opening

aus|schöpfen *tr. V.* (**a**) scoop out (**aus** from); (mit dem Schöpflöffel) ladle out (**aus** of); (**b**) (leeren) bale the water *etc.* out of ‹*basin, bath, tank, etc.*›; bale ‹*boat*› out; (**c**) (fig.: ausnutzen) exhaust

aus|schreiben *unr. tr. V.* (**a**) write ‹*word, name, etc.*› out in full; write ‹*number*› out in words; (**b**) (ausstellen) write *or* make out ‹*cheque, invoice, receipt*›; (**c**) (bekannt geben) announce, call ‹*election, meeting*›; advertise ‹*flat, job*›; put ‹*supply order etc.*› out to tender; organize ‹*competition*›

Aus·schreibung *die* ⇒ **ausschreiben c:** announcement; calling; advertisement; invitation to tender; organization

aus|schreiten *unr. itr. V.* (geh.)*; mit sein* step out

Ausschreitung *die;* ~, ~**en;** *meist Pl.* act of violence; **es kam zu ~en** violence broke out

Aus·schuss, *****Aus·schuß** *der* (**a**) (Kommission) committee; (**b**) *o. Pl.* (Aussortiertes) rejects *pl.*

aus|schütteln *tr. V.* shake ‹*dust, tablecloth, etc.*› out

aus|schütten *tr. V.* (**a**) tip out ‹*water, sand, etc.*›; (leeren) empty ‹*bucket, bowl, container*›; (verschütten) spill; **sich vor Lachen ~ [wollen]** (ugs.) split one's sides laughing; die laughing (coll.); *s. auch* **Herz b;** (**b**) (auszahlen) distribute ‹*dividends, prizes, etc.*›

aus|schwärmen *itr. V.; mit sein* (auch fig.) swarm out; ‹*soldiers*› deploy; (fächerartig) fan out

ausschweifend 1 *Adj.* wild ‹*imagination, emotion, hope, desire, orgy*›; extravagant ‹*idea*›; riotous, wild ‹*enjoyment*›; dissolute, dissipated ‹*life*›; dissolute ‹*person*›. 2 *adv.* ~ **leben** lead a dissolute life

Ausschweifung *die;* ~, ~**en** dissolution; dissipation

aus|schweigen *unr. refl. V.* remain silent

aus|schwenken *tr. V.* (**a**) swing out; (**b**) (ausspülen) rinse out

aus|schwitzen *tr. V.* sweat out

aus|sehen *unr. itr. V.* look; **gut ~:** look good; ‹*person*› be good-looking; (gesund ~) look well; **es sieht nach Regen aus** it looks like rain; **wie sieht ein Okapi aus?** what does an okapi look like?; **ich habe vielleicht ausgesehen!** I looked a real sight!; **es sieht danach** *od.* **so aus, als ob ...:** it looks as if ...; **so siehst du aus!** (ugs.) you've got another think coming (coll.); that's what you think!

Aussehen *das;* ~s appearance; **etw. nach dem ~ beurteilen** judge sth. by appearances

*****aus|sein** ⇒ aus 2

außen /ˈausn̩/ *Adv.* outside; ~ **bemalt** painted on the outside; ~ **an der Windschutzscheibe** on the outside of the windscreen; **nach ~ hin** on the outside; outwardly; **das Fenster geht nach ~ auf** the window opens outwards; **von dem Skandal darf nichts nach ~ dringen** (fig.) nothing must get out about the scandal; **von ~:** from the outside; **Hilfe von ~:** (fig.) outside help

Außen-: ~**arbeiten** *Pl.* outside work *sing.;* ~**bahn** *die* (Sport) outside lane

Außenbord·motor *der* outboard motor

aus|senden *unr.* (auch regelm.) *tr. V.* send out

außen-, Außen-: ~**dienst** *der:* **im ~dienst sein** *od.* **arbeiten**, ~**dienst machen** be working out of the office; ‹*salesman*› be on the road ~**handel** *der; o. Pl.* foreign trade *no art.;* ~**minister** *der* Foreign Minister;

Foreign Secretary (Brit.); Secretary of State (Amer.); ~**ministerium** *das* Foreign Ministry; Foreign and Commonwealth Office (Brit.); Foreign Office (Brit. coll.); State Department (Amer.); ~**politik** *die* foreign politics *sing.;* (bestimmte) foreign policy/policies *pl.;* ~**politiker** *der* politician concerned with foreign affairs; ~**politisch** 1 *Adj.* foreign-policy *attrib.* ‹*debate*›; ‹*question*› relating to foreign policy; ‹*mistake*› in foreign policy; ‹*reporting*› of foreign affairs; ‹*experience*› in foreign affairs; ‹*expert, speaker*› on foreign affairs; **auf ~politischem Gebiet** in foreign affairs; 2 *adv.* as regards foreign policy; ~**politisch gesehen** from the point of view of foreign policy; ~**posten** *der* outpost; ~**seite** *die* outside

Außenseiter *der;* ~s, ~, **Außenseiterin** *die;* ~, ~**nen** (Sport, fig.) outsider

Außen-: ~**spiegel** *der* exterior mirror; ~**stände** *Pl.* outstanding debts *or* accounts

Außenstehende *der/die; adj. Dekl.* outsider

Außen-: ~**stelle** *die* branch; ~**stürmer** *der* (Ballspiele) winger; outside forward; ~**tasche** *die* outside pocket; ~**temperatur** *die* outside temperature; ~**wand** *die* external *or* outside wall; ~**welt** *die* outside world; ~**winkel** *der* exterior angle; ~**wirtschaft** *die; o. Pl.* foreign trade and investment

außer /ˈausɐ/ 1 *Präp. mit Dat.* (**a**) *auch mit Gen.* (außerhalb) out of; ~ **Atem** out of breath; ~ **Haus sein** be out of the house; ~ **Zweifel stehen** be beyond doubt; ~ **sich sein** be beside oneself (**vor** + *Dat.* with); (**b**) (abgesehen von) apart from; **alle ~ mir** all except [for] me; (**c**) (zusätzlich zu) in addition to. 2 *Präp. mit Akk.* **etw. ~ jeden Zweifel stellen** make sth. very clear *or* clear beyond all doubt; ~ **sich geraten** become beside oneself (**vor** + *Dat.* with). 3 *Konj.* ⇒ **ausgenommen.** 4 *Adv.* except

äußer... /ˈɔysɐ.../ *Adj.; nicht präd.* (**a**) outer; outer, outside ‹*wall, door*›; external ‹*diameter, injury, cause, force, form, circumstances*›; outside ‹*pocket*›; outlying ‹*district, area*›; outward ‹*appearance, similarity, effect, etc.*›; (**b**) (auswärtig) foreign

außer-: ~**dem** /auch: -ˈ-/ *Adv.* as well; besides; (im übrigen) besides; anyway; **er ist Politiker und ~ Schriftsteller** he is a politician and a writer as well; ~**dienstlich** 1 *Adj.* private; social, unofficial ‹*event*›; unofficial ‹*commitment, activity*›; 2 *adv.* out of working hours; **mit jmdm. ~dienstlich verkehren** meet with sb. on a social basis

Äußere *das;* ~**n** [outward] appearance; **das ~ täuscht oft** appearances are often deceptive; **der Minister des ~n** the Foreign Minister

außer-: ~**ehelich** 1 *Adj.* extra-marital ‹*relationship*›; illegitimate ‹*child, birth*›; 2 *adv.* outside marriage; **ein ~ehelich geborenes Kind** a child born out of wedlock, ~**fahrplan·mäßig** /-ˈ----/ 1 *Adj.* unscheduled ‹*train, bus*›; 2 *adv.* **dieser Zug verkehrt ~fahrplanmäßig** this train is not a scheduled one; ~**gewöhnlich** 1 *Adj.* (**a**) unusual; (**b**) (das Gewohnte übertreffend) exceptional; 2 *adv.* (**a**) unusually; (**b**) (sehr) exceptionally; ~**halb** 1 *Präp. mit Gen.* outside; ~**halb der Sprechstunde** out of *or* outside consulting hours; 2 *Adv.* (**a**) outside; ~ **von** outside; (**b**) (~halb der Stadt) out of town; **von ~halb** from out of town

äußerlich 1 *Adj.* (**a**) external ‹*use, injury*›; (**b**) (nach außen hin) outward ‹*appearance, calm, similarity, etc.*›. 2 *adv.* externally; (nach außen hin) outwardly; ~ **gesehen** on the face of it

Äußerlichkeit *die;* ~, ~**en** (**a**) (Umgangsform) formality; (**b**) (Unwesentliches) minor point

äußern 1 *tr. V.* express, voice ‹*opinion, view, criticism, reservations, disapproval, doubt*›; express ‹*joy, happiness, wish*›; voice ‹*suspicion*›. 2 *refl. V.* (**a**) (Stellung nehmen) **sich über etw.** (*Akk.*) ~**:** give one's view on sth.; **ich möchte mich dazu jetzt nicht ~:** I don't want to comment on that at present; (**b**) (in Erscheinung treten) ‹*illness*› manifest itself; ‹*emotion*› show itself, be expressed

außer-: ~**ordentlich** 1 *Adj.* (**a**) extraordinary; (**b**) (das Gewohnte übertreffend) exceptional; *s. auch* **Professor;** 2 *adv.* (sehr) exceptionally; ‹*value*› highly; extremely ‹*pleased, relieved*›; ~**ordentlich viel Mühe** an enormous *or* exceptional amount of trouble; **∼plan·mäßig** *Adj.* (a) unscheduled; unbudgeted ⟨*expenditure*⟩; (b) ⇒ **∼fahrplanmäßig**

äußerst *Adv.* extremely; extremely, exceedingly ⟨*important*⟩; **∼ knapp gewinnen/entkommen** *usw.* only just win/escape *etc.*

äußerst... *Adj.; nicht präd.* (a) farthest; (b) (größt...) extreme; **mit ∼er Umsicht** with extreme *or* the utmost circumspection; **aufs ∼e erschrocken/angestrengt/verwirrt** frightened in the extreme/strained to the utmost/utterly confused; **von ∼er Wichtigkeit sein** be of extreme *or* the utmost importance; (c) (letztmöglich) latest *or* last possible ⟨*date, deadline*⟩; **das Äußerste wagen/versuchen** risk/try everything; (d) (schlimmst...) worst; **im ∼en Fall** if the worst comes/came to the worst; **auf das Äußerste gefasst sein** be prepared for the worst

außerstande *Adv.* **∼ sein, etw. zu tun** (nicht befähigt) be unable to do sth.; (nicht in der Lage) not be in a position to *or* not be able to do sth.

Äußerung *die;* **∼, ∼en** comment; remark

aus|setzen 1 *tr. V.* (a) expose (*Dat.* to); **Belastungen ausgesetzt sein** be subject to strains; (b) (sich selbst überlassen) abandon ⟨*baby, animal*⟩; (auf einer einsamen Insel) maroon; (c) (hinaussetzen) release ⟨*animal*⟩ [into the wild]; plant out ⟨*plants, seedlings*⟩; launch, lower ⟨*boat*⟩; (d) **an jmdm./etw. nichts auszusetzen haben** have no objection to sb./sth.; **an jmdm./etw./allem etwas auszusetzen haben** find fault with sb./sth./everything; **daran war nichts auszusetzen** there was nothing wrong with that; (e) (in Aussicht stellen) offer ⟨*reward, prize*⟩; **eine große Summe für etw. ∼:** provide a large sum for sth.; (f) (Kaufmannsspr.) prepare ⟨*consignment*⟩ [for packing]. 2 *itr. V.* (a) (aufhören) stop; ⟨*engine, machine*⟩ cut out, stop; ⟨*heart*⟩ stop [beating]; (b) (eine Pause machen) ⟨*player*⟩ miss a turn; **er muss solange ∼, bis er eine Sechs würfelt** he must wait until he throws a six; **mit seinem Studium ∼:** interrupt one's studies; **mit den Tabletten ∼:** stop taking the tablets

Aus·setzer *der* (Kaufmannsspr.) *employee who prepares consignments etc. for packing*

Ausfuhr·verbot *das* (Wirtsch.) export embargo

Aus·sicht *die* (a) view (**auf** + *Akk.* of); **ein Zimmer mit ∼ aufs Meer** a room overlooking the sea; **jmdm. die ∼ nehmen/versperren** block *or* obstruct sb.'s view; (b) (fig.) prospect (**auf** + *Akk.* of); **das sind ja vielleicht [heitere] ∼en!** (iron.) that's a fine prospect! (iron.); **∼ auf etw.** (*Akk.*) **haben** have the prospect of sth.; **er hat gute ∼en, gewählt zu werden** he stands a good chance of being elected; **etw. in ∼ haben** have the prospect of sth.; have sth. in prospect

aussichts-, Aussichts-: ∼los 1 *Adj.* hopeless; 2 *adv.* hopelessly; **∼losigkeit** *die;* **∼:** hopelessness; **∼reich** *Adj.* promising; **∼turm** *der* lookout *or* observation tower

aus|sieben *tr. V.* sift out; screen ⟨*coal*⟩

aus|siedeln *tr. V.* move out and resettle; (evakuieren) evacuate

Aus·siedler *der;* **Aus·siedlerin** *die* emigrant

aus|söhnen 1 *refl. V.:* ⇒ **versöhnen** 1. 2 *tr. V.:* ⇒ **versöhnen** 2 a

Aussöhnung *die;* **∼, ∼en** reconciliation

aus|sondern *tr. V.* (a) (ausscheiden) weed out; (b) (auswählen) sort *or* pick out; select

aus|sortieren *tr. V.* sort out

aus|spannen 1 *tr. V.* (a) unharness, unhitch ⟨*horse, mule*⟩; unyoke ⟨*oxen*⟩; (b) (salopp: wegnehmen) **jmdm. etw. ∼:** get sb. to part with sth.; **jmdm. den Freund/die Freundin ∼:** pinch sb.'s boyfriend/girlfriend (esp. Brit. coll.). 2 *itr. V.* (ausruhen) take *or* have a break

aus|sparen *tr. V.* leave ⟨*line etc.*⟩ blank; (fig.) leave out; omit

aus|sperren 1 *tr. V.* lock out; shut ⟨*animal*⟩ out. 2 *itr. V.* organize a lockout; lock the workforce out

Aus·sperrung *die* lockout

aus|spielen 1 *tr. V.* (a) (Kartenspiel) lead; **sein ganzes Wissen ∼** (fig.) make use of all one's knowledge; (b) (manipulieren) **jmdn./etw. gegen jmdn./etw. ∼:** play sb./sth.

off against sb./sth. 2 *itr. V.* (Kartenspiel) lead; **wer spielt aus?** whose lead is it?

aus|spionieren *tr. V.* spy out

Aus·sprache *die* (a) pronunciation; (Artikulation) articulation; (Akzent) accent; (b) (Gespräch) discussion; (zwangloseres) talk

Aussprache·wörterbuch *das* pronouncing dictionary

aussprechbar *Adj.* pronounceable

aus|sprechen 1 *unr. tr. V.* (a) pronounce; (b) (ausdrücken) express; voice ⟨*suspicion, request*⟩; grant ⟨*divorce*⟩; **der Regierung das Vertrauen ∼:** pass a vote of confidence in the government. 2 *unr. refl. V.* (a) (ausgesprochen werden) be pronounced; (b) (sich äußern) speak; **sich lobend/missbilligend über jmdn./etw. ∼:** speak highly/disapprovingly of sb./sth.; **er hat sich nicht näher darüber ausgesprochen** he did not say anything further about it; **sich für jmdn./etw. ∼:** declare *or* pronounce oneself in favour of sb./sth.; **sich gegen jmdn./etw. ∼:** declare *or* pronounce oneself against sb./sth.; (c) (offen sprechen) say what's on one's mind; **sich mit** *od.* **bei jmdm. ∼:** have a heart-to-heart talk with sb.; (d) (Strittiges klären) have it out, talk things out (mit with); **wir haben uns über alles ausgesprochen** we had everything out. 3 *unr. itr. V.* finish [speaking]

Aus·spruch *der* remark; (Sinnspruch) saying

aus|spucken 1 *itr. V.* spit. 2 *tr. V.* (a) spit out; (fig. ugs.) spew out ⟨*products, data, results, etc.*⟩; cough up (coll.) ⟨*money*⟩; (b) (ugs.: erbrechen) throw up

aus|spülen *tr. V.* (a) flush *or* wash out; (b) (reinigen) rinse out; (Med.) irrigate; wash out; **sich** (*Dat.*) **den Mund ∼:** rinse one's mouth out

aus|staffieren /'aʊsʃtafiːrən/ *tr. V.* kit *or* rig out; fit out, furnish ⟨*room etc.*⟩; (verkleiden) dress up

Aus·stand *der* strike; **im ∼ sein** be on strike; **in den ∼ treten** go on strike

aus|statten /'aʊsʃtatn̩/ *tr. V.* provide (**mit** with); (mit Kleidung) provide; fit out; (mit Gerät) equip; (mit Möbeln, Teppichen usw.) furnish; **mit Befugnissen ausgestattet sein** be vested with authority *sing.;* **ein prächtig ausgestatteter Band** a splendidly produced volume

Ausstattung *die;* **∼, ∼en** (a) (das Ausstatten) ⇒ **ausstatten:** provision; fitting out; equipping; furnishing; vesting; production; (b) (Ausrüstung) equipment; (Innen eines Autos) trim; (c) (Einrichtung) furnishings *pl.;* (d) (Film, Theater) décor and costumes; (e) (Buchw.) design and layout; (typographisch) design

aus|stechen *unr. tr. V.* (a) **jmdm. die Augen ∼:** put *or* gouge sb.'s eyes out; (b) (entfernen) dig up ⟨*plants*⟩; cut ⟨*turf*⟩; (c) (herstellen) dig [out] ⟨*trench, hole, etc.*⟩ (Kochk.) press *or* cut out ⟨*biscuits*⟩; (d) (übertreffen) outdo; **jmdn. bei jmdm. ∼:** oust sb. in sb.'s affections/esteem/favour

aus|stehen 1 *unr. itr. V.* **noch ∼** ⟨*money, amount*⟩ be outstanding; ⟨*decision*⟩ be still to be taken, have not yet been taken; ⟨*solution*⟩ be still to be found; **ihre Antwort steht noch aus** I am/we are *etc.* still awaiting their reply; **∼de Forderungen** outstanding demands. 2 *unr. tr. V.* endure ⟨*pain, suffering*⟩; suffer ⟨*worry, anxiety*⟩; **ausgestanden sein** be all over; **ich kann ihn/das nicht ∼:** I can't stand *or* bear him/it

aus|steigen *unr. itr. V.; mit sein;* (a) (aus einem Auto, Boot) get out (**aus** of); (aus einem Zug, Bus) get off; alight (formal); (Fliegerspr.: abspringen) bale out; **aus einem Zug/Bus ∼:** get off a train/bus; alight from a train/bus (formal); (b) (ugs.: sich nicht mehr beteiligen) **∼ aus** opt out of; give up ⟨*show business, job*⟩; leave ⟨*project*⟩; (c) (Sport: aus einem Rennen o. Ä.) drop out (**aus** of); retire (**aus** from); (d) (ugs.: der Gesellschaft den Rücken kehren) drop out

Aussteiger *der;* **∼s, ∼** (ugs.) drop-out (coll.)

aus|stellen *tr. V.* (a) *auch itr.* put on display; display; (im Museum, auf einer Messe) exhibit; **ausgestellt sein** ⟨*goods*⟩ be on display/be exhibited; ⟨*painting*⟩ be exhibited; (b) (ausfertigen) make out, write [out] ⟨*cheque, prescription, receipt*⟩; make out ⟨*bill*⟩; issue ⟨*visa, passport, certificate*⟩; (c) (ugs.: ausschalten) turn *or* switch off

Aussteller *der;* ~s, ~, **Ausstellerin** *die;* ~, ~nen (a) (auf Messen) exhibitor; (b) (eines Dokuments) issuer; (Behörde) issuing authority; (eines Schecks) drawer

Aus·stellung *die* (a) exhibiting; (b) (das Ausfertigen) ⇒ **ausstellen b:** making out; writing [out]; issuing; (c) (Veranstaltung) exhibition

Ausstellungs-: ~gelände *das* exhibition site; ~halle *die* exhibition hall; ~raum *der* exhibition room; ~stück *das* display item; (in Museen usw.) exhibit

aus|sterben *unr. itr. V.; mit sein* (auch fig.) die out; ‹species› die out, become extinct; **ein ~des Handwerk** (fig.) a dying craft

Aus·steuer *die* trousseau (consisting mainly of household linen)

aus|steuern *tr. V.* (Elektronik) modulate ‹signal, wave›; (bei der Aufnahme) control the recording level of; control the power level of ‹amplifier›

Ausstieg *der;* ~[e]s, ~e (a) (Ausgang) exit; (Tür) door[s]; (~luke) hatch; (b) *o. Pl.* (das Aussteigen) climbing out (**aus** of); „Kein ~" 'no exit'

aus|stopfen *tr. V.* stuff

aus|stoßen *unr. tr. V.* (a) expel; give off, emit ‹gas, fumes, smoke›; (b) give ‹cry, whistle, laugh, etc.›; let out ‹cry, scream, yell›; heave, give ‹sigh›; utter ‹curse, threat, accusation, etc.›; (c) jmdm. ein Auge ~: put sb.'s eye out; (d) (ausschließen) expel (**aus** from); (aus der Armee) drum out (**aus** of); **sich ausgestoßen fühlen** feel an outcast

aus|strahlen 1 *tr. V.* (a) (auch fig.) radiate; radiate, give off ‹heat›; ‹lamp› give out ‹light›; (b) (Rundf., Ferns.) broadcast; transmit. 2 *itr. V.* (a) radiate; ‹heat› radiate, be given off; ‹light› be given out; (fig.) ‹pain› spread, extend; (b) (fig.) **auf jmdn./etw. ~:** communicate itself to sb./influence sth.

Aus·strahlung *die* (a) radiation; (eines Menschen) charisma; (b) (Rundf., Ferns.) transmission

aus|strecken 1 *tr. V.* extend, stretch out ‹arms, legs›; stretch out ‹hand›; put out ‹feelers›; stick *or* put out ‹tongue›; **mit ausgestreckten Armen** with arms extended; with outstretched arms. 2 *refl. V.* stretch [oneself] out; **ausgestreckt am Boden liegen** lie stretched out on the floor

aus|streichen *unr. tr. V.* (a) (durchstreichen) cross *or* strike out; delete; (b) (verstreichen) spread; (c) (Kochk.) grease ‹tin, pan, etc.›; (d) (füllen) fill, smooth over ‹cracks›

aus|strömen 1 *tr. V.* radiate ‹warmth›; give off ‹scent›; (fig.) radiate ‹optimism, confidence, etc.›. 2 *itr. V.; mit sein* stream *or* pour out; ‹gas, steam› escape

aus|suchen *tr. V.* choose; pick; **such dir was aus!** choose what you want; take your pick

Aus·tausch *der* (a) exchange; **im ~ gegen** in exchange for; (b) (das Ersetzen) replacement (**gegen** with); (Sport) substitution (**gegen** by)

austauschbar *Adj.* interchangeable; (ersetzbar) replaceable

aus|tauschen *tr. V.* (a) exchange (**gegen** for); (b) (ersetzen) replace (**gegen** with); (Sport) substitute (**gegen** by)

Austausch-: ~motor *der* (Kfz-W.) replacement engine; ~schüler *der* exchange pupil *or* student

aus|teilen *tr. V.* (verteilen) distribute (**an** + Akk. to); (ausgeben) hand *or* give out ‹books, post, etc.› (**an** + Akk. to); issue, give ‹orders›; deal [out] ‹cards›; give out ‹marks, grades›; administer ‹sacrament›; serve ‹food etc.›; give ‹blessing›; **Prügel ~** (fig.) hand out beatings

Auster /'austɐ/ *die;* ~, ~n oyster

aus|tilgen *tr. V.* exterminate ‹pests, race›; eradicate ‹weeds›; wipe out, eradicate ‹disease›

aus|toben *refl. V.* romp about; have a good romp

aus|tragen *unr. tr. V.* (a) (zustellen) deliver ‹newspapers, post›; (b) (im Mutterleib) carry ‹child› to full term; (nicht abtreiben) have ‹child›; (c) (ausfechten) settle; settle, resolve ‹conflict, differences›; fight out ‹battle›; **einen Streit mit jmdm. ~:** have it out with sb.; (d) (bes. Sport) hold ‹competition, race, event›

Australien /aus'traːli̯ən/ *(das);* ~s Australia

Australier *der;* ~s, ~, **Australierin** *die;* ~, ~nen ▶388 Australian

australisch *Adj.* ▶388 Australian

aus|treiben 1 *unr. tr. V.* (a) exorcize, cast out ‹evil spirit, demon›; (b) jmdm. etw. ~: cure sb. of sth.; (c) (geh.: vertreiben) drive out (**aus** from). 2 *unr. itr. V.* ‹plant› sprout

aus|treten 1 *unr. tr. V.* (a) tread out ‹spark, cigarette end›; trample out ‹fire›; (b) (bahnen) tread out ‹path›; **ausgetretene Pfade** (fig.) well-trodden paths; (c) (abnutzen) wear down; **ausgetretene Stufen** worn-down steps; (d) (weiten) wear out ‹shoes›; break in ‹new shoes›. 2 *unr. itr. V.; mit sein* (a) (ugs.: zur Toilette gehen) pay a call (coll.); **der Schüler fragte, ob er ~ dürfe** the pupil asked to be excused; (b) (ausscheiden) leave; **aus etw. ~:** leave sth.; **aus einer Vereinigung ~:** resign from a society; (c) (nach außen gelangen) come out; (entweichen) escape

aus|tricksen *tr. V.* (ugs.) trick

aus|trinken 1 *tr. V.* finish, drink up ‹drink›; finish, drain ‹glass, cup, etc.›. 2 *itr. V.* drink up

Aus·tritt *der* leaving; (aus einer Vereinigung) resignation (**aus** from); **seinen ~ aus der Partei/Kirche erklären** announce that one is leaving the party/church

aus|trocknen 1 *tr. V.* dry out; dry up ‹river bed, marsh›; parch ‹throat›. 2 *itr. V.; mit sein* dry out; ‹river bed, pond, etc.› dry up; ‹skin, hair› become dry; ‹throat› become parched

aus|trudeln *itr. V.* (ugs.) ⇒ **auswürfeln**

aus|tüfteln *tr. V.* (ugs.) work out; (ersinnen) think up

aus|üben *tr. V.* practise ‹art, craft›; follow ‹profession›; carry on ‹trade›; do ‹job›; wield, exercise ‹power›; exercise ‹right, control›; exert ‹influence, pressure›; **welche Tätigkeit üben Sie aus?** what is your occupation?

Aus·übung *die o. Pl.;* ⇒ **ausüben:** practising; following; carrying on; doing; wielding; exercising; exertion

aus|ufern *itr. V.; mit sein* get out of hand

Aus·verkauf *der* [clearance] sale; (wegen Geschäftsaufgabe) closing-down (Brit.) *or* (Amer.) liquidation sale; (fig.) sell-out; **etw. im ~ kaufen** buy sth. at the sale[s]

ausverkauft *Adj.* sold out; **Bier ist ~:** there is no beer left [in stock]; **wir sind ~:** we are sold out; **vor ~em Haus spielen** play to a full house

aus|wachsen 1 *unr. refl. V.* (a) (verschwinden) right *or* correct itself; (b) (sich entwickeln) grow (**zu** into). 2 *unr. itr. V.* **zum Auswachsen sein** (ugs.) be enough to drive you up the wall (coll.)

Aus·wahl *die* (a) (das Auswählen) choice; selection; **Sie haben die [freie] ~:** the choice is yours; you can choose whichever you like; **bei uns stehen Ihnen mehr als 600 Wagen zur ~:** we offer you a choice of over 600 cars; **eine ~ treffen** make a selection; (b) (Auslese) selection; (von Texten) anthology; selection; (c) (Sortiment) range; **viel/wenig ~ haben** have a wide/limited selection (**an** + Dat., **von** of); **Spirituosen in reicher ~:** a wide selection of spirits; (d) (Sport: Mannschaft) [selected] team

aus|wählen *tr. V.* choose, select (**aus** from); **sich** (Dat.) **etw. ~:** choose *or* select sth. [for oneself]

aus|walzen *tr. V.* roll out; (fig. ugs.) drag out ‹subject›

Aus·wanderer *der* emigrant

aus|wandern *itr. V.; mit sein* emigrate

Aus·wanderung *die* emigration

auswärtig /'ausvɛrtɪç/ *Adj.; nicht präd.* (a) non-local; (b) (von auswärts stammend) ‹student, guest, etc.› from out of town; (c) (das Ausland betreffend) foreign

auswärts *Adv.* (a) (nach außen) outwards; (b) (nicht zu Hause) ‹sleep› away from home; ~ **essen** eat out; (c) (nicht am Ort) in another town; (Sport) away; **von/nach ~:** from/to another town

Auswärts- (Sport) away ‹match, win, etc.›

aus|waschen *unr. tr. V.* (a) wash out; (ausspülen) rinse out; (b) (Geol.) erode

auswechselbar *Adj.* changeable; exchangeable; (untereinander) interchangeable; (ersetzbar) replaceable

aus|wechseln *tr. V.* (a) change (**gegen** + Akk. for); (b) (ersetzen) replace (**gegen** with); (Sport) substitute ‹player›; **A gegen B ~:** replace A by B; **sie war wie ausgewechselt** she was a different person

Aus·weg der way out (**aus** of); **der letzte ~ für jmdn. sein** be a last resort for sb.

ausweg·los 1 Adj. hopeless. 2 adv. hopelessly

Ausweglosigkeit die; ~: hopelessness

aus|weichen unr. itr. V.; mit sein (a) (Platz machen) make way (Dat. for); (wegen Gefahren, Hindernissen) get out of the way (Dat. of); [nach] **rechts/nach der Seite ~**: move to the right/move aside to make way/get out of the way; **einem Schlag/ Angriff ~**: dodge a blow/evade an attack; **dem Feind ~**: avoid [contact with] the enemy; **einer Frage/Entscheidung ~**: evade a question/decision; **~de Antworten** evasive answers; (b) (zurückgreifen) **auf etw.** (Akk.) **~**: switch [over] to sth.

Ausweich·manöver das evasive manœuvre; ~ Pl. evasive action sing.

aus|weinen refl. V. have a good cry

Ausweis /ˈausvais/ der; ~es, ~e card; (Personal~) identity card; (Mitglieds~) membership card

aus|weisen 1 unr. tr. V. (a) (aus dem Land) expel (**aus** from); (b) (erkennen lassen) **jmdn. als etw. ~**: show that sb. is/was sth.; **seine Papiere wiesen ihn als … aus** his papers proved or established his identity as … 2 unr. refl. V. prove or establish one's identity [by showing one's papers]; **können Sie sich ~?** do you have any means of identification?

Ausweis·papiere Pl. identity papers

Aus·weisung die expulsion (**aus** from)

aus|weiten 1 tr. V. stretch. 2 refl. V. (a) stretch; (b) (fig.: sich vergrößern) expand; **sich zur Krise ~**: develop or grow into a crisis

aus·wendig Adv. etw. **~ können/lernen** know/learn sth. [off] by heart; **etw. ~ aufsagen** recite sth. from memory; s. auch **inwendig**

Auswendig·lernen das learning by heart

aus|werfen unr. tr. V. cast ‹net, anchor, rope, line, etc.›

aus|werten tr. V. (a) analyse and evaluate; (b) (nutzen) utilize

Aus·wertung die (a) analysis and evaluation; (Nutzung) utilization; (b) (Ergebnis) analysis

aus|wickeln tr. V. unwrap (**aus** from)

aus|wiegen unr. tr. V. weigh

aus|wirken refl. V. have an effect (**auf** + Akk. on); **sich in etw.** (Dat.) **~**: result in sth.; **sich günstig/negativ** usw. **~**: have a favourable/an unfavourable etc. effect (**auf** + Akk. on); **sich zu jmds. Vorteil ~**: work to sb.'s advantage

Aus·wirkung die effect (**auf** + Akk. on); (Folge) consequence (**auf** + Akk. for)

aus|wischen tr. V. (a) wipe ‹dirt etc.› out (**aus** of); (b) (säubern) wipe [clean]; **sich** (Dat.) **die Augen ~**: wipe one's eyes; (c) in **jmdm. eins ~** (ugs.) get one's own back on sb. (coll.)

aus|wringen unr. tr. V. (bes. nordd.) wring out

Aus·wuchs der (a) growth; excrescence (Med., Bot.); (b) (fig.) unhealthy product; (Folge) harmful consequence; (Übersteigerung, Missstand) excess

aus|wuchten tr. V. (Technik) balance

Aus·wurf der (Med.) sputum

aus|würfeln tr. V. **eine Runde Bier** usw. **~**: throw dice to decide who will pay for a round of beer etc.; **~, wer anfangen soll** throw dice to decide who will start

aus|zahlen 1 tr. V. pay [out] ‹sum, wages, etc.›; pay off ‹worker, employee›; buy out ‹partner›; **ausgezahlt bekommt er 1 650 Mark** his take-home pay is 1,650 marks. 2 refl. V. pay off; ‹investment etc.› pay; **Verbrechen zahlen sich nicht aus** crime doesn't pay

aus|zählen tr. V. (a) count [up] ‹votes etc.›; (b) (Boxen) count out

Aus·zahlung die ⇨ auszahlen1: paying [out]; paying off; buying out

Aus·zählung die counting [up]; **mit der ~ wurde bereits begonnen** the count has already started

aus|zehren tr. V. (geh.) exhaust; **ein ausgezehrtes Gesicht/eine ausgezehrte Gestalt** an emancipated face/figure

aus|zeichnen 1 tr. V. (a) (mit einem Preisschild) mark, price; (b) (ehren) honour; **jmdn. mit einem Orden ~**: decorate sb. [with a medal]; **jmdn./etw. mit einem Preis/Titel ~**: award a prize/title to sb./sth.; (c) (bevorzugt behandeln) single out for special favour; (ehren) single out for special honour; (d) (kennzeichnen) distinguish (**gegenüber, vor** + Dat. from). 2 refl. V. (durch eine Eigenschaft) stand out (**durch** for); (durch Leistung) ‹person› distinguish oneself (**durch** by)

Aus·zeichnung die (a) o. Pl. (von Waren) marking; (b) (Ehrung) honouring; (mit Orden) decoration; (c) (Orden) decoration; (Preis) award; prize; (d) in **mit ~**: with distinction

ausziehbar Adj. extendible; telescopic ‹aerial›; extending attrib. ‹ladder›; sliding-leaf attrib. ‹table›

aus|ziehen 1 unr. tr. V. (a) (vergrößern) pull out ‹couch›; extend ‹table, tripod, etc.›; (b) (ablegen) take off, remove ‹clothes›; (c) (entkleiden) undress; **sich ~**: undress; get undressed; **sich ganz/nackt ~**: strip off or undress completely; (d) (auszupfen) pull out ‹hair etc.›. 2 unr. itr. V.; mit sein move out (**aus** of)

Auszieh·tisch der extending table; sliding-leaf table

Auszubildende der/die; adj. Dekl. ▶ 85| (bes. Amtsspr.) trainee; (im Handwerk) apprentice

Aus·zug der (a) (Extrakt) extract; (b) (Exzerpt) extract; excerpt; (c) (Konto~) statement; (d) (aus Wohnung) move

auszugs·weise Adv. in extracts or excerpts; **etw. ~ lesen** read extracts from sth.

aus|zupfen tr. V. pluck out; pull out ‹weeds›

autark /auˈtark/ Adj. (Wirtsch., fig. geh.) self-sufficient

Autarkie /autarˈkiː/ die; ~, ~n (Wirtsch., fig. geh.) self-sufficiency

authentisch /auˈtɛntɪʃ/ 1 Adj. authentic. 2 adv. authentically

Authentizität /autɛntitsiˈtɛːt/ die; ~ (geh.) authenticity

Auto /ˈauto/ das; ~s, ~s car; automobile (Amer.); **~ fahren** drive; (mitfahren) go in the car; **mit dem ~ fahren** go by car

Auto-: **~atlas** der road atlas; **~bahn** die motorway (Brit.); expressway (Amer.)

Autobahn- motorway (Brit.), expressway (Amer.) ‹exit, intersection, junction, service area, etc.›

Auto·biographie die autobiography

auto·biographisch 1 Adj. autobiographical. 2 adv. autobiographically

Auto·bus der ⇨ Bus

Auto·didakt /-diˈdakt/ der; ~en, ~en autodidact

auto-, Auto-: **~fähre** die car ferry; **~fahren** das driving; motoring; **~fahrer** der [car-]driver; **~fahrt** die ▶ 160| drive; **~fokus** der autofocus; **~frei** Adj. ‹place› where no cars are/were allowed; **X ist ~frei** no cars are allowed in X; **~fried·hof** das (ugs.) car dump

auto·gen 1 Adj. (a) (Technik) **~es Schneiden/Schweißen** gas or oxyacetylene cutting/welding; (b) (Psych.) **~es Training** autogenic training; autogenics; 2 adv. (Technik) **~ schweißen/schneiden** weld/cut using an oxyacetylene flame

Auto·gramm das; ~s, ~e autograph

Autogramm·jäger der (ugs.) autograph-hunter

Auto-: **~karte** die road map; **~kino** das drive-in cinema; **~knacker** der (ugs.) car thief; **~kolonne** die line of cars

Auto·krat /-ˈkraːt/ der; ~en, ~en autocrat

auto·kratisch 1 Adj. autocratic. 2 adv. autocratically

Auto·mat /-ˈmaːt/ der; ~en, ~en (a) (Verkaufs~) [slot-]machine; vending machine; (b) (in der Produktion, fig.: Mensch) robot; automaton

Automaten·knacker der (ugs.) thief who breaks into slot machines

Automatik die; ~, ~en automatic control mechanism; (Getriebe~) automatic transmission

automatisch 1 Adj. automatic. 2 adv. automatically

automatisieren tr. V. automate

Automatisierung die; ~, ~en automation

Automatismus der; ~, **Automatismen** (Med., Biol., Psych.) automatism no art.

Auto-: ~**mechaniker** *der* ▶85⌋ motor mechanic; ~**minute** *die:* **zehn** ~**minuten entfernt sein** be ten minutes [away] by car; be ten minutes' drive [away]
Auto·mobil *das;* ~**s,** ~**e** (geh.) motor car; automobile (Amer.)
Automobil-: ~**aus·stellung** *die* motor show (Brit.); automobile show (Amer.); ~**industrie** *die* motor industry; ~**klub** *der* motoring organization
auto·nom /-'noːm/ **1** *Adj.* autonomous. **2** *adv.* autonomously
Auto·nomie /-noˈmiː/ *die;* ~, ~**n** autonomy
Auto-: ~**nummer** *die* [car] registration number; ~**papiere** *Pl.* car documents
Autopsie /autɔˈpsiː/ *die;* ~, ~**n** (Med.) autopsy; postmortem [examination]
Autor /ˈautɔr/ *der;* ~**s,** ~**en** /-ˈtoːrən/ author
Auto-: ~**radio** *das* car radio; ~**reifen** *der* car tyre; ~**reisezug** *der* Motorail train (Brit.); auto train (Amer.); ~**rennen** *das* (Sportart) motor (Brit.) *or* (Amer.) auto racing; (Veranstaltung) motor (Brit.) *or* (Amer.) auto race; ~**reparatur** *die* car repair; repair to the/a car
Autorin *die;* ~, ~**nen** authoress; author
autoritär /autoriˈtɛːɐ/ **1** *Adj.* authoritarian. **2** *adv.* in an authoritarian manner
Autorität /autoriˈtɛːt/ *die;* ~, ~**en** authority
autoritäts·gläubig *Adj.* trusting in authority *pred.*
Auto-: ~**schlange** *die* queue *or* line of cars; ~**schlüssel** *der* car key; ~**skooter** /~skuːtɐ/ *der* dodgem; bumper car; ~**stopp** *der* hitch-hiking; hitching (coll.); **per** *od.* **mit** ~**stopp fahren,** ~**stopp machen** hitch-hike; hitch (coll.); ~**telefon** *das* car telephone; ~**tür** *die* car door; ~**unfall** *der* car accident; ~**verkehr** *der* [motor] traffic; ~**verleih** *der,* ~**vermietung** *die* car hire (Brit.) *or* rental firm *or* service; ~**werkstatt** *die* garage; car repair shop; ~**zubehör** *das* car accessories *pl.*
autsch /autʃ/ *Interj.* ouch; ow
Au·wald *der* riverside forest
auwei[a] /auˈvai(a)/ *Interj.* (ugs.) oh dear
avancieren /avãˈsiːrən/ *itr. V.; mit sein* (geh.) be promoted (also iron.); rise
Avantgarde /avãˈgardə/ *die;* ~, ~**n** avant-garde; (Politik) vanguard (fig.)
avantgardistisch **1** *Adj.* avant-garde. **2** *adv.* ‹paint etc.› in an avant-garde style
AvD /aːfauˈdeː/ *der;* ~ *Abk.:* **Automobilclub von Deutschland**
Ave-Maria /aˈvemaˈriːa/ *das;* ~[s], ~[s] (kath. Kirche) Ave Maria; Hail Mary
Aversion /averˈzjoːn/ *die;* ~, ~**en** aversion
Avis /aˈviː/ *der od. das;* ~ (Kaufmannsspr., Bankw.) advice; (schriftlich) advice note
avisieren /aviˈziːrən/ *tr. V.* (bes. Wirtsch.) send notification of; advise *or* notify of
Aviso /aˈviːzo/ *das;* ~**s,** ~**s** (österr.) ⇒ **Avis**
Avocado /avoˈkaːdo/ *die;* ~, ~**s** avocado [pear]
Axel /ˈaksl̩/ *der;* ~**s,** ~ (Eis-, Rollkunstlauf) axel
Axiom /aˈksjoːm/ *das;* ~**s,** ~**e** axiom
Axt /akst/ *die;* ~, **Äxte** /ˈɛkstə/ axe
Azalee /atsaˈleːa/ *die;* ~, ~**n** azalea
Azteke /atsˈteːkə/ *der;* ~**n,** ~**n** Aztec
Azubi /aˈtsubi/ *der;* ~**s,** ~**s**/*die;* ~, ~**s** (ugs.) ⇒ **Auszubildende**
azur·blau /aˈtsuːɐ-/ *Adj.* (geh.) azure[-blue]

B b

b, B /beː/ *das;* ~, ~ (a) (Buchstabe) b/B; (b) (Musik) [key of] B flat; *s. auch* **a, A**
B *Abk.* **Bundesstraße**
BAB *Abk.* **Bundesautobahn**
Babel /ˈbaːbl̩/ *(das);* ~**s** Babel; **der Turmbau zu** ~: the building of the Tower of Babel
Baby /ˈbeːbi/ *das;* ~**s,** ~**s** baby
Baby·ausstattung *die* layette
babylonisch *Adj.* Babylonian; **ein** ~**es Sprachengewirr** a babel of languages
baby-, Baby-: ~|**sitten** /~sɪtn̩/ *itr. V.; nur im Inf.* (ugs.) babysit; ~**sitter** /~sɪtɐ/ *der;* ~**s,** ~: babysitter; ~**sitting** /~sɪtɪŋ/ *das;* ~**s** babysitting; ~**wäsche** *die* baby clothes
Bach /bax/ *der;* ~[e]s, **Bäche** /ˈbɛçə/ stream; brook; (fig.) stream [of water]; **den** ~ **runtergehen** (ugs.) get pushed into the background
Bache /ˈbaxə/ (Jägerspr.) *die;* ~, ~**n** wild sow
Bach·stelze *die* wagtail
Back·blech *das* baking sheet
Back·bord *das* (Seew., Luftf.) port [side]; **über** ~: over the port side
backbord[s] /ˈbakbɔrt(s)/ *Adv.* (Seew., Luftf.) on the port side
Bäckchen /ˈbɛkçən/ *das;* ~**s,** ~: [little] cheek
Backe /ˈbakə/ *die;* ~, ~**n** (a) ▶326⌋ (Wange) cheek; *s. auch* **voll 1 a**; (b) ▶326⌋ (ugs.: Gesäß~) buttock; cheek (sl.)
backen /ˈbakn̩/ **1** *unr. itr. V.* (a) bake; (b) ‹cake etc.› bake. **2** *unr. tr. V.* (a) bake ‹cakes, bread, etc.›; **ich backe vieles selbst** I do a lot of my own baking; (fig.) **das frisch gebackene Ehepaar** (ugs.) the newly-weds *pl.* (coll.); **ein frisch gebackener Arzt** (ugs.) a newly-fledged doctor; (b) (bes. südd.: braten) roast; (in der Bratpfanne) fry
Backen-: ~**bart** *der* side-whiskers *pl.;* sideboards *pl.* (sl.); ~**knochen** *der* ▶326⌋ cheek-bone ~**zahn** *der* ▶326⌋ molar
Bäcker /ˈbɛkɐ/ *der;* ~**s,** ~ ▶85⌋ (a) baker; ~ **lernen** learn the baker's trade; learn to be a baker; **er will** ~ **werden/ist** ~: he wants to be/is a baker; (b) (Geschäft) baker's [shop]; **zum** ~ **gehen** go to the baker's; **beim** ~: at the baker's
Bäckerei *die;* ~, ~**en** baker's [shop]
Bäckerin *die;* ~, ~**nen** baker
Bäcker-: ~**laden** *der* baker's shop; ~**lehre** *die* baker's apprenticeship; ~**meister** *der* master baker
Bäckers·frau *die* baker's wife
Back-: ~**fisch** *der* (bes. südd.) fried fish (*in breadcrumbs*); ~**form** *die* baking tin (Brit.); baking pan (Amer.)
Background /ˈbɛkgraunt/ *der;* ~**s,** ~**s** background
Back-: ~**hähnchen** *das* (bes. südd.), ~**hendl** *das* (österr.) fried chicken (*in breadcrumbs*); ~**obst** *das* dried fruit; ~**ofen** *der* oven; ~**pfeife** *die* (bes. nordd.) slap in the face; ~**pulver** *das* baking powder; ~**röhre** *die* oven; ~**stein** *der* brick; ~**stube** *die* bakery; bakehouse; ~**waren** *Pl.* bread, cakes, and pastries
Bad /baːt/ *das;* ~[e]s, **Bäder** /ˈbɛːdɐ/ (a) (Wasser) bath; [**sich** (*Dat.*)] **ein** ~ **einlaufen lassen** run [oneself] a bath; (b) (das Baden) bath; (das Schwimmen) swim; (im Meer o. ä.) bathe; **ein** ~ **nehmen** (geh.) have *or* take a bath; (schwimmen) go for a swim; (im Meer o. ä.) bathe; **nach dem** ~: after bathing; (c) (Badezimmer) bathroom; **ein Zimmer mit** ~: a room with [private] bath; (d) (Schwimm~) [swimming] bath; swimming bath; (e) (Heil~) spa; (See~) [seaside] resort; (f) (Technik) bath
Bade-: ~**anstalt** *die* swimming baths *pl.* (Brit.); public pool (Amer.); ~**an·zug** *der* swimming *or* bathing costume; swimsuit; ~**gast** *der* bather; swimmer; ~**hose** *die*

swimming or bathing trunks pl; ~**mantel** der dressing gown; bathrobe; ~**meister** der swimming pool attendant; ~**mütze** die swimming or bathing cap

baden 1 itr. V. (a) (in der Wanne) have or take a bath; bath; **warm** ~: have or take a hot bath; (b) (schwimmen) bathe; swim; ~ **gehen** go for a bathe or a swim; go bathing or swimming; [**bei** od. **mit etw.**] ~ **gehen** (fig. ugs.) come a cropper (coll.) [over sth.]. 2 tr. V. bath ‹person›; bathe ‹wound, face, eye, etc.›; **in Schweiß gebadet** (fig.) bathed in sweat

Baden-Württemberg /'ba:dn̩'vʏrtəmbɛrk/ (das); ~s Baden-Württemberg

Baden-Württemberger 1 indekl. Adj.; nicht präd. Baden-Württemberg attrib. 2 der; ~s, ~: native of Baden-Württemberg; (Einwohner) inhabitant of Baden-Württemberg

baden-württembergisch Adj. of Baden-Württemberg postpos.; ‹produce, wine, etc.› from Baden-Württemberg

Bade-: ~**ofen** der bathwater heater; ~**ort** der (a) (Seebad) [seaside] resort; (b) (Kurort) spa; ~**platz** der bathing-place; ~**sachen** Pl. bathing or swimming things; ~**salz** das bath salts pl.; ~**strand** der bathing-beach; ~**tuch** das bath towel; ~**wanne** die bath[-tub]; ~**wasser** das bath water; ~**zeug** das (ugs.) bathing or swimming things pl.; ~**zimmer** das bathroom

baff /baf/ in ~ **sein** (ugs.) be flabbergasted

Bagage /ba'ga:ʒə/ die; ~, ~**n** (abwertend) (Familie) tribe (derog.); (Gesindel) rabble; crowd (coll.); **die ganze** ~: the whole lot of them

Bagatelle /baga'tɛlə/ die; ~, ~**n** trifle; bagatelle

Bagger /'bagɐ/ der; ~**s**, ~: excavator; digger; (Schwimm~) dredger

baggern tr., itr. V. excavate; (mit dem Schwimmbagger) dredge

Bagger·see der flooded gravel-pit

Baguette /ba'gɛt/ die; ~, ~**n** baguette

bah /ba:/ Interj. ugh

bäh /bɛ:/ Interj. (bei Ekel) ugh; (schadenfroh) hee-hee; tee-hee

Bahama·inseln /ba'ha:ma-/, **Bahamas** Pl. die ~: the Bahamas

Bahn /ba:n/ die; ~, ~**en** (a) (Weg) path; way; (von Wasser) course; (fig.) **einer Sache** (Dat.) ~ **brechen** pave or prepare the way for sth.; **jmdn. aus der** ~ **werfen** od. **bringen** od. **schleudern** knock sb. sideways; **auf die schiefe** ~ **geraten** go astray; (b) (Strecke) path; (Umlauf~) orbit; (einer Rakete) [flight-] path; (eines Geschosses) trajectory; **etw. [wieder] in die richtige** ~ **lenken** (fig.) get sth. [back] on the right track; (c) (Sport) track; (für Pferderennen) course (Brit.); track (Amer.); (für einzelne Teilnehmer) lane; (Kegel~) alley; (Schlitten~, Bob~) run; (Bowling~) lane; ~ **frei!** make way!; get out of the way!; (d) (Fahrspur) lane; (e) (Eisen~) railways pl.; railroad (Amer.); (Zug) train; **jmdn. zur** ~ **bringen/an der** ~ **abholen** take sb. to/pick sb. up from the station; **mit der** ~: by train; ~ **fahren** go by train; (f) (Straßen~) tram; streetcar (Amer.); (g) (Schienenweg) railway [track]; (h) (Streifen) (Stoff~) length; (Tapeten~) strip; length

bahn-, Bahn-: ~**beamte** der railway or (Amer.) railroad official; ~**brechend** Adj. pioneering; ~**brechend für etw. sein** pave or prepare the way for sth.; ~**bus** der railway bus

Bähnchen /'bɛ:nçən/ das; ~**s**, ~: little train

Bahn·damm der railway or (Amer.) railroad embankment

bahnen tr. V. clear ‹way, path›; **jmdm./einer Sache einen Weg** ~: clear the or a way for sb./sth.; (fig.) pave or prepare the way for sb./sth.; **sich** (Dat.) **einen Weg durch etw.** ~: force a or one's way through sth.

Bahn-: ~**fahrt** die train or rail journey; ~**gleis** das railway or (Amer.) railroad track or line

Bahn·hof der [railway or (Amer.) railroad] station; ~ **Käfertal** Käfertal station; **ich verstehe nur** ~ (ugs.) it's [all] double Dutch to me

Bahnhofs-: ~**gast·stätte** die station restaurant; ~**halle** die station concourse; ~**hotel** das station hotel; ~**mission** die ≈ Travellers' Aid (charitable organization for helping rail travellers in need of care or assistance)

bahn-, Bahn-: ~**lagernd** (a) Adj. to be collected from the station postpos.; (b) adv. **Waren** ~**lagernd schicken** send goods to await collection at the station; ~**linie** die railway or (Amer.) railroad line; ~**polizei** die railway or (Amer.) railroad police; ~**reise** die train or rail journey; ~**schranke** die level-crossing (Brit.) or (Amer.) grade crossing barrier/gate; ~**steig** /~ʃtaik/ der; ~[**e**]**s**, ~**e** [station] platform; ~**über·gang** der level crossing (Brit.); grade or railroad crossing (Amer.); ~**ver·bindung** die rail (Brit.) or train connection; ~**wärter** der level-crossing keeper (Brit.)

Bahre /'ba:rə/ die; ~, ~**n** (a) (Kranken~) stretcher; (b) (Toten~) bier

bairisch /'bairɪʃ/ Adj. Bavarian

Baiser /bɛ'ze:/ das; ~**s**, ~**s** meringue

Bajonett /bajo'nɛt/ das; ~[**e**]**s**, ~**e** bayonet

Bajuware /baju'va:rə/ der; ~**n**, ~**n** (scherzh.) Bavarian

Bakkarat /'bakara(t)/ das; ~**s** baccarat

Bakterie /bak'te:riə/ die; ~, ~**n** bacterium

bakteriell Adj. bacterial

bakteriologisch 1 Adj. bacteriological. 2 adv. bacteriologically

Balalaika /bala'laika/ die; ~, ~**s** od. **Balalaiken** balalaika

Balance /ba'laŋsə/ die; ~, ~**n** balance; **die** ~ **halten/ verlieren** keep/lose one's balance

balancieren /balaŋ'si:rən/ 1 itr. V.; mit sein (auch fig.) balance 2 tr. V. balance

bald /balt/ Adv. (a) soon; **das wird er so** ~ **nicht vergessen** he won't forget that in a hurry; **wirds** ~? get a move on, will you; **bis** ~: see you soon; (b) (ugs.: fast) almost; nearly; (c) (veralt.) **in** ~ ..., ~ ...: now ..., now ...; ~ **so,** ~ **so** now this way, now that

Baldachin /'baldaxi:n/ der; ~**s**, ~**e** baldachin; (über dem Bett) canopy

baldig Adj.; nicht präd. speedy; quick

bald·möglichst Adv. (Papierdt.) as soon as possible

Baldrian /'baldria:n/ der; ~**s**, ~**e** valerian

Balearen /bale'a:rən/ Pl. die ~: the Balearic Islands

Balg das; ~[**e**]**s**, **Bälger** /'bɛlgɐ/ od. **Bälge** /'bɛlgə/ (ugs., oft abwertend) kid (coll.); brat (derog.)

balgen refl. V. (ugs.) scrap (coll.) (**um** over); (fig.) fight (**um** over)

Balgerei die; ~, ~**en** (ugs.) scrap (coll.)

Balkan /'balka:n/ der; ~**s: der** ~: the Balkans pl.; (Gebirge) the Balkan Mountains pl.; **auf dem** ~: in the Balkans

Balkan- Balkan ‹Peninsula, country, etc.›

Balken /'balkn̩/ der; ~**s**, ~: beam; **lügen, dass sich die** ~ **biegen** (ugs.) tell a [complete] pack of lies; (b) (Schwebe~) beam; (c) (Musik) cross-stroke

Balken·überschrift die banner headline

Balkon /bal'koŋ, bal'ko:n/ der; ~**s**, ~**s** /bal'kɔŋs/ od. ~**e** /bal'ko:nə/ (a) balcony; (b) (in Theater) [dress] circle; (im Kino) circle

Ball /bal/ der; ~[**e**]**s**, **Bälle** /'bɛlə/ (a) (auch fig.: Kugel) ball; ~ **spielen** play ball; **am** ~ **sein** have the ball; (fig. ugs.) be in touch; be on the ball (coll.); **am** ~ **bleiben** (fig. ugs.) stick (coll.) or keep at it; (b) (Sportjargon: Schuss, Wurf) ball; (aufs Tor) shot; (c) (Fest) ball

ballaballa /bala'bala/ Adj.; nicht attr. (salopp) crackers (sl.); daft

Ballade /ba'la:də/ die; ~, ~**n** ballad

balladenhaft Adj. ballad-like

Ballast /ba'last/ der; ~[**e**]**s**, ~**e** ballast; (fig.: in Text) padding; ~ **abwerfen** od. **über Bord werfen** (fig.) rid oneself of unnecessary burdens

Bällchen /'bɛlçən/ das; ~**s**, ~: [little] ball

ballen 1 tr. V. clench ‹fist›; crumple ‹paper› into a ball; press ‹snow etc.› into a ball. 2 refl. V. ‹clouds› gather, build up; ⟨*crowd*⟩ gather; ⟨*fist*⟩ clench; (fig.) ⟨*problems, difficulties, etc.*⟩ accumulate, mount up

Ballen *der;* ~s, ~ (a) bale; (b) (Hand~, Fuß~) ball

Ballerei *die;* ~, ~en (ugs.) shoot-out

Baller·mann *der; Pl.* -männer (ugs.) shooting-iron (sl.); shooter (coll.)

ballern (ugs.) **1** *itr. V.* (a) (schießen) fire [away]; bang away; (b) (schlagen) bang, hammer (gegen on). **2** *tr. V.* (a) jmdm. **eine** ~: sock sb. one (sl.); (b) (Sportjargon) fire ⟨*ball*⟩

Ballett /ba'lɛt/ *das;* ~[e]s, ~e ballet; **beim** ~ **sein** (ugs.) be a ballet dancer

Ballistik *die;* ~: ballistics *sing., no art.*

ballistisch *Adj.* ballistic

Ball-: ~**junge** *der* ballboy; ~**kleid** *das* ball dress *or* gown

Ballon /ba'lɔŋ/ *der;* ~s, ~s (a) balloon; (b) (salopp: Kopf) nut (coll.)

Ball-: ~**saal** *der* ballroom; ~**spiel** *das* ball game; ~**spielen** *das;* ~s playing ball *no art.;* ~**spielen verboten** no ball games

Ballungs·gebiet *das* conurbation

Ball·wechsel *der* (Tennis, Tischtennis, Badminton) rally

Balsam /'balza:m/ *der;* ~s, ~e balsam; balm; (fig.) balm

Balsam·essig *der* balsamic vinegar

Balte /'baltə/ *der;* ~n, ~n, **Baltin** *die;* ~, ~nen Balt; **er ist Balte** he is from one of the Baltic states

Baltikum /'baltikʊm/ *das;* ~s: **das** ~: the Baltic States *pl.*

baltisch *Adj.* Baltic

Balz /balts/ *die;* ~, ~en (a) courtship display; (b) (Zeit) mating season

balzen *itr. V.* perform its/their courtship display

Bambus /'bambʊs/ *der;* ~ *od.* ~ses, ~se bamboo

Bambus·rohr *das* bamboo [cane]

Bammel /'baml/ *der;* ~s (ugs.) ~ **vor** jmdm./etw. **haben** be scared stiff of sb./sth. (coll.)

banal /ba'na:l/ **1** *Adj.* (a) (abwertend: platt) banal; trite, banal ⟨*speech, reply, etc.*⟩; (b) (gewöhnlich) commonplace; ordinary. **2** *adv.* (a) (abwertend: platt) banally; tritely; (b) (gewöhnlich) ~ **gesagt** to put it plainly and simply

Banalität *die;* ~, ~en (a) *o. Pl.* ⇒ **banal 1**: banality; triteness; commonplaceness; ordinariness; (b) (Äußerung) banality

Banane /ba'na:nə/ *die;* ~, ~n banana

Banause /ba'nauzə/ *der;* ~n, ~n (abwertend) philistine

band /bant/ *1. u. 3. Pers. Sg. Prät. v.* binden

Band¹ *das;* ~[e]s, **Bänder** /'bɛndɐ/ (a) (Schmuck~; auch fig.) ribbon; (Haar~, Hut~) band; (Schürzen~) string; (b) (Mess~) measuring tape; tape measure; (Farb~) ribbon; (Klebe~, Isolier~) tape; (c) (Ton~) [magnetic] tape; **etw. auf** ~ (*Akk.*) **aufnehmen** tape[-record] sth.; (d) ⇒ **Förderband;** (e) ⇒ **Fließband;** (f) **am laufenden** ~ (ugs.) nonstop; continuously; (g) (Anat.) ligament

Band² *der;* ~[e]s, **Bände** /'bɛndə/ volume; **etw. spricht Bände** (ugs.) sth. speaks volumes

Band³ /bɛnt/ *die;* ~, ~s band

Bandage /ban'da:ʒə/ *die;* ~, ~n bandage; **mit harten** ~**n kämpfen** (fig.) fight with the gloves off

Band-: ~**aufnahme** *die* tape recording; ~**breite** *die* (fig.) range

Bändchen¹ /'bɛntçən/ *das;* ~s, ~ (kleines Band) little ribbon

Bändchen² *das;* ~s, ~ (kleiner Band) little volume

Bande¹ /'bandə/ *die;* ~, ~n (a) gang; (b) (ugs.: Gruppe) mob (sl.); crew

Bande² *die;* ~, ~n (Sport) [perimeter] barrier; (mit Reklame) billboards *pl.;* (Billard) cushion; (der Eisbahn) boards *pl.*

Banden·werbung *die advertising on hoardings around the perimeter of a football pitch etc.*

Bänder-: ~**riss,** *~**riß** *der* (Med.) torn ligament; ~**zerrung** *die* (Med.) pulled ligament

-bändig /-bɛndɪç/ *adj.* -volume

bändigen /'bɛndɪgŋ/ *tr. V.* tame ⟨*animal, sea, river, natural forces*⟩; control ⟨*person, anger, urge*⟩; bring ⟨*fire*⟩ under control

Bändigung *die;* ~: ⇒ **bändigen:** taming; controlling; bringinmg under control

Bandit /ban'di:t/ *der;* ~en, ~en bandit; brigand; (fam. scherzh.) rascal

Band-: ~**säge** *die* band-saw; ~**scheibe** *die* (Anat.) [intervertebral] disc; ~**wurm** *der* tapeworm

bang /baŋ/ ⇒ **bange**

bange; banger, bangst... od. bänger /bɛŋɐ/, **bängst...** /bɛŋst.../ **1** *Adj.* afraid; scared; (besorgt) anxious; worried; **mir ist/wurde** ~ [**zumute**] I am *or* feel/became scared *or* frightened. **2** *adv.* anxiously

Bange *die;* ~ (bes. nordd.) fear; [**nur**] **keine** ~! don't be afraid; (sei nicht besorgt) don't worry; jmdm. ~ **machen** scare *or* frighten sb.

bangen *itr. V.* **um** jmdn./etw. ~: be anxious *or* worried about sb./sth.; worry about sb./sth.

Banjo /'banjo/ *das;* ~s, ~s banjo

Bank¹ /baŋk/ *die;* ~, **Bänke** /'bɛŋkə/ bench; (mit Lehne) bench seat; (Kirchen~) pew; (Anklage~) dock; **etw. auf die lange** ~ **schieben** (ugs.) put sth. off; **durch die** ~ (ugs.) every single one; the whole lot of them

Bank² *die;* ~, ~en bank; **Geld auf der** ~ **haben** have money in the bank; **ein Konto bei einer** ~ **eröffnen** open an account with a bank

Bank-: ~**angestellte** *der/die; adj. Dekl.,* (veralt.) ~**beamte** *der* bank employee

Bänkchen /'bɛŋkçən/ *das;* ~s, ~: little *or* small bench; (mit Lehne) little *or* small seat

Bank·direktor *der* director of a/the bank

Bänkel- /'bɛŋkl-/: ~**lied** *das* street ballad; ~**sänger** *der* singer of street ballads

Bankert /'baŋkɐt/ *der;* ~s, ~e (veralt. abwertend) bastard

Bankett /ban'kɛt/ *das;* ~[e]s, ~e banquet

Bankier /ban'kie:/ *der;* ~s, ~s banker

Bank-: ~**konto** *das* bank account; ~**leit·zahl** *die* bank sorting code number; ~**note** *die* banknote; bill (Amer.); ~**raub** *der* bank robbery; ~**räuber** *der* bank robber

bankrott /ban'krɔt/ *Adj.* bankrupt; jmdn./etw. ~ **machen** bankrupt sb./sth.

Bankrott *der;* ~[e]s, ~e bankruptcy; **seinen** ~ **erklären** declare oneself bankrupt; **spellbound**); ~ **machen** *od.* **gehen** go bankrupt

Bankrotteur /baŋkrɔ'tø:ɐ/ *der;* ~s, ~e hankrupt

Bank-: ~**überfall** *der* bank raid; ~**verbindung** *die* particulars of one's bank account

Bann /ban/ *der;* ~[e]s (a) (kath. Kirche) excommunication; (b) (fig. geh.) spell; **in jmds.** ~/**im** ~ **einer Sache** (*Gen.*) **stehen** be under sb.'s spell/under the spell of sth.; **jmdn. in seinen** ~ **schlagen** cast one's/its spell over sb.

bannen *tr. V.* (a) (festhalten) entrance; captivate; [**wie**] **gebannt** ⟨*watch, listen, etc.*⟩ spellbound; (b) (vertreiben) exorcize ⟨*spirit*⟩; avert, ward off ⟨*danger*⟩

Banner *das;* ~s, ~: banner

Bantu /'bantu/ *der;* ~[s], ~[s] Bantu

bar /ba:ɐ̯/ **1** *Adj.* (a) ▶215 *nicht präd.* cash; ~**es Geld** cash; **in** ~: in cash; **Verkauf nur gegen** ~: cash sales only; *s. auch* **Münze a;** (b) *nicht präd.* (pur) pure; sheer. **2** *adv.* ▶215 in cash; ~ **auf die Hand** (ugs.) *od.* (salopp) **Kralle** cash on the nail

Bar *die;* ~, ~s (a) (Nachtlokal) nightclub; bar; (b) (Theke) bar

Bär /bɛ:ɐ̯/ *der;* ~en, ~en bear; **der Große/ Kleine** ~ (Astron.) the Great/Little Bear (*Gen.*); **jmdm. einen** ~**en aufbinden** have sb. on (coll.); pull sb.'s leg

Baracke /ba'rakə/ *die;* ~, ~n hut

Barbar /bar'ba:ɐ̯/ *der;* ~en, ~en barbarian

Barbarei *die;* ~, ~en (a) (Rohheit) barbarity; (b) (Kulturlosigkeit) barbarism *no indef. art.*

Barbarin *die;* ~, ~**nen** (auch hist.) barbarian

barbarisch 1 *Adj.* (a) (roh) barbarous; savage; barbarous, brutal ‹*torture*›; (b) (unzivilisiert) barbaric; barbaric, uncivilized ‹*person*›. 2 *adv.* (a) (roh) barbarously; ‹*torture*› barbarously, brutally; (b) (unzivilisiert) barbarically; in an uncivilized manner

Bar·bestand *der* (Buchf.) cash in hand; (Finanzw.) cash reserve

bar·busig /-buːzɪç/ *Adj.* topless

Bar·dame *die* barmaid

Barde /'bardə/ *der;* ~**n**, ~**n** bard

bären-, Bären-: ~**dienst** *der in* jmdm. einen ~**dienst erweisen** do sb. a disservice; ~**fell** *das* bearskin; ~**hunger** *der* (ugs.) einen ~**hunger haben/kriegen** be famished (coll.) *or* starving (coll.) / get famished (coll.) *or* ravenous (coll.); ~**stark** *Adj.* as strong as an ox *postpos.*

Barett /ba'rɛt/ *das;* ~**[e]s**, ~**e** (eines Geistlichen) biretta; (eines Richters, Professors) cap; (Baskenmütze) beret

bar-: ~**fuß** *indekl. Adj.* barefooted; ~**fuß herumlaufen/gehen** run about/go barefoot; ~**füßig** /~fyːsɪç/ *Adj.* (geh.) barefooted

barg /bark/ *1. u. 3. Pers. Sg. Prät. v.* **bergen**

bar-, Bar-: ~**geld** *das* cash; ~**geld·los** 1 *Adj.* ▶215⃓ cashless; 2 *adv.* ▶215⃓ without using cash; ~**geschäft** *das* (Kaufmannsspr.) cash transaction; ~**hocker** *der* bar stool

Bärin /'bɛːrɪn/ *die;* ~, ~**nen** she-bear

Bariton /'ba(ː)riton/ *der;* ~**s**, ~**e** baritone; (im Chor) baritones *pl.*

Bark /bark/ *die;* ~, ~**en** barque

Barkasse /bar'kasə/ *die;* ~, ~**n** launch

Bar·kauf *der* (Kaufmannsspr.) cash purchase

Barke /'barkə/ *die;* ~, ~**n** [small] rowing-boat

barmherzig /barm'hɛrtsɪç/ (geh.) 1 *Adj.* merciful; compassionate; ~**er Gott/Himmel!** merciful God/Heaven!; *s. auch* **Samariter.** 2 *adv.* mercifully; compassionately

Barmherzigkeit *die;* ~ (geh.) mercy; compassion

Bar·mittel *Pl.* cash resources

Bar·mixer *der* barman; barkeeper (Amer.)

barock /ba'rɔk/ *Adj.* baroque

Barock *das od. der;* ~**[s]** baroque; (Zeit) baroque period *or* age

Barometer /baro'meːtɐ/ *das* barometer; **das** ~ **steht auf Sturm** (fig.) the atmosphere is very strained

Baron /ba'roːn/ *der;* ~**s**, ~**e** ▶34⃓ baron; (als Anrede) [**Herr**] ~: ≈ my lord

Baronin *die;* ~, ~**nen** ▶34⃓ baroness; (als Anrede) [**Frau**] ~: ≈ my lady

Barras /'baras/ *der;* ~ (Soldatenspr.) army; **beim** ~: in the army

Barren /'barən/ *der;* ~**s**, ~ (a) bar; (b) (Turngerät) parallel bars *pl.*

Barriere /ba'rie̯ːrə/ *die;* ~, ~**n** (auch fig.) barrier

Barrikade /bari'kaːdə/ *die;* ~, ~**n** barricade; **auf die** ~**n gehen** *od.* **steigen** (ugs.) go on the warpath

barsch /barʃ/ 1 *Adj.* curt. 2 *adv.* curtly; **jmdn.** ~ **anfahren** snap at sb.

Barsch *der;* ~**[e]s**, ~**e** (Zool.) perch

Barschaft *die;* ~, ~**en** [ready] cash; **seine ganze** ~ **bestand aus 20 Mark** all he had was 20 marks

Bar·scheck *der* open *or* uncrossed cheque

barst /barst/ *1. u. 3. Pers. Sg. Prät. v.* **bersten**

Bart /baːɐt/ *der;* ~**[e]s**, **Bärte** /'bɛːɐtə/ (a) beard; (Oberlippen~, Schnurr~) moustache; (ugs.: Schnurrhaare) whiskers *pl.*; **sich** (*Dat.*) **einen** ~ **wachsen** *od.* **stehen lassen** grow a beard; (fig.) **der** ~ **ist ab** (ugs.) it's all over; **der Witz hat [so] einen** ~ (ugs.) that joke is as old as the hills; **etw. in seinen** ~ **brummen** *od.* **murmeln** mumble sth.; **jmdm. um den** ~ **gehen** (abwertend) butter sb. up; (b) (am Schlüssel) bit

Bärtchen /'bɛːɐtçən/ *das;* ~**s**, ~: [small] beard; (Schnurr~) [thin] moustache

---

*alte Schreibung (vgl. Hinweise auf S. xvi–xvii)

Bart·haar *das* hair from sb.'s/one's beard

bärtig /'bɛːɐtɪç/ *Adj.* bearded

bart-, Bart-: ~**los** *Adj.* beardless; ~**stoppel** *die* piece of stubble; ~**stoppeln** stubble *sing.*; ~**tracht** *die* style of beard; ~**träger** *der* man with a beard; ~**wuchs** *der* growth of beard

Bar-: ~**zahlung** *die* cash payment; ~**zahlungs·rabatt** *der* cash discount

Basalt /ba'zalt/ *der;* ~**[e]s**, ~**e** basalt

Basar /ba'zaːɐ/ *der;* ~**s**, ~**e** bazaar

Base¹ /'baːzə/ *die;* ~, ~**n** (a) (veralt.: Cousine) cousin; (b) (schweiz.: Tante) aunt

Base² *die;* ~, ~**n** (Chemie) base

Baseball /'beɪsbɔːl/ *der;* ~**s** baseball

Basedow-Krankheit /'baːzədo-/ *die,* **Basedowsche Krankheit** *die* ▶329⃓ (Med.) exophthalmic goitre; Graves' disease

Basel /'baːzl̩/ *(das);* ~**s** ▶490⃓ Basle

Basen ⇨ **Basis**

basieren *itr. V.* **auf etw.** (*Dat.*) ~: be based on sth.

Basilika /ba'ziːlika/ *die;* ~, **Basiliken** (Kunstwiss.) basilica

Basilikum /ba'ziːlikʊm/ *das;* ~**s** basil

Basis /'baːzɪs/ *die;* ~, **Basen** (a) (Grundlage) basis; **auf einer festen** ~ **ruhen** have a firm basis; (b) (Math., Archit., Milit., marx.) base; (c) (Politik) grass roots *pl.;* **an der** ~: at grass-roots level

basisch (Chemie) 1 *Adj.* basic. 2 *adv.* ‹*react*› as a base

Basis·demokratie *die* (Politik) grass-roots democracy

Baske /'baskə/ *der;* ~**n**, ~**n** ▶388⃓ Basque

Basken-: ~**land** *das* Basque region; ~**mütze** *die* beret

Basket·ball /'ba(ː)skət-/ *der* basketball

Baskin *die;* ~, ~**nen** Basque

baskisch *Adj.* ▶388⃓, ▶487⃓ Basque

bass, *baß /bas/ *Adv.* **in** ~ **erstaunt sein** (veralt.) be quite taken aback

Bass, *Baß *der;* **Bässe** /'bɛsə/ (a) bass; (im Chor) basses *pl.;* (b) (Instrument) double bass; bass (coll.)

Bass·geige, *Baß·geige *die* (volkst.) double bass

Bassin /ba'sɛ̃ː/ *das;* ~**s**, ~**s** ⇨ **Becken b**

Bassist *der;* ~**en**, ~**en** (Musik) (a) (Sänger) bass; (b) (Instrumentalist) double bass player; bassist; (Gitarrist) bass guitarist

Bass-, *Baß-: ~**schlüssel** *der* (Musik) bass clef; ~**stimme** *die* bass voice

Bast /bast/ *der;* ~**[e]s**, ~**e** bast; (Raffia~) raffia

basta /'basta/ *Interj.* (ugs.) that's enough; **und damit** ~**!** and that's that

Bastard /'bastart/ *der;* ~**s**, ~**e** (a) (veralt., salopp) bastard; (b) (Biol.) hybrid

Bastel·arbeit *die* piece of handicraft work; ~**en** handicraft work *sing.*

Bastelei *die;* ~, ~**en** (a) handicraft work *no pl.;* (b) (Gegenstand) piece of handicraft work

basteln /'bastl̩n/ 1 *tr. V.* make; make, build ‹*model, device*›. 2 *itr. V.* make things [with one's hands]; do handicraft work; **an etw.** (*Dat.*) ~: be working on sth.; (etw. herstellen) be making sth.; (etw. laienhaft bearbeiten) tinker with sth.

Bastion /bas'ti̯oːn/ *die;* ~, ~**en** bastion

Bastler /'bastlɐ/ *der;* ~**s**, ~: handicraft enthusiast

bat /baːt/ *1. u. 3. Pers. Sg. Prät. v.* **bitten**

Bataillon /batal'jo:n/ *das;* ~**s**, ~**e** (Milit.) battalion

Batik /'baːtɪk/ *der;* ~**s**, ~**en** *od. die;* ~, ~**en** batik

batiken 1 *tr. V.* **etw.** ~: decorate sth. with batik work. 2 *itr. V.* do batik work

Batist /ba'tɪst/ *der;* ~**[e]s**, ~**e** batiste

Batterie /batə'riː/ *die;* ~, ~**n** battery; **eine ganze** ~ **von leeren Flaschen** (fig. ugs.) rows of empties (coll.)

batterie-, Batterie-: ~**betrieb** *der; o. Pl.* battery operation; ~**betrieben** *Adj.* battery-operated

Batzen /'batsṇ/ *der;* ~s, ~ (a) (ugs.: Klumpen) lump; (b) (ugs.: Menge) pile (coll.); **ein [schöner** *od.* **ganzer] ~ Geld** a pile (coll.) [of money]

Bau¹ /bau/ *der;* ~[e]s, ~ten (a) *o. Pl.* building; construction; **im ~ sein** be under construction; **mit dem ~ [von etw.] beginnen** start construction [of sth.]; start building [sth.]; (b) (Gebäude) building; (c) *o. Pl.* (~stelle) building site; **auf dem ~ arbeiten** (Bauarbeiter sein) be in the building trade; (d) *o. Pl.* (Struktur) structure; (e) *o. Pl.* (Körper~) build; **von schmalem ~ sein** be slenderly built; have a slender physique

Bau² /bau/ *der;* ~[e]s, ~e (Kaninchen~) burrow; hole; (Fuchs~) earth; (Wolfs~) lair; (Dachs~) sett; earth; **nicht aus dem ~ gehen/kommen** (fig. ugs.) not stick *or* put one's nose outside the door (coll.)

Bau-: ~**arbeiten** *Pl.* building *or* construction work *sing.;* (Straßenarbeiten) roadworks; ~**bude** *die* site hut

Bauch /baux/ *der;* ~[e]s, **Bäuche** /'bɔyçə/ (a) ▶326⌐ stomach; belly; abdomen (Anat.); tummy (coll.); (fig.: von Schiffen, Flugzeugen) belly; **mir tut der ~ weh** I have [a] stomach ache *or* (coll.) tummy ache; **sich** (*Dat.*) **den ~ vollschlagen** (ugs.) stuff oneself (sl.); **ich habe nichts im ~** (ugs.) I haven't had anything to eat; **sich** (*Dat.*) **[vor Lachen] den ~ halten** (ugs.) split one's sides [with laughing]; (fig.) **auf den ~ fallen** (ugs.) come a cropper (sl.) (**mit** with); **aus dem hohlen ~** (salopp) off the top of one's head (sl.); (b) (Wölbung des ~s) paunch; corporation (coll.); (c) (Kochk.) (vom Schwein) belly; (vom Kalb) flank

Bauch·binde *die* (a) woollen body belt; (b) (ugs.: bei Zigarren, Büchern) band

bauchig *Adj.* bulbous

Bauch-: ~**klatscher** /~klatʃɐ/ *der;* ~s, ~ (ugs.) belly-flop (coll.); ~**laden** *der* vendor's tray; ~**landung** *die* belly-landing

Bäuchlein /'bɔyçlaɪn/ *das;* ~s, ~: stomach; tummy (coll.)

bauch-, Bauch-: ~**muskel** *der* stomach muscle; ~**nabel** *der* ▶326⌐ (ugs.) belly button (coll.); tummy button (coll.); ~**reden** *itr. V.; nur Inf. gebr.* ventriloquize; ~**redner** *der* ventriloquist; ~**schmerz** *der; meist Pl.* stomach pain; ~**schmerzen** stomach ache *sing.;* stomach pains; ~**speichel·drüse** *die* pancreas; ~**tanz** *der* belly dance; ~**tanzen** *itr. V.; nur Inf. gebr.* belly dance; ~**tänzerin** *die* belly dancer; ~**weh** *das* (ugs.) tummy ache (coll.); stomach ache

Bau-: ~**denkmal** *das* architectural monument; ~**element** *das* component

bauen 1 *tr. V.* (a) build; build, construct ‹house, road, bridge, etc.›; make ‹violin, piano, burrow›; s. *auch* **Bett a**; (b) (ugs.) **seinen Doktor ~:** do one's Ph.D.; (c) (ugs.: verursachen) **einen Unfall ~:** have an accident. 2 *itr. V.* (a) build; **wir wollen ~:** we want to build a house; (bauen lassen) we want to have a house built; **an etw.** (*Dat.*) **~:** do building work on sth.; (b) (fig.) **auf jmdn./etw. ~:** rely on sb./sth.

Bauer¹ /'bauɐ/ *der;* ~n, ~n (a) farmer; (mit niedrigem sozialem Status, auch ugs. abwertend) peasant; **die dümmsten ~n haben die dicksten Kartoffeln** (abwertend) fortune favours fools (prov.); (b) (Schachfigur) pawn; (c) (Spielkarte) jack

Bauer² *das od. der;* ~s, ~: bird-cage; cage

Bäuerchen /'bɔyɐçən/ *das;* ~s, ~: **[ein] ~ machen** (Kinderspr.) burp

Bäuerin /'bɔyərɪn/ *die;* ~, ~nen [lady] farmer; (Frau eines Bauern) farmer's wife; (mit niedrigem sozialem Status) peasant [woman]

Bäuerlein /'bɔyɐlaɪn/ *das;* ~s, ~: [simple] peasant

bäuerlich /'bɔyɐlɪç/ 1 *Adj.* farming *attrib.;* (ländlich) rural. 2 *adv.* rurally

bauern-, Bauern-: ~**fang** *der* **in auf ~fang ausgehen** (ugs. abwertend) set out to con people out of their money (coll.); ~**fänger** *der* (ugs. abwertend) con man (coll.); ~**frühstück** *das* (Kochk.) fried potatoes mixed with scrambled egg and bacon; ~**haus** *das* farmhouse; ~**hoch·zeit** *die* country wedding; ~**hof** *der* farm; ~**krieg** *der* (hist.) **der Große ~krieg, die ~kriege** the Peasant[s'] War; ~**regel** *die* country saying; ~**schlau**

1 *Adj.* cunning; sly; crafty; **2** *adv.* cunningly; slyly; craftily

Bauers-: ~**frau** *die,* ⇒ **Bäuerin;** ~**leute** *Pl.* (Bauer und Bäuerin) **die [beiden] ~leute** the farmer and his wife

bau-, Bau-: ~**erwartungs·land** *das o. Pl.* land shortly to be made available for building; ~**fällig** *Adj.* ramshackle; badly dilapidated; unsafe ‹roof, ceiling›; ~**fälligkeit** *die; o. Pl.* bad state of dilapidation; badly dilapidated state; ~**firma** *die* building *or* construction firm; ~**gerüst** *das* scaffolding; ~**gewerbe** *das* building trade; ~**hütte** *die* (MA.) stonemasons' lodge; ~**ingenieur** *der* building engineer; ~**jahr** *das* year of construction; (bei Autos) year of manufacture; ~**kasten** *der* construction set *or* kit; (mit Holzklötzen) box of bricks; ~**kasten·system** *das; o. Pl.* unit construction system; ~**klotz** *der* building-brick; ~**klötze[r] staunen** (salopp) be staggered (coll.) *or* flabbergasted; ~**kosten** *Pl.* building *or* construction costs; ~**kran** *der* construction crane; ~**kunst** *die; o. Pl.* (geh.) architecture; ~**land** *das; o. Pl.* building land

baulich 1 *Adj.; nicht präd.* structural. 2 *adv.* **etw. ~ verändern** carry out structural alterations to sth.

Baulichkeit *die;* ~, ~en building

Bau-: ~**löwe** *der* (ugs. abwertend) building speculator; ~**lücke** *die* vacant lot

Baum /baum/ *der;* ~[e]s, **Bäume** /'bɔymə/ tree; **er ist stark wie ein ~:** he's as strong as an ox; **Bäume ausreißen können** (fig. ugs.) be *or* feel ready to tackle anything

Bau-: ~**markt** *der* (Kaufhaus) DIY hypermarket; ~**maschine** *die* piece of construction plant *or* machinery; ~**maschinen** construction plant *sing. or* machinery; ~**material** *das* building material

Bäumchen /'bɔymçən/ *das;* ~s, ~: small tree; (junger Baum) sapling; young tree; **~, wechsle dich** (Kinderspiel) puss in the corner

Bau·meister *der* (hist.) [architect and] master builder

baumeln /'bauml̩n/ *itr. V.* (a) (ugs.) dangle (**an** + *Dat.* from); **die Beine ~ lassen** dangle one's legs; (b) (derb: gehängt werden) swing (sl.)

baum-, Baum-: ~**grenze** *die* ▶277⌐ treeline; timberline; ~**gruppe** *die* clump of trees; ~**krone** *die* treetop; crown [of the/a tree]; ~**lang** *Adj.* (ugs.) tremendously tall (coll.); ~**rinde** *die* bark [of trees]; ~**schule** *die* [tree] nursery; ~**stamm** *der* tree trunk; ~**sterben** *das* dying-off of trees; ~**stumpf** *der* tree-stump; ~**wolle** *die* cotton; ~**wollen** *Adj.; nicht präd.* cotton

Bau-: ~**plan** *der* (Zeichnung) building plans *pl.;* (für eine Maschine) designs *pl.;* ~**planung** *die* building design; ~**platz** *der* site for building *or* construction

bäurisch /'bɔyrɪʃ/ (abwertend) 1 *Adj.* boorish; oafish. 2 *adv.* boorishly; oafishly

Bau-: ~**ruine** *die* (ugs.) building abandoned only half-finished; ~**satz** *der* kit

Bausch /bauʃ/ *der;* ~[e]s, ~e *od.* **Bäusche** /'bɔyʃə/ (a) (am Kleid, Ärmel) puff; (b) **ein ~ Watte** a wad of cotton wool; (c) **etw. in ~ und Bogen verwerfen/verdammen** reject/condemn sth. wholesale

bauschen 1 *tr. V.* billow, fill ‹sail, curtains, etc.›; **gebauschte Ärmel** puffed *or* puff sleeves. 2 *refl. V.* ‹dress, sleeve› puff out; (ungewollt) bunch up; become bunched up; (im Wind) ‹curtain, flag, etc.› billow [out]

bauschig *Adj.* puffed ‹dress›; baggy ‹trousers›

bau-, Bau-: ~**sparen** *itr. V.; nur Inf. gebr.* save with a building society; ~**sparer** *der* building-society investor; ~**spar·kasse** *die* ≈ building society; ~**spar·vertrag** *der* savings contract with a building society (*to save a specified sum which earns interest and is later used to pay for the building of a house*); ~**stein** *der* (a) building stone; (b) (Bestandteil) element; component; (Elektronik, DV) module; **die ~steine der Materie** the constituents of matter; (c) (~klotz) building-brick; ~**stelle** *die* building site; (beim Straßenbau) roadworks *pl.;* (bei der Eisenbahn) site of engineering works; ~**stil** *der* architectural style; ~**stoff** *der* building material; ~**teil** *das* component

Bauten ⇒ **Bau**

Bau-: ~**tischler** *der* ▶85⌐ [building] joiner; ~**unternehmen** *das* building firm; ~**unternehmer** *der*

building contractor; builder; **~vorhaben** *das* building project; **~weise** *die* method of building *or* construction; **~werk** *das* building; (Brücke, Staudamm) structure; **~wirtschaft** *die; o. Pl.* building *or* construction industry

Bauxit /bau'ksi:t/ *der;* **~s,** **~e** bauxite

Bau·zaun *der* site fence

Bayer /'baiɐ/ *der;* **~n,** **~n ▶ 388**| Bavarian

bay[e]risch *Adj.* **▶ 388**| Bavarian

Bayern /'baiɐn/ *(das);* **~s** Bavaria

Bazille /ba'tsılə/ *die;* **~,** **~n** (ugs.) ⇒ **Bazillus**

Bazillus /ba'tsılus/ *der;* **~,** **Bazillen** **(a)** bacillus; **(b)** (fig.) cancer

Bd. *Abk.* **Band** Vol.

B-Dur /'be:-/ *das;* **~** (Musik) B flat major

beabsichtigen /bə'|apzıçtıgņ/ *tr. V.* intend; **~, etw. zu tun** intend *or* mean to do sth.; **die beabsichtigte Wirkung** the intended *or* desired effect

beachten *tr. V.* **(a)** observe, follow ‹*rule, regulations*›; follow ‹*instruction*›; heed, follow ‹*advice*›; obey ‹*traffic signs*›; observe ‹*formalities*›; **(b)** (berücksichtigen) take account of; (Aufmerksamkeit schenken) pay attention to *or* take notice of sth.; **es ist zu ~, dass ...:** please note that ...; **jmdn. nicht ~:** ignore sb.

beachtens·wert *Adj.* remarkable

beachtlich 1 *Adj.* considerable; marked, considerable ‹*change, increase, improvement, etc.*›; notable, considerable ‹*success*›; **Beachtliches leisten** make one's mark. **2** *adv.* considerably; ‹*change, increase, improve, etc.*› markedly, considerably

Beachtung *die* **(a)** ⇒ **beachten a:** observance; following; heeding; obeying; **bei ~ der Regeln** if one observes *or* follows the rules; **(b)** (Berücksichtigung) consideration; **unter ~ aller Umstände** taking all the circumstances into account; **(c)** (Aufmerksamkeit) attention; **~/keinerlei ~ finden** receive attention/be ignored completely

Beamte /bə'|amtə/ *der;* **▶ 85**| *adj. Dekl.* official; (Staats~) [permanent] civil servant; (Kommunal~) [established] local government officer *or* official; (Polizei~) [police] officer; (Zoll~) [customs] officer *or* official

Beamten-: **~beleidigung** *die* insulting a public servant; **~laufbahn** *die* career in the civil service *or* as a civil servant

beamtet *Adj.* **~ sein** have permanent civil-servant status

Beamtin *die;* **~,** **~nen ▶ 85**| ⇒ **Beamte**

beängstigend 1 *Adj.* worrying ‹*feeling*›; unsettling ‹*sign*›; eerie ‹*silence*›; **ein ~es Gedränge** a frightening crush of people; **sein Zustand ist ~:** his condition is giving cause for anxiety. **2** *adv.* alarmingly; **~ schnell** at an alarming speed

beanspruchen *tr. V.* **(a)** claim; **etw. ~ können** be entitled to expect sth.; **(b)** (ausnutzen) make use of ‹*person, equipment*›; take advantage of ‹*hospitality, services*›; **(c)** (erfordern) demand ‹*energy, attention, stamina*›; take up ‹*time, space, etc.*›

Beanspruchung *die;* **~,** **~en** demands *pl.* (*Gen.* on); **die ~ durch den Beruf** the demands of his/her job

beanstanden *tr. V.* object to; take exception to; (sich beklagen über) complain about; **an der Arbeit ist nichts/allerlei zu ~:** there ist nothing/there are all sorts of things wrong with the work; **~, dass ...:** complain that ...

Beanstandung *die;* **~,** **~en** complaint; **Anlass zu ~en geben** give cause for complaint *sing.*

beantragen *tr. V.* **(a)** apply for; **ich beantrage, mich zu versetzen** I apply to be transferred; **(b)** (fordern) call for; demand; **(c)** (vorschlagen) propose

beantworten *tr. V.* answer; reply to, answer ‹*letter*›; respond to ‹*insult*›; return ‹*greeting*›; **jmdm. eine Frage ~:** answer a question for sb.

Beantwortung *die;* **~,** **~en: zur ~ dieser Frage bist du nicht verpflichtet** you are not obliged to answer this question; **in ~** (Amtsspr.) in reply (*Gen.* to); **zur ~ Ihrer Frage** in order to answer your question

bearbeiten *tr. V.* **(a)** deal with; work on, handle ‹*case*›; treat ‹*subject*›; edit ‹*book*›; **ein Buch völlig neu ~:** revise a book completely; **(b)** (adaptieren) adapt; **ein Stück für Klavier ~:** arrange a piece for the piano; **(c)** (behandeln) treat; work ‹*wood, metal, leather, etc.*›; **etw. mit einer Bürste ~:** work on sth. with a brush; **den Boden ~:** work the soil; **(d)** (ugs.: traktieren) beat [repeatedly]; hammer away on ‹*piano, typewriter keys, etc.*›; **jmdn. mit den Fäusten ~:** pummel sb.; **(e)** (ugs.: überreden) work on

Bearbeiter *der,* **Bearbeiterin** *die* **(a)** der zuständige Bearbeiter the person who is dealing/who dealt with the matter *etc.;* **(b)** (eines Romans, Schauspiels) adapter; (eines Musikstücks) arranger; **(c)** (eines Buches) editor

Bearbeitung *die;* **~,** **~en (a)** die **~** eines Antrags/eines Falles *usw.* dealing with an application/working on or handling a case *etc.;* **die ~ eines Themas** the treatment of a subject; **die ~ eines Buches** editing a book; **(b)** (bearbeitete Fassung) adaptation; (eines Musikstücks) arrangement; **(c)** (Behandlung) treatment; (von Holz, Metall, Leder usw.) working; **die ~ des Metalls ist schwer** it is difficult to work the metal; **zur weiteren ~:** in order to be worked further/for further treatment

Bearbeitungs·gebühr *die* handling charge; (bei Behörden) administrative charge

beargwöhnen *tr. V.* **jmdn./etw. ~:** be suspicious of sb./sth.; **beargwöhnt werden** be regarded with suspicion

Beat /bi:t/ *der;* **~[s]** beat

beatmen *tr. V.* (Med.) **jmdn. [künstlich] ~:** administer artificial respiration to sb.; (während einer Operation) ventilate sb.

beaufsichtigen *tr. V.* supervise; mind, look after ‹*child*›

Beaufsichtigung *die;* **~,** **~en** supervision

beauftragen *tr. V.* **(a)** **jmdn. mit etw. ~:** entrust sb. with sth.; charge sb. with sth.; **jmdn. ~, etw. zu tun** give sb. the job *or* task of doing sth.; **einen Künstler/Architekten ~, etw. zu tun** commission an artist/architect to do sth.; **(b)** (anweisen) **jmdn. ~, etw. zu tun** order sb. to do sth.

Beauftragte *der/die; adj. Dekl.* representative

beäugen *tr. V.* eye ‹*person*›; inspect ‹*thing*›

bebauen *tr. V.* **(a)** build on; develop; **ein Gelände mit Häusern ~:** build houses on a site; **(b)** (für den Anbau nutzen) cultivate

Bebauung *die;* **~,** **~en (a)** (mit Gebäuden) development; **(b)** (Gebäude) buildings *pl.;* **(c)** (eines Ackers) cultivation

beben /'be:bņ/ *itr. V.* shake; tremble

Beben *das;* **~s,** **~ (a)** shaking; trembling; **(b)** (Erd~) earthquake; quake (coll.)

bebildern *tr. V.* illustrate

Becher /'bɛçɐ/ *der;* **~s,** **~** (Glas~, Porzellan~) glass; tumbler; (Plastik~) beaker; cup; (Eis~) (aus Glas, Metall) sundae dish; (aus Pappe) tub; (Joghurt~) carton

bechern *tr., itr. V.* (ugs. scherzh.) **[einen] ~:** have a few (coll.)

Becken /'bɛkņ/ *das;* **~s,** **~ (a)** (Wasch~) basin; (Abwasch~) sink; (Toiletten~) pan; bowl; **(b)** (Schwimm~) pool; (Plansch~) paddling pool; (eines Brunnens) basin; (Fisch~) pond; **(c)** **▶ 326**| (Anat.) pelvis; **(d)** *Pl.* (Musik) cymbals *pl.*

Becken-: **~bruch** *der* (Med.) pelvic fracture; **~knochen** *der* pelvic bone

bedacht 1 *Adj.* **(a)** carefully considered; (umsichtig) circumspect; **(b)** **auf etw.** (*Akk.*) **~ sein** be intent on sth.; **darauf ~/sehr ~ sein, etw. zu tun** be intent on doing sth./be [most] anxious to do sth. **2** *adv.* in a carefully considered way; (umsichtig) circumspectly

Bedacht *der* **in ohne ~:** rashly; without thinking *or* forethought; **mit ~:** in a carefully considered way; (umsichtig) circumspectly

bedächtig /bə'dɛçtıç/ **1** *Adj.* **(a)** deliberate; measured ‹*steps, stride, speech*›; **(b)** (besonnen) thoughtful; well-considered ‹*words*›; (vorsichtig) careful. **2** *adv.* **(a)** deliberately;

∼ **reden** speak in measured tones; (b) (besonnen) thoughtfully; (vorsichtig) carefully

Bedächtigkeit *die;* ∼ (a) deliberateness; (b) (Besonnenheit) thoughtfulness; (Vorsichtigkeit) carefulness

bedanken *refl. V.* say thank you; express one's thanks; **sich bei jmdm. [für etw.]** ∼**:** thank sb. *or* say thank you to sb. [for sth.]; **sich bei jmdm.** ∼**, dass er etw. getan hat** thank sb. for doing sth.; **dafür kannst du dich bei ihm** ∼ (iron. ugs.) you've got him to thank for that (iron.)

Bedarf /bə'darf/ *der;* ∼**[e]s** (a) need (**an** + *Dat.* of); requirement (**an** + *Dat.* for); (Bedarfsmenge) needs *pl.;* requirements *pl.;* **Dinge des täglichen** ∼**s** everyday necessities; **bei** ∼**:** if and when the need arises; if required; ∼ **an etw.** (*Dat.*) **haben** (Kaufmannsspr.) require sth.; **je nach** ∼**:** as required; **kein** ∼**!** (salopp) I don't feel like it; (b) (Nachfrage) demand (**an** + *Dat.* for)

Bedarfs-: ∼**ampel** *die* (Verkehrsw.) traffic-controlled lights; (Fußgängerampel) pedestrian-controlled *or* -operated lights; ∼**fall** *der in* **im** ∼**fall[e]** if required; if the need arises/arose; ∼**güter** *Pl.* consumer goods; ∼**halte·stelle** *die* request stop

bedauerlich *Adj.* regrettable; unfortunate

bedauerlicher·weise *Adv.* regrettably; unfortunately

bedauern *tr., itr. V.* (a) feel sorry for; **sie lässt sich gerne** ∼**:** she likes being pitied; (b) ▶ 163 | (schade finden) regret; **ich bedaure sehr, dass** ...: I am very sorry that ...; **wir** ∼**, Ihnen mitteilen zu müssen** we regret to [have to] inform you; **bedaure!** sorry!

Bedauern *das;* ∼**s** (a) sympathy; **jmdm. sein** ∼ **ausdrücken** offer one's sympathy to sb.; (b) ▶ 163 | (Betrübnis) regret; **zu meinem** ∼**:** to my regret; **zu unserem** ∼ **müssen wir Ihnen mitteilen, dass** ...: we regret to [have to] inform you that ...; **mit** ∼**:** with regret

bedauerns·wert *Adj.* unfortunate

bedecken 1 *tr. V.* cover; **von Schlamm/Schmutz bedeckt sein** be covered in mud/dirt. 2 *refl. V.* cover oneself up

bedeckt *Adj.* (a) overcast ⟨*sky*⟩; **bei** ∼**em Himmel** when the sky is overcast; (b) **sich** ∼ **halten** (fig.) keep a low profile

Bedeckung *die;* ∼, ∼**en** (a) covering; (b) (Schutz) guard

bedenken *unr. tr. V.* (a) consider; think about; **wenn ich es recht bedenke/wenn man es recht bedenkt** when I/you stop and think about it; (b) (beachten) take into consideration; **du musst** ∼**, dass** ...: you should bear in mind that *or* take into consideration the fact that ...; **ich gebe [dir]/er gab [uns] zu** ∼**, dass** ...: I would ask you/he asked us to bear in mind that *or* take into consideration the fact that ...; (c) (geh.: beschenken) **jmdn. reich** ∼**:** shower sb. with gifts; **jmdn. mit etw.** ∼**:** present sb. with sth.; (d) (im Testament berücksichtigen) remember

Bedenken *das;* ∼**s**, ∼**:** doubt, reservation (**gegen** about); **aber jetzt kommen mir** ∼**:** but now I'm having second thoughts; **ohne** ∼**:** without hesitation

bedenken·los 1 *Adj.* unhesitating; (skrupellos) unscrupulous. 2 *adv.* without hesitation; (skrupellos) unscrupulously

bedenkens·wert *Adj.* ⟨*argument, suggestion*⟩ worthy of consideration; ∼ **sein** be worth considering *or* worthy of consideration

bedenklich 1 *Adj.* (a) (fragwürdig) dubious, questionable ⟨*methods, transactions, etc.*⟩; (b) (besorgniserregend) alarming; disturbing; ∼ **sein/werden** be giving/be starting to give cause for concern; (c) (besorgt) concerned; apprehensive; anxious; **das machte od. stimmte mich** ∼**:** that gave me cause for concern. 2 *adv.* (a) alarmingly; disturbingly; (b) (besorgt) apprehensively; anxiously

Bedenklichkeit *die;* ∼**:** dubiousness; questionableness

Bedenk·zeit *die* time for reflection; **ich gebe Ihnen vierundzwanzig Stunden** ∼**:** I'll give you twenty-four hours to think about it

bedeppert /bə'dɛpɐt/ *Adj.* (salopp) (a) (verwirrt) confused and embarrassed; (b) (dumm) gormless (coll.)

bedeuten *tr. V.* (a) mean; **was soll das** ∼**?** what does that mean?; „**Ph. D.**" **bedeutet Doktor der Philosophie** 'Ph.D.' stands for Doctor of Philosophy; (b) (darstellen) represent; **das bedeutet ein Wagnis** that is being really daring; **einen Eingriff in die Pressefreiheit** ∼**:** amount to *or* represent an attack on press freedom; (c) (hindeuten auf) mean; **das bedeutet nichts Gutes** that bodes ill; that's a bad sign; **schönes Wetter** ∼**:** mean good weather; **das hat nichts zu** ∼**:** that doesn't mean anything; (d) (wert sein) mean; **Geld bedeutet ihm nichts** money means nothing to him; (e) (geh.) **jmdm.** ∼**, etw. zu tun** intimate to sb. that he/she should do sth.

bedeutend 1 *Adj.* (a) significant, important ⟨*step, event, role, etc.*⟩; important ⟨*city, port, artist, writer, etc.*⟩; (b) (groß) considerable. 2 *adv.* considerably

bedeutsam 1 *Adj.* (a) ⇒ **bedeutend** 1; (b) (viel sagend) meaningful; significant. 2 *adv.* meaningfully; significantly

Bedeutung *die;* ∼, ∼**en** (a) *o. Pl.* meaning; significance; **einer Sache** (*Dat.*) **zu große** ∼ **beimessen** attach too much significance to sth.; (b) (Wort∼) meaning; (c) *o. Pl.* (Wichtigkeit) importance; (Tragweite) significance; importance; [**an**] ∼ **gewinnen** become more significant; **nichts von** ∼**:** nothing important *or* significant; nothing of [any] importance *or* significance

bedeutungs-, Bedeutungs-: ∼**los** *Adj.* insignificant; unimportant; ∼**losigkeit** *die;* ∼**:** insignificance; unimportance; ∼**voll** 1 *Adj.* (a) significant; (b) (vielsagend) meaningful; meaning ⟨*look*⟩; 2 *adv.* meaningfully

bedienen 1 *tr. V.* (a) wait on; ⟨*waiter, waitress*⟩ wait on, serve; ⟨*sales assistant*⟩ serve; **jmdn. vorn und hinten** ∼ (ugs.) wait on sb. hand and foot; **werden Sie schon bedient?** are you being served?; (b) operate ⟨*machine*⟩; (c) [**mit etw.**] **gut/schlecht bedient sein** (ugs.) be well-served/illserved [by sth.]; **bedient sein** (salopp) have had enough; (d) (Kartenspiel) play; **Kreuz/Trumpf** ∼**:** play a club/trump. 2 *itr. V.* (a) serve; **wer bedient hier?** who is serving here?; (b) (Kartenspiel) follow suit. 3 *refl. V.* (a) help oneself; **sich selbst** ∼ (im Geschäft, Restaurant usw.) serve oneself; (b) **sich einer Sache** (*Gen.*) ∼ (geh.) make use of sth.; use sth.

Bedienstete *der/die; adj. Dekl.* (a) (Amtsspr.) employee; (b) (veralt.: Diener) servant

Bediente /bə'di:ntə/ *der/die; adj. Dekl.* (veralt.) servant

Bedienung *die;* ∼, ∼**en** (a) *o. Pl.* (das Bedienen) service; ∼ **inbegriffen** service included; (b) *o. Pl.* (Handhabung) operation; (c) (Person) waiter/waitress; **hallo,** ∼**!** waiter/waitress!; (d) (österr.) cleaning woman

Bedienungs-: ∼**an·leitung** *die* operating instructions *pl.;* (Heft) instruction book; ∼**auf·schlag** *der,* ∼**geld** *das,* ∼**zu·schlag** *der* service charge

bedingen /bə'dɪŋən/ *tr. V.* cause; **einander** ∼**:** be interdependent *or* mutually dependent; **psychisch bedingt sein** be psychologically determined

bedingt /bə'dɪŋt/ 1 *Adj.* conditional; qualified ⟨*praise, approval*⟩; *s. auch* **Reflex.** 2 *adv.* partly ⟨*true*⟩; **nur** ∼ **tauglich** fit for certain duties only

-bedingt *adj.* **krankheitsbedingte Abwesenheit** absence due to illness; **berufsbedingte Krankheiten** occupational illnesses; **witterungsbedingte Schäden** damage caused by the weather

Bedingung *die;* ∼, ∼**en** condition; **etw. zur** ∼ **machen** make sth. a condition; **zu annehmbaren** ≳**en** on acceptable terms; **unter diesen** ∼**en** on these conditions; **unter keiner** ∼**:** under no circumstances; **unter der** ∼**, dass** ...: on condition that ...

bedingungs·los 1 *Adj.* unconditional ⟨*surrender, acceptance, etc.*⟩; absolute, unquestioning ⟨*obedience, loyalty, devotion*⟩. 2 *adv.* ⟨*surrender, accept, etc.*⟩ unconditionally; ⟨*subordinate oneself*⟩ unquestioningly

Bedingungs·satz *der* (Sprachw.) conditional clause

bedrängen *tr. V.* (a) besiege ⟨*town, fortress, person*⟩; put ⟨*opposing player*⟩ under pressure; **vom Feind bedrängt**

sein be hard pressed by the enemy; **mit Fragen bedrängt werden** be assailed with questions; **in einer bedrängten Lage sein** be hard-pressed *or* in a difficult situation; **(b)** (belästigen) pester

Bedrängnis *die;* ~, ~**se** (geh.) (innere Not) distress; (wirtschaftliche Not) [great] difficulties *pl.;* **in** ~ **geraten/sein** get into/be in great difficulties *pl.*

bedrohen *tr. V.* **(a)** threaten; **(b)** (gefährden) threaten; endanger; **den Frieden** ~: be a threat *or* danger to peace; **vom Aussterben bedroht sein** be threatened with extinction

bedrohlich **1** *Adj.* threatening, menacing ⟨*gesture*⟩; (Unheilverkündend) ominous; (gefährlich) dangerous. **2** *adv.* threateningly; menacingly; (Unheil verkündend) ominously; (gefährlich) dangerously

Bedrohung *die* threat (*Gen.,* **für** to); **in ständiger** ~: under a constant threat

bedrucken *tr. V.* print; **etw. mit einer Adresse** ~: print an address on sth.

bedrücken *tr. V.* depress; **es bedrückt mich, dass ...:** I feel depressed that ...; **bedrückt dich etwas?** is something weighing on your mind?

bedrückend *Adj.* depressing; oppressive ⟨*atmosphere*⟩

bedruckt *Adj.* printed; print *attrib.* ⟨*dress etc.*⟩

bedrückt *Adj.* depressed

Bedrückung *die;* ~, ~**en** depression

Beduine /bedu'i:nə/ *der;* ~**n**, ~**n** Bed[o]uin

bedürfen *unr. itr. V.* (geh.) **jmds./einer Sache** ~: require *or* need sb./sth.; **es bedarf einiger Mühe** some effort is needed *or* required

Bedürfnis *das;* ~**ses**, ~**se** need (**nach** for); **das** ~ **haben, etw. zu tun** feel a need to do sth.; **ein** ~ **nach etw. haben** be in need of sth.; **es war mir ein** ~, **das zu tun** I felt the need to do it

bedürfnis-, Bedürfnis-: ~**anstalt** *die* (Amtsspr.) public convenience; ~**los** *Adj.* ⟨*person*⟩ with few [material] needs; modest, simple ⟨*life*⟩; ~**los sein** have few [material] needs; ~**losigkeit** *die;* ~: lack of [material] needs

bedürftig *Adj.* needy; **die Bedürftigen** the needy; those in need

Bedürftigkeit *die;* ~: neediness

Beef·steak /'bi:fste:k/ *das* [beef]steak; **deutsches** ~: ≈ beefburger

beehren *tr. V.* **jmdn. mit etw.** ~ (geh., auch iron.) honour sb. with sth.; ~ **Sie uns bald wieder** (gespreizt: besuchen) we hope to have the pleasure of your custom/company again

beeiden /bə'|aidn̩/ *tr. V.* ~, **dass ...:** swear [on oath] that ...; **eine Aussage** ~: swear to the truth of a statement

beeilen *refl. V.* hurry [up (coll.)]; **beeil dich!** hurry [up]; **sich bei** *od.* **mit etw.** ~: hurry over sth.; **sich** ~, **etw. zu tun** hasten to do sth.

Beeilung: [**los,/ein bisschen**] ~! (ugs.) get a move on! (coll.); hurry up! (coll.)

beeindrucken *tr. V.* impress; **sich von etw.** ~ **lassen** be impressed by sth.; ~**d** impressive

beeinflussbar, **beeinflußbar* *Adj.* **jmd./etw. ist** [**nicht**] ~: sb./sth. can[not] be influenced; **leicht/schwer** ~ **sein** ⟨*person*⟩ be easily influenced/hard *or* difficult to influence

beeinflussen /bə'|ainflʊsn̩/ *tr. V.* influence; influence, affect ⟨*result, process, etc.*⟩; **jmdn./etw. positiv** ~: have a positive influence on sb./sth.; **sich leicht** ~ **lassen** be easily influenced

Beeinflussung *die;* ~, ~**en** influencing; **seine** ~ **durch die Schule** the influence of the school on him

beeinträchtigen /bə'|aintreçtign̩/ *tr. V.* restrict ⟨*rights, freedom*⟩; detract from, spoil ⟨*pleasure, enjoyment*⟩; spoil ⟨*appetite, good humour*⟩; detract from, diminish ⟨*value*⟩; diminish, impair ⟨*quality*⟩; impair ⟨*efficiency, vision, hearing*⟩; damage, harm ⟨*sales, reputation*⟩; reduce

⟨*production*⟩; **jmdn. in seiner Freiheit** ~: restrict sb.'s freedom; **sich beeinträchtigt fühlen** feel hampered

Beeinträchtigung *die;* ~, ~**en:** ⇒ **beeinträchtigen:** restriction (*Gen.* on); detraction (*Gen.* from); spoiling; diminution; impairment; damage (*Gen.* to); harm (*Gen.* to); reduction

Beelzebub /'be:ltsə-/ *(der)* Beelzebub; **den Teufel mit** *od.* **durch** ~ **austreiben** (fig.) replace one evil by *or* with another

beenden *tr. V.* end; finish ⟨*piece of work*⟩; end, conclude ⟨*negotiations, letter, lecture*⟩; complete, finish ⟨*studies*⟩; end, bring to an end ⟨*meeting, relationship, dispute, strike*⟩; **damit** ~ **wir unser heutiges Programm** that brings to an end our programmes for today

Beendigung *die;* ~: **zur** ~ **der Unruhen wurde die Armee eingesetzt** the army was called in to put an end to the unrest; **sie wurden zur** ~ **der Kampfhandlungen aufgefordert** they were called upon to cease *or* stop hostilities

beengen *tr. V.* hinder; restrict; (fig.) restrict ⟨*freedom [of action]*⟩; **beengt wohnen** live in cramped surroundings *or* conditions; **sich beengt fühlen** feel cramped; (fig.) feel constricted

Beengtheit *die;* ~: crampedness; **ein Gefühl der** ~: a feeling of being cramped

beerben *tr. V.* **jmdn.** ~: inherit something from sb.; (allein) inherit sb's estate

beerdigen /bə'|eːɐdɪgn̩/ *tr. V.* bury; **jmdn. kirchlich** ~: give sb. a Christian burial

Beerdigung *die;* ~, ~**en** burial; (Trauerfeier) funeral

Beerdigungs·institut *das* [firm *sing.* of] undertakers *pl. or* funeral directors *pl.*

Beere /'be:rə/ *die;* ~, ~**n** berry

Beet /be:t/ *das;* ~[**e**]**s**, ~**e** (Blumen~) bed; (Gemüse~) plot

befähigen /bə'fɛːɪgn̩/ *tr. V.* **jmdn.** ~, **etw. zu tun** enable sb. to do sth.; ⟨*qualifications, training, etc.*⟩ qualify sb. to do sth.

befähigt *Adj.* **(a)** able; capable (**zu** of); **(b)** (qualifiziert) qualified

Befähigung *die;* ~ **(a)** ability; **(b)** (Qualifikation) qualification; **die** ~ **zum Internisten/Hochschulstudium/ Richteramt** the qualifications *pl.* for becoming an internist/studying at university/being a judge

befahrbar *Adj.* passable; navigable ⟨*canal, river*⟩; **nicht** ~: impassable/unnavigable

befahren *unr. tr. V.* drive on, use ⟨*road*⟩; drive across, use ⟨*bridge, pass*⟩; use ⟨*railway line*⟩; sail ⟨*sea*⟩; navigate ⟨*river, canal*⟩; **die Straße ist nur in einer Richtung zu** ~: traffic can only use the road in one direction; „**Seitenstreifen nicht** ~!" 'keep off verges'; **die Straße ist stark/wenig** ~: the road is heavily/little used; **eine stark** ~**e Straße/Wasserstraße** a busy road/waterway

Befall *der;* ~[**e**]**s** attack (*Gen.* on; **durch, von, mit** by)

befallen *unr. tr. V.* **(a)** overcome; ⟨*misfortune*⟩ befall; **Fieber/eine Grippe befiel ihn** (geh.) he was stricken by fever/influenza; **von Panik/Angst/Heimweh** *usw.* **werden** be seized *or* overcome with *or* by panic/fear/ homesickness *etc.;* **(b)** ⟨*pests*⟩ attack

befangen **1** *Adj.* **(a)** self-conscious, awkward; **(b)** (bes. Rechtsw.: voreingenommen) biased; **einen Richter als** ~ **ablehnen** challenge a judge on grounds of bias; **(c)** **in einem Glauben/Irrtum** ~ **sein** (geh.) labour under a belief/misapprehension. **2** *adv.* self-consciously; awkwardly

Befangenheit *die;* ~ **(a)** self-consciousness; awkwardness; **(b)** (bes. Rechtsw.: Voreingenommenheit) bias

Befangenheits·antrag *der* (Rechtsw.) challenge on grounds of bias

befassen **1** *refl. V.* **sich mit etw.** ~: occupy oneself with sth.; (studieren) study sth.; ⟨*article, book*⟩ deal with sth.; **sich mit jmdm./einer Angelegenheit** ~: deal with *or* attend to sb./a matter. **2** *tr. V.* (bes. Amtsspr.) **jmdn. mit etw.** ~: get *or* instruct sb. to deal with sth.

befehden /bə'fe:dn̩/ *tr. V.* (hist., fig. geh.) feud with; **sich** ~: feud

---

*alte Schreibung (vgl. Hinweise auf S. xvi–xvii)

Befehl /bəˈfeːl/ *der;* ∼[e]s, ∼e (a) order; command; jmdm. den ∼ geben, etw. zu tun order *or* command sb. to do sth.; den ∼ haben, etw. zu tun be under orders *or* have been ordered to do sth.; auf jmds. ∼ *(Akk.)* on sb.'s orders; auf ∼ *(Akk.)* handeln act under orders; ∼ ist ∼: orders are orders; zu ∼! yes, sir!; aye, aye, sir! (Navy); dein Wunsch ist mir ∼ (ugs. scherzh.) your wish is my command; (b) (Befehlsgewalt) command; den ∼ über jmdn./etw. haben have command of *or* be in command of sb./sth.; (c) (DV) instruction; command

befehlen 1 *unr. tr. V.* (a) *auch itr.* order; (Milit.) order; command; von Ihnen lasse ich mir nichts ∼: I don't take orders from you; (b) (beordern) order; (zu sich) summon; jmdn. zum Rapport ∼: order/summon sb. to report; (c) (geh. veralt.: anvertrauen) commend. 2 *unr. itr. V.* über jmdn./etw. ∼: have command of *or* be in command of sb./sth.

befehligen *tr. V.* have command of; be in command of; von jmdm. befehligt werden be commanded by sb.; be under the command of sb.

befehls-, Befehls-: ∼**empfänger** *der* recipient of an order/orders; bloße ∼empfänger sein just follow *or* take orders; ∼**form** *die* (Sprachw.) imperative [form]; ∼**gewalt** *die; o. Pl.* command (über + *Akk.* of); ∼**haber** /∼haːbɐ/ *der;* ∼s, ∼ (Milit.) commander; ∼**ton** *der; o. Pl.* peremptory tone; ∼**verweigerung** *die* refusal to obey an order/orders

befestigen *tr. V.* (a) fix; etw. mit Stecknadeln/ Bindfaden ∼: fasten sth. with pins/string; etw. mit Schrauben/Leim ∼: fasten *or* fix sth. with screws/fix *or* stick sth. with glue; etw. an der Wand ∼: fix sth. to the wall; einen Anhänger an einem Koffer ∼: attach *or* fasten a label to a case; (b) (haltbar machen) stabilize ⟨bank, embankment⟩; make up ⟨road, path, etc.⟩; (c) (sichern) fortify ⟨town etc.⟩; strengthen ⟨border⟩

Befestigung *die;* ∼, ∼en (a) ⇒ befestigen a: fixing; fastening; attachment; (b) ⇒ befestigen b: stabilization; making up; (c) (Milit.) fortification

Befestigungs·anlage *die* fortifications *pl.*

befeuchten /bəˈfɔʏçtn̩/ *tr. V.* moisten; damp ⟨hair, cloth⟩

befeuern *tr. V.* (a) (beheizen) fuel; (b) (beschießen) shoot at; fire on; (c) (ugs.: bewerfen) pelt

befiehlst /bəˈfiːlst/, **befiehlt** /bəˈfiːlt/ 2., 3. Pers. Sg. Präsens v. **befehlen**

befinden 1 *unr. refl. V.* be; unter ihnen befand sich jemand, der ...: among them there was somebody who ... 2 *unr. tr. V.* (geh.) etw. für *od.* als gut/richtig ∼: find *or* consider sth. [to be] good/right; jmdn. für *od.* als schuldig ∼: find sb. guilty. 3 *unr. itr. V.* darüber habe ich nicht zu ∼: that's not for me to decide

Befinden *das,* ∼s health; (eines Patienten) condition; sich nach jmds. ∼ erkundigen enquire after *or* about sb.'s health

befindlich *Adj.; nicht präd.* to be found *postpos.;* das in der Kasse ∼e Geld the money in the till; die im Bau ∼en Häuser the houses [which are/were] under construction

befingern *tr. V.* (salopp) finger

beflaggen *tr. V.* etw. ∼: decorate *or* [be]deck sth. with flags; ein Schiff ∼: dress a ship

beflecken *tr. V.* stain; sich mit Blut ∼ (verhüll. geh.) stain one's hands with blood

befleißigen *refl. V.* (geh.) sich eines klaren Stils/höflicheren Tons *usw.* ∼: make a great effort to cultivate a clear style/to adopt a more polite tone of voice *etc.;* sich größter Zurückhaltung ∼: endeavour to exercise the greatest restraint

beflissen /bəˈflɪsn̩/ (geh.) 1 *Adj.* keen; eager; (emsig) assiduous; zealous. 2 *adv.* keenly; eagerly; (emsig) assiduously; zealously

beflügeln *tr. V.* (geh.) jmdn. ∼: inspire sb.; ⟨success, praise⟩ spur sb. on, inspire sb.

befohlen /bəˈfoːlən/ 2. Part. v. **befehlen**

befolgen *tr. V.* follow, obey ⟨instruction⟩; obey, comply with ⟨law, regulation⟩; follow, take ⟨advice⟩; follow ⟨suggestion⟩

Befolgung *die;* ∼: ⇒ **befolgen**: following; obedience (Gen. to); compliance (Gen. with)

befördern *tr. V.* (a) carry; transport; convey; jmdn. ins Freie *od.* an die Luft ∼ (ugs.) chuck (coll.) *or* throw sb. out; (b) (aufrücken lassen) promote; zum Direktor befördert werden be promoted to director

Beförderung *die* (a) *o. Pl.* carriage; transport; conveyance; die ∼ per Luft/zu Lande carriage *or* transport by air/road; (b) (das Aufrückenlassen) promotion (zu to)

Beförderungs·mittel *das* means of transport

befrachten *tr. V.* load (mit with); mit Emotionen befrachtet (fig.) ⟨discussion etc.⟩ charged with emotion

befragen *tr. V.* (a) question (über + *Akk.* about); einen Zeugen ∼: question *or* examine a witness; auf Befragen when questioned; (b) (konsultieren) ask; consult; jmdn. nach seiner Meinung ∼: ask sb. for his/her opinion; ein Orakel/die Karten ∼: consult an oracle/ the cards

Befragung *die;* ∼, ∼en (a) questioning; (vor Gericht) questioning; examination; (b) (Konsultation) consultation; (c) (Umfrage) opinion poll

befreien 1 *tr. V.* (a) free ⟨prisoner⟩; set ⟨animal⟩ free; liberate ⟨country, people⟩; jmdn. aus den Händen seiner Entführer ∼: rescue sb. from the hands of his/ her abductors; (b) (freistellen) exempt; jmdn. vom Turnunterricht/Wehrdienst/von einer Pflicht ∼: excuse sb. [from] physical education/exempt sb. from military service/release sb. from an obligation; (c) (erlösen) jmdn. von Schmerzen ∼: free sb. from pain; von seinen Leiden befreit werden (durch den Tod) be released from one's sufferings; ein ∼des Lachen a laugh which breaks/broke the tension. 2 *refl. V.* free oneself (von from); sich von Vorurteilen ∼: rid oneself of prejudice *sing.*

Befreier *der,* **Befreierin** *die;* ∼, ∼nen liberator

befreit *Adj.* (erleichtert) relieved

Befreiung *die;* ∼ (a) ⇒ befreien 1 a: freeing; liberation; die ∼ der Frau the emancipation of women; (b) (Erlösung) die ∼ von Schmerzen release from pain; (c) (Erleichterung) relief; (d) (Freistellung) exemption; um ∼ vom Sportunterricht/von einer Pflicht bitten ask to be excused [from] sport/released from an obligation

Befreiungs-: ∼**bewegung** *die* liberation movement; ∼**kampf** *der* liberation struggle; ∼**krieg** *der* war of liberation; die ∼**kriege** (hist.) the Wars of Liberation (1813–1815)

befremden /bəˈfrɛmdn̩/ 1 *tr. V.* jmdn. ∼: put sb. off; (erstaunen) take sb. aback; es befremdete ihn, dass ...: he was taken aback [to find] that ... 2 *itr. V.* be disturbing

Befremden *das;* ∼s surprise and displeasure

befremdlich *Adj.* (geh.) strange; odd

befreunden /bəˈfrɔʏndn̩/ *refl. V.* ⇒ **anfreunden**

befreundet *Adj.* [gut *od.* eng] ∼ sein be [good *or* close] friends (mit with); meine Frau und ich und ein ∼es Ehepaar/ein ∼er Schauspieler my wife and I and a couple with whom we are friends/an actor who is a friend of ours; ∼e Familien/Kinder families which are friendly with each other/children who are friends; das ∼e Ausland friendly [foreign] countries

befrieden *tr. V.* (geh.) bring peace to ⟨country⟩

befriedigen /bəˈfriːdɪgn̩/ *tr. V.* (a) *auch itr.* satisfy; satisfy, meet ⟨demand, need⟩; satisfy, fulfil ⟨wish⟩; satisfy, gratify ⟨lust⟩; seine Gläubiger ∼: satisfy one's creditors; das Ergebnis befriedigte mich the result satisfied me *or* was satisfactory to me; seine Leistung befriedigte [nicht] his performance was [un]satisfactory; (b) *auch itr.* (ausfüllen) ⟨job, occupation, etc.⟩ fulfil; (c) (sexuell) satisfy; sich [selbst] ∼: masturbate

befriedigend 1 *Adj.* (a) satisfactory; satisfactory; adequate ⟨reply, performance⟩; nicht ∼ sein be unsatisfactory/inadequate; (b) fulfilling ⟨job, occupation, etc.⟩. 2 *adv.* satisfactorily; ⟨answer⟩ satisfactorily, adequately

befriedigt 1 *Adj.* satisfied. 2 *adv.* with satisfaction

Befriedigung *die;* ∼: ⇒ **befriedigen** a: satisfaction; meeting; fulfilment; gratification; sexuelle ∼: sexual satisfaction; ∼ darin finden, etw. zu tun get satisfaction from doing sth.

befristen *tr. V.* limit the duration of (**auf** + *Akk.* to)
befristet *Adj.* temporary ⟨*visa*⟩; fixed-term ⟨*ban, contract*⟩; **ein auf zwei Jahre ~er Vertrag** a two-year fixed-term contract; **~ sein** ⟨*visa, permit*⟩ be valid for a limited period [only]; **auf ein Jahr ~ sein** ⟨*visa, permit*⟩ be valid for one year
befruchten *tr. V.* (**a**) fertilize ⟨*egg*⟩; pollinate ⟨*flower*⟩; impregnate ⟨*female*⟩; **ein Tier künstlich ~:** artificially inseminate an animal; (**b**) (geh.) **jmdn./etw. ~, einen ~den Einfluss auf jmdn./etw. haben** have *or* be a stimulating *or* inspiring influence [up]on sb./sth.
Befruchtung *die;* **~, ~en:** ⇒ **befruchten a:** fertilization; pollination; impregnation; **künstliche ~:** artificial insemination
befugen *tr. V.* authorize; **[dazu] befugt sein, etw. zu tun** be authorized to do sth.
Befugnis *die;* **~, ~se** authority; **seine ~se überschreiten** exceed one's authority *sing.*
befühlen *tr. V.* feel
befummeln *tr. V.* (ugs.) (**a**) paw (coll.); (**b**) (sexuell berühren) grope (sl.); feel up (sl.)
Befund *der* (bes. Med.) result[s *pl.*]; **ohne ~ sein** be negative
befürchten *tr. V.* fear; **ich befürchte, dass ...:** I am afraid that ...; **das ist nicht zu ~:** there is no fear of that
Befürchtung *die;* **~, ~en** fear; **die ~ haben, dass ...:** be afraid that ...
befürworten /bə'fy:ɐvɔrtn̩/ *tr. V.* support
Befürworter *der;* **~s, ~:** supporter
Befürwortung *die;* **~, ~en** support
begabt /bə'ga:pt/ *Adj.* talented; gifted; **vielseitig ~ sein** be multi-talented; have many talents; **für etw. ~ sein** have a gift *or* talent for sth.
Begabte *der/die; adj. Dekl.* gifted *or* talented person/man/woman *etc.*
Begabung *die;* **~, ~en** talent; gift; **eine ~ [für etw.] haben** have a gift *or* talent [for sth.]
begaffen *tr. V.* (ugs. abwertend) gawp at (coll.); stare at
begann /bə'gan/ *1. u. 3. Pers. Sg. Prät. v.* **beginnen**
begatten /bə'gatn̩/ **1** *tr. V.* mate with; ⟨*man*⟩ copulate with; ⟨*stallion, bull*⟩ cover. **2** *refl. V.* mate; ⟨*persons*⟩ copulate
Begattung *die* mating; (bei Menschen) copulation
begeben *unr. refl. V.* (geh.) (**a**) proceed; make one's way; go; **sich nach Hause ~:** proceed *or* make one's way *or* go home; **sich zu Bett ~:** retire to bed; **sich in ärztliche Behandlung ~:** get medical treatment; go to a doctor for treatment; **sich an die Arbeit ~:** commence work; (**b**) (geschehen) happen; occur
Begebenheit *die;* **~, ~en** (geh.) event; occurrence
begegnen /bə'ge:gnən/ *itr. V.; mit sein* (**a**) **jmdm. ~:** meet sb.; **sich** (*Dat.*) **~:** meet [each other]; **ihre Blicke begegneten sich** (*Dat.*) (geh.) their eyes met; (**b**) **etw. begegnet jmdm.** (jmd. trifft etw. an) sb. comes across *or* encounters sth.; (geh.: etw. passiert jmdm.) sth. happens to sb.; (**c**) **jmdm. freundlich/höflich** *usw.* **~** (geh.) behave in a friendly/polite *etc.* way towards sb.; (**d**) (geh.: entgegentreten) counter ⟨*accusation, attack*⟩; combat ⟨*illness, disease; misuse of drugs, alcohol, etc.*⟩; meet ⟨*difficulty, danger*⟩; deal with ⟨*emergency*⟩
Begegnung *die;* **~, ~en** (**a**) meeting; **eine Stätte internationaler ~en** an international meeting place; (**b**) (Sport) match
begehen *unr. tr. V.* (**a**) commit ⟨*crime, adultery, indiscretion, sin, suicide, faux-pas, etc.*⟩; make ⟨*mistake*⟩; **eine [furchtbare] Dummheit/Taktlosigkeit ~:** do something [really] stupid/tactless; (**b**) (geh.: feiern) celebrate; **ein Fest würdig ~:** celebrate an occasion fittingly; (**c**) (abgehen) inspect [on foot]; (**d**) (betreten) walk on
begehren *tr. V.* desire; *s. auch* **Herz b**
Begehren *das;* **~s** (geh.) desire, wish (**nach** for); (Bitte) request

begehrens·wert *Adj.* desirable
begehrlich **1** *Adj.* greedy. **2** *adv.* greedily
begehrt *Adj.* much sought-after
begeistern **1** *tr. V.* **jmdn. [für etw.] ~:** fill *or* fire sb. with enthusiasm [for sth.]; **das Publikum ~:** fire the audience. **2** *refl. V.* get enthusiastic; (begeistert sein) be enthusiastic (**für** about)
begeistert **1** *Adj.* enthusiastic; **von jmdm./etw. ~ sein** be taken by *or* with sb./be enthusiastic about sth. **2** *adv.* enthusiastically
Begeisterung *die;* **~:** enthusiasm; **in ~ geraten** become *or* get enthusiastic
begeisterungs-, Begeisterungs-: **~fähig** *Adj.* ⟨*children, people, etc.*⟩ who are able to get enthusiastic *or* are capable of enthusiasm; **~fähig sein** be able to get enthusiastic; **~fähigkeit** *die; o. Pl.* capacity for enthusiasm; **~sturm** *der* storm of enthusiastic applause
Begierde /bə'gi:ɐdə/ *die;* **~, ~n** desire (**nach** for)
begierig **1** *Adj.* eager; (gierig) greedy; hungry; **~ sein, etw. zu tun** be [desperately] eager to do sth.; **mit ~en Blicken** with hungry *or* greedy glances. **2** *adv.* eagerly; (gierig) greedily; hungrily
begießen *unr. tr. V.* (**a**) water ⟨*plants*⟩; baste ⟨*meat*⟩; **jmdn./etw. mit Wasser ~:** pour water over sb./sth.; (**b**) (ugs.) **etw. ~:** celebrate sth. with a drink; **das muss begossen werden** that calls for a drink
Beginn /bə'gɪn/ *der;* **~[e]s** start; beginning; **zu ~:** at the start *or* beginning
beginnen **1** *unr. itr. V.* start; begin; **mit einer Arbeit/dem Studium ~:** start *or* begin a piece of work/one's studies; **mit dem Bau ~:** start *or* begin building; **dort beginnt der Wald** the forest starts there. **2** *unr. tr. V.* (**a**) start; begin; start ⟨*argument*⟩; (**b**) **es ~, etw. zu tun** go *or* set about doing sth.; **was hättet ihr nur ohne mich begonnen?** what would you have done without me?
beginnend *Adj.; nicht präd.* incipient; **mit der ~en Morgendämmerung** as dawn begins/began to break; **im ~en 19. Jahrhundert** at the beginning of the 19th century
beglaubigen /bə'glaʊbɪgn̩/ *tr. V.* certify
Beglaubigung *die;* **~, ~en** certification
Beglaubigungs·schreiben *das* letter of accreditation
begleichen *unr. tr. V.* settle, pay ⟨*bill, debt*⟩; pay ⟨*sum*⟩; **mit jmdm. eine Rechnung zu ~ haben** (fig.) have a score to settle with sb.
Begleit·brief *der* covering *or* accompanying letter
begleiten *tr. V.* (auch Musik, fig.) accompany; **jmdn. zur Tür ~:** show sb. to the door; **jmdn. nach Hause ~:** see sb. home
Begleiter *der;* **~s, ~, Begleiterin** *die;* **~, ~nen** companion; (zum Schutz) escort
Begleit-: **~erscheinung** *die* concomitant; (einer Krankheit) accompanying symptom; **~musik** *die* (fig.) accompaniment; **~papiere** *Pl.* accompanying documents; **~person** *die* escort; **~schreiben** *das* ⇒ **~brief**
Begleitung *die;* **~, ~en** (**a**) *o. Pl.* **er bot uns seine ~ an** he offered to accompany us; **in ~ einer Frau/eines Erwachsenen** in the company of *or* accompanied by a woman/an adult; **er ist in ~ hier** he's here with someone; (**b**) (Musik) accompaniment; **ohne ~:** unaccompanied *or* without accompaniment; (**c**) (Person[en]) companion[s *pl.*]; (zum Schutz) escort
beglücken *tr. V.* (geh.) **jmdn. ~:** make sb. happy; delight sb.; **jmdn. mit etw. ~** (oft iron.) favour sb. with sth.; **die Frauen/Männer ~:** gratify women/men; **ein ~des Erlebnis** a gladdening experience
beglückt **1** *Adj.* happy; delighted. **2** *adv.* happily; delightedly
Beglückung *die;* **~:** **zur ~ der Menschheit beitragen** contribute to the sum of human happiness
beglück·wünschen *tr. V.* congratulate (**zu** on)
begnadet *Adj.* (geh.) divinely gifted
begnadigen *tr. V.* pardon; reprieve
Begnadigung *die;* **~, ~en** pardonning; reprieving; (Straferlass) pardon; reprieve

begnügen /bə'gny:gn̩/ *refl. V.* content oneself (**mit** with)

Begonie /be'go:niə/ *die;* ~, ~**n** begonia

begonnen /bə'gɔnən/ *2. Part. v.* **beginnen**

begraben *unr. tr. V.* (**a**) bury; **dort möchte ich nicht** ~ **sein** (ugs.) I wouldn't live there if you paid me (coll.); **du kannst dich** ~ **lassen** (ugs.) you may as well give up; (**b**) (fig.) abandon ‹*hope, plan, etc.*›

Begräbnis /bə'grɛ:pnɪs/ *das;* ~**ses**, ~**se** burial; (~feier) funeral

begradigen /bə'gra:dɪgn̩/ *tr. V.* straighten

Begradigung *die;* ~, ~**en** straightening

begreifen 1 *unr. tr. V.* (**a**) understand; understand, grasp, comprehend ‹*connection, problem, meaning*›; **er konnte nicht** ~, **was geschehen war** he could not grasp what had happened; **kaum zu** ~ **sein** be almost incomprehensible; **das begreife, wer will** it's beyond me; (**b**) (geh.: betrachten) regard, see (**als** as). 2 *itr. V.* understand; **schnell** *od.* **leicht/langsam** *od.* **schwer** ~: be quick/slow on the uptake; be quick/slow to grasp things

begreiflich *Adj.* understandable; **das ist mir nicht** ~: I can't understand it; **jmdm. etw.** ~ **machen** make sb. understand sth.

begreiflicher·weise *Adv.* understandably

begrenzen *tr. V.* (**a**) limit, restrict (**auf** + *Akk.* to); (**b**) (die Grenze bilden von) mark the boundary of; **durch etw. begrenzt sein** be bounded by sth.

begrenzt *Adj.* limited; restricted

Begrenzung *die;* ~, ~**en** (**a**) (Grenze) boundary; (**b**) (das Begrenzen) limiting; restriction; (der Geschwindigkeit) restriction

Begriff *der* (**a**) concept; (Terminus) term; (**b**) (Auffassung) idea; **einen/keinen** ~ **von etw. haben** have an idea/no idea of sth.; **sich** (*Dat.*) **keinen** ~ **von etw. machen können** not be able to imagine sth.; **für meine** ~**e** in my estimation; **ein/kein** ~ **sein** be/not be well known; (**c**) **im** ~ **sein** *od.* **stehen, etw. zu tun** be about to do sth.; (**d**) **schwer von** ~ **sein** (ugs.) be slow on the uptake

begriffen /bə'grɪfn̩/ *Adj.* **in im Aufbruch/Fallen** *usw.* ~ **sein** be leaving/falling *etc.*

begrifflich 1 *Adj.* conceptual. 2 *adv.* conceptually

begriffs-, Begriffs-: ~**bestimmung** *die* definition [of the/a concept]; ~**stutzig** *Adj.* obtuse; slow-witted; gormless (coll.); slow-wittedly; gormlessly (coll.); ~**stutzigkeit** *die;* ~: obtuseness; slow-wittedness; gormlessness (coll.); ~**verwirrung** *die* conceptual confusion

begründen *tr. V.* (**a**) substantiate ‹*statement, charge, claim*›; give reasons for ‹*decision, refusal, opinion*›; (**b**) (gründen) found; establish ‹*fame, reputation*›; **einen Hausstand** ~: set up house

Begründer *der* founder

begründet *Adj.* well-founded; (berechtigt) reasonable; **sachlich** ~: objectively based; **in etw.** (*Dat.*) ~ **sein** be the result of sth.

Begründung *die;* ~, ~**en** (**a**) reason[s *pl.*]; **mit der** ~, **dass** ...: on the grounds that ...; **seine** ~ **war** ...: the reason/reasons he gave was/were ...; **ohne jede** ~: without giving any reasons; (**b**) (Gründung) founding; establishment; (eines Hausstands) setting up

begrünen *tr. V.* **etw.** ~: plant greenery in/on sth.; (mit Rasen) grass sth.

begrüßen *tr. V.* (**a**) greet; ‹*host, hostess*› greet, welcome; (**b**) (gutheißen) welcome ‹*suggestion, proposal*›; **ich begrüße es, dass** ...: I am glad that ...

begrüßens·wert *Adj.* welcome

Begrüßung *die;* ~, ~**en** greeting; (von Gästen) welcoming; (Zeremonie) welcome (*Gen.* for); **jmdm. zur** ~ **etw. überreichen** welcome sb. with sth.; **sich zur** ~ **die Hand schütteln** shake hands by way of greeting

Begrüßungs-: ~**an·sprache** *die*, ~**rede** *die* speech of welcome; welcoming speech

begucken *tr. V.* (ugs.) look at; have *or* take a look at; **sich** (*Dat.*) **jmdn./etw.** ~: have *or* take a look at sb./sth.

begünstigen /bə'gʏnstɪgn̩/ *tr. V.* (**a**) favour; encourage ‹*exports, trade, growth*›; further ‹*plan*›; (**b**) (bevorzugen)

favour; show favour to; **vom Schicksal begünstigt werden** be blessed by fate

Begünstigung *die;* ~, ~**en** (**a**) ⇒ **begünstigen a:** favouring; encouragement; furthering; (**b**) (Bevorzugung) preferential treatment

begutachten *tr. V.* (**a**) examine and report on; (**b**) (ugs.: ansehen) look at; have *or* take a look at; **lass dich mal** ~! let's have *or* take a look at you

begütert /bə'gy:tɐt/ *Adj.* wealthy; affluent

begütigen /bə'gy:tɪgn̩/ *tr. V.* placate; mollify; pacify; ~**d auf jmdn. einreden** speak soothingly to sb.

behaart /bə'ha:ɐt/ *Adj.* hairy; **schwarz/stark** ~ **sein** be covered with black hair/covered with hair

Behaarung *die;* ~, ~**en** hair *no indef. art.*

behäbig /bə'hɛ:bɪç/ 1 *Adj.* stolid and portly; (langsam) slow and ponderous. 2 *adv.* slowly and ponderously

Behäbigkeit *die;* ~ (**a**) stolidness and portliness; (**b**) (Langsamkeit) slowness and ponderousness

behaftet *Adj.* (geh.) **mit einem Makel/Laster** ~ **sein** be marked with a blemish/tainted with a vice; **mit einem schlechten Ruf/einem Fehler** ~ **sein** have a bad name/a defect

behagen /bə'ha:gn̩/ *itr. V.* **etw. behagt jmdm.** sth. pleases sb.; sb. likes sth.; **er behagt mir gar nicht** I don't like him at all

Behagen *das;* ~**s** pleasure; **etw. mit** ~ **essen** eat sth. with relish

behaglich 1 *Adj.* comfortable; comfortable, cosy ‹*atmosphere, room, home, etc.*›; **es jmdm./sich** ~ **machen** make sb./oneself comfortable. 2 *adv.* comfortably, cosily ‹*warm, furnished*›

Behaglichkeit *die;* ~: ⇒ **behaglich 1:** comfortableness; cosiness

behalten *unr. tr. V.* (**a**) keep; keep on ‹*employees*›; keep, retain ‹*value, expressive power, etc.*›; **etw. für sich** ~: keep sth. to oneself; **die Nerven/die Ruhe** ~: keep one's nerve/keep calm; (**b**) ⇒ **zurückbehalten b;** (**c**) (sich merken) remember; *s. auch* **Recht d**

Behälter /bə'hɛltɐ/ *der;* ~**s**, ~: container; (für Abfälle) receptacle

Behältnis *das;* ~**ses**, ~**se** (geh.) container

behämmert *Adj.* (salopp) ⇒ **bekloppt**

behände /bə'hɛndə/ 1 *Adj.* (geschickt) deft; adroit; (flink) nimble; agile. 2 *adv.* (geschickt) deftly; adroitly; (flink) nimbly; agilely

behandeln *tr. V.* (**a**) treat ‹*person*›; handle ‹*matter, thing*›; (**b**) (bearbeiten) treat ‹*material, wood, etc.*›; (**c**) (sich befassen mit) deal with, treat ‹*subject, question; theme*›; (**d**) ▶ 329 (ärztlich) treat (**auf** + *Akk.*, **wegen** for)

Behändigkeit *die;* ~: ⇒ **behände 1:** deftness; adroitness; nimbleness; agility

Behandlung *die;* ~, ~**en** ▶ 329 treatment; **in** [**ärztlicher**] ~ **sein** be under medical treatment; **er ist bei Dr. N. in** ~: he is under Dr N.

Behandlungs-: ~**methode** *die* method of treatment; ~**stuhl** *der* chair for the patient; (beim Zahnarzt) [dentist's] chair

Behang *der;* ~[**e**]**s**, **Behänge** hanging

behangen *Adj.* **ein mit Äpfeln** ~**er Baum** a tree laden with apples; **mit Schmuck** ~: festooned with jewellery

behängen *tr. V.* (**a**) **etw. mit etw.** ~: hang *or* decorate sth. with sth.; (**b**) (ugs. abwertend) **jmdn./sich mit etw.** ~: festoon sb./oneself with sth.

beharren *itr. V.* **auf etw.** (*Dat.*) ~: persist in sth.; „**...**", **beharrte er** '...', he insisted

beharrlich 1 *Adj.* dogged; persistent. 2 *adv.* doggedly; persistently

Beharrlichkeit *die;* ~: doggedness; persistence

behauchen *tr. V.* breathe on

behauen *unr. tr. V.* hew; **roh** ~**e Steine** rough-hewn stone blocks

behaupten /bə'haʊptn̩/ 1 *tr. V.* (**a**) maintain; assert; ~, **jmd. zu sein/etw. zu wissen** claim to be sb./know sth.;

das kann man nicht ∼: you cannot say that; **(b)** (verteidigen) maintain ⟨*position*⟩; *s. auch* **Feld** f. 2 *refl. V.* **(a)** hold one's ground; (sich durchsetzen) assert oneself; (fortbestehen) survive; **die Kirche/der Dollar konnte sich ∼:** the church/the dollar was able to maintain its position; **(b)** (Sport) win through

Behauptung *die;* ∼, ∼**en (a)** claim; assertion; **(b)** (das Sichdurchsetzen) assertion

Behausung *die;* ∼, ∼**en** (oft abwertend: Wohnung) dwelling

beheben *unr. tr. V.* remove; repair ⟨*damage*⟩; remedy ⟨*abuse, defect*⟩

Behebung *die;* ∼, ∼**en** ⇒ **beheben:** removal; repair; remedying

beheimatet *Adj.* **an einem Ort/in einem Land ∼ sein** ⟨*plant, animal, tribe, race*⟩ be native *or* indigenous to a place/country; ⟨*person*⟩ come from a place/country

beheizbar *Adj.* heatable

beheizen *tr. V.* heat

Behelf /bə'hɛlf/ *der;* ∼**[e]s,** ∼**e** stopgap; makeshift

behelfen *unr. refl. V.* get by; manage; **sich mit etw. ∼:** make do *or* manage with sth.

Behelfs- temporary ⟨*exit, dwelling, etc.*⟩

behelfs·mäßig 1 *Adj.* makeshift; temporary. **2** *adv.* in a makeshift way *or* fashion

behelligen /bə'hɛlɪɡn̩/ *tr. V.* bother

*behende ⇒ **behände**

*Behendigkeit ⇒ **Behändigkeit**

beherbergen *tr. V.* accommodate, put up ⟨*guest*⟩; (fig.) contain

Beherbergung *die;* ∼: accommodation

Beherbungs·gewerbe *das* hotel trade

beherrschen 1 *tr. V.* **(a)** rule; **den Markt ∼:** dominate *or* control the market; **(b)** (meistern) control ⟨*vehicle, animal*⟩; be in control of ⟨*situation*⟩; **(c)** (bestimmen, dominieren) dominate ⟨*townscape, landscape, discussions, relationship*⟩; **(d)** (zügeln) control ⟨*feelings*⟩; control, curb ⟨*impatience*⟩; **(e)** (gut können) have mastered ⟨*instrument, trade*⟩; have a good command of ⟨*language*⟩. **2** *refl. V.* control oneself; **ich kann mich ∼** (iron.) I can resist the temptation (iron.)

Beherrscher *der;* ∼**s,** ∼: ruler

beherrscht 1 *Adj.* self-controlled. **2** *adv.* with self-control

Beherrschtheit *die;* ∼: self-control

Beherrschung *die;* ∼ **(a)** control; (eines Volks, Landes usw.) rule; (eines Markts) domination; control; **(b)** (das Meistern) control; **(c)** (Beherrschtheit) self-control; **seine** *od.* **die ∼ verlieren** lose one's self-control; **(d)** (das Können) mastery

beherzigen /bə'hɛrtsɪɡn̩/ *tr. V.* **etw. ∼:** take sth. to heart; heed sth.

beherzt 1 *Adj.* spirited; **einige Beherzte** a few brave souls. **2** *adv.* spiritedly

behexen *tr. V.* bewitch

behilflich /bə'hɪlflɪç/ *in* **jmdm. [beim Aufräumen usw.] ∼ sein** help sb. [clear up *or* with the clearing-up *etc.*]; **kann ich [Ihnen] ∼ sein?** can I help [you]?

behindern *tr. V.* **(a)** hinder; hamper, impede ⟨*movement*⟩; hold up ⟨*traffic*⟩; impede ⟨*view*⟩; **(b)** (Sport, Verkehrsw.) obstruct

behindert *Adj.* handicapped

Behinderte *der/die; adj. Dekl.* handicapped person; **die ∼n** the handicapped; **WC für ∼:** toilet for disabled persons

Behinderung *die;* ∼, ∼**en (a)** hindrance; **(b)** (Sport, Verkehrsw.) obstruction; **auf der Autobahn A 8 kommt es zu ∼en** there are delays on the A 8 motorway; **(c)** (Gebrechen) handicap

Behörde /bə'hø:ɐdə/ *die;* ∼, ∼**n** authority; (Amt, Abteilung) department; **die ∼n** the authorities

behördlich 1 *Adj.; nicht präd.* official. **2** *adv.* officially

behüten *tr. V.* (bewahren, beschützen) protect (**vor** + *Dat.* from); (bewachen) guard; **jmdn. vor einer Gefahr ∼:**

keep *or* safeguard sb. from a danger; **[Gott] behüte!** God *or* Heaven forbid!

Behüter *der;* ∼**s,** ∼ (geh.) protector

behütet *Adj.* sheltered ⟨*life, upbringing*⟩

behutsam /bə'hu:tza:m/ **1** *Adj.* careful; cautious; (zartfühlend) gentle. **2** *adv.* carefully; cautiously; (zartfühlend) gently

Behutsamkeit *die;* ∼: care; caution; (Zartgefühl) gentleness

bei /baɪ/ *Präp. mit Dat.* **(a)** (nahe) near; (dicht an, neben) by; **die Schlacht ∼ Leipzig** the battle of Leipzig; **∼ den Fahrrädern/Kindern bleiben** stay with the bicycles/children; **etw. ∼ sich haben** have sth. with *or* on one; **nicht [ganz] ∼ sich sein** (fig.) be not quite with it; **sich ∼ jmdm. entschuldigen/erkundigen** apologize to sb./ask sb.; **wir haben Physik ∼ Herrn Meyer** we do physics with Mr Meyer; **(b)** (unter) among; **war heute ein Brief für mich ∼ der Post?** was there a letter for me in the post today?; **(c)** (an) by; **jmdn. ∼ der Hand nehmen** take sb. by the hand; **(d)** (im Wohn-/Lebens-/Arbeitsbereich von) **∼ uns tut man das nicht** we don't do that; **∼ mir [zu Hause]** at my house; **∼ uns um die Ecke/gegenüber** round the corner from us/opposite us; **∼ seinen Eltern leben** live with one's parents; **wir sind ∼ ihr eingeladen** we have been invited to her house; **wir treffen uns ∼ uns/Peter** we'll meet at our/Peter's place; **∼ uns in Österreich** in Austria [where I/we come from/live]; **∼ uns in der Firma** in our company; **∼ Schmidt** (auf Briefen) c/o Schmidt; **∼ einer Firma sein** be with a company; **∼ jmdm./einem Verlag arbeiten** work for sb./a publishing house; **(e)** (im Bereich eines Vorgangs) at; **∼ einer Hochzeit/einem Empfang** *usw.* at a wedding/reception *etc.;* **∼ einem Unfall** in an accident; **(f)** (im Werk von) **∼ Goethe** in Goethe; **∼ Schiller heißt es …:** Schiller says *or* writes that …; **(g)** (im Falle von) in the case of; **∼ bestimmten Pflanzen** in certain plants; **∼ der Hauskatze** in the domestic cat; **wie ∼ den Römern** as with the Romans; **hoffentlich geht es nicht wie ∼ mir** I hope the same thing doesn't happen as happened in my case; **(h)** (Zeitpunkt) **∼ seiner Ankunft** on his arrival; **∼ diesen Worten errötete er** at this he blushed; **∼ Sonnenaufgang/-untergang** at sunrise/sunset; **∼ unserer Begegnung** at our meeting; **(i)** (modal) **∼ Tag/Nacht** by day/night; **∼ Tag und [∼] Nacht** day and night; **∼ Tageslicht** by daylight; **∼ Nebel** in fog; **∼ Kälte** when it's cold; **∼ offenem Fenster schlafen** sleep with the window open; **(j)** (im Falle des Auftretens von) „**∼ Feuer Scheibe einschlagen**" 'in case of fire, break glass'; „**∼ Regen Schleudergefahr**" 'slippery when wet'; **∼ hohem Fieber** when sb. has a high temperature; **(k)** (angesichts) with; **∼ dieser Hitze** in this heat; **∼ diesem Sturm/Lärm** with this storm blowing/noise going on; **(l)** (trotz) **∼ all seinem Engagement/seinen Bemühungen** in spite of *or* despite *or* for all his commitment/efforts; **∼ allem Verständnis, aber ich kann das nicht** much as I sympathize, I cannot do that; **(m)** (in Beteuerungsformeln) by; **∼ Gott!** by God!; **∼ meiner Ehre!** (veralt.) upon my honour!

bei|behalten *unr. tr. V.* keep; retain; keep up ⟨*custom, habit*⟩; continue, maintain ⟨*way of life*⟩; keep to ⟨*course, method*⟩; preserve, maintain ⟨*attitude*⟩

Beibehaltung *die;* ∼: ⇒ **beibehalten:** keeping; retention; keeping up; continuance; maintenance; preservation

Bei·boot *das* ship's boat

bei|bringen *unr. tr. V.* **(a) jmdm. etw. ∼:** teach sb. sth.; **jmdm. Gehorsam ∼:** teach sb. obedience; **(b)** (ugs.: mitteilen) **jmdm. ∼, dass …:** break it to sb. that …; **(c)** (zufügen) **jmdm./sich etw. ∼:** inflict sth. on sb./oneself; **(d)** (beschaffen) produce ⟨*witness, evidence*⟩; provide, supply ⟨*reference, proof*⟩; produce, furnish ⟨*money*⟩

Beichte /'baɪçtə/ *die;* ∼, ∼**n** confession *no def. art.;* **zur ∼ gehen** go to confession; **jmdm. die ∼ abnehmen** hear sb.'s confession

beichten 1 *itr. V.* confess; **∼ gehen** go to confession. **2** *tr. V.* (auch fig.) confess

Beicht-: ∼**geheimnis** *das* seal of confession; ∼**stuhl** *der* confessional; ∼**vater** *der* father confessor

beide /'baɪdə/ *Indefinitpron. u. Zahlw.* **1** *Pl.* **die** ~n the two; ~: both; (der/die/das eine oder der/die/das andere von den ~n) either *sing;* **die/seine** ~n **Brüder** the/his two brothers; **die ersten** ~n **Strophen** the first two verses; **kennst du die** ~n? do you know those two?; **alle** ~: both of you/them; **sie sind alle** ~ **sehr schön** they're both very nice; both of them are very nice; **sie sind** ~ **nicht hübsch** neither of them is pretty; **ihr/euch** ~: you two; **Ihr/euch** ~ **nicht** neither of you; **wir/uns** ~: the two of us/both of us; **er hat** ~ **Eltern verloren** he has lost both [his] parents; **mit** ~n **Händen** with both hands; ~ **Male** both times; **ich habe** ~ **gekannt** I knew both of them; **einer/eins von** ~n one of the two; **keiner/ keins von** ~n neither [of them]. **2** *Neutr. Sg.* **both** *pl.;* (das eine oder das andere) either; ~s **ist möglich** either is possible; **ich glaube** ~s/~s **nicht** I believe both things/ neither thing; **das ist** ~s **nicht richtig** neither of those is correct; **er hat sich in** ~m **geirrt** he was wrong on both counts; **er hatte von** ~m **wenig Ahnung** he had little idea of either

beiderlei /'baɪdɐ'laɪ:/ *Gattungsz., indekl.* ~ **Geschlechts** of both sexes; **von** ~ **Art** of both kinds

beider·seitig *Adj.* mutual ⟨*decision, agreement*⟩; **zur** ~en **Überraschung** to the surprise of both of us/them; **in** ~em **Einverständnis** by mutual agreement

beider·seits **1** *Präp. mit Gen.* on both sides of. **2** *Adv.* on both sides

bei|drehen *itr. V.* (Seemannsspr.) heave to

beid·seitig **1** *Adj.* mutual. **2** *adv.* ⟨*be printed etc.*⟩ on both sides; ~ **gelähmt** paralysed down both sides

bei·einander *Adv.* together; ~ **Trost suchen** seek comfort from each other; **du hast/er hat** *usw.* **[sie] nicht alle** ~ (ugs.) he's/you're *etc.* not all there (coll.); **gut/ schlecht** ~ **sein** (ugs.) be in good/bad shape; **nicht ganz** ~ **sein** (ugs.) be not quite all there (coll.)

*beieinander|haben *usw.:* s. beieinander

Bei·fahrer *der,* **Bei·fahrerin** *die* (a) [front-seat] passenger; (auf dem Motorrad) pillion passenger; (im Beiwagen) sidecar passenger; (b) (berufsmäßig) co-driver; (im LKW) driver's mate

Beifahrer·sitz *der* passenger seat; (eines Motorrads) pillion

Bei·fall *der; o. Pl.* (a) applause; (Zurufe) cheers *pl.;* cheering; ~ **klatschen/spenden** applaud; (b) (Zustimmung) approval; ~ **finden** meet with approval

bei·fällig **1** *Adj.* approving; favourable ⟨*judgement*⟩. **2** *adv.* approvingly; ~ **nicken** nod approvingly *or* in approval

Beifalls-: ~**äußerung** *die* expression of approval; ~**bekundung** *die* demonstration of approval; ~**ruf** *der* shout of approval; cheer; ~**sturm** *der* storm of applause

bei|fügen *tr. V.* **einer Bewerbung etw.** ~: enclose sth. with an application; **einem Paket eine Zollerklärung** ~: attach a customs declaration to a parcel

Bei·gabe *die* (a) *o. Pl.* **unter** ~ (*Dat.*) **von etw.** adding sth.; (b) (Hinzugefügtes) addition

beige /be:ʃ/ *Adj.* beige

Beige *das;* ~, ~ *od.* (ugs.) ~s beige

bei|geben **1** *unr. tr. V.* add (*Dat.* to). **2** *unr. itr. V.* **in klein** ~ (ugs.) give in

Bei·geschmack *der; o. Pl.* **einen bitteren** *usw.* ~ **haben** have a slightly bitter *etc.* taste [to it]; taste slightly bitter *etc.;* **dieses Wort hat einen negativen** ~ (fig.) this word has slightly negative overtones *pl.*

Bei·hilfe *die* (a) [financial] aid *or* assistance; (Zuschuss) allowance; (Subvention) subsidy; (b) *o. Pl.* (Rechtsw.: Mithilfe) aiding and abetting; **jmdn. wegen** ~ **zum Mord anklagen** charge sb. with aiding and abetting a murder *or* with acting as accessory to a murder

bei|kommen *unr. itr. V.; mit sein* **jmdm.** ~: get the better of sb.; **den Schwierigkeiten/jmds. Sturheit** ~: overcome the difficulties/cope with sb.'s obstinacy

Beil /baɪl/ *das;* ~[e]s, ~e axe; (kleiner) hatchet; (Fleischer~) cleaver

Bei·lage *die* (a) (Zeitungs~) supplement; (b) (zu Speisen) side dish; (Gemüse~) vegetables *pl.;* **ein Fleischgericht**

mit diversen ~n a meat dish with a selection of trimmings

bei·läufig **1** *Adj.* casual; casual, passing ⟨*remark, mention*⟩. **2** *adv.* casually; **etw.** ~ **erwähnen** mention sth. casually *or* in passing

Beiläufigkeit *die;* ~ casualness

bei|legen *tr. V.* (a) (dazulegen) enclose; (einem Buch, einer Zeitschrift) insert (*Dat.* in); **einem Brief** *usw.* **etw.** ~: enclose sth. with a letter *etc.;* (b) (schlichten) settle ⟨*dispute, controversy, etc.*⟩; (c) ⇒ **beimessen**

Beilegung *die;* ~, ~**en** settlement

beileibe /baɪ'laɪbə/ *Adv.* ~ **nicht** certainly not; **er ist** ~ **kein Genie** he is by no means a genius

Bei·leid *das* sympathy; **[mein] herzliches** *od.* **aufrichtiges** ~! please accept my sincere condolences; **jmdm. sein [aufrichtiges]** ~ **[zu etw.] aussprechen** offer one's [sincere] condolences *pl.* to sb. [on sth.]

Beileids-: ~**besuch** *der* visit of condolence; ~**bezeigung** *die;* ~, ~**en,** ~**bezeugung** *die* expression of sympathy

bei|liegen *unr. itr. V.* **einem Brief** ~: be enclosed with a letter; **dem Buch liegt ein Prospekt bei** the book contains a catalogue as an insert

bei·liegend *Adj.* (Amtsspr.) enclosed; ~ **senden wir** ...: please find enclosed ...

beim /baɪm/ *Präp. + Art.* (a) = **bei dem;** (b) ~ **Bäcker** at the baker's; **jmdn.** ~ **Arm packen** seize sb. by the arm; ~ **Film sein** be in films; ~ **Ahorn/ Menschen** in the maple/in man; (c) (zeitlich) **er will** ~ **Arbeiten nicht gestört werden** he doesn't want to be disturbed when *or* while [he's] working; ~ **Essen spricht man nicht** you shouldn't talk while [you're] eating; ~ **Verlassen des Gebäudes** when *or* on leaving the building; ~ **Fasching** at carnival time; **[gerade]** ~ **Duschen sein** be taking a shower

bei|mengen *tr. V.* add (*Dat.* to)

bei|messen *unr. tr. V.* attach (*Dat.* to)

bei|mischen *tr. V.* add (*Dat.* to)

Bei·mischung *die* (a) *o. Pl.* (das Beimischen) addition; (b) (Zusatz) admixture

Bein /baɪn/ *das;* ~[e]s, ~e (a) ▸326↓ leg; **jmdm.** ~e **machen** (ugs.) make sb. get a move on (coll.); **er hat sich** (*Dat.*) **kein** ~ **ausgerissen** (ugs.) he didn't overexert himself; **jmdm. ein** ~ **stellen** trip sb.; (fig.) put *or* throw a spanner *or* (Amer.) a monkey wrench in sb.'s works; **jmdm. [einen] Knüppel** *od.* **Prügel zwischen die** ~e **werfen** (fig.) put *or* throw a spanner *or* (Amer.) a monkey wrench in sb.'s works; **das hat** ~e **gekriegt** (fig. ugs.) it seems to have [grown legs and] walked (coll.); **die** ~e **in die Hand** *od.* **unter die Arme nehmen** (fig. ugs.) step on it (coll.); **[wieder] auf die** ~e **kommen** (ugs.) get back on one's/ its feet [again]; **jmdn./etw. [wieder] auf die** ~e **bringen** (ugs.) put sb./sth. back on his/her/its feet again; **jmdm. auf die** ~e **helfen** help sb. to his/her feet; **ich kann mich nicht mehr/kaum noch auf den** ~en **halten** I can't/can hardly stand up; **auf eigenen** ~en **stehen** (fig.) stand on one's own two feet; support oneself; **mit beiden** ~en **im Leben** *od.* **[fest] auf der Erde stehen** have both feet [firmly] on the ground; **mit dem linken** ~ **zuerst aufgestanden sein** (ugs.) have got out of bed on the wrong side; **mit einem** ~ **im Gefängnis/ Grab[e] stehen** (fig.) stand a good chance of ending up in prison/have one foot in the grave; **von einem** ~ **aufs andere treten** (ugs.) shift from one foot to the other; (b) (Hosen~, Tisch~, Stuhl~ usw.) leg

bei·nah[e] /'baɪna:(ə)/ *Adv.* almost; nearly; **wir wären** ~ **zu spät gekommen** we were nearly too late

Beinahe·zusammenstoß *der* (Flugw.) airmiss

Bei·name *der* epithet

Bein·bruch *der* broken leg; **das ist [doch] kein** ~**bruch!** (ugs.) it's not the end of the world (coll.)

beinhalten /bə'|ɪnhaltn/ *tr. V.* (Papierdt.) involve

-beinig *adj.* -legged

Bein·schiene *die* [long] shin pad; (Cricket, Hockey) pad

Beipack·zettel *der* instruction leaflet

bei|pflichten /'baɪpflɪçtn/ *itr. V.* **jmdm. [in etw.** (*Dat.*)] ~: agree with sb. [on sth.]; **einem Vorschlag** *usw.* ~: agree with a proposal *etc.*

Bei·rat der advisory committee or board

beirren tr. V. sich durch nichts/von niemandem ∼ lassen not be put off or deterred by anything/anybody; not let anything/anybody put one off or deter one; nichts konnte ihn in seinen Ansichten ∼: nothing could shake him in his views

beisammen /bai'zamən/ Adv. together

beisammen-, Beisammen-: ∼|haben unr. tr. V. er hat sie nicht alle ∼ (ugs.) he's not all there (coll.); ∼|halten unr. tr. V. keep together; hold on to ⟨money⟩; ∼|sein unr. itr. V.; mit sein; (nur im Inf. und 2. Part. zusammengeschrieben) [gut] ∼sein (ugs.) be in good health or shape; ∼sein das get-together; ∼|sitzen unr. itr. V. sit together

Bei·schlaf der (geh., Rechtsw.) sexual intercourse

bei|schließen unr. tr. V. (österr.) einem Brief usw. etw. ∼: enclose sth. with a letter etc.

Bei·schluss, *Bei·schluß der (österr.: Anlage) enclosure

Bei·sein das in im ∼ von jmdm., in jmds. ∼: in the presence of sb. or in sb.'s presence

bei·seite Adv. aside; jmdn. ∼ ziehen/schieben draw/push sb. to one side or aside; etw. ∼ bringen get sth. hidden away; hide sth. away; etw. ∼ lassen (fig.) leave sth. aside; etw. ∼ legen put or lay sth. aside; (sparen) put sth. by; jmdn./etw. ∼ schaffen (ugs.) get rid of sb./sth.

Beis[e]l /'baizl/ das; ∼s, ∼ od. ∼n (österr.) ⇒ **Kneipe**

bei|setzen tr. V. bury; inter; lay to rest; inter ⟨ashes⟩

Bei·setzung die; ∼, ∼en (geh.) funeral; burial

Bei·sitzer der; ∼s, ∼, **Bei·sitzerin** die; ∼, ∼nen assessor; (bei Ausschüssen) committee member

Bei·spiel das (a) example (für of); zum ∼: for example or instance; wie zum ∼: as for example; such as; ohne ∼ sein be without parallel; be unparalleled; (b) (Vorbild) example; ein warnendes ∼: a warning; jmdm. ein ∼ geben set an example to sb.; sich (Dat.) an jmdm./etw. ein ∼ nehmen follow sb.'s example/take sth. as one's example; mit gutem ∼ vorangehen set a good example

beispielhaft Adj. exemplary

beispiel·los 1 Adj. unparalleled. 2 adv. incomparably ⟨well, badly, etc.⟩; ∼ erfolgreich with unparalleled success

beispiels-: ∼halber Adv. for example or instance; ∼weise Adv. for example or instance

bei|springen unr. itr. V.; mit sein jmdm. [in der Not] ∼: leap or rush to sb.'s aid or assistance [in an emergency]; jmdm. mit Geld ∼: help sb. out with money

beißen /'baisn/ 1 unr. tr., itr. V. (a) bite; (kauen) chew; in etw. (Akk.) ∼: bite into sth.; an den Nägeln ∼: bite one's nails; ich habe mich od. mir auf die Zunge/in die Lippe gebissen I've bitten my tongue/lip; der Hund hat mir od. mich ins Bein gebissen the dog bit me in the leg; nichts/nicht viel zu ∼ haben (fig.) have nothing/not have much to eat; (b) (ätzen) sting; in die od. in den Augen ∼: sting one's eyes; make one's eyes sting; auf der Zunge ∼: burn the tongue. 2 unr. refl. V. (ugs.) ⟨colours⟩ clash (mit with)

beißend Adj.; nicht präd. biting ⟨cold⟩; acrid ⟨smoke, fumes⟩; sharp ⟨frost⟩; pungent, sharp ⟨smell, taste⟩; (fig.) biting ⟨ridicule⟩; cutting ⟨irony⟩

Beiß-: ∼ring der teething-ring; ∼zange die ⇒ Kneifzange

Bei·stand der o. Pl. (geh.) aid; assistance; help; jmdm. ∼ leisten give sb. aid or assistance; come to sb.'s aid or assistance

bei|stehen unr. itr. V. jmdm. ∼: aid or assist or help sb.; (zur Seite stehen) stand by sb.

Beistell-: ∼tisch der, ∼tischchen das occasional table; (im Restaurant) side table

bei|steuern tr. V. contribute; make ⟨contribution⟩

bei|stimmen itr. V.: ⇒ zustimmen

Bei·strich der (veralt.) comma

Beitrag /'baitra:k/ der; ∼[e]s, Beiträge /'baitre:gə/ contribution; (Versicherungs∼) premium; (Mitglieds∼) subscription; einen ∼ zu etw. leisten make a contribution to sth.

*alte Schreibung (vgl. Hinweise auf S. xvi–xvii)

bei|tragen unr. tr., itr. V. contribute (zu to); das Seine/viel zu etw. ∼: contribute one's share/a great deal to sth.

beitrags-: ∼frei Adj. non-contributory; ⟨person⟩ not liable to pay contributions; ∼pflichtig Adj. (Sozialw.) ⟨employee⟩ liable to pay contributions; ⟨earnings⟩ on which contributions are payable

bei|treiben unr. tr. V. (Rechtsw.) enforce payment of

bei|treten unr. itr. V.; mit sein join; einem Verein usw. ∼: join a club etc.; einem Abkommen/Pakt ∼: accede to an agreement/a pact

Bei·tritt der joining; seinen ∼ erklären apply for membership

Beitritts·erklärung die application for membership

Bei·wagen der sidecar

Bei·werk das; o. Pl. accessories pl.

bei|willigen itr. V. (schweiz.) ⇒ zustimmen

bei|wohnen itr. V. einer Sache (Dat.) ∼: be present at or attend sth.

Beize¹ /'baitsə/ die; ∼, ∼n (Holzbearb.) [wood] stain

Beize² die; ∼, ∼n (Jagdw.) hawking

Beize³ die; ∼, ∼n (schweiz.) ⇒ **Kneipe**

beizeiten /bai'tsaitn/ Adv. in good time

beizen /'baitsn/ tr. V. (Holzbearb.) stain

bei|ziehen unr. tr. V. (südd., österr., schweiz.) call in ⟨lawyer, psychologist, expert, etc.⟩; bring in, enlist ⟨helpers⟩

Bei·ziehung die (südd., österr., schweiz.) calling in

Beiz·jagd die ⇒ **Beize²**

bejahen /bə'ja:ən/ tr. V. (a) etw. ∼: give an affirmative answer to sth.; answer sth. in the affirmative; (b) (gutheißen, befürworten) approve of; das Leben ∼: have a positive or affirmative attitude to life

bejahend 1 Adj. affirmative; affirmative, positive ⟨attitude⟩. 2 adv. ⟨answer⟩ in the affirmative; ⟨nod⟩ affirmatively

bejahrt /bə'ja:et/ Adj. (geh.) advanced in years

Bejahung die; ∼, ∼en (a) affirmative answer or reply; (b) (das Gutheißen) approval

bejammern tr. V. lament

bejubeln tr. V. cheer; acclaim

bekämpfen tr. V. (a) fight against; sich [gegenseitig] ∼: fight [one another or each other]; (b) (fig.) combat, fight ⟨disease, epidemic, pest⟩; combat ⟨unemployment, crime, alcoholism⟩; curb ⟨curiosity, prejudice⟩

Bekämpfung die; ∼ (a) fight (Gen. against); (b) ⇒ bekämpfen b: combating; fighting; curbing

bekannt /bə'kant/ Adj. (a) well-known; etw. ∼ geben announce sth.; etw. ∼ machen announce sth.; (der Öffentlichkeit) make sth. public; ∼ werden become known; become public knowledge; für etw. ∼ sein be well known for sth.; ∼er sein be better known; (b) jmd./etw. ist jmdm. ∼: sb. knows sb./sth.; davon ist mir nichts ∼: I know nothing about that; mit jmdm. ∼ sein/werden know or be acquainted with sb./get to know or become acquainted with sb.; jmdn./sich mit jmdm. ∼ machen introduce sb./oneself to sb.; Darf ich ∼ machen? Meine Eltern may I introduce my parents?; jmdn./sich mit etw. ∼ machen acquaint sb./oneself with sth.; jmdm. ∼ vorkommen seem familiar to sb.; der Witz kommt mir ∼ vor I think I've heard that joke somewhere before

Bekannte der/die adj. Dekl. acquaintance

Bekannten·kreis der circle of acquaintances

bekannter·maßen Adv. (Papierdt.) ⇒ bekanntlich

Bekannt·gabe die; ∼: announcement

***bekannt|geben** ⇒ bekannt a

Bekanntheit die; ∼: trotz der ∼ dieser Tatsache although this fact is widely known; wegen Brandts großer ∼: because Brandt is so well known

bekanntlich Adv. as is well known; etw. ist ∼ der Fall sth. is known to be the case; der Wal ist ∼ ein Säugetier it is well known that the whale is a mammal

***bekannt|machen** ⇒ bekannt a

Bekannt·machung die; ∼, ∼en (a) o. Pl. announcement; (Veröffentlichung) publication; (b) (Mitteilung) announcement; notice

Bekanntschaft *die;* ~, ~**en** (a) *o. Pl.* acquaintance; **bei näherer** ~: on closer acquaintance; **jmds.** ~ **machen** make sb.'s acquaintance; (**b**) (Bekannter, Bekannte) acquaintance; (Bekanntenkreis) circle of acquaintances

*bekannt|werden ⇒ bekannt a

bekehren 1 *tr. V.* convert (**zu** to). 2 *refl. V.* become converted (**zu** to)

Bekehrte *der/die; adj. Dekl.* convert

Bekehrung *die;* ~, ~**en** conversion (**zu** to)

bekennen 1 *unr. tr. V.* (**a**) admit ‹*mistake, defeat*›; confess ‹*sin*›; admit, confess ‹*guilt, truth*›; (**b**) (Rel.) profess; **die Bekennende Kirche** (hist.) the Confessional Church. 2 *refl. V.* **sich zum Islam** *usw.* ~: profess Islam *etc.;* **sich zu Buddha/Mohammed** ~: profess one's faith in Buddha/Muhammad; **seine Freunde bekannten sich zu ihm** his friends stood by him; **sich zu einer Verfehlung** ~: amit to a misdemeanour; **sich zu seiner Vergangenheit** ~: acknowledge one's past; **sich zu seiner Schuld** ~: admit *or* confess one's guilt; **sich schuldig/nicht schuldig** ~: admit *or* confess/not admit *or* not confess one's guilt; (vor Gericht) plead guilty/not guilty; **sich zu einem Bombenanschlag** ~: claim responsibility for a bomb attack

Bekenner-: ~**brief,** *der* letter claiming responsibility; ~**geist** *der,* ~**mut** *der; o. Pl.* courage of one's convictions

Bekenntnis *das;* ~**ses,** ~**se** (**a**) confession; **ein** ~ **ablegen** make a confession; (**b**) **ein** ~ **zum Frieden** a declaration for peace; **ein** ~ **zum Christentum/zur Demokratie ablegen** profess one's faith in Christianity/declare one's belief in democracy; (**c**) (Konfession) denomination

Bekenntnis-: ~**freiheit** *die; o. Pl.* religious freedom; freedom of worship; ~**schule** *die* denominational school

bekiffen *refl. V.* get stoned (sl.)

bekifft /bə'kɪft/ *Adj.* (ugs.) stoned (coll.)

beklagen 1 *tr. V.* (geh.) (**a**) (betrauern) mourn; **Menschenleben waren nicht zu** ~: there were no fatalities; (**b**) (bedauern) lament; **sein/jmds. Los** ~: lament *or* bewail one's fate/deplore sb.'s fate; **wir haben einen großen Umsatzrückgang zu** ~: we have to note with regret a large drop in sales. 2 *refl. V.* complain (**bei** to); **ich kann mich nicht** ~: I can't complain

beklagens·wert *Adj.* pitiful ‹*sight, impression*›; pitiable ‹*person*›; lamentable, pitiable, deplorable ‹*condition, state*›; wretched ‹*situation*›

Beklagte *der/die; adj. Dekl.* defendant; (bei Ehescheidungen) respondent

beklatschen *tr. V.* clap; applaud

beklauen *tr. V.* (salopp) rob; do (sl.)

bekleben *tr. V.* **eine Wand** *usw.* **mit etw.** ~: stick sth. all over a wall *etc.*

bekleckern (ugs.) 1 *tr. V.* **seinen Schlips** *usw.* **mit Soße** *usw.* ~: drop *or* spill sauce *etc.* down one's tie *etc.* 2 *refl. V.* **sich [mit Soße** *usw.*] ~: drop *or* spill sauce *etc.* down oneself

bekleiden *tr. V.* (**a**) clothe; **mit etw. bekleidet sein** be dressed in *or* be wearing sth.; (**b**) (geh.: innehaben) occupy, hold ‹*office, position*›

Bekleidung *die* clothing; clothes *pl.;* garments *pl.*

beklemmend 1 *Adj.* oppressive. 2 *adv.* oppressively

Beklemmung *die;* ~, ~**en** oppressive feeling; (Angst) [feeling of] unease; (stärker) [feeling of] apprehension

beklommen /bə'klɔmən/ 1 *Adj.* uneasy; (stärker) apprehensive. 2 *adv.* uneasily; (stärker) apprehensively

Beklommenheit *die;* ~: uneasiness; (stärker) apprehensiveness

bekloppt /bə'klɔpt/ *Adj.* (salopp) barmy (Brit. coll.); loony (coll.); **ein Bekloppter** a nutcase (Brit. coll.); a nut (coll.)

beknackt *Adj.* (salopp) lousy (coll.); **ein** ~**er Typ** a berk (Brit. sl.)

beknien *tr. V.* (ugs.) beg

bekommen 1 *unr. tr. V.* (**a**) get; get, receive ‹*money, letter, reply, news, orders*›; (erlangen) get; obtain; (erreichen)

catch ‹*train, bus, flight, etc.*›; **eine Flasche** *usw.* **an den Kopf** ~: get hit on the head with a bottle *etc.;* **was** ~ **Sie?** (im Geschäft) can I help you?; (im Lokal, Restaurant) what would you like?; **was** ~ **Sie [dafür]?** how much is that?; **noch Geld von jmdm.** ~: be owed money by sb.; **wir** ~ **Regen/besseres Wetter** we're going to get some rain/some better weather; there's rain/better weather on the way; **ich bekomme keine Verbindung** I can't get through; **Besuch** ~: have a visitor/visitors; **sie bekommt ein Kind** she's expecting a baby; **Hunger/Durst** ~: get hungry/thirsty; **einen roten Kopf/eine Glatze** ~: go red/bald; **eine Erkältung** ~: catch a cold; **Krebs** ~: get cancer; **Mut/Angst** ~: take heart/become frightened; **er bekommt einen Bart** he's growing a beard; **sie bekommt eine Brust** her breasts are developing; **Zähne** ~ ‹*baby*› teethe; **wo bekomme ich etwas zu essen/trinken?** where can I get something to eat/drink?; **etw./jmdn. zu fassen** ~: get hold of sth./lay one's hands on sb.; **etw. zu sehen** ~: set eyes on sth.; *s. auch* **hören; spüren;** (**b**) **etw. durch die Tür/ins Auto** ~: get sth. through the door/into the car; **jmdn. nicht aus dem Bett** ~: be unable to get sb. out of bed *or* up; **jmdn. dazu** ~, **die Wahrheit zu sagen** get sb. to tell the truth; **etw. sauber** ~: get sth. clean; **jmdn. satt** ~: feed sb.; (**c**) **es nicht über sich** (*Akk.*) ~, **etw. zu tun** be unable to bring oneself to do sth. 2 *unr. V.; der Funktion eines Hilfsverbs zur Umschreibung des Passivs* get; **etw. geschenkt** ~: get [given] sth. *or* be given sth. as a present; **etw. gestohlen** ~: have sth. stolen; **etw. geliehen** ~: be lent sth.; **einen Zahn gezogen** ~: have a tooth out. 3 *unr. itr. V.; mit sein* **jmdm. [gut]** ~: do sb. good; be good for sb.; ‹*food, medicine*› agree with sb.; **jmdm. schlecht** *od.* **nicht** ~: not be good for sb.; not do sb. any good; ‹*food, medicine*› not agree with sb.; **wohl bekomms!** your [very good] health!

bekömmlich /bə'kœmlɪç/ *Adj.* easily digestible; **leicht/schwer** ~ be easily digestible/difficult to digest

Bekömmlichkeit *die;* ~: easy digestibility

beköstigen /bə'kœstɪgn/ *tr. V.* cater for; **er wird von seiner Tante beköstigt** he gets his meals provided by his aunt

Beköstigung *die;* ~: catering *no indef. art.*

bekräftigen *tr. V.* reinforce ‹*statement*›; reaffirm ‹*promise*›

Bekräftigung *die:* **zur** ~ **seiner Worte** to reinforce his words; **zur** ~ **seines Versprechens** to reaffirm his promise

bekreuzigen *refl. V.* cross oneself

bekriegen *tr. V.* wage war on; (fig.) fight; **sich** ~: be at war; (fig.) fight [each other *or* one another]

bekritteln *tr. V.* (abwertend) find fault with (in a petty way)

bekritzeln *tr. V.* scribble on; **die Wände waren von oben bis unten bekritzelt** the walls were covered with graffiti

bekümmern *tr. V.* **jmdn.** ~: cause sb. worry

bekümmert /bə'kʏmɐt/ *Adj.* worried; troubled; (stärker) distressed

bekunden /bə'kʊndn̩/ *tr. V.* (geh.) express

Bekunden *das:* **nach eigenem** ~: according to his/her *etc.* own statement[s]

Bekundung *die;* ~, ~**en** expression; (Aussage) statement

belächeln *tr. V.* smile [pityingly/tolerantly *etc.*] at; **belächelt werden** meet with a pitying smile

beladen[1] *unr. tr. V.* load [up] ‹*car, wagon*›; load up ‹*horse, donkey, etc.*›; **Be- und Entladen gestattet/verboten** loading and unloading permitted/no loading or unloading

beladen[2] *Adj.* loaded, laden (**mit** with); **mit etw.** ~ **sein** be laden with sth.; **sie war schwer mit Paketen** ~: she was loaded *or* laden down with parcels; **mit Sorgen/Schuld** ~ **sein** (fig.) ‹*person*› be burdened with cares/guilt

Belag /bə'la:k/ *der;* ∼[e]s, **Beläge** /bə'lɛ:gə/ (a) coating; film; (Zahn∼) film; (b) (Fußboden∼) covering; (Straßen∼) surface; (Brems∼) lining; (c) (von Kuchen, Pizza, Scheibe Brot usw.) topping; (von Sandwich) filling

Belagerer /bə'la:gərə/ *der;* ∼s, ∼: besieger

belagern *tr. V.* (Milit.) besiege; lay siege to; (fig.) besiege

Belagerung *die;* ∼, ∼en (Milit.) siege; (fig.) besieging

belämmert *Adj.* (ugs.) miserable; **er stand [wie]** ∼ **da** he stood there miserably

Belang /bə'laŋ/ *der;* ∼[e]s, ∼e (a) *o. Pl.* (Bedeutung) [**für etw.**] **von/ohne** ∼ **sein** be of importance/of no importance [for sth.]; **für jmdn. von/ohne** ∼ **sein** be important/not be important to sb.; (b) *Pl.* (Interessen) interests; **jmds.** ∼e **wahrnehmen/vertreten** look after/represent sb.'s interests

belangen *tr. V.* (Rechtsw.) sue; (strafrechtlich) prosecute; **jmdn. wegen etw.** ∼: sue/prosecute sb. for sth.

belang·los *Adj.* of no importance (**für** for); (trivial) trivial

Belang·losigkeit *die;* ∼, ∼en unimportance; (Trivialität) triviality

belassen *unr. tr. V.* leave; ∼ **wir es dabei** let's leave it at that

belastbar *Adj.* (a) tough, resilient 〈*material*〉; 〈*material*〉 able to withstand stress *pred.;* [**nur**] **mit 3,5 t** ∼ **sein** be able to take a load of [only] 3.5 t; (b) (beanspruchbar) tough, resilient 〈*person*〉; **seelisch/körperlich** ∼ **sein** be emotionally/physically tough *or* resilient; be able to stand emotional/physical stress

Belastbarkeit *die;* ∼, ∼n (a) (von Material) ability to withstand stress; (von Konstruktionen) load-bearing capacity; (b) (von Menschen) toughness; resilience

belasten *tr. V.* (a) **etw.** ∼: put sth. under strain; (durch Gewicht) put weight on sth.; (b) (beeinträchtigen) pollute 〈*atmosphere*〉; put pressure on 〈*environment*〉; (c) (in Anspruch nehmen) burden (**mit** with); (d) (zu schaffen machen) **jmdn.** ∼ 〈*responsibility, guilt*〉 weigh upon sb.; 〈*thought*〉 weigh upon sb.'s mind; **Fett belastet den Magen** fat puts a strain on the stomach; (e) (Rechtsw.: schuldig erscheinen lassen) incriminate; ∼**des Material** incriminating evidence; (f) (Geldw.) **jmds. Konto mit 100 DM** ∼: debit sb.'s account with 100 DM; **den Staatshaushalt** ∼: place a burden on the national budget; **das Haus ist mit einer Hypothek belastet** the house is encumbered with a mortgage

belästigen /bə'lɛstɪgn̩/ *tr. V.* bother; (sehr aufdringlich) pester; (sexuell) molest; **sich von etw. belästigt fühlen** regard sth. as a nuisance

Belästigung *die;* ∼, ∼en: **die** ∼ **durch die Reporter/Insekten** being pestered by reporters/bothered by insects; **etw. als** ∼ **empfinden** regard sth. as a nuisance

Belastung /bə'lastʊŋ/ *die;* ∼, ∼en (a) strain; (das Belasten) straining; (durch Gewicht) loading; (Last) load; (b) **die** ∼ **der Atmosphäre/Umwelt durch Schadstoffe** the pollution of the atmosphere by harmful substances/the pressure on the environment caused by harmful substances; (c) (Bürde, Sorge) burden; **das stellte eine schwere seelische** ∼ **für sie dar** it was causing her great strain and distress; (d) (Rechtsw.) incrimination

Belastungs-: ∼**material** *das* (Rechtsw.) incriminating evidence; ∼**probe** *die* (bei Menschen) endurance test; (bei Materialien) stress test; (bei Konstruktionen) load test; ∼**zeuge** *der* (Rechtsw.) witness for the prosecution

belauern *tr. V.* **jmdn.** ∼: eye *or* watch sb. carefully; keep a watchful eye on sb.; (aus einem Versteck heraus) watch sb. from hiding

belaufen *unr. refl. V.* **sich auf ...** (*Akk.*) ∼: amount *or* come to ...; 〈*rent, price*〉 come to ..., be ...

belauschen *tr. V.* eavesdrop on

beleben 1 *tr. V.* (a) enliven; liven up (coll.) 〈*drink*〉 revive; **neu** ∼: put new life into; stimulate 〈*economy*〉; (b) (lebendig gestalten) enliven; brighten up; (c) (lebendig machen) give life to. **2** *refl. V.* (a) 〈*eyes*〉 light up; 〈*face*〉 brighten [up]; 〈*market, economic activity*〉 revive, pick up; (b) (lebendig, bevölkert werden) come to life

belebend 1 *Adj.* stimulating; invigorating. **2** *adv.* ∼ **wirken** have a stimulating *or* invigorating effect

belebt *Adj.* (a) (lebhaft, bevölkert) busy 〈*street, crossing, town, etc.*〉; (b) (lebendig) living; **die** ∼**e Natur** the living world

Belebtheit *die;* ∼: bustle; bustling activity

Belebung *die;* ∼: **zur** ∼ **ein Glas Sekt trinken** have a glass of champagne to revive oneself; **die** ∼ **der Konjunktur** the stimulation of the economy

belecken *tr. V.* lick

Beleg /bə'le:k/ *der;* ∼[e]s, ∼e (a) (Beweisstück) piece of [supporting] documentary evidence; (Quittung) receipt; **als** ∼ **für etw.** as evidence for sth.; (b) (Sprachw.: Zitat) quotation; **für dieses Wort gibt es zwei** ∼**e** there are two instances of this word

belegbar *Adj.* verifiable

belegen *tr. V.* (a) (Milit.: beschießen) bombard; (mit Bomben) attack; (b) (mit Belag versehen) cover 〈*floor*〉 (**mit** with); fill 〈*flan base, sandwich*〉; top 〈*open sandwich*〉; **eine Scheibe Brot mit Schinken/Käse** ∼: put some ham/cheese on a slice of bread; (c) (in Besitz nehmen) occupy 〈*seat, room, etc.*〉; (d) (Hochschulw.) enrol for, register for 〈*seminar, lecture-course*〉; (e) (Sport) **den ersten/letzten Platz** ∼: come first *or* take first place/come last; (f) (nachweisen) prove; give a reference for 〈*quotation*〉; **etw. mit** *od.* **durch Quittungen** ∼: support sth. with receipts; (g) (versehen) **jmdn./etw. mit etw.** ∼: impose sth. on sb./sth.

Belegschaft *die;* ∼, ∼en staff; employees *pl.*

belegt *Adj.* (a) **ein** ∼**es Brot** an open *or* (Amer.) openface sandwich; (zugeklappt) a sandwich; **ein** ∼**es Brötchen** a roll with topping; an open-face roll (Amer.); (zugeklappt) a filled roll; a sandwich roll (Amer.); (b) (mit Belag bedeckt) coated, furred 〈*tongue, tonsils*〉; (c) (heiser) husky 〈*voice*〉; (d) (nicht mehr frei) occupied; 〈*[telephone] line, number*〉 engaged, (Amer.) busy; **voll** ∼ 〈*hotel, hospital*〉 full

belehren *tr. V.* (a) teach; instruct; (aufklären) enlighten; (informieren) inform; advise; **jmdn. über etw.** (*Akk.*) ∼: inform sb. about sth.; (b) (von einer irrigen Meinung abbringen) **sich** ∼ **lassen müssen** learn otherwise; **ich lasse mich gern** ∼: I'm quite willing to believe otherwise; *s. auch* **besser**

belehrend *Adj.* didactic

Belehrung *die;* ∼, ∼en (a) (das Belehrtwerden) instruction; (b) (Zurechtweisung) lecture

beleibt /bə'laipt/ *Adj.* (geh.) stout; portly; corpulent

Beleibtheit *die;* ∼ (geh.) stoutness; portliness; corpulence

beleidigen /bə'laidign̩/ *tr. V.* insult; offend; (fig.) offend 〈*sb.'s honour, ear, eye*〉; ∼**d** offensive

beleidigt *Adj.* insulted; offended; (gekränkt) offended; **er ist schnell** ∼: he easily takes offence

Beleidigung *die;* ∼, ∼en insult; (Rechtsw.) (schriftlich) libel; (mündlich) slander; **eine** ∼ **für das Auge/Ohr** (fig.) an offence to the eye/ear

beleihen *unr. tr. V.* grant a loan on the security of; grant a mortgage on 〈*home, property*〉; raise money on 〈*insurance, policy*〉

Beleihung *die;* ∼, ∼en: **die** ∼ **von etw.** raising a loan on sth.

*belemmert ⇒ **belämmert**

belesen *Adj.* well-read

Belesenheit *die;* ∼: [**große**] ∼: [very] wide reading

beleuchten *tr. V.* (a) illuminate; light up; light 〈*stairs, room, street, etc.*〉; **festlich beleuchtet** festively lit; (b) (fig.: untersuchen) examine 〈*topic, problem*〉

Beleuchter *der;* ∼s, ∼ (Theater, Film) lighting technician

Beleuchtung *die;* ∼, ∼en (a) (Licht) light; **die** ∼ **fiel aus** all the lights *pl.* went out; (b) (das Beleuchten) lighting; (Anstrahlung) illumination; (c) (fig.: Untersuchung) examination

beleumdet /bə'lɔymdət/, **beleumundet** /bə'lɔymʊndət/ *Adj.* **übel/gut** ∼ **sein** have a bad/good reputation

---

Belgien /'bɛlgiən/ (das); ~s Belgium
Belgier /'bɛlgiɐ/ der; ~s, ~ ▶388| Belgian
belgisch /'bɛlgiʃ/ Adj. ▶388| Belgian
belichten 1 tr. V. (Fot.) expose; **eine Aufnahme richtig/falsch** ~: give a shot the right/wrong exposure. **2** itr. V. (Fot.) **richtig/falsch/kurz** ~: use the right/wrong exposure/a short exposure time
Belichtung die; ~, ~en (Fot.) exposure
Belichtungs-: ~**messer** der (Fot.) exposure meter; ~**zeit** die (Fot.) exposure time
belieben itr. V. (geh.) **ihr könnt tun, was euch** (Dat.) **beliebt** you can do what you like; (unpers.) **[ganz] wie es dir beliebt** [just] as you like
Belieben das; ~s: **es steht in deinem** ~/es **bleibt Ihrem** ~ **überlassen** it is up to you; **nach** ~: just as you/they etc. like
beliebig 1 Adj. any; **du kannst ein** ~es **Beispiel wählen** you can choose any example you like; **fünf** ~e **Personen** any five people; **in** ~er **Reihenfolge** in any order. **2** adv. as you like/he likes etc.; ~ **viele** as many as you like/he likes etc.; **wähle eine** ~ **große Zahl** choose any number[, as high as] you like
beliebt Adj. popular; favourite attrib.; **sich [bei jmdm.]** ~ **machen** make oneself popular [with sb.]
Beliebtheit die; ~: popularity
beliefern tr. V. supply; **jmdn. mit etw.** ~: supply sb. with sth.
Belieferung die supply; **jmds.** ~ **mit etw.** supplying sb. with sth.
bellen /'bɛlən/ **1** itr. V. (a) ⟨dog, fox⟩ bark; ⟨hound⟩ bay; (fig.) ⟨cannon⟩ boom; (b) (laut husten) have a hacking cough. **2** tr. V. (abwertend) bark out ⟨orders⟩
Belletristik /bɛle'trɪstɪk/ die; ~: belles-lettres pl.
belletristisch Adj. belletristic ⟨literature⟩; **ein** ~er **Verlag** a publishing house specializing in belletristic literature
belobigen /bə'lo:bɪgn̩/ tr. V. commend
Belobigung die; ~, ~en commendation
belohnen tr. V. reward
Belohnung die; ~, ~en (a) (Lohn) reward; **eine** ~ **für etw. aussetzen** offer a reward for sth.; (b) o. Pl. (das Belohnen) rewarding
belüften tr. V. ventilate
Belüftung die; ~: ventilation
belügen unr. tr. V. **jmdn.** ~: lie to sb; tell lies to sb.; **sich selbst** ~: deceive oneself
belustigen tr. V. amuse
belustigt 1 Adj. amused. **2** adv. in amusement
Belustigung die; ~: amusement; **der allgemeinen** ~ **dienen** serve to amuse everybody
bemächtigen /bə'mɛçtɪgn̩/ refl. V. (geh.) **sich jmds./einer Sache** ~: seize sb./sth.; **Angst bemächtigte sich seiner** he was seized by fear
bemäkeln tr. V. (ugs.) find fault with
bemalen 1 tr. V. paint; (verzieren) decorate ⟨porcelain etc.⟩; **sich** (Dat.) **das Gesicht** ~ (ugs.) paint one's face. **2** refl. V. (ugs.) paint one's face; put on one's warpaint (coll.)
Bemalung die; ~, ~en (a) o. Pl. painting; (Verzierung) decorating; (b) (Farbschicht) painting
bemängeln /bə'mɛŋl̩n/ tr. V. find fault with; **die Reifen** ~: find the tyres to be faulty; **etw. an jmdm./etw.** ~: criticize sth. about sb./sth.
bemannen tr. V. man
bemänteln /bə'mɛntl̩n/ tr. V. cover up
bemerkbar Adj. noticeable; perceptible; **sich** ~ **machen** (auf sich aufmerksam machen) attract attention [to oneself]; (spürbar werden) become apparent; ⟨tiredness⟩ make itself felt
bemerken tr. V. (a) (wahrnehmen) notice; **ich wurde nicht bemerkt** I was unobserved; **sie bemerkte zu spät, dass …:** she realized too late that …; (b) (äußern) remark; **nebenbei bemerkt** by the way; incidentally
bemerkenswert 1 Adj. remarkable; notable. **2** adv. remarkably

Bemerkung die; ~, ~en (a) remark; comment; (b) (schriftliche Anmerkung) note
bemessen 1 unr. tr. V. etw. nach etw. ~: measure sth. according to sth.; **die Zeit ist kurz/sehr knapp** ~: time is short or limited/very limited **2** unr. refl. V. (Amtsspr.) **sich** ~ **nach** be measured on the basis of
Bemessung die calculation; **die** ~ **der Strafe richtet sich nach der Schwere des Deliktes** the penalty is fixed in accordance with the seriousness of the offence
Bemessungs·grundlage die (Amtsspr.) basis for assessment
bemitleiden tr. V. pity; feel sorry for; **er ist zu** ~: he is to be pitied; **sich selbst** ~: feel sorry for oneself
bemitleidens·wert Adj. pitiable
bemogeln tr. V. (ugs.) cheat; diddle (coll.); con (sl.)
bemühen 1 refl. V. (a) (sich anstrengen) try; make an effort; **sich sehr** ~: try hard; **bemüht sein, etw. zu tun** endeavour to do sth.; **bitte,** ~ **Sie sich nicht [weiter]!** please do not trouble yourself [any further]; (b) (sich kümmern) **sich um jmdn./etw.** ~: seek to help sb./endeavour or strive to achieve sth.; **um das Wohl der Hotelgäste bemüht sein** make every effort to ensure the comfort and enjoyment of the hotel patrons; (c) (zu erlangen suchen) **sich um etw.** ~: try or endeavour to obtain sth.; **sich um eine Stelle/Wohnung** ~: try to get a job/a flat (Brit.) or (Amer.) apartment; **sich um einen Regisseur/Trainer** ~: try or endeavour to obtain the services of a director/manager; (d) (geh.: sich begeben) proceed (formal). **2** tr. V. (geh.) trouble; call in, call upon the services of ⟨lawyer, architect, etc.⟩; (zum Beweis heranziehen) bring in a quotation/quotations from ⟨author, philosopher, etc.⟩
Bemühen das; ~s (geh.) effort; endeavour; **trotz jahrelangen** ~s despite years of effort
Bemühung die; ~, ~en effort; endeavour; **alle** ~en **waren vergeblich** all efforts were in vain; **trotz aller** ~en in spite of or despite all our/his etc. efforts; **vielen Dank für Ihre** ~en thank you very much for your efforts or trouble
bemüßigt /bə'my:sɪçt/ (geh. iron.) in sich ~ **fühlen, etw. zu tun** feel obliged to do sth.; feel it incumbent on oneself to do sth.
bemuttern tr. V. mother
benachbart Adj. neighbouring attrib.; ~e **Fachgebiete** related fields of study
benachrichtigen /bə'na:xrɪçtɪgn̩/ tr. V. inform, notify (von of, about)
Benachrichtigung die; ~, ~en notification; **ich bitte um sofortige** ~: I wish to be informed or notified immediately
benachteiligen tr. V. put at a disadvantage; (diskriminieren) discriminate against; **sich benachteiligt fühlen** feel at a disadvantage/feel discriminated against; **sozial benachteiligt** underprivileged
Benachteiligte der/die; adj. Dekl. disadvantaged person; **die sozial** ~n the underprivileged; the socially deprived
Benachteiligung die; ~, ~en (Vorgang) discrimination (Gen. against); (Zustand) disadvantage (Gen. to); **der Firma wurde eine** ~ **der Frauen vorgeworfen** the firm was accused of discriminating against women
benagen tr. V. gnaw [at]
benebeln tr. V. befuddle
Benefiz- /bene'fi:t̮s/: ~**konzert** das charity concert; ~**spiel** das charity match; ~**vorstellung** die charity performance
benehmen unr. refl. V. behave; (in Bezug auf Umgangsformen) behave [oneself]; **sich schlecht** ~: behave badly; misbehave
Benehmen das; ~s (a) behaviour; **kein** ~ **haben** have no manners pl.; (b) (Amtsspr.) in sich mit jmdm. ins ~ **setzen** make contact with sb.
beneiden tr. V. envy; be envious of; **jmdn. um etw.** ~: envy sb. sth.; **du bist [nicht] zu** ~: I [don't] envy you

beneidens·wert 1 *Adj.* enviable. 2 *adv.* enviably

Benelux·länder /'be:neluks-/ *Pl.* Benelux countries

benennen *unr. tr. V.* (a) name; **etw./jmdm. nach jmdm. ~:** name sth./name *or* call sb. after *or* (Amer.) for sb.; (b) (namhaft machen) call ‹*witness*›; **jmdn. als Kandidaten ~:** nominate sb. as a candidate

Benennung *die* (a) *o. Pl.* naming; (b) *o. Pl.* **durch ~ zweier weiterer Zeugen** by calling two more witnesses; (c) (Name) name

benetzen *tr. V.* (geh.) moisten; ‹*dew*› cover

Bengale /bɛŋ'ga:lə/ *der;* **~n, ~n** Bengali; Bengalese

Bengalen (*das*); **~s** Bengal

bengalisch *Adj.* ▶ 487 Bengalese; Bengali, Bengalese ‹*people, language*›; **~e Beleuchtung** Bengal light *or* fire

Bengel /'bɛŋl/ *der;* **~s, ~** (a) (abwertend: junger Bursche) young rascal; (b) (fam.: kleiner Junge) little lad *or* boy

Benimm /bə'nɪm/ *der;* **~s** (ugs.) manners *pl.;* **jmdm. ~ beibringen** teach sb. some manners

benommen /be'nɔmən/ *Adj.* bemused; dazed; (durch Fieber, Alkohol) muzzy (von from)

Benommenheit *die;* **~:** bemused *or* dazed state; (durch Fieber, Alkohol) muzziness

benoten *tr. V.* mark (Brit.); grade (Amer.); **einen Test mit „gut“ ~:** mark a test 'good' (Brit.); assign a grade of 'good' to a test (Amer.)

benötigen *tr. V.* need; require; **das benötigte Geld** the necessary money

Benotung *die;* **~, ~en** (a) *o. Pl.* marking (Brit.); grading (Amer.); (b) (Note) mark (Brit.); grade (Amer.)

benutzbar *Adj.* usable

benutzen *tr. V.* use; take, use ‹*car, lift*›; take ‹*train, taxi*›; use, consult ‹*reference book*›

Benutzer *der;* **~s, ~** user

Benutzung *die;* **~:** use; **jmdm. etw. zur ~ überlassen** give sb. the use of sth.

Benutzungs·gebühr *die* charge; (Maut) toll

Benzin /bɛn'tsi:n/ *das;* **~s** petrol (Brit.); gasoline (Amer.); gas (Amer. coll.); (Wasch~) benzine

Benziner *der;* **~s, ~** (ugs.) car that runs on petrol (Brit.) *or* (Amer.) gasoline

Benzin-: **~feuerzeug** *das* petrol (Brit.) *or* (Amer.) gasoline lighter; **~gut·schein** *der* petrol (Brit.) *or* (Amer.) gasoline coupon; **~kanister** *der* petrol (Brit.) *or* (Amer.) gasoline can; **~motor** *der* petrol (Brit.) *or* (Amer.) gasoline engine; **~preis** *der* price of petrol (Brit.) *or* (Amer.) gasoline; **~pumpe** *die* petrol (Brit.) *or* (Amer.) gasoline pump; **~verbrauch** *der* fuel consumption

Benzol /bɛn'tso:l/ *das;* **~s, ~e** (Chemie) benzene

beobachten /bə'|o:baxtn̩/ *tr. V.* (a) observe; watch; (als Zeuge) see; **er hat beobachtet, wie sie das Radio stahl** he watched her steal the radio; **jmdn. ~ lassen** put sb. under surveillance; have sb. watched; (b) (bemerken) notice; observe; **etw. an jmdm. ~:** notice sth. about sb.

Beobachter *der;* **~s, ~:** observer

Beobachtung *die;* **~, ~en** observation; **zur ~:** for observation; **unter ~ stehen** be kept under surveillance

Beobachtungs-: **~gabe** *die; o. Pl.* powers *pl.* of observation; **~posten** *der* observation post

beordern *tr. V.* order; **jmdn. nach Hause/ins Ausland ~:** order *or* summon sb. home/order sb. [to go] abroad

bepacken *tr. V.* load; **etw./jmdn./sich mit etw. ~:** load sth. up with/sb. with/oneself with sth.

bepflanzen *tr. V.* plant

Bepflanzung *die* planting

bepinseln *tr. V.* (a) (ugs.: einpinseln) paint ‹*gums*›; brush ‹*dough, cake-mixture*›; (b) (ugs. abwertend: anstreichen) paint; **etw. mit Farbe ~:** paint sth.

bepudern *tr. V.* powder

bequatschen *tr. V.* (salopp) (a) (bereden) have a jaw about (coll.); (b) (überreden) persuade; **jmdn. ~, dass er mitkommt** talk sb. into coming along

bequem /bə'kve:m/ 1 *Adj.* (a) comfortable; **es sich** (*Dat.*) **~ machen** make oneself comfortable; **machen**

Sie es sich ~: make yourself at home; (b) (mühelos) easy; **ein ~es Leben führen** have an easy *or* comfortable life; (c) (abwertend: träge) lazy; idle. 2 *adv.* (a) comfortably; **liegen/sitzen Sie ~ so?** are you comfortable like that?; (b) (mühelos) easily; comfortably

bequemen *refl. V.* (geh.) deign; **sich zu einer Antwort ~:** deign to answer; **sich dazu ~, etw. zu tun** deign to do sth.

Bequemlichkeit *die;* **~, ~en** (a) comfort; (b) *o. Pl.* (Trägheit) laziness; idleness; **aus [reiner] ~:** out of [sheer] laziness *or* idleness

berappen /bə'rapn̩/ *tr., itr. V.* ⇨ **blechen**

beraten 1 *unr. tr. V.* (a) advise; **jmdn. gut/schlecht ~:** give sb. good/bad advice; **sich ~ lassen** take *or* get advice (von from); (b) (besprechen) discuss ‹*plan, matter*›. 2 *unr. itr. V.* **über etw.** (*Akk.*) **~:** discuss sth.; **sie berieten lange** they were a long time in discussion. 3 *unr. refl. V.* **sich mit jmdm. ~, ob …:** discuss with sb. whether …; **sich mit seinem Anwalt ~:** consult one's lawyer

beratend *Adj.* advisory, consultative ‹*function, role, etc.*›

Berater *der;* **~s, ~, Beraterin** *die;* **~, ~nen** adviser

beratschlagen /bə'ra:tʃla:gn̩/ 1 *tr. V.* discuss. 2 *itr. V.* **über etw.** (*Akk.*) **~:** discuss sth.

Beratung *die;* **~, ~en** (a) advice *no indef. art.;* (durch Arzt, Rechtsanwalt) consultation; **ohne juristische ~:** without [taking] legal advice; (b) (Besprechung) discussion; **Gegenstand der ~ war …:** the subject under discussion was …; **sich zur ~ zurückziehen** withdraw for discussions *pl.*

Beratungs·stelle *die* advice centre (Brit.); counseling center (Amer.)

berauben *tr. V.* (auch fig.) rob; **jmdn. einer Sache** (*Gen.*) **~** (geh.) rob sb. of sth.; **jmdn. seiner Freiheit/Hoffnungen ~** (fig.) deprive sb. of his/her freedom/hopes

Beraubung *die;* **~:** robbing *no indef. art.*

berauschen (geh.) 1 *tr. V.* (auch fig.) intoxicate; ‹*alcohol*› intoxicate, inebriate; ‹*drug*› make euphoric; ‹*speed*› exhilarate; **der Erfolg/die Macht berauschte ihn** he was intoxicated *or* drunk with success/drunk with power. 2 *refl. V.* become intoxicated; **sich an etw.** (*Dat.*) **~:** become intoxicated with sth.

berauschend 1 *Adj.* intoxicating, heady, intoxicating ‹*perfume, scent*›; **das ist nicht ~** (ugs.) it's nothing very special *or* (coll.) nothing to write home about. 2 *adv.* **~ schön** enchantingly beautiful; **~ wirken** have an intoxicating effect

Berber /'bɛrbɐ/ *der;* **~s, ~** (a) Berber; (b) (Teppich) Berber carpet/rug

Berber·teppich *der* Berber carpet/rug

berechenbar /bə'rɛçn̩ba:ɐ̯/ *Adj.* calculable; predictable ‹*behaviour*›

berechnen *tr. V.* (a) calculate; predict ‹*consequences, behaviour*›; (b) (anrechnen) charge; **jmdm. 10 Mark für etw. od. jmdm. etw. mit 10 Mark ~:** charge sb. 10 marks for sth.; **jmdm. etw. nicht ~:** not charge sb. for sth.; **jmdm. zu viel ~:** overcharge sb.; charge sb. too much; (c) (kalkulieren) calculate; (vorsehen) intend; **für sechs Personen berechnet sein** ‹*recipe, buffet*› be for six people

berechnend *Adj.* calculating

Berechnung *die* (a) calculation; **nach meiner ~, meiner ~ nach** according to my calculations *pl.*; (b) *o. Pl.* (abwertend: Eigennutz) [calculating] self-interest; **etw. aus ~ tun** do sth. from motives of self-interest; (c) *o. Pl.* (Überlegung) deliberation; calculation; **mit kühler ~ vorgehen** act with cool deliberation

berechtigen /bə'rɛçtɪgn̩/ 1 *tr. V.* entitle; **jmdn. ~, etw. zu tun** entitle sb. *or* give sb. the right to do sth.; **das berechtigt ihn zu dieser Kritik** it entitles him *or* gives him the right to criticize [in this way]. 2 *itr. V.* **die Karte berechtigt zum Eintritt** the ticket entitles the bearer to admission; **das berechtigt zu der Annahme, dass …:** it justifies the assumption that …

berechtigt *Adj.* (a) (gerechtfertigt) justified, legitimate; (b) (befugt) authorized

Berechtigung *die;* ~, ~**en** (a) (Befugnis) entitlement; (Recht) right; **mit welcher ~ kritisiert er mich?** what right has he to criticize me?; (b) (Rechtmäßigkeit) legitimacy; **seine/ihre ~ haben** be justified *or* legitimate

bereden 1 *tr. V.* (a) (besprechen) talk over; discuss; (b) (überreden) **jmdn.** ~, **etw. zu tun** talk sb. into doing sth.; **sich ~ lassen, etw. zu tun** let oneself be talked into doing sth. 2 *refl. V.* **sich [mit jmdm.] über etw.** (*Akk.*) ~: talk sth. over *or* discuss sth. [with sb.]

beredsam /bə're:tza:m/ 1 *Adj.* eloquent. 2 *adv.* eloquently

Beredsamkeit *die;* ~: eloquence

beredt /bə're:t/ *Adj.* (auch fig.) eloquent

Bereich *der;* ~**[e]s,** ~**e** (a) area; **im ~ der Stadt** within the town; (b) (fig.) sphere; area; (Fachgebiet) field; area; **in jmds.** ~ (*Akk.*) **fallen** be [within] sb.'s province; **im ~ des Möglichen liegen** be within the bounds *pl.* of possibility; **aus dem ~ der Kunst/Politik** from the sphere of art/politics; **im privaten/staatlichen ~:** in the private/public sector

bereichern /bə'raiçɐn/ 1 *refl. V.* make a profit; **sich an jmdm./etw.** ~: make a great deal of money at sb.'s expense/out of sth. 2 *tr. V.* enrich

Bereicherung *die;* ~, ~**en** enrichment; **eine wertvolle ~ der koreanischen Literatur** a valuable addition to Korean literature

bereifen *tr. V.* put tyres on ⟨*car*⟩; put a tyre on ⟨*wheel*⟩; **neu bereift sein** ⟨*car*⟩ have new tyres

Bereifung *die;* ~, ~**en** [set *sing.* of] tyres *pl.*

bereinigen *tr. V.* clear up ⟨*misunderstanding*⟩; settle, resolve ⟨*dispute*⟩; **mit jmdm. etw. zu ~ haben** have sth. to sort out with sb.

Bereinigung *die* ⇒ **bereinigen:** clearing up; settlement; resolution

bereisen *tr. V.* travel around *or* about; (beruflich) ⟨*representative etc.*⟩ cover ⟨*area*⟩; **fremde Länder ~:** travel in foreign countries; **ganz Afrika ~:** travel throughout Africa

bereit /bə'rait/ *Adj.* (a) (fertig, gerüstet) ~ **sein** be ready; **sich ~ halten** be ready; **etw. ~ haben** have sth. ready; (b) (gewillt) ~ **sein, etw. zu tun** be willing *or* ready *or* prepared to do sth.; **sich ~ zeigen/finden, etw. zu tun** show oneself/be willing *or* ready *or* prepared to do sth.; **sich ~ erklären, etw. zu tun** declare oneself willing *or* ready to do sth.; **zu einem Kompromiss ~ sein** be ready to compromise

bereiten *tr. V.* (a) prepare (*Dat.* for); make ⟨*tea, coffee*⟩ (*Dat.* for); (b) (fig.) **[jmdm.] Schwierigkeiten/Ärger/Kummer ~:** cause [sb.] difficulty/trouble/sorrow; **jmdm. Freude/einen begeisterten Empfang ~:** give sb. great pleasure/an enthusiastic reception; **einer Sache** (*Dat.*) **ein Ende ~:** put an end to sth.

bereit-: ~|**halten** *unr. tr. V.* have ready; (für Notfälle) keep ready; ~|**legen** *tr. V.* lay out ready (*Dat.* for); ~|**liegen** *unr. itr. V.* be ready; ⟨*surgical instruments, tools, papers*⟩ be laid out ready; ~|**machen** *tr. V.* get ready

bereits *Adv.* ⇒ **schon 1 a, d**

Bereitschaft *die;* ~ (a) willingness; readiness; preparedness; **etw. in ~ haben** have sth. ready; (b) (ugs.) ⇒ **Bereitschaftsdienst**

Bereitschafts-: ~**arzt** *der* doctor on call; ~**dienst** *der:* ~**dienst haben** ⟨*doctor, nurse*⟩ be on call; ⟨*policeman, fireman*⟩ be on standby duty; ⟨*chemist's*⟩ be on rota duty (for dispensing outside normal hours)

bereit-: ~|**stehen** *unr. itr. V.* be ready; ⟨*car, train, aircraft*⟩ be waiting; ⟨*troops*⟩ be standing by; **für uns steht ein Auto ~:** a car is/will be waiting for us; ~|**stellen** *tr. V.* place ready; get ready ⟨*food, drinks*⟩; provide, make available ⟨*money, funds*⟩

bereit·willig 1 *Adj.* willing. 2 *adv.* readily

Bereitwilligkeit *die;* ~: willingness

bereuen 1 *tr. V.* regret; **seine Sünden ~:** repent [of] one's sins. 2 *itr. V.* be sorry; (Rel.) repent

Berg /bɛrk/ *der;* ~**[e]s,** ~**e** (a) ▶ 277| hill; (im Hochgebirge) mountain; **in die ~e fahren** go up into the mountains; **über ~ und Tal** up hill and down dale; ~ **Heil!** *greeting*

---

between mountaineers; **mit etw. hinter dem** *od.* **hinterm ~ halten** (fig.) keep sth. to oneself; **über den ~ sein** (ugs.) be out of the wood (Brit.) *or* (Amer.) woods; ⟨*patient*⟩ be on the mend, have turned the corner; **[längst] über alle ~e sein** (ugs.) be miles away; (b) (Haufen) enormous *or* huge pile; (von Akten, Abfall auch) mountain

berg·ab *Adv.* downhill; **einen steilen Weg ~ fahren** go down a steep path; **mit dem Patienten/der Firma geht es ~** (fig. ugs) the patient's getting worse/the firm's going downhill

berg·an *Adv.* ⇒ **bergauf**

Berg·arbeiter *der* ▶ 85| miner; mineworker

berg·auf *Adv.* uphill; **es geht ~ mit der Firma** (fig. ugs.) things are looking up for the firm; **mit dem Patienten geht es ~:** the patient's on the mend

Berg-: ~**bahn** *die* mountain railway; (Seilbahn) mountain cableway; ~**bau** *der; o. Pl.* mining; ~**bauer** *der* mountain farmer

bergen *unr. tr. V.* (a) (retten) rescue, save ⟨*person*⟩; salvage ⟨*ship, wrecked car*⟩; salvage, recover ⟨*cargo, belongings*⟩; **jmdn. tot/lebend ~:** recover sb.'s body/rescue sb. alive; (b) (geh.: enthalten) hold; **Gefahren [in sich** (*Dat.*)**] ~** (fig.) hold dangers

Berg-: ~**fried** /-fri:t/ *der;* ~[e]s, ~e keep; ~**führer** *der* ▶ 85| mountain guide; ~**gipfel der** mountain peak *or* top; summit; ~**hütte** *die* mountain hut

bergig *Adj.* hilly; (mit hohen Bergen) mountainous

berg-, Berg-: ~**kessel** *der* corrie; cirque; ~**kette** *die* range *or* chain of mountains; mountain range *or* chain; ~**kristall** *der* rock crystal; ~**kuppe** *die* [rounded] peak *or* mountain-top; ~**land** *das* hilly country *no indef. art;* (mit hohen Bergen) mountainous country *no indef. art.;* **das spanische ~land** the hill country of Spain; **das Schottische ~land** the Highlands *or* Scotland; ~**mann** *der; Pl.* **Bergleute** ▶ 85| miner; mineworker; ~**männisch** /-mɛnɪʃ/ *Adj.* miner's *attrib.;* ~**not** *die:* **in ~not sein/geraten** ⟨*climber*⟩ be/get into difficulties while climbing [in the mountains]; **jmdn. aus ~not retten** rescue sb. who has got into difficulties while climbing [in the mountains]; ~**predigt** *die; o. Pl.* Sermon on the Mount; ~**rücken** *der* mountain ridge; ~**rutsch** *der* landslide; landslip; ~**sattel** *der* saddle; col; ~**see** *der* mountain lake; ~**spitze** *die* [mountain] peak; mountain top; ~**station** *die* top station; ~**steigen** *unr. itr. V.; mit haben od. sein; nur im Inf. und Part.* go mountaineering *or* mountain climbing; ~**steigen** *das;* ~s mountaineering *no art.;* mountain climbing *no art.;* ~**steiger** *der,* ~**steigerin** *die* ~, ~**nen** ▶ 85| mountaineer; mountain climber; ~**tour** *die* mountain tour; (kürzere Wanderung) hike in the mountains; (Klettertour) mountain climb; ~**-und-Tal-Bahn** *die* roller coaster

Bergung *die;* ~, ~**en** (a) (von Verunglückten) rescue; saving; (b) (von Schiffen, Gut) salvaging; salvage

Bergungs·arbeiten *Pl.* rescue work *sing.*

Berg-: ~**volk** *das* mountain people; ~**wacht** *die; o. Pl.* mountain rescue service; ~**wand** *die* mountain face; ~**wanderung** *die* hike in the mountains; ~**werk** *das* mine; **im ~ arbeiten** work down the mine; ~**wiese** *die* mountain pasture

Bericht /bə'rɪçt/ *der;* ~[e]s, ~e report; **über etw.** (*Akk.*) **geben** give a report on sth.

berichten *tr., itr. V.* report (**von, über** + *Akk.* on); **jmdm. etw.** ~: report sth. to sb.; **es wird soeben berichtet, dass ...:** reports are coming in that ...

Bericht-: ~**erstatter** /-ɛɐʃtatɐ/ *der;* ~s, ~: ▶ 85| reporter; ~**erstattung** *die* reporting *no indef. art.;* **die ~erstattung durch Presse und Rundfunk über diese Ereignisse** press and radio coverage of these events

berichtigen *tr. V.* correct

Berichtigung *die;* ~, ~**en** correction

Berichts·heft *das* (Schulw.) (apprentice's/trainee's) record book

beriechen *unr. tr. V.* (a) smell; sniff [at]; (b) (fig. ugs.) **sich [gegenseitig] ~:** size each other *or* one another up

berieseln *tr. V.* **(a)** (bewässern) irrigate; **(b)** (ugs. abwertend) **mit Werbung/Musik berieselt werden** be subjected to a constant [unobtrusive] stream of advertisements/to constant background music; **sich die ganze Zeit [mit Musik]** ～ **lassen** constantly have music on in the background

Berieselung *die;* ～ **(a)** (Bewässerung) irrigation; **(b)** (ugs. abwertend) **die ständige** ～ **mit Musik** subjection to constant background music

Bering·straße /'be:rɪŋ-/ *die* (Geogr.) Bering Strait

beritten *Adj.* mounted

Berlin /bɛr'li:n/ *(das);* ～**s ▶ 490」** Berlin

Berliner /bɛr'li:nɐ/ **▶ 490」 1** *Adj.; nicht präd.* Berlin; ～ **Weiße [mit Schuss]** light, very fizzy beer flavoured with a dash of raspberry juice or woodruff. **2** *der;* ～**s,** ～ **(a)** Berliner; **(b)** (～ Pfannkuchen) [jam (Brit.) or (Amer.) jelly] doughnut

Berlinerin *die;* ～**,** ～**nen** Berliner

berlinern *itr. V.* (ugs.) speak [in] Berlin dialect

berlinisch *Adj.* **▶ 490」** Berlin *attrib.*

Bermuda·inseln /bɛr'mu:da-/ *Pl.* Bermuda *sing., no art.;* Bermudas

Bermudas *Pl.* **(a)** Bermudas; Bermuda *sing., no art.;* **(b)** ⇒ **Bermudashorts**

Bermuda·shorts *Pl.* Bermuda shorts

Bern /bɛrn/ *(das);* ～**s ▶ 490」** Bern[e]

Berner ▶ 490」 1 *Adj.; nicht präd.* Bernese; **eine** ～ **Zeitung** a Bern[e] newspaper. **2** *der;* ～**s,** ～**:** Bernese

Bernerin *die;* ～**,** ～**nen** Bernese

Bernhardiner /bɛrnhar'di:nɐ/ *der;* ～**s,** ～**:** St. Bernard [dog]

Bern·stein /'bɛrn-/ *der* **(a)** *o. Pl.* amber; **(b)** (Stück ～) piece of amber

bernstein·farben *Adj.* amber[-coloured]

Berserker /bɛr'zɛrkɐ/ *der;* ～**s,** ～**: wie ein** ～ **arbeiten** work like mad (coll.); **wie ein** ～ **auf jmdn. einschlagen** go berserk and attack sb.

bersten /'bɛrstn̩/ *unr. itr. V.; mit sein* (geh.) ‹ice› break or crack up; ‹glass› shatter [into pieces]; ‹wall› crack up; **zum Bersten voll sein** be full to bursting-point; **vor Neugier/Ungeduld/Zorn** ～ (fig.) be bursting with curiosity/impatience/rage

berüchtigt /bə'rʏçtɪçt/ *Adj.* notorious **(wegen** for); (verrufen) disreputable

berücksichtigen /bə'rʏkzɪçtɪgn̩/ *tr. V.* **(a)** take into account or consideration, take account of ‹fact›; **(b)** consider ‹applicant, application, suggestion›

Berücksichtigung *die;* ～ **(a) bei** ～ **aller Umstände** taking all the circumstances into account; **unter** ～ **(Dat.) der Vor- und Nachteile** taking account of all the advantages and disadvantages; **(b)** (Beachtung) consideration; **eine** ～ **Ihres Antrags ist nicht möglich** we cannot consider your application

Beruf *der;* ～**[e]s,** ～**e ▶ 85」** occupation; (akademischer, wissenschaftlicher, medizinischer) profession; (handwerklicher) trade; (Stellung) job; (Laufbahn) career; **was sind Sie von** ～**?** what do you do for a living?; what is your occupation?; **er ist von** ～ **Bäcker/Lehrer** he's a baker by trade/a teacher by profession; **den** ～ **verfehlt haben** (scherzh.) have missed one's vocation

berufen¹ 1 *unr. tr. V.* **(a)** (einsetzen) appoint; **jmdn. auf einen Lehrstuhl/in ein Amt** ～**:** appoint sb. to a chair/an office; **(b) berufe es nicht!** (ugs.) don't speak too soon! **2** *unr. refl. V.* **sich auf etw.** (Akk.) ～**:** refer to sth.; **sich auf jmdn.** ～**:** quote or mention sb.'s name; (jmdn. zitieren) quote or cite sb.

berufen² ** *Adj.* **(a) competent; **aus** ～**em Munde** from somebody or one competent or qualified to speak; **(b)** (prädestiniert) **sich dazu** ～ **fühlen, etw. zu tun** feel called to do sth.; feel one has a mission to do sth.; **zum Dichter/zu Höherem** ～ **sein** have a vocation as a poet/be destined for greater things

beruflich 1 *Adj.; nicht präd.* occupational, vocational ‹training etc.›; (bei akademischen Berufen) professional ‹training etc.›; **seine** ～**e Tätigkeit** his occupation. **2** *adv.*

～ **erfolgreich sein** be successful in one's career; ～ **viel unterwegs sein** be away a lot on business; **sich** ～ **weiterbilden** undertake further job training; ～ **verhindert sein** be detained by one's work

berufs-, Berufs-: ～**armee** *die* ⇒ ～**heer;** ～**ausbildung** *die* occupational or vocational training; (als Lehrer, Wissenschaftler, Arzt) professional training; ～**aussichten** *Pl.* job prospects (in a particular profession etc.); ～**bedingt** *Adj.* occupational ‹disease›; ‹expenses, difficulties› connected with one's job; ～**berater** *der* **▶ 85」** vocational adviser; ～**beratung** *die* vocational guidance; ～**bezeichnung** *die* job title; ～**bild** *das* outline of a/the profession/trade as a career; ～**boxer** *der* **▶ 85」** professional boxer; ～**erfahrung** *die; o. Pl.* [professional] experience; ～**fachschule** *die* vocational college (providing full-time vocational training); ～**feuerwehr** *die* [professional] fire service; ～**geheimnis** *das* professional secret; ～**gruppe** *die* occupational group; ～**heer** *das* regular or professional army; ～**kleidung** *die* [prescribed] work[ing] clothes *pl.;* ～**krankheit** *die* occupational disease; ～**leben** *das* working life; **im** ～**leben stehen** be working; ～**politiker** *der* **▶ 85」** professional politician; ～**richter** *der* **▶ 85」** full-time salaried judge; ～**risiko** *das* occupational risk; ～**schule** *die* vocational school; ～**schüler** *der* student at a vocational school; ～**soldat** *der* **▶ 85」** regular or professional soldier; ～**stand** *der* profession; ～**tätig** *Adj.* working *attrib.;* ～**tätig sein** work; ～**tätige** *der/die; adj. Dekl.* working person; ～**tätige** *Pl.* working people; ～**verbrecher** *der* professional criminal; ～**verkehr** *der* rush hour traffic; ～**wahl** *die; o. Pl.* choice of career

Berufung *die;* ～**,** ～**en (a)** (für ein Amt) offer of an appointment **(auf, in, an** + *Akk.* to); **(b)** (innerer Auftrag) vocation; **die** ～ **zum Künstler in sich** (Dat.) **verspüren** feel one has a vocation as an artist; **(c)** (das Sichberufen) **unter** ～ (Dat.) **auf jmdn./etw.** referring or with reference to sb./sth.; **(d)** (Rechtsw.: Einspruch) appeal; ～ **einlegen** lodge an appeal; appeal; **in die** ～ **gehen** appeal

beruhen *itr. V.* **auf etw.** (Dat.) ～**:** be based on sth.; **etw. auf sich** (Dat.) ～ **lassen** let sth. rest

beruhigen /bə'ru:ɪgn̩/ **1** *tr. V.* calm [down]; quieten, pacify ‹child, baby›; salve, soothe ‹conscience›; (trösten) soothe; (die Befürchtung nehmen) reassure; **die Nerven/den Magen** ～**:** calm one's nerves/settle the stomach; **beruhigt schlafen/nach Hause gehen können** be able to sleep/go home with one's mind set at ease. **2** *refl. V.* ‹person› calm down; ‹sea› become calm; ‹struggle, traffic› lessen; ‹rush of people› subside; ‹prices, stock exchange, stomach› settle down

Beruhigung *die;* ～ **(a)** ⇒ **beruhigen 1:** calming [down]; quietening; pacifying; salving; soothing; reassurance; **jmdm. etw. zur** ～ **geben** give sb. sth. to calm him/her [down]; **(b)** (das Ruhigwerden) **eine** ～ **des Wetters ist vorauszusehen** the weather can be expected to become more settled; **zu Ihrer** ～ **kann ich sagen, ...:** you'll be reassured to know that ...; **eine** ～ **der politischen Lage ist nicht zu erwarten** we should not expect that the political situation will become more stable

Beruhigungs-: ～**mittel** *das* sedative; tranquillizer; ～**pille** *die* sedative [pill]; tranquillizer; ～**spritze** *die* sedative injection; ～**zelle** *die* cooling-off cell

berühmt /bə'ry:mt/ *Adj.* famous; **wegen** od. **für etw.** ～ **sein** be famous for sth.

berühmt-berüchtigt *Adj.* notorious

Berühmtheit *die;* ～**,** ～**en (a)** *o. Pl.* fame; ～ **erlangen/gewinnen** become famous/win fame; **zu trauriger** ～ **gelangen** become notorious; **(b)** (Mensch) celebrity

berühren *tr. V.* **(a)** touch; (fig.) touch on ‹topic, issue, question›; **sich** od. (geh.) **einander** ～**:** touch; „Bitte Waren nicht ～!" 'please do not touch the merchandise'; **(b)** (beeindrucken) affect; **wir fühlten uns davon unangenehm/peinlich berührt** it made an unpleasant impression on us/made us feel embarrassed; **das berührt mich [überhaupt] nicht** it's a matter of [complete] indifference to me

Berufe

Was machen Sie beruflich?, Was sind Sie von Beruf?	= What's your job?, What do you do for a living?
In welcher Branche sind Sie tätig?	= What's your field [of work]?, What's your line of business?
Ich arbeite bei einer Bank/in einer Buchhandlung/bei einem Verlag	= I work in od. for a bank/in a bookshop/at a publisher's od. for a publisher
Er ist in der Textilindustrie/ Versicherungsbranche tätig	= He is in textiles/ insurance
Ich arbeite bei einem kleinen Unternehmen/ einem großen Konzern	= I am with od. work for a small company od. firm/a large combine od. group
Sie besitzt/leitet einen kleinen Betrieb	= She owns/runs a small business
Mein Mann ist bei der gleichen Firma angestellt	= My husband works for od. is employed by the same firm
Sie arbeitet ganztags od. hat eine Ganztagsstelle	= She works full time od. has a full-time job
Er arbeitet halbtags od. hat eine Halbtagsstelle/ Teilzeitstelle	= He works part time od. has a part-time job
Ich arbeite freiberuflich/ bin selbstständig	= I work freelance/am self-employed

Beachten Sie, dass bei der Angabe des Berufs im Englischen der unbestimmte Artikel **a/an** verwendet wird. Auch wird mit der Berufsbezeichnung keine Aussage über das Geschlecht gemacht; es gibt zwar ein paar Ausnahmen (**authoress, manageress**), diese Formen werden aber meist als sexistisch vermieden:

Er ist [von Beruf] Bäcker	= He's a baker [by trade]
Sie ist Lehrerin [von Beruf]	= She's a teacher [by profession]
Michael will System-analytiker werden	= Michael wants to be a systems analyst
Bettina ist als Journalistin tätig	= Bettina works as a journalist

Wenn man ausdrücklich von einer Frau in einem bestimmten Beruf spricht, stellt man der Berufs-bezeichnung das Wort **woman** oder **female** voran:

Sie möchte lieber von einer Ärztin behandelt werden	= She prefers to be treated by a woman doctor
Es gibt mehr und mehr Anwältinnen	= There are more and more women od. female lawyers

Aber:

Sie ist Ärztin/Anwältin	= She's a doctor/lawyer

Stellensuche

Ich suche eine Stelle als Sekretärin	= I am looking for a job as a secretary
Bei den Stellenanzeigen habe ich nichts Geeignetes gefunden	= I didn't find anything suitable in the situations vacant
Ich will mich um diese Stelle bewerben	= I want to apply for this job
Der Bewerbung sind ein Lebenslauf und ein Foto beizulegen	= A CV and a photograph should be sent with the application
Können Sie am 24. März zu einem Vorstellungsgespräch kommen?	= Could you come for an interview on March 24th?
Wann wäre Ihr frühestmöglicher Einstellungstermin?	= What is the earliest [date] you could start?

Berührung *die; ~, ~en* (a) (das Berühren) touch; **bei der geringsten ~:** at the slightest touch; (b) (Kontakt) contact; **mit jmdm./etw. in ~** (*Akk.*) **kommen** come into contact with sb./sth.

Berührungs-: **~angst** *die* fear of contact; **~punkt** *der* (a) (Math.) point of contact *or* tangency; (b) (fig.: Gemein-samkeit) point of contact

Berufungs-: **~instanz** *die* (Rechtsw.) court of appeal; **~verfahren** *das* (Rechtsw.) appeal proceedings *pl.*

besagen *tr. V.* say; (bedeuten) mean; **das besagt noch gar nichts** that doesn't mean anything

besagt *Adj.; nicht präd.* (Amtsspr.) aforementioned

besamen /bə'zaːmən/ *tr. V.* fertilize; (künstlich) inseminate

Besamung *die; ~, ~en* fertilization; (künstlich) insem-ination

besänftigen /bə'zɛnftɪɡn̩/ *tr. V.* calm [down]; pacify; calm, soothe ⟨*temper*⟩

Besänftigung *die; ~:* calming [down]; pacifying; (von jmds. Zorn) calming; soothing

besät /bə'zɛːt/ *Adj.* sown (**mit** with); (fig.) covered (**mit, von** with); **mit Sternen ~:** studded with stars

Besatz *der* (Mode: Borte) trimming *no indef. art.*

Besatzung *die* (a) (Mannschaft) crew; (b) (Milit.) occupying troops *pl. or* forces *pl.*

Besatzungs-: **~macht** *die* occupying power; **~zone** *die* occupied zone

besaufen *unr. refl. V.* (salopp) get boozed up (Brit. sl.) *or* canned (Brit. sl.) *or* bombed (Amer. sl.)

Besäufnis /bə'zɔyfnɪs/ *das; ~ses, ~se* (salopp) booze-up (Brit. sl.): blast (Amer. sl.)

beschädigen *tr. V.* damage

Beschädigung *die* (a) *o. Pl.* (das Beschädigen) damaging; (b) (Schaden) damage; **zahlreiche ~en** a lot of damage *sing.*

beschaffen[1] *tr. V.* obtain; get; get ⟨job⟩; **ein Quartier ~:** find accommodation; **jmdm. etw. ~:** obtain/get sb. sth. *or* sth. for sb.; **sich** (*Dat.*) **Geld/die Genehmigung ~:** get [hold of] money/get *or* obtain the permit/licence

beschaffen[2] *Adj.* **so ~ sein, dass …:** be such that …; ⟨product⟩ be made in such a way that …; **ähnlich ~ wie Leder** similar in nature to leather

Beschaffenheit *die; ~:* properties *pl.*; (Konsistenz) consistency

Beschaffung *die* ⇒ **beschaffen:** obtaining; getting; finding

Beschaffungs·kriminalität *die* crime in the pur-suit of drug acquisition

beschäftigen /bə'ʃɛftɪɡn̩/ **1** *refl. V.* occupy *or* busy one-self; **sich viel mit Musik/den Kindern ~:** devote a great deal of one's time to music/the children; **sich mit den Schriften Hegels ~:** be engaged in a study of the writings of Hegel; **sehr beschäftigt sein** be very busy. **2** *tr. V.* (a) occupy; **jmdn. mit etw. ~:** give sb. sth. to oc-cupy him/her; **du musst die Kinder ~:** you must keep the children occupied; (b) (angestellt haben) employ ⟨workers, staff⟩; **bei einer Firma beschäftigt sein** work for a firm; (c) (jmdn. geistig in Anspruch nehmen) be on sb.'s mind; preoccupy sb.

Beschäftigte *der/die; adj. Dekl.* employee; **die Fabrik/ das Kaufhaus hat 500 ~:** the factory has a workforce/ the department store has a staff of 500

Beschäftigung *die;* ~, ~**en** (a) (Tätigkeit) activity; occupation; **bei dieser** ~ **solltest du ihn nicht stören** you shouldn't disturb him while he's occupied with that; **(b)** (Anstellung, Stelle) job; **ohne** ~ **sein** not be working; (unfreiwillig) be unemployed; **(c)** *o. Pl.* (geistige Auseinandersetzung) consideration (**mit** of); (Studium) study (**mit** of); **(d)** *o. Pl.* (von Arbeitskräften) employment

beschämen *tr. V.* shame; **jmdn. durch seine Großmütigkeit** ~: make sb. ashamed by one's generosity

beschämend **1** *Adj.* **(a)** (schändlich) shameful; **(b)** (demütigend) humiliating. **2** *adv.* shamefully

beschämt *Adj.* ashamed; abashed

Beschämung *die;* ~: shame

beschatten *tr. V.* **(a)** (geh.) shade; **(b)** (überwachen) shadow

beschaulich /bə'ʃaulɪç/ **1** *Adj.* peaceful, tranquil ‹*life, manner, etc.*›; meditative, contemplative ‹*person, character*›. **2** *adv.* peacefully; tranquilly

Beschaulichkeit *die;* ~: peacefulness; tranquillity

Bescheid /bə'ʃait/ *der;* ~[e]s, ~e **(a)** (Auskunft) information; (Antwort) answer; reply; **jmdm.** ~ **geben** *od.* **sagen**[, **ob** …] let sb. know or tell sb. [whether …]; **sage bitte im Restaurant** ~, **dass** …: please let the restaurant know *or* let them know in the restaurant that …; **jmdm.** ~ **sagen** (ugs.: sich beschweren) give sb. a piece of one's mind (coll.); [**über etw.** (*Akk.*)] ~ **wissen** know [about sth.]; **(b)** (Entscheidung) decision; **ein abschlägiger/positiver** ~: a refusal/a positive reply

bescheiden[1] **1** *unr. tr. V.* **(a)** (inform, notify ‹*person*›; **jmdn./etw. abschlägig** ~: turn sb./sth. down; refuse sb./sth., **(b)** **es war ihm nicht beschieden, … zu …** (geh.) it was not granted to him to … **2** *unr. refl. V.* (geh.) be content

bescheiden[2] **1** *Adj.* **(a)** modest; unassuming ‹*person, behaviour*›; **(b)** (einfach) modest; simple ‹*meal*›; **in** ~**en Verhältnissen aufwachsen** grow up in humble circumstances; **(c)** (dürftig) modest ‹*salary, results, pension, etc.*›; **(d)** (ugs. verhüll.: sehr schlecht) lousy (coll.); bloody awful (Brit. sl.). **2** *adv.* modestly

Bescheidenheit *die;* ~: modesty

bescheinen *unr. tr. V.* shine [up]on; **vom Mond/von der Sonne beschienen** moonlit/sunlit

bescheinigen /bə'ʃainɪɡn̩/ *tr. V.* **etw.** ~: confirm sth. in writing; **jmdm. den Empfang des Geldes** ~: acknowledge receipt of the money; **sich** (*Dat.*) ~ **lassen, dass man arbeitsunfähig ist** get oneself certified as unfit for work

Bescheinigung *die;* ~, ~**en** written confirmation *no indef. art.;* (Schein, Attest) certificate

bescheißen *unr. tr. V.* (derb) **jmdn.** ~: rip sb. off (sl.); screw sb. (coarse)

beschenken *tr. V.* **jmdn.** ~: give sb. a present/presents; **jmdn. reich** ~: shower sb. with presents; **jmdn. mit etw.** ~: give sb. sth. as a present

bescheren **1** *tr. V.* **(a)** **jmdn.** [**mit etw.**] ~ (zu Weihnachten beschenken) give sb. [sth. as] a Christmas present/Christmas presents; **(b)** **ich bin gespannt, was uns dieser Tag** ~ **wird** I wonder what today will bring. **2** *itr. V.* **nach dem Abendessen wird beschert** the presents are given out after supper

Bescherung *die;* ~, ~**en** **(a)** (zu Weihnachten) giving out of the Christmas presents; **die Kinder konnten die** ~ **kaum erwarten** the children could hardly wait for the presents to be given out; **(b)** (ugs. iron.: unangenehme Überraschung) **das ist ja eine schöne** ~: this is a pretty kettle of fish; **jetzt haben wir die** ~: that's done it, I told you so

bescheuert *Adj.* (salopp) **(a)** barmy (Brit. coll.); nuts (sl.); **(b)** (unangenehm) stupid ‹*task, party, etc.*›; **etw.** ~ **finden** find sth. a real pain [in the neck] (coll.)

beschichten *tr. V* (Technik) coat; **mit Kunststoff beschichtet** plastic-coated

Beschichtung *die;* ~, ~ (Technik) coating

beschicken *tr. V.* (Technik: füllen) charge ‹*furnace*›

beschickert /bə'ʃɪkɐt/ *Adj.* (ugs.) tipsy; merry (Brit. coll.)

Beschickung *die;* ~, ~**en** (Technik: eines Hochofens) (das Beschicken) charging; (Füllung) charge

beschießen *unr. tr. V.* fire *or* shoot at; (mit Artillerie) bombard

Beschießung *die;* ~, ~**en** ⇒ **beschießen:** firing (*Gen.* at); shooting (*Gen.* at); bombardement (*Gen.* of)

beschimpfen *tr. V.* abuse; swear at

Beschimpfung *die;* ~, ~**en** insult; ~**en** abuse *sing.;* insults

Beschiss, *Beschiß *der;* (derb) rip-off (coll.)

beschissen /bə'ʃɪsn̩/ (derb) **1** *Adj.* lousy (coll.); shitty (coarse). **2** *adv.* ‹*behave*› in a bloody awful manner (Brit. sl.), shittily (coarse); **ihm geht es** ~: he's having a (coll.) lousy *or* (Brit.) bloody awful time of it (sl.)

Beschlag *der* **(a)** fitting; **(b)** **jmdn./etw. mit** ~ **belegen** *od.* **in** ~ **nehmen** monopolize sb./sth.

beschlagen[1] **1** *unr. tr. V.* shoe ‹*horse*›; **Schuhsohlen mit Nägeln** ~: stud the soles of shoes with [hob]nails. **2** *unr. itr. V.; mit sein* ‹*window*› mist up (Brit.), fog up (Amer.); (durch Dampf) steam up; ~**e Scheiben** misted-up/fogged-up/steamed-up windows

beschlagen[2] *Adj.* knowledgeable; **in etw.** (*Dat.*) [**gut**] ~ **sein** be knowledgeable about sth.

Beschlagenheit *die;* ~: thorough *or* sound knowledge

Beschlag·nahme /-naːmə/ *die;* ~, ~**n** seizure; confiscation

beschlagnahmen *tr. V.* seize; confiscate

beschleichen *unr. tr. V.* **(a)** creep up on *or* to; steal up to; ‹*hunter*› stalk ‹*game, prey*›; **(b)** (geh.: überkommen) creep over

beschleunigen /bə'ʃlɔynɪɡn̩/ **1** *tr. V.* accelerate; quicken ‹*pace, step[s], pulse*›; speed up, expedite ‹*work, delivery*›; hasten ‹*departure, collapse*›; accelerate, speed up, expedite ‹*process*›. **2** *refl. V.* ‹*speed, heart-rate*› increase; ‹*pulse*› quicken. **3** *itr. V.* ‹*driver, car, etc.*› accelerate

Beschleunigung *die;* ~, ~**en** **(a)** ⇒ **beschleunigen 1:** speeding up; quickening; acceleration; expedition; hastening; **(b)** (ugs.: ~svermögen) acceleration; **eine gute** ~ **haben** have good acceleration; **(c)** (Physik) acceleration

beschließen **1** *unr. tr. V.* **(a)** ~, **etw. zu tun** decide *or* resolve to do sth.; ‹*committee, council, etc.*› resolve to do sth.; **den Bau einer Brücke** ~: decide to build a bridge; **das ist beschlossene Sache** it's settled; **(b)** (beenden) end; end, conclude ‹*lecture*›; end, close ‹*letter*›. **2** *unr. itr. V.* **über etw.** (*Akk.*) ~: decide concerning sth.

Beschluss, *Beschluß *der* decision; (gemeinsam gefasst) resolution; **einen** ~ **fassen** come to a decision/pass a resolution; **gemäß dem** ~ **des Gerichtes** in accordance with the decision of the court

beschluss-, *beschluß-, Beschluss-, *Beschluß-: ~**fähig** *Adj.* quorate; **~fähig sein** have a quorum; be quorate; ~**fähigkeit** *die; o. Pl.* presence of a quorum; ~**unfähig** *Adj.* inquorate; ~**unfähig sein** not have a quorum; be inquorate

beschmeißen *unr. tr. V.* (salopp) **jmdn. mit etw.** ~: pelt sb. with sth.; **jmdn./etw. mit Dreck** ~ (fig.) fling mud at sb./sth.

beschmieren *tr. V.* **(a)** **etw./sich** ~: get sth./oneself in a mess; **sich** (*Dat.*) **die Kleidung/Hände mit etw.** ~: smear *or* get sth. [smeared] all over one's clothes/ hands; **(b)** (abwertend) (bemalen) daub paint all over; (bekritzeln) scrawl *or* scribble all over; **(c)** (bestreichen) **sein Brot mit etw.** ~: spread sth. on one's bread; **etw. mit Fett/Salbe** ~: grease sth./smear ointment on sth.; **(d)** (abwertend: voll schreiben) cover ‹*paper*›

beschmutzen *tr. V.* **etw.** ~: make sth. dirty; **ganz beschmutzt sein** be covered in dirt; **jmds. Namen/Gedenken** ~ (fig.) besmirch sb.'s name/memory

beschneiden *unr. tr. V.* **(a)** cut, trim, clip ‹*hedge*›; prune, cut back ‹*bush*›; cut back ‹*tree*›; clip ‹*bird's wings*›;

(b) (Med., Rel.) circumcise; **(c)** (fig.) cut ⟨*salary, income, wages*⟩; restrict ⟨*rights*⟩

Beschneidung *die;* ∼, ∼**en** **(a)** ⇒ **beschneiden a:** trimming; cutting; clipping; pruning; cutting back; **(b)** ⇒ **beschneiden c:** cutting; restriction; **(c)** (Med., Rel.) circumcision

beschönigen /bəˈʃøːnɪɡn̩/ *tr. V.* gloss over

Beschönigung *die;* ∼, ∼**en** glossing over; **das wäre eine** ∼: that would be to gloss over the true situation

beschränken /bəˈʃrɛŋkn̩/ **1** *tr. V.* restrict; limit; **etw. auf etw.** (*Akk.*) ∼: restrict *or* limit sth. to sth.; **jmdn. in seinen Rechten** ∼: restrict sb.'s rights. **2** *refl. V.* tighten one's belt (fig.); **sich auf etw.** (*Akk.*) ∼: restrict *or* confine oneself to sth.

beschrankt *Adj.* ⟨*level crossing*⟩ with barriers; ∼ **sein** have barriers

beschränkt **1** *Adj.* **(a)** (abwertend: dumm) dull-witted; **(b)** (engstirnig) narrow-minded ⟨*person*⟩; narrow[-minded] ⟨*views, outlook*⟩. **2** *adv.* narrow-mindedly; in a narrow-minded way

Beschränktheit *die;* ∼: **(a)** (Dummheit) lack of intelligence; **(b)** ⇒ **beschränkt b:** narrow-mindedness; narrowness; **(c)** (das Begrenztsein) limitedness; restrictedness

Beschränkung *die;* ∼, ∼**en** restriction; **jmdm./einer Sache** ∼**en auferlegen** impose restrictions on sb./sth.

beschreiben *unr. tr. V.* **(a)** write on; (voll schreiben) write ⟨*page, sheet, etc.*⟩; **eng beschriebene Seiten** closely written pages; **(b)** (darstellen) describe; **ich kann dir [gar] nicht** ∼**, wie** ...: I [simply] can't tell you how ...; **(c) einen Kreis/Bogen** *usw.* ∼: describe a circle/curve *etc.*

Beschreibung *die;* ∼, ∼**en** description

beschreien *unr. tr. V.:* ⇒ **berufen¹ 1 b**

beschreiten *unr. tr. V.* (geh.) walk along ⟨*path etc.*⟩; **neue Wege** ∼ (fig.) tread new paths

Beschrieb *der* (schweiz.) description

beschriften /bəˈʃrɪftn̩/ *tr. V.* label; inscribe ⟨*stone*⟩; letter ⟨*sign, label, etc.*⟩; (mit Adresse) address

Beschriftung *die;* ∼, ∼**en (a)** *o. Pl.* labelling; (eines Steines) inscribing; (eines Etiketts) lettering; (mit Adresse) addressing; **(b)** (Aufschrift) label; (eines Steines) inscription; (eines Etiketts usw.) lettering

beschuldigen /bəˈʃʊldɪɡn̩/ *tr. V.* accuse (*Gen.* of); **jmdn.** ∼**, etw. getan zu haben/etw. zu sein** accuse sb. of doing/being sth.

Beschuldigte *der/die; adj. Dekl.* accused

Beschuldigung *die;* ∼, ∼**en** accusation

beschummeln *tr. V.* (ugs.) cheat; diddle (coll.); burn (Amer. sl.)

Beschuss, *Beschuß *der* fire; (aus Kanonen) shelling; (mit Pfeilen) shooting; **unter** ∼ **nehmen** fire at/shell/shoot at; (fig.: kritisieren) attack; **unter** ∼ **geraten/liegen** (auch fig.) come/be under fire

beschützen *tr. V.* protect (**vor** + *Dat.* from)

Beschützer *der;* ∼**s**, ∼, **Beschützerin** *die;* ∼, ∼**nen** protector (**vor** from)

beschwatzen *tr. V.* (ugs.) **(a) jmdn.** ∼: talk sb. round; **jmdn. zu etw.** ∼: talk sb. into sth.; **jmdn.** ∼**, etw. zu tun** talk sb. into doing sth.; **(b)** (bereden) chat about *or* over

Beschwerde /bəˈʃveːɐdə/ *die;* ∼, ∼**n (a)** complaint (**gegen, über** + *Akk.* about); ∼ **führen** (Amtsspr.) *od.* einlegen (Rechtsw.) lodge a complaint; (gegen einen Entscheid) lodge an appeal; **(b)** ▶ **329** *Pl.* (Schmerz) pain *sing.;* (Leiden) trouble *sing.*

beschwerde-, Beschwerde-: ∼**buch** *das* complaints book; ∼**frei** **1** *Adj.* trouble-free; (ohne Schmerz) free from pain *postpos.;* **2** *adv.* without pain; ∼**führer** *der* complainant; (gegen einen Entscheid) apellant

beschweren /bəˈʃveːrən/ **1** *refl. V.* complain (**über** + *Akk., wegen about*); **sich bei jmdm.** ∼: complain to sb. **2** *tr. V.* weight; (durch Auflegen eines schweren Gegenstands) weight down

beschwerlich *Adj.* arduous; (ermüdend) exhausting

beschwichtigen /bəˈʃvɪçtɪɡn̩/ *tr. V.* pacify; calm ⟨*excitement*⟩; placate, mollify ⟨*anger etc.*⟩

Beschwichtigung *die;* ∼, ∼**en** pacification; (des Zorns, Hasses) mollification

beschwindeln *tr. V.* (ugs.) **jmdn.** ∼: tell sb. a fib/fibs; (betrügen) hoodwink sb.

beschwingt /bəˈʃvɪŋt/ *Adj.* elated, lively ⟨*mood*⟩; lively, lilting ⟨*tune, melody*⟩; ∼ **sein/sich** ∼ **fühlen** ⟨*person*⟩ be/feel elated

beschwipst /bəˈʃvɪpst/ *Adj.* (ugs.) tipsy

beschwören *unr. tr. V.* **(a)** swear to; ∼**, dass** ...: swear that ...; **eine Aussage** ∼: swear a statement on *or* unter oath; **(b)** charm ⟨*snake*⟩; **(c)** (erscheinen lassen) invoke, conjure up ⟨*spirit*⟩; (fig.) evoke, conjure up ⟨*pictures, memories, etc.*⟩; **(d)** (bitten) beg; implore; **in** ∼**dem Ton** in a beseeching *or* imploring tone

Beschwörung *die;* ∼, ∼**en (a)** ⇒ **beschwören b, c:** charming; invoking; conjuring up; evoking; **(b)** (Zauberformel) spell; incantation; **(c)** (Bitte) entreaty

besehen *unr. tr. V.* have a look at; **sich** (*Dat.*) **etw. genau** ∼: have a close look at sth.; inspect sth. closely; **er besah sich im Spiegel** he looked at himself in the mirror

beseitigen /bəˈzaitɪɡn̩/ *tr. V.* **(a)** remove; eliminate ⟨*error, difficulty*⟩; dispose of ⟨*rubbish*⟩; eradicate ⟨*injustice, abuse*⟩; **(b)** (verhüll.: ermorden) dispose of; eliminate

Beseitigung *die;* ∼ **(a)** ⇒ **beseitigen a:** removal; elimination; disposal; eradication; **(b)** (verhüll.: Ermordung) elimination

Besen /ˈbeːzn̩/ *der;* ∼**s**, ∼ **(a)** broom; (Reisig∼) besom; (Hand∼) brush; **ich fress einen** ∼**, wenn das stimmt** (salopp) I'll eat my hat if that's right (coll.); **neue** ∼ **kehren gut** (Spr.) a new broom sweeps clean (prov.); **(b)** (salopp abwertend. Frau) battleaxe (coll.)

besen-, Besen-: ∼**kammer** *die* broom cupboard; broom closet (Amer.); ∼**rein** *Adj.* swept clean *postpos.;* ∼**schrank** *der* ⇒ ∼**kammer;** ∼**stiel** *der* broom handle; (eines Reisigbesens) broomstick

besessen /bəˈzɛsn̩/ *Adj.* **(a)** possessed; **vom Teufel** ∼ **sein** be possessed by *or* (dated) of the Devil; **wie** ∼ *od.* **ein Besessener/eine Besessene** like one possessed; **(b)** (fig.) obsessive ⟨*gambler*⟩; **von einer Idee** *usw.* ∼ **sein** be obsessed with an idea *etc.*

Besessenheit *die;* ∼ **(a)** possession; **(b)** (fig.) obsessiveness; **mit wahrer** ∼: in a truly obsessive manner

besetzen *tr. V.* **(a)** (mit Pelz, Spitzen) edge; trim; **mit Perlen/Edelsteinen besetzt** set with pearls/ precious stones; **(b)** (belegen; auch Milit.: erobern) occupy; (füllen) fill (**mit** with); **(c)** (vergeben) fill ⟨*post, position, role, etc.*⟩

besetzt *Adj.* occupied; ⟨*table, seat*⟩ taken *pred.;* (gefüllt) full; filled to capacity; **es** *od.* **die Leitung/die Nummer ist** ∼: the line/number is engaged *or* (Amer.) busy

Besetzt·zeichen *das* (Fernspr.) engaged tone (Brit.); busy signal (Amer.)

Besetzung *die;* ∼, ∼**en (a)** (einer Stellung) filling; **(b)** (Mitwirkende) (Film, Theater usw.) cast; **(c)** (Eroberung) occupation

besichtigen /bəˈzɪçtɪɡn̩/ *tr. V.* see ⟨*sights*⟩; see the sights of ⟨*town*⟩; look round ⟨*building*⟩; ⟨*prospective buyer or tenant*⟩ view ⟨*house, flat*⟩

Besichtigung *die;* ∼, ∼**en** viewing; (Rundgang, -fahrt) tour; (von Truppen) inspection; **die** ∼ **der Kirche ist zwischen 10 und 16 Uhr möglich** the church is open to visitors between 10 a.m. and 4 p.m.

besiedeln *tr. V.* settle (**mit** with); **ein dicht/dünn besiedeltes Land** a densely/thinly populated country

Besiedlung *die* settlement

besiegeln *tr. V.* set the seal on

Besieg[e]lung *die;* ∼, ∼**en** sealing; **die** ∼ **von etw. sein** seal sth.; **zur** ∼ **unserer Freundschaft** to seal our friendship

besiegen *tr. V.* **(a)** defeat; **(b)** (fig.) overcome ⟨*doubts, curiosity, etc.*⟩

Besiegte *der/die; adj. Dekl.* loser

besingen *unr. tr. V.* **(a)** (geh.) celebrate in verse; (durch ein Lied) celebrate in song; **(b) eine Platte** ∼: make a record [of songs]

besinnen *unr. refl. V.* (a) think it *or* things over; **sich anders/eines Besseren** ~: change one's mind/think better of it; (b) (sich erinnern) **sich [auf jmdn./etw.]** ~: remember *or* recall [sb./sth.]

besinnlich *Adj.* contemplative; thoughtful ‹*person*›; reflective ‹*story*›; **ein** ~**er Abend** an evening of reflection

Besinnung *die;* ~ (a) consciousness; **die** ~ **verlieren** lose consciousness; **ohne** *od.* **nicht bei** ~: unconscious; **[wieder] zur** ~ **kommen** come to; regain consciousness; (b) (Nachdenken) reflection; **zur** ~ **kommen** stop and think things over; **jmdn. zur** ~ **bringen** bring sb. to his/her senses

besinnungs·los 1 *Adj.* (a) unconscious; (b) (fig.) mindless, blind ‹*rage, hatred*›. 2 *adv.* mindlessly

Besitz *der* (a) property; **nur wenig** ~ **haben** have only a few possessions *pl.;* (b) (das Besitzen) possession; **sich in jmds.** ~ **(***Dat.***) befinden, in jmds.** ~ **(***Dat.***) sein** be in sb.'s possession; **sich in privatem** ~ **befinden** be privately owned; be in private ownership *or* hands; **im** ~ **einer Sache (***Gen.***) sein** be in possession of sth.; possess sth.; **etw. in** ~ **(***Akk.***) nehmen, von etw.** ~ **ergreifen** take possession of sth.; (c) (Landgut) estate

Besitz·anspruch *der* claim to ownership; **einen** ~ **auf etw. (***Akk.***) anmelden** file a claim to ownership of sth.

besitz·anzeigend *Adj.* (Sprachw.) possessive

besitzen *unr. tr. V.* own; have ‹*quality, talent, right, etc.*›; (nachdrücklicher) possess; **keinen Pfennig** ~ (ugs.) not have a penny to one's name; **er besaß die Frechheit, zu …:** he had the cheek *or* nerve to …

Besitzer *der;* ~**s,** (a) owner; (eines Betriebs usw.) owner; proprietor; **den** ~ **wechseln** change hands *pl.;* (b) (österr.) property-owner

Besitzerin *die;* ~**, ~nen** ⇒ **Besitzer**

Besitzer·stolz *der* pride of ownership

besitz·los *Adj.* destitute

Besitz·stand *der* standard of living; **den** ~**stand wahren** maintain living standards

Besitztum *das;* ~**s, Besitztümer** /-ty:mɐ/ possession

besoffen /bə'zɔfn̩/ 1 2. *Part. v.* **besaufen.** 2 *Adj.* (salopp) boozed [up] (sl.); plastered (sl.); pissed *pred.* (sl.); **völlig** ~: completely stoned (coll.); blind drunk

Besoffene *der/die; adj. Dekl.* (salopp) drunk

besohlen *tr. V.* sole; **neu** ~: resole

Besoldung /bə'zɔldʊŋ/ *die;* ~**, ~en** pay

besonder... /bə'zɔndɐ.../ *Adj.; nicht präd.* special; (größer als gewohnt) particular ‹*pleasure, enthusiasm, effort, etc.*›; (hervorragend) exceptional ‹*quality, beauty, etc.*›; **im Besonderen** in particular; **ein** ~**es Ereignis** an unusual *or* a special event; **keine** ~**en Vorkommnisse wurden gemeldet** no incidents of any particular note were reported; ~**e Merkmale** (im Pass usw.) distinguishing marks; **keine** ~**e Leistung** no great achievement

Besondere *das; adj. Dekl.* **etwas [ganz]** ~**s** something [really] special; **nichts** ~**s** nothing special; **das ist doch nichts** ~**s** there's nothing special *or* unusual about that

Besonderheit *die;* ~**, ~en** special *or* distinctive feature; (Eigenart) peculiarity

besonders 1 *Adv.* (a) particularly; ~ **du solltest das wissen** you of all people should know that; ~ **bei schönem Wetter** especially in fine weather; (b) **nur verneint** (ugs.: besonders gut) particularly well; **es geht ihm nicht** ~: he doesn't feel too well. 2 *Adj.; nicht attr.; nur verneint* (ugs.) **nicht** ~ **sein** be nothing special; be nothing to write home about

besonnen /bə'zɔnən/ 1 *Adj.* prudent; (umsichtig) circumspect; **ruhig und** ~: calm and collected. 2 *adv.* prudently; (umsichtig) circumspectly

Besonnenheit *die;* ~: prudence (Umsichtigkeit); circumspection

besorgen *tr. V.* (a) get; (kaufen) buy; **jmdm. etw.** ~: get/buy sb. sth. *or* sth. for sb.; **sich (***Dat.***) etw.** ~: get/buy sth.; (ugs. verhüll.: stehlen) help oneself to sth.; (b) (erledigen)

take care of; deal with; **jmdm. den Haushalt/die Wäsche** ~: keep house/do the washing for sb.

Besorgnis *die;* ~**, ~se** concern; **jmds.** ~ **erregen** cause sb. concern

besorgnis·erregend *Adj.* serious; ~ **sein** give cause for concern

besorgt 1 *Adj.* worried (**über** + *Akk.*, **um** about); concerned *usu. pred.* (**über** + *Akk.*, **um** about); **sie war rührend um das Wohl ihrer Gäste** ~: she showed a touching concern for the well-being of her guests. 2 *adv.* with concern; (ängstlich) anxiously

Besorgung *die;* ~**, ~en** (a) purchase; **[einige] ~en machen** do some shopping; (b) *o. Pl.* (das Beschaffen) getting; (das Kaufen) buying .

bespannen *tr. V.* cover ‹*wall, chair, car, etc.*›; string ‹*racket, instrument*›

Bespannung *die;* ~**, ~en** covering; (eines Schlägers, eines Instruments) stringing

bespielbar *Adj.* (Sport) playable ‹*ground, tennis court*›

bespielen *tr. V.* record on ‹*tape, cassette*›; **ein Band mit etw.** ~: record sth. on a tape; **bespielt** used ‹*tape, cassette*›; (vom Hersteller) prerecorded ‹*cassette*›; **ist dieses Band bespielt?** is there anything on this tape?

bespitzeln *tr. V.* spy on

Bespitz[e]lung *die;* ~**, ~en** spying

besprechen 1 *unr. tr. V.* (a) discuss; talk over; (b) (rezensieren) review; **gut/schlecht besprochen werden** get a good/bad review; (mehrfach) get good/bad reviews; (c) **eine Kassette** ~: make a [voice] recording on a cassette; (statt eines Briefes) record a message on a cassette; (d) **etw.** ~ (beschwören) utter a magic incantation *or* spell over sth. 2 *unr. refl. V.* confer (**über** + *Akk.* about); **sich mit jmdm.** ~: have a talk with sb.

Besprechung *die;* ~**, ~en** (a) discussion; (Konferenz) meeting; **in einer** ~ **sein, [gerade] eine** ~ **haben** be in a meeting; (b) (Rezension) review (*Gen.,* **von** of)

bespritzen *tr. V.* (a) splash; (mit einem Wasserstrahl) spray; (b) (beschmutzen) bespatter

besprühen *tr. V.* spray

bespucken *tr. V.* **jmdn. [mit etw.]** ~: spit [sth.] at sb.

besser /'bɛsɐ/ 1 *Adj.* (a) better; ~ **werden** get better; ‹*work etc.*› improve; **um so** ~: so much the better; all the better; that wasn't the best of it (iron.); **ich habe Besseres zu tun** I've got better things to do; **jmdn. eines Besseren belehren** (geh.) put sb. right; *s. auch* **besinnen** a; (b) (sozial höher gestellt) superior; upper-class; ~**e** *od.* **die** ~**en Kreise** more elevated circles; **eine** ~**e Gegend/Adresse** a smart[er] *or* [more] respectable area/address; (c) (abwertend) glorified; **wir arbeiten in einer** ~**en Baracke** we work in a glorified hut. 2 *adv.* better; [immer] **alles** ~ **wissen** always know better; **es** ~ **haben** be better off; (es leichter haben) have an easier time of it; **es geht ihr** ~: she feels better; **es kommt noch** ~ (iron.) it gets even better (iron.); ~ **gesagt** to be [more] precise; **er täte** ~ **daran, zu …:** he would do better to … 3 *Adv.* (lieber) **das lässt du** ~ **sein** *od.* (ugs.) bleiben you'd better not do that

***besser|gehen** ⇒ **besser** 2

bessern 1 *refl. V.* improve; ‹*person*› mend one's ways. 2 *tr. V.* improve; reform ‹*criminal*›

Besserung *die;* ~: (a) (Genesung) recovery; **[ich wünsche dir] gute** ~: [I hope you] get well soon; **sich auf dem Wege der** ~ **befinden** be on the road to recovery *or* on the mend; (b) (Verbesserung) improvement (*Gen.* in); (eines Kriminellen) reform; ~ **geloben** promise to mend one's ways

Besser-: ~**wisser** *der;* ~**s,** ~ (abwertend) know-all; smart aleck; ~**wisserei** /----'-/ *die;* ~ (abwertend) superior attitude

best... /'bɛst.../ 1 *Adj.* (a) best; **bei** ~**er Gesundheit/Laune sein** be in the best of health/spirits *pl.;* **im** ~**en Falle** at best; **in den** ~**en Jahren, im** ~**en Alter** in one's prime; ~**e** *od.* **die** ~**en Grüße an …** (*Akk.*) best wishes to …; **mit den** ~**en Grüßen** *od.*

Wünschen with best wishes; (als Briefschluss) ≈ yours sincerely; **~en Dank** many thanks *pl.;* **der/die/das nächste ~e ...:** the first ... one comes across; **es steht nicht zum Besten mit etw.** things are not going too well for sth.; **eine Geschichte/einen Witz zum Besten geben** entertain [those present] with a story/a joke; **jmdn. zum Besten halten** *od.* **haben** pull sb.'s leg; **das Beste vom Besten** the very best; **sein Bestes tun** do one's best; **das Beste aus etw. machen** make the best of sth.; **das Beste hoffen** hope for the best; **ich will nur dein Bestes** I am doing this for your own good; **zu deinem Besten** for your benefit; in your best interests *pl.;* **(b) es ist** *od.* **wäre das Beste** *od.* **am ~en, wenn ...:** it would be best if ...; **es wäre das Beste, ... zu ...:** it would be best to ... **2** *adv.* **(a) am ~en** the best; **(b) am ~en fährst du mit dem Zug** you'd best go by train

Bestand *der* (a) *o. Pl.* existence; (Fort~) continued existence; survival; **keinen ~ haben, nicht von ~ sein** not last; not last long; **(b)** (Vorrat) stock **(an + Dat. of)**

bestanden /bə'ʃtandn̩/ *Adj.* **von** *od.* **mit etw. ~ sein** have sth. growing on it; **mit Tannen ~e Hügel** fir-covered hills

beständig 1 *Adj.* **(a)** *nicht präd.* (dauernd) constant; **(b)** (gleich bleibend) constant; steadfast ⟨*person*⟩; settled ⟨*weather*⟩; (Chemie) stable ⟨*compound*⟩; (zuverlässig) reliable; **(c)** (widerstandsfähig) resistant **(gegen, gegenüber** to). **2** *adv.* **(a)** (dauernd) constantly; **(b)** (gleich bleibend) consistently

-beständig *adj.* **hitze~/wetter~/säure~:** heat-/weather-/acid-resistant

Beständigkeit *die;* ~ **(a)** constancy; steadfastness; (bei der Arbeit) consistency; (Zuverlässigkeit) reliability; **(b)** (Widerstandsfähigkeit) resistance **(gegen, gegenüber** to)

Bestands·aufnahme *die* stocktaking; **[eine] ~ machen** do a stocktaking; take inventory (Amer.); (fig.) take stock

Bestand·teil *der* component; **sich in seine ~e auflösen** fall apart; fall to pieces; **etw. in seine [sämtlichen] ~e zerlegen** dismantle sth. [completely]

bestärken *tr. V.* confirm; **jmdn. in seinem Plan** *od.* **Vorsatz** *od.* **darin ~, etw. zu tun** strengthen sb.'s resolve *or* confirm sb. in his/her resolve to do sth.

bestätigen /bə'ʃtɛ:tɪgn̩/ **1** *tr. V.* confirm; endorse ⟨*document*⟩; acknowledge ⟨*receipt of letter, money, goods, etc.*⟩; **ein Urteil ~** (Rechtsw.) uphold a judgement; **jmdn. [im Amt] ~:** confirm sb.'s appointment; **einen Brief/eine Bestellung ~** (Kaufmannsspr.) acknowledge [receipt of] a letter/an order. **2** *refl. V.* be confirmed; ⟨*rumour*⟩ prove to be true

Bestätigung *die;* ~, **~en** confirmation; (des Empfangs) acknowledgement; (schriftlich) letter of confirmation; **die ~ in seinem Amt** the confirmation of his appointment

bestatten /bə'ʃtatn̩/ *tr. V.* (geh.) inter (formal); bury; **bestattet werden** be laid to rest

Bestatter *der;* ~s, ~: undertaker; mortician (Amer.); (bei Firmennamen) funeral director

Bestattung *die;* ~, **~en** (geh.) interment (formal); burial; (Feierlichkeit) funeral

Bestattungs-: **~institut**, *das*, **~unternehmen** *das* [firm of] undertakers *pl. or* funeral directors *pl.;* funeral parlor (Amer.)

bestäuben /bə'ʃtɔybn̩/ *tr. V.* **(a)** dust; **(b)** (Biol.) pollinate

Bestäubung *die;* ~, **~en** (Biol.) pollination

bestaunen *tr. V.* marvel at; (bewundernd anstarren) gaze in wonder at

bestechen 1 *unr. tr. V.* bribe. **2** *unr. itr. V.* be attractive **(durch** on account of)

bestechend *Adj.* attractive; captivating; winning ⟨*smile, charm*⟩; persuasive ⟨*argument, logic*⟩; tempting ⟨*offer*⟩

bestechlich *Adj.* corruptible; open to bribery *postpos.*

Bestechlichkeit *die;* ~: corruptibility

Bestechung *die;* ~, **~en** bribery *no indef. art.;* **eine ~:** a case of bribery; **aktive ~** (Rechtsw.) giving bribes; **passive ~** (Rechtsw.) accepting bribes

Bestechungs-: **~geld** *das* bribe; **~versuch** *der* attempted bribery

Besteck /bə'ʃtɛk/ *das;* ~[e]s, **~e (a)** cutlery setting; (ugs.: Gesamtheit der Bestecke) cutlery; **(b)** (Med.) [set *sing.* of] instruments *pl.*

Besteck-: **~kasten** *der* cutlery-box; (größer) canteen; **~schublade** *die* cutlery-drawer

bestehen 1 *unr. itr. V.* **(a)** exist; ~ **bleiben** remain; ⟨*doubt*⟩ persist; ⟨*regulation*⟩ remain in force; **die Schule besteht noch nicht sehr lange** the school has not been in existence *or* has not been going for very long; **es besteht [die] Aussicht/Gefahr, dass ...:** there is a prospect/danger that ...; **noch besteht die Hoffnung, dass ...:** there is still hope that ...; **(b)** (fortdauern) survive; last; (standhalten) hold one's own; **in einer Gefahr** *usw.* ~: prove oneself in a dangerous situation *etc.;* **(c) aus etw.** ~: consist of sth.; (aus einem Material) be made of sth.; **(d) ihre Aufgabe besteht in der Aufstellung der Liste** her task is to draw up the list; **der Unterschied besteht darin, dass ...:** the difference is that ...; **eine Möglichkeit besteht darin, zu beweisen ...:** one possibility would be to prove ...; **(e) auf etw. (Dat.)** ~: insist on sth.; **er bestand darauf, den Chef zu sprechen** he insisted on seeing the boss; **(f)** (die Prüfung ~) pass [the examination]. **2** *unr. tr. V.* pass ⟨*test, examination*⟩; **nach bestandener Prüfung** after passing one's examination

Bestehen *das;* **~s** existence; **die Firma feiert ihr 10jähriges ~:** the firm is celebrating its tenth anniversary; **seit ~ der Bundesrepublik** since the Federal Republic came into existence

*bestehen|bleiben ⇒ **bestehen 1 a**

bestehend *Adj.* existing; current ⟨*conditions*⟩

bestehlen *unr. tr. V.* rob

besteigen *unr. tr. V.* **(a)** climb; mount ⟨*horse, bicycle*⟩; ascend ⟨*throne*⟩; **(b)** (betreten) board ⟨*ship, aircraft*⟩; get on ⟨*bus, train*⟩

Besteigung *die* ascent

bestellen 1 *tr. V.* **(a)** order **(bei** from); **sich (Dat.) etw.** ~: order sth. [for oneself]; **würden Sie mir bitte ein Taxi ~?** would you order me a taxi?; **(b)** (reservieren lassen) reserve ⟨*table, tickets*⟩; **(c)** (kommen lassen) **jmdn. [für 10 Uhr] zu sich ~:** ask sb. to go/come to see one [at 10 o'clock]; **beim** *od.* **zum Arzt bestellt sein** have an appointment with the doctor; **(d)** (ausrichten) **jmdm. etw.** ~: pass on sth. to sb.; tell sb. sth.; **bestell ihm schöne Grüße von mir** give him my regards; **er lässt dir ~, dass ...:** he left a message [for you] that ...; **nichts/nicht viel zu ~ haben** have no say/little *or* not much say; **(e)** (ernennen) appoint **(zu, als** as); **(f)** (bearbeiten) cultivate, till ⟨*field*⟩; **(g) es ist um jmdn./etw.** *od.* **mit jmdm./etw. schlecht bestellt** sb./sth. is in a bad way; **mit seiner Gesundheit ist es schlecht bestellt** he is in poor health. **2** *itr. V.* order

Besteller *der;* ~s, ~: customer (*who has ordered sth.*)

Bestell-: **~nummer** *die* order number; **~schein** *der* order form

Bestellung *die* **(a)** order **(über + Akk.** for); (das Bestellen) ordering *no indef. art.;* **auf ~:** to order; **(b)** (Reservierung) reservation; **(c)** (das Ernennen) appointment; **(d)** (das Bearbeiten) cultivation; tilling

Bestell·zettel *der* order form

besten·falls *Adv.* at best

bestens *Adv.* excellently; extremely well; **sich ~ verstehen** get on splendidly; **jmdn. ~ grüßen** give sb. one's best wishes

besteuern *tr. V.* tax

Besteuerung *die* taxation

Best·form *die; o. Pl.* (Sport) best form; **in ~form** in top form

best·gehasst, *best·gehaßt *Adj.; nicht präd.* (ugs. iron.) most heartily disliked

bestialisch /bɛs'tja:lɪʃ/ **1** *Adj.* **(a)** bestial; **(b)** *nicht präd.* (ugs.: schrecklich) ghastly (coll.); awful (coll.). **2** *adv.* **(a)** in a bestial manner; **(b)** (ugs.: schrecklich) awfully (coll.); unbearably

Bestialität /bɛstjali'tɛ:t/ *die;* ~, **~en (a)** *o. Pl.* bestiality; **ein Verbrechen von solcher ~:** a crime of such a bestial nature *or* of such brutality; **(b)** (Tat) brutality; atrocity

besticken *tr. V.* embroider

Bestie /'bɛstiə/ *die;* ~, ~**n** (auch fig. abwertend) beast

bestimmbar *Adj.* ascertainable; (identifizierbar) identifiable; **nicht [genau]** ~ **sein** be impossible to ascertain/identify [precisely]

bestimmen 1 *tr. V.* **(a)** (festsetzen) decide on; fix ⟨*price, time, etc.*⟩; **jmdn. zum** *od.* **als Nachfolger** ~: decide on sb. as one's successor; (nennen) name sb. as one's successor; **(b)** (vorsehen) destine; intend; set aside ⟨*money*⟩; **das ist für dich bestimmt** that is meant for you; **er ist zu Höherem bestimmt** he is destined for higher things; **(c)** (ermitteln, definieren) identify ⟨*part of speech, find, plant, etc.*⟩; determine ⟨*age, position*⟩; define ⟨*meaning*⟩; **(d)** (prägen) determine the character of; give ⟨*landscape, townscape*⟩ its character. 2 *itr. V.* **(a)** make the decisions; **hier bestimme ich** I'm in charge *or* the boss here; my word goes around here; **(b)** (verfügen) **über jmdn.** ~: tell sb. what to do; **[frei] über etw.** *(Akk.)* ~: do as one wishes with sth.

bestimmend 1 *Adj.* decisive; determining. 2 *adv.* decisively

bestimmt 1 *Adj.* **(a)** *nicht präd.* (speziell) particular; (gewiss) certain; (genau) definite; **ich habe nichts Bestimmtes vor** I am not doing anything in particular; **(b)** (festgelegt) fixed; given ⟨*quantity*⟩; **(c)** (Sprachw.) definite ⟨*article etc.*⟩; **(d)** (entschieden) firm. 2 *adv.* (entschieden) firmly. 3 *Adv.* for certain; **du weißt es doch [ganz]** ~ **noch** I'm sure you must remember it; **ganz** ~, **ich komme** I'll definitely come; yes, certainly, I'll come; **ich habe das** ~ **liegen gelassen** I must have left it behind

Bestimmtheit *die;* ~ **(a)** (Entschiedenheit) firmness; (im Auftreten) decisiveness; **etw. mit aller** ~ **sagen/ablehnen** say sth. very firmly/reject sth. categorically; **(b)** (Gewissheit) **mit** ~: for certain

Bestimmung *die* **(a)** *o. Pl.* (das Festsetzen) fixing; **(b)** (Vorschrift) regulation; **gesetzliche** ~**en** legal requirements; **(c)** *o. Pl.* (Zweck) purpose; **eine Brücke** *usw.* **ihrer** ~ **übergeben** [officially] open a bridge *etc.;* **(d)** (das Ermitteln) identification; (eines Begriffs, der Bedeutung) definition; (des Alters, der Position) determination; **(e)** (Sprachw.) **adverbiale** ~: adverbial qualification

bestimmungs-, Bestimmungs-: ~**bahnhof** *der* (Eisenb.) destination; ~**gemäß** *Adv.* in accordance with the regulations *or* requirements [of the law]; ~**hafen** *der* [port of] destination; ~**ort** *der; Pl.* **-orte** destination

Best·leistung *die* (Sport) best performance; **persönliche** ~: personal best

best·möglich *Adj.* best possible; **das Bestmögliche tun** do the best one can

bestrafen *tr. V.* punish **(für, wegen** for); **es wird mit Gefängnis bestraft** it is punishable by imprisonment

Bestrafung *die;* ~, ~**en** punishment; (Rechtsw.) penalty

bestrahlen *tr. V.* **(a)** illuminate; floodlight ⟨*building*⟩; (scheinen auf) ⟨*sun etc.*⟩ shine on; **(b)** (Med.) treat ⟨*tumour, part of body*⟩ using radiotherapy; (mit Höhensonne) use sunlamp treatment on ⟨*part of body*⟩

Bestrahlung *die;* ~, ~**en** (Med.) radiation [treatment] *no indef. art.;* (mit Röntgenstrahlen) radiotherapy *no art.;* (mit Höhensonne) sunlamp treatment

Bestreben *das* endeavour[s *pl.*]

bestrebt *Adj.* ~ **sein, etw. zu tun** endeavour to do sth.

Bestrebung *die;* ~, ~**en** effort; (Versuch) attempt

bestreichen *unr. tr. V.* **A mit B** ~: spread B on A; **sein Brot mit Butter** ~: spread butter on one's bread; butter one's bread

bestreiken *tr. V.* take strike action against; **diese Firma wird bestreikt** there is a strike [on] at this firm

bestreitbar *Adj.* disputable; **es ist nicht** ~**[, dass ...]:** it is indisputable *or* cannot be denied [that ...]

bestreiten *unr. tr. V.* **(a)** dispute; contest; (leugnen) deny; **er bestreitet, dass ...:** he denies that ...; **es lässt sich nicht** ~, **dass ...:** it cannot be denied *or* there is no disputing that ...; **jmdm. das Recht auf etw.** *(Akk.)* ~:

dispute *or* challenge sb.'s right to sth.; **(b)** (finanzieren) finance ⟨*studies*⟩; pay for ⟨*studies, sb.'s keep, etc.*⟩; meet ⟨*costs, expenses*⟩; **(c)** (gestalten) carry ⟨*programme, conversation, etc.*⟩

bestreuen *tr. V.* etw. mit Zucker ~: sprinkle sth. with sugar; **einen Weg mit Sand/Salz** ~: scatter sand on a path/salt a path

Bestseller /'bɛstzɛlɐ/ *der;* ~**s**, ~: best seller

bestücken *tr. V.* fit; equip; (mit Waffen) arm; (mit Waren) stock [up]

Bestückung *die;* ~, ~**en** equipment; (mit Waffen) armament; (mit Waren) stocking

Bestuhlung *die;* ~, ~**en (a)** fitting of [the] seats (*Gen.* in); **(b)** (Stühle) seating

bestürmen *tr. V.* **(a)** storm; **(b)** (bedrängen) besiege **(mit** with)

bestürzen *tr. V.* dismay; (erschüttern) shake

bestürzend *Adj.* disturbing

bestürzt 1 *Adj.* dismayed **(über** + *Akk.* about). 2 *adv.* with dismay *or* consternation; **jmdn. [sehr]** ~ **ansehen** look at sb. in *or* with [great] consternation

Bestürzung *die;* ~: dismay; consternation; **mit** ~ **feststellen, dass ...:** find to one's consternation that ...

Best·zeit *die* (Sport) best time; **persönliche** ~**zeit** personal best [time]

Besuch /bə'zu:x/ *der;* ~**[e]s**, ~**e (a)** visit; **ein** ~ **bei jmdm.** a visit to sb.; (kurz) a call on sb.; ~ **eines Museums** *usw.* visit to a museum *etc.;* **bei seinem letzten** ~: on his last visit; ~ **von jmdm. bekommen** receive a visit from sb.; **ich bekomme gleich** ~: I've got visitors/a visitor coming any minute; **auf** *od.* **zu** ~ **kommen** come for a visit; (für länger) come to stay; **(b)** (das Besuchen) visiting; (Teilnahme) attendance (*Gen.* at); **(c)** (Gast) visitor; (Gäste) visitors *pl.*

besuchen *tr. V.* **(a)** visit ⟨*person*⟩; (weniger formell) go to see, call on ⟨*person*⟩; **(b)** visit ⟨*place*⟩; go to ⟨*exhibition, theatre, museum, etc.*⟩; (zur Besichtigung) go to see ⟨*church, exhibition, etc.*⟩; **die Schule/Universität** ~: go to *or* (formal) attend school/university

Besucher *der;* ~**s**, ~, **Besucherin** *die;* ~, ~**nen** visitor (*Gen* to); **die Besucher der Vorstellung** those attending the performance

Besuchs-: ~**erlaubnis** *die* visiting permit; ~**tag** *der* visiting day; ~**zeit** *die* visiting time *or* hours *pl.*

besucht *Adj.* **gut/schlecht** ~: well/poorly attended ⟨*lecture, performance, etc.*⟩; much/little frequented ⟨*restaurant etc.*⟩

besudeln *tr. V.* (geh. abwertend) besmirch; **jmds. Andenken/Namen** ~ (fig.) cast a slur on sb.'s memory/name

Beta /'be:ta/ *das;* ~**[s]**, ~**s** beta

Beta·blocker /-blɔkɐ/ *der;* ~**s**, ~ (Med.) betablocker

betagt /bə'ta:kt/ *Adj.* (geh.) elderly; (scherzh.) ancient ⟨*car etc.*⟩

betasten *tr. V.* feel [with one's fingers]

betätigen 1 *refl. V.* busy *or* occupy oneself; **sich politisch/literarisch/körperlich** ~: engage in political/literary/physical activity; **sich als etw.** ~: act as sth. 2 *tr. V.* operate ⟨*lever, switch, flush, etc.*⟩; apply ⟨*brake*⟩

Betätigung *die;* ~, ~**en (a)** activity; **(b)** *o. Pl.* (das Bedienen) operation; (einer Bremse) application

Betätigungs·feld *das* sphere of activity

betäuben /bə'tɔybn̩/ *tr. V.* **(a)** (Med.) anaesthetize; make numb, deaden ⟨*nerve*⟩; **jmdn. örtlich** ~: give sb. a local anaesthetic; **(b)** (unterdrücken) ease, deaden ⟨*pain*⟩; quell, still ⟨*unease, fear*⟩; **seinen Kummer mit Alkohol** ~ (fig.) drown one's sorrows [in drink]; **(c)** (benommen machen) daze; (mit einem Schlag) stun; **ein** ~**der Duft** a heady *or* intoxicating scent

Betäubung *die;* ~, ~**en (a)** (Med.) anaesthetization; (Narkose) anaesthesia; **(b)** (Benommenheit) daze

Betäubungs·mittel *das* narcotic; (Med.) anaesthetic

Betäubungsmittel·gesetz *das* narcotics law

Bete /'be:tə/ *die;* ~, ~**n** *in* **Rote** ~: beetroot (Brit.); [red] beet (Amer.)

beteiligen 1 *refl. V.* **sich an etw.** (*Dat.*) ∼: participate *or* take part in sth.; **er hat sich kaum an der Diskussion beteiligt** he took hardly any part in the discussion; **sich an einem Geschäft** ∼: take a share in *or* come in on a deal. **2** *tr. V.* **jmdn.** [**mit 10 %**] **an etw.** (*Dat.*) ∼: give sb. a [10 %] share of sth.

beteiligt *Adj.* (**a**) involved (**an** + *Dat.* in); (**b**) (finanziell) **an einem Unternehmen/am Gewinn** ∼ **sein** have a share in a business/in the profit; **er ist mit 20 000 DM** ∼: he has a 20,000 mark share

Beteiligte *der/die; adj. Dekl.* (**a**) person involved (**an** + *Dat.* in); (**b**) ⇒ **Teilnehmer**

Beteiligung *die;* ∼, ∼**en** (**a**) participation (**an** + *Dat.* in); (an einem Verbrechen) involvement (**an** + *Dat.* in); **unter** ∼ **von** with the participation of; (**b**) (Anteil) share (**an** + *Dat.* in)

beten /'beːtn̩/ **1** *itr. V.* pray (**für, um** for). **2** *tr. V.* say ⟨*prayer*⟩

beteuern /bəˈtɔyɐn/ *tr. V.* affirm; assert, protest ⟨*one's innocence*⟩

Beteuerung *die;* ∼, ∼**en** ⇒ **beteuern**: affirmation; assertion; protestation

betiteln /bəˈtiːtl̩n/ *tr. V.* (**a**) give ⟨*book etc.*⟩ a title; (**b**) ⇒ **titulieren**

Beton /beˈtɔŋ, *bes. österr.:* beˈtoːn/ *der;* ∼**s**, ∼**s** /beˈtɔŋs/ *od.* ∼**e** /beˈtoːnə/ concrete

Beton-: ∼**bau** *der; Pl.* ∼**bauten** concrete building; ∼**bunker** *der* (abwertend: ∼bau) concrete box

betonen /bəˈtoːnən/ *tr. V.* (**a**) stress ⟨*word, syllable*⟩; accent ⟨*syllable, beat*⟩; **ein Wort falsch** ∼: put the wrong stress on a word; (**b**) (hervorheben) emphasize; **die Taille** ∼: accentuate the waist

betonieren /betoni'rən/ *tr. V.* concrete; surface ⟨*road etc.*⟩ with concrete

Beton-: ∼**klotz** *der* (abwertend: massiver ∼bau) concrete monolith; ∼**kopf** *der* (abwertend) hardliner

betont /bəˈtoːnt/ **1** *Adj.* (**a**) stressed; accented; (**b**) (bewusst) pointed, studied; deliberate, studied ⟨*simplicity, elegance*⟩. **2** *adv.* pointedly; deliberately; **sich** ∼ **sportlich kleiden** wear clothes with a strong *or* pronounced sporting character; **sich** ∼ **zurückhaltend verhalten** behave with studied reserve

Betonung *die;* ∼, ∼**en** (**a**) *o. Pl.* stressing; accenting; (**b**) (Akzent) stress; accent (esp. Mus.); (Intonation) intonation; (**c**) *o. Pl.:* ⇒ **betonen b**; emphasis (*Gen.* on); accentuation

betören /bəˈtøːrən/ *tr. V.* (geh.) captivate; bewitch

betr. *Abk.* **betreffs, betrifft** re

Betr. *Abk.* **Betreff** re

Betracht /bəˈtraxt/ *in* **jmdn./etw. in** ∼ **ziehen** consider sb./sth.; **jmdn./etw. außer** ∼ **lassen** discount *or* disregard sb./sth.; **sie kommt/kommt nicht in** ∼: she can/cannot be considered

betrachten *tr. V.* (**a**) look at; **sich** (*Dat.*) **etw.** [**genau**] ∼: take a [close] look at sth.; watch *or* observe sth. [closely]; **sich im Spiegel** ∼: look at oneself in the mirror; (längere Zeit) contemplate oneself in the mirror; **genau/bei Licht betrachtet** (fig.) upon closer consideration/seen in the light of day; **objektiv betrachtet** viewed objectively; from an objective point of view; **so betrachtet** seen in this light *or* from this point of view; (**b**) **jmdn./etw. als etw.** ∼: regard sb./sth. as sth.

Betrachter *der;* ∼**s**, ∼: observer

beträchtlich /bəˈtrɛçtlɪç/ **1** *Adj.* considerable; **um ein Beträchtliches** to a considerable degree. **2** *adv.* considerably

Betrachtung *die;* ∼, ∼**en** (**a**) *o. Pl.* contemplation; (Untersuchung) examination; **bei genauer[er]** ∼: upon close[r] examination; (fig.) upon close[r] consideration; (**b**) (Überlegung) reflection; ∼**en über etw.** (*Akk.*) **anstellen** reflect on sth.

Betrachtungs·weise *die* way of looking at things

Betrag /bəˈtraːk/ *der;* ∼[**e**]**s**, **Beträge** /bəˈtrɛːgə/ sum; amount; ∼ **dankend erhalten** (auf Quittungen) received *or* paid with thanks

betragen **1** *unr. itr. V.* be; (bei Geldsummen) come to; amount to. **2** *unr. refl. V.* ⇒ **benehmen**

Betragen *das;* ∼**s** behaviour; (in der Schule) conduct

betrauen *tr. V.* **jmdn. mit etw.** ∼: entrust sb. with sth.; **jmdn. damit** ∼, **etw. zu tun** entrust sb. with the task of doing sth.

betrauern *tr. V.* mourn ⟨*death, loss*⟩; mourn for ⟨*person*⟩

Betreff /bəˈtrɛf/ *der;* ∼[**e**]**s**, ∼**e** (Amtsspr., Kaufmannsspr.) subject; matter; (∼zeile) heading; reference line; ∼: **Ihr Schreiben vom 26. d. M.** (im Brief) re: your letter of the 26th inst.

betreffen *unr. tr. V.* concern; ⟨*new rule, change, etc.*⟩ affect; **was mich betrifft, ...:** as far as I'm concerned ...; **was das betrifft, ...:** as regards that; as far as that goes

betreffend *Adj.* concerning; **der** ∼**e Sachbearbeiter** the person concerned with *or* dealing with this matter; **in dem** ∼**en Fall** in the case concerned *or* in question

Betreffende *der/die; adj. Dekl.* person concerned; **die** ∼**n** the people concerned

betreffs *Präp. mit Gen.* (Amtsspr., Kaufmannsspr.) concerning

betreiben *unr. tr. V.* (**a**) tackle ⟨*task*⟩; proceed with, (energisch) press ahead with ⟨*task, case, etc.*⟩; pursue ⟨*policy, studies*⟩; carry on ⟨*trade*⟩; **auf jmds./sein Betreiben** (*Akk.*) [**hin**] at the instigation of sb./at his instigation; (**b**) (führen) run ⟨*business, shop*⟩; **Radsport** ∼: go in for cycling as a sport; (**c**) (in Betrieb halten) operate (**mit** by); **die Kühlbox kannst du auch mit Gas** ∼: the fridge runs on *or* you can run the fridge on gas

betreten¹ *unr. tr. V.* (eintreten in) enter; (treten auf) walk *or* step on to; (begehen) walk on ⟨*carpet, grass, etc.*⟩; **er hat das Haus nie wieder** ∼: he never set foot in the house again; „**Betreten verboten**" 'Keep off'; (kein Eintritt) 'Keep out'; „**Betreten der Baustelle verboten**" 'Building site. No entry *or* Keep out'; **den Rasen nicht** ∼: keep off the grass; **jmds. Grundstück unerlaubt** ∼: trespass on sb.'s property

betreten² **1** *Adj.* embarrassed; **ein** ∼**es Gesicht machen** look embarrassed. **2** *adv.* with embarrassment

Betretenheit *die;* ∼: embarrassment

betreuen /bəˈtrɔyən/ *tr. V.* look after; care for ⟨*invalid*⟩; supervise ⟨*youth group*⟩; see to the needs of ⟨*tourists, sportsmen*⟩

Betreuer *der;* ∼**s**, ∼, **Betreuerin** *die;* ∼, ∼**nen** ⇒ **betreuen:** person who looks after/cares for/etc. others; (einer Jugendgruppe) supervisor

Betreuung *die;* ∼: care *no indef. art.;* **zwei Reiseleiter waren zu unserer** ∼ **vorhanden** there were two couriers *or* travel guides to see to our needs

Betrieb *der;* ∼[**e**]**s**, ∼**e** (**a**) business; (Firma) firm; **ein landwirtschaftlicher** ∼: an agricultural holding; **im** ∼ (am Arbeitsplatz) at work; (**b**) *o. Pl.* (das In-Funktion-Sein) operation; **in** ∼ **sein** be running; be in operation; **außer** ∼ **sein** not operate; (wegen Störung) be out of order; **in/außer** ∼ **setzen** start up/stop ⟨*machine etc.*⟩; **in** ∼ **nehmen** put into operation; put ⟨*bus, train*⟩ into service; **den** ∼ **einstellen** close down *or* cease operations; (in einer Fabrik) stop work; **den** [**ganzen**] ∼ **aufhalten** (ugs.) hold everybody up; (**c**) *o. Pl.* (ugs.: Treiben) bustle; commotion; (Verkehr) traffic; **es herrscht großer** ∼: it's very busy

betrieblich *Adj.; nicht präd.* firm's; company

betriebsam **1** *Adj.* busy; (ständig) ∼ constantly on the go *postpos.* **2** *adv.* busily

Betriebsamkeit *die;* ∼: [bustling] activity; **eine hektische** ∼ **an den Tag legen** become frantically busy

betriebs-, Betriebs-: ∼**angehörige** *der/die* employee; ∼**an·leitung** *die* operating instructions *pl.*; (Heft) instruction manual; ∼**aus·flug** *der* staff outing; ∼**blind** *Adj.* inured to the shortcomings of working methods *postpos.*; professionally blinkered; ∼**blind werden** get into a rut *or* become blinkered in one's work; ∼**eigen** *Adj.* company-owned; ∼**ferien** *Pl.* firm's annual close-down *sing.*; „**Wegen** ∼**ferien geschlossen**" 'closed for annual holidays'; ∼**fest** *das* firm's party; ∼**frieden** *der* harmonious relationship between employer and employed (*which all parties are obliged to uphold*); industrial peace; ∼**geheimnis** *das* company secret; trade secret (also fig.); ∼**gruppe** *die* trade union membership (*within the company*); ∼**intern** 1 *Adj.* internal; internal company *attrib.;* 2 *adv.* internally; within the company; ∼**klima** *das* working atmosphere; ∼**kosten** *Pl.* running costs; (einer Firma) operating costs; ∼**leiter** *der* manager; (einer Fabrik) works manager; ∼**leitung** *die* management [of the firm]; ∼**prüfung** *die* audit of a/the firm's accounts (*by the tax authorities*); ∼**rat** *der* (**a**) works committee; (**b**) (Person) member of a/the works committee; ∼**rente** *die* company pension; ∼**ruhe** *die;* ∼**ruhe haben** ⟨*business, factory*⟩ be closed; ∼**stilllegung** *die* closure [of a/the firm]; (eines Werks) works closure; ∼**system** *das* (DV) operating system; ∼**unfall** *der* (veralt.) industrial accident; ∼**vereinbarung** *die agreement between 'Betriebsrat' and management;* ∼**verfassungs·gesetz** *das* industrial relations law (*for the private sector*); ∼**versammlung** *die* meeting of the workforce; ∼**wirt** *der* graduate in business management; ∼**wirtschaft** *die; o. Pl.* business management; ∼**wirtschaftlich** *Adj.* business management *attrib.;* ∼**wirtschafts·lehre** *die; o. Pl.* [theory of] business management; (Fach) management studies *sing., no art.*

betrinken *unr. refl. V.* get drunk; **sich fürchterlich/sinnlos** ∼: get terribly/blind drunk

betroffen /bəˈtrɔfn̩/ 1 *Adj.* upset; (bestürzt) dismayed. 2 *adv.* in dismay *or* consternation; ∼ **schweigen** be too upset/dismayed to say anything

Betroffene *der/die; adj. Dekl.* person affected; **die von ... ∼n** those affected by ...

Betroffenheit *die;* ∼: dismay; consternation

betrüben *tr. V.* sadden

betrüblich *Adj.* gloomy; (deprimierend) depressing

betrübt /bəˈtryːpt/ 1 *Adj.* sad (**über** + *Akk.* about); (deprimiert) dismayed, depressed (**über** + *Akk.* about); gloomy ⟨*face etc.*⟩. 2 **sadly**; (schwermütig) gloomily

Betrug *der;* ∼**[e]s** deception; (Mogelei) cheating *no indef. art.;* (Rechtsw.) fraud; **das ist [glatter]** ∼: that's [plain] fraud/cheating

betrügen 1 *unr. tr. V.* deceive; be unfaithful to ⟨*husband, wife*⟩; (Rechtsw.) defraud; (beim Spielen) cheat; **sich selbst** ∼: deceive oneself; **jmdn. um 100 DM** ∼: cheat *or* (coll.) do sb. out of 100 marks; (arglistig) swindle sb. out of 100 marks. 2 *unr. itr. V.* cheat; (bei Geschäften) swindle people

Betrüger *der;* ∼**s,** ∼: swindler; (Hochstapler) con man (coll.); (beim Spielen) cheat

Betrügerei *die;* ∼, ∼**en** deception; (beim Spielen usw.) cheating; (bei Geschäften) swindling

Betrügerin *die;* ∼, ∼**nen** swindler; (beim Spielen) cheat

betrügerisch *Adj.* deceitful; (Rechtsw.) fraudulent

betrunken /bəˈtrʊŋkn̩/ *Adj.* drunken *attrib.;* drunk *pred.*

Betrunkene *der/die; adj. Dekl.* drunk; **eine** ∼: a drunken woman

Bett /bɛt/ *das;* ∼**[e]s,** ∼**en** (**a**) bed; **die** ∼**en machen** *od.* (ugs. scherzh.) bauen make the beds; **jmdm. das Frühstück ans** ∼ **bringen** bring sb. breakfast in bed; **jmdn. aus dem** ∼ **holen** (ugs.) get sb. out of bed; **er kommt nur schwer aus dem** ∼: he doesn't like getting up; **im** ∼: in bed; **ins** ∼ *od.* **zu** ∼ **gehen, sich ins** *od.* **zu** ∼ **legen** go to bed; **ins** ∼ **fallen** (ugs.) fall into bed; **die Kinder ins** ∼ **bringen** put the children to bed; **das** ∼ **hüten [müssen]** (fig.) [have to] stay in bed; **mit jmdm. ins** ∼ **gehen** *od.* **steigen** (fig. ugs.) go to bed with sb.; (**b**) (Feder∼) duvet; (**c**) (Fluss∼) bed

Bet·tag *der* ⇒ **Buß- und Bettag**

Bett-: ∼**bezug** *der* duvet cover; ∼**couch** *die* bed-settee; studio couch; ∼**decke** *die* blanket; (gesteppt) [continental] quilt; (Federbett) duvet

Bettel /ˈbɛtl̩/ *der;* ∼**s** (ugs.) junk (coll.)

bettel·arm *Adj.* destitute; penniless

Bettelei *die;* ∼, ∼**en** begging *no art.*

Bettel·mönch *der* mendicant friar

betteln /ˈbɛtl̩n/ *itr. V.* beg (**um** for); „Betteln verboten!" 'No begging'; **bei jmdm. um etw.** ∼: beg sb. for sth.

Bettel-: ∼**orden** *der* mendicant order; ∼**stab** *der in* **jmdn. an den** ∼**stab bringen** reduce sb. to penury

betten (geh.) 1 *tr. V.* lay; **jmdn. flach** ∼: lay sb. [down] flat. 2 *refl. V.* (fig.) **wie man sich bettet, so liegt man** as you make your bed, so you must lie on it

bett-, Bett-: ∼**hupferl** /∼hʊpfɐl/ *das;* ∼**s,** ∼[**n**]: bedtime treat; ∼**kante** *die* edge of the bed; ∼**kasten** *der* bedding box (under a bed); ∼**lägerig** /∼lɛːɡərɪç/ *Adj.* bedridden; ∼**laken** *das* sheet; ∼**lektüre** *die* bedtime reading *no indef. art.*

Bettler /ˈbɛtlɐ/ *der;* ∼**s,** ∼: beggar

Bettlerin *die;* ∼, ∼**nen** beggar [woman]

Bett-: ∼**nässer** *der;* ∼**s,** ∼: bed-wetter; ∼**pfanne** *die* bedpan; ∼**ruhe** *die* bed rest; ∼**tuch** *das* sheet

*****Bettuch** ⇒ **Betttuch**

Bett-: ∼**vorleger** *der* bedside rug; ∼**wäsche** *die* bedlinen; ∼**zeug** *das; o. Pl.* (ugs.) bedclothes *pl.*

betucht /bəˈtuːxt/ *Adj.* (ugs.) [**gut**] ∼: well-heeled (coll.); well-off

betulich /bəˈtuːlɪç/ 1 *Adj.* (**a**) fussy; (**b**) (gemächlich) leisurely; unhurried. 2 *adv.* (**a**) fussily; (**b**) (gemächlich) in a calm unhurried way

Betulichkeit *die;* ∼ (**a**) fussiness; (Besorgtheit) agitation; (**b**) (Gemächlichkeit) calm unhurried manner

betupfen *tr. V.* dab

Beuge /ˈbɔʏɡə/ *die;* ∼, ∼**n** (einer Gliedmaße) crook; **in der** ∼ **des linken Arms** in the crook of his/her *etc.* left arm

beugen 1 *tr. V.* (**a**) bend; bow ⟨*head*⟩; **den Rumpf** ∼: bend from the waist; **gebeugt gehen** walk with a stoop; **vom Alter/vom Kummer gebeugt** (geh.) bent *or* bowed with age *postpos.*/bowed down with grief *postpos.*; (**b**) (geh.: brechen) **jmdn.** ∼: break sb.'s resistance; **jmds. Starrsinn/Stolz** ∼: break sb.'s stubborn/proud nature; (**c**) (Sprachw.) ⇒ **flektieren** 1; (**d**) (Rechtsw.) bend ⟨*law*⟩; **das Recht** ∼: pervert the course of justice. 2 *refl. V.* (**a**) bend over; (sich bücken) stoop; **sich nach vorn/hinten** ∼: bend forwards/bend over backwards; **sich aus dem Fenster** ∼: lean out of the window; (**b**) (sich fügen) give way; give in; **sich der Mehrheit** ∼: bow to the will of the majority

Beugung *die;* ∼, ∼**en** (**a**) bending; (**b**) (Sprachw.) ⇒ **Flexion**

Beule /ˈbɔʏlə/ *die;* ∼, ∼**n** bump; (Vertiefung) dent; (eiternd) boil

beulen *itr. V.* bulge

beunruhigen /bəˈ|ʊnruːɪɡn̩/ 1 *tr. V.* worry; **es beunruhigte ihn sehr** it made him very worried; **über etw.** (*Akk.*) **beunruhigt sein** be worried about sth. 2 *refl. V.* worry (**um, wegen** about)

Beunruhigung *die;* ∼, ∼**en** worry; concern

beurkunden /bəˈ|uːɐkʊndn̩/ *tr. V.* record; (belegen) document, provide a record of

beurlauben /bəˈ|uːɐlaʊbn̩/ *tr. V.* (**a**) jmdn. [**für zwei Tage**] ∼: give sb. [two days'] leave of absence; **sich** ∼ **lassen** obtain leave of absence; (**b**) (suspendieren) suspend

Beurlaubung *die;* ∼, ∼**en** (**a**) leave of absence *no indef. art.;* (**b**) (Suspendierung) suspension

beurteilen *tr. V.* judge; assess ⟨*situation etc.*⟩; **etw. falsch** ∼: misjudge sth./assess sth. wrongly

Beurteilung *die;* ∼, ∼**en** (**a**) judgement; (einer Lage usw.) assessment; (**b**) (Gutachten) assessment

Beute /ˈbɔʏtə/ *die;* ∼, ∼**n** (**a**) (Gestohlenes) haul; loot *no indef. art.;* (Kriegs∼) booty; spoils *pl.;* **fette** ∼ **machen** get rich pickings *pl.;* (**b**) (eines Tiers) prey; (eines Jägers) bag; [**seine**] ∼ **schlagen** catch its prey; (**c**) (geh.: Opfer) prey (+ *Gen.* to); **eine** ∼ **der Flammen werden** be consumed by the flames

Beutel /ˈbɔʏtl̩/ *der;* ∼**s,** ∼ (**a**) bag; (kleiner, für Tabak usw.) pouch; (**b**) (ugs.: Geld∼) purse; (**c**) (Zool.) pouch

beuteln *tr. V.* (**a**) (südd., österr.: schütteln) shake; (**b**) **das Leben hat ihn gebeutelt** (fig.) life has given him some hard knocks

Beutel-: ∼**ratte** *die* opossum; ∼**schneider** *der* (veralt., geh.: Nepper) shark; racketeer; ∼**tier** *das* marsupial

---

bevölkern /bə'fœlkɐn/ **1** *tr. V.* populate; inhabit; (fig.) fill; invade; **ein stark/dünn** *od.* **wenig bevölkertes Land** a densely/thinly *or* sparsely populated country. **2** *refl. V.* become populated; ‹*bar, restaurant, etc.*› fill up

Bevölkerung *die;* ~, ~**en** population; (Volk) people

Bevölkerungs-: ~**dichte** *die* population density; ~**explosion** *die* population explosion; ~**schicht** *die* section *or* stratum of society

bevollmächtigen /bə'fɔlmɛçtɪgn̩/ *tr. V.* **jmdn. [dazu]** ~, **etw. zu tun** authorize sb. to do sth.; (in Rechtshandlungen) give sb. power of attorney to do sth.

Bevollmächtigte *der/die; adj. Dekl.* authorized representative

Bevollmächtigung *die;* ~, ~**en** authorization; (Rechtsw.) power of attorney

bevor /bə'fo:ɐ̯/ *Konj.* before; ~ **du nicht unterschrieben hast** until you sign/have signed

bevormunden *tr. V.* **jmdn.** ~: impose one's will on sb.; **bevormundet werden** be dictated to

Bevormundung *die;* ~, ~**en** imposing one's will (+ *Gen.* on); **wie kann sie sich diese** ~ **durch ihre Eltern gefallen lassen?** how can she put up with her parents telling her what to do?

bevor|stehen *unr. itr. V.* be near; be about to happen; (unmittelbar) be imminent; **mir steht etwas Unangenehmes bevor** there's something unpleasant in store for me

bevorstehend *Adj.* forthcoming; (unmittelbar) imminent

bevorzugen /bə'fo:ɐ̯tsu:gn̩/ *tr. V.* **(a)** prefer (**vor** + *Dat.* to); **(b)** (begünstigen) favour; give preference *or* preferential treatment to (**vor** + *Dat.* over)

bevorzugt 1 *Adj.* favoured; preferential ‹*treatment*›; (privilegiert) privileged. **2** *adv.* **jmdn.** ~ **behandeln** give sb. preferential treatment; **jmdn.** ~ **abfertigen** give sb. priority *or* precedence

Bevorzugung *die;* ~, ~**en** preferenzial treatment; preference (+ *Gen.*, **von** for)

bewachen *tr. V.* guard; (Ballspiele) mark; **bewachter Parkplatz** car park with an attendant

Bewacher *der;* ~**s**, ~: guard; (Ballspiele) marker

bewachsen *unr. tr. V.* grow over; cover; **mit Efeu** ~: overgrown with ivy *postpos.;* ivy-covered

Bewachung *die;* ~: guarding; (Ballspiele) marking; **unter scharfer** ~: closely guarded; **jmdn. unter** ~ **stellen** put sb. under guard

bewaffnen /bə'vafnən/ **1** *tr. V.* arm; **ein Heer [neu]** ~: supply an army with [new] weapons. **2** *refl. V.* (auch fig.) arm oneself

bewaffnet *Adj.* (auch fig.) armed

Bewaffnete *der/die; adj. Dekl.* armed man/woman/person

Bewaffnung *die;* ~, ~**en** **(a)** arming; **(b)** (Waffen) weapons *pl.*

bewahren *tr. V.* **(a) jmdn. vor etw.** (*Dat.*) ~: protect *or* preserve sb. from sth.; **[Gott** *od.* **i] bewahre!** good Lord, no!; (Gott behüte) God forbid!; **(b)** (erhalten) **seine Fassung** *od.* **Haltung** ~: keep *or* retain one's composure; **Stillschweigen/Treue** ~: remain silent/faithful; **sich** (*Dat.*) **etw.** ~: retain *or* preserve sth.; **etw. im Gedächtnis** ~ (fig. geh.) preserve the memory of sth.

bewähren *refl. V.* prove oneself/itself; prove one's/its worth; **sich als [guter] Freund** ~: prove to be a [good] friend; **sich im Leben** ~: make a success of one's life; **sich gut/schlecht** ~: prove/not prove to be worthwhile *or* a success

bewahrheiten /bə'va:ɐ̯haitn̩/ *refl. V.* prove to be true

bewährt *Adj.* proven ‹*method, design, etc.*›; well-tried, tried and tested ‹*recipe, cure*›; reliable ‹*worker*›

Bewährung *die;* ~, ~**en** (Rechtsw.) probation; **3 Monate Gefängnis mit** ~: three months suspended sentence [with probation]; **eine Strafe zur** ~ **aussetzen** [conditionally] suspend a sentence on probation

Bewährungs-: ~**auf·lage** *die* (Rechtsw.) *obligation imposed as a condition of sentence being suspended*; ~**frist** *die* period of probation; ~**helfer** *der* probation officer

bewaldet /bə'valdət/ *Adj.* wooded

Bewaldung *die;* ~, ~**en** tree cover; (Wälder) woodlands *pl.*

bewältigen /bə'vɛltɪgn̩/ *tr. V.* deal with; cope with; overcome ‹*difficulty, problem*›; cover ‹*distance*›; (innerlich verarbeiten) get over ‹*experience*›

Bewältigung *die;* ~, ~**en** ⇨ **bewältigen:** coping with; overcoming; covering; getting over; **zur** ~ **der Arbeit** *usw.* to deal *or* cope with the work *etc.*

bewandert /bə'vandɐt/ *Adj.* well-versed; knowledgeable; **auf einem Gebiet/in etw.** (*Dat.*) ~ **sein** be well-versed *or* well up in a subject/in sth.

Bewandtnis /bə'vantnɪs/ *die;* ~, ~**se: mit etw. hat es [s]eine eigene/besondere** ~: there's a particular explanation for sth. *or* a [special] story behind sth.; **damit hat es folgende** ~: the story behind *or* reason for it is this

bewässern *tr. V.* irrigate

Bewässerung *die;* ~, ~**en** irrigation

Bewässerungs-: ~**an·lage** *die* irrigation system; (für Grünflächen usw.) watering system; ~**graben** *der* irrigation ditch; ~**kanal** *der* irrigation channel; ~**system** *das* irrigation system

bewegbar *Adj.* movable

bewegen[1] /bə've:gn̩/ **1** *tr. V.* **(a)** move; **etw. von der Stelle** ~: move *or* shift sth. [from the spot]; **(b)** (ergreifen) move; **eine** ~**de Rede** a moving speech; **(c)** (innerlich beschäftigen) preoccupy; **das bewegt mich schon lange** I have been preoccupied with this *or* this has exercised my mind for a long time. **2** *refl. V.* **(a)** move; **(b)** (ugs.: sich Bewegung verschaffen) **ich muss mich ein bisschen** ~: I must get some exercise; **du solltest/musst dich mehr** ~: you ought to/must take more exercise; **(c) seine Ausführungen** ~ **sich in der gleichen Richtung** (fig.) his comments have the same drift *or* are on the same lines; **(d)** (sich verhalten) behave

bewegen[2] *unr. tr. V.* **jmdn. dazu** ~, **etw. zu tun** ‹*thing*› make sb. do sth., induce sb. to do sth.; ‹*person*› prevail upon *or* persuade sb. to do sth.; **jmdn. zur Teilnahme** ~ ‹*person*› talk sb. into taking part; ‹*thing*› make sb. take part; induce sb. to take part

Beweg·grund *der* motive

beweglich *Adj.* **(a)** movable; moving ‹*target*›; **seine** ~**e Habe** one's goods and chattels *pl.;* one's personal effects *pl.;* ~**e Feste** movable feasts; **etw. ist leicht/schwer** ~: sth. is easy/difficult to move; **(b)** (rege) agile, active ‹*mind*›; **geistig** ~ **sein** be nimble-minded; have an agile mind

Beweglichkeit *die;* ~ **(a)** mobility; **(b)** (Regheit) agility

bewegt /bə've:kt/ *Adj.* **(a)** eventful; (unruhig) turbulent; **ein** ~**es Leben** an eventful/turbulent life; **(b)** (gerührt) moved *pred.;* *emotional ‹words, voice›;* **mit tief** ~**en Worten/** ~**er Stimme** in words/a voice heavy with emotion; **(c)** (unruhig) **leicht/stark** ~ ‹*sea*› slightly choppy/very rough

Bewegung *die;* ~, ~**en (a)** movement; (bes. Technik, Physik) motion; **in** ~ **sein** ‹*person*› be on the move; ‹*thing*› be in motion; **eine Maschine in** ~ **setzen** start [up] a machine; **sich in** ~ **setzen** ‹*train etc.*› start to move; ‹*procession*› move off; ‹*person*› get moving; **(b)** (körperliche ~) exercise; **(c)** (Ergriffenheit) emotion; **(d)** (Bestreben, Gruppe) movement

bewegungs-, Bewegungs-: ~**freiheit** *die; o. Pl.* freedom of movement; ~**los 1** *Adj.* motionless; **vor Schreck** ~**los** paralysed with fright; **2** *adv.* without moving; ~**los liegen/sitzen/stehen** lie/sit/stand motionless; ~**unfähig** *Adj.* unable to move *postpos.;* (gelähmt) paralysed; ‹*vehicle*› immobilized

beweih·räuchern /bə'vai̯rɔyçɐn/ *tr. V.* surround with incense; (fig. abwertend) idolize; **sich selbst** ~: sing one's own praises

Beweis /bə'vai̯s/ *der;* ~**es**, ~**e** proof (*Gen.*, **für** of); (Zeugnis) evidence; **einen** ~/~**e für etw. haben** have proof/evidence of sth.; **als** *od.* **zum** ~ **seiner Aussage/Theorie** to substantiate *or* in support of his statement/theory; **aus Mangel an** ~**en** owing to lack of evidence;

jmdm. einen ~ seines Vertrauens/seiner Hochachtung geben give sb. a token of one's trust/esteem
Beweis-: ~**antrag** der (Rechtsw.) application to produce evidence; ~**aufnahme** die (Rechtsw.) hearing of [the] evidence
beweisbar Adj. provable; susceptible of proof postpos.
beweisen 1 unr. tr. V. (a) prove; (b) (zeigen) show. **2** unr. refl. V. prove oneself or one's worth (**vor** + Dat. to)
Beweis-: ~**führung** die (a) (Rechtsw.) presentation of the evidence or case; (b) (Argumentation) reasoning; argumentation; ~**last** die; o. Pl. (Rechtsw.) (a) (Beweispflicht) burden of proof; (b) (Nachteil) disadvantage due to one's inability to prove a fact material to one's case; ~**material** das evidence; ~**mittel** das (Rechtsw.) form of evidence
bewenden unr. V. es bei od. mit etw. ~ lassen content oneself with sth.
bewerben 1 unr. refl. V. apply (**um** for); **sich bei einer Firma** usw. ~: apply to a company etc. [for a job]; **sich als Buchhalter** usw. ~: apply for a job as a bookkeeper etc. **2** unr. tr. V. advertise; promote
Bewerber der; ~s, ~, **Bewerberin** die; ~, ~**nen** applicant
Bewerbung die application (**um** for)
Bewerbungs-: ~**schreiben** das letter of application; ~**unterlagen** Pl. documents in support of an/the application
bewerfen unr. tr. V. jmdn./etw. mit etw. ~: throw sth. at sb./sth.; jmdn. mit [faulen] Eiern ~: pelt sb. with [rotten] eggs
bewerkstelligen /bə'vɛrkʃtɛlɪgn̩/ tr. V. manage
bewerten tr. V. assess; rate; (dem Geldwert nach) value (**mit** at); (Schulw., Sport) mark; grade (Amer.); **einen Aufsatz mit [der Note] „gut"** ~: mark or (Amer.) grade an essay 'good'
Bewertung die (a) ⇒ **bewerten:** assessment; valuation; marking; grading (Amer.); (b) (Note) mark; grade (Amer.)
Bewertungs·maß·stab der criterion of assessment
bewilligen /bə'vɪlɪgn̩/ tr. V. grant; award ‹salary, grant›; (im Parlament usw.) approve ‹sum, tax increase, etc.›
Bewilligung die; ~, ~**en** granting; (Zustimmung) approval; (eines Gehalts, Stipendiums) award
bewirken tr. V. bring about; cause; ~, **dass etw. geschieht** cause sth. to happen; **das bewirkt bei ihm nichts/das Gegenteil** it has no effect/the opposite effect on him
bewirten /bə'vɪrtn̩/ tr. V. feed; jmdn. mit etw. ~: serve sth. to sb.; serve sb. sth.
bewirtschaften tr. V. (a) run, manage ‹estate, farm, restaurant, business, etc.›; (b) (bestellen) farm ‹fields, land›; cultivate ‹field›
Bewirtung die; ~, ~**en** provision of food and drink; **die ~ der Gäste** catering for the guests
bewog /bə'vo:k/ 1. u. 3. Pers. Sg. Prät. v. **bewegen²**
bewohnbar Adj. habitable
bewohnen tr. V. inhabit, live in ‹house, area›; live in ‹room, flat›; live on ‹floor, storey›; ‹animal, plant› be found in
Bewohner der; ~s, ~, **Bewohnerin** die; ~, ~**nen** (eines Hauses, einer Wohnung) occupant; (einer Stadt, eines Gebietes) inhabitant; **ein ~ des Waldes** a forest-dweller; (Tier) a woodland creature
bewohnt Adj. occupied ‹house etc.›; inhabited ‹area›; **ist das Haus noch ~?** is the house still lived in or occupied?
bewölken /bə'vœlkn̩/ refl. V. cloud over; become overcast
bewölkt Adj. cloudy; overcast; **dicht** od. **stark** ~: heavily overcast; **der Himmel ist nur leicht** ~: there is only a light cloud cover
Bewölkung die; ~, ~**en** (a) o. Pl. clouding over; (b) (Wolkendecke) cloud [cover]; **wechselnde** ~: variable amounts pl. of cloud
Bewunderer der; ~s, ~, **Bewunderin** die; ~, ~**nen** admirer

bewundern tr. V. admire (**wegen, für** for)
bewunderns·wert 1 Adj. admirable; worthy of admiration postpos. **2** adv. admirably; in an admirable fashion
Bewunderung die; ~: admiration
bewunderungs·würdig ⇒ **bewundernswert**
bewusst, *bewußt /bə'vʊst/ **1** Adj. (a) conscious ‹reaction, behaviour, etc.›; (absichtlich) deliberate ‹lie, deception, attack, etc.›; jmdm./sich etw. ~ **machen** make sb. realize sth./realize sth.; **etw. ist/wird jmdm.** ~: sb. is/becomes aware of sth.; sb. realizes sth.; (b) (denkend) **ein** ~**er Mensch** a thinking person; **sich** (Dat.) **einer Sache** (Gen.) ~ **sein/werden** be/become aware or conscious of something; (c) nicht präd. (bekannt) particular; (fraglich) in question postpos. **2** adv. consciously; (absichtlich) deliberately; ~**er leben** live with greater awareness
bewusst·los, *bewußt·los Adj. unconscious
Bewusstlosigkeit, *Bewußtlosigkeit die; ~: unconsciousness; **bis zur** ~ (ugs.) ad nauseam
***bewußt|machen** ⇒ **bewusst 1 a**
Bewusst·sein, *Bewußt·sein das (a) (deutliches Wissen) awareness; **etw. mit** ~ **erleben** be fully aware of sth. [one is experiencing]; **jetzt erst kam ihr zu** ~, **dass** ...: only now did she realize that ...; (b) (geistige Klarheit) consciousness; **das** ~ **verlieren** lose consciousness; **wieder zu** ~ **kommen, das** ~ **wiedererlangen** regain consciousness; **bei [vollem]** ~ **sein** be [fully] conscious
bewusstseins-, *bewußtseins-, Bewusstseins-, *Bewußtseins-: ~**erweiternd 1** Adj. mind-expanding; psychedelic; **2** adv. ~**erweiternd wirken** have a mind-expanding effect; ~**spaltung** die (Med., Psych.) split consciousness; schizophrenia
bez. Abk. bezahlt pd.
bezahlbar Adj. affordable
bezahlen 1 tr. V. ▶216 | pay ‹person, bill, taxes, rent, amount›; pay for ‹goods etc.›; jmdm. etw. ~: pay for sth. for sb.; **bekommst du das Essen bezahlt?** do you get your meals paid for?; **gut bezahlt** well-paid; **bezahlter Urlaub** paid leave; holiday[s] with pay; **er musste seinen Leichtsinn teuer** ~ (fig.) he had to pay dearly for his carelessness; **das macht sich bezahlt** it pays off. **2** itr. V. ▶216 | pay; **Herr Ober, ich möchte** ~ od. **bitte** ~: waiter, the bill or (Amer.) check please
Bezahlung die payment; (Lohn, Gehalt) pay; **die ~ der Waren** the payment for the goods; **gegen** ~ ‹work› for payment or money
bezähmen 1 tr. V. contain, control ‹wrath, curiosity, impatience›; restrain ‹desire›. **2** refl. V. restrain oneself
bezaubern tr. V. enchant; **von etw. bezaubert** enchanted with or by sth.
bezaubernd 1 Adj. enchanting. **2** adv. enchantingly
bezeichnen tr. V. (a) jmdn./sich/etw. als etw. ~: call sb./oneself/sth. sth.; describe sb./oneself/sth. as sth.; **wie bezeichnet man das?** what is it called?; **mit dem Wort bezeichnet man eine Art Jacke** this word is used to denote or describe a kind of jacket; (b) (Name sein für) denote; (c) (markieren) mark; (durch Zeichen angeben) indicate
bezeichnend Adj. characteristic, typical (**für** of); (bedeutsam) significant
bezeichnender·weise Adv. characteristically; typically
Bezeichnung die (a) o. Pl. marking; (Angabe durch Zeichen) indication; (b) (Name) name; **mir fällt die richtige ~ dafür nicht ein** I can't think of the right word for it/them
bezeugen tr. V. testify to; ~, **dass** ...: testify that ...
bezichtigen /bə'tsɪçtɪgn̩/ tr. V. accuse; jmdn. des Verrats ~: accuse sb. of treachery; jmdn. ~, etw. getan zu haben accuse sb. of having done sth.
Bezichtigung die; ~, ~**en** accusation
beziehbar Adj. (a) ‹flat, house, etc.› ready for occupation; (b) auf jmdn./etw. ~: applicable to sb./sth. postpos.
beziehen 1 unr. tr. V. (a) cover, put a cover/covers on ‹seat, cushion, umbrella, etc.›; **die Betten frisch** ~: put

clean sheets on the beds; **das Sofa ist mit Leder bezogen** the sofa is upholstered in leather; **(b)** (einziehen in) move into ⟨*house, office*⟩; **(c)** (Milit.) take up ⟨*position, post*⟩; **einen klaren Standpunkt ~** (fig.) adopt a clear position; take a definite stand; **(d)** (erhalten) receive, obtain [one's supply of] ⟨*goods*⟩; take ⟨*newspaper*⟩; draw, receive ⟨*pension, salary*⟩; **Prügel ~** (ugs.) get a hiding (coll.); **(e)** (in Beziehung setzen) apply **(auf** + *Akk.* to); **etw. auf sich** (*Akk.*) **~:** take sth. personally; **bezogen auf jmdn./etw.** [seen] in relation to sb./sth. **2** *unr. refl. V.* **(a) es/der Himmel bezieht sich** it/the sky is clouding over *or* becoming overcast; **(b) sich auf jmdn./etw. ~** ⟨*person, letter, etc.*⟩ refer to sb./sth.; ⟨*question, statement, etc.*⟩ relate to sb./sth.; **wir ~ uns auf Ihr Schreiben vom 28. 8. und ...:** with reference to your letter of 28 August, we ...

Bezieher *der;* ~**s**, ~, **Bezieherin** *die;* ~, ~**nen** (einer Zeitung) subscriber (*Gen.*, **von** to); (einer Rente, eines Gehalts) recipient

Beziehung *die* **(a)** relation; (Zusammenhang) connection (**zu** with); **gute ~en** *od.* **eine gute ~ zu jmdm. haben** have good relations with sb.; be on good terms with sb.; **~en haben** (gewisse Leute kennen) have [got] connections; **etw. durch ~en bekommen** get sth. through connections; **seine ~en spielen lassen** pull some strings; **zu jmdm. keine ~ haben** be unable to relate to sb.; **er hat keine ~ zur Kunst** he has a blind spot where the arts are concerned; the arts are a closed book to him; **zwischen A und B besteht keine ~/eine ~:** there is no/a connection between A and B; **A zu B in ~** (*Akk.*) **setzen** relate A to B; see A in relation to B; **A und B in ~** (*Akk.*) **zueinander setzen** relate A and B to each other; connect *or* link A and B; **(b)** (Freundschaft, Liebes~) relationship; **(c)** (Hinsicht) respect; **in mancher ~:** in many respects

beziehungs-, Beziehungs-: ~**kiste** *die* (ugs.) relationship; ~**los 1** *Adj.* unconnected; unrelated; **2** *adv.* without any connection; ~**reich** *Adj.* evocative; rich in associations *postpos.*; ~**weise** *Konj.* **(a)** and ... respectively; (oder) or; **die beiden Münzen waren aus Kupfer ~weise aus Nickel** the two coins were made of copper and of nickel respectively; **(b)** (ugs.: oder vielmehr) that is; or; to be precise

beziffern /bə'tsɪfən/ **1** *tr. V.* **(a)** (nummerieren) number; **(b)** (angeben) estimate **(auf** + *Akk.* at). **2** *refl. V.* **sich auf 10 Millionen** (*Akk.*) **DM ~:** come *or* amount to 10 million marks

Bezirk /bə'tsɪrk/ *der;* ~**[e]s**, ~**e** district

*bezug /bə'tsuːk/ ⇨ **Bezug d**

Bezug *der* **(a)** (für Kissen usw.) cover; (für Polstermöbel) loose cover; slip cover (Amer.); (für Betten) duvet cover; (für Kopfkissen) pillowcase; **(b)** *o. Pl.* (Erwerb) obtaining; (Kauf) purchase; **~ einer Zeitung** taking a newspaper; **(c)** *Pl.* salary *sing.;* **die Bezüge der Beamten** the salaries of the civil servants; **(d)** (Papierdt.) *in* **mit** *od.* **unter ~ auf etw.** (*Akk.*) with reference to sth.; **auf etw.** (*Akk.*) **~ nehmen** refer to sth.; **~ nehmend auf unser Telex** with reference to our telex; **in ~ auf jmdn./etw.** concerning *or* regarding sb./sth.; **(e)** (Verbindung) connection; link

bezüglich /bə'tsyːklɪç/ **1** *Präp. mit Gen.* concerning; regarding. **2** *Adj.* **auf etw.** (*Akk.*) **~:** relating to sth.; **die darauf ~en Paragraphen** the relevant paragraphs

Bezugnahme /bə'tsuːknaːmə/ *die;* ~, ~**n** (Papierdt.) reference; **unter ~ auf etw.** (*Akk.*) with reference to sth.

Bezugs-: ~**person** *die* (Psych., Soziol.) **jedes Kind braucht eine ~person** every child needs someone it can relate to and take as an example; ~**quelle** *die* source of supply; (Firma) supplier; ~**recht** *das* (Wirtsch.) preemptive *or* subscription right

bezuschussen /bə'tsuː∫ʊsn̩/ *tr. V.* (Papierdt.) subsidize

bezwecken /bə'tsvɛkn̩/ *tr. V.* aim to achieve; aim at; **was willst du damit ~?** what do you expect to achieve by [doing] that?

bezweifeln *tr. V.* doubt; question; **ich bezweifle nicht, dass ...:** I do not doubt that ...; **das ist nicht zu ~:** there is no doubt about that

bezwingen *unr. tr. V.* conquer ⟨*enemy, mountain, pain, etc.*⟩; defeat ⟨*opponent*⟩; take, capture ⟨*fortress*⟩; master

⟨*pain, hunger*⟩; **seinen Zorn/seine Neugier ~:** keep one's anger/curiosity under control

Bezwinger *der,* **Bezwingerin** *die;* ~, ~**nen** conqueror

BGB /beːgeː'beː/ *Abk.:* **Bürgerliches Gesetzbuch**

BH /beː'haː/ *der;* ~**[s]**, ~**[s]** *Abk.:* **Büstenhalter** bra

Biathlon /'biːatlɔn/ *das;* ~**s**, ~**s** (Sport) biathlon

bibbern /'bɪbən/ *itr. V.* (ugs.) (vor Kälte) shiver (**vor** with); (vor Angst) shake, tremble (**vor** with); **um jmdn./etw. ~:** fear *or* tremble for sb./sth.

Bibel /'biːbl̩/ *die;* ~, ~**n** (auch fig.) Bible

Bibel-: ~**spruch** *der* biblical saying; ~**vers** *der* verse from the Bible

Biber¹ /'biːbɐ/ *der;* ~**s**, ~**:** beaver

Biber² *der od. das;* ~**s** (Stoff) flannelette

Bibliographie *die;* ~, ~**n** bibliography

Bibliothek /biblio'teːk/ *die;* ~, ~**en** library

Bibliothekar /bibliote'kaːɐ̯/ *der;* ~**s**, ~**e**, **Bibliothekarin** *die;* ~, ~**nen** librarian

biblisch /'biːblɪʃ/ *Adj.* biblical; **ein ~es Alter** a grand old age

Bidet /bi'deː/ *das;* ~**s**, ~**s** bidet

bieder /'biːdɐ/ **1** *Adj.* **(a)** unsophisticated; (langweilig) stolid; **(b)** (veralt.: rechtschaffen) upright. **2** *adv.* in an unsophisticated manner

Bieder·mann *der; Pl.* **Biedermänner (a)** (veralt.) man of integrity *or* probity; **(b)** (Spießer) petty bourgeois

Biedermeier *das;* ~**s** Biedermeier [period/style]

biegen /'biːgn̩/ **1** *unr. tr. V.* bend. **2** *unr. refl. V.* bend; (nachgeben) give; sag; **der Tisch bog sich unter der Last der Speisen** the table sagged *or* groaned under the weight of the food. **3** *unr. itr. V.; mit sein* turn; **um die Ecke ~:** turn the corner; ⟨*car*⟩ take the corner. **4** *in* **auf Biegen oder Brechen** (ugs.) at all costs; by hook or by crook; **es geht auf Biegen oder Brechen** (ugs.) it has come to the crunch *or* (Amer.) showdown

biegsam *Adj.* flexible; pliable ⟨*material*⟩; (gelenkig) supple

Biegsamkeit *die;* ~ ⇒ **biegsam:** flexibility; pliability; suppleness

Biegung *die;* ~, ~**en** bend; **eine [scharfe] ~ nach rechts machen** bend [sharply] to the right

Biene /'biːnə/ *die;* ~, ~**n (a)** bee; **(b)** (ugs. veralt.: Mädchen) bird (Brit. +l.); dame (Amer. sl.)

Bienen-: ~**fleiß** *der* unflagging industry; ~**honig** *der* bees' honey; ~**königin** *die* queen bee; ~**korb** *der* straw hive; ~**schwarm** *der* swarm of bees; ~**stich** *der* **(a)** bee-sting; **(b)** (Kuchen) *cake with a topping of sugar and almonds (and sometimes a cream filling)* ; ~**stock** *der* beehive

Bier /biːɐ̯/ *das;* ~**[e]s**, ~**e** beer; **ein kleines/großes ~:** a small/large [glass of] beer; **zwei ~:** two beers; two glasses of beer; **das ist [nicht] mein ~** (ugs.) that is [not] my affair *or* business

Bier·bauch *der* (ugs. spött.) beer belly (coll.)

Bierchen *das;* ~**s**, ~ (ugs.) little [glass of] beer

bier-, Bier-: ~**deckel** *der* beer mat; ~**dose** *die* beer can; ~**ernst** (ugs.) **1** *Adj.* deadly serious; solemn; **2** *adv.* solemnly; ~**fass, *~faß** *das* beer barrel; ~**filz** *der* beer mat; ~**flasche** *die* beer bottle; ~**garten** *der* beer garden; ~**glas** *das* beer glass; ~**kasten** *der* beer crate; ~**keller** *der* beer cellar; ~**krug** *der* beer mug; (aus Glas, Zinn) tankard; ~**laune** *die* (ugs.) **in einer ~laune, aus einer ~laune heraus** in an exuberant mood; ~**schinken** *der* slicing sausage containing pieces of ham; ~**selig** (scherzh.) **1** *Adj.* beery ⟨*mood*⟩; ~**selig, wie er war** in his beerily happy state; **2** *adv.* in a beerily happy state; ⟨*laugh*⟩ in beery merriment; ~**tisch** *der:* **am ~tisch** over a glass of beer; in the pub (Brit.) *or* (Amer.) bar; ~**trinker** *der,* ~**trinkerin** *die* beer-drinker; ~**zeitung** *die* joke newspaper *(made up for a closed group)*; ~**zelt** *das* beer tent

Biest /biːst/ *das;* ~**[e]s**, ~**er** (ugs. abwertend) **(a)** (Tier, Gegenstand) wretched thing; (Bestie) creature; **(b)** (Mensch) beast (derog.); wretch; **das freche ~:** the cheeky devil (coll.)

bieten /'biːtṇ/ *unr. tr. V.* **(a)** offer; put on ‹*programme etc.*›; provide ‹*shelter, guarantee, etc.*›; (bei Auktionen, Kartenspielen) bid **(für, auf** + *Akk.* for); **jmdm. Geld/eine Chance** ~: offer sb. money/a chance; **jmdm. den Arm** ~ (geh.) offer sb. one's arm; **eine hervorragende Leistung** ~: put up an outstanding performance; **das bietet keine Schwierigkeiten** that presents no difficulties; **das Stadion bietet 40 000 Personen Platz** the stadium has room for *or* can hold 40,000 people; **(b)** **ein schreckliches/gespenstisches** *usw.* **Bild** ~: present a terrible/eerie *etc.* picture; be a terrible/eerie *etc.* sight; **einen prächtigen Anblick** ~: look splendid; be a splendid sight; **(c)** (zumuten) **das lasse ich mir nicht** ~: I won't put up with *or* stand for that. **2** *unr. refl. V.* **sich jmdm.** ~: present itself to sb.; **hier bietet sich dir eine Chance** this is an opportunity for you; this offers you an opportunity; **ihnen bot sich ein Bild des Grauens** a horrific sight confronted them. **3** *unr. itr. V.* bid **(auf** + *Akk.* for)

Bigamie /biga'miː/ *die;* ~, ~n bigamy *no def. art.*

Bigband /'bɪg ˈbænd/ *die;* ~ ~, ~ ~s big band

bigott /bi'gɔt/ *Adj.* (abwertend) **(a)** religiose; over-devout; **(b)** (scheinheilig) sanctimonious; holier-than-thou

Bigotterie /bigɔtə'riː/ *die;* ~ (abwertend) religious bigotry; religiosity; (Scheinheiligkeit) sanctimoniousness

Bike /baik/ *das;* ~s, ~s, (Jargon) bike

Biker /'baikɐ/ *der;* ~s, ~, (Jargon) biker

Bikini /bi'kiːni/ *der;* ~s, ~s bikini

Bilanz /bi'lants/ *die;* ~, ~en **(a)** (Kaufmannsspr., Wirtsch.) balance sheet; **eine** ~ **aufstellen** make up the accounts *pl.;* draw up a balance sheet; **(b)** (Ergebnis) outcome; (Endeffekt) net result; ~ **ziehen** take stock; sum things up; **die** ~ **aus etw. ziehen** draw conclusions *pl.* about sth.; (rückblickend) take stock of sth.

Bilanz-: ~**analyse** *die* (Wirtsch., Kaufmannsspr.) balance sheet analysis; ~**buchhalter** *der* (Wirtsch., Kaufmannsspr.) [stewardship] accountant

bilanzieren (Wirtsch., Kaufmannsspr.) **1** *itr. V.* balance; **mit … DM** ~: show a balance of … marks. **2** *tr. V.* balance ‹*account*›; show ‹*turnover*› in the balance sheet; (fig.) sum up

Bilanz-: ~**prüfer** *der* (Wirtsch., Kaufmannsspr.) auditor; ~**summe** *die* (Wirtsch., Kaufmannsspr.) balance-sheet total

bilateral (Politik) **1** *Adj.* bilateral. **2** *adv.* bilaterally

Bild /bɪlt/ *das;* ~[e]s, ~er **(a)** picture; (in einem Buch usw.) illustration; (Spielkarte) picture *or* court card; **ein** ~ [**von einem Mann/einer Frau sein** be a fine specimen of a man/woman; be a fine-looking man/woman; **(b)** (Aussehen) appearance; (Anblick) sight; **ein** ~ **des Jammers** a pathetic sight; **ein** ~ **für** [**die**] **Götter** (scherzh.) a sight for sore eyes; **(c)** (Metapher) image; metaphor; **(d)** (Abbild) image; (Spiegel~) reflection; **(e)** (Vorstellung) image; **ein falsches/merkwürdiges** ~ **von etw. haben** have a wrong impression/curious idea of sth.; **sich** (*Dat.*) **ein** ~ **von jmdm./etw. machen** form an impression of sb./sth.; **(f)** *in* **jmdn.** [**über etw.** (*Akk.*)] **ins** ~ **setzen** put sb. in the picture [about sth.]; [**über etw.** (*Akk.*)] **im** ~**e sein** be in the picture [about sth.]; **(g)** (Theater) scene

Bild·band *der* copiously illustrated book

bildbar *Adj.* formable (aus from); malleable ‹*personality, mind*›

Bild-: ~**bei·lage** *die* pictorial *or* illustrated supplement; ~**beschreibung** *die* picture description

bilden 1 *tr. V.* **(a)** form (aus from); (modellieren) mould (aus from); **den Charakter** ~: form *or* mould sb.'s/one's personality; **eine Gasse** ~: make a path *or* passage; **sich** (*Dat.*) **ein Urteil** [**über jmdn./etw.**] ~: form an opinion [of sb./sth.]; **(b)** (ansammeln) build up ‹*fund, capital*›; **(c)** (darstellen) be, represent ‹*exception etc.*›; constitute ‹*rule etc.*›; **den Höhepunkt des Abends bildete sein Auftritt** his appearance was the high spot of the evening; **(d)** (erziehen) educate; *itr.* **Reisen bildet** travel broadens the mind. **2** *refl. V.* **(a)** (entstehen) form; **(b)** (lernen) educate oneself

bildend *Adj.* **(a)** **die** ~**e Kunst** the plastic arts *pl.* (including painting and architecture); **(b)** (belehrend) educational

Bilder·buch *das* picture book (*for children*); **aussehen wie im** *od.* **aus dem** ~: look a picture

Bilderbuch- perfect ‹*landing, weather*›; picture book ‹*weather, village*›; story book ‹*marriage, career*›

Bilder-: ~**geschichte** *die* picture story; (Comic) strip cartoon; ~**rahmen** *der* picture frame; ~**rätsel** *das* picture puzzle; (Rebus) rebus

bild-, Bild-: ~**fläche** *die:* **auf der** ~**fläche erscheinen** (ugs.) appear on the scene; (auftauchen) turn up; **von der** ~**fläche verschwinden** (ugs.) (rasch weggehen) make oneself scarce (coll.); (aus der Öffentlichkeit verschwinden) disappear from the scene; ~**frequenz** *die* (Film, Ferns.) picture frequency; ~**geschichte** *die* ⇒ **Bildergeschichte;** ~**haft 1** *Adj.* graphic; pictorial, illustrative ‹*language, sense, etc.*›; vivid ‹*imagination, clarity, etc.*›; **2** *adv.* graphically; (lebhaft) vividly; ~**hauer** *der* sculptor; ~**hauerei** /---ʹ-/ *die* sculpture *no def. art.;* ~**hauerin** *die;* ~, ~**nen** sculptress; ~**hübsch** *Adj.* really lovely; stunningly beautiful ‹*girl*›

bildlich 1 *Adj.* **(a)** pictorial; **(b)** (übertragen) figurative; ~**er Ausdruck,** ~**e Wendung** figure of speech; image. **2** *adv.* **(a)** pictorially; **sich etw.** ~ **vorstellen** picture sth. to oneself; **(b)** (übertragen) figuratively; ~ **gesprochen** metaphorically speaking

Bild·material *das* pictures *pl.;* (Fotos/Film) photographic/film material

bildnerisch *Adj.* artistic; creative ‹*abilities*›

Bildnis /'bɪltnɪs/ *das;* ~ses, ~se portrait; (Plastik) sculpture

Bild-: ~**platte** *die* video disc; ~**reportage** *die* photo-reportage; ~**röhre** *die* (Ferns.) picture tube; ~**schirm** *der* screen; **am** ~**schirm arbeiten** work at *or* with a VDU

Bildschirm-: ~**arbeit** *die* VDU work *no art., no pl.;* ~**gerät** *das* VDU; visual display unit; ~**schirm·schoner** *der;* ~, ~ (DV) screen saver; ~**zeitung** *die* teletext

bild·schön *Adj.* really lovely; stunningly beautiful ‹*girl, woman*›

Bild·störung *die* interference *no def. art.* on vision

Bildung *die;* ~, ~en **(a)** (Erziehung) education; (Kultur) culture; [**keine**] ~ **haben** be [un]educated; ([un]kultiviert sein) be [un]cultivated *or* [un]cultured; **(b)** (Schaffung) formation; **die** ~ **einer Kommission** setting up a committee

bildungs-, Bildungs-: ~**chancen** *Pl.* educational opportunities ~**hunger** *der* thirst for education; ~**hungrig** *Adj.* eager to be educated *postpos.;* ~**lücke** *die* gap in one's education; **das ist eine** ~**lücke!** that's culpable ignorance!; ~**politik** *die* educational policy; ~**urlaub** *der* educational leave

Bild-: ~**unter·schrift** *die* caption; ~**wörter·buch** *das* pictorial dictionary

Billard /'bɪljart, *österr.:* bi'jaːɐ/ *das;* ~s, ~e billiards

Billard-: ~**kugel** *die* billiard ball; ~**stock** *der* billiard cue; ~**tisch** *der* billiard table

Billett /bɪl'jɛt/ *das;* ~[e]s, ~e *od.* ~s (schweiz., veralt.) ticket

Billiarde /bɪl'jardə/ *die;* ~, ~n thousand million million; quadrillion (Amer.)

billig /'bɪlɪç/ **1** *Adj.* **(a)** cheap; **(b)** (abwertend: primitiv) shabby, cheap ‹*trick*›; feeble ‹*excuse*›; **ist dir das nicht zu** ~? isn't that beneath you? **2** *adv.* cheaply; ~ **einkaufen** shop cheaply; ~ **abzugeben** (in Anzeigen) for sale cheap

Billig·angebot *das* special *or* cut-price offer

billigen *tr. V.* approve; ~, **dass jmd. etw. tut** approve of sb.'s doing sth.; **etw. stillschweigend** ~: give sth. one's tacit approval

Billig-: ~**flug** *der* cheap flight; ~**lohn·land** *das* low-wage country

Billigung *die;* ~: approval; **jmds.** ~ **finden** meet with *or* receive sb.'s approval

Billig·ware *die* cheap goods *pl.*

Billion /bɪˈljoːn/ *die;* ~, ~en ▶600⏌ trillion; million million

bim /bɪm/ *Interj.* ding; ~, **bam** ding dong

Bimbam *in* [**ach du**] **heiliger** ~! (ugs.) [oh] my sainted aunt! (sl.); glory be! (sl.)

Bimmel /ˈbɪml/ *die;* ~, ~n (ugs.) [tɪŋ-a-lɪŋ] bell

Bimmel·bahn *die* (ugs. scherzh.) narrow-gauge railway (*with a warning bell*)

Bimmelei *die;* ~ (ugs. abwertend) constant ringing

bimmeln *itr. V.* (ugs.) ring

Bims·stein /ˈbɪms-/ *der* pumice stone

bin /bɪn/ *1. Pers. Sg. Präsens v.* **sein**[1]

Binde /ˈbɪndə/ *die;* ~, ~n (a) (Verband) bandage; (Augen~) blindfold; (b) (Arm~) armband; (c) (veralt.: Krawatte) tie; **sich** (*Dat.*) **einen hinter die** ~ **gießen** *od.* **kippen** (ugs.) have a drink or two

Binde-: ~**gewebe** *das* (Anat.) connective tissue; ~**glied** *das* [connecting] link; ~**haut** *die* (Anat.) conjunctiva; ~**haut·entzündung** *die* (Med.) conjunctivitis *no art.;* ~**mittel** *das* binder

binden 1 *unr. tr. V.* (a) (bündeln) tie; **etw. zu etw.** ~: tie sth. into sth.; (b) (herstellen) make up ⟨*wreath, bouquet*⟩; make ⟨*broom*⟩; (c) (fesseln) bind; (d) (verpflichten) bind; (e) (befestigen, auch fig.) tie (**an** + *Dat.* to); **nicht an einen Ort gebunden sein** (fig.) not be tied to one place; **jmdn. an sich** (*Akk.*) ~ (fig.) make sb. dependent on one; (f) (knüpfen) tie ⟨*knot, bow, etc.*⟩; knot ⟨*tie*⟩; (festhalten) bind ⟨*soil, mixture, etc.*⟩; thicken ⟨*sauce*⟩; (h) (Buchw.) bind. 2 *unr. itr. V.* (als Bindemittel wirken) bind. 3 *unr. refl. V.* tie oneself down; **ich bin zu jung, um mich schon zu** ~: I am too young to be tied down

bindend *Adj.* binding (**für** on); definite ⟨*answer*⟩

Binder *der;* ~s, ~ (a) (Krawatte) tie; (b) (Bindemittel) binder

Binde-: ~**strich** *der* hyphen; ~**wort** *das* (Sprachw.) conjunction

Bind·faden *der* string; **ein** [**Stück**] ~: a piece of string; **es regnet Bindfäden** (ugs.) it's raining cats and dogs (coll.)

Bindung *die;* ~, ~en (a) (Beziehung) relationship (**an** + *Akk.* to); (b) (Verbundenheit) attachment (**an** + *Akk.* to); (c) (Ski~) binding; (d) (Chemie) bond

binnen /ˈbɪnən/ *Präp. mit Dat. od.* (geh.) *Gen.* within; ~ **Jahresfrist** within a year

Binnen-: ~**gewässer** *das* inland water; ~**hafen** *der* inland port; ~**land** *das; o. Pl.* interior; ~**markt** *der* (Wirtsch.) domestic *or* home market; **europäischer** ~**markt** single European market; ~**meer** *das* inland sea; ~**see** *der* lake; ~**zoll** *der* internal duty *or* tariff

Binom /biˈnoːm/ *das;* ~s, ~e (Math.) binomial

binomisch *Adj.* (Math.) binomial

Binse /ˈbɪnzə/ *die;* ~, ~n (Bot.) rush; **in die** ~n **gehen** (ugs.) fall through

Binsen·weisheit *die* truism

Bio /ˈbiːo/ *o. Art.* (Schülerspr.) biol (school sl.); biology

Bio- (ugs.) organic ⟨*farmer, garden, vegetables, etc.*⟩; ~**laden** health food shop

bio-, Bio-: ~**chemie** *die* biochemistry; ~**chemisch** *Adj.* biochemical; ~**ethik** /---/ *die* bioethics *sing.;* ~**gas** /---/ *das* biogas; ~**graph** *der;* ~en, ~en biographer; ~**graphie** *die;* ~, ~n biography; ~**graphisch** *Adj.* biographical; ~**loge** /-ˈloːgə/ *der;* ~n, ~n ▶85⏌ biologist; ~**logie** *die;* ~: biology *no art.;* ~**login** *die;* ~, ~nen biologist; ~**logisch** *Adj.* (a) biological; (b) (natürlich) natural ⟨*medicine, cosmetic, etc.*⟩; ~**masse** /---/ *die* biomass

Bionik /biːˈonɪk/ *die;* ~: bionics *sing., no art.*

Bio-: ~**rhythmus** *der* biorhythm; ~**sphäre** /--ˈ--/ *die* biosphere

Biotop /bioˈtoːp/ *der od. das;* ~s, ~e (Biol.) biotope

Bio·wissenschaften *Pl.* life sciences

Birke /ˈbɪrkə/ *die;* ~, ~n (a) birch [tree]; (b) *o. Pl.* (Holz) birch[wood]

Birk-: ~**hahn** *der* blackcock; ~**huhn** *das* black grouse

Birma /ˈbɪrma/ ⟨*das*⟩; ~s Burma

Birn·baum *der* pear tree

Birne /ˈbɪrnə/ *die;* ~, ~n (a) pear; (b) (Glüh~) [light-]bulb; (c) (salopp: Kopf) nut (coll.)

bis /bɪs/ ▶119⏌ 1 *Präp. mit Akk.* (a) (zeitlich) until; till; (die ganze Zeit über und bis zu einem bestimmten Zeitpunkt) up to; up until; up till; (nicht später als) by; **ich muss** ~ **fünf Uhr warten** I have to wait until *or* till five o'clock; ~ **gestern glaubte ich …:** [up] until yesterday I had thought …; **von Dienstag** ~ **Donnerstag** from Tuesday to Thursday; Tuesday through Thursday (Amer.); **von sechs** ~ **sieben** [**Uhr**] from six until *or* till seven [o'clock]; ~ **Ende März ist er zurück/verreist** he'll be back by/away until the end of March; ~ **wann dauert das Konzert?** till *or* until when does the concert go on?; ~ **dann/gleich/später/morgen/nachher!** see you then/in a while/later/tomorrow/later!; (b) (räumlich, fig.) to; **dieser Zug fährt nur** ~ **Offenburg** this train only goes to *or* as far as Offenburg; ~ **wohin fährt der Bus?** how far does the bus go?; **nur** ~ **Seite 100** only up to *or* as far as page 100; ~ **5 000 Mark** up to 5,000 marks; **Kinder** ~ **6 Jahre** children up to the age of six *or* up to six years of age. 2 *Adv.* (a) **Städte** ~ **zu 50 000 Einwohnern** towns of up to 50,000 inhabitants; ~ **zu 6 Personen** up to six people; ~ **nach Köln** to Cologne; ~ **an die Decke** up to the ceiling; (b) ~ **auf** (einschließlich) down to; (mit Ausnahme von) except for. 3 *Konj.* (a) (nebenordnend) to; **vier** ~ **fünf** four to five; (b) (unterordnend) until; till; (österr.: sobald) when

Bisam·ratte *die* muskrat

Bischof /ˈbɪʃof/ *der;* ~s, **Bischöfe** /ˈbɪʃœfə/ bishop

bischöflich *Adj.* episcopal

Bischofs-: ~**mütze** *die* [bishop's] mitre; ~**sitz** *der* seat of a/the bishopric; ~**stab** *der* [bishop's] crosier *or* crook

Bi·sexualität *die* bisexuality

bi·sexuell 1 *Adj.* bisexual. 2 *adv.* bisexually

bis·her *Adv.* up to now; (aber jetzt nicht mehr) until now; till now; **er hat sich** ~ **nicht gemeldet** he hasn't been in touch up to now *or* as yet

bisherig *Adj.; nicht präd.* (vorherig) previous; (momentan) present; **sie ziehen um, ihre** ~**e Wohnung wird zu klein** they are moving — their present flat is getting too small; **sie sind umgezogen, ihre** ~**e Wohnung wurde zu klein** they have moved — their previous flat became too small

Biskaya /bɪsˈkaːja/ *die;* ~: **die** ~/**der Golf von** ~: the Bay of Biscay

Biskuit /bɪsˈkviːt/ *das od. der;* ~[e]s, ~s *od.* ~e (a) sponge biscuit; (b) (~teig) sponge

bis·lang *Adv.:* ⇒ **bisher**

Bismarck·hering /ˈbɪsmark-/ *der* Bismarck herring

Bison /ˈbiːzɔn/ *der;* ~s, ~s bison

biss, *biß /bɪs/ *1. u. 3. Pers. Sg. Prät. v.* **beißen**

Biss, *Biß /bɪs/ *der;* **Bisses, Bisse** bite

bisschen, *bißchen *indekl. Indefinitpron.* 1 *adj.* **ein** ~ **Geld/Brot/Milch/Wasser** a bit of *or* a little money/bread/a drop of *or* a little milk/water; **ich würde ihm kein** ~ **Geld mehr leihen** I wouldn't lend him any more money at all; **ein/kein** ~ **Angst haben** be a bit/not a bit frightened. 2 *adv.* **ein/kein** ~: a bit *or* a little/not a *or* one bit; **ich werde mich ein** ~ **aufs Ohr legen** I'm going to lie down for a bit; **ein klein** ~: a little bit; **ein** ~ **zu viel/mehr** a bit too much/a bit more. 3 *subst.* **ein** ~: a bit; a little; (bei Flüssigkeiten) a drop; a little; **von dem** ~ **werde ich nicht satt** that little bit/drop won't fill me up; **das/kein** ~: the little [bit]/not a *or* one bit

Bissen *der;* ~s, ~ mouthful; **sie bekam keinen** ~ **herunter** she couldn't eat a thing; **ihm blieb der** ~ **im Hals[e] stecken** (ugs.) the food stuck in his throat; **sich** (*Dat.*) **den letzten** ~ **vom Munde absparen** scrimp [and save]

bissig 1 *Adj.* (a) ~ **sein** ⟨*dog*⟩ bite; **ein** ~**er Hund** a dog that bites; „**Vorsicht,** ~**er Hund**" 'beware of the dog'; (b) (fig.) cutting, caustic ⟨*remark, tone, etc.*⟩. 2 *adv.* (fig.) ⟨*say*⟩ cuttingly, caustically

Biss·wunde, *Biß·wunde die bite

bist /bɪst/ 2. Pers. Sg. Präsens v. **sein**

biste (ugs.) = bist du; s. auch **haste**

Bistum /'bɪstu:m/ das; ~s, **Bistümer** /'bɪsty:mɐ/ bishopric; diocese

bis·weilen Adv. (geh.) from time to time; now and then

Bitt·brief der letter of request; (Bittgesuch) petition

bitte /'bɪtə/ 1 Adv. please; **können Sie mir** ~ **sagen ...?** could you please tell me ...?; ~ **nicht!** no, please don't!; ~ **nach Ihnen** after you. 2 Interj. (a) (Bitte, Aufforderung) please; ~[, **nehmen sie doch Platz]!** do take a seat; ~[, **treten sie ein]!** come in!; **zwei Tassen Tee,** ~: two cups of tea, please; **Noch eine Tasse Tee?** — **[Ja]** ~! Another cup of tea? — Yes, please; (b) (Aufforderung etw. entgegenzunehmen) ~ **[schön od. sehr]!** there you are!; **na** ~! (da siehst du es!) there you are!; (c) (Ausdruck des Einverständnisses) ~ **[gern]!** certainly; of course; **aber** ~! yes do; ~, **macht doch, was ihr wollt** just [go ahead and] do what you want; **Entschuldigung! — Bitte!** [I'm] sorry! — That's all right!; (d) (Aufforderung, sich zu äußern) ~ **[schön od. sehr]!** (im Laden, Lokal) yes, please?; **ja,** ~? (am Telefon) hello?; yes?; (e) (Nachfrage) **[wie]** ~? sorry; (überrascht, empört) what?; (f) (Erwiderung einer Dankesformel) ~ **[schön od. sehr]** not at all; you're welcome

Bitte die; ~, ~n request; (inständig) plea; **eine große** ~ **[an jmdn.]/nur die eine** ~ **haben** have a [great] favour to ask [of sb.]/have [just] one request or just one thing to ask

bitten 1 unr. itr. V. (a) **um etw.** ~: ask for or request sth.; (inständig) beg for sth.; **der Blinde bat um eine milde Gabe** the blind man begged for alms; **ich bitte einen Moment um Geduld/Ihre Aufmerksamkeit** I must ask you to be patient for a moment/may I ask for your attention for a moment; (b) (einladen) ask; **ich lasse** ~: [please] ask him/her/them to come in. 2 unr. tr. V. (a) **jmdn. um etw.** ~: ask sb. for sth.; **darf ich Sie um Feuer/ein Glas Wasser** ~? could I ask you for a light/a glass of water, please?; **darf ich die Herrschaften um Geduld/Ruhe** ~? could I ask you to be patient/silent?; [aber] **ich bitte dich/Sie!** [please] don't mention it; (b) (einladen) ask, invite; **jmdn. zum Tee [zu sich]** ~: ask or invite sb. to tea; **jmdn. ins Haus/Zimmer** ~: ask or invite sb. [to come] in

bitter 1 Adj. (a) bitter; plain ‹chocolate›; (b) (schmerzlich) bitter ‹experience, disappointment, etc.›; painful, hard ‹loss›; painful, bitter, hard ‹truth›; hard ‹time, fate, etc.›; **eine** ~**e Lehre** a hard lesson; (c) (beißend) bitter ‹irony, sarcasm›; (d) (verbittert) bitter; **ein** ~**es Gefühl** a feeling of bitterness; (e) (groß, schwer) bitter ‹cold, tears, grief, remorse, regret›; dire ‹need›; desperate ‹poverty›; grievous ‹injustice, harm›. 2 adv. (a) (verbittert) bitterly; (b) (sehr stark) desperately; ‹regret› bitterly

bitter-: böse 1 Adj. furious; **2** adv. furiously; ~**ernst** 1 Adj. deadly serious; **damit ist es mir** ~**ernst!** I am deadly serious; **2** adv. **ich meine das** ~**ernst** I mean it deadly seriously; ~**kalt** Adj.; präd. getrennt geschr. bitterly cold

Bitterkeit die; ~ (auch fig.) bitterness

bitterlich 1 Adj. slightly bitter ‹taste›. 2 adv. (heftig) ‹cry, complain, etc.› bitterly

Bitter·mandel die bitter almond

bitter·süß Adj. (auch fig.) bitter-sweet

Bitt-: gang der: **einen** ~ **zu jmdm. machen** go to sb. with a request; ~**gesuch** das petition; ~**schrift** die petition; ~**steller** /~ʃtɛlɐ/ der; ~s, ~: petitioner

Bitumen /bi'tu:mən/ das ~s, ~ (auch) **Bitumina** /-mina/ (Chemie) bitumen

Biwak /'bi:vak/ das; ~s, ~s (bes. Milit., Bergsteigen) bivouac

bizarr /bi'tsar/ 1 Adj. bizarre; (fantastisch) fantastic. 2 adv. bizarrely

Bizeps /'bi:tsɛps/ der; ~[es], ~e biceps

BKA /be:ka:'|a:/ das; ~[s] Abk.: **Bundeskriminalamt**

Blackout /'blɛkaut/ das od. der; ~[s], ~s blackout

blaffen /'blafn̩/, **bläffen** /'blɛfn̩/ itr. V. (a) bark; give a short bark; (kläffen) yap; (b) (schimpfen) snap

blähen /'blɛ:ən/ 1 tr. V. (a) billow, fill, belly [out] ‹sail›; billow ‹sheet, curtain, clothing›; (b) (aufblasen) flare ‹nostrils›. 2 refl. V. ‹sail› billow or belly out; ‹nostrils› dilate. 3 itr. V. (Blähungen verursachen) cause flatulence or wind; ~**de Speisen** flatulent foods

Blähung die; ~, ~en flatulence no art., no pl.; wind no art., no pl.; ~**en** flatulence sing.; wind sing.

blamabel /bla'ma:bl̩/ 1 Adj. shameful, disgraceful ‹behaviour etc.›. 2 adv. shamefully; disgracefully

Blamage /bla'ma:ʒə/ die; ~, ~n disgrace

blamieren /bla'mi:rən/ 1 tr. V. disgrace. 2 refl. V. disgrace oneself; (sich lächerlich machen) make a fool of oneself

blanchieren /blã'ʃi:rən/ tr. V. (Kochk.) blanch

blank /blaŋk/ Adj. (a) (glänzend) shiny; etw. ~ **reiben/polieren** rub/polish sth. till it shines; ~ **poliert** brightly polished; (b) (unbekleidet) bare; naked; (c) (ugs.: mittellos) ~ **sein** be broke (coll.); (d) (bloß) bare ‹wood, plaster, earth, etc.›; (e) (rein) pure; sheer; utter ‹mockery›

Blanko- /'blaŋko-/: ~**scheck** der (Wirtsch., fig.) blank cheque; ~**vollmacht** die (Wirtsch., fig.) carte blanche

*blank poliert ⇨ **blank a**

Blank·vers der blank verse

Bläschen /'blɛ:sçən/ das; ~s, ~ (a) [small] bubble; (b) (in der Haut) [small] blister

Blase /'bla:zə/ die; ~, ~n (a) bubble; (in einem Anstrich) blister; ~**n werfen od. ziehen** ‹paint› blister; ‹wallpaper› bubble; (b) (in der Haut) blister; **sich** (Dat.) ~**n laufen** get blisters [from walking/running]; (c) (Harn~) ▸ 326 bladder; (d) (salopp: Leute) mob (sl.)

Blase·balg der bellows pl.; pair of bellows

blasen 1 unr. itr. V. (a) blow; (b) **auf dem Kamm** ~: play the comb; (c) **zum Angriff/Rückzug/Aufbruch** ~: sound the charge/retreat/departure; (d) (wehen) ‹wind› blow; unpers.: **es bläst** it's windy or blowy. 2 unr. tr. V. (a) blow; (b) (spielen) play ‹musical instrument, tune, melody, etc.›; (c) (wehen) ‹wind› blow

Blasen-: bildung die blistering ~**katarrh** der ▸ 329 (Med.) cystitis no indef. art.

Bläser /'blɛ:zɐ/ der; ~s, ~ (Musik) wind player

blasiert /bla'zi:ɐt/ (abwertend) 1 Adj. blasé. 2 adv. in a blasé way

Blas-: instrument das wind instrument; ~**kapelle** die brass band; ~**musik** die brass band music; (~kapelle) brass band; ~**orchester** das brass band

Blasphemie /blasfe'mi:/ die; ~, ~n blasphemy

blasphemisch /blas'fe:mɪʃ/ Adj. blasphemous

Blas·rohr das blowpipe

blass, *blaß /blas/ 1 Adj. (a) pale; (fig.) colourless ‹account, portrayal, etc.›; ~ **werden** turn or go pale; **Rot macht dich** ~: red makes you look pale [in the face]; ~ **vor Neid sein/werden** (fig.) be/turn or go green with envy; (b) (schwach) faint ‹recollection, hope›. 2 adv. palely

Blässe /'blɛsə/ die; ~: paleness

Bläss·huhn, *Bläß·huhn /'blɛs-/ das coot

blässlich, *bläßlich /'blɛslɪç/ 1 Adj. (a) rather pale; palish; (b) (fig.) colourless ‹person, account, portrayal, etc.›. 2 adv. (fig.) colourlessly

Blatt /blat/ das; ~[e]s, **Blätter** /'blɛtɐ/ (a) (von Pflanzen) leaf; **kein** ~ **vor den Mund nehmen** not mince one's words; (b) (Papier) sheet; **ein** ~ **Papier** a sheet of paper; [noch] **ein unbeschriebenes** ~ **sein** (ugs.) (unerfahren sein) be inexperienced; (unbekannt sein) be an unknown quantity; (c) (Buchseite usw.) page; leaf; etw. **vom** ~ **spielen** sight-read sth.; **auf einem anderen** ~ **stehen** (fig.) be [quite] another or a different matter; (d) (Zeitung) paper; (e) (Spielkarten) hand; (f) (am Werkzeug, Ruder) blade; (g) (Grafik) print

Blättchen /'blɛtçən/ das; ~s, ~ (a) (von Pflanzen) [small] leaf; (b) (Papier) [small] sheet; (c) (abwertend: Zeitung) rag (derog.)

Blạttern *Pl.* ▶ 329 | smallpox *sing.*

blạttern /'blɛtɐn/ **1** *itr. V.* **in einem Buch** ∼: leaf through a book. **2** *tr. V.* put down [one by one]; **er blätterte mir 50 Mark auf den Tisch** he counted me out fifty marks in notes on the table

Blạtter·teig *der* puff pastry

Blạtt-: ∼**gold** *das; o. Pl.* gold leaf; ∼**laus** *die* aphid; greenfly; ∼**pflanze** *die* foliage plant; ∼**säge** *die* wide-bladed [hand]saw; ∼**salat** *der* green salad

blau /blau/ *Adj.* blue; **ein** ∼**es Auge** (ugs.) a black eye; **mit einem** ∼**en Auge davonkommen** (fig. ugs.) get off fairly lightly; **ein** ∼**er Fleck** a bruise; **ein** ∼**er Brief** (ugs.) (Kündigung) one's cards *pl.*; (Schulw.) *letter informing parents that their child is in danger of having to repeat a year;* **einen** ∼**en Montag einlegen** *od.* **machen** (ugs.) skip work on Monday; **sein** ∼**es Wunder erleben** (ugs.) get a nasty surprise; ∼ **sein** (fig. ugs.) be tight (coll.) *or* canned (sl.)

Blau *das;* ∼**s,** ∼ *od.* (ugs.:) ∼**s** blue

blau-, Blau-: ∼**alge** *die* blue-green alga; ∼**äugig** *Adj.* **(a)** blue-eyed; **(b)** (naiv) naive; ∼**beere** *die* bilberry; whortleberry; ∼**blütig** *Adj.* (meist iron.) blue-blooded

Blaue[1] /'blauə/ *das;* ∼**n** blue; **das** ∼ **vom Himmel [herunter]lügen** (ugs.) lie like anything; tell a pack of lies; **wir wollen einfach ins** ∼ **fahren** we'll just set off and see where we end up; *s. auch* **Fahrt c**

Blaue[2] *der;* ∼**n,** ∼**n** (ugs.) hundred-mark note

Bläue /'blɔyə/ *die;* ∼ (geh.) blue; blueness; (des Himmels) blue

blau-, Blau-: ∼**filter** *der od. das* (Fot.) blue filter; ∼**grau** *Adj.* blue-grey; bluish grey; ∼**grün** *Adj.* blue-green; bluish green; ∼**kraut** *das* (südd., österr.) ⇒ **Rotkohl**

bläulich *Adj.* bluish

blau-, Blau-: ∼**licht** *das* flashing blue light; **ein Krankenwagen raste mit** ∼ **vorbei** an ambulance raced past with [its] blue light flashing; ∼|**machen** *itr. V.* (ugs.) skip work; ∼**mann** *der; Pl.* ∼**männer** (ugs.) boiler suit; ∼**meise** *die* blue tit; ∼**papier** *das* [blue] carbon paper; ∼**pause** *die* blueprint; ∼**rot** *Adj.* purple; ∼**säure** *die; o. Pl.* (Chemie) prussic acid; hydrocyanic acid; ∼**stichig** /ʃtɪçɪç/ *Adj.* (Fot.) with a blue cast *postpos., not pred.;* ∼**stichig sein** have a blue cast; ∼**strumpf** *der* (abwertend) bluestocking; ∼**tanne** *die* blue spruce; Colorado spruce; ∼**wal** *der* blue whale

Blazer /'ble:zɐ/ *der;* ∼**s,** ∼: blazer

Blech /blɛç/ *das;* ∼**[e]s,** ∼**e (a)** sheet metal; (Stück Blech) metal sheet; **(b)** (Back∼) [baking] tray; **(c)** *o. Pl.* (ugs.: Unsinn) rubbish; nonsense; tripe (coll.)

Blech-: ∼**blas·instrument** *das* brass instrument; ∼**büchse** *die,* ∼**dose** *die* can; tin (Brit.)

blechen *tr., itr. V.* (ugs.) cough up (coll.); fork out (coll.)

blechern /'blɛçɐn/ **1** *Adj.* **(a)** nicht präd. (aus Blech) metal; **(b)** (metallisch klingend) tinny ⟨sound, voice⟩. **2** *adv.* (metallisch) tinnily

Blech-: ∼**kiste** *die* (ugs. abwertend) crate (sl.); ∼**musik** *die* (abwertend) brass band music; ∼**napf** *der* metal bowl

Blechner *der;* ∼**s,** ∼ (südd.) ⇒ **Klempner**

Blech-: ∼**schaden** *der* (Kfz-W.) damage *no indef. art.* to the bodywork; ∼**trommel** *die* tin drum

blecken /'blɛkṇ/ *tr. V.* **die Zähne** ∼: bare one's/its teeth

Blei[1] /blai/ *das;* ∼**[e]s,** ∼**e** lead

Blei[2] *der od. das;* ∼**[e]s,** ∼**e** (ugs.:stift) pencil

Bleibe *die;* ∼, ∼**n** place to stay; **keine** ∼ **haben** have nowhere to stay

bleiben /'blaibṇ/ *unr. itr. V.; mit sein* **(a)** stay; remain; ∼ **Sie bitte am Apparat** hold the line please; **wo bleibt er so lange?** where has he got to?; **wo bleibst du denn so lange?** where have you been *or* what's been keeping you all this time?; **zum Abendessen** ∼: stay for supper; **auf dem Weg** ∼: keep *or* stay on the path; **bei etw.** ∼ (fig.: an etw. festhalten) keep *or* stick to sth.; **jmdm. in Erinnerung** *od.* **im Gedächtnis** ∼: stay in sb.'s mind *or* memory; **das bleibt unter uns** (*Dat.*) that's [just] between ourselves; **zusehen können, wo man bleibt** (ugs.) have to fend for oneself; **jmdn. zum Bleiben auffordern** ask sb. to stay; **im Feld/im Krieg/auf See** ∼ (verhüll. geh.) die *or* fall in action/die in the war/die at sea; **der Kuchen bleibt mehrere Tage frisch** the cake will keep for several days; **bleib ruhig!** keep calm!; **das Geschäft bleibt heute geschlossen** the shop is closed today; **unbestraft/unbemerkt** ∼: go unpunished/go unnoticed *or* escape notice; **sitzen** ∼: stay *or* remain sitting down *or* seated; **dabei bleibt es!** (ugs.: daran wird nichts mehr geändert) that's that; that's the end of it; **(b) das bleibt abzuwarten** that remains to be seen; **es bleibt zu hoffen, dass …:** we can only hope that …; **(c)** (übrig bleiben) be left; remain; **uns** (*Dat.*) **bleibt noch Zeit** we still have time; **es blieb ihm keine Hoffnung mehr** he had no hope left; **(d) etw.** ∼ **lassen** give sth. a miss; forget sth.; **das Rauchen** ∼ **lassen** (aufgeben) give up *or* stop smoking

bleibend *Adj.* lasting; permanent ⟨damage⟩

*****bleiben|lassen** ⇒ **bleiben d**

bleich /blaiç/ *Adj.* pale; ∼ **werden** turn *or* go pale; (vor Angst, Schreck) pale; turn *or* go pale

bleichen[1] *tr. V.* bleach

bleichen[2] *regelm.* (veralt. auch unr.) *itr. V.* become bleached; **in der Sonne** ∼: be bleached by the sun

Bleich-: ∼**gesicht** *das Pl.* ∼**gesichter** (scherzh.: Weißer) pale-face; ∼**mittel** *das* bleach; bleaching agent

bleiern /'blaiɐn/ *Adj.* **(a)** nicht präd. lead; **(b)** (geh.: bleifarben) leaden ⟨sky, grey⟩; **(c)** (schwer) heavy ⟨sleep, tiredness, etc.⟩; leaden ⟨heaviness⟩

blei-, Blei-: ∼**frei** *Adj.* unleaded ⟨fuel⟩; ∼**frei** *das;* ∼**s** unleaded; ∼**gießen** *das;* ∼**s** pouring lead into cold water to tell one's fortune for the coming year; ∼**kristall** *das* lead crystal; ∼**kugel** *die* lead ball; (Geschoss) lead bullet; ∼**schwer 1** *Adj.* heavy as lead *postpos.;* **2** *adv.* heavily; like a heavy *or* lead weight; ∼**soldat** *der* lead soldier

Blei·stift *der* pencil; **mit** ∼: in pencil

Bleistift-: ∼**absatz** *der* stiletto heel; ∼**mine** *die* [pencil] lead; ∼**spitzer** *der* pencil sharpener

Blei·vergiftung *die* lead poisoning

Blende *die;* ∼, ∼**n (a)** (Lichtschutz) shade; (im Auto) [sun-]visor; **(b)** (Optik, Film, Fot.) diaphragm; **die** ∼ **öffnen/schließen** open up the aperture/stop down; **(c)** (Film, Fot.: Blendenzahl) aperture setting; f-number; **mit** *od.* **bei** ∼ **8** at [an aperture setting of] f/8

blenden 1 *tr. V.* **(a)** (auch fig.) dazzle; **(b)** (blind machen) blind. **2** *itr. V.* (light) be dazzling

blendend 1 *Adj.* splendid; brilliant ⟨musician, dancer, speech, achievement, etc.⟩; **es geht mir** ∼: I feel wonderfully well *or* wonderful. **2** *adv.* **wir haben uns** ∼ **amüsiert** we had a wonderful *or* marvellous time

Blendung *die;* ∼, ∼**en (a)** dazzling; **(b)** (das Blindmachen) blinding

Blesse /'blɛsə/ *die;* ∼, ∼**n** blaze

blich /blɪç/ *1. u. 3. Pers. Sg. Prät. v.* **bleichen**[2]

Blick /blɪk/ *der;* ∼**[e]s,** ∼**e (a)** look; (flüchtig) glance; **jmdm. einen** ∼/**sich** ∼**e zuwerfen** give sb. a look/exchange glances; **einen kurzen** ∼ **auf etw.** (*Akk.*) **werfen** take a quick look at *or* glance [briefly] at sth.; **auf den ersten** ∼: at first glance; **auf den zweiten** ∼: looking at it again *or* a second time; **mein** ∼ **fiel auf den Brief** my eye fell on the letter; the letter caught my eye; **(b)** *o. Pl.* (Ausdruck) look in one's eyes; **mit misstrauischem** ∼: with a suspicious look in one's eye; **(c)** (Aussicht) view; **ein Zimmer mit** ∼ **aufs Meer** a room with a sea view; **jmdn./etw. aus dem** ∼ **verlieren** lose sight of sb./sth.; **etw. im** ∼ **haben** be able to see sth.; **(d)** *o. Pl.* (Urteil[skraft]) eye; **einen sicheren/geschulten** ∼ **für etw. haben** have a sure/trained eye for sth.; **keinen** ∼ **für etw. haben** have no eye for sth.

blicken 1 *itr. V.* look; (flüchtig) glance; **jmdm. gerade in die Augen** ∼: look sb. straight in the eye. **2** *tr. V.: in sich* ∼ **lassen** put in an appearance; **lass dich mal wieder** ∼: come again some time

Blick-: ∼**fang** *der* eye-catcher; ∼**feld** *das* field of vision *or* view; ∼**kontakt** *der* eye contact; ∼**punkt** *der* view; field of vision; **jmdn. in den** ∼**punkt rücken** (fig.) single sb. out; ∼**richtung** *die* line of sight *or* vision; ∼**winkel** *der* **(a)** angle of vision; **(b)** (fig.) point of view; perspective

blieb /bliːp/ *1. u. 3. Pers. Sg. Prät. v.* **bleiben**

blies /bliːs/ *1. u. 3. Pers. Sg. Prät. v.* **blasen**

blind /blɪnt/ **1** *Adj.* **(a)** blind; ~ **werden** go blind; **auf einem Auge** ~ **sein** be blind in one eye; ~ **für etw. sein** be blind to sth.; **(b)** (maßlos) blind ⟨*rage, hatred, fear, etc.*⟩; indiscriminate ⟨*violence*⟩; **(c)** (kritiklos) blind ⟨*obedience, enthusiasm, belief, etc.*⟩; **(d)** (trübe) clouded ⟨*glass*⟩; dull, tarnished ⟨*metal*⟩; **(e)** (verdeckt) concealed; invisible ⟨*seam*⟩; **ein** ~**er Passagier** a stowaway; **(f)** ~**er Alarm** a false alarm; **(g) der** ~**e Zufall** pure *or* sheer chance. **2** *adv.* **(a)** (ohne hinzusehen) without looking; (wahllos) blindly; wildly; **(b)** (unkritisch) ⟨*trust*⟩ implicitly; ⟨*obey*⟩ blindly

Blind·darm *der* ▶326 **(a)** (Anat.) caecum; **(b)** (volkst.: Wurmfortsatz) appendix

Blind·darm-: ~**entzündung** *die* (volkst.) ▶329 appendicitis; ~**operation** *die* (volkst.) appendix operation ~**reizung** *die* (volkst.) ▶329 grumbling appendix

Blinde *der/die; adj. Dekl.* blind person; blind man/woman; **die** ~**n** the blind; **das sieht doch ein** ~**r [mit dem Krückstock]** (ugs.) anyone *or* any fool can see that

Blinde·kuh *o. Art.* blind man's buff

Blinden-: ~**hund** *der* guide dog; ~**schrift** *die* Braille

Blind·gänger *der* **(a)** (Geschoss) unexploded shell; dud (sl.); **(b)** (salopp: Versager) dead loss (coll.)

Blindheit *die;* ~ (auch fig.) blindness

blindlings /ˈblɪntlɪŋs/ *Adv.* blindly; ⟨*trust*⟩ implicitly

Blind·schleiche /~ʃlaiçə/ *die;* ~, ~**n** slowworm; blindworm

blind·wütig 1 *Adj.* raging ⟨*anger, hatred, fury, etc.*⟩; wild ⟨*rage*⟩. **2** *adv.* in a blind rage *or* fury

blinken /ˈblɪŋkn̩/ **1** *itr. V.* **(a)** ⟨*light, glass, crystal*⟩ flash; ⟨*star*⟩ twinkle; ⟨*metal, fish*⟩ gleam; **(b)** (Verkehrsw.) indicate. **2** *tr. V.* flash; **SOS** ~: flash an SOS [signal]

Blinker *der;* ~**s,** ~ **(a)** (am Auto) indicator [light]; winker; **(b)** (Angeln) spoon[-bait]

Blink-: ~**feuer** *das* (Seew.) flashing light; ~**licht** *das* (Verkehrsw.) flashing light; (Blinker) indicator light; ~**licht·anlage** *die* (Verkehrsw.) flashing lights *pl.* ~**zeichen** *das* flashlight signal

blinzeln /ˈblɪntsl̩n/ *itr. V.* blink; (mit einem Auge, um ein Zeichen zu geben) wink

Blitz /blɪts/ *der;* ~**es,** ~**e (a)** lightning *no indef. art.;* **ein** ~: a flash of lightning; **der** ~ **hat eingeschlagen** lightning has struck; **[schnell] wie der** ~: like lightning; as fast as lightning; **wie ein geölter** ~ (ugs.) like greased lightning; **wie ein** ~ **aus heiterem Himmel** like a bolt from the blue; **(b)** (Fot.) flash

blitz-, Blitz-: ~**ab·leiter** *der* lightning conductor; ~**aktion** *die* lightning operation; ~**angriff** *der* (Milit.) lightning attack; ~**artig 1** *Adj.; nicht präd.* lightning ⟨*disappear*⟩ in a flash; **2** *adv.* like lightning; ⟨*disappear*⟩ in a flash; ~**blank** *Adj.* (ugs.) ~**blank [geputzt]** sparkling clean; brightly polished ⟨*shoes*⟩

blitzeblank ⇒ **blitzblank**

blitzen 1 *itr. V.* **(a)** *unpers.* **es blitzte** (einmal) there was a flash of lightning; (mehrmals) there was lightning; there were flashes of lightning; **(b)** (glänzen) ⟨*light, glass, crystal*⟩ flash; ⟨*metal*⟩ gleam; **das Haus blitzte vor Sauberkeit** the house was sparkling clean; **(c)** (ugs.: mit Blitzlicht) use [a] flash. **2** *tr. V.* (ugs.) take a flash photo of

blitz-, Blitz-: ~**gerät** *das* (Fot.) flash [unit]; flashgun; ~**krieg** *der* (Milit.) blitzkrieg; ~**licht** *das; Pl.* ~**lichter** flash[light]; ~**sauber** *Adj.* sparkling clean; ~**schlag** *der* flash of lightning; **von einem** ~**schlag getroffen werden** be struck *or* hit by lightning; ~**schnell 1** *Adj.* lightning *attrib.;* ~**schnell sein** be like lightning; **2** *adv.* like lightning; ⟨*disappear*⟩ in a flash; ~**sieg** *der* (Milit.) lightning victory; ~**start** *der* lightning start; ~**um·frage** *die* lightning poll; ~**würfel** *der* (Fot.) flashcube

Block /blɔk/ *der;* ~**[e]s,** **Blöcke** /ˈblœkə/ *od.* ~**s (a)** *Pl.* **Blöcke** (Brocken) block; (Fels~) boulder; **(b)** (Wohn~) block;

(c) *Pl.* **Blöcke** (Gruppierung von politischen Kräften, Staaten) bloc; **(d)** (Schreib~) pad

Blockade /blɔˈkaːdə/ *die;* ~, ~**n** blockade

block-, Block-: ~**buchstabe** *der* block capital *or* letter; ~**flöte** *die* recorder; ~**frei** *Adj.* non-aligned ⟨*country, state*⟩; **die Blockfreien** the non-aligned countries *or* states; ~**haus** *das,* ~**hütte** *die* log cabin

blockieren 1 *tr. V.* block; jam ⟨*telephone line*⟩; stop, halt ⟨*traffic*⟩; lock ⟨*wheel, machine, etc.*⟩. **2** *itr. V.* ⟨*wheels*⟩ lock; ⟨*gears*⟩ jam

Block-: ~**schokolade** *die* cooking chocolate; ~**schrift** *die* block capitals *pl. or* letters *pl.;* ~**stunde** *die* (Schulw.) double period

blöd[e] /ˈbløːt, ˈbløːdə/ **1** *Adj.* **(a)** (schwachsinnig) mentally deficient; imbecilic; **(b)** (ugs.: dumm) stupid; idiotic (coll.); **(c)** (ugs.: unangenehm) stupid; **das Blöde ist nur, dass …:** the stupid thing is that … **2** *adv.* **(a)** (schwachsinnig) imbecilically; **(b)** (ugs.: dumm) stupidly; idiotically (coll.); **frag doch nicht so** ~: don't ask such stupid *or* (coll.) idiotic questions; **(c)** (ärgerlich) stupidly

Blödel /ˈbløːdl̩/ *der;* ~**s,** ~ (ugs. abwertend) ⇒ **Blödian**

Blödelei *die;* ~, ~**en (a)** *o. Pl.* messing *or* fooling about *no indef. art.;* **(b)** (Äußerung) silly joke

blödeln *itr. V.* **(a)** mess *or* fool about; **(b)** (alberne Witze machen) make silly jokes

blöder·weise *Adv.* (ugs.) stupidly

Blöd·hammel *der* (salopp abwertend) stupid fool *or* (coll.) idiot *or* (Brit. coll.) twit *or* (Amer. sl.) jerk

Blödheit *die;* ~, ~**en (a)** *o. Pl.* (Dummsein) stupidity; **(b)** (dumme Äußerung) stupid remark; (dumme Tat) stupid act; **(c)** *o. Pl.* (Schwachsinnigkeit) mental deficiency; imbecility

Blödian /ˈbløːdiaːn/ *der;* ~**s,** ~**e** (ugs. abwertend) idiot (coll.); fool

blöd-, Blöd-: ~**mann** *der; Pl.* ~**männer** (salopp) stupid idiot (coll.) *or* fool; ~**sinn** *der; o. Pl.* (ugs. abwertend) nonsense; **jetzt habe ich** ~**sinn gemacht** now I've [gone and] messed it up; **mach doch keinen** ~**sinn!** don't be stupid; ~**sinnig 1** *Adj.* **(a)** (ugs.) stupid; idiotic (coll.); **(b)** (schwachsinnig) mentally deficient; imbecilic; **2** *adv.* (ugs.) stupidly; idiotically (coll.)

blöken /ˈbløːkn̩/ *itr. V.* ⟨*sheep*⟩ bleat; ⟨*cattle*⟩ low

blond /blɔnt/ **1** *Adj.* fair-haired, blond ⟨*man, race*⟩; blonde, fair-haired ⟨*woman*⟩; blond/blonde, fair ⟨*hair*⟩ **2** *adv.* ~ **gelocktes Haar** fair curly hair; **ein** ~ **gelocktes Kind** with fair curly hair

Blond *das;* ~**s** blond; (von Frauenhaar) blonde

*blond·gelockt ⇒ **blond 2**

blondieren *tr. V.* bleach; (mit Färbemittel) dye blond/blonde; **sich** ~ **lassen** have one's hair bleached/dyed blond/blonde

Blondine /blɔnˈdiːnə/ *die;* ~, ~**n** blonde

bloß /bloːs/ **1** *Adj.* **(a)** (nackt) bare; naked; **mit** ~**em Oberkörper** stripped to the waist; **mit** ~**em Kopf** bareheaded; **mit** ~**en Händen** with one's bare hands; **(b)** (nichts als) mere ⟨*words, promises, triviality, suspicion, etc.*⟩; **der** ~**e Gedanke daran** the mere *or* very thought of it; **ein** ~**er Zufall** mere *or* pure chance; ~**es Gerede** mere gossip. **2** *Adv.* (ugs.: nur) only. **3** *Partikel* **was hast du dir** ~ **dabei gedacht?** what on earth *or* whatever were you thinking of?; **wie konnte das** ~ **geschehen?** how on earth did it happen?; **wenn ich das** ~ **wüsste!** if only I knew!; **sei** ~ **pünktlich!** just make sure you're on time

Blöße /ˈbløːsə/ *die;* ~, ~**n (a)** (geh.: Nacktheit) nakedness; **(b) in sich** (Dat.) **eine/keine** ~ **geben** show a/not show any weakness

bloß-: ~**|legen** *tr. V.* uncover; expose; (fig.) expose; reveal ⟨*error, defect, etc.*⟩; ~**|liegen** *unr. itr. V.; mit sein* be uncovered *or* exposed; ~**|stellen** *tr. V.* show up; ~**|strampeln** *refl. V.* kick the *or* one's covers off

Blouson /bluˈzõ/ *das od. der;* ~**s,** ~**s** blouson; bomber jacket

blubbern /ˈblʊbɐn/ *itr. V.* (ugs.) bubble

Blücher /ˈblyçɐ/ *in* **er/sie geht ran wie** ~ (ugs.) he/she really goes hard at it

Bluejeans, Blue Jeans /ˈbluːdʒiːns/ *Pl. od. die;* ~, ~: [blue] jeans *pl.;* denims *pl.*

---

*alte Schreibung (vgl. Hinweise auf S. xvi–xvii)

Blues /blu:s/ *der;* ~, ~ (Musik, Tanz) blues; **der** ~: the blues *sing. or pl.*

Bluff /blʊf/ *der;* ~s, ~s bluff

bluffen *tr., itr. V.* bluff

blühen /'bly:ən/ *itr. V.* (**a**) ⟨*plant*⟩ flower, bloom, be in flower *or* bloom; ⟨*flower*⟩ bloom, be in bloom, be out; ⟨*tree*⟩ be in blossom; **blau** ~: have blue flowers; ~**de Gärten** gardens full of flowers; **es blüht** there are flowers in bloom; (**b**) (florieren) flourish; thrive; (**c**) (ugs.: bevorstehen) jmdm. ~: be in store for sb.; **das kann dir auch noch** ~: the same may *or* could happen to you; **sonst blüht dir was!** otherwise you'll catch it!

blühend *Adj.* (**a**) (frisch, gesund) glowing ⟨*colour, complexion, etc.*⟩; radiant ⟨*health*⟩; **sie starb im** ~**en Alter von 20 Jahren** she died at 20, in the full bloom of youth; (**b**) (übertrieben) vivid, lively ⟨*imagination*⟩

Blümchen /'bly:mçən/ *das;* ~s, ~: [little] flower

Blume /'blu:mə/ *die;* ~, ~n (**a**) flower; **etw. durch die** ~ **sagen** say sth. in a roundabout way; (**b**) (des Weines) bouquet; (**c**) (des Biers) head

blumen-, Blumen-: ~**beet** *das* flower bed; ~**erde** *die* potting compost; ~**frau** *die* flower-woman; ~**garten** *der* flower garden; ~**geschäft** *das* florist's; flower shop; ~**geschmückt** *Adj.* flower-bedecked; adorned with flowers *postpos.;* ~**kasten** *der* flower box; (vor einem Fenster) window box; ~**kohl** *der* cauliflower; ~**laden** *der* ⇒ ~**geschäft;** ~**mädchen** *das* flower-girl; ~**muster** *das* floral pattern; ~**rabatte** *die* flower border; herbaceous border; ~**stock** *der* [flower-ing] pot plant; ~**strauß** *der* bunch of flowers; (Bukett) bouquet of flowers; ~**topf** *der* flowerpot; ~**vase** *die* [flower] vase; ~**zwiebel** *die* bulb

blümerant /blymə'rant/ *Adj.* queasy

Bluse /'blu:zə/ *die;* ~, ~n blouse

Blut /blu:t/ *das;* ~[e]s ▶ 326 | blood; **gleich ins** ~ **gehen** pass straight into the bloodstream; **es wurde viel** ~ **ver-gossen** there was a great deal of bloodshed; **den Zuschauern gefror** *od.* **stockte** *od.* **gerann das** ~ **in den Adern** (fig.) the spectators' blood ran cold; **an jmds. Händen klebt** ~ (fig. geh.) there is blood on sb.'s hands (fig.); **blaues** ~ **in den Adern haben** (fig.) have blue blood in one's veins (fig.); **böses** ~ **machen** *od.* **schaffen** (fig.) cause *or* create bad blood; ~ **und Wasser schwitzen** (fig. ugs.) sweat blood (fig. coll.); **[nur/immer] ruhig** ~! (ugs.) keep your hair on! (Brit. coll.); keep your cool! (coll.); **jmdn. bis aufs** ~ **quälen** *od.* **peinigen** (fig.) torment sb. merci-lessly; **jmdm. im** ~ **liegen** (fig.) be in sb.'s blood (fig.)

blut-, Blut-: ~**alkohol** *der* blood alcohol level; ~**apfelsine** *die* ⇒ ~**orange;** ~**arm** *Adj.* (Med.) an-aemic; ~**armut** *die* ▶ 329 | (Med.) anaemia; ~**bad** *das* bloodbath; ~**bahn** *die* bloodstream; ~**befleckt** *Adj.* bloodstained; **seine Hände sind** ~**befleckt** (fig.) he has blood on his hands; ~**beschmiert** *Adj.* smeared with blood *postpos.;* ~**bild** *das* (Med.) blood picture; ~**buche** *die* copper beech; ~**druck** *der; o. Pl.* blood pressure

Blüte /'bly:tə/ *die;* ~, ~n (**a**) flower; bloom; (eines Baums) blossom; ~**n treiben** flower; bloom; (tree) blossom; (**b**) (das Blühen) flowering; blooming; (Baum~) blossoming; **in [voller]** ~ **stehen** be in [full] flower *or* bloom/blossom; (**c**) (fig. geh.) **seine** ~ **erreichen** ⟨*culture*⟩ reach its full flowering; **die Renaissance war für die Kunst eine Zeit der** ~: art flourished during the Renaissance; (**d**) (ugs.: falsche Banknote) dud note (sl.)

Blut·egel *der* leech

bluten *itr. V.* (**a**) bleed (**aus** from); (**b**) (ugs.: viel bezahlen) **[ganz schön]** ~: cough up (coll.) *or* fork out (coll.) a[n aw-ful] lot of money

Blüten-: ~**blatt** *das* petal; ~**honig** *der* blossom honey; ~**kelch** *der* (Bot.) calyx; ~**knospe** *die* flower bud; ~**pflanze** *die* (Bot.) flowering plant; ~**stand** *der* (Bot.) inflorescence; ~**staub** *der* (Bot.) pollen

Blut·entnahme *die* taking of a blood sample; **zur** ~ **zum Arzt gehen** go to the doctor to have a blood sample taken

blüten·weiß *adj.* sparkling-white

Bluter /'blu:tɐ/ *der;* ~s, ~ (Med.) haemophiliac

Blut·erguss, *Blut·erguß *der* haematoma; (blauer Fleck) bruise

Bluter·krankheit *die* ▶ 329 | haemophilia *no art.*

Blüte·zeit *die* (**a**) **die** ~ **der Geranien ist von Mai bis Oktober** geraniums flower *or* are in flower from May to October; **während der** ~ **der Obstbäume** when the fruit trees are/were in blossom; (**b**) (fig.) heyday; **seine** ~ **erleben** ⟨*culture, empire*⟩ be in its heyday

Blut-: ~**fleck[en]** *der* bloodstain; ~**gefäß** *das* ▶ 326 | (Anat.) bloodvessel; ~**gerinnsel** *das* blood clot; ~**gruppe** *die* (Med.) blood group; blood type; **jmds.** ~**gruppe bestimmen** blood-type sb.'s type; **er hat** ~**gruppe 0** he is blood group 0; ~**hochdruck** *der* ▶ 329 | (Med.) high blood pressure; ~**hund** *der* blood-hound

blutig (**a**) bloody; **jmdn.** ~ **schlagen** beat sb. to a pulp; ~ **geschlagen werden** be left battered and bleeding; (**b**) *nicht präd.* (fig. ugs.) absolute, complete ⟨*beginner, layman, etc.*⟩

blut-, Blut-: ~**jung** *Adj.* very young; ~**konserve** *die* (Med.) container of stored blood; ~**konserven** stored blood; ~**körperchen** *das* (Anat.) blood corpuscle; **rote/weiße** ~**körperchen** red/white corpuscles; ~**krebs** *der* (Med.) leukaemia; ~**kreislauf** *der* (Physiol.) blood cir-culation; ~**lache** *die* pool of blood; ~**leer** *Adj.* (auch fig.) anaemic; ~**orange** *die* blood orange; ~**plasma** *das* (Physiol.) blood plasma; ~**probe** *die* (Med.) (**a**) blood sample; (**b**) (~untersuchung) blood test; ~**rache** *die* blood revenge; blood vengeance; ~**rausch** *der* (geh.) mur-derous frenzy; ~**rot** *Adj.* blood-red; ~**rünstig** /-rʏns tɪç/ **1** *Adj.* bloodthirsty; **2** *adv.* bloodthirstily; ~**sauger** *der* (auch fig.) bloodsucker

Bluts·brüderschaft *die* blood brotherhood

blut-, Blut-: ~**schande** *die* incest; ~**serum** *das* (Physiol.) blood serum; ~**spende** *die* (das Spenden) giving *no indef. art.* of blood; donation of blood; (~menge) blood-donation; ~**spender** *der* blood donor; ~**spur** *die* (**a**) trail of blood; (**b**) *Pl.* (auf Kleidung o. ä.) traces of blood; ~**stillend** *Adj.* styptic; ~**stillende Mittel** styptics

bluts-, Bluts-: ~**tropfen** *der* drop of blood; ~**ver-wandt** *Adj.* related by blood *postpos.;* **sie sind nicht** ~**verwandt** they are not blood relations; ~**verwandt-schaft** *die* blood relationship

blut-, Blut-: ~**tat** *die* (geh.) bloody deed; ~**transfu-sion** *die* blood transfusion; ~**triefend** *Adj.;* **nicht** *präd.* dripping with blood *pred.;* ~**überströmt** *Adj.* streaming with blood *pred.;* covered in blood *pred.*

Blutung *die;* ~, ~en (**a**) bleeding *no indef. art., no pl.;* haemorrhage; **innere/äußere** ~**en** internal/external bleeding *sing.;* (**b**) (Regel~) period

blut-, Blut-: ~**unterlaufen** *Adj.* suffused with blood *postpos.;* bloodshot ⟨*eyes*⟩; ~**untersuchung** *die* (Med.) blood test; ~**vergießen** *das;* ~s bloodshed; ~**vergiftung** *die* ▶ 329 | blood poisoning *no indef. art., no pl.;* ~**verlust** *der* loss of blood; ~**verschmiert** *Adj.* bloodstained, smeared with blood *pred.;* ~**wurst** *die* black pudding; ~**zucker** *der* (Physiol.) blood sugar

b-Moll /'be:mɔl/ *das;* ~: B flat minor

BMX-Rad /beɛm'ɪks:.../ *das* BMX [bike]

Bö /bø:/ *die;* ~, ~en gust [of wind]

Bob /bɔp/ *der;* ~s, ~s bob[-sleigh]

Bob-: ~**bahn** *die* bob[-sleigh] run; ~**fahrer** *der* bobber; ~**rennen** *das* bob[-sleigh] racing; (Veranstaltung) bob [-sleigh] race

Bock¹ /bɔk/ *der;* ~[e]s, Böcke /'bœkə/ (**a**) (Reh~, Kanin-chen~) buck; (Ziegen~) billy goat; he-goat; (Schafs~) ram; **stur wie ein** ~ **sein** (ugs.) be as stubborn as a mule; **einen** ~ **schießen** (fig. ugs.) boob (Brit. sl.); make a boo-boo (Amer. coll.); (einen Fauxpas begehen) drop a clanger (Brit. sl.); **den** ~ **zum Gärtner machen** (ugs.) be asking for trouble; **einen/keinen** ~ **auf etw.** (*Akk.*) **haben** (ugs.) fancy/not fancy sth.; (**b**) (ugs.: Schimpfwort) **der geile alte** ~: the randy old goat; **sturer** ~! you stubborn git (sl. de-rog.); (**c**) (Gestell) trestle; (**d**) (Turnen) buck; (**e**) (Kutsch~) box

Bock² *das;* ∼**s**, **Bock·bier** *das* bock [beer]

bocken *itr. V.* (a) (nicht weitergehen) refuse to go on; (vor einer Hürde) refuse; (sich aufbäumen) buck; rear; (b) (fam.: trotzig sein) be stubborn and awkward; play up (coll.); (fig. ugs.) ⟨*car*⟩ play up (coll.)

bockig 1 *Adj.* stubborn and awkward; contrary (coll.). **2** *adv.* stubbornly [and awkwardly]; contrarily (coll.)

Bock·mist *der* (salopp) bilge *no indef. art.* (sl.); bullshit *no indef. art.* (coarse)

Bocks-: ∼**beutel** *der* (a) bocksbeutel; *wide, bulbous bottle for fine Franconian wines;* (b) (Wein) *o. Pl.* bocksbeutel wine; ∼**horn** *das in* sich ins ∼**horn** jagen lassen (ugs.) let oneself be browbeaten

Bock-: ∼**springen** *das* (Turnen) vaulting [over the buck]; (ohne Gerät) leapfrog; ∼**sprung** *der* (ungelenker Sprung) [ungainly] jump *or* leap; ∼**sprünge machen** jump *or* leap about; ∼**wurst** *die* bockwurst

Boden /'bo:dn̩/ *der;* ∼**s**, **Böden** /'bø:dn̩/ (a) (Erde) ground; soil; **etw. [nicht] aus dem** ∼ **stampfen können** [not] be able to conjure sth. up [out of thin air]; (b) (Fuß∼) floor; **zu** ∼ **fallen/sich zu** ∼ **fallen lassen** fall/drop to the ground; **der Boxer ging zu** ∼: the boxer went down; **jmdn. zu** ∼ **schlagen** *od.* (geh.) strecken knock sb. down; floor sb.; (fig.) **sich auf unsicherem** ∼ **bewegen** be on shaky ground (fig.); **am** ∼ **liegen** be bankrupt; **am** ∼ **zerstört [sein]** (ugs.) [be] shattered (coll.); **bleiben wir doch auf dem** ∼ **der Tatsachen!** let's stick to the facts; (c) *o. Pl.* (Terrain) **heiliger** ∼: holy ground; **feindlicher** ∼: enemy territory; **auf französischem** ∼: on French soil; **[an]** ∼ **gewinnen/verlieren** gain/lose ground; (d) (unterste Fläche) bottom; (Hosen∼) seat; (Torten∼) base; *s. auch* **doppelt**; (e) (Dach∼) loft; **auf dem** ∼: in the loft

boden-, Boden-: ∼**belag** *der* (Teppich, Linoleum) floor-covering; (Fliesen, Parkett) flooring; ∼**erosion** *die* soil erosion; ∼**frost** *der* ground frost; ∼**haltung** *die o. Pl.* (Landw.) deep-litter system (*of poultry farming*); ∼**kammer** *die* attic; ∼**los** *Adj.* (a) (tief) bottomless; **ins Bodenlose fallen** fall into a bottomless abyss; (b) (ugs.: unerhört) incredible, unbelievable ⟨*foolishness, meanness, etc.*⟩; ∼**nebel** *der* ground mist; (dichter) ground fog; ∼**personal** *das* (Flugw.) ground staff; ∼**reform** *die* land reform; ∼**satz** *der* sediment; ∼**schätze** *Pl.* mineral resources

Boden·see *der;* ∼**s** Lake Constance

boden-, Boden-: ∼**ständig** *Adj.* indigenous, native ⟨*culture, population, etc.*⟩; local ⟨*custom, craft, cuisine, tradition*⟩; ⟨*novel*⟩ rooted in the soil; ∼**station** *die* (Raumf.) ground station; ∼**streitkräfte** *Pl.,* ∼**truppen** *Pl.* ground forces *or* troops; ∼**turnen** *das* floor exercises *pl.;* ∼**vase** *die* large vase (standing on the floor); ∼**welle** *die* bump

Bodybuilding /'bɔdibildɪŋ/ *das;* ∼**s** body-building *no art.*

Bodycheck /'bɔditʃɛk/ *der;* ∼**s**, ∼**s** (Eishockey) bodycheck

Böe /'bø:ə/ *die;* ∼, ∼**n** ⇒ **Bö**

Bofist /'bo:fɪst/ *der;* ∼**[e]s**, ∼**e** puff-ball

bog /bo:k/ *1. u. 3. Pers. Sg. Prät. v.* **biegen**

Bogen /'bo:gn̩/ *der;* ∼**s**, ∼ (südd., österr.:) **Bögen** /'bø:gn̩/ (a) (gebogene Linie) curve; (Math.) arc; (Skifahren) turn; (Schlittschuhlaufen) curve; **einen** ∼ **schlagen** move in a curve; **der Weg macht/beschreibt einen** ∼: the path bends/the path describes a curve; **immer, wenn ich sie auf der Straße sehe, mache ich einen großen** ∼ (fig. ugs.) whenever I see her in the street I make a detour [round her]; **einen großen** ∼ **um jmdn./etw. machen** (fig. ugs.) give sb./sth. a wide berth; **in hohem** ∼ **hinausfliegen** (fig. ugs.) be chucked out (sl.); (b) (Archit.) arch; (c) (Waffe) bow; **den** ∼ **überspannen** (fig.) go too far; (d) (Musik: Geigen∼ usw.) bow; (e) (Papier∼) sheet; **ein** ∼ **Packpapier** a sheet of wrapping paper; **ein A4-**∼: a sheet of A4 paper; (f) (Musik: Zeichen) slur; (bei gleicher Notenhöhe) tie

bogen-, Bogen-: ∼**fenster** *das* arched window; ∼**förmig** *Adj.* arched; ∼**gang** *der* arcade;

∼**schießen** *das* (Sport) archery *no art.;* ∼**schütze** *der* (Sport) archer

Boheme /bo'e:m/ *die;* ∼: bohemian world *or* society

Bohemien /boe'mjɛ̃:/ *der;* ∼**s**, ∼**s** bohemian

Bohle /'bo:lə/ *die;* ∼, ∼**n** [thick] plank

Böhme /'bø:mə/ *der;* ∼**n**, ∼**n** Bohemian

Böhmen /'bø:mən/ (das); ∼**s** Bohemia

Böhmer·wald *der* Bohemian Forest

Böhmin *die;* ∼, ∼**nen** Bohemian

böhmisch *Adj.* Bohemian

Böhnchen /'bø:nçən/ *das;* ∼**s**, ∼: [small] bean

Bohne /'bo:nə/ *die;* ∼, ∼**n** bean; **grüne** ∼**n** green beans; French beans (Brit.); **dicke/weiße** ∼**n** broad/haricot beans; **blaue** ∼**n** (scherzh.) bullets; **nicht die** ∼ (ugs.) not one little bit

Bohnen-: ∼**ein·topf** *der* bean stew; ∼**kaffee** *der* real coffee; ∼**kraut** *das* savory; ∼**salat** *der* bean salad; ∼**stange** *die* (auch ugs.: Mensch) beanpole; ∼**stroh** *in* **dumm wie** ∼**stroh** (ugs.) as thick as two short planks (coll.); ∼**suppe** *die* bean soup

bohnern *tr., itr. V.* polish; „**Vorsicht, frisch gebohnert!**" 'freshly polished floor/stairs *etc.*'

Bohner·wachs *das* floor polish

bohren /'bo:rən/ **1** *tr. V.* (a) bore; (mit Bohrer, Bohrmaschine) drill, bore ⟨*hole*⟩; sink ⟨*well, shaft*⟩; bore, drive ⟨*tunnel*⟩; sink ⟨*pole, post etc.*⟩ (**in** + *Akk.* into); (b) (bearbeiten) drill ⟨*wood, concrete, etc.*⟩; (c) (drücken in) poke (**in** + *Akk.* in[to]). **2** *itr. V.* (a) (eine Bohrung vornehmen) drill; **in der Nase** ∼ pick one's nose; **nach Öl/Wasser** usw. ∼ drill for oil/water *etc.;* (b) (ugs.: drängen, fragen) keep on; **jetzt hört auf zu** ∼: now, don't keep on. **3** *refl. V.* **sich in/durch etw.** ∼ bore its way into/through sth.

bohrend *Adj.* (a) gnawing ⟨*pain, hunger, remorse*⟩; (b) (hartnäckig) piercing ⟨*look etc.*⟩; probing ⟨*question*⟩

Bohrer *der;* ∼**s**, ∼: drill; (zum Vorbohren) gimlet

Bohr-: ∼**insel** *die* drilling rig; ∼**kern** *der* (Technik) drill core; ∼**maschine** *die* drill; ∼**meißel** *der* bit; ∼**schrauber** *der* power drill/screwdriver; ∼**turm** *der* derrick

Bohrung *die;* ∼, ∼**en** (a) ⇒ **bohren 1 a:** boring; drilling; sinking; driving; (b) (Loch) drill-hole

böig *Adj.* gusty

Boiler /'bɔylɐ/ *der;* ∼**s**, ∼: water heater

Boje /'bo:jə/ *die;* ∼, ∼**n** buoy

Bolero /bo'le:ro/ *der;* ∼**s**, ∼**s** bolero

Bolivianer /boli'vja:nɐ/ *der;* ∼**s**, ∼, **Bolivianerin** *die;* ∼, ∼**nen** ▶ 388 | Bolivian

bolivianisch *Adj.* ▶ 388 | Bolivian

Bolivien /bo'li:vjən/ (das); ∼**s** Bolivia

Böller·schuss, *°***Böller·schuß** /'bœlɐ-/ *der* gun salute; **der Admiral wurde mit fünf Böllerschüssen begrüßt** the admiral was greeted with a five-gun salute

Boll·werk *das* bulwark; (fig.) bulwark; bastion; stronghold

Bolschewik /bɔlʃe'vɪk/ *der;* ∼**en**, ∼**i**, (abwertend:) ∼**en** Bolshevik

Bolschewismus /bɔlʃe'vɪsmʊs/ *der;* ∼: Bolshevism *no art.*

Bolschewist *der;* ∼**en**, ∼**en** Bolshevist

bolschewistisch *Adj.* Bolshevik

bolzen /'bɔltsn̩/ *itr. V.* (ugs.) kick the ball about

Bolzen *der;* ∼**s**, ∼ (a) pin; bolt; (mit Gewinde) bolt; (b) (Geschoss) bolt

Bolzerei *die;* ∼, ∼**en** (ugs.) [aimless] kick-about

Bolz·platz *der* [children's] football area

bombardieren /bɔmbar'di:rən/ *tr. V.* (a) (Milit.) bomb; (b) (fig. ugs.) bombard

Bombardierung *die;* ∼, ∼**en** (a) (Milit.) bombing; (b) (fig. ugs.) bombardment

bombastisch (abwertend) **1** *Adj.* bombastic ⟨*speech, language, style, etc.*⟩; ostentatious ⟨*architecture, theatrical, production*⟩. **2** *adv.* ⟨*speak, write*⟩ bombastically; ostentatiously ⟨*dressed*⟩

Bombe /'bɔmbə/ *die;* ~, ~**n** (a) bomb; **die Nachricht schlug uns wie eine** ~: the news came as a bombshell; **die** ~ **ist geplatzt** (fig. ugs.) the balloon has gone up (fig.); (b) (Sportjargon: Schuss) thunderbolt; tremendous shot (coll.)

bomben-, Bomben-: ~**angriff** *der* bomb attack; bombing raid; ~**an·schlag** *der.,* ~**attentat** *das* bomb attack; ~**drohung** *die* bomb threat; ~**erfolg** *der* (ugs.) smash hit (sl.); ~**form** *die* (ugs.) top form; ~**ge·halt** *das* (ugs.) tremendous salary (coll.); ~**geschäft** *das* (ugs.) **ein** ~**geschäft machen** do a roaring trade; ~**krater** *der* bomb crater; ~**sicher** *Adj.* (a) bomb-proof; (b) /'--'--/ (ugs.: gewiss) dead certain (coll.); ~**stim·mung** *die* (ugs.) tremendous *or* fantastic atmosphere (coll.)

Bomber *der;* ~**s,** ~ (ugs.) bomber

bombig *Adj.* (ugs.) super (coll.); smashing (coll.); terrific (coll.); fantastic (coll.)

Bommel /'bɔml/ *die;* ~, ~**n** *od. der;* ~**s,** ~ (bes. nordd.) bobble; pompom

Bon /bɔŋ/ *der;* ~**s,** ~**s** (a) voucher; coupon; (b) (Kassen~) sales slip

Bonbon /bɔŋ'bɔŋ/ *der od.* (österr. nur) *das;* ~**s,** ~**s** sweet; candy (Amer.); (fig.) treat

bonbon-: ~**farben,** ~**farbig** *Adj.* (abwertend) candy-coloured

bongen /'bɔŋən/ *tr. V.* (ugs.) ring up; **gebongt sein** (fig.) be fine

Bongo /'bɔŋgo/ *das;* ~**s,** ~**s** *od. die;* ~, ~**s** bongo [drum]

Bonität /boni'tɛ:t/ *die;* ~ (Kaufmannsspr.) creditworthiness; [good] credit rating

Bonmot /bõ'mo:/ *das;* ~**s,** ~**s** bon mot

Bonsai *der;* ~**s,** ~**s** bonsai [tree]

Bonus /'bo:nʊs/ *der;* ~ *od.* **Bonusses,** ~ *od.* **Bonusse** (a) (Kaufmannsspr.) (Rabatt) discount; (Dividende) extra dividend; (Versicherungsw.) bonus; (b) (Punktvorteil) bonus points *pl.*

Bonze /'bɔntsə/ *der;* ~**n,** ~**n** (abwertend: Funktionär) bigwig (coll.); big noise (coll.); big wheel (Amer. sl.)

Boogie-Woogie /'bʊgi'vʊgi/ *der;* ~[**s**], ~**s** boogie-woogie

Boom /bu:m/ *der;* ~**s,** ~**s** boom

Boot /bo:t/ *das;* ~[**e**]**s,** ~**e;** **wir sitzen alle in einem** *od.* **im selben** ~ (fig. ugs.) we're all in the same boat

booten /'bu:tn/ *tr. V.* (DV) boot [up]; **neu** ~: reboot

Boots-: ~**fahrt** *die* boat trip; ~**haus** *das* boathouse; ~**länge** *die* [boat's] length; ~**mann** *der Pl.* ~**leute** (a) ≈ boatswain, bosun; (b) (Milit.: Rang) ≈ petty officer; ~**steg** *der* landing stage; ~**verleih** *der* boat hire [business]

Bor /bo:ɐ/ *das;* ~**s** (Chemie) boron

Bord¹ /bɔrt/ *das;* ~[**e**]**s,** ~**e** shelf

Bord² *der;* ~[**e**]**s,** ~**e: an** ~: on board; **an** ~ **eines Schiffes/der „Baltic"** on board *or* aboard a ship/the 'Baltic'; **alle Mann an** ~! all aboard!; **über** ~: overboard; **etw. über** ~ **werfen** (auch fig.) throw sth. overboard; **von** ~ **gehen** leave the ship/aircraft

Bord-: ~**buch** *das* log[-book]; ~**computer** *der* on-board computer

Bordeaux /bɔr'do:/ *der;* ~ /bɔr'do:s/, ~ /bɔr'do:s/ ⇒ **Bordeauxwein**

bordeaux·rot *Adj.* bordeaux-red; claret

Bordeaux·wein *der* Bordeaux [wine]; **roter** ~: claret

Bordell /bɔr'dɛl/ *das;* ~**s,** ~**e** brothel

Bord-: ~**funk** *der* [ship's/aircraft] radio; ~**funker** *der* radio operator; ~**personal** *das* (Flugw.) cabin crew; ~**stein** *der* kerb; ~**stein·kante** *die* [edge of the] kerb

Bordüre /bɔr'dy:rə/ *die;* ~, ~**n** edging

borgen /'bɔrgn/ *tr. V.:* ⇒ **leihen**

Borke /'bɔrkə/ *die;* ~, ~**n** bark

Borken·käfer *der* bark beetle

borkig *Adj.* cracked ⟨earth⟩; chapped, cracked ⟨skin⟩

borniert /bɔr'ni:ɐt/ (abwertend) **1** *Adj.* narrow-minded; bigoted. **2** *adv.* in a narrow-minded *or* bigoted way

Borniertheit *die;* ~: narrow-mindedness; bigotry

Borretsch /'bɔrɛtʃ/ *der;* ~[**e**]**s** borage

Bor·salbe *die* boric acid ointment

Börse /'bœrzə/ *die;* ~, ~**n** (a) (Aktien~) stock market; **an der** ~: on the stock market; (b) (Gebäude) stock exchange; (c) (geh. veralt.: Geld~) purse

Börsen-: ~**beginn** *der* opening of the [stock] market; ~**fähig,** ~**gängig** *Adj.* (Wirtsch.) ⟨commodity, security, etc.⟩ negotiable on the stock market; ~**gang** *der* (Wirtsch.) [stock market] flotation; ~**krach** *der* stock market crash; collapse of the [stock] market; ~**kurs** *der* [stock-]market price; ~**makler** *der* stockbroker; ~**speku·lation** *die* speculation on the stock market; ~**tendenz** *die* [stock-]market trend

Börsianer *der;* ~**s,** ~ (ugs.) (a) (Makler) stockbroker; (b) (Spekulant) stock market speculator

Borste /'bɔrstə/ *die;* ~, ~**n** bristle

borstig *Adj.* bristly

Borte /'bɔrtə/ *die;* ~, ~**n** braiding *no indef. art.;* trimming *no indef. art.;* edging *no indef. art.*

Bor·wasser *das* boric acid lotion

bös /bø:s/ ⇒ **böse 1 c, d, 2**

bös·artig 1 *Adj.* (a) malicious ⟨person, remark, etc.⟩; vicious ⟨animal⟩; (b) (Med.) malignant. **2** *adv.* maliciously

Bös·artigkeit *die* (a) maliciousness; (von Tieren) viciousness; (b) (Med.) malignancy

Böschung /'bœʃʊŋ/ *die;* ~, ~**en** (an der Straße) bank; embankment; (am Bahndamm) embankment; (am Fluss) bank

böse /'bø:zə/ **1** *Adj.* (a) wicked; evil; **jmdm. Böses tun** (geh.) do sb. harm; **ich will dir doch nichts Böses** I don't mean you any harm; (b) *nicht präd.* (schlimm, übel) bad ⟨times, illness, dream, etc.⟩; nasty ⟨experience, affair, situation, trick, surprise, etc.⟩; **ein** ~ **Ende nehmen** end in disaster; **eine** ~ **Geschichte** a bad *or* nasty business; **nichts Böses ahnend** unsuspectingly; (c) (ugs.) (wütend) mad (coll.); (verärgert) cross (coll.); ~ **auf jmdm.** *od.* **mit jmdm. sein** be mad at/cross with sb. (coll.); ~ **über etw.** (*Akk.*) **sein** be mad at/cross about sth. (coll.); (d) (fam.: ungezogen) naughty; (e) *nicht präd.* (ugs.: arg) terrible (coll.) ⟨pain, fall, shock, disappointment, storm, etc.⟩. **2** *adv.* (a) (schlimm, übel) ⟨end⟩ badly; **mit ihm wird es noch** ~ **enden** he'll come to a bad end; **das wird** ~ **enden** it is bound to end in disaster; **es war nicht** ~ **gemeint** I didn't mean it nastily; (b) (ugs.) (wütend) angrily; (verärgert) crossly (coll.); (c) (ugs.: sehr) terribly (coll.) ⟨hurt⟩ badly

Böse·wicht *der;* ~[**e**]**s,** ~**er** (a) (ugs. scherzh.: Schlingel) rascal; (b) (veralt., fig.: Schuft) villain

boshaft /'bo:shaft/ **1** *Adj.* malicious. **2** *adv.* maliciously

Boshaftigkeit *die;* ~, ~**en** (a) *o. Pl.* maliciousness; (b) (Bemerkung) malicious remark; (Handlung) piece of maliciousness

Bosheit *die;* ~, ~**en** (a) *o. Pl.* (Art) malice; (b) (Bemerkung) malicious remark; (Handlung) piece of maliciousness

Boskop /'bɔskɔp/, **Boskoop** /'bɔsko:p/ *der;* ~**s,** ~: russet

Bosnien /'bɔsniən/ ⟨*das*⟩; ~**s** Bosnia

Bosnien und Herzegowina /--hertse'go:vina/ ⟨*das*⟩; ~**s** Bosnia-Herzegovina

Boss, *Boß /bɔs/ *der;* ~**es,** ~**e** (ugs.) boss (coll.)

Bossa Nova /'bɔsa'no:va/ *der;* ~~, ~~**s** bossa nova

bosseln /'bɔsln/ *tr., itr. V.* (ugs.) **etw./an etw.** (*Dat.*) ~: beaver away (Brit.) *or* slave away making sth.; **er braucht immer was zu** ~: he always needs to be working on *or* making something

bös·willig 1 *Adj.* malicious; wilful ⟨desertion⟩. **2** *adv.* maliciously; wilfully ⟨desert⟩

Böswilligkeit *die;* ~: malice; maliciousness

bot /bo:t/ *1. u. 3. Pers. Sg. Prät. v.* **bieten**

Botanik /bo'ta:nɪk/ *die;* ~: botany *no art.*

Botaniker *der;* ~**s,** ~: botanist

botanisch 1 *Adj.* botanical. **2** *adv.* botanically

Bötchen /'bø:tçən/ *das;* ~**s,** ~: little boat

Bote /'bo:tə/ *der;* ~**n,** ~**n** (a) messenger; (fig.) herald; harbinger; (b) (Laufbursche) errand boy; messenger [boy]

Boten-: ∼**dienst** der job as a messenger [boy]/an errand boy; ∼**gang** der errand; ∼**gänge erledigen** run errands

bot·mäßig (geh. veralt.) **1** Adj. (gehorsam) obedient; (untertänig) submissive. **2** adv. (gehorsam) obediently; (untertänig) submissively

Botschaft die; ∼, ∼**en** (a) message; **die Frohe** ∼ (das Evangelium) the Gospel; (b) (diplomatische Vertretung) embassy

Botschafter der; ∼s, ∼, **Botschafterin** die; ∼, ∼**nen** ambassador; **der irische Botschafter in Japan** the Irish ambassador to Japan

Böttcher /'bœtçɐ/ der; ∼s, ∼: ▶ 85 | cooper

Böttcherei die; ∼, ∼**en** (a) o. Pl. (Handwerk) cooper's trade; cooperage no art.; (b) (Werkstatt) cooper's workshop; cooperage

Bottich /'bɔtɪç/ der; ∼s, ∼e tub

Bouillon /bul'jɔŋ/ die; ∼, ∼s bouillon; consommé

Bouillon·würfel der bouillon cube

Boulevard /bulə'vaːɐ/ der; ∼s, ∼s boulevard

Boulevard-: ∼**blatt** das ⇒ ∼**zeitung**; ∼**presse** die (abwertend) popular press; ∼**theater** das light theatre; ∼**zeitung** die (abwertend) popular rag (derog.); tabloid

bourgeois /bʊr'ʒoa/ Adj. (abwertend, Soziol.) bourgeois

Bourgeois der; ∼, ∼ (abwertend, Soziol.) bourgeois

Bourgeoisie /bʊrʒoa'ziː/ die; ∼, ∼**n** (abwertend, Soziol.) bourgeoisie

Boutique /bu'tiːk/ die; ∼, ∼**n** /---kn̩/ boutique

Bovist ⇒ **Bofist**

Bowden·zug /'baʊdn̩-/ der (Technik) Bowden cable

Bowle /'boːlə/ die; ∼, ∼**n** punch (made of wine, champagne, sugar, and fruit or spices)

Bowling /'boʊlɪŋ/ das; ∼s, ∼s [ten-pin] bowling

Bowling·bahn die [ten-pin] bowling alley

Box /bɔks/ die; ∼, ∼**en** (a) box; (b) (Lautsprecher∼) speaker; (c) (Pferde∼) [loose] box; (d) (Motorsport) pit; **an den** ∼**en** in the pits

boxen 1 itr. V. box; **gegen jmdn.** ∼: fight sb.; **box [against] sb.**; **jmdm. in den Magen** ∼: punch sb. in the stomach. **2** tr. V. (a) (ugs.) punch; (b) (Sportjargon: boxen gegen) fight. **3** refl. V. (a) **sich ins Freie/durch die Menge** usw. ∼ (ugs.) fight one's way outside/through the crowd etc.; (b) (ugs.: sich prügeln) have a punch-up (coll.) or fight

Boxer der; ∼s, ∼ (Sportler, Hund) boxer

Boxer-: ∼**motor** der (Technik) horizontally opposed engine; ∼**nase** die boxer's nose

Box·hand·schuh der boxing glove

Box·kalf /-kalf/ das; ∼s, ∼s boxcalf

Box-: ∼**kampf** der boxing match; (Prügelei) fist-fight; ∼**ring** der boxing ring; ∼**sport** der; o. Pl. boxing no art.

Boy /bɔy/ der; ∼s, ∼s servant; (im Hotel) pageboy

Boykott /bɔy'kɔt/ der; ∼[e]s, ∼s boycott

boykottieren tr. V. boycott

brabbeln /'brabl̩n/ tr., itr. V. (ugs.) mutter; mumble; ⟨baby⟩ babble

brach /braːx/ 1. u. 3. Pers. Sg. Prät. v. **brechen**

brachial /bra'xiaːl/ Adj. violent; ∼**e Gewalt** brute force

Brachial·gewalt die; o. Pl. brute force

Brach·land das fallow [land]; (auf Dauer) uncultivated or waste land

brach|liegen unr. itr. V. (auch fig.) lie fallow; (auf Dauer) lie waste

brachte /'braxtə/ 1. u. 3. Pers. Sg. Prät. v. **bringen**

Brach·vogel der curlew

Brahmane /bra'maːnə/ der; ∼n, ∼n Brahmin

Branche /'brãːʃə/ die; ∼, ∼**n** [branch of] industry; **er kennt sich in der** ∼ **am besten aus** he has the most knowledge of the industry

Branchen·verzeichnis das classified directory; (Telefonbuch) yellow pages pl.

Brand /brant/ der; ∼[e]s, **Brände** /'brɛndə/ (a) fire; (b) (Brennen) **beim** ∼ **der Scheune** when the barn caught fire; **in** ∼ **geraten** catch fire; **etw. in** ∼ **setzen** od. **stecken** set fire to sth.; set sth. on fire; (c) (ugs.: Durst) raging thirst

brand-, Brand-: ∼**aktuell** Adj. up-to-the-minute ⟨report⟩; red-hot ⟨news item, issue⟩; highly topical ⟨book⟩; ∼**binde** die dressing [for burns]; ∼**blase** die [burn] blister; ∼**eilig** Adj. (ugs.) extremely urgent

branden itr. V. (geh.) break

Branden·burg (das); ∼s Brandenburg

Brandenburger 1 indekl. Adj.; nicht präd. Brandenburg attrib.; **das** ∼ **Tor** the Brandenburg Gate. **2** der; ∼s, ∼: native of Brandenburg; (Einwohner) inhabitant of Brandenburg; **die** ∼: the people of Brandenburg

brandenburgisch Adj. Brandenburg attrib.

brand-, Brand-: ∼**fleck** der burn mark; ∼**gefahr** die danger of fire; ∼**geruch** der smell of burning; ∼**herd** der source of the fire; ∼**mal** das (geh.) burn mark; ∼**marken** tr. V. brand ⟨person⟩; denounce ⟨thing⟩; **jmdn. als Verräter** ∼**marken** brand sb. as a traitor; ∼**neu** Adj. (ugs.) brand-new; ∼**rede** die fiery tirade; ∼**salbe** die ointment for burns; ∼**schaden** der fire damage no pl., no indef. art.; ∼**schatzen** tr. V. (hist.) pillage and threaten to burn; ∼**sohle** die insole; ∼**stelle** die (verbrannte Stelle) burn; (größer) burnt patch; ∼**stifter** der arsonist; ∼**stiftung** die arson no pl., no indef. art.

Brandung die; ∼, ∼**en** surf; breakers pl.

Brandungs·welle die breaker

Brand·wunde die burn; (Verbrühung) scald

brannte /'brantə/ 1. u. 3. Pers. Sg. Prät. v. **brennen**

Brannt·wein der (a) spirit; (b) o. Pl. (Spirituosen) spirits pl.

Brasil die; ∼, ∼[s] Brazil cigar

Brasilianer /brazi'liaːnɐ/ der; ∼s, ∼, **Brasilianerin** die; ∼, ∼**nen** ▶ 388 | Brazilian

brasilianisch Adj. ▶ 388 | Brazilian

Brasilien /bra'ziːliən/ (das) ∼s Brazil

brät /brɛːt/ 3. Pers. Sg. Präsens v. **braten**

Brat·apfel der baked apple

braten /'braːtn̩/ unr. tr., itr. V. fry; (im Backofen, am Spieß) roast

Braten der; ∼s, ∼ (a) joint; (b) o. Pl. roast [meat] no indef. art.; **kalter** ∼: cold meat; (c) **den** ∼ **riechen** (fig. ugs.) get wind of what's going on; (merken, dass etwas nicht stimmt) smell a rat

Braten-: ∼**saft** der meat juice[s pl.]; ∼**soße** die gravy

Brat-: ∼**fett** das [cooking] fat; ∼**fisch** der fried fish; ∼**hähnchen** das, (südd., österr.) ∼**hendl** das (a) roast chicken; (gegrillt) broiled chicken; (b) (Hähnchen zum Braten) roasting chicken; (zum Grillen) broiling chicken; ∼**hering** der fried herring; ∼**huhn** das, ∼**hühnchen** das ⇒ ∼**hähnchen**; ∼**kartoffeln** Pl. fried potatoes; home fries (Amer.); ∼**ofen** der oven; ∼**pfanne** die frying pan; ∼**röhre** die ⇒ ∼**ofen**; ∼**rost** der grill

Bratsche /'braːtʃə/ die; ∼, ∼**n** (Musik) viola

Bratschist der; ∼en, ∼en violist; viola-player

Brat-: ∼**spieß** der spit; ∼**wurst** die (a) [fried/grilled] sausage; (b) (Wurst zum Braten) sausage [for frying/grilling]

Brauch /braux/ der; ∼[e]s, **Bräuche** /'brɔyçə/ custom; **das ist bei ihnen so** ∼: that's their custom; **nach altem** ∼: in accordance with an old custom

brauchbar 1 Adj. useful; (benutzbar) usable; wearable ⟨clothes⟩. **2** adv. **er schreibt/arbeitet ganz** ∼: he's a useful writer/he does useful work

brauchen 1 tr. V. (a) (benötigen) need; **alles, was man zum Leben braucht** everything one needs in order to live reasonably; (b) (aufwenden müssen) **mit dem Auto braucht er nur zehn Minuten** it only takes him ten minutes by car; **er hat für die Arbeit Jahre gebraucht** the work took him years; **wie lange hast du dafür gebraucht?** how long did it take you?; (c) (benutzen, gebrauchen) use; **ich könnte es gut ∼:** I could do with it. **2** *mod. V.;* **2.** *Part.* ∼: need; **du brauchst nicht zu helfen** there is no need [for you] to help; you don't need to help; **du brauchst doch nicht gleich zu weinen** there's no need to start crying; **das hättest du nicht zu tun ∼:** there was no need to do it; you needn't have done that; **du brauchst es [mir] nur zu sagen** you only have to tell me

Brauchtum *das;* ∼s, **Brauchtümer** /-ty:mɐ/ custom

Braue /'brauǝ/ *die;* ∼, ∼n ▶ 326 ┃ [eye]brow

brauen *tr. V.* **(a)** brew; **(b)** (ugs.: aufbrühen, zubereiten) brew [up] ⟨*tea, coffee*⟩; concoct ⟨*potion etc.*⟩

Brauerei *die;* ∼, ∼en **(a)** *o. Pl.* brewing; **(b)** (Betrieb) brewery

braun /braun/ *Adj.* **(a)** brown; ∼ **werden** (sonnengebräunt) get brown; get a tan; ∼ **gebrannt** [sun]tanned; **(b)** (abwertend: nationalsozialistisch) Nazi; ∼ **sein** ⟨*person*⟩ be a Nazi; **die Zeitung ist ziemlich ∼:** the paper has definite Nazi tendencies

Braun *das;* ∼s, ∼, (ugs.) ∼s brown

braun·äugig *Adj.* brown-eyed; ∼ **sein** have brown eyes

Braun·bär *der* brown bear

Bräune /'brɔynǝ/ *die;* ∼: [sun-]tan

bräunen **1** *tr. V.* **(a)** tan ⟨*skin, body, etc.*⟩; **sich ∼:** get a tan; **(b)** (Kochk.) brown. **2** *itr. V.* **die Sonne bräunt stark** the sun gives you a good tan. **3** *refl. V.* go brown; ⟨*skin*⟩ tan

***braun·gebrannt** ⇨ **braun** a

Braun·kohle *die* brown coal; lignite

bräunlich *Adj.* brownish

Bräunung *die;* ∼, ∼en browning

Braus /braus/ ⇨ **Saus**

Brause /'brauzǝ/ *die;* ∼, ∼n **(a)** fizzy drink; (∼pulver) sherbet; **(b)** (veralt.: Dusche) shower

brausen **1** *itr. V.* **(a)** ⟨*wind, water, etc.*⟩ roar; (fig.) ⟨*organ, applause, etc.*⟩ thunder; **(b)** (sich schnell bewegen) race; **(c)** *auch refl.:* ⇨ **duschen** 1. **2** *tr. V.* ⇨ **duschen** 2

Brausen *das;* ∼s roar

Brause-: ∼**pulver** *das* sherbet; ∼**tablette** *die* effervescent tablet

Braut /braut/ *die;* ∼, **Bräute** /'brɔytǝ/ **(a)** bride; **(b)** (Verlobte) fiancée; bride-to-be; **(c)** (ugs.: Freundin) girl[-friend]

Braut·eltern *Pl.* bride's parents

Bräutigam /'brɔytigam/ *der;* ∼s, ∼e **(a)** [bride]groom; **(b)** (veralt.: Verlobter) fiancé; husband-to-be

Braut-: ∼**jungfer** *die* bridesmaid; ∼**kleid** *das* wedding dress; ∼**kranz** *der* bridal wreath; ∼**mutter** *die* bride's mother; ∼**paar** *das* bridal couple; bride and groom; ∼**schleier** *der* bridal veil; ∼**vater** *der* bride's father

brav /bra:f/ **1** *Adj.* **(a)** (artig) good; **sei [schön] ∼:** be good; **(b)** (redlich) honest; upright; **(c)** (hausbacken) plain and conservative ⟨*clothes*⟩. **2** *adv.* **nun iss schön ∼ deine Suppe** be a good boy/girl and eat up your soup; eat up your soup like a good boy/girl

bravo /'bra:vo/ *Interj.* bravo

Bravo *das;* ∼s, ∼s cheer; **ein ∼ für ...:** three cheers for ...

Bravo·ruf *der* cheer

Bravour /bra'vu:ɐ/ *die;* ∼: stylishness; **mit ∼:** with style and élan

Bravour·leistung *die* brilliant performance

bravourös /bravu'rø:s/ **1** *Adj.* brilliant. **2** *adv.* brilliantly

Bravour·stück *das* piece of bravura; brilliant performance

BRD /be:|ɛr'de:/ *die;* ∼ *Abk.* **Bundesrepublik Deutschland** FRG

Breakdance /'breikdæns/ *der;* ∼[s] breakdancing

Brech-: ∼**bohne** *die* French bean (Brit.); green bean; ∼**eisen** *das* crowbar

brechen /'brɛçn̩/ ▶ 329 ┃ **1** *unr. tr. V.* **(a)** break; **sich** (*Dat.*) **den Arm/das Genick ∼:** break one's arm/neck; **(b)** (abbauen) cut ⟨*marble, slate, etc.*⟩; **(c)** (ablenken) break

the force of ⟨*waves*⟩; refract ⟨*light*⟩; **(d)** (bezwingen) overcome ⟨*resistance*⟩; break ⟨*will, silence, record, blockade, etc.*⟩; **(e)** (nicht einhalten) break ⟨*agreement, contract, promise, the law, etc.*⟩; **(f)** (ugs.: erbrechen) bring up. **2** *unr. itr. V.* **(a)** *mit sein* break; **mir bricht das Herz** (fig.) it breaks my heart; **brechend voll sein** be full to bursting; **(b)** *mit jmdm.* ∼: break with sb.; **(c)** *mit sein* **durch etw. ∼:** break through sth.; **(d)** (ugs.: sich erbrechen) throw up. **3** *unr. refl. V.* ⟨*waves etc.*⟩ break; ⟨*rays etc.*⟩ be refracted

Brecher *der;* ∼s, ∼: breaker

Brech-: ∼**mittel** *das* emetic; ∼**reiz** *der* nausea; ∼**stange** *die* crowbar; **mit der ∼stange vorgehen** (fig.) go about it with a sledgehammer

Brechung *die;* ∼, ∼en (Physik) refraction

Brechungs·winkel *der* (Physik) angle of refraction

Bredouille /bre'dʊljǝ/ *die;* ∼, ∼n (ugs.) **in der ∼ sein** *od.* **sitzen** be in real trouble; **in die ∼ kommen** get into real trouble

Brei /brai/ *der;* ∼[e]s, ∼e (Hafer∼) porridge (Brit.), oatmeal (Amer.) *no indef. art.;* (Reis∼) rice pudding (Grieß∼) semolina *no indef. art.;* **etw. zu einem ∼ verrühren** make sth. into a mash *or* purée; **um den heißen ∼ herumreden** (fig. ugs.) beat about the bush

breiig *Adj.* mushy

breit /brait/ **1** *Adj.* **(a)** ▶ 340 ┃ wide; broad, wide ⟨*hips, shoulders, forehead, etc.*⟩; **etw. ∼er machen** widen sth.; **die Beine ∼ machen** open one's legs; **ein ∼es Lachen** a guffaw; **ein 5 cm ∼er Saum** a hem 5 cm wide; **(b)** (groß) **die ∼e Masse** the general public; most people *pl.;* **die ∼e Öffentlichkeit** the general public; **ein ∼es Interesse finden** arouse a great deal of interest; **(c) sich ∼ machen** (ugs.) take up room; (sich ausbreiten) be spreading. **2** *adv.* ∼ **gebaut** sturdily *or* well built; ∼ **lachen** guffaw; **etw. ∼ darstellen** (fig.) describe sth. in great detail

breit·beinig *Adj.; nicht attr.* with one's legs apart; **er stand ∼ vor uns** he stood squarely in front of us

Breite /'braitǝ/ *die;* ∼, ∼n **(a)** ▶ 340 ┃ ⇨ **breit** 1 a: width; breadth; **in die ∼ gehen** (ugs.) put on weight; **(b)** (Geogr.) latitude; **auf/unter 50° nördlicher ∼:** at/below latitude 50° north; **in diesen ∼n** in these latitudes

breiten *tr., refl. V.* (geh.) spread

Breiten-: ∼**grad** *der* degree of latitude; **der 30. ∼grad** the 30th parallel; ∼**kreis** *der* [line of] latitude; parallel; ∼**sport** *der* popular sport

***breit|machen** ⇨ **breit** 1 c

breit-, Breit-: ∼|**schlagen** *unr. tr. V.* (ugs.) **sich zu etw. ∼schlagen lassen** let oneself be talked into sth.; **er ließ sich ∼schlagen** he let himself be persuaded; ∼**schult[e]rig** *Adj.* broad-shouldered; ∼**seite** *die* long side; ∼|**treten** *unr. tr. V.* (fig. ugs. abwertend) go on about; ∼**wand** *die* (Kino) wide *or* big screen; ∼**wand·film** *der* wide-screen *or* big-screen film

Bremen (*das*) ∼s ▶ 490 ┃ Bremen

Bremer **1** *indekl. Adj.; nicht präd.* Bremen; **der ∼ Hafen** the Port of Bremen. **2** *der;* ∼s, ∼: native/inhabitant of Bremen; *s. auch* **Kölner**

Brems-: ∼**backe** *die* brake shoe; ∼**belag** *der* brake lining

Bremse[1] /'brɛmzǝ/ *die;* ∼, ∼n brake; **auf die ∼ treten** put on the brakes

Bremse[2] *die;* ∼, ∼n (Insekt) horsefly

bremsen **1** *itr. V.* brake. **2** *tr. V.* **(a)** brake; (um zu halten) stop; **(b)** (fig.) slow down ⟨*rate, development, production, etc.*⟩; restrict ⟨*imports etc.*⟩; **jmdn. ∼** (ugs.) stop sb. **3** *refl. V.* (ugs.) stop oneself; hold oneself back

Brems-: ∼**flüssigkeit** *die* brake fluid; ∼**hebel** *der* brake lever; ∼**klotz** *der* brake pad; ∼**licht** *das; Pl.* ∼**lichter** brake light; ∼**pedal** *das* brake pedal; ∼**scheibe** *die* brake disc; ∼**spur** *die* skid mark; ∼**trommel** *die* brake drum

Bremsung *die;* ∼, ∼en braking

Brems-: ∼**weg** *der* braking distance; ∼**zug** *der* brake cable; ∼**zylinder** *der* (Kfz-W.) brake cylinder

brenn·bar *Adj.* [in]flammable; combustible; **leicht ∼:** highly [in]flammable *or* combustible

brennen /'brɛnən/ **1** *unr. itr. V.* **(a)** burn; ⟨*house etc.*⟩ burn, be on fire; **schnell/leicht** ~: catch fire quickly/ easily; **es brennt!** fire!; **wo brennt's denn?** (fig. ugs.) what's the panic?; **(b)** (glühen) be alight; **(c)** (leuchten) be on; **in ihrem Zimmer brennt Licht** there is a light on in her room; **das Licht** ~ **lassen** leave the light on; **(d)** (scheinen) **die Sonne brannte** the sun was burning down; **(e)** (schmerzen) ⟨*wound etc.*⟩ burn, sting; ⟨*feet etc.*⟩ hurt, be sore; **mir** ~ **die Augen** my eyes are stinging *or* smarting; **(f) darauf** ~, **etw. zu tun** be dying *or* longing to do sth. **2** *unr. tr. V.* **(a)** burn ⟨*hole, pattern, etc.*⟩; **einem Tier ein Zeichen ins Fell** ~: brand an animal; **(b)** (mit Hitze behandeln) fire ⟨*porcelain etc.*⟩; distil ⟨*spirits*⟩; **gebrannter Kalk** quicklime; **(c)** (rösten) roast ⟨*coffee beans, almonds, etc.*⟩

brennend 1 *Adj.* (auch fig.) burning; lighted ⟨*cigarette*⟩; raging ⟨*thirst*⟩; urgent ⟨*topic, subject*⟩. **2** *adv.* **es scheint dich ja** ~ **zu interessieren, was besprochen wurde** you seem to be dying to know what was discussed

Brennerei *die;* ~, ~**en (a)** *o. Pl.* distilling; **(b)** (Betrieb) distillery

*Brennessel ⇨ Brennnessel

Brenn-: ~**glas** *das* burning-glass; ~**holz** *das; o. Pl.* firewood; ~**material** *das* fuel; ~**nessel** *die* stinging nettle; ~**punkt** *der* (Math., Optik, fig.) focus; **im** ~**punkt des Interesses stehen** be the focus of attention *or* interest; ~**schere** *die* curling-tongs *pl.* (Brit.); curling iron (Amer.); ~**spiritus** *der* methylated spirits *pl.;* ~**stab** *der* (Kerntechnik) fuel rod; ~**stoff** *der* fuel; ~**weite** *die* (Optik) focal length

Brenn·nessel /'brɛnnɛsl̩/ *die;* ~, ~**n** stinging nettle

brenzlig /'brɛntslɪç/ *Adj.* **(a)** ⟨*smell, taste, etc.*⟩ of burning *not pred.;* ~ **riechen/schmecken** smell of burning/ taste burnt; **(b)** (ugs.: bedenklich) dicey (coll.); **mir wird die Sache zu** ~: things are getting too hot for me (coll.)

Bresche /'brɛʃə/ *die;* ~, ~**n** gap; breach; (fig.) [**für jmdn.**] **in die** ~ **springen** stand in [for sb.]; **für jmdn./ etw. eine** ~ **schlagen** give one's backing to sb./sth.

Bretagne /bre'tanjə/ *die;* ~: Brittany

Brett /brɛt/ *das;* ~**[e]s**, ~**er (a)** board; (lang und dick) plank; **schwarzes** ~: noticeboard; **ein** ~ **vor dem Kopf haben** (fig. ugs.) be thick; **(b)** (für Spiele) board; **(c)** *Pl.* (Ski) skis; **(d)** *Pl.* (Bühne) stage *sing.;* boards; **die** ~**er, die die Welt bedeuten** the stage *sing.;* the boards; **(e)** *Pl.* (Boxen) floor *sing.;* canvas *sing.*

Brettchen *das;* ~**s**, ~ **(a)** *wooden board used for breakfast;* **(b)** (zum Schneiden) board

Bretter-: ~**boden** *der* wooden floor; ~**bude** *die* [wooden] hut, shack; ~**verschlag** *der* [wooden] shed; ~**wand** *die* wooden wall *or* partition; ~**zaun** *der* wooden fence

Brett·spiel *das* board game

Brezel /'bre:tsl̩/ *die;* ~, ~**n**, (österr.) **Brezen** /'bre:tsn̩/ *der;* ~**s**, ~ *od. die;* ~, ~: pretzel

Bridge /brɪtʃ/ *das;* ~[e]s: bridge

Brief /bri:f/ *der;* ~**[e]s**, ~**e** ▶ **107** letter; **jmdm.** ~ **und Siegel** [**auf etw.** (*Akk.*)] **geben** (fig.) promise sb. faithfully *or* give sb. one's word [on sth.]

Brief-: ~**beschwerer** *der;* ~**s**, ~: paperweight; ~**block** *der; Pl.* ~**blöcke** *od.* ~**blocks** writing pad; letter pad; ~**bogen** *der* sheet of writing paper *or* note-paper; ~**bombe** *die* letter bomb

Briefchen *das;* ~**s**, ~ **(a) ein** ~ **Streichhölzer** a book of matches; **ein** ~ **Nähnadeln** a packet of needles; **(b)** (kurzer Brief) note

Brief-: ~**druck·sache** *die* (Postw.) printed paper (*sent as a letter*); ~**freund** *der*, ~**freundin** *die* penfriend; pen-pal (coll.); ~**geheimnis** *das* privacy of the post; secrecy of correspondence; ~**karte** *die* correspondence card; ~**kasten** *der* **(a)** postbox; **(b)** (privat) letter box

Briefkasten-: ~**firma** *die* accommodation address; ~**tante** *die* (ugs. scherzh.) agony aunt (coll.)

Brief-: ~**kopf** *der* **(a)** letter-heading; **(b)** (aufgedruckt) letterhead; ~**kuvert** *das* (veralt.) ⇨ ~**umschlag**

---

brieflich 1 *Adj.; nicht präd.* written. **2** *adv.* by letter

Brief·marke *die* [postage] stamp

Briefmarken-: ~**album** *das* stamp album; ~**sammler** *der* stamp collector; philatelist; ~**sammlung** *die* stamp collection

Brief-: ~**öffner** *der* letter-opener; ~**papier** *das* writing paper; notepaper; ~**partner** *der*, ~**partnerin** *die* penfriend; ~**schreiber** *der* [letter-]writer; ~**tasche** *die* wallet; ~**taube** *die* carrier pigeon; ~**träger** *der* ▶ **85** postman; letter-carrier (Amer.); ~**trägerin** *die* ▶ **85** postwoman; ~**um·schlag** *der* envelope; ~**waage** *die* letter-scales *pl.;* ~**wahl** *die* postal vote; ~**wechsel** *der* **(a)** correspondence; **einen** ~**wechsel führen** have a *or* be in correspondence; **(b)** (gesammelte Briefe) correspondence

Bries /bri:s/ *das;* ~**es**, ~**e** (Kochk.) sweetbreads *pl.*

briet /bri:t/ *1. u. 3. Pers. Sg. Prät. v.* **braten**

Brigade /bri'ga:də/ *die;* ~, ~**n** (Milit.) brigade

Brikett /bri'kɛt/ *das;* ~**s**, ~**s** briquette

brillant /brɪl'jant/ **1** *Adj.* brilliant. **2** *adv.* brilliantly

Brillant /brɪl'jant/ *der;* ~**en**, ~**en** brilliant

Brillant-: ~**ring** *der* (brilliant-cut) diamond ring; ~**schmuck** *der; o. Pl.* (brilliant-cut) diamond jewellery

Brillanz /brɪl'jants/ *die;* ~: brilliance

Brille /'brɪlə/ *die;* ~, ~**n (a)** glasses *pl.;* spectacles *pl.;* specs (coll.) *pl.;* **eine** ~: a pair of glasses *or* spectacles; **eine** ~ **tragen** wear glasses *or* spectacles; **etw. durch eine rosa[rote]** ~ **sehen** *od.* **betrachten** (fig.) see sth. through rose-coloured *or* rose-tinted spectacles; **(b)** (ugs.: Klosett~) [lavatory *or* toilet] seat

Brillen-: ~**etui** *das*, ~**futteral** *das* glasses case; spectacle case; ~**glas** *das* [spectacle] lens; ~**schlange** *die* spectacled cobra; ~**träger** *der* spectacle user *or* spectacle wearer; person who wears glasses; ~**träger sein** wear glasses

brillieren /brɪl'ji:rən/ *itr. V.* (geh.) be brilliant

Brimborium /brɪm'bo:ri̯ʊm/ *das;* ~**s** (ugs. abwertend) hoo-ha (coll.)

bringen /'brɪŋən/ *unr. tr. V.* **(a)** (her~) bring; (hin~) take; **sie brachte mir/ich brachte ihr ein Geschenk** she brought me/I took her a present; **Unglück/Unheil** [**über jmdn.**] ~: bring misfortune/disaster [upon sb.]; **jmdm. Glück/Unglück** ~: bring sb. [good] luck/bad luck; **jmdm. eine Nachricht** ~: bring sb. news; **(b)** (begleiten) take; **jmdn. nach Hause/zum Bahnhof** ~: take sb. home/to the station; **die Kinder ins Bett** *od.* **zu Bett** ~: put the children to bed; **(c) es zu etwas/nichts** ~: get somewhere/get nowhere *or* not get anywhere; **es bis zum Direktor** ~: make it to director; **es weit** ~: get on *or* do very well; **es im Leben weit** ~: go far in life; **(d) jmdn. ins Gefängnis** ~ ⟨*crime, misdeed*⟩ land sb. in prison *or* gaol; **eine Sache vor Gericht** ~: take a matter to court; **das Gespräch auf etw./ein anderes Thema** ~: bring the conversation round to sth./change the topic of conversation; **jmdn. wieder auf den rechten Weg** ~ (fig.) get sb. back on the straight and narrow; **jmdn. zum Lachen/zur Verzweiflung** ~: make sb. laugh/ drive sb. to despair; **jmdn. dazu** ~, **etw. zu tun** get sb. to do sth.; **du hast mich auf eine gute Idee gebracht** you have given me a good idea; **etw. hinter sich** ~ (ugs.) get sth. over and done with; **es nicht über sich** (*Akk.*) ~ [**können**], **etw. zu tun** not be able to bring oneself to do sth.; **etw. an sich** (*Akk.*) ~ (ugs.) collar sth. (sl.); **(e) jmdn. um seinen Besitz** ~: do sb. out of his property; **jmdn. um den Schlaf/Verstand** ~: rob sb. of his/her sleep/drive sb. mad; **(f)** (veröffentlichen) publish; **alle Zeitungen brachten Berichte über das Massaker** all the papers carried reports of the massacre; **(g)** (senden) broadcast; **das Fernsehen bringt eine Sondersendung** there is a special programme on television; **das Fernsehen hat nichts darüber gebracht** there was nothing about it on television; **(h)** (darbringen) **das/ein Opfer** ~: make the/a sacrifice; **eine Nummer/ein Ständchen** ~: perform a number/a serenade; **das kannst du nicht** ~ (ugs.) you can't do that; **(i)** (erbringen) **einen großen Gewinn/hohe Zinsen** ~: make a large profit/earn high interest; **das Gemälde brachte 50 000**

Briefeschreiben

Der Umschlag

Im Gegensatz zu deutschen Anschriften steht der Titel des Adressaten zusammen mit dem Namen auf der ersten Zeile. Vor allem in Großbritannien haben Häuser oft einen Namen anstelle einer oder zusätzlich zur (vor dem Straßennamen stehenden!) Hausnummer. In GB folgt dann die Stadt, aber bei einer kleineren Ortschaft oder einem Stadtteil steht diese(r) davor auf einer eigenen Zeile; nach der Stadt folgt meist die Grafschaft, es sei denn, es handelt sich um eine 'county town', die der Grafschaft ihren Namen gibt, oder eine Großstadt mit eigener Postleitzahl (**postcode**). Letztere steht dann allein auf der letzten Zeile. Britische Adressen können also leicht sieben oder sogar acht Zeilen einnehmen. In den USA dagegen werden die Adressen einfacher gehalten; hier steht auch die Postleitzahl (**Zip code**) an letzter Stelle, davor aber der Staat, auf zwei Buchstaben abgekürzt (CA = California, NJ = New Jersey usw.).

GB:

Mr James Bainbridge	Ms B. Gordon
oder: James Bainbridge Esq.	Kirkbrae
5 Avon Crescent	10 Strathmore Road
Kenilworth	Cults
Warwickshire	Aberdeen
CV8 2PQ	AB1 9TJ

Sir Alan and Lady Weston
Aberdare House
Llanyre
Llandrindod Wells
Powys
LD1 6DX

USA:

Robert J. Hale Jr.	Mrs Nancy Bright
1496 Pacific Boulevard	PO Box 731
Monterey	Milville
CA 93940	NJ 08332

Miss Abigail Schott
c/o Floyd
1100 North Street
Harrisburg
PA 17105

PO Box = *Postfach*, **c/o** (für *care of*) = *bei*. Zu den verschiedenen Anreden (Mr, Mrs, Miss, Ms usw.) siehe □ **Anreden und Titel.**

Bei Geschäftsbriefen kann der Name des Adressaten entweder vor oder nach der Firma bzw. Organisation

stehen, im letzteren Fall oft mit **FAO** (**for the attention of**) oder **Attn.** (**attention**) davor. In den USA ist es üblich, nach dem Namen des Inhabers einer leitenden Position diese anzugeben. Partnerschaften und Firmen mit dem Zusatz "& Co." kann **Messrs.** = *Herren* vorangestellt werden.

Messrs. Gibbons & Prestwick	John C. Wagner
FAO Anita Dobby	President
45 Albright Way	Bix Corporation
London	222 Madison Avenue
W11 2BJ	New York
	NY 10016

Der Absender steht, wenn überhaupt, links oben oder auf der Rückseite.

Der Brief selbst

Die Adresse des Absenders steht oben entweder rechts oder in der Mitte, darunter das Datum:

> 10 Copthall Avenue
> West Drayton
> Middlesex
> UB7 2FL
>
> 24th September 1997

Anrede

Es gibt fast nur die eine Möglichkeit – **Dear** und der Name des Adressaten, bloß der Vorname bei Freunden und Verwandten oder wenn man weniger formell erscheinen will, sonst Titel und Familienname:

Dear Charles/Mary/Mr Churchill/Dr Watson/ Professor Andrews

Bei Geschäftsbriefen schreibt man, wenn man den Namen des Adressaten nicht kennt, **Dear Sir or Madam**, und wenn man eine Firma oder andere Organisation anschreibt, **Dear Sirs**.

Zum Schluss

Informell:	Yours	Love	All our love
	Charles	Mary	Brian and Wendy
Etwas formeller:	With best wishes	Kind regards	
Formeller Schluss:	Yours sincerely *(brit.)*		
	Yours truly *(amerik.)*		
Sehr formell:	Yours faithfully *(brit.)*		
	Yours very truly *(amerik.)*		

DM the painting fetched 50,000 marks; **das bringt nichts** *od.* **bringts nicht** (ugs.) it's pointless; **(j) das bringt es mit sich, dass …:** that means that …; **(k)** (verursachen) cause ‹*trouble, confusion*›; **es kann dir doch nur Vorteile ~:** it can only be to your advantage; **(l)** (salopp: schaffen, erreichen) **das bringst du doch nicht** you'll never do it; **(m)** (bes. südd.) ⇒ **bekommen 1 b**

brisant /briˈzant/ *Adj.* explosive

Brisanz /briˈzants/ *die;* ~ explosiveness; explosive nature

Brise /ˈbriːzə/ *die;* ~, ~n breeze

Britannien /briˈtaniən/ (*das*); ~s Britain; (hist.) Britannia

Brite /ˈbriːtə/ *der;* ~n, ~n ▶ 388 | Briton; **die** ~n the British; **er ist [kein]** ~: he is [not] British

Britin *die;* ~, ~nen Briton; British girl/woman; **die** ~nen the British [girls/women]; **sie ist [keine]** ~: she is [not] British

britisch *Adj.* ▶ 388 | British; **die Britischen Inseln** the British Isles

bröckelig *Adj.* crumbly

bröckeln /ˈbrœkl̩n/ **1** *itr. V.* **(a)** crumble; **(b)** *mit sein* **von der Decke/Wand** ~: crumble away from the ceiling/wall. **2** *tr. V.* crumble

Brocken /ˈbrɔkn̩/ *der;* ~s, ~ **(a)** (von Brot) hunk, chunk; (von Fleisch) chunk; (von Lehm, Kohle, Erde) lump; **(b)** (fig.) **ein paar** ~ **Englisch** a smattering of English; **ein harter** ~ (ugs.) a tough *or* hard nut to crack; **(c)** (ugs.: dicke Person) lump

brocken·weise *Adv.* (auch fig.) bit by bit

bröcklig ⇒ **bröckelig**

brodeln /ˈbroːdl̩n/ *itr. V.* bubble

Broiler /ˈbrɔylɐ/ *der;* ~s, ~ (regional) ⇒ **Brathähnchen**

Brokat /broˈkaːt/ *der;* ~[e]s, ~e brocade

Brokkoli /ˈbrɔkoli/ *Pl.* broccoli *sing.*

Brom /broːm/ *das;* ~s (Chemie) bromine

Brom·beere /ˈbrɔm-/ *die* blackberry

Bronchial-: ~**katarrh** *der* (Med.) ⇒ **Bronchitis;** ~**tee** *der* bronchial tea

Bronchie /ˈbrɔnçiə/ *die;* ~, ~n (Med.) bronchial tube; bronchus

Bronchitis /brɔnˈçiːtɪs/ *die;* ~, **Bronchitiden** ▶ 329 | (Med.) bronchitis

Bronze /ˈbrõːsə/ *die;* ~: bronze

Bronze·medaille *die* bronze medal

Bronze·zeit *die* Bronze Age

Brosche /ˈbrɔʃə/ *die;* ~, ~n brooch

broschiert /brɔ'ʃi:rt/ *Adj.* paperback; **eine ∼e Ausgabe** a paperback or soft-cover edition

Broschüre /brɔ'ʃy:rə/ *die;* ∼, ∼n booklet; pamphlet

Brösel /'brø:zl/ *der;* ∼s, ∼: breadcrumb

bröselig *Adj.* crumbly

bröseln *itr., tr. V.* crumble

Brot /bro:t/ *das;* ∼[e]s, ∼e (a) bread *no pl., no indef. art.;* (Laib ∼) loaf [of bread]; (Scheibe ∼) slice [of bread]; (b) (Lebensunterhalt) daily bread (fig.); **das ist ein hartes ∼**: it's a hard way to earn a *or* your living

Brot-: ∼**aufstrich** *der* spread; ∼**belag** *der* topping; (im zusammengeklappten Brot) filling

Brötchen /'brø:tçən/ *das;* ∼s, ∼: roll; **kleinere ∼ backen [müssen]** (fig. ugs.) [have to] lower one's sights; **seine/die ∼ verdienen** (ugs.) earn one's/the daily bread

Brötchen·geber *der;* ∼s, ∼ (scherzh.) employer

brot-, Brot-: ∼**erwerb** *der* way to earn a living; ∼**fabrik** *die* bakery (*producing bread on a large scale*); ∼**kasten** *der* bread bin; ∼**korb** *der* bread basket; **jmdm. den ∼korb höher hängen** (fig. ugs.) put sb. on short rations; ∼**krume** *die,* ∼**krümel** *der* breadcrumb; ∼**kruste** *die* [bread] crust; ∼**laib** *der* loaf [of bread]; ∼**los** *Adj.* unemployed; ∼**maschine** *die* bread slicer; ∼**messer** *das* bread knife; ∼**rinde** *die* [bread] crust; ∼**teig** *der* bread dough; ∼**zeit** *die* (südd.) (a) (Pause) [tea-/coffee-/lunch-]break; (b) *o. Pl.* (Vesper) snack; (Vesperbrot) sandwiches *pl.*

Browser /'brauzɐ/ *der;* ∼s, ∼ (DV) browser

BRT *Abk.* **Bruttoregistertonne** grt

Bruch /brʊx/ *der;* ∼[e]s, **Brüche** /'bryçə/ ▶ 329 |, ▶ 600 | (a) (auch fig.) break; (eines Versprechens) breaking; **der ∼ des Deiches/Dammes** the breaching (Brit.) *or* (Amer.) breaking of the dike/dam; ∼ **machen** (ugs.) break things; **in die Brüche gehen** (zerbrechen) break; get broken; (enden) break up; **zu ∼ gehen** break; get broken; **etw. zu ∼ fahren** smash sth. up; (b) (∼stelle) break; **die Brüche im Deich** the breaches (Brit.) *or* (Amer.) breaks in the dike; (c) (Med.: Knochen∼) fracture; break; (d) (Med.: Eingeweide∼) hernia; rupture; **sich** (*Dat.*) **einen ∼ heben** rupture oneself *or* give oneself a hernia [by lifting sth.]; (e) (Math.) fraction; (f) (Kaufmannsspr.: beschädigte Ware) **diese Schokolade ist ∼**: this chocolate is broken

Bruch·bude *die* (ugs. abwertend) hovel; dump (coll.)

brüchig /'bryçɪç/ *Adj.* (a) brittle, crumbly ⟨*rock, brickwork*⟩; **der Stoff ist ziemlich ∼**: the material is splitting quite a bit; (b) (fig.) crumbling ⟨*relationship, marriage, etc.*⟩

bruch-, Bruch-: ∼**landung** *die* crash-landing; ∼**rechnen** *itr. V.; nur im Inf.* do fractions; ∼**rechnen** *das* fractions *pl.;* **beim ∼rechnen …:** when doing fractions …; ∼**rechnung** *die* fractions *pl.;* ∼**strich** *der* fraction line; ∼**stück** *das* fragment; ∼**stückhaft** 1 *Adj.* fragmentary; 2 *adv.* in a fragmentary way; **im ∼teil** *der* fraction; **im ∼teil einer Sekunde** in a fraction of a second; in a split second

Brücke /'brykə/ *die;* ∼, ∼n (a) (auch: Schiffs∼, Zahnmed., Turnen, Ringen) bridge; **die od. alle ∼n hinter sich** (*Dat.*) **abbrechen** (fig.); burn one's bridges (fig.); **jmdm. eine [goldene] od. [goldene] ∼n bauen** (fig.) make things easier for sb.; (b) (Teppich) rug

Brücken-: ∼**bogen** *der* arch [of a/the bridge]; ∼**geländer** *das* parapet; railing; ∼**kopf** *der* (Milit., fig.) bridgehead; ∼**pfeiler** *der* pier [of a/the bridge]

Bruder /'bru:dɐ/ *der;* ∼s, **Brüder** /'bry:dɐ/ (a) (auch fig.) brother; **die Brüder Müller** the Müller brothers; the brothers Müller; **der große ∼** (fig.) Big Brother; **unter Brüdern** (fig. ugs. scherzh.) between *or* amongst friends; (b) (ugs. abwertend: Mann) guy (coll.)

Brüderchen /'bry:dɐçən/ *das;* ∼s, ∼: little brother

Bruder-: ∼**krieg** *der* fratricidal war; ∼**kuss,** *∼***kuß** *der* brotherly kiss

brüderlich 1 *Adj.* brotherly; (im politischen Bereich) fraternal. 2 *adv.* in a brotherly way; (im politischen Bereich) fraternally; **etw. ∼ [mit jmdm.] teilen** share sth. [with sb.] in a fair and generous way

Brüderlichkeit *die;* ∼: brotherliness; (im politischen Bereich) fraternity

Brüderschaft *die;* ∼: [mit jmdm.] ∼ **trinken** drink to close friendship [with sb.] (*agreeing to use the familiar 'du' form*)

Brühe /'bry:ə/ *die;* ∼, ∼n (a) stock; (als Suppe) clear soup; broth; (b) (ugs. abwertend) (Getränk) muck; (verschmutztes Wasser) dirty *or* filthy water

brühen *tr. V.* (a) blanch; (b) (auf∼) brew, make ⟨*tea*⟩; make ⟨*coffee*⟩

brüh-, Brüh-: ∼**warm** *Adj. in* **etw. ∼warm weitererzählen** (ugs.) pass sth. on *or* spread sth. around straight away; ∼**würfel** *der* stock cube; ∼**wurst** *die* sausage (*which is heated in boiling water*)

brüllen /'brylən/ 1 *itr. V.* (a) ⟨*bull, cow, etc.*⟩ bellow; ⟨*lion, tiger, etc.*⟩ roar; ⟨*elephant*⟩ trumpet; (b) (ugs.: schreien) roar; shout; **vor Schmerzen/Lachen ∼**: roar with pain/laughter; **nach jmdm. ∼**: shout to *or* for sb.; **das ist [ja] zum Brüllen** (ugs.) it's a [real] scream (coll.); what a scream (coll.); (c) (ugs.: weinen) howl; bawl; **er brüllte wie am Spieß** he bawled his head off. 2 *tr. V.* yell; shout

Brumm-: ∼**bär** *der* (ugs.) grouch (coll.); ∼**bass,** *∗***∼baß** *der* (ugs.) deep *or* bass voice

brummeln /'brʊmln/ *tr., itr. V.* (ugs.) mumble; mutter

brummen /'brʊmən/ *tr., itr. V.* (a) ⟨*insect*⟩ buzz; ⟨*bear*⟩ growl; ⟨*engine etc.*⟩ drone; **mir brummt der Schädel** *od.* **Kopf** (ugs.) my head is buzzing; (b) (unmelodisch singen) drone; (c) (mürrisch sprechen) mumble; mutter

Brummer *der;* ∼s, ∼ (ugs.) (a) (Fliege) bluebottle; (b) (Lkw) heavy lorry (Brit.) *or* truck

Brummi *der;* ∼s, ∼s (ugs.) lorry (Brit.); truck

brummig (ugs.) 1 *Adj.* grumpy. 2 *adv.* grumpily

Brumm-: ∼**kreisel** *der* humming top; ∼**schädel** *der* (ugs.) thick head

brünett /bry'nɛt/ *Adj.* dark-haired ⟨*person*⟩; dark ⟨*hair*⟩; **sie ist ∼**: she's [a] brunette

Brünette *die;* ∼, ∼n brunette

Brunft /brʊnft/ *die;* ∼, **Brünfte** /'brynftə/ (Jägerspr.) ⇒ **Brunst**

Brunnen /'brʊnən/ *der;* ∼s, ∼ (a) well; (b) (Spring∼) fountain; (c) (Heilwasser) spring water

Brunnen-: ∼**kresse** *die* watercress; ∼**vergifter** *der;* ∼s, ∼: water-poisoner; (fig. abwertend) troublemaker; ∼**vergiftung** *die* water-poisoning; (fig. abwertend) trouble-making

Brunst /brʊnst/ *die;* ∼, **Brünste** /'brynstə/ (von männlichen Tieren) rut; (von weiblichen Tieren) heat; **Männchen/Weibchen in der ∼** rutting males/females in *or* on heat

Brunst·zeit *die* (bei männlichen Tieren) rut; rutting season; (bei weiblichen Tieren) [season of] heat

brüsk /brysk/ 1 *Adj.* brusque; abrupt. 2 *adv.* brusquely; abruptly

brüskieren *tr. V.* offend; (stärker) insult; (schneiden) snub

Brüssel /'brysl/ (*das*) ∼s ▶ 490 | Brussels

Brüsseler ▶ 490 | 1 *indekl. Adj.; nicht präd.* Brussels; **∼ Spitzen** Brussels lace *sing.* 2 *der;* ∼s, ∼ inhabitant of Brussels; (von Geburt) native of Brussels; *s. auch* **Kölner**

Brust /brʊst/ *die;* ∼, **Brüste** /'brystə/ (a) ▶ 326 | chest; (fig. geh.) breast; heart; **sich in die ∼ werfen** puff oneself up; (b) ▶ 326 | (der Frau) breast; **einem Kind die ∼ geben** breastfeed a baby; (c) (Hähnchen∼) breast; (Rinder∼) brisket; (d) *o. Pl.:* ⇒ **Brustschwimmen**

Brust-: ∼**bein** *das* breastbone; ∼**beutel** *der* purse (worn around the neck)

brüsten /'brystn/ *refl. V.* (abwertend) **sich mit etw. ∼**: boast *or* brag about sth.

Brust-: ∼**flosse** *die* (Zool.) pectoral fin; ∼**kasten** (ugs.) chest; ∼**korb** *der* (Anat.) thorax *pl.*; ∼**krebs** *der* breast cancer; cancer of the breast; ∼**schwimmen** *unr. itr. V.; nur im Inf.* do [the] breaststroke; ∼**schwimmen** *das* breaststroke; ∼**stück** *das* (Kochk.) breast; (vom Rind) brisket; ∼**tasche** *die* breast pocket; (Innentasche) inside breast pocket; ∼**ton** *der in* **im ∼ton der Überzeugung** (fig.) with utter conviction; ∼**umfang** *der* chest measurement; (bei Frauen) bust measurement

---

Brüstung *die;* ~, ~**en** parapet; (Balkon~) balustrade

Brust-: ~**warze** *die* ▶ 326 | nipple; ~**wickel** *der* (Med.) chest compress; ~**wirbel** *der* (Anat.) thoracic vertebra

Brut /bruːt/ *die;* ~, ~**en** (a) (das Brüten) brooding; (b) (Jungtiere, auch fig. scherzh.: Kinder) brood

brutal /bruˈtaːl/ **1** *Adj.* brutal; violent ‹*attack, film, etc.*›; brute ‹*force*›. **2** *adv.* brutally

brutalisieren *tr. V.* brutalize

Brutalität /brutaliˈtɛːt/ *die;* ~, ~**en** (a) *o. Pl.* brutality; (b) (Handlung) act of brutality *or* violence

brüten /ˈbryːtn̩/ *itr. V.* (a) brood; ~**de Hitze** (fig.) stifling heat; ~**d heiß** boiling *or* stifling hot; (b) (grübeln) ponder (**über** + *Dat.* over); **über einem Plan** ~: work on a plan

***brütend·heiß** ⇒ brüten a

Brüter *der;* ~**s**, ~ (Kerntechnik) breeder

Brut-: ~**kasten** *der* incubator; ~**reaktor** *der* (Kernphysik) breeder reactor; ~**stätte** *die* breeding ground; (fig.) breeding ground (*Gen.*, **für** for); hotbed (*Gen.*, **für** for)

brutto /ˈbruto/ *Adv.* gross; ~ **4 000 DM, 4 000 DM** ~: 4,000 marks gross; ~ **800 kg** 800 kilos gross

Brutto- gross ‹*income, weight, etc.*›; full ‹*price*›

brutzeln /ˈbrutsln̩/ **1** *itr. V.* sizzle. **2** *tr. V.* (ugs.) fry [up]

BSE /beɛsˈeː/ *die;* ~ ▶ 329 | BSE

Btx /beːteːˈɪks/ *Abk.* **Bildschirmtext**

Bub /buːp/ *der;* ~**en**, ~**en** (südd., österr., schweiz.) boy; lad

Bube /ˈbuːbə/ *der;* ~**n**, ~**n** (Kartenspiele) jack; knave

Buben·streich *der* childish prank

Bubi /ˈbuːbi/ *der;* ~**s**, ~**s** (a) [little] boy *or* lad *or* fellow; (b) (salopp abwertend: Schnösel) young lad

Bubi·kopf *der* bobbed hair[cut]; bob; **sich** (*Dat.*) **einen** ~**kopf schneiden lassen** have one's hair bobbed

Buch /buːx/ *das;* ~[e]s, **Bücher** /ˈbyːçɐ/ (a) book; **das** ~ **der Bücher** the Book of Books; **wie ein** ~ **reden** (ugs.) talk nineteen to the dozen; **ein Detektiv/ein Faulpelz, wie er im** ~ **steht** a classic [example of a] detective/a complete lazybones; **ein** ~ **mit sieben Siegeln** a closed book; a complete mystery; **ein schlaues** ~ (ugs.) a reference book/textbook; (b) (Dreh~) script; (c) (Geschäfts~) book; **über etw.** (*Akk.*) ~ **führen/genau** ~ **führen** keep a record/an exact record of sth.; **zu** ~[e] **schlagen** be reflected in the budget; (fig.) have a big influence; **mit 200 DM zu** ~[e] **schlagen** make a difference of 200 marks

Buch-: ~**besprechung** *die* book-review; ~**binder** *der* ▶ 85 | bookbinder; ~**deckel** *der* [book] cover (front or back); ~**druck** *der; o. Pl.* letterpress printing; **im** ~**druck** in letterpress; ~**drucker** *der* ▶ 85 | printer; ~**druckerei** *die* (a) *o. Pl.* letterpress printing; (b) (Betrieb) printing works; ~**drucker·kunst** *die; o. Pl.* art of printing

Buche *die;* ~, ~**n** (a) beech[-tree]; (b) *o. Pl.* (Holz) beech[wood]

Buch·ecker *die* beech-nut

buchen *tr. V.* (a) enter; **etw. auf ein Konto** ~: enter sth. into an account; **etw. als Erfolg** ~ (fig.) count sth. as a success; (b) (vorbestellen) book

Buchen-: ~**holz** *das* beechwood; ~**wald** *der* beechwood

Bücher-: ~**bord** *das* (a) ⇒ ~**brett**; (b) ⇒ ~**regal**; ~**brett** *das* bookshelf

Bücherei *die;* ~, ~**en** library

Bücher-: ~**regal** *das* bookshelves *pl.*; ~**schrank** *der* bookcase; ~**stütze** *die* book-end; ~**verbrennung** *die* burning of books; ~**wand** *die* (a) (Möbel) bookshelf unit; (b) (Wand mit ~regal) wall of bookshelves; ~**wurm** *der* (scherzh.) bookworm

Buch-: ~**fink** *der* chaffinch; ~**führung** *die* bookkeeping; ~**halter** *der*, ~**halterin** *die* ▶ 85 | bookkeeper; ~**haltung** *die* (a) accountancy; (b) (Abteilung) accounts department; ~**handel** *der; o. Pl.* book trade; **im** ~**handel erhältlich** available from bookshops;

~**händler** *der* ▶ 85 | bookseller; ~**handlung** *die* bookshop; ~**klub** *der* book club; ~**laden** *der* bookshop; ~**messe** *die* book fair; ~**prüfer** *der* auditor; ~**rücken** *der* spine

Buchs·baum /ˈbuks-/ *der* box tree; box

Buchse /ˈbuksə/ *die;* ~, ~**n** (a) (Elektrot.) socket; (b) (Technik) bush; liner

Büchse /ˈbyksə/ *die;* ~, ~**n** (a) can; tin (Brit.); (b) (ugs.: Sammel~) box; (c) (Gewehr) rifle; (Schrot~) shotgun

Büchsen-: ~**fleisch** *das* tinned (Brit.) *or* (Amer.) canned meat; ~**milch** *die* tinned (Brit.) *or* (Amer.) canned milk; ~**öffner** *der* tin-opener (Brit.); can opener (Amer.)

Buchstabe /ˈbuːxʃtaːbə/ *der;* ~**ns**, ~**n** letter; (Druckw.) character; **ein großer/kleiner** ~: a capital [letter]/small letter; **sich auf seine vier** ~**n setzen** (ugs. scherzh.) sit [oneself] down

buchstaben·getreu 1 *Adj.* literal. **2** *adv.* to the letter

buchstabieren *tr. V.* (a) spell; (b) (mühsam lesen) spell out

buchstäblich /ˈbuːxʃtɛːplɪç/ *Adv.* literally

Buch·stütze *die* ⇒ **Bücherstütze**

Bucht /buxt/ *die;* ~, ~**en** bay

Buchung *die;* ~, ~**en** (a) entry; (b) (Vorbestellung) booking

Buch-: ~**weizen** *der* buckwheat; ~**wissen** *das* book-learning; ~**zeichen** *das* bookmark[er]

Buckel /ˈbukl̩/ *der;* ~**s**, ~ (a) (ugs.: Rücken) back; **einen** ~ **machen** ‹*cat*› arch its back; ‹*person*› hunch one's shoulders; **rutsch mir den** ~ **runter!** (fig. salopp) get lost! (sl.); **den** ~ **hinhalten** (fig.) take the blame; carry the can (fig. coll.); **einen krummen** ~ **machen** (fig.) bow and scrape; kowtow; **schon 40 Jahre auf dem** ~ **haben** be 40 already; (b) (Rückenverkrümmung) hunchback; hump; (c) (ugs.: Hügel) hillock; (d) (ugs.: gewölbte Stelle) bump

buckeln *itr. V.* (ugs.) (abwertend) bow and scrape; kowtow; **vor jmdm.** ~: kowtow to sb.; **nach oben** ~ **und nach unten treten** bow to superiors and kick underlings

bücken /ˈbykn̩/ *refl. V.* bend down; **sich nach etw.** ~: bend down to pick sth. up

bucklig *Adj.* (a) hunchbacked; humpbacked; (b) (ugs.: uneben) bumpy

Bucklige *der/die; adj. Dekl.* hunchback; humpback

Bückling¹ /ˈbyklɪŋ/ *der;* ~**s**, ~**e** (ugs. scherzh.: Verbeugung) bow

Bückling² *der;* ~**s**, ~**e** (Hering) bloater

Buddel /ˈbudl̩/ *die;* ~, ~**n** (nordd.) bottle

buddeln *itr. V.* (ugs.) dig; **die Kinder** ~ **im Sand** the children are digging about in the sand

Buddha /ˈbuda/ *der;* ~**s**, ~**s** Buddha

Buddhismus *der;* ~: Buddhism *no art.*

Buddhist *der;* ~**en**, ~**en** Buddhist

buddhistisch *Adj.* Buddhist *attrib.*

Bude /ˈbuːdə/ *die;* ~, ~**n** (a) kiosk; (Markt~) stall; (Jahrmarkts~) booth; (b) (Bau~) hut; (c) (ugs.: Haus) dump (coll.); (d) (ugs.: Zimmer) room; digs *pl.* (Brit. coll.); **Leben in die** ~ **bringen** liven the place up; (e) (ugs. abwertend: Laden, Lokal) outfit (coll.)

Budget /byˈdʒeː/ *das;* ~**s**, ~**s** budget

Büfett /byˈfɛt/ *das;* ~[e]s, ~**s** *od.* ~**e** (a) sideboard; (b) (Schanktisch) bar; (c) (Verkaufstisch) counter; (d) **kaltes** ~: cold buffet

Büffel /ˈbyfl̩/ *der;* ~**s**, ~: buffalo

Büffelei *die;* ~ (ugs.) swotting *no pl.* (Brit. sl.)

büffeln (ugs.) **1** *itr. V.* swot (Brit. sl.); cram. **2** *tr. V.* swot up (Brit. sl.); cram

Buffet /byˈfeː/ *das;* ~**s**, ~**s** ⇒ **Büfett**

Bug /buːk/ *der;* ~[e]s, ~**e** *u.* **Büge** /ˈbyːgə/ (a) (Schiffs~) bow; (Flugzeug~) nose; (b) (Schulterstück) shoulder

Bügel /ˈbyːgl̩/ *der;* ~**s**, ~ (a) (Kleider~) hanger; (b) (Brillen~) ear-piece; (c) (an einer Tasche, Geldbörse) frame

bügel-, Bügel-: ~**brett** *das* ironing board; ~**eisen** *das* iron; ~**falte** *die* [trouser] crease; ~**frei** *Adj.* non-iron

bügeln *tr., itr. V.* iron; *s. auch* **gebügelt**

Buggy /'bagi/ *der;* ~s, ~s buggy

Bügler *der;* ~s, ~, **Büglerin** *die;* ~, ~**nen** ironer

bugsieren /buˈksiːrən/ *tr. V.* (ugs.) shift; manœuvre; steer ⟨*person*⟩

Bug·welle *die* bow wave

buh /buː/ *Interj.* boo; ~ **rufen** boo

Buh *das;* ~s, ~s (ugs.) boo

buhen *itr. V.* (ugs.) boo

buhlen /'buːlən/ *itr. V.* (abwertend) **um jmds. Gunst** ~: court sb.'s favour; **um jmds. Anerkennung** ~: strive for recognition by sb.

Buh·mann *der; Pl.* **Buhmänner** (ugs.) (a) whipping-boy; scapegoat; (b) (Schreckgestalt) bogyman

Bühne /'byːnə/ *die;* ~, ~**n** (a) stage; **ein Stück auf die** ~ **bringen** put on *or* stage a play; **auf der politischen** ~ (fig.) on the political scene; **über die** ~ **bringen** (ugs.) finish ⟨*process*⟩; get ⟨*event*⟩ over; **über die** ~ **gehen** (ugs.) go off; (b) (Theater) theatre; **die Städtischen** ~**n Köln** the Cologne municipal theatres; **zur** ~ **gehen** go on the stage *or* into the theatre

bühnen-, Bühnen-: ~**anweisung** *die* stage direction; ~**arbeiter** *der* stagehand; ~**autor** *der* playwright; ~**bearbeitung** *die* stage adaptation; ~**bildner** *der;* ~s, ~, ~**bildnerin** *die;* ~, ~**nen** stage *or* set designer; ~**reif** *Adj.* ⟨*play etc.*⟩ ready for the stage; ⟨*imitation etc.*⟩ worthy of the stage; dramatic ⟨*entrance etc.*⟩; ~**stück** *das* stage play

Buh·ruf *der* boo

buk /buːk/ *1. u. 3. Pers. Sg. Prät. v.* **backen**

Bukett /buˈkɛt/ *das;* ~s, ~s *od.* ~e (geh.) bouquet

Bulette /buˈlɛtə/ *die;* ~, ~**n** (bes. berl.) rissole

Bulgare /bʊlˈɡaːrə/ *der;* ~**n**, ~**n** ▸ 388 | Bulgarian

Bulgarien /bʊlˈɡaːriən/ *(das);* ~s Bulgaria

bulgarisch *Adj.* ▸ 388 | Bulgarian

Bull- /bʊl-/: ~**auge** *das* circular porthole; ~**dogge** *die* bulldog

Bulldozer /'bʊldoːzɐ/ *der;* ~s, ~: bulldozer

Bulle[1] /'bʊlə/ *der;* ~**n**, ~**n** (a) bull; (b) (ugs. abwertend: Mann) great ox; big bull; (c) (salopp abwertend: Polizist) cop (coll.)

Bulle[2] *die;* ~, ~**n** (päpstlicher Erlass) bull

Bullen·hitze *die* (ugs.) sweltering *or* boiling heat

Bulletin /bylˈtɛ̃/ *das;* ~s, ~s bulletin

bullig 1 *Adj.* (a) beefy, stocky ⟨*person, appearance, etc.*⟩; chunky, hefty ⟨*car*⟩; (b) (drückend) sweltering, boiling ⟨*heat*⟩. **2** *adv.* ~ **heiß** boiling hot

Bull·terrier *der* bull terrier

bum /bʊm/ *Interj.* bang

Bumerang /'buːməraŋ/ *der;* ~s, ~e *od.* ~s boomerang; **es erwies sich als** ~ (fig.) it boomeranged [on him/her/them]

Bummel /'bʊml/ *der;* ~s, ~: stroll (**durch** around); (durch Lokale) pub crawl (coll.)

Bummelant /bʊməˈlant/ *der;* ~en, ~en (ugs.) (a) slowcoach (Brit.); slowpoke (Amer.); dawdler; (b) (Faulenzer) idler; loafer

Bummelei *die;* ~, ~en (ugs.) (a) dawdling; (b) (Faulenzerei) idling *or* loafing about

bummelig (ugs. abwertend) **1** *Adj.* slow. **2** *adv.* slowly

bummeln *itr. V.* (a) *mit sein* (ugs.) stroll (**durch** around); ~ **gehen** go for *or* take a stroll; **durch die Kneipen** ~: go round the pubs (Brit. coll.); go on a pub crawl (Brit. coll.); (b) (ugs.: trödeln) dawdle; **bei den Schulaufgaben** ~: dawdle over one's homework; (c) (ugs.: faulenzen) laze about; do nothing

Bummel-: ~**streik** *der* go-slow; (bei Beamten usw.) work to rule; **in einen** ~**streik treten** go on a go-slow; ~**zug** *der* (ugs.) slow *or* stopping train

bums /bʊms/ *Interj.* bang!; **es machte laut** ~: there was a loud bang *or* thud

Bums *der;* ~es, ~e (ugs.) bang; (dumpfer) thud; thump

bumsen 1 *itr. V.* (ugs.) (a) *unpers.* **es bumste ganz furchtbar** there was a terrible bang/thud *or* thump; **an dieser Kreuzung bumst es mindestens einmal am**

Tag (fig.) there's at least one smash *or* crash a day at this junction; (b) (schlagen) bang; (dumpfer) thump; **gegen die Tür** ~: bang/thump on the door; (c) *mit sein* (stoßen) bang; bash; **er ist mit dem Kopf gegen die Wand gebumst** he banged *or* bashed his head on the wall; (d) (salopp: koitieren) have it off (sl.); screw (coarse). **2** *tr. V.* (salopp: koitieren mit) have it off with (sl.); screw (coarse)

Bums-: ~**lokal** *das* (ugs. abwertend) dive (coll.); ~**musik** *die* (ugs. abwertend) oompah music (coll.)

Bund[1] /bʊnt/ *der;* ~[e]s, **Bünde** /'byndə/ (a) (Verband, Vereinigung) association; society; (Bündnis, Pakt) alliance; **der Dritte im** ~**e** (fig.) the third in the trio; **den** ~ **der Ehe eingehen, den** ~ **fürs Leben schließen** (geh.) enter into the bond of marriage; (b) (föderativer Staat) federation; (c) (ugs.: Bundeswehr) forces *pl;* **beim** ~: in the forces *pl.;* (d) (an Röcken od. Hosen) waistband

Bund[2] *das;* ~[e]s, ~e bunch; **ein** ~ **Petersilie** a bunch of parsley

Bündchen /'byntçən/ *das;* ~s, ~: band

Bündel /'byndl/ *das;* ~s, ~: bundle; **ein** ~ **von Fragen** (fig.) a set *or* cluster of questions; **sein** ~ **packen** *od.* **schnüren** pack one's bags *pl.*

bündeln *tr. V.* bundle up ⟨*newspapers, old clothes, rags, etc.*⟩; tie ⟨*banknotes etc.*⟩ into bundles/a bundle; tie ⟨*flowers, carrots, etc.*⟩ into bunches/a bunch; sheave ⟨*straw, hay, etc.*⟩

bündel·weise *Adv.* by the bundle; in bundles; (bei Blumen, Möhren usw.) by the bunch; in bunches

Bundes- federal ⟨*motorway, civil servant, territory, capital, state, authority, etc.*⟩; (in Namen, Titeln) Federal ⟨*Railway, Government, Republic, Chancellor, etc.*⟩

bundes-, Bundes-: ~**bürger** *der* (Bürger der alten BRD) West German citizen; ~**deutsch** *Adj.* (auf die alte BRD bezogen) West German; ~**ebene** *die:* **auf** ~**ebene** at federal *or* national level; ~**genosse** *der* ally; ~**grenzschutz** *der* Federal Border Police; ~**haus** *das* Federal Parliament building; ~**kabinett** *das* Federal Cabinet; ~**kanzler** *der* Federal Chancellor; ~**kanzleramt** *das* Federal Chancellery; ~**lade** *die* (jüd. Rel.) Ark of the Covenant; ~**land** *das* federal state; (österr.) province; ~**liga** *die* national *or* federal division; ~**ligist** /~liɡɪst/ *der;* ~en, ~en team in the national *or* federal division; ~**präsident** *der* (a) [Federal] President; (b) (schweiz.) President of the Confederation; ~**rat** *der* (a) Bundesrat; (b) (österr., schweiz.) Federal Council; ~**republik** *die* federal republic; ~**republik Deutschland** Federal Republic of Germany; ~**staat** *der* (a) federal state; (b) (Gliedstaat) state; ~**straße** *die* federal highway; ≈ A road (Brit.); ~**tag** *der* Bundestag

Bundestags-: ~**abgeordnete** *der/die* member of parliament; member of the Bundestag; ~**wahl** *die* parliamentary *or* general election

bundes-, Bundes-: ~**trainer** *der* national team manager; national coach; ~**wehr** *die* [Federal] Armed Forces *pl.;* ~**weit 1** *Adj.;* **nicht präd.** nationwide; national; **2** *adv.* nationwide; nationally

Bund-: ~**falten** *Pl.* pleats; ~**hose** *die* knee-breeches *pl.*

bündig /'byndɪç/ **1** *Adj.* (a) concise; succinct; (b) (schlüssig) conclusive. **2** *adv.* (a) concisely; succinctly; (b) (schlüssig) conclusively

Bündnis /'byntnɪs/ *das;* ~ses, ~se alliance

Bündnis·grüne *der/die* (Politik) ⇒ **Grüne**[2]

Bund·weite *die* waist; (Maß) waist measurement

Bungalow /'bʊŋɡalo/ *der;* ~s, ~s bungalow

Bunker /'bʊŋkɐ/ *der;* ~s, ~ (a) (auch Behälter) bunker; (b) (Luftschutz~) air-raid shelter; (c) (salopp: Gefängnis) clink (sl.)

Bunsen·brenner /'bʊnzn-/ *der* Bunsen burner

bunt /bʊnt/ **1** *Adj.* (a) colourful; (farbig) coloured; ~**e Farben/Kleidung** bright colours/brightly coloured *or* colourful clothes; (b) (fig.) colourful ⟨*sight*⟩; varied ⟨*programme etc.*⟩; **ein** ~**er Abend** a social [evening]; *s. auch* **Hund** a; (c) (ungeordnet) confused ⟨*muddle etc.*⟩; **ein** ~**es Treiben** a real hustle and bustle; **jetzt wird es mir zu** ~ (ugs.) that's *or* it's too much. **2** *adv.* (a) colourfully;

die Vorhänge waren ~ geblümt the curtains had a colourful floral pattern; **etw. ~ bemalen** paint sth. in bright colours; **~ bemalt** brightly or colourfully painted; **~ gekleidet sein** be colourfully dressed; have colourful clothes; **(b) ein ~ gemischtes Programm** a varied programme; **(c) ~ durcheinander liegen** be in a complete muddle; **es zu ~ treiben** (ugs.) go too far; overdo it

bunt-, Bunt-: *~**bemalt** ⇒ **bunt** 2 a; **~papier** das coloured paper; **~sand·stein** der red sandstone; **~scheckig** Adj. spotted; **~specht** der spotted woodpecker; **~stift** der coloured pencil/crayon; **~wäsche** die coloureds pl.

Bürde /ˈbʏrdə/ die; ~, ~n (geh.) weight; load; (fig.) burden

Burg die; ~, ~en (a) castle; **(b)** (Strand~) wall of sand

Bürge /ˈbʏrgə/ der; ~n, ~n guarantor

bürgen itr. V. **(a) für jmdn./etw. ~:** vouch for or act as guarantor for sb./vouch for or guarantee sth.; **(b)** (fig.) guarantee; **der Name bürgt für Qualität** the name is a guarantee of quality

Bürger der; ~s, ~: citizen

Bürger-: **~begehren** das public petition; **~entscheid** der local referendum

Bürgerin die; ~, ~nen citizen

Bürger-: **~initiative** die citizens' action group; **~krieg** der civil war

bürgerlich 1 Adj. **(a)** nicht präd. (staats~) civil 〈rights, marriage, etc.〉; civic 〈duties〉; **das Bürgerliche Gesetzbuch** the [German] Civil Code; **sein ~er Name** his real name; **(b)** (dem Bürgertum zugehörig) middle-class; **die ~e Küche** good plain cooking; good home cooking; **(c)** (Polit.) non-socialist; (nicht marxistisch) non-Marxist; **(d)** (abwertend: spießerhaft) bourgeois. 2 adv. **(a)** 〈think, etc.〉 in a middle-class way; **~ leben** live a middle-class life; **gut ~ essen** have a good plain meal; (gewohnheitsmäßig) eat good plain food; **(b)** (abwertend: spießerhaft) in a bourgeois way

Bürgerliche der/die; adj. Dekl. **(a)** (Nichtadlige) commoner; **(b)** (Polit.) non-socialist

bürger-, Bürger-: **~meister** der ▶ 34 ͩ mayor; **~meisterin** die mayor; **~nah** Adj. which/who reflects the general public's interests postpos., not pred.; **~pflicht** die civic duty; duty as a citizen; **~recht** das one of the civil rights; **~rechte** civil rights; **~rechtler** der; ~s, ~: civil-rights campaigner

Bürgerschaft die; ~, ~en **(a)** citizens pl.; **(b)** (Stadtparlament) city parliament

Bürger·schreck der bogey of the middle classes

Bürger·steig der pavement (Brit.); sidewalk (Amer.)

Bürgertum das; ~s **(a)** middle class; **(b)** (Groß~) bourgeoisie

Bürger·wehr die vigilante group

Burg-: **~friede** der truce; **~graben** der [castle] moat

Bürgin /ˈbʏrgɪn/ die; ~, ~nen ⇒ **Bürge**

Bürgschaft die; ~, ~en **(a)** (Rechtsw.) guarantee; security; **die ~ für jmdn./etw. übernehmen** agree to act as sb.'s guarantor/to guarantee sth.; **(b)** (Garantie) guarantee; **(c)** (Betrag) penalty

Burgund /bʊrˈgʊnt/ (das); ~s Burgundy

Burgunder der; ~s, ~ (Wein) burgundy

burlesk /bʊrˈlɛsk/ Adj. burlesque

Burma /ˈbʊrma/ (das); ~s Burma

Büro /byˈroː/ das; ~s, ~s office

Büro-: **~angestellte** der/die office worker; **~bedarf** der office supplies pl.; **~haus** das office block; **~klammer** die paper clip; **~kraft** die clerical worker

Bürokrat /byroˈkraːt/ der; ~en, ~en (abwertend) bureaucrat

Bürokratie /byrokraˈtiː/ die; ~, ~n bureaucracy

bürokratisch 1 Adj. bureaucratic. 2 adv. bureaucratically

Büro-: **~maschine** die office machine; **~zeit** die office hours pl.; **während der ~zeit** during office hours

Bürschchen /ˈbʏrʃçən/ das; ~s, ~: little fellow; little chap; **ein freches ~:** a cheeky little devil

Bursche /ˈbʊrʃə/ der; ~n, ~n **(a)** boy; lad; **(b)** (veralt.: junger Mann) young man; **die jungen ~n aus dem Dorf** the village youths; **er ist ein toller ~** (ugs.) he's a reckless devil; **(c)** (abwertend: Kerl) guy (coll.); **(d)** (ugs.: Prachtexemplar) specimen; **(e)** (Milit. hist.) batman; orderly

Burschenschaft die; ~, ~en students' duelling society

burschikos /bʊrʃiˈkoːs/ **1** Adj. **(a)** sporty 〈clothes, look〉; [tom]boyish 〈behaviour, girl, haircut〉; **(b)** (ungezwungen) casual 〈comment, behaviour, etc.〉. **2** adv. **(a)** [tom]boyishly; **(b)** (ungezwungen) 〈express oneself〉 in a colloquial way

Bürste /ˈbʏrstə/ die; ~, ~n **(a)** brush; **(b)** (Haarschnitt) crew cut

bürsten tr. V. brush

Bürsten·schnitt der crew cut

Bus /bʊs/ der; ~ses, ~se bus; (Privat- und Reisebus) coach; bus

Bus·bahn·hof der bus station; (für Reisebusse) coach station; bus station

Busch /bʊʃ/ der; ~[e]s, **Büsche** /ˈbʏʃə/ **(a)** bush; (fig.) **auf den ~ klopfen** (ugs.) sound things out; **bei jmdm. auf den ~ klopfen** (ugs.) sound sb. out; **es ist etw. im ~** (ugs.) something's up; **(b)** (Geogr.) bush; **(c)** (ugs.: Urwald) jungle

Büschel /ˈbʏʃl̩/ das; ~s, ~ (von Haaren, Federn, Gras usw.) tuft; (von Heu, Stroh) handful

buschig Adj. bushy

Busch-: **~mann** der Bushman; **~messer** das machete; **~wind·röschen** das wood anemone

Busen /ˈbuːzn̩/ der; ~s, ~: bust; **sie hat wenig ~** (ugs.) she has very little bosom

busen-, Busen-: **~frei** Adj. topless; **~freund** der, **~freundin** die (oft iron.) bosom friend

Bus-: **~fahrer** der ▶ 85 ͩ bus/coach driver; **~halte·stelle** die bus/coach stop; **~linie** die bus/coach route

Bussard /ˈbʊsart/ der; ~s, ~e (Zool.) buzzard

Buße /ˈbuːsə/ die; ~, ~n **(a)** (Rel.) penance no art.; **(b)** (Rechtsw.) damages pl.

büßen /ˈbyːsn̩/ **1** tr. V. **(a)** (Rel.: sühnen) atone for; expiate; **(b)** (bestraft werden für) atone for; **(c)** (fig.) pay for; **das sollst du mir ~:** you'll pay for that. **2** itr. V. **(a)** (Rel.) **für etw. ~:** atone for or expiate sth.; **(b)** (bestraft werden) suffer; **(c)** (fig.) pay

Büßer der; ~s, ~ (Rel.) penitent

Buß-: **~geld** das fine; **~geld·bescheid** der official demand for payment of a fine; **~prediger** der repentance-preacher

Büsten·halter der bra; brassière (formal)

Bus-: **~verbindung** die **(a)** (Linie) bus service; **(b)** (Anschluss) bus/coach connection; **~verkehr** der bus/coach service

Butan·gas das butane gas

Butt /bʊt/ der; ~[e]s, ~e flounder; butt

Büttel /ˈbʏtl̩/ der; ~s, ~ (abwertend) lackey

Bütten das; ~s ⇒ **~papier**

Bütten-: **~papier** das handmade paper (with deckle-edge); **~rede** die carnival speech

Butter /ˈbʊtɐ/ die; ~: butter; (fig.) **es ist alles in ~** (ugs.) everything's fine; **sie lässt sich** (Dat.) **nicht die ~ vom Brot nehmen** (ugs.) she doesn't let anyone put one over on her

Butter-: **~blume** die (Sumpfdotterblume) marsh marigold; (Hahnenfuß) buttercup; **~brot** das piece or slice of bread and butter; (zugeklappt) sandwich; **ein ~brot mit Schinken** a slice of bread and butter with ham on it/a ham sandwich; **~brot·papier** das greaseproof paper; **~creme** die butter-cream; **~creme·torte** die butter-cream cake; **~dose** die butter dish

Butterfly /ˈbʌtɐflai/ der; ~s (Schwimmen) butterfly [stroke]

Butter-: **~käse** der rich creamy cheese; **~keks** der butter biscuit; **~milch** die buttermilk

buttern 1 *itr. V.* make butter. **2** *tr. V.* **(a)** butter; grease ‹*baking tray*› with butter

butter·weich *Adj.* **(a)** beautifully soft; **(b)** (fig.) vague ‹*agreement, promise*›

Button /ˈbʌtn/ *der;* ∼s, ∼s badge

Bụtzen·scheibe *die* bull's-eye pane

b.w. *Abk.* **bitte wenden** p.t.o.

bzw. *Abk.* **beziehungsweise**

....

C c

....

c, C /t͡seː/ *das;* ∼, ∼: **(a)** (Buchstabe) c/C; **(b)** (Musik) [key of] C; *s. auch* **a, A**

C *Abk.* **Celsius** C

ca. *Abk.* **cirka** c.

Café /kaˈfeː/ *das;* ∼s, ∼s café

Cafeteria /kafetəˈriːa/ *die;* ∼, ∼s cafeteria

cal *Abk.* **[Gramm]kalorie** cal.

Callgirl /ˈkɔːlɡøːl/ *das;* ∼s, ∼s call-girl

Calypso /kaˈlɪpso/ *der;* ∼[s], ∼s calypso

Camcorder /ˈkamkɔrdɐ/ *der;* ∼s, ∼ ⇨ **Kamerare-korder**

Camembert /ˈkaməmbɛːɐ/ *der;* ∼s, ∼s Camembert

Camp /kɛmp/ *das;* ∼s, ∼s camp

campen /ˈkɛmpn̩/ *itr. V.* camp

Camper *der;* ∼s, ∼, **Camperin** *die;* ∼, ∼nen camper

Camping /ˈkɛmpɪŋ/ *das;* ∼s camping; **zum** ∼ **[nach X] fahren** go camping [in X]

Camping-: ∼**bus** *der* motor caravan; camper; ∼**platz** *der* campsite; campground (Amer.)

Campus /ˈkampʊs/ *der;* ∼ (Hochschulw.) campus

Canasta /kaˈnasta/ *das;* ∼s canasta

Cantilever·bremse /ˈkæntiliːvɐ-/ *die* cantilever brake

Cape /keːp/ *das;* ∼s, ∼s cape

Caravan /ˈka(ː)ravan/ *der;* ∼s, ∼s **(a)** (Kombi) estate car; station wagon (Amer.); **(b)** (Wohnwagen) caravan; trailer (Amer.)

Caritas /ˈkaːritas/ *die;* ∼: Caritas (*Catholic welfare organization*)

Cartoon /karˈtuːn/ *der od. das;* ∼[s], ∼s cartoon

Casanova /kazaˈnoːva/ *der;* ∼[s], ∼s Casanova

Cäsar /ˈt͡seːzar/ (*der*) Caesar

Cassata /kaˈsaːta/ *die od. das;* ∼, ∼s cassata

catchen /ˈkɛt͡ʃn̩/ *itr. V.* do all-in wrestling

Catcher /ˈkɛt͡ʃɐ/ *der;* ∼s, ∼: all-in wrestler

Cayenne·pfeffer /kaˈjɛn-/ *der* cayenne [pepper]

CB-Funk /t͡seːˈbeː-/ *der;* ∼s CB radio

ccm *Abk.* **Kubikzentimeter** c.c.

CD /t͡seːˈdeː/ *die;* ∼, ∼s CD

CD-ROM /t͡seːdeːˈrɔm/ *die;* ∼, ∼[s] (DV) CD-ROM

CD-ROM-Lauf·werk *das* (DV) CD-ROM drive

CD-Spieler *der* CD-player

CDU /t͡seːdeːˈʔuː/ *die;* ∼ *Abk.* **Christlich-Demokratische Union [Deutschlands]** [German] Christian Democratic Party

C-Dur /ˈt͡seː-/ *das;* ∼: C major; *s. auch* **A-Dur**

Cedille /seˈdiːjə/ *die;* ∼, ∼n (Sprachw.) cedilla

Cellist /t͡ʃɛˈlɪst/ *der;* ∼en, ∼en cellist

Cello /ˈt͡ʃɛlo/ *das;* ∼s, ∼s *od.* **Cẹlli** cello

Celsius /ˈt͡sɛlziʊs/ **▶511** *o. Art.* **1 Grad/20 Grad** ∼: 1 degree/20 degrees Celsius *or* centigrade

Cembalo /ˈt͡ʃɛmbalo/ *das;* ∼s, ∼s *od.* **Cẹmbali** harpsichord

Ceylon /ˈt͡saɪlɔn/ (*das*); ∼s (hist.) Ceylon (Hist.)

C-Flöte /ˈt͡seː-/ *die* soprano recorder

Chamäleon /kaˈmɛːleɔn/ *das;* ∼s, ∼s (auch fig.) chameleon

Champagner /ʃamˈpanjɐ/ *der;* ∼s, ∼: champagne

Champignon /ˈʃampɪnjɔn/ *der;* ∼s, ∼s mushroom

Champion /ˈt͡ʃɛmpiən/ *der;* ∼s, ∼s (Sport) champion

Chance /ˈʃãːsə/ *die;* ∼, ∼n **(a)** (Gelegenheit) chance; **die** ∼**n [zu gewinnen] stehen eins zu hundert** the chances [of winning] are one in a hundred; (bes. beim Wetten) the odds [against winning] are 100:1 *or* a hundred to one; **(b)** *Pl.* (Aussichten) prospects; **[bei jmdm]** ∼**n haben** stand a chance [with sb.]

Chạncen·gleichheit *die; o. Pl.* (Päd., Soziol.) equality of opportunity *no art.*

changieren /ʃãˈʒiːrən/ *itr. V.* shimmer (in different colours); iridesce

Chanson /ʃãˈsõː/ *das;* ∼s, ∼s chanson; cabaret-style song

Chaos /ˈkaːɔs/ *das;* ∼: chaos *no art.*

Chạos·theorie *die* (Physik) chaos theory

Chaot /kaˈoːt/ *der;* ∼en, ∼en **(a)** (Politik) anarchist (*trying to undermine society*); (bei Demonstrationen) violent demonstrator; **(b)** (salopp: unordentlicher Mensch) **ein [furchtbarer]** ∼ **sein** be [terribly] disorganized

chaotisch 1 *Adj.* chaotic. **2** *adv.* chaotically; **es geht** ∼ **zu** there is chaos

Charakter /kaˈrakte/ *der;* ∼s, ∼e /...ˈteːrə/ **(a)** character; (eines Menschen) character; personality; **Geld verdirbt den** ∼: money spoils people; **(b)** *o. Pl.* (∼stärke) [strength of] character; **keinen** ∼ **haben** lack [strength of] character; be spineless

charakter-, Charakter-: ∼**darsteller** *der* actor of complex parts; ∼**darstellerin** *die* actress of complex parts; ∼**eigenschaft** *die* characteristic; trait; ∼**fest** *Adj.* steadfast

charakterisieren *tr. V.* characterize

charakteristisch *Adj.* characteristic, typical (**für** of)

Charạkter·kopf *der* striking head

charakterlich 1 *Adj.* character *attrib.* ‹*defect, development, training*›; personal ‹*qualities*›. **2** *adv.* in [respect of] character

charakter-, Charakter-: ∼**los 1** *Adj.* unprincipled; (niederträchtig) despicable; (labil) spineless; **2** *adv.* (niederträchtig) despicably; (labil) spinelessly; ∼**losigkeit** *die;* ∼: lack of principle; (Niederträchtigkeit) despicableness; (Labilität) weakness of character; spinelessness; ∼**schwäche** *die* weakness of character; spinelessness *no pl.;* ∼**schwein** *das* (salopp abwertend) unprincipled bastard (sl.); ∼**stärke** *die; o. Pl.* strength of character; ∼**voll** *Adj.* **(a)** (∼fest) steadfast; showing strength of character *postpos., not pred.;* **(b)** (ausdrucksvoll) distinctive; ‹*house etc.*› of character; strongly characterized, individual ‹*features*›; ∼**zug** *der* characteristic

Charge /ˈʃarʒə/ *die;* ∼, ∼n rank; **die unteren** ∼**n** the lower ranks (Mil.) /orders; **die oberen** ∼**n** the upper ranks (Mil.) /echelons

charmant /ʃarˈmant/ **1** *Adj.* charming. **2** *adv.* charmingly; with much charm

Charme /ʃarm/ *der;* ∼s charm; **seinen ganzen** ∼ **aufwenden** use all one's charms

Charta /ˈkarta/ *die;* ∼, ∼s (Politik) charter

Charter- /ˈt͡ʃartɐ-/: ∼**flug** *der* charter flight; ∼**maschine** *die* chartered aircraft

chartern *tr. V.* charter ‹*aircraft, boat*›; hire (the services of] ‹*guide, firm*›

Chassis /ʃaˈsiː/ *das;* ∼ /ʃaˈsiː(s)/, ∼ /ʃaˈsiːs/ (Kfz-W., Elektrot.) chassis

chatten /ˈt͡ʃɛtn̩/ *itr. V.* (DV Jargon) chat

Chauffeur /ʃɔˈføːɐ/ *der;* ∼s, ∼e **▶85]** driver; (privat angestellt) chauffeur

Chauffeuse /ʃɔˈføːzə/ *die;* ∼n, ∼n, (bes. schweiz.) driver; (privat angestellt) chauffeur; chauffeuse (dated)

chauffieren *tr., itr. V.* (veralt.) drive

Chaussee /ʃoˈseː/ *die;* ∼, ∼n (veralt.) (surfaced) [high] road; highway (Amer.)

Chauvi /ˈʃoːvi/ *der;* ∼s, ∼s (ugs. abwertend) male chauvinist (coll. derog.)

Chauvinismus /ʃovi'nɪsmʊs/ *der;* ~ (auch fig. abwertend) chauvinism

Chauvinist *der;* ~en, ~en (auch fig. abwertend) chauvinist

chauvinistisch *Adj.* (auch fig. abwertend) chauvinistic; (männlich~~) male chauvinist

Check (schweiz.) ⇨ **Scheck**

checken /'tʃɛkn̩/ *tr. V.* (a) (bes. Technik: kontrollieren) check; examine; (b) (salopp: begreifen) twig (coll.); (bemerken) spot

Check·liste /'tʃɛk-/ *die* checklist

Chef /ʃɛf/ *der;* ~s, ~s (a) (Leiter) (einer Firma, Abteilung, Regierung) head; (der Polizei, des Generalstabs) chief; (einer Partei, Bande) leader; (Vorgesetzter) superior; boss (coll.); **wer ist denn hier der** ~**?** who's in charge here?; (b) (salopp: Anrede) **hallo,** ~**:** hey, chief *or* squire (Brit. coll.); hey mister (Amer. coll.)

Chef- chief ⟨*editor, ideologist, etc.*⟩

Chef-: ~**arzt** *der* head of one or more specialist departments in a hospital; (Direktor) superintendent (*of a small hospital*); ~**etage** *die* management floor

Chefin *die;* ~, ~nen (a) (Leiterin) (einer Firma, Abteilung, Regierung) head; (einer Partei, Bande) leader; (Vorgesetzte) superior; boss (coll.); (b) (ugs.: Frau des Chefs) boss's wife (coll.); (c) (salopp: Anrede) missis (sl.); ma'am (Amer.)

Chef-: ~**koch** *der* ▶ 85 ⏐ chef; head cook; ~**redakteur** *der* chief editor; ~**sekretärin** *die* director's secretary

Chemie /çe'mi:/ *die;* ~ (a) chemistry *no art.;* (b) (ugs.: Chemikalien) chemicals *pl.*

Chemie-: ~**arbeiter** *der* chemical worker; ~**betrieb** *der* chemical firm; ~**faser** *die* synthetic *or* man-made fibre; ~**laborant** *der,* ~**laborantin** *die* chemical laboratory assistant

Chemikalie /çemi'ka:liə/ *die;* ~, ~n chemical

Chemiker /'çe:mikɐ/ *der;* ~s, ~, **Chemikerin** *die;* ~, ~nen ▶ 85 ⏐ (graduate) chemist

chemisch 1 *Adj.* chemical; ~**er Versuch** chemistry experiment. 2 *adv.* chemically

Chemo·therapie *die* (Med.) chemotherapy

Chester·käse /'tʃɛstɐ-/ *der* (*usu. processed*) Cheddar cheese

Chicorée /'ʃikore/ *der;* ~s *od. die;* ~: chicory

Chiffon /'ʃɪfõ/ *der;* ~s, ~s chiffon

Chiffre /'ʃɪfrə/ *die;* ~, ~n (a) (Zeichen) symbol; (b) (Geheimzeichen) cipher; ~**n** cipher *sing.;* (c) (in Annoncen) box number; **Zuschriften unter** ~ **...:** reply quoting box no. ...

chiffrieren *tr. V.* [en]code; **chiffriert** in code *postpos.*

Chile /'tʃi:le, 'çi:lə/ (*das*); ~s Chile

Chilene /tʃi'le:nə, çi'le:nə/ *der;* ~n, ~n, **Chilenin** *die;* ~, ~nen ▶ 388 ⏐ Chilean

chilenisch *Adj.* ▶ 388 ⏐ Chilean

Chili /'tʃi:li/ *der;* ~s, ~es (a) *Pl.* (Schoten) chillies; (b) *o. Pl.* (Gewürz) chilli [powder]

Chimäre /çi'mɛ:rə/ *die;* ~, ~n ⇨ **Schimäre**

China /'çi:na/ (*das*); ~s China

China-: ~**kohl** *der* Chinese cabbage; ~**kracher** *der* Chinese cracker

Chinese /çi'ne:zə/ *der;* ~n, ~n, **Chinesin** *die;* ~, ~nen ▶ 388 ⏐ Chinese

chinesisch *Adj.* ▶ 388 ⏐, ▶ 487 ⏐ Chinese; **die Chinesische Mauer** the Great Wall of China

Chinin /çi'ni:n/ *das;* ~s quinine

Chip /tʃɪp/ *der;* ~s, ~s (a) (Spielmarke) chip; (b) (Kartoffel~) [potato] crisp (Brit.) *or* (Amer.) chip; (c) (Elektronik) [micro]chip

Chip·karte *die* smart card

Chiropraktiker /çiro.../ *der;* ~s, ~ (Med.) chiropractor

Chirurg /çi'rʊrk/ *der;* ~en, ~en surgeon

Chirurgie /çirʊr'gi:/ *die;* ~, ~n (a) *o. Pl.* (Disziplin) surgery *no art.;* (b) (Abteilung) surgical department; (Station) surgical ward

Chirurgin *die;* ~, ~nen surgeon

chirurgisch 1 *Adj.; nicht präd.* surgical. 2 *adv.* (operativ) surgically; by surgery

Chitin /çi'ti:n/ *das;* ~s chitin

Chitin·panzer *der* (Zool.) chitinous exoskeleton

Chlor /klo:ɐ̯/ *das;* ~s chlorine

chloren *tr. V.* chlorinate

Chloroform /kloro'fɔrm/ *das;* ~s chloroform

Chlorophyll /kloro'fʏl/ *das;* ~s (Bot.) chlorophyll

Choke /tʃoʊk/ *der;* ~s, ~s (Kfz-W.) [manual] choke

Cholera /'ko:lera/ *die;* ~ ▶ 329 ⏐ (Med.) cholera

Choleriker /ko'le:rikɐ/ *der;* ~s, ~ (a) choleric type; (b) (ugs.: jähzorniger Mensch) irascible person; **ein** ~ **sein** have a short fuse

cholerisch 1 *Adj.* irascible; choleric ⟨*temperament*⟩. 2 *adv.* irascibly

Cholesterin /çolɛste'ri:n/ *das;* ~s (Med.) cholesterol

Chor /ko:ɐ̯/ *der;* ~[e]s, **Chöre** /'kø:rə/ (auch Archit.) choir; (in Oper, Sinfonie, Theater; Komposition) chorus; **im** ~ **rufen** shout in chorus

Choral /ko'ra:l/ *der;* ~s, **Choräle** /ko'rɛ:lə/ (a) chorale; (b) (gregorianischer ~) [Gregorian] chant

Choreograph /koreo'gra:f/ *der;* ~en, ~en ▶ 85 ⏐ choreographer

Choreographie *die;* ~, ~n choreography

Chor-: ~**knabe** *der* choirboy; chorister; ~**leiter** *der* chorus-master; (eines Kirchenchors) choirmaster; ~**musik** *die* choral music; ~**sänger** *der,* ~**sängerin** *die* member of the chorus

Chose /'ʃo:zə/ *die;* ~, ~n (ugs.) (a) (Angelegenheit) business (derog.); (b) (Gegenstände) stuff; **die ganze** ~**:** the whole lot (coll.) *or* (coll.) shoot *or* (coll.) caboodle

Chow-Chow /tʃ:aʊ 'tʃ:aʊ/ *der;* ~s, ~s chow

Christ /krɪst/ *der;* ~en, ~en Christian

christ-, Christ-: ~**baum** *der* (bes. südd.) Christmas tree; ~**demokrat** *der* (Politik) Christian Democrat; ~**demokratisch** *Adj.* (Politik) Christian-Democrat

Christen·gemeinde *die* Christian community

Christenheit *die;* ~: Christendom *no art.*

Christentum *das;* ~s Christianity *nu art.;* (Glaube) Christian faith

Christen·verfolgung *die* persecution of Christians

Christ·fest *das* (veralt., noch südd., österr.) ⇨ **Weihnachtsfest**

christianisieren /kristjani'zi:rən/ 1 *tr. V.* Christianize; convert to Christianity. 2 *itr. V.* make conversions to Christianity

Christianisierung *die* ~: Christianization

Christin *die;* ~, ~nen Christian

Christ·kind *das; o. Pl.* Christ-child (as bringer of Christmas gifts)

christlich 1 *Adj.* Christian. 2 *adv.* in a [truly] Christian spirit; **Kinder** ~ **erziehen** give children a Christian upbringing

Christ-: ~**messe** *die* (kath. Rel.) Christmas Mass; ~**mette** *die* (kath. Rel.) Christmas Mass; (ev. Rel.) midnight service [on Christmas Eve]; ~**rose** *die* Christmas rose; ~**stollen** *der* stollen; [German] Christmas loaf (*with candied fruit, almonds, etc.*)

Christus /'krɪstʊs/ (*der*); ~ *od.* **Christi** Christ

Christ·vesper *die* (christl. Rel.) Christmas Eve vespers (*with music*)

Chrom /kro:m/ *das;* ~s chromium

Chromatik /kro'ma:tɪk/ *die;* ~ (Musik) chromaticism

chromatisch *Adj.* chromatic

Chromosom /kromo'zo:m/ *das;* ~s, ~en (Biol.) chromosome

Chronik /'kro:nɪk/ *die;* ~, ~en chronicle

chronisch *Adj.* chronic

Chronist /kro'nɪst/ *der;* ~en, ~en chronicler

Chronologie *die;* ~: chronology

chronologisch 1 *Adj.* chronological. 2 *adv.* chronologically; in chronological order

Chrysantheme /kryzan'te:mə/ *die;* ~, ~n chrysanthemum

CIA /'siːaɪ'eɪ/ *der od. die;* ~: CIA

circa ⇨ **zirka**

cis, Cis /tsɪs/ *das;* ~, ~, (Musik) C sharp

City /'sɪti/ *die;* ~, ~s city centre

City·ruf *der* area paging service

clever /'klɛvɐ/ **1** *Adj.* (raffiniert) shrewd; (intelligent, geschickt) clever; smart. **2** *adv.: s. Adj.:* shrewdly; cleverly; smartly

Clinch /klɪntʃ/ *der;* ~[e]s **(a)** (Boxen) clinch; **(b)** (ugs.: Auseinandersetzung) conflict; **mit jmdm. im** ~ **liegen** be locked in dispute with sb.

Clique /'klɪkə/ *die;* ~, ~n **(a)** (abwertend: Interessengemeinschaft) clique; **(b)** (Freundeskreis) set; lot (coll.); (größere Gruppe) crowd (coll.); (Jugendliche) gang (coll.)

Clou /klu:/ *der;* ~s, ~s (ugs.) main point; **der besondere** ~: the really special thing [about it]

Clown /klaʊn/ *der;* ~s, ~s clown

Club ⇨ **Klub**

cm *Abk.:* **Zentimeter** cm.

Co. *Abk.:* **Compagnie** Co.

Coach /koʊtʃ/ *der;* ~[s], ~s (Sport) coach; (bes. Fußball: Trainer) manager

coachen /koːtʃn̩/ *tr., itr. V.* (Sport) coach; (Trainer sein) manage

Coaching /'koːtʃɪŋ/ *das;* ~s coaching

Cocker·spaniel /'kɔkɐ-/ *der;* ~s, ~s cocker spaniel

Cockpit /'kɔkpɪt/ *das;* ~s, ~s cockpit

Cocktail /'kɔkteɪl/ *der;* ~s, ~s **(a)** (Getränk; auch Salat usw.) cocktail; **(b)** (Party) cocktail party

Cocktail-: ~**kleid** *das* cocktail dress; ~**party** *die* cocktail party

Cognac *der;* ~s, ~s Cognac

Collage /kɔ'laːʒə/ *die;* ~, ~n collage

Color- /ko'loːɐ̯-/ (Fot.) colour ‹*film, slide, etc.*›

Colt ⓌⓏ /kɔlt/ *der;* ~s, ~s Colt **(P)** [revolver]

Combo /'kɔmbo/ *die;* ~, ~s small (jazz *or* dance) band; combo (sl.)

Come-back /kam'bɛk/ *das;* ~s, ~s comeback; **ein** ~ **feiern** stage a comeback

Comic /'kɔmɪk/ *der;* ~s, ~s comic strip; (Heft) comic

Comic·heft *das* comic

Computer /kɔm'pjuːtɐ/ *der;* ~s, ~: computer; **auf** ~ (Akk.) **umstellen** computerize

computer-, Computer-: ~**animation** *die* (DV) computer animation; ~**anlage** *die* computer system; ~**ausdruck** *der;* ~s, ~e computer printout; ~**gesteuert** *Adj.* computer-controlled; ~**gestützt** *Adj.* computer-assisted

computerisieren *tr. V.* computerize

Computer-: ~**kriminalität** *die* computer crime; ~**kunst** *die; o. Pl.* computer art; ~**satz** *der; o. Pl.* (Druckw.) computer setting; ~**spiel** *das* computer game; ~**tomographie** *die* (Med.) **(a)** (Methode) computer tomography; computed tomography; **(b)** (Bild) computed tomogram

Conférencier /kõferã'sjeː/ *der;* ~s, ~s compère (Brit.); master of ceremonies

Container /kɔn'teːnɐ/ *der;* ~s, ~: container; (für Müll) [refuse] skip

Container-: ~**hafen** *der* container port *or* terminal; ~**schiff** *das* container ship; ~**verkehr** *der; o. Pl.* container traffic *no art.*

Contergan·kind *das* thalidomide child

cool /ku:l/ (ugs.) **1** *Adj.* cool; ~ **bleiben** keep one's cool (sl.). **2** *adv.* coolly

Copyright /'kɔpiraɪt/ *das;* ~s, ~s copyright

Copyshop /'kɔpiʃɔp/ *der* photocopy[ing] shop; copyshop

Cord /kɔrt/ *der;* ~[e]s, ~e *od.* ~s cord; (~samt) corduroy

Cord-: ~**anzug** *der* cord/corduroy suit; ~**hose** *die* [pair *sing.* of] corduroy trousers *pl. or* cords *pl.;* ~**jeans** *Pl.* corduroy jeans; cords

Cordon bleu /kɔrdõ'blø/ *das;* ~ ~, ~s ~s /kɔrdõ'blø/ (Kochk.) veal escalope cordon bleu

Cord·samt *der* corduroy

Cornedbeef /'kɔːnd 'biːf/ *das;* ~ ~: corned beef

Corn-flakes /'kɔːnfleɪks/ *Pl.* cornflakes

Corpus Delicti /'kɔrpʊs de'lɪkti/ *das;* ~ ~, **Corpora** /'kɔrpora/ **Delicti (a)** (Rechtsspr.) weapon [used]; **(b)** (meist scherzh.: Beweisstück) piece of incriminating evidence

Couch /kaʊtʃ/ *die;* ~, ~es sofa

Couch-: ~**garnitur** *die* three-piece suite; ~**tisch** *der* coffee table

Couleur /ku'løːɐ̯/ *die;* ~, ~s *o. Pl.* shade [of opinion]; persuasion

Count-down /'kaʊnt'daʊn/ *der od. das;* ~s, ~s (Raumf., *auch* fig.) countdown

Countrymusic /'kʌntrɪmjuːzɪk/ *die;* ~: country music

Coup /ku:/ *der;* ~s, ~s coup; **einen** ~ **landen** (ugs.) pull off a coup

Coupé /ku'pe:/ *das;* ~s, ~s (Auto) coupé

Coupon /ku'põ:/ *der;* ~s, ~s **(a)** coupon; voucher; **auf** *od.* **für** *od.* **gegen diesen** ~ **bekommen Sie ...:** for this voucher you will receive ...; **(b)** (Finanzw.) [interest] coupon

Courage /ku'raːʒə/ *die;* ~ (ugs.) courage

couragiert /kura'ʒiːɐ̯t/ **1** *Adj.* (mutig) courageous; (beherzt) spirited. **2** *adv.* ⇨ **1:** courageously; spiritedly

Courtage /kʊr'taːʒə/ *die;* ~, ~n brokerage; broker's commission

Cousin /ku'zɛ̃:/ *der;* ~s, ~s (male) cousin

Cousine /ku'ziːnə/ *die;* ~, ~n (female) cousin

Cover /'kavɐ/ *das;* ~s, ~s **(a)** (von Illustrierten) cover; **(b)** (von Schallplatten) sleeve

covern /'kavɐn/ *tr. V.* cover ‹*song, record*›

Cover·version /'kavɐ.../ *die* cover [version]

Cowboy /'kaʊbɔy/ *der;* ~s, ~s cowboy

Cox Orange /'kɔks|orã:ʒə/ *der;* ~ ~, ~ ~: Cox's orange pippin

Crack /krɛk/ *der;* ~s, ~s ace; crack player; (Athlet) crack athlete; **ein** ~ **im Schwimmen/Radfahren** a crack swimmer/cyclist

Cracker /'krɛkɐ/ *der;* ~s, ~ cracker

Crash·kurs /'krɛʃ.../ *der* crash course

Credo ⇨ **Kredo**

Creme /kreːm/ *die;* ~, ~s, (schweiz.:) ~n **(a)** (cream); **(b)** *o. Pl.* (oft iron.: Oberschicht) cream; top people

creme·farben *Adj.* cream[-coloured]

Creme·torte *die* cream cake *or* gateau

cremig *Adj.* creamy; **etw.** ~ **schlagen** beat sth. into a cream

Creutzfeldt-Jakob-Krankheit /'krɔytsfɛlt 'jaːkɔp-/ *die* ▶ 329 | (Med.) Creutzfeldt-Jakob disease

Crew /kru:/ *die;* ~, ~s team; (eines Schiffs/Flugzeugs) crew

C-Schlüssel /'tse:-/ *der* (Musik) C clef

ČSFR /tʃe:|ɛs|ɛf'|ɛr/ *die;* ~ (1990-1992) **die** ~: Czechoslovakia

ČSSR /tʃe:|ɛs|ɛs'|ɛr/ *die;* ~ (1960-1990) **die** ~: Czechoslovakia

CSU /tse:|ɛs'|u:/ *die;* ~ *Abk.:* **Christlich-Soziale Union** CSU

CT (Med.) *Abk.* **Computertomographie** CT

Cup /kap/ *der;* ~s, ~s (Sport) cup

Curriculum /kʊ'riːkulʊm/ *das;* ~s, **Curricula** (Päd.) curriculum

Curry /'kœri/ *das;* ~s, ~s curry powder

Curry-: ~**sauce**, ~**soße** *die* curry sauce; ~**wurst** *die* sliced fried sausage sprinkled with curry powder and served with ketschup

Cutter /'katɐ/ *der;* ~s, ~, **Cutterin** *die;* ~, ~nen ▶ 85 | (Film, Ferns., Rundf.) editor

CVJM /tse:faʊjɔt'|ɛm/ *der;* ~ *Abk.:* **(a) Christlicher Verein Junger Männer** YMCA; **(b) Christlicher Verein Junger Menschen** combined form of YMCA and YWCA

Cyber·sex /'saɪbɐ-/ *der* cybersex

Cyberspace /'saɪbɐspeɪs/ *der;* ~ (DV) cyberspace

---

*alte Schreibung (vgl. Hinweise auf S. xvi–xvii)

Dd

d, D /de:/ *das;* ~, ~ **(a)** (Buchstabe) d/D; **(b)** (Musik) [key of] D

D *Abk.* **Damen**

da /da:/ **1** *Adv.* **(a)** (dort) there; **da draußen/drüben/unten** out/over/down there; **da hinten/vorn[e]** [there] at the back/front; **he, Sie da!** hey, you there!; **der Kerl da** that fellow [over there]; **halt, wer da?** (Milit.) halt, who goes there?; **da bist du ja!** there you are [at last]!; **da, ein Reh!** look, [there's] a deer!; **da, wo die Straße nach X abzweigt** where the road to X turns off; at the turning for X; **da und da** at such-and-such a place; **da und dort** here and there; (manchmal) now and again *or* then; **(b)** (hier) here; **da hast du das Buch** here's the book; **da, nimm schon!** here [you are], take it!; *s. auch* **dahaben**; **(c)** (zeitlich) then; (in dem Augenblick) at that moment; **von da an** from then on; **in meiner Jugend, da war alles besser** back in my young days, everything was better [then]; **(d)** (deshalb) **der Zug war schon weg, da habe ich den Bus genommen** the train had already gone, so I took the bus; **(e)** (ugs.: in diesem Fall) **da kann man nichts machen** there's nothing one can do about it *or* that; **da kann ich [ja] nur lachen!** that's plain ridiculous!; **was tut man da?** what does one do in a case like this?; **(f)** (altertümelnd: nach Relativpronomen; wird nicht übersetzt) ..., **der da sagt** ..., who says; **(g)** (hervorhebend; wird meist nicht übersetzt) **ich habe da einen Kollegen, der** ...: I have a colleague who ...; **da fällt mir noch was ein** [oh yes] another thought strikes me; **(h) da sein** (existieren) exist; (übrig sein) be left; (anwesend sein) be about *or* around; (im Haus, zu Hause sein) be in; (zu sprechen sein) be available; (angekommen, eingetroffen sein) have arrived; (fig.) ‹*case*› have occurred; ‹*moment*› have arrived; ‹*situation*› have arisen; **ich bin gleich wieder da** I'll be right *or* straight back; **dafür** *od.* **dazu ist es ja da!** (coll.) that's what it's [there] for!; **ganz** *od.* **voll da sein** (klar bei Bewusstsein sein) be completely with it. **2** *Konj.* (weil) as; since

d. Ä. *Abk.:* **der Ältere**

da|behalten *unr. tr. V.* keep [there]; (hier behalten) keep here

da·bei /(hinweisend:) '--/ *Adv.* **(a)** with it/him/her/them; **eine Tankstelle mit einer Werkstatt** ~: a filling station with its own workshop [attached]; **nahe** ~: near it; close by; ~ **sein** (anwesend sein) be there; be present (**bei** at); (teilnehmen) take part (**bei** in); **Dabeisein ist alles** it's taking part that counts; **(b)** (währenddessen) at the same time; (bei diesem Anlass) then; on that occasion; **die** ~ **entstehenden Kosten** the expense involved; **er ist** ~ **gesehen worden, wie er das Geld nahm** he was seen [in the act of] taking the money; **ein Unfall** — ~ **gab es zwei Tote** an accident — two people were killed [in it]; **er suchte nach dem Brief,** ~ **hatte er ihn in der Hand** he was looking for the letter and all the time he had it in his hand; **[gerade]** ~ **sein, etw. zu tun** be just doing sth.; **(c)** (außerdem) ~ **[auch]** what is more; **er ist sehr beschäftigt, aber** ~ (dennoch) **immer freundlich** he is very busy but even so always friendly; **(d)** (hinsichtlich dessen) **ich fühle mich gar nicht wohl** ~: I'm not at all happy about it; **was hast du dir denn** ~ **gedacht?** what were you thinking of?; what came over you?; **er hat sich nichts** ~ **gedacht** he saw no harm in it; **(e) da ist doch nichts** ~! there's really no harm in it!; (es ist nicht schwierig) there's nothing to it!; *s. auch* **bleiben a**

dabei-: ~|**bleiben** *unr. itr. V.; mit sein* (dort) stay there; be there; (bei einer Tätigkeit) stick to it; ~|**haben** *unr. tr. V.* have with one; **ich habe kein Geld** ~: I haven't got any money with me *or* on me;

***dabei|sein** ⇨ dabei a, b

dabei-: ~|**sitzen** *unr. itr. V.* sit there; ~|**stehen** *unr. itr. V.* stand by; stand there

da|bleiben *unr. itr. V.; mit sein* stay there; (hier bleiben) stay here; **[noch]** ~: stay on

Dach /dax/ *das;* ~[e]s, **Dächer** /'dɛçɐ/ **(a)** roof; [ganz oben] **unterm** ~ [right up] in the attic; **ein/kein** ~ **über dem Kopf haben** (ugs.) have a/no roof over one's head; **etw. unter** ~ **und Fach bringen** get sth. [safely] under cover; bring in sth.; (fig.: erfolgreich beenden) get sth. all wrapped up; **(b)** (fig. ugs.) **jmdm. aufs** ~ **steigen** give sb. a piece of one's mind; **jmdm. eins aufs** ~ **geben** bash sb. over the head; (tadeln) give sb. a dressing down; tear a strip off sb. (Brit. coll.); **eins aufs** ~ **kriegen** get a bash on the head; (eine Rüge erhalten) get it in the neck (coll.)

Dach-: ~**boden** *der* loft; **auf dem** ~**boden** in the loft; ~**decker** /~dɛkɐ/ *der;* ~**s**, ~: ▶ 85| roofer ~**fenster** *das* skylight; (Dachgaube) dormer window ~**garten** *der* roof-garden; ~**gepäckträger** *der* (Kfz-W.) roof-rack; ~**geschoss,** ***~**geschoß** *das* attic [storey]; ~**kammer** *die* attic [room]; (ärmlich) garret; ~**lawine** *die mass of snow sliding from a roof;* ~**luke** *die* skylight; ~**rinne** *die* gutter

Dachs /daks/ *der;* ~**es**, ~**e** badger

Dachs·bau *der; Pl.* ~**e** badger's earth *or* set

Dach-: ~**schaden** *der* **(a)** *o. Pl.* (ugs.) **einen** ~**schaden haben** be not quite right in the head; be slightly screwy (coll.); **(b)** (Schaden am Dach) roof-damage; ~**stube** *die* (veralt.) ⇨ ~**kammer;** ~**stuhl** *der* roof-truss

dachte /'daxtə/ *1. u. 3. Pers. Sg. Prät. v.* **denken**

Dach-: ~**terrasse** *die* roof-terrace; ~**wohnung** *die* attic flat (Brit.) *or* (Amer.) apartment; ~**ziegel** *der* roof-tile; ~**zimmer** *das* attic room

Dackel /'dakl̩/ *der;* ~**s**, ~: dachshund

Dackel·beine *Pl.* (ugs. scherzh.) [stumpy] bow legs

da·durch /(hinweisend:) '--/ *Adv.* **(a)** through it/them; **(b)** (durch diesen Umstand) as a result; (durch dieses Mittel) in this way; by this [means]; **ich nehme den D-Zug,** ~ **bin ich zwanzig Minuten eher da** I'll take the express, that way I'll get there twenty minutes earlier; ~, **dass er älter ist, hat er einige Vorteile** he has several advantages by virtue of being older *or* because he is older; ~ **gekennzeichnet sein, dass** ... be characterized by the fact that ...

da·für /(hinweisend:) '--/ *Adv.* **(a)** for it/them; ~, **dass** ... (damit) so that ...; ~ **sorgen [, dass** ...] see to it [that ...]; **der Grund** ~, **dass** ... the reason why ...; ~ **sein** be in favour [of it]; **ich bin ganz** ~: I'm all for it; **das ist ein Beweis** ~, **dass** ...: this is proof that ...; **ein Beispiel** ~ **ist** ...: an example of this is ...; **alles spricht** ~, **dass** ...: all the evidence *or* everything suggests that ...; **(b)** (als Gegenleistung) in return [for it]; (beim Tausch) in exchange; (statt dessen) instead; **heute hat er keine Zeit,** ~ **will er morgen kommen** he has no time today, so he wants to come tomorrow instead; **(c) er ist schon 60, aber** ~ **hält ihn niemand** he is 60 but nobody would think so; **(d)** (wenn man das berücksichtigt) ~ **ist sein Französisch nicht sehr gut** his French is not very good, considering; ~ **dass** ... considering that ...; **(e) etwas/nichts** ~ **können** be/not be responsible; ~ **kann er nichts[, dass** ...]: it can't help it [that ...]

dafür-: ~|**halten** *unr. itr. V.* (geh.) consider; be of the opinion; **nach meinem Dafürhalten** in my opinion; ~|**können** ⇨ **dafür e**

dagegen /(hinweisend:) '---/ *Adv.* **(a)** against it/them; **er stieß aus Versehen** ~: he knocked into it by mistake; **ich protestiere energisch** ~, **dass Sie mich verleumden** I must protest strongly against this slander; **ich habe nichts** ~: I've no objection; I don't mind; **was hat er** ~, **dass wir Freunde sind?** why does he object to our being friends?; ~ **sein** be opposed to it *or* against it; ~ **sein, etw. zu tun** be opposed to doing sth.; **was spricht** ~? what is the objection?; ~ **kann man nichts machen** there is nothing one can do about it; **(b)** (im Vergleich dazu) by *or* in comparison; compared with that; (jedoch) on the other hand; **(c)** (als Gegenwert) in exchange

dagegen-: ~|**halten** *unr. tr. V.* **(a)** (entgegnen) counter; (einwenden) object; **(b)** (ugs.: vergleichen) hold it/them against; compare it/them with; ~|**stellen** *refl. V.* oppose it

da|haben *unr. tr. V. (Zusschr. nur im Inf. u. 2. Part.)* (ugs.) have [here]; (im Hause) have in the house; **mal sehen, ob ich noch eins dahabe** I'll see whether I've got one left

da·heim *Adv.* (bes. südd., österr., schweiz.) (a) (zu Hause) at home; (*nach Präp.*) home; ∼ **anrufen** phone *or* ring home; **bei mir** ∼: at my place; (b) (in der Heimat) [back] home; **bei uns** ∼: back home where I/we come from

da·her *Adv.* (a) from there; ∼ **habe ich meine neuen Stiefel** that's where I got my new boots from; ∼ **weht also der Wind!** (ugs.) so 'that's the way the wind blows'; (fig.); (b) (durch diesen Umstand) hence; ∼ **kommt seine gute Laune** that's why he's in a good mood; ∼ **wusste er das** *od.* **hat er das** that's how he knew; that's where he got it from; (c) (deshalb) therefore; so

daher-: ∼**gelaufen** *Adj.; nicht präd.* (abwertend) that nobody's heard of *postpos.;* **jeder** ∼**gelaufene Kerl** any guy who comes along (coll.); any Tom, Dick, or Harry; ∼|**kommen** *unr. itr. V.* come along; ∼**reden** (abwertend) **1** *itr. V.* talk off the cuff; [**so**] **dumm** ∼**reden** talk [such] rubbish; **2** *tr. V.* say off the cuff

da·hin *Adv.* (a) there; (b) (fig.) ∼ **musste es kommen** it had to come to that; **du wirst es** ∼ **bringen, dass ...:** you'll carry things *or* matters so far that ...; (c) *in* **bis** ∼: to there; (zeitlich) until then; **bis** ∼ **sind es 75 km** it's 75 km from here; **es steht mir bis** ∼ (ugs.) I am sick and tired of it *or* fed up to the back teeth with it (coll.); (d) /-'-/ (verloren, vorbei) ∼ **sein** be *or* have gone; (e) (in diesem Sinne) ∼ [**gehend**], **dass ...:** to the effect that ...; **man kann dieses Schreiben auch** ∼ [**gehend**] **auslegen, dass ...:** one can also interpret this letter as meaning that ...

da-: ∼**hinab** *Adv.* down there; down that way; ∼**hinauf** *Adv.* up there; up that way; ∼**hinaus** *Adv.* out there; (in die Richtung) out that way

dahin-: ∼|**dämmern** *itr. V.; mit sein* be semi-conscious; ∼|**eilen** *itr. V.; mit sein* (geh.) hurry along *or* on one's way; ⟨*time*⟩ fly [past]

da·hinein *Adv.* in there; (hier hinein) in here

dahin-: ∼|**gehen** *unr. itr. V.; mit sein* (geh.: vergehen) pass; ⟨*years*⟩ go by; ∼**gestellt** *in* **es ist** *od.* **bleibt** ∼**gestellt** it remains to be seen; **etw.** ∼**gestellt sein lassen** leave sth. open [for the moment]; ∼|**jagen** *itr. V.; mit sein* (geh.) tear *or* race along; ∼|**sagen** *tr. V.* say without thinking; **das war nur so** ∼**gesagt** that was just a casual *or* off-the-cuff remark

da·hinten *Adv.* over there

da·hinter /(hinweisend:) '---/ *Adv.* behind it/them; (folgend) after it/them; **ein Haus mit einem Garten** ∼: a house with a garden behind *or* at the back; **sich** ∼ **klemmen** (ugs.) buckle down to it; pull one's finger out (sl.); ∼ **kommen** (ugs.) find out; ∼ **stecken** (ugs.) (als Grund, Urheber) be behind it/them; **es steckt nichts/nicht viel** ∼: there is nothing/not much to it/them; ∼ **stehen** (fig.) be behind it/ them

***dahinter|klemmen** *usw.:* ⇒ **dahinter**

dahin|ziehen 1 *unr. itr. V.; mit sein* go *or* move on one's/ its way; ⟨*clouds*⟩ drift by; **2** *unr. refl. V.* ⟨*path*⟩ pass along

Dahlie /'da:li̯ə/ *die;* ∼, ∼**n** dahlia

da-: ∼|**lassen** *unr. tr. V.* (ugs.) leave there; (hier lassen) have [there]; ∼|**liegen** *unr. itr. V.* lie there

dalli /'dali/ *Adv.* (ugs.) **aber [ein bisschen]** ∼**!** and make it snappy (coll.); [∼] ∼**!** get a move on!

damalig /'da:ma:lɪç/ *Adj.; nicht präd.* at that *or* the time *postpos.;* **der** ∼**e Bundeskanzler** the then Federal Chancellor; the Federal Chancellor at that *or* the time; **die** ∼**e Regierung** the government of the day; **im** ∼**en Gallien** in what was then Gaul

damals /'da:ma:ls/ *Adv.* then; at that time; ∼, **als ...:** at the time *or* in the days when ...; **von** ∼: of that time *or* those days; (aus dieser Zeit) from that time *or* those days; **seit** ∼: since then

Damast /'da'mast/ *der;* ∼[**e**]**s**, ∼**e** damask

Dame /'da:mə/ *die;* ∼, ∼**n** (a) ▶ 34, ▶ 107 lady; **sehr verehrte** *od.* **meine** ∼**n und Herren!** ladies and gentlemen; **die Abfahrt/die 200 Meter der** ∼**n** (Sport) the women's downhill/200 metres; (b) (Schach, Kartenspiele)

queen; (c) *o. Pl.* (Spiel) draughts (Brit.); checkers (Amer.); (d) (Doppelstein im Damespiel) king

Damen-: ∼**binde** *die* sanitary towel (Brit.) *or* (Amer.) napkin; ∼**fahr·rad** *das* lady's bicycle; ∼**friseur** *der* ladies' hairdresser

damenhaft 1 *Adj.* ladylike. **2** *adv.* like a lady; in a lady-like manner

Damen-: ∼**mannschaft** *die* women's team; ∼**rad** *das* lady's bicycle; ∼**salon** *der* ladies' hairdressing salon (Brit.); beauty salon (Amer.); ∼**sitz** *der* (Reiten) **im** ∼**sitz reiten** ride side-saddle; ∼**toilette** *die* ladies' toilet; ∼**wahl** *die; o. Pl.* ladies' choice

Dame·spiel *das* draughts (Brit.); checkers (Amer.)

Dam·hirsch /'dam-/ *der* fallow deer; (männliches Tier) fallow buck

da·mit /(hinweisend:) '--/ **1** *Adv.* (a) (mit dieser Sache) with it/ them; **ich bin gleich** ∼ **fertig** I'll be finished in a moment; **er hatte nicht** ∼ **gerechnet** he had not expected that *or* reckoned with that; **was ist denn** ∼**?** what's the matter with it/them?; what about it/them?; **wie wäre es** ∼**?** how about it?; (b) (gleichzeitig) with that; thereupon; (c) (daher) thus; as a result. **2** *Konj.* so that

dämlich /'dɛ:mlɪç/ (ugs. abwertend) **1** *Adj.* stupid. **2** *adv.* stupidly; ∼**fragen** ask stupid questions

Dämlichkeit *die;* ∼ (ugs. abwertend) stupidity

Damm /dam/ *der;* ∼[**e**]**s**, **Dämme** /'dɛmə/ (a) embankment; levee (Amer.); (Deich) dike; (Stau∼) dam; (fig.) bulwark; (b) (Straßen∼, Bahn∼) embankment

Dämmer·licht *das; o. Pl.* twilight; (trübes Licht) dim light

dämmern /'dɛmɐn/ *itr. V.* (a) **es dämmert** (morgens) it is getting light; (abends) it is getting dark; **der Morgen dämmert** the day is dawning *or* breaking; **der Abend dämmert** dusk is falling; (b) (ugs.: klar werden) **jmdm.** ∼: dawn upon sb.; **mir dämmert da etwas** the penny is beginning to drop; (ich habe einen Verdacht) I am beginning to smell a rat; (c) (halb schlafen) doze

Dämmerung *die;* ∼, ∼**en** (Abend∼) twilight; dusk; (Morgen∼) dawn; daybreak

dämmrig *Adj.* (a) **es ist/wird schon** ∼ (morgens) it is beginning to get light; day is breaking; (abends) it is beginning to get dark; night is falling; (b) (halbdunkel) gloomy; dim ⟨*light*⟩

Dämon /'dɛ:mɔn/ *der;* ∼**s**, ∼**en** /dɛ'mo:nən/ demon

dämonisch 1 *Adj.* daemonic. **2** *adv.* daemonically

dämonisieren *tr. V.* demonize; portray as a demon/demons

Dampf /dampf/ *der;* ∼[**e**]**s**, **Dämpfe** /'dɛmpfə/ steam *no pl., no indef. art.;* (Physik) [water] vapour *as tech. term, no pl., no indef. art.;* ∼ **dahinter/hinter etw.** (Akk.) **machen** (ugs.) (sich beeilen) get a move on/get a move on with sth.; (andere zur Eile treiben) get things *pl.*/sth. moving

Dampf·bügeleisen *das* steam iron

dampfen *itr. V.* steam

dämpfen /'dɛmpfn/ *tr. V.* (a) (mit Dampf garen) steam ⟨*fish, vegetables, potatoes*⟩; (b) (mildern) muffle, deaden ⟨*sound*⟩; lower ⟨*voice*⟩; dim, turn down ⟨*lights*⟩; cushion, absorb ⟨*blow, impact, shock*⟩; (fig.) temper, diminish ⟨*joy*⟩; dampen ⟨*enthusiasm*⟩; assuage ⟨*sb.'s wrath*⟩; calm ⟨*anger, excitement*⟩

Dampfer *der;* ∼**s**, ∼: steamer; **auf dem falschen** ∼ **sein** (fig. ugs.) be barking up the wrong tree; have got it wrong

Dämpfer *der;* ∼**s**, ∼: (a) (beim Klavier) damper; (bei Streich- u. Blasinstrumenten) mute; (b) (fig.) **einen** ∼ **bekommen** (ugs.) have one's enthusiasm dampened; (gerügt werden) be taken down a peg or two

Dampf-: ∼**kessel** *der* boiler; ∼**kochtopf** *der* pressure cooker; ∼**lok[omotive]** *die* steam locomotive *or* engine; ∼**maschine** *die* steam engine; ∼**nudel** *die* (südd., Kochk.) steamed yeast dumpling; ∼**schiff** *das* steamer

Dämpfung *die;* ∼, ∼**en** (a) (der Stimme) lowering; (von Licht) dimming; (b) (Stoß∼) cushioning; absorption; (von Schwingungen) damping; (fig.) (von Freude, Leidenschaft) tempering; diminishing; (von Begeisterung) dampening; (von Wut, Aufregung) calming

---

*alte Schreibung (vgl. Hinweise auf S. xvi–xvii)

Dampf·walze *die* steamroller

da·nach /(hinweisend:) '--/ *Adv.* **(a)** (zeitlich) after it/that; then; **noch tagelang** ~: for days after[wards]; **eine Stunde** ~: an hour later; **(b)** (räumlich: dahinter) after it/them; **voran gingen die Eltern,** ~ **kamen die Kinder** the parents went in front, the children following after *or* behind; **(c)** (ein Ziel angebend) towards it/them; **er griff** ~: he made a grab for it/them; ~ **lasst uns alle streben** let us all strive for that; ~ **fragen** ask about it/them; **(d)** (entsprechend) in accordance with it/them; **ein Brief ist gekommen;** ~ **ist sie schon unterwegs** a letter has arrived, according to which she is already on her way; **ihr kennt die Regeln, nun richtet euch** ~! you know the rules, so stick to *or* abide by them

Däne /'dɛːnə/ *der;* ~**n,** ~**n** ▶ 388| Dane; **er ist** ~: he is Danish *or* a Dane

da·neben /(hinweisend:) '---/ *Adv.* **(a)** next to *or* beside him/her/it/them *etc.;* **(b)** (im Vergleich dazu) in comparison; **(c)** (außerdem) in addition [to that]; besides [that]; **(d)** ~ **sein** (ugs.) ‹reaction, remark› be out of order (coll.); **die Entscheidung war total** ~: the decision was all wrong; **er sah völlig** ~ **aus** he looked a real freak (coll.)

daneben-: ~|**benehmen** *unr. refl. V.* (ugs.) blot one's copybook (coll.); spoil one's record; (sich aufführen) make an exhibition of oneself; ~|**gehen** *unr. itr. V.; mit sein* **(a)** (das Ziel verfehlen) miss [the target]; **(b)** (ugs.: fehlschlagen) misfire; be a flop (sl.); ~|**schießen** *unr. itr. V.* miss [the target]; **mit Absicht** ~ **schießen** shoot to miss; ~|**tippen** *itr. V.* (ugs.) guess wrong

Dänemark /'dɛːnəmark/ *(das);* ~**s** Denmark

dang /daŋ/ *1. u. 3. Pers. Sg. Prät. v.* **dingen**

danieder|liegen *unr. itr. V.* (geh.) **(a)** (krank sein) be laid low; **schwer [krank]/sterbend** ~: lie seriously ill/dying; **(b)** (fig.) ‹trade, economy› be depressed

Dänin *die;* ~, ~**nen** Dane; Danish woman/girl

dänisch /'dɛːnɪʃ/ *Adj.* ▶ 388|, ▶ 487| Danish

dank /daŋk/ *Präp. mit Dat. u. Gen.* thanks to

Dank *der;* ~**[e]s (a)** thanks *pl.;* **jmdm. seinen** ~ **abstatten** offer one's thanks to sb.; **jmdm. [großen]** ~ **schulden** *od.* **schuldig sein** (geh.), **jmdm. zu [großem]** ~ **verpflichtet sein** owe sb. a [great] debt of gratitude; **und das ist nun der** ~ **dafür** (iron.) so that's all the thanks I get!; **mit vielem** *od.* **bestem** ~ **zurück** thanks for the loan; (bes. geschrieben) returned with thanks!; **(b)** (in Dankesformeln) **vielen/besten/herzlichen** ~! thank you very much!; many thanks; **vielen** ~, **dass du mir geholfen hast** thank you very much for helping me; **tausend** ~! (ugs.) very many thanks [indeed]

dankbar 1 *Adj.* **(a)** grateful; (anerkennend) appreciative ‹child, audience, etc.›; **sich** ~ **zeigen** show one's gratitude *or* appreciation; **für eine baldige Antwort wären wir** ~: we should be grateful for an early reply; **(b)** (lohnend) rewarding ‹job, part, task, etc.›. **2** *adv.* gratefully; **jmdm.** ~ **anblicken** give sb. a look of gratitude

Dankbarkeit *die;* ~; gratitude

danke /'daŋkə/ *Interj.* thank you; (ablehnend) no, thank you; **ja** ~[, **gern**] yes, please; **nein** ~: no, thank you; ~ **schön/sehr/vielmals** thank you very much; ~ **schön sagen** say 'thank you'; **sonst geht's dir [wohl]** ~! (ugs.) what do you think you're doing?; have you taken leave of your senses?

danken 1 *itr. V.* thank; **ich danke Ihnen vielmals** thank you very much; **Betrag** ~**d erhalten** [payment] received with thanks; **na, ich danke!** (ugs.) no, 'thank you!. **2** *tr. V.* [aber bitte,] **nichts zu** ~: don't mention it; not at all; **sie hat ihm seine Hilfe schlecht gedankt** she gave him a poor reward for his help

dankens·wert *Adj.* commendable ‹effort etc.›; **es ist** ~, **dass er uns hilft** it is kind *or* very good of him to help [us]

dankenswerter·weise *Adv.* kindly; generously; ~ **haben sich viele freiwillig gemeldet** commendably many have volunteered

Danke·schön *das;* ~**s** thank-you; **ein [herzliches]** ~ **sagen** express one's [sincere] thanks

Dankes·wort *das* word of thanks

dann /dan/ *Adv.* **(a)** then; **was** ~? what happens then?; **noch drei Tage,** ~ **ist Ostern** another three days and it will be Easter; **bis** ~: see you then; ~ **und wann** now and then; **er ist der Klassenbeste,** ~ **kommt sein Bruder** he is top of the class, followed by his brother *or* then comes his brother; **(b)** (unter diesen Umständen) then; in that case; [na,] ~ **eben nicht!** in that case, forget it!; ~ **bis morgen** see you tomorrow, then; **nur** ~, **wenn** ...: only if ...; **(c)** (außerdem) ~ **noch** ...: then ... as well; **zuletzt fiel** ~ **noch der Strom aus** finally to top it all there was a power failure

dannen /'danən/ *Adv. in* **von** ~ (veralt.) from thence (arch./literary)

daran /da'ran, (hinweisend:) '--/ *Adv.* **(a)** on it/them; **es hängt etwas** ~: something is hanging from it/them; **er klammert sich** ~ (auch fig.) he clings to it; ~ **riechen** take a sniff at it/them; **dicht** ~: close to it/them; **nahe** ~ **sein, etw. zu tun** be on the point of doing sth.; **(b)** ~ **ist nichts zu machen** there's nothing one can do about it; ~ **wird sich nichts ändern** nothing will alter this fact; **kein Wort** ~ **ist wahr** not a word of it is true; ~ **arbeiten** work on it/them; **wir haben keinen Bedarf mehr** ~: we no longer have any need of it/them; **mir liegt viel** ~: it means a lot to me; **ich wäre beinahe** ~ **erstickt** I almost choked on it; it almost made me choke; **er ist** ~ **gestorben** he died of it; **(d)** **im Anschluss** ~ **fand eine Diskussion statt** after that there was a discussion

daran-: ~|**gehen** *unr. itr. V.; mit sein* set about it; ~**gehen, etw. zu tun** set about doing sth.; ~|**machen** *refl. V.* (ugs.) set about it; (energisch) get down to it; ~|**setzen** *tr. V.* devote ‹energy etc.› to it; summon up ‹ambition› for it; (aufs Spiel setzen) risk ‹one's life, one's honour› for it

darauf /da'rauf, (hinweisend:) '--/ *Adv.* **(a)** on it/them; (oben ~) on top of it/them; **(b)** **er hat** ~ **geschossen** he shot at it/them; ~ **müsst ihr zugehen** that's what you must head towards *or* make for; **er ist ganz versessen** ~: he is mad [keen] on 1t (coll.); **also** ~ **willst du hinaus** so 'that's what you're getting at; **(c)** **wie kommst du nur** ~? what makes you think that?; **(d)** (danach) after that; **ein Jahr** ~ / **kurz** ~ **starb er** he died a year later/shortly afterwards; **zuerst kamen die Kinder,** ~ **folgten die Festwagen** first came the children, then followed *or* followed by the floats; ~ **folgend** following; **am** ~ **folgenden Tag** the following day; [the] next day; **(e)** (infolgedessen, daraufhin) because of that; as a result

***darauf·folgend** ⇨ darauf d

darauf·hin *Adv.* **(a)** (infolgedessen) as a result [of this/that]; consequently; (danach) thereupon; **(b)** (unter diesem Gesichtspunkt) with a view to this/that; **etw.** ~ **prüfen, ob es geeignet ist** examine sth. to see whether it is suitable

daraus /da'raus, (hinweisend:) '--/ *Adv.* **(a)** from it/them; out of it/them; **(b)** **mach dir nichts** ~ don't worry about it; ~ **ist eine große Firma geworden** it has become *or* turned into a large business; **was ist** ~ **geworden?** what has become of it?; ~ **wird nichts** nothing will come of it

darben /'darbn/ *itr. V.* (geh.) live in want; (hungern) go hungry

dar|bieten (geh.) **1** *unr. tr. V.* perform. **2** *unr. refl. V.* **sich jmds. Blicken** ~: expose oneself to sb.'s gaze

Darbietung *die;* ~, ~**en** (geh.) **(a)** presentation; **(b)** (Aufführung) performance; (beim Varieté usw.) act

darf /darf/ *1. u. 3. Pers. Sg. Präsens v.* **dürfen**

darfst /darfst/ *2. Pers. Sg. Präsens v.* **dürfen**

darin /da'rɪn, (hinweisend:) '--/ *Adv.* **(a)** in it/them; (drinnen) inside [it/them]; **(b)** (in dieser Hinsicht) in that respect; ~ **stimme ich völlig mit Ihnen überein** I entirely agree with you there

dar|legen *tr. V.* explain (Dat. to); set forth ‹reasons, facts›; expound ‹theory›

Darlegung *die;* ~, ~**en** explanation

Darlehen /'daːʁleːən/ *das;* ~**s,** ~: loan; **ein** ~ **aufnehmen** get *or* raise a loan

Darlehens-: ~**kasse** *die* credit bank; ~**nehmer** *der* (Bankw.) borrower

Darm /darm/ *der;* ~[e]s, **Därme** /'dɛrmə/ (**a**) ▶ 326 | intestines *pl.;* bowels *pl.;* (**b**) (Wursthaut) skin; (**c**) *o. Pl.* (Material) gut

Darm-: ~**grippe** *die* ▶ 329 | gastric influenza; ~**trägheit** *die* (Med.) constipation

dar|stellen 1 *tr. V.* (**a**) depict; portray; **etw. grafisch** ~: present sth. graphically; (**b**) (verkörpern) play; act; **etwas/nichts** ~: make [a bit of] an impression/not make any sort of an impression; ⟨*gift etc.*⟩ look good/not look anything special; (**c**) (schildern) describe ⟨*person, incident, etc.*⟩; present ⟨*matter, argument*⟩; (**d**) (sein, bedeuten) represent; constitute. 2 *refl. V.* (**a**) (sich erweisen, sich zeigen) prove [to be]; turn out to be; **sich jmdm. als ...** ~: appear to sb. as ...; (**b**) (sich selbst schildern) portray oneself

Darsteller *der;* ~s, ~ actor

Darstellerin *die;* ~, ~**nen** actress

darstellerisch *Adj.; nicht präd.* acting *attrib.;* **ihre** ~**en Fähigkeiten** her abilities as an actress

Darstellung *die* (**a**) representation; (Schilderung) portrayal; (Bild) picture; **grafische/schematische** ~: diagram; (Graph) graph; (**b**) (Beschreibung, Bericht) description; account; (**c**) (Theater) interpretation; performance

darüber /da'ry:bɐ, (hinweisend:) '---/ *Adv.* (**a**) (über diesem/diesen) over *or* above it/them; (über dies/diese) over it/them; **wir wohnen im zweiten Stock und er** ~: we live on the second floor and he lives above us; ~ **fahren** run over it/them; ~ **liegen** be higher; ~ **stehen** (fig.) be above such things; ~ **steigen** climb over it/them; (**b**) ~ **hinaus** in additon [to that]; (noch obendrein) what is more; (**c**) (über dieser/diese Angelegenheit) about it/them; ~ **wollen wir hinwegsehen** we will overlook it; (**d**) (über diese Grenze, dieses Maß hinaus) above [that]; over [that]; **Ist es schon 12 Uhr? — Aber ja, es ist schon 10 Minuten** ~: Is it twelve o'clock yet? — Oh yes, it's already ten past; (**e**) (währenddessen) meanwhile; (**f**) (währenddessen und deshalb) because of it/them; as a result

*****darüber|fahren** *usw.:* ⇒ **darüber a**

darum /da'rʊm, (hinweisend:) '--/ *Adv.* (**a**) (**a**)round it/them; (**b**) **ich werde mich** ~ **bemühen** I will try to deal with it; (versuchen, es zu bekommen) I'll try to get it; **sie wird nicht** ~ **herumkommen, es zu tun** she won't get out of *or* avoid doing it; **es geht mir** ~, **eine Einigung zu erzielen** my concern *or* aim is to reach an agreement; (**c**) /'--/ (deswegen) because of that; for that reason; **ach,** ~ **ist er so schlecht gelaunt!** so that's why he's in such a bad mood!; **Warum weinst du? — Darum!** Why are you crying? — Because!

darum|legen *tr. V.* put around it/them

darunter /da'rʊntɐ, (hinweisend:) '---/ *Adv.* (**a**) under *or* beneath it/them; **wir wohnen im 2. Stock und er** ~: we live on the second floor and he lives below us *or* on the floor below; **etw.** ~ **schreiben** write sth. underneath *or* at the bottom; **eine Unterschrift/einen Namen** ~ **setzen** put a signature/a name to it; (**b**) 10° **oder etwas** ~: 10° or a bit less; **Bewerber im Alter von 40 Jahren und** ~: applicants aged 40 and under; ~ **bleiben** keep below this; ~ **liegen** be lower; (**c**) **was verstehen Sie** ~? what do you understand by that?; **sie hat sehr** ~ **gelitten** she suffered a great deal from *or* because of it/that; (**d**) (dabei, dazwischen) amongst them; **in vielen Ländern,** ~ **der Schweiz** in many countries, including Switzerland; (**e**) ~ **fallen** (fig.) be included; be amongst them; (in diese Kategorie) come under it; **etw.** ~ **mischen** mingle with it/them

*****darunter|bleiben** *usw.:* ⇒ **darunter**

das /das/ 1 *best. Art. Nom. u. Akk.* the; **das Leben im Dschungel** life in the jungle; **das Weihnachtsfest** Christmas; **das Laufen fällt ihm schwer** walking is difficult for him. 2 *Demonstrativpron.* (**a**) *attr.* **das Kind war es** it was that child; (**b**) *allein stehend* **das** [da] that one; **das** [hier] this one [here]; **das mit dem blonden Haar** the one with the fair hair. 3 *Relativpron.* (Mensch)

*alte Schreibung (vgl. Hinweise auf S. xvi–xvii)

who; that; (Sache, Tier) which; that; **das Mädchen, das da drüben entlanggeht** the girl walking along over there

*****da|sein** ⇒ **da** 1 h

Da·sein *das* existence

Daseins·berechtigung *die* right to exist

da|sitzen *unr. itr. V.* (**a**) sit there; (**b**) (ugs.: in Schwierigkeiten sein) be left [there]; **ich saß ohne Geld da** I was stuck there without any money

dasjenige ⇒ **derjenige**

dass, *daß /das/ *Konj.* (**a**) that; **entschuldigen Sie bitte,** ~ **ich mich verspätet habe** please forgive me for being late; **please forgive my being late; ich weiß,** ~ **du Recht hast** I know [that] you are right; **ich verstehe nicht,** ~ **sie ihn geheiratet hat** I don't understand why she married him; **es ist schon 3 Jahre her,** ~ **wir zum letzten Mal im Theater waren** it is three years since *or* it was three years ago when we last went to the theatre; (**b**) (nach Pronominaladverbien o. dergl.) [the fact] that; **Wissen erwirbt man dadurch,** ~ **man viel liest** one acquires knowledge by reading a great deal; **das liegt daran,** ~ **du nicht aufgepasst hast** that is due to the fact that you did not pay attention; that comes from your not paying attention; **ich bin dagegen,** ~ **er geht** I am against his going; (**c**) (im Konsekutivsatz) that; **er lachte so [sehr],** ~ **ihm die Tränen in die Augen traten** he laughed so much that he almost cried; (**d**) (im Finalsatz) so that; (**e**) (im Wunschsatz) **if only;** ~ **mir das nicht noch einmal passiert!** see that it doesn't happen again!; (**f**) (im Ausruf) ~ **er so jung sterben musste!** how terrible *or* it's so sad that he had to die so young!; ~ **mir das passieren musste!** why did it have to [go and] happen to me!; *s. auch* **als; [an]statt; auf; außer; nur; ohne; kaum**

dasselbe ⇒ **derselbe**

da|stehen *unr. itr. V.* (**a**) ([untätig] stehen) [just] stand there; **krumm** ~: slouch; ~ **wie der Ochs vorm Berg** (salopp) be completely baffled; (**b**) (in einer bestimmten Lage sein) find oneself; **gut** ~: be in a good position; [**ganz**] **allein** ~: be [all] alone in the world; **mit leeren Händen/als Lügner** *usw.* ~: be left empty-handed/looking like a liar *etc.*

Datei /da'tai̯/ *die;* ~, ~**en** data file

Daten /'da:tn̩/ 1 ⇒ **Datum**. 2 *Pl.* data; **die technischen** ~ **eines Typs** the technical specification *sing.* of a model

Daten-: ~**autobahn** *die* (DV) data highway; ~**bank** *die; Pl.* ~**banken** data bank; ~**erfassung** *die;* data capture; ~**handschuh** *der* dataglove; ~**helm** *der* data helmet; virtual reality helmet; ~**highway** /...hai̯wei̯/ *der;* ~s, ~s ⇒ **Datenautobahn;** ~**schutz** *der* data protection; ~**schutz·beauftragte** *der/die* data protection officer; ~**träger** *der* data carrier; ~**verarbeitung** *die* data processing *no def. art.;* ~**verarbeitungs·anlage** *die* data processor; (größeres System) data processing system

datieren /da'ti:rən/ *tr. V.* date; **vom 1. Mai datiert** dated 1 May

Dativ /'da:ti:f/ *der;* ~s, ~e (Sprachw.) dative [case]

Dativ·objekt *das* (Sprachw.) indirect object

dato /'da:to/ *in* **bis** ~ (Kaufmannsspr., sonst ugs.) to date

Dattel /'datl/ *die;* ~, ~**n** date

Dattel·palme *die* date palm

Datum /'da:tʊm/ *das;* ~s, **Daten** /'da:tn̩/ ▶ 119 |, ▶ 107 | date; **welches** ~ **haben wir heute?** what is the date today?

Dauer /'dau̯ɐ/ *die;* ~: (**a**) length; duration; **die** ~ **eines Vertrags** the term of a contract; **von kurzer** *od.* **nicht von [langer]** ~ **sein** not last long; be short-lived; **für die** ~ **eines Jahres** *od.* **von einem Jahr** for a period of one year; (**b**) **von** ~ **sein** last [long]; **auf die** ~: in the long run; **auf** ~: permanently; for good; **er hat die Stelle jetzt auf** ~: his job is now permanent

dauer-, Dauer-: ~**auftrag** *der* (Finanzw.) standing order; ~**frost** *der* long period of frost; ~**gast** *der* (im Hotel usw.) long-stay guest *or* resident; ~**haft** 1 *Adj.* (**a**) [long-]lasting, enduring ⟨*peace, friendship, etc.*⟩; (**b**) (haltbar)

Datum

Im Englischen gibt es mehrere Möglichkeiten, das Datum zu schreiben oder zu sagen:

der 10. Mai = *(geschrieben)* May 10, 10 May,
May 10th, 10th May

= *(gesprochen)* May the tenth,
the tenth of May *od. (amerik.)*
May tenth

Die folgenden Beispiele beziehen sich auf die häufigsten Versionen, die überall in der englischsprachigen Welt verwendet werden: May 10 bzw. May 10th für die schriftliche Form, die auch so im Briefkopf erscheint, und May the tenth für die gesprochene Form.

Selbstverständlich werden Daten auch nur mit Ziffern angegeben, vor allem in Geschäftsbriefen. Hier ist zu beachten, dass in den USA die Reihenfolge Monat, Tag, Jahr (mit Bindestrich) ist. Der Monat erscheint also an erster Stelle (May 10th 1995 = 5-10-1995). Im britischen Gebrauch hingegen ist die Reihenfolge wie auch im deutschen Tag, Monat, Jahr (10.5.1995), oft auch mit Schrägstrich: 10/5/1995).

Der Wievielte?

Der Wievielte ist heute? = What's the date [today]?

Heute ist der zehnte Mai = Today is *od.* It's May the tenth

Am Wievielten ist die Hochzeit? = What date is the wedding?

Die Hochzeit ist am 22. = The wedding is on the 22nd *(gesprochen:* twenty-second)

	GESCHRIEBEN	GESPROCHEN
der 1. Mai	May 1st, May 1	May the first
der 21. Mai	May 21st, May 21	May the twenty-first
der 30. Mai 1994	May 30th *od.* May 30 1994 *od. (amerik.)* May 30, 1994	May the thirtieth nineteen ninety-four
Montag, der 3. Mai	Monday May 3rd *od.* May 3	Monday May the third
21.5.1966	21.5.66 *od. (amerik.)* 5-21-66	twenty-one five *od. (amerik.)* five twenty-one sixty-six

In welchem Jahr?

1900	1900	nineteen hundred
1905	1905	nineteen [oh] five, nineteen hundred and five
1920	1920	nineteen twenty[1]
das Jahr 2000	the year 2000	the year two thousand
im Jahr 2000	in the year 2000	in the year two thousand
2001	2001	two thousand and one
230 n.Chr.	230 AD[2]	two hundred and thirty AD [ei'di:]
55 v.Chr.	55 BC[3]	fifty-five BC [bi'si:]
das 16. Jahrhundert	the 16th century	the sixteenth century

[1] Meist wird das **hundred and** bei der Jahresangabe weggelassen; es wird aber manchmal doch hinzugefügt, vor allem bei den Jahren 01 bis 09 des Jahrhunderts.

[2] = anno domini

[3] = before Christ

Wann?

am Freitag = on Friday

am 6. März = on March 6th *(gesprochen:* on March the sixth)

am Freitag, dem 6. März = on Friday March 6th *(gesprochen:* on Friday March the sixth)

Beachten Sie, dass **the** nicht geschrieben und nur vor der Ordinalzahl für das Datum gesprochen wird.

Ausnahme: Wenn nur die Zahl (ohne Angabe des Monats) genannt wird, wird **the** auch geschrieben:

Wir treffen uns am 6. = We're meeting on the 6th

Der Termin ist am Ersten = The deadline is on the first

Sie kommen am nächsten Ersten = They are coming on the first of next month

Auch bei der Angabe des Monats wird **the** nicht verwendet:

im Juni = in June

letztes Jahr im Juni = last June

im Juni nächsten Jahres = next June

Mitte Juni = in the middle of June

Ende/Anfang Juni = at the end/beginning of June

Vor Jahresangaben steht immer **in**:

1945 kam er aus dem Krieg zurück = In 1945 he came back from the war

Für "im Jahr[e]" sagt man meist einfach **in**; **in the year ...** ist stilistisch etwas gehoben und bezieht sich meist auf geschichtliche Daten:

im Jahr[e] 55 v.Chr. = in [the year] 55 BC

im Jahr[e] 27 n.Chr. = in [the year] 27 AD

Sonstige Ausdrücke

vom 5. November an = from November 5th [onwards]

ab kommendem Dienstag = from next Tuesday

vom 21. bis zum 30. = from the 21st to the 30th

Es wird bis Freitag/ bis zum 14. fertig = It will be ready by Friday/by the 14th

Es wird erst am Freitag fertig = It won't be ready until Friday

um den 16. Mai [herum] = around May 16th

in den Sechzigerjahren = in the sixties *od.* 60s

in den Achtzigerjahren des 19. Jahrhunderts = in the 1880s

der Roman des 19. Jahrhunderts = the 19th century novel

ein Komponist des 17. Jahrhunderts = a 17th century composer

ein Gebäude aus dem 14. Jahrhundert = a 14th century building

Das Auto ist ein 1990er Modell|ist Baujahr 1990 = The car's a 1990 model

der Aufstand von 1912 = the 1912 uprising

durable; hard-wearing; **2** *adv.* lastingly; with long-lasting effect; **~karte** *die* season ticket; **~lauf** *der* jogging *no art.;* **einen ~lauf machen** go for a jog; go jogging; **im ~lauf** at a jog; **~lutscher** *der* large lollipop; all-day sucker (Amer.)

dauern *itr. V.* last; ⟨*job etc.*⟩ take; **der Film dauert zwei Stunden** the film lasts [for] *or* goes on for two hours; **bei ihm dauert alles furchtbar lange** everything takes him a terribly long time; **einen Moment, es dauert nicht lange** just a minute, it won't take long; **das dauert** (ugs.) that will take [some] time

dauernd 1 *Adj.; nicht präd.* constant, perpetual ⟨*noise, interruptions, etc.*⟩; permanent ⟨*institution*⟩. **2** *adv.* constantly; (immer) always; the whole time; **er kommt ~ zu spät** he is for ever *or* keeps on arriving late

Dauer-: **~regen** *der* continuous rain; **~stellung** *die* permanent position; **~welle** *die* perm; permanent wave; **~wurst** *die* smoked sausage **~zustand** *der* permanent state [of affairs]

Däumchen /ˈdɔymçən/ *das;* **~s, ~:** little thumb; **~ drehen** (ugs.) twiddle one's thumbs

Daumen /ˈdaumən/ *der;* **~s, ~:** ▶ 326⎮ thumb; **am ~ lutschen** suck one's thumb; **jmdm. den** *od.* **die ~ drücken** *od.* **halten** keep one's fingers crossed for sb.; **auf etw.** (*Dat.*) **den ~ haben, auf etw.** (*Akk.*) **den ~ halten** (ugs.) keep a careful eye *or* check on sth.; **[etw.] über den ~ peilen** (ugs.) make a guesstimate [of sth.] (coll.)

daumen·breit *Adj.* as wide as your thumb *postpos.;* ≈ an inch across *postpos.*

Daumen·nagel *der* thumbnail

Daune /ˈdaunə/ *die;* **~, ~n** down [feather]; **~n** down *sing.*

Daunen·bett *das* down-filled quilt

da·von /(hinweisend:) '--/ *Adv.* **(a)** from it/them; (von dort) from there; (mit Entfernungsangabe) away [from it/them]; **wir sind noch weit ~ entfernt** (fig.) we are still a long way from that; **(b) dies ist die Hauptstraße, und ~ zweigen einige Nebenstraßen ab** this is the main road and a few side roads branch off it; **(c)** (darüber) about it/ them; **(d)** (dadurch) by it/them; thereby; **~ wirst du krank** it will make you ill; **~ kriegt man Durchfall** you get diarrhoea from [eating] that/those; **das kommt ~!** (ugs.) [there you are,] that's what happens; **(e) das Gegenteil ~ ist wahr** the opposite [of this] is true; **geben Sie mir vier ~:** give me four of them; **(f)** (aus diesem Material, man dieser Grundlage) from *or* out of it/them; **~ kann man nicht leben** you can't live on that

davon-: **~|fahren** *unr. itr. V.; mit sein* leave; (mit dem Auto) drive away *or* off; (mit dem Fahrrad, Motorrad) ride away *or* off; **jmdm. ~fahren** leave sb. behind; **~|kommen** *unr. itr. V.; mit sein* get away; escape; (mit dem Schrecken/einer Geldstrafe **~kommen** get off with a fright/a fine; **~|laufen** *unr. itr. V.; mit sein* **(a)** run away; **er ist mir ~gelaufen** he's made off; **es ist zum Davonlaufen** (ugs.) it really turns you off (coll.); it makes you want to run a mile; **(b)** (ugs.: überraschend verlassen) **jmdm. ~laufen** walk out on sb.; **~|machen** *refl. V.* make off (mit with); **~|stehlen** *unr. refl. V.* (geh.) steal away; **~|tragen** *unr. tr. V.* **(a)** carry away; **(b)** (geh.: erringen) win, gain ⟨*a victory, fame*⟩; **(c)** (geh.: sich zuziehen) receive, suffer ⟨*injuries*⟩

da·vor /(hinweisend:) '--/ *Adv.* **(a)** in front of it/them; **sich ~ legen** lie down in front of it/them; **(b)** (zeitlich) before [it/them]; **kurz ~ stehen** (vor diesem Ereignis usw.) be close to it; (vor dieser Tat) be about to do it; **(c) jmdn. ~ warnen** warn sb. of *or* about it/them.; **er hat Angst ~, erwischt zu werden** he is afraid of being caught; **wir sind ~ geschützt** we are protected from it/them

*****davor|legen** *usw.:* ⇒ davor

da·zu /(hinweisend:) '--/ *Adv.* **(a)** with it/them; (gleichzeitig) at the same time; (außerdem) what is more; **~ reicht man am besten Salat** it's/they're best served with lettuce/salad; **(b)** (darüber) about *or* on it/them; **(c)** (zu diesem Zweck) for it; (es zu tun) to do it; **~ reicht das Geld nicht** we haven't enough money for that; **(d) im Widerspruch** *od.*

Gegensatz ~: contrary to this/that; **~ war sie nicht in der Lage** she was not in a position to do it *or* do so; **er hatte ~ keine Lust** he didn't want to *or* didn't feel like it; **wie komme ich ~?** (ugs.) it would never occur to me; why on earth should I?

dazu-: **~|geben** *unr. tr. V.* **(a)** (beisteuern) give towards it; **(b)** (zusätzlich geben) add; give as well; **~|gehören** *tr. V.* **(a)** belong to it/them; (als Zusatz) go with it/them; **(b)** (erforderlich sein); **es gehört Mut/schon einiges ~:** it takes courage/quite something; **~gehörig** *Adj.; nicht präd.* appropriate; which goes/go with it/them *postpos.;* **~|kommen** *unr. itr. V.; mit sein* **(a)** (hinkommen) arrive [on the scene]; turn up; **(b)** (hinzukommen) **kommt noch etwas ~?** (fig.) is there anything else [you would like]?; **~ kommt, dass …** (fig.) what's more, …; on top of that, …; **~|lernen** *tr., itr. V.* **[etwas] ~ lernen** learn [something new]; **~|rechnen** *tr., itr. V.* add on; **~|setzen** *refl. V.* sit down next to him/her/you/them; **~|tun** *unr. tr. V.* (ugs.) add; **das Seine ~tun** do one's bit; **ohne jmds. Dazutun** without sb.'s help; **~|verdienen** *tr., itr. V.* earn ⟨*sth.*⟩ extra; (durch Nebenbeschäftigung) earn ⟨*sth.*⟩ on the side

da·zwischen /(hinweisend:) '--/ *Adv.* in between; between them; (darunter) among them

dazwischen-: **~|fahren** *unr. itr. V.; mit sein* (eingreifen) step in [and sort things out]; **~|funken** *itr. V.* (ugs.) put a spanner in the works; (sich einmischen) put one's oar in; **~|kommen** *unr. itr. V.; mit sein* **(a) mit dem Finger ~kommen** get one's finger caught [in it]; **(b)** (als Hindernis auftreten) **mir ist etwas ~gekommen** I had problems; **~|liegen** *unr. itr. V.;* lie in between; **Jahre lagen ~:** years had passed; **die ~liegende Zeit/Strecke** the intervening period/distance; **~|reden** *itr. V.* interrupt; **~|rufen 1** *unr. itr. V.* interrupt [by shouting]; **2** *unr. tr. V.* interrupt [loudly] with; interject

DDR /de:de:'|ɛr/ *die;* **~** *Abk.* (1949–1990) **Deutsche Demokratische Republik** GDR; East Germany (*in popular use*)

Deal /di:l/ *der od. das;* **~s, ~s** (salopp) deal

dealen /ˈdi:lən/ *itr. V.* (ugs.) push drugs

Dealer /ˈdi:lɐ/ *der;* **~s, ~** (ugs.) pusher

Debatte /deˈbatə/ *die;* **~, ~n** debate (**über** + *Akk.* on); **etw. in die ~ werfen** introduce *or* bring sth. into the debate; **[nicht] zur ~ stehen** [not] be under discussion

debattieren *tr., itr. V.* debate; [mit jmdm.] **über etw. ~:** discuss sth. [with sb.]

Debet /ˈde:bɛt/ *das;* **~s, ~s** (Finanzw.) debit [side].

Debitor /ˈde:bitɔr/ *der;* **~s, ~en** /debiˈto:rən/ (Finanzw.) debtor

Debüt /deˈby:/ *das;* **~s, ~s** debut; **sein ~ geben** make one's debut

Debütant /debyˈtant/ *der;* **~en, ~en, Debütantin** *die;* **~, ~nen** newcomer [making his debut]

dechiffrieren *tr. V.* decipher ⟨*code, message*⟩

Deck /dɛk/ *das;* **~[e]s, ~s** (a) deck; **alle Mann an ~!** all hands on deck!; **(b)** (Park~) storey; level

Deck-: **~adresse** *die* accommodation *or* (Amer.) cover address; **~anstrich** *der* top coat; **~bett** *das* ⇒ **Oberbett**

Decke /ˈdɛkə/ *die;* **~, ~n** **(a)** (Tisch~) tablecloth; **(b)** (Woll~, Pferde~, auch fig.) blanket; (Reise~) rug; (Deckbett, Stepp~) quilt; **mit jmdm. unter einer ~ stecken** (ugs.) be hand in glove with sb.; be in cahoots with sb. (sl.); **(c)** (Zimmer~) ceiling; **mir fällt die ~ auf den Kopf** (ugs.) I get sick of [the sight of] these four walls; **an die ~ gehen** (ugs.) hit the roof (coll.)

Deckel /ˈdɛk(ə)l/ *der;* **~s, ~** **(a)** lid; (von Flaschen, Gläsern usw.) top; (Schacht~, Uhr~, Buch~ usw.) cover; **(b)** (Bier~) beer mat; **(c) jmdm. eins auf den ~ geben** (ugs.) haul sb. over the coals; take sb. to task

decken 1 *tr. V.* **(a) etw. über etw.** (*Akk.*) **~:** spread sth. over sth.; **(b)** roof ⟨*house*⟩; cover ⟨*roof*⟩; **ein Dach/ Haus mit Ziegeln/Stroh ~:** tile/thatch a roof/house; **(c) den Tisch ~:** lay *or* set the table; **(d)** (schützen) cover ⟨*player*⟩; (vor Gericht usw.) cover up for ⟨*accomplice, crime, etc.*⟩; **(e)** (befriedigen) satisfy, meet ⟨*need, demand*⟩; **mein Bedarf ist gedeckt** (ugs.) I've had enough; **(f)** (Finanzw., Versicherungsw.) cover; **(g)** (begatten) cover; ‹*stallion*› serve ‹*mare*›. **2** *itr. V.* **(a)** (Fußball) mark; (Boxen) keep up one's guard; **(b)** (den Tisch ∼) lay *or* set the table; **(c)** ‹*colour*› cover. **3** *refl. V.* coincide; tally

Decken-:   ∼**beleuchtung** *die* ceiling light; ∼**fluter** *der;* ∼**s,** ∼**:** uplighter; ∼**gemälde** *das* ceiling painting; ∼**malerei** *die* ceiling painting

Deck-:   ∼**farbe** *die* paint (*which covers well*); body-colour; ∼**hengst** *der* stud-horse; breeding stallion; ∼**mantel** *der; o. Pl.* (abwertend) cover; **unter dem** ∼**mantel der Entwicklungshilfe** using development aid as a blind *or* cover; under the guise of development aid; ∼**name** *der* alias; assumed name

Deckung *die;* ∼, ∼**en (a)** (Schutz; auch fig.) cover (esp. Mil.); (Schach) defence; (Boxen) guard; (bes. Fußball: die deckenden Spieler) defence; ∼ **nehmen, in** ∼ **gehen** take cover; **(b)** (Finanzw.: das Begleichen) *o. Pl.* (von Schulden) meeting; (von Schecks) cover[ing]; **als** ∼ **für seine Schulden** as security for his debts; **(c)** (Befriedigung) satisfaction; **(d)** (Übereinstimmung) **Pläne** *usw.* **zur** ∼ **bringen** make plans *etc.* agree; bring plans *etc.* into line

deckungs·gleich *Adj.* (Geom.) congruent

Deck·weiß *das* opaque white

Decoder /de'ko:dɐ/ *der;* ∼**s,** ∼ (Elektronik) decoder

de facto /de: 'fakto/ *Adv.* de facto (esp. Polit., Law); in reality

defekt /de'fɛkt/ *Adj.* defective; faulty; ∼ **sein** have a defect; be faulty; (nicht funktionieren) not be working

Defekt *der;* ∼**[e]s,** ∼**e** defect, fault (**an** + *Dat.* in)

defensiv /defɛn'zi:f/ **1** *Adj.* defensive. **2** *adv.* defensively

Defensive *die;* ∼, ∼**n** defensive; **in der** ∼**:** on the defensive

Defensiv·krieg *der* defensive war

definierbar *Adj.* definable

definieren /defi'ni:rən/ *tr. V.* define

Definition /defini'tsio:n/ *die;* ∼, ∼**en** definition

definitiv /defini'ti:f/ **1** *Adj.* definitive; final ‹*answer, decision*›. **2** *adv.* finally

Defizit /'de:fitsɪt/ *das;* ∼**s,** ∼**e (a)** deficit; **(b)** (Mangel) deficiency

Deformation *die* deformation; (Missbildung) deformity

deformieren *tr. V.* **(a)** distort; put out of shape; **(b)** (entstellen) deform (also fig.); (verunstalten) disfigure ‹*face etc.*›; (verstümmeln) mutilate

deftig /'dɛftɪç/ *Adj.* (ugs.) **(a)** [good] solid *attrib.*, good and solid *pred.* ‹*meal etc.*›; [nice] big, [nice] fat ‹*sausage etc.*›; **(b)** (derb) crude, coarse ‹*joke, speech, etc.*›

Degen /'de:gn̩/ *der;* ∼**s,** ∼ **(a)** (Waffe) [light] sword; **(b)** (Sportgerät) épée

degenerieren /degene'ri:rən/ *itr. V.; mit sein* degenerate (**zu** into)

degeneriert *Adj.* degenerate

degradieren /degra'di:rən/ *tr. V.* demote; **jmdn./etw. zu etw.** ∼ (fig.) reduce sb./sth. to [the level of] sth.

Degradierung *die;* ∼, ∼**en** demotion; (fig.) degradation; reduction (**zu** to the level of)

dehnbar *Adj.* **(a)** elastic ‹*waistband etc.*›; stretch ‹*fabric*›; **etw. ist** ∼**:** sth. can be stretched; **(b)** (fig.: vage) elastic; **das ist ein** ∼**er Begriff** it's a loose concept

Dehnbarkeit *die;* ∼ (auch fig.) elasticity

dehnen /'de:nən/ **1** *tr. V.* **(a)** stretch; lengthen, draw out ‹*vowel, word*›. **2** *refl. V.* stretch

Dehnung *die;* ∼, ∼**en** stretching

Deich /daiç/ *der;* ∼**[e]s,** ∼**e** dike

Deichsel /'daiks̩l/ *die;* ∼, ∼**n** shaft; (in der Mitte) pole; (aus zwei Stangen) shafts *pl.*

deichseln *tr. V.* (ugs.) fix; (durch eine List) wangle (sl.)

dein /dain/ *Possessivpron.* your; (Rel., auch altertümelnd) thy; **viele Grüße von** ∼**em Emil** with best wishes, yours Emil; **das Buch dort, ist das** ∼**[e]s?** that book over there, is it yours?; **du und die Deinen** (geh.) you and yours *or* your family; **der/die Deine** *od.* ∼**e** (geh.) your husband/wife; **das Deine** *od.* ∼**e** (geh.) your possessions

pl. or property; **du musst das Deine** *od.* ∼**e tun** you must do your bit *or* share

deiner *Gen. von* **du** (geh.) of you; **ich gedenke** ∼ **auf ewig** I will always remember you

deiner·seits /'dainɐ'zaits/ *Adv.* (von deiner Seite) on your part; (auf deiner Seite) for your part

deines·gleichen *indekl. Pron.* people *pl.* like you; (abwertend) the likes *pl.* of you; your sort *or* kind; **unter** ∼**:** amongst your own sort *or* kind

deinet·wegen *Adv.* **(a)** because of you; on your account; (für dich) on your behalf; (dir zuliebe) for your sake; **(b)** (von dir aus) **du hast gesagt,** ∼ **könnten wir gehen** you said we could go as far as you were concerned

deinet·willen *Adv. in* **um** ∼**:** for your sake

de jure /de: 'ju:rə/ *Adv.* de jure; legally

Dekade /de'ka:də/ *die;* ∼, ∼**n** decade

dekadent /deka'dɛnt/ *Adj.* decadent

Dekadenz /deka'dɛnts/ *die;* ∼**:** decadence

Dekan /de'ka:n/ *der;* ∼**s,** ∼**e** dean

Dekanat /deka'na:t/ *das;* ∼**s,** ∼**e** dean's office

dekartellisieren /dekartɛli'zi:rən/ *tr. V.* (Wirtsch.) decartelize

deklamieren /dekla'mi:rən/ *tr.,* *itr. V.* recite

Deklaration /deklara'tsio:n/ *die;* ∼, ∼**en** declaration

deklarieren /dekla'ri:rən/ *tr. V.* declare; **etw. als etw.** ∼**:** declare sth. to be sth.

deklassieren *tr. V.* **(a)** (herabsetzen) reduce; downgrade; **(b)** (Sport) outclass; (beim Rennen) leave standing

Deklination /deklina'tsio:n/ *die;* ∼, ∼**en** (Sprachw.) declension

deklinierbar *Adj.* (Sprachw.) declinable

deklinieren /dekli'ni:rən/ *tr. V.* (Sprachw.) decline; **ein Wort schwach/stark** ∼**:** decline a word as weak/strong

Dekolleté /dekɔl'te:/ *das;* ∼**s,** ∼**s** low[-cut] neckline; décolletage

Dekor /de'ko:ɐ̯/ *das;* ∼**s,** ∼**s** *od.* ∼**e** decoration; (Muster) pattern

Dekorateur /dekora'tø:ɐ̯/ *der;* ∼**s,** ∼**e, Dekorateurin** *die;* ∼, ∼**nen ▶ 85 |** (Schaufenster∼) window-dresser; (von Innenräumen) interior decorator *or* designer

Dekoration /dekora'tsio:n/ *die;* ∼, ∼**en (a)** *o. Pl.* decoration; (von Schaufenstern) window-dressing; **(b)** (Schmuck, Ausstattung) decorations *pl.;* (Schaufenster∼) window display; (Theater, Film) set; scenery *no pl.*

dekorativ /dekora'ti:f/ **1** *Adj.* decorative. **2** *adv.* decoratively

dekorieren /deko'ri:rən/ *tr. V.* **(a)** decorate ‹*room etc.*›; dress ‹*shop window*›; **(b)** (mit Orden auszeichnen) decorate (**mit** with)

Dekostoff /'de:ko-/ *der* furnishing fabric

Dekret /de'kre:t/ *das;* ∼**[e]s,** ∼**e** decree

dekretieren *tr. V.* decree

Delegation /delega'tsio:n/ *die;* ∼, ∼**en** delegation

delegieren /dele'gi:rən/ *tr. V.* **(a)** send as a delegate/as delegates (**zu** to); **jmdn. ins Komitee** ∼**:** select sb. as one's representative on the committee; **(b)** delegate ‹*task etc.*› (**an** + *Akk.* to)

Delegierte *der/die; adj. Dekl.* delegate

Delegierten·konferenz *die* delegates' *or* delegate conference

delikat /deli'ka:t/ *Adj.* **(a)** (wohlschmeckend) delicious; (fein) subtle, delicate ‹*bouquet, aroma*›; **(b)** (heikel) delicate

Delikatesse /delika'tɛsə/ *die;* ∼, ∼**n** delicacy; (fig.) treat

Delikatess[en]·geschäft,   ***Delikateß·geschäft** *das* delicatessen

Delikt /de'lɪkt/ *das;* ∼**[e]s,** ∼**e** offence

Delinquent *der;* ∼**en,** ∼**en** offender

delirieren /deli'ri:rən/ *itr. V.* be delirious

Delirium /de'li:riʊm/ *das;* ∼**s, Delirien** delirium

Delle /'dɛlə/ *die;* ∼, ∼**n** (ugs.) dent

Delphin[1] /dɛl'fi:n/ *der;* ∼**s,** ∼**e** dolphin

Delphin[2] *das;* ∼**s** (Schwimmen) butterfly [stroke]

Delphin·schwimmen *das* butterfly

Delta[1] /'dɛlta/ *das;* ∼**[s],** ∼**[s]** (Buchstabe) delta

Delta² *das;* ~s, ~s *od.* **Delten** (Fluss~) delta
Delta·mündung *die* delta
dem /deːm/ **1** *best. Art., Dat. Sg. v.* **der¹ 1** *u.* **das 1:** the; **ich gab dem Mann das Buch** I gave the man the book; I gave the book to the man; **er hat sich dem Okkultismus zugewandt** he turned to occultism; **aus dem Libanon** from Lebanon. **2** *Demonstrativpron., Dat. Sg. v.* **der¹ 2** *u.* **das 2:** (a) *attr.* that; **gib es dem Mann** give it to 'that man; (b) *allein stehend* **gib es nicht dem, sondern dem da!** don't give it to him, give it to that man/child *etc.;* **Zwiebeln schneide ich nicht mit dem [hier], sondern mit dem da** I chop onions with 'that knife, not with this one. **3** *Relativpron., Dat. Sg. v.* **der¹** *u.* **das 3** (Person) that/whom; (Sache) that/which; **der Mann, dem ich das Geld gab** the man to whom I gave the money *or* (coll.) [that] I gave the money to; **der Mann, dem ich geholfen habe** the man [whom *or* that] I helped
Demagoge /dema'goːgə/ *der;* ~n, ~n (abwertend) demagogue
demagogisch (abwertend) **1** *Adj.* demagogic. **2** *adv.* by demagogic means
Demarkations·linie *die* demarcation line
demaskieren 1 *refl. V.* (fig.) reveal oneself. **2** *tr. V.* (fig.) unmask; expose
Dementi /de'mɛnti/ *das;* ~s, ~s denial
dementieren 1 *tr. V.* deny. **2** *itr. V.* deny it
dem-: ~**entsprechend 1** *Adj.* appropriate; **das Wetter war schlecht und die Stimmung** ~**entsprechend** the weather was bad and the general mood was correspondingly bad *or* bad too. **2** *adv.* accordingly; (vor Adjektiven) correspondingly; ~**gegenüber** *Adv.* in contrast; (jedoch) on the other hand; ~**gemäß** *Adv.* (a) (infolgedessen) consequently; (b) (entsprechend) accordingly; ~**jenigen** ⇒ **derjenige;** ~**nach** *Adv.* therefore; ~**nächst** *Adv.* in the near future; shortly
Demo /'dɛmo/ *die;* ~, ~s (ugs.) demo
Demo·graphie *die* demography *no art.*
demo·graphisch 1 *Adj.* demographic. **2** *adv.* demographically
Demokrat /demo'kraːt/ *der;* ~en, ~en democrat
Demokratie /demokra'tiː/ *die;* ~, ~n (a) o. Pl. (Prinzip) democracy *no art.;* (b) (Staat) democracy
demokratisch 1 *Adj.* democratic. **2** *adv.* democratically; **es wurde** ~ **gewählt** democratic elections were held; **bei uns geht es** ~ **zu** we run things on democratic lines
demokratisieren *tr. V.* democratize
Demokratisierung *die;* ~ democratization
demolieren /demo'liːrən/ *tr. V.* (a) wreck; smash up ⟨*furniture*⟩; (b) (österr.: abreißen) demolish
Demonstrant /demɔn'strant/ *der;* ~en, ~en, **Demonstrantin** *die;* ~, ~nen demonstrator
Demonstration /demɔnstra'tsi̯oːn/ *die;* ~, ~en demonstration (**für** in support of, **gegen** against)
Demonstrations-: ~**recht** *das* right to demonstrate; ~**verbot** *das* ban on demonstrations; ~**zug** *der* column *or* procession of demonstrators
demonstrativ /demɔnstra'tiːf/ **1** *Adj.* (a) demonstrative; pointed; **ein** ~**es Nein** an emphatic no; (b) (Sprachw.) demonstrative. **2** *adv.* pointedly; **ich sah** ~ **weg** I intentionally looked the other way
Demonstrativ·pronomen *das* (Sprachw.) demonstrative pronoun
demonstrieren /demɔn'striːrən/ **1** *itr. V.* demonstrate (**für** in support of, **gegen** against). **2** *tr. V.* demonstrate
demontieren *tr. V.* (a) dismantle; break up ⟨*ship, aircraft*⟩; (b) (abmontieren) take off
demoralisieren *tr. V.* demoralize
Demoralisierung *die;* ~, ~en demoralization
Demoskop /demo'skoːp/ *der;* ~en, ~en opinion pollster
Demoskopie /demosko'piː/ *die;* ~: [public] opinion research *no art.*

demoskopisch 1 *Adj.; nicht präd.* opinion research ⟨*institute, methods, data, etc.*⟩; ⟨*data etc.*⟩ from opinion polls *or* opinion research; ~**e Umfrage** [public] opinion poll. **2** *adv.* through opinion polls *or* research
dem·selben ⇒ **derselbe**
Demut /'deːmuːt/ *die;* ~: humility
demütig /'deːmyːtɪç/ **1** *Adj.* humble. **2** *adv.* humbly
demütigen 1 *tr. V.* humiliate; humble ⟨*sb.'s pride*⟩. **2** *refl. V.* humble oneself
Demütigung *die;* ~, ~en humiliation
Demuts·gebärde *die* (Verhaltensf.) attitude of submission
dem·zufolge *Adv.* therefore; consequently
den¹ /deːn/ **1** *best. Art., Akk. Sg. v.* **der¹ 1:** the; **ich sah den Mann** I saw the man; **wir haben den „Faust" gelesen** we read 'Faust'; **in den Libanon reisen** travel to Lebanon; **den Sozialismus ablehnen** reject socialism. **2** *Demonstrativpron., Akk. Sg. v.* **der¹ 2:** (a) *attr.* 'that; **ich meine den Mann, nicht den anderen** I mean 'that man, not the other; (b) *allein stehend* **ich meine den [da]** I mean 'that one. **3** *Relativpron., Akk. Sg. v.* **der¹ 3:** (Person) that/whom; (Sache) that/which; **der Mann, den ich gesehen habe** the man [that] I saw
den² **1** *best. Art., Dat. Pl. v.* **der¹ 1, die¹ 1, das 1:** the; **ich gab es den Männern** I gave it to the men. **2** *Demonstrativpron., Dat. Pl. v.* **der¹ 2 a; die¹ 2 a, das 2 a** those
denen 1 *Demonstrativpron., Dat. Pl. v.* **der¹ 2 b, die¹ 2 b, das 2 b:** them; **gib es** ~, **nicht den anderen** give it to 'them, not to the others. **2** *Relativpron., Dat. Pl. v.* **der¹ 3, die¹ 3, das 3:** (Person) that/whom; (Sache) that/which; **die Menschen,** ~ **wir Geld gegeben haben** the people to whom we gave money; **die Tiere,** ~ **er geholfen hat** the animals that he helped
Den Haag /deːn 'haːk/ *(das);* ~ ~s ▶ 490 The Hague
denjenigen ⇒ **derjenige**
denkbar *Adj.* conceivable; **in einem Zustand, wie er schlimmer nicht** ~ **ist** in the worst state imaginable. **2** *adv.* (äußerst) extremely; **die Lösung ist** ~ **leicht** the solution could not be easier
denken /'dɛŋkn̩/ **1** *unr. itr. V.* think (**an** *od.* [südd., österr.] **auf** + *Akk.* of, **über** + *Akk.* about); **liberal** ~**:** be liberal-minded; **wie denkst du darüber?** what do you think about it?; what's your opinion of it?; **erst** ~, **dann handeln** think before you act; **Denken ist Glückssache** you/ he/ she *etc.* thought wrong; **jmdm. zu** ~ **geben** make sb. think; (stutzig machen) make sb. suspicious; **denk daran, dass …/zu …:** don't forget that …/to …; **ich denke nicht daran!** no way!; not on your life!; **ich denke nicht daran, das zu tun** I've no intention *or* I wouldn't dream of doing that. **2** *unr. tr. V.* think; **er dachte den gleichen Gedanken** the same thought occurred to him; **ich denke es** I think so; **denkste!** (ugs.) how wrong can one be!; (da irrst du dich) that's what 'you think!; **eine gedachte Linie** an imaginary line. **3** *unr. refl. V.* (sich vorstellen) imagine; **das kann ich mir** ~/**nicht** ~**:** I can well believe/cannot believe that; **das hast du dir so gedacht!** that's what you thought; **du hättest dir doch** ~ **können, dass …:** you should have realized that …; **das habe ich mir [gleich] gedacht** that's [just] what I thought; (bei Verdacht) I thought *or* suspected as much; **ich denke mir mein[en] Teil** I can put two and two together *or* work things out for myself; (b) **sich** (*Dat.*) **bei etw. etwas** ~ (etw. ganz bewusst tun) mean something by sth.; **ich habe mir nichts [Böses] dabei gedacht** I didn't mean any harm [by it]
Denken *die;* ~s thinking; (Denkweise) thought
Denker *der;* ~s, ~: thinker
denk- Denk-: ~**faul** *Adj.* mentally lazy; **sei nicht so** ~**faul** use your brains; ~**fehler** *der* flaw in one's reasoning; ~**mal** *das;* ~s, **Denkmäler** *od.* **Denkmale** (a) monument; memorial; (b) (historisches Zeugnis) monument; ~**pause** *die* pause for thought; ~**sport·aufgabe** *die* brain-teaser; ~**vermögen** *das:* [kreatives] ~**vermögen** ability to think [creatively]; ~**weise** *die* way of thinking; [mental] attitude; ~**würdig** *Adj.* memorable; ~**zettel** *der* warning; lesson; **jmdm. einen** ~**zettel verpassen** teach sb. a lesson

---

denn /dɛn/ **1** *Konj.* **(a)** (kausal) for; because; **(b)** (geh.: als) than; **schöner ~ je [zuvor]** more beautiful than ever. **2** *Adv.*: **in es sei ~, [dass]** ...: unless ...; *s. auch* **geschweige. 3** *Partikel* **(a)** (in Fragesätzen): oft nicht übersetzt); **was ist ~ da los?** what 'is going on there?; **wie geht es dir ~?** tell me, how are you?; **ist das ~ so wichtig?** is that really so important?; **was muss ich ~ machen?** what am I to do, then?; **wie heißt du ~?** tell me your name; **warum ~ nicht?** why ever not?; **was soll das ~?** what's all this about?; **was ~ [sonst]?** well, what [else] then?; **(b)** (verstärkend) **das ist ~ doch die Höhe!** that really is the limit!

dennoch /'dɛnɔx/ *Adv.* nevertheless; even so; **ein höfliches und ~ eisiges Lächeln** a polite yet frosty smile

denselben ⇨ **derselbe**

Denunziant /denʊn'tsi̯ant/ *der;* **~en, ~en** (abwertend) informer; grass (Brit. coll.)

Denunziation /denʊntsi̯a'tsi̯oːn/ *die;* **~, ~en** (abwertend) denunciation

denunzieren /denʊn'tsiːrən/ *tr. V.* (abwertend) (anzeigen) denounce; (bei der Polizei) inform against; grass on (Brit. coll.) **(bei** to)

Deo /'deːo/ *das;* **~s, ~s, Deodorant** /deˈodoˈrant/ *das;* **~s, ~s** (auch:) **~e** deodorant

Deo·spray *das* deodorant spray

deplaciert, deplatziert, *deplaziert /depla'tsiːɐt/ *Adj.* out of place *pred.;* misplaced ‹*remark etc.*›

Deponie /depo'niː/ *die;* **~, ~n** tipp (Brit.); dump

deponieren *tr. V.* put (im Safe o. Ä.) deposit **(bei** with)

Deportation /depɔrta'tsi̯oːn/ *die;* **~, ~en** transportation **(in** + *Akk.,* **nach** to); (ins Ausland) deportation **(in** + *Akk.,* **nach** to)

deportieren /depɔr'tiːrən/ *tr. V.* transport **(in** + *Akk.,* **nach** to); (ins Ausland) deport **(in** + *Akk.,* **nach** to)

Deportierte *der/die; adj. Dekl.* transportee; (ins Ausland) deportee

Depot /de'poː/ *das;* **~s, ~s (a)** depot; (Lagerhaus) warehouse; (für Möbel usw.) depository; (im Freien, für Munition o. Ä.) dump; (in einer Bank) strongroom; safe deposit; **(b)** (hinterlegte Wertgegenstände) deposits *pl.*

Depp /dɛp/ *der;* **~en, ~en** (bes. südd., österr., schweiz. abwertend) ⇨ **Dummkopf**

Depression /deprɛ'si̯oːn/ *die;* **~, ~en** depression

depressiv /deprɛ'siːf/ **1** *Adj.* depressive. **2** *adv.* **~ veranlagt sein** have a tendency towards depression

deprimieren /depri:mi'rən/ *tr. V.* depress

deprimierend *Adj.* depressing

deprimiert *Adj.* depressed

Deputierte *der/die; adj. Dekl.* (Abgeordnete[r]) deputy

der¹ /deːɐ̯/ **1** *best. Art. Nom.* the; **der Kleine** the little boy; **der Tod** death; **der April/Winter** April/winter; **der „Faust"** 'Faust'; **der Dieter** (ugs.) Dieter; **der Kapitalismus/Islam** capitalism/Islam; **der Bodensee/Mount Everest** Lake Constance/Mount Everest; **der Iran** Iran. **2** *Demonstrativpron.* **(a)** *attr.* that; **der Mann war es** it was 'that man; **(b)** *allein stehend* he; **der war es** it was 'him; **der und arbeiten!** (ugs.) [what,] him work! (coll.); **der [da]** (Mann) that man; (Gegenstand, Tier) that one; **der [hier]** (Mann) this man; (Gegenstand, Tier) this one. **3** *Relativpron.* (Mensch) who/that; (Sache) which/that; **der Mann, der da drüben entlanggeht** the man walking along over there. **4** *Relativ- u. Demonstrativpron.* the one who

der² **1** *best. Art.* **(a)** *Gen. Sg. v.* **die¹ 1: der Hut der Frau** the woman's hat; **der Henkel der Tasse** the handle of the cup; **(b)** *Dat. Sg. v.* **die¹ 1:** to the; (nach Präp.) the; **in der Türkei** in Turkey; **(c)** *Gen. Pl. v.* **der¹ 1, die¹ 1, das¹ 1: das Haus der Freunde** our/their *etc.* friends' house; **das Bellen der Hunde** the barking of the dogs. **2** *Demonstrativpron.* **(a)** *Gen. Sg. v.* **die¹ 2 a:** of the; of that; **(b)** *Dat. Sg. v.* **die¹ 2** *attr.* **der Frau [da/hier] gehört es** it belongs to that woman there/this woman here; *allein stehend* **gib es der da!** (ugs.) give it to 'her; **(c)** *Gen. Pl. v.* **der¹ 2 a, die¹ 2 a, das 2 a:** of those. **3** *Relativpron.; Dat. Sg. v.* **die¹ 3** (Person) whom; **die Frau, der ich es gegeben habe** the woman to whom I gave it; the woman I

gave it to; (Sache) that/which; **die Katze, der er einen Tritt gab** the cat [that] he kicked

der·art *Adv.* jmdn. **~ schlecht/unfreundlich behandeln, dass** ...; treat sb. so badly/in such an unfriendly way that ...; **es hat lange nicht mehr ~ geregnet** it hasn't rained as hard as that for a long time; **sie hat ~ geschrien, dass** ...: she screamed so much that ...

der·artig 1 *Adj.; nicht präd.* such; **etwas Derartiges** a thing like that; such a thing. **2** *adv.* ⇨ **derart**

derb /dɛrp/ **1** *Adj.* **(a)** strong, tough ‹*material*›; stout, strong, sturdy ‹*shoes*›; **(b)** (kraftvoll, deftig) earthy ‹*scenes, humour*›; **(c)** (unverblümt) crude, coarse ‹*expression, language*›. **2** *adv.* **(a)** strongly ‹*made, woven, etc.*›; **(b)** (kraftvoll, deftig) earthily; **(c)** (unverblümt) crudely; coarsely

Derbheit *die;* **~:** ⇨ **derb 1 b, c:** earthiness; crudity; coarseness

Derby /'dɛrbi/ *das;* **~s, ~s (a)** (Pferdesport) Derby; **(b)** (Fußball) derby

Deregulierung /'deregu:li'rʊŋ/ *die;* **~, ~en** deregulation

deren /'deːrən/ **1** *Relativpron.* **(a)** *Gen. Sg. v.* **die¹ 3** (Menschen) whose; (Sachen) of which; **die Katastrophe, ~ Folgen furchtbar waren** the disaster, the consequences of which were frightful; **die Großmutter, ~ wir uns gerne erinnern** our grandmother, of whom we have fond memories; **(b)** *Gen., Pl. v.* **der¹ 3, die¹ 3, das 3** (Menschen) whose; (Sachen) **Maßnahmen, ~ Folgen wir noch nicht absehen können** measures, the consequences of which we cannot yet foresee. **2** *Demonstrativpron.* **(a)** *Gen. Sg. v.* **die¹ 2: meine Tante, ihre Freundin und ~ Hund** my aunt, her friend and 'her dog; **(b)** *Gen. Pl. v.* **der¹ 2 b, die¹ 2 b, das 2 b: meine Verwandten und ~ Kinder** my relatives and their children; **Bücher? Deren hat er genug** (geh.) Books? He's got enough of those

derent-: ~wegen *Adv.* **1** *relativ* on whose account; on account of whom; because of whom; (von Sachen) on account of which; because of which; **2** *demonstrativ* because of them; **~willen** *Adv.* **1** *relativ* **um ~willen** for whose sake; for the sake of whom; (von Sachen) for the sake of which; **die Erbstücke, um ~willen sich die Kinder zerstritten** the heirlooms over which the children fell out; **2** *demonstrativ* **um ~willen** for her/their sake

derer /'deːrɐ/ *Demonstrativpron.; Gen. Pl. v.* **der¹ 2 b, die¹ 2 b, das 2 b** of those; **die Zahl ~, die das glauben, nimmt ab** the number of people who believe that is declining

der·gestalt *Adv.* (geh.) **~, dass** ...: in such a way that ...

der·gleichen *indekl. Demonstrativpron.* **(a)** *attr.* such; like that *postpos., not pred.;* **(b)** *allein stehend* that sort of thing; such things *pl.;* things *pl.* like that; **nichts ~:** nothing of the sort; **und ~ [mehr]** and suchlike

Derivat /deri'va:t/ *das;* **~[e]s, ~e** (Chemie, Biol., Sprachw., Bankw.) derivative

der·jenige /-je:nɪgə/, **die·jenige, das·jenige** *Demonstrativpron.* **(a)** *attr.* that; *Pl.* those; **diejenige Person, die** ...: the *or* that person who ...; **(b)** *allein stehend* that one; *Pl.* those; **derjenige, der** .../**diejenige, die** ...: the person who ...; **diejenigen, die** ...: those [poeple] who ...; **dasjenige, was** ...: that which ...

derlei /'deːrlai/ *indekl. Demonstrativpron.* **(a)** *attr.* such; like that *postpos., not pred.;* **(b)** *allein stehend* that sort of thing; such things *pl.;* things *pl.* like that

der·maßen *Adv.* **~ schön** *usw.,* **dass** ...: so beautiful *etc.* that ...; **ein ~ intelligenter Mensch** such an intelligent person

derselbe /deːɐ̯'zɛlbə/, **dieselbe, dasselbe,** *Pl.* **dieselben** *Demonstrativpron.* **(a)** *attr.* the same; **(b)** *allein stehend* the same one; **sie ist immer noch [ganz] dieselbe** she is still [exactly] the same; **es sind immer dieselben, die** ...: it's always the same people *or* ones who ...; **noch einmal dasselbe, bitte** (ugs.) [the] same again please; **er sagt immer dasselbe** he always says the same thing

der·weil[en] (veralt.) **1** *Adv.* ⇨ **inzwischen** c. **2** *Konj.* while

der·zeit *Adv.* at present; at the moment

der·zeitig *Adj.; nicht präd.* present; current

des¹ /dɛs/ **1** *best. Art.; Gen. Sg. v.* **der¹** 1, **das** 1: **die Mütze des Jungen** the boy's cap; **das Klingeln des Telefons** the ringing of the telephone. **2** *Demonstrativpron.; Gen. Sg. v.* **der¹** 2 a, **das** 2 a: **er ist der Sohn des Mannes, der** ... he's the son of the man who ...

des², **Des** *das;* ~, ~ (Musik) D flat

Desaster /de'zastɐ/ *das;* ~s, ~: disaster

Deserteur /dezɛr'tøːɐ/ *der;* ~s, ~e (Milit.) deserter

desertieren *itr. V.; mit sein* (Milit., fig.) desert

des·gleichen *Adv.* likewise; **er ist Arzt,** ~ **sein Sohn** he is a doctor, as is *or* and so is his son; **es fehlt an Papier,** ~ **an Bleistiften** there's a shortage of paper and also [of] pencils

des·halb *Adv.* for that reason; because of that; ~ **bin ich zu dir gekommen** that is why I came to you; **aber** ~ **ist sie nicht dumm** but that doesn't mean she is stupid

Design /di'zaɪn/ *das;* ~s, ~s design

Designer /di'zaɪnɐ/ *der;* ~s, ~, **Designerin** *die;* ~, ~nen ▶ 85 ⏐ designer

Designer·droge /di'zaɪnɐ.../ *die;* designer drug

desillusionieren /dɛs|iluzjo'niːrən/ *tr. V.* disillusion

Des·infektion /dɛs|-/ *die* disinfection

Desinfektions·mittel *das* disinfectant

des·infizieren *tr. V.* disinfect

Des·information *die* disinformation *no indef. art.*

Des·interesse *das* lack of interest (**an** + *Dat.* in)

des·interessiert **1** *Adj.* uninterested. **2** *adv.* uninterestedly

deskriptiv /dɛskrɪp'tiːf/ **1** *Adj.* descriptive. **2** *adv.* descriptively

Desktoppublishing /'dɛsktɔp'pʌblɪʃɪŋ/ *das;* ~s (DV) desktop publishing

desodorierend /dɛs|odo'riːrənt/ *Adj.* deodorant

desolat /dezo'laːt/ *Adj.* (geh.) wretched

Desperado /dɛspe'raːdo/ *der;* ~s, ~s desperado

Despot /dɛs'poːt/ *der;* ~en, ~en despot; (fig. abwertend) tyrant

Despotie /dɛspo'tiː/ *die;* ~, ~n despotism

despotisch **1** *Adj.* despotic. **2** *adv.* despotically

des·selben ⇨ **derselbe**

dessen /'dɛsn/ **1** *Relativpron.; Gen. Sg. v.* **der¹** 3, **das** 3 (Mensch) whose; (Sache, Tier) of which; **unser Großvater,** ~ **wir uns gern erinnern** our grandfather, of whom we have fond memories. **2** *Demonstrativpron.; Gen. Sg. v.* **der¹** 2 b, **das** 2 b: **mein Onkel, sein Sohn und** ~ **Hund** my uncle, his son, and 'his dog; **das Waldsterben und** ~ **Folgen** the death of the forests and its consequences; **Onkel August?** **Dessen erinnere ich mich noch sehr gut** Uncle August? I remember 'him well

dessent-: ~**wegen** *Adv.* **1** *relativ* on whose account; on account of whom; because of whom; (von Sachen) on account of which; because of which; **das Verbrechen,** ~**wegen er verurteilt wurde** the crime of which he was convicted; **2** *demonstrativ* because of him; (von Sachen) because of this; ~**willen** *Adv.* **1** *relativ* **um** ~**willen** for whose sake; for the sake of whom; (von Sachen) for the sake of which; **2** *demonstrativ* **um** ~**willen** for his sake

*****dessen·ungeachtet** ⇨ **ungeachtet**

Dessert /dɛ'seːɐ/ *das;* ~s, ~s dessert

Dessin /dɛ'sɛ̃/ *das;* ~s, ~s design; pattern

destabilisieren *tr. V.* (Politik) destabilize

Destabilisierung *die;* ~, ~en (Politik) destabilization

destillieren *tr. V.* (Chemie) distil; **destilliertes Wasser** distilled water

desto *Konj., nur vor Komp.* **je eher,** ~ **besser** the sooner the better; ~ **ängstlicher** the more anxious/anxiously;

ich schätzte ihn ~ **mehr** I appreciated him all the more

Destruktion /dɛstrʊk'tsjoːn/ *die;* ~, ~en destruction

destruktiv /dɛstrʊk'tiːf/ **1** *Adj.* destructive. **2** *adv.* destructively

des·wegen *Adv.* ⇨ **deshalb**

Detail /de'taɪ/ *das;* ~s, ~s detail; **ins** ~ **gehen** go into detail; **in allen** ~s in the fullest detail

detailliert /deta'jiːɐt/ **1** *Adj.* detailed. **2** *adv.* in detail; **sehr** ~: in great detail

Detektei /detɛk'taɪ/ *die;* ~, ~en [private] detective agency

Detektiv /detɛk'tiːf/ *der;* ~s, ~e, **Detektivin** *die;* ~, ~nen ▶ 85 ⏐ [private] detective

Detektiv·roman *der* detective novel

Detonation /detona'tsjoːn/ *die;* ~, ~en detonation; explosion; **etw. zur** ~ **bringen** detonate sth.

detonieren /deto'niːrən/ *itr. V.; mit sein* detonate

Deut /dɔʏt/ **in kein[en]** ~ **besser** not one bit *or* whit better

deutbar *Adj.* interpretable

deuteln /'dɔʏtln̩/ *itr. V.* quibble (**an** + *Dat.* about); **daran gibt es nichts zu** ~: there are no ifs and buts about it

deuten /'dɔʏtn̩/ **1** *itr. V.* point; [**mit dem Finger**] **auf jmdn./etw.** ~: point [one's finger] at sb./sth. **2** *tr. V.* interpret

deutlich **1** *Adj.* (a) clear; **daraus wird** ~, **dass/wie** ...: this makes it clear that/how ...; (b) (eindeutig) clear, distinct ‹*recollection, feeling*›; ~ **werden** make oneself plain *or* clear. **2** *adv.* (a) clearly; (b) (eindeutig) clearly; plainly; **jmdm. etw.** ~ **zu verstehen geben** make sth. clear *or* plain to sb.

Deutlichkeit *die;* ~: (a) clarity; (b) (Eindeutigkeit) clearness; distinctness; **in** *od.* **mit aller** ~ **sagen, dass** ...: make it perfectly clear *or* plain that ...

deutsch /dɔʏtʃ/ ▶ 388 ⏐, ▶ 487 ⏐ **1** *Adj.* (a) German; **Deutsche Mark** Deutschmark; German mark; **Deutsche Demokratische Republik** (1949 bis 1990) German Democratic Republic; **das Deutsche Reich** (hist.) the German Reich *or* Empire; **alles Deutsche** all things *pl.* or everything German; **das typisch Deutsche daran** what is/was typically German about it; (b) (die Sprache betreffend) German; **etw. auf Deutsch sagen** say sth. in German; **was heißt das Wort auf Deutsch?** what is the word in German?; what is the German for that word?; **auf [gut] Deutsch** (ugs.) in plain English; **die** ~**e Schweiz** German-speaking Switzerland. **2** *adv.;* ~ **sprechen/schreiben** speak/write German; ~ **geschrieben sein** be written in German

Deutsch *das;* ~[s] ▶ 487 ⏐ (a) German; **gutes/fließend** ~ **sprechen** speak good/fluent German; **kein** ~ [**mehr**] **verstehen** (ugs.) not understand plain English; (b) *o. Art.* (Unterrichtsfach) German *no art.;* **er ist gut in** ~: he's good at German

Deutsch·amerikaner *der* German-American

deutsch-amerikanisch *Adj.; nicht präd.* German-American

deutsch-deutsch *Adj.; nicht präd.* intra-German

Deutsche¹ /'dɔʏtʃə/ *der/die; adj. Dekl.* ▶ 388 ⏐ German; ~[**r**] **sein** be German

Deutsche² *das;* ▶ 487 ⏐ *adj. Dekl.* **das** ~: German; **aus dem** ~**n/ins** ~ **übersetzen** translate from/into German

deutsch-französisch *Adj.* Franco-German ‹*relations, border, etc.*›; German-French ‹*dictionary, anthology, etc.*›

Deutschland (*das*); ~s Germany

Deutschland-: ~**lied** *das* the song 'Deutschland, Deutschland über alles'; ~**politik** *die* policy towards Germany

deutsch-, **Deutsch-:** ~**lehrer** *der* German teacher; ~**sprachig** *Adj.* (a) German-speaking; **Deutschsprachige** *Pl.* German speakers; (b) (in deutscher Sprache) German-language *attrib.* ‹*newspaper, edition, broadcast*›; ‹*teaching*› in German; German ‹*literature*›; ~**stämmig** *Adj.* of German origin *postpos.*

Deutschtum *das;* ~s Germanness
Deutsch·unterricht *der* German teaching; (Unterrichtsstunde) German lesson; ~ **erteilen** *or* **geben** teach German
Deutung *die;* ~, ~**en** interpretation
Devalvation /devalvaˈtsi̯oːn/ *die;* ~, ~**en** (Finanzw.) devaluation
Devise /deˈviːzə/ *die;* ~, ~**n** motto
Devisen *Pl.* foreign exchange *sing.;* (Sorten) foreign currency *sing. or* exchange *sing.*
Devisen-: ~**börse** *die* foreign exchange market; ~**geschäft** *das* foreign exchange business *or* dealings *pl.;* (einzelne Transaktion) foreign exchange transaction; ~**schmuggel** *der* [foreign] currency smuggling
Devisen-: ~**markt** *der* foreign exchange market; ~**vergehen** *das* currency offence; breach of exchange control regulations
devot /deˈvoːt/ (geh. abwertend) **1** *Adj.* obsequious. **2** *adv.* obsequiously
Dextrose /dɛksˈtroːzə/ *die;* ~: dextrose
Dezember /deˈtsɛmbɐ/ *der;* ~s, ~: ▶ 119 December
dezent /deˈtsɛnt/ **1** *Adj.* quiet ⟨*colour, pattern, suit*⟩; subdued ⟨*lighting, music*⟩; discreet ⟨*smile, behaviour*⟩. **2** *adv.* discreetly; ⟨*dress*⟩ unostentatiously
dezentralisieren *tr. V.* decentralize
Dezentralisierung *die;* ~, ~**en** decentralization
Dezernat /detsɛrˈnaːt/ *das;* ~[e]s, ~e department
Dezernent /detsɛrˈnɛnt/ *der;* ~en, ~en head of department
Dezi- /ˈdeːtsi-/: deci⟨*litre, metre, etc.*⟩
Dezibel /detsiˈbɛl/ *das;* ~s, ~: decibel
dezimal /detsiˈmaːl/ *Adj.* decimal
Dezimal-: ~**rechnung** *die* decimal arithmetic *no art.;* ~**stelle** *die* decimal place; ~**system** *das* decimal system; ~**zahl** *die* ▶ 600 decimal [number]
dezimieren /detsiˈmiːrən/ *tr. V.* decimate
Dezimierung *die;* ~, ~**en** decimation
DFB /deːɛfˈbeː/ *der;* ~ *Abk.* **Deutscher Fußball-Bund**
DGB /deːgeːˈbeː/ *der;* ~ *Abk.* **Deutscher Gewerkschaftsbund** West German Trade Union Federation
dgl. *Abk.* **dergleichen, desgleichen**
d. Gr. *Abk.* **der/die Große**
d. h. *Abk.* **das heißt** i. e.
Di. *Abk.* **Dienstag** Tue[s].
Dia /ˈdiːa/ *das;* ~s, ~s slide
Diabetes /diaˈbeːtɛs/ *der;* ~: ▶ 329 diabetes
Diabetiker /diaˈbeːtikɐ/ *der;* ~s, ~, **Diabetikerin**, *die;* ~, ~**nen** diabetic
diabolisch (geh.) **1** *Adj.* diabolic. **2** *adv.* with diabolic malevolence
Diadem /diaˈdeːm/ *das;* ~s, ~e diadem
Diagnose /diaˈgnoːzə/ *die;* ~, ~**n** diagnosis; **eine** ~ **stellen** make a diagnosis
diagnostisch **1** *Adj.* diagnostic. **2** *adv.* diagnostically
diagnostizieren /diagnɔstiˈtsiːrən/ *tr. V.* diagnose
diagonal /diagoˈnaːl/ **1** *Adj.* diagonal. **2** *adv.* diagonally; **etw.** ~ **lesen** (ugs.) skim through sth.
Diagonale *die;* ~, ~n diagonal
Diagramm *das* graph; (schematische Darstellung) diagram
Diakon /diaˈkoːn/ *der;* ~s *od.* ~en, ~e[n] (christl. Kirche) deacon
Diakonisse /diakoˈnɪsə/ *die;* ~, ~n (ev. Kirche) deaconess
Dialekt /diaˈlɛkt/ *der;* ~[e]s, ~e dialect
Dialekt·ausdruck *der; Pl.* ~**ausdrücke** dialect expression
dialekt·frei **1** *Adj.* ~**es Deutsch sprechen** speak German without a trace of [any] dialect. **2** *adv.* ⟨*speak*⟩ without a trace of [any] dialect
Dialog /diaˈloːk/ *der;* ~[e]s, ~e dialogue
Dialyse /diaˈlyːzə/ *die;* ~, ~**n** (fachspr.) dialysis
Diamant /diaˈmant/ *der;* ~en, ~en diamond
diametral /diameˈtraːl/ (fig. geh.) **1** *Adj.* diametrical ⟨*opposition*⟩. **2** *adv.* diametrically

Dia-: ~**positiv** *das* slide; ~**projektor** *der* slide projector
Diät *die;* ~, ~**en** diet; **eine** ~ **einhalten** keep to a diet; ~ **kochen** cook according to a/one's diet; ~ **essen** be on a diet
Diäten *Pl.* [parliamentary] allowance *sing.*
dich /dɪç/ **1** *Akk. von* **du** you. **2** *Akk. des Reflexivpron. der 2. Pers. Sg.* yourself; **wäschst du dich?** are you washing [yourself]?; **entschuldige dich!** apologize!
dicht /dɪçt/ **1** *Adj.* **(a)** thick ⟨*hair, fur, plumage, moss*⟩; thick, dense ⟨*foliage, fog, cloud*⟩; dense ⟨*forest, thicket, hedge, crowd*⟩; heavy, dense ⟨*traffic*⟩; densely ranked, close-ranked ⟨*rows of houses*⟩; heavy ⟨*snowstorm, traffic*⟩; (fig.) full, packed ⟨*programme*⟩; **in** ~**er Folge** in rapid *or* quick succession; **(b)** (undurchlässig) (für Luft) airtight; (für Wasser) watertight ⟨*shoes*⟩; (für Licht) heavy ⟨*curtains, shutters*⟩; ~ **machen** seal ⟨*crack*⟩; seal the crack[s]/ leak[s] in ⟨*roof, window, etc.*⟩; waterproof ⟨*material, umbrella, etc.*⟩; **nicht ganz** ~ **sein** (salopp) have a screw loose (coll.); **(c)** (ugs.: geschlossen) shut; closed. **2** *adv.* **(a)** densely ⟨*populated*⟩; tightly ⟨*packed*⟩; thickly, densely ⟨*wooded*⟩; heavily ⟨*built up*⟩; ~ **verschneit** thick with snow; ~ **besetzt** full; packed; ~ **bewachsen** covered with dense vegetation; ~ **bebaut** heavily built-up; ~ **gedrängt** tightly *or* closely packed; ~ **behaart** [very] hairy; ~ **an** ~ *od.* ~ **gedrängt stehen/sitzen** stand/sit close together; **(b)** (undurchlässig) tightly; **(c)** *mit Präp.* (nahe) ~ **neben** right next to; ~ **daran** hard by; ~ **beieinander** close together; ~ **vor/hinter ihm** right *or* just in front of/behind him; **die Polizei ist ihm** ~ **auf den Fersen** the police are hard *or* close on his heels; **(d)** (zeitlich: unmittelbar) **ich war** ~ **daran, es zu tun** I was just about to do it; ~ **bevorstehen** be imminent
***dicht·bebaut** *usw.:* ⇒ **dicht** 2 a
Dichte /ˈdɪçtə/ *die;* ~ (Physik, fig.) density
dichten¹ /ˈdɪçtn̩/ **1** *itr. V.* [**gut**] ~: make a good seal. **2** ⇒ **abdichten**
dichten² **1** *itr. V.* write poetry. **2** *tr. V.* write; compose
Dichter *der;* ~s, ~: poet; (Schriftsteller) writer; author
Dichterin *die;* ~, ~**nen** poet[ess]; (Schriftstellerin) writer; author[ess]
dichterisch **1** *Adj.* poetic; (schriftstellerisch) literary. **2** *adv.;* ⇒ **1:** poetically; literarily
***dicht·gedrängt** ⇒ **dicht** 2 a
dicht|halten *unr. itr. V.* (ugs.) keep one's mouth shut (fig. sl.)
dicht|machen *tr., itr. V.* (ugs.) shut; close; (endgültig) shut *or* close down
Dichtung¹ *die;* ~, ~**en** **(a)** *o. Pl.* sealing; **(b)** (dichtendes Teil) seal; (am Hahn usw.) washer; (am Vergaser, Zylinder usw.) gasket
Dichtung² *die;* ~, ~**en** **(a)** literary work; work of literature; (in Versform) poetic work; poem; (fig. ugs.) fiction; ~ **und Wahrheit** fact and fiction; truth and fantasy; **(b)** *o. Pl.* (Dichtkunst) literature; (in Versform) poetry
dick /dɪk/ **1** *Adj.* **(a)** thick; thick, chunky ⟨*pullover*⟩; stout ⟨*tree*⟩; fat ⟨*person, arms, legs, behind, etc.*⟩; big ⟨*bust*⟩; ~ **und rund** *od.* **fett sein** (ugs.) be round and fat; ~ **machen** ⟨*drink, food*⟩ be fattening; **das Kleid macht** ~: the dress makes you look fat; **im** ~**sten Verkehr** (fig. ugs.) in the heaviest traffic; **mit jmdm. durch** ~ **und dünn gehen** stay *or* stick with sb. through thick and thin; **(b)** (ugs.: angeschwollen) swollen ⟨*cheek, ankle, tonsils, etc.*⟩; **(c)** (ugs.: groß) big ⟨*mistake, order*⟩; hefty, (coll.) fat ⟨*fee, premium, salary*⟩; **ein** ~**es Auto** (ugs.) a great big car (coll.); **jmdm. ein** ~**es Lob aussprechen** give sb. a great deal of prise *or* high praise; **das** ~**e Ende kommt noch** (ugs.) the worst is yet to come; **(d)** (ugs.: eng) close ⟨*friends, friendship, etc.*⟩. **2** *adv.* **(a)** thickly; **etw. 5 cm** ~ **schneiden/auftragen** *usw.* cut/apply sth. 5 cm. thick; **etw.** ~ **unterstreichen** underline sth. heavily; **sich** ~ **anziehen** wrap up warm[ly]; ~ **geschminkt** heavily made up; ~ **auftragen** (ugs. abwertend) lay it on thick (sl.); **(b)** ~ **geschwollen** (ugs.) badly swollen; **(c)** ~ **befreundet sein** (ugs.) be close friends

Dick-: ∼**bauch** der (scherzh.) fatty; (mit Spitzbauch) potbelly; ∼**darm** der (Anat.) large intestine

dicke Adv. (ugs.) easily; **jmdn./etw.** ∼ **haben** (salopp) have had a bellyful of sb./sth.

Dicke¹ die; ∼: thickness; (von Menschen, Körperteilen) fatness

Dicke² der/die; adj. Dekl. (ugs.) fatty (coll.); fat man/woman; **die** ∼**n** fatties (coll.); fat people

Dickerchen das; ∼**s**, ∼ (ugs. scherzh.) podge (coll.)

dick-, Dick-: ∼**fellig** (ugs. abwertend) **1** Adj. thickskinned. **2** adv. in a thick-skinned way; ∼**felligkeit** die; ∼ (ugs. abwertend) insensitivity; ∼**flüssig** Adj. thick; ∼**häuter** der; ∼**s**, ∼: pachyderm

Dickicht /'dɪkɪçt/ das; ∼[e]**s**, ∼**e** thicket; (fig.) jungle

Dick·kopf der (ugs.) mule (coll.); **du bist ein** ∼ you're as stubborn as a mule

dick·köpfig (ugs.) **1** Adj. stubborn; pigheaded; **2** adv. stubbornly; pigheadedly

dicklich Adj. plumpish; chubby

Dick-: ∼**milch** die sour milk; ∼**schädel** der ⇒ ∼**kopf**

Didaktik /di'daktɪk/ die; ∼, ∼**en (a)** o. Pl. didactics sing., no art.; **(b)** (Unterrichtsmethode) teaching method

didaktisch 1 Adj. didactic. **2** adv. didactically

die¹ 1 best. Art. Nom. the; **die Kleine** the little girl; **die Liebe/Freundschaft** love/friendship; **die „Iphigenie"/** (ugs.) Helga 'Iphigenia'/Helga; **die Demokratie** democracy; **die Marktstraße** Market Street; **die Schweiz** Switzerland; **die Frau/Menschheit** women pl./mankind; **die „Concorde"/„Klaus Störtebeker"** 'Concorde'/the 'Klaus Störtebeker'; **die Kunst/Oper** art/opera. **2** Demonstrativpron. **(a)** attr. **die Frau war es** it was 'that woman; **(b)** allein stehend she; **die war es** it was 'her; **die und arbeiten!** (ugs.) [what,] her work!; **die mit dem Hund** (ugs.) her with the dog; **die [da]** (Frau, Mädchen) that woman/girl; (Gegenstand, Tier) that one; **die blöde Kuh, die!** (fig. salopp) what a silly cow! (sl. derog.). **3** Relativpron. Nom. (Mensch) who; that; (Sache, Tier) which; that; **die Frau, die da drüben entlanggeht** the woman walking along over there. **4** Relativ- u. Demonstrativpron. the one who; **die das getan hat** the woman etc. who did it

die² 1 best. Art. **(a)** Akk. Sg. v. **die¹ 1**: the; **hast du die Ute gesehen?** (ugs.) have you seen Ute?; **(b)** Nom. u. Akk. Pl. v. **der¹ 1, die¹ 1, das 1**: the. **2** Demonstrativpron. Nom. u. Akk. Pl. v. **der¹ 1, die¹ 1, das 1**: attr. **ich meine die Männer, die gestern hier waren** I mean those men who were here yesterday; allein stehend **ich meine die [da]** I mean 'them. **3** Relativpron. **(a)** Akk. Sg. v. **die¹ 3**: (bei Menschen) who; that; (bei Sachen, Tieren) which; that; **(b)** Nom. u. Akk. Pl. v. **der¹ 3, die¹ 3, das 3**: (bei Menschen) whom; **die Männer, die ich gesehen habe** the men I saw; (bei Sachen, Tieren) which; **die Bücher, die da liegen** the books lying there

Dieb /di:p/ der; ∼[e]**s**, ∼**e** thief; **haltet den** ∼**!** stop thief!

Diebes-: ∼**bande** die (abwertend) gang of thieves; ∼**gut** das stolen goods pl. or property

Diebin die; ∼, ∼**nen** [woman] thief

diebisch 1 Adj. **(a)** thieving; **(b)** (verstohlen) mischievous. **2** adv. mischievously; **sich** ∼ **über etw.** (Akk.) **freuen** take a mischievous pleasure in sth.

Diebstahl /'di:p-ʃta:l/ der; ∼[e]**s**, **Diebstähle** /'di:p ʃtɛ:lə/ theft

Diebstahl·versicherung die insurance against theft

die·jenige, diejenigen ⇒ **derjenige**

Diele /'di:lə/ die; ∼, ∼**n (a)** hall[way]; **(b)** (Fußbodenbrett) floorboard

dienen /'di:nən/ itr. V. **(a)** be in service; **jmdm. als Magd** ∼: serve sb. as a maid; **(b)** (veralt.: Militärdienst tun) do military service; **beim Heer** ∼: serve in the army; **(c)** (dienlich sein) serve; **das dient einer guten Sache** it is in a good cause; **(d)** (helfen) help **(in + Dat.** in); **womit kann ich** ∼**?** what can I do for you?; can I help you?; **mit 20 DM wäre mir schon gedient** 20 marks would do; **(e)**

(verwendet werden) serve; **als Museum** ∼: serve or be used as a museum; **das soll dir als Warnung** ∼: let that serve as or be a warning to you

Diener der; ∼**s**, ∼ servant; **einen** ∼ **machen** (ugs.) bow; make a bow

Dienerin /'di:nərɪn/ die; ∼, ∼**nen** maid; servant

dienern itr. V. (abwertend) bow; (fig.) bow and scrape

Dienerschaft die; ∼: servants pl.; domestic staff

dienlich Adj. helpful; useful; **jmdm./einer Sache** ∼ **sein** be helpful or of help to sb./sth.; **kann ich Ihnen mit etwas** ∼ **sein?** (geh.) can I be of any assistance to you?

Dienst /di:nst/ der; ∼[e]**s**, ∼**e (a)** (Tätigkeit) work; (von Soldaten, Polizeibeamten, Krankenhauspersonal usw.) duty; **seinen** ∼ **antreten** start work/go on duty; ∼ **haben** be at work/on duty; ⟨chemist⟩ be open; ∼ **habender** od. **tuender Offizier** duty officer; ∼ **habender** od. **tuender Arzt/Beamter** doctor/official on duty; **außerhalb des** ∼**es** outside work/when off duty; **seinen** ∼ **tun** ⟨machine, appliance⟩ serve its purpose; ∼ **ist** ∼**, und Schnaps ist Schnaps** (ugs.) you shouldn't mix business and pleasure; **(b)** (Arbeitsverhältnis) post; **den** od. **seinen** ∼ **quittieren** resign one's post; (Milit.) leave the service; ⟨officer⟩ resign one's commission; **Major** usw. **außer** ∼: retired major etc.; **in** ∼ **stellen** put sth. into service or commission; **(c)** o. Pl. (Tätigkeitsbereich) service; **der höhere** ∼ **der Beamtenlaufbahn** the senior civil service; **(d)** (Hilfe) service; ∼ **am Kunden** (ugs.) customer service; **jmdm. mit etw. einen schlechten** ∼ **erweisen** do sb. a disservice or a bad turn with sth.; **zu jmds.** ∼**en** od. **jmdm. zu** ∼ **sein** od. **stehen** (geh.) be at sb.'s disposal or service; **(e)** (Hilfs∼) service; (Nachrichten∼, Spionage∼) [intelligence] service

Diens·tag /di:ns-/ der ▶119, ▶595 Tuesday; **am** ∼: on Tuesday; ∼**, der 1. Juni** Tuesday the first of June; Tuesday, 1 June; **er kommt** ∼: he is coming on Tuesday; **eines** ∼**s** one Tuesday; **den ganzen** ∼ **über** all day Tuesday; the whole of Tuesday; **ab nächsten** od. **nächstem** ∼: from next Tuesday [onwards]; **die Nacht von** ∼ **auf** od. **zum Mittwoch** Tuesday night; ∼ **in einer Woche** od. **in acht Tagen** Tuesday week; a week on Tuesday; ∼ **vor einer Woche** a week last Tuesday

Dienstag·abend der ▶595 Tuesday evening or (coll.) night

dienstag·abends Adv. ▶595 [on] Tuesday evenings

dienstäglich ▶595 **1** Adj.; nicht präd. [regular] Tuesday. **2** adv. on Tuesday

dienstag-, Dienstag-: ∼**mittag** der ▶595 Tuesday lunchtime; ∼**mittags** Adv. ▶595 [at] lunchtime on Tuesdays; ∼**morgen** der ▶595 Tuesday morning; ∼**morgens** Adv. ▶595 [on] Tuesday mornings; ∼**nachmittag** der ▶595 Tuesday afternoon; ∼**nachmittags** Adv. ▶595 [on] Tuesday afternoons; ∼**nacht** die ▶595 Tuesday night; ∼**nachts** Adv. ▶595 [on] Tuesday nights

diens·tags Adv. ▶595 on Tuesday[s]; ∼ **abends/morgens** on Tuesday evening[s]/morning[s]; on a Tuesday evening/morning

Dienstag·vormittag der ▶595 Tuesday morning

dienstag·vormittags Adv. ▶595 [on] Tuesday mornings

dienst-, Dienst-: ∼**alter** das length of service; ∼**ältest…** adj. longest-serving; ∼**an·tritt** der commencement of one's duties; ∼**auf·fassung** die conception of duty; ∼**aufsichtsbeschwerde** die complaint to the supervising authority (about a public servant or government department); ∼**ausweis** der [official] identity card; ∼**beflissen 1** Adj. zealous; eager; **2** adv. zealously; eagerly; ∼**beginn** der start of work; ∼**bereit** Adj. ⟨chemist⟩ open pred.; ⟨doctor⟩ on call or duty; ⟨dentist⟩ on duty; ∼**bezüge** Pl. salary sing.; ∼**bote** der servant; ∼**boten·eingang** der tradesmen's entrance; ∼**eid** der official oath; ∼**eifer** der zeal; eagerness; ∼**eifrig 1** Adj. zealous; eager; **2** adv. zealously; eagerly; ∼**fähig** Adj. fit for work postpos.; (Milit.) fit for service postpos.; ∼**fahrt** die ⇒ ∼**reise**; ∼**frei** Adj. free ⟨time⟩; **an** ∼**freien Tagen** on days off; ∼**frei haben/**

bekommen have/get time off; **~geheimnis** das **(a)** professional secret; (im Staatsdienst) official secret; **(b)** o. Pl. professional secrecy; (im Staatsdienst) official secrecy; **unter das ~geheimnis fallen** be a professional/official secret; **~grad** der (Milit.) rank; *~**habend** ⇒ **Dienst** a; **~hund** der dog used for police/security work; **~jahr** das year of service; **~jubiläum** das anniversary; **~kleidung** die uniform; **~leister** der; **~s**, **~**: service provider; **~leistung** die (auch Wirtsch.) service

Dienstleistungs-: **~abend** der late opening evening; **~betrieb** der (Wirtsch.) business in the service sector; **~gewerbe** das (Wirtsch.) service industries pl.; **~sektor** der (Wirtsch.) service sector

dienstlich 1 Adj. **(a)** business ‹call›; (im Staatsdienst) official ‹letter, call, etc.›; **(b)** (offiziell) official; **~ werden** (ugs.) get businesslike and formal. **2** adv. on business; (im Staatsdienst) on official business

dienst-, Dienst-: **~mädchen** das (veralt.) maid; **~marke** die [police] identification badge; ≈ warrant card (Brit.) or (Amer.) ID card; **~ordnung** die official regulations pl.; **~pflicht** die **(a)** o. Pl. compulsory service; **(b)** (bei Beamten) duty; **~pistole** die service pistol; **~reise** die business trip; **~schluss,** *~**schluß** der; o. Pl. end of work; **um 17 Uhr ist ~schluss** work finishes at 5 o'clock; **nach ~schluss** after work; **~stelle** die office; (Abteilung) department; **~stunden** Pl. **(a)** working hours; **(b)** (Öffnungszeiten) **~stunden haben** be open; *~**tuend** ⇒ **Dienst** a; **~unfähig** Adj. unfit for work postpos.; (Milit.) unfit for service postpos.; **~vergehen** das offence against [official] regulations; **~vorschrift** die regulations pl.; (Milit.) service regulations; **~wagen** der official car; (Geschäftswagen) company car; **~weg** der proper or official channels pl.; **den ~weg gehen** od. **einhalten** go through the proper or official channels; **~wohnung** die (von Firmen) company flat (Brit.) or (Amer.) apartment; (von staatlichen Stellen) government flat (Brit.) or (Amer.) apartment; (vom Militär) army/navy/air force flat (Brit.) or (Amer.) apartment; **~zeit** die **(a)** period of service; **(b)** (tägliche Arbeitszeit) working hours pl.; **~zimmer** das office

dies /diːs/ ⇒ **dieser**

dies·bezüglich 1 Adj.; nicht präd. relating to or regarding this postpos., not pred. **2** adv. regarding this; on this matter

diese /ˈdiːzə/ ⇒ **dieser**

Diesel /ˈdiːzl̩/ der; **~s**, **~** diesel

die·selbe ⇒ **derselbe**

Diesel-: **~lokomotive** die diesel locomotive; **~motor** der diesel engine

dieser /ˈdiːzɐ/, **diese, dieses, dies** Demonstrativpron. **(a)** attr. this; Pl. these; **dieses Buch/diese Bücher [da]** that book/those books [there]; **in dieser Nacht wird es noch schneien/begann es zu schneien** it will snow tonight/it started to snow that night; **er hat dieser Tage Geburtstag** it's his birthday within the next few days; **ich habe ihn dieser Tage noch gesehen** I saw him the other day; **diese Inge ist doch ein Goldschatz** that Inge is a treasure, isn't she?; **(b)** allein stehend **diese[r] [hier/da]** this one [here]/that one [there]; **diese** Pl. **[hier/da]** these [here]/those [there]; **dies alles** all this; **diese …, jene …** (geh.) the latter …, the former …; **dies und das,** (geh.) dieses und jenes this and that; **dieser und jener** (geh.) (einige) some [people] pl.; (ein paar) a few [people] pl.

dieser·art indekl. Demonstrativpron. (geh.) of this/that kind postpos.

dieses ⇒ **dieser**

diesig Adj. hazy

dies-: **~jährig** Adj.; nicht präd. this year's; **unser ~jähriges Treffen** our meeting this year; **~mal** Adv. this time; **~seitig** Adj.; nicht präd. **das ~seitige Rheinufer** this side of the Rhine; **~seits** 1 Präp. mit Gen. on this side of; **2** Adv. **~seits von** on this side of

Diesseits das; **~:** **das ~:** this world

Dietrich /ˈdiːtrɪç/ der; **~s**, **~e** picklock

die·weil (veralt.) 1 Konj. **(a)** (zeitlich) while; **(b)** (kausal) because. **2** adv. in the mean time or the mean while

diffamieren /dɪfaˈmiːrən/ tr. V. defame; **~de Äußerungen** defamatory utterances

Diffamierung die; **~**, **~en** defamation; (Bemerkung) defamatory statement

Differential usw. ⇒ **Differenzial** usw.

Differenz /dɪfəˈrɛnts/ die; **~**, **~en** difference; (Meinungsverschiedenheit) difference [of opinion]

Differenz·betrag der difference

Differenzial das; **~s**, **~e (a)** (Math.) differential; **(b)** (Technik) differential [gear]

Differenzial- differential ‹gear, equation, calculus, etc.›

differenzieren 1 tr. V. (Math.) differentiate. **2** itr. V. differentiate; make a distinction/distinctions **(zwischen** between); (bei einem Urteil, einer Behauptung) be discriminating

differenziert 1 Adj. subtly differentiated ‹methods, colours›; complex ‹life, language, person, emotional life›; sophisticated ‹taste›; diverse ‹range›. **2** adv. **~ urteilen** be discriminating in one's judgement

differieren /dɪfəˈriːrən/ itr. V. (geh.) differ **(um** by)

diffizil /dɪfiˈtsiːl/ Adj. (geh.) difficult

diffus /dɪˈfuːs/ 1 Adj. **(a)** (Physik, Chemie) diffuse; **(b)** (geh.) vague; vague and confused ‹idea, statement, etc.›. **2** adv. in a vague and confused way

digital /digiˈtaːl/ (fachspr.) 1 Adj. digital. **2** adv. digitally

Digital- digital ‹clock, display, recording, etc.›

digitalisieren tr. V. (DV) digitalize

Diktat /dɪkˈtaːt/ das; **~[e]s**, **~e (a)** dictation; **nach ~ schreiben** take dictation; **(b)** (geh.: Befehl) dictate; (Politik) diktat

Diktator /dɪkˈtaːtɔr/ der; **~s**, **~en** /-ˈtoːrən/ (auch fig.) dictator

diktatorisch (auch fig.) 1 Adj. dictatorial. **2** adv. dictatorially

Diktatur /dɪktaˈtuːɐ̯/ die; **~**, **~en** (auch fig.) dictatorship

diktieren /dɪkˈtiːrən/ tr. V. dictate

Diktier·gerät das dictating machine

Dilemma /diˈlɛma/ das; **~s**, **~s** dilemma

Dilettant /dileˈtant/ der; **~en**, **~en, Dilettantin** die; **~**, **~nen** (auch abwertend) dilettante

dilettantisch (abwertend) 1 Adj. dilettante; amateurish. **2** adv. amateurishly

Dill /dɪl/ der; **~[e]s**, **~e** dill

Dimension /dimɛnˈzi̯oːn/ die; **~**, **~en** (Physik, fig.) dimension

-dimensional /dimɛnzi̯oˈnaːl/ Adj. -dimensional

DIN /diːn/ Abk. **Deutsche Industrie-Norm[en]** German Industrial Standard[s]; DIN; **DIN-Format** DIN size; **DIN-A4-Format** A4

Ding¹ /dɪŋ/ das; **~[e]s**, **~e (a)** thing; **jedes ~ hat zwei Seiten** (fig.) there are two sides to everything; **(b)** meist Pl. **nach Lage der ~e** the way things are; **über den ~en stehen** be above such things; **persönliche/private ~e** personal/private matters; **ein ~ der Unmöglichkeit sein** be quite impossible; **das geht nicht mit rechten ~en zu** there's something funny about it; **vor allen ~en** above all; **(c) guter ~e sein** (geh.) be in good spirits

Ding² das; **[e]s**, **~er** (ugs.) **(a)** thing; **das ist ja ein ~!** that's really something; **ein ~ drehen** ‹criminal› pull a job (sl.); **mach keine ~er!** stop having me on (Brit. coll.); stop putting me on (Amer. coll.); **(b)** (Mädchen) thing; creature

dingen unr. tr. V. (geh.) hire

ding·fest in jmdn. **~ machen** arrest or apprehend sb.

Dings¹ /dɪŋs/ (der/die) **~** (ugs.: für einen Personennamen) thingamy (coll.); thingumajig (coll.); what's-his-name/-her-name

Dings² (ugs.) 1 das; **~** (Gegenstand) thingamy (coll.); thingumajig (coll.) what-d'you-call-it. **2** (das); **~** (für einen Ortsnamen) what's-its-name; what's-it-called

Dings·bums ⇨ Dings¹; Dings²
Dino *der;* ∼**s**, ∼**s** (ugs.) dinosaur
Dinosaurier /dino'zaurie/ *der;* ∼**s**, ∼ dinosaur
Diode /di'o:də/ *die;* ∼, ∼**n** (Elektrot.) diode
Dioden·rücklicht *das* LED rear light
Dioxid /'di:|ɔksy:t/ *das;* ∼**s**, ∼**e** (Chemie) dioxide
Dioxin /di:|ɔ'ksi:n/ *das;* ∼**s** (Chemie) dioxin
Diözese /diø'tse:zə/ *die;* ∼, ∼**n** diocese
Diphtherie /dɪfte'ri:/ *die;* ∼, ∼**n** (Med.) diphtheria
Dipl.-Ing. *Abk.* **Diplomingenieur** *academically quali-fied engineer*
Diplom /di'plo:m/ *das;* ∼**s**, ∼**e** (a) ≈ [first] degree (*in a scientific or technical subject*); (für einen Handwerksberuf) dip-loma; (b) (Urkunde) ≈ degree certificate (*in a scientific or technical subject*); (für einen Handwerksberuf) diploma
Diplom-: qualified
Diplom·arbeit *die* ≈ degree dissertation (*for a first de-gree in a scientific or technical subject*); (für einen Handwerksberuf) dissertation [submitted for a/the diploma]
Diplomat /diplo'ma:t/ *der;* ∼**en**, ∼**en** (auch fig.) diplomat
Diplomaten-: ∼**koffer** *der* attaché case; executive case; ∼**viertel** *das* embassy district
Diplomatie /diploma'ti:/ *die;* ∼ diplomacy
Diplomatin *die;* ∼, ∼**nen** (auch fig.) diplomat
diplomatisch (auch fig.) **1** *Adj.* diplomatic. **2** *adv.* dip-lomatically
diplomiert *Adj.* qualified
Diplom·prüfung *die* ≈ degree examination (*in a scien-tific or technical subject*); (für einen Handwerksberuf) diploma examination
dir /di:ɐ/ **1** *Dat. von* **du** to you; (nach Präp.) you; **ich gab ∼ das Buch** I gave you the book; **Freunde von ∼:** friends of yours; **gehen wir zu ∼:** let's go to your place. **2** *Dat. des Reflexivpron. der 2. Pers. Sg.* yourself; **hast du ∼ gedacht, dass ...:** did you think that ...; **nimm ∼ noch von dem Braten** help yourself to some more roast
direkt /di'rɛkt/ **1** *Adj.* direct. **2** *adv.* (a) (geradewegs, sofort) straight; directly; ‹*broadcast sth.*› live; (b) (nahe) directly; **∼ am Marktplatz** right by the market square; (c) (unmit-telbar) direct; **sich ∼ mit jmdm. verbinden lassen** get a direct line to sb.; (d) (unverblümt) directly; (e) (ugs.: geradezu) really, positively ‹*dangerous, witty*›
Direkt·flug *der* direct flight
Direktheit *die;* ∼: directness
Direktion /dirɛk'tsio:n/ *die;* ∼, ∼**en** (a) *o. Pl.* manage-ment; (von gemeinnützigen, staatlichen Einrichtungen) administra-tion; (b) (die Geschäftsleiter) management; (c) (Büroräume) managers' offices *pl.*
Direktor /di'rɛktor/ *der;* ∼**s**, ∼**en** /...'to:rən/, **Direkto-rin** /dirɛk'to:rɪn/ *die;* ∼, ∼**nen** ▶ 34 director; (einer Schule) headmaster/headmistress; (einer Fachschule) principal; (einer Strafanstalt) governor; (einer Abteilung) manager
Direkt-: ∼**sendung** *die,* ∼**übertragung** *die* live transmission *or* broadcast; ∼**verbindung** *die* (a) (Ei-senb.) direct connection; through train; (Flugw.) direct flight; (b) (Fernspr.) direct [telephone] connection; ∼**wahl** *die* (a) (Polit.) direct election; (b) *o. Pl.* (Fernspr.) direct dialling
Direx /'di:rɛks/ *der;* ∼, ∼**e**./die;* ∼, ∼**en** (Schülerspr.) head
Dirigent /diri'gɛnt/ *der;* ∼**en**, ∼**en** conductor
Dirigenten-: ∼**pult** *das* conductor's rostrum; ∼**stab** *der,* ∼**stock** *der* [conductor's] baton
dirigieren /diri'gi:rən/ *tr. V.* (a) (Musik) *auch itr.* conduct; (b) (führen) steer ‹*vehicle, person*›; **jmdn. an einen Ort ∼:** send sb. to a place
Dirigismus /diri'gismʊs/ *der;* ∼ (Wirtsch.) dirigisme
dirigistisch (Wirtsch.) **1** *Adj.* dirigiste. **2** *adv.* in a diri-giste manner
Dirndl /'dɪrndl/ *das;* ∼**s**, ∼, **Dirndl·kleid** *das* dirndl
Dis /dɪs/ *das;* ∼, ∼ (Musik) D sharp
Disco /'dɪsko:/ *die;* ∼, ∼**s** disco
Discount- /dɪs'kaunt-/ discount ‹*shop, price, etc.*›
Diskette /dɪs'kɛtə/ *die;* ∼, ∼**n** (DV) floppy disc
Disketten·lauf·werk *das* (DV) [floppy-]disc drive
Disk·jockey /'dɪskdʒɔke/ *der* disc jockey
Diskont /dɪs'kɔnt/ *der;* ∼**s**, ∼**e** (Finanzw.) discount
Diskonten *Pl.* (Finanzw.) inland *or* domestic bills of ex-change

Diskont·satz *der* (Finanzw.) discount rate
Diskothek /dɪsko'te:k/ *die;* ∼, ∼**en** (a) (Tanzlokal) disco-thèque; (b) (Schallplatten) record collection
diskreditieren /dɪskredi'ti:rən/ *tr. V.* discredit
Diskrepanz /dɪskre'pants/ *die;* ∼, ∼**en** discrepancy
diskret /dɪs'kre:t/ **1** *Adj.* (a) (vertraulich) confidential ‹*discussion, report*›; (unauffällig) discreet ‹*action*›; (b) (taktvoll) discreet; tactful ‹*behaviour, reserve*›; (c) (Technik, Physik, Math.) discrete. **2** *adv.* (a) (vertraulich) confidentially; **etw. ∼ behandeln** treat sth. in confidence; (b) (taktvoll) discreetly; tactfully
Diskretion /dɪskre'tsio:n/ *die;* ∼ (a) (Verschwiegenheit, Takt) discretion; **∼ [ist] Ehrensache** you can rely on my discretion; (b) (Unaufdringlichkeit) discreetness
diskriminieren /dɪskrimi'ni:rən/ *tr. V.* (a) discrimin-ate against; (b) (herabwürdigen) disparage
diskriminierend *Adj.* disparaging
Diskriminierung *die;* ∼, ∼**en** discrimination (*Gen.* against)
Diskus /'dɪskʊs/ *der;* ∼ *od.* ∼**ses**, **Disken** *od.* ∼**se** (Leichtathletik) discus
Diskussion /dɪsku'sio:n/ *die;* ∼, ∼**en** discussion; **etw. zur ∼ stellen** put sth. up for discussion; **[nicht] zur ∼ stehen** [not] be under discussion
Diskussions-: ∼**beitrag** *der* contribution to a/the discussion; ∼**leiter** *der* chairman [of the discussion]; ∼**teilnehmer** *der* participant [in a/the discussion]
Diskus·werfen *das;* ∼**s** (Leichtathletik) [throwing the] dis-cus
diskutieren /dɪsku'ti:rən/ **1** *itr. V.* **über etw.** (*Akk.*) ∼: discuss sth.; **wir haben stundenlang diskutiert** our dis-cussion went on for hours. **2** *tr. V.* discuss
Disponent /dɪspo'nɛnt/ *der;* ∼**en**, ∼**en** (Wirtsch.) junior departmental manager
disponieren *itr. V.* make plans; (vorausplanen) plan ahead; **anders ∼:** make other plans
Dispositions·kredit *der* (Finanzw.) overdraft facility
Disput /dɪs'pu:t/ *der;* ∼[**e**]**s**, ∼**e** (geh.) dispute, argument
Disqualifikation *die* (auch Sport) disqualification
disqualifizieren *tr. V.* (auch Sport) disqualify
Dissertation /dɪsɛrta'tsio:n/ *die;* ∼, ∼**en** [doctoral] dis-sertation *or* thesis
Dissonanz /dɪso'nants/ *die;* ∼, ∼**en** (Musik, fig.) disson-ance
Distanz /dɪs'tants/ *die;* ∼, ∼**en** (auch Sport, fig.) distance; **∼ zu etw. gewinnen** (fig.) distance oneself from sth.; **auf ∼** (*Akk.*) **gehen,** ∼ **wahren** *od.* **halten** (fig.) keep one's distance
distanzieren *refl. V.* dissociate (**von** from) oneself
distanziert **1** *Adj.* distant; reserved. **2** *adv.* in a distant *or* reserved manner; with reserve
Distel /'dɪstl/ *die;* ∼, ∼**n** thistle
distinguiert /dɪstɪŋ'gi:ɐt/ (geh.) **1** *Adj.* distinguished. **2** *adv.* in a distinguished manner
Distribution /dɪstribu'tsio:n/ *die;* ∼, ∼**en** (auch Wirtsch., Math., Sprachw.) distribution
Disziplin /dɪstsi'pli:n/ *die;* ∼, ∼**en** (a) *o. Pl.* discipline; (Selbstbeherrschung) [self-]discipline; ∼ **halten** keep discip-line; (sich diszipliniert verhalten) behave in a disciplined way; (b) (Wissenschaftszweig, Sportart) discipline
Disziplinar- disciplinary ‹*measure, proceedings, etc.*›
disziplinarisch **1** *Adj.* disciplinary. **2** *adv.* **gegen jmdn. ∼ vorgehen** take disciplinary action against sb.
disziplinieren **1** *tr. V.* discipline. **2** *refl. V.* discipline oneself
diszipliniert **1** *Adj.* (a) well-disciplined; (b) (beherrscht) disciplined. **2** *adv.* (a) in a well-disciplined way; (b) (be-herrscht) in a disciplined way
disziplin-, Disziplin-: ∼**los** **1** *Adj.* undisciplined; **2** *adv.* in an undisciplined way; ∼**losigkeit** *die;* ∼: lack of discipline; ∼**schwierigkeiten** *Pl.* discipline prob-lems; problems in maintaining discipline

dito /'di:to/ *Adv.* (Kaufmannsspr., auch ugs.) ditto

Diva /'di:va/ *die;* ~, ~s *u.* D**i**ven (a) prima donna; diva; (Film~) great [film] star; (b) (eingebildeter Mensch) prima donna

divers... /di'vɛrs.../ *Adj.; nicht präd.* various; (mehrer...) several

Diversifikation /divɛrzifika'tsi̯o:n/ *die;* ~, ~en (Wirtsch.) diversification

diversifizieren /divɛrzifi'tsi:rən/ *tr., itr. V.* (Wirtsch.) diversify

Dividende /divi'dɛndə/ *die;* ~, ~n (Börsenw., Wirtsch.) dividend

dividieren /divi'di:rən/ *tr. V.* (Math.) divide

Division /divi'zi̯o:n/ *die;* ~, ~en (Math., Milit.) division

Diwan /'di:va:n/ *der;* ~s, ~e (veralt.) divan

d. J. *Abk.* (a) dieses Jahres; (b) der/die Jüngere

dm *Abk.* Dezimeter dm

DM *Abk.* Deutsche Mark DM

DNS /de:ʔɛn'ʔɛs/ *die;* ~ *Abk.* (Chemie) Desoxyribonukleinsäure DNA

Do. *Abk.* Donnerstag Thur[s].

Dobermann /'do:bɐman/ *der;* ~s, D**o**bermänner Dobermann [pinscher]

doch /dɔx/ **1** *Konj.* but. **2** *Adv.* (a) (jedoch) but; (b) (dennoch) all the same; still; (wider Erwarten) after all; **und ~:** and yet; (c) (geh.: nämlich) **wusste er ~, dass ...:** because he knew that ...; (d) (als Antwort) [oh] yes; **Hast du keinen Hunger? — Doch!** Aren't't you hungry? — Yes [I am]!; (e) (trotz allem, was dagegen sprechen/gesprochen haben mag) **er war also ~ der Mörder!** so he 'was the murderer'!; **sie hat es also ~ gesagt** so she 'did say it; (f) (ohnehin) in any case; **du kannst mir ~ nicht helfen** there's nothing you can do to help me. **3** *Interj.* (a) (widersprechende Antwort auf eine verneinte Aussage) **Das stimmt nicht. — Doch!** That's not right. — [Oh] yes it is!; (b) (negative Antwort auf eine verneinte Frage) **Hast du keinen Hunger? — Doch!** Aren't you hungry? — Yes [I am]! **4** *Partikel* (a) (auffordernd, Ungeduld, Empörung ausdrückend) **das hättest du ~ wissen müssen** you [really] should have known that; **du hast ~ selbst gesagt, dass ...** (rechtfertigend) you did say yourself that ...; **gib mir ~ bitte mal die Zeitung** pass me the paper, please; **reg dich ~ nicht so auf!** don't get so worked up!; **pass ~ auf!** [oh.] do be careful!; **das ist ~ nicht zu glauben** that's just incredible; (b) (Zweifel ausdrückend) **du hast ~ meinen Brief erhalten?** you did get my letter, didn't you?; (c) (Überraschung ausdrückend) **das ist ~ Karl!** there's Karl! (d) (an Bekanntes erinnernd) **er ist ~ nicht mehr der Jüngste** he's not as young as he used to be[, you know]; (e) (nach Vergessenem fragend) **wie war ~ sein Name?** now what was his name?; (f) (verstärkt Bejahung/Verneinung ausdrückend) **gewiss/sicher ~:** [why] certainly; of course; **ja ~:** [yes,] all right *or* (coll.) OK; **nicht ~!** (abwehrend) [no,] don't!; (g) (Wunsch verstärkend) **wäre es ~ ...:** if only it were ...

Docht /dɔxt/ *der;* ~[e]s, ~e wick

Dock /dɔk/ *das;* ~s, ~s dock

docken 1 *itr. V.* (Seew., Raumf.) dock. **2** *tr. V.* (Seew.) dock ‹ship›; put ‹ship› in dock

Dogge /'dɔgə/ *die;* ~, ~n (a) Deutsche ~: Great Dane; (b) **Englische** ~: mastiff

Dogma /'dɔgma/ *das;* ~s, D**o**gmen (auch fig.) dogma

dogmatisch (auch fig.) **1** *Adj.* dogmatic. **2** *adv.* dogmatically

Dohle /'do:lə/ *die;* ~, ~n jackdaw

Doktor /'dɔktɔr/ *der;* ~s, ~en /-'to:rən/ (a) *o. Pl.* (Titel) doctorate; doctor's degree; **den/seinen ~ machen** do a/one's doctorate; (b) ▸ 34 | (Träger) doctor; **Herr ~ Krause** Doctor Krause; (c) (ugs.: Arzt) doctor; **der Onkel ~** (Kinderspr.) the nice doctor

Doktorand /dɔktoˈrant/ *der;* ~en, ~en, D**o**ktor**a**ndin *die;* ~, ~nen student taking his/her doctorate

Doktor·arbeit *die* doctoral thesis *or* dissertation

Doktorin *die;* ~, ~nen doctor

Doktor·ingenieur *der* doctor of engineering science

Doktor-: ~**titel** *der* title of doctor; ~**vater** *der* (ugs.) [thesis] supervisor

Doktrin /dɔk'tri:n/ *die;* ~, ~en doctrine

Dokument /doku'mɛnt/ *das;* ~[e]s, ~e document

Dokumentar·film *der* documentary [film]

dokumentarisch 1 *Adj.* 2 *adv.* etw. ~ belegen provide documentary evidence of *or* for sth.; **etw.** ~ **festhalten** make a documentary record of sth.

Dokumentation /dɔkumɛnta'tsi̯o:n/ *die;* ~, ~en (a) *o. Pl.* documentation; (fig.) demonstration; (b) (Material) documentary account; (Bericht) documentary report

dokumentieren *tr. V.* (a) (belegen) document; (fig.) demonstrate; (b) (festhalten, darstellen) record ‹behaviour, event›

Dolch /dɔlç/ *der;* ~[e]s, ~e dagger

Dolde /'dɔldə/ *die;* ~, ~n (Bot.) umbel

doll /dɔl/ (bes. nordd., salopp) **1** *Adj.* (a) (ungewöhnlich) incredible; amazing; (b) (großartig) fantastic (coll.); great (coll.). **2** *adv.* (a) (großartig) fantastically [well] (coll.); (b) (sehr) ‹hurt› dreadfully (coll.); ‹shake, rain› good and hard (coll.)

Dollar /'dɔla:ɐ̯/ *der;* ~[s], ~s ▸ 216 | dollar

Dollar·kurs *der* dollar rate

dolmetschen *itr. V.* act as interpreter (**bei** at)

Dolmetscher *der;* ~s, ~, D**o**lmetscher**i**n *die;* ~, ~nen ▸ 85 | interpreter

Dom /do:m/ *der;* ~[e]s, ~e cathedral; (fig.) dome; **der Kölner** ~, **der** ~ **zu Köln** Cologne Cathedral

Domäne /do'mɛ:nə/ *die;* ~, ~n (fig.) domain

domestizieren /domɛsti'tsi:rən/ *tr. V.* domesticate

dominant /domi'nant/ *Adj.* (auch Biol.) dominant

Dominante *die;* ~, ~n (Musik) (Quint) dominant; (Akkord) dominant chord

Dominanz /domi'nants/ *die;* ~, ~en (auch Biol.) dominance

dominieren /domi'ni:rən/ *itr. V.* dominate; ~**d** dominant

Dominikaner /domini'ka:nɐ/ *der;* ~s, ~, Dominik**a**ner**i**n *die;* ~, ~nen (Mönch/Nonne, Einwohner/Einwohnerin der Dominikanischen Republik) Dominican

Dominikaner·orden *der o. Pl.* Dominican order

dominikanisch *Adj.* Dominican; **die Dominikanische Republik** the Dominican Republic

Domino *das;* ~s, ~s dominoes *sing.*

Domino·stein *der* (a) domino; (b) (Gebäck) *small chocolate-covered cake with layers of marzipan, jam, and gingerbread*

Domizil /domi'tsi:l/ (a) *das;* ~s, ~e (geh.) domicile; residence; (b) (Finanzw.) place of payment

domizilieren *tr. V.* (Finanzw.) domicile

Dompteur /dɔmp'tøːɐ̯/ *der;* ~s, ~e, Dompt**eu**se /dɔmp'tøːzə/ *die;* ~, ~n tamer

Donau /'do:nau̯/ *die;* ~: Danube

Donner /'dɔnɐ/ *der;* ~s, ~ (auch fig.) thunder; **wie vom** ~ **gerührt dastehen** *od.* **sein** be thunderstruck

donnern 1 *itr. V.* (a) (unpers.) thunder; **es hat gedonnert und geblitzt** there was thunder and lightning; (b) (fig.) ‹gun› thunder, boom [out]; ‹engine› roar; ‹hooves› thunder; ~**der Applaus** thunderous applause; (c) *mit sein* (sich laut fortbewegen) ‹train, avalanche, etc.› thunder; (d) (ugs.: schlagen) thump, hammer (**an** + *Akk.*, **gegen** on); (e) *mit sein* (ugs.: prallen) **gegen etw.** ~: smash into sth. **2** *tr. V.* (a) (ugs.: schleudern) sling (coll.); hurl

Donner·schlag *der* clap *or* peal of thunder; **die Nachricht traf uns wie ein** ~: the news completely stunned us

Donners·tag *der* ▸ 119 |, ▸ 595 | Thursday; *s. auch* **Dienstag**

donnerstags *Adv.* ▸ 595 | on Thursday[s]; *s. auch* **dienstags**

Donner·wetter *das* (ugs.) (a) (Krach) row; (b) /'--'--/ **zum** ~ **[noch einmal]!** (Ausruf der Verärgerung) damn it!; ~**!** (Ausruf der Bewunderung) my word; wow

doof /do:f/ (ugs. abwertend) **1** *Adj.* (a) (einfältig) stupid; dumb (coll.); dopey (coll.); (b) (langweilig) boring; (c) *nicht präd.* (ärgerlich) stupid. **2** *adv.* stupidly

Doofheit *die;* ~ (ugs. abwertend) stupidity; dumbness (coll.)

Doofmann *der;* ~[e]s, **Doofmänner** (ugs. abwertend) dope (coll.); dummy; [stupid] twit (Brit. coll.)

dopen /'do:pn̩/ *tr. V.* dope ‹ *horse etc.* ›; **jmdn.** ~: give sb. drugs; **gedopt sein** ‹ *athlete* › have taken drugs

Doping /'do:pɪŋ/ *das;* ~s, ~s **(a)** (bei Sportlern) taking drugs; **(b)** (von Pferden usw.) doping

Doping·kontrolle *die* (Sport) drug[s] test

Doppel /'dɔpl̩/ *das;* ~s, ~ **(a)** (Kopie) duplicate; copy; **(b)** (Sport) doubles *sing. or pl.;* **ein** ~: a game of doubles; (im Turnier) a doubles match

doppel-, Doppel-: ~**album** *das* double album *or* LP; ~**besteuerung** *die* double taxation; ~**bett** *das* double bed; ~**bock** *das* extra-strong bock beer; ~**decker** *der;* ~s, ~ **(a)** (Flugzeug) biplane; **(b)** (Omnibus) double-decker [bus]; ~**deutig** /~dɔytɪç/ **1** *Adj.* ambiguous; **2** *adv.* ambiguously; ~**deutigkeit** *die;* ~, ~**en** ambiguity; ~**fenster** *das* double-glazed window; ~**gänger** *der;* ~s, ~, ~**gängerin** *die;* ~, ~**nen** double; ~**haus** *das* pair of semi-detached houses; ~**haus·hälfte** *die* semi[-detached house]; ~**kinn** *das* double chin; ~**klick** *der;* ~s, ~s (DV) double click; ~**kopf** *der; o. Pl.* (Kartenspiel) Doppelkopf; ~**leben** *das* double life; ~**moral** *die* double standards *pl.;* ~**mord** *der* double murder; ~**name** *der* double-barrelled name (Brit.); hyphenated name; ~**pass**, ***~**paß** *der* (Fußball) one-two; ~**punkt** *der* colon; ~**rolle** *die* dual role; ~**seitig** *Adj.* (Med.) double ‹ *pleurisy, pneumonia* ›; bilateral ‹ *paralysis* ›; ~**sinnig 1** *Adj.* ambiguous; **2** *adv.* ambiguously; ~**stecker** *der* (Elektrot.) twoway plug *or* adapter; ~**stunde** *die* (Schulw.) double period

doppelt 1 *Adj.* **(a)** (zweifach) double; dual ‹ *nationality* ›; **die** ~**e Länge** double *or* twice the length; **ein** ~**er Klarer** (ugs.) a double schnapps; **ein** ~**er Boden** a false bottom; ~**e Buchführung** (Kaufmannsspr.) double-entry bookkeeping; **(b)** (besonders groß, stark) redoubled ‹ *enthusiasm, attention* ›; **mit** ~**er Kraft arbeiten** work with twice as much energy; **2** *adv.* (zweimal) twice; ~ **genäht hält besser** (Spr.) it's better to be on the safe side; better safe than sorry; **das ist** ~ **gemoppelt** (ugs.) that's just saying the same thing twice over; ~ **so viel** twice as much; **das habe ich** ~: I have two of them; ~ **sehen** see double; **(b)** (ganz besonders, noch mehr) ~ **einsam** twice as lonely; **sich** ~ **anstrengen** try twice as hard

Doppelte[1] *das; adj. Dekl.* **das** ~ **bezahlen** pay twice as much; pay double; **auf das** ~ **steigen** double

Doppelte[2] *der; adj. Dekl.* (ugs.) double

doppel-, Doppel-: ~**zentner** *der* 100 kilograms; quintal; ~**zimmer** *das* double room; ~**züngig** /-tsyŋɪç/ (abwertend) **1** *Adj.* two-faced; **2** *adv.* ~**züngig reden** be two-faced

Dorf /dɔrf/ *das;* ~[e]s, **Dörfer** /'dœrfɐ/ village; **auf dem** ~: in the country; **vom** ~ from the country; **über die Dörfer** from village to village; **das sind für mich böhmische Dörfer** (ugs.) it's all Greek to me

Dorf-: ~**bewohner** *der* villager; ~**jugend** *die* young people *pl.* of the village; village youth

dörflich *Adj.* village *attrib.* ‹ *life, traditions, etc.* ›; (ländlich) rural ‹ *character* ›

Dorn /dɔrn/ *der;* ~[e]s, ~**en** thorn; **jmdm. ein** ~ **im Auge sein** annoy sb. intensely

Dornen-: ~**krone** *die* crown of thorns; ~**strauch** *der* thorn-bush

dornig *Adj.* thorny

Dorn·röschen *(das)* the Sleeping Beauty

dorren /'dɔrən/ *itr. V.; mit sein* (geh.) dry up

dörren /'dœrən/ **1** *tr. V.* dry. **2** *itr. V.; mit sein* dry

Dörr-: ~**fleisch** *das* (südd.) ≈ streaky bacon; ~**obst** *das* dried fruit; ~**pflaume** *die* prune

Dorsch /dɔrʃ/ *der;* ~[e]s, ~**e** cod; (junger Kabeljau) codling

dort /dɔrt/ *Adv.* there; **jmdn./etw.** ~ **behalten** keep sb./ sth. there; ~ **bleiben** stay there

**alte Schreibung (vgl. Hinweise auf S. xvi–xvii)

****dort|behalten** *usw.:* ⇒ **dort**

dort-: ~**her** *Adv.* [von] ~**her** from there; ~**hin** *Adv.* there; **bis** ~**hin** as far as there; ~**hin, wo** … to where …; ~**hinab** *Adv.* down there; down that way; ~**hinauf** *Adv.* up there; up that way; ~**hinaus** *Adv.* **(a)** out there; (in diese Richtung) out that way; **(b)** /'---/ **frech bis** ~**hinaus** (ugs.) [as] cheeky as anything; ~**hinein** *Adv.* in there

dortig *Adj.; nicht präd.* there *postpos.*

Dose /'do:zə/ *die;* ~, ~**n** **(a)** (Blech~) tin; (Pillen~) box; (Zucker~) bowl; **(b)** (Konserven~) can; tin (Brit.); (Bier~) can

dösen /'dø:zn̩/ *itr. V.* (ugs.) doze

Dosen-: ~**bier** *das* canned beer; ~**milch** *die* canned *or* (Brit.) tinned milk; ~**öffner** *der* can opener; tin-opener (Brit.)

dosieren *tr. V.* **etw.** ~: measure out the required dose of sth.; **sorgfältig dosierte Mengen** carefully measured doses

Dosierung *die;* ~, ~**en** **(a)** *o. Pl.* measuring out; **(b)** ⇒ **Dosis**

dösig /'dø:zɪç/ (ugs.) **1** *Adj.* drowsy; dozy. **2** *adv.* drowsily

Dosimeter /dozi'me:tɐ/ *das;* ~s, ~ (Physik) dosimeter

Dosis /'do:zɪs/ *die;* ~, **Dosen** (auch fig.) dose; **die tägliche** ~: the daily dosage

Döskopp /'dø:skɔp/ *der;* ~s, **Dösköppe** /'dø:skœpə/ (salopp) dozy twit (Brit. coll.); dimwit

Dossier /dɔ'sie:/ *das;* ~s, ~s dossier

dotieren /do'ti:rən/ *tr. V.* **eine Position gut/mit 5 000 DM** ~: offer a good salary/a salary of 5,000 marks with a position; **eine gut dotierte Stellung** a well-paid position

Dotierung *die* ~, ~**en** *o. Pl.* (das Dotieren) **die** ~ **des Wettbewerbs/Rennens** putting up the prize money for the competition/race; **(b)** (Entgelt) remuneration; salary; (Preis, Gewinn) prize

Dotter /'dɔtɐ/ *der od. das;* ~s, ~: yolk

Double /'du:bl̩/ *das;* ~s, ~s **(a)** (Ersatzdarsteller[in]) stand-in; **(b)** (Doppelgänger) double

Dozent /do'tsɛnt/ *der;* ~en, ~en, **Dozentin** *die;* ~, ~**nen** lecturer (**für** in)

dozieren /do'tsi:rən/ *itr. V.* (auch fig.) lecture

dpa /de:pe:'|a:/ *Abk.* **Deutsche Presse-Agentur** German Press Agency

Dr. *Abk.:* ▶ 34 | **Doktor** Dr

Drache /'draxə/ *der;* ~n, ~n (Myth.) dragon

Drachen *der;* ~s, ~ **(a)** (Papier~) kite; **einen** ~ **steigen lassen** fly a kite; **(b)** (salopp: zänkische Frau) dragon

Drachen·fliegen *das;* ~s (Sport) hang-gliding

Dragee, Dragée /dra'ʒe:/ *das;* ~s, ~s dragee

Draht /dra:t/ *der;* ~[e]s, **Drähte** /'drɛ:tə/ **(a)** wire; **(b)** (Leitung) wire; cable; (Telefonleitung) line; wire; **heißer** ~: hot line; **(c) auf** ~ **sein** (ugs.) be on the ball (coll.)

Draht·bürste *die* wire brush

Draht-: ~**esel** *der* (ugs. scherzh.) bike (coll.); ~**geflecht** *das* wire mesh

drahtig *Adj.* wiry ‹ *person, hair* ›

draht-, Draht-: ~**los** (Nachrichtenw.) **1** *Adj.* wireless; **2** *adv.* **etw.** ~**los telegrafieren/übermitteln** radio sth.; ~**schere** *die* wire-cutters *pl.;* ~**seil** *das* [steel] cable; ~**seil·bahn** *die* cable railway; ~**zieher** /-tsi:ɐ/ *der* (fig.) wire puller

drakonisch /dra'ko:nɪʃ/ **1** *Adj.* Draconian. **2** *adv.* in a Draconian way

drall /dral/ *Adj.* strapping ‹ *girl* ›; full, rounded ‹ *cheeks, bottom* ›

Drall *der;* ~[e]s, ~**e** spin

Drama /'dra:ma/ *das;* ~s, **Dramen** drama; (fig. ugs.: Katastrophe) disaster

Dramatik /dra'ma:tɪk/ *die;* ~: drama

Dramatiker *der;* ~s, ~: dramatist

dramatisch 1 *Adj.* dramatic. **2** *adv.* dramatically

dramatisieren *tr. V.* dramatize

Dramaturg /drama'tʊrk/ *der;* ~en, ~en (Theater) literary and artistic director; (Rundf., Fems.) script editor

Dramaturgie /dramatʊrˈgiː/ *die;* ~, ~n (a) dramaturgy; (b) (Abteilung) (Theater) literary and artistic director's department; (Rundf., Ferns.) script department

dramaturgisch 1 *Adj.* dramaturgical. **2** *adv.* ~ **wirkungsvoll in Szene gesetzt** staged effectively

dran /dran/ *Adv.* (ugs.) (a) **das Schild bleibt** ~: the sign stays up; **häng das Schild** ~! put the sign up!; **ich komme/kann nicht** ~: I can't reach; (b) **arm** ~ **sein** be in a bad way; **gut/schlecht** ~ **sein** be well off/badly off; **früh/spät** ~ **sein** be early/late; **an dem Gerücht ist was** ~: there is something in the rumour; **ich bin** ~ *od.* (scherzh.) **am** ~**sten** (ich bin an der Reihe) it's my turn; I'm next; (ich werde zur Verantwortung gezogen) I'll be for the high jump *or* (sl.) I'll be under the gun (Amer.); **nicht wissen, wo man** ~ **ist** not know where one stands; *s. auch* **daran; dranbleiben; dranhängen** *usw.;* **glauben**

dran|bleiben *unr. itr. V.; mit sein* (ugs.) (am Telefon) hold *or* (coll.) hang on; (das Programm weiter verfolgen) stay tuned; (an der Arbeit) stick at it (coll.)

drang /draŋ/ *1. u. 3. Pers. Sg. Prät. v.* **dringen**

Drang *der;* ~[e]s, **Dränge** /ˈdrɛŋə/ urge; **ein** ~ **nach Bewegung/Freiheit** an urge to move/be free

dränge /ˈdrɛŋə/ *1. u. 3. Pers. Sg. Konjunktiv II v.* **dringen**

dran-: ~**|geben** *unr. tr. V.* give up ⟨*time*⟩; give, sacrifice ⟨*one's life*⟩; ~**|gehen** *unr. tr. V.; mit sein* (ugs.) (a) (berühren) touch; (b) (in Angriff nehmen) ~**gehen, etw. zu tun** get down to doing sth.

Drängelei *die;* ~, ~**en** (abwertend) (a) pushing [and shoving]; (b) (mit Wünschen, Bitten) pestering

drängeln /ˈdrɛŋln/ (ugs.) **1** *itr. V.* (a) push [and shove]; (b) (auf jmdn. einreden) go on (coll.); **zum Aufbruch** ~: go on about it being time to leave (coll.). **2** *tr. V.* (a) push; shove; (b) (einreden auf) pester; go on at (coll.). **3** *refl. V.* **sich nach vorn** ~: push one's way to the front

drängen /ˈdrɛŋən/ **1** *itr. V.* (a) (schieben) push; **die Menge drängte zum Ausgang** the crowd pressed towards the exit; (b) **auf etw.** (*Akk.*) ~: press for sth.; **zum Aufbruch** ~: insist that it is/was time to leave; **zur Eile** ~: hurry us/them *etc.* up; **die Zeit drängt** time is pressing. **2** *tr. V.* (a) push; (b) (antreiben) press; urge. **3** *refl. V.* ⟨*visitors, spectators, etc.*⟩ crowd, throng; ⟨*crowd*⟩ throng; **sich nach vorn** ~: push one's way to the front; **sich in den Vordergrund** ~ (fig.) make oneself the centre of attention

Drangsal /ˈdraŋzaːl/ *die;* ~, ~**e** (geh.) (Not) hardship; (Qual) suffering

drangsalieren *tr. V.* (abwertend) (quälen) torment; (plagen) plague

dran-: ~**|halten** *unr. refl. V.* (ugs.) get a move on (coll.); ~**|hängen** (ugs.) **1** *tr. V.* (a) (aufwenden) invest; **viel Zeit/Geld** ~**hängen** put a lot of time/money into it; (b) (anschließen) add ⟨**an** + *Akk.* to⟩. **2** *refl. V.* (verfolgen) stay *or* (coll.) stick close behind; ~**|kommen** *unr. itr. V.; mit sein* (ugs.) have one's turn; **ich kam als Erste/Erster** ~: it was my turn first; (beim Arzt, Zahnarzt usw.) I was the first one; **wer kommt jetzt** ~? who's next?; **ich bin heute in Latein** ~**gekommen** (aufgerufen worden) I got picked on to answer in Latin today (coll.); ~**|kriegen** *tr. V.* (ugs.) **jmdn.** ~**kriegen** get sb.; (zum Handeln bringen) get sb. at it (coll.); ~**|machen** *refl. V.* (ugs.) **sich** ~**machen, etw. zu tun** get down to doing sth.; **wenn sich die Kinder** ~**machen, ist der Kuchen gleich weg** once the children get started on it the cake won't last long; ~**|nehmen** *unr. tr. V.* (ugs.) (beim Friseur usw.) see to; (beim Arzt) see; (in der Schule) pick on; ~**|setzen** (ugs.) **1** *tr. V.* (einsetzen) **seine ganze Kraft** ~**setzen, etw. zu erreichen** put all one's energy into achieving sth.; **2** *refl. V.* (beginnen) get down to it

drastisch 1 *Adj.* (a) (grob) crudely explicit ⟨*joke, story, etc.*⟩; graphic ⟨*report, account*⟩; (b) (empfindlich spürbar) drastic ⟨*measure, means*⟩. **2** *adv.* (a) (grob) with crude explicitness; (deutlich) graphically; (b) (einschneidend) drastically

drauf /drauf/ *Adv.* (ugs.) on it; **den Deckel** ~ **machen** put the lid on; **die dollsten Sprüche** ~ **haben** (fig.) have the most amazing patter; **90 Sachen** ~ **haben** (fig.) be doing 90; ~ **und dran sein, etw. zu tun** be just about to do *or* be on the verge of doing sth.

drauf-, Drauf-: ~**|bekommen** *unr. tr. V.* (ugs.) *in* **eins** ~**bekommen** (gescholten werden) get it in the neck (coll.); (geschlagen werden) get a smack; ~**gänger** *der* daredevil; ~**gängerisch** *Adj.* daring; audacious; ~**|geben** *unr. tr. V.* (ugs.) (a) (dazugeben) add; (b) jmdm. **eins** ~**geben** (schlagen) give sb. a smack; (zurechtweisen) put sb. in his/her place; ~**|gehen** *unr. itr. V.; mit sein* (ugs.) (a) (umkommen) kick the bucket (fig. sl.); (b) (verbraucht werden) go; **für etw.** ~**gehen** ⟨*money*⟩ go on sth.; (c) (entzweigehen) get busted (coll.) *or* broken; ~**|legen** (ugs.) **1** *tr. V.* **150 DM/noch etwas** ~**legen** fork out (coll.) an extra 150 marks/a bit more; **2** *itr. V.* lay out (sl.); **ich lege dabei noch** ~: it's costing me money

drauf·los *Adv.* nichts wie ~! go on!

drauflos-: ~**|arbeiten** *itr. V.* work away; (anfangen zu arbeiten) get straight down to work; ~**|gehen** *unr. itr. V.; mit sein* (ugs.) get going; ~**|reden** *itr. V.* talk away; (anfangen zu reden) start talking away

drauf-: ~**|machen** *in* **einen** ~**machen** (ugs.) paint the town red (fig. coll.); ~**|stehen** *unr. itr. V.* (ugs.) be on it; ~**|zahlen** (ugs.) **1** *tr. V.* **noch etwas/1 250 DM** ~**zahlen** fork out (coll.) *or* pay a bit more/an extra 1,250 marks; **2** *itr. V.* (Unkosten haben) **ich zahle dabei noch** ~: it's costing me money

draus /draus/ *Adv.* (ugs.) ⇒ **daraus**

draußen /ˈdrausn̩/ *Adv.* outside; **hier/da** ~: out here/there; ~ **vor der Tür** at the door; **nach/von** ~: outside/from outside; ~ **in der Welt** (fig.) in the world outside

drechseln /ˈdrɛksln̩/ *tr. V.* turn

Dreck /drɛk/ *der;* ~[e]s (ugs.) dirt; (sehr viel/ekelerregend) filth; (Schlamm) mud; **vor** ~ **starren** be covered in dirt; be filthy [dirty]; ~ **machen** make a mess; (b) (salopp abwertend: Angelegenheit) **bei/wegen jedem** ~ **regt er sich auf** he gets worked up about every piddling little thing (coll.); **mach deinen** ~ **allein** do it yourself; **kümmere dich um deinen eigenen** ~: mind your own damn business; **das geht dich einen** ~ **an** (salopp) none of your damned business (sl.); **jmdn. wie [den letzten]** ~ **behandeln** (ugs.) treat sb. like dirt; (c) (salopp: Zeug) rubbish *no indef. art.;* junk *no indef. art.*

Dreck-: ~**arbeit** *die* (salopp) (a) dirty *or* messy work *no indef. art., no pl./*job; (b) (fig.) dirty *or* menial work *no indef. art., no pl./*job; ~**fink** *der* (ugs.) ⇒ **Schmutzfink**

dreckig *Adj.* (a) (ugs.: schmutzig, ungepflegt, auch fig.) dirty; (sehr/ekelerregend schmutzig, auch fig.) filthy; **mach dich nicht** ~: don't get yourself dirty; (b) (salopp abwertend: unverschämt) cheeky; (c) (salopp abwertend: gemein) dirty, filthy ⟨*swine etc.*⟩. **2** *adv.* (a) **es geht ihm** ~ (ugs.) he's in a bad way; (b) (salopp abwertend: unverschämt) cheekily; ~ **grinsen** have a cheeky grin on one's face

Dreck-: ~**loch** *das* (salopp abwertend) dump (coll.); ~**sack** *der* (derb) bastard (sl.); ~**sau** *die* (derb) dirty *or* filthy swine; ~**schleuder** *die* (a) (derb abwertend) (Mundwerk) foul mouth; (Mensch) foul-mouth; (b) (ugs. abwertend: Quelle schädlicher Emissionen) factory/power station pumping out clouds of pollutants; (Fahrzeug) car/lorry *etc.* belching clouds of exhaust fumes; ~**schwein** *das* ⇒ ~**sau**

Drecks·kerl *der* (derb abwertend) dirty *or* filthy swine

Dreck·spatz *der* (fam.: Kind) grubby little so-and-so (coll.); (Kind, das etw. schmutzig macht) mucky pup (Brit. coll.)

Dreh /dreː/ *der;* ~s, ~s (ugs.) (a) **den** ~ **heraushaben** have [got] the knack; (b) [so] **um den** ~ (so ungefähr) about that

Dreh-: ~**arbeiten** *Pl.* (Film) shooting *sing.;* ~**bank** *die* lathe

drehbar 1 *Adj.* revolving *attrib.* ⟨*stand, stage*⟩; swivel *attrib.* ⟨*chair*⟩; ~ **sein** revolve/swivel. **2** *adv.* ~ **gelagert** pivoted

Dreh-: ~**bewegung** *die* rotary motion; rotation; ~**bleistift** *der* propelling pencil (Brit.); mechanical pencil (Amer.); ~**buch** *das* screenplay; [film] script

drehen 1 *tr. V.* (a) turn; (b) (ugs.: einstellen) **das Radio laut/leise** ~: turn the radio up/down; **die Flamme klein/die Heizung auf klein** ~: turn the heat/heating down; (c) (formen) twist ⟨*rope, thread*⟩; roll ⟨*cigarette*⟩; (d) (Film) shoot; film ⟨*report*⟩; (e) (ugs. abwertend: beeinflussen) **es so** ~, **dass** ...: work it so that ... (coll.). **2** *itr. V.* (a) ⟨*car,* *driver*⟩ turn; ⟨*wind*⟩ change, shift; **(b) an etw.** (*Dat.*) ~: turn sth.; **da muss einer dran gedreht haben** (salopp) somebody must have fiddled about *or* messed around with it; **(c)** (Film) shoot [a/the film]; film. **3** *refl. V.* **(a)** turn; ⟨*wind*⟩ change, shift; (um eine Achse) turn; rotate; revolve; (um einen Mittelpunkt) revolve (**um** around); (sehr schnell) spin; **mir dreht sich alles** (ugs.) everything's going round and round; **sich auf den Bauch** ~: turn over on to one's stomach; **(b) sich um etw.** ~ (fig. ugs.) be about sth.

Dreher *der;* ~s, ~ ▶ 85 | lathe-operator

Dreh-: ~**orgel** *die* barrel organ; ~**punkt** *der* pivot; **der** ~- **und Angelpunkt einer Sache** (fig.) the key element in sth.; ~**scheibe** *die* (fig.) hub; ~**stuhl** *der* swivel chair; ~**tür** *die* revolving door

Drehung *die;* ~, ~**en** **(a)** (um eine Achse) turn; rotation; revolution; (um einen Mittelpunkt) revolution; (sehr schnell) spin; **eine halbe/ganze** ~: a half/complete turn; **eine** ~ **um 180°** [**machen**] [do] a 180° turn; (fig.) [do] a complete about-face; **(b)** (das Drehen) turning; (sehr schnell) spinning

Dreh-: ~**wurm** *der in* **einen** *od.* **den** ~**wurm kriegen/haben** (salopp) get/feel giddy; ~**zahl** *die* number of revolutions *or* (coll.) revs [per minute]; ~**zahl·messer** *der* revolution counter; rev counter (coll.); tachometer

drei *Kardinalz.* ▶ 22 |, ▶ 530 |, ▶ 600 | three; **aller guten Dinge sind** ~! all good things come in threes; (nach zwei missglückten Versuchen) third time lucky!; **nicht bis** ~ **zählen können** (ugs.) be as thick as two [short] planks (Brit. coll.); be dead from the neck up (coll.); *s. auch* **acht¹**

Drei *die;* ~, ~**en** three; **eine** ~ **schreiben/bekommen** (Schulw.) get a C; *s. auch* **Acht¹** a, b, d, e; **Zwei** b

drei-, Drei-: ~**achtel·takt** *der* (Musik) three-eight time; ~**akter** *der* three-act play; ~**dimensional 1** *Adj.* three-dimensional; **2** *adv.* three-dimensionally; in three dimensions; ~**eck** *das;* ~s, ~e triangle; ~**eckig** *Adj.* triangular; three-cornered; ~**ecks·verhältnis** *das* eternal triangle; ~**ein·halb** *Bruchz.* ▶ 600 | three and a half; ~**einigkeit** *die* (christl. Rel.) trinity

Dreier *der;* ~s, ~ **(a)** (ugs.) ⇨ **Drei; (b)** (ugs.: im Lotto) three winning numbers; **(c)** (ugs.: Sprungbrett) three-metre board

dreierlei *Gattungsz.; indekl.* **(a)** *attr.* three kinds *or* sorts of; three different ⟨*sorts, kinds, sizes, possibilities*⟩; **(b)** *subst.* three [different] things

drei-, Drei-: ~**fach** *Vervielfältigungsz.* triple; **die** ~**fache Menge** three times *or* triple the amount; three times as much; *s. auch* **achtfach;** ~**fache** *das; adj. Dekl.* **das** ~**fache von 3 ist 9** three times three is nine; **auf ein** ~**faches** *od.* **auf das** ~**fache steigen** treble; triple; ~**gang·schaltung** *die* three-speed gearbox *or* gears *pl. or* (Amer.) gear shift; ~**hundert** *Kardinalz.* ▶ 600 | three hundred; ~**jährig** *Adj.* (3 Jahre alt) three-year-old *attrib.;* (3 Jahre dauernd) three-year *attrib.;* ~**kampf** *der* (Sport) triathlon; ~**käse·hoch** /-'--/ *der;* ~s, ~s (ugs. scherzh.) [little] nipper (Brit. sl.); little kid (coll.); ~**klang** *der* triad; ~**könige** ~ *das;* ~ Epiphany *sing.;* ~**köpfig** *Adj.* ⟨*family, crew*⟩ of three; ~**ländereck** /-'--/ *das;* ~s, ~e region where three countries meet; ~**mal** *Adv.* three times; ~**malig** *Adj.; nicht präd.* **eine** ~**malige Warnung** three warnings; ~**meilenzone** /-'---/ *die* three-mile zone; ~**meter·brett** /-'--/ *das* three-metre board

drein (ugs.) ⇨ **darein**

drein-: ~|**blicken,** ~|**schauen** *itr. V.* look

drei-, Drei-: ~**rad** *das* tricycle; ~**räd[e]rig** *Adj.* three-wheeled; ~**satz** *der* (Math.) rule of three; ~**seitig** *Adj.* three-sided ⟨*figure*⟩; three-page ⟨*letter, leaflet, etc.*⟩; ~**silbig** *Adj.* trisyllabic; three-syllable *attrib.;* ~**spaltig** *Adj.* (Druckw.) three-column *attrib.;* ~**sprachig** *Adj.* trilingual; ~**sprung** *der* triple jump

dreißig /'draɪsɪç/ *Kardinalz.* ▶ 22 |, ▶ 600 | thirty

dreißiger *indekl. Adj.; nicht präd.* **die** ~ **Jahre** the thirties

Dreißiger¹ *der;* ~s, ~ (30jähriger) thirty-year-old

Dreißiger² *die;* ~, ~ (ugs.) (Briefmarke) thirty-pfennig/schilling *etc.* stamp

Dreißiger·jahre *Pl.* ▶ 22 |, ▶ 119 | thirties *pl.*

dreißigjährig *Adj.* (30 Jahre alt) thirty-year-old *attrib.;* (30 Jahre dauernd) thirty-year *attrib.*

dreißigst... /'draɪsɪçst.../ *Ordinalz.* ▶ 119 |, ▶ 600 | thirtieth

Dreißigstel *das;* ~s, ~: ▶ 600 | thirtieth

dreist /draɪst/ **1** *Adj.* brazen; barefaced ⟨*lie*⟩. **2** *adv.* brazenly

drei·stellig *Adj.* three-figure *attrib.* ⟨*number, sum*⟩

Dreistigkeit *die;* ~, ~**en** **(a)** *o. Pl.* (Art) brazenness; **(b)** (Handlung) brazen act; (Bemerkung) brazen remark

drei-, Drei-: ~**stimmig 1** *Adj.* ⟨*song*⟩ for three voices; three-voice ⟨*choir*⟩; three-part ⟨*singing*⟩; **2** *adv.* ⟨*sing*⟩ in three voices; ⟨*play*⟩ in three parts; ~**stöckig 1** *Adj.* three-storey *attrib.;* **2** *adv.* ⟨*build*⟩ three storeys high; ~**stündig** *Adj.* three-hour *attrib.; s. auch* **achtstündig;** ~**tägig** *Adj.* (3 Tage alt) three-day-old *attrib.;* (3 Tage dauernd) three-day *attrib.; s. auch* **achttägig;** ~**tausend** *Kardinalz.* ▶ 600 | three thousand; ~**tausender** *der* mountain more than three thousand metres high; ~**teilig** *Adj.* three-part *attrib.* ⟨*documentary, novel, etc.*⟩; three-piece *attrib.* ⟨*suit*⟩;*~**viertel** ⇨ **viertel; (b)** ~**viertel·liter·flasche** /--'---/ *die* three-quarter-litre bottle; ~**viertel·mehrheit** /-'---/ *die* three-quarters majority; ~**viertel·stunde** /--'---/ *die* three-quarters of an hour; ~**viertel·takt** /-'---/ *der* three-four time; ~**wege·katalysator** *der* (Kfz-W.) three-way catalytic converter; ~**wertig** *Adj.* (Chemie) trivalent; ~**zehn** *Kardinalz.* ▶ 22 |, ▶ 530 |, ▶ 600 | thirteen; **jetzt schlägt's aber** ~**zehn!** (ugs.) that's going too far; *s. auch* **achtzehn**

Dresche /'drɛʃə/ *die;* ~ (salopp) walloping (sl.); thrashing

dreschen 1 *unr. tr. V.* **(a)** thresh; **(b)** (salopp: prügeln) wallop (sl.); thrash; **(c)** (salopp: schießen) wallop (sl.) ⟨*ball*⟩. **2** *unr. itr. V.* **(a)** thresh; **(b)** (salopp: schlagen) thump; bang

Dresch-: ~**flegel** *der* flail; ~**maschine** *die* threshing-machine

Dress, *Dreß /drɛs/ *der;* **Dresses, Dresse;** (österr. auch *die;* ~, **Dressen**) (Sportkleidung) kit (Brit.)

dressieren *tr. V.* train ⟨*animal*⟩

Dressman /'drɛsmən/ *der;* ~s, **Dressmen** male model

Dressur /drɛ'suːɐ/ *die;* ~, ~**en** **(a)** training; **(b)** (Kunststück) trick; **(c)** (Dressurreiten) dressage

Dressur·pferd *das* dressage horse

dribbeln /'drɪblṇ/ *itr. V.* (Ballspiele) dribble [the ball]

Dribbling /'drɪblɪŋ/ *das;* ~s, ~s (Ballspiele) piece of dribbling

Drill /drɪl/ *der;* ~[e]s drilling; (Milit.) drill

drillen *tr. V.* (auch Milit.) drill

Drillich /'drɪlɪç/ *der;* ~s, ~e drill

Drilling /'drɪlɪŋ/ *der;* ~s, ~e triplet

drin /drɪn/ *Adv.* **(a)** (ugs.: darin) in it; **mehr als 2 000 DM ist nicht** ~: any more than 2,000 marks is not on (Brit. coll.) *or* (Amer. coll.) is no go; **es ist noch alles** ~ (bei einem Fußballspiel usw.) there's still everything to play for; **nach drei Tagen ist man wieder** ~ (wieder eingearbeitet) after three days you're back in the swing of things; **(b)** (ugs.: drinnen) inside; **hier/da** ~: in here/there

dringen /'drɪŋən/ *unr. itr. V.* **(a)** *mit sein* (gelangen) ⟨*water, smell, etc.*⟩ penetrate, come through; ⟨*news*⟩ get through; **in etw.** (*Akk.*) ~: get into *or* penetrate sth.; **durch etw.** ~: come through *or* penetrate sth.; ⟨*person*⟩ push one's way through sth.; **(b)** *mit sein* **in jmdn.** ~ (geh.) press *or* urge sb.; **(c) auf etw.** (*Akk.*) ~: insist upon sth.

dringend 1 *Adj.* **(a)** (eilig) urgent; **(b)** (eindringlich, stark) urgent ⟨*appeal*⟩; strong ⟨*suspicion, advice*⟩; compelling ⟨*need*⟩. **2** *adv.* **(a)** (sofort) urgently; **(b)** (zwingend) ⟨*recommend, advise, suspect*⟩ strongly; ~ **erforderlich sein** be imperative *or* essenzial

dringlich /'drɪŋlɪç/ **1** *Adj.* urgent. **2** *adv.* urgently; **jmdn.** ~ **bitten, etw. zu tun** plead hard with sb. to do sth.

Dringlichkeit *die;* ~: urgency

Drink /drɪŋk/ *der;* ~s, ~s drink

drinnen /'drɪnən/ *Adv.* inside; (im Haus) indoors; inside; **nach** ~ **gehen** go in[side]/indoors; **hier/da** ~: in here/there

---

*alte Schreibung (vgl. Hinweise auf S. xvi–xvii)

drin-: ~|**sitzen** *unr. itr. V.* (ugs.) be right in it (coll.); ~|**stecken** *itr. V.* (ugs.) (a) [bis über beide Ohren] in etw. (*Dat.*) ~**stecken** be up to one's ears in sth. (coll.); (b) **ich bin überzeugt, dass viel in ihm ~steckt** I am convinced he has a lot in him; **da steckt viel Arbeit ~:** there's a lot of work in that; (**c**) **da steckt man nicht ~** (das kann man nicht wissen) there's no [way of] telling

dritt /drɪt/ **wir waren zu ~:** there were three of us; *s. auch* **acht²**

dritt... *Ordinalz.* ▶ 119 |, ▶ 600 | third; **in Gegenwart Dritter** in the presence of other people; **der lachende Dritte** the one to benefit (*from a dispute between two others*); *s. auch* **acht...**

dritt·best... *Adj.* third-best

Drittel *das,* (*schweiz. meist der*); ~**s,** ~**:** ▶ 600 | third

dritteln *tr. V.* split *or* divide ⟨*cost, profit*⟩ three ways; divide ⟨*number*⟩ by three

drittens *Adv.* thirdly

Dritt·klässler *der;* ~**s** ~**:** third-former

Drive /draif/ *der;* ~**s,** ~**s** (auch Jazz, Golf, Tennis) drive

Dr. jur. *Abk.* doctor juris LL D

DRK /de:|ɛr'ka:/ *das;* ~ *Abk.* **Deutsches Rotes Kreuz** German Red Cross

Dr. med. *Abk.* doctor medicinae MD

droben /'dro:bn̩/ *Adv.* (südd., österr., sonst geh.) up there

Droge /'dro:gə/ *die;* ~, ~**n** drug; **unter** ~**n stehen** be on drugs

drogen-, Drogen-: ~**abhängig** *Adj.* addicted to drugs *postpos.;* ~**abhängige** *der/die; adj. Dekl.* drug addict; ~**süchtig** *Adj.* ⇨ ~**abhängig;** ~**szene** *die* drug scene

Drogerie /drogə'ri:/ *die;* ~, ~**n** chemist's [shop] (Brit.); drugstore (Amer.)

Drogist *der;* ~**en,** ~**en, Drogistin** *die;* ~, ~**nen** ▶ 85 | chemist (Brit.); druggist (Amer.)

Droh·brief *der* threatening letter

drohen /'dro:ən/ **1** *itr. V.* (a) threaten; **er drohte mit [seiner] Kündigung** he threatened to give notice; **er drohte ihm mit erhobenem Zeigefinger** he raised a warning finger to him; (**b**) (bevorstehen) be threatening; **jmdm. droht etw.** sb. is threatened with sth. **2** *mod. V.* **etw. zu tun ~:** threaten to do sth.

drohend *Adj.* (a) threatening; (**b**) (bevorstehend) impending ⟨*danger, strike, disaster*⟩

Drohne *die;* ~, ~**n** drone

dröhnen /'drø:nən/ *itr. V.* (a) ⟨*voice, music*⟩ boom; ⟨*machine*⟩ roar; ⟨*room etc.*⟩ resound (**von** with); ~**er Applaus** thunderous applause

Drohung *die;* ~, ~**en** threat; **eine ~ wahr machen** carry out a threat

drollig /'drɔlɪç/ **1** *Adj.* (a) (spaßig) funny; comical; (niedlich) sweet; cute (Amer.); (**b**) (seltsam) odd; peculiar. **2** *adv.* (a) (spaßig) comically; (niedlich) sweetly; cutely (Amer.); (**b**) (seltsam) oddly; peculiarly

Dromedar /'dro:meda:ɐ̯/ *das;* ~**s,** ~**e** dromedary

Drops /drɔps/ *der od. das;* ~, ~**:** fruit *or* (Brit.) acid drop; **saurer** *od.* **saures ~:** acid drop (Brit.); sour ball (Amer.)

drosch /drɔʃ/ *1. u. 3. Pers. Sg. Prät. v.* **dreschen**

Droschke /'drɔʃkə/ *die;* ~, ~**n** (a) hackney carriage; (**b**) (veralt.: Taxi) [taxi-]cab

Drossel /'drɔsl̩/ *die;* ~, ~**n** thrush

drosseln *tr. V.* (a) turn down ⟨*heating, air-conditioning*⟩; throttle back ⟨*engine*⟩; reduce *or* restrict the flow of ⟨*steam, air*⟩; check ⟨*flow*⟩; (**b**) (herabsetzen) reduce; cut back *or* down

Dr. phil. *Abk.* doctor philosophiae Dr; ~ ~ **Hans Schulz** Dr Hans Schulz; Hans Schulz, Ph. D.

drüben /'dry:bn̩/ *Adv.* (a) dort **u. da ~:** over there; ~ **auf der anderen Seite** over on the other side; **von ~ kommen** come from across the border/sea *etc.;* (**b**) (veralt.) (in der DDR) in the East; (in der BRD, in West-Berlin) in the West

drüber /'dry:bɐ/ (ugs.) ⇨ **darüber**

drüber- (ugs.) ⇨ **darüber-**

Druck¹ /drʊk/ *der;* ~**[e]s, Drücke** /'drʏkə/ (a) (Physik) pressure; **einen ~ im Kopf haben** (fig.) have a feeling of pressure in one's head; (**b**) *o. Pl.* (das Drücken) **ein ~ auf den Knopf** a touch of *or* on the button; (**c**) *o. Pl.* (Zwang) pressure; **auf jmdn.** ~ **ausüben** put pressure on sb.; **unter ~ stehen** be under pressure; **jmdn. unter ~ setzen** put pressure on sb.; ~ **dahinter machen** (ugs.) put some pressure on

Druck² *der;* ~**[e]s,** ~**e** (a) *o. Pl.* (das Drucken) printing; (Art des Drucks) print; **in ~ gehen** go to press; **im ~ sein** be being printed; (**b**) (Bild, Grafik usw.) print

Druck-: ~**abfall** *der* (Physik) drop *or* fall in pressure; ~**buchstabe** *der* printed letter

Drückeberger /'drʏkəbɛrgɐ/ *der;* ~**s,** ~ (ugs.) shirker

druck·empfindlich *Adj.* pressure-sensitive ⟨*material*⟩; easily bruised ⟨*fruit*⟩

drucken *tr., itr. V.* print

drücken /'drʏkn̩/ **1** *tr. V.* (a) press; press, push ⟨*button*⟩; squeeze ⟨*juice, pus*⟩ (aus out of); **jmdm. die Hand ~:** squeeze sb.'s hand; **jmdn. an die Wand ~:** push sb. against the wall; **jmdn. ans Herz** *od.* **an sich** (*Akk.*) ~: clasp sb. to one's breast; **jmdm. etw. in die Hand ~:** press sth. into sb.'s hand; (**b**) (liebkosen) **jmdn.** ~**:** hug [and squeeze] sb.; (**c**) (Druck verursachen, quetschen) ⟨*shoe, corset, bandage, etc.*⟩ pinch; (**d**) (geh.: be~) ⟨*consience*⟩ weigh heavily [up]on sb.; (**e**) (herabsetzen) push *or* force down ⟨*price, rate*⟩; depress ⟨*sales*⟩; bring down ⟨*standard*⟩; (**f**) (Gewichtheben) press. **2** *itr. V.* (a) press; **auf den Knopf ~:** press *or* push the button; „**[bitte]** ~**":** 'push'; **das drückte auf die Stimmung/unsere gute Laune** (fig.) it spoilt the atmosphere/dampened our spirits; (**b**) (Druck verursachen) ⟨*shoe, corset, bandage*⟩ pinch; **mein Rucksack drückt** my rucksack is pressing *or* digging into me; (**c**) **auf etw.** (*Akk.*) ~ (fig.: etw. sinken lassen) push *or* force sth. down. **3** *refl. V.* (a) **sich in die Ecke ~:** squeeze [oneself] into the corner; (**b**) (ugs.) shirk; **sich vor etw.** (*Dat.*) ~**:** get out of *or* dodge sth.

drückend *Adj.* (a) burdensome ⟨*responsibility*⟩; grinding ⟨*poverty*⟩; heavy ⟨*debt, taxes*⟩; serious ⟨*worries*⟩; (**b**) (schwül) oppressive

Drucker *der;* ~**s,** ~**:** ▶ 85 | printer

Drücker *der;* ~**s,** ~ (a) (Tür~) handle; **auf den letzten** ~ (ugs.) at the very last minute; (**b**) (Knopf) [push-]button; **am ~ sitzen** *od.* **sein** (fig. ugs.) be in charge

Druckerei *die;* ~, ~**en** printing-works; (Firma) printing house; printer's

Drucker·schwärze *die* printing *or* printer's ink

druck-, Druck-: ~**farbe** *die* printer's *or* printing ink; ~**fehler** *der* misprint; printer's error; ~**fest** *Adj.* pressure-resistant; ~**knopf** *der* (a) press stud (Brit.); snap-fastener; (**b**) (an Geräten) push-button; ~**luft** *die* (Physik) compressed air; ~**maschine** *die* printing press; ~**mittel** *das* means of bringing pressure to bear (**gegenüber** on); ~**reif** **1** *Adj.* ready for publication; (fig.) polished, perfectly formulated ⟨*phrase, reply*⟩; **2** *adv.* ⟨*speak*⟩ in a polished manner; ~**sache** *die* (a) (Postw.) printed matter; (**b**) (Druckw.) printed stationery; ~**schrift** *die* (a) printed writing; (**b**) (Schriftart) type-[-face]; (**c**) (Schriftwerk) pamphlet

drucksen /'drʊksn̩/ *itr. V.* (ugs.) hum and haw (coll.)

druck-, Druck-: ~**stelle** *die* mark (*where pressure has been applied*); (an Obst) bruise; ~**taste** *die* push-button; ~**verband** *der* pressure bandage; ~**verfahren** *das* printing process; ~**welle** *die* (Physik) shock wave

Druckwasser·reaktor *der* pressurized-water reactor

drum /drʊm/ *Adv.* (ugs.) (a) ⇨ **darum;** (**b**) [a]round; **um etw.** ~ **herum** [all] [a]round sth.; ~ **rumreden** beat about *or* (Amer.) around the bush; **seis** ~**:** never mind; [that's] too bad; **alles** *od.* **das [ganze] Drum und Dran** (bei einer Mahlzeit) all the trimmings; (bei einer Feierlichkeit) all the palaver that goes with it (coll.)

Drum·herum *das;* ~**s** everything that goes/went with it

Drummer /'dramɐ/ *der;* ~**s,** ~ (Musik) drummer

drunter /'drʊntɐ/ *Adv.* (ugs.) underneath; **es** *od.* **alles geht ~ und drüber** everything is topsy-turvy; things are completely chaotic

Drüse /'dry:zə/ *die;* ~, ~n gland
Dschungel /'dʒʊŋl/ *der;* ~s, ~ (auch fig.) jungle
Dschungel·krieg *der* jungle war; (Kriegsführung) jungle warfare
dt. *Abk.* **deutsch** G.
Dtzd. *Abk.* **Dutzend** doz.
du /du:/ *Personalpron.;* 2. *Pers. Sg. Nom.* you; thou (arch.); **mit jmdm. auf du und du stehen** be on familiar terms with sb.; **du bist es** it's 'you; **mach du das doch** 'you do it; *s. auch* (*Gen.*) **deiner,** (*Dat.*) **dir,** (*Akk.*) **dich**
Du *das;* ~[s], ~[s] 'du' *no art.;* the familiar form 'du'; **jmdm. das** ~ **anbieten** suggest to sb. that he/she use [the familiar form] 'du' *or* the familiar form of address
Dübel /'dy:bl/ *der;* ~s, ~: plug
dübeln *tr. V.* etw. ~: fix sth. using a plug/plugs
dubios /du'bi̯o:s/ *Adj.* (geh.) dubious
Dublette /du'blɛtə/ *die;* ~, ~n duplicate
ducken /'dʊkn̩/ **1** *refl. V.* duck; (vor Angst) cower. **2** *tr. V.* (abwertend) (einschüchtern) intimidate; (demütigen) humiliate. **3** *itr. V.* humble oneself
Duckmäuser /'dʊkmɔyzɐ/ *der;* ~s, ~ (abwertend) moral coward
Dudel·kasten *der* (salopp abwertend) (Radio) radio; (Plattenspieler) record player
dudeln /'du:dl̩n/ **1** *tr. V.* (auf Blasinstrument) tootle; (singen) sing tunelessly. **2** *itr. V.* ‹*radio, television, etc.*› drone on; ‹*barrel organ*› grind away
Dudel·sack *der* bagpipes *pl.*
Duell /du'ɛl/ *das;* ~s, ~e (a) duel; (b) (Sport) contest
duellieren *refl. V.* fight a duel
Duett /du'ɛt/ *das;* ~[e]s, ~e (Musik) duet; **im** ~ **singen** sing a duet
Dufflecoat /'dʌfəlkoʊt/ *der;* ~s, ~s duffle-coat
Duft /dʊft/ *der;* ~[e]s, **Düfte** /'dyftə/ pleasant smell; scent; (Zool.) scent; (von Parfüm, Blumen) scent; fragrance; (von Kaffee, frischem Brot, Tabak) aroma; (iron.) beautiful smell (iron.); **den** ~ **der großen, weiten Welt schnuppern** (fig.) get a taste of the big, wide world
dufte /'dʊftə/ (ugs.) **1** *Adj.* great (coll.). **2** *adv.* ‹*dressed, behave*› smashingly (coll.); ‹*taste*› great (coll.)
duften /'dʊftn̩/ *itr. V.* smell (**nach** of); **die Rosen** ~ **gut** the roses smell lovely *or* have a lovely scent
duftend *Adj.* sweet-smelling; fragrant
Duft-: ~**stoff** *der* (a) aromatic substance; (b) (Biol.) scent; ~**wasser** *das; Pl.* ~**wässer** (scherzh.: Parfüm) perfume; scent; ~**wolke** *die* cloud of perfume
dulden /'dʊldn̩/ **1** *tr. V.* (a) tolerate; put up with; **die Arbeit duldet keinen Aufschub** the work will admit no delay; (b) (Aufenthalt gestatten) **jmdn.** ~: tolerate *or* put up with sb.'s presence. **2** *itr. V.* (geh.) suffer
duldsam /'dʊldza:m/ **1** *Adj.* tolerant (**gegen** towards). **2** *adv.* tolerantly
Duldsamkeit *die;* ~: tolerance
Duldung *die;* ~: toleration
dumm /dʊm/, **dümmer** /'dymɐ/, **dümmst**... /'dymst.../ **1** *Adj.* (a) stupid; stupid, thick, dense ‹*person*›; **sich** ~ **stellen** act stupid; **sich nicht für** ~ **verkaufen lassen** (ugs.) not be taken in; **sich** ~ **und dämlich** *od.* **dusselig reden/verdienen** (ugs.) talk till one is blue in the face/ earn a fortune; (b) (unvernünftig) foolish; stupid; daft; **so etwas Dummes!** how stupid!; (c) (ugs.: töricht, albern) idiotic; silly; stupid; **das ist mir [einfach] zu** ~ (ugs.) I've had enough of it; (d) (ugs.: unangenehm) nasty ‹*feeling, suspicion*›; annoying ‹*habit*›; awful (coll.) ‹*coincidence*›; **so etwas Dummes!** how annoying! **2** *adv.* (a) (ugs.: töricht) foolishly; stupidly; **frag nicht so** ~: don't ask such silly *or* stupid questions; (b) (ugs.: unangenehm) ‹*end*› badly *or* unpleasantly; **jmdm.** ~ **kommen** be cheeky *or* insolent to sb.
Dumme *der/die; adj. Dekl.* fool; **einen** ~**n finden, der etw. macht** find somebody stupid enough to do sth.; **der** ~ **sein** (ugs.) be the loser

---

Dumme·jungen·streich *der* (ugs.) silly prank
dummer·weise *Adv.* (a) (leider) unfortunately; (ärgerlicherweise) annoyingly; irritatingly; (b) (törichterweise) foolishly; like a fool; stupidly
Dummheit *die;* ~, ~**en** (a) *o. Pl.* stupidity; (b) (unkluge Handlung) stupid *or* foolish thing; [**mach**] **keine** ~**en!** don't do anything stupid *or* foolish; **lauter** *od.* **nur** ~**en im Kopf haben** have a head full of silly ideas
Dumm·kopf *der* (ugs.) [silly] fool *or* idiot
dümmlich /'dymlɪç/ **1** *Adj.* simple-minded. **2** *adv.* ‹*grin, smile*› [rather] foolishly *or* stupidly
dumpf /dʊmpf/ **1** *Adj.* (a) dull ‹*thud, rumble of thunder*›; muffled ‹*sound, thump*›; (b) (muffig) musty; (c) (stumpfsinnig) dull; numb ‹*indifference*›; (d) (undeutlich) dull ‹*pain, anger*›. **2** *adv.* (a) ‹*echo*› hollowly; ~ **auf etw.** (*Akk.*) **aufschlagen** land with a dull thud on sth.; (b) (stumpfsinnig) apathetically; numbly
Dumpfheit *die;* ~ (Stumpfsinn) torpor; apathy
Dumping·preis *der* dumping price
Dünn-: ~**bier** *das* (veralt.) small beer; ~**darm** *der* (Anat.) small intestine
Düne /'dy:nə/ *die;* ~, ~n dune
Dung /dʊŋ/ *der;* ~[e]s dung; manure
Dünge·mittel *das* fertilizer
düngen /'dyŋən/ **1** *tr. V.* fertilize ‹*soil, lawn, etc.*›; spread fertilizer on ‹*field*›; scatter fertilizer around ‹*plants*›. **2** *itr. V.* ‹*person*› put on fertilizer; **gut** ~ ‹*substance*› be a good fertilizer
Dünger *der;* ~s, ~: fertilizer
Dung·haufen *der* dunghill; dung *or* manure heap
Düngung *die;* ~, ~**en** use of fertilizers
dunkel /'dʊŋkl/ **1** *Adj.* (a) dark; **es wird um 22 h** ~: it gets dark about 10 o'clock; **im Dunkeln** in the dark; **im Dunkeln bleiben** (fig.) remain a mystery; remain unidentified; **im Dunkeln tappen** (fig.) grope around *or* about in the dark; (b) (unerfreulich) dark ‹*chapter in one's life*›; black ‹*day*›; (c) (tief schwarz) dark; **dunkles Brot** brown bread; (d) (tief) deep ‹*voice, sound*›; (e) (unbestimmt) vague; dim; faint; vague ‹*recollection*›; dark ‹*hint, foreboding, suspicion*›; (f) (abwertend: zweifelhaft) dubious; shady. **2** *adv.* (a) ‹*dress, paint sth., etc.*› in a dark colour/in dark colours; (b) (unbestimmt) vaguely
Dunkel *das;* ~s (geh.) darkness; **in** ~ **gehüllt sein** (fig.) be shrouded in mystery
Dünkel /'dyŋkl/ *der;* ~s (geh. abwertend) (Überheblichkeit) arrogance; haughtiness; (Einbildung) conceit[edness]
dunkel- dark ‹*blue, grey, etc.*›
dunkel-: ~**blond** *Adj.* light brown ‹*hair*›; ‹*person*› with light brown hair; ~**haarig** *Adj.* dark-haired; ~**häutig** *Adj.* dark-skinned
Dunkelheit *die;* ~: darkness; **bei** ~: during the hours of darkness; **bei Einbruch der** ~: at nightfall
Dunkel-: ~**kammer** *die* darkroom; ~**mann** *der; Pl.* ~**männer** (abwertend) shady character
dunkeln *itr. V.* (a) *unpers.* **es dunkelt** (geh.) it is growing dark; (b) *mit sein* grow *or* go darker; darken
Dunkel·ziffer *die* number of unrecorded cases
dünken /'dyŋkn̩/ (geh. veralt.) **1** *tr. V.* **jmdn. gut/ schlecht/gerecht** *usw.* ~: strike sb. as good/bad/just *etc.*; **mich dünkt, er hat recht** me thinks he is right (arch.). **2** *refl. V.* **er dünkt sich etwas Besseres/ein Held** he thinks of himself as superior/a hero; **ich dünkte mich sicher** *od.* **in Sicherheit** I imagined I was safe
dünn /dyn/ **1** *Adj.* (a) thin ‹*slice, layer, etc.*›; slim ‹*book*›; (b) (mager) thin ‹*person*›; **sich** ~ **machen** (scherzh.) squash *or* (Amer.) scrunch up [a bit]; (c) (leicht) thin, light ‹*clothing, fabric*›; fine ‹*stocking*›; (fig.) thin, rarefied ‹*air*›; fine ‹*rain*›; (d) (spärlich) thin ‹*hair*›; sparse ‹*tree, cover, vegetation*›; (e) (wenig gehaltvoll) thin ‹*soup*›; weak, watery ‹*coffee, tea*›; watery ‹*beer*›; (f) (~flüssig) thin ‹*paint, lubricating oil*›; runny ‹*batter*›; (g) (schwach) thin ‹*voice*›; weak, faint ‹*smile*›; faint ‹*scent*›. **2** *adv.* (a) thinly (b) (leicht) lightly ‹*dressed*›; (c) ~ **besiedelt** thinly *or* sparsely populated *or* inhabited; ~ **gesät** rare; (d) (schwach) ‹*smile*› weakly, faintly

---

*dünn·besiedelt ⇨ **dünn 2 c**

Dünne *der/die; adj. Dekl.* (ugs.) thin man/woman

dünn-: ~**flüssig** *Adj.* thin; runny ‹*batter etc.*›; ***gesät** ⇨ **dünn;** ~**|machen** *refl. V.* (ugs.) make oneself scarce (coll.)

Dunst /dʊnst/ *der;* ~[e]s, **Dünste** /ˈdʏnstə/ (a) *o. Pl.* haze; (Nebel) mist; (b) (Geruch) smell; (Ausdünstung) fumes *pl.;* (stickige, dumpfe Luft) fug (coll.); (c) **keinen [blassen]** ~ **von etw. haben** (ugs.) have not the foggiest *or* faintest idea about sth.

Dunst·abzugs·haube *die* extractor hood

dünsten /ˈdʏnstn̩/ *tr. V.* steam ‹*fish, vegetables*›; braise ‹*meat*›; stew ‹*fruit*›

Dunst·glocke *die* pall of haze

dunstig *Adj.* (a) hazy; (neblig) misty; (b) (verräuchert) smoky

Dunst·kreis *der* (fig.) orbit

Dunst·schleier *der* veil of haze; (Nebelschleier) veil of mist

Duo /ˈduːo/ *das;* ~s, ~s (Musik) (a) duet; (b) (fig. scherzh.) duo; pair

Duplikat /dupliˈkaːt/ *das;* ~[e]s, ~e duplicate

Dur /duːɐ̯/ *das;* ~ (Musik) major [key]; **C-**~: C major

durch /dʊrç/ **1** *Präp. mit Akk.* (a) (räumlich) through; ~ **ganz Europa reisen** travel all over *or* throughout Europe; ~ **einen Fluss waten** wade across a river; (b) (modal) by; **etw.** ~ **die Post schicken** send sth. by post (Brit.) *or* mail; **etw.** ~ **das Fernsehen bekannt geben** announce sth. on television; **etw.** ~ **jmdn. bekommen** get *or* obtain sth. through sb.; **zehn [geteilt]** ~ **zwei** ten divided by two. **2** *Adv.* (a) (hin~) **das ganze Jahr** ~: throughout the whole year; all year; **die ganze Zeit** ~: the whole time; (b) (ugs.: vorbei) **es war 3 Uhr** ~: it was past *or* gone 3 o'clock; (c) ~ **und** ~ **nass** wet through [and through]; **er ist ein Lügner** ~ **und** ~: he's an out and out liar; (d) **[durch etw.]** ~ **sein** be through *or* have got through [sth.]; **ist die Post/der Briefträger schon** ~? has the postman (Brit.) *or* (Amer.) mailman been?; (e) ~ **sein** (vorbeigefahren sein) ‹*train, cyclist*› have gone through; (abgefahren sein) ‹*train, bus, etc.*› have gone; (f) ~ **sein** (fertig sein) have finished; **durch/mit etw.** ~ **sein** have got through sth.; (g) ~ **sein** (durchgescheuert sein) have worn through; (h) ~ **sein** (reif sein) ‹*cheese*› be ripe; (i) ~ **sein** (durchgebraten sein) ‹*meat*› be well done; (j) ~ **sein** (angenommen sein) ‹*law, regulation*› have gone through; ‹*35-hour week etc.*› have been adopted; (k) ~ **sein** (gerettet sein) ‹*sick or injured person*› be out of danger; (l) **bei jmdm. unten** ~ **sein** be in sb.'s bad books

durch|arbeiten 1 *tr. V.* (a) work *or* go through ‹*book, article*›; (b) (durchkneten) work *or* knead thoroughly ‹*dough*›; massage *or* knead thoroughly ‹*muscles*›. **2** *itr. V.* work through; **die Nacht/Pause** ~: work through the night/break. **3** *refl. V.* (auch fig.) work one's way through

durch|atmen *itr. V.* breathe deeply

durch·aus *Adv.* (a) (ganz und gar) absolutely; perfectly, quite ‹*correct, possible, understandable*›; **das ist** ~ **richtig** that is entirely right; **ich bin** ~ **Ihrer Meinung** I am entirely of your opinion; **das hat** ~ **nichts damit zu tun** that's got nothing at all *or* whatsoever to do with it; **es ist** ~ **nicht so einfach wie** …: it is by no means as easy as …; (b) (unbedingt) ~ **mitkommen wollen** [absolutely] insist on coming too; ~ **nicht ins Wasser wollen** absolutely refuse to go into the water

durch|beißen 1 *unr. tr. V.* bite through. **2** *unr. refl. V.* (ugs.) [manage to] struggle through

durch|bekommen *unr. tr. V.* (a) (hindurchbekommen) **etw.** ~: get sth. through; (b) (zerteilen) get *or* cut through ‹*rope, branch, etc.*›; (c) (durchlesen) get through; finish

durch|biegen *unr. refl. V.* sag

durch|blasen 1 *unr. tr. V.* (a) (reinigen) **etw.** ~: clear sth. by blowing through it; (b) (treiben) **etw. durch etw.** ~: blow sth. through sth. **2** *unr. itr. V.* **durch etw.** ~ ‹*wind*› blow through sth.

durch|blättern *tr. V.* leaf through ‹*book, file, etc.*›

Durch·blick *der* (ugs.) **den [absoluten]** ~ **haben** know [exactly] what's going on; **den** ~ **verlieren** no longer know what's going on

durch|blicken *itr. V.* (a) look through; **durch etw.** ~: look through sth.; (b) (ugs.) **ich blicke da nicht durch** I can't make head or tail of it; (c) **etw.** ~ **lassen** hint at sth.

durch·bluten *tr. V.* supply ‹*body, limb, etc.*› with blood; **seine Beine sind schlecht durchblutet** the circulation in his legs is poor

Durch·blutung *die; o. Pl.* flow *or* supply of blood (Gen. to); [blood-]circulation

Durchblutungs·störung *die* disturbance of the blood supply

durch|bohren[1] **1** *tr. V.* drill *or* bore through ‹*wall, plank*›. **2** *itr. V.* **durch etw.** ~: drill *or* bore through sth.

durch·bohren[2] *tr. V.* pierce; **jmdn. mit Blicken** ~ (fig.) look piercingly *or* penetratingly at sb.

durch|boxen (ugs.) **1** *refl. V.* fight one's way through; (fig.) battle through. **2** *tr. V.* force *or* push through ‹*law, measure, bill, etc.*›

durch|braten *unr. tr. V.* **etw.** ~: cook *or* roast sth. till it is well done; **ich möchte mein Steak durchgebraten** I'd like my steak well done

durch|brechen[1] **1** *unr. tr. V.* break in two. **2** *unr. itr. V.; mit sein* (a) break in two; **der Blinddarm/das Magengeschwür ist durchgebrochen** (Med.) the appendix has burst/the gastric ulcer has perforated; (b) (hervorkommen) ‹*sun*› break through; (c) (einbrechen) fall through; **durch etw.** ~: fall through sth.

durch·brechen[2] *unr. tr. V.* break through ‹*sound barrier*›; break *or* burst through ‹*crowd barrier*›; ‹*car*› crash through ‹*railings etc.*›

durch|brennen *unr. itr. V.; mit sein* (a) ‹*heating coil, light bulb*› burn out; ‹*fuse*› blow; (b) (ugs.: weglaufen) (von zu Hause) run away; (mit der Kasse) run off; abscond; (mit dem Geliebten/der Geliebten) run off

durch|bringen *unr. tr. V.* (a) ⇨ **durchbekommen;** (b) (durch eine Kontrolle) **etw.** ~: get sth. through; (c) (bei Wahlen) **jmdn.** ~: get sb. elected; (d) (durchsetzen) get ‹*bill*› through; get ‹*motion*› passed; get ‹*proposal*› accepted; (e) (versorgen) **seine Familie** ~: support one's family; (f) (verschwenden) get through

Durch·bruch *der* (fig.) breakthrough; **einer Idee** (Dat.) **zum** ~ **verhelfen** get an idea generally accepted

durch|bürsten *tr. V.* brush ‹*hair*› thoroughly

durch|checken *tr. V.* check ‹*list, documents*› thoroughly; over thoroughly

durch·dacht *Adj.* **wenig/gut** ~: badly/well thought-out

durch·denken *unr. tr. V.* think over *or* through

durch|drängen *refl. V.* **sich [durch etw.]** ~: push *or* force one's way through [sth.]

durch|drehen 1 *tr. V.* put ‹*meat etc.*› through the mincer *or* (Amer.) grinder; chop ‹*nuts etc.*› in the blender. **2** *itr. V.* (a) **auch mit sein** (ugs.) crack up (coll.); go to pieces; (b) ‹*wheels*› spin

durch|dringen[1] *unr. itr. V.; mit sein* ‹*rain, sun*› come through; **durch etw.** ~: penetrate sth.; come through sth.; **der Redner drang mit seiner Stimme nicht durch** the speaker couldn't make himself heard

durch·dringen[2] *unr. tr. V.* penetrate

durch·dringend *Adj.* (a) (intensiv) piercing, penetrating ‹*voice, look, scream, sound*›; (b) (penetrant) pungent, penetrating ‹*smell*›. **2** *adv.* piercingly; penetratingly

Durchdringung *die;* ~ (a) penetration; (Verschmelzung) fusion; (b) (Erfassung) comprehension

durch|drücken *tr. V.* (a) **etw. [durch etw.]** ~: press sth. through [sth.]; (b) (strecken) straighten ‹*limb, back*›; (c) (ugs.: durchsetzen) manage to get ‹*extra holiday etc.*›; manage to force ‹*application*› through

durch|dürfen *unr. itr. V.* (ugs.); **darf ich mal [hier] durch?** can I get through here?

durch·einander *Adv.* ~ **sein** ⟨*papers, desk, etc.*⟩ be in a mess *or* a muddle; (verwirrt sein) be confused *or* in a state of confusion; (aufgeregt sein) be flustered *or* (coll.) in a state; ~ **bringen** get ⟨*room, flat*⟩ into a mess; get ⟨*papers, file*⟩ into a muddle; muddle up ⟨*papers, file*⟩; (verwechseln) confuse ⟨*names etc.*⟩; get ⟨*names etc.*⟩ mixed up *or* muddled; **jmdn.** ~ **bringen** confuse sb.; ~ **geraten/kommen** get into a muddle; ~ **laufen** run [around] in all directions; ~ **reden** all talk at once

Durcheinander *das;* ~**s** (a) muddle; mess; (b) (Wirrwarr) confusion

*durcheinander|bringen *usw.:* ⇒ durcheinander

durch|exerzieren *tr. V.* (ugs.) rehearse ⟨*situation etc.*⟩

durch|fahren¹ *unr. itr. V.; mit sein* (a) [durch etw.] ~: drive through [sth.]; (b) (nicht anhalten) go straight through; (mit dem Auto) drive straight through; (fahren, ohne umsteigen zu müssen) travel direct; go straight through; **der Zug fährt [in H.] durch** the train doesn't stop [at H.]; **der Zug fährt bis München durch** the train is nonstop to Munich

durch·fahren² *unr. tr. V.* (a) travel through; ⟨*train*⟩ pass through; (mit dem Auto) drive through; (b) (zurücklegen) cover ⟨*distance*⟩; complete ⟨*course, lap*⟩; (c) **plötzlich durchfuhr ihn ein Schreck** he was seized with sudden fright

Durch·fahrt *die* (a) *o. Pl.* (das Durchfahren) passage; „~ verboten" 'no entry except for access' **die** ~ **freigeben** allow vehicles through; (b) *o. Pl.* (Durchreise) **auf der** ~ **sein** be passing through; be on the way through; (c) (Weg) thoroughfare; „**bitte [die]** ~ **freihalten**" 'please do not obstruct'

Durch·fall *der* ▶ 329┃ diarrhoea *no art.*

durch|fallen *unr. itr. V.; mit sein* (a) fall through; **durch etw.** ~: fall through sth.; (b) (ugs.: nicht bestehen) fail; flunk (Amer. coll.); **bei etw./in etw.** (*Dat.*) /**durch etw.** ~: fail *or* flunk sth.; (c) (ugs.: erfolglos sein) ⟨*play, performance*⟩ flop (sl.); be a flop (sl.) *or* failure; (d) (ugs.: die Wahl verlieren) lose the election

durch|finden *unr. refl. V.* **sich** [durch etw.] ~: find one's way through [sth.]

durch|fliegen *unr. itr. V.; mit sein* (a) [durch etw.] ~: fly through [sth.]; **unter der Brücke** ~: fly under the bridge; (b) (nicht zwischenlanden) fly non-stop

durch|fließen *unr. itr. V.; mit sein* [durch etw.] ~: flow through [sth.]

durch·fluten *tr. V.* (geh.) ⟨*warmth, pleasant feeling*⟩ flood through ⟨*person*⟩; ⟨*light*⟩ flood ⟨*room*⟩

durch·forsten *tr. V.* (fig.) sift through

durch|fragen *refl. V.* **sich** [zum Museum] ~: find one's way [to the museum] by asking

durch|fressen 1 *unr. tr. V.* eat through; ⟨*moths*⟩ eat holes in ⟨*pullover etc.*⟩. 2 *unr. refl. V.* ⟨*maggot, woodworm*⟩ eat [its way] through; ⟨*rust*⟩ eat through

durch|frieren *unr. itr. V.; mit sein* (a) **durchgefroren sein** ⟨*person*⟩ be frozen stiff *or* chilled to the bone; (b) ⟨*water, lake*⟩ freeze solid

durchführbar *Adj.* practicable; feasible; workable; **ein leicht** ~**er Plan** a plan that is easy to carry out

Durchführbarkeit *die;* ~: practicability; feasibility; workability

durch|führen 1 *tr. V.* carry out; carry out, put into effect, (einer Operation) per- implement ⟨*plan*⟩; perform, carry out ⟨*operation*⟩; take ⟨*measurement*⟩; make ⟨*charity collection*⟩; hold ⟨*meeting, election, examination*⟩. 2 *itr. V.* **durch etw./unter etw.** (*Dat.*) ~ ⟨*track, road*⟩ go *or* run *or* pass through/ under sth.

Durchfuhr-: ~**handel** *der* (Wirtsch.) transit trade; ~**land** *das* (Wirtsch.) country of transit

Durch·führung *die* carrying out; (einer Operation) performing; (einer Messung) taking; (eines Kongresses usw.) holding

durch|füttern *tr. V.* (ugs.) feed; support; **sich von jmdm.** ~ **lassen** live off sb.

Durch·gang *der* (a) „kein ~", „ ~ verboten" 'no thoroughfare'; (b) (Weg) passage[way]; (c) (Phase) stage; (einer Versuchsreihe) run; (Sport, bei Wahlen, Wettbewerb) round

durch·gängig 1 *Adj.* general; (universell) universal; constant ⟨*feature*⟩. 2 *adv.* generally, universally ⟨*accepted*⟩

Durchgangs-: ~**lager** *das* transit camp; ~**straße** *die* through road; thoroughfare; ~**verkehr** *der* through traffic

durch|geben *unr. tr. V.* announce ⟨*news*⟩; give ⟨*results, winning numbers, weather report*⟩; make ⟨*announcement*⟩

durch|gehen 1 *unr. itr. V.; mit sein* (a) [durch etw.] ~: go *or* walk through [sth.]; „**bitte** ~!" 'pass *or* move right down, please'; (b) [durch etw.] ~: ⟨*rain, water*⟩ come through [sth.]; ⟨*wind*⟩ go through [sth.]; (c) ⟨*train, bus, flight*⟩ go [right] through (**bis** to); go direct; (d) ⟨*path etc.*⟩ go *or* run through (**bis zu** to); ⟨*stripe*⟩ go *or* run right through; (e) (angenommen werden) ⟨*application, claim*⟩ be accepted; ⟨*law*⟩ be passed; ⟨*motion*⟩ be carried; ⟨*bill*⟩ be passed, get through; (f) (hingenommen werden) ⟨*discrepancy*⟩ be tolerated; ⟨*mistake, discourtesy*⟩ be allowed to *or* let pass, be overlooked; **[jmdm.] etw.** ~ **lassen** let sb. get away with sth.; (g) (davonstürmen) ⟨*horse*⟩ bolt; (h) (ugs.: davonlaufen) run off; (i) (außer Kontrolle geraten) **die Nerven gehen mit ihm durch** he loses his temper; **ihr Temperament/ihre Begeisterung geht mit ihr durch** her temperament/enthusiasm gets the better of her; (j) (ugs.: durchgebracht werden können) [durch etw.] ~: go through [sth.]; (k) (gehalten werden für) **für neu/30 Jahre** usw. ~: be taken to be *or* pass for new/thirty etc.. 2 *unr. tr. V.; mit sein* go through ⟨*newspaper, text*⟩

durch·gehend 1 *Adj.* (a) continuous ⟨*line, pattern, etc.*⟩; (constantly recurring ⟨*motif*⟩; (b) (direkt) through attrib. ⟨*train, carriage*⟩; direct ⟨*flight, connection*⟩. 2 *adv.* ~ **geöffnet haben** be open all day

durchgeknallt *Adj.* (ugs.) crazy

durch·geschwitzt *Adj.* ⟨*person*⟩ soaked *or* bathed in sweat; ⟨*clothes*⟩ soaked with sweat; sweat-soaked *attrib.* ⟨*clothes*⟩

durch|gießen *unr. tr. V.; etw.* [durch etw.] ~: pour sth. through [sth.]

durch|greifen *unr. itr. V.* (a) [hart] ~: take drastic measures *or* steps; (b) [durch etw.] ~: reach through [sth.]

durch|gucken *itr. V.* (ugs.) [durch etw.] ~: peep *or* look through [sth.]

durch|haben *unr. tr. V.* (ugs.) have finished with ⟨*book, newspaper*⟩

durch|hacken *tr. V.* hack *or* chop through

durch|halten 1 *unr. itr. V.* (bei einem Kampf) hold out; (bei einer schwierigen Aufgabe) see it through; (beim Rennen) stay the course. 2 *unr. tr. V.* stand

durch|hängen *unr. itr. V.* sag;

durch|hauen 1 *regelm.* (auch unr.) *tr. V.:* ⇒ **durch·schlagen** 1 a. 2 *tr. V.* (ugs.) **jmdn.** ~: give sb. a good hiding (coll.) *or* (sl.) walloping

durch|heizen 1 *tr. V.* heat ⟨*house, offices, etc.*⟩ through. 2 *itr. V.* have *or* keep the heating on

durch|kämmen¹ *tr. V.* comb ⟨*hair*⟩ through

durch·kämmen² *tr. V.* comb ⟨*area etc.*⟩

durch|kämpfen 1 *tr. V.* (a) fight ⟨*case*⟩ [right] to the end; fight one's way through ⟨*adversity*⟩; (b) (durchsetzen) force through. 2 *refl. V.* **sich** [durch etw.] ~: fight *or* battle one's way through [sth.]

durch|kauen *tr. V.* (a) etw. [gut] ~: chew sth. thoroughly *or* well; (b) (ugs.: besprechen) go over and over

durch|kneten *tr. V.* knead ⟨*dough etc.*⟩ thoroughly

durch|kommen *unr. itr. V.; mit sein* (a) come through; (mit Mühe hindurchgelangen) get through; **es gab kein Durchkommen** there was no way through; (b) (ugs.: beim Telefonieren) get through; (c) (durchgehen, -fahren usw.) **durch etw.** ~: come *or* pass through sth.; (d) (sich zeigen) ⟨*sun*⟩ come out; ⟨*character trait, upbringing*⟩ come through, become apparent; (e) (erfolgreich sein) **damit kommst du bei mir nicht durch** you won't get anywhere with me like that; (f) (ugs.: überleben) pull through; (g) (ugs.: durchdringen) [durch etw.] ~ ⟨*water, sand, etc.*⟩ come through [sth.];

(h) (bestehen) get through; pass; **(i)** (auskommen) manage; get by

durch|können *unr. itr. V.* (ugs.) **[durch etw.]** ~: be able to go/come through [sth.]; **kann ich bitte mal durch?** can I get by, please?; excuse me, please

durch·kreuzen *tr. V.* thwart, frustrate ‹*plan, policy*›

durch|kriechen *unr. itr. V.; mit sein* **[durch etw.]** ~: crawl through [sth.]; **unter etw.** *(Dat.)* ~: crawl [through] under sth.

durch|kriegen *tr. V.* (ugs.) ⇒ **durchbekommen**

durch|laden 1 *unr. V.* cock ‹*pistol etc.*› and rotate the cylinder. **2** *unr. itr. V.* cock the trigger and rotate the cylinder

Durchlass, *Durchlaß /'dʊrçlas/ *der;* **Durchlasses, Durchlässe** /'dʊrçlɛsə/ (Öffnung) gap; opening

durch|lassen *unr. tr. V.* **(a)** jmdn. **[durch etw.]** ~: let *or* allow sb. through [sth.]; **den Ball** ~ (Sport) ‹*goalkeeper*› let a goal in; **(b)** let ‹*light, water, etc.*› through

durchlässig /'dʊrçlɛsɪç/ *Adj.* permeable; **die Grenzen müssen** ~**er werden** (fig.) the borders must be opened up further

Durchlässigkeit *die;* ~ permeability

Durch·lauf *der* **(a)** (Sport, DV) run; **(b)** (von Wasser) flow

durch|laufen¹ 1 *unr. itr. V.; mit sein* **(a)** **[durch etw.]** ~: run through [sth.]; **(b)** (durchrinnen) **[durch etw.]** ~: trickle through [sth.]; **der Kaffee ist durchgelaufen** the coffee is filtered; **(c)** (ohne Pause laufen) run without stopping. **2** *unr. tr. V.* go through ‹*socks, soles of shoes*›

durch·laufen² *unr. tr. V.* go *or* pass through ‹*phase, stage*›

durchlaufend 1 *Adj.* continuous. **2** *adv.* ‹*numbered, marked*› in sequence

Durchlauf·erhitzer *der;* ~**s,** ~: geyser; instantaneous water heater

durch·leben *tr. V.* live through; experience; experience ‹*moments of bliss, terror, fright*›

durch|lesen *unr. tr. V.* etw. **[ganz]** ~: read sth. [all the way] through; **sich** *(Dat.)* **etw.** ~: read sth. through

durch·leuchten *tr. V.* **(a)** x-ray ‹*patient, part of body*›; **sich** ~ **lassen** have an x-ray; **(b)** (fig.: analysieren) investigate ‹*case, matter, problem, sb.'s past, etc.*› thoroughly; vet ‹*applicant*›

Durchleuchtung *die;* ~, ~**en (a)** x-ray examination; **(b)** (fig.: Analyse) [thorough] investigation; (von Bewerbern usw.) vetting

durch·löchern *tr. V.* **(a)** make holes in; **völlig durchlöchert sein** be full of holes; **(b)** (fig.: schwächen) undermine ‹*system*› completely; render ‹*principle*› meaningless

durch|lüften 1 *tr. V.* air ‹*room, flat, etc.*› thoroughly. **2** *itr. V.* air the place

durch|machen (ugs.) **1** *tr. V.* **(a)** undergo ‹*change*›; go through ‹*stage, phase*›; **(b)** (erleiden) go through; suffer ‹*illness*›. **2** *itr. V.* (durcharbeiten) work [right] through; (durchfeiern) celebrate all night/day *etc.;* keep going all night/day *etc.*

durch|marschieren *itr. V.; mit sein* **[durch etw.]** ~: march through [sth.]

durch·messen *unr. tr. V.* (geh.) cross ‹*room*›

Durchmesser *der;* ~**s,** ~: diameter

durch|mischen *tr. V.* mix ‹*ingredients etc.*› thoroughly

durch|mogeln *refl. V.* (ugs. abwertend) cheat one's way through; **sich bei einer Prüfung** *usw.* ~: get through an examination *etc.* by cheating

durch|müssen *unr. itr. V.* (ugs.) **[durch etw.]** ~: have to go through [sth.]; **da werden wir** ~ (fig.) we'll have to see it *or* the thing through

durch|nagen *tr. V.* gnaw through

durch·nässen *tr. V.* soak; drench; **[völlig] durchnässt sein** be soaking wet *or* wet through

durch|nehmen *unr. tr. V.* (Schulw.: behandeln) deal with; do

*durch|numerieren, durch|nummerieren *tr. V.* number ‹*pages, seats, etc.*› consecutively from beginning to end

durch|organisieren *tr. V.* organize sth. well; **etw. perfekt** ~: organize sth. down to the last detail

durch|pausen *tr. V.* trace

durch|peitschen *tr. V.* (ugs. abwertend) railroad ‹*law, application, etc.*› through

durch|probieren *tr. V.* taste *or* try ‹*wines, cakes, etc.*› one after another; try on ‹*dresses, suits, etc.*› one after another

durch|prügeln *tr. V.* (ugs.) give ‹*child*› a good hiding *or* (sl.) walloping

durch·queren *tr. V.* cross; travel across ‹*country*›

durch|rechnen *tr. V.* calculate

durch|regnen *itr. V.* (unpers.) **in der Küche** *usw.* **regnet es durch** the rain is coming through in the kitchen *etc.;* **die ganze Nacht** ~: rain all [through the] night

Durchreiche *die;* ~, ~**n** [serving] hatch

durch|reichen *tr. V.* etw. **[durch etw.]** ~: pass *or* hand sth. through [sth.]

Durch·reise *die* journey through; **auf der** ~ **sein** be on the way through *or* passing through

durch|reisen *itr. V.; mit sein* travel *or* pass through

Durch·reisende *der/die* person travelling through

Durchreise·visum *das* transit visa

durch|reißen 1 *unr. tr. V.* etw. ~: tear sth. in two *or* in half. **2** *unr. itr. V.; mit sein* ‹*fabric, garment*› rip, tear; ‹*thread, rope*› snap *or* break [in two]

durch|reiten *unr. itr. V.;* **[durch etw.]** ~: ride through [sth.]

durch|rennen *unr. itr. V.; mit sein* **[durch etw.]** ~: run through [sth.]

durch|ringen *unr. refl. V.* **sie hat sich endlich [zu einem Entschluss] durchgerungen** finally she managed to come to a decision; **wann wirst du dich dazu** ~, **es zu tun?** when are you going to bring yourself to do it?

durch|rosten *itr. V.; mit sein* rust through

durch|rühren *tr. V.* etw. **[gut]** ~: stir sth. [well]

durch|rutschen *itr. V.; mit sein* **[durch etw.]** ~ slip through [sth.]

durchs /dʊrçs/ *Präp. + Art.* = **durch das**

Durch·sage *die* announcement

durch|sagen *tr. V.* announce

durch|sägen *tr. V.* saw through

durchschaubar *Adj.* transparent; **leicht** ~ easy to see through

durch·schauen *tr. V.* see through ‹*lie, plan, intention, person, etc.*›; see ‹*situation*› clearly; **du bist durchschaut** I've/we've seen through you; I/we know what you're up to

durch|scheinen *unr. itr. V.* **[durch etw.]** ~ ‹*sun, light*› shine through [sth.]; ‹*colour, pattern*› show through [sth.]

durchscheinend *Adj.* translucent

durch|scheuern 1 *tr. V.* wear through; **ein durchgescheuertes Kabel** a worn cable. **2** *refl. V.* wear through

durch|schimmern *itr. V.* **[durch etw.]** ~ ‹*light*› shimmer through [sth.]; ‹*colour*› gleam through [sth.]; **(b)** (fig.) ‹*qualities, emotions*› show through

durch|schlafen *unr. itr. V.* sleep [right] through; **die ganze Nacht** ~: sleep all night [without waking]

Durch·schlag *der* carbon [copy]

durch|schlagen¹ 1 *unr. tr. V.* **(a)** etw. ~: chop *or* split sth. in two; **(b)** (schlagen) **einen Nagel [durch etw.]** ~: knock *or* drive a nail through [sth.]. **2** *unr. itr. V.* mit sein **[durch etw.]** ~ ‹*dampness, water*› come through [sth.]; **das schlägt auf die Preise durch** (fig.) it has an effect on prices. **3** *refl. V.* **(a)** struggle along; **(b)** (ein Ziel erreichen) (mit Gewalt) fight one's way through; (mit List) make one's way through

durch·schlagen² *unr. tr. V.* smash

durchschlagend *Adj.* resounding ‹*success*›; decisive ‹*effect*›

Durchschlag·papier *das* copy paper

Durchschlags·kraft *die* (fig.: Wirkung) power; force

durch|schlängeln *refl. V.* **sich [durch etw.]** ∼ (auch fig.) thread one's way through [sth.]

durch|schleusen *tr. V.* (ugs.) **jmdn./etw. [durch etw.]** ∼: guide sb./sth. through [sth.]; (durchschmuggeln) get sb./sth. through [sth.]

Durchschlupf /'dʊrçʃlʊpf/ *der;* ∼[e]s, ∼e gap; (Loch) hole

durch|schlüpfen *itr. V.; mit sein* **[durch etw.]** ∼: slip through [sth.]

durch|schmuggeln *tr. V.* **etw. [durch etw.]** ∼: smuggle sth. through [sth.]

durch|schneiden *unr. tr. V.* cut through ‹thread, cable›; cut ‹ribbon, sheet of paper› in two; cut ‹throat, umbilical cord›; **etw. in der Mitte** ∼: cut sth. in half

Durch·schnitt *der* average; **im** ∼: on average; **im** ∼ **110 km/h fahren** average 110 k.p.h.; do 110 k.p.h. on average; **über/unter dem** ∼ **liegen** be above/below average

durchschnittlich **1** *Adj.* (a) *nicht präd.* average ‹growth, performance, output›; (b) (ugs.: nicht außergewöhnlich) ordinary ‹life, person, etc.›; (c) (mittelmäßig) modest ‹intelligence, talent, performance, achievements›; ordinary ‹appearance›. **2** *adv.* ‹produce, spend, earn, etc.› on [an] average; ∼ **groß sein** be of average height; ∼ **begabt sein** be moderately talented

Durchschnitts- average ‹age, speed, person, etc.›

durch·schreiten *unr. tr. V.* (geh.) stride across ‹room›; stride through ‹door, hall›

Durch·schrift *die* carbon [copy]

Durch·schuss, **Durch·schuß der* bullet *or* gunshot wound (*where the bullet has passed right through*)

durch|schütteln *tr. V.* **jmdn.** ∼: give sb. a good shaking; **wir wurden im Bus tüchtig durchgeschüttelt** we were shaken about all over the place in the bus

durch|schwimmen¹ *unr. itr. V.; mit sein* **[durch etw.]** ∼: swim through [sth.]

durch·schwimmen² *unr. tr. V.* swim ‹the Channel, course, etc.›

durch|schwitzen *tr. V.* **ich habe mein Hemd** *usw.* **durchgeschwitzt** my shirt *etc.* is soaked in sweat

durch|sehen 1 *unr. itr. V.* (a) **[durch etw.]** ∼: look through [sth.]; (b) ⇒ **durchblicken b. 2** *unr. tr. V.* look through ‹essay, homework, newspaper, etc.›; **etw. auf Fehler** ∼: look *or* check through sth. for mistakes

durch|seihen *tr. V.* (Kochk.) strain; pass ‹sauce, gravy› through a sieve

***durch|sein** ⇒ **durch 2**

durchsetzbar *Adj.* enforceable ‹demand, claim›

durch|setzen¹ 1 *tr. V.* carry *or* put through ‹programme, reform›; carry through ‹intention, plan›; accomplish, achieve ‹objective›; enforce ‹demand, claim›; get ‹resolution› accepted; **seinen Willen** ∼: have one's [own] way. **2** *refl. V.* assert oneself (**gegen** against); ‹idea› find *or* gain acceptance, become generally accepted *or* established; ‹fashion› catch on (coll.), find *or* gain acceptance

durch·setzen² *tr. V.* **ein Land mit Spionen** ∼: infiltrate spies into a country; **mit Nadelbäumen durchsetzt sein** be interspersed with conifers

Durchsetzung *die;* ∼ ⇒ **durchsetzen¹:** carrying through; putting through; accomplishment; achievement; enforcement

Durchsetzungs-: ∼**kraft** *die,* ∼**vermögen** *das* ability to assert oneself

Durch·sicht *die:* **nach [einer]** ∼ **der Unterlagen** after looking *or* checking through the documents; **jmdm. etw. zur** ∼ **geben** give sb. sth. to look *or* check through

durchsichtig *Adj.* (auch fig.) transparent; see-through, transparent ‹night-dress, blouse›

durch|sickern *itr. V.; mit sein* (a) seep through; (b) (bekannt werden) ‹news› leak out; **es ist durchgesickert, dass ...:** news has leaked out that ...

**alte Schreibung (vgl. Hinweise auf S. xvi–xvii)

durch|sieben¹ *tr. V.* sift, sieve ‹flour etc.›; strain ‹tea etc.›

durch·sieben² *tr. V.* ‹bullets› riddle

durch|spielen *tr. V.* (a) act ‹scene› through; play ‹piece of music› through; (b) (fig.) go through ‹alternatives, options›

durch|sprechen *unr. tr. V.* talk ‹matter etc.› over; discuss ‹matter etc.› thoroughly

durch|springen *unr. itr. V.; mit sein* **[durch etw.]** ∼: jump *or* leap through [sth.]

durch|spülen *tr. V.* **etw. [gut/gründlich]** ∼: rinse sth. thoroughly

durch|starten *itr. V.; mit sein* (a) (Flugw.) begin climbing again; (b) (Kfz-W.) accelerate away again

durch|stechen *unr. tr. V.* pierce

durch|stecken *tr. V.* **etw. [durch etw.]** ∼: put *or* (coll.) stick sth. through [sth.]

durch|stehen *unr. tr. V.* stand ‹pace, boring job›; come through ‹adventure, difficult situation›; pass ‹test›; get over ‹illness›

durch|steigen *unr. itr. V.; mit sein* (a) **[durch etw.]** ∼: climb through [sth.]; (b) (salopp: verstehen) get it (coll.)

durch|stellen *tr. V.* put ‹call› through

durch|stöbern¹ *tr. V.* (ugs.) search all through ‹house›; rummage through ‹cupboard, case, etc.›; scour ‹wood, area›

durch·stöbern² *tr. V.* (ugs.) (a) ⇒ **durch|stöbern¹;** (b) rummage through (**nach** in search of); rummage around ‹shop› (**nach** in search of)

durch|stoßen¹ *unr. itr. V.* (a) **durch etw.** ∼: knock a hole through sth.; break through sth.; (b) *mit sein* (Milit.) break through (**bis zu** to)

durch·stoßen² *unr. tr. V.* break through

durch|streichen *unr. tr. V.* cross through *or* out; (in Formularen) delete

durch·streifen *tr. V.* (geh.) roam, wander through ‹fields, countryside›

durch·strömen *tr. V.* flow through

durch|stylen *tr. V.* give a completely integrated design/ style to ‹premises, rooms etc.›

durch|suchen¹ *tr. V.* search through

durch·suchen² *tr. V.* search (**nach** for)

Durchsuchung *die;* ∼, ∼**en** search

Durchsuchungs·befehl *der* search warrant

durch|trainieren *tr. V.* get ‹athlete, team, body› into condition; **ein gut durchtrainierter Körper** a body in peak condition

durch|trennen¹, **durch·trennen²** *tr. V.* cut [through] ‹wire, rope›; sever ‹nerve etc.›

durch|treten 1 *unr. tr. V.* press ‹clutch pedal, brake pedal› right down; depress ‹clutch pedal, brake pedal› completely. **2** *unr. itr. V. mit sein* **[durch etw.]** ∼ ‹liquid, gas› come through [sth.]

durchtrieben (abwertend) **1** *Adj.* crafty; sly. **2** *adv.* craftily; slyly

Durchtriebenheit *die;* ∼: craftiness; slyness

durch·wachen *tr. V.* **die Nacht** ∼: stay awake all night

durch|wachsen¹ *unr. itr. V.; mit sein* **[durch etw.]** ∼ ‹plant› grow through sth.

durch·wachsen² 1 *Adj.* (a) ∼**er Speck** streaky bacon; (b) *nicht attr.* (ugs. scherzh.) so-so. **2** *adv.* **ihr geht es** ∼: she has her ups and downs

Durchwahl *die; o. Pl.* (a) direct dialling; (b) **mein Apparat hat keine** ∼: I don't have an outside line; (c) ⇒ **Durchwahlnummer**

durch|wählen *itr. V.* (a) dial direct; **direkt nach Nairobi** ∼: dial Nairobi direct; (b) (bei Nebenstellenanlagen) dial straight through

Durchwahl·nummer *die* number of the/one's direct line

durch|wandern¹ *itr. V.; mit sein* walk *or* hike without a break

dürfen

1. Erlaubnis

ich darf = I may od. **can**

Wann darf ich nach Hause gehen?	= When may od. can I go home?
Er sagte mir, ich dürfte sofort nach Hause gehen	= He told me I could go home right away

Bei der Übersetzung von *dürfte* in dieser Konstruktion (indirekter Rede) ist **could** vorzuziehen, da **might** sich etwas gespreizt anhört.

In der Vergangenheit und in Fällen, wo *dürfen* qualifiziert wird, arbeitet man am besten mit **be allowed to**:

Sie durfte die Katze streicheln	= She was allowed to stroke the cat
Ich darf nur bis hierher kommen	= I am only allowed to come this far
Ich darf nie meine Meinung sagen	= I'm never allowed to say what I think, I can never speak my mind
Er darf nicht reiten, weil er es mit dem Rücken hat	= He isn't allowed to od. He can't ride because he has back trouble

(Weiteres zum negativen Gebrauch finden Sie unter 2.).

Wenn *dürfen* ohne zweites Verb allein steht, übersetzt man auch am besten mit **be allowed [to]**:

Wir haben nicht gedurft	= We weren't allowed to
Darf man das?	= Is that allowed?

Bei Höflichkeitsformeln mit *darf/dürfte ich …* handelt es sich um höfliche Bitten um Erlaubnis, logischerweise ist die Übersetzung also **may/might I …**:

Darf/Dürfte ich Sie begleiten?	= May/Might I accompany you?

Lediglich bei der Formel *darf ich Sie bitten …* kommen andere Übersetzungen in Betracht:

Darf ich Sie bitten, hereinzukommen?	= Would you please come in?

Im erweiterten Sinne von "Grund haben zu" = **can**:

Wir dürfen annehmen, dass …	= We can assume that …
Ich darf mich nicht beklagen	= I can't od. mustn't complain

2. Verbot

Das darf man/darfst du/dürfen Sie nicht tun

Solche Beispiele lassen sich auf verschiedene Art übersetzen, je nachdem, welcher Aspekt betont wird. Will man betonen, dass die Handlung nicht erlaubt ist, sagt man "That's not allowed". Ist man entsetzt über einen Verstoß gegen die Sitten, sagt man "You can't do that!". Aber vor allem wenn man ein Verbot ausspricht oder jemandem von etwas abrät, heißt es "You mustn't do that":

Das darfst du unter keinen Umständen erwähnen	= You mustn't mention that under any circumstances

Das gilt aber nicht nur für die Anrede in der zweiten Person:

Sie darf nicht alleine fahren	= She mustn't go on her own
Er darf es nicht wissen	= He must not know about it

Auch bei Vorschriften oder dergleichen sagt man **must not**:

Hier darf man nicht rauchen	= You must not smoke here, There's no smoking here
Dieser Stoff darf nicht nass werden	= This material must not get wet

Ähnliche Beispiele in der Vergangenheit, die Missbilligung ausdrücken, werden mit **should not have** übersetzt:

Das hätte sie nicht sagen dürfen	= She shouldn't have said that

3. dürfte

Außer in Höflichkeitsformeln, wird dieser Konjunktiv 2 meist mit **should** oder **ought to** übersetzt:

Jetzt dürften sie dort angekommen sein	= They should be there by now
Das dürfte schon möglich sein	= That should od. ought to be possible

Bei einer Schätzung sagt man aber **must**:

Sie dürfte in den Achtzigern sein	= She must be in her eighties

Und bei einer Vorhersage kann man **will probably** sagen:

Es dürfte ein Gewitter geben	= There will probably be a storm

---

durch·wandern[2] *tr. V.* walk or hike through

durch|waschen *unr. tr. V.* (ugs.) **etw.** ~: wash sth. through

durch|waten[1] *itr. V.; mit sein* [durch etw.] ~: wade through [sth.]

durch·waten[2] *tr. V.* wade across

durchweg /'dʊrçvɛk/ *Adv.* without exception

durch|weichen[1] *itr. V.; mit sein* ⟨*cardboard, paper*⟩ become or go [soft and] soggy

durch·weichen[2] *tr. V.* make ⟨*earth, path, etc.*⟩ sodden

durch|werfen *unr. tr. V.* **etw.** [durch etw.] ~: throw sth. through [sth.]

durch|wetzen wear through ⟨*sleeves, knees, elbows, etc.*⟩

durch|wollen *unr. itr. V.* (ugs.) [durch etw.] ~: want to go/come/get through [sth.]

durch|wühlen[1] **1** *tr. V.* rummage through, ransack ⟨*drawers, cupboard, case*⟩ (**nach** in search of, looking for); turn ⟨*room, house*⟩ upside down (**nach** in search of, looking for). **2** *refl. V.* (ugs.) **sich durch die Erde** ~ ⟨*mole*⟩ burrow through the earth; **sich durch einen Aktenstoß** ~ (fig.) plough through a pile of documents

durch·wühlen[2] *tr. V.* ⇒ **durchwühlen**[1] **1**

durch|zählen *tr. V.* count; count up ⟨*money, people*⟩

durch|ziehen[1] **1** *unr. tr. V.* (a) **jmdn./etw.** [durch etw.] ~: pull sb./sth. through [sth.]; **ein Gummiband** [durch etw.] ~: draw an elastic through [sth.]; (b) (ugs.: durchführen) get through ⟨*sylabus, programme*⟩; **wir müssen die Sache** ~: we must see the matter through; (c) (salopp: rauchen) smoke. **2** *unr. itr. V.; mit sein* (a) [durch ein Gebiet *usw.*] ~: pass through [an area *etc.*]; ⟨*soldiers*⟩ march through [an area *etc.*]; (b) (Kochk.) ⟨*fruit, meat, etc.*⟩ soak

durch·ziehen[2] *unr. tr. V.* ⟨*river, road, ravine*⟩ run through, traverse ⟨*landscape*⟩; ⟨*theme, motif, etc.*⟩ run through ⟨*book etc.*⟩

durch·zucken *tr. V.* ⟨*lightning, beam of light*⟩ flash across; **jmdn.** ~ (fig.) ⟨*thought*⟩ flash through or cross sb.'s mind

Durch·zug *der* (a) *o. Pl.* draught; ~ **machen** create a draught; **die Ohren auf** ~ **stellen** (ugs.) let it go in one ear and out the other; (b) (das Durchziehen) passage through; (von Truppen) march through

dürfen /'dʏrfn̩/ **1** *unr. Modalverb; 2. Part.* ~ (a) (Erlaubnis haben zu) **etw. tun** ~: be allowed or permitted to do sth.;

darf ich [das tun]? may I [do that]?; **das darf man nicht tun** that is not allowed; one mustn't do that; **er hat es nicht tun ~:** he was not allowed *or* permitted to do it; **nein, das darfst du nicht** no, you may not; **ich darf morgen nicht verschlafen** I mustn't oversleep tomorrow; **du darfst nicht lügen/jetzt nicht aufgeben!** you mustn't tell lies/give up now!; **ihm darf nichts geschehen** nothing must happen to him; **das darf nicht wahr sein** (ugs.) that's incredible; **hier darf man nicht rauchen** smoking is prohibited here; **(b)** (in Höflichkeitsformeln) **darf ich rauchen?** may I smoke?; **darf ich Sie bitten, das zu tun?** could I ask you to do that?; **darf od. dürfte ich mal Ihre Papiere sehen?** may I see your papers?; **darf ich um diesen Tanz bitten?** may I have [the pleasure of] this dance?; **was darf es sein?** (im Laden) can I help you?; (was möchten Sie zu trinken haben) what can I get you to drink?; **darf ich bitten?** (um einen Tanz) may I have the pleasure?; (einzutreten) won't you come in?; **Ruhe, wenn ich bitten darf!** will you please be quiet!; **(c)** (Grund haben zu) **ich darf Ihnen mitteilen, dass …:** I am able to inform you that …; **darf ich annehmen, dass …?** can I assume that …?; **sie darf sich nicht beklagen** she can't complain; she has no reason to complain; **das darfst du mir glauben** you can take my word for it; **(d)** *Konjunktiv II + Inf.* **das dürfte der Grund sein** that is probably the reason; (ich nehme an, dass das der Grund ist) that must be the reason; **das dürfte reichen** that should be enough. **2** *unr. tr., itr. V.* **er hat nicht gedurft** he was not allowed *or* permitted to; **darf ich ins Theater?** may I go to the theatre?; **darfst du das?** are you allowed to?

durfte /'dʊrftə/ *1. u. 3. Pers. Sg. Prät. v.* **dürfen**

dürfte /'dʏrftə/ *1. u. 3. Pers. Sg. Konjunktiv II v.* **dürfen**

dürftig /'dʏrftɪç/ **1** *Adj.* **(a)** (ärmlich) poor; scanty, meagre ⟨*meal*⟩; scanty, poor ⟨*clothing*⟩; **(b)** (abwertend: unzulänglich) poor ⟨*substitute, performance, light*⟩; feeble, poor ⟨*explanation*⟩; lame, feeble ⟨*excuse*⟩; scanty ⟨*knowledge, evidence, results*⟩; sparse ⟨*growth of hair*⟩; paltry, meagre ⟨*income*⟩. **2** *adv.* **(a)** ⟨*live*⟩ poorly; scantily ⟨*dressed*⟩; **(b)** (abwertend: unzulänglich) skimpily, scantily ⟨*furnished*⟩; poorly ⟨*attended*⟩; ⟨*report, formulate*⟩ sketchily; thinly ⟨*concealed*⟩

Dürftigkeit *die;* ~ ⇒ **dürftig:** **(a)** (Ärmlichkeit) poorness; scantiness; meagreness; **(b)** (abwertend: Unzulänglichkeit) poorness; feebleness; lameness; scantiness; sparseness; paltriness; meagreness

dürr /dʏr/ *Adj.* **(a)** withered ⟨*branch*⟩; dry, dried up, withered ⟨*grass, leaves*⟩; arid, barren ⟨*ground, earth*⟩; **(b)** (mager) skinny, scraggy, scrawny ⟨*legs, arms, body, person*⟩; **(c)** (unergiebig) lean ⟨*years*⟩; bare ⟨*words, description*⟩

Dürre *die;* ~, ~n drought

Dürre-: ~**katastrophe** *die* catastrophic drought; ~**periode** *die* period of drought

Durst /dʊrst/ *der;* ~[e]s thirst; ~ **haben** be thirsty; ~ **bekommen** get *or* become thirsty; **seinen** ~ **löschen** *od.* **stillen** quench *or* slake one's thirst; **ich habe** ~ **auf ein Bier** I could just drink a beer; ~ **nach Wissen** (fig. geh.) a thirst for knowledge; **ein Glas** *od.* **einen über den** ~ **trinken** (ugs. scherzh.) have one too many

dursten *itr. V.* (geh.) thirst; ~ **müssen** have to go thirsty

dürsten /'dʏrstn̩/ *tr. V.* (unpers.) **mich dürstet** (geh.) I am thirsty

durstig *Adj.* thirsty

durst-, Durst-: ~**löschend**, ~**stillend** *Adj.* thirst-quenching; ~**strecke** *die* (fig.) lean period *or* time

Dusch·bad *das* shower[-bath]

Dusche /'du:ʃə/ *die;* ~, ~n shower; **unter die** ~ **gehen** take *or* have a shower; **unter der** ~ **sein** be in the shower; **eine kalte** ~ **[für jmdn.] sein** (fig. ugs.) be like a cold douche *or* a douche of cold water [on sb.]

duschen **1** *itr., refl. V.* take *or* have a shower; **kalt** ~: take *or* have a cold shower. **2** *tr. V.* **jmdn.** ~: give sb. a shower

Düse /'dy:zə/ *die;* ~, ~n (Technik) nozzle; (eines Vergasers) jet

**alte Schreibung (vgl. Hinweise auf S. xvi–xvii)

Dusel /'du:zl̩/ *der;* ~s (ugs.) luck; ~ **haben** be jammy (Brit. coll.) *or* lucky

düsen *itr. V.; mit sein* (ugs.) dash

Düsen-: ~**an·trieb** *der* jet propulsion; ~**flugzeug** *das* jet aeroplane *or* aircraft *or* plane; ~**trieb·werk** *das* jet power plant; jet engine

Dussel /'dʊsl̩/ *der;* ~s, ~ (ugs.) dope (coll.); idiot (coll.); clot (Brit. coll.)

dusselig, dusslig, *dußlig (ugs.) **1** *Adj.* gormless (Brit. coll.); stupid; idiotic. **2** *adv.* gormlessly (Brit. coll.); stupidly

düster /'dy:stɐ/ **1** *Adj.* **(a)** dark; gloomy; dim ⟨*light*⟩; **(b)** (fig.) gloomy; sombre ⟨*colour, music*⟩; dark ⟨*foreboding*⟩. **2** *adv.* (fig.) gloomily

Düsterheit, Düsterkeit *die;* ~ **(a)** ⇒ **düster** a: darkness; gloom; dimness; **(b)** ⇒ **düster** b: gloominess; sombreness; darkness

Dutt /dʊt/ *der;* ~[e]s, ~e *od.* ~s bun

Dutzend /'dʊtsn̩t/ *das;* ~s, ~e dozen; **zwei** ~: two dozen; **ein** ~ **Eier** a dozen eggs; **das** ~ **Schnecken kostet 16 Mark, Schnecken kosten 16 Mark das Dutzend** snails cost 16 marks a dozen; **sie kamen zu** ~**en** they came in [their] dozens (coll.)

dutzend-, Dutzend-: ~**fach**, ~**mal** *Adv.* a dozen times; dozens of times; ~**ware** *die* (abwertend) cheap mass-produced item ~**weise** *Adv.* ⟨*arrive, leave*⟩ in [their] dozens (coll.); **etw.** ~**weise verkaufen** sell sth. by the dozen

duzen /'du:tsn̩/ *tr. V.* call ⟨*sb., each other*⟩ 'du' (the familiar form of address); **sich** ~: call each other 'du'; **sich mit jmdm.** ~: call sb. 'du'

Duz·freund *der* good friend (whom one addresses with 'du')

Dynamik /dy'na:mɪk/ *die;* ~ **(a)** (Physik) dynamics *sing.,* no *art.;* **(b)** (Triebkraft) dynamism; **(c)** (Musik) dynamics *pl.*

dynamisch /dy'na:mɪʃ/ **1** *Adj.* dynamic; ~**e Renten** ≈ index-linked pensions (linked to changes in the national product). **2** *adv.* dynamically

Dynamit /dyna'mi:t/ *das;* ~s dynamite

Dynamo /dy'na:mo/ *der;* ~s, ~s dynamo

Dynastie *die;* ~, ~n dynasty

D-Zug /'de:-/ *der* fast *or* express train; **ein alter Mann/ eine alte Frau ist doch kein** ~**!** (salopp) I'm too old to hurry

D-Zug-Zuschlag *der* fast train supplement

Ee

e, E /e:/ *das;* ~, ~ (Buchstabe) e/E

E *Abk.* Europastraße

Ebbe /'ɛbə/ *die;* ~, ~n **(a)** (Bewegung) ebb tide; **es ist** ~**:** the tide is going out; **bei** ~**:** at ebb tide; when the tide is going out; ~ **und Flut** ebb and flow; **(b)** (Zustand) low tide; **es ist** ~**:** the tide is out; **bei** ~**:** at low tide; when the tide is/was out; **es herrschte** ~ **in seinem Portemonnaie** (fig. ugs.) he was short of cash (coll.)

eben /'e:bn̩/ **1** *Adj.* **(a)** (flach) flat; **(b)** (glatt) level ⟨*ground, path, stretch*⟩. **2** *Adv.* **(a)** (gerade jetzt) just; **(b)** (kurz) [for] a moment; **(c)** (gerade noch) just [about]; **etw.** ~ **noch schaffen** only just manage sth.; **(d)** (genau) precisely; **ja,** ~**:** yes, exactly *or* precisely; **ja,** ~ **das meine ich auch** yes, that's just *or* exactly what I think. **3** *Partikel* **(a)** **nicht** ~**:** not exactly; **(b)** (nun einmal) simply; **das ist** ~ **so** that's just the way it is

eben-, Eben-: ~**bild** *das* image; **ganz jmds.** ~**bild sein** be the spitting image of sb.; ~**bürtig** /~bʏrtɪç/ *Adj.* equal (*Dat.* to); ~**da** *Adv.* there; (bei Literaturangaben) ibid *adv.;* ibidem; ~**der,** ~**die,** ~**das** *Demonstrativpron.* ~**das meine ich** that's exactly what I mean; ~**die, von der wir sprachen** the very one we were talking about; ~**der war krank** he was the very one who was ill; **∼derselbe**, **∼dieselbe**, **∼dasselbe** *Demonstrativpron.; attr.* the very same ‹*person, thing*›; *allein stehend* **∼dieselbe meine ich** she's just the one I mean; **∼dieser**, **∼diese**, **∼dieses** *Demonstrativpron.; attr.* **∼dieses Thema wurde behandelt** this very topic was discussed; *allein stehend* **∼dieser wurde genannt** he was the very one who was mentioned

Ebene *die; ∼, ∼n* (a) (flaches Land) plain; **in der ∼:** on the plain; (b) (Geom., Physik) plane; (c) (fig.) level

eben-: **∼erdig 1** *Adj.* ground-level; **2** *adv.* at ground level; **∼falls** *Adv.* likewise; as well; **danke, ∼falls** thank you, [and] [the] same to you

Eben·holz *das* ebony

Eben·maß *das; o. Pl.* (der Gesichtszüge) regularity; (des Körperbaus) symmetry; even proportions *pl.;* (von Versen) regularity; harmony

eben·mäßig *Adj.* regular ‹*features*›; well-proportioned ‹*figure*›; regular, harmonious ‹*verse*›; even ‹*proportions*›

eben·so *Adv.* (a) *mit Adjektiven u. Adverbien, Indefinitpromina* just as; **∼ groß wie … sein** be just as big as …; **ein ∼ frecher wie dummer Kerl** a fellow who is/was as impudent as he is/was stupid; **∼ gern mag ich Erdbeeren** [**wie** …] I like strawberries just as much [as …]; **∼ gern würde ich an den Strand gehen** I would just as soon go to the beach; **∼ gut** just as well; **ich kann ∼ gut ein Taxi nehmen** I can just as easily take a taxi; **∼ oft** just as often *or* frequently; **∼ sehr** just as much; **∼ viel** just as much; **∼ wenig** just as little; **man kann dieses ∼ wenig tun** one cannot do this, any more than that; (b) *mit Verben* in exactly the same way; (in demselben Maße) just as much; **mir geht es ∼:** its just the same for me

*****ebenso·gern** *usw.:* ⇒ **ebenso** a

eben·solch… *Demonstrativpron.* the same; **ich habe ebensolche Angst wie du** I am just as afraid as you are

*****ebenso·sehr** *usw.:* ⇒ **ebenso** a

Eber /'e:bɐ/ *der; ∼s, ∼:* boar

ebnen *tr. V.* level ‹*ground*›; **jmdm. den Weg** *od.* **die Bahn ∼** (fig.) smooth the way for sb.

Echo /'ɛço/ *das; ∼s, ∼s* echo; (fig.) response (**auf** + *Akk.* to); **das ∼ in der Presse** (fig.) the press reaction; the reaction in the press

Echo·lot *das* echo sounder

Echse /'ɛksə/ *die; ∼, ∼n* (Zool.) (a) saurian; (b) (Eid∼) lizard

echt /ɛçt/ **1** *Adj.* (a) genuine; authentic, genuine ‹*signature, document*›; (b) (wahr) true, real ‹*love, friendship*›; real, genuine ‹*concern, sorrow, emergency*›; (c) *nicht präd.* (typisch) real, typical ‹*Bavarian, American, etc.*›; (d) (Math.) proper ‹*fraction*›. **2** *adv.* (a) **∼ golden/italienisch** *usw.* real gold/real *or* genuine Italian *etc.;* (b) (ugs.: wirklich) really; **das ist ∼ wahr/blöd** that's absolutely true/stupid; (c) (typisch) typically

echt- real ‹*silver, silk, leather, etc.*›

Echtheit *die; ∼* genuineness; (einer Unterschrift, eines Dokuments) authenticity

Eck /ɛk/ *das; ∼s, ∼e* (bes. südd., österr.) corner; **über[s] ∼:** diagonally

Eck-: **∼ball** *der* (Sport) corner [kick/hit/throw]; **einen ∼ball treten** take a corner; **∼bank** *die* corner seat; **∼daten** *Pl.* basic information *sing.*

Ecke /'ɛkə/ *die; ∼, ∼n* (a) corner; **Nietzschestraße, ∼ Goethestraße** on the corner of Nietzschestrasse and Goethestrasse; **um die ∼ biegen** turn the corner; go/come round the corner; **die lange/kurze ∼** (Ballspiele) the far/near corner; **jmdn. um die ∼ bringen** (fig. salopp) bump sb. off (sl.); **mit jmdm. um** *od.* **über sieben ∼n verwandt sein** (fig. ugs.) be distantly related to sb.; **an allen ∼n** [**und Enden** *od.* **Kanten**] (ugs.) everywhere; (b) (Ballspiele) corner; **eine ∼ treten** take a corner; (c) (ugs.: Gegend) corner; **eine schöne ∼:** a lovely spot; (d) (ugs., bes. nordd.: Strecke) **bis dahin ist es noch eine ganze ∼:** it's still quite some way there

Ecker /'ɛkɐ/ *die; ∼, ∼n* beech-nut

Eck·haus *das* corner house; house on the/a corner; (einer Häuserreihe) end house

eckig 1 *Adj.* (a) square; angular ‹*features*›; (b) (ruckartig) jerky ‹*movement, walk, gait*›. **2** *adv.* jerkily

Eck-: **∼kneipe** *die* small friendly pub on a street corner; **∼lohn** *der* (Wirtsch.) basic *or* minimum wage; **∼pfeiler** *der* corner pillar; (fig.) cornerstone; **∼schrank** *der* corner cupboard; **∼stoß** *der* (Fußball) corner kick; **∼wert** *der* (Wirtsch.) standard [of value]; **∼zahn** *der* ▶ 326 | canine tooth; **∼zimmer** *das* corner room; **∼zins** *der* (Finanzw.) official minimum interest rate on savings

Economy·klasse /ɪ'kɔnəmɪ-/ *die* economy class; tourist class

Ecstasy /'ɛkstəsi/ *das; ∼s* Ecstasy

edel /'e:dl̩/ **1** *Adj.* (a) *nicht präd.* thoroughbred ‹*horse*›; (b) (großmütig) noble[-minded], high-minded ‹*person*›; noble ‹*thought, gesture, deed*›; honourable ‹*motive*›; **edle Gesinnung** nobility of mind; noble-mindedness; (c) (geh.: wohlgeformt) finely-shaped; **von edlem Wuchs** of noble stature; (d) (geh.: vortrefflich) fine ‹*wine*›; high-grade ‹*wood, timber*›; (e) *nicht präd.* (veralt.: adlig) noble. **2** *adv.* nobly

Edel-: **∼holz** *das* high-grade wood; high-grade timber; **∼kitsch** *der* grandly pretentious kitsch; **∼mann** *der; Pl.* **∼leute** *od.* **∼männer** (hist.) nobleman; noble; **∼metall** *das* noble metal; **∼mut** *der* (geh.) nobility of mind; noble-mindedness; magnanimity; **∼schnulze** *die* (abwertend) example of pretentious schmaltz; **∼stahl** *der* stainless steel; **∼stein** *der* precious stone; gem[stone]; **∼tanne** *die* silver fir; **∼weiß** *das;* **∼[es]**, **∼e** edelweiss

Eden /'e:dn̩/ *in* **der Garten ∼** (bibl.) the Garden of Eden

Edikt /e'dɪkt/ *das; ∼[e]s, ∼e* (hist.) edict

Edition /edi'tsi̯oːn/ *die; ∼, ∼en* edition

EDV *Abk.* **elektronische Datenverarbeitung** EDP

EEG /e:e:'ge:/ *das; ∼[s], ∼[s]* *Abk.* **Elektroenzephalogramm** EEG

Efeu /'e:fɔy/ *der; ∼s* ivy

efeu·bewachsen *Adj.* ivy-covered; ivy-clad

Effeff /ɛf'|ɛf/ *in* **etw. aus dem ∼ beherrschen** know sth. inside out

Effekt /ɛ'fɛkt/ *der; ∼[e]s, ∼e* effect

Effekten /ɛ'fɛktn̩/ *Pl.* (Finanzw.) securities

Effekten-: **∼börse** *die* stock exchange; **∼geschäft** *das* dealing in securities; **∼makler** *der* stockbroker

Effekt·hascherei /-haʃə'rai̯/ *die; ∼, ∼en* (abwertend) straining for effect; showiness

effektiv /ɛfɛk'tiːf/ **1** *Adj.* effective. **2** *adv.* effectively

Effektivität /ɛfɛktivi'tɛːt/ *die; ∼:* effectiveness

Effektiv·lohn *der* real wage[s]

effekt·voll 1 *Adj.* effective ‹*speech, poem, contrast, pattern*›; dramatic ‹*pause, gesture, entrance*›. **2** *adv.* effectively

Effet /ɛ'fe:/ *der; ∼s, ∼s* spin; (Billard) side; **den Ball mit ∼ schlagen** put spin/side on the ball

effizient /ɛfi'tsi̯ɛnt/ **1** *Adj.* (geh.) efficient. **2** *adv.* efficiently

EG /'e:'ge:/ *Abk.* (a) *die; ∼:* **Europäische Gemeinschaft** EC; (b) **Erdgeschoss**

egal /e'ga:l/ *Adj.* (a) *nicht attr.* (ugs.: einerlei) **es ist jmdm. ∼:** it's all the same to sb.; **das ist ∼:** that doesn't make any difference; [**ganz**] **∼, wie/wer/ob** *usw.* …: no matter how/who/whether *etc.* …; (b) (ugs.: gleich[artig]) identical

egalisieren *tr. V.* (Sport) equal ‹*record*›

egalitär /egali'tɛːɐ̯/ **1** *Adj.* egalitarian. **2** *adv.* in an egalitarian way

Egel /'e:gl̩/ *der; ∼s, ∼:* leech

Egge /'ɛgə/ *die; ∼, ∼n* (Landw.) harrow

eggen *tr. V.* (Landw.) harrow

Ego /'e:go/ *das; ∼, ∼s* (Psych.) ego

Egoismus /ego'ɪsmʊs/ *der; ∼:* egoism

Egoist /ego'ɪst/ *der; ∼en, ∼en*, **Egoistin** *die; ∼, ∼nen* egoist

egoistisch 1 *Adj.* egoistic[al]. **2** *adv.* egoistically

Egozentriker *der; ∼s, ∼*, **Egozentrikerin** *die; ∼, ∼nen* egocentric

egozentrisch *Adj.* egocentric

eh¹ /eː/ *Interj.* (ugs.) **(a)** hey; **(b) das hast du nicht erwartet, ∼?** you didn't expect that, did you [,eh]?

eh² *Adv.* **(a)** (bes. südd., österr.: sowieso) anyway; in any case; **es ist ∼ alles zu spät** it's too late anyway *or* in any case; **(b) seit ∼ und je** for as long as anyone can remember; for donkey's years (coll.); **wie ∼ und je** just as before

ehe /ˈeːə/ *Konj.* ⇒ **bevor**

Ehe /ˈeːə/ *die;* ∼, ∼n marriage; **eine glückliche ∼ führen** be happily married; lead a happy married life; **die ∼ brechen** commit adultery (geh. veralt.); **jmdm. die ∼ versprechen** promise to marry sb.; **aus erster ∼:** from his/her first marriage

ehe-, Ehe-: ∼**beratung** *die* marriage guidance (Brit.); marriage counselling; ∼**bett** *das* marriage-bed; (Doppelbett) double bed; ∼**brecher** *der;* ∼s, ∼: adulterer; ∼**brecherin** *die;* ∼, ∼nen adulteress; ∼**brecherisch** *Adj.* adulterous; ∼**bruch** *der* adultery

ehe·dem *Adv.* (geh.) formerly; in former times

Ehe-: ∼**frau** *die* wife; (verheiratete Frau) married woman; ∼**gatte** *der* (geh.) husband; (∼mann od. ∼frau) spouse; **beide** ∼**gatten** both husband and wife; ∼**glück** *das* wedded *or* married bliss; ∼**hälfte** *die* (scherzh.) better half (joc.); ∼**hindernis** *das* (Rechtsw.) impediment to marriage; ∼**krach** *der* (ugs.) row; quarrel; ∼**leben** *das* married life; ∼**leute** *Pl.* married couple; **die beiden** ∼**leute** the husband and wife

ehelich *Adj.* marital; matrimonial; conjugal ⟨rights, duties⟩; legitimate ⟨child⟩; ∼**e Gemeinschaft** marriage partnership

ehelichen *tr. V.* (veralt., scherzh.) wed

ehemalig /ˈeːəmaliç/ *Adj.* former; **seine** ∼**e Frau** his ex-wife; **seine Ehemalige/ihr Ehemaliger** (ugs.) his/her ex (coll.)

ehe-, Ehe-: ∼**mann** *der; Pl.* ∼**männer** husband; (verheirateter Mann) married man; ∼**müde** *Adj.* tired of married life *postpos.;* ∼**mündig** *Adj.* (Rechtsspr.) of marriageable age *postpos.;* ∼**mündig sein** be of marriageable age *or* of an age to marry; ∼**paar** *das* married couple

eher /ˈeːɐ/ *Adv.* **(a)** (früher) earlier; sooner; **je** ∼, **desto lieber** *od.* **besser** the sooner the better; **(b)** (lieber) rather; sooner; **alles** ∼ **als das** anything but that; (c) (wahrscheinlicher) more likely; (leichter) more easily; **das ist schon** ∼ **möglich** that's more likely; **(d)** (mehr) **er ist** ∼ **faul als dumm** he is lazy rather than stupid; he's more lazy than stupid (coll.); **alles** ∼ **sein als …:** be anything but …

Ehe-: ∼**ring** *der* wedding ring; ∼**scheidung** *die* divorce; ∼**schließung** *die* wedding *or* marriage ceremony

ehest… /ˈeːəst/ **1** *Adj.; nicht präd.* earliest; **zum** ∼**en Termin** at the earliest possible date. **2** *adv.* **am** ∼**en** (am liebsten) best of all; (am wahrscheinlichsten) most likely

Ehe·stand *der; o. Pl.* marriage *no art.;* matrimony *no art.*

ehestens /ˈeːəstn̩s/ *Adv.* ⇒ **frühestens**

Ehe-: ∼**streit** *der* marital *or* matrimonial dispute; ∼**vermittlungs·institut** *das* marriage bureau; ∼**vertrag** *der* (Rechtsw.) marriage contract

ehrbar **1** *Adj.* (geh.) respectable, worthy ⟨person, occupation⟩; honourable ⟨intentions⟩. **2** *adv.* respectably

Ehre /ˈeːrə/ *die;* ∼, ∼n **(a)** honour; **es ist mit eine ∼, … zu …:** it is an honour for me to …; **die ∼ haben, etw. zu tun** have the ∼ of doing sth.; **jmdm./einer Sache [alle] ∼ machen** do sb./sth. [great] credit; **jmds. Andenken** (Akk.) **in** ∼**n halten** honour sb.'s memory; **auf ∼ und Gewissen** in all truthfulness *or* honesty; **jmds./einer Sache zu viel ∼ antun** (fig.: jmdn./etw. überschätzen) overvalue sb./sth.; **jmdm. zur ∼ gereichen** (geh.) bring honour to sb.; ∼, **wem ∼ gebührt** [give] credit where credit is due; **jmdm. die letzte ∼ erweisen** pay one's last respects to sb.; **um der Wahrheit die ∼ zu geben** (fig.) to tell the truth; to be [perfectly] honest; **zu** ∼**n des Königs, dem König zu** ∼**n** in honour of the king; **wieder zu** ∼**n kommen** (fig.) come back into favour; **damit kannst du keine ∼ einlegen** that does you no credit;

(b) *o. Pl.* (Ehrgefühl) sense of honour; **er hat keine ∼ im Leib[e]** he doesn't have an ounce of integrity in him

ehren *tr. V.* **(a)** (Ehre erweisen) honour; **jmdn. mit einem Orden ∼:** award sb. a medal; **sehr geehrter Herr Müller/sehr geehrte Frau Müller** *usw.* Dear Herr Müller/Dear Frau Müller *etc.;* **(b)** (Ehre machen) **deine Hilfsbereitschaft ehrt dich** your willingness to help does you credit; **sein Vertrauen ehrt mich** I'm honoured by his confidence in me

ehren-, Ehren-: ∼**abzeichen** *das* medal; ∼**amt** *das* honorary position *or* post; ∼**amtlich** **1** *Adj.* honorary ⟨position, membership⟩; voluntary ⟨help, worker⟩; **2** *adv.* in an honorary capacity; (freiwillig) on a voluntary basis

Ehren-: ∼**bürger** *der,* ∼**bürgerin** *die* honorary citizen; **jmdn. zum** ∼**bürger der Stadt ernennen** give sb. the freedom *or* make sb. a freeman of the town/city; ∼**doktor** *der* **(a)** honorary doctor; **(b)** (Titel) honorary doctorate; ∼**gast** *der* guest of honour; ∼**geleit** *das* official escort

ehrenhaft **1** *Adj.* honourable ⟨intentions, person⟩. **2** *adv.* ⟨act⟩ honourably

ehren-, Ehren-: ∼**halber** *Adv.* **jmdm. den Doktortitel** ∼**halber verleihen** confer an honorary doctorate on sb.; **Doktor** ∼**halber** honorary doctor; ∼**kodex** *der* code of honour; ∼**mal** *das* monument; ∼**mann** *der; Pl.* ∼**männer** man of honour; ∼**mitglied** *das* honorary member; ∼**platz** *der* place of honour; ∼**preis** *der* special prize; ∼**rechte** *Pl.* **die bürgerlichen** ∼**rechte** civil rights *or* liberties; ∼**rettung** *die:* **zu ihrer** ∼**rettung muss ich sagen, dass …:** it must be said in her defence that …; ∼**rührig** *Adj.* defamatory ⟨allegations⟩; insulting ⟨behaviour⟩; ∼**runde** *die* lap of honour; ∼**sache** *die:* **das ist** ∼**sache** that is a point of honour; **Verschwiegenheit ist** ∼**sache** I/we feel honour bound to stay silent; ∼**sache!** you can count on me!; ∼**tag** *der* (geh.) special day; ∼**tor** *das,* ∼**treffer** *der* (Sport) consolation goal; ∼**tribüne** *die* VIP stand; ∼**urkunde** *die* certificate; ∼**voll** **1** *Adj.* honourable ⟨peace, death, compromise, occupation⟩; creditable, gallant ⟨attempt, conduct⟩; **2** *adv.* ⟨act⟩ honourably; ∼**vorsitzender** *der/die* honorary chairman; ∼**wert** *Adj.* (geh.) worthy, honourable ⟨person, occupation⟩; **die Ehrenwerte Gesellschaft** the Mafia; ∼**wort** *das; pl.* ∼**worte/**∼**wort** [!/?] word of honour [!/?]; **sein** ∼**wort brechen** break one's word

ehrerbietig /ˈeːɐʔɛɐbiːtɪç/ **1** *Adj.* (geh.) respectful. **2** *adv.* ⟨greet⟩ respectfully

Ehrerbietung *die;* ∼ (geh.) respect

Ehr·furcht *die* reverence (**vor** + *Dat.* for); [**große**] ∼ **vor jmdm./etw. haben** have [a great] respect for sb./sth.; **jmdm.** ∼ **einflößen** fill sb. with awe

ehrfürchtig **1** *Adj.* reverent. **2** *adv.* reverently

ehr-, Ehr-: ∼**gefühl** *das; o. Pl.* sense of honour; ∼**geiz** *der* ambition; ∼**geizig** **1** *Adj.* ambitious; **2** *adv.* ambitiously

ehrlich **1** *Adj.* honest ⟨person, face, answer, deal⟩; genuine ⟨concern, desire, admiration⟩; upright ⟨character⟩; honourable ⟨intentions⟩; (wahrheitsgetreu) truthful ⟨answer, statement⟩; **der** ∼**e Finder gab die Brieftasche ab** the person who found the wallet handed (Brit.) *or* (Amer.) turned it in; ∼ **währt am längsten** (Spr.) honesty is the best policy (prov.). **2** *adv.* honestly; **etw.** ∼ **teilen** share sth.; ∼ **spielen** play fairly; **es** ∼ **mit jmdm. meinen** play straight with sb.; ∼ **gesagt** quite honestly; to be honest

Ehrlichkeit *die;* ∼ ⇒ **ehrlich 1:** honesty; genuineness; uprightness; honourableness; truthfulness

ehr·los **1** *Adj.* dishonourable; **2** *adv.* dishonourably

Ehr·losigkeit *die;* ∼: dishonourableness

Ehrung *die;* ∼, ∼**en (a) die** ∼ **der Preisträger** the prize-giving (Brit.) *or* (Amer.) awards ceremony; **bei der** ∼ **der Sieger** when the winners were awarded their medals/trophies; **(b)** (etw. Ehrendes) honour

ehr·würdig *Adj.* **(a)** venerable ⟨person⟩; **ein** ∼**es Alter haben** ⟨person⟩ have reached a grand old age; ⟨building⟩ be of great age; **(b)** (kath. Kirche) ∼**er Vater/** ∼**e Mutter** Reverend Father/ Mother

ei /ai̯/ *Interj.* hey; (abschätzig) oho

Ei /ai̯/ *das;* ~[e]s, ~er (a) egg; (Physiol., Zool.) ovum; **aus dem ~ schlüpfen** hatch [out]; **verlorene** *od.* **pochierte** ~er poached eggs; **russische** ~er egg mayonnaise; Russian eggs; **sie geht wie auf [rohen]** ~ern (fig.) she is walking very carefully; **ach, du dickes** ~! (ugs.) dash it! (Brit. coll.); darn it! (Amer. coll.); **das ~ des Kolumbus** (fig.) an inspired discovery; **wie aus dem ~ gepellt sein** (fig.) be dressed to the nines; **sich gleichen wie ein ~ dem anderen** be as like as two peas in a pod; *s. auch* **Apfel;** (b) (derb: Hoden) *meist Pl.* ~er balls (coarse); nuts (Amer. coarse)

Eibe /'ai̯bə/ *die;* ~, ~n yew[-tree]

Eiche /'ai̯çə/ *die;* ~, ~n oak[-tree]; (Holz) oak[-wood]

Eichel /'ai̯çl̩/ *die;* ~, ~n (a) (Frucht) acorn; (b) ▶326┤ (Anat.) glans

Eichel·häher *der* jay

eichen *tr. V.* calibrate ‹*measuring instrument, thermometer*›; standardize ‹*weights, measures*›

Eichen-: ~**holz** *das* oak[-wood]; ~**wald** *der* oak-wood; (größer) oak forest

Eich·hörnchen *das*, (landsch.) **Eich·kätzchen** *das* squirrel

Eid /ai̯t/ *der;* ~[e]s, ~e oath; **einen ~ leisten** *od.* **ablegen** swear *or* take an oath; **einen ~ auf die Verfassung schwören** solemnly swear to preserve, protect, and defend the constitution

Eid·bruch *der* breach of one's oath; (Rechtsw.) perjury *no indef. art.;* **einen ~ begehen** break one's oath

eid·brüchig *Adj.* treacherous ‹*ally*›; ~ **werden** break one's oath; (Rechtsw.) perjure oneself

Eidechse /'ai̯dɛksə/ *die;* ~, ~n lizard

Eides·formel *die* (jur.) wording of the oath

eides·stattlich (Rechtsw.) 1 *Adj.* ~**e Erklärung** statutory declaration. 2 *adv.* ~ **erklären** *od.* **versichern, dass …:** attest in a statutory declaration that …

eid-, Eid-: ~**genosse** *der* Swiss; ~**genossenschaft** *die; o. Pl.* **die Schweizerische** ~**genossenschaft** the Swiss Confederation; ~**genössisch** *Adj.* Swiss

eidlich 1 *Adj.* made under oath *postpos.* 2 *adv.* on oath

Ei·dotter *der od. das* egg yolk

Eier-: ~**becher** *der* eggcup; ~**farbe** *die* paint for decorating eggs as Easter gifts; ~**kuchen** *der* pancake; (Omelett) omelette; ~**laufen** *das* egg-and-spoon race; ~**likör** *der* egg-liqueur; ~**löffel** *der* egg-spoon

eiern *itr. V.* (ugs.) wobble

eier-, Eier-: ~**nudel** *die* egg noodle; ~**pfann·kuchen** *der* ⇨ ~**kuchen;** ~**schale** *die* eggshell; ~**schalen·farben** *Adj.* off-white; ~**speise** *die* (a) egg dish; (b) (österr.) scrambled egg; ~**stock** *der* (Anat.) ▶326┤ ovary; ~**uhr** *die* egg-timer

Eifer /'ai̯fɐ/ *der;* ~s eagerness; (Emsigkeit) zeal; (Begeisterung) enthusiasm; **im ~ des Gefechts** in the *or* with all the excitement

Eiferer *der;* ~s, ~ (geh.) zealot

eifern *itr. V.* **für/gegen etw.** ~: agitate for/against sth.

Eifer·sucht *die* jealousy (**auf** + *Akk.* of)

eifer·süchtig 1 *Adj.* jealous (**auf** + *Akk.* of). 2 *adv.* jealously

ei·förmig *Adj.* egg-shaped

eifrig 1 *Adj.* eager; enthusiastic ‹*supporter, collector*›; (fleißig) assiduous; ~ **bei etw. sein** show keen interest in doing sth. 2 *adv.* eagerly; ~ **dabei sein, etw. zu tun** be busy doing sth.; ~ **bemüht sein, etw. zu tun** be eager to do sth.

Ei·gelb *das;* ~[e]s, ~e egg yolk; **drei** ~: the yolks of three eggs

eigen /'ai̯gn̩/ *Adj.* (a) *nicht präd.* own; **eine** ~**e Wohnung haben** have one's own flat (Brit.) *or* (Amer.) apartment; **ein Zimmer mit** ~**em Eingang** a room with a separate entrance; **auf** ~**en Füßen** *od.* **Beinen stehen** stand on one's own two feet; ***sich** (*Dat.*) **etw. zu eigen machen** ⇨ **Eigen;** (b) (kennzeichnend) characteristic; (c) (landsch.: penibel) particular (**mit** about)

Eigen *in* **sich** (*Dat.*) **etw. zu** ~ **machen** adopt sth.

eigen-, Eigen-: ~**art** *die* peculiarity; **eine** ~**art dieser Stadt** one of the characteristic features of this city; ~**artig** *Adj.* peculiar; strange; odd; ~**artigerweise** *Adv.* strangely [enough]; oddly [enough]; ~**brötler** /~brøːtlɐ/ *der;* ~s, ~: loner; lone wolf; ~**brötlerisch** 1 *Adj.* solitary; 2 *adv.* **sich** ~**brötlerisch verhalten** behave like a loner *or* a lone wolf; ~**gewicht** *das* own weight; ~**händig** 1 *Adj.* personal ‹*signature*›; personally inscribed ‹*dedication*›; holographic ‹*will, document*›; 2 *adv.* personally; ~**heim** *das* house of one's own

Eigenheit *die;* ~, ~en peculiarity

eigen-, Eigen-: ~**initiative** *die* initiative of one's own; ~**interesse** *das* personal interest; ~**kapital** *das* (Wirtsch.) equity capital; ~**leben** *das; o. Pl.* life of one's own; ~**liebe** *die* amour propre; ~**lob** *das* self-praise; ~**lob stinkt!** (ugs.) self-praise is no recommendation; ~**mächtig** 1 *Adj.* unauthorized ‹*decision*›; (selbstherrlich) high-handed; 2 *adv.* ~**mächtig handeln** act on one's own authority; (selbstherrlich) act high-handedly; **etw.** ~**mächtig tun** do sth. without asking; ~**mächtigkeit** *die;* ~, ~en (a) *o. Pl.* high-handedness; (b) (Handlung) unauthorized action; ~**name** *der* proper name; (Ling.) proper noun; ~**nutz** *der;* ~es self-interest; ~**nützig** /~nʏtsɪç/ 1 *Adj.* self-interested, self-seeking ‹*person*›; selfish ‹*motive*›; 2 *adv.* selfishly

eigens *Adv.* specially; ~ **für diesen Zweck** specifically for this purpose

Eigenschaft *die;* ~, ~en (von Lebewesen) quality; characteristic; (von Sachen, Stoffen) property; **in seiner** ~ **als Mann/Vorsitzender** as a man/in his capacity as chairman

Eigenschafts·wort *das* adjective

eigen-, Eigen-: ~**sinn** *der; o. Pl.* obstinacy; stubbornness; ~**sinnig** 1 *Adj.* obstinate; stubborn; 2 *adv.* obstinately; stubbornly; ~**sinnigkeit** *die* ⇨ ~**sinn;** ~**ständig** 1 *Adj.* independent; 2 *adv.* independently; ~**ständigkeit** *die;* ~: independence; ~**süchtig** 1 *Adj.* selfish; 2 *adv.* selfishly

eigentlich /'ai̯gn̩tlɪç/ 1 *Adj.; nicht präd.* (wirklich) actual; real; (wahr) true; (ursprünglich) original; **das Eigentliche** the essential thing. 2 *Adv.* (tatsächlich, genau genommen) actually; really; ~ **müsste ich ja jetzt gehen, aber …:** really, I ought to go now, but …; **es ist** ~ **schade, dass …:** actually, it's a pity that… 3 *Partikel* **wann erscheint** ~ **der letzte Band?** tell me, when will the last volume come out; **sind sie** ~ **verheiratet?** are they in fact married?; **wer sind Sie** ~? who do you think you are?; **was willst du** ~? what exactly do you want?

Eigen·tor *das* (Ballspiele, fig.) own goal

Eigentum *das;* ~s, ~s property; (einschließlich Geld usw.) assets *pl.;* **geistiges** ~: [one's own] intellectual creation; (b) (Recht des Eigentümers) ownership (**an** + *Dat.* of)

Eigentümer /'ai̯gn̩tyːmɐ/ *der;* ~s, ~: owner; (Hotel~, Geschäfts~) proprietor; owner

Eigentümerin *die* owner; (Hotel~, Geschäfts~) proprietress; proprietor; owner

eigentümlich /'ai̯gn̩tyːmlɪç/ 1 *Adj.* (a) (typisch) peculiar; characteristic; (b) (eigenartig) peculiar; strange; odd. 2 *adv.* peculiarly; strangely; oddly

Eigentümlichkeit *die;* ~, ~en (a) *o. Pl.* (Eigenartigkeit) peculiarity; strangeness; (b) (typischer Zug) peculiarity

Eigentums-: ~**delikt** *das* offence against property; ~**wohnung** *die* owner-occupied flat (Brit.); condominium *or* co-op apartment (Amer.); **eine** ~**wohnung kaufen** buy a flat (Brit.) *or* (Amer.) an apartment

eigen-, Eigen-: ~**verantwortlich** 1 *Adj.* responsible; 2 *adv.* ~**verantwortlich handeln** act on one's own authority; **etw.** ~**verantwortlich bestimmen/entscheiden** decide sth. on one's own responsibility; ~**wert** *der* intrinsic value; ~**willig** *Adj.* (a) self-willed ‹*person*›; individual ‹*style, idea*›; (b) (~sinnig) obstinate; stubborn; ~**willigkeit** *die;* ~, ~en (a) *o. Pl.* individualism; independence of mind; (b) (Handlung) display of self-will

eignen *refl. V.* be suitable; **sich als** *od.* **zum Lehrer** ~: be suitable as a teacher; **das Buch eignet sich gut als**

Geschenk this book makes a good present; **für solche Arbeiten eignet er sich besonders** he is particularly well suited for that kind of work; *s. auch* **geeignet**

Eigner *der;* ~s, ~: owner

Eignung *die;* ~: suitability; aptitude; **seine** ~ **zum Fliegen** his aptitude for flying

Eignungs-: ~**prüfung** *die,* ~**test** *der* aptitude test

Ei·klar *das;* ~s, ~ (österr.) ⇒ **Eiweiß a**

Ei·land *das;* ~[e]s, ~e (veralt., dichter.) isle (poet.)

Eil- /ail-/: ~**bote** *der* special messenger; „**durch** *od.* **per** ~**boten**" (veralt.) 'express'; ~**brief** *der* express letter

Eile /'ailə/ *die;* ~: hurry; **ich habe keine** *od.* **bin nicht in** ~: I'm not in a *or* any hurry; **die Sache hat keine** ~: there's no hurry; it's not urgent; **in aller** ~: in great haste; **jmdn. zur** ~ **antreiben** hurry sb. up

Ei·leiter *der* (Anat.) ▶ 326 Fallopian tube

eilen 1 *itr. V.* (a) *mit sein* hurry; hasten; (besonders schnell) rush; **nach Hause** ~: hurry/rush home; **jmdm. zu Hilfe** ~: rush to sb.'s aid; (b) (dringend sein) ⟨*matter*⟩ be urgent; „**eilt!**" 'urgent'; „**eilt sehr!**" 'immediate'. 2 *refl. V.* hurry; make haste

eilends *Adv.* (geh.) hastily

Eil·gut *das* fast freight; express goods *pl.*

eilig 1 *Adj.* (a) (schnell) hurried; **mit** ~**en Schritten** hurriedly; **es** ~ **haben** be in a hurry; (b) (dringend) urgent ⟨*news*⟩; **es** [**sehr**] ~ **mit etw. haben** be in a [great] hurry about sth.; **nichts Eiligeres zu tun haben, als ...** (iron) have nothing better to do than... 2 *adv.* hurriedly

Eil-: ~**schritt** *der:* **im** ~**schritt laufen** walk with short, quick steps; ~**sendung** *die* express consignment; ~**tempo** *das* (ugs.) **im** ~**tempo** in a rush; ~**zug** *der* semi-fast train; stopping train (Brit.); ~**zustellung** *die* (Postw.) express delivery

Eimer /'aimə/ *der;* ~s, ~ bucket; (Abfall~) bin; **ein** ~ [**voll**] **Wasser** a bucket of water; **es gießt wie aus** ~**n** (ugs.) it's raining cats and dogs (coll.); it's coming down in buckets (coll.); **im** ~ **sein** (salopp) be up the spout (coll.)

eimer·weise *Adv.* by the bucketful; in bucketfuls

ein¹, **eine**, **ein** /ain/ 1 *Kardinalz.* ▶ 600 **ich will dir noch** ~[**e**]**s sagen** there's one more thing I'd like to tell you; ~**er von beiden** one of the two; one or the other; ~**er für alle, alle für** ~**en** one for all and all for one; ~ **allemal** once and for all; ~ **und derselbe** one and the same; ~**er Meinung sein** be of the same opinion. 2 *unbest. Art.* a/an; ~ **Kleid/Apfel** a dress/an apple; ~ **bisschen** *od.* **wenig** a little [bit]; ~ **anderer** somebody else; ~ **jeder** (geh.) each and every one; ~**e Kälte ist das hier!** it's freezing here! 3 *Indefinitpron.:* ⇒ **irgendein** a; *s. auch* **einer**

ein² (elliptisch) ~ – **aus** (an Schaltern) on – off; ~ **und aus gehen** go in and out; **bei jmdm.** ~ **und aus gehen** be a regular visitor at sb.'s house; **ich wusste nicht** ~ **noch aus** I didn't know where to turn *or* what to do

Einakter /'ain|aktə/ *der;* ~s, ~: one-act play

einander /ai'nandə/ *reziprokes Pron.; Dat u. Akk.* (geh.) each other; one another

ein|arbeiten *tr. V.* (a) (ausbilden) train ⟨*employee*⟩; **sich in etw.** (*Akk.*) ~: become familiar *or* familiarize oneself with sth.; (b) (einfügen) incorporate ⟨*quotation etc.*⟩ (**in** + *Akk.* into)

Einarbeitung *die;* ~, ~**en** training

ein·armig *Adj.* one-armed; **ein Einarmiger** a one-armed man

ein|äschern /'ain|ɛʃən/ *tr. V.* (a) reduce ⟨*building etc.*⟩ to ashes; (b) cremate ⟨*corpse*⟩

Einäscherung *die;* ~, ~**en** (a) (das Niederbrennen) burning down; **die** ~ **der Stadt** the destruction of the town by fire; (b) (Leichenverbrennung) cremation

ein|atmen *tr., itr. V.* breathe in

ein·äugig *Adj.* one-eyed; single-lens ⟨*camera*⟩

Ein·bahn·straße *die* one-way street

ein|balsamieren *tr. V.* embalm

Ein·band *der; Pl.* **-bände** binding; [book-] cover

ein·bändig *Adj.* one-volume

Ein·bau *der; o. Pl.* (a) fitting; (eines Motors) installation; (b) ⇒ **einbauen b**: insertion; incorporation

---

ein|bauen *tr. V.* (a) build in, fit ⟨*cupboard, kitchen*⟩; install ⟨*engine, motor*⟩; (b) (einfügen) insert, incorporate ⟨*chapter*⟩

Einbau-: ~**küche** *die* fitted kitchen; ~**möbel** *Pl.* built-in furniture *sing.;* (Regale) fitted shelves; ~**schrank** *der* built-in cupboard; (für Kleidung) built-in wardrobe

ein|behalten *unr. tr. V.* withhold

ein·beinig *Adj.* one-legged

ein|berufen *unr. tr. V.* (a) summon; call; **den Bundestag** ~: summon the Bundestag; (b) (zur Wehrpflicht) call up; conscript; draft (Amer.)

Ein·berufung *die* (a) calling; **die** ~ **des Parlaments** the summoning of Parliament; (b) (zur Wehrpflicht) call-up; conscription; draft (Amer.)

Einberufungs-: ~**befehl** *der,* ~**bescheid** *der* call-up papers *pl.;* draft card (Amer.)

ein|bestellen *tr. V.* (Amtsspr.) summon

ein|betonieren *tr. V.* concrete in

ein|betten *tr. V.* embed (**in** + *Akk.* in)

Einbett-: ~**kabine** *die* single-berth cabin; ~**zimmer** *das* single room

ein|beulen *tr. V. etw.* ~: dent sth.; make a dent in sth.

ein|beziehen *unr. tr. V.* include (**in** + *Akk.* in)

Ein·beziehung *die o. Pl.* inclusion (**in** + *Akk.* in)

ein|biegen 1 *unr. itr. V.; mit sein* ▶ 595 turn (**in** + *Akk.* into); [**nach**] **links/rechts** ~: turn left/right. 2 *unr. tr. V.* bend

ein|bilden *refl. V.* (a) **sich** (*Dat.*) **etw.** ~: imagine sth.; **eine eingebildete Krankheit** an imaginary illness; **was bildest du dir eigentlich ein?** (ugs.) what do you think you are doing?; (b) (ugs.) **sich etwas** ~: be conceited (**auf** + *Akk.* about); **er bildet sich** (*Dat.*) **ganz schön viel ein** he thinks no end of himself (coll.); **darauf brauchst du dir nichts einzubilden** there's no need to be stuck-up about it

Ein·bildung *die;* ~, ~**en** (a) *o. Pl.* (Fantasie) imagination; (b) (falsche Vorstellung) fantasy; **das ist alles nur** ~: it's all in the mind; (c) *o. Pl.* (Hochmut) conceitedness

Einbildungs-: ~**kraft** *die,* ~**vermögen** *das* [powers *pl.* of] imagination; imaginative powers *pl.*

ein|binden *unr. tr. V.* (a) bind ⟨*book*⟩; **etw. neu** ~: re-bind sth.; (b) (fig.: integrieren) link (**in** + *Akk.* into); **in ein System eingebunden bleiben** remain part of a system

ein|bläuen *tr. V.* **jmdm. etw.** ~: drum *or* hammer sth. into sb.

ein|blenden (Rundf., Ferns., Film) 1 *tr. V.* insert; **eine Nachricht in eine Sendung** ~: interrupt a programme with a news flash; **Musik nachträglich** ~: dub in music. 2 *refl. V.* **sich in ein Fußballspiel** ~: go over to a football match

Ein·blendung *die* (Rundf., Ferns., Film) insertion

*ein|bleuen ⇒ **einbläuen**

Ein·blick *der* (a) view (**in** + *Akk.* into); ~ **in etw.** (*Akk.*) **haben** be able to see into sth.; (b) ⇒ **Einsicht b**; (c) (fig.: Kenntnis) insight (**in** + *Akk.* into)

ein|brechen *unr. itr. V.* (a) *mit haben od. sein* break in; **in eine Bank** ~: break into a bank; **bei jmdm.** ~: burgle sb.; (b) *mit sein* (einstürzen) ⟨*roof, ceiling*⟩ fall in, cave in; (c) *mit sein* (durchbrechen) fall through; (d) *mit sein* (eindringen) **in ein Land** ~: invade a country; (e) *mit sein* (geh.: beginnen) ⟨*night, darkness*⟩ fall; ⟨*winter*⟩ set in

Ein·brecher *der;* ~s, ~: burglar

ein|bringen 1 *unr. tr. V.* (a) bring *or* gather in ⟨*harvest*⟩; (b) (verschaffen) yield ⟨*profit*⟩ bring in ⟨*interest, money*⟩; bring ⟨*fame, honour*⟩; **das bringt nichts ein** it isn't worth it; (c) (Parl.: vorlegen) introduce ⟨*bill*⟩; (d) (in eine Gemeinschaft, Gesellschaft usw.) invest ⟨*capital, money*⟩; **etw. in eine Ehe** ~: bring sth. into a marriage. 2 *unr. refl. V.* **sich in eine Beziehung** ~: make one's own contribution to a relationship

ein|brocken *tr. V.* (ugs.) **sich/jmdm. etwas** [**Schönes**] ~, **sich/jmdm. eine schöne Suppe** ~: land oneself/sb. in the soup (fig. coll.) *or* (coll.) in it; **das hast du dir**

selbst eingebrockt you've only yourself to thank for that (coll.)

Ein·bruch *der* (a) burglary; break-in (**in** + *Akk.* at); (b) (das Einstürzen) collapse; **ein ∼ der Börsenkurse** (fig.) a slump in stock market prices; (c) ⇨ **einbrechen d**: invasion (**in** + *Akk.* of); (d) (Beginn) **vor ∼ der Dunkelheit** before it gets dark; **der ∼ des Winters** the onset of winter; **bei ∼ der Nacht** at nightfall; when night closes/closed in

einbruch[s]·sicher *Adj.* burglar-proof

ein|buchten *tr. V.* (salopp) **jmdn. ∼:** lock sb. up (coll.); put sb. away (coll.)

Einbuchtung *die; ∼, ∼en* (a) (Bucht) bay; inlet; (b) (Delle) dent

einbürgern ▶388⏐ 1 *tr. V.* naturalize ⟨*person, plant, animal*⟩; introduce ⟨*custom, practice*⟩. 2 *refl. V.* ⟨*custom, practice*⟩ become established; ⟨*person, plant, animal*⟩ become naturalized

Einbürgerung *die; ∼, ∼en* naturalization

Ein·buße *die* loss (**an** + *Dat.* of)

ein|büßen 1 *tr. V.* lose; (durch eigene Schuld) forfeit. 2 *itr. V.* **sie büßte an Ansehen ein** her reputation suffered

ein|checken *tr., itr. V.* (Flugw.) check in

ein|cremen *tr. V.* put cream on ⟨*hands, back*⟩; **sich ∼:** put cream on

ein|dämmen *tr. V.* (fig.) check; stem

Eindämmung *die; ∼, ∼en* ⇨ **eindämmen**: checking, stemming

ein|decken 1 *refl. V.* stock up. 2 *tr. V.* (ugs.: überhäufen) swamp

ein|dellen *tr. V.* (ugs.) dent [in]

eindeutig /'aindɔytɪç/ 1 *Adj.* (a) (klar) clear; clear, definite ⟨*proof*⟩; (b) (nicht mehrdeutig) unambiguous. 2 *adv. s. Adj.* clearly; unambiguously

Eindeutigkeit *die; ∼:* ⇨ **eindeutig**: clarity; unambiguity

ein|deutschen *tr. V.* Germanize

Eindeutschung *die; ∼, ∼en* (a) *o. Pl.* Germanization; (b) (Wort) Germanized word

ein·dimensional *Adj.* one-dimensional

ein|dösen *itr. V.* (ugs.) *mit sein* doze off

ein|drängen *itr. V.; mit sein* **auf jmdn. ∼:** crowd around sb.; **Eindrücke/Erinnerungen drängten auf ihn ein** (fig.) impressions/memories crowded in [up]on him

ein|drehen *tr. V.* (a) screw in ⟨*light bulb*⟩ (**in** + *Akk.* into); (b) **sich** (*Dat.*) **die Haare ∼:** put one's hair in curlers *or* rollers

ein|dringen *unr. itr. V.; mit sein* (a) **in etw.** (*Akk.*) **∼:** penetrate into sth.; ⟨*vermin*⟩ get into sth.; ⟨*bullet*⟩ pierce sth.; (allmählich) ⟨*water, sand, etc.*⟩ seep into sth.; (b) (einbrechen) **in ein Gebäude ∼:** force an entry *or* one's way into a building; **Feinde sind in das Land eingedrungen** (geh.) enemies invaded the country; (c) **∼ auf** (+ *Akk.*) set upon, attack ⟨*person*⟩; **mit Fragen auf jmdn. ∼:** besiege *or* ply sb. with questions

ein·dringlich 1 *Adj.* urgent ⟨*warning, entreaty*⟩; impressive ⟨*voice*⟩; forceful, powerful ⟨*speech, words*⟩. 2 *adv.* ⟨*urge*⟩ strongly; ⟨*talk*⟩ insistently

Ein·dringlichkeit *die; ∼* ⇨ **eindringlich**: urgency; impressiveness; forcefulness

Eindringling /'aindrɪŋlɪŋ/ *der; ∼s, ∼e* intruder

Ein·druck *der; ∼[e]s, Eindrücke* (Druckstelle, fig.) impression; **∼ auf jmdn. machen** make an impression on sb.; **er tat es nur, um [bei ihr] ∼ zu schinden** (ugs.) he only did it to impress [her]

ein|drücken *tr. V.* (a) smash in ⟨*mudguard, bumper*⟩; stave in ⟨*side of ship*⟩; smash ⟨*pier, support*⟩; break ⟨*window*⟩; crush ⟨*ribs*⟩; flatten ⟨*nose*⟩; (b) (hineindrücken) **etw. [in etw.** (*Akk.*)**] ∼:** press *or* push sth. in[to sth.]

eindrucks·voll 1 *Adj.* impressive; 2 *adv.* impressively

eine ⇨ **einer**

ein|ebnen *tr. V.* level (fig.) eliminate ⟨*difference*⟩

Einebnung *die; ∼, ∼en* levelling; (fig.) elimination

eineiig /'ain|ai:ɪç/ *Adj.* identical ⟨*twins*⟩

ein·ein·halb *Bruchz.* ▶600⏐ one and a half; **∼ Stunden** an hour and a half; one and a half hours; **∼ Jahre** eighteen months

ein·ein·halb·fach *Vervielfältigungsz.* one and a half times; **die ∼e Anzahl** one and a half times the number

ein|engen *tr. V.* (a) **jmdn. ∼:** restrict sb.'s movement[s]; **sich eingeengt fühlen** feel hemmed in *or* shut in; (b) (fig.: einschränken) restrict; **jmdn. in seiner Freiheit ∼:** restrict *or* curb sb.'s freedom

einer, eine, eines, eins *Indefinitpron.* (man) one; (jemand) someone; somebody; (fragend, verneint) anyone; anybody; **das mach mal einem verständlich** try explaining that to anybody; **eine/einer/ein[e]s der besten** one of the best [people/things]; **kaum einer** hardly anybody; **einer nach dem anderen** one after the other; one by one; **die einen …, die anderen …:** some …, the others …; **er trinkt ganz gerne einen** (ugs.) he likes [to have] a drink; **ein[e]s ist sicher** one thing is for sure

Einer *der; ∼s, ∼* (a) (Math.) unit; (b) (Sport) single sculler; **im ∼:** in the single sculls

einerlei /'ainɐlai/ *Adj.; nicht attr.* (unwichtig) **∼, ob/wo/wer** *usw.* no matter whether/where/who *etc.;* **es ist ∼:** it makes no difference; **es ist ihm ∼:** it is all the same *or* all one to him

Einerlei *das; ∼s* monotony

einerseits /'ainɐzaits/ *Adv.* on the one hand

Einer·stelle *die* (Math.) units place

eines ⇨ **einer**

ein·fach 1 *Adj.* (a) simple; simple, easy ⟨*task*⟩; plain, simple ⟨*food*⟩; (b) (nicht mehrfach) single ⟨*knot, ticket, journey*⟩. 2 *adv.* (a) simply; (b) (nicht mehrfach) **etw. ∼ falten** fold sth. once; **zweimal ∼ [nach Köln]** two singles [to Cologne]. 3 *Partikel* simply; just

Einfachheit *die; ∼* simplicity; (der Nahrung) plainness; simplicity; **der ∼ halber** for the sake of simplicity; for simplicity's sake

ein|fädeln 1 *tr. V.* (a) thread ⟨*needle, film, tape*⟩ (**in** + *Akk.* into); thread up ⟨*sewing machine*⟩; **einen [neuen] Faden ∼:** (re)thread the needle; (b) (ugs.: geschickt einleiten) engineer ⟨*scheme, plot*⟩; **das hat sie fein/schlau eingefädelt** she worked that nicely/craftily (coll.). 2 *refl. V.* (Verkehrsw.) filter in; **sich in den fließenden Verkehr ∼:** filter into the flow of traffic

ein|fahren 1 *unr. itr. V.; mit sein* come in; ⟨*train*⟩ come *or* pull in; **in den Bahnhof ∼:** come *or* pull into the station; **der Zug nach Hamburg ist soeben auf Gleis 5 eingefahren** the Hamburg train has just arrived at platform 5. 2 *unr. tr. V.* (a) bring in ⟨*harvest*⟩; (b) (beschädigen) knock down ⟨*wall*⟩; smash in ⟨*mudguard*⟩; (c) (Kfz-W.) run in ⟨*car*⟩; (d) (Technik) retract ⟨*undercarriage, antenna, aerial, etc.*⟩; *s. auch* **eingefahren**

Ein·fahrt *die* (a) (Weg, Straße, Stelle zum Hineinfahren) entrance; (Autobahn∼) slip road; (b) (das Hineinfahren) entry; **Vorsicht bei der ∼ des Zuges!** stand clear [of the edge of the platform], the train is approaching

Ein·fall *der* (a) (Idee) idea; (b) *o. Pl.* (Licht∼) incidence (Optics); (c) (in ein Land usw.) invasion (**in** + *Akk.* of)

ein|fallen *unr. itr. V.; mit sein* (a) **jmdm. fällt etw. ein** sb. thinks of sth.; sth. occurs to sb.; **ihm fallen immer wieder neue Ausreden ein** he can always think of *or* (coll.) come up with new excuses; **was fällt dir denn ein!** what do you think you're doing?; how dare you?; (b) (in Erinnerung kommen) **ihr Name fällt mir nicht ein** I cannot think of her name; **es wird dir schon [wieder] ∼:** it will come [back] to you; **plötzlich fiel ihr ein, dass …** suddenly she remembered that …; (c) (von Licht) come in; (d) (gewaltsam eindringen) **in ein Land ∼:** invade a country; (e) (einstimmen, mitreden usw.) join in

einfalls-, Einfalls-: ∼los 1 *Adj.* unimaginative; lacking in ideas; 2 *adv.* unimaginatively; without imagination; **∼losigkeit** *die; ∼:* unimaginativeness; lack of ideas; **~reich 1** *Adj.* imaginative; full of ideas; **2** *adv.* imaginatively; with imagination; **~reichtum** *der; o. Pl.* imaginativeness; wealth of ideas

Einfalt /'ainfalt/ *die;* **~:** simpleness; simple-mindedness

einfältig /'ainfɛltɪç/ *Adj.* **(a)** (arglos) simple; naïve; artless; naïve ⟨*remarks*⟩; **sei nicht so ~!** don't be so naïve!; **(b)** (beschränkt) simple; simple-minded

Einfältigkeit *die;* **~ (a)** (Arglosigkeit) simplicity; naïvety; **(b)** (Beschränktheit) simpleness; simple-mindedness

Einfalts·pinsel *der* (ugs. abwertend) nincompoop

Ein·familien·haus *das* [detached] house

ein|fangen 1 *unr. tr. V.* **(a)** catch, capture ⟨*fugitive, animal*⟩; **(b)** (fig. geh.) capture ⟨*atmosphere, aura, etc.*⟩. **2** *unr. refl. V.* (ugs.: bekommen) **sich** (*Dat.*) **eine Erkältung** *usw.* **~:** catch *or* get a cold *etc.*

ein|färben *tr. V.* dye

ein·farbig *Adj.* single-colour; of one colour *postpos.;* (ohne Muster) plain

ein|fassen *tr. V.* border, hem, edge ⟨*material, dress, tablecloth*⟩; set ⟨*gem*⟩; edge ⟨*lawn, flower bed, grave*⟩; curb ⟨*source, spring*⟩

Ein·fassung *die* ⇒ **einfassen:** border; hem; edging; setting; (von Brunnen, Quelle) enclosure

ein|fetten *tr. V.* grease; dubbin ⟨*leather*⟩; **sich** (*Dat.*) **die Haut/Hände ~:** rub cream into one's skin/hands

ein|finden *unr. refl. V.* arrive; ⟨*crowd*⟩ gather

ein|flechten *unr. tr. V.* **Episoden in einen Roman ~:** weave episodes into a novel; **wenn ich das kurz ~ darf** if I could turn to this for a moment

ein|fliegen 1 *unr. tr. V.* fly in ⟨*supplies, troops*⟩. **2** *unr. itr. V.; mit sein* fly in; **in etw. ~:** fly into sth.

ein|fließen *unr. itr. V.; mit sein* flow in; **von Norden fließt Kaltluft nach Westeuropa ein** (fig.) a cold northerly airstream is moving into Western Europe; **etw. in ein Gespräch ~ lassen** (fig.) slip sth. into a conversation

ein|flößen *tr. V.* **(a)** jmdm. Tee/Medizin **~:** pour tea/medicine into sb.'s mouth; **(b)** (fig.) **jmdm. Angst ~:** put fear into sb.; arouse fear in sb.

Einflug·schneise *die* (Flugw.) approach path

Ein·fluss, *Ein·fluß *der* influence (**auf** + *Akk.* on); **unter jmds. ~** (*Dat.*) **stehen** be under sb.'s influence

Einfluss·bereich, *Einfluß·bereich *der* sphere of influence

einfluss·reich, *einfluß·reich *Adj.* influential

ein·förmig 1 *Adj.* monotonous. **2** *adv.* monotonously

Ein·förmigkeit *die;* **~, ~en** monotony

ein|fressen *unr. refl. V.* **sich in etw.** (*Akk.*) **~:** eat into sth.

ein|frieren 1 *unr. itr. V.; mit sein* ⟨*water*⟩ freeze, turn to ice; ⟨*pond*⟩ freeze over; ⟨*pipes*⟩ freeze up; ⟨*ship*⟩ be frozen in. **2** *unr. tr. V.* **(a)** deep-freeze ⟨*food*⟩; **(b)** (fig.) freeze

ein|fügen 1 *tr. V.* fit in; **etw. in etw.** (*Akk.*) **~:** fit sth. into sth.; **etw. in einen Text ~:** insert sth. into a text. **2** *refl. V.* adapt; **sich in etw.** (*Akk.*) **~:** adapt oneself to sth.; **sich überall gut ~:** fit in well anywhere

ein|fühlen *refl. V.* **sich in jmdn. ~:** empathize with sb.; **ich kann mich gut in deine Lage ~:** I know exactly how you feel; **er kann sich gut in eine Rolle ~:** he is good at getting into a part

einfühlsam *Adj.* understanding; sensitive ⟨*interpretation, performance*⟩

Einfühlungs·vermögen *das* ability to empathize

Ein·fuhr *die;* **~, ~en** import

ein|führen 1 *tr. V.* **(a)** (importieren) import; **(b)** (als Neuerung) introduce ⟨*method, technology*⟩; **(c)** (ein-, unterweisen) introduce (**in** + *Akk.* to); **jmdn. in sein Amt ~:** install sb. in office; **(d)** (hineinschieben) introduce, insert ⟨*catheter etc.*⟩ (**in** + *Akk.* into). **2** *refl. V.* (Kaufmannsspr.) ⟨*shop, company*⟩ become established

Einfuhr-: **~erlaubnis, ~genehmigung** *die* import licence; **~sperre** *die,* **~stopp** *der* embargo or ban on imports

---

Ein·führung *die* **(a)** introduction; **die ~ in sein Amt** his installation in office; **(b)** (Einarbeitung) introduction; initiation; induction; **(c)** (das Hineinschieben) introduction; insertion

Einführungs-: **~kurs[us]** *der* (Schulw.) introductory course; **~preis** *der* (Kaufmannsspr.) introductory price

Einfuhr- **~verbot** *das* ⇒ **~sperre; ~zoll** *der* import duty

ein|füllen *tr. V.* etw. in etwas (*Akk.*) **~:** pour *or* put sth. into something

Ein·gabe *die* **(a)** (Gesuch) petition; (Beschwerde) complaint; **(b)** (DV) input

Eingabe·gerät *das* (DV) input device

Ein·gang *der* **(a)** (Zutritt) entrance; „**kein ~**" 'no entry'; **in etw.** (*Akk.*) **~ finden** (fig.) become established in sth.; **(b)** *o. Pl.* (von Post, Geld) receipt; **(c)** (Elektrot.) input

ein·gängig *Adj.* catchy ⟨*song, melody*⟩

eingangs *Adv.* at the beginning; at the start

Eingangs-: **~buch** *das* (Buchf.) 'goods inward' book; **~datum** *das* (Bürow.) date of receipt; **~halle** *die* entrance hall; (eines Hotels, Theaters) foyer; **~tür** *die* [entrance] door; (von Wohnung, Haus usw.) front door

ein|geben *unr. tr. V.* (DV) feed in; **etw. in den Computer ~:** feed sth. into the computer

ein·gebildet *Adj.* **(a)** (imaginär) imaginary ⟨*illness*⟩; **ein ~er Kranker** a malade imaginaire; **~e Schwangerschaft** false pregnancy; **(b)** (arrogant) conceited

ein·geboren *Adj.* native ⟨*population etc.*⟩

Eingeborene *der/die; adj. Dekl.* (veralt.) native

Eingebung *die;* **~, ~en** inspiration; **einer ~ folgend** acting on a sudden impulse

eingedenk /'aingədɛŋk/ *Adj.; nicht attr.* **einer Sache** (*Gen.*) **~ sein** (geh.) be mindful of sth.; **~ der Tatsache, dass …:** bearing in mind that …

ein·gefahren *Adj.* long-established; **sich auf** *od.* **in ~en Bahnen** *od.* **Gleisen bewegen** go on in the same old way

ein·gefallen *Adj.* gaunt ⟨*face*⟩; sunken, hollow ⟨*cheeks*⟩

eingefleischt /'aingəflaiʃt/ *Adj., nicht präd.* confirmed ⟨*bachelor*⟩; inveterate ⟨*smoker*⟩

ein|gehen 1 *unr. itr. V.; mit sein* **(a)** (eintreffen) arrive; be received; **(b)** (fig.) **in die Geschichte ~:** go down in history; **in die Weltliteratur ~:** find one's/its place in world literature; **(c)** (schrumpfen) shrink; **(d) auf eine Frage/ein Problem ~/nicht ~:** go into *or* deal with/ignore a question/problem; **auf jmdn. ~:** be responsive to sb.; **auf jmdn. nicht ~:** ignore sb.'s wishes; **auf ein Angebot ~/nicht ~:** accept/reject an offer; **(e)** (sterben) die; **(f)** (bankrott gehen) close down. **2** *unr. tr. V.* enter into ⟨*contract, matrimony*⟩; take ⟨*risk*⟩; accept ⟨*obligation*⟩; **darauf gehe ich jede Wette ein** (ugs.) I'll bet you anything on that (coll.)

eingehend 1 *Adj.* detailed. **2** *adv.* in detail

ein·gekeilt *Adj.* (von beiden Seiten) wedged in (**in**, **zwischen** + *Dat.* between); (von allen Seiten) hemmed in (**in** among)

Ein·gemachte *das; adj. Dekl.* preserved fruit/vegetables; (fig.: Substanz) **ans ~ gehen** (ugs.) draw on one's reserves

ein|gemeinden *tr. V.* incorporate ⟨*village*⟩ (**in** + *Akk.*, **nach** into)

ein·genommen (*Adj.*) **von sich ~ sein** be conceited; **von etw. ~ sein** be conceited about sth.

ein·geschnappt *Adj.* (ugs.: beleidigt) huffy

ein·geschossig *Adj.* single-storey; one-storey

ein·geschränkt *Adj.* reduced; **~es Haltverbot** prohibition of stopping except for certain purposes

ein·geschrieben *Adj.* registered ⟨*letter, member*⟩; enrolled ⟨*student*⟩

ein·geschworen *Adj.* dedicated (**auf** + *Akk.* to)

ein·gespannt *Adj.* **stark ~:** very busy

ein·gespielt *Adj.* in practice; **aufeinander ~:** playing well together

Ein·geständnis *das* confession; admission

ein|gestehen *unr. tr. V.* admit, confess ⟨*guilt*⟩; admit, confess to ⟨*mistake, theft*⟩; **[sich] ~, dass …:** admit [to oneself] that …

ein·gestellt *Adj.* **fortschrittlich** ~: progressively minded; **wie ist er [politisch]** ~? what are his [political] views?

Eingeweide /'aɪngəvaɪdə/ *das;* ~s, ~; *meist Pl.* entrails *pl.;* innards *pl.*

ein|gewöhnen 1 *refl. V.* get used *or* accustomed to one's new surroundings; accustom oneself to one's new surroundings; **sich an seinem neuen Arbeitsplatz/in eine neue Tätigkeit** ~: settle in at one's new place of work/get used to a new job. **2** *tr. V.* **jmdn. in etw.** (*Akk.*) ~: get sb. used *or* accustomed to sth.

Ein·gewöhnung *die; o. Pl.* settling in *no art.;* **die** ~ **in seiner neuen Umgebung/an seinem neuen Arbeitsplatz fiel ihm schwer** he found it difficult to get used to his new surroundings/job

ein|gießen *unr. tr.* (*auch itr.*) *V.* pour in; **etw. in etw.** (*Akk.*) ~: pour sth. into sth.; **den Kaffee** ~: pour [out] the coffee

ein|gipsen *tr. V.* (a) fix ⟨*nail, hook, etc.*⟩ in with plaster; (b) put *or* set ⟨*arm, leg, etc.*⟩ in plaster

eingleisig /'aɪnglaɪzɪç/ *Adj.* single-track ⟨*railway line*⟩

ein|gliedern 1 *tr. V.* integrate (**in** + *Akk.* into); incorporate ⟨*village, company*⟩ (**in** + *Akk.* into); (einordnen) include (**in** + *Akk.* in). **2** *refl. V.* **sich in etw.** (*Akk.*) ~: fit into sth.

Ein·gliederung *die* ⇒ **eingliedern 1**: integration; incorporation; inclusion

ein|graben *unr. tr. V.* bury (**in** + *Akk.* in); sink ⟨*pile, pipe*⟩ (**in** + *Akk.* into)

ein|gravieren *tr. V.* engrave (**in** + *Akk.* on)

ein|greifen *unr. itr. V.* intervene (**in** + *Akk.* in)

ein|grenzen *tr. V.* (a) enclose; (b) (fig.: beschränken) limit; restrict (**auf** + *Akk.* to)

Ein·griff *der* (a) intervention (**in** + *Akk.* in); **ein** ~ **in jmds. Rechte** an infringement of sb.'s rights; (b) ▶ 329 (Med.) operation

ein|gruppieren *tr. V.* **jmdn. in eine Gehaltsstufe** ~: place sb. on a step on the salary scale

ein|hacken *itr. V.* **auf jmdn./etw.** ~: peck at sb./sth.

ein|haken 1 *tr. V.* (a) (mit Haken befestigen) fasten; (b) *reziprok* **sich** ~: link arms; **sie gingen eingehakt** they walked arm in arm. **2** *refl. V.* link arms (**bei** with). **3** *itr. V.* (fig. ugs.) butt in

Ein·halt *der;* **jmdm./einer Sache** ~ **gebieten** *od.* **tun** (geh.) stop *or* halt sb./sth.

ein|halten 1 *unr. tr. V.* keep ⟨*appointment*⟩; meet ⟨*deadline, commitments*⟩; keep to ⟨*diet, speed-limit, agreement*⟩; observe ⟨*regulation*⟩; obey ⟨*laws*⟩. **2** *unr. itr. V.* (geh.) stop

Ein·haltung *die; o. Pl.* (einer Verabredung) keeping; (einer Vorschrift) observance; **die** ~ **einer Frist** meeting a deadline

ein|hämmern 1 *itr. V.* **auf etw.** (*Akk.*) ~: hammer on sth. **2** *tr. V.* **jmdm. etw.** ~: hammer *or* drum sth. into sb. *or* sb.'s head

ein|handeln *refl. V.* **sich** (*Dat.*) **etw.** ~ (fig. ugs.) let oneself in for sth. (coll.)

einhändig /'aɪnhɛndɪç/ **1** *Adj.* one-handed. **2** *adv.* with [only] one hand

ein|hängen 1 *tr. V.* hang ⟨*door*⟩; fit ⟨*window*⟩; put down ⟨*receiver*⟩. **2** *itr. V.* hang up. **3** *refl. V.* **sich bei jmdm.** ~: take sb.'s arm

ein|hauen 1 *unr. tr. V.* ⇒ **einschlagen 1 a, b. 2** *unr. itr. V.* ⇒ **einschlagen 2 b**

ein|heften *tr. V.* file

ein·heimisch *Adj.* native; indigenous ⟨*population, plant*⟩

Einheimische *der/die; adj. Dekl.* local

ein|heimsen /'aɪnhaɪmzn̩/ *tr. V.* (ugs.) rake in (coll.) ⟨*profits*⟩

ein|heiraten *itr. V.* **in eine Familie** ~: marry into a family

Einheit *die;* ~, ~en (a) unity; (b) (Maß~, Milit.) unit

einheitlich 1 *Adj.* (a) (in sich geschlossen) unified; integrated; (b) (unterschiedslos) uniform ⟨*dress*⟩; standardized

⟨*education*⟩; standard ⟨*procedure, practice*⟩. **2** *adv.* ~ **gekleidet sein** be dressed the same; ~ **gestaltet sein** be designed along the same lines

Einheits-: ~**format** *das* standard size; ~**front** *die* united front; ~**gewerkschaft** *die* general trade union; ~**staat** *der* centralized state; ~**wert** *der* (Steuerw.) rateable value

ein|heizen 1 *tr. V.* put on ⟨*stove, boiler*⟩; heat ⟨*room*⟩. **2** *itr. V.* (ugs.: bedrängen) **jmdm.** ~: give sb. a kick up the backside (coll.)

einhellig /'aɪnhɛlɪç/ **1** *Adj.* unanimous. **2** *adv.* unanimously

Einhelligkeit *die;* ~: unanimity

ein·her|gehen *unr. itr. V.; mit sein* (fig.: begleitet sein) **mit etw.** ~: be accompanied by sth.

ein|holen 1 *tr. V.* (a) (erreichen) **jmdn./ein Fahrzeug** ~: catch up with sb./a vehicle; (b) (ausgleichen) make up ⟨*arrears, time*⟩; (c) (einziehen) haul in, pull in ⟨*nets*⟩; lower ⟨*flag*⟩; (d) (ugs.: einkaufen) buy, get ⟨*groceries*⟩; (e) (erbitten) ask for, seek ⟨*reference, advice*⟩; make ⟨*enquiries*⟩. **2** *itr. V.* (ugs.) ~ **gehen** go shopping

Ein·horn *das* unicorn

ein|hüllen *tr. V.* **sich/jmdn. in etw.** (*Akk.*) ~: wrap oneself/sb. up in sth.

ein·hundert *Kardinalz.* ▶ 600 | a *or* one hundred; *s. auch* **hundert**

einig /'aɪnɪç/ *Adj.* **sich** (*Dat.*) ~ **sein** be agreed *or* in agreement; **sich** (*Dat.*) ~ **werden** reach agreement; **mit jmdm. über etw.** (*Akk.*) ~ **sein** be in agreement *or* agree with sb. about *or* on sth.

einig... /'aɪnɪg.../ *Indefinitpron. u. unbest. Zahlwort* some ⟨*effort, hope, courage*⟩; **in** ~**er Entfernung** some distance away; ~**e wenige** a few; ~**e hundert** several hundred; ~**er Ärger** (viel Ärger) quite a bit *or* quite a lot of trouble

einigen 1 *tr. V.* unite. **2** *refl. V.* come to *or* reach an agreement (**mit** with, **über** + *Akk.* about); **sich auf jmdn./etw.** ~: agree on sb./sth.

einigermaßen *Adv.* rather, somewhat; ~ **zufrieden** fairly *or* reasonably satisfied; **Wie geht's dir? — Einigermaßen** How are you? — Not too bad

Einigkeit *die;* ~ (a) unity; (b) (Übereinstimmung) agreement

Einigung *die;* ~, ~**en** (a) (Übereinkunft) agreement; (b) (Vereinigung) unification

Einigungs·vertrag *der* (Politik) unification treaty

ein|impfen *tr. V.* (ugs.) **jmdm. etw.** ~: drum sth. into sb.

ein|jagen *tr. V.* **jmdm. Angst/einen Schrecken** ~: give sb. a fright

ein·jährig *Adj.* (a) (ein Jahr alt) one-year-old *attrib.;* one year old *pred.;* (ein Jahr dauernd) one-year *attrib.;* **eine** ~**e Abwesenheit** a year's absence; (b) (Bot.) annual

Einjährige *der/die; adj. Dekl.* one-year-old

ein|kalkulieren *tr. V.* take into account

ein|kassieren *tr. V.* (a) collect; (b) (ugs.: entwenden) pinch (esp. Brit. coll.); nick (Brit. coll.); (c) (salopp: festnehmen) pinch (sl.); nab (coll.)

Ein·kauf *der* (a) buying; (für eine Firma) buying; purchasing; **[einige] Einkäufe machen** do some shopping; (b) (eingekaufte Ware) purchase; **ein guter/schlechter** ~: a good/bad buy; (c) *o. Pl.* (Kaufmannsspr.) buying *or* purchasing department

ein|kaufen 1 *itr. V.* (a) shop; ~ **gehen** go shopping; **beim Bäcker/im Supermarkt** ~: shop at the baker's/the supermarket; (b) (Kaufmannsspr.) do the buying *or* purchasing. **2** *tr. V.* buy; purchase; buy in ⟨*stores, provisions*⟩

Ein·käufer *der,* **Ein·käuferin** *die* ▶ 85 | (Berufsbez.) buyer; purchaser

Einkaufs-: ~**abteilung** *die* ⇒ **Einkauf c;** ~**bummel** *der:* **einen** ~**bummel machen** go on a shopping expedition; ~**korb** *der* shopping basket; (im Geschäft) [wire]basket; ~**netz** *das* string bag; ~**tasche** *die* shopping bag; ~**wagen** *der* [shopping] trolley (Brit.) *or* (Amer.) cart; ~**zentrum** *das* shopping centre; ~**zettel** *der* shopping list

Einkehr /'ainkeːɐ̯/ *die;* ~ (geh.: Selbstbesinnung) ~ **halten** take stock of oneself and one's attitudes

ein|kehren *itr. V.; mit sein* stop; **in einem Wirtshaus** ~: stop at an inn

ein|kellern *tr. V.* store in the/a cellar

ein|kerben *tr. V.* cut *or* carve a notch/notches in; notch

Einkerbung *die;* ~, ~**en** notch

ein|klagen *tr. V.* sue for (*damages, compensation, etc.*); sue for the recovery of (*debts*)

ein|klammern *tr. V.* etw. ~: put sth. in brackets; bracket sth.

Ein·klang *der* harmony; **im** ~ **mit jmdm. sein** be in accord *or* agreement with sb.; **im** *od.* **in** ~ **mit etw. stehen** accord with sth.; **zwei Dinge in** ~ **bringen** harmonize two things

ein·klassig *Adj.* (Schulw.) one-room (*school*)

ein|kleben *tr. V.* stick in; **etw. in etw.** (*Akk.*) ~: stick sth. into sth.

ein|kleiden *tr. V.* **(a)** sich/jmdn. ~: clothe oneself/sb.; sich/jmdn. neu ~: fit oneself/sb. out with a new set of clothes; **(b)** (Milit.) kit out (*soldier*)

ein|klemmen *tr. V.* **(a)** (quetschen) catch; **jmdm./sich die Hand [in etw.** (*Dat.*)**]** ~: catch *or* trap sb.'s/one's hand [in sth.]; **(b)** (fest einfügen) clamp

ein|klicken *refl. V.* (DV) **sich in das Netz** ~: go on-line

ein|klopfen *tr. V.* knock in (*nail*)

ein|knicken 1 *tr. V.* bend; (brechen) snap. **2** *itr. V.; mit sein* bend; (brechen) snap; **sie knickte beim Gehen ein** she went over on her ankle while walking along

ein|kochen 1 *tr. V.* preserve (*fruit, vegetables*). **2** *itr. V.* thicken

Einkommen *das;* ~**s,** ~: income

einkommens-: ~**schwach** *Adj.* low-income *attrib.;* ~**stark** *Adj.* high-income *attrib.*

einkommenssteuerpflichtig /-pflɪçtɪç/ *Adj.* liable for income tax *postpos.*

Einkommen·steuer *die* income tax

ein|kreisen *tr. V.* **(a)** (markieren) **etw.** ~: put a circle round sth.; **(b)** (umzingeln) surround; **(c)** (fig.: eingrenzen) circumscribe (*problem*)

ein|kriegen (ugs.) **1** *tr. V.* ⇒ **einholen 1 a. 2** *refl. V.* control oneself; **sie konnte sich vor Lachen nicht** ~: she couldn't stop laughing

Einkünfte /'ainkynftə/ *Pl.* income *sing.*

ein|laden¹ *unr. tr. V.* load (**in** + *Akk.* into) (*goods*)

ein|laden² 1 *unr. tr. V.* **(a)** invite; **jmdn. zum Essen** ~: invite sb. for a meal; (im Restaurant) invite sb. out for a meal; **sich einladen** (scherzh.) invite oneself; **jmdn. zu sich nach Hause** ~: invite sb. over; **(b)** (freihalten) treat (**zu** to); **ich lade euch ein** this is on me. **2** *unr. itr. V.* **(a) die Feuerwehr lädt zu einem Tag der offenen Tür ein** the fire station is having an open day; **der Direktor des Goethe-Instituts lädt zu einem Empfang ... ein** the Director of the Goethe-Institut requests the pleasure of your company at a reception ...; **(b)** (fig.) **das Meer lädt zum Baden ein** the sea looks inviting; **das lädt zum Diebstahl geradezu ein** that's inviting theft

einladend 1 *Adj.* inviting; tempting, appetizing (*meal*). **2** *adv.* invitingly

Ein·ladung *die* invitation

Ein·lage *die* **(a)** (in einem Brief) enclosure; **(b)** (Kochk.) *vegetables, meat balls, dumplings, etc. added to a clear soup;* **eine Brühe mit** ~: a clear soup with meat balls/dumpling *etc.;* **(c)** (Schuh~) arch-support; **(d)** (Darbietung) **eine witzige** ~: a witty *or* humorous aside; **eine musikalische** ~: a musical interlude; **(e)** (Finanzw.) (Guthaben) deposit; (Beteiligung) investment

ein|lagern *tr. V.* store; lay in (*stores*). **2** *refl. V.* **sich [in etw.** (*Akk.*)**]** ~: be deposited [in sth.]

Ein·lagerung *die* storage

Einlass, *Einlaß /'ainlas/ *der;* **Einlasses, Einlässe** /'ainlɛsə/ admission, admittance (**in** + *Akk.* to); „~ **ab 20 Uhr"** 'doors open 8 p.m.'

*alte Schreibung (vgl. Hinweise auf S. xvi–xvii)

ein|lassen 1 *unr. tr. V.* **(a)** admit; let in; **(b)** (einfüllen) run (*water*); **(c)** (einpassen) **etw. in etw.** (*Akk.*) ~: set sth. into sth. **2** *unr. refl. V.* **(a)** (meist abwertend) **sich mit jmdm.** ~: get mixed up *or* involved with sb.; **(b) sich auf etw.** (*Akk.*) ~: get involved in sth.

Ein·lauf *der* **(a)** (Med.) enema; **jmdm. einen** ~ **machen** give sb. an enema; **(b)** *o. Pl.* (Sport) **beim** ~ **in die Gerade/das Stadion** entering the straight/the stadium

ein|laufen 1 *unr. itr. V.; mit sein* **(a)** (Sport) **ins Stadion** ~: run into *or* enter the stadium; **in die letzte Runde** ~: start the last lap; **(b)** (ankommen) **das Schiff läuft ein** the ship is coming in; **in den Hafen** ~: come into *or* enter port; **(c)** (kleiner werden) (*clothes*) shrink; **(d)** (hineinfließen) run in; **(e)** (eingehen) (*news, information*) come in. **2** *unr. tr. V.* **(a)** wear in (*shoes*); **(b)** ⇒ **einrennen 1 b. 3** *unr. refl. V.* (Sport) warm up

ein|läuten *tr. V.* ring in (*Sunday, New Year*)

ein|leben *refl. V.* settle down; (in einem Haus) settle in

Einlege·arbeit *die* (Kunsthandwerk) inlaid work; (Gegenstand) piece of inlaid work

ein|legen *tr. V.* **(a)** put in; **etw. in etw.** (*Akk.*) ~: put sth. in sth.; **den ersten Gang** ~: engage first gear; **(b) jmdm./sich das Haar** ~: set sb.'s/one's hair; **(c)** (Kunsthandwerk) inlay; **eingelegte Muster** inlaid patterns; **(d)** (Kochk.) pickle; **(e)** (fig.: einschieben) **eine Rast** ~: stop for a rest; **einen Spurt** ~: put on a spurt; **eine Pause** ~: take a break; **(f)** (geltend machen) lodge (*protest, appeal*); **Widerspruch** ~: protest; *s. auch* **Ehre a; Veto; Wort b**

Einlege·sohle *die* insole

ein|leiten *tr. V.* **(a)** introduce; institute, start (*search*); open (*negotiations, investigation*); launch, open (*campaign*); induce (*birth*); **einige** ~**de Worte** a few introductory remarks; **(b) etw. in etw.** (*Akk.*) ~: lead sth. into sth.

Ein·leitung *die;* ⇒ **einleiten a:** introduction; institution; opening; launching; induction

ein|lenken *itr. V.* give way; make concessions

ein|lesen 1 *unr. refl. V.* **sich in ein Buch** ~: get into a book. **2** *unr. tr. V.* (DV) read in; **etw. in den Speicher** ~: read sth. into the memory

ein|leuchten *itr. V.* **jmdm.** ~: be clear to sb.; **es leuchtet ihr nicht ein, dass sie es machen soll** she doesn't see why she should do it

ein·leuchtend 1 *Adj.* plausible. **2** *adv.* plausibly

ein|liefern *tr. V.* **(a)** post (Brit.), mail (*letter, parcel*); **(b) jmdn. ins Krankenhaus/Gefängnis** ~: take sb. to hospital/jail

Ein·lieferung *die* **(a)** ⇒ **einliefern a:** posting (Brit.); mailing; **(b) die** ~ **eines Verurteilten [ins Gefängnis]** taking a convicted prisoner to jail

Einlieferungs·schein *der* (Postw.) certificate of posting

ein·liegend *Adj.* (Papierdt.) enclosed; ~ **übersenden wir Ihnen ...** please find enclosed ...

Einlieger·wohnung *die* ≈ granny flat

ein|lochen *tr. V.* (salopp) **jmdn.** ~: put sb. away (coll.)

ein|loggen *refl. V.* (DV) log in *or* on

ein|lösen *tr. V.* **(a)** cash (*cheque*); cash [in] (*token, voucher, bill of exchange*); redeem (*pawned article*); **(b)** (geh.: erfüllen) redeem (*pledge*); **sein Wort** ~: keep one's word

ein|machen *tr. V.* preserve (*fruit, vegetables*); (in Gläser) bottle

Einmach·glas *das* preserving jar

einmal 1 *Adv.* **(a)** (ein Mal) once; **noch** ~ **so groß [wie]** twice as big [as]; **etw. noch** ~ **tun** do sth. again; ~ **sagt er dies, ein andermal das** first he says one thing, then another; ~ **ist keinmal** (Spr.) it won't matter just this once; **auf** ~: all at once; suddenly; (zugleich) at once; **(b)** /'-'-/ (später) some day; one day; (früher) once; **es war** ~ **ein König, der ...:** once upon a time there was a king who ... **2** *Partikel* **(a) daran ist nun** ~ **nichts mehr zu ändern** there's nothing more that can be done about it; **nicht** ~: not even; **wieder** ~: yet again; **(b) alle** ~ **zuhören!** listen everybody!

Einmal·eins *das;* ~**:** [multiplication] tables *pl.;* **das kleine/große** ~**:** tables from 1 to 10/11 to 20; (fig. Anfangsgründe) fundamentals *pl.*

Einmal·hand·tuch *das* disposable towel

einmalig 1 *Adj.* (a) unique ‹*opportunity, chance*›; one-off, single ‹*payment, purchase*›; (b) (hervorragend) superb ‹*film, book, play, etc.*›; (ugs.) fantastic (coll.) ‹*girl, woman*›. 2 *adv.* (ugs.) really fantastic *or* superb (coll.)

Ein·mann·betrieb *der* (a) (Firma) one-man business; (b) (Arbeitsweise) one-man operation

Ein·mark·stück *das* ▶216⌡ one-mark piece

Ein·marsch *der* (a) entry; **der** ~ **ins Stadion** the march into the stadium; (b) (Besetzung) invasion (**in** + *Akk.* of)

ein|marschieren *itr. V.; mit sein* (a) march in; **in etw.** (*Akk.*) ~**:** march into sth.; (b) **in ein Land** ~ (Milit.) march into *or* invade a country

ein|mauern *tr. V.* (a) immure ‹*prisoner, traitor*›; wall in ‹*relic, treasure*›; (b) (ins Mauerwerk einfügen) **etw. in die Wand** *usw.* ~**:** set sth. into the wall *etc.*

Ein·meter·brett *das* one-metre board

ein|mieten *refl. V.* **sich in einer Villa/Pension** ~**:** rent a villa/a room in a boarding house

ein|mischen *refl. V.* interfere (**in** + *Akk.* in)

Ein·mischung *die* interference (**in** + *Akk.* in)

einmonatig *Adj.; nicht präd.* (a) (einen Monat alt) one-month-old *attrib.;* (b) (einen Monat dauernd) one-month *attrib.; s. auch* **achtmonatig**

ein·monatlich 1 *Adj.* monthly; *s. auch* **achtmonatlich** 1. 2 *adv.* monthly; once a month

ein·motorig *Adj.* single-engined

ein|motten *tr. V.* (fig.) mothball

ein|mumme[l]n *tr. V.* (ugs.) wrap up; **sich** ~**:** wrap [oneself] up

ein|münden *itr. V.; auch mit sein* flow in; enter; **in etw.** ~**:** flow into *or* enter sth.

Ein·mündung *die* (von Straßen) junction; **die** ~ **der Straße in die Hauptstraße** the junction of the street and the main road

einmütig /'ainmy:tɪç/ 1 *Adj.* unanimous. 2 *adv.* unanimously

Einmütigkeit *die;* ~**:** unanimity

ein|nähen *tr. V.* sew in; **etw. in etw.** (*Akk.*) ~**:** sew sth. into sth.

Einnahme *die;* ~, ~**en** (a) *meist Pl.* income; (Staats~) revenue; (Kassen~) takings *pl.;* (b) *o. Pl.* (von Arzneimitteln, einer Mahlzeit) taking; (c) *o. Pl.* (einer Stadt, Burg) capture; taking

Einnahme·quelle *die* source of income; (des Staates) source of revenue

ein|nehmen *unr. tr. V.* (a) (kassieren) take; (b) (zu sich nehmen) take ‹*medicine, tablets, meal*›; (c) (besetzen) capture, take ‹*town, fortress*›; (d) **seinen Platz** ~**:** take one's place; (sich setzen) take one's seat *or* place; **einen Standpunkt** ~ (fig.) take up *or* adopt a position; **eine wichtige Stellung** ~ (fig.) occupy an important place; (e) (ausfüllen) take up ‹*amount of room*›; (f) (beeinflussen) **jmdn. für sich** ~**:** win sb. over; **gegen jmdn. eingenommen sein** be prejudiced against sb.; **von sich eingenommen sein** think a lot of oneself (coll.)

einnehmend *Adj.* winning ‹*manner*›

ein|nisten *refl. V.* (a) **sich bei jmdm.** ~ (fig. abwertend) park oneself on sb. (coll.); (b) (ein Nest bauen) build a nest/their nests; nest

Ein·öde *die* barren *or* featureless waste; (Einsamkeit) isolation

ein|ölen *tr. V.* (a) oil; (b) **sich/jmdn.** ~**:** put *or* rub oil on oneself/sb.

ein|ordnen 1 *tr. V.* (a) arrange; put in order; (b) (klassifizieren) classify; categorize, classify ‹*writer, thinker, artist*›. 2 *refl. V.* (a) (Verkehrsw.) get into the correct lane; **sich rechts/links** ~**:** get into the right-hand/left-hand lane; „**bitte** ~" 'get in lane'; (b) **sich [in die Gemeinschaft]** ~**:** fit in[to the community]

ein|packen 1 *tr. V.* (a) pack (**in** + *Akk.* in); (einwickeln) wrap [up]; (b) (ugs.: warm anziehen) wrap up. 2 *itr. V.* (ugs.)

er kann ~**:** he's had it (coll.); **pack ein!** pack it in! (coll.); give it a rest! (coll.)

ein|parken *tr., itr. V.* park

ein|pauken *tr. V.* **etw.** ~**:** mug up (Brit.) *or* (Amer.) bone up on sth. (coll.); **jmdm. etw.** ~**:** drum *or* hammer sth. into sb.

ein|pendeln 1 *refl. V.* settle down. 2 *itr. V.; mit sein* commute; **die aus dem Umland** ~**den Beschäftigen** the workers commuting in from the surrounding area

Ein·pendler *der* commuter; *s. auch* **Auspendler**

Ein·pfennig·stück *das* ▶216⌡ one-pfennig piece

ein|pferchen *tr. V.* **eingepfercht stehen/sein** stand/be crammed *or* crushed together

ein|pflanzen *tr. V.* (a) plant ‹*flowers, shrubs, etc.*›; (b) (Med.) implant; **jmdm. ein Organ** ~**:** implant an organ in[to] sb.

ein|planen *tr. V.* **etw.** ~**:** include sth. in one's plans; **das war nicht eingeplant** we/they *etc.* didn't plan on that

ein|pökeln *tr. V.* (Kochk.) salt

ein·polig *Adj.* (Physik, Elektrot.) single-pole

ein|prägen 1 *tr. V.* (a) stamp (**in** + *Akk.* into, on); (b) (fig.) **sich** (*Dat.*) **etw.** ~**:** memorize sth.; commit sth. to memory. 2 *refl. V.* **das prägte sich ihm [für immer] ein** it made an [indelible] impression on him

einprägsam 1 *Adj.* easily remembered. 2 *adv.* **er hat das sehr** ~ **dargelegt** he expounded it in a way that made it easy to remember

ein|programmieren *tr. V.* (DV) programme in

ein|prügeln 1 *itr. V.* **auf jmdn.** ~**:** beat sb. 2 *tr. V.* **jmdm. etw.** ~ (fig.) drub *or* beat sth. into sb.

ein|pudern *tr. V.* powder

ein|quartieren 1 *tr. V.* quarter, billet ‹*troops*›; **die Opfer wurden vorläufig in Hotels einquartiert** the victims were given temporary accommodation in hotels. 2 *refl. V.* **sich bei jmdm.** ~ (Milit.) be quartered with *or* billeted on sb.

Ein·rad *das* unicycle

ein|rahmen *tr. V.* frame

ein|rammen *tr. V.* ram in

ein|rasten *itr. V.; mit sein* engage

ein|räuchern *tr. V.* envelope in smoke; fill ‹*room*› with smoke

ein|räumen *tr. V.* (a) put away; **etw. in etw.** (*Akk.*) ~**:** put sth. away in sth.; **Bücher wieder [ins Regal]** ~**:** put books back [on the shelf]; (b) **er musste seinen Schrank** ~**:** he had to put his things away in his cupboard; **das Zimmer wieder** ~**:** put everything *or* all the furniture back into the room; (c) (zugestehen) admit; concede; **jmdm. ein Recht/einen Kredit** ~**:** give *or* grant sb. a right/loan

ein|rechnen *tr. V.* include, take account of ‹*costs etc.*›

ein|reden 1 *tr. V.* **jmdm. etw.** ~**:** talk sb. into believing sth.; **sich** (*Dat.*) ~, **dass** …**:** persuade oneself that…; **das redest du dir bloß ein** you're just imagining it. 2 *itr. V.* **auf jmdn.** ~**:** talk insistently to sb.

ein|regnen *refl. V.* (unpers.) **es hat sich eingeregnet** it's begun to rain steadily

ein|reiben *unr. tr. V.* **Salbe [in die Haut]** ~**:** rub ointment in[to one's skin]; **jmdm. den Rücken** ~**:** rub lotion/ointment *etc.* into sb.'s back; **sich** (*Dat.*) **das Gesicht mit etw.** ~**:** rub sth. into one's face

ein|reichen *tr. V.* (a) submit ‹*application*›; hand in, submit ‹*piece of work, dissertation, thesis*›; lodge, make ‹*complaint*›; tender ‹*resignation*›; (b) (jur.) file ‹*suit, petition for divorce*›

ein|reihen 1 *refl. V.* **sich in etw.** (*Akk.*) ~**:** join sth. 2 *tr. V.* place (**in** + *Akk.* in)

Einreiher *der;* ~**s,** ~**:** single-breasted suit/jacket/coat

einreihig /'ainraihɪç/ *Adj.* single-breasted ‹*suit, jacket, coat*›

Ein·reise *die* entry; **bei der** ~ **nach Frankreich** on entry into France

ein|reisen *itr. V.; mit sein* enter; **nach Schweden** ~**:** enter Sweden

Einreise-: ~**verbot** das: jmdm. ~**verbot erteilen** refuse sb. entry; ~**visum** das entry visa

ein|reißen 1 unr. tr. V. **(a)** tear; rip; **(b)** ⇒ **abreißen 1 b. 2** unr. itr. V.; mit sein **(a)** tear; rip; **(b)** (ugs.: zur Gewohnheit werden) become a habit

ein|reiten 1 unr. itr. V.; mit sein ride in. **2** unr. tr. V. break in ⟨horse⟩

ein|renken 1 tr. V. **(a)** (Med.) set; reduce (Med.); jmdm. **den Fuß/Arm [wieder]** ~: [re]set sb.'s foot/arm; **(b)** (ugs.: bereinigen) etw. ~: sort or straighten sth. out. **2** refl. V. **das renkt sich ein** that will sort or straighten itself out

ein|rennen 1 unr. tr. V. **(a)** break down ⟨door⟩; s. auch **offen 1 a; (b)** jmdm. **das Haus** od. **die Tür** od. **die Bude** ~ (ugs.) pester sb. all the time. **2** unr. refl. V. (ugs.: sich verletzen) **sich** (Dat.) **den Kopf an etw.** (Dat.) ~: bash or bang one's head on or against sth.

ein|richten 1 refl. V. **(a) sich gemütlich/schön** ~: furnish one's home comfortably/beautifully; **sich häuslich** ~: make oneself at home; **(b)** (auskommen) **sich [mit seinem Gehalt]** ~: get by or make ends meet [on one's salary]; **(c)** (sich vorbereiten) **sich auf etw.** ~: prepare for sb./sth.. **2** tr. V. **(a)** furnish ⟨flat, house⟩; fit out ⟨shop, restaurant⟩; equip ⟨laboratory⟩; **(b)** (ermöglichen) arrange; **das lässt sich** ~: that can be arranged; **(c)** (eröffnen) open ⟨branch, shop⟩; set up ⟨advisory centre⟩; start, set up ⟨business⟩

Ein·richtung die **(a)** o. Pl. (das Einrichten) furnishing; **(b)** (Mobiliar) furnishings pl.; **(c)** (Geräte) ~**en** (Geschäfts~) fittings; (Labor~) equipment sing.; **sanitäre** ~**en** sanitation sing.; **(d)** (Institution, Gewohnheit) institution

Einrichtungs·gegen·stand der piece of furniture

ein|ritzen tr. V. carve

ein|rollen tr. V. roll up ⟨carpet etc.⟩; **sich/jmdm. die Haare** ~: put one's/sb.'s hair in curlers or rollers; **sich** ~: ⟨hedgehog, cat⟩ curl up

ein|rosten itr. V.; mit sein go rusty; rust up

ein|rücken 1 itr. V.; mit sein (Milit.: einmarschieren) move in; **in ein Land** ~: march into a country. **2** tr. V. indent ⟨line, heading, etc.⟩

ein|rühren tr. V. stir in

eins /aıns/ ▶22◀, ▶530◀, ▶600◀ **1** Kardinalz. one; **es ist** ~: it is one o'clock; ~ **zu null für dich!** (ugs.) that's one up to you!; **die Nummer** ~ **sein** (fig.) be number one; „~**, zwei, drei!"** 'ready, steady, go'; s. auch **acht¹, ein. 2** Adj.; nicht attr. **mir ist alles** ~: it's all the same or all one to me; **mit jmdm. über etw.** (Akk.) ~ **sein/werden** be in/reach agreement with sb. about or on sth. **3** Indefinitpron.: ⇒ **einer**

Eins die; ~, ~**en (a)** one; **wie eine** ~ **stehen** (ugs.) stand as straight as a ramrod; s. auch **Acht¹ a, e; (b)** (Schulnote) one; A

ein|sacken¹ tr. V. **(a)** (in Säcke füllen) **etw.** ~: put sth. into sacks; **(b)** (ugs.: einstecken) grab; pocket ⟨money⟩

ein|sacken² itr. V.; mit sein sink in; ⟨building, pavement⟩ subside

einsam Adj. **(a)** (verlassen) lonely ⟨person, decision⟩; ~ **leben** live a lonely or solitary life; **(b)** (einzeln) solitary ⟨rock, tree, wanderer⟩; **(c)** (abgelegen) isolated; ~ **liegen** be situated miles from anywhere; **(d)** (menschenleer) empty; deserted

Einsamkeit die; ~, ~**en (a)** (Verlassenheit) loneliness; **(b)** (Alleinsein) solitude; **(c)** (Abgeschiedenheit) isolation

ein|sammeln tr. V. **(a)** (auflesen) pick up; gather up; **(b)** (sich aushändigen lassen) collect in; collect ⟨tickets⟩

Ein·satz der **(a)** (eingesetztes Teil) (in Tischdecke, Kopfkissen usw.) inset; (in Kochtopf, Nähkasten usw.) compartment; **(b)** (eingesetzter Betrag) stake; **den** ~ **erhöhen** raise the stakes pl.; **(c)** (das Einsetzen) (von Maschinen, Waffen usw.) use; (von Truppen) deployment; **unter** ~ **seines Lebens** at the risk of his life; **zum** ~ **kommen** od. **gelangen** (Papierdt.) ⟨machine⟩ come into operation; ⟨police, troops⟩ be used; **jmdn./etw. zum** ~ **bringen** use sb./sth.; **(d)** (Engagement) commitment; dedication; **(e)** (Milit.) **im** ~ **sein/fallen** be in action or on active service/die in action; **einen** ~ **fliegen** fly a

mission; **(f)** (Musik) **der** ~ **der Instrumente** the entry of the instruments

einsatz-, Einsatz-: ~**befehl** der order to go into action; ~**bereit** Adj. **(a)** ready for use; **(b)** (Milit.) combat-ready attrib.; ready for action postpos.; ~**gruppe** die, ~**kommando** das task force; ~**leiter** der head of operations; ~**plan** der plan of action; ~**wagen** der (der Polizei) police car; (der Feuerwehr) fire engine; (Notarztwagen) ambulance; (der Straßenbahn) relief; ~**zentrale** die operations centre

ein|saugen unr. (auch regelm.) tr. V. suck in ⟨air, liquid⟩

ein|scannen tr. V. (DV) scan in

ein|schalten 1 tr. V. **(a)** switch on; turn on; **einen anderen Sender** ~: switch to another station; **(b)** (fig.: beteiligen) call in ⟨press, police, expert, etc.⟩; **jmdn. in die Verhandlungen** ~: bring sb. into the negotiations. **2** refl. V. **(a)** switch [itself] on; come on; **(b)** (eingreifen) intervene **(in** + Akk. in)

Einschalt·quote die (Rundf.) listening figures pl.; (Ferns.) viewing figures pl.

ein|schärfen tr. V. **jmdm. etw.** ~: impress sth. [up]on sb.

ein|schätzen tr. V. judge ⟨person⟩; assess ⟨situation⟩; (schätzen) estimate; **jmdn./eine Situation falsch** ~: misjudge sb./a situation

Ein·schätzung die ⇒ **einschätzen:** judging; assessment; estimation; **nach meiner** ~: in my estimation or judgement

ein|schäumen tr. V. lather

ein|schenken tr., itr. V. **(a)** pour [out]; **jmdm. etw.** ~: pour out sth. for sb.; **(b)** (füllen) fill [up] ⟨glass, cup⟩

ein|scheren itr. V.; mit sein (Verkehrsw.) **in** od. **auf eine Fahrspur** ~: get or move into a lane

ein|schicken tr. V. send in

ein|schieben unr. tr. V. **(a)** (hineinschieben) push in; **(b)** (einfügen) put in; insert; put on ⟨trains, buses⟩; fit in ⟨client, patient⟩; **etw. in etw.** (Akk.) ~: put or insert sth. into sth.

ein|schießen 1 unr. tr. V. **(a)** (zerstören) demolish ⟨wall, building⟩ by gunfire; **das Fenster [mit einem Ball]** ~ (fig.) smash the window [with a ball]; **(b)** (treffsicher machen) try out, test ⟨gun etc.⟩; **(c)** (Sport) kick in ⟨ball⟩; **den Ball zum 1:1** ~: shoot a goal to make it or the score 1–1. **2** unr. refl. V. (auch Sport) find or get the range **(auf** + Akk. of)

ein|schiffen 1 tr. V. embark ⟨passengers⟩; load ⟨cargo⟩. **2** refl. V. embark **(nach** for)

Einschiffung die; ~, ~**en** ⇒ **einschiffen:** embarkation; loading

ein|schlafen unr. itr. V.; mit sein **(a)** fall asleep; go to sleep; **ich kann nicht** ~: I can't get to sleep; **(b)** (verhüll.: sterben) pass away (euphem.); **(c)** (gefühllos werden) ⟨arm, leg⟩ go to sleep; **(d)** (aufhören) peter out

ein|schläfern tr. V. **(a)** (in Schlaf versetzen) jmdn. ~: send sb. to sleep; **(b)** (betäuben) jmdn. ~: put sb. to sleep; **(c)** (schmerzlos töten) **ein Tier** ~: put an animal to sleep; **(d)** (beruhigen) soothe, salve ⟨conscience⟩; dull ⟨critical faculties⟩

einschläfernd 1 Adj. soporific. **2** adv. ~ **wirken** have a soporific effect

Ein·schlag der **(a)** (Einschlagen) **wir sahen den** ~ **des Blitzes/der Bomben** we saw the lightning strike/the bombs land; **(b)** (Stelle) **wir sahen die Einschläge der Kugeln/der Bomben** we saw the bullet holes/where the bombs had fallen or landed; **(c)** (Anteil) element; **eine Familie mit südländischem** ~: a family with southern blood in it; **(d)** (Kfz-W.) (des Lenkrads) turning; (der Räder) lock

ein|schlagen 1 unr. tr. V. **(a)** (hineinschlagen) knock in; hammer in; **etw. in etw.** (Akk.) ~: knock or hammer sth. into sth.; **(b)** (zertrümmern) smash [in]; **(c)** (einwickeln) wrap up ⟨present⟩; cover ⟨book⟩; **(d)** (wählen) take ⟨route, direction⟩; take up ⟨career⟩; adopt ⟨policy⟩; **einen Kurs** ~ (auch fig.) follow a course; **einen anderen Kurs** ~ (auch fig.) change or alter course; **(e)** (Kfz-W.) turn ⟨[steering-]wheel⟩. **2** unr. itr. V. **(a)** (auftreffen) ⟨bomb⟩ land; ⟨lightning⟩ strike; **bei uns hat es eingeschlagen** our house

was struck by lightning; **(b)** (einprügeln) **auf jmdn./etw.
~:** rain blows on *or* beat sb./sth.; **(c)** (durch Händedruck)
shake [hands] on it; (fig.) accept; **schlag ein!** shake on it!;
(d) (Kfz-W.) **nach links/rechts ~:** steer to the left/right
einschlägig /'aɪnʃlɛːgɪç/ **1** *Adj.* relevant. **2** *adv.* **er ist
~ vorbestraft** he has previous convictions for a similar
offence/similar offences
ein|schleichen *unr. refl. V.* steal *or* sneak *or* creep in;
(fig.) creep in; **sich in etw.** (*Akk.*) **~:** steal *or* sneak *or*
creep into sth.
ein|schleifen *unr. tr. V.* cut in
ein|schleppen *tr. V.* bring in, introduce ⟨*disease, pest*⟩
ein|schleusen *tr. V.* smuggle in; infiltrate ⟨*agents*⟩ (**in**
+ *Akk.* into)
ein|schließen *unr. tr. V.* **(a)** **etw. in etw.** (*Dat.*) **~:**
lock sth. up [in sth.]; **jmdn./sich ~:** lock sb./oneself in;
(b) (umgeben) ⟨*wall*⟩ surround, enclose; ⟨*people*⟩ surround,
encircle; **(c)** (einbeziehen) **etw. in etw.** (*Akk.*) **~:** include
sth. in sth.
einschließlich 1 *Präp. mit Gen.* including; inclusive
of; **~ der Unkosten** including expenses. **2** *adv.* **bis ~
30. Juni/Montag** up to and including 30 June/Monday
Ein·schluss, ***Ein·schluß** *der* **(a)** (Einbeziehung) inclusion; **unter od. mit ~ von** including; **(b)** (Geol.) inclusion
ein|schmeicheln *refl. V.* ingratiate oneself (**bei** with)
einschmeichelnd *Adj.* beguiling ⟨*music, voice*⟩; ingratiating ⟨*manner*⟩
ein|schmelzen *unr. tr. V.* melt down
ein|schmieren *tr. V.* (ugs.) (mit Creme) cream ⟨*face,
hands, etc.*⟩; (mit Fett) grease; (mit Öl) oil
ein|schmuggeln *tr. V.* **(a)** smuggle in; **(b)** **sich in
etw.** (*Akk.*) **~** (ugs.) sneak into sth.
ein|schnappen *itr. V.; mit sein* **(a)** ⟨*door, lock*⟩ click to;
(b) (ugs.: schmollen) go into a huff
ein|schneiden 1 *unr. tr. V.* make a cut in; cut. **2** *unr.
itr. V.* **das Kleid schneidet an den Schultern ein** the
dress cuts into my shoulders
einschneidend *Adj.* drastic, radical ⟨*measure,
change*⟩; drastic, far-reaching ⟨*effect*⟩
ein|schneien *itr. V.; mit sein* get snowed in; **einge-
schneit sein** be snowed in
Ein·schnitt *der* **(a)** cut; (Med.) incision; (im Gebirge) cleft;
(b) (Zäsur) break; **(c)** (einschneidendes Ereignis) [decisive] turning point; decisive event
ein|schnüren *tr. V.* **(a)** **sich/ jmdm. die Taille ~:**
lace one's/sb.'s waist; **(b)** (einengen) ⟨*belt, elastic*⟩ cut in
ein|schränken 1 *tr. V.* **(a)** reduce, curb ⟨*expenditure,
consumption, power*⟩; **das Trinken/Rauchen ~:** cut
down on the amount one drinks/smokes; **(b)** (einengen) limit; restrict; **jmdn. in seinen Rechten/seiner Bewegungsfreiheit ~:** limit *or* restrict sb.'s rights/freedom
of movement; **(c)** (relativieren) qualify, modify ⟨*remark*⟩. **2**
refl. V. economize; cut back on spending; **sich finanziell
~ müssen** have to cut back on one's spending; **sich im
Rauchen/Trinken ~:** cut down on the amount one
smokes/drinks
Einschränkung *die;* **~, ~en** **(a)** restriction; limitation; **jmdm. ~en auferlegen** impose restrictions on
sb.; **(b)** (Vorbehalt) reservation; **nur mit ~[en]** only with
reservations *pl.;* **ohne ~[en]** without reservation; **mit
der ~, dass...:** with the [one] reservation that ...
ein|schrauben *tr. V.* screw in
Einschreibe-: **~brief** *der* registered letter; **~ge-
bühr** *die* (Postw., Hochschulw.) registration fee
ein|schreiben *unr. tr. V.* **(a)** (hineinschreiben) write up;
(b) (Postw.) register ⟨*letter*⟩; **(c)** (eintragen) **sich/jmdn. [in
eine Liste] ~:** enter sb.'s/one's name [on a list]; **sich an
einer Universität ~:** register at a university; **sich für
einen Abendkurs ~:** enrol for an evening class
Ein·schreiben *das* (Postw.) registered letter; **per ~:** by
registered mail
Ein·schreibung *die* (Hochschulw.) registration; (für einen
Abendkurs) enrolment
ein|schreiten *unr. itr. V.* intervene; **gegen jmdn./etw.
~:** take action against sb./sth.

ein|schrumpfen *itr. V.; mit sein* shrivel up
Ein·schub *der* insertion
ein|schüchtern *tr. V.* intimidate
ein|schulen *tr. V.* eingeschult werden start school
Ein·schuss, ***Ein·schuß** *der* bullet wound; wound at
point of entry
ein|schütten *tr. V.* pour in
ein|schweißen *tr. V.* **(a)** weld in; **(b)** (in Klarsichtfolie)
etw. ~: seal sth. in transparent film
ein|schwenken *itr. V.; mit sein* **(a)** turn in; **in die Tor-
einfahrt ~:** turn into the gateway; **nach links ~:** wheel
left; **(b)** (fig.) fall into line
ein|sehen *unr. tr. V.* **(a)** see into ⟨*building, garden, etc.*⟩;
(b) (prüfend lesen) look at, see ⟨*files*⟩; **(c)** (erkennen) see;
realize; **(d)** (begreifen) understand; see
Einsehen *das;* **~s:** **ein ~ haben** show [some] understanding
ein|seifen *tr. V.* **(a)** lather; **jmdn. mit Schnee ~:** rub
snow in sb.'s face; **(b)** (ugs.: betrügen) con (coll.)
ein·seitig 1 *Adj.* **(a)** on one side *postpos.;* unrequited
⟨*love*⟩; one-sided ⟨*friendship*⟩; **er hat eine ~e Lähmung**
he's paralysed down one side; **(b)** one-sided, biased ⟨*view,
statement, etc.*⟩; one-sided ⟨*person*⟩; **(c)** unbalanced ⟨*diet*⟩;
one-sided ⟨*education*⟩. **2** *adv.* **(a)** **etw. ~ bedrucken**
print sth. on one side; **(b)** ⟹ **einseitig 1 b:** one-sidedly;
(c) **sich ~ ernähren** have an unbalanced diet
Einseitigkeit *die;* **~, ~en** ⟹ **einseitig 1 b:** one-sid-
edness; bias
ein|senden *unr.* (auch regelm.) *tr. V.* send [in]; **etw. ei-
nem Verlag od. an einen Verlag ~:** send sth. to a publisher
Ein·sender *der* sender; (bei einem Preisausschreiben) entrant
Einsende·schluss, ***Einsende·schluß** *der* closing date
Ein·sendung *die* letter/card/contribution/article *etc.;*
(bei einem Preisausschreiben) entry
Einser *der;* **~s, ~** (ugs.: Schulnote) one; A
ein|setzen 1 *tr. V.* **(a)** (hineinsetzen) put in; put in, fit
⟨*window*⟩; insert, put in ⟨*tooth, piece of fabric, value,
word*⟩; **etw. in etw.** (*Akk.*) **~:** put/fit/insert sth. into sth.;
(b) (Verkehrsw.) put on ⟨*special train etc.*⟩; **(c)** (ernennen, in
eine Position setzen) appoint; **jmdn. in ein Amt ~:** appoint
sb. to an office; **(d)** (in Aktion treten lassen) use ⟨*weapon,
machine, strength*⟩; bring into action, use ⟨*troops, police*⟩;
bring on, use ⟨*reserve player*⟩; **(e)** (aufs Spiel setzen) stake
⟨*money*⟩; **(f)** (riskieren) risk ⟨*life, reputation*⟩. **2** *itr. V.* start;
begin; ⟨*storm*⟩ break; **mit etw. ~:** start *or* begin sth.. **3**
refl. V. **(a)** (sich engagieren) **ich werde mich dafür ~,
dass ...:** I shall do what I can to see that ...; **der Schüler/
Minister setzt sich nicht genug ein** the pupil is lacking application/the minister is lacking in commitment; **(b)**
(Fürsprache einlegen) **sich für jmdn. ~:** support sb.'s cause
Einsetzung *die;* **~, ~en** appointment (**in** + *Akk.* to)
Ein·sicht *die* **(a)** (das Einsehen) view (**in** + *Akk.* into); **(b)**
o. Pl. (Einblick) **~ in die Akten nehmen** take *or* have a
look at the files; **jmdm. ~ in etw.** (*Akk.*) **gewähren** allow sb. to look at *or* see sth.; **(c)** (Erkenntnis) insight; **zu der
~ kommen, dass ...:** come to realize that ...; **(d)** *o. Pl.*
(Vernunft) sense; reason; (Verständnis) understanding; **zur ~
kommen** come to one's senses
einsichtig 1 *Adj.* **(a)** (verständnisvoll) understanding; **(b)**
(verständlich) comprehensible, understandable, clear; **ihm
war nicht ~, warum ...:** he was not clear why ... **2** *adv.*
sehr ~ vorgehen show a great deal of understanding
Einsichtnahme *die;* **~, ~n** (Papierdt.) **nach ~ in die
Akten** after studying the files; **die Baupläne liegen zur
~ aus** the building plans are available for inspection
ein|sickern *itr. V.; mit sein* seep in
Einsiedelei /aɪnziːdəˈlaɪ/ *die;* **~, ~en** hermitage
Ein·siedler *der* hermit; (fig.) recluse
ein·silbig *Adj.* **(a)** monosyllabic ⟨*word*⟩; **(b)** (fig.) taciturn ⟨*person*⟩; monosyllabic ⟨*answer*⟩
ein|sinken *unr. itr. V.* sink in; **in etw.** (*Dat.*) **~:** sink
into sth.; **eingesunkene Wangen** sunken cheeks

ein|sortieren *tr. V.* sort ⟨*books, papers, etc.*⟩ and put them away; **Karteikarten** ∼: file cards; **Briefe in Fächer** ∼: sort letters into pigeon-holes

ein·spaltig (Druckw.) **1** *Adj.* single-column *attrib.* **2** *adv.* ⟨*print, set*⟩ in one column

ein|spannen *tr. V.* **(a)** harness ⟨*horse*⟩; **(b)** (in etw. spannen); **den Bogen [in die Schreibmaschine]** ∼: put the sheet of paper in[to the typewriter]; **das Werkstück [in den Schraubstock]** ∼: clamp the work [in the vice]; **(c)** (ugs.: heranziehen) rope in (coll.)

ein|sparen *tr. V.* save, cut down on ⟨*costs, expenditure*⟩; save ⟨*time*⟩; save, economize on ⟨*energy, materials*⟩; **Stellen/Arbeitsplätze** ∼: cut down on the number of posts/cut down on staff

Einsparung *die;* ∼, ∼en saving; ∼en an Kosten/ Energie savings *or* economies in costs/energy; **durch** ∼ **von Material** by economizing on *or* saving materials

ein|speichern *tr. V.* (DV) feed in; input

ein|speisen *tr. V.* (Technik, DV) feed in; **etw. in etw.** (*Akk.*) ∼: feed sth. into sth.

ein|sperren *tr. V.* lock ⟨*sb.*⟩ up

ein|spielen 1 *refl. V.* **(a)** ⟨*musician, athlete, team, etc.*⟩ warm up; **sich aufeinander** ∼ (fig.) get used to each other's ways *or* one another; **(b)** (fig.) get going [properly]. **2** *tr. V.* **(a)** (einbringen) make; bring in; **(b)** play *or* break in ⟨*musical instrument*⟩; **(c)** (aufnehmen) record

einsprachig /ˈainʃpraːxɪç/ **1** *Adj.* monolingual. **2** *adv.* ∼ **aufwachsen** grow up speaking only one language

ein|springen *unr. itr. V.; mit sein* (als Stellvertreter) stand in; (fig.: aushelfen) step in and help out

ein|spritzen *tr. V.* inject; **jmdm. etw.** ∼: inject sb. with sth.

Einspritz-: ∼**motor** *der* fuel-injection engine; ∼**pumpe** *die* injection pump

Ein·spruch *der* (bes. Rechtsw.) objection; (gegen Urteil, Entscheidung) appeal; **[gegen etw.]** ∼ **einlegen/erheben** raise an objection [to sth.]; (gegen Urteil, Entscheidung) lodge an appeal [against sth.]

ein|sprühen *tr. V.* **x mit y** ∼: spray y on [to] x; **sich** (*Dat.*) **das Haar** ∼: put hair-spray on one's hair

einspurig /ˈainʃpuːrɪç/ **1** *Adj.* single-track ⟨*road*⟩. **2** *adv.* **die Straße ist nur** ∼ **befahrbar** only one lane of the road is open

einst /ainst/ *Adv.* (geh.) **(a)** (früher) once; **(b)** (der∼) some *or* one day

ein|stampfen *tr. V.* pulp ⟨*books*⟩

Ein·stand *der* **(a)** **seinen** ∼ **geben/feiern** celebrate starting a new job; **(b)** *o. Pl.* (Sport: erstes Spiel) début; **(c)** *o. Pl.* (Tennis) deuce

ein|stanzen *tr. V.* stamp in

ein|stauben *itr. V.; mit sein* get dusty; get covered in dust

ein|stechen 1 *unr. itr. V.* **auf jmdn.** ∼: stab sb. **2** *unr. tr. V.* prick

ein|stecken *tr. V.* **(a)** put in; **das Bügeleisen** ∼: plug in the iron; **er steckte die Pistole/das Messer wieder ein** he put the pistol back in the holster/the knife back in the sheath; **(b)** (mitnehmen) **[sich** (*Dat.*)**] etw.** ∼: take sth. with one; **(c)** mail ⟨*letter*⟩; **(d)** (abwertend: für sich behalten) pocket ⟨*money, profits*⟩; **(e)** (hinnehmen) take ⟨*criticism, defeat, etc.*⟩; take, swallow ⟨*insult*⟩

ein|stehen *unr. itr. V.* **für jmdn.** ∼: vouch for sb.; **für etw.** ∼: take responsibility for *or* assume liability for sth.

ein|steigen *unr. itr. V.; mit sein* (in ein Fahrzeug) get in; **in ein Auto** ∼: get into a car; **in den Bus** ∼: get on the bus; **vorn/hinten** ∼ (ins Auto) get into the front/back; (in den Bus) get on at the front/back; **(b)** (eindringen) **durch ein Fenster/über den Balkon** ∼: climb in *or* get in through a window/over the balcony; **(c)** (ugs.: sich engagieren) **in ein Geschäft/die Politik** ∼: go into a business/into politics

einstellbar *Adj.* adjustable

ein|stellen 1 *tr. V.* **(a)** (einordnen) put away ⟨*books etc.*⟩; **(b)** (unterstellen) put in ⟨*car, bicycle*⟩; **(c)** (auch itr.) (beschäftigen) take on, employ ⟨*workers*⟩; **(d)** (regulieren) adjust; set;

focus ⟨*camera, telescope, binoculars*⟩; adjust ⟨*headlights*⟩; **(e)** (beenden) stop; call off ⟨*search, strike*⟩; **das Feuer** ∼: cease fire; **ein Gerichtsverfahren** ∼: abandon court proceedings; **die Arbeit** ∼ ⟨*factory*⟩ close; ⟨*workers*⟩ stop work; **(f)** (Sport) equal ⟨*record*⟩. **2** *refl. V.* **(a)** (ankommen, auch fig.) arrive; **(b)** (eintreten) ⟨*pain*⟩ begin; ⟨*success*⟩ come; ⟨*symptoms, consequences*⟩ appear; **(c)** **sich auf jmdn./ etw.** ∼: adapt to sb./prepare oneself *or* get ready for sth.; **sich schnell auf neue Situationen** ∼: adjust quickly to new situations

ein·stellig *Adj.* single-figure *attrib.* ⟨*number*⟩

Einstell·platz *der* parking space; (auf eigenem Grundstück) carport

Ein·stellung *die* **(a)** (von Arbeitskräften) employment; taking on; **(b)** (Regulierung) adjustment; setting; (eines Fernglases, einer Kamera) focusing; **(c)** (Beendigung) stopping; (einer Suchaktion, eines Streiks) calling off; **(d)** (Sport) **die** ∼ **eines Rekordes** the equalling of a record; **(e)** (Ansicht) attitude; **ihre politische/religiöse** ∼: her political/religious views *pl.*; **(f)** (Film) take

Einstellungs-: ∼**gespräch** *das* interview; ∼**stopp** *der* freeze on recruitment

Ein·stich *der* puncture; prick

Ein·stieg *der;* ∼[e]s, ∼e **(a)** (Eingang) entrance; (Tür) door/doors; **(b)** *o. Pl.* (das Einsteigen) entry; „**kein** ∼" 'exit only'; **(c)** (fig.) **der** ∼ **in diese Problematik ist schwierig** these are difficult problems to approach

Einstiegs·droge *die* come-on drug

einstig *Adj.; nicht präd.* former

ein|stimmen 1 *itr. V.* join in; **in den Gesang** ∼: join in the singing. **2** *tr. V.* **jmdn. auf etw.** (*Akk.*) ∼: get sb. in the [right] mood for sth.

einstimmig 1 *Adj.* **(a)** (Musik) **ein** ∼**es Lied** a song for one voice; **(b)** (einmütig) unanimous ⟨*decision, vote*⟩. **2** *adv.* **(a)** (Musik) ∼ **singen** sing in unison; **(b)** (einmütig) unanimously

Einstimmigkeit *die;* ∼: unanimity; ∼ **erzielen** achieve unanimity

Ein·stimmung *die;* **zur** ∼: to get in the [right] mood (**auf** + *Akk.* for)

ein·stöckig *Adj.* single-storey *attrib.;* one-storey *attrib.;* ∼ **sein** have one storey

ein|stöpseln *tr. V.* plug in ⟨*telephone, electrical device*⟩

ein|stoßen *unr. tr. V.* break down ⟨*door, wall*⟩; smash [in] ⟨*window*⟩

Ein·strahlung *die* irradiation; (Sonnen∼) insolation

ein|streichen *unr. tr. V.* (ugs.) pocket ⟨*money, winnings, etc.*⟩; (abwertend) rake in (coll.) ⟨*money, profits, etc.*⟩

ein|streuen *tr. V.* **(a)** **etw. mit Sand** ∼: strew *or* scatter sand on sth.; **(b)** (einfügen) **er streute witzige Bemerkungen in seinen Vortrag ein** he sprinkled his lecture with witty remarks

ein|strömen *itr. V.* ⟨*water*⟩ pour *or* flood *or* stream in; ⟨*air, light*⟩ stream in; (fig.) ⟨*crowd, supporters*⟩ stream *or* pour in

ein|studieren *tr. V.* rehearse

Einstudierung *die;* ∼, ∼en **(a)** *o. Pl.* rehearsal; **(b)** (Inszenierung) production

ein|stufen *tr. V.* classify; categorize; **jmdn. in eine Kategorie** ∼: put sb. in a category

Einstufung /ˈainʃtuːfʊŋ/ *die;* ∼, ∼en classification; categorization

ein·stündig *Adj.* one-hour *attrib.* ⟨*wait, delay*⟩; *s. auch* **achtstündig**

ein|stürmen *itr. V.* **mit Fragen/Bitten auf jmdn.** ∼: besiege sb. with questions/requests

Ein·sturz *der* collapse

ein|stürzen *itr. V.; mit sein* **(a)** collapse; **eine Welt stürzte für sie ein** (fig.) her whole world collapsed *or* fell apart; **(b)** (fig.) **auf jmdn.** ∼ ⟨*worries, problems*⟩ crowd in [up]on sb.

Einsturz·gefahr *die; o. Pl.* danger of collapse; „**Achtung,** ∼**!**" 'danger – building unsafe'

einst·weilen *Adv.* for the time being; temporarily

ein·suggerieren *itr. V.* **jmdm. etw. ~:** instil sth. into sb. by suggestion

ein·tägig *Adj.* one-day *attrib.; s. auch* **achttägig**

Eintags·fliege *die* (Zool.) mayfly; (fig. ugs.) seven-day wonder

ein|tauchen 1 *tr. V.* dip; (untertauchen) immerse. **2** *itr. V.; mit sein* dive in

ein|tauschen *tr. V.* exchange (**gegen** for)

ein·tausend *Kardinalz.* **▶ 600 |** a *or* one thousand; *s. auch* **acht**[1]

ein|teilen *tr. V.* **(a)** divide up; classify ‹*plants, species*›; **(b)** (disponieren, verplanen) organize; plan [out] ‹*work, time*›; **sein Geld [besser] ~:** plan *or* organize one's finances [better]; **(c)** (delegieren, abkommandieren) **jmdn. für** *od.* **zu etw. ~:** assign sb. to sth.

einteilig /'aintailɪç/ *Adj.* one-piece ‹*dress, bathing suit*›

Ein·teilung *die* **(a)** (Gliederung) division; dividing up; (Biol.) classification; **(b)** (planvolles Disponieren) organization; planning; **(c)** (Delegierung, Abkommandierung) assignment

Eintel /'aintl/ *das* (*schweiz. meist der*); **~s, ~:** whole

ein|tippen *tr. V.* (in die Kasse) register; (in einen Rechner) key in

eintönig /'aintø:nɪç/ **1** *Adj.* monotonous. **2** *adv.* monotonously

Eintönigkeit *die; ~:* monotony

Ein·topf *der,* **Eintopf·gericht** *das* (Kochk.) stew

Ein·tracht *die; o. Pl.* harmony; concord

ein·trächtig 1 *Adj.* harmonious. **2** *adv.* harmoniously; **~ zusammenleben** live together in harmony

Eintrag /'aintra:k/ *der;* ~[e]s, **Einträge** /'aintrɛːgə/ entry

ein|tragen *unr. tr. V.* **(a)** (einschreiben) enter; copy out ‹*essay*›; (einzeichnen) mark in; enter; **seinen Namen** *od.* **sich [in eine Liste] ~:** enter one's name [on a list]; **(b)** (Amtsspr.) register; **sich ~ lassen** register; **etw. auf seinen Namen ~ lassen** have sth. registered in one's name; **ein eingetragenes Warenzeichen** a registered trade mark; **(c)** (einbringen) bring in ‹*money*›; bring ‹*criticism*›; win ‹*goodwill*›; **das Geschäft trägt [einen] Gewinn ein** the business makes a profit

einträglich /'aintrɛːklɪç/ *Adj.* profitable, lucrative ‹*business, sideline*›; lucrative ‹*work, job*›

Eintragung *die; ~,* ~en **(a)** (das Eintragen) entering; **(b)** (Eingetragenes) entry

ein|treffen *unr. itr. V.; mit sein* **(a)** arrive; **(b)** ‹*prophecy*› come true

Ein·treffen *das; o. Pl.* arrival

ein|treiben *unr. tr. V.* collect ‹*taxes, debts*›; (durch Gerichtsverfahren) recover ‹*debts, money*›

Eintreibung *die; ~,* ~en collection; (durch Gerichtsverfahren) recovery

ein|treten 1 *unr. itr. V.; mit sein* **(a)** (auch fig.) enter; **bitte, treten Sie ein!** please come in; **in Verhandlungen ~:** enter into negotiations; **(b)** (Mitglied werden) **in einen Verein/einen Orden ~:** join a club/enter a religious order; **(c)** (sich ereignen) occur; **(d)** (sich einsetzen) **für jmdn./etw. ~:** stand up for sb./sth.; (vor Gericht) speak in sb.'s defence. **2** *unr. tr. V.* kick in ‹*door, window, etc.*›

ein|trichtern *tr. V.* **jmdm. etw. ~** (salopp) drum sth. into sb.

Ein·tritt *der* **(a)** entry; entrance; **sich** (*Dat.*) **[in etw.** (*Akk.*)**] ~ verschaffen** gain entry [to sth.]; **vor dem ~ in die Verhandlungen** (fig.) before entering into negotiations; **(b)** (Beitritt) **der ~ in einen Verein/Orden** joining a club/entering a religious order; **(c)** (Zugang, Eintrittsgeld) admission; **[der] ~ [ist] frei** admission [is] free; **(d)** (Beginn) onset; **(e)** (eines Ereignisses) occurrence; **bei ~ des Todes** when death occurs

Eintritts-: **~geld** *das* admission charge *or* fee; entrance charge *or* fee; **~karte** *die* admission *or* entrance ticket; **~preis** *der* admission *or* entrance charge

ein|trocknen *itr. V.; mit sein* **(a)** ‹*paint, blood*› dry; ‹*water, toothpaste*› dry up; **(b)** (verdorren) ‹*leather*› dry out; ‹*berry, fruit*› shrivel

ein|trudeln *itr. V.; mit sein* (ugs.) drift in (coll.)

ein|tüten *tr. V.* bag

ein|üben *tr. V.* practise

ein·und·ein·halb ⇒ **anderthalb**

ein|verleiben /-fɛɐlaibn/ **1** *tr. V.* annex ‹*land, country*›. **2** *refl. V.* assimilate, absorb ‹*knowledge, experience*›; (scherzh.: zu sich nehmen) put away (coll.)

Ein·vernehmen *das;* ~s harmony; (Übereinstimmung) agreement

ein·vernehmlich (Amtsspr.) **1** *Adv.* conjointly. **2** *adj.* conjoint

einverstanden *Adj.; nicht attr.* **~ sein** agree; **mit jmdm./etw. ~ sein** approve of sb./sth.; **~!** (ugs.) okay! (coll.); agreed!

Ein·verständnis *das* **(a)** (Billigung) consent, approval (**zu** of); **(b)** (Übereinstimmung) agreement

Ein·waage *die* (Amtsspr.) contents *pl.*

Einwand *der;* ~[e]s, **Einwände** /'ainvɛndə/ objection (**gegen** to)

Ein·wanderer *der* immigrant

ein|wandern *itr. V.; mit sein* immigrate (**in** + *Akk.* into)

Ein·wanderung *die* immigration

Einwanderungs·land *das* country of immigration

einwand·frei 1 *Adj.* flawless; perfect; impeccable ‹*behaviour*›; indisputable, definite ‹*proof*›; watertight ‹*alibi*›. **2** *adv.* perfectly; flawlessly; ‹*behave*› impeccably; **es ist ~ erwiesen, dass ...:** it has been proved beyond question *or* doubt that ...

einwärts /'ainvɛrts/ *Adv.* inwards

ein|wechseln *tr. V.* **(a)** change ‹*money*›; **(b)** (Sport) substitute ‹*player*›

ein|wecken *tr. V.* preserve; preserve, bottle ‹*fruit, vegetables*›

Einweck·glas *das* preserving-jar

Ein·weg·flasche *die* non-returnable bottle

ein|weichen *tr. V.* soak

ein|weihen *tr. V.* **(a)** open [officially] ‹*bridge, road*›; consecrate ‹*church*›; dedicate ‹*monument*›; **(b)** (ugs. scherzh.: zum erstenmal benutzen) christen (coll.); **(c)** (vertraut machen) **jmdn. in etw.** (*Akk.*) **~:** let sb. in on sth.

Einweihung *die; ~,* ~en [official] opening

ein|weisen *unr. tr. V.* **(a)** **jmdn. in ein Krankenhaus ~:** have sb. admitted to hospital; **(b)** (in eine Tätigkeit) **jmdn. [in eine/die Arbeit] ~:** show sb. what a/the job involves; **(c)** (in ein Amt) install; **jmdn. in sein Amt ~:** install sb.; **(d)** (Verkehrsw.) direct

Ein·weisung *die* **(a)** **~ in ein Krankenhaus** admission to a hospital; **(b)** (in eine Tätigkeit) introduction

ein|wenden *unr. (auch regelm.) tr. V.* **gegen etw. nichts einzuwenden haben** have no objection to sth.; **dagegen lässt sich manches ~:** there are a number of things to be said against that; „....", **wandte er ein** '....,' he objected

Ein·wendung *die* objection (**gegen** to)

ein|werfen 1 *unr. tr. V.* **(a)** put in, insert ‹*coin*›; mail ‹*letter, mail*›; **(b)** (zertrümmern) smash, break ‹*window*›; **(c)** (Ballspiele) throw in ‹*ball*›; **(d)** (bemerken, sagen) throw in ‹*remark*›; „....", **warf sie ein** '....,' she interjected. **2** *unr. itr. V.* (Ballspiele) (vom Rand) take the throw-in; (ins Tor) score

ein|wickeln *tr. V.* **(a)** wrap [up]; **(b)** **jmdn. ~** (ugs.) take sb. in

ein|willigen *itr. V.* agree, consent (**in** + *Akk.* to)

Einwilligung *die; ~,* ~en agreement; consent; **seine ~ zu etw. geben** give one's consent to sth.

ein|winken *tr. V.* (Verkehrsw.) guide in ‹*aircraft*›; guide *or* direct in ‹*car*›

ein|wirken (a) **auf jmdn. ~:** influence sb.; **beruhigend auf jmdn. ~:** exert a soothing *or* calming influence on sb.; **(b)** (eine Wirkung ausüben) have an effect (**auf** + *Akk.* on); **die Creme ~ lassen** let the cream work in

Ein·wirkung *die* (Einfluss) influence; (Wirkung) effect; **unter ~ von Drogen stehen** be under the influence of drugs

ein·wöchig Adj. one-week attrib.; week-old ⟨baby⟩; week-long ⟨conference⟩

Einwohner der; ~s, ~, **Einwohnerin** die; ~, ~nen inhabitant; **die Stadt hat 3 Millionen Einwohner:** the town has 3 million inhabitants or a population of 3 million

Einwohner·meldeamt das local government office for registration of residents

Einwohnerschaft die; ~: population; inhabitants pl.

Einwohner·zahl die population

Ein·wurf der (a) (Einwerfen) insertion; (von Briefen) mailing; (b) (Ballspiele) throw-in; (c) (Öffnung) (eines Briefkastens) slit; (einer Tür) letter box; (d) (Zwischenbemerkung) interjection; (kritisch) objection

Ein·zahl die; o. Pl. (Sprachw.) singular

ein|zahlen tr. V. pay in; deposit; **Geld auf sein Konto ~:** pay or deposit money into one's account

Ein·zahlung die payment; deposit; (Überweisung) payment

Einzahlungs·beleg der counterfoil

ein|zäunen tr. V. fence in; enclose

Einzäunung die; ~, ~en (a) (das Einzäunen) fencing-in; enclosure; (b) (Zaun) fence; enclosure

ein|zeichnen tr. V. draw or mark in; **etw. in eine Karte ~:** draw or mark sth. in on a map

ein·zeilig Adj. one-line attrib.

Einzel /'aintsl/ das; ~s, ~ (Sport) singles pl.; ~ **spielen** to play a singles match

Einzel-: ~**aktion** die independent action; ~**anfertigung** die custom-made article; ~**ausgabe** die separate edition; ~**band** der individual or single volume; ~**bett** das single bed; ~**erscheinung** die isolated occurrence; ~**fahrschein** der single; ~**fall** der (a) particular case; **im ~fall** in particular cases; (b) (Ausnahme) isolated case; exception; ~**frage** die individual question

Einzelgänger /-ɡɛŋɐ/ der; ~s, ~ (a) solitary person; loner; (b) (Tier) lone animal

Einzel-: ~**gewerkschaft** die member union; ~**haft** die solitary confinement

Einzel·handel der retail trade; **etw. im ~ kaufen** buy sth. retail

Einzelhandels-: ~**geschäft** das retail shop; retail store (Amer.); ~**preis** der retail price

Einzel·händler der retailer; retail trader

Einzelheit die; ~, ~en (a) detail; (b) (einzelner Umstand) particular

Einzel·kind das only child

einzeln Adj. (a) individual; **die ~en Bände des Werkes** the individual or separate volumes of the work; **jede ~e Insel** each individual island; **ein ~er Schuh/Handschuh** an odd shoe/glove; **schon ein ~es von diesen Gläsern** just one of these glasses on its own; (b) solitary ⟨building, tree⟩; **eine ~e Dame/ein ~er Herr** a single lady/gentleman; (c) ~e (wenige) a few; (einige) some; ~**e Regenschauer** scattered or isolated showers; (d) substantivisch (~er Mensch) **der/jeder Einzelne** the/each individual; **als Einzelner** as an individual; **jeder Einzelne der Betroffenen** every [single] one of those concerned; **ein Einzelner** one individual; (e) substantivisch **Einzelnes** (manches) some things pl.; **etw. im Einzelnen besprechen** discuss sth. in detail; **ins Einzelne gehen** go into detail[s pl.]; **bis ins Einzelne** right down to the last detail

Einzel-: ~**person** die one person; individual; **als ~person** as an individual; ~**richter** der judge sitting singly; ~**schicksal** das individual fate or destiny; ~**stück** das individual piece or item; ~**teil** das [individual or separate] part; **etw. in [seine] ~teile zerlegen** take sth. to pieces; ~**unterricht** der individual tuition; ~**zelle** die single cell; ~**zimmer** das single room

Einzieh·decke die duvet (Brit.); continental quilt (Brit.); stuffed quilt (Amer.)

ein|ziehen 1 unr. tr. V. (a) put in ⟨duvet⟩; thread in ⟨tape, elastic⟩; (b) (einbauen) put in ⟨wall, ceiling⟩; (c) (einholen) haul in, pull in ⟨net⟩; retract, draw in ⟨feelers, claws⟩;

den Kopf ~: duck; **der Hund zog den Schwanz ein** the dog put its tail between its legs; (d) (einatmen) breathe in ⟨scent, fresh air⟩; inhale ⟨smoke⟩; (e) (einberufen) call up, conscript ⟨recruits⟩; (f) (beitreiben) collect; **er lässt die Miete vom Konto ~:** he pays his rent by direct debit; (g) (beschlagnahmen) confiscate; seize; (h) (aus dem Verkehr ziehen) withdraw, call in ⟨coins, banknotes⟩; (i) (Papierdt.: einholen) **Informationen/Erkundigungen ~:** gather information/make enquiries. **2** unr. itr. V.; mit sein (a) ⟨liquid⟩ soak in; (b) (einkehren) enter; **der Frühling zieht ein** (geh.) spring comes or arrives; (c) (in eine Wohnung) move in

Ein·ziehung die (a) (Einberufung) call-up; conscription; drafting (Amer.); (b) (Beitreibung) collection; (c) (von Eigentum) confiscation, seizure; (von Münzen, Banknoten usw.) withdrawal

einzig /'aintsɪç/ **1** Adj. (a) only; **nur ein ~er Besucher** only one visitor; **kein** od. **nicht ein ~es Stück** not one single piece; **ihre ~e Freude** her one and only joy; **das Einzige** the only thing; (b) nicht präd. (völlig) complete; absolute; **eine ~e Qual** one long torment; (c) nicht attr. (geh.: unvergleichlich) unique; unparalleled. **2** adv. (a) (intensivierend bei Adj.) singularly; extraordinarily; (b) (ausschließlich) only; **das ~ Wahre** the only thing; **das ~ Vernünftige/Richtige** the only sensible/right thing [to do]; ~ **und allein** nobody/nothing but; solely

einzig·artig 1 Adj. unique. **2** adv. uniquely; ~ **schön** extraordinarily beautiful

Einzigartigkeit die uniqueness

Ein·zimmer-: ~**appartement** das, ~**wohnung** die one-room flat or (Amer.) apartment

Ein·zug der (a) entry (**in** + Akk. into); **der ~ des Winters** (geh.) the advent of winter; **[seinen] ~ halten** make one's entrance; (b) (in eine Wohnung) move

Einzugs-: ~**bereich** der, ~**gebiet** das catchment area

ein|zwängen tr. V. squeeze or hem in; ⟨corset⟩ constrict

Eis /ais/ das; ~es (a) ice; **ein Whisky mit ~:** a whisky with ice or on the rocks; **etw. auf ~ legen** (auch fig. ugs.) put sth. on ice; ~ **laufen** ice-skate; (b) (Speise~) ice cream; **ein ~ am Stiel** an ice lolly (Brit.) or (Amer.) ice pop

Eis-: ~**bahn** die ice rink; ~**bär** der polar bear; ~**becher** der (a) (~portion) ice cream sundae; (b) (Gefäß) [ice cream] sundae dish; ~**bein** das (Kochk.) knuckle of pork; ~**berg** der iceberg; **die Spitze des ~bergs** (fig.) the tip of the iceberg; ~**beutel** der ice-bag; ice pack; ~**blume** die frost flower; ~**bombe** die (Gastr.) bombe glacée; ~**brecher** der ice-breaker; ~**café** das ice cream parlour

Ei·schnee der stiffly beaten egg white

Eisen /'aizn̩/ das; ~s, ~: (a) o. Pl. iron; **aus ~ sein** be made of iron; **die ~ verarbeitende Industrie** the iron-processing industry; (b) (Werkzeug, Golf~) iron; (fig.) **das ist ein heißes ~:** that is a hot potato (coll.); **noch ein ~ im Feuer haben** have another iron in the fire; **zum alten ~ gehören** belong on the scrap heap

Eisen·bahn die (a) railway; railroad (Amer.); **mit der ~ fahren** go or travel by train or rail; **es ist [aller]höchste ~** (ugs.) it's high time; its' getting late; (b) (Bahnstrecke) railway line; railroad track (Amer.); (c) (Spielbahn) train set

Eisenbahn·abteil das railway or (Amer.) railroad compartment

Eisenbahner der; ~s, ~: ▸ 85 ⏋ railwayman; railroader (Amer.)

Eisenbahn-: ~**fähre** die train ferry; ~**knotenpunkt** der railway or (Amer.) railroad junction; ~**netz** das railway or (Amer.) railroad network; ~**schaffner** der railway guard; railroad conductor (Amer.); ~**tunnel** der railway or (Amer.) railroad tunnel; ~**unglück** das train crash; railway carriage; railroad car (Amer.); (Güterwagen) railway wagon; railroad car (Amer.)

eisen-, Eisen-: ~**berg·werk** das iron mine; ~**erz** das iron ore; ~**haltig** Adj. iron-bearing ⟨stone⟩; ⟨food⟩ containing iron; ~**hütte** die ironworks sing. or pl.; iron foundry; ~**mangel** der (Med.) iron deficiency; ~**nagel** der iron nail; ~**säge** die hacksaw; ~**stange** die iron bar; ~**teil** das iron part; ~**träger** der iron girder;

---

*~verarbeitend ⇨ **Eisen** a; **~waren** *Pl.* iron-mongery *sing.;* **~waren·händler** *der* ironmonger; **~zeit** *die* Iron Age

eisern /ˈaizɐn/ **1** *Adj.* **(a)** *nicht präd.* (aus Eisen) iron; **~e Lunge** (Med.) iron lung; **der Eiserne Vorhang** (Politik) the Iron Curtain; **(b)** (unerschütterlich) iron ‹*discipline*›; unflagging ‹*energy*›; **mit ~em Willen** with a will of iron; **(c)** (unerbittlich) iron; unyielding; iron ‹*discipline*›; **(d)** (bleibend) **~er Bestand/~e Reserve** emergency stock/reserves *pl.;* **die ~e Ration** the iron rations *pl.;* (fig.) one's last reserves *pl. or* standby. **2** *adv.* **(a)** (unerschütterlich) resolutely; **~ bei etw. bleiben** stick tenaciously to sth.; **sich ~ an etw.** (*Akk.*) **halten** keep resolutely to sth.; **~ sparen/trainieren** save/train with iron determination; **(b)** (unerbittlich) **~ durchgreifen** take drastic measures *or* action

eis-, Eis-: **~fach** *das* freezing compartment; **~fläche** *die* sheet *or* surface of ice; **~frei** *Adj.* ice-free; free of ice *postpos.;* **~gekühlt** *Adj.* iced ‹*drink*›; **~glatt** *Adj.* icy ‹*road*›; **~glätte** *die* black ice; **~hockey** *das* ice hockey

eisig 1 *Adj.* **(a)** icy ‹*wind, cold*›; icy [cold] ‹*water*›; **(b)** (fig.) frosty, icy ‹*atmosphere*›; frosty ‹*smile*›. **2** *adv.* **(a)** **~ kalt sein** be icy cold; **(b)** (fig.) ‹*smile*› frostily; **~ schweigen** maintain an icy silence

eis-, Eis-: **~kaffee** *der* iced coffee; **~kalt 1** *Adj.* **(a)** ice-cold ‹*drink*›; freezing cold ‹*weather*›; **(b)** (fig.) icy; ice-cold ‹*technocrat, businessman*›; **ein ~kalter Blick** a cold look. **2** *adv.* (fig.) **(a) es lief mir ~kalt über den Rücken** a cold shiver went down my spine; **(b) etw. ~kalt tun** (kaltblütig) do sth. in cold blood; (lässig) do sth. without turning a hair; **~kristall** *das* ice crystal; **~kübel** *der* ice bucket

Eis·kunst-: **~lauf** *der* figure skating; **~laufen** *das* figure skating; **~läufer** *der* figure skater

eis-, Eis-: **~lauf** *der* ice-skating;***~laufen** ⇨ **Eis** a; **~laufen** *das* ice-skating; **~läufer** *der* ice-skater; **~mann** *der; Pl.* **~männer** (ugs.) ice cream man; **~maschine** *die* ice cream maker; freezer (Amer.); **~meer** *das:* **das Nördliche/Südliche ~meer** the Arctic/Antarctic Ocean; **~pickel** *der* (Bergsteigen) ice-pick

Ei·sprung *der* (Physiol.) ovulation

eis-, Eis-: **~regen** *der* sleet; **~revue** *die* ice show; **~schicht** *die* layer of ice; **~scholle** *die* ice floe; **~schrank** *der* (ugs.) refrigerator; **~sport** *der* ice sports *pl.;* **~stadion** *das* ice rink; **~stock-schießen** *das* (Sport) ice-stick shooting; **~tanz** *der* (Sport) ice-dancing; **~wasser** *das; o. Pl.* iced water; **~wein** *der* wine made from grapes frozen on the vine; **~würfel** *der* ice cube; **~zapfen** *der* icicle; **~zeit** *die* ice age; **~zeit·lich** *Adj.* ice-age *attrib.,* of the ice age *postpos.*

eitel /ˈaitl̩/ *Adj.* **(a)** (abwertend) vain; **(b)** (veralt.: nichtig) vain ‹*hope*›; futile, vain ‹*endeavour*›; **(c)** indekl., *nicht präd.* (veralt.: rein) pure

Eitelkeit *die;* **~, ~en** vanity

Eiter /ˈaitɐ/ *der;* **~s** pus

Eiter-: **~beule** *die* boil; abscess; **~pickel** *der* spot; pimple

eitern *itr. V.* suppurate

eitrig *Adj.* suppurating; festering

Ei·weiß *das* **(a)** egg white; **(b)** (Chemie, Biol.) protein

eiweiß-, Eiweiß-: **~arm** *Adj.* low-protein *attrib.;* low in protein *postpos.;* **~haltig** *Adj.* ‹*food*› containing protein; **~mangel** *der* protein deficiency; **~reich** *Adj.* high-protein *attrib.;* rich in protein *postpos.*

Ejakulation /eʒakulaˈtsi̯oːn/ *die;* **~, ~en** ejaculation

EKD /eːkaːˈdeː/ *die;* **~** *Abk.* **Evangelische Kirche in Deutschland**

Ekel¹ *der;* **~s** disgust; loathing; revulsion; **[einen] ~ vor etw.** (*Dat.*) **haben** have a loathing *or* revulsion for sth.; **~ erregend** disgusting; nauseating; revolting

Ekel² *das;* **~s, ~** (ugs. abwertend) horror; **er ist ein [altes] ~:** he is a perfect horror *or* quite obnoxious

*ekel·erregend ⇨ **Ekel¹**

ekelhaft ⇨ eklig 1 a, 2

ekelig ⇨ eklig

ekeln /ˈeːkl̩n/ **1** *refl. V.* be *or* feel disgusted *or* sickened; **sie ekelt sich vor Spinnen** she finds spiders repulsive;

sich vor jmdm./etw. **~:** find sb./sth. disgusting *or* revolting. **2** *tr., itr. V.; unpers.* **mich** *od.* **mir ekelt davor** I find it disgusting *or* revolting. **3** *tr. V.* **(a) Hunde ~ ihn** he finds dogs repulsive; **(b)** (vertreiben) **jmdn. aus dem Haus ~:** hound sb. out of the house

EKG /eːkaːˈgeː/ *das;* **~[s], ~[s]** *Abk.* **Elektrokardiogramm** ECG

Eklat /eˈkla(ː)/ *der;* **~s, ~s** (geh.) (Aufsehen, Skandal) sensation; stir; (Konfrontation) row; altercation

eklatant /eklaˈtant/ *Adj.* (geh.) striking ‹*difference*›; flagrant, scandalous ‹*offence*›

eklig /ˈeːklɪç/ **1** *Adj.* **(a)** disgusting, revolting, nauseating ‹*sight*›; nasty (coll.), horrible ‹*weather, person*›; **~ riechen/schmecken** smell/taste disgusting *or* revolting; **(b)** (ugs.: gemein) mean; nasty; **sich ~ benehmen** be mean *or* nasty. **2** *adv.* **(a)** in a disgusting *or* revolting *or* nauseating way; **(b)** (ugs.: sehr) terribly (coll.), dreadfully (coll.) ‹*hot, cold*›

Eklipse /eˈklɪpsə/ *die;* **~, ~n** (Astron.) eclipse

Ekstase /ɛkˈstaːzə/ *die;* **~, ~n** ecstasy; **in ~ geraten** go into ecstasies; **jmdn. in ~ versetzen** send sb. into ecstasies

ekstatisch **1** *Adj.* ecstatic. **2** *adv.* ecstatically

Ekzem *das;* **~s, ~e ▶ 329 |** (Med.) eczema

Elan /eˈlaːn/ *der;* **~s** zest; vigour

Elaste /eˈlastə/ *Pl.* (Chemie) elastomers

elastisch *Adj.* **(a)** elastic; (Textilw.: Gummifäden o. Ä. enthaltend) elasticated ‹*fabric*›; (federnd) springy, resilient; **(b)** (geschmeidig) supple, lithe ‹*person, body*›

Elastizität /elastitsiˈtɛːt/ *die;* **~:** **(a)** elasticity; (Federkraft) springiness; **(b)** (Geschmeidigkeit) suppleness

Elch /ɛlç/ *der;* **~[e]s, ~e** elk; (in Nordamerika) moose

Elch·test *der* (ugs.) elk test

Eldorado /ɛldoˈraːdo/ *das;* **~s, ~s** eldorado; **ein ~ der** *od.* **für Taucher** (fig.) a divers' paradise

Elefant /eleˈfant/ *der;* **~en, ~en** elephant; **wie ein ~ im Porzellanladen** (ugs.) like a bull in a china shop; *s. auch* **Mücke**

Elefanten-: **~bulle** *der* bull elephant; **~herde** *die* elephant herd; **~kuh** *die* cow elephant

elegant /eleˈgant/ **1** *Adj.* elegant, stylish ‹*dress, appearance*›; elegant ‹*society*›; elegant, graceful ‹*movement*›; neat ‹*solution*›; elegant, civilized ‹*taste*›; elegant ‹*style*›; civilized ‹*manner*›. **2** *adv.* elegantly, stylishly ‹*dressed*›

Eleganz /eleˈgants/ *die;* **~** elegance

Elegie /eleˈgiː/ *die;* **~, ~n** elegy

elektrifizieren /elɛktrifiˈtsiːrən/ *tr. V.* electrify

Elektrifizierung *die;* **~, ~en** electrification

Elektrik /eˈlɛktrɪk/ *die;* **~, ~en** electrics *pl.*

Elektriker *der;* **~s, ~:** electrician

elektrisch **1** *Adj.* electric ‹*current, light, heating, shock*›; electrical ‹*resistance, wiring, system*›; **der ~e Stuhl** the electric chair. **2** *adv.* **~ kochen** cook with electricity; **~ geladen sein** be charged with electricity; **sich ~ rasieren** use an electric shaver

elektrisieren **1** *tr. V.* (fig.) electrify. **2** *refl. V.* give oneself *or* get an electric shock

Elektrizität /elɛktritsiˈtɛːt/ *die;* **~** (Physik) electricity; (elektrische Energie) electricity; [electric] power

Elektrizitäts-: **~versorgung** *die* [electric] power supply; **~werk** *das* power station

Elektro-: **~antrieb** *der* electric drive; **~auto** *das* electric car

Elektrode /elɛkˈtroːdə/ *die;* **~, ~n** electrode

elektro-, Elektro-: **~fahrzeug** *das* electric vehicle; **~gerät** *das* electrical appliance; **~geschäft** *das* electrical shop *or* (Amer.) store; **~herd** *der* electric cooker; **~industrie** *die* electrical goods industry; **~ingenieur** *der* **▶ 85 |** electrical engineer; **~installateur** *der* **▶ 85 |** electrical fitter; electrician; **~konzern** *der* electrical company; **~magnet** *der* electromagnet; **~magnetisch** *Adj.* electromagnetic; **~mobil** *das* electric car; **~motor** *der* electric motor

Elektron /e'lɛktrɔn/ *das;* ~s, ~en /-'tro:nən/ (Kernphysik) electron

Elektronen-: ~**blitz** *der* electronic flash; ~**[ge]hirn** *das* (ugs.) electronic brain (coll.); ~**mikroskop** *das* electron microscope; ~**röhre** *die* electron tube *or* valve

Elektronik /elɛk'tro:nɪk/ *die;* ~ (a) *o. Pl.* electronics *sing., no art.;* (b) (elektronisches System) electronics *pl.*

Elektroniker *der;* ~s, ~: ▶ 85 ⎮ electronics engineer

Elektronik·schrott *der* scrapped electrical appliances *pl.*

elektronisch 1 *Adj.* electronic. **2** *adv.* electronically

elektro-, Elektro-: ~**ofen** *der* (Technik) electric furnace; ~**rasierer** *der* electric shaver *or* razor; ~**schock** *der* (Med.) electric shock; ~**smog** *der* electronic smog; ~**statisch 1** *Adj.* electrostatic; **2** *adv.* electrostatically; ~**technik** *die* electrical engineering *no art.*

Element /ele'mɛnt/ *das;* ~[e]s, ~e (a) element; **er war/fühlte sich in seinem** ~: he was/felt in his element; **zwielichtige/kriminelle** ~e shady/criminal elements; (b) (Bauteil) element; (einer Schrankwand) unit; (c) (Elektrot.) cell

elementar /elemɛn'ta:ɐ̯/ **1** *Adj.* (a) (grundlegend) fundamental ‹*requirement, right, condition, etc.*›; (b) (einfach) elementary, rudimentary ‹*knowledge*›; (c) (naturhaft) elemental ‹*force, forces*›. **2** *adv.* with elemental force

Elementar-: ~**kenntnisse** *Pl.* elementary *or* rudimentary knowledge *sing.;* ~**stufe** *die* (Schulw.) preschool level; ~**teilchen** *das* (Physik) elementary particle; ~**unterricht** (a) elementary instruction; (b) (Unterricht in der ~stufe) preschool teaching

elend /'e:lɛnt/ **1** *Adj.* (a) wretched, miserable ‹*existence, life conditions, environment*›; (b) (krank) **sich** ~ **fühlen** feel wretched *or* (coll.) awful; **mir ist/wird** ~: I feel/I am beginning to feel awful *or* terrible (coll.); (c) (gemein) despicable ‹*person, coward, allegation*›; (d) *nicht präd.* (ugs.: besonders groß) dreadful (coll.) ‹*hunger, pain*›. **2** *adv.* (a) (jämmerlich) wretchedly; miserably; ~ **zugrunde gehen** come to a miserable *or* wretched end; (b) (ugs.: intensivierend) dreadfully (coll.)

Elend *das;* ~s (a) (Leid) misery; wretchedness; *s. auch* **Häufchen;** (b) (Armut) misery; destitution

elendig, elendiglich *Adv.* (geh.) miserably; wretchedly

Elends-: ~**quartier** *das* slum [dwelling]; ~**viertel** *das* slum area

Eleve /e'le:və/ *der;* ~n, ~n, **Elevin** *die;* ~, ~nen (Theater, Ballett) student

elf /ɛlf/ *Kardinalz.* ▶ 22 ⎮, ▶ 530 ⎮, ▶ 600 ⎮ eleven; *s. auch* **acht**[1]

Elf[1] *die;* ~, ~en (a) eleven; *s. auch* **Acht**[1] a, e; (b) (Sport) team; side

Elf[2] *der;* ~en, ~en elf

Elfe /'ɛlfə/ *die;* ~, ~n fairy

Elfen·bein *das* ivory

elfenbein-, Elfenbein-: ~**farben** *Adj.* ivory-coloured; ~**küste** *die* Ivory Coast; ~**schnitzerei** *die* (a) *o. Pl.* ivory-carving; (b) (Gegenstand) ivory carving; ~**turm** *der* (fig.) ivory tower

Eifer *der;* ~s, ~ (a) (Fußballjargon) penalty; (b) (landsch.: Zahl Elf) eleven; (c) (Buslinie) number eleven

elf-: ~**fach** *Vervielfältigungsz.* elevenfold; *s. auch* **achtfach;** ~**mal** *Wiederholungsz.* eleven times; *s. auch* **achtmal**

Elf·meter *der* (Fußball) penalty; **einen** ~ **schießen** take a penalty

Elfmeter-: ~**punkt** *der* (Fußball) penalty spot; ~**schießen** *das* (Fußball) **durch** ~**schießen** by *or* on penalties

elft: wir waren zu ~: there were eleven of us; *s. auch* **acht**[2]

elft... *Ordinalz.* ▶ 119 ⎮, ▶ 600 ⎮ eleventh; *s. auch* **acht**...

elf·tausend *Kardinalz.* eleven thousand

Elftel /'ɛlft̩/ *das;* ~s, ~: eleventh

elftens *Adv.* eleventh

Elimination /elimina'tsio:n/ *die;* ~, ~en elimination

eliminieren /elimi'ni:rən/ *tr. V.* eliminate

Eliminierung *die;* ~, ~en elimination

Elisabeth /e'li:zabɛt/ *die* Elizabeth

elisabethanisch *Adj.* Elizabethan

elitär /eli'tɛ:ɐ̯/ **1** *Adj.* élitist. **2** *adv.* in an élitist fashion

Elite /e'li:tə/ *die;* ~, ~n élite

Elite-: ~**denken** *das* élitist thinking; élitism; ~**truppe** *die* (Milit.) élite *or* crack force

Elixier /elɪ'ksi:ɐ̯/ *das;* ~s, ~e elixir

Ell·bogen *der;* ~s, ~: ▶ 326 ⎮ elbow; **er/sie hat keine** ~ (fig. ugs.) he/she isn't pushy enough (coll.)

Ellbogen-: ~**freiheit** *die* elbow room; ~**gesellschaft** *die* (abwertend) society where the weakest go to the wall

Elle /'ɛlə/ *die;* ~, ~n (a) ▶ 326 ⎮ (Anat.) ulna; (b) (frühere Längeneinheit) cubit; (c) (veralt.: Maßstock) ≈ yardstick; **alles mit einer** ~ **messen** (fig.) measure everything by the same yardstick

Ellen·bogen ⇒ **Ellbogen**

ellen·lang *Adj.* (ugs.) ‹*list*› as long as your arm; interminable ‹*lecture, sermon*›; terribly long (coll.) ‹*letter*›

Ellipse /ɛ'lɪpsə/ *die;* ~, ~n ellipse; (Sprachw., Rhet.) ellipsis

elliptisch *Adj.* elliptical

eloquent /elo'kvɛnt/ *Adj.* (geh.) eloquent

Elsass, *Elsaß /'ɛlzas/ *das;* ~ *od.* **Elsasses: das** ~: Alsace; **im/aus dem** ~: in/from Alsace

Elsässer /'ɛlzɛsɐ/ **1** *indekl. Adj.; nicht präd.* Alsatian. **2** *der;* ~s, ~: Alsatian

Elster /'ɛlstɐ/ *die;* ~, ~n (Zool.) magpie; **wie eine** ~ **stehlen** be light-fingered; **eine diebische** ~ (fig.) a pilferer

Elter /'ɛltɐ/ *das od. der;* ~s, ~n (Biol.) parent

elterlich *Adj.; nicht präd.* parental

Eltern *Pl.* parents

eltern-, Eltern-: ~**abend** *der* parents' evening; ~**beirat** *der* (Schulw.) parents' association; ~**haus** *das* parental home; **aus einem armen/katholischen** ~**haus kommen** come from a poor/Catholic home; ~**liebe** *die* parental love; ~**los 1** *Adj.* parentless; orphaned; **ein** ~**loses Kind** a child without parents; an orphan; **2** *adv.* ~**los aufwachsen** grow up an orphan *or* without parents; ~**sprech·tag** *der* parents' day; ~**teil** *der* parent; ~**versammlung** *die* parents' meeting

Email /e'mai/ *das;* ~s, ~s, **Emaille** /e'maljə/ *die;* ~, ~n enamel

E-Mail *die;* ~, ~s (DV) e-mail

emaillieren /ema'ji:rən/ *tr. V.* enamel

Emanze /e'mantsə/ *die;* ~, ~n (ugs. abwertend) women's libber (coll.)

Emanzipation /emantsipa'tsio:n/ *die;* ~, ~en emancipation

Emanzipations·bewegung *die* liberation movement

emanzipieren /emantsi'pi:rən/ *refl. V.* emancipate oneself (**von** from)

emanzipiert *Adj.* emancipated; emancipated, liberated ‹*woman*›

Embargo /ɛm'bargo/ *das;* ~s, ~s embargo

Emblem /ɛm'ble:m/ *das;* ~s, ~e emblem

Embolie /ɛmbo'li:/ *die;* ~, ~n (Med.) embolism

Embryo /'ɛmbryo/ *der;* ~s, ~nen /-y'o:nən/ *od.* ~s embryo

embryonal *Adj.; nicht präd.* (auch fig.) embryonic

emeritieren /emeri'ti:rən/ *tr. V.* confer emeritus status on; **emeritierter Professor** emeritus professor; professor emeritus

Emigrant /emi'grant/ *der;* ~en, ~en emigrant; (politischer Flüchtling) emigré

---

*alte Schreibung (vgl. Hinweise auf S. xvi–xvii)

Emigration /emigra'tsi̯oːn/ *die;* ~, ~**en** emigration; **in der** ~ **leben** live in exile

emigrieren /emiˈɡriːrən/ *itr. V.; mit sein* emigrate

eminent /emiˈnɛnt/ **1** *Adj.* (geh.) eminent; **von** ~**er Bedeutung sein** be of the utmost significance. **2** *adv.* eminently

Eminenz /emiˈnɛnts/ *die;* ~, ~**en ▶ 34⌋** (kath Kirche) eminence; **Eure/Seine** ~**:** Your/His Eminence

Emir /ˈeːmɪr/ *der;* ~**s,** ~**e** emir

Emirat *das;* ~**[e]s,** ~**e** emirate

Emission /emiˈsi̯oːn/ (fachspr.) **(a)** emission; **(b)** (Ausgabe [von Briefmarken, Wertpapieren]) issue

Emissions·schutz·gesetz *das* anti-pollution law

emittieren *tr. V.* (fachspr.) **(a)** emit; **(b)** issue ⟨*stamps, shares*⟩

e-Moll *das* E minor

Emotion /emoˈtsi̯oːn/ *die;* ~, ~**en** emotion

emotional 1 *Adj.* emotional. **2** *adv.* emotionally

Emotionalität *die;* ~**:** emotionalism

empfahl /ɛmˈpfaːl/ *1. u. 3. Pers. Sg. Prät. v.* **empfehlen**

empfand /ɛmˈpfant/ *1. u. 3. Pers. Sg. Prät. v.* **empfinden**

Empfang /ɛmˈpfaŋ/ *der;* ~**[e]s, Empfänge (a)** (auch Funkw., Rundf., Ferns.) reception; **(b)** (Entgegennahme) receipt; **bei** ~**:** on receipt; **etw. in** ~ **nehmen** accept sth.

empfangen *unr. tr. V.* **(a)** (auch Funkw., Rundf., Ferns.) receive; receive, greet ⟨*person*⟩; **(b)** (geh.: erhalten) conceive ⟨*idea*⟩; **(c)** *auch itr.* (geh.) **[ein Kind]** ~**:** conceive [a child]

Empfänger /ɛmˈpfɛŋɐ/ *der;* ~**s,** ~ **(a)** recipient; (eines Briefs) addressee; ~ **unbekannt** not known at this address; **(b)** (Empfangsgerät) receiver

Empfängerin *die;* ~, ~**nen** ⇒ **Empfänger** a

empfänglich *Adj.* **(a)** receptive **(für** to); **(b)** (anfällig, auch fig.) susceptible **(für** to)

Empfänglichkeit *die;* ~**: (a)** (Zugänglichkeit) receptivity, receptiveness **(für** to); **(b)** (Auffälligkeit, auch fig.) susceptibility **(für** to)

Empfängnis *die;* ~**:** conception

empfängnis·verhütend *Adj.* **ein** ~**es Mittel** a contraceptive

Empfängnis·verhütung *die* contraception

Empfängnisverhütungs·mittel *das* contraceptive

Empfangs-: ~**antenne** *die* [receiving] aerial (Brit.) *or* (Amer.) antenna; ~**bestätigung** *die* receipt; ~**chef** *der* head receptionist; ~**dame** *die* receptionist; ~**gerät** *das* receiver; ~**halle** *die* reception lobby

empfehlen /ɛmˈpfeːlən/ **1** *unr. tr. V.* **jmdm. etw./ jmdn.** ~**:** recommend sth./sb. to sb.; **etw. ist sehr zu** ~**:** sth. is to be highly recommended. **2** *unr. refl. V.* **(a)** (geh.: sich verabschieden und gehen) take one's leave; **darf ich mich** ~**?** may I take my leave?; **(b)** (ratsam sein) be advisable; **es empfiehlt sich, … zu …:** it is advisable to …; **(c)** (geh.: sich als geeignet ausweisen) **sich [durch/wegen etw.]** ~**:** commend oneself/itself [because of sth.]

empfehlens·wert *Adj.* **(a)** to be recommended *postpos.;* recommendable; **(b)** (ratsam) advisable

Empfehlung *die;* ~, ~**en (a)** recommendation; **(b)** (Empfehlungsschreiben) letter of recommendation; **(c)** (höflicher Gruß) „**mit freundlicher** ~“ 'with kindest regards'

Empfehlungs·schreiben *das* letter of recommendation

empfiehl /ɛmˈpfiːl/ *Imperativ Sg. v.* **empfehlen**

empfiehlst *2. Pers. Sg. Präsens v.* **empfehlen**

empfiehlt *3. Pers. Sg. Präsens v.* **empfehlen**

empfinden /ɛmˈpfɪndn̩/ *unr. tr. V.* feel ⟨*pain, pleasure, bitterness, etc.*⟩; **etwas/nichts für jmdn.** ~**:** feel something/nothing for sb.; **etw. als Beleidigung** ~**:** feel sth. to be an insult

Empfinden *das;* ~**s** feeling; **für mein** *od.* **nach meinem** ~**:** to my mind

empfindlich 1 *Adj.* **(a)** (sensibel, feinfühlig, auch fig.) sensitive; fast ⟨*film*⟩; **eine** ~**e Stelle** a tender spot; **(b)** (leicht beleidigt) sensitive, touchy ⟨*person*⟩; **(c)** (anfällig) delicate; ~ **gegen Viruserkrankungen** prone to virus infections; **(d)** (spürbar) severe ⟨*punishment, shortage*⟩; harsh

⟨*punishment, measure*⟩; sharp ⟨*increase*⟩. **2** *adv.* **(a)** ~ **auf etw. (***Akk.***) reagieren** (sensibel) be susceptible to sth.; (beleidigt) react oversensitively to sth.; **(b)** (spürbar) ⟨*punish*⟩ severely, harshly; ⟨*increase*⟩ sharply; **(c)** (intensivierend) ⟨*hurt*⟩ badly; bitterly ⟨*cold*⟩

Empfindlichkeit *die;* ~, ~**en** ⇒ **empfindlich:** sensitivity; touchiness; severity; harshness; (eines Films) speed

empfindsam 1 *Adj.* sensitive ⟨*nature*⟩; (gefühlvoll) sentimental. **2** *adv.* sensitively; (gefühlvoll) sentimentally

Empfindsamkeit *die;* ~**:** sensitivity; (Literaturw.) sentimentality

Empfindung *die;* ~, ~**en (a)** (sinnliche Wahrnehmung) sensation; sensory perception; **(b)** (Gefühl) feeling; emotion

empfindungs-, Empfindungs-: ~**los** *Adj.* **(a)** (körperlich) numb; **(b)** (seelisch) insensitive; unfeeling; ~**losigkeit** *die;* ~ **(a)** (körperlich) numbness; **(b)** (seelisch) insensitivity

empfing /ɛmˈpfɪŋ/ *1. u. 3. Pers. Sg. Prät. v.* **empfangen**

empfohlen /ɛmˈpfoːlən/ *Adj.* recommended

empirisch /ɛmˈpiːrɪʃ/ **1** *Adj.* empirical. **2** *adv.* empirically

empor /ɛmˈpoːɐ̯/ *Adv.* (geh.) upwards; up

empor-: ~**arbeiten** *refl. V.* (geh.) work one's way up; ~**blicken** *itr. V.* (geh.) look upwards *or* (literary) heavenwards

Empore *die;* ~, ~**n** gallery

empören /ɛmˈpøːrən/ **1** *tr. V.* fill with indignation; incense; outrage. **2** *refl. V.* become indignant *or* incensed *or* outraged **(über** + *Akk.* about)

empörend *Adj.* outrageous

empor-: ~**heben** *unr. tr. V.* (geh.) raise; ~**kommen** *unr. itr. V.; mit sein* (geh.) **(a)** (nach oben kommen) come up; **(b)** (fig.: aufsteigen) rise

Emporkömmling /-kœmlɪŋ/ *der;* ~**s,** ~**e** (abwertend) upstart; parvenu

empor-: ~**ragen** *itr. V.* (geh.) rise [up]; ~**schauen** *itr. V.* (geh.) raise one's eyes; ~**schwingen** *unr. refl. V.* (geh.) swing oneself aloft; ~**steigen** *unr. itr. V.; mit sein* (geh.) **(a)** climb up; **(b)** ⟨*balloon, kite*⟩ rise aloft

empört 1 *Adj.* outraged ⟨*letter, look*⟩; **über jmdn./etw.** ~ **sein** be outraged at sth./about sb. **2** *adv.* **jmdn./etw.** ~ **zurückweisen** reject sb./sth. indignantly *or* angrily

Empörung *die;* ~ outrage

emsig /ˈɛmzɪç/ **1** *Adj.* (fleißig) industrious, busy ⟨*person*⟩; (geschäftig) bustling ⟨*activity*⟩; (übereifrig) sedulous; **ein** ~**es Treiben** bustling activity; a hustle and bustle. **2** *adv.* (fleißig) industriously; busily; (übereifrig) sedulously

Emsigkeit *die;* ~ (Fleiß) industriousness; business; (Übereifer) sedulousness

Emu /ˈeːmu/ *der;* ~**s,** ~**s** (Zool.) emu

Emulgator /emʊlˈɡaːtor/ *der;* ~**s,** ~**en** /-ɡaˈtoːrən/ (Chemie) emulsifying agent; emulsifier

Emulsion /emʊlˈzi̯oːn/ *die;* ~, ~**en** (fachspr.) emulsion

E-Musik *die;* ~**:** serious music

End-: ~**abnehmer** *der* (Wirtsch.) ultimate buyer; ~**abrechnung** *die* final account; ~**bahnhof** *der* terminus

Ende /ˈɛndə/ *das;* ~**s,** ~**n ▶ 22⌋, ▶ 119⌋ (a)** end; **am** ~**:** at the end; (schließlich) in the end; **am** ~ **der Welt** (scherzh.) at the back of beyond; **am/bis/gegen** ~ **des Monats/ der Woche** at/by/towards the end of the month/week; ~ **April** at the end of April; **bis** ~ **der Woche** by the end of the week; **zu** ~ **sein** ⟨*patience, hostility, war*⟩ be at an end; **die Schule/das Kino/das Spiel ist zu** ~**:** school is over/the film/game has finished; **zu** ~ **gehen** ⟨*period of time*⟩ come to an end; ⟨*supplies, savings*⟩ run out; ⟨*contract*⟩ expire; **etw. zu** ~ **führen** *od.* **bringen** finish sth.; **ein Buch zu** ~ **lesen** read a book to the end; ~ **gut, alles gut** all's well that ends well (prov.); **ein/kein** ~ **nehmen** come to an end/never come to an end; **einer Sache/seinem Leben ein** ~ **machen** *od.* **setzen** (geh.) put an end to sth./take one's life; **am** ~ **sein** (ugs.) be at the end of one's tether; **ich bin mit meiner Geduld am** ~**:** my patience is at an end; **(b)** (ugs.: kleines Stück) bit; piece; **(c)** (ugs.: Strecke) **ein ganzes** ~**:** a pretty long way; **(d)** (Jägerspr.) point

End·effekt *der:* **im** ~**:** in the end; in the final analysis
endemisch /ɛn'de:mɪʃ/ **1** *Adj.* (Biol., Med.) endemic. **2** *adv.* endemically
enden *itr. V.* **(a)** end; ‹*programme*› end, finish; **der Zug endet hier** this train terminates here; **gut** ~**:** end well; **nicht** ~ **wollender Beifall** unending applause; **(b)** (sterben) *mit sein* **in der Gosse/im Gefängnis** ~**:** die in the gutter/end one's days in prison
End·ergebnis *das* final result
en détail /ãde'taj/ *Adv.* **(a)** (im Einzelnen) in detail; **(b)** (Kaufmannsspr. veralt.) retail
end·gültig 1 *Adj.* final ‹*consent, answer, decision*›; conclusive ‹*evidence*›; **etwas/nichts Endgültiges sagen/hören** say/hear something/nothing definite. **2** *adv.* **das ist** ~ **vorbei** that's all over and done with; **sich** ~ **trennen** separate for good
Endivie /ɛn'di:vjə/ *die;* ~**,** ~**n** endive
Endivien·salat *der* **(a)** endive; **(b)** (Speise) endive salad
end-, End-: ~**kampf** *der* (Sport) final; (Milit.) final battle; ~**lager** *das* [permanent] disposal site; [permanent] depository; ~**lagern** *tr. V.* dispose of [permanently]; ~**lagerung** *die* permanent disposal (*of nuclear waste*); ~**lauf** *der* final
endlich 1 *Adv.* **(a)** (nach langer Zeit) at last; **na** ~ [**kommst du**]**!** [so you've arrived] at [long] last; **(b)** (schließlich) in the end; eventually. **2** *Adj.* finite ‹*size, number*›
end·los 1 *Adj.* **(a)** (ohne Ende) infinite; (ringförmig) endless, continuous ‹*belt, chain*›; **(b)** (nicht enden wollend) endless ‹*road, desert, expanse, etc.*›; interminable ‹*speech*›. **2** *adv.* ~ **lange dauern** be interminably long
endogen /ɛndoge:n/ *Adj.* (Med., Psych., Bot.) endogenous
End-: ~**phase** *die* final stages *pl.*; ~**produkt** *das* final *or* end product; ~**punkt** *der* end; ~**resultat** *das* final result; ~**runde** *die* (Sport) final; ~**runden·teilnehmer** *der* (Sport) finalist; ~**sieg** *der* (bes. ns.) final *or* ultimate victory; ~**spiel** *das* **(a)** (Sport) final; **(b)** (Schach) end-game; ~**spurt** *der* (bes. Leichtathletik) final spurt; **einen guten** ~**spurt haben** have a good finish; ~**stadium** *das* final stage; (Med.) terminal stage; **Krebs im** ~**stadium** terminal cancer; ~**stand** *der* (Sport) final result; ~**station** *die* terminus; ~**stück** *das* end; (eines Brotes) crust
Endung *die;* ~**,** ~**en** (Sprachw.) ending
End-: ~**verbraucher** *der* (Wirtsch.) consumer; ~**ziel** *das* (einer Reise) final destination; (Zweck) ultimate aim *or* goal; ~**zweck** *der* ultimate purpose *or* object
Energie /enɛr'gi:/ *die;* ~**,** ~**n** **(a)** (Physik) energy; **(b)** *o. Pl.* (Tatkraft) energy; vigour
energie-, Energie-: ~**bedarf** *der* energy requirement; ~**geladen** *Adj.* energetic, dynamic ‹*person*›; ~**gewinnung** *die* energy production; ~**haushalt** *der* (Physiol.) energy balance; ~**krise** *die* energy crisis; ~**los** *Adj.* lacking [in] energy *postpos.*; sluggish; ~**politik** *die* energy policy; ~**quelle** *die* energy source; source of energy; ~**spar·lampe** *die* energy-saving lamp; ~**sparend** *Adj.* energy-saving; ~**verbrauch** *der* energy consumption; ~**verschwendung** *die* wasting of energy; ~**versorgung** *die* energy supply; ~**wirtschaft** *die* energy sector
energisch /e'nɛrgɪʃ/ **1** *Adj.* **(a)** (tatkräftig) energetic, vigorous ‹*person*›; firm ‹*action*›; ~ **werden** put one's foot down; **(b)** (von starkem Willen zeugend) determined; forceful; strong ‹*chin*›; **(c)** (entschlossen) forceful, firm ‹*voice, words*›. **2** *adv.* **(a)** (tatkräftig) ~ **durchgreifen** take drastic action; **(b)** (entschlossen) ‹*reject, say*› forcefully, firmly; ‹*stress*› emphatically; ‹*deny*› strenuously
eng /ɛŋ/ **1** *Adj.* **(a)** (schmal) narrow ‹*valley, road, bed*›; **einen** ~**en Horizont haben** (fig.) have a narrow *or* limited outlook; **(b)** (fest anliegend) close-fitting, tight; **der Anzug/Rock ist zu** ~**:** the suit/skirt is too tight; **(c)** (beschränkt) narrow, restricted ‹*interpretation, concept*›; cramped, constricted ‹*room, space*›; **(d)** *im Komp. u. Sup.* (begrenzt) **in die** ~**ere Wahl kommen** be short-listed (Brit.); **im** ~**eren Sinne** in the stricter sense; **(e)** (nahe)

close ‹*friend*›; **im** ~**sten Freundeskreis** among close friends; **die** ~**ere Verwandtschaft** one's immediate relatives. **2** *adv.* **(a)** (dicht) ~ **schreiben** write closely together; ~ [**zusammen**] **sitzen/stehen** sit/stand close together; ~ **bedruckte Seiten** closely printed pages; **(b)** (fest anliegend) ~ **anliegen/sitzen** fit closely; ~ **anliegend** close-fitting; **(c)** (beschränkt) **etw. zu** ~ **auslegen** interpret sth. too narrowly; **(d)** (nahe) closely; **mit jmdm.** ~ **befreundet sein** be a close friend of sb.
Engadin /'ɛŋgadi:n/ *das;* ~**s** Engadine
Engagement /ãgaʒə'mã:/ *das;* ~**s,** ~**s** **(a)** *o. Pl.* (Einsatz) involvement; **sein** ~ **für etw.** his commitment to sth.; **sein** ~ **gegen etw.** his committed stand against sth.; **(b)** (eines Künstlers) engagement
engagieren /ãgaʒi:rən/ **1** *refl. V.* commit oneself, become committed (**für** to); **sich politisch** ~**:** become politically involved. **2** *tr. V.* engage ‹*artist, actor, etc.*›
engagiert *Adj.* committed ‹*literature, film, director*›; **politisch/sozial** ~ **sein** be politically/socially committed *or* involved
***eng·anliegend** *usw.:* ⇒ **eng 2**
Enge /'ɛŋə/ *die;* ~**,** ~**n** **(a)** *o. Pl.* confinement; restriction; **(b)** **jmdn. in die** ~ **treiben** (fig.) drive sb. into a corner
Engel /'ɛŋl/ *der;* ~**s,** ~**:** angel; **sie ist mein guter/ein rettender** ~**:** she is my good/a guardian angel
Engel-: ~**macher** *der,* ~**macherin** *die;* ~**,** ~**nen** (ugs. verhüll.) backstreet abortionist; ~**schar** *die* heavenly host; host of angels
Engels-: ~**geduld** *die* patience of a saint; ~**miene** *die* innocent look; ~**zungen** *Pl.:* **mit** ~**zungen auf jmdn. einreden** use all one's powers of persuasion on sb.
eng·herzig 1 *Adj.* petty. **2** *adv.* in a petty way
Eng·herzigkeit *die;* ~**:** pettiness
England (*das*)*;* ~**s (a)** England; **(b)** (ugs.: Großbritannien) Britain
Engländer /'ɛŋlɛndɐ/ *der;* ~**s,** ~ ▶388▏ **(a)** Englishman/English boy; **er ist** ~**:** he is English *or* an Englishman; **die** ~**:** the English; **(b)** (ugs.: Brite) British person/man; Britisher (Amer.); **die** ~**:** the British; **(c)** (Schraubenschlüssel) monkey wrench
Engländerin *die;* ~**,** ~**nen** ▶388▏ **(a)** Englishwoman/ English girl; **sie ist** ~**:** she is English *or* an Englishwoman; **(b)** (ugs.: Britin) British person/woman; **die** ~**nen sind** …**:** British women are …
englisch ▶388▏, ▶487▏ **1** *Adj.* English; ~**-deutsch** Anglo-German; English-German ‹*dictionary*›; **die** ~**e Sprache/Literatur** the English language/English literature; **die** ~**e Krankheit** (veralt.) rickets. **2** *adv.* ~ [**gebraten**] rare; underdone; **ein** ~ **abgefasster Artikel** an article in English; *s. auch* **deutsch; Deutsche²**
Englisch *das;* ~[**s**] ▶487▏ English; **ein gutes/fehlerfreies** ~ **sprechen** speak good/perfect English; *s. auch* **Deutsch**
englisch-, Englisch-: ~**horn** *das* (Musik) cor anglais; ~**lehrer** *der* 'English teacher; ~**sprachig** *Adj.* **(a)** (in ~er Sprache) English-language ‹*book, magazine*›; **die** ~**sprachige Literatur** English literature; **(b)** (Englisch sprechend) English-speaking ‹*population, country*›; ~**unterricht** *der* English teaching; (Unterrichtsstunde) English lesson; **er gibt** ~**unterricht** he teaches English
eng·maschig *Adj.* close-meshed ‹*fabric*›
Eng·pass, *****Eng·paß** *der* **(a)** [narrow] pass; defile; **(b)** (fig.: in der Versorgung usw.) bottleneck
en gros /ã'gro/ (Kaufmannsspr.) wholesale
eng·stirnig 1 *Adj.* (abwertend) narrow-minded ‹*person*›. **2** *adv.* ~**stirnig handeln** be narrow-minded in the way one acts
Eng·stirnigkeit *die;* ~**:** narrow-mindedness
Enkel *der;* ~**s,** ~ **(a)** grandson; **(b)** (Nachfahr) grandchild
Enkelin *die;* ~**,** ~**nen** granddaughter
Enkel-: ~**kind** *das* grandchild; ~**sohn** *der* grandson; ~**tochter** *die* granddaughter
Enklave /ɛn'kla:və/ *die;* ~**,** ~**en** enclave
en masse /ã'mas/ (ugs.) en masse
enorm /e'nɔrm/ **1** *Adj.* enormous ‹*sum, costs*›; tremendous (coll.) ‹*effort*›; immense ‹*strain*›; vast ‹*knowledge,*

sum⟩. **2** *adv.* tremendously (coll.) ⟨*expensive, practical*⟩; ∼
viel/viele a tremendous (coll.) *or* an enormous amount/
number

en passant /āpa'sã/ en passant; in passing

Ensemble /ā'sã:bļ/ *das* **(a)** (auch fig. geh.) ensemble; (von
Schauspielern) company; **(b)** (Kleidungsstücke) outfit

entarten *itr. V.; mit sein* degenerate; **entartet** degenerate; **zu** *od.* **in** (*Akk.*) **etw.** ∼**:** degenerate into sth.

Entartung *die;* ∼, ∼**en** degeneration

entäußern *refl. V.* (geh.) **sich einer Sache** (*Gen.*) ∼
(entsagen) renounce sth.; (weggeben) relinquish *or* give up
sth.

entbehren /ɛnt'be:rən/ **1** *tr. V.* **(a)** (geh.: vermissen) miss
⟨*person*⟩; **(b)** (verzichten) do without; spare; **etw./jmdn.
nicht** ∼ **können** not be able to do without sth./sb.; **vieles**
od. **viel** ∼ **müssen** have to go without [a lot of things]. **2**
itr. V. (geh.: ermangeln) **einer Sache** (*Gen.*) ∼**:** lack *or* be
without sth.

entbehrlich *Adj.* dispensable

Entbehrung *die;* ∼, ∼**en** privation; **große** ∼**en auf
sich** (*Akk.*) **nehmen** make great sacrifices

entbehrungs-: ∼**reich,** ∼**voll** *Adj.* ⟨*life, years*⟩ of
privation

entbinden **1** *unr. tr. V.* **(a)** (befreien) **jmdn. von einem
Versprechen** ∼**:** release sb. from a promise; **seines
Amtes** *od.* **von seinem Amt entbunden werden** be
relieved of [one's] office; **(b)** (Geburtshilfe leisten) **jmdn.** ∼**:**
deliver sb.; deliver sb.'s baby; **von einem Jungen/
Mädchen entbunden werden** give birth to a boy/girl.
2 *unr. itr. V.* (gebären) give birth; **zu Hause** ∼**:** have one's
baby at home

Entbindung *die* **(a)** (das Gebären) birth; delivery; **bei der**
∼ **anwesend sein** be present at the birth; **(b)** (Befreiung)
release

Entbindungs·station *die* maternity ward

entblättern *refl. V.* **(a)** ⟨*trees, shrubs*⟩ shed its/their
leaves; **(b)** (scherzh.: sich ausziehen) strip; take one's clothes
off

entblößen **1** *refl. V.* take one's clothes off; ⟨*exhibitionist*⟩
expose oneself. **2** *tr. V.* **(a)** uncover; **entblößt** bare; **(b)**
(fig.) reveal ⟨*feelings, thoughts*⟩

entbrennen *unr. itr. V.; mit sein* (geh.) **(a)** (beginnen)
⟨*battle*⟩ break out; ⟨*quarrel*⟩ flare up; **(b) in Liebe ent-
brannt sein** be passionately in love

Entchen /'ɛntçən/ *das;* ∼**s,** ∼**:** duckling

entdecken *tr. V.* **(a)** (finden) discover; **(b)** (ausfindig
machen) **jmdn.** ∼**:** find *or* spot sb.; **etw.** ∼**:** find *or* discover sth.; **(c)** (überraschend bemerken) discover ⟨*theft*⟩; come
across ⟨*acquaintance*⟩

Entdecker *der;* ∼**s,** ∼**:** discoverer; (Forschungsreisender)
explorer

Entdeckung *die;* ∼, ∼**en** discovery

Entdeckungs·reise *die* voyage of discovery; (zu Lande)
expedition

Ente /'ɛntə/ *die;* ∼, ∼**n (a)** duck; **eine lahme** ∼ (ugs.) a
slow-coach (coll.); **(b)** (ugs.: Falschmeldung) canard; spoof (coll.);
(c) kalte ∼**:** [cold] punch; **(d)** (ugs.: Auto) Citroën 2 CV
car; (e) (ugs.: Uringefäß) [bed-]bottle

enteignen *tr. V.* expropriate

Enteignung *die* expropriation

enteisen *tr. V.* de-ice

enteisenen *tr. V.* remove the iron from; **stark/
schwach enteisent** with a very low/slightly reduced iron
content

Enten-: ∼**braten** *der* roast duck; ∼**ei** *das* duck's egg;
∼**küken** *das* duckling

Entente /ā'tã:t(ə)/ *die;* ∼, ∼**n** (Politik) entente

Enten·teich *der* duck pond

enterben *tr. V.* disinherit

Enter·haken *der* grapnel; grappling iron

Enterich /'ɛntərɪç/ *der;* ∼**s,** ∼**e** drake

entern /'ɛntən/ *tr. V.* board ⟨*ship*⟩

entfachen *tr. V.* (geh.) **(a)** kindle, light ⟨*fire*⟩; **einen
Brand** ∼**:** start a fire; **(b)** (fig.) provoke, start ⟨*quarrel,
argument*⟩; arouse ⟨*passion, enthusiasm*⟩

entfahren *unr. itr. V.; mit sein* **ihm entfuhr ein Fluch/
ein Seufzer** he swore inadvertently/he let out a sigh

entfallen *unr. itr. V.; mit sein* **(a) der Name/das Wort
ist mir** ∼**:** the name/word escapes me *or* has slipped my
mind; **(b) auf jmdn./etw.** ∼**:** be allotted to sb./sth.; **auf
jeden Erben/Miteigentümer entfielen 10 000 Mark**
each heir received/each of the joint owners had to pay
10,000 marks; **(c)** (wegfallen) lapse; **für Kinder** ∼ **diese
Gebühren** these charges do not apply to children

entfalten **1** *tr. V.* **(a)** open [up]; unfold, spread out ⟨*map
etc.*⟩; **(b)** (fig.) show, display ⟨*ability, talent*⟩; **(c)** (fig.) expound ⟨*ideas, thoughts*⟩; present ⟨*plan*⟩. **2** *refl. V.* **(a)**
⟨*flower, parachute*⟩ open [up]; **(b)** (fig.) ⟨*personality, talent*⟩
develop; **sich frei** ∼**:** develop one's own personality to the
full

Entfaltung *die;* ∼ (fig.) **(a)** (Entwicklung) development; **zur**
∼ **kommen** develop; **(b)** ⇒ **entfalten 1 b:** display; **(c)**
⇒ **entfalten 1 c:** exposition; presentation

entfärben **1** *tr. V.* take the colour out of ⟨*material,
clothing*⟩. **2** *refl. V.* ⟨*material, clothing, etc.*⟩ fade

Entfärber *der* colour *or* dye remover

entfernen **1** *tr. V.* **(a)** remove ⟨*stain, wart, etc.*⟩; take out
⟨*tonsils etc.*⟩; **jmdn. aus seinem Amt** ∼**:** dismiss sb.
from office; **(b)** (geh.: fortbringen) remove. **2** *refl. V.* go away;
sich vom Weg ∼**:** go off *or* leave the path; **sich unerlaubt von der Truppe** ∼**:** go absent without leave

entfernt **1** *Adj.* **(a)** ▶ **160** away (**von** from); **voneinander** ∼**:** apart; **das ist** *od.* **liegt weit** ∼ **von der
Stadt** it is a long way from the town *or* out of town; **er ist
weit davon** ∼, **das zu tun** (fig.) he does not have the
slightest intention of doing that; **(b)** (fern, entlegen) remote;
(c) *nicht präd.* (weitläufig) slight ⟨*acquaintance*⟩; distant
⟨*relation*⟩; **(d)** (schwach) slight, vague ⟨*resemblance*⟩; **(e)
nicht im Entferntesten** not in the slightest *or* in the
least. **2** *adv.* **(a)** (fern) remotely; **(b)** (weitläufig) slightly
⟨*acquainted*⟩; distantly ⟨*related*⟩; **(c)** (schwach) slightly,
vaguely

Entfernung *die;* ∼, ∼**en** ▶ **160 (a)** (Abstand) distance;
(beim Schießen) range; **in einer** ∼ **von 100 m** at a distance/
range of 100 m.; **auf eine** ∼ **von 100 m** from a distance
of 100 m.; **aus der** ∼**:** from a distance; **(b)** (das Beseitigen)
removal

entfesseln *tr. V.* unleash ⟨*war, riot, etc.*⟩; **entfesselt**
raging ⟨*elements*⟩

entfetten *tr. V.* skim ⟨*milk*⟩

Entfettungs·kur *die* diet to remove one's excess fat

entflammbar *Adj.* inflammable

entflammen **1** *tr. V.* arouse ⟨*enthusiasm etc*⟩; **jmdn.
für etw.** ∼**:** arouse sb.'s enthusiasm for sth. **2** *itr. V.; mit
sein* ⟨*hatred etc.*⟩ flare up; ⟨*battle, strike*⟩ break out; **für
jmdn. entflammt sein** be passionately in love with sb.

entflechten *tr. V.* (*auch regelm.*) *tr. V.* **(a)** (entwirren) disentangle; **(b)** (Wirtsch.) break up ⟨*cartel etc.*⟩

Entflechtung *die;* ∼, ∼**en** (Wirtsch.) breaking-up; break-
up

entfliegen *unr. itr. V.; mit sein* fly away

entfliehen *unr. itr. V.; mit sein* **jmdm./einer Sache** ∼**:**
escape sb./sth.; **dem Alltag** ∼ (geh.) escape from the daily
routine

entfremden **1** *tr. V.* **jmdn. einer Sache** (*Dat.*) ∼**:**
alienate *or* estrange sb. from sth.; **etw. seinem Zweck**
∼**:** use sth. for a different purpose. **2** *refl. V.* **sich jmdm./
einer Sache** ∼**:** become estranged from sb./unfamiliar
with sth.

entfremdet *Adj.* (Philos., Soziol.) alienated

Entfremdung *die;* ∼, ∼**en (a)** alienation; estrange-
ment; **(b)** (Philos., Soziol.) alienation

entfrosten *tr. V.* defrost

Entfroster *der;* ∼**s,** ∼**:** defroster

entführen *tr. V.* **(a)** kidnap, abduct ⟨*child etc.*⟩; hijack
⟨*plane, lorry, etc.*⟩; **(b)** (scherzh.: mitnehmen) steal; make off
with

Entführer *der* ⇒ **entführen a:** kidnapper; abducter; hijacker

Entführung *die* ⇒ **entführen a:** kidnap; kidnapping;
abduction; hijack; hijacking

Entfernung

1 Meter = one metre = 3 feet 3.4 inches *od.* 1.094 yards.
1 Kilometer = one kilometre = 1094 yards *od.* 0.6214 mile

Wie weit ist es von A nach B?	= How far is it *od.* What's the distance from A to B?	*A und B sind gleich weit entfernt*	= A and B are the same distance away
Es sind/Die Entfernung beträgt beinahe 600 Kilometer	= It's/The distance is nearly 600 kilometres ≈ It's/The distance is nearly 370 miles	*Er traf das Ziel aus einer Entfernung von 50 Metern*	= He hit the target from a distance of 50 metres
Es ist ziemlich weit [entfernt]	= It's quite a long way [away]	*eine Autofahrt von achtzig Kilometern/ zwanzig Minuten*	= an eighty-kilometre *od.* ≈ a fifty-mile/twenty-minute drive
Hannover liegt weiter vom Meer entfernt als Bremen	= Hanover is further from the sea than Bremen	*eine Stunde/zwei Stunden Fahrt [mit dem Auto]*	= an hour's/two hours' drive, a one-hour/two-hour drive
Magdeburg liegt näher an Berlin als Braunschweig	= Magdeburg is closer to Berlin than Brunswick	*Es sind nur zehn Minuten zu Fuß*	= It's only a ten-minute walk *od.* ten minutes on foot

entgegen 1 *Adv.* towards; **der Sonne** ∼**!** on towards the sun! **2** *Präp. mit Dat.* ∼ **meinem Wunsch** against my wishes; ∼ **dem Befehl** contrary to orders
entgegen-, Entgegen-: ∼|**bringen** *unr. tr. V.* (fig.) **jmdm. Liebe/Verständnis** ∼**bringen** show sb. love/understanding; ∼|**gehen** *unr. itr. V.; mit sein* (a) **jmdm. [ein Stück]** ∼**gehen** go [a little way] to meet sb.; (b) (fig.) **einer Katastrophe/schweren Zeiten** ∼**gehen** be heading for *or* towards a catastrophe/hard times; **der Vollendung/dem Ende** ∼**gehen** be approaching completion/its end; ∼**gesetzt 1** *Adj.* (a) opposite ⟨*end, direction*⟩; (b) (gegensätzlich) opposing; ∼**gesetzter Meinung sein** hold opposing views; **das Entgegengesetzte tun** do the opposite; **2** *adv.* **genau** ∼**gesetzt handeln/denken** do/think exactly the opposite; ∼|**halten** *unr. tr. V.* (a) **jmdm. etw.** ∼**halten** offer sth. to sb.; (b) (fig.: einwenden) **einem Argument ein anderes** ∼**halten** counter an argument with another; ∼|**kommen** *unr. itr. V.; mit sein* (a) **jmdm.** ∼**kommen** come to meet sb.; **der** ∼**kommende Verkehr** oncoming traffic; (b) (fig.) **jmdm.** ∼**kommen** be accommodating towards sb.; (in Verhandlungen) make concessions; **sie/das kam unseren Wünschen** ∼**:** she complied with our wishes/it was what we wanted; ∼**kommen** *das* (a) (Konzilianz) cooperation; (b) (Zugeständnis) concession; ∼**kommend** *Adj.* obliging; ∼**kommenderweise** *Adv.* obligingly; ∼**nahme** *die* (Amtsdt.) receipt; ∼|**nehmen** *unr. itr. V.* receive; accept ⟨*parcel*⟩; ∼|**sehen** *unr. itr. V.* **einer Sache** (*Dat.*) [freudig] ∼**sehen** look forward [eagerly] to sth.; ∼|**setzen** *tr. V.* (a) **einer Sache** (*Dat.*) **etw.** ∼**setzen** oppose sth. with sth.; **einer Sache** (*Dat.*) **Widerstand** ∼**setzen** resist sth.; (b) **einer Behauptung/einem Argument etw.** ∼**setzen** counter a claim/an argument with sth.; ∼|**stellen** *tr. V.* ⇒ ∼**setzen b**; ∼|**treten** *unr. itr. V.; mit sein* go/come up to; (fig.) **Schwierigkeiten** (*Dat.*) ∼**treten** stand up to difficulties; **einem Angriff** ∼**treten** answer an attack; **Vorwürfen/Anschuldigungen** ∼**treten** answer reproaches/ accusations; ∼|**wirken** *itr. V.* **einer Sache** (*Dat.*) ∼**wirken** [actively] oppose sth.
entgegnen /ɛntˈgeːgnən/ *tr. V.* retort; reply; **auf etw.** (*Dat.*) *od.* **einer Sache** (*Dat.*) **etw.** ∼**:** say sth. in reply to sth.; **jmdm.** ∼**, dass** ...: reply that ...
Entgegnung *die;* ∼**,** ∼**en** retort; reply; **als** ∼ **darauf** in reply
entgehen *unr. itr. V.; mit sein* (a) **einer Gefahr/Strafe** (*Dat.*) ∼**:** escape *or* avoid danger/punishment; **das darf man sich** (*Dat.*) **nicht** ∼ **lassen** (fig.) that is not to be missed; (b) **jmdm. entgeht etw.** sb. misses sth.; **ihm ist nicht entgangen, dass** ...: it has not escaped his notice that ...
entgeistert /ɛntˈgaistɐt/ *Adj.* dumbfounded; **jmdn.** ∼ **anstarren** stare at sb. in amazement *or* astonishment
Entgelt /ɛntˈgɛlt/ *das;* ∼**[e]s,** ∼**e** payment; fee; **gegen** *od.* **für ein geringes** ∼**:** for a small fee

entgelten *unr. tr. V.* (geh.) pay for (also fig.); **jmdm. eine Arbeit** ∼**:** pay sb. a job
entgleisen *itr. V.; mit sein* (a) be derailed; **der Zug ist entgleist** the train was derailed; (b) (fig.: aus der Rolle fallen) make *or* commit a/some faux pas
Entgleisung *die;* ∼**,** ∼**en** ⇒ **entgleisen:** (a) derailment; (b) (fig.) faux pas
entgleiten *unr. itr. V.; mit sein* (geh.) (a) slip; **jmds. Händen** ∼**:** slip from sb.'s hands; (b) (fig.) **jmdm. entgleitet etw.** sb. loses his/her grip on sth.
entgräten *tr. V.* fillet; bone; **entgräteter Fisch** filleted fish
enthaaren *tr. V.* remove hair from; depilate (formal)
Enthaarungs·mittel *das* hair remover; depilatory
enthalten¹ 1 *unr. tr. V.* contain. **2** *unr. refl. V.* **sich einer Sache** (*Gen.*) ∼**:** abstain from sth.; **sich der Stimme** ∼**:** abstain; **sich jeder Meinung/Äußerung** ∼**:** refrain from giving any opinion/making any comment
enthalten² *Adj.* **in etw.** (*Dat.*) ∼ **sein** be contained in sth.; **das ist im Preis** ∼**:** that is included in the price
enthaltsam 1 *Adj.* abstemious; (sexuell) abstinent. **2** *adv.* ∼ **leben** live in abstinence
Enthaltsamkeit *die;* ∼**:** abstinence
Enthaltung *die* abstention
enthärten *tr. V.* soften ⟨*water*⟩
enthaupten *tr. V.* (geh.) behead
Enthauptung *die;* ∼**,** ∼**en** (geh.) beheading
enthäuten *tr. V.* skin
entheben *unr. tr. V.* (geh.) relieve; **jmdn. seines Amtes** ∼**:** relieve sb. of his/her office
enthemmen *tr. V.* **jmdn.** ∼**:** make sb. lose his/her inhibitions
enthemmend 1 *Adj.* disinhibitory ⟨*effect, etc.*⟩. **2** *adv.* ∼ **wirken** take away sb.'s inhibitions
enthemmt *Adj.* uninhibited
Enthemmung *die* loss of inhibition[s]; disinhibition (Psych.)
enthüllen 1 *tr. V.* (a) unveil ⟨*monument etc.*⟩; reveal ⟨*face, etc.*⟩; (b) (offenbaren) reveal ⟨*truth, secret*⟩; disclose ⟨*secret*⟩; (Zeitungsw.) expose ⟨*scandal*⟩. **2** *refl. V.* **sich [jmdm.]** ∼**:** be revealed [to sb.]
Enthüllung *die;* ∼**,** ∼**en** ⇒ **enthüllen 1:** unveiling; revelation; disclosure; exposé
enthülsen *tr. V.* shell; pod
Enthusiasmus /ɛntuˈziasmʊs/ *der;* ∼**:** enthusiasm
Enthusiast *der;* ∼**en,** ∼**en** enthusiast
enthusiastisch 1 *Adj.* enthusiastic. **2** *adv.* enthusiastically
entjungfern *tr. V.* deflower
entkalken *tr. V.* decalcify
entkernen *tr. V.* core ⟨*apple etc.*⟩; stone, remove stone from ⟨*plum etc.*⟩; remove pips from ⟨*grape etc.*⟩

entkleiden *tr. V.* jmdn./sich ~ (geh.) undress sb./undress

entkoffeiniert /ɛntkɔfeiˈniːɐt/ *Adj.* decaffeinated

entkommen *unr. itr. V.; mit sein* escape; **jmdm./einer Sache** ~: escape *or* get away from sb./sth.; **es gibt kein Entkommen** there is no escape

entkorken *tr. V.* uncork ‹bottle›

entkräften /ɛntˈkrɛftn̩/ *tr. V.* **(a)** weaken; **völlig** ~: exhaust; [**völlig**] **entkräftet sein** be [utterly] exhausted; **(b)** (fig.) refute, invalidate ‹argument etc.›; remove ‹suspicion etc.›

Entkräftung *die;* ~, ~**en (a)** debility; **völlige** ~: exhaustion; **(b)** (fig.) refutation; invalidation

entkrampfen 1 *tr. V.* **(a)** relax; **(b)** (fig.) ease ‹situation, tension›. 2 *refl. V.* **(a)** relax; **(b)** (fig.) ‹atmosphere etc.› become relaxed

Entkrampfung *die;* ~, ~**en** ⇨ **entkrampfen:** relaxation; easing

entkriminalisieren *tr. V.* decriminalize; legalize

entladen 1 *unr. tr. V.* unload; discharge ‹battery›. 2 *unr. refl. V.* **(a)** ‹storm› break; **(b)** (fig.: hervorbrechen) ‹anger etc.› erupt; ‹aggression etc.› be released; **(c)** (Elektrot.) ‹battery› run down

Entladung *die* ⇨ **entladen** 1, 2 b: unloading; discharge; eruption; release

entlang 1 *Präp. mit Akk. u. Dat.* along; **den Weg** ~, ~ **dem Weg** along the path. 2 *Adv.* along; **dort** ~, **bitte!** that way please!

entlang-: ~**|fahren** *unr. itr. V.; mit sein* **(a)** drive along; **die Straße/den** *od.* **am Fluss** ~**fahren** drive *or* go down the street/along the river; **(b)** (streichen) go along; ~**|führen** 1 *tr. V.* lead along; **jmdn. die Straße** ~**führen** lead sb. along *or* down the street; 2 *itr. V.* (verlaufen) run *or* go along; ~**|gehen** *unr. itr. V.; mit sein* ‹person› go *or* walk along; **bitte gehen Sie hier** ~: [go] this way please; ~**|laufen** *unr. itr. V.; mit sein* **(a)** go *or* walk/run along; **(b)** (verlaufen) go *or* run along

entlarven *tr. V.* expose

Entlarvung *die;* ~, ~**en** exposure

entlassen *unr. tr. V.* **(a)** (aus dem Gefängnis) release; (aus dem Krankenhaus, der Armee) discharge; **jmd. wird aus der Schule** ~: sb. leaves school; **(b)** (aus einem Arbeitsverhältnis) dismiss; (wegen Arbeitsmangels) make redundant (Brit.); lay off; **bei einer Firma** ~ **werden** be dismissed from/be made redundant (Brit.) *or* laid off by a company; **(c)** (geh.: gehen lassen) release

Entlassung *die;* ~, ~**en (a)** (aus dem Gefängnis) release; (aus dem Krankenhaus, der Armee) discharge; (aus der Schule) leaving; **(b)** (aus einem Arbeitsverhältnis) dismissal; (wegen Arbeitsmangels) redundancy (Brit.); laying off; **(c)** ⇨ **Entlassungsschreiben**

Entlassungs-: ~**feier** *die* (Schulw.) school-leaving *or* (Amer.) graduation ceremony; ~**schreiben** *das* (Arbeitsw.) notice of dismissal; (wegen Arbeitsmangels) redundancy notice (Brit.); pink slip (Amer.)

entlasten *tr. V.* **(a)** relieve; **jmdn.** ~: relieve *or* take the load off sb.; **den Kreislauf** ~: relieve the strain on the circulation; **sein Gewissen** ~: ease *or* relieve one's conscience; **(b)** (Rechtsspr.) exonerate ‹defendant›; **(c)** (Kaufmannsspr.) approve the actions of ‹chairman, board, etc.›

Entlastung *die;* ~, ~**en (a)** (Rechtsspr.) exoneration; defence; **zu jmds.** ~: in sb.'s defence; **(b)** (Minderung der Belastung) relief; **die** ~ **eines Menschen/des Körpers/der Straßen** relief of the burden on a person/the body/the roads; **(c)** (Erleichterung) easing; relief; **(d)** (Kaufmannsspr.) approval of the actions (of chairman, board, etc.)

Entlastungs-: ~**material** *das* (Rechtsspr.) evidence for the defence; ~**zeuge** *der* (Rechtsspr.) witness for the defence; defence witness; ~**zug** *der* (Eisenb.) relief train

entlauben *tr. V.* strip ‹branch›; defoliate ‹forest, area›

entlaufen *unr. itr. V.; mit sein* run away; **jmdm.** ~: run away from sb.; **ein** ~**er Sträfling/Sklave** an escaped convict/a runaway slave

entledigen *refl. V.* (geh.) **(a) sich jmds./einer Sache** (*Gen.*) ~: dispose of *or* rid oneself of sb./sth.; **(b) sich eines Kleidungsstücks** ~: remove an item of clothing;

(c) sich einer Aufgabe/einer Schuld/seiner Pflichten ~: carry out a task/discharge a debt/one's duty

entleeren 1 *tr. V.* empty ‹ashtray etc.›; evacuate ‹bowels, bladder›. 2 *refl. V.* empty; become empty

Entleerung *die* emptying

entlegen *Adj.* (entfernt) remote, out-of-the-way ‹place›

entlehnen *tr. V.* (Sprachw.) borrow (*Dat.*, **aus** from)

entleihen *tr. V.* borrow

Entleiher *der;* ~**s**, ~: borrower

Entlein /ˈɛntlain/ *das;* ~**s**, ~: duckling; **ein hässliches** ~ (ugs. scherzh.) an ugly duckling

entloben *refl. V.* break off one's *or* the engagement

entlocken *tr. V.* (geh.) **jmdm. etw.** ~: elicit sth. from sb.; **jmdm. ein Geheimnis** ~: worm a secret out of sb.

entlohnen, (bes. schweiz.) **entlöhnen** *tr. V.* pay

Entlohnung *die;* ~, ~**en** payment; (Lohn) pay

entlüften *tr. V.* **(a)** ventilate; **(b)** (Technik) bleed ‹brakes, radiator, etc.›

Entlüftung *die* **(a)** ventilation; (Anlage) ventilation [system]; **(b)** (Technik) bleeding

entmachten *tr. V.* deprive of power

Entmachtung *die;* ~, ~**en** deprivation of power

entmannen *tr. V.* castrate

entmilitarisieren *tr. V.* demilitarize

Entmilitarisierung *die* demilitarization

entmündigen *tr. V.* (Rechtsw.) incapacitate; (fig.) deprive of the right of decision

Entmündigung *die;* ~, ~**en** (Rechtsw.) incapacitation; (fig.) deprivation of the right of decision

entmutigen *tr. V.* discourage; dishearten; **lass dich nicht** ~: don't be discouraged

Entmutigung *die;* ~, ~**en** discouragement

Entnahme *die;* ~, ~**n** (von Wasser) drawing; (von Geld, Blutprobe) taking; (von Blut) extraction; (von Organen) removal

entnehmen *unr. tr. V.* **(a) etw. [einer Sache (*Dat.*)]** ~: take sth. [from sth.]; **der Kasse Geld** ~: take money out of the till; **jmdm. Blut/eine Blutprobe** ~: take a blood sample from sb.; **Organe** ~: remove organs; **(b)** (ersehen aus) gather (*Dat.* from)

entnerven *tr. V.* jmdn. ~: be nerve-racking for sb.

entnervend *Adj.* nerve-racking

entpuppen *refl. V.* **sich als etw.** ~: turn out to be sth.

entrahmen *tr. V.* skim ‹milk›

enträtseln *tr. V.* decipher ‹code etc.›; understand, fathom ‹behaviour etc.›

entrechten *tr. V.* jmdn. ~: deprive sb. of his/her rights

entreißen *unr. tr. V.* **jmdm. etw.** ~: snatch sth. from sb.; **jmdn. dem Tod** ~ (fig.) save sb. from imminent death

entrichten *tr. V.* (Amtsspr.) pay ‹fee›

entriegeln *tr. V.* unbolt

entrinnen *unr. itr. V.; mit sein* (geh.) **einer Sache** (*Dat.*) ~: escape sth.

entrosten *tr. V.* derust

entrückt *Adj.* (geh.) carried away; (gedankenverloren) lost in reverie

entrümpeln /ɛntˈrʏmpl̩n/ *tr. V.* clear out

Entrümpelung *die;* ~, ~**en** clear-out; clearing out

entrußen *tr. V.* clear of soot

entrüsten 1 *refl. V.* **sich [über etw. (*Akk.*)]** ~: be indignant [at *or* about sth.]. 2 *tr. V.* jmdn. ~: make sb. indignant; **über etw.** (*Akk.*) **entrüstet/aufs Höchste entrüstet sein** be indignant/outraged at sth.

Entrüstung *die* indignation (**über** + *Akk.* at, about)

entsaften *tr. V.* extract the juice from

Entsafter *der;* ~**s**, ~: juice-extractor

entsagen *itr. V.* (geh.) **einem Genuss** ~: renounce *or* forgo a pleasure

Entsagung *die;* ~, ~**en** (geh.) renunciation

entsagungs·voll *Adj.* **(a)** full of self-denial *postpos.*; **(b)** (Entsagungen verlangend) full of privation *postpos.*

entsalzen *tr. V.* desalinate

Entsalzungs·anlage *die* desalination plant

entschädigen *tr. V.* compensate (**für** for); **jmdn. für etw.** ~ (fig.) make up for sth.

Entschädigung *die* compensation *no indef. art.*

Entschädigungs·summe *die* compensation *no indef. art.*

entschärfen *tr. V.* (a) defuse, deactivate ‹*bomb etc.*›; (b) (fig.) defuse ‹*situation*›; tone down ‹*discussion, criticism*›

Entschärfung *die;* ~, ~**en** (a) (von Bomben usw.) defusing; deactivation; (b) (fig.) defusing; toning down

Entscheid /ɛnt'ʃait/ *der;* ~[e]s, ~e decision

entscheiden 1 *unr. refl. V.* (a) decide; **sich für/gegen jmdn./etw.** ~: decide on *or* in favour of/against sb./sth.; **sich nicht** ~ **können** be unable to make up one's mind; (b) (entschieden werden) be decided; **morgen entscheidet es sich, ob ...**: I/we/you will know tomorrow whether ... 2 *unr. itr. V.* **über etw.** (*Akk.*) ~: decide on *or* settle sth. 3 *unr. tr. V.* (a) (bestimmen) decide on ‹*dispute*›; **der Richter entschied, dass ...**: the judge decided *or* ruled that ...; (b) (den Ausschlag geben für) decide ‹*outcome, result*›

entscheidend 1 *Adj.* crucial ‹*problem, question, significance*›; decisive ‹*action*›; **die** ~**e Stimme** the deciding vote. 2 *adv.* **jmdn./etw.** ~ **beeinflussen** have a crucial *or* decisive influence on sb./sth.

Entscheidung *die* decision; (Gerichts~) ruling; (Schwurgerichts~) verdict; **etw. steht vor der** ~: sth. is just about to be decided

Entscheidungs-: ~**befugnis** *die* decision-making powers *pl.;* ~**kampf** *der* decisive struggle; ~**schlacht** *die* decisive battle; ~**spiel** *das* deciding match; (bei gleichem Rang) play-off

entschieden 1 *Adj.* (a) (entschlossen) determined; resolute; (b) (eindeutig) definite. 2 *adv.* resolutely; **etw.** ~/**auf das Entschiedenste ablehnen** reject sth. emphatically *or* categorically; **das geht** ~ **zu weit** that is going much too far

Entschiedenheit *die;* ~: decisiveness; **etw. mit** ~ **fordern** demand sth. emphatically

entschlacken *tr. V.* cleanse

entschlafen *unr. itr. V.; mit sein* (verhüll.: sterben) pass away; fall asleep (euphem.)

entschleiern *tr. V.* (geh.) (a) (fig.) reveal; uncover; (b) unveil ‹*face*›

entschließen *unr. refl. V.* decide; make up one's mind; **sich** ~, **etw. zu tun** decide *or* resolve to do sth.; **sich dazu** ~: decide to do it

Entschließung *die* resolution

entschlossen 1 *Adj.* determined, resolute ‹*person*›; determined ‹*look etc.*›; **fest** ~ [**sein**], **etw. zu tun** [be] absolutely determined to do sth. 2 *adv.* ~ **handeln** act resolutely *or* with determination; **kurz** ~: on the spur of the moment; (als Reaktion) immediately

Entschlossenheit *die;* ~: determination; resolution

entschlummern *itr. V.; mit sein* (dichter.: einschlafen) fall asleep

entschlüpfen *itr. V.; mit sein* (a) escape; slip away; (b) ‹*remarks, words*› slip out

Entschluss, ***Entschluß** *der* decision; **seinen** ~ **ändern** change one's mind; **aus eigenem** ~: of one's own volition

entschlüsseln *tr. V.* decipher; decode

Entschlüsselung *die;* ~, ~**en** deciphering; decoding

Entschluss·kraft, ***Entschluß·kraft** *die* decisiveness

entschuldbar *Adj.* excusable; pardonable

entschuldigen 1 *refl. V.* ▶163 apologize; **sich bei jmdm. wegen** *od.* **für etw.** ~: apologize to sb. for sth. 2 *tr., auch itr. V.* ▶163 excuse ‹*person*›; **sich** ~ **lassen** ask to be excused; ~ **Sie** [**bitte**]! (bei Fragen, Bitten) excuse me; (bedauernd) excuse me; I'm sorry

Entschuldigung *die;* ~, ~**en** (a) (Rechtfertigung) excuse; **etw. zu seiner** ~ **sagen/anführen** say sth. in one's defence; (b) (schriftliche Mitteilung) [excuse] note; letter of excuse; (c) ▶163 **jmdn. für** *od.* **wegen etw. um** ~ **bitten** apologize to sb. for sth.; ~! (bei Fragen, Bitten) excuse me; (bedauernd) excuse me; [I'm] sorry; (d) (entschuldigende Äußerung) apology

Entschuldigungs-: ~**grund** *der* excuse; ~**schreiben** *das* letter of apology

entschwinden *unr. itr. V.; mit sein* (geh.) disappear; vanish

entsenden *unr., auch regelm. tr. V.* dispatch

entsetzen 1 *refl. V.* be horrified; **sich vor** *od.* **bei dem Anblick von etw.** ~: be horrified at the sight of sth. 2 *tr. V.* (a) (erschrecken) horrify; **über etw.** (*Akk.*) **entsetzt sein** be horrified by sth.; (b) (Milit.) relieve

Entsetzen *das;* ~**s** horror; **er bemerkte mit** ~, **dass ...**: he noticed to his horror that ...

entsetzlich 1 *Adj.* (a) horrible, dreadful ‹*accident, crime, etc.*›; (b) *nicht präd.* (ugs.: stark) terrible ‹*thirst, hunger*›. 2 *adv.* terribly (coll.); awfully

entseuchen *tr. V.* decontaminate

entsichern *tr. V.* release the safety catch of ‹*pistol etc.*›

entsinnen *unr. refl. V.* **sich jmds./einer Sache** ~, **sich an jmdn./etw.** ~: remember sb./sth.

entsorgen *tr. V.* (Amtsspr., Wirtsch.) dispose of ‹*waste etc.*›; **eine Stadt/ein Kernkraftwerk** ~: dispose of a town's/ a nuclear power station's waste

Entsorgung *die;* ~, ~**en** (Amtsspr., Wirtsch.) waste disposal

entspannen 1 *tr. V.* relax ‹*body etc.*›; relax, loosen ‹*muscles*›. 2 *refl. V.* (a) ‹*person*› relax; (b) (fig.) ‹*situation, tension*› ease

Entspannung *die; o. Pl.* (a) relaxation; (b) (politisch) easing of tension; détente

Entspannungs-: ~**politik** *die* policy of détente; ~**übung** *die* relaxation exercise

entspiegeln *tr. V.* bloom; **entspiegeltes Glas** coated glass

entsprechen *unr. itr. V.* **einer Sache** (*Dat.*) ~: correspond to sth.; **der Wahrheit/den Tatsachen** ~: be in accordance with the truth/the facts; **den Erwartungen** ~: live up to one's expectations; **sich** (*Dat.*) *od.* (geh.) **einander** ~: correspond; **einem Wunsch/einer Bitte** ~: comply with a wish/request; **den Anforderungen** ~: meet the requirements; **dem Anlass** ~: be appropriate for the occasion; **dem Zweck** ~: suit the purpose

entsprechend 1 *Adj.* (a) corresponding; (angemessen) appropriate ‹*payment, reply, etc.*›; (b) *nicht attr.* (dem~) in accordance *postpos.;* **das Wetter war schlecht und die Stimmung** ~: the weather was bad and the mood was the same; (c) *nicht präd.* (betreffend, zuständig) relevant ‹*department etc.*›; ‹*person*› concerned. 2 *adv.* (a) (angemessen) appropriately; (b) (dem~) accordingly. 3 *Präp. mit Dativ* in accordance with; **es geht ihm den Umständen** ~: he is as well as can be expected [in the circumstances]

Entsprechung *die;* ~, ~**en** (a) correspondence; (b) (Analogie) parallel

entspringen *unr. itr. V.; mit sein* (a) ▶193 ‹*river*› rise, have its source; (b) (entstehen aus) **einer Sache** (*Dat.*) ~: spring from sth.; (c) (entweichen aus) escape

entstammen *itr. V.; mit sein* **einer Sache** (*Dat.*) ~: come from sth.; (von etw. herrühren) derive from sth.

entstehen *unr. itr. V.; mit sein* (a) originate, ‹*quarrel, friendship, etc.*› arise; ‹*work of art*› be created; ‹*building, town, etc.*› be built; ‹*industry*› emerge; ‹*novel etc.*› be written; (b) (gebildet werden) be formed (**aus** from, **durch** by); (c) (sich ergeben) occur; (als Folge) result; **jmdm.** ~ **Kosten** sb. incurs costs; **hoffentlich ist nicht der Eindruck entstanden, dass ...**: I/we hope I/we have not given the impression that ...

Entstehung *die;* ~: origin; **die** ~ **dieser Industrie** the emergence of this industry

Entstehungs-: ~**geschichte** *die* history of the origin[s]; ~**ort** *der* place of origin; ~**zeit** *die* time of origin

---

*alte Schreibung (vgl. Hinweise auf S. xvi–xvii)

Entschuldigungen

Ziemlich formell

Wir bedauern, Ihnen mitteilen zu müssen, dass ...	= We regret to have to inform you that ...
Ich muss Ihnen leider mitteilen, dass ...	= I am sorry to have to inform you that ...
Ich bedaure sehr, dass ich Sie enttäuschen musste	= I greatly *od.* very much regret that I have had to disappoint you
Es tut mir aufrichtig Leid, dass ich Sie im Stich gelassen habe	= I am really sorry to have let you down *od.* that I have let you down
Ich muss mich bei Ihnen [in aller Form] entschuldigen, dass ich Sie fälschlich beschuldigt habe	= I owe you an [unreserved] apology *od.* I must apologize [unreservedly] for accusing you wrongly
Ich muss Sie für meinen Fehler um Entschuldigung/ Verzeihung bitten	= I must ask you to excuse/forgive my mistake
Wir bitten Sie für unser Versehen um Entschuldigung	= We apologize for our oversight
Sie müssen entschuldigen, dass ich erst heute schreibe	= You must forgive me *od.* Please forgive me for not writing earlier
Bitte entschuldigen Sie unser Versehen	= Please excuse our oversight
Entschuldigen Sie bitte, können Sie mir sagen, wie spät es ist?	= Excuse me, can you tell me the time?
Entschuldigen Sie die Störung, aber haben Sie meine Uhr gesehen?	= I'm sorry to bother you, but have you seen my watch?

Weniger formell

Tut mir Leid, da kann ich nicht helfen	= Sorry, I can't help you there
Tut mir Leid, dass ich dir so viel Mühe mache	= [I'm] sorry to be such a nuisance
Verzeihung! od. Tut mir Leid! Es war alles nur ein dummes Missverständnis!	= Sorry! It was all a stupid misunderstanding
Leider muss ich jetzt gehen	= I'm afraid I'll have to go now
Sei mir nicht böse! Ich konnte nichts dafür	= Don't be cross [with me]! I couldn't help it

---

entsteinen *tr. V.* stone

entstellen *tr. V.* **(a)** disfigure ‹*person*›; distort ‹*face*›; **(b)** (fig.) distort ‹*text, facts*›

Entstellung *die* **(a)** disfigurement; **(b)** (fig.) distortion

entstören *tr. V.* (Elektrot.) suppress ‹*engine, distributor, electrical appliance*›

enttarnen *tr. V.* uncover; (fig.) discover; **etw. als etw. ∼:** reveal sth. as sth.

Enttarnung *die* uncovering

enttäuschen **1** *tr. V.* disappoint; **unsere Hoffnungen wurden enttäuscht** our hopes were dashed. **2** *itr. V.* be a disappointment

enttäuscht *Adj.* disappointed; dashed ‹*hopes*›; **von jmdm. ∼ sein** be disappointed in sb.; **von** *od.* **über etw. ∼ sein** be disappointed by *or* at sth.

Enttäuschung *die* disappointment (**für** to); **jmdm. eine ∼ bereiten** be a disappointment to sb.

entthronen *tr. V.* (geh.) dethrone

entvölkern /ɛnt'fœlkɐn/ **1** *tr. V.* depopulate. **2** *refl. V.* become depopulated *or* deserted

ent·wachsen *unr. itr. V.; mit sein* **einer Sache** (*Dat.*) **∼:** grow out of *or* outgrow sth.

entwaffnen *tr. V.* (auch fig.) disarm

entwaffnend **1** *Adj.* disarming. **2** *adv.* disarmingly

Entwaffnung *die;* **∼:** disarming

entwarnen *itr. V.* sound *or* give the all-clear

Entwarnung *die* [sounding of the] all-clear

entwässern *tr. V.* drain ‹*area, meadow*›

Entwässerung *die;* **∼, ∼en** drainage

entweder *Konj.:* **∼ ... oder ...:** either ... or ...

entweichen *unr. itr. V.; mit sein* escape

entweihen *tr. V.* desecrate; profane

entwenden *tr. V.* (geh.) purloin (*Dat.* **from**)

entwerfen *unr. V.* design ‹*furniture, dress*›; draft ‹*novel, text, etc.*›; draw up ‹*plans etc.*›

entwerten *tr. V.* **(a)** cancel ‹*ticket, postage stamp*›; **(b)** (Finanzw.) devalue ‹*currency*›

Entwerter *der;* **∼s, ∼:** ticket-cancelling machine

Entwertung *die* ⇒ **entwerten:** cancellation; cancelling; devaluation

entwickeln **1** *refl. V.* develop (**aus** from, **zu** into). **2** *tr. V.* **(a)** (auch Fot.) develop; **(b)** (hervorbringen) give off, produce

‹*vapour, smell*›; show, display ‹*ability, characteristic*›; elaborate ‹*theory, ideas*›

Entwickler *der;* **∼s, ∼** (Fot.) developer

Entwicklung *die;* **∼, ∼en** **(a)** (auch Fot.) development; **in der ∼ sein** ‹*young person*› be adolescent *or* in one's adolescence; **in seiner [körperlichen] ∼ zurückbleiben** be physically underdeveloped; **etw. befindet sich in der ∼:** sth. is [still] in the development stage; **(b)** (einer Theorie usw.) elaboration

entwicklungs-, Entwicklungs-: **∼dienst** *der* development aid service; **∼fähig** *Adj.* capable of development; **∼geschichte** *die* history of the development; **die ∼geschichte der Menschheit/der Meerestiere** the evolution of man/of marine animals; **∼helfer** *der* development aid worker; **∼hilfe** *die* [development] aid; **∼land** *das; Pl.* **∼länder** developing country; **∼politik** *die* development aid policy; **∼störung** *die* developmental disturbance; **∼zeit** *die* period of development

entwirren *tr. V.* **(a)** unravel, disentangle ‹*wool etc.*›; **(b)** (fig.) unravel, sort out ‹*situation etc.*›

entwischen *itr. V.; mit sein* (ugs.) get away; **jmdm. ∼:** give sb. the slip (coll.)

entwöhnen /ɛnt'vø:nən/ *tr. V.* **(a)** wean ‹*baby*›; **(b)** (geh.) **jmdn. einer Sache** (*Dat.*) **∼:** break sb. of the habit of [doing] sth.; **jmdn. [von einer Sucht] ∼:** cure sb. [of an addiction]

entwürdigen *tr. V.* degrade

entwürdigend **1** *Adj.* degrading. **2** *adv.* ‹*treat sb.*› in a degrading manner

Entwurf *der* **(a)** design; **(b)** (Konzept) draft; **der ∼ zu einem Roman** the outline *or* draft of a novel

entwurzeln *tr. V.* (auch fig.) uproot

entzerren *tr. V.* **(a)** (Technik) correct; rectify; **(b)** (Fot.) rectify

entziehen **1** *unr. tr. V.* **(a)** take away; **etw. jmdm./ einer Sache ∼:** take sth. away from sb./sth.; **jmdm. den Führerschein ∼:** take sb.'s driving licence away; **jmdm. das Wort ∼:** ask sb. to stop [speaking]; **jmdm. das Vertrauen/seine Unterstützung ∼:** withdraw one's confidence in sb./one's support from sb.; **(b)** etw. **einer Sache** (*Dat.*) **∼** (entfernen von, aus) remove sth. from sth.; (herausziehen aus) extract sth. from sth.. **2** *unr. refl. V.* **sich der Gesellschaft** (*Dat.*) **∼** (geh.) withdraw from society; **sich seinen Pflichten** (*Dat.*) **∼:** shirk *or* evade

one's duty; **das entzieht sich meiner Kontrolle/ Kenntnis** that is beyond my control/knowledge
Entziehung *die* **(a)** withdrawal; **(b)** (Entziehungskur) withdrawal treatment *no indef. art.*
Entziehungs·kur *die* course of withdrawal treatment; withdrawal programme
entzifferbar *Adj.* decipherable
entziffern *tr. V.* decipher
entzücken *tr. V.* delight
entzückend 1 *Adj.* delightful; **das ist ja ∼!** (iron.) [that's] charming! **2** *adv.* delightfully
entzückt *Adj.* delighted; **von/über etw. (Akk.) ∼ sein** be delighted by/at sth.
Entzug *der;* ∼[e]s **(a)** withdrawal; (das Herausziehen) extraction; **(b)** ⇒ **Entziehung b**
Entzugs·erscheinung *die* withdrawal symptom
entzündbar *Adj.* [in]flammable
entzünden 1 *tr. V.* **(a)** (geh.: anzünden) light ⟨*fire*⟩; strike, light ⟨*match*⟩; **(b)** (geh.: erregen) kindle, arouse ⟨*passion*⟩; arouse ⟨*hatred*⟩. **2** *refl. V.* **(a)** catch fire; ignite; **(b)** ▶ 329 (anschwellen) become inflamed; **entzündet** inflamed; **(c)** (geh.: entstehen) **sich an etw. (Dat.) ∼:** ⟨*quarrel*⟩ be sparked off by sth.; ⟨*temper*⟩ flare at sth.
entzündlich *Adj.* **(a)** [in]flammable ⟨*substance*⟩; **leicht ∼** highly inflammable; **(b)** ▶ 329 (Med.) inflammatory
Entzündung *die;* ∼, ∼**en** ▶ 329 inflammation
entzwei *Adj.; nicht attr.* (geh.) in pieces
entzweien 1 *refl. V.* **sich [mit jmdm.]** ∼: fall out [with sb.]. **2** *tr. V.* cause ⟨*persons*⟩ to fall out
entzwei·gehen *unr. itr. V.; mit sein* (geh.) break; ⟨*machine*⟩ break down; ⟨*shoes, clothes*⟩ fall to pieces
Enzian /'ɛntsia:n/ *der;* ∼**s,** ∼**e (a)** (Bot.) gentian; **(b)** (Schnaps) enzian liqueur
Enzyklika /ɛn'tsy:klika/ *die;* ∼, **Enzykliken** encyclical
Enzyklopädie /ɛntsyklopɛ'di:/ *die;* ∼, ∼**n** encyclopaedia
enzyklopädisch *Adj.* encyclopaedic
Enzym /ɛn'tsy:m/ *das;* ∼**s,** ∼**e** (Chemie) enzyme
Epen ⇒ **Epos**
Epidemie /epide'mi:/ *die;* ∼, ∼**n** (auch fig.) epidemic
epidemisch *Adj.* epidemic
Epik /'e:pɪk/ *die;* ∼ (Literaturw.) epic poetry
Epiker *der;* ∼**s,** ∼: epic poet
Epilepsie /epilɛ'psi:/ *die;* ∼, ∼**n** ▶ 329 (Med.) epilepsy *no art.*
Epileptiker /epi'lɛptikɐ/ *der;* ∼**s,** ∼: epileptic
epileptisch *Adj.* epileptic
Epilog /epi'lo:k/ *der;* ∼**s,** ∼**e** epilogue
episch /'e:pɪʃ/ *Adj.* epic
Episkopat /episko'pa:t/ *das od. der;* ∼[e]s, ∼**e** episcopate
Episode /epi'zo:də/ *die;* ∼, ∼**n** episode
episodenhaft *Adj.* episodic
Epistel /e'pɪstl/ *die;* ∼, ∼**n (a)** (bibl.) epistle; **(b)** (kath. Kirche) epistle; lesson;
Epitaph /epi'ta:f/ *das;* ∼**s,** ∼**e** (geh.) epitaph
Epi·zentrum *das* (Geol.) epicentre
epochal /epo'xa:l/ *Adj.* epochal; epoch-making ⟨*invention*⟩; (fig. iron.) world-shattering; monumental
Epoche /e'pɔxə/ *die;* ∼, ∼**n** epoch; ∼ **machend** epoch-making
*****epoche·machend** ⇒ **Epoche**
Epos /'e:pɔs/ *das;* ∼, **Epen** epic [poem]; epos
Equipe /e'kɪp/ *die;* ∼, ∼**n** team
er /e:ɐ/ *Personalpron.; 3. Pers. Sg. Nom. Mask.* he; (betont) him; (bei Dingen/Tieren) it; (bei männlichen Tieren) he/him; it; „**Er**" (auf Handtüchern, an Türen) 'His'; **bring Er den Wein!** (veralt.) fetch the wine!; *s. auch* **ihm; ihn; seiner**
Er *der;* ∼, ∼**s** (ugs.) he; **ist es ein Er oder eine Sie?** is it a he or a she?

───────

*alte Schreibung (vgl. Hinweise auf S. xvi–xvii)

erachten *tr. V.* (geh.) consider; **etw. als** *od.* **für seine Pflicht** ∼: consider sth. [to be] one's duty; **etw. als** *od.* **für notwendig** ∼: consider *or* think sth. necessary
Erachten *das:* **meines** ∼**s** in my opinion
erahnen *tr. V.* imagine; guess
erarbeiten *tr. V.* **(a)** (erwerben) work for; [**sich** (*Dat.*)] **ein Vermögen** ∼: make [oneself] a fortune; **(b)** (zu Eigen machen) work on; study; **(c)** (erstellen) work out ⟨*plan, programme, etc.*⟩
Erb- /'ɛrp-/: ∼**adel** *der* hereditary nobility; ∼**anlage** *die* (Biol.) hereditary disposition
erbarmen /ɛɐ'barmən/ (geh.) **1** *refl. V.* **sich jmds./einer Sache** ∼: take pity on sb./sth.; **Herr, erbarme dich unser!** Lord, have mercy upon us. **2** *tr. V.* **jmdn.** ∼: arouse sb.'s pity; move sb. to pity
Erbarmen *das;* ∼**s** pity; **mit jmdm.** ∼ **haben** take pity on *or* feel pity for sb.; **er kennt kein** ∼: he knows no pity *or* mercy; **zum** ∼ **sein** be pitiful *or* pathetic
erbärmlich /ɛɐ'bɛrmlɪç/ **1** *Adj.* **(a)** (elend) wretched; **(b)** (unzulänglich) pathetic; **(c)** (abwertend: gemein) mean; wretched; **(d)** *nicht präd.* (sehr groß) terrible ⟨*hunger, thirst, fear, etc.*⟩. **2** *adv.* (intensivierend) terribly ⟨*cold, thirsty, etc.*⟩
Erbärmlichkeit *die;* ∼: **(a)** (Elend) wretchedness; **(b)** (abwertend: Gemeinheit) meanness; wretchedness
erbarmungs·los *Adj.* merciless
erbauen 1 *tr. V.* **(a)** build; **(b)** (geh.: erheben) uplift; edify; **wir waren von seinen Plänen wenig erbaut** we were not exactly delighted about his plans. **2** *refl. V.* **sich an etw. (Dat.)** ∼ (geh.) be uplifted *or* edified by sth.
Erbauer *der;* ∼**s,** ∼: architect
erbaulich *Adj.* edifying
Erbauung *die;* ∼ (fig. geh.) edification
erb·berechtigt *Adj.* entitled to inherit; entitled to an/ the inheritance
Erbe¹ /'ɛrbə/ *das;* ∼**s (a)** (Vermögen) inheritance; **das väterliche/mütterliche** ∼: patrimony/maternal inheritance; **sein** ∼ **antreten** come into one's inheritance; **(b)** (Vermächtnis) heritage; legacy
Erbe² *der;* ∼**n** ∼**n** heir; **jmdn. zum** *od.* **als** ∼**n einsetzen** appoint sb. as one's heir; **die lachenden** ∼**n** (ugs.) my/his *etc.* heirs and successors
erbeben *itr. V.; mit sein* (geh.) **(a)** shake; tremble; **(b)** (fig.: erregt werden) shake; quiver
Erb·eigenschaft *die* (Biol.) hereditary characteristic
erben *tr., auch itr. V.* inherit; **bei mir ist nichts zu** ∼ (ugs.) you won't get anything out of me
Erben·gemeinschaft *die* community of joint heirs
erbetteln *tr. V.* get by begging
erbeuten /ɛɐ'bɔytn/ *tr. V.* carry off, get away with ⟨*valuables, prey, etc.*⟩; (Milit.) capture
Erb-: ∼**feind** *der* traditional enemy; ∼**folge** *die* succession; **die gesetzliche** ∼: intestate succession; ∼**forschung** *die* genetics *sing., no art.;* ∼**gut** *das* (Biol.) genotype; genetic make-up; ∼**hof** *der* ancestral estate
erbieten *unr. refl. V.* (geh.) **sich** ∼, **etw. zu tun** offer to do sth.
Erbin *die;* ∼, ∼**nen** heiress
erbitten *unr. tr. V.* (geh.) request
erbittern *tr. V.* enrage; incense
erbittert 1 *Adj.* bitter ⟨*resistance, struggle*⟩. **2** *adv.* ∼ **kämpfen** wage a bitter struggle
Erbitterung *die;* ∼: bitterness
Erb·krankheit *die* hereditary disease
erblassen /ɛɐ'blasn/ *itr. V.; mit sein* (geh.) ⇒ **erbleichen**
Erblasser /'ɛrplasɐ/ *der;* ∼**s,** ∼ (Rechtsw.) testator
erbleichen *itr. V.; mit sein* (geh.) go *or* turn pale; blanch (literary)
erblich 1 *Adj.* hereditary ⟨*title, disease*⟩. **2** *adv.* **er ist** ∼ **belastet** he suffers from a hereditary condition; (scherzh.) it runs in his family

erblicken *tr. V.* (geh.) (**a**) catch sight of; see; (**b**) (fig.) see

erblinden *itr. V.; mit sein* go blind; lose one's sight

Erblindung *die;* ∼: loss of sight

erblühen *itr. V.; mit sein* (geh.) bloom; blossom

Erb·masse *die* (**a**) (Biol.) genotype; genetic make-up; (**b**) (Rechtsspr.) estate

erbosen /ɛɐ̯ˈboːzn̩/ *tr. V.* (geh.) infuriate

erbost *Adj.* angry, furious (**über** + *Akk.* at)

Erb·pacht *die* (Rechtsw.) hereditary lease

erbrechen 1 *unr. tr. V.* bring up ⟨*food*⟩. 2 *unr. itr., refl. V.* vomit; be sick

Erbrechen *das;* ∼s vomiting; **bis zum** ∼ (ugs.) ad nauseam

Erb·recht *das o. Pl.* law of inheritance

erbringen *unr. tr. V.* (**a**) produce ⟨*proof, evidence*⟩; (**b**) (liefern) produce ⟨*result etc.*⟩; yield ⟨*amount*⟩; result in ⟨*savings etc.*⟩; **die vorgesehene Leistung** ∼: do the required work

Erb·schaden *der* (Genetik) hereditary defect

Erbschaft *die;* ∼, ∼en inheritance; **eine** ∼ **machen** come into an inheritance

Erbschaft[s]·steuer *die* estate *or* death duties *pl.*

Erb-: ∼**schein** *der* certificate of inheritance; ∼**schleicher** *der;* ∼s, ∼ (abwertend) legacy hunter

Erbse /ˈɛrpsə/ *die;* ∼, ∼n pea

erbsen·groß *Adj.* pea-size; the size of a pea *postpos.*

Erbsen·suppe *die* (**a**) pea soup; (**b**) (ugs.: Nebel) pea-souper

Erb-: ∼**stück** *das* heirloom; ∼**sünde** *die* original sin; ∼**teil** *das* share of an/the inheritance

Erd-: ∼**achse** *die* earth's axis; ∼**anziehung** *die* earth's gravitational pull; ∼**apfel** *der* (bes. österr.) potato; ∼**atmosphäre** *die* earth's atmosphere; ∼**ball** *der* (geh.) globe; earth; ∼**beben** *das* earthquake

erdbeben·sicher *Adj.* earthquake-proof ⟨*building, construction*⟩; ⟨*region etc.*⟩ free from earthquakes

Erd·beere *die* strawberry

Erd-: ∼**bevölkerung** *die* earth's population; ∼**bewohner** *der* inhabitant of the earth; ∼**boden** *der* ground; earth; **etw. dem** ∼**boden gleichmachen** raze sth. to the ground; **vom** ∼**boden verschwinden** disappear from *or* off the face of the earth

Erde /ˈeːɐ̯də/ *die;* ∼, ∼n (**a**) (Erdreich) soil; earth; **ein Klumpen** ∼: a lump of earth; **etw. in die** ∼ **rammen** ram sth. into the ground; (**b**) *o. Pl.* (fester Boden) ground; **etw. auf die** ∼ **legen/stellen** put sth. down [on the ground]; **zu ebener** ∼: on the ground floor *or* (Amer.) the first floor; **auf der** ∼ **bleiben** (fig.) keep one's feet on the ground (fig.); **unter der** ∼ **liegen** (geh. verhüll.) be in one's grave; **jmdn. unter die** ∼ **bringen** (ugs.) bury sb.; (fig.: töten) be the death of sb. (coll.); (**c**) *o. Pl.* (Welt) earth; world; **auf** ∼n (bibl.), **auf der** ∼: on earth; **auf der ganzen** ∼: throughout the world; **ein ruhiges/idyllisches Fleckchen** ∼: a peaceful/idyllic spot; (**d**) *o. Pl.* (Planet) Earth; (**e**) (Elektrot.) earth

erden *tr. V.* (Elektrot.) earth

Erden·bürger *der* earth-dweller

erdenken *unr. tr. V.* think *or* make up

erdenklich *Adj.* conceivable; imaginable; **sich** (*Dat.*) **alle** *od.* **jede** ∼**e Mühe geben** take the greatest possible trouble

Erd-: ∼**gas** *das* natural gas; ∼**geist** *der* earth spirit; ∼**geschichte** *die; o. Pl.* history of the earth; ∼**geschoss**, *∗*∼**geschoß** *das* ground floor; first floor (Amer.); ∼**hörnchen** *das* (Zool.) chipmunk; ground-squirrel

erdig *Adj.* (**a**) earthy ⟨*mass, smell, taste*⟩; (**b**) (geh.: mit Erde beschmutzt) muddy

erd-, Erd-: ∼**innere** *das* interior of the earth; ∼**kabel** *das* underground cable; ∼**kruste** *die* earth's crust; ∼**kugel** *die* terrestrial globe; earth; ∼**kunde** *die* geography; ∼**magnetismus** *der* terrestrial magnetism; ∼**mittelpunkt** *der* centre of the earth; ∼**nuss**, *∗*∼**nuß** *die* peanut; ground-nut; ∼**nuss·butter**, *∗*∼**nuß·butter** *die* peanut butter; ∼**nuss·öl**, *∗*∼**nuß·öl** *das* ground-nut oil; ∼**ober·fläche** *die*

earth's surface; ∼**öl** *das* oil; petroleum (as tech. term); ∼**öl exportierend** oil-exporting;

erdolchen *tr. V.* (geh.) stab to death

erdöl-, Erdöl-: *∗*∼**exportierend** ⇒ **Erdöl**; ∼**feld** *das* oilfield; ∼**gewinnung** *die* oil production; ∼**leitung** *die* oil pipeline; ∼**produzent** *der* oil-producing country; ∼**raffinerie** *die* oil refinery

Erd·reich *das* soil

erdreisten *refl. V.* **sich** ∼, **etw. zu tun** have the audacity to do sth.

erdrosseln *tr. V.* strangle

erdrücken *tr. V.* (**a**) crush; (**b**) (fig.) overwhelm

erdrückend *Adj.* overwhelming ⟨*evidence, superiority*⟩

Erd-: ∼**rutsch** *der* landslide; landslip; **ein politischer** ∼**rutsch** a political landslide; ∼**rutsch·sieg** *der* (Politik) landslide victory; ∼**schicht** *die* (**a**) layer of earth; (**b**) (Geol.) stratum; ∼**stoß** *der* earth tremor; ∼**teil** *der* continent

erdulden *tr. V.* endure ⟨*sorrow, misfortune*⟩; tolerate ⟨*insults*⟩; (mitmachen) undergo

Erd-: ∼**um·drehung** *die* rotation of the earth; ∼**um·fang** *der* circumference of the earth; ∼**umlaufbahn** *die* orbit [of the earth]; **in die** ∼**umlaufbahn eintreten** enter into orbit

Erdung *die;* ∼, ∼en (Elektrot.) (**a**) earthing; (**b**) (Leitung) earth [connection]

Erd-: ∼**wall** *der* wall of earth; (Milit., Straßenbau) earthwork; ∼**zeit·alter** *das* geological era

ereifern *refl. V.* get excited (**über** + *Akk.* about)

ereignen *refl. V.* happen; ⟨*accident, mishap*⟩ occur

Ereignis /ɛɐ̯ˈʔaɪɡnɪs/ *das;* ∼ses, ∼se event; occurrence; **die** ∼**se überstürzten sich** everything seemed to happen at once; **ein freudiges** ∼: a happy event

ereignis-: ∼**los** *Adj.* uneventful; ∼**reich** *Adj.* eventful

ereilen *tr. V.* (geh.) **der Tod ereilte ihn** he died [suddenly]; **das gleiche Schicksal ereilte ihn** he met the same fate

Erektion /erɛkˈtsi̯oːn/ *die;* ∼, ∼en erection

Eremit /ereˈmiːt/ *der;* ∼en, ∼en hermit

ererbt *Adj.* inherited

erfahren[1] *unr. tr. V.* (**a**) find out; learn; (hören) hear; **etw. von jmdm.** ∼: find sth. out from sb.; **etw. über jmdn./etw.** ∼: find out *or* hear sth. about sb./sth.; **etw. von etw.** ∼: find out *or* learn/hear sth. about sth.; **etw. durch jmdn./etw.** ∼: learn of sth. from sb./sth.; (**b**) (geh.: erleben) experience; **viel Leid/Kummer** ∼: suffer much sorrow/anxiety; (**c**) (mitmachen) undergo ⟨*change, development, etc.*⟩; suffer ⟨*setback*⟩

erfahren[2] *Adj.* experienced

Erfahrung *die;* ∼, ∼en (**a**) experience; **über reiche/langjährige** ∼**en verfügen** have extensive/years of experience; ∼**en sammeln** gain experience *sing.;* **die** ∼ **machen, dass …:** learn by experience that …; **wir haben schlechte** ∼**en mit ihm/damit gemacht** our experience of him/it has not been very good; (**b**) **etw. in** ∼ **bringen** discover sth.

erfahrungs-, Erfahrungs-: ∼**austausch** *der* exchange of experiences ∼**gemäß** *Adv.* in our/my experience; ∼**gemäß ist es so, dass …:** experience shows that …

erfassen *tr. V.* (**a**) (mitreißen) catch; (**b**) (begreifen) grasp ⟨*situation, implications, etc.*⟩; (**c**) (registrieren) record; (**d**) (einbeziehen) cover; (**e**) (packen) seize; **Angst/Freude erfasste ihn** he was seized by fear/overcome with joy

Erfassung *die* registration

erfinden *unr. tr. V.* (**a**) invent; (**b**) (ausdenken) make up ⟨*story, words*⟩; make up, invent ⟨*excuse*⟩; **eine erfundene Geschichte** a fictional story; **das ist alles erfunden** it is pure fabrication; *s. auch* **Pulver b**

Erfinder *der;* ∼s, ∼ (**a**) inventor; (**b**) (Urheber) creator; **das ist nicht im Sinne des** ∼s (ugs.) that's not what it was meant for

erfinderisch *Adj.* inventive; *s. auch* **Not b**

Erfindung *die;* ~, ~en (a) invention; **eine** ~ **machen** invent something; **er hat viele** ~**en gemacht** he has many inventions to his credit; (b) (Ausgedachtes) invention; fabrication

erfindungs-, Erfindungs-: ~**gabe** *die* inventiveness; ~**reich** *Adj.* imaginative

erflehen *tr. V.* (geh.) beg; **jmds. Hilfe/Hilfe von jmdm.** ~: beg sb.'s help/beg help from sb.

Erfolg /ɛɐ̯'fɔlk/ *der;* ~[e]s, ~e ▶240| success; **viel/ keinen** ~ **haben** be very successful/be unsuccessful; **viel** ~! good luck!; **etw. mit/ohne** ~ **tun** do something successfully/without success; **der** ~ **blieb aus** success was not forthcoming; **der** ~ **war, dass** ... (ugs.) the upshot was that ...; ~ **versprechend** promising

erfolgen *itr. V.; mit sein* take place; occur; **auf seine Beschwerden erfolgte keine Reaktion** there was no reaction to his complaints

erfolg-, Erfolg-: ~**los** 1 *Adj.* unsuccessful; 2 *adv.* unsuccessfully; ~**losigkeit** *die;* ~: lack of success; ~**reich** 1 *Adj.* successful; 2 *adv.* successfully

Erfolgs-: ~**aus·sicht** *die; meist Pl.* prospect of success; ~**autor** *der* successful author; ~**erlebnis** *das* feeling of achievement; ~**mensch** *der* successful individual; ~**prämie** *die* (eines Vertreters) commission; (eines Arbeiters) bonus; ~**quote** *die* success rate; (bei Prüfungen) pass rate; ~**rezept** *das* recipe for success; ~**roman** *der* successful novel; ~**zwang** *der* pressure to succeed

*erfolg·versprechend ⇒ **Erfolg**

erforderlich *Adj.* necessary; required;

erfordern *tr. V.* require; demand

Erfordernis *das;* ~**ses,** ~**se** requirement

erforschen *tr. V.* discover ⟨*facts, causes, etc.*⟩; explore ⟨*country*⟩; find out ⟨*truth*⟩; **sein Gewissen** ~: search one's conscience

Erforschung *die* research (*Gen.* into); (der Erde, des Weltalls usw.) exploration

erfragen *tr. V.* ascertain [by asking]

erfreuen 1 *tr. V.* please; **sehr erfreut!** pleased to meet you. 2 *refl. V.* (a) **sich an etw.** (*Dat.*) ~: take pleasure in sth.; (b) **sich einer Sache** (*Gen.*) ~ (geh.) enjoy sth.

erfreulich *Adj.* pleasant; **eine** ~**e Mitteilung** a piece of good news

erfreulicherweise *Adv.* happily

erfrieren *unr. itr. V.; mit sein* (a) ▶329| ⟨*person, animal*⟩ freeze to death; ⟨*plant, harvest, etc.*⟩ be damaged by frost; suffer frost-damage; **ihm sind die Zehen erfroren** he got frostbite in his toes; **er ist ganz erfroren** (ugs.) he's absolutely frozen; (b) (fig.: erstarren) freeze

Erfrierung *die;* ~, ~**en** ▶329| frostbite *no pl.;* ~**en an den Händen/Füßen** frostbitten hands/feet

erfrischen 1 *tr., auch itr. V.* refresh; **ein Spaziergang erfrischt sehr** a walk is very refreshing. 2 *refl. V.* freshen oneself up

erfrischend (auch fig.) 1 *Adj.* refreshing. 2 *adv.* refreshingly

Erfrischung *die;* ~, ~**en** (auch fig.) refreshment

Erfrischungs-: ~**getränk** *das* soft drink; ~**raum** *der* refreshment room; ~**tuch** *das; Pl.* ~**tücher** tissue wipe; towelette

erfüllbar *Adj.* ⟨*wish*⟩ which can be granted; ⟨*condition*⟩ which can be met

erfüllen 1 *tr. V.* (a) grant ⟨*wish, request*⟩; fulfil ⟨*contract*⟩; carry out ⟨*duty*⟩; serve ⟨*condition*⟩; serve ⟨*purpose*⟩; (b) (füllen) fill; (fig. geh.) **ein erfülltes Leben** a full life; **eine Sehnsucht erfüllte sein Herz** a longing came over him; **jmdn. mit etw.** ~: fill sb. with sth.. 2 *refl. V.* come true

Erfüllung *die* (einer Pflicht) performance; (eines Wunsches) fulfilment; **in** ~ **gehen** come true

ergänzen /ɛɐ̯'gɛntsn̩/ *tr. V.* (a) (vervollständigen) complete; (erweitern) add to; replenish ⟨*supply*⟩; amplify ⟨*remark, statement, etc.*⟩; amend ⟨*statute*⟩; (b) (hinzufügen) add

⟨*remark*⟩; (c) (hinzukommen zu) complement; (d) **sich** *od.* (geh.) **einander** ~: complement each other

Ergänzung *die;* ~, ~**en** (a) (Vervollständigung) completion; (Erweiterung) enlargement; (von Vorräten) replenishment; **zur** ~ **des Gesagten/einer Sammlung** to amplify what has been said/in order to enlarge a collection; (b) (Zusatz) addition; (zu einem Gesetz) amendment; (c) (zusätzliche Bemerkung) further remark; (d) (Sprachw.: Objekt) object

Ergänzungs·band *der; Pl.* ~**bände** supplementary volume; supplement

ergattern *tr. V.* (ugs.) manage to grab

ergaunern *tr. V.* get by underhand means

ergeben[1] 1 *unr. refl. V.* (a) (sich fügen) **sich in etw.** (*Akk.*) ~: submit to sth.; **sich in sein Schicksal** ~: resign oneself *or* become resigned to one's fate; (b) (kapitulieren) surrender (*Dat.* to); (c) (entstehen) ⟨*opportunity, difficulty, problem*⟩ arise (**aus** from); **bald ergab sich ein angeregtes Gespräch** soon a lively discussion was taking place; (d) **sich dem Alkohol**/(ugs.) **Suff** ~ (fig.) take to alcohol/drink *or* the bottle. 2 *unr. tr. V.* result in; **die Ernte ergab rund 400 Zentner Kartoffeln** the harvest produced about 400 hundredweight of potatoes; **eins und eins ergibt zwei** one and one makes two

ergeben[2] 1 *Adj.* devoted; **Ihr sehr** ~**er** ... (geh.) yours most obediently, ... 2 *adv.* devotedly

Ergebenheit *die;* ~: devotion

Ergebnis *das;* ~**ses,** ~**se** result; (von Verhandlungen, Überlegungen usw.) conclusion; **zu einem** ~ **führen** produce a result

ergebnis·los 1 *Adj.* fruitless ⟨*discussion*⟩; **die Verhandlungen blieben** ~/**wurden** ~ **abgebrochen** negotiations remained inconclusive/were broken off without a conclusion having been reached. 2 *adv.* fruitlessly

ergehen 1 *unr. refl. V.* (a) **sich in etw.** (*Dat.*) ~: indulge in sth.; (b) (geh.: lustwandeln) take a turn. 2 *unr. itr. V.; mit sein* (a) (geh.: erlassen werden) ⟨*law*⟩ be enacted; **die Einladungen ergingen an alle Mitglieder** the invitations went to all members; (b) *unpers.* **jmdm. ist es gut/ schlecht** *usw.* **ergangen** things went well/badly *etc.* for someone; (c) **etw. über sich** (*Akk.*) ~ **lassen** let sth. wash over one

ergiebig /ɛɐ̯'giːbɪç/ *Adj.* rich ⟨*deposits, resources*⟩; productive ⟨*mine*⟩; fertile ⟨*fisheries, topic*⟩

Ergiebigkeit *die;* ~: ⇒ **ergiebig:** richness; productivity; fertility

ergießen *unr. refl. V.* pour

ergo /'ɛrgo/ *Adv.* ergo

ergonomisch 1 *Adj.* ergonomic. 2 *adv.* ergonomically

ergötzen (geh.) 1 *tr. V.* enthrall; captivate. 2 *refl. V.* **sich an etw.** (*Dat.*) ~: be delighted by sth.

Ergötzen *das;* ~**s** (geh.) delight

ergötzlich *Adj.* (geh.) delightful

ergrauen *itr. V.; mit sein* go *or* turn grey

ergreifen *unr. tr. V.* (a) grab; **jmds. Hand** ~: grasp sb.'s hand; **die Macht** ~ (fig.) seize power; (b) (festnehmen) catch ⟨*thief etc.*⟩; (c) (fig.: erfassen) seize; **von blindem Zorn ergriffen** (geh.) in the grip of blind anger; (d) (fig.: aufnehmen) **einen Beruf** ~: take up a career; **die Initiative/eine Gelegenheit** ~: take the initiative/an opportunity; (e) (fig.: bewegen) move

ergreifend 1 *Adj.* moving. 2 *adv.* movingly

Ergreifung *die;* ~ (a) (Festnahme) capture; (b) (der Macht) seizure

ergriffen *Adj.* moved

Ergriffenheit *die;* ~: **vor** ~ **schweigen** be too moved to speak; **vor** ~ **weinen** be moved to tears

ergründen *tr. V.* ascertain; discover ⟨*cause*⟩; fathom ⟨*mystery*⟩

Ergründung *die* ⇒ **ergründen:** ascertainment; discovery; fathoming

Erguss, *Erguß *der* (a) (Med.) (Blut~) bruise; contusion; (Samen~) ejaculation; (b) (geh. abwertend) outburst

erhaben *Adj.* (a) solemn ⟨*moment*⟩; awe-inspiring ⟨*sight*⟩; sublime ⟨*beauty*⟩; (b) **über etw.** (*Akk.*) ~ **sein**

be above sth.; **über jeden Zweifel** ∼: beyond all criticism

Erhabenheit *die;* ∼: grandeur

Erhalt *der;* ∼[e]s (Amtsdt.) (a) receipt; **bei** ∼ **zahlen** pay on receipt; (b) ⇒ **Erhaltung**

erhalten 1 *unr. tr. V.* (a) (bekommen) receive ⟨*letter, news, gift*⟩; be given ⟨*order*⟩; get ⟨*good mark, impression*⟩; **eine hohe Geldstrafe** ∼: be fined heavily; **er erhielt 3 Jahre Gefängnis** he was sentenced to 3 years in prison; (b) (bewahren) preserve ⟨*town, building*⟩; conserve ⟨*energy*⟩; **gut** ∼ **sein** ⟨*clothes etc.*⟩ be in good condition; **jmdn. am Leben** ∼: keep sb. alive. 2 *unr. refl. V.* survive

erhältlich /ɛɐ̯'hɛltlɪç/ *Adj.* obtainable

Erhaltung *die;* ∼ (des Friedens) maintenance; (der Arten, von Kunstschätzen) preservation; (der Energie) conservation

erhängen *tr. V.* **jmdn./sich** ∼: hang sb./oneself; **Tod durch Erhängen** death by hanging

erhärten *tr. V.* strengthen ⟨*suspicion, assumption*⟩; substantiate ⟨*claim*⟩

erheben 1 *unr. tr. V.* (a) (emporheben) raise ⟨*one's arm/hand/glass*⟩; **erhobenen Hauptes** with head held high; **die Stimme** ∼: raise one's voice; (b) levy ⟨*tax*⟩; charge ⟨*fee*⟩; (c) **jmdn. in den Adelsstand** ∼: elevate sb. to the nobility; (d) gather, collect ⟨*data, material*⟩; (e) **Anklage** ∼: bring *or* prefer charges. 2 *unr. refl. V.* (a) rise; (b) (rebellieren) rise up (**gegen** against)

erhebend *Adj.* uplifting

erheblich /ɛɐ̯'he:plɪç/ 1 *Adj.* considerable. 2 *adv.* considerably

Erhebung *die;* ∼, ∼en (a) (Anhöhe) elevation; (b) (Aufstand) uprising; (c) (Umfrage) survey; (d) (von Steuern) levying; (von Gebühren) charging

erheitern *tr. V.* **jmdn.** ∼: cheer sb. up

Erheiterung *die;* ∼, ∼en amusement

erhellen 1 *tr. V.* (a) light up, illuminate ⟨*room, sky*⟩; (b) (erklären) shed light on, illuminate ⟨*reason, relationship*⟩. 2 *refl. V.* (geh.) ⟨*eyes, face*⟩ brighten

Erhellung *die;* ∼ (Erklärung) illumination

erhitzen *tr. V.* (a) heat ⟨*liquid*⟩; **jmdn.** ∼: make sb. hot; (b) (fig.: erregen) **die Gemüter** ∼: make feelings run high. 2 *refl. V.* (a) heat up; ⟨*person*⟩ become hot; (b) (fig.: sich erregen) ⟨*feelings*⟩ become heated

Erhitzung *die;* ∼, ∼en heating; (Hitze) heat

erhoffen *tr. V.* **sich** (*Dat.*) **viel/wenig von etw.** ∼: expect a lot/little from sth.; **die erhoffte Änderung/Lohnerhöhung** the change/pay rise we/they had expected

erhöhen 1 *tr. V.* increase, raise ⟨*prices, productivity, etc.*⟩; increase ⟨*dose*⟩; **erhöhte Temperatur haben** have a temperature; **erhöhter Blutdruck** somewhat high blood pressure; **erhöhte Vorsicht** extra care. 2 *refl. V.* ⟨*rent, prices*⟩ rise

Erhöhung *die;* ∼, ∼en: **eine** ∼ **der Preise/Steuern** an increase in prices/taxes; **eine Erhöhung des Blutdrucks** a rise in blood pressure; **die** ∼ **einer Dosis** the increasing of a dose

erholen *refl. V.* (a) ▶329┘ recover (**von** from); (nach Krankheit) recuperate; (sich ausruhen) rest; have a rest; (sich entspannen, ausspannen) relax; (b) (fig.) recover

erholsam *Adj.* restful ⟨*weekend, holiday*⟩; **Wandern ist sehr** ∼: walking is very refreshing

Erholung *die;* ∼ ▶329┘ ⇒ **erholen:** recovery; recuperation; rest; relaxation; ∼ **brauchen** need a rest; **nach der langen Krankheit hat er** ∼ **nötig** he needs to recuperate after his long illness; **zur** ∼ **fahren** go on holiday to rest/relax; (nach Krankheit) go on holiday to convalesce; **eine** ∼ **sein** be relaxing; (fig.) be a refreshing change

erholungs-, Erholungs-: ∼**bedürftig** *Adj.* in need of a rest *postpos.;* ∼**bedürftig sein** need a rest; ∼**gebiet** *das* holiday area; ∼**heim** *das* holiday home; ∼**ort** *der; Pl.* ∼e resort; ∼**pause** *die* break

erhören *tr. V.* (geh.) hear ⟨*plea, prayer*⟩; **jmdn.** ∼ (veralt.) yield to sb.

erigieren /eri'gi:rən/ *itr. V.; mit sein* become erect; **erigiert** erect

Erika /'e:rika/ *die;* ∼, ∼s *od.* **Eriken** /-kən/ (Bot.) erica

erinnern /ɛɐ̯'|mɛn/ 1 *refl. V.* **sich an jmdn./etw. [gut/genau]** ∼: remember sb./sth. [well/clearly]; **sich [daran]** ∼, **dass** …: remember *or* recall that …; **wenn ich mich recht erinnere** if I remember rightly. 2 *tr. V.* (a) jmdn. an etw./jmdn. ∼: remind sb. of sth./sb.; **jmdn. daran** ∼, **etw. zu tun** remind sb. to do sth.; (b) (bes. nordd.: sich erinnern an) remember. 3 *itr. V.* (a) **jmd./etw. erinnert an jmdn./etw.** sb./sth. reminds one of sb./sth.; (b) (zu bedenken geben) **an etw.** (*Akk.*) ∼: remind sb. of sth.; **ich möchte daran** ∼, **dass** …: let us not forget *or* overlook that …

Erinnerung *die;* ∼, ∼en (a) memory (**an** + *Akk.* of); **etw.** [noch gut] **in** ∼ **haben** [still] remember sth. [well]; **wenn mich die** ∼ **nicht täuscht** if my memory does not deceive me; **nach meiner** ∼, **meiner** ∼ **nach** as far as I remember; **jmdn./etw. in guter** ∼ **behalten** have pleasant memories of sb./sth.; **zur** ∼ **an jmdn./etw.** in memory of sb./sth.; (b) (Erinnerungsstück) remembrance; souvenir; (c) *Pl.* (Memoiren) memoirs

Erinnerungs-: ∼**lücke** *die* gap in one's memory; ∼**stück** *das* keepsake; (von einer Reise) souvenir; ∼**wert** *der* sentimental value

erkalten *tr. V. mit sein* cool; ⟨*limbs*⟩ grow cold; (fig.) ⟨*passion, feeling*⟩ cool

erkälten *refl. V.* ▶329┘ catch cold

Erkältung *die;* ∼, ∼en ▶329┘ cold; **sich** (*Dat.*) **eine** ∼ **zuziehen** *od.* (ugs.) **holen** catch a cold

Erkältungs·krankheit *die* cold

erkämpfen *tr. V.* win; **sich** (*Dat.*) **etw.** ∼ **müssen** have to fight for sth.

erkaufen *tr. V.* (a) buy; (b) (fig.) win; **etw. teuer** ∼: win something at great cost

erkennbar *Adj.* recognizable; (sichtbar) visible; (schwach sichtbar) discernible

erkennen 1 *unr. tr. V.* (a) (deutlich sehen) make out; **deutlich zu** ∼ **sein** be clearly visible; (b) (identifizieren) recognize (**an** + *Dat.* by); **sich zu** ∼ **geben** reveal one's identity; (c) (fig.) recognize; realize. 2 *unr. itr. V.* (a) (Rechtsspr.) **auf Freispruch** ∼: grant an acquittal; (b) (Sport) **auf Elfmeter/Freistoß** ∼: award a penalty/free kick

erkenntlich *Adj.* **sich [für etw.]** ∼ **zeigen** show one's appreciation [for sth.]

Erkenntnis *die;* ∼, ∼se (a) discovery; **wissenschaftliche/gesicherte** ∼**se** scientific findings/firm insights; **zu der** ∼ **kommen, dass** …: come to the realization that …; (b) *o. Pl.* (das Erkennen) cognition

erkennungs-, Erkennungs-: ∼**dienst** *der* police records department; ∼**dienstlich** 1 *Adj.* ∼**dienstliche Behandlung** fingerprinting and photographing; 2 *adv.* **jmdn.** ∼**dienstlich behandeln** take sb.'s fingerprints and photograph; ∼**melodie** *die* (einer Sendung) theme music; (eines Senders) signature tune; ∼**zeichen** *das* sign [to recognize sb. by]

Erker /'ɛrkɐ/ *der;* ∼s, ∼: bay window

Erker-: ∼**fenster** *das* bay window; ∼**zimmer** *das* room with a bay window

erklärbar *Adj.* explicable; **etw. ist** ∼: sth. can be explained

erklären 1 *tr. V.* (a) explain (*Dat.* to, **durch** by); (b) (mitteilen) state; declare; announce ⟨*one's resignation*⟩; **jmdm. den Krieg** ∼: declare war on sb.; (c) (bezeichnen) **jmdn. für tot** ∼: pronounce someone dead; **etw. für ungültig/verbindlich** ∼: declare something to be invalid/binding; **jmdn. zu etw.** ∼: name sb. as sth. 2 *refl. V.* (a) **sich einverstanden/bereit** ∼: declare oneself [to be] in agreement/willing; **sich für/gegen jmdn./etw.** ∼ (geh.) declare one's support for/opposition to sb./sth.; (b) (seine Begründung finden) be explained; **das erklärt sich einfach/von selbst** that is easily explained/self-evident

erklärend *Adj.* explanatory; **mit einigen** ∼**en Worten** with a few words of explanation

erklärlich *Adj.* understandable; **es ist mir einfach nicht** ∼, **wie** …: I just can't understand how …

erklärt *Adj.; nicht präd.* declared ⟨*opponent, intention*⟩

Erklärung *die;* ~, ~**en** (a) explanation; (b) (Mitteilung) statement

Erklärungs·versuch *der* attempt at an explanation

erklecklich /ɛɐ̯'klɛklɪç/ *Adj.* considerable ⟨*sum, profit*⟩

erklettern *tr. V.* climb to the top of ⟨*rock, wall, mountain*⟩; climb to ⟨*summit*⟩

erklimmen *unr. tr. V.* (geh.) climb ⟨*wall, tree*⟩

erklingen *unr. itr. V.; mit sein* ring out

erkranken *itr. V.* ▶ 329 ; *mit sein* become ill (**an** + *Dat.* with); **er ist an einer Lungenentzündung erkrankt** he's got pneumonia; **schwer erkrankt sein** be seriously ill; **ein erkrankter Kollege** a sick colleague

Erkrankung *die;* ~, ~**en** ▶ 329 (eines Menschen, Tieres) illness; (eines Körperteils) disease

Erkrankungs·fall *der:* **im** ~: in event of illness

erkunden *tr. V.* reconnoitre ⟨*terrain*⟩; **die Situation** ~: find out what the situation is

erkundigen *refl. V.* **sich nach jmdm./etw.** ~: ask after sb./enquire about sth.; **sich** ~**, wann …:** enquire when …

Erkundigung *die;* ~, ~**en** enquiry; ~**en einholen** *od.* **einziehen** make enquiries

Erkundung *die;* ~, ~**en** (meist Milit.) reconnaissance; **auf** ~ **gehen** go out on reconnaissance

Erlag·schein /ɛɐ̯'la:k-/ *der* (österr.) ⇒ **Zahlkarte**

erlahmen *itr. V.; mit sein* tire; become tired; ⟨*strength*⟩ flag; ⟨*enthusiasm etc.*⟩ wane

erlangen *tr. V.* gain; obtain ⟨*credit, visa*⟩; reach ⟨*age*⟩

Erlass, ***Erlaß*** /ɛɐ̯'las/ *der;* **Erlasses, Erlasse** (a) (Anordnung) decree ⟨*Gen.* by⟩; (b) (Straf~, Schulden~ usw.) remission; (c) *o. Pl.* (eines Gesetzes, einer Bestimmung) enactment; (eines Dekrets) issue; (eines Verbots) imposition

erlassen *unr. tr. V.* (a) (verkünden) enact ⟨*law*⟩; declare ⟨*amnesty*⟩; issue ⟨*warrant*⟩; (b) remit ⟨*sentence*⟩

erlauben 1 *tr. V.* (a) allow; **jmdm.** ~**, etw. zu tun** allow sb. to do sth.; ~ **Sie mir, das Fenster zu öffnen?** (geh.) would you mind if I opened the window?; [**na,**] ~ **Sie mal!** (ugs.) do you mind! (coll.); (b) (ermöglichen) permit; **meine Zeit erlaubt es mir nicht** time does not allow. 2 *refl. V.* (a) (sich die Freiheit nehmen) **sich** (*Dat.*) **etw.** ~: permit oneself sth.; **sich** (*Dat.*) **Freiheiten** ~: take liberties; **sich** (*Dat.*) **über jmdn./etw. kein Urteil** ~ **können** not feel free to comment on sb./sth.; **sich** (*Dat.*) **einen Scherz** [**mit jmdm.**] ~: play a trick [on someone]; (b) (sich leisten) **sich** (*Dat.*) **etw.** ~: treat oneself to sth.

Erlaubnis *die;* ~, ~**se** permission; (Schriftstück) permit; **jmdn. um** ~ **bitten, etw. zu tun** ask sb.'s permission to do sth.; **jmdm. die** ~ **erteilen/verweigern, etw. zu tun** give/refuse sb. permission to do sth.

erläutern *tr. V.* explain; comment on ⟨*picture etc.*⟩; annotate ⟨*text*⟩; **näher** ~: clarify; ~**de Anmerkungen** explanatory notes

Erläuterung *die* explanation; (zu einem Bild usw.) commentary; (zu einem Text) [explanatory] note

Erle /'ɛrlə/ *die;* ~, ~**n** alder

erleben *tr. V.* experience; **etwas Schönes/Schreckliches** ~: have a pleasant/terrible experience; **das habe ich noch nie erlebt!** I've never heard of such a thing!; **große Abenteuer** ~: have great adventures; **so ängstlich hatte er sie noch nie erlebt** he had never seen her so afraid before; **etw. bewusst/intensiv** ~: be fully aware of sth./experience sth. to the full; **sie wünschte sich nur, die Hochzeit ihrer Tochter noch zu** ~: her only remaining wish was to be at her daughter's wedding; **er wird das nächste Jahr nicht mehr** ~: he won't see next year; **du kannst was** ~! (ugs.) you won't know what's hit you!

Erlebens·fall *der* (Versicherungsw.) **im** ~: in the event of survival; **eine Versicherung auf den** ~: endowment assurance

Erlebnis *das;* ~**ses**, ~**se** experience; **das war ein** ~: what an experience!

erledigen 1 *tr. V.* (a) **einen Auftrag** ~: deal with a task; **ich muss noch einige Dinge erledigen** I must see to a few things; **die Angelegenheit ist erledigt** the matter is settled; **sie hat alles pünktlich erledigt** she got everything done on time; **schon erledigt!** that's already done; (b) (erschöpfen) finish (coll.) ⟨*person*⟩; (ugs.: töten) knock off (sl.); (fig.: zerstören) destroy. 2 *refl. V.* ⟨*matter, problem*⟩ resolve itself; **damit hat sich die Sache erledigt** that's that; **sich von selbst** ~: sort it'self out

erledigt *Adj.* (a) closed ⟨*case*⟩; (b) (ugs.) worn out ⟨*person*⟩

Erledigung *die;* ~, ~**en** (a) *o. Pl.* carrying out; (Beendigung) completion; (einer Angelegenheit) settling; **um baldige** ~ **wird gebeten** please give this matter your prompt attention; (b) (Besorgung) **er hat einige** ~**en zu machen** he's got one or two things to see to

erlegen *tr. V.* (a) shoot ⟨*animal*⟩; (b) (österr.: entrichten) pay ⟨*fee, charge*⟩

erleichtern 1 *tr. V.* (a) (einfacher machen) make easier;' **jmdm./sich die Arbeit** ~: make sb.'s/one's work easier; (b) (befreien) relieve; **das hat ihn erleichtert** that came as a relief to him; **erleichtert aufatmen** breathe a sigh of relief; (c) (Gewicht verringern, fig.) lighten; **sein Herz/sein Gewissen** ~: open one's heart/unburden one's conscience; **jmdn. um etw.** ~ (ugs. scherzh.) relieve sb. of sth. 2 *refl. V.* (verhüll.: seine Notdurft verrichten) relieve oneself

Erleichterung *die;* ~, ~**en** (a) *o. Pl.* (Vereinfachung) **zur** ~ **der Arbeit** to make the work easier; (b) *o. Pl.* (Befreiung) relief; ~ **empfinden** feel relieved; (c) (Verbesserung, Milderung) alleviation

erleiden *unr. tr. V.* suffer

erlernen *tr. V.* learn

erlesen *Adj.* superior ⟨*wine*⟩; choice ⟨*dish*⟩; select ⟨*circle*⟩

erleuchten *tr. V.* (a) light; **Blitze erleuchteten den Himmel** the sky was lit up by flashes of lightning; **hell erleuchtet** brightly lit; (b) (geh.: inspirieren) inspire

Erleuchtung *die;* ~, ~**en** inspiration

erliegen *unr. itr. V.; mit sein* (a) succumb (*Dat.* to); **einem Irrtum** ~: be misled; (b) (zum Opfer fallen) **einer Krankheit** (*Dat.*) ~: die from an illness; (c) **zum Erliegen kommen** come to a standstill

erlisch /ɛɐ̯'lɪʃ/, **erlischst, erlischt** *Imperativ, 2. u. 3. Pers. Sg. Präsens v.* **erlöschen**

erlogen *Adj.* made up; untruthful ⟨*story*⟩

Erlös /ɛɐ̯'lø:s/ *der;* ~**es**, ~**e** proceeds *pl.*

erlosch /ɛɐ̯'lɔʃ/ *1. u. 3. Pers. Sg. Präteritum v.* **erlöschen**

erloschen *2. Part. v.* **erlöschen**

erlöschen *unr. itr. V.; mit sein* (a) ⟨*fire*⟩ go out; **ein erloschener Vulkan** an extinct volcano; **die Lichter waren schon erloschen** the lights were already out; (b) (fig.) ⟨*hope, feelings*⟩ wane; ⟨*family, clan*⟩ die out; ⟨*claim, obligation*⟩ cease; ⟨*firm, membership*⟩ cease to exist

erlösen *tr. V.* save, rescue (**von** from); **jmdn. von seinen Schmerzen** ~: release sb. from pain; **und erlöse uns von dem Übel** *od.* **Bösen** (bibl.) and deliver us from evil

erlösend *Adj.* **das** ~**e Wort sprechen** say the magic word

Erlöser *der;* ~**s**, ~ (a) saviour; (b) (christl. Rel.) redeemer

Erlösung *die* release (**von** from); (christl. Rel.) redemption

ermächtigen *tr. V.* authorize

Ermächtigung *die;* ~, ~**en** authorization

ermahnen *tr. V.* admonish; tell (coll.); (warnen) warn

Ermahnung *die* admonition; (Warnung) warning

Ermang[e]lung *die;* ~: **in** ~ **einer Sache** (*Gen.*) (geh.) in the absence of sth.; **in** ~ **eines Besseren** for lack of anything better

ermannen *refl. V.* (geh.) **sich** ~, **etw. zu tun** pluck up courage to do sth.

---

*alte Schreibung (vgl. Hinweise auf S. xvi–xvii)

ermäßigen 1 *tr. V.* reduce. **2** *refl. V.* be reduced
Ermäßigung *die* reduction
ermatten (geh.) **1** *itr. V.; mit sein* ‹person› become exhausted; (fig.) ‹enthusiasm› wane. **2** *tr. V.* exhaust, tire ‹person›
ermessen *unr. tr. V.* estimate, gauge ‹consequences›
Ermessen *das;* ∼s estimation; **nach eigenem** ∼: in one's own estimation; **in jmds.** ∼ (*Dat.*) **liegen** be at sb.'s discretion; **nach menschlichem** ∼: as far as anyone can judge
Ermessens-:   ∼**frage** *die* matter of discretion; ∼**spielraum** *der* powers *pl.* of discretion
ermitteln 1 *tr. V.* (a) ascertain, determine ‹facts›; discover ‹culprit, hideout, address›; establish, determine ‹identity, origin›; decide ‹winner›; (b) (errechnen) calculate ‹quota, rates, data›. **2** *itr. V.* investigate; **gegen jmdn.** ∼: investigate sb.; **in einer Sache** ∼: investigate sth.
Ermittlung *die;* ∼, ∼en (a) ⇒ **ermitteln a:** ascertainment; determination; discovery; establishment; **die** ∼ **eines Gewinners** deciding a winner; (b) *meist Pl.* (der Polizei, Staatsanwaltschaft) investigation
Ermittlungs-:   ∼**arbeit** *die* investigatory work; ∼**beamte** *der* investigating officer; ∼**verfahren** *das* (Rechtsw.) preliminary inquiry
ermöglichen *tr. V.* enable; **jmdm. etw.** ∼: make sth. possible for sb.; **es jmdm.** ∼, **etw. zu tun** enable sb. to do sth.
ermorden *tr. V.* murder; (aus politischen Gründen) assassinate
Ermordung *die;* ∼, ∼en ⇒ **ermorden:** murder; assassination
ermüden 1 *itr. V.; mit sein* tire; become tired. **2** *tr. V.* tire; make tired
ermüdend *Adj.* tiring
Ermüdung *die;* ∼, ∼en tiredness
ermuntern *tr. V.* encourage; **jmdn. zu etw.** ∼, **jmdn. [dazu]** ∼, **etw. zu tun** encourage sb. to do sth.
ermunternd *Adj.* encouraging
Ermunterung *die;* ∼, ∼en (a) encouragement; **zur** ∼: to encourage; (b) (ermunternde Worte) words *pl.* of encouragement
ermutigen *tr. V.* ⇒ **ermuntern a**
ermutigend *Adj.* encouraging
Ermutigung *die;* ∼, ∼en ⇒ **Ermunterung**
ernähren 1 *tr. V.* (a) feed ‹young, child›; **mit der Flasche ernährt werden** be bottle-fed; (b) (unterhalten) keep ‹family, wife›. **2** *refl. V.* feed oneself; **sich von etw.** ∼: live on sth.; ‹animal› feed on sth.
Ernährer *der;* ∼s, ∼, **Ernährerin** *die;* ∼, ∼nen breadwinner; provider
Ernährung *die;* ∼: (a) feeding; (b) (Ernährungsweise) diet; **gesunde/ungesunde** ∼: a healthy/an unhealthy diet
Ernährungs-: ∼**weise** *die* diet; ∼**wissenschaft** *die* dietetics *sing., no art.*
ernennen *unr. tr. V.* appoint ‹deputy, ambassador, etc.›; **jmdn. zu etw.** ∼: make sb. sth.
Ernennung *die* appointment (**zu** as)
erneuern 1 *tr. V.* (a) (auswechseln) replace; (b) (wiederherstellen) renovate ‹roof, building›; (fig.) thoroughly reform ‹system›; (c) (verlängern lassen) extend, renew ‹permit, licence, contract›. **2** *refl. V.* ‹nature, growth› renew itself
Erneuerung *die* (a) (Auswechslung) replacement; (b) (Wiederherstellung) renovation; (fig.) thorough reform; **demokratische/religiöse** ∼: democratic/religious revival; (c) (Verlängerung eines Vertrages usw.) renewal; extension
erneut 1 *Adj.; nicht präd.* renewed. **2** *adv.* once again
erniedrigen *tr. V.* humiliate; **sich [selbst]** ∼: lower oneself
erniedrigend *Adj.* humiliating
Erniedrigung *die;* ∼, ∼en humiliation
ernst /ɛrnst/ **1** *Adj.* (a) serious ‹face, expression, music, doubts›; (b) (aufrichtig) genuine ‹intention, offer›; (c) (schlimm) serious ‹injury›; grave ‹situation›. **2** *adv.* seriously; **jmdn./etw.** ∼ **nehmen** take sb./sth. seriously; ∼

gemeinte Angebote serious offers; ∼ **gemeinte Wünsche** sincere wishes
Ernst *der;* ∼[e]s (a) seriousness; **das ist mein [voller]** ∼: I mean that [quite] seriously; **es ist mir [bitterer]** ∼ **damit** I'm [deadly] serious about it; **allen** ∼**es** in all seriousness; (b) **daraus wurde** [blutiger/bitterer] ∼: it became [deadly] serious; **der** ∼ **des Lebens** the serious side of life; **der** ∼ **der Lage** the seriousness of the situation; **er wird mit seiner Drohung** ∼ **machen** he will carry out his threat; **er wird** ∼ **machen** he will carry it out; (c) (gemessene Haltung) gravity
Ernst·fall *der;* **im** ∼: when the real thing happens
*ernst·gemeint ⇒ **ernst 2**
ernsthaft 1 *Adj.* serious; **etwas/nichts Ernsthaftes** something/nothing serious. **2** *adv.* seriously
Ernsthaftigkeit *die;* ∼: seriousness
ernstlich 1 *Adj.* serious; genuine ‹wish›. **2** *adv.* seriously; genuinely ‹sorry, repentant›
Ernte /'ɛrntə/ *die;* ∼, ∼n (a) harvest; **bei der** ∼ **sein** be bringing in the harvest; **während der** ∼: at harvest time; (b) (Ertrag) crop; **die** ∼ **einbringen** bring in the harvest
Ernte-: ∼**aus·fall** *der* crop failure; ∼**dank·fest** *das* harvest festival; ∼**ertrag** *der* yield; ∼**maschine** *die* harvester
ernten *tr. V.* harvest ‹cereal, fruit›; (fig.) get ‹mockery, ingratitude›; win ‹fame, praise›
ernüchtern *tr. V.* (a) sober up; (b) (fig.) **jmdn. [völlig]** ∼: bring sb. down to earth [with a bang]; ∼**d** sobering
Ernüchterung *die;* ∼, ∼en (fig.) disillusionment
Eroberer /ǀoːbərə/ *der;* ∼s, ∼, **Eroberin** *die;* ∼, ∼nen conqueror
erobern *tr. V.* (a) conquer ‹country›; take ‹town, fortress›; (b) (fig.) conquer ‹woman, market›; seize ‹power›; [sich (*Dat.*)] **die Herzen** ∼: win hearts; **eine Stadt/ein Land** ∼ (scherzh.) take a town/country by storm
Eroberung *die;* ∼, ∼en (auch fig. scherzh.) conquest; (einer Stadt, Festung) taking; (der Macht) seizing; ∼**en machen** make conquests
eröffnen 1 *tr. V.* (a) open ‹shop, gallery, account›; start ‹business, practice›; (b) (beginnen) open ‹meeting, conference›; begin ‹event›; **das Feuer** ∼: open fire; (c) **jmdm. etw.** ∼ (mitteilen) reveal sth. to sb.; (d) **ein Testament** ∼: read a will; (e) (Rechtsw., Wirtsch.) **den Konkurs** ∼: institute bankruptcy proceedings; **das Verfahren** ∼: begin proceedings; (f) **jmdm. neue Möglichkeiten** ∼: open up new possibilities to sb.. **2** *refl. V.* (sich bieten) **sich jmdm.** ∼ ‹opportunity, possibility› present itself
Eröffnung *die* (a) opening; (einer Sitzung) start; (einer Schachpartie) opening [move]; (b) (Mitteilung) revelation; (c) (Testaments∼) reading; (d) (Wirtsch.) **die** ∼ **des Konkurses** the institution of bankruptcy proceedings
Eröffnungs-: ∼**an·sprache** *die* opening speech; ∼**feier** *die* opening ceremony
erogen /ǀero'geːn/ *Adj.* erogenous
erörtern /ɛɐ'œrtɛn/ *tr. V.* discuss
Erörterung *die;* ∼, ∼en discussion
Erosion /ǀero'zjoːn/ *die;* ∼, ∼en erosion
Erotik /ǀe'roːtɪk/ *die;* ∼: eroticism
erotisch 1 *Adj.* erotic. **2** *adv.* erotically
erotisieren *tr. V.* arouse sexual desire in; ∼**d wirken** have an erotic effect
Erotomane /ǀeroto'maːnə/ *der;* ∼n, ∼n erotomaniac
Erpel /'ɛrpl/ *der;* ∼s, ∼: drake
erpicht /ɛɐ'pɪçt/ *Adj.:* **auf etw.** (*Akk.*) ∼ **sein** be keen on sth.
erpressen *tr. V.* (a) blackmail ‹person›; (b) extort ‹money, confession› (**von** from)
Erpresser *der;* ∼s, ∼, **Erpresserin** *die;* ∼, ∼nen blackmailer
erpresserisch *Adj.* blackmailing *attrib.;* **in** ∼**er Absicht** for the purpose of blackmail
Erpressung *die* blackmail *no indef. art.;* (von Geld, Geständnis) extortion

erproben *tr. V.* test ⟨*medicine*⟩ (**an** + *Akk.* on); put ⟨*reliability etc.*⟩ to the test; **ein erprobter Soldat** an experienced soldier

Erprobung *die;* ~, ~**en** testing

erquicken /ɛɐ̯'kvɪkn̩/ *tr. V.* (geh.) refresh

erquickend *Adj.* (geh.) refreshing

erraten *unr. tr. V.* guess

errechenbar *Adj.* calculable

errechnen *tr., auch itr. V.* calculate

erregbar *Adj.* excitable

erregen 1 *tr. V.* (a) annoy; (b) (sexuell) arouse; (c) (verursachen) arouse; **Ärgernis/Aufsehen** ~: cause annoyance/a stir. **2** *refl. V.* **sich über etw.** (*Akk.*) ~: get excited about sth.

erregend *Adj.* exciting; (sexuell) arousing

Erreger *der;* ~**s**, ~ (Med.) pathogen

erregt *Adj.* excited; hot ⟨*temper*⟩ (sexuell) aroused

Erregung *die* (a) excitement; (sexuell) arousal; **in** ~ **geraten** become excited; (b) ~ **öffentlichen Ärgernisses** (Rechtsspr.) causing a public nuisance

erreichbar *Adj.* (a) within reach *postpos.;* reachable; **der Ort ist mit dem Auto/Zug** ~: the place can be reached by car/train; **leicht** ~ **sein** be easy to reach; (b) **er ist [telefonisch]** ~: he can be contacted [by telephone]

erreichen *tr. V.* (a) reach; **den Zug** ~: catch the train; **etw. ist zu Fuß zu** ~: sth. can be reached on foot; (b) **er ist telefonisch zu** ~: he can be contacted by telephone; (c) achieve ⟨*goal, aim*⟩; **[bei jmdm.] etwas/nichts** ~: get somewhere/not get anywhere [with sb.]

erretten *tr. V.* (geh.) save

Erretter *der* (geh.) saviour

errichten *tr. V.* (a) build ⟨*house, bridge, etc.*⟩; (b) erect, put up ⟨*rostrum, barrier, etc.*⟩; (c) found ⟨*company*⟩; set up ⟨*fund*⟩

erringen *unr. tr. V.* gain ⟨*victory*⟩; reach ⟨*first etc. place*⟩; win ⟨*majority*⟩; gain, win ⟨*sb.'s trust*⟩

erröten *itr. V.; mit sein* blush (**vor** with)

Errungenschaft /ɛɐ̯'rʊŋənʃaft/ *die;* ~, ~**en** achievement

Ersatz *der;* ~**es** (a) replacement; (nicht gleichartig) substitute; **als** ~ **für jmdn.** in place of sb.; (b) (Entschädigung) compensation

ersatz-, Ersatz-: ~**befriedigung** *die* (Psych.) vicarious satisfaction; ~**dienst** *der community service as an alternative to military service;* ~**kasse** *die* private health insurance company; ~**los 1** *Adj.* without replacement *postpos.;* **2** *adv.* **etw.** ~**los streichen** cancel sth.; ~**mann** *der; Pl.* ~**männer**, ~**leute** replacement (Sport) substitute; ~**spieler** *der* (Sport) substitute [player]; ~**teil** *das* spare part; spare (Brit.); ~**weise** *Adv.* as an alternative

Ersatzteil-: ~**lager** *das* [spares] store; ~**medizin** *die* spare-part surgery

ersaufen *unr. itr. V.; mit sein* (salopp) drown

ersäufen /ɛɐ̯'zɔyfn̩/ *tr. V.* drown; **seinen Kummer [im Alkohol]** ~ (fig.) drown one's sorrows [in drink]

erschaffen *unr. tr. V.* create

Erschaffung *die* creation

erschallen *unr. od. regelm. itr. V.; mit sein* ⟨*song, call*⟩ ring out; ⟨*music*⟩ sound

erschaudern *itr. V.; mit sein* (geh.) shudder (**bei** at)

erschauern *itr. V.; mit sein* (geh.) tremble (**vor** + *Dat.* with)

erscheinen *unr. itr. V.; mit sein* (a) appear; **jmdm.** ~: appear to sb.; **vor Gericht** ~: appear in court; **um rechtzeitiges/zahlreiches Erscheinen wird gebeten** a punctual arrival/a full turnout is requested; (b) ⟨*newspaper, periodical*⟩ appear; ⟨*book*⟩ be published; (c) (zu sein scheinen) seem (*Dat.* to)

Erscheinung *die;* ~, ~**en** (a) (Phänomen) phenomenon; **in** ~ **treten** become evident; (b) (äußere Gestalt) appearance; **eine stattliche/elegante** ~ **sein** be an imposing/elegant figure; (c) (Vision) apparition; **eine** ~/~**en haben** see a vision/visions

Erscheinungs-: ~**bild** *das* appearance; ~**form** *die* manifestation; ~**jahr** *das* year of publication

erschießen *unr. tr. V.* shoot dead; **Tod durch Erschießen** death by firing squad; **erschossen sein** (fig. ugs.) be completely whacked (Brit. coll.)

Erschießung *die;* ~, ~**en** shooting

Erschießungs·kommando *das* firing squad

erschlaffen *itr. V.; mit sein* (a) ⟨*muscle, limb*⟩ become limp; (fig.) ⟨*resistance, will*⟩ weaken; (b) ⟨*skin*⟩ grow slack

erschlagen[1] *unr. tr. V.* strike dead; kill; **jmdn. mit Argumenten** ~ (fig.) defeat sb. with arguments

erschlagen[2] *Adj.* (ugs.) (a) (erschöpft) worn out; (b) (verblüfft) **wie** ~ **sein** be flabbergasted (coll.) *or* thunderstruck

erschleichen *unr. refl. V.* (abwertend) **sich** (*Dat.*) **etw.** ~: get sth. by devious means

erschließen 1 *unr. tr. V.* (a) (zugänglich machen) develop ⟨*area, building land*⟩; open up ⟨*market*⟩; (fig.) make sth. accessible to sb.; (b) (nutzbar machen) tap ⟨*resources, energy sources*⟩; (c) (ermitteln) deduce ⟨*meaning, wording*⟩. **2** *unr. refl. V.* **sich jmdm.** ~: become accessible to sb.

Erschließung *die* (a) (eines Gebiets, von Bauland) development; (von Märkten) opening up; (b) (von Rohstoffen) tapping

erschöpfen 1 *tr. V.* (auch fig.) exhaust. **2** *refl. V.* **darin** ~ **sich ihre Kenntnisse** her knowledge does not go beyond that

erschöpfend 1 *Adj.* exhaustive. **2** *adv.* exhaustively

erschöpft *Adj.* exhausted

Erschöpfung *die* exhaustion; **bis zur** ~: to the point of exhaustion

erschrecken[1] *unr. itr. V.; mit sein* be startled; **vor etw.** (*Dat.*) *od.* **über etw.** (*Akk.*) ~: be startled by sth.

erschrecken[2] *tr. V.* frighten; scare; **du hast mich erschreckt!** you gave me a scare

erschrecken[3] *unr. od. regelm. refl. V.* get a fright; **erschrick dich nicht!** don't be frightened

erschreckend *Adj.* **1** alarming. **2** *adv.* alarmingly

erschrocken *Adj.* frightened; **sie wandte sich** ~ **ab** she turned away in fright

erschüttern *tr. V.* (auch fig.) shake; **über etw.** (*Akk.*) **erschüttert sein** be shaken by sth.; **das kann mich nicht** ~ (ugs.) that doesn't worry me

erschütternd *Adj.* deeply distressing ⟨*account, picture, news*⟩; deeply shocking ⟨*conditions*⟩

Erschütterung *die;* ~, ~**en** (a) vibration; (der Erde) tremor; **wirtschaftliche** ~**en** (fig.) economic upheavals; (b) (Ergriffenheit) shock; (Trauer) distress

erschweren *tr. V.* **etw.** ~: make sth. more difficult; **etw. durch etw.** ~: impede *or* hinder sth. by sth.

erschwerend 1 *Adj.* complicating ⟨*factor*⟩. **2** *adv.* **es kommt** ~ **hinzu, dass er ...:** to make matters worse he ...; **das kommt** ~ **hinzu** that is an added problem

Erschwerung *die;* ~, ~**en** impediment (*für* to); **das ist eine** ~ **seiner Arbeit** that makes his job more difficult

erschwindeln *refl. V.* get by swindling; **sich** (*Dat.*) **etw. von jmdm.** ~: swindle sb. out of sth.

erschwinglich *Adj.* reasonable ⟨*price*⟩; affordable ⟨*rent*⟩; **für jmdn. nicht** ~ **sein** not be within sb.'s reach

ersehen *unr. tr. V.* see; **aus etw. [klar] zu** ~ **sein** be evident from sth.

ersehnen *tr. V.* (geh.) long for

ersetzbar *Adj.* replaceable

ersetzen *tr. V.* (a) replace; **etw./jmdn. durch etw./jmdn.** ~: replace sth./sb. by sth./sb.; **Talent durch Fleiß** ~: substitute hard work for talent; (b) (erstatten) reimburse ⟨*expenses etc.*⟩; **jmdm. einen Schaden** ~: compensate sb. for damages

Ersetzung *die;* ~, ~**en** (Erstattung) reimbursement; **die** ~ **von Schäden** compensation for damage

---

*alte Schreibung (vgl. Hinweise auf S. xvi–xvii)

ersichtlich *Adj.* apparent

ersinnen *unr. tr. V.* (geh.) devise

ersparen *tr. V.* (a) save ⟨*money*⟩; **mein erspartes Geld** *od.* **Erspartes** my savings; (b) jmdm./sich etw. ∼: save *or* spare sb./oneself sth.; **das würde mir viel Arbeit** ∼: that would save me a lot of work; **es bleibt einem nichts erspart** (ugs.) at least I/you *etc.* could have been spared that

Ersparnis *die;* ∼, ∼se (a) (österr. auch das; ∼ses, ∼se) (ersparte Summe) savings *pl.;* (b) (Einsparung) saving

Ersparnis·kasse *die* (schweiz.) savings bank

erst /eːɐ̯st/ 1 *Adv.* (a) (zu∼) first; ∼ **einmal** first [of all]; ∼ **noch** first; **eine solche Frau muss** ∼ **noch geboren werden** such a woman has not yet been born; (b) (nicht aber als) **eben** ∼: not only just; **er will** ∼ **in drei Tagen/einer Stunde zurückkommen** he won't be back for three days/an hour; ∼ **nächste Woche/um 12 Uhr** not until next week/12 o'clock; **er war** ∼ **zufrieden, als** ...: he was not satisfied until ...; (c) (noch nicht mehr als) only; ∼ **eine Stunde/halb soviel** only an hour/half as much; **sie ist mit ihrer Arbeit** ∼ **am Anfang** she is only just beginning her work. 2 *Partikel* **so was lese ich gar nicht** ∼: I don't even start reading that sort of stuff; **jetzt tue ich es** ∼ **recht!** that makes me even more determined to do it

erst... *Ordinalz.* ▶ 119 | (a) ▶ 600 | first; **der** ∼**e Stock** the first *or* (Amer.) second floor; **etw. das** ∼**e Mal tun** do sth. for the first time; **am Ersten [des Monats]** on the first [of the month]; **als Erstes** first of all; **als Erster/Erste etw. tun** be the first to do sth.; **Karl der Erste** Charles the First; **fürs Erste** for the moment; **sie kam als Erste ins Ziel** she was the first to reach the finish; (b) (best...) **das** ∼**e Hotel** the best hotel

erstarren *itr. V.; mit sein* (a) ⟨*jelly, plaster*⟩ set; (b) ⟨*limbs, fingers*⟩ grow stiff; (c) **vor Schreck/Entsetzen** ∼: be paralysed by fear/with horror

erstatten *tr. V.* (a) reimburse ⟨*expenses*⟩; (b) **Anzeige gegen jmdn.** ∼: report sb. [to the police]; **jmdm. Bericht über etw.** (*Akk.*) ∼: report on sth. to sb.

Erstattung *die;* ∼, ∼en (a) (von Kosten) reimbursement; (b) **die** ∼ **einer Anzeige** the reporting of sth. [to the police]

Erst-: ∼**aufführung** *die* première; ∼**auflage** *die* first impression

erstaunen *tr. V.* astonish; amaze; **es erstaunte ihn nicht** he wasn't surprised

Erstaunen *das;* ∼s astonishment; amazement; **jmdn. in** ∼ **versetzen** astonish *or* amaze sb.

erstaunlich 1 *Adj.* astonishing, amazing ⟨*achievement, number, amount*⟩. 2 *adv.* astonishingly; amazingly

erstaunlicher·weise *Adv.* astonishingly *or* amazingly [enough]

erstaunt *Adj.* astonished; amazed

erst-, Erst-: ∼**aus·gabe** *die* first edition; ∼**best...** *Adj.* der/die/das ∼**beste** ... the first suitable ...; **der** ∼**beste Wagen, der ihr angeboten wurde** the first car she was offered

erstechen *unr. tr. V.* stab [to death]

erstehen 1 *unr. tr. V.* (geh.: kaufen) purchase. 2 *unr. itr. V.; mit sein* (geh.) (a) (entstehen) ⟨*difficulties, problems*⟩ arise; (b) (auferstehen) rise

Erste-Hilfe-Ausrüstung *die* first-aid kit

ersteigen *unr. tr. V.* climb

ersteigern *tr. V.* buy [at an auction]

Ersteigung *die* ascent

erstellen *tr. V.* (Papierdt.) (a) (bauen) build; (b) (anfertigen) make ⟨*assessment*⟩; draw up ⟨*plan, report, list*⟩

***erste·mal,** ***ersten·mal** ⇒ **Mal¹**

erstens /ˈeːɐ̯stn̩s/ *Adv.* firstly; in the first place

erster... /ˈeːɐ̯stɐ.../ *Adj.* ∼**er**/∼**e**/∼**es** ... the former ...; **der/die/das Erstere** the former

Erste[r]-Klasse-Abteil *das* first-class compartment

erst-: ∼**geboren** *Adj.; nicht präd.* first-born; **der/die Erstgeborene** the first-born child; ∼**genannt** *Adj.; nicht präd.* mentioned first *postpos.*

ersticken 1 *itr. V.; mit sein* suffocate; (sich verschlucken) choke; **an einem Knochen** ∼: choke on a bone; **vor Lachen** ∼ (ugs.) choke with laughter; **zum Ersticken sein** ⟨*heat*⟩ be stifling; **in Arbeit** ∼ (ugs.) be swamped with work. 2 *tr. V.* (a) suffocate; **der Widerstand wurde erstickt** (fig.) resistance was suppressed; **etw. sofort** *od.* **im Keim** ∼ (fig.) nip sth. in the bud; (b) (löschen) smother ⟨*flames*⟩

Erstickung *die;* ∼: suffocation; asphyxiation

Erstickungs-: ∼**gefahr** *die* danger of suffocation; ∼**tod** *der* death from suffocation

erst-, Erst-: ∼**klassig** 1 *Adj.* first-class; ∼**klassige Bedingungen** excellent conditions; 2 *adv.* superbly; **da kann man** ∼**klassig essen** you can get a first-class meal there; ∼**klässler**, *∼**kläßler** *der;* ∼**s**, ∼ (südd., schweiz.) *pupil in first class of primary school;* first-year pupil; ∼**kommunion** *die* (kath. Rel.) first communion

Erstling *der;* ∼**s**, ∼**e** first work

Erstlings-: ∼**film** *der* first film; ∼**roman** *der* first novel; ∼**werk** *das* first work

erstmalig 1 *Adj.* first. 2 *adv.* for the first time

erstmals *Adv.* for the first time

erstrahlen *itr. V.; mit sein* shine

erstrangig *Adj.* (a) (vordringlich) of top priority *postpos.;* **von** ∼**er Bedeutung** of the utmost importance; (b) ⇒ **erstklassig 1**

erstreben *tr. V.* strive for

erstrebens·wert *Adj.* ⟨*ideals etc.*⟩ worth striving for; desirable ⟨*situation*⟩

erstrecken *refl. V.* (a) stretch; **sich bis an etw.** (*Akk.*) ∼: extend as far as sth.; **sich über ein Gebiet** ∼: extend over *or* cover an area; (b) (dauern) **sich über 10 Jahre** ∼: carry on for 10 years; (c) (betreffen) **sich auf jmdn./etw.** ∼: affect sb./sth.; ⟨*laws, regulations*⟩ apply to sb./sth.

Erst-: ∼**schlag** *der* first strike; ∼**schlag·waffe** *die* first-strike weapon; ∼**stimme** *die* first vote

Ersttags-: ∼**brief** *der* (Philat.) first-day cover; ∼**stempel** *der* (Philat.) first-day stamp

erstunken /ɛɐ̯ˈʃtʊŋkn̩/: ∼ **und erlogen sein** (salopp) be a pack of lies

erstürmen *tr. V.* take ⟨*fortress, town*⟩ by storm

Erst·wähler *der* first-time voter

ersuchen *tr. V.* (geh.) ask; **jmdn. um etw.** ∼: request sth. of sb.; **jmdn.** ∼, **etw. zu tun** request sb. to do sth.

Ersuchen *das;* ∼**s**, ∼: request (**an** + *Akk.* to); **auf** ∼ **von** .../**des** ...: at the request of ...

ertappen *tr. V.* catch ⟨*thief, burglar*⟩; **jmdn. dabei** ∼, **wie er etw. tut** catch sb. in the act of doing sth.; **sich bei etw.** ∼: catch oneself doing sth.; *s. auch* **frisch 1 a**

erteilen *tr. V.* give ⟨*advice, information*⟩; give, grant ⟨*permission*⟩; **Unterricht** ∼: teach; **Deutschunterricht** ∼: give German lessons

Erteilung *die* giving; (einer Genehmigung) granting

ertönen *itr. V.; mit sein* sound

Ertrag /ɛɐ̯ˈtraːk/ *der;* ∼**[e]s**, **Erträge** /ɛɐ̯ˈtrɛːɡə/ yield

ertragen *unr. tr. V.* bear ⟨*pain, shame, uncertainty*⟩; **es ist nicht mehr zu** ∼: I can't stand it any longer

erträglich /ɛɐ̯ˈtrɛːklɪç/ 1 *Adj.* (a) bearable ⟨*pain*⟩; tolerable ⟨*conditions, climate*⟩; **die Grenze des Erträglichen erreichen** be as much as one can endure; (b) (ugs.: annehmbar) tolerable. 2 *adv.* (ugs.: annehmbar) tolerably

ertrag·reich *Adj.* lucrative ⟨*business*⟩; productive ⟨*land, soil*⟩

Ertrag[s]·steuer *die* (Wirtsch.) tax on profits

ertränken *tr. V.* drown; **seinen Kummer [im Alkohol]** ∼ (fig.) drown one's sorrows [in drink]

erträumen *refl. V.* dream of

ertrinken *unr. itr. V.; mit sein* be drowned; drown; (fig.) be inundated

Ertrinkende *der/die; adj. Dekl.* drowning person

Ertrunkene *der/die; adj. Dekl.* drowned person

ertüchtigen 1 *tr. V.* toughen up ⟨*body*⟩. 2 *refl. V.* **sich körperlich** ∼: get/keep oneself fit

Ertüchtigung *die;* ∼, ∼**en** getting/keeping fit

erübrigen 1 *tr. V.* spare ‹*money, time*›; **etw. Geld/Zeit** ∼ **können** have some money/time to spare. **2** *refl. V.* be unnecessary; **es erübrigt sich, etw. zu tun** there's no point in doing sth.

eruieren /eru'i:rən/ *tr. V.* (geh.) find out; **jmdn.** ∼: (österr.) trace sb.

Eruierung *die;* ∼, ∼**en** (geh.) investigation; **die** ∼ **des Täters** (österr.) the tracing of the culprit

Eruption /erʊp'tsi̯o:n/ *die;* ∼, ∼**en** (Geol., Med.) eruption

erwachen *itr. V.; mit sein* (geh.) awake; wake up; (fig.) awake; **aus tiefem Schlaf** ∼: awake from a deep sleep; **aus der Narkose** ∼: come round; **ein neuer Tag erwacht** (geh.) a new day dawns

Erwachen *das;* ∼**s** (auch fig.) awakening; **es wird ein böses** ∼ **[für ihn] geben** (fig.) it'll be a rude awakening [for him]

erwachsen[1] *unr. itr. V.; mit sein* (a) grow (**aus** out of); (b) (sich ergeben) ‹*difficulties, tasks*› arise

erwachsen[2] **1** *Adj.* grown-up *attrib.;* ∼ **sein** be grown up. **2** *adv.* ‹*behave*› in an adult way

Erwachsene *der/die; adj. Dekl.* adult; grown-up

Erwachsenen·bildung *die; o. Pl.* adult education *no art.*

Erwachsen·sein *das* being an adult/adults *no art.*

erwägen *unr. tr. V.* consider

Erwägung *die;* ∼, ∼**en** consideration; **etw. in** ∼ **ziehen** consider sth.; take sth. into consideration

erwählen *tr. V.* (geh.) choose

Erwählte *der/die; adj. Dekl.* (Freund[in]) sweetheart; (Bevorrechtigte) **er gehört zu den wenigen** ∼**n** he belongs to the select few

erwähnen *tr. V.* mention; **etw. mit keinem Wort** ∼: make no mention of sth.; **jmdn. lobend** ∼: speak in praise of sb.

erwähnens·wert *Adj.* worth mentioning *postpos.*

Erwähnung *die;* ∼, ∼**en** mention; ∼ **verdienen** be worth mentioning

erwandern *tr., refl. V.* **er hat [sich** (*Dat.*)**] ganz Frankreich erwandert** he's walked all round France

erwärmen 1 *tr. V.* (a) heat; (b) **jmdn. für etw.** ∼ (fig.) win sb. over to sth. **2** *refl. V.* (a) warm up; (b) **sich für jmdn./etw.** ∼ (fig.) warm to sb./sth.

erwarten *tr. V.* (a) expect ‹*guests, phone call, post*›; **etw. ungeduldig/sehnlich** ∼: wait impatiently/eagerly for sth; **jmdn. am Bahnhof** ∼: wait for sb. at the station; **wir** ∼ **ihn um 7 Uhr** we are expecting him at 7 o'clock; **ein Kind** ∼: be expecting a baby; be expecting (coll.); (b) (rechnen mit) **etw. von jmdm.** ∼: expect sth. of sb.; **von jmdm.** ∼, **dass er etw. tut** expect sb. to do sth.; **es ist** *od.* (geh.) **steht zu** ∼, **daß** …: it is to be expected that …; **wider Erwarten** contrary to expectation; **[sich** (*Dat.*)**] von etw. viel/wenig/nichts** ∼: expect a lot/little/nothing from sth.

Erwartung *die;* ∼, ∼**en** expectation; ∼**en in etw.** (*Akk.*) **setzen** have expectations of sth.; **in freudiger** ∼: in joyful anticipation; **die** ∼**en [nicht] erfüllen** [not] come up to one's expectations

erwartungs-: ∼**gemäß** *Adv.* as expected; ∼**voll 1** *Adj.* expectant; **2** *adv.* expectantly

erwecken *tr. V.* (a) resurrect; (b) (fig.) arouse ‹*longing, mistrust, pity*›; **den Eindruck** ∼, **als** …: give the impression that …

Erweckung *die;* ∼, ∼**en** (a) resurrection; (b) (fig.) arousal

erwehren *refl. V.* (geh.) **sich jmds./einer Sache** ∼: fend *or* ward sb./sth. off; **sie konnte sich des Gefühls/des Eindrucks nicht** ∼, **dass** …: she could not help feeling/thinking that …

erweichen *tr. V.* soften; **jmdn./jmds. Herz** ∼ (fig.) soften sb.'s heart

Erweichung *die;* ∼, ∼**en** softening

erweisen 1 *unr. tr. V.* (a) prove; (b) **jmdm. Achtung** ∼: show respect to sb.; **jmdm. einen Gefallen** ∼: do sb. a favour. **2** *unr. refl. V.* **sich als etw.** ∼: prove to be sth.; **sich als falsch** ∼: prove false

erweitern 1 *tr. V.* widen ‹*river, road*›; expand ‹*library, business*›; enlarge ‹*collection*›; dilate ‹*pupil, blood vessel*›; extend ‹*power*›; broaden ‹*horizons, knowledge*›; **eine erweiterte Neuauflage** a new, expanded edition; **erweiterte Oberschule** (DDR) (Stufe) ≈ sixth form; (Schule) ≈ sixth-form college. **2** *refl. V.* ‹*road, river*› widen; ‹*pupil, blood vessel*› dilate; **sich zu etw.** ∼: widen into sth.

Erweiterung *die;* ∼, ∼**en** ⇒ **erweitern:** widening; expansion; enlargement; dilation; extension; broadening

Erwerb /ɛg'vɛrp/ *der;* ∼**[e]s** (a) **der** ∼ **des Lebensunterhaltes** earning a living; (b) (Arbeit) occupation; **ohne** ∼ **sein** be unemployed; (c) (Aneignung) acquisition; (d) (Kauf) purchase

erwerben *unr. tr. V.* (a) (verdienen) earn; (fig.) win ‹*fame*›; **sich** (*Dat.*) **großen Ruhm** ∼: win great fame; (b) (sich aneignen) gain ‹*experience, influence*›; acquire, gain ‹*knowledge*›; (c) acquire ‹*property, works of art, etc.*›; **etw. käuflich** ∼ (Papierdt.) purchase sth.; (d) (Biol., Psych.) acquire

erwerbs-, Erwerbs-: ∼**fähig** *Adj.* capable of gainful employment *postpos.;* able to work *postpos.;* ∼**fähigkeit** *die; o. Pl.* ability to work; ∼**leben** *das* working life; ∼**los** *Adj.;* ⇒ **arbeitslos;** ∼**lose** *der/die; adj. Dekl.;* ⇒ **Arbeitslose;** ∼**tätig** *Adj.* gainfully employed; ∼**tätige** *der/die; adj. Dekl.* person in work; **die** ∼**tätigen** those in work; ∼**unfähig** *Adj.* incapable of gainful employment *postpos.;* unable to work *postpos.;* ∼**unfähigkeit** *die* inability to work

Erwerbung *die* acquisition

erwidern /ɛg'vi:dən/ *tr. V.* (a) reply; **etw. auf etw.** (*Akk.*) ∼: say sth. in reply to sth.; (b) (reagieren auf) return ‹*greeting, visit*›; reciprocate ‹*sb.'s feelings*›

Erwiderung *die;* ∼, ∼**en** (Antwort) reply (**auf** + *Akk.* to); (b) ⇒ **erwidern b:** return; reciprocation

erwiesen *Adj.* proved; **eine** ∼**e Tatsache** a proven fact

erwiesener·maßen *Adv.* as has been proved; **er hat** ∼ **gelogen** it has been proved that he lied

erwirtschaften *tr. V.* **etw.** ∼: obtain sth. by careful management

erwischen *tr. V.* (ugs.) (a) (fassen, ertappen, erreichen) catch ‹*culprit, train, bus*›; **jmdn. beim Abschreiben** ∼: catch sb. copying; (b) (greifen) grab; **jmdn. am Ärmel** ∼: grab sb. by the sleeve; (c) (bekommen) manage to catch *or* get; (d) *unpers.* **es hat ihn erwischt** (ugs.) (er ist tot) he has bought it (sl.); (er ist krank) he has got it; (er ist verletzt) he's been hurt; (scherzh.: er ist verliebt) he's got it bad (coll.)

erwünscht /ɛg'vynʃt/ *Adj.* wanted; desired ‹*result*›

erwürgen *tr. V.* strangle

Erz /ɛrts *od.* e:ɐ̯ts/ *das;* ∼**es,** ∼**e** ore

erzählen *tr., auch itr. V.* tell ‹*joke, story*›; recount ‹*dream, experience*›; **jmdm. etw.** ∼: tell sb. sth.; **erzähl keine Märchen!** (ugs.) don't tell stories!; **jmdm. von etw.** ∼: tell sb. about sth.; **von etw.** ∼: talk about sth.; **etw. über jmdn.** ∼: tell sth. about sb.

Erzähler *der* (a) storyteller; **der** ∼ **eines Romans** the narrator of a novel; (b) (Autor) writer [of stories]; narrative writer

erzählerisch *Adj.* narrative *attrib.*

Erzählung *die;* ∼, ∼**en** (a) narration; (Bericht) account; (b) (Literaturw.) story; (märchenhafte Geschichte) tale

Erz-: ∼**bergbau** *der* ore-mining *no art.;* ∼**bergwerk** *das* ore mine; ∼**bischof** *der* archbishop; ∼**bistum** *das,* ∼**diözese** *die* archbishopric; archdiocese; ∼**engel** *der* archangel

erzeugen *tr. V.* (a) produce; generate ‹*electricity*›; (b) (österr.: anfertigen) manufacture

Erzeuger *der;* ∼**s,** ∼ (a) (Vater) father; (b) (Produzent) producer; (c) (österr.: Hersteller) manufacturer

Erzeuger-: ∼**land** *das* country of origin; ∼**preis** *der* manufacturer's price

---

Erzeugnis das (auch fig.) product; **landwirtschaftliche** ~se agricultural products or produce

Erzeugung die (a) (von Lebensmitteln usw.) production; (von Industriewaren) manufacture; (von Strom) generation; (b) (österr.: Herstellung) manufacture

erz-, Erz-: ~**feind** der arch enemy; ~**gang** der lode of ore; ~**grube** die ore mine; ~**haltig** Adj. ore-bearing; ~**herzog** der archduke; ~**herzogin** die archduchess; ~**hütte** die ore-smelting works sing.

erziehbar Adj. educable; **der Junge ist sehr schwer** ~: the boy is a very difficult child

erziehen unr. tr. V. (a) bring up; (in der Schule) educate; **ein Kind streng/sehr frei** ~: give a child a strict/very liberal upbringing/education; **gut/schlecht erzogen sein** have been brought up/not have been brought up properly; (b) jmdn. **zum Verbrecher** ~: bring sb. up to criminal ways; **ein Kind zur Ordnung** ~: bring a child up to be tidy; **jmdn./sich dazu** ~, **etw. zu tun** train sb./oneself to do sth.

Erzieher der; ~**s**, ~, **Erzieherin** die; ~, ~**nen** ▶ 85 | educator; (Lehrer[in]) teacher; (Kindergärtner[in]) nursery-school teacher

erzieherisch ⇒ pädagogisch 1, 2

Erziehung die; o. Pl. (a) upbringing; (Schul~) education; (b) (Manieren) upbringing; breeding; **seine gute** ~ **vergessen** (fig.) forget oneself

erziehungs-, Erziehungs-: ~**anstalt** die (veralt.) approved school; Borstal (Brit.); ~**beratung** die (a) child guidance; (b) (Beratungsstelle) child guidance clinic; ~**berechtigt** Adj. having parental authority postpos., not pred.; ~**berechtigte** der/die; adj. Dekl. parent or [legal] guardian; ~**heim** das community home; ~**methode** die educational method; teaching method; ~**wesen** das educational system; education; ~**wissenschaft** die education

erzielen tr. V. reach ⟨agreement, compromise, speed⟩; achieve ⟨result, effect⟩; make ⟨profit⟩; obtain ⟨price⟩; score ⟨goal⟩

erzittern itr. V.; mit sein [begin to] shake or tremble; **etw.** ~ **lassen** shake sth.

erz·konservativ Adj. ultra-conservative

erzürnen (geh.) **1** tr. V. anger; (stärker) incense; **erzürne ihn nicht** don't make him angry. **2** refl. V. **sich über jmdn./etw.** ~: become or grow angry with sb./about sth.

erzwingen unr. tr. V. force; **sich** (Dat.) **den Zutritt** ~: force an entry

es¹ /ɛs/ Personalpron.; 3. Pers. Sg. Nom. u. Akk. Neutr. (a) (s. auch Gen. **seiner;** Dat. **ihm**) (bei Dingen) it; (bei weiblichen Personen) she/her; (bei männlichen Personen) he/him; (b) ohne Bezug auf ein bestimmtes Subst., mit unpers. konstruierten Verben, als formales Satzglied it; **keiner will es gewesen sein** no one will admit to it; **ich bin es** it's me; it is I (formal); **wir sind traurig, ihr seid es auch** we are sad, and you are too or so are you; **er hatte es nicht anders erwartet** he hadn't expected anything else; **es war einmal ein König** once upon a time there was a king; **es gibt keinen anderen Weg** there is no other way; **es wundert mich, dass** ...: I'm surprised that ...; **es sei denn, [dass]** ...: unless ...; **es ist genug!** that's enough; **wir schaffen es** we'll manage it; **es regnet/schneit/donnert** it rains/snows/thunders; (jetzt) it is raining/snowing/thundering; **es hat geklopft** there was a knock; **es klingelte** there was a ring; **es klingelt** someone is ringing; **es friert mich** I am cold; **es ist 9 Uhr/spät/Nacht** it is 9 o'clock/late/night-time; **es wird schöner** the weather is improving; **es wird kälter** it's getting colder; **es wird Frühling** spring is on the way; **es geht ihm gut/schlecht** he is well/unwell; **es wird gelacht** there is laughter; **es wird um 6 Uhr angefangen** we/they etc. start at 6 o'clock; **es lässt sich aushalten** it is bearable; **es bleit sich gut hier** it's a good life here; **er hat es gut** he has it good; it's all right for him; **er meinte es gut** he meant well; **sie hat es mit dem Herzen** (ugs.) she has got heart trouble or something wrong with her heart; s. auch **haben 1** n

es², Es das; ~, ~ (Musik) E flat

E-Saite die E-string

Esche /'ɛʃə/ die; ~, ~**n** (Bot.) ash

Esel /'e:zl/ der; ~**s**, ~ (a) donkey; ass; (b) (ugs.: Dummkopf) ass (coll.); idiot (coll.); **so ein alter** ~! what a stupid ass or idiot (coll.); **du** ~! you ass!

Eselin die; ~, ~**nen** she-donkey; jenny-ass

Esels-: ~**brücke** die (ugs.) mnemonic; ~**ohr** das (ugs.) (a) ~**ohren haben** (fig.) have donkey's ears; (b) (umgeknickte Ecke) dog-ear; **ein Buch voller** ~**ohren** a dog-eared book

Esel·treiber der donkey-driver

Eskalation /ɛskala'tsi̯o:n/ die; ~, ~**en** escalation

eskalieren tr., itr. V. escalate

Eskapade /ɛska'pa:də/ die; ~, ~**n** escapade; (Seitensprung) amorous adventure

Eskapismus /ɛska'pɪsmʊs/ der; ~ (Psych.) escapism no art.

eskapistisch Adj. escapist

Eskimo /'ɛskimo/ der; ~[**s**], ~[**s**] Eskimo

Eskorte /ɛs'kɔrtə/ die; ~, ~**n** escort; (fig.) entourage

eskortieren tr. V. escort

esoterisch /ezo'te:rɪʃ/ Adj. esoteric

Espe /'ɛspə/ die; ~, ~**n** aspen

Espen·laub das: **wie** ~ **zittern** shake like a leaf

Esperanto /ɛspe'ranto/ das; ~[**s**] ▶ 487 | Esperanto

Esplanade /ɛspla'na:də/ die; ~, ~**n** esplanade

Espresso /ɛs'prɛso/ der; ~[**s**], ~**s** espresso [coffee]; **zwei** ~, **bitte** two espressos, please

Esprit /ɛs'pri:/ der; ~**s** esprit

Essay /'ɛse/ der od. das; ~**s**, ~**s** essay

essbar, *eßbar Adj. edible; **ist etwas Essbares im Haus?** (ugs.) is there anything to eat in the house?; **nicht** ~ **sein** be inedible

Ess·besteck, *Eß·besteck das knife, fork, and spoon

Ess·ecke, *Eß·ecke die dining area

essen /'ɛsn̩/ unr. tr., itr. V. eat; eat, drink ⟨soup⟩; **etw. gern** ~: like sth.; **möchten Sie ein Stück Kuchen** ~? would you like a piece of cake?; **was gibt es zu** ~? what's for lunch/dinner/supper?; **von etw.** ~: eat some of sth.; **jmdm. etwas zu** ~ **machen** get sb. something to eat; **sich satt** ~: eat one's fill; **den Teller leer** ~: clear one's plate; **gut** ~: have a good meal; (immer) eat well; **warm/kalt** ~: have a hot/cold meal; **das Kind isst sehr schlecht** the child doesn't eat very much or has a poor appetite; ~ **gehen** got out for a meal; **er isst bei seiner Tante** he has his meals with his aunt; **es wird nichts so heiß gegessen, wie es gekocht wird** (Spr.) nothing is ever as bad as it seems; **selber** ~ **macht fett** (ugs.) I'm all right, Jack (coll.); s. auch **Abend; Mittag**

Essen das; ~**s**, ~ (a) o. Pl. **beim** ~ **sein** be having lunch/dinner/supper; **zum** ~ **gehen** go to lunch; **jmdn. zum** ~ **einladen** invite sb. for a meal; (b) (Mahlzeit) meal; (Fest~) banquet; (c) (Speise) food; [**das**] ~ **machen/kochen** get/cook the meal; **das** ~ **warm stellen** keep the lunch/dinner/supper hot; ~ **auf Rädern** meals on wheels; (d) (Verpflegung) o. Pl. food; ~ **und Trinken** food and drink

Essen[s]-: ~**ausgabe** die (a) (das Ausgeben) serving of meals; **die** ~**ausgabe ist um 12 Uhr** meals are or lunch is served at 12 [o'clock]; (b) (Stelle) serving hatch; ~**marke** die meal ticket; ~**zeit** die mealtime

***essentiell** ⇒ essenziell

Essenz /ɛ'sɛnts/ die; ~, ~**en** essence

essenziell /ɛsɛn'tsi̯ɛl/ Adj. (geh., fachspr.) essential

Esser der; ~**s**, ~: **er ist ein guter/schlechter** ~: he has a healthy/poor appetite

Ess·geschirr, *Eß·geschirr das (a) pots and pans; (b) (Milit.) mess kit

Essig /'ɛsɪç/ der; ~**s**, ~**e** vinegar; ~ **und Öl** oil and vinegar; **es ist mit etw.** ~ (ugs.) sth. has fallen through completely (coll.)

Essig-: ~**essenz** die vinegar essence; ~**gurke** die pickled gherkin; ~**sauer** Adj. acetic; ~**saure Tonerde**

basic aluminium acetate; ~**säure** die (Chemie) acetic acid
ess-, *****eß-**, **Ess-**, *****Eß-**: ~**kastanie** die sweet
chestnut; ~**löffel** der soup spoon; ~**lokal** das restaurant; ~**stäbchen** das chopstick; ~**teller** der dinner
plate; ~**tisch** der dining table; ~**waren** Pl. food sing.;
~**zimmer** das dining room; (Möbel) dining room suite
Establishment /ɪsˈtɛblɪʃmənt/ das; ~s, ~s Establishment
Este /ˈeːstə/ der; ~n, ~n, **Estin** die; ~, ~nen Estonian
Est·land (das); ~s Estonia
estnisch Adj. ▶ 388 | Estonian
Estragon /ˈɛstragɔn/ der; ~s tarragon
Estrich /ˈɛstrɪç/ der; ~s, ~e composition or jointless
floor
Eszett /ɛsˈtsɛt/ das; ~, ~: (the letter) ß
etablieren /etaˈbliːrən/ **1** tr. V. establish; set up. **2** refl.
V. **(a)** (sich niederlassen) ‹shop› open up; ‹chain store› open
up or set up branches; **(b)** (sich einrichten) settle in; **(c)** (ge-
sellschaftlich) become established
etabliert Adj. established
Etablissement /etablɪs(ə)ˈmɑ̃ː/ das; ~s, ~s establish-
ment
Etage /eˈtaːʒə/ die; ~, ~n floor; storey; **in** od. **auf der
dritten** ~ **wohnen** live on the third or (Amer.) fourth floor
Etagen-: ~**bett** das bunk bed; ~**wohnung** die flat
(Brit.) or (Amer.) apartment occupying an entire floor
Etappe /eˈtapə/ die; ~, ~n **(a)** (Teilstrecke) stage; leg;
(Rennsport) stage; **(b)** (Stadium) stage; **(c)** (Milit.) back area;
base
Etappen-: ~**sieg** der (Rennsport) stage-win; ~**wertung** die (Rennsport) daily points classification
Etat /eˈtaː/ der; ~s, ~s budget
Etat·kürzung die cut in the budget
etc. Abk. et cetera etc.
et cetera /ɛtˈtseːtera/ et cetera
etepetete /eˈtəpeˈteːtə/ Adj.; nicht attrib. (ugs.) fussy;
finicky; pernickety (coll.)
Eternit Ⓦ /eterˈniːt/ das od. der; ~s asbestos cement
Ethik /ˈeːtɪk/ die; ~, ~en **(a)** (Sittenlehre) ethics sing.; **(b)**
o. Pl. (sittliche Normen) ethics pl.; **(c)** (Werk über Ethik) ethical
work
ethisch Adj. ethical
Ethnie /ɛtˈniː/ die; ~, ~n (Völkerk.) ethnos
ethnisch /ˈɛtnɪʃ/ Adj. ethnic
Ethno der ethnic music
Ethnologe /ɛtnoˈloːgə/ der; ~n, ~n ethnologist
Ethnologie die; ~, ~n ethnology no art.
ethnologisch Adj. ethnological
Ethno·pop der ethnic pop [music]
Ethologie /etoloˈgiː/ die; ~, ~n ethology no art.
Ethos /ˈeːtɔs/ das; ~: ethos
Etikett /etiˈkɛt/ das; ~[e]s, ~en od. ~e od. ~s label;
jmdn./etw. mit einem ~ versehen (fig.) pin a label on
sb./sth.
Etikette die; ~, ~n etiquette; **die ~ wahren** observe
the proprieties
Etiketten·schwindel der (abwertend) playing with
names
etikettieren /etikɛˈtiːrən/ tr. V. label
etlich... /ˈɛtlɪç.../ Indefinitpron. u. unbest. Zahlwort (ugs.)
Sg. quite a lot of; Pl. quite a few; a number of; **vor** ~**en
Wochen** several or some weeks ago
Etrusker /eˈtrʊskɐ/ der; ~s, ~: Etruscan
etruskisch Adj. Etruscan
Etüde /eˈtyːdə/ die; ~, ~n (Musik) étude
Etui /ɛtˈviː/ das; ~s, ~s case
etwa /ˈɛtva/ **1** Adv. **(a)** (ungefähr) about; approximately; ~
so groß wie ...: about as large as ...; ~ **so** roughly like
this; **in** ~: to some or a certain extent or degree; **(b)** (beispielsweise) for example; for instance; **vergleicht man** ~
...: for example, if one compares ...; **wie** ~ ...: as, for

example ... **2** Part. (womöglich) **hast du das** ~ **vergessen?**
you haven't forgotten that, have you?; **störe ich** ~? am I
disturbing you at all?
etwaig... /ˈɛtva(ː)ɪg.../ Adj. (Papierdt.) possible ‹delays›;
~**e Mängel/Beschwerden** any faults/complaints
[which might arise]
etwas /ˈɛtvas/ Indefinitpron. **(a)** something; (fragend, verneint) anything; ~ **gegen jmdn. haben** have something
against sb.; **sie haben ~ miteinander** (ugs.) there is
something going on between them; ~ **für sich haben**
(ugs.) have sth. in it; **so** ~: a thing like that; **so** ~ **habe
ich noch nie gesehen** I've never seen anything like it;
so ~ **Schönes habe ich noch nie gesehen** I've never
seen anything so beautiful before; ~ **anderes** something
else; (fragend, verneinend) anything else; **(b)** (Bedeutsames) **aus
ihm wird** ~: he'll make something of himself or his life;
es zu ~ **bringen** get somewhere; **das will** ~ **heißen**
that really is something; **(c)** (ein Teil) some; (fragend, verneinend) any; ~ **von dem Geld/davon** some of the money/
it; **(d)** (ein wenig) a little; **noch** ~ **Milch** a little more or
some more milk; **kannst du mir** ~ **Geld leihen?** can
you lend me some money?; **[noch]** ~ **spielen/lesen** play/
read for a little while [longer]; ~ **Englisch** a little or some
English
Etwas das; ~, ~: something; **das gewisse** ~: that certain something
Etymologe /etymoˈloːgə/ der; ~n, ~n etymologist
Etymologie die; ~, ~n etymology
etymologisch (Sprachw.) **1** Adj. etymological. **2** adv.
etymologically
Et-Zeichen /ˈɛt-/ das ampersand
euch /ɔʏç/ **1** Dat. u. Akk. von **ihr** you; **ich gebe** ~ **das**
I'll give you it; I'll give it to you. **2** Dat. u. Akk. Pl. des
Reflexivpron. der 2. Pers. Pl. **(a)** refl. yourselves; **(b)** reziprok one another; s. auch **uns**
Eucharistie /ɔʏçarɪsˈtiː/ die; ~, ~n (kath. Rel.) Eucharist
eucharistisch Adj. (kath. Rel.) Eucharistic
euer¹ /ˈɔʏɐ/ Possessivpron. der 2. Pers. Pl. your; **Grüße
von eu[e]rer Helga/eu[e]rem Hans** Best wishes,
Yours, Helga/Hans; **Eu[e]re** od. **Euer Exzellenz** Your
Excellency; **ist das/sind das eure?** is that/are they
yours?; s. auch **unser¹**
euer² Gen. von **ihr** (geh.) of you; **wir werden** ~ **gedenken** we will remember you
Eukalyptus /ɔʏkaˈlʏptʊs/ der; ~, **Eukalypten** od. ~:
eucalyptus
Eule /ˈɔʏlə/ die; ~, ~n owl; ~**n nach Athen tragen**
carry coals to Newcastle
Eulen-: ~**spiegel** der joker; s. auch **Till;** ~**spiegelei** die; ~, ~en caper (coll.)
Eumel /ˈɔʏml/ der; ~s, ~ (Jugendspr.) twerp (coll.)
Eunuch /ɔʏˈnuːx/ der; ~en, ~en eunuch
Euphorie /ɔʏfoˈriː/ die; ~, ~n (geh., fachspr.) euphoria
euphorisch (geh., fachspr.) **1** Adj. euphoric. **2** adv. eu-
phorically
Eurasien /ɔʏˈraːzịən/ (das); ~s Eurasia
eurasisch Adj. Eurasian
eure /ˈɔʏrə/ ⇒ **euer¹**
eurer·seits Adv. (von eurer Seite) on your part; (auf eurer
Seite) for your part
eures·gleichen indekl. Pron. people pl. like you; (abwertend) the likes pl. of you; your sort or kind; s. auch **deines-
gleichen**
euret-: ~**halben** /-halbn/ (veralt.), ~**wegen** Adv.
(wegen euch) because of you; on your account; (für euch) on
your behalf; (euch zuliebe) for your sake; **ich mache mir**
~**wegen keine Sorgen** I don't worry about you;
~**willen** Adv. um ~**willen** for your sake
Euro der; ~s, ~s Euro
Eurocheque /ˈɔʏroʃɛk/ der; ~s, ~s Eurocheque
Euro-: ~**dollar** der (Wirtsch.) Eurodollar; ~**krat**
/~ˈkraːt/ der; ~en, ~en Eurocrat

Europa /ɔy'roːpa/ (*das*); ⁓s Europe
Europa·cup *der* (Sport) European cup
Europäer /ɔyro'pɛːɐ/ *der;* ⁓s, ⁓, **Europäerin** *die;* ⁓, ⁓nen European
Europa·flagge *die* flag of the Council of Europe
europäisch /ɔyro'pɛːɪʃ/ *Adj.* European; **die Europäische Gemeinschaft** the European Community; **Europäische Wirtschaftsgemeinschaft** European Economic Community
europäisieren *tr. V.* Europeanize
Europa-: ⁓**meister** *der* (Sport) European champion; ⁓**meisterschaft** *die* (Sport) **(a)** (Wettbewerb) European Championship; **(b)** (Titel) championship of Europe, European title; ⁓**minister** *der* minister for Europe; ⁓**parlament** *das; o. Pl.* European Parliament *or* Assembly; ⁓**pokal** *der* (Sport) European cup; ⁓**politik** *die* policy towards the EC; ⁓**rat** *der; o. Pl.* Council of Europe; ⁓**rekord** *der* (Sport) European record; ⁓**straße** *die* European long-distance road; ⁓**wahlen** *Pl.* European elections
Euro·scheck *der* Eurocheque
Euro·vision *die* Eurovision
Euter /'ɔytɐ/ *das od. der;* ⁓s, ⁓: udder
Euthanasie /ɔytana'ziː/ *die;* ⁓: euthanasia *no art.*
e. V., E. V. *Abk.* **eingetragener Verein**
ev. *Abk.* **evangelisch** ev.
Eva /'eːfa *od.* 'eːva/ (*die*) Eve; *s. auch* **Adam**
evakuieren /evaku'iːrən/ *tr. V.* evacuate
Evakuierte *der/die; adj. Dekl.* evacuee
Evakuierung *die;* ⁓, ⁓en evacuation
Evaluation /evalua'tsioːn/ *die;* ⁓, ⁓en **(a)** (geh.) valuation; **(b)** (Päd.) evaluation
evangelisch /evaŋ'geːlɪʃ/ *Adj.* Protestant; **die** ⁓**e Kirche** the Protestant Church
evangelisch-lutherisch *Adj.* Lutheran
evangelisch-reformiert *Adj.* Reformed
Evangelist *der;* ⁓en, ⁓en evangelist
Evangelium /evaŋ'geːliʊm/ *das;* ⁓s, **Evangelien (a)** *o. Pl.* (auch fig.) gospel; **(b)** (christl. Rel.) Gospel; **das** ⁓ **des Johannes** St. John's Gospel
Evas- /'eːfas- *od.* 'eːvas-/**:** ⁓**kostüm** *das:* **im** ⁓**kostüm** (ugs. scherzh.) in her birthday suit/their birthday suits (coll. joc.); ⁓**tochter** *die* (scherzh.) **eine echte** ⁓**tochter** a real little Eve
Eventual·fall /even'tuaːl-/ *der* eventuality; contingency; **für den** ⁓**fall** should the eventuality arise
Eventualität /evɛntualiˈtɛːt/ *die;* ⁓, ⁓n eventuality; contingency
eventuell /evɛn'tuɛl/ **1** *Adj.; nicht präd.* possible ⟨*objections, difficulties, applicants*⟩; ⟨*objections, difficulties*⟩ which might occur; **bei** ⁓**en Schäden** in the event *or* case of damage. **2** *adv.* possibly; perhaps
Evergreen /'ɛvəɡriːn/ *der;* ⁓s, ⁓s old favourite
evident /evi'dɛnt/ *Adj.* (geh.) **(a)** (einleuchtend) convincing ⟨*argument, proof*⟩; evident, self-evident ⟨*truth*⟩; **(b)** (offenkundig) evident, obvious ⟨*disadvantage*⟩
Evidenz /evi'dɛnts/ *die;* ⁓, ⁓en (geh.) (einer Behauptung, eines Beweises) convincingness; (eines Satzes, einer Wahrheit) self-evidence
Evolution /evolu'tsioːn/ *die;* ⁓, ⁓en evolution
evolutionär /evolutsio'nɛːɐ/ **1** *Adj.* evolutionary. **2** *adv.* by evolution
Evolutions·theorie *die* theory of evolution
evtl. *Abk.* **eventuell**
E-Werk *das* power station
EWG /eːveː'geː/ *die;* ⁓: EEC
ewig /'eːvɪç/ **1** *Adj.* eternal, everlasting ⟨*life, peace*⟩; eternal, undying ⟨*love*⟩; (abwertend) never-ending; **die Ewige Stadt** the Eternal City; **ein** ⁓**er Student** (scherzh.) an eternal student; **seit** ⁓**en Zeiten** for ages (coll.); for donkey's years (coll.); **das Ewige Licht** (kath. Rel.) the Sanctuary Lamp. **2** *adv.* eternally; for ever; ⁓ **warten** wait for ever; ⁓ **dauern** take ages; ⁓ **halten** last for ever *or* indefinitely; **auf** ⁓: for ever

Ewig·gestrige *der/die; adj. Dekl.* (abwertend) **ein** ⁓**r sein** be an old reactionary
Ewigkeit *die;* ⁓, ⁓en **(a)** eternity; **in** ⁓: for ever and ever; **in die** ⁓ **eingehen** (geh. verhüll.) find eternal rest; **(b) eine [halbe]** ⁓, ⁓**en** (ugs.) ages; **es dauert eine** ⁓: it takes ages (coll.); **in alle** ⁓: for ever
ex /ɛks/ *Adv.* (ugs.) **etw. ex trinken** down sth. in one (coll.); **ex!** down in one! (sl.)
Ex- (vor Personenbez.: vormalig) ex-⟨*wife, husband, president, etc.*⟩
exakt /ɛ'ksakt/ **1** *Adj.* exact; precise. **2** *adv.* ⟨*work etc.*⟩ accurately; ⁓ **um 12 Uhr** at 12 o'clock precisely
Exaktheit *die;* ⁓: precision; exactness
exaltiert **1** *Adj.* (hysterisch) overexcited; (überspannt) exaggerated ⟨*behaviour, gestures*⟩; (überschwänglich) effusive. **2** *adv.* (hysterisch) overexcitedly; (überschwänglich) effusively
Examen /ɛ'ksaːmən/ *das;* ⁓s, ⁓ *od.* **Examina** /ɛ'ksaːmina/ examination; exam (coll.); **ein** ⁓ **machen** *od.* **ablegen** sit *or* take an examination; ⁓ **haben** (ugs.) have examinations
Examens-: ⁓**angst** *die* examination nerves *pl.;* ⁓**arbeit** *die written work presented for an examination;* ⁓**kandidat** *der* examination candidate
examinieren *tr. V.* **(a)** examine; **(b)** (ausfragen) question
Exegese /ɛkse'geːzə/ *die;* ⁓, ⁓n (Theol.) exegesis
exekutieren /ɛkseku'tiːrən/ *tr. V.* execute
Exekution /ɛkseku'tsioːn/ *die;* ⁓, ⁓en execution
Exekutions·kommando *das* firing squad
exekutiv /ɛkseku'tiːf/ *Adj.* (bes. Politik, Rechtsw.) executive
Exekutive /ɛkseku'tiːvə/ *die;* ⁓, ⁓n (Rechtsw., Politik) executive
Exempel /ɛ'ksɛmpl̩/ *das;* ⁓s, ⁓: example; **ein** ⁓ **[an jmdm.] statuieren** make an example [of sb.]
Exemplar /ɛksɛm'plaːɐ/ *das;* ⁓s, ⁓e specimen; (Buch, Zeitung, Zeitschrift) copy
exemplarisch /ɛksɛm'plaːrɪʃ/ *Adj.* exemplary
exerzieren /ɛksɛr'tsiːrən/ (Milit.) **1** *itr. V.* drill. **2** *tr. V.* drill ⟨*soldiers*⟩
Exerzier-: ⁓**munition** *die* (Milit.) dummy ammunition; ⁓**platz** *der* (Milit.) parade ground
Exerzitien /ɛksɛr'tsiːtsiən/ *Pl.* (kath. Rel.) religious *or* spiritual exercises
Exhibitionismus *der;* ⁓ (Psych., fig.) exhibitionism
Exhibitionist *der;* ⁓en, ⁓en exhibitionist
exhibitionistisch *Adj.* exhibitionist
exhumieren /ɛkshu'miːrən/ *tr. V.* exhume
Exhumierung *die;* ⁓, ⁓en exhumation
Exil /ɛ'ksiːl/ *das;* ⁓s, ⁓e exile; **ins** ⁓ **gehen** go into exile
Exilant /ɛksi'lant/ *der;* ⁓en, ⁓en exile
exiliert /ɛksi'liːɐt/ *Adj.* exiled
Exilierte *der/die; adj. Dekl.* exile
Exil-: ⁓**literatur** *die* literature written in exile; ⁓**regierung** *die* government in exile
existent /ɛksɪs'tɛnt/ *Adj.* existing; existent
Existentialismus *usw.* ⇨ **Existenzialismus** *usw.*
Existenz /ɛksɪs'tɛnts/ *die;* ⁓, ⁓en **(a)** existence; **(b)** (Lebensgrundlage) livelihood; **sich** (*Dat.*) **eine** ⁓ **aufbauen** build a life for oneself; **(c)** (Mensch) **zweifelhafte** ⁓**en** dubious characters
Existenz-: ⁓**berechtigung** *die* right to exist; ⁓**fähig** *Adj.* able to exist *or* to survive *postpos.;* ⁓**grund·lage** *die* basis of one's livelihood; ⁓**gründung** *die* [business] start-up;
Existenzialismus *der;* ⁓: existentialism *no art.*
Existenzialist *der;* ⁓en, ⁓en existenzialist
existenzialistisch *Adj.* existentialist
existenziell *Adj.* existential; **in etw.** (*Dat.*) **eine** ⁓**e Bedrohung sehen** see in sth. a threat to one's existence
existenz-, Existenz-: ⁓**kampf** *der* struggle for existence; ⁓**minimum** *das* subsistence level; **am Rande des** ⁓**minimums leben** live at subsistence level; ⁓**philosophie** *die* existential philosophy *no art.*

existieren /ɛksɪs'tiːrən/ *itr. V.* exist
Exitus /'ɛksitʊs/ *der;* ~ (Med.) death
exkl. *Abk.* **exklusiv[e]** excl.
exklusiv /ɛksklu'ziːf/ **1** *Adj.* exclusive. **2** *adv.* exclusively
Exklusiv·bericht *der* exclusive [report]
exklusive /ɛksklu'ziːvə/ *Präp.* + *Gen.* (Kaufmannsspr.) exclusive of; excluding
Exklusivität /ɛkskluzivi'tɛːt/ *die;* ~: exclusiveness; exclusivity
Ex·kommunikation *die* (kath. Kirche) excommunication
ex·kommunizieren *tr. V.* (kath. Kirche) excommunicate
Exkrement /ɛkskre'mɛnt/ *das;* ~[e]s, ~e (fachspr., geh.) excrement
Exkurs /ɛks'kʊrs/ *der;* ~es, ~e digression; (in einem Buch) excursus
Exkursion /ɛkskʊr'zioːn/ *die;* ~, ~en study trip *or* tour
Exmatrikulation /ɛksmatrikula'tsioːn/ *die;* ~, ~en (Hochschulw.) *removal of a student's name from the register on leaving a university*
exmatrikulieren /ɛksmatriku'liːrən/ *tr. V.* (Hochschulw.) **jmdn./sich** ~: remove sb.'s name/have one's name removed from the university register
Exodus /'ɛksodʊs/ *der;* ~, ~se (geh.) exodus
exogen /ɛkso'geːn/ *Adj.* (Med., Psych., Bot.) exogenous
exorbitant /ɛksɔrbi'tant/ **1** *Adj.* (geh.) exorbitant ⟨price⟩. **2** *adv.* exorbitantly
Exorzismus /ɛksɔr'tsɪmʊs/ *der;* ~, **Exorzismen** (Rel.) exorcism
Exot /ɛ'ksoːt/ *der;* ~en, ~en, **Exotin** *die;* ~, ~nen strange foreigner
exotisch **1** *Adj.* exotic. **2** *adv.* exotically
Expander /ɛks'pandɐ/ *der;* ~s, ~ (Sport) chest expander
expandieren /ɛkspan'diːrən/ *tr., itr. V.* expand
Expansion /ɛkspan'zioːn/ *die;* ~, ~en expansion
expansionistisch *Adj.* (Polit.) expansionist
expansiv /ɛkspan'ziːf/ *Adj.* (a) (Politik) expansionist; (b) (Wirtsch.) expansionary
Expedient /ɛkspe'diɛnt/ *der;* ~en, ~en (a) dispatch clerk; (b) (im Reisebüro) travel agency clerk
Expedition /ɛkspedi'tsioːn/ *die;* ~, ~en expedition
Experiment /ɛksperi'mɛnt/ *das;* ~[e]s, ~e experiment
Experimental·physik /ɛksperɪmɛn'taːl-/ *die* experimental physics
experimentell /ɛksperɪmɛn'tɛl/ **1** *Adj.; nicht präd.* experimental. **2** *adv.* experimentally
experimentieren *itr. V.* experiment
Experte /ɛks'pɛrtə/ *der;* ~n, ~n, **Expertin** *die;* ~, ~nen expert (**für** in)
Expertise /ɛkspɛr'tiːzə/ *die;* ~, ~n expert's report
explizit /ɛkspli'tsiːt/ (geh.) **1** *Adj.* explicit. **2** *adv.* explicitly
explodieren /ɛksplo'diːrən/ *itr. V.; mit sein* (auch fig.) explode; ⟨costs⟩ rocket
Explosion /ɛksplo'zioːn/ *die;* ~, ~en explosion; **etw. zur** ~ **bringen** detonate sth.
explosions-, Explosions-: ~**artig 1** *Adj.* explosive, astronomical ⟨growth, increase⟩; **2** *adv.* ⟨rise⟩ astronomically; ~**gefahr** *die; o. Pl.* danger of explosion; „~**gefahr!**" '[Danger,] Explosives!'; ~**welle** *die* shock wave
explosiv /ɛksplo'ziːf/ **1** *Adj.* (auch fig.) explosive. **2** *adv.* explosively; ~ **reagieren** (fig.) react violently
Explosivität /ɛksplozivi'tɛːt/ *die* explosiveness
Exponat /ɛkspo'naːt/ *das;* ~[e]s, ~e exhibit
Exponent /ɛkspo'nɛnt/ *der;* ~en, ~en (Math.) exponent; (fig.) leading exponent
Exponential- /ɛksponɛn'tsiaːl-/ (Math.) exponential ⟨function, equation, curve⟩
exponieren /ɛkspo'niːrən/ *tr. V.* **jmdn./sich** ~ (geh.) (der Aufmerksamkeit aussetzen) draw attention to sb./oneself; (der Gefahr aussetzen) lay sb./oneself open to attack

exponiert *Adj.* exposed
Export¹ /ɛks'pɔrt/ *der;* ~[e]s, ~e (a) *o. Pl.* (das Exportieren) export; exporting; **der** ~ **nach Afrika** exports to Africa; (b) (das Exportierte) export
Export² *das;* ~[s], ~: export; **zwei** ~: two export
Export-: ~**artikel** *der* export; ~**bier** *das* export beer
Exporteur /ɛkspɔr'tøːɐ̯/ *der;* ~s, ~e (Wirtsch.) exporter
Export-: ~**firma** *die* exporter; ~**geschäft** *das* (a) export business; (b) (geschäftlicher Abschluss) export deal; ~**handel** *der* export trade; ~**händler** *der* exporter
exportieren *tr., itr. V.* export
Exposé /ɛkspo'zeː/ *das;* ~s, ~s (a) exposé; report; (b) (eines Drehbuchs, Romans usw.) outline
Exposition /ɛkspozi'tsioːn/ *die;* ~, ~en exposition
express, *expreß /ɛks'prɛs/ *Adv.* (veralt.) express
Express, *Expreß *der;* **Expresses, Expresse** (bes. österr.) express [train]
Express·gut, *Expreß·gut *das* express freight; express goods *pl.;* **etw. als** ~**gut schicken** send sth. by express goods
Expressionismus /ɛksprɛsio'nɪsmʊs/ *der;* ~ expressionism *no art.*
Expressionist /der;* ~en, ~en expressionist
expressionistisch **1** *Adj.* expressionist. **2** *adv.* expressionistically; ⟨influenced⟩ by expressionism
Express·zug *der* (bes. schweiz.) express [train]
exquisit /ɛkskvi'ziːt/ **1** *Adj.* exquisite. **2** *adv.* exquisitely
extensiv /ɛkstɛn'ziːf/ **1** *Adj.* (auch Landw.) extensive. **2** *adv.* (auch Landw.) extensively
extern /ɛks'tɛrn/ (Schulw.) **1** *Adj.* external; **ein** ~**er Schüler** a day boy/girl. **2** *adv.* **eine Prüfung** ~ **ablegen** take an examination as an external candidate
exterritorial /ɛkstɛrito'riaːl/ *Adj.* (Völkerr.) extraterritorial
extra /'ɛkstra/ *Adv.* (a) (gesondert) ⟨pay⟩ separately; **Getränke werden** ~ **berechnet** drinks are extra; (b) (zusätzlich, besonders) extra; **dafür brauche ich aber noch 10 DM** ~: but I need another 10 marks for that; (c) (eigens) especially; **etw.** ~ **für jmdn. tun** do sth. especially *or* just for sb.; ~ **deinetwegen** just because of you; (d) (ugs.: absichtlich) **etw.** ~ **tun** do sth. on purpose
Extra *das;* ~s, ~s; *meist Pl.* extra
Extra-: ~**ausgabe** *die* (a) (Zeitung) special edition; extra; (b) (Geldausgabe) extra *or* additional expense; ~**blatt** *das* special edition; extra; ~**fahrt** *die* (bes. schweiz.) special excursion
Extrakt /ɛks'trakt/ *der;* ~[e]s, ~e (a) *fachspr. auch das* extract; (b) (Zusammenfassung) summary; synopsis
Extra·ration *die* extra ration
extraterrestrisch /-tɛ'rɛstrɪʃ/ *Adj.* (Astron.) extraterrestrial
extravagant /-va'gant/ **1** *Adj.* flamboyant. **2** *adv.* flamboyantly
Extravaganz /-va'gants/ *die;* ~, ~en (a) *o. Pl.* flamboyance; (b) (Sache) ~en flamboyance *sing.*
extravertiert /-vɛr'tiːɐ̯t/ *Adj.* (Psych.) extrovert[ed]
Extra·wurst *die* (fig. ugs.) **eine** ~ **bekommen** get special treatment *or* special favours
extrem /ɛks'treːm/ **1** *Adj.* extreme. **2** *adv.* extremely; ~ **reagieren** react in an extreme manner
Extrem *das;* ~s, ~e extreme; **von einem** ~ **ins andere fallen** go from one extreme to another
Extrem·fall *der* extreme case
Extremismus *der;* ~, **Extremismen** extremism
Extremist *der;* ~en, ~en, **Extremistin** *die;* ~, ~nen extremist
extremistisch *Adj.* extremist
Extremität /ɛkstremi'tɛːt/ *die;* ~, ~en extremity
Extrem-: ~**punkt** *der,* ~**wert** *der* (Math.) extremum
extrovertiert /ɛkstrovɛr'tiːɐ̯t/ ⇒ **extravertiert**
exzellent /ɛkstsɛ'lɛnt/ (geh.) **1** *Adj.* excellent. **2** *adv.* excellently

---

*alte Schreibung (vgl. Hinweise auf S. xvi–xvii)

Exzellenz /ɛkstsɛ'lɛnts/ *die;* ∼, ∼**en** ▶ 34╵ Excellency;
Eure/Seine ∼**:** Your/His Excellency
Exzentriker /ɛks'tsɛntrike/ *der;* ∼**s**, ∼**:** eccentric
exzentrisch 1 *Adj.* eccentric. **2** *adv.* eccentrically
Exzentrizität /ɛkstsɛntritsi'tɛ:t/ *die;* ∼, ∼**en** eccentricity
Exzess, ***Exzeß** /ɛks'tsɛs/ *der;* **Exzesses, Exzesse**
excess; **etw. bis zum** ∼ **treiben** carry sth. to excess
exzessiv /ɛkstsɛ'si:f/ *Adj.* excessive
E-Zug *der* ⇒ **Eilzug**

....

....

f, F /ɛf/ *das;* ∼, ∼ **(a)** (Buchstabe) f/F; **nach Schema F**
according to a set pattern *or* routine; **(b)** (Musik) [key of] F;
s. auch **a/A**
f. *Abk.* **folgend** f.
F *Abk.* **Fahrenheit** F
Fa. *Abk.* **Firma**
Fabel /'fa:bḷ/ *die;* ∼, ∼**n (a)** (Literaturw.) (Gattung) fable;
(Kern einer Handlung) plot; **(b)** (Erfundenes) story; tale; fable;
ins Reich der ∼ **gehören** belong in the realm of fantasy
fabelhaft 1 *Adj.* **(a)** (ugs.: großartig) fantastic (coll.); **(b)**
nicht präd. (unglaublich) fabulous ⟨*riches*⟩. **2** *adv.* (ugs.) fantastically (coll.); fabulously (coll.)
Fabel·tier *das* mythological *or* fabulous creature
Fabrik /fa'bri:k/ *die;* ∼, ∼**en** factory; (Papier∼, Baumwollspinnerei) mill; **eine chemische** ∼**:** a chemical works
Fabrik·anlage *die* factory; (Maschinen) factory plant
Fabrikant /fabri'kant/ *der;* ∼**en**, ∼**en** manufacturer
Fabrik·arbeiter *der* factory-worker
Fabrikat /fabri'ka:t/ *das;* ∼[**e**]**s**, ∼**e** product; (Marke)
make
Fabrikation /fabrika'tsio:n/ *die;* ∼**:** production
Fabrikations·fehler *der* manufacturing fault
Fabrik-: ∼**besitzer** *der* factory-owner; ∼**direktor**
der works *or* production manager; ∼**gebäude** *das* factory building; ∼**gelände** *das* factory site
fabrizieren /fabri'tsi:rən/ *tr. V.* **(a)** (ugs. abwertend) knock
together (coll.); **(b)** (veralt.: herstellen) manufacture; produce
fabulieren /fabu'li:rən/ *itr. V.* invent stories; spin yarns
Facette /fa'sɛtə/ *die;* ∼, ∼**n** facet
Fach /fax/ *das;* ∼[**e**]**s**, **Fächer** /'fɛçɐ/ **(a)** compartment;
(für Post) pigeon-hole; (im Schrank) shelf; **(b)** (Studienrichtung,
Unterrichts∼) subject; (Wissensgebiet) field; (Berufszweig) trade;
ein Meister seines ∼**es** a master of his trade; **vom** ∼
sein be an expert; **ein Mann vom** ∼**:** an expert
fach-, Fach-: ∼**arbeiter** *der* skilled worker; craftsman; ∼**arzt** *der* specialist **(für** in); ∼**ausdruck** *der*
technical *or* specialist term; ∼**bezogen** *Adj.* specialized ⟨*training*⟩; ∼**buch** *das* specialist book
fächeln /'fɛçḷn/ *tr. V.* fan
Fächer /'fɛçɐ/ *der;* ∼**s**, ∼**:** fan
fächer·artig *Adj.* fan-like
fach-, Fach-: ∼**frau** *die* expert; ∼**gebiet** *das* field;
∼**gelehrte** *der/die* specialist **(für** in); ∼**gerecht** 1
Adj. correct; **2** *adv.* correctly; ∼**geschäft** *das* specialist
shop; **ein** ∼**geschäft für Sportartikel/Eisenwaren** a
specialist sports shop/ironmonger's; ∼**hochschule**
die college (*offering courses in a special subject*); ∼**idiot**
der (abwertend) *person who has no interests outside his/her
subject;* ∼**jargon** *der* (abwertend) technical jargon;
∼**kenntnis** *die* specialized *or* specialist knowledge;
∼**kraft** *die* skilled worker; ∼**kreise** *Pl.* **in** ∼**kreisen**
in specialist circles; ∼**kundig** 1 *Adj.* knowledgeable; **2**
adv. jmdn. ∼**kundig beraten** give sb. informed *or* expert advice
fachlich 1 *Adj.* specialist ⟨*knowledge, work*⟩; technical
⟨*problem, explanation, experience*⟩; ∼**e Ausbildung/**

Qualifikation training/qualification in the subject. **2**
adv. **etw.** ∼ **beurteilen** give a professional opinion on
sth.; ∼ **qualifiziert** qualified in the subject
fach-, Fach-: ∼**literatur** *die* specialist literature;
(bes. naturwissenschaftlich auch) technical literature; **in der
medizinischen** ∼**literatur** in the specialist medical
literature; ∼**mann** *der* expert; ∼**männisch** 1 *Adj.*
expert; **2** *adv.* jmdn. ∼**männisch beraten** give sb. expert advice
Fachschaft *die;* ∼, ∼**en (a)** (einer Berufsgruppe) professional association; **(b)** (von Studenten) student body of the/a
faculty
fach-, Fach-: ∼**schule** *die* technical college;
∼**simpelei** /∼zɪmpə'lai/ *die;* ∼, ∼**en** (ugs.) shop-talk;
∼**simpeln** /∼zɪmpḷn/ *itr. V.* (ugs.) talk shop; ∼**sprache** *die* technical terminology *or* language; ∼**sprachlich** *Adj.* technical; ∼**übergreifend** *Adj.* interdisciplinary; ∼**welt** *die; o. Pl.* experts *pl.;* **in der** ∼**welt**
among experts
Fach·werk *das o. Pl.* (Bauweise) half-timbered construction
Fachwerk·haus *das* half-timbered house
Fach-: ∼**wissenschaftler** *der* specialist; ∼**wort**
das; Pl. ∼**wörter** technical *or* specialist term;
∼**zeitschrift** *die* ⇒ ∼**literatur:** specialist/technical
journal
Fackel /'fakḷ/ *die;* ∼, ∼**n** torch
fackeln *itr. V.* (ugs.) shilly-shally (coll.); dither; **nicht
lange gefackelt!** no shilly-shallying! (coll.); don't dither
about!
Fackel-: ∼**schein** *der* torchlight; ∼**zug** *der* torchlight procession
fade /'fa:də/ *Adj.* **(a)** (schal) insipid; **ein** ∼**r Beigeschmack** (fig.) a flat after-taste; **(b)** (bes. südd., österr.: langweilig) dull
Faden¹ /'fa:dn̩/ *der;* ∼**s**, **Fäden** /'fɛ:dn̩/ **(a)** (Garn) thread;
ein ∼**:** a piece of thread; **der rote** ∼ (fig.) the central
theme; **den** ∼ **verlieren** (fig.) lose the thread; **er hat** *od.*
hält alle Fäden in der Hand (fig.) he holds the reins; **an
einem dünnen** *od.* **seidenen** ∼ **hängen** (fig.) hang by a
single thread; **Fäden ziehen** ⟨*cheese etc.*⟩ be soft and
stringy; **(b)** (Med.) suture; **die Fäden ziehen** remove the
stitches
Faden² *der;* ∼**s**, ∼ (Seemannsspr.) fathom
faden-, Faden-: ∼**kreuz** *das* cross-hairs *pl.;*
∼**scheinig** /∼ʃainɪç/ *Adj.* **(a)** (fig. abwertend) threadbare
⟨*morality*⟩; flimsy ⟨*argument, reason, excuse*⟩; **(b)** (abgewetzt)
threadbare ⟨*clothes*⟩; ∼**wurm** *der* (Zool.) threadworm
Fagott /fa'gɔt/ *das;* ∼[**e**]**s**, ∼**e** bassoon
Fagottist *der;* ∼**en**, ∼**en**, bassoonist
fähig /'fɛ:ɪç/ *Adj.* **(a)** (begabt) able; capable; **ein** ∼**er Kopf
sein** have an able mind; **(b)** (bereit, in der Lage) **zu etw.** ∼
sein be capable of sth.; ∼ **sein, etw. zu tun** be capable
of doing sth.
Fähigkeit *die;* ∼, ∼**en (a)** *meist Pl.* (Tüchtigkeit) ability;
capability; **geistige** ∼**en** intellectual faculties *or* abilities;
praktische ∼**en** practical skills; **jmds.** ∼**en wecken**
awaken sb.'s talents; **(b)** *o. Pl.* (Imstandesein) ability **(zu** to)
fahl /fa:l/ *Adj.* pale; pallid; wan ⟨*light, smile*⟩
Fähnchen /'fɛ:nçən/ *das;* ∼**s**, ∼ **(a)** little flag; **(b)** (ugs.
abwertend: Kleid) **ein billiges** ∼**:** a cheap frock (Brit.) *or* dress
fahnden /'fa:ndn̩/ *itr. V.* search **(nach** for)
Fahndung *die;* ∼, ∼**en** search
Fahne /'fa:nə/ *die;* ∼, ∼**n (a)** flag; **(b)** (fig.) **etw. auf
seine** ∼**n schreiben** espouse the cause of sth.; **seine** ∼
nach dem Wind[e] hängen trim one's sails to the wind;
mit fliegenden ∼**n zu jmdm./etw. überlaufen**
openly and suddenly turn one's coat; **(c)** *o. Pl.* (ugs.: Alkoholgeruch) **eine** ∼ **haben** reek of alcohol
fahnen-, Fahnen-: ∼**eid** *der* oath of allegiance;
∼**flucht** *die* desertion; ∼**flucht begehen** desert;
∼**flüchtig** *Adj.* ∼**flüchtig werden/sein** desert/be a
deserter; ∼**mast** *der*, ∼**stange** *die* flagpole;
∼**träger** *der* standard-bearer
Fähnrich /'fɛ:nrɪç/ *der;* ∼**s**, ∼**e** (Milit.) ensign; ∼ **zur
See** ensign

Fahr·ausweis der (a) (Amtsspr.: Fahrschein) ticket; (b) (schweiz.: Führerschein) driving licence

Fahr·bahn die carriageway; **beim Überqueren der ~:** when crossing the road

Fahrbahn·markierung die road-marking

fahrbar Adj. ⟨table, bed⟩ on castors; mobile ⟨crane, kitchen, etc.⟩; **ein ~er Untersatz** (ugs.) wheels pl. (joc.)

Fähre /'fɛːrə/ die; ~, ~n ferry

fahren /'faːrən/ 1 unr. itr. V.; mit sein (a) (als Fahrzeuglenker) drive; (mit dem Fahrrad, Motorrad usw.) ride; **mit dem Auto ~:** drive; (her~ auch) come by car; (hin~ auch) go by car; **mit dem Fahrrad/Motorrad ~:** cycle/motorcycle; come/go by bicycle/motorcycle; **mit 80 km/h ~:** drive/ride at 80 k.p.h.; **links/rechts ~:** drive on the left/right; (abbiegen) bear or turn left/right; **langsam ~:** drive/ride slowly; **gegen etw. ~:** go into sth.; (b) (mit dem Auto usw. als Mitfahrer; mit öffentlichen Verkehrsmitteln usw. als Fahrgast) go **(mit** by); (mit dem Aufzug/der Rolltreppe/der Seilbahn/dem Skilift) take the lift (Brit.) or (Amer.) elevator/escalator/cable-car/ski lift; (mit der Achterbahn, dem Karussell usw.) ride **(auf** + Dat. on); (per Anhalter) hitch-hike; **erster/zweiter Klasse/zum halben Preis ~:** travel or go first/second class/at half-price; **ich fahre nicht gern [im] Auto/Bus** I don't like travelling in cars/buses; **fährst du mit mir?** are you coming with me?; (c) (reisen) go; **in Urlaub ~:** go on holiday; (d) (los~) go; leave; (e) ⟨motor vehicle, train, lift, cable-car⟩ go; ⟨ship⟩ sail; **mein Auto fährt nicht** my car won't go; **der Aufzug fährt heute nicht** the lift (Brit.) or (Amer.) elevator is out of service today; (f) (verkehren) run; **der Bus fährt alle fünf Minuten/bis Goetheplatz** the bus runs or goes every five minutes/goes to Goetheplatz; **von München nach Passau fährt ein D-Zug** there's a fast train from Munich to Passau; (g) (betrieben werden) **mit Diesel/Benzin ~:** run on diesel/petrol (Brit.) or (Amer.) gasoline; **mit Dampf/Atomkraft ~:** be steam-powered/atomic-powered; (h) (schnelle Bewegungen ausführen) **in die Kleider ~:** leap into one's clothes; **in die Höhe ge~:** jump up [with a start]; **der Blitz ist in einen Baum ge~:** the lightning struck a tree; **jmdm. an die Kehle ~:** leap at sb.'s throat; **sich** (Dat.) **mit der Hand durchs Haar ~:** run one's fingers through one's hair; **was ist denn in dich ge~?** (fig.) what's got into you?; **der Schreck fuhr ihm in die Glieder** (fig.) the shock went right through him; **jmdm. über den Mund ~** (fig.) shut sb. up; **aus der Haut ~** (ugs.) blow one's top (coll.); **etw. ~ lassen** (loslassen) let sth. go; (fig.: aufgeben) abandon sth.; (i) (Erfahrungen machen) **gut/schlecht mit jmdm./einer Sache ~:** get on well/badly with sb./sth. 2 unr. tr. V. (a) (fortbewegen) drive ⟨car, lorry, train, etc.⟩; ride ⟨bicycle, motorcycle⟩; **ein Boot ~:** sail a boat; **Auto/Motorrad/Roller ~:** drive [a car]/ride a motorcycle/scooter; **Bahn/Bus** usw. **~: go by train/bus** etc.; **Kahn** od. **Boot/Kanu ~:** go boating/canoeing; **Ski ~:** ski; **Schlitten ~:** toboggan; **Rollschuh ~:** [roller-]skate; **Schlittschuh ~:** [ice-]skate; **Aufzug/Rolltreppe ~:** take the lift (Brit.) or (Amer.) elevator/use the escalator; **Sessellift ~:** ride in a/the chairlift; **U-Bahn ~:** ride on the underground (Brit.) or (Amer.) subway; **Karussell ~:** ride on the merry-go-round; (b) mit sein ([als Strecke] zurücklegen) drive; (mit dem Motorrad, Fahrrad) ride; take ⟨curve⟩; **einen Umweg/eine Umleitung ~:** make a detour/follow a diversion; **der Zug fährt jetzt eine andere Strecke** the train takes a different route now; (c) (befördern) drive, take ⟨person⟩; take ⟨thing⟩; ⟨vehicle⟩ take; ⟨ship, lorry, etc.⟩ carry ⟨goods⟩; (herbringen) drive, bring ⟨person⟩; bring ⟨thing⟩; ⟨vehicle⟩ bring; (d) ▶224| mit sein **80 km/h ~:** do 80 k.p.h.; **hier muss man 50 km/h ~:** you've got to keep to 50 k.p.h. here; (e) meist mit sein **ein Rennen ~:** take part in a race; (f) meist mit sein **einen Rekord ~:** set a record; **1:23:45/eine gute Zeit ~:** do or clock 1.23.45/a good time; (g) **ein Auto schrottreif ~:** write off a car; (durch lange Beanspruchung) run or drive a car into the ground; **eine Beule in den Kotflügel ~:** dent the wing; (h) (als Treibstoff benutzen) use ⟨diesel, regular⟩. 3 unr. refl. V. (a) **sich gut ~** ⟨car⟩ handle well, be easy to drive; (b) unpers. **in dem Wagen/mit dem Zug fährt es sich bequem** the car gives a comfortable ride/it is comfortable travelling by train

fahrend Adj. itinerant; **~es Volk** travelling people pl.

***fahren|lassen** ⇒ fahren 1 h

Fahrer der; ~s, ~: ▶85| driver

Fahrer·flucht die: **~flucht begehen** fail to stop after [being involved in] an accident

Fahrerin die; ~, ~nen driver

Fahr-: **~erlaubnis** die (Amtsspr.) driving licence; **jmdm. die ~ entziehen** disqualify sb. from driving; **~gast** der passenger; **~geld** das fare; **~gemein·schaft** die car pool; **~gestell** das (Kfz-W.) chassis

fahrig /'faːrɪç/ Adj. nervous, agitated ⟨movements⟩

Fahr·karte die ticket

Fahrkarten-: **~ausgabe** die ticket office; **~auto·mat** der ticket machine; **~schalter** der ticket window

fahr-, Fahr-: **~lässig** 1 Adj. negligent ⟨behaviour⟩; **~e Tötung/Körperverletzung** (Rechtsw.) causing death/injury through or by [culpable] negligence; 2 adv. negligently; **~lässigkeit** die negligence; **~lehrer** der ▶85| driving instructor

Fähr·mann der ▶85| ferryman

Fahr·plan der (a) timetable; schedule (Amer.); **den ~ einhalten** run to schedule or on time; (b) (ugs.: Programm) plans pl.

fahrplan·mäßig 1 Adj. scheduled ⟨departure, arrival⟩. 2 adv. ⟨depart, arrive⟩ according to schedule, on time

Fahr-: **~praxis** die driving experience; **~preis** der fare; **~prüfung** die driving test

Fahr·rad das bicycle; cycle; **mit dem ~ fahren** cycle; ride a bicycle

Fahrrad-: **~computer** der cycle computer; **~fahrer** der cyclist; **~geschäft** das bicycle shop; **~händler** der bicycle dealer; **etw. beim ~händler kaufen** buy sth. from a/the bicycle shop; **~kurier** der bicycle or bike messenger; bicycle or bike courier; **~ständer** der bicycle rack or stand

Fahr·rinne die shipping channel; fairway

Fahr·schein der ticket

Fahrschein-: **~automat** der ticket machine; **~entwerter** der ticket cancelling machine; **~heft** das book of tickets

Fahr-: **~schule** die (a) (Unternehmen) driving school; (b) (ugs.: Unterricht) driving lessons pl; **~schüler** der (a) learner driver; (b) pupil who must use transport to get to school; **~spur** die traffic-lane; **die ~spur wechseln/beibehalten** change lanes/stay in one's lane

fährst /fɛːɐ̯st/ 2. Pers. Sg. Präsens v. fahren

Fahr-: **~stil** der style of driving; (mit dem Rad) style of riding; **~streifen** der ⇒ **~spur;** **~stuhl** der lift (Brit.); elevator (Amer.); (für Lasten) hoist; **mit dem ~ fahren** take the lift/elevator; **~stunde** die driving lesson

Fahrt /faːɐ̯t/ die; ~, ~en (a) ▶160| o. Pl. (das Fahren) journey; **freie ~ haben** have a clear run; (fig.) have been given the green light; (b) (Reise) journey; (Schiffsreise) voyage; **auf der ~:** on the journey; (c) (kurze Reise, Ausflug) trip; (Wanderung) hike; **eine ~ [nach/zu X] machen** go on or take a trip [to X]; **eine ~ ins Blaue machen** (mit dem Auto) go for a drive; (Veranstaltung) go on a mystery tour; **auf ~ gehen** (veralt.) go hiking; (d) o. Pl. (Bewegung) **~ machen** (Seemannsspr.) make way; **in voller ~:** at full speed; **die ~ verlangsamen** slow down; decelerate; **die ~ beschleunigen** speed up; accelerate; **~ aufnehmen** gather speed; pick up speed; **in ~ kommen** od. **geraten** (ugs.) get going; (böse werden) get worked up

fährt /fɛːɐ̯t/ 3. Pers. Sg. Präsens v. fahren

fahr·tauglich Adj. fit to drive postpos.

Fahr·tauglichkeit die fitness to drive

Fährte /'fɛːɐ̯tə/ die tracks pl.; trail; **jmds. ~ verfolgen** track sb.; **die richtige ~ finden** (fig.) get on the right track; **die falsche ~ verfolgen** (fig.) be on the wrong track

Fahrten·messer das sheath knife

Fahrt·kosten Pl. (für öffentliche Verkehrsmittel) fare/fares; (für Autoreisen) travel costs; **die ~ erstatten** pay travelling expenses

---

*alte Schreibung (vgl. Hinweise auf S. xvi–xvii)

Fahr·treppe *die* escalator

Fahrt·richtung *die* direction; **in ~ parken** park in the direction of the traffic; **gegen die ~ sitzen** (im Zug) sit with one's back to the engine; (im Bus) sit facing backwards; **in ~ sitzen** (im Zug) sit facing the engine; (im Bus) sit facing forwards

Fahrtrichtungs·anzeiger *der* (Kfz-W.) [direction] indicator

fahr·tüchtig *Adj.* ⟨*driver*⟩ fit to drive; roadworthy ⟨*vehicle*⟩

Fahr·tüchtigkeit *die* (des Fahrers) fitness to drive; (des Fahrzeugs) roadworthiness

Fahrt-: **~unterbrechung** *die* break [in the journey]; stop; **~wind** *der* airflow; **~ziel** *das* destination

fahr-, Fahr-: **~untüchtig** *Adj.* ⟨*driver*⟩ unfit to drive; unroadworthy ⟨*vehicle*⟩; **~verbot** *das* disqualification from driving; driving ban; **jmdm. [ein] ~verbot erteilen** ban *or* disqualify sb. from driving; **~wasser** *das* shipping channel; fairway; **in ein gefährliches ~wasser geraten** (fig.) get on to dangerous ground; **in jmds. ~wasser schwimmen** *od.* **segeln** (fig.) follow [along] in sb.'s wake; **~werk** *das* (Flugw.) undercarriage; **~zeit** *die* travelling time

Fahr·zeug *das* vehicle; (Luft~) aircraft; (Wasser~) vessel

Fahrzeug-: **~bau** *der* motor manufacturing industry; **~führer** *der* driver of a/the motor vehicle; **~halter** *der* registered keeper [of a/the vehicle]; **~papiere** *Pl.* vehicle documents *pl.*

Faible /ˈfɛːbl̩/ *das;* **~s, ~s** liking; (Schwäche) weakness (**für** for)

fair /fɛːɐ̯/ **1** *Adj.* fair (**gegen** to). **2** *adv.* fairly; **~ spielen** play fairly *or* (coll.) fair

Fairness, *Fairneß /ˈfɛːɐ̯nɛs/ *die;* **~:** fairness

Fakir /ˈfaːkiːɐ̯, österr.: faˈkiːɐ̯/ *der;* **~s, ~e** fakir

Faksimile /fakˈziːmile/ *das;* **~s, ~s** facsimile

Fakten ⇒ **Faktum**

faktisch 1 *Adj.; nicht präd.* real; actual; practical ⟨*disadvantage, usefulness*⟩. **2** *adv.* **(a) das bedeutet ~ ...:** it means in effect ...; **es ist ~ möglich/unmöglich** it is in actual fact possible/impossible; **(b)** (bes. österr. ugs.: praktisch, eigentlich) more or less; virtually

Faktor /ˈfaktɔr/ *der;* **~s, ~en** /-ˈtoːrən/ factor

Faktotum /fakˈtoːtʊm/ *das;* **~s, ~s** *od.* **Faktoten** (scherzh.) factotum

Faktum /ˈfaktʊm/ *das;* **~s, Fakten** fact

Faktur /fakˈtuːɐ̯/ *die;* **~, ~en** (Kaufmannsspr. veralt.) invoice

Fakultät /fakʊlˈtɛːt/ *die;* **~, ~en** (Hochschulw.) faculty

fakultativ /fakʊltaˈtiːf/ *Adj.* optional ⟨*subject, participation*⟩

Falke /ˈfalkə/ *der;* **~n, ~n** (auch Politik fig.) hawk

Falkland·inseln *Pl.* Falkland Islands; Falklands

Falkner *der;* **~s, ~:** falconer

Fall /fal/ *der;* **~[e]s, Fälle** /ˈfɛlə/ **(a)** (Sturz) fall; **zu ~ kommen** have a fall; (fig.) come to grief; **jmdn. zu ~ bringen** (fig.) bring about sb.'s downfall; **etw. zu ~ bringen** (fig.) stop sth.; **der ~ einer Stadt** (fig.) the fall of a town; **(b)** (das Fallen) descent; **der freie ~:** free fall; **(c)** (Ereignis, Vorkommnis) case; (zu erwartender Umstand) eventuality; **für den äußersten** *od.* **schlimmsten ~, im schlimmsten ~:** if the worst comes to the worst; **im besten ~:** at best; **es ist [nicht] der ~:** it is [not] the case; **gesetzt den ~:** assuming; supposing; **auf jeden ~, in jedem ~, auf alle Fälle** in any case; **auf keinen ~:** on no account; **das ist doch ein ganz klarer ~:** it's perfectly clear; **nicht jmds. ~ sein** (fig. ugs.) not be sb.'s cup of tea; **(d)** (Rechtsw., Med., Grammatik) case; **der 1./2./3./4. ~** (Grammatik) the nominative/genitive/dative/accusative case

Fall·beil *das* guillotine

Falle /ˈfalə/ *die;* **~, ~n (a)** (auch fig.) trap; **in die ~ gehen** walk into the trap; **jmdm. eine ~ stellen** (fig.) set a trap for sb.; **jmdm. in die ~ gehen** (fig.) fall into sb.'s trap; **(b)** (salopp: Bett) **in die ~ gehen** turn in (coll.)

fallen *unr. itr. V.; mit sein* **(a)** fall; **etw. ~ lassen** drop sth.; **sich ins Gras/Bett/Heu ~ lassen** fall on to the grass/into bed/into the hay; (fig.) **in Trümmer ~:** collapse in ruins; **in Schwermut ~:** be overcome by melancholy; **jmdn. ~ lassen** drop sb.; **eine Bemerkung ~ lassen** let fall a remark; **einen Hinweis ~ lassen** drop a hint; **einen Plan ~ lassen** abandon a plan; **(b)** (hin~, stürzen) fall [over]; **auf die Knie/in den Schmutz ~:** fall to one's knees/in the dirt; **über einen Stein ~:** trip over a stone; **(c)** (sinken) ⟨*prices*⟩ fall; ⟨*temperature, water level*⟩ fall, drop; ⟨*fever*⟩ subside; **im Preis ~:** go down *or* fall in price; **(d)** (an einen bestimmten Ort gelangen) ⟨*light, shadow, glance, choice, suspicion*⟩ fall; **die Wahl fiel auf ihn** the choice fell on him; **(e)** (abgegeben werden) ⟨*shot*⟩ be fired; (Sport: erzielt werden) ⟨*goal*⟩ be scored; (geäußert werden) ⟨*word*⟩ be spoken; ⟨*remark*⟩ be made; (getroffen werden) ⟨*decision*⟩ be taken *or* made; **(f)** (nach unten hängen) ⟨*hair*⟩ fall; **die Haare ~ ihr ins Gesicht/auf die Schulter** her hair falls over her face/to her shoulders; **(g)** (im Kampf sterben) die; fall (literary); **im Krieg ~:** die in the war; **(h)** (aufgehoben, beseitigt werden) ⟨*ban*⟩ be lifted; ⟨*tax*⟩ be abolished; ⟨*obstacle*⟩ be removed; ⟨*limitation*⟩ be overcome; **(i)** (zu einer bestimmten Zeit stattfinden) **in eine Zeit ~:** occur at a time; **mein Geburtstag fällt auf einen Samstag** my birthday falls on a Saturday; **(j)** (zu einem Bereich gehören) **in/unter eine Kategorie ~:** fall into *or* within a category; **unter ein Gesetz/eine Bestimmung ~:** come under a law/a regulation; **(k)** (zu~, zuteil werden) ⟨*inheritance, territory*⟩ fall (**an** + *Akk.* to); **jmdm. in die Hände ~:** fall into the hands of sb.

fällen /ˈfɛlən/ *tr. V.* **(a)** fell ⟨*tree, timber*⟩; **(b) ein Urteil ~** ⟨*judge*⟩ pass sentence; ⟨*jury*⟩ return a verdict; **einen Schiedsspruch ~:** make a ruling

***fallen|lassen** ⇒ **fallen** a

fällig /ˈfɛlɪç/ *Adj.* **(a)** due; **eine ~e Reform** an overdue reform; **(b)** ⟨*sum of money*⟩ payable, due; **ein ~er Wechsel/~e Zinsen** a bill to mature/interest payable

Fall·obst *das* windfalls *pl.*

Fall·rückzieher *der* (Fußball) bicycle kick

falls /fals/ *Konj.* if; (für den Fall, dass) in case; **~ es regnen sollte** in case it should rain

Fall·schirm *der* parachute; **mit dem ~ abspringen** (im Notfall) parachute out; (als Sport) make a [parachute] jump

Fallschirm-: **~springen** *das* parachuting *no art.*; **~springer** *der* parachutist

Fall-: **~strick** *der* trap; snare; **jmdm. ~stricke legen** (fig.) set traps for sb.; **~studie** *die* case study; **~tür** *die* trapdoor

falsch /falʃ/ **1** *Adj.* **(a)** (unecht, imitiert) false ⟨*teeth, plait*⟩; imitation ⟨*jewellery*⟩; **~er Hase** (Kochk.) meat loaf; **(b)** (gefälscht) counterfeit, forged ⟨*banknote*⟩; false, forged ⟨*passport*⟩; assumed ⟨*name*⟩; **(c)** (irrig, fehlerhaft) wrong ⟨*impression, track, pronunciation*⟩; wrong, incorrect ⟨*answer*⟩; **logisch ~ sein** be logically false; **an den Falschen geraten** come to the wrong man; **etw. in die ~e Kehle** *od.* **den ~en Hals bekommen** (fig. ugs.) take sth. the wrong way; **(d)** (unangebracht) false ⟨*shame, modesty*⟩; **(e)** (irreführend) false ⟨*statement, promise*⟩; **unter Vorspiegelung ~er Tatsachen** under false pretences; **(f)** (abwertend: hinterhältig) false ⟨*friend*⟩; **ein ~er Hund** (salopp) a two-faced so-and-so (sl.); **eine ~e Schlange** (fig.) a snake in the grass; **ein ~es Spiel [mit jmdm.] treiben** play false with sb. **2** *adv.* **(a)** (fehlerhaft) wrongly; incorrectly; **~ singen** sing wrongly; **~ gehen/fahren** go the wrong way; **etw. ~ verstehen** misunderstand sth.; **die Uhr geht ~:** the clock is wrong; **~ informiert** *od.* **unterrichtet sein** be misinformed; **~ herum** (verkehrt) back to front; the wrong way round; (auf dem Kopf) upside down; (links) inside out; **~ liegen** (ugs.) be mistaken; **(b)** (irreführend) **~ schwören** lie on oath

Falsch·aus·sage *die* (Rechtsspr.) **[eidliche] ~aussage** false testimony *or* evidence; **uneidliche ~aussage** false statement [not on oath]

fälschen /ˈfɛlʃn̩/ *tr. V.* forge, fake ⟨*signature, document, passport*⟩; forge, counterfeit ⟨*coin, banknote*⟩

Fälscher *der;* **~s, ~** ⇒ **fälschen:** forger; counterfeiter

Falsch·geld *das* counterfeit money

Falschheit *die;* **~:** duplicity; deceitfulness

fälschlich /ˈfɛlʃlɪç/ **1** *Adj.; nicht präd.* false ⟨*claim, accusation*⟩; (irrtümlich) mistaken, false ⟨*assumption, suspicion*⟩. **2** *adv.*

falsely, wrongly ⟨*claim, accuse*⟩; mistakenly, falsely ⟨*assume, suspect*⟩

fälschlicher·weise *Adv.* by mistake; mistakenly

falsch-, Falsch-: *~|**liegen** ⇨ **falsch 2 a;** *~* **meldung** *die* false report; ~**münzer** /'~myntsɐ/ *der* forger; counterfeiter

Fälschung *die;* ~, ~**en (a)** fake; counterfeit; **(b)** (das Fälschen) ⇨ **fälschen:** forging; counterfeiting

Falsett /fal'zɛt/ *das;* ~[e]s, ~e (Musik) falsetto [voice]

Falt-: ~**blatt** *das* leaflet; (in Zeitungen, Zeitschriften, Büchern) insert; ~**boot** *das* collapsible boat

Falte /'faltə/ *die;* ~, ~**n (a)** crease; ~**n schlagen** crease; **(b)** (im Stoff) fold; (mit scharfer Kante) pleat; **(c)** (Haut~) wrinkle; line; **die Stirn in** ~**n legen** *od.* **ziehen** (nachdenklich) knit one's brow; (verärgert) frown; **(d)** (Geol.) fold

fälteln /'fɛltln/ *tr. V.* pleat

falten 1 *tr. V.* fold; **die Hände** ~**:** fold one's hands. **2** *refl. V.* (auch Geol.) fold; ⟨*skin*⟩ wrinkle, become wrinkled

falten-, Falten-: ~**bildung** *die* folding; (der Haut) wrinkling; ~**gebirge** *das* [range *sing.* of] fold mountains *pl.*; ~**los** *Adj.* uncreased ⟨*garment*⟩; unwrinkled ⟨*skin*⟩; ~**rock** *der* pleated skirt

Falter *der;* ~s, ~ (Nacht~) moth; (Tag~) butterfly

faltig (a) *Adj.* ⟨*clothes*⟩ gathered [in folds]; wrinkled ⟨*skin, hands*⟩; **(b)** (zerknittert) creased

-fältig /-fɛltɪç/ *Adj., adv.* -fold

Falz /falts/ *der;* ~es, ~e (Buchbinderei) (scharfe Faltlinie) fold; (Übergang zwischen Buchdeckel und -rücken) groove

falzen *tr. V.* (Buchbinderei) fold; (Technik) seam

familiär /fami'liːɐ̯/ **1** *Adj.* **(a)** family ⟨*problems, worries*⟩; **aus** ~**en Gründen** for family reasons; **(b)** (zwanglos) familiar; informal; informal ⟨*tone, relationship*⟩. **2** *adv.* (zwanglos) **sich** ~ **ausdrücken** to talk in a familiar way

Familie /fa'miːliə/ *die;* ~, ~**n (a)** family; ~ **Meyer** the Meyer family; ~ **haben** (ugs.) have a family; **eine** ~ **gründen** (heiraten) marry; (Kinder bekommen) start a family; **das bleibt in der** ~**:** it will stay in the family; **das kommt in den besten** ~**n vor** it happens in the best families; **das liegt in der** ~**:** it runs in the family; **(b)** (Biol.) family

familien-, Familien-: ~**angehörige** *der/die; adj. Dekl.* member of the family; ~**angelegenheit** *die* family affair *or* matter; ~**anschluss,** *~*~**anschluß** *der* personal contact [with a/the family]; ~**anzeigen** *Pl.* births, deaths, and marriages; ~**besitz** *der* family property; **im** ~**besitz** in the family's possession; ~**betrieb** *der* family business *or* firm; ~**feier** *die* family party; ~**krach** *der* (ugs.) family row; ~**kreis** *der* family circle; **im engsten** ~**kreis** in the immediate family; ~**leben** *das; o. Pl.* family life; ~**mit·glied** *das* member of the family; ~**name** *der* surname; family name; ~**ober·haupt** *das* head of the family; ~**planung** *die; o. Pl.* family planning *no art.;* ~**politik** *die; o. Pl.* policy/policies relating to the family; ~**stand** *der* marital status; ~**vater** *der:* ~**vater sein** be the father of a family; **ein guter** ~**vater** a good husband and father; ~**verhältnisse** *Pl.* family circumstances; family background

famos /fa'moːs/ (veralt.) **1** *Adj.* splendid. **2** *adv.* splendidly

Fan /fɛn/ *der;* ~s, ~s fan

Fanal /fa'naːl/ *das;* ~s, ~e (geh.) torch

Fanatiker /fa'naːtikɐ/ *der;* ~s, ~: fanatic; (religiös) fanatic; zealot

fanatisch 1 *Adj.* fanatical. **2** *adv.* fanatically

Fanatismus *der;* ~: fanaticism

fand /fant/ *1. u. 3. Pers. Sg. Prät. v.* **finden**

Fanfare /fan'faːrə/ *die;* ~, ~**n (a)** herald's trumpet; **(b)** (Signal) fanfare; flourish

Fang /faŋ/ *der;* ~[e]s, **Fänge** /'fɛŋə/ **(a)** *o. Pl.* (Tier~) trapping; (von Fischen) catching; **(b)** *o. Pl.* (Beute) bag; (von Fischen) catch; haul; **einen guten** ~ **machen** *od.* **tun** (fig.) make a good catch

Fang·arm *der* (Zool.) tentacle

fangen 1 *unr. tr. V.* **(a)** (ergreifen, fassen) catch, trap ⟨*bird, animal*⟩; catch ⟨*fish*⟩; **die Katze fängt eine Maus** the cat catches a mouse; **eine** ~ (südd., österr. ugs.) get a clip round the ear (coll.); **(b)** (gefangen nehmen) catch, capture ⟨*fugitive etc.*⟩; **gefangene Soldaten** captured soldiers; **von etw. [ganz] gefangen sein** (fig.) be [quite] enthralled by sth.; **jmdn./ein Tier gefangen halten** hold sb. prisoner *or* captive/keep an animal in captivity; **jmdn. gefangen nehmen** capture sb.; take sb. prisoner; **jmdn. gefangen halten** (fig. geh.: fesseln) hold sb. enthralled; **(c)** *auch itr.* (auffangen) catch ⟨*ball*⟩; **er kann gut/nicht** ~**:** he's good/not good at catching. **2** *unr. refl. V.* **(a)** (in eine Falle geraten, nicht mehr frei kommen) get *or* be caught; **(b)** (wieder in die normale Lage kommen) **sich [gerade] noch** ~**:** [just] manage to steady oneself; **sich wieder** ~ (fig.) recover

Fangen *das;* ~**s:** ~ **spielen** play tag *or* catch

Fänger /'fɛŋɐ/ *der;* ~s, ~: catcher; (von Großwild) hunter

Fang-: ~**frage** *die* catch question; trick question; ~**netz** *das* (Fischereiw.) [fishing] net; ~**schuss,** *~*~**schuß** *der* (Jägerspr.) coup de grâce

Fan- /fɛn-/: ~**klub** *der* fan club; ~**post** *die* fan mail

Fantasie /fanta'ziː/ *die;* ~, ~**n (a)** *o. Pl.* imagination; **eine schmutzige** ~ **haben** have a dirty mind; **(b)** *meist Pl.* (Produkt der ~) fantasy

fantasie·los 1 *Adj.* unimaginative. **2** *adv.* unimaginatively

Fantasie·losigkeit *die;* ~**:** lack of imagination; (Eintönigkeit) dullness

fantasieren 1 *itr. V.* **(a)** indulge in fantasies, fantasize (von about); **(b)** (Med.: irrereden) talk deliriously. **2** *tr. V.* **was fantasierst du da?** what's all that nonsense?

fantasie·voll 1 *Adj.* imaginative. **2** *adv.* imaginatively

fantastisch 1 *Adj.* **(a)** fantastic; ⟨*idea*⟩ divorced from reality; **(b)** (ugs.: großartig) fantastic (coll.); terrific (coll.). **2** *adv.* (ugs.) fantastically (coll.); ~ **tanzen** (ugs.) dance fantastically (coll.) *or* incredibly well

Farb-: ~**band** *das* [typewriter] ribbon; ~**bild** *das* **(a)** (Foto) colour photo; **(b)** (Illustration) colour picture; ~**dia** *das* colour slide; colour transparency

Farbe /'farbə/ *die;* ~, ~**n (a)** colour; ~ **bekommen/ verlieren** get some colour/lose one's colour; **an** ~ **gewinnen/verlieren** (fig.) become more/less colourful; **(b)** (Substanz) (zum Malen, Anstreichen) paint; (zum Färben) dye; ~**n mischen/auftragen** mix/apply paint; **(c)** *o. Pl.* (Farbigkeit) colour; **der Film ist in** ~**:** the film is in colour; **(d)** (Kartenspiel) suit; **eine** ~ **bedienen** follow suit; ~ **bekennen** (fig. ugs.) come clean (coll.)

farb·echt *Adj.* colour-fast

Färbe·mittel *das* dye

färben /'fɛrbn/ **1** *tr. V.* **(a)** dye ⟨*wool, material, hair*⟩; **etw. grün** ~**:** dye sth. green; **(b)** **eine politisch gefärbte Rede** a speech with a political slant. **2** *refl. V.* **sich schwarz/rot** *usw.* ~**:** turn black/red etc. **3** *itr. V.* (ugs.: ab~) ⟨*material, blouse etc.*⟩ run

-farben *Adj., adv.* -coloured; **creme**~ angestrichen painted cream

farben-, Farben-: ~**blind** *Adj.* colour-blind; ~**freudig** *Adj.,* ~**froh** *Adj.* colourful; ~**pracht** *die* colourful splendour; ~**prächtig** *Adj.* vibrant with colour; postpos.

Färber *der;* ~s, ~: ▶ 85 dyer

Färberei *die;* ~, ~**en** dye-works *sing.*

Färberin *die;* ~, ~**nen** dyer

Farb-: ~**fernsehen** *das* colour television; ~**fernseher** *der* (ugs.) colour telly (coll.) *or* television; ~**fernsehgerät** *das* colour television [set]; ~**film** *der* colour film; ~**foto** *das* colour photo; ~**fotografie** *die o. Pl.* colour photography

farbig 1 *Adj.* **(a)** coloured; **(b)** (bunt, fig.) colourful ⟨*dress, picture, description, tale*⟩; ~**e [Kirchen]fenster** stained-glass [church-]windows. **2** *adv.* colourfully

-farbig *Adj., adv.* ⇨ **-farben**

Farbige *der/die; adj. Dekl.* coloured man/woman; coloured; **die** ~**n** the coloured people; (in Südafrika) the Coloureds

farblich 1 *Adj.* in colour *postpos.;* as regards colour *postpos.* **2** *adv.* **etw. ~ aufeinander abstimmen** match sth. in colour

farb-, Farb-: **~los** *Adj.* (auch fig.) colourless; clear ‹*varnish*›; neutral ‹*shoe polish*›; **~schicht** *die* layer of paint; (Anstrich) coat of paint; **~stift** *der* (a) (Buntstift) coloured pencil; **(b)** (Filzstift) coloured felt-tip *or* pen; **~stoff** *der* (a) (Med., Biol.) pigment; **(b)** (für Lebensmittel) colouring; **~ton** *der* shade

Färbung *die;* **~, ~en** (a) (Farbgebung) colouring; colour; **(b)** (das Färben) dyeing; **(c)** (fig.: Tendenz) slant

Farce /'farsə/ *die;* **~, ~n** farce

Farm /farm/ *die;* **~, ~en** farm

Farmer *der;* **~s, ~:** farmer

Farn /farn/ *der;* **~[e]s, ~e** fern

Farn·kraut *das* fern

Fasan /fa'za:n/ *der;* **~[e]s, ~e[n]** pheasant

Faschierte *das; adj. Dekl.* (österr.) minced meat; mince

Fasching /'faʃɪŋ/ *der;* **~s, ~e** *od.* **~s** [pre-Lent] carnival

Faschismus /fa'ʃɪsmʊs/ *der;* **~:** fascism *no art.*

Faschist *der;* **~en, ~en** fascist

faschistisch *Adj.* fascist

faseln /'fa:zḷn/ *itr. V.* (ugs. abwertend) drivel; blather

Faser /'fa:zɐ/ *die;* **~, ~n** fibre

faserig *Adj.* fibrous ‹*paper*›; stringy ‹*meat*›

fasern *itr. V.* fray

Faser·pflanze *die* fibre-plant

Fas·nacht /'fas-/ *die; o. Pl.* (bes. südd.) ⇒ **Fastnacht**

Fass, *Faß /fas/ *das;* **Fasses, Fässer** /'fɛsɐ/ barrel; (Öl~, Benzin~ usw.) drum; (kleines Bier~) keg; (kleines Sherry~, Portwein~ usw.) cask; **Bier vom ~:** draught beer; **das schlägt dem ~ den Boden aus** (ugs.) that takes the biscuit (Brit. coll.) *or* (coll.) cake; **ein ~ ohne Boden sein** be an endless drain on sb.'s resources; **ein ~ aufmachen** (ugs.) paint the town red (fig. coll.)

Fassade /fa'sa:də/ *die;* **~, ~n** (a) façade; frontage; **(b)** (abwertend: äußere Erscheinung) façade; front

fassbar, *faßbar *Adj.* (a) (greifbar, konkret) tangible; concrete ‹*results*›; **(b)** (verständlich) comprehensible

Fass·bier, *Faß·bier *das* beer on draught; (Bier vom Fass) draught beer

Fässchen, *Fäßchen /'fɛsçən/ *das;* **~s, ~:** small barrel; [small] cask

fassen /'fasḏ/ **1** *tr. V.* (a) (greifen) grasp; take hold of; **jmdn. am Arm ~:** take hold of sb.'s arm; **jmdn. bei der Hand ~:** take sb. by the hand; **etw. zu ~ bekommen** get a hold on sth.; **(b)** (festnehmen) catch ‹*thief, culprit*›; **(c)** ▶ 427 | (aufnehmen können) ‹*hall, tank*› hold; **(d)** (begreifen) **ich kann es nicht ~:** I cannot take it in; **das ist [doch] nicht zu fassen!** it's incredible; **(e)** (in verblasster Bedeutung) make, take ‹*decision*›; **Vertrauen** *od.* **Zutrauen zu jmdm. ~:** begin to feel confidence in *or* to trust sb.; **Mut ~:** take courage; **(f)** (in eine Fassung bringen) set, mount ‹*jewel*›; curb ‹*spring, well*›; **(g)** (formulieren, gestalten) **etw. in Worte/Verse ~:** put sth. into words/verse; **einen Begriff eng/weit ~:** define a concept narrowly/widely; **(h)** (fachspr.: aufnehmen) take on ‹*load, goods*›; **(i)** (Soldatenspr.) draw ‹*rations, supplies, ammunition*›. **2** *itr. V.* (a) (greifen) **nach etw. ~:** reach for sth.; **in etw. (Akk.) ~:** put one's hand in sth.; **an etw. (Akk.) ~:** touch sth.; **ins Leere ~:** grasp thin air; **(b)** (einrasten) ‹*screw*› bite; ‹*cog*› mesh. **3** *refl. V.* (a) pull oneself together; recover [oneself]; **(b) sich kurz ~:** be brief

Fasson /fa'sõ:/ *die;* **~, ~s** style; shape; **jeder muss nach seiner [eigenen]** *od.* **auf seine [eigene] ~ selig werden** everyone has to work out his own salvation

Fasson·schnitt *der* short back and sides

Fassung *die;* **~, ~en** (a) (Version) version; **(b)** *o. Pl.* (Selbstbeherrschung, Haltung) composure; self-control; **die ~ bewahren** keep one's composure; **die ~ verlieren** lose one's self-control; **jmdn. aus der ~ bringen** upset *or* ruffle sb.; **etw. mit ~ tragen** bear sth. calmly; **(c)** (für Glühlampen) holder; **(d)** (von Juwelen) setting; (Bilder~, Brillen~) frame

fassungs-, Fassungs-: **~los** *Adj.* stunned; **jmdn. ~los anstarren** gaze at sb. in bewilderment; **~losigkeit** *die* state of bewilderment; **~vermögen** *das;* ▶ 427 | *o. Pl.* capacity

fast /fast/ *Adv.* almost; nearly; **~ nie** almost never; hardly ever; **~ nirgends** hardly anywhere

fasten *itr. V.* fast

Fasten-: **~kur** *die* drastic reducing diet; **~zeit** *die* (a) (Rel.) time of fasting; **(b)** (kath. Rel.) Lent

Fast·nacht *die* (a) (Faschingsdienstag) Shrove Tuesday; **(b)** (Karneval) carnival; Shrovetide

Fastnachts-: **~dienstag** *der* Shrove Tuesday; **~zug** *der* carnival procession

Faszination /fastsina'tsi̯o:n/ *die;* **~:** fascination; **eine ~ auf jmdn. ausüben** fascinate sb.

faszinieren /fastsi'ni:rən/ *tr. V.* fascinate

fatal /fa'ta:l/ *Adj.* (a) fatal; **(b)** (peinlich, misslich) awkward; embarrassing; **~e Folgen haben** have unfortunate consequences

Fatalismus *der;* **~:** fatalism

Fatalist *der;* **~en, ~en** fatalist

fatalistisch *Adj.* fatalistic

Fata Morgana /'fa:ta mɔr'ga:na/ *die;* **~ ~, ~ Morganen** *od.* **~s** fata morgana; mirage; (fig.) illusion

Fatzke /'fatskə/ *der;* **~n** *od.* **~s, ~n** *od.* **~s** (ugs. abwertend) twit (Brit. coll.); jerk (sl.)

fauchen /'fauxn/ *itr. V.* (a) ‹*cat*› hiss; ‹*tiger*› snarl; (fig.) ‹*engine*› hiss; **(b)** (sich gereizt äußern) snarl

faul /faul/ **1** *Adj.* (a) (verdorben) rotten, bad ‹*food*›; bad ‹*tooth*›; rotten ‹*wood*›; foul, stale ‹*air*›; foul ‹*water*›; **(b)** (träge) lazy; idle; **zu ~ zu etw. sein/zu ~ sein, etw. zu tun** be too lazy *or* idle for sth./to do sth.; **auf der ~en Haut liegen/sich auf die ~e Haut legen** take it easy; **(c)** (ugs.: nicht einwandfrei) bad ‹*joke*›; dud ‹*cheque*›; false ‹*peace*›; lame ‹*excuse*›; shabby ‹*compromise*›; shady ‹*business, customer*›; **das ist doch [alles] ~er Zauber** it's [all] quite bogus; **etwas ist ~ im Staate Dänemark** something is rotten in the state of Denmark; **(d)** (säumig) bad ‹*debtor*›. **2** *adv.* (träge) lazily; idly

faulen *itr. V.; meist mit sein* rot; ‹*water*› go foul, stagnate; ‹*meat*› go off, putrefy; ‹*fish*› go off, go bad

faulenzen /'faulɛntsn̩/ *itr. V.* laze about; loaf about (derog.)

Faulenzer *der;* **~s, ~:** idler; lazybones *sing.* (coll.)

Faulenzerei *die;* **~, ~en** (abwertend) idleness; laziness

Faulheit *die;* **~:** laziness; idleness

faulig *Adj.* stagnating ‹*water*›; putrefying ‹*meat*›; ‹*meat*› which is going bad; rotting ‹*vegetables, fruit*›; foul, putrid ‹*smell*›; **~ schmecken/riechen** taste/smell bad *or* off

Fäulnis /'fɔylnɪs/ *die;* **~:** rottenness; **in ~ übergehen** begin to rot

Faul-: **~pelz** *der* (fam.) lazybones *sing.* (coll.); **~tier** *das* (a) (Zool.) sloth; **(b)** (ugs.: Faulenzer) ⇒ **~pelz**

Fauna /'fauna/ *die;* **~, Faunen** (Zool.) fauna

Faust /faust/ *die;* **~, Fäuste** /'fɔystə/ fist; **eine ~ machen, die Hand zur ~ ballen** clench one's fist; **die ~ ballen/öffnen** clench/unclench one's fist; **jmdm. mit der ~ ins Gesicht schlagen** punch sb. in the face; **das passt wie die ~ aufs Auge** (ugs.) (passt nicht) that clashes horribly; (passt) that matches perfectly; **die ~/Fäuste in der Tasche ballen** (fig.) be seething inwardly; **auf eigene ~:** on one's own initiative; off one's own bat (coll.); **mit der ~ auf den Tisch schlagen** *od.* **hauen** (fig.) put one's foot down

Faust·ball *der* faustball

Fäustchen /'fɔystçən/ *das;* **~s, ~:** fist; **sich (Dat.) ins ~ lachen** laugh up one's sleeve; (aus finanziellen Gründen) laugh all the way to the bank

faust·dick 1 *Adj.* as thick as a man's fist *postpos.;* **eine ~e Lüge** (fig.) a bare-faced lie. **2** *adv.* **er hat es ~ hinter den Ohren** (ugs.) he's a crafty *or* sly one

fausten *tr. V.* fist, punch ‹*ball*›

faust-, Faust-: **~groß** *Adj.* as big as a fist *postpos.;* **~handschuh** *der* mitten; **~kampf** *der* (geh.) pugilism; boxing; (Wettkampf) boxing contest; **~kämpfer** *der* (geh.) pugilist; boxer

Fäustling /'fɔystlɪŋ/ *der;* ~s, ~e mitten

Faust-: ~**pfand** *das* security; ~**recht** *das; o. Pl.* rule of force; ~**regel** *die* rule of thumb; ~**schlag** *der* punch

Fauxpas /fo'pa/ *der;* ~ /fo'pas/, ~ /fo'pas/ faux pas

Favorit /favo'ri:t/ *der;* ~en, ~en favourite

Fax /faks/ *das;* ~es, ~e fax

faxen *tr. V.* fax

Faxen *Pl.* (ugs.) (a) (dumme Späße) fooling around; **lass die** ~! stop fooling around *or* playing the fool!; (b) (Grimassen) ~ **machen** *od.* **schneiden** make *or* pull faces

Fax-: ~**gerät** *das* fax machine; ~**nummer** *die* fax number

Fazit /'fa:tsɪt/ *das;* ~s, ~s *od.* ~e result; **das** ~ [**aus etw.**] **ziehen** sum [sth.] up

FDJ /ɛfde:'jɔt/ *die;* ~ *Abk.* (DDR) **Freie Deutsche Jugend** Free German Youth

F.D.P. /'ɛfde:pe:/ *die;* ~ *Abk.* **Freie Demokratische Partei**

F-Dur /'ɛf-/ *das;* ~ (Musik) [key of] F major

Feature /'fi:tʃɐ/ *das;* ~s, ~s *od.* *die;* ~, ~s (Rundf., Ferns., Zeitungsw.) feature

Februar /'fe:brua:ɐ̯/ *der;* ~[s], ~e ▶119 February; *s. auch* **April**

fechten /'fɛçtn̩/ *unr. itr., tr. V.* fence; (fig. geh.) fight

Fechter *der;* ~s, ~, **Fechterin** *die;* ~, ~nen fencer

Fecht·kampf *der* rapier fight; (Sport) fencing bout

Feder /'fe:dɐ/ *die;* ~, ~n (a) (Vogel~) feather; (Gänse~) quill; (lange Hut~) plume; [**noch**] **in den** ~**n liegen** (ugs.) [still] be in one's bed; **sich mit fremden** ~**n schmücken** strut in borrowed plumes; (b) (zum Schreiben) nib; (mit Halter) pen; (Gänse~) quill[-pen]; **eine spitze** ~ **führen** (geh.) wield a sharp pen; **zur** ~ **greifen** (geh.) take up one's pen; (c) (Technik) spring

feder-, Feder-: ~**ball** *der* (a) *o. Pl.* (Spiel) badminton; (b) (Ball) shuttlecock; ~**bett** *das* duvet (Brit.); continental quilt (Brit.); stuffed quilt (Amer.); ~**fuchser** /~fʊksɐ/ *der;* ~s, ~ (abwertend) pen-pusher; ~**führend** *Adj.* in charge *postpos.;* ~**führung** *die:* **unter der** ~**führung des Ministers** under the overall control of the minister; ~**gewicht** (Schwerathletik) featherweight; *s. auch* **Fliegengewicht a;** ~**halter** *der* fountain pen; ~**kiel** *der* quill; ~**kissen** *das* feather cushion; (im Bett) feather pillow; ~**kraft** *die* tension [of a/the spring]; ~**leicht 1** *Adj.* ⟨*person*⟩ as light as a feather; featherweight ⟨*object*⟩; **2** *adv.* as lightly as a feather; ~**lesen** *das:* **nicht viel** ~**lesen[s] mit jmdm./etw. machen** make short work of sb./sth.; **ohne viel** ~**lesen[s], ohne langes** ~**lesen** without much ado; **viel zu viel** ~**lesen[s] machen** make far too much fuss; ~**mappe** *die* pen and pencil case

federn 1 *itr. V.* ⟨*springboard, floor, etc.*⟩ be springy; **in den Knien** ~: bend at the knees. **2** *tr. V.* (a) spring; **das Auto ist gut/schlecht gefedert** the car has good/poor suspension; **das Bett ist gut gefedert** the bed is well-sprung; (b) *s. auch* **teeren**

Feder·strich *der* stroke of the pen

Federung *die;* ~, ~en (in Möbeln) springs *pl.;* (Kfz-W.) suspension

Feder-: ~**vieh** *das* (ugs.) poultry; ~**zeichnung** *die* pen-and-ink drawing

Fee /fe:/ *die;* ~, ~n fairy

Fege·feuer *das* purgatory

fegen /'fe:gn̩/ **1** *tr. V.* (a) (bes. nordd.: säubern) sweep; (mit einem Handfeger) brush; (b) (schnell entfernen) brush; **etwas vom Tisch** ~: brush sth. off the table; (fig.) brush sth. aside; (c) (schnell treiben) sweep; drive. **2** *itr. V.* (a) sweep; do the sweeping; (b) *mit sein* (rasen, stürmen) sweep; tear (coll.)

Fehde /'fe:də/ *die;* ~, ~n feud; **mit jmdm. in** ~ **liegen** be at feud with sb.

fehl /fe:l/ *Adv.* ~ **am Platz[e] sein** be out of place

Fehl·anzeige *die* (a) ~! (ugs.) no chance (coll.); (b) (Milit.) nil return

fehlbar *Adj.* fallible

Fehl-: ~**besetzung** *die:* [als Ophelia] **eine** ~**besetzung sein** be miscast [in the role of Ophelia]; ~**betrag** *der* (bes. Kaufmannsspr.) deficit; ~**diagnose** *die* incorrect diagnosis; ~**einschätzung** *die* false assessment; (einer Entwicklung) misjudgement

fehlen *itr. V.* (a) (nicht vorhanden sein) be lacking; **ihm fehlt der Vater/das Geld** he has no father/no money; **ihr fehlt der Sinn dafür** she lacks a *or* has no feeling for it; (b) (ausbleiben) be missing; be absent; [**un**]**entschuldigt** ~: be absent with[out] permission; **du darfst bei dieser Party nicht** ~: you mustn't miss this party; **Knoblauch darf bei dieser Soße nicht** ~: garlic is a must in this sauce; (c) (verschwunden sein) be missing; be gone; **in der Kasse fehlt Geld** money is missing *or* has gone from the till; (d) (vermisst werden) **er/das wird mir** ~: I shall miss him/that; (e) (erforderlich sein) be needed; **ihm** ~ **noch zwei Punkte zum Sieg** he needs only two points to win; **es fehlte nicht viel, und ich wäre eingeschlafen** I all but fell asleep; **das fehlte mir gerade noch** [**zu meinem Glück**], **das hat mir gerade noch gefehlt** (ugs.) that's all I needed; (f) *unpers.* (mangeln) **es fehlt an Lehrern** there is a lack of teachers; **bei ihnen fehlt es am Nötigsten** they lack what is most needed; **es an nichts** ~ **lassen** provide everything that is needed; **es fehlt an allen Ecken und Enden** *od.* **Kanten** [**bei jmdm.**] sb. is short of everything; (g) **was fehlt Ihnen?** what seems to be the matter?; **fehlt dir etwas?** is there something wrong?; are you all right?; (h) **weit gefehlt!** (geh.) far from it!

Fehl·entscheidung *die* wrong decision

Fehler *der;* ~s, ~ (a) mistake; error; (falsches Verhalten, Sport) fault; (b) (schlechte Eigenschaft) fault; shortcoming; (Gebrechen) [physical] defect; (c) (schadhafte Stelle) flaw; blemish; **Porzellan mit kleinen** ~**n** porcelain with small flaws *or* imperfections

fehler·frei 1 *Adj.* faultless, perfect ⟨*piece of work, dictation, etc.*⟩; correct ⟨*measurement*⟩; **ein** ~**es Deutsch sprechen/schreiben** speak/write faultless *or* perfect German; (Reiten) **ein** ~**er Durchgang** a clear round. **2** *adv.* without any mistakes; (Reiten) without any faults

fehlerhaft *Adj.* faulty; defective; incorrect ⟨*measurement*⟩; **eine** ~**e Stelle im Material** a defect in the material

fehler-, Fehler-: ~**los 1** *Adj.* flawless; **2** *adv.* flawlessly; without a mistake; ~**quelle** *die* source of error; ~**quote** *die* (Statistik, Schulw.) error rate; ~**zahl** *die* number of mistakes *or* errors

fehl-, Fehl-: ~**farbe** *die* (Kartenspiel) (Farbe, die einem Spieler fehlt) void suit; (Farbe, die nicht Trumpf ist) plain suit; ~**geburt** *die* miscarriage; ~**gehen** *unr. itr. V.; mit sein* (geh.) (a) (sich irren) go *or* be wrong; (b) (sich verlaufen) lose one's way; **Sie können nicht** ~**gehen** you cannot go [far] wrong; ~**griff** *der* mistake; wrong choice; ~**information** *die* piece of wrong information; **auf einer** ~**information beruhen** be based on [a piece of] incorrect information; ~**interpretation** *die* misinterpretation; ~**investition** *die* bad investment; ~**konstruktion** *die:* **eine** ~**konstruktion sein** be badly designed; ~**pass,** ***~**paß** *der* (Ballspiele) bad pass; ~**planung** *die* [piece of] bad planning *no art.;* ~**schlag** *der* failure; ~**schlagen** *unr. itr. V.; mit sein* fail; ~**start** *der* (a) (Leichtathletik) false start; (b) (Flugw.) faulty start; (c) (Raumf.) abortive launch; ~**tritt** *der* (a) false step; (b) (geh.: Verfehlung) slip; indiscretion; ~**urteil** *das* (a) (Rechtsw.) **ein** ~**urteil fällen** ⟨*jury*⟩ return a wrong verdict; ⟨*judge*⟩ pass a wrong judgement; (b) (falsche Beurteilung) error of judgement; ~**zündung** *die* (Technik) misfire

feien /'faɪən/ *tr. V.* (geh.) protect ⟨**gegen** against⟩

Feier /'faɪɐ/ *die;* ~, ~n (a) (Veranstaltung) party; (aus festlichem Anlass) celebration; **eine** ~ **in kleinem Rahmen/im Familienkreis** a small/family celebration/party; (b) (Zeremonie) ceremony; **zur** ~ **des Tages** (oft scherzh.) in honour of the occasion

Feier·abend *der* (a) (Zeit nach der Arbeit) evening; **schönen** ~! have a nice evening; (b) (Arbeitsschluss) finishing time; **nach** ~: after work; ~ **machen** finish work;

knock off (coll.); **für mich ist** ∼, **dann ist** *od.* **mache ich** ∼ (fig. ugs.) I'm finished; I've had enough (coll.)

feierlich 1 *Adj.* (a) ceremonial; solemn; **eine** ∼e Handlung a ceremonial act; **das ist ja [schon] nicht mehr** ∼ (ugs.) it's got beyond a joke; (b) (emphatisch) solemn ⟨*declaration*⟩. 2 *adv.* (a) solemnly; ceremoniously; ∼ **verabschiedet werden** be given a ceremonious farewell; (b) (emphatisch) solemnly ⟨*declare, swear, etc.*⟩

Feierlichkeit *die;* ∼, ∼**en** (a) *o. Pl.* solemnity; (b) *meist Pl.* (Veranstaltung) celebration; festivity

feiern 1 *tr. V.* (a) (festlich begehen) celebrate ⟨*birthday, wedding, etc.*⟩; **man muss die Feste** ∼, **wie sie fallen** you have to enjoy yourself while you can; (b) (ehren, umjubeln) acclaim ⟨*artist, sportsman, etc.*⟩. 2 *itr. V.* celebrate; have a party

Feier-: ∼**schicht** *die* (Arbeitswelt) cancelled shift; **eine** ∼**schicht einlegen müssen** have one's shift cancelled; ∼**tag** *der* holiday; **ein gesetzlicher/kirchlicher** ∼**tag** a public holiday/religious festival; **an Sonn- und** ∼**tagen** on Sundays and public holidays

feig /faik/, **feige** /ˈfaigə/ 1 *Adj.* cowardly. 2 *adv.* like a coward/like cowards; in a cowardly way

Feige *die;* ∼, ∼**n** fig

Feigen-: ∼**baum** *der* fig tree; ∼**blatt** *das* (a) fig leaf; (b) (fig.) front; cover

Feigheit *die;* ∼: cowardice; cowardliness

Feigling *der;* ∼**s**, ∼**e** coward

feil /fail/ *Adj.* (veralt.) for sale *postpos.;* (fig.) venal

feil|bieten *unr. tr. V.* (geh.) offer ⟨*goods*⟩ for sale

Feile *die;* ∼, ∼**n** file

feilen *tr., itr. V.* file

feilschen /ˈfailʃn/ *itr. V.* (ugs.) haggle (**um** over)

fein /fain/ 1 *Adj.* (a) (zart) fine ⟨*material, line, etc.*⟩; (b) (∼körnig) fine ⟨*sand, powder*⟩; finely-ground ⟨*flour*⟩; finely-granulated ⟨*sugar*⟩; **etw.** ∼ **mahlen** grind sth. fine; (c) (hochwertig) high-quality ⟨*fruit, soap, etc.*⟩; fine ⟨*silver, gold, etc.*⟩; fancy ⟨*cakes, pastries, etc.*⟩; **nur das Feinste vom Feinen kaufen** buy only the best; (d) (ugs.: erfreulich) great (coll.); marvellous; (e) (∼ geschnitten) finely shaped, delicate ⟨*hands, features, etc.*⟩; (f) (scharf, exakt) keen, sensitive ⟨*hearing*⟩; keen ⟨*sense of smell*⟩; (g) (ugs.: anständig, nett) great (coll.), splendid ⟨*person*⟩; **eine** ∼**e Verwandtschaft/Gesellschaft** (iron.) a fine *or* nice family/crowd; (h) (einfühlsam) delicate ⟨*sense of humour*⟩; keen ⟨*sense, understanding*⟩; (i) (gediegen, vornehm) refined ⟨*gentleman, lady*⟩; **sich** ∼ **machen** (ugs.) dress up. 2 *adv.* (a) ∼ **[he]raus sein** (ugs.) be sitting pretty (coll.); **Unterschiede** ∼ **herausarbeiten** bring out subtle differences; (b) (ugs.: bekräftigend) **etw.** ∼ **säuberlich aufschreiben** write sth. down nice and neatly

Fein·arbeit *die* detailed work; (Technik) precision work

Feind *der;* ∼**[e]s**, ∼**e** (a) enemy; **sich** (*Dat.*) ∼**e machen** make enemies; **sich** (*Dat.*) **jmdn. zum** ∼ **machen** make an enemy of sb.; (b) **der** ∼ (Milit.) the enemy *constr. as pl.*

Feind·berührung *die* (Milit.) contact with the enemy

Feindin *die;* ∼, ∼**nen** ⇒ Feind a

feindlich 1 *Adj.* (a) hostile; (b) *nicht präd.* (Milit.) enemy ⟨*attack, broadcast, activity*⟩. 2 *adv.* in a hostile manner; with hostility

Feindschaft *die;* ∼, ∼**en** enmity; **sich** (*Dat.*) **jmds.** ∼ **zuziehen** make an enemy of sb.

feind·selig 1 *Adj.* hostile. 2 *adv.* **sich** ∼ **ansehen** look at each other in a hostile manner *or* with hostility

Feind·seligkeit *die;* ∼, ∼**en** hostility; ∼**en** (Milit.) hostilities

fein-, Fein-: ∼**frost** *der; o. Pl.* (regional) deep-frozen foods *pl.;* ∼**fühlig** 1 *Adj.* sensitive; 2 *adv.* sensitively; ∼**fühligkeit** *die;* ∼: sensitivity; ∼**gebäck** *das* [fancy] cakes and pastries *pl.;* ∼**gefühl** *das* sensitivity; ∼**gold** *das* fine gold

Feinheit *die;* ∼, ∼**en** (a) *o. Pl.* fineness; delicacy; (b) (Nuance) subtlety; **die stilistischen** ∼**en** the stylistic subtleties *or* nuances

fein-, Fein-: ∼**körnig** *Adj.* (a) fine-grained, fine ⟨*sand, gravel, etc.*⟩; finely-granulated ⟨*sugar*⟩; (b) (Fot.) fine-grain ⟨*film*⟩; ∼**kost** *die* delicatessen *pl.;* ∼**kost·geschäft** *das* delicatessen; ***∼**|machen** ⇒ **fein** 1 i; ∼**maschig** *Adj.* finely meshed, fine-mesh *attrib.* ⟨*net etc.*⟩; ∼**mechaniker** *der* ▶ 85| precision engineer; ∼**schmecker** *der;* ∼**s**, ∼: gourmet; ∼**schmecker·lokal** *das* gourmet restaurant; ∼**schnitt** *der* (Tabak) fine cut; ∼**sinnig** 1 *Adj.* sensitive and subtle; 2 *adv.* in a sensitive and subtle manner; ∼**strumpfhose** *die* sheer tights *pl.* or pantihose; ∼**wäsche** *die* delicates *pl.;* ∼**waschmittel** *das* mild detergent

feist *Adj.* (meist abwertend) fat ⟨*face, fingers, etc.*⟩

feixen /ˈfaiksn/ *itr. V.* (ugs.) smirk

Feld /fɛlt/ *das;* ∼**[e]s**, ∼**er** (a) *o. Pl.* (geh.: unbebaute Bodenfläche) country[side]; freies ∼: open country[side]; (b) (bebaute Bodenfläche) field; **auf dem** ∼ **arbeiten** work in the field; **das** ∼ **bestellen** till the field; (c) (Sport: Spiel∼) pitch; field [of play]; (d) (auf Formularen) box; space; (bei Brettspielen) space; (auf dem Schachbrett) square; (e) *o. Pl.* (Tätigkeitsbereich) field; sphere; **das** ∼ **der Wissenschaften** the field of science; **ein weites** ∼ **[sein]** (fig.) [be] a wide sphere; (f) *o. Pl.* (veralt.: Schlacht) ∼ field [of battle]; **gegen/für jmdn./etw. ins** ∼ **ziehen** (fig.) crusade against/for sb./sth.; **das** ∼ **räumen** leave; get out; **jmdn. aus dem** ∼**[e] schlagen** eliminate sb.; get rid of sb.; (g) (Sport: geschlossene Gruppe) field

feld-, Feld-: ∼**arbeit** *die* (a) work in the field; (b) (Wissensch.) field work; ∼**blume** *die* field flower; wild flower; ∼**flasche** *die* (Milit.) canteen; water bottle; ∼**forschung** *die* (Wirtsch.) fieldwork; ∼**frucht** *die* arable crop; ∼**gottesdienst** *der* field service; ∼**hase** *der* common hare; European hare; ∼**herr** *der* (veralt.) commander; ∼**jäger** *der* military policeman; **die** ∼: the military police; ∼**küche** *die* (bes. Milit.) field kitchen; ∼**marschall** *der* ▶ 34| Field Marshal; ∼**maus** *die* [European] common vole; ∼**post** *die* forces' (Brit.) or (Amer.) military postal service; ∼**salat** *der* corn salad; lamb's lettuce; ∼**spat** /∼ʃpaːt/ *der;* ∼**[e]s**, ∼**späte** /∼ʃpɛːtə/ *od.* ∼**spate** feldspar; ∼**spieler** *der* player (excluding goalkeeper); ∼**stecher** *der* binoculars *pl.;* field glasses *pl.;* ∼**verweis** *der* (Sport) sending-off

Feld-Wald-und-Wiesen- (ugs.) run-of-the-mill; common-or-garden

Feld-: ∼**webel** /-veːbl/ *der;* ∼**s**, ∼ ▶ 34| (Milit.) sergeant; ∼**weg** *der* path; track; ∼**zug** *der* (Milit., fig.) campaign

Felge /ˈfɛlgə/ *die;* ∼, ∼**n** (a) [wheel] rim; (b) (Turnen) circle

Fell /fɛl/ *das;* ∼**[e]s**, ∼·**e** (a) (Haarkleid) fur; (Pferde∼, Hunde∼, Katzen∼) coat; (Schaf∼) fleece; skin; **einem Tier das** ∼ **abziehen** skin an animal; **jmdm. das** ∼ **über die Ohren ziehen** (fig. salopp) take sb. for a ride (fig. coll.); (b) *o. Pl.* (Material) fur; furskin; (c) (abgezogene behaarte Haut) skin; hide; (d) (salopp: Haut des Menschen) skin; (fig.) **ihm** *od.* **ihn juckt das** ∼ (ugs.) he is asking for a good hiding (coll.); **ein dickes** ∼ **haben** (ugs.) be thick-skinned *or* have a thick skin

Fell-: ∼**jacke** *die* fur jacket; ∼**mütze** *die* fur cap

Fels /fɛls/ *der;* ∼**en**, ∼**en** (a) *o. Pl.* rock; (b) (geh.: Felsen) rock; **wie ein** ∼ **in der Brandung stehen** stand as firm as a rock

Fels·block *der; Pl.* ∼**blöcke** rock; boulder

Felsen /ˈfɛlzn/ *der;* ∼**s**, ∼: rock; (an der Steilküste) cliff

felsen-, Felsen-: ∼**fest** 1 *Adj.* firm; unshakeable ⟨*opinion, belief*⟩; 2 *adv.* ⟨*believe, be convinced*⟩ firmly; ∼**klippe** *die* rocky cliff; ∼**riff** *das* rocky reef

felsig *Adj.* rocky

Fels-: ∼**spalte** *die* crevice [in the rock]; ∼**vorsprung** *der* ledge; ∼**wand** *die* rock face

Feme /ˈfeːmə/ *die;* ∼, ∼**n** (a) (hist.) vehmgericht; (b) (Geheimbünde) kangaroo court

Feme·mord *der* lynching

feminin /femiˈniːn/ *Adj.* (a) (geh.: weiblich) feminine ⟨*characteristic, behaviour*⟩; (b) (abwertend: unmännlich) effeminate ⟨*man, type*⟩; (c) (Sprachw.) feminine

Femininum /'feːminiˑnʊm/ *das;* ~s, **Feminina** feminine noun

Feminismus *der;* ~, **Feminismen** feminism *no art.*

Feminist *der;* ~en, ~en, **Feministin** *die;* ~, ~nen feminist

feministisch *Adj.* feminist

Fenchel /'fɛnçl/ *der;* ~s fennel

Fenn /fɛn/ *das;* ~[e]s, ~e (bes. nordd.) fen

Fenster /'fɛnstɐ/ *das;* ~s, ~ (auch DV) window; [sein] Geld zum ~ hinauswerfen (fig.) throw [one's] money down the drain; weg vom ~ sein (ugs.) be right out of it

Fenster-: ~bank *die,* ~brett *das* window sill; window ledge; ~[brief]umschlag *der* window envelope; ~glas *das; Pl.* ~gläser (a) window glass; (b) (ungeschliffenes Glas) plain glass; ~heber *der* (Kfz.-W.) window regulator; (elektrisch) window [regulator] mechanism; das Auto hat elektrische ~heber this car has electric windows; ~kreuz *das* mullion and transom; ~laden *der* [window] shutter; ~leder *das* wash leather

fensterln /'fɛnstɐln/ *itr. V.* (bes. südd., österr.) climb through one's sweetheart's window

fenster-, Fenster-: ~los *Adj.* windowless; ~putzer *der* ▶ 85 | window cleaner; ~rahmen *der* window frame; ~scheibe *die* window pane

Ferial·tag /fe'riˑaːl-/ *der* (österr.) ⇒ **Ferientag**

Ferien /'feːriˑən/ *Pl.* (a) holiday (Brit.); vacation (Amer.); (Werks~) shutdown; holiday (Brit.); (Parlaments~) recess; (Hochschul~) vacation; ~ haben have a *or* be on holiday/ vacation; (b) (Urlaub) holiday[s *pl.*] (Brit.); vacation (Amer.); in die ~ fahren go on holiday/vacation

Ferien-: holiday… (Brit.); vacation… (Amer.) ‹house, camp, resort, trip, etc.›; *s. auch* **Urlaubs-**

Ferien-: ~arbeit *die* vacation work; eine ~arbeit a vacation job; ~kolonie *die* [children's] holiday/vacation camp; ~lager *das* holiday/vacation camp; ~reise *die* holiday/vacation trip

Ferkel /'fɛrkl/ *das;* ~s, ~ (a) piglet; (b) (ugs. abwertend) pig

Ferkelei *die;* ~, ~en (ugs. abwertend) (Benehmen) filthy behaviour; (Bemerkung) dirty remark

ferkeln *itr. V.* farrow

Ferment /fɛr'mɛnt/ *das;* ~[e]s, ~e (veralt.) ferment (arch.); enzyme

fern /fɛrn/ **1** *Adj.* (a) (räumlich) distant, far-off, faraway ‹country, region, etc.›; jmdn./etw. von jmdm./etw. ~ halten keep sb./sth. away from sb./sth.; sich von jmdm./etw. ~ halten keep away from sb./sth.; (b) (zeitlich) distant ‹past, future›; in [nicht allzu] ~er Zukunft in the [not too] distant future; der Tag ist nicht mehr ~: the day is not far off. **2** *adv.* ~ von der Heimat [sein/leben] [be/live] far from home; das liegt mir ~ (fig.) that is the last thing I want to do; etw. von ~ betrachten look at sth. from a distance; *s. auch* **Osten c**; nahe **2 a**. **3** *Präp. mit Dat.* (geh.) far [away] from; a long way from; ~ der Heimat [leben] [live] far from home *or* a long way from home

fern-, Fern-: ~ab /·'·-/ (geh.) **1** *Adv.* far away; **2** *Präp. mit Dat.* ~ab aller Zivilisation far [away] from all civilization; ~amt *das* (veralt.) telephone exchange; ~bedienung *die* remote control; ~|bleiben *unr. itr. V.; mit sein* (geh.) stay away (Dat. from)

ferne: von ~ (geh.) from far off *or* away

Ferne *die;* ~, ~n (a) distance; etw. in weiter ~ erblicken see sth. in the far distance; (b) das liegt noch/ schon in weiter ~ (zeitlich) that is still a long time away/ that was a long time ago

ferner *Adv.* (a) in addition; furthermore; er rangiert unter „~ liefen" (fig.) he is an also-ran; (b) (geh.: künftig) in [the] future

fern-, Fern-: ~fahrer *der* long-distance lorry driver (Brit.) *or* (Amer.) trucker; ~gelenkt *Adj.* remote-controlled; (fig.: durch Geheimdienste usw.) controlled; ~gespräch *das* long-distance call; trunk call; ein ~gespräch mit jmdm./London führen speak to *or*

with sb./London long-distance; ~glas *das* binoculars *pl.;* *~|halten ⇒ fern 1 a; ~heizung *die* district heating system; ~kopierer *der* fax machine; ~kurs[us] *der* correspondence course; ~laster *der* (ugs.) long-distance lorry (Brit.) *or* (Amer.) truck; ~last·zug *der* [long-distance] articulated lorry; ~leitung *die* (a) (Postw.) long-distance line; (b) (Energiewirtsch.) long-distance cable; ~|lenken *tr. V.* operate by remote control; ~lenkung *die* remote control; ~licht *das* (Kfz-W.) full beam; das ~licht anhaben drive on full beam; *~|liegen ⇒ fern 2

Fern·melde-: ~amt *das* local telephone headquarters; ~gebühren *Pl.* telephone charges; ~technik *die; o. Pl.* telecommunications *sing., no art.*

fern-, Fern-: ~ost *o. Art.* Far East; in/nach ~ost in/ to the Far East; ~östlich *Adj.; nicht präd.* Far Eastern; ~rohr *das* telescope; ~ruf *der* telephone number; ~schreiben *das* telex [message]; ~schreiber *der* telex [machine]; teleprinter

Fernseh-: ~ansager *der,* ~ansagerin *die* television announcer; ~antenne *die* television aerial (Brit.) *or* (Amer.) antenna; ~apparat *der* television [set]

fern|sehen *unr. itr. V.* watch television

Fern·sehen *das;* ~s television; im ~: on television; vom *od.* im ~ übertragen werden be televised; be shown on television

Fern·seher *der;* ~s, ~ (ugs.) (a) (Gerät) telly (Brit. coll.); TV; television; (b) (Zuschauer) [television] viewer

Fernseh-: ~film *der* television film; ~gebühren *Pl.* television licence fee; ~gerät *das* television [set]; ~kamera *die* television camera; ~kanal *der* television channel; ~programm *das* (a) (Sendungen) television programmes *pl.;* (b) (Kanal) television channel; (c) (Blatt, Programmheft) television [programme] guide; ~sendung *die* television programme; ~spiel *das* television play; ~studio *das* television studio; ~turm *der* television tower; ~übertragung *die* television broadcast; ~werbung *die* television advertising; ~zuschauer *der* television viewer

Fern·sicht *die* (Aussicht) view; (gute Sicht) visibility

fern·sichtig *Adj.* ⇒ **weitsichtig**

Fern·sprech- (bes. Amtsspr.) ⇒ **Telefon-**

Fernsprech·auskunft *die* directory enquiries *sing., no art.*

Fern·sprecher *der* telephone

Fernsprech·teilnehmer *der* telephone subscriber; telephone customer (Amer.)

fern-, Fern-: ~|steuern *tr. V.* ⇒ ~lenken; ~steuerung *die* (Technik) remote control; (fig.: durch Geheimdienste usw.) control; ~straße *die* [principal] trunk road; major road; ~studium *das* correspondence course; ~unterricht *der* correspondence courses *pl.;* ~verkehr *der* long-distance traffic; ~wärme *die* district heating; ~weh *das* (geh.) wanderlust; ~ziel *das* (a) (zeitlich) long-term aim; (b) (räumlich) distant destination

Ferse /'fɛrzə/ *die;* ~, ~n ▶ 326| heel; (fig.) sich an jmds. ~n (Akk.) /sich jmdm. an die ~n heften stick [hard] on sb.'s heels; jmdm. [dicht] auf den ~n sitzen *od.* sein (ugs.) be [hard *or* close] on sb.'s heels

Fersen·geld *das;* ~geld geben (ugs. scherzh.) take to one's heels

fertig /'fɛrtiç/ *Adj.* (a) (völlig hergestellt) finished ‹manuscript, picture, etc.›; das Essen ist ~: lunch/ dinner etc. is ready; und ~ ist der Lack *od.* die Laube (ugs.) and there you are; and bob's your uncle (Brit. coll.); etw. ~ bringen/bekommen manage sth.; ich brächte es nicht fertig, das zu tun I couldn't bring myself to do that; der bringt das fertig! (iron.) I wouldn't put it past him; etw. ~ stellen complete *or* finish sth.; (b) *nicht attr.* (zu Ende) finished; [mit etw.] ~ sein/werden have finished/finish [sth.]; etw. ~ bringen/bekommen/ machen finish sth.; bist du ~? have you finished?; mit jmdm. ~ sein (ugs.) be finished *or* through with sb.; mit etw. ~ werden (fig.) cope with sth.; (c) *nicht attr.* (bereit, verfügbar) ready (zu, für for); das Essen ~ machen get the meal ready; sich für etw. ~ machen get ready for sth.; zum Abmarsch/Start ~ sein be ready to march/

ready for take-off; **auf die Plätze — ~ — los!** on your marks, get set, go! (Sport); (bei Kindern auch:) ready, steady, go!; **(d)** *nicht attr.* (ugs.: erschöpft) shattered (coll.); **mit den Nerven ~ sein** be at the end of one's tether; **jmdn. ~ machen** wear sb. out; (durch Schikanen) wear sb. down; (deprimieren) get sb. down; (salopp: zusammenschlagen, töten) do sb. in (sl.); (ugs.: zurechtweisen) tear sb. off a strip (sl.); **(e)** (reif) mature ‹*person, artist, etc.*›

fertig-, Fertig-: **~bau** *der; Pl.* **~ten** prefabricated building; **~bauweise** *die* prefabricated construction; prefabrication; ***~|bekommen** ⇨ **fertig a;** ***~|bringen** ⇨ **fertig a;**

fertigen *tr. V.* make; **von Hand/maschinell gefertigt** hand-made/machine-produced

Fertig-: **~gericht** *das* ready-to-serve meal; **~haus** *das* prefabricated house; prefab (coll.)

Fertigkeit *die;* **~, ~en** skill

***fertig|machen** *usw.:* ⇨ **fertig**

Fertig·stellung *die* completion

Fertigung *die;* **~:** production; manufacture

Fertig.ware *die* finished product

Fes /fe:s/ *der;* **~[es], ~[e]** fez

fesch /fɛʃ/ *Adj.* (bes. österr.: hübsch) smart ‹*woman, suit, etc.*›

Fessel¹ /'fɛsl/ *die;* **~, ~n** *meist Pl.* (auch fig.) fetter; shackle; (Kette) chain; **jmdm. ~n anlegen** fetter sb./put sb. in chains

Fessel² *die;* **~, ~n** (Anat.) **(a)** (bei Huftieren) pastern; **(b)** (bei Menschen) ankle

fesseln *tr. V.* **(a)** tie up; (mit Ketten) chain up; **jmdn. an Händen und Füßen ~:** tie sb. hand and foot; **jmdm. die Hände auf den Rücken ~:** tie sb.'s hands behind his/her back; **ans Bett/Haus/an den Rollstuhl gefesselt sein** (fig.) be confined to [one's] bed/tied to the house/confined to a wheelchair; **(b)** (faszinieren) ‹*book*› grip; ‹*work, person*› fascinate; ‹*personality*› captivate; ‹*idea*› possess; **das Buch hat mich so gefesselt** I was so gripped by the book

fest /fɛst/ **1** *Adj.* **(a)** (nicht flüssig od. gasförmig) solid; **~e Nahrung** solid food; **~e Gestalt** *od.* **Form[en] annehmen** take on a definite shape; **(b)** (straff) firm, tight ‹*bandage*›; **(c)** (kräftig) firm ‹*handshake*›; (tief) sound ‹*sleep*›; **(d)** (haltbar, solide) sturdy ‹*shoes*›; tough, strong ‹*fabric*›; solid ‹*house, shell*›; **(e)** (energisch) firm ‹*tread*›; steady ‹*voice*›; **eine ~e Hand brauchen** (fig.) need a firm hand; **(f)** (unbeirrbar) **der ~en Überzeugung/Meinung sein, dass …:** be firmly convinced/of the firm opinion that …; **(g)** (endgültig) firm ‹*appointment, date*›; firm, definite ‹*commitment*›; **(h)** *nicht präd.* (konstant) fixed, permanent ‹*address*›; fixed ‹*income*›; **einen ~en Platz in etw.** (*Dat.*) **haben** (fig.) be firmly established in sth.. **2** *adv.* **(a)** (straff) ‹*tie, grip*› tight[ly]; **(b)** (ugs. auch **~e**) (tüchtig) ‹*work*› with a will; ‹*eat*› heartily; ‹*sleep*› soundly; **~ zuschlagen** plant a solid punch; **er schläft ~:** he is fast asleep; **(c)** (unbeirrbar) ‹*believe, be convinced*› firmly; **sich auf jmdn./etw. ~ verlassen** rely one hundred per cent on sb./sth.; **(d)** (endgültig) firmly; definitely; **etw. ~ vereinbaren** come to a firm *or* definite arrangement about sth.; **(e)** (auf Dauer) permanently; **~ angestellt sein** be permanently employed; **~ befreundet sein** be close friends; (als Paar) be going steady

Fest *das;* **~[e]s, ~e (a)** (Veranstaltung) celebration; (Party) party; **(b)** (Feiertag) festival; (Kirchen~) feast; festival; **frohes ~!** happy Christmas/Easter!

fest-, Fest-: **~akt** *der* ceremony; **~ansprache** *die* address; **~beißen** *unr. refl. V.* **sich in etw.** (*Dat.*) **~beißen** ‹*dog etc.*› sink its teeth firmly into sth.; **~beleuchtung** *die* festive lighting; **in ~beleuchtung erstrahlen** be ablaze with festive illuminations; **~|binden** *unr. tr. V.* tie [up] **(an** + *Dat.*)

feste *Adv.* (ugs.) ⇨ **fest 2 b**

fest-, Fest-: **~essen** *das* banquet; **~|fahren** *unr. itr., refl. V.* (itr. mit sein) get stuck; (fig.) get bogged down; **~halle** *die* festival hall; **~|halten 1** *unr. tr. V.* **(a)** (halten, packen) hold on to; **jmdn. am Arm ~halten** hold on to sb.'s arm; **etw. mit den Händen ~halten** hold

sth. in one's hands; **(b)** (nicht weiterleiten) withhold ‹*letter, parcel, etc.*›; **(c)** (verhaftet haben) hold, detain ‹*suspect*›; **(d)** (aufzeichnen, fixieren) record; capture; **etw. mit der Kamera ~halten** capture sth. with the camera; **(e)** (konstatieren) record; **2** *unr. refl. V.* (sich anklammern) **sich an jmdm./etw. ~halten** hold on to sb./sth.; **halt dich ~!** hold tight!; (fig. ugs.) brace yourself!; **3** *unr. itr. V.* **an jmdm./etw. ~halten** stand by sb./sth.

festigen /'fɛstɪɡn/ **1** *tr. V.* strengthen ‹*friendship, alliance, marriage, etc.*›; consolidate ‹*position*›; **in sich** (*Dat.*) **gefestigt sein** be strong. **2** *refl. V.* ‹*friendship, ties*› become stronger

Festigkeit *die;* **~ (a)** (Entschlossenheit) firmness; **(b)** (Standhaftigkeit) steadfastness; resolution; **(c)** (von Stoffen) strength

Festigung *die;* **~:** strengthening; (einer Stellung) consolidation

Festival /'fɛstivəl/ *das;* **~s, ~s** festival

Festivität /fɛstivi'tɛːt/ *die;* **~, ~en** (veralt., scherzh.) festivity; celebration

fest-, Fest-: **~|klammern** *refl. V.* **sich an jmdm./etw. ~klammern** cling [on] to sb./sth.; **~|kleben 1** *itr. V.; mit sein* stick **(an** + *Dat.* to); **2** *tr. V.* stick; **etw. an etw.** (*Dat.*) **~kleben** stick sth. to sth.; **~|klemmen 1** *itr. V.; mit sein* **~geklemmt sein** be stuck *or* jammed; **2** *tr. V.* wedge; jam; **~körper** *der* (Physik) solid; **~krallen** *refl. V.* **sich in etw.** (*Dat.*) **~krallen** ‹*cat etc.*› dig its claws into sth.; **sich an jmdm. ~krallen** ‹*cat etc.*› cling to sb. with its claws; ‹*person*› cling [on] to sb.; **~land** *das; o. Pl.* mainland; **das europäische ~land** the continent of Europe/the European mainland; **~ländisch** *Adj.; nicht präd.* **(a)** mainland *attrib.*; **(b)** (kontinental) continental ‹*climate, shelf, etc.*›; **~land·sockel** *der* (Geogr.) continental shelf; **~|legen** *tr. V.* **(a)** (verbindlich regeln) fix ‹*time, deadline, price*›; arrange ‹*programme*›; **etw. gesetzlich ~legen** prescribe sth. by law; **(b)** (verpflichten) **sich [auf etw.** (*Akk.*)**] ~legen [lassen]** commit oneself [to sth.]; **jmdn. [auf etw.** (*Akk.*)**] ~legen** tie sb. down [to sth.]; **(c)** (Bankw.) tie up ‹*money*›; **~legung** *die;* **~, ~en** ⇨ **~legen: (a)** fixing; arrangement; **(b)** commitment

festlich 1 *Adj.* **(a)** festive ‹*atmosphere*›; **(b)** (einem Fest gemäß) formal ‹*dress*›. **2** *adv.* **(a)** festively; **(b)** (einem Fest gemäß) formally; **etw. ~ begehen** celebrate sth.

Festlichkeit *die;* **~, ~en (a)** (Feier) celebration; **(b)** (der Stimmung, Atmosphäre) festiveness; (Feierlichkeit, Würde) solemnity

fest-, Fest-: **~|liegen** *unr. itr. V.* **(a)** (nicht weiterkommen) be stuck; **(b)** (~stehen) have been fixed; **(c)** (Bankw.) ‹*money*› be tied up; **~|machen 1** *tr. V.* **(a)** (befestigen) fix; **(b)** (fest vereinbaren) arrange ‹*meeting etc.*›; **(c)** (Seemannsspr.) moor ‹*boat*›; **2** *itr. V.* (Seemannsspr.) moor; **~|nageln** *tr. V.* **(a)** (befestigen) nail **(an** + *Dat.* to); (fig. ugs.: festlegen) **jmdn. [auf etw.** (*Akk.*)**] ~nageln** tie sb. down [to sth.]; **sich auf etw.** (*Akk.*) **~nageln lassen** let oneself be tied [down] to sth.; **~nahme** *die;* **~, ~n** arrest; **bei seiner ~nahme** when he was/is arrested; **~|nehmen** *unr. tr. V.* arrest; **jmdn. vorläufig ~nehmen** take sb. into custody; **~platte** *die* (DV) hard disc; **~platz** *der* fairground; **~preis** *der* (Wirtsch.) fixed price; **~rede** *die* speech; **~redner** *der* speaker; **~saal** *der* banqueting hall; (Ballsaal) ballroom; **~|saugen** *regelm.* (*auch unr.*) *refl. V.* attach itself **(an** + *Dat.* to); **~|schrauben** *tr. V.* screw [up] tight; **~|schreiben** *unr. tr. V.* establish; **~schrift** *die* commemorative volume; **~|setzen 1** *tr. V.* **(a)** (~legen) fix ‹*time, deadline, price*›; lay down ‹*duties*›; **(b)** (in Haft nehmen) detain; **2** *refl. V.* ‹*dust*› collect, settle; (fig.) ‹*idea*› take root; **~setzung** *die;* **~, ~en** ⇨ **~setzen 1:** fixing; laying down; **~|sitzen** *unr. itr. V.* be stuck; **~spiel** *das* **(a)** *Pl.* festival sing.; **(b)** (Bühnenstück) festival production; **~|stehen** *unr. itr. V.* **(a)** (~gelegt sein) ‹*order, appointment, etc.*› have been fixed; **(b)** (unumstößlich sein) ‹*decision*› be definite; ‹*fact*› be certain; **es steht ~, dass …:** it is certain *or* definite that …; **~stellbar** *Adj.* **(a)** (zu ermitteln) ascertainable; **(b)** (wahrnehmbar) detectable; diagnosable ‹*illness*›; **~|stellen** *tr. V.* **(a)** (ermitteln) establish ‹*identity, age,* *facts*); (**b**) (wahrnehmen) detect; diagnose ‹*illness*›; **er stellte** ∼, **dass er sich geirrt hatte** he realized that he was wrong; **die Ärzte konnten nur noch den Tod** ∼**stellen** all the doctors could do was [to] confirm that the patient/victim *etc.* was dead; (**c**) (aussprechen) state ‹*fact*›; **ich muss** ∼**stellen, dass** …: I must *or* am bound to say that …

Fest·stellung *die* (**a**) (Ermittlung) establishment; (**b**) (Wahrnehmung) realization; **die** ∼ **machen, dass** …: realize that …; (**c**) (Erklärung) statement; **die** ∼ **treffen, dass** …: observe that …

Fest·tag *der* holiday; (Kirchenfest) [religious] feast-day; (Ehrentag) special day

Festung *die;* ∼, ∼**en** fortress

Festungs-: ∼**anlage** *die* fortification; ∼**mauer** *die* wall of a/the fortress

fest-, Fest-: ∼**verzinslich** *Adj.* (Bankw.) fixed-interest *attrib.;* fixed-income *attrib.;* ∼**vortrag** *der* lecture; ∼**wiese** *die* festival site; ∼**zelt** *das* marquee; ∼|**ziehen** *unr. tr. V.* pull tight; ∼**zug** *der* procession

Fete /'fe:tə/ *die;* ∼, ∼**n** (ugs.) party; **eine** ∼ **geben** *od.* **feiern** have *or* throw a party

Fetisch /'fe:tɪʃ/ *der;* ∼**s**, ∼**e** (Völkerk., fig.) fetish

Fetischismus *der;* ∼: fetishism *no art.*

Fetischist *der;* ∼**en**, ∼**en** fetishist

fett /fɛt/ **1** *Adj.* (**a**) fatty ‹*food*›; ∼**er Speck** fat bacon; (**b**) (sehr dick) fat; (**c**) (ugs.: üppig, reich) fat ‹*inheritance, wallet*›; ∼**e Jahre/Zeiten** rich years/good times; ∼**e Beute machen** make a rich haul; (**d**) (ertragreich) rich ‹*soil*›; luxuriant ‹*vegetation*›; (**e**) (Druckw.) bold; (breiter, größer) extra bold; **etw.** ∼ **drucken** print sth. in bold/extra bold [type]; ∼ **gedruckt** bold. **2** *adv.* ∼ **essen** eat fatty foods; ∼ **kochen** use a lot of fat [in cooking]

Fett *das;* ∼[**e**]**s**, ∼**e** (**a**) fat; **sein** ∼ [**ab**]**bekommen** *od.* [**ab**]**kriegen** (ugs.) get one's come-uppance (Amer.); **sein** ∼ [**weg**]**haben** (ugs.) have been put in one's place *or* taught a lesson; (**b**) *o. Pl.* (∼**gewebe**) fat; ∼ **ansetzen** ‹*animal*› fatten up; ‹*person*› put on weight; ∼ **schwimmt oben** (Spr.) fat people never drown!; (fig.) the rich never suffer; (**c**) (Schmiermittel, Pflegemittel) grease

fett-, Fett-: ∼**arm 1** *Adj.* low-fat ‹*food*›; low in fat *pred.;* **2** *adv.* ∼**arm essen** eat low-fat foods; ∼**auge** *das* speck of fat; ∼**creme** *die* enriched [skim] cream; ∼**druck** *der* bold type; **in** ∼**druck** in bold [type]

fetten 1 *tr. V.* (mit Fett einreiben) grease. **2** *itr. V.* (Fett absondern) be greasy

fett-, Fett-: ∼**fleck[en]** *der* grease mark *or* spot; ∼**frei** *Adj.* fat-free; grease-free ‹*surface*›; ∼ **sein** be fat-free/be free of grease;*∼**gedruckt** ⇒ **fett 1 e**; ∼**haltig** *Adj.* fatty; [sehr] ∼**haltig sein** contain [a lot of] fat

fettig *Adj.* greasy; oily; greasy ‹*skin, saucepan, etc.*›

fett-, Fett-: ∼**kloß** *der* (ugs. abwertend) fatty; fatso (sl.); ∼**leibig** *Adj.* obese; ∼**leibigkeit** *die;* ∼: obesity; ∼**näpfchen** *das:* [bei **jmdm.**] **ins** ∼**näpfchen treten** (scherzh.) put one's foot in it [with sb.]; ∼**reich 1** *Adj.* high-fat ‹*food*›; **2** *adv.* ∼**reich essen** eat high-fat foods; ∼**sack** *der* (salopp abwertend) fatso (sl.); ∼**schicht** *die* layer of fat; ∼**stift** *der* (**a**) (Schreibgerät) grease pencil; lithographic pencil; (**b**) (Lippenstift) lip salve; ∼**sucht** *die* (Med.) obesity; ∼**wanst** *der* (salopp abwertend) fatso (sl.)

Fetus /'fe:tʊs/ *der;* ∼ *od.* ∼**ses**, ∼**se** *od.* **Feten** (Med.) foetus

Fetzen *der;* ∼**s**, ∼ (**a**) scrap; **etw. in** ∼ [**zer**]**reißen** tear sth. to pieces *or* shreds; **in** ∼ (ugs.) fall apart *or* to pieces; **dass die** ∼ **fliegen** (ugs.) like mad (coll.); (**b**) (abwertend: Kleid) **ein billiger** ∼: cheap rags *pl.*

feucht /fɔʏçt/ *Adj.* damp ‹*cloth, wall, hair*›; tacky ‹*paint*›; humid ‹*climate*›; sweaty, clammy ‹*hands*›; moist ‹*lips*›; **eine** ∼**e Aussprache haben** (scherzh.) spit when one speaks; ∼**e Augen bekommen** be close to tears

feucht-, Feucht-: ∼**fröhlich** *Adj.* (ugs. scherzh.) merry ‹*company*›; boozy (coll.) ‹*evening*›; ∼**gebiet** *das* wet area; ∼**heiß** *Adj.* hot and humid

Feuchtigkeit *die* (**a**) (leichte Nässe) moisture; (**b**) (das Feuchtsein) dampness; (des Bodens) wetness; (Luft∼) humidity

Feuchtigkeits·creme *die* (Kosmetik) moisturizing cream; moisturizer

feucht-: ∼**kalt** *Adj.* cold and damp; ∼**warm** *Adj.* muggy; humid

feudal /fɔʏ'da:l/ **1** *Adj.* (**a**) feudal ‹*system*›; (**b**) (aristokratisch) aristocratic ‹*regiment etc.*›; (**c**) (ugs.: vornehm) plush ‹*hotel etc.*›. **2** *adv.* (ugs.: vornehm) ∼ **essen** have a slap-up meal (coll.)

Feudalismus *der;* ∼: feudalism *no art.*

Feuer /'fɔʏɐ/ *das;* ∼**s**, ∼ (**a**) fire; [**ein Gegensatz**] **wie** ∼ **und Wasser sein** be as different as chalk and cheese; **das Essen aufs** ∼ **stellen/vom** ∼ **nehmen** put the food on to cook/take the food off the heat; **jmdn. um** ∼ **bitten** ask sb. for a light; **jmdm.** ∼ **geben** give sb. a light; **mit dem** ∼ **spielen** play with fire; **er ist absolut ehrlich, für ihn** *od.* **dafür lege ich die Hand ins** ∼: he is totally honest, I'd swear to it; [**für etw.**] ∼ **und Flamme sein** be full of enthusiasm [for sth.]; ∼ **fangen** catch fire; (fig.: sich verlieben) be smitten; (fig.: sich schnell begeistern) be fired with enthusiasm; **für jmdn. durchs** ∼ **gehen** go through hell and high water for sb.; **ein** ∼ **speiender Drache** a fire-breathing dragon; **ein** ∼ **speiender Vulkan** a volcano spewing fire; (**b**) (Brand) fire; blaze; ∼**!** fire!; (**c**) *o. Pl.* (Milit.) fire; **unter feindliches** ∼ **geraten** come under enemy fire; **das** ∼ **einstellen** cease fire; **jmdn./etw. unter** ∼ **nehmen** fire on sb./sth.; (**d**) *o. Pl.* (Leuchten, Funkeln) sparkle; blaze; **ihre Augen sprühten** ∼: her eyes blazed [with fire]; (**e**) *o. Pl.* (innerer Schwung) fire; passion

feuer-, Feuer-: ∼**alarm** *der* fire alarm; ∼**bekämpfung** *die* fire-fighting; ∼**beständig** *Adj.* fire-resistant; ∼**bestattung** *die* cremation; ∼**eifer** *der* enthusiasm; zest; ∼**fest** *Adj.* heat-resistant ‹*dish, plate*›; fire-proof ‹*material*›; ∼**gefahr** *die* fire hazard *or* risk; **bei** ∼**gefahr** when there is a risk of fire; ∼**gefährlich** *Adj.* [in]flammable; ∼**haken** *der* poker

Feuer·land (*das*)*;* ∼**s** Tierra del Fuego

Feuer-: ∼**leiter** *die* (bei Häusern) fire escape; (beim ∼**wehrauto**) [fireman's] ladder; (fahrbar) turntable ladder; ∼**löscher** *der;* ∼**s**, ∼: fire extinguisher; ∼**melder** *der* fire alarm

feuern 1 *tr. V.* (**a**) (ugs.: entlassen) fire (coll.); sack (coll.); (**b**) (ugs.: schleudern, werfen) fling; **jmdm. eine** ∼ (salopp) belt sb. one (coll.); (**c**) (heizen) fire ‹*stove*›; **mit Holz** ∼: have wood fires. **2** *itr. V.* (Milit.) fire (**auf** + *Akk.* at)

feuer-, Feuer-: ∼**polizei** *die authorities responsible for fire precautions and fire-fighting;* ∼**probe** *die* (fig.) test; **die** ∼**probe bestehen** pass the [acid] test; ∼**rot** *Adj.* fiery red; flaming red

Feuers·brunst *die* (geh.) great fire; conflagration

feuer-, Feuer-: ∼**schein** *der* glow of the/a fire; ∼**schiff** *das* lightship; ∼**schlucker** *der* fire-eater; ∼**schutz** *der* (**a**) (Brandschutz) fire prevention *or* protection; (**b**) (Milit.) covering fire; **jmdm.** ∼**schutz geben** cover sb.;*∼**speiend** ⇒ **Feuer a**; ∼**spritze** *die* fire hose; ∼**stein** *der* flint; ∼**stelle** *die* [camp]fire; ∼**stuhl** *der* (ugs. scherzh.) [motor]bike (coll.); machine; ∼**taufe** *die* baptism of fire; ∼**tod** *der* (geh.) [death at] the stake; ∼**treppe** *die* fire escape

Feuerung *die;* ∼, ∼**en** (**a**) (Vorrichtung) firing [system]; (**b**) *o. Pl.* (das Heizen) heating

Feuer-: ∼**versicherung** *die* fire insurance; ∼**wache** *die* fire station; ∼**waffe** *die* firearm

Feuer·wehr *die;* ∼, ∼**en** fire service

Feuerwehr-: ∼**auto** *das* fire engine; ∼**mann** *der; Pl.* ∼**männer** *od.* ∼**leute** fireman

Feuer-: ∼**werk** *das* firework display; (∼**werkskörper**) fireworks *pl.;* (fig.) barrage; ∼**werks·körper** *der* firework; ∼**zangen·bowle** *die: burnt rum and red wine punch;* ∼**zeug** *das* lighter

Feuilleton /fœjə'tõ:/ *das;* ∼**s**, ∼**s** (**a**) arts section; (**b**) (literarischer Beitrag) [literary] article

feurig *Adj.* fiery ‹*horse, spice, wine*›; passionate ‹*speech*›
Fez /fe:ts/ *der;* ~**es** (ugs.) lark (coll.); ~ **machen** lark about (coll.); **hört mit dem** ~ **auf!** stop larking about (coll.)
ff /ɛf'ɛf/ *Abk.* **sehr fein** superior-quality ‹*sweets, pastries, etc.*›
ff. *Abk.* **folgende [Seiten]** ff.
Fiaker /'fi̯akɐ/ *der;* ~**s**, ~ (österr.) hackney carriage; cab
Fiasko /'fi̯asko/ *das;* ~**s**, ~**s** fiasco; **unser Urlaub war ein einziges** ~: our holiday was a total disaster (coll.)
Fibel /'fi:bl̩/ *die;* ~, ~**n** (a) (Lesebuch) reader; primer; (b) (Lehrbuch) handbook; guide
Fiber /'fi:bɐ/ *die;* ~, ~**n** fibre
ficht /fɪçt/ *Imperativ Sg. u. 3. Pers. Sg. Präsens v.* **fechten**
Fichte *die;* ~, ~**n** (a) spruce; (b) (Rottanne) Norway spruce
Fichten-: ~**holz** *das* spruce [wood]; ~**nadel** *die* spruce needle; ~**wald** *der* spruce forest
Fick /fɪk/ *der;* ~**s**, ~**s** (vulg.) fuck (coarse)
ficken *tr., itr. V.* (vulg.) fuck (coarse); **mit jmdm.** ~: fuck sb.
fidel /fi'de:l/ *Adj.* (ugs.) jolly, merry ‹*company, person*›
Fidschi·inseln /'fɪdʒi-/ *Pl.* Fiji Islands
Fieber /'fi:bɐ/ *das;* ~**s** (a) ▶329⌋, ▶511⌋ [high] temperature; (über 38 °C) fever; ~ **haben** have a [high] temperature/a fever; ~ **messen/bei jmdm.** ~ **messen** take one's/sb.'s temperature; **im** ~: in one's fever; (b) (geh.: Besessenheit) fever
fieber-, Fieber-: ~**anfall** *der* attack *or* bout of fever; ~**frei** *Adj.* ‹*person*› free from fever; **er ist wieder** ~**frei** his temperature is back to normal; ~**haft 1** *Adj.* (a) feverish, febrile ‹*infection, state, condition*›; (b) (fig.) feverish ‹*activity*›. **2** *adv.* (fig.) feverishly
fieberig *Adj.* ⇒ **fiebrig**
Fieber·kurve *die* temperature chart
fiebern *itr. V.* (a) have *or* run a temperature; (b) (fig.) **vor Aufregung/Erwartung** (*Dat.*) ~: be in a fever of excitement/anticipation; **nach etw.** ~: long desperately for sth.
fieber-, Fieber-: ~**senkend** *Adj.* antipyretic; ~**senkende Mittel** antipyretics; ~**thermometer** *das* [clinical] thermometer
fiebrig *Adj.* (auch fig.) feverish
Fiedel /'fi:dl̩/ *die;* ~, ~**n** (veralt., scherzh.) fiddle
fiedeln *tr., itr. V.* (scherzh., abwertend) fiddle
fiel /fi:l/ *1. u. 3. Pers. Sg. Prät. v.* **fallen**
fiepen /'fi:pn̩/ *itr. V.* ‹*dog*› whimper; ‹*bird*› cheep
fies /fi:s/ **1** *Adj.* (ugs.) (a) (charakterlich) nasty ‹*person, character*›; **das finde ich** ~: I think that's mean; (b) (geschmacklich) horrid (coll.); awful (coll.). **2** *adv.* in a nasty way
Fifa, FIFA /'fi:fa/ *die;* ~: FIFA; International Football Federation
Figur /fi'ɡuːɐ/ *die;* ~, ~**en** (a) (Wuchs, Gestalt) (einer Frau) figure; (eines Mannes) physique; **eine gute/schlechte** ~ **machen** cut a good/poor *or* sorry figure; (b) (Bildwerk) figure; (c) (geometrisches Gebilde) shape; (d) (Spielstein) piece; (e) (Persönlichkeit) figure; (f) (literarische Gestalt) character; **die komische** ~ (Theater) the comic character *or* figure; (g) (Tanzen, Eissport usw.) figure; ~**en laufen** skate figures
figurativ /fiɡura'ti:f/ (Sprachw., Kunstw.) **1** *Adj.* figurative. **2** *adv.* figuratively
figürlich /fi'ɡy:ɐlɪç/ **1** *Adj.* (Kunstwiss.) figured. **2** *adv.* (in Bezug auf die Figur) as far as her figure/his physique is concerned
Fiktion /fik'tsi̯oːn/ *die;* ~, ~**en** fiction
fiktiv /fik'ti:f/ *Adj.* (geh.) fictitious
Filet[1] /fi'le:/ *das;* ~**s**, ~**s** (Textilw.) filet; netting
Filet[2] *das;* ~**s**, ~**s** fillet; (Rinder~, Schweine~) fillet; filet
Filet·steak *das* fillet steak
Filial·betrieb *der* branch
Filiale /fi'li̯a:lə/ *die;* ~, ~**n** branch
Filialist *der;* ~**en**, ~**en** (Wirtsch.) chain-store owner
Filial·leiter *der* branch manager
Filius /'fi:li̯ʊs/ *der;* ~, ~**se** (scherzh.) son
Film /fɪlm/ *der;* ~**[e]s**, ~**e** (a) (Fot.) film; (b) (Kino~) film; movie (Amer. coll.); **da ist bei ihm der** ~ **gerissen** (fig.

ugs.) he's had a mental blackout; (**c**) *o. Pl.* (~branche) films *pl.;* **beim** ~ **sein** be in films; (**d**) (dünne Schicht) film
Film·atelier *das* film studio
Filme·macher *der;* ~**s**, ~, **Filme·macherin** *die;* ~, ~**nen** film-maker
filmen 1 *tr. V.* (a) film; (b) (ugs.: hereinlegen) **jmdn.** ~: take sb. for a ride (fig. coll.). **2** *itr. V.* film; make a film/films
Film·festspiele *Pl.* film festival *sing.*
filmisch 1 *Adj.* cinematic ‹*art etc.*›. **2** *adv.* cinematically
Film-: ~**kamera** *die* film camera; (Schmalfilmkamera) cine-camera; ~**kritik** *die* (a) (Besprechung) film review; (**b**) (~kritiker) film critics *pl.;* ~**musik** *die* film music; (eines einzelnen Films) theme music; ~**preis** *der* film award; ~**produzent** *der* film producer; ~**regisseur** *der* film director; ~**rolle** *die* (a) (schauspielerische Rolle) film part *or* role; (**b**) (Spule) reel of film; ~**schauspieler** *der* ▶85⌋ film actor; ~**schauspielerin** *die* ▶85⌋ film actress; ~**star** *der* film star; ~**verleih** *der* film distributor[s]; ~**vorstellung** *die* film show
Filou /fi'lu:/ *der* (abwertend) (**a**) (Spitzbube) dog (derog.); rogue; (**b**) (Verführer) devil (derog.)
Filter /'fɪltɐ/ *der,* (fachspr. meist) *das;* ~**s**, ~: filter; **Zigarette ohne/mit** ~: plain/[filter-]tipped cigarette
filter·fein *Adj.* finely-ground *attrib.*, filter-fine *attrib.* ‹*coffee*›
Filter·kaffee *der* filter coffee
filtern *tr. V.* filter
Filter-: ~**papier** *das* filter paper; ~**tüte** *die* filter; ~**zigarette** *die* [filter-]tipped cigarette
Filtration /filtra'tsi̯oːn/ *die;* ~, ~**en** (Technik) filtration
filtrieren *tr. V.* filter
Filz /fɪlts/ *der;* ~**es**, ~**e** (a) felt; (**b**) (filzartig Verschlungenes) mass; mat; (**c**) (Bierdeckel) beer mat
filzen 1 *itr. V.* felt. **2** *tr. V.* (ugs.: durchsuchen) search ‹*room, car, etc.*›; frisk ‹*person*›
Filz·hut *der* felt hat
filzig *Adj.* felted ‹*wool*›; matted ‹*hair*›
Filzokratie /filtsokra'ti:/ *die;* ~, ~**n** (abwertend) corruption; graft (coll.)
Filz-: ~**pantoffel** *der* slipper; ~**schreiber** *der,* ~**stift** *der* felt-tip pen
Fimmel /'fɪml̩/ *der;* ~**s**, ~ (ugs. abwertend) **einen** ~ **für etw. haben** have a thing about sth. (coll.); **du hast wohl einen** ~**!** there must be something the matter with you; you must be dotty (Brit.)
Finale /fi'na:lə/ *das;* ~**s**, ~**[s]** (a) (Sport) final; (**b**) (Musik, fig.) finale
Final·satz *der* (Sprachw.) final clause
Finanz /fi'nants/ *die;* ~ (a) (Geldwesen) finance *no art.;* (**b**) (~leute) financial world
Finanz-: ~**amt** *das* (a) (Behörde) ≈ Inland Revenue; *das* ~**amt** (ugs.: die Steuerbehörden) the taxman; (**b**) (Gebäude) tax office; ~**beamte** *der* tax officer
Finanzen *Pl.* (a) finance *sing.;* (**b**) (ugs.: finanzielle Verhältnisse) finances; (**c**) (Einkünfte des Staates) [government] finances
Finanz·hoheit *die* fiscal prerogative
finanziell /finan'tsi̯ɛl/ **1** *Adj.* financial. **2** *adv.* financially
finanzieren *tr. V.* (a) finance; (fig.: bezahlen) pay for; **frei/staatlich finanziert sein** be privately financed/financed by the state; (**b**) (Kaufmannsspr.: auf Kredit kaufen) buy on credit; **etw. langfristig** ~: obtain long-term credit for sth.
Finanzierung *die;* ~, ~**en** financing
finanz-, Finanz-: ~**kontrolle** *die* (Wirtsch.) financial control; ~**kraft** *die; o. Pl.* financial strength; ~**kräftig** *Adj.* financially powerful; ~**minister** *der* minister of finance; ≈ Chancellor of the Exchequer (Brit.); ≈ Secretary of the Treasury (Amer.); ~**ministerium** *das* Ministry of Finance; (in GB u. USA) ≈ Treasury; ~**politik** *die* politics of finance; **eine neue** ~**politik** a new financial policy; ~**politisch 1** *Adj.* ‹*questions etc.*› relating to financial policy; **2** *adv.* from the point of view of financial policy; ~**stark** *Adj.* financially strong; ~**wesen** *das o. Pl.* system of public finances

Findel·kind /'fɪndl-/ *das* foundling

finden /'fɪndn̩/ 1 *unr. tr. V.* (**a**) (entdecken) find; **eine Spur von jmdm. ~:** get a lead on sb.; **keine Spur von jmdm. ~:** find no trace of sb.; (**b**) (erlangen, erwerben) find ‹*work, flat, wife, etc.*›; **Freunde ~:** make friends; (**c**) (heraus~) find ‹*solution, mistake, pretext, excuse, answer*›; (**d**) (einschätzen, beurteilen) **etw. gut ~:** think sth. is good; **nichts bei etw. ~:** not mind sth.; **ich finde nichts dabei** I don't mind; (**e**) (erhalten) **Hilfe [bei jmdm.] ~:** get help [from sb.]. 2 *unr. refl. V.* **sich ~:** turn up; **es fand sich niemand/jemand, der das tun wollte** nobody wanted to do that/ there was somebody who wanted to do that; **das/es wird sich alles ~** it will all work out all right. 3 *unr. itr. V.* **zu jmdm. ~:** find sb.; **nach Hause ~:** find the way home; **zu sich selbst ~** (fig.) come to terms with oneself

Finder *der;* ~s, ~, **Finderin** *die;* ~, ~nen finder

Finder·lohn *der* reward [for finding sth.]

findig *Adj.* resourceful

Finesse /fi'nɛsə/ *die;* ~, ~n (**a**) *meist Pl.* (Kunstgriff) trick; (**b**) *meist Pl.* (in der Ausstattung) refinement; **mit allen ~n** with every refinement; (**c**) (Schlauheit) flair

fing /fɪŋ/ *1. u. 3. Pers. Sg. Prät. v.* **fangen**

Finger /'fɪŋɐ/ *der;* ~s, ~ (**a**) ▶ 326 | finger; **mit dem ~ auf jmdn./etw. zeigen** (auch fig.) point one's finger at sb./ sth.; (**b**) (fig.) **wenn man ihm den kleinen ~ reicht, nimmt er gleich die ganze Hand** if you give him an inch he takes a mile; **die ~ davonlassen/von etw. lassen** (ugs.) steer clear of it/of sth.; **sie macht keinen ~ krumm** (ugs.) she never lifts a finger; **er rührte keinen ~:** he wouldn't lift a finger; **lange ~ machen** (ugs.) get itchy fingers; **ich würde mir alle [zehn] ~ danach lecken** (ugs.) I'd give my eye-teeth for it; **die ~ in etw.** (*Dat.*) **/im Spiel haben** (ugs.) have a hand in sth./have one's finger in the pie; **sich** (*Dat.*) **die ~ verbrennen** (ugs.) burn one's fingers (fig.); **sich** (*Dat.*) **die ~ schmutzig machen** get one's hands dirty; **sich** (*Dat.*) **etw. an den [fünf od. zehn] ~n abzählen können** be able to see sth. straight away; **jmdm. auf die ~ klopfen** (ugs.) rap sb. across the knuckles; **sich** (*Dat.*) **etw. aus den ~n saugen** (ugs.) make sth. up; **ihm od. ihn juckt es in den ~n** [, **etw. zu tun**] (ugs.) he is itching [to do sth.]; **wenn ich den in die ~ kriege!** (ugs.) wait till I get my hands on him (coll.); **jmdn. um den [kleinen] ~ wickeln** (ugs.) wrap sb. round one's little finger

finger-, Finger-: **~abdruck** *der* fingerprint; **~breit** *der;* ~, ~ (fig.) inch; **~fertigkeit** *die; o. Pl.* dexterity; **~hakeln** /~ha:kl̩n/ *das;* ~s finger-wrestling; **~handschuh** *der* glove [with fingers]; **~hut** *der* (**a**) thimble; (**b**) (Bot.) foxglove; **~knöchel** *der* knuckle; **~kuppe** *die* fingertip

fingern *itr. V.* fiddle; **an etw.** (*Dat.*) **~:** fiddle with sth.; **nach etw. ~:** fumble [around] for sth.

Finger-: **~nagel** *der* ▶ 326 | fingernail; **~spitze** *die* fingertip; **das muss man in den ~n haben** (fig.) you have to have a feel for it; **~spitzen·gefühl** *das; o. Pl.* feeling; **~zeig** /~tsaik/ *der;* ~s, ~e hint; (an die Polizei) tip-off

fingieren /fɪn'giːrən/ *tr. V.* fake

Fink /fɪŋk/ *der;* ~en, ~en finch

Finne /'fɪnə/ *der;* ~n, ~n, **Finnin** *die;* ~, ~nen ▶ 388 | Finn

finnisch *Adj.* ▶ 388 |, ▶ 487 | Finnish

Finnland /'fɪnlant/ (*das*); ~s Finland

finster /'fɪnstɐ/ 1 *Adj.* (**a**) dark; **im Finstern** in the dark; (**b**) (düster) dark ‹*house, forest, alleyway*›; dimly-lit ‹*pub, district*›; (**c**) (dubios) shady ‹*plan, affair*›; sinister ‹*figure*›; (**d**) (verdüstert, feindselig) **eine ~e Miene** a black expression; (**e**) (fig.) **im Finstern tappen** be groping in the dark. 2 *adv.* **jmdn. ~ ansehen** give sb. a black look

Finsternis *die;* ~, ~se (**a**) darkness; (bibl., fig.) dark; (**b**) (Astron.) eclipse

Finte /'fɪntə/ *die;* ~, ~n (**a**) (List) trick; (**b**) (Fechten) feint

Firlefanz /'fɪrləfants/ *der;* ~es (ugs. abwertend) (**a**) (Tand, Flitter) frippery; trumpery; (**b**) (Unsinn) nonsense; ~ **machen** fool around

firm /fɪrm/ *Adj.* **in etw.** (*Dat.*) **~ sein** be well up in sth.; know sth. thoroughly

Firma /'fɪrma/ *die;* ~, **Firmen** firm; company

Firmament /fɪrma'mɛnt/ *das;* ~[e]s (dichter.) firmament

firmen *tr. V.* (kath. Rel.) confirm

Firmen-: **~inhaber** *der* owner of the/a company; **~name** *der* name of a/the company *or* firm; **~schild** *das* company's name plate; **~wagen** *der* company car; **~zeichen** *das* trademark

firmieren *itr. V.* trade

Firmung *die;* ~, ~en confirmation; **jmdm. die ~ erteilen** confirm sb.

Firn *der;* ~[e]s firn

Firnis /'fɪrnɪs/ *der;* ~ses, ~se varnish

First /fɪrst/ *der;* ~[e]s, ~e ridge

Fis /fɪs/ *das;* ~, ~ (Musik) F sharp

Fisch /fɪʃ/ *der;* ~[e]s, ~e (**a**) fish; [fünf] ~e fangen catch [five] fish; **gesund und munter wie ein ~ im Wasser** as fit as a fiddle; **stumm wie ein ~ sein** keep a stony silence; (fig.) **kleine ~e** (ugs.) small fry; (**b**) *o. Pl.* (Nahrungsmittel) fish; **das ist weder ~ noch Fleisch** (fig.) that's neither fish nor fowl; (**c**) (Astrol.) **die ~e** Pisces; the Fishes; **er ist [ein] ~:** he is a Piscean; **im Zeichen der ~e geboren sein** be born under [the sign of] Pisces

Fisch-: **~becken** *das* fish-pond; **~dampfer** *der* steam trawler

fischen 1 *tr. V.* (**a**) fish for; (**b**) (ugs.) **etw. aus etw. ~:** fish sth. out of sth. 2 *itr. V.* fish (**nach** for); **~ gehen** go fishing; *s. auch* **trüb** 1 a

Fischer *der;* ~s, ~ ▶ 85 | fisherman

Fischer-: **~boot** *das* fishing boat; **~dorf** *das* fishing village

Fischerei *die;* ~: fishing

Fisch·fang *der; o. Pl.* **vom ~ leben** make a/one's living by fishing; **auf ~ gehen** go fishing

Fisch-: **~filet** *das* fish fillet; **~geruch** *der* smell of fish; **~geschäft** *das* fishmonger's [shop] (Brit.); fish store (Amer.); **~grät[en]·muster** *das* (Textilw.) herringbone pattern; **~gründe** *Pl.* fishing grounds; **~händler** *der* fishmonger (Brit.); fish dealer (Amer.); **~konserve** *die* canned fish; **~kutter** *der* fishing trawler; **~laden** *der* ⇨ **~geschäft**; **~markt** *der* fish market; **~mehl** *das* fish-meal; **~otter** *der* otter; **~schuppe** *die* fish scale; **~stäbchen** *das* (Kochk.) fish finger; **~sterben** *das* death of the fish; **~zucht** *die* fish farming; **~zug** *der* (ugs.) killing

Fis-Dur /auch: '-'-/ *das;* ~ (Musik) F sharp major

Fisimatenten /fizima'tɛntn̩/ *Pl.* (ugs.) messing about *sing.;* **mach keine ~!** stop messing about

fiskalisch /fɪs'kaːlɪʃ/ *Adj.* fiscal

Fiskus /'fɪskʊs/ *der;* ~, **Fisken** *od.* ~se Government (*as managing the State finances*)

fis-Moll /auch: '-'-/ *das;* ~ (Musik) F sharp minor

Fistel /'fɪstl̩/ *die;* ~, ~n (Med.) fistula

Fistel·stimme *die* thin high-pitched voice

fit /fɪt/ *Adj.; nicht attr.* fit; **sich ~ halten** keep fit; **das hält ~:** it keeps you fit

Fitness, *Fitneß /'fɪtnɛs/ *die;* ~: fitness

Fittich /'fɪtɪç/ *der;* ~[e]s, ~e (dichter.) wing; pinion; **jmdn. unter seine ~e nehmen** (ugs. scherzh.) take sb. under one's wing

Fitzelchen /'fɪtsl̩çən/ *das;* ~s, ~ (ugs.) scrap

fix /fɪks/ 1 *Adj.* (**a**) (ugs.: flink, wendig) quick; **ein ~er Bursche** a bright lad; (**b**) (ugs.) **~ und fertig** (fertig vorbereitet) quite finished; (völlig erschöpft) completely shattered (coll.); (**c**) (festgelegt) fixed ‹*cost, salary*›; **eine ~e Idee** an idée fixe. 2 *adv.* (ugs.) quickly; **das geht ganz ~:** it won't take a jiffy (coll.); [**mach**] ~! hurry up!

fixen /'fɪksn̩/ *itr. V.* (Drogenjargon) fix (sl.)

Fixer *der;* ~s, ~, **Fixerin,** *die* ~, ~nen (Drogenjargon) fixer

Fixier·bad *das* (Fot.) fixer

fixieren /fɪ'ksiːrən/ *tr. V.* (**a**) (scharf ansehen) fix one's gaze on; (**b**) (geh.: schriftlich niederlegen) take down; (**c**) (Fot.) fix

Fläche

1 Quadratzentimeter	= one square centimetre (sq. cm)	= 0.155 square inch (sq. in.)
1 Quadratmeter	= one square metre (sq. m)	= 10.764 square feet (sq. ft) *od.* 1.196 square yards (sq. yds)
1 Hektar	= one hectare (ha)	= 2.471 acres
1 Quadratkilometer	= one square kilometre (sq. km)	= 0.386 square mile

Wie viel Wohnfläche hat die Wohnung?	=	What is the floor area of the flat *od. (amerik.)* apartment?
Das Zimmer hat 16 m² [Fläche]	=	The room has an area of 16 sq. m, ≈ the room has an area of 170 sq. ft.
ein Gebäude mit 8 000 m² Bürofläche	=	a building with 8,000 sq. m, ≈ a building with 86,000 sq. ft of office space
Er bewirtschaftet 400 Hektar [Land]	=	He farms 400 hectares [of land], ≈ he farms 1,000 acres [of land]
ein Gut von 400 ha	=	an estate of 400 ha, ≈ an estate of 1,000 acres
eine Fläche von etwa 100 km²	=	an area of about 100 sq. km, ≈ an area of about 40 square miles

Fixierung *die;* ~, ~**en** (a) (starres Festlegen, -halten) **die** ~ **auf seine Mutter** his mother-fixation; (b) (Festlegung) determination

Fix·stern *der* (Astron.) fixed star

Fixum /'fɪksʊm/ *das;* ~**s**, **Fixa** basic salary

Fjord /fjɔrt/ *der;* ~[e]**s**, ~**e** fiord

FKK /ɛf ka: 'ka:/ *Abk.* **Freikörperkultur** nudism *no art.;* naturism *no art.*

FKK-: ~**-Anhänger** *der* nudist; naturist; ~**-Strand** *der* nudist beach

flach /flax/ *Adj.* (a) flat ‹countryside, region, roof›; ~ **liegen** lie flat; **die** ~**e Hand** the flat of one's hand; (b) ▶ 277 ‹(niedrig) low ‹heels, building›; flat ‹shoe›; (c) ▶ 277 (nicht tief) shallow ‹water, river, dish›; (d) (fig. abwertend) shallow

flach·brüstig *Adj.* flat-chested

Flach·dach *das* flat roof

Fläche /'flɛçə/ *die;* ~, ~**n** (a) (ebenes Gebiet) area; (b) (Ober~, Außenseite) surface; (c) ▶ 189 (Math.) area; (einer dreidimensionalen Figur) side; face; (d) (weite Land~, Wasser~) expanse

Flächen-: ~**brand** *der* extensive blaze; ~**inhalt** *der* (Math.) area; ~**maß** *das* (Math.) unit of square measure

flach-, Flach-: ~|**fallen** *itr. V.; mit sein* (ugs.) ‹trip› fall through; ‹event› be cancelled; ~**hang** *der* slip-off slope; ~**land** *das; o. Pl.* lowland; ~|**legen** 1 *refl. V.* (ugs.) lie down; 2 *tr. V.* (zu Boden strecken) floor ‹opponent›; ~|**liegen** *unr. V.* (ugs.) be flat on one's back; ~**mann** *der; Pl.* ~**männer** (ugs. scherzh.) hip flask

Flachs /flaks/ *der;* ~**es** (a) flax; (b) (ugs.: Ulk) **das war doch nur** ~: I/he *etc.* was just having you on (Brit. coll.) *or* (Amer. coll.) putting you on; **ganz ohne** ~: no kidding (coll.)

flachs·blond *Adj.* flaxen ‹hair›

flachsen /'flaksn̩/ *itr. V.* (ugs.) **mit jmdm.** ~: joke with sb.; **gerne** ~: like a joke

Flach·zange *die* flat tongs *pl.*

flackern /'flakɐn/ *itr. V.* flicker

Fladen /'fla:dn̩/ *der;* ~**s**, ~ (a) *flat, round unleavened cake made with oat or barley flour;* ≈ [large] oatcake (Scot.); (b) (Kuh~) cowpat

Fladen·brot *das* unleavened bread

Flagge /'flaɡə/ *die;* ~, ~**n** flag; **die** ~ **streichen** (fig.) strike the flag (fig.); ~ **zeigen** (fig.) show one's colours

flaggen *itr. V.* put out the flags

Flaggen-: ~**alphabet** *das* international code of signals; ~**gruß** *der* flag salute; ~**mast** *der* flagstaff

Flagg-: ~**leine** *die* halyard; ~**offizier** *der* flag officer; ~**schiff** *das* flagship

Flair /flɛːɐ̯/ *das od. der;* ~**s** (a) (Fluidum, Aura) air; (b) (Talent) flair

Flak /flak/ *die;* ~, ~ (Milit.) anti-aircraft gun; AA gun

Flakon /fla'kõ/ *das od. der;* ~**s**, ~**s** bottle

flambieren /flam'biːrən/ *tr. V.* flambé

Flame /'fla:mə/ *der;* ~**n**, ~**n** ▶ 388 Fleming

Flamenco /fla'mɛŋko/ *der;* ~[s], ~**s** flamenco

Flämin /'flɛːmɪn/ *die;* ~, ~**nen** Fleming

Flamingo /fla'mɪŋɡo/ *der;* ~**s**, ~**s** flamingo

flämisch *Adj.* ▶ 388 , ▶ 487 Flemish

Flamme /'flamə/ *die;* ~, ~**n** (a) flame; **in** ~**n stehen/ aufgehen** be/go up in flames; (b) (Brennstelle) burner; (c) (ugs. veralt.: Freundin) flame

flammen /'flamən/ *itr. V.* (geh.) blaze

flammend *Adj.* (a) flaming; ~**es Haar** flaming red hair; (b) (fig.) fiery ‹speech›

Flammen-: ~**meer** *das* (geh.) sea of flame[s]; ~**tod** *der* (geh.) death by burning; ~**werfer** *der* (Milit.) flamethrower

Flandern /'flandɐn/ (*das*); ~**s** Flanders

Flanell /fla'nɛl/ *der;* ~**s**, ~**e** flannel

Flanell·anzug *der* flannel suit

Flaneur /fla'nøːɐ̯/ *der;* ~**s**, ~**e** (geh.) flâneur

flanieren /fla'niːrən/ *itr. V.; mit Richtungsangabe mit sein* stroll

Flanke /'flaŋkə/ *die;* ~, ~**n** (a) (auch Milit.) flank; (b) (Ballspiele) (Flankenball) centre; (Teil des Spielfeldes) wing; (c) (Turnen) flank vault

flanken *itr. V.* (a) (Ballspiele) [**in die Mitte**] ~: centre the ball; (b) (Turnen) flank vault

Flanken-: ~**ball** *der* (Ballspiele) centre; ~**deckung** *die* (Milit.) flank defence

flankieren *tr. V.* flank; ~**de Maßnahmen** (fig.) additional measures

Flansch /flanʃ/ *der;* ~[e]**s**, ~**e** (Technik) flange

flapsig /'flapsɪç/ (ugs.) **1** *Adj.* rude. **2** *adv.* rudely

Flasche /'flaʃə/ *die;* ~, ~**n** (a) bottle; **ein Tier mit der** ~ **großziehen** rear an animal by bottle; **ich muss dem Kind noch die** ~ **geben** I must just feed the baby; **zur** ~ **greifen** (fig.) take to the bottle; (b) (ugs. abwertend) (Feigling) wet (coll.); (unfähiger Mensch) **eine** ~ **sein** be useless; **du** ~! you useless item! (coll.)

Flaschen-: ~**bier** *das* bottled beer; ~**hals** *der* (auch fig.) bottleneck; ~**halter** *der* bottle cage; ~**kind** *das* bottle-fed baby; ~**milch** *die* bottled milk; ~**öffner** *der* bottle opener; ~**pfand** *das* deposit [on a/the bottle]; ~**post** *die* message in a/the bottle; ~**wein** *der* wine by the bottle; ~**zug** *der* block and tackle

Flaschner /'flaʃnɐ/ *der;* ~**s**, ~ (südd., schweiz.) plumber

flatterhaft *Adj.* fickle

Flatterhaftigkeit *die;* ~: fickleness

Flatter·mann *der; Pl.* ~**männer** (salopp) (a) *o. Pl.* (nervöse Unruhe) jitters *pl.* (coll.); (b) (scherzh.: Brathuhn) roast chicken

flattern *itr. V.* (a) *mit Richtungsangabe mit sein* flutter; (b) (zittern) ‹hands› shake; ‹eyelids› flutter; **seine Nerven flatterten** (fig.) he got in a flap (coll.)

flau /flau/ **1** *Adj.* **(a)** (schwach, matt) slack ‹*breeze*›; flat ‹*atmosphere*›; **(b)** (leicht übel) queasy ‹*feeling*›; **mir ist ∼:** I feel queasy. **2** *adv.* (Kaufmannsspr.) **das Geschäft geht ∼:** business is slack

Flaum /flaum/ *der;* ∼[e]s **(a)** fuzz; **(b)** (∼federn) down

Flaum·bart *der* downy beard

Flaum·feder *die* down feather

flaumig *Adj.* downy

Flausch /flauʃ/ *der;* ∼[e]s, ∼e brushed wool

flauschig *Adj.* fluffy

Flause /'flauzə/ *die;* ∼, ∼n; *meist Pl.* (ugs.) **er hat nur ∼n im Kopf** he can never think of anything sensible; **jmdm. die ∼n austreiben** knock some sense into sb.

Flaute /'flautə/ *die;* ∼, ∼n **(a)** (Seemannsspr.) calm; **(b)** (Kaufmannsspr.) fall[-off] in trade; **in der ∼:** in the doldrums

Flecht·arbeit *die* piece of wickerwork; ∼en wickerwork *sing.*

Flechte /'flɛçtə/ *die;* ∼, ∼n **(a)** (Bot.) lichen; **(b)** (Med.) eczema

flechten *unr. tr. V.* plait ‹*hair*›; weave ‹*basket, mat*›

Flechter *der;* ∼s, ∼, **Flechterin** *die;* ∼, ∼nen basket-weaver

Flecht·werk *das* **(a)** (Geflecht) wickerwork; **(b)** (Archit.) wattle and daub

Fleck /flɛk/ *der;* ∼[e]s, ∼e **(a)** (verschmutzte Stelle) stain; **∼e machen** leave stains; **einen ∼ auf der [weißen] Weste haben** (fig. ugs.) have blotted one's copybook; **(b)** (andersfarbige Stelle) patch; *s. auch* **blau**; **(c)** (Stelle, Punkt) spot; **sich nicht vom ∼ rühren** not to move an inch; **auf demselben ∼:** in the same place; **wir kriegten den Stein nicht vom ∼:** we couldn't budge the stone; **ich bin nicht vom ∼ gekommen** (fig.) I didn't get anywhere; **vom ∼ weg** (fig.) on the spot; *s. auch* **Herz a**

Fleckchen *das;* ∼s, ∼: spot; **ein schönes ∼ Erde** a lovely little spot

flecken *itr. V.* stain

Flecken *der;* ∼s, ∼ **(a)** ⇒ **Fleck a, b**; **(b)** (Ortschaft) little place

Fleck·entferner *der,* **Flecken·wasser** *das* stain *or* spot remover

fleckig /'flɛkɪç/ *Adj.* **(a)** (verschmutzt) stained; **(b)** (gepunktet) speckled ‹*apple*›; blotchy ‹*face, skin*›

fleddern /'flɛdɐn/ *tr. V.* plunder, rob ‹*person*›

Fleder·maus /'fleːdɐ-/ *die* bat

Fleder·wisch *der* feather duster

Flegel /'fleːgl̩/ *der;* ∼s, ∼ (abwertend) lout

Flegel·alter *das* ⇒ **Flegeljahre**

flegelhaft *Adj.* (abwertend) loutish; boorish ‹*tone of voice*›

Flegel·jahre *Pl.* uncouth adolescence *sing.;* **in die ∼ kommen/aus den ∼n heraus sein** reach/be past the awkward age *sing.*

flegeln *refl. V.* (abwertend) **sich auf ein Sofa ∼:** flop on to a sofa

flehen /'fleːən/ *itr. V.* plead; **[bei jmdm.] um etw. ∼:** plead [with sb.] for sth.; **zu Gott ∼:** beg God

flehentlich *Adv.* (geh.) pleadingly

Fleisch /flaiʃ/ *das;* ∼[e]s **(a)** (Muskelgewebe) flesh; **das nackte/rohe ∼:** one's bare/raw flesh; **∼ fressend** (Biol.) carnivorous; (fig.) **sein eigen[es] ∼ und Blut** (geh.) his own flesh and blood; **jmdm. in ∼ und Blut übergehen** become second nature to sb.; **sich** (*Dat.*) **ins eigene ∼ schneiden** cut off one's nose to spite one's face; **vom ∼ fallen** (ugs.) waste away; **(b)** (Nahrungsmittel) meat; **(c)** (Frucht∼) flesh

fleisch-, Fleisch-: **∼arm** *Adj.* ‹*diet*› low in meat; **∼beschau** *die* meat inspection; **∼brocken** *der* chunk of meat; **∼brühe** *die* bouillon; consommé

Fleischer /'flaiʃɐ/ *der;* ∼s, ∼: ▶ 85 butcher; *s. auch* **Bäcker**

Fleischerei *die;* ∼, ∼en butcher's shop; **in der ∼:** at the butcher's; *s. auch* **Bäckerei**

Fleischer-: **∼haken** *der* meat hook; **∼meister** *der* master butcher; **∼messer** *das* butcher's knife

fleisch-, Fleisch-: **∼farben**, **∼farbig** *Adj.* flesh-coloured; **∼fondue** *das* (Kochk.) meat fondue;*∼fressend** ⇒ **Fleisch**; **∼fresser** *der;* ∼s, ∼ (Biol.) carnivore; **∼gang** *der* (Gastr.) meat course; **∼gericht** *das* meat dish

fleischig *Adj.* plump ‹*hands, face*›; fleshy ‹*leaf, fruit*›

fleisch-, Fleisch-: **∼käse** *der* meat loaf; **∼kloß** *der* **(a)** (Kochk.) meat ball; **(b)** ⇒ **∼klumpen**; **∼klößchen** *das* small meat ball; **∼klumpen** *der* (ugs.) chunk of meat; **∼konserve** *die* tin of meat (Brit.); can of meat (Amer.); **∼los** *Adj.* **(a)** without meat ‹*meal*›; **(b)** (hager, mager) bony ‹*hands, face*›; **∼pastete** *die* (Kochk.) pâté; **∼salat** *der* (Kochk.) meat salad; **∼vergiftung** *die* food poisoning [from meat]; **∼waren** *Pl.* meat products; **∼wolf** *der* mincer; **∼wunde** *die* flesh wound; **∼wurst** *die* pork sausage

Fleiß /flais/ *der;* ∼es **(a)** (eifriges Streben) hard work; (Eigenschaft) diligence; **viel ∼ auf etw.** (*Akk.*) **verwenden** put a lot of effort into sth.; **durch ∼ etw. erreichen** achieve sth. by hard work; **ohne ∼ kein Preis** (Spr.) success never comes easily; **(b)** (veralt., südd.: Absicht) **mit ∼:** on purpose

fleißig /'flaisɪç/ **1** *Adj.* **(a)** (arbeitsam) hard-working; willing ‹*hands*›; **(b)** *nicht präd.* (von Fleiß zeugend) diligent ‹*piece of work*›; **(c)** (regelmäßig, häufig) frequent ‹*visitor*›; **(d)** (unermüdlich) indefatigable ‹*collector*›; great ‹*walker*›. **2** *adv.* **(a)** ‹*work, study*› hard; **(b)** (unermüdlich) ‹*drink, spend*› steadily; ‹*collect*› regularly; **(c)** (regelmäßig) frequently

flektieren /flɛk'tiːrən/ (Sprachw.) **1** *tr. V.* inflect. **2** *itr. V.* be inflected

flennen /'flɛnən/ *itr. V.* (ugs. abwertend) blubber

fletschen /'flɛtʃn̩/ *tr. V.* **die Zähne ∼:** bare one's/its teeth

Fleurop Ⓦ /'flɔyrɔp/ *die* Interflora (**P**)

Flex *die;* ∼, ∼e (ugs.) angle grinder [with cutting disc]

flexibel /flɛ'ksiːbl̩/ **1** *Adj.* flexible. **2** *adv.* flexibly

Flexibilität /flɛksibili'tɛːt/ *die;* ∼: flexibility

Flexion /flɛ'ksioːn/ *die;* ∼, ∼en (Sprachw.) inflexion

Flexions·endung *die;* (Sprachw.) inflectional suffix *or* ending

flicht *Imperativ Sg. u. 3. Pers. Sg. Präsens v.* **flechten**

flicken /'flɪkn̩/ *tr. V.* mend ‹*trousers, dress*›; repair ‹*engine, cable*›; mend, repair ‹*wall, roof*›

Flicken *der;* ∼s, ∼: patch

Flicken·decke *die* patchwork quilt

Flickflack /'flɪkflak/ *der;* ∼s, ∼s (Turnen) flik-flak

Flick-: **∼werk** *das; o. Pl.* (abwertend) botched-up job; **∼zeug** *das* repair kit

Flieder /'fliːdɐ/ *der;* ∼s, ∼: lilac

flieder·farben, **flieder·farbig** *Adj.* lilac

Fliege /'fliːgə/ *die;* ∼, ∼n **(a)** fly; **sie starben wie die ∼n** they were dying like flies; **er tut keiner ∼ etwas zuleide/könnte keiner ∼ etwas zuleide tun** he wouldn't/couldn't hurt a fly; (fig.) **ihn stört die ∼ an der Wand** the least little thing annoys him; **zwei ∼n mit einer Klappe schlagen** kill two birds with one stone (coll.); **die od. ne ∼ machen** (salopp) beat it (sl.); **(b)** (Schleife) bow tie; **(c)** (Bärtchen) shadow

fliegen 1 *unr. itr. V.* **(a)** *mit sein* fly; **das ∼de Personal** the air-crew; **in die Luft ∼** (durch Explosion) blow up; **(b)** *mit sein* (ugs.: geworfen werden) **aus der Kurve ∼:** skid off a/the bend; **vom Pferd ∼:** fall off a/the horse; **(c)** *mit sein* (ugs.: entlassen werden) be sacked (coll.); get the sack (coll.); **auf die Straße/aus einer Stellung ∼:** get the sack (coll.); **von der Schule ∼:** be chucked out [of the school] (coll.); **(d)** *mit sein* (ugs.: hinfallen, stürzen) fall; **über etw.** (*Akk.*) **∼:** trip over sth.; **durch das Examen ∼** (fig.) fail the exam; **(e)** *mit sein* **auf jmdn./etw. ∼** (ugs.) go for sb./sth.. **2** *unr. tr. V.* **(a)** (steuern, fliegend befördern) fly ‹*aircraft, passengers, goods*›; **(b)** *auch mit sein* (fliegend ausführen) **einen Einsatz ∼:** fly a mission; **einen Umweg ∼:** make a detour

fliegend *Adj.; nicht präd.* flying; **ein ∼er Händler** a pedlar

Fliegen-: ~**fänger** der fly- paper; ~**fenster** das wire-mesh window; ~**gewicht** das (Schwerathletik) flyweight; **im** ~**gewicht starten** compete at flyweight; ~**klatsche** die fly swat; ~**pilz** der fly agaric

Flieger der; ~**s**, ~ (a) pilot; **er ist bei den** ~**n** (Milit.) he's in the air force; (b) (Radsport) sprinter

Flieger·alarm der air-raid warning

Fliegerei die; ~; flying nω art.

Fliegerin die; ~, ~**nen** [woman] pilot

fliehen /'fli:ən/ **1** unr. itr. V.; mit sein (flüchten) flee (**vor** + Dat. from); (entkommen) escape (**aus** from); **ins Ausland/ über die Grenze** ~: flee the country/escape over the border. **2** unr. tr. V. (geh.: meiden) shun

fliehend Adj.; nicht präd. sloping ⟨forehead⟩; receding ⟨chin⟩

Flieh·kraft die (Physik) centrifugal force

Fliese /'fli:zə/ die; ~, ~**n** tile; **etw. mit** ~**n auslegen** tile sth.

Fliesenleger /-le:gɐ/ der; ~**s**, ~: ▶ 85 tiler

Fließ-: ~**band** das conveyor belt; **am** ~**band arbeiten** work on the assembly line; ~**band·arbeit** die assembly-line work

fließen /'fli:sn̩/ unr. itr. V.; mit sein flow; **es floss Blut** blood was shed; **die Gaben flossen reichlich** donations were pouring in

fließend 1 Adj. running ⟨water⟩; moving ⟨traffic⟩; fluid ⟨transition⟩; fluent ⟨English, French, etc.⟩; **die Grenzen sind** ~: the dividing-line ist blurred. **2** adv. ⟨speak a language⟩ fluently

Fließ·heck das (Kfz-W.) fastback

Fließ-: ~**heck** das (Kfz-W.) fastback; ~**komma** das (DV) floating point

Flimmer-: ~**kasten** der, ~**kiste** die (ugs.) telly (coll.); box (coll.)

flimmern /'flɪmɐn/ itr. V. ⟨water, air, surface⟩ shimmer; ⟨film⟩ flicker; **ihm flimmerte es vor den Augen** everything was swimming in front of his eyes

flink /flɪŋk/ **1** Adj. nimble ⟨fingers⟩; sharp ⟨eyes⟩; quick ⟨hands⟩; ~ **wie ein Wiesel** as quick as a flash. **2** adv. quickly

Flinkheit die; ~ ⇒ **flink 1**: nimbleness; sharpness; quickness

Flinte /'flɪntə/ die; ~, ~**n** shotgun; **der soll mir nur vor die** ~ **kommen!** (fig. salopp) if I can just get my hands on him; **die** ~ **ins Korn werfen** (fig.) throw in the towel

Flinten-: ~**kugel** die shotgun pellet; ~**lauf** der shotgun barrel

Flip /flɪp/ der; ~**s**, ~**s** flip

Flipper /'flɪpɐ/ der; ~**s**, ~, **Flipper·automat** der pinball machine

flippern /'flɪpɐn/ itr. V. (ugs.) play pinball

Flirt /flʊ't/ der; ~**s**, ~**s** flirtation; **einen** ~ **mit jmdm. haben** flirt with sb.

flirten itr. V. flirt

Flittchen /'flɪtçən/ das; ~**s**, ~ (ugs. abwertend) floozie

Flitter /'flɪtɐ/ der; ~**s**, ~ (a) o. Pl. frippery; trumpery; (b) (Metallplättchen) sequin

Flitter·kram der (ugs. abwertend) frippery; trumpery

Flitter·wochen Pl. honeymoon sing.; **in die** ~**wochen fahren** go on one's honeymoon

Flitz[e]·bogen /'flɪts(ə)-/ der bow; (fig.) **gespannt sein wie ein** ~: be on tenterhooks

flitzen /'flɪtsn̩/ itr. V.; mit sein (ugs.) shoot; dart; **ich flitze mal eben zum Fleischer** I'll just dash to the butcher's

Flitzer der; ~**s**, ~ (ugs.: kleines, schnelles Auto) sporty job (coll.)

floaten /'floʊtn̩/ tr., itr. V. (Wirtsch.) float

Floating /'floʊtɪŋ/ das; ~**s**, ~**s** (Wirtsch.) floating

flocht /flɔxt/ 1. u. 3. Pers. Sg. Prät. v. **flechten**

Flocke /'flɔkə/ die; ~, ~**n** (a) flake; **eine** ~ **Watte/ Wolle** a bit of cottonwool/tuft of wool; (b) (Staub~) piece of fluff

flockig Adj. fluffy

flog /flo:k/ 1. u. 3. Pers. Sg. Prät. v. **fliegen**

floh /flo:/ 1. u. 3. Pers. Sg. Prät. v. **fliehen**

Floh /flo:/ der; ~**[e]s**, **Flöhe** /'flø:ə/ (a) flea; **jmdm. einen** ~ **ins Ohr setzen** (ugs.) put an idea into sb.'s head; (b) Pl. (salopp: Geld) dough sing. (sl.); bread sing. (sl.)

Floh-: ~**biss**, *~**biß** der flea bite; ~**kino** das (ugs.) flea-pit (sl.); ~**markt** der flea market; ~**zirkus** der flea-circus

Flor[1] /flo:ɐ/ der; ~**s**, ~**e** (geh.) (a) (Blütenpracht) **im** ~ **stehen** be in full bloom; (b) (Blumenfülle) display

Flor[2] der; ~**s**, ~**e** (a) (zartes Gewebe) gauze; (b) (Faserenden) pile; (c) ⇒ **Trauerflor**

Flora /'flo:ra/ die; ~, **Floren** flora

Florentiner[1] /florɛn'ti:nɐ/ der; ~**s**, ~: ▶ 490 Florentine

Florentiner[2] der; ~**s**, ~ (a) (Hut) picture hat; (b) (Gebäck) florentine

Florentinerin die; ~, ~**nen** Florentine

Florenz /flo'rɛnts/ (das); **Florenz'** ▶ 490 Florence

Florett /flo'rɛt/ das; ~**[e]s**, ~**e** (a) foil; (b) o. Pl. (~fechten) foils sing.; foil fencing no art.

florieren /flo'ri:rən/ itr. V. ⟨business⟩ flourish

Florist /flo'rɪst/ der; ~**en**, ~**en**, **Floristin** die; ~, ~**nen** ▶ 85 (a) (Blumenbinder) flower-arranger; (b) (Blumenhändler) florist

Floskel /'flɔskl̩/ die; ~, ~**n** cliché

floskelhaft Adj. cliché-ridden; clichéd

floss, *](**floß** /flɔs/ 1. u. 3. Pers. Sg. Prät. v. **fließen**

Floß /flo:s/ das; ~**es**, **Flöße** /'flø:sə/ raft

Flosse /'flɔsə/ die; ~, ~**n** (a) (Zool., Flugw.) fin; (b) (zum Tauchen) flipper; (c) (ugs. scherzh. od. abwertend: Hand) paw

flößen /'flø:sn̩/ tr., itr. V. float; **Baumstämme** ~: raft tree trunks

Flößer /'flø:sɐ/ der; ~**s**, ~: ▶ 85 raftsman

Flößerei die; ~: rafting

Flöte /'flø:tə/ die; ~, ~**n** (a) (Musik) flute; (Block~) recorder; (b) (Skat) **die [ganze]** ~ **herunterspielen** play a [straight] flush

flöten[1] /'flø:tn̩/ **1** itr. V. (a) play the flute; (Blockflöte spielen) play the recorder; ⟨bird⟩ flute; (b) (ugs.: piepfen) whistle; (c) (ugs.: affektiert sprechen) pipe. **2** tr. V. (a) play ⟨tune etc.⟩ on the flute/recorder; (b) (ugs.: piepfen) whistle ⟨tune etc.⟩

flöten[2] **in** ~ **gehen** (ugs.) ⟨money⟩ go down the drain; ⟨time⟩ be wasted; **seine Illusionen gingen** ~: his illusions went for a burton (Brit. sl.)

flöten-, Flöten-: *~**gehen** ⇒ **flöten**[2]; ~**konzert** das (a) (Musikstück) flute concerto; (b) (Veranstaltung) flute concert; ~**spiel** das flute-playing; ~**spieler** der flute-player; ~**ton** der: **jmdm. die** ~**töne beibringen** (fig. ugs.) teach sb. a thing or two (coll.)

Flötist /flø'tɪst/ der; ~**en**, ~**en**, **Flötistin** die; ~, ~**nen** ▶ 85 flautist

flott /flɔt/ **1** Adj. (a) (ugs.: schwungvoll) lively ⟨music, dance, pace, style⟩; snappy ⟨dialogue⟩; (b) (ugs.: schick, modisch) smart ⟨hat, suit, car⟩; (c) (munter, hübsch) stylish; smart; ~ **aussehen** look attractive; (d) (leichtlebig) **ein** ~**es Leben führen** be fast-living; (e) nicht attr. (fahrbereit, wiederhergestellt) seaworthy ⟨vessel⟩; (ugs.) roadworthy ⟨vehicle⟩; airworthy ⟨aircraft⟩; **mein Auto ist wieder** ~: my car is back on the road again. **2** adv. ⟨work⟩ quickly; ⟨dance, write⟩ in a lively manner; ⟨be dressed⟩ smartly

Flotte /'flɔtə/ die; ~, ~**n** fleet

Flotten-: ~**stützpunkt** der naval base; ~**verband** der naval unit

flott-: ~**kriegen** tr. V. get ⟨boat⟩ afloat; get ⟨car⟩ going; ~**machen** tr. V. refloat ⟨ship⟩; get ⟨car⟩ back on the road

Flöz /flø:ts/ das; ~**es**, ~**e** (Bergbau) seam

Fluch /flu:x/ der; ~**[e]s**, **Flüche** /'fly:çə/ (a) (Kraftwort) curse; oath; (b) (Verwünschung) curse; (c) o. Pl. (Unheil, Verderben) curse; **ein** ~ **liegt über/lastet auf jmdm.** there's a curse on sb.

fluchen itr. V. curse; swear; **auf/über jmdn./etw.** ~: swear at or curse sb./sth.

Flucht¹ /fluxt/ *die;* ~ (a) flight; **auf/während der** ~: while fleeing; (von Gefangenen) on the run; **jmdn. auf der** ~ **erschießen** shoot sb. while he/she is trying to escape; **die** ~ **ergreifen** ‹*prisoner*› make a dash for freedom; (fig.: weglaufen) make a dash for it; **jmdn. in die** ~ **schlagen** put sb. to flight; (b) (fig.) refuge; **die** ~ **in die Anonymität** taking refuge in anonymity; **die** ~ **aus der Wirklichkeit** escape from reality; **die** ~ **nach vorn antreten** take the bull by the horns

Flucht² *die;* ~, ~**en** (a) (Bauw.: Häuser~, Arkaden~) row; **die** ~ **der Fenster** the line of the windows; (b) (Zimmer~) suite

flucht·artig 1 *Adj.* hurried; hasty; 2 *adv.* hurriedly; hastily

Flucht·auto *das* getaway car

flüchten /'flʏçtn̩/ 1 *itr. V.; mit sein* **vor jmdm./etw.** ~: flee from sb./sth.; **vor der Polizei** ~: run away from the police; (mit Erfolg) escape from the police; **zu jmdm.** ~: take refuge with sb.; **ins Ausland** ~: escape abroad. 2 *refl. V.* **sich in ein Bauernhaus** ~: take refuge in a farmhouse; **sich aufs Dach** ~: escape on to the roof

Flucht-: ~**fahrzeug** *das* getaway vehicle; ~**gefahr** *die* risk of an escape attempt; ~**helfer** *der* person who aids/aided an/the escape

flüchtig /'flʏçtɪç/ 1 *Adj.* (a) (flüchtend) fugitive; wanted ‹*thief, criminal*› ~ **sein** be at large; (b) (oberflächlich) cursory; superficial ‹*insight*›; hurried ‹*piece of work*›; (c) (eilig, schnell) quick; short ‹*visit, greeting*›; fleeting ‹*glance*›; (d) (vergänglich) fleeting ‹*moment*›. 2 *adv.* (a) (oberflächlich) cursorily; (b) (eilig) hurriedly

Flüchtigkeit *die;* ~, ~**en** (a) (Oberflächlichkeit) cursoriness; (b) ⇒ **Flüchtigkeitsfehler;** (c) (Vergänglichkeit) fleetingness

Flüchtigkeits·fehler *der* slip; (tadelnswert) careless mistake

Flucht·kapital *das* (Wirtsch.) *capital which has been sent out of the country to evade tax*

Flüchtling /'flʏçtlɪŋ/ *der;* ~**s,** ~**e** refugee

Flüchtlings-: ~**lager** *das* refugee camp; ~**treck** *der* long stream of refugees

Flucht-: ~**linie** *die* vanishing-line; ~**plan** *der* escape plan; ~**versuch** *der* escape attempt; ~**weg** *der* escape route

Flug /fluːk/ *der;* ~**[e]s,** **Flüge** /'flyːɡə/ (a) *o. Pl.* flight; **im** ~: in flight; **etw. vergeht [wie] im** ~**e** sth. flows by; (b) (Flugreise) flight

Flug-: ~**abwehr** *die* (Milit.) anti-aircraft defence; ~**angst** *die* fear of flying; ~**bahn** *die* trajectory; ~**ball** *der* (Tennis) volley; ~**begleiter** *der* steward; ~**begleiterin** *die* stewardess; ~**blatt** *das* pamphlet; leaflet; ~**boot** *das* flying boat

Flügel /'flyːɡl̩/ *der;* ~**s,** ~ (a) wing; **die** ~ **hängen lassen** (fig. ugs.) become disheartened; **jmdm. die** ~ **stutzen** (fig.) clip sb.'s wings; (b) (Altar~) wing; (Fenster~) casement; (Nasen~) nostril; (c) (Klavier) grand piano; (d) (Milit., Ballspiele) wing

flügel-, Flügel-: ~**horn** *das* (Musik) flugelhorn; ~**lahm** *Adj.* (a) ‹*bird*› with an injured wing; (b) (fig.: mutlos, kraftlos) lacking energy *postpos.;* limping ‹*organization*›; ~**spannweite** *die* (Flugw., Zool.) wing span; ~**stürmer** *der* (Ballspiele) wing forward; winger; ~**tür** *die* double door

Flug·gast *der* [air] passenger

flügge /'flʏɡə/ *Adj.* fully-fledged; (fig.: selbstständig) independent

Flug-: ~**geschwindigkeit** *die* (eines Flugzeugs) flying speed; (eines Vogels) speed of flight; ~**gesellschaft** *die* airline; ~**hafen** *der* airport; ~**höhe** *die* altitude; ~**kapitän** *der* ▶ 85⌋ captain; ~**lärm** *der* aircraft noise; ~**lehrer** *der* ▶ 85⌋ flying instructor; ~**linie** *die* (a) (Strecke) air route; (b) (Gesellschaft) airline; ~**lotse** *der* ▶ 85⌋ air traffic controller; ~**objekt** *das* flying object; **ein unbekanntes** ~**objekt** an unidentified flying object; ~**personal** *das* flight personnel; ~**plan** *der* flight

schedule; ~**platz** *der* airfield; aerodrome; ~**preis** *der* air fare; ~**reise** *die* air journey

flugs /fluːks/ *Adv.* (veralt.) swiftly

flug-, Flug-: ~**sand** *der* wind-borne sand; ~**schein** *der* air ticket; ~**schreiber** *der* flight recorder; ~**schrift** *die* pamphlet; ~**sicherung** *die* air traffic control; ~**steig** *der* pier; (Ausgang) ~**steig 5 gate 5;** ~**ticket** *das* air ticket; ~**verkehr** *der* air traffic; ~**zeit** *die* flight time

Flug·zeug *das;* ~**[e]s,** ~**e** aeroplane (Brit.); airplane (Amer.); aircraft; **mit dem** ~ **reisen** travel by plane or air

Flugzeug-: ~**absturz** *der* plane crash; ~**bau** *der;* *o. Pl.* aircraft construction; ~**besatzung** *die* crew; ~**entführer** *der* [aircraft] hijacker; ~**entführung** *die* [aircraft] hijack[ing]; ~**modell** *das* model aeroplane; ~**träger** *der* aircraft carrier; ~**unglück** *das* plane crash; ~**wrack** *das* wreckage of the/a plane

Fluidum /'fluːidʊm/ *das;* ~**s, Fluida** aura; atmosphere

Fluktuation /flʊktua'tsi̯oːn/ *die;* ~, ~**en** fluctuation (*Gen.* in)

fluktuieren /flʊktu'iːrən/ *itr. V.* fluctuate

Flunder /'flʊndɐ/ *die;* ~, ~**n** flounder

Flunkerei /flʊŋkə'rai̯/ *die;* ~, ~**en** (ugs.) (a) *o. Pl.* story-telling; (b) (Lügengeschichte) tall story

flunkern /'flʊŋkɐn/ *itr. V.* tell stories

Flunsch /flʊnʃ/ *der;* ~**[e]s,** ~**e** *od. die;* ~, ~**en** (ugs.) pout; **eine[n]** ~ **ziehen** *od.* **machen** pout

Fluor /'fluːɔr/ *das;* ~**s** (Chemie) fluorine

Fluoreszenz /fluoreˈstsɛnts/ *die;* ~: fluorescence

fluoreszieren *itr. V.* fluoresce; be fluorescent

Flur¹ /fluːɐ̯/ *der;* ~**[e]s,** ~**e** corridor; (Diele) [entrance] hall

Flur² *die;* ~, ~**en** (a) (landwirtschaftliche Nutzfläche) farmland *no indef. art.;* **die** ~**en** the fields; (b) (geh.: offenes Kulturland) fields *pl.;* **allein auf weiter** ~ **sein** *od.* **stehen** (fig.) be all alone in the world

Flur-: ~**bereinigung** *die* reallocation of land; ~**garderobe** *die* hall stand; ~**schaden** *der* damage *no pl., no indef. art.* to farmland; ~**tür** *die* front door

Fluss, *Fluß /flʊs/ *der;* **Flusses, Flüsse** /'flʏsə/ (a) ▶ 193⌋, ▶ 277⌋ river; (b) *o. Pl.* (fließende Bewegung) flow; **die Dinge sind im** ~: things are in a state of flux; **etw. in** ~ **bringen** get sth. going

fluss-, *fluß-, Fluss-, *Fluß-: ~**aal** *der* freshwater eel; ~**ab[wärts]** *Adv.* ▶ 193⌋ downstream; ~**arm** *der* river branch; river arm; ~**auf[wärts]** *Adv.* ▶ 193⌋ upstream; ~**bett** *das* river bed

Flüsschen, *Flüßchen /'flʏsçən/ *das;* ~**s,** ~: small river

Fluss·diagramm, *Fluß·diagramm *das* (DV, Arbeitswiss.) flow chart

flüssig /'flʏsɪç/ 1 *Adj.* (a) liquid ‹*nourishment, fuel*›; molten ‹*ore, glass*›; melted ‹*butter*›; runny ‹*honey*›; **etw.** ~ **machen** melt sth.; (b) (fließend, geläufig) fluent; free-flowing ‹*traffic*›; (c) (verfügbar, solvent) ready ‹*capital, money*›; liquid ‹*assets*›; **Geld** ~ **machen** make money available; **wieder** ~ **sein** (ugs.) have got some cash to play with again (coll.); **nicht** ~ **sein** (ugs.) be skint (Brit. coll.) *or* (coll.) [flat] broke. 2 *adv.* ‹*write, speak*› fluently

Flüssiggas *das* liquid gas

Flüssigkeit *die;* ~, ~**en** (a) liquid; (Körper~, Brems~ usw.) fluid; (b) (Geläufigkeit) fluency

Flüssigkeits·maß *das* liquid measure

Flüssig·kristall·anzeige *die* (Technik) liquid crystal display

***flüssig|machen** ⇒ **flüssig** 1 c

Flüssigseife *die* liquid soap

Fluss-, *Fluß-: ~**krebs,** *der* (Zool.) crayfish; ~**landschaft** *die* (Geogr.) fluvial topography; ~**mündung** *die* river mouth; ~**pferd** *das* hippopotamus; ~**schifffahrt** *die* river traffic; (Navigation) river navigation; ~**tal** *das* river valley; ~**ufer** *das* river bank; **das diesseitige/jenseitige** ~**ufer** the near/opposite bank [of the river]

flüstern /'flʏstɐn/ 1 *itr. V.* whisper; **sich** ~**d unterhalten** speak in whispers. 2 *tr. V.* whisper; **jmdm.**

Flüsse

Im Englischen gibt es nur das eine Wort **river,** das (oft großgeschrieben) vor dem Flussnamen eingesetzt werden kann:

die Seine = the [river *od.* River] Seine

Eine Ausnahme im Englischen wie im Deutschen:

der Sankt-Lorenz-Strom = the St Lawrence River

Bei Ortsnamen steht einfach **on** ohne Artikel:

*Walton-on-Thames   Stockton-on-Tees
Ross-on-Wye*

Heute fehlt oft der Bindestrich.

Flusssprache

flussaufwärts/ flussabwärts fahren	= to go upstream/ downstream *od.* up/ down [the] river
rheinaufwärts/ rheinabwärts fahren	= to go up/down the Rhine
die linksrheinischen Landesteile	= the parts of the country on the left bank of the Rhine
am rechten Weserufer	= on the right bank of the Weser
ein Haus am Fluss	= a house by *od.* on the river

Der Fluss führt Hochwasser	= The river is in flood *od.* in full spate
Der Fluss führt sehr wenig Wasser	= The river is very low
Die Drau, ein rechter Nebenfluss der Donau, ist in ihrem Unterlauf schiffbar	= The Drava, a tributary of the Danube on its right bank, is navigable in its lower reaches
Der Rhein entspringt in der Schweiz und mündet in die Nordsee	= The Rhine rises in Switzerland and flows into the North Sea
Das Schiff ist in der Elbmündung gesunken	= The ship sank in the mouth of the Elbe *od.* the Elbe estuary
An der Mündung der Mosel in den Rhein befindet sich das Deutsche Eck	= At the point where the Moselle flows into the Rhine is the Deutsche Eck
Münden liegt am Zusammenfluss von Werra und Fulda [zur Weser]	= Münden lies at the confluence of the Werra and Fulda [which then become the Weser]

[et]was ~ (ugs.) give sb. something to think about; **das kann ich dir** ~ (ugs.) I can promise you that

Flüster-: **~propaganda** *die* underground propaganda; **~ton** *der* whisper; **im ~ton sprechen** speak in whispers; **~tüte** *die* (ugs.) megaphone; **~witz** *der* underground joke

Flut /flu:t/ *die;* ~, **~en** **(a)** *o. Pl.* tide; **es ist** ~: the tide is coming in; **(b)** *meist Pl.* (geh.: Wassermasse) flood; **schmutzige ~en** dirty waters; **eine ~ von Protesten** (fig.) a flood of protests

flu̱ten **1** *itr. V.; mit sein* (geh.) flood; **in etw.** (*Akk.*) ~: flood sth.. **2** *tr. V.* (Seemannsspr.: unter Wasser setzen) flood

Flut·licht *das; o. Pl.* floodlight

flutschen /ˈflʊtʃn̩/ *itr. V.* (ugs., bes. nordd.) **(a)** *mit sein* (gleiten) slip; **(b)** (glatt vonstatten gehen) go smoothly; **es flutscht nur so** it's going extremely well

Flut·welle *die* tidal wave

fluvial /fluˈvi̯a:l/ *Adj.* (Geol.) fluvial

Flyer /ˈflai̯ɐ/ *der;* ~s, ~: flyer

f-Moll /ˈɛf-/ F minor

focht /fɔxt/ *1. u. 3. Pers. Sg. Prät. v.* **fechten**

Fock /fɔk/ *die;* ~, **~en** (Seew.) foresail; (auf einer Jacht) jib

Föderalismus *der;* ~: federalism *no art.*

föderalistisch *Adj.* federalist

Föderation /føderaˈtsi̯o:n/ *die;* ~, **~en** federation

föderativ /føderaˈti:f/ *Adj.* federal

Fohlen *das;* ~s, ~: foal

Föhn /fø:n/ *der;* ~[e]s, ~e **(a)** (Wind) föhn; **(b)** (Haartrockner) hair-drier

föhnen /ˈfø:nən/ *tr. V.* blow-dry ⟨hair⟩

Föhre /ˈfø:rə/ *die;* ~, **~n** (landsch.) ⇒ **Kiefer²**

Fokus /ˈfo:kʊs/ *der;* ~, **~se** (Optik, Med.) focus

Folge /ˈfɔlgə/ *die;* ~, **~n (a)** consequence; (Ergebnis) result; **an den ~n eines Unfalls sterben** die as a result of an accident; **etw. zur ~ haben** result in sth.; lead to sth.; **(b)** (Aufeinander~) succession; (zusammengehörend) sequence; **in rascher ~:** in quick succession; **in ~:** in a row; in succession; **das dritte Mal in ~:** the third time in a row *or* running; **(c)** (Fortsetzung) (einer Sendung) episode; (eines Romans) instalment; **(d)** **einem Aufruf/einem Befehl/einer Einladung ~ leisten** (Papierdt.) respond to an appeal/obey *or* follow an order/accept an invitation

Folge·erscheinung *die* consequence

folgen /ˈfɔlgn̩/ *itr. V.* **(a)** *mit sein* follow; **jmdm. im Amt ~:** succeed sb. in office; **auf etw.** (*Akk.*) ~: follow sth.; come after sth.; **kannst du mir ~?** (oft scherzh.) do you follow me?; **daraus folgt, dass ...:** it follows from this that ...; **(b)** *auch mit sein* jmds. Anordnungen/Befehlen ~: follow *or* obey sb.'s orders; **seiner inneren Stimme/seinem Gefühl ~:** listen to one's inner voice/ be ruled by one's feelings

folgend *Adj.* following; **der/die/das Folgende** the next in order; **er sagte Folgendes** *od.* **das Folgende ...:** he said this ...; **Folgendes, das Folgende** the following [passage *etc.*]; **im Folgenden, in Folgendem** in [the course of] the following passage *etc.*

folgendermaßen *Adv.* as follows; (in folgender Weise) in the following way

folgen-: **~los** *Adj.* without consequences *postpos.; das ist nicht ~los geblieben* that hasn't been without its consequences; **~reich** *Adj.* ⟨decision, event⟩ fraught with consequences; **~schwer** *Adj.* with serious consequences *postpos.*

folge·richtig **1** *Adj.* logical ⟨decision, conclusion⟩; consistent ⟨behaviour, action⟩. **2** *adv.* ⟨think, develop, conclude⟩ logically; ⟨act, behave⟩ consistently

Folge·richtigkeit *die* ⇒ **folgerichtig**: logicality; consistency

folgern /ˈfɔlgɐn/ **1** *tr. V.* deduce (aus from); ~, **dass ...:** conclude that ... **2** *itr. V.* **richtig ~:** draw a/the correct conclusion

Folgerung *die;* ~, **~en** conclusion

Folge·schaden *der* (Versicherungsw.) consequential damage

folglich /ˈfɔlklɪç/ *Adv.* consequently; as a result; (ugs.: deshalb) consequently; therefore

folgsam **1** *Adj.* obedient. **2** *adv.* obediently

Folie /ˈfo:li̯ə/ *die;* ~, **~n** (Metall~) foil; (Plastik~) film

Folklore /fɔlkˈlo:rə/ *die;* ~ **(a)** folklore; **(b)** (Musik) folk music

folkloristisch **1** *Adj.* folkloric. **2** *adv.* in a folkloric way

Follikel /fɔˈli:kl̩/ *der;* ~s, ~ (Med., Bot.) follicle

Follikel·sprung *der* (Med.) ovulation

Folter /ˈfɔltɐ/ *die;* ~, **~n** torture; **jmdn. auf die ~ spannen** (fig.) keep sb. in an agony of suspense

Folterer *der;* ∼s, ∼: torturer
Folter·kammer *die* torture chamber
foltern **1** *tr. V.* torture. **2** *itr. V.* use torture
Folterung *die;* ∼, ∼en torture
Fön Ⓦz /føːn/ *der;* ∼[e]s, ∼e hairdrier
Fond[1] /fõː/ *der;* ∼s, ∼s (geh.) rear compartment; back
Fond[2] *der;* ∼s, ∼s (Kochk.) juices *pl.*
Fonds /fõː/ *der;* ∼ /fõː(s)/, ∼ /fõːs/ fund
Fondue /fõˈdyː/ *die;* ∼, ∼s *od. das;* ∼s, ∼s (Kochk.) fondue
*****fönen** /ˈføːnən/ ⇒ **föhnen**
Fontäne /fɔnˈtɛːnə/ *die;* ∼, ∼n jet; (Springbrunnen) fountain
foppen /ˈfɔpn̩/ *tr. V.* **jmdn.** ∼ (ugs.) pull sb.'s leg (coll.); put sb. on (Amer. coll.)
forcieren /fɔrˈsiːrən/ *tr. V.* step up ‹*production*›; redouble, intensify ‹*efforts*›; speed up, push forward ‹*developments*›; **das Tempo** ∼ (Sport) force the pace
Forcierung *die;* ∼, ∼en ⇒ **forcieren:** stepping up; redoubling, intensification; speeding up; pushing forward; forcing
Förde /ˈføːɐdə/ *die;* ∼, ∼n long narrow inlet
Förder-: ∼**anlage** *die* (Technik) conveyor; ∼**band** *das* (Technik) conveyor belt
Förderer /ˈfœrdərɐ/ *der;* ∼s, ∼ (Gönner) patron
Förder·korb *der* (Bergbau) cage
förderlich *Adj.* beneficial (*Dat.* to); **guten Beziehungen** ∼ **sein** be conducive to *or* promote good relations
fordern /ˈfɔrdɐn/ *tr. V.* **(a)** demand; **Rechenschaft von jmdm.** ∼**:** call sb. to account; **(b)** (fig.: kosten) claim ‹*lives*›; **(c)** (in Anspruch nehmen) make demands on; **von etw. gefordert werden** be stretched by sth.; **(d)** **jmdn.** [**zum Duell**] ∼**:** challenge sb. [to a duel]
fördern /ˈfœrdɐn/ *tr. V.* **(a)** promote ‹*trade, plan, project, good relations*›; patronize, support ‹*artist, art*›; further ‹*investigation*›; foster ‹*talent, tendency, new generation*›; improve ‹*appetite*›; aid ‹*digestion, sleep*›; **(b)** (Bergbau) mine ‹*coal, ore*›; extract ‹*oil*›
Förder·schacht *der* (Bergbau) winding shaft
Forderung *die;* ∼, ∼en **(a)** (Anspruch) demand; (in bestimmter Höhe) claim; **(b)** (Kaufmannsspr.) claim (**an** + *Akk.* against); **eine** ∼ **einklagen** sue for payment of a debt; **(c)** (zum Duell) challenge
Förderung *die;* ∼ **(a)** ⇒ **fördern a:** promotion; patronage; support; furthering; fostering; improvement; aiding; **(b)** (Bergbau) ⇒ **fördern b:** mining; extraction; **(c)** (Bergbau: geförderte Menge) output
Förder·wagen *der* (Bergbau) mine car
Forelle /foˈrɛlə/ *die;* ∼, ∼n trout
forensisch /foˈrɛnzɪʃ/ *Adj.* forensic
Forke /ˈfɔrkə/ *die;* ∼, ∼n (bes. nordd.) fork
Form /fɔrm/ *die;* ∼, ∼en **(a)** (Gestalt) shape; **die Demonstration nahm hässliche** ∼**en** the demonstration began to look ugly; **in** ∼ **von Tabletten** in the form of tablets; **(b)** (bes. Sport: Verfassung) form; **in** ∼ **sein/sich in** ∼ **bringen** be/get on form; **in guter/schlechter** ∼ **sein** be in good/off form; **(c)** (vorgeformtes Modell) mould; (Back∼) baking tin; **(d)** (Gestaltungsweise, Erscheinungs∼) form; **(e)** (Umgangs∼) form; **die** ∼**[en] wahren** observe the proprieties; **in aller** ∼**:** formally
formal /fɔrˈmaːl/ **1** *Adj.* formal; **ein** ∼**er Fehler** a technical error; (Rechtsw.) procedural error. **2** *adv.* formally; ∼ **im Recht sein** be technically in the right
Formalin Ⓦz /fɔrmaˈliːn/ *das;* ∼s formalin
formalisieren *tr. V.* formalize
Formalisierung *die;* ∼, ∼en formalization
Formalismus *der;* ∼, **Formalismen** formalism
Formalist *der;* ∼en, ∼en formalist
Formalität /fɔrmaliˈtɛːt/ *die;* ∼, ∼en formality
formal·juristisch **1** *Adj.* technical; **ein rein** ∼**er Standpunkt** a narrowly legalistic view. **2** *adv.* technically

Format /fɔrˈmaːt/ *das;* ∼[e]s, ∼e **(a)** size; (Buch∼, Papier∼, Bild∼) format; **(b)** *o. Pl.* (Persönlichkeit) stature; **(c)** *o. Pl.* (besonderes Niveau) quality; **etw. hat/ist ohne** ∼**:** sth. has/lacks class
Formation /fɔrmaˈtsi̯oːn/ *die;* ∼, ∼en **(a)** (Herausbildung, Anordnung) formation; (einer Generation, Gesellschaft) development; **(b)** (Gruppe) group; **(c)** (Milit.) (von Flugzeugen) formation; (von Soldaten) unit
Formations·flug *der* formation flying
formbar *Adj.* malleable; soft ‹*bone*›; (fig.) malleable, pliable ‹*character, person*›
Formbarkeit *die;* ∼**:** malleability; (fig.) malleability; pliability
Form·blatt *das* form
Formel /ˈfɔrml̩/ *die;* ∼, ∼n formula; ∼ **1** (Motorsport) Formula One
formelhaft *Adj.* stereotyped ‹*style, mode of expression, phrase*›
formell /fɔrˈmɛl/ **1** *Adj.* formal. **2** *adv.* formally; **die Einladung wurde rein** ∼ **ausgesprochen** the invitation was made only as a matter of form; **er ist nur** ∼ **im Recht** he's only technically in the right
Formel·zeichen *das* symbol
formen **1** *tr. V.* form; shape; mould, form ‹*character, personality*›; mould ‹*person*›. **2** *refl. V.* take on a shape; (fig.) form; take shape
formen-, Formen-: ∼**lehre** *die* (Sprachw., Biol.) morphology; ∼**reich** *Adj.* with its/their great variety of forms *postpos.*
form-, Form-: ∼**fehler** *der* **(a)** (in einem Verfahren, Dokument) irregularity; **(b)** (Taktlosigkeit) faux pas; breach of etiquette; ∼**frage** *die* formality; ∼**gebung** *die;* ∼, ∼en design; ∼**gerecht** **1** *Adj.* correct; proper; **2** *adv.* correctly; properly
formieren **1** *tr. V.* form ‹*team, party, organization*›. **2** *refl. V.* **(a)** form; **(b)** (sich zusammenschließen) be formed
Formierung *die;* ∼, ∼en formation; (von Truppen) drawing up
-förmig /-fœrmɪç/ -shaped
förmlich /ˈfœrmlɪç/ **1** *Adj.* **(a)** formal; **(b)** *nicht präd.* (regelrecht) positive; **ein** ∼**er Schreck** a real fright. **2** *adv.* **(a)** (steif, unpersönlich, offiziell) formally; **(b)** (geradezu) positively; **sich** ∼ **fürchten** be really afraid
Förmlichkeit *die;* ∼, ∼en formality
form-, Form-: ∼**los** **1** *Adj.* **(a)** informal; **einen** ∼**losen Antrag stellen** make an application without the official form[s]; apply informally; **(b)** (gestaltlos) shapeless; **2** *adv.* informally; ∼**losigkeit** *die;* ∼ **(a)** informality; **(b)** (Gestaltlosigkeit) shapelessness; ∼**sache** *die* formality; ∼**schön** *Adj.* elegant
Formular /fɔrmuˈlaːɐ̯/ *das;* ∼s, ∼e form
formulieren /fɔrmuˈliːrən/ *tr. V.* formulate
Formulierung *die;* ∼, ∼en **(a)** *o. Pl.* (das Formulieren) formulation; (eines Entwurfes, Gesetzes) drafting; **(b)** (formulierter Text) formulation
Formung *die;* ∼, ∼en **(a)** design; **die strenge** ∼ **des Sonetts** strict sonnet form; **(b)** *o. Pl.* (Bildung, Erziehung) moulding
form·vollendet **1** *Adj.* perfectly executed ‹*pirouette, bow, etc.*›; perfect in form ‹*poem*›; **2** *adv.* **etw.** ∼ **tun** do sth. faultlessly
forsch /fɔrʃ/ **1** *Adj.* self-assertive; forceful. **2** *adv.* self-assertively; forcefully
forschen *itr. V.* **(a)** **nach jmdm./etw.** ∼**:** search *or* look for sb./sth.; **jmdn.** ∼**d** *od.* **mit** ∼**dem Blick betrachten** look at sb. searchingly; give sb. a searching look; **(b)** (als Wissenschaftler) research; do research
Forscher *der;* ∼s, ∼, **Forscherin** *die;* ∼, ∼nen **(a)** researcher; research scientist; **(b)** (Forschungsreisender) explorer
Forscher-: ∼**drang** *der* **(a)** (Wissensdurst) thirst for new knowledge; **(b)** (Entdeckerfreude) urge to explore; ∼**team** *das* research team

---

*****alte Schreibung (vgl. Hinweise auf S. xvi–xvii)

Forschheit *die;* ~: self-assertiveness; forcefulness

Forschung *die;* ~, ~**en** research; ~**en [auf einem Gebiet]** betreiben do research [in a field]; ~ **und Lehre** teaching and research

Forschungs-: ~**auftrag** *der* research assignment; ~**bericht** *der* research report; ~**gebiet** *das* field of research; ~**programm** *das* research programme; ~**reise** *die* expedition; ~**reisende** *der/die* explorer; ~**satellit** *der* research satellite; ~**tätigkeit** *die* research work; ~**zweck** *der* purpose of the research; **für** ~**zwecke** for research purposes

Forst /fɔrst/ *der;* ~**[e]s,** ~**e[n]** forest

Forst-: ~**amt** *das* forestry office; ~**beamte** *der* forestry official

Förster /ˈfœrstɐ/ *der;* ~**s,** ~ ▸ 85 forest warden; forester; ranger (Amer.)

Forst-: ~**frevel** *der* offence against the forest law; ~**frevel begehen** break the forest law; ~**haus** *das* forester's house; ~**revier** *das* forest district; ~**wirtschaft** *die* forestry

Forsythie /fɔrˈzyːtsjə/ *die;* ~, ~**n** forsythia

fort /fɔrt/ *Adv.* (a) ⇒ **weg a;** (b) (weiter) **nur immer so** ~: just carry on as you are *or* like that; **und so** ~: and so on; and so forth; **in einem** ~: continuously

Fort /foːɐ̯/ *das;* ~**s,** ~**s** fort

fort-, Fort-: ~**an** /-'-/ *Adv.* from now/then on; ~**bestand** *der; o. Pl.* continuation; (eines Staates) continued existence; ~**bestehen** *unr. itr. V.* remain; continue; ⟨nation⟩ remain in existence; ~**bewegen** 1 *tr. V.* move; shift; 2 *refl. V.* move [along]; ~**bewegung** *die; o. Pl.* locomotion; ~**bilden** *tr. V.* jmdn./sich ~**bilden** continue sb.'s/one's education; ~**bildung** *die; o. Pl.* further education; (beruflich) further training; ~**bildungs·kurs** *der* further education course; (beruflich) training course; ~**bleiben** *unr. itr. V.; mit sein* ⇒ **wegbleiben;** ~**bringen** *unr. tr. V.:* ⇒ **wegbringen;** ~**dauer** *die* continuation; ~**dauern** *itr. V.* continue

forte /ˈfɔrtə/ *Adv.* (Musik, Pharm.) forte

fort-, Fort-: ~**|eilen** *itr. V.; mit sein* (geh.) hurry off *or* away; hasten away; ~**|entwickeln** 1 *tr. V.* etw. ~**entwickeln** develop sth. further; 2 *refl. V.* develop; ~**|fahren** 1 *unr. itr. V.* (a) *mit sein* ⇒ **wegfahren 1;** (b) *auch mit sein* (weitermachen) continue, go on (mit with); ~**fahren, etw. zu tun** continue *or* go on doing sth. 2 *unr. tr. V.:* ⇒ **wegfahren 2;** ~**|fallen** *unr. itr. V.; mit sein* ⇒ **wegfallen;** ~**|fliegen** *unr. itr. V.; mit sein:* ⇒ **wegfliegen;** ~**|führen** *tr. V.* (a) lead away; (b) (fortsetzen) continue, keep up ⟨tradition, business⟩; continue, carry on ⟨another's work⟩; ~**führung** *die* ⇒ **fortsetzen;** (b) (Weiterentwicklung) progress; ~**|geben** *unr. tr. V.* ⇒ **weggeben;** ~**|gehen** *unr. itr. V.; mit sein* (a) ⇒ **weggehen;** (b) (andauern, verlaufen) continue; go on; ~**geschritten** *Adj.* advanced ⟨age, stage of illness⟩; **zu** ~**geschrittener Tageszeit** at a late hour; ~**geschrittene** *der/die; adj. Dekl.* advanced student/player; ~**geschrittenen·kurs[us]** *der* advanced course; ~**gesetzt** 1 *Adj.; nicht präd.* continual; constant; ~**gesetzter Betrug** repeated fraud; 2 *adv.* continually; constantly

fortissimo /fɔrˈtɪsimo/ *Adv.* (Musik) fortissimo

fort-, Fort-: ~**|jagen** *tr. V.:* ⇒ **wegjagen;** ~**|kommen** *unr. itr. V.; mit sein* (a) ⇒ **wegkommen a, b, d, f;** (b) (Erfolg haben) get on; do well; ~**|kommen** *das;* ~**s** progress; ~**|können** *unr. itr. V.:* ⇒ **wegkönnen;** ~**|lassen** *unr. tr. V.:* ⇒ **weglassen;** ~**|laufen** *unr. itr. V.; mit sein* (a) ⇒ **weglaufen;** (b) (sich ~setzen) continue; ~**laufend** 1 *Adj.* continuous; ongoing ⟨plot of a series⟩; consecutive ⟨numbers, issues⟩. 2 *adv.* continuously; consecutively ⟨numbered⟩; ~**|leben** *itr. V.:* ⇒ **weiterleben c;** ~**|legen** *tr. V.* ⇒ **weglegen;** ~**|machen** *refl. V.* (ugs.) get away; ~**|müssen** *unr. itr. V.:* ⇒ **wegmüssen;** ~**|nehmen** *unr. tr. V.* take away; ~**|pflanzen** *refl. V.* (a) (sich vermehren) reproduce [oneself/itself]; (b) (sich verbreiten) ⟨idea, mood⟩ spread; ⟨sound, light⟩ travel, propagate; ~**pflanzung** *die* (a) (Vermehrung) reproduction; (b) (Verbreitung) transmission;

(von Schall, Licht) propagation; (von Ideen) spread; ~**pflanzungs·fähig** *Adj.* capable of reproduction *postpos.;* ~**|reißen** *unr. tr. V.* (a) tear away; ⟨floods⟩ sweep away; (b) (fig.) jmdn. ~**reißen** carry *or* sweep sb. along; ~**|rennen** *unr. itr. V.; mit sein* (ugs.) run off *or* away; ~**|schaffen** *tr. V.* take *or* carry away; ~**|scheren** *refl. V.* (ugs.) clear off (coll.); ~**|scheuchen** *tr. V.* shoo *or* chase away; ~**|schicken** *tr. V.:* ⇒ **wegschicken;** ~**|schleichen** *unr. itr., refl. V.:* ⇒ **wegschleichen;** ~**|schleppen** *refl., tr. V.:* ⇒ **wegschleppen;** ~**|schleudern** *tr. V.* fling away; ~**|schreiben** *unr. tr. V.* update; (in die Zukunft) project forward; ~**schreibung** *die* updating; (in die Zukunft) forward projection; ~**|schreiten** *unr. itr. V.; mit sein* ⟨process⟩ progress, continue; ⟨time⟩ move on; **der Sommer ist [weit]** ~**geschritten** we are well into summer; ~**schreitend** *Adj.* progressive; advancing ⟨age⟩; **mit** ~**schreitender Jahreszeit** as the year goes/went on; ~**schritt** *der* progress; ~**schritte** progress *sing.;* **ein** ~**schritt** a step forward; ~**schrittlich** 1 *Adj.* progressive; 2 *adv.* progressively; ~**schritts·feindlich** *Adj.* anti-progressive; ~**schritts·gläubig** *Adj.* ~**schrittsgläubig sein** put one's faith in progress; ~**|setzen** 1 *tr. V.* continue; carry on; 2 *refl. V.* continue; ~**setzung** *die;* ~, ~**en** (a) (das ~setzen) continuation; **[s]eine** ~**setzung finden** resume; (b) (anschließender Teil) instalment; ~**setzung folgt** to be continued; ~**setzungs·roman** *der* serial; serialized novel; ~**|spülen** *tr. V.:* ⇒ **wegspülen;** ~**|stehlen** *unr. refl. V.* steal *or* sneak away; ~**|stoßen** *unr. tr. V.:* ⇒ **wegstoßen;** ~**|tragen** *unr. tr. V.:* ⇒ **wegtragen;** ~**|treiben** 1 *unr. tr. V.* drive off *or* away; 2 *itr. V.; mit sein* float away

Fortuna /fɔrˈtuːna/ (die) Fortune

fort-: ~**|währen** *itr. V.* (geh.) continue; ~**|während** 1 *Adj.; nicht präd.* continual; incessant; 2 *adv.* continually; incessantly; ~**|werfen** *unr. tr. V.:* ⇒ **wegwerfen;** ~**|wollen** *unr. itr. V.:* ⇒ **wegwollen;** ~**|ziehen** *unr. tr., itr. V.:* ⇒ **wegziehen**

Forum /ˈfoːrʊm/ *das;* ~**s,** **Foren** forum; (Diskussionsveranstaltung) forum discussion

fossil /fɔˈsiːl/ *Adj.* fossilized; fossil *attrib.*

Fossil *das;* ~**s,** ~**ien** fossil

Foto /ˈfoːto/ *das;* ~**s,** ~**s** photo; ~**s machen** *od.* (ugs.) schießen take photos; **auf einem** ~: in a photo

Foto-: ~**album** *das* photo album; ~**apparat** *der* camera; ~**atelier** *das* photographic studio; ~**ecke** *die* [mounting] corner

fotogen /fotoˈgeːn/ *Adj.* photogenic

Foto·geschäft *das* photographic shop

Fotograf *der;* ~**en,** ~**en** ▸ 85 photographer

Fotografie *die;* ~, ~**n** (a) *o. Pl.* photography *no art.;* (b) (Lichtbild) photograph

fotografieren 1 *tr. V.* photograph; take a photograph/photographs of 2 *itr. V.* take photographs

Fotografin *die;* ~, ~**nen** ▸ 85 photographer

fotografisch 1 *Adj.* photographic. 2 *adv.* photographically

foto-, Foto-: ~**kopie** *die* photocopy; ~**kopieren** *tr., itr. V.* photocopy; ~**kopierer** *der,* ~**kopier·gerät** *das* photocopier; photocopying machine; ~**labor** *das* photographic laboratory; ~**modell** *das* ▸ 85 photographic model; ~**montage** *die* photomontage; ~**reporter** *der* ▸ 85 press photographer; newspaper photographer; ~**wettbewerb** *der* photographic competition; ~**zeitschrift** *die* photographic magazine

Fotze /ˈfɔtsə/ *die;* ~, ~**n** (vulg.) cunt (coarse)

Foul *das;* ~**s,** ~**s** (Sport) foul (**an** + *Dat.* on)

foulen /ˈfaulən/ (Sport) 1 *tr. V.* foul. 2 *itr. V.* commit a foul

Fox /fɔks/ *der;* ~**[es],** ~**e** (a) ⇒ **Foxterrier;** (b) ⇒ **Foxtrott**

Fox·terrier *der* fox terrier

Fox·trott /-trɔt/ *der;* ~**s,** ~**e** *od.* ~**s** foxtrot

Foyer /foaˈjeː/ *das;* ~**s,** ~**s** foyer

FPÖ *Abk.* **Freiheitliche Partei Österreichs**

Fr.¹ *Abk.* **Franken** SFr.

Fr.² *Abk.* **Frau**

Fr.³ *Abk.* **Freitag** Fri.

Fracht /fraxt/ *die;* ~, ~en (a) (Schiffs~, Luft~) cargo; freight; (Bahn~, LKW~) goods *pl.;* freight; (b) (~kosten) (Schiffs~, Luft~) freight; freightage; (Bahn~, LKW~) carriage

Fracht·brief *der* consignment note; waybill

Frachter *der;* ~s, ~: freighter

Fracht-: ~**geld** *das* ⇒ **Fracht** b; ~**gut** *das* slow freight; slow goods *pl.;* ~**raum** *der; o. Pl.* [cargo] hold; (Platz) [cargo] space; ~**schiff** *das* cargo ship

Frack /frak/ *der;* ~[e]s, **Fräcke** /'frɛkə/ tails *pl.;* evening dress; **im** ~: in tails *or* evening dress

Frack-: ~**hemd** *das* dress shirt; ~**sausen** *das in* ~**sausen haben** (ugs.) get the wind up (coll.); ~**schoß** *der; meist Pl.* coat-tail; ~**weste** *die* waistcoat (worn with evening dress)

Frage /'fra:gə/ *die;* ~, ~**n** (a) question; **jmdm.** *od.* **an jmdn. eine** ~ **stellen** put a question to sb.; **jmdm. eine** ~ **beantworten/auf jmds.** ~ (*Akk.*) **antworten** reply to *or* answer sb.'s question; **eine** ~ **verneinen/bejahen** give a negative/positive answer to a question; (b) (Problem) question; (Angelegenheit) issue; **das ist [nur] eine** ~ **der Zeit** that is [only] a question *or* matter of time; (c) *in* **das ist noch sehr die** ~: that is still very much the question; **das ist die große** ~: that is the big question; **das ist gar keine** ~: there's no doubt *or* question about it; **ohne** ~: without question

Frage·bogen *der* questionnaire; (Formular) form

fragen 1 *tr., itr. V.* (a) ask; **er fragt immer so klug he** always asks *or* puts such astute questions; **frag nicht so dumm!** (ugs.) don't ask such silly questions; **das fragst du noch?** (ugs.) need you ask?; **da fragst du mich zu viel** that I don't know; I really can't say; **jmdn.** ~**d an-sehen** look at sb. inquiringly; give sb. a questioning look; (b) (sich erkundigen) **nach etw.** ~: ask *or* inquire about sth.; **jmdn. nach/wegen etw.** ~: ask sb. about sth.; **nach dem Weg/jmds. Meinung** ~: ask the way/[for] sb.'s opinion; **nach jmdm.** ~ (jmdn. suchen) ask for sb.; (nach jmds. Befinden ~) ask after *or* about sb.; (c) (nachfragen) ask for; **jmdn. um Rat** ~: ask sb. for advice; (d) (verneint: sich nicht kümmern) **nach jmdm./etw. nicht** ~: not care about sb./sth.. 2 *refl. V.* **sich** ~, **ob** ...: wonder whether ...; **das frage ich mich auch** I was wondering that, too

Frage-: ~**satz** *der* interrogative sentence/clause; **ein direkter/indirekter** ~**satz** a direct/an indirect question; ~**stellung** *die* (a) (Formulierung) formulation of a/ the question; **durch eine geschickte** ~**stellung** by skilled questioning; (b) (Problem) problem; ~**stunde** *die* (Parl.) question time; ~**und-Antwort-Spiel** *das* question-and-answer game; ~**zeichen** *das* question mark

fragil /fra'gi:l/ *Adj.* (geh.) fragile

fraglich /'fra:klɪç/ *Adj.* (a) doubtful; (b) *nicht präd.* (betreffend) in question *postpos.;* relevant

frag·los *Adv.* without question; unquestionably

Fragment /fra'gmɛnt/ *das;* ~[e]s, ~e fragment

fragmentarisch /fragmɛn'ta:rɪʃ/ *Adj.* fragmentary

frag·würdig *Adj.* (a) questionable; (b) (zwielichtig) dubious

Fragwürdigkeit *die;* ~, ~en (a) questionableness; (b) (Zwielichtigkeit) dubiousness

Fraktion /frak'tsjo:n/ *die;* ~, ~en (a) (Parl.) parliamentary party; (mit zwei Parteien) parliamentary coalition; (b) (Sondergruppe) faction

fraktionell /fraktsjo'nɛl/ *Adj.* within a/the party/group *postpos.;* internal ⟨*conflict, agreement*⟩

fraktions-, Fraktions- (Parl.): ~**beschluss**, ***~**beschluß** *der* party/coalition decision; ~**los** *Adj.* independent; ~**sitzung** *die* meeting of the parliamentary party/coalition; ~**vorsitzende** *der/die* leader of the parliamentary party/coalition; ~**zwang** *der* obligation to vote in accordance with party policy; **den** ~**zwang aufheben** allow a free vote

*alte Schreibung (vgl. Hinweise auf S. xvi–xvii)

Fraktur /frak'tu:ɐ/ *die;* ~, ~en (a) ▶ 329⏐ (Med.) fracture; (b) (Schriftart) Fraktur; **mit jmdm.** ~ **reden** (ugs.) talk straight with sb.

Franc /frã/ *der;* ~, ~s franc

Franchise /'frænʃaɪz/ *das;* ~ (Wirtsch.) franchise

frank /fraŋk/ *Adv.* ~ **und frei** frankly and openly; openly and honestly

Franke *der;* ~n, ~n (a) Franconian; (b) (hist.) Frank

Franken¹ (*das*); ~s Franconia

Franken² *der;* ~s, ~: /ʃwiss/ franc

Frankfurter¹ /'fraŋkfʊrtɐ/ *die;* ~, ~ (Wurst) frankfurter

Frankfurter² ▶ 490⏐ 1 *indekl. Adj.; nicht präd.* Frankfurt. 2 *der;* ~s, ~: Frankfurter

frankieren /fraŋ'ki:rən/ *tr. V.* frank

fränkisch /'frɛŋkɪʃ/ *Adj.* (a) Franconian; (b) (hist.) Frankish

franko /'fraŋko/ *Adv.* (Kaufmannsspr. veralt.) carriage paid; (mit der Post) post-free

Frank·reich (*das*); ~s France

Franse /'franzə/ *die;* ~, ~**n** strand [of a/the fringe]; **die** ~**n des Teppichs** the fringe of the carpet

Franz /frants/ (*der*) Francis

Franz·branntwein *der; o. Pl.* (veralt.) alcoholic liniment

Franziskaner /frantsɪs'ka:nɐ/ *der;* ~s, ~: Franciscan

Franzose /fran'tso:zə/ *der;* ~n, ~n ▶ 388⏐ (a) Frenchman; **die** ~**n** the French; (b) (ugs.: Schraubenschlüssel) screw wrench

Französin /fran'tsøːzɪn/ *die;* ~, ~**nen** Frenchwoman

französisch ▶ 388⏐, ▶ 487⏐ 1 *Adj.* French; **ein** ~**es Bett** a double bed; **die Französische Schweiz** French-speaking Switzerland. 2 *adv.* **sich [auf]** ~ **empfehlen** *od.* **verabschieden** (ugs.) take French leave

Französisch *das;* ~[s] ▶ 487⏐ French

frappant /fra'pant/ *Adj.* striking ⟨*similarity*⟩; remarkable ⟨*success, discovery*⟩

frappieren /fra'pi:rən/ *tr. V.* (geh.) astonish; astound

frappierend *Adj.* astonishing; remarkable

Fräse /'frɛːzə/ *die;* ~, ~**n** (a) (für Holz) moulding machine; (für Metall) milling machine; (b) (Boden~) rotary cultivator

fräsen *tr. V.* shape ⟨*wood*⟩; mill ⟨*metal*⟩; form ⟨*groove, thread*⟩

Fräser *der;* ~s, ~ (a) (Werkzeug) cutter; (b) ▶ 85⏐ (Metallbearb.) milling-machine operator; (Holzverarb.) moulding-machine operator

fraß /fra:s/ *1. u. 3. Pers. Sg. Prät. v.* **fressen**

Fraß *der;* ~**es** (a) food; **einem Tier etw. zum** ~ **vorwerfen** feed an animal with sth.; **jmdm. etw. zum** ~ **vorwerfen** (fig. abwertend) let sb. have sth.; (b) (derb: schlechtes Essen) muck; swill

Fratz /frats/ *der;* ~**es**, ~**e**, (österr.:) ~**en**, ~**en** (a) (ugs.: niedliches Kind) [little] rascal; (b) (bes. südd., österr.: ungezogenes Kind) brat

Fratze /'fratsə/ *die;* ~, ~**n** (a) (hässliches Gesicht) hideous features *pl.;* (abwertend) mug (sl.); (b) (ugs.: Grimasse) grimace; **jmdm.** ~**n schneiden** pull faces at sb.

Frau *die;* ~, ~**en** (a) woman; (b) (Ehe~) wife; (c) ▶ 34⏐, ▶ 107⏐ (Titel, Anrede) ~ **Schulze** Mrs Schulze; ~ **Professor/Dr. Schulze** Professor/Dr Schulze; ~ **Ministerin/ Direktorin/Studienrätin Schulze** Mrs/Miss/Ms Schulze; ~ **Ministerin/Professor/Doktor** Minister/Professor/doctor; ~ **Vorsitzende/Präsidentin** Madam Chairman/President; (in Briefen) **Sehr geehrte** ~ **Schulze** Dear Madam; (bei persönlicher Bekanntschaft) Dear Mrs/Miss/Ms Schulze; [**Sehr verehrte**] **gnädige** ~: [Dear] Madam; **Ihre** ~ **Mutter** your mother; (d) (Herrin) lady; mistress; **die** ~ **des Hauses** the lady of the house

Frauchen /'frauçən/ *das;* ~s, ~ (a) (ugs.: Ehefrau) wifie (coll.); (b) (Herrin eines Hundes) mistress

frauen-, Frauen-: ~**arbeit** *die* (a) *o. Pl.* (Erwerbstätigkeit) women's employment; (b) (für ~ geeignete Arbeit) women's work; ~**arzt** *der,* ~**ärztin** *die* gynaecologist; ~**beruf** *der* women's occupation; ~**bewegung** *die; o. Pl.* women's movement; ~**emanzipation** *die* female emancipation; women's emancipation; ~**feind** der misogynist; ~**feindlich** Adj. anti-women; ~**haus** das battered wives' refuge; ~**held** der ladykiller; ~**mörder** der killer of women; ~**rechtlerin** /-rɛçtlərɪn/ die; ~, ~**nen** feminist; Women's Libber (coll.) **Frauens·person** die (veralt.) female

Frauen-: ~**sport** der women's sport; ~**station** die women's ward; ~**stimme** die woman's voice; ~**wahl·recht** das women's franchise; women's right to vote; ~**zeitschrift** die women's magazine; ~**zimmer** das (abwertend) female

Fräulein /'frɔylaɪn/ das; ~s, ~ (ugs. ~s) (a) (junges ~) young lady; (ältliches ~) spinster; (b) ▶107|, ▶34| (Titel, Anrede) ~ **Mayer** Miss Mayer; [**sehr verehrtes**] **gnädiges** ~ [**X**] Dear Miss X; **Ihr** ~ **Tochter** your daughter; (c) (Kellnerin) waitress; ~, **wir möchten zahlen** [Miss,] could we have the bill (Brit.) or (Amer.) check, please?; (d) **das** ~ **vom Amt** (veralt.) the operator

fraulich 1 Adj. feminine; (reif) womanly. 2 adv. in a feminine/womanly way

Fraulichkeit die; ~: femininity; (reifes Wesen) womanliness

frech /frɛç/ 1 Adj. (a) (respektlos, unverschämt) impertinent; impudent; cheeky; bare-faced ‹lie›; etw. mit ~**er Stirn behaupten** (fig.) have the bare-faced cheek to say sth.; (b) (keck, kess) saucy. 2 adv. (respektlos, unverschämt) impertinently; impudently; cheekily; **jmdn.** ~ **anlügen** tell sb. bare-faced lies

Frech·dachs der (ugs., meist scherzh.) cheeky little thing

Frechheit die; ~, ~**en** (a) o. Pl. (Benehmen) impertinence; impudence; cheek; **die** ~ **haben, etw. zu tun** have the impertinence etc. to do sth.; (b) (Äußerung) impertinent or impudent or cheeky remark; **sich** (Dat.) ~**en erlauben** be impertinent

Freesie /'freːziə/ die; ~, ~**n** freesia

Fregatte /fre'gatə/ die; ~, ~**n** frigate

Fregatten·kapitän der commander

frei /fraɪ/ 1 Adj. (a) free ‹man, will, life, people, decision, etc.›; (b) (nicht angestellt) freelance ‹writer, worker, etc.›; **die** ~**en Berufe** the independent professions; (c) (ungezwungen) free and easy; lax (derog.); (d) (nicht eingesperrt, gefangen) free; at liberty pred.; (e) (offen) open; **unter** ~**em Himmel** in the open [air]; outdoors; **auf** ~**er Strecke** (Straße) on the open road; (Eisenbahn) between stations; **ins Freie gehen** walk out into the open; ~ **lebende Tiere** animals living in the wild; ~ **herumlaufen** ‹person› run around scot-free; (f) (unbesetzt) vacant; unoccupied; free; **ein** ~**er Stuhl/Platz** a vacant or free chair/seat; **Entschuldigung, ist hier noch** ~? excuse me, is this anyone's seat etc.?; **eine** ~**e Stelle** a vacancy; **ein Bett ist [noch]** ~: one bed is [still] free or not taken; **ist der Tisch** ~? is this table free?; **einige Seiten** ~ **lassen** leave some pages blank; (g) (kostenlos) free ‹food, admission›; **20 kg Gepäck** ~ **haben** have or be allowed a 20 kilogram baggage allowance; **Lieferung** ~ **Haus** carriage free; (h) (ungenau) **eine** ~**e Übersetzung** a free or loose translation; (i) (ohne Vorlage) improvised; (j) (uneingeschränkt) free; **der Zug hat** ~**e Fahrt** the train can proceed; **der** ~**e Fall** (Physik) free fall; (k) **von etw.** ~/~ **von etw. sein** be free of sth.; ~ **von Fehlern** without faults; (l) (verfügbar) spare; free; **ich habe heute** ~/ **meinen** ~**en Abend** I've got today off/this is my evening off; **sich** (Dat.) ~ **nehmen** (ugs.) take some time off; **er ist noch/nicht mehr** ~: he is still/no longer unattached; (m) (ohne Hilfsmittel) **eine** ~**e Rede** an extempore speech; (n) (unbekleidet) bare; (o) (bes. Fußball) unmarked; ~ **stehen** be unmarked; (p) (Chemie, Physik) free; ~ **werden** (bei einer Reaktion) be given off; (q) (in festen Wendungen) ~**e Hand haben/jmdm.** ~**e Hand lassen** have/give a free hand; **aus** ~**en Stücken** (ugs.) of one's own accord; voluntarily; **jmdn. auf** ~**en Fuß setzen** set sb. free; **auf** ~**em Fuß** (von Verbrechern etc.) at large. 2 adv. ‹act, speak, choose› freely; ‹translate› freely, loosely; **etw.** ~ **heraus sagen** say sth. freely; **eine Rede** ~ **halten** make a speech without notes

frei-, Frei-: ~**bad** das open-air or outdoor swimming pool; ~|**bekommen** 1 unr. itr. V. (ugs.) get time off; 2

unr. tr. V. **jmdn./etw.** ~**bekommen** get sb./sth. released; ~**beruflich** ▶85| 1 Adj. self-employed; freelance ‹journalist, editor, architect, etc.›; ‹doctor, lawyer› in private practice; 2 adv. ~**beruflich tätig sein/arbeiten** work freelance/practise privately; ~**betrag** der (Steuerw.) [tax] allowance; ~**beuter** /-bɔytɐ/ der; ~s, ~ (hist.: Pirat) freebooter; 1 Adj. ~**bier** das free beer; ~**bleibend** (Kaufmannsspr.) 1 Adj. ~**bleibendes Angebot** provisional offer; 2 adv. **die Preise verstehen sich** ~**bleibend** prices are subject to alteration; ~**brief** der: **kein** ~**brief für etw. sein** be no excuse for sth.; **jmdm. einen** ~**brief für etw. ausstellen** give sb. a licence for sth.

freien 1 tr. V. (veralt.) marry; wed. 2 itr. V. **um ein Mädchen** ~: court or woo a girl

Freier der; ~s, ~ (a) (veralt.) suitor; (b) (salopp: Kunde einer Dirne) punter (sl.)

Freiers·füße Pl. **in auf** ~**n gehen** (scherzh.) be courting

frei-, Frei-: ~**exemplar** das (Buch) free copy; (Zeitung) free issue; ~**frau** die baroness; ~**gabe** die (a) release; (der Wechselkurse) floating; (b) (einer Straße, Brücke usw.) opening (für to); (eines Films) passing; ~|**geben** 1 unr. tr. V. (a) release ‹prisoner, footballer›; float ‹exchange rates›; **jmdm. den Weg** ~**geben** let sb. through; (b) open ‹road, bridge, etc.› (für to); pass ‹film›; **der Film ist ab 18 freigegeben** the film has been passed 18; 2 unr. tr. etc. V. **jmdm.** ~**geben** give sb. time off; ~**gebig** /-geːbɪç/ Adj. generous; open-handed; ~**gebigkeit** die generosity; open-handedness; ~**gehege** das outdoor or open-air enclosure; ~|**haben** unr. tr., itr. V. (ugs.) **ich habe [am** od. **den] Montag** ~: I've got Monday off; ~**hafen** der free port; ~|**halten** unr. tr. V. (a) treat; **er hielt das ganze Lokal** ~: he stood drinks for everyone in the pub (Brit.) or (Amer.) bar; (b) (offenhalten) keep ‹entrance, roadway› clear; **Einfahrt** ~**halten!** no parking in front of entrance; keep clear; (c) (reservieren) **jmdn.** od. **für jmdn. einen Platz** ~**halten** keep a place for sb.; ~**handel** der free trade; ~**handels·zone** die free-trade zone; ~**händig** /-hɛndɪç/ 1 Adj. free-hand ‹drawing›, 2 adv. ‹cycle› without holding on; ‹draw› free-hand

Freiheit die; ~, ~**en** (a) freedom; **die persönliche** ~: personal freedom or liberty; **jmdm. völlige** ~ **lassen** give sb. a completely free hand; (b) (Vorrecht) freedom; privilege; **sich** (Dat.) ~**en herausnehmen** take liberties (gegen with); **die dichterische** ~: poetic licence

freiheitlich 1 Adj. liberal ‹philosophy, conscience›; ~ **und demokratisch** free and democratic. 2 adv. liberally

Freiheitliche der/die; adj. Dekl. (Politik) member of the Freedom Party; **die** ~**n** the Freedom Party

Freiheits-: ~**beraubung** die (jur.) wrongful detention; ~**bewegung** die liberation movement; ~**entzug** der imprisonment; ~**kampf** der struggle for freedom; ~**kämpfer** der freedom fighter; ~**liebe** die; o. Pl. love of freedom or liberty; ~**liebend** Adj. freedom-loving; ~**rechte** Pl. civil rights; ~**statue** die Statue of Liberty; ~**strafe** die (Rechtsw.) term of imprisonment; prison sentence

frei·heraus Adv. frankly; openly

frei-, Frei-: ~**herr** der ▶34| baron; ~|**kämpfen** tr. V. liberate; **sich** ~**kämpfen** fight one's way out; ~**karte** die complimentary or free ticket; ~|**kaufen** tr. V. ransom ‹hostage›; buy the freedom of ‹slave›; **sich von der Verantwortung** ~**kaufen** (fig.) buy off one's responsibility; ~|**kommen** unr. itr. V.; mit sein **aus dem Gefängnis** ~**kommen** be released from prison; leave prison; **aus jmds. Fängen** ~**kommen** escape from sb.'s clutches; ~**körper·kultur** die; o. Pl. nudism no art.; naturism no art.; ~**land·gemüse** das outdoor vegetables pl.; ~|**lassen** unr. tr. V. set free; release; ~**lassung** die release; ~**lauf** der (Technik) freewheel; **im** ~**lauf fahren** freewheel;*~**lebend** ⇒ **frei** 1 d; ~|**legen** tr. V. uncover

freilich Adv. (a) (einschränkend) **er arbeitet schnell,** ~ **nicht sehr gründlich** he works quickly, though admittedly he's not very thorough; **sie hat sehr viel Talent,** ~ **fehlt es ihr an Ausdauer** she has a great deal of talent, but she does lack staying power; (b) (einräumend)

man muss ∼ bedenken, dass …: one must of course
bear in mind that …; ∼ scheinen die Tatsachen gegen
meine Überlegungen zu sprechen …: admittedly the
facts seem to contradict my ideas, but …; **(c)** (bes. südd.:
selbstverständlich) of course; **ja** ∼**:** [why] yes; of course
Frei·licht-: ∼**bühne** die, ∼**theater** das open-air
or outdoor theatre
frei-, Frei-: ∼|**machen** 1 refl. V. (ugs.: frei nehmen)
sich ∼machen take time off; 2 tr. V. **(a)** (entkleiden) **den**
Oberkörper ∼**machen** strip to the waist; **sich** ∼
machen strip; **(b)** (Postw.) put a stamp on; (freistempeln);
frank. ∼**maurer** der Freemason; ∼**maurer·loge** die
Freemasons' lodge; ∼**mut** der candidness; frankness;
∼**mütig** 1 Adj. candid; frank; 2 adv. candidly; frankly;
∼**mütigkeit** die; ∼: candidness; frankness; ∼**raum**
der (Psych., Soziol.) space no indef. art. to be oneself;
∼**schaffend** Adj. freelance; ∼**schärler** /-ʃɛːɐlɐ/
der; ∼s, ∼: irregular [soldier]; ∼|**schwimmen** unr.
refl. V. pass the 15-minute swimming test; ∼|**setzen** tr.
V. **(a)** (Physik, Chemie) release ⟨energy⟩; emit ⟨rays, electrons,
neutrons⟩; release, give off ⟨gas⟩; **(b)** (Wirtsch.) release
⟨staff⟩; ∼**spiel** das free turn; ∼|**spielen** tr. V. (Ballspiele)
le) jmdn./sich ∼spielen create space for sb./oneself;
∼|**sprechen** unr. tr. V. **(a)** (Rechtsw.) acquit; jmdn. von
einer Anklage ∼sprechen acquit sb. of a charge; **(b)**
(fig.) exonerate (von from); ∼**spruch** der (Rechtsw.) ac-
quittal; ∼|**stehen** unr. itr. V. **(a) es steht jmdm.** ∼,
etw. zu tun sb. is free to do sth.; **(b)** ⟨flat, house⟩ be empty
or vacant; ⟨storeroom etc.⟩ be empty; ∼**stehend** Adj.
detached ⟨house⟩; ∼|**stellen** tr. V. **(a)** jmdm. etw.
∼stellen leave sth. up to sb.; let sb. decide sth.; **(b)** (befreien) release ⟨person⟩; jmdn. vom Wehrdienst
∼stellen exempt sb. from military service; ∼**stellung**
die release; (befristet) leave
Frei·stil der; o. Pl. (Sport) **(a)** ⇒ **Freistilringen; (b)** ⇒
Freistilschwimmen
Freistil-: ∼**ringen** das free-style wrestling;
∼**schwimmen** das free-style swimming
Frei-: ∼**stoß** der (Fußball) free kick; ∼**stunde** die
(Schulw.) free period
Frei·tag der ▸ 119 |, ▸ 595 | Friday; s. auch **Dienstag,**
Dienstag-
freitags Adv. ▸ 595 | on Friday[s]; s. auch **dienstags**
frei-, Frei-: ∼**tod** der (verhüll.) suicide no art.; **den**
∼**tod wählen** choose to take one's own life; ∼**tragend**
Adj. (Bauw.) sus- pended ⟨floor⟩; cantilever ⟨bridge⟩;
∼**treppe** die [flight of] steps; ∼**übung** die; meist Pl.
(Sport) keep-fit exercise; ∼**umschlag** der stamped addressed envelope; s.a.e.; ∼**weg** Adv. (ugs.) openly; freely
⟨talk⟩ sag es ∼weg say it straight out; ∼**wild** das fair
game; ∼**willig** 1 Adj. voluntary ⟨decision⟩; optional
⟨subject⟩; 2 adv. voluntarily; of one's own accord; sich
∼**willig melden** volunteer; ∼**willige** der/die; adj.
Dekl. volunteer; ∼**wurf** der free throw; ∼**zeichen** das
ringing tone
Frei·zeit die; o. Pl. **(a)** spare time; leisure time; **(b)** (Zusammenkunft) [holiday/weekend] course; (der Kirche) retreat
Freizeit-: ∼**anzug** der leisure suit; ∼**beschäfti-**
gung die leisure pursuit or activity; ∼**gesellschaft**
die (Soziol.) leisure society; ∼**wert** der: **eine Stadt mit**
hohem ∼**wert** a town with many leisure amenities
frei-, Frei-: ∼**zügig** 1 Adj. **(a)** (großzügig) generous,
liberal ⟨dosage, spending⟩; liberal, flexible ⟨interpretation
of rule etc.⟩; **(b)** (gewagt, unmoralisch) risqué, daring ⟨remark,
film, dress⟩; permissive ⟨attitude⟩; 2 adv. **Geld** ∼zügig
ausgeben be generous with one's money; **ein Gesetz**
∼**zügig auslegen** interpret a law flexibly; ∼**zügig-**
keit die; ∼ **(a)** (Großzügigkeit) liberalness; (in Geldsachen)
generosity; (von Interpretation) flexibility; **(b)** (von Einstellung)
permissiveness; **(c)** (freie Wahl des Wohnsitzes) freedom of
domicile
fremd /frɛmt/ Adj. **(a)** strange; foreign ⟨country, government, customs, language⟩; **(b)** nicht präd. (nicht eigen) other
people's; of others postpos.; **ohne** ∼**e Hilfe** without anyone else's help; **(c)** (unbekannt) strange; strange, unknown
⟨surroundings⟩; **sich sehr** ∼ **fühlen** feel very much a

stranger; **einander** ∼ **werden** become estranged; grow
apart
fremd·artig Adj. strange
Fremd·artigkeit die strangeness
Fremde[1] /'frɛmdə/ der/die; adj. Dekl. **(a)** stranger; **(b)**
(Ausländer) foreigner; alien (Admin. lang.); **(c)** (Tourist) visitor
Fremde[2] die; ∼ (geh.) foreign parts pl.; **in die** ∼ **ziehen**
go off to foreign parts; go abroad
fremden-, Fremden-: ∼**feindlich** Adj. hostile to
strangers/foreigners postpos.; ∼**feindlichkeit** die; ∼:
xenophobia; ∼**heim** das guest house; boarding house;
∼**legion** die; o. Pl. foreign legion; ∼**pass,** *∼**paß**
der alien's passport; ∼**verkehr** der tourism no art.;
∼**zimmer** das room; ∼**zimmer frei** vacancies (Brit.);
vacancy (Amer.)
fremd|gehen unr. itr. V.; mit sein (ugs.) be unfaithful
Fremdheit die; ∼: strangeness
fremd-, Fremd-: ∼**herrschaft** die foreign domination no art. or rule no art.; ∼**körper** der (Med., Biol.)
foreign body; **ein** ∼**körper sein** (fig.) be out of place;
∼**ländisch** /-lɛndɪʃ/ Adj. foreign; (exotisch) exotic
Fremdling der; ∼s, ∼e (veralt.) stranger
Fremd·sprache die foreign language
Fremdsprachen-: ∼**korrespondentin** die
▸ 85 | bilingual/multilingual secretary; ∼**unterricht**
der teaching of foreign languages
fremd-, Fremd-: ∼**sprachig** Adj. foreign
⟨literature⟩; foreign-language ⟨edition, teaching⟩;
∼**sprachlich** Adj.; nicht präd. foreign-language
⟨teaching⟩; foreign ⟨word⟩; ∼**wort** das; Pl. ∼**wörter**
foreign word; **Liebe ist für ihn ein** ∼**wort** (fig.) he
doesn't know the meaning of the word love; ∼**wörter·**
buch das dictionary of foreign words
frenetisch /fre'neːtɪʃ/ 1 Adj. frenetic. 2 adv. fren-
etically
frequentieren tr. V. frequent ⟨pub, café⟩; use ⟨library⟩
Frequenz /fre'kvɛnts/ die; ∼, ∼**en** (fachspr.) frequency;
(Med.: Puls∼) rate
Fresko /'frɛsko/ das; ∼s, **Fresken** (Kunstwiss.) fresco
Fressalien /frɛ'saːliən/ Pl. (ugs. scherzh.) grub (sl.)
Fresse /'frɛsə/ die; ∼, ∼**n** (derb) **(a)** (Mund) gob (sl.); trap
(sl.); **eine große** ∼ **haben** (fig.) have a big mouth (coll.);
[**ach**] **du meine** ∼**!** bloody hell! (sl.); **die** ∼ **halten** keep
one's trap or gob shut (sl.); **(b)** (Gesicht) mug (sl.); **jmdm.**
die ∼ **polieren** smash sb.'s face in (sl.)
fressen 1 unr. tr. V. **(a)** ⟨animal⟩ eat; (sich ernähren von)
feed on; **sich satt** ∼**:** eat its/her/his fill; (sl.) (ugs.: verschlingen) swallow up ⟨money, time, distance⟩; drink
⟨petrol⟩; **(c)** (zerstören) eat away; **(d)** (derb: von Menschen)
guzzle; (fig.) **er wird dich schon nicht** ∼ (salopp) he won't
eat you (coll.); **etw. ge**∼ **haben** (ugs.) have understood sth.;
jmdn. ge∼ **haben** (ugs.) hate sb.'s guts (coll.); **jmdn. zum**
Fressen gern haben like sb. so much one could eat him/
her. 2 unr. itr. V. **(a)** (von Tieren) feed; **einem Tier zu** ∼
geben feed an animal; **(b)** (zerstören) **an etw.** (Dat.) ∼**:**
⟨rust⟩ eat away at sth.; ⟨fire⟩ begin to consume sth.; **(c)**
(derb: von Menschen) stuff oneself or one's face (sl.). 3 unr. refl.
V. **sich durch/in etw.** (Akk.) ∼**:** eat its way through/into
sth.
Fressen das; ∼s **(a)** (für Hunde, Katzen usw.) food; (für Vieh)
feed; **(b)** (derb: Essen) grub (sl.); **das ist ein gefundenes**
∼ **für sie** (fig.) that's just what she needed; that's a real
gift for her
Fresserei die; ∼, ∼**en** (derb abwertend) guzzling; stuffing;
eine große ∼**:** a big blow-out (sl.)
Fress-, *Freß-:** ∼**korb** der (ugs.) **(a)** (Verpflegungskorb)
picnic basket; **(b)** (Geschenkkorb) hamper; ∼**napf** der feed-
ing-bowl; ∼**paket** das (ugs.) food parcel; ∼**sack** der
(derb) greedy pig (sl.)
Frettchen /'frɛtçən/ das; ∼s, ∼ ferret
Freude /'frɔydə/ die; ∼, ∼**n** joy; (Vergnügen) pleasure;
(Wonne) delight; ∼ **an etw.** (Dat.) **haben** take pleasure in
sth.; ∼ **am Leben haben** enjoy life; **das war eine**
große ∼ **für uns** that was a great pleasure for us; **jmdm.**
eine ∼ **machen** od. **bereiten** make sb. happy; **zu un-**
serer ∼**:** to our delight; **mit** ∼**n** with pleasure; **die** ∼**n**

---

*alte Schreibung (vgl. Hinweise auf S. xvi–xvii)

des Alltags/der Liebe the pleasures of everyday life/the joys of love

Freuden-: ~**fest** das celebration; ~**feuer** das bonfire; ~**haus** das house of pleasure; ~**mädchen** das (verhüll.) woman of easy virtue; ~**schrei** der cry or shout of joy; ~**tanz** der in einen [wilden od. wahren] ~tanz aufführen od. vollführen dance for joy; ~**taumel** der transport of delight or joy; ~**tränen** Pl. tears of happiness or joy

freude·strahlend Adj. beaming or radiant with joy

freudig 1 Adj. (a) joyful, happy ‹face, feeling, greeting›; joyous ‹heart›; **in** ~**er Erwartung** in joyful anticipation; (b) (erfreulich) delightful ‹surprise›; **ein** ~**es Ereignis** (verhüll.) a happy event. 2 adv. ~ **erregt** happy and excited; **von etw.** ~ **überrascht sein** be surprised and delighted about sth.; **etw.** ~ **erwarten** look forward to sth. with pleasure

freud·los 1 Adj. joyless ‹days, existence›; cheerless ‹surroundings›. 2 adv. joylessly

freuen /'frɔyən/ 1 refl. V. be pleased or glad (**über** + Akk. about); (froh sein) be happy; **sich zu früh** ~: get carried away or rejoice too soon; **sich auf etw.** (Akk.)/**jmdn.** ~: look forward to sth./to seeing sb.; **sich mit jmdm.** ~: rejoice with sb. 2 tr. V. please; **es freut mich, dass** ...: I am pleased or glad that ...; **freut mich!** pleased to meet you

Freund der; ~es, ~e (a) friend; **alter** ~! (ugs. scherzh. drohend) mate!; (b) (Geliebter) boyfriend; (älter) gentleman-friend; (c) (Anhänger, Liebhaber) lover; **ich bin kein** ~ **von großen Worten** (fig.) I am not one for fine words

Freundchen das; ~s, ~ (Anrede; scherzh. drohend) mate

Freundes·kreis der circle of friends; **im engen** ~**kreis** among close friends

Freundin die; ~, ~**nen** (a) friend; (b) (Geliebte) girlfriend; (älter) lady-friend; (c) ⇒ **Freund** c

freundlich 1 Adj. (a) kind ‹face›; kind, friendly ‹reception›; friendly ‹smile›; fond ‹farewell›; **zu jmdm.** ~ **sein** be kind to sb.; **er war so** ~, **mir zu helfen** he was kind or good enough to help me; **würden Sie bitte so** ~ **sein und das Fenster schließen?** would you be so kind or good as to close the window?; (b) (angenehm) pleasant ‹weather, surroundings›; pleasant, congenial ‹atmosphere›; pleasant, mild ‹climate›; (c) (freundschaftlich) friendly, amiable ‹person, manner›; friendly ‹disposition, attitude, warning›. 2 adv. **jmdn.** ~ **begrüßen** greet sb. amiably; **jmdm.** ~ **danken** thank sb. kindly; **jmdm.** ~ **gesinnt sein** be well-disposed towards sb.

freundlicher·weise Adv. kindly

Freundlichkeit die; ~, ~**en** (a) kindness; **jmdm. ein paar** ~**en sagen** make a few kind remarks to sb.; (b) o. Pl. (angenehme Art) pleasantness; friendliness; (eines Zimmers, Hauses) cheerfulness

Freundschaft die; ~, ~**en** friendship; **mit jmdm.** ~ **schließen** make or become friends with sb.; **jmdm. etw. in aller** ~ **sagen** tell sb. sth. as a friend

freundschaftlich 1 Adj. friendly; amicable. 2 adv. in a friendly way; amicably

Freundschafts-: ~**besuch** der (bes. Politik) goodwill visit; ~**dienst** der service rendered out of friendship; ~**spiel** das (Sport) friendly match or game; friendly (coll.); ~**vertrag** der (Politik) treaty of friendship

Frevel /'fre:fl/ der; ~s, ~ (geh., veralt.) crime; outrage; ~ **gegen Gott** sacrilege

frevelhaft (geh.) 1 Adj. wicked ‹deed, rebellion, person›; criminal ‹stupidity›. 2 adv. wickedly

freveln itr. V. (geh.) **an jmdm./gegen etw.** ~: commit a crime against sb./sth.

Friede /'fri:də/ der; ~ns, ~n (a) (älter, geh.) ⇒ **Frieden;** (b) (geh.) ~ **seiner Asche** (Dat.) God rest his soul; ~ **auf Erden** peace on earth

Frieden der; ~s, ~ peace; ~ **schließen/stiften** make peace; **mit jmdm.** ~ **schließen** make one's peace with sb.; **mitten im** ~: in the middle of peace-time; **um des lieben** ~**s willen** for the sake of peace and quiet; **lass mich in** ~! (ugs.) leave me in peace!; leave me alone!; **ich traue dem** ~ **nicht** (ugs.) it's too good to be true

friedens-, Friedens-: ~**bedingungen** Pl. peace terms; terms for peace; ~**bewegung** die peace movement; ~**bruch** der violation of the peace; ~**diktat** das dictated peace terms pl.; ~**forschung** die peace studies pl., no art.; ~**göttin** die goddess of peace; ~**konferenz** die peace conference; ~**liebe** die love of peace; ~**nobelpreis** der Nobel Peace Prize; ~**pfeife** die pipe of peace; ~**politik** die policy of peace; ~**richter** der lay magistrate dealing with minor offences; ≈ Justice of the Peace; ~**schluss**, *~**schluß** der peace settlement; ~**sicherung** die peacekeeping; ~**stifter** der peacemaker; ~**taube** die dove of peace; ~**truppe** die peacekeeping force; ~**verhandlungen** Pl. peace negotiations; peace talks; ~**vertrag** der peace treaty; ~**zeiten** Pl. peace-time sing.

fried·fertig Adj. peaceable ‹person, character›; peaceful ‹intentions›

Fried·fertigkeit die; ~: peaceableness

Fried·hof der cemetery; (Kirchhof) graveyard; churchyard

Friedhofs-: ~**gärtner** der cemetery gardener; ~**kapelle** die cemetery chapel

friedlich /'fri:tlɪç/ 1 Adj. (a) peaceful; **auf** ~**em Wege** by peaceful means; (b) (ruhig, verträglich) peaceable, peaceful ‹character, person›; peaceful, tranquil ‹life, atmosphere, valley›; **sei** ~! (ugs.) be quiet!. 2 adv. ‹live, sleep› peacefully

fried·liebend Adj. peace-loving

Friedrich Wilhelm der; ~ ~s, ~ ~s (ugs. scherzh.: Unterschrift) monicker (coll. joc.)

frieren /'fri:rən/ unr. itr. V. (a) be or feel cold; **erbärmlich/sehr** ~: be freezing/terribly cold; **er fror an den Händen** he had [freezing] cold hands; unpers.: **jmdn. friert [es]** sb. is cold; (b) mit sein (ge~) freeze; **das Wasser ist gefroren** the water is or has frozen; **steif gefroren sein** be frozen stiff; **blau gefroren sein** be blue with cold; (c) (unpers.) **es friert** it is freezing; s. auch **Stein**

frigid[e] /fri'gi:d(ə)/ Adj. frigid

Frikadelle /frika'dɛlə/ die; ~, ~**n** rissole

Frikassee /frika'se:/ das; ~s, ~s (Kochk.) fricassee

frisch /frɪʃ/ 1 Adj. (a) fresh; new-laid ‹egg›; fresh, clean ‹linen›; clean ‹underwear›; wet ‹paint›; **mit** ~**en Kräften with renewed strength; sich** ~ **machen** freshen oneself up; **jmdn. auf** ~**er Tat ertappen** catch sb. redhanded; (b) (munter) fresh; ~ **und munter sein** (ugs.) be bright and cheerful. 2 adv. freshly; ~ **gewaschen sein** ‹person› have just had a wash; ‹garment› have just been washed; ~ **von der Universität kommen** have come straight from the university; ~ **gestrichene Bänke** newly painted seats; „**Vorsicht,** ~ **gestrichen!**" 'wet paint'; **die Betten** ~ **beziehen** put fresh or clean sheets on the beds; **ein** ~ **gebackenes Ehepaar** (ugs.) a newly-wed couple; newly-weds pl.; **ein** ~ **gebackener Doktor** (ugs.) a newly-qualified doctor; ~ **gewagt ist halb gewonnen** (Spr.) nothing ventured, nothing gained (prov.)

Frische die; ~: freshness; **geistige** ~: mental alertness; **körperliche** ~: physical fitness; vigour

frisch-, Frisch-: ~**fisch** der fresh fish; ~**fleisch** das fresh meat; *~**gebacken** ⇒ frisch 2; ~**gemüse** das fresh vegetables pl.; ~**halte·beutel** der airtight bag; ~**halte·packung** die airtight pack; ~**käse** der curd cheese

Frischling der; ~s, ~e (a) (Jägerspr.) young boar; (b) (scherzh.) new boy or girl

Frisch-: ~**luft** die fresh air ~**milch** die fresh milk; ~**obst** das fresh fruit; ~**zelle** die (Med.) living cell

Friseur /fri'zø:ɐ/ der; ~s, ~e ▶85⌋ hairdresser; (Herren~) hairdresser; barber; s. auch **Bäcker**

Friseurin /fri'zø:rɪn/ die; ~, ~**nen** ▶85⌋ hairdresser

Friseur·salon der hairdressing or hairdresser's salon (Brit.); beauty salon (Amer.); (für Herren) barber shop (Amer.)

Friseuse /fri'zø:zə/ die; ~, ~**n** ▶85⌋ hairdresser

Frisier·creme die hair cream

frisieren /fri'zi:rən/ tr. V. (a) **jmdn./sich** ~: do sb.'s/one's hair; **sich** ~ **lassen** have one's hair done; (b) (ugs.: verfälschen) doctor ‹reports, statistics›; fiddle (coll.) ‹accounts›; (c) (Kfz-W.) soup up (coll.) ‹engine, vehicle›

Frisör ⇨ Friseur

friss /frɪs/ *Imperativ Sg. v.* **fressen**

Frist /frɪst/ *die;* ~, ~**en** time; period; [**sich** (*Dat.*)] **eine** ~ **von 3 Wochen setzen** set [oneself] a time limit of 3 weeks; **die** ~ **verlängern** extend the deadline; **in kürzester** ~: within a very short time; **jmdm. eine** ~ **von drei Tagen geben** give sb. three days' time; **eine letzte** ~ (Aufschub) a final extension

fristen *tr. V.* **ein kümmerliches Dasein** *od.* **Leben** ~: eke out a wretched existence; barely manage to survive

frist-: ~**gemäß**, ~**gerecht** *Adj., adv.* within the specified time *postpos.;* (bei Anmeldung usw.) before the closing date *postpos.;* ~**los 1** *Adj.* instant ‹*dismissal*›; **2** *adv.* without notice; **jmdm.** ~ **kündigen** dismiss sb. without notice; **jmdm.** ~**los die Wohnung kündigen** ask sb. to quit without notice

Frisur /fri'zuːɐ̯/ *die;* ~, ~**en** hairstyle; hairdo (coll.)

***Friteuse** ⇨ Fritteuse

***fritieren** ⇨ frittieren

Fritte /'frɪtə/ *die;* ~, ~**n** (ugs.) chip

Fritteuse /fri'tøːzə/ *die;* ~, ~**n** deep fryer

frittieren /fri'tiːrən/ *tr. V.* deep-fry

frivol /fri'voːl/ *Adj.* (a) (schamlos) suggestive ‹*picture, etc.*›; risqué ‹*remark, joke*›; earthy ‹*man*›; flighty ‹*woman*›; (b) (leichtfertig) frivolous; irresponsible

Frivolität /frivoli'tɛːt/ *die;* ~, ~**en** *o. Pl.* ⇨ **frivol a:** suggestiveness; risqué nature; earthiness; flightiness; (b) (frivole Bemerkung) risqué remark

froh /froː/ **1** *Adj.* (a) (glücklich) happy; cheerful ‹*person, mood*›; **jmdn.** ~ **machen** make sb. happy; cheer sb. up; (b) (ugs.: erleichtert) pleased, glad (**über** + *Akk.* about); **du kannst** ~ **sein, dass ...:** you can be thankful *or* glad that ...; **da bin ich aber** ~ [**, dass...**] I am glad [that ...]; **seines Lebens nicht mehr** ~ **werden** not enjoy life any more; (c) ▶**240**| *nicht präd.* (erfreulich) good ‹*news*›; happy ‹*event*›. **2** *adv.* ~ **gelaunt** cheerful

froh-: *****~**gelaunt** ⇨ **froh 2;** ~**gemut 1** *Adj.* happy; **2** *adv.* happily; in good spirits

fröhlich /'frøːlɪç/ **1** *Adj.* ▶**240**| cheerful; happy; ~**es Treiben** merrymaking. **2** *adv.* (unbekümmert) blithely; cheerfully

Fröhlichkeit *die;* ~: cheerfulness; (eines Festes, einer Feier) gaiety

froh·locken *itr. V.* (geh.) rejoice; exult; **frohlocket dem Herrn** sing joyfully unto the Lord

Froh-: ~**natur** *die* (Mensch) cheerful person; ~**sinn** *der; o. Pl.* cheerfulness; gaiety

fromm /frɔm/; ~**er** *od.* **frömmer** /'frœmɐ/, ~**st...** *od.* **frömmst...** **1** *Adj.* (a) pious, devout ‹*person*›; devout ‹*life, Christian*›; (b) (scheinheilig) ~**es Getue** pious affectation; (c) (wohl gemeint) **eine** ~ **Lüge** a white lie; **ein** ~**er Wunsch** a pious hope. **2** *adv.* piously

Frömmelei *die;* ~ (abwertend) affected piety

Frömmigkeit /'frœmɪçkai̯t/ *die;* ~: piety; devoutness

Frömmler /'frœmlɐ/ *der;* ~**s**, ~ (abwertend) [pious] hypocrite

Fron /froːn/ *die;* ~, ~**en** (a) (hist.) corvée; (b) (geh.: aufgezwungene Mühsal) drudgery

frönen /'frøːnən/ *itr. V.* (geh.) **einer Neigung/einem Laster** ~: indulge an inclination/in a vice

Fron·leichnam *o. Art.* [the feast of] Corpus Christi

Front /frɔnt/ *die;* ~, ~**en** (a) (Gebäude~) front; façade; (b) (Kampfgebiet) front [line]; **an die** ~ **gehen/an der** ~ **sein** go to the front/fight at the front; (c) (Milit.: vorderste Linie) front line; **in vorderster** ~ **kämpfen** fight at the very front; **die** ~**en haben sich verhärtet** (fig.) attitudes have hardened; **an zwei** ~**en kämpfen** (fig.) fight on two fronts; (d) (Milit.: inner Truppe) **die** ~ **abnehmen/abschreiten** inspect the troops/guard of honour *etc.;* **gegen jmdn./ etw.** ~ **machen** (fig.) make a stand against sb./sth.; (e) (Sport) **in** ~ **liegen/gehen** be in front *or* in the lead/go in front; (f) (Met.) front

---

*****alte Schreibung (vgl. Hinweise auf S. xvi–xvii)

frontal /frɔn'taːl/ **1** *Adj.; nicht präd.* (a) (von vorn) head-on ‹*collision*›; (b) (nach vorn) frontal ‹*attack*›. **2** *adv.* ‹*collide*› head-on; ‹*attack*› from the front

Frontal-: ~**angriff** *der* frontal attack; ~**zusammenstoß** *der* head-on collision

Front-: ~**antrieb** *der* (Kfz-W.) front-wheel drive; ~**scheibe** *die* windscreen (Brit.); windshield (Amer.); ~**urlaub** *der* (Milit.) leave from the front; ~**wechsel** *der* (fig.) U-turn; volte-face

fror /froːɐ̯/ *1. u. 3. Pers. Sg. Prät. v.* **frieren**

Frosch /frɔʃ/ *der;* ~[**e**]**s**, **Frösche** /'frœʃə/ (a) frog; **sei kein** ~ (ugs.) don't be a spoilsport; (b) (Musik) nut

Frosch-: ~**könig** *der* Frog Prince; ~**mann** *der; Pl.* ~**männer** frogman; ~**perspektive** *die* worm's-eye view; ~**schenkel** *der* frog's leg

Frost /frɔst/ *der;* ~[**e**]**s**, **Fröste** /'frœstə/ frost; **es herrscht** [**strenger**] ~: there is a [severe] frost; it is [very] frosty

frost·beständig *Adj.* frost-resistant

Frost·beule *die* chilblain

frösteln /'frœstl̩n/ *itr. V.* feel chilly; **vor Kälte** ~: shiver with cold; *unpers.:* **es fröstelt ihn, ihn fröstelt** he feels chilly

Froster *der;* ~**s**, ~: freezing compartment

frostig /'frɔstɪç/ *1 Adj.* (auch fig.) frosty. **2** *adv.* frostily

Frost-: ~**schaden** *der* frost damage; ~**schutz** *der* frost protection; protection from frost; ~**schutz·mittel** *das* (a) frost protection agent; (b) (Kfz-W.) anti-freeze; ~**warnung** *die* (Met.) frost warning

Frottee /frɔ'teː/ *das* u. *der;* ~**s**, ~**s** terry towelling

Frottee-: ~**handtuch** *das* terry towel; ~**kleid** *das* towelling dress

frottieren /frɔ'tiːrən/ *tr. V.* rub; towel; **sich** ~: rub oneself down

Frotzelei *die;* ~, ~**en** (ugs.) (a) *o. Pl.* teasing; (b) (Bemerkung) teasing remark

frotzeln /'frɔtsl̩n/ **1** *tr. V.* tease. **2** *itr. V.* **über jmdn./ etw.** ~: make fun of sb./sth.

Frucht /fruxt/ *die;* ~, **Früchte** /'fryçtə/ (a) (auch fig. geh.) fruit; **Früchte tragen** (auch fig.) bear fruit; (b) *o. Pl.* (landsch.: Getreide) corn; crops *pl.*

frucht·bar *Adj.* fertile ‹*soil, field, man, woman*›; prolific ‹*breed*›; fruitful ‹*work, idea*›; fruitful, rewarding ‹*conversation*›; **eine Idee** *usw.* **für etw.** ~ **machen** allow sth. to benefit from an idea *etc.*

Fruchtbarkeit *die;* ~ ⇨ **fruchtbar:** fertility; prolificness; fruitfulness

Frucht-: ~**becher** *der* (a) (Eisbecher) fruit sundae; (b) (Bot.) cupule; ~**blase** *die* (Anat.) amniotic sac; ~**bonbon** *das od. der* fruit drop

Früchtchen /'fryçtçən/ *das;* ~**s**, ~ (ugs. abwertend: Tunichtgut) good-for-nothing

Frucht-: ~**ein·waage** *die* net weight [of fruit]; ~**eis** *das* fruit ice-cream

fruchten *itr. V.* **nichts** ~: be [of] no use; be of no avail; [**bei jmdm.**] **nicht**[**s**] ~: have no effect [on sb.]

Frucht·fleisch *das* flesh; pulp

fruchtig *Adj.* fruity

frucht-, Frucht-: ~**joghurt** *der od. das* fruit yoghurt; ~**los** *Adj.* fruitless, vain ‹*efforts*›; ~**saft** *der* fruit juice; ~**wasser** *das* (Anat.) amniotic fluid; waters *pl.* (coll.); ~**zucker** *der* fruit sugar; fructose

früh /fryː/ **1** *Adj.* (a) early; **am** ~**en Morgen** early in the morning; (b) (vorzeitig) premature; **ein** ~**es Ende finden** come to an untimely end; **einen** ~**en Tod sterben** die an untimely *or* premature death. **2** *adv.* (a) early; ~ **am Tage** early in the day; ~ **genug kommen** arrive in [good] time; ~**er oder später** sooner or later; **seine** ~ **verstorbene Mutter** his mother, who died young; **von** ~ **auf** from early childhood on[wards]; (b) (morgens) in the morning; **heute/morgen/gestern** ~: this/tomorrow/yesterday morning; **von** ~ **bis spät** from morning till night; from dawn to dusk; *s. auch* **früher**

früh-, Früh-: ~**auf** ⇨ **früh 2 a;** ~**aufsteher** *der;* ~**s**, ~: early riser; early bird (coll.); ~**dienst** *der* early duty; (im Betrieb) early shift

Frühe *die;* ~: **in der** ~: (geh.) in the early morning; **in aller** ~: at the crack of dawn

früher *Adv.* formerly; ~ **war er ganz anders** he used to be quite different at one time; **meine Bekannten von** ~: my former acquaintances; **ich kenne ihn [noch] von** ~ **[her]** I know him from some time ago; **an** ~ **denken** think back

früher... *Adj., nicht präd.* **(a)** (vergangen) earlier; former; **in** ~**en Zeiten** in the past; in former times; **aus** ~**en Jahrhunderten** from past centuries; **(b)** (ehemalig) former ⟨*owner, occupant, friend*⟩

Früh·erkennung *die* (Med.) early recognition *or* diagnosis

frühestens /'fry:əstns/ *Adv.* at the earliest

frühest·möglich /'fry:əst'mø:klɪç/ *Adj.; nicht präd.* earliest possible

Früh-: ~**geburt** *die* **(a)** premature birth; **(b)** (Kind) premature baby; ~**invalide** *der/die* premature invalid

Früh·jahr *das* ▶ 293 | spring

Frühjahrs-: ~**müdigkeit** *die* springtime tiredness; ~**putz** *der* spring-cleaning

Früh-: ~**kapitalismus** *der* early capitalism *no art.;* ~**kartoffel** *die* early potato

Frühling /'fry:lɪŋ/ *der;* ~**s,** ~**e** ▶ 293 | spring; **im** ~: [the] spring; **der** ~ **kommt** spring is coming; **im** ~ **des Lebens** (geh.) in the springtime of one's life; **seinen zweiten** ~ **erleben** (fig. iron.) relive one's youth

frühlings-, Frühlings-: ~**anfang** *der* first day of spring; ~**haft** *Adj.* ▶ 293 | springlike; ~**tag** *der* spring day

früh-, Früh-: ~**messe,** ~**mette** *die* (kath. Kirche) early [morning] mass; ~**morgens** /-'--/ *Adv.* early in the morning; ~**nebel** *der* early morning fog/mist; ~**reif** *Adj.* precocious ⟨*child*⟩; ~**rentner** *der* person who has retired early; ~**rentner werden/sein** retire/ have retired early; ~**schicht** *die* early shift; ~**schoppen** *der* morning drink; (um Mittag) lunchtime drink; ~**sport** *der* early-morning exercise; ~**stadium** *das* early stage; ~**start** *der* (Sport) false start

Früh·stück *das;* ~**s,** ~**e** breakfast; **zweites** ~: mid-morning snack

frühstücken 1 *itr. V.* breakfast; have breakfast; **ausgiebig** ~: have a hearty breakfast. 2 *tr. V.* **etw.** ~: breakfast on sth.; have sth. for breakfast

Frühstücks-: ~**fernsehen** *das* breakfast television; ~**fleisch** *das* luncheon meat; ~**pause** *die* morning break; coffee break

früh-, Früh-: *~**verstorben** ⇒ **früh 2 a;** ~**werk** *das* early work; (gesamtes) early works *pl.;* ~**zeit** *die* early period; ~**zeitig** 1 *Adj.* early; (vorzeitig) premature; untimely ⟨*death*⟩; 2 *adv.* early; (im Leben, in der Entwicklung) at an early stage; (vorzeitig) prematurely; **jmdn.** ~**zeitig benachrichtigen** let someone know in good time; ~**zug** *der* early [morning] train

Frust /frʊst/ *der;* ~**[e]s** (ugs.) frustration; **ihre Arbeit war der absolute** ~: her work was a real drag (coll.); **der große** ~ **überkam ihn** he began to feel really browned off (Brit. coll.)

Frustration /frʊstra'tsi̯o:n/ *die;* ~**,** ~**en** (Psych.) frustration

frustrieren /frʊs'tri:rən/ *tr. V.* frustrate

FU[B] /'ɛf|'u:('be:)/ *die;* ~ *Abk.* **Freie Universität [Berlin]**

Fuchs /fʊks/ *der;* ~**es, Füchse** /'fʏksə/ **(a)** (auch Pelz) fox; **dort sagen sich** ~ **und Hase** *od.* **die Füchse gute Nacht** (scherzh.) it's in the middle of nowhere *or* at the back of beyond; **(b)** (ugs.: schlauer Mensch) **ein [schlauer]** ~: a sly *or* cunning devil; **(c)** (Pferd) chestnut; (heller) sorrel

Fuchs·bau *der; Pl.* ~**baue** fox-den

fuchsen 1 *tr. V.* annoy; vex. 2 *refl. V.* **sich [über etw. (*Akk.*)]** ~: be annoyed [about sth.]

Fuchsie /'fʊksi̯ə/ *die;* ~**,** ~**n** (Bot.) fuchsia

Füchsin /'fʏksɪn/ *die;* ~**,** ~**nen** vixen

fuchs-, Fuchs-: ~**jagd** *die* fox-hunt; (Schleppjagd) drag-hunt; ~**pelz** *der* fox-fur; ~**rot** *Adj.* ginger;

~**schwanz** *der* **(a)** [fox's] brush; foxtail; **(b)** (Bot.) amaranth; love-lies-bleeding; **(c)** (Werkzeug) handsaw; ~**teufels·wild** *Adj.* (ugs.) livid (coll.); hopping mad (coll.)

Fuchtel /'fʊxtl/ *die;* ~**,** ~**n** *o. Pl.* (ugs.: strenge Zucht) **jmdn. unter der/seiner** ~ **haben/halten** have/keep sb. under one's thumb

fuchteln *itr. V.* **mit etw.** ~ (ugs.) wave sth. about

Fuder /'fu:dɐ/ *das;* ~**s,** ~ **(a)** (Wagenladung) cart-load; **(b)** (ugs.: große Menge) load (coll.)

Fuffziger *der;* ~**s,** ~ (ugs.) fifty-pfennig piece; **ein falscher** ~ (salopp) a real crook

Fug /fu:k/ *der* **in mit** ~ **[und Recht]** rightly; justifiably

Fuge¹ /'fu:gə/ *die;* ~**,** ~**n** joint; (Zwischenraum) gap; **der Tisch kracht in allen** ~**n** (ugs.) every joint in the table creaks; **aus den** ~**n gehen** *od.* **geraten/sein** (fig.) be turned completely upside down (fig.)

Fuge² *die;* ~**,** ~**n** (Musik) fugue

fügen /'fy:gn/ 1 *tr. V.* **(a)** (hinzu~) place; set; **Wort an Wort** ~: string words together; **(b)** (geh.: zusammen~) put together; **lose gefügte Bretter** loosely joined boards; **(c)** (geh.: bewirken) ⟨*fate*⟩ ordain, decree; ⟨*person*⟩ arrange. 2 *refl. V.* **(a)** (sich ein~) **sich in etw. (*Akk.*)** ~: fit into sth.; **(b)** (gehorchen) **sich** ~: fall into line; **sich jmdm./einer Sache (*Dat.*)** ~: fall into line with sb./sth.; **er muss lernen, sich zu** ~: he must learn to toe the line; **sich in sein Schicksal** ~: submit to *or* accept one's fate; **(c)** (geh.: geschehen) **es fügt sich gut, dass** ...: it is fortunate that ...

fügsam 1 *Adj.* obedient. 2 *adv.* obediently

Fügsamkeit *die;* ~: obedience

Fügung *die;* ~**,** ~**en (a)** **eine** ~ **Gottes** divine providence; **eine** ~ **des Schicksals** a stroke of fate; **(b)** (Sprachw.) construction

fühlbar 1 *Adj.* **(a)** noticeable; **(b)** (wahrnehmbar) perceptible. 2 *adv.* **(a)** noticeably; **(b)** (wahrnehmbar) perceptibly

fühlen /'fy:lən/ 1 *tr. V.* feel. 2 *refl. V.* **sich krank/bedroht/schuldig** ~: feel sick/threatend/guilty; **sich zu etw. berufen** ~: feel called to be sth.; **sich als Künstler** ~: feel oneself to be an artist; feel one is an artist. 3 *itr. V.* feel; **nach etw.** ~: feel for sth.

Fühler *der;* ~**s,** ~ feeler; antenna; **seine/die** ~ **ausstrecken** (fig.) put out feelers

Fühlung *die;* ~: contact; **mit jmdm.** ~ **bekommen/ [auf]nehmen** get into contact with sb.

Fühlungnahme *die;* ~: initial contact

fuhr /fu:ɐ/ *1. u. 3. Pers. Sg. Prät. v.* **fahren**

Fuhre /'fu:rə/ *die;* ~**,** ~**n (a)** (Wagenladung) load; **(b)** (Transport) trip; journey; (mit Taxi) fare

führen /'fy:rən/ 1 *tr. V.* **(a)** lead; **ein Tier an der Leine** ~: walk an animal on a lead; **jmdn. durch eine Stadt** ~: show sb. around a town; **durch das Programm führt [Sie] Klaus Frank** Klaus Frank will present the programme; **jmdn. auf die richtige Spur** ~: put sb. on the right track; **(b)** (Kaufmannsspr.) stock, sell ⟨*goods*⟩; **(c)** (durch~) **Gespräche** ~: hold conversations; **ein Orts-/ Ferngespräch** ~: make a local/long-distance call; **ein unruhiges Leben** ~: lead a turbulent life; **eine glückliche Ehe** ~: be happily married; **einen Prozess [gegen jmdn.]** ~: take legal action [against sb.]; **(d)** (verantwortlich leiten) manage, run ⟨*company, business, pub, etc.*⟩; lead ⟨*party, country*⟩; command ⟨*regiment*⟩; chair ⟨*committee*⟩; **eine Reisegruppe** ~: be courier to a group of tourists; **(e)** (gelangen lassen) ⟨*journey, road*⟩ take; **was führt Sie zu mir?** what brings you to me?; **(f)** (Amtsspr.) drive ⟨*train, motor, vehicle*⟩; navigate ⟨*ship*⟩; fly ⟨*aircraft*⟩; **(g)** (verlaufen lassen) take ⟨*road, cable, etc.*⟩; **(h)** (als Kennzeichnung, Bezeichnung haben) bear; **einen Titel/Künstlernamen** ~: have a title/use a stage name; **den Titel „Professor"** ~: use the title of professor; **(i)** (angelegt haben) keep ⟨*diary, list, file*⟩; **(j)** (befördern) carry; **der Zug führt einen Speisewagen** the train has a dining car; **der Fluss führt Hochwasser** the river is in flood; **(k)** (registriert haben) **jmdn. in einer Kartei** ~: have sb. on file; **(l)** (tragen) **etw. bei** *od.* **mit sich** ~: have sth. on one; **eine Waffe bei sich** ~: carry a weapon. 2 *itr. V.* **(a)** lead; **die Straße führt nach .../durch .../über ...:** the road leads *or* goes to …/goes through …/goes over …; **das würde zu weit** ~ (fig.) that would be taking things too far; **(b)** (an der Spitze liegen) lead; be ahead; **nach Punkten** ~: be ahead on points; **in der Tabelle** ~: be the league leaders; be at the top of the league; **(c) zu etw.** ~ (etw. bewirken) lead to sth.; **zum Ziel** ~: bring the desired result; **das führt zu nichts** (ugs.) that won't get you/us *etc.* anywhere (coll.). **3** *refl. V.* **sich gut/schlecht** ~: conduct oneself *or* behave well/badly

führend *Adj.* leading ⟨*politician, figure, role*⟩; prominent ⟨*position*⟩; **auf einem Gebiet** ~ **sein** be a leader in a field

Führer *der;* ~**s,** ~ **(a)** leader; **der** ~ (ns.) the Führer; **(b)** (Fremden~) guide; **(c)** (Handbuch) guide, guidebook **(durch** to)

Führer·haus *das* driver's cab

Führerin *die;* ~, ~**nen (a)** leader; **(b)** (Fremden~) guide

führer·los 1 *Adj.* **(a)** leaderless; **(b)** (ohne Lenker) driverless ⟨*car*⟩; pilotless ⟨*aircraft*⟩; **2** *adv.* **(a)** without a leader; **(b)** (ohne Lenker) ⇒ **1b**: without a driver; without a pilot

Führer·schein *der* driving licence (Brit.); driver's license (Amer.); **den** ~ **machen** (ugs.) learn to drive

Fuhr·park *der* transport fleet

Führung *die;* ~, ~**en (a)** *o. Pl.* ⇒ **führen 1 d:** management; running; leadership; command; chairmanship; **(b)** (Fremden~) guided tour; **(c)** *o. Pl.* (führende Position) lead; **in etw.** (*Dat.*) **die** ~ **haben** be leading *or* the leader/leaders in sth.; **in** ~ **liegen/gehen** (Sport) be in/go into the lead; **(d)** *o. Pl.* (Erziehung) guidance; **eine feste** ~: a firm hand; firm guidance; **(e)** *o. Pl.* (leitende Gruppe) leaders *pl.;* (einer Partei) leadership; (einer Firma) directors *pl.;* (eines Regiments) commanders *pl.;* **(f)** *o. Pl.* (Betragen) conduct; **(g)** *o. Pl.* (eines Registers, Protokolls usw.) keeping

Führungs-: ~**anspruch** *der* claim to leadership; **einen** ~**anspruch erheben** lay claim to the leadership; ~**aufgabe** *die* (im Betrieb) management function; (Politik) leadership function; ~**kraft** *die* manager; ~**spitze** *die* (Politik) top leadership; (im Betrieb) top management; ~**zeugnis** *das document issued by police certifying that holder has no criminal record*

Fuhr-: ~**unternehmen** *das* haulage business; ~**unternehmer** *der* haulage contractor; ~**werk** *das* cart (*drawn by horse[s], ox[en], etc.*)

Fülle /ˈfʏlə/ *die;* ~ **(a)** wealth; abundance; **eine** ~ **von Arbeit** an enormous amount of work; **in** ~: in plenty; in abundance; **(b)** (Körper~) corpulence

füllen 1 *tr. V.* **(a)** fill; **bis zum Rand gefüllt sein** be full to the brim; **der Saal ist bis auf den letzten Platz gefüllt** the hall is completely full; *s. auch* **gefüllt; (b)** (fig.) fill in ⟨*gap, time*⟩; **(c)** (mit einer Füllung versehen) stuff ⟨*fowl, tomato, apple, mattress, toy*⟩; fill ⟨*tooth*⟩; *s. auch* **gefüllt; (d)** (schütten) pour; **etw. in Flaschen/Säcke** ~: bottle sth./put sth. into sacks; **(e)** (einnehmen) fill ⟨*space etc.*⟩. **2** *refl. V.* fill [up]; **sich mit etw.** ~: fill up with sth.

Füller *der;* ~**s,** ~, **Füll·federhalter** *der;* ~**s,** ~ [fountain-]pen

Füll·gewicht *das* net weight

füllig *Adj.* corpulent, portly ⟨*person*⟩; ample, portly ⟨*figure*⟩; full ⟨*face*⟩; ample ⟨*bosom*⟩

Füllung *die;* ~, ~**en (a)** (in Geflügel, Paprika usw., in Kissen, Matratzen) stuffing; (in Pasteten, Kuchen) filling; (in Schokolade, Pralinen) centre; **(b)** (Zahnmed.) filling; **(c)** (Teil der Tür) panel

Füll·wort *das; Pl.* **-wörter** filler; (Sprachw., Literaturw.) expletive

Fummel /ˈfʊml/ *der;* ~**s,** ~ (salopp) rags *pl.*

Fummelei *die;* ~, ~**en** (ugs.) **(a)** twiddling; **das ist eine furchtbare** ~: it's terribly fiddly; **(b)** (Petting) petting; groping (coll.)

fummeln *itr. V.* **(a)** (ugs.: fingern) fiddle; **an etw.** (*Dat.*) ~: fiddle [around] with sth.; **nach etw.** ~: grope for *or* feel for sth.; **(b)** (ugs.: erotisch) pet

Fund /fʊnt/ *der;* ~**[e]s,** ~**e** find

Fundament /fʊndaˈmɛnt/ *das;* ~**[e]s,** ~**e (a)** (Bauw.) foundations *pl.;* **das** ~ **legen** *od.* **mauern** lay the foundations; **etw. in seinen** ~**en erschüttern** (fig.) strike at the very foundations of sth.; **(b)** (Basis) base; basis

fundamental /fʊndamɛnˈtaːl/ *Adj.* fundamental

Fundamentalismus *der;* ~: fundamentalism

Fundamentalist *der;* ~**en,** ~**en, Fundamentalistin** *die;* ~, ~**nen** fundamentalist

Fund-: ~**büro** *das* lost property office (Brit.); lost and found office (Amer.); ~**grube** *die* treasure house

fundieren /fʊnˈdiːrən/ *tr. V.* underpin; **ein wissenschaftlich fundierter Vortrag** a scientifically sound lecture

fündig /ˈfʏndɪç/ *Adj.* ~ **sein** yield something; ~ **werden** make a find; (bei Bohrungen) make a strike

Fund-: ~**ort** *der,* ~**stelle** *die* place *or* site where sth. is/was found

Fundus /ˈfʊndʊs/ *der;* ~, ~ **(a)** (Requisition) equipment store; **(b)** (Bestand) **einen** ~ **von/an etw.** (*Dat.*) **haben** have a fund of sth.

fünf /fʏnf/ *Kardinalz.* ▶ 22 , ▶ 530 , ▶ 600 five; ~**[e] gerade sein lassen** (fig. ugs.) let sth. pass; **man muss manchmal** ~**[e] gerade sein lassen** (ugs.) one has to turn a blind eye sometimes; **[um]** ~ **Minuten vor zwölf** (fig.) at the eleventh hour; at the last minute; *s. auch* **acht¹; Sinn a**

Fünf *die;* ~, ~**en** five; **eine** ~ **schreiben/bekommen** (Schulw.) get an E; *s. auch* **Acht¹ a, d, e**

fünf-, Fünf- (*s. auch* **acht-, Acht-**)*:* ~**eck** *das;* ~**s,** ~**e** pentagon; ~**eckig** *Adj.* pentagonal; five-cornered

Fünfer *der;* ~**s,** ~ (ugs.) **(a)** (Geldschein, Münze) five; **(b)** (ugs.: Ziffer) five; **(c)** (Lottogewinn) five out of six; **(d)** (ugs.: Sprungturm) five-metre platform

fünf-, Fünf-: ~**fach** *Vervielfältigungsz.* fivefold; quintuple; *s. auch* **achtfach;** ~**fache** *das; adj. Dekl.* five times as much; quintuple; *s. auch* **Achtfache;** ~**hundert** *Kardinalz.* ▶ 600 five hundred; ~**hundert·jahr·feier** *die* quincentenary; ~**jahres·plan** *der* five-year plan; ~**jährig** *Adj.* (~ Jahre alt) five-year-old; (~ Jahre dauernd) five-year; ~**kampf** *der* (Sport) pentathlon; ~**kämpfer** *der,* ~**kämpferin** *die* (Sport) pentathlete; ~**köpfig** *Adj.* ⟨*family, crew*⟩ of five; five-headed ⟨*monster*⟩

Fünfling /ˈfʏnflɪŋ/ *der;* ~**s,** ~**e** quintuplet; quin (coll.)

fünf-, Fünf-: ~**mal** *Adv.* five times; *s. auch* **achtmal;** ~**markstück** *das* ▶ 216 five-mark piece; ~**meter·raum** *der* (Fußball) goal area; ~**pfennig·stück** *das* ▶ 216 five-pfennig piece; ~**prozentig** *Adj.* five per cent; ~**stellig** *Adj.* five-figure ⟨*number, sum*⟩; *s. auch* **achtstellig;** ~**stöckig** *Adj.* five-storey *attrib.; s. auch* **achtstöckig**

fünft /fʏnft/ ▶ 600 **in wir/sie waren zu** ~: there were five of us/them; *s. auch* **acht²**

fünft... *Ordinalz.* ▶ 600 fifth; *s. auch* **acht…**

fünf-, Fünf-: ~**tage·woche** *die* five-day [working] week; ~**tägig** *Adj.* five-day; *s. auch* **achttägig;** ~**tausend** *Kardinalz.* ▶ 600 five thousand; ~**teilig** *Adj.* five-part; *s. auch* **achtteilig**

fünftel /ˈfʏnftl/ *Bruchz.* ▶ 600 fifth; *s. auch* **achtel**

Fünftel *das* (schweiz. meist *der*) ▶ 600 ; ~**s,** ~: fifth

fünftens /ˈfʏnftn̩s/ *Adv.* fifthly; in the fifth place

fünf-: ~**zehn** *Kardinalz.* ▶ 22 , ▶ 530 , ▶ 600 fifteen; *s. auch* **achtzehn;** ~**zehn·jährig** *Adj.* (15 Jahre alt) fifteen-year-old *attrib.;* (15 Jahre dauernd) fifteen-year *attrib.*

fünfzig /ˈfʏnftsɪç/ *Kardinalz.* ▶ 22 , ▶ 600 fifty; *s. auch* **achtzig**

fünfziger *indekl. Adj.; nicht präd.* **die** ~ **Jahre** the fifties; *s. auch* **achtziger**

Fünfziger *der;* ~**s,** ~ **(a)** fifty-year-old; **(b)** (Münze, Geldschein) fifty

Fünfziger·jahre *Pl.* ▶ 22 , ▶ 119 fifties *pl.*

fünfzig·jährig *Adj.* (50 Jahre alt) fifty-year-old *attrib.;* (50 Jahre dauernd) fifty-year *attrib.*

fünfzigst... /ˈfʏnftsɪçst.../ *Ordinalz.* ▶ 600 fiftieth; *s. auch* **acht…**

fungieren /fʊŋˈgiːrən/ *itr. V.* **als etw.** ~ ⟨*person*⟩ act as sth.; ⟨*word etc.*⟩ function as sth.

Funk /fʊŋk/ *der;* ~**s (a)** (drahtlose Übermittlung) radio; **über** ~: by radio; **(b)** (Rund~) radio; **beim** ~ **sein** (ugs.) *od.* arbeiten be (coll.) *or* work in radio

Funk·amateur *der* radio ham

Fünkchen /'fʏŋkçən/ *das;* ~s, ~: ⇨ **Funke b**

Funke /'fʊŋkə/ *der;* ~ns, ~n (a) spark; ~n sprühen send out a shower of sparks; (fig.) ⟨*eyes*⟩ flash; (b) (fig.) **der** ~ **der Begeisterung** the spark of enthusiasm; **kein** ~ *od.* **Fünkchen [von] Verstand/Ehrgefühl/Mitleid** not a glimmer of understanding/shred of honour/scrap of sympathy

funkeln /'fʊŋkln̩/ *itr. V.* ⟨*light, star*⟩ twinkle, sparkle; ⟨*gold, diamonds*⟩ glitter, sparkle; ⟨*eyes*⟩ blaze

funkel·nagel·neu *Adj.* (ugs.) brand new; spanking new (coll.)

funken /'fʊŋkn̩/ **1** *tr. V.* radio; ⟨*transmitter*⟩ broadcast; **SOS** ~: send out an SOS. **2** *itr. V.; unpers.* (fig. ugs.) **es hat gefunkt** (es hat Streit gegeben) the sparks flew; (man hat sich verliebt) something clicked between them/us (coll.); **es hat bei ihm gefunkt** the penny's dropped [with him] (coll.)

Funker *der;* ~s, ~: ▶ 85 radio operator

Funk-: ~**gerät** *das* radio set; (tragbar) walkie-talkie; ~**haus** *das* broadcasting centre; ~**kolleg** *das* radio-based [adult education] course; ~**sprech·gerät** *das* radiophone; (tragbar) walkie-talkie; ~**sprech·verkehr** *der* radio telephony; ~**spruch** *der* radio signal; (Nachricht) radio message; ~**stille** *die* radio silence; **bei ihm herrscht** ~**stille** (fig.) he's keeping quiet; ~**streife** *die* [police] radio patrol; ~**taxi** *das* radio taxi; ~**technik** *die* radio technology

Funktion /fʊnk'tsi̯oːn/ *die;* ~, ~en (a) function; (b) *o. Pl.* (Tätigkeit, Arbeiten) functioning, working; **in** ~ **sein/in** ~ (*Akk.*) **treten** be in operation/come into operation; **jmdn./etw. außer** ~ **setzen** put sb./sth. out of operation

funktional /fʊŋktsi̯oˈnaːl/ **1** *Adj.* functional. **2** *adv.* functionally

Funktionär /fʊŋktsi̯oˈnɛːɐ̯/ *der;* ~s, ~e, **Funktionärin** *die;* ~, ~nen official; functionary

funktionieren *itr. V.* work; function

funktions-, Funktions-: ~**fähig** *Adj.* able to function *or* work *pred.;* ~**störung** *die* (Med.) functional disorder; dysfunction; ~**tüchtig** *Adj.* working ⟨*equipment, part*⟩; sound ⟨*organ*⟩

Funk-: ~**turm** *der* radio tower; ~**verbindung** *die* radio contact; ~**verkehr** *der* radio communication

Funzel /'fʊntsl̩/ *die;* ~, ~n (ugs., abwertend) useless lamp *or* light; **bei dieser** ~: in this gloomy light

für /fyːɐ̯/ *Präp. mit Akk.* (a) for; ~ **jmdn. bestimmt sein** be meant for sb.; **das ist nichts** ~ **mich** that's not for me; **Lehrer** ~ **etw. sein** be a teacher of sth.; ~ **sich** by oneself; on one's own; **sich** ~ **jmdn. freuen** be pleased for sb.; ~ **immer** for ever; for good; ~ **gewöhnlich** usually; ~ **nichts und wieder nichts** for absolutely nothing; (b) (zugunsten) for; ~ **jmdn./etw. sein** be for *or* in favour of sb./sth.; **das hat etwas** ~ **sich** it has something to be said for it; **das Für und Wider** the pros and cons *pl.;* (c) (als) etw. ~ **zulässig erklären** declare sth. admissible; **jmdn.** ~ **tot erklären** declare sb. dead; (d) (anstelle) for; ~ **jmdn. einspringen** take sb.'s place; ~ **zwei arbeiten** do the work of two people; (e) (als Stellvertreter) for; on behalf of; (f) (um) **Jahr** ~ **Jahr** year after year; **Wort** ~ **Wort** word for word; **Schritt** ~ **Schritt** step by step *s. auch* **was 1**

Für·bitte *die* intercession; **[bei jmdm.] für jmdn.** ~ **einlegen** intercede [with sb.] for sb.

Furche /'fʊrçə/ *die;* ~, ~n (a) furrow; ~n **auf der Stirn haben** have a furrowed brow; (b) (Rille) groove

furchen *tr. V.* (geh.) furrow

Furcht /fʊrçt/ *die;* ~: fear; ~ **vor jmdm./etw. haben** fear sb./sth.; **jmdm.** ~ **einflößen** frighten sth.; **aus** ~ **vor jmdm./etw.** for fear of sb./sth.; **jmdn. in** ~ **und Schrecken versetzen** fill sb. with terror; terrify sb.

furchtbar 1 *Adj.* (a) awful; frightful; dreadful; **es war mir** ~, **das tun zu müssen** it was awful [for me] to have to do it; (b) (ugs.: unangenehm) awful (coll.); terrible (coll.); **ein** ~**er Angeber** an awful *or* frightful show-off (coll.). **2** *adv.* (ugs.) awfully (coll.); terribly (coll.); ~ **lachen [müssen]**

laugh oneself silly (coll.); **es dauerte** ~ **lange** it took an awfully long time

furcht·einflößend *Adj.* fearsome; frightening

fürchten 1 *refl. V.* **sich [vor jmdm./etw.]** ~: be afraid *or* frightened [of sb./sth.]; **es ist zum Fürchten** it is quite frightening. **2** *tr. V.* fear; be afraid of; **ein gefürchteter Kritiker** a feared critic; **ich fürchte, [dass]** …: I'm afraid [that] … **3** *itr. V.* **für** *od.* **um jmdn./etw.** ~: fear for sb./sth.

fürchterlich *Adj.* ⇨ **furchtbar**

furcht·erregend *Adj.* frightening

furcht·los 1 *Adj.* fearless. **2** *adv.* fearlessly

Furcht·losigkeit *die;* ~: fearlessness

furchtsam /'fʊrçtzaːm/ **1** *Adj.* timid; fearful. **2** *adv.* timidly; fearfully

Furchtsamkeit *die;* ~, ~en timidity; fearfulness

für·einander *Adv.* for one another; for each other

Furie /'fuːri̯ə/ *die;* ~, ~n Fury; **sie wurde zur** ~ (fig.) she started acting like a woman possessed

Furnier /fʊrˈniːɐ̯/ *das;* ~s, ~e veneer

Furore /fuˈroːrə/ **in** ~ **machen** cause a sensation *or* stir

fürs /fyːɐ̯s/ *Präp. + Art.* (a) = **für das**; (b) ~ **erste** for the time being

Für·sorge *die;* ~ (a) care; (b) (veralt.: Sozialhilfe) welfare; (c) (veralt.: Sozialamt) social services *pl.;* (d) (ugs.: Unterstützungsgeld) social security (Brit.); welfare (Amer.)

für·sorgend 1 *Adj.* caring; thoughtful. **2** *adv.* caringly; thoughtfully

für·sorglich 1 *Adj.* considerate; thoughtful. **2** *adv.* considerately; thoughtfully

Fürsorglichkeit *die;* ~: considerateness; thoughtfulness

Für·sprache *die* support; **bei jmdm. für jmdn.** ~ **einlegen** put in a good word for sb. with sb.

Für·sprecher *der,* **Für·sprecherin** *die* advocate

Fürst /fʏrst/ *der;* ~en, ~en prince

Fürsten-: ~**geschlecht** *das,* ~**haus** *das* royal house

Fürstentum *das;* ~s, **Fürstentümer** /-tyːmɐ/ principality

Fürstin *die;* ~, ~nen princess

fürstlich 1 *Adj.* (a) *nicht präd.* royal; (b) (fig.: üppig) handsome; lavish. **2** *adv.* (a) handsomely; (b) (fig.) handsomely; lavishly

Furt /fʊrt/ *die;* ~, ~en ford

Furunkel /fuˈrʊŋkl̩/ *der od. das;* ~s, ~: boil; furuncle

Für·wort *das;* *Pl.* -**wörter** pronoun

Furz /fʊrts/ *der;* ~es, **Fürze** /'fʏrtsə/ (derb) fart (coarse)

furzen *itr. V.* (derb) fart (coarse)

Fusel /'fuːzl̩/ *der;* ~s, ~ (ugs. abwertend) rotgut (coll. derog.)

Fusion /fuˈzi̯oːn/ *die;* ~, ~en (a) amalgamation; (von Konzernen) merger; (b) (Naturw.) fusion

fusionieren *itr. V.* merge

Fusionmusic /'fjuːʒənmjuːzɪk/ *die;* ~: fusion

Fuß /fuːs/ *der;* ~es, **Füße** /'fyːsə/ (*Dat.*) ▶ 326 foot; **sich** (*Dat.*) **den** ~ **verstauchen/brechen** sprain one's ankle/break a bone in one's foot; **mit bloßen Füßen** barefoot; with bare feet; **jmdm. auf den** ~ **treten** tread on sb.'s foot; **zu** ~ **gehen** go on foot; walk; **gut/schlecht zu** ~ **sein** be a good/bad walker; **jmdm. auf dem** ~**e folgen** follow at sb.'s heels; **bei** ~! heel!; **nimm die Füße weg!** (ugs.) move your feet!; (b) (fig.) **stehenden** ~**es** (veralt., geh.) without delay; instanter (arch.); **sich die Füße nach etw. ablaufen** *od.* **wund laufen** chase round everywhere for sth.; **[festen]** ~ **fassen** find one's feet; **kalte Füße kriegen** (ugs.) get cold feet (coll.); **auf freiem** ~ **sein** be at large; **jmdn. auf freien** ~ **setzen** set sb. free; **auf großem** ~ **leben** live in great style; **jmdm. auf die Füße treten** (ugs.) give sb. a good talking-to; **jmdn./etw. mit Füßen treten** trample on sb./sth.; **jmdm. etw. vor die Füße werfen** throw sth. in sb.'s face; **jmdn. zu Füßen liegen** (geh.: bewundern) adore *or* worship sb.; (c) (tragender Teil) (einer Lampe) base; (eines Weinglases) foot; (eines

Schranks, Sessels, Klaviers) leg; **auf tönernen Füßen stehen** (fig.) be unsoundly based; **(d)** o. Pl. (eines Berges) foot; (einer Säule) base; **(e)** ▶ 159 |, ▶ 277 |, ▶ 340 | Pl.: ~ (Längenmaß) foot; **zwei/drei ~:** two/three feet or foot; **(f)** (Teil des Strumpfes) foot

fuß-, Fuß-: **~abdruck** der footprint; **~abstreifer** der, **~abtreter** der shoe scraper; **~angel** die mantrap; (fig.) trap; **~bad** das foot-bath

Fuß·ball der **(a)** o. Pl. (Ballspiel) [Association] football; soccer (coll.); **(b)** (Ball) football; soccer ball (coll.)

Fuß·ballen der the ball of the/one's foot

Fußballer der; ~s, ~, **Fußballerin** die; ~, ~nen: footballer; soccer player (coll.)

Fußball-: **~mannschaft** die football team; **~meisterschaft** die football championship; **~platz** der football ground; (Spielfeld) football pitch; **~schuh** der football boot; **~spiel** das **(a)** football match; **(b)** o. Pl. (Sportart) football no art.; **~spieler** der football player; **~toto** das od. der football pools pl.; **~verein** der football club

Fuß-: **~bank** die foot-stool; **~boden** der floor

Fußboden-: **~belag** der floor covering; **~heizung** die underfloor heating

Fuß·breit der; ~, ~: foot

Füßchen /'fy:sçən/ das; ~s, ~: [little] foot

Fussel /'fʊsl̩/ die; ~, ~n od. der; ~s, ~[n] fluff; ein[e] ~: a piece of fluff; some fluff

fusselig Adj. covered in fluff postpos.; (ausgefranst) frayed; **sich** (Dat.) **den Mund ~ reden** (salopp) talk till one is blue in the face (coll.)

fusseln itr. V. make fluff

fußen itr. V. **auf etw.** (Dat.) ~: be based on sth.

Fuß·ende das foot

Fußgänger /-gɛŋɐ/ der; ~s, ~, **Fußgängerin**, die; ~, ~nen: pedestrian

Fußgänger-: **~brücke** die foot bridge; **~übergang** der, **~überweg** der pedestrian crossing; **~unterführung** die pedestrian subway; **~zone** die pedestrian precinct

fuß-, Fuß-: **~gelenk** das ankle; **~hebel** der foot pedal; **~kalt** Adj. **das Zimmer ist ~kalt** the room has a cold floor; **~kettchen** das anklet; **~leiste** die skirtingboard (Brit.); baseboard (Amer.); **~marsch** der march; **~matte** die doormat; **~nagel** der toenail; **~note** die footnote; **~pflege** die foot treatment; (beruflich) chiropody; **~pfleger** der, **~pflegerin** die ▶ 85 | chiropodist; **~pilz** der ▶ 329 | athlete's foot; **~schweiß** der foot perspiration; **~sohle** die sole [of the/one's foot]; **~spitze** die: **auf den ~spitzen** walk on tiptoe; **~spur** die footprint; (Fährte) line of footprints; tracks pl.; **~stapfen** der; ~s, ~: footprint; **in jmds. ~stapfen** (Akk.) **treten** (fig.) follow in sb.'s footsteps; **~tritt** der kick; **jmdm./einer Sache einen ~tritt geben** od. **versetzen** (fig.) give sb./sth. a kick; **einen ~tritt bekommen** (fig.) get a kick in the teeth (coll.); **~volk** das **(a)** (hist.) footmen pl.; **(b)** (abwertend: Untergeordnete) lower ranks pl.; dogsbodies pl. (coll.); **~wanderung** die ramble; **~weg** der **(a)** (Gehweg, Bürgersteig) footpath; **(b)** (Gehen zu ~) walk; **eine Stunde/zwei Stunden ~weg** one hour's/two hours' walk

Futon /'fu:tɔn/ der; ~s, ~s futon

futsch /fʊtʃ/ Adj.; nicht attr. (salopp) **~ sein** have gone for a burton (Brit. coll.)

Futter[1] /'fʊtɐ/ das; ~s (Tiernahrung) feed; (für Pferde, Kühe) fodder; **dem Vieh ~ geben** feed the cattle; **gut im ~ sein** od. **stehen** (ugs.) be well-fed

Futter[2] das; ~s (von Kleidungsstücken) lining

Futteral /fʊtəˈraːl/ das; ~s, ~e case

Futter·krippe die manger; (fig.) **an der ~krippe sitzen** (ugs.) be in clover

futtern (ugs.) **1** tr. V. eat. **2** itr. V. feed

füttern[1] /'fʏtɐn/ tr. V. feed

füttern[2] tr. V. (mit Futter[2] ausstatten) line

Futter-: **~napf** der bowl; **~neid** der **(a)** (Verhaltensf.) jealousy [as regards food]; **(b)** (fig. ugs.: Neid) jealousy; envy;

~pflanze die fodder plant; forage plant; **~suche** die search for food; **auf ~suche/bei der ~suche** searching for food; **~trog** der feeding trough

Fütterung die; ~, ~en feeding

Futur /fu'tu:ɐ̯/ das; ~s, ~e (Sprachw.) future [tense]; **das erste/zweite ~:** future/future perfect [tense]

futuristisch (a) futuristic; (b) (den Futurismus betreffend) Futurist

g, G /ge:/ das; ~, ~ **(a)** (Buchstabe) g/G; **(b)** (Musik) [key of] G; s. auch **a, A**

gab /ga:p/ 1. u. 3. Pers. Sg. Prät. v. **geben**

Gabardine /'gabardi:n/ der; ~s od. die; ~: gabardine

Gabe /'ga:bə/ die; ~, ~n **(a)** (geh.: Geschenk) gift; present; **eine ~ Gottes** a gift of God; **(b)** (Almosen, Spende) alms pl.; (an eine Sammlung) donation; **(c)** (geh.: Begabung, Talent) gift; **die ~ haben, etw. zu tun** have the gift or (iron.) knack of doing sth.

gäbe /'gɛ:bə/ 1. u. 3. Pers. Sg. Konjunktiv II v. **geben**; s. auch **gang**

Gabel /'ga:bl̩/ die; ~, ~n **(a)** fork; **(b)** (Heu~, Mist~) pitchfork; **(c)** (Telefon~) rest; cradle; **(d)** (Fahrrad~) fork; **(e)** (Ast~) fork

gabel·förmig Adj. forked

Gabel·frühstück das cold buffet; fork lunch

gabeln refl. V. fork; (fig.: sich teilen) divide

Gabel·stapler /-ʃtaːplɐ/ der; ~s, ~: fork-lift truck

Gabelung die; ~, ~en fork

Gaben·tisch der gift table (at Christmas and on birthdays)

gackern /'gakɐn/ itr. V. **(a)** cluck; **(b)** (ugs.: kichern, lachen) cackle

gaffen /'gafn̩/ itr. V. (abwertend) gape; gawp (coll.)

Gaffer der; ~s, ~: gaper; starer

Gag /gɛk/ der; ~s, ~s **(a)** (Theater, Film) gag; **(b)** (Besonderheit) gimmick

Gage /'ga:ʒə/ die; ~, ~n salary; (für einzelnen Auftritt) fee

gähnen /'gɛ:nən/ itr. V. **(a)** yawn; **im Saal herrschte ~de Leere** the hall was totally empty; **(b)** (geh.: sich auftun) ⟨chasm, abyss⟩ yawn; ⟨hole⟩ gape

Gala /'ga:la, auch 'gala/ die; ~ **(a)** (Festkleidung) formal or gala dress; **(b)** (Veranstaltung) gala

Gala-: **~abend** der [evening] gala; **~diner** das formal dinner; banquet; **~empfang** der gala or formal reception

galaktisch /ga'laktɪʃ/ Adj. galactic; **~er Nebel** [galactic] nebula

galant /ga'lant/ **1** Adj. **(a)** (veralt.) gallant; **(b)** (amourös) amorous ⟨adventure⟩. **2** adv. gallantly

Gala·vorstellung die gala performance

Galaxie /gala'ksi:/ die; ~, ~n (Astron.) galaxy

Galeere /ga'le:rə/ die; ~, ~n galley

Galerie /galə'ri:/ die; ~, ~n **(a)** gallery; **(b)** (bes. österr., schweiz.: Tunnel) tunnel

Galerist /galə'rɪst/ der; ~en, ~en gallery-owner

Galgen /'galgn̩/ der gallows sing.; gibbet; **jmdn. an den ~ bringen** (ugs.) bring sb. to the gallows

Galgen-: **~frist** die reprieve; **~humor** der gallows humour; **~strick** der, **~vogel** der (ugs. abwertend) rogue

Galions·figur /ga'lio:ns-/ die figurehead

Galle /'galə/ die; ~, ~n **(a)** ▶ 326 | (Gallenblase) gall[-bladder]; **(b)** (Sekret) (bei Tieren) gall; (bei Menschen) bile; **bitter wie ~:** extremely bitter; **mir lief die ~ über** od. **kam die ~ hoch** (fig.) my blood boiled

Gallen-: ~**blase** *die* ▶326⌋ gall-bladder; ~**kolik** *die* ▶329⌋ biliary colic; ~**leiden** *das* ▶329⌋ gall-bladder complaint; ~**stein** *der* ▶329⌋ gallstone

Gallert /'galɐt/ *das;* ~[e]s jelly

Galopp /ga'lɔp/ *der;* ~s, ~s *od.* ~e gallop; **im/in gestrecktem** ~: at a/at full gallop; **in** ~ **fallen** break into a gallop; **etw. im** ~ **machen** (fig. ugs.) race through sth.

Galopp·bahn *die* (Pferdesport) racetrack; racecourse

Galopper *der;* ~s, ~ (Pferd) racehorse; (Reiter) jockey

galoppieren *itr. V.; meist mit sein* gallop; **die** ~**de Inflation** galloping inflation

Galopp·rennen *das* (Pferdesport) race

galt /galt/ *1. u. 3. Pers. Sg. Prät. v.* **gelten**

galvanisch /gal'vaːnɪʃ/ *Adj.* galvanic

galvanisieren *tr. V.* electroplate

Gamasche /ga'maʃə/ *die;* ~, ~n gaiter; (bis zum Knöchel) spat

Gambe /'gambə/ *die;* ~, ~n (Musik) viola da gamba

Gamma /'gama/ *das;* ~[s], ~s gamma

Gamma·strahlen *Pl.* (Physik, Med.) gamma rays

Gammel /'gaml̩/ *der;* ~s (ugs.) junk (coll.)

gammelig /'gam(ə)lɪç/ *Adj.* (ugs.) (a) bad; rotten; (b) (unordentlich) scruffy

gammeln /'gaml̩n/ *itr. V.* (ugs.) (a) go bad; go off; (b) (nichts tun) loaf around; bum around (Amer. coll.)

Gammler /'gamlɐ/ *der;* ~s, ~, **Gammlerin** *die;* ~, ~**nen** (ugs.) drop-out (coll.)

Gämse /'gɛmzə/ *die;* ~, ~n chamois

gang /gaŋ/ *in* ~ **und gäbe sein** be quite usual; be the usual *or* accepted thing

Gang¹ /gaŋ/ *der;* ~[e]s, **Gänge** /'gɛŋə/ (a) (Gehweise) walk; gait; **jmdn. am** ~ **erkennen** recognise sb. by the way he/she walks; (b) (zu einem Ort) **einen** ~ **in die Stadt machen** go to town; **einen schweren** ~ **tun** *od.* **gehen [müssen]** (fig.) [have to] do a difficult thing; (c) (Besorgung) errand; (d) *o. Pl.* (Bewegung) running; **etw. in** ~ **bringen** *od.* **setzen/halten** get/keep sth. going; **in** ~ **sein** be going; (Maschine) be running; **in** ~ **kommen** get going; get off the ground; (e) *o. Pl.* (Verlauf) course; **seinen [gewohnten]** ~ **gehen** go on as usual; **im** ~[e] **sein** be in progress; (f) (Technik) gear; **den ersten** ~ **einlegen** engage first gear; **in den ersten** ~ **[zurück]schalten** change [down] into first gear; **einen** ~ **zulegen** (fig. ugs.) get a move on (coll.); (g) (Flur) (in Zügen, Gebäuden usw.) corridor; (Verbindungs~) passage[-way]; (im Theater, Kino, Flugzeug) aisle; (h) (unterirdisch) tunnel; passage[way]; (im Bergwerk) gallery; (eines Tierbaus) tunnel; (i) (Kochk.) course

Gang² /gɛŋ/ *die;* ~, ~s (Bande) gang

Gang·art *die* walk; way of walking; gait; (eines Pferdes) gait; **eine schnellere** ~ **anschlagen** step up the pace

gangbar *Adj.* passable; **ein** ~**er Weg** (fig.) a feasible *or* practicable way

Gängel·band /'gɛŋəl-/ *das in* **jmdn. am** ~ **führen** keep sb. in leading-reins

gängeln /'gɛŋl̩n/ *tr. V.* **jmdn.** ~ (ugs.) boss sb. around; tell sb. what to do

gängig /'gɛŋɪç/ *Adj.* (a) (üblich) common; (b) (leicht verkäuflich) popular; in demand *postpos.*

Gang·schaltung *die* gear change; **ein Fahrrad mit** ~: a bicycle with gears

Gangster /'gɛŋstɐ/ *der;* ~s, ~ (abwertend) gangster

Gangster-: ~**bande** *die* gang [of criminals]; ~**boss,** ***~**boß** *der* (ugs.) gang boss

Gangway /'gæŋweɪ/ *die;* ~, ~s gangway

Ganove /ga'noːvə/ *der;* ~n, ~n (ugs. abwertend) crook (coll.)

Gans /gans/ *die;* ~, **Gänse** /'gɛnzə/ (a) goose; (b) (abwertend: weibliche Person) **eine [dumme/alberne/blöde]** ~: a silly goose

Gänse-: ~**blümchen** *das* daisy; ~**braten** *der* roast goose; ~**feder** *die* goose-feather; goose-quill; ~**füßchen** *das; meist Pl.* (ugs.) ⇒ **Anführungszeichen;** ~**haut** *die* (fig.) goose-flesh; goose pimples *pl.;* ~**leber·pastete** *die* pâté de foie gras; ~**marsch** *in* **im** ~**marsch** in single *or* Indian file

Gänserich /'gɛnzərɪç/ *der;* ~s, ~e gander

Gänse·schmalz *das* goose dripping

ganz /gants/ ▶600⌋ **1** *Adj.* (a) *nicht präd.* (gesamt) whole; entire; **den** ~**en Tag** all day; **die** ~**e Welt** the whole world; **die** ~**e Straße** (alle Bewohner) everybody in the street; ~ **Europa** the whole of Europe; **wir fuhren durch** ~ **Frankreich** we travelled all over France; ~**e Arbeit leisten** do a complete *or* proper job; **die** ~**e Geschichte** *od.* **Sache** (ugs.) the whole story *or* business; (b) *nicht präd.* (ugs.: sämtlich) **die** ~**e Milch** all the milk; **die** ~**en Leute** *usw.* all the people *etc.;* (c) *nicht präd.* (vollständig) whole ⟨*number, truth*⟩; **eine** ~**e Note** (Musik) a semibreve (Brit.); a whole note (Amer.); **im Ganzen sechs Tage** six days in all *or* altogether; **im [Großen und] Ganzen** on the whole; all in all; (d) *nicht präd.* (ugs.: ziemlich groß) **eine** ~**e Menge/ein** ~**er Haufen** quite a lot/quite a pile; (e) (ugs.: unversehrt) intact; **etw. wieder** ~ **machen** mend sth.; (f) *nicht präd.* (ugs.: nur) all of; ~ **e 14 Jahre alt** all of fourteen [years old]. **2** *adv.* (a) (vollkommen) quite; **das ist mir** ~ **egal** it's all the same to me; I don't care; **etw.** ~ **vergessen** completely *or* quite forget sth.; **etwas** ~ **anderes** something quite different; **etw.** ~ **allein tun** *od.* **machen** do sth. entirely on one's own; **nicht** ~: not quite; ~ **besonders** especially; **sie ist** ~ **die Mutter** she's the image of *or* just like her mother; ~ **und gar** totally; utterly; (b) (sehr, ziemlich) quite; **es ist mir** ~ **recht** it's quite all right with me

Ganze *das; adj. Dekl.* (a) (Einheit) whole; (b) (alles) **das** ~: the whole thing; **aufs** ~ **gehen** (ugs.) go the whole hog (coll.)

Gänze /'gɛntsə/ *in* **in seiner/ihrer** ~ (geh.) in its/their entirety

ganz·jährig 1 *Adj.; nicht präd.* **die** ~**e Trockenperiode** the dry period lasting all year. **2** *adv.* ~ **geöffnet** open throughout the year *or* all the year round

gänzlich /'gɛntslɪç/ **1** *Adv.* completely; entirely. **2** *Adj.* complete; total

ganz·tägig 1 *Adj.; nicht präd.* all-day; **eine** ~**tägige Arbeit** a full-time job; **2** *adv.* all day

ganz·tags *Adv.* ~ **arbeiten** work full-time

Ganztags-: ~**beschäftigung** *die; o. Pl.* full-time job; ~**schule** *die* all-day school; (System) all-day schooling *no art.*

gar¹ /gaːɐ̯/ *Adj.* cooked; done *pred.;* **etw.** ~ **kochen** cook sth. [until it is done]

gar² *Partikel* (a) (überhaupt) ~ **nicht [wahr]** not [true] at all; ~ **nichts** nothing at all *or* whatsoever; ~ **niemand** *od.* **keiner** nobody at all *or* whatsoever; ~ **keines** not a single one; (b) (südd., österr., schweiz.: verstärkend) ~ **zu** only too; **er wäre** ~ **zu gern gekommen** he would so much have liked to come; (c) (geh.: sogar) even; (d) (veralt.: sehr) very

Garage /ga'raːʒə/ *die;* ~, ~n garage

Garantie /garan'tiː/ *die;* ~, ~n (a) (Gewähr) guarantee (**für** of); (b) (Kaufmannsspr.) guarantee; warranty; **eine** ~ **auf etw.** (*Akk.*) **geben** guarantee sth.; **für** *od.* **auf etw.** (*Akk.*) **ein Jahr** ~ **erhalten** get a one year guarantee on sth.; (c) (Sicherheit) guarantee; surety

Garantie·frist *die* guarantee period

garantieren 1 *tr. V.* guarantee; **jmdm. etw.** ~: guarantee sb. sth. **2** *itr. V.* **für etw.** ~: guarantee sth.

garantiert *Adv.* (ugs.) **wir kommen** ~ **zu spät** we're dead certain to arrive late (coll.)

Garantie·schein *der* guarantee [certificate]

Garaus /'gaːɐ̯|aʊs/ *in* **jmdm. den** ~ **machen** do sb. in (coll.); **dem Unkraut den** ~ **machen** get rid of the weeds

Garbe /'garbə/ *die;* ~, ~n (a) (Getreide~) sheaf; (b) (Geschoss~) burst [of fire]

Garde /'gardə/ *die;* ~, ~n (a) (Milit., Leib~) guard; (b) (Gruppe) team

Garderobe /gardə'roːbə/ *die;* ~, ~n (a) *o. Pl.* (Oberbekleidung) wardrobe; clothes *pl.;* **die passende** ~: suitable clothes; **für** ~ **wird nicht gehaftet!** clothes are left at the owner's risk; (b) (Flur~) coat-rack; (c) (im Theater o. Ä.) cloakroom; checkroom (Amer.); (d) (Ankleideraum) dressing room

Garderoben-: ~**frau** *die* ▶85┃ cloakroom *or* (Amer.) checkroom attendant; ~**marke** *die* cloakroom *or* (Amer.) checkroom ticket; ~**ständer** *der* coat-stand

Gardine /gar'di:nə/ *die;* ~, ~**n** (a) net curtain; (b) (landsch., veralt.) curtain; *s. auch* **schwedisch**

Gardinen-: ~**leiste** *die* curtain rail; ~**predigt** *die* (ugs.) telling-off (coll.); (einer Ehefrau zu ihrem Mann) curtain lecture; ~**stange** *die* curtain rail

garen /'ga:rən/ *tr., itr. V.* cook

gären /'gɛ:rən/ *regelm.* (*auch unr.*) *itr. V.* ferment; (fig.) seethe

Garn /garn/ *das;* ~[e]s, ~**e** (a) thread; (Näh~) cotton; (b) (fig.) [s]ein ~ spinnen spin a yarn; **jmdm. ins** ~ **gehen** fall *or* walk into sb.'s trap

Garnele /gar'ne:lə/ *die;* ~, ~**n** shrimp

garnieren /gar'ni:rən/ *tr. V.* (a) (schmücken) decorate (*mit* with); (b) (Gastr.) garnish

Garnierung *die;* ~, ~**en** (a) garnish; (b) (Vorgang) garnishing

Garnison /garni'zo:n/ *die;* ~, ~**en** garrison

Garnison·stadt *die* garrison town

Garnitur /garni'tu:ɐ̯/ *die;* ~, ~**en** (a) set; (Wäsche) set of [matching] underwear; (Möbel) suite; **eine zweiteilige** ~: a two-piece suite; (b) (ugs.) **die erste/zweite** ~: the first/ second-rate people *pl.;* **zur ersten/zweiten** ~ **gehören** be first-/second-rate; (c) (Gastr.) garnishing; garniture

Garn-: ~**knäuel** *das od. der* ball of thread; ~**rolle** *die* reel; bobbin; (von Nähgarn) cotton reel

garstig /'garstɪç/ *Adj.* (a) (boshaft) nasty (**zu** to); bad ‹*behaviour*›; nasty, naughty, (coll.) horrid ‹*child*›; (b) (abscheulich) horrible; nasty

Garten /'gartn̩/ *der;* ~s, **Gärten** /'gɛrtn̩/ garden; *s. auch* **zoologisch**

Garten-: ~**arbeit** *die* gardening; ~**bau** *der o. Pl.* horticulture; ~**erde** *die* garden mould; ~**fest** *das* garden party; ~**gerät** *das* garden tool; ~**haus** *das,* ~**laube** *die* summer house; garden house; ~**lokal** *das* beer garden; (Restaurant) open-air café; ~**party** ⇒ ~**fest;** ~**schlauch** *der* garden hose; ~**stuhl** *der* garden chair; ~**zaun** *der* garden fence; ~**zwerg** *der* garden gnome

Gärtner /'gɛrtnɐ/ *der;* ~s, ~: ▶85┃ gardener

Gärtnerei *die;* ~, ~**en** nursery

Gärtnerin *die;* ~, ~**nen** ▶85┃ gardener

Gärung *die;* ~, ~**en** (a) fermentation; (b) (fig.: Unruhe) ferment

Gas /ga:s/ *das;* ~**es**, ~**e** (a) gas; (b) (Kfz.-W.) ~ **wegnehmen** decelerate; take one's foot off the accelerator; ~ **geben** accelerate; put one's foot down (coll.); (c) (ugs.) ⇒ **Gaspedal**

gas-, Gas-: ~**anzünder** *der* gas-lighter; ~**explosion** *die* gas explosion; ~**feuerzeug** *das* gas lighter; ~**flamme** *die* gas flame; ~**flasche** *die* gas-cylinder; (für einen Herd, Ofen) gas bottle; gas container; ~**förmig** *Adj.* gaseous; ~**hahn** *der* gas tap; **den** ~**hahn aufdrehen** (ugs. verhüll.) end it all (coll. euphem.); ~**heizung** *die* gas heating; ~**herd** *der* gas cooker; ~**kammer** *die* gas chamber; ~**kocher** *der* camping stove; ~**laterne** *die* gas lamp; ~**leitung** *die* gas pipe; (Hauptrohr) gas main; ~**licht** *das* gaslight; ~**mann** *der* (ugs.) gas man; ~**maske** *die* gas mask; ~**ofen** *der* gas heater; ~**pedal** *das* accelerator [pedal]; gas pedal (Amer.); ~**rechnung** *die* gas bill

Gasse /'gasə/ *die;* ~, ~**n** (a) lane; narrow street; (österr.) street; **[für jmdn.] eine** ~ **bilden** (fig.) make way *or* clear a path [for sb.]; (b) (Fußball) opening

Gassen-: ~**hauer** *der* (ugs.) popular song; ~**junge** *der* (abwertend) street urchin

Gassi /'gasi/ *in* ~ **gehen** (ugs.) go walkies (Brit. coll.)

Gast /gast/ *der;* ~[e]s, **Gäste** /'gɛstə/ (a) guest; **ungebetene Gäste** (auch fig.) uninvited guests; **bei jmdm. zu** ~ **sein** be sb.'s guest/guests; **jmdn. zu** ~ **haben** have sb. as one's guest/guests; (b) (Besucher eines Lokals) patron; (c) (Besucher) visitor

Gast·arbeiter *der* immigrant *or* foreign *or* guest worker

Gäste-: ~**buch** *das* guest book; ~**handtuch** *das* guest-towel; ~**zimmer** *das* (privat) guest room; spare room; (im Hotel) room

gast-, Gast-: ~**freundlich** *Adj.* hospitable; ~**freundlichkeit** *die,* ~**freundschaft** *die* hospitality; ~**geber** *der* host; ~**geberin** *die;* ~, ~**nen** hostess; ~**haus** *das,* ~**hof** *der* inn; ~**hörer** *der* auditor (Amer.)

gastieren *itr. V.* give a guest performance

gastlich **1** *Adj.* hospitable. **2** *adv.* hospitably

Gastlichkeit *die;* ~: hospitality

Gast-: ~**mahl** *das* (geh.) banquet; ~**mannschaft** *die* (Sport) visiting team; ~**recht** *das* right to hospitality; ~**recht genießen** enjoy the privileges of a guest; **das** ~**recht missbrauchen** abuse one's position as a guest

Gastritis /gas'tri:tɪs/ *die;* ~, **Gastritiden** ▶329┃ (Med.) gastritis

gastro-, Gastro- /gastro:-/: ~**nom** /~'no:m/ *der;* ~**en**, ~**en** restaurateur; ~**nomie** /~no'mi:/ *die;* ~ (a) restaurant trade; (Versorgung, Service) catering *no art.;* (b) (Kochk.) gastronomy; ~**nomisch** /~'no:mɪʃ/ *Adj.* gastronomic

Gast·spiel *das* guest performance; **ein [kurzes]** ~ **geben** (fig. scherzh.) stay for a short time

Gastspiel·reise *die* tour; **eine** ~ **durch Japan** a tour of Japan

Gast-: ~**stätte** *die* public house (Brit.); pub (Brit.); bar (Amer.); (Speiselokal) restaurant; ~**stube** *die* bar; (in einem Speiselokal) restaurant; ~**vorlesung** *die* guest lecture; ~**wirt** *der* publican; landlord; (eines Restaurants) [restaurant] proprietor *or* owner; (Pächter) restaurant manager; ~**wirtschaft** *die* ⇒ ~**stätte**

Gas-: ~**uhr** *die* gas meter; ~**verbrauch** *der* gas consumption; ~**vergiftung** *die* gas-poisoning *no indef. art.;* ~**versorgung** *die* gas supply; ~**werk** *das* gasworks *sing.;* ~**zähler** *der* gas meter

Gatte /'gatə/ *der;* ~**n**, ~**n** (geh.) husband

Gatter /'gatɐ/ *das;* ~**s**, ~ (a) (Zaun) fence; (Lattenzaun) fence; paling; (b) (Tor) gate

Gattin /'gatɪn/ *die;* ~, ~**nen** (geh.) wife

Gattung /'gatʊŋ/ *die;* ~, ~**en** (a) kind; sort; (Kunst~) genre; form; (b) (Biol.) genus; (c) (Milit.) service

GAU /gau/ *der;* ~**s**, ~**s** (Kerntechnik) MCA

Gaucho /'gautʃo/ *der;* ~[s], ~**s** gaucho

Gaudi /'gaudi/ *das;* ~**s** (bayr., österr.: *die;* ~) (ugs.) bit of fun; **ein[e]** ~ **sein** be great fun

Gaukelei *die;* ~, ~**en** (coll.) (a) (Vorspiegelung) trickery *no indef. art., no pl.;* (b) (Possenspiel) trick

Gaukler *der;* ~**s**, ~ (a) (veralt.: Taschenspieler) itinerant entertainer; (b) (geh.: Betrüger) charlatan; mountebank; trickster

Gaul /gaul/ *der;* ~[e]s, **Gäule** /'gɔylə/ (a) (abwertend) nag (derog.); hack (derog.); (b) (veralt.) horse; **einem geschenkten** ~ **schaut man nicht ins Maul** (Spr.) never look a gift-horse in the mouth

Gaumen /'gaumən/ *der;* ~**s**, ~: palate; roof of the mouth; **das ist etwas für einen verwöhnten** ~: this is something for the real gourmet

Gaumen-: ~**freude** *die; meist Pl.* (geh.), ~**kitzel** *der* (geh.) delicacy

Gauner /'gaunɐ/ *der;* ~**s**, ~ (a) (abwertend) crook (coll.); rogue; **ein kleiner** ~: a small-time crook (coll.); (b) (ugs.: schlauer Mensch) cunning devil (coll.); sly customer (coll.)

Gaunerei *die;* ~, ~**en** swindle; (das Gaunern) swindling

Gauner-: ~**sprache** *die* thieves' cant *or* Latin; ~**streich** *der* swindle

Gaze /'ga:zə/ *die;* ~, ~**n** gauze; (Draht~) gauze; [wire-]mesh

Gazelle /ga'tsɛlə/ *die;* ~, ~**n** gazelle

Gazette /ga'tsɛtə/ *die;* ~, ~**n** newspaper; rag (coll. derog.)

G-Dur /'ge:-/ *das;* ~ (Musik) G major

geachtet *Adj.* respected; **bei jmdm.** ~ **sein** be respected *or* held in esteem by sb.

Geächtete *der/die; adj. Dekl.* outlaw

geadert, **geädert** *Adj.* veined

geartet *Adj.* **kein wie auch immer ~er Reiz** no stimulus of any kind; **besonders ~:** special; **sie ist so ~, dass ...:** her nature is such that ...; **sie ist ganz anders ~:** she is quite different; she has quite a different nature

Geäst /gə'|ɛst/ *das;* **~[e]s** branches *pl.;* boughs *pl.*

geb. *Abk.* (a) **geboren;** (b) **geborene**

Gebäck /gə'bɛk/ *das;* **~[e]s**, **~e** cakes and pastries *pl.;* (Kekse) biscuits *pl.;* (Törtchen) tarts *pl.*

gebacken *2. Part. v.* **backen**

Gebälk /gə'bɛlk/ *das;* **~[e]s**, **~e** (a) beams *pl.;* (Dach~) rafters *pl.;* **es knistert im ~** (fig.) there are signs that things are beginning to fall apart (fig.)

Geballere *das;* **~s** (ugs. abwertend) banging

geballt /gə'balt/ *Adj.; nicht präd.* concentrated; **jmdm. eine ~e Ladung Sand ins Gesicht werfen** (ugs.) chuck a load of sand in sb.'s face (coll.)

gebar *1. u. 3. Pers. Sg. Prät. v.* **gebären**

Gebärde /gə'bɛ:ɐdə/ *die;* **~**, **~n** gesture; **mit vielen ~n** with much gesticulation

gebärden *refl. V.* **sich seltsam/wie ein Rasender/ wie toll ~:** behave *or* act oddly/like a madman/as if one were mad

Gebärden·sprache *die* sign language; (Taubstummen- sprache) deaf-and-dumb language

Gebaren *das;* **~s** (oft abwertend) conduct; behaviour

gebären /gə'bɛ:rən/ **1** *unr. tr. V.* bear; give birth to; **jmdm. ein Kind ~** (geh.) bear sb. a child; **wo bist du geboren?** where were you born?; **er ist blind/taub ge- boren** he was born blind/deaf; *s. auch* **geboren. 2** *unr. itr. V.* give birth

Gebär·mutter *die;* **~**, **-mütter ▶326」** womb

gebauchpinselt /gə'bauxpɪnzl̩t/ *in* **sich ~ fühlen** (ugs. scherzh.) feel flattered

Gebäude /gə'bɔydə/ *das;* **~s**, **~** (a) building; (b) (fig.) structure; **ein ~ von Lügen** a tissue of lies

Gebäude·komplex *der* complex of buildings

gebaut *Adj.* **gut ~ sein** have a good figure; **so wie du ~ bist ...** (ugs.) with a figure like yours ...; (fig.) you being what you are ... (coll.)

Gebein *das;* **~s**, **~e** (a) (geh.: Skelett) bones *pl.;* (b) *Pl.* (sterbliche Reste) [mortal] remains

Gebell *das;* **~[e]s** barking; (der Jagdhunde) baying; (fig.: von Geschützen) booming

geben /'ge:bn̩/ **1** *unr. tr. V.* (a) give; (reichen) give; hand; pass; **jmdm. zu essen ~:** give sb. sth. to eat; **~ Sie mir bitte Herrn N.** please put me through to Mr N.; **ich gäbe viel darum, wenn ich das machen könnte** I'd give a lot to be able to do that; **jmdm. etw. in die Hand ~:** give sb. sth.; **etw. [nicht] aus der Hand ~:** [not] let go of sth.; **~ Sie mir bitte ein Bier** I'll have a beer, please; **Geben ist seliger denn Nehmen** (Spr.) it is more blessed to give than to receive (prov.); (b) (über~) **jmdn. zu jmdm. in die Lehre ~:** apprentice sb. to sb.; **etw. in Druck** (*Akk.*) *od.* **zum Druck ~:** send sth. to press *or* to be printed; *s. auch* **Pflege;** (c) (gewähren) give; **einen Elfmeter ~** (Sport) award a penalty; (d) (bieten) give; **jmdm. ein gutes Beispiel ~:** set sb. a good example; (e) (versetzen) give ⟨*slap, kick, etc.*⟩; **es jmdm. ~** (ugs.: jmdm. die Meinung sagen) give sb. what for (sl.); (jmdn. verprügeln) let sb. have it; **gib [es] ihm!** (ugs.) let him have it!; (f) (erteilen) give; **Unterricht ~:** teach; **Französisch ~:** teach French; (g) (hervorbringen) give ⟨*milk, shade, light*⟩; (h) (veranstalten) give, throw ⟨*party*⟩; lay on ⟨*banquet*⟩; give ⟨*dinner party, ball*⟩; (i) (aufführen) give ⟨*concert, performance*⟩; **das Theater gibt den „Faust"** the the- atre is putting on 'Faust'; **was wird heute ge~?** what's on today?; **sein Debüt ~:** make one's debut; (j) (er~) **drei mal drei gibt neun** three threes are nine; three times three is *or* makes nine; **eins plus eins gibt zwei** one and one is *or* makes two; **das gibt [k]einen Sinn** that makes [no] sense; **ein Wort gab das andere** one word led to another; (k) *in* **etw. ist jmdm. nicht ge~:** sb. just hasn't got sth.; (l) (äußern) **etw. von sich ~:** utter sth.;

Unsinn/dummes Zeug von sich ~ (abwertend) talk non- sense/rubbish; **keinen Laut/Ton von sich ~:** not make a sound; (m) *in* **viel/wenig auf etw.** (*Akk.*) **~:** set great/ little store by sth.; (n) (hinzu~) add; put in; **etw. an das Essen ~:** add sth. to *or* put sth. into the food; (o) (ugs.: erbrechen) **alles wieder von sich ~:** bring *or* (coll.) sick everything up again. **2** *unr. tr. V.; unpers.* (a) (vorhanden sein) **es gibt** there is/are; **das gibt es wohl häufiger** it happens all the time; **dass es so etwas heutzutage überhaupt noch gibt!** I'm surprised that such things still go on nowadays; **zu meiner Zeit gab es das nicht** it wasn't like that in my day; **das gibt es ja gar nicht** I don't believe it; you're joking (coll.); **Ein Hund mit fünf Beinen? Das gibt es ja gar nicht** A dog with five legs? There's no such thing!; **Kommen Sie herein. Was gibt es?** Come in. What's the matter *or* (coll.) what's up?; **was gibts denn da?** what's going on over there?; **was es nicht alles gibt!** (ugs.) what will they think of next?; **da gibts nichts** (ugs.) there's no denying it *or* no doubt about it; **da gibts nichts, da würde ich sofort protestieren** there's nothing else for it, I'd protest immediately in that case; (b) (angeboten werden) **was gibt es zu essen/ trinken?** what is there to eat/drink?; **was gibt es denn zum Mittagessen?** what's for lunch?; **heute gibts Schweinefleisch** we're having pork today; (c) (kommen zu) **morgen gibt es Schnee/Sturm** it'll snow tomorrow/ there'll be a storm tomorrow; **gleich/sonst gibts was** (ugs.) there'll be trouble in a minute/otherwise. **3** *unr. intr. V.* (a) (Karten austeilen) deal; **wer gibt?** whose deal is it?; (b) (Sport: aufschlagen) serve. **4** *unr. refl. V.* (a) **sich [natürlich] ~:** act *or* behave [naturally]; **sich nach außen hin ge- lassen geben** give the appearance of being relaxed; **deine Art, dich zu ~:** the way you behave; (b) (nachlassen) **das Fieber wird sich ~:** his/her *etc.* temperature will drop; **sein Eifer wird sich bald ~:** his enthusiasm will soon wear off *or* cool; **das gibt sich/wird sich noch ~:** it will get better

Geber *der;* **~s**, **~**, **Geberin** *die;* **~**, **~nen** (a) (veralt.) giver; donor

Gebet /gə'be:t/ *das;* **~[e]s**, **~e** prayer; **sein ~ ver- richten** say one's prayers *pl.;* **jmdn. ins ~ nehmen** (ugs.) give sb. a dressing down; take sb. to task

Gebet·buch *das* prayer-book

gebeten *2. Part. v.* **bitten**

gebierst /gə'be:ɐst/, **gebiert** /gə'bi:ɐt/ *2., 3. Pers. Sg. Präsens v.* **gebären**

Gebiet /gə'bi:t/ *das;* **~[e]s**, **~e** (a) region; area; (b) (Staats~) territory; (c) (Bereich) field; sphere; (d) (Fach) field; **auf einem ~:** in a field

gebieten (geh.) **1** *unr. tr. V.* (a) command; order; **jmdm. ~, etw. zu tun** command *or* order sb. to do sth.; **eine Respekt ~de Persönlichkeit** a figure who commands/ commanded respect; (b) (erfordern) demand; bid; *s. auch* **Einhalt. 2** *unr. itr. V.* (a) **über etw.** (*Akk.*) **~:** command sth.; have command over sth.; **über ein Land ~:** hold sway over a country; (b) (verfügen) **über Geld ~:** have money at one's disposal

Gebieter *der;* **~s**, **~** (veralt.) master

Gebieterin *die;* **~**, **~nen** (veralt.) mistress

gebieterisch (geh.) **1** *Adj.* imperious; (herrisch) dom- ineering; overbearing; peremptory ⟨*tone*⟩. **2** *adv.* imperi- ously

Gebiets-: **~anspruch** *der* territorial claim; **~kör- perschaft** *die* (Rechtsw.) regional authority

Gebilde /gə'bɪldə/ *das;* **~s**, **~** object; (Bauwerk) construc- tion; structure; **diese Dinge sind ~ seiner Fantasie** (fig.) these things are products of his imagination

gebildet *Adj.* educated; (kultiviert) cultured

Gebimmel *das;* **~s** (ugs.) ringing; (von kleinen Glocken) tinkling

Gebinde *das;* **~s**, **~** (Blumenarrangement) arrangement; (Bund, Strauß) bunch; (von kleinen Blumen) posy

Gebirge /gə'bɪrgə/ *das;* **~s**, **~** (a) mountain range; range of mountains; **ein ~ von Schutt** (fig.) a mountain of rubble (fig.); (b) (Gebirgsgegend) mountains *pl.*

gebirgig *Adj.* mountainous

Gebirgs-: ~**ausläufer** *der* foothill; ~**bach** *der* mountain stream; ~**kette** *die* mountain chain *or* range; ~**landschaft** *die* mountainous region; (Ausblick) mountain scenery; (Gemälde) mountain landscape; ~**massiv** *das* massif; ~**pass**, *** ~**paß** *der* mountain pass; ~**zug** *der* mountain range

Gebiss, ***Gebiß** *das;* **Gebisses**, **Gebisse** ▶ 326 | (a) set of teeth; teeth *pl.;* (b) (Zahnersatz) denture; plate (coll.); (für beide Kiefer) dentures *pl.;* set of false teeth; false teeth *pl.*

gebissen /gə'bɪsn̩/ *2. Part. v.* **beißen**

Gebläse /gə'blɛːzə/ *das;* ~**s**, ~ (Technik) fan

geblasen *2. Part. v.* **blasen**

geblichen /gə'blɪçn̩/ *2. Part. v.* **bleichen**

Geblödel *das;* ~**s** (ugs.) silly chatter; twaddle (coll.)

geblümt /gə'blyːmt/ *Adj.* flowered

Geblüt /gə'blyːt/ *das;* ~**[e]s** (geh.) blood; **von königlichem** ~ **sein** be of royal blood; **eine Prinzessin von** ~: a princess of the blood

gebogen 1 *2. Part. v.* **biegen**. 2 *Adj.* bent; **eine aufwärts** ~**e Nase** an upturned nose

geboren /gə'boːrən/ 1 *2. Part. v.* **gebären**. 2 *Adj.* **Frau Anna Schmitz** ~**e Meyer** Mrs Anna Schmitz née Meyer; **sie ist eine** ~**e von Schiller** she is a von Schiller by birth; **der** ~**e Schauspieler** *usw.* **sein** be a born actor *etc.*

geborgen 1 *2. Part. v.* **bergen**. 2 *Adj.* safe; secure; **sich bei jmdm.** ~ **fühlen** feel safe and secure with sb.

Geborgenheit *die;* ~: security

geborsten /gə'bɔrstn̩/ *2. Part. v.* **bersten**

gebot *1. u. 3. Pers. Sg. Prät. v.* **gebieten**

Gebot *das;* ~**[e]s**, ~**e** (a) precept; **die Zehn** ~**e** (Rel.) the Ten Commandments; (b) (Vorschrift) regulation; (c) (geh.: Befehl) command; (Verordnung) decree; **auf jmds.** ~ (*Akk.*) [**hin**] at sb.'s command; (d) *in* **jmdm. zu** ~**[e] stehen** (geh.) be at sb.'s command/disposal; (e) (Erfordernis) **ein** ~ **der Klugheit** a dictate of good sense; (f) (Kaufmannsspr.) bid; **verkaufe X gegen** ~: offers [are] invited for X

geboten 1 *2. Part. v.* **bieten**, **gebieten**. 2 *Adj.* (ratsam) advisable; (notwendig) necessary; (unbedingt ~) imperative; **mit der** ~**en Sorgfalt/mit dem** ~**en Respekt** with all due care/respect

Gebots·schild *das* (Verkehrsw.) regulatory sign

Gebr. *Abk.* **Gebrüder** Bros.

gebracht /gə'braxt/ *2. Part. v.* **bringen**

gebrannt /gə'brant/ *2. Part. v.* **brennen**

gebraten *2. Part. v.* **braten**

Gebräu /gə'brɔy/ *das;* ~**[e]s**, ~**e** (meist abwertend) brew; concoction (derog.)

Gebrauch *der* (a) *o. Pl.* use; **vor** ~ **gut schütteln** shake well before use; **von etw.** ~ **machen** make use of sth.; **von seinem Recht** ~ **machen** avail oneself of *or* exercise one's rights *pl.;* **außer** ~ **kommen** fall into disuse; **etw. in** ~ (*Akk.*) **nehmen/in** *od.* **im** ~ **haben** start/be using sth.; **in** *od.* **im** ~ **sein** be in use; (b) *meist Pl.* (Brauch) custom

gebrauchen *tr. V.* use; **das kann ich gut** ~: I can make good use of that; I can just do with that (coll.); **er ist zu nichts zu** ~ (ugs.) he is useless; **den Verstand** ~: use one's common sense; **er könnte einen neuen Mantel** ~ (ugs.) he could do with *or* (coll.) use a new coat; **ich kann jetzt keine Störung** ~ (ugs.) I don't want to be disturbed just now

gebräuchlich /gə'brɔyçlɪç/ *Adj.* (a) (üblich) normal; usual; customary; (b) (häufig) common

gebrauchs-, **Gebrauchs-:** ~**anleitung** *die*, ~**anweisung** *die* instructions *pl.* or directions *pl.* [for use]; ~**fähig** *Adj.* usable; in working order *pred.;* ~**fertig** *Adj.* ready for use *pred.;* ~**gegenstand** *der* item of practical use

gebraucht *Adj.* second-hand ⟨*bicycle, clothes, etc.*⟩; used; second-hand ⟨*car*⟩; used ⟨*handkerchief*⟩; **etw.** ~ **kaufen** buy sth. second-hand

Gebraucht-: ~**wagen** *der* used *or* second-hand car; ~**wagen·händler** *der* used-car dealer; second-hand car dealer; ~**waren** *Pl.* second-hand goods

Gebrechen *das;* ~**s**, ~ (geh.) affliction

gebrechlich *Adj.* infirm; frail

Gebrechlichkeit *die;* ~: infirmity; frailty

gebrochen /gə'brɔxn̩/ 1 *2. Part. v.* **brechen**. 2 *Adj.* (a) (fehlerhaft) ~**es Englisch** broken English; (b) (niedergedrückt) broken; (c) (gestört) **ein** ~**es Verhältnis zu jmdm./etw. haben** have a disturbed relationship to sb./sth. 3 *adv.* ~ **Deutsch sprechen** speak broken German

Gebrüder *Pl.* (a) (Kaufmannsspr.) **die** ~ **Meyer** Meyer Brothers; (b) (veralt.) **die** ~ **Schulze** the brothers Schulze

Gebrüll *das;* ~**[e]s** (a) roaring; (von Rindern) bellowing; (b) (ugs.) (lautes Schreien) bellowing; yelling; (einer Menschenmenge) roaring; **auf sie mit** ~**!** (scherzh.) go for *or* get them!; (c) (ugs.: lautes Weinen) bawling

gebückt *Adj.* **in** ~**er Haltung** bending forward; ~ **gehen** walk with a stoop

Gebühr /gə'byːɐ̯/ *die;* ~, ~**en** (a) charge; (Maut) toll; (Anwalts~) fee; (Fernseh~) licence fee; (Vermittlungs~) commission *no pl.;* fee; (Post~) postage *no pl.;* ~ **bezahlt Empfänger** postage will be paid by addressee; (b) **über** ~ (*Akk.*) unduly; excessively

gebühren (geh.) 1 *itr. V.* **jmdm. gebührt Achtung** *usw.* [**für etw.**] sb. deserves respect *etc.* [for sth.]; respect *etc.* is due to sb. [for sth.]. 2 *refl. V.* **wie es sich gebührt** as is fitting *or* proper

gebührend 1 *Adj.* fitting; proper; (angemessen) fitting; suitable; **mit** ~**er Sorgfalt** with due care. 2 *adv.* fittingly; in a fitting manner

gebühren-, **Gebühren-:** ~**einheit** *die* (Fernspr.) [tariff] unit; ~**erhöhung** *die* increase in charges; (der Anwaltsgebühren) increase in fees; (der Fernsehgebühren) licence fee increase; ~**ermäßigung** *die* reduction of charges; (der Anwaltsgebühren) reduction of fees; ~**frei** 1 *Adj.* free of charge *pred.;* post-free ⟨*letter, packet, etc.*⟩; 2 *adv.* free of charge; (postfrei) post-free

gebunden 1 *2. Part. v.* **binden**. 2 *Adj.* (a) (verpflichtet) bound; **an ein Versprechen/das Haus** ~ **sein** be bound by a promise/tied to one's home; **sich [an etw. (*Akk.*)]** ~ **fühlen** feel bound by sth.; (b) (verlobt) engaged; (verheiratet) married

Geburt /gə'buːɐ̯t/ *die;* ~, ~**en** ▶ 388 | birth; **von** ~ **an** from birth; **vor/nach Christi** ~: before/after the birth of Christ; **das war eine schwere** ~ (fig. ugs.) it wasn't easy; it took some doing (coll.)

Geburten·kontrolle *die; o. Pl.* birth control

gebürtig /gə'byrtɪç/ *Adj.* **ein** ~**er Schwabe** a Swabian by birth; **aus Ungarn/Paris** ~ **sein** be Hungarian/Parisian by birth

Geburts-: ~**datum** *das* date of birth; ~**haus** *das:* **das** ~**haus Beethovens** the house where Beethoven was born; Beethoven's birthplace; ~**helfer** *der* (Arzt) obstetrician; (Laie) assistant [at a/the birth]; ~**helferin** *die* obstetrician; (Hebamme) midwife; ~**jahr** *das* year of birth; ~**ort** *der* place of birth; birthplace; ~**stunde** *die* hour of birth

Geburts·tag *der* (a) ▶ 240 | birthday; **jmdm. zum** ~ **gratulieren** wish sb. [a] happy birthday *or* many happy returns of the day; **er hat morgen** ~: it's his birthday tomorrow; (b) (Geburtsdatum) date of birth

Geburtstags-: ~**feier** *die* birthday party; ~**geschenk** *das* birthday present; ~**kind** *das* (scherzh.) birthday boy/girl; ~**überraschung** *die* birthday surprise

Geburts·ur·kunde *die* birth certificate

Gebüsch /gə'byʃ/ *das;* ~**[e]s**, ~**e** bushes *pl.;* clump of bushes; **ein niedriges** ~: a clump of low bushes; some low bushes *pl.*

Geck /gɛk/ *der;* ~**en**, ~**en** (abwertend) dandy; fop

geckenhaft 1 *Adj.* dandyish; foppish. 2 *adv.* **er kleidet sich** ~: he dresses like a dandy

gedacht /gə'daxt/ 1 *2. Part. v.* **denken**, **gedenken**. 2 *Adj.* **für jmdn./etw.** ~ **sein** be meant *or* intended for sb./sth.; **so war das nicht** ~: that wasn't what I intended

---

Gedächtnis /gə'dɛçtnıs/ *das;* ~ses, ~se (a) memory; **sich** (*Dat.*) **etw. ins** ~ [**zurück**]**rufen** recall sth.; **aus dem** ~: from memory; **ein** ~ **wie ein Sieb** (ugs.) a memory like a sieve (coll.); (b) (Andenken) memory; remembrance; **zum** ~ **an jmdn.** in memory *or* remembrance of sb.

Gedächtnis-: ~**lücke** *die* gap in one's memory; ~**schwund** *der* loss of memory; amnesia; ~**stütze** *die* memory aid; mnemonic

gedämpft *Adj.* subdued ⟨*mood*⟩; subdued, soft ⟨*light*⟩; subdued, muted ⟨*colour*⟩; muffled ⟨*sound*⟩; low, hushed ⟨*voice*⟩

Gedanke *der;* ~ns, ~n (a) thought; **seinen** ~n **nachhängen** abandon oneself to one's thoughts; **jmdn. auf andere** ~n **bringen** take sb.'s mind off things; **in** ~n **verloren** *od.* **versunken** [**sein**] [be] lost *or* deep in thought; **mit seinen** ~n **nicht bei der Sache sein** have one's mind on something else; **sich mit einem** ~n **vertraut machen/einen** ~n **aufgreifen** get used to/take up an idea; ~n **lesen können** be able to read people's thoughts *or* to mind-read; **sich** (*Dat.*) [**um jmdn./etw.** *od.* **wegen jmds./etw.**] ~n **machen** be worried [about sb./sth.]; **sich über etw.** (*Akk.*) ~n **machen** (länger nachdenken) think about *or* ponder sth.; (b) *o. Pl.* **der** ~ **an etw.** (*Akk.*) the thought of sth.; **bei dem** ~n, **hingehen zu müssen** at the thought of having to go; **kein** ~ [**daran**]! (ugs.) out of the question!; no way! (coll.); (c) *Pl.* (Meinung) ideas; **seine** ~n [**über etw.** (*Akk.*)] **austauschen** exchange views [about sth.]; (d) (Einfall) idea; **das bringt mich auf einen** ~n that gives me an idea; **mir kam der** ~, **wir könnten ...**: it occurred to me that we could ...; **auf dumme** ~n **kommen** (ugs.) get silly ideas (coll.); **mit dem** ~n **spielen**[, **etw. zu tun**] be toying with the idea [of doing sth.]; (e) (Idee) idea; **der** ~ **des Friedens** the idea of peace

gedanken-, Gedanken-: ~**austausch** *der* exchange of ideas; ~**blitz** *der* (ugs. scherzh.) brainwave (coll.); ~**freiheit** *die; o. Pl.* freedom of thought; ~**gang** *der* train of thought; ~**gut** *das* thought; ~**lesen** *das* mind-reading; ~**los 1** *Adj.* unconsidered; thoughtless; **2** *adv.* without thinking; thoughtlessly; ~**losigkeit** *die* lack of thought; thoughtlessness; ~**strich** *der* dash; ~**übertragung** *die* telepathy *no indef. art.;* thought-transference *no indef. art.;* ~**verloren** *Adv.* lost in thought; ~**voll 1** *Adj.* pensive; thoughtful; **2** *adv.* pensively; thoughtfully

gedanklich /gə'daŋklıç/ **1** *Adj.; nicht präd.* intellectual. **2** *adv.* intellectually

Gedärm /gə'dɛrm/ *das;* ~[e]s, ~e ▶ 326 intestines *pl.;* bowels *pl.,* (eines Tieres) entrails *pl.*

Gedeck *das;* ~[e]s, ~e (a) place setting; cover; **ein** ~ **auflegen** lay *or* set a place; (b) (Menü) set meal; (c) (Getränk) drink [with a cover charge]

gedeckt *Adj.* subdued, muted ⟨*colour*⟩

Gedeih *in* **auf** ~ **und Verderb** for good or ill; for better or [for] worse; **jmdm. auf** ~ **und Verderb ausgeliefert sein** be entirely at sb.'s mercy

gedeihen /gə'daıən/ *unr. itr. V.; mit sein* (a) thrive; (wirtschaftlich) flourish; prosper; (b) (fortschreiten) progress

gedeihlich *Adj.* (geh.) thriving, flourishing, successful ⟨*business*⟩; successful ⟨*development, cooperation*⟩; beneficial ⟨*effect etc.*⟩

gedenken *unr. itr. V.* (a) **jmds./einer Sache** ~ (geh.) remember sb./sth.; (erwähnen) recall sb./sth.; (in einer Feier) commemorate sb./sth.; (b) **etw. zu tun** ~: intend to do *or* doing sth.

Gedenken *das;* ~s (geh.) remembrance; memory; **zum** ~ **an jmdn./etw.** in memory *or* remembrance of sb./sth.

Gedenk-: ~**feier** *die* commemoration; commemorative ceremony; ~**minute** *die* minute's silence; **eine** ~**minute einlegen** observe a minute's silence; ~**stätte** *die* memorial; ~**stein** *der* memorial *or* commemorative stone; ~**tag** *der* day of remembrance; commemoration day

Gedicht *das;* ~[e]s, ~e poem; **Goethes** ~e Goethe's poetry *sing. or* poems; **das Steak/Kleid ist ein** ~ (fig. ugs.) the steak is just superb/the dress is just heavenly

Gedicht·sammlung *die* collection of poems; (von mehreren Dichtern) anthology of poetry *or* verse; poetry anthology

gediegen /gə'di:gn/ **1** *Adj.* (a) (solide) solid, solidly-made ⟨*furniture*⟩; sound, solid ⟨*piece of work*⟩; well-made ⟨*clothing*⟩; sound ⟨*knowledge*⟩; (b) (rein) pure ⟨*gold, silver, etc.*⟩. **2** *adv.* ~ **gebaut/verarbeitet** solidly built/made

gedieh /gə'di:/ *1. u. 3. Pers. Sg. Prät. v.* **gedeihen**

gediehen *2. Part. v.* **gedeihen**

gedient /gə'di:nt/ *Adj.* **ein** ~**er Soldat** a former soldier

Gedränge *das;* ~s (a) pushing and shoving; (Menschenmenge) crush; crowd; (b) **ins** ~ **kommen** *od.* **geraten** (fig. ugs.) get into difficulties

gedrängt *Adj.* compressed, condensed ⟨*account*⟩; terse, succinct ⟨*style, description*⟩; crowded ⟨*timetable, agenda*⟩

gedroschen /gə'drɔʃn/ *2. Part. v.* **dreschen**

gedrückt *Adj.* dejected, depressed ⟨*mood*⟩

gedrungen /gə'drʊŋən/ **1** *2. Part. v.* **dringen. 2** *Adj.* stocky; thick-set ⟨*build*⟩

Gedudel *das;* ~s (ugs. abwertend) tootling; (im Radio) noise

Geduld /gə'dʊlt/ *die;* ~: patience; **keine** ~ [**zu etw.**] **haben** have no patience [with sth.]; **mit jmdm.** ~ **haben** be patient with sb.

gedulden *refl. V.* be patient; ~ **Sie sich bitte ein paar Minuten** please be so good as to wait a few minutes

geduldig 1 *Adj.* patient. **2** *adv.* patiently

Gedulds-: ~**faden** *der in* **mir/ihm** *etc.* **reißt der** ~**faden** (ugs.) my/his *etc.* patience is wearing thin; ~**probe** *die* trial of one's patience; **auf eine harte** ~**probe gestellt werden** have one's patience sorely tried; ~**spiel** *das* puzzle; (fig.) Chinese puzzle

gedungen /gə'dʊŋən/ *2. Part. v.* **dingen**

gedunsen /gə'dʊnzn/ *Adj.* ⇒ **aufgedunsen**

gedurft /gə'dʊrft/ *2. Part. v.* **dürfen**

geeignet *Adj.* suitable; (richtig) right

Gefahr *die;* ~, ~en danger; (Bedrohung) danger; threat; (Risiko) risk; **die** ~**en meines Berufs** the hazards of my job; **die** ~**en des Dschungels** the perils of the jungle; **eine** ~ **für jmdn./etw.** a danger to sb./sth.; **in** ~ **kommen/geraten** get into danger; **jmdn./etw. in** ~ **bringen** put sb./sth. in danger; **sich in** ~ **begeben** put oneself in danger; expose oneself to danger; **in** ~ **sein/schweben** be in danger; ⟨*rights, plans*⟩ be in jeopardy *or* peril; **außer** ~ **sein** be out of danger; **bei** ~: in case of emergency; **jmdn./sich einer** ~ **aussetzen** run *or* take a risk; **es besteht die Gefahr, dass ...**: there is a danger *or* risk that ...; **auf die** ~ **hin, dass das passiert** at the risk of that happening; ~ **laufen, etw. zu tun** risk *or* run the risk of doing sth.; **auf eigene** ~: at one's own risk; **wer sich in** ~ **begibt, kommt darin um** if you keep on taking risks, you'll come to grief eventually

gefährden /gə'fɛːɐdn/ *tr. V.* endanger; jeopardize ⟨*enterprise, success, position, etc.*⟩; (aufs Spiel setzen) put at risk

gefährdet *Adj.* ⟨*people, adolescents, etc.*⟩ at risk *postpos.*

Gefährdung *die;* ~, ~en (a) *o. Pl.* endangering; (eines Unternehmens, einer Position usw.) jeopardizing; (b) (Gefahr) threat (*Gen.* to)

gefahren *2. Part. v.* **fahren**

Gefahren-: ~**bereich** *der* danger area *or* zone; ~**herd** *der,* ~**quelle** *die* source of danger; ~**zone** *die* ⇒ ~**bereich;** ~**zulage** *die* danger money *no indef. art.*

gefährlich /gə'fɛːɐlıç/ **1** *Adj.* dangerous; (gewagt) risky; [**für jmdn./etw.**] ~ **sein** be dangerous [for sb./sth.]; **er könnte mir** ~ **werden** he could be a threat *or* a danger to me; (fig.) I could fall for him [in a big way]. **2** *adv.* dangerously

Gefährlichkeit *die;* ~: dangerousness; (Gewagtheit) riskiness

gefahr·los 1 *Adj.* safe. **2** *adv.* safely

Gefährt *das;* ~[e]s, ~e (geh.) vehicle

Gefährte *der;* ~n, ~n, **Gefährtin** *die;* ~, ~en (geh.) companion; (Lebens~) partner in life

Gefälle /gə'fɛlə/ *das;* ~s, ~ slope; incline; (eines Flusses) drop; (einer Straße) gradient

gefallen[1] *unr. itr. V.* **(a)** das gefällt mir [gut]/[gar] nicht I like it [very much *or* (coll.) a lot]/ don't like it [at all]; **es gefiel ihr, wie er sich bewegte** she liked the way he moved; **weißt du, was mir an dir/dem Bild so gut gefällt?** do you know what I like so much about you/ the picture?; **mir gefällt es hier** I like it here; **er gefällt mir [ganz und gar] nicht** (ugs.: sieht krank aus) he looks in a bad way to me (coll.); **die Sache gefällt mir nicht** (ugs.) I don't like [the look of] it (coll.); **(b)** sich (*Dat.*) etw. ∼ lassen put up with sth.; **(c)** (abwertend) sich (*Dat.*) in einer Rolle ∼: enjoy *or* like playing a role; fancy oneself in a role (coll.); **er gefällt sich in Übertreibungen** he likes to exaggerate

gefallen[2] 1 *2. Part. v.* **fallen, gefallen.** **2** *Adj.* fallen ‹*angel etc.*›; **ein** ∼**es Mädchen** (veralt.) a fallen woman

Gefallen[1] *der;* ∼**s,** ∼: favour; **jmdm. einen** ∼ **tun** *od.* **erweisen** do sb. a favour; **tu mir den** *od.* **einen** ∼, **und ...!** (ugs.) do me a favour and ...; **jmdn. um einen** ∼ **bitten** ask a favour of sb.

Gefallen[2] *das;* ∼**s** pleasure; ∼ **an jmdm./aneinander finden** like sb./each other; **an etw.** (*Dat.*) ∼ **finden** get *or* derive pleasure from sth.; enjoy sth.; **etw. jmdm. zu** ∼ **tun** do sth. to please sb.

Gefallene *der/die; adj. Dekl.* soldier killed in action; **die** ∼**n** the fallen; those killed *or* those who fell in action

ge·fällig 1 *Adj.* **(a)** (hilfsbereit) obliging; helpful; **jmdm.** ∼ **sein** oblige *or* help sb.; **(b)** (anziehend) pleasing; agreeable; pleasant, agreeable ‹*programme, behaviour*›; **(c)** *nicht attr.* **noch ein Kaffee** ∼? would you like *or* care for another coffee?. **2** *adv.* pleasingly; agreeably

Gefälligkeit *die;* ∼, ∼**en** **(a)** (Hilfeleistung) favour; **jmdm. eine** ∼ **erweisen** do sb. a favour; **(b)** *o. Pl.* (Hilfsbereitschaft) obligingness; helpfulness; **etw. aus reiner** ∼ **tun** do sth. just to be obliging

Gefälligkeits·akzept *das,* **Gefälligkeits·wechsel** *der* (Bankw.) accommodation bill

gefälligst /gə'fɛlɪçst/ *Adv.* (ugs.) kindly; **lass das** ∼! kindly stop that

gefangen *2. Part. v.* **fangen**

Gefangene *der/die; adj. Dekl.* **(a)** prisoner; captive; ∼ **machen** take prisoners; **(b)** (Häftling, Kriegs∼) prisoner

Gefangenen·lager *das* prisoner of war camp; prison camp

gefangen-, Gefangen-: *∗∼|halten* ⇒ **fangen** 1 b; ∼**nahme** *die;* ∼: capture;*∗∼|nehmen* ⇒ **fangen** 1 b

Gefangenschaft *die;* ∼, ∼**en** captivity; **in** ∼ **sein/geraten** be a prisoner/be taken prisoner

Gefängnis /gə'fɛŋnɪs/ *das;* ∼**ses,** ∼**se** **(a)** prison; gaol; **jmdn.** ∼ **bringen/werfen** put/throw sb. in[to] prison; **im** ∼ **sein** *od.* **sitzen** be in prison; **ins** ∼ **kommen** be sent to prison; **(b)** (Strafe) imprisonment; **darauf steht** ∼: that is punishable by imprisonment *or* a prison sentence; **jmdn. zu zwei Jahren** ∼ **verurteilen** sentence sb. to two years' imprisonment *or* two years in prison

Gefängnis-: ∼**direktor** *der* prison governor; ∼**kleidung** *die* prison uniform; ∼**mauer** *die* prison wall; ∼**strafe** *die* prison sentence; **eine** ∼**strafe verbüßen** serve a prison sentence; ∼**wärter** *der* prison officer; [prison] warder; ∼**zelle** *die* prison cell

Gefasel *das;* ∼**s** (ugs. abwertend) twaddle (coll.); drivel (derog.)

Gefäß /gə'fɛːs/ *das;* ∼**es,** ∼**e** **(a)** (Behälter) vessel; container; **(b)** ▶ 326 ⟨ (Med.) vessel

gefasst, *gefaßt /gə'fast/ **1** *Adj.* **(a)** calm; composed; **mit** ∼**er Haltung** with composure; **(b)** *in* **auf etw.** (*Akk.*) **[nicht]** ∼ **sein** [not] be prepared for sth.; **sich auf etw.** (*Akk.*) ∼ **machen** prepare oneself for sth.; **der kann sich auf was** ∼ **machen** (ugs.) he'll catch it *or* be for it (coll.). **2** *adv.* calmly; with composure

Gefecht *das;* ∼**[e]s,** ∼**e** **(a)** battle; engagement (Milit.); **ein schweres/kurzes** ∼: fierce fighting/a skirmish; **sich** (*Dat.*) **/dem Feind ein** ∼ **liefern** engage each other/the enemy in battle; **jmdn./etw. außer** ∼ **setzen** put sb./ sth. out of action; **(b)** (Fechten) bout; *s. auch* **Eifer**

gefechts-, Gefechts-: ∼**bereit,** ∼**klar** *Adj.* (Milit.) ready for action *or* battle *postpos.;* combat-ready; ∼**stand** *der* (Milit.) battle headquarters *pl.;* command post; (Luftw.) operations room

gefehlt *Adj.* **weit** ∼! wide of the mark!

gefestigt *Adj.* assured ‹*beliefs*›; secure ‹*person*›; established ‹*tradition*›

Gefieder /gə'fiːdɐ/ *das;* ∼**s,** ∼: plumage; feathers *pl.*

gefiedert *Adj.* **(a)** feathered; **(b)** (Bot.) pinnate

Gefilde /gə'fɪldə/ *das;* ∼**s,** ∼ (geh.) **sonnige** ∼: sunny climes (literary); **wieder in heimatlichen** ∼**n sein** (scherzh.) be back under one's native skies

Geflecht *das;* ∼**[e]s,** ∼**e** **(a)** wickerwork *no art.;* **(b)** (fig.) tangle; **ein wirres/dichtes** ∼ **von Zweigen** a tangled/dense network of twigs

gefleckt *Adj.* spotty, blotchy ‹*skin, face*›; spotted ‹*leopard skin*›

geflissentlich /gə'flɪsṇtlɪç/ **1** *Adj.; nicht präd.* deliberate. **2** *adv.* deliberately

geflochten /gə'flɔxtṇ/ *2. Part. v.* **flechten**

geflogen /gə'floːgṇ/ *2. Part. v.* **fliegen**

geflohen /gə'floːən/ *2. Part. v.* **fliehen**

geflossen /gə'flɔsṇ/ *2. Part. v.* **fließen**

Geflügel *das;* ∼**s** poultry

Geflügel-: ∼**farm** *die* poultry farm; ∼**schere** *die* poultry shears *pl.*

geflügelt *Adj.* winged ‹*insect, seed*›; **ein** ∼**es Wort** (fig.) a standard *or* familiar quotation

Geflüster *das;* ∼**s** whispering

gefochten /gə'fɔxtṇ/ *2. Part. v.* **fechten**

Gefolge *das;* ∼**s,** ∼ **(a)** (Begleitung) entourage; retinue; **(b)** (Trauergeleit) cortège

Gefolgschaft *die;* ∼: allegiance; **jmdm.** ∼ **leisten** give one's allegiance to sb.

gefragt *Adj.* ‹*artist, craftsman, product*› in great demand; sought-after ‹*artist, craftsman, product*›

gefräßig /gə'frɛːsɪç/ *Adj.* (abwertend) greedy; gluttonous; voracious ‹*animal, insect*›

Gefräßigkeit *die;* ∼ (abwertend) greediness; gluttony; (von Tieren) voracity

Gefreite /gə'fraɪtə/ *der;* ▶ 34 ⟨ *adj. Dekl.* (Milit.) lance corporal (Brit.); private first class (Amer.); (Marine) able seaman; (Luftw.) aircraftman first class (Brit.); airman third class (Amer.)

gefressen *2. Part. v.* **fressen**

gefrieren **1** *unr. itr. V.; mit sein* freeze. **2** *unr. tr. V.* [deep-]freeze ‹*food*›

gefrier-, Gefrier-: ∼**fach** *das* freezing compartment; ∼**punkt** *der* ▶ 511 ⟨ freezing point; **Temperaturen über/unter dem** ∼**punkt** temperatures above/ below freezing; ∼**schrank** *der* [upright] freezer; ∼**|trocknen** *tr. V.; meist im Inf. u. 2. Part.* freeze-dry; ∼**truhe** *die* [chest] freezer

gefroren /gə'froːrən/ *2. Part. v.* **frieren, gefrieren**

Gefüge *das;* ∼**s,** ∼: structure; **das soziale** ∼: the social fabric

gefügig *Adj.* submissive; compliant; docile ‹*animal*›; **ein** ∼**es Werkzeug** (fig.) a willing tool; **sich** (*Dat.*) **jmdn.** ∼ **machen** make sb. submit to one's will

Gefühl *das;* ∼**s,** ∼**e** **(a)** sensation; feeling; **ein** ∼ **des Schmerzes** a sensation of pain; **(b)** (Gemütsregung) feeling; **ein** ∼ **der Einsamkeit** a sense *or* feeling of loneliness; **kein** ∼ **haben** have no feelings; **das ist das höchste der** ∼**e** (ugs.) that's the absolute limit; **(c)** (Ahnung) feeling; **etw. im** ∼ **haben** have a feeling *or* a premonition of sth.; **(d)** (Verständnis, Gespür) sense; instinct; **sich auf sein** ∼ **verlassen** trust one's feelings *or* instinct; **etw. nach** ∼ **tun** do sth. by instinct

gefühl·los *Adj.* **(a)** numb; **(b)** (herzlos) unfeeling; callous

Gefühllosigkeit *die;* ∼ **(a)** numbness; lack of sensation; **(b)** (Herzlosigkeit) unfeelingness; callousness

gefühls-, Gefühls-: ∼**arm** *Adj.* lacking in feeling; ∼**ausbruch** *der* outburst [of emotion]; ∼**betont** 1

Adj. emotional ‹*speech, argument*›; **2** *adv.* ∼**betont handeln** be guided by one's emotions; ∼**duselei** /-du:zə'laị/ *die;* ∼ (ugs. abwertend) mawkishness; mawkish sentimentality; ∼**leben** *das* emotional life; ∼**mäßig 1** *Adj.* emotional ‹*reaction*›; ‹*action*› based on emotion; **2** *adv.* **rein** ∼**mäßig würde ich sagen, dass …**: my own, purely instinctive, feeling would be to say that …; ∼**regung** *die* emotion

gefühl·voll 1 *Adj.* **(a)** (empfindsam) sensitive; **(b)** (ausdrucksvoll) expressive. **2** *adv.* sensitively; expressively; with feeling

gefüllt *Adj.* full ‹*wallet*›; double ‹*lilac, geraniums*›; stuffed ‹*fowl, tomato etc.*›; ∼**e Bonbons** sweets (Brit.) *or* (Amer.) candies with centres

gefunden /gə'fʊndṇ/ *2. Part. v.* **finden;** *s. auch* **Fressen** b

gefurcht *Adj.* lined; wrinkled

gefürchtet *Adj.* dreaded; feared ‹*despot, opponent*›

gegangen *2. Part. v.* **gehen**

gegeben 1 *2. Part. v.* **geben. 2** *Adj.* **(a)** given; **etw. als** ∼ **voraussetzen/hinnehmen** take sth. for granted; **aus** ∼**em Anlass** for certain reasons (*specified or not*); **unter den** ∼**en Umständen** in these circumstances; **(b)** (passend) right; proper; **das ist das Gegebene** that's the best thing; **zu** ∼**er Zeit** in due course; at the appropriate time

gegebenen·falls *Adv.* should the occasion arise

Gegebenheit *die;* ∼, ∼**en;** *meist Pl.* condition; fact

gegen /'ge:gṇ/ ▶530 | **1** *Präp. mit Akk.* **(a)** towards; (on) against; **das Dia** ∼ **das Licht halten** hold the slide up to *or* against the light; ∼ **die Tür schlagen** bang on the door; ∼ **etw. stoßen** knock into *or* against sth.; **ein Mittel** ∼ **Husten/Krebs** a cough medicine/a cure for cancer; ∼ **die Abmachung** contrary to *or* against the agreement; ∼ **alle Vernunft/bessere Einsicht** against all reason/ one's better judgement; **(b)** (ungefähr um) around ‹*midnight, 4 o'clock, etc.*›; ∼ **Abend/Morgen** towards evening/dawn; **(c)** (im Vergleich zu) compared with; in comparison with; **ich wette hundert** ∼ **eins, dass er …**: I'll bet you a hundred to one he …; **(d)** (im Ausgleich für) for; **etw.** ∼ **bar verkaufen** sell sth. for cash; **etw.** ∼ **Quittung erhalten** receive sth. against a receipt; **(e)** (veralt.: gegenüber) to; towards; ∼ **jmdn./sich streng sein** be strict with sb./oneself. **2** *Adv.* (ungefähr) about; around

Gegen-: ∼**angriff** *der* counter-attack; ∼**argument** *das* counter-argument; ∼**beispiel** *das* example to the contrary; counter-example; ∼**besuch** *der* return visit; ∼**bewegung** *die* counter-movement; ∼**beweis** *der* evidence to the contrary, counter-evidence *no indef. art.*, *no pl.;* **den** ∼**beweis antreten** *od.* **führen** produce evidence to the contrary *or* counter-evidence

Gegend /'ge:gṇt/ *die;* ∼, ∼**en (a)** (Landschaft) landscape; (geographisches Gebiet) region; **durch die** ∼ **latschen/ kurven** (salopp) traipse around (coll.) /drive around; **(b)** (Umgebung) area; neighbourhood; **in der** ∼ **von/um Hamburg** in the Hamburg area; **in der** ∼ **des Parks** in the neighbourhood of the park; **(c) in der** ∼ **des Magens** in the region of the stomach

Gegen·darstellung *die:* **eine** ∼**darstellung [der Sache]** an account [of the matter] from an opposing point of view

gegen·einander *Adv.* **(a)** against each other *or* one another; ∼ **prallen** collide; **zwei Dinge** ∼ **halten** hold two things up together *or* side by side; (fig.: vergleichen) compare two things; put two things together side by side; **man tauschte die Geiseln** ∼ **aus** the hostages were exchanged; **zwei Begriffe/Epochen** ∼ **abgrenzen** distinguish two concepts/divide two periods from each other; **(b)** (zueinander) to[wards] each other *or* one another

***gegeneinander|halten** *usw.:* ⇒ **gegeneinander a**

gegen-, Gegen-: ∼**entwurf** *der* alternative draft; ∼**fahrbahn** *die* opposite carriageway; ∼**frage** *die* question in return; counter-question; ∼**gewicht** *das* counterweight; **ein** ∼**gewicht zu** *od.* **gegen etw. bilden** (fig.) counterbalance sth.; ∼**gift** *das* antidote; ∼**grund** *der* ⇒ **Grund** d; ∼**kandidat** *der* opposing candidate;

rival candidate; ∼**leistung** *die* service in return; consideration; **als** ∼**leistung für etw.** in return for sth.; ∼**lenken** *itr. V.* turn the wheel to correct the line

Gegen·licht *das; o. Pl.* (bes. Fot.) back-lighting

Gegenlicht·aufnahme *die* (Fot.) photograph taken against the light; contre-jour photograph

gegen-, Gegen-: ∼**liebe** *die in* [**bei jmdm.**] ∼**liebe finden** *od.* **auf** ∼**liebe stoßen** find favour [with sb.]; ∼**maßnahme** *die* countermeasure; ∼**mittel** *das* (gegen Gift) antidote; ∼**partei** *die* opposing side; other side; ∼**pol** *der* (auch fig.) opposite pole; (Math.) antipole; ∼**probe** *die* cross-check; **die** ∼**probe machen** (bei einer Behauptung, These) carry out a cross-check; (bei einer Rechnung) work the sum the other way round; (bei Abstimmungen) *carry out a recount in which the opposite motion is put;* ∼**rede** *die* **(a)** (geh.: Erwiderung) reply; rejoinder; **(b)** (Widerrede) contradiction; (Einspruch) objection; ∼**richtung** *die* opposite direction; ∼**satz** *der* **(a)** opposite; **einen schroffen/diametralen** ∼**satz zu etw./jmdm. bilden** contrast sharply with/be diametrically opposed to sth./sb.; **im** ∼**satz zu** in contrast to *or* with; unlike; **(b)** (Widerspruch) conflict; **im krassen/scharfen** ∼**satz zu etw. stehen** be in stark/sharp conflict with sth.; **(c)** *Pl.* (Meinungsverschiedenheiten) differences *Pl.;* ∼**sätzlich 1** *Adj.* conflicting ‹*views, opinions, etc.*›; opposing ‹*alignments*›; **2** *adv.* **etw.** ∼**sätzlich beurteilen** judge sth. completely differently; ∼**schlag** *der* counterstroke; **zum** ∼**schlag ausholen** prepare to counter-attack *or* strike back; ∼**seite** *die* **(a)** other side; far side; **(b)** ⇒ ∼**partei;** ∼**seitig 1** *Adj.* mutual ‹*aid, consideration, love, consent, services*›; reciprocal ‹*aid, obligation, services*›; **in** ∼**seitiger Abhängigkeit stehen** be mutually dependent; be dependent on each other *or* one another; **in** ∼**seitigem Einvernehmen** by mutual agreement; **2** *adv.* **sich** ∼**seitig helfen** help each other *or* one another; ∼**seitigkeit** *die* reciprocity; **auf** ∼**seitigkeit** (*Dat.*) **beruhen** be mutual; ∼**spieler** *der* **(a)** (Widersacher) opponent; **(b)** (Sport) opposite number; **(c)** (Theater) antagonist; ∼**sprechanlage** *die* intercom [system]; (Fernspr.) duplex system

Gegen·stand *der* **(a)** object; **Gegenstände des täglichen Bedarfs** objects *or* articles of everyday use; **(b)** *o. Pl.* (Thema) subject; topic; **etw. zum** ∼ **haben** deal with sth.; be concerned with sth.; **(c)** (Ziel) (der Zuneigung, des Hasses) object; (der Kritik) target; butt

gegenständlich /'ge:gṇʃtɛntlɪç/ *Adj.* (Kunst) representational

gegenstands·los *Adj.* **(a)** (hinfällig) invalid; **(b)** (grundlos) unsubstantiated, unfounded ‹*accusation, complaint*›; baseless ‹*fear*›; unfounded ‹*jealousy*›

gegen-, Gegen-: ∼**stimme** *die* **(a)** vote against; **ohne** ∼**stimme** unanimously; **(b)** (gegenteilige Meinung) dissenting voice; ∼**stück** *das* companion piece; (fig.) counterpart; ∼**teil** *das* opposite; **im** ∼**teil** on the contrary; ∼**teilig** *Adj.* opposite; contrary; ∼**teiliger Meinung sein** be of the opposite opinion; ∼**tor** *das,* ∼**treffer** *der* (Ballspiele) goal for the other side

gegen·über 1 *Präp. mit Dat.* **(a)** ▶583 | opposite; ∼ **dem Bahnhof, dem Bahnhof** ∼: opposite the station; **(b)** (in Bezug auf) ∼ **jmdm.** *od.* **jmdm.** ∼ **freundlich/ streng sein** be kind to/strict with sb.; ∼ **einer Sache** *od.* **einer Sache** ∼ **skeptisch sein** be sceptical about sth.; **(c)** (im Vergleich zu) compared with; in comparison with; ∼ **jmdm. im Vorteil sein** have an advantage over sb. **2** *Adv.* ▶583 | opposite

Gegen·über *das;* ∼**s,** ∼ person [sitting/standing] opposite

gegenüber-, Gegenüber-: ∼**|liegen** *unr. itr. V.* **sich** (*Dat.*) *od.* **einander** ∼**liegen** face each other *or* one another; **auf der** ∼**liegenden Seite** on the opposite side; ∼**|sitzen** *unr. itr. V.* **jmdm./sich** ∼**sitzen** sit opposite or facing sb./each other; ∼**|stehen** *unr. itr. V.* **(a)** jmdm./**einer Sache** ∼**stehen** stand facing sb./sth.; **Schwierigkeiten** ∼**stehen** (fig.) be faced *or* confronted with difficulties; **(b)** **jmdm./einer Sache feindlich/ wohlwollend** ∼**stehen** (fig.) be ill/well disposed towards sb./sth.; *s. auch* **ablehnend 2;** **(c)** **sich** ∼**stehen** (Sport) face each other *or* one another; meet; **(d)** **sich** (*Dat.*)

~stehen (fig.: im Widerstreit stehen) stand directly opposed to each other or one another; ~|**stellen** tr. V. (a) confront; jmdn. einem Zeugen ~stellen to confront sb. with a witness; (b) (vergleichen) compare; ~**stellung** die (a) confrontation; (b) (Vergleich) comparison; ~|**treten** unr. itr. V.; mit sein (auch fig.) face ⟨person, difficulties⟩

Gegen-: ~**verkehr** der oncoming traffic; ~**vorschlag** der counter-proposal

Gegenwart /-vart/ die; ~ (a) present; (heutige Zeit) present [time or day]; die Musik der ~: contemporary music; (b) (Anwesenheit) presence; in ~ von anderen in the presence of others; (c) (Grammatik) present [tense]

gegenwärtig /-vɛrtɪç/ 1 Adj. (a) nicht präd. present; (heutig) present[-day]; current; (b) (veralt.: anwesend, zugegen) present; bei etw. ~ sein be present at sth.. 2 adv. at present; at the moment; (heute) at present; currently

gegenwarts-, Gegenwarts-: ~**bezogen** 1 Adj. relevant to the present day or to today postpos.; (aktuell) topical; 2 adv. ~**bezogen unterrichten** teach in accordance with contemporary ideas; ~**kunst** die contemporary art no art.; ~**literatur** die contemporary literature no art.; ~**nah** adj., adv. ⇒ ~**bezogen**; ~**sprache** die present-day language

gegen-, Gegen-: ~**wehr** die; o. Pl. resistance; [keine] ~**wehr leisten** put up [no] resistance; ~**wert** der equivalent; ~**wind** der head wind; ~|**zeichnen** tr. V. countersign; ~**zug** der (a) (Brettspiele, fig.) countermove; (Politik) reciprocal gesture; (b) (entgegenkommender Zug) train in the opposite direction

gegessen /gəˈɡɛsn̩/ 2. Part. v. **essen**

geglichen /gəˈɡlɪçn̩/ 2. Part. v. **gleichen**

geglitten /gəˈɡlɪtn̩/ 2. Part. v. **gleiten**

geglommen /gəˈɡlɔmən/ 2. Part. v. **glimmen**

Gegner /ˈɡeːɡnɐ/ der; ~s, ~ (a) adversary; opponent; (Rivale) rival; ein ~ einer Sache (Gen.) sein oppose sth.; be an opponent of sth.; (b) (Sport) opponent; (Mannschaft) opposing team; (c) (Milit.) enemy

Gegnerin die; ~, ~nen (a) ⇒ **Gegner** a; (b) (Sport) opponent

gegnerisch Adj.; nicht präd. (a) opposing; (b) (Sport) opposing ⟨team, player, etc.⟩; opponents' ⟨goal⟩; (c) (Milit.) enemy

Gegnerschaft die; ~ hostility; antagonism

gegolten /gəˈɡɔltn̩/ 2. Part. v. **gelten**

gegoren /gəˈɡoːrən/ 2. Part. v. **gären**

gegossen /gəˈɡɔsn̩/ 2. Part. v. **gießen**

gegriffen /gəˈɡrɪfn̩/ 2. Part. v. **greifen**

Gegröle das; ~s (ugs. abwertend) [raucous] bawling and shouting; (Gesang) raucous singing

Gehabe das; ~s (abwertend) affected behaviour

gehaben refl. V. (veralt., noch scherzh.) in gehab dich wohl!/gehabt euch wohl! farewell!

gehabt 1 2. Part. v. **haben.** 2 Adj.; nicht präd. (ugs.: schon da gewesen) same old (coll.); usual; wie ~: as before

Gehackte /gəˈhaktə/ das; adj. Dekl. mince[meat]; ~s vom Rind/Schwein minced beef/pork

Gehalt¹ der; ~[e]s, ~e (a) (gedanklicher Inhalt) meaning; religiöser ~: religious content; (b) (Anteil) content; ein hoher ~ an Gold a high gold content

Gehalt² das, österr. auch: der; ~[e]s, Gehälter /gəˈhɛltɐ/ salary; 1 000 DM ~, ein ~ von 1 000 DM beziehen draw a salary of 1,000 marks

gehalten 1 2. Part. v. **halten.** 2 Adj. (geh.) ~ sein, etw. zu tun be obliged or required to do sth.

gehalt·los Adj. unnutritious ⟨food⟩; ⟨wine⟩ lacking in body; (fig.) vacuous; empty; lacking in substance postpos., not pred.

Gehalts-: ~**anspruch** der salary claim; pay claim; ~**aufbesserung** die increase in salary; ~**empfänger** der salary earner; ~**erhöhung** die salary increase; rise [in salary]; ~**liste** die payroll; auf jmds. ~**liste** (Dat.) stehen (fig.) be on sb.'s payroll; be in sb.'s pocket; ~**vorschuss** der advance [on one's salary]

gehalt·voll Adj. nutritious, nourishing ⟨food⟩; full-bodied ⟨wine⟩; ⟨novel, speech⟩ rich in substance postpos.

Gehänge das; ~s, ~ (Girlande) festoon; (Kranz) garland

geharnischt /gəˈharnɪʃt/ Adj. (a) (scharf, energisch) strongly-worded; (b) (hist.: gepanzert) ein ~er Ritter a knight in armour

gehässig /gəˈhɛsɪç/ Adj. (abwertend) spiteful; ~ von jmdm. reden be spiteful about sb.

Gehässigkeit die; ~, ~en (a) o. Pl. (Wesen) spitefulness; (b) meist Pl. (Äußerung) spiteful remark

gehauen 2. Part. v. **hauen**

gehäuft 1 Adj. heaped ⟨spoon⟩. 2 adv. in large numbers

Gehäuse /gəˈhɔyzə/ das; ~s, ~ (a) (einer Maschine, Welle) casing; housing; (einer Kamera, Uhr) case; casing; (einer Lampe) housing; (b) (Schnecken~ usw.) shell; (c) (Kern~) core; (d) (Sportjargon: Tor) goal

geh·behindert Adj. able to walk only with difficulty postpos.; disabled; sie ist stark ~behindert she can walk only with great difficulty

Gehege das; ~s, ~ (a) (Jägerspr.: Revier) preserve; jmdm. ins ~ kommen (fig.) poach on sb.'s preserve; sich (Dat.) [gegenseitig] ins ~ kommen (fig.) encroach on each other's territory; (b) (im Zoo) enclosure

geheim 1 Adj. (a) secret; streng ~: top or highly secret; etw. ~ halten keep sth. secret; (b) (mysteriös) mysterious. 2 adv. ~ abstimmen vote by secret ballot

Geheim- secret ⟨agent, society, code, service, etc.⟩

*geheim|halten ⇒ geheim 1 a

Geheim·haltung die; o. Pl. observance of secrecy

Geheimnis das; ~ses, ~se (a) secret; vor jmdm. [keine] ~se haben have [no] secrets from sb.; das ist das ganze ~: that's all there is to it; (b) (Unerforschtes) mystery; secret; die ~se der Natur the mysteries or secrets of nature

geheimnis-, Geheimnis-: ~**krämer** der (ugs.) mystery-monger; ~**krämerei** die; ~, ~**tuerei** die; ~ (ugs. abwertend) secretiveness; mystery-mongering; ~**voll** 1 Adj. mysterious; auf ~**volle Weise** in a mysterious way; mysteriously; 2 adv. mysteriously; ~**voll tun** be mysterious; act mysteriously

Geheim·nummer die (a) (Bankw.) personal identification number; PIN; (b) (Telefonnummer) ex-directory number; unlisted number (Amer.)

Geheim·polizei die secret police

Geheimrats·ecken Pl. (ugs. scherzh.) receding hairline sing.

Geheim-: ~**rezept** das secret recipe; *~**tip**, ~**tipp** der inside tip; ~**tür** die secret door; ~**waffe** die (Milit.) secret weapon

Geheiß das; ~es (geh.) behest (literary); command; auf jmds. ~: at sb.'s behest or command

gehemmt Adj. inhibited

gehen /ˈɡeːən/ 1 unr. itr. V.; mit sein (a) (sich zu Fuß fortbewegen) walk; go; auf und ab ~: walk up and down; über die Straße ~: cross the street; wo er geht und steht wherever he goes or is; no matter where he goes or is; etw. geht durch die Presse (fig.) sth. is in the papers; (b) (sich irgendwohin begeben) go; tanzen ~: go dancing; schlafen ~: go to bed; zu jmdm. ~: go to see sb.; go and see sb. (coll.); zum Arzt ~: go to the doctor; nach London ~: move to London; an die Arbeit ~ (fig.) get down to work; in sich (Akk.) ~ (fig.) take stock of oneself; (c) (regelmäßig besuchen) attend; in die od. zur Schule ~: be at or attend school; (d) (weg~) go; leave; Sie können ~: you may go; der Minister musste ~: the Minister had to resign; er ist von uns gegangen (verhüll.) he has passed away or passed over (euphem.); jmdn. ~ lassen (ugs.) leave sb. alone; (e) (ugs.: [ab]fahren) ⟨train⟩ leave; (f) (in Funktion sein) work; meine Uhr geht falsch/richtig my watch is wrong/right; das Telefon geht ununterbrochen the telephone never stops ringing; (g) (möglich sein) ja, das geht yes, I/we can manage that; das geht nicht that can't be done; that's impossible; (ist nicht zulässig) that's not on (Brit. coll.); no way (coll.); Donnerstag geht auch Thursday's a possibility or all right too; es geht einfach nicht, dass du so spät nach Hause kommst it simply won't do for you to come home so late; **es geht leider nicht anders** unfortunately there's nothing else for it; **das wird schwer/schlecht** ~: that will be difficult; **auf diese Weise geht es nicht/sicher** it won't/is bound to work this way; **(h)** (ugs.: angehen) **es geht so** it could be worse; **das Essen ging ja noch, aber der Wein war ungenießbar** the food was passable, but the wine was undrinkable; **Hast du gut geschlafen? — Es geht** Did you sleep well? — Not too bad *or* So-so; **(i)** (ablaufen) **das Geschäft geht gut/gar nicht** business is doing well/not doing well at all; **gut gehend** flourishing; thriving; **es geht alles nach Plan** everything is going according to plan; **alles geht drunter und drüber** (ugs.) everything's at sixes and sevens; **wie geht die Melodie?** (fig.) how does the tune go?; what's the tune?; **vor sich ~:** go on; happen; **gut ~** (gut ausgehen) turn out well; **es ist noch einmal ~ gegangen** it worked out all right again this time; **schief ~** (ugs.: schlecht ausgehen) go wrong; **es wird schon schief ~** (iron.) it'll all turn out OK (coll.); **(j)** (reichen) **das Wasser geht mir bis an die Knie** the water comes up to *or* reaches my knees; **ich gehe ihm bis zu den Schultern** I come up to his shoulders; **in die Hunderte ~:** run into [the] hundreds; **das geht über mein Vermögen/meinen Horizont** (fig.) that is beyond me; **es geht [doch] nichts über ...** (+ *Akk.*) (fig.) there is nothing like *or* nothing to beat ...; **nothing beats ...; das geht zu weit** (fig.) that's going too far; **(k)** *unpers.* **jmdm. geht es gut/schlecht** (gesundheitlich) sb. is well *or* (coll.) fine/not well; (geschäftlich) sb. is doing well/badly; **wie geht es dir/Ihnen?** how are you?; **wie gehts, wie stehts?** (ugs.) how are things?; **wenn sie das herausfindet, gehts dir schlecht!** (ugs.) if she finds out, you'll be [in] for it; **(l)** *unpers.* (sich um etw. handeln) **es geht um mehr als ...:** there is more at stake than ...; **jmdm. geht es um etw.** sth. matters to sb.; **worum geht es hier?** what is this all about?; **(m)** (tätig werden) **in den Staatsdienst/in die Politik ~:** join the Civil Service/go into politics; **zum Film/Theater ~:** go into films/on the stage; **(n)** (ugs.: sich kleiden) **in Hosen ~:** wear trousers; **in kurz/lang ~:** wear a short/long dress/skirt; **als Zigeuner ~:** go as a gypsy; **(o)** (ugs.: sich zu schaffen machen an) **du sollst nicht an meine Sachen ~** you must not mess around with my things; (benutzen) you must not take my things; **die Kinder sind an den Kuchen gegangen** the children have been at the cake (coll.); **(p)** **mit jmdm. ~:** go out with sb.; **(q)** (absetzbar sein) **[gut/schlecht] ~:** sell [well/slowly]; **(r)** (passen) go; **(s)** (verlaufen) go; **die Straße geht geradeaus/nach links** the road goes *or* runs straight ahead/turns to the left; **wohin geht diese Straße?** where does this road go *or* lead to?; **(t)** (gerichtet sein auf) **nach der Straße/nach Süden ~** ‹*room, window, etc.*› face the road/face south; **gegen jmdn./etw. ~** (fig.) be aimed *or* directed at sb./sth.; **das geht gegen meine Überzeugung** that goes against my convictions; **(u)** (als Maßstab nehmen) **nach jmdm./etw. ~:** go by sb./sth.; **(v)** **in Stücke/Scherben ~:** get smashed; **(w)** **etw. geht auf jmdn./jmds. Rechnung** sb. is paying for sth.; **(x)** (geschickt werden) **an jmdn. ~:** go to sb.; **die Briefe ~ nach Oxford** the letters are going to Oxford; **(y)** **sich ~ lassen** lose control of oneself; (sich vernachlässigen) let oneself go. **2** *unr. tr. V.* (zurücklegen) **eine Strecke ~:** cover *or* do a distance; **einen Umweg ~:** make a detour; **einen Weg in 30 Minuten ~:** do a walk in 30 minutes; **seine eigenen Wege ~** (fig.) go one's own way

Gehen *das;* ~s **(a)** walking; **er hat Schmerzen beim ~:** it hurts him to walk; **(b)** (Leichtathletik) walking; **der Sieger im 50-km-~:** the winner of the 50 km walk

*gehen|lassen ⇒ **gehen 1 d, 1 y**

Geher /ˈgeːɐ/ *der;* ~s, ~ (Leichtathletik) walker

geheuer /gəˈhɔyɐ/ *Adj.* **(a)** **in diesem Gebäude ist es nicht ~:** this building is eerie; this building feels as if it's haunted (coll.); **(b)** **ihr war doch nicht [ganz] ~:** she felt [a little] uneasy; **(c)** **die Sache ist [mir] nicht ganz ~:** [I feel] there's something odd *or* suspicious about this business

Geheul *das;* ~[e]s **(a)** (auch fig.) howling; **(b)** (ugs. abwertend: Weinen) bawling; wailing

Geheule *das;* ~s ⇒ **Geheul b**

Gehilfe /gəˈhɪlfə/ *der;* ~n, ~n, **Gehilfin** *die;* ~, ~nen **(a)** qualified assistant; **(b)** (veralt.: Helfer/Helferin) helper; assistant

Gehirn *das;* ~[e]s, ~e **(a)** brain; **(b)** ▶ 326 | (ugs.: Verstand) mind; **sein ~ anstrengen, sich** (*Dat.*) **das ~ zermartern** rack one's brain[s]

Gehirn-: ~**erschütterung** *die* ▶ 329 | (Med.) concussion; ~**schlag** *der* ▶ 329 | (Med.) stroke; [cerebral] apoplexy *no art.* (Med.); ~**wäsche** *die* brainwashing *no indef. art.;* **jmdn. einer ~wäsche unterziehen** brainwash sb.; ~**zelle** *die* brain cell

gehoben /gəˈhoːbn̩/ **1** *2. Part. v.* **heben. 2** *Adj.* **(a)** higher ‹*income*›; senior ‹*position*›; **der ~e Dienst** the higher [levels of the] Civil Service; **der ~e Mittelstand** the upper middle class; **(b)** (anspruchsvoll) **Kleidung für den ~en Geschmack** clothes for those with discerning taste; **Artikel für den ~en Bedarf** luxury goods; **(c)** (gewählt) elevated, refined ‹*language, expression*›; **(d)** (feierlich) festive ‹*mood*›. **3** *adv.* **sich ~ ausdrücken** use elevated *or* refined language

Gehöft /gəˈhœft, -ˈhøːft/ *das;* ~[e]s, ~e farm[stead]

geholfen /gəˈhɔlfn̩/ *2. Part. v.* **helfen**

Gehölz /gəˈhœlts/ *das;* ~es, ~e **(a)** copse; spinney (Brit.); **(b)** *meist Pl.* (Holzgewächs) woody plant

Gehör /gəˈhøːɐ̯/ *das;* ~[e]s [sense of] hearing; **ein gutes ~ haben** have good hearing; **[etw.] nach dem ~ singen/spielen** sing/play [sth.] by ear; **das absolute ~ haben** (Musik) have absolute pitch; **~/kein ~ finden** meet with *or* get a/no response; **jmdm./einer Sache [kein] ~ schenken** [not] listen to sb./sth.

gehorchen /gəˈhɔrçn̩/ *itr. V.* **jmdm. ~:** obey sb.; **einer Sache** (*Dat.*) **~:** respond to sth.; **einer Laune** (*Dat.*) **~:** yield to a caprice

gehören /gəˈhøːrən/ **1** *itr. V.* **(a)** (Eigentum sein) **jmdm. ~:** belong to sb.; **das Haus gehört uns nicht** the house doesn't belong to us; we don't own the house; **wem gehört das Buch?** whose book is it?; who does the book belong to?; **(b)** (Teil eines Ganzen sein) **zu jmds. Freunden ~:** be one of sb.'s friends; **zu jmds. Aufgaben ~:** be part of sb.'s duties; **(c)** (passend sein) **dein Roller gehört doch nicht in die Küche!** your scooter does not belong in the kitchen!; **das gehört nicht/durchaus zur Sache** that is not to the point/is very much to the point; **(d)** (sein sollen) **du gehörst ins Bett** you should be in bed; **(e)** (nötig sein) **es hat viel Fleiß dazu gehört** it took *or* called for a lot of hard work; **dazu gehört sehr viel/einiges** that takes a lot/something; **dazu gehört nicht viel** that doesn't take much; **(f)** (bes. südd.) **das gehört verboten** that should be forbidden; that shouldn't be allowed; **er gehört geohrfeigt** he deserves *or* (coll.) needs a box round the ears. **2** *refl. V.* (sich schicken) be fitting; **es gehört sich [nicht], ... zu ...:** it is [not] good manners to ...; **wie es sich gehört** comme il faut

gehörig 1 *Adj.* **(a)** *nicht präd.* (gebührend) proper; **jmdm. den ~en Respekt/die ~e Achtung erweisen** show sb. proper *or* due respect; **(b)** *nicht präd.* (ugs.: beträchtlich) **ein ~er Schrecken/eine ~e Portion Mut** a good fright/a good deal of courage. **2** *adv.* **(a)** (gebührend) properly; **(b)** (ugs.: beträchtlich) **essen** eat properly *or* heartily; **er hat ~ geschimpft** he didn't half grumble (coll.)

gehör·los *Adj.* deaf

gehörnt *Adj.* **(a)** horned; (mit einem Geweih) antlered; **(b)** (scherzh. verhüll.: betrogen) cuckolded; **ein ~er Ehemann** a cuckold

gehorsam /gəˈhoːɐ̯zaːm/ *Adj.* obedient

Gehorsam *der;* ~s obedience; **jmdm. ~ leisten/den ~ verweigern** obey/refuse to obey sb.

Gehorsams·verweigerung *die; o. Pl.* (Milit.) insubordination; refusal to obey orders

Geh-: ~**steig** *der* pavement (Brit.); sidewalk (Amer.); ~**versuch** *der; meist Pl.* attempt at walking; (nach einem Unfall) attempt at walking again

Geier /ˈgaiɐ/ *der;* ~s, ~: vulture; **hols der ~** (ugs.) to hell with it (coll.); **weiß der ~** (salopp) God only knows (sl.); Christ knows (sl.)

Geifer /'gaifɐ/ *der;* ~s (a) slaver; slobber; (b) (geh. abwertend: Gehässigkeit) venom; vituperation

geifern *itr. V.* (a) slaver; slobber; (b) (abwertend: gehässig reden) **gegen jmdn./über etw.** (*Akk.*) ~: discharge one's venom at sb./sth.

Geige /'gaigə/ *die;* ~, ~n violin; **die erste** ~ **spielen** (fig. ugs.) play first fiddle; call the tune

geigen 1 *itr. V.* (a) (ugs.: Geige spielen) play the fiddle (coll.) *or* the violin; (b) (ugs.: von Insekten) chirp; chirr. 2 *tr. V.* (a) (ugs.: auf der Geige spielen) **einen Walzer** ~: play a waltz on the fiddle (coll.) *or* violin

Geigen-: ~**bauer** *der* ▶ 85 | violin-maker; ~**bogen** *der* violin bow; ~**kasten** *der* violin case

Geiger *der;* ~s, ~, **Geigerin** *die;* ~, ~**nen:** violin-player; violinist

Geiger·zähler *der* (Physik) Geiger counter

geil /gail/ 1 *Adj.* (a) (oft abwertend) (sexuell erregt) randy; horny (sl.); (lüstern) lecherous; **auf jmdn.** ~ **sein** lust for *or* after sb.; (b) (Jugendspr.) great (coll.). 2 *adv.* (oft abwertend) lecherously

Geisel /'gaizl/ *die;* ~, ~n hostage; **jmdn. als** *od.* **zur** ~ **nehmen** take sb. hostage

Geisel-: ~**drama** *das* (Pressejargon) hostage drama; ~**gangster** *der* (Pressejargon) ⇒ ~**nehmer;** ~**nahme** *die* taking of hostages; ~**nehmer** *der* terrorist/guerrilla *etc.* holding the hostages

Geiß /gais/ *die;* ~, ~**en** (a) (südd., österr., schweiz.: Ziege) [nanny-]goat; (b) (Jägerspr.) doe

Geißel /'gaisl/ *die;* ~, ~**n** (auch fig.) scourge

geißeln *tr. V.* (a) (tadeln) castigate; (b) (züchtigen) scourge

Geißelung *die;* ~, ~**en** (a) (Tadelung) castigation; (b) (Züchtigung) scourging

Geist /gaist/ *der;* ~**[e]s,** ~**er** (a) *o. Pl.* (Verstand) mind; **jmds.** ~ **ist verwirrt/gestört** sb. is mentally deranged/disturbed; **jmdm. mit etw. auf den** ~ **gehen** (salopp) get on sb.'s nerves with sth.; **den** ~ **aufgeben** (geh./ugs. scherzh., auch fig.) give up the ghost; **im** ~**[e]** in my/his *etc.* mind's eye; (b) *o. Pl.* (Scharfsinn) wit; (c) *o. Pl.* (innere Einstellung) spirit; (d) (denkender Mensch) mind; intellect; **ein großer/kleiner** ~: a great mind/a person of limited intellect; **hier** *od.* **da scheiden sich die** ~**er** this is where opinions differ; (e) (überirdisches Wesen) spirit; **der Heilige** ~ (christl. Rel.) the Holy Ghost *or* Spirit; **der böse** ~: the evil spirit; **von allen guten** ~**ern verlassen sein** have taken leave of one's senses; be out of one's mind; (f) (Gespenst) ghost; ~**er gehen im Schloss um/spuken im Schloss** the castle is haunted

Geister-: ~**bahn** *die* ghost train; ~**fahrer** *der* (ugs.) ghost-driver (Amer.); *person driving on the wrong side of the road or the wrong carriageway;* ~**geschichte** *die* ghost story

geisterhaft *Adj.* ghostly; spectral; eerie ‹*atmosphere*›

Geister·hand *die in* **wie von** ~: as if by an invisible hand

geistern /'gaistɐn/ *itr. V.; mit sein* ‹*ghost*› wander; (fig.) wander like a ghost; **diese Idee geisterte immer noch durch seinen Kopf** he still had this idea in his head

Geister-: ~**stadt** *die* ghost town; ~**stunde** *die* witching hour

geistes-, Geistes-: ~**abwesend** 1 *Adj.* absent-minded; 2 *adv.* absent-mindedly; ~**abwesenheit** *die* absent-mindedness; ~**blitz** *der* (ugs.) brainwave; flash of inspiration; ~**gaben** *Pl.* intellectual gifts; ~**gegenwart** *die* presence of mind; ~**gegenwärtig** 1 *Adj.* quick-witted; 2 *adv.* with great presence of mind; ~**geschichte** *die* history of ideas; intellectual history; ~**gestört** *Adj.* mentally disturbed; ~**haltung** *die* attitude [of mind]; ~**krank** *Adj.* mentally ill; [mentally] deranged; ~**kranke** *der/die* mentally ill person; (im Krankenhaus) mental patient; ~**krankheit** *die* mental illness; ~**schwäche** *die; o. Pl.* feeble-mindedness; mental deficiency; ~**wissenschaften** *Pl.* arts; humanities; ~**wissenschaftler** *der* arts scholar; scholar in the humanities; ~**wissenschaftlich** *Adj.* ~**wissenschaftliche Fächer** arts subjects; ~**zustand** *der* mental condition; mental state

geistig 1 *Adj.; nicht präd.* (a) intellectual; spiritual ‹*legacy, father, author*›; (Psych.) mental; ~**e Arbeit** brainwork; ~**er Diebstahl** plagiarism; (b) (alkoholisch) ~**e Getränke** alcoholic drinks *or* beverages. 2 *adv.* intellectually ‹*superior*›; mentally ‹*lazy, active, retarded, disabled*›; ~ **weggetreten sein** (ugs.) be miles away (coll.)

geistlich *Adj.; nicht präd.* sacred ‹*song, music*›; religious ‹*order*›; religious, devotional ‹*book, wrIttngs*›; spiritual ‹*matter, support*›; spiritual, religious ‹*leader*›; ecclesiastical ‹*office, dignitary*›; **der** ~**e Stand** the clergy

Geistliche *der; adj. Dekl.* clergyman; priest; (einer Freikirche) minister; (Militär~, Gefängnis~) chaplain

geist-, Geist-: ~**los** *Adj.* dim-witted; witless; (trivial) trivial; ~**losigkeit** *die;* ~ dim-wittedness; witlessness; (Trivialität) triviality; ~**reich** 1 *Adj.* witty; (klug) clever; 2 *adv.* wittily; (klug) cleverly; ~**tötend** *Adj.* soul-destroying ‹*work, job*›; stupefyingly boring ‹*chatter, drivel*›; ~**voll** *Adj.* brilliantly witty ‹*joke, satire*›; brilliant ‹*idea*›; intellectually stimulating ‹*conversation, book*›

Geiz /gaits/ *der;* ~**es** meanness; (Knauserigkeit) miserliness

geizen *itr. V.* be mean; **mit etw.** ~: be mean *or* stingy with sth.; **mit Lob** ~ (fig.) be sparing with one's praise

Geiz·hals *der* (abwertend) skinflint

geizig *Adj.* mean; (knauserig) miserly

Geiz·kragen *der* (ugs. abwertend) skinflint

gekannt /gə'kant/ 2. *Part. v.* **kennen**

Gekicher *das;* ~**s** giggling

Geklimper *das;* ~**s** (abwertend) plunking

geklungen /gə'kluŋən/ 2. *Part. v.* **klingen**

geknickt *Adj.* (ugs.) dejected; downcast

gekniffen 2. *Part. v.* **kneifen**

Geknister *das;* ~**s** rustling; rustle; (von Holz, Feuer) crackling; crackle

gekommen 2. *Part. v.* **kommen**

gekonnt /gə'kɔnt/ 1 2. *Part. v.* **können.** 2 *Adj.* accomplished; (hervorragend ausgeführt) masterly. 3 *adv.* in an accomplished manner; (hervorragend) in masterly fashion

gekoren /gə'ko:rən/ 2. *Part. v.* **küren, kiesen**

Gekreisch[e] *das;* ~**s** (von Vögeln) screeching; (von Menschen) shrieking; squealing; (von Rädern, Bremsen) squealing

Gekritzel[e] *das;* ~**s** (abwertend) scribble; scrawl

gekrochen 2. *Part. v.* **kriechen**

gekünstelt /gə'kʏnstlt/ 1 *Adj.* artificial; forced ‹*smile*›; affected ‹*behaviour*›. 2 *adv.* ~ **lächeln** give a forced smile; ~ **sprechen** talk affectedly

Gel /ge:l/ *das;* ~**s,** ~**e** (Chemie) gel

Gelaber[e] *das;* ~**s** (ugs. abwertend) rabbiting (coll.) *or* babbling on

Gelächter /gə'lɛçtɐ/ *das;* ~**s,** ~: laughter; **in** ~ **ausbrechen** burst out laughing

gelackmeiert /gə'lakmaiɐt/ *Adj.; nicht attr.* (salopp scherzh.) had (sl.); conned (coll.); **der Gelackmeierte sein** be the one who's been had (sl.)

geladen 1 2. *Part. v.* **laden.** 2 *in* ~ **sein** be furious *or* (Brit. coll.) livid

Gelage *das;* ~**s,** ~: feast; banquet; (abwertend) orgy of eating and drinking

Gelähmte *der/die; adj. Dekl.* paralytic

Gelände /gə'lɛndə/ *das;* ~**s,** ~ (a) ground; terrain; **das** ~ **steigt an/fällt ab** the ground rises/falls; (b) (Grundstück) site; (von Schule, Krankenhaus usw.) grounds *pl.*

gelände-, Gelände-: ~**fahrt** *die* cross-country drive; (das Fahren) cross-country driving; ~**fahrzeug** *das* cross-country vehicle; ~**gängig** *Adj.* cross-country *attrib.* ‹*vehicle*›; ‹*vehicle*› suitable for cross-country driving

Geländer /gə'lɛndɐ/ *das;* ~**s,** ~: banisters *pl.;* handrail; (am Balkon, an einer Brücke) railing[s *pl.*]; (aus Stein) balustrades; parapet

Gelände·wagen *der* ⇒ **Geländefahrzeug**

gelang 3. *Pers. Sg. Prät. v.* **gelingen**

gelangen *itr. V.; mit sein* (a) **an etw.** (*Akk.*) **/zu etw.** ~: arrive at *or* reach sth.; **an die Öffentlichkeit** ~:

reach the public; leak out; **in jmds. Besitz ~:** come into sb.'s possession; **(b)** (fig.) **zu Ansehen ~:** gain esteem or standing; **zu Ruhm ~:** achieve fame; **zu der Erkenntnis ~, dass ...:** come to the realization that ...; realize that ...; **(c)** als Funktionsverb **zur Aufführung ~:** be presented or performed; **zur Auszahlung ~:** be paid [out]

gelassen 1 2. Part. v. **lassen. 2** Adj. calm; (gefasst) composed; **~ bleiben** keep calm or cool. **3** adv. calmly

Gelassenheit die; ~: calmness; (Gefasstheit) composure

Gelatine /ʒelaˈtiːnə/ die; ~: gelatine

gelaufen 2. Part. v. **laufen**

geläufig Adj. **(a)** (vertraut) familiar, common ⟨expression, concept⟩; **etw. ist jmdm. ~:** sb. is familiar with sth.; **(b)** (fließend, perfekt) fluent

gelaunt /ɡəˈlaʊnt/ **gut ~:** good-humoured; cheerful; **schlecht ~:** ill-tempered; bad-tempered; **übel ~:** ill; ill-tempered; **gut/schlecht ~ sein** be in a good/bad mood; **wie ist sie ~?** what sort of mood is she in?

gelb /ɡɛlp/ Adj. yellow; **vor Neid ~ werden** turn green with envy; **das ist nicht das Gelbe vom Ei** (fig. ugs.) that's no great shakes (sl.)

Gelb das; ~s, ~ od. (ugs.) ~s yellow; **bei ~ über die Ampel fahren** go through or crash the lights on amber

gelb-, Gelb-: **~braun** Adj. yellowish-brown; **~fieber** das ▸329┃ (Med.) yellow fever; **~grün** Adj. yellowish-green

gelblich Adj. yellowish; yellowed ⟨paper⟩; sallow ⟨skin⟩

Gelb·sucht die; ▸329┃ o. Pl. (Med.) jaundice; icterus (Med.)

Geld /ɡɛlt/ das; ~es, ~er money; **großes ~:** large denominations pl.; **kleines/bares ~:** change/cash; **es ist für ~ nicht zu haben** money cannot buy it; **das ist hinausgeworfenes ~:** that is a waste of money or (coll.) money down the drain; **ins ~ gehen** (ugs.) run away with the money (coll.); **~ stinkt nicht** (Spr.) money has no smell; **~ regiert die Welt** (Spr.) money makes the world go round; **~ allein macht nicht glücklich** [(scherzh.), aber es hilft] (Spr.) money isn't everything[, but it helps]; **das große ~ machen** make a lot of money; **~ wie Heu haben, im ~ schwimmen** be rolling in money or in it (coll.), **nicht für ~ und gute Worte** (ugs.) not for love or money; **zu ~ kommen** get hold of [some] money; **etw. zu ~ machen** turn sth. into money or cash; **öffentliche ~er** public money sing. or funds

geld-, Geld-: **~angelegenheit** die; meist Pl. money or financial matter; **~anlage** die investment; **~automat** der cash dispenser; **~betrag** der sum or amount [of money]; **~beutel** der (bes. südd.), **~börse** die purse; **~geber** der financial backer; (für Forschungen usw.) sponsor; **~gier** die (abwertend) greed; avarice; **~gierig** Adj. (abwertend) greedy; avaricious; **~hahn** der in [jmdm.] den **~hahn zudrehen** (ugs.) cut off sb.'s supply of money; **~institut** das financial institution

geldlich Adj.; nicht präd. financial

Geld-: **~mittel** Pl. financial resources; funds; **~prämie** die cash bonus; (~preis) cash prize; **~preis** der cash prize; (bei einem Turnier) prize money; **~quelle** die source of income; (für den Staat) source of revenue; **~schein** der ▸216┃ banknote; bill (Amer.); **~schrank** der safe; **~schrank·knacker** der (ugs.) safe-breaker; safe-cracker; **~schwierigkeiten** Pl. financial difficulties or straits; **~sorgen** Pl. money troubles; financial worries; **~strafe** die fine; **jmdn. zu einer ~strafe verurteilen** fine sb.; **~stück** das ▸216┃ coin; **~verschwendung** die waste of money; **~waschanlage** die (ugs.) money-laundering scheme; **~wechsel** der ex- changing of money; „~wechsel" 'bureau de change'; 'change'

geleckt Adj. in **wie ~ aussehen** (ugs.) look all spruced up

Gelee /ʒeˈleː/ der od. das; ~s, ~s jelly; **Aale in ~:** jellied eels

gelegen 1 2. Part. v. **liegen. 2** Adj. **(a)** (passend) convenient; **das kommt mir ~:** that comes just at the right time for me; **(b)** (liegend) situated

Gelegenheit die; ~, ~en **(a)** opportunity; **die ~ nutzen** make the most of the opportunity; **bei nächster ~:** at the next opportunity; **bei ~:** some time; **die ~ beim Schopf[e] fassen** od. **ergreifen** grab or seize the opportunity with both hands; **(b)** (Anlass) occasion

Gelegenheits-: **~arbeit** die casual work; **~arbeiter** der casual worker; **~kauf** der bargain

gelegentlich 1 Adj.; nicht präd. occasional. **2** adv. **(a)** (manchmal) occasionally; **(b)** (bei Gelegenheit) some time

gelehrig /ɡəˈleːrɪç/ Adj. ⟨child⟩ who is quick to learn or quick at picking things up; ⟨animal⟩ that is quick to learn

gelehrt Adj. **(a)** (kenntnisreich) learned; erudite; **(b)** (wissenschaftlich) scholarly

Gelehrte der/die; adj. Dekl. scholar; **darüber streiten sich die ~n** the experts disagree on that; (fig.) that's a moot point

Geleit das; ~[e]s, ~e (geh.) **jmdm. sein ~ anbieten** offer to accompany or escort sb.; **freies** od. **sicheres ~:** (Rechtsw.) safe-conduct; **jmdm. das letzte ~ geben** (geh. verhüll.) attend sb.'s funeral

geleiten tr. V. (geh.) escort; (begleiten) accompany; escort; **jmdn. zur Tür ~:** see sb. to the door; show sb. out

Geleit·schutz der (Milit.) escort; **jmdm. ~schutz geben** provide an escort for sb.

Gelenk /ɡəˈlɛŋk/ das; ~[e]s, ~e ▸326┃ (Anat., Technik) joint; (Scharnier) hinge

gelenkig 1 Adj. agile ⟨person⟩; (geschmeidig) supple ⟨limb⟩. **2** adv. agilely

Gelenkigkeit die; ~: agility; (von Gliedmaßen) suppleness

gelernt Adj.; nicht präd. qualified

gelesen 2. Part. v. **lesen**

Geliebte der/die; adj. Dekl. **(a)** lover/mistress; **(b)** (geh. veralt.) beloved

geliefert 1 2. Part. v. **liefern. 2** Adj. **in ~ sein** (salopp) be sunk (coll.); have had it (coll.)

geliehen 2. Part. v. **leihen**

gelieren /ʒeˈliːrən/ itr. V. set

gelind[e] 1 Adj. **(a)** (schonend) mild; **(b)** (geh. veralt.: mild, sanft) mild ⟨climate⟩; light ⟨punishment⟩; slight ⟨pain⟩. **2** adv. mildly; **~e gesagt** to put it mildly

gelingen /ɡəˈlɪŋən/ unr. itr. V.; mit sein succeed; **es gelang ihr, es zu tun** she succeeded in doing it; **es gelang ihr nicht, es zu tun** she did not succeed in doing it; she failed to do it; **eine gelungene Arbeit** a successful piece of work; s. auch **gelungen 2**

Gelingen das; ~s success; **auf ein gutes ~ hoffen** hope for success; **jmdm. gutes ~ wünschen** wish sb. every success; **gutes ~!** the best of luck!

gelitten /ɡəˈlɪtn/ 2. Part. v. **leiden**

gell[e] /ˈɡɛl(ə)/ Interj. (südd.) ⇒ **gelt**

gellen /ˈɡɛlən/ itr. V. ring out; **ein Schrei gellte durch die Nacht** a scream or shriek pierced the night; **jmdm. in den Ohren ~:** make sb.'s ears ring; **~des Gelächter** shrill peals of laughter

geloben tr. V. (geh.) vow; **Besserung ~:** promise solemnly to improve; **jmdm. Treue ~:** vow to be faithful to sb.; **sich** ⟨Dat.⟩ **~, etw. zu tun** vow to oneself or make a solemn resolve to do sth.; **das Gelobte Land** the Promised Land

Gelöbnis /ɡəˈløːpnɪs/ das; ~ses, ~se (geh.) vow; **ein ~ ablegen** od. **leisten** make or take a vow

gelockt /ɡəˈlɔkt/ Adj. curly

gelogen 2. Part. v. **lügen**

gelöst /ɡəˈløːst/ Adj. relaxed

gelt /ɡɛlt/ Interj. (südd., österr. ugs.) **~, du bist mir doch nicht böse?** you're not angry with me, are you?; **er kommt doch morgen zurück, ~?** he'll be coming back tomorrow, won't he? or (coll.) right?

gelten /ˈɡɛltn̩/ **1** unr. itr. V. **(a)** (gültig sein) be valid; ⟨banknote, coin⟩ be legal tender; ⟨law, regulation, agreement⟩ be in force; ⟨price⟩ be effective; **etw. gilt für jmdn.** sth. applies to sb.; **das gilt auch für dich/Sie!** (ugs.) that includes you!; that goes for you too!; **das gilt nicht!** that doesn't count!; **nach ~dem Recht** in accordance with the law as it [now] stands; **die ~de Meinung**

Geld

Britisches Geld

GESCHRIEBEN	GESPROCHEN
1p	one p
2p	two p *od.* pence
50p	fifty p *od.* pence
£1	one pound, a pound
£1.03	one pound three p *od.* three pence*
£1.20	one pound twenty [p *od.* pence]*
£1.99	one pound ninety-nine
£20	twenty pounds
£100	one hundred *od.* a hundred pounds
£1,000	one thousand *od.* a thousand pounds
£1,000,000	one million *od.* a million pounds
£5,000,000	five million pounds

100 Pence sind ein Pfund = 100 pence make one pound, there are 100 pence in a pound

* Normalerweise sagt man immer 'p' bzw 'pence' nach einer Zahl zwischen 1 und 19, die auf eine Pfundzahl folgt; bei 20 Pence oder mehr wird das 'p' bzw 'pence' hier meist weggelassen.

Amerikanisches Geld

GESCHRIEBEN	GESPROCHEN
1c	one cent, a cent
10c	ten cents, a dime*
25c	twenty-five cents, a quarter*
$1	one dollar, a dollar
$1.50	one dollar fifty [cents]
$5.99	five dollars ninety-nine
$200	two hundred dollars
$1,000	one thousand *od.* a thousand dollars
$1,000,000	one million *od.* a million dollars
$100,000,000	one hundred *od.* a hundred million dollars

100 Cent sind ein Dollar = 100 cents make one dollar, There are 100 cents in a dollar

* Diese Bezeichnungen beziehen sich meist auf die Münzen mit diesen Werten.

Deutsches Geld

GESCHRIEBEN	GESPROCHEN
1Pf	one pfennig, a pfennig
25Pf	twenty-five pfennigs
DM1	one [Deutsch]mark, a [Deutsch]mark*
DM1.50	one mark fifty [pfennigs]
DM2	two marks
DM2.75	two marks seventy-five [pfennigs]
DM100	one hundred *od.* a hundred marks
DM200	two hundred marks
DM1,000	one thousand *od.* a thousand marks
DM1,000,000	one million *od.* a million marks
DM50,000,000	fifty million marks

100 Pfennig sind eine Mark = 100 pfennigs make one mark, there are 100 pfennigs in a mark

* Die Bezeichnung 'Deutschmark' wird meist für die Währung verwendet, z.B.

der Wert des Pfundes gegenüber der Deutschen Mark = the value of the pound against the Deutschmark

Österreichisches Geld

GESCHRIEBEN	GESPROCHEN
90g	ninety groschen
1S, 1 Sch.	one schilling, a schilling
100S, 100 ATS	one hundred *od.* a hundred schillings

Schweizerisches Geld

GESCHRIEBEN	GESPROCHEN
90c	ninety centimes
1 SF	one [Swiss] franc, a [Swiss] franc
2,000 SF	two thousand [Swiss] francs

Allgemeine Bemerkungen: 1. Im Englischen steht bei Zahlen über tausend ein Komma dort, wo im Deutschen ein Spatium steht. 2. Das Wort 'million' ist kein Substantiv (wie *Million* im Deutschen), sondern ein Adjektiv. Deshalb kein **s** bei mehreren Millionen (zwei Millionen Pfund = two million pounds).

Siehe auch □ **Zahlen**.

Münzen und Scheine

GB:

ein Zwanzigpencestück	= a 20p *od.* 20 pence piece
ein Fünfzigpencestück	= a 50p *od.* 50 pence piece
ein Pfundstück	= a pound coin
ein Fünfpfundschein	= a five-pound note

USA:

ein Fünfcentstück	= a nickel
ein Zehncentstück	= a dime
ein Vierteldollarstück	= a quarter
ein Dollarstück	= a dollar coin
ein Dollarschein	= a dollar bill
ein Zehndollarschein	= a ten-dollar bill

Man sieht, dass für die kleineren Werte (unter 1 Pfund bzw. 1 Dollar) *Stück* durch 'piece' übersetzt wird, sonst durch 'coin'. Auch dass die Währungseinheit (pound, dollar, mark usw.) vor 'piece', 'coin', 'note' oder 'bill' im Singular bleibt. Das gilt ebenfalls für deutsche Münzen:

ein Fünfzigpfennigstück	= a 50 pfennig piece
ein Markstück	= a one-mark coin
ein Fünfmarkstück	= a five-mark coin
ein Zwanzigmarkschein	= a twenty-mark note *od.* (amerik.) bill

Sonstige Ausdrücke

Was od. Wie viel kostet das?	= What *od.* How much does it cost?
Es kostet knapp 200 DM/etwas über 200 DM	= It costs just under/just over 200 DM
Die Kartoffeln kosten 30p das Pfund	= The potatoes are 30p a pound
100 Mark in bar	= 100 marks in cash
etwas bar/in Pfund bezahlen	= to pay for something in cash/in pounds
bargeldlose Zahlung	= cashless payment
Kann ich mit Scheck/ mit Kreditkarte zahlen?	= Can I pay by cheque/by credit card?
ein Scheck über 50 Pfund	= a cheque for £50
ein Reisescheck in Dollar/Pfund [Sterling]	= a dollar/sterling traveller's cheque *od.* (amerik.) traveler's check
Können Sie auf einen Zwanzigmarkschein herausgeben?	= Can you change *od.* give me change for a twenty-mark note *od.* (amerik.) bill?
Ich will Mark in Dollar wechseln	= I want to change marks into dollars
Es gehen … Mark auf ein Pfund	= There are … marks to the pound

the generally accepted opinion; **etw. [nicht]** ~ **lassen** [not] accept sth.; **(b)** (angesehen werden) **als etw.** ~**:** be regarded as sth.; be considered [to be] sth.; **(c)** (+ *Dat.*) (bestimmt sein für) be directed at; **die Bemerkung gilt dir** the remark is aimed at you; **der Beifall galt auch dem Regisseur** the applause was also for the director. **2** *unr. tr. V.* **(a)** (wert sein) **sein Wort gilt viel/wenig** his word carries a lot of/little weight; **was gilt die Wette?** what do you bet?; **etw. gilt jmdm. mehr als …:** sth. is worth *or* means more to sb. than …; **(b)** (darauf ankommen, dass) **es gilt, rasch zu handeln** it is essential to act swiftly; **(c)** *unpers.* (geh.: auf dem Spiel stehen) **es gilt dein Leben** *od.* **deinen Kopf** your life is at stake

geltend *in etw.* ~ **machen** assert sth.; **einige Bedenken/einen Einwand** ~ **machen** express some doubts/raise an objection; *s. auch* **gelten 1 a**

Geltung *die;* ~ **(a)** (Gültigkeit) validity; ~ **haben** ⟨*banknote, coin*⟩ be legal tender; ⟨*law, regulation, agreement*⟩ be in force; ⟨*price*⟩ be effective; **für jmdn.** ~ **haben** apply to sb.; **(b)** (Wirkung) recognition; **jmdm./ sich/einer Sache** ~ **verschaffen** gain *or* win recognition for sb./oneself/sth.; **an** ~ **verlieren** ⟨*value, principle, etc.*⟩ lose its importance, become less important; **etw. zur** ~ **bringen** show sth. to its best advantage; **zur** ~ **kommen** show to [its best] advantage

Geltungs-: ~**bedürfnis** *das* need for recognition; ~**bereich** *der* scope; ~**dauer** *die* period of validity; ~**drang** *der* ⇒ ~**bedürfnis;** ~**sucht** *die* [pathological] craving for recognition

gelungen /gə'lʊŋən/ **1** *2. Part. v.* **gelingen. 2** *Adj.* **(a)** (ugs.: spaßig) priceless; **das finde ich** ~**:** what a laugh!; **(b)** (ansprechend) inspired

Gelüst *das;* ~[e]s, ~e, **Gelüste** *das;* ~s, ~ (geh.) longing; strong desire; (zwingend, krankhaft) craving; **ein** ~ **nach** *od.* **auf etw.** (*Akk.*) **haben** have a longing *or* a strong desire/a craving for sth.

gelüsten *tr. V.; unpers.* **es gelüstet ihn nach …:** he has a longing for …; (zwingend, krankhaft) he has a craving for …

Gemach /gə'ma(ː)x/ *das;* ~[e]s, **Gemächer** /gə'mɛ(ː)çɐ/ (veralt. geh.) apartment

gemächlich /gə'mɛ(ː)çlɪç/ **1** *Adj.* leisurely; **ein** ~**es Leben führen** take life easily. **2** *adv.* in a leisurely manner

gemacht *Adj.* **in ein** ~**er Mann sein** (ugs.) be a made man

Gemahl *der;* ~s, ~e (geh.) consort; husband; **bitte grüßen Sie Ihren Herrn** ~**:** please give my regards to your husband

Gemahlin *die;* ~, ~**nen** (geh.) consort; wife; **eine Empfehlung an Ihre Frau** ~**:** my compliments to your wife

gemahnen *tr., itr. V.* (geh.) **jmdn. an etw.** (*Akk.*) ~**:** remind sb. of sth.

Gemälde /gə'mɛ:ldə/ *das;* ~s, ~**:** painting

Gemälde-: ~**ausstellung** *die* exhibition of paintings; ~**galerie** *die* picture gallery

gemäß /gə'mɛ:s/ **1** *Präp.* + *Dat.* in accordance with. **2** *Adj.* **jmdm./einer Sache** ~ **sein** be appropriate for sb./ to sth.

gemäßigt *Adj.* moderate; temperate ⟨*climate*⟩

Gemäuer /gə'mɔyɐ/ *das;* ~s, ~**:** walls *pl.;* ⟨*Ruine*⟩ ruin

Gemecker[e] *das;* ~s **(a)** (von Schafen, Ziegen) bleating; **(b)** (ugs.: Nörgelei) griping (coll.); grousing (sl.); moaning

gemein 1 *Adj.* **(a)** (abstoßend) coarse, vulgar ⟨*joke, expression*⟩; nasty ⟨*person*⟩; **(b)** (niederträchtig) mean; base, dirty ⟨*lie*⟩; mean, dirty ⟨*trick*⟩; **du bist** ~**!/das ist** ~ **[von dir]!** you're mean *or* nasty!/that's mean *or* nasty [of you]!; **(c)** (ärgerlich) infuriating; damned annoying (coll.); **(d)** *nicht präd.* (Bot., Zool., sonst veralt.: allgemein vorkommend) common; **der** ~**e Mann** the ordinary man; the man in the street; **(e)** (veralt.: allgemein) general; **etw. mit jmdm./etw.** ~ **haben** have sth. in common with sb./sth.. **2** *adv.* **(a)** jmdn. ~ **behandeln** treat sb. in a mean *or* nasty way; **(b) es hat ganz** ~ **weh getan** (ugs.) it hurt like hell (coll.)

Gemeinde /gə'maɪndə/ *die;* ~, ~**n (a)** (staatliche Verwaltungseinheit) municipality; (ugs.: ~**amt**) local authority; **die**

~ **X** the municipality of X; **(b)** (Seelsorgebezirk) (christlich) parish; (nichtchristlich) community; **(c)** (Einwohnerschaft) community; local population; **(d)** (Gottesdienstteilnehmer) congregation; **(e)** (Anhängerschaft) body of followers; **die** ~ **seiner Anhänger** his following

Gemeinde-: ~**haus** *das* parish hall; ~**mitglied** *das* parishioner; ~**rat** *der* **(a)** (Gremium) local council; **(b)** (Mitglied) local councillor; ~**schwester** *die* district nurse; ~**verwaltung** *die* local administration; ~**zentrum** *das* community centre

gemein·gefährlich *Adj.* dangerous to the public; dangerous ⟨*criminal*⟩; ~ **sein** be a danger to the public

Gemein·gut *das; o. Pl.* (geh.) common property

Gemein·heit *die;* ~, ~**en (a)** *o. Pl.* meanness; nastiness; **(b)** (gemeine Handlung) mean *or* nasty *or* dirty trick; **das war eine** ~**:** that was a mean *or* nasty thing to do/ say

gemein-, Gemein-: ~**hin** *Adv.* commonly; generally; ~**kosten** *Pl.* (Wirtsch.) overheads; ~**nutz** *der;* ~**es** public good; ~**nützig** /-nʏtsɪç/ *Adj.* serving the public good *postpos., not pred.;* (wohltätig) charitable; **eine** ~**nützige Institution** a charitable *or* non-profit-making institution; ~**platz** *der* platitude; commonplace

gemeinsam 1 *Adj.* **(a)** common ⟨*interests, characteristics*⟩; mutual ⟨*acquaintance, friend*⟩; joint ⟨*property, account*⟩; shared ⟨*experience*⟩; **der Gemeinsame Markt** the Common Market; ~**e Interessen haben** have interests in common; ~**e Kasse machen** pool funds *or* resources; **(b)** *nicht präd.* (miteinander unternommen) joint ⟨*undertaking, consultations*⟩; joint, concerted ⟨*efforts, action, measures*⟩; **[mit jmdm.]** ~**e Sache machen** join forces *or* up [with sb.]; **(c)** *nicht attr.* **viel Gemeinsames haben, viel[es]** ~ **haben** have a lot in common; **das ist ihnen** ~**:** that is something they have in common. **2** *adv.* together; **es gehört ihnen** ~**:** it is owned by them jointly

Gemeinsamkeit *die;* ~, ~**en (a)** (gemeinsames Merkmal) common feature; point in common; **(b)** *o. Pl.* (Verbundenheit) community of interest; **ein Gefühl der** ~**:** a sense of community

Gemeinschaft *die;* ~, ~**en (a)** community; **die Europäische** ~**:** the European Community; **(b)** *o. Pl.* (Verbundenheit) coexistence; **in unserer Klasse herrscht keine echte** ~**:** there is no real sense of community in our class; **in** ~ **mit jmdm.** together with sb.

gemeinschaftlich 1 *Adj.; nicht präd.* common ⟨*interests, characteristics*⟩; joint ⟨*property, undertaking*⟩; joint, concerted ⟨*efforts, action*⟩. **2** *adv.* together; **wir führen die Firma** ~**:** we run the firm jointly *or* together

Gemeinschafts-: ~**antenne** *die* communal aerial (Brit.) *or* (Amer.) antenna; ~**arbeit** *die* **(a)** *o. Pl.* joint work; **(b)** (Ergebnis) joint product *or* effort; ~**gefühl** *das; o. Pl.* community spirit; ~**kunde** *die; o. Pl.* social studies *sing.;* ~**raum** *der* common room (Brit.)

gemein-, Gemein-: ~**sinn** *der; o. Pl.* public spirit; ~**verständlich 1** *Adj.* generally comprehensible *or* intelligible; **2** *adv.* **sich** ~**verständlich ausdrücken** make oneself generally comprehensible *or* intelligible; ~**wesen** *das* community; (staatlich) political unit; polity; ~**wohl** *das* public *or* common good; **etw./jmd. dient dem** ~**wohl** sth. is/sb. acts in the public interest

Gemenge *das;* ~s, ~ mixture

gemessen 1 *2. Part. v.* **messen. 2** *Adj.* measured ⟨*steps, tones, language*⟩; deliberate ⟨*words, manner of speaking*⟩; ~**en Schrittes** with measured tread *or* steps *pl.*

Gemetzel *das;* ~s, ~ (abwertend) bloodbath; massacre

gemieden /gə'miːdn̩/ *2. Part. v.* **meiden**

Gemisch *das;* ~[e]s, ~**e** mixture (aus, von of); mix (coll.)

gemischt *Adj.* **(a)** mixed; ~**e Kost** a varied diet; **eine** ~**e Klasse** a mixed *or* coeducational *or* (coll.) coed class; **(b)** (abwertend: anrüchig) disreputable ⟨*crowd*⟩

gemocht /gə'mɔxt/ 2. Part. v. **mögen**

gemolken 2. Part. v. **melken**

gemoppelt /gə'mɔplt/ ⇒ **doppelt 2 a**

Gemotze das; ~s (salopp) grouching (coll.); belly-aching (sl.)

***Gemse** ⇒ **Gämse**

Gemurmel das; ~s murmuring

Gemüse /gə'my:zə/ das; ~s, ~: vegetables pl.; **ein** ~: a vegetable; **junges** ~ (fig. ugs.) youngsters pl.

Gemüse-: ~**beet** das vegetable patch or plot; ~**bei-lage** die vegetables pl.; ~**eintopf** der vegetable stew; ~**frau** die vegetable seller; ~**garten** der vegetable or kitchen garden; (Teil eines Gartens) vegetable patch or plot; ~**händler** der greengrocer; ~**laden** der greengrocer's [shop]; ~**saft** der vegetable juice; ~**suppe** die vegetable soup

gemusst, *gemußt /gə'mʊst/ 2. Part. v. **müssen**

Gemüt /gə'my:t/ das; ~[e]s, ~er (a) nature; disposition; **ein sonniges/kindliches** ~ **haben** (iron.) be [really] naive; (b) (Empfindungsvermögen) heart; soul; **das rührt ans** od. **ist etw. fürs** ~ it touches the heart or tears at one's heart-strings; **jmdm. aufs** ~ **schlagen** od. **gehen** make sb. depressed; (c) (Mensch) soul; **etw. erhitzt/erregt die** ~**er** sth. makes feelings run high

gemütlich 1 Adj. (a) (behaglich) snug; cosy; gemütlich (literary); (bequem) comfortable; **mach es dir** ~! make yourself comfortable or at home!; (b) (ungezwungen) informal ‹get-together›; (c) (umgänglich) sociable; friendly; (d) (gemächlich) leisurely; comfortable ‹pace›. 2 adv. (a) (behaglich) cosily; (bequem) comfortably; (b) (ungezwungen) ~ **beisammensitzen** sit pleasantly together; **sich** ~ **unterhalten** have a pleasant chat; (c) (gemächlich) at a leisurely or comfortable pace; unhurriedly

Gemütlichkeit die; ~ (a) (Behaglichkeit) snugness; (b) (Ungezwungenheit) informality; **die** ~ **stören** disturb the atmosphere or mood of informality; (c) (Gemächlichkeit) **in aller** ~: quite unhurriedly; (d) **da hört die** ~ **auf** (fig. ugs.) that's going too far

gemüts-, Gemüts-: ~**bewegung** die emotion; ~**krank** Adj. emotionally disturbed; ~**mensch** der (ugs.) good-natured or even-tempered person; ~**regung** die emotion; ~**ruhe** die peace of mind; **in aller** ~**ruhe** (ugs.) (ohne Sorge) completely unconcerned; (ohne Hast) as if there were all the time in the world

gemüt·voll Adj. warm-hearted; (empfindsam) sentimental

gen /gɛn/ Präp. + Akk. (veralt., bibl., dichter.) toward[s]; ~ **Süden** southwards

Gen /ge:n/ das; ~s, ~e (Biol.) gene

genannt /gə'nant/ 2. Part. v. **nennen**

genas /gə'na:s/ 1. u. 3. Pers. Sg. Prät. v. **genesen**

genau /gə'nau/ 1 Adj. (a) exact; precise; accurate ‹scales›; exact, right ‹time›; **Genaues/Genaueres wissen** know the/more exact or precise details; **ich weiß nichts Genaues/Genaueres** I don't know anything definite/more definite; (b) (sorgfältig, gründlich) meticulous, painstaking ‹person›; careful ‹study›; precise ‹use of language›; detailed, thorough ‹knowledge›. 2 adv. (a) exactly; precisely; ~ **um 8⁰⁰** at 8 o'clock precisely; at exactly 8 o'clock; **die Uhr geht [auf die Minute]** ~: the watch/clock keeps perfect time; (b) (gerade, eben) just; ~ **reichen** be just enough; (c) (als Verstärkung) just; exactly; precisely; (d) (als Zustimmung) exactly; precisely; quite [so]; (e) (sorgfältig) **etw.** ~ **durchdenken** think sth. out carefully or meticulously; **jmdn.** ~ **kennen** know exactly what sb. is like; **etw.** ~ **beachten** observe sth. meticulously or painstakingly; **es mit etw. [nicht so]** ~ **nehmen** be [not too] particular about sth.; ~ **genommen** strictly speaking

***genau·genommen** ⇒ **genau 2 e**

Genauigkeit die; ~ (a) exactness; exactitude; precision; (einer Waage) accuracy; (b) (Sorgfalt) meticulousness

genau·so Adv. ⇒ **ebenso**

Gendarm /ʒan'darm/ der; ~en, ~en (österr., sonst veralt.) village or local policeman or constable

Gendarmerie /ʒandarmə'ri:/ die; ~, ~n (österr., sonst veralt.) village or local constabulary

genehm /gə'ne:m/ Adj. jmdm. ~ **sein** (geh.) be convenient to or suit sb.; (für jmdn. annehmbar sein) be acceptable to sb.

genehmigen tr. V. approve ‹plan, alterations›; grant, approve ‹application›; authorize ‹stay›; grant, agree to ‹request›; give permission for ‹demonstration›; **sich** (Dat.) **etw.** ~ (ugs.) treat oneself to sth.; **sich** (Dat.) **einen** ~ (ugs.) have a drink

Genehmigung die; ~, ~en (a) (eines Plans, Antrags, einer Veränderung) approval; (eines Aufenthalts) authorization; (einer Bitte) granting; (einer Demonstration) permission (Gen. for); (b) (Schriftstück) permit; (Lizenz) licence

geneigt /gə'naikt/ Adj. ~ **sein** od. **sich** ~ **zeigen, etw. zu tun** be inclined to do sth.; (bereit sein) be ready or willing to do sth.

Genera ⇒ **Genus**

General /genə'ra:l/ der; ~s, ~e od. **Generäle** /genə're:lə/ ▶ 34 | general; **Herr** ~: General

general-, General-: ~**amnestie** die general amnesty; ~**bass, *~baß** der (Musik) [basso] continuo; thorough-bass; ~**direktor** der chairman; president (Amer.); ~**probe** die (a) (auch fig.) dress or final rehearsal; (b) (Sport: letztes Testspiel) final trial; ~**sekretär** der Secretary General; (einer Partei) general secretary; ~**stab** der (Milit.) general staff; ~**streik** der general strike; ~**überholen** tr. V.; nur im Inf. und 2. Part. gebr. (bes. Technik) **etw.** ~**überholen** give sth. a general overhaul; ~**versammlung** die general meeting; **die** ~**versammlung der Vereinten Nationen** the General Assembly of the United Nations; ~**vertreter** der general representative; ~**vollmacht** die (Rechtsw.) full or unlimited power of attorney

Generation /genəra'tsi̯o:n/ die; ~, ~en generation

Generations-: ~**konflikt** der generation gap; ~**problem** das generation problem; ~**wechsel** der (a) new generation; (b) (Biol.) alternation of generations

Generator /genə'ra:tor/ der; ~s, ~en /---'--/ generator

generell /genə'rɛl/ 1 Adj. general. 2 adv. generally; **man kann ganz** ~ **sagen, dass** ...: generally speaking or in general, it can be said that ...; **es sollte sonnabends** ~ **schulfrei sein** all schools should close on Saturdays

genesen /gə'ne:zn̩/ unr. itr. V.; mit sein (geh.) recover; recuperate; (fig.) recover

Genesende der/die; adj. Dekl. convalescent

Genesung die; ~, ~en ▶ 240 | (geh.) recovery

Genetik /ge'ne:tik/ die; ~ (Biol.) genetics sing., no art.

genetisch (Biol.) 1 Adj. genetic. 2 adv. genetically

Genf /gɛnf/ (das); ~s ▶ 490 | Geneva

Genfer ▶ 490 | 1 der; ~s, ~: Genevese. 2 Adj. Genevese; **der** ~ **See** Lake Geneva

Genferin die; ~, ~nen Genevese

genial /ge'ni̯a:l/ 1 Adj. brilliant ‹idea, invention, solution, etc.›; **ein** ~**er Musiker** an inspired musician; a musician of genius. 2 adv. brilliantly

Genialität /geniali'tɛ:t/ die; ~: genius

Genick /gə'nik/ das; ~[e]s, ~e ▶ 326 | back or nape of the neck; **sich das** ~ **brechen** (auch fig.) break one's neck; **am** ~: by the scruff of the neck; **jmdm./einer Sache das** ~ **brechen** (ugs.) ruin sb./sth.

Genick·starre die stiffness of the neck

Genie /ʒe'ni:/ das; ~s, ~s genius; **sie ist ein** ~ **im Kochen** she is a brilliant cook

genieren /ʒe'ni:rən/ refl. V. be or feel embarrassed (wegen about); **sich vor jmdm.** ~: be or feel embarrassed or shy in sb.'s presence

genießbar Adj. (essbar) edible; (trinkbar) drinkable; **er ist heute nicht** ~ (fig. ugs.) he is unbearable today

genießen /gə'ni:sn̩/ unr. tr. V. (a) enjoy; **er hat eine gute Ausbildung genossen** he had [the benefit of] a good education; (b) (geh.: essen/trinken) eat/drink; **nicht mehr zu** ~ **sein** be no longer edible/drinkable

Genießer der; ~s, ~: **er ist ein richtiger** ~: he is a regular 'bon viveur'; he really knows how to enjoy life [to

---

the full]; **er ist ein stiller** ∼**:** he enjoys life [to the full] in his own quiet way

genießerisch 1 *Adj.* appreciative. **2** *adv.* appreciatively; ⟨*drink, eat*⟩ with relish

Genitale /geni'ta:lə/ *das;* ∼**s**, **Genitalien** /geni'ta:liən/ ▶326⌡ genital organ

Genitiv /'ge:niti:f/ *der;* ∼**s**, ∼**e** (Sprachw.) genitive [case]

Genius /'ge:niʊs/ *der;* ∼, **Genien** /'ge:niən/ (geh.) genius

Gen·manipulation *die* genetic manipulation

genmanipuliert *Adj.* genetically engineered; genetically manipulated

Genom /ge'no:m/ *das;* ∼**s**, ∼**e** (Biol.) genome

genommen /gə'nɔmən/ *2. Part. v.* **nehmen**

genoppt /gə'nɔpt/ *Adj.* knop ⟨*yarn, wool*⟩; pimpled ⟨*rubber*⟩; made of knop yarn ⟨*suit*⟩

genoss /gə'nɔs/ *1. u. 3. Pers. Sg. Prät. v.* **genießen**

Genosse /gə'nɔsə/ *der;* ∼**n**, ∼**n** (a) ▶34⌡ comrade; (als Titel, Anrede) Comrade; (b) (veralt.: Kamerad) comrade; companion

genossen /gə'nɔsn̩/ *2. Part. v.* **genießen**

Genossenschaft *die;* ∼, ∼**en** cooperative

genossenschaftlich 1 *Adj.* cooperative; collective ⟨*ownership*⟩; jointly owned ⟨*property*⟩. **2** *adv.* on a cooperative basis

Genossin *die;* ∼, ∼**nen** (a) ⇒ **Genosse** a; (b) (veralt.: Kameradin) companion

Genozid /-'tsi:t/ *der od. das;* ∼**[e]s**, ∼**e** genocide

Genre /'ʒã:rə/ *das;* ∼**s**, ∼**s** genre

Gen-: ∼**technik** *die,* ∼**technologie** *die* genetic engineering *no art.*

gentechnisch 1 *Adj.* genetic engineering ⟨*techniques, research etc.*⟩; ⟨*research, developments etc.*⟩ in genetic engineering. **2** *adv.* by genetic engineering; ∼ **verändert** genetically altered *or* modified; altered *or* modified by genetic engineering

genug /gə'nu:k/ *Adv.* enough; ∼ **Geld/Geld** ∼ **haben:** have enough *or* sufficient money; **das ist** ∼**:** that's enough *or* sufficient; ∼ **gearbeitet haben** have done enough work; **ich habe jetzt** ∼ **[davon]** now I've had enough [of it] **nicht** ∼ **damit, dass er faul ist, er ist auch frech** not only is he lazy, he is cheeky as well; **das ist ihm nicht gut** ∼**:** that is not good enough for him; **sich** (*Dat.*) **selbst** ∼ **sein** be quite happy in one's own company; **er kann nie** ∼ **kriegen** (ugs.) he is very greedy; **davon kann er nicht** ∼ **kriegen** (ugs.) he can't get enough of it (fig. coll.)

Genüge /gə'ny:gə/ (geh.) jmdm. ∼ **tun** *od.* **leisten** satisfy sb.; **einer Anordnung/einer Pflicht** ∼ **tun** *od.* **leisten** comply with an order; **zur** ∼ (ausreichend) enough; sufficiently; (im Übermaß) quite enough; **etw. zur** ∼ **kennen** know sth. only too well; be only too familiar with sth.

genügen *itr. V.* (a) be enough *or* sufficient; **das genügt mir** that is enough *or* sufficient [for me]; that will do [for me]; (b) (erfüllen) satisfy; **den Bestimmungen** ∼**:** comply with the regulations

genügend 1 *Adj.* (a) enough; sufficient; (b) (befriedigend) satisfactory. **2** *adv.* enough; sufficiently; ∼ **Geld haben** have enough *or* sufficient money

genügsam /gə'ny:kza:m/ 1 *Adj.* modest ⟨*life*⟩; **ein** ∼**er Mensch** a person who lives modestly; **Schafe sind sehr** ∼**e Tiere** sheep can live *or* subsist on very little. **2** *adv.* ∼ **leben** live modestly

Genügsamkeit *die;* ∼**:** **wegen ihrer** ∼ **sind Schafe** ...**:** as they can live *or* subsist on very little, sheep are ...

Genugtuung /-tu:ʊŋ/ *die;* ∼, ∼**en** satisfaction; **es ist mir eine** ∼**, das zu hören** it gives me satisfaction to hear that

Genus /'gɛnʊs/ *das;* ∼, **Genera** /'gɛnera/ (Sprachw.) gender

Genuss, *Genuß /gə'nʊs/ *der;* **Genusses, Genüsse** /gə'nʏsə/ (a) *o. Pl.* consumption; (b) (Wohlbehagen) **etw. mit/ohne** ∼ **essen/trinken** eat/drink sth. with/without relish; **etw. mit** ∼ **lesen** enjoy reading sth.; **das Konzert/der Kuchen ist ein** ∼**:** the concert is thoroughly

enjoyable/the cake is delicious; **in den** ∼ **von etw. kommen** enjoy sth.

genüsslich, *genüßlich /gə'nʏslıç/ 1 *Adj.* appreciative; comfortable ⟨*feeling*⟩; (schadenfroh) gleeful. **2** *adv.* appreciatively; ⟨*eat, drink*⟩ with relish; (schadenfroh) ⟨*smile*⟩ gleefully; **sich** ∼ **im Sessel zurücklehnen** lie back luxuriously in the armchair

genuss-, *genuß-, Genuß-, *Genuss-: ∼**mittel** *das* tea, coffee, alcoholic drinks, tobacco, etc.; ∼**sucht** *die; o. Pl.* (oft abwertend) craving for pleasure; ∼**süchtig** *Adj.* (oft abwertend) pleasure-seeking

Geograph /-'gra:f/ *der;* ∼**en**, ∼**en** geographer

Geographie *die;* ∼**:** geography *no art.*

geographisch 1 *Adj.* geographic[al]. **2** *adv.* geographically

Geologe /-'lo:gə/ *der;* ∼**n**, ∼**n** geologist

Geologie *die;* ∼**:** geology *no art.*

geologisch 1 *Adj.; nicht präd.* geological; **2** *adv.* geologically

Geometrie *die;* ∼**:** geometry *no art.*

geometrisch 1 *Adj.* geometric[al]. **2** *adv.* geometrically

geo·politisch *Adj.; nicht präd.* geopolitical

geordnet *Adj.* **in** ∼**en Verhältnissen leben, ein** ∼**es Leben führen** live a settled life

Geo·wissenschaft *die* geoscience *no art.*

Gepäck /gə'pɛk/ *das;* ∼**[e]s** luggage (Brit.); baggage (Amer.)

Gepäck-: ∼**abfertigung** *die* (a) *o. Pl.* checking in the luggage/baggage; (b) (Schalter) (am Bahnhof) luggage office (Brit.); baggage office (Amer.); (am Flughafen) baggage check-in; ∼**ablage** *die* luggage rack (Brit.); baggage rack (Amer.); ∼**annahme** *die* (a) *o. Pl.* checking in the luggage/baggage; (b) (Schalter) [in-counter of the] luggage office (Brit.) *or* (Amer.) baggage office; (zur Aufbewahrung) [in-counter of the] left-luggage office (Brit.) *or* (Amer.) checkroom; (am Flughafen) baggage check-in; ∼**aufbewahrung** *die* left-luggage office (Brit.); checkroom (Amer.); ∼**ausgabe** *die* [out-counter of the] luggage office (Brit.) *or* (Amer.) baggage office; (zur Aufbewahrung) [out-counter of the] left-luggage office (Brit.) *or* (Amer.) checkroom; (am Flughafen) baggage reclaim; ∼**kontrolle** *die* baggage check; ∼**netz** *das* ⇒ ∼**ablage**; ∼**raum** *der* luggage/baggage compartment; ∼**schein** *der* luggage ticket (Brit.); baggage check (Amer.); ∼**stück** *das* piece *or* item of luggage/baggage; ∼**träger** *der* (a) porter; (b) (am Fahrrad) carrier; rack; ∼**wagen** *der* luggage van (Brit.); baggage car (Amer.)

Gepard /'ge:part/ *der;* ∼**s**, ∼**e** cheetah; hunting leopard

gepfeffert *Adj.* (ugs.) steep (coll.) ⟨*price, rent, etc.*⟩

gepfiffen /gə'pfɪfn̩/ *2. Part. v.* **pfeifen**

gepflegt 1 *Adj.* (a) well-groomed, spruce ⟨*appearance*⟩; neat ⟨*clothing*⟩; cultured ⟨*conversation*⟩; cultured, sophisticated ⟨*atmosphere, environment*⟩; stylish ⟨*living*⟩; well-kept, well-tended ⟨*garden, park*⟩; well cared-for ⟨*hands, house*⟩; (b) (hochwertig) choice ⟨*food, drink*⟩. **2** *adv.* ∼ **essen** dine in style; **sich** ∼ **ausdrücken** express oneself in a cultured manner

Gepflogenheit *die;* ∼, ∼**en** (geh.) (Sitte, Brauch) custom; tradition; (Gewohnheit) habit; (Verfahrensweise) practice

Geplänkel /gə'plɛŋkl̩/ *das;* ∼**s**, ∼ (a) (Wort∼) banter *no indef. art.;* (b) (Milit. veralt.) skirmish

Geplapper *das;* ∼**s** (ugs., oft abwertend) prattling; **das** ∼ **des Babys** the baby's babbling

Gepolter *das;* ∼**s** (a) clatter; **mit** ∼ **die Treppe hinunterrennen** clatter down the stairs; (b) (Schimpfen) grumbling; moaning

Gepräge *das;* ∼**s**, ∼ (fig. geh.) [special] character; **einer Sache** (*Dat.*) **ihr** ∼ **geben** give sth. its character

gepriesen *2. Part. v.* **preisen**

gepunktet *Adj.* spotted ⟨*tie, blouse, etc.*⟩; (regelmäßig) polka-dot; dotted ⟨*line*⟩

gequält *Adj.* forced ⟨*smile, gaiety*⟩; pained ⟨*expression*⟩

Gequassel, *das,* **Gequatsche** *das;* ∼**s** (ugs. abwertend) jabbering

gequollen 2. *Part. v.* **quellen**

gerade /gə'ra:də/, (ugs.) **grade** /'gra:də/ 1 *Adj.* (a) straight; bend straight; straighten [out]; **etw. ~ biegen** bend sth. straight; straighten sth. [out]; **etw. ~ halten** hold sth. straight; **den Kopf ~ halten** hold one's head up; **sich ~ halten** hold oneself [up] straight; **~ sitzen** sit up straight; **etw. ~ machen** straighten sth. out; **etw. ~ richten** straighten sth. out; put *or* set sth. straight; **den ~n Weg verfolgen** (fig.) keep to the straight and narrow; (b) (nicht schief) upright; **~ gewachsen sein** ⟨*plant*⟩ have grown straight; ⟨*person*⟩ have grown up straight; (c) (aufrichtig) forthright; direct; (d) *nicht präd.* (genau) **das ~ Gegenteil** the direct *or* exact opposite; (e) (Math.) even ⟨*number*⟩. 2 *Adv.* (a) just; **haben Sie ~ Zeit?** do you have time just now?; **~ erst** only just; **ich frage ihn ~ [mal]** (bes. südd.: mal eben) I'll just ask him; (b) (direkt) right; **~ gegenüber/um die Ecke** right opposite/just round the corner; (c) (knapp) just; **~ noch** only just; **er hat das Examen ~ so bestanden** he just scraped through the examination; **~ so viel, dass ...:** just enough to ...; **~ noch rechtzeitig** only just in time; (d) (genau) **~ diese Angelegenheit** precisely *or* just this matter; (e) (ausgerechnet) **~ du/dieser Idiot** you/this idiot, of all people; **warum ~ ich/heute?** why me of all people/today of all days?. 3 *Partikel* (a) (besonders) particularly; **nicht ~:** not exactly; (b) (ugs.: erst recht) **jetzt [tue ich es] ~:** [you] just watch me; [you] just try and stop me now

Gerade *die; adj. Dekl.* (a) (Geom.) straight line; (b) (Leichtathletik) straight; (c) (Boxen) straight-arm punch; **linke/rechte ~:** straight left/right

gerade·aus *Adv.* ▶ 583 | straight ahead; ⟨*walk, drive*⟩ straight on, straight ahead; **immer ~ gehen/fahren** carry straight on

gerade-: **~|biegen** *unr. tr. V.* (ugs.: bereinigen) straighten out; put right; *s. auch* **gerade** 1 a; **~|halten* ⇒ **gerade** 1 a; **~heraus** /----'-/ (ugs.) 1 *Adv.* **etw. ~heraus sagen** say sth. straight out; **jmdm. ~heraus sagen/jmdn. ~heraus fragen** tell/ask sb. straight; 2 *adj.; nicht präd.* straightforward; direct; **~|machen usw.:* ⇒ **gerade** 1 a

gerädert *Adj.* (ugs.) whacked (coll.); tired out

gerade-: **~|sitzen* ⇒ **gerade** 1 a; **~so** *Adv.* **etw. ~so machen wie jmd. anderes** do sth. just like sb. else; **~so gut** just as well; equally well; **~so gut/groß/lang wie ...:** just as well/big/long as ...; **~sogut* ⇒ **geradeso**; **~|stehen** *unr. itr. V.*(fig.: einstehen) **für etw. ~stehen** accept responsibility for sth.; **für jmdn. ~stehen** answer for sb.; *s. auch* **gerade** 1 a; **~wegs** *Adv.* (a) straight; (b) (ohne Umschweife) straight away; directly; **~wegs zum Thema kommen** come straight to the point; **~zu** *Adv.* really; perfectly; **das ist ~zu lächerlich** that is downright ridiculous; **ein ~zu ideales Beispiel** an absolutely perfect example

gerad·linig /~li:nɪç/ 1 *Adj.* (a) straight; direct; lineal ⟨*descent, descendant*⟩; (b) (fig.) straightforward; 2 *adv.* (a) **~linig verlaufen** run in a straight line; (b) (fig.) **~linig handeln/denken** be straightforward

gerammelt *Adv.* **in ~ voll** (ugs.) [jam-]packed (coll.); packed out (coll.)

Gerangel /gə'raŋl/ *das; ~s* (ugs.) (a) scrapping (coll.); (b) (abwertend: Kampf) free-for-all; scramble

Geranie /ge'ra:niə/ *die; ~, ~n* geranium

gerann /gə'ran/ 3. *Pers. Sg. Prät. v.* **gerinnen**

gerannt /gə'rant/ 2. *Part. v.* **rennen**

Geraschel *das; ~s* (ugs.) rustling

Gerät /gə'rɛ:t/ *das; ~[e]s, ~e* (a) piece of equipment; (Fernseher, Radio) set; (Garten~) tool; (Küchen~) utensil; (Mess~) instrument; **elektrische ~e** electrical appliances; (b) (Turnen) piece of apparatus; **an den ~en turnen** do gymnastics on the apparatus; (c) *o. Pl.* (Ausrüstung) equipment *no pl.*

geraten¹ *unr. itr. V.; mit sein* (a) get; **in ein Unwetter ~:** be caught in a storm; **an jmdn. ~:** meet sb.; **an den Richtigen/Falschen ~:** come to the right/wrong person;

in Panik ~: panic *or* get into a panic; (b) (gelingen) turn out well; **sie ist zu kurz/lang ~** (scherzh.) she has turned out on the short/tall side; (c) (ähneln) **nach jmdm. ~:** take after sb.

geraten² *Adj.; nicht attr.* advisable; **es scheint mir ~, ...:** I think it advisable ...

Geräte-: **~schuppen** *der* tool shed; **~turnen** *das* apparatus gymnastics *sing.*

Geratewohl *in* **wir fuhren aufs ~ los** (ugs.) we went for a drive just to see where we ended up; **er hat sich aufs ~ einige Firmen ausgewählt** (ugs.) he selected a few firms at random

Geratter *das; ~s* (ugs.) clatter

geraum *Adj.; nicht präd.* (geh.) considerable; **nach ~er Zeit** after some [considerable] time

geräumig /gə'rɔymɪç/ *Adj.* roomy; spacious ⟨*room*⟩

Geräusch /gə'rɔyʃ/ *das; ~[e]s, ~e** sound; (unerwünscht) noise

geräusch-, Geräusch-: **~empfindlich** *Adj.* sensitive to noise *pred.*; **~empfindliche Menschen** people who are sensitive to noise; **~los** 1 *Adj.* silent; noiseless; 2 *adv.* (a) silently; without a sound; noiselessly; (b) (fig. ugs.: ohne Aufsehen) without [any] fuss; quietly; **~pegel** *der* noise level; **~voll** 1 *Adj.* noisy; 2 *adv.* noisily

gerben /'gɛrbn/ *tr. V.* tan ⟨*hides, skins*⟩; **von Wind und Wetter gegerbte Haut** (fig.) skin tanned by wind and sun

Gerberei *die; ~, ~en* tannery

gerecht 1 *Adj.* just ⟨*teacher, cause, verdict, punishment*⟩; (unparteiisch) just; fair; impartial ⟨*judge*⟩; righteous ⟨*anger*⟩; **der ~e Gott** (bibl.) our righteous Lord; **~ gegen jmdn. sein** be fair *or* just to sb.; **jmdm./einer Sache ~ werden** do justice to sb./sth.; **einer Aufgabe ~ werden** cope with a task. 2 *adv.* justly; ⟨*judge, treat*⟩ fairly

gerechtfertigt *Adj.* justified

Gerechtigkeit *die; ~* (a) justice; **die ~ Gottes** (christl. Rel.) the righteousness of God; **~ üben** (geh.) act justly; be just; **jmdm. ~ widerfahren lassen** (geh.) treat sb. justly; (b) **die ~ nimmt ihren Lauf** the law takes its course

gerechtigkeits-, Gerechtigkeits-: **~gefühl** *das* sense of justice; **~liebend** *Adj.* **~liebend sein** have a love of justice; **~sinn** *der* ⇒ **~gefühl**

Gerede *das; ~s* (abwertend) (a) (ugs.) talk; (b) (Klatsch) gossip; **ins ~ kommen/jmdn. ins ~ bringen** get into/bring sb. into disrepute

geregelt *Adj.; nicht präd.* regular, steady ⟨*job*⟩; orderly, well-ordered ⟨*life*⟩; computer-controlled ⟨*catalytic converter*⟩

gereichen *itr. V.* (geh.) **jmdm. zur Ehre/zum Vorteil ~:** redound to sb.'s honour *or* credit/advantage

gereift *Adj.; nicht präd.* mature

gereizt *Adj.* irritable; touchy

geriatrisch *Adj.* geriatric

Gericht¹ /gə'rɪçt/ *das; ~[e]s, ~e* (a) (Institution) court; **jmdn. vor ~ laden** summon sb. to appear in court; **vor ~ erscheinen/aussagen** appear/testify in court; **vor ~ stehen** be on *or* stand trial; (b) (Richter) bench; **Hohes ~!** Your Honour!; (c) (Gebäude) court[-house]; (d) *in* **das Jüngste** *od.* **Letzte ~** (Rel.) the Last Judgement; **mit jmdm. [hart** *od.* **scharf] ins ~ gehen** take sb. [severely] to task

Gericht² *das; ~[e]s, ~e* dish

gerichtlich 1 *Adj.; nicht präd.* judicial; forensic ⟨*psychology, medicine*⟩; legal ⟨*proceedings*⟩; court ⟨*order*⟩; **ein ~es Nachspiel haben** have legal consequences. 2 *adv.* **jmdn. ~ verfolgen** prosecute sb.; take sb. to court; **gegen jmdn. ~ vorgehen** take legal action against sb.; take sb. to court

gerichts-, Gerichts-: **~beschluss**, **~beschluß* *der* decision of the/a court; the/a court's decision; **~hof** *der* Court of Justice; **~kosten** *Pl.* legal costs; costs of the case; **~notorisch** *Adj.* (Rechtsspr.) ⟨*person, event, fact*⟩ known to the court; **~saal** *der* courtroom; **~stand** *der* (Rechtsspr.) place of jurisdiction; **~urteil** *das* judgement [of the court]; **~verfahren** *das* legal proceedings *pl.*; **ein ~verfahren einleiten** institute legal *or* court proceedings; **~verhandlung** *die* (strafrechtlich) trial; (zivil) hearing; **~vollzieher** *der;* ~**s**, ~**:** bailiff

gerieben 1 *2. Part. v.* **reiben.** **2** *Adj.* (ugs.) artful

geriffelt *Adj.* corrugated ⟨*surface, sheet metal*⟩; fluted ⟨*column*⟩; ribbed ⟨*glass*⟩

gering /gə'rɪŋ/ *Adj.* **(a)** low ⟨*temperature, pressure, price*⟩; low, small ⟨*income, fee*⟩; little ⟨*value*⟩; small ⟨*quantity, amount*⟩; short ⟨*distance, time*⟩; **in ~er Höhe** low down; **(b)** (unbedeutend) slight; minor ⟨*role*⟩; **meine ~ste Sorge** the least of my worries; **nicht das Geringste** nothing at all; **nicht im Geringsten** not in the slightest *or* least; **jmdn./jmds. Leistung ~ achten** *od.* **schätzen** have a low opinion of *or* think very little of sb./sb.'s achievement; **den Erfolg/Reichtümer ~ achten** *od.* **schätzen** set little store by success/riches; **die Gefahr ~ achten** *od.* **schätzen** make light of the danger; **sein eigenes Leben ~ achten** *od.* **schätzen** have scant regard for one's own life; **(c)** (veralt.: niedrigstehend) humble ⟨*origin, person*⟩; **kein Geringerer als ...:** no less a person than ...; **(d)** (geh.: schlecht) poor, low, inferior ⟨*quality, opinion*⟩

***gering|achten** ⇒ **gering b**

geringelt *Adj.* curly; ⟨*hair*⟩ in ringlets; ⟨*pattern, socks, jumper*⟩ with horizontal stripes

gering·fügig /-fy:gɪç/ **1** *Adj.* slight ⟨*difference, deviation, improvement*⟩; slight, minor ⟨*alteration, injury*⟩; small, trivial ⟨*amount*⟩; minor, trivial ⟨*detail*⟩. **2** *adv.* slightly

Geringfügigkeit *die;* ~, ~**en** **(a)** *o. Pl.* triviality; insignificance;; **(b)** (Kleinigkeit) triviality; trifle

***gering|schätzen** ⇒ **gering b**

gering·schätzig /-ʃɛtsɪç/ **1** *Adj.* disdainful; contemptuous; disparaging ⟨*remark*⟩. **2** *adv.* disdainfully; contemptuously; **von jmdm. ~ sprechen** speak disparagingly of sb.

Gering·schätzung *die; o. Pl.* disdain; contempt

gerinnen *unr. itr. V.; mit sein* coagulate; ⟨*blood*⟩ coagulate, clot; ⟨*milk*⟩ curdle; *s. auch* **Blut**

Gerinnsel /gə'rɪnzl̩/ *das;* ~**s**, ~ (Blut) clot

Gerinnung *die;* ~, ~**en** coagulating; (von Blut auch) clotting; (von Milch) curdling

Gerippe *das;* ~**s**, ~ **(a)** skeleton; **sie ist bis zum ~ abgemagert** (fig.) she has lost so much weight that she is only skin and bones; **(b)** (fig.) framework; (von Schiffen, Gebäuden) skeleton

gerippt /gə'rɪpt/ *Adj.* ribbed ⟨*fabric, garment*⟩; fluted ⟨*glass, column*⟩; laid ⟨*paper*⟩

gerissen /gə'rɪsn̩/ **1** *2. Part. v.* **reißen.** **2** *Adj.* (ugs.) crafty

geritten *2. Part. v.* **reiten**

geritzt *Adj.* (salopp) *in* **etw. ist ~:** sth. is [all] settled; **ist ~!** will do! (coll.)

Germane /gɛr'ma:nə/ *der;* ~**n**, ~**n**, **Germanin** *die;* ~, ~**nen** (hist.) ancient German; Teuton

germanisch *Adj.* Germanic; Teutonic

Germanist *der;* ~**en**, ~**en** Germanist; German scholar

Germanistik *die;* ~: German studies *pl., no art.*

Germanistin *die;* ~, ~**nen** ⇒ **Germanist**

gern[e] /'gɛrn(ə)/; **lieber** /'li:bɐ/, **am liebsten** /-'li:pstn̩/ *Adv.* **(a)** (mit Vergnügen) **etw. ~ tun** like *or* enjoy *or* be fond of doing sth.; **er spielt lieber Tennis als Golf** he prefers playing tennis to golf; **etw. ~ essen/trinken** like sth.; **am liebsten trinkt er Wein** he likes wine best; **ja, ~/aber ~:** yes, of course; certainly!; **Kommst du mit? – Ja, ~!** Are you coming too? – Yes I'd like to!; **[das ist] ~ geschehen** it is *or* was a pleasure; **jmdn./etw. ~ haben** like *or* be fond of sb./sth.; **jmdn./etw. am liebsten haben** *od.* **mögen** like sb./sth. best; **~ gesehen sein** be welcome; **der kann mich ~ haben!** (ugs.) he can go to hell! (coll.); he can get stuffed (sl.); **(b)** (drückt Billigung aus: durchaus) **das glaube ich ~:** I can quite *or* well believe that; **das kannst du ~ tun** you are welcome to do that; **(c)** (drückt Wunsch aus) **ich hätte ~ einen Apfel** I would like an apple; **er wäre ~ mitgekommen** he would have liked to come along; **das hättest du lieber nicht tun sollen** it would have been better if you had not done that; **lass das lieber** better not do that; **noch ein Stück**

Kuchen? — Lieber nicht Another piece of cake? — I'd better not; **ich bleibe heute lieber im Bett** I'd better stay in bed today; **(d) etw. ~ tun** (etw. oft tun) usually do sth.

Gerne·groß *der;* ~, ~**e** (ugs. scherzh.) **er ist ein [kleiner] ~:** he likes to act big (coll.)

gerochen *2. Part. v.* **riechen**

Geröll /gə'rœl/ *das;* ~**s**, ~**e** detritus; debris; (größer) boulders *pl.;* (im Gebirge auch) scree

geronnen /gə'rɔnən/ *2. Part. v.* **rinnen, gerinnen**

Gerste /'gɛrstə/ *die;* ~, ~**n:** barley

Gersten·korn *das* **(a)** (Frucht) barleycorn; **(b)** (Augenentzündung) sty

Gerte /'gɛrtə/ *die;* ~, ~**n** switch

Geruch /gə'rʊx/ *der;* ~**[e]s**, **Gerüche** /gə'rʏçə/ smell; odour; (von Blumen) scent; fragrance; (von Brot, Kuchen) smell; aroma; **einen unangenehmen ~ verbreiten** give off an unpleasant smell *or* odour *or* a stench

geruch·los *Adj.* odourless; (ohne Duft) unscented, scentless ⟨*flower etc.*⟩

Geruchs-: ~**organ** *das* olfactory organ; ~**sinn** *der; o. Pl.* sense of smell; olfactory sense

Gerücht /gə'rʏçt/ *das;* ~**[e]s**, ~**e** rumour; **ein ~ in die Welt** *od.* **in Umlauf setzen** start a rumour; **das halte ich für ein ~!** (ugs.) I can't believe that!

gerücht·weise *Adv.* **ich habe ~ vernommen** *od.* **gehört, dass ...:** I've heard it rumoured that ...

gerufen *2. Part. v.* **rufen**

gerührt *Adj.* touched (also iron.); moved

geruhsam **1** *Adj.* peaceful; quiet; leisurely ⟨*stroll*⟩. **2** *adv.* leisurely; (ungestört) quietly

Gerümpel /gə'rʏmpl̩/ *das;* ~**s** (abwertend) junk; [useless] rubbish

Gerundium /ge'rʊndiǔm/ *das;* ~**s**, **Gerundien** (Sprachw.) gerund

gerungen /gə'rʊŋən/ *2. Part. v.* **ringen**

Gerüst /gə'rʏst/ *das;* ~**[e]s**, ~**e** scaffolding *no pl., no in-def. art.;* (fig.: eines Romans usw.) framework

gerüttelt *Adj.: in* **ein ~ Maß** (veralt.) a good measure

ges, Ges /gɛs/ *das;* ~, ~ (Musik) [key of] G flat; *s. auch* **a, A**

gesalzen *Adj.* (salopp) steep (coll.) ⟨*price, bill*⟩

gesammelt *Adj.* concentrated ⟨*attention, energy*⟩; ~**e Werke** collected works

gesamt *Adj.; nicht präd.* whole; entire; **das ~e Vermögen** the entire *or* total wealth

gesamt-, Gesamt-: ~**auflage** *die* (Druckw.) total edition; (einer Zeitung) total circulation; ~**ausgabe** *die* (Buchw.) complete edition; ~**betrag** *der* total amount; ~**eindruck** *der* general *or* overall impression; ~**ergebnis** *das* overall result; ~**gewicht** *das* total weight; **das zulässige ~gewicht** the permissible maximum weight

Gesamtheit *die;* ~ **die ~ der Beamten** all civil servants; **die ~ der Bevölkerung** the whole of the *or* the entire population; **die Lehrer in ihrer ~:** teachers as a whole

gesamt-, Gesamt-: ~**hoch·schule** *die* (Hochschulw.) institution with colleges teaching at various levels, so that students can more readily extend their courses; ~**note** *die* overall mark; ~**schule** *die* comprehensive [school]; ~**sieger** *der,* ~**siegerin** *die* (Sport) overall winner; ~**summe** *die* ⇒ ~**betrag**; ~**werk** *das* œuvre; (Bücher) complete works *pl.;* ~**zahl** *die* total number

gesandt /gə'zant/ *2. Part. v.* **senden**

Gesandte *der/die; adj. Dekl.* envoy; **der päpstliche ~:** the papal legate *or* nuncio

Gesandtschaft *die;* ~, ~**en** legation

Gesang /gə'zaŋ/ *der;* ~**[e]s**, **Gesänge** /gə'zɛŋə/ **(a)** *o. Pl.* singing; **(b)** (Lied) song; **(c)** (Literaturw.) canto

Gesang·buch *das* hymn book

Gesang[s]-: ~**stunde** *die* singing-lesson; ~**unter·richt** *der* singing instruction; ~**unterricht nehmen/geben** take/give singing-lessons *pl.*

Gesang·verein *der* choral society
Gesäß /gə'zɛːs/ *das;* **~es, ~e ▶ 326** backside; buttocks *pl.*
Gesäß·tasche *die* back pocket
gesättigt *Adj.* (Chemie) saturated
Geschädigte /gə'ʃɛːdɪçtə/ *der/die; adj. Dekl.* injured party
geschaffen 2. *Part. v.* **schaffen** 1
geschafft 1 2. *Part. v.* **schaffen** 2, 3. 2 *Adj.; nicht attr.* (ugs.) all in (coll.)
Geschäft /gə'ʃɛft/ *das;* **~[e]s, ~e** (a) business; (Abmachung) [business] deal *or* transaction; **mit jmdm. ~e/ein ~ machen** do business/strike a bargain *or* do a deal with sb.; **mit etw. ein gutes/schlechtes ~ machen** make a good/poor profit on sth.; (b) *o. Pl.* (Absatz) business *no art.;* **das ~ blüht** business *or* trade is booming; (c) (Firma) business; **im ~** (südd.) at work; **ein ~ führen** run *or* manage a business; (d) (Laden) shop; store (Amer.); (Kaufhaus) store; (e) (Aufgabe) task; duty; **seinen ~en nachgehen** go about one's business; (f) **sein großes/kleines ~ erledigen** *od.* **machen** (ugs. verhüll.) do big jobs *or* number two/small jobs *or* number one (child language)
Geschäfte·macher *der* (abwertend) profit-seeker
geschäftig 1 *Adj.* bustling; **ein ~es Treiben** bustling activity; hustle and bustle. 2 *adv.* **~ hin und her laufen** bustle about
Geschäftigkeit *die; ~:* bustle
geschäftlich 1 *Adj.* (a) business *attrib.* ‹*conference, appointment*›; (b) (sachlich, kühl) businesslike. 2 *adv.* (a) on business; **er hat dort ~ zu tun** he has [some] business to do there; (b) (sachlich, kühl) in a businesslike way *or* manner
geschäfts-, Geschäfts-: **~abschluss,** *****~abschluß** *der* conclusion of the/a business transaction *or* deal; **~aufgabe** *die* closure of the/a business; **~bedingungen** *Pl.* terms [and conditions] of trade; **~bericht** *der* company report; (jährlich) annual report; **~beziehungen** *Pl.* business dealings; **~brief** *der* business letter; **~bücher** *Pl.* books; accounts; **~eröffnung** *die* opening of a/the shop *or* (Amer.) store; **~fähig** *Adj.* (Rechtsspr.) legally competent; **~fähigkeit** *die* (Rechtsspr.) legal competence; **~frau** *die* businesswoman; **~freund** *der* business associate; **~führend** *Adj.; nicht präd.* managing ‹*director*›; executive ‹*chairman*›; **~führer** *der* (a) manager; (b) (Vereinswesen) secretary; **~führung** *die* management; **~gebaren** *das* business *no art.;* business practices *pl.;* **~haus** *das* office block (*with or without shops*); **~interesse** *das; meist Pl.* **das ~interesse/die ~interessen** the interests *pl.* of the business; **~kosten** *Pl.:* **in auf ~kosten** on expenses; **~lage** *die* (a) die **~lage der Firma** the [business] position of the firm; **die allgemeine ~lage** the general business situation; (b) (Ort) **in guter ~lage** well situated [for business]; **~leben** *das* business [life]; **~leitung** *die ⇒* **~führung;** **~mann** *der; Pl.* **~leute** businessman; **~methoden** *Pl.* business methods; **~ordnung** *die* standing orders *pl.;* (im Parlament) [rules *pl.* of] procedure; **Fragen zur ~ordnung** questions on points of order; **~partner** *der* business partner; **~räume** *Pl.* business premises; (Büroräume) offices; **~reise** *die* business trip; **~rückgang** *der* fall-off in business; **~schädigend** *Adj.* bad for business; ‹*conduct*› damaging to the interests of the company; **~schluss,** *****~schluß** *der* closing time; **nach ~schluss** after business hours; (im Büro) after office hours; **~sinn** *der; o. Pl.* business sense *or* acumen; **~stelle** *die* (einer Bank, Firma) branch; (einer Partei, eines Vereins) office; **~straße** *die* shopping street; **~stunden** *Pl.* business hours; (im Büro) office hours; **~tüchtig** *Adj.* able, capable, efficient ‹*businessman, landlord, etc.*›; **~verbindung** *die* business connection; **~wagen** *der* company car; **~zeit** *die ⇒* **~stunden**
gescheckt /gə'ʃɛkt/ *Adj.* spotted ‹*cow, bull, rabbit, etc.*›; skewbald ‹*horse*›
geschehen /gə'ʃeːən/ *unr. itr. V.; mit sein* (a) (passieren) happen; occur; **er ließ es ~:** he let it happen; **~ ist ~:**

what's done is done; (b) (ausgeführt werden) ‹*deed*› be done; **der Mord geschah aus Eifersucht** the murder was committed out of jealousy; **es muss etwas ~:** something must be done; **was geschieht damit?** what's to be done with it?; (c) (widerfahren) **jmdm. geschieht etw.** sth. happens to sb.; **es geschieht dir nichts** nothing will happen to you; **das geschieht ihm recht** it serves him right; (d) **es ist um ihn ~:** it's all up with him; **es ist um seine Gesundheit/Stellung ~:** his health is ruined/he has lost his job
Geschehen *das;* **~s, ~** (geh.) (a) (Ereignisse) events *pl.;* happenings *pl.;* (b) (Vorgang) action
gescheit /gə'ʃait/ 1 *Adj.* (a) (intelligent) clever; **daraus werde ich nicht ~:** I can't make head or tail of it; (b) (ugs.: vernünftig) sensible; **sei doch ~:** be sensible; **du bist wohl nicht ganz** *od.* **nicht recht ~:** you can't be quite right in the head; (c) (ugs.: ordentlich, gut) decent. 2 *adv.* cleverly
Geschenk /gə'ʃɛŋk/ *das;* **~[e]s, ~e** present; gift; **jmdm. ein ~ machen** give sb. a present; **ein ~ des Himmels** a godsend
Geschenk-: **~artikel** *der* gift; **~packung** *die* gift pack; **~papier** *das* gift wrapping paper
Geschichte /gə'ʃɪçtə/ *die;* **~, ~n** (a) *o. Pl.* history; **~ machen** make history; **in die ~ eingehen** (geh.) go down in history; (b) (Erzählung) story; (Fabel, Märchen) story; tale; (c) (ugs.: Sache) **das sind alte ~n** that's old hat (coll.); **das ist [wieder] die alte ~:** it's the [same] old story [all over again]; **das sind ja schöne ~n!** (iron.) that's a fine thing *or* state of affairs! (iron.); **die ganze ~:** the whole business *or* thing; **mach keine ~n!** don't do anything silly; **mach keine langen ~n** don't make a [great] fuss
geschichtlich 1 *Adj.* (a) historical; (b) (bedeutungsvoll) historic. 2 *adv.* historically
Geschichts-: **~atlas** *der* historical atlas; **~bewusstsein,** *****~bewußtsein** *das* awareness of history; historical awareness; **~buch** *das* history book; **~lehrer** *der* history teacher; **~schreibung** *die* historiography; **~unterricht** *der* history teaching; (Unterrichtsstunde) history lesson; **im ~unterricht** in history; **~wissenschaftler** *der* [academic] historian
Geschick[1] /gə'ʃɪk/ *das;* **~[e]s, ~e** (a) (geh.) fate; **ihn ereilte sein ~:** he met his fate; **ein glückliches ~:** a kindly Providence; (b) *Pl.* (Lebensumstände) destiny *sing.*
Geschick[2] *das;* **~[e]s** skill; **ein ~ für etw. haben** be skilled at sth.
Geschicklichkeit *die; ~:* skilfulness; skill
Geschicklichkeits·spiel *das* game of skill
geschickt 1 *Adj.* (a) skilful; (fingerfertig) skilful; dexterous; (beweglich) agile ‹*climber*›; (b) (klug) clever; adroit. 2 *adv.* (a) skilfully; (fingerfertig) skilfully; dexterously; (b) (klug) cleverly; adroitly
geschieden 2. *Part. v.* **scheiden**
Geschiedene *der/die; adj. Dekl.* divorcee; **seine ~:** his ex-wife
geschienen 2. *Part. v.* **scheinen**
Geschirr /gə'ʃɪr/ *das;* **~[e]s, ~e** (a) (Riemenzeug) harness; **dem Pferd das ~ anlegen** harness the horse; **sich ins ~ legen** (kräftig ziehen) pull hard; (angestrengt arbeiten) work like a slave; (b) (Teller, Tassen usw.) crockery; (benutzt) dishes *pl.;* (zusammenpassend) [dinner/tea] service; (Küchen~) pots and pans *pl.;* kitchenware; **das gute ~:** the good china; **das ~ abwaschen** wash up *or* do the dishes
Geschirr-: **~reiniger** *der* dishwasher detergent; **~schrank** *der* china cupboard; **~spülen** *das; ~s* washing-up; **~spüler** *der,* **~spül·maschine** *die* dish-washing machine; dishwasher; **~spülmittel** *das* washing-up liquid; **~tuch** *das; Pl.* **-tücher** tea towel; drying-up cloth (Brit.); dish towel (Amer.)
geschissen /gə'ʃɪsn̩/ 2. *Part. v.* **scheißen**
geschlafen 2. *Part. v.* **schlafen**
geschlagen 2. *Part. v.* **schlagen**
Geschlecht *das;* **~[e]s, ~er** (a) sex; **männlichen/weiblichen ~s sein** be male/female; **das starke ~** (ugs. scherzh.) the stronger sex; **das schwache/schöne/zarte**

~ (ugs. scherzh.) the weaker/fair/gentle sex; (b) (Sippe) family; **von altem ~:** of ancient lineage; **das ~ der Habsburger** the house of Habsburg; (c) (Sprachw.) gender; (d) *o. Pl.* (Geschlechtsteil) sex

geschlechtlich 1 *Adj.* sexual. **2** *adv.* **mit jmdm. ~ verkehren** have sexual intercourse with sb.

geschlechts-, Geschlechts-: **~akt** *der* sex[ual] act; **~hormon** *das* sex hormone; **~krank** *Adj.* ⟨*person*⟩ suffering from VD *or* a venereal disease; **~krank sein** have VD; be suffering from a venereal disease; **~krankheit** *die* ▶329⟩ venereal disease; **~leben** *das* sex life; **~los** *Adj.* (Biol.) asexual; (fig.) sexless; **~merkmal** *das* sex[ual] characteristic; **~organ** *das* ▶326⟩ sex[ual] organ; genital organ; **~reif** *Adj.* sexually mature; **~reife** *die* sexual maturity; **~spezifisch** *Adj.* (Soziol.) sex-specific; **~teil** *das;* ▶326⟩ **die ~teile/ das ~teil** the genitals *pl.;* **~trieb** *der* sex[ual] drive *or* urge; **~verkehr** *der* sexual intercourse; **~wort** *das* (Sprachw.) article

geschlichen *2. Part. v.* **schleichen**

geschliffen 1 *2. Part. v.* **schleifen. 2** *Adj.* polished, refined ⟨*style, manners, etc.*⟩; polished ⟨*sentence*⟩. **3** *adv.* in a polished manner

geschlossen 1 *2. Part. v.* **schließen. 2** *Adj.* (a) (gemeinsam) united ⟨*action, front*⟩; unified ⟨*procedure*⟩; *s. auch* **Gesellschaft c;** (b) (zusammenhängend) **eine ~e Ortschaft** a built-up area; (c) (abgerundet) full; complete ⟨*picture, impression*⟩. **3** *adv.* ~ **für etw. stimmen/sein** vote/be unanimously in favour of sth.; **wir verließen ~ unser Büro** we walked out in a body *or* en masse; ~ **gegen etw. vorgehen** take concerted action against sth.; ~ **hinter jmdm. stehen** be solidly behind sb.

Geschlossenheit *die;* ~ (a) (Gemeinschaft) unity; (b) (Einheitlichkeit) unity; uniformity

geschlungen /ɡə'ʃlʊŋən/ *2. Part. v.* **schlingen**

Geschmack /ɡə'ʃmak/ *der;* ~[e]s, **Geschmäcke** /ɡə'ʃmɛkə/ *od. ugs. scherzh.:* **Geschmäcker** /ɡə'ʃmɛkɐ/ (a) taste; **einen guten/schlechten ~ haben** have good/ bad taste; **das ist [nicht] mein** *od.* **nach meinem ~:** that is [not] to my taste; **das verstößt gegen den guten ~:** that offends against good taste; **im ~ jener Zeit** in the style of that period; **über ~ lässt sich nicht streiten** there's no accounting for taste[s]; **an etw.** (*Dat.*) ~ **finden** *od.* **gewinnen** acquire a taste for sth.; take a liking to sth.; **sie kann solchen Bildern keinen ~ abgewinnen** she cannot appreciate such pictures; **auf den ~ kommen** acquire the taste for it; get to like it; (b) *o. Pl.* (Geschmackssinn) sense of taste

geschmacklos 1 *Adj.* (a) tasteless; insipid; (b) (fig.) tasteless; ~ **sein** be in bad taste; ⟨*person*⟩ be lacking in taste. **2** *adv.* tastelessly

Geschmacklosigkeit *die;* ~, ~en (a) lack of [good] taste; bad taste; (b) *o. Pl.* (fig.) tastelessness; bad taste; (c) (fig.) (Äußerung) tasteless remark; (Handlung) tasteless behaviour *sing., no indef. art.*

geschmacks-, Geschmacks-: **~frage** *die* question *or* matter of taste; **~neutral** *Adj.* tasteless; flavourless; **~richtung** *die* (a) flavour; (b) (fig.) taste; **Geschmack[s]·sache** *die in* **das ist ~:** that is a question *or* matter of taste

Geschmacks-: **~sinn** *der; o. Pl.* sense of taste; **~verirrung** *die* (abwertend) lapse of taste; **an** *od.* **unter ~verirrung** (*Dat.*) **leiden** (ugs.) suffer from a lapse in taste; **~verstärker** *der* flavour enhancer

geschmack·voll 1 *Adj.* tasteful; **die Bemerkung war nicht sehr ~:** the remark was not in very good taste. **2** *adv.* tastefully

Geschmeide /ɡə'ʃmaɪdə/ *das;* ~s, ~ (geh.) jewellery *no pl.*

geschmeidig 1 *Adj.* (a) sleek ⟨*hair, fur*⟩; supple, soft ⟨*leather, boots, skin*⟩; smooth ⟨*dough*⟩; (b) (gelenkig) supple ⟨*fingers*⟩; supple, lithe ⟨*body, movement, person*⟩; (c) (fig.: anpassungsfähig) adaptable. **2** *adv.* (a) (gelenkig) agilely; (b) (fig.) adaptably

Geschmeidigkeit *die;* ~: ⇒ **geschmeidig 1:** sleekness; suppleness; softness; smoothness; litheness

Geschmiere *das;* ~s (ugs. abwertend) (a) [filthy] mess; (b) (Geschriebenes) scribble; scrawl; (c) (Machwerk) rubbish; bilge (sl.)

geschmissen /ɡə'ʃmɪsn̩/ *2. Part. v.* **schmeißen**

geschmolzen *2. Part. v.* **schmelzen**

Geschnatter *das;* ~s (ugs.) (a) (das Schnattern) cackling; cackle; (b) (abwertend: das Sprechen) chatter[ing]; nattering (coll.)

geschniegelt *Adj.* (ugs. abwertend) nattily dressed; ~ **und gebügelt** *od.* **gestriegelt** all spruced up

geschnitten /ɡə'ʃnɪtn̩/ *2. Part. v.* **schneiden**

geschnoben *2. Part. v.* **schnauben**

geschoben /ɡə'ʃoːbn̩/ *2. Part. v.* **schieben**

geschollen *2. Part. v.* **schallen**

gescholten /ɡə'ʃɔltn̩/ *2. Part. v.* **schelten**

Geschöpf /ɡə'ʃœpf/ *das;* ~[e]s, ~e (a) creature; (b) (erfundene Gestalt) creation

geschoren *2. Part. v.* **scheren**

Geschoss¹, *Geschoß *das;* **Geschosses, Geschosse** projectile; (Kugel) bullet; (Rakete) rocket; missile; (Granate) shell; grenade

Geschoss², *Geschoß *das;* **Geschosses, Geschosse** (Etage) floor; (Stockwerk) storey

geschossen /ɡə'ʃɔsn̩/ *2. Part. v.* **schießen**

-geschossig 1 *Adj.* -storey; **ein~/mehr~:** single-storey/multi-storey; **zwei~ sein:** have two storeys. **2** *adv.* **drei~ bauen** build three storeys high

geschraubt *Adj.* (ugs. abwertend) stilted ⟨*language*⟩; (schwülstig) affected, pretentious ⟨*way of speaking, style*⟩

Geschrei *das;* ~s (a) shouting; shouts *pl.;* (durchdringend) yelling; yells *pl.;* (schrill) shrieking; shrieks *pl.;* (von Verletzten, Tieren) screaming; screams *pl.;* (b) (ugs.: das Lamentieren) fuss; to-do; **ein großes ~ wegen etw. machen** make *or* kick up a great fuss about sth.; make a great to-do about sth.

geschrieben *2. Part. v.* **schreiben**

*geschrieen, geschrien /ɡə'ʃriː(ə)n/ *2. Part. v.* **schreien**

geschritten *2. Part. v.* **schreiten**

geschunden *2. Part. v.* **schinden**

Geschütz *das;* ~es, ~e [big] gun; piece of artillery; **die ~e** the artillery *sing.;* the [big] guns; **schweres ~ auffahren** (fig. ugs.) bring up the big guns *or* heavy artillery (fig.)

Geschütz·feuer *das* artillery-fire; shell-fire

geschützt *Adj.* (a) sheltered; (b) (unter Naturschutz) protected

Geschwader /ɡə'ʃvaːdɐ/ *das;* ~s, ~ (Marine) squadron; (Luftwaffe) wing (Brit.); group (Amer.)

Geschwafel *das;* ~s (ugs. abwertend) waffle

Geschwätz *das;* ~es (ugs. abwertend) (a) prattle; prattling; (b) (Klatsch) gossip; tittle-tattle

geschwätzig *Adj.* (abwertend) talkative

Geschwätzigkeit *die;* ~ (abwertend) talkativeness

geschweift *Adj.* curved; **~e Klammer** (Druckw.) brace

geschweige *Konj.* ~ **[denn]** let alone; never mind

geschwiegen *2. Part. v.* **schweigen**

geschwind /ɡə'ʃvɪnt/ (bes. südd.) **1** *Adj.* swift; quick. **2** *adv.* swiftly; quickly; **ich laufe ~ zum Kaufmann** I'm just dashing to the grocer's

Geschwindigkeit *die;* ~, ~en speed; **mit großer ~:** at great speed; **mit einer ~ von 50 km/h** at a speed of 50 km/h

Geschwindigkeits-: **~begrenzung** *die,* **~beschränkung** *die* speed limit; **die ~beschränkung nicht beachten** exceed the speed limit; **~kontrolle** *die* speed check

Geschwister /ɡə'ʃvɪstɐ/ *das;* ~s, ~ (a) *Pl.* brothers and sisters; **Hans und Maria sind ~:** Hans and Maria are brother and sister; (b) (bes. Biol., Psych.) sibling

geschwisterlich *Adj.* brotherly/sisterly ⟨*affection, love*⟩

Geschwindigkeiten

In Großbritannien und den USA werden Geschwindigkeiten im Straßenverkehr sowie im Schienenverkehr und im Luftverkehr noch meist in Meilen in der Stunde (**miles per hour** *oder* **miles an hour, mph**) gemessen.

100 km/h = 62,14 Meilen in der Stunde

Aber immer öfter werden diese Geschwindigkeiten auch als Kilometer in der Stunde (**kilometres** *od.* *(amerik.)* **kilometers per hour, kph**) angegeben.

Das britische Tempolimit in geschlossenen Ortschaften liegt bei 30 Meilen in der Stunde (ungefähr 50 km/h). Andere Grenzen liegen bei 40 ($\approx$ 65 km/h), 50 (= 80 km/h), 60 ($\approx$ 100 km/h), und auf der Autobahn 70 Meilen in der Stunde ($\approx$ 110 km/h).

Wie schnell od. Mit welcher Geschwindigkeit fuhr der Wagen?	= How fast was the car going?, What speed was the car doing?
Der Wagen fuhr mit 120 Stundenkilometern	$\approx$ The car was going at *od.* doing 75 [miles an hour]
Sie fuhr mit Vollgas/mit Höchstgeschwindigkeit	= She was driving flat out/at full speed

Das Auto fährt 200 Kilometer Spitze	$\approx$ The car will do 125 [miles an hour] flat out, The car's top speed is 125 [miles an hour]
Du hast das Tempolimit überschritten	= You were exceeding the speed limit
Sie rasten dahin/fuhren in rasendem Tempo	= They were tearing along/going at a crazy speed
Wir mussten im Kriechtempo fahren	= We had to go at a crawl *od.* were reduced to a crawl

Lichtgeschwindigkeit, Schallgeschwindigkeit

Die Schallgeschwindigkeit beträgt 330 Meter pro Sekunde	= The speed of sound is 330 metres per second (m/s)
die Schallmauer durchbrechen	= to break the sound barrier
Die Lichtgeschwindigkeit beträgt 300 000 Kilometer pro Sekunde	= The speed of light is 186,300 miles per second
mit Lichtgeschwindigkeit	= at the speed of light

Geschwister·paar *das* brother and sister

geschwollen 1 *2. Part. v.* **schwellen. 2** *Adj.* (abwertend) pompous; bombastic. **3** *adv.* (abwertend) pompously; bombastically

geschwommen /gə'ʃvɔmən/ *2. Part. v.* **schwimmen**

geschworen 1 *2. Part. v.* **schwören. 2** *Adj.; nicht präd.* sworn ⟨*enemy*⟩

Geschworene *der/die; adj. Dekl.* juror; **die** ~**n** the jury

Geschworenen-: ~**bank** *die* jury box; (fig.) jury; ~**gericht** *das* ⇒ **Schwurgericht**

Geschwulst /gə'ʃvʊlst/ *die;* ~, **Geschwülste** /gə'ʃvʏlstə/ tumour

geschwunden *2. Part. v.* **schwinden**

geschwungen 1 *2. Part. v.* **schwingen. 2** *Adj.* curved

Geschwür /gə'ʃvyːɐ̯/ *das;* ~**s**, ~**e** ▸ **326**⌟ ulcer; (Furunkel) boil; (fig.) running sore

Geselle /gə'zɛlə/ *der;* ~**n**, ~**n** (a) journeyman; (b) (Kerl) fellow

gesellen *refl. V.* **sich zu jmdm.** ~: join sb.

Gesellen·brief *der* journeyman's diploma *or* certificate

gesellig 1 *Adj.* (a) sociable; gregarious; **ein** ~**er Abend/ein** ~**es Beisammensein** a convivial *or* sociable evening/a friendly get-together; (b) (Biol.) gregarious. **2** *adv.* ~ **leben** live gregariously; be gregarious; ~ **zusammensitzen** sit [together] and chat [sociably]

Geselligkeit *die;* ~: **die** ~ **lieben** enjoy [good] company

Gesellschaft *die;* ~, ~**en** (a) society; **jmdn. in die** ~ **einführen** introduce sb. into society; (b) (Anwesenheit anderer) company; ~ **bekommen** get company; **in schlechte** ~ **geraten** get into bad company; **jmdm.** ~ **leisten** keep sb. company; (c) (Veranstaltung) party; **eine** ~ **geben** give a party; **eine geschlossene** ~: a private function *or* party; (d) (Kreis von Menschen) group of people; crowd; (abwertend) crew; lot (coll.); (e) (Wirtschaft) company

Gesellschafter *der;* ~**s**, ~ (a) partner; **ein guter** ~ **sein** be good company; (b) (Wirtsch.) partner; (Teilhaber) shareholder; **stiller** ~: sleeping partner; silent partner (Amer.)

Gesellschafterin *die;* ~, ~**nen** (a) [lady] companion; (b) (Wirtsch.) partner; (Teilhaber) shareholder

gesellschaftlich 1 *Adj.; nicht präd.* (a) social; (b) (Soziol.) society; **die** ~**e Produktion** production by society; ~**es Eigentum an etw.** (*Dat.*) social ownership of sth. **2** *adv.* socially

gesellschafts-, Gesellschafts-: ~**anzug** *der* dress-suit; ~**fähig** *Adj.* (auch fig.) socially acceptable; ~**form** *die* form of society; social system; ~**klasse** *die* social class; ~**kritik** *die* social criticism; ~**kritisch** *Adj.* critical of society *postpos.;* ~**ordnung** *die* social order; ~**politik** *die* social policy; ~**politisch** *Adj.* socio-political; ~**reise** *die* group tour; ~**schicht** *die* stratum of society; ~**spiel** *das* parlour *or* party game; ~**system** *das* social system; ~**tanz** *der* ballroom dance; (das Tanzen) ballroom dancing; ~**wissenschaften** *Pl.* social sciences; ~**wissenschaftlich** *Adj.* sociological ⟨*studies, analyses*⟩

gesessen /gə'zɛsn̩/ *2. Part. v.* **sitzen**

Gesetz /gə'zɛts/ *das;* ~**es**, ~**e** (a) law; (geschrieben) statute; **ein** ~ **verabschieden/einbringen** pass/introduce a bill; **das** ~ **des Handelns an sich reißen** seize the initiative; **etw. hat seine eigenen** ~**e** (fig.) sth. is a law unto itself; (b) (Regel) rule; law

Gesetz-: ~**blatt** *das* law gazette; ~**buch** *das* statute book; **das Bürgerliche** ~**buch** the Civil Code; ~**entwurf** *der* bill

gesetzes-, Gesetzes-: ~**brecher** *der* lawbreaker; ~**hüter** *der* (iron.) guardian of the law; ~**kraft** *die* force of law; legal force; ~**lücke** *die* loophole in the law; ~**novelle** *die* amendment; ~**text** *der* wording of the/a law; ~**treu 1** *Adj.* law-abiding. **2** *adv.* in accordance with the law; ~**übertretung** *die* violation of the law; ~**vorlage** *die* bill

gesetz-, Gesetz-: ~**gebend** *Adj.* legislative; **die** ~**gebende Gewalt** the legislative power; ~**geber** *der* legislator; law-maker; (Organ) legislature; ~**gebung** *die;* ~: legislation; law-making

gesetzlich 1 *Adj.* legal ⟨*requirement, definition, representative, interest*⟩; legal, statutory ⟨*obligation*⟩; statutory ⟨*period of notice, holiday*⟩; lawful, legitimate ⟨*heir, claim*⟩. **2** *adv.* legally; ~ **verankert sein** be established in law; ~ **geschützt** registered ⟨*patent, design*⟩; ⟨*symbol*⟩ registered as a trade mark

gesetz-, Gesetz-: ~**los** *Adj.* lawless; ~**mäßig 1** *Adj.* (a) law-governed ⟨*development, process*⟩; ~**mäßig sein** be governed by *or* obey a [natural] law/ [natural] laws; (b) (gesetzlich) legal; (rechtmäßig) lawful; legitimate; **2** *adv.* in accordance with a [natural] law/[natural] laws; ~**mäßigkeit** *die* (a) conformity to a [natural] law/[natural] laws; (b) (Gesetzlichkeit) legality; (Rechtmäßigkeit) lawfulness; legitimacy

gesetzt *Adj.* staid; **eine Dame** ~**en Alters** a woman of mature years

gesetz·widrig 1 *Adj.* illegal; unlawful. 2 *adv.* illegally; unlawfully

Gesicht /gə'zɪçt/ *das;* ~[e]s, ~er (a) face; ein fröhliches ~ machen look pleasant *or* cheerful; über das ganze ~ strahlen (ugs.) beam all over one's face; (fig.) sein wahres ~ zeigen show oneself in one's true colours; show one's true character; jmdm. wie aus dem ~ geschnitten sein be the [very *or* (coll.) dead] spit [and image] of sb.; das ist ein Schlag ins ~: that is a slap in the face; jmdm. ins ~ lachen/lügen laugh in/lie to sb.'s face; jmdm. etw. ins ~ sagen say sth. to sb.'s face; jmdm. ins ~ sehen to look sb. in the face; den Tatsachen ins ~ sehen face the facts; jmdm. [nicht] zu ~[e] stehen [not] become sb.; ein anderes ~ aufsetzen *od.* machen put on a different expression; das ~ verlieren lose face; ein ~ machen wie drei *od.* acht *od.* vierzehn Tage Regenwetter look as miserable as sin; ein langes ~/lange ~er machen pull a long face; ~er schneiden pull *or* make faces; das stand ihm im ~ geschrieben it was written all over his face; (b) (fig.: Aussehen) das ~ einer Stadt the appearance of a town; die vielen ~er Chinas the many faces of China; ein anderes ~ bekommen take on a different complexion; (c) *o. Pl.* (geh., veralt.: Sehvermögen) sight; das Zweite ~ [haben] [have] second sight; jmdm./etw. zu ~ bekommen set eyes on *or* see sb./sth.

Gesichts-: ~ausdruck *der* expression; look; ~creme *die* face cream; ~farbe *die* complexion; ~kreis *der* (veralt.) field of view; field *or* range of vision; (fig.) horizon; outlook; ~lotion *die* face lotion; ~maske *die* (a) (Larve) mask; (b) (Kosmetik) face-mask; face-pack; ~puder *der* face-powder; ~punkt *der* point of view; ~verlust *der* loss of face; ~wasser *das* face-lotion; ~winkel *der* (a) angle of vision; visual angle; (b) ⇒ ~punkt; ~züge *Pl.* features

Gesindel /gə'zɪndl̩/ *das;* ~s (abwertend) rabble; riff-raff *pl.*

gesinnt /gə'zɪnt/ *Adj.* christlich/sozial ~ [sein] [be] Christian-minded/public-spirited; jmdm. freundlich/übel ~ sein be well-disposed/ill-disposed towards sb.

Gesinnung *die;* ~, ~en [basic] convictions *pl.;* [fundamental] beliefs *pl.;* eine niedrige ~: a low cast of mind

gesinnungs-, Gesinnungs-: ~genosse *der* like-minded person; ~los (abwertend) 1 *Adj.* unprincipled; 2 *adv.* in an unprincipled manner; ~losigkeit *die;* ~: lack of principle; ~wandel *der* change *or* shift of attitude *or* views

gesittet /gə'zɪtət/ 1 *Adj.* (a) well-behaved; well-mannered ⟨behaviour⟩; (b) (zivilisiert) civilized. 2 *adv.* (a) sich ~ benehmen be well-behaved; (b) (zivilisiert) in a civilized manner

Gesöff /gə'zœf/ *das;* ~[e]s, ~e (salopp abwertend) muck (coll.); awful stuff (coll.)

gesogen 2. *Part. v.* saugen

gesondert /gə'zɔndɐt/ 1 *Adj.* separate. 2 *adv.* separately

gesonnen 1 2. *Part. v.* sinnen. 2 *Adj.* ~ sein, etw. zu tun feel disposed to do sth.

gesotten 2. *Part. v.* sieden

Gespann /gə'ʃpan/ *das;* ~[e]s, ~e (a) (Zugtiere) team; (b) (Wagen) horse and carriage; (zur Güterbeförderung) horse and cart; (c) (Menschen) couple; pair

gespannt 1 *Adj.* (a) eager; expectant; rapt ⟨attention⟩; ich bin ~, ob …: I'm keen *or* eager to know/see whether …; (b) (konfliktbeladen) tense ⟨situation, atmosphere⟩; strained ⟨relations, relationships⟩. 2 *adv.* eagerly; expectantly; einer Geschichte ~ zuhören listen with rapt attention to a story

Gespenst /gə'ʃpɛnst/ *das;* ~[e]s, ~er (a) ghost; ~er sehen (fig.) be imagining things; (b) (geh.: Gefahr) spectre

Gespenster-: ~geschichte *die* ghost story; ~stunde *die* witching hour

gespenstisch *Adj.* ghostly; ghostly, eerie ⟨appearance⟩; eerie ⟨building, atmosphere⟩

gespie[e]n /gə'ʃpiː(ə)n/ 2. *Part. v.* speien

Gespiele *der;* ~n, ~n, **Gespielin** *die;* ~, ~nen (geh. veralt.) playmate

Gespinst /gə'ʃpɪnst/ *das;* ~[e]s, ~e gossamer-like material; das ~ der Seidenraupe the cocoon of the silkworm; ein ~ von Lügen (fig.) a tissue of lies

gesponnen /gə'ʃpɔnən/ 2. *Part. v.* spinnen

gespornt *Adj.* ⇒ gestiefelt

Gespött /gə'ʃpœt/ *das;* ~[e]s mockery; ridicule; jmdn./sich zum ~ machen make sb./oneself a laughing stock

Gespräch /gə'ʃprɛːç/ *das;* ~[e]s, ~e (a) conversation; (Diskussion) discussion; der Gegenstand des ~[e]s the subject *or* topic under discussion; ein ~ mit jmdm. führen have a conversation *or* talk with sb.; jmdn. in ein ~ verwickeln engage sb. in conversation; mit jmdm. ins ~ kommen get into *or* engage in conversation with sb.; (fig.: sich annähern) enter into a dialogue with sb.; im ~ sein be under discussion;; (b) (Telefonanruf) call

gesprächig *Adj.* talkative; der Alkohol machte ihn ~: the alcohol loosened his tongue

gesprächs-, Gesprächs-: ~bereit *Adj.* ready to talk *postpos.;* (zu Verhandlungen bereit auch) ready for discussions *postpos.;* ~bereitschaft *die* readiness for discussions; ~fetzen *der* fragment *or* snatch of conversation; ~gegenstand *der* topic of conversation; ~kreis *der* discussion group ~partner *der:* mein heutiger ~partner wird der Innenminister sein today I shall be talking to the Minister of the Interior; ~pause *die* break in the discussions *or* talks; ~stoff *der* subjects *pl. or* topics *pl.* of conversation; ~teilnehmer *der* participant in the discussion; ~thema *das* topic of conversation; ~zeit *die* (Fernspr.) call-time

gespreizt *Adj.* (abwertend) stilted; affected

gesprenkelt *Adj.* mottled; speckled ⟨egg⟩

Gespritzte *der; adj. Dekl.* (südd.) wine with soda water

gesprochen /gə'ʃprɔxn̩/ 2. *Part. v.* sprechen

gesprossen /gə'ʃprɔsn̩/ 2. *Part. v.* sprießen

gesprungen 2. *Part. v.* springen

Gespür /gə'ʃpyːɐ̯/ *das;* ~s feel

Gestade /gə'ʃtaːdə/ *das;* ~s, ~ (dichter.) shore(s)

Gestagen /ɡɛsta'geːn/ *das;* ~s, ~e (Med.) gestagen

Gestalt /gə'ʃtalt/ *die;* ~, ~en (a) build; (b) (Mensch, Persönlichkeit) figure; eine zwielichtige ~: a shady character; (c) (in der Dichtung) character; (d) (Form) form; ~ annehmen *od.* gewinnen take shape; in ~ von etw. *od.* einer Sache (Gen.) in the form of sth.

gestalten 1 *tr. V.* fashion, shape, form ⟨vase, figure, etc.⟩; design ⟨furnishings, stage-set, etc.⟩; lay out ⟨public gardens⟩; dress ⟨shop window⟩; mould, shape ⟨character, personality⟩; arrange ⟨party, conference, etc.⟩; frame ⟨sentence, reply, etc.⟩. 2 *refl. V.* turn out; sich schwieriger ~ als erwartet turn out *or* prove to be more difficult than had been expected

gestalterisch *Adj.;* nicht präd. creative; artistic

gestalt·los *Adj.* shapeless; formless

Gestaltung *die;* ~, ~en ⇒ gestalten: fashioning; shaping; forming; designing; laying out; dressing; moulding; shaping; arranging; framing

Gestaltungs·prinzip *das* formal principle

Gestammel *das;* ~s stammering; stuttering

gestand 1. u. 3. *Pers. Sg. Prät. v.* gestehen

gestanden 1 2. *Part. v.* stehen, gestehen. 2 *Adj.* ein ~er Mann a grown man

geständig *Adj.* ~ sein have confessed

Geständnis /gə'ʃtɛntnɪs/ *das;* ~ses, ~se confession

Gestänge /gə'ʃtɛŋə/ *das;* ~s, ~ (a) (Stangen) struts *pl.;* (b) (Technik) linkage; (des Kolbens) connecting rod

Gestank /gə'ʃtaŋk/ *der;* ~[e]s (abwertend) stench; stink

gestatten /gə'ʃtatn̩/ 1 *tr., itr. V.* permit; allow; „Rauchen nicht gestattet!" 'no smoking'; ~ Sie, dass ich …: may I …?; wenn Sie ~: if I may. 2 *refl. V.* (geh.) sich (Dat.) etw. ~: allow oneself sth.

Geste /'ɡɛstə, 'ɡeːstə/ *die;* ~, ~n (auch fig.) gesture

Gesteck /gə'ʃtɛk/ *das;* ~[e]s, ~e flower arrangement

gestehen *tr., itr. V.* confess; die Tat usw. ~: confess to the deed etc.; jmdm. seine Gefühle ~: confess one's feelings to sb.; offen gestanden …: frankly *or* to be honest …

Gestein *das;* ~[e]s, ~e rock

Gesteins·kunde *die* petrology

Gestell /gə'ʃtɛl/ *das;* ~[e]s, ~e (a) (für Weinflaschen) rack; (zum Wäschetrocknen) horse; (für Pflanzen) planter; (b) (Unterbau) frame; (eines Wagens) chassis

gestelzt *Adj.* stilted; affected

gestern /'gɛstɐn/ *Adv.* (a) yesterday; ~ **Morgen/ Abend/Mittag** yesterday morning/evening/[at] midday yesterday; ~ **vor einer Woche** a week ago yesterday; **die Zeitung von ~:** yesterday's [news]paper; **von ~ sein** be outdated *or* outmoded; **sie ist nicht von ~** (ugs.) she wasn't born yesterday (coll.)

gestiefelt *Adj.* booted; **der gestiefelte Kater** Puss in Boots; ~ **und gespornt** (ugs. scherzh.) ready and waiting

gestiegen 2. *Part. v.* **steigen**

Gestik /'gɛstɪk/ *die;* ~: gestures *pl.*

Gestikulation /gɛstikula'tsi̯oːn/ *die;* ~, ~en gesticulation

gestikulieren /gɛstiku'liːrən/ *itr. V.* gesticulate

gestimmt *Adj.* **freudig/heiter ~:** in a joyful/cheerful mood *pred.*

Gestirn *das;* ~[e]s, ~e heavenly body; (Stern) star

gestoben /gə'ʃtoːbn̩/ 2. *Part. v.* **stieben**

gestochen /gə'ʃtɔxn̩/ 1 2. *Part. v.* **stechen.** 2 *Adj.* **eine ~e Handschrift** extremely neat *or* careful handwriting. 3 *adv.* ~ **scharfe Bilder** crystal clear photographs

gestohlen /gə'ʃtoːlən/ 1 2. *Part. v.* **stehlen.** 2 *Adj.* **der/das kann mir ~ bleiben** (ugs.) he can get lost (sl.)/ you can keep it (coll.)

gestorben /gə'ʃtɔrbn̩/ 2. *Part. v.* **sterben**

gestört /gə'ʃtøːɐ̯t/ *Adj.* disturbed

gestoßen 2. *Part. v.* **stoßen**

Gestotter /gə'ʃtɔtɐ/ *das;* ~s (ugs., meist abwertend) stuttering

Gesträuch /gə'ʃtrɔy̯ç/ *das;* ~[e]s, ~e shrubbery; bushes *pl.*

gestreift *Adj.* striped

gestrichen 1 2. *Part. v.* **streichen.** 2 *Adj.* level ‹*measure*›; **ein ~er Teelöffel [Zucker *usw.*]** a level teaspoon[ful] [of sugar *etc.*]

gestrig /'gɛstrɪç/ *Adj.; nicht präd.* yesterday's; **der ~e Abend** yesterday evening; (spät) last night; **der ~e Tag** yesterday

gestritten /gə'ʃtrɪtn̩/ 2. *Part. v.* **streiten**

Gestrüpp /gə'ʃtrʏp/ *das;* ~[e]s, ~e undergrowth

Gestühl /gə'ʃtyːl/ *das;* ~[e]s, ~e seats *pl.;* (Kirchen~) pews *pl.*

gestunken /gə'ʃtʊŋkn̩/ 2. *Part. v.* **stinken**

Gestüt /gə'ʃtyːt/ *das;* ~[e]s, ~e stud[-farm]

Gesuch /gə'zuːx/ *das;* ~[e]s, ~e request (**um** for); (Antrag) application (**um** for); **ein ~ einreichen/zurückziehen** submit/withdraw a request/an application

gesucht *Adj.* (a) (begehrt) [much] sought-after; (b) (gekünstelt) affected ‹*style*›; laboured ‹*expression*›; far-fetched ‹*comparison*›

Gesumm /gə'zʊm/ *das;* ~[e]s buzzing; humming

gesund /gə'zʊnt/, **gesünder** /gə'zʏndɐ/, *seltener:* **gesunder, gesündest...** /gə'zʏndəst.../, *seltener:* **gesundest...** *Adj.* (a) ▶329 | healthy; (fig.) viable, financially sound ‹*company, business*›; **wieder ~ werden** get better; recover; ~ **sein** ‹*person*› be healthy; (im Augenblick) be in good health; **jmdn. ~ pflegen** nurse sb. back to health; ~ **und munter** hale and hearty; **bleib ~!** look after yourself!; (b) (natürlich, normal) healthy ‹*mistrust, ambition, etc.*›; sound ‹*construction*›; healthy, sound ‹*attitude, approach*›; **der ~e Menschenverstand** common sense

gesund|beten *tr. V.* jmdn. ~beten heal sb. *or* restore sb. to health by prayer

gesunden *itr. V.; mit sein* ‹*person*› recover, get well, regain one's health; ‹*tissue*› heal; (fig.) ‹*economy etc.*› recover

Gesundheit *die;* ~: ▶329 | health; **bei bester ~ sein** be in the best of health; ~**!** (ugs.: Zuruf beim Niesen) bless you!

gesundheitlich 1 *Adj.; nicht präd.* **aus ~en Gründen** for reasons of health. 2 *adv.* ~ **geht es ihm nicht sehr gut** he is not in very good health

gesundheits-, Gesundheits-: ~**amt** *das* [local] public health department; ~**attest** *das* health certificate; ~**gefährdung** *die* risk to health; ~**schaden** *der* ▶329 | damage *no pl., no indef. art.* to [one's] health; **das kann ~schäden bewirken** that can damage one's health; ~**schädlich** *Adj.* detrimental to [one's] health *postpos.;* unhealthy; **Rauchen ist ~schädlich** smoking can damage your health; ~**wesen** *das* [public] health service; ~**zeugnis** *das* certificate of health; health certificate; ~**zustand** *der* state of health

gesund-: ~|**schreiben** *unr. tr. V.* pass ‹*patient*› fit; ~|**schrumpfen** *itr. (auch refl.) V.* (ugs.) ‹*industry, firm*› be slimmed down; ~|**stoßen** *unr. refl. V.* (salopp) grow fat (coll.)

Gesundung *die;* ~ (geh., auch fig.) recovery

gesungen /gə'zʊŋən/ 2. *Part. v.* **singen**

gesunken /gə'zʊŋkn̩/ 2. *Part. v.* **sinken**

getäfelt 2. *Part. v.* **täfeln**

getan /gə'taːn/ 2. *Part. v.* **tun**

Getier *das;* ~[e]s (geh.) animals *pl.;* wildlife

getigert /gə'tiːgɐt/ *Adj.* (a) (mit ungleichen Flecken) patterned like a tiger *postpos.;* (b) (mit Querstreifen) striped

Getöse *das;* ~s [thunderous] roar; (von vielen Menschen) din

getragen 1 2. *Part. v.* **tragen.** 2 *Adj.* solemn ‹*music, voice, etc.*›. 3 *adv.* solemnly

Getrampel *das;* ~s (ugs.) tramping

Getränk /gə'trɛŋk/ *das;* ~[e]s, ~e drink; beverage (formal)

Getränke-: ~**automat** *der* drinks machine *or* dispenser; ~**karte** *die* list of beverages; (in einem Restaurant) wine list

Getratsch[e] *das;* ~s (ugs. abwertend) gossip; gossiping

getrauen *refl. V.* ⇒ **trauen** 2

Getreide /gə'trai̯də/ *das;* ~s grain; corn

Getreide-: ~**anbau** *der* growing of cereals *or* grain; ~**art** *die* kind of grain *or* cereal; ~**ernte** *die* grain harvest; ~**feld** *das* cornfield; ~**handel** *der* corn-trade; ~**speicher** *der* grain silo

getrennt 1 *Adj.* separate. 2 *adv.* ‹*pay*› separately; ‹*sleep*› in separate rooms; [**von jmdm.**] ~ **leben** live apart [from sb.]

Getrennt·schreibung *die* writing a lexical item as two or more separate words

getreten 2. *Part. v.* **treten**

getreu 1 *Adj.* (geh.) (a) (genau entsprechend) exact ‹*wording*›; true, faithful ‹*image*›; (b) (treu) faithful, loyal ‹*friend, servant*›. 2 *adv.* (geh.) (a) (genau entsprechend) ‹*report, describe*› faithfully, accurately; (b) (treu) faithfully, loyally. 3 *präpositional* (geh.) ~ **einer Abmachung handeln** act in accordance with an agreement

getreulich *Adv.* ⇒ **getreu** 2

Getriebe *das;* ~s, ~ (a) gears *pl.;* (in einer Maschine) gear system; (~kasten) gearbox; (b) (Betriebsamkeit) hustle and bustle

getrieben 2. *Part. v.* **treiben**

Getriebe·schaden *der* gearbox damage

getroffen 2. *Part. v.* **treffen, triefen**

getrogen /gə'troːgn̩/ 2. *Part. v.* **trügen**

getrost 1 *Adj.* confident. 2 *adv.* (a) (zuversichtlich) confidently; (b) (ruhig) **du kannst das Kind ~ allein lassen** you need have no qualms about leaving the child on its own

getrunken 2. *Part. v.* **trinken**

Getto /'gɛto/ *das;* ~s, ~s ghetto

Getue /gə'tuːə/ *das;* ~s (ugs. abwertend) fuss (**um** about)

Getümmel /gə'tʏml/ *das;* ~s tumult; **mitten im dichtesten** *od.* **dicksten ~:** in the thick of it

---

*alte Schreibung (vgl. Hinweise auf S. xvi–xvii)

getupft *Adj.* speckled ⟨*garment, fabric, etc.*⟩

Getuschel *das;* ~**s** (ugs.) whispering

geübt /gə'ly:pt/ *Adj.* experienced, accomplished, proficient ⟨*horseman, speaker, etc.*⟩; trained, practised ⟨*eye, ear*⟩; **in etw.** (*Dat.*) ~ **sein** be proficient at sth.

Gewächs /gə'vɛks/ *das;* ~**es**, ~**e** (a) (Pflanze) plant; (b) (Weinsorte) wine; (Weinjahrgang) vintage; (c) (Med.: Geschwulst) growth

gewachsen 1 *2. Part. v.* **wachsen.** 2 *Adj.* **jmdm./ einer Sache** ~ **sein** be a match for sb./be equal to sth.

Gewächs·haus *das* greenhouse

gewagt *Adj.* (a) (kühn) daring; (gefährlich) risky; (b) (fast anstößig) risqué ⟨*joke, song, etc.*⟩; daring ⟨*neckline etc.*⟩

gewählt 1 *Adj.* refined, elegant. 2 *adv.* in a refined manner; elegantly

gewahr /gə'vaːɐ̯/ *in* **jmdn./etw.** *od.* (geh.) **jmds./einer Sache** ~ **werden** catch sight of sb./sth.; **etw.** (*Akk.*) *od.* (geh.) **einer Sache** (*Gen.*) ~ **werden** (etw. erkennen, feststellen) become aware of sth.

Gewähr /gə'vɛːɐ̯/ *die;* ~: guarantee; **die** ~ **für etw. übernehmen** guarantee sth.; **keine** ~ **übernehmen** be unable to guarantee anything; **die Angaben erfolgen ohne** ~: no responsibility is accepted for the accuracy of this information; **ohne** ~ (auf Fahrplänen usw.) subject to change

gewahren *tr. V.* (geh.) become aware of

gewähren 1 *tr. V.* (a) (zugestehen) give; grant, give ⟨*asylum, credit, loan*⟩; **jmdm. einen Aufschub** ~: grant *or* allow sb. a period of grace; (b) (erfüllen) grant. 2 *itr. V.* **in jmdn.** ~ **lassen** let sb. do as he/she likes

gewähr·leisten *tr. V.* guarantee

Gewähr·leistung *die* guarantee; (von Sicherheit) ensuring

Gewahrsam /gə'vaːɐ̯zaːm/ *der;* ~**s** (a) (Obhut) safe-keeping; **etw. in** ~ **nehmen/behalten** take sth. into safekeeping/keep sth. safe; (b) (Haft) custody

Gewährs·mann *der; Pl.* ...**männer** *od.* ...**leute** source

Gewährung *die;* ~: ⇒ **gewähren** 1: granting; giving; offering

Gewalt /gə'valt/ *die;* ~, ~**en** (a) (Macht, Befugnis) power; **jmdn./ein Land in seine** ~ **bekommen/bringen** catch sb./bring a country under one's control; **die** ~ **über sein Fahrzeug verlieren** (fig.) lose control of one's vehicle; **sich/seine Beine in der** ~ **haben** have oneself under control/have control over one's legs; (b) *o. Pl.* (Willkür) force; **er versuchte mit aller** ~, **seinen Ehrgeiz zu befriedigen** he did everything he could to achieve his ambition; (c) *o. Pl.* (körperliche Kraft) force; violence; ~ **anwenden** use force *or* violence; **etw. mit** ~ **öffnen** force sth. open; (d) (geh.: elementare Kraft) force; **höhere** ~ [**sein**] [be] an act of God

Gewalt-: ~**akt** *der* act of violence; ~**anwendung** *die* use of force *or* violence

Gewalten·teilung *die* separation of powers

Gewalt·herrschaft *die; o. Pl.* tyranny; despotism

gewaltig 1 *Adj.* (a) (immens) enormous, huge ⟨*sum, amount, difference, loss*⟩; tremendous ⟨*progress*⟩; (b) (imponierend) mighty, huge, massive ⟨*wall, pillar, building, rock*⟩; monumental ⟨*literary work etc.*⟩; mighty ⟨*spectacle of nature*⟩; (c) (mächtig; auch fig.) powerful. 2 *adv.* (ugs.: sehr, überaus) **sich** ~ **irren/täuschen** be very much mistaken

gewalt-, Gewalt-: ~**los** 1 *Adj.* non-violent; 2 *adv.* without violence; ~**losigkeit** *die;* ~: non-violence; ~**marsch** *der* forced march

gewaltsam 1 *Adj.* forcible ⟨*expulsion*⟩; enforced ⟨*separation*⟩; violent ⟨*death*⟩. 2 *adv.* forcibly; ~ **die Tür öffnen** open the door by force

gewalt-, Gewalt-: ~**tat** *die* ⇒ ~**verbrechen;** ~**tätig** *Adj.* violent; ~**tätigkeit** *die* (a) *o. Pl.* (gewalttätige Art) violence; (b) ~**akt;** ~**verbrechen** *das* crime of violence; ~**verbrecher** *der* violent criminal; ~**verzicht** *der* renunciation of the use of force; ~**verzichts·abkommen** *das* non-aggression treaty

Gewand *das;* ~[**e**]**s, Gewänder** /gə'vɛndɐ/ (geh.) robe; gown; (Abendkleid) gown; **im neuen** ~ (fig.) dressed up as new

gewandt /gə'vant/ 1 *2. Part. v.* **wenden.** 2 *Adj.* skilful; (körperlich) agile; expert ⟨*skier*⟩; ~**e Umgangsformen** easy social manners. 3 *adv.* skilfully; (körperlich) agilely

Gewandtheit *die;* ~: ⇒ **gewandt** 2: skill; skilfulness; agility; expertness; easiness

gewann /gə'van/ *1. u. 3. Pers. Sg. Prät. v.* **gewinnen**

gewärtig /gə'vɛrtɪç/ *Adj.* **einer Sache** (*Gen.*) ~ **sein** (geh.) be prepared for sth.

Gewäsch /gə'vɛʃ/ *das;* ~[**e**]**s** (ugs. abwertend) twaddle; garbage (Amer. coll.)

gewaschen *2. Part. v.* **waschen**

Gewässer /gə'vɛsɐ/ *das;* ~**s**, ~: stretch of water; **sich in arktische** ~ **wagen** venture into Arctic waters

Gewässer-: ~**kunde** *die* hydrography *no art.;* ~**schutz** *der* prevention of water pollution

Gewebe *das;* ~**s**, ~ (a) (Stoff) fabric; (b) (Med., Biol.) tissue

Gewehr /gə'veːɐ̯/ *das;* ~[**e**]**s**, ~**e** rifle; (Schrot~) shotgun; **mit dem** ~ **auf jmdn./etw. zielen** aim [one's rifle/shotgun] at sb./sth.

Gewehr-: ~**feuer** *das; o. Pl.* rifle fire; ~**kolben** *der* rifle/shotgun butt; ~**kugel** *die* rifle bullet; ~**lauf** *der* rifle/shotgun barrel; ~**schuss,** ***~**schuß** *der* rifle shot

Geweih /gə'vai/ *das;* ~[**e**]**s**, ~**e** antlers *pl.;* **ein** ~: a set of antlers

Geweih·stange *die* (Jägerspr.) beam; main trunk

Gewerbe *das;* ~**s**, ~ (a) (Handel, Handwerk) business; (b) *o. Pl.* (kleine Betriebe) [small and medium-sized] businesses and industries

Gewerbe-: ~**aufsicht** *die enforcement of laws governing health and safety and conditions of work;* ~**freiheit** *die* right to carry on a business *or* trade; ~**gebiet** *das* trading estate; ~**schein** *der* licence to carry on a business *or* trade; ~**schule** *die* trade school; ~**steuer** *die* trade tax; ~**treibende** *der/die; adj. Dekl.* tradesman/tradeswoman

gewerblich 1 *Adj.; nicht präd.* commercial; business *attrib.;* (industriell) industrial; trade *attrib.* ⟨*union, apprentice*⟩; ~**e Nutzung** use for commercial *or* business/industrial purposes. 2 *adv.* ~ **tätig sein** work; **etw.** ~ **nutzen** use sth. for commercial *or* business/industrial purposes

gewerbs·mäßig 1 *Adj.; nicht präd.* professional. 2 *adv.* **etw.** ~ **betreiben** do sth. professionally *or* for gain

Gewerkschaft /gə'vɛrkʃaft/ *die;* ~, ~**en** trade union

Gewerkschaft[l]er *der;* ~**s**, ~, **Gewerkschaft[l]erin** *die;* ~, ~**nen** trade unionist

gewerkschaftlich 1 *Adj.* [trade] union *attrib.;* ⟨*rights, duties*⟩ as a [trade] union member; ~**er Vertrauensmann**/~**e Vertrauensfrau** shop steward. 2 *adv.* ~ **organisiert sein** belong to a [trade] union; **sich** ~ **engagieren** devote oneself to trade union work

Gewerkschafts-: ~**bewegung** *die; o. Pl.* [trade] union movement; ~**bund** *der* federation of trade unions; ≈ Trades Union Congress (Brit.); ≈ AFL–CIO (Amer.) ~**führer** *der* [trade] union leader; ~**funktionär** *der* [trade] union official; ~**kongress** *der* ⇒ ~**tag;** ~**mitglied** *das* member of a [trade] union; ~**tag** *der* [trade] union conference

gewesen *2. Part. v.* **sein**[1]

gewichen *2. Part. v.* **weichen**

Gewicht /gə'vɪçt/ *das;* ~[**e**]**s**, ~**e** ▶ 228 (auch Physik, auch fig.) weight; **ein** ~ **von 75 kg/ein großes** ~ **haben** weigh 75 kg/be very heavy; **das spezifische** ~ (Physik) the specific gravity; **sein** ~ **halten** stay the same weight; **einer Sache** (*Dat.*) [**kein**] ~ **beimessen** *od.* **beilegen** attach [no] importance to sth.; [**nicht**] **ins** ~ **fallen** be of [no] consequence

gewichten *tr. V.* (a) (Statistik) weight; (b) (Schwerpunkte festsetzen) evaluate

Gewicht-: ~**heben** *das;* ~**s** weightlifting; ~**heber** *der;* ~**s**, ~ weightlifter

gewichtig *Adj.* (a) (veralt.: schwer) heavy; weighty; (b) (bedeutungsvoll) weighty, important ⟨*reason, question, decision, etc.*⟩

Gewichte

```
1 Gramm      = one gram      = 0.035 ounce (oz)
1 Kilogramm  = one kilogram  = 2.205 pounds (lb)
1 Tonne      = one tonne     = 2, 205 lb od. 19.684 hundredweight (cwt)
```
Es ist zu beachten, dass das britische Pfund (**pound**) nur 454 Gramm wiegt. Dagegen ist die britische Tonne (**ton**) etwas schwerer als die metrische (1 016 kg).

Personen

Wie viel wiegen Sie?	= How much do you weigh?, What's your weight?
Ich wiege 76 Kilo	≈ I weigh 12 stone (brit.) od. 168 pounds (amerik.)
Er hat zugenommen	= He has put on weight
Sie hat stark abgenommen	= She has lost a lot of weight
Mit mehr als 114 Kilo hat er Übergewicht	= At over 18 stone (brit.) od. 250 pounds (amerik.) he is overweight

Dinge

Wie viel wiegt das Paket?	= How much does the parcel weigh?, What's the weight of the parcel?

Es wiegt ungefähr zwei Kilo	= It weighs about two kilograms, ≈ it weighs about four pounds
Mein Gepäck hat fünf Kilo Übergewicht	= My baggage is five kilograms over weight, ≈ My baggage is ten pounds over weight
A hat das gleiche Gewicht wie B	= A is the same weight as B
A und B sind gleich schwer	= A and B are the same weight
125 Gramm Leberwurst	= 125 grams of liver sausage, ≈ 4 oz of liver sausage
6 Pfund Kartoffeln	≈ 6 pounds of potatoes
They are sold by the kilo	= Sie werden kiloweise verkauft
eine 500-Gramm-Schachtel Pralinen	≈ a pound box of chocolates

---

Gewichts-: ∼**klasse** die (a) (Sport) weight [division or class]; (b) (Kaufmannsspr.) weight class; ∼**verlagerung** die shift or transfer of weight; (fig.) shift in or of emphasis; ∼**verlust** der loss of weight

Gewichtung die; ∼, ∼**en** evaluation

gewieft /ɡə'viːft/ Adj. (ugs.) cunning; wily

gewiesen 2. Part. v. **weisen**

gewillt /ɡə'vɪlt/ Adj. in ∼/nicht ∼ sein, etw. zu tun be willing/unwilling to do sth.

Gewimmel das; ∼**s** throng; milling crowd; (von Insekten) teeming mass

Gewimmer das; ∼**s** whimpering

Gewinde das; ∼**s**, ∼ (Technik) thread

Gewinde-: ∼**bohrer** der [screw] tap; ∼**stift** der grub-screw

Gewinn /ɡə'vɪn/ der; ∼[e]s, ∼e (a) (Reinertrag) profit; etw. mit ∼ verkaufen sell sth. at a profit; (b) (Preis einer Lotterie) prize; (beim Wetten, Kartenspiel usw.) winnings pl.; die ∼e auslosen draw the winners or winning numbers; (c) (Nutzen) gain; profit; (d) (Sieg) win

gewinn-, Gewinn-: ∼**beteiligung** die (Wirtsch.) profit-sharing; (Betrag) profit-sharing bonus; ∼**bringend** Adj. profitable; lucrative; ∼**chance** die chance of winning

gewinnen /ɡə'vɪnən/ **1** unr. tr. V. (a) (siegen in) win ‹contest, race, etc.›; s. auch **Spiel b**; (b) (erringen, erreichen, erhalten) gain, win ‹respect, sympathy, etc.›; gain ‹time, lead, influence, validity, confidence›; win ‹prize›; **wie gewonnen, so zerronnen** (Spr.) easy come, easy go; s. auch **Oberhand**; (c) (Unterstützung erlangen) **jmdn. für etw. ∼**: win sb. over [to sth.]; (d) (abbauen, fördern) mine, extract ‹coal, ore, metal›; recover ‹oil›; (e) (erzeugen) produce (**aus** from); (durch Recycling) reclaim; recover. **2** unr. itr. V. (a) win (**bei** at); **jedes zweite Los gewinnt!** every other ticket [is] a winner!; (b) (sich vorteilhaft verändern) improve; (c) (zunehmen) **an Höhe/ Fahrt ∼:** gain height/gain or pick up speed; **an Bedeutung ∼:** gain in importance

gewinnend 1 Adj. winning, engaging, winsome ‹manner, smile, way›. **2** adv. ‹smile› winningly, engagingly, winsomely

Gewinner der; ∼**s**, ∼, **Gewinnerin** die; ∼, ∼**nen** winner

gewinn-, Gewinn-: ∼**spanne** die profit margin; ∼**streben** das pursuit of profit; ∼**sucht** die; o. Pl. greed for profit; ∼**süchtig** Adj. greedy for profits pred.; ∼**trächtig** Adj. profitable; lucrative

Gewinn-und-Verlust-Rechnung die (Wirtsch.) profit and loss account

Gewinnung die; ∼ (a) (von Kohle, Erz usw.) mining; extraction; (von Öl) recovery; (von Metall aus Erz) extraction; (b) (Erzeugung) production

Gewinn·zahl die winning number

Gewinsel das; ∼**s** whimpering; whining

Gewirr das; ∼[e]s tangle; **ein ∼ von Paragraphen** a maze or jungle of regulations; **ein ∼ von Stimmen** a [confused] babble of voices

Gewisper das; ∼**s** whispering

gewiss, *gewiß /ɡə'vɪs/ **1** Adj. (a) nicht präd. (nicht sehr viel/groß) certain; **in gewisser Beziehung** in some respects; s. auch **Etwas; Maß¹ d**; (b) (sicher) certain (Gen. of); **etw. ist jmdm. ∼:** sb. is certain or sure of sth. **2** adv. certainly; **ja** od. **aber ∼ [doch]**! but of course!

Gewissen das; ∼**s**, ∼: conscience; **ruhigen ∼s etw. tun** do sth. with a clear conscience; **mit gutem ∼:** with a clear conscience; **etw./jmdn. auf dem ∼ haben** have sth./sb. on one's conscience; **jmdm. ins ∼ reden** [, etw. zu tun] have a serious talk with sb. [and persuade him/her to do sth.]

gewissenhaft 1 Adj. conscientious. **2** adv. conscientiously

Gewissenhaftigkeit die; ∼: conscientiousness

gewissen·los 1 Adj. conscienceless; unscrupulous. **2** adv. ∼ **handeln** act with a complete lack of conscience

Gewissenlosigkeit die; ∼ lack of conscience

Gewissens-: ∼**bisse** Pl. pangs of conscience; ∼**frage** die question or matter of conscience; matter for one's conscience; ∼**freiheit** die; o. Pl. freedom of conscience; ∼**gründe** Pl. reasons of conscience; ∼**konflikt** der moral conflict

gewissermaßen Adv. (sozusagen) as it were; (in gewissem Sinne) to a certain extent

Gewissheit, *Gewißheit die; ∼, ∼**en** certainty; **sich (Dat.) ∼ verschaffen** find out for certain

Gewitter /ɡə'vɪtɐ/ das; ∼**s**, ∼: thunderstorm; (fig.) storm

Gewitter·front die storm front

gewittern itr. V. (unpers.) **es gewitterte/wird bald ∼:** there was/will soon be thunder and lightning

---

Gewitter-: ∼**neigung** *die; o. Pl.* likelihood of thunderstorms; ∼**regen** *der* thundery shower; ∼**wolke** *die* thundercloud

gewittrig /gə'vɪtrɪç/ *Adj.* thundery; ∼e **Schwüle** sultry heat

gewitzt /gə'vɪtst/ *Adj.* shrewd; **ein** ∼**er Junge** a smart lad

gewoben /gə'vo:bn̩/ *2. Part. v.* **weben**

gewogen 1 *2. Part. v.* **wiegen.** 2 *Adj.* (geh.) well disposed, favourably inclined (*Dat.* towards)

gewöhnen /gə'vø:nən/ 1 *tr. V.* **jmdn. an jmdn./etw.** ∼: get sb. used *or* accustomed to sb./sth.; accustom sb. to sb./sth.; **an jmdn./etw. gewöhnt sein** be used *or* accustomed to sb./sth.. 2 *refl. V.* **sich an jmdn./etw.** ∼: get used *or* get *or* become accustomed to sb./sth.; accustom oneself to sb./sth.

Gewohnheit /gə'vo:nhait/ *die;* ∼, ∼**en** habit; **die** ∼ **haben, etw. zu tun** be in the habit of doing sth.; **sich** (*Dat.*) **etw. zur** ∼ **machen** make a habit of sth.; **nach alter** ∼: from long-established habit

gewohnheits-, Gewohnheits-: ∼**mäßig** 1 *Adj.* habitual ⟨*drinker etc.*⟩; automatic ⟨*reaction etc.*⟩; 2 *adv.* (a) (regelmäßig) habitually; (b) (einer Gewohnheit folgend) as is/was my/his *etc.* habit; ∼**recht** *das* (Rechtsw.) (a) *o. Pl.* (System) common law; (b) (einzelnes Recht) established right; ∼**sache** *die* matter *or* question of habit; ∼**tier** *das* (scherzh.) creature of habit; ∼**trinker** *der* habitual drinker; ∼**verbrecher** *der* (Rechtsw.) habitual criminal

gewöhnlich /gə'vø:nlɪç/ 1 *Adj.* (a) *nicht präd.* (alltäglich) normal; ordinary; (b) *nicht präd.* (gewohnt, üblich) usual; normal; customary; (c) (abwertend: ordinär) common. 2 *adv.* (a) [**für**] ∼: usually; normally; **wie** ∼: as usual; (b) (abwertend: ordinär) in a common way

gewohnt *Adj.* (a) *nicht präd.* (vertraut) usual; (b) **es** ∼ **sein, etw. zu tun** be used *or* accustomed to doing sth.

Gewöhnung *die;* ∼ (a) habituation (**an** + *Akk.* to); (b) (Sucht) habit; addiction

Gewölbe /gə'vœlbə/ *das;* ∼**s**, ∼: vault

gewonnen /gə'vɔnən/ *2. Part. v.* **gewinnen**

geworben /gə'vɔrbn̩/ *2. Part. v.* **werben**

geworfen /gə'vɔrfn̩/ *2. Part. v.* **werfen**

gewrungen /gə'vrʊŋən/ *2. Part. v.* **wringen**

Gewühl *das;* ∼**[e]s** (a) milling crowd; (b) (das Wühlen) rooting about

gewunden *2. Part. v.* **winden**

gewunken /gə'vʊŋkn̩/ *2. Part. v.* **winken**

gewürfelt *Adj.* (kariert) check; checked

Gewürz *das;* ∼**es**, ∼**e** spice; (würzende Zutat) seasoning; condiment; (Kraut) herb

Gewürz-: ∼**gurke** *die* pickled gherkin; ∼**mischung** *die* mixed spices *pl.*/herbs *pl.;* ∼**nelke** *die* clove

gewusst, *gewußt *2. Part. v.* **wissen**

Geysir /'gaizr/ *der;* ∼**s**, ∼**e** geyser

gez. *Abk.* **gezeichnet** sgd.

Gezänk /gə'tsɛŋk/ *das;* ∼**[e]s, Gezanke** /gə'tsaŋkə/ *das;* ∼**s** (abwertend) quarrelling

Gezappel *das;* ∼**s** (ugs., oft abwertend) wriggling

Gezeit *die;* ∼, ∼**en** tide

Gezeiten·kraft·werk *das* tidal powerstation

Gezeter *das;* ∼**s** (abwertend) scolding; nagging

geziehen /gə'tsi:ən/ *2. Part. v.* **zeihen**

gezielt 1 *Adj.* specific ⟨*questions, measures, etc.*⟩; deliberate ⟨*insult, indiscretion*⟩; well-directed ⟨*advertising campaign*⟩. 2 *adv.* ⟨*proceed, act*⟩ purposefully, in a purposeful manner; ∼ **nach etw. forschen** search specifically for sth.

geziemen *refl. V.* (geh. veralt.) be proper *or* right; **sich für jmdn.** ∼: befit sb.

geziemend (geh.) 1 *Adj.* fitting; proper, due ⟨*respect*⟩. 2 *adv.* in a fitting manner

geziert 1 *Adj.* affected. 2 *adv.* affectedly

Geziertheit *die;* ∼ (abwertend) affectedness

Gezirp[e] *das;* ∼**s** (oft abwertend) chirping; chirruping

gezogen /gə'tso:gn̩/ *2. Part. v.* **ziehen**

Gezwitscher *das;* ∼**s** twittering; chirping; chirruping

gezwungen /gə'tsvʊŋən/ 1 *2. Part. v.* **zwingen.** 2 *Adj.* forced ⟨*laugh, smile, etc.*⟩; stiff ⟨*behaviour*⟩. 3 *adv.* ⟨*laugh*⟩ in a forced way *or* manner; ⟨*behave*⟩ stiffly

gezwungenermaßen *Adv.* of necessity; **etw.** ∼ **machen** be forced to do sth.

GG *Abk.* **Grundgesetz**

ggf. *Abk.* **gegebenenfalls**

gib /gi:p/ *Imperativ Sg. Präsens v.* **geben**

Gibbon /'gɪbɔn/ *der;* ∼**s**, ∼**s** (Zool.) gibbon

gibst /gi:pst/ *2. Pers. Sg. Präsens v.* **geben**

gibt /gi:pt/ *3. Pers. Sg. Präsens v.* **geben**

Gicht *die;* ∼**:** ▶ **329** gout

gichtig, gichtisch *Adj.* gouty

Giebel /'gi:bl̩/ *der;* ∼**s**, ∼ (a) gable; (b) (von Portalen) pediment

Giebel-: ∼**dach** *das* gable roof; ∼**fenster** *das* gable-window

Gier /gi:ɐ̯/ *die;* ∼ greed (**nach** for); **mit solcher** ∼: so greedily; ∼ **nach Macht/Ruhm** lust *or* craving for power/craving for fame

gierig 1 *Adj.* greedy; avid ⟨*desire, reader*⟩; **nach etw.** ∼ **sein** be greedy for sth. 2 *adv.* greedily

gießen /'gi:sn̩/ 1 *unr. tr. V.* (a) (rinnen lassen/schütten) pour (**in** + *Akk.* into, **über** + *Akk.* over); (b) (verschütten) spill (**über** + *Akk.* over); (c) (begießen) water ⟨*plants, flowers, garden*⟩; (d) cast ⟨*machine part, statue, candles, etc.*⟩; cast, found ⟨*metal*⟩; found ⟨*glass*⟩. 2 *unr. itr. V.* (unpers., ugs.) pour [with rain]; **es gießt in Strömen** it is coming down in buckets; it's raining cats and dogs

Gießer *der;* ∼**s**, ∼**:** ▶ **85** caster; founder

Gießerei *die;* ∼, ∼**en** (a) (Betrieb) foundry; (b) *o. Pl.* (Zweig der Metallindustrie) casting; founding

Gießkannen·prinzip *das; o. Pl.* (scherzh.) principle of 'equal shares for all'

Gift /gɪft/ *das;* ∼**[e]s**, ∼**e** (a) poison; (Schlangen∼) venom; (b) (fig.) ∼ **für jmdn./etw. sein** be extremely bad for sb./sth.; ∼ **und Galle speien** *od.* **spucken** (sehr wütend sein) be in a terrible rage; (gehässig reagieren) give vent to one's spleen

gift-, Gift-: ∼**frei** *Adj.* non-toxic; non-poisonous; ∼**gas** *das* poison gas; ∼**grün** *Adj.* garish green

giftig 1 *Adj.* (a) poisonous; venomous, poisonous ⟨*snake*⟩; toxic, poisonous ⟨*substance, gas, chemical*⟩; (b) (ugs.: bösartig) venomous, spiteful ⟨*remark, person, words, etc.*⟩; venomous ⟨*look*⟩; ∼ **werden** turn nasty; (c) (grell, schreiend) garish, loud ⟨*colour*⟩. 2 *adv.* venomously

Gift-: ∼**mischer** *der* (ugs.) (a) maker of poisons; (b) (scherzh.: Apotheker) chemist; ∼**mord** *der* [murder by] poisoning; ∼**mörder** *der* poisoner; ∼**müll** *der* toxic waste; ∼**müll·deponie** *die* toxic [waste] tip *or* dump; ∼**pfeil** *der* poisoned arrow; ∼**pilz** *der* poisonous mushroom; [poisonous] toadstool; ∼**schlange** *die* poisonous *or* venomous snake; ∼**stachel** *der* poisonous sting; ∼**stoff** *der* poisonous *or* toxic substance; ∼**zahn** *der* poison fang; ∼**zwerg** *der* (ugs. abwertend) [nasty] spiteful little man

Giga- /giga-/ giga⟨*hertz etc.*⟩

Gigant /gi'gant/ *der;* ∼**en**, ∼**en** giant

gigantisch *Adj.* gigantic; huge ⟨*success*⟩

Gigolo /'ʒi:golo/ *der;* ∼**s**, ∼**s** gigolo

gilt /gɪlt/ *3. Pers. Sg. Präsens v.* **gelten**

Gimpel /'gɪmpl̩/ *der;* ∼**s**, ∼ (a) (Vogel) bullfinch; (b) (ugs. abwertend: einfältiger Mensch) ninny

ging /gɪŋ/ *1. u. 3. Pers. Sg. Prät. v.* **gehen**

Ginster /'gɪnstɐ/ *der;* ∼**s**, ∼**:** broom; (Stech∼) gorse; furze

Gipfel /'gɪpfl̩/ *der;* ∼**s**, ∼ (a) peak; (höchster Punkt des Berges) summit; (b) (Höhepunkt) height; (von Begeisterung, Glück, Ruhm, Macht auch) peak; **auf dem** ∼ **der Macht/des**

Ruhmes at the height of one's power/fame; **das ist [doch] der ~!** (ugs.) that's the limit!; **(c)** (~konferenz) summit

Gipfel-: **~konferenz** die summit conference; **~kreuz** das cross on the summit of a/the mountain

gipfeln itr. V. **in etw.** (Dat.) **~:** culminate in sth.

Gipfel·punkt der highest point; top; (fig.) high point; **der ~ seines künstlerischen Schaffens** the peak of his artistic powers

Gips /gɪps/ der; **~es, ~e** plaster; gypsum (Chem.); (zum Modellieren) plaster of Paris

Gips-: **~abdruck** der, **~abguss, *~abguß** der plaster cast; **~bein** das (ugs.) **ich komme mit meinem ~bein nicht mit** I can't keep up, with this plaster on my leg

gipsen tr. V. **(a)** plaster ‹wall, ceiling›; put ‹leg, arm, etc.› in plaster; **(b)** (ausbessern) repair with plaster

Gipser der; **~s, ~:** ▶ 85 plasterer

Gips-: **~figur** die plaster [of Paris] figure; **~verband** der plaster cast

Giraffe /gi'rafə/ die; **~, ~n** giraffe

Girlande /gɪr'landə/ die; **~, ~n** festoon

Girlie /'gœrli/ das; **~s, ~s** girlie

Giro /'ʒi:ro/ das; **~s, ~s,** österr. auch **Giri** (Finanzw.) giro

Giro·konto das (Finanzw.) current account

girren /'gɪrən/ itr. V. (auch fig.) coo

Gis, gis /gɪs/ das; **~, ~** (Musik) G sharp

Gischt /gɪʃt/ der; **~[e]s, ~e** od. die; **~, ~en (a)** (Schaumkronen) foam; surf; **(b)** (Sprühwasser) spray

Gis-Dur /auch: '-'-/ das; **~** (Musik) G sharp major

gis-Moll /auch: '-'-/ das; **~** (Musik) G sharp minor

Gitarre /gi'tarə/ die; **~, ~n** guitar

Gitarrist der; **~en, ~en** guitarist

Gitter /'gɪtɐ/ das; **~s, ~ (a)** (parallele Stäbe) bars pl.; (Drahtgeflecht) grille; (in der Straßendecke, im Fußboden) grating; (Geländer) railing[s pl.]; (Spalier) trellis; (feines Draht~) mesh; **hinter ~n** (ugs.) behind bars; **(b)** (Physik, Chemie) lattice

Glace /'glasə/ die; **~, ~n** (schweiz.) ice cream

Glacé·handschuh /gla'se:.../ der kid glove; **jmdn./etw. mit ~en anfassen** (ugs.) handle sb./sth. with kid gloves

Gladiator /gla'dia:tor/ der; **~s, ~en** /-'to:rən/ gladiator

Gladiole /gla'dio:lə/ die; **~, ~n** gladiolus

Glanz /glants/ der; **~es (a)** (von Licht, Sternen) brightness; brilliance; (von Haar, Metall, Perlen, Leder usw.) shine; lustre; sheen; (von Augen) shine; brightness; lustre; **den ~ verlieren** ‹diamonds, eyes› lose their sparkle; ‹metal, leather› lose its shine; **(b) mit ~ und Gloria** (ugs. iron.) in grand style

glänzen /'glɛntsn̩/ itr. V. **(a)** (Glanz ausstrahlen) shine; ‹car, hair, metal, paintwork, etc.› gleam; ‹elbows, trousers, etc.› be shiny; **vor Sauberkeit ~:** be so clean [that] it shines; **(b)** (Bewunderung erregen) shine (**bei** at); **durch Abwesenheit ~** (iron.) be conspicuous by one's absence

glänzend (ugs.) **1** Adj. **(a)** shining; gleaming ‹car, hair, metal, paintwork, etc.›; shiny ‹elbows, trousers, etc.›; **(b)** (bewundernswert) brilliant ‹idea, career, victory, pupil, prospects, etc.›; splendid, excellent, outstanding ‹references, marks, results, etc.›. **2** adv. **~ mit jmdm. auskommen** get on very well with sb.; **es geht mir/uns ~:** I am/we are very well; (finanziell) I am/we are doing very well or very nicely; **eine Aufgabe ~ lösen** solve a problem brilliantly

glanz-, Glanz-: **~leistung** die (auch iron.) brilliant performance; **~licht** das (bild. Kunst) highlight; **einer Sache** (Dat.) **[noch einige] ~lichter aufsetzen** give sth. [more] sparkle; **~los** Adj. dull; lacklustre; **~nummer** die star turn; **~papier** das glossy paper; **~rolle** die star role; **~stück** das **(a)** (Meisterwerk) pièce de résistance; **(b)** (der kostbarste Gegenstand) showpiece; **~voll 1** Adj. **(a)** (ausgezeichnet) brilliant; sparkling ‹variety number›; **(b)** (prachtvoll) magnificent; **2** adv. **(a)** (ausgezeichnet) brilliantly; **(b)** (prachtvoll) **Louis XIV pflegte ~voll Hof zu halten** Louis XIV used to hold court in glittering style; **~zeit** die heyday

Glas¹ /'gla:s/ das; **~es, Gläser** /'glɛːzɐ/ **(a)** o. Pl. glass; **unter ~:** behind glass; ‹plants› under glass; **(b)** (Trinkgefäß) glass; **ein ~ über den Durst trinken, zu tief ins ~ gucken** (ugs. scherzh.) have one too many or one over the eight; **(c)** (Behälter aus ~) jar

Glas² das; **~es, ~en** (Seemannsspr.) bell; **es schlug acht ~en** it struck eight bells

Glas-: **~auge** das glass eye; **~baustein** der glass brick or block; **~bläser** der ▶ 85 glass-blower

Gläschen /'glɛːsçən/ das; **~s, ~:** [little] glass

Glaser der; **~s, ~:** ▶ 85 glazier

Glaserei die; **~, ~en** glazing business

gläsern /'glɛːzɐn/ Adj.; nicht präd. (aus Glas) glass

glas-, Glas-: **~fabrik** die glassworks sing. or pl.; **~faser** die; meist Pl. glass fibre; **~fenster** das [glass] window; **bemalte ~fenster** stained glass windows; **~fiber** die ⇒ **~faser; ~fiber·stab** der (Leichtathletik) glass-fibre pole; **~flasche** die glass bottle; **~haus** das greenhouse; glasshouse; **wer [selbst] im ~haus sitzt, soll nicht mit Steinen werfen** (Spr.) those who live in glass houses shouldn't throw stones (prov.)

glasieren tr. V. **(a)** (glätten und haltbar machen) glaze; **(b)** (Kochk.) ice ‹cake etc.›; glaze ‹meat›

glasig Adj. **(a)** (starr) glassy ‹stare, eyes, etc.›; **(b)** (Kochk.: durchsichtig) transparent

Glas-: **~kasten** der glass case; (kleiner) glass box; **~keramik** die devitrified glass; **~kugel** die glass ball; (einer Wahrsagerin) crystal ball; (Murmel) marble; **~malerei** die stained glass; (Verfahren) glass-staining; **~perle** die glass bead; **~platte** die glass plate; (eines Tisches) glass top; (im Fenster) pane of glass; **~scheibe** die sheet of glass; (im Fenster) pane of glass; **~scherbe** die piece of broken glass; **~schneider** der glass-cutter; **~splitter** der splinter of glass; **~tür** die glass door

Glasur /gla'zuːɐ/ die; **~, ~en (a)** (Schmelz) glaze; **(b)** (Kochk.) (auf Kuchen) icing; (auf Fleisch) glaze

Glas·wolle die glass wool

glatt /glat/ **1** Adj. **(a)** smooth; straight ‹hair›; **eine ~e Eins/Fünf** a clear A/E; **etw. ~ hobeln/bügeln** plane/iron sth. smooth; **etw. ~ machen** smooth sth. out; **den Boden ~ machen** level the ground; **etw. ~ ziehen** pull sth. straight; **~ rasiert** clean-shaven; **(b)** (rutschig) slippery; **(c)** nicht präd. (komplikationslos) smooth ‹landing, journey›; clean, straightforward ‹fracture›; **(d)** nicht präd. (ugs.: offensichtlich) downright, outright ‹lie›; outright ‹deception, fraud›; sheer, utter ‹nonsense, madness, etc.›; pure, sheer ‹invention›, flat ‹refusal›; complete ‹failure›; **(e)** (allzu gewandt) smooth. **2** adv. **(a) die Rechnung geht ~ auf** the calculation works out exactly; **(b)** (komplikationslos) smoothly; **~ gehen** (ugs.) go smoothly; **(c)** (ugs.: rückhaltlos) **jmdm. etw. ~ ins Gesicht sagen** tell sb. sth. straight to his/her face

***glatt|bügeln** ⇒ **glatt 1a**

Glätte /'glɛtə/ die; **~ (a)** smoothness; **(b)** (Rutschigkeit) slipperiness

Glatt·eis das glaze; ice; (auf der Straße) black ice; **jmdn. aufs ~ führen** (fig.) catch sb. out

Glatteis·gefahr die; o. Pl. danger of black ice

glätten **1** tr. V. smooth out ‹piece of paper, banknote, etc.›; smooth [down] ‹feathers, fur, etc.›; plane ‹wood etc.›. **2** refl. V. ‹waves› subside; ‹sea› become calm or smooth; (fig.) subside; die down

glatt-: *~|**gehen** ⇒ **glatt 2 b;*~|hobeln** usw.: ⇒ **glatt 1 a; ~weg** Adv. (ugs.) etw. **~weg ablehnen/ignorieren** turn sth. down flat/just or simply ignore sth.; *~|**ziehen** ⇒ **glatt 1 a**

Glatze /'glatsə/ die; **~, ~n** bald head; **eine ~ haben/bekommen** be/go bald

Glatz·kopf der **(a)** (Kopf) bald head; **(b)** (ugs.: Person) baldhead

glatz·köpfig Adj. bald[-headed]

Glaube /'glaʊbə/ der; **~ns** faith (**an** + Akk. in); (Überzeugung, Meinung) belief (**an** + Akk. in); **jmdm./jmds. Worten ~n schenken** believe sb./what sb. says; **[bei jmdm.] ~n finden** be believed [by sb.]; **in dem ~n leben, dass ...:** live in the belief that ...; **lass ihn in**

seinem ∼n don't disillusion him; [der] ∼ versetzt Berge faith can move mountains

glauben 1 tr. V. (a) (annehmen, meinen) think; believe; **ich glaube, ja** I think or believe so; (b) (für wahr halten) believe; **das glaubst du doch selbst nicht!** [surely] you can't be serious; **ob du es glaubst oder nicht …:** believe it or not …; **wer hätte das [je] geglaubt?** who would [ever] have thought it?; **du glaubst [gar] nicht, wie …:** you have no idea how …; **wers glaubt, wird selig** (ugs. scherzh.) if you believe that, you'll believe anything; **das ist doch kaum zu** ∼ (ugs.) it's incredible. 2 itr. V. (a) (vertrauen) **an jmdn./etw./sich [selbst]** ∼: believe in or have faith in sb./sth./oneself; (b) (gläubig sein) hold religious beliefs; believe; **fest/unbeirrbar** ∼: have a strong/unshakeable religious belief; (c) (von der Existenz von etw. überzeugt sein) believe (**an** + Akk. in); (d) **dran** ∼ **müssen** (salopp: getötet werden) buy it (sl.); (salopp: sterben) peg out (coll.); kick the bucket (fig. sl.)

Glaubens-: ∼**bekenntnis** das o. Pl. (auch fig.: Überzeugung) creed; ∼**frage** die question of faith or belief; ∼**freiheit** die; o. Pl. religious freedom; freedom of worship; ∼**gemeinschaft** die religious sect; denomination; ∼**streit** der religious dispute

Glauber·salz /ˈglaubɐ-/ das; ∼es (Chemie) Glauber's salt

glaubhaft 1 Adj. credible; believable. 2 adv. convincingly

Glaubhaftigkeit die; ∼: credibility

gläubig /ˈglɔybɪç/ 1 Adj. (a) (religiös) devout; **sehr/zutiefst** ∼ **sein** be very/deeply religious; (b) (vertrauensvoll) trusting. 2 adv. (a) (religiös) devoutly; (b) (vertrauensvoll) trustingly

Gläubige der/die; adj. Dekl. believer; **die** ∼n the faithful

Gläubiger der; ∼s, ∼, **Gläubigerin** die; ∼, ∼**nen** creditor

Gläubigkeit die; ∼ (a) (religiöse Überzeugung) religious faith; (b) (Vertrauen) trustfulness

glaub·würdig 1 Adj. credible; believable. 2 adv. convincingly

Glaubwürdigkeit die credibility

Glaukom /glauˈkoːm/ das; ∼s, ∼e ▶ 329 | (Med.) glaucoma

glazial /glaˈtsi̯aːl/ Adj. (Geol.) glacial

gleich /glaiç/ 1 Adj. (a) (identisch, von derselben Art) same; (∼berechtigt, ∼wertig, Math.) equal; ∼**er Lohn für** ∼**e Arbeit** equal pay for equal work; ∼**es Recht für alle** equal rights for all; **dreimal zwei [ist]** ∼ **sechs** three times two equals or is six; ∼ **bleiben** remain or stay the same; (konstant) remain or stay constant or steady; **das** (Dat.) ∼ **bleiben** remain the same; **das bleibt sich [doch]** ∼ (ugs.) it makes no difference; ∼ **bleibend** (konstant) constant; steady; **das Gleiche wollen/beabsichtigen** have the same objective[s pl.]/intentions pl.; **das kommt auf das Gleiche** od. **aufs Gleiche heraus** it amounts or comes to the same thing; **Gleiches mit Gleichem vergelten** pay sb. back in his/her own coin or in kind; **Gleich und Gleich gesellt sich gern** (Spr.) birds of a feather flock together (prov.); (b) (ugs.: gleichgültig; **ganz** ∼, **wer anruft,** …: no matter who calls, … 2 adv. (a) (übereinstimmend) ∼ **groß/alt** usw. **sein** be the same height/age etc.; ∼ **gut/schlecht** usw. equally good/bad etc.; ∼ **gesinnt** like-minded; ∼ **lautend** identical; identically worded; (b) (in derselben Weise) ∼ **aufgebaut/gekleidet** having the same structure/wearing identical clothes; **alle Menschen** ∼ **behandeln** treat everyone alike; (c) (sofort) at once; right or straight away; (bald) in a moment or minute; **ich komme** ∼: I'm just coming; **es muss nicht** ∼ **sein** there's no immediate hurry; **es ist** ∼ **zehn Uhr** it is almost or nearly ten o'clock; **das habe ich [euch]** ∼ **gesagt** I told you so; what did I tell you?; **bis** ∼! see you later!; (d) (räumlich) right; immediately; just; ∼ **rechts/links** just or immediately on the right/left. 3 Präp. + Dat. (geh.) like. 4 Partikel (a) **nun wein nicht** ∼**/sei nicht** ∼ **böse** don't start crying/don't get cross; (b) (in Fragesätzen) **wie hieß er** ∼? what was his name [again]?

gleich-, Gleich-: ∼**alt[e]rig** /∼alt[ə]rıç/ Adj. of the same age (**mit** as); **die beiden sind** ∼**alt[e]rig** they are

both the same age; ∼**artig** 1 Adj. of the same kind postpos. (Dat. as); (sehr ähnlich) very similar (Dat. to); 2 adv. in the same way; ∼**bedeutend** Adj. ∼**bedeutend mit** synonymous with; (action) tantamount to; ∼**berechtigt** Adj. having or enjoying or with equal rights postpos.; ∼**berechtigte Partner/Mitglieder** equal partners/members; ∼**berechtigt sein** have or enjoy equal rights; ∼**berechtigung** die equal rights pl.; *∼|**bleiben** usw.: ⇒ **gleich 1 a**

gleichen unr. itr. V. **jmdm./einer Sache** ∼: be like or resemble sb./sth.; (sehr ähnlich aussehen) closely resemble sb./sth.; **sich** (Dat.) ∼: be alike; (sehr ähnlich aussehen) closely resemble each other

gleichen·orts Adv. (schweiz.) in the same place

gleichermaßen Adv. equally

gleich-, Gleich-: ∼**falls** Adv. (auch) also; (ebenfalls) likewise; **danke** ∼**falls!** thank you, [and] the same to you; ∼**förmig** 1 Adj. (a) (einheitlich) uniform; steady (development); (b) (langweilig, monoton) monotonous; 2 adv. (a) (einheitlich) uniformly; (b) (langweilig, monoton) monotonously; ∼**förmigkeit** die; ∼ (a) (Einheitlichkeit) uniformity; (b) (Monotonie) monotony; ∼**geschlechtlich** Adj. homosexual; *∼**gesinnt** ⇒ **gleich 2 a**

Gleich·gewicht das; o. Pl. (a) balance; **das** ∼ **halten/verlieren** keep/lose one's balance; **im** ∼ **sein** be in equilibrium; (b) (Ausgewogenheit) balance; **das europäische** ∼: the balance of power in Europe; **das** ∼ **der Kräfte** the balance of power; (c) (innere Ausgeglichenheit) equilibrium; **jmdn. aus dem** ∼ **bringen** throw sb. off balance

Gleichgewichts-: ∼**organ** das (Anat.) organ of equilibrium; ∼**sinn** der sense of balance; ∼**störung** die disturbance of one's sense of balance

gleich·gültig 1 Adj. (a) indifferent (**gegenüber** towards); (b) (egal) **sie war ihm [nicht]** ∼ (verhüll.) he was [by no means] indifferent to her; **das ist mir [vollkommen]** ∼: it's a matter of [complete] indifference to me; **es ist** ∼, **ob** …: it does not matter whether … 2 adv. indifferently; (look on) with indifference

Gleich·gültigkeit die indifference (**gegenüber** towards)

Gleichheit die; ∼, ∼**en** (a) (Identität) identity; (Ähnlichkeit) similarity; (b) o. Pl. (gleiche Rechte) equality

Gleichheits-: ∼[**grund**]**satz** der principle of equality before the law; ∼**zeichen** das equals sign

gleich-, Gleich-: ∼**klang** der harmony; ∼|**kommen** unr. itr. V.; mit sein amount to; be tantamount to; **jmdm./einer Sache [an etw.** (Dat.)] ∼**kommen** equal sb./sth. [in sth.]; ∼**laufend** Adj. parallel (**mit** with); *∼**lautend** ⇒ **gleich 2 a**; ∼|**machen** tr. V. make equal; s. auch **Erdboden**; ∼**macherei** die; ∼, ∼**en** (abwertend) levelling down (derog.); egalitarianism; ∼**macherisch** Adj. (abwertend) egalitarian; ∼**maß** das; o. Pl. (a) (Ebenmaß) (von Bewegung, Strophen) regularity; (von Zügen, Proportionen) symmetry; (b) (Ausgeglichenheit) equilibrium; ∼**mäßig** 1 Adj. regular (interval, rhythm); uniform (acceleration, distribution); even (heat); 2 adv. (breathe) regularly; **etw.** ∼**mäßig verteilen/auftragen** distribute sth. equally/apply sth. evenly; ∼**mäßig hohe Temperaturen** constantly high temperatures; ∼**mäßigkeit** die ⇒ ∼**mäßig:** regularity; uniformity; evenness; ∼**mut** der equanimity; calmness; composure; ∼**mütig** 1 Adj. calm; composed; unruffled (calm); 2 adv. calmly; ∼**namig** /-naːmɪç/ Adj. (a) of the same name postpos.; (b) (Math.) ∼**namige Brüche** fractions with a common denominator; **Brüche** ∼**namig machen** reduce fractions to a common denominator

Gleichnis das; ∼**ses**, ∼**se** (Allegorie) allegory; (Parabel) parable

gleich·rangig /-raŋɪç/ 1 Adj. (principle, problem, etc.) of equal importance or status; equally important (principle, problem, etc.); (official, job) of equal rank. 2 adv. **alle Punkte** ∼ **behandeln** give all points equal treatment

Gleich·richter der (Elektrot.) rectifier

gleichsam Adv. (geh.) as it were; so to speak; ∼ **als [ob]** …: just as if …

gleich-, Gleich-: ~|**schalten** *tr. V.* (abwertend) force *or* bring into line; ~**schenk[e]lig** *Adj.* (Math.) isosceles; ~**schritt** *der; o. Pl.* marching in step; ~**seitig** *Adj.* (Math.) equilateral; ~|**setzen** *tr. V.* **zwei Dinge** ~**setzen** equate two things; **etw. einer Sache** (*Dat.*) *od.* **mit etw.** ~**setzen** equate sth. with sth.; ~**stand** *der; o. Pl.* (a) (Sport: gleicher Spielstand) **den** ~**stand herstellen/erzielen** level the score; ~|**stellen** *tr. V.* **etw. einer Sache** (*Dat.*) *od.* **mit etw.** ~**stellen** equate sth. with sth.; ~**stellung** *die:* **die rechtliche** ~**stellung unehelicher Kinder** giving equal rights to illegitimate children; **soziale** ~**stellung** social equality; ~**strom** *der* (Elektrot.) direct current; ~|**tun** *unr. tr. V.* **es jmdm.** ~**tun** match *or* equal sb.; (jmdn. nachahmen) copy sb.

Gleichung *die;* ~, ~**en** equation

gleich-, Gleich-: ~**viel** /-'- *od.* '--/ *Adv.* no matter; ~**wertig** *Adj.* (a) of equal *or* the same value *postpos.;* (b) (Sport: gleich stark) evenly matched ⟨*opponents, teams*⟩; ~**wink[e]lig** *Adj.* equiangular; ~**wohl** /-'- *od.* '--/ *Adv.* nevertheless; ~**zeitig** 1 *Adj.; nicht präd.* simultaneous; 2 *adv.* (a) simultaneously; at the same time; (b) (auch noch) at the same time; ~**zeitigkeit** *die* simultaneity; simultaneousness; ~|**ziehen** *unr. itr. V.* catch up; draw level

Gleis /glais/ *das;* ~**es,** ~**e** (a) (Fahrspur) track; line; rails *pl.;* permanent way *as Brit. tech. term;* (Bahnsteig) platform; (einzelne Schiene) rail; **auf** ~ **5 einlaufen** ⟨*train*⟩ arrive at platform 5; **jmdn. aufs tote** ~ **schieben** put sb. out of harm's way (fig.); **jmdn. aus dem** ~ **bringen** *od.* **werfen** put sb. off [his/her stroke]; (von jmdm. psychisch nicht bewältigt werden) upset *or* affect sb. deeply

Gleis-: ~**an·lage** *die* [railway] lines *pl. or* tracks *pl.;* ~**anschluss,** *****~**anschluß** *der* siding

gleißen /'glaisn̩/ *itr. V.* (dichter.) blaze

gleiten /'glaitn̩/ *unr. itr. V.; mit sein* (a) glide; ⟨*hand*⟩ slide; **aus dem Sattel/ins Wasser** ~: slide out of the saddle/slide *or* slip into the water; **jmdm. aus den Händen** ~: slip from sb.'s hands; (b) (ugs.: in Bezug auf Arbeitszeit) work flexitime

gleitend *Adj.; nicht präd.* ~**e Arbeitszeit** flexitime; flexible working hours *pl.;* ~**e Lohnskala** index-linked wage scale

Gleit-: ~**flug** *der* glide; **im** ~**flug landen** glide-land; ~**zeit** *die* flexible working hours *pl.*

Gletscher /'glɛtʃɐ/ *der;* ~**s,** ~: glacier

Gletscher-: ~**bach** *der* glacial stream; ~**eis** *das* glacial ice; ~**spalte** *die* crevasse

glich /glɪç/ *1. u. 3. Pers. Sg. Prät. v.* **gleichen**

Glied /gli:t/ *das;* ~**[e]s,** ~**er** (a) ▶ 326 | (Körperteil) limb; (Finger~, Zehen~) joint; **der Schreck sitzt** *od.* **steckt ihm noch in den** ~**ern** he is [still] shaking with the shock; **der Schreck fuhr ihr in die** *od.* **durch alle** ~**er** the shock made her shake all over; (b) (Ketten~, auch fig.) link; (c) (Teil eines Ganzen) section; part; (Mitglied) member; (eines Satzes) part; (einer Gleichung) term; (d) ▶ 326 | (Penis) penis; (e) (Mannschaftsreihe) rank

Glieder·füßer *der* (Zool.) arthropod

gliedern /'gli:dɐn/ 1 *tr. V.* structure; organize ⟨*thoughts*⟩; **nach Eigenschaften** ~: classify according to properties. 2 *refl. V.* **sich in Gruppen/Abschnitte** *usw.* ~: divide *or* be divided into groups/sections *etc.*

Glieder-: ~**puppe** *die* jointed doll; ~**schmerz** *der* rheumatic pains *pl.*

Gliederung *die;* ~, ~**en** (a) (Aufbau, Einteilung) structure; (b) (das Gliedern) structuring; (von Gedanken) organization; (nach Eigenschaften) classification; (in Teile) arrangement

Glied-: ~**maße** /-ma:sə/ *die;* ~, ~**n** limb; ~**satz** *der* (Sprachw.) subordinate clause

glimmen /'glɪmən/ *unr. od. regelm. itr. V.* glow

Glimmer *der;* ~**s,** ~: mica

glimmern *itr. V.* glimmer; ⟨*lake etc.*⟩ glisten

Glimm·stängel, *****Glimm·stengel** *der* (ugs. scherzh.) fag (coll.); ciggy (coll.)

glimpflich /'glɪmpflɪç/ 1 *Adj.* (a) **der Unfall nahm ein** ~**es Ende** the accident turned out not to be too serious; (b) (mild) lenient ⟨*sentence, punishment*⟩. 2 *adv.* (a) (ohne

Schaden) ~ **davonkommen** get off lightly; **es ist** ~ **abgegangen** it turned out not to be too bad; (b) (mild) mildly; leniently

glitschen /'glɪtʃn̩/ *itr. V.; mit sein* (ugs.) slip

glitschig /'glɪtʃɪç/ *Adj.* (ugs.) slippery

glitt /glɪt/ *1. u. 3. Pers. Sg. Prät. v.* **gleiten**

glitzern /'glɪtsɐn/ *itr. V.* ⟨*star*⟩ twinkle; ⟨*diamond, decorations*⟩ sparkle, glitter; ⟨*snow, eyes, tears*⟩ glisten

global /glo'ba:l/ 1 *Adj.* (a) (weltweit) global; worldwide; (b) (umfassend) general, all-round ⟨*education*⟩; overall ⟨*control, planning, etc.*⟩; (c) (allgemein) general. 2 *adv.* (a) (weltweit) worldwide; globally; (b) (umfassend) in overall terms; (c) (allgemein) in general terms

globalisieren *tr. V.* globalize

Globalisierung *die;* ~, ~**en** globalization

Global·steuerung *die* (Wirtsch.) overall control

Globen ⇒ **Globus**

Globetrotter /'glo:bətrɔtɐ/ *der;* ~**s,** ~: globetrotter

Globus /'glo:bʊs/ *der;* ~ *od.* ~**ses,** ~**se** *od.* **Globen** /'glo:bn̩/ globe

Glöckchen /'glœkçən/ *das;* ~**s,** ~: [little] bell

Glocke /'glɔkə/ *die;* ~, ~**n** (a) (auch: Tür~, Taucher~, Blüte) bell; **etw. an die große** ~ **hängen** (ugs.) tell the whole world about sth.; (b) (Hut) cloche; (c) (Käse~, Butter~, Kuchen~) cover; bell

glocken-, Glocken-: ~**blume** *die* (Bot.) bell-flower; campanula; ~**förmig** *Adj.* bell-shaped; widely flared ⟨*skirt etc.*⟩; ~**hell** *Adj.* bell-like; **eine** ~**helle Stimme** a high, clear voice; ~**läuten** *das* pealing *or* ringing of bells; ~**rock** *der* widely flared skirt; ~**schlag** *der* stroke; **mit dem** *od.* **auf den** ~**schlag** (ugs.) on the dot (coll.); ~**spiel** *das* (a) carillon; (mit einer Uhr gekoppelt auch) chimes *pl.;* (b) (Musikinstrument) glockenspiel; ~**turm** *der* bell tower; belfry

glockig /'glɔkɪç/ ⇒ **glockenförmig**

Glöckner /'glœknɐ/ *der;* ~**s,** ~ (veralt.) bellringer; **der** ~ **von Notre Dame** the Hunchback of Notre Dame

glomm /glɔm/ *1. u. 3. Pers. Sg. Prät. v.* **glimmen**

glorifizieren /glorifi'tsi:rən/ *tr. V.* glorify

Glorifizierung *die;* ~, ~**en** glorification

Gloriole /glo'rio:lə/ *die;* ~, ~**n** (a) (auch fig.) glory; (b) (um den Kopf) halo; aura

glor·reich /'glo:ɐ̯-/ 1 *Adj.* glorious. 2 *adv.* gloriously

Glossar /glɔ'sa:ɐ̯/ *das;* ~**s,** ~**e** glossary

Glosse /'glɔsə/ *die;* ~, ~**n** (a) (in den Medien) commentary; (b) (spöttische Bemerkung) sneering *or* (coll.) snide comment

glossieren *tr. V.* (a) commentate on; (b) (bespötteln) sneer at

Glotz·augen *Pl.* (salopp abwertend) goggle eyes; ~ **machen/kriegen** go goggle-eyed; goggle

Glotze /'glɔtsə/ *die;* ~, ~**n** (salopp) box (coll.); goggle-box (Brit. coll.)

glotzen *itr. V.* (abwertend) goggle; gawk, gawp (coll.)

Glotz·kiste *die* (salopp) box (coll.); goggle-box (Brit. coll.)

Glück /glʏk/ *das;* ~**[e]s,** ~ (a) luck; **ein großes/unverdientes** ~ a great/an undeserved stroke of luck; **[es ist/war] ein** ~**, dass …:** it's/it was lucky that …; **er hat [kein]** ~ **gehabt** he was [un]lucky; ~ **bei Frauen haben** be successful with women; **jmdm.** ~ **wünschen** wish sb. [good] luck; **viel** ~**!** [the] best of luck!; good luck!; ~ **bringen** bring [good] luck; **mehr** ~ **als Verstand haben** have more luck than judgement; **sein** ~ **versuchen** *od.* **probieren** try one's luck; **auf gut** ~**:** trusting to luck; **zum** *od.* **zu meinem/seinem** *usw.* ~**:** luckily *or* fortunately [for me/him *etc.*]; ~ **bringend** lucky; (b) (Hochstimmung) happiness; **das häusliche** ~**:** domestic bliss; **jmdn. zu seinem** ~ **zwingen** make sb. do what is good for him/her; **jeder ist seines** ~**es Schmied** (Spr.) life is what you make it; (c) (Fortuna) fortune; luck

*****glück·bringend** ⇒ **Glück** a

Glucke /'glʊkə/ *die;* ~, ~**n** brood-hen; mother hen

glucken *itr. V.* (a) (brüten) brood; (b) (ugs.: herumsitzen) sit around; (c) (Laut hervorbringen) cluck

---

glücken *tr. V.; mit sein* succeed; be successful; **etw. glückt jmdm.** sb. is successful with sth.; **ein geglückter Versuch** a successful attempt; **die Flucht ist nicht geglückt** the escape[-attempt] failed

gluckern /'glʊkɐn/ *itr. V.* gurgle; glug

glücklich 1 *Adj.* (a) ▶ 240 ǀ (von Glück erfüllt) happy (**über** + Akk. about); (b) (erfolgreich) lucky ⟨winner⟩; successful ⟨outcome⟩; safe ⟨journey⟩; happy ⟨ending⟩; (c) (vorteilhaft) fortunate; **ein ~er Zufall** a happy coincidence; a lucky chance; s. auch **Hand** f. 2 *adv.* (a) (erfolgreich) successfully; (b) (vorteilhaft, zufrieden) happily ⟨chosen, married⟩; (c) (endlich) at last; eventually

glücklicher·weise *Adv.* fortunately; luckily

glück·los *Adj.* luckless ⟨enterprise⟩; unhappy ⟨existence etc.⟩

Glücks·bringer *der* lucky or good-luck charm; [lucky] mascot

glück·selig *Adj.* blissfully happy; blissful

Glück·seligkeit *die; ~:* bliss; blissful happiness

glucksen /'glʊksn̩/ *itr. V.* (a) ⇨ **gluckern**; (b) (lachen) chuckle

Glücks-: **~fall** *der* piece or stroke of luck; **~göttin** *die* goddess of fortune; Fortune no art.; **~käfer** *der* ⇨ **Marienkäfer**; **~kind** *das* lucky person; **~klee** *der* four-leaf or four-leaved clover; **~pfennig** *der* lucky penny; **~pilz** *der* (ugs.) lucky devil (coll.) or beggar (coll.); **~sache** *die:* **das ist ~sache** it's a matter of luck

Glücks-: **~spiel** *das* (a) game of chance; **dem ~spiel verfallen sein** be addicted to gambling; (b) (fig.) matter of luck; lottery; **~spieler** *der* gambler; **~stern** *der* lucky star; **~strähne** *die* lucky streak; **eine ~strähne haben** have hit a lucky streak; have a run of good luck; **~tag** *der* lucky day

glück·strahlend *Adj.* radiant; radiantly happy; **sie verkündete uns ~, dass sie heiraten werde** she was radiant with happiness or radiantly happy as she told us she was going to get married

Glücks-: **~treffer** *der* (a) (Gewinn) bit or piece of luck; (b) (beim Schießen) lucky hit; fluke; **~zahl** *die* lucky number

Glück·wunsch *der* ▶ 240 ǀ congratulations *pl.*; **herzlichen ~ zum Geburtstag!** happy birthday!; many happy returns of the day!

Glückwunsch-: **~karte** *die* congratulations card; (zum Geburtstag) greetings card; **~telegramm** *das* telegram of congratulations; congratulatory telegram; (zum Geburtstag) greetings telegram

Glucose /glu'ko:zə/ *die; ~* (Chemie) glucose

Glüh·birne *die* lightbulb

glühen /'gly:ən/ 1 *itr. V.* (a) (leuchten) glow; (fig.) ⟨eyes, cheeks, etc.⟩ glow; (b) (geh.: erregt sein) burn. 2 *tr. V.* (zum Leuchten bringen) heat until red-hot

glühend 1 *Adj.* (a) (heiß) red-hot ⟨metal etc.⟩; (fig.) blazing ⟨heat⟩; burning ⟨hatred⟩; flushed, burning ⟨cheeks⟩; **~ heiß** scorching or blazing hot; **~ rot** red-hot; (b) (begeistert) ardent ⟨admirer etc.⟩; passionate ⟨words, letter, etc.⟩. 2 *adv.* ⟨love⟩ passionately; ⟨admire⟩ ardently

*glühendheiß *usw.:* ⇨ **glühend** 1 a

Glüh-: **~faden** *der* filament; **~lampe** *die* light bulb; **~wein** *der* mulled wine; glühwein; **~würmchen** *das* (ugs.) (weiblich) glow-worm; (männlich) firefly

Glukose ⇨ **Glucose**

Glupsch·augen /'glʊpʃ-/ *Pl.* (nordd.) goggle-eyes

Glut /glu:t/ *die; ~, ~en* (a) embers *pl.*; (fig.) [blazing] heat; (b) (geh.: Leidenschaft) passion

Glutamat /gluta'ma:t/ *das; ~[e]s, ~e* (Chemie) glutamate

Glut·hitze *die* blazing or sweltering heat

Glycerin (fachspr.), **Glyzerin** /glytse'ri:n/ *das; ~s* glycerine

GmbH *Abk.* **Gesellschaft mit beschränkter Haftung** ≈ p.l.c.

g-Moll /'ge:mɔl/ *das; ~* (Musik) G minor

Gnade /'gna:də/ *die; ~, ~n* (a) (Gewogenheit) favour; **vor jmdm. od. vor jmds. Augen ~ finden** find favour with sb. or in sb.'s eyes; **jmdm. auf ~ und od. oder Ungnade ausgeliefert sein** be [completely] at sb.'s mercy; **in ~n wieder aufgenommen werden** be restored to favour; (b) (Rel.: Güte) grace; (c) (Milde) mercy; **~ vor od. für Recht ergehen lassen** temper justice with mercy; (d) (veraltete Anrede) **Euer od. Ihro od. Ihre ~n** Your Grace

gnaden *itr. V.* in **gnade mir/dir** *usw.* **Gott!** God or Heaven help me/you *etc.*!

gnaden-, Gnaden-: **~akt** *der* act of mercy; **~brot** *das:* **jmdm./einem Tier das ~brot geben** keep sb./an animal in his/ her/its old age; **~frist** *die* reprieve; **~gesuch** *das* plea for clemency; **~los** (auch fig.) 1 *Adj.* merciless; 2 *adv.* mercilessly; **~losigkeit** *die; ~:* mercilessness; **~schuss, *~schuß** *der* coup de grâce (by shooting), **~stoß** *der* coup de grâce (with sword etc.); **~tod** *der* euthanasia; mercy killing **~weg** *der:* **auf dem ~weg** by a pardon

gnädig /'gnɛːdɪç/ 1 *Adj.* (a) (oft iron.) gracious; **~er Herr** (veralt.) sir; **die ~e Frau/das ~e Fräulein/der ~e Herr** (veralt.) madam/the young lady/the master; (b) (glimpflich) lenient, light ⟨sentence etc.⟩; (c) (Rel.) gracious ⟨God⟩; **Gott sei uns ~:** [may] the good Lord preserve us. 2 *adv.* (a) (oft iron.) graciously; (b) (glimpflich) **das ist ~ abgegangen** it turned out not to be too bad

Gneis /gnais/ *der; ~es, ~e* (Geol.) gneiss

Gnom /gno:m/ *der; ~en, ~en* gnome; (fig.: ugs.) little twerp (coll.)

Gnu /gnu:/ *das; ~s, ~s* gnu

Gobelin /gobə'lɛ̃:/ *der; ~s, ~s* Gobelin [tapestry]

Gockel /'gɔkl̩/ *der; ~s, ~* (bes. südd., sonst ugs. scherzh.) cock

Go-go-Girl /'go:gogø:ɐl/ *das* go-go girl or dancer

Gokart /'go:kart/ *der; ~s, ~s* go-kart (Brit.); kart

Golan·höhen /go'la:n-/ *Pl.* Golan Heights

Gold *das; ~[e]s* gold; **das schwarze ~** (fig.) black gold (fig.); **es ist nicht alles ~, was glänzt** (Spr.) all that glitters or glistens is not gold (prov.); **~ in der Kehle haben** (fig.) have a golden voice; **olympisches ~:** Olympic gold

gold-, Gold-: **~ader** *die* vein of gold; **~barren** *der* gold bar or ingot; **~bestickt** *Adj.* embroidered with gold [thread] postpos.; **~dublee** *das* rolled gold

golden 1 *Adj.* (a) gold ⟨bracelet, watch, etc.⟩; **der Tanz ums Goldene Kalb** the worship of the golden calf or Mammon; **eine ~e Schallplatte** a gold disc; **das Goldene Vlies** (Myth.) the Golden Fleece; (b) (dichter.: goldfarben) golden; (c) (herrlich) golden ⟨memories, days, etc.⟩; blissful ⟨freedom etc.⟩; **die ~e Mitte od. den ~en Mittelweg finden/wählen** find/strike a happy medium; **die goldenen zwanziger Jahre** the roaring twenties; **der goldene Schnitt** (Math.) the golden section. 2 *adv.* like gold

gold-, Gold-: **~farben, ~farbig** *Adj.* gold-coloured; (dichter.) gold filling; **~füllung** *die* gold filling; **~fund** *der* gold find or strike; **~gehalt** *der* gold content; **~gelb** *Adj.* golden yellow; **~glänzend** *Adj.* shining gold; **~gräber** *der* gold-digger; **~grube** *die* (auch fig.) gold mine; **~haltig** *Adj.* gold-bearing; auriferous; **~hamster** *der* golden hamster

goldig 1 *Adj.* (niedlich, landsch.: nett) sweet. 2 *adv.* sweetly

Gold-: **~junge** *der* (Kosewort) good [little] boy; **~kette** *die* gold chain; **~klumpen** *der* gold nugget; **~krone** *die* (Zahnmed.) gold crown; **~kurs** *der* (Börsenw.) price of gold; gold price; **~küste** *die; ~* (Geogr.) Gold Coast; **~lack** *der* (a) gold lacquer; (b) (Bot.) wallflower; **~macher** *der* alchemist

Gold·medaille *die* gold medal

Goldmedaillen-: **~gewinner** *der*, **~gewinnerin** *die* gold medallist; gold-medal winner

gold-, Gold-: **~mine** *die* gold mine; **~münze** *die* gold coin; **~rausch** *der* gold fever; **~regen** *der* (a) (Bot.) laburnum; golden rain; (b) (Feuerwerk) golden rain; (c) (Reichtum) riches *pl.*; wealth; **~reserve** *die* gold reserve; **~richtig** (ugs.) 1 *Adj.* absolutely or (coll.) dead right; 2 *adv.* absolutely right; **~schatz** *der* gold treasure; (verborgen auch) hoard of gold

Gold·schmied der ▶85| goldsmith
Goldschmiede·kunst die; o. Pl. goldsmith's art; gold-work no art.
Gold-: ~**schmuck** der gold jewelry or (Brit.) jewellery; ~**schnitt** der gilt edging; ~**staub** der gold dust; ~**stück** das (hist.) gold piece; **sie ist ein** ~**stück** (fig.) she is a [real] treasure; ~**sucher** der gold prospector; ~**vorkommen** das gold deposit; ~**waage** die gold balance; **alles** od. **jedes Wort auf die** ~**waage legen** (wörtlich nehmen) take everything or every word [too] literally; (vorsichtig äußern) weigh one's words very carefully; ~**während** die (Wirtsch.) currency tied to the gold standard; ~**zahn** der (ugs.) gold tooth
Golf¹ /gɔlf/ der; ~[e]s, ~e gulf; **der** ~ **von Neapel** the Bay of Naples
Golf² das; ~s (Sport) golf
Golf·ball der golf ball
Golfer der; ~s, ~, **Golferin** die; ~, ~nen golfer
Golf-: ~**krieg** der Gulf War; ~**mütze** die golf[ing] cap; ~**platz** der golfcourse; ~**schläger** der golf club; ~**spieler** der, ~**spielerin** die golfer; ~**staat** der Gulf State; ~**strom** der Gulf Stream; ~**turnier** das golf tournament
Golgatha /'gɔlgata/ das; ~s (Bibl.) Golgotha
Gomorrha /go'mɔra/ ⇒ **Sodom**
Gondel /'gɔndl/ die; ~, ~n gondola
gondeln itr. V.; mit sein (ugs.) **durch die Stadt/die Ägäis** ~: cruise around town/the Aegean; **durch die Gegend** ~: cruise around
Gong /gɔŋ/ der; ~s, ~s gong
Gong·schlag der stroke of the/a gong; **beim** ~: when the gong sounds/sounded
gönnen /'gœnən/ tr. V. (a) jmdm. etw. ~: not begrudge sb. sth.; **ich gönne ihm diesen Erfolg von ganzem Herzen** I'm delighted or very pleased for him that he has had this success; (b) (zukommen lassen) **sich/jmdm. etw.** ~: give or allow oneself/sb. sth.; **sie gönnte ihm keinen Blick** she didn't spare him a single glance
Gönner der; ~s, ~: patron
gönnerhaft (abwertend) **1** Adj. patronizing. **2** adv. patronizingly; in a patronizing manner
Gönnerin die; ~, ~nen patroness
Gönner·miene die (abwertend) patronizing expression
Gonorrhö[e] /gɔnɔ'røː/ die; ~, **Gonorrhöen** ▶329| (Med.) gonorrhoea
Gopher /'goʊfɐ/ der; ~s, ~ (DV) gopher
gor /goːɐ̯/ 3. Pers. Sg. Prät. v. **gären**
gordisch /'gɔrdɪʃ/ Adj. **der Gordische Knoten** the Gordian knot
Göre /'gøːrə/ die; ~, ~n (nordd., oft abwertend) (a) (Kind) child; kid (coll.); brat (coll. derog.); (b) (freches Mädchen) [cheeky or saucy] little madam (coll.)
Gorilla /go'rɪla/ der; ~s, ~s (a) gorilla; (b) (ugs.: Leibwächter) heavy (coll.)
Gosch[e] /'gɔʃ(ə)/, **Goschen** /'gɔʃn/ die; ~, **Goschen** (südd., österr. meist abwertend) mouth
Gospel /'gɔspl/ das od. der; ~s, ~s, **Gospel·song** der; ~s, ~s gospel song
goss /gɔs/ 1. u. 3. Pers. Sg. Prät. v. **gießen**
Gosse /'gɔsə/ die; ~, ~n gutter; (fig. abwertend) **in der** ~ **enden** end up in the gutter
Gote /'goːtə/ der; ~n, ~n Goth
Gotik /'goːtɪk/ die; ~ (Stil) Gothic [style]; (Epoche) Gothic period
gotisch Adj. Gothic; **die** ~**e Schrift** Gothic [script]
Gott /gɔt/ der; ~es, **Götter** /'gœtɐ/ (a) o. Pl.; o. Art. God; ~ **Vater** God the Father; **vergelts** ~! (landsch.) thank you! God bless you!; **großer** od. **mein** ~! good God!; **o** od. **ach [du lieber]** ~! goodness me!; ~ **behüte** God or Heaven forbid; ~ **und die Welt** all the world and his wife; **über** ~ **und die Welt quatschen** (ugs.) talk about everything under the sun (coll.); ~ **sei Dank!** (ugs.) thank God!; **um**

~**es Willen** (bei Erschrecken) for God's sake; (bei einer Bitte) for heaven's or goodness' sake; **tue es in** ~**es Namen** (ugs.) do it and have done with it; **wie** ~ **in Frankreich leben** (ugs.) live in the lap of luxury; **den lieben** ~ **einen guten Mann sein lassen** (ugs.) take things as they come; (b) (übermenschliches Wesen) god; **wie ein junger** ~ **spielen/tanzen** play/dance divinely; **das wissen die Götter** (ugs.) God or heaven only knows
gott·ähnlich Adj. godlike
Gott·erbarmen das **in zum** ~ **sein** (mitleiderregend) be pitiful; (schlecht) be pathetic
gott·ergeben 1 Adj. meek. **2** adv. meekly
Götter·speise die (a) o. Pl. (Myth.) food of the gods; (b) (Kochk.) jelly
gottes-, Gottes-: ~**dienst** der service; **den** ~**dienst besuchen** go to church; ~**furcht** die fear of God; ~**haus** das (geh.) house of God; ~**lästerer** der blasphemer; ~**lästerlich 1** Adj. blasphemous; **2** adv. blasphemously; ~**lästerung** die blasphemy; ~**mutter** die; o. Pl. Mother of God; ~**staat** der theocracy; ~**urteil** das (hist.) trial by ordeal
gott-: ~**gefällig** Adj. (geh.) pleasing to God postpos.; ~**gewollt** Adj. ordained by God postpos.
Gottheit die; ~, ~en (a) (Gott, Göttin) deity; (b) o. Pl. (geh.: Gottsein) divinity
Göttin /'gœtɪn/ die; ~, ~nen goddess
göttlich /'gœtlɪç/ **1** Adj. (a) (Gott eigen od. ähnlich; herrlich) divine ⟨grace, beauty, etc.⟩; (b) (einem Gott zukommend) godlike ⟨status etc.⟩. **2** adv. (herrlich) divinely
gott-: ~**lob** adv. thank goodness; ~**los 1** Adj. (a) (verwerflich) ungodly, wicked ⟨life etc.⟩; impious ⟨words, speech, etc.⟩; (pietätlos) irreverent; (b) (Gott leugnend) godless ⟨theory etc.⟩; **2** adv. (verwerflich) irreverently
gott-, Gott-: ~**vater** der; o. Pl. God the Father; ~**verdammt** Adj.; nicht präd. (salopp), ~**verflucht** Adj.; nicht präd. (salopp) goddamn[ed] (sl.); ~**verlassen** Adj. (a) (ugs.: abseits) godforsaken; (b) (von Gott verlassen) forsaken by God postpos.; ~**vertrauen** das trust in God
Götze /'gœtsə/ der; ~n, ~n (auch fig.) idol
Götzen-: ~**bild** das idol; graven image (bibl.); (fig.) idol; ~**diener** der idolater; (fig.) worshipper
Götz·zitat /'gœts-/ das: the insulting remark 'du kannst mich am Arsch lecken' or the like, frequently used in altercations; a verbal equivalent of the V-sign
Goulasch ⇒ **Gulasch**
Gouvernante /guvɛr'nantə/ die; ~, ~n governess
Gouverneur /guvɛr'nøːɐ̯/ der; ~s, ~e governor
Grab-: ~**stätte** die tomb; grave; ~**stein** der gravestone; tombstone; ~**stelle** die burial plot
Grab /graːp/ das; ~[e]s, **Gräber** /'grɛːbɐ/ grave; **er würde sich im** ~[e] **herumdrehen** (fig. ugs.) he would turn in his grave; **das** ~ **des Unbekannten Soldaten** the tomb of the Unknown Soldier or Warrior; **verschwiegen wie ein** od. **das** ~ **sein** (ugs.) keep absolutely mum (coll.); **sich** (Dat.) **selbst sein** ~ **schaufeln** (fig.) dig one's own grave (fig.); **mit einem Fuß** od. **Bein im** ~[e] **stehen** (fig.) have one foot in the grave (fig.); **jmdn. ins** ~ **bringen** be the death of sb.; **etw. mit ins** ~ **nehmen** (geh.) take sth. with one to the grave; **jmdn. zu** ~ **tragen** (geh.) bury sb.; **seine Hoffnungen zu** ~**e tragen** (fig. geh.) abandon one's hopes; **jmdn. an den Rand des** ~**es bringen** (fig. geh.) drive sb. to distraction
graben 1 unr. tr. V. dig. **2** unr. itr. V. dig (**nach** for). **3** unr. refl. V. (geh.) **sich in etw.** (Akk.) ~: dig into sth.
Graben der; ~s, **Gräben** /'grɛːbn/ (a) ditch; (b) (Schützengraben) trench; (c) (Festungsgraben) moat
Gräber-: ~**feld** das [large] cemetery; ~**fund** der grave find
Grabes-: ~**kälte** die (geh.) deathly cold; ~**stille** die deathly silence or hush; ~**stimme** die (ugs.) sepulchral voice
Grab-: ~**hügel** der grave mound; ~**inschrift** die inscription [on a/the gravestone]; epitaph; ~**kammer** die burial chamber; ~**kreuz** das cross [on the/a grave]; ~**mal** das; Pl. ~**mäler**, (geh.) ~**male** monument;

(~stein) gravestone; **das ~mal des Unbekannten Soldaten** the tomb of the Unknown Soldier *or* Warrior;
~platte *die* memorial slab; (aus Metall) memorial plate;
~rede *die* funeral oration *or* speech; **~schändung**
die desecration of a/the grave/of [the] graves

grabschen /'grapʃn̩/ **1** *tr. V.* grab; snatch. **2** *itr. V.* **nach
etw. ~:** grab at sth.

gräbst /grɛ:pst/ *2. Pers. Sg. Präsens v.* **graben**

gräbt *3. Pers. Sg. Präsens v.* **graben**

Grabung *die;* ~, ~en (bes. Archäol.) excavation

Grab·urne *die* funeral urn

Gracht /graxt/ *die;* ~, ~en canal

Grad /gra:t/ *der;* ~[e]s, ~e (a) degree; **Verbrennungen
ersten/zweiten ~es** first-/second-degree burns; **ein Verwandter ersten/zweiten ~es** an immediate relation/a
relation once removed; **in hohem ~e** to a great *or* large
extent; (b) (akademischer ~) degree; (Milit.) rank; (c) ▶ 511│
(Maßeinheit, Math., Geogr.) degree; **10 ~ Wärme/Kälte** 10
degrees above zero/below [zero]; **39 ~ Fieber haben**
have a temperature of 39 degrees; **minus 5 ~/5 ~ minus**
minus 5 degrees; **null ~:** zero; **Gleichungen zweiten
~es** equations of the second degree; quadratic equations;
sich um hundertachtzig ~ drehen (fig.) completely
change [one's views]; **der 50. ~ nördlicher Breite** [lati-
tude] 50 degrees North

grad-, Grad-¹ ⇒ **gerad[e]-, Gerad[e]-**

graduell /gra'dʊɛl/ **1** *Adj.* gradual ⟨*development etc.*⟩;
slight ⟨*difference etc.*⟩. **2** *adv.* gradually; by degrees;
⟨*different*⟩ in degree

graduiert *Adj.* graduate; **ein ~er Ingenieur/eine ~e
Ingenieurin** an engineering graduate

Graf /gra:f/ *der;* ~en, ~en (a) count; (britischer ~) earl;
(b) *o. Pl.* (Titel) Count; (britischer ~) Earl; **~ Koks** [**von der
Gasanstalt**] (salopp) Lord Muck (Brit. joc.)

Grafik /'gra:fɪk/ *die;* ~, ~en (a) *o. Pl.* graphic art[s *pl.*];
(b) (Kunstwerk) graphic; (Druck) print; (c) (Illustration) diagram

Grafiker *der;* ~s, ~, **Grafikerin** *die;* ~, ~nen
[graphic] designer; (Künstler[in]) graphic artist

Gräfin /'grɛ:fɪn/ *der;* ~, ~nen countess; (Titel) Countess

grafisch **1** *Adj.* (a) graphic; **das ~e Gewerbe** (veralt.)
the printing trade; (b) (schematisch) graphic; diagrammatic;
eine ~e Darstellung a diagram. **2** *adv.* graphically

gräflich /'grɛ:flɪç/ *Adj.* count's *attrib.;* of the count *postpos., not pred.;* (in Großbritannien) earl's; of the earl

Grafschaft *die;* ~, ~en (a) (Amtsbezirk des Grafen) count's
land; (in Großbritannien) earldom; (b) (Verwaltungsbezirk) county

Graham·brot /'gra:ham-/ *das* wholemeal (Brit.) *or* (Amer.)
wheatmeal bread

Gral /gra:l/ *der;* ~[e]s: **der [Heilige] ~:** the [Holy] Grail

Grals·ritter *der* knight of the [Holy] Grail

gram /gra:m/ *in* **jmdm. ~ sein** be aggrieved at sb.

Gram *der;* ~[e]s (geh.) grief; sorrow; **aus ~ um** *od.* **über
etw.** (Akk.) out of grief *or* sorrow at sth.

grämen /'grɛ:mən/ **1** *tr. V.* grieve. **2** *refl. V.* grieve (**über**
+ Akk., **um** over)

gram·gebeugt *Adj.* bowed down with grief *or* sorrow
postpos.

grämlich /'grɛ:mlɪç/ **1** *Adj.* morose; sullen; morose
⟨*thought*⟩. **2** *adv.* morosely; sullenly

Gramm /gram/ *das;* ~s, ~e ▶ 228│ gram; **250 ~ Käse**
250 grams of cheese

Grammatik /gra'matɪk/ *die;* ~, ~en (a) grammar; (b)
(Lehrbuch) grammar [book]

grammatikalisch /gramati'ka:lɪʃ/, **grammatisch**
1 *Adj.* grammatical. **2** *adv.* grammatically

GrammophonⓌ /gramo'fo:n/ *das;* ~s, ~e gramophone

Granat /gra'na:t/ *der;* ~[e]s, ~e (a) (Schmuckstein) gar-
net; (b) (Garnele) [common] shrimp

Granat·apfel *der* pomegranate

Granate /gra'na:tə/ *die;* ~, ~n shell; (Hand~) grenade

Granat-: **~feuer** *das* shell-fire *no pl., no indef. art.;*
~splitter *der* shell splinter; **~werfer** *der* (Milit.) mortar

Grand /grã: *od.* graŋ/ *der;* ~s, ~s (Skat) grand

Grand·hotel /'grã:-/ *das* luxury *or* five-star hotel

grandios /gran'djo:s/ **1** *Adj.* magnificent. **2** *adv.* magnificently

Grand Prix /grã'pri:/ *der;* ~ ~ /-pri:(s)/, ~ ~ /-pri:s/
Grand Prix

Granit /gra'ni:t/ *der;* ~s, ~e granite; **auf ~** (Akk.)
beißen (fig.) bang one's head against a brick wall (fig.); **bei
jmdm. auf ~** (Akk.) **beißen** (fig.) get nowhere with sb.
(fig.)

Granit·block *der; Pl.* **-blöcke** block of granite; granite
block

Granne /'granə/ *die;* ~, ~n awn; beard

grantig /'grantɪç/ (südd., österr. ugs.) **1** *Adj.* bad-tempered;
grumpy. **2** *adv.* bad-temperedly; grumpily

Granulat /granu'la:t/ *das;* ~[e]s, ~e (bes. Chemie)
granules *pl.*

granulieren *itr., tr. V.* (bes. Chemie) granulate

Grapefruit /'gre:pfru:t/ *die;* ~, ~s grapefruit

Graphik usw. ⇒ **Grafik** usw.

Graphit /gra'fi:t/ *der;* ~s, ~e graphite

Graphologe /grafo'lo:gə/ *der;* ~n, ~n graphologist

Graphologie *die;* ~: graphology *no art.*

Graphologin *die;* ~, ~en graphologist

graphologisch **1** *Adj.* graphological. **2** *adv.* grapho-
logically

grapschen /'grapʃn̩/ ⇒ **grabschen**

Gras /gra:s/ *das;* ~es, **Gräser** /'grɛ:zə/ grass; **das ~
wachsen hören** (ugs. spött.) read too much into things;
über etw. (Akk.) **~ wachsen lassen** (ugs.) let the dust
settle on sth.; **ins ~ beißen** [**müssen**] (salopp) bite the
dust (coll.)

gras-: **~bedeckt, ~bewachsen** *Adj.* grass-
covered; grassy

Gras·büschel *das* tuft of grass

grasen *itr. V.* graze

gras-, Gras-: **~fläche** *die* area of grass; (Rasen) lawn;
~fleck *der* (a) patch of grass; (b) (auf der Kleidung) grass
stain; **~grün** *Adj.* grass-green; **~halm** *der* blade of
grass; **~hüpfer** *der* (ugs.) grasshopper; **~land** *das; o.
Pl.* grassland; **~mücke** *die* warbler; **~narbe** *die* turf

grassieren /gra'si:rən/ *itr. V.* ⟨*disease etc.*⟩ rage, be
rampant; ⟨*craze etc.*⟩ be [all] the rage; ⟨*rumour*⟩ be rife

grässlich, *gräßlich /'grɛslɪç/ **1** *Adj.* (a) (abscheulich)
horrible; terrible ⟨*accident*⟩; (b) (ugs.: unangenehm) dreadful
(coll.); awful; (c) (ugs.: sehr stark) terrible (coll.); awful. **2** *adv.*
(a) (abscheulich) horribly; terribly; (b) (ugs.: unangenehm) terribly (coll.); (c) (ugs.: sehr) terribly (coll.); dreadfully (coll.)

Grässlichkeit, *Gräßlichkeit *die;* ~ (a) (Abscheulichkeit) horribleness; (eines Unfalls) terribleness; (b) (unangenehme Art) dreadfulness (coll.); awfulness

Gras-: **~steppe** *die* (Geogr.) [grassy] steppe; **~strei-
fen** *der* strip of grass; (längs einer Straße) grass verge

Grat /gra:t/ *der;* ~[e]s, ~e (a) (Bergrücken) ridge; (b) (Archit.) hip; (c) (Technik) burr

Gräte /'grɛ:tə/ *die;* ~, ~n bone (*of fish*)

gräten·los *Adj.* boneless

Gräten·muster *das* herring-bone [pattern]

Gratifikation /gratifika'tsio:n/ *die;* ~, ~en bonus

gratis /'gra:tɪs/ *Adv.* free [of charge]; gratis

Gratis-: **~muster** *das,* **~probe** *die* free sample;
~vorstellung *die* free performance

Grätsche /'grɛ:tʃə/ *die;* ~, ~n (Turnen) straddle; (Sprung)
straddle-vault; **in die ~ gehen** go into the straddle position

grätschen **1** *tr. V.* **die Beine ~:** straddle one's legs. **2**
itr. V.; mit sein straddle; do *or* perform a straddle; **über
etw.** (Akk.) **~:** do a straddle-vault over sth.

Gratulant /gratu'lant/ *der;* ~en, ~en, **Gratulantin**
die; ~, ~nen well-wisher

Gratulation /gratula'tsio:n/ *die;* ~, ~en congratulations *pl.*

Gratulations·schreiben *das* congratulatory letter

gratulieren *itr. V.* jmdm. ~: congratulate sb.; **jmdm. zum Geburtstag** ~: wish sb. many happy returns [of the day]; **[ich] gratuliere!** congratulations!

Grat·wanderung *die* ridge walk; (fig.) balancing act

grau /grau/ **1** *Adj.* (a) grey; ~ **werden** go grey; ~ **in** ~: grey and drab; (b) (trostlos) dreary; drab; depressing; **der** ~**e Alltag** the dull routine *or* monotony of daily life; (c) (zwischen legal und illegal) grey; (d) (unbestimmt) vague; **in** ~**er Vorzeit** in the dim and distant past. **2** *adv.* ~ **meliert** greying

Grau *das;* ~**s,** ~ (a) grey; (b) *o. Pl.* (Trostlosigkeit) dreariness; drabness

grau·blau *Adj.* grey-blue

Grau·brot *das* bread made with rye- and wheat-flour

Grau·bünden /-'byndn̩/ (*das*); ~**s** the Grisons

Gräuel /'grɔyəl/ *der;* ~**s,** ~ (geh.) (a) *o. Pl.* (Abscheu) horror; **er/sie/es ist mir ein** ~: I loathe *or* detest him/her/it; (b) *meist Pl.* (~tat) atrocity

Gräuel-: ~**märchen** *das* horror story; ~**propaganda** *die* atrocity propaganda; stories *pl.* of atrocities; ~**tat** *die* atrocity

grauen[1] *itr. V.* (geh.) **der Morgen/der Tag graut** morning is breaking; day is dawning *or* breaking

grauen[2] *itr. V.* (unpers.) **ihm graut [es] davor/vor ihr** he dreads [the thought of] it/he's terrified of her; **mir graut es, wenn ich nur daran denke** I dread the [mere] thought of it

Grauen *das;* ~**s,** ~ (a) *o. Pl.* horror (**vor** + *Dat.* of); **ein Bild des** ~**s** a scene of horror; (b) (Schreckbild) horror

grauen·haft, grauen·voll **1** *Adj.* (a) horrifying; (b) (ugs.: sehr unangenehm) terrible (coll.); dreadful (coll.). **2** *adv.* (a) horrifyingly; (b) (ugs.: sehr unangenehm) terribly (coll.); dreadfully (coll.)

grau-, Grau-: ~**gans** *die* grey goose; greylag [goose]; ~**grün** *Adj.* grey-green; ~**haarig** *Adj.* grey-haired

gräulich[1] /'grɔylɪç/ *Adj.* greyish

gräulich[2] ⇒ **grässlich**

*****grau·meliert** ⇒ **grau 2**

Graupe /'graupə/ *die;* ~, ~**n** grain of pearl barley; ~**n** pearl barley *sing.*

Graupel /'graupl̩/ *die;* ~, ~**n** soft hail pellet; ~**n** soft hail; graupel

Graupel·schauer *der* shower of soft hail

Graupen·suppe *die* barley soup *or* broth

Graus /graus/ *der;* ~**es: es ist ein** ~: it's terrible; **o** ~**!** (ugs. scherzh.) oh horror! (joc.)

grausam **1** *Adj.* (a) cruel; ~ **gegen jmdn. sein** be cruel to sb.; (b) (furchtbar) terrible; dreadful; (c) (ugs.: sehr schlimm) terrible (coll.); dreadful (coll.). **2** *adv.* (a) cruelly; **sich** ~ **für etw. rächen** take cruel revenge for sth.; (b) (furchtbar) terribly, dreadfully; (c) (ugs.: sehr stark) terribly (coll.); dreadfully (coll.)

Grausamkeit *die;* ~, ~**en** (a) *o. Pl.* cruelty; (b) (Handlung) act of cruelty; (Gräueltat) atrocity

Grau·schimmel *der* (a) (Pferd) grey [horse]; (b) (Pilz) grey mould

grau·schwarz *Adj.* grey-black

grausen ⇒ **grauen**[2]

Grausen *das;* ~**s** horror; **das kalte** ~ **kriegen** (ugs.) be scared stiff *or* to death (coll.)

grausig ⇒ **grauenhaft**

grauslich (bes. bayr., österr.) ⇒ **grässlich**

grau-, Grau-: ~**tier** *das* (ugs. scherzh.) (Esel) ass; donkey; (Maultier) mule; ~**weiß** *Adj.* greyish white; ~**zone** *die* grey area (fig.)

Graveur /gra'vøːɐ̯/ *der;* ~**s,** ~**e, Graveurin** *die;* ~, ~**nen** ▶ 85 engraver

gravieren /gra'viːrən/ *tr. V.* engrave

gravierend *Adj.* serious, grave ‹*matter, accusation, error, etc.*›; important ‹*difference, decision*›

Gravierung *die;* ~, ~**en** engraving

Gravitation /gravita'tsi̯oːn/ *die;* ~ (Physik, Astron.) gravitation

Gravitations-: ~**feld** *das* (Physik, Astron.) gravitational field; ~**gesetz** *das* (Physik, Astron.) law of gravitation

gravitätisch **1** *Adj.* grave; solemn. **2** *adv.* gravely; solemnly

Gravur /gra'vuːɐ̯/ *die;* ~, ~**en, Gravüre** /gra'vyːrə/ *die;* ~, ~**n** engraving

Grazie /'graːtsi̯ə/ *die;* ~, ~**n** (a) *o. Pl.* (Anmut) grace; gracefulness; (b) *Pl.* (Myth.) Graces; (c) *Pl.* (fig. scherzh.) beauties

grazil /gra'tsiːl/ *Adj.* (auch fig.) delicate

graziös /gra'tsi̯øːs/ **1** *Adj.* graceful. **2** *adv.* gracefully

Gregor /'greːgɔr/ (*der*) Gregory

gregorianisch /grego'ri̯aːnɪʃ/ *Adj.* Gregorian; ~**er Gesang** Gregorian chant

Greif /graif/ *der;* ~**[e]s** *od.* ~**en,** ~**en** (a) (Wappentier) griffin; gryphon; (b) ⇒ **Greifvogel**

greif·bar **1** *Adj.* (a) etw. ~ **haben** have sth. to hand; ~ **sein** be within reach; **in** ~**er Nähe** (fig.) within reach; (b) (deutlich) tangible; concrete; (c) *nicht attr.* (ugs.: verfügbar) available. **2** *adv.* ~ **nahe** (fig.) within reach

greifen **1** *unr. tr. V.* (a) (er~) take hold of; grasp; (rasch ~) grab; seize; **sich** (*Dat.*) etw. ~: help oneself to sth.; **von hier scheint der See zum Greifen nah[e]** from here the lake seems close enough to reach out and touch; **zum Greifen nahe sein** ‹*end, liberation*› be imminent; ‹*goal, success*› be within sb.'s grasp; (b) (fangen) catch; (c) **einen Akkord** ~ (auf dem Klavier usw.) play a chord; (auf der Gitarre usw.) finger a chord; (d) (schätzen) **tausend ist zu hoch/niedrig gegriffen** one thousand is an overestimate/underestimate. **2** *unr. itr. V.* (a) **in/unter/hinter etw./sich** (*Akk.*) ~: reach into/under/behind sth./one; **nach etw.** ~: reach for sth.; (hastig) make a grab for sth.; **zu Drogen/zur Zigarette** ~: turn to drugs/reach for a cigarette; **nach der Macht** ~ (fig.) try to seize power; **etw. greift um sich** sth. is spreading; (b) (Technik) grip; (c) (ugs.: spielen) **in die Tasten/Saiten** ~: sweep one's hand over the keys/across the strings

Greifer *der;* ~**s,** ~ (Technik) grab[-bucket]

Greif-: ~**vogel** *der* (Zool.) diurnal bird of prey; ~**zange** *die* tongs *pl.*

greis /grais/ *Adj.* (geh.) aged; white ‹*hair, head*›

Greis *der;* ~**es,** ~**e** old man

Greisen·alter *das* old age

greisen·haft *Adj.* old man's/woman's *attrib.;* aged; (von jüngerem Menschen) ‹*face etc.*› like that of an old man/woman

Greisin *die;* ~, ~**nen** old woman *or* lady

grell /grɛl/ **1** *Adj.* (a) (hell) glaring, dazzling ‹*light, sun, etc.*›; (b) (auffallend) garish, gaudy ‹*colour etc.*›; flashy, loud ‹*dress, pattern, etc.*›; (c) (schrill) shrill, piercing ‹*cry, voice, etc.*›. **2** *adv.* (a) (hell) with glaring *or* dazzling brightness; ~ **beleuchtet** dazzlingly lit; (b) (schrill) shrilly; piercingly

grell-: *****~**beleuchtet** ⇒ **grell 2** a; ~**bunt** *Adj.* gaudily coloured; ~**rot** *Adj.* garish *or* bright red

Gremium /'greːmi̯um/ *das;* ~**s, Gremien** committee

Grenadier /grena'diːɐ̯/ *der;* ~**s,** ~**e** (Milit.) (a) (Infanterist) infantryman; (b) (hist.) grenadier

Grenz-: ~**abfertigung** *die* (Zollw.) passport control and customs clearance [at the/a border]; ~**beamte** *der* border official; ~**befestigung** *die* (Milit.) border fortification; ~**bereich** *der* (a) *o. Pl.* border *or* frontier zone *or* area; (b) (äußerster Bereich) limit[s *pl.*]; ~**bezirk** *der* border *or* frontier district

Grenze /'grɛntsə/ *die;* ~, ~**n** (a) (zwischen Staaten) border; frontier; **die** ~ **zu Italien** the border with Italy; **an der** ~ **wohnen** live on the border *or* frontier; (b) (zwischen Gebieten) boundary; (c) (gedachte Trennungslinie) borderline; dividing line; (d) (Schranke) limit; **jmdm. [keine]** ~**n setzen** impose [no] limits on sb.; **an seine** ~**n stoßen** reach its limit[s]; **sich in** ~**n halten** (begrenzt sein) keep *or* stay within limits; **seine Leistungen hielten sich in** ~**n** his achievements were not [all that (coll.)] outstanding

grenzen *itr. V.* **an etw.** (*Akk.*) ~: border [on] sth.; (fig.) verge on sth.

---

grenzen·los 1 *Adj.* boundless; endless; (fig.) boundless, unbounded ⟨*joy, wonder, jealousy, grief, etc.*⟩; unlimited ⟨*wealth, power*⟩; limitless ⟨*patience, ambition*⟩; extreme ⟨*tiredness, anger, foolishness*⟩. **2** *adv.* endlessly; (fig.) beyond all measure

Grenzen·losigkeit *die;* ∼**:** boundlessness; immensity

grenz-, Grenz-: ∼**fall** *der* (nicht eindeutiger Fall) borderline case; (Sonderfall) limiting case; ∼**formalitäten** *Pl.* passport and customs formalities [at the/a border]; ∼**gänger** *der;* ∼**s,** ∼**:** [regular] commuter across the border *or* frontier; ∼**gebiet** *das* (a) border *or* frontier area *or* zone; (b) (Sachgebiet zwischen Disziplinen) adjacent field; ∼**konflikt** *der* border *or* frontier conflict; ∼**kontrolle** *die* border *or* frontier check; ∼**linie** *die* border; ∼**nah** *Adj.; nicht präd.* close to the border *or* frontier *postpos.;* ∼**posten** *der* border *or* frontier guard; ∼**schutz** *der* (a) border *or* frontier protection; (b) (ugs.: Bundesgrenzschutz) border *or* frontier police; ∼**soldat** *der* border *or* frontier guard; ∼**stadt** *die* border *or* frontier town; ∼**stein** *der* boundary stone; ∼**streitigkeit** *die* boundary dispute; (wegen einer Staatsgrenze) border *or* frontier dispute; ∼**übergang** *der* (a) border crossing-point; frontier crossing-point; [border] checkpoint; (b) (das Passieren der Grenze) crossing of the border *or* frontier; ∼**verkehr** *der* [cross-]border traffic; frontier traffic; ∼**verletzung** *die* border *or* frontier violation; ∼**wall** *der* border *or* frontier rampart; ∼**wert** *der* (Math.) limit; ∼**zwischenfall** *der* border incident

Gretchen·frage *die;* ∼**:** crucial question; sixty-four-thousand-dollar question (coll.)

*Greuel *usw.:* ⇒ **Gräuel** *usw.*

Griebe /ˈgriːbə/ *die;* ∼, ∼**n** crackling *no indef. art.;* greaves *pl.*

Grieben·schmalz *das* dripping with crackling *or* greaves

Grieche /ˈgriːçə/ *der;* ∼**n,** ∼**n** ▶ 388 Greek

Griechen·land *(das);* ∼**s** Greece

Griechin *die;* ∼, ∼**nen** Greek

griechisch ▶ 388, ▶ 487 1 *Adj.* Greek ⟨*language, mythology, island, etc.*⟩; Grecian, Greek ⟨*vase, style, etc.*⟩; **die** ∼**e Tragödie** Greek tragedy. **2** *adv.* ∼ **sprechen/schreiben** speak/write in Greek; *s. auch* **deutsch**

Griechisch *das;* ∼**[s]** ▶ 487 Greek *no art.; s. auch* **Deutsch**

griechisch-: ∼**-orthodox** *Adj.* Greek Orthodox; ∼**-römisch** *Adj.* (Ringen) Graeco-Roman

Griesgram /ˈgriːsɡraːm/ *der;* ∼**[e]s,** ∼**e** grouch (coll.)

griesgrämig /ˈgriːsɡrɛːmɪç/ **1** *Adj.* grouchy (coll.); grumpy. **2** *adv.* in a grouchy (coll.) *or* grumpy manner

Grieß /griːs/ *der;* ∼**es,** ∼**e** semolina

Grieß·brei *der* semolina

griff /grɪf/ *1. u. 3. Pers. Sg. Prät. v.* **greifen**

Griff *der;* ∼**[e]s,** ∼**e** (a) grip; grasp; **mit eisernem/festem** ∼**:** with a grip of iron/a firm grip; **der** ∼ **nach etw./in etw.** (*Akk.*)/**an etw.** (*Akk.*) reaching for sth./dipping into sth./taking hold of *or* grasping sth.; [**mit jmdm./etw.] einen guten/glücklichen** ∼ **tun** make a good choice [with sb./sth.]; (b) (beim Ringen, Bergsteigen) hold; (beim Turnen) grip; **etw. im** ∼ **haben** (etw. routinemäßig beherrschen) have the hang of sth. (coll.); (etw. unter Kontrolle haben) have sth. under control; (c) (Knauf, Henkel) handle; (eines Gewehrs, einer Pistole) butt; (eines Schwerts) hilt; (d) (Musik) finger-placing

griff·bereit *Adj.* ready to hand *postpos.*

Griff·brett *das* (Musik) fingerboard

Griffel /ˈgrɪfl̩/ *der;* ∼**s,** ∼ (a) (Schreibgerät) slate-pencil; (b) (Bot.) style

griffig *Adj.* (a) (handlich) handy; ⟨*tool etc.*⟩ that is easy to handle; (b) (gut greifend) that grips well *postpos., not pred.;* non-slip ⟨*surface, floor*⟩

Grill /grɪl/ *der;* ∼**s,** ∼**s** grill; (Rost) barbecue

Grille /ˈgrɪlə/ *die;* ∼, ∼**n** (a) (Insekt) cricket; (b) (sonderbarer Einfall) whim; fancy

grillen 1 *tr. V.* grill. 2 *itr. V.* **im Garten** ∼**:** have a barbecue in the garden

Grill·platz *der* barbecue area

Grimasse /griˈmasə/ *die;* ∼, ∼**n** grimace; **eine** ∼ **schneiden** *od.* **machen** grimace; pull a face

Grimm /grɪm/ *der;* ∼**[e]s** (geh.) fury

grimmig 1 *Adj.* (a) (zornig) furious ⟨*person*⟩; grim ⟨*face; expression*⟩; fierce, ferocious ⟨*enemy, lion, etc.*⟩; (b) (heftig) fierce, severe ⟨*cold, hunger, pain, etc.*⟩. **2** *adv.* (a) (wütend) furiously; ∼ **lachen** laugh grimly; (b) (heftig) fiercely

Grind /grɪnt/ *der;* ∼**[e]s,** ∼**e** (Wundschorf) scab

grindig *Adj.* scabby

grinsen /ˈgrɪnzn̩/ *itr. V.* grin; (höhnisch) smirk

Grinsen *das;* ∼**s:** ein fröhliches/unverschämtes ∼**:** a happy grin/an insolent smirk

Grippe /ˈgrɪpə/ *die;* ∼, ∼**n** ▶ 329 (a) influenza; flu (coll.); (b) (volkst.: Erkältung) cold

Grippe·welle *die* wave of influenza *or* (coll.) flu

Grips /grɪps/ *der;* ∼**es** brains *pl.;* nous (coll.); **streng deinen** ∼ **an** use your brains *or* nous

Grisli·bär, *Grisly·bär, Grizzly·bär /ˈgrɪsli-/ *der* grizzly bear

grob /groːp/ **1** *Adj.* (a) coarse ⟨*sand, gravel, paper, sieve, etc.*⟩; thick ⟨*wire*⟩; rough, dirty ⟨*work*⟩; (b) (ungefähr) rough; **in** ∼**en Umrissen** in rough outline; (c) (schwerwiegend) gross; flagrant ⟨*lie*⟩; **ein** ∼**er Fehler/Irrtum** a bad mistake *or* gross error; **aus dem Gröbsten heraus sein** (ugs.) be over the worst; (d) (barsch) coarse; rude; ∼ **werden** become abusive *or* rude; (e) (nicht sanft) rough; ∼ [**zu jmdm.] sein** be rough [with sb.]. **2** *adv.* (a) (coarsely) ∼**gemahlen** coarsely ground; coarse-ground; (b) (ungefähr) roughly; ∼ **geschätzt** at a rough estimate; (c) (schwerwiegend) grossly; (d) (barsch) coarsely; rudely; (e) (nicht sanft) roughly

*grob·gemahlen ⇒ **grob** 2 a

Grobheit *die;* ∼, ∼**en** (a) *o. Pl.* rudeness; coarseness; (b) (Äußerung) rude remark

Grobian /ˈgroːbiaːn/ *der;* ∼**[e]s,** ∼**e** boor; lout

grob-: ∼**körnig** *Adj.* coarse ⟨*sand, flour, etc.*⟩ (Fot.) coarse-grained ⟨*film*⟩; ∼**maschig** *Adj.* wide-meshed ⟨*sieve, net, etc.*⟩; loose-knit ⟨*pullover etc.*⟩; ∼**schlächtig** /∼ʃlɛçtɪç/ *Adj.* heavily built

Grog /grɔk/ *der;* ∼**s,** ∼**s** grog

groggy /ˈgrɔgi/ *Adj.; nicht attr.* (a) (Boxen) groggy; (b) (ugs.: erschöpft) whacked [out] (coll.); all in (coll.)

grölen /ˈgrøːlən/ **1** *tr. V.* (ugs. abwertend) bawl [out]; roar, howl ⟨*approval*⟩. **2** *itr. V.* bawl

Groll /grɔl/ *der;* ∼**[e]s** (geh.) rancour; resentment; **einen** ∼ **gegen jmdn./etw. hegen** harbour resentment *or* a grudge against sb./sth.

grollen *itr. V.* (geh.) (a) (verstimmt sein) be sullen; [**mit] jmdm.** ∼**:** bear a grudge against sb.; bear sb. a grudge; (b) (dröhnen) rumble; ⟨*thunder*⟩ roll, rumble

Grön·land /ˈgrøːn-/ *(das);* ∼**s** Greenland

Gros /groː/ *das;* ∼, ∼**:** (s); ∼ /groːs/ bulk; main body

Groschen /ˈgrɔʃn̩/ *der;* ∼**s,** ∼**:** ▶ 215 (a) (österreichische Münze) groschen; (b) (ugs.: Zehnpfennigstück) ten-pfennig piece; (fig.) penny; cent (Amer.); [**sich** (*Dat.*)] **ein paar** ∼ **verdienen** (ugs.) earn [oneself] a few pennies *or* pence; **der** ∼ **ist [bei ihm] gefallen** (fig.) the penny has dropped

Groschen·roman *der* (abwertend) cheap novel; dime novel (Amer.)

groß /groːs/ **größer** /ˈgrøːsɐ/, **größt...** /ˈgrøːst.../ **1** *Adj.* (a) big; big, large ⟨*house, window, area, room, etc.*⟩; large ⟨*pack, size, can, etc.*⟩; great ⟨*length, width, height*⟩; tall ⟨*person*⟩; ∼**e Eier/Kartoffeln** large eggs/potatoes; **eine** ∼**e Terz/Sekunde** (Musik) a major third/second; **ein** ∼**es Bier, bitte** a pint, please; (b) (eine bestimmte Größe aufweisend) 1 m²/2 ha ∼**:** 1 m²/2 ha in area; **sie ist 1,75 m** ∼**:** she is 1.75 m tall; **doppelt/dreimal so** ∼ **wie ...:** twice/three times the size of ...; (c) (älter) big ⟨*brother, sister*⟩; **seine größere Schwester** his elder sister; **unsere Große/unser Großer** our eldest *or* oldest daughter/son; (d) (erwachsen) grown-up ⟨*children, son, daughter*⟩; [**mit etw.]** ∼ **werden** grow up [with sth.]; **die Großen** (Erwachsene) the grown-ups; (ältere Kinder) the older children; **Groß und Klein** old and young [alike]; (e) (lange dauernd) long, lengthy ‹*delay, talk, explanation, pause*›; **die ~en Ferien** (Schulw.) the summer holidays *or* (Amer.) long vacation *sing.*; **die ~e Pause** (Schulw.) [mid-morning] break; **(f)** (beträchtlich) **~e Summen/Kosten** large sums/heavy costs; **eine ~e Auswahl** a wide selection *or* range; **(g)** (außerordentlich) great ‹*pleasure, pain, hunger, anxiety, hurry, progress, difficulty, mistake, importance*›; intense ‹*heat, cold*›; high ‹*speed*›; **mit dem größten Vergnügen** with the greatest of pleasure; **~en Hunger haben** be very hungry; **ihre/seine ~e Liebe** her/his great love; **(h)** (gewichtig) great; major ‹*producer, exporter*›; great, major ‹*event*›; **ein ~er Augenblick/Tag** a great moment/day; **~e Worte** grand *or* fine words; **[k]eine ~e Rolle spielen** [not] play a great *or* an important part; **die Großen [der Welt]** the great figures [of our world]; **(i)** *nicht präd.* (glanzvoll) grand ‹*celebration, ball, etc.*›; **die ~e Dame/den ~en Herrn spielen** (iron.) play the fine lady/gentleman; **(j)** (bedeutend) great, major ‹*artist, painter, work*›; **Katharina die Große** Catherine the Great; *s. auch* **Karl**; **(k)** (wesentlich) **die ~e Linie/der ~e Zusammenhang** the basic line/the overall context; **in ~en Zügen** *od.* **Umrissen** in broad outline; **im Großen [und] Ganzen** by and large; on the whole; **(l)** (geh.: selbstlos) noble ‹*deed etc.*›; **ein ~es Herz haben** be great-hearted; **(m)** (ugs.: ~spurig) **~e Reden schwingen** *od.* (salopp) Töne spucken talk big (coll.). **2** *adv.* **(a) ~ geschrieben werden** (fig. ugs.) be stressed *or* emphasized; **bei ihm wird Verdienen ~ geschrieben** earning money comes high on his list of priorities; **jmdn. ~ ansehen** stare hard at sb.; **~ machen** (Kinderspr.) do number two (child lang.); **~ und breit** at great length; **(b)** (ugs.: aufwendig) **~ ausgehen** go out for a big celebration; **etw. ~ feiern** celebrate sth. in a big way; **ein ~ angelegtes Projekt** a large-scale project; **ein ~ angelegter Angriff** a full-scale attack; **(c)** (ugs.: besonders) greatly; particularly; **(d)** (ugs.: ~artig) **sie steht ganz ~ da** she has made it big (coll.) *or* made the big time (coll.)

groß-, Groß-: ~abnehmer *der* bulk buyer *or* purchaser;*~**angelegt** ⇒ **groß 2 b**; ~**artig 1** *Adj.* magnificent; splendid; wonderful ‹*person*›; **2** *adv.* magnificently; splendidly; ~**aufnahme** *die* (Film) close-up

Groß·británnien (*das*) the United Kingdom; [Great] Britain

Groß·búchstabe *der* capital [letter]; upper-case letter (Printing)

Größe /'grø:sə/ *die;* **~, ~n (a)** size; (Kleider~) **in ~ 38** in size 38; **(b)** ► 277 | (Höhe, Körper~) height; **der ~ nach** by height; **(c)** (Bedeutsamkeit, sittlicher Wert) greatness; **(d)** (Genie) outstanding *or* important figure; **(e)** (Math., Physik) quantity

Groß-: ~ein·kauf *der* bulk purchase; ~**eltern** *Pl.* grandparents; ~**enkel** *der* great-grandchild; (Junge) great-grandson; ~**enkelin** *die* great-granddaughter

größen-, Größen-: ~ordnung *die* order [of magnitude]; ~**verhältnis** *das* **(a)** (Maßstab) scale; **(b)** (Proportion) proportions *pl.;* ~**wahn** *der* (abwertend) megalomania; delusions *pl.* of grandeur; ~**wahnsinnig** *Adj.* megalomaniacal

größer ⇒ **groß**

groß-, Groß-: ~fahndung *die* large-scale search *or* manhunt; ~**grund·besitzer** *der* big landowner; ~**handel** *der* wholesale trade; ~**händler** *der* wholesaler; ~**handlung** *die* wholesale business; ~**herzig** (geh.) **1** *Adj.* magnanimous; **2** *adv.* magnanimously; ~**herzog** *der* Grand Duke; ~**herzogin** *die* Grand Duchess; ~**herzogtum** *das* grand duchy; ~**herzogtum Luxemburg** Grand Duchy of Luxembourg; ~**hirn** *das* (Anat.) cerebrum; ~**industrielle** *der/die; adj. Dekl.* big industrialist

Grossíst *der;* ~**en,** ~**en** (Kaufmannsspr.) wholesaler

groß-, Groß-: ~kapital *das* (Wirtsch.) big business *or* capital; ~**konzern** *der* big *or* large combine; ~**kotzig** /~kɔtsɪç/ **1** *Adj.* (salopp abwertend) pretentious ‹*style*›; swanky (coll.) ‹*present etc.*›; **2** *adv.* boastfully; ~**kundgebung** *die* mass rally *or* meeting; ~**macht** *die* great power; ~**mama** *die* (ugs.) grandma (coll./child lang.); granny (coll./child lang.); ~**markt** *der* central market; ~**mast** *der* (Seemannsspr.) mainmast; ~**maul** *das* (ugs.

*alte Schreibung (vgl. Hinweise auf S. xvi–xvii)

abwertend) big-mouth (coll.); braggart; ~**mäulig** /~mɔylɪç/ *Adj.* (ugs. abwertend) big-mouthed (coll.); ~**meister** *der* Grand Master; ~**mut** *die;* ~: magnanimity; generosity; ~**mütig** /~my:tɪç/ **1** *Adj.* magnanimous; generous; **2** *adv.* magnanimously; generously; ~**mutter** *die* **(a)** grandmother; **das kannst du deiner ~mutter erzählen** (ugs.) tell that to the marines; **(b)** (ugs.: alte Frau) old lady; ~**neffe** *der* great-nephew; grandnephew; ~**nichte** *die* great-niece; grandniece; ~**onkel** *der* great-uncle; granduncle; ~**papa** *der* (ugs.) grandpa (coll./child lang.); granddad (coll./child lang.); ~**raum** *der* area; **im ~raum Hamburg** in the [Greater] Hamburg area; ~**raum·büro** *das* open-plan office

großräumig /-rɔymɪç/ **1** *Adj.* extensive; over a wide *or* large area *postpos., not pred.;* (viel Platz bietend) spacious, roomy ‹*office, house, etc.*›. **2** *adv.* over a wide *or* large area

groß-, Groß-: ~reinemachen *das* (ugs.) thorough cleaning; spring clean; ~|**schreiben** *unr. tr. V.* write ‹*word*› with a capital [initial] letter; write ‹*word*› with a capital; *s. auch* **groß 2 a;** ~**schreibung** *die* capitalization; ~**segel** *das* (Seemannsspr.) mainsail; ~**sprecherisch** *Adj.* (abwertend) boastful; ~**spurig** (abwertend) **1** *Adj.* boastful; (hochtrabend) pretentious ‹*word, language*›; grandiose ‹*plan*›; **2** *adv.* boastfully; (hochtrabend) pretentiously; ~**stadt** *die* city; large town; ~**städter** *der* urbanite; city-dweller; ~**städtisch** *Adj.* [big-]city attrib. ‹*life*›

größt... ⇒ **groß**

Groß-: ~tante *die* great-aunt; grandaunt; ~**tat** *die* (geh.) great feat; ~**teil** *der* large part; (Hauptteil) major part; **zum ~teil** mostly; for the most part

größten·teils *Adv.* for the most part

größt·möglich *Adj.; nicht präd.* greatest possible

groß-, Groß-: ~|**tun** *unr. itr. V.* boast; brag; ~**unternehmen** *das* (Wirtsch.) large-scale enterprise; big concern; ~**vater** *der* grandfather; ~**verdiener** *der* big earner; ~**wild** *das* big game; ~**wildjagd** *die* big-game hunting *no art.;* ~|**ziehen** *unr. tr. V.* bring up; raise; rear ‹*animal*›; ~**zügig 1** *Adj.* **(a)** generous; generous, handsome ‹*tip*›; **(b)** (in großem Stil) grand and spacious ‹*building, gardens, etc.*›; generous, liberal ‹*working conditions*›; large-scale ‹*measures*›; **2** *adv.* **(a)** generously; **sich ~zügig über etw.** (*Akk.*) **hinwegsetzen** be broad-minded enough to disregard sth.; **(b)** (in großem Stil) **ein ~zügig eingerichtetes Büro** a handsomely equipped office; ~**zügigkeit** *die* **(a)** generosity; **(b)** (großes Ausmaß) grand scale

grotesk /gro'tɛsk/ **1** *Adj.* grotesque. **2** *adv.* grotesquely

Groteske *die;* ~, ~**n (a)** (Ornamentik) grotesque; **(b)** (Literaturwiss.) grotesque tale

Grotte /'grɔtə/ *die;* ~, ~**n** grotto

grub /gru:p/ *1. u. 3. Pers. Sg. Prät. v.* **graben**

Grübchen /'gry:pçən/ *das;* ~**s,** ~: dimple

Grube *die;* ~, ~**n (a)** pit; hole; **wer andern eine ~ gräbt, fällt selbst hinein** (Spr.) take care that you are not hoist with your own petard; **(b)** (Bergbau) mine; pit; **(c)** (veralt.: offenes Grab) grave; **in die ~ fahren** (veralt.) yield up the ghost (arch.)

Grübelei *die;* ~, ~**en** pondering

grübeln /'gry:bļn/ *itr. V.* ponder (**über** + *Dat.* on, over)

Gruben-: ~arbeiter *der* miner; mineworker; ~**unglück** *das* pit *or* mine disaster

Grübler *der;* ~**s,** ~ meditative person

grüezi /'gry:ɛtsi/ *Adv.* (schweiz.) hallo

Gruft /gruft/ *die;* ~, **Grüfte** /'gryftə/ vault; (in einer Kirche) crypt

grummeln /'grʊmļn/ *itr. V.* **(a)** (dröhnen) rumble; **(b)** (murmeln) mumble

grün /gry:n/ *Adj.* **(a)** green; ~**er Salat** lettuce; **die Ampel ist ~** (ugs.) the lights are green; **die Grüne Insel** the Emerald Isle; ~**e Bohnen/Erbsen** French beans/green peas; ~**e Heringe** fresh herrings; **ein ~er Junge** (abwertend) a greenhorn; ~**es Licht geben** give the go-ahead; **jmdn. ~ und blau** *od.* **gelb schlagen** (ugs.) beat sb. black and blue; **sich ~ und blau** *od.* **gelb ärgern** (ugs.)

be livid (coll.) *or* furious; **(b)** (ugs.: wohlgesinnt) **ich bin ihr nicht** ~: she's not someone I care for; **(c)** (Politik) Green; *s. auch* **Grüne²**

Grün *das;* ~**s**, ~ *od.* (ugs.) ~**s (a)** green; **die Ampel zeigt** ~: the lights *pl.* are at green; **das ist dasselbe in** ~ (ugs.) it makes *or* there is no real difference; **(b)** *o. Pl.* (Pflanzen) greenery; **(c)** (Golf) green

Grün·anlage *die* green space; (Park) park

grün·blau *Adj.* greenish blue

Grund /grʊnt/ *der;* ~[e]s, **Gründe** /ˈgrʏndə/ **(a)** (Erdoberfläche) ground; **etw. bis auf den** ~ **abreißen** raze sth. to the ground; **sich in** ~ **und Boden schämen** be utterly ashamed; **(b)** *o. Pl.* (eines Gewässers, geh.: eines Gefäßes) bottom; **auf** ~ **laufen** run aground; **im** ~ **e seines Herzens/seiner Seele** (fig. geh.) at heart *or* deep down/in his innermost soul; **der Sache** *(Dat.)* **auf den** ~ **gehen/kommen** get to the bottom *or* root of the matter; **im** ~**e [genommen]** basically; **(c)** (Ursache, Veranlassung) reason; (Beweg~) grounds *pl.;* reason; **[k]einen** ~ **zum Feiern/Klagen haben** have [no] cause for [a] celebration/to complain *or* for complaint; **aus dem einfachen** ~, **weil ...** (ugs.) for the simple reason that ...; **ohne ersichtlichen** ~: for no obvious *or* apparent reason; **(d) Gründe und Gegengründe** pros and cons; arguments for and against; **(e)** (Land) land; ~ **und Boden** land; **(f) auf** ~ ⇒ **aufgrund; (g) zu** ~**e** ⇒ **zugrunde**

grund-, Grund-: ~**ausbildung** *die* (Milit.) basic training; ~**ausstattung** *die* basic equipment; ~**besitz** *der* **(a)** (Eigentum an Land) ownership of land; **(b)** (Land) land; landed property; ~**besitzer** *der* landowner; ~**bestandteil** *der* [basic] element; ~**buch** *das* land register; ~**ehrlich** *Adj.* thoroughly honest; ~**einheit** *die* fundamental unit

gründen /ˈgrʏndn̩/ **1** *tr. V.* **(a)** (neu schaffen) found, set up, establish ⟨*organization, party, etc.*⟩; set up, establish ⟨*business*⟩; start [up] ⟨*club*⟩; **eine Familie/ein Heim** ~: start a family/set up home; **(b)** (aufbauen) base ⟨*plan, theory, etc.*⟩ **(auf** + *Akk.* on). **2** *refl. V.* **sich auf etw.** *(Akk.)* ~: be based on sth.

Gründer *der;* ~**s**, ~, **Gründerin** *die;* ~, ~**nen:** founder

grund-, Grund-: ~**falsch** *Adj.* utterly wrong; ~**festen** *Pl. in* **etw. in seinen** *od.* **bis in seine** ~**festen erschüttern** shake sth. to its [very] foundations; ~**fläche** *die* **(a)** (eines Zimmers) [floor] area; **(b)** (Math.) base; ~**form** *die* **(a)** (Hauptform) basic form; **(b)** (Urform) original form; **(c)** (Sprachw.) infinitive; ~**gebühr** *die* basic *or* standing charge; ~**gedanke** *der* basic idea; ~**gesetz** *das* **(a)** (Verfassung) Basic Law; **(b)** (wichtiges Gesetz) fundamental *or* basic law

grundieren /grʊnˈdiːrən/ *tr. V.* prime; (Ölmalerei) ground; apply the ground to

Grundierung *die;* ~, ~**en** (erster Anstrich) priming coat; (Ölmalerei) ground coat

Grund-: ~**kapital** *das* (Wirtsch.) equity *or* share capital; ~**kenntnis** *die; meist Pl.* basic knowledge *no pl.* **(in** + *Dat.* of); ~**kurs** *der* basic course

Grund·lage *die* basis; foundation; **auf der** ~: on the basis; **jeder** ~ **entbehren** be completely unfounded *or* without any foundation

grund·legend **1** *Adj.* fundamental, basic **(für** to); seminal ⟨*idea, work*⟩. **2** *adv.* fundamentally

gründlich /ˈgrʏntlɪç/ **1** *Adj.* thorough. **2** *adv.* **(a)** (gewissenhaft) thoroughly; **(b)** (ugs.: gehörig) **sich** ~ **täuschen** be sadly *or* greatly mistaken; ~ **mit etw. aufräumen** do away completely with sth.

Gründlichkeit *die;* ~: thoroughness

grund-, Grund-: ~**linie** *die* **(a)** (Math.) base; **(b)** (Sport) baseline; **(c)** (Hauptzug) main *or* principal feature *or* characteristic; ~**los** **1** *Adj.* **(a)** (unbegründet) groundless; unfounded; **(b)** (ohne festen Boden) bottomless ⟨*sea, depths, etc.*⟩; **2** *adv.* ~**los lachen** laugh for no reason [at all]; **jmdn.** ~**los verdächtigen** be suspicious of sb. without reason; ~**mauer** *die* foundation wall; **das Haus war bis auf die** ~**mauern abgebrannt** the house had burnt to the ground; ~**nahrungsmittel** *das* basic food-[stuff]

Grün·donnerstag *der* Maundy Thursday

Grund-: ~**prinzip** *das* fundamental *or* basic principle; ~**recht** *das* basic *or* fundamental *or* constitutional right; ~**regel** *die* fundamental *or* basic rule; ~**riss**, *** ~**riß** *der* **(a)** (Bauw.) [ground-] plan; **(b)** (Leitfaden) outline; ~**satz** *der* principle; **aus** ~**satz** on principle

grund·sätzlich **1** *Adj.* ~ **(a)** fundamental ⟨*difference, question, etc.*⟩; **(b)** (aus Prinzip) ⟨*rejection, opponent, etc.*⟩ on principle; **(c)** (allgemein) ⟨*agreement, readiness, etc.*⟩ in principle. **2** *adv.* ~ **(a)** fundamentally; **zu etw.** ~ **Stellung nehmen** make a statement of principle on sth.; **(b)** (aus Prinzip) as a matter of principle; on principle; **(c)** (allgemein) in principle

Grund-: ~**schule** *die* primary school; ~**schüler** *der* primary school pupil; ~**schul·lehrer** *der* primary-school teacher; ~**stein** *der* foundation stone; ~**stein·legung** *die* ~, ~**en** laying of the foundation stone; ~**stellung** *die* (Sport) basic position; ~**steuer** *die* (Steuerw.) property tax [under German law]; ~**stock** *der* basis; foundation; ~**stoff** *der* **(a)** (Chemie: Element) element; **(b)** (Rohstoff) [basic] raw material

Grund·stück *das* piece of land; (Bau~) plot of land; (größer) site; **jmds.** ~ **betreten** enter sb.'s property

Grundstücks·makler *der* estate agent

Grund-: ~**studium** *das* basic course; ~**tendenz** *die* basic trend; ~**ton** *der* **(a)** (Farbton) basic colour; **(b)** (~stimmung) basic *or* prevailing tone *or* mood; **(c)** (Musik) fundamental [tone]; root; ~**übel** *das* basic evil

Gründung *die;* ~, ~**en** (Partei~, Vereins~) foundation; establishment; setting up; (Geschäfts~) setting up; establishing; (Klub~) starting [up]

grund-, Grund-: ~**verkehrt** *Adj.* completely *or* entirely wrong; ~**verschieden** *Adj.* totally *or* completely different; ~**wasser** *das* (Geol.) ground water; ~**wasser·spiegel** *der* water table; ground-water level; ~**wehr·dienst** *der* basic military service; national service; ~**zug** *der* essential feature

Grüne¹ *das; adj. Dekl.* **(a)** green; **(b) im** ~**n/ins** ~: [out] in/into the country; **(c)** (ugs.) ⇒ **Grün b**

Grüne² *der/die; adj. Dekl.* (Politik) member of the Green Party; **die** ~**n** the Greens

grünen *itr. V.* (goh.) be green; (grün werden) turn green

grün-, Grün-: ~**fink** *der* greenfinch; ~**fläche** *die* green space; (im Park) lawn; ~**gelb** *Adj.* greenish yellow; ~**gürtel** *der* green belt; ~**kohl** *der* curly kale

grünlich *Adj.* greenish

Grün-: ~**schnabel** *der* (abwertend) [young] whippersnapper; (Neuling) greenhorn; ~**span** *der* verdigris; ~**streifen** *der* central reservation; centre strip (*grassed and often with trees and bushes*))

grunzen /ˈgrʊntsn̩/ *tr., itr. V.* grunt

Grün·zeug *das* (ugs.) ⇒ **Grüne¹ c**

Gruppe /ˈgrʊpə/ *die;* ~, ~**n (a)** (auch fachspr.) group; **(b)** (Kategorie, Klasse) class; category

Gruppen-: ~**arbeit** *die; o. Pl.* group work; ~**bild** *das* group photograph; ~**reise** *die* (Touristik) group travel *no pl., no art.;* **eine** ~**reise nach London machen** travel to London with a group; ~**sex** *der* group sex; ~**sieg** *der* (Sport) top place in the group; **den** ~**sieg erreichen** win the group; ~**sieger** *der* (Sport) winner of the/a group; ~**therapie** *die* (Psych.) group therapy

gruppieren **1** *tr. V.* arrange. **2** *refl. V.* form a group/groups

Gruppierung *die;* ~, ~**en (a)** (Personengruppe) grouping; group; (Politik) faction; **(b)** (Anordnung) arrangement; grouping

Grusel·geschichte *die* horror story

gruselig /ˈgruːzəlɪç/ *Adj.* eerie; creepy; blood-curdling ⟨*apparition, scream*⟩; spine-chilling ⟨*story, film*⟩

gruseln **1** *tr., itr. V.* (unpers.) **es gruselt jmdn.** *od.* **jmdm.** sb.'s flesh creeps. **2** *refl. V.* be frightened; get the creeps (coll.)

Gruß /gruːs/ *der;* ~**es**, **Grüße** /ˈgryːsə/ **▶240] (a)** greeting; (Milit.) salute; **bestell Barbara bitte viele Grüße von mir** please give Barbara my regards; please remember me to Barbara; **einen [schönen]** ~ **an jmdn./von**

Grüße

Auf einer Postkarte

Schöne od. Herzliche Grüße aus Freiburg	= Greetings od. Best wishes from Freiburg
Es gefällt uns hier ausgezeichnet	= We're having a wonderful time
Bis bald	= See you soon
Es grüßen recht herzlich Stephan und Inge	= All best wishes, Stephan and Inge

Zum Geburtstag

Herzlichen Glückwunsch zum Geburtstag	= Many happy returns [of the day], Happy birthday
Alles Gute zum 60. Geburtstag	= All best wishes on your 60th birthday

Zu Weihnachten und zum neuen Jahr

Frohe Weihnachten!	= Happy Christmas!
Ein gesegnetes Weihnachtsfest und viel Glück im neuen Jahr	= Best wishes for a Happy od. Merry Christmas and a Prosperous New Year
Glückliches neues Jahr!, Prost Neujahr!	= Happy New Year!

Zu Ostern

Frohe Ostern!	= [Best wishes for a] Happy Easter

Zu einer Hochzeit

Dem glücklichen Paar alles Gute am Hochzeitstag und viel Glück in der Zukunft	= Every good wish to the happy couple od. to the bride and groom on their wedding day and in the years to come

Zu einer Prüfung

Viel Erfolg bei der bevorstehenden Prüfung	= Every success in your exams, The best of luck with your exams

Alles Gute zum/Viel Glück beim Abitur	≈ All good wishes/The best of luck with your A levels

Zum Umzug

Viel Glück im neuen Heim	= Every happiness in your new home

Bei einem Krankheitsfall

Gute Besserung!	= Get well soon!
Die besten Wünsche zur baldigen Genesung	= Best wishes for a speedy recovery

Gesprochene Grüße

Hier gibt es manchmal keine genauen bzw. gar keine richtigen Entsprechungen.

Bei Begegnungen

Guten Tag!	= Good morning/afternoon/evening (je nach Tageszeit); Hello! (wirkt ungezwungener)
Hallo!	= Hello [there]!, Hi [there]!
Guten Morgen!	= Good morning!
Guten Abend!	= Good evening!
Wie geht es Ihnen?/Wie gehts?	= How are you?
Freut mich! (bei Vorstellungen)	= How do you do?

Beim Abschied

Auf Wiedersehen!	= Goodbye!
Tschüs!	= 'Bye now!
Bis bald!	= See you soon!
Machs gut!	= Look after yourself!, Take care!

Siehe auch □ **Briefeschreiben**

---

jmdm. [best] regards *pl.* to/from sb.; **(b)** (im Brief) **mit herzlichen Grüßen** [with] best wishes; **viele liebe Grüße euer Hans** love, Hans

grüßen /'gry:sn̩/ ▶ 240 **1** *tr. V.* **(a)** greet; (Milit.) salute; **grüß [dich] Gott!** (südd.) hello; **(b)** (Grüße senden) **grüße deine/grüßen Sie Ihre Eltern [ganz herzlich] von mir** please give your parents my [kindest] regards; **jmdn. ∼ lassen** send one's regards to sb. **2** *itr. V.* say hello; (Milit.) salute

gruß·los *Adv.* without a word of greeting/farewell

Grütze /'grʏtsə/ *die;* ∼, ∼**n (a)** groats *pl.;* **rote** ∼**:** red fruit pudding (*made with fruit juice, fruit and cornflour,* etc.); **(b)** *o. Pl.* (ugs.: Verstand) brains *pl.;* nous (coll.)

G-Schlüssel /'ge:-/ *der* (Musik) ⇒ **Violinschlüssel**

Guatemala /ɡuate'ma:la/ *(das),* ∼**s** Guatemala

Guatemalteke /ɡuatemal'te:kə/ *der;* ∼**n,** ∼**n** Guatemalan

gucken /'ɡʊkn̩/ **1** *itr. V.* (ugs.) **(a)** look; (heimlich) peep; **jmdm. über die Schulter** ∼**:** look *or* peer over sb.'s shoulder; **lass [mich] mal** ∼**!** let's have a look! (coll.); **(b)** (hervorsehen) stick out; **(c)** (dreinschauen) look; **finster/freundlich** ∼**:** look grim/affable. **2** *tr. V.* (ugs.) **Fernsehen** ∼**:** watch TV *or* (coll.) telly *or* (coll.) the box

Guck·loch *das* spy-hole; peephole

Guerilla /ɡe'rɪlja/ *die;* ∼, ∼**s (a)** (Krieg) guerrilla war; **(b)** (Einheit) guerrilla unit

Guerilla-: ∼**kämpfer** *der* guerrilla; ∼**krieg** *der* guerrilla war

Gugel·hupf /-hʊpf/ *der;* ∼**[e]s,** ∼**e** (südd., österr.) gugelhupf

Guillotine /ɡijo'ti:nə/ *die;* ∼, ∼**n** guillotine

Guinea /ɡi'ne:a/ *(das),* ∼**s** Guinea

Gulasch /'ɡʊlaʃ, 'ɡu:laʃ/ *das od. der;* ∼**[e]s,** ∼**e** *od.* ∼**s** goulash

Gulasch·suppe *die* goulash soup

Gulden /'ɡʊldn̩/ *der;* ∼**s,** ∼**:** guilder; florin

Gully /'ɡʊli/ *der;* ∼**s,** ∼**s** drain

gültig /'ɡʏltɪç/ *Adj.* valid; current ‹*note, coin*›; **diese Münze/dieser Geldschein ist nicht mehr** ∼**:** this coin/note is no longer legal tender; **der Fahrplan ist ab 1. Oktober** ∼**:** the timetable comes into operation on 1 October

Gültigkeit *die;* ∼**:** validity; ∼ **haben/erlangen** be/become valid; **die** ∼ **verlieren** become invalid

Gummi¹ /'ɡʊmi/ *der od. das;* ∼**s,** ∼**[s] (a)** [india] rubber; **(b)** (∼ring) rubber *or* elastic band

Gummi² *der;* ∼**s,** ∼**s (a)** (Radier∼) rubber; eraserrubber (sl.); **(b)** (salopp: Präservativ) rubber (sl.)

Gummi³ *das;* ∼**s,** ∼**s** (∼band) elastic *no indef. art.*

gummi-, Gummi-: ∼**artig** *Adj.* rubbery; rubber-like ‹*material*›; ∼**ball** *der* rubber ball; ∼**band** *das; Pl.* ∼**bänder (a)** rubber *or* elastic band; **(b)** (in Kleidung) elastic *no indef. art.;* ∼**bär** *der,* ∼**bärchen** *das* jelly baby; ∼**baum** *der* rubber plant; ∼**bonbon** *das* gumdrop

gummieren *tr. V.* gum

Gummierung *die;* ∼, ∼**en** gum

Gummi-: ∼**hand·schuh** *der* rubber glove; ∼**knüp·pel** *der* [rubber] truncheon; ∼**paragraph** *der* (ugs.)

---

paragraph *or* section with an elastic interpretation; ～**reifen** *der* rubber tyre; ～**ring** *der* (a) rubber band; (b) (Spielzeug) rubber ring; quoit; (c) (Weckglasring) rubber seal; ～**sohle** *die* rubber sole; ～**stiefel** *der* rubber boot; (für Regenwetter) wellington [boot] (Brit.); ～**zelle** *die* padded cell

Gunst /gʊnst/ *die;* ～ (a) favour; goodwill; **die** ～ **der Stunde nutzen** (fig.) take advantage of the favourable *or* propitious moment; **zu jmds.** ～**en** in sb.'s favour; (b) **zu** ～**en** ⇒ **zugunsten**

günstig /ˈgʏnstɪç/ **1** *Adj.* (a) (vorteilhaft) favourable; propitious ‹*sign*›; auspicious ‹*moment*›; beneficial ‹*influence*›; good, reasonable ‹*price*›; **bei** ～**em Wetter** if the weather is favourable; weather permitting; (b) (wohlwollend) well-disposed; favourably disposed. **2** *adv.* (a) (vorteilhaft) favourably; *etw.* ～ **beeinflussen** have *or* exert a beneficial influence on sth.; *etw.* ～ **kaufen/verkaufen** buy/sell sth. at a good price; (b) (wohlwollend) **jmdn./etw.** ～ **aufnehmen** receive sb./sth. well *or* favourably

günstig[st]en·falls *Adv.* at best

Günstling /ˈgʏnstlɪŋ/ *der;* ～**s**, ～**e** favourite

Guppy /ˈgʊpi/ *der;* ～**s**, ～**s** (Zool.) guppy

Gurgel /ˈgʊrgl̩/ *die;* ～, ～**n** throat; **jmdm. die** ～ **zudrücken** strangle *or* throttle sb.; **jmdm. die** ～ **durchschneiden** cut sb.'s throat; **jmdm. an die** ～ **wollen** fly at sb.

gurgeln *itr. V.* (a) (spülen) gargle; (b) (blubbern) gurgle

Gürkchen /ˈgʏrkçən/ *das;* ～**s**, ～ [cocktail] gherkin

Gurke /ˈgʊrkə/ *die;* ～, ～**n** (a) cucumber; (eingelegt) gherkin; **saure** ～**n** pickled gherkins; (b) (salopp: Nase) hooter (sl.); snout (coll.)

Gurken-: ～**hobel** *der* cucumber-slicer; ～**salat** *der* cucumber salad; ～**truppe** *die* (salopp) useless *or* feeble bunch (coll.)

gurren /ˈgʊrən/ *itr. V.* coo

Gurt /gʊrt/ *der;* ～**[e]s**, ～**e** strap; (im Auto, Flugzeug) [seat-]belt

Gürtel /ˈgʏrtl̩/ *der;* ～**s**, ～**:** belt; **den** ～ **enger schnallen** (fig. ugs.) tighten one's belt (fig.)

Gürtel-: ～**linie** *die* waist[line]; **ein Schlag unter die** ～**linie** (Boxen) a punch *or* blow below the belt; ～**reifen** *der* radial[-ply] tyre; ～**schnalle** *die* belt buckle; ～**tier** *das* armadillo

gürten /ˈgʏrtn̩/ (geh. verall.) **1** *tr. V.* gird (arch./literary). **2** *refl. V.* **sich [zum Kampf]** ～**:** gird oneself

Gurtstraffer *der;* ～**s**, ～ (Kfz.-W.) [seat]belt tensioner

Guru /ˈgʊru/ *der;* ～**s**, ～**s** guru

Guss, *￾**Guß** /gʊs/ *der;* **Gusses**, **Güsse** /ˈgʏsə/ (a) (das Gießen) casting; founding; **[wie] aus einem** ～**:** forming a unified *or* an integrated whole; fully coordinated ‹*plan*›; (b) (ugs.: Regenschauer) downpour; (c) (gegossenes Erzeugnis) casting; cast; (d) (das Begießen) stream

guss-, *￾**Guß-**, **Guss-**, *￾**Guß-:** ～**eisen** *das* cast iron; ～**eisern** *Adj.* cast-iron; ～**form** *die* casting mould

Gusto /ˈgʊsto/ *der;* ～**s**, ～**s** taste; liking

gut /guːt/; **besser** /ˈbɛsɐ/, **best...** /ˈbɛst.../ **1** *Adj.* (a) good; fine ‹*wine*›; **in Französisch** ～ **sein** be good at French; **ist der Kuchen** ～ **geworden?** did the cake turn out all right?; **es wäre** ～, **wenn** ...: it would be as well if ...; **also** ～**:** very well; all right; **schon** ～**:** [it's] all right *or* (coll.) OK; **das ist ja alles** ～ **und schön** that's all very well *or* all well and good; **etwas Gutes zu essen/trinken** something good to eat/drink; **es** ～ **sein lassen** (ugs.) leave it at that; **das ist** ～ **gegen** *od.* **für Kopfschmerzen** it's good for headaches; ～**en Tag!** good morning/afternoon!; ～**en Morgen!** good morning!; ～**en Abend!** good evening!; ～**e Nacht!** good night!; **ein** ～**es neues Jahr!** a happy new year!; **er hat es doch** ～ **bei uns** he's well enough off with us; **mir ist nicht** ～**:** I'm not feeling well; **alles Gute!** all the best!; ～**en Appetit!** enjoy your lunch/dinner *etc.!*; **es dürfte eine** ～**e Stunde [von hier] sein** it must be a good hour [from here]; **sich** (*Dat.*) **zu** ～ **für etw. sein** consider sth. beneath one *or* beneath one's dignity; **du bist** ～**!** (iron.) you're joking!; you must be joking!; **sei [bitte] so** ～ **und reich mir das Buch** would you be good *or* kind enough to pass me the book?; **im Guten auseinander gehen** part amicably *or* on amicable terms; ～ **aussehend** good-looking; ～ **tun** do good; (b) (besonderen Anlässen vorbehalten) best; **sein** ～**er**

Anzug his best suit. **2** *adv.* (a) well; ～ **reiten/schwimmen** be a good rider/swimmer; *etw.* ～ **können** be good at sth.; **seine Sache** ～ **machen** do well; ～ **hören/sehen** [be able to] hear/see well *or* clearly; **[das hast du]** ～ **gemacht!** well done!; **der Laden/das Geschäft geht** ～**:** the shop/business is doing well; ～ **bezahlt** well-paid; ～ **gemeint** well-meant; ～ **zwei Pfund wiegen** weigh a good two pounds; ～ **und gern** (ugs.) easily; at least (ugs.); **so** ～ **wie nichts** next to nothing; **so** ～ **ich kann** as best I can; **jmdm.** ～ **zureden** coax sb. [gently]; **es** ～ **meinen** mean well; (b) (mühelos) easily; ～ **zu Fuß sein** (ugs.) be a strong walker; **hinterher hat** *od.* **kann man** ～ **reden** it's easy to be wise after the event; **du hast** ～ **lachen** it's all right for you to laugh; **es kann** ～ **sein, dass** ...: it may well be that ...; *s. auch* **besser**, **best**...

Gut *das;* ～**[e]s**, **Güter** /ˈgyːtɐ/ (a) (Eigentum) property; (Besitztum, auch fig.) possession; **irdische Güter** earthly goods *or* possessions; **unrecht** ～ **gedeihet nicht** (Spr.) ill-gotten goods *or* gains never *or* seldom prosper; (b) (landwirtschaftlicher Grundbesitz) estate; (c) (Fracht～, Ware) item; **Güter** goods; (Fracht～) freight *sing.;* goods (Brit.); (d) (das Gute) ～ **und Böse** good and evil; **jenseits von** ～ **und Böse sein** (iron.) be past it (coll.)

gut-, **Gut-:** ～**achten** *das;* ～**s**, ～**:** [expert's] report; ～**achter** *der;* ～**s**, ～**:** expert; (in einem Prozess) expert witness; ～**artig** *Adj.* (a) good-natured; (b) (nicht gefährlich) benign; *￾*～**aussehend** ⇒ **gut 1 a;** *￾*～**bezahlt** ⇒ **gut 2 a;** ～**bürgerlich** *Adj.* good middle-class; ～**bürgerliche Küche** good plain cooking; ～**dünken** *das;* ～**s** discretion; judgement; **nach [eigenem]** ～**dünken** at one's own discretion

Güte /ˈgyːtə/ *die;* ～ (a) goodness; kindness; (～ Gottes) lovingkindness; goodness; **ein Vorschlag zur** ～**:** a suggestion for an amicable agreement; **[ach] du meine** *od.* **liebe** ～**!** (ugs.) my goodness!; goodness me; (b) (Qualität) quality

Gute·nacht·kuss, *￾**Gute·nacht·kuß** *der* good-night kiss

Güter-: ～**abfertigung** *die* (a) dispatch of freight *or* (Brit.) goods; (b) (Annahmestelle) freight *or* (Brit.) goods office; ～**bahnhof** *der* freight depot; goods station (Brit.); ～**trennung** *die* (Rechtsw.) separation of property; ～**wagen** *der* goods wagon (Brit.); freight car (Amer.); ～**zug** *der* goods train (Brit.); freight train (Amer.)

gut-, **Gut-:** *￾*～**|gehen** ⇒ **gehen i, k;** *￾*～**gehend** ⇒ **gehen i;** *￾*～**gelaunt** ⇒ **gelaunt***￾**; ～**gemeint** ⇒ **gut 2 a;** ～**gläubig** *Adj.* innocently trusting; ～**gläubigkeit** *die* innocent trust; ～**|haben** *unr. tr. V.* **etw. bei jmdm.** ～**haben** be owed sth. by sb.; ～**haben** *das;* ～**s**, ～**:** credit balance; **Sie haben ein** ～**haben von 450 DM auf Ihrem Konto** your account is 450 marks in credit; ～**|heißen** *unr. tr. V.* approve of; ～**herzig** *Adj.* kind-hearted; good-hearted

gütig /ˈgyːtɪç/ **1** *Adj.* kindly; kind ‹*heart*›. **2** *adv.* ～ **lächeln/nicken** give a kindly smile/nod

gütlich /ˈgyːtlɪç/ **1** *Adj.; nicht präd.* amicable. **2** *adv.* amicably; **sich** ～ **an etw.** (*Dat.*) **tun** regale oneself with sth.

gut-, **Gut-:** ～**|machen** *tr. V.* (a) (in Ordnung bringen) make good ‹*damage*›; put right, correct ‹*omission, mistake, etc.*›; (b) (Überschuss erzielen) make [a profit of] (**bei** on); ～**mütig 1** *Adj.* good-natured; **2** *adv.* good-naturedly; ～**mütigkeit** *die;* ～ good nature; goodnaturedness; ～**nachbarlich 1** *Adj.* good-neigbourly ‹*relations etc.*›; **2** *adv.* as good neighbours

Guts·besitzer *der* owner of a/the estate; landowner

gut-, **Gut-:** ～**schein** *der* voucher, coupon (**für, auf** + *Akk.* for); ～**|schreiben** *unr. tr. V.* credit; **etw. jmdm./jmds. Konto** ～**schreiben** credit sb./sb.'s account with sth.; ～**schrift** *die* credit

Guts-: ～**herr** *der* lord of the manor; ～**hof** *der* estate; manor; ～**verwalter** *der* steward; bailiff

gut-, **Gut-:** *￾*～**|tun** ⇒ **gut 1 a;** ～**willig 1** *Adj.* willing; (entgegenkommend) obliging; **sich** ～**willig zeigen** be obliging; show willing (coll.); **2** *adv.* **etw.** ～**willig herausgeben** hand sth. over voluntarily; ～**willigkeit** *die* willingness; (Entgegenkommen) obligingness

Gymnasiast /gʏmnaˈzi̯ast/ *der;* ～**en**, ～**en**, **Gymnasiastin** *die;* ～, ～**nen** ≈ grammar-school pupil

Gymnasium /gym'na:zjʊm/ *das;* ~s, **Gymnasien** ≈ grammar school; **aufs** ~ **gehen** ≈ be at *or* attend grammar school

Gymnastik /gym'nastɪk/ *die;* ~: physical exercises *pl.;* (Turnen) gymnastics *sing.*

gymnastisch *Adj.* gymnastic

Gynäkologe /gynɛko'lo:gə/ *der;* ~n, ~n gynaecologist

Gynäkologie *die;* ~: gynaecology *no art.*

Gynäkologin *die;* ~, ~nen gynaecologist

gynäkologisch *Adj.; nicht präd.* gynaecological

....

Hh

....

h, H /ha:/ *das;* ~, ~ (a) (Buchstabe) h/H; (b) (Musik) [key of] B; *s. auch* **a, A**

H *Abk.* (a) **Herren;** (b) **Haltestelle**

ha¹ /ha(:)/ *Interj.* ha!; oh!; ah!; (Triumph) aha!

ha² *Abk.* **Hektar** ha

Haag /ha:k/ *(das) od. der;* ~s ▶ 490 The Hague

Haar /ha:ɐ̯/ *das;* ~[e]s, ~e (a) (auch Zool., Bot.) hair; **blonde** ~e *od.* **blondes** ~ **haben** have fair hair; [**sich** (*Dat.*)] **das** ~ *od.* **die** ~e **waschen** wash one's hair; **sich** (*Dat.*) **das** ~ *od.* **die** ~e **schneiden lassen** have *or* get one's hair cut; **ihm geht das** ~ **aus** he's losing his hair; **sich** (*Dat.*) **die** ~e [**aus**]**raufen** (ugs.) tear one's hair [out]; (b) (fig.) **ihr stehen die** ~e **zu Berge** *od.* **sträuben sich die** ~e (ugs.) her hair stands on end; **ein** ~ **in der Suppe finden** (ugs.) find something to quibble about *or* find fault with; **kein gutes** ~ **an jmdm./etw. lassen** (ugs.) pull sb./sth. to pieces (fig. coll.); ~e **auf den Zähnen haben** (ugs. scherzh.) be a tough customer; **sich** (*Dat.*) **über** *od.* **wegen etw. keine grauen** ~e **wachsen lassen** not lose any sleep over sth.; not worry one's head about sth.; **er wird dir kein** ~ **krümmen** (ugs.) he won't harm a hair of your head; **das ist an den** ~**en herbeigezogen** (ugs.) that's far-fetched; **jmdm. aufs** ~ **gleichen** be the spitting image of sb.; **sich in die** ~e **kriegen** (ugs.) quarrel, squabble (**wegen** over); **sich** (*Dat.*) **in den** ~**en liegen** (ugs.) be at loggerheads; **um ein** ~ (ugs.) very nearly

Haar-: ~**ausfall** *der* loss of hair; hair loss; ~**bürste** *die* hairbrush; ~**büschel** *das* tuft of hair

haaren *itr. V.* moult; lose *or* shed its hair

Haares·breite *die in* **um** ~: by a hair's breadth

haar-, Haar-: ~**farbe** *die* hair colour; ~**fein** *Adj.* fine as a hair *postpos.;* ~**festiger** *der* setting lotion; ~**genau** (ugs.) **1** *Adj.* exact; **2** *adv.* exactly; **das stimmt** ~**genau** that is absolutely right

haarig *Adj.* (a) (behaart) hairy; (b) (ugs.: heikel) tricky

haar-, Haar-: ~**klammer** *die* hairgrip; ~**klein** **1** *Adj.* minute; **2** *adv.* in minute detail; ~**klemme** *die* hairgrip; ~**kranz** *der* (a) fringe *or* circle of hair; (b) (Frisur) chaplet [of plaited hair]; ~**los** *Adj.* hairless; ~**mode** *die* hairstyle; ~**nadel** *die* hairpin; ~**nadel·kurve** *die* hairpin bend; ~**netz** *das* hairnet; ~**scharf** *Adv.* (a) (sehr nah) **die Kugel flog** ~**scharf an ihm vorbei** the bullet missed him by a hair's breadth; (b) (sehr genau) with great precision; ~**schleife** *die* bow; hair-ribbon; ~**schnitt** *der* (a) haircut; (modisch) hairstyle; ~**schopf** *der* mop *or* shock of hair; ~**spalter** *der;* ~s, ~ (abwertend) hair-splitter; ~**spalterei** *die;* ~ (abwertend) hair-splitting; **das ist doch** ~**spalterei** that's splitting hairs; ~**spange** *die* hairslide; ~**spray** *der od. das* hair spray; ~**sträubend** *Adj.* (a) (grauenhaft) hair-raising; horrifying; (b) (empörend) outrageous; shocking; ~**teil** *das* hairpiece; ~**wasch·mittel** *das* shampoo; ~**wasser** *das; Pl.* ~**wässer** hair lotion; ~**wuchs** *der* hair growth; growth of hair; **einen spärlichen/starken** ~**wuchs haben** have little/a lot of hair; ~**wuchs·mittel** *das* hair-restorer

*alte Schreibung (vgl. Hinweise auf S. xvi–xvii)

Hab /ha:p/ *in* ~ **und Gut** (geh.) possessions *pl.;* belongings *pl.*

Habe /'ha:bə/ *die;* ~ (geh.) possessions *pl.;* belongings *pl.*

haben **1** *unr. tr. V.* (a) have; have got; **er hat nichts** (ugs.) he has nothing; **da hast du das Geld** there's the money; **ich habe Zeit/keine Zeit** I have [got] [the] time/I have [got] no time *or* I haven't [got] any time; **die Sache hat Zeit** it's not urgent; it can wait (coll.); **heute** ~ **wir schönes Wetter/30°** the weather is fine/it's 30° today; **wann hast du Urlaub?** when is your holiday?; *s. auch* **Schuld** b; (b) (empfinden) **Hunger/Durst** ~: be hungry/thirsty; **Sehnsucht nach etw.** ~: long for sth.; **Heimweh/Furcht** ~: be homesick/afraid; **Husten/Fieber/Schmerzen** ~: have [got] a cough/a temperature/have pain; **was hast du denn?** (ugs.) what's the matter?; what's wrong?; **ich kann das nicht** ~ (ugs.) I can't stand it; (c) *mit Adj. u. „es"* **es gut/schlecht/schwer/eilig** ~: have it good (coll.) /have a bad time [of it]/have a difficult *or* tough time/be in a hurry; (d) *mit „zu" u. Inf.* **nichts zu essen/trinken** ~: have nothing to eat/drink; (müssen) **du hast zu gehorchen** you must obey; **etw. zu tun/erledigen** ~: have [got] sth. to do *or* that one must do; **er hat zu tun** he's busy; (dürfen) **er hat mir nichts zu befehlen** he has [got] no right to order me about; (e) (sich zusammensetzen aus) **das Jahr hat 12 Monate** there are 12 months in a year; **ein Kilometer hat 1 000 Meter** there are 1,000 metres in a kilometre; **diese Stadt hat 10 000 Einwohner** this town has 10,000 inhabitants; (f) (bekommen) have; **zu** ~ **sein** (ugs.) be unattached; **dafür ist er immer zu** ~: he's always game for that; **da hast dus** (ugs.) there you are; (g) (ugs.: in der Schule) **morgen** ~ **wir Geschichte** we've got history tomorrow; (h) (ugs.: gebrauchen) **man hat das nicht mehr** it is no longer in use/in fashion; (i) (ugs.: gefasst) **have ‹ thief etc. ›; jetzt hab ich dich** now I've got you; (j) (bekommen) **Nachricht von jmdm.** ~: have heard from sb.; **was** (ugs.) /**welche Note hast du diesmal in Physik?** what did you get in *or* for physics this time?; (k) (gefunden) **ich habs!** (ugs.) I've got it!; **das werden wir gleich** ~ (ugs.) we'll soon find out; (l) (ugs.: repariert, beendet) **das werden wir gleich** ~: we'll soon fix that; (m) *mit Präp.* **wir** ~ **viele Bilder an der Wand [hängen]** we have quite a lot of pictures up; **etwas/nichts gegen jmdn.** *od.* **etw.** ~: have something/nothing against sb. *or* sth.; **etwas mit jmdm.** ~ (ugs.) have a thing *or* something going with sb. (coll.); **viel/wenig von jmdm.** ~: see a lot/little of sb.; **etw. von etw.** ~: get sth. out of sth.; (bes. österr., südd.: vorhanden sein) **es hat ...:** there is/are ... **2** *refl. V.* (a) (ugs.) **hab dich nicht so!** don't make *or* stop making such a fuss!; (b) (ugs.: sich erledigt ~) **und damit hat es sich** *od.* **hat sich die Sache** then that's that; **hat sich was!** far from it! **3** *Hilfsverb* have; **ich habe/hatte ihn eben gesehen** I have *or* I've/I had *or* I'd just seen him; **sie** ~ **gelacht** they laughed; **er hat das gewusst** he knew it; **das hättest du früher machen können** you could have done that earlier

Haben *das;* ~s, ~ (Kaufmannsspr.) credit; *s. auch* **Soll** a

Habe·nichts *der;* ~, ~e pauper

Haben-: ~**seite** *die* (Kaufmannsspr.) credit side; ~**zinsen** *Pl.* interest *sing.* on deposits

Haber *der;* ~s (südd., österr., schweiz.) ⇒ **Hafer**

Hab·gier *die* (abwertend) greed

hab·gierig **1** *Adj.* (abwertend) greedy. **2** *adv.* greedily

habhaft *in* jmds./einer Sache ~ **werden** catch *or* apprehend sb./get hold of sth.

Habicht /'ha:bɪçt/ *der;* ~s, ~e hawk

Habilitation /habilita'tsi̯o:n/ *die;* ~, ~en habilitation (*qualification as a university lecturer*)

habilitieren /habili'ti:rən/ *refl. V.* habilitate (*qualify as a university lecturer*)

Habsburger /'ha:psbʊrgɐ/ *der;* ~s, ~ (hist.) Habsburg

hab-, Hab-: ~**seligkeiten** *Pl.* [meagre] possessions *or* belongings; ~**sucht** *die;* ~ (abwertend) greed; avarice; ~**süchtig** (abwertend) **1** *Adj.* greedy; avaricious. **2** *adv.* greedily; avariciously

hach /hax/ *Interj.* oh!

Hachse /'haksə/ *die;* ~, ~n (südd.) (a) knuckle; (b) (ugs. scherzh.) leg

Hack /hak/ *das;* ~**s** (ugs., bes. nordd.) mince; minced meat

Hack-: ~**beil** *das* chopper; cleaver; ~**braten** *der* (Kochk.) meat loaf

Hacke¹ *die;* ~, ~**n** hoe; (Pickel) pick[axe]

Hacke² *die;* ~, ~**n** (bes. nordd. u. md.) heel; **sich** (*Dat.*) **die** ~**n nach etw. ablaufen** wear oneself out running around looking for sth.

hacken 1 *itr. V.* (a) (mit der Hacke arbeiten) hoe; (b) **sich** (*Dat.*) **ins Bein** ~: cut one's leg [with an axe *etc.*]; (c) (picken) peck. 2 *tr. V.* (a) (mit der Hacke bearbeiten) hoe ‹*garden, flower bed, etc.*›; (b) (zerkleinern) chop ‹*wood etc.*›; chop [up] ‹*meat, vegetables, etc.*›; **etw. in Stücke** ~: chop sth. up; (c) **ein Loch in etw.** (*Akk.*) ~: chop *or* hack a hole in sth.

Hacker *der;* ~**s** ~ (DV-Jargon) hacker

Hack-: ~**fleisch** *das* minced meat; mince; **aus** jmdm. ~**fleisch machen** (fig. ugs.) make mincemeat of sb.; ~**klotz** *der* chopping-block

Häcksel /'hɛksl̩/ *der od. das;* ~**s** (Landw.) chaff

Hader /'ha:dɐ/ *der;* ~**s** (geh.) discord

hadern *itr. V.* (geh.) **mit etw.** ~: be at odds with sth.; **er haderte mit seinem Schicksal** he railed against his fate

Hafen /'ha:fn̩/ *der;* ~**s, Häfen** harbour; port; **der Hamburger** ~: the port of Hamburg; **ein Schiff läuft den** ~ **an/aus dem** ~ **aus/in den** ~ **ein** a ship is putting into/ leaving/entering port *or* harbour

Hafen-: ~**anlagen** *Pl.* docks; ~**arbeiter** *der* dock-worker; docker; ~**kneipe** *die* dockland pub (Brit.) *or* (Amer.) bar; ~**polizei** *die* port *or* dock police; ~**rund-fahrt** *die* trip round the harbour; ~**stadt** *die* port; ~**viertel** *das* dock area; dockland *no art.*

Hafer /'ha:fɐ/ *der;* ~**s** oats *pl.;* **jmdn. sticht der** ~ (ugs.) sb. is feeling his oats

Hafer-: ~**brei** *der* porridge; ~**flocken** *Pl.* rolled oats; porridge oats; ~**grütze** *die* (a) oat groats; (b) (Brei) porridge; ~**schleim** *der* gruel

Haff /haf/ *das;* ~[**e**]**s,** ~**s** *od.* ~**e** lagoon

Haft /haft/ *die;* ~: custody; (aus politischen Gründen) detention; **jmdn. aus der** ~ **entlassen** release sb. from custody/detention; **jmdn. zu zwei Jahren** ~ **verurteilen** sentence sb. to two years in prison *or* two years' imprisonment

-haft *Adj., adv.* -like

Haft·anstalt *die* prison

haftbar *Adj.* [legally] liable; **jmdn. für etw.** ~ **machen** make *or* hold sb. [legally] liable for sth.

Haft-: ~**befehl** *der* (Rechtsw.) warrant [of arrest]; ~**creme** *die* (Pharm.) fixative cream

haften¹ *itr. V.* (a) (festkleben) stick; **an/auf etw.** (*Dat.*) ~: stick to sth.; ~ **bleiben** stick (**an/auf** + *Dat.* to); (b) (sich festsetzen) ‹*smell, dirt, etc.*› cling (**an** + *Dat.* to); **an ihm haftet ein Makel** (fig.) he carries a stigma

haften² *itr. V.* (Rechtsw., Wirtsch.) be liable

*haften|bleiben ⇨ **haften¹** a

Häftling /'hɛftlɪŋ/ *der;* ~**s,** ~**e** prisoner

Häftlings·kleidung *die* prison clothing

Haft·pflicht *die* (a) liability (**für** for); (b) ⇨ **Haftpflichtversicherung**

Haftpflicht·versicherung *die* personal liability insurance; (für Autofahrer) third party insurance

haft-, Haft-: ~**reibung** *die* (Physik) static friction; ~**richter** *der* (Rechtsw.) magistrate; ~**schale** *die; meist Pl.* contact lens; ~**strafe** *die* (Rechtsspr. veralt.) prison sentence; ~**unfähig** *Adj.* unfit to be kept in prison *postpos.*

Haftung¹ *die;* ~: adhesion; (von Reifen) grip

Haftung² *die;* ~, ~**en** (a) (Verantwortlichkeit) liability; responsibility; *s. auch* **Garderobe**; (b) (Rechtsw., Wirtsch.) liability; **Gesellschaft mit [un]beschränkter** ~: [un]limited [liability] company

Hagebutte /'ha:gəbʊtə/ *die;* ~, ~**n** (a) (Frucht) rose-hip; (b) (ugs.: Heckenrose) dog-rose

Hagel /'ha:gl̩/ *der;* ~**s,** ~ (auch fig.) hail

Hagel·korn *das* hailstone

hageln *itr., tr. V.* (unpers.) hail; **es hagelt** it is hailing; **es hagelte Steine und leere Bierdosen** (fig.) there was a hail of stones and empty beer cans

Hagel-: ~**schauer** *der* [short] hailstorm; ~**schlag** *der* hail

hager /'ha:gɐ/ *Adj.* gaunt ‹*person, figure, face*›; thin ‹*neck, arm, fingers*›

Häher /'hɛ:ɐ/ *der;* ~**s,** ~: jay

Hahn¹ /ha:n/ *der;* ~[**e**]**s, Hähne** /'hɛ:nə/ (a) cock; ~ **im Korb sein** (ugs.) be cock of the walk; **nach ihr/danach kräht kein** ~ (ugs.) no one could care less about her/it; (b) (Wetter~) weathercock

Hahn² *der;* ~[**e**]**s, Hähne,** *fachspr.:* ~**en** (a) tap; faucet (Amer.); (b) (bei Waffen) hammer; **den** ~ **spannen** cock a/ the gun

Hähnchen /'hɛ:nçən/ *das;* ~**s,** ~: chicken

Hahnen-: ~**fuß** *der* buttercup; ~**kampf** *der* cock-fighting; (einzelner Wettkampf) cock-fight; ~**schrei** *der* cock-crow; **beim ersten** ~**schrei** at cock-crow; ~**tritt·muster** *das* dog-tooth *or* dog's tooth check

Hai /hai/ *der;* ~**s,** ~**e** shark

Hai·fisch *der* shark

Haifisch·flossen·suppe *die* (Kochk.) shark-fin soup

Hain /hain/ *der;* ~[**e**]**s,** ~**e** (dichter. veralt.) grove

Hain·buche *die* hornbeam

Haiti /ha'i:ti/ (*das*); ~**s** Haiti

haitianisch *Adj.* Haitian

Häkchen /'hɛ:kçən/ *das;* ~**s,** ~ (a) [small] hook; (b) (Zeichen) mark; (beim Abhaken) tick

Häkel·garn *das* crochet thread *or* yarn

häkeln /'hɛ:kl̩n/ *tr., itr. V.* crochet

Häkel·nadel *die* crochet-hook

haken /'ha:kn̩/ 1 *tr. V.* hook (**an** + *Akk.* on to). 2 *itr. V.* (klemmen) be stuck

Haken *der;* ~**s,** ~ (a) hook; ~ **und Öse** hook and eye; **einen** ~ **schlagen** dart sideways; (b) (Zeichen) tick; (c) (ugs.: Schwierigkeit) catch; snag; **der** ~ **an etw.** (*Dat.*) the catch in sth.; (d) (Boxen) hook

haken-, Haken-: ~**förmig** *Adj.* hooked; hook-shaped; ~**kreuz** *das* swastika; ~**nase** *die* hooked nose; hook-nose

halb /halp/ ▸ 600⌋ 1 *Adj. u. Bruchz.* (a) half; **eine** ~**e Stunde/ein** ~**er Meter/ein** ~**es Glas** half an hour/a metre/a glass; **zum** ~**en Preis** [at] half price; ~ **Europa/die** ~**e Welt** half of Europe/half the world; **es ist** ~ **eins** it's half past twelve; **5 Minuten vor/nach** ~: 25 [minutes] past/to; *s. auch* **Weg** d; (b) (unvollständig, vermindert) **die** ~**e Wahrheit** half [of] *or* part of the truth; **nichts Halbes und nichts Ganzes [sein]** [be] neither one thing nor the other; (c) (fast) [**noch**] **ein** ~**es Kind sein** be hardly *or* scarcely more than a child; **die** ~**e Stadt** half the town. 2 *adv.* (a) ~ **voll/leer** half-full/-empty; ~ **lachend,** ~ **weinend** half laughing, half crying; (b) (unvollständig) ~ **gar/angezogen/wach/offen/fertig** half-done *or* -cooked/half dressed/half-awake/half-open/half-finished; ~ **links/rechts** (Fußball) [at] inside left/ right; (c) (fast) ~ **blind/verhungert/tot** half blind/ starved/dead; ~ **nackt** half-naked; ~ **roh** half-cooked; half-done; ~ **und** ~ (ugs.) more or less

halb-, Halb-: ~**amtlich** *Adj.* semi-official; ~**bil-dung** *die* (abwertend) superficial education; ~**bitter** *Adj.* plain ‹*chocolate*›; ~**blut** *das* (a) (bei Pferden) cross-breed; (b) (Mischling) half-caste; half-breed; ~**bruder** *der* half-brother; ~**dunkel** *das* semi-darkness

Halbe *die od. das; adj. Dekl.* (ugs.) half litre (*of beer etc.*)

Halb·edelstein *der* (veralt.) semi-precious stone

halbe-halbe *in* [**mit jmdm.**] ~ **machen** (ugs.) go halves [with sb.]

halber /'halbɐ/ *Präp. mit Gen.* (wegen) on account of; (um ... willen) for the sake of; **der Ordnung** ~: as a matter of form

halb-, Halb-: *~**fertig** ⇨ **halb** 2 b; ~**fett** 1 *Adj.* (Druckw.) bold ‹*type*›; (schmaler, kleiner) semibold; 2 *adv.* **etw.** ~**fett drucken** print sth. in bold/semibold [type]; ~**fi-nale** *das* (Sport) semi-final;*~**gar** ⇨ **halb** 2 b; ~**ge-bildet** *Adj.* (abwertend) half-educated; ~**gefror[e]ne** *das; adj. Dekl.* soft ice cream; ~**gott** *der* (Myth., fig. iron.) demigod

Halbheit *die;* ~, ~en (abwertend) half-measure

halb-: ~**herzig 1** *Adj.* half-hearted; **2** *adv.* half-heartedly; ~**hoch** *Adj.* calf-length ‹*boot*›

halbieren *tr. V.* cut/tear ‹*object*› in half; halve ‹*amount, number*›; (Math.) bisect

halb-, Halb-: ~**insel** *die* peninsula; ~**jahr** *das* six months *pl.;* half year; **im ersten/zweiten** ~**jahr** in the first/last six months [of the year]; ~**jährig** *Adj.; nicht präd.* **(a)** (ein halbes Jahr alt) six-months-old ‹*baby, pony, etc.*›; **(b)** (ein halbes Jahr dauernd) six-month ‹*contract, course, etc.*›; ~**jährlich 1** *Adj.* half-yearly; six-monthly; **2** *adv.* every six months; twice a year; ~**kreis** *der* semicircle; **sich im** ~**kreis aufstellen** form a semicircle; ~**kreis- förmig 1** *Adj.* semicircular; **2** *adv.* in a semicircle; ~**kugel** *die* hemisphere; ~**kugel·förmig** *Adj.* hemispherical; ~**lang** *Adj.* mid-length ‹*hair*›; mid-calf length ‹*coat, dress, etc.*›; ~**laut 1** *Adj.* low; quiet; **2** *adv.* in a low voice; in an undertone; ~**leder** *das* (Buchw.) half-leather; ~**leinen** *das* **(a)** (Gewebe) fifty-per-cent linen material; **(b)** (Buchw.) half-cloth; ~**leiter** *der* (Elektronik) semiconductor;*~**links** ⇨ halb 2 b; ~**mast** *Adv.* at half mast; ~**mast flaggen** fly a flag/the flags at half mast; ~**messer** *der* (Math.) radius; ~**monatlich** *Adj.* fortnightly; twice-monthly; ~**mond** *der* **(a)** (Mond) half-moon; **(b)** (Figur) crescent;*~**nackt** ⇨ **halb 2 c;** *~**offen** ⇨ **halb 2 b;** ~**part** *Adv. in* [mit jmdm.] ~**part machen** (ugs.) go halves [with sb.]; ~**pension** *die; o. Pl., meist o. Art.* half-board;*~**rechts** ⇨ **halb 2 b;** ~**roh** ⇨ **halb 2 c;** ~**rund** *Adj. (präd. getrennt geschrieben)* semicircular; ~**rund** *das* semicircle; ~**schatten** *der* half shadow ~**schlaf** *der* light sleep; **im** ~**schlaf liegen** be half asleep; doze; ~**schuh** *der* shoe; ~**schwer·gewicht** *das* (Schwerathletik) light-heavyweight; ~**schwergewichtler** /-ɡəvɪçtlɐ/ *der;* ~**s,** ~ (Schwerathletik) light-heavyweight; ~**schwester** *die* half-sister; ~**seiden** *Adj.* **(a)** fifty-per-cent silk; **(b)** (ugs. abwertend: unmännlich) poofy (coll.); pansyish (coll.); **(c)** (ugs. abwertend: anrüchig) dubious ‹*business practice etc.*›; fast ‹*woman*›; ~**seitig 1** *Adv.* **(a)** half-page ‹*advertisement, article, etc.*›; **(b)** (Med.: einseitig) of one side of the body *postpos.;* **2** *adv.* **(a)** ~ **annoncieren** place a half-page advert; **(b)** (Med.: einseitig) ~ **gelähmt** paralysed down one side; ~**starke** *der; adj. Dekl.* (ugs. abwertend) young rowdy; [young] hooligan; ~**stiefel** *der* half-boot; ankle boot; ~**stündig** *Adj.; nicht präd.* half-hour; lasting half an hour *postpos., not ·pred.;* ~**stündlich 1** *Adj.; nicht präd.* half-hourly; **2** *adv.* half-hourly; every half an hour; ~**stürmer** *der* (bes. Fußball) midfield player

halb·tags *Adv.* ▶ 85⌋ ‹*work*› part-time; (morgens/nachmit-tags) ‹*work*› [in the] mornings/afternoons

Halbtags-: ~**arbeit** *die; o. Pl.* part-time job; (morgens/nachmittags) morning/afternoon job; ~**kraft** *die* part-time worker; part-timer

halb-, Halb-: ~**ton** *der; Pl.* ~**töne (a)** (Musik) semitone; halftone (Amer.); **(b)** (Malerei) half-tone;*~**verhung- ert** ⇨ **halb 2 c;** *~**voll** ⇨ **halb 2 a;*~**wach** ⇨ **halb 2 b;** ~**wahrheit** *die* half-truth; ~**wegs** /'~'ve:ks/ *Adv.* to some extent; reasonably ‹*good, clear, etc.*›; ~**welt** *die; o. Pl.* demi-monde; ~**wüchsig** /~vy:ksɪç/ *Adj.* adolescent; teenage; ~**wüchsige** *der/ die; adj. Dekl.* adolescent; teenager; ~**zeit** *die* (bes. Fußball) **(a)** half; **die erste/zweite** ~**zeit** the first/second half; **(b)** (Pause) half-time

Halde /'haldə/ *die;* ~, ~n **(a)** (Bergbau) slag heap; (von Vor-räten) pile; (fig.) mountain; pile; **(b)** (geh.: Hang) slope

half /half/ *1. u. 3. Pers. Sg. Prät. v.* **helfen**

Hälfte /'hɛlftə/ *die;* ~, ~n **(a)** half; **die** ~ **einer Sache** *(Gen.) od. von* **etw.** half [of] sth.; **Studenten bezahlen die** ~ **des Preises** students pay *or* (coll.) are half-price; **er füllte sein Glas nur bis zur** ~: he only half-filled his glass; **über die** ~: more than *or* over half; **um die** ~ **größer/kleiner** half as big/small again; **etw. zur** ~ **zahlen** pay half of sth.; **die gegnerische** ~ (Sport) the opponents' half; **ich habe die** ~ **vergessen** I've forgotten half of it; **meine bessere** ~ (ugs. scherzh.) my better half (coll. joc.); **(b)** (ugs.: Teil) part

*alte Schreibung (vgl. Hinweise auf S. xvi–xvii)

Halfter¹ /'halftɐ/ *der od. das;* ~**s,** ~; *veralt. auch die;* ~, ~**n** halter

Halfter² *die;* ~, ~**n;** *auch das;* ~**s,** ~: holster

Hall /hal/ *der;* ~[e]s, ~e **(a)** (geh.) reverberation; **(b)** (Echo) echo

Halle /'halə/ *die;* ~, ~**n** (Saal, Gebäude) hall; (Fabrik~) shed; (Hotel~, Theater~) lobby; foyer; (Sport~) [sports] hall

halleluja /hale'lu:ja/ *Interj.* hallelujah!; (scherzh.: hurra) hurrah!

Halleluja *das;* ~**s,** ~**s** hallelujah

hallen *itr. V.* **(a)** reverberate; ring; ‹*shot, bell, cry*› ring out; **(b)** (widerhallen) echo

Hallen- indoor ‹*swimming pool, handball, football, hockey, tennis, etc.*›

Hallig /'halɪç/ *die;* ~, ~**en** small low island (*off the North Sea coast of Schleswig-Holstein*)

hallo *Interj.* **(a)** *meist* /'halo/ (am Telefon) hello; ~, **warte doch mal auf mich!** hey! wait for me!; ~, **gehört Ihnen diese Tasche?** excuse me! is this your bag?; **(b)** *meist* /ha'lo:/ (überrascht) hello

Hallo /ha'lo:/ *das;* ~**s,** ~**s** cheering; cheers *pl.;* **mit großem** ~: with loud cheering *or* cheers

Halluzination /halutsina'tsio:n/ *die;* ~, ~**en** hallucination

Halm /halm/ *der;* ~[e]s, ~**e** stalk; stem

Halma /'halma/ *das;* ~**s** halma

Halogen /halo'ge:n/ *das;* ~**s,** ~**e** (Chemie) halogen

Halogen- halogen ‹*lamp, headlamp*›

Hals /hals/ *der;* ~**es, Hälse** **(a)** ▶ 326⌋ neck; **sich** *(Dat.)* **den** ~ **brechen** break one's neck; **jmdm. um den** ~ **fallen** throw *or* fling one's arms around sb.['s neck]; ~ **über Kopf** (ugs.) in a rush *or* hurry: **sich** ~ **über Kopf verlieben** fall head over heels in love; **einen langen** ~ **machen** (ugs.) crane one's neck; **jmdm. den** ~ **brechen** (ugs.) drive sb. to the wall; **das kostete ihn** *od.* **ihm den** ~ (ugs.) that did for him (coll.); **sich jmdm. an den** ~ **werfen** (ugs.) throw oneself at sb.; **jmdm. jmdn. auf den** ~ **schicken** *od.* **hetzen** (ugs.) get *or* put sb. on [to] sb.; **sich** *(Dat.)* **jmdn./etw. auf den** ~ **laden** (ugs.) lumber *or* saddle oneself with sb./sth. (coll.); **jmdm. steht das Wasser bis zum** ~ (ugs.: jmd. hat Schulden) sb. is up to his/her eyes in debt; (ugs.: jmd. hat Schwierigkeiten) sb. is up to his/her neck in it; **(b)** ▶ 326⌋ (Kehle) throat; **aus vollem** ~[e] at the top of one's voice; **er hat es in den falschen** ~ **bekommen** (ugs.: falsch verstanden) he took it the wrong way; (ugs.: sich verschluckt) it went down [his throat] the wrong way; **er kann den** ~ **nicht voll [genug] kriegen** (ugs.) he can't get enough; he's insatiable; **das hängt/wächst mir zum** ~[e] **heraus** (ugs.) I'm sick and tired of it (coll.); **(c)** (einer Flasche) neck; **(d)** (Musik) (einer Note) stem; (eines Saiteninstruments) neck

hals-, Hals-: ~**abschneider** *der* (ugs. abwertend) shark; ~**ausschnitt** *der* neckline; ~**band** *das; Pl.* ~**bänder** **(a)** (für Tiere) collar; **(b)** (Samtband) choker; neck-band; ~**brecherisch** /~brɛçərɪʃ/ *Adj.* dangerous; risky ‹*climb, action, etc.*›; hazardous ‹*road*›; breakneck *attrib.* ‹*speed*›; ~**entzündung** *die* ▶ 329⌋ inflam-mation of the throat; ~**kette** *die* necklace; ~**krause** *die* ruff; ~**-Nasen-Ohren-Arzt** *der* ear, nose, and throat specialist; ~**schlagader** *die* ▶ 326⌋ carotid [ar-tery]; ~**schmerzen** *Pl.* ▶ 329⌋ sore throat *sing.;* [**starke**] ~**schmerzen haben** have a[n extremely] sore throat; ~**starrig** /~ʃtarɪç/ (abwertend) **1** *Adj.* stubborn; obstinate; **2** *adv.* stubbornly; obstinately; ~**starrig- keit** *die* (abwertend) stubbornness; obstinacy; ~**tuch** *das* cravat; (des Cowboys) neckerchief; ~**- und Beinbruch** *Interj.* (scherzh.) good luck!; best of luck!; ~**weh** *das;* (ugs.) ⇨ ~**schmerzen;** ~**wirbel** *der* (Anat.) cervical vertebra

halt¹ /halt/ *Partikel* (südd., österr., schweiz.) ⇨ **eben 3 b**

halt² *Interj.* stop; (Milit.) halt

Halt *der;* ~[e]s, ~**e (a)** *o. Pl.* (Stütze) hold; **seine Füße/ Hände fanden keinen** ~: he couldn't find *or* get a foot-hold/handhold; **den** ~ **verlieren** lose one's hold; **(b)** (An-halten) stop; **ohne** ~: non-stop; without stopping; ~ **machen** stop; **vor jmdm./etw. nicht** ~ **machen** (fig.) not spare sb./sth.

haltbar *Adj.* (a) (nicht verderblich) ∼ **sein** ⟨*food*⟩ keep [well]; **etw.** ∼ **machen** preserve sth.; ∼ **bis 5. 3.** use by 5 March; (b) (nicht verschleißend) hard-wearing, durable ⟨*material, clothes*⟩; (c) (aufrechtzuerhalten) tenable ⟨*hypothesis etc.*⟩; (d) (Ballspiele) stoppable, savable ⟨*shot*⟩

Haltbarkeit *die;* ∼ (a) **Lebensmittel von beschränkter** ∼: perishable foods; (b) (Strapazierfähigkeit) durability; (c) ⇒ **haltbar c:** tenability

Halte-: ∼**griff** *der* (a) [grab] handle; (Riemen) [grab] strap; (b) (Budo, Ringen) pinning hold; ∼**linie** *die* (Verkehrsw.) stop line

halten 1 *unr. tr. V.* (a) (auch Milit.) hold; **etw. an einem Ende** ∼: hold one end of sth.; **sich** (*Dat.*) **den Kopf/den Bauch** ∼: hold one's head/stomach; **jmdn. an** *od.* **bei der Hand** ∼: hold sb.'s hand; hold sb. by the hand; **die Hand vor den Mund** ∼: put one's hand in front of one's mouth; **etw. ins Licht/gegen das Licht** ∼: hold sth. to/ up to the light; (b) (Ballspiele) save ⟨*shot, penalty, etc.*⟩; (c) (bewahren) keep; (beibehalten, aufrechterhalten) keep up ⟨*speed etc.*⟩; maintain ⟨*temperature, equilibrium*⟩; **einen Ton** ∼: stay in tune; (lange an∼) sustain a note; **den Takt** ∼: keep time; **Diät** ∼: keep to a diet; **den Kurs** ∼: stay on course; **diese Behauptung lässt sich nicht** ∼: this statement does not hold up; **Ordnung/Frieden** ∼: keep order/the peace; (d) (erfüllen) keep; **sein Wort/ein Versprechen** ∼: keep one's word/a promise; (e) (besitzen, beschäftigen, beziehen) keep ⟨*chickens etc.*⟩; take ⟨*newspaper, magazine, etc.*⟩; **ein Auto** ∼: run a car; (f) (einschätzen) **jmdn. für reich/ehrlich** ∼: think sb. is *or* consider sb. to be rich/honest; **ich halte es für das Beste/möglich/ meine Pflicht** I think it best/possible/my duty; **viel/ nichts/wenig von jmdm./etw.** ∼: think a lot/nothing/ not think much of sb./sth.; (g) (ab∼, veranstalten) give, make ⟨*speech*⟩; give, hold ⟨*lecture*⟩; **Unterricht** ∼: give lessons; teach; **seinen Mittagsschlaf** ∼: have one's *or* an afternoon nap; (h) (Halt geben) hold up, support ⟨*bridge etc.*⟩; hold back ⟨*curtain, hair*⟩; fasten ⟨*dress*⟩; (i) (zurück∼) keep; **ihn hält hier nichts** there's nothing to keep him here; **es hält dich niemand** nobody's stopping you; (j) (bei sich be∼) **das Wasser** ∼: hold one's water; (k) (nicht aufgeben) **ein Geschäft** *usw.* ∼: keep a business *etc.* going; (l) (behandeln) treat; **jmdn. streng** ∼: be strict with sb., (m) (vorziehen) **es mehr** *od.* **lieber mit jmdm./etw.** ∼: prefer sb./sth.; (n) (verfahren) **es mit einer Sache so/anders** ∼: deal with *or* handle sth. like this/differently; (o) (gestalten) **das Badezimmer ist in Grün ge**∼: the bathroom is decorated in green; **die Rede war sehr allgemein ge**∼: the speech was very general. **2** *unr. intr. V.* (a) (stehen bleiben) stop; (b) (unverändert, an seinem Platz bleiben) last; **der Nagel/das Seil hält nicht mehr länger** the nail/rope won't hold much longer; **diese Freundschaft hält nicht** [lange] (fig.) this friendship won't last [long]; (c) (Sport) save; **er hat gut ge**∼: he made some good saves; (d) (beistehen) **zu jmdm.** ∼: stand *or* stick by sb.; (e) (zielen) an **(auf** + *Akk.* at); (f) (Seemannsspr.) head; **auf etw.** (*Akk.*) ∼: head for *or* towards sth.; (g) (sich beherrschen) **an sich** (*Akk.*) ∼: control oneself; (h) (achten) **auf Ordnung** ∼: attach importance to tidiness. **3** *unr. refl. V.* (a) (sich durchsetzen, behaupten) **wir werden uns nicht länger** ∼ **können** we won't be able to hold out much longer; **das Geschäft wird sich nicht** ∼ **können** the shop won't keep going [for long]; (b) (sich bewähren) **sich gut** ∼: do well; make a good showing; **halte dich tapfer** be brave; (c) (unverändert bleiben) ⟨*weather, flowers, etc.*⟩ last; ⟨*milk, meat, etc.*⟩ keep; (d) (Körperhaltung haben) **sich schlecht/gerade/aufrecht** ∼: hold *or* carry oneself badly/straight/erect; (e) (bleiben) **sich auf den Beinen/ im Sattel** ∼: stay on one's feet/in the saddle; (f) (gehen, bleiben) **sich links/rechts** ∼: keep [to the] left/right; **sich an jmds. Seite** (*Dat.*) **/hinter jmdm.** ∼: stay *or* keep next to/behind sb.; (g) (befolgen) **sich an etw.** (*Akk.*) ∼: keep to *or* follow sth.; (h) (sich wenden) **sich an jmdn.** ∼: ask sb.; (i) (ugs.: jung, gesund bleiben) **sie hat sich gut ge**∼: she is well preserved for her age (coll.)

Halter *der;* ∼**s,** ∼ (a) (Fahrzeug∼) keeper; (b) (Tier∼) owner; (c) (Vorrichtung) holder; (d) (ugs.: Feder∼) pen

Halterin *die;* ∼, ∼**nen** ⇒ **Halter a, b**

Halterung *die;* ∼, ∼**en** support

Halte-: ∼**signal** *das* stop signal; ∼**stelle** *die* stop; ∼**verbot** *das* (a) „∼**verbot**" 'no stopping'; „**absolutes/eingeschränktes** ∼**verbot**" 'no stopping/no

waiting'; (b) (Stelle) no-stopping zone; ∼**verbots·- schild** *das* no-stopping sign

-haltig /-halтıç/, (österr.) **-hältig** /-hɛltıç/ **vitamin**∼/**silber**∼ *usw.* containing vitamins/silver *etc. postpos.*, *not pred.;* **vitamin**∼ **sein** contain vitamins

halt-, Halt-: ∼**los** *Adj.* (a) (labil) **ein** ∼**loser Mensch** a weak character; (b) (unbegründet) unfounded; ∼**losigkeit** *die;* ∼ (a) (Labilität) weakness of character; (b) (mangelnde Begründung) unfoundedness;*∼|**machen** ⇒ **Halt b**

Haltung *die;* ∼, ∼**en** (a) (Körper∼) posture; (Sport) stance; (in der Bewegung) style; ∼ **annehmen** (Milit.) stand to attention; (b) (Pose) manner; (c) (Einstellung) attitude; (d) *o. Pl.* (Fassung) composure; ∼ **zeigen/bewahren** keep one's composure; (e) (Tier∼) keeping

Haltungs·fehler *der* (a) (Med.) bad posture; (b) (Sport) style fault

Halunke /ha'lʊnkə/ *der;* ∼**n,** ∼**n** (a) scoundrel; villain; (b) (scherzh.: Lausbub) rascal; scamp

Hamburg /'hambʊrk/ *(das);* ∼**s** ▶ 490 | Hamburg

Hamburger¹ ▶ 490 | **1** *der;* ∼**s,** ∼: native of Hamburg; (Einwohner) inhabitant of Hamburg; **Schmidt ist** ∼: Schmidt comes from Hamburg. **2** *indekl. Adj.* Hamburg; **der** ∼ **Hafen** the harbour at Hamburg; Hamburg harbour

Hamburger² *der;* ∼**s,** ∼ (Frikadelle) hamburger

hamburgisch *Adj.* Hamburg *attrib.;* of Hamburg *postpos.*

hämisch /'hɛːmıʃ/ **1** *Adj.* malicious. **2** *adv.* maliciously

Hammel /'haml/ *der;* ∼**s,** ∼ (a) wether; (b) (Fleisch) mutton; (c) (salopp abwertend) oaf; dolt

Hammel-: ∼**bein** *das:* **jmdm. die** ∼**beine lang ziehen** (ugs.) give sb. a good telling-off; ∼**fleisch** *das* mutton; ∼**herde** *die* (salopp abwertend) flock of sheep; ∼**keule** *die* leg of mutton; ∼**sprung** *der* (Parl.) division

Hammer /'hame/ *der;* ∼**s, Hämmer** /'hɛme/ (a) hammer; (Holz∼) mallet; ∼ **und Sichel** hammer and sickle; **unter den** ∼ **kommen** come under the hammer; (b) (Technik) tup; ram; (c) (Musik) hammer; (d) (Leichtathletik) hammer; (e) (ugs.: Fehler) bad mistake; (in einor Aufgabe) howler (coll.); **ein dicker** ∼: an awful blunder

Hämmerchen /'hɛmeçən/ *das;* ∼**s,** ∼: [small] hammer

hämmern /'hɛmen/ **1** *itr. V.* (a) hammer; **es hämmert** sb. is hammering; (b) (schlagen) hammer; (mit der Faust) hammer; pound; **gegen die Wand/die Tür** ∼: hammer/ pound on the wall/door; (c) (klopfen) pound; ⟨*pulse*⟩ race. **2** *tr. V.* (a) hammer; beat, hammer ⟨*tin, silver, etc.*⟩; beat ⟨*jewellery*⟩; (b) (ugs.) hammer *or* pound out ⟨*melody etc.*⟩; (c) (ugs.: einprägen) **jmdm. etw. in den Schädel** ∼: hammer *or* knock sth. into sb.'s head (coll.)

Hammer-: ∼**werfen** *das* (Leichtathletik) throwing the hammer; **er ist Weltmeister im** ∼**werfen** he's world champion in the hammer; ∼**werfer** *der;* ∼**s,** ∼ (Leichtathletik) hammer-thrower; ∼**wurf** *der* (Leichtathletik) ⇒ ∼**werfen**

Hammond·orgel /'hæmənd-/ *die* Hammond organ

Hämorrhoiden /hɛmɔro'iːdn/ *Pl.* (Med.) haemorrhoids; piles

Hampel·mann /'hampl-/ *der;* ∼[e]s, **Hampel·männer** a) jumping jack; (b) (ugs. abwertend) puppet

hampeln *itr. V.* (ugs.) jump about

Hamster /'hamste/ *der;* ∼**s,** ∼: hamster

Hamsterer *der;* ∼**s,** ∼, **Hamstererin** *die;* ∼, ∼**nen** (ugs.) hoarder

Hamster-: ∼**fahrt** *die* foraging trip; **auf** ∼**fahrt gehen** go foraging; ∼**kauf** *der* panic-buying *no pl.;* ∼**käufe machen** panic-buy

hamstern *tr., itr. V.* (horten) hoard; (Hamsterkäufe machen) panic-buy

Hand /hant/ *die;* ∼, **Hände** /'hɛndə/ (a) ▶ 326 | hand; **eine** ∼ **voll** a handful; **mit der rechten/linken** ∼: with one's right/left hand; **jmdm. die** ∼ **geben** *od.* (geh.) **reichen** shake sb.'s hand; shake sb. by the hand; **jmdm. die** ∼ **drücken/schütteln** press/shake sb.'s hand; **eine** ∼ **frei haben** have a free hand; **Hände hoch!** hands up!; **jmdn. an die** *od.* (geh.) **bei der** ∼ **nehmen** take sb. by the hand; **jmdm. etw. aus der** ∼ **nehmen** take sth. out of sb.'s hand/hands; **etw. aus der** ∼ **legen** put sth. down;

jmdm. aus der ∼ lesen read sb.'s hand or palm; etw. in die/zur ∼ nehmen pick sth. up; etw. in der ∼/den Händen haben od. (geh.) halten have got or hold sth. in one's hand/hands; in die Hände klatschen clap one's hands; mit Händen und Füßen reden use gestures to make oneself understood; etw. mit der ∼ schreiben/nähen write/sew sth. by hand; von ∼: by hand; ∼ in ∼ gehen go or walk hand-in-hand; jmdm. etw. in die ∼ versprechen promise sb. sth. faithfully; (b) o. Pl. (Fußball) handball; (c) (in Wendungen) was hältst du davon – ∼ aufs Herz! what do you think? – be honest; eine ∼ wäscht die andere you scratch my back and I'll scratch yours; jmdm. sind die Hände gebunden sb.'s hands are tied; ∼ und Fuß/weder ∼ noch Fuß haben (ugs.) make sense/no sense; [bei etw. selbst mit] ∼ anlegen lend a hand [with sth.]; die od. seine ∼ aufhalten (ugs.) hold out one's hand; letzte ∼ an etw. (Akk.) legen put the finishing touches pl. to sth.; die (Dat.) od. (geh.) alle od. beide Hände damit voll haben, etw. zu tun (ugs.) have one's hands full doing sth.; die Hände in den Schoß legen sit back and do nothing; bei etw. die od. seine Hände [mit] im Spiel haben have a hand in sth.; die Hände über dem Kopf zusammenschlagen (ugs.) throw up one's hands in horror; zwei linke Hände haben (ugs.) have two left hands (coll.); eine lockere od. lose ∼ haben (ugs.) hit out at the slightest provocation; eine glückliche ∼ bei etw. haben have a feel for the right choice in sth.; linker/rechter ∼: on or to the left/right; [klar] auf der ∼ liegen (ugs.) be obvious; jmdn. auf Händen tragen lavish every kind of care and attention on sb.; ein Auto/Möbel aus erster ∼: a car/furniture which has/had had one [previous] owner; etw. aus erster ∼ wissen know sth. at first hand; have first-hand knowledge of sth.; Kleidung aus zweiter ∼: second-hand clothes pl.; jmdm. aus der ∼ fressen eat out of sb.'s hand (fig.); etw. aus der ∼ geben (weggeben) let sth. out of one's hands; (aufgeben) give sth. up; jmdm. etw. aus der ∼ nehmen relieve sb. of sth.; etw. bei der ∼ haben (greifbar haben) have sth. handy; (parat haben) have sth. ready; mit etw. schnell od. rasch bei der ∼ sein (ugs.) be ready [with sth.]; ∼ in ∼ arbeiten work hand in hand; mit etw. ∼ in ∼ gehen go hand in hand with sth.; hinter vorgehaltener ∼: off the record; in die Hände spucken spit on one's hands; (fig. ugs.) roll up one's sleeves (fig.); jmdm./etw. in die ∼ od. Hände bekommen lay or get one's hands on sb./get one's hands on sth.; jmdm. in die Hände fallen fall into sb.'s hands; jmdn. in der ∼ haben have or hold sb. in the palm of one's hand; etw. in die ∼ nehmen take sth. in hand; in jmds. ∼ (Dat.) sein od. (geh.) liegen be in sb.'s hands; in sicheren od. guten Händen sein be in safe or good hands; sich mit Händen und Füßen gegen etw. sträuben od. wehren (ugs.) fight tooth and nail against sth.; mit leeren Händen emptyhanded; das Geld mit vollen Händen ausgeben spend money like water; um jmds. ∼ anhalten od. bitten (geh. veralt.) ask for sb.'s hand [in marriage]; unter der ∼ (fig.) on the quiet; etw. unter der ∼ erfahren hear sth. on the grapevine; das geht ihm gut/leicht von der ∼: he finds that no trouble; etw. von langer ∼ vorbereiten plan sth. well in advance; die Nachteile/seine Argumente sind nicht von der ∼ zu weisen the disadvantages cannot be denied/his arguments cannot [simply] be dismissed; von der ∼ in den Mund leben live from hand to mouth; jmdm. zur ∼ gehen lend sb. a hand; zu Händen [von] Herrn Müller for the attention of Herr Müller; s. auch öffentlich 1; (d) an ∼ ⇒ anhand

Hand·arbeit die (a) o. Pl. handicraft; craft work; etw. in ∼ herstellen make sth. by hand; (b) (Gegenstand) hand-made article; (c) (Arbeit aus Stoff, Wolle usw.) sie macht gerne ∼en she likes doing needlework/knitting/crocheting; (d) o. Pl. (ugs.: ∼arbeitsunterricht) needlework

hand·arbeiten itr. V. do needlework

Handarbeits-: ∼geschäft das wool and needlework shop; ∼korb der workbasket; ∼lehrerin die needlework teacher

*alte Schreibung (vgl. Hinweise auf S. xvi–xvii)

hand-, Hand-: ∼auflegen das; ∼s (bes. Rel.) laying on or imposition of hands; ∼ball der handball; ∼ballen der ball of the thumb; ∼bedienung die; o. Pl. ⇒ ∼betrieb; ∼besen der brush; ∼betrieb der; o. Pl. manual operation; mit ∼betrieb manually operated or hand-operated; ∼bewegung die (a) movement of the hand; (b) (Geste) gesture; ∼bibliothek die (a) reference library; (b) (∼apparat) set of reference books; reference collection; ∼bohrer der (mit Kurbel) hand-drill; (zum Vorbohren) gimlet; ∼bohr·maschine die hand-drill; (elektrisch) drill; ∼brause die shower handset; ∼breit Adj. ⟨seam etc.⟩ a few inches wide; ∼breit die; ∼, ∼: eine/zwei ∼breit a few/several inches; ∼bremse die handbrake; ∼buch das handbook; (technisches ∼buch) manual

Händchen /'hɛntçən/ das; ∼s, ∼: [little] hand; ∼ halten (ugs. scherzh.) hold hands

Hand·creme die hand cream

Hände ⇒ Hand

Hände-: ∼druck der; Pl. ∼drücke handshake; ∼klatschen das; ∼s clapping; applause

Handel¹ /'handḷ/ der; ∼s (a) (Wirtschaft) trade; commerce; (b) (Handeln) trade; der ∼ mit Waffen/Drogen the traffic in arms/drugs; ∼ treibende Nationen trading nations; (c) (Geschäftsverkehr) trade; das ist [nicht mehr] im ∼: it is [no longer] on the market; (d) (Vereinbarung) deal

Handel² der; ∼s, Händel /'hɛndḷ/; meist Pl. (geh.) Händel suchen [try to] pick a quarrel

Hand·elfmeter der (Fußball) penalty for handball

handeln 1 itr. V. (a) trade; deal; mit od. in Gemüse/Gebrauchtwagen ∼: deal in vegetables/second-hand cars; (b) (feilschen) haggle; bargain; um den Preis ∼: haggle over the price; mit ihm lässt sich [nicht] ∼: he is [not] open to negotiation; (c) (eingreifen) act; auf Befehl/aus Überzeugung ∼: act on orders/out of conviction; im Affekt/in Notwehr ∼: act in the heat of the moment/in self-defence; (d) (verfahren) act; eigenmächtig/richtig/fahrlässig ∼: act on one's own authority/correctly/carelessly; (e) (sich verhalten) behave; (f) von etw. od. über etw. (Akk.) ∼ ⟨book, film, etc.⟩ be about or deal with sth. 2 refl. V. (unpers.) bei dem Besucher handelte es sich um einen entfernten Verwandten the visitor was a distant relative; es handelt sich um ...: it is a matter of ...; (es dreht sich um) it's about or it concerns ... 3 tr. V. sell (für at, for); diese Papiere werden nicht an der Börse gehandelt these securities are not traded on the stock exchange

Handeln das; ∼s (a) (das Feilschen) haggling; bargaining; (b) (das Eingreifen) action; (c) (Verhalten) action[s pl.]

handels-, Handels-: ∼abkommen das trade agreement; ∼bank die merchant bank; ∼beziehungen Pl. trade relations; ∼bilanz die (a) (eines Betriebes) balance sheet; (b) (eines Staates) balance of trade; eine aktive/passive ∼bilanz a balance of trade surplus/deficit; ∼boykott der trade boycott; ∼einig, ∼eins in mit jmdm. ∼einig od. ∼eins werden/sein agree/have agreed terms or come/have come to an agreement with sb.; ∼firma die [business or commercial] firm; business concern; ∼flagge die merchant flag; ∼flotte die merchant fleet; ∼gesellschaft die company; offene ∼gesellschaft general partnership; ∼gesetz·buch das; o. Pl. commercial code; ∼größe die (Kaufmannsspr.) commercial size; ∼hafen der commercial or trading port; ∼kammer die ⇒ Industrie- und ∼kammer; ∼kette die (Kaufmannsspr.) (a) (Weg der Ware) channel of distribution; (b) (Zusammenschluss von Händlern) voluntary chain; ∼klasse die grade; ∼macht die trading power; ∼marine die merchant navy; ∼marke die trade mark; ∼minister der minister of trade; (in UK) Secretary of State for Trade; Trade Secretary (coll.); ∼ministerium das ministry of trade; (in UK) Department of Trade; ∼mission die trade mission; ∼name der trade or business name; ∼niederlassung die branch; ∼organisation die (a) trading organization; (b) (DDR) [state-owned] commercial concern running shops, hotels, etc.; ∼partner der trading partner; ∼politik die trade or commercial policy; ∼recht das; o. Pl.

commercial law; ~**rechtlich 1** *Adj.; nicht präd.* relating to commercial law *postpos.; ‹offence›* against commercial law; **2** *adv.* from the point of view of commercial law; ~**register** *das* register of companies; ~**reisende** *der/ die; adj. Dekl.* ⇨ ~**vertreter**; ~**schiff** *das* merchant ship; trading vessel; ~**schifffahrt** *die* merchant shipping; (Schiffsverkehr) movement of merchant shipping; ~**schranke** *die; meist Pl.* trade barrier; ~**schule** *die* commercial college; ~**spanne** *die* (Kaufmannsspr.) margin; ~**straße** *die* (hist.) trade route; ~**üblich** *Adj.* ~**übliche Größen** standard [commercial] sizes; ~**unternehmen** *das* trading concern; ~**verbindung** *die; meist Pl.* trade link; ~**vertreter** *der* [sales] representative; travelling salesmann/saleswoman; commercial traveller; ~**vertretung** *die* ⇨ ~**mission**; ~**volumen** *das* (Wirtsch.) volume of trade; ~**ware** *die* commodity; ~**ware** (Postw.) 'no commercial value'; ~**wert** *der* (Kaufmannsspr.) commercial value; ~**zentrum** *das* trading or commercial centre

***handel·treibend** ⇨ Handel b

hände-, Hände-: ~**ringend** *Adv.* (a) wringing one's hands; (b) (ugs.: dringend) ~**ringend nach jmdm./ etw. suchen** search desperately for sb./sth.; ~**schütteln** *das;* ~s hand-shaking *no pl.;* ~**waschen** *das;* ~s washing *no art.* one's hands

hand-, Hand-: ~**feger** *der* brush; ~**fest** *Adj.* (a) (kräftig) robust; sturdy; (b) (deftig) substantial ‹*meal etc.*›; **etwas Handfestes** something substantial; (c) (gewichtig) solid, tangible ‹*proof*›; concrete ‹*suggestion*›; full-blooded, violent ‹*row*›; complete ‹*lie*›; well-founded ‹*argument*›; real, thorough ‹*beating*›; ~**fläche** *die* ▶ 326 | palm [of one's/the hand]; flat of one's/the hand; ~**gearbeitet** *Adj.* hand-made ‹*furniture, jewellery, etc.*›; ~**geld** *das* lump sum [payment]; ~**gelenk** *das* ▶ 326 | wrist; **ein loses od. lockeres** ~**gelenk haben** (ugs.) lash out at the slightest provocation; **etw. aus dem** ~**gelenk schütteln** (ugs.) do sth. just like that (coll.); ~**gemacht** *Adj.* hand-made; ~**gemenge** *das* fight; ~**gepäck** *das* hand baggage; ~**geschöpft** *Adj.* handmade; ~**geschrieben** *Adj.* handwritten; ~**gesteuert** *Adj.* manually operated; manually controlled ‹*vehicle*›; ~**gewebt** *Adj.* hand-woven; ~**granate** *die* hand grenade; ~**greiflich** *Adj.* (a) (tätlich) **eine** ~**greifliche Auseinandersetzung** a scuffle; ~**greiflich werden** start using one's fists; (b) tangible ‹*success, advantage, proof, etc.*›; palpable ‹*contradiction, error*›; obvious ‹*fact*›; ~**greiflichkeit** *die;* ~, ~**en: es kam zu** ~**greiflichkeiten** a fight broke out; ~**griff** *der* (a) **ein falscher** ~**griff** a false move; **mit einem** ~**griff/wenigen** ~**griffen** in one movement/without much trouble; (schnell) in no time at all/ next to no time; **jeder** ~**griff muss sitzen** every movement must be exactly right; (b) (am Koffer, an einem Werkzeug) handle; ~**habe** *die;* ~, ~**n: eine [rechtliche]** ~**habe [gegen jmdn.]** a legal handle [against sb.]; ~**haben** *tr. V.* (a) handle; operate ‹*machine; device*›; (b) (praktizieren) implement ‹*law etc.*›; ~**habung** *die;* ~, ~**en** (a) handling; (eines Gerätes, einer Maschine) operation; (b) (Durchführung) implementation

Handikap /'hɛndɪkɛp/ *das;* ~s, ~s (auch Sport) handicap

hand-, Hand-: ~**kante** *die* edge of the/one's hand; **Handkanten·schlag** *der* chop; ~**käse** *der* (landsch.) small, *hand-formed curd cheese;* ~**käse mit Musik** (landsch.) marinaded hand-formed curd cheese; ~**koffer** *der* [small] suitcase; ~**koloriert** *Adj.* hand-coloured; ~**kuss,** *~**kuß** *der* kiss on sb.'s hand; **etw. mit** ~**kuss tun** (fig. ugs.) do sth. with [the greatest of] pleasure; ~**langer** *der;* ~s, ~ (a) (ungelernter Arbeiter) labourer; (abwertend) lackey; general dogsbody; (b) (abwertend: Büttel) henchman; ~**lauf** *der* handrail

Händler /'hɛndlɐ/ *der;* ~s, ~, **Händlerin** *die;* ~, ~**nen** trader; tradesman/tradeswoman; **ein fliegender** ~: a hawker or street-trader

handlich /'hantlɪç/ **1** *Adj.* handy; easily carried ‹*parcel, suitcase*›. **2** *adv.* ~ **verpackt** wrapped as a manageable parcel

Handlichkeit *die;* ~: handiness; (eines Buches) handy size

Handlung *die;* ~, ~**en** (a) (Vorgehen) action; (Tat) act; **eine symbolische/feierliche** ~: a symbolic/ceremonial act; (b) (Fabel) plot; **Einheit der** ~: unity of action

handlungs-, Handlungs-: ~**fähig** *Adj.* able to act *pred.;* working *attrib.* ‹*majority*›; ~**fähigkeit** *die; o. Pl.* ability to act; (Rechtsw.) employee (*on the business side of a firm*); ~**spiel·raum** *der* scope for action; ~**unfähig** *Adj.* (a) unable to act *pred.;* (b) (Rechtsw.) unable to act on one's own account *pred.;* ~**unfähigkeit** *die* inability to act; ~**weise** *die* behaviour; conduct

hand-, Hand-: ~**presse** *die* hand-press; ~**puppe** *die* glove or hand puppet; ~**puppen·spiel** *das* glove puppet or hand puppet show; ~**rücken** *der* ▶ 326 | the back of the/one's hand; ~**säge** *die* hand-saw; ~**schelle** *die* handcuff; jmdm. ~**schellen anlegen** handcuff sb.; put handcuffs on sb.; ~**schlag** *der* (a) handshake; **etw. durch einen** ~**schlag besiegeln** shake hands on sth.; (b) **in er tat keinen** ~**schlag** (ugs.) he did not lift a finger; ~**schrift** *die* (a) handwriting; (b) (Ausdrucksweise) personal style; (c) (Text) manuscript; ~**schriftlich 1** *Adj.* handwritten; ~**schriftliche Quellen** manuscript sources; **2** *adv.* by hand; ~**schuh** *der* glove; ~**schuh·fach** *das* glove compartment or box; ~**signiert** *Adj.* signed; ~**spiegel** *der* hand-mirror; ~**spiel** *das* (Fußball) handball; ~**stand** *der* (Turnen) handstand; **einen** ~**stand machen** do a handstand; ~**stand·überschlag** *der* (Turnen) handspring; ~**steuerung** *die* (a) *o. Pl.* manual operation or control; (b) (Apparatur) manual control; ~**streich** *der* (bes. Milit.) lightning or surprise attack; ~**tasche** *die* handbag; ~**teller** *der* palm [of the/one's hand]; ~**tuch** *das; Pl.* -tücher towel; **das** ~**tuch werfen** (Boxen, fig.) throw in the towel; ~**tuch·halter** *der* towel rail; ~**umdrehen: im** ~**umdrehen** in no time at all; *~**voll** ⇨ Hand a; ~**waffe** *die* hand weapon; ~**wagen** *der* handcart; ~**warm 1** *Adj.* hand-hot; **2** *adv.* **etw.** ~**warm waschen** wash sth. in hand-hot water

Handwerk *das* (a) craft; (als Beruf) trade; **ein** ~ **ausüben/betreiben** carry on/ply a trade; (b) (Beruf) **sein** ~ **verstehen/beherrschen** know one's job; ‹*tradesman*› know/be master of one's trade; **jmdm. das** ~ **legen** put a stop to sb.'s activities; **jmdm. ins** ~ **pfuschen** try to do sb.'s job for him/her; (c) *o. Pl.* (Berufsstand) craft professions *pl.*

Handwerker *der;* ~**s,** ~: tradesman; craftsman; **die** ~ **im Haus haben** have the workmen in

handwerklich *Adj.; nicht präd.* (a) ‹*training, skill, ability*› as a craftsman; **ein** ~**er Beruf** a [skilled] trade; (b) (fig.) technical

Handwerks-: ~**betrieb** *der* workshop; ~**bursche** *der* (veralt.) travelling journeyman (arch.); ~**kammer** *die* Chamber of Crafts; ~**zeug** *das* tools *pl.;* (fig.) tools *pl.* of the trade

Hand-: ~**wörter·buch** *das* concise dictionary; ~**zeichen** *das* (a) sign [with one's hand]; (eines Autofahrers) hand signal; (b) (Abstimmung) show of hands; **durch** ~**zeichen** by a show of hands; ~**zettel** *der* handbill; leaflet

Handy /'hɛndi/ *das;* ~s, ~s mobile [phone]

hanebüchen /'ha:nəby:çn̩/ *Adj.* outrageous

Hanf /hanf/ *der;* ~[e]s (a) hemp; (b) (Samen) hempseed

Hänfling /'hɛnflɪŋ/ *der;* ~s, ~e (a) (Vogel) linnet; (b) (abwertend) weakling

Hang /haŋ/ *der;* ~[e]s, **Hänge** /'hɛŋə/ (a) (Berg~) slope; hillside/mountainside; (Ski~) slope; **das Haus am** ~: the house on the hillside; (b) (Neigung) tendency; **einen** ~ **zum Träumen/Lügen usw. haben** have a tendency to dream/lie etc.; (c) (Turnen) hang

Hangar /'haŋga:ɐ̯/ *der;* ~s, ~s hangar

Hänge-: ~**backe** *die* flabby cheek; ~**bauch** *der* paunch; ~**brücke** *die* suspension bridge; ~**brust** *die,* ~**busen** *der* sagging breasts *pl.;* ~**lampe** *die* pendant-light; drop-light

hangeln /'haŋl̩n/ *itr., refl. V.; meist mit sein* make one's way hand over hand; **[sich] an einem Seil über die**

Schlucht ∼: make one's way hand over hand along a rope over the ravine

Hänge·matte *die* hammock

hängen[1] /'hɛŋən/ *unr. itr. V.; südd., österr., schweiz. mit sein* **(a)** hang; **die Bilder** ∼ **[schon]** the pictures are [already] up; **der Schrank hängt voller Kleider** the wardrobe is full of clothes; **der Weihnachtsbaum hängt voller Süßigkeiten** the Christmas tree is laden with sweets; **an einem Faden** ∼: be hanging by a thread; **etw.** ∼ **lassen** (vergessen) leave sth. behind; **(b)** (sich festhalten) hang, dangle **(an** + *Dat.* from); **jmdm. am Hals** ∼: hang round sb.'s neck; *s. auch* **Rockzipfel; (c)** (erhängt werden) hang; be hanged; **(d)** (an einem Fahrzeug) be hitched *or* attached **(an** + *Dat.* to); **(e)** (herab∼) hang down; **bis auf den Boden** ∼: hang down to the ground; **die Beine ins Wasser** ∼ **lassen** let one's legs dangle in the water; **sich** ∼ **lassen** (fig.) let oneself go; **lass dich nicht so** ∼**!** (fig.) [you must] pull yourself together!; **(f)** (unordentlich sitzen) **im Sessel** ∼ (erschöpft, betrunken) be *or* sit slumped in one's/ the chair; (flegelhaft) lounge in one's/the chair; **(g)** (geh.: schweben, auch fig.) hang **(über** + *Dat.* over); **jmdn.** ∼ **lassen** (fig. ugs.: jmdm. nicht helfen) let sb. down; **(h)** (haften) cling, stick **(an** + *Dat.* to); **an/auf etw.** *(Dat.)* ∼ **bleiben** stick to sth.; **von dem Vortrag blieb [bei ihm] nicht viel** ∼ (fig.) not much of the lecture stuck (coll.); **ein Verdacht bleibt an ihr** ∼ (fig.) suspicion rests on her; **(i)** (fest∼) **sie hing mit dem Rock am Zaun/in der Fahrradkette** her skirt was caught on the fence/in the bicycle chain; **[mit dem Ärmel** *usw.***] an/in etw.** *(Dat.)* ∼ **bleiben** get one's sleeve *etc.* caught on/in sth.; **(j)** (ugs.: sich aufhalten, sein) hang around (coll.); **[schon wieder] am Telefon/vorm Fernseher** ∼: be on the telephone [again]/be in front of the television [again]; **(k)** (sich nicht trennen wollen) **an jmdm./etw.** ∼: be very attached to sb./ sth.; **(l)** (sich neigen) lean; **(m)** (ugs.: angeschlossen sein) **an etw.** *(Dat.)* ∼: be on sth.; **(n)** (ugs.: nicht weiterkommen) be stuck; **(o)** (ugs.: zurück sein) be behind; ∼ **bleiben** (ugs.: verweilen) get stuck (coll.); (ugs.: nicht versetzt werden) stay down; have to repeat a year; **(p)** (entschieden werden) **an/bei jmdm./etw.** ∼: depend on sb./sth.

hängen[2] **1** *tr. V.* **(a)** etw. in/über etw. *(Akk.)* ∼: hang sth. in/over sth.; **etw. an/auf etw.** *(Akk.)* ∼: hang sth. on sth.; **(b)** (befestigen) hitch up **(an** + *Akk.* to); couple on ‹*railway carriage, trailer, etc.*› **(an** + *Akk.* to); **(c)** (∼ lassen) hang; **die Beine ins Wasser** ∼: let one's legs dangle in the water; **(d)** (er∼) hang; **Tod durch Hängen** death by hanging; **mit Hängen und Würgen** by the skin of one's teeth; **(e)** (ugs.: aufwenden) **an/in etw.** *(Akk.)* ∼: put ‹*work, time, money*› into sth.; spend ‹*time, money*› on sth.; **(f)** (ugs.: anschließen) **jmdn./etw. an etw.** *(Akk.)* ∼: put sb./sth. on sth.; *s. auch* **Glocke a; Nagel b. 2** *refl. V.* **(a)** (ergreifen) **sich an etw.** *(Akk.)* ∼: hang on to sth.; **sich jmdm. an den Hals** ∼: cling to sb.'s neck; **sich ans Telefon** ∼ (fig. ugs.) get on the telephone; **(b)** (sich festsetzen) ‹*smell*› cling **(an** + *Akk.* to); ‹*burr, hairs, etc.*› cling, stick **(an** + *Akk.* to); **(c)** (anschließen) **sich an jmdn.** ∼: attach oneself to sb.; latch on to sb. (coll.); **(d)** (verfolgen) **sich an jmdn./ein Auto** ∼: follow *or* (coll.) tail sb./a car

***hängen|bleiben** ⇨ **hängen**[1] h, i, n

hängend *Adj.* hanging; **mit** ∼**em Kopf** with head hanging

***hängen|lassen** ⇨ **hängen**[1] a, e, g

Hänge-: ∼**ohr** *das* lop ear; ∼**partie** *die* (Schach) adjourned game; ∼**schrank** *der* wall cupboard

Hannover /ha'noːfɐ/ *(das);* ∼**s** ▶ 490 Hanover

Hannoveraner ▶ 490 **1** *der;* ∼**s,** ∼ Hanoverian. **2** *indekl. Adj.* Hanover

Hans /hans/ *der;* ∼, **Hänse** /'hɛnzə/ ∼ **im Glück** lucky devil; (Märchenfigur) Hans in Luck

Hansaplast ⓦ /hanza'plast/ *das;* ∼**[e]s** sticking plaster; Elastoplast (P)

Hans·dampf *der;* ∼**[e]s,** ∼**e:** ∼ **[in allen Gassen]** Jack of all trades

Hanse /'hanzə/ *die;* ∼ (hist.) Hanse; Hanseatic league

Hanseat /hanze'aːt/ *der;* ∼**en,** ∼**en (a)** citizen of a Hanseatic city; **(b)** (hist.) member of the Hanseatic League

hanseatisch *Adj.* Hanseatic

Hänselei *die;* ∼**:** teasing

hänseln /'hɛnzl̩n/ *tr. V.* tease

Hanse·stadt *die* Hanseatic city

Hans·wurst *der;* ∼**[e]s,** ∼**e (a)** (dummer Mensch) clown; **(b)** (Theater) fool; hanswurst

Hantel /'hantl̩/ *die;* ∼, ∼**n** (Sport) (kurz) dumb-bell; (lang) barbell

hantieren /han'tiːrən/ *itr. V.* be busy

hapern /'haːpɐn/ *itr. V. (unpers.)* **(a)** (fehlen) **es hapert bei jmdm. an etw.** sb. is short of sth.; **(b)** (nicht klappen) **es hapert mit etw.** there's a problem with sth.

Häppchen /'hɛpçən/ *das;* ∼**s,** ∼ [small] morsel; **(b)** (Appetithappen) canapé

Happen /'hapn̩/ *der;* ∼**s,** ∼**:** morsel; **einen** ∼ **essen** have a bite to eat; **ein fetter** ∼ (fig.) a real plum

happig /'hapɪç/ *Adj.* (ugs.) ∼**e Preise** fancy prices (coll.)

Happyend, Happy-End /'hɛpi'|ɛnt/ *das;* ∼**[s],** ∼**s** happy ending

Härchen /'hɛːɐçən/ *das;* ∼**s,** ∼**:** little *or* tiny hair

Hardware /'haːdwɛɐ/ *die;* ∼, ∼**s** (DV) hardware

Harem /'haːrɛm/ *der;* ∼**s,** ∼**s** (auch ugs. scherzh.) harem

Harems-: ∼**dame** *die* lady of the harem; ∼**wächter** *der* guardian of the harem

Häretiker /hɛ're:tikɐ/ *der;* ∼**s,** ∼**:** heretic

Harfe /'harfə/ *die;* ∼, ∼**n** harp

Harke /'harkə/ *die;* ∼, ∼**n** rake; **jmdm. zeigen, was eine** ∼ **ist** (fig. salopp) give sb. what for (sl.)

harken *tr. V.* rake

Harlekin /'harlekiːn/ *der;* ∼**s,** ∼**e** harlequin

härmen /'hɛrmən/ *refl. V.* (geh.) grieve **(um** over)

harm·los 1 *Adj.* **(a)** harmless; slight ‹*injury, cold, etc.*›; mild ‹*illness*›; safe ‹*medicine, bend, road, etc.*›; **eine** ∼**e Grippe** a mild bout of flu; **(b)** (arglos) innocent; harmless ‹*fun, pastime, etc.*›. **2** *adv.* **(a)** harmlessly; **(b)** (arglos) innocently; **ganz** ∼ **tun** act innocent

Harmlosigkeit *die;* ∼ **(a)** harmlessness; (einer Krankheit) mildness; (eines Medikaments) safety; **(b)** (Arglosigkeit) innocence

Harmonie /harmo'niː/ *die;* ∼, ∼**n** (auch fig.) harmony

Harmonie·lehre *die; o. Pl.* theory of harmony

harmonieren *itr. V.* harmonize; go together; match; **mit etw.** ∼: harmonize *or* go together with sth.

Harmonik /har'moːnɪk/ *die;* ∼**:** harmony

Harmonika /har'moːnika/ *die;* ∼, ∼**s** *od.* **Harmoniken** harmonica

harmonisch 1 *Adj.* **(a)** (Musik) harmonic ‹*tone, minor*›; **(b)** (wohlklingend, übereinstimmend) harmonious; **(c)** (Math.) ∼**e Teilung** harmonic division. **2** *adv.* **(a)** (Musik) harmonically; **(b)** (wohlklingend, übereinstimmend) harmoniously; ∼ **zusammenleben** live together in harmony

harmonisieren *tr. V.* **(a)** (Musik) harmonize; **(b)** (in Einklang bringen) coordinate

Harmonium /har'moːniʊm/ *das;* ∼**s, Harmonien** harmonium

Harn /harn/ *der;* ∼**[e]s,** ∼**e** (Med.) urine; ∼ **lassen** (ugs.) pass water; urinate

Harn-: ∼**blase** *die* bladder; ∼**drang** *der* desire to urinate *or* pass water

Harnisch /'harnɪʃ/ *der;* ∼**s,** ∼**e (a)** armour; **(b)** jmdn. **in** ∼ **bringen** get sb.'s hackles up; make sb. see red

harn·treibend *Adj.* diuretic

Harpune /har'puːnə/ *die;* ∼, ∼**n** harpoon

Harpunier /harpu'niːɐ/ *der;* ∼**s,** ∼**e** harpooner

harpunieren 1 *tr. V.* harpoon. **2** *itr. V.* throw/fire the harpoon

harren /'harən/ *itr. V.* (geh.) **jmds./einer Sache** ∼**:** wait for *or* await sb./sth.; (fig.) await sb./sth.; **der Dinge** ∼**, die da kommen sollen** wait and see what happens

harsch /harʃ/ **1** *Adj.* **(a)** (vereist) crusted ‹*snow*›; **(b)** (barsch) harsh. **2** *adv.* harshly

---

Harsch *der;* ~[e]s crusted *or* hard snow

hart /hart/; **härter** /'hɛrtɐ/, **härtest**... /'hɛrtəst.../ **1** *Adj.* **(a)** hard; ~e/~ **gekochte Eier** hard-boiled eggs; **Eier** ~ **kochen** hard-boil eggs; ~ **gefroren** frozen solid; *s. auch* **Nuss a**; **(b)** (abgehärtet) tough; ~ **im Nehmen sein** (Schläge ertragen können) be able to take a punch; (Enttäuschungen ertragen können) be able to take the rough with the smooth; **(c)** (schwer erträglich) hard ⟨*work, life, fate, lot, times*⟩; tough ⟨*childhood, situation, job*⟩; harsh ⟨*reality, truth*⟩; **ein** ~**er Schlag für jmdn. sein** be a heavy *or* severe blow for sb.; **(d)** (streng) severe, harsh ⟨*penalty, punishment, judgement*⟩; tough ⟨*measure, law, course*⟩; harsh ⟨*treatment*⟩; severe, hard ⟨*features*⟩; **(e)** (heftig) hard, violent ⟨*impact, jolt*⟩; heavy ⟨*fall*⟩; **(f)** (rau, scharf) rough ⟨*game, opponent*⟩; hard, severe ⟨*winter, frost*⟩; harsh ⟨*accent, contrast*⟩. **2** *adv.* **(a)** (mühevoll) ⟨*work*⟩ hard; **es kommt mich** ~ **an** it is hard for me; **(b)** (streng) severely; harshly; ~ **durchgreifen** take tough measures; **jmdn.** ~ **anfassen** be tough with sb.; **(c)** (heftig) **jmdm.** ~ **zusetzen, jmdn.** ~ **bedrängen** press sb. hard; **es geht** ~ **auf** ~: the chips are down; **(d)** (nahe) close (**an** + *Dat.* to); ~ **am Wind segeln** (Seemannsspr.) sail near *or* close to the wind

Härte /'hɛrtə/ *die;* ~, ~**n (a)** (auch Physik) hardness; **(b)** *o. Pl.* (Widerstandsfähigkeit) toughness; **(c)** (schwere Belastung) hardship; **eine soziale** ~: a case of social hardship; **(d)** *o. Pl.* (Strenge) severity; **(e)** *o. Pl.* (Heftigkeit) (eines Aufpralls usw.) force; (eines Streits) violence; **(f)** (Rauheit) roughness; **(g)** *o. Pl.* (Stabilität) hardness; **(h)** (von Wasser) hardness; **(i)** (von Licht, Farbe) harshness; (von Frost) hardness

Härte-: ~**fall** *der* **(a)** case of hardship; **(b)** (ugs.: Person) hardship case; ~**grad** *der* degree of hardness

härten **1** *tr. V.* harden; harden, temper ⟨*steel*⟩. **2** *itr. V.* harden

härter, härtest... ⇨ **hart**

hart-, Hart-: ~**faser·platte** *die* hardboard;*~**gekocht** ⇨ **hart 1 a**; ~**geld** *das* coins *pl.*; small change; ~**gesotten** *Adj.* **(a)** (gefühllos) hard-bitten; hard-boiled; **(b)** (unbelehrbar) hardened; ~**gummi** *das* hard rubber; ~**herzig** **1** *Adj.* hard-hearted; **2** *adv.* hard-heartedly; ~**herzigkeit** *die;* ~: hard-heartedness; ~**holz** *das* hardwood; ~**metall** *das* hard metal; ~**näckig** /~nɛkɪç/ **1** *Adj.* **(a)** obstinate; stubborn; **(b)** (ausdauernd) persistent; dogged; inveterate ⟨*liar*⟩; stubborn, dogged ⟨*resistance*⟩; persistent ⟨*questioning, questioner*⟩; **2** *adv.* **(a)** obstinately; stubbornly; **(b)** (ausdauernd) persistently; doggedly; ~**näckigkeit** *die;* ~ **(a)** obstinacy; stubbornness; **(b)** (Ausdauer) persistence; doggedness; ~**platz** *der* (Sport) (Tennis) hard court; (Fußball) asphalt pitch; ~**schalig** /~ʃaːlɪç/ *Adj.* hardshell; hard-shelled; thick-skinned ⟨*apple, pear, etc.*⟩

Härtung *die;* ~, ~**en** hardening; (von Stahl auch) tempering

Hart·wurst *die* dry sausage

Harz /haːɐts/ *das;* ~**es**, ~**e** resin

Harzer Käse *der;* ~ ~**s**, ~ ~: Harz [Mountain] cheese

harzig *Adj.* resinous

Hasch /haʃ/ *das;* ~**s** (ugs.) hash (coll.)

Haschee /ha'ʃeː/ (Kochk.) *das;* ~**s**, ~**s** hash

haschen[1] (veralt.) **1** *tr. V.* catch. **2** *itr. V.* **nach etw.** ~: make a grab for sth.

haschen[2] *itr. V.* (ugs.) smoke [hash] (coll.)

Häschen /'hɛːsçən/ *das;* ~**s**, ~: bunny

Häscher /'hɛʃɐ/ *der;* ~**s**, ~ (geh. veralt.) pursuer

Haschisch /'haʃɪʃ/ *das od. der;* ~**s** hashish

Hase /'haːzə/ *der;* ~**n**, ~**n** hare; **ein alter** ~ **sein** (ugs.) be an old hand; **falscher** ~ (Kochk.) meat loaf; **da liegt der** ~ **im Pfeffer** (ugs.) that's the real trouble; **sehen/wissen wie der** ~ **läuft** (ugs.) see/know which way the wind blows; **mein Name ist** ~ (ugs. scherzh.) I'm not saying anything

Hasel-: ~**kätzchen** *das* hazel catkin; ~**nuss**, *~**nuß** *die* **(a)** hazelnut; **(b)** hazel [tree]; ~[nuss]·**strauch**, *~[nuß]·**strauch** *der* hazel [tree]

hasen-, Hasen-: ~**fuß** *der* (spöttisch abwertend) coward; chicken (coll.); ~**jagd** *die* hare shoot; ~**panier** *in* **das** ~**panier ergreifen** take to one's heels; ~**pfeffer**

der (Kochk.) marinaded and stewed trimmings *pl.* of hare; ~**rein** *Adj.* **er/das ist nicht ganz** ~**rein** (fig.) there's something fishy (coll.) about him/it; ~**scharte** *die* (Med.) harelip

Haspel /'haspl/ *die;* ~, ~**n** (Technik) **(a)** (für Garn) reel; bobbin; (für ein Seil, Kabel) drum; **(b)** (Seilwinde) windlass

Hass, ***Haß** /has/ *der;* **Hasses** hate; hatred (**auf** + *Akk.*, **gegen** of, for); **sein [ganzer]** ~: [all] his hatred

hassen *tr., itr. V.* hate; *s. auch* **Pest**

hass·erfüllt, ***haß·erfüllt** **1** *Adj.* filled with hatred *or* hate *postpos.* **2** *adv.* **jmdn.** ~ **ansehen** look at sb. with [one's] eyes full of hatred *or* hate

hässlich, ***häßlich** /'hɛslɪç/ **1** *Adj.* **(a)** ugly; ~ **wie die Nacht** as ugly as sin (coll.); **(b)** (gemein) nasty; hateful; **(c)** (unangenehm) terrible (coll.), awful ⟨*weather, cold, situation, etc.*⟩. **2** *adv.* **(a)** ⟨*dress*⟩ unattraively; **(b)** (gemein) nastily; hatefully

Hässlichkeit, ***Häßlichkeit** *die;* ~, ~**en (a)** *o. Pl.* (Aussehen) ugliness; **(b)** *o. Pl.* (Gesinnung) meanness; nastiness; hatefulness

Hass·liebe, ***Haß·liebe** *die* love-hate relationship

hast /hast/ *2. Pers. Sg. Präsens v.* **haben**

Hast *die;* ~: haste; **etw. in** *od.* **mit größter** ~ **tun** do sth. in great haste; **ohne** ~: unhurriedly; without hurrying *or* haste

haste /'hastə/ (ugs.) = **hast du:** [**was**] ~ **was kannste** as fast as he/you/they *etc.* can/could; ~ **was, biste was** money talks

hasten *itr. V.; mit sein* hurry; hasten

hastig **1** *Adj.* hasty; hurried. **2** *adv.* hastily; hurriedly; **nur nicht so** ~! not so fast!

hat /hat/ *3. Pers. Sg. Präsens v.* **haben**

Hätschel·kind *das* pampered child; (fig.) darling

hätscheln /'hɛːtʃln/ *tr. V.* **(a)** (liebkosen) fondle; caress; **(b)** (verwöhnen) pamper; (fig.) lionize

hatschi /ha'tʃiː/ *Interj.* atishoo; atchoo

hatte /'hatə/ *1. u. 3. Pers. Sg. Prät. v.* **haben**

hätte /'hɛtə/ *1. u. 3. Pers. Sg. Konjunktiv II v.* **haben**

Hatz /hats/ *die;* ~, ~**en (a)** (Hetzjagd, auch fig. ugs.) hunt; **(b)** (ugs., bes. bayr.: Eile) mad rush

Haube /'haubə/ *die;* ~, ~**n (a)** bonnet; (einer Krankenschwester) cap; **unter die** ~ **kommen** (ugs. scherzh.) get hitched (coll.); **(b)** (Kfz-W.) bonnet (Brit.); hood (Amer.); **(c)** (Zool.) crest; **(d)** (Bedeckung) cover; (über Teekanne, Kaffeekanne, Ei) cosy

Hauben·taucher *der* great crested grebe

Haubitze /hau'bɪtsə/ *die;* ~, ~**n** (Milit.) howitzer

Hauch /haux/ *der;* ~[e]s, ~**e** (geh.) **(a)** (Atem, auch fig.) breath; **(b)** (Luftzug) breath of wind; breeze; **(c)** (leichter Duft) delicate smell; waft; **(d)** (dünne Schicht) [gossamer-]thin layer

hauch·dünn **1** *Adj.* gossamer-thin ⟨*material, dress*⟩; wafer-thin, paper-thin ⟨*layer, slice, majority*⟩. **2** *adv.* **etw.** ~ **auftragen** apply sth. very sparingly; **etw.** ~ **schneiden** cut sth. wafer-thin *or* into wafer-thin slices

hauchen **1** *itr. V.* breathe (**gegen, auf** + *Akk.* on). **2** *tr. V.* (auch fig.: flüstern) breathe; **jmdm. etw. ins Ohr** ~: breathe sth. in sb.'s ear

hauch-: ~**fein** *Adj.* extremely fine; ~**zart** *Adj.* extremely delicate; gossamer-thin

Hau·degen *der;* [**alter**] ~: old soldier *or* warhorse

Haue /'hauə/ *die;* ~, ~**n (a)** (südd., österr.: Hacke) hoe; **(b)** *o. Pl.* (ugs.: Prügel) a hiding (coll.)

hauen **1** *unr. tr. V.* **(a)** (ugs.: schlagen) belt (coll.); clobber (coll.); beat; **jmdn. windelweich/grün und blau** ~ beat sb. black and blue; **(b)** (ugs.: auf einen Körperteil) belt (coll.); hit; (mit der Faust auch) smash (sl.); punch; (mit offener Hand auch) slap; smack; **(c)** (ugs.: hineinschlagen) knock; **(d)** (herstellen) carve ⟨*figure, statue, etc.*⟩ (**in** + *Akk.* in); cut, chop ⟨*hole*⟩; **Stufen in den Fels** ~: cut steps in the rock; **(e)** (mit einer Waffe schlagen) **jmdn. aus dem Sattel/vom Pferd** ~: knock sb. out of the saddle/off his/her horse; **(f)** (salopp: schleudern) sling (coll.); fling; **(g)** (landsch.: fällen) fell; cut down; **(h)** (Bergbau) cut ⟨*coal, ore*⟩. **2** *unr. itr. V.* **(a)** **jmdm. auf die Schulter** ~: slap *or* clap sb. on the shoulder; **jmdm. ins Gesicht** ~: belt (coll.)/slap sb. in the face; **mit der**

Faust auf den Tisch ∼**:** thump the table [with one's fist]; **(b)** *mit sein* (ugs.: stoßen) bump; **mit dem Kopf/Bein gegen etw.** ∼**:** bang *or* hit *or* bump one's head/leg against sth. **3** *unr. refl. V.* **(a)** (ugs.: sich prügeln) have a punch-up (coll.) *or* a fight; fight; **(b)** (salopp: sich setzen, legen) fling *or* throw oneself; **sich ins Bett** ∼**:** hit the sack (coll.)

Hauer *der;* ∼**s,** ∼ **(a)** ▶ 85⌋ (Bergmannsspr.) face-worker; **(b)** (Jägerspr.) tusk; (fig.) fang

Häufchen /'hɔyfçən/ *das;* ∼**s,** ∼**:** [small *or* little] pile *or* heap; **nur noch ein** ∼ **Unglück** *od.* **Elend sein** (ugs.) be nothing but a small bundle of misery

Haufen /'haufn̩/ *der;* ∼**s,** ∼ **(a)** heap; pile; **etw. zu** ∼ **aufschichten** stack sth. up in piles; **alles auf einen** ∼ **werfen** throw everything in a heap; **der Hund hat da einen** ∼ **gemacht** (ugs.) the dog has done his business there (coll.); **etw. über den** ∼ **werfen** (ugs.) (aufgeben) chuck sth. in (coll.); (zunichte machen) mess sth. up; **jmdn. über den** ∼ **fahren/rennen** (ugs.) knock sb. down; run sb. over; **jmdn. über den** ∼ **schießen** *od.* **knallen** (ugs.) gun *or* shoot sb. down (coll.); **(b)** (ugs.: große Menge) heap (coll.); pile (coll.); load (coll.); **ein** ∼ **Arbeit/Bücher** a load *or* heap *or* pile of work/books (coll.); loads *or* heaps *or* piles of work/books (coll.); **ein** ∼ **Geld** loads of money (coll.); **(c)** (Ansammlung von Menschen) crowd; **so viele Idioten auf einem** ∼ (ugs.) so many idiots in one place

häufen /'hɔyfn̩/ **1** *tr. V.* heap, pile (**auf** + *Akk.* on to). **2** *refl. V.* (sich mehren) pile up

haufen·weise *Adv.* (ugs.) ∼ **Geld ausgeben/Eis essen** spend loads of money/eat heaps *or* loads of ice cream (coll.)

häufig /'hɔyfɪç/ **1** *Adj.* frequent. **2** *adv.* frequently; often

Häufigkeit *die;* ∼**,** ∼**en** frequency

Häufung *die;* ∼**,** ∼**en** increasing frequency

Haupt /haupt/ *das;* ∼**[e]s, Häupter** /'hɔyptɐ/ **(a)** (geh.: Kopf) head; **erhobenen** ∼**es** with one's head [held] high; **gesenkten** ∼**es** with head bowed; **gekrönte Häupter** crowned heads; **(b)** (geh.: wichtigste Person) head

haupt-, Haupt-: ∼**aktionär** *der* principal shareholder; ∼**akzent** *der* (Phon.) main *or* primary stress; (fig.) main emphasis; ∼**amtlich 1** *Adj.* full-time; **2** *adv.* ∼**amtlich tätig sein** work full-time *or* on a full-time basis; ∼**arbeit** *die* main part of the work; ∼**bahnhof** *der* main station; Amsterdam ∼**bahnhof** Amsterdam Central; ∼**beruflich 1** *Adj.* seine ∼**berufliche Tätigkeit** his main occupation; **2** *adv.* **er ist** ∼**beruflich als Elektriker tätig** his main occupation is that of electrician; ∼**beschäftigung** *die* main occupation; ∼**buch** *das* (Kaufmannsspr.) ledger; ∼**darsteller** *der* (Theater, Film) leading man; male lead; ∼**darstellerin** *die* (Theater, Film) leading lady; female lead; ∼**eingang** *der* main entrance; ∼**einnahme·quelle** *die* main *or* principal source of income; (eines Staates) main *or* principal source of revenue; ∼**fach** *das* **(a)** (Universität) main subject; major; **etw. im** ∼**fach studieren** study sth. as one's main subject; **(b)** (Schule) main subject; ∼**fehler** *der* main *or* principal *or* chief mistake/(im Charakter) fault/(in einer Theorie, einem Argument) flaw; ∼**feld** *das* (Sport) [main] bunch; ∼**feldwebel** *der* ▶ 34⌋ (Milit.) ≈ staff sergeant (Brit.); ≈ sergeant first class (Amer.); ∼**figur** *die* main *or* principal character; ∼**film** *der* main feature *or* film; ∼**gang** *der* **(a)** main corridor; **(b)** ⇒ ∼**gericht**; ∼**gebäude** *das* main building; ∼**gericht** *das* main course; ∼**geschäft** *das* **(a)** (Laden) main branch; **(b)** (größter Umsatz) peak sales *pl.;* (wichtigster Geschäftszweig) main line; ∼**geschäftsstraße** *die* main shopping street; ∼**gewicht** *das* main emphasis; ∼**gewinn** *der* first *or* top prize; ∼**grund** *der* main *or* principal *or* chief reason; ∼**hahn** *der* mains stopcock; ∼**interesse** *das* main interest; ∼**last** *die* main burden; ∼**leitung** *die* (Gas-, Wasserleitung) main; (Stromleitung) main[s *pl.*]

Häuptling /'hɔyptlɪŋ/ *der;* ∼**s,** ∼**e** chief[tain]; (iron.) bigwig (coll.)

haupt-, Haupt-: ∼**mahlzeit** *die* main meal; ∼**mann** *der; Pl.* ∼**leute** **(a)** ▶ 34⌋ (Milit.) captain; **(b)** (hist.) leader; ∼**merkmal** *das* main *or* principal *or* chief

characteristic; ∼**motiv** *das* **(a)** (Gegenstand) main *or* principal motif; **(b)** (Beweggrund) main *or* principal *or* chief motive; ∼**person** *die* central figure; **sie will immer und überall die** ∼**person sein** (fig.) she always wants to be the centre of everything *or* of attention; ∼**post** *die,* ∼**post·amt** *das* main post office; ∼**problem** *das* main *or* chief problem; ∼**quartier** *das* (Milit., auch fig.) headquarters *sing. or pl.;* ∼**redner** *der* main *or* principal speaker; ∼**reise·zeit** *die* high season; peak [holiday] season; ∼**rolle** *die* leading *or* main role; lead; **die** ∼**rolle spielen** play the leading role *or* the lead (**in** + *Dat.* in); **die** ∼**rolle** [**in** *od.* **bei etw.**] **spielen** (fig.) play the leading role [in sth.]; ∼**sache** *die* main *or* most important thing; **in der** ∼**sache** mainly; in the main; ∼**sächlich 1** *Adv.* mainly; principally; chiefly; **2** *Adj.; nicht präd.* main; principal; chief; ∼**saison** *die* high season; ∼**satz** *der* (Sprachw.) main clause; (allein stehend) sentence; ∼**schalter** *der* (Elektrot.) mains switch; ∼**schlagader** *die* aorta; ∼**schlüssel** *der* master key; pass key; ∼**schul·abschluss,** *∗*∼**schul·abschluß** *der* ≈ secondary school leaving certificate; ∼**schuld** *die* main share of the blame; ∼**schuldige** *der/die* person mainly to blame; (an einem Verbrechen) main *or* chief offender; ∼**schule** *die* ≈ secondary modern school; ∼**schul·lehrer** *der* ≈ secondary modern school teacher; ∼**sicherung** *die* (Elektrot.) mains fuse; ∼**sitz** *der* head office; headquarters *pl.;* ∼**stadt** *die* capital [city]; ∼**städtisch** *Adj.* metropolitan; ∼**straße** *die* ▶ 583⌋ **(a)** (wichtigste Geschäftsstraße) high *or* main street; **(b)** (Durchgangsstraße) main road; ∼**strecke** *die* (Eisenb.) main line; ∼**teil** *der* major part; ∼**treffer** *der* ⇒ ∼**gewinn**; ∼**tribüne** *die* (Sport) main stand; ∼**unterschied** *der* main *or* principal *or* chief difference; ∼**ursache** *die* main *or* principal *or* chief cause; ∼**verantwortliche** *der/die* person mainly responsible; ∼**verhandlung** *die* (Rechtsw.) main hearing

Hauptverkehrs-: ∼**straße** *die* main road; ∼**zeit** *die* rush hour

Haupt-: ∼**versammlung** *die* (Wirtsch.) shareholders' meeting; ∼**verwaltung** *die* head office; ∼**wohn·sitz** *der* main place of residence; ∼**wort** *das* (Sprachw.) noun

hau ruck /'hau'ruk/ *Interj.* heave[-ho]

Haus /haus/ *das;* ∼**es, Häuser** /'hɔyzɐ/ **(a)** house; (Firmengebäude) building; **er ist gerade aus dem** ∼ **gegangen** he has just gone out; **ins** ∼ **spielen** play indoors; **kommt ins** ∼**, es regnet** come inside, it's raining; ∼ **und Hof** (fig.) house and home; **jmdm. ins** ∼ **stehen** (fig. ugs.) be in store for sb.; **(b)** (Heim) home; **jmdm. das** ∼ **verbieten** not allow sb. in one's *or* the house; **etw. ins** ∼**/frei** ∼ **liefern** deliver sth. to sb.'s door/free of charge; **das** ∼ **auf den Kopf stellen** (ugs.) turn the place upside down; **außer** ∼[**e**] **sein/essen** be/eat out; **ist Ihre Frau im** ∼[**e**]**?** is your wife at home?; **nach** ∼**e** home; **zu** ∼**e** at home; **fühlt euch wie zu** ∼**e** make yourselves at home; **das** ∼ **hüten** stay at home *or* indoors; **jmdm. das** ∼ **einrennen** (ugs.) be constantly on sb.'s doorstep; **auf einem Gebiet/in etw.** (*Dat.*) **zu** ∼**e sein** (ugs.) be at home in a field/in sth.; **(c)** (Theater) theatre; (Publikum) house; **das große/kleine** ∼**:** the large/small theatre; **vor vollen/ausverkauften Häusern spielen** play to full *or* packed houses; **(d)** (Gasthof, Geschäft) **das erste** ∼ **am Platze** the best shop of its kind/hotel in the town/village *etc.;* **eine Spezialität des** ∼**es** a speciality of the house; **(e)** (Firma) firm; business house; **das** ∼ **Meyer** the firm of Meyer; **(f)** (geh.: Parlament) **das Hohe** ∼**:** the House; **(g)** (geh.: Familie) household; **der Herr/die Dame des** ∼**es** the master/lady of the house; **aus gutem** ∼**e kommen** come from a *or* be of good family; **der Herr im eigenen** ∼ **sein** be master in one's own house; **von** ∼[**e**] **aus** (von der Familie her) by birth; (eigentlich) really; actually; **(h)** (∼**halt**) household; **jmdm. das** ∼ **führen** keep house for sb.; **(i)** (Dynastie) **das** ∼ **Tudor/[der] Hohenzollern** the House of Tudor/Hohenzollern; **(j)** **ein gelehrtes/lustiges** ∼**:** (ugs. scherzh.) a scholarly/ amusing *etc.* sort (coll.); **(k)** (Schnecken∼) shell; **(l)** ∼ **halten** be economical (**mit** with)

haus-, Haus-: ∼**angestellte** *der/die* domestic servant; ∼**apotheke** *die* medicine cabinet; ∼**arbeit** *die*

(a) housework; (b) (Schulw.) item of homework; **~arrest** *der* (a) house arrest; (b) (in der Familie) **mein Bruder hat ~arrest** my brother is being kept in; **~arzt** *der* family doctor; **~aufgabe** *die* piece of homework; **~aufgaben aufhaben** (ugs.) have homework *sing.*; **~aufsatz** *der* homework essay; **~backen** 1 *Adj.* plain; unadventurous, boring ⟨*clothes*⟩; 2 *adv.* ⟨*dress*⟩ unadventurously; **~bau** *der* house-building; **beim ~bau** when building a/one's house; **~besetzer** *der* squatter; **~besetzung** *die* (Vorgang) squatting; (Ergebnis) squat; **~besitzer** *der* house-owner; (Vermieter) landlord; **~besitzerin** *die* house-owner; (Vermieterin) landlady; **~besuch** *der* house-call; **~bewohner** *der* occupant [of the house]; **~boot** *das* houseboat

Häuschen /ˈhɔysçən/ *das*; **~s, ~:** (a) little *or* small house; (b) [**ganz** *od.* **rein**] **aus dem ~ sein** (ugs.) be [completely] over the moon (coll.); (c) (ugs.: Toilette) privy

haus-, Haus-: **~dame** *die* housekeeper; **~detektiv** *der* house detective; **~diener** *der* domestic servant; **~drachen** *der* (ugs. abwertend) dragon (coll.); **~ecke** *die* corner of the house; **~eigen** *Adj.* the **~eigene Kindergarten** the company's/hotel's *etc.* own kindergarten; **das Hotel hat einen ~eigenen Swimming-pool/Strand** the hotel has its own swimming pool/[private] beach; **~eigentümer** *der* ⇒ **~besitzer; ~eingang** *der* entrance [to the house]

hausen *itr. V.* (ugs.) (a) (wohnen) live; (b) (Verwüstungen anrichten) [**furchtbar**] **~:** cause *or* wreak havoc

Häuser·block *der* block [of houses]

Haus-: **~flur** *der* hall[way]; entrance-hall; (im Obergeschoss) landing; **~frau** *die* ▶ 85] housewife

hausfraulich *Adj.* housewifely; **ihre ~en Fähigkeiten** her abilities as a housewife

Haus·freund *der* (a) friend of the family; family friend; (b) (verhüll.: Liebhaber) man-friend (euphem.)

Hausfriedens·bruch *der* (Rechtsw.) trespass

haus-, Haus-: **~gebrauch** *der* domestic use; **das reicht für den ~gebrauch** (ugs.) it's good enough to get by (coll.); **~gehilfin** *die* [home] help; **~gemacht** *Adj.* home-made; **~gemeinschaft** *die* (a) (gemeinsamer ~halt) household; (b) (Bewohner eines Hauses) occupants *pl.* of the block

Haus·halt *der* (a) household; **einen ~ gründen/auflösen** set up home/break up a household; (b) (Arbeit im ~) housekeeping; **jmdm. den ~ führen** keep house for sb.; **im ~ helfen** help with the housework; (c) (Politik) budget

haus|halten *unr. itr. V.* be economical (**mit** with)

Haushälterin *die*; **~, ~nen** ▶ 85] housekeeper

Haushalts-: **~artikel** *der* household article; **~auflösung** *die* house clearance; **~buch** *das* housekeeping book; **~debatte** *die* (Politik) budget debate; **~defizit** *das* budgetary deficit; **~führung** *die* housekeeping; **~geld** *das; o. Pl.* housekeeping money; **~gerät** *das* household appliance; **~hilfe** *die* home help; **~jahr** *das* (Rechnungsjahr) financial year; **~kasse** *die* housekeeping money; **die ~kasse war leer** there was no housekeeping money left; **~plan** *der* budget; **~politik** *die* budgetary policy; **~waren** *Pl.* household goods

haus-, Haus-: **~haltung** *die* (a) ⇒ **Haushalt** a; (b) (Haushaltsführung) housekeeping; **~herr** *der* (a) (Familienoberhaupt) head of the household; (b) (als Gastgeber) host; (c) (Rechtsspr.) (Eigentümer) owner; (Mieter) occupier; (d) (südd., österr.) ⇒ **~besitzer; ~herrin** *die* (a) (Familienoberhaupt) lady of the house; (b) (als Gastgeberin) hostess; (c) (südd., österr.) ⇒ **~besitzerin; ~hoch** 1 *Adj.* ⟨*flames, waves etc.*⟩ as high as a house; (fig.) overwhelming ⟨*superiority etc.*⟩; **die ~hohe Favoritin** the hot favourite; 2 *adv.* **~hoch gewinnen/jmdm. ~hoch schlagen** win hands down/beat sb. hands down; **jmdm. ~hoch überlegen sein** be vastly superior to sb.

hausieren *itr. V.* [**mit etw.**] **~:** hawk [sth.]; peddle [sth.]; **„Hausieren verboten"** 'no hawkers'

Hausierer *der*; **~s, ~:** ▶ 85] pedlar; hawker

haus-, Haus-: **~intern** 1 *Adj.* internal ⟨*regulations, purposes, information*⟩; ⟨*agreement, custom*⟩ within the company; 2 *adv.* internally; within the company;

~katze *die* domestic cat; **~kleid** *das* house dress; **~lehrer** *der* private tutor

häuslich /ˈhɔyslɪç/ 1 *Adj.* (a) *nicht präd.* domestic ⟨*bliss, peace, affairs, duties, etc.*⟩; **am ~en Kaminfeuer** at one's own fireside; *s. auch* **Herd** a; (b) (das Zuhause liebend) home loving. 2 *adv.* **sich [bei jmdm./irgendwo] ~ niederlassen** (ugs.) make oneself at home [in sb.'s house/somewhere]

Hausmacher-: **~art** *die in* **nach ~art** home-made-style *attrib.*; **~wurst** *die* home-made sausage

Haus-: **~macht** *die* (hist.) allodium; (fig.) power base; **~mädchen** *das* ▶ 85] [home] help

Haus·mann *der* ▶ 85] man who stays at home and does the housework; (Ehemann) househusband

Hausmanns·kost *die* plain cooking

Haus-: **~marke** *die* (a) (Wein, Sekt) house wine; (b) (ugs.: bevorzugtes Getränk) usual *or* favourite tipple (coll.); **~meister** *der*, **~meisterin** *die* ▶ 85] caretaker; **~mittel** *das* household remedy; **~musik** *die* music at home; **~mütterchen** *das* (ugs. scherzh.) little housewife; **~nummer** *die* ▶ 107] house number; **ihre ~nummer** the number of her house; **~ordnung** *die* house rules *pl.*; **~putz** *der* spring clean; (regelmäßig) clean-out; **~putz halten** *od.* **machen** spring-clean the house

Haus·rat *der* household goods *pl.*

Hausrat·versicherung *die* [household *or* home] contents insurance

Haus-: **~recht** *das* (Rechtsw.) right of a householder or owner of a property to forbid sb. entrance or order sb. to leave; **~schlachtung** *die* home slaughtering; **~schlüssel** *der* front-door key; house-key; **~schuh** *der* slipper

Hausse /ˈhoːs(ə)/ *die*; **~, ~n** (Börsenw.) rise [in prices]; (fig.) boom

Haus-: **~segen** *der:* **bei ihnen hängt der ~segen schief** (ugs. scherzh.) they've been having a row; **~stand** *der* household; **einen [eigenen] ~stand gründen** set up home [on their own]; **~suchung** *die;* **~, ~en** house search; **~suchungs·befehl** *der* search warrant; **~tier** *das* (a) pet; (b) (Nutztier) domestic animal; **~tür** *die* front door; **etw. direkt vor der ~tür haben** (ugs. fig.) have sth. on one's doorstep; **~tyrann** *der* (ugs.) tyrant [in one's own home]; **~verbot** *das* ban on entering the house/pub/restaurant *etc.;* **jmdm. ~verbot erteilen** ban sb. [from the house/pub/restaurant *etc.*]; **~verwalter** *der* manager [of the block]; **~verwaltung** *die* management [of the block]; **~wand** *die* [house] wall; **~wirt** *der* landlord; **~wirtin** *die* landlady

Haus·wirtschaft *die; o. Pl.* domestic science and home economics

hauswirtschaftlich *Adj.; nicht präd.* domestic

Hauswirtschafts-: **~lehrerin** *die* ▶ 85] home economics and domestic science teacher; **~schule** *die* college of domestic science and home economics

Haut /haut/ *die;* **~, Häute** /ˈhɔytə/ ▶ 326] (a) skin; **sich** (*Dat.*) **die ~ abschürfen** graze oneself; **viel ~ zeigen** (ugs. scherzh.) show a lot of bare flesh (coll.); **nass bis auf die ~:** soaked to the skin; wet through; **nur noch ~ und Knochen sein** (ugs.) be nothing but skin and bone; **seine eigene ~ retten** save one's own skin; **seine ~ so teuer wie möglich verkaufen** (ugs.) sell oneself as dearly as possible; **sich seiner ~** (*Gen.*) **wehren** (ugs.) stand up for oneself; **aus der ~ fahren** (ugs.) go up the wall (coll.); **er/sie kann nicht aus seiner/ihrer ~ heraus** (ugs.) a leopard cannot change its spots (prov.); **sich in seiner ~ nicht wohl fühlen** (ugs.) feel uneasy; (unzufrieden sein) feel discontented [with one's lot]; **ich möchte nicht in deiner ~ stecken** (ugs.) I shouldn't like to be in your shoes (coll.); **mit heiler ~ davonkommen** (ugs.) get away with it; (b) (Fell) skin; (von größerem Tier auch) hide; **auf der faulen ~ liegen** (ugs.) sit around and do nothing; (c) (Schale, dünne Schicht, Bespannung) skin; (d) (ugs.) **eine gute/ehrliche ~** a good/honest sort (coll.)

Haut-: **~abschürfung** *die* graze; **~arzt** *der* ▶ 85] skin specialist; dermatologist; **~ausschlag** *der* [skin-] rash; **~creme** *die* skin cream

häuten /'hɔytn̩/ **1** tr. V. skin, flay ‹animal›; skin ‹tomato, almond, etc.›. **2** refl. V. shed its skin/their skins; ‹snake› shed or slough its skin

haut-, Haut-: ~**eng** Adj. skintight; ~**farbe** die [skin] colour; **wegen seiner** ~**farbe** because of the colour of his skin; ~**freundlich** Adj. kind to the/one's skin pred.; ~**krankheit** die skin disease; ~**krebs** der skin cancer ~**nah 1** Adj. **(a)** (unmittelbar) immediate ‹contact›; eyeball-to-eyeball ‹confrontation›; **(b)** (ugs.: packend, anschaulich) realistic and gripping ‹description›; **2** adv. (unmittelbar) **mit etw.** ~**nah in Berührung/Kontakt kommen** come into very close contact with sth.; ~**pflege** die skin care; ~**transplantation** die (Med.) skin graft

Häutung die; ~, ~**en (a)** ⇒ **häuten 1**: skinning; flaying; **(b)** (das Sichhäuten) **Schlangen machen viele** ~**en durch** snakes shed or slough their skin many times

Havarie /hava'ri:/ die; ~, ~**n** (Seew., Flugw., österr. auch: ~ eines Autos) accident; (Schaden) damage no indef. art.

havarieren itr. V. (Seew., Flugw.) ‹aircraft› crash; ‹ship› have an accident; **ein havariertes Schiff** a damaged ship

Hawaii /ha'vai/ (das); ~**s** Hawaii

Haxe die; ~, ~**n** ⇒ **Hachse**

H-Bombe /'ha:-/ die H-bomb

H-Dur /'ha:-/ das; ~ (Musik) B major

he /he:/ Interj. (ugs.) **(a)** (Zuruf, Ausruf) hey; ~ **[du], komm mal her!** hey [you], come here!; **(b)** (zur Verstärkung einer Frage) eh

Heb·amme die ▶ 85| midwife

Hebe-: ~**balken** der lever; ~**bühne** die hydraulic lift; ~**figur** die (Eis-, Rollkunstlauf) lift

Hebel /'he:bl̩/ der; ~**s**, ~ (auch Griff, Physik) lever; **den** ~ **ansetzen** position the lever; **alle** ~ **in Bewegung setzen** (ugs.) move heaven and earth; **am längeren** ~ **sitzen** (ugs.) have the whip hand

Hebel-: ~**gesetz** das (Physik) principle of the lever; ~**kraft**, die ~**wirkung** die leverage

heben /'he:bn̩/ **1** unr. tr. V. **(a)** (nach oben bewegen) lift; raise; raise ‹baton, camera, glass›; **eine Last** ~: lift a load; **die Hand/den Arm** ~: raise one's hand/arm; **schlurft nicht, hebt die Füße!** pick your feet up!; **die Stimme** ~ (geh.) raise one's voice; **einen** ~ (ugs.) have a drink; **(b)** (an eine andere Stelle bringen) lift; **jmdn. auf die Schulter/von der Mauer** ~: lift sb. [up] on to one's shoulders/[down] from the wall; **(c)** (heraufholen) dig up ‹treasure etc.›; raise ‹wreck›; **(d)** (verbessern) raise, improve ‹standard, level›; increase ‹turnover, self-confidence›; improve ‹mood›; enhance ‹standing›; boost ‹morale›; **(e)** (unpers.) **es hebt jmdm. den Magen** sb.'s stomach heaves. **2** unr. refl. V. **(a)** (geh.: sich recken, sich er~) rise; **(b)** (hochgehen, hochsteigen) rise; ‹curtain› rise, go up; ‹mist, fog› lift; **sich** ~ **und senken** rise and fall; ‹sea, chest› rise and fall, heave; **(c)** (sich verbessern) ‹mood› improve; ‹trade› pick up; ‹standard, level› rise, improve, go up

Heber der; ~**s**, ~ **(a)** (Technik) jack; **(b)** (Chemie) pipette; **(c)** (Sport: Gewicht~) weightlifter

hebräisch /he'brɛɪʃ/ ▶ 487| Hebrew

Hebung die; ~, ~**en (a) die** ~ **eines Schiffes** the raising of a ship; **bei der** ~ **des Schatzes …:** when the treasure is/was dug up …; **(b)** o. Pl. (Verbesserung) raising; improvement; **zur** ~ **des Selbstvertrauens/der Moral** to improve sb.'s self-confidence/morale; **(c)** (Geol.) uplift; **(d)** (Verslehre) stressed syllable

hecheln itr. V. pant [for breath]

Hecht /hɛçt/ der; ~**[e]s**, ~**e (a)** pike; **der** ~ **im Karpfenteich sein** (ugs.) be the kingpin; **(b)** (ugs.: Bursche) **ein toller** ~: an incredible fellow; **(c)** (Tabaksqualm) fug (coll.)

hechten itr. V.; mit sein dive headlong; make a headlong dive; (schräg nach oben) throw oneself sideways; (vom Sprungturm) perform or do a pike-dive; (Turnen) do a long-fly

Hecht-: ~**sprung** der **(a)** (Turnen) Hecht vault; **(b)** (Schwimmen) racing dive; (vom Sprungturm) pike-dive;

---

*alte Schreibung (vgl. Hinweise auf S. xvi–xvii)

~**suppe** die in **es Licht wie** ~**suppe** (ugs.) there's a terrible draught (coll.)

Heck /hɛk/ das; ~**[e]s**, ~**e** od. ~**s (a)** (Schiffs~) stern; **(b)** (Flugzeug~) tail; **im** ~ **der Maschine** at the rear of the plane; **(c)** (Auto~) rear; back

Heck·antrieb der (Kfz-W.) rear-wheel drive

Hecke die; ~, ~**n (a)** hedge; **(b)** (wild wachsend) thicket

Hecken-: ~**rose** die dogrose; ~**schere** die hedge shears pl.; (elektrisch) hedge trimmer; ~**schütze** der sniper

Heck·fenster das rear or back window

Heckmeck /'hɛkmɛk/ der; ~**s** (ugs. abwertend) **(a)** (Getue) fuss; **(b)** (Unsinn) rubbish

Heck-: ~**motor** der rear engine; ~**scheibe** die rear or back window

Heer /he:ɐ̯/ das; ~**[e]s**, ~**e (a)** (Gesamtheit der Streitkräfte) armed forces pl.; **das stehende** ~: the standing army; **(b)** (für den Landkrieg, auch fig.) army

Heeres·leitung die (Milit.) army command staff; **die oberste** ~ the high command

Heer·schar die (veralt., noch fig.) host (arch.); s. auch **himmlisch 1 a**

Hefe /'he:fə/ die; ~, ~**n** yeast; (fig.) driving force

Hefe-: ~**gebäck** das pastry ‹made with yeast dough›; ~**kloß** der dumpling made with yeast dough; **aufgehen od. auseinander gehen wie ein** ~**kloß** (ugs. scherzh.) blow up like a balloon; ~**kuchen** der yeast cake; ~**teig** der yeast dough; ~**zopf** der plaited bun

Heft¹ /hɛft/ das; ~**[e]s**, ~**e** (geh.) (am Dolch, Messer) haft; handle; (am Schwert) hilt; **das** ~ **in der Hand haben/behalten** (geh.) be in/keep control

Heft² das; ~**[e]s**, ~**e (a)** (geh.) exercise book; **(b)** (Nummer einer Zeitschrift) issue; **Jahrgang 10, Heft 12** Volume 10, No. 12; **(c)** (kleines Buch) (small stapled) book

Heftchen das; ~**s**, ~ **(a)** (Comic) comic; (Groschenroman) novelette; **(b)** (Block) book [of tickets/stamps etc.]

heften 1 tr. V. **(a)** (mit einer Nadel) pin; fix; (mit einer Klammer) clip; fix; (mit Klebstoff) stick; **etw. an/in etw.** (Akk.) ~: pin/stick/clip sth. to/into sth.; **(b)** (richten) **den Blick auf jmdn./etw.** ~: fasten one's gaze on sb./sth.; **(c)** (Schneiderei) tack; baste; **(d)** (Buchbinderei) stitch; (mit Klammern) staple. **2** refl. V. **sich an jmds. Fersen** (Akk.) ~: stick hard on sb.'s heels

Hefter der; ~**s**, ~: [loose-leaf] file

Heft·garn das tacking-thread; basting-thread

heftig 1 Adj. violent; heavy ‹rain, shower, blow›; intense, burning ‹hatred, desire›; fierce ‹controversy, criticism, competition›; severe ‹pain, cold›; loud ‹bang›; rapid ‹breathing›; bitter ‹weeping›; heated, vehement ‹tone, words›; ~ **werden** fly into a temper. **2** adv. ‹rain, snow, breathe› heavily; ‹hit› hard; ‹hurt› a great deal; ‹answer› angrily, heatedly; ‹react› angrily, violently

Heftigkeit die; ~ **(a)** ⇒ **heftig 1**: violence; heaviness; intensity; fierceness; severity; loudness; rapidity; bitterness; **(b)** (Unbeherrschtheit) vehemence

Heft-: ~**klammer** die staple; ~**maschine** die stapler; (Buchbinderei) stitcher; ~**pflaster** das sticking plaster; ~**zwecke** die ⇒ **Reißzwecke**

Hege /'he:gə/ die; ~ (Forstw., Jagdw.) care and protection; (fig.) care

hegen tr. V. **(a)** (bes. Forstw., Jagdw.) look after, tend ‹plants, animals›; **(b)** (geh.: umsorgen) look after; take care of; preserve ‹old customs›; **jmdn./etw.** ~ **und pflegen** lavish care and attention on sb./sth.; **(c)** (in sich tragen) feel ‹contempt, hatred, mistrust›; cherish ‹hope, wish, desire›; harbour, nurse ‹grudge, suspicion›; **eine Abneigung gegen jmdn.** ~: have a dislike for sb.; **ich hege den Verdacht, dass …:** I have a suspicion that …

Hehl /he:l/ in **kein[en]** ~ **aus etw. machen** make no secret of sth.

Hehler der; ~**s**, ~: fence (coll.); receiver [of stolen goods]

Hehlerei die; ~, ~**en** (Rechtsw.) receiving [stolen goods] no art.

hehr /he:ɐ̯/ Adj. (geh.) majestic ‹sight›; glorious ‹moment›; noble ‹ideal›

heia /'haia/ (Kinderspr.) *in* ~ **machen** go bye-byes *or* beddy-byes (child lang.)

Heia *die;* ~, ~s, **Heia·bett** *das* (Kinderspr.) bye-byes, beddy-byes (child lang.); **ab in die Heia:** off to bye-byes *or* beddy-byes

Helde[1] /'haidə/ *der;* ~n, ~n heathen; pagan

Heide[2] *die;* ~, ~n **(a)** moor; heath; (~landschaft) moorland; heathland; **die Lüneburger** ~: the Luneburg Heath; **(b)** ⇒ ~**kraut**

Heide-: ~**kraut** *das; o. Pl.* heather; ling; ~**land** *das* moorland; heathland

Heidel·beere /'haidl-/ *die* bilberry; blueberry; whortleberry

Heiden-: ~**angst** *die; o. Pl.* (ugs.) **eine** ~**angst vor etw.** (*Dat.*) **haben** be scared stiff of sth. (coll.); ~**arbeit** *die; o. Pl.* (ugs.) a heck of a lot of work (coll.); ~**krach** *der; o. Pl.* (ugs.) **(a)** ⇒ ~**lärm; (b)** (Streit) flaming row (coll.); ~**lärm** *der* (ugs.) unholy *or* dreadful din *or* row (coll.); dreadful racket (coll.); ~**respekt** *der* (ugs.) healthy respect (**vor** + *Dat.* for); ~**spaß** *der; o. Pl.* (ugs.) terrific fun (coll.); **es macht einen** ~**spaß** it's terrific fun (coll.); ~**spektakel** *der* (ugs.) (Lärm) unholy *or* dreadful din *or* row (coll.); (Aufregung) great *or* (coll.) dreadful commotion

Heidentum *das;* ~s heathenism; paganism

Heidin *die;* ~, ~nen heathen; pagan

heidnisch *Adj.* heathen; pagan

Heid·schnucke *die;* ~, ~n German Heath [sheep]

heikel /'haikl/ *Adj.* **(a)** (schwierig) delicate, ticklish ⟨*matter, subject*⟩; ticklish, awkward, tricky ⟨*problem, question, situation*⟩; **(b)** (wählerisch, empfindlich) finicky, fussy, fastidious (**in Bezug auf** + *Akk.* about)

heil /hail/ *Adj.* **(a)** (unverletzt) unhurt, unharmed ⟨*person*⟩; ~ **ankommen** arrive safely *or* safe and sound; **etw.** ~ **überstehen** survive sth. unscathed; *s. auch* **Haut a; (b)** *nicht attr.* (wieder gesund) ~ **werden/wieder** ~ **sein** ⟨*injured part*⟩ heal [up]/have healed [up]; **(c)** (nicht entzwei) intact; in one piece; **eine** ~**e Welt** (fig.) an ideal *or* a perfect world

Heil *das;* ~s **(a)** (Wohlergehen) benefit; **bei jmdm./irgendwo sein** ~ **versuchen** try one's luck with sb./somewhere; **sein** ~ **in der Flucht suchen** seek refuge in flight; **(b)** (Rel.) salvation

Heiland /'hailant/ *der;* ~[e]s, ~e **(a)** (Christus) Saviour; Redeemer; **(b)** (geh.: Retter) saviour

Heil-: ~**anstalt** *die* **(a)** (Anstalt für Kranke, Süchtige) sanatorium; **(b)** (psychiatrische Klinik) mental hospital *or* home; ~**bad** *das* **(a)** (Kurort) spa; watering-place; **(b)** (medizinisches Bad) medicinal bath

heilbar *Adj.* curable

Heil·butt *der* halibut

heilen **1** *tr. V.* **(a)** ▶329 cure ⟨*disease*⟩; heal ⟨*wound*⟩; **jmdn.** ~: cure sb.; restore sb. to health; **(b)** (befreien) **jmdn. von etw.** ~: cure sb. of sth.; **davon/von ihm bin ich geheilt** (ugs.) I've been cured of it/my attachment to him. **2** *itr. V.; mit sein* ▶329 ⟨*wound*⟩ heal [up]; ⟨*infection*⟩ clear up; ⟨*fracture*⟩ mend

heil·froh *Adj.; nicht attr.* very *or* (Brit. coll.) jolly glad

heilig *Adj.* **(a)** holy; **der Heilige Vater** the Holy Father; **die Heilige Jungfrau** the Blessed Virgin; **die** ~**e Barbara/der** ~**e Augustinus** Saint Barbara/Saint Augustine; **die Heilige Familie/Dreifaltigkeit** the Holy Family/Trinity; **der Heilige Geist** the Holy Spirit; **die Heiligen Drei Könige** the Three Kings *or* Wise Men; the Magi; **die Heilige Schrift** the Holy Scriptures *pl.; das* **Heilige Römische Reich** (hist.) the Holy Roman Empire; **jmdn.** ~ **sprechen** (kath. Kirche) canonize sb.; **(b)** (besonders geweiht) holy; sacred; ~**e Stätten** holy *or* sacred places; **der Heilige Abend/die Heilige Nacht** Christmas Eve/Night; **das Heilige Land** the Holy Land; **(c)** (geh.: unantastbar) sacred ⟨*right, tradition, cause, etc.*⟩; sacred, solemn ⟨*duty*⟩; gospel ⟨*truth*⟩; solemn ⟨*conviction, oath*⟩; righteous ⟨*anger, zeal*⟩; awed ⟨*silence*⟩; **etw. ist jmdm.** ~: sth. is sacred to sb.; **bei allem, was mir** ~ **ist** by all that I hold sacred; *s. auch* **hoch 2 d; (d)** (ugs.: groß) incredible (coll.); healthy ⟨*respect*⟩

Heilig·abend *der* Christmas Eve

Heilige *der/die; adj. Dekl.* saint; **ein sonderbarer** *od.* **komischer** ~**r** (ugs. iron.) a queer fish (coll.)

heiligen *tr. V.* keep, observe ⟨*tradition, Sabbath, etc.*⟩; **der Zweck heiligt die Mittel** the end justifies the means

Heiligen-: ~**bild** *das* picture of a saint; ~**legende** *die* life of a saint; ~**schein** *der* gloriole; aureole; (um den Kopf) halo; **jmdn. mit einem** ~**schein umgeben** (fig.) be unable to see sb.'s faults

Heiligkeit *die;* ~ **(a)** holiness; **Seine/Euere** ~ (Anrede) His/Your Holiness; **(b)** (der Ehe, Taufe usw.) sanctity; sacredness

*****heilig|sprechen** ⇒ **heilig a**

Heilig·sprechung *die;* ~, ~**en** (kath. Kirche) canonization

Heiligtum *das;* ~s, **Heiligtümer** shrine; **sein Arbeitszimmer ist sein** ~ (fig.) his study is his sanctuary *or* sanctum

heil-, Heil-: ~**kraft** *die* healing *or* curative power; ~**kräftig** *Adj.* medicinal ⟨*herb, plant, etc.*⟩; curative ⟨*effect*⟩; ~**kraut** *das* medicinal *or* officinal herb; ~**kunde** *die* medicine; ~**kundig** *Adj.* skilled in medicine *or* the art of healing *postpos.;* ~**los 1** *Adj.* hopeless, awful ⟨*mess, muddle*⟩; utter, (coll.) terrible ⟨*confusion*⟩; **2** *adv.* hopelessly; ~**methode** *die* method of treatment; ~**mittel** *das* (auch fig.) remedy (**gegen** for); (Medikament) medicament; ~**pflanze** *die* medicinal *or* officinal plant *or* herb; ~**praktiker** *der* ▶85 non-medical practitioner; ~**quelle** *die* mineral spring

heilsam *Adj.* salutary ⟨*lesson, effect, experience, etc.*⟩

Heils-: ~**armee** *die* Salvation Army; ~**botschaft** *die* message of salvation; ~**lehre** *die* (auch fig.) doctrine of salvation

Heilung *die;* ~, ~**en** ▶329 healing; (von Krankheit, Kranken) curing; **wenig Hoffnung auf** ~ **haben** have little hope of being cured; **diese Salbe wird die** ~ **der Wunde beschleunigen** this ointment will help the wound to heal faster

Heilungs·prozess, ***Heilungs·prozeß** *der* healing process

heim /haim/ *Adv.* home

Heim *das;* ~[e]s, ~e **(a)** (Zuhause) home; **ein eigenes** ~: a home of his/their *etc.* own; **(b)** (Anstalt, Alters~) home; (für Obdachlose) hostel; (für Studenten) hall of residence; hostel

Heim-: ~**arbeit** *die* outwork; **etw. in** ~**arbeit herstellen lassen** have sth. produced by home-workers; ~**arbeiter** *der,* ~**arbeiterin** *die* home-worker; outworker

Heimat /'haima:t/ *die;* ~, ~**en** home; homeland

Heimat-: ~**dichter** *der* regional writer; ~**erde** *die* native soil; ~**film** *der* [sentimental] film in a[n idealized] regional setting; ~**hafen** *der* home port; ~**kunde** *die* local history, geography, and natural history; ~**land** *das* homeland; native land; (fig.) home

heimatlich *Adj.* native ⟨*dialect*⟩; **die** ~**en Berge** the mountains of [one's] home; ~**e Klänge** sounds which evoke memories of home

heimat-, Heimat-: ~**los** *Adj.* homeless; **durch den Krieg** ~**los werden** be displaced by the war; ~**lose** *der/die; adj. Dekl.* homeless person; **die** ~**losen** the homeless; ~**museum** *das* museum of local history; ~**stadt** *die* home town; ~**vertriebene** *der/die; adj. Dekl.* expellee [from his/her homeland]

heim-: ~|**begleiten** *tr. V.* **jmdn.** ~**begleiten** take *or* see sb. home; ~|**bringen** *unr. tr. V.* **(a)** ⇒ ~**begleiten; (b)** bring home

Heimchen *das;* ~s, ~ **(a)** (ugs. abwertend: Frau) ~ **[am Herd]** little hausfrau *or* housewife; **(b)** (Grille) house cricket

Heim·computer *der* home computer

heim|dürfen *unr. itr. V.* be allowed [to go] home; **darf ich heim?** may I go home?

heimelig /'haiməliç/ *Adj.* cosy

heim-, Heim-: ~**erzieher** *der* ▶85 counsellor in a home for children or young people; ~|**fahren 1** *unr.*

itr. V.; mit sein go home; **2** *unr. tr. V.* (mit dem Auto) drive ⟨*person*⟩ home; **∼fahrt** *die* way home; (∼reise) journey home; **∼|finden** *unr. itr. V.* find one's way home; **∼|führen** *tr. V.* (a) (geleiten) take home; (b) (geh. veralt.: heiraten) **er führte sie ∼:** he took her to wife (arch.); **∼|gehen** *unr. itr. V.; mit sein* (a) go home; (b) (geh. verhüll.: sterben) pass away; **∼|holen** *tr. V.* (a) fetch home; (b) (geh. verhüll.) **Gott hat ihn [zu sich] ∼geholt** he has been called to his Maker

heimisch *Adj.* (a) (einheimisch) indigenous, native ⟨*plants, animals, etc.*⟩ (in + *Dat.* to); domestic, home ⟨*industry*⟩; **die ∼en Flüsse und Seen** the rivers and lakes of his/her *etc.* native land; **vor ∼em Publikum** (Sport) in front of a home crowd; (b) *nicht präd.* (zum Heim gehörend) **an den ∼en Herd zurückkehren** go back home; (c) **∼ sein/sich ∼ fühlen** be/feel at home

heim-, Heim-: ∼kehr *die;* ∼: return home; homecoming; **∼|kehren** *itr. V.; mit sein* return home (aus from); **∼kehrer** *der* home-comer; **die ∼kehrer aus dem Urlaub/Krieg** the holidaymakers returning home/ the soldiers returning from the war; **∼kind** *das* child brought up in a home; **∼|kommen** *unr. itr. V.; mit sein* come *or* return home; **∼|laufen** *unr. itr. V.; mit sein* run [back] home; **schnell ∼laufen** dash home; **∼leiter** *der* warden; (eines Kinderheims/Jugendheims) superintendent; (eines Pflegeheims) director; **∼leiterin** *die* warden; (eines Kinderheims/Jugendheims) superintendent; (eines Pflegeheims) matron

heimlich **1** *Adj.* secret. **2** *adv.* secretly; ⟨*meet*⟩ secretly, in secret; **er ist ∼ weggelaufen** he slipped *or* stole away; **∼, still und leise** (ugs.) on the quiet; quietly

Heimlichkeit *die;* ∼, ∼en; *meist Pl.* secret; **in aller ∼:** in secret; secretly

Heimlichtuer /-tu:ɐ/ *der;* ∼s, ∼ (abwertend) secretive person

heim-, Heim-: ∼mannschaft *die* (Sport) home team *or* side; **∼|müssen** *unr. itr. V.* have to go home; **∼niederlage** *die* (Sport) home defeat; **∼reise** *die* journey home; **∼|schicken** *tr. V.* send home; **∼sieg** *der* (Sport) home win; **∼spiel** *das* (Sport) home match *or* game; **∼|suchen** *tr. V.* (a) ⟨*storm, earthquake, epidemic*⟩ strike; ⟨*disease*⟩ afflict; ⟨*nightmares, doubts*⟩ plague; ⟨*catastrophe, fate*⟩ overtake; **von Dürre ∼gesucht** drought-ridden; (b) (aufsuchen) ⟨*visitor, salesman, etc.*⟩ descend [up]on; **∼suchung** *die;* ∼, ∼en affliction; visitation

Heim·tücke *die;* ∼ (Bösartigkeit) [concealed] malice; (Hinterlistigkeit, fig.: einer Krankheit) insidiousness

heim·tückisch **1** *Adj.* (bösartig) malicious; (fig.) insidious ⟨*disease*⟩; (hinterlistig) insidious. **2** *adv.* maliciously

heim-, Heim-: ∼vorteil *der* (Sport) advantage of playing at home; home advantage; **∼wärts** /∼vɛrts/ (nach Hause zu) home; (in Richtung Heimat) homeward[s]; **∼weg** *der* way home; **sich auf den ∼weg machen** set off [for] home

Heim·weh *das* homesickness; **nach einem Ort ∼ haben** be homesick for a place

heimweh·krank *Adj.* homesick

Heim·werker *der* handyman; do-it-yourselfer

heim|zahlen *tr. V.* **jmdm. etw. ∼** pay sb. back *or* get even with sb. for sth.; **es jmdm. in gleicher Münze ∼** pay sb. back in the same coin

Heini /ˈhaini/ *der;* ∼s, ∼s (ugs. Schimpfwort) idiot; clot (Brit. coll.)

Heinzel·männchen /ˈhaintsl̩-/ *das;* ∼s, ∼: brownie

Heirat /ˈhaɪraːt/ *die;* ∼, ∼en marriage

heiraten **1** *itr. V.* marry; get married; **∼ müssen** (verhüll.) have to get married. **2** *tr. V.* marry

heirats-, Heirats-: ∼absichten *Pl.* marriage plans; **∼annonce** *die* advertisement for a marriage partner; **∼antrag** *der* proposal *or* offer of marriage; **jmdm. einen ∼antrag machen** propose to sb.; **∼anzeige** *die* (a) (Anzeige, dass jemand heiratet) announcement of a/the forthcoming marriage; (b) = **∼annonce**; **∼fähig** *Adj.* ⟨*person*⟩ of marriageable age;

∼schwindler *der* person who makes a spurious offer of marriage for purposes of fraud; **∼urkunde** *die* marriage certificate; **∼vermittler** *der,* **∼vermittlerin** *die* ▶ 85 marriage broker

heischen /ˈhaɪʃn̩/ *tr. V.* (geh.) demand

heiser /ˈhaɪzɐ/ **1** *Adj.* hoarse. **2** *adv.* hoarsely; in a hoarse voice

Heiserkeit *die;* ∼: hoarseness

heiß /haɪs/ **1** *Adj.* (a) hot; hot, torrid ⟨*zone*⟩; **brennend/ glühend ∼:** burning/scorching hot; **kochend** *od.* **siedend ∼:** boiling hot; piping hot ⟨*soup etc.*⟩; **jmdm. ist ∼:** sb. feels hot; **es überläuft mich ∼ und kalt** I feel hot and cold all over; **sie haben sich die Köpfe ∼ geredet** the conversation/debate became heated; (b) (heftig) heated ⟨*debate, argument*⟩; impassioned ⟨*anger*⟩; burning, fervent ⟨*desire*⟩; fierce ⟨*fight, battle*⟩; (c) (innig) ardent, passionate ⟨*wish, love*⟩; **∼e Tränen weinen** weep bitterly; cry one's heart out; **∼en Dank** (ugs.) thanks a lot! (coll.); (d) (aufreizend) hot ⟨*rhythm etc.*⟩; sexy ⟨*blouse, dress, etc.*⟩; **was fürn ∼er Typ!** (salopp) what a guy! (coll.); (e) (ugs.: gefährlich) hot (sl.) ⟨*goods, money*⟩; **ein ∼es Thema** a controversial subject; *s. auch* **Eisen b;** (f) *nicht präd.* (ugs.: Aussichten habend) hot ⟨*favourite, tip, contender, etc.*⟩; **auf einer ∼en Spur sein** be hot on the scent; (g) *nicht präd.* (ugs.: schnell) hot; *s. auch* **Ofen e;** (h) (ugs.: brünstig) on heat; (i) (salopp: aufgereizt) **jmdn. ∼ machen** turn sb. on (coll.). **2** *adv.* (a) (heftig) ⟨*fight*⟩ fiercely; **∼ umkämpft** fiercely contested *or* disputed; **ein ∼ umstrittenes Thema** a hotly debated subject; **der ∼ umstrittene Direktor** the highly controversial director; **es ging ∼ her** things got heated; sparks flew (coll.); (auf einer Party usw.) things got wild; (b) (innig) **jmdn. ∼ und innig lieben** love sb. dearly *or* with all one's heart; **ihr ∼ geliebter Gatte/Sohn** her dearly beloved husband/son; **sein ∼ geliebtes Auto** his beloved car; **das ∼ ersehnte Fahrrad** the bicycle he/ she has/had longed for so fervently

heiß·blütig *Adj.* hot-blooded; ardent, passionate ⟨*lover*⟩; (leicht erregbar) hot-tempered

heißen¹ **1** *unr. itr. V.* (a) (den Namen tragen) be called; **ich heiße Hans** I am called Hans; my name is Hans; **er heißt mit Nachnamen Müller** his surname is Müller; **so wahr ich … heiße** (ugs.) as sure as I'm standing here; **dann will ich Emil ∼** (ugs.) then I'm a Dutchman (coll.); (b) (bedeuten) mean; **was heißt „danke" auf Französisch?** what's the French for 'thanks'?; **das will viel/ nicht viel ∼:** that means a lot/doesn't mean much; **was soll das denn ∼?** what's that supposed to mean?; **was heißt hier: morgen?** what do you mean, tomorrow?; **das heißt** that is [to say]; (c) (lauten) ⟨*saying*⟩ go; **der Titel/ sein Motto heißt …:** the title/his motto is …; (d) *unpers.* **es heißt, dass …:** they say *or* it is said that …; **es heißt, dass sie unheilbar krank ist** she is said to be incurably ill; **es soll nicht ∼, dass …:** never let it be said that …; (e) *unpers.* **in dem Gedicht/Roman/Artikel heißt es …:** in the poem/novel/article it says that …; (f) *unpers.* **jetzt heißt es aufgepasst!** (ugs.) you'd better watch out now! **2** *unr. tr. V.* (a) (geh.: auffordern) tell; bid; **jmdn. etw. tun ∼:** tell sb. to do sth.; bid sb. do sth.; (b) (geh.: bezeichnen als) call; **jmdn. einen Lügner ∼:** call sb. a liar; **jmdn. willkommen ∼:** bid sb. welcome; (c) (veralt.: nennen) name; call

heißen² *tr. V.* ⇒ **hissen**

heiß-, Heiß-: *∗**∼ersehnt** ⇒ **heiß 2 b;** *∗**∼geliebt** ⇒ **heiß 2b;** **∼hunger** *der:* einen **∼hunger auf etw.** (*Akk.*) *od.* **nach etw. [haben]** [have] a craving for sth.; **etw. mit [wahrem] ∼hunger verschlingen** devour sth. ravenously; [absolutely (coll.)] wolf sth. down; **∼hungrig** **1** *Adj.* ravenous; **2** *adv.* ravenously; voraciously; **∼|laufen** **1** *unr. itr. V.; mit sein* run hot; ⟨*engine*⟩ run hot, overheat; **sie hat soviel telefoniert, dass die Drähte heißliefen** she made so many telephone calls that the wires were buzzing; **2** *unr. refl. V.* run hot; ⟨*engine*⟩ run hot, overheat

Heiß·luft *die* hot air

Heißluft: ∼backofen *der* fan oven; **∼ballon** *der* hot-air balloon

heiß-, Heiß-: ~**mangel** *die* rotary ironer; ~**sporn** *der* hothead;*~**umkämpft,** *~**umstritten** ⇨ **heiß 2 a**

Heißwasser·bereiter *der* water heater

heiter /ˈhaɪtɐ/ *Adj.* **(a)** (fröhlich) cheerful, happy ‹*person, nature*›; happy, merry ‹*laughter*›; **(b)** (froh stimmend) cheerful ‹*music etc.*›; (amüsant) funny, amusing ‹*story etc.*›; **einer Sache** (*Dat.*) **eine** ~**e Seite abgewinnen** look on the bright side of sth.; **das kann ja** ~ **werden!** (ugs. iron.) that'll be fun (iron.); **(c)** (sonnig) fine ‹*weather*›

Heiterkeit *die;* ~ **(a)** (Frohsinn) cheerfulness; **(b)** (Belustigung) merriment; **allgemeine** ~ **erregen** provoke *or* cause general merriment

heizbar *Adj.* heated ‹*windscreen, room, etc.*›; **das Zimmer ist nicht/schwer** ~: the room has no heating/ is difficult to heat

Heiz·decke *die* electric blanket

heizen /ˈhaɪtsn̩/ **1** *itr. V.* have the heating on; **der Ofen heizt gut** the stove gives off *or* throws out a good heat; **mit Kohle** ~: use coal for heating. **2** *tr. V.* **(a)** heat ‹*room etc.*›; **(b)** stoke ‹*furnace, boiler, etc.*›; **sie** ~ **ihre Öfen mit Öl** their boilers are oil-fired

Heizer *der;* ~**s,** ~ (einer Lokomotive) fireman; stoker; (eines Schiffes) stoker

Heiz-: ~**gerät** *das* heater; ~**kessel** *der* boiler; ~**kissen** *das* heating pad; ~**körper** *der* radiator; ~**kosten** *Pl.* heating costs; ~**lüfter** *der* fan heater; ~**ofen** *der* stove; heater; **ein elektrischer** ~**ofen** an electric heater; ~**öl** *das* heating oil; fuel oil; ~**periode** *die* heating period; ~**strahler** *der* radiant heater

Heizung *die;* ~, ~**en (a)** [central] heating *no pl., no indef. art.;* **(b)** (ugs.: Heizkörper) radiator

Heizungs-: ~**anlage** *die* heating system; ~**keller** *der* boiler room (in the basement); ~**monteur** *der* ▶ 85 ▌ heating engineer

Hektar /ˈhɛktaːɐ̯/ *das od. der;* ~**s,** ~**e** ▶ 189 ▌ hectare

Hektik /ˈhɛktɪk/ *die;* ~: hectic rush; (des Lebens) hectic pace; **nur keine** ~**!** (ugs.) take it easy!

hektisch 1 *Adj.* hectic; **nun mal nicht so** ~**!** take it easy!. **2** *adv.* ‹*work, run to and fro*› frantically; ~ **zugehen** be hectic; ~ **leben** lead a hectic life

Hekto: ~**liter** *der od. das* hectolitre; ~**pascal** *das* hectopascal

helau /heˈlaʊ/ *Interj.: cheer or greeting used at Carnival time*

Held /hɛlt/ *der;* ~**en,** ~**en** hero; **du bist mir ein schöner** ~ (scherzh.) a fine one you are!

Helden-: ~**dichtung** *die* (Literaturw.) epic *or* heroic poetry; ~**epos** *das* (Literaturw.) heroic epic

heldenhaft 1 *Adj.* heroic. **2** *adv.* heroically

helden-, Helden-: ~**mut** *der* heroism; ~**mütig 1** *Adj.* heroic; **2** *adv.* heroically; ~**sage** *die* (Literaturw.) heroic legend; (aus Norwegen, Island) heroic saga; ~**tat** *die* heroic feat *or* deed; **das war keine** ~**tat** (spött.) that was nothing to be proud of

Heldentum *das;* ~**s** heroism

Heldin *die;* ~, ~**nen** heroine

helfen /ˈhɛlfn̩/ *unr. itr. V.* **(a)** help; **jmdm.** ~ **[etw. zu tun]** help *or* assist sb. [to do sth.]; lend *or* give sb. a hand [in doing sth.]; **jmdm. bei etw.** ~**:** help *or* assist sb. with sth.; **jmdm. in den/aus dem Mantel** ~**:** help sb. into *or* on with/out of *or* off with his/her coat; **jmdm. über die Straße/in den Bus** ~**:** help sb. across the road/on to the bus; **dem Kranken war nicht mehr zu** ~**:** the patient was beyond [all] help; **dir ist nicht zu** ~ (ugs.) you're a hopeless case; **sich** (*Dat.*) **nicht mehr zu** ~ **wissen** be at one's wits' end; **dem werde ich** ~**, einfach die Schule zu schwänzen!** (ugs.) I'll teach him to play truant; **ich kann mir nicht** ~**, aber …:** I'm sorry, but [I have to say that] …; **hilf dir selbst, so hilft dir Gott** (Spr.) God helps those who help themselves; **(b)** (hilfreich sein, nützen) help; **das hilft gegen** *od.* **bei Kopfschmerzen** it is good for *or* helps to relieve headaches; **da hilft alles nichts** there's nothing *or* no help for it; **es hilft nichts** it's no use *or* good; **was hilfts?** what's the use *or* good?;

damit ist uns nicht geholfen that is no help to us; that doesn't help us

Helfer *der;* ~**s,** ~, **Helferin** *die;* ~, ~**nen** helper; (Mitarbeiter) assistant; (bei einem Verbrechen) accomplice; **ein** ~ **in der Not** a friend in need

Helfers·helfer *der;* ~**s,** ~ (abwertend) accomplice

Helikopter /heliˈkɔptɐ/ *der;* ~**s,** ~**:** helicopter

Helium /ˈheːli̯ʊm/ *das;* ~**s** helium

hell /hɛl/ **1** *Adj.* **(a)** (von Licht erfüllt) light ‹*room etc.*›; well-lit ‹*stairs*›; **es wird** ~**:** it's getting light; **es war schon** ~**er Morgen/Tag** it was already broad daylight; **am** ~**en Tag** (ugs.) in broad daylight; **in** ~**en Flammen stehen** be in flames *or* ablaze; **(b)** (klar, viel Licht spendend) bright; **(c)** (blass) light ‹*colour*›; fair ‹*skin, hair*›; light-coloured ‹*clothes*›; ~**es Bier** ≈ lager; **(d)** (akustisch) **ein** ~**er Ton/Klang** a high, clear sound; **eine** ~**e Stimme** a high, clear voice; **ein** ~**es Lachen** a ringing laugh; **(e) ein** ~**er Kopf sein** be bright; **(f)** (voll bewusst) lucid ‹*moment, interval*›; **(g)** *nicht präd.* (ugs.: absolut) sheer, utter ‹*madness, foolishness, despair, nonsense*›; unbounded, boundless ‹*enthusiasm*›; unrestrained ‹*jubilation*›; **in** ~**e Wut geraten** fly into a blind rage; **er hat seine** ~**e Freude an ihr/daran** she/it is his great joy. **2** *adv.* **(a)** brightly ‹*lit*›; ‹*shine, blaze*› brightly; **ein** ~ **erleuchtetes Zimmer** a brightly-lit room; ~ **lodernd** blazing; ~ **lodernde Flammen** raging flames; **(b)** (in hoher Tonlage) ~ **läuteten die Glocken** the bells rang out high and clear; ~ **lachen** give a ringing laugh; **(c)** (sehr) highly ‹*enthusiastic, delighted, indignant, etc.*›

hell-: ~**auf** *Adv.* highly ‹*enthusiastic, indignant, etc.*›; ~**auf lachen** laugh out loud; ~**blau** *Adj.* light blue; ~**blond** *Adj.* very fair; light blonde; ~**braun** *Adj.* light brown

helle *Adj.; nicht attr.* (landsch.) bright; intelligent

Helle *das; adj. Dekl.* ≈ lager

Hellebarde /hɛləˈbardə/ *die;* ~, ~**n** (hist.) halberd

Heller *der;* ~**s,** ~**:** heller; **bis auf den letzten** ~/**bis auf** ~ **und Pfennig** (ugs.) down to the last penny *or* (Amer.) cent

hell-: *~**erleuchtet** ⇨ **hell 2 a;** ~**gelb** *Adj.* light yellow; ~**grau** *Adj.* light grey; ~**grün** *Adj.* light green; ~**haarig** *Adj.* fair[-haired]; ~**häutig** *Adj.* fair[-skinned]; fair-skinned, pale-skinned ‹*race*›; ~**hörig** *Adj.* **(a)** (aufmerksam) ~**hörig werden** sit up and take notice (coll.); **jmdn.** ~**hörig machen** make sb. sit up and take notice (coll.); **(b)** (schalldurchlässig) badly *or* poorly sound-proofed

***hellicht** ⇨ **helllicht**

Helligkeit *die;* ~, ~**en** (auch Physik) brightness

helllicht /ˈhɛllɪçt/ *Adj.* **es ist** ~**er Tag** it's broad daylight; **am** ~**en Tag** in broad daylight

***hellodernd** /ˈhɛloːdɐnt/ ⇨ **hell 2 a**

hell-, Hell-: ~**rot** *Adj.* light red; ~**sehen** *unr. itr. V.; nur im Inf.* ~**sehen können** have second sight; be clairvoyant; ~**seher** *der,* ~**seherin** *die* clairvoyant; ~**seherisch** *Adj.* clairvoyant; ~**sichtig** *Adj.* **(a)** (durchschauend) perceptive; **(b)** (weitblickend) far-sighted; ~**wach** *Adj.* **(a)** (ganz wach) wide awake; **(b)** (ugs.: klug) bright

Helm /hɛlm/ *der;* ~**[e]s,** ~**e** helmet; ~ **ab zum Gebet!** (Milit.) helmets off for prayers!

Helm·busch *der* plume; crest

Hemd /hɛmt/ *das;* ~**[e]s,** ~**en (a)** (Oberhemd) shirt; **(b)** (Unterhemd) [under]vest; undershirt; **(c)** *in* **etw. wechseln wie sein** ~ (ugs. abwertend) change sth. as often as one changes one's clothes; **das** ~ **ist mir näher als der Rock** for me charity begins at home; **mach dir nicht ins** ~ (salopp) don't get [all] uptight (coll.); **für sie gibt er sein letztes** *od.* **das letzte** ~ **her** (ugs.) he'd sell the shirt off his back to help her; **jmdn. bis aufs** ~ **ausziehen** (ugs.) have the shirt off sb.'s back (coll.)

Hemd-: ~**bluse** *die* shirt; ~**blusen·kleid** *das* shirt-waist dress

Hemds·ärmel *der* shirtsleeve; **in** ~**n** in [one's] shirtsleeves

hemdsärmelig /~ɛrməlɪç/ *Adj.* **(a)** (im Hemd) shirtsleeved *attrib.;* in [one's] shirtsleeves *postpos.;* **(b)** (ugs.: leger) casual ‹*manner*›; informal ‹*style*›

Hemisphäre /hemi'sfɛːrə/ *die;* ~, ~**n** hemisphere
hemmen /'hɛmən/ *tr. V.* (a) (verlangsamen) slow [down]; retard; (b) (aufhalten) check; stem ‹*flow*›; (c) (beeinträchtigen) hinder; hamper
Hemmnis *das;* ~**ses**, ~**se** obstacle, hindrance (**für** to)
Hemm·schuh *der* (a) (Hemmnis) obstacle, hindrance (**für** to); (b) (Eisenb.) slipper [brake]
Hemmung *die;* ~, ~**en** (a) inhibition; ~**en haben** have inhibitions; be inhibited; (b) (Skrupel) scruple
hemmungs·los 1 *Adj.* unrestrained; unrestrained, unbridled ‹*passion*›; (skrupellos) unscrupulous. 2 *adv.* unrestrainedly; without restraint; ‹*cry, laugh, scream*› uncontrollably; (skrupellos) unscrupulously
Hemmungslosigkeit *die;* ~: lack of restraint; (Skrupellosigkeit) unscrupulousness
Hendl /'hɛndl/ *das;* ~**s**, ~**[n]** (bayr., österr.) chicken
Hengst /hɛŋst/ *der;* ~**[e]s**, ~**e** (Pferd) stallion; (Kamel) male; (Esel) male; jackass
Hengst-: ~**fohlen** *das,* ~**füllen** *das* colt; [male] foal
Henkel /'hɛnkl/ *der;* ~**s**, ~: handle
Henkel-: ~**kanne** *die* jug; (größer) pitcher; ~**mann** *der* (ugs.) *portable set of stacked containers for taking a hot meal to one's work*
henken /'hɛŋkn̩/ *tr. V.* (veralt.) hang
Henker *der;* ~**s**, ~ hangman; (Scharfrichter, auch fig.) executioner; **hols der** ~! damn [it]! (coll.); **the devil take it!** (coll.); **weiß der** ~! the devil only knows (coll.)
Henkers-: ~**knecht** *der* hangman's assistant; (eines Scharfrichters) executioner's assistant; (fig.) henchman; ~**mahlzeit** *die* last meal (before execution)
Henna /'hɛna/ *die;* ~ *od. das;* ~**[s]** henna
Henne /'hɛnə/ *die;* ~, ~**n** hen
her /heːɐ̯/ *Adv.* (a) ~ **damit** give it to me; give it here (coll.); ~ **mit dem Geld** hand over *or* give me the money; **vom Fenster** ~: from the window; **von weit** ~: from far away *or* a long way off; **er ist von Köln** ~: he is *or* comes from Cologne; (b) (zeitlich) **jmdn. von früher/von der Schulzeit** ~ **kennen** know sb. from earlier times/ from one's schooldays; (c) **von der Konzeption** ~: as far as the basic design is concerned; **das ist von der Sache** ~ **nicht vertretbar** it is unjustifiable in the nature of the matter; (d) **einen Monat/einige Zeit/lange** ~ **sein** be a month/some time/a long time ago; **es ist lange** ~, **dass wir** …: it is a long time since we …; **es muss 5 Jahre** ~ **sein, dass wir** …: it must be five years since we …; (e) **es ist nicht weit** ~ **mit jmdm./etw.** (ugs.) sb./sth. isn't all that hot (coll.); (f) **hinter jmdm.** (ugs.)/etw. ~ **sein** be after sb./sth.
herab /hɛ'rap/ *Adv.* **bis** ~ **auf etw.** (*Akk.*) down to sth.; **die Treppe/den Berg** ~: down the stairs/the mountain; **von oben** ~ (fig.) condescendingly
herab-, Herab- (*s. auch* **herunter-**)*:* ~**fließen** *unr. itr. V.; mit sein* (geh.) flow down; ~**hängen** *unr. itr. V.* (a) (nach unten hängen) hang [down] (**von** from); (fig.) ‹*clouds*› hang low [in the sky]; (b) (schlaff hängen) ‹*hair, arms, etc.*› hang down; ~**lassen** 1 *unr. tr. V.* let down; lower; 2 *unr. refl. V.* **sich** ~**lassen, etw. zu tun** condescend *or* deign to do sth.; ~**lassend** 1 *Adj.* condescending; patronizing (**zu** towards); 2 *adv.* condescendingly; patronizingly; in a condescending *or* patronizing manner; ~**lassung** *die* condescension; ~**mindern** *tr. V.* (a) reduce; (b) (schlechtmachen) belittle, disparage ‹*achievement, qualities, etc.*›; ~**minderung** *die* belittlement; disparagement; ~**regnen** *itr. V.; mit sein* ‹*drops of rain*› fall; (fig.) rain down; ~**rieseln** *itr. V.; mit sein* (geh.) trickle down; ‹*snow*› fall gently; ‹*snowflakes*› float down; ~**sehen** *unr. itr. V.* (a) (nach unten sehen) look down (**auf** + *Akk.* on); (b) (geringschätzig betrachten) **auf jmdn.** ~**sehen** look down on sb.; ~**senken** *refl. V.* (geh.) ‹*night, evening*› fall; ‹*mist, fog*› settle, descend (**auf** + *Akk.* on, over); ~**setzen** *tr. V.* (a) (reduzieren) reduce, cut ‹*cost, price, working hours, etc.*›; reduce ‹*speed*›; **zu** ~**gesetzten Preisen** at reduced prices; (b) (abwerten) belittle; disparage; ~**setzung** *die;* ~: ⇨ ~**setzen:** (a) reduction, cut (*Gen.* in); (b) belittling; disparagement; ~**sinken** *unr. itr. V.; mit sein* sink [down]; (fig.) ‹*night*›

fall; descend; ‹*mist, fog*› settle, descend (**auf** + *Akk.* on, over); ~**steigen** *unr. itr. V.; mit sein* (geh.) descend; climb down; (vom Pferd) dismount; ~**stürzen** *unr. itr. V.; mit sein* plummet down; **er stürzte vom Gerüst** ~: he fell from *or* off the scaffolding; ~**stürzende Felsbrocken** falling rocks; 2 *refl. V.* throw oneself (**von** from *or* off); ~**würdigen** *tr. V.* belittle; disparage ~**würdigung** *die; o. Pl.* belittling; disparagement; ~**ziehen** *unr. tr. V.* (geh.) (a) pull down; (b) (moralisch) **jmdn. zu sich/auf sein eigenes Niveau** ~**ziehen** drag sb. down to one's own level
heran /hɛ'ran/ *Adv.* **an etw.** (*Akk.*) ~: close to *or* right up to sth.; **nur** ~ **zu mir!, immer** ~**!** come closer!
heran-, Heran-: ~**bilden** *tr. V.* train [up]; (auf der Schule, Universität) educate; 2 *refl. V.* (sich entwickeln) develop; ~**bringen** *unr. tr. V.* (a) (zu jmdm. bringen) bring [up] (**an** + *Akk.,* **zu** to); (b) (vertraut machen) **jmdn. an etw.** (*Akk.*) ~**bringen** introduce sb. to sth.; ~**fahren** *unr. itr. V.; mit sein* drive up (**an** + *Akk.* to); ~**führen** 1 *tr. V.* (a) (in die Nähe führen) lead up; bring up ‹*troops*›; (b) (nahe bringen) bring up (**an** + *Akk.* to); (c) (vertraut machen) **jmdn. an etw.** (*Akk.*) ~**führen** introduce sb. to sth.; 2 *itr. V.* **an etw.** (*Akk.*) ~**führen** lead to sth.; ~**gehen** *unr. itr. V.; mit sein* (a) go up (**an** + *Akk.* to); **näher** ~**gehen** go [up] closer; (b) (anpacken) **an ein Problem/eine Aufgabe/die Arbeit** *usw.* ~**gehen** tackle a problem/a task/ the work *etc.;* ~**holen** *tr. V.* fetch; ~**kommen** *unr. itr. V.; mit sein* **an etw.** (*Akk.*) ~**kommen** come *or* draw near to sth.; approach sth.; **ganz nahe an etw.** (*Akk.*) ~**kommen** come right up to sth.; (b) (zeitlich) **der große Tag war** ~**gekommen** the big day had arrived; (c) **an etw.** (*Akk.*) ~**kommen** (erreichen) reach sth.; (erwerben) obtain sth.; get hold of sth.; **an jmdn.** ~**kommen** (fig.) get hold of sb.; **an jmds. Erfolg/Rekord** ~**kommen** (fig.) equal sb.'s success/record; ~**machen** *refl. V.* (ugs.) (a) (beginnen) **sich an etw.** (*Akk.*) ~**machen** get down to *or* (coll.) get going on sth.; (b) (nähern) **sich an jmdn.** ~**machen** chat sb. up (coll.); ~**nehmen** *unr. tr. V.* **die Lehrlinge werden ganz schön** ~**genommen** the apprentices are really made to work [hard]; **der Lehrer nahm den Schüler tüchtig** ~: the teacher took the boy firmly in hand; ~**nahen** *itr. V.; mit sein* (geh.) approach; draw near; ~**reichen** *tr. V.* (a) [**an etw.** (*Akk.*)] ~ **reichen** reach [sth.]; (b) **an jmdn./etw.** ~**reichen** (fig.) come *or* measure up to the standard of sb.'s sth.; ~**reifen** *itr. V.; mit sein* ‹*fruit, crops*› ripen; (fig.) ‹*plan*› mature; **zur Frau/zum Mann/zu einer großen Malerin** ~**reifen** mature into a woman/man/great painter; ~**rücken** 1 *tr. V.* pull up ‹*table*›; draw *or* pull *or* bring up ‹*chair*›; 2 *itr. V.; mit sein* move *or* come closer *or* nearer; ‹*troops*› advance (**an** + *Akk.* towards); **dicht od. nah** ~**rücken** move up close (**an** + *Akk.* to); **mit seinem Stuhl** ~**rücken** draw *or* pull *or* bring one's chair up closer; ~**schaffen** *tr. V.* bring; (liefern) supply; ~**schleichen** *unr. itr. V. mit sein; refl. V.* [**sich an jmdn./etw.**] ~**schleichen** creep *or* sneak up [on sb./to sth.]; ~**tasten** *refl. V.* **sich [an etw.** (*Akk.*)] ~**tasten** grope *or* feel one's way [over to sth.]; (fig.) feel one's way [towards sth.]; ~**tragen** *unr. tr. V.* (a) bring [over]; (b) **eine Bitte/Beschwerde an jmdn.** ~**tragen** (jmdm. vortragen) go/come to sb. with a request/complaint; ~**treten** *unr. itr. V.; mit sein* (a) (an eine Stelle treten) come/ go up (**an** + *Akk.* to); (b) (sich wenden) **an jmdn.** ~**treten** approach sb.; ~**wachsen** *unr. itr. V.; mit sein* grow up; (fig.) develop; **zum Mann/zur Frau** ~**wachsen** grow up into *or* to be a man/woman; **die** ~**wachsende Generation** the rising *or* up-and-coming generation; ~**wachsende** *der/die; adj. Dekl.* (a) young person; (b) (Rechtsw.) adolescent; ~**wagen** *refl. V.* venture near; dare to go near; **sich an etw.** (*Akk.*) ~**wagen** venture near sth.; dare to go near sth.; (fig.) venture *or* dare to tackle *or* attempt sth.; ~**ziehen** 1 *unr. tr. V.* (a) (an eine Stelle ziehen) pull *or* draw over; pull *or* draw up ‹*chair*›; **etw. zu sich** ~**ziehen** pull *or* draw sth. towards one; (b) (fig.: beauftragen) call *or* bring in; **weitere Arbeitskräfte** ~**ziehen** bring in more labour; (c) (fig.) (in Betracht ziehen) refer to; (geltend machen) invoke; quote; 2 *unr. itr. V.; mit sein* (auch fig.) approach; (Milit.) advance

herauf /hɛ'rauf/ *Adv.* up; **vom Tal** ~: up from the valley
herauf-: ~|**arbeiten** *refl. V.* (a) work one's/its way
up; (b) (hocharbeiten) work one's way up; ~|**be-
schwören** *tr. V.* (a) (verursachen) cause, bring about
‹disaster, war, crisis›; cause, provoke ‹dispute, argument›;
give rise to ‹criticism›; (b) (erinnern) evoke ‹memories etc.›;
~|**bringen** *unr. tr. V.* bring up; ~|**fahren** 1 *unr. itr.
V.; mit sein* drive up; (mit einem Motorrad, Rad) ride up; 2 *unr.
tr. V.* jmdn. ~**fahren** drive sb. up; ~|**führen** 1 *itr. V.*
es führen zwei Wege ~: there are two paths up; 2 *tr.
V.* show ‹person› up; ~|**kommen** *unr. itr. V.; mit sein*
(a) (nach oben kommen) come up; **auf den Baum/die
Mauer** ~**kommen** climb *or* get up the tree/up on the
wall; (b) (aufsteigen) rise; come up; (c) (bevorstehen) ‹storm›
be approaching *or* gathering *or* brewing; ~|**setzen** *tr.
V.* increase, raise, put up ‹prices, rents, interest rates, etc.›;
~|**steigen** *unr. itr. V.; mit sein* (a) (nach [hier] oben kom-
men) climb [up]; (b) (aufsteigen) rise; come up; ~|**ziehen**
1 *unr. tr. V.* pull up; 2 *unr. itr. V.; mit sein* ‹storm› be
approaching *or* gathering *or* brewing; ‹disaster› be approaching

heraus /hɛ'raus/ *Adv.* ~ **aus dem Bett!** out of bed!; ~
mit dir! get out of here!; ~ **damit!** (gib her!) hand it over!;
(weg damit!) let's have it!; ~ **mit der Sprache!** out with it!;
aus einem Gefühl der Einsamkeit ~: out of a feeling
of loneliness; [**aus etw.**] ~ **sein** (auch fig.) be out [of sth.];
aus dem Gröbsten ~ **sein** (ugs.) be over the worst; **fein
~ sein** (ugs.) be sitting pretty (coll.)

heraus-, Heraus-: ~|**arbeiten** *tr. V.* (a) (aus Stein,
Holz) fashion, carve (**aus** out of); (b) (hervorheben) bring out
‹difference, aspect, point of view, etc.›; develop ‹observation,
remark›; ~|**bekommen** 1 *unr. tr. V.* (a) (entfernen) get
out (**aus** of); (b) (ugs.: lösen) work out ‹problem, answer,
etc.›; solve ‹puzzle›; (c) (ermitteln) find out; **etw. aus
jmdm.** ~**bekommen** get sth. out of sb.; (d) (als Wechselgeld bekommen) 5 **DM** ~**bekommen** get back 5 marks
change; (e) (von sich geben) utter; say; 2 *unr. itr. V.* (Wechselgeld bekommen) **richtig/falsch** ~**bekommen** (ugs.) get the
right/wrong change; ~|**bilden** *refl. V.* develop;
~|**bitten** *unr. tr. V.* jmdn. ~**bitten** ask sb. to come out-
[side]; ~|**boxen** *tr. V.* (a) (Fußball, Handball) punch out;
(b) (befreien) bail out; ~|**brechen** 1 *unr. tr. V.* knock
out; (mit brutaler Gewalt) wrench out; pull up ‹paving stone›;
2 *unr. itr. V.; mit sein* ‹anger, hatred› burst forth, erupt;
~|**bringen** *unr. tr. V.* (a) (nach außen bringen) bring out
(**aus** of); (b) (nach draußen begleiten) show out; (c) (veröffentlichen) bring out; publish; (aufführen) put on, stage ‹play›;
screen ‹film›; (d) (auf den Markt bringen) bring out; launch;
(e) (populär machen) make widely known; **jmdn./etw. ganz
groß** ~**bringen** launch sb./sth. in a big way; (f) (ugs.: ermitteln) ⇒ ~**bekommen** 1 c; (g) (ugs.: lösen) ⇒ ~**bekom-
men** 1 b; (h) (von sich geben) utter; say; ~|**drehen** *tr. V.*
unscrew; ~|**drücken** *tr. V.* (a) etw. ~**drücken**
squeeze sth. out (**aus** of); squeeze *or* press ‹juice, oil› out
(**aus** of); (b) (vorwölben) stick out ‹chest etc.›; ~|**fahren**
1 *unr. itr. V.; mit sein* (a) (nach außen fahren) aus etw.
~**fahren** drive out of sth.; (mit dem Rad, Motorrad) ride out
of sth.; **der Zug fuhr aus dem Bahnhof** ~: the train
pulled out of the station; (b) (fahrend ~**kommen**) come out;
(c) (ugs.: entschlüpfen) ‹word, remark, etc.› slip out; 2 *unr.
tr. V.* (a) **den Wagen/das Fahrrad** [**aus dem Hof**]
~**fahren** drive the car/ride the bicycle out [of the yard];
(b) (Sport) **eine gute Zeit/einen Sieg** ~**fahren** record a
good *or* fast time/a victory; ~|**finden** 1 *unr. tr. V.* (a)
(entdecken) find out; trace ‹fault›; **man fand** ~, **dass** ...:
it was found *or* discovered that ...; (b) (aus einer Menge) pick
out (**aus** from ‹among›); find (**aus** among); 2 *unr. tr. V.*
find one's way out (**aus** of); ~|**fliegen** 1 *unr. itr. V.; mit
sein* (a) fly out (**aus** of); (b) (aus etw. fallen) be thrown out
(**aus** of); (c) (ugs.: entlassen werden) be fired *or* (coll.) sacked
(**bei** from); 2 *unr. tr. V.* fly out (**aus** of); ~|**forderer** *der;*
~**s,** ~ (auch Sport) challenger; ~|**fordern** 1 *tr. V.* (a)
(auch Sport) (zu etw.) (b) (heraufbeschwören) provoke ‹person,
resistance, etc.›; invite ‹criticism›; court ‹danger›; **sein
Schicksal** ~**fordern** tempt fate *or* providence; 2 *itr. V.*
(provozieren) **zu etw.** ~**fordern** provoke sth.; ~|**for-
dernd** 1 *Adj.* provocative; (Streit suchend) challenging, defiant ‹words, speech, look›; 2 *adv.: s. Adj.*: provocatively;
challengingly; defiantly

Heraus·forderung *die* (auch Sport) challenge; (Prokation) provocation

heraus-, Heraus-: ~|**fühlen** *tr. V.* sense; fee...
~|**führen** *tr., itr. V.* lead out (**aus** of); ~|**gabe** *die; o.
Pl.* (a) (von Eigentum, Personen, Geiseln usw.) handing over;
(Rückgabe) return; (b) (das Veröffentlichen) publication; (Redak-
tion) editing; ~|**geben** 1 *unr. tr. V.* (a) (nach außen geben)
hand *or* pass out; (b) (aushändigen) hand over ‹property, person, hostage, etc.›; (zurückgeben) return; give back; (c) (als
Wechselgeld zurückgeben) 5 **DM/zu viel** ~**geben** give 5
marks/too much change; (d) (veröffentlichen) publish; (für die
Veröffentlichung bearbeiten) edit [for publication]; (e) issue
‹stamp, coin, etc.›; (f) (erlassen) issue; 2 *itr. V.* give change;
können Sie [**auf 100 DM**] ~**geben?** do you have *or*
can you give me change [for 100 marks]?; ~|**geber** *der,*
~**geberin** *die* publisher; (Redakteur[in]) editor;
~|**gehen** *unr. itr. V.; mit sein* (a) (nach außen) go out;
leave; **aus sich** ~**gehen** come out of one's shell; (b) (sich
entfernen lassen) ‹stain, cork, nail, etc.› come out; ~|**grei-
fen** *unr. tr. V.* pick out; select; **sich** (*Dat.*) jmdn. ~**greifen** pick *or* single sb. out (**aus** from); (fig.) take ‹example,
aspect, etc.› (**aus** from); ~|**haben** *unr. tr. V.* (ugs.) (a)
(entfernt haben) have got ‹stain, nail, cork, etc.› out; **ich will
ihn aus dem Verein** ~**haben** I want him out of the club;
(b) (~gefunden haben) have found out; (c) (gelöst haben) have
worked out *or* solved ‹problem›; have solved ‹puzzle›; **wir
hat etwas anderes** ~ **als ich** we arrived at *or* got differ-
ent answers; **ich habs** ~! I've done it!; ~|**halten** 1
unr. tr. V. (a) (nach außen halten) put *or* stick out (**aus** of);
(b) (ugs.: fernhalten, nicht verwickeln) keep out (**aus** of); 2 *unr.
refl. V.* keep *or* stay out; ~|**hängen¹** *unr. itr. V.* hang out
(**aus** of); ~|**hängen²** *tr. V.* hang out (**aus** of);
~|**hauen** *unr. tr. V.* (a) (durch Hauen fertigen) carve ‹figure,
letters, relief, etc.› (**aus** from, out of); (b) (ugs.: befreien) get
out; (aus Schwierigkeiten) bail out; ~|**heben** 1 *unr. tr. V.*
(a) (nach außen heben) lift out (**aus** of); (b) (hervorheben) bring
out; **es ist diese Eigenschaft, die ihn aus der Masse**
~**hebt** it is this quality that raises him above *or* sets him
apart from the rest; 2 *unr. refl. V.* stand out (**aus** from);
~|**helfen** *unr. tr. V.* jmdm. ~**helfen** (auch fig.) help sb.
out (**aus** of); ~|**holen** *tr. V.* (a) (nach außen holen) bring
out; (b) (ugs.: abgewinnen) get out; gain, win ‹victory, points›;
er holte das Letzte aus sich ~: he made an all-out *or*
supreme effort; (c) (ugs.: erwirken) gain, win ‹wage increase,
advantage, etc.›; get, achieve ‹result›; (d) (ugs.: durch Fragen)
get out; (e) (ugs.: ~arbeiten) bring out ‹difference, aspect,
point of view›; ~|**hören** *tr. V.* (a) hear; (b) (erkennen)
detect, sense (**aus** in); ~|**kehren** *tr. V.* parade; **den Vor-
gesetzten** ~**kehren** parade the fact that one is in charge;
~|**kommen** *unr. itr. V.; mit sein* (a) (nach außen kommen)
come out (**aus** of); (b) (ein Gebiet verlassen) **er ist nie aus
seiner Heimatstadt** ~**gekommen** he's never been out
of *or* never left his home town; **wir kamen aus dem
Staunen/Lachen nicht** ~ (fig.) we couldn't get over our
surprise/stop laughing; (c) (ugs.: einen Ausweg finden) get out
(**aus** of); (d) (ugs.: auf den Markt kommen) come out; **mit einem Produkt** ~**kommen** bring out *or* launch a product;
(e) (erscheinen) ‹book, timetable, etc.› come out; be published, appear; ‹postage stamp, coin› be issued; ‹play› be
staged; (f) (ugs.: bekannt werden) come out; (g) (ugs.: zur Sprache kommen) **mit etw.** ~**kommen** come out with sth.; (h)
(ugs.: sich erfolgreich produzieren) **ganz groß** ~**kommen**
make a big splash; (i) (deutlich werden) come out; ‹colour›
show up; (j) (ugs.: sich als Resultat ergeben) **bei etw.** ~**kommen** come out of *or* emerge from sth.; **auf dasselbe**
~**kommen** amount to the same thing; **was kommt bei
der Aufgabe** ~? what is the answer to the question?;
dabei kommt nichts ~: nothing will come of it; **was
soll dabei** ~**kommen?** what's that supposed to achieve?;
(k) (ugs.: ausspielen) lead; **wer kommt** ~? whose lead is
it?; **mit etw.** ~**kommen** lead sth.; ~|**kriegen** *tr. V.*
(ugs.) ⇒ ~**bekommen**; ~|**kristallisieren** 1 *tr. V.*
(a) (Chemie) crystallize [out]; (b) (zusammenfassen) extract;
2 *refl. V.* (a) (Chemie) crystallize [out]; ‹crystal› form; (b)
(entwickeln) crystallize (**aus** out of); ~|**lassen** *unr. tr. V.*
(ugs.) (a) (nach außen kommen lassen) let out (**aus** of); release
(**aus** from); (b) (weglassen) leave out (**aus** of); ~|**laufen**
unr. itr. V.; mit sein (a) run out (**aus** of); (Fußball)

ɔalkeeper› come out; **(b)** (nach außen fließen) run out **(aus .)**; ∼**lesen** unr. tr. V. **(a)** (entnehmen) tell **(aus** from); **(b)** ɪnterpretieren) etw. aus etw. ∼**lesen** read sth. into sth.; **(c)** (auswählen) pick out **(aus** from); ∼**locken** tr. V. entice out **(aus** of); lure ‹enemy, victim, etc.› out **(aus** of); jmdn. aus seiner Reserve ∼**locken** draw sb. out of his/her shell; ∼**machen** (ugs.) **1** tr. V. take out; get out ‹stain›; **2** refl. V. come on well; ∼**müssen** unr. itr. V. (ugs.) **(a)** aus etw. ∼**müssen** have to leave sth.; **dieser Zahn muss** ∼: this tooth has to come out; **(b)** (aufstehen müssen) have to get up; **(c)** (gesagt werden müssen) **das musste einfach** ∼! I simply had to get that off my chest (coll.); ∼**nehmbar** Adj. removable; detachable ‹lining›; ∼**nehmen** unr. tr. V. **(a)** take out **(aus** of); **den Gang** ∼**nehmen** (fig.) put the car into neutral; **(b)** (ugs.: entfernen) take out, remove ‹appendix, tonsils, tooth, etc.›; **sich** (Dat.) **die Mandeln** ∼**nehmen lassen** have one's tonsils out; **(c)** (ugs.) **sich** (Dat.) **Freiheiten** ∼**nehmen** take liberties; **sich** (Dat.) **zuviel** ∼**nehmen** go too far; ∼**picken** tr. V. (fig.) pick out **(aus** of); ∼**platzen** itr. V.; mit sein (ugs.) **(a)** (∼lachen) burst out laughing; **(b)** (spontan äußern) **mit etw.** ∼**platzen** blurt sth. out; ∼**pressen** tr. V. **(a)** (aus etw. pressen) ⇒ ∼**drücken a**; **(b)** (erpressen) squeeze out ‹money› (aus from); wring out ‹confession, concession› **(aus** from); ∼**putzen** tr. V. **(a)** (festlich kleiden) dress up; **sich** ∼**putzen** get dressed up; **(b)** (festlich schmücken) deck out; **sich** ∼**putzen** be decked out; ∼**ragen** itr. V. **(a)** jut out, project **(aus** from); **(sich erheben über) aus etw.** ∼**ragen** rise above sth.; **(b)** (hervortreten) stand out **(aus** from); ∼**ragend** Adj. outstanding; ∼**reden** refl. V. (ugs.) talk one's way out **(aus** of); ∼**reißen** unr. tr. V. **(a)** tear or rip out **(aus** of); pull up or out ‹plant›; pull out ‹hair›; pull up ‹floor›; rip out ‹tiles›; **(b)** (aus der Umgebung, der Arbeit) tear away **(aus** from); jmdn. aus einem Gespräch/seiner Lethargie ∼**reißen** drag sb. away from a conversation/jolt or shake sb. out of his/her lethargy; **(c)** (ugs.: befreien) save; ∼**rücken 1** tr. V. **(a)** (nach außen rücken) move out **(aus** of); **(b)** (ugs.: hergeben) hand over; cough up (coll.) ‹money›; **2** itr. V.; mit sein **mit etw./der Sprache** ∼**rücken** come out with sth./it; ∼**rufen 1** unr. itr. V. call or shout out **(aus** of); **2** unr. tr. V. call out; **jmdn. aus einer Sitzung** ∼**rufen** call sb. out of a meeting; ∼**rutschen** itr. V.; mit sein **(a)** slip out **(aus** of); **(b)** (ugs.: entschlüpfen) ‹remark etc.› slip out; **die Bemerkung war ihr nur so** ∼**gerutscht** the remark just slipped out somehow; ∼**saugen** unr. (auch regelm.) tr. V. suck out **(aus** of); ∼**schälen** refl. V. **(a)** (erkennbar werden) emerge **(aus** from); **(b)** (sich erweisen) **sich als etw.** ∼**schälen** turn out or prove to be sth.; ∼**schlagen 1** unr. tr. V. **(a)** knock out; **(b)** (ugs.: gewinnen) get ‹discount, advantage, etc.›; make ‹money, profit›; **2** unr. itr. V.; mit sein ‹flames› leap out **(aus** of); ∼**schleudern** tr. V. hurl or fling out **(aus** of); ∼**schlüpfen** itr. V.; mit sein slip out **(aus** of); ∼**schmecken 1** tr. V. **etw.** ∼**schmecken** [**können**] be able to taste sth.; **2** itr. V. taste; ∼**schmuggeln** tr. V. smuggle out **(aus** of); ∼**schneiden** unr. V. cut out **(aus** of); ∼**schrauben** tr. V. unscrew; ∼**schreiben** unr. V. copy out **(aus** from); ∼**schreien** unr. itr. V. **seine Wut/seinen Zorn/seinen Hass** ∼**schreien** vent or give vent to one's anger/rage/hatred in a loud outburst; *∼**sein** ⇒ **heraus**; ∼**springen** unr. itr. V.; mit sein **(a)** jump or leap out **(aus** of); **(b)** (sich lösen) come out; **(c)** (ugs.: zu erwarten sein) **dabei springt nicht viel für ihn** ∼: there's not much in it for him; ∼**sprudeln 1** itr. V.; mit sein bubble out **(aus** of); **2** tr. V. **sie sprudelte die Worte** ∼: the words tumbled from her lips; ∼**stehen** unr. itr. V. protrude; stick out; ∼**stellen 1** tr. V. **(a)** put out[side]; **einen Spieler** ∼**stellen** (Sport) send a player off; **(b)** (hervorheben) emphasize; bring out; present, set out ‹principles etc.›; **2** refl. V. **es stellte sich** ∼, **dass** ...: it turned out or emerged that ...; **wie sich später** ∼**stellte, hatte er** ...: it turned out later that he had ...; **sich als falsch/wahr** usw. ∼**stellen** turn out or prove to be wrong/true etc.; ∼**strecken** tr. V. stick out **(aus**

of); jmdm. die Zunge ∼**strecken** stick or put one's tongue out at sb.; **seinen Arm/Kopf zum Fenster** ∼**strecken** stick or put one's arm/head out of the window; ∼**streichen** unr. tr. V. **(a)** (ausstreichen) cross out; delete **(aus** from); **(b)** (hervorheben) point out; ∼**strömen** itr. V.; mit sein **(a)** (ausströmen) ‹water etc.› pour out **(aus** of); ‹gas› escape **(aus** from); **(b)** (herauskommen) ‹Menschenmenge› pour out **(aus** of); ∼**stürzen** itr. V.; mit sein **(a)** (∼fallen) fall out **(aus** of); **(b)** (eilen) rush or dash out **(aus** of); ∼**suchen** tr. V. pick out; look out ‹file›; ∼**treten** unr. itr. V.; mit sein **(a)** come out **(aus** of); **auf den Balkon** ∼**treten** come or step out onto the balcony; **(b)** (sich abzeichnen) ‹veins etc.› stand out; ∼**trommeln** tr. V. (ugs.) get out; ∼**wachsen** itr. unr. V.; mit sein grow out **(aus** of); ∼**werfen** unr. tr. V. **(a)** throw out **(aus** of); **(b)** ⇒ **hinauswerfen**; ∼**winden** unr. refl. V. wriggle out **(aus** of); ∼**wirtschaften** tr. V. make ‹profit etc.› **(aus** out of); ∼**ziehen 1** unr. tr. V. **(a)** pull out **(aus** of); **(b)** (wegbringen) pull out, withdraw ‹troops etc.›; **2** unr. itr. V.; mit sein move out **(aus** of)

herb /hɛrp/ Adj. **(a)** [slightly] sharp or astringent ‹taste›; dry ‹wine›; [slightly] sharp or tangy ‹smell, perfume›; **(b)** bitter ‹disappointment, loss›; severe ‹face, features›; austere ‹beauty›; **(c)** (unfreundlich) harsh ‹words, criticism›

herbei /hɛr'bai/ Adv. ∼ [**zu mir**]! come [over] here!

herbei-: ∼|**bringen** unr. tr. V. bring [over]; ∼|**eilen** itr. V.; mit sein hurry over; come hurrying up; ∼|**führen** tr. V. produce, bring about ‹decision›; bring about, cause ‹downfall›; cause ‹accident, death›; ∼|**holen** tr. V. fetch; ∼|**kommen** unr. itr. V.; mit sein come up or along; ∼|**lassen** unr. refl. V. (iron.) **sich** ∼**lassen, etw. zu tun** condescend to do sth.; ∼|**laufen** unr. itr. V.; mit sein come running up; ∼|**reden** tr. V. talk ‹crisis, problem, etc.› into existence; ∼|**rufen** unr. tr. V. call over; **Hilfe/einen Arzt** ∼**rufen** summon help/call a doctor; ∼|**schaffen** tr. V. bring; (besorgen) get; ∼|**sehnen** tr. V. long for; ∼|**strömen** itr. V.; mit sein come in crowds; come flocking; ∼|**wünschen** tr. V. long for; **jmdn.** ∼**wünschen** long for sb. to come

her-: ∼|**bekommen** unr. tr. V. get; ∼|**bemühen** (geh.) **1** tr. V. **jmdn.** ∼:**bemühen** trouble sb. to come.; **2** refl. V. take the trouble to come; ∼|**beordern** tr. V. summon; send for

Herberge /'hɛrbɛrgə/ die; ∼, ∼**n (a)** (veralt.: Gasthaus) inn; **(b)** (Jugend∼) [youth] hostel

Herbergs-: ∼**mutter** die, ∼**vater** der warden [of the/a youth hostel]

her-: ∼|**bestellen** tr. V. **jmdn.** ∼**bestellen** ask sb. to come; (∼beordern) summon sb.; ∼|**bitten** unr. tr. V. **jmdn.** ∼**bitten** ask sb. to come; ∼|**bringen** tr. V. **etw.** ∼**bringen** bring sth. [here]

Herbst /hɛrpst/ der; ∼[**e**]**s**, ∼**e** ▶ 293| autumn; fall (Amer.); s. auch **Frühling**

Herbst-: ∼**anfang** der beginning of autumn; ∼**blume** die autumn flower; ∼**ferien** Pl. autumn half-term holiday sing.

herbstlich 1 Adj. ▶ 293| autumn attrib.; autumnal; **es wird** ∼: autumn is coming. **2** adv. ▶ 293| **sich** ∼ **färben** take on the colours of autumn

Herbst-: ∼**tag** der autumn day; ∼**zeit·lose** die; ∼, ∼**n** (Bot.) meadow saffron

Herd /he:ɐt/ der; ∼[**e**]**s**, ∼**e (a)** (Kochstelle) cooker; stove; **das Essen auf dem** ∼ **haben** (ugs.) be cooking something; **eigener** ∼ **ist Goldes wert** there's no place like home (prov.); **(b)** (Ausgangspunkt) centre (of disturbance/rebellion); **(c)** (Med.) focus; seat

Herde /'he:ɐdə/ die; ∼, ∼**n** herd; **eine** ∼ **Schafe** a flock of sheep

Herden-: ∼**tier** das **(a)** gregarious animal; **(b)** (abwertend: Mensch) sheep; ∼**trieb** der (auch fig. abwertend) herd instinct

Herd·platte die hotplate; (eines Kohlenherds) top

herein /hɛ'rain/ Adv. ∼! come in!; [**immer**] **nur** ∼ **mit dir!** come on in!

herein-: ∼|**bekommen** unr. tr. V. (ugs.) get in ‹fresh stocks›; pick up ‹radio station›; recover ‹investment›;

~|**bemühen** (geh.)   **1** *tr. V.* **jmdn.** ~**bemühen** trouble sb. to come in;   **2** *refl. V.* take the trouble to come in; ~|**bitten** *unr. tr. V.* **jmdn.** ~**bitten** ask *or* invite sb. in; ~|**brechen** *unr. itr. V.; mit sein* **(a)** (geh.: hart treffen) **über jmdn./etw.** ~**brechen** ⟨*fate, disaster, misfortune, etc.*⟩ befall *or* overtake sb./sth.; **(b)** (geh.: beginnen) ⟨*night, evening, dusk*⟩ fall; ⟨*winter*⟩ strike, break; ~|**bringen** *unr. tr. V.* **(a)** bring in; **(b)** (wettmachen) make up ⟨*loss*⟩;   make up for ⟨*delay*⟩;   recoup ⟨*costs*⟩; ~|**drängen** *itr. V.; mit sein* push one's way in; **in etw.** (*Akk.*) ~**drängen** push one's way into sth.; ~|**dürfen** *unr. itr. V.* (ugs.) be allowed in; **in etw. (**_Akk._**)** ~**dürfen** be allowed into sth.; **darf er** ~? may *or* can he come in?; ~|**fallen** *unr. itr. V.; mit sein* **(a)** ⟨*light*⟩ shine in; **(b)** (ugs.: betrogen werden) be taken for a ride (fig. coll.); be done (coll.); **bei/mit etw.** ~**fallen** be taken for a ride with sth. (fig. coll.); **auf jmdn./etw.** ~**fallen** be taken in by sb./sth.; ~|**führen** *tr. V.* **jmdn.** ~**führen** show sb. in; ~|**holen** *tr. V.* **(a)** bring in; **(b)** (ugs.: verdienen) make (coll.); ~|**kommen** *unr. itr. V.; mit sein* come in; **in das Haus/ zur Tür** ~**kommen** come into the house/in through the door; ~|**kriegen** *tr. V.* (ugs.) ⇒ ~**bekommen;** ~|**lassen** *unr. tr. V.* let *or* allow in; ~|**legen** *tr. V.* (ugs.) **jmdn.** ~**legen** take sb. for a ride (fig. coll.) **(mit, bei** with); ~|**nehmen** *tr. V.* **(a)** bring in; **etw. ins Haus** ~**nehmen** bring sth. into the house; **(b)** (in eine Liste) include; **etw. in sein Sortiment** ~**nehmen** start selling sth. as well; ~|**platzen** *itr. V.; mit sein* (ugs.) burst in; come bursting in; ~|**regnen** *itr. V.* (unpers.) **es regnet** ~: the rain's coming in; ~|**reichen** *tr. V.* hand *or* pass in; ~|**rufen** *unr. tr. V.* **jmdn.** ~**rufen** call sb. in; ~|**schauen** *itr. V.* (landsch.) ⇒ ~**sehen;** ~|**schleichen** *unr. itr. V. mit sein, unr. refl. V.* creep *or* steal in; ~|**schneien** *unr. itr. V.* **(a)** *mit sein* (ugs.) turn up out of the blue (coll.); **(b)** (unpers.) **es schneit** ~: the snow's coming in; ~|**sehen** *unr. itr. V.* **(a)** see in; (hereinblicken) look in; **(b)** (kurz besuchen) look *or* drop in (**bei** on); ~|**spazieren** *itr. V.; mit sein* (ugs.) walk in; stroll in; **nur** ~**spaziert!** come right in!; ~|**stecken** *tr. V.* **den Kopf zur Tür** ~**stecken** put one's head round the door; ~|**strömen** *itr. V.; mit sein* ⟨*water etc.*⟩ pour in; ⟨*people*⟩ pour *or* stream in; **in etw.** (*Akk.*) ~**strömen** pour *or* stream into sth.; ~|**stürmen** *itr. V.; mit sein* rush *or* dash in; come rushing *or* dashing in; (wütend) storm in; come storming in; ~|**stürzen** *itr. V.; mit sein* rush in; burst in; **ins Zimmer** ~**stürzen** rush *or* burst into the room; ~|**tragen** *unr. tr. V.* carry in; **etw. ins Haus** ~**tragen** carry sth into the house; ~|**wagen** *refl. V.* venture to come in; ~|**wollen** *unr. itr. V.* (ugs.) want to come in; **ins Haus** ~**wollen** want to come into the house

her-, Her-: ~|**fahren** **1** *unr. itr. V.; mit sein* come here; (mit einem Auto) drive *or* come here; (mit einem [Motor]rad) ride *or* come here; **hinter/vor jmdm./etw.** ~**fahren** drive/ride along behind/in front of sb./sth.;   **2** *unr. tr. V.* **jmdn.** ~**fahren** drive sb. here; ~**fahrt** *die* journey here; ~|**fallen** *unr. itr. V.; mit sein* **(a)** **über jmdn.** ~**fallen** set upon *or* attack sb.; ⟨*animal*⟩ attack sb.; **(b)** **über etw.** (*Akk.*) ~**fallen** (etw. gierig zu essen beginnen) fall upon sth.; ~|**finden** *unr. itr. V.* find one's way here; ~|**führen** *tr. V.* **jmdn.** ~**führen** bring sb. here; ~**gang** *der:* **den** ~**gang der Ereignisse** the sequence of events; **schildern Sie den** ~**gang des Überfalls** describe what happened during the attack; ~|**geben** *unr. tr. V.* **(a)** hand over; (weggeben) give away; **sein Geld für etw.** ~**geben** put one's money into sth.; **er hat sein Letztes** ~**gegeben** he gave everything he had; **dazu gebe ich mich nicht** ~: I won't have anything to do with it; **(b)** (reichen) give; **gib es** ~! hand it over!; **(c)** (erbringen); **was seine Beine** ~**gaben** as fast as his legs could carry him; ~**gebracht** *Adj.; nicht präd.* time-honoured; ~|**gehen** *unr. itr. V.; mit sein* **(a)** (begleiten) **neben/vor/hinter jmdm.** ~**gehen** walk along beside/in front of/behind sb.; **(b)** (ugs.) ~**gehen und etw. tun** just [go and] do sth.; **(c)** (unpers.) (ugs.) **bei der Debatte ging es heiß** ~: the sparks really flew in the debate; ~|**gehören** ⇒ **hierhergehören;** ~**gelaufen** *Adj.; nicht präd.* **dieser** ~**gelaufene Strolch** this good-for-nothing rascal from Heaven knows where; ~|**haben**

unr. tr. V. (ugs.) **wo hat er/sie das** ~? where did he/she get that from?; ~|**halten** **1** *unr. itr. V.* ~**halten müssen [für jmdn./etw.]** be the one to suffer [for sb./ sth.]; **2** *unr. tr. V.* hold out; ~|**holen** *tr. V.* fetch; **etw. von weit** ~**holen** get sth. from a long way away; **weit** ~**geholt** far-fetched; ~|**hören** *itr. V.* listen; **alle mal** ~**hören!** listen everybody

Hering /'heːrɪŋ/ *der;* ~**s,** ~**e** **(a)** herring; **wie die** ~**e** (fig.) packed together like sardines; **(b)** (Zeltpflock) peg

Herings-: ~**filet** *das* herring fillet; ~**salat** *der* herring salad

herinnen /hɛ'rɪnən/ *Adv.* (südd., österr.) in here

her-: ~**jagen** **1** *tr. V.* **jmdn./ein Tier vor sich** (*Dat.*) ~**jagen** drive *or* chase sb./an animal along ahead of one;   **2** *itr. V.; mit sein* **hinter jmdm.** ~**jagen** chase *or* pursue sb.; **hinter etw.** ~**jagen** (fig.) pursue sth.; ~|**kommen** *unr. itr. V.; mit sein* **(a)** come here; **komm [mal]** ~! come here!; **(b)** (stammen) come; ~**kommen das;** ~ **(a)** (Brauch, Sitte) tradition; **(b)** ⇒ **Herkunft a;** ~**kömmlich** /~kœmlɪç/ *Adj.* conventional; traditional ⟨*custom*⟩

Herkunft /'heːʀkʊnft/ *die;* ~**, Herkünfte** /'heːʀkʏnftə/ origin[s *pl.*]; **einfacher** (*Gen.*) *od.* **von einfacher** ~ **sein** be of humble origin *or* stock

Herkunfts-: ~**bezeichnung** *die* indication of country of origin; ~**land** *das* country of origin

her-: ~|**laufen** *unr. itr. V.; mit sein* **(a)** **vor/hinter/ neben jmdm.** ~**laufen** run [along] in front of/behind/ alongside sb.; **(b)** (nachlaufen) **hinter jmdm.** ~**laufen** run after sb.; (fig.) chase sb. up; **(c)** (zum Sprechenlaufen laufen) come on foot; (schneller) come running up; ~|**leiten** **1** *tr. V.* derive (**aus, von** from); **etw. von jmdm.** ~**leiten** derive sth. from sb.;   **2** *refl. V.* **sich von/aus etw.** ~**leiten** derive *or* be derived from sth.; ~|**locken** *tr. V.* **jmdn./ ein Tier** ~**locken** lure sb./an animal here; ~|**machen** (ugs.) **1** *refl. V.* **(a)** **sich über etw.** (*Akk.*) ~**machen** get stuck into sth. (coll.); **sich über das Essen** ~**machen** fall upon the food; **(b)** (~fallen) **sich über jmdn.** ~**machen** set on *or* attack sb.; **2** *tr. V.* **wenig** ~**machen** not look much (coll.); **viel** ~**machen** look great (coll.)

Hermelin /hɛrmə'liːn/ *das;* ~**s,** ~**e** ermine; (im Sommerfell) stoat

hermetisch /hɛr'meːtɪʃ/ **1** *Adj.* hermetic. **2** *adv.* hermetically; **ein Dorf** *usw.* ~ **abriegeln** seal a village *etc.* off completely

her|müssen *unr. itr. V.* (ugs.) **das muss her** I/we have to *or* must have it

her·nach *Adv.* (veralt.) after that

her|nehmen *unr. tr. V.* **wo soll ich das Geld** ~? where am I supposed to get the money from *or* find the money?

heroben /hɛ'roːbn̩/ *Adv.* (südd., österr.) up here

Heroin /hero'iːn/ *das;* ~**s** heroin

heroin·süchtig *Adj.* addicted to heroin *postpos.*

heroisch *Adj.* heroic

Herold /'heːrolt/ *der;* ~**[e]s,** ~**e** herald

Herr /hɛr/ *der;* ~**n** (selten: ~**en**), ~**en** **(a)** (Mann) gentleman; **ein feiner** ~: a refined gentleman; **das Kugelstoßen der** ~**en** (Sport) the men's shot-put; **mein Alter** ~ (ugs. scherzh.: Vater) my old man (coll.); **Alter** ~ (Studentenspr.) former member; **(b)** ▶ **34** (Titel, Anrede) ~ **Schulze** Mr Schulze; ~ **Professor/Dr. Schulze** Professor/Dr Schulze; ~ **Minister/Direktor/Studienrat Schulze** Mr Schulze; ~ **Minister/Professor/Doktor** Minister/Professor/doctor; ~ **Vorsitzender/Präsident** Mr Chairman/President; **Sehr geehrter** ~ **Schulze!** Dear Sir; (bei persönlicher Bekanntschaft) Dear Mr Schulze; **Sehr geehrte** ~**en!** Dear Sirs; ~ **Ober!** waiter!; **mein** ~: sir; **meine** ~**en** gentlemen; **bitte sehr, der** ~! there you are, sir; **Ihr** ~ **Vater/Sohn** your father/son; **(c)** (Gebieter) master; **mein** ~ **und Gebieter** (scherzh.) my lord and master (joc.); **die** ~**en der Schöpfung** (ugs. scherzh.) their lordships (coll. joc.); **sein eigener** ~ **sein** be one's own master; ~ **der Lage sein/bleiben** be/remain master of the situation; **nicht mehr** ~ **seiner Sinne sein** be no longer in control of oneself; **aus aller** ~**en Länder[n]** (geh.) from the four corners of the earth; from all over the world; **(d)** (Besitzer) master (**über** + *Akk.* of); **(e)** (christl. Rel.: Gott) Lord; **Gott der** ~: Lord God

Herrchen *das;* ~**s**, ~: master

herren-, Herren-: ~**abend** *der* stag evening; ~**ausstatter** *der* [gentle]men's outfitter; ~**bekanntschaft** *die* gentleman acquaintance; ~**besuch** *der* gentleman visitor/visitors; ~**besuch haben** have a gentleman visitor/gentlemen visitors; ~**friseur** *der* men's hairdresser; ~**los** *Adj.* abandoned (*car, luggage*); stray (*dog, cat*); ~**mode** *die* men's fashion; ~**schuh** *der* man's shoe; ~**schuhe** men's shoes; ~**toilette** *die* [gentle]men's toilet

Herr·gott *der;* ~**s** **(a)** (ugs.: Gott) **der [liebe]/unser** ~: the Lord [God]; God; ~ **noch mal!** for Heaven's sake!; for God's sake!; **(b)** (südd., österr.: Kruzifix) crucifix

Herrgotts·frühe *die* **in in aller** ~: at the crack of dawn

her·richten **1** *tr. V.* **(a)** (bereitmachen) get (*room, refreshments, etc.*) ready; dress (*shop window*); arrange (*table*); **(b)** (in Ordnung bringen) renovate; do up (coll.). **2** *refl. V.* get ready

Herrin *die;* ~, ~**en** mistress; (als Anrede) my lady

herrisch **1** *Adj.* overbearing; peremptory; imperious. **2** *adv.* peremptorily; imperiously

herr·je, herrjemine /hɛrˈjeːminə/ *Interj.* (ugs.) goodness gracious [me]; heavens [above]

herrlich **1** *Adj.* marvellous; marvellous, glorious (*weather*); magnificent, splendid (*view*); magnificent, gorgeous (*clothes*); (*sth. tastes, looks, sounds*) wonderful, marvellous. **2** *adv.* marvellously; ~ **und in Freuden leben** live in clover

Herrlichkeit *die;* ~, ~**en** **(a)** *o. Pl.* (Schönheit) magnificence; splendour; **die** ~ **Gottes** the glory of God; **(b)** *meist Pl.* (herrliche Sache) marvellous *or* wonderful thing

Herrschaft *die;* ~, ~**en** **(a)** *o. Pl.* rule; (Macht) power; **die** ~ **an sich reißen/erringen** seize/gain power; **die** ~ **über sich/das Auto verlieren** (fig.) lose control of oneself/the car; **(b)** *Pl.* (Damen u. Herren) ladies and gentlemen; **meine** ~**en!** ladies and gentlemen!

herrschaftlich *Adj.* **(a)** (zu einer Herrschaft gehörend) master's/mistress's (*coach etc.*); **(b)** (einer Herrschaft gemäß) grand

Herrschafts·form *die* system of government

herrschen /ˈhɛrʃn̩/ *itr. V.* **(a)** (regieren) rule; (*monarch*) reign, rule; **(b)** (vorhanden sein) **draußen** ~ **30° Kälte** it's 30° below outside; **überall herrschte große Freude/Trauer** there was great joy/sorrow everywhere; **jetzt herrscht hier wieder Ordnung** order has been restored here; **(c)** (unpers.) prevail; **es herrscht jetzt Einigkeit** there is now agreement

herrschend *Adj., nicht präd.* **(a)** ruling (*power, party, etc.*); reigning (*monarch*); **die Herrschenden** the rulers; those in power; **(b)** (vorhanden) prevailing (*opinion, view, conditions, etc.*)

Herrscher *der;* ~**s**, ~: ruler; ~ **über ein Volk sein** be [the] ruler of a people

Herrscher-: ~**geschlecht** *das* ruling dynasty; ~**haus** *das* ruling house

Herrscherin *die;* ~, ~**nen** ⇒ **Herrscher**

Herrsch·sucht *die* thirst for power; (herrisches Wesen) domineering nature

herrsch·süchtig *Adj.* domineering

her-: ~**rufen** *unr. tr. V.* call (*dog*); jmdn. ~**rufen** call sb. [over]; **etw. hinter jmdm.** ~**rufen** call sth. after sb.; ~**rühren** *itr. V.* **von jmdm./etw.** ~**rühren** come from sb./stem from sth.; ~**sagen** *tr. V.* **etw.** ~**sagen** recite sth. mechanically; ~**schaffen** *tr. V.* jmdn./etw. ~**schaffen** bring sb./sth. here; **das Geld** ~**schaffen** get the money; ~**schicken** *tr. V.* jmdn./etw. ~**schicken** send sb./sth. here; **jmdn./etw. hinter jmdm.** ~**schicken** send sb./sth. after sb.; ~**schieben** *unr. tr. V.* **etw.** ~**schieben** push sth. here; **etw. vor sich** (*Dat.*) ~**schieben** push sth. along in front of one; (fig.) put sth. off; ~**sehen** *unr. itr. V.* look [over] here *or* this way;

seht mal alle ~! look here *or* this way, everyone!; ***~**|sein** ⇒ **her a, d, e;** ~**|stellen** **1** *tr. V.* **(a)** (anfertigen) produce; manufacture; make; **in Deutschland** ~**gestellt** made in Germany; **etw. serienmäßig** ~**stellen** mass-produce sth.; **(b)** (zustande bringen) establish (*contact, relationship, etc.*); bring about (*peace, order, etc.*); **(c)** (gesund machen) **sie** *od.* **ihre Gesundheit ist [ganz]** ~**gestellt** she has [quite] recovered; **(d)** (zum Sprechenden stellen) **etw.** ~**stellen** put sth. [over] here; **2** *refl. V.* **stell dich** ~ **[zu mir]** [come and] stand over here [next to *or* by me]

Her·steller *der;* ~**s**, ~: producer; manufacturer

Her·stellung *die* **(a)** (Anfertigung) production; manufacture; **(b)** ⇒ **herstellen b**: establishment; bringing about

Herstellungs-: ~**kosten** *Pl.* production *or* manufacturing costs; ~**land** *das* country of manufacture

her|tragen *unr. tr. V.* **(a)** (zum Sprecher) **etw.** ~: carry sth. here; **(b)** (begleiten und tragen) **etw. hinter/vor jmdm.** ~: carry sth. along behind/in front of sb.;

herüben /hɛˈryːbn̩/ *Adv.* (südd., österr.) over here

herüber /hɛˈryːbɐ/ *Adv.* over

herüber-: ~**|bringen** *unr. tr. V.* jmdn./etw. ~**bringen** bring sb./sth. over; ~**|fahren** **1** *unr. itr. V.;* *mit sein* drive *or* come over; (mit dem Motorrad, Rad) come *or* ride over; **2** *unr. tr. V.* jmdn./etw. ~**fahren** drive sb./sth. over; ~**|geben** *unr. tr. V.* pass *or* hand over; ~**|holen** *tr. V.* jmdn./etw. ~**holen** bring sb./sth. over; ~**|kommen** *unr. itr. V.; mit sein* come over; **über den Zaun/Fluss** ~**kommen** get over the fence/across the river; **kommt doch** ~! come over!; ~**|laufen** *unr. itr. V.; mit sein* run *or* come running over; ~**|reichen** **1** *tr. V.* ⇒ **herübergeben;** **2** *intr. V.* **[über etw.** (*Akk.*)] ~**reichen** reach across [sth.]; ~**|retten** **1** *tr. V.* retain; **etw. in die Gegenwart** ~**retten** preserve sth. [until the present day]; **2** *refl. V.* (*customs, hopes, etc.*) survive; ~**|schicken** *tr. V.* jmdn./etw. ~**schicken** send sb./sth. over; ~**|sehen** *unr. itr. V.* **[zu jmdm.]** ~**sehen** look across [at sb.]; ~**|wechseln** *itr. V.; mit sein od. haben* come across

herum /hɛˈrʊm/ *Adv.* **(a)** (Richtung) round; **im Kreis** ~: round in a circle; **verkehrt/richtig** ~: the wrong/right way round; (mit Ober- und Unterseite) upside down/the right way up; **etw. falsch** *od.* **verkehrt** ~ **anziehen** put sth. on back-to-front/(Innenseite nach außen) inside out; **(b)** (Anordnung) **um jmdn./etw.** ~: around sb./sth.; **(c)** (in enger Umgebung) **um jmdn.** ~: around sb.; **um München** ~: around Munich; **(d)** (ugs.: ungefähr) **um Weihnachten/Ostern** ~: around Christmas/Easter; **um das Jahr 1050** ~: around *or* about the year 1050; **(e)** (ugs.: vorüber) ~ **sein** have passed *or* gone by; **seine Probezeit ist noch nicht** ~: his probationary period is not yet over

herum-, Herum-: ~**|albern** *itr. V.* (ugs.) fool around *or* about; ~**|ärgern** *refl. V.* (ugs.) **sich mit jmdm./etw.** ~**ärgern** keep getting annoyed with sb./sth.; ~**|blättern** *itr. V.* **in etw.** (*Dat.*) ~**blättern** keep leafing through sth.; ~**|brüllen** *itr. V.* (ugs.) go on shouting one's head off (coll.); ~**|bummeln** *itr. V.* (ugs.) **(a)** *mit sein* (spazieren) stroll *or* wander around; **(b)** (trödeln) **[mit etw.]** ~**bummeln** dawdle [over sth.]; ~**|doktern** *itr. V.* (ugs.) **an jmdm./etw.** ~**doktern** have a go at treating sb./sth.; **an etw.** (*Dat.*) ~**doktern** (fig.) fiddle *or* tinker around *or* about with sth.; ~**|drehen** **1** *tr. V.* (ugs.) turn (*key*); turn over (*coin, mattress, hand, etc.*); **den Kopf** ~**drehen** turn one's head; **2** *refl. V.* turn [a]round; **sich [auf die andere Seite]** ~**drehen** turn over [on to one's other side]; **3** *itr. V.* (ugs.) **an etw.** (*Dat.*) ~**drehen** fiddle [around *or* about] with sth.; ~**|drücken** *refl. V.* **(a)** (ugs.: vermeiden) **sich um etw.** ~**drücken** get out of *or* (coll.) dodge sth.; **(b)** (ugs.: sich aufhalten) hang around; **wo hast du dich** ~**gedrückt?** where have you been?; ~**|drucksen** *itr. V.* (ugs.) hum and haw (coll.); ~**|erzählen** *tr. V.* (ugs.) **etw.** ~**erzählen** spread sth. around; **er erzählte überall** ~, **dass ...:** he went around telling everyone that ...; ~**|experimentieren** *tr. V.* **[an jmdm./etw.]** ~**experimentieren** carry out experiments [on sb./etw.]; ~**|fahren** (ugs.) **1** *unr. itr. V.; mit sein* **(a) um etw.** ~**fahren** drive *or* go round sth.; (mit einem Motorrad, Rad) ride *or* go round sth.; (mit einem Schiff) sail round sth.; **(b)**

(irgendwohin fahren) drive/ride/sail around; **(c)** (sich plötzlich herumdrehen) spin round; **2** *unr. tr. V.* **jmdn. [in der Stadt]** ~**fahren** drive sb. around the town; ~**|fragen** *itr. V.* (ugs.) ask around (**bei** among); ~**|fuchteln** *itr. V.* (ugs.) **mit den Armen/einem Messer** *usw.* ~**fuchteln** wave one's arms/a knife *etc.* around or about; ~**|führen** **1** *tr. V.* **(a)** **jmdn. [in der Stadt]** ~**führen** show sb. around the town; *s. auch* **Nase**; **(b)** (rund um etw. führen) **jmdn. um etw.** ~**führen** lead or take sb. round sth.; **(c)** (um etw. bauen) **die Straße um etw.** ~**führen** take the road round the town; **2** *itr. V.* **um etw.** ~**führen** ‹road *etc.*› go round sth.; ~**|fuhr·werken** *itr. V.* (ugs.) mess about; ~**|fummeln** *itr. V.* (ugs.) **(a) an etw.** (*Dat.*) ~**fummeln** fiddle about with sth.; **(b)** (sich handwerklich beschäftigen) fiddle or mess around with something; **(c)** (betasten) **an jmdm.** ~**fummeln** touch sb. up (sl.); ~**|gehen** *unr. itr. V.; mit sein* **(a) um etw.** ~**gehen** go or walk round sth.; **(b)** (ziellos gehen) walk around; **im Garten** ~**gehen** walk around the garden; **(c)** (die Runde machen) go around; (~gereicht werden) be passed or handed around; **etw.** ~**gehen lassen** circulate sth.; **(d)** (vergehen) pass; go by; ~**|geistern** *itr. V.; mit sein* (ugs.) wander around or about; (fig.) ‹idea, rumour, *etc.*› go round; **jmdm. im Kopf** ~**geistern** go round in sb.'s mind; ~**|hacken** *itr. V.* (ugs.) **auf jmdm.** ~**hacken** keep getting at sb. (coll.); ~**|hängen** *unr. itr. V.* (ugs.) **(a)** (aufgehängt sein) **überall** ~**hängen** be hung up all over the place; **(b)** ⇒ **rumhängen a;** ~**|horchen** *itr. V.* (ugs.) keep one's ears open; ~**|irren** *itr. V.; mit sein* wander around or about; **im Wald** ~**irren** wander about the wood; ~**|kommandieren** *tr. V.* (ugs.) **jmdn.** ~**kommandieren** boss (coll.) or order sb. around or about; ~**|kommen** *unr. itr. V.; mit sein* (ugs.) **(a)** (vorbeikommen können) get round; **(b)** (sich herumbewegen) come round; **um die Ecke** ~**kommen** come round the corner; **(c)** (vermeiden können) **um etw. [nicht]** ~**kommen** [not] be able to get out of sth.; **(d)** (viel reisen) get around or about; **in der Welt** ~**kommen** see a lot of the world; **viel** ~**kommen** get around or about a lot or a great deal; ~**|kramen** *itr. V.* (ugs.) keep rummaging around or about; ~**|krebsen** *itr. V.* (ugs.) struggle; ~**|kriegen** *tr. V.* (salopp) **jmdn.** ~**kriegen** talk sb. into it; (verführen) get sb. into bed (coll.); ~**|kritisieren** *itr. V.* (ugs.) **an jmdm./etw.** ~**kritisieren** pick holes in sb./sth.; ~**|laufen** *unr. itr. V.; mit sein* **(a)** walk/(schneller) run around or about; **in der Stadt** ~**laufen** walk/(schneller) run around the town; **(b) um etw.** ~**laufen** walk or go round sth.; **(c)** (gekleidet sein) **wie läufst du wieder** ~**!** what do you look like!; ~**|liegen** *unr. itr. V.* (ugs.) lie around or about; ~**|lungern** *itr. V.* (salopp) loaf around; ~**|machen** *itr. V.* (ugs.) be busy; (abwertend) mess about or around; ~**|mäkeln** *itr. V.* (ugs.) **[an jmdm./etw.]** ~**mäkeln** pick holes [in sb./sth.]; **am Essen** ~**mäkeln** moan (*coll.*) or grumble about the food; ~**|nörgeln** *itr. V.* (ugs. abwertend) moan; grumble; **an jmdm./etw.** ~**nörgeln** moan or grumble about sb./sth.; ~**|posaunen** *tr. V.* (ugs.) broadcast; **sie posaunte im ganzen Dorf** ~**, dass …** she broadcast to the whole village the fact that …; ~**|quälen** *refl. V.* (ugs.) **sich [mit einem Problem]** ~**quälen** struggle [with a problem]; ~**|reden** *itr. V.* (ugs.) **um etw.** ~**reden** talk round sth.; **red nicht lange um die Sache** ~**!** don't beat about the bush!; ~**|reichen** *tr. V.* (ugs.) **etw.** ~**reichen** pass sth. round; ~**|reißen** *unr. tr. V.* **den Wagen/das Pferd** ~**reißen** swing the car/horse round; *s. auch* **Steuer¹;** ~**|reiten** *unr. itr. V.; mit sein* **(a) in der Gegend** ~**reiten** ride around the area; **(b)** (salopp: auf dasselbe zurückkommen) **auf etw.** (*Dat.*) ~**reiten** go on about sth. (coll.); harp on sth.; ~**|rennen** *unr. itr. V.; mit sein* (ugs.) **(a)** (ziellos rennen) run around or about; **(b)** (im Bogen rennen) **um etw.** ~**rennen** run round sth.; **im Kreis** ~**rennen** run round in a circle; ~**|rutschen** *itr. V.; mit sein* (ugs.) slide around or about; ~**|schlagen** *unr. refl. V.* (ugs.) **(a)** (sich schlagen) **sich mit jmdm.** ~**schlagen** keep fighting or getting into fights with sb.; **(b)** (sich auseinander setzen) **sich mit Problemen/Einwänden** ~**schlagen** grapple with problems/battle against objections; ~**|schleichen** *unr. itr. V.; mit sein* (ugs.) creep around or about; **um etw.** ~**schleichen** creep round sth.; ~**|schlendern** *itr. V.;*

mit sein (ugs.) stroll around or about; **in der Stadt** ~**schlendern** stroll around or about the town; ~**|schleppen** *tr. V.* (ugs.) **etw. um etw.** ~**schleppen** lug sth. round sth.; **eine Erkältung/ein Problem mit sich** (*Dat.*) ~**schleppen** (fig.) go around with a cold/be worried by a problem; ~**|schnüffeln** *itr. V.* (ugs. abwertend) nose or snoop around or about (coll.); ~**|schubsen** *tr. V.* (ugs.) **jmn.** ~**schubsen** push sb. around; **(a)** ***~**|sein** ⇒ **herum;** ~**|sitzen** *unr. itr. V.* (ugs.) **(a)** sit around or about; **tatenlos** ~**sitzen** sit around or about doing nothing; **(b) um etw.** ~**sitzen** sit round sth.; ~**|spielen** *itr. V.* (ugs.) **an/mit etw.** ~**spielen** keep playing [around or about] with sth.; **an seinen Knöpfen** ~**spielen** fiddle with one's buttons; ~**|spionieren** *itr. V.* (ugs.) snoop around or about (coll.); ~**|sprechen** *unr. refl. V.* get around or about; **schnell hatte sich** ~**gesprochen, dass …**: it had quickly got around that …; ~**|spuken** *itr. V.* (ugs.) **in/auf etw.** (*Dat.*) ~**spuken** haunt sth.; ~**|stehen** *unr. itr. V.* (ugs.) stand around or about; ~**|stöbern** *itr. V.* (ugs.) (in einem Schreibtisch usw.) keep rummaging around or about (**in** + *Dat.* in); ~**|stochern** *itr. V.* poke around or about; **im Essen** ~**stochern** pick at one's food; ~**|stoßen** *unr. tr. V.* (ugs.) **jmdn.** ~**stoßen** push sb. around; ~**|streichen** *unr. itr. V.* (abwertend) **(a)** (umherstreifen) roam around or about; **(b)** (lauernd umkreisen) **um jmdn./etw.** ~**streichen** prowl round sb./sth.; ~**|streiten** *unr. refl. V.* (ugs.) **sich [mit jmdm./etw.]** ~**streiten** keep quarrelling [with sb.]; ~**|streunen** *itr. V.; mit sein* (abwertend) roam around or about; **auf den Feldern** ~**streunen** roam the fields; ~**|stromern** *itr. V.; mit sein* (salopp abwertend) roam around or about; ~**|tanzen** *itr. V.; mit sein* dance around or about; *s. auch* **Nase b;** ~**|tollen** *itr. V.; mit sein* romp around or about; **auf dem Hof** ~**tollen** romp around the yard; ~**|tragen** *unr. tr. V.* (ugs.) **(a)** (überallhin tragen) **jmdn./etw.** ~**tragen** carry sb./sth. around or about; **(b) eine Idee/einen Plan mit sich** ~**tragen** nurse an idea/a plan; **(c)** (abwertend: weitererzählen) **etw.** ~**tragen** spread sth. around; ~**|trampeln** *itr. V.; mit haben od. sein* **auf etw.** (*Dat.*) ~**trampeln** trample [around] on sth.; trample all over sth.; **auf jmds. Nerven/Gefühlen** ~**trampeln** (fig.) really get on sb.'s nerves/trample on sb.'s feelings; ~**|treiben** *unr. refl. V.* (ugs. abwertend) **sich auf den Straßen/in Spelunken** ~**treiben** hang around the streets/(coll.) in dives; **mit Männern** ~**treiben** hang around with men; **wo hast du dich nur** ~**getrieben?** where have you been?; ~**treiber** *der* (ugs.) layabout; (Streuner) vagabond; ~**|trödeln** *itr. V.* (ugs.) dawdle around or about (**mit** over); ~**|wälzen** (ugs.) **1** *tr. V.* **etw.** ~**wälzen** roll sth. over; **2** *refl. V.* roll around or about; **sich im Bett** ~**wälzen** toss and turn in bed; ~**|werfen** **1** *unr. tr. V.* **(a)** (ugs.: umherwerfen) **etw.** ~**werfen** chuck (coll.) or throw sth. around or about; **(b)** (in eine andere Richtung drehen) throw ‹helm, steering wheel, *etc.*› [hard] over; **den Kopf** ~**werfen** turn one's head quickly; **2** *unr. refl. V.* **sich im Bett** ~**werfen** toss and turn in bed; ~**|wirbeln** **1** *tr. V.* **jmdn./etw.** ~**wirbeln** whirl or spin sb./sth. [a]round; **der Wind wirbelte die Blätter** ~**:** the wind whirled the leaves around or about; **2** *itr. V.; mit sein* spin or whirl [a]round; ~**|wühlen** *itr. V.* **in etw.** (*Dat.*) ~**wühlen** rummage or root around or about in sth.; **in jmds. Vergangenheit** ~**wühlen** (fig.) dig into sb.'s past; ~**|wurschteln,** ~**|wursteln** *itr. V.* (salopp) **mit etw.** ~**wurschteln** *od.* ~**wursteln** mess or fiddle around or about with sth.; ~**|zeigen** *tr. V.* (ugs.) **etw.** ~**zeigen** show sth. round; ~**|ziehen** **1** *unr. itr. V.* move around or about; **im Land** ~**ziehen** move around or about the country; **2** *unr. tr. V.* (ugs.: mit sich ziehen) **jmdn./etw.** ~**ziehen** drag sb./sth. round (coll.).

herunten /hɛˈrʊntn̩/ *Adv.* (südd., österr.) down here

herunter /hɛˈrʊntɐ/ *Adv.* **(a)** (nach unten, unten) down; **von Kiel nach München** ~ (fig.) from Kiel down to Munich; **(b)** (fort) off; ~ **vom Sofa!** [get] off the sofa!; **(c)** [körperlich] ~ sein be in poor health

herunter-: ~**|bekommen** *unr. tr. V.* (ugs.) **(a)** (essen können) be able to eat; (~schlucken) swallow; **(b)** (entfernen können) **etw. [von etw.]** ~**bekommen** be able to get sth.

off [sth.]; ~|**beten** *tr. V.* (abwertend) **etw. ~beten** recite sth. mechanically; ~|**brennen** *unr. itr. V.* (a) *mit sein* (vollkommen abbrennen) ‹*house, fire, etc.*› burn down; (b) ‹*sun*› burn or beat down; ~|**bringen** *unr. tr. V.* (a) (nach unten bringen) bring down; (b) (zugrunde richten) ruin; (c) (ugs.: herunterschlucken) ⇒ **bekommen a;** ~|**drücken** *tr. V.* (a) (nach unten drücken) **etw. ~drücken** press sth. down; (b) (auf ein niedriges Niveau bringen, verringern) force down ‹*prices, wages, etc.*›; bring down ‹*temperature*›; reduce ‹*marks*›; ~|**fahren** **1** *unr. itr. V.; mit sein* drive or come down; ‹*skier*› ski down; (mit einem Motorrad, Rad) ride down; **2** *unr. tr. V.* (a) **jmdn./etw. ~fahren** drive or bring sb. down/bring sth. down; (b) (DV) shut down; ~|**fallen** *unr. itr. V.; mit sein* fall down; **vom Tisch/Stuhl ~fallen** fall off the table/chair; **die Treppe ~fallen** fall down the stairs; **jmdm. fällt etw. ~:** sb. drops sth.; ~|**geben** *unr. tr. V.* (ugs.) pass or hand down; ~|**gehen** *unr. itr. V.; mit sein* (a) (nach unten gehen) come down; (b) (niedriger werden) ‹*temperature*› go down, drop, fall; ‹*prices*› come down, fall; (c) (die Höhe senken) **auf eine Flughöhe von 2 000 m ~gehen** descend to 6,000 ft.; **mit den Preisen ~gehen** reduce one's/its prices; (d) **von etw. ~gehen** (ugs.: räumen) get off sth.; (e) (ugs.: sich lösen) come off; ~**gekommen** **1** *2. Part. v.* ~**kommen; 2** *Adj.* poor ‹*health*›; dilapidated, run-down ‹*building*›; run-down ‹*area*›; down and out ‹*person*›; ~|**handeln** *tr. V.* (ugs.) **einen Preis ~handeln** beat down a price; **den Preis um 100 Mark ~handeln** get 100 marks knocked off the price (coll.); ~|**hängen** *unr. itr. V.* hang down; ~|**hauen** *unr. tr. V.* (ugs.) (a) (ohrfeigen) **jmdm. eine ~hauen** give sb. a clout round the ear (coll.); (b) (schlecht ausführen) dash off; ~|**holen** *tr. V.;* **jmdn./etw. ~holen** fetch sb./sth. down; ~|**klappen** *tr. V.* pull or put down ‹*seat*›; close ‹*lid*›; **seinen Kragen ~klappen** turn down one's collar; ~|**kommen** *unr. itr. V.; mit sein* (a) (kommen) come down; (nach unten kommen können) manage to come down; (b) (ugs.: verfallen) go to the dogs (coll.); **er ist so weit ~gekommen, dass ...:** he has sunk so low that ...; (c) (ugs.: wegkommen) **von Drogen/vom Alkohol ~kommen** come off drugs/alcohol; kick the habit (coll.); ~|**können** *unr. itr. V.* (ugs.) be able to get down; ~|**laden** *unr. tr. V.* (DV) download; ~|**lassen** *unr. tr. V.* (schließen) let down, lower ‹*blind, shutter*›; lower ‹*barrier*›; shut ‹*window*›; (nach unten gleiten lassen) wind down ‹*car window*›; **jmdn./etw. an etw.** (*Dat.*) ~**lassen** lower sb./sth. by sth.; **die Hose ~lassen** take one's trousers down; ~|**leiern** *tr. V.* (salopp) (a) (abwertend) drone out (coll.); (b) (wind down ‹*car window*›; ~**machen** *tr. V.* (salopp) (a) (zurechtweisen) **jmdn. ~machen** give sb. a rocket (sl.); tear sb. off a strip (Brit. coll.); (b) (herabsetzen) slate (coll.); run down (coll.); ~|**nehmen** *unr. tr. V.* take down; ~**etw. von etw. ~nehmen** take sth. off sth.; ~|**putzen** *tr. V.* (salopp) ⇒ ~**machen a;** ~|**reißen** *unr. tr. V.* (ugs.) (a) (nach unten reißen) pull down; (b) (abreißen) pull off ‹*plaster, wallpaper*›; tear down ‹*poster*›; (c) (salopp: ableisten) get through; ~|**rutschen** *itr. V.; mit sein* (ugs.) slide down; ‹*trousers, socks*› slip down; ~|**schalten** *itr. V.* (Kfz-Jargon) change down; ~|**schlagen** *unr. itr. V.* (a) knock off; (b) turn ‹*collar etc.*› down; ~|**schlucken** *tr. V.* swallow; ~|**schrauben** *tr. V.* turn down ‹*wick etc.*›; **seine Ansprüche/Erwartungen ~schrauben** (fig.) reduce one's requirements/lower one's expectations; ~|**sehen** *unr. itr. V.* (a) (nach unten sehen) look down; (b) (geringschätzig betrachten) **auf jmdn. ~sehen** look down [up]on sb.; **~|**sein** ⇒ **herunter;** ~|**spielen** *tr. V.* (ugs.) (a) (als unbedeutend darstellen) play down (coll.); (b) (ausdruckslos spielen) **etw. ~spielen** play sth. through mechanically; ~|**steigen** *unr. itr. V.; mit sein* climb down; ~|**stürzen** **1** *itr. V.; mit sein* fall down; (steil herabfallen) ‹*aircraft, person, etc.*› plunge down; (~eilen) rush down; **vom Dach ~stürzen** fall off the roof; **2** *tr. V.* (a) (schnell trinken) gulp down; (b) **jmdn. ~stürzen** throw sb. down; ~|**tragen** *unr. tr. V.* **etw. ~tragen** carry sth. down; ~|**werfen** *unr. tr. V.* (a) (nach unten werfen) throw down; **~werfen** throw sth. down; (b) (ugs.: herunterfallen lassen)

drop; ~|**wirtschaften** *tr. V.* (ugs.) **etw. ~wirtschaften** ruin sth./bring sth. to the brink or edge of ruin [by mismanagement]; ~|**ziehen** **1** *unr. tr. V.* pull down; **2** *unr. itr. V.; mit sein* go or move down

her·**vor** *Adv.* **aus etw. ~:** out of sth.; **aus der Ecke ~ kam ...:** from out of the corner came ...

hervor-, Hervor-: ~|**bringen** *unr. tr. V.* (a) (zum Vorschein bringen) bring out (**aus** of); produce (**aus** from); (b) (wachsen, entstehen lassen; auch fig.) produce; (c) (von sich geben) say; produce ‹*sound*›; ~|**gehen** *unr. itr. V.; mit sein* (geh.) (a) (seinen Ursprung haben) **viele große Musiker gingen aus dieser Stadt ~:** this city produced many great musicians; **drei Kinder gingen aus der Ehe ~:** the marriage produced three children; there were three children from the marriage; (b) (herauskommen, sich ergeben) emerge (**aus** from); **aus seinem Brief geht klar ~, dass ...:** it is clear from his letter that ...; (c) (zu folgern sein) follow; **daraus geht ~, dass ...:** from this it follows that ...; ~|**gucken** *itr V.* (ugs.) look out; **unter etwas** (*Dat.*) ~**gucken** peep out from under sth.; ~|**heben** *unr. tr. V.* emphasize; stress; ~|**holen** *tr. V.* take out (**aus** of); ~|**kehren** *tr. V.* ⇒ **herauskehren;** ~|**kommen** *unr. itr. V.; mit sein* come out (**aus** of, **unter** + *Dat.* from under); ~|**locken** *tr. V.* lure or entice ‹*person, animal*› out (**aus** of); ~|**quellen** *unr. itr. V.; mit sein* well up; ‹*smoke*› pour out; **aus etw. ~quellen** stream from sth.; ~|**ragen** *itr. V.* (a) (aus etw. ragen) project; jut out; ‹*cheekbones*› stand out; (b) (sich auszeichnen) stand out; ~**ragend** **1** *Adj.* outstanding[ly good]; **2** *adv.* ~**ragend geschult** outstandingly well trained; ~**ragend spielen/arbeiten** play/work outstandingly well or excellently; ~**ruf** *der* curtain call; ~|**rufen** *unr. tr. V.* (a) (nach vorn rufen) **jmdn. ~rufen** call for sb. to come out; (Theater usw.) call sb. back; (b) (verursachen) elicit, provoke ‹*response*›; arouse ‹*admiration*›; cause ‹*unease, disquiet, confusion, merriment, disease*›; provoke ‹*protest, displeasure*›; ~|**springen** *unr. itr. V.; mit sein* (a) (springend hervorkommen) leap or jump out (**hinter** + *Dat.* from behind); (b) (vorspringen) project; jut out; ‹*nose*› stick out; ~|**stechen** *unr. itr. V.* stick out (**aus** of); ~**stechend** *Adj.* outstanding; striking; ~|**stehen** *unr. itr. V.* protrude; stick out; ‹*cheekbones*› stand out; ~|**stürzen** *itr. V.; mit sein* rush or burst out (**hinter** + *Dat.* from behind); ~|**suchen** *tr. V.* look out; ~|**treten** *unr. itr. V.; mit sein* emerge, step out (**hinter** + *Dat.* from behind); ‹*veins, ribs, etc.*› stand out; ‹*similarity etc.*› become apparent or evident; ‹*eyes*› bulge, protrude; ~|**tun** *unr. refl. V.* (Besonderes leisten) distinguish oneself; **sich mit/als etw. ~tun** make one's mark with/as sth.; (b) (wichtig tun) show off; ~|**wagen** *refl. V.* dare to come out (**aus** of); **du kannst dich wieder ~wagen** you can come out again; ~|**zaubern** *tr. V.* conjure up

Her·weg *der:* **auf dem ~weg** on the way here

Herz /hɛrts/ *das;* ~**ens,** ~**en** (a) **▶ 326 |** (auch: herzförmiger Gegenstand, zentraler Teil) heart; **sie hat es am ~en** (ugs.) she has a bad heart; (fig.) **komm an mein ~, Geliebter** come into my arms, my darling; **mir blutet das ~** (auch iron.) my heart bleeds; **ihm rutschte** *od.* **fiel das ~ in die Hose[n]** (ugs., oft scherzh.) his heart sank into his boots; **jmds. ~ höher schlagen lassen** make sb.'s heart beat faster; **jmdm. das ~ brechen** (geh.) break sb.'s heart; **das ~ auf dem rechten Fleck haben** have one's heart in the right place; **jmdn./etw. auf ~ und Nieren prüfen** (ugs.) grill sb./go over sth. with a fine tooth-comb; (b) (meist geh.: Gemüt) heart; **die ~en bewegen/rühren** touch people's hearts; **von ~en kommen** come from the heart; **im Grunde seines Herzens** in his heart of hearts; **ein ~ und eine Seele sein** be bosom friends; **jmds. ~ hängt an etw.** (*Dat.*) (jmd. möchte etw. sehr gerne behalten) sb. is attached to sth.; (jmd. möchte etw. sehr gerne haben) sb.'s heart is set on sth.; **ihm war/wurde das ~ schwer** his heart was/grew heavy; **alles, was das ~ begehrt** everything one's heart desires; **sich** (*Dat.*) **ein ~ fassen** pluck up one's courage; take one's courage in both hands; **sein ~ für etw. entdecken** (geh.) discover a passion for sth.; **ein ~ für Kinder/die Kunst haben** have a love of children/art; **jmdm. sein ~ ausschütten** pour out one's heart to sb.; **das ~ auf der Zunge tragen** wear one's heart on one's sleeve; **seinem ∼en einen Stoß geben** [suddenly] pluck up courage; **seinem ∼en Luft machen** (ugs.) give vent to one's feelings; **leichten ∼ens** easily; happily; **schweren ∼ens** with a heavy heart; **jmd./etw. liegt jmdm. am ∼en** sb. has the interests of sb./sth. at heart; **jmdm. etw. ans ∼ legen** entrust sb. with sth.; **jmd./etw. ist jmdm. ans ∼ gewachsen** sb. has grown very fond of sb./sth.; **etw. auf dem ∼en haben** have sth. on one's mind; **jmdn. ins od. in sein ∼ schließen** take to sb.; **mit halbem ∼en** (geh.) half-heartedly; **es nicht übers ∼ bringen, etw. zu tun** not have the heart to do sth.; **von ∼en gern** [most] gladly; **von ganzem ∼en** (aufrichtig) with all one's heart; (aus voller Überzeugung) whole-heartedly; **sich** (*Dat.*) **etw. zu ∼en nehmen** take sth. to heart; **mit ganzem ∼en** (geh.) whole-heartedly; **jmdm. aus dem ∼en sprechen** express just what sb. is/was thinking; *s. auch* **Luft c; Stein b; Stich e;** **(c)** (Kartenspiel) hearts *pl.;* (Karte) heart; *s. auch* **Pik²;** **(d)** (Kosewort) **mein ∼:** my dear

herz-, Herz-: **∼an·fall** *der* heart attack; ***∼as,** **∼ass** *das* ace of hearts; **∼beklemmend** *Adj.* oppressive; **∼beschwerden** *Pl.* heart trouble *sing.;* **∼bube** *der* jack of hearts

Herzchen *das;* **∼s, ∼** (a) (abwertend: naive/unzuverlässige Person) simpleton/unreliable person; (b) (Kosewort) darling; sweetheart; (c) (kleines Herz) little heart

Herz-: **∼chirurgie** *die* heart *or* cardiac surgery; **∼dame** *die* queen of hearts

Herzegowina /hɛrtse'go:vina/ *die;* **∼:** Herzegovina

her|zeigen *tr. V.* (ugs.) show; **zeig** [es] **mal her!** let me see [it]!

herzen *tr. V.* (veralt.) hug

herzens-, Herzens-: **∼angelegenheit** *die* (Liebesangelegenheit) affair of the heart; (Leidenschaft) passion; **∼bedürfnis** *das* in **jmdm. ein ∼bedürfnis sein** (geh.) be very important to sb.; **∼brecher** *der* ladykiller; **∼gut** /'--'-/ *Adj.* kind-hearted; good-hearted; **∼lust** *die;* **etw. nach ∼lust tun** do sth. to one's heart's content; **∼wunsch** *der* dearest *or* fondest wish

herz-, Herz-: **∼erfrischend** 1 *Adj.* refreshing; 2 *adv.* refreshingly; **∼ergreifend** 1 *Adj.* heart-rending; 2 *adv.* heart-rendingly; **∼erquickend** *Adj.* ⇨ **∼erfrischend;** **∼fehler** *der* heart defect; **∼flimmern** *das* (Med.) (Kammerflimmern) ventricular fibrillation; (Vorhofflimmern) auricular fibrillation; **∼förmig** *Adj.* heart-shaped

herzhaft 1 *Adj.* (a) (kräftig) hearty; (b) (nahrhaft) hearty, substantial ⟨meal⟩; (von kräftigem Geschmack) tasty; **ein ∼er Eintopf** a substantial/tasty stew. 2 *adv.* (kräftig) heartily; **∼ gähnen** give a wide yawn

her|ziehen 1 *unr. itr. V.* (a) *mit sein od. haben* (ugs.: abfällig reden) **über jmdn./etw. ∼:** run sb./sth. down; pull sb./sth. to pieces; (b) *mit sein* (mitgehen) **vor/hinter/neben jmdm./etw. ∼:** march along in front of/behind/beside sb./sth.; (c) (umziehen) *mit sein* move here. 2 *unr. tr. V.* (a) (ugs.: zum Sprechenden bewegen) **etw. ∼:** pull sth. over [here]; (b) (mit sich führen) **jmdn./etw. hinter sich** (*Dat.*) **∼:** pull sb./sth. along behind one

herzig 1 *Adj.* sweet; dear; delightful. 2 *adv.* sweetly; delightfully

herz-, Herz-: **∼infarkt** *der* ▶ 329 | heart attack; cardiac infarction (Med.); **∼insuffizienz** *die* ▶ 329 | (Med.) cardiac insufficiency; **∼kammer** *die* (Anat.) ventricle; **∼klappe** *die* (Anat.) heart-valve; **∼klopfen** *das;* **∼s: jmd. bekommt ∼klopfen** sb.'s heart starts to pound; **mit ∼klopfen** with a pounding heart; **∼könig** *der* king of hearts; **∼krank** *Adj.* ⟨person⟩ with *or* suffering from a heart condition; **∼kranke** *der/die* person with *or* suffering from a heart condition; (Patient) cardiac patient; **∼kranz·gefäß** *das; meist Pl.* coronary vessel

herzlich 1 *Adj.* ▶ 240 | warm ⟨smile, reception⟩; kind ⟨words⟩; **∼e Grüße/∼en Dank** kind regards/many thanks; **sein ∼es Beileid zum Ausdruck bringen** express one's sincere condolences *pl.; s. auch* **Glückwunsch.** 2 *adv.* ▶ 240 | (a) (warmly) ⟨congratulate⟩ heartily; **es grüßt euch ∼ Eure Viktoria** (als Briefschluss)

kind regards, Victoria; (b) (sehr) **∼ wenig** very *or* (coll.) precious little; **∼ gern!** gladly

Herzlichkeit *die* ⇨ **herzlich:** warmth; kindness

herz-, Herz-: **∼los** 1 *Adj.* heartless; callous; 2 *adv.* heartlessly, callously; **∼losigkeit** *die;* **∼, ∼en** (a) *o. Pl.* heartlessness; callousness; (b) (herzlose Tat/Bemerkung) heartless act/remark; **∼-Lungen-Maschine** *die* heart-lung machine; **∼massage** *die* cardiac massage; heart massage; **∼mittel** *das* (ugs.) heart pills *pl.;* **∼muskel** *der* (Anat.) heart muscle; cardiac muscle

Herzog /'hɛrtso:k/ *der;* **∼s, Herzöge** /'hɛrtsø:gə/ duke; [**Herr**] **Friedrich ∼ von Meiningen** Frederick, Duke of Meiningen

Herzogin *die;* **∼, ∼nen** duchess

herzoglich *Adj.; nicht präd.* ducal; of the duke *postpos., not pred.;* **die ∼e Familie** the family of the duke

Herzogtum *das;* **∼s, Herzogtümer** duchy

herz-, Herz-: **∼rhythmus·störung** *die* (Med.) disturbance of the heart *or* cardiac rhythm; **∼schlag** *der* (a) heartbeat; **einen ∼schlag lang** (geh.) for a *or* one fleeting moment; (b) *o. Pl.* (Abfolge der Herzschläge, auch fig. geh.) pulse; (c) (Herzversagen) heart failure; **an einem ∼schlag sterben** die of heart failure; **∼schmerz** *der; meist pl.* pain in the region of the heart; **∼schrittmacher** *der* (Anat., Med.) [cardiac] pacemaker; **∼spezialist** *der* heart specialist; **∼stärkend** *Adj.* **ein ∼stärkendes Mittel** a cardiac tonic; **∼still·stand** *der* (Med.) cardiac arrest; **∼stück** *das* (geh.) heart; **∼ton** *der; meist Pl.* (Med.) heart *or* cardiac sound; **∼transplantation** *die* (Med.) heart transplantation; **∼versagen** *das;* **∼s** ▶ 329 | heart failure; **∼zerreißend** 1 *Adj.* heart-rending; 2 *adv.* heart-rendingly

Hesse /'hɛsə/ *der;* **∼n, ∼n** Hessian

Hessen (*das*); **∼s** Hesse

hessisch *Adj.* Hessian

hetero-, Hetero- /hetero-/ hetero-

Hetero *der;* **∼s, ∼s** (ugs.) hetero (coll.)

heterogen /-'ge:n/ *Adj.* heterogeneous

hetero·sexuell *Adj.* heterosexual

Hetz /hɛts/ *die;* **∼, ∼en** (österr. ugs.) **das war eine ∼!** that was a [good] laugh; **aus ∼:** for fun

Hetz·blatt *das* (abwertend) political smear-sheet

Hetze /'hɛtsə/ *die;* **∼** (a) (große Hast) [mad] rush; **in großer ∼:** in a mad rush *or* hurry; (b) *o. Pl.* (abwertend: Aufhetzung) smear campaign; (gegen eine Minderheit) hate campaign

hetzen 1 *tr. V.* (a) hunt; **die Hunde/die Polizei auf jmdn. ∼:** set the dogs on [to] sb./get the police on to sb.; (b) (antreiben) rush; hurry. 2 *itr. V.* (a) (in großer Eile sein) rush; **den ganzen Tag ∼:** be in a rush all day long; (b) *mit sein* (hasten) rush; hurry; (rennen) dash; race; (c) (abwertend: Hass entfachen) stir up hatred; (schmähen) say malicious things; **gegen jmdn./etw. ∼:** smear sb./agitate against sth.

Hetzer *der;* **∼s, ∼, Hetzerin** *die;* **∼, ∼nen** malicious agitator

Hetz-: **∼jagd** *die* (a) (Jagdw.) hunting (*with hounds*); (einzelne Jagd) hunt (*with hounds*); (b) (Hast) [mad] rush; **∼kampagne** *die* (abwertend) smear campaign; **∼rede** *die* (abwertend) inflammatory speech

Heu /hɔy/ *das;* **∼[e]s** hay; **∼ machen** make hay

Heu·boden *der* hayloft

Heuchelei *die;* **∼** (abwertend) hypocrisy

heucheln /'hɔyçln/ 1 *itr. V.* be a hypocrite. 2 *tr. V.* feign

Heuchler *der;* **∼s, ∼, Heuchlerin** *die;* **∼, ∼nen** hypocrite

heuchlerisch 1 *Adj.* (a) (unaufrichtig) hypocritical; (b) (geheuchelt) feigned ⟨interest, sympathy, etc.⟩. 2 *adv.* hypocritically

heuer /'hɔyɐ/ *Adv.* (südd., österr., schweiz.) this year

Heuer *die;* **∼, ∼n** (Seemannsspr.) (a) (Lohn) pay; wages *pl.;* (b) (Anstellung) **auf einem Frachter ∼ nehmen** ship on board a freighter; **eine ∼ bekommen** get hired

Heu-: ~**ernte** *die* (**a**) hay harvest; haymaking; (**b**) (Ertrag) hay crop; ~**gabel** *die* hay-fork; ~**haufen** *der* haystack; hayrick

Heul·boje *die* (Seew.) whistling-buoy

heulen /'hɔylən/ *itr. V.* (**a**) ⟨*wolf, dog, jackal, etc.*⟩ howl; (fig.) ⟨*wind, gale*⟩ howl; ⟨*storm*⟩ roar; (**b**) ⟨*siren, buoy, etc.*⟩ wail; (**c**) (ugs.: weinen) howl; bawl; **vor Wut/Schmerz/ Freude** ~: howl and weep with rage/pain/howl with delight; **das ist zum Heulen** (ugs.) it's enough to make you weep

Heulsuse /'hɔylzu:zə/ *die;* ~, ~**n** (ugs. abwertend) crybaby

Heu·pferd *das* grasshopper

Heurige *der; adj. Dekl.* (bes. österr.) new wine; **sie saßen beim** ~**n** they sat drinking the new wine

Heu-: ~**schnupfen** *der* hay fever; ~**schober** *der* (südd., österr.) haystack; hayrick; ~**schrecke** *die* grasshopper; (in Afrika, Asien) locust; grasshopper

heut /hɔyt/ (ugs.), **heute** /'hɔytə/ *Adv.* today; ~ **früh** early this morning; ~ **Morgen/Abend** this morning/ evening; ~ **Mittag** [at] midday today; ~ **Nacht** tonight; (letzte Nacht) last night; ~ **in einer Woche** a week [from] today; today week; ~ **vor einer Woche** a week ago today; **seit** ~: from today; **ab** ~, **von** ~ **an** from today [on]; **bis** ~: until today; **bis** ~ **nicht** (erst ~) not until today; (überhaupt noch nicht) not to this day; (bis jetzt noch nicht) not as yet; **für** ~: for today; **lieber** ~ **als morgen** (ugs.) the sooner, the better; **von** ~ **auf morgen** from one day to the next; **du Frau von** ~: the woman of today

heutig *Adj.; nicht präd.* (**a**) (von diesem Tag) today's; **der** ~**e Tag/am** ~**en Tage** today; **bis zum** ~**en Tag** until the present day *or* today; (**b**) (gegenwärtig) today's; of today *postpos.;* **die** ~**e Jugend/Generation** today's youth/generation; the youth/generation of today; **in der** ~**en Zeit** today; nowadays

heut·zu·tage *Adv.* nowadays

Hexe /'hɛksə/ *die;* ~, ~**n** (**a**) witch; (**b**) **diese kleine** ~ (abwertend) this little minx

hexen *itr. V.* work magic; **ich kann doch nicht** ~ (ugs.) I'm not a magician (coll.)

Hexen-: ~**jagd** *die* (auch fig.) witch-hunt; ~**kessel** *der:* **ein [wahrer]** ~**kessel** be [absolute] bedlam; **das Fußballstadion glich einem** ~**kessel** there was pandemonium *or* bedlam in the football-ground; ~**meister** *der* sorcerer; ~**schuss**, ***~**schuß** *der; o. Pl.* lumbago *no indef. art.;* ~**verbrennung** *die* (hist.) burning of a witch/of witches; ~**verfolgung** *die* (hist.) witchhunt

Hexer *der;* ~**s**, ~: sorcerer

Hexerei *die;* ~, ~**en** sorcery; witchcraft; (Zauberkunststücke) magic; **das ist doch keine** ~: there's no magic about it

Hickhack /'hɪkhak/ *das od. der;* ~**s**, ~**s** (ugs.) squabbling; bickering

hie /hi:/ *Adv.* ~ **und da** (an manchen Stellen) here and there; (manchmal) [every] now and then

hieb /hi:p/ *1. u. 3. Pers. Sg. Prät. v.* **hauen**

Hieb *der;* ~**[e]s**, ~**e** (**a**) (Schlag) blow; (mit der Peitsche) lash; (im Fechten) cut; (fig.) dig (**gegen** at); **jmdm. einen** ~ **mit der Faust versetzen** punch sb.; (**b**) *Pl.* (ugs.: Prügel) ~**e bekommen/kriegen** get a hiding *or* beating *or* (sl.) walloping; **es gibt/setzt** ~**e!** you'll get a hiding *or* beating *or* (sl.) walloping

hieb·fest *Adj. in* **hieb- und stichfest** watertight; castiron

hielt /hi:lt/ *1. u. 3. Pers. Sg. Prät. v.* **halten**

hier /hi:ɐ/ *Adv.* (**a**) here; ~ **sein/bleiben** be/stay here; **etw.** ~ **lassen** leave sth. here; **[von]** ~ **oben/unten** [from] up/down here; ~ **vorn[e]** here in front; ~ **draußen/drinnen** out/in here; ~ **entlang** along here; **von** ~ **[aus]** from here; **er ist nicht von** ~: he's not from this area *or* around here; ~ **spricht Hans Schulze** this is Hans Schulze [speaking]; ~ **und da** *od.* **dort** (an manchen Stellen) here and there; (manchmal) [every] now and

then; ~ **und jetzt** *od.* **heute** (geh.) here and now; (**b**) (zu diesem Zeitpunkt) now; **von** ~ **an** from now on

hieran /'hi:'ran/ *Adv.* (**a**) (an dieser/diese Stelle) here; (**b**) (fig.) **im Anschluss** ~: immediately after this

Hierarchie /hierar'çi:/ *die;* ~, ~**n** hierarchy

hierarchisch **1** *Adj.* hierarchical. **2** *adv.* hierarchically

hierauf /'hi:'rauf/ *Adv.* (**a**) (auf dieser/diese Stelle) on here; (**b**) (darauf) on this; **wir werden** ~ **zurückkommen** we'll come back to this; (**c**) (danach) after that; then; (**d**) (infolgedessen) whereupon

hierauf·hin *Adv.* hereupon

hieraus /'hi:'raus/ *Adv.* (**a**) (aus dem eben Erwähnten) out of *or* from here; (**b**) (aus dieser Tatsache, Quelle) from this; (**c**) (aus diesem Material) out of this

hier|behalten *unr. tr. V.* **jmdn./etw.** ~: keep sb./sth. here

hier·bei *Adv.* (**a**) (bei dieser Gelegenheit) **Diese Übung ist sehr schwierig. Man kann sich** ~ **leicht verletzen.** This exercise is very difficult. You can easily injure yourself doing it; **Ich habe ihn gestern getroffen. Hierbei habe ich gleich** ...: I met him yesterday, and straightaway I ...; (**b**) (bei der erwähnten Sache) here

*****hier|bleiben** ⇒ **hier a**

hier·durch *Adv.* (**a**) (hier hindurch) through here; (**b**) (aufgrund dieser Sache) because of this; as a result of this

hier·für *Adv.* for this

hier·her *Adv.* here; **wie bist du** ~ **gekommen?** how did you get here?; **ich gehe bis** ~ **und nicht weiter** I'm going this far and no further; **bis** ~ **und nicht weiter** (als Warnung) so far and no further; **das gehört nicht** ~ (fig.) that is not relevant [here]

*****hierher|gehören**, *****hierher|kommen** ⇒ **hierher**

hier·hin *Adv.* here; **sie blickte bald** ~, **bald dorthin** she looked this way and that; **bis** ~: up to here *or* this point

hierin /'hi:rɪn/ *Adv.* in this

*****hier|lassen** ⇒ **hier a**

hier·mit *Adv.* with this/these; ~ **ist der Fall erledigt** that puts an end to the matter; ~ **erkläre ich, dass** ... (Amtsspr.) I hereby declare that ...

hier·nach *Adv.* (**a**) (zeitlich, räumlich) after this *or* that; (**b**) (diesem entsprechend) in accordance with this/these; (**c**) (demnach) according to this/these

Hieroglyphe /hiero'gly:fə/ *die;* ~, ~**n** hieroglyph; ~**n** hieroglyphics

*****hier|sein** ⇒ **hier a**

hierüber /'hi:'ry:bɐ/ *Adv.* (**a**) (über dem Erwähnten) above here; (**b**) (über das Erwähnte) over here; (**c**) (das Erwähnte betreffend) about this/these; (**d**) (geh.: währenddessen) **er war** ~ **eingeschlafen** he had fallen asleep while doing so

hierum /'hi:'rʊm/ *Adv.* about this; ~ **geht es gar nicht** that's not the point; it's not a question of that

hierunter /'hi:'rʊntɐ/ *Adv.* (**a**) (unter diese[r] Stelle) under here; (**b**) ~ **leiden** suffer from this; **etw.** ~ **verstehen** *od.* **sich** (*Dat.*) **etw.** ~ **vorstellen** understand sth. by this; (**c**) (unter die genannte/der genannten Gruppe) among these

hier·von *Adv.* (**a**) (von dieser Sache) of this; ~ **zeugen** bear witness to this; (**b**) (dadurch) because of this; (**c**) (aus dieser Menge) of this/these; (**d**) (aus diesem Material) out of this

hier·vor *Adv.* (**a**) (vor dieser/diese Stelle) in front of this *or* here; (**b**) **Respekt** ~ **haben** have respect for this; **Angst** ~ **haben** be afraid of this

hier·zu *Adv.* (**a**) (zu dieser Sache) with this; **vgl.** ~: cf.; (**b**) (zu dieser Gruppe) ~ **gehört/gehören** ...: this includes/ these include; (**c**) **ich kann dir** ~ **nur raten** I can only recommend you to do this/buy this/go *etc.;* **ich wünsche dir** ~ **viel Erfolg** I wish you every success with this; ~ **reicht mein Geld nicht** I haven't got enough money for that; (**d**) (hinsichtlich dieser Sache) about this

---

**alte Schreibung (vgl. Hinweise auf S. xvi–xvii)

hierzu·lande *Adv.* (in diesem Land) [here] in this country

hiesig /'hi:zɪç/ *Adj.; nicht präd.* local

hieß /hi:s/ *1. u. 3. Pers. Sg. Prät. v.* **heißen**

hieven /'hi:vn̩/ *tr. V.* heave

Hi-Fi- /'haifai, 'haifi-/ hi-fi ‹*system, unit, etc.*›

high /haɪ/ *Adj.; nur präd.* (ugs.) high (coll.)

Highlife /'haɪlaɪf/ *das;* ∼[s] (ugs.) high life; ∼ **machen** live it up

High·society /haɪsə'saɪətɪ/ *die;* ∼: high society

High·tech- /'haɪ'tɛk-/ high-tech ‹*equipment, device, etc.*›

hihi /hi'hi:/, **hihihi** /hihi'hi:/ *Interj.* he-he[-he]

Hilfe /'hɪlfə/ *die;* ∼, ∼**n (a)** help; (für Notleidende) aid; relief; **wirtschaftliche/finanzielle** ∼: economic aid/financial assistance; **jmdm.** ∼ **leisten** help sb.; **sein** ∼ **suchender Blick ging zum Fenster** he looked towards the window, seeking help; **sich** ∼ **suchend umsehen** look round for help; **mit** ∼ (+ *Gen.*) with the help *or* aid of; **jmdn. um** ∼ **bitten** ask sb. for help *or* assistance; **um** ∼ **rufen** shout for help; **jmdn. zu** ∼ **rufen** call on sb. for help; **jmdm. zu** ∼ **kommen/eilen** come/hurry to sb.'s aid *or* assistance; **[zu]** ∼**!** help!; **erste** ∼: first aid; **(b)** (Hilfskraft) help; (im Geschäft) assistant

hilfe-, Hilfe-: ∼**leistung** *die* help; assistance; **unterlassene** ∼**leistung** (Rechtsspr.) failure to render assistance in an emergency; ∼**ruf** *der* cry for help; (Notsignal) distress signal; ∼**stellung** *die* (Turnen) **jmdm.** ∼**stellung geben** act as spotter for sb.; ***∼**suchend** ⇒ Hilfe a

hilf-, Hilf-: ∼**los 1** *Adj.* helpless; **2** *adv.* helplessly; ∼**losigkeit** *die;* ∼: helplessness; ∼**reich** *Adj.* (geh.) helpful

hilfs-, Hilfs-: ∼**aktion** *die* relief programme; ∼**arbeiter** *der* labourer; (in einer Fabrik) unskilled worker; ∼**bedürftig** *Adj.* **(a)** (schwach) in need of help *postpos.*; **(b)** (Not leidend) in need; needy; ∼**bedürftigkeit** *die* need; neediness; ∼**bereit** *Adj.* helpful; ∼**bereitschaft** *die* helpfulness; readiness *or* willingness to help; ∼**dienst** *der* (Organisation) emergency service; (bei Katastrophen) [emergency] relief service; (für Autofahrer) [emergency] breakdown service; ∼**kraft** *die* assistant; ∼**maßnahme** *die* aid *or* relief measure; ∼**mittel** *das* aid; ∼**organisation** *die* aid *or* relief organization; ∼**schule** *die* (veralt., ugs.) special school; ∼**schüler** *der* (veralt., ugs.) pupil at a special school; ∼**verb** *das*, ∼**zeitwort** *das* (Sprachw.) auxiliary [verb]

Himalaja /hi'ma:laja/ *der;* ∼[s]: **der/im** ∼: the/in the Himalayas *pl.*

Him·beere /'hɪm-/ *die* raspberry

Himbeer-: ∼**eis** *das* raspberry ice [cream]; ∼**strauch** *der* raspberry bush

Himmel /'hɪml̩/ *der;* ∼**s, (a)** sky; **am** ∼: in the sky; **unter freiem** ∼: in the open [air]; outdoors; **aus heiterem** ∼ (ugs.) out of the blue; **(b)** (Aufenthalt Gottes) heaven; **in den** ∼ **kommen** go to heaven; **im** ∼ **sein** (verhüll.) be in heaven; **gen** ∼ **fahren** (geh.) ascend into heaven; ∼ **und Hölle in Bewegung setzen** (ugs.) move heaven and earth; **im sieb[en]ten** ∼ **sein/sich im sieb[en]ten** ∼ **fühlen** (ugs.) be in the seventh heaven; **zum** ∼ **schreien** be scandalous *or* a scandal; **zum** ∼ **stinken** (salopp) stink to high heaven; **(c)** (verhüll.: Schicksal) Heaven; **gerechter/gütiger/[ach] du lieber** ∼**!** good Heavens!; Heavens above!; **dem** ∼ **sei Dank** thank Heaven[s]; **weiß der** ∼**!** (ugs.) Heaven knows; **um [des]** ∼**s willen!** (Ausruf des Schreckens) good Heavens!; good God!; (inständige Bitte) for Heaven's sake; ∼ **noch [ein]mal!** for Heaven's *or* goodness' sake!; ∼, **Arsch und Zwirn!** (derb) bloody hell! [Brit. sl.); **(d)** (Baldachin) canopy; **(e)** (im Auto) roof lining

himmel-, Himmel-: ∼**angst** *Adj.* **in mir ist/wird** ∼**angst** I am scared to death; ∼**bett** *das* four-poster bed; ∼**blau** *Adj.* sky-blue; azure; clear blue ‹*eyes*›

Himmel·fahrt *die* (Rel.) **(a) Christi** ∼: the Ascension of Christ; **die** ∼ **Mariäs** the Assumption of the Virgin Mary; **(b)** (Festtag) **[Christi** ∼: Ascension Day *no art.;* **Mariä** ∼: the [feast of the] Assumption

Himmelfahrts·kommando *das* suicide mission *or* operation

Himmel·herrgott *in* ∼**herrgott noch [ein]mal!** (salopp) hell's bells! (sl.)

himmel-, Himmel-: ∼**hoch 1** *Adj.* soaring; towering; **2** *adv.* ‹*rise up etc.*› high into the sky; ∼**hoch jauchzend, zu Tode betrübt** up one minute, down the next; on top of the world one minute, down in the dumps the next; ∼**reich** *das* (christl. Rel.) kingdom of heaven; ∼**schreiend** *Adj.* scandalous; outrageous; scandalous, appalling ‹*conditions, disgrace*›; arrant *attrib.* ‹*nonsense*›; **eine** ∼**e Ungerechtigkeit** an injustice that cries out to heaven

Himmels-: ∼**gabe** *die* (geh.) gift from heaven; ∼**karte** *die* (Astron.) star map; ∼**körper** *der* celestial body; ∼**kunde** *die* astronomy; ∼**macht** *die* (geh.) heavenly power; ∼**richtung** *die* point of the compass; cardinal point; **aus allen** ∼**richtungen** from all directions; **in alle** ∼**richtungen verstreut sein** be scattered to all four corners of the earth; ∼**schlüssel** *der*, ∼**schlüsselchen** *das* cowslip; (Waldschlüsselblume) oxlip; ∼**stürmer** *der* (geh.) unshakeable idealist

himmel·stürmend *Adj.; nicht präd.* (geh.) boundless ‹*enthusiasm*›; wildly ambitious ‹*plan*›

Himmels·zelt *das* (dichter.) firmament

himmel·weit *Adj.* enormous, vast ‹*difference*›

himmlisch 1 *Adj.* **(a)** *nicht präd.* heavenly; **die** ∼**en Heerscharen** the heavenly host[s]; **der** ∼**e Vater** our Heavenly Father; **eine** ∼**e Fügung** divine providence; **(b)** (herrlich) heavenly; divine; wonderful ‹*weather, day, view*›. **2** *adv.* divinely; wonderfully, gloriously ‹*comfortable, warm*›

hin /hɪn/ *Adv.* **(a)** (räumlich) **zur Straße** ∼ **liegen** face the road; **nach Frankfurt** ∼: in the direction of Frankfurt; **bis zu dieser Stelle** ∼: [up] to this point; as far as here; **(b)** (zeitlich) **gegen Mittag** ∼: towards midday; **zum Herbst** ∼: towards the autumn; as autumn approaches/approached; **(c)** (in Verbindungen) **nach außen** ∼: outwardly; **auf meinen Rat** ∼: on my advice; **auf seine Bitte** ∼: at his request; **selbst/auch auf die Gefahr** ∼, **einen Fehler zu machen** even at the risk of making a mistake; **(d)** ∼ **und zurück** there and back; **einmal Köln** ∼ **und zurück** a return [ticket] to Cologne; **Hin und zurück? – Nein, nur** ∼: Return? - No, just a single; ∼ **und her** to and fro; back and forth; ∼ **und her beraten/reden** go backwards and forwards over the same old ground; **das Hin und Her** the toing and froing; **nach langem Hin und Her** after a great deal of argument; ∼ **und wieder** [every] now and then; **(e)** (elliptisch) **nichts wie** ∼**!** what are we waiting for?; ∼ **zu ihm!** [hurry up,] to him!; ∼ **sein** (ugs.: hingegangen, -gefahren sein) have gone; **(f) das ist noch lange** ∼: that's not for a long time yet; **bis zu dem Termin ist es noch einige Zeit** ∼: there's some time to go before the deadline; **(g) von jmdm./etw. ganz** ∼ **sein** (ugs.: hingerissen sein) be mad about sb./bowled over by sth.; **(h)** ∼ **sein** (ugs.: nicht mehr brauchbar sein) have had it (coll.); **das Auto ist** ∼ (ugs.) the car is a write-off; **er ist** ∼ (salopp: tot) he has snuffed it (sl.); **wenn er richtig zuschlägt, bist du** ∼ (salopp: tot) if he really hits you you've had it (coll.)

hinab /hɪ'nap/ *Adv.* ⇒ **hinunter**

hinab|- ⇒ **hinunter|-**

hinan /hɪ'nan/ *Adv.* (geh.) ⇒ **hinauf**

hin|arbeiten *itr. V.* **auf etw.** (*Akk.*) ∼: work towards sth.

hinauf /hɪ'nauf/ *Adv.* up; **den Hügel** ∼: up the hill

hinauf|- ‹*go, walk, take, throw, look, let, etc.*› up; (in ein weiter oben gelegenes Stockwerk) ‹*go, take, etc.*› upstairs; **auf einen Berg** ∼**steigen** climb up a mountain

hinauf-: ∼**|arbeiten** *refl. V.* ⇒ **hocharbeiten**; ∼**|bemühen 1** *tr. V.* **jmdn.** ∼**bemühen** trouble sb. to go up; **2** *refl. V.* take the trouble to go up; ∼**|bitten** *unr. tr. V.* **jmdn.** ∼**bitten** ask sb. to go up; ∼**|fahren 1** *unr. itr. V.; mit sein* go up; (im Auto) drive up; (mit einem Motorrad) ride up; **2** *unr. tr. V.* **jmdn.** ∼**fahren** drive *or* take sb. up; ∼**|fallen** *unr. itr. V.; mit sein* ⇒ **Treppe** a; ∼**|führen 1** *itr. V.* lead up; **2** *tr. V.* **jmdn.** ∼**führen** show sb. up; ∼**|gehen** *unr. itr. V.; mit sein* **(a)** go up; (in ein höheres Stockwerk) go upstairs; **die Treppe** ∼**gehen** go

Himmelsrichtungen

Die vier Himmelsrichtungen haben im Englischen nur die eine Form, die auch adjektivisch verwendet wird. (Es gibt andere Übersetzungen für die deutschen Adjektive *nördlich, südlich* usw.; s. unten):

Nord, Norden, Nord-	north
Ost, Osten, Ost-	east
Süd, Süden, Süd-	south
West, Westen, West-	west

Die weiteren, zusammengesetzten Bezeichnungen werden ähnlich wie im Deutschen gebildet:

Nordost, Nordosten	north-east
Nordwest, Nordwesten	north-west
Südost, Südosten	south-east
Südwest, Südwesten	south-west
Nordnordost, Nordnordosten	north-north-east
Nordnordwest, Nordnordwesten	north-north-west
Südsüdost, Südsüdosten	south-south-east
Südsüdwest, Südsüdwesten	south-south-west
Ostnordost, Ostnordosten	east-north-east
Westnordwest, Westnordwesten	west-north-west
Ostsüdost, Ostsüdosten	east-south-east
Westsüdwest, Westsüdwesten	west-south-west

Richtung

Der Wind kommt von Norden/Nordosten	= The wind is from the north/north-east
Wir fahren morgen nach Norden	= We are going north tomorrow
Die Nadel weist nach Norden	= The needle points to the north
der Zug nach Norden	= the northbound train
Das Schiff fährt nach Süden	= The ship is southward bound
Die Straße führt nach Südwesten	= The road runs south-west/south-westwards
Sie fuhren in Richtung Osten od. in östliche Richtung	= They were travelling eastwards od. in an easterly direction
Das Wohnzimmer geht nach Norden	= The sitting room faces north

Lage

Sie wohnen im Südwesten	= They live in the South-West
im Süden Englands, in Südengland	= in the South of England, in southern England
Im Norden ballten sich Gewitterwolken zusammen	= To the north storm clouds were gathering
Sie stammt aus dem Nordosten	= She comes from the North-East
Es liegt ein paar Kilometer westlich	= It's a few kilometres to the west
Es liegt weiter östlich	= It's further east
30 Kilometer südlich von Passau	= 30 kilometres [to the] south of Passau
etwas westlich der Insel	= a little to the west of the island

Adjektive

Nord-, Süd-, Ost-, West- bei geographischen Namen werden durch **North, South, East, West** übersetzt, solange es sich um ein ziemlich genau umgrenztes Gebiet handelt, also:

Nordamerika/ Südamerika	= North America/South America
Westafrika/Ostafrika	= West Africa/East Africa
Nordkorea/Südkorea	= North Korea/South Korea
Westberlin/Ostberlin	= West Berlin/East Berlin

Aber:

Norditalien/Süditalien	= Northern/Southern Italy,

da es sich hier nicht um ein genau umgrenztes Gebiet handelt. Man kann auch sagen 'the North/South of Italy'; vor allem *Südfrankreich* = the South of France. Allerdings:

die Südstaaten	= the southern States
die Westmächte	= the Western Powers
Ostdeutschland/ Westdeutschland	= East od. Eastern Germany/West od. Western Germany

(hierbei bezieht sich die jeweils erste Bezeichnung hauptsächlich auf die ehemalige DDR bzw. die alte BRD)

Man beachte ferner:

die Westküste	= the West Coast
die Südseite	= the south side; *(eines Hauses)* the south front
die Eigernordwand	= the north face of the Eiger

Aber:

die Westfront/Ostfront	= the Western/Eastern Front

Da sie im Deutschen schon weniger spezifisch sind, liegt es nahe, die Adjektive *nördlich, südlich, westlich, östlich* mit **northern, southern, western, eastern** zu übersetzen, etwa in:

das südliche Afrika	= southern Africa (im Gegensatz zu *Südafrika* = South Africa)

Sofern die Adjektive eine politische Bedeutung haben, werden sie groß geschrieben:

westliche Journalisten	= Western journalists
die westlichen Länder	= the Western countries

Bei Winden (und Richtungen) hingegen verwendet man die Formen **northerly, southerly, westerly, easterly:**

nördliche Winde	= northerly winds, northerlies (im Gegensatz zu *der Nordwind* = the north wind)
Winde aus östlicher Richtung	= winds from an easterly direction, easterly winds

Für den Superlativ kann im Englischen auch eine mit den Adjektiven **northern, southern** usw. und dem Suffix **-most** gebildete Form stehen:

der östlichste Punkt	= the easternmost point, the most easterly point

up the stairs; **(b)** (nach oben führen) ⟨*path, road, etc.*⟩ lead up; **es geht steil ∼:** the road/path climbs steeply; **(c)** (ugs.: steigen) ⟨*prices, taxes, etc.*⟩ go up; rise; **(d) mit dem Preis/der Miete ∼gehen** (ugs.) put the price/rent up; **∼|gelangen** *itr. V.; mit sein* [manage to] get up; **auf etw.** (*Akk.*) **∼gelangen** [manage to] get up sth.;

~|**helfen** *unr. itr. V.* jmdm. [die Treppe] ~helfen help sb. up [the stairs]; ~|**klettern** *itr. V.; mit sein* climb up; [auf] den Baum ~klettern climb up the tree; ~|**kommen** *unr. itr. V.; mit sein* (a) (nach oben kommen) come up; (b) (nach oben kommen können) [manage to] get up; ~|**laufen** *unr. itr. V.; mit sein* run up; die Treppe ~laufen run up the stairs; ~|**schicken** *tr. V.* send up; ~|**setzen** *tr. V.* (erhöhen) raise; increase; put up; die Preise ~setzen increase *or* raise prices; ~|**steigen** *unr. itr. V.; mit sein* climb up; (hinaufgehen) go up; ~|**tragen** *unr. tr. V.* carry *or* take up; ~|**werfen** *unr. tr. V.* etw. ~werfen throw sth. up (auf + *Akk.* on to)

hinaus /hɪˈnaus/ *Adv.* (a) (räumlich) out; ~ [mit dir]! out you go!; out with you!; zum Fenster ~: out of the window; hier/dort ~: this/that way out; nach hinten/vorne ~ liegen ‹*room*› be situated at the back/front; (b) (zeitlich) auf Jahre ~: for years to come; (c) über etw. (*Akk.*) ~: beyond sth.; (zusätzlich zu etw.) over and above *or* in addition to sth.; (d) über etw. (*Akk.*) ~ sein be past *or* beyond sth.; *s. auch* **darüber**

hinaus- ‹go, look, drive, ride, let, carry, etc.› out; (ins Freie) ‹go, look, carry, etc.› outside; aus etw. ~gehen/~sehen usw. go/look etc. out of sth.; etw. aus etw. ~bringen/~werfen usw. take/throw *etc.* sth. out of sth.; zur Tür ~laufen run out of the door; etw. zum Fenster ~werfen throw sth. out of the window; über etw. (*Akk.*) ~gehen/~kommen go/get beyond sth.

hinaus-: ~|**befördern** *tr. V.* jmdn. ~befördern throw *or* (coll.) chuck sb. out; ~|**begeben** *unr. refl. V.* go out; ~|**begleiten** *tr. V.* jmdn. ~begleiten see sb. out; ~ |**blicken** *itr. V.* look out (aus of); ~|**bringen** *tr. V.* jmdn./etw. ~bringen take *or* see sb. out/take sth. out (aus of); ~|**bugsieren** *tr. V.* (ugs.) jmdn. ~bugsieren (mit Geschick) steer sb. out (aus of); (hinausbefördern) hustle sb. out (aus of); ~|**drängen** 1 *itr. V.; mit sein* push one's way out (aus of); ‹*crowd*› push its way out (aus of); 2 *tr. V.* jmdn. ~drängen push sb. out (aus of); (fig.) push sb. out (aus of); oust sb. (aus from); ~|**ekeln** *tr. V.* (ugs.) jmdn. ~ekeln drive sb. out; ~|**fahren** 1 *unr. itr. V.; mit sein* (a) etw. ~fahren (mit dem Auto) drive out of sth.; (mit dem Zweirad) ride out of sth.; ‹*car, bus*› go out of sth.; ‹*train*› pull out of sth.; zum Flugplatz ~fahren drive out to the airport; aufs Meer ~fahren head for the sea; (b) (herauskommen) shoot out (aus of); (c) über etw. (*Akk.*) ~fahren go past sth.; 2 *unr. tr. V.* jmdn./etw. ~fahren drive *or* take sb./take sth. out; ~|**fallen** *unr. itr. V.; mit sein* fall sth. out (aus of); ‹*light*› come out (aus of); ~|**finden** *unr. itr. V.* find one's way out (aus of); er wird alleine ~finden he'll find his own way out; ~|**fliegen** 1 *unr. itr. V.; mit sein* (a) ⇒ **hinaus**|-; (b) (fig. ugs.) ~geworfen werden be chucked out (coll.); (als Arbeitnehmer) get the sack (coll.); be fired (coll.); (als Mieter) be thrown out (coll.); 2 *unr. tr. V.* ⇒ **hinaus**|-; ~|**führen** 1 *tr. V.* (a) jmdn. ~führen show sb. out; (b) (retten) die Partei aus der Krise ~führen lead the party out of the crisis; (c) jmdn. über etw. (*Akk.*) ~führen take sb. beyond sth.; 2 *itr. V.* (a) (verlaufen) lead out (aus of); (b) (nach draußen gerichtet sein) lead out; (c) über etw. (*Akk.*) ~führen go beyond sth.; ~|**gehen** *unr. itr. V.; mit sein* (a) ⇒ **hinaus**|-; (b) das Zimmer geht zum Garten/nach Westen ~: the room looks out on to *or* faces the garden/faces west; die Tür geht auf den Hof ~: the door leads *or* opens into the yard; die Schlafzimmer gehen nach hinten ~: the bedrooms are at the back; (c) *unpers.* wo geht es ~? which is the way out?; hier/da geht es ~: this/that is the way out; ~|**gelangen** *itr. V.; mit sein* (a) (nach draußen gelangen, auch fig.) [manage to] get out (aus of); (b) über etw. (*Akk.*) ~gelangen progress *or* get beyond sth.; ~|**gucken** *itr. V.* (ugs.) ⇒ ~blicken; ~|**hängen**¹ *unr. itr. V.* hang out (aus of); ~|**hängen**² *tr. V.* hang out (aus of); ~|**jagen** 1 *tr. V.* drive *or* chase out; jmdn. ~jagen (fig.: aus dem Haus) drive *or* turn sb. out; 2 *itr. V.; mit sein* rush *or* race out (aus of); ~|**katapultieren** *tr. V.* (a) (mit dem Schleudersitz) eject; (b) (salopp: verdrängen) jmdn. ~katapultieren push sb. out (aus of); ~|**kommen** *unr. itr. V.; mit sein* (a) ⇒ **hinaus**|-; (b) ich bin schon seit zwei Tagen nicht mehr ~gekommen I've not got *or* been out of the house for two days; er ist nie aus dem Dorf ~gekommen he has never been out of *or* outside his village;

~|**komplimentieren** *tr. V.* jmdn. ~komplimentieren usher sb. out; ~|**lassen** *unr. tr. V.* jmdn. ~lassen let sb. out; ~|**laufen** *unr. itr. V.; mit sein* (a) ⇒ **hinaus**|-; (b) auf etw. (*Akk.*) ~laufen lead to sth.; das läuft auf dasselbe ~: it comes to the same thing; ~|**lehnen** *refl. V.* lean out; sich zum Fenster ~lehnen lean out of the window; ~|**posaunen** *tr. V.* (ugs.) broadcast; ~|**ragen** *itr. V.* über etw. (*Akk.*) ~ragen rise up above sth.; (horizontal) jut out *or* project beyond sth.; ~|**reichen** 1 *tr. V.* etw. ~reichen hand *or* pass sth. out (aus of); 2 *itr. V.* (a) (bis nach draußen reichen) reach *or* stretch (bis zu as far as); (b) über etw. (*Akk.*) ~reichen go beyond sth.; ~|**rennen** *unr. itr. V.; mit sein* run out; ~|**schaffen** *tr. V.* jmdn. ~schaffen get sb./sth. out (aus of); ~|**scheuchen** *tr. V.* chase sb. out; ~|**schicken** *tr. V.* (a) jmdn. ~schicken send sb. out; (b) (senden) send out; ~|**schieben** 1 *unr. tr. V.* (a) ⇒ **hinaus**|-; (b) (aufschieben) put off; postpone; eine Entscheidung [um einen Tag] ~schieben put off *or* postpone *or* defer a decision [by one day]; 2 *unr. refl. V.:* ⇒ **hinaus**|-; ~|**schießen** *unr. itr. V.* (a) aus dem Auto/zum Fenster ~schießen fire from the car/the window; (b) *mit sein* (sich schnell hinausbewegen) shoot out (aus of); ‹*water*› rush out (aus of); (c) über das Ziel ~schießen (fig.) go too far; ~|**schmuggeln** *tr. V.* smuggle out (aus of); ~|**schreien** 1 *unr. tr. V.* shout out; 2 *unr. refl. V.* (geh.) seinen Hass/Zorn ~schreien vent *or* give vent to one's hate/rage in a loud outburst; ~|**schwimmen** *unr. itr. V.; mit sein* ‹*person*› swim out; ‹*object*› float out; ~|**sehen** *unr. itr. V.* look out; zum Fenster ~sehen look out of the window; **~|sein* ⇒ **hinaus** d; ~|**setzen** 1 *tr. V.* ⇒ **hinaus**|-; 2 *refl. V.* go and sit outside; ~|**stehlen** *unr. refl. V.* sneak *or* steal out (aus of); ~|**steigen** *unr. itr. V.; mit sein* climb out (aus of); zum Fenster ~steigen climb out of the window; ~|**stellen** 1 *tr. V.* ⇒ **hinaus**|-; 2 *refl. V.* go and stand outside; ~|**stürzen** 1 *unr. itr. V.; mit sein* (a) (hinausfallen) fall (aus out of); (b) (hinauseilen) rush *or* dash out (aus of); zur Tür ~stürzen rush *or* dash out of the door; 2 *refl. V.* throw oneself out (aus of); ~|**tragen** *unr. tr. V.* (a) jmdn./etw. ~tragen carry sb./sth. out; (b) etw. in alle Welt ~tragen spread sth. throughout the world; (c) über etw. ~getragen werden be carried across sth.; ~|**trauen** *refl. V.* venture out; dare to go out; ~|**treiben** 1 *unr. tr. V.* drive out (aus of); 2 *unr. itr. V.; mit sein* drift out; ~|**treten** *unr. itr. V.; mit sein* step out (aus of); ~|**trompeten** *tr. V.* ⇒ ~posaunen; ~|**wagen** *refl. V.* (a) venture out (aus of); sich in die Dunkelheit ~wagen dare [to] go out into the dark; (b) sich über etw. (*Akk.*) ~wagen venture beyond *or* dare [to] go beyond sth.; ~|**wachsen** *unr. itr. V.; mit sein* (a) über etw. (*Akk.*) ~wachsen grow taller than *or* up above sth.; (b) (fig.) über etw. (*Akk.*) ~wachsen outgrow sth.; über jmdn./sich [selbst] ~wachsen surpass sb./rise above oneself; ~|**werfen** *unr. tr. V.* (a) ⇒ **hinaus**|-; (b) (ugs.: ausschließen, die Wohnung kündigen) jmdn. ~werfen throw sb. out (aus of); (ugs.: entlassen) sack sb. (coll.); ~|**wollen** *unr. itr. V.* (a) want to get *or* go out (aus of); (b) [zu] hoch ~wollen (fig.) aim [too] high; set one's sights [too] high; (c) worauf willst du ~? (fig.) what are you getting *or* driving at?; auf etwas Bestimmtes ~wollen (fig.) have something particular in mind

Hinaus·wurf *der* (ugs.) throwing out; (eines Angestellten) sacking (coll.)

hinaus-: ~|**ziehen** 1 *unr. tr. V.* (a) ⇒ **hinaus**|-; (b) (verzögern) put off; delay; (c) *unpers.* es zog sie in die Natur ~: she felt the urge to get out into the countryside; 2 *unr. itr. V.; mit sein* ⇒ **hinaus**|-; 3 *unr. refl. V.* (sich verzögern) be delayed; ~|**zögern** 1 *tr. V.* delay; put off; 2 *refl. V.* be delayed; be put off

hin-, Hin-: ~|**bauen** *tr. V.* build; put up; ~|**begeben** *unr. refl. V.* ⇒ hingehen a; ~|**begleiten** *tr. V.* jmdn. ~begleiten accompany sb. [there]; ~|**bekommen** *unr. tr. V.* (ugs.) ⇒ hinkriegen; ~|**bemühen** 1 *tr. V.* jmdn. ~bemühen trouble sb. to go; 2 *refl. V.* take the trouble to go; ~|**beordern** *tr. V.* jmdn. ~beordern order sb. [to go] there; ~|**bestellen** *tr. V.* jmdn. ~**bestellen** tell sb. to be there; ~|**biegen** *unr. tr. V.* (ugs.) etw. ~biegen sort sth. out; **wie hat er das bloß** ~**gebogen?** how did he manage *or* (sl.) wangle that?; ~|**blättern** *tr. V.* (ugs.) fork *or* shell out (coll.), pay out ‹sum of money›; ~**blick** der in im od. in ~blick auf etw. (*Akk.*) (wegen) in view of; (hinsichtlich) with regard to; ~|**blicken** *itr. V.* look; **zu jmdm.** ~**blicken** look [across] at sb.; ~|**bringen** *unr. tr. V.* jmdn./etw. ~bringen take sb./sth. [there]

hin|denken *unr. itr. V.* wo denkst du hin? (ugs.) whatever are you thinking of?; what an idea!

hinderlich *Adj.* ~ sein get in the way; jmdm. ~ sein get in sb.'s way; **einer Sache** (*Dat.*) **sein** be an obstacle to sth.

hindern /'hɪndɐn/ *tr. V.* jmdn. ~: stop *or* prevent sb.; jmdn. [daran] ~, etw. zu tun prevent *or* stop sb. [from] doing sth.; jmdn. am Sprechen ~: prevent *or* stop sb. [from] speaking; ich werde dich nicht ~ (iron.) I'm not stopping you

Hindernis *das;* ~ses, ~se obstacle; (Springreiten) jump; obstacle; (Pferderennen) fence

Hindernis-: ~**lauf** *der,* ~**laufen** *das* (Leichtathletik) steeplechase; ~**rennen** *das* (Pferdesport) steeplechase

Hinderung *die;* ~, ~en hindrance

Hinderungs·grund *der:* das ist kein ~ für mich it does not prevent *or* stop me

hin|deuten *itr. V.* (a) auf jmdn./etw. od. zu jmdm./etw. ~: point to sb./sth.; (b) auf etw. (*Akk.*) ~ (fig.) suggest sth.; point to sth.; alles deutet darauf hin, dass …: everything suggests that …

hin|drängen 1 *tr. V.* jmdn. zu etw. ~: force sb. towards sth. 2 *itr. V.; mit sein; refl. V.* [**sich**] zu jmdm./etw. ~: push [one's way] towards sb./sth.

Hindu /'hɪndu/ *der;* ~[s], ~[s] Hindu

Hinduismus *der;* ~: Hinduism *no art.*

hinduistisch *Adj.* Hindu

hin·durch *Adv.* (a) (räumlich) **durch den Wald** ~: through the wood; **mitten/quer durch etw.** ~: straight through sth.; (b) (zeitlich) **das ganze Jahr** ~: throughout the year; **die ganze Nacht** ~: all night [long]; throughout the night; all through the night

hindurch|- ‹go, run, look, throw, etc.› through; **durch etw.** ~**laufen** run through sth.; **etw. durch etw.** ~**werfen** throw sth. through sth.; **sich durch etw.** ~**finden** find one's way through sth.; **unter etw.** (*Dat.*) ~**gehen** walk under sth.; **durch etw.** ~**müssen** have to go through sth.

hin-: ~|**dürfen** *unr. itr. V.* (ugs.) be allowed to go (**zu** to); **ihr dürft nicht mehr** ~: you're not to go there any more; ~|**eilen** *itr. V.; mit sein* (a) hurry (**zu** to); **alle eilten** ~: everyone hurried there

hinein /hɪ'naɪn/ *Adv.* (a) (räumlich) in; ~ **mit euch!** in you go!; in with you!; **in etw.** (*Akk.*) ~: into sth.; **nur** ~! go *or* walk right in!; (b) (zeitlich) **bis in den Morgen/tief in die Nacht** ~: till morning/far into the night

hinein|- ‹go, drive, ride, run, look, throw, etc.› in; **in etw.** (*Akk.*) ~**gehen/**~**sehen** go/look into sth.; **etw. in etw.** (*Akk.*) ~**legen/**~**kriegen** put/get sth. in[to] sth.; **sich in etw.** (*Akk.*) ~**bohren** bore one's/its way into sth.; **in etw.** (*Akk.*) ~**dürfen** be allowed into sth.

hinein-: ~|**bekommen** *unr. tr. V.* (ugs.) etw. [in etw. (*Akk.*)] ~**bekommen** get sth. in[to sth.]; ~|**bemühen** 1 *tr. V.* jmdn. ~**bemühen** trouble sb. to go in; 2 *refl. V.* take the trouble to go in; ~|**bitten** *unr. tr. V.* ask *or* invite sb. in; ~|**blicken** *itr. V.* look in; **in etw.** (*Akk.*) ~**blicken** look into sth.; ~|**bohren** 1 *tr. V.* **Löcher in die Wand** ~**bohren** drill holes in the wall; **den Finger in den Kuchen** ~**bohren** stick *or* poke one's finger into the cake; 2 *refl. V.* sich in etw. (*Akk.*) ~**bohren** bore one's/its way into sth.; ~|**bringen** *unr. tr. V.* take in; **Ordnung in etw.** ~**bringen** bring [some] order into sth.; **Schwung in etw.** (*Akk.*) ~**bringen** put [some] life into sth.; liven sth. up; (b) (ugs.) ⇒ ~**bekommen;** ~|**denken** *unr. refl. V.* sich in jmdn./in jmds. Lage

~**denken** put oneself in sb.'s position; ~|**drängen** 1 *itr. V. mit sein; refl. V.* [**sich**] **in etw.** (*Akk.*) ~**drängen** push one's way into sth.; [**sich**] **in den Bus** ~**drängen** push one's way on to the bus; 2 *tr. V.* jmdn. in etw. (*Akk*) ~**drängen** push sb. into sth.; **jmdn. in eine Rolle** ~**drängen** ((fig.) force sb. into a role; ~|**dürfen** *unr. itr. v.* be allowed in; **in etw.** (*Akk.*) ~**dürfen** be allowed into sth.; ~|**fahren** 1 *unr. itr. V.; mit sein* (a) (mit dem Auto) drive in; (mit dem Zweirad) ride in; **in etw.** (*Akk.*) ~**fahren** drive/ride into sth.; **der Zug fuhr [in den Bahnhof]** ~: the train pulled in[to the station]; (b) (ugs.) **in ein anderes Auto** ~**fahren** run into another car; 2 *unr. tr. V.* **den Wagen in etw.** (*Akk.*) ~**fahren** drive one's car into sth.; (b) **jmdn. in die Stadt** ~**fahren** drive sb. into town; ~|**fallen** *unr. itr. V.; mit sein* fall in; **in etw.** (*Akk.*) ~**fallen** fall into sth.; **jmdn. in einen Sessel** ~**fallen lassen** drop into a chair; ~|**finden** *unr. refl. V.* sich in etw. (*Akk.*) ~**finden** get used to sth.; (sich abfinden) come to terms with sth.; ~|**fressen** 1 *unr. tr. V.* etw. in sich ~**fressen** ‹animal, (derb) person› gobble sth. down *or* up, wolf sth. down; **seine Sorgen/seinen Ärger in sich** ~**fressen** (fig.) bottle up one's worries/anger; 2 *unr. refl. V.* sich in etw. (*Akk.*) ~**fressen** eat into sth.; ~|**ge-bären** *unr. tr. V.* in eine Zeit/Umwelt *usw.* ~**geboren werden/sein** be/have been born into an age/environment *etc.;* ~|**gehen** *unr. itr. V.; mit sein* (a) go in; **in etw.** (*Akk.*) ~**gehen** go into sth.; (b) (~passen) **in den Eimer gehen drei Liter** ~: the bucket holds three litres; ~|**geraten** *unr. itr. V.; mit sein* **in eine Schlägerei** ~**geraten** get into a fight; ~|**gießen** *unr. tr. V.* pour in; **etw. in etw.** (*Akk.*) ~**gießen** pour sth. into sth.; ~|**gucken** *itr. V.* (ugs.) look in; **in etw.** (*Akk.*) ~**gucken** look in[to] sth.; ~|**helfen** *unr. itr. V.* jmdm. in den Mantel ~**helfen** help sb. on with his/her coat; jmdn. in den Bus ~**helfen** help sb. on to the bus; ~|**interpretieren** *tr. V.* etw. in etw. (*Akk.*) ~**interpetieren** read sth. into sth.; ~|**knien** *refl. V.* (ugs.) sich in etw. (*Akk.*) ~**knien** get one's teeth into sth.; ~|**kommen** *unr. itr. V.; mit sein* (a) come in; **in etw.** (*Akk.*) ~**kommen** come into sth.; (b) (gelangen, auch fig.) get in; **in etw.** (*Akk.*) ~**kommen** get into sth.; (c) (sich hineinfinden) **in eine Sprache/ein Fach [wieder]** ~**kommen** get [back] into a language/subject; (d) (ugs.: hinzugefügt werden) **in etw.** (*Akk.*) ~**kommen** go into sth.; ~|**kriegen** *tr. V.* (ugs.) ⇒ ~**bekommen;** ~|**laufen** *unr. itr. V.; mit sein* (a) run in; (gehen) walk in; **in etw.** (*Akk.*) ~**laufen** run/walk into sth.; **in sein Verderben** ~**laufen** (fig.) be heading [straight] for disaster; **in ein Fahrzeug** ~**laufen** run under a vehicle; (b) (fließen) **in etw.** (*Akk.*) ~**laufen** run into sth.; ~|**leuchten** *itr. V* shine in; **in etw.** (*Akk.*) ~**leuchten** shine into sth.; **mit einer Lampe in den Keller** ~**leuchten** shine a light into the cellar; ~|**manövrieren** *tr. V.* (a) etw. in etw. (*Akk.*) ~**manövrieren** manoeuvre sth. into sth.; (b) jmdn./sich in eine verzwickte Lage ~**manövrieren** get *or* put sb./oneself into a tricky situation; ~|**reden** *itr. V.* (abwertend: sich einmischen) **jmdm. in seine Angelegenheiten/Entscheidungen** *usw.* ~**reden** meddle *or* interfere in sb.'s affairs/decisions *etc.;* ~|**regnen** (unpers.) es regnet [ins Zimmer] ~: the rain is coming in[to] the room; ~|**reißen** *unr. V.* jmdn. in etw. (*Akk.*) ~**reißen** (auch fig.) drag sb. into sth.; ~|**reiten** 1 *unr. itr. V.; mit sein* ride in; **in etw.** (*Akk.*) ~**reiten** ride into sth.; 2 *unr. tr. V.* (ugs.) ⇒ **reinreiten;** ~|**rennen** *unr. itr. V.; mit sein* (ugs.) run in; race in; **in etw.** (*Akk.*) ~**rennen** run *or* race into sth.; **in sein Verderben** ~**rennen** (fig.) be heading [straight] for disaster; ~|**riechen** *unr. itr. V.* (ugs.) **in eine Arbeit/eine Firma** ~**riechen** get a taste of a job/a firm; ~|**schaffen** *tr. V.* jmdn./etw.[in etw. (*Akk.*)] ~**schaffen** get sb./sth. in[to sth.]; ~|**schauen** *itr. V.* (a) (bes. südd., österr.) ⇒ ~**sehen;** (b) (bes. südd., österr.: kurz besuchen) **bei jmdm.** ~**schauen** look in on sb.; ~|**schlagen** *unr. tr. V.* **einen Nagel/Pfahl [in etw.** (*Akk.*)] ~**schlagen** knock *or* drive a nail/stake in[to sth.]; **ein Loch in etw.** (*Akk.*) ~**schlagen** knock *or* cut a hole in sth.; ~|**schleichen** 1 *unr. itr. V.; mit sein* slip in; [in etw. (*Akk.*)] ~**schleichen** creep *or* steal in[to sth.]; 2 *unr. refl. V.* sich [in etw. (*Akk.*)] ~**schleichen** creep *or* steal in[to sth.]; (fig.) ‹*error*› creep in[to sth.]; ∼|**schlüpfen** *itr. V.; mit sein* slip in; **ins Zimmer/in seinen Mantel** ∼**schlüpfen** slip into the room/one's coat; ∼|**schmuggeln** *tr. V.* smuggle in; **jmdn./etw. [in etw. (*Akk.*)]** ∼**schmuggeln** smuggle sb.sth. in[to sth.]; ∼|**schneien** *itr. V.* (**a**) (unpers.) **es schneit [in die Hütte]** ∼: the snow is coming in[to the hut]; (**b**) *mit sein* ⇒ **hereinschneien** a; ∼|**schütten** *tr. V.* pour in; **etw. (*Akk.*)** ∼**schütten** pour sth. into sth.; **etw. in sich** ∼**schütten** (fig.) knock sth. back (sl.); pour sth. down one's throat; ∼|**sehen** *unr. itr. V.* look in; **in etw. (*Akk.*)** ∼**sehen** look into sth; **in jmds. Zeitung** ∼**sehen** have a look at sb.'s paper; ∼|**stecken** *tr. V.* (**a**) **etw. [in etw. (*Akk.*)]** ∼**stecken** put sth. in[to sth.]; (**b**) **viel Geld in etw. (*Akk.*)** ∼**stecken** (ugs.) put *or* sink a lot of money into sth.; **viel Arbeit in etw. (*Akk.*)** ∼**stecken** (ugs.) put a lot of work into sth.; ∼|**steigern** *refl. V.* **sich in große Erregung/seine Wut** ∼**steigern** work oneself up into a state of great excitement/into a rage; ∼|**stoßen** **1** *unr. tr. V.* (**a**) thrust in; **etw. in etw. (*Akk.*)** ∼**stoßen** thrust sth. into sth.; (**b**) (hineinbringen) **jmdn. in etw. (*Akk.*)** ∼**stoßen** push sb. into sth.; (fig.) plunge sb. into sth.; **2** *unr. itr. V.; mit sein* **in etw. (*Akk.*)** ∼**stoßen** (vordringen) push *or* thrust into sth. (hineinsteuern) drive (or) turn into sth.; ∼|**stürzen** **1** *itr. V.; mit sein* (**a**) (hineinfallen) **in etw. (*Akk.*)** ∼**stürzen** fall *or* plunge into sth.; (**b**) (nach innen eilen) rush *or* burst in; **2** *tr. V.* **jmdn. in etw. (*Akk.*)** ∼**stürzen** hurl sb. into sth.; **3** *refl. V.* **sich in etw. (*Akk.*)** ∼**stürzen** throw oneself *or* plunge into sth.; **sich in die Arbeit** ∼**stürzen** (fig.) throw oneself into one's work; ∼|**tappen** *itr. V.; mit sein* (ugs.) **in etw. (*Akk.*)** ∼**tappen** grope one's way into sth.; (hineingeraten) walk [right] into sth.; ∼|**tragen** *unr. tr. V.* (**a**) carry in; **etw. in etw. (*Akk.*)** ∼**tragen** carry sth. into sth.; **Schmutz ins Haus** ∼**tragen** bring dirt into the house; (**b**) (verbreiten) **etw. in etw. (*Akk.*)** ∼**tragen** bring sth. into sth.; **Unruhe in einen Betrieb** ∼**tragen** spread unrest in a firm; ∼|**treiben** *unr. tr. V.* (**a**) **jmdn./etw. in etw. (*Akk.*)** ∼**treiben** drive sb./sth. into sth.; (**b**) (in etw. schlagen) **etw. [in etw. (*Akk.*)]** ∼**treiben** drive sth. in[to sth.]; ∼|**versetzen** *refl. V.* **sich in jmdn. od. jmds. Lage** ∼**versetzen** put oneself in sb.'s position; ∼|**wachsen** *unr. itr. V.; mit sein* (**a**) **in etw. (*Akk.*)** ∼**wachsen** grow into sth.; (**b**) (ugs.) **in ein Kleid usw.** ∼**wachsen** grow into a dress *etc.*; (**c**) (fig.) **in eine Aufgabe/Rolle** ∼**wachsen** get to know a job/get into *or* inside a part; ∼|**wagen** *refl. V.* venture in; dare to go in; **sich in etw. (*Akk.*)** ∼**wagen** venture into sth.; dare to go into sth.; ∼|**werfen** *unr. tr. V.* (**a**) **etw. [in etw. (*Akk.*)]** ∼**werfen** throw sth. in[to sth.]; (**b**) (fallen lassen) **einen Blick [in etw. (*Akk.*)]** ∼**werfen** glance at sth.; ∼|**wollen** *unr. itr. V.* (ugs.: ∼gelangen wollen) want to get *or* go in; **in etw. (*Akk.*)** ∼**wollen** want to go/get into sth.; **das will mir nicht in den Kopf** ∼: I just *or* simply can't understand it; ∼|**ziehen** **1** *unr. tr. V.* (**a**) ⇒ **hinein|-**; (**b**) (fig.) **jmdn. in eine Angelegenheit/einen Streit/Skandal** ∼**ziehen** drag sb. into an affair/a dispute/scandal; **2** *unr. itr. V.; mit sein:* ⇒ **hinein|-**; ∼|**zwängen** **1** *tr. V.* **etw. [in etw. (*Akk.*)]** ∼**zwängen** squeeze *or* force sth. in[to sth.]; **2** *refl. V.* squeeze in; **sich in die Hose** ∼**zwängen** squeeze [oneself] into one's trousers; ∼|**zwingen** *unr. tr. V.* **jmdn. [in etw. (*Akk.*)]** ∼**zwingen** force sb. to go in[to sth.]; **jmdn. in ein Schema/eine Rolle** ∼**zwingen** force sb. into rigid pattern/a role.

hin-, Hin-: ∼|**fahren** **1** *unr. itr. V.; mit sein* go/drive/ride there; **wo ist er** ∼**gefahren?** where has he gone?; **2** *unr. tr. V.* **jmdn.** ∼**fahren** drive *or* take sb. there; **jmdn. zum Bahnhof** ∼**fahren** drive *or* take sb. to the station; ∼**fahrt** *die* journey there; (Seereise) voyage out; **auf der** ∼**fahrt** on the way *or* journey there/the voyage out; ∼|**fallen** *unr. itr. V.; mit sein* (**a**) fall down *or* over; **lang** ∼**fallen** fall flat [on one's face/back]; (**b**) **jmdm. fällt etw.** ∼: sb. drops sth.; ∼**fallen lassen** drop sth.; ∼**fällig** *Adj.* (**a**) (schwächlich) infirm; frail; (**b**) (ungültig) invalid; ∼**fälligkeit** *die;* ∼ (**a**) (Schwäche) infirmity; frailty; (**b**) (Ungültigkeit) invalidity; ∼|**finden** *unr. itr. V.* find one's way there; **zu jmdm./zu einem Ort** ∼**finden**

find one's way to sb./a place; ∼|**flegeln** *refl. V.* (ugs. abwertend) loll around *or* about; ∼|**fliegen** **1** *unr. itr. V.;* *mit sein* (**a**) fly there; **er fliegt heute** ∼: he's flying [out] there today; (**b**) (ugs.: fallen) come a cropper (coll.); fall over; **2** *unr. tr. V.* **jmdn./etw.** ∼**fliegen** fly sb./sth. [out] there; ∼**flug** *der* outward flight; ∼|**führen** **1** *tr. V.* **jmdn.** ∼: lead *or* take sb. there; **jmdn. zu etw.** ∼: lead sb. to sth. **2** *itr. V.* **zu etw.** ∼: lead to sth.

hing /hɪŋ/ *1. u. 3. Pers. Sg. Prät. v.* **hängen**[1]

Hin·gabe *die;* ∼ (**a**) devotion; (Eifer) dedication; **etw. mit** ∼ **tun** do sth. with dedication; (**b**) (geh.: das Opfern) **unter** ∼ **des Lebens** at the cost of one's life

hin|geben **1** *unr. tr. V.* (geh.) give; sacrifice; **sein Leben** ∼: lay down *or* sacrifice one's life. **2** *unr. refl. V.* (**a**) **sich einer Illusion/einem Genuss** ∼: entertain an illusion/ abandon oneself to a pleasure; (**b**) (verhüll.) **sich einem Mann** ∼: give oneself to a man

hingebungs·voll **1** *Adj.* devoted. **2** *adv.* devotedly; with devotion; ‹*listen*› raptly, with rapt attention; ‹*dance, play*› with abandon

hin·gegen *Adv.* however; (andererseits) on the other hand

hin-: ∼**gegossen** *Adj.* (ugs. scherzh.) **wie** ∼**gegossen auf der Couch liegen/sitzen** have draped oneself over the couch; ∼|**gehen** *unr. itr. V.; mit sein* (**a**) go [there]; **zu jmdm./etw.** ∼**gehen** go to sb./sth.; **wo gehst du** ∼? where are you going?; (**b**) (verstreichen) ‹*years, time*› pass, go by; **darüber gingen Jahre** ∼: it took years; (**c**) (∼genommen werden) pass; **diesmal mag das noch** ∼**gehen** I'll/ we'll *etc.* let it pass this time; ∼|**gehören** *itr. V.* (ugs.) go; belong; ‹*person*› belong; **wo gehört das** ∼? where does this go *or* belong *or* (coll.) live?; ∼|**gelangen** *itr. V.;* *mit sein* get there; **zu jmdm./etw.** ∼**gelangen** get to sb./ sth.; ∼|**geraten** *unr. itr. V.; mit sein* get there; **wo ist er/der Brief** ∼**geraten?** where has he/the letter got to?; ∼**gerissen** *Adj.; nicht attr.* carried away; spellbound; ∼**gerissen der Musik lauschen** listen spellbound to the music; ∼|**halten** *unr. tr. V.* (**a**) hold out (*Dat.* to); (**b**) (warten lassen) **jmdn.** ∼**halten** put sb. off; keep sb. waiting

hin-: ∼|**hängen** *tr. V.* (ugs.) hang up; ∼|**hauen** **1** *unr. tr. V.* (**a**) (salopp) ⇒ ∼**schmeißen** b; (**b**) (salopp abwertend: flüchtig anfertigen) knock off (coll.); dash off; (**c**) unpers. (salopp) **es hat mich** ∼**gehauen** I came a cropper (coll.); **2** *unr. tr. V.* (**a**) (ugs.: schlagen) take a swipe (coll.); (**b**) *mit sein* (hinfallen) fall [down] heavily; (**c**) (salopp: gut gehen) ‹*plan*› work [all right]; **es wird schon** ∼**hauen** it'll work out *or* be all right *or* (coll.) OK; (**d**) (salopp: richtig sein) ‹*calculation*› be right; **3** *unr. refl. V.* (salopp) lie down and have a kip (Brit. coll.); ∼|**hören** *itr. V.* listen

hinken /'hɪŋkn̩/ *itr. V.* (**a**) limp; walk with a limp; **auf od. mit dem rechten Bein** ∼: have a limp in one's right leg; (**b**) *mit sein* limp; hobble; (**c**) (fig.) ‹*comparison*› be poor *or* feeble

hin-, Hin-: ∼|**knallen** (ugs.) **1** *tr. V.* slam down; **2** *itr. V.; mit sein* fall [down] heavily; come a cropper (coll.); ∼|**knien** *refl. V.* kneel [down]; ∼|**kommen** *unr. itr. V.; mit sein* (**a**) get there; **wie kommt man zu ihm** ∼? how do you get to his place?; (**b**) (an einen Ort gehören) go; belong; **wo kommen die Gläser** ∼? where do the glasses go *or* belong?; (**c**) (∼geraten) **wo ist meine Uhr** ∼**gekommen?** where has my watch got to *or* gone?; **wo kommen od. kämen wir** ∼**, wenn ...** (fig.) where would we be if ...; (**d**) (ugs.: auskommen) manage; (**e**) (ugs.: in Ordnung kommen) work out *or* turn out all right *or* (coll.) OK; (**f**) (ugs.: stimmen) be right; ∼|**kriegen** *tr. V.* (ugs.) (**a**) (fertig bringen) **das hat sie toll** ∼**gekriegt** she made a great job of that (coll.); **das wird er schon** ∼**kriegen** he'll manage it all right *or* (coll.) OK; (**b**) **etw. wieder** ∼**kriegen** fix sth.; **jmdn. wieder** ∼**kriegen** put sb. right; ∼|**langen** *itr. V.* (**a**) (ugs.: fassen) **er langte** ∼ **und steckte einige Uhren in seine Tasche** he reached over and stuck some watches in his pocket (coll.); (**b**) (salopp: zuschlagen) [**kräftig**] ∼**langen** take a [hefty] swipe (coll.); (**c**) (salopp: sich bedienen) help oneself; **schön/ ordentlich** ∼**langen** help oneself in a big way (coll.); ∼|**länglich** **1** *Adj.* sufficient; (angemessen) adequate; **2** *adv.* sufficiently; (angemessen) adequately; ∼|**lassen** *unr. tr. V.* (ugs.) **jmdn.** ∼**lassen** allow sb. to go there; let sb. go there; **jmdn. zu etw.** ∼**lassen** allow

sb. to go to sth.; let sb. go to sth.; ~|**laufen** *unr. itr. V.;*
mit sein (a) run there; **zu jmdm./zu einer Stelle**
~**laufen** run to sb./a place; (b) (zu Fuß hingehen) walk [there];
~|**legen** 1 *tr. V.* (a) put; **sie legte den Kindern fri-
sche Wäsche** ~: she put out clean underwear for the children; (b) (weglegen) put down; (c) (zu Bett bringen) **jmdn.**
~**legen** lay sb. down; (d) (ugs.: zahlen) pay *or* (coll.) shell
out; (e) (salopp: ausführen) **eine hervorragende Rede**
~**legen** do a brilliant speech; **eine gekonnte Übung
auf dem Trampolin** ~**legen** turn in a splendid performance on the trampoline; 2 *refl. V.* (a) lie down; **da
legst du dich [lang]** ~ (ugs.) you won't believe your ears;
(b) (sich schlafen legen) lie down; (c) (ugs.: hinfallen) come a
cropper (coll.); fall [down *or* over]; ~|**leiten** *tr. V.* lead
there; **etw. zu etw.** ~**leiten** lead sth. to sth.; ~|**lenken**
tr. V. (a) **etw. zu etw.** ~**lenken** steer sth. to sth.; (b) (fig.)
steer ‹*conversation*› (**auf** + *Akk.* round to); direct
‹*attention*› (**auf** + *Akk.* towards); turn ‹*gaze*› (**auf** +
Akk. towards); ~|**machen** (ugs.) 1 *tr. V.* put up
‹*curtain, picture, fence, etc.*›; put on ‹*paint, oil, cream*›; put
in ‹*comma etc.*›; put ‹*cross, ring, etc.*›; make ‹*dirty mark
etc.*›; 2 *itr. V.* (seine Notdurft verrichten) do one's/its business
(coll.); ~|**marschieren** *itr. V.; mit sein* march there;
~|**metzeln**, ~|**morden** *tr. V.* (geh.) massacre; slaugh-
ter; butcher ~|**nehmen** *unr. tr. V.* (a) (annehmen) accept;
take; put up with, swallow, accept ‹*insult*›; (b) (ugs.: mitnehmen) **kannst du das Buch mit** ~**nehmen** can you take
the book with you?; **kannst du mich mit** ~**nehmen?**
can you take me there?; ~|**neigen** 1 *tr. V.* incline; **den
Kopf zu jmdm.** ~**neigen** incline *or* bend one's head to-
wards sb.; 2 *refl. V.* lean [over]; ~|**passen** *itr. V.* (ugs.)
(a) fit *or* go in; (b) (harmonieren) fit in; go; ~|**reichen** 1
tr. V. hand; pass; **jmdm. etw.** ~**reichen** hand *or* pass sth.
to sb.; 2 *itr. V.* (a) reach; **bis zu etw.** ~**reichen** reach
to *or* as far as sth.; (b) (ausreichen) be enough *or* sufficient;
~**reichend** 1 *Adj.* sufficient; (angemessen) adequate; 2
adv. sufficiently; (angemessen) adequately; ~**reise** *die*
journey there; outward journey; (mit dem Schiff) voyage out;
outward voyage; **[die] Hin- und Rückreise** the journey
there and back; ~|**reisen** *itr. V.; mit sein* travel there;
~|**reißen** *unr. tr. V.* (a) **jmdn. zu sich** ~**reißen** pull
sb. to one; (b) (begeistern) enrapture; **das Publikum zu
Beifallsstürmen** ~**reißen** elicit thunderous *or* rapturous applause from the audience; (c) **jmdn. zu etw.**
~**reißen** drive sb. to sth.; **sich dazu** ~**reißen lassen,
etw. zu tun** let oneself get *or* be carried away and do sth.;
er ließ sich zu einer Beleidigung ~**reißen** he let himself be carried away and insulted him/her *etc.*; ~**reißend** 1 *Adj.* enchanting ‹*person, picture, view*›;
captivating ‹*speaker, play*›; 2 *adv.* enchantingly;
~|**richten** *tr. V.* execute; ~**richtung** *die* execution;
~|**rücken** 1 *tr. V.* **etw.** ~**rücken** move *or* push sth.
over; 2 *itr. V.; mit sein* move over; ~|**sagen** *tr. V.* say
without thinking; (nur beiläufig sagen) say casually; **das hat
er nur so** ~**gesagt** he just said it without thinking; ~|
schaffen *unr. tr. V.* **etw.** ~**schaffen** get sth. there;
etw. zum Bahnhof ~**schaffen** get sth. to the station;
~|**schauen** *itr. V.* (bes. südd., österr.) ⇒ ~**sehen;**
~|**scheiden** *das;* ~**s** (geh. verhüll.) decease; demise;
~|**scheißen** *unr. itr. V.* (derb) crap (coarse);
~|**schicken** *tr. V.* send; ~|**schieben** *unr. tr. V.*
jmdm. etw. ~**schieben** push sth. over to sb.;
~|**schielen** *itr. V.* steal a glance/glances (**zu** at);
~|**schlagen** *unr. tr. V.* (a) strike; hit; (b) **mit sein** (ugs.:
fallen) **[der Länge nach** *od.* **lang]** ~**schlagen** fall flat on
one's face/back; ~|**schleichen** *unr. itr. V.; mit sein;
unr. refl. V.* creep *or* steal over; ~|**schleppen** 1 *refl.
V.* drag oneself along; **sich zu etw.** ~**schleppen** drag
oneself to sth.; 2 *tr. V.* **etw.** ~**schleppen** drag sth. there;
etw. zu etw. ~**schleppen** drag sth. to sth.;
~|**schmelzen** *unr. itr. V.; mit sein* (a) ⇒ **zerschmel-
zen;** (b) (ugs. scherzh.: vergehen) swoon; **vor Rührung**
~**schmelzen** be overcome with emotion; ~|**schmei-
ßen** *unr. tr. V.* (salopp) (a) chuck down (coll.); (b) (aufgeben)
chuck in (coll.); (c) (fallen lassen) drop; ~|**schreiben** 1
unr. tr. V. write down; 2 *unr. itr. V.* write; ~|**sehen** *unr.*

itr. V. look; **ich kann nicht** ~**sehen** I can't [bear to] look;
bei genauerem Hinsehen on closer inspection;
*ᵃ~|**sein** ⇒ **hin;** ~|**setzen** 1 *tr. V.* put; seat, put
‹*person*›; **das Kind** ~**setzen** sit the child/baby down; 2
refl. V. (a) sit down; **setz dich doch** ~! do sit down!; **sich
gerade** ~**setzen** sit up straight; **sich** ~**setzen und
etw. tun** (fig.) sit down and do sth.; get down to doing sth.;
(b) (ugs.: fallen) land on one's backside; (c) (salopp: überrascht
sein) **er wird sich** ~**setzen** he won't believe his ears;
~**sicht** *die; o. Pl.* respect; **in finanzieller** ~**sicht**
financially; ~**sichtlich** *Präp. mit Gen.* (Amtsspr.) with
regard to; ~|**sollen** *unr. itr. V.* (ugs.) **wo sollen die
Sachen** ~? where do these things go?; where do you want
these things [to go]?; **sie weiß nicht, wo sie** ~**soll** she
doesn't know where to go; ~**spiel** *das* (Sport) first leg;
~|**starren** *itr. V.* stare (**zu, nach** at); ~|**stellen** 1
tr. V. (a) put; put up ‹*building*›; put, park ‹*car*›; (b) (auf
den Boden stellen) put down; (c) (darstellen) **etw. als falsch**
~**stellen** make sth. out to be *or* represent sth. as false;
jmdn. als Lügner ~**stellen** make sb. out to be *or* represent sb. as a liar; **jmdn. als Vorbild** ~**stellen** hold sb. up
as an example; **sich als Opfer/als unschuldig**
~**stellen** make out that one is a victim/is innocent; 2
refl. V. stand; ‹*driver*› park; (aufstehen) stand up; **sich ge-
rade** ~**stellen** stand up straight; ~|**strecken** 1 *tr. V.*
(a) stretch out; hold out; **jmdm. die Hand** ~**strecken**
hold out one's hand to sb.; (b) (geh. veralt.: töten) fell; slay
(liter.); 2 *refl. V.* stretch [oneself] out; lie down full length;
~|**strömen** *itr. V.; mit sein* ‹*people*› flock there; **zu etw.**
~**strömen** flock to sth.; ~|**stürzen** *itr. V.; mit sein* (a)
fall down [heavily]; (b) (hineilen) rush *or* dash there; **zum
Ausgang** ~**stürzen** rush *or* dash towards the exit
Hinrichtungs-: ~**kommando** *das* firing squad;
~**stätte** *die* place of execution
hintan-, Hintan- /hɪnt|'an/: ~|**setzen** *tr. V.* **etw.**
~**setzen** put sth. last; **Differenzen** ~**setzen** put *or* set
aside differences; ~**setzung** *die;* ~: **nur unter** ~**setzung persönlicher Interessen** only by putting personal
interests last; ~|**stellen** *tr. V.* ⇒ ~**setzen**
hinten /'hɪntn̩/ *Adv.* at the back; in *or* at the rear; ~ **im
Bus** in the back of the bus; ~ **einsteigen** get on at the
back; **sich** ~ **anstellen** join the back of the queue (Brit.)
or (Amer.) line; ~ **im Buch** at the back *or* end of the book;
weiter ~: further back; (in einem Buch) further on; **von** ~
nach vorne backwards; (in einem Buch) from back to front;
nach ~ gehen go *or* walk to the room be-
hind; **die Adresse steht** ~ **auf dem Brief** the address
is on the back of the envelope; ~ **am Haus** at the back
or rear of the house; **von** ~ **kommen/jmdn. von** ~
erstechen come from behind/stab sb. from behind; **von**
~ **sah sie jünger aus** she looked younger from the back;
jmdm. ~ **drauffahren** (ugs.) run into the back of sb.; **die
anderen sind ganz weit** ~: the others are a long way
back *or* behind; ~ **in Sibirien** far away in Siberia; ~
und vorn[e] bedient werden (ugs.) be waited on hand
and foot; **jmdn. am liebsten von** ~ **sehen** (ugs.) be glad
to see the back of sb.
hinten-: ~**drauf** *Adv.* (ugs.) on the back; **jmdm. eins
od. ein paar** ~**drauf geben** (ugs.) smack sb.'s bottom;
~**herum** /'---/, ~**rum** /'---/ *Adv.* (ugs.) (a) round the
back; **mir ist** ~**herum kalt** my back's cold; (b) **etw.**
~**herum erfahren** hear sth. indirectly
hinten·über *Adv.* backwards
hintenüber-: ~|**fallen** *unr. tr. V.; mit sein* fall [over]
backwards; ~|**kippen** *itr. V.; mit sein* tipp [over] back-
wards; ~|**stürzen** *itr. V.; mit sein:* ⇒ ~**fallen**
hinter /'hɪntɐ/ 1 *Präp. mit Dat.* (a) behind; ~ **dem
Haus** behind *or* at the back of the house; ~ **jmdm.
zurückbleiben** lag behind sb.; **eine große Strecke** ~
sich haben have put a good distance behind one; ~
jmdm. stehen (fig.) be behind sb.; back *or* support sb.;
etw. (*Dat.*) **stehen** (fig.) support sth.; **jmdn.** ~ **sich
haben** (fig.) have sb.'s backing; **3 km** ~ **der Grenze** 3 km
beyond the frontier; **die nächste Station** ~ **Mannheim**
the next stop after Mannheim; ~ **der Entwicklung/der
Zeit zurückbleiben** lag behind in development/be behind in times; **er ist** ~ **unseren Erwartungen zurückgeblieben** he has fallen short of our expectations; (b)

eine Prüfung/Aufgabe ∼ sich haben (fig.) have got an examination/a job over [and done] with; **viele Enttäu-schungen/eine Krankheit** ∼ **sich haben** have experienced many disappointments/have got over an illness; **wenn er das Studium** ∼ **sich hat** when he's finished his studies. **2** *Präp. mit Akk.* **(a)** behind; ∼ **das Haus gehen** go behind the house; **(b)** etw. ∼ **sich bringen** get sth. over [and done] with; **(c)** (fig.) ∼ **ein Geheimnis/ die Wahrheit/seine Geschichte kommen** find out a secret/get to the truth/get to the bottom of his story

hinter... *Adj.; nicht präd.* back; **das** ∼**e Ende des Ganges/des Zimmers** the far end of the corridor/the far end or the back of the room; **das** ∼**e Ende des Zuges** the back or rear [end] of the train; **die** ∼**ste Reihe** the back row

Hinter-: ∼**achse** die rear or back axle; ∼**an·sicht** die rear or back view; ∼**ausgang** der rear or back exit; ∼**bänkler** /∼bɛŋklɐ/ der; ∼**s**, ∼ (ugs.) inconspicuous backbencher; ∼**bein** das hind leg; **sich auf die** ∼**beine stellen** (ugs.) put up a fight

Hinterbliebene /-'bliːbənə/ der/die; adj. Dekl. **(a)** Pl. **die** ∼**n** the bereaved [family]; **(b)** (Rechtsspr.) surviving dependant

hinter·bringen unr. tr. V. **jmdm. etw.** ∼**bringen** inform sb. [confidentially] of sth.

hinter·einander Adv. **(a)** (räumlich) one behind the other; **sie liefen dicht** ∼: they were running close behind one another; **(b)** (zeitlich) one after another or the other; **an drei Tagen** ∼: for three days running or in succession

hinter-, Hinter-: ∼**ein·gang** der rear or back entrance; ∼**fragen** /-'--/ tr. V. examine; analyse; ∼**fuß** der hind foot; ∼**gebäude** das ⇒ ∼**haus;** ∼**gedanke** der ulterior motive; **einen** ∼**gedanken bei etw. haben** have an ulterior motive for sth.; ∼**gehen** /-'--/ unr. tr. V. deceive

Hinter·grund der (auch fig.) background; **der akusti-sche/musikalische** ∼: the background sounds/music; **etw. im** ∼ **haben** have sth. up one's sleeve

hinter·gründig **1** Adj. enigmatic; cryptic. **2** adv. enigmatically; cryptically

Hintergründigkeit die; ∼ enigmaticness; crypticness

Hintergrund-: ∼**information** die item or piece of background information; ∼**informationen** [items or pieces of] background information sing.; ∼**musik** die background music

hinter-, Hinter-: ∼**halt** der ambush; **in einen** ∼**halt geraten** be ambushed; **jmdn. aus dem** ∼**halt überfallen** ambush sb.; **im** ∼**halt lauern** lie in ambush; ∼**hältig** **1** Adj. underhand; **2** adv. in an underhand fashion or manner; ∼**hältigkeit** die; ∼, ∼**en** **(a)** o. Pl. underhandedness; **(b)** (Handlung) underhand act; ∼**hand** die **(a)** (bei Tieren) hindquarters pl.; **(b)** etw. in der ∼**hand haben** have sth. up one's sleeve or in reserve; ∼**haus** das dwelling situated at or forming the rear of a house [and accessible only from a courtyard]

hinter·her Adv. **(a)** (räumlich) behind; **nichts wie ihm** ∼! quick, after him!; **(b)** (zeitlich) afterwards; **es** ∼ **besser wissen** be wise after the event; **(c)** ∼ **sein** (ugs.: zurückgeblieben sein) be behind (**mit** with); **(d)** **jmdm.** ∼ **sein** (ugs.) be after sb.

hinterher-: ∼|**blicken** itr. V. **jmdm.** ∼**blicken** follow sb. with one's eyes; gaze after sb.; ∼|**fahren** unr. itr. V.; mit sein **(a)** go/drive/ride [along] behind; **jmdm.** ∼**fahren** drive/ride [along] behind sb.; **(b)** ⇒ **nach-fahren;** ∼|**gehen** unr. itr. V.; mit sein **(a)** walk [along] behind; **jmdm.** ∼**gehen** walk [along] behind sb.; **(b)** (nachgehen) **jmdm.** ∼**gehen** follow sb.; ∼|**hinken** itr. V.; mit sein **(a)** limp or hobble [along] behind; **jmdm.** ∼**hinken** limp or hobble [along] behind sb.; **(b)** (fig.) **einer Sache** (Dat.) ∼**hinken** lag behind sth.; **mit etw.** ∼**hinken** be behind with sth.; ∼|**kommen** unr. itr. V.; mit sein follow behind; ∼|**laufen** unr. itr. V.; mit sein **(a)** run [along] behind; **jmdm.** ∼**laufen** run[along] behind sb.; **(b)** (nachlaufen) **jmdm.** ∼**laufen** follow sb.; **(c)** ⇒ ∼**gehen; (d)** (fig. ugs.) ⇒ **nachlaufen b;** ∼|**schicken** tr. V. **jmdm. jmdn./etw.** ∼**schicken** send sb. after sb./

send sth. on to sb.; *∼**sein** ⇒ **hinterher** c, d; ∼|**spionieren** itr. V. **jmdm.** ∼**spionieren** spy on sb.

hinter-, Hinter-: ∼**hof** der courtyard; ∼**kopf** der back of the/one's head; **etw. im** ∼**kopf haben/behalten** (ugs.) have/keep sth. at the back of one's mind; ∼**land** das hinterland; (Milit.) back area; ∼**lassen** /-'--/ unr. tr. V. leave; (testamentarisch) leave; bequeath; **die** ∼**lassenen Schriften** the posthumous works; **keine Spuren** ∼**lassen** leave no trace[s] [behind]; ∼**lassenschaft** /-'--/ die; ∼, ∼**en** estate; **jmds.** ∼**lassenschaft an-treten** inherit sb.'s estate; ∼**legen** /-'--/ tr. V. deposit (**bei** with); (als Pfand) deposit, leave (**bei** with)

Hinterlegung die; ∼, ∼**en** ⇒ **hinterlegen:** depositing; leaving; **jmdn. gegen** ∼ **einer Kaution frei-lassen** release sb. on bail

Hinter·list die o. Pl. guile; deceit

hinter·listig Adj. deceitful

hinterm /'hɪntɐm/ Präp. + Art. (ugs.) = **hinter dem**

Hinter-: ∼**mann** der; Pl. ∼**männer** **(a)** person behind; **sein** ∼**mann** the person behind [him]; **(b)** (jmd., der aus dem Hintergrund lenkt) **der** ∼**mann/die** ∼**männer** the brains behind the operation; ∼**mannschaft** die (Sport) defence

hintern Präp. + Art. (ugs.) = **hinter den**

Hintern /'hɪntɐn/ der; ∼**s**, ∼ (ugs.) behind; backside; bottom; **jmdm. den** ∼ **verhauen** od. **versohlen** tan sb.'s hide (sl.); **jmdm.** od. **jmdm. in den** ∼ **treten** kick sb. in the pants (coll.) or up the backside; (fig.) kick sb. in the teeth (fig.); **sich [vor Wut** od. **Ärger] in den** ∼ **beißen** (salopp) kick oneself; **jmdm. in den** ∼ **kriechen** (derb) lick sb.'s arse (coarse); suck up to sb. (coll.); **sich auf den** ∼ **setzen** (salopp) (sich anstrengen) get or knuckle down to it; (aufs Gesäß fallen) fall on one's behind; (überrascht sein) be flabbergasted

Hinter-: ∼**pfote** die hind paw; ∼**rad** das back or rear wheel; ∼**rad·antrieb** der rear-wheel drive

hinter·rücks /'hɪntɐryks/ Adv. from behind

hinters /'hɪntɐs/ Präp. + Art. (ugs.) = **hinter das**

hinter-, Hinter-: ∼**seite** die ⇒ **Rückseite;** ∼**sinn** der deeper meaning; ∼**sinnig** Adj. ⟨remark, story, etc.⟩ with a deeper meaning; subtle ⟨sense of humour⟩; ∼**teil** das (ugs.) backside; behind; ∼**treffen** das (ugs.) in **ins** ∼**treffen geraten** od. **kommen** fall behind; ∼**treiben** /-'--/ unr. tr. V. foil, thwart, frustrate ⟨plan⟩; prevent ⟨marriage, promotion⟩; block ⟨law, investigation, reform⟩; ∼**treppe** die back stairs pl.; ∼**tupfingen** /-'tʊpfŋən/ (das); ∼**s** (ugs. spött.) the back of beyond; ∼**tür** die back door; **durch die** ∼**tür** (auch fig.) by the back door; **sich** (Dat.) **eine** ∼**tür offenhalten** (fig.) leave oneself a way out (fig.); ∼**wäldler** /∼vɛltlɐ/ der; ∼**s**, ∼ (spött.) backwoodsman; ∼**wäldlerisch** Adj. (spött.) backwoods attrib. ⟨views, attitudes, manners, etc.⟩; ∼**ziehen** /-'--/ unr. tr. V. misappropriate ⟨materials, goods⟩; **Steuern** ∼**ziehen** evade [payment of] tax; ∼**zie-hung** die ⇒ ∼**ziehen:** misappropriation; evasion; ∼**zimmer** das back room

hin-: ∼|**tragen** unr. tr. V. **jmdn./etw.** ∼**tragen** carry sb./take or carry sth. there; **etw. zu jmdm.** od. **jmdm. etw.** ∼**tragen** take sth. to sb.; ∼|**treiben** **1** unr. tr. V. **(a)** drive ⟨animals⟩ there; **die Strömung/der Wind trieb das Boot zum Ufer** ∼: the current carried/the wind blew the boat to the shore; **(b)** unpers. **es trieb ihn immer wieder zu ihr** ∼: something always drove him back to her; **2** unr. V.; mit sein drift or float there; ∼|**treten** unr. itr. V.; mit sein **vor jmdn.** ∼**treten** go up to sb.

hin|tun unr. tr. V. (ugs.) put; **wo soll ich ihn bloß** ∼? (fig.) I can't place him

hinüber /hɪ'nyːbɐ/ Adv. **(a)** over; across; **bis zur anderen Seite** ∼: over or across to the other side; ∼ **und herüber** back and forth; **(b)** ∼ **sein** (ugs.: tot, unbrauchbar sein) have had it (coll.); **er ist** ∼ (ugs.) he's had it; **(c)** ∼ **sein** (ugs.: verdorben sein) be or have gone off; **(d)** ∼ **sein** (ugs.: eingeschlafen sein) have dropped off; (ugs.: bewusstlos sein) be out for the count (coll.); (ugs.: betrunken sein) be well away (coll.) or plastered (sl.)

hinüber-: ∼|**blicken** itr. V. look across; **zu** od. **nach jmdm.** ∼**blicken** look across at sb.; ∼|**bringen** unr. tr. V. jmdn./etw. ∼**bringen** take sb./sth. across or over; ∼|**dämmern** itr. V.; mit sein (a) (einschlafen) drift off; (b) (geh. verhüll.: sterben) pass away in one's sleep; ∼|**fahren** 1 unr. itr. V.; mit sein (mit dem Auto/Fahrrad) drive/ride or go over or across; **über den Fluss** ∼**fahren** cross the river; 2 unr. tr. V. jmdn./ein Auto ∼**fahren** drive or take sb./drive a car over or across; ∼|**führen** 1 tr. V. jmdn. über die Straße/in den Saal ∼**führen** take sb. across the road/take or show sb. across to the hall; 2 itr. V. ⟨street, path, etc.⟩ lead or go over or across; **über etw.** (Akk.) ∼**führen** lead or go over or across; ∼|**gehen** unr. itr. V.; mit sein walk or go over or across; ∼|**helfen** unr. itr. V. jmdm. [über etw. (Akk.)] ∼**helfen** help sb. over or across [sth.]; ∼|**kommen** unr. itr. V.; mit sein (a) come over or across [sth.]; (∼kommen können) get across; **über etw.** (Akk.) ∼**kommen** get across sth.; (b) (ugs.: Besuch machen) come over; pop over (coll.); ∼|**lassen** unr. tr. V. jmdn. ∼**lassen** allow or let sb. over or across; ∼|**reichen** tr. V. [jmdm.] etw. ∼**reichen** pass or hand sth. across [to sb.]; ∼|**retten** tr. V. (fig.) preserve ⟨tradition etc.⟩; ∼|**rufen** 1 unr. tr. V. call over; call out ⟨greeting, order, etc.⟩; 2 unr. itr. V. call over; ∼|**schauen** itr. V. ⇒ ∼**blicken**; ∼|**schicken** tr. V. jmdn./etw. ∼**schicken** send sb./sth. over; ∼|**schwimmen** unr. itr. V.; mit sein swim over or across; ∼|**sehen** unr. itr. V. ⇒ ∼**blicken**;*∼|**sein** ⇒ hinüber; ∼|**spielen** itr. V. (Sport) cross ⟨ball⟩; ∼|**springen** unr. itr. V.; mit sein jump over; **über etw.** (Akk.) ∼**springen** jump over sth.; ∼|**steigen** unr. itr. V.; mit sein climb over; **über etw.** (Akk.) ∼**steigen** climb over sth.; ∼|**wechseln** itr. V.; mit haben od. sein cross over; **zu einer anderen Partei** ∼**wechseln** go over or switch to another party; ∼|**werfen** unr. tr. V. throw ⟨sth.⟩ over or across; **einen Blick** ∼**werfen** (fig.) glance over or across; ∼|**ziehen** 1 unr. tr. V. draw or pull ⟨sb./sth.⟩ over or across; 2 unr. itr. V.; mit sein move across

hin- und her-|- ⟨move, travel, go, walk, etc.⟩ to and fro, back and forth

Hin- und Rück-: ∼**fahrt** die journey there and back; round trip (Amer.); ∼**flug** der outward and return flight; ∼**reise** die, ∼**weg** der journey there and back

hinunter /hɪˈnʊntɐ/ Adv. down; **den Hang** ∼: down the slope

hinunter-|- ⟨go, walk, fall, take, throw, let, etc.⟩ down; (in ein weiter unten gelegenes Stockwerk) ⟨go, take, etc.⟩ downstairs

hinunter-: ∼|**begeben** unr. refl. V. sich ∼**begeben** go down; ∼|**blicken** itr. V. look down; **auf jmdn.** ∼**blicken** (fig.) look down on sb.; ∼|**bringen** unr. tr. V. jmdn./etw. ∼**bringen** take sb./sth. down; ∼|**fahren** 1 unr. itr. V.; mit sein go down; (mit dem Auto) drive down; (mit dem Fahrrad) ride down; 2 unr. tr. V. jmdn./ein Auto/eine Ladung ∼**fahren** drive or take sb. down; take a car down/take a load down; ∼|**fallen** unr. itr. V.; mit sein fall down; **etw.** ∼**fallen lassen** drop sth.; **mir ist die Vase** ∼**gefallen** I dropped the vase; ∼|**führen** 1 tr. V. jmdn. ∼**führen** lead or guide sb. down; 2 itr. V. ⟨path, road, etc.⟩ lead or run down; ∼|**klettern** itr. V.; mit sein climb down; ∼|**kommen** unr. itr. V.; mit sein come down; **die Treppe** ∼**kommen** come downstairs; ∼|**lassen** unr. tr. V. (a) (mit einem Seil usw.) jmdn./etw. ∼**lassen** lower sb./sth.; let sb./sth. down; (b) (∼gehen lassen) jmdn. ∼**lassen** let sb. [go] down; ∼|**reichen** 1 tr. V. pass or hand down; 2 itr. V. (a) (sich bis hinunter erstrecken) reach down (**bis auf** + Akk. to); (b) (bis zu einer Stufe reichen) **bis zu jmdm.** ∼**reichen** reach or extend down to sb.; ∼|**rutschen** itr. V.; mit sein slide down; ∼|**schauen** itr. V. (landsch.) ⇒ ∼**blicken**; ∼|**schlingen** unr. tr. V. gulp or gobble down; ∼|**schlucken** tr. V. (a) swallow; (b) (hinnehmen) swallow ⟨insult etc.⟩; (c) (unterdrücken) bite back ⟨remark, oath, etc.⟩; choke back ⟨tears, anger⟩; ∼|**sehen** unr. itr. V. ⇒ ∼**blicken**; ∼|**springen** unr. itr. V.; mit sein (a) jump down; (b) (ugs.: schnell ∼laufen) run down; ∼|**spülen** tr. V. (a) etw. **[den Ausguss]** ∼**spülen** swill sth. down [the

sink]; **etw. [die Toilette]** ∼**spülen** flush sth. down [the toilet]; (b) (ugs.: hinunterschlucken) wash down ⟨tablets etc.⟩; **seinen Kummer [mit Alkohol]** ∼**spülen** (fig.) drown one's sorrows [in drink]; ∼|**stürzen** 1 itr. V.; mit sein (a) fall or plunge down; (b) (ugs.: eilen) rush or race down; 2 refl. V. throw or fling oneself down; **sich von etw.** ∼**stürzen** throw or fling oneself off sth.; 3 tr. V. jmdn. ∼**stürzen** throw or hurl sb. down; ∼|**tragen** unr. itr. V. etw. ∼**tragen** carry sth. down; ∼|**werfen** unr. tr. V. throw down; **einen Blick** ∼**werfen** (fig.) glance down; ∼|**ziehen** 1 unr. itr. V.; mit sein (a) (umziehen) move down; (b) (sich nach unten bewegen) move or go down; 2 unr. tr. V. jmdn./etw. ∼**ziehen** pull sb./sth. down; 3 unr. refl. V. stretch or extend down

hin|wagen refl. V. dare [to] go there; venture there

hin·weg Adv. (a) (geh.) ∼ **mit diesem Unrat!** away with this rubbish!; ∼ **mit dir!** away with you!; (b) **über etw.** ∼: over sth.; **über den Brillenrand** ∼: over [the top of] his/her spectacles; **über jmdn.** ∼ (fig.) over sb.'s head; **über Jahre/lange Zeit** ∼: for many years/a long time

Hin·weg der way there

hinweg-: ∼|**brausen** itr. V.; mit sein **über etw.** (Akk.) ∼**brausen** roar over sth.; ∼|**gehen** unr. itr. V.; mit sein **über etw.** (Akk.) ∼**gehen** (auch fig.) pass over sth.; ∼|**helfen** unr. itr. V. jmdm. **über etw.** (Akk.) ∼**helfen** help sb. [to] get over sth.; ∼|**kommen** unr. itr. V.; mit sein **über etw.** (Akk.) ∼**kommen** get over sth.; ∼|**lesen** unr. itr. V. **über etw.** (Akk.) ∼**lesen** read past sth. without noticing it; ∼|**raffen** tr. V. (geh.) carry off; ∼|**sehen** unr. itr. V. (a) **über jmdn./etw.** ∼**sehen** see over sb. or sb.'s head/sth.; (b) **über etw.** (fig.) overlook sth.; ∼|**setzen** 1 itr. V.; auch mit sein **über etw.** (Akk.) ∼**setzen** leap or jump over sth.; 2 refl. V. **sich über etw.** (Akk.) ∼**setzen** ignore or disregard sth.; ∼|**täuschen** tr. V. **jmdn. über etw.** (Akk.) ∼**täuschen** blind sb. to sth.; deceive or mislead sb. about sth.; **darüber** ∼**täuschen, dass** …: hide or obscure the fact that …; ∼|**trösten** tr. V. **jmdn. über etw.** (Akk.) ∼**trösten** console sb. for sth.

Hinweis /ˈhɪnvaɪs/ der; ∼**es**, ∼**e** (a) (Wink) hint; tip; **jmdm. einen** ∼ **geben** give sb. a hint; **wenn ich mir den** ∼ **erlauben darf** if I may [just] point something out or draw your attention to something; (b) **unter** ∼ **auf** (+ Akk.) with reference to; (c) (Anzeichen) hint; indication

hin-: ∼|**weisen** 1 unr. itr. V. (a) ⇒ hindeuten a; (b) ⇒ hindeuten b; (c) **auf etw.** ∼**weisen** (fig.: aufmerksam machen) point sth. out; refer to sth.; **darauf** ∼**weisen, dass** …: point out that; 2 unr. tr. V. jmdn. auf etw. (Akk.) ∼**weisen** point sth. out to sb.; draw sb.'s attention to sth.; ∼**weisend** Adj. (Sprachw.) demonstrative ⟨pronoun, adjective, etc.⟩

Hinweis-: ∼**schild** das sign; (Straßenschild) [road] sign; ∼**tafel** die information board

hin-: ∼|**wenden** 1 unr. tr. V. turn (**zu** towards); 2 unr. refl. V. turn (**zu** to, towards); ∼|**werfen** 1 unr. tr. V. (a) throw down; (b) (ugs.: aufgeben) chuck in (coll.); (c) (flüchtig schreiben) jot down; (flüchtig zeichnen) dash off; (d) (beiläufig äußern) drop [casually] ⟨remark⟩; ask casually ⟨question⟩; say casually ⟨words⟩; (e) (ugs.: fallen lassen) drop; 2 unr. refl. V. sich **[vor jmdm.]** ∼**werfen** throw oneself down [before sb.]

hin|wirken itr. V. **auf etw.** (Akk.) ∼: work towards sth.

Hinz /hɪnts/ in ∼ **und Kunz** (ugs. abwertend) every Tom, Dick and Harry

hin-: ∼|**zählen** tr. V. count out; ∼|**zaubern** tr. V. (ugs.) etw. ∼**zaubern** produce sth. as if by magic; ∼|**zeigen** itr. V. point (**zu** to, towards); ∼|**ziehen** 1 unr. tr. V. (a) pull, draw (**zu** to, towards); **sich zu jmdm./etw.** ∼**gezogen fühlen** be or feel attracted to sb./sth.; (b) (in die Länge ziehen) draw out; protract; 2 unr. itr. V.; mit sein move there; **wo ist sie** ∼**gezogen?** where did she move to?; 3 unr. refl. V. drag on (**über** + Akk. for); ∼|**zielen** itr. V. **auf etw.** (Akk.) ∼**zielen** aim at sth.; ⟨policies, efforts, etc.⟩ be aimed at sth.

hinzu-, Hinzu-: ∼|**bekommen** unr. tr. V. get in addition; ∼|**denken** unr. refl. V. sich (Dat.) etw.

~**denken** add sth. in one's imagination; ~|**fügen** *tr. V.* add; ~**fügung** *die* addition; **unter** ~**fügung** (*Dat.*) **einer Sache** (*Gen.*) *od.* **von etw.** with the addition of sth.; ~|**geben** *unr. tr. V.* add; ~|**gesellen** *refl. V.* **sich** [**zu**] **jmdm./etw.** ~**gesellen** join sb./sth.; ~|**gewinnen** *unr. tr. V.* gain in addition; ~|**kommen** *unr. itr. V.; mit sein* (**a**) ⇒ **dazukommen a**; (**b**) (hinzugefügt werden) **zu etw.** ~**kommen** be added to sth.; **es kommt noch** ~, **dass** ... (fig.) there is also the fact that ...; ~|**nehmen** *unr. tr. V.* add; ~|**setzen** 1 *refl. V.* ⇒ **dazusetzen**; 2 *tr. V.* add; ~|**tun** *unr. tr. V.* (ugs.) add; ~|**verdienen** *tr. V.* earn <*sth.*> extra; ~|**zählen** *tr. V.* add [on]; ~|**ziehen** *unr. tr. V.* consult; call in; ~**ziehung** *die;* ~: consultation; **unter** ~**ziehung einschlägiger Literatur** by consulting the relevant literature

Hiob /'hiːɔp/ (*der*) Job

Hiobs·botschaft *die* bad news

Hippe /'hɪpə/ *die;* ~, ~**n** pruning-knife; (des Todes) scythe

hipp, hipp, hurra /'hɪp'hɪphʊ'ra:/ *Interj.* hip, hip, hooray *or* hurrah

Hippie /'hɪpi/ *der;* ~**s**, ~**s** hippie (coll.)

Hirn /hɪrn/ *das;* ~[**e**]**s**, ~**e** (**a**) brain; (**b**) (Speise; ugs.: Verstand) brains *pl.;* **sich** (*Dat.*) **das** ~ **zermartern** rack one's brains

hirn-, Hirn-: ~**gespinst** *das* (abwertend) fantasy; ~**haut·entzündung** *die* (Med.) meningitis; ~**los** (abwertend) 1 *Adj.* brainless; 2 *adv.* brainlessly; ~**rissig** *Adj.* (salopp abwertend) ⇒ ~**verbrannt;** ~**tod** *der* (Med.) brain death; ~**tot** *Adj.* brain-dead; ~**tumor** *der* (Med.) brain tumour; ~**verbrannt** *Adj.* (ugs. abwertend) crazy; crack-brained (coll.)

Hirsch /hɪrʃ/ *der;* ~[**e**]**s**, ~**e** (**a**) deer; (**b**) (Rothirsch) red deer; (**c**) (männlicher Hirsch) stag; hart (literary, in pub names etc.); (**d**) (Speise) venison; (**e**) (Schimpfwort) bastard (sl.)

Hirsch-: ~**brunft**, ~**brunst** *die* rut [of the stags]; **während der** ~**brunft** *od.* ~**brunst** while the stags are in rut; ~**geweih** *das* [stag's] antlers *pl.;* **ein** ~**geweih** a set of antlers; ~**horn** *das* stag-horn; ~**kalb** *das* [male] deer calf; [male] fawn; ~**kuh** *die* hind; ~**leder** *das* buckskin

Hirse /'hɪrzə/ *die;* ~, ~**n** millet

Hirse·brei *der* millet gruel

Hirt /hɪrt/ *der;* ~**en**, ~**en** ⇒ **Hirte**

Hirte *der;* ~**n**, ~**n** herdsman; (Schaf~) shepherd; **der Gute** ~: the Good Shepherd

Hirten-: ~**amt** *das* (kath. Rel.) pastorate; pastoral office; ~**brief** *der* (kath. Rel.) pastoral letter; ~**hund** *der* sheepdog; ~**stab** *der* (**a**) (geh.) shepherd's crook; (**b**) (kath. Rel.) pastoral staff; crosier

his, His /hɪs/ *das;* ~, ~ (Musik) B sharp; *s. auch* **a, A**

hissen /'hɪsn̩/ *tr. V.* hoist, run up <*flag*>

Historiker /hɪs'toːrikɐ/ *der;* ~**s**, ~: historian

historisch /hɪs'toːrɪʃ/ 1 *Adj.* (**a**) historical; (**b**) (geschichtlich bedeutungsvoll) historic. 2 *adv.* historically

Hit /hɪt/ *der;* ~[**s**], ~**s** (ugs.) hit

Hitler- /'hɪtlɐ-/: ~**gruß** *der* Nazi salute; ~**jugend** *die* Hitler Youth; ~**junge** *der* member of the Hitler Youth

Hit-: ~**liste** *die* top ten/twenty *etc.;* ~**parade** *die* hit parade

Hitze /'hɪtsə/ *die;* ~ heat; **bei dieser** ~: in this heat; **etw. bei mittlerer/mäßiger** ~ **backen** bake sth. in a medium/moderate oven; **die fliegende** ~: the hot flushes; **in der** ~ **des Gefechts** in the heat of the moment

hitze-, Hitze-: ~**beständig** *Adj.* heat-resistant, heat-resisting <*metal etc.*>; heat-proof, heat-resistant <*glass etc.*>; ~**bläschen** *das* heat spot; ~**empfindlich** *Adj.* sensitive to heat *postpos.;* heat-sensitive <*material*>; ~**frei** *Adj.* ~ **frei haben/bekommen** have/be given the rest of the day off [school/work] because of excessively hot weather; ~**periode** *die* hot spell; spell *or* period of hot weather; ~**welle** *die* heat wave

hitzig *Adj.* (**a**) (heftig) hot-tempered; quick-tempered; ~ **werden** flare up; fly into a temper; (**b**) (leidenschaftlich) hot-blooded <*person, race, etc.*>; hot <*blood*>; (**c**) (erregt) heated <*discussion, argument, words, etc.*>

Hitzigkeit *die;* ~ hot *or* quick temper

hitz-, Hitz-: ~**kopf** *der* hothead; ~**köpfig** *Adj.* hotheaded; ~**schlag** *der* heatstroke

Hiwi /'hiːvi/ *der;* ~**s**, ~**s** laboratory *or* (coll.) lab/departmental/library assistant

HJ *die;* ~ *Abk.* (ns.) **Hitlerjugend**

hl. *Abk.* **heilig** St.

hm /hmʃ/ *Interj.* h'm; hem

H-Milch /'haː-/ *die;* ~: long-life *or* UHT milk

h-Moll /'haːmɔl/ *das;* ~ (Musik) B minor; *s. auch* **a-Moll**

HNO-Arzt /haː|en'|oː-/ *der* ENT specialist

hob /hoːp/ 1. u. 3. Pers. Sg. Prät. v. **heben**

Hobby /'hɔbi/ *das;* ~**s**, ~**s** hobby

Hobby- amateur <*gardener, archaeologist, astronomer, etc.*>

Hobby·raum *der* hobby room

Hobel /'hoːbl̩/ *der;* ~**s**, ~ (**a**) plane; (**b**) (Gemüse~) [vegetable] slicer

Hobel·bank *die* carpenter's *or* woodworker's bench

hobeln *tr., itr. V.* (**a**) plane; **an etw.** (*Dat.*) ~: plane sth.; (**b**) slice <*vegetables etc.*>

Hobel·span *der* shaving

hoch /hoːx/; **höher** /'høːɐ/, **höchst...** /'høːçst.../ ▶ 277|
1 *Adj.* (**a**) high; high, tall <*building*>; tall <*tree, mast*>; long <*grass*>; deep <*snow, water*>; long, tall <*ladder*>; high-ceilinged <*room*>; **10 m** ~ 10 m high; **eine hohe Stirn** a high forehead; **von hoher Gestalt** (geh.) tall in stature; of tall stature; **hohe Absätze** high heels; **hohe Schuhe** (mit hohem Schaft) high boots; (mit hohen Absätzen) high-heeled shoes; **der hohe Norden** (fig.) the far North; (**b**) (mengenmäßig groß) high <*price, wage, rent, speed, pressure, temperature, sensitivity*>; heavy <*fine*>; great <*weight*>; large <*sum, amount*>; high, large, big <*profit*>; severe, extensive <*damage*>; (**c**) (zeitlich fortgeschritten) great <*age*>; **ein hohes Alter erreichen** live to *or* reach a ripe old age; **es ist höchste Zeit, dass ...:** it is high time that ...; (**d**) (oben in einer Rangordnung) high <*birth, office*>; high-ranking <*officer, civil servant*>; senior <*official, officer, post*>; high-level <*diplomacy, politics*>; important <*guest, festival*>; great <*honour, discretion, urgency*>; **Verhandlungen auf höchster Ebene** top-level negotiations; **der hohe Adel** the higher ranks of the nobility; **höchste Gefahr** extreme danger; **im höchsten Fall**[**e**] at the most; (qualitativ ~**stehend**) high <*standard, opinion*>; great <*responsibility, concentration, talent, happiness, good, importance*>; **die hohe Schule** (Reiten) haute école; (**f**) (Musik) high <*voice, note*>; **das hohe C** top C; (**g**) (Math.) **vier** ~ **fünf** four to the power [of] five; (**h**) (auf dem Höhepunkt) **das hohe Mittelalter** the High Middle Ages; (**i**) *in* **das ist mir zu** ~ (ugs.) that's beyond me; that went over my head. 2 *adv.* (**a**) high; ~ **gelegen** high-lying; ~ **oben am Himmel** high up in the sky; ~ **über uns** high above us; **die Sonne steht** ~: the sun ist high in the sky; ~ **zu Ross** (geh.) on horseback; **er wohnt drei Treppen** ~: he lives on the third (Brit.) *or* (Amer.) fourth floor; ~ **auf etw.** (*Dat.*) **sitzen** sit high up on sth.; **eine** ~ **gestellte Persönlichkeit** (fig.) a person in a high position; an important person; **eine** ~ **stehende Person** (fig.) a person of high standing; **eine geistig** ~ **stehende Person** a person of high intellect; **ein geistig** ~ **stehendes Buch** an intellectually distinguished book; **sittlich** ~ **stehend** high-minded; (**b**) (nach oben) up; **Kopf** ~**!** chin up!; **mit** ~ **erhobenen Armen** with arms raised *or* held high; ~ **erhobenen Hauptes** with head held high; **die Flammen loderten** ~: the flames leapt up high; **ein** ~ **aufgeschossener Junge** a very tall lad; ~ **gewachsen** tall; **einen Ball** ~ **in die Luft werfen** throw a ball high in the air; **die Nase** ~ **tragen** walk around with one's nose in the air; (**c**) (zahlenmäßig viel) highly <*taxed, paid*>; ~ **verschuldet/versichert** heavily in debt/insured for a large sum [of money]; ~ **gewinnen/verlieren** (Sport) win/lose by a large margin; **wenn es** ~ **kommt** at [the] most; (**d**) (sehr) ~ **angesehen/begabt/befriedigt/dotiert/erfreut/geehrt/qualifiziert** *usw.* highly respected *or* regarded/gifted/satisfied/paid/delighted/honoured/qualified *etc.;* ~

geschätzt highly *or* greatly esteemed or respected; ~ willkommen most welcome; **ein ~ empfindlicher Film** a high-speed *or* fast film; **eine ~ entwickelte Methode** a [highly] sophisticated method; **jmdm. etw. ~ anrechnen** consider sth. [to be]greatly to sb.'s credit; **jmdn. ~ verehren** esteem sb. highly *or* greatly; **jmdn./ etw. ~ achten** respect sb./sth. greatly; have a high regard for sb./sth.; **(e)** (zeitlich fortgeschritten) **~ in den Siebzigern** well into his/her seventies; **(f)** (Musik) high; **(g)** (in Wendungen) **etw. ~ und heilig versprechen** promise sth. faithfully; **das Herz höher schlagen lassen** make sb.'s heart beat faster; **es ging ~ her** things were pretty lively; **sie kamen drei Mann ~:** three of them came; there were three of them

Hoch *das; ~s, ~s* **(a)** (Hochruf) **ein [dreifaches] ~ auf jmdn. ausbringen** give three cheers for sb.; **ein ~ dem Gastgeber!** three cheers for the host!; **(b)** (Met.) high

*****hoch|achten** ⇨ hoch 2 d

Hoch·achtung *die* great respect; high esteem; **~ vor jmdn. haben** have a great respect for sb.; hold sb. in high esteem; **meine ~!** may I congratulate you

hochachtungs·voll *Adv.* (Briefschluss) yours faithfully

hoch-, Hoch-: **~adel** *der* higher ranks *pl.* of the nobility; **~aktuell** *Adj.* highly topical; **~alpin** *Adj.* high alpine *attrib.* ‹landscape, flora, fauna, etc.›; **~altar** *der* high altar; **~amt** *das* (kath. Rel.) high mass;*****~ange-sehen** ⇨ hoch 2 d; **~anständig** 1 *Adj.* very decent; 2 *adv.* very *or* most decently; **~arbeiten** *refl. V.* work one's way up; **~bahn** *die* overhead railway; elevated railroad (Amer.); **~barren** *der* (Sport) parallel bars *pl.* (set at international height of 180 cm.); **~bau** *der; o. Pl.* [building] construction *no art.; ~-* **und Tiefbau** [building] construction and civil engineering *no art.;* *****~be-friedigt, ~begabt** ⇨ hoch 2 d; **~beinig** *Adj.* long-legged ‹person, animal›; ‹table, sofa, etc.› with long legs; **~|bekommen** *unr. tr. V.* [manage to] lift; **~berühmt** *Adj.* very famous; **~betagt** *Adj.* aged; ‹person› advanced in years *postpos.;* **~betrieb** *der; o. Pl.* (ugs.) **es herrschte ~betrieb im Geschäft** the shop was at its busiest; **~|biegen** 1 *unr. tr. V.* **etw. ~bie-gen** bend sth. up[wards]; 2 *unr. refl. V.* bend up; **~|binden** *unr. tr. V.* tie up ‹plant›; put up ‹hair›; **~|blicken** *itr. V.* look up; **~blüte** *die* golden age; **~|bringen** *unr. tr. V.* **(a)** bring up; (ugs.: in die Wohnung bringen) bring in[to the flat (Brit.) *or* (Amer.) apartment]; **(b)** (gesund machen) **jmdn. ~bringen** put sb. on his/her feet; **(c)** (ugs.: ärgern) **jmdn. ~bringen** put sb.'s back up; **~burg** *die* stronghold; **~deutsch** *Adj.* standard *or* High German; **~deutsch** *das, ~deutsche das* standard *or* High German; **~|dienen** *refl. V.* work one's way up;*****~dotiert** ⇨ hoch 2 d; **~|drehen** *tr. V.* **(a)** wind up ‹window, barrier, etc.›; **(b)** rev [up] (coll.) ‹engine›

Hoch·druck[1] *der; Pl.* **Hochdrücke (a)** (Technik, Met.) high pressure; **(b)** (Geschäftigkeit) **mit** *od.* **unter ~ ar-beiten** (ugs.) work flat out *or* at full stretch; **(c)** (Med.) high blood pressure; hypertension (Med.)

Hoch·druck[2] *der; Pl.* **~e** (Druckw.) **(a)** (Verfahren) relief *or* letterpress printing; **etw. im ~ herstellen/drucken** produce/print sth. by letterpress; **(b)** (Erzeugnis) piece of letterpress work

Hochdruck·gebiet *das* high-pressure area

hoch-, Hoch-: **~ebene** *die* plateau; tableland;*****~empfindlich,** *****~entwickelt** ⇨ hoch 2 d;*****~erhoben** ⇨ hoch 2 d; **~explosiv** *Adj.* (auch fig.) highly explosive; **~|fahren** 1 *unr. itr. V.; mit sein* **(a)** (ugs.) go/drive/ride up; **(b)** (auffahren) start up; **aus dem Sessel ~fahren** start [up] from one's chair; **aus dem Schlaf ~fahren** wake up with a start; **(c)** (aufbrausen) flare up; 2 *unr. tr. V.* (ugs.) drive ‹sb./sth.› up; **~fah-rend** *Adj.* arrogant; supercilious; **~finanz** *die* high finance; **~|fliegen** *unr. itr. V.; mit sein* fly up [into the air]; **~fliegend** *Adj.* ambitious ‹plan, idea, etc.›; **~form** *die* peak *or* top form; **~format** *das* upright format; **in ~format** with an upright format; **~fre-quenz** *die* (Physik) high frequency; **~frisur** *die* upswept hairstyle; *****~geachtet** ⇨ hoch 2 d; **~gebildet**

*alte Schreibung (vgl. Hinweise auf S. xvi–xvii)

Adj. (präd. getrennt geschrieben) highly cultured; **~ge-birge** *das* [high] mountains *pl.;* *****~geehrt** ⇨ hoch 2 d; **~gefühl** *das* [feeling of] elation; **im ~gefühl des Erfolges/Sieges** in his/her *etc.* elation at success/victory; **~|gehen** *unr. itr. V.; mit sein* (ugs.) **(a)** ⇨ hinaufgehen; **(b)** (zornig werden) blow one's top (coll.); explode; (explodieren) ‹bomb, mine› go off; ‹bridge, building, etc.› go up; **etw. ~gehen lassen** (salopp) blow sth. up; **(d)** (aufgedeckt werden) get caught *or* (sl.) nabbed; **jmdn. ~gehen lassen** ‹informer› grass (Brit. coll.) *or* (sl.) squeal on sb; **~geistig** *Adj.* highly intellectual;*****~gelegen** ⇨ hoch 2 a; **~gelehrt** *Adj.* extremely *or* very learned *or* erudite; **~genuss,** *****~genuß** *der in ein* **~genuss sein** be a real delight; ‹meal, concert, etc.› be a real treat; *****~ge-schätzt** ⇨ hoch 2 d; **~geschlossen** *Adj.* high-necked ‹dress›; **~gespannt** *Adj.* great, high ‹expectations›;*****~gestellt** ⇨ hoch 2 a; **~ge-stochen** (ugs. abwertend) 1 *Adj.* highbrow (coll.); 2 *adv.* in a highbrow way (coll.);*****~gewachsen** ⇨ hoch 2 b; **~gezüchtet** *Adj.* highly-bred ‹animal›; highly sophisticated ‹engine, system›

Hoch·glanz *der:* **ein Foto in ~** (Dat.) a high-gloss print; **etw. auf ~** (Akk.) **polieren** polish sth. until it shines *or* gleams; **etw. auf ~** (Akk.) **bringen** give sth. a high polish; (fig.) make sth. spick and span

hoch-, Hoch-: **~gradig** 1 *Adj.; nicht präd.* extreme; 2 *adv.* extremely; **~hackig** *Adj.* high-heeled ‹shoe›; **~|halten** *unr. tr. V.* **(a)** hold up ‹arms›; **(b)** (fig. geh.) uphold ‹truth, tradition, etc.›; **~haus** *das* high-rise-building; **~|heben** *unr. tr. V.* lift up; raise ‹arm, leg, etc.›; raise, hold up ‹hand›; **~herrschaftlich** *Adj.* palatial ‹house, apartment›; **~herzig** *Adj.* (geh.) magnanimous; generous; **~intelligent** *Adj.* highly intelligent; **~interessant** *Adj.* extremely *or* most interesting; fascinating; **~|jagen** *tr. V.* scare up ‹birds›; forcibly rouse ‹sleeper›; **~|jubeln** *tr. V.* (ugs.) **jmdn./ etw. ~jubeln** build sb. up as a star/sth. up as a hit; **~kant** *Adv.* **(a)** on end; **(b)** (ugs.) *in* **jmdn. ~kant raus-werfen** chuck sb. out (sl.); throw sb. out on his/her ear (coll.); **~kant rausfliegen** be chucked out (sl.); be thrown out on one's ear (coll.); **~kantig** *Adv.* (ugs.) ⇨ **~kant b;** **~karätig** ~ka'rɛ:tɪç/ *Adj.* **(a)** high-carat ‹gold, diamond›; **(b)** (fig.) top-flight (coll.); **~|klappen** 1 *tr. V.* fold up ‹chair, table›; raise, lift up ‹lid, car-bonnet›; turn up ‹collar›; 2 *itr. V.; mit sein* (ugs.) fold up; **~|klettern** *itr. V.; mit sein* (ugs.) climb up; **den Baum ~klettern** climb [up] the tree; **~|kommen** *unr. itr. V.; mit sein* (ugs.) **(a)** come up; **(b)** (fig.: vorwärts kommen) get on; **(c)** (aus dem Magen) **ihr kam das Essen ~** she threw up (coll.) *or* brought up her meal; **es kommt einem ~, wenn ...** (fig.) it makes you sick when ...; **(d)** (sich erheben) get up; (sich erheben können) be able to get up; **~konjunktur** *die* (Wirtsch.) boom; **auf dem Automarkt herrscht ~konjunktur** the car market is booming; **~|können** *unr. V.* (ugs.) be able to get up; **~|krempeln** *tr. V.* roll up ‹sleeve, trouserleg›; **~|kriegen** *tr. V.* (ugs.) ⇨ **~bekommen; einen ~kriegen** (salopp) get it up (sl.); **~kultur** *die* advanced civilization *or* culture; **~land** *das; Pl.* **~länder** highlands *pl.;* **~|leben** *itr. V. in* **jmdn./etw. ~leben lassen** cheer sb./sth.; **er lebe ~!** three cheers for him!; **der König lebe ~!** long live the king!; **~|legen** *tr. V.* **ein gebrochenes Bein ~legen** support a broken leg in a raised position; **die Beine ~legen** put one's feet up

Hoch·leistung *die* outstanding performance

Hochleistungs·sport *der* top-level sport

hoch-, Hoch-: **~mittel·alter** *das* High Middle Ages; **~modern** *Adj.* ultra-modern; **~moor** *das* (Geogr.) high-moor bog; **~motiviert** *Adj.* highly motivated; **~mut** *der* arrogance; **~mut kommt vor dem Fall** (Spr.) pride goes before a fall (prov.); **~mütig** *Adj.* arrogant; **~näsig** /~nɛ:zɪç/ *Adj.* (abwertend) stuck-up; conceited; **~näsigkeit** *die;* (abwertend) conceitedness; **~|nehmen** *unr. tr. V.* **(a)** lift *or* pick up; **(b)** (ugs.: verspotten) **jmdn. ~nehmen** pull sb.'s leg; **(c)** (ugs.: nach oben nehmen) **jmdn./etw. mit ~nehmen** take sb./sth. up with one; **(d)** (salopp: verhaften) run in; **~ofen** *der* blast furnace; **~|päppeln** *tr. V.* (salopp) feed up; **~parterre** *das* upper ground floor; **~politisch** *Adj.* highly political;

∼prozentig *Adj.* high-proof ⟨*spirits*⟩;***∼qualifi-ziert** ⇨ **hoch 2 d; ∼|ragen** *itr. V.* rise *or* tower up; **∼|rappeln** *refl. V.* ⇨ **aufrappeln; ∼rechnung** *die* (Statistik) projection; **∼|reißen** *unr. tr. V.* whip up; pull up ⟨*aircraft*⟩; **die Arme ∼reißen** throw one's arms up; **∼rot** *Adj.* bright red; **∼rot im Gesicht werden** (aus Verlegenheit) go as red as a beetroot; **∼ruf** *der* cheer; **∼|rutschen** *itr. V.; mit sein* (ugs.) ⟨*dress, shirt, etc.*⟩ ride up; **∼saison** *die* high season; **∼|schaukeln** *tr. V.* (ugs.) blow up ⟨*problem, incident, etc.*⟩; **∼|scheuchen** *tr. V.* ⇨ **aufscheuchen; ∼|schieben** *unr. tr. V.* (ugs.) push up; **∼|schießen** **1** *unr. tr. V.* send up, launch ⟨*rocket, space probe, etc.*⟩; **2** *unr. itr. V.; mit sein* (auch fig.) shoot up; **∼|schlagen** **1** *unr. tr. V.* turn up ⟨*collar, brim*⟩; **2** *unr. itr. V.; mit sein* ⟨*waves*⟩ surge up; ⟨*flames*⟩ leap up; **∼|schnellen** *itr. V.; mit sein* leap up; **∼|schrauben** **1** *tr. V.* **(a)** raise ⟨*seat*⟩ ⟨*by screwing*⟩; **(b)** (fig.) force up ⟨*prices*⟩; step up, increase ⟨*demands*⟩; raise ⟨*expectations*⟩; **2** *refl. V.* circle up[wards]; **∼|schrecken** *tr. V.* ⇨ **aufschrecken**

Hoch-: **∼schule** *die* college; (Universität) university; **∼schüler** *der* college/university student

Hochschul-: **∼lehrer** *der* ▶85⎮ college/university lecturer *or* teacher; **∼studium** *das* college/university studies *pl.*, *no art.*

hoch·schwanger *Adj.* in an advanced stage of pregnancy *postpos.;* very pregnant (coll.)

Hoch·see *die; o. Pl.* open sea

Hochsee-: **∼fischerei** *die* deep-sea fishing *no art.;* **∼flotte** *die* deep sea fleet; **∼jacht** *die* ocean-going yacht

Hoch·seil *das* high wire

Hochseil·akrobat *der* ▶85⎮ performer on the high wire

hoch-, Hoch-: **∼sitz** *der* (Jagdw.) raised hide; **∼sommer** *der* high summer; midsummer; **∼sommerlich** *Adj.* very summery ⟨*weather etc.*⟩

Hoch·spannung *die* **(a)** (Elektrot.) high voltage *or* tension; Vorsicht, **∼spannung!** danger – high voltage; **(b)** *o. Pl.* (gespannte Stimmung) high tension

Hochspannungs-: **∼leitung** *die* high voltage *or* high tension [transmission] line; power line; **∼mast** *der* electricity pylon

hoch-, Hoch-: **∼|spielen** *tr. V.* blow up ⟨*incident, affair, etc.*⟩; **∼sprache** *die* standard language; **∼|springen** *unr. itr. V.; mit sein* jump *or* leap up; **an jmdm. ∼springen** ⟨*dog etc.*⟩ jump up at sb.; **∼springer** *der* (Sport) high jumper; **∼sprung** *der* (Sport) high jump

höchst /høːçst/ *Adv.* extremely; most

höchst... ⇨ **hoch**

hoch-, Hoch-: **∼stand** *der* (Jagdw.) raised stand; **∼stapelei** /∼ʃtaːpəˈlaɪ/ *die;* ∼, ∼en **(a)** fraud; **eine ∼stapelei** a confidence trick; **(b)** (Aufschneiderei) empty boasting; **(c)** ⟨*collar*⟩ make up; **∼staplen** *itr. V.* **(a)** perpetrate a fraud/frauds; **(b)** (aufschneiden) make empty boasts; **∼stapler** /∼ʃtaːplɐ/ *der;* ∼s, ∼ **(a)** confidence trickster; conman (coll.); **(b)** (Aufschneider) fraud

Höchst-: **∼betrag** *der* maximum amount; **∼bietende** *der/die; adj. Dekl.* highest bidder

hoch-: ***∼stehend** ⇨ **hoch 2 a; ∼|steigen** *unr. itr. V.; mit sein* **(a)** climb; **die Treppe/Stufen ∼steigen** climb the stairs/steps; **(b)** ⟨*bubbles, smoke, etc.*⟩ rise; ⟨*rocket*⟩ go up; **(c)** (langsam entstehen) rise up ⟨*tears*⟩ well up ∼|**stellen** *tr. V.* **(a)** put up; **(b)** (hochklappen) turn up ⟨*collar*⟩; **∼|stemmen** *tr. V.* **(a)** lift; **(b)** (aufrichten) **sich/seine Oberkörper ∼stemmen** raise oneself [up]

höchsten·falls /ˈhøːçstn̩-/ *Adv.* at [the] most *or* the outside; at the very most

höchstens *Adv.* at most; (bestenfalls) at best

Höchst-: **∼fall** *der in* **im ∼fall[e]** at [the] most *or* the outside; at the very most; **∼form** *die* (bes. Sport) peak *or* top form; **∼gebot** *das* highest bid *or* offer; **∼geschwindigkeit** *die* ▶224⎮ top *or* maximum speed **hoch|stilisieren** *tr. V.* (abwertend) build up (**zu** into)

Hoch·stimmung *die* festive mood; high spirits *pl.;* **in ∼ sein** be in a festive mood

---

höchst-, Höchst-: **∼leistung** *die* supreme performance; (Ergebnis) supreme achievement; (Technik) maximum performance; **∼maß** *das:* **ein ∼maß an etw.** (*Dat.*) a very high degree of sth.; **ein ∼maß von etw.** (*Dat.*) a maximum [amount] of sth.; **∼möglich** *Adj.; nicht präd.* highest possible; **∼persönlich** **1** *Adj.; nicht präd.* personal; **2** *adv.* in person; **∼preis** *der* (höchstmöglicher Preis) highest price; (höchstzulässiger Preis) maximum price

Hoch·straße *die* elevated road; flyover (Brit.); overpass

hoch|streifen *tr. V.* pull up

höchst-, Höchst-: **∼satz** *der* maximum *or* top rate; **∼stand** *der* highest level; **∼strafe** *die* maximum penalty; **∼wahrscheinlich** *Adv.* very probably; **∼wert** *der* maximum value; **∼zulässig** /auch: ˈˈ‑ˈ‑/ *Adj.; nicht präd.* maximum [permissible] ⟨*weight, speed, etc.*⟩

hoch-, Hoch-: **∼tour** *die in* **auf ∼touren laufen** run at top *or* full speed; (intensiv betrieben werden) be in full swing; **∼tourig** /‑tuːrɪç/ (Technik) **1** *Adj.* fast-revving (coll.) ⟨*engine*⟩; **2** *adv.* **∼tourig fahren** drive at high revs (coll.); **∼trabend** (abwertend) **1** *Adj.* pretentious; high-flown; **2** *adv.* pretentiously; in a high-flown manner; **∼|tragen** *unr. tr. V.* carry up; **∼|treiben** *unr. tr. V.* **(a)** (ugs.: hinauftreiben) drive up; **(b)** (fig.) force *or* push up ⟨*prices etc.*⟩; **∼verdient** *Adj.* (präd. getrennt geschrieben) **(a)** ⟨*scientist etc.*⟩ of outstanding merit; **(b)** richly deserved ⟨*victory, success, etc.*⟩; **∼verehrt** *Adj.; nicht präd.* highly respected *or* esteemed; (als Anrede) **meine ∼verehrten Damen und Herren!** ladies and gentlemen!; **∼verrat** *der* high treason; **∼verräter** *der* traitor; person guilty of high treason; ***∼verschuldet** ⇨ **hoch 2 c**

Hoch·wasser *das* ▶193⎮ (Flut) high tide *or* water; (Überschwemmung) flood; **der Fluss hat** *od.* **führt ∼:** the river is in flood; **er hat ∼** (ugs. scherzh.) his trousers are at half mast (coll.)

hoch-, Hoch-: **∼|werfen** *unr. tr. V.* **etw. ∼werfen** throw sth. up; **∼wertig** *Adj.* high-quality ⟨*goods*⟩; highly nutritious ⟨*food*⟩; **∼willkommen** *Adj.* (präd. getrennt geschrieben) very *or* most welcome; **∼|winden** **1** *unr. tr. V.* wind up; weigh ⟨*anchor*⟩; **2** *unr. refl. V.* wind its way up; **∼wirksam** *Adj.* (präd. getrennt geschrieben) highly *or* extremely effective; **∼wohlgeboren** *Adj.* ▶34⎮ (veralt.) high-born; **Euer Hochwohlgeboren** Your Honour; **∼|wollen** *unr. itr. V.* (ugs.) want to get up; **∼wuchten** *tr. V.* (ugs.) heave up; **∼würden** ▶34⎮ *o. Art.; ∼*[s] (veralt.) Reverend Father; **∼zahl** *die* (Math.) exponent

Hoch·zeit¹ *die* (geh.) Golden Age

Hochzeit² /ˈhɔxtsaɪt/*die;* ∼, ∼en ▶240⎮ wedding; **silberne/goldene ∼:** silver/golden wedding [anniversary]; **man kann nicht auf zwei ∼en tanzen** (fig. ugs.) you can't be in two places at once

Hochzeiter *der;* ∼s, ∼ (landsch.) [bride] groom; **die ∼:** the bride and groom

Hochzeiterin *die;* ∼, ∼nen (landsch.) bride

Hochzeits-: **∼feier** *die* wedding; **∼geschenk** *das* wedding gift *or* present; **∼kleid** *das* (Zool.) nuptial coloration; (von Vögeln) nuptial plumage; **∼nacht** *die* wedding night; **∼reise** *die* honeymoon [trip]; **wir haben unsere ∼reise nach Berlin gemacht** we went to Berlin for our honeymoon; **∼tag** *der* (a) ▶240⎮ wedding day; **(b)** ▶240⎮ (Jahrestag) wedding anniversary

hoch-: **∼|ziehen** **1** *unr. tr. V.* **(a)** pull up; pull up, raise ⟨*shutters, blind*⟩; hoist, raise, run up ⟨*flag*⟩; hoist ⟨*sail*⟩; **die Schultern/Brauen ∼ziehen** hunch one's shoulders/raise one's eyebrows; **die Nase ∼ziehen** sniff [loudly]; **(b)** **ein Flugzeug ∼ziehen** put an aircraft into a steep climb; **(c)** (bauen) put up, build ⟨*wall, building*⟩; **2** *unr. refl. V.* **sich [an etw. (*Dat.*)] ∼ziehen** pull oneself up [by hanging on to sth.]; **sich an etw.** (*Dat.*) **∼ziehen** (fig.) latch on to sth.

Hocke /ˈhɔkə/ *die;* ∼, ∼n **(a)** squat; crouch; **in der ∼ sitzen** squat; crouch; **in die ∼ gehen** squat [down]; crouch down; **(b)** (Turnen) squat vault

hocken **1** *itr. V.* **(a)** *mit haben od.* (südd.) *sein* squat; crouch; **(b)** *mit sein* (südd.: sitzen) sit; **(c)** *mit sein* (Turnen) perform *or* do a squat vault (**über** + *Akk.* over). **2** *refl. V.* (**a**) crouch down; squat [down]; (**b**) (südd.: sich setzen) sit down

Hocker *der;* ~s, ~: stool

Höcker /'hœkɐ/ *der;* ~s, ~: hump; (auf der Nase) bump; (auf dem Schnabel) knob

Hockey /'hɔki/ *das;* ~s hockey

Hockey-: ~**schläger** *der* hockey stick; ~**spieler** *der* hockey player

Hoden /'hoːdn̩/ *der;* ~s, ~: ▶ 326 | testicle

Hoden·sack *der* ▶ 326 | scrotum

Hof /hoːf/ *der;* ~[e]s, **Höfe** /'høːfə/ (**a**) courtyard; (Schul~) playground; (Gefängnis~) [prison] yard; (**b**) (Bauern~) farm; (**c**) (eines Herrschers) court; **am** ~[**e**] at court; (**d**) jmdm. **den** ~ **machen** (veralt.) pay court to sb.; (**e**) (Aureole) corona; aureole; (**f**) ~ **halten** hold court

hof-, Hof-: ~**amt** *das* (hist.) [hereditary] office at court; ~**dame** *die* lady of the court; (Begleiterin der Königin) lady-in-waiting; ~**fähig** *Adj.* presentable at court *pred.;* (fig.) [socially] acceptable

Hoffart /'hɔfart/ *die;* ~ (veralt.) overweening pride; haughtiness

hoffärtig /'hɔfɛrtɪç/ (veralt. abwertend) **1** *Adj.* haughty. **2** *adv.* haughtily

hoffen /'hɔfn̩/ **1** *tr. V.* hope; **ich hoffe es/will es** ~: I hope so/can only hope so; **ich will es nicht** ~, **ich hoffe es nicht** I hope not; **es bleibt zu** ~, **dass** ...: let us hope that ...; ~ **wir das Beste** let's hope for the best. **2** *itr. V.* (**a**) hope; **auf etw.** (*Akk.*) ~: hope for sth.; (**b**) (Vertrauen setzen auf) **auf jmdn./etw.** ~: put one's trust *or* faith in sb./sth.

hoffentlich /'hɔfn̩tlɪç/ *Adv.* hopefully; ~! let's hope so; ~ **ist ihr nichts passiert** I do hope nothing's happened to her; **es ist dir doch** ~ **recht** I hope it's all right with you

Hoffnung /'hɔfnʊŋ/ *die;* ~, ~**en** hope; **seine** ~ **auf** jmdn./etw. **setzen** pin one's hopes *pl.* on sb./sth.; **keine** ~ **mehr haben** have given up [all] hope; **sich** (*Dat.*) [falsche] ~**en machen** have [false] hopes; **jmdm.** ~**en machen** raise sb.'s hopes

hoffnungs-, Hoffnungs-: ~**los 1** *Adj.* hopeless; despairing ⟨*person*⟩; **2** *adv.* hopelessly; ~**losigkeit** *die;* ~: hopelessness; (Verzweiflung) despair; ~**schimmer** *der* (geh.) glimmer of hope; ~**voll 1** *Adj.* (**a**) hopeful; full of hope *pred.;* jmdn. ~**voll stimmen** give sb. cause to hope *or* make sb. hopeful; (**b**) (erfolgversprechend) promising; **2** *adv.* (**a**) full of hope; (**b**) (erfolgversprechend) promisingly

*hof|halten ⇒ Hof f

Hof·hund *der* watchdog

hofieren /ho'fiːrən/ *tr. V.* (geh.) pay court to

höfisch /'høːfɪʃ/ *Adj.* courtly

höflich /'høːflɪç/ **1** *Adj.* polite; courteous; **etw. in** ~**em Ton fragen/sagen** ask/say sth. politely. **2** *adv.* politely; courteously

Höflichkeit *die;* ~, ~**en** (**a**) *o. Pl.* politeness; courteousness; **etw. [nur] aus** ~ **tun/sagen** do/say sth. [only] to be polite *or* out of politeness; (**b**) *meist Pl.* (höfliche Redensart) civility; courtesy

Höflichkeits-: ~**besuch** *der* courtesy visit; ~**floskel** *die* polite phrase

Höfling /'høːflɪŋ/ *der;* ~s, ~e courtier

Hof-: ~**marschall** *der* ▶ 34 | major-domo; ~**narr** *der* (hist.) court jester; ~**rat** *der* ▶ 34 | (veralt., noch österr.) honorary title conferred on senior civil servant; ~**schranze** *die od. der* (veralt. abwertend) fawning courtier; ~**staat** *der; o. Pl.* court; ~**tor** *das* courtyard gate

hoh... /'hoː.../ ⇒ hoch

Höhe /'høːə/ *die;* ~, ~**n** (**a**) ▶ 277 | height; (Entfernung nach oben) height; altitude; **in einer** ~ **von 4 000 m fliegen** fly at a height *or* altitude of 4,000 m.; **an** ~ **gewinnen/verlieren** gain/lose height *or* altitude; **auf halber** ~: at mid-altitude; (**b**) (Richtung) **etw. in die** ~ **heben** lift sth. up; **in die** ~ [**auf**]**steigen** rise up[wards]; (**c**) (Gipfelpunkt)

---

height; **auf der** ~ **seines Ruhmes/Könnens/Erfolges sein** be at the height of one's fame/ability/success; **auf der** ~ **sein** (fig. ugs.) (gesund sein) be fit; (sich wohl fühlen) feel fine; **nicht [ganz] auf der** ~ **sein** (fig. ugs.) be/feel a bit under the weather (coll.); not be/feel quite oneself; **das ist ja die** ~! (fig. ugs.) that's the limit; (**d**) (messbare Größe) level; (von Einkommen) size; level; **die** ~ **der Geschwindigkeit/Temperatur** the speed/temperature level; **Unkosten in** ~ **von 5 000 DM** expenses of 5,000 DM; (**e**) (Linie) **auf gleicher** ~ **sein/fahren** be in line abreast *or* be level/travel in line abreast; **auf** ~ **des Leuchtturms/von Hull sein** (Seemannsspr.) be level with *or* abreast of the lighthouse/be off Hull; (**f**) (Anhöhe) hill; **die** ~**n und Tiefen des Lebens** (fig.) the ups and downs of life; (**g**) (Math., Astron.) altitude; (**h**) *Pl.* (Akustik) treble *sing.*

Hoheit /'hoːhait/ *die;* ~, ~**en** (**a**) *o. Pl.* (Souveränität) sovereignty (**über** + *Akk.* over); **unter der** ~ **eines Staates stehen** be under the sovereignty of a state; (**b**) ▶ 34 | **Seine/Ihre** ~: His/Your Highness

Hoheits-: ~**ab·zeichen** *das* national emblem; ~**gebiet** *das* [sovereign] territory; ~**gewässer** *das; meist Pl.* territorial waters *pl.;* ~**recht** *das; meist Pl.* right of the state; ~**zeichen** *das* national emblem

Hohe·lied *das* (fig. geh.) song of praise; *s. auch* **Lied**

Höhen-: ~**angst** *die; o. Pl.* fear of heights; ~**flug** *der* (Flugw.) high-altitude flight; (fig.) flight; ~**krankheit** *die* altitude sickness; ~**lage** *die* altitude; **in** ~**lage** at high altitude; ~**luft** *die; o. Pl.* mountain air; air at high altitude; ~**messer** *der* altimeter; ~**ruder** *das* (Flugw.) elevator; ~**sonne** *die* (**a**) (Gerät) sun lamp; (**b**) (Bestrahlung) sun lamp treatment; ~**unterschied** *der* altitude difference; difference in altitude; ~**zug** *der* (Geogr.) range of hills

*Hohe·priester ⇒ **Priester**

Höhepunkt *der* high point; (einer Veranstaltung) high spot; highlight; (einer Laufbahn, des Ruhms) peak; pinnacle; (einer Krankheit) crisis; critical point; (einer Krise) turning point; (der Macht) summit; pinnacle; (des Glücks) height; (Orgasmus; eines Stückes) climax; **auf dem** ~ **seiner Laufbahn stehen** be at the peak of one's career

höher /'høːɐ/ (**a**) ⇒ **hoch**; (**b**) **ein** ~ **gestellter Beamter** a senior official/civil servant

höher-: *~**gestellt** ⇒ höher b; ~|**schrauben** *tr. V.* force *or* push up ⟨*prices*⟩

hohl /hoːl/ **1** *Adj.* (**a**) hollow; **sich innerlich** ~ **fühlen** (fig.) feel empty inside; (eingewölbt) cupped ⟨*hand*⟩; sunken, hollow ⟨*cheeks, eyes*⟩; **ein** ~**es Kreuz** a hollow back; (**c**) (dumpf) hollow ⟨*sound, voice, etc.*⟩; (**d**) (abwertend: geistlos) hollow, empty ⟨*phrases, slogans*⟩; empty ⟨*talk, chatter*⟩. **2** *adv.* (**a**) (dumpf) hollowly; (**b**) (abwertend: geistlos) inanely

hohl·äugig *Adj.* hollow-eyed; sunken-eyed

Höhle /'høːlə/ *die;* ~, ~**n** (**a**) cave; (größer) cavern; (**b**) (Tierbau) den; lair; **sich in die** ~ **des Löwen begeben** enter the lion's den; (**c**) (abwertend: Wohnung) hole; (**d**) *meist Pl.* (Augen~) socket

höhlen /'høːlən/ *tr. V.* hollow out; **steter Tropfen höhlt den Stein** (Spr.) these things take their toll eventually

Höhlen-: ~**forscher** *der* speleologist; (Sportler) caver; ~**malerei** *die* cave-painting; ~**mensch** *der* cave dweller; caveman

hohl-, Hohl-: ~**kopf** *der* (abwertend) idiot (coll.); dimwit; ~**köpfig** *Adj.* (abwertend) idiotic (coll.); blockheaded; ~**körper** *der* hollow body; ~**kreuz** *das* hollow back; lordosis (Med.); ~**kugel** *die* hollow sphere; ~**maß** *das* ▶ 427 | measure of capacity; ~**raum** *der* cavity; [hollow] space; ~**saum** *der* (Handarb.) hem-stitch; ~**spiegel** *der* concave mirror

Höhlung *die;* ~, ~**en** hollow

hohl·wangig *Adj.* hollow-cheeked; sunken-cheeked

Hohl·weg *der* defile

Hohn /hoːn/ *der;* ~[e]s scorn; derision; **jmdn. mit** ~ **und Spott überschütten** pour *or* heap scorn on sb.; ~ **lachen** laugh scornfully *or* derisively; **einer Sache** (*Dat.*) ~ **sprechen** fly in the face of sth.

Höhe und Tiefe

Höhe

Wie hoch ist es?	= How high od. What height is it?
Es ist ungefähr neun Meter hoch	– It's about nine metres od. ≈ thirty feet high od. in height
A ist niedriger/höher als B	= A is lower/higher than B
A ist [genau]so hoch wie B	= A is [just] the same height od. as high as B
Die Türme sind gleich hoch	= The towers are the same height
Die Maschine flog in einer Höhe von 3 000 Metern	≈ The aircraft was flying at a height od. an altitude of 10,000 feet
Die Baumgrenze liegt bei etwa 2 000 Metern	≈ The treeline is at [a height of] about 6,500 feet
drei Meter hohe Wellen	≈ waves ten feet high
ein Berg von über 6 000 Metern od. von über 6 000 Meter Höhe	≈ a mountain of over 20,000 feet od. over 20,000 feet in height

Körpergröße

Wie groß ist sie?	= How tall od. What height is she?
Sie ist ein od. einen Meter achtundsechzig groß	≈ She's five foot six
ein 1,80 Meter großer Athlet	≈ an athlete six foot od. feet tall

Er ist kleiner als sein Bruder	= He's shorter od. smaller than his brother
A ist [genau]so groß wie B	= A is [just] the same height od. as tall as B
Sie sind gleich groß	= They are the same height

Tiefe

Wie tief ist od. Welche Tiefe hat der Fluss?	= How deep od. What depth is the river?
Er ist drei Meter tief od. hat eine Tiefe von drei Metern	= It's three metres deep, ≈ It's ten feet deep
Der Schatz liegt in einer Tiefe von fünfzehn Metern od. fünfzehn Meter tief	= The treasure is at a depth of fifteen metres od. is fifteen metres down, ≈ The treasure is at a depth of fifty feet od. is fifty feet down
A hat die gleiche Tiefe wie B	= A is the same depth as od. as deep as B
A und B sind gleich tief	= A and B are the same depth
A ist flacher od. seichter als B	= A is shallower than B
ein drei Meter tiefes Loch	= a hole three metres deep, ≈ a hole ten feet deep

---

höhnen /'høːnən/ *itr. V.* (geh.) jeer; sneer

Hohn·gelächter *das* derisive *or* scornful laughter

höhnisch /'høːnɪʃ/ **1** *Adj.* scornful; derisive. **2** *adv.* scornfully; derisively

hohn-: ~**lachen** *itr. V.* laugh scornfully *or* derisively; **ein Hohnlachen** a scornful *or* derisive laugh; *s. auch* **Hohn;** ~|**sprechen** *unr. itr. V.* **einer Sache** (*Dat.*) ~**sprechen** fly in the face of sth.; *s. auch* **Hohn**

Hokuspokus /hoːkʊs'poːkʊs/ *der;* ~**:** hocus-pocus; (abwertend: Getue) fuss

hold /hɔlt/ **1** *Adj.* **(a)** (dichter. veralt.) fair; lovely; lovely ‹sight›; sweet, lovely ‹smile›; **die** ~**e Weiblichkeit** (scherzh.) the fair sex; **(b) das Glück war uns** (*Dat.*) ~ (geh.) fortune smiled upon us. **2** *adv.* sweetly

Holder *der;* ~**s,** ~ (bes. südd.) ⇒ **Holunder**

holen /'hoːlən/ **1** *tr. V.* **(a)** fetch; get; **sich** (*Dat.*) **Hilfe/Rat** *usw.* ~**:** get [some] help/advice *etc.;* **jmdn. aus dem Bett** ~**:** get *or* (coll.) drag sb. out of bed; **da/bei ihr ist nichts zu** ~ (fig.) you won't get anything there/out of her; **(b)** (ab~) fetch; pick up; collect; (ugs. verhüll.: verhaften) take away; **(c)** (ugs.: erlangen) get, win ‹prize›; get, carry off, win ‹medal, trophy, etc.›; get, score ‹points›; **sich** (*Dat.*) **die Meisterschaft/den Preis** *usw.* ~**:** win *or* take the championship/prize *etc.;* **(d)** (ugs. landsch.: kaufen) get; **sich** (*Dat.*) **etw.** ~**:** get [oneself] sth. **2** *refl. V.* (ugs.: sich zuziehen) catch; **sich** (*Dat.*) **[beim Baden** *usw.***] einen Schnupfen/die Grippe** ~**:** catch a cold/the flu [swimming *etc.*]; **sich** (*Dat.*) **den Tod** ~ (fig.) catch one's death [of cold]

Holland /'hɔlant/ (*das*) ~**s** Holland

Holländer /'hɔlɛndɐ/ *der;* ~**s,** ~ ▶ 388 (a) Dutchman; **er ist** ~**:** he is Dutch *or* a Dutchman; **die** ~**:** the Dutch; **(b)** (Käse) Dutch cheese

Holländerin *die;* ~, ~**nen** Dutchwoman/Dutch girl

holländisch *Adj.* ▶ 388 Dutch

Hölle /'hœlə/ *die;* ~, ~**n (a)** hell *no art.;* **in die** ~ **kommen** go to hell; **zur** ~ **fahren** (geh.) descend into hell; **jmdn. zur** ~ **wünschen** (geh.) wish sb. to hell; **zur** ~ **mit ihm/damit!** to hell with him/it (coll.); **(b)** (fig.) **die** ~ **ist los** (ugs.) all hell has broken loose (coll.); **die** ~ **auf Erden haben** suffer hell on earth; **jmdm. das Leben**

zur ~ **machen** make sb.'s life hell (coll.); **jmdm. die** ~ **heiß machen** give sb. hell (coll.)

Höllen-: ~**angst** *die* (salopp) **eine** ~**angst vor etw.** (*Dat.*) **haben** be scared to death of sth. (coll.); be terrified of sth.; ~**lärm** *der* (ugs.) diabolical noise *or* row (coll.); ~**maschine** *die* infernal machine (arch.); time bomb; ~**pein,** ~**qual** *die* agony; ~**qualen erleiden** suffer the torments of hell (fig.); suffer terrible agony *sing.;* ~**spektakel** *das* (ugs.) ⇒ ~**lärm;** ~**tempo** *das* (ugs.) breakneck speed

Holler /'hɔlɐ/ *der;* ~**s,** ~ (bes. südd., österr.) ⇒ **Holunder**

höllisch /'hœlɪʃ/ **1** *Adj.* **(a)** *nicht präd.* infernal; ‹spirits, torments› of hell; **(b)** (schrecklich) terrible ‹war, situation›; fiendish, diabolical ‹invention, laughter›; ~**e Schmerzen** terrible agony *sing.;* **(c)** (ugs.: sehr groß) tremendous (coll.) ‹noise, shock, respect› (coll.); enormous (coll.) ‹pleasure›; ~**e Angst vor etw.** (*Dat.*) **haben** be scared stiff of sth. (coll.). **2** *adv.* (ugs.: sehr) terribly, hellishly (coll.) ‹cold, difficult›; **sich** ~ **zusammennehmen** make a tremendous effort to control oneself (coll.); **es tut** ~ **weh** it hurts like hell (coll.)

Hollywood·schaukel /'hɔlɪwʊd-/ *die* swinging garden hammock

Holm /hɔlm/ *der;* ~**[e]s,** ~**e (a)** (Turnen) bar; **(b)** (Leiter~) upright; side-piece

Holocaust /holo'kaʊst/ *der;* ~**s,** ~**s** Holocaust

holperig ⇒ **holprig**

holpern /'hɔlpɐn/ *itr. V.* **(a)** jolt; **(b)** *mit sein* (holpernd fahren) jolt; bump

holprig /'hɔlprɪç/ **1** *Adj.* **(a)** (uneben) bumpy; uneven; rough; **(b)** (stockend) stumbling, halting ‹speech›; clumsy ‹verses, translation, language, style, wording, etc.›. **2** *adv.* haltingly; ~ **lesen** stumble over one's words when reading

Holster /'hɔlstɐ/ *das;* ~**s,** ~**:** holster

holterdiepolter /hɔltɐdiˈpɔltɐ/ *Adv.* (ugs.) helter-skelter; **alles ging** ~**:** there was a mad rush

Holunder /hoˈlʊndɐ/ *der;* ~**s,** ~ **(a)** (Strauch) elder; **(b)** *o. Pl.* (Früchte) elderberries *pl.*

Holunder-: ~**beere** die elderberry; ~**strauch** der elder[berry] bush

Holz /hɔlts/ das; ~**es**, **Hölzer** /'hœltsɐ/ (a) wood; (Bau~, Tischler~) timber; wood; **bearbeitetes** ~: timber (Brit.); lumber (Amer.); **die** ~ **verarbeitende Industrie** the timber processing industry; **ein Festmeter** ~: a cubic metre of timber; [**viel**] ~ **vor der Hütte** od. **Tür haben** (fig. ugs. scherzh.) be well stacked (coll.) or well endowed; **aus dem** ~ **sein, aus dem man Helden macht** be of the stuff heroes are made of; **aus dem gleichen** ~ [**geschnitzt**] **sein** (fig.) be cast in the same mould; (**b**) (Streich~) match; (zweckentfremdet) matchstick

Holz-: ~**bein** das wooden leg; ~**bläser** der woodwind player; ~**blas·instrument** das woodwind instrument; ~**block** der; Pl. ~**blöcke** block of wood; ~**bock** der (**a**) (Gestell) wooden stand or trestle; (**b**) (Zecke) castor-bean tick

Hölzchen /'hœltsçən/ das; ~**s**, ~ (**a**) small piece of wood; (Stöckchen) stick; (**b**) ⇒ **Holz b**

holzen itr. V. (Fußballjargon) play dirty (coll.)

hölzern /'hœltsɐn/ Adj.; nicht präd. (auch fig.) wooden

holz-, Holz-: ~**fäller** der woodcutter; lumberjack (Amer.); ~**feuer** das wood fire; ~**frei** Adj. wood-free ‹paper›; ~**gas** das wood-gas; ~**hacker** der (**a**) (bes. österr.) ⇒ **fäller**; (**b**) (Fußballjargon) dirty player; ~**haltig** Adj. woody ‹paper›; ‹paper› containing mechanical wood pulp; ~**hammer** der [wooden] mallet

Holzhammer·methode die (ugs.) sledgehammer method

Holz·haus das timber or wooden house

holzig Adj. woody

holz-, Holz-: ~**kitt** der plastic wood; ~**klotz** der block of wood; (als Spielzeug) wooden block; ~**kohle** die charcoal; ~**kopf** der (salopp abwertend) blockhead; numskull; ~**kreuz** das wooden cross; ~**leim** der woodglue; ~**leiste** die batten; ~**nagel** der wooden nail; ~**pantine** die (landsch.), ~**pantoffel** der clog; ~**pflock** der wooden stake; ~**scheit** das piece of wood; (Brenn~) piece of firewood; ~**schnitt** der (**a**) o. Pl. woodcutting no art.; (**b**) (Bild) woodcut; ~**schnitt·artig** Adj. (fig.) simplistic; ~**schnitzer** der wood carver; ~**schnitzerei** die wood carving; ~**schuh** der clog; ~**span** der (**a**) (zum Feueranzünden) stick of firewood; (zum Rühren usw.) small stick [of wood]; (**b**) meist Pl. (Hobelspan) [wood] shaving; ~**spielzeug** das wooden toy; ~**splitter** der splinter of wood; ~**stab** der wooden rod; ~**stoß** der pile of wood;*~**verarbeitend** ⇒ **Holz a**; ~**weg** der (fig.) in **auf dem** ~**weg sein** od. **sich auf dem** ~**weg befinden** be on the wrong track (fig.); be barking up the wrong tree (fig.); ~**wirtschaft** die timber industry; ~**wolle** die; o. Pl. wood wool; ~**wurm** der woodworm

Homburg /'hɔmbʊrk/ der; ~**s**, ~**s** Homburg

Homepage /'hoʊmpeɪʤ/ die; ~, ~**s** (DV) home page

Homo /'ho:mo/ der; ~**s**, ~**s** (ugs.) queer (sl. derog.), homo (coll.)

homo-, Homo-: ~**gen** /~'ge:n/ Adj. homogeneous; ~**genisieren** tr. V. (fachspr.) homogenize; ~**genität** /~geni'tɛ:t/ die; ~ (geh.) homogeneity

homöo-, Homöo- /homøo-/: ~**path** /~'pa:t/ der; ~**en**, ~**en** homoeopath; ~**pathie** die; ~: homoeopathy no art.; ~**pathisch** Adj. homoeopathic

homo-, Homo-: ~**sexualität** die; ~: homosexuality; ~**sexuell** 1 Adj. homosexual; 2 adv. ~**sexuell veranlagt sein** have homosexual tendencies; ~**sexuelle** der/die; adj. Dekl. homosexual

Honduras /hɔn'du:ras/ (das); **Honduras'** Honduras

Hongkong /'hɔŋkɔŋ/ (das); ~**s** ▶ 490 Hong Kong

Honig /'ho:nɪç/ der; ~**s**, ~**e** honey; **jmdm.** ~ **um den Bart** (ugs.) od. (salopp) **ums Maul schmieren** (fig.) butter sb. up

honig-, Honig-: ~**biene** die honey bee; ~**brot** das bread and honey; ~**kuchen** der honey cake; ~**kuchen·pferd** das in **grinsen wie ein** ~**kuchenpferd** (ugs. scherzh.) grin like a Cheshire cat; ~**lecken** das; das

---

*alte Schreibung (vgl. Hinweise auf S. xvi–xvii)

ist kein ~**lecken** (ugs.) it is not a bed of roses; ~**melone** die honeydew melon; ~**schlecken** das ⇒ ~**lecken**; ~**süß** 1 Adj. ‹grapes, taste, etc.› as sweet as honey; (fig.) honey-sweet ‹voice›; **ein** ~**süßes Lächeln** (fig.) the sweetest of smiles; 2 adv. (fig.) ~**süß lächeln/antworten** smile a honey-sweet smile/answer in honeyed tones

Honorar /hono'ra:ɐ/ das; ~**s**, ~**e** fee; (Autoren~) royalty

Honoratioren /honora'tsjo:rən/ Pl. notabilities

honorieren tr. V. (würdigen) appreciate; (belohnen) reward

honorig Adj. honourable; respectable

Hopfen der; ~**s**, ~: hop; (Blüten) hops pl.; **bei ihm ist** ~ **und Malz verloren** (ugs.) he's a hopeless case

hopp /hɔp/ Interj. quick; look sharp

hoppeln /'hɔpl̩n/ itr. V.; mit sein hop (über + Akk. across, over); (fig.) bump, jolt (über + Akk. across, over)

hopp·hopp 1 Interj. ⇒ **hopp.** 2 Adv. in double-quick time

hoppla /'hɔpla/ Interj. oops; whoops

hopp|nehmen unr. tr. V. (salopp) nab (sl.); nick (Brit. coll.)

hops /hɔps/ Interj. up; jump

hopsen itr. V.; mit sein (ugs.) ⇒ **hüpfen**

Hopser der; ~**s**, ~ (ugs.) [little] jump

hops-: ~|**gehen** unr. itr. V.; mit sein (salopp) (**a**) (umkommen) buy it (sl.); (**b**) (entzweigehen) get broken; (abhanden kommen) go missing; ~|**nehmen** unr. tr. V. ⇒ **hoppnehmen**

hörbar 1 Adj. audible. 2 adv. audibly; (geräuschvoll) noisily

horchen /'hɔrçn̩/ itr. V. listen (**auf** + Akk. to); (heimlich zuhören) eavesdrop; listen; **an der Tür/Wand** ~: listen at the door/through the wall

Horcher der; ~**s**, ~: ⇒ **Lauscher a**

Horde¹ /'hɔrdə/ die; ~, ~**n** (auch Völkerk.) horde; (von Halbstarken) mob; crowd

Horde² die; ~, ~**n** (Gestell) rack

hören /'hø:rən/ 1 tr. V. (**a**) hear; **jmdn. kommen/sprechen** ~: hear sb. coming/speaking; **ich höre nichts** I can't hear anything; s. auch **Gras**; (**b**) (anhören) listen to, hear ‹programme, broadcast, performance, etc.›; hear ‹singer, musician›; **Radio** ~: listen to the radio; **den Angeklagten/Zeugen** ~: hear the accused/witness; **das lässt sich** ~: that's good news; (**c**) (erfahren) hear; **ich habe gehört, dass**… I hear that…; **etw. von jmdm.** ~: hear sth. from sb.; **er lässt nichts von sich** ~: I/we etc. haven't heard from him; **lass mal etwas von dir** ~! keep in touch; **von jmdm. etwas zu** ~ **bekommen** od. (ugs.) **kriegen** get a good talking-to from sb. (coll.); (**d**) (erkennen) **an etw. (Dat.)** ~, **dass** …: hear or tell by sth. that … 2 itr. V. (**a**) hear; **gut** ~: have good hearing; **schlecht** ~: have bad hearing; be hard of hearing; **nur auf einem Ohr** ~: be deaf in one ear; (**b**) (aufmerksam verfolgen) **auf etw. (Akk.)** ~: listen to sth.; (**c**) (zuhören) listen; **ich höre** I'm listening; **hörst du!** listen [here]!; **hörst du?** are you listening?; **man höre und staune** would you believe it!; wonders will never cease (iron.); **hör mal!/** ~ **Sie mal!** listen [here]!; (**d**) **auf jmdn./jmds. Rat** ~: listen to or heed sb./sb.'s advice; **auf den Namen Monika** ~: answer to the name [of] Monika; **alles hört auf mein Kommando!** (Milit.) I'm taking command; (scherzh.) everyone do as I say; (**e**) (Kenntnis erhalten) **von jmdm./etw.** ~: hear of sb./sth.; **von jmdm.** ~ (Nachricht bekommen) hear from sb.; **Sie hören noch von mir** you'll be hearing from me again; you haven't heard the last of this; (**f**) (ugs.: gehorchen) do as one is told; **wer nicht** ~ **will, muss fühlen** (Spr.) if you don't do as you're told, you'll suffer for it

Hören·sagen das; ~**s** in **vom** ~: by or from hearsay

Hörer der; ~**s**, ~ (**a**) listener; (**b**) (Telefon~) receiver

Hörer·brief der listener's letter

Hörerin die; ~, ~**nen** listener

Hör-: ~**fehler** der (**a**) **das war ein** ~**fehler** he/she etc. misheard; (**b**) (Schwerhörigkeit) hearing defect; ~**folge** die radio series; (in Fortsetzungen) radio serial; ~**funk** der radio; **im** ~**funk** on the radio; ~**gerät** das hearing aid

hörig *Adj.* **(a)** *in* **jmdm.** ~ **sein** be submissively dependent on sb.; (sexuell) be sexually dependent on *or* enslaved to sb.; be sb.'s sexual slave; **(b)** (hist.) **die** ~**en Bauern** the serfs; ~ **sein** be in bondage

Hörige *der/die; adj. Dekl.* (hist.) serf; bondsman/bondswoman

Hörigkeit *die;* ~ **(a)** enslavement; (sexuell) sexual dependence; **(b)** (hist.) bondage; serfdom

Horizont /hori'tsɔnt/ *der;* ~[e]s, ~e (auch fig.) horizon; **am** ~: on the horizon; **seinen** ~ **erweitern** (fig.) widen *or* expand one's horizons *pl.;* **hinter dem** ~: below the horizon; **über jmds.** ~ *(Akk.)* **gehen** (fig.) be beyond sb.; go over sb.'s head

horizontal /horitsɔn'ta:l/ **1** *Adj.* horizontal. **2** *adv.* horizontally

Horizontale *die;* ~, ~**n** **(a)** (Linie) horizontal line; **(b)** *o. Pl.* (Lage) **die** ~: the horizontal; **sich in die** ~ **begeben** (scherzh.) lie down

Hormon /hɔr'mo:n/ *das;* ~**s**, ~**e** hormone

hormonal /hɔrmo'na:l/ **1** *Adj.* hormonal. **2** *adv.* hormonally

Hör·muschel *die* ear-piece

Horn /hɔrn/ *das;* ~[e]s, **Hörner** /'hœrnɐ/ **(a)** horn; **jmdm. Hörner aufsetzen** (fig. ugs.) cuckold sb.; **sich** *(Dat.)* **die Hörner abstoßen** (fig.) sow one's wild oats; **(b)** (Blasinstrument) horn; (Milit.) bugle; **ins gleiche** ~ **stoßen** (fig.) take the same line; **(c)** *o. Pl.* (Substanz) horn; **(d)** (Signal~) (eines Autos usw.) horn; hooter (Brit.); (eines Zuges) horn

Hornberger /'hɔrnbɛrgɐ/ *in* **wie das** ~ **Schießen ausgehen** all come to nothing

Horn·brille *die* horn-rimmed spectacles *pl. or* glasses *pl.*

Hörnchen /'hœrnçən/ *das;* ~**s**, ~ **(a)** small *or* little horn; **(b)** (Gebäck) croissant; **(c)** ⇒ **Lenkerhörnchen**

Horn·haut *die* **(a)** callus; hard *or* callused skin *no indef. art.;* **(b)** (am Auge) cornea

Hornisse /hɔr'nɪsə/ *die;* ~, ~**n** hornet

Hornist *der;* ~**en**, ~**en** **(a)** horn player; **(b)** (Milit.) bugler

Horn-: ~**kamm** *der* horn comb; ~**ochse** *der* (ugs.) stupid ass

Horoskop /horo'sko:p/ *das;* ~**s**, ~**e** horoscope

horrend /hɔ'rɛnt/ *Adj.* shocking (coll.), horrendous (coll.) ⟨price⟩; colossal (coll.) ⟨sum, amount, rent⟩

Hör·rohr *das* **(a)** (Stethoskop) stethoscope; **(b)** (Hörgerät) ear-trumpet

Horror /'hɔrɔr/ *der;* ~**s** horror; **einen** ~ **vor jmdm./etw. haben** loathe and fear sb./have a horror of sth.

Horror·film *der* horror film

Hör·saal *der* **(a)** lecture theatre *or* hall *or* room; **(b)** *o. Pl.* (Zuhörerschaft) audience

Hör·spiel *das* radio play

Horst /hɔrst/ *der;* ~[e]s, ~e (Nest) eyrie

Hör·sturz *der* (Med.) acute hearing loss

Hort /hɔrt/ *der;* ~[e]s, ~e (a) (dichter.: Goldschatz) hoard [of gold]; **(b)** (geh.: sicherer Ort) refuge; sanctuary; **ein** ~ **der Freiheit** a stronghold *or* bulwark of liberty; **(c)** ⇒ **Kinderhort**

horten *tr. V.* hoard; stockpile ⟨raw materials⟩

Hortensie /hɔr'tɛnziə/ *die;* ~, ~**n** hydrangea

Hör-: ~**test** *der* hearing test; ~**vermögen** *das; o. Pl.* hearing; ~**weite** *die* hearing range; **in/außer** ~**weite** in/out of hearing range *or* of earshot

Höschen /'hœːsçən/ *das;* ~**s**, ~ **(a)** trousers *pl.;* pair of trousers; (kurze Hose) short trousers *pl.;* shorts *pl.;* pair of shorts; **(b)** (Slip) panties *pl.;* pair of panties

Hose /'ho:zə/ *die;* ~, ~**n (a)** trousers *pl.;* pants *pl.* (Amer.); (Unter~) pants *pl.;* (Freizeit~) slacks *pl.;* (Bund~) breeches *pl.;* (Reit~) jodhpurs *pl.;* riding breeches *pl.;* **eine** ~: a pair of trousers/pants/slacks *etc.;* **eine kurze/lange** ~: [a pair of] short trousers *or* shorts/long trousers; **ein/zwei Paar** ~**n** one pair/two pairs of trousers; **das Kind hat in die** ~[**n**] **gemacht** the child has made a mess in its pants; **(b)** (fig.) **die** ~**n anhaben** (ugs.) wear the trousers; **jmdm. die** ~**n stramm ziehen** (ugs.) give sb. a good hiding (coll.);

sich [vor Angst] **in die** ~[**n**] **machen** (salopp) shit oneself (coarse); get into a blue funk (coll.); **es ist tote** ~ (Jugendspr.) there's nothing doing (coll.)

Hosen-: ~**an·zug** *der* trouser suit (Brit.); pant suit; ~**aufschlag** *der* [trouser *or* (Amer.) pants] turn-up; ~**bein** *das* trouser leg; pants leg (Amer.); ~**boden** *der* seat of the/one's/sb.'s trousers *or* (Amer.) pants; **sich auf den** ~**boden setzen** (fig.) knuckle down to it; **jmdm. den** ~**boden stramm ziehen** (fig. ugs.) give sb. a good hiding (coll.); ~**bügel** *der* trouser-hanger; ~**bund** *der* waistband; ~**klammer** *die* bicycle-clip; ~**knopf** *der* trouser-button; pants button (Amer.); ~**matz** *der* (ugs. scherzh.) toddler; [tiny] tot; ~**rock** *der* culottes *pl.;* divided skirt; ~**schlitz** *der* fly; flies *pl.;* ~**tasche** *die* trouser-pocket; pants pocket (Amer.); **etw. wie seine** ~**tasche kennen** (fig. ugs.) know sth. like the back of one's hand; ~**träger** *Pl.* braces; suspenders (Amer.); pair of braces/suspenders

hosianna /ho'zjana/ *Interj.* (christl. Rel.) hosanna

Hospital /hɔspi'ta:l/ *das;* ~**s**, ~**e** *od.* **Hospitäler** /hɔspi'tɛ:lɐ/ hospital

hospitieren *itr. V.* **bei jmdm.** ~: sit in on sb.'s lectures/seminars; **in einem Seminar/einer Vorlesung** ~: sit in on a seminar/lecture

Hostess, *Hosteß /hɔs'tɛs/ *die;* ~, **Hostessen** ▶ 85 ǀ hostess

Hostie /'hɔstiə/ *die;* ~, ~**n** (christl. Rel.) host

Hotel /ho'tɛl/ *das;* ~**s**, ~**s** hotel

Hotel-: ~**boy** *der* ▶ 85 ǀ page[-boy]; bellboy (Amer.); ~**führer** *der* hotel guide

Hotel garni /- gar'ni:/ *das;* ~ ~, ~**s** ~**s** bed-and-breakfast hotel

Hotel·halle *die* hotel lobby

Hotelier /hotɛ'lie:/ *der;* ~**s**, ~**s** ▶ 85 ǀ hotelier

Hotel-: ~**page** *der* ▶ 85 ǀ ⇒ ~**boy**; ~**portier** *der* ▶ 85 ǀ [hotel] commissionaire; ~**zimmer** *das* hotel room

Hotline /'hɔtlaɪn/ *die;* ~, ~**s** hotline

hott /hɔt/ *Interj.* gee[-up]; *s. auch* **hü**

hrsg. *Abk.* **herausgegeben** ed.

Hrsg. *Abk.* **Herausgeber** ed.

hu /hu/ *Interj.* **(a)** ugh; **(b)** (bei Kälte) brrr; **(c)** (zum Erschrecken) boo

hü /hy/ *Interj.* **(a)** (vorwärts) giddap; gee[-up]; **(b)** (halt) whoa; **einmal sagt sie** ~ **und einmal hott** (fig. ugs.) first she says one thing, then another

Hub /hu:p/ *der;* ~[e]s, **Hübe** /'hy:bə/ (Technik: Weg des Kolbens) stroke

Hubbel /'hʊbl/ *der;* ~**s**, ~ (bes. südd.) bump

hubbelig *Adj.* (bes. südd.) bumpy

Hub·brücke *die* lift bridge

hüben /'hy:bn̩/ *Adv.* on this side; over here; ~ **und drüben** on both sides

Hub·raum *der* ▶ 426 ǀ (Technik) cubic capacity

hübsch /hʏpʃ/ **1** *Adj.* **(a)** pretty; nice-looking ⟨boy, person⟩; nice, pleasant ⟨area, flat, voice, tune, etc.⟩; nice ⟨phrase, expression, present⟩; **sich** ~ **machen** make oneself look nice; **(b)** *nicht präd.* (ugs.: ziemlich groß) **eine** ~**e Stange Geld kosten** cost a pretty penny; **ein** ~**es Sümmchen** a tidy sum (coll.); a nice little sum; **ein** ~**es Stück Arbeit** a fair amount *or* quite a lot of work; **(c)** (ugs. iron.: unangenehm) **das ist eine** ~**e Geschichte/hier herrschen** ~**e Zustände** this is a fine *or* pretty kettle of fish (coll.) *or* a fine state of affairs. **2** *adv.* **(a)** prettily; **sich** ~ **anziehen** dress nicely; wear nice clothes; **eingerichtet/gekleidet** nicely *or* attractively furnished/dressed; **(b)** (ugs.: sehr) [ganz] ~ **kalt** perishing cold; **(c)** (ugs.: ordentlich) **immer** ~ **der Reihe nach** everybody must take his turn; **sei** ~ **brav** be a good boy/girl

Hub·schrauber *der;* ~**s**, ~: helicopter

Hubschrauber·landeplatz *der* heliport; (kleiner) helicopter pad; landing pad

huch /hʊx/ *Interj.* ugh; (bei Kälte) brrr

Hucke /'hʊkə/ *die;* ~, ~**n** pannier; **jmdm. die** ~ **voll hauen** (fig. ugs.) give sb. a good hiding (coll.); (bei einer Prügelei) beat hell out of sb. (coll.); **jmdm. die** ~ **voll lügen** (fig.

ugs.) tell sb. a pack of lies; **die ~ voll kriegen** (fig. ugs.) get a good hiding (coll.); (bei einer Prügelei) get a proper beating (coll.)

huckepack /'hʊkəpak/ *Adv.* (ugs.) *in* **jmdn. ~ tragen** carry sb. piggyback; give sb. a piggyback; **etw. ~ tragen** carry sth. piggyback; **jmdn./etw. ~ nehmen** take sth. up on one's back

Hudelei *die; ~, ~en* (bes. südd., österr.) (a) (Arbeitsweise) sloppiness; (b) (Pfuscharbeit) sloppy *or* slapdash work *no indef. art.*

hudeln /'huːdl̩n/ *itr. V.* (bes. südd., österr.) work sloppily; be sloppy *or* slapdash (**bei in**); **nur nicht ~!** don't be in such a hurry!; take it easy!

Huf /huːf/ *der;* ~**[e]s,** ~**e** hoof; **einem Pferd die ~e beschlagen** shoe a horse

huf-, Huf-: ~**eisen** *das* horseshoe; ~**eisenförmig** *Adj.* horseshoe-shaped; ~**lattich** *der* coltsfoot; ~**nagel** *der* horseshoe nail; ~**schmied** *der* farrier; blacksmith

Hüft·bein *das* (Anat.) hip bone; innominate bone (Anat.)

Hüfte /'hʏftə/ *die; ~,* ~**n** ▶ 326⌐ hip; **aus der ~ schießen** shoot from the hip

hüft-, Hüft-: ~**gelenk** *das* (Anat.) hip joint; ~**gürtel** *der,* ~**halter** *der* girdle; ~**hoch** *Adj.* ≈ waist-high; ~**hoch sein** be almost waist-high

Huf·tier *das* hoofed animal; ungulate (Zool.)

Hüft·weite *die* hip size

Hügel /'hyːgl̩/ *der;* ~**s,** ~**:** hill; (fig.) heap; pile

Hügel·grab *das* (Archäol.) barrow; tumulus

hügelig *Adj.* hilly

Hügel·kette *die* chain *or* range of hills

Hugenotte /hugə'nɔtə/ *der;* ~**n,** ~**n** Huguenot

Huhn /huːn/ *das;* ~**[e]s,** **Hühner** /'hyːnɐ/ (a) chicken; [domestic] fowl; (Henne) chicken; hen; **gebratenes ~:** roast chicken; **herumlaufen wie ein aufgescheuchtes ~** (ugs.) run about in a great panic (coll.); **da lachen [ja] die Hühner** (ugs.) you/he *etc.* must be joking (coll.); **ein blindes ~ findet auch mal ein Korn** (Spr.) anyone can have a stroke of luck once in a while; **mit den Hühnern zu Bett gehen/aufstehen** (scherzh.) go to bed early/get up with the lark; (b) (ugs.: Mensch) **ein dummes/fideles ~:** a stupid twit (Brit. coll.) *or* an idiot/a cheerful sort (coll.)

Hühnchen /'hyːnçən/ *das;* ~**s,** ~**:** little *or* small chicken; **mit jmdm. [noch] ein ~ zu rupfen haben** (ugs.) [still] have a bone to pick with sb.

Hühner-: ~**auge** *das* (am Fuß) corn; **jmdm. auf die ~augen treten** (fig. ugs.) tread on sb.'s corns *or* toes; ~**brühe** *die* chicken broth; ~**brust** *die* (a) (Med.) chicken-breast; pigeon-breast; (b) (ugs.: flacher Brustkorb) scrawny chest; ~**dieb** *der* chicken-thief; ~**ei** *das* hen's egg; ~**farm** *die* chicken farm; ~**frikassee** *das* chicken fricassee; fricassee of chicken; ~**futter** *das* chicken feed; ~**habicht** *der* [northern] goshawk; ~**hof** *der* chicken-run; ~**klein** *das;* ~**s** trimmings *pl.* of chicken (in stew etc.); ~**leiter** *die* chicken-ladder; ~**stall** *der* chicken-coop; hen-coop; ~**suppe** *die* chicken soup

hui /hui/ *Interj.* whoosh; **außen ~ und innen pfui** (von Dingen) the outside's fine but inside it's a different story; (von Personen) he/she seems very nice on the surface, but underneath it's a different story

huldigen /'hʊldɪgn̩/ *itr. V.* (a) **jmdm. ~:** pay tribute to *or* honour sb.; (b) (geh.: anhängen) **einem Grundsatz/ einer Ansicht/Mode ~:** hold [devotedly] to a principle/ a point of view/follow a fashion

Huldigung *die; ~,* ~**en** tribute; homage

Hülle /'hʏlə/ *die; ~,* ~**n** (a) cover; (für Ausweis, Zeitkarte) cover; holder; (Schallplatten~) cover; sleeve; **die sterbliche ~** (geh. verhüll.) the mortal remains *pl.;* (b) (ugs. scherzh.: Kleidung) **seine** *od.* **die ~ fallen lassen** strip off [one's clothes]; (c) **in ~ und Fülle** in abundance; in plenty

hüllen *tr. V.* (geh.) wrap; **jmdn./sich in etw.** (*Akk.*) ~**:** wrap sb./oneself in sth.; **in Wolken** (*Akk.*) **gehüllt** (fig.) enveloped in clouds

hüllenlos *Adj.* (a) *nicht präd.* (unverhüllt) plain; clear; (b) (scherzh.: nackt) naked

Hülse /'hʏlzə/ *die; ~,* ~**n** (a) (für Füllhalter, Thermometer, Patrone) case; (für Film) [cassette] container; (b) (Bot.) pod; hull

Hülsen·frucht *die; meist Pl.* (a) fruit of a leguminous plant; **Hülsenfrüchte** pulse *sing.;* (b) (Pflanze) legume; leguminous plant

human /hu'maːn/ 1 *Adj.* (a) humane; (b) (nachsichtig) considerate; (c) (Med.) human. 2 *adv.* (a) humanly; (b) (nachsichtig) considerately

humanisieren *tr. V.* humanize

Humanisierung *die;* ~**:** humanization

Humanismus *der;* ~**:** humanism; (Epoche) Humanism *no art.*

Humanist *der;* ~**en,** ~**en** (a) humanist; (hist.) Humanist; (b) (Altsprachler) classical scholar

humanistisch *Adj.* (a) humanist[ic]; (hist.) Humanist; (b) (altsprachlich) classical; **ein ~es Gymnasium** *secondary school emphasizing classical languages*

humanitär /humani'tɛːɐ̯/ *Adj.* humanitarian

Humanität /humani'tɛːt/ *die;* ~**:** respect for humanity

Human·medizin *die* human medicine *no art.*

Humbug /'hʊmbʊk/ *der;* ~**s** (ugs. abwertend) humbug

Hummel /'hʊml̩/ *die; ~,* ~**n** bumble-bee; humble-bee; **eine wilde ~** (scherzh.) a proper tomboy

Hummer /'hʊmɐ/ *der;* ~**s,** ~**:** lobster

Hummer·krabbe *die* king prawn

Humor /hu'moːɐ̯/ *der;* ~**s** humour; (Sinn für ~) sense of humour; **etw. mit ~ tragen/nehmen** bear/take sth. with a sense of humour *or* cheerfully; **den ~ nicht verlieren** remain good-humoured

humorig *Adj.* humorous

Humorist *der;* ~**en,** ~**en** (a) humorist; (b) (Komiker) comedian

humoristisch 1 *Adj.* humorous. 2 *adv.* with humour

humor-, Humor-: ~**los** 1 *Adj.* humourless; 2 *adv.* without humour; ~**losigkeit** *die;* ~**:** humourlessness; lack of humour; ~**voll** 1 *Adj.* humorous; 2 *adv.* humorously; in a humorous way

humpeln /'hʊmpl̩n/ *itr. V.* (a) *auch mit sein* walk with *or* have a limp; (b) *mit sein* (sich ~d fortbewegen) hobble; limp

Humpen /'hʊmpn̩/ *der;* ~**s,** ~**:** tankard; [beer-]mug; (aus Ton auch) stein

Humus /'huːmʊs/ *der;* ~**:** humus

Hund /hʊnt/ *der;* ~**es,** ~**e** (a) dog; (Jagd~) hound; dog; **bekannt sein wie ein bunter ~** (ugs.) be a well-known figure; **bei diesem Wetter würde man keinen ~ vor die Tür schicken** I wouldn't turn a dog out in weather like this; **da liegt der ~ begraben** (fig. ugs.) (Ursache) that's what's causing it; (Grund) that's the real reason; **da wird der ~ in der Pfanne verrückt** (salopp) it's quite incredible; ~**e, die bellen, beißen nicht** (Spr.) barking dogs seldom bite; **den letzten beißen die ~e** (fig.) latecomers must expect to be unlucky; **ein dicker ~** (ugs.: grober Fehler) a real bloomer (Brit. sl.) *or* (sl.) goof; **das ist ein dicker ~** (ugs.: Frechheit) that's a bit thick (coll.); **wie ~ und Katze leben** (ugs.) lead a cat-and-dog life; **damit kannst du keinen ~ hinter dem Ofen hervorlocken** that won't tempt anybody; **auf den ~ kommen** (ugs.) go to the dogs (coll.); **vor die ~e gehen** (ugs.) go to the dogs (coll.); (sterben) die; kick the bucket (fig. sl.); (b) (salopp: Mann) bloke (Brit. coll.); (abwertend) bastard (sl.); **so ein blöder ~!** [what a] stupid bastard!

Hündchen /'hʏntçən/ *das;* ~**s,** ~ (kleiner Hund) little dog; (Koseform) doggie (coll.); (junger Hund) puppy; pup

hunde-, Hunde-: ~**dreck** *der* (ugs.) dog's mess *or* muck; ~**elend** *Adj.; nicht attr.* [really] wretched *or* awful; ~**futter** *das* dog food; ~**halsband** *das* dog collar; ~**hütte** *die* (auch fig. abwertend) [dog-]kennel; ~**kalt** *Adj.; nicht attr.* (ugs.) freezing cold; ~**kälte** *die* (ugs.) freezing cold; ~**kot** *der* (ugs.) dog-dirt; ~**kuchen** *der* dog biscuit; ~**leben** *das* (ugs.) dog's life; ~**marke** *die* dog-licence disc; dog-tag; ~**müde** *Adj.; nicht attr.* (ugs.) dog-tired; ~**rasse** *die* breed of dog; ~**rennen** *das* dog-racing; greyhound-racing

hundert /'hʊndɐt/ *Kardinalz.* ▶ 600⌐ (a) ▶ 22⌐ a *or* one hundred; **mehrere/einige ~ /Hundert Menschen** several/a few hundred people; (b) (ugs.: viele) hundreds of

Hundert *das; ~s, ~e od.* (nach unbest. Zahlwörtern) ~ **(a)** hundred; **ein halbes** ~: fifty; **fünf vom** ~: five per cent; **(b)** *Pl.* (große Anzahl) ~**e von Menschen** hundreds of people; **in die** ~**e gehen** (ugs.) run into hundreds

hundert·ein[s] *Kardinalz.* ▶ 22 |, ▶ 600 | a *or* one hundred and one

Hunderter *der; ~s, ~* **(a)** (ugs.) hundred-mark/-dollar *etc.* note; **(b)** (Math.) hundred

hunderterlei *Gattungsz.; indekl.* (ugs.) **(a)** *attr.* a hundred and one different ⟨*answers, kinds, etc.*⟩; **(b)** *attr.* (viele) a hundred and one; **(c)** *subst.* a hundred and one different things; **(d)** *subst.* (vieles) a hundred and one things

hundert·fach *Vervielfältigungsz.* hundredfold; **die** ~**e Menge/der** ~**e Preis** a hundred times the amount/price; **das Hundertfache** a hundred times as much; *s. auch* **achtfach**

Hundert·jahr·feier *die* centenary; centennial

hundert·jährig *Adj.* **(a)** (100 Jahre alt) [one-]hundred-year-old; **(b)** (100 Jahre dauernd) **nach** ~**em Kampf** after a hundred years of war; **der Hundertjährige Krieg** (hist.) the Hundred Years' War

hundert·mal *Adv.* a hundred times; **auch wenn du dich** ~ **beschwerst** (ugs.) however much *or* no matter how much you complain; *s. auch* **achtmal**

Hundert-: ~**mark·schein** *der* ▶ 216 | hundred-mark note; ~**meterhürden·lauf** *der* (Leichtathletik) hundred-metres hurdles *sing.;* ~**meter·lauf** *der* (Leichtathletik) hundred metres *sing.*

hundert·prozentig **1** *Adj.* **(a)** [one-]hundred per cent *attrib.;* **(b)** (ugs.: völlig) a hundred per cent, complete, absolute ⟨*certainty, agreement, etc.*⟩. **2** *adv.* (ugs.) **ich bin nicht** ~ **sicher** I'm not a hundred per cent sure; **etw.** ~ **wissen** know sth. for sure

Hundertschaft *die; ~, ~en* group of a hundred; **einige** ~**en Polizei** several hundred police

hundertst... ~ /'hʊndɛtst.../ *Ordinalz.* hundredth; **zum** ~**en Mal fragen** (ugs.) ask for the hundredth time; **vom Hundertsten ins Tausendste kommen** get carried away so that one subject just leads another

hundertstel /'hʊndɛtstl̩/ *Bruchz.* ▶ 600 | hundredth; *s. auch* **achtel**

Hundertstel... *das* (schweiz. meist der) ▶ 600 |; ~s, ~: hundredth

Hundertstel·sekunde *die* hundredth of a second

hundert·tausend *Kardinalz.* ▶ 600 | a *or* one hundred thousand

hundert·und·ein[s] *Kardinalz.* ▶ 22 |, ▶ 600 | a *or* one hundred and one

hundert·zehn *Kardinalz.* ▶ 22 |, ▶ 600 | a *or* one hundred and ten

Hunde-: ~**scheiße** *die* (derb) dog-shit (coarse); ~**schlitten** *der* dog-sledge; dog-sled (Amer.); ~**steuer** *die* dog-licence fee; ~**wetter** *das* (ugs.) filthy *or* (coll.) lousy weather; ~**zwinger** *der* dog run

Hündin /'hʏndɪn/ *die; ~, ~nen* bitch

hündisch /'hʏndɪʃ/ **1** *Adj.* **(a)** (würdelos) doglike, servile ⟨*obedience*⟩; doglike ⟨*devotion*⟩; fawning, abject ⟨*submissiveness*⟩; **(b)** (gemein) mean; nasty. **2** *adv.* **jmdm.** ~ **ergeben sein** have a doglike devotion to sb.

hunds-, Hunds-: ~**erbärmlich** (ugs.) **1** *Adj.* **(a)** [really] dreadful (coll.); **(b)** (verabscheuenswürdig) dirty *attrib.* ⟨*lie, coward*⟩; **2** *adv.* **(a)** (sehr) terribly (coll.), dreadfully (coll.) ⟨*cold*⟩; **(b)** (sehr schlecht) [really] abysmally (coll.) *or* dreadfully (coll.); ~**gemein** (ugs.) **1** *Adj.* **(a)** (abwertend: überaus gemein) really mean *or* shabby; dirty ⟨*liar*⟩; **(b)** (sehr stark) terrible (coll.), dreadful (coll.) ⟨*cold, weather, pain, etc.*⟩; **2** *adv.* **(a)** (gemein) ⟨*deceive, behave*⟩ really meanly *or* shabbily; **(b)** (sehr stark) **das tut** ~**gemein weh** it hurts like hell (coll.) *or* terribly (coll.); ~**miserabel** (salopp abwertend) **1** *Adj.* [really] lousy *or* dreadful (coll.); **2** *adv.* ⟨*behave*⟩ [really] appallingly (coll.) *or* dreadfully (coll.); ~**tage** *Pl.* dog-days

Hüne /'hy:nə/ *der; ~n, ~n* giant

Hünen·grab *das* megalithic tomb; (Hügelgrab) barrow; tumulus

hünenhaft *Adj.* gigantic ⟨*build, stature*⟩

Hunger /'hʊŋɐ/ *der; ~s* **(a)** ~ **bekommen/haben** get/ be hungry; **ich habe** ~ **wie ein Bär** *od.* **Wolf** I'm so hungry I could eat a horse; **sein** ~ **war groß** he was very hungry; ~ **auf etw.** (Akk.) **haben** fancy sth.; feel like sth. (coll.); ~ **leiden** go hungry; starve; **vor** ~ **sterben** die of starvation *or* hunger; **starve to death**; **(b)** (Hungersnot) famine; **(c)** (geh.: Verlangen) hunger; (nach Ruhm, Macht) craving; thirst

Hunger-: ~**gefühl** *das* feeling of hunger; ~**kur** *die* starvation diet; ~**leider** *der* (ugs. abwertend) starving pauper; ~**lohn** *der* (abwertend) starvation wage[s *pl.*]

hungern /'hʊŋɐn/ **1** *itr. V.* **(a)** go hungry; starve; **(b)** (verlangen) **nach etw.** ~: hunger *or* be hungry for sth.; (nach Macht, Ruhm) crave sth.; thirst for sth. **2** *refl. V.* **sich zu Tode** ~: starve oneself to death; **sich schlank** ~: slim by going on a starvation diet

Hungers·not *die* famine

Hunger-: ~**streik** *der* hunger strike; ~**tod** *der* death from starvation; ~**tuch** *das in* **am** ~**tuch nagen** (ugs. scherzh.) be on the breadline

hungrig *Adj.* hungry; **das macht [einen]** ~: it makes you hungry *or* gives you an appetite; ~ **nach etw. sein** fancy sth.; feel like sth. (coll.)

Hunne /'hʊnə/ *der; ~n, ~n* (hist.) Hun

Hupe /'hu:pə/ *die; ~, ~n* horn

hupen *itr. V.* sound the *or* one's horn; **dreimal** ~: hoot three times; give three toots on the horn

hupfen /'hʊpfn̩/ *itr. V.; mit sein* (südd., österr.) hop; **das ist gehupft wie gesprungen** (ugs.) it doesn't make any difference; it doesn't matter either way

hüpfen /'hʏpfn̩/ *itr. V.; mit sein* hop; ⟨*child*⟩ skip; ⟨*ball*⟩ bounce; **Hüpfen spielen** play [at] hopscotch; **mein Herz hüpfte vor Freude** my heart leapt for joy; **das ist gehüpft wie gesprungen** (ugs.) ⇒ **hupfen**

Hüpfer *der; ~s, ~*: skip; (auf einem Bein) hop

Hup·konzert *das* (ugs. scherzh.) chorus of hooting

Hürde /'hʏrdə/ *die; ~, ~n* **(a)** (Leichtathletik, fig.) hurdle; **eine** ~ **nehmen** clear a hurdle; (fig.) get over a hurdle

Hürden-: ~**lauf** *der* (Leichtathletik) hurdling; (Wettbewerb) hurdles *pl.;* hurdle race; ~**läufer** *der* (Leichtathletik) hurdler

Hure /'hu:rə/ *die; ~, ~n* (abwertend) whore

huren *itr. V.* (abwertend) whore; fornicate

Huren·sohn *der* (abwertend) bastard (coll.); son of a bitch (derog.)

hurra /hʊ'ra:/ *Interj.* hurray; hurrah; ~/**Hurra schreien** cheer; *s. auch* **hipp, hipp, hurra**

Hurra *das; ~s, ~s* cheer; **jmdn. mit** ~ **begrüßen** greet sb. with cheering *or* cheers *pl.*

Hurra·ruf *der* cheering; cheers *pl.*

Hurrikan /'hʌrɪkən/ *der; ~s, ~s* hurricane

hurtig /'hʊrtɪç/ **1** *Adj.; nicht präd.* rapid. **2** *adv.* quickly; ⟨*work*⟩ fast, quickly

husch /hʊʃ/ *Interj.* quick; quickly; ~, ~! away with you!; be off with you!; (zu einem Tier) shoo!

huschen *itr. V.; mit sein* ⟨*person*⟩ flit, dart; ⟨*mouse, lizard, etc.*⟩ dart; ⟨*smile*⟩ flit; ⟨*light*⟩ flash; ⟨*shadow*⟩ slide *or* glide quickly

hüsteln /'hy:stl̩n/ *itr. V.* cough slightly; give a slight cough

husten /'hu:stn̩/ **1** *itr. V.* **(a)** cough; **(b)** (Husten haben) have a cough; be coughing. **2** *tr. V.* cough up ⟨*blood, phlegm*⟩; **jmdm. etwas** ~ (salopp spött.) tell sb. where he/she can get off (coll.)

Husten *der; ~s, ~*: ▶ 329 | cough; ~ **haben** have a cough

Husten-: ~**an·fall** *der* ▶ 329 | coughing-fit; fit of coughing; ~**bonbon** *das* cough sweet (Brit.); cough-drop; ~**reiz** *der* tickling in the throat; ~**saft** *der* cough-syrup; cough mixture

Hut¹ /hu:t/ *der; ~es, Hüte* /'hy:tə/ **(a)** hat; **den** ~ **ziehen** raise one's hat; **in** ~ **und Mantel** wearing one's hat and coat; with one's hat and coat on; **(b)** (fig.) **da geht einem/mir der** ~ **hoch** (ugs.) it makes you/me mad *or* wild (coll.); ~ **ab!** (ugs.) hats off to him/her *etc.;* I take my hat off to him/her *etc.;* **ein alter** ~ **sein** (ugs.) be old hat; **seinen** ~ **nehmen** (ugs.) pack one's bags and go; **vor jmdm./etw. den** ~ **ziehen** (ugs.) take off one's hat to sb./ sth.; **das kann er sich** (*Dat.*) **an den** ~ **stecken** (ugs. abwertend) he can keep it (coll.) *or* (sl.) stick it; **mit etw. nichts am** ~ **haben** (ugs.) have nothing to do with sth.; **jmdm. eins auf den** ~ **geben** (ugs.) give sb. a dressing down *or* (Brit. coll.) rocket; **eins auf den** ~ **kriegen** (ugs.) get a dressing down *or* (Brit. coll.) rocket; **verschiedene Interessen/Personen unter einen** ~ **bringen** (ugs.) reconcile different interests/the interests of different people; **(c)** (Bot.: eines Pilzes) cap

Hut² *die;* ~: *in* **auf der** ~ **sein** (geh.) be on one's guard
Hut-: ~**ab·lage** *die* hat rack; ~**band** *das* hat-band; (eines Damenhutes) hat-ribbon
hüten /'hyːtn̩/ **1** *tr. V.* look after; take care of; tend, keep watch over ‹*sheep, cattle, etc.*›; **ein Geheimnis** ~ (fig.) keep *or* guard a secret; *s. auch* **Bett a. 2** *refl. V.* (vorsehen) be on one's guard; **sich vor jmdm./etw.** ~: be on one's guard against sb./sth.; **sich** ~, **etw. zu tun** take [good] care not to do sth.; **ich werde mich** ~! (ugs.) no fear! (coll.); not likely! (coll.)
Hüter *der;* ~**s,** ~, **Hüterin** *die;* ~, ~**nen** guardian; custodian
Hut-: ~**feder** *die* hat feather; ~**geschäft** *das* hat shop; hatter's [shop]; (für Damen) hat shop; milliner's (shop); ~**größe** *die* hat size; size of hat; ~**krempe** *die* [hat] brim; ~**macher** *der,* ~**macherin** *die;* ~, ~**nen** ▶ 85◀ hatter; hat maker; (für Damen) milliner; ~**nadel** *die* hat-pin; ~**schachtel** *die* hat-box; ~**schnur** *die:* **das geht mir über die** ~**schnur** (ugs.) that's going too far
Hütte /'hyːtə/ *die;* ~, ~**n (a)** hut; (Holz~) cabin; hut; (ärmliches Haus) shack; hut; **(b)** (Eisen~) iron [and steel] works *sing. or pl.;* (Glas~) glassworks *sing. or pl.;* (Blei~) lead works *sing. or pl.;* **(c)** (Jagd~) [hunting-]lodge
Hütten-: ~**käse** *der* cottage cheese; ~**schuh** *der* slipper-sock
hutzelig *Adj.* (ugs.) wizened ‹*person, face*›; shrivelled, dried-up ‹*fruit*›
Hyäne /'hyː‐nə/ *die;* ~, ~**n** hyena
Hyazinthe /haia'tsɪntə/ *die;* ~, ~**n** hyacinth
Hydrant /hy'drant/ *der;* ~**en,** ~**en** hydrant
Hydrat /hy'draːt/ *das;* ~[e]**s,** ~**e** (Chemie) hydrate
hydraulisch /hy'draulɪk/ *die;* ~ (Technik) **(a)** hydraulics *sing., no art.;* **(b)** (System) hydraulics *pl.;* hydraulic system
hydraulisch 1 *Adj.* hydraulic. **2** *adv.* hydraulically
Hydrid /hy'driːt/ *das;* ~[e]**s,** ~**e** (Chemie) hydride
hydrieren /hy'driːrən/ *tr. V.* (Chemie) hydrogenate
hydro-, Hydro- /hydro‐/: ~**kultur** *die;* ~, ~**en** (Gartenbau) hydroponics *sing.;* ~**lyse** /‐'lyːzə/ *die;* ~, ~**n** (Chemie) hydrolysis; ~**pneumatisch** *Adj.* (Technik) hydropneumatic
Hygiene /hy'giːnə/ *die;* ~ hygiene
hygienisch 1 *Adj.* hygienic. **2** *adv.* hygienically
Hymen /'hyːmən/ *das od. der;* ~**s,** ~ (Anat.) hymen
Hymne /'hʏmnə/ *die;* ~, ~**n (a)** hymn; **(b)** (Nationalhymne) national anthem
hymnisch *Adj.* hymnic
Hyperbel /hy'pɛrbl̩/ *die;* ~, ~**n** (Geom.) hyperbola
hyper·korrekt /hypɐ‐/ (ugs. abwertend, Sprachw.) **1** *Adj.* hypercorrect. **2** *adv.* in a hypercorrect way
Hyper·link /'haipɐ‐/ *der* (DV) hyperlink
hyper- /hypɐ‐/: ~**modern 1** *Adj.* ultra-modern; ultra-fashionable ‹*clothes*›; **2** *adv.* ultra-modernly; ‹*dress*› ultra-fashionably; ~**sensibel** *Adj.* hypersensitive
Hyper·text /'haipɐ‐/ *der* (DV) hypertext
Hypnose /hyp'noːzə/ *die;* ~, ~**n** hypnosis; **jmdn. in** ~ **versetzen** put sb. under hypnosis; **unter** ~ **stehen** be under hypnosis
hypnotisch *Adj.* hypnotic; hypnotic, soporific ‹*drug*›
Hypnotiseur /hypnoti'zøː/ *der;* ~**s,** ~**e** hypnotist
hypnotisieren *tr. V.* hypnotize
Hypochonder /hypo'xɔndɐ/ *der;* ~**s,** ~: hypochondriac

Hypochondrie *die;* ~, ~**n** (Med.) hypochondria *no art.*
hypochondrisch *Adj.* hypochondriac
Hypo- /hypo‐/: ~**physe** /‐'fyːzə/ *die;* ~, ~**n** (Anat.) hypophysis; ~**tenuse** /‐te'nuːzə/ *die;* ~, ~**n** (Math.) hypotenuse
Hypothek /‐'teːk/ *die;* ~, ~**en (a)** (Bankw.) mortgage; **eine** ~ **aufnehmen** take out a mortgage; **etw. mit einer** ~ **belasten** encumber sth. with a mortgage; mortgage sth.; **(b)** (fig.: Bürde) burden
Hypotheken·zins *der; meist Pl.* mortgage interest
Hypo·these /‐'teːzə/ *die;* ~, ~**n** hypothesis
hypo·thetisch 1 *Adj.* hypothetical; **2** *adv.* hypothetically
Hysterie /hystə'riː/ *die;* ~, ~**n** /‐iːən/ hysteria
Hysteriker /hys'teːrikɐ/ *der;* ~**s,** ~, **Hysterikerin** *die;* ~, ~**nen** hysterical person; hysteric
hysterisch 1 *Adj.* hysterical. **2** *adv.* hysterically
Hz *Abk.* **Hertz** Hz

I i

i, I /iː/ *das;* ~, ~: i/I; **das Tüpfelchen auf dem i** (fig.) the final touch; *s. auch* **a, A**
i. A. *Abk.* **im Auftrag[e]** p.p.
iah /'iː'aː/ *Interj.* hee-haw
iahen /'iː'aːən/ *itr. V.* hee-haw; bray
iberisch /i'beːrɪʃ/ *Adj.* Iberian; **Iberische Halbinsel** Iberian Peninsula
Ibis /'iːbɪs/ *der;* ~**ses,** ~**se** (Zool.) ibis
IC *Abk.* **Intercity** IC
ich /ɪç/ *Personalpron.; 1. Pers. Sg. Nom.* I; **Wer ist da? — Ich bins!** Who's there? — It's me!; **Wer hat das gemacht? — Ich wars** Who did that? — I did *or* It was me; **Hat sie mich gerufen? — Nein,** ~: Was it she who called me? — No, I did; **und** ~ **Esel/Idiot habe es gemacht** and I, silly ass/idiot that I am, did it; and, like a fool, I did it; **immer** ~ (ugs.) [it's] always me; ~ **selbst** I myself; ~ **nicht** not me; **Menschen wie du und** ~: people like you and I *or* me; *s. auch* (*Gen.*) **meiner,** (*Dat.*) **mir,** (*Akk.*) **mich**
Ich *das;* ~[s], ~[s] **(a)** self; **das eigene** ~: one's own self; **(b)** (Psych.) ego
ich-, Ich-: ~**bezogen 1** *Adj.* egocentric; **2** *adv.* ~**bezogen denken** think in an egocentric way; ~**bezogenheit** *die;* ~: egocentricity; ~**form,** *~**Form** *die; o. Pl.* first person; ~**laut,** *~**-Laut** *der* (Sprachw.) palatal fricative; ich-laut
Ichthyo·saurier /ɪçtyo‐/ *der* ichthyosaurus
Icon /'aikən/ *das;* ~**s,** ~**s** (DV) icon
ideal /ide'aːl/ **1** *Adj.* ideal. **2** *adv.* ideally
Ideal *das;* ~**s,** ~**e** ideal
Ideal-: ~**bild** *das* ideal; ~**fall** *der* ideal case; **im** ~**fall** in ideal circumstances *pl.;* ~**figur** *die* ideal figure; ~**gewicht** *das* ideal weight
idealisieren *tr. V.* idealize
Idealismus *der;* ~: idealism
Idealist *der;* ~**en,** ~**en** idealist
idealistisch 1 *Adj.* idealistic. **2** *adv.* idealistically
Ideal·vorstellung *die* ideal
Idee /i'deː/ *die;* ~, ~**n (a)** idea; **du hast [vielleicht]** ~**n** (iron.) you do get some ideas, don't you! (coll.); **auf eine** ~ **kommen** hit [up]on an idea; **jmdn. auf eine** ~ **bringen** give sb. an idea; **eine fixe** ~: an obsession; an idée fixe; **(b)** (ein bisschen) **eine** ~: a shade *or* trifle; **eine** ~ **Salz** a touch of salt
ideell /ide'ɛl/ **1** *Adj.* non-material; (geistig-seelisch) spiritual. **2** *adv.* **etw.** ~ **unterstützen** support sth. in non-material ways

---

*alte Schreibung (vgl. Hinweise auf S. xvi–xvii)

ideen·reich *Adj.* full of ideas *postpos.;* inventive

Identifikation /idɛntifika'tsi̯oːn/ *die;* ~, ~**en** identification

identifizierbar *Adj.* identifiable

identifizieren /idɛntifi'tsiːrən/ **1** *tr. V.* identify. **2** *refl. V.* **sich mit jmdm./etw.** ~: identify with sb./sth.

Identifizierung *die;* ~, ~**en** identification

identisch /i'dɛntɪʃ/ *Adj.* identical

Identität /idɛnti'tɛːt/ *die;* ~: identity

Identitäts-: ~**krise** *die* identity crisis; ~**verlust** *der* loss of identity

Ideologe /ideo'loːgə/ *der;* ~**n**, ~**n** ideologue

Ideologie *die;* ~, ~**n** /-iːən/ ideology

ideologisch **1** *Adj.* ideological. **2** *adv.* ideologically; **jmdn.** ~ **schulen** give sb. ideological instruction

Idiom /i'di̯oːm/ *das;* ~**s**, ~**e** (Sprachw.) idiom

idiomatisch **1** *Adj.* idiomatic. **2** *adv.* idiomatically

Idiot /i'di̯oːt/ *der;* ~**en**, ~**en** (a) idiot; (b) (ugs. abwertend) fool; (stärker) idiot (coll.)

idioten-, **Idioten-:** ~**hang** *der*, ~**hügel** *der* (ugs. scherzh.) nursery slope; ~**sicher** *Adj.* (ugs. scherzh.) foolproof; ~**test** *der* (ugs.) *range of medical and psychological tests designed to test suitability to hold a driving licence*

Idiotie /idi̯o'tiː/ *die;* ~, ~**n** /-iːən/ (a) idiocy; (b) (ugs. abwertend: Dummheit) lunacy; madness

Idiotin *die;* ~, ~**nen** (a) idiot; (b) (ugs. abwertend) fool; (stärker) idiot

idiotisch **1** *Adj.* (a) severely subnormal; idiotic (as tech. term); (b) (ugs. abwertend: unsinnig) stupid; (stärker) idiotic. **2** *adv.* (a) idiotically; (b) (ugs. abwertend: unsinnig) stupidly; (stärker) idiotically

Idol /i'doːl/ *das;* ~**s**, ~**e** idol

Idyll /i'dʏl/ *das;* ~**s**, ~**e** idyll

Idylle *die;* ~, ~**n** idyll

idyllisch **1** *Adj.* idyllic. **2** *adv.* ~ **gelegen** in an idyllic spot

IG *Abk.* **Industriegewerkschaft**

Igel /'iːgl̩/ *der;* ~**s**, ~: hedgehog

igitt[igitt] /i'gɪt(i'gɪt)/ *Interj.* ugh

Iglu /'iːglu/ *der od. das;* ~**s**, ~**s** igloo

Ignorant *der;* ~**en**, ~**en** (abwertend) ignoramus

Ignoranz /ɪgno'rants/ *die;* ~ (abwertend) ignorance

ignorieren *tr. V.* ignore

ihm /iːm/ *Dat. von* **er**, **es** (bei Personen) him; (bei Dingen, Tieren) it; (bei männlichen Tieren) him; it; **gib es** ~: give it to him; **give him it**; (dem Tier) give it to it/him; ~ **geht es gut** he's well; **sie sah** ~ **ins Gesicht** she looked him in the face; **Freunde von** ~: friends of his

ihn /iːn/ *Akk. von* **er** (bei Personen) him; (bei Dingen, Tieren) it; (bei männlichen Tieren) him; it

ihnen /'iːnən/ *Dat. von* **sie**, *Pl.* them; **gib es** ~: give it to them; **give them it; Freunde von** ~: friends of theirs; *s. auch* **ihm**

Ihnen *Dat. von* **Sie** (Anrede) you; **ich habe es** ~ **gegeben** I gave it to you; I gave you it; **geht es** ~ **gut?** are you well?; **Freunde von** ~: friends of yours; *s. auch* **ihm**

ihr[1] /iːɐ̯/ *Dat. von* **sie**, *Sg.* (bei Personen) her; (bei Dingen, Tieren) it; (bei weiblichen Tieren) her; it; *s. auch* **ihm**

ihr[2] *Personalpron.;* 2. *Pers. Pl. Nom.* (Anrede an vertraute Personen) you; ~ **Lieben** (im Brief) dear all; *s. auch* (*Gen.*) **euer**, (*Dat., Akk.*) **euch**

ihr[3] *Possessivpron.* (a) (einer Person) her; **Ihre Majestät** Her Majesty; **das Buch dort, ist das** ~**[e]s?** that book there, is it hers?; is that book hers?; **das ist nicht mein Mann, sondern** ~**er** that is not my husband, but hers; **der/die/das** ~**e** hers; **die** ~**en** hers; **die Ihren** their family; **sie haben das Ihre** *od.* ~**e getan** they did their bit

Ihr *Possessivpron.* (Anrede) your; ~ **Hans Meier** (Briefschluss) yours, Hans Meier; **das Buch dort, ist das** ~**[e]s?** that book there, is it yours?; **welcher Mantel ist** ~**er?** which coat is yours?; **der/die/das** ~**e** yours; **die** ~**en** yours; *s. auch* **ihr**[3]

ihrer /'iːrɐ/ (a) *Gen. von* **sie**, *Sg.* (geh.) **wir gedachten** ~: we remembered her; (b) *Gen. von* **sie**, *Pl.* (geh.) **wir werden** ~ **gedenken** we will remember them; **es waren** ~ **zwölf** there were twelve of them

Ihrer *Gen. von* **Sie** (Anrede) (geh.) **wir werden** ~ **gedenken** we will remember you

ihrerseits /-zaits/ *Adv.* (a) *Sg.* (von ihrer Seite) on her part; (auf ihrer Seite) for her part; (b) *Pl.* (von ihrer Seite) on their part; (auf ihrer Seite) for their part

Ihrerseits *Adv.* (von Ihrer Seite) on your part; (auf Ihrer Seite) for your part

ihres·gleichen *indekl. Pron.* (a) *Sg.* people *pl.* like her; (abwertend) the likes of her; her sort *or* kind; **sie fühlt sich nur unter** ~ **wohl** she only feels at home among people like herself *or* her own kind; (b) *Pl.* people like them; (abwertend) the likes of them; their sort *or* kind; **sie sollten unter** ~ **bleiben** they should stay among their own kind

Ihresgleichen *indekl. Pron.* people *pl.* like you; (abwertend) the likes of you; your sort *or* kind; **Sie sollten besser unter** ~ **bleiben** you should stay among your own kind

ihret·halben (veralt.), **ihretwegen** *Adv.* (a) *Sg.* (wegen ihr) because of her; on her account; (für sie) on her behalf; (ihr zuliebe) for her sake; (b) *Pl.* (wegen ihnen) because of them; on their account; (für sie) on their behalf; (ihnen zuliebe) for their sake[s]

Ihrethalben (veralt.), **Ihretwegen** *Adv.* (wegen Ihnen) because of you; on your account; (für Sie) on your behalf; (Ihnen zuliebe) for your sake; *Pl.* for your sake[s]

ihret·willen *Adv. in* **um** ~ (Sg.) for her sake; (Pl.) for their sake[s]

Ihret·willen *Adv. in* **um** ~ (Sg.) for your sake; (Pl.) for your sake[s]

ihrige /'iːrɪgə/ *Possessivpron.* (geh. veralt.) (a) *Sg.* **der/die/das** ~: hers; (b) *Pl.* **der/die/das** ~: theirs

Ihrige *Possessivpron.* (Anrede) (geh. veralt.) **der/die/das** ~: yours

Ikone /i'koːnə/ *die;* ~, ~**n** icon

illegal /'ɪlegaːl/ **1** *Adj.* illegal. **2** *adv.* illegally

Illegalität /ɪlegali'tɛːt/ *die;* ~, ~**en** illegality

Illumination /ɪlumina'tsi̯oːn/ *die;* ~, ~**en** illumination

illuminieren *tr. V.* illuminate

Illuminierung *die;* ~, ~**en** illumination

Illusion /ɪlu'zi̯oːn/ *die;* ~, ~**en** illusion; **sich** (*Dat.*) ~**en machen** delude oneself

illusionär /ɪluzi̯o'nɛːɐ̯/ *Adj.* (geh.) illusory ‹conception, expectation, thing›

Illusionist *der;* ~**en**, ~**en** (a) (geh.) dreamer; (b) (Zauberkünstler) illusionist

illusionistisch *Adj.* (Kunstw.) illusionistic

illusions·los *Adj.* [sober and] realistic; ~ **sein** have no illusions

illusorisch /ɪlu'zoːrɪʃ/ *Adj.* illusory

Illustration /ɪlustra'tsi̯oːn/ *die;* ~, ~**en** illustration

Illustrator /ɪlus'traːtɔr/ *der;* ~**s**, ~**en** /-'toːrən/ illustrator

illustrieren *tr. V.* (auch fig.) illustrate; **eine illustrierte Zeitschrift** a magazine

Illustrierte *die; adj. Dekl.* magazine

Iltis /'ɪltɪs/ *der;* ~**ses**, ~**se** polecat; (Pelz) fitch

im /ɪm/ *Präp. + Art.* (a) = **in dem**; (b) (räumlich) in the; **im vierten Stock** on the fourth floor; **im Theater** at the theatre; **im Fernsehen** on television; **im Bett** in bed; (c) (zeitlich) **im Mai/Januar** in May/January; **im Jahre 1648**

in [the year] 1648; **im letzten Jahr** last year; **im Alter von 50 Jahren** at the age of 50; **(d)** (Verlauf) **etw. im Sitzen tun** do sth. [while] sitting down; **im Kommen sein** be coming

Image /'ɪmɪtʃ/ das; ~[s], ~s image

imaginär /imagi'nɛːɐ̯/ Adj. (geh., Math.) imaginary

Imagination /imagina'tsi̯oːn/ die; ~, ~en (geh.) imagination

Imam /i'maːm/ der; ~s, ~s od. ~e imam

Imbiss, *Imbiß/'ɪmbɪs/ der; **Imbisses, Imbisse** (a) snack; **(b)** ⇒ **Imbisslokal**

Imbiss-, *Imbiß- ~**bude** die (ugs.) ≈ hot-dog stall or stand; ~**lokal** das café; ~**stand** der ⇒ ~**bude**; ~**stube** die café

Imitation /imita'tsi̯oːn/ die; ~, ~en imitation

Imitator /imi'taːtɔr/ der; ~s, ~en /-ta'toːrən/ imitator; mimic; (im Kabarett usw.) impressionist

imitieren tr. V. imitate

Imker /'ɪmkɐ/ der; ~s, ~: ▶ 85 ◀ bee-keeper

Imkerei die; ~, ~en (a) o. Pl. bee-keeping no art.; **(b)** (Betrieb) apiary

immanent /ima'nɛnt/ Adj. (geh.) inherent; **einer Sache** (Dat.) ~ **sein** be inherent in sth.

Immatrikulation /ɪmatrikula'tsi̯oːn/ die; ~, ~en (a) (an der Hochschule) registration; **(b)** (schweiz.: eines Fahrzeugs) registration

immatrikulieren 1 tr. V. **(a)** (an der Hochschule) register; **(b)** (schweiz.) register ⟨vehicle⟩. **2** refl. V. (an der Hochschule) register

immens /ɪ'mɛns/ **1** Adj. immense. **2** adv. immensely

immer /'ɪmɐ/ Adv. **(a)** always; **wie ~:** as always; as usual; ~ **dieser Streit!** you're/they're etc. always arguing; ~ **diese Kinder!** these wretched children!; **schon ~:** always; ~ **und ewig** for ever; (jedesmal) always; **auf od. für ~ [und ewig]** for ever [and ever]; ~ **wieder** again and again; time and time again; ~ **wieder von vorne anfangen** keep on starting from the beginning again; ~, **wenn** every time that; whenever; ~ **während** perpetual; **(b)** ~ **dunkler/häufiger** darker and darker/ more and more often; ~ **mehr** more and more; **(c)** (ugs.: jeweils) **es durften ~ zwei auf einmal eintreten** we/ they were allowed in two at a time; **(d) wo/wer/wann/ wie [auch]** ~: wherever/whoever/whenever/however; **(e)** (verstärkend) ~ **noch, noch ~:** still; **(f)** (ugs.: bei Aufforderung) ~ **langsam!/mit der Ruhe!** take it easy!; ~ **der Nase nach!** keep following your nose!

immer-, Immer-: ~**fort** Adv. all the time; constantly; ~**grün** Adj. evergreen; ~**grün** das periwinkle; ~**hin** Adv. **(a)** (wenigstens) at any rate; anyhow; at least; **er ist zwar nicht reich, aber ~hin!** he's not rich, it's true, but still; **(b)** (trotz allem) nevertheless; all the same; **(c)** (schließlich) after all;*~**während** ⇒ **immer a;** ~**zu** Adv. (ugs.) the whole time; all the time; constantly

Immigrant /imi'grant/ der; ~en, ~en, **Immigrantin** die; ~, ~nen immigrant

Immigration /ɪmigra'tsi̯oːn/ die; ~, ~en immigration

immigrieren itr. V.; mit sein immigrate

Immission /ɪmɪ'si̯oːn/ die; ~, ~en (fachspr.) air pollution, noise, noxious substances, radiation, etc. constituting a private nuisance

Immissions·schutz der protection against the effects of air pollution, noise, noxious substances, radiation, etc.

Immobilie /ɪmo'biːli̯ə/ die; ~, ~n [piece of] property; **mit ~n handeln** deal in real estate sing.

Immobilien-: ~**geschäft** das real-estate business; ~**makler** der estate agent (Brit.); realtor (Amer.); ~**markt** der property market

Immortelle /ɪmɔr'tɛlə/ die; ~, ~n everlasting [flower]; immortelle

immun /ɪ'muːn/ **(a)** (Med., fig.) immune (**gegen** to); **(b)** (Rechtsspr.) ~ **sein** have or enjoy immunity

immunisieren tr. V. immunize (**gegen** against)

Immunisierung die; ~, ~en immunization (**gegen** against)

Immunität /ɪmuni'tɛːt/ die; ~, ~en **(a)** (Med.) immunity (**gegen** to); **(b)** (Rechtsspr.) immunity

Immun-: ~**schwäche** die (Med.) immunodeficiency; immune deficiency; **eine ~schwäche haben** be immunodeficient; ~**system** das (Med.) immune system

Imperativ /'ɪmperatiːf/ der; ~s, ~e (Sprachw.) imperative

imperativisch Adj. (Sprachw.) imperative

Imperator /ɪmpe'raːtɔr/ der; ~s, ~en /-'toːrən/ (hist.) **(a)** (Feldherr) imperator; **(b)** (Kaiser) emperor

Imperfekt /'ɪmpɛrfɛkt/ das; ~s, ~e (Sprachw.) imperfect [tense]

Imperialismus /ɪmperi̯a'lɪsmus/ der; ~: imperialism no art.

Imperialist der; ~en, ~en imperialist

imperialistisch Adj. imperialistic

Imperium /ɪm'peːri̯ʊm/ das; ~s, **Imperien** (auch fig.) empire

impertinent /ɪmpɛrti'nɛnt/ **1** Adj. impertinent; impudent. **2** adv. impertinently; impudently

Impertinenz /ɪmpɛrti'nɛnts/ die; ~, ~en impertinence; impudence

Impetus /'ɪmpetʊs/ der; ~: impetus; (Schwung) verve; zest

Impf·ausweis der vaccination certificate

impfen /'ɪmpfn̩/ tr. V. ▶ 329 ◀ vaccinate, inoculate; **sich ~ lassen** be vaccinated or inoculated

Impf-: ~**pass, *~paß** der vaccination certificate; ~**schutz** der protection given by vaccination; ~**stoff** der vaccine

Impfung die; ~, ~en ▶ 329 ◀ vaccination; inoculation

Impf·zeugnis das ⇒ ~**ausweis**

Implantat /ɪmplan'taːt/ das; ~[e]s, ~e (Med.) implant

implantieren tr. V. (Med.) implant; **jmdm. etw. implantieren** implant sth. in sb.

implementieren tr. V. (DV) implement

Implikation /ɪmplika'tsi̯oːn/ die; ~, ~en (geh.) implication

implizieren /ɪmpli'tsiːrən/ tr. V. (geh.) imply

implizit /ɪmpli'tsiːt/ (geh.) **1** Adj. implicit. **2** adv. implicitly

imponieren /ɪmpo'niːrən/ itr. V. impress; **jmdm. durch etw./mit etw.** ~: impress sb. by sth.

imponierend **1** Adj. impressive. **2** adv. impressively

Imponier·gehabe das (Verhaltensf.) display

Import /ɪm'pɔrt/ der; ~[e]s, ~e import; **den ~ erhöhen** increase imports; **eine Firma für ~ und Export** an import/export firm

Importeur /ɪmpɔr'tøːɐ̯/ der; ~s, ~e importer

importieren tr., itr. V. import

imposant /ɪmpo'zant/ **1** Adj. imposing; impressive ⟨achievement⟩. **2** adv. imposingly

impotent /'ɪmpotɛnt/ Adj. impotent

Impotenz /'ɪmpotɛnts/ die; ~: impotence

imprägnieren /ɪmprɛ'gniːrən/ tr. V. impregnate; (wasserdicht machen) waterproof

Imprägnierung die; ~, ~en ⇒ **imprägnieren a, b:** impregnation; waterproofing

Impresario /ɪmpre'zaːri̯o/ der; ~s, ~s od. **Impresari** (veralt.) impresario

Impressen ⇒ **Impressum**

Impression /ɪmprɛ'si̯oːn/ die; ~, ~en impression

Impressionismus der; ~: impressionism no art.

impressionistisch Adj. impressionistic

Impressum /ɪm'prɛsum/ das; ~s, **Impressen** imprint

Improvisation /ɪmproviza'tsi̯oːn/ die; ~, ~en improvisation

Improvisations·gabe die gift or talent for improvisation

improvisieren tr., itr. V. improvise; **über ein Thema** ~ (Musik) improvise on a theme

---

*alte Schreibung (vgl. Hinweise auf S. xvi–xvii)

Impuls /ɪm'pʊls/ *der;* ~**es**, ~**e** (**a**) (Anstoß) stimulus; einer Sache (*Dat.*) neue ~**e** geben give sth. fresh stimulus *sing. or* impetus *sing.*; (**b**) (innere Regung) impulse; einem ~ folgen act on [an] impulse; etw. aus einem ~ heraus tun do sth. on impulse; (**c**) (Physik) impulse; (**d**) (Elektrot.) pulse

impulsiv /ɪmpʊl'ziːf/ **1** *Adj.* impulsive. **2** *adv.* impulsively

Impulsivität /ɪmpʊlzivi'tɛːt/ *die;* ~: impulsiveness

imstande /ɪm'ʃtandə/ *Adv.* ~ sein, etw. zu tun (fähig sein) be able to do sth.; be capable of doing sth.; (die Möglichkeit haben) be in a position to do sth.; zu etw. ~ sein be capable of sth.; er ist ~ und schiebt mir die Schuld in die Schuhe he's [quite] capable of putting the blame on to me

in[1] /ɪn/ **1** *Präp. mit Dat.* (**a**) (räumlich, fig.) in; er hat ~ Tübingen studiert he studied at Tübingen; ~ Deutschland/der Schweiz in Germany/Switzerland; sind Sie schon mal ~ China gewesen? have you ever been to China?; ~ der Schule/Kirche at school/church; ~ der Schule/Kirche steht noch eine alte Orgel there's still an old organ in the school/church; ~ einer Partei in a party; (**b**) (zeitlich) in; ~ zwei Tagen/einer Woche in two days/a week; ~ diesem Sommer this summer; [gerade] ~ dem Moment, als er kam the [very] moment he came; ~ diesem Jahr/Monat this/that year/month; (**c**) (modal) in; ~ Farbe/Schwarzweiß in colour/black and white; ~ deutsch/englisch in German/English; ~ Mathematik/Englisch in mathematics/English; sich ~ jmdm. täuschen be wrong about sb.; (**d**) er hat es ~ sich (ugs.) he's got what it takes (coll.); der Schnaps/diese Übersetzung hat es ~ sich (ugs.) this schnapps packs a punch (coll.) /this translation is a tough one; (**e**) (Kaufmannsspr.) ~ etw. handeln deal in sth.; *s. auch* **im. 2** *Präp. mit Akk.* (**a**) (räumlich, fig.) into; ~ die Stadt/das Dorf into town/the village; ~ die Schweiz to Switzerland; ~ die Kirche/Schule gehen go to church/school; ~ eine Partei eintreten join a party; (**b**) (zeitlich) into; bis ~ den Herbst into the autumn; (**c**) (fig.) ~ die Millionen gehen run into millions; sich ~ jmdm. verlieben fall in love with sb.; ~ etw. einwilligen agree *or* consent to sth.; *s. auch* **ins**

in[2] *Adj.* (ugs.) ~ sein be in

in·adäquat 1 *Adj.* (geh.) inadequate. **2** *adv.* inadequately

in·akzeptabel *Adj.* (geh.) unacceptable

In·angriffnahme /-naːmə/ *die;* ~, ~**n** (Papierdt.) commencement; (eines Problems) tackling

In·anspruchnahme *die;* ~, ~**n** (**a**) (Papierdt.) use; bei häufiger ~ der Versicherung if frequent [insurance] claims are made; (**b**) (starke Belastung) demands *pl.;* die starke berufliche ~: the heavy demands made on him/her by his/her job; (**c**) (von Maschinen, Material) use; (von Einrichtungen) utilization

In·begriff *der* quintessence; der ~ des Spießers the epitome of the petit bourgeois; the quintessential petit bourgeois

inbegriffen *Adj.* included

In·besitznahme *die;* ~, ~**n** (Papierdt.) appropriation

In·betriebnahme *die;* ~, ~**n**, **In·betriebsetzung** /-zɛtsʊŋ/ *die;* ~, ~**en** (Papierdt.) (**a**) (von [öffentlichen] Einrichtungen) opening; (**b**) (von Maschinen) bringing into service; vor ~ der Maschine before bringing the machine into service; (**c**) (eines Kraftwerks) commissioning

In·brunst *die;* ~ (geh.) fervour; (der Liebe) ardour; jmdn. mit ~ lieben love sb. ardently

in·brünstig (geh.) **1** *Adj.* fervent; ardent ‹love›. **2** *adv.* fervently; ‹love› ardently

Inbus·schlüssel ⓦ /'ɪnbʊs-/ *der* (Technik) Allen key

in·dem *Konj.* (**a**) (während) while; (gerade als) as; (**b**) (dadurch, dass) ~ man etw. tut by doing sth.

Inder /'ɪndɐ/ *der;* ~**s**, ~, **Inderin** *die;* ~, ~**nen** ▶ 388 | Indian

in·des (veralt.), **in·dessen** *Adv.* (**a**) (inzwischen) meanwhile; in the mean time; (**b**) (jedoch) however

Index /'ɪndɛks/ *der;* ~ *od.* ~**es**, ~**e** *od.* Indizes /'ɪn ditsesːs/ index; der ~ (kath. Kirche) the Index

Index·schaltung *die* index gears *pl.*

Indianer /ɪn'diaːnɐ/ *der;* ~**s**, ~: ▶ 388 | [American] Indian

Indianer·häuptling *der* Indian chief

Indianerin *die;* ~, ~**nen** [American] Indian

Indianer·krapfen *der* (österr.) ⇒ **Mohrenkopf b**

indianisch *Adj.* ▶ 388 | Indian

Indien /'ɪndiən/ *(das);* ~**s** India

in·different (geh.) **1** *Adj.* indifferent. **2** *adv.* indifferently

indigniert /ɪndɪ'gniːɐt/ *Adj.* (geh) indignant

Indigo /'ɪndigo/ *der od. das;* ~**s**, ~**s** indigo

Indikation /ɪndika'tsioːn/ *die;* ~, ~**en** (**a**) (Med.) indication; (**b**) (Rechtsw.) [**medizinische/soziale/ethische**] ~: [medical/social/ethical] grounds *pl.* for abortion

Indikativ /'ɪndikatiːf/ *der;* ~**s**, ~**e** /-iːvə/ (Sprachw.) indicative [mood]

indikativisch *Adj.* (Sprachw.) indicative

Indikator /ɪndi'kaːtɔr/ *der;* ~**s**, ~**en** /-ka'to:rən/ indicator

Indio /'ɪndio/ *der;* ~**s**, ~**s** (*Central/South American*) Indian

in·direkt 1 *Adj.* indirect; ~**e** Rede (Sprachw.) indirect *or* reported speech. **2** *adv.* indirectly; einen Freistoß ~ ausführen (Sport) take an indirect free kick

indisch /'ɪndɪʃ/ *Adj.* ▶ 388 | Indian

in·diskret *Adj.* indiscreet

In·diskretion *die;* ~, ~**en** indiscretion

in·disponiert *Adj.* indisposed

Individualismus /ɪndividua'lɪsmʊs/ *der;* ~ individualism

Individualist *der;* ~**en**, ~**en** individualist

individualistisch *Adj.* individualistic

Individualität /ɪndividuali'tɛːt/ *die;* ~ (geh.) individuality

Individual·verkehr *der* private transport

individuell /ɪndivi'duɛl/ **1** *Adj.* (**a**) individual; (**b**) *nicht präd.* (privat) private ‹property, vehicle, etc.›. **2** *adv.* individually; etw. ~ gestalten give sth. one's own personal touch

Individuum /ɪndi'viːduʊm/ *das;* ~**s**, **Individuen** (auch fachspr.) individual

Indiz /ɪn'diːts/ *das;* ~**es**, ~**ien** (**a**) (Rechtsw.) piece of circumstantial evidence; ~**ien** circumstantial evidence *sing.;* (**b**) (geh.: Anzeichen) sign (**für** of)

Indizien-: ~**beweis** *der* (Rechtsw.) circumstantial evidence *no pl., no art.;* ~**prozess**, ***~**prozeß** *der* (Rechtsw.) trial based on circumstantial evidence

indizieren /ɪndi'tsiːrən/ *tr. V.* (**a**) (Med.) indicate; (**b**) (kath. Kirche) ein Buch ~: place a book on the Index

indo-, Indo- /ɪndo-/: ~**china** (*das*) Indo-China; ~**europäer** *Pl.* ⇒ ~**germanen**; ~**europäisch** *Adj.* ⇒ ~**germanisch**; ~**germanen** *Pl.* Indo-Europeans; ~**germanisch** *Adj.* Indo-European; Indo-Germanic

Indoktrination /ɪndɔktrina'tsioːn/ *die;* ~, ~**en** (geh.) indoctrination

indoktrinieren *tr. V.* (geh.) indoctrinate

Indonesien /ɪndo'neːziən/ *(das);* ~**s** Indonesia

Indonesier *der;* ~**s**, ~, **Indonesierin** *die;* ~, ~**nen** ▶ 388 | Indonesian

indonesisch *Adj.* ▶ 388 | Indonesian

Induktion /ɪndʊk'tsioːn/ *die;* ~, ~**en** (fachspr.) induction

Induktions-: ~**spule** *die* (Elektrot.) induction coil; ~**strom** *der* (Elektrot.) induced current

industrialisieren /ɪndʊstriali'ziːrən/ *tr. V.* industrialize

Industrialisierung *die;* ~: industrialization

Industrie /ɪndʊs'triː/ *die;* ~, ~**n** industry

Industrie- industrial ‹plant, product, area, etc.›; ‹branch› of industry

industriell /ɪndʊstri'ɛl/ **1** *Adj.; nicht präd.* industrial; die ~**e** Revolution (hist.) the Industrial Revolution. **2** *adv.* industrially

Industrielle der/die; adj. Dekl. industrialist
Industrie- und Handels·kammer die Chamber of Industry and Commerce
induzieren /ɪndu'tsiːrən/ tr. V. (fachspr.) induce
in·einander Adv. ~ fließen flow together; **die Farben fließen** ~: the colours run into each other or one another; **zwei Dinge** ~ **fügen** fit two things into each or one another; ~ **passen/sich** ~ **fügen** fit into each other or one another; ~ **greifen** mesh or engage [with each other or one another]; mesh together (lit. or fig.); **zwei Dinge** ~ **schieben** telescope two things; **sich** ~ **schieben** telescope; ~ **verliebt sein** be in love with each other or one another; ~ **verschlungene Ornamente** intertwined decorations
***ineinander|fließen** usw.: ⇨ **ineinander**
infam /ɪn'faːm/ (geh.) **1** Adj. disgraceful. **2** adv. disgracefully
Infamie /ɪnfa'miː/ die; ~, ~n (geh.) (a) o. Pl. disgracefulness; (b) (Äußerung) disgraceful remark; (Handlung) disgraceful action
Infanterie /'ɪnfant(ə)riː/ die; ~, ~n (Milit.) infantry
Infanterist der; ~en, ~en (Milit.) infantryman
infantil /ɪnfan'tiːl/ (Psych., Med., sonst abwertend) **1** Adj. infantile. **2** adv. in an infantile way
Infarkt /ɪn'farkt/ der; ~[e]s, ~e ▶ 329] (Med.) infarct; infarction
Infekt /ɪn'fɛkt/ der; ~[e]s, ~e (Med.) infection
Infektion /ɪnfɛk'tsioːn/ die; ~, ~en (Med.) infection
Infektions-: ~**gefahr** die (Med.) danger or risk of infection; ~**herd** der (Med.) seat of the/an infection; ~**krankheit** die (Med.) infectious disease
infektiös /ɪnfɛk'tsioːs/ Adj. (Med.) infectious
infernalisch /ɪnfɛr'naːlɪʃ/ (geh.) **1** Adj. infernal. **2** adv. infernally; ~ **stinken** stink dreadfully
Inferno /ɪn'fɛrno/ das; ~s (geh.) inferno
Infiltration /ɪnfɪltra'tsioːn/ die; ~, ~en infiltration
infiltrieren tr. V. infiltrate
in·finit Adj. (Sprachw.) infinite
Infinitesimal·rechnung /ɪnfinitezi'maːl-/ die (Math.) infinitesimal calculus
Infinitiv /'ɪnfinitiːf/ der; ~s, ~e /-tiːvə/ (Sprachw.) infinitive
infizieren /ɪnfi'tsiːrən/ **1** tr. V. (auch fig.) infect. **2** refl. V. become or get infected; **sich bei jmdm.** ~: be infected by sb.; catch an infection from sb.
in flagranti /ɪn fla'granti/ Adv. (geh.) in flagrante [delicto]
Inflation /ɪnfla'tsioːn/ die; ~, ~en (Wirtsch.) inflation; (Zeit der ~) period of inflation; **eine schleichende** ~: creeping inflation
inflationär /ɪnflatsio'nɛːɐ̯/ Adj. inflationary
Info[1] /'ɪnfo/ das; ~s, ~s (ugs.) handout
Info[2] die; ~, ~s (ugs.) info no pl., no indef. art. (coll.); **eine** ~: a piece of info; **weitere** ~s more info
in·folge 1 Präp. + Gen. as a result of; owing to. **2** Adv. ~ **von etw.** (Dat.) as a result of or owing to sth.
infolge·dessen Adv. consequently; as a result of this
Informant /ɪnfɔr'mant/ der; ~en, ~en informant
Informatik /ɪnfɔr'maːtɪk/ die; ~: computer science no art.
Informatiker der; ~s, ~: computer scientist
Information /ɪnfɔrma'tsioːn/ die; ~, ~en (a) information no pl., no indef. art. (über + Akk. about, on); **eine** ~: [a piece of] information; **zu Ihrer** ~: for your information; **nach neuesten** ~en according to the latest information; **nähere** ~en **erhalten Sie** ...: you can obtain more information ...; (b) (Büro) information bureau; (Stand) information desk
Informations-: ~**aus·tausch** der exchange of information; ~**büro** das information bureau or office; ~**material** das informational literature; ~**quelle** die source of information; ~**stand** der (a) information

stand; (b) (Grad der Informiertheit) **bei meinem jetzigen** ~**stand** with the information I have at present
informativ /ɪnfɔrma'tiːf/ **1** Adj. informative. **2** adv. informatively
in·formell Adj. informal
informieren 1 tr. V. inform (über + Akk. about); **falsch/einseitig informiert sein** be misinformed/have biased information; **aus gut informierten Kreisen** from well-informed circles. **2** refl. V. obtain information; **sich über etw.** (Akk.) ~: inform oneself or find out about sth.
infrage in etw. ~ **stellen** call sth. into question; question sth.; ~ **kommen** be possible; **für ein Stipendium kommen nur gute Schüler** ~: only good pupils can be considered for a grant; **dieses Kleid kommt für mich nicht** ~: I couldn't possibly wear this dress; **das kommt nicht** ~ (ugs.) that is out of the question
infra·rot /'ɪnfra-/ Adj. (Physik) infra-red
Infra·rot das; ~s (Physik) infra-red radiation
Infra·struktur die infrastructure
Infusion /ɪnfu'zioːn/ die; ~, ~en (Med.) infusion
Ing. Abk. **Ingenieur**
Ingenieur /ɪnʒe'nioːɐ̯/ der; ~s, ~e ▶ 85] [qualified] engineer
Ingenieur·büro das firm of consulting engineers
Ingenieurin die; ~, ~nen ▶ 85] [qualified] engineer
Ingredienz /ɪngre'diɛnts/ die; ~, ~en; meist Pl. ingredient
In·grimm der (geh.) inward rage or wrath
Ingwer /'ɪŋvɐ/ der; ~s, ~: ginger
Inhaber /'ɪnhaːbɐ/ der; ~s, ~, **Inhaberin** die; ~, ~nen (a) holder; (b) (Besitzer) owner
inhaftieren /ɪnhaf'tiːrən/ tr. V. take into custody; detain
Inhaftierte der/die; adj. Dekl. prisoner
Inhaftierung die; ~, ~en detention
Inhalation /ɪnhala'tsioːn/ die; ~, ~en (Med.) inhalation
inhalieren tr. V. inhale
In·halt der; ~[e]s, ~e (a) contents pl.; (b) (das Dargestellte/geistiger Gehalt) content; **ein Buch politischen** ~s a political book; (c) (Flächen~) area; (Raum~) volume
inhaltlich 1 Adj. **die** ~**e Struktur des Dramas** the plot-structure of the drama; **an** ~**en Gesichtspunkten gemessen** from the point of view of content. **2** adv. ~ **ist der Aufsatz gut** the essay is good as regards content; ~ **übereinstimmen** be the same in content
inhalts-, Inhalts-: ~**angabe** die summary [of contents]; synopsis; (eines Films, Dramas) [plot] summary; synopsis; ~**los** Adj. lacking in content postpos.; meaningless ‹word, phrase›; empty ‹life›; ~**verzeichnis** das table of contents; (auf einem Paket) list of contents; (als Überschrift) [table of] contents
in·human Adj. (a) inhuman; (b) (rücksichtslos) inhumane
In·humanität die; ~: inhumanity
Initiale die; ~, ~n initial [letter]
Initial·zündung die detonation
initiativ /initsia'tiːf/ Adj. ~ **werden** take the initiative
Initiative die; ~, ~n (a) initiative; **die** ~ **ergreifen** take the initiative; **auf jmds.** ~ (Akk.) [hin] on sb.'s initiative; ~ **entwickeln/entfalten** develop initiative; **nur der** ~ (Dat.) **der Opposition ist es zu verdanken, daß** ...: it is only thanks to the Opposition that ...; (b) ⇒ **Bürgerinitiative**
Initiator /ini'tsiaːtɔr/ der; ~s, ~en, **Initiatorin** die; ~, ~nen initiator; (einer Organisation) founder
initiieren /initsi'iːrən/ tr. V. (geh.) initiate
Injektion /ɪnjɛk'tsioːn/ die; ~, ~en (Med.) injection
Injektions-: ~**nadel** die hypodermic needle; ~**spritze** die hypodermic syringe
injizieren /ɪnji'tsiːrən/ tr. V. (Med.) inject; **jmdm. etw.** ~: inject sb. with sth.
Inkarnation /ɪnkarna'tsioːn/ die; ~, ~en incarnation
inkl. Abk. **inklusive** incl.

---

*alte Schreibung (vgl. Hinweise auf S. xvi–xvii)

inklusive /ɪnklu'ziːvə/ **1** *Präp.* + *Gen.* (bes. Kaufmannsspr.) inclusive of; including; **der Preis versteht sich ~ der Verpackung** the price includes *or* is inclusive of packing; **wir bezahlten ~ Frühstück 40 DM** we paid 40 DM, breakfast included *or* including breakfast. **2** *Adv.* inclusive

inkognito /ɪn'kɔgnito/ *Adv.* (geh.) incognito

Inkognito *das;* ~s, ~s incognito

in·kompetent *Adj.* incompetent

In·kompetenz *die* incompetence

in·konsequent 1 *Adj.* inconsistent. **2** *adv.* inconsistently

In·konsequenz *die* inconsistency

in·korrekt 1 *Adj.* incorrect. **2** *adv.* incorrectly

Inkorrektheit *die;* ~, ~en (a) *o. Pl.* incorrectness; (b) (Fehler) mistake

In·kraft·treten *das;* ~s: **mit dem ~ des Gesetzes** when the law comes/came into effect *or* force

Inkubation /ɪnkuba'tsi̯oːn/ *die;* ~, ~en (Med.) incubation

Inkubations·zeit *die* (Med.) incubation period

in·kulant *Adj.* (Kaufmannsspr.) unaccommodating; disobliging

Inkulanz /'ɪnkulants/ *die;* ~ (Kaufmannsspr.) disobligingness

In·land *das;* ~[e]s (a) **im ~:** at home; **im ~ hergestellte Waren, Produktionen des ~es** home-produced goods; **im In- und Ausland** at home and abroad

Inländer /'ɪnlɛndɐ/ *der;* ~s, ~, **Inländerin** *die;* ~, ~nen native citizen

inländisch *Adj.* domestic; internal, domestic ‹trade, traffic›; home, domestic ‹market›; home-produced, domestic ‹goods›

Inlands-: ~**markt** *der* home *or* domestic market; ~**porto** *das* inland postage

Inlett /'ɪnlɛt/ *das;* ~[e]s, ~e *od.* ~s (Stoff) tick; ticking; (Hülle) tick

Inliner /'ɪnlaɪnɐ/ *der;* ~s, ~: Rollerblade (P); in-liner

Inlineskate /'ɪnlaɪnskeːt/ *der;* ~s, ~s Rollerblade (P); in-line skate

Inlineskater /'ɪnlaɪnskeːtɐ/ *der;* ~s, ~: rollerblader; in-line skater

in·mitten 1 *Präp.* + *Gen.* (geh.) in the midst of; surrounded by. **2** *Adv.* ~ **von** in the midst of; surrounded by

inne- /'ɪnə-/: ~|**haben** *unr. tr. V.* hold, occupy ‹position›; hold ‹office›; **die Führung/Leitung ~haben** be in charge; ~|**halten** *unr. itr. V.* pause; **in** *od.* **mit etw.** ~**halten** stop sth. for a moment

innen /'ɪnən/ *Adv.* (a) inside; (auf/an der Innenseite) on the inside; **etw. von ~ nach außen kehren** turn sth. inside out; **die Leitung verlief von ~ nach außen** the cable ran from the inside to the outside; ~ **und außen** inside and out[side]; **nach ~ aufgehen** open inwards; **etw. von ~ besichtigen/ansehen** look round/look at the inside of sth.; **von ~ heraus** from within; (b) (österr.: drinnen) indoors (im Haus)

innen-, Innen-: ~**arbeiten** *Pl.* interior work *sing.*; ~**architekt** *der* interior designer; ~**aufnahme** *die* (Fot.) indoor photo[graph]; (Film) indoor *or* interior shot; ~**ausstattung** *die;* [eine] ~ausstattung decoration and furnishings; (eines Autos) [an] interior trim; ~**bahn** *die* (Sport) inside lane; ~**dienst** *der:* ~dienst haben be working in the office; ‹policeman› be on station duty; **im** ~**dienst tätig sein** work in the office; ‹policeman› do station duty; ~**einrichtung** *die* furnishings *pl.;* ~**hof** *der* inner courtyard; ~**lager** *das* (Jargon) ⇒ Tretlager; ~**leben** *das; o. Pl.* (a) [inner] thoughts and feelings *pl.;* (b) (oft scherzh.: Ausstattung) inside; (eines Hauses) interior; (eines Autos, Fernsehers usw.) inner workings *pl.;* ~**minister** *der* Minister of the Interior; ≈ Home Secretary (Brit.); ≈ Secretary of the Interior (Amer.); ~**ministerium** *das* Ministry of the Interior; ≈ Home Office (Brit.); ≈ Department of the Interior (Amer.); ~**politik** *die* domestic politics *sing.;* (bestimmte) domestic policy/policies *pl.;* ~**politiker** *der* politician concerned with home affairs;

~**politisch 1** *Adj.* ‹question› relating to domestic policy; ‹mistake› in domestic policy; ‹experience› in home affairs; **eine** ~**politische Debatte** a debate on domestic policy; *s. auch* **außenpolitisch 1; 2** *adv.* as regards domestic policy; ~**politisch betrachtet** from the point of view of domestic policy; ~**raum** *der* (a) inner room; (b) *o. Pl.* (Platz im Innern) room inside; **ein Auto/Haus mit großem** ~**raum** a car/house with a spacious interior; ~**seite** *die* inside; ~**spiegel** *der* rear-view mirror; ~**stadt** *die* town centre; downtown (Amer.); (einer Großstadt) city centre; ~**tasche** *die* inside pocket; ~**temperatur** *die* inside temperature; ~**wand** *die* interior wall; ~**winkel** *der* interior angle

inner... /'ɪnɐ.../ *Adj.; nicht präd.* (a) inner; internal ‹organs, structure, stability, etc.›; inside ‹pocket, lane›; (b) (inländisch) internal

inner-: ~**betrieblich 1** *Adj.* internal ‹problem, question, regulation, agreement›; **2** *adv.* internally; ~**deutsch** *Adj.* (hist.) ‹trade, relations, border› between the two German states

Innere /'ɪnərə/ *das; adj. Dekl.; o. Pl.* (a) inside; (eines Gebäudes, Wagens, Schiffes) interior; inside; (eines Landes) interior; **der Minister des Innern** the Minister of the Interior; (b) (Empfindung) inner being; **in seinem tiefsten** ~**n** in his heart of hearts; deep [down] inside; (c) (Kern) heart

Innereien /ɪnə'raɪən/ *Pl.* entrails; (Kochk.) offal *sing.*

inner·halb 1 *Präp.* + *Gen.* (a) (räumlich; fig.) within, inside; ~ **der Familie/Partei** (fig.) within the family/party; (b) (zeitlich) within; ~ **einer Woche** within a week; ~ **der Arbeitszeit** during *or* in working hours. **2** *Adv.* (a) (räumlich; fig.) ~ **von** within; inside; (b) (zeitlich) ~ **von** within

innerlich 1 *Adj.* (a) inner; (von außen nicht erkennbar) inward; (b) (im Körper) internal ‹use, effect›. **2** *adv.* (a) inwardly; ~ **lachen** laugh inwardly *or* to oneself; (b) (im Körper) internally

inner-: ~**parteilich** *Adj.* ~**parteiliche Auseinandersetzungen** internal [party] disputes; disputes within the party; ~**parteiliche Diskussionen** discussions within the party; ~**staatlich** *Adj.* internal; domestic

innerst... *Adj.; nicht präd.* inmost; innermost; **ihre** ~**e Überzeugung** her deepest *or* most profound conviction

Innerste *das; adj. Dekl.; o. Pl.* innermost being; **in meinem** ~**n** in my heart of hearts; deep [down] inside

innert /'ɪnɐt/ *Präp.* + *Gen. od. Dat.* (schweiz., österr.) within

inne|wohnen *itr. V.* (geh.) **etw. wohnt jmdm./einer Sache** ~: sb./sth. possesses sth.

innig /'ɪnɪç/ **1** *Adj.* (a) heartfelt, deep ‹affection, sympathy›; heartfelt, fervent ‹wish›; intimate ‹relation, relationship, friendship›; (b) (Chemie) intimate. **2** *adv.* ‹hope› fervently; ‹love› deeply, with all one's heart

Innigkeit *die;* ~: depth; (einer Beziehung) intimacy

inniglich /'ɪnɪklɪç/ *Adj., adv.* (geh.) ⇒ **innig 1 a, 2**

Innovation /ɪnova'tsi̯oːn/ *die;* ~, ~en innovation

innovativ *Adj.* innovative

Innung /'ɪnʊŋ/ *die;* ~, ~en [trade] guild; **die ganze** ~ **blamieren** (ugs. scherzh.) let the side down

in·offiziell 1 *Adj.* unofficial. **2** *adv.* unofficially

in petto /ɪn 'pɛto/ *in etw.* ~ ~ **haben** (ugs.) have sth. up one's sleeve

in puncto /ɪn 'pʊŋkto/ ~ ~ **Pünktlichkeit** *usw.* as regards punctuality *etc.;* where punctuality *etc.* is concerned

Input /'ɪnpʊt/ *der od. das;* ~s, ~s (fachspr.) input

Inquisition /ɪnkvizi'tsi̯oːn/ *die;* ~ (hist.) Inquisition

Inquisitor /ɪnkvi'ziːtɔr/ *der;* ~s, ~en /-zi'toːrən/ (hist.) inquisitor

ins /ɪns/ *Präp.* + *Art.* (a) = **in das;** (b) ~ **Bett/Theater gehen** go to bed/the theatre; **er kam** ~ **Stottern** he began to stutter

Insasse /'ɪnzasə/ *der;* ~n, ~n, **Insassin** *die;* ~, ~nen (a) (Fahrgast) passenger; **die** ~**n eines Autos/ Flugzeuges** the passengers in a car/an aircraft; (b) (Bewohner) inmate

ins·besond[e]re *Adv.* (Papierdt.) ⇒ **besonders 1**

In·schrift *die* inscription

Insekt /ɪn'zɛkt/ *das;* ~s, ~en insect; ~en fressend insectivorous; insect-eating

insekten-, Insekten-: *~fressend ⇒ **Insekt;** ~plage *die* plague of insects; ~stich *der* (einer Wespe, Biene) insect sting; (einer Mücke) insect bite

Insektizid /ɪnzɛkti'tsi:t/ *das;* ~s, ~e (fachspr.) insecticide

Insel /'ɪnzl̩/ *die;* ~, ~n (auch fig.) island; **die ~ Helgoland** the island of Heligoland; **die ~ Man** the Isle of Man

Insel-: ~gruppe *die* group of islands ~volk *das* island race *or* people; ~welt *die* islands *pl.*

Inserat /ɪnze'ra:t/ *das;* ~[e]s, ~e advertisement (in a newspaper); **sich auf ein ~ melden** reply to an advertisement; **ein ~ aufgeben** put in an advertisement

Inserent /ɪnze'rɛnt/ *der;* ~en, ~en advertiser

inserieren *itr., tr. V.* advertise; **[wegen etw.] in einer Zeitung ~**: advertise [sth.] in a newspaper

ins·geheim *Adv.* secretly

ins·gesamt *Adv.* (a) in all; altogether; **es waren ~ 500** there were 500 in all *or* altogether; (b) (alles in allem) all in all; **~ gesehen** all in all

Insider /'ɪnsaɪdɐ/ *der;* ~s, ~: insider

Insigne /ɪn'zɪɡnə/ *das;* ~s, **Insignien;** *meist Pl.* insignia

insistieren /ɪnzɪs'ti:rən/ *itr. V.* (geh.) insist (**auf** + *Dat.* on)

insofern **1** *Adv.* /ɪn'zo:fɐrn/ (in dieser Hinsicht) in this respect; to this extent; **~, als** in so far as. **2** *Konj.* /ɪnzo'fɛrn/ (falls) provided [that]; so *or* as long as

insoweit /ɪn'zo:vaɪt, ɪnzo'vaɪt/ *Adv./Konj.* ⇒ **insofern**

in spe /ɪn 'spe:/ **mein Schwiegersohn ~ ~**: my future son-in-law

Inspekteur /ɪnspɛk'tø:ɐ/ *der;* ~s, ~e (Milit.) Chief of Staff

Inspektion /ɪnspɛk'tsio:n/ *die;* ~, ~en (a) inspection; (b) (Kfz-W.) service; **das Auto zur ~ bringen** take the car in for a service

Inspektor /ɪns'pɛktor/ *der;* ~s, ~en /-'to:rən/, **Inspektorin** *die;* ~, ~nen inspector; (als Titel) Inspector

Inspiration /ɪnspira'tsio:n/ *die;* ~, ~en inspiration

inspirieren *tr. V.* inspire; **das inspirierte ihn zu einem Roman** it inspired him to write a novel; **sich von jmdm./etw. ~ lassen** be inspired by sb./sth.

Inspizient /ɪnspi'tsiɛnt/ *der;* ~en, ~en (Theater) stage-manager; (Ferns., Rundf.) studio manager

inspizieren *tr. V.* inspect

Inspizierung *die;* ~, ~en inspection

in·stabil *Adj.* (geh., fachspr.) unstable

Installateur /ɪnstala'tø:ɐ/ *der;* ~s, ~e, **Installateurin** *die;* ~, ~nen ▶ 85 | (a) (Klempner) plumber; (b) (Gas~) [gas-]fitter; (c) (Heizungs~) heating engineer; (d) (Elektro~) electrician

Installation /ɪnstala'tsio:n/ *die;* ~, ~en (a) *o. Pl.* installation; (b) (Anlage) installation; ~en (installierte Rohre) plumbing *no pl.*

installieren 1 *tr. V.* (a) install; (b) (einrichten) set up. **2** *refl. V.* settle in

in·stand *Adv.* **etw. ist gut/schlecht ~**: sth. is in good/poor condition; **etw. ~ halten** keep sth. in good condition *or* repair; (funktionsfähig halten) keep sth. in working order; **etw. ~ setzen/bringen** repair sth.; (funktionsfähig machen) get sth. into working order; **ein Haus ~ besetzen** occupy and renovate a house (*illegally to prove that its demolition is not desirable*)

instand-, Instand-: *~besetzen ⇒ **instand;** ~besetzung *die* (illegal) occupation and renovation; ~haltung *die* maintenance; upkeep

in·ständig 1 *Adj.* urgent. **2** *adv.* urgently; **~ um etw. bitten** beg for sth.; **jmdn. ~ bitten, etw. zu tun** beg *or* implore *or* beseech sb. to do sth.; **~ auf etw.** (*Akk.*) **hoffen** hope fervently for sth.

---

*alte Schreibung (vgl. Hinweise auf S. xvi–xvii)

Instandsetzung *die;* ~, ~en (Papierdt.) repair

Instanz /ɪn'stants/ *die;* ~, ~en (a) authority; **durch alle ~en gehen** *od.* **alle ~en durchlaufen** go *or* pass through all the official channels; (b) (Rechtsw.) **[die] erste/zweite/letzte ~**: the court of first instance *or* of original jurisdiction/the appeal court/the court of final appeal; **durch alle ~en gehen** go through all the courts

Instinkt /ɪn'stɪŋkt/ *der;* ~[e]s, ~e instinct; **einen ~ für etw. haben** have a flair for sth.; **seinem ~ folgen** follow one's instincts *pl.*

Instinkt·handlung *die* instinctive action

instinktiv /ɪnstɪŋk'ti:f/ **1** *Adj.* instinctive. **2** *adv.* instinctively

instinkt·los 1 *Adj.* insensitive. **2** *adv.* insensitively

Instinktlosigkeit *die;* ~, ~en insensitivity

Institut /ɪnsti'tu:t/ *das;* ~[e]s, ~e institute

Institution /ɪnstitu'tsio:n/ *die;* ~, ~en (auch fig.) institution

institutionalisieren /ɪnstitutsionali'zi:rən/ *tr. V.* (geh.) institutionalize

institutionell /ɪnstitutsio'nɛl/ *Adj.* institutional

instruieren /ɪnstru'i:rən/ *tr. V.* (a) inform; (b) (anweisen) instruct

Instruktion /ɪnstrʊk'tsio:n/ *die;* ~, ~en instruction

instruktiv /ɪnstrʊk'ti:f/ **1** *Adj.* instructive; informative. **2** *adv.* instructively; informatively

Instrument /ɪnstru'mɛnt/ *das;* ~[e]s, ~e instrument

instrumental /ɪnstrumɛn'ta:l/ (Musik) **1** *Adj.* instrumental. **2** *adv.* instrumentally

Instrumental- instrumental ‹*music, accompaniment, etc.*›

Instrumentarium /ɪnstrumɛn'ta:riʊm/ *das;* ~s, **Instrumentarien** (a) (Technik) equipment; instruments *pl.;* (b) (Musik) instruments *pl.;* (c) (geh.: Gesamtheit der Mittel) apparatus

Instrumenten-: ~brett *das* instrument panel; ~flug *der* (Flugw.) flying on instruments; instrument-flying

instrumentieren *tr. V.* (Musik) instrument

Insuffizienz /'ɪnzʊfitsiɛnts:/ *die;* ~, ~en (Med.) insufficiency

Insulin /ɪnzu'li:n/ *das;* ~s insulin

inszenieren /ɪnstse'ni:rən/ *tr. V.* (a) stage, put on ‹*play, opera*›; (Regie führen bei) direct; (Ferns.) direct; produce; (b) (oft abwertend) (einfädeln) engineer; (organisieren) stage

Inszenierung *die;* ~, ~en (a) staging; (Regie) direction; (b) (Produktion) production; (c) (oft abwertend) (das Einfädeln) engineering; (das Organisieren) staging

intakt /ɪn'takt/ *Adj.* (a) intact; (b) (funktionsfähig) in [proper] working order *postpos.*

Intarsie /ɪn'tarziə/ *die;* ~, ~n intarsia

integer /ɪn'te:ɡɐ/ *Adj.* **eine integre Persönlichkeit** a person of integrity; **~ sein** be a person of integrity

integral /ɪnte'ɡra:l/ *Adj.* (geh.) integral

Integral *das;* ~s, ~s (Math.) integral

Integral-: ~helm *der* integral helmet; ~rechnung *die* (a) integral calculus; (b) (einzelne Rechnung) problem in integral calculus

Integration /ɪnteɡra'tsio:n/ *die;* ~, ~en (auch Math.) integration

integrieren *tr. V.* (auch Math.) integrate

Integrierung *die;* ~, ~en (auch Math.) integration

Integrität /ɪnteɡri'tɛ:t/ *die;* ~: integrity

Intellekt /ɪntɛ'lɛkt/ *der;* ~[e]s intellect

intellektuell /ɪntɛlɛk'tuɛl/ *Adj.* intellectual

Intellektuelle *der/die; adj. Dekl.* intellectual

intelligent /ɪntɛli'ɡɛnt/ **1** *Adj.* intelligent. **2** *adv.* intelligently

Intelligenz /ɪntɛli'ɡɛnts/ *die;* ~ (a) intelligence; (b) (Gesamtheit der Intellektuellen) intelligentsia

Intelligenz-: ~bestie *die* (ugs.) egghead (coll.); brain (coll.); ~quotient *der* intelligence quotient; ~test *der* intelligence test

Intendant /ɪntɛnˈdant/ *der;* ∼**en,** ∼**en** manager and artistic director; (Fernseh∼, Rundfunk∼) director-general
Intendanz /ɪntɛnˈdants/ *die;* ∼, ∼**en (a)** (Amt) management and artistic directorship; (Ferns., Rundf.) director-generalship; **(b)** (Büro) office of the manager and artistic director; (Ferns., Rundf.) director-general's office
intendieren /ɪntɛnˈdiːrən/ *tr. V.* (geh.) intend
Intensität /ɪntɛnziˈtɛːt/ *die;* ∼: intensity
intensiv /ɪntɛnˈziːf/ **1** *Adj.* intensive ‹*research, efforts, cultivation, etc.*›; (kräftig) intense; strong ‹*smell, taste*›. **2** *adv.* intensively; ‹*think*› hard; (kräftig) intensely; ‹*smell, taste*› strongly; **sich** ∼ **mit etw. beschäftigen** be deeply involved with sth.
-intensiv ‹*time, labour, etc.*›-intensive
intensivieren *tr. V.* intensify
Intensivierung *die;* ∼, ∼**en** intensification
Intensiv-: ∼**kurs** *der* intensive course; ∼**station** *die* intensive-care unit
Intention /ɪntɛnˈtsi̯oːn/ *die;* ∼, ∼**en** (geh.) intention
interaktiv *Adj.* interactive
Interaktivität *die;* ∼: interactivity
Inter·city *der;* ∼**s,** ∼**s** inter-city [train]
inter·disziplinär 1 *Adj.* interdisciplinary. **2** *adv.* ∼ **forschen** do interdisciplinary research
interessant /ɪntərɛˈsant/ **1** *Adj.* interesting; **sich** ∼ **machen** attract attention to oneself. **2** *adv.* ∼ **schreiben** write in an interesting way
interessanterweise *Adv.* interestingly enough
Interesse /ɪntəˈrɛsə/ *das;* ∼**s,** ∼**n** interest; **[großes]** ∼ **an jmdm./etw. haben** be [very] interested in sb./sth.; **für jmdn./etw. haben/zeigen** have/show an interest in sb./sth.; **gemeinsame** ∼**n haben** have interests in common; **im eigenen** ∼ **handeln** act in one's own interest; **jmds.** ∼**n wahrnehmen** look after *or* represent sb.'s interests; **in jmds.** ∼ (*Dat.*) **liegen** be in sb.'s interest
interesse-, Interesse-: ∼**halber** /∼halbɐ/ *Adv.* out of interest; ∼**los 1** *Adj.* uninterested; **2** *adv.* without interest; uninterestedly; ∼**losigkeit** *die;* ∼: lack of interest
Interessen-: ∼**ausgleich** *der* reconciliation of [conflicting] interests; ∼**gegensatz** *der* ⇒ ∼**konflikt;** ∼**gruppe** *die* interest group; ∼**konflikt** *der* conflict of interests; ∼**lage** *die* interests *pl.*
Interessent /ɪntərɛˈsɛnt/ *der;* ∼**en,** ∼**en, Interessentin** *die;* ∼, ∼**nen (a)** interested person; **wenn es genug Interessenten gibt** if enough people are interested; **(b)** (möglicher Käufer) potential buyer
Interessen·vertretung *die* **(a)** representation; **(b)** (Gremium, Organisation) representative body
interessieren 1 *refl. V.* **sich für jmdn./etw.** ∼: be interested in sb./sth. **2** *tr. V.* interest; **jmdn. für etw.** ∼: interest sb. in sth.; **interessiert dich denn nicht, was passiert ist?** aren't you interested to know what happened?; **das interessiert mich nicht** I'm not interested [in it]; it doesn't interest me
interessiert *Adj.* interested; **an jmdm./etw.** ∼ **sein** be interested in sb./sth.; **er ist daran** ∼, **dass sie nichts davon erfahren** he doesn't want them to find out anything about it; **vielseitig** ∼ **sein** have a wide range of interests; ∼ **zuhören** listen with interest
Inter·feron /-feˈroːn/ *das;* ∼**s,** ∼**e** (Med.) interferon
Interim /ˈɪntərɪm/ *das;* ∼**s,** ∼**s** (geh.) interim measure
Interims·lösung *die* (geh.) interim solution
Interjektion /ɪntɐjɛkˈtsi̯oːn/ *die;* ∼, ∼**en** (Sprachw.) interjection
inter-, Inter-: ∼**kontinental** *Adj.* (geh.) intercontinental; ∼**kontinental·rakete** *die* (Milit.) intercontinental ballistic missile; ∼**mezzo** /∼ˈmɛtso/ *das;* ∼**mezzos,** ∼**mezzos** *od.* ∼**mezzi** (Theat., Musik) intermezzo; (fig.) interlude; intermezzo
intern /ɪnˈtɛrn/ **1** *Adj.* **(a)** internal; **(b)** (im Internat wohnend) **ein** ∼**er Schüler** a boarder. **2** *adv.* internally; **wir haben das Jubiläum nur** ∼ **gefeiert** we only celebrated the anniversary among ourselves

internalisieren /ɪntɛnaliˈziːrən/ *tr. V.* (Soziol., Psych.) internalize
Internalisierung *die;* ∼, ∼**en** (Soziol., Psych.) internalization
Internat /ɪntəˈnaːt/ *das;* ∼**[e]s,** ∼**e (a)** boarding school; **(b)** (einer Schule angeschlossenes Heim) dormitory block
inter-, Inter-: ∼**national 1** *Adj.* international; **2** *adv.* internationally; ∼**nationale** *die;* ∼, ∼**n (a)** (Internationale Arbeiterassoziation) International; Internationale; **(b)** (Lied) Internationale; ∼**nationalismus** *der o. Pl.* (Politik) internationalism
Internats-: ∼**schule** *die* boarding school; ∼**schüler** *der,* ∼**schülerin** *die* boarding school pupil; boarder
Internet /ˈɪntənɛt/ *das;* ∼**s** Internet; **im** ∼: on the Internet
Internet·anschluss *der,* ***Internet·anschluß** *der* Internet connection; connection to the Internet; **einen** ∼ **haben** be connected to the Internet;
internieren *tr. V.* (Milit.) intern
Internierte *der/die; adj. Dekl.* (Milit.) internee
Internierung *die;* ∼, ∼**en** internment
Internierungs·lager *das* internment camp
Internist *der;* ∼**en,** ∼**en** (Med.) internist
Interpol /ˈɪntɛpoːl/ (*die*); ∼ Interpol
Interpolation /ɪntɛpolaˈtsi̯oːn/ *die;* ∼, ∼**en** (fachspr.) interpolation
interpolieren *itr., tr. V.* (fachspr.) interpolate
Interpret /ɪntɛˈpreːt/ *der;* ∼**en,** ∼**en** interpreter
Interpretation /ɪntɛpretaˈtsi̯oːn/ *die;* ∼, ∼**en** interpretation
interpretieren *tr. V.* interpret; **etw. falsch** ∼: misinterpret sth.; interpret sth. wrongly
Interpretin *die;* ∼, ∼**nen** ⇒ **Interpret**
Interpunktion /ɪntɛpʊŋkˈtsi̯oːn/ *die;* ∼ (Sprachw.) punctuation
Interrail·karte /ˈɪntəreɪl-/ *die* (Eisenbahnw.) Interrail card
interrogativ /ɪntɛrogaˈtiːf/ *Adj.* (Sprachw.) interrogative
Interrogativ·pronomen *das* interrogative pronoun
Intervall /ɪntɛˈval/ *das;* ∼**s,** ∼**e** interval
intervenieren /ɪntɛveˈniːrən/ *itr. V.* (geh., Politik) intervene; (protestieren) make representations (**bei** to)
Intervention /ɪntɛvɛnˈtsi̯oːn/ *die;* ∼, ∼**en** (geh., Politik) intervention; (Protest) representations *pl.*
Interventions·krieg *der* war of intervention
Interview /ˈɪntɐvjuː/ *das;* ∼**s,** ∼**s** interview
interviewen /ɪntɐˈvjuːən/ *tr. V.* interview
Interviewer /ɪntɐˈvjuːɐ/ *der;* ∼**s,** ∼, **Interviewerin** *die;* ∼, ∼**nen** interviewer
Inthronisation /ɪntroːnizaˈtsi̯oːn/ *die;* ∼, ∼**en** enthronement
inthronisieren *tr. V.* enthrone
intim /ɪnˈtiːm/ **1** *Adj.* intimate; **mit jmdm.** ∼ **sein/werden** (verhüll.) be/become intimate with sb. (euphem.). **2** *adv.* **mit jmdm.** ∼ **verkehren** (verhüll.) have intimate relations with sb. (euphem.)
Intim-: ∼**bereich** *der* **(a)** ⇒ ∼**sphäre; (b)** (Genitalbereich) genital area; ∼**hygiene** *die* intimate personal hygiene
Intimität /ɪntimiˈtɛːt/ *die;* ∼, ∼**en** intimacy; **es ist zu** ∼**en gekommen** (verhüll.) intimacy took place (euphem.); ∼**en austauschen** (verhüll.) be engaged in intimacy (euphem.)
Intim-: ∼**leben** *das* (verhüll.) intimate life; ∼**pflege** *die* ⇒ ∼**hygiene;** ∼**sphäre** *die* private life; **jmds.** ∼**sphäre verletzen** invade sb.'s privacy; ∼**spray** *der od. das* intimate deodorant
Intimus /ˈɪntimʊs/ *der;* ∼, **Intimi** intimate friend; (Vertrauter) confidant
Intim·verkehr *der* (verhüll.) intimate relations *pl.* (euphem.)
in·tolerant 1 *Adj.* intolerant (**gegenüber** of). **2** *adv.* intolerantly

In·toleranz *die;* ~, ~**en** intolerance (**gegenüber** of)

Intonation /ɪntona'tsi̯o:n/ *die;* ~, ~**en** (Sprachw., Musik) intonation

intonieren *tr. V.* (**a**) (Musik) (anstimmen) **etw.** ~: sing/play the first few bars of sth.; start to sing/play sth.; (**b**) (Sprachw.) **etw. richtig/anders** ~: say sth. with the right/a different intonation

intransitiv 1 *Adj.* (Sprachw.) intransitive. 2 *adv.* intransitively

Intrigant *der;* ~**en**, ~**en**, **Intrigantin** *die;* ~, ~**nen** schemer; intriguer

Intrige /ɪn'tri:gə/ *die;* ~, ~**n** intrigue

intrigieren *itr. V.* intrigue; scheme; **gegen jmdn.** ~: intrigue *or* scheme against sb.

introvertiert /ɪntrovɛr'ti:ɐt/ *Adj.* (Psych.) introverted

Intuition /ɪntu̯i'tsi̯o:n/ *die;* ~, ~**en** intuition

intuitiv /ɪntu̯i'ti:f/ 1 *Adj.* intuitive. 2 *adv.* intuitively

intus /'ɪntʊs/ *in* **etw.** ~ **haben** (ugs.) (begriffen haben) have got sth. into one's head; (gegessen od. getrunken haben) have put sth. away (coll.)

invalid /ɪnva'li:t/, **invalide** /ɪnva'li:də/ *Adj.* invalid *attrib.;* ~ **sein** be an invalid

Invalide *der; adj. Dekl.* invalid

Invalidität /ɪnvalidi'tɛ:t/ *die;* ~: invalidity

in·variabel *Adj.* invariable

Invasion /ɪnva'zi̯o:n/ *die;* ~, ~**en** (auch fig. scherzh.) invasion

Inventar /ɪnvɛn'taːɐ̯/ *das;* ~**s**, ~**e** (**a**) [totes] ~ (einer Firma) fittings and equipment *pl.;* (eines Hauses, Büros) furnishings and fittings *pl.;* (eines Hofes) machinery and equipment; **lebendes** ~: livestock; **zum** ~ **gehören** (fig.) ⟨person⟩ be part of the scenery; (**b**) (Verzeichnis) inventory

Inventur /ɪnvɛn'tuːɐ̯/ *die;* ~, ~**en** stocktaking; ~ **machen** carry out a stocktaking

Inversion /ɪnvɛr'zi̯o:n/ *die;* ~, ~**en** (fachspr.) inversion

investieren *tr., itr. V.* (auch fig.) invest (**in** + *Akk.* in)

Investition /ɪnvɛsti'tsi̯o:n/ *die;* ~, ~**en** investment; **die privaten** ~**en sind zurückgegangen** private investment has fallen

Investitions-: ~**güter** *Pl.* (Wirtsch.) capital goods; ~**lenkung** *die* investment control

Investment /ɪn'vɛstmɛnt/ *das;* ~**s**, ~**s** (Finanzw.) ⇨ **Investition**

Investment·fonds *der* investment fund

Investor /ɪn'vɛstɔr/ *der;* ~**s**, ~**en** /-'toːrən/ (Wirtsch.) investor

in·wendig 1 *Adj.* inside ⟨pocket⟩; inner ⟨part⟩; (fig.) inner, inward ⟨happiness, strength⟩. 2 *adv.* (on the) inside; (fig.) inwardly; deep down [inside]; **etw./jmdn. in- und auswendig kennen** (ugs.) know sb./sth. inside out

in·wie·fern *Adv.* (in welcher Hinsicht) in what way; (bis zu welchem Grade) to what extent; how far

in·wie·weit *Adv.* to what extent; how far

In·zahlungnahme *die;* ~, ~**n** part exchange; trade in (Amer.)

Inzest /ɪn'tsɛst/ *der;* ~[**e**]**s**, ~**e** incest

In·zucht *die;* ~: inbreeding

in·zwischen *Adv.* (**a**) (seither) in the meantime; since [then]; **es hatte sich** ~ **nichts geändert** nothing had changed in the meantime *or* since; (**b**) (bis zu einem Zeitpunkt) (in der Gegenwart) by now; (in der Vergangenheit) by then; (in der Zukunft) by then; by that time; (**c**) (währenddessen) meanwhile; in the meantime

IOK /iːoː'kaː/ *das;* ~[**s**] **Internationales Olympisches Komitee** IOC

Ion /joːn/ *das;* ~**s**, ~**en** (Physik, Chemie) ion

Ionen-: ~**austauscher** *der* (Physik, Chemie) ion exchanger; ~**gitter** *das* (Chemie) ionic lattice

Ionisation /joniza'tsi̯o:n/ *die;* ~, ~**en** (Physik, Chemie) ionization

Iono·sphäre /jono-/ *die* ionosphere

i-Punkt, ·I-Punkt /'iː-/ *der* dot over *or* on the i; **bis auf den** ~ (fig.) down to the last detail

---

IQ /iː'kuː: *od.* aɪ'kjuː/ *der;* ~[**s**], ~[**s**] IQ

i. R. /iː'ɛr/ *Abk.* retd.

IRA /iː|ɛr'|aː/ *die;* ~: IRA

Irak /i'raːk/ (*das*); ~**s** *od. der;* ~[**s**] Iraq; **in/nach/aus** *od.* **im/in den/aus dem** ~: in/to/from Iraq

Iraker *der;* ~**s**, ~, **Irakerin** *die;* ~, ~**nen** ▶ 388 | Iraqi

irakisch ▶ 388 | Iraqi

Iran /i'raːn/ (*das*); ~**s** *od. der;* ~[**s**] Iran; *s. auch* **Irak**

Iraner *der;* ~**s**, ~, **Iranerin** *die;* ~, ~**nen** ▶ 388 | Iranian

iranisch *Adj.* ▶ 388 | Iranian

irden /'ɪrdn̩/ *Adj.* earthen[ware] ⟨bowl, pot, jug⟩; ~**es Geschirr** earthenware

irdisch *Adj.* (**a**) earthly ⟨joys, paradise, love⟩; mortal, earthly ⟨creature, being⟩; temporal ⟨power, justice⟩; worldly ⟨goods, pleasures, possessions⟩; **den Weg alles Irdischen gehen** go the way of all flesh; ⟨object⟩ go the way of all things; (**b**) (zur Erde gehörig) terrestrial; **das** ~**e Leben** life on earth

Ire /'iːrə/ *der;* ~**n**, ~**n** ▶ 388 | Irishman; **die** ~**n** the Irish; **er ist** ~: he is Irish *or* an Irishman

irgend /'ɪrgn̩t/ *Adv.* (**a**) ~ **so ein Politiker** (ugs.) some politician [or other]; ~ **so etwas** something like that; something of the sort *or* kind; *s. auch* **irgendetwas, irgendjemand**; (**b**) (irgendwie) **wenn** ~ **möglich** if at all possible

irgend-: ~**ein** *Indefinitpron.* (**a**) *attr.* some; (fragend, verneint) any; ~**ein Idiot** some idiot [or other]; **in** ~**einer Zeitung habe ich neulich gelesen, dass** ...: I read in one of the papers recently that ...; **Welche Zeitung soll es sein? — Irgendeine** What newspaper do you want? — Just any; ~**ein anderer/**~**eine andere** someone *or* somebody else; (fragend, verneint) anyone *or* anybody else; **mehr als** ~**ein anderer** more than anyone *or* anybody else; (**b**) (allein stehend) ~**einer/**~**eine** someone; somebody; (fragend, verneint) anyone; anybody; ~**eines** *od.* (ugs.) ~**eins** any one; ~**einer muss es machen** someone *or* somebody [or other] must do it; **nicht** ~**einer** not just anyone; ~**etwas** *Indefinitpron.* something; (fragend, verneint) anything; ~**jemand** *Indefinitpron.* someone; somebody; somebody or another; (coll.) (fragend, veneint) anyone; anybody; ~**wann** *Adv.* [at] some time [or other]; somewhen; (zu jeder beliebigen Zeit) [at] any time; ~**wann einmal** [at] some time [or other]; ~**was** *Indefinitpron.* (ugs.) something [or other]; (fragend, verneint) anything; [**nimm**] ~**was** [take] anything [you like]; **ist** ~**was?** is [there] something wrong *or* the matter?; ~**welch...** *Indefinitpron.* some; (fragend, verneint) any; ~**wer** *Indefinitpron.* (ugs.) somebody or other (coll.); someone; somebody; (fragend, verneint) anyone; anybody; ~**wie** *Adv.* somehow; somehow or other (coll.); **kann man das** ~**wie anders/besser machen?** is there some other/better way of doing this?; **er tut mir** ~**wie leid, aber** ...: I feel sorry for him in a way, but ...; ~**wo** *Adv.* (**a**) somewhere; some place [or other] (coll.); (fragend, verneint) anywhere; **ist hier** ~**wo ein Lokal?** is there a pub anywhere around here?; ~**wo anders** somewhere/anywhere else; (**b**) (ugs.: irgendwie) **er tut mir** ~**wo leid, aber** ...: I feel sorry for him in a way, but ...; ~**woher** *Adv.* from somewhere; from some place; from somewhere or other (coll.); (fragend, verneint) from anywhere; from any place; ~**wohin** *Adv.* somewhere; somewhere or other (coll.); (fragend, verneint) anywhere

Irin *die;* ~, ~**nen** Irishwoman; **sie ist** ~: she is Irish *or* an Irishwoman

Iris /'iːrɪs/ *die;* ~, ~ ▶ 326 | (Bot., Anat.) iris

irisch *Adj.* ▶ 388 |, ▶ 487 | Irish; **Irisch/das Irische** Irish

irisieren *itr. V.* iridesce; be iridescent; ~**d** iridescent

Irland /'ɪrlant/ (*das*); ~**s** Ireland; (die Republik) Ireland; Eire

Ironie /iro'niː/ *die;* ~, ~**n** irony; **es war eine** ~ **des Schicksals, dass** ...: it was one of the ironies of fate *or* an irony of fate that ...

ironisch 1 *Adj.* ironic; ironical. **2** *adv.* ironically
ironischer·weise *Adv.* ironically
ironisieren *tr. V.* ironize
Ironisierung *die;* ~, ~**en** ironizing
irr /ɪr/ *Adj.* ⇨ **irre 1 a**
irrational /'ɪratsi̯onaːl/ **1** *Adj.* irrational. **2** *adv.* irrationally
Irrationalismus *der;* ~, **Irrationalismen** irrationalism
Irrationalität *die;* ~: irrationality
irre /'ɪrə/ **1** *Adj.* (a) (geistesgestört) mad, insane ‹*person*›; insane ‹*laughter*›; demented ‹*grin, look*›; insane, crazy ‹*idea, thought, suggestion*›; **davon kann man ja** ~ **werden** it's enough to drive you mad or crazy; (b) *nicht präd.* (salopp: stark) terrific (coll.); terrible (coll.); **eine** ~ **Arbeit** a hell of a job (coll.); (c) (salopp: faszinierend) amazing (coll.); *s. auch* **irrewerden. 2** *adv.* (salopp) terrifically (coll.); terribly (coll.); **sich** ~ **freuen** be thrilled to bits (coll.)
Irre[1] /'ɪrə/ *der/die; adj. Dekl.* madman/madwoman; lunatic; (fig.) fool; idiot; lunatic; **sie fährt wie eine** ~: she drives like a maniac or lunatic; **er schreit/arbeitet wie ein** ~**r** he shouts/works like mad (coll.)
Irre[2] *die* (geh.) **in die** ~ **gehen** go astray; (fig.: sich irren) make a mistake; **jmdn. in die** ~ **führen** mislead sb./ (täuschen) deceive sb.
irreal /'ɪreaːl/ *Adj.* unreal
irre-, Irre-: ~**|führen** *tr. V.* mislead; (täuschen) deceive; ~**führend** *Adj.* misleading; (täuschend) deceptive; ~**führung** *die:* **das war eine bewusste** ~**führung** that was a deliberate attempt to mislead; ~**führung der Öffentlichkeit** misleading the public; ~**|gehen** *unr. V.; mit sein* (geh.) be mistaken; ~**|leiten** *tr. V.* (geh.) lead astray; **irregeleitete Emotionen/Jugend** misguided emotions/ youth
irrelevant /'ɪrelevant/ *Adj.* irrelevant (**für** to)
Irrelevanz *die* irrelevance (**für** to)
irre|machen *tr. V.* (a) (verwirren) disconcert; put off; **lass dich durch ihn nicht** ~: don't be disconcerted or (coll.) put off by him; (b) (zweifeln lassen) **jmdn. in seinem Glauben** ~: shake sb.'s faith; **sie ließ sich in ihrer Hoffnung/ihrem Plan nicht** ~: she would not let anything confound her hopes/her plan
irren /'ɪrən/ **1** *refl. V.* be mistaken; **man kann sich auch mal** ~ everybody makes or we all make mistakes [sometimes]; **Sie** ~ **sich, wenn** ...: you are making a mistake if ...; **er hat sich in einigen Punkten geirrt** he got a few things wrong; **Sie haben sich in der Person/Hausnummer geirrt** you've got the wrong person/number; **sich um 1 DM** ~: be out by 1 DM; be 1 DM out. **2** *itr. V.* (a) (sich irren) **da** ~ **Sie** you are mistaken or wrong there; **Irren ist menschlich** to err is human (prov.); (b) *mit sein* **durch die Straßen/den Park** ~: wander the streets/about in the park
Irren-: ~**anstalt** *die* (veralt.) mental home; madhouse (derog.); ~**arzt** *der* (veralt.) mad-doctor (arch.); ~**haus** *das* (abwertend) [lunatic] asylum; madhouse (derog.); **das war das reinste** ~**haus** (ugs.) it was bedlam or an absolute madhouse; **er ist reif fürs** ~**haus** (ugs.) he'll crack up soon (coll.)
irreparabel /ɪrepa'raːbl̩/ *Adj.* irreparable; beyond repair *pred.*
irreversibel *Adj.* (fachspr.) irreversible
irre|werden *unr. itr. V.* (geh.) **an jmdm.** ~: lose faith in sb.; **an sich** (*Dat.*) **selbst** ~: doubt oneself
Irr-: ~**fahrt** *die* wandering; **meine Reise wurde zu einer endlosen** ~**fahrt** my journey turned into an endless series of wanderings; ~**glaube[n]** *der* (Irrtum) misconception
irrig /'ɪrɪç/ *Adj.* erroneous
irrigerweise *Adv.* mistakenly; erroneously
Irritation /ɪrita'tsi̯oːn/ *die;* ~, ~**en** (Med., geh.) irritation
irritieren *tr., itr. V.* (a) (verwirren) bother; put off; **das irritiert** it's off-putting; **lass dich dadurch nicht** ~: don't be put off by it; (b) (stören) disturb; (c) (befremden) annoy; irritate

irr-, Irr-: ~**licht** *das* will o' the wisp; jack o' lantern; ~**lichter entstehen durch** ...: will o' the wisp or jack o' lantern is caused by ...; ~**sinn** *der; o. Pl.* (a) insanity; madness; (b) (ugs. abwertend) madness; lunacy; **so ein** ~**sinn!** what lunacy!; ~**sinnig 1** *Adj.* (a) insane; mad; (absurd) idiotic; **bist du** ~**sinnig?** are you mad?; **wie** ~**sinnig schreien/rasen** scream/rush like mad (coll.); (b) (ugs.: extrem) terrible (coll.), horrific (coll.) ‹*pain, screams, prices, etc.*›; terrific (coll.) ‹*speed, heat, cold*›; **2** *adv.* (ugs.) terribly (coll.); frightfully (coll.); ~**sinnig schuften** slog away like mad or crazy (coll.); ~**sinnige** *der/die; adj. Dekl.* madman/madwoman; lunatic
Irrtum *der;* ~**s**, **Irrtümer** /'ɪrtyːmɐ/ (a) fallacy; misconception; **im** ~ **sein, sich im** ~ **befinden** be wrong or mistaken; (b) (Fehler) mistake; error
irrtümlich /'ɪrtyːmlɪç/ **1** *Adj.; nicht präd.* incorrect; wrong. **2** *adv.* by mistake; **wie man oft** ~ **meint** as is often erroneously or mistakenly thought
Irrung *die;* ~, ~**en** (geh.) **die** ~**en und Wirrungen seiner verfehlten Jugend** the vagaries of his misspent youth
irr-, Irr-: ~**weg** *der* error; **diese Methode hat sich als** ~**weg erwiesen** this method has proved to be wrong; ~**witzig** *Adj.* (geh.) mad
Ischias /'ɪʃi̯as/ *der od. das od.* (Med.) *die;* ~: ▶ **329** sciatica
Ischias·nerv *der* ▶ **326** sciatic nerve
Isegrim /'iːzəɡrɪm/ *der;* ~**s**, ~**e** (Myth.) [**Meister**] ~: Isegrim; Isgrin
Islam /ɪs'laːm *od.* 'ɪslam/ *der;* ~[**s**]: **der** ~ Islam; **die Welt des** ~[**s**] the Islamic world; the world of Islam
islamisch *Adj.* Islamic; Islamitic
Islamismus *der;* ~: Islamic fundamentalism; Islamism
Islamist *der;* ~**en**, ~**en** Islamic fundamentalist; Islamist
islamistisch *Adj.* Islamic fundamentalist; Islamist
Island /'iːs-/ (*das*); ~**s** Iceland
Isländer /'iːslɛndɐ/ *der;* ~**s**, ~, **Isländerin** *die;* ~, ~**nen** ▶ **388** Icelander
isländisch /'iːslɛndɪʃ/ *Adj.* ▶ **388**, ▶ **487** Icelandic; Isländisch/das Isländische Icelandic
Iso·bare /izo'baːrə/ *die;* ~, ~**n** (Met.) isobar
Isolation /izola'tsi̯oːn/ *die;* ~, ~**en** ⇨ **Isolierung**
Isolations·haft *die* solitary confinement
Isolator /izo'laːtɔr/ *der;* ~**s**, ~**en** /-'toːren/ insulator
Isolier·band *das; Pl.* ~**bänder** insulating tape
isolieren *tr. V.* (a) isolate ‹*prisoner, patient, bacterium, element*›; **von der Umwelt isoliert** cut off from the outside world; **etw. isoliert betrachten** look at sth. out of context; (b) (Technik) insulate ‹*wiring, wall, etc.*›; lag ‹*boilers, pipes, etc.*›; (gegen Schall) soundproof; insulate ‹*room, door, window, etc.*›
Isolier-: ~**kanne** *die* Thermos jug (**P**); vacuum jug; ~**schicht** *die* insulating layer; ~**station** *die* (Med.) isolation ward
Isolierung *die;* ~, ~**en** (a) (auch fig.) isolation; **in der** ~: in isolation; **in die** ~ **geraten** (fig.) become isolated or detached; (b) (Technik) insulation; insulating; (von Kesseln, Röhren) lagging; (gegen Schall) soundproofing; (c) (Isoliermaterial) insulation; (für Kessel, Röhren) lagging
Isotherme /izo'tɛrmə/ *die;* ~, ~**n** (Met.) isotherm
Isotop /izo'toːp/ *das;* ~**s**, ~**e** isotope
Israel /'ɪsraeːl/ (*das*); ~**s** Israel; **das Volk** ~ (bibl.) the Israelites; the people of Israel; **die Kinder** ~[**s**] (bibl.) the Children of Israel
Israeli *der;* ~[**s**], ~[**s**]/**die;** ~, ~[**s**] ▶ **388** Israeli
israelisch *Adj.* ▶ **388** Israeli
Israelit *der;* ~**en**, ~**en**, **Israelitin** *die;* ~, ~**nen** Israelite
israelitisch *Adj.* Israelite
iss, *iß /ɪs/ *Imperativ Sg. v.* **essen**
isst, *ißt /ɪst/ *2. u. 3. Pers. Sg. Präsens v.* **essen**
ist /ɪst/ *3. Pers. Sg. Präsens v.* **sein**[1]
Ist-: ~**bestand, *~-Bestand** *der* (Kaufmannsspr.) actual stocks *pl.*; ~**stärke, *~-Stärke** *die* (Milit.) actual strength

Isthmus /'ɪstmʊs/ *der;* ~, **Isthmen** isthmus

Italien /i'ta:liən/ *(das);* ~s Italy

Italiener /ita'lie:nɐ/ *der;* ~s, ~, **Italienerin** *die;* ~, ~nen ▶ 388 | Italian

italienisch *Adj.* ▶ 388 |, ▶ 487 | Italian; **Italienisch/ das Italienische** Italian

Italo·western /'i:talo-/ *der* Italian-made Western; spaghetti western (derog.)

i-Tüpfel[chen], **I-Tüpfel[chen]* *das;* ~s, ~, (österr.) **i-Tüpferl**, **I-Tüpferl* /'i:typfl/ *das;* ~s, ~n final *or* finishing touch; **bis aufs [letzte]** ~: down to the last *or* smallest detail

i. V. /i:'fau/ *Abk.* **in Vertretung**

i. w. S. *Abk.* **im weiteren Sinne**

....

Jj

....

j, J /jɔt, österr.: je:/ *das;* ~, ~: j/J; *s. auch* **a, A**

ja /ja:/ **1** *Interj.* (**a**) yes; **Wohnen Sie hier? — Ja** Do you live here? — Yes[, I do]; **Hast du ihm Bescheid gesagt? — Ja** Have you told him? — Yes[, I have]; (**b**) (Bitte um Bestätigung) **du bleibst doch noch ein bisschen, ja?** but you'll stay on a bit, won't you *or* surely?; **Sie kommen. — Ja?** They're coming. — Are they?; (ungläubig) **Der König ist tot. — Ja?** The King is dead. — [Is he] really? (**c**) (Antwort auf Anrede, Anruf usw.) yes; **ja [bitte]?** (am Telefon) yes? **2** *Partikel* (**a**) (beschwichtigend) **ich komme ja schon** I'm [just] coming; (**b**) (Bekanntheit unterstellend) **die Delphine, die ja Säugetiere sind** dolphins, which are known to be mammals; **ich habe es ja gleich gesagt** I said that in the first place, didn't I?; **Sie wissen ja, dass ...:** you know, of course, that ...; **du kennst ihn ja** you know what he's like; you know him; (**c**) (Überraschung ausdrückend) **es schneit ja!** it's [actually] snowing!; **da seid ihr ja!** there you are!; (**d**) (einräumend) **er mag ja recht haben** he may [well] be right. **3** *Adv.* (**a**) (unbedingt) **lass ja die Finger davon!** [just you] leave it alone!; **sag das ja nicht weiter!** don't [you dare] pass it on, whatever you do!; **damit er ja alles mitbekommt** to make sure he knows all *or* everything that's going on; **damit wir ja nicht zu spät kommen** so that there's no risk of us being late; (**b**) konjunktional (sogar) indeed; even; **ich schätze, ja bewundere ihn** I like him, indeed admire him *or* admire him even

Ja *das;* ~[s], ~[s] yes; **mit ~ stimmen** vote yes

Jacht /jaxt/ *die;* ~, ~en yacht

Jacht·hafen *der* yacht harbour; marina

Jäckchen /'jɛkçən/ *das;* ~s, ~: jacket; (gestrickt) cardigan

Jacke /'jakə/ *die;* ~, ~n jacket; (gestrickt) cardigan; **das ist ~ wie Hose** (ugs.) it makes no odds (coll.)

Jacken·tasche *die* jacket pocket

Jacket·krone /'dʒɛkɪt-/ *die* (Zahnmed.) jacket crown

Jackett /ʒa'kɛt/ *das;* ~s, ~s jacket

Jade /'ja:də/ *der;* ~[s] od. *die;* ~: jade

Jagd /ja:kt/ *die;* ~, ~en (**a**) o. *Pl.* (Weidwerk) **die** ~ shooting; hunting; **die ~ auf Hasen** hare-hunting; ~ **auf Fasanen/Wildschweine machen** shoot pheasant/ hunt wild boar; **auf der ~ sein** be hunting/shooting; **auf die ~ gehen** go hunting/shooting; (**b**) (Veranstaltung) hunt; (Hetzjagd) hunt; (**c**) (Revier) preserve; shoot; **eine ~ pachten** rent a hunting-preserve *or* shoot; (**d**) (Verfolgung) hunt; (Verfolgungsjagd) chase; **auf jmdn./etw.** ~ **machen** hunt for sb./sth.; **die ~ nach Geld/Besitz** (fig.) the constant pursuit of money/possessions

jagdbar *Adj.* ~e **Tiere** animals that can be hunted/shot

Jagd-: ~**beute** *die* bag; kill; ~**bomber** *der* (Luftwaffe) fighter-bomber; ~**falke** *der* falcon; ~**fieber** *das* hunting-fever; **vom ~fieber gepackt** in the fever of the hunt; ~**flugzeug** *das* (Luftwaffe) fighter aircraft; ~**frevel** *der* poaching; ~**gesellschaft** *die* shooting party; hunting-party; ~**gewehr** *das* sporting gun; ~**glück** *das:* ~glück/kein ~glück **haben** be lucky/ unlucky [in the hunt]; ~**grund** *der; meist Pl.* hunting-ground; **in die ewigen Jagdgründe eingehen** (verhüll.) go to the happy hunting-grounds; ~**haus** *das* hunting *or* shooting lodge; hunting *or* shooting box; ~**horn** *das* hunting-horn; ~**hund** *der* gun-dog; (bei Hetzjagden) hunting-dog; hound; ~**hütte** *die* hunting *or* shooting box; ~**messer** *das* hunting-knife; ~**revier** *das* preserve; shoot; (fig.) hunting-ground; ~**schein** *der* game licence; ~**wurst** *die* chasseur sausage; ~**zeit** *die* open *or* hunting *or* shooting season

jagen /'ja:gn̩/ **1** *tr. V.* (**a**) hunt ⟨*game, fugitive, criminal, etc.*⟩; shoot ⟨*game, game birds*⟩; (hetzen) chase, pursue ⟨*fugitive, criminal, etc.*⟩; (wegscheuchen) chase; run after; **von Todesangst gejagt** stricken by the fear of death; **ein Gedanke jagte den anderen** thoughts raced through his/her *etc.* mind; (**b**) (treiben) drive; **jmdn. aus dem Haus** ~: throw sb. out of the house; **jmdn. aus dem Bett** ~: turn sb. out of bed; **jmdn. in die Flucht** ~: put sb. to flight; (**c**) (ugs.) **sich/jmdm. eine Spritze in den Arm** ~: jab *or* stick a needle in one's/sb.'s arm; **sich/ jmdm. eine Kugel durch den Kopf** ~: blow one's/sb.'s brains out. **2** *itr. V.* (**a**) (die Jagd ausüben) go shooting *or* hunting; (auf Hetzjagd gehen) go hunting; (**b**) *mit sein* (eilen) race; rush; **Wolken ~ am Himmel** (fig.) clouds race *or* scud across the sky; **mit ~dem Puls** (fig.) with his/her *etc.* pulse racing

Jäger /'jɛːgɐ/ *der;* ~s, ~ (**a**) hunter; (bei Hetzjagden) huntsman; (**b**) (Jagdflugzeug) fighter

Jäger·art *die* (Kochk.) **Schnitzel nach** ~: escalope chasseur

Jägerin *die;* ~, ~nen huntress; huntswoman

Jäger-: ~**latein** *das* (scherzh.) [hunter's *or* huntsman's] tall story/stories; ~**schnitzel** *das* (Kochk.) escalope chasseur; ~**sprache** *die* hunting language

Jaguar /'ja:gua:ɐ̯/ *der;* ~s, ~e jaguar

jäh /jɛː/ **1** *Adj.* (geh.) (**a**) sudden; sudden, abrupt ⟨*change, movement, stop*⟩; sudden, sharp ⟨*pain*⟩; **er fand einen ~en Tod** he met his death suddenly; **ein ~es Erwachen** (fig.) a rude awakening; (**b**) (steil) steep; precipitous ⟨*slope, ravine, ridge*⟩. **2** *adv.* (**a**) **die Stimmung schlug ~ um** the mood changed suddenly *or* abruptly; (**b**) (steil) ⟨*fall, drop*⟩ steeply, abruptly

Jahr /ja:ɐ̯/ *das;* ~[e]s, ~e ▶ 119 | (**a**) year; **ein halbes** ~: six months; **anderthalb ~e** eighteen months; a year and a half; **im ~[e] 1908** in [the year] 1908; **jedes** ~: every year; **jedes zweite** ~: [once] every two years; **alle ~e** every year; **lange ~e [hindurch]** for many years; ~ **für od. um** ~: year after year; **von ~ zu** ~: from one year to the next; **from year to year**; **zwischen den ~en** between Christmas and the New Year; **auf ~ und Tag** to the exact day; **nach ~ und Tag** after many years; **vor ~ und Tag** (meist Plusquamperfekt) many years ago; (mit Plusquamperfekt) many years before; (**b**) ▶ 22 | (Lebens~) year; **er ist zwanzig ~e [alt]** he is twenty years old *or* of age; **Kinder bis zu zwölf ~en** children up to the age of twelve *or* up to twelve years of age; **Kinder über 14 ~e** children over the age of 14 *or* over 14 years of age; **Kinder ab zwei ~en** children of two years and over; **alle Männer zwischen 18 und 45 ~en** all men between the ages of 18 and 45; **mit 65 ~en od. im Alter von 65 ~en** at the age of 65; **das hat er schon in jungen ~en gelernt** he learned that at an early age *or* while he was still young; **mit den ~en** as he/she *etc.* grows/grew older; **er ist um ~e gealtert** he's put on years; **in die ~e kommen** reach middle age

jahr·aus *Adv.* ~, **jahrein** year in, year out

Jahr·buch *das* yearbook

Jährchen /'jɛːɐ̯çən/ *das;* ~s, ~ (scherzh.) year; **die paar ~, die ich noch zu leben habe!** the few short years I have left to live; **einige ~ auf dem Buckel haben** be knocking on a bit (coll.)

Die Jahreszeiten

der Frühling, das = spring
Frühjahr
der Sommer = summer
der Herbst = autumn *(brit.)*, **fall** *(amerik.)*
der Winter = winter

Spricht man von einer Jahreszeit im Allgemeinen oder als Phänomen, verwendet man im Englischen oft keinen Artikel:

Der Frühling ist früh = Spring came early
eingetroffen

Der Sommer ist meine = Summer *od.* The
Lieblingsjahreszeit   summer is my favourite
                        time of year

Im Winter bleibe ich = In [the] winter I stay at
die meiste Zeit zu   home most of the time
Hause

Sie blühen zu Anfang/ = They flower in [the]
zu Ende des Frühjahrs   early/late spring

Eine Ausnahme bildet der amerikanische Ausdruck **fall**, der stets mit dem Artikel verwendet wird.

Im Herbst verfärbt sich = The leaves change
das Laub   colour in [the] autumn
                          od. (amerik.) in the fall

Spricht man aber von einem bestimmten Sommer usw., ist der Gebrauch ähnlich wie im Deutschen:

Der Sommer war = The summer was wet
verregnet

nächsten/letzten Winter = next/last winter

Er blieb den ganzen = He stayed all summer
Sommer   od. [for] the whole
                      summer

Sie kommen diesen = They are coming this
Herbst   autumn *od. (amerik.)*
                    this fall

Er macht jeden Winter = He goes skiing every
Skiurlaub   winter

Die letzten beiden = The last two summers
Sommer waren wir   we were in Greece
in Griechenland

Adjektive

frühlingshaft = springlike
sommerlich = summery
herbstlich = autumnal
winterlich = wintry

In ganz wenigen Fällen lässt sich das Adjektiv durch ein attributives **summer**, **winter** usw. übersetzen. Bei Kleidung etwa unterscheidet man nicht zwischen *winterlich/sommerlich* und *Winter-/Sommer-:*

Winterkleidung/ = winter clothing
winterliche Kleidung

Sommerkleidung/ = summer clothing
sommerliche Kleidung

Allerdings:

ein sommerliches Kleid = a summery dress

Beachten Sie auch:

winterliche/sommerliche = winter/summer
Temperaturen   temperatures

---

jahr·ein *Adv.;* ⇨ **jahraus**

jahre·lang 1 *Adj.; nicht präd.* [many] years of 〈 *practice, imprisonment, experience, etc.* 〉; long-standing 〈 *feud, friendship* 〉; **mit** ⁓**er Verspätung** years late; **nach** ⁓**er Abwesenheit** after being away for years. **2** *adv.* for [many] years

jähren /'jɛːrən/ *refl. V.* **heute jährt sich [zum fünften Male] sein Todestag** today is the [fifth] anniversary of his death; **heute jährt [es] sich zum zehntenmal, dass ...:** it is ten years ago today that ...; it is ten years since ...

jahres-, Jahres-: ⁓**ab·schluss,** *⁎*⁓**abschluß** *der* **(a)** (Wirtsch., Kaufmannsspr.) annual accounts *pl.*; **(b)** ⇨ ⁓**ende;** ⁓**durch·schnitt** *der* yearly *or* annual average; ⁓**anfang** *der* beginning *or* start of the year; ⁓**ausgleich** *der* (Steuerw.) end-of-year adjustment; **den** ⁓**ausgleich beantragen** send in one's tax return; ⁓**beginn** *der* beginning *or* start of the new year; ⁓**bei·trag** *der* annual *or* yearly subscription; ⁓**bilanz** *die* (Wirtsch., Kaufmannsspr.) annual balance [of accounts]; (Dokument) annual balance sheet; ⁓**einkommen** *das* annual income; ⁓**ende** *das* end of the year; ⁓**frist** *die in* in *od.* innerhalb *od.* binnen ⁓**frist** within [a period of] a *or* one year; **vor** ⁓**frist** in less than a year; (vor einem Jahr) a year ago; **nach** ⁓**frist** after [a period of] a *or* one year; ⁓**gehalt** *das* annual salary; **zwei** ⁓**gehälter** two years' salary; ⁓**hälfte** *die:* **die erste/zweite** ⁓**hälfte** the first/second half *or* six months of the year; ⁓**haupt·versammlung** *die* (Wirtsch.) annual general meeting; ⁓**karte** *die* yearly season ticket; ⁓**miete** *die* annual *or* yearly rent; ⁓**mittel** *das* annual mean; **im** ⁓**mittel fallen 3,2 cm Niederschlag** the mean annual precipitation is 3.2 cm; ⁓**ring** *der; meist Pl.* (Bot.) annual ring; ⁓**tag** *der* anniversary; ⁓**umsatz** *der* annual turnover; ⁓**urlaub** *der* annual holiday *or* (formal) leave *or* (Amer.) vacation; ⁓**versammlung** *die* annual [general] meeting; ⁓**wechsel** *der* turn of the year; **zum** ⁓**wechsel die besten Wünsche** best wishes for the New Year; ⁓**wende** *die* turn of the year; ⁓**zahl** *die* date;

⁓**zeit** *die* season; **für die** ⁓**zeit ist es kalt** it's cold for the time of the year; **trotz der vorgerückten** ⁓**zeit** although it is/was late in the year; ⁓**zeitlich 1** *Adj.; nicht präd.* seasonal; **2** *adv.* ⁓**zeitlich schwanken** vary with the seasons *or* according to the time of year; ⁓**zeitlich bedingt sein** be governed by seasonal factors

Jahr·gang *der* **(a)** year; **der** ⁓ **1900** those *pl.* born in 1900; **sie ist** ⁓ **1943** she was born in 1943; **er ist mein** ⁓: he was born in the same year as I was; **(b)** (eines Weines) vintage; **der 81er soll ein guter** ⁓ **werden** 81 should be a vintage year; **ein Edelzwicker** ⁓ **1978** a 1978 Edelzwicker; **(c)** (einer Zeitschrift) set [ot issues] for a/the year; **die beiden letzten Jahrgänge** the sets of back numbers for the past two years

Jahr·hundert *das* ▶ 119 | century; **im 19. und 20.** ⁓: in the 19th and 20th centuries; **durch die** ⁓**e** over *or* through the centuries; **im ersten** ⁓ **vor/nach Christi Geburt** in the first century BC/AD; **die Literatur des 19.** ⁓**s** 19th-century literature; the literature of the 19th century

Jahrhundert·wende *die* turn of the century; **aus der Zeit um die** ⁓**wende** from the turn of the century

-jährig /'jɛːrɪç/ **(a)** ▶ 22 | (... *Jahre alt*) **ein elfjähriges/halbjähriges Kind** an eleven-year-old/a six-month-old child; **kaum achtjährig:** hardly eight years old; **(b)** (... *Jahre dauernd*) ... year's/years'; -year; **nach vierjähriger/halbjähriger Vorbereitung** after four years'/six months' preparation; **mit dreijähriger/halbjähriger Verspätung** three years/six months late

jährlich /'jɛːrlɪç/ **1** *Adj.; nicht präd.* annual; yearly. **2** *adv.* annually; yearly; **einmal/zweimal** ⁓: once/twice a *or* per year; **ein Umsatz von 5 Millionen** ⁓: a turnover of five million per annum

Jahr·markt *der* fair; funfair

Jahr·millionen *Pl.* millions of years

Jahr·tausend *das* thousand years; millennium; **vor** ⁓**en** thousands of years ago; **das dritte** ⁓ **nach Christi Geburt** the third millennium AD

Jahrtausend·wende *die* turn of the millennium

Jahr·zehnt *das* decade

jahrzehnte·lang 1 *Adj.; nicht präd.* decades of ⟨*practice, experience, etc.*⟩; **mit ~er Verspätung** decades late; **nach ~er Abwesenheit** after being away for decades. **2** *adv.* for decades

Jäh·zorn *der* violent anger; **er neigt zum ~:** he tends towards violent fits *or* outbursts of temper *or* anger; **in wildem ~:** in blind anger *or* a blind rage

jäh·zornig 1 *Adj.* violent-tempered; **ein ~es Temperament** a violent temper. **2** *adv.* in blind anger; in a blind rage

ja·ja *Partikel* (ugs.) **(a)** (seufzend) ~[, **so ist das Leben**] o well[, that's life]; **(b)** (ungeduldig) ~[, **ich komme schon**]! OK, OK *or* all right, all right[, I'm coming]!

Jakob /ˈjaːkɔp/ (*der*) James; (in der Bibel) Jacob; **ich weiß ja nicht, ob das der wahre ~ ist** (ugs.) I don't know if that is really quite the thing

Jakobiner /jakoˈbiːnɐ/ *der;* ~s, ~ (hist.) Jacobin

Jalousette /ʒaluˈzɛtə/ *die;* ~, ~n, **Jalousie** /ʒaluˈziː/ *die;* ~, ~n Venetian blind

Jamaika /jaˈmaɪka/ (*das*) ~s Jamaica

Jamaikaner *der;* ~s, ~, **Jamaikanerin** *die;* ~, ~nen Jamaican

jamaikanisch *Adj.* Jamaican

Jamaika·rum *der* Jamaica rum

jambisch *Adj.* (Verslehre) iambic

Jambus /ˈjambʊs/ *der;* ~, **Jamben** (Verslehre) iambus; iamb; **ein Drama in Jamben** a drama in iambic verse *or* in iambics

Jammer /ˈjamɐ/ *der;* ~s **(a)** (Wehklagen) [mournful] wailing; **(b)** (Elend) misery; **ein Bild des ~s** a picture of misery; **es ist ein ~, dass** ... (ugs.) it's a crying shame that ...

Jammer-: ~**bild** *das* miserable sight; ~**gestalt** *die* **(a)** pitiful creature; **(b)** (ugs. abwertend) miserable wretch; ~**lappen** *der* (ugs. abwertend) (Feigling) coward; (Schwächling) sniveller

jämmerlich /ˈjɛmɐlɪç/ **1** *Adj.* **(a)** (Jammer ausdrückend) pathetic; pitiful; **(b)** (beklagenswert) miserable ⟨*existence, conditions, etc.*⟩; wretched ⟨*appearance, existence, etc.*⟩; **(c)** (ärmlich) pathetic; pitiful ⟨*conditions, clothing, housing*⟩; paltry, meagre ⟨*quantity*⟩; pitiful, sorry ⟨*state*⟩; **(d)** (abwertend: minderwertig) contemptible ⟨*person*⟩; pathetic, paltry ⟨*wages, sum*⟩; pathetic, useless ⟨*piece of work etc.*⟩. **2** *adv.* **(a)** (Jammer ausdrückend) pathetically; pitifully; **(b)** (beklagenswert) miserably; hopelessly; pitifully; ~ **versagen** fail miserably *or* hopelessly; **(c)** (ärmlich) pitifully; miserably; **(d)** (abwertend: schlecht) pathetically; hopelessly; **(e)** (sehr, stark) terribly (coll.); ~ **frieren** be frozen stiff

jammern *itr. V.* **(a)** wail; **ohne zu ~:** without so much as a groan; **(b)** (sich beklagen) moan; grumble; **über sein Schicksal ~:** bemoan one's fate; **(c)** (verlangen) cry [out]; **die Kinder jammerten nach einem Stück Brot** the children were crying out for *or* crying after a piece of bread

jammer-, Jammer-: ~**schade** *Adj.; nicht attr.* (ugs.) **es ist ~schade, dass** ...: it's a crying shame that ...; **es ist ~schade um ihn** it's a great pity about him; ~**tal** *das; o. Pl.* (geh.) vale of tears; ~**voll 1** *Adj.* **(a)** pathetic; pitiful ⟨*cry etc.*⟩; **(b)** (beklagenswert) miserable; **2** *adv.* **(a)** pathetically; pitifully; **(b)** (beklagenswert) miserably; wretchedly

Janker /ˈjaŋkɐ/ *der;* ~s, ~ (südd., österr.) Alpine jacket

Jänner /ˈjɛnɐ/ *der;* ~s, ~ (österr.), **Januar** /ˈjanuaːɐ/ *der;* ~[s], ~e ▶ 119 │ January; *s. auch* **April**

Japan /ˈjaːpan/ (*das*) ~s Japan

Japaner *der;* ~s, ~, **Japanerin** *die;* ~, ~nen ▶ 388 │ Japanese

japanisch *Adj.* ▶ 388 │, ▶ 487 │ Japanese; **Japanisch/ das Japanische** Japanese; *s. auch* **Deutsch**

Japs /japs/ *der;* ~es, ~e (ugs. abwertend) Jap (derog.)

japsen /ˈjapsn̩/ *itr. V.* (ugs.) pant; **ich kann kaum noch ~:** I'm gasping for breath

Japser *der;* ~s, ~ (ugs.) gasp of breath

Jargon /jarˈgõː/ *der;* ~s, ~s **(a)** jargon; **der ~ der Juristen/Mediziner** legal/medical jargon; **der Berliner ~:** Berlin slang; **im „Spiegel"-~:** in the jargon of the 'Spiegel'; **(b)** (abwertend) language; **er redet in einem ganz ordinären ~:** he uses very vulgar language

Ja·sager /-zaɡɐ/ *der;* ~s, ~ (abwertend) yes-man

Jasmin /jasˈmiːn/ *der;* ~s, ~e **(a)** jasmine; **(b)** (Falscher ~) mock orange

Jasmin·tee *der* jasmine-tea

Jass, *Jaß /jas/ *der;* **Jasses** (schweiz.) jass

jassen *itr. V.* (schweiz.) play jass

Ja·stimme *die* yes-vote; **die ~n** the votes in favour; the ayes (Brit. Parl.)

jäten /ˈjɛːtn̩/ **1** *tr. V.* weed [out]; ⟨*dandelions, thistles, etc.*⟩; weed ⟨*flower bed*⟩; **Unkraut ~:** weed. **2** *itr. V.* weed

Jauche /ˈjaʊxə/ *die;* ~, ~n **(a)** liquid manure; **(b)** (ugs. abwertend) muck

Jauche·grube *die* liquid-manure reservoir

jauchzen /ˈjaʊxtsn̩/ *itr. V.* **(a)** cheer; **vor Freude ~:** shout for joy; **das Publikum jauchzte** the audience was in raptures; **(b)** (veralt.) rejoice; **jauchzet dem Herrn** rejoice in the Lord

Jauchzer *der;* ~s, ~: cry of delight

jaulen /ˈjaʊlən/ *itr. V.* ⟨*dog, cat, etc.*⟩ howl, yowl; ⟨*wind*⟩ howl; ⟨*engine*⟩ scream

Jause /ˈjaʊzə/ *die;* ~, ~n (österr.) **(a)** snack; **eine ~ machen** have a snack; **(b)** (Nachmittagskaffee) [afternoon] tea

Jausen·station *die* (österr.) café

jausnen *itr. V.* (österr.) have a snack

ja·wohl 1 *Interj.* certainly; ~, **Herr Oberst!** yes, sir! **2** *Partikel* certainly, ~ **Kant** Kant, no less

jawoll /jaˈvɔl/ (ugs.) ⇒ **jawohl**

Ja·wort *das* consent; **jmdm. das ~ geben** consent to marry sb.; **sich** (*Dat.*) **das ~ geben** accept each other in marriage

Jazz /dʒæz od. dʒɛs od. jats/ *der;* ~: jazz

Jazz-: ~**band** *die,* ~**kapelle** *die* jazz band; ~**keller** *der* jazz cellar; ~**musik** *die* jazz music; ~**rock** *der* jazz-rock

Jazzer /ˈdʒɛːzɐ od. ˈjatsɐ/ *der;* ~s, ~: jazz musician

jazzig /ˈdʒɛːzɪç/ *Adj.* (ugs.) jazzy

je¹ /jeː/ **1** *Adv.* **(a)** (jemals) ever; **mehr/besser denn je** more/better than ever; **seit** *od.* **von je** always; for as long as anyone can remember; *s. auch* **eh²** b; **(b)** (jeweils) **je zehn Personen** ten people at a time; **die Kinder stellen sich je zwei und zwei auf** the children arrange themselves in twos *or* in pairs; **sie kosten je 30 DM** they cost 30 DM each; **er gab den Mädchen je eine Birne** he gave each of the girls a pear; **in Schachteln mit** *od.* **zu je 10 Stück verpackt** packed in boxes of ten; **(c) je nach Gewicht/Geschmack** according to weight/taste. **2** *Präp. mit Akk.* for each; **je angebrochene Stunde** for each *or* per hour or part of an hour. **3** *Konj.* **(a) je länger, je lieber** the longer the better; **je früher du kommst, desto** *od.* **um so mehr Zeit haben wir** the earlier you come, the more time we'll have; **(b) je nachdem** it all depends; **wir gehen hin, je nachdem [, ob] wir Zeit haben oder nicht** we'll go, depending on whether we have the time or not

je² *Interj.* **ach je, wie schade!** oh dear *or* dear me, what a shame!

Jeans /dʒiːnz/ *Pl. od. die;* ~, ~ jeans *pl.;* denims *pl.*

Jeans-: ~**hose** *die* [pair of] jeans; ~**jacke** *die* denim jacket; ~**stoff** *der* denim; jean[s] material

jeck /jɛk/ *Adj.* (rhein., meist abwertend) (leicht verrückt) stupid; daft; (wahnsinnig) crazy

Jeck *der;* ~en, ~en (rhein.) **(a)** (abwertend: Verrückter) idiot; **(b)** (Fastnachter) carnival clown

jede ⇒ **jeder**

jeden·falls *Adv.* **(a)** in any case; at any rate; anyway; **das steht ~ fest** that much is certain, in any case *or* at any rate *or* anyway; **(b)** (zumindest) at any rate; **ich ~ habe**

keine Lust mehr I at any rate *or* for one have had enough

jeder /'je:dɐ/, **jede**, **jedes** *Indefinitpron. u. unbest. Zahlwort* **1** *attr.* **(a)** (alle) every; **jeder einzelne Schüler** every single pupil; **jeder zweite Bürger** one out of *or* in every two citizens; **der Zug fährt jeden Tag/viermal jeden Tag** the train runs every day/four times a day; **das kann Ihnen jedes Kind sagen** any child could tell you that; **ohne jeden Zweifel** without any doubt; **ohne jeden Grund** without any reason whatever; for no reason whatever; **(b)** (alle einzeln) each; **(c)** (jeglicher) all; **jede Hilfe kam zu spät** all help came too late; **hier wurde jedes Maß überschritten** that went beyond all bounds; **Menschen jeden** *od.* **jedes Alters** people of all ages. **2** *allein stehend* **(a)** (alle) everyone; everybody; **jeder** *od.* (geh.) **ein jeder darf mitkommen** everyone *or* everybody can come; **hier kennt jeder jeden** everybody knows everybody else here; (verstärkend) **jeder, der Lust hat, ist willkommen** anyone who wants to come is welcome; **das kann ja jeder** anyone can do that; **(b)** (alle einzeln) **jedes der Kinder** every one *or* each of the children; **jeder von uns kann helfen** each *or* every one of us can help; **jedem nach seinem Verdienst** to each according to his merits

jeder-: ~**art** *unbest. Gattungsz.; indekl.; nicht präd.* any kind *or* sort *or* type of; ~**lei** *unbest. Gattungsz.; indekl.; nicht präd.* (geh.) all kinds *or* sorts of; ~**mann** *Indefinitpron.* everyone; everybody; **hier kann** ~**mann mitmachen** everyone *or* everybody *or* anyone *or* anybody can come along and join in; **Schnecken sind nicht** ~**manns Sache/Geschmack** snails are not to everyone's *or* everybody's taste; ~**zeit** *Adv.* [at] any time

jedes ⇒ **jeder**

*****jedes·mal** ⇒ **Mal**[1]

je·doch *Konj., Adv.* however; **es war** ~ **zu spät** it was too late, however; it was, however, too late

Jeep ⓌⓏ /dʒiːp/ *der;* ~**s**, ~**s** jeep (P)

jeglicher /'je:klɪçɐ/, **jegliche**, **jegliches** *Indefinitpron. u. unbest. Zahlw.* ⇒ **jeder 1 c, 2 b**

je·her /*od.* ˈ--/ *Adv.* **seit** *od.* **von** ~: always; since *or* from time immemorial

Jehova /je'ho:va/ ⇒ **Zeuge**

jemals /'je:ma:ls/ *Adv.* ever

jemand /'je:mant/ *Indefinitpron.* someone; somebody; (fragend, verneint) anyone; anybody; **ich kenne** ~**[en], der …:** I know someone *or* somebody who …; **sich mit** ~**[em] treffen** to meet someone *or* somebody; **ist da** ~**?** is anybody there?; **ich glaube nicht, dass da** ~ **ist** I don't think there's anybody there; ~ **anders/Fremdes** someone *or* somebody else/strange; **kaum** ~**:** hardly *or* scarcely anyone *or* anybody

Jemen /'je:mən/ *(das);* ~**s** *od.* **der;** ~**[s]** Yemen; *s. auch* **Irak**

jener /'je:nɐ/, **jene**, **jenes** *Demonstrativpron.* (geh.) **1** *attr.* that; *Pl.* those; **in jenem Haus dort** in that house [over] there; **zu jenem Zeitpunkt** at that time; **in jenen Tagen** in those days. **2** *allein stehend* that one; *Pl.* those; **jene, die …:** those who …

jenseitig /'je:n- *od.* 'jɛn-/ *Adj.; nicht präd.* opposite; far, opposite ‹ *bank, shore* ›

jenseits /'je:n-/ **1** *Präp. mit Gen.* on the other side of; (in größerer Entfernung) beyond; ~ **des Flusses** on the other *or* far *or* opposite side of the river. **2** *Adv.* beyond; on the other side; ~ **von** on the other side of; beyond; **eine Welt** ~ **von Hass und Gewalt** a world free from hatred and violence

Jenseits *das;* ~**:** hereafter; beyond; **jmdn. ins** ~ **befördern** (salopp) bump sb. off (sl.)

Jersey[1] /'dʒø:ɐzi/ *der;* ~**[s]**, ~**s** jersey

Jersey[2] *das;* ~**s**, ~**s** jersey

Jersey·kleid *das* jersey dress

Jesuit /je'zui:t/ *der;* ~**en**, ~**en** (Rel., auch fig. abwertend) Jesuit

Jesus /'je:zʊs/ *(der);* **Jesu** /'je:zu/ Jesus; ~ **Christus** Jesus Christ

Jesus·kind *das:* **das** ~**:** the Infant Jesus; baby Jesus (child lang.)

Jet /dʒɛt/ *der;* ~**[s]**, ~**s** jet

Jetset /'dʒɛtsɛt/ *der;* ~**[s]**, ~**s** jet set

jetten /'dʒɛtn̩/ *itr. V.; mit sein* (ugs.) jet

jetzig /'jɛtsɪç/ *Adj.; nicht präd.* present; current

jetzt /jɛtst/ *Adv.* **(a)** at the moment; just now; **bis** ~: up to now; **bis** ~ **noch nicht** not yet; not so far; **von** ~ **an** *od.* **ab** from now on[wards]; ~ **noch** still; **was,** ~ **[so spät] noch?** what, now?; ~ **oder nie!** it's now or never; ~ **ist aber Schluss!** that's [quite] enough!; ~ **ist es aus mit uns** we've had it now; ~ **endlich** [now,] at last; **erst** ~ *od.* ~ **erst** only just; **schon** ~: already; **er ist** ~ **schon drei Wochen krank** he has been ill for three weeks now; **(b)** (heutzutage) now; these days; nowadays

Jetzt *das;* ~ (geh.) **das** ~: the present

jeweilig /'je:vaɪlɪç/ *Adj.; nicht präd.* **(a)** (in einem bestimmten Fall) particular; **(b)** (zu einer bestimmten Zeit) current; of the time *postpos., not pred.;* **(c)** (zugehörig, zugewiesen) respective

jeweils /'je:vaɪls/ *Adv.* **(a)** (jedesmal) ~ **am ersten/ letzten Mittwoch des Monats** on the first/last Wednesday of each month; **(b)** (zur Zeit) currently; at the time

Jh. *Abk.* **Jahrhundert** c.

jiddisch /'jɪdɪʃ/ *Adj.* ▶ 487 ◀ Yiddish; **Jiddisch/das Jiddische** Yiddish; *s. auch* **Deutsch**

Jiu-Jitsu /dʒiːuˈdʒɪtsu/ *das;* ~**[s]** j[i]u-jitsu

Job /dʒɔp/ *der;* ~**s**, ~**s** ▶ 85 ◀ (ugs.; auch DV) job

jobben *itr. V.* (ugs.) do a job/jobs; **als Taxifahrer** ~: do [some] taxi-driving

Jobber *der;* ~**s**, ~ (Börsenw.) [stock] jobber

Joch /jɔx/ *das;* ~**[e]s**, ~**e (a)** (auch fig.) yoke; **Ochsen ins/unters** ~ **spannen** yoke oxen; **(b)** (Geogr.) col; saddle

Joch·bein *das* (Anat.) zygomatic bone; malar bone

Jockei, Jockey /'dʒɔke *od.* 'dʒɔki/ *der;* ~**s**, ~**s** jockey

Jod /jo:t/ *das;* ~**[e]s** iodine

Jodel·lied *das* yodelling song

jodeln /'jo:dl̩n/ *itr., tr. V.* yodel

Jodler *der;* ~**s**, ~ **(a)** (Person) yodeller; **(b)** (kurzes Jodeln) yodel

Jodlerin *die;* ~, ~**nen** yodeller

Jod·tinktur *die* tincture of iodine; iodine tincture

Joga /'jo:ga/ *der od. das;* ~**[s]** yoga

Joga·übung *die* yoga exercise

joggen /'dʒɔgn̩/ *itr. V.; mit Richtungsangabe mit sein* jog; **[zwei Kilometer]** ~: go jogging [for two km]

Jogging /'dʒɔgɪŋ/ *das;* ~**s** jogging *no art.*

Joghurt /'jo:gʊrt/ *der od. das;* ~**[s]**, ~**[s]** yoghurt

Joghurt·becher *der* yoghurt pot (Brit.) *or* (Amer.) container

Jogi /'jo:gi/ *der;* ~**s**, ~**s** yogi

Johann /'jo:han/ *(der)* John

Johanna /jo'hana/ *(die)* Joan; ~ **von Orléans** Joan of Arc

Johannes /jo'hanəs/ *(der);* **Johannes'** John; ~ **der Täufer** John the Baptist

Johanni /jo'hani/ *(das); indekl.* ⇒ **Johannistag**

Johannis·beere *die* currant; **rote/weiße/schwarze** ~**n** redcurrants/white currants/blackcurrants

Johannisbeer-: ~**saft** *der* currant juice; ~**strauch** *der* currant bush

Johannis-: ~**brot** *das* (Bot.) Saint-John's-bread; carob [bean]; ~**feuer** *das* Saint John's fire; ~**käfer** *der* (südd.) ⇒ **Leuchtkäfer;** ~**tag** *der* Saint John the Baptist's day

Johanniter·orden *der* Order of [the Hospital of] St. John of Jerusalem

johlen /'jo:lən/ *itr. V.* yell; (vor Wut) howl

Joint /dʒɔɪnt/ *der;* ~**s**, ~**s** (ugs.) joint (sl.)

Jointventure, Joint Venture /'dʒɔɪntˈventʃə/ *das;* ~**s**, ~**s** (Wirtsch.) joint venture

Jo-Jo /joː(ː)'joː/ *das;* ~s, ~s yo-yo

Joker /'joːkɐ *od.* dʒoːkɐ/ *der;* ~s, ~ (Kartensp.) joker

Jolle /'jɔlə/ *die;* ~, ~n keel-centre-board yawl

Jollen·kreuzer *der* dinghy cruiser

Jongleur /ʒɔŋg'løːɐ̯/ *der;* ~s, ~e juggler

jonglieren *tr., itr. V.* juggle; **Bälle** *od.* **mit Bällen** ~: juggle with balls; **mit Zahlen** ~ (fig.) juggle [about] with figures

Jordan /'jɔrdan/ *der;* ~[s] Jordan; **über den** ~ **gehen** (verhüll.) go the way of all flesh

Jordanien /jɔr'daːniən/ *(das);* ~s Jordan

Jordanier *der;* ~s, ~, **Jordanierin** *die;* ~, ~nen Jordanian

jordanisch *Adj.* Jordanian

Jot /jɔt/ *das;* ~, ~: j, J; *s. auch* **a, A**

Jota /'joːta/ *das;* ~[s], ~s iota; **kein/nicht ein/um kein** ~ (geh.) not an iota; not one jot

Joule /dʒuːl *od.* dʒaul/ *das;* ~[s], ~ (Physik) joule

Journal /ʒʊr'naːl/ *das;* ~s, ~e **(a)** (veralt.: Tageszeitung) journal (dated); newspaper; **(b)** (geh.: Zeitschrift) journal; periodical; **(c)** (veralt.: Tagebuch) journal (dated); diary

Journal·beamte *der* (österr.) official *or* officer [on duty]

Journalismus *der;* ~: journalism *no art.*

Journalist *der;* ~en, ~en, **Journalistin** *die;* ~, ~nen journalist

journalistisch 1 *Adj.; nicht präd.* journalistic; **eine** ~e **Ausbildung** a training in journalism. **2** *adv.* journalistically; ~ **tätig sein** work as *or* be a journalist

jovial /jo'viaːl/ *Adj.* jovial

Jovialität /joviali'tɛːt/ *die;* ~: joviality

Joystick /'dʒɔɪstɪk/ *der;* ~s, ~s (DV) joystick

jr. *Abk.* **junior** Jr.

Jubel /'juːbl̩/ *der;* ~s rejoicing; jubilation; (laut) cheering; **großer** ~ **brach aus** a loud cheer went up; **unter dem** ~ **der Zuschauer** amid the cheering *or* cheers of the spectators

Jubel-: ~**feier** *die* jubilee; anniversary; (Feierlichkeiten) jubilee *or* anniversary celebrations *pl.* ~**jahr** *das* jubilee; **alle** ~**jahre [einmal]** once in a blue moon

jubeln *itr. V.* cheer; **über etw.** *(Akk.)* ~: rejoice over sth.

Jubel-: ~**paar** *das* couple celebrating their wedding anniversary; ~**ruf** *der* cheer; joyful shout

Jubilar /jubi'laːɐ̯/ *der;* ~s, ~e man celebrating his anniversary/birthday

Jubilarin *die;* ~, ~nen woman celebrating her anniversary/birthday

Jubiläum /jubi'lɛːʊm/ *das;* ~s, **Jubiläen** anniversary; (eines Monarchen) jubilee; **fünfundzwanzigjähriges/ fünfzigjähriges** ~: twenty-fifth/fiftieth anniversary/jubilee; **hundertjähriges** ~: hundredth anniversary; centenary

Jubiläums-: ~**aus·gabe** *die* jubilee edition; ~**aus·stellung** *die* jubilee exhibition

jubilieren *itr. V.* (geh. veralt.) jubilate (literary); rejoice

juchhe /jʊx'heː/, **juchheißa** /jʊx'haisa/ *Interj.* (veralt.) hurrah

Juchten /'jʊxtn̩/ *der od. das;* ~s **(a)** (Leder) Russia [leather]; **(b)** (Duftstoff) Russian leather

juchzen /'jʊxtsn̩/ *itr. V.* (ugs.) shout with glee

Juchzer *der;* ~s, ~ (ugs.) shout of glee; **einen** ~ **aus·stoßen** shout with glee

jucken /'jʊkn̩/ **1** *tr., itr. V.* **(a)** **mir juckt die Haut** I itch; **es juckt mir** *od.* **mich auf dem Kopf** my head itches; **es juckt mich hier** I've got an itch here; **(b)** (Juckreiz verursachen) irritate; **die Wolle juckt ihn** *od.* **ihm auf der Haut** the wool makes him itch; the wool irritates his skin; **ein** ~**der Hautausschlag** an itching rash. **2** *tr. V.* (ugs.) **(a)** (reizen) **es juckt mich, das zu tun** I am itching *or* dying to do it; **(b)** (stören) **das juckt mich nicht** I couldn't care less (coll.). **3** *refl. V.* (ugs.: sich kratzen) scratch

Jucken *das;* ~s itching; **ein** ~ **verspüren** feel an itch

Juck-: ~**pulver** *das* itching powder; ~**reiz** *der* itch

Judaist *der;* ~en, ~en, **Judaistin** *die;* ~, ~nen specialist in Jewish studies

Judaistik *die;* ~: Jewish studies *pl., no art.*

Judas /'juːdas/ **1** (*der*) **Judas'** Judas; ~ **Ischariot** Judas Iscariot. **2** *der;* ~, ~**se** (fig.) Judas

Jude /'juːdə/ *der;* ~n, ~n Jew; **er ist** ~: he is a Jew; he is Jewish

Juden-: ~**hass**, *~**haß** *der* anti-Semitism; hatred of [the] Jews; ~**hetze** *die* Jew-baiting; ~**pogrom** *der od. das* pogrom against the Jews; ~**stern** *der* (ns.) Star of David

Judentum *das;* ~s **(a)** (Volk) Jewry; Jews *pl.;* **das gesamte** ~: the whole of Jewry; **(b)** (Kultur u. Religion) Judaism

Juden-: ~**verfolgung** *die* persecution of [the] Jews; ~**viertel** *das* Jewish quarter; (hist.) Jewry

Judikative /judika'tiːvə/ *die;* ~, ~n (Rechtsw., Politik) judiciary

Jüdin /'jyːdɪn/ *die;* ~, ~nen Jewess; **sie ist** ~: she is Jewish *or* a Jewess

jüdisch *Adj.* Jewish

Judo /'juːdo/ *das;* ~[s] judo *no art.*

Judo·griff *der* judo throw

Judoka /ju'doːka/ *der;* ~[s], ~[s] judoka; judoist

Jugend /'juːgn̩t/ *die;* ~ **(a)** youth; **in ihrer** ~: in her youth; when she was young; **schon in früher** ~: at an early age; **schon von** ~ **auf** from an early age; from his/ her *etc.* youth; **(b)** (Jugendliche) young people; **die weibliche/männliche** ~: girls *pl.*/boys *pl.*

jugend-, Jugend-: ~**alter** *das* adolescence; ~**amt** *das* youth office (agency responsible for education and welfare of young people); ~**arrest** *der* detention in a community home; **vier Wochen** ~**arrest** four weeks in a community home; ~**buch** *das* book for young people; ~**frei** *Adj.* (film, book, etc.) suitable for persons under 18; **nicht** ~**frei** (film) not U-certificate *pred.;* (scherzh.) (joke, story, etc.) not for young ears *pred.;* ~**freund** *der* friend of [the days of] one's youth; **er ist ein** ~**freund von ihr** he used to be a friend of hers when she was young; ~**gefährdend** *Adj.* liable to have an undesirable influence on the moral development of young people *postpos.;* ~**gericht** *das* juvenile court; ~**gruppe** *die* youth group; ~**heim** *das* youth centre; ~**herberge** *die* youth hostel; ~**klub** *der* youth club; ~**kriminalität** *die* juvenile delinquency

jugendlich /'juːgn̩tlɪç/ **1** *Adj.* **(a)** *nicht präd.* young (offender, customer, etc.); **noch in** ~**em Alter sein** still be a youngster; still be young; **(b)** (jung, für Jugendliche charakteristisch) youthful; **in** ~**er Begeisterung** fired by the spirit of youth *or* by youthful enthusiasm; **sie wirkt noch sehr** ~: she still looks very young; **(c)** (bes. Werbespr.) young (fashions, dress, hairstyle, etc.). **2** *adv.* **sich** ~ **kleiden** dress young

Jugendliche /'juːgn̩tlɪçə/ *der/die; adj. Dekl.* **(a)** young person; **für** ~: for young people; **(b)** (Rechtsspr.) juvenile; young person; **zwei** ~: two juveniles; two young persons; **ein 16jähriger** ~**r/eine 16jährige** ~: a 16-year-old youth/girl

Jugendlichkeit *die* youth; (jugendliche Wirkung) youthfulness

Jugend-: ~**liebe** *die* love *or* sweetheart of one's youth; ~**mannschaft** *die* (Sport) youth team *or* side; ~**meister** *der* youth champion; (Mannschaft) youth champions; ~**psychologie** *die* psychology of adolescence; adolescent psychology *no art.;* ~**schutz** *der* protection of young people; ~**sprache** *die* young people's language *no art.;* ~**stil** *der* art nouveau; (in Deutschland) Jugendstil; ~**straf·anstalt** *die* detention centre; ~**strafe** *die* youth custody sentence; **sechs Monate** ~**strafe** get six months in a detention centre; ~**sünde** *die*, ~**torheit** *die* youthful folly; ~**weihe** *die* (ehem. DDR) ceremony in which fourteen-year-olds are given adult social status; ~**werk** *das* early *or* youthful work; (gesamtes) early *or* youthful works *pl.;* juvenilia *pl.;* ~**zeit** *die* youth; younger days *pl.;* ~**zentrum** *das* youth centre

Jugo·sl̯a̲we /jugo-/ *der* ▶388| Yugoslav
Jugo·sl̯a̲wien (*das*)*;* ∼**s** Yugoslavia
Jugo·sl̯a̲win *die* Yugoslav
jugo·sl̯a̲wisch *Adj.* ▶388| Yugoslav[ian]
Juice /d̮ʒuːs/ *der od. das;* ∼, ∼**s** /'d̮ʒuːsɪs/ (bes. österr.) [fruit] juice
Julei /ju:'la̲i̯/ *der;* ∼[s], ∼**s** (ugs.; bes. zur Verdeutlichung) ⇒ **Juli**
Juli /'ju:li/ *der;* ∼[s], ∼**s** ▶119| July; *s. auch* **April**
Jumper /'d̮ʒampɐ/ *der;* ∼**s**, ∼**:** jumper (Brit.); pullover
jun. *Abk.* **junior** Jr.
jung /jʊŋ/ *Adj.; jünger* /'jʏŋɐ/, **jüngst**... /'jʏŋst.../ ▶22| young; new ⟨*project, undertaking, sport, marriage, etc.*⟩; **er ist ∼ gestorben** he died young; **∼ an Jahren** young in years; **Cato der Jüngere** Cato the Younger; **[ganze] 30 Jahre ∼** (ugs. scherzh.) 30 years young; **Sport hält ∼** sport keeps you young; **die Nacht ist noch ∼:** the night is young; **der ∼e Tag** (geh.) the new day; **in jüngster Zeit** recently; lately; **ein Ereignis der jüngeren/ jüngsten Geschichte** an event in recent/very recent history; **die jüngsten Geschehnisse** the latest *or* [most] recent happenings; **der Jüngste Tag** (Rel.) doomsday
Jung-: ∼**brunnen** *der* Fountain of Youth; **das ist ein wahrer** ∼**brunnen** (fig.) that's a real tonic; ∼**bürger** *der* (bes. österr.) first-time voter; new voter
Jungchen *das;* ∼**s**, ∼ (bes. ostd.) little boy; little lad; **mein** ∼**:** my boy *or* lad
Junge¹ /'jʊŋə/ *der;* ∼**n**, ∼**n** *od.* (ugs.) Jung[en]s boy; **Tag, alter** ∼**!** (ugs.) hello, old pal! (coll.); **jmdn. wie einen dummen** ∼**n behandeln** (ugs.) treat sb. like a child; ∼, ∼**!** (ugs.) [boy], oh boy!; *s. auch* **schwer 1 e**
Junge² *das; adj. Dekl.* **ein** ∼ one of the young; ∼ **kriegen** give birth to young; **eine Löwin und ihr** ∼**s** a lioness and her cub
Jüngelchen /'jʏŋl̩çən/ *das;* ∼**s**, ∼ (ugs. abwertend) young puppy *or* cub
jungenhaft *Adj.* boyish
Jungen-: ∼**klasse** *die* boys' class; **wir waren eine reine** ∼**klasse** our class was all boys; ∼**schule** *die* boys' school; school for boys; ∼**streich** *der* boyish prank
jünger /'jʏŋɐ/ *Adj.* youngish; **sie ist noch** ∼**:** she is still quite young; **Jüngere** (jüngere Menschen) [the] younger people; **die Jüngeren unter Ihnen** the younger ones amongst you; *s. auch* **jung**
Jünger *der;* ∼**s**, ∼**:** follower; disciple; (der Kunst, Literatur) devotee; **Jesus und seine** ∼**:** Jesus and his disciples
Jungfer /'jʊŋfɐ/ *die;* ∼, ∼**n** (a) (veralt.) young lady; (b) (abwertend: ältere ledige Frau) spinster; **eine alte** ∼**:** an old maid
Jungfern-: ∼**fahrt** *die* ma̲i̯den voyage; ∼**flug** *der* ma̲i̯den flight; ∼**häutchen** *das* hymen
Jung·frau *die* (a) virgin; **sie ist noch** ∼**:** she is still a virgin; **die** ∼ **Maria** the Virgin Mary; (b) (Astrol.) Virgo; (c) (veralt.: junges Mädchen) young maid *or* maiden (arch.)
jung·fräulich /-frɔ̯yliç/ *Adj.* (geh., auch fig.) virgin; ∼ **in die Ehe gehen** be a virgin bride
Jungfräulichkeit *die* (geh.) virginity; (fig.) virgin state
Jung·geselle *der* bachelor
Jung·gesellen-: ∼**bude** *die* (ugs.) bachelor pad (coll.); ∼**leben** *das* bachelor['s] life; ∼**wohnung** *die* bachelor flat; ∼**zeit** *die* bachelor days *pl.;* bachelorhood
Jung·gesellin *die* bachelor girl; **sie ist** ∼**gesellin geblieben** she never married
Jüngling /'jʏŋlɪŋ/ *der;* ∼**s**, ∼**e** (geh./spött.) youth; boy
jüngst /jʏŋst/ *Adv.* (geh.) recently
jüngst... ⇒ **jung**
Jüngste *der/die; adj. Dekl.* (Sohn, Tochter) youngest [one]
Jung-: ∼**steinzeit** *die* Neolithic period; New Stone Age; ∼**tier** *das* young animal; ∼**verheiratete** *der/ die; adj. Dekl.,* (geh.) ∼**vermählte** *der/die; adj. Dekl.* young married man/woman; **die** ∼**verheirateten** the newly-weds; ∼**volk** *das; o. Pl.* (veralt., scherzh.) young folk; ∼**wähler** *der* first-time voter; new voter

Juni /'ju:ni/ *der;* ∼[s], ∼**s** ▶119| June; *s. auch* **April**
junior /'ju:nịor/ *indekl. Adj.; nach Personennamen* junior
Junior *der;* ∼**s**, ∼**en** /-'nịo:rən/ (a) (oft scherzh.) junior (joc.); **mit seinem** ∼**:** with junior; (b) (Kaufmannsspr.) junior partner
Junior·chef *der* owner's *or* (coll.) boss's son
Junioren-: ∼**mannschaft** *die* youth team; ∼**meister** *der* junior champion; (Mannschaft) junior champions
Junior·partner *der* junior partner
Junker /'jʊŋkɐ/ *der;* ∼**s**, ∼ (hist., oft abwertend) junker; squire
Junkie /d̮ʒʌŋki/ *der;* ∼**s**, ∼**s** (Drogenjargon) junkie (sl.)
Junktim *das;* ∼**s**, ∼**s** package [deal]; **zwischen den beiden Abkommen besteht ein** ∼**:** the two agreements form one package
Juno /ju'no:/ *der;* ∼[s], ∼**s** (ugs.; bes. zur Verdeutlichung) June
Junta /'xʊnta/ *die;* ∼, **Junten** junta
Jupiter /'ju:pitɐ/ *der;* ∼**s** (Astron.) Jupiter
Jura¹ /'ju:ra/ *o. Art., o. Pl.* law; ∼ **studieren** read *or* study Law
Jura² *der;* ∼**s** (Geol.) Jurassic [period/system]
juridisch /ju'ri:dɪʃ/ *Adj.* (österr., veralt.) ⇒ **juristisch**
Jurisdiktion /jurɪsdɪk'tsi̯o:n/ *die;* ∼, ∼**en** (geh.) jurisdiction
Jurisprudenz /jurɪspru'dɛnts/ *die;* ∼**:** jurisprudence *no art.*
Jurist *der;* ∼**en**, ∼**en** ▶85| lawyer; jurist
Juristerei *die;* ∼ (oft scherzh.) law *no art.*
Juristin *die;* ∼, ∼**nen** ▶85| ⇒ **Jurist**
juristisch 1 *Adj.* legal ⟨*wrangle, term, training, career*⟩; law ⟨*examination*⟩; **die Juristische Fakultät** the Law Faculty. 2 *adv.* ∼ **denken** think in legal terms; ∼ **argumentieren** use legal arguments
Juror /'ju:ror/ *der;* ∼**s**, ∼**en** /-'ro:ren/, **Jurorin** *die;* ∼, ∼**nen** judge
Jury /ʒy'ri:/ *die;* ∼, ∼**s** panel [of judges]; jury
Jus /ju:s/ *das;* ∼ (österr., schweiz.) ⇒ **Jura¹**
just /jʊst/ *Adv.* (veralt., scherzh.) just; ∼ **an jenem Tag** on that very day
justieren *tr. V.* adjust
Justitiar: ⇒ **Justiziar**
Justiz /jʊs'ti:ts/ *die;* ∼**:** justice; (Behörden) judiciary; **ein Vertreter der** ∼**:** a representative of justice *or* of the law
Justiz-: ∼**beamte** *der* court official; ∼**behörde** *die* judicial authority;
Justiziar /jʊsti'tsi̯a:ɐ/ *der;* ∼**s**, ∼**e** company lawyer
Justiz-: ∼**irrtum** *der* miscarriage of justice; ∼**minister** *der* Minister of Justice; ∼**ministerium** *das* Ministry of Justice; ∼**mord** *der* judicial murder; ∼**vollzugs·anstalt** *die* (Amtsspr.) penal institution (formal)
Jute /'ju:tə/ *die;* ∼**:** jute
Jute·sack *der* jute *or* gunny sack
Jüt·land /'jy:t-/ (*das*)*;* ∼**s** Jutland
Juwel¹ /ju've:l/ *das od. der;* ∼**s**, ∼**en** piece *or* item of jewellery; (Edelstein) jewel; gem
Juwel² *das;* ∼**s**, ∼**e** (fig.) gem; **ein** ∼ **gotischer Baukunst** a gem *or* jewel of Gothic architecture
Juwelen·raub *der* jewel robbery
Juwelier /juvə'li:ɐ/ *der;* ∼**s** ▶85| jeweller; *s. auch* **Bäcker**
Juwelier·geschäft *das* jeweller's shop
Jux /jʊks/ *der;* ∼**es**, ∼**e** (ugs.) joke; **aus** ∼**:** as a joke; for fun; **sie machten sich** (*Dat.*) **einen** ∼ **daraus, das zu tun** they did it as a joke *or* for a lark
jwd /jɔtve:'de:/ *Adv.* (ugs. scherzh.) in *or* at the back of beyond; miles out

Kk

k, K /ka:/ *das;* ~, ~: k/K; *s. auch* **a, A**

Kabarett /kaba'rɛt/ *das;* ~s, ~s *od.* ~e **(a)** satirical cabaret [show]; satirical revue; **ein politisches** ~: a satirical political revue; **(b)** (Ensemble) cabaret act

Kabarettist *der;* ~en, ~en, **Kabarettistin** *die;* ~, ~nen revue performer

kabarettistisch *Adj.* [satirical] revue *attrib.;* ~e Szenen scenes in the style of a [satirical] revue

Kabäuschen /ka'bɔysçən/ *das;* ~s, ~ (ugs.) (Zimmer) cubbyhole; (Häuschen) little hut

Kabbelei *die;* ~, ~en squabble

kabbeln /'kabl̩n/ *refl. V.* (ugs.) squabble, bicker (**mit** with)

Kabel /'ka:bl̩/ *das;* ~s, ~ (auch veralt.: Telegramm) cable; (für kleineres Gerät) flex

Kabel·fernsehen *das* cable television

Kabeljau /'ka:bl̩jau/ *der;* ~s, ~e *od.* ~s cod

kabeln *tr., itr. V.* (veralt.) cable

Kabine /ka'bi:nə/ *die;* ~, ~n **(a)** cabin; **(b)** (Umkleideraum, abgeteilter Raum) cubicle; **in die** ~**n gehen** (Fußball) go back into the dressing rooms; **(c)** (einer Seilbahn) [cable-]car

Kabinen-: ~**bahn** *die* cableway; ~**roller** *der* bubble car

Kabinett /kabi'nɛt/ *das;* ~s, ~e **(a)** Cabinet; **(b)** (österr.: kleines Zimmer) small room with one window; boxroom (Brit.); **(c)** *o. Art.; o. Pl.* (Weinprädikat) Kabinett

Kabinetts-: ~**beschluss**, *~**beschluß** *der* Cabinet decision; ~**bildung** *die* formation of a/the Cabinet; ~**sitzung** *die* Cabinet meeting

Kabinett·stück[chen] *das* tour de force

Kabrio /'ka:brio/ *das;* ~s, ~s, **Kabriolett** /kabrio'lɛt/ *das;* ~s, ~s convertible

Kabuff /ka'bʊf/ *das;* ~s, ~s (ugs., oft abwertend) [poky little] cubbyhole

Kachel /'kaxl̩/ *die;* ~, ~n [glazed] tile; **etw. mit** ~**n auslegen** tile sth.

kacheln *tr. V.* tile; **eine grün gekachelte Wand** a wall covered with green tiles

Kachel·ofen *der* tiled stove

Kacke /'kakə/ *die;* ~ (derb; auch fig.) shit (coarse); crap (coarse); **so eine** ~! shit! (coarse)

kacken /'kakn̩/ *itr. V.* (derb) shit (coarse); crap (coarse)

Kadaver /ka'da:vɐ/ *der;* ~s, ~ (auch fig., abwertend) carcass

Kadaver·gehorsam *der* (abwertend) blind obedience

Kadenz /ka'dɛnts/ *die;* ~, ~en (Musik) cadence; (solistische Paraphrasierung) cadenza

Kader /'ka:dɐ/ *der od.* (schweiz.) *das;* ~s, ~ **(a)** cadre; **(b)** (Sport) squad

Kader-: ~**abteilung** *die* (DDR) personnel department; ~**akte** *die* (DDR) personal file; ~**arbeit** *die* (DDR) cadre work; ~**leiter** *der* (DDR) [chief] personnel officer

Kadi /'ka:di/ *der;* ~s, ~s cadi; **jmdn. vor den** ~ **schleppen** (ugs.) haul sb. up before a judge *or* (Brit. sl.) the beak

Kadmium /'katmiʊm/ *das* ~s (Chemie) cadmium

Käfer /'kɛ:fɐ/ *der;* ~s, ~: beetle

Kaff /kaf/ *das;* ~s, ~s *od.* **Käffer** /'kɛfɐ/ (ugs. abwertend) dump (coll.); hole (coll.)

Kaffee /'kafe *od.* (österr.) ka'fe:/ *der;* ~s, ~s **(a)** coffee; ~ **kochen** make coffee; ~ **mit Milch** white coffee (Brit.); coffee with milk; **dir haben sie wohl was in den** ~ **getan?** (ugs.) have you gone soft in the head? (coll.); **das ist**

kalter ~ (ugs.) (ist längst bekannt) that's old hat (coll.); (ist Unsinn) that's a load of old rubbish (coll.); **(b)** (Nachmittags~) afternoon coffee; ~ **trinken** have afternoon coffee

kaffee-, Kaffee-: ~**bohne** *die* coffee bean; ~**braun** *Adj.* coffee-coloured; ~**filter** *der* coffee filter; (Filtertüte) filter [paper]

Kaffee·haus *das* (bes. österr.) coffee-house

Kaffee-: ~**kanne** *die* coffee pot; ~**klatsch** *der* (ugs. scherzh.) get-together and a chat over coffee; coffeeklatsch (Amer.); ~**kränzchen** *das* (veralt.) **(a)** (Zusammentreffen) coffee afternoon; **(b)** (Gruppe) coffee circle; ~**löffel** *der* coffee-spoon; ~**maschine** *die* coffee-maker; ~**mühle** *die* coffee grinder; ~**pulver** *das* coffee powder; ~**satz** *der* coffee grounds *pl.;* ~**service** *das* coffee-service *or* -set; ~**sieb** *das* coffee-strainer; ~**tante** *die* (ugs. scherzh.) coffee addict; ~**tasse** *die* coffee cup; ~**tisch** *der:* **sie saßen gerade am** ~**tisch** they were [sitting] having coffee and cakes; ~**wärmer** *der* coffee pot cosy *or* cover; ~**wasser** *das:* ~**wasser/das** ~**wasser aufsetzen** put on some water for coffee/the water for the coffee

Kaffer /'kafɐ/ *der;* ~s, ~n **(a)** Xhosa; **(b)** (Schimpfwort) blockhead; thickhead

Käfig /'kɛ:fɪç/ *der;* ~s, ~e cage; **in einem goldenen** ~ **sitzen** (fig.) be a bird in a gilded cage

Kaftan /'kaftan/ *der;* ~s, ~e caftan

kahl /ka:l/ *Adj.* **(a)** (ohne Haare, Federn) bald; ~ **werden** go bald; **jmdn.** ~ **scheren** shave sb.'s hair off; shave sb.'s head; **sein** ~ **geschorener Kopf** his shaven head; **(b)** (ohne Grün, schmucklos) bare; **etw.** ~ **fressen** strip sth. bare

*****kahl|fressen** ⇒ kahl b

Kahlheit *die;* ~: ⇒ kahl a, b: baldness; bareness

kahl-, Kahl-: ~**kopf** *der* **(a)** bald head; **(b)** (ugs.: Person) baldhead; ~**köpfig** *Adj.* bald[-headed]; *****~|scheren** ⇒ kahl a; ~**schlag** *der* **(a)** clear-felling *no indef. art.;* clear-cutting *no indef. art.;* **(b)** (Waldfläche) clear-felled area; **(c)** (fig.) clearance

Kahn /ka:n/ *der;* ~[e]s, **Kähne** /'kɛ:nə/ **(a)** (Ruder~) rowing-boat; (Stech~) punt; ~ **fahren** go rowing/punting; **(b)** (Lastschiff) barge; **(c)** (ugs.: Schiff) tub

Kahn·fahrt *die;* ~, ~en trip in a rowing-boat/punt

Kai /kai/ *der;* ~s, ~s quay

Kai·anlage *die* quays *pl.*

Kaiman /'kaiman/ *der;* ~s, ~e (Zool.) cayman

Kai·mauer *die* quay wall

Kairo /'kairo/ *(das);* ~s ▶ 490◀ Cairo

Kaiser /'kaizɐ/ *der;* ~s, ~: emperor; **sich um des** ~**s Bart streiten** engage in pointless argument

Kaiserin *die;* ~, ~nen empress

Kaiser·krone *die* **(a)** imperial crown; **(b)** (Zierpflanze) crown imperial

kaiserlich *Adj.* imperial

kaiserlich-königlich *Adj.; nicht präd.* imperial and royal

Kaiser-: ~**reich** *das* empire; ~**schmarren** *der* (österr., südd.) pancake pulled to pieces and sprinkled with powdered sugar and raisins; ~**schnitt** *der* Caesarean section; ~**wetter** *das* (scherzh.) glorious, sunny weather (for an event)

Kajak /'kajak/ *der;* ~s, ~s kayak

Kajüte /ka'jy:tə/ *die;* ~, ~n (Seemannsspr.) cabin

Kakadu /'kakadu/ *der;* ~s, ~s cockatoo

Kakao /ka'kau/ *der;* ~s, ~s cocoa; **jmdn./etw. durch den** ~ **ziehen** (ugs.) make fun of sb./sth.; take the mickey out of sb./sth. (Brit. coll.)

Kakao·pulver *das* cocoa powder

Kakerlak /'ka:kɐlak/ *der;* ~s *od.* ~en, ~en cockroach; black-beetle

Kaktee /kak'te:ə/ *die;* ~, ~n, **Kaktus** /'kaktʊs/ *der;* ~, **Kakteen** cactus

Kalauer /'ka:lauɐ/ *der;* ~s, ~: laboured *or* (coll.) corny joke; (Wortspiel) atrocious *or* (coll.) corny pun

kalauern *itr. V.* tell laboured *or* (coll.) corny jokes; (mit Wortspielen) make atrocious *or* (coll.) corny puns

Kalb /kalp/ *das;* ~[e]s, **Kälber** /'kɛlbɐ/ (a) calf; (Hirsch~) fawn; (b) (~fleisch) veal

Kälbchen /'kɛlpçən/ *das;* ~s, ~: little calf

kalben *itr. V.* (auch Geogr.) calve

kalbern /'kalbɐn/ *itr. V.* (ugs.) mess *or* fool about *or* around

Kalb·fleisch *das* veal

Kalbs-: ~**braten** *der* roast veal *no indef. art.;* (Gericht) roast of veal; ~**brust** *die* breast of veal; ~**frikassee** *das* fricassee of veal; ~**hachse**, (südd.:) ~**haxe** *die* knuckle of veal; ~**leder** *das* calfskin; calf-leather; ~**schnitzel** *das* veal cutlet

Kaldaune /kal'daʊnə/ *die;* ~, ~**n** entrails *pl.*

Kaleidoskop /kalaido'sko:p/ *das;* ~**s**, ~**e** (auch fig.) kaleidoscope

Kalender /ka'lɛndɐ/ *der;* ~**s**, ~: calendar; (Taschen~) diary; **sich** (*Dat.*) **etw./einen Tag im** ~ [rot] **anstreichen** (oft iron.) mark sth. in red on the calendar/mark a day as a red-letter day

Kalender-: ~**blatt** *das* calendar sheet; ~**jahr** *das* calendar year

Kali /'ka:li/ *das;* ~**s**, ~**s** potash

Kaliber /ka'li:bɐ/ *das;* ~**s**, ~ (a) (Technik, Waffenkunde) calibre; (b) (ugs., oft abwertend) sort; kind

Kali·dünger *der* potash fertilizer

Kalif /ka'li:f/ *der;* ~**en**, ~**en** (hist.) caliph

Kalifornien /kali'fɔrnjən/ (*das*); ~**s** California

kalifornisch *Adj.* Californian

Kalium /'ka:liʊm/ (Chemie) *das;* ~**s** potassium

Kalk /kalk/ *der;* ~[e]s, ~**e** (a) (Kalziumkarbonat) calcium carbonate; (b) (Baustoff) lime; quicklime; burnt lime; **bei ihm rieselt schon der** ~ (salopp) he's going a bit senile

Kalk-: ~**ablagerung** *die* deposit of calcium carbonate; ~**boden** *der* limy soil; lime soil

kalken /'kalkn/ *tr. V.* (tünchen) whitewash

kalk-, Kalk-: ~**erde** *die* (a) (gebrannter Kalk) lime; quicklime; burnt lime; (b) ⇒ ~**boden**; ~**haltig** *Adj.* (bes. Geol., Mineral.) limy ⟨*soil*⟩; calcareous ⟨*soil, rock*⟩ (Geol., Min.); ⟨*water*⟩ containing calcium carbonate; **das Wasser ist sehr** ~**haltig** the water is high in calcium carbonate; ~**mangel** *der; o. Pl.* (a) (Mangel an Kalzium) calcium deficiency; (b) (Mangel an Kalk) deficiency of lime; ~**stein** *der* limestone

Kalkül /kal'ky:l/ *das od. der;* ~**s**, ~**e** (geh.) calculation

Kalkulation /kalkula'tsio:n/ *die;* ~, ~**en** (auch Wirtsch.) calculation; **nach meiner** ~: according to my calculations *pl.*

kalkulieren 1 *tr. V.* (a) (Kaufmannsspr.) calculate ⟨*cost, price*⟩; cost ⟨*product, article*⟩; (b) (abschätzen) calculate. 2 *itr. V.* calculate; **falsch** ~: miscalculate

Kalkutta /kal'kʊta/ *das;* ~**s** ▶ 490 ◄ Calcutta

kalk·weiß *Adj.* (a) chalk-white; (b) (sehr bleich) deathly pale; chalky white; ~ **sein** be as white as a sheet

Kalorie /kalo'ri:/ *die;* ~, ~**n** calorie

kalorien-, Kalorien-: ~**arm** 1 *Adj.* low-calorie *attrib.;* ~**arm sein** be low in calories; 2 *adv.* ~**arm kochen/essen** cook low-calorie meals/eat low-calorie foods; ~**gehalt** *der* calorie content; ~**reich** 1 *Adj.* high-calorie *attrib.;* ~**reich sein** be high in calories; 2 *adv.* ~**reich kochen/essen** cook high-calorie meals/eat high-calorie foods

kalt /kalt/; **kälter** /'kɛltɐ/, **kältest...** /'kɛltəst.../ 1 *Adj.* cold; chilly, frosty ⟨*atmosphere, smile*⟩; **ein** ~**es Buffet** a cold buffet; **mir ist/wird** ~: I am/am getting cold; **das Essen wird** ~: the food is getting cold; **im Kalten sitzen** sit in the cold; ~ **und berechnend sein** be cold and calculating; **es packte uns das** ~**e Grausen/Entsetzen** our blood ran cold; **jmdm. die** ~**e Schulter zeigen** give sb. the cold shoulder; cold-shoulder sb.; ~ **bleiben** (fig.) remain unmoved; **jmdn.** ~ **lassen** (ugs.) leave sb. unmoved; (nicht interessieren) leave sb. cold (coll.). 2 *adv.* (a) ~ **duschen** have *or* take a cold shower; ~ **schlafen** sleep in a cold room; **Getränke/Sekt** ~ **stellen** cool drinks/chill champagne; **jmdn.** ~ **erwischen** (bes.

Sportjargon) catch sb. on the hop; (b) (nüchtern) coldly; (c) (abweisend, unfreundlich) coldly; frostily; **jmdn.** ~ **anblicken** look at sb. coldly; ~ **lächeln** smile coldly *or* frostily; **etw.** ~ **lächelnd tun** (ugs.) take callous pleasure in doing sth.; (d) **mich überlief** *od.* **durchrieselte es** ~: cold shivers ran down my spine

kalt-, Kalt-: ***~**|bleiben** ⇒ **kalt** 1; ~**blüter** /-bly:tɐ/ *der* (Zool.) cold-blooded animal; ~**blütig** 1 *Adj.* (a) (beherrscht) cool-headed; (b) (abwertend: skrupellos) cold-blooded; (c) (Zool.) cold-blooded; 2 *adv.* (a) (beherrscht) coolly; calmly; (b) (abwertend: skrupellos) cold-bloodedly; ~**blütigkeit** *die;* ~ ⇒ **blütig a, b:** cool-headedness; cold-bloodedness

Kälte /'kɛltə/ *die;* ~ (a) cold; **10 Grad** ~: 10 degrees of frost; 10 degrees below freezing; **vor** ~ **zittern** shiver with cold; **bei dieser** ~: in this cold; when it's as cold as this; (b) (fig.) coldness

kälte-, Kälte-: ~**beständig** *Adj.* cold-resistant; ~**beständig sein** be resistant to cold; ~**einbruch** *der* (Met.) sudden onset of cold weather; ~**empfindlich** *Adj.* sensitive to cold *pred.;* ~**empfindliche Pflanzen** plants which are sensitive to cold; ~**grad** *der* degree of frost

kälter, kältest... ⇒ **kalt**

Kälte-: ~**technik** *die* refrigeration engineering *no art.;* ~**tod** *der:* **den** ~**tod erleiden** freeze to death; die of cold; ~**welle** *die* cold wave *or* spell

kalt-, Kalt-: ~**front** *die* (Met.) cold front; ~**herzig** *Adj.* cold-hearted;***~**lächelnd** ⇒ **kalt** 1;***~**|lassen** ⇒ **kalt** 1; ~**luft** *die; o. Pl.* cold air; ~**|machen** *tr. V.* (salopp) **jmdn.** ~**machen** do sb. in (sl.); ~**mamsell** *die* ▶ 85 ◄ *girl/woman who prepares and serves cold dishes in a restaurant, hotel, etc.;* ~**miete** *die* rent exclusive of heating; ~**schale** *die cold sweet soup made with fruit, beer, wine, or milk;* ~**schnäuzig** /~ʃnɔʏtsɪç/ (ugs.) 1 *Adj.* cold and insensitive; 2 *adv.* coldly and insensitively; ~**schnäuzigkeit** *die;* ~ (ugs.) coldness and insensitivity; (Frechheit) insolence; ~**|stellen** *tr. V.* (ugs.) **jmdn.** ~**stellen** put sb. out of the way (coll. joc.); **den Mittelstürmer** ~**stellen** cut the centre forward out of the game

Kalvinismus /kalvi'nɪsmʊs/ *der;* ~: Calvinism *no art.*

Kalvinist *der;* ~**en**, ~**en**, **Kalvinistin** *die;* ~, ~**nen** Calvinist

kalvinistisch *Adj.* Calvinist

Kalzium /'kaltsiʊm/ *das;* ~**s** calcium

kam /ka:m/ *1. u. 3. Pers. Prät. v.* **kommen**

Kambodscha /kam'bɔdʒa/ (*das*); ~**s** Cambodia

Kambodschaner /kambo'dʒa:nɐ/ *der;* ~**s**, ~: Cambodian

käme /'kɛ:mə/ *1. u. 3. Pers. Konjunktiv II v.* **kommen**

Kamel /ka'me:l/ *das;* ~**s**, ~**e** (a) camel; (b) (salopp) clot (Brit. coll.); twit (Brit. coll.); fathead

Kamel-: ~**haar** *das* camel-hair; ~**haar·mantel** *der* camel-hair coat

Kamelie /ka'me:liə/ *die;* ~, ~**n** camellia

Kamellen /ka'mɛlən/ *Pl.* (ugs.) *in* **alte** *od.* **olle** ~: old hat *sing.* (coll.)

Kamera /'kaməra/ *die;* ~, ~**s** camera

Kamerad /kamə'ra:t/ *der;* ~**en**, ~**en** (Gefährte) companion; (Freund) friend; (Mitschüler) mate; friend; (Soldat) comrade; (Sport) team-mate

Kameraderie /kamərada'ri:/ *die;* ~ (meist abwertend) loyalty to a/the clique

Kameradin *die;* ~, ~**nen** ⇒ **Kamerad**

Kameradschaft *die;* ~: comradeship; **die** ~ **zwischen ihnen** the sense of comradeship between them

kameradschaftlich 1 *Adj.* comradely. 2 *adv.* in a comradely way

Kameradschaftlichkeit *die;* ~: comradeliness

Kamera-: ~**führung** *die* (Film) camerawork *no indef. art.;* ~**mann** *der Pl.* ~**männer** *od.* ~**leute** ▶ 85 ◄ cameraman; ~**rekorder** *der* camcorder

Kamerun /'kaməru:n/ (*das*); ~**s** Cameroon; the Cameroons *pl.*

Kameruner *der;* ~s, ~: ▶ 388 | Cameroonian

Kamille /ka'mɪlə/ *die;* ~, ~n camomile

Kamillen·tee *der* camomile tea

Kamin /ka'miːn/ *der, schweiz.: das;* ~s, ~e (a) fireplace; **sie saßen am** ~: they sat by the hearth *or* the fireside; (b) (bes. südd.: Schornstein; Felsspalt) chimney

Kamin-: ~**feger** *der* (bes. südd.) ⇒ **Schornsteinfeger;** ~**feuer** *das* [open] fire; ~**kehrer** *der* (bes. südd.) ⇒ **Schornsteinfeger;** ~**sims** *der od. das* mantelpiece; mantelshelf

Kamm /kam/ *der;* ~[e]s, **Kämme** /'kɛmə/ (a) comb; **alle/alles über einen** ~ **scheren** lump everyone/everything together; (b) (bei Hühnern usw.) comb; (bei Reptilien, Amphibien) crest; **ihm schwillt der** ~ (ugs.) he gets cocky and big-headed (coll.); (c) (Gebirgs~) ridge; crest; (d) (Wellen~) crest; (e) (Rinder~) neck; (Schweine~) spare rib

kämmen /'kɛmən/ *tr. V.* comb; **jmdm./sich die Haare** ~, **jmdn./sich** ~: comb sb.'s/one's hair; **jmdm. einen Scheitel/Pony** ~: put a parting in sb.'s hair/comb sb.'s hair into a fringe

Kammer /'kamɐ/ *die;* ~, ~n (a) storeroom; (veralt.: Schlafraum) chamber; (b) (Biol., Med., Technik) chamber; (c) (Parl.) chamber; House; **die erste/zweite** ~: the upper/lower chamber *or* House; (d) (Rechtsw.) court (*dealing with a particular branch of judicial business*); (e) (gewerbliche Vereinigung) professional association; (f) (Milit.) stores *pl.*

Kämmerchen /'kɛmɐçən/ *die;* ~s, ~: small room; (Abstellkammer) [small] storeroom

Kammer·chor *der* chamber choir

Kammer·diener *der* (veralt.) valet

Kämmerer /'kɛmɐrɐ/ *der;* ~s, ~ (veralt.) [town/city] treasurer

Kammer-: ~**jäger** *der* pest controller; ~**konzert** *das* chamber concert

Kämmerlein /'kɛmɐlain/ *das;* ~s, ~ (oft scherzh.) **im stillen** ~ **über etw.** (*Akk.*) **nachdenken** think about sth. in peace and quiet

Kammer-: ~**musik** *die; o. Pl.* chamber music; ~**orchester** *das* chamber orchestra; ~**ton** *der* (Musik) standard pitch; ~**zofe** *die* (veralt.) lady's maid

Kamm·garn *das* worsted

Kampagne /kam'panjə/ *die;* ~, ~n campaign (**für** for, on behalf of; **gegen** against)

Kämpe /'kɛmpə/ *der;* ~n, ~n (veralt.) [brave] warrior *or* fighter; **ein alter** ~ (scherzh.) an old campaigner; a seasoned veteran

Kampf /kampf/ *der;* ~[e]s, **Kämpfe** (a) (militärisch) battle (**um** for); **nach wochenlangen erbitterten Kämpfen** after weeks of bitter fighting; **er ist im** ~ **gefallen** he fell *or* was killed in action *or* combat; (b) (zwischen persönlichen Gegnern) fight; (fig.) struggle; **ein** ~ **aller gegen alle** a free-for-all; **ein** ~ **Mann gegen Mann** a hand-to-hand fight; **ein** ~ **auf Leben und Tod** a fight to the death; (c) (Wett~) contest; (Boxen) contest; fight; bout; **sich einen spannenden** ~ **liefern** produce an exciting contest; (d) (fig.) struggle, fight (**um, für** for; **gegen** against); **der** ~ **ums Dasein** the struggle for existence; **jmdm./einer Sache den** ~ **ansagen** declare war on sb./sth.; **der** ~ **zwischen den Geschlechtern** the battle of the sexes

kampf-, Kampf-: ~**ab·stimmung** *die* (Politik) crucial vote; ~**an·sage** *die* declaration of war; ~**bahn** *die* (für Gladiatoren) arena; (für Stiere) ring; ~**bereit** *Adj.* (a) (vorbereitet) ready to fight *postpos.;* (*army*) ready for battle; (*troops*) ready for battle *or* action; (b) (willens) willing to fight *postpos.;* ~**bereitschaft** *die* ⇒ ~**bereit a, b**: readiness for battle; readiness for battle *or* action; willingness to fight

kämpfen /'kɛmpfn̩/ **1** *itr. V.* (a) fight (**um, für** for); **mit jmdm.** ~: fight [with] sb.; **gegen jmdn.** ~: fight [against] sb.; **mit den Tränen** ~ (fig.) fight back one's tears; **mit dem Schlaf** ~ (fig.) struggle to keep awake; **mit dem Tod** ~ (fig.) fight for one's life *or* to stay alive; **mit etw. zu** ~ **haben** (fig.) have to contend with sth.; **[lange] mit sich** (*Dat.*) ~: have a [long] struggle with oneself; (b) (Sport: sich messen) (*team*) play; (*wrestler, boxer*) fight; **gegen jmdn.** ~: play/fight sb. **2** *refl. V.* (auch fig.)

fight one's way. **3** *tr. V.* **einen Kampf** ~ (auch fig.) fight a battle

Kampfer /'kampfɐ/ *der;* ~s camphor

Kämpfer /'kɛmpfɐ/ *der;* ~s, ~, **Kämpferin** *die;* ~, ~nen fighter

kämpferisch 1 *Adj.* (a) fighting (*spirit, mood*); (*person*) full of fighting spirit; **eine** ~**e Natur sein** be full of fighting spirit; (b) (Sport) spirited. **2** *adv.* (a) in a fighting spirit; (b) (Sport) spiritedly

Kämpfer·natur *die* fighter

kampf·erprobt *Adj.* battle-tried; battle-tested (*equipment*)

kampf-, Kampf-: ~**flugzeug** *das* bomber; ~**gas** *das* war gas; ~**gebiet** *das* battle area; combat zone; ~**geist** *der; o. Pl.* fighting spirit; ~**gericht** *das* (Sport) [panel of] judges *pl.;* ~**hahn** *der* (a) fighting cock; (b) (fig. ugs.) fighter; brawler; ~**handlungen** *Pl.* fighting *sing.;* **die** ~**handlungen einstellen** cease hostilities *or* fighting; ~**kraft** *die* fighting power *or* strength; ~**lied** *das* battle song; (einer Bewegung) battle anthem; ~**los 1** *Adj.* **an eine** ~**lose Übergabe der Stadt war nicht zu denken** to hand over the town without a fight was unthinkable; **2** *adv.* without a fight; ~**lustig 1** *Adj.* belligerent; **2** *adv.* belligerently; ~**maßnahme** *die; meist Pl.* active measure; ~**maßnahmen [beschließen]** [decide to take] action *sing.;* ~**platz** *der* battlefield; ~**richter** *der* (Sport) judge; ~**stark** *Adj.* powerful (*army*); efficient (*troops*); strong, powerful (*team*); ~**stärke** *die* (eines Heeres) fighting strength *or* power; (einer Mannschaft) strength; ~**stoff** *der; meist Pl.* warfare agent; ~**unfähig** *Adj.* (*troops*) unfit for action *or* battle; (*boxer etc.*) unfit to fight; **jmdn./etw.** ~**unfähig machen** put sb./sth. out of action; ~**zone** *die* (Milit.) battle zone; combat zone

kampieren /kam'piːrən/ *itr. V.* camp; (ugs.: wohnen) camp down *or* out; (ugs.: übernachten) bed *or* (Brit. sl.) doss down

Kanada /'kanada/ (*das*); ~s Canada

Kanadier /ka'naːdiɐ/ *der;* ~s, ~ ▶ 388 | (a) (Einwohner Kanadas) Canadian; (b) (Boot) Canadian canoe

kanadisch /ka'naːdɪʃ/ *Adj.* ▶ 388 | Canadian

Kanaille /ka'naljə/ *die;* ~, ~n (abwertend) scoundrel; villain

Kanal /ka'naːl/ *der;* ~s, **Kanäle** /ka'nɛːlə/ (a) canal; (b) (Geogr.) **der** ~: the [English] Channel; (c) (für Abwässer) sewer; (d) (zur Entwässerung, Bewässerung) channel; (Graben) ditch; (e) (Rundf., Ferns., Weg der Information) channel; (f) (salopp) **den** ~ **voll haben** (betrunken sein) be canned *or* plastered (sl.); (überdrüssig sein) have had a bellyful *or* as much as one can take

Kanal-: ~**arbeiter** *der* sewerage worker; ~**deckel** *der* manhole cover; ~**inseln** *Pl.* **die** ~**inseln** the Channel Islands

Kanalisation /kanaliza'tsɪ̯oːn/ *die;* ~, ~en (a) (System der Abwasserkanäle) sewerage system; sewers *pl.;* (b) (Ausbau eines Flusses) canalization

kanalisieren *tr. V.* (a) (lenken) channel (*energies, goods, etc.*); (b) (schiffbar machen) canalize

Kanalisierung *die;* ~, ~en (a) (Lenkung) channelling; (b) (Schiffbarmachen) canalization

Kanal·tunnel *der der* ~: the Channel Tunnel

Kanapee /'kanape/ *das;* ~s, ~s (a) (veralt., scherzh.: Sofa) sofa; settee; (b) (belegtes Weißbrotschnittchen) canapé

Kanaren /ka'naːrən/ *Pl.* **die** ~: the Canaries

Kanarien·vogel /ka'naːrɪ̯ən-/ *der* canary

Kanarische Inseln *Pl.* **die** ~n, ~: the Canary Islands

Kandare /kan'daːrə/ *die;* ~, ~n curb bit; **jmdn. an die** ~ **nehmen** (fig.) take sb. in hand

Kandelaber /kande'laːbɐ/ *der;* ~s, ~: candelabrum

Kandidat /kandi'daːt/ *der;* ~en, ~en, **Kandidatin** *die;* ~, ~nen (a) candidate; (b) (beim Quiz usw.) contestant

Kandidatur /kandida'tuːɐ/ *die;* ~, ~en candidature (**auf** + *Akk.* for)

kandidieren *itr. V.* stand [as a candidate] (**für** for)

kandieren /kan'diːrən/ *tr. V.* candy; **kandiert** crystallized (*orange, petal*); glacé (*cherry, pear*); candied (*peel*)

Kandis /'kandɪs/ *der;* ~, **Kandis·zucker** *der* rock candy

Känguru /'kɛŋguru/ *das;* ~s, ~s kangaroo

Kanin /ka'niːn/ *das;* ~s, ~e (fachspr.) rabbit [fur]

Kaninchen /ka'niːnçən/ *das;* ~s, ~: rabbit

Kaninchen-: ~**bau** *der; Pl.* ~**baue** rabbit burrow; rabbit hole; ~**fell** *das* rabbit fur; ~**stall** *der* rabbit hutch

Kanister /ka'nɪstɐ/ *der;* ~s, ~: can; [metal/plastic] container

kann /kan/ *1. u. 3. Pers. Sg. Präsens v.* **können**

Kännchen /'kɛnçən/ *das;* ~s, ~: [small] pot; (für Milch) [small] jug; **ein ~ Kaffee/Milch** a [small] pot of coffee/jug of milk

Kanne /'kanə/ *die;* ~, ~**n** (a) (Krug) (Tee~, Kaffee~) pot; (Milch~, Wasser~) jug; (b) (Henkel~) can; (große Milch~) churn; (Gieß~) watering can

kannen·weise *Adv.* by the jugful

Kannibale /kani'baːlə/ *der;* ~**n**, ~**n** cannibal

kannibalisch *Adj.* cannibalistic

Kannibalismus *der;* ~ (auch Zool.) cannibalism *no art.*

kannst /kanst/ *2. Pers. Sg. Präsens v.* **können**

kannste /'kanstə/ (ugs.) = **kannst du;** *s. auch* **haste**

kannte /'kantə/ *1. u. 3. Pers. Sg. Prät. v.* **kennen**

Kanon /'kaːnɔn/ *der;* ~s, ~s (Musik, Lit., Theol., geh.) canon

Kanonade /kano'naːdə/ *die;* ~, ~**n** (Milit.) cannonade; (fig. ugs.) barrage

Kanone /ka'noːnə/ *die;* ~, ~**n** (a) cannon; big gun; **mit** ~**n auf Spatzen** (*Akk.*) **schießen** (fig.) take a sledge-hammer to crack a nut; **das ist unter aller ~** (ugs.) it's appallingly bad *or* indescribably dreadful (coll.); (b) (ugs.: Könner) ace; (c) (salopp: Revolver) shooting-iron (sl.); rod (Amer. sl.)

Kanonen·boot *das* gunboat

Kanonen-: ~**donner** *der* [rumble of] gunfire; ~**futter** *das* (ugs.) cannon fodder; ~**kugel** *die* cannon ball; ~**ofen** *der* cylindrical [iron] stove; ~**rohr** *das* gun-barrel

Kanonier /kano'niːɐ/ *der;* ~s, ~e (Milit.) gunner; artilleryman

kanonisch *Adj.* (kath. Kirche) canonical; ~**es Recht** canon law

kanonisieren *tr. V.* canonize

Kanossa·gang /ka'nɔsa-/ *der* (geh.) humiliation; **einen ~ antreten/machen** eat humble pie; go to Canossa (literary)

Kantate /kan'taːtə/ *die;* ~, ~**n** (Musik) cantata

Kante /'kantə/ *die;* ~, ~**n** edge; (bei Stoffen) selvedge; **etw. auf die hohe ~ legen** (ugs.) put sth. away *or* by; **etw. auf der hohen ~ haben** (ugs.) have sth. put away *or* by; *s. auch* **Ecke a**

kantig *Adj.* square-cut ‹timber, stone›; rough-edged ‹rock›; angular ‹face, figure, etc.›; sharp ‹nose›; square ‹chin›; jerky, awkward ‹movement›

Kantine /kan'tiːnə/ *die;* ~, ~**n** canteen

Kanton /kan'toːn/ *der;* ~s, ~e canton

kantonal /kanto'naːl/ **1** *Adj.* cantonal. **2** *adv.* on a cantonal basis

Kantons-: ~**rat** *der* (schweiz.) cantonal great council; ~**regierung** *die* (schweiz.) cantonal government

Kantor /'kantɔr/ *der;* ~s, ~**en** /-'toːrən/ ▶85| choirmaster and organist

Kant·stein *der* kerb

Kanu /'kaːnu/ *das;* ~s, ~s canoe

Kanüle /ka'nyːlə/ *die;* ~, ~**n** (Med.) cannula; (einer Injektionsspritze) [hypodermic] needle

Kanute /ka'nuːtə/ *der;* ~**n**, ~**n** (Sport) canoeist

Kanzel /'kantsl̩/ *die;* ~, ~**n** (a) pulpit; **auf der ~:** in the pulpit; (b) (Flugw.) cockpit

kanzerogen /kantsero'geːn/ *Adj.* (Med.) carcinogenic

Kanzlei /kants'lai/ *die;* ~, ~**en** (a) (veralt.: Büro) office; (b) (Anwalts~) chambers *pl.* (*of barrister*); office (*of lawyer*)

Kanzlei·sprache *die; o. Pl.* language of officialdom; officialese

Kanzler /'kantslɐ/ *der;* ~s, ~ (a) chancellor; (b) (an Hochschulen) vice-chancellor

Kanzler-: ~**amt** *das* Chancellery; ~**kandidat** *der* candidate for the chancellorship

Kap /kap/ *das;* ~s, ~s cape; **das ~ der Guten Hoffnung** Cape of Good Hope; ~ **Hoorn** Cape Horn

Kapazität /kapatsi'tɛːt/ *die;* ~, ~**en** (a) (auch Wirtsch.) capacity; **ungenutzte ~en** (Wirtsch.) unused capacity; (b) (Experte) expert

Kapee /ka'peː/ **in schwer von ~ sein** (salopp) be slow on the uptake

Kapelle /ka'pɛlə/ *die;* ~, ~**n** (a) (Archit.) chapel; (b) (Musik) band; [light] orchestra

Kapell·meister *der* band-leader; bandmaster; (im Orchester) conductor; (im Theater usw.) musical director

Kaper /'kaːpɐ/ *die;* ~, ~**n** caper *usu. in pl.*

kapern *tr. V.* (hist.) capture, seize ‹ship›

Kapern·soße *die* caper sauce

Kaper·schiff *das* (hist.) privateer

kapieren /ka'piːrən/ (ugs.) **1** *tr. V.* (ugs.) get (coll.); understand; **kapier das endlich!** get that into your thick skull! (coll.). **2** *itr. V.* **schnell ~:** be quick to catch on (coll.); **kapiert?** got it? (coll.)

kapital /kapi'taːl/ *Adj.; nicht präd.* major ‹error, blunder, etc.›; (Jägerspr.) large and powerful; royal ‹stag›

Kapital *das;* ~s, ~e *od.* ~**ien** (a) capital; (b) (fig.) asset; **~ aus etw. schlagen** make capital out of sth.; capitalize on sth.

Kapital-: ~**anlage** *die* (Wirtsch.) capital investment; ~**flucht** *die* flight of capital

Kapitalismus *der;* ~ capitalism *no art.*

Kapitalist *der;* ~**en**, ~**en** capitalist

kapitalistisch **1** *Adj.* capitalistic. **2** *adv.* capitalistically

Kapital-: ~**markt** *der* (Wirtsch.) capital market; ~**verbrechen** *das* serious offence *or* crime; (mit Todesstrafe bedroht) capital offence *or* crime; ~**verbrecher** *der* serious/capital offender; ~**verflechtung** *die* interlacing of capital interests

Kapitän /kapi'tɛːn/ *der;* ~s, ~e ▶34| (Seew., Flugw., Sport) captain; ~ **der Landstraße** (ugs.) knight of the road

Kapitäns·patent *das* master's certificate

Kapitel /ka'pɪtl̩/ *das;* ~s, ~ (auch fig.) chapter; **das ist ein anderes ~** (fig.) that's another story; **das ist ein ~ für sich** (fig.) that's a complicated subject

Kapitell /kapi'tɛl/ *das;* ~s, ~e capital

Kapitulation /kapitula'tsi̯oːn/ *die;* ~, ~**en** (a) (Milit.) surrender; capitulation; (Vertrag) surrender *or* capitulation document; **seine ~ erklären** admit defeat; (b) (fig.) giving up

kapitulieren *itr. V.* (a) (Milit.) surrender; capitulate; **vor dem Feind ~:** surrender to the enemy; (b) (fig.) give up; **vor etw.** (*Dat.*) ~**:** give up in the face of sth.

Kaplan /ka'plaːn/ *der;* ~s, **Kapläne** (kath. Kirche) (a) (Hilfsgeistlicher) curate; (b) (Geistlicher mit besonderen Aufgaben) chaplain

Kappe /'kapə/ *die;* ~, ~**n** cap; **etw. auf seine [eigene] ~ nehmen** (ugs.) take the responsibility for sth.

kappen *tr. V.* (a) (Seemannsspr.) cut; (b) (beschneiden) cut back ‹hedge etc.›; (fig.) cut; (c) (abschneiden) cut off ‹branches, shoots, crown, etc.›

Kappes /'kapəs/ *der;* ~ (bes. westd.) (a) (Weißkohl) cabbage; (b) (ugs.: Unsinn) rubbish; nonsense

Käppi /'kɛpi/ *das;* ~s, ~s overseas cap; garrison cap

Kaprice /ka'priːsə/ *die;* ~, ~**n** (geh.) caprice; whim

Kapriole /kapri'oːlə/ *die;* ~, ~**n** (a) caper; capriole; ~**n schlagen** cut capers; (b) (Streich) trick

kapriziös /kapri'tsi̯øːs/ **1** *Adj.* capricious. **2** *adv.* capriciously

Kapsel /'kapsl̩/ *die;* ~, ~**n** capsule

kaputt /ka'pʊt/ *Adj.* (a) (entzwei) broken ‹toy, cup, plate, arm, leg, etc.›; **die Maschine/das Auto ist ~:** the machine/car has broken down; (ganz und gar) the machine/car has had it (coll.); **irgendetwas ist am Auto ~:** there's something wrong with the car; **diese Jacke ist** ~: this jacket needs mending; (ist zerrissen) this jacket's torn; **die Birne ist** ~: the bulb has gone; (ist zerbrochen) the bulb is smashed; **das Telefon ist** ~: the phone is not working *or* is out of order; **der Fernseher ist** ~: the television has gone wrong; **sein Leben ist** ~: his life is in ruins; **ein** ~**er Typ** (fig. ugs.) a down-and-out; **eine** ~**e Lunge/ ein** ~**es Herz haben** (ugs.) have bad lungs/a bad heart; **die Ehe ist** ~: the marriage has failed *or* (coll.) is on the rocks; **was ist denn jetzt** ~**?** (ugs.) what's wrong *or* the matter now?; **(b)** (ugs.: erschöpft) shattered (coll.); whacked (Brit. coll.); pooped (coll.); **(c)** (salopp: abartig) sick

kaputt-: ~**|arbeiten** *refl. V.* (ugs.) work oneself into the ground (coll.); ~**|fahren** *unr. tr. V.* **(a)** (ugs.) smash up ‹*car etc.*›; **(b)** (salopp) ⇒ **totfahren**; ~**|gehen** *unr. itr. V.; mit sein* (ugs.) **(a)** (entzweigehen) break; ‹*machine*› break down, (sl.) pack up; ‹*clothes, shoes*› fall to pieces; ‹*lightbulb*› go; (zerbrechen) be smashed; (eingehen) ‹*plant*› die; (verderben) ‹*fish, fruit, etc.*› go off; (fig.) ‹*marriage*› fail; ‹*community, relationship, etc.*› break up; **(b)** (zugrunde gehen) ‹*firm*› go bust (coll.); ‹*person*› go to pieces; ~**|kriegen** *tr. V.* (ugs.) break; **wie hast du das** ~**gekriegt?** how did you [manage to] break it?; ~**|lachen** *refl. V.* (ugs.) kill oneself [laughing] (coll.); **das ist ja zum Kaputtlachen!** that's a laugh!; ~**|machen (ugs.) 1** *tr. V.* break ‹*watch, spectacles, plate, etc.*›; spoil ‹*sth. made with effort*›; ruin ‹*clothes, furniture, etc.*›; burst ‹*balloon*›; drive ‹*business, company*› to the wall; destroy ‹*political party*›; finish ‹*person*› off; **2** *refl. V.* wear oneself out; ~**|schlagen** *unr. tr. V.* (ugs.) smash

Kapuze /ka'puːtsə/ *die;* ~, ~**n** hood; (bei Mönchen) cowl; hood

Kapuziner /kapu'tsiːnɐ/ *der;* ~**s**, ~: Capuchin [friar]

Karabiner /kara'biːnɐ/ *der;* ~**s**, ~ **(a)** (Gewehr) carbine; **(b)** (österr.) ⇒ **Karabinerhaken**

Karabiner·haken *der* snap hook; spring hook; (Bergsteigen) karabiner

Karacho /ka'raxo/ *das;* ~**s** *in* **mit** ~ *od.* **in vollem** ~ (ugs.) hell for leather (coll.)

Karaffe /ka'rafə/ *die;* ~, ~**n** carafe; (mit Glasstöpsel) decanter

Karambolage /karambo'laːʒə/ *die;* ~, ~**n** (ugs.) crash; collision

***Karamel** *usw.:* ⇒ **Karamell** *usw.*

Karamell /kara'mɛl/ *der (schweiz.: das);* ~**s** caramel

Karamell-: ~**bonbon** *der od. das* caramel [toffee]; ~**creme** *die* crème caramel

Karamelle /kara'mɛlə/ *die;* ~, ~**n** caramell [toffee]

Karaoke /kara'oːkə/ *das;* ~**[s]** karaoke

Karat /ka'raːt/ *das;* ~**[e]s**, ~**e** carat; **ein Diamant von 5** ~: a 5-carat diamond; **reines Gold hat 24** ~: pure gold is 24 carats

Karate /ka'raːtə/ *das;* ~**[s]** karate

-karäter /-karɛːtɐ/ **der Zehnkaräter/Fünfkaräter** ten-carat/five-carat diamond/stone

Karate·schlag *der* karate chop

-karätig /-karɛːtɪç/ **zehnkarätig/fünfkarätig** ten-carat/five-carat

Karavelle /kara'vɛlə/ *die;* ~, ~**n** (hist.) caravel

Karawane /kara'vaːnə/ *die;* ~, ~**n** caravan

Karawanen·straße *die* caravan route

Karbid /kar'biːt/ *das;* ~**[e]s**, ~**e** (Chem.) carbide

Karbol /kar'boːl/ *das;* ~**s** carbolic acid

Karbunkel /kar'buŋkl/ *der;* ~**s**, ~ (Med.) carbuncle

Kardan- /kar'daːn-/ (Technik) cardan ‹*drive, shaft, tunnel, etc.*›

Kardinal /kardi'naːl/ *der;* ~**s**, **Kardinäle** /kardi'nɛːlə/ cardinal

Kardinal-: ~**fehler** *der* cardinal error; ~**tugend** *die; meist Pl.* cardinal virtue; ~**zahl** *die* cardinal [number]

Kardiogramm /kardio'gram/ *das;* ~**s**, ~**e** (Med.) cardiogram

Kardiologie *die;* ~ (Med.) cardiology *no art.*

Karenz /ka'rɛnts/ *die;* ~, ~**en**, **Karenz·zeit** *die* waiting period

karfiol /kar'fioːl/ *der;* ~**s** (südd., österr.) cauliflower

Kar·freitag /kaːɐ̯-/ *der* Good Friday

Karfunkel /kar'fuŋkl/ *der;* ~**s**, ~ (Edelstein; volkst.: Geschwür) carbuncle

karg /kark/ **1** *Adj.* meagre ‹*wages, pay, etc.*›; frugal ‹*meal etc.*›; poor ‹*light, accommodation*›; scanty ‹*supply*›; meagre, scant ‹*applause*›; sparse ‹*furnishings*›; barren, poor ‹*soil*›. **2** *adv.* ~ **bemessen sein** ‹*helping*› be mingy (Brit. coll.); ‹*supply*› be scanty; ~ **leben** live frugally; ~ **möbliert** sparsely furnished; ~ **ausgestattet** scantily equipped

Kargheit *die;* ~: ⇒ **karg 1:** meagreness; frugality; poorness; scantiness; sparseness; barrenness

kärglich /'kɛrklɪç/ **1** *Adj.* meagre, poor ‹*wages, pension, etc.*›; poor ‹*light*›; frugal ‹*meal*›; scanty ‹*supply*›; meagre ‹*existence*›; meagre, scant ‹*applause*›; sparse ‹*furnishing*›. **2** *adv.* sparsely ‹*furnished*›; poorly ‹*lit, paid, rewarded*›

Karibik /ka'riːbɪk/ *die;* ~: **die** ~: the Caribbean; **in die** ~: to the Caribbean

karibisch *Adj.* Caribbean

kariert /ka'riːɐ̯t/ **1** *Adj.* check, checked ‹*material, pattern*›; check ‹*jacket etc.*›; squared ‹*paper*›. **2** *adv.* (ugs.) ~ **reden** *od.* **quatschen** talk rubbish

Karies /'kaːriɛs/ *die;* ~ ► **329|** (Zahnmed.) caries

Karikatur /karika'tuːɐ̯/ *die;* ~, ~**en (a)** cartoon; (Porträt) caricature; **(b)** (abwertend: Zerrbild) caricature

Karikaturist *der;* ~**en**, ~**en** cartoonist; (Porträtist) caricaturist

karikaturistisch 1 *Adj.* caricatural; **eine** ~**e Darstellung** a caricature. **2** *adv.* **etw.** ~ **überzeichnen** caricature sth.

karikieren /kari'kiːrən/ *tr. V.* caricature

kariös /ka'riøːs/ *Adj.* (Zahnmed.) carious

karitativ /karita'tiːf/ **1** *Adj.* charitable. **2** *adv.* **sich** ~ **betätigen** do work for charity

Karl /karl/ *(der)* Charles; ~ **der Große** Charlemagne

Karmeliter /karme'liːtɐ/ *der;* ~**s**, ~: Carmelite [friar]

Karmelit[er]in *die;* ~, ~**nen** Carmelite [nun]

Karmin /kar'miːn/ *das;* ~**s** carmine

karmin·rot *Adj.* carmine

Karneval /'karnəval/ *der;* ~**s**, ~**e** *od.* ~**s** carnival; **im** ~: at carnival time; ~ **feiern** join in the carnival festivities

Karnevalist *der;* ~**en**, ~**en** carnival reveller; (Vortragender) carnival performer

karnevalistisch *Adj.* carnival *attrib.* ‹*festivities etc.*›

Karnevals- carnival ‹*costume, society, procession, etc.*›

Karnickel /kar'nɪkl/ *das;* ~**s**, ~ (landsch.) rabbit

Kärnten /'kɛrntn̩/ *(das)* ~**s** Carinthia

Kärnt[e]ner *der;* ~**s**, ~, **Kärntnerin** *die;* ~, ~**nen** Carinthian

Karo /'kaːro/ *das;* ~**s**, ~**s (a)** square; (Raute) diamond; **(b)** *o. Pl.* (~**muster**) check; **(c)** (Kartenspiel) (Farbe) diamonds *pl.*; (Karte) diamond; *s. auch* **Pik²**

Karo-: *•*~**as**, ~**ass** *das* ace of diamonds; ~**bube** *der* jack of diamonds; ~**dame** *die* queen of diamonds; ~**könig** *der* king of diamonds; ~**muster** *das* check; check[ed] pattern

Karolinger /'kaːrolɪŋɐ/ *der;* ~**s**, ~ (hist.) Carolingian

Karosse /ka'rɔsə/ *die;* ~, ~**n (a)** (Prunkwagen) [state-] coach; **(b)** (scherzh. iron.: Auto) limousine

Karosserie /karɔsə'riː/ *die;* ~, ~**n** bodywork; coachwork

Karotin /karo'tiːn/ *das;* ~**s** carotene

Karotte /ka'rɔtə/ *die;* ~, ~**n** small carrot

Karpaten /kar'paːtn̩/ *Pl.* **die** ~: the Carpathians; the Carpathian Mountains

Karpfen /'karpfn̩/ *der;* ~**s**, ~: carp

Karpfen·teich *der* carp pond; *s. auch* **Hecht a**

Karre /'karə/ *die;* ~, ~**n** (bes. nordd.) **(a)** ⇒ **Karren**; **(b)** (abwertend: Fahrzeug) [old] heap (coll.)

Karree /ka're:/ *das;* ~s, ~s (a) (Rechteck) rectangle; (Quadrat; auch Milit.: Formation) square; (b) (Häuserblock) block

karren *tr. V.* (a) cart; (b) (salopp: mit einem Auto) run (coll.)

Karren *der;* ~s, ~ (bes. südd., österr.) cart; (zweirädrig) barrow; (Schubkarren) [wheel]barrow; (für Gepäck usw.) trolley; **ein ~ voll Sand** a cartload/barrowload of sand; (fig.) **den ~ in den Dreck fahren** (ugs.) get things into a mess; **mess things up; den ~ [für jmdn.] aus dem Dreck ziehen** (ugs.) sort out the mess [for sb.]; **jmdm. an den ~ fahren** (ugs.) tell sb. where he/she gets off (coll.)

Karriere /ka'rie:rə/ *die;* ~, ~n career; ~ **machen** make a [successful] career for oneself

Karriere-: ~**frau** *die* career woman/girl; ~**macher** *der* (abwertend) careerist

Karrierist *der;* ~en, ~en (abwertend) careerist

Kar·samstag /ka:ɐ̯-/ *der* Easter Saturday; Holy Saturday

Karst *der;* ~[e]s, ~e (Geol.) karst

karstig *Adj.* karstic

Karst·landschaft *die* karst landscape

Kartäuser /kar'tɔʏ̯zɐ/ *der;* ~s, ~ (a) (Mönch) Carthusian [monk]; (b) (Likör) chartreuse

Karte /'kartə/ *die;* ~, ~n (a) **card; die gelbe/rote ~** (Fußball) the yellow/red card; (b) (Speise~) menu; (Wein~) wine-list; **nach der ~ essen** eat à la carte; (Fahr~, Flug~, Eintritts~) ticket; (d) (Lebensmittel~) ration-card; **auf ~n** on coupons; (e) (Land~) map; (See~) chart; ~**n lesen** map-read; (f) (Spiel~) card; **jmdm. die ~n legen** read sb.'s fortune from the cards; **die** *od.* **seine ~n aufdecken** *od.* **[offen] auf den Tisch legen** *od.* **offen legen** put one's cards on the table; **alles auf eine ~ setzen** stake everything on one chance; **auf die falsche ~ setzen** back the wrong horse; **jmdm. in die ~n sehen** *od.* (ugs.) gucken find out or see what sb. is up to; **sich** (*Dat.*) **nicht in die ~n sehen** *od.* (ugs.) gucken lassen play one's cards close to one's chest; not show one's hand; **mit offenen/verdeckten ~n spielen** put one's cards on the table/play one's cards close to one's chest; (g) (Anzahl von Spielkarten) hand; **eine schlechte ~ haben** have a poor hand

Kartei /kar'taɪ̯/ *die;* ~, ~en card file *or* index

Kartei-: ~**karte** *die* file *or* index card; ~**kasten** *der* file-card *or* index-card box; ~**leiche** *die* (ugs. scherzh.: passives Mitglied) inactive member

Kartell /kar'tɛl/ *das;* ~s, ~e (Wirtsch., Politik) cartel

Kartell-: ~**amt** *das,* ~**behörde** *die government body concerned with the control and supervision of cartels;* ≈ Monopolies and Mergers Commission (Brit.); ~**recht** *das* law relating to cartels; ≈ monopolies law (Brit.)

Karten-: ~**gruß** *der* greeting *or* short message on a [post]card; **an jmdn. einen ~gruß schicken** send sb. a card; ~**haus** *das* house of cards; ~**legen** *das;* reading the cards *no art.;* cartomancy; ~**leger** *der,* ~**legerin** *die* fortune-teller (*who tells fortunes by reading the cards*); ~**lesen** *das* map-reading; ~**spiel** *das* (a) card game; (b) (Satz Spielkarten) pack *or* (Amer.) deck [of cards]; (c) (das Kartenspielen) card-playing *no art.;* ~**spieler** *der* card-player; ~**telefon** *das* cardphone; ~**vorverkauf** *der; o. Pl.* advance booking

Karthager /kar'ta:gɐ/ *der;* ~s, ~: Carthaginian

Karthago /kar'ta:go/ (*das*); ~s Carthage

Kartoffel /kar'tɔfl̩/ *die;* ~, ~n potato

Kartoffel-: ~**acker** *der* potato-field; ~**brei** *der* mashed *or* creamed potatoes *pl.;* mash (coll.); ~**chips** *Pl.* [potato] crisps (Brit.) *or* (Amer.) chips; ~**käfer** *der* Colorado beetle; potato-beetle; ~**kloß** *der,* ~**knödel** *der* (südd.) potato dumpling; ~**puffer** *der* potato pancake (*made from grated raw potatoes*); ~**püree** *das* ⇒ ~**brei;** ~**salat** *der* potato salad; ~**suppe** *die* potato soup

Kartograph /karto'gra:f/ *der;* ~en, ~en ▶ 85 cartographer

Kartographie /-'fi:/ *die;* ~: cartography *no art.*

kartographisch *Adj.* cartographic

Karton /kar'tɔŋ/ *der;* ~s, ~s (a) (Pappe) card[board]; (b) (Behälter) cardboard box; (kleiner und dünner) carton; **zwei ~[s] Seife** two boxes *or* packs of soap

kartonieren /karto'ni:rən/ *tr. V.* (Buchw.) bind in [paper] boards

Karussell /karʊ'sɛl/ *das;* ~s, ~s *od.* ~e merry-go-round; carousel (Amer.); (kleineres) roundabout; ~ **fahren** have a ride on *or* go on the merry-go-round/roundabout

Kar·woche /'ka:ɐ̯vɔxə/ *die* Holy Week; Passion Week

Karzer /'kartsɐ/ *der;* ~s, ~ (hist.) (Raum) detention room (in university, school); (Strafe) detention (often lasting several days)

karzinogen /kartsino'ge:n/ *Adj.* (Med.) carcinogenic

Karzinom /kartsi'no:m/ *das;* ~s, ~e ▶ 329 (Med.) carcinoma

Kaschemme /ka'ʃɛmə/ *die;* ~, ~n (abwertend) [low] dive (coll.)

kaschen /'kaʃn̩/ *tr. V.* (salopp) nab (sl.); nick (Brit. coll.)

kaschieren /ka'ʃi:rən/ *tr. V.* (a) (geh.) conceal; hide; disguise ⟨*fault*⟩; (b) (Buchw.) laminate ⟨*jacket etc.*⟩; line ⟨*cover etc.*⟩ [with paper]

Kaschmir¹ /'kaʃmi:ɐ̯/ (*das*); ~s Kashmir

Kaschmir² *der;* ~s, ~e (Textilw.) cashmere

Käse /'kɛ:zə/ *der;* ~s, ~ (a) cheese; (b) (ugs. abwertend: Unsinn) rubbish; nonsense; codswallop (Brit. sl.)

Käse-: ~**blatt** *das* (salopp abwertend) rag; ~**brot** *das* slice of bread and cheese; (zugeklappt) cheese sandwich; ~**fondue** *das* cheese fondue; ~**gebäck** *das* cheese savouries *pl.;* ~**glocke** *die* cheese dome; ~**kuchen** *der* cheesecake

Kasematte /kazə'matə/ *die;* ~, ~n (Milit., Marine) casemate

Käse·platte *die* (Gericht) [selection of] assorted cheeses *pl.*

Käserei /kɛzə'raɪ̯/ *die;* ~, ~en (a) *o. Pl.* (Herstellung von Käse) cheese-making *no art.* (b) (Betrieb) cheese-factory

Kaserne /ka'zɛrnə/ *die;* ~, ~n barracks *sing. or pl.*

Kasernen·hof *der* barrack square

kasernieren *tr. V.* quarter in barracks

Kasernierung *die;* ~, ~en quartering in barracks *no art.*

käse-, Käse-: ~**stange** *die* cheese straw; ~**torte** *die* cheesecake; ~**weiß** *Adj.* (ugs.) [as] white as a sheet

käsig *Adj.* (a) (ugs.: bleich) pasty; pale; (vor Schreck) as white as a sheet; (b) (wie Käse) cheesy; cheeselike

Kasino /ka'zi:no/ *das;* ~s, ~s (a) (Spiel~) casino; (b) (Offiziers~) [officers'] mess

Kaskade /kas'ka:də/ *die;* ~, ~n (auch fig.) cascade; **eine ~ von Verwünschungen/Flüchen** (fig.) a barrage of curses

Kasko·versicherung *die* (Voll~) comprehensive insurance; (Teil~) *insurance against theft, fire, or act of God*

Kasper /'kaspɐ/ *der;* ~s, ~ (a) (Kasette) ≈ Punch; (b) (ugs.: alberner Mensch) clown; fool

Kasperl /'kaspɐl/ *das;* ~s, ~[n] (österr.), **Kasperle** /'kaspɐlə/ *das od. der;* ~s, ~ ⇒ **Kasper**

Kasper-: ~**puppe** *die* ≈ Punch and Judy puppet; ~**theater** *das* ≈ Punch and Judy show; (Puppenbühne) ≈ Punch and Judy theatre

Kaspische Meer /'kaspɪʃə -/ *das* Caspian Sea

Kasse /'kasə/ *die;* ~, ~n (a) (Kassette) cash box; (Registrier~) till; cash register; **in die ~ greifen** *od.* **einen Griff in die ~ tun** (ugs.; auch fig.) help oneself from the till; **er wurde beim Griff in die ~ ertappt** (auch fig.) he was caught with his fingers in the till; (b) (Ort zum Bezahlen) cash *or* pay desk; (im Supermarkt) checkout; (in einer Bank) counter; ~ **machen** (Kaufmannsspr.) cash up; **jmdn. zur ~ bitten** (ugs.) ask sb. to pay up; (c) (Geld) cash; **gemeinsame ~ führen** *od.* **machen** share expenses; **getrennte ~ haben** pay separately; **gut/knapp bei ~ sein** be well-off *or* flush; be short of cash *or* money; **etw. reißt ein Loch in die ~** (ugs.) sth. makes a hole in sb.'s pocket *or* a dent in sb.'s finances; **die ~ führen** be in charge of the money *or* finances *pl.;* (d) (Kassenraum) cashier's office; (e) (Theater~, Kino~, Stadion~) box office; (f) ⇒ **Krankenkasse;** (g) (Kaufmannsspr.: Barzahlung) [payment in] cash; **wir liefern nur gegen ~:** we deliver only if payment is made in cash

Kasseler /'kasələ/ *das;* ~s smoked loin of pork

kassen-, Kassen-: ~**arzt** *der doctor who treats members of health insurance schemes;* ~**bon** *der* sales slip; receipt; ~**buch** *das* cash-book; ~**erfolg** *der* box office success; ~**magnet** *der* (ugs.) box office draw; ~**patient** *der patient who is a member of a health insurance scheme;* ~**raum** *der* counter hall; ~**schlager** *der* (ugs.) (a) (Film, Theater) box office hit; (b) (von Waren) top seller; ~**stunden** *Pl.* hours of business, business hours (of bank, cashier's office, etc.); ~**sturz** *der* (ugs.) ~**sturz machen** check up on one's ready cash; ~**wart** *der* treasurer; ~**zettel** *der* receipt; (~bon) sales slip

Kasserolle /kasə'rolə/ *die;* ~, ~**n** saucepan

Kassette /ka'sɛtə/ *die;* ~, ~**n** (a) (für Geld u. Wertsachen) box; case; (b) (mit Büchern, Schallplatten) boxed set; (c) (Tonband~, Film~) cassette; **etw. auf** ~ **aufnehmen** record *or* tape sth. on cassette

Kassetten·rekorder *der* cassette recorder

kassieren[1] **1** *tr. V.* (a) (einziehen) collect ‹rent etc.›; (b) (ugs.: einnehmen) collect ‹money, fee, etc.›; (fig.) receive, get ‹recognition, praise, etc.›; **bei der Transaktion hat er 100 000 DM kassiert** he made 100,000 marks on the deal; (c) (ugs.: hinnehmen müssen) receive, get ‹penalty points, scorn, ingratitude, etc.›; (d) (ugs.: wegnehmen) confiscate; take away ‹driving licence›; (e) (ugs.: verhaften/gefangen nehmen) pick up; nab (sl.); nick (Brit. coll.). **2** *itr. V.* (a) **bei jmdm.** ~ ‹waiter› give sb. his/her bill *or* (Amer.) check; (ohne Rechnung) ‹waiter› settle up with sb.; **darf ich bei Ihnen** ~? would you like your bill?/can I settle up with you?; (b) (ugs.: Geld einnehmen) collect the money; **[bei einem Geschäft] ganz schön** ~: make a packet (coll.) *or* (coll.) a bomb [on a deal]

kassieren[2] *tr. V.* (Rechtsw.) quash ‹judgement etc.›

Kassierer *der;* ~s, ~, **Kassiererin** *die;* ~, ~**nen** ▶ 85 cashier; teller

Kastagnette /kastan'jɛtə/ *die;* ~, ~**n** castanet

Kastanie /kas'ta:niə/ *die;* ~, ~**n** chestnut; **[für jmdn.] die** ~**n aus dem Feuer holen** (ugs.) pull the chestnuts out of the fire [for sb.]

Kastanien·baum *der* chestnut tree

kastanien·braun *Adj.* chestnut

Kästchen /'kɛstçən/ *das;* ~s, ~ (a) small box; (b) (vorgedrucktes Quadrat) square; (auf Fragebögen) box

Kaste /'kastə/ *die;* ~, ~**n** caste

kasteien /kas'taiən/ *refl. V.* chastise oneself; (fig.) deny oneself

Kasteiung *die;* ~, ~**en** self-chastisement; (fig.) self-denial

Kastell /kas'tɛl/ *das;* ~s, ~**e** (a) (hist.: röm. Lager) fort; (b) (Burg) castle

Kasten /'kastn̩/ *der;* ~s, **Kästen** /'kɛstn̩/ (a) box; (b) (für Flaschen) crate; (c) (ugs.: Briefkasten) postbox; (d) (ugs. abwertend: Gebäude) barracks *sing. or pl.;* **das ist ja ein furchtbarer alter** ~: that's a terrible old barracks of a place; (e) (ugs. abwertend: Fernseher, Radio) box (coll.); (f) (ugs.: Kamera) **ein Bild im** ~ **haben** have got a picture; **eine Szene im** ~ **haben** have a picture in the can; (g) **etw. auf dem** ~ **haben** (ugs.) have got it up top (coll.); have plenty of grey matter; (h) (Schaukasten) showcase; display case; (i) (Turnen) box; (j) (Ballspiele Jargon) goal; (k) (bes. nordd.: Schublade) drawer; (l) (südd., österr., schweiz.: Schrank) cupboard

Kasten-: ~**brot** *das* tin[-loaf]; ~**form** *die* (Backform) [rectangular] tin; ~**wagen** *der* van; ~**wesen** *das; o. Pl.* caste system

Kastrat /kas'tra:t/ *der;* ~**en**, ~**en** (a) (Eunuch) eunuch; (b) (Musik hist.) castrato

Kastraten·stimme *die* (a) (Musik) castrato voice; (b) (abwertend) falsetto voice

Kastration /kastra'tsio:n/ *die;* ~, ~**en** castration

kastrieren *tr. V.* castrate

Kasus /'ka:zʊs/ *der;* ~, ~ /'ka:zu:s/ (Sprachw.) case

Kat /kat/ *der;* ~s, ~s (ugs.) ⇒ **Katalysator b**

Katafalk /kata'falk/ *der;* ~s, ~**e** catafalque

Katakombe /kata'kɔmbə/ *die;* ~, ~**n;** *meist Pl.* catacomb

Katalog /kata'lo:k/ *der;* ~[e]s, ~**e** (auch fig.) catalogue

katalogisieren *tr. V.* catalogue

Katalysator /kataly'za:tor/ *der;* ~s, ~**en** /-za'to:rən/ (a) (Chemie, fig. geh.) catalyst; (b) (Kfz-W.) catalytic converter; *s. auch* **geregelt 2**

Katamaran /katama'ra:n/ *der od. das;* ~s, ~**e** catamaran

Katapult /kata'pʊlt/ *das od. der;* ~[e]s, ~**e** catapult

katapultieren *tr. V.* (auch fig.) catapult; eject ‹pilot›

Katarakt /kata'rakt/ *der;* ~[e]s, ~**e** (Stromschnelle) rapids *pl.;* (Wasserfall) cataract

Katarrh /ka'tar/ *der;* ~s, ~**e** (Med.) catarrh; **einen** ~ **haben** have catarrh

Kataster /ka'tastɐ/ *der od. das;* ~s, ~: land register

Kataster·amt *das* land registry

katastrophal /katastro'fa:l/ **1** *Adj.* disastrous; (stärker) catastrophic. **2** *adv.* disastrously; (stärker) catastrophically; **sich** ~ **auswirken** have a disastrous/catastrophic effect; ~ **enden** end in disaster/catastrophe

Katastrophe /katas'tro:fə/ *die;* ~, ~**n** disaster; (stärker) catastrophe; **jmd. ist eine** ~ (ugs.) sb. is a disaster

Katastrophen-: ~**alarm** *der* emergency *or* disaster alert; ~**dienst** *der* emergency services *pl.;* ~**einsatz** *der:* **den** ~**einsatz üben** practise procedures in case of a disaster; ~**fall** *der* disaster [situation]; ~**gebiet** *das* disaster area; ~**schutz** *der* (a) (Organisation) emergency services *pl.;* (b) (Maßnahmen) disaster procedures *pl.;* **dem** ~**schutz dienen** be useful in the event of a disaster

Kate /'ka:tə/ *die;* ~, ~**n** (bes. nordd.) small cottage

Katechismus /kate'çısmʊs/ *der;* ~, **Katechismen** (christl. Kirche) catechism

Kategorie /katego'ri:/ *die;* ~, ~**n** /-i:ən/ category

kategorisch **1** *Adj.* categorical. **2** *adv.* categorically

kategorisieren *tr. V.* categorize

Kater /'ka:tɐ/ *der;* ~s, ~ (a) tom-cat; **wie ein verliebter** ~: like an amorous tom-cat; (b) (ugs.: schlechte Verfassung) hangover; **einen** ~ **haben** have a hangover; be hung-over

Kater-: ~**frühstück** *das* breakfast, usually of pickled herrings and gherkins, supposed to cure a hangover; ~**stimmung** *die* morning-after feeling

Katheder /ka'te:dɐ/ *das od. der;* ~s, ~: lectern; (Pult des Lehrers) teacher's desk

Kathedrale /kate'dra:lə/ *die;* ~, ~**n** cathedral

Kathete /ka'te:tə/ *die;* ~, ~**n** (Math.) leg (of a right-angled triangle)

Katheter /ka'te:tɐ/ *der;* ~s, ~ (Med.) catheter

Kathode /ka'to:də/ *die;* ~, ~**n** (Physik) cathode

Katholik /kato'li:k/ *der;* ~**en**, ~**en**, **Katholikin** *die;* ~, ~**nen** [Roman] Catholic

katholisch *Adj.* [Roman] Catholic

Katholizismus /katoli'tsısmʊs/ *der;* ~: [Roman] Catholicism *no art.*

Kattun /ka'tu:n/ *der;* ~s, ~**e** calico

Katz /kats/ *die in* ~ **und Maus [mit jmdm.] spielen** (ugs.) play cat and mouse [with sb.]; **für die** ~ **sein** (salopp) be a waste of time; *s. auch* **Katze**

katzbuckeln *itr. V.* (abwertend) bow and scrape (**vor** + *Dat.* to)

Kätzchen /'kɛtsçən/ *das;* ~s, ~ (a) little cat; (liebkosend) pussy; (junge Katze) kitten; (b) (Blüte der Birke, Erle u. a.) catkin

Katze /'katsə/ *die;* ~, ~**n** cat; **die** ~ **lässt das Mausen nicht** (Spr.) a leopard cannot change its spots (prov.); **bei Nacht sind alle** ~**n grau** it's impossible to see any details in the dark; **wenn die** ~ **aus dem Haus ist, tanzen die Mäuse [auf dem Tisch]** (Spr.) when the cat's away the mice will play (prov.); **die** ~ **aus dem Sack lassen** (ugs.) let the cat out of the bag; **die** ~ **im Sack kaufen** (ugs.) buy a pig in a poke; **um etw. herumgehen wie die** ~ **um den heißen Brei** (ugs.) beat about the bush; *s. auch* **Katz**

katzen-, Katzen-: ~**auge** *das* (a) (ugs.: Rückstrahler) reflector; (b) (Mineral.) cat's-eye; ~**buckel** *der* hunched back; **einen** ~**buckel machen** hunch one's back; ~**fell**

das cat's skin; **~haft** *Adj.* catlike; **~jammer** *der* (fig.) mood of depression; **~klo** *das* (ugs.) cat's [litter] tray; **~kopf** *der* (ugs.) cobble[-stone]; **~musik** *die* (ugs. abwertend) terrible row (coll.); cacophony; **~sprung** *der* (fig.) stone's throw; **bis zum Strand ist es nur ein ~sprung** the beach is only a stone's throw away; **~tisch** *der* (ugs. scherzh.) children's table; **~wäsche** *die* (ugs.) lick and a promise (coll.); catlick (coll.)

Kauderwelsch /'kaʊdɐvɛlʃ/ *das;* ~[s] gibberish *no indef. art.;* double Dutch *no indef. art.;* juristisches ~: legal jargon; **ein ~ aus Deutsch, Englisch und Französisch** an incomprehensible hotchpotch of German, English, and French

kauen /'kaʊən/ **1** *tr. V.* chew; **Nägel** ~: bite *or* chew one's nails. **2** *itr. V.* (a) chew; **an etw.** (*Dat.*) ~: chew [on] sth.; **mit vollen Backen** ~ (ugs.) chew with one's mouth [stuffed] full; (b) (nagen, knabbern) chew; bite; **an einem Bleistift/den Fingernägeln** ~: chew a pencil/bite *or* chew one's nails

kauern /'kaʊɐn/ *itr., refl. V.* crouch [down]; (ängstlich) cower

Kauf /kaʊf/ *der;* ~[e]s, **Käufe** /'kɔyfə/ (a) (das Kaufen) buying; purchasing (formal); **einen ~ abschließen/tätigen** complete/make a purchase; **jmdn. zum ~ ermuntern** encourage sb. to buy; **jmdm. etw. zum ~ anbieten** offer sb. sth. for sale; **etw. in ~ nehmen** (fig.) accept sth.; (b) (Gekauftes) purchase

kaufen 1 *tr. V.* (a) buy; purchase; **etw. billig/zu teuer** ~: buy sth. cheaply/pay too much for sth.; **sich/jmdm. etw.** ~: buy sth. for oneself/sb.; buy oneself/sb. sth.; **etw. auf Raten** *od.* **Abzahlung** ~: buy sth. on hire purchase (Brit.) *or* (Amer.) the installment plan; **etw. für viel** *od.* **teures Geld** ~: pay a lot of money for sth.; **das wird viel** *od.* **gern gekauft** it sells well; **sich** (*Dat.*) **jmdn.** ~ (ugs.) give sb. what for (sl.); let sb. have *or* (sl.) give sb. a piece of one's mind; (b) (ugs.: bestechen) buy. **2** *itr. V.* (einkaufen) shop; **in diesem Laden kaufe ich nicht mehr** I'm not getting anything in that shop again

Käufer /'kɔyfɐ/ *der;* ~s, ~, **Käuferin** *die;* ~, ~nen buyer; purchaser; (Kunde/Kundin) customer

Kauf-: **~frau** *die* businesswoman; (Händlerin) trader; merchant; **~haus** *das* department store; **~haus·detektiv** *der* store detective; **~kassette** *die* [commercially produced] video; **den Film/die Reihe gibt es auch als ~kassette** you can buy that film/series on video too; **~kraft** *die* (Wirtsch.) (a) (des Geldes) purchasing power; (b) (von Personen) spending power; **~laden** *der* (Kinderspielzeug) toy shop

käuflich /'kɔyflɪç/ **1** *Adj.* (a) for sale *postpos.;* **ein ~es Mädchen** (fig.) a woman/girl of easy virtue; **~e Liebe** prostitution *no art.;* (b) (bestechlich) venal; **~ sein** be easily bought. **2** *adv.* **etw.** ~ **erwerben/erstehen** buy *or* purchase sth.; **~ zu erwerben sein** be for sale

kauf·lustig *Adj.* eager to buy *pred.;* **die Kauflustigen** the eager shoppers

Kauf·mann *der; Pl.* **Kaufleute** (a) (Geschäftsmann) businessman; (Händler) trader; merchant; **gelernter** ~: *person who has completed a course of training in some branch of business;* (b) (veralt.: Lebensmittelhändler) grocer; **zum ~ gehen** go to the grocer's

kaufmännisch 1 *Adj.* commercial; business *attrib.;* commercial ⟨bookkeeping⟩; **~er Angestellter** clerk; employee in business; **einen ~en Beruf ergreifen/erlernen** go into business/receive a business training; **~es Geschick/~e Erfahrung haben** possess business skill/experience. **2** *adv.* **~ tätig sein** be in business; **~ denken** think along commercial lines

Kaufmanns·sprache *die* business parlance

Kauf-: **~preis** *der* purchase price; **~rausch** *der* frantic urge to spend; (beim Hauskauf) title-deed; **~vertrag** *der* contract of sale; **~zwang** *der* obligation to buy *or* purchase

Kau·gummi *der od. das;* ~s, ~s chewing gum

Kaukasus /'kaʊkazʊs/ *der;* ~: **der** ~ the Caucasus

Kaulquappe /'kaʊlkvapə/ *die;* ~, ~n tadpole

kaum /kaʊm/ *Adv.* (a) (fast gar nicht) hardly; scarcely; ~ **jemand/etwas** hardly anybody *or* anyone/anything; **älter/größer/besser** hardly *or* scarcely any older/bigger/

better; **ich kann es** ~ **glauben/erwarten** I can hardly believe it/wait; **ich konnte** ~ **rechtzeitig damit fertig werden** I could hardly *or* barely finish it in time; **diese Schrift ist** ~ **zu entziffern** this writing is barely decipherable; (b) (vermutlich nicht) hardly; scarcely; **er wird [wohl]** ~ **zustimmen** he is hardly likely to agree; **ich glaube** ~: I hardly *or* scarcely think so; (c) (eben erst) ~ **hatte er Platz genommen, als ...:** no sooner had he sat down than ...; (d) ~ **dass** almost as soon as; ~ **dass er aus dem Gefängnis gekommen war ...:** hardly *or* scarcely had he left prison when ...

kausal /kau'za:l/ *Adj.* (geh., Sprachw.) causal

Kausal- causal ⟨*clause, connection, etc.*⟩

Kausalität /kauzali'tɛ:t/ *der;* ~, ~en causality

Kau·tabak *der* chewing tobacco

Kaution /kau'tsio:n/ *die;* ~, ~en (a) (für Gefangenen) bail; **eine** ~ **stellen** stand bail *or* surety; **gegen** ~: on bail; **jmdn. gegen** ~ **freibekommen** bail sb. out; (b) (für Wohnung) deposit

Kautschuk /'kautʃʊk/ *der;* ~s, ~e [india] rubber

Kauz /kauts/ *der;* ~es, **Käuze** /'kɔytsə/ (a) owl; (Stein~) little owl; (b) (Sonderling) odd *or* strange fellow; oddball (coll.); **ein komischer** ~: an odd *or* a queer bird (coll.)

Käuzchen /'kɔytsçən/ *das;* ~s, ~: ⇒ **Kauz a**

kauzig *Adj.* odd; queer; funny (coll.)

Kavalier /kava'li:ɐ/ *der;* ~s, ~e gentleman

Kavaliers·delikt *das* trifling offence; peccadillo

Kavalier[s]·start *der* racing start

Kavallerie /kavalə'ri:/ *die;* ~, ~n (Milit. hist.) cavalry

Kaviar /'ka:viar/ *der;* ~s, ~e caviare

kcal *Abk.* **Kilo[gramm]kalorie** kcal

keck /kɛk/ **1** *Adj.* (a) impertinent; cheeky; saucy (Brit.); (b) (flott) jaunty, pert ⟨hat etc.⟩. **2** *adv.* (a) impertinently; cheekily; saucily (Brit.); (b) (flott) jauntily

Keckheit *die;* ~, ~en impertinence; cheek; sauce (Brit.)

Kefir /'ke:fir/ *der;* ~s kefir

Kegel /'ke:gl̩/ *der;* ~s, ~ (a) (das Kaufen... cone; (b) (Spielfigur) skittle; (beim Bowling) pin; ~ **schieben** play skittles *or* ninepins; (c) (Licht~) beam

kegel-, Kegel-: **~bahn** *die* skittle alley; **~förmig** *Adj.* conical; cone-shaped; **~klub** *der* skittle club

kegeln 1 *itr. V.* play skittles *or* ninepins. **2** *tr. V.* **eine Partie** ~: play a game of skittles *or* ninepins; **eine Neun** ~: score a nine

Kegel-: **~schnitt** *der* (Geom.) conic section; **~stumpf** *der* truncated cone; frustum of a cone

Kegler *der;* ~s, ~: skittle player

Kehle /'ke:lə/ *die;* ~, ~n ▶326 throat; **sich** (*Dat.*) **die** ~ **anfeuchten** wet one's whistle (coll.); **sich** (*Dat.*) **die** ~ **aus dem Hals schreien** (ugs.) shout *or* yell one's head off; **aus voller** ~: at the top of one's voice; **sein ganzes Geld durch die** ~ **jagen** pour all one's money down one's throat; **jmdm. in der** ~ **stecken bleiben** stick in sb.'s throat *or* gullet; **etw. in die falsche** ~ **bekommen** (ugs.) (fig.: etw. missverstehen) take sth. the wrong way; (sich an etw. verschlucken) have sth. go down the wrong way

kehlig 1 *Adj.* guttural ⟨speech, sound, etc.⟩; throaty, guttural ⟨voice, laugh, etc.⟩. **2** *adv.* throatily; gutturally; in a throaty *or* guttural voice

Kehl·kopf *der* (Anat.) larynx

Kehlkopf·krebs *der* ▶329 (Med.) cancer of the larynx

Kehl·laut *der* (a) guttural sound; (b) (Sprachw.) guttural

Kehr-: **~aus** *der;* ~: last dance; **~blech** *das* (landsch.) dustpan

Kehre /'ke:rə/ *die;* ~, ~n (a) sharp bend *or* turn; (Haarnadelkurve) hairpin bend; (b) (Turnen) back *or* rear vault

kehren[1] **1** *tr. V.* turn; **die Innenseite von etw. nach außen** ~: turn sth. inside out; **jmdm. den Rücken** ~: turn one's back on sb. **2** *refl. V.* (a) turn; **sich gegen jmdn./etw.** ~: turn against sb./sth.; (b) **sich an etw.** (*Dat.*) ~: pay no attention to *or* not care about sth. **3** *itr. V.* **in sich** (*Akk.*) **gekehrt** lost in thought; in a brown study

kehren[2] (bes. südd.) **1** *itr. V.* sweep; do the sweeping. **2** *tr. V.* sweep; (mit einem Handfeger) brush

Kehricht /'ke:rɪçt/ der od. das; ~s (a) (geh.) rubbish; **das geht dich einen feuchten ~ an!** (salopp) mind your own damned business!; (b) (schweiz.: Müll) refuse; garbage (Amer.)

Kehricht-: ~**eimer** der dustbin; garbage can (Amer.); ~**haufen** der pile or heap of rubbish

Kehr-: ~**maschine** die [mechanical] road sweeper; ~**reim** der refrain; ~**schaufel** die dustpan; ~**seite** die (a) back; (einer Münze, Medaille) reverse; **die ~seite der Medaille** (fig.) the other side of the coin; (b) (scherzh.: Gesäß) backside; (c) (nachteiliger Aspekt) drawback; disadvantage

kehrt Interj. (Milit.) about turn; about face (Amer.)

kehrt|machen itr. V. (ugs.) turn [round and go] back; (plötzlich) turn in one's tracks; **auf dem Absatz ~:** turn on one's heel

Kehrt·wendung die (bes. Milit.; fig.) about-turn; about-face (Amer.)

keifen /'kaifn/ itr. V. (abwertend) nag; scold

Keil /kail/ der; ~[e]s, ~e wedge; **einen ~ zwischen die beiden Freunde treiben** (fig.) drive a wedge between the two friends

Keil·absatz der wedge [heel]

Keile /'kailə/ die; ~ (nordd.) walloping (sl.); thrashing; ~ **kriegen** get a walloping (sl.) or thrashing

keilen 1 refl. V. (ugs.: sich prügeln) fight; scrap; **sich um etw. ~:** fight over sth. **2** tr. V. (ugs.: anwerben) rope in (coll.); recruit

Keiler der; ~s, ~ (Jägerspr.) wild boar

Keilerei die; ~, ~en (ugs.) punch-up (coll.); brawl; fight

keil-, Keil-: ~**förmig** Adj. wedge-shaped; ~**hose** die tapering trousers; ~**kissen** das wedge-shaped bolster; ~**riemen** der (Technik) V-belt; (Kfz-W.: zum Antrieb des Kühlergebläses) fan belt; ~**schrift** die cuneiform script

Keim /kaim/ der; ~[e]s, ~e (a) (Bot.: erster Trieb) shoot; (b) (Biol.: befruchtete Eizelle) embryo; (c) (fig.: Ursprung) seed[s pl.]; **etw. im ~ ersticken** nip sth. in the bud; (d) (Biol., Med.: Krankheitserreger) germ

Keim-: ~**bahn** die (Biol.) germ line; ~**bahn·therapie** die (Med.) germ-line therapy; ~**blatt** das cotyledon; seed leaf; ~**drüse** die (Zool., Med.) gonad

keimen itr. V. (a) germinate; sprout; (b) (fig.) ‹hope› stir; ‹thought, belief, decision› form; ‹love, yearning› awaken

keim-, Keim-: ~**fähig** Adj. viable; capable of germinating postpos.; ~**fähigkeit** die; o. Pl. viability; ability to germinate; ~**frei** Adj. germ-free; sterile; **etw. ~ frei machen** sterilize sth.

Keimling /'kaimlɪŋ/ der; ~s, ~e (Bot.) embryo

Keim·zelle die (a) (fig.) nucleus; (b) (Bot.) germ-cell

kein /kain/ Indefinitpron.; attr. (a) no; **ich habe ~ Geld/ ~e Zeit** I have no money/time; I don't have any money/ time; **er hat ~ Wort gesagt** he didn't say a word; he said not a word; **er konnte ~e Arbeit finden** he could find no work; he could not find any work; **~ Mensch/~ einziger** nobody or no one/not a single one; **in ~er Weise/ unter ~en Umständen** in no way/in or under no circumstances; **das ist ~ schlechter Vorschlag** that's not a bad suggestion; **~ anderer als er kann es gewesen sein** it can't have been anybody else but him; (b) (ugs.: weniger als) less than; **es ist ~e drei Tage her, dass ich zuletzt dort war** it's not or it's less than three days since I was last there; **es dauert ~e fünf Minuten** it won't take five minutes; (c) nachgestellt (ugs.) **Lust habe ich ~e** I don't feel like it; **Kinder waren ~e da** there weren't any children there; s. auch **kein**...

kein... Indefinitpron. (niemand, nichts) ~**er**/~**e** nobody; no one; ~**er von uns** not one of us; none of us; **ich kenne ~en, der dir helfen kann** I don't know anyone who can help you; ~**[e]s von beiden** neither [of them]; **ich wollte ~[e]s von beiden** I didn't want either of them; **mir kann ~er!** (salopp) I can look after myself!

keinerlei indekl. unbest. Gattungsz. no ... at all; no ... what[so]ever

---

keines·falls Adv. on no account; **die Aufgabe ist schwer, aber ~ unlösbar** the problem is difficult but by no means insoluble

keines·wegs Adv. by no means; not by any means; not at all; **sein Einfluss darf ~ unterschätzt werden** his influence must in no way be underestimated

kein·mal Adv. not [even] once; s. auch **einmal** a

Keks /ke:ks/ der; ~ od. ~es, ~ od. ~e biscuit (Brit.); cookie (Amer.)

Kelch /kɛlç/ der; ~[e]s, ~e (a) goblet; **der ~ ist an ihm vorübergegangen** (geh.) he was spared that ordeal; (b) (Rel.) chalice; communion cup; (c) (Bot.) calyx

Kelch·blatt das (Bot.) sepal

kelch·förmig Adj. goblet-shaped

Kelle /'kɛlə/ die; ~, ~n (a) (Schöpflöffel) ladle; (b) (Signalstab) signalling disc; (c) (Maurer~) trowel

Keller /'kɛlɐ/ der; ~s, ~ (a) cellar; (~geschoss) basement; **der Dollar[kurs] ist in den ~ gegangen** (fig.) the dollar has gone through the floor (fig.); **im ~ sein** (Skat Jargon) have a minus score or minus points; (b) (Luftschutz~) [air-raid] shelter; (c) ⇒ **Kellerlokal**

Keller·assel die woodlouse

Kellerei die; ~, ~en winery; wine producer's

Keller-: ~**fenster** das cellar window; (von ~geschoss) basement window; ~**geschoss**, *~**geschoß** das basement; ~**gewölbe** das underground vault; ~**lokal** das cellar bar/disco/restaurant etc.; ~**treppe** die cellar stairs pl.; ~**wohnung** die basement flat (Brit.) or (Amer.) apartment

Kellner /'kɛlnɐ/ der; ~s, ~: ▶ 85 ǀ waiter

Kellnerin die; ~, ~nen waitress

kellnern itr. V. (ugs.) work as a waiter/waitress

Kelte /'kɛltə/ der; ~n, ~n Celt

Kelter /'kɛltɐ/ die; ~, ~n fruit-press; (für Trauben) wine-press

keltern tr. V. press ‹grapes etc.›

keltisch Adj. ▶ 487 ǀ Celtic

Keltisch das; ~[s] ▶ 487 ǀ Celtic

Kenia /'ke:nia/ (das); ~s Kenya

Kenianer /ke'nianɐ/ der; ~s, ~, **Kenianerin** die; ~, ~nen ▶ 388 ǀ Kenyan

kennen /'kɛnən/ unr. tr. V. (a) know; **das Leben ~:** know about life; know the ways of the world; **das ~ wir gar nicht anders** it's always been like that; **kennst du ihn?** do you know who he is?; (bist du mit ihm bekannt?) are you acquainted with him?; **kennst du den?** (diesen Witz) have you heard this one?; **jmds. Bücher/Werk ~:** know or be acquainted with sb.'s books/work; **da kennst du mich aber schlecht** (ugs.) that just shows you don't know me very well; **das kennen wir [schon]** (ugs. abwertend) we've heard all that before; **sich nicht mehr ~ [vor ...]** be beside oneself [with ...]; **da kenne ich/da kennt er nichts** (ugs.) and to hell with everything else (coll.); (b) (bekannt sein mit) know; be acquainted with; **jmdn. flüchtig/ persönlich ~:** know sb. slightly/personally; **die beiden ~ sich nicht mehr** (fig.) the two are no longer on speaking terms; **ich glaube, wir beide ~ uns noch nicht** I don't think we've been introduced; (c) (haben) have; **keinen Winter/Sommer ~:** have no winter/summer; **er kennt keine Kopfschmerzen** he never gets a headache; **kein Mitleid ~:** know or have no pity; (d) (wiedererkennen) know; recognize; **na, kennst du mich noch?** well, do you remember me?; (e) **jmdn./etw. [näher] ~ lernen** get to know sb./sth. [better]; become [better] acquainted with sb./sth.; **jmdn. ~ lernen** (jmdm. erstmals begegnen) meet sb.; **jmdn. von einer bestimmten Seite ~ lernen** see a particular side of sb.; **jmdn. als einen bescheidenen Menschen usw. ~ lernen** come to know sb. as a modest person etc.; **du wirst mich noch ~ lernen!** you'll find out I don't stand for any nonsense; **[es] freut mich, Sie ~ zu lernen** pleased to meet you; pleased to make your acquaintance (formal)

***kennen|lernen** ⇒ **kennen** e

Kenner der; ~s, ~ (a) expert, authority (+ Gen. on); (b) (von Wein, Speisen) connoisseur

Kẹnnerblick *der* expert eye; **mit** ∿: with an expert eye
Kẹnner·miene *die* air of an expert/connoisseur; **mit** ∿: with the air of an expert/connoisseur
Kẹnnerschaft *die;* ∿: connoisseurship; (Sachkenntnis) expertise
Kẹnn-: ∿**karte** *die* identity card; ∿**marke** *die* [police] identification badge; ≈ (police) warrant card *or* (Amer.) ID card; ∿**melodie** *die* (Rundf.) signature tune; ∿**nummer** *die* reference number
kenntlich /'kɛntlɪç/ *Adj. in* ∿ **sein** be recognizable *or* distinguishable (**an** by); **jmdn./etw.** ∿ **machen** mark sth./make sb. [easily] identifiable; **etw. als Gift** ∿ **machen** mark *or* label sth. as a poison
Kenntnis /'kɛntnɪs/ *die;* ∿, ∿**se (a)** *o. Pl.* knowledge; **von etw.** ∿ **haben/erhalten** be informed on sth. *or* have knowledge of sth./learn *or* hear about sth.; **das entzieht sich meiner** ∿ (geh.) I have no knowledge of that; **von etw.** ∿ **nehmen, etw. zur** ∿ **nehmen** take note of sth.; **jmdn. von etw. in** ∿ **setzen** inform *or* notify sb. of sth.; **jmdn. zur** ∿ **nehmen** take notice of sb.; **(b)** *Pl.* knowledge *sing.;* **oberflächliche/gründliche** ∿**se in etw.** (*Dat.*) **haben** have a superficial/thorough knowledge of sth.
Kẹnntnisnahme *die;* ∿ (Papierdt.) **jmdm. etw. zur** ∿ **vorlegen** submit sth. to sb. for his/her attention; **nach** ∿ **der Akten** after giving the documents my/his *etc.* attention
kenntnis·reich *Adj.* well-informed; knowledgeable
*****Kẹnnummer** ⇨ **Kennnummer**
kẹnn-, Kẹnn-: ∿**wort** *das; Pl.* ∿**wörter (a)** (Erkennungszeichen) code word; reference; **(b)** (Parole) password; code word; ∿**zahl** *die* **(a)** ⇨ ∿**ziffer;** **(b)** (Fernspr.) code; ∿**zeichen** *das* **(a)** (Merkmal) sign; mark; **ein** ∿**zeichen eines Genies** a [hall]mark of a genius; **besondere** ∿**zeichen** distinguishing marks; **(b)** (Erkennungszeichen) badge; (auf einem Behälter, einer Ware usw.) label; **(c)** (Kfz-W.) registration number; ∿**zeichnen** *tr. V.* **(a)** mark; label ⟨*container, goods, etc.*⟩; mark, signpost ⟨*way*⟩; tag ⟨*bird, animal*⟩; **etw. als ...** ∿**zeichnen** mark *or* identify sth. as ...; **(b)** (charakterisieren) characterize; **jmdn. als ...** ∿**zeichnen** characterize sb. as ...; **(c)** (in seiner Eigenart erkennen lassen) typify; **jmdn. als ...** ∿**zeichnen** mark sb. out as ...; ∿**zeichnend** *Adj.* typical, characteristic (**für** of); ∿**zeichnung** *die* **(a)** marking; (von Behältern, Waren) labelling; (von Vögeln, Tieren) tagging; **(b)** (Charakterisierung) characterization; **(c)** (Kennzeichen) mark; ∿**ziffer** *die* reference number; (bei einem Zeitungsinserat) box number
kẹntern /'kɛntɐn/ *itr. V.; mit sein* capsize
Keramik /ke'raːmɪk/ *die;* ∿, ∿**en (a)** *o. Pl.* (gebrannter Ton) ceramics *pl.;* pottery; **(b)** (∿gegenstand) ceramic; piece of pottery; **(c)** (Material) fired clay; **(d)** *o. Pl.* (Technik) ceramics *sing.;* pottery
keramisch *Adj.; nicht präd.* ceramic
Kerbe /'kɛrbə/ *die;* ∿, ∿**n** notch; **in dieselbe** *od.* **die gleiche** ∿ **hauen** (ugs.) take the same line
Kerbel /'kɛrbl̩/ *der;* ∿**s** chervil
kẹrben *tr. V.* notch; **etw. in etw.** (*Akk.*) ∿: carve sth. into sth.
Kẹrb-: ∿**holz** *das in* **etwas/einiges auf dem** ∿**holz haben** (ugs.) have done a job/a job or two (sl.); ∿**tier** *das* insect
Kerker /'kɛrkɐ/ *der;* ∿**s,** ∿ **(a)** (hist.) (Gefängnis) dungeons *pl.;* (Zelle) dungeon; **(b)** (österr., hist.) (Strafe) imprisonment
Kerl /kɛrl/ *der;* ∿**s,** ∿**e** (nordd., md. auch: ∿**s) (a)** (ugs.: männliche Person) guy (coll.); chap (coll.); bloke (Brit. sl.); **ein ganzer** *od.* **richtiger** ∿: a splendid fellow (coll.) *or* chap (coll.); **ein gemeiner/frecher** ∿ (abwertend) a nasty so-and-so (coll.) /an impudent fellow (coll.); **(b)** (ugs.: sympathische Mensch) **er ist ein feiner** ∿: he's a fine chap (coll.) *or* (sl.) a good bloke; **sie ist ein netter/feiner** ∿: she's a nice/fine woman
Kern /kɛrn/ *der;* ∿**[e]s,** ∿**e (a)** (Fruchtsamen) pip; (von Steinobst) stone; (von Nüssen, Mandeln usw.) kernel; **der** ∿ **eines Problems/Vorschlags** (fig.) the crux *or* gist of a problem/gist of a suggestion; **er hat einen guten** *od.* **in ihm steckt ein guter** ∿ (fig.) he is good at heart; **zum** ∿

einer Sache (*Gen.*) **kommen** (fig.) get to the heart of a matter; **(b)** (wichtigster Teil einer Gruppe) core; nucleus; **der harte** ∿: the hard core; **(c)** (Physik: Atom∿) nucleus; **(d)** (einer elektrischen Spule, eines Reaktors) core
kern-, Kẹrn-: ∿**brenn·stoff** *der* nuclear fuel; ∿**energie** *die* nuclear energy *no art.;* ∿**explosion** *die* nuclear explosion; ∿**fach** *das* (Schulw.) core subject; ∿**forschung** *die* nuclear research; ∿**frage** *die* central question; ∿**fusion** *die* (Phys., Biol.) nuclear fusion *no art.;* ∿**gehäuse** *das* core; ∿**gesund** *Adj.* fit as a fiddle *pred.;* sound as a bell *pred.*
kẹrnig 1 *Adj.* **(a)** (urwüchsig, markig) robust, earthy ⟨*language*⟩; down-to-earth ⟨*remarks*⟩; (kraftvoll) powerful, forceful ⟨*speech*⟩; pithy ⟨*saying*⟩; **ein** ∿**er Mann/Typ** (ugs.) a robust and athletic man/type; **(b)** (gehaltvoll, kräftig) full-bodied ⟨*wine*⟩. **2** *adv.* (urwüchsig, markig) robustly; (kraftvoll) forcefully
Kẹrn·kraft *die* **(a)** nuclear power *no art.;* **(b)** *Pl.* (Physik) nuclear forces
Kẹrnkraft-: ∿**gegner** *der* opponent of nuclear power; ∿**werk** *das* nuclear power station *or* plant
kern-, Kẹrn-: ∿**los** *Adj.* seedless; ∿**obst** *das* pomaceous fruit; pomes *pl.;* ∿**pflicht·fach** *das* (Schulw.) core-curriculum subject; ∿**physik** *die* nuclear physics *sing., no art.;* ∿**physiker** *der* nuclear physicist; ∿**punkt** *der* central point; ∿**reaktor** *der* nuclear reactor; ∿**satz** *der* key sentence *or* statement; ∿**seife** *die* washing soap; hard soap; ∿**spaltung** *die* (Physik) nuclear fission *no art.*
Kẹrnspin·tomographie /'kɛrnspɪn.../ *die* (Med.) [nuclear] magnetic resonance imaging
kern-, Kẹrn-: ∿**stück** *das* centrepiece; ∿**technik** *die* nuclear engineering *no art.;* ∿**waffe** *die; meist Pl.* nuclear weapon; ∿**waffen·frei** *Adj.* nuclear-free; ∿**zeit** *die* core time
Kerosin /kero'ziːn/ *das;* ∿**s** kerosene
Kerze /'kɛrtsə/ *die;* ∿, ∿**n (a)** candle; **elektrische** ∿: candle bulb; **(b)** (Zünd∿) spark plug; sparking plug; **(c)** (Turnen) shoulder stand
kẹrzen-, Kẹrzen-: ∿**beleuchtung** *die* candlelight *no indef. art.;* ∿**docht** *der* [candle] wick; ∿**gerade,** (ugs.) ∿**grade 1** *Adj.* dead straight ⟨*tree, post, etc.*⟩; very stiff ⟨*bow*⟩; **2** *adv.* bolt upright; ⟨*rise*⟩ straight upwards; ∿**halter** *der* candle-holder; ∿**leuchter** *der* candlestick; (für mehrere Kerzen) candelabrum; ∿**licht** *das; o. Pl.* the light of a candle/of candles; **bei** ∿**licht** by candlelight; ∿**schein** *der; o. Pl.* candlelight *no pl.;* ∿**stummel** *der,* ∿**stumpf** *der* stump of a/the candle
kess, *****keß** /kɛs/ **1** *Adj.* **(a)** (flott) pert; pert, jaunty ⟨*hat, dress, etc.*⟩; **(b)** (frech) cheeky. **2** *adv.* **(a)** (flott) jauntily; **(b)** (frech) cheekily
Kessel /'kɛsl̩/ *der;* ∿**s,** ∿ **(a)** (Tee∿) kettle; **(b)** (zum Kochen) pot; (für offenes Feuer) cauldron; (in einer Brauerei) vat; (Wasch∿) copper; wash-boiler; **(c)** (Berg∿) basin-shaped valley; **(d)** (Milit.) encircled area; (kleiner) pocket; **(e)** (Dampf∿, Heiz∿) boiler
Kẹssel-: ∿**fleisch** *das* ⇨ **Wellfleisch;** ∿**pauke** *die* kettledrum; ∿**schlacht** *die* battle of encirclement; ∿**stein** *der; o. Pl.* fur; scale; ∿**treiben** *das* **(a)** (Jägerspr.) battue (*using a circle of hunters and beaters*); **(b)** (fig.) witch-hunt
Ketchup, Ketschup /'kɛtʃap/ *der od. das;* ∿**[s],** ∿**s** ketchup
Kẹttchen /'kɛtçən/ *das;* ∿**s,** ∿: [neck-]chain (*with cross etc. attached*); (Fuß∿) anklet; (Arm∿) bracelet
Kette /'kɛtə/ *die;* ∿, ∿**n (a)** chain; (von Kettenfahrzeugen) track; **die** ∿ **[an der Tür] vorlegen** put the chain across [the door]; **an der** ∿ **liegen** ⟨*dog*⟩ be chained up; **jmdn. in** ∿**n legen** put sb. in chains; **die** ∿ **n abwerfen/zerreißen** (fig. geh.) cast off *or* throw off/break one's chains *or* shackles; **jmdn. an die** ∿ **legen** (fig.) keep sb. on a [tight *or* short] leash; **(b)** (Halsschmuck) necklace; (eines Bürgermeisters usw.) chain; **(c)** (fig.: Reihe) chain; (von Ereignissen) string; series; ∿**rauchen** (ugs.) chain-smoke; **(d)** (Weberei) warp
ketten *tr. V.* **(a)** chain (**an** + *Akk.* to); **(b)** (fig.) bind; **jmdn. an sich** (*Akk.*) ∿: bind sb. to oneself; **sich an jmdn.** ∿: tie oneself to sb.

Ketten-: ~**blatt** das chain wheel; front sprocket; ~**glied** das [chain-]link; ~**hemd** das (hist.) coat of chain mail; ~**hund** der watchdog or guard dog (kept on a chain); ~**laden** der chain store; ~**panzer** der chain mail; chain-armour; ~**rad** das sprocket [wheel]; ~**rauchen** das; ~**s** chain-smoking no art.; ~**raucher** der chain-smoker; ~**reaktion** die chain reaction; **eine** ~**reaktion auslösen** trigger a chain reaction; ~**ritzel** das [rear] sprocket; [rear] sprocket wheel; ~**schaltung** die derailleur gears pl.; ~**schutz** der chain guard; ~**werfer** der ⇒ **Umwerfer**

Ketzer /'kɛtsɐ/ der; ~**s**, ~ (auch fig.) heretic

Ketzerei die; ~, ~**en** (auch fig.) heresy

Ketzerin die; ~, ~**nen** (auch fig.) heretic

ketzerisch (auch fig.) **1** Adj. heretical. **2** adv. heretically

keuchen /'kɔʏçn̩/ itr. V. **(a)** pant; gasp for breath; **(b)** mit sein (sich keuchend fortbewegen) puff or pant one's way; come/ go puffing or panting along

Keuch·husten der ▶329┃ whooping cough no art.

Keule /'kɔʏlə/ die; ~, ~**n (a)** club; cudgel; **chemische** ~: Chemical Mace (P); **(b)** (Gymnastik) [Indian] club; **(c)** (Kochk.) leg; (Reh~, Hasen~) haunch; (Gänse~, Hühner~) drumstick; leg

Keulen-: ~**hieb** der, ~**schlag** der blow with a club or cudgel; ~**schwingen** das; ~**s** (Gymnastik) club swinging; swinging [Indian] clubs

keusch /kɔʏʃ/ **1** Adj. **(a)** chaste; pure; **(b)** (geh. veralt.) (sittsam) modest; demure; (sittlich rein) pure. **2** adv. **(a)** ~ **leben** lead a chaste life; **(b)** (sittsam) modestly; demurely; (sittlich rein) in a pure manner

Keuschheit die; ~ **(a)** chastity; **(b)** (geh. veralt.) (Sittsamkeit) modesty; (sittliche Reinheit) purity

Keuschheits-: ~**gelübde** das vow of chastity; ~**gürtel** der chastity belt

Kfz /ka:|ɛf'tsɛt/ Abk. **Kraftfahrzeug**

kg Abk. **Kilogramm** kg

KG Abk. **Kommanditgesellschaft**

khaki·farben Adj. khaki[-coloured]

Kibbuz /kɪ'buːts/ der; ~, ~**im** /kɪbuˈtsiːm/ od. ~**e** kibbutz

Kicher·erbse die chickpea

kichern /'kɪçɐn/ itr. V. giggle; **vor sich hin** ~: giggle to oneself

kicken (ugs.) **1** itr. V. play football. **2** tr. V. kick

Kicker der; ~**s**, ~**[s]** (ugs.) footballer; [football-]player

kidnappen /'kɪtnɛpn̩/ tr. V. kidnap

Kidnapper der; ~**s**, ~: kidnapper

Kidnapping /'kɪtnɛpɪŋ/ das; ~**s**, ~**s** kidnapping

kiebig /'kiːbɪç/ Adj. (bes. nordd.) (frech) cheeky; impertinent; (gereizt) touchy

Kiebitz /'kiːbɪts/ der; ~**es**, ~**e (a)** lapwing; peewit; **(b)** (ugs.: Zuschauer beim Spiel) kibitzer (coll.)

kiebitzen itr. V. (ugs. scherzh.) kibitz (coll.)

Kiefer¹ /'kiːfɐ/ der; ~**s**, ~: ▶326┃ jaw; (~knochen) jawbone

Kiefer² die; ~, ~**n (a)** pine[tree]; **(b)** o. Pl. (Holz) pine[-wood]

Kiefer-: ~**höhle** die ▶326┃ (Anat.) maxillary sinus; ~**knochen** der ▶326┃ jaw-bone

Kiefern-: ~**holz** das pine[-wood]; ~**nadel** die pine-needle; ~**zapfen** der pine cone

Kiefer·orthopädie die orthodontics sing., no art.

kieken /'kiːkn̩/ itr. V. (nordd.) look

Kieker /'kiːkɐ/ der; ~**s**, ~ in **jmdn. auf dem** ~ **haben** (ugs.) have it in for sb. (coll.)

Kiel¹ /kiːl/ der; ~**[e]s**, ~**e** keel; **ein Schiff auf** ~ **legen** lay down a ship; lay the keel of a ship

Kiel² der; ~**[e]s**, ~**e** (Feder~) quill

kiel-, Kiel-: ~**holen** tr. V. (Seemannsspr.) keel-haul ⟨person⟩; ~**oben** /-'--/ Adv. bottom up; ~**raum** der bilge; ~**wasser** das wake; **in jmds.** ~**wasser segeln** (fig.) follow in sb.'s wake

Kieme /'kiːmə/ die; ~, ~**n;** meist Pl. gill

Kien /kiːn/ der; ~**[e]s** resinous wood; (Kiefernholz) resinous pine-wood

Kien-: ~**fackel** die pine[-wood] torch; ~**span** der pine-wood chip; (zum Anzünden) pine-wood spill

Kiepe /'kiːpə/ die; ~, ~**n** (nordd., md.) dosser; pannier

Kies /kiːs/ der; ~**es**, ~**e (a)** gravel; (auf dem Strand) shingle; **(b)** (Mineral.) pyrites sing.; **(c)** (salopp: Geld) dough (sl.); bread (sl.)

Kiesel /'kiːzl̩/ der; ~**s**, ~: pebble

Kiesel-: ~**erde** die siliceous earth; ~**säure** die (Chemie) silicic acid; ~**stein** der pebble

kiesen /'kiːzn̩/ unr., auch regelm. tr. V. (dichter.) choose; select

Kies·grube die gravel pit

Kiez /kiːts/ der; ~**es**, ~**e** (bes. berlin.) neighbourhood

kiffen /'kɪfn̩/ itr. V. (ugs.) smoke pot (sl.) or grass (sl.)

Kiffer der; ~**s**, ~ (ugs.) pot-head (sl.)

kikeriki /kikəri'kiː/ Interj. (Kinderspr.) cock-a-doodle-doo

killen /'kɪlən/ tr. V. (salopp) do in (sl.); bump off (sl.)

Killer der; ~**s**, ~ (salopp) killer; (gedungener) hit man (coll.)

Kilo /'kiːlo/ das; ~**s**, ~**[s]** ▶228┃ kilo

Kilo-: ~**gramm** das ▶228┃ kilogram; ~**hertz** das; ~, ~ (Physik) kilohertz; ~**meter** der; ~**s**, ~: ▶160┃, ▶340┃ kilometre

kilometer-, Kilometer-: ~**fresser** der (ugs.) **er ist ein** ~**fresser** he really burns up the miles (coll.); ~**geld** das mileage allowance; ~**lang 1** Adj. miles long pred.; **eine** ~**lange Autoschlange** a traffic jam stretching [back] for miles; **2** adv. for miles [and miles]; ~**stand** der mileage reading; ~**weit 1** Adj.; nicht präd. to ~**weiter Entfernung** miles away in the distance; **2** adv. for miles [and miles]; ~**weit entfernt** miles away

Kilowatt·stunde die (Physik; bes. Elektrot.) kilowatt-hour

Kimme /'kɪmə/ die; ~, ~**n** sighting notch

Kimono /'kiːmoːno/ der; ~**s**, ~**s** kimono

Kind /kɪnt/ das; ~**[e]s**, ~**er (a)** child; kid (coll.); (Kleinkind) child; infant; (Baby) child; baby; **jmdm. ein** ~ **machen** (ugs.) put sb. in the family way (coll.) or in the club (sl.); **ein** ~ **erwarten/bekommen** od. (ugs.) **kriegen** be expecting/ have a baby; **ein** ~ **zur Welt bringen** (geh.) give birth to a child; **ein** ~/~**er in die Welt setzen** bring a child/ children into the world; **wir werden das** ~ **schon** [**richtig**] **schaukeln** (ugs.) we'll soon sort things out or have things sorted out; **das** ~ **mit dem Bade ausschütten** (fig.) throw the baby out with the bathwater; **das** ~ **beim Namen nennen** (fig.) call a spade a spade; **jmdn. wie ein** [**kleines**] ~ **behandeln** treat sb. like a [small] child; **das weiß/kann doch jedes** ~: any child or five-year old knows/can do that; **von** ~ **an** od. **auf** from childhood; **sich wie ein** ~ **freuen** be [as] pleased as Punch; **dann kommt bei ihm das** ~ **im Manne durch** (scherzh.) then he shows that he is [still] a child at heart; **sich bei jmdm. lieb** ~ **machen** (ugs.) get on the right side of sb.; **einziges** ~ **sein** be an only child; **armer/reicher Leute** ~ **sein** be the child of poor/wealthy parents; come from a poor/ wealthy family; **ein** ~ **der Liebe** (geh. verhüll.) a love-child; **er ist/du bist** usw. **kein** ~ **von Traurigkeit** (ugs.) he knows/you know etc. how to enjoy himself/yourself etc.; **jmdn. an** ~**es Statt annehmen** (veralt.) adopt sb.; s. auch **totgeboren;** **(b)** (ugs.: als Anrede) **mein** [**liebes**] ~: my [dear] child; ~**er, hört mal alle her!** listen to this, all of you (coll.); [~**er,**] ~**er!** my goodness!

Kindchen /'kɪntçən/ das; ~**s**, ~ **(a)** [small or little] child; **(b)** (Anrede) dear child

kinder-, Kinder-: ~**arbeit** die; o. Pl. child labour; ~**arzt** der ▶85┃ paediatrician; ~**bett** das cot; (für größeres Kind) child's bed; ~**bild** das (Foto) photograph of a child; (Malerei usw.) portrait of a child; **ein** ~**bild von jmdm.** a photograph/portrait of sb. as a child; ~**buch** das children's book; ~**chor** der children's choir; ~**dorf** das children's village

Kinderei die; ~, ~**en** childishness no indef. art., no pl.; **eine** ~: a childish prank; ~**en** childishness sing.; childish behaviour sing.

---

*alte Schreibung (vgl. Hinweise auf S. xvi–xvii)

kinder-, Kinder-: ~**erziehung** *die* bringing up of children; ~**fahrrad** *das* child's bicycle; ~**feindlich** 1 *Adj.* hostile to children *pred.;* anti-children *pred.;* 2 *adv.* sich ~**feindlich verhalten** act in a manner hostile to children; ~**feindlichkeit** *die; o. Pl.* hostility to children; (von Planung, Politik) failure to cater for children; ~**fest** *das* children's party; children's fête; ~**film** *der* children's film; ~**freund** *der:* ein [großer] ~**freund/** [große] ~**freunde** sein be [very] fond of children; ~**freundlich** 1 *Adj.* fond of children *pred.;* ‹planning, policy› which caters for the needs of children; 2 *adv.* sich ~**freundlich verhalten** act in a manner friendly to children; ~**freundlichkeit** *die* fondness for children; ~**funk** *der* children's programmes *pl.;* ~**garten** *der* kindergarten; nursery school; ~**gärtnerin** *die* ▸ 85 ⌡ kindergarten teacher; nursery-school teacher; ~**geld** *das* child benefit; ~**gesicht** *das* child's face; (eines Erwachsenen) childlike face; baby-face; ~**glaube** *der* childlike belief *or* faith; (abwertend) childish belief *or* faith; ~**gottes·dienst** *der* children's service; ~**heim** *das* children's home; ~**hort** *der* day-home for schoolchildren; ~**karussell** *das* children's roundabout; ~**kleidung** *die* children's clothes *pl.;* children's wear; ~**krankheit** *die* (a) children's disease *or* illness; welche ~**krankheiten hatten Sie?** what childhood diseases have you had?; (b) *Pl.* (fig.) teething troubles; ~**kriegen** *das;* ~s (ugs.) having children; ~**krippe** *die* crèche; day nursery; ~**lähmung** *die* ▸ 329 ⌡ poliomyelitis; infantile paralysis *no art.;* ~**leicht** (ugs.) 1 (Adj.) childishly simple *or* easy; dead easy (coll.); **das ist** ~**leicht** it's child's play *or* (coll.) kid's stuff; 2 *adv.* es ist ~**leicht zu bedienen** it's childishly simple to use; ~**lieb** *Adj.* fond of children *pred.;* ~**liebe** *die* love of children; ~**lied** *das* nursery rhyme; ~**los** *Adj.* childless; ~**losigkeit** *die* childlessness; ~**mädchen** *das* nursemaid; nanny; ~**märchen** *das* [children's] fairy tale; ~**mord** *der* child-murder; ~**mund** *der* child's mouth; ~**mund tut Wahrheit kund** (Prov.) it takes a child to point out the truth; ~**narr** *der:* **er ist ein** ~**narr** he adores children; ~**popo** *der* (ugs.) [baby's] bottom; **glatt wie ein** ~**popo** [as] smooth as a baby's bottom; ~**reich** *Adj.* with many children *postpos., not pred.;* **eine** ~**reiche Familie** a large family; ~**reichtum** *der; o. Pl.* large number of children; ~**reim** *der* nursery rhyme; ~**schreck** *der;* bogyman; ~**schuh** *der* child's shoe; **ich bin/du bist den** ~**schuhen entwachsen** (fig.) I'm/you're not a child any more; **noch in den** ~**schuhen stecken** ‹process, technique, etc.› be still in its infancy; ~**schwester** *die* children's nurse; ~**segen** *der; o. Pl.* (oft scherzh.) **eine Familie mit reichem** ~**segen** a family blessed with a large number of children; ~**sitz** *der* child's seat; (an einem Fahrrad) child carrier [seat]; (im Auto) child's safety seat; ~**spiel** *das* children's game; [für jmdn.] **ein** ~**spiel sein** be child's play [to sb.]; ~**spielplatz** *der* [children's] playground; ~**spielzeug** *das* [children's] toys *pl.* or playthings *pl.;* (einzeln) [child's] toy *or* plaything; ~**sterblichkeit** *die* child mortality; ~**stimme** *die* child's voice; ~**stube** *die; o. Pl.* **eine gute/schlechte** ~**stube gehabt** *od.* **genossen haben** have been well/ badly brought up; **hast du gar keine** ~**stube?** didn't you ever learn any manners?; ~**teller** *der* (a) child's plate; (b) (Gericht) children's menu; ~**wagen** *der* (Brit.) baby carriage (Amer.); (Sportwagen) pushchair (Brit.); stroller (Amer.); ~**zimmer** *das* children's room; (für Kleinkinder) nursery

Kindes-: ~**alter** *das; o. Pl.* childhood; **im** ~**alter** at an early age; ~**beine** *Pl.* in **von** ~**beinen an** from *or* since childhood; from an early age; ~**entführung** *die* kidnapping [of a child]; child abduction; ~**kind** *das* (veralt.) grandchild; **unsere Kinder und** ~**kinder** our children and our children's children; ~**misshandlung,** *~**mißhandlung** *die* (Rechtsw.) child abuse; ~**mord** *der* child murder; (Mord am eigenen Kind) infanticide; ~**mörderin** *die* infanticide; ~**tötung** *die* (Rechtsw.) infanticide

kind·gemäß *Adj.* suitable for children *postpos.*

Kindheit *die;* ~: childhood; **seit frühester** ~: from earliest childhood; from infancy

Kindheits·erinnerung *die* childhood memory

kindisch 1 *Adj.* childish, infantile ‹behaviour, enjoyment›; naïve ‹ideas›; ~ **werden** become childish; **werd nicht** ~! do behave sensibly. 2 *adv.* childishly; **sich** ~ **an etw.** (Dat.) **freuen** take childish pleasure in sth.

kindlich 1 *Adj.* childlike. 2 *adv.* ‹behave› in a childlike way *or* manner; **sich** ~ **über etw.** (Akk.) **freuen** take a childlike pleasure in sth.

Kindlichkeit *die;* ~: childlike quality

Kinds·kopf *der* overgrown child; **sei doch kein** ~! don't be so childish!; act your age!

Kind·taufe *die* christening

Kinematographie /kinematogra'fi:/ *die;* ~: cinematography *no art.*

Kinetik /ki'ne:tik/ *die;* ~ (Physik) kinetics *sing., no art.*

Kinkerlitzchen /'kıŋkɐlıtsçən/ *Pl.* (ugs.) trifles

Kinn /kın/ *das;* ~[e]s, ~e ▸ 326 ⌡ chin

Kinn-: ~**backe** *die,* ~**backen** *der* (südd.) cheek; ~**bart** *der* chin-beard; chin-tuft; ~**haken** *der* hook to the chin; ~**lade** *die* jaw

Kino /'ki:no/ *das;* ~s, ~s (a) cinema (Brit.); movie theatre *or* house (Amer.); **in die [deutschen]** ~s **kommen** go on general release [in Germany]; (b) (Vorstellung) film; movie (Amer.); **ins** ~ **gehen** go to the cinema (Brit.) *or* pictures (Brit.) *or* (Amer.) movies *pl.;* (c) *o. Pl.* (Film als Medium) cinema

Kino-: ~**karte** *die* cinema ticket (Brit.); movie ticket (Amer.); ~**kasse** *die* cinema (Brit.) *or* (Amer.) movie box office; ~**programm** *das* cinema guide

Kintopp /'ki:ntɔp/ *der od. das;* ~s, ~s *od.* **Kintöppe** /'ki:ntœpə/ (ugs.) cinema

Kiosk /ki:ɔsk/ *der;* ~[e]s, ~e kiosk

Kipfel /'kıpfl/ *das;* ~s, ~, **Kipferl** /'kıpfɐl/ *das;* ~s, ~n (bayr., österr.) ⇒ **Hörnchen b**

Kippe¹ /'kıpə/ *die;* ~, ~n (ugs.) cigarette end; fag end (coll.); dog-end (sl.)

Kippe² *die;* ~, ~n (a) (Müll...) tip; dump; (b) *in* **auf der** ~ **stehen** (ugs.) be balanced precariously; **etw. steht auf der** ~ (fig.) (etw. befindet sich in einer kritischen Lage) it's touch and go with sth.; (etw. ist noch nicht entschieden) sth. hangs in the balance

kippelig /'kıpəlıç/ *Adj.* (ugs.) wobbly; rickety, wobbly ‹chair, table›

kippeln /'kıpln/ *itr. V.* (ugs.) wobble; ‹chair, table› wobble; be wobbly *or* rickety; [**mit seinem Stuhl**] ~: rock one's chair backwards and forwards

kippen 1 *tr. V.* (a) (neigen) tip [up]; tilt; (b) (ausschütten) tip; (c) (ugs.: trinken) knock back (sl.); **einen** ~: have a quick one (coll.) *or* a drink; (d) (ugs.: abbrechen) give ‹project, series› the chop (sl.). 2 *itr. V.; mit sein* tip over; ‹top-heavy object› topple over; ‹person› fall, topple; ‹boat› overturn; ‹car› roll over; **von etw.** ~: topple *or* fall off sth.

Kipper *der;* ~s, ~: tipper lorry *or* truck; dump truck; (Eisenb.) tipper *or* tipping wagon; dump car (Amer.)

Kipp-: ~**fenster** *das* horizontally pivoted window; ~**lore** *die* tipper *or* tipping wagon; ~**schalter** *der* tumbler *or* toggle switch; ~**wagen** *der* ⇒ ~**lore**

Kirche /'kırçə/ *die;* ~, ~n (a) church; (fig.) **die** ~ **im Dorf lassen** keep a sense of proportion; **mit der** ~ **ums Dorf gehen/fahren** do things in a roundabout way; (b) *o. Pl.* (Gottesdienst) church *no art.;* **in der** ~ **sein** be at church; **in die** ~ **gehen** go to church; (c) (Institution) Church; **aus der** ~ **austreten** secede from *or* leave the Church

kirchen-, Kirchen-: ~**älteste** *der/die* (ev. Kirche) [church-]elder; ~**bank** *die* [church-]pew; ~**chor** *der* church choir; ~**feindlich** *Adj.* hostile to the Church *postpos.;* ~**fenster** *das* church window; ~**fürst** *der* (geh.) high ecclesiastical dignitary; high dignitary of the Church; (kath. Kirche: Kardinal) Prince of the Church; ~**gemeinde** *die* parish; ~**glocke** *die* church bell; ~**jahr** *das* ecclesiastical year; Church year; ~**lied** *das* hymn); ~**maus** *die in* **arm sein wie eine** ~**maus** (ugs. scherzh.) be as poor as a church mouse; ~**musik** *die* church music; sacred music; ~**portal** *das* portal *or* main door of the/a church; ~**schiff** *das* (Archit.) nave; ~**steuer**

die church tax; ~**tag** *der* Church congress; ~**tür** *die* church door

Kirch-: ~**gang** *der:* der sonntägliche ~**gang** going to church on Sunday; ~**gänger** *der* churchgoer; ~**hof** *der* (veralt.) churchyard; graveyard

kirchlich 1 *Adj.* ecclesiastical; Church *attrib.;* ecclesiastical ‹*law, building*›; religious, church ‹*festival*›; church *attrib.* ‹*wedding, funeral*›. 2 *adv.* ~ **getraut/begraben werden** have a church wedding *or* be married in church/ have a church funeral

Kirch·turm *der* church tower; (mit Spitze) [church] steeple

Kirchturm-: ~**spitze** *die* church spire; ~**uhr** *die* church clock

Kirch-: ~**weih** *die;* ~, ~**en** fair; ~**weihe** *die* consecration of a/the church

Kirmes /ˈkɪrməs/ *die;* ~, **Kirmessen** /ˈkɪrmɛsn̩/ (bes. md., niederd.) ⇒ **Kirchweih**

kirre /ˈkɪrə/ *Adj.; nicht attr.* **jmdn.** ~ **machen** (ugs.) bring sb. to heel

Kirsch /kɪrʃ/ *der;* ~[e]s, ~: ⇒ **Kirschwasser**

Kirsch-: ~**baum** *der* (a) cherry[-tree]; (b) (Holz) *o. Pl.* cherry[-wood]; ~**blüte** *die* (a) (Blüte des ~baums) cherry blossom; (b) (Zeit der ~blüte) cherry blossom time

Kirsche /ˈkɪrʃə/ *die;* ~, ~**n** cherry; **mit ihm ist nicht gut** ~**n essen** (ugs.) it's best not to tangle with him

kirsch-, Kirsch-: ~**kern** *der* cherry stone; ~**likör** *der* cherry liqueur; (Weinbrand) cherry brandy; ~**saft** *der* cherry juice; ~**stein** *der* ⇒ ~**kern;** ~**torte** *die* cherry gateau; (mit Tortenboden) cherry flan; **Schwarzwälder** ~**torte** Black Forest gateau; ~**wasser** *das* kirsch

Kissen /ˈkɪsn̩/ *das;* ~s, ~: cushion; (Kopf~) pillow

Kissen-: ~**bezug** *der* cushion cover; (für Kopfkissen) pillow-case; pillowslip; ~**schlacht** *die* (ugs.) pillow-fight

Kiste /ˈkɪstə/ *die;* ~, ~**n** (a) box; (Truhe) chest; (Latten~) crate; (für Obst) case; box; (für Wein) case; (b) (salopp) (Flugzeug, Auto) bus (coll.); (Fernseher) box (coll.); (c) (ugs., bes. berlin.: Sache, Angelegenheit) affair; business

Kitsch /kɪtʃ/ *der;* ~[e]s kitsch

kitschig *Adj.* kitschy

Kitt /kɪt/ *der;* ~[e]s, ~**e** (Fenster~) putty; (für Porzellan, Kacheln usw.) cement; (Füllmasse) filler

Kittchen *das;* ~s, ~ (ugs.) clink (sl.); jug (sl.); jail; **im** ~ **sitzen** be inside (sl.); be in clink *or* jug (sl.)

Kittel /ˈkɪtl̩/ *der;* ~s, ~ (a) overall; (eines Arztes, Laboranten usw.) white coat; (b) (hemdartige Bluse) smock

kitten *tr. V.* cement [together]; stick [together] with cement; (fig.) mend ‹*breach*›; patch up ‹*broken marriage, friendship*›

Kitz /kɪts/ *das;* ~**es,** ~**e** (Reh~) fawn; (Ziegen~, Gämsen~) kid

Kitzel /ˈkɪtsl̩/ *der;* ~s, ~ (Reiz, Antrieb) itch; urge; (freudige Erregung) thrill

kitzelig ⇒ **kitzlig**

kitzeln 1 *tr. V.* tickle; **es kitzelt mich in der Nase** my nose tickles. 2 *itr. V.* tickle; **auf der Haut** ~: tickle [the skin]

Kitzler *der;* ~s, ~ (Anat.) clitoris

kitzlig *Adj.* (a) ticklish; (b) (schwierig, heikel) ticklish

Kiwi /ˈkiːvi/ *die;* ~, ~**s** kiwi [fruit]

KKW *Abk.* **Kernkraftwerk**

Klacks /klaks/ *der;* ~**es,** ~**e** (ugs.) (~ Schlagsahne, Kartoffelbrei) dollop (coll.); (~ Senf) blob; dab; **etw. ist ein** ~ **[für jmdn.]** (fig.) sth. is no trouble at all [for sb.]

Kladde /ˈklada/ *die;* ~, ~**n** rough book; **etw. in** ~ **schreiben** write sth. in rough

klaffen *itr. V.* gape; yawn; ‹*hole, wound*› gape; ‹*gap*› yawn; **in der Mauer klaffte ein großes Loch** there was a gaping hole in the wall

kläffen /ˈklɛfn̩/ *itr. V.* (abwertend) yap

klaffend *Adj.* gaping; yawning; gaping ‹*hole, wound*›; yawning ‹*gap*›

---

*alte Schreibung (vgl. Hinweise auf S. xvi–xvii)

Kläffer *der;* ~s, ~ (ugs. abwertend) yapping dog; yapper

Klage /ˈklaːgə/ *die;* ~, ~**n** (a) (aus Trauer) lamentation; lament; (wegen Schmerzen) complaint; (b) (Beschwerde) complaint; **keinen Grund zur** ~ **geben/haben** give/have no grounds *pl. or* reason for complaint; **bei jmdm. über jmdn./etw.** ~ **führen** make a complaint to sb. *or* lodge a complaint with sb. about sb./sth.; (c) (Rechtsw.) (im Zivilrecht) action; suit; (im Strafrecht) charge; **[öffentliche]** ~ **gegen jmdn. einreichen/erheben** bring an action against sb.; institute [criminal] proceedings against sb.

Klage-: ~**laut** *der* plaintive cry; (von Schmerzen verursacht) cry of pain; (stöhnend) moan; ~**lied** *das* lament; ~**mauer** *die* Wailing Wall

klagen 1 *itr. V.* (a) (geh.: jammern) wail; (stöhnend) moan; ‹*animal*› cry plaintively; (b) (sich beschweren) complain; **über etw.** (*Akk.*) ~: complain about sth.; **über Rückenschmerzen** ~: complain of backache *sing.;* **[ich] kann nicht** ~: [I] can't complain; [I] mustn't grumble; (c) (geh.) **um jmdn./jmds. Tod** ~: mourn sb./sb.'s death; **über den Verlust seines Vermögens** ~: lament *or* bewail the loss of one's fortune; (d) (bei Gericht) sue; take legal action; **auf Schadenersatz** ~: sue for damages; bring an action for damages; **gegen jmdn.** ~: sue sb.; take legal action against sb. 2 *tr. V.* **jmdm. sein Leid** ~: pour out one's sorrows *pl.* to sb.

Kläger /ˈklɛːgə/ *der;* ~s, ~, **Klägerin** *die;* ~, ~**nen** (im Zivilrecht) plaintiff; (im Strafrecht) prosecuting party; (bei einer Scheidung) petitioner

Klage·schrift *die* (Rechtsw.) (im Zivilrecht) statement of claim; (im Strafrecht) charge/list of charges; (bei einer Scheidung) petition

kläglich /ˈklɛːklɪç/ *Adj.* (a) (mitleiderregend) pitiful ‹*expression, voice, cry*›; pitiful, wretched ‹*condition, appearance*›; (b) (minderwertig) pathetic ‹*achievement, result, etc.*›; (c) (erbärmlich) despicable, wretched ‹*behaviour, role, compromise*›; pathetic ‹*result, defeat*›

klaglos 1 *Adj.* uncomplaining. 2 *adv.* uncomplainingly; without complaint

Klamauk /klaˈmaʊk/ *der;* ~s (ugs. abwertend) fuss; to-do; (Lärm, Krach) row (coll.); racket; (im Theater) slapstick

klamm /klam/ *Adj.* (a) (feucht) cold and damp; (b) (steif) numb

Klammer *die;* ~, ~**n** (a) (Wäsche~) peg; (b) (Haar~) [hair-] grip; (c) (Zahn~) brace; (d) (Wund~) clip; (e) (Büro~) paper clip; (Heft~) staple; (f) (Schriftzeichen) bracket; ~ **auf/zu** open/close brackets

klammern 1 *refl. V.* **sich an jmdn./etw.** ~ (auch fig.) cling to sb./sth. 2 *tr. V.* (a) **eine Wunde** ~: close a wound with a clip/clips; (b) (mit Büroklammer) clip; (mit einer Heftmaschine) staple; (mit einer Wäscheklammer) peg. 3 *itr. V.* (Boxen) clinch

klamm·heimlich 1 *Adj.; nicht präd.* (ugs.) on the quiet *postpos.* 2 *adv.* on the quiet

Klamotte /klaˈmɔtə/ *die;* ~, ~**n** (a) *Pl.* (salopp: Kleidung) clobber *sing.* (sl.); gear *sing.* (sl.); (b) *Pl.* (salopp: Kram) junk *sing.;* stuff *sing.;* (c) (ugs. abwertend: Schwank) rubbishy play/ film etc.

klang /klaŋ/ *1. u. 3. Pers. Sg. Prät. v.* **klingen**

Klang *der;* ~[e]s, **Klänge** /ˈklɛŋə/ (a) (Ton) sound; (b) (~farbe) tone; (c) *Pl.* (Melodie) **alte, wohl bekannte Klänge** old familiar tunes; **nach den Klängen eines Walzers tanzen** dance to the strains of a waltz

Klang·farbe *die* tone colour *or* quality

klanglich 1 *Adj.; nicht präd.* tonal ‹*beauty, quality, etc.*›; tonal, tone *attr.* ‹*characteristics*›. 2 *adv.* tonally

klanglos 1 *Adj.* toneless ‹*voice*›. 2 *adv.* tonelessly; *s. auch* **sanglos**

klang·voll *Adj.* sonorous ‹*voice, language*›; (fig.) illustrious ‹*name, title*›

Klapp·bett *das* folding bed

Klappe *die;* ~, ~**n** (a) [hinged] lid; (am Briefkasten) flap; (b) (am LKW) tail-board; tailgate; (seitlich) side-gate; (am Kombiwagen) back; (c) (an Kleidertaschen) flap; (d) (am Ofen) [drop-]door; (e) (an Musikinstrumenten) key; (an einer Trompete) valve; (f) (Herz~) valve; (g) (Augen~) [eye-] patch; (h) (Achselstück) shoulder strap; (i) (Filmjargon) clapper-board; (j) (salopp:

Mund) trap (sl.); *die od.* **seine ~ halten** shut one's trap (sl.); **eine große ~ haben** (abwertend) have a big mouth; **(k)** (ugs.: Bett) ⇒ **Falle b**

klappen 1 *tr. V.* **nach oben/unten ~:** turn up/down ‹*collar, hat-brim*›; lift up/put down *or* lower ‹*lid*›; **nach vorne/hinten ~:** tilt forward/back ‹*seat*›. **2** *itr. V.* **(a)** ‹*door, shutter*› bang; **(b)** (stoßen) bang; **(c)** (ugs.: gelingen) work out all right; ‹*rehearsal, performance, etc.*› go [off] all right; **hat es mit den Karten geklappt?** did you get the tickets all right?

Klappen·text *der* (Buchw.) blurb

Klapper *die;* ~, ~n rattle

Klapper·kiste *die* (ugs.) rattletrap

klappern *itr. V.* **(a)** rattle; **(b)** (ein Klappern erzeugen) make a clatter; **vor Kälte klapperte er mit den Zähnen** his teeth were chattering with cold; **mit den Augen ~** (ugs.) keep blinking; (kokettieren) flutter one's eyelashes

Klapper-: ~**schlange** *die* rattlesnake; ~**storch** *der* (Kinderspr.) stork

Klapp-: ~**fahrrad** *das* folding bicycle; ~**fenster** *das* top-hung window; ~**messer** *das* clasp-knife; ~**rad** *das* folding bicycle

klapprig *Adj.* **(a)** (alt) rickety; ramshackle; **(b)** (wenig stabil) rickety; wobbly; **(c)** (ugs.: hinfällig) decrepit

Klapp-: ~**sitz** *der* folding seat; tip-up seat; ~**stuhl** *der* folding chair; ~**tisch** *der* folding table

Klaps /klaps/ *der;* ~**es,** ~**e (a)** (ugs.: leichter Schlag) smack; slap; **(b)** (salopp) **einen ~ haben** have a screw loose (coll.); be a bit bonkers (sl.)

Klaps·mühle *die* (salopp) loony-bin (coll.); nut-house (sl.)

klar /klaːɐ̯/ **1** *Adj.* **(a)** clear; ~**er Sicht** when it's clear; **on a clear day; ein ~er Verstand** clear judgement; ~ **[im Kopf] sein** have a clear head; be able to think clearly *or* straight; **er ist nicht ganz ~ im Kopf** (salopp) he's not quite right in the head (sl.); **(b)** (eindeutig) clear ‹*decision, aim, objective*›; straight ‹*question, answer*›; ~**e Verhältnisse schaffen** set things straight; **[ist] alles ~?** [is] everything clear?; **jetzt ist mir alles ~:** now I understand; **na ~!** (ugs.), **aber ~!** (ugs.) of course!; **ist dir ~, dass ...?** are you aware that ...?; **sich** (*Dat.*) **über etw.** (*Akk.*) **im Klaren sein** realize *or* be aware of sth.; **sich** (*Dat.*) **über etw.** (*Akk.*) ~ **werden** realize *or* grasp sth.; **jmdm.** ~ **werden** become clear to sb.; **(c)** *nicht attr.* (fertig) ready. **2** *adv.* clearly; **etw.** ~ **und deutlich sagen** say sth. clearly and unambiguously; ~ **sehen** understand the matter

Klär·anlage *die* sewage treatment plant; (einer Fabrik) wastewater treatment plant

Klare *der;* ~**n,** ~**n** schnapps

klären /ˈklɛːrən/ **1** *tr. V.* **(a)** (aufklären) settle, resolve ‹*question, issue, matter*›; clarify ‹*situation*›; clear up ‹*case, affair, misunderstanding*›; **(b)** (reinigen) purify; treat ‹*effluent, sewage*›; clear ‹*beer, wine*›. **2** *refl. V.* **(a)** (klar werden) ‹*situation*› become clear; ‹*question, issue, matter*› be settled *or* resolved; **(b)** (rein werden) ‹*liquid, sky*› clear. **3** *itr. V.* (Ballspiele) clear [the ball]

klar·gehen *unr. itr. V.; mit sein* (ugs.) go OK (coll.); **es wird schon ~:** it'll be OK (coll.)

Klarheit *die;* ~, ~**en (a)** *o. Pl.* clarity; (von Ausführungen, Rede usw.) clarity; lucidity; **(b)** *o. Pl.* (Gewissheit) **sich** (*Dat.*) **über etw.** (*Akk.*) ~ **verschaffen** clarify sth.; **(c)** (ugs. scherzh.) **jetzt sind alle** ~**en beseitigt** now I'm/everyone's *etc.* totally confused

Klarinette /klariˈnɛtə/ *die;* ~, ~**n** clarinet

Klarinettist *der;* ~**en,** ~**en, Klarinettistin** *die;* ~, ~**nen** clarinettist

klar-, Klar-: ~**|kommen** *unr. itr. V.; mit sein* (ugs.) manage; cope; **mit jmdm.** ~**kommen** get on with sb.; ~**|machen** *tr. V.* **(a)** (ugs.) make clear; **jmdm./sich etw.** ~**machen** make sth. clear to sb./realize sth.; **(b)** (Seemannsspr.) get ready; prepare; ~**schriftleser** *der* (DV) optical character reader;*~**|sehen** ⇒ **klar 2**

Klarsicht-: ~**folie** *die* transparent film; ~**packung** *die* transparent pack

klar-, Klar-: ~**|spülen** *itr. V.* rinse; ~**spüler** *der,* ~**spülmittel** *das* rinse aid; ~**|stellen** *tr. V.* clear up;

clarify; **ich möchte** ~**stellen, dass ...:** I should like to make it clear that ...; ~**stellung** *die* clarification; ~**text** *der* (auch DV) clear *or* plain text; **im** ~**text** (fig.) in plain language

Klärung *die;* ~, ~**en (a)** clarification; **(b)** (Reinigung) purification; (von Abwässern) treatment

*****klar|werden** ⇒ **klar 1 b**

Klär·werk *das* sewage works *sing. or pl.;* (einer Fabrik) wastewater treatment works *sing. or pl.*

klasse /ˈklasə/ (ugs.) **1** *indekl. Adj.* great (coll.); marvellous. **2** *adv.* marvellously

Klasse *die;* ~, ~**n (a)** (Schul~) class; form (esp. Brit.); (Raum) classroom; (Stufe) year; grade (Amer.); **(b)** (Bevölkerungsgruppe) class; **die** ~ **der Werktätigen** the working class; **(c)** (Sport) league; (Boxen) division; class; **(d)** (Kategorie) class; **eine Fahrkarte erster ~:** a first-class ticket; **zweiter ~ liegen** occupy a second-class hospital-bed; **er ist ein Künstler erster ~** (ugs.) he is a first-class *or* first-rate artist; **das ist [einsame od. ganz große]** ~**!** (ugs.) that's [just] great (coll.) *or* marvellous!; **(e)** (Biol.) class

Klasse-: ~**frau** *die* (ugs.) stunner (coll.); smasher (coll.); ~**mann** *der* (ugs.) marvellous man; fantastic guy (coll.)

klassen-, Klassen-: ~**arbeit** *die* [written] class test; ~**ausflug** *der* class outing; ~**beste** *der/die; adj. Dekl.* top pupil in the class; ~**bewusstsein,** *****bewußtsein** *das* (Soziol.) classconsciousness; ~**buch** *das* (Schulw.) ≈ [class-]register; ~**fahrt** *die* ⇒ ~**ausflug;** ~**feind** *der* (marx.) class enemy; ~**gegensatz** *der* class difference; ~**gesellschaft** *die* (Soziol.) class society; ~**justiz** *die* (Soziol.) legal system with a built-in class bias; ~**kamerad** *der,* ~**kameradin** *die* class-fellow; classmate; ~**kampf** *der* (marx.) class struggle; ~**lehrer** *der,* ~**lehrerin** *die* class *or* form teacher; form master/mistress; ~**los** *Adj.* (Soziol.) classless; ~**sprecher** *der,* ~**sprecherin** *die* class spokesman; ≈ form leader *or* captain; ~**treffen** *das* class reunion; ~**unterschied** *der* (Soziol.) class difference; ~**ziel** *das* (Schulw.) required standard (for pupils in a particular class); **das** ~**ziel erreichen** reach the required standard; (fig.) make the grade; come up to scratch; ~**zimmer** *das* classroom

Klassifikation /klasifikaˈtsi̯oːn/ *die;* ~, ~**en** classification

klassifizieren /klasifiˈtsiːrən/ *tr. V.* classify (**als** as)

Klassifizierung *die;* ~, ~**en** classification

Klassik /ˈklasɪk/ *die;* ~ **(a)** (Antike) classical antiquity *no art.;* **(b)** (Zeit kultureller Höchstleistung) classical period *or* age

Klassiker *der;* ~**s,** ~ classic; (Schriftsteller) classic; classical writer; (Komponist) classic; classical composer

klassisch *Adj.* **(a)** classical; **(b)** (vollendet, zeitlos; auch iron.) classic

Klassizismus /klasiˈtsɪsmʊs/ *der;* ~: classicism

klassizistisch *Adj.* classical

klatsch *Interj.* smack

Klatsch /klatʃ/ *der;* ~**[e]s,** ~**e (a)** *o. Pl.* (ugs. abwertend: Gerede) gossip; tittle-tattle; **(b)** (Geräusch) smack

Klatsch·base *die* (ugs. abwertend) gossip

klatschen 1 *itr. V.* **(a)** *auch mit sein* ‹*waves, wet sails*› slap (**gegen** against); **der Regen klatscht gegen die Scheiben** the rain beats against the windows; **jmdm. eine Ohrfeige geben, dass es nur so klatscht** give sb. a resounding smack *or* slap round the face; **(b)** (mit den Händen; applaudieren) clap; **in die Hände ~:** clap one's hands; **lautes Klatschen** loud applause; **(c)** (schlagen) slap; **jmdm.** (*Dat.*) **auf die Schenkel ~:** slap one's thighs; **(d)** (ugs. abwertend: reden) gossip (**über** + *Akk.* about). **2** *tr. V.* **(a)** (ugs.: werfen) slap; chuck (coll.) ‹*book etc.*›; **(b)** **den Takt ~** clap time; **jmdm. Beifall ~:** clap *or* applaud sb.; **(c)** (ugs.: schlagen) **jmdm. eine ~:** slap sb. *or* give sb. a slap across the face

Klatscherei *die;* ~, ~**en** (ugs. abwertend) gossiping

klatsch-, Klatsch-: ~**mohn** *der* corn-poppy; field poppy; ~**nass,** *****naß** *Adj.* soaking *or* sopping wet ‹*clothes*›; dripping wet ‹*hair*›; ~**nass werden** get soaked [to the skin] *or* drenched; ~**spalte** *die* (ugs. abwertend) gossip column; ~**süchtig** *Adj.* extremely gossipy;

~**süchtig sein** be a compulsive gossip/compulsive gossips; ~**tante** *die* (ugs. abwertend), ~**weib** *das* (ugs. abwertend) gossip

Klaue /'klaʊə/ *die;* ~, ~**n** (a) claw; (von Raubvögeln) talon; (fig. geh.) **in den** ~**n eines Erpressers** in the clutches of a blackmailer; (b) (Huf) hoof; (c) (salopp: Hand) mitt (sl.); paw (coll.); (d) *o. Pl.* (salopp abwertend: Handschrift) scrawl

klauen (ugs.) **1** *tr. V.* pinch (sl.); nick (Brit. sl.); (fig.) pinch (sl.), nick (Brit. coll.), crib ⟨*idea*⟩; **jmdm. etw.** ~: pinch *or* (Brit. coll.) nick/crib sth. from sb. **2** *itr. V.* pinch (sl.) *or* nick (Brit. coll.) things

Klauen·seuche *die* ⇒ **Maul- und Klauenseuche**

Klausel /'klaʊzl̩/ *die;* ~, ~**n** clause; (Bedingung) stipulation; condition; (Vorbehalt) proviso

Klausur /klaʊ'zuːɐ̯/ *die;* ~, ~**en** (a) **in** ~: ⟨*meet*⟩ in private; (b) (Klausurarbeit) [examination] paper; **eine** ~ **schreiben** take a[n examination] paper

Klausur·tagung *die* private meeting

Klaviatur /klavia'tuːɐ̯/ *die;* ~, ~**en** keyboard

Klavier /kla'viːɐ̯/ *das;* ~**s**, ~**e** piano

Klavier-: ~**begleitung** *die* piano accompaniment; ~**hocker** *der* piano stool; ~**konzert** *das* (a) (Komposition) piano concerto; (b) (Veranstaltung) piano recital; ~**lehrer** *der*, ~**lehrerin** *die* piano teacher; ~**sonate** *die* piano sonata; ~**spiel** *das* piano-playing; ~**spieler** *der*, ~**spielerin** *die* pianist; piano player; ~**stunde** *die* piano-lesson; ~**unterricht** *der* piano lessons *pl.*

Klebe-: ~**band** *das* adhesive *or* sticky tape; ~**folie** *die* adhesive film

kleben 1 *itr. V.* (a) stick (**an** + *Dat.* to); ~ **bleiben** stick; remain stuck; **das Hemd klebte ihm am Körper** his shirt stuck *or* clung to his body; **an seinen Händen klebt Blut** (fig.) he has blood on his hands (fig.); his hands are stained with blood (fig.); (b) (ugs.: klebrig sein) be sticky (**von, vor** + *Dat.* with); (c) (ugs.: sich klammern) **an seinem Stuhl/an der Theke** ~: stay put in one's chair (coll.)/ prop the bar up (coll.). (d) ~ **bleiben** (ugs.: nicht versetzt werden) stay down [a year]; have to repeat a year. **2** *tr. V.* (a) (befestigen) stick; (mit Klebstoff) stick; glue; (mit Leim) stick; paste; **jmdm. eine** ~ (salopp) belt sb. one (coll.); (b) (mit Klebstoff reparieren) stick *or* glue ⟨*vase etc.*⟩ back together

*****kleben|bleiben** ⇒ **kleben 1 a, d**

Kleber *der;* ~**s**, ~: adhesive; glue

Kleb·pflaster *das* adhesive plaster; sticking plaster

klebrig *Adj.* sticky; (von Schweiß) clammy ⟨*hands etc.*⟩

Kleb-: ~**stelle** *die* join; (eines Films, Tonbandes) splice; ~**stoff** *der* adhesive; glue; ~**streifen** *der* adhesive *or* sticky tape

kleckern /'klɛkɐn/ (ugs.) **1** *itr. V.* (a) (Flecken machen) make a mess; **oje, jetzt habe ich gekleckert** oh dear, now I've gone and spilled something (coll.); (b) *mit sein* (heruntertropfen) drip; spill; (c) **nicht** ~**, sondern klotzen** (ugs.) not mess about with half-measures, but do the thing properly. **2** *tr. V.* spill; splash ⟨*paint*⟩

kleckerweise *Adv.* (ugs.) in dribs and drabs

Klecks /klɛks/ *der;* ~**es**, ~**e** (a) stain; (nicht aufgesogen) blob; (Tintenfleck) [ink-]blot; (b) (ugs.: kleine Menge) spot; (von Senf, Mayonnaise) dab

klecksen 1 *itr. V.* (a) make a stain/stains; (mit Tinte) make a blot/blots; ⟨*pen*⟩ blot; (b) (ugs. abwertend: schlecht malen) daub. **2** *tr. V.* (ugs.) daub ⟨*paint*⟩

Klee /kleː/ *der;* ~**s** clover; **jmdn./etw. über den grünen** ~ **loben** praise sb./sth. to the skies

Klee·blatt *das* (a) cloverleaf; **ein vierblättriges** ~: a four-leaf *or* four-leaved clover; (b) (ugs.: drei Personen) trio; threesome

Kleid /klaɪt/ *das;* ~**es**, ~**er** (a) dress; **ein zweiteiliges** ~: a two-piece [suit]; (b) *Pl.* (Kleidung) clothes; ~**er machen Leute** (Spr.) clothes make the man; the apparel oft proclaims the man (literary)

kleiden 1 *refl. V.* dress. **2** *tr. V.* (a) dress; (b) suit; look well on; **die Farbe kleidet dich gut** the colour suits you *or* looks well on you; (c) **etw. in Worte** ~: express sth. in words; put sth. into words

Kleider-: ~**ablage** *die* (a) (Ablage) coat rack; (b) (Raum) cloakroom; checkroom (Amer.); ~**bügel** *der* clothes hanger; coat-hanger; ~**bürste** *die* clothes brush; ~**größe** *die* size; ~**haken** *der* coat hook; ~**schrank** *der* wardrobe; ~**ständer** *der* coat-stand; ~**stange** *die* clothes-rail

kleidsam *Adj.* becoming

Kleidung *die;* ~: clothes *pl.;* clothing

Kleidungs·stück *das* garment; article of clothing

Kleie /'klaɪə/ *die;* ~**:** bran

klein /klaɪn/ **1** *Adj.* (a) ▶277 little; small ⟨*format, letter*⟩; little ⟨*finger, toe*⟩; small, short ⟨*steps*⟩; **das Kleid ist mir zu** ~: the dress is too small for me; **ein** ~**es Bier** a small beer; ≈ a half[-pint]; **sich** ~ **machen** make oneself small; **etw.** ~ **hacken** chop sth. up [small]; **etw.** ~ **schneiden** cut sth. up small; **Zwiebeln** ~ **schneiden** chop up onions [small]; **etw.** ~ **machen** cut sth. up small; (ugs.: aufbrauchen) get through *or* (sl.) blow sth.; **auf** ~**stem Raum** in the minimum of space; **sie ist** ~ [von Gestalt/ für ihr Alter] she is small [in stature/for her age]; **er ist** [einen Kopf] ~**er als ich** he is [a head] shorter than me *or* shorter than I am [by a head]; **im Kleinen** in miniature; on a small scale; ~**, aber oho** he/she may be small, but he/she certainly makes up for it; ~**, aber fein** little, but very nice; (b) (jung) little ⟨*brother, sister*⟩; **als ich** [noch] ~ **war** when I was small *or* little; **für die Kleinen** for the little ones; **von** ~ **auf** from an early age; *s. auch* **Kleine**[1, 2, 3]; (c) (von kurzer Dauer) little, short ⟨*while*⟩; short ⟨*walk, break*⟩; short, brief ⟨*delay, introduction*⟩; brief ⟨*moment*⟩; (d) (von geringer Menge) little ⟨*family, amount, audience, staff*⟩; small, low ⟨*salary*⟩; low ⟨*price*⟩; ~**es Geld haben** have some [small] change; **einen Schein** ~ **machen** (ugs.: wechseln) change a note; **kann mir jemand ein 5-Mark-Stück** ~ **machen?** (ugs.) can anyone give me change for a five-mark piece?; **haben Sie es** ~? (ugs.) do you have the right money?; ~**er habe ich es nicht** I don't have anything smaller; (e) (von geringem Ausmaß) light ⟨*refreshment*⟩; small ⟨*party, gift*⟩; scant, little ⟨*attention*⟩; slight ⟨*cold, indisposition*⟩; slight, small ⟨*mistake, irregularity*⟩; minor ⟨*event, error*⟩; **die** ~**en Dinge des Alltags** the little everyday things; **das** ~**ere Übel** the lesser evil; the lesser of the two evils; **ein** ~[es] **bisschen** a little *or* tiny bit; **ein** ~ **wenig** a little bit; **im Kleinen wie im Großen** in little things as well as in big ones; **bis ins Kleinste** down to the smallest *or* ·tiniest detail; (f) (unbedeutend) lowly ⟨*employee, sales assistant*⟩; minor ⟨*official*⟩; **der** ~**e Mann** the ordinary citizen; the man in the street; **der** ~**en Leute** ordinary people; the man *sing.* in the street; ~ **anfangen** (ugs.) start off in a small way; (g) **ganz** ~ [**und hässlich**] **werden** become meek and subdued; (h) **ein** ~**er Geist** (engstirnig) a narrow-minded person; (beschränkt) a person of limited intellect. **2** *adv.* **die Heizung** ~/~**er** [**ein**]**stellen** turn the heating down low/lower; ~ **gedruckt** in small print *postpos.;* **das** ~ **Gedruckte** the small print; ~ **gemustert** small-patterned; ~ **kariert** ⟨*skirt, shirt, etc.*⟩ with a small check; ~ **machen** (Kinderspr.) do number one (child lang.); ~ **geschrieben werden** (ugs.) count for [very] little (bei with); *s. auch* **beigeben 2**

klein-, Klein-: ~**aktionär** *der* (Wirtsch.) small shareholder; ~**anzeige** *die* (Zeitungsw.) small *or* classified advertisement *or* (coll.) ad; ~**arbeit** *die; o. Pl.* painstaking and detailed work; ~**asien** (*das*) Asia Minor; ~**bauer** *der* small farmer; smallholder; ~|**bekommen** *unr. tr. V.:* ⇒ ~**kriegen**; ~**betrieb** *der* (a) (Industrie) small business; (b) (Landw.) small farm; smallholding; ~**bild·kamera** *die* (Fot.) miniature camera; 35 mm camera; ~**buchstabe** *der* small letter; lower-case letter (Printing); ~**bürger** *der* lower middle-class person; (abwertend: Spießbürger) petit bourgeois; ~**bürgerlich 1** *Adj.* (a) lower middle-class; (b) (abwertend: spießbürgerlich) petit bourgeois; **2** *adv.* (abwertend: spießbürgerlich) ~**bürgerlich denken** have a petit-bourgeois way of thinking; ~**bürgertum** *das* lower middle class; petite bourgeoisie; ~**bus** *der* minibus

Kleine[1] *der; adj. Dekl.* (a) (kleiner Junge) little boy; (b) (ugs.: Anrede) little man

Kleine[2] *die; adj. Dekl.* **(a)** (kleines Mädchen) little girl; **(b)** (ugs. Anrede) love; (abwertend) little madam; **(c)** (ugs.: Freundin) girl[-friend]

Kleine[3] *das; adj. Dekl.* **(a)** (ugs. scherzh.) little boy/girl (joc.); **(b)** (von Tieren) baby; little one

klein-, Klein-: ~**familie** *die* (Soziol.) nuclear family; ~**format** *das* small size; (bei Büchern) small format *or* size; ~**garten** *der* ≈ allotment; ~**gärtner** *der* ≈ allotment-holder; *~**gedruckt** ⇒ **klein 2**; ~**gedruckte** *das; adj. Dekl.* small print; ~**geist** *der* (abwertend) small-minded person; ~**geld** *das; o. Pl.* [small] change; *~**gemustert** ⇒ **klein 2**; ~**gläubig** *Adj.* of little faith *postpos.;* sceptical; (ängstlich, zweifelnd) faint-hearted; ~**gläubigkeit** *die* ⇒ ~**gläubig**: lack of faith; scepticism; faint-heartedness; *~**hacken** ⇒ **klein 1 a**

Kleinheit *die;* ~ smallness; small size

Klein·hirn *das* (Anat.) cerebellum; little brain

Klein·holz *das; o. Pl.* chopped wood; ~ **aus etw./ jmdm. machen, etw./jmdn. zu** ~ **machen** (ugs.) smash sth. to pieces/make mincemeat of sb.

Kleinigkeit *die;* ~, ~**en (a)** (kleine Sache) small thing; (kleines Geschenk) small *or* litte gift *or* present (Einzelheit) [small] detail; minor point; **ich habe noch eine** ~ **zu erledigen** I still have a small matter to attend to; **eine** ~ **essen** have a [small] bite to eat; **das kostet eine** ~ (ugs. iron.) that costs a bob *or* two (Brit. coll.) *or* a tidy sum (coll.); **die** ~ **von 50 000 DM** (ugs. iron.) the small *or* little matter of 50,000 marks; **sich nicht mit** ~**en abgeben** not concern oneself with details *or* trifles; **(b)** (leichte Aufgabe) **eine** ~ **für jmdn. sein** be no trouble for sb.; be a simple matter for sb.; **das war eine** ~**:** it was nothing; **(c) eine** ~ (ugs.: ein bisschen) a little bit

Kleinigkeits·krämer *der* (abwertend) pettifogger

klein-, Klein-: ~**kaliber·gewehr** *das* small-bore rifle; ~**kariert** (ugs. abwertend) **1** *Adj.*narrow-minded; **2** *adv.* narrow-mindedly; in a narrow-minded way; *s. auch* **klein 2;** ~**kind** *das* small child; ~**kram** *der* (ugs.) **(a)** (kleine Dinge) odds and ends *pl.;* **(b)** (unbedeutende Dinge) trivial matters *pl.;* (Einzelheiten) trivial details; ~**kredit** *der* (Bankw.) personal loan; ~**krieg** *der* (fig.) running battle; ~**kriegen** *tr. V.* (ugs.) **(a)** (zerkleinern) crush [to pieces]; (zerkauen) get one's teeth through ⟨*tough meat*⟩; **(b)** (zerstören) smash; break; **nicht** ~**zukriegen sein** be indestructible; **(c)** (aufbrauchen) get through, (coll.) blow ⟨*money*⟩; get through, (joc.) demolish ⟨*sweets, cakes, etc.*⟩; **(d) jmdn.** ~**kriegen** get sb. down (coll.); ~**kunst** *die; o. Pl.* cabaret; ~**laut 1** *Adj.* subdued; **2** *adv.* in a subdued fashion

kleinlich (abwertend) **1** *Adj.* pernickety; (ohne Großzügigkeit) mean; (engstirnig) small-minded; petty; (in Bezug auf Sauberkeit und Ordnung) pernickety; fussy; petty ⟨*regulations*⟩. **2** *adv.* meticulously; punctiliously

Kleinlichkeit *die;* ~ (abwertend) ⇒ **kleinlich**: pernickiness; meanness; small-mindedness; pettiness; fussiness

klein-, Klein-: *~|**machen** ⇒ **klein 1 a, d**; ~**mut** *der* (geh.) faint-heartedness; timidity; ~**mütig** *Adj.* (geh.) faint-hearted; timid

Kleinod /'klaino:t/ *das;* ~[e]s, ~e *od.* ~**ien** /-'no:diən/ (geh.) **(a)** (Schmuckstück) piece of jewellery; (Edelstein) jewel; **(b)** (fig.: Kostbarkeit) gem

klein-, Klein-: ~|**schneiden** ⇒ **klein 1 a**; ~|**schreiben** *unr. tr. V.* write ⟨*word*⟩ with a small *or* (Printing) lower-case letter; *s. auch* **klein 2;** ~**staat** *der* small state; ~**stadt** *die* small town; ~**städter** *der*, ~**städterin** *die* small-town dweller; ~**städtisch** *Adj.* small-town *attrib.;* ~|**stellen** *tr. V.* turn down [low]

Kleinst·lebewesen *das* micro-organism

kleinst·möglich *Adj.; nicht präd.* smallest possible

Klein·tier *das* pet; (Nutztier) small domestic animal

Kleintier·zucht *die* [professional] breeding of small animals

Klein·vieh *das* small farm *or* domestic animals *pl.;* small livestock; ~ **macht auch Mist** (ugs.) many a mickle makes a muckle (prov.); every little helps

Klein·wagen *der* small car

klein·wüchsig /-vy:ksɪç/ *Adj.* ⟨*person*⟩ of small stature; small, short ⟨*person, race*⟩; small ⟨*variety, species*⟩

Kleister /'klaistɐ/ *der;* ~**s**, ~**:** paste

kleistern *tr. V.* (ugs.) **(a)** (kleben) paste, stick (**an** + *Akk.* on); **(b)** (reparieren) stick; **(c)** (dick auftragen) plaster

Klementine /klemɛn'ti:nə/ *die;* ~, ~**n** clementine

Klemme /'klɛmə/ *die;* ~, ~**n (a)** (Haar~) [hair-]clip; (Med.) clip; **(b)** (ugs.: schwierige Lage) **in der** ~ **sein** *od.* **sitzen be in a fix** *or* jam (coll.); **jmdm. aus der** ~ **helfen** help sb. out of a fix *or* jam (coll.)

klemmen 1 *tr. V.* **(a)** (befestigen) tuck; stick (coll.); etw. **unter den Arm** ~**:** tuck *or* (coll.) stick sth. under one's arm; **(b)** (quetschen) **sich** (*Dat.*) **die Hand** ~**:** get one's hand caught *or* trapped; catch *or* trap one's hand. **2** *refl. V.* **sich hinter etw.** (*Akk.*) ~**:** wedge oneself behind sth.; (fig. ugs.: sich einsetzen) put some hard work into sth.; **sich hinter jmdn.** ~**:** (fig. ugs.) get to work on sb. (coll.). **3** *itr. V.* ⟨*door, drawer, etc.*⟩ stick

Klempner /'klɛmpnɐ/ *der;* ~**s**, ~**:** ▶ 85 tinsmith; (Installateur) plumber

Kleptomane /klɛpto'ma:nə/ *der;* ~**n**, ~**n** (Psych.) kleptomaniac

Kleptomanie /klɛptoma'ni:/ *die;* ~ (Psych.) kleptomania *no art.*

Kleptomanin *die;* ~, ~**nen** kleptomaniac

klerikal /kleri'ka:l/ *Adj.* clerical

Kleriker /'kle:rikɐ/ *der;* ~**s**, ~**:** cleric

Klerus /'kle:rʊs/ *der;* ~**:** clergy

Klette /'klɛtə/ *die;* ~, ~**n** bur; (Pflanze) burdock; **sich wie eine** ~ **an jmdn. hängen** (ugs.) stick like a bur to sb.

Kletterer *der;* ~**s**, ~**:** climber

Kletter-: ~**gerüst** *das* climbing frame; ~**maxe** *der* (ugs. scherzh.) climbing-mad child

klettern /'klɛtɐn/ *itr. V.; mit sein* (auch fig.) climb; (mit Mühe) clamber; **auf einen Baum** ~**:** climb a tree

Kletter-: ~**partie** *die* **(a)** (Bergsteigen) climb; **(b)** (ugs.: anstrengende Wanderung) climbing expedition; ~**pflanze** *die* creeper; (Bot.) climbing plant; climber; ~**seil** *das* climbing-rope; ~**stange** *die* (Turnen) climbing pole; ~**tour** *die* ⇒ ~**partie**; ~**wand** *die* (Turnen) climbing wall

Klett·verschluss, *Klett·verschluß *der* Velcro (P) fastening

klick /klɪk/ *Interj.* click; ~ **machen** click; go click

klicken *itr. V.* **(a)** click; **es klickte** there was a click; **(b)** (DV) click

Klient /kli'ɛnt/ *der;* ~**en**, ~**en, Klientin** *die;* ~, ~**nen** client

Kliff /klɪf/ *das;* ~**[e]s**, ~**e** cliff

Klima /'kli:ma/ *das;* ~**s**, ~**s** *od.* **Klimate** /kli'ma:tə/ climate; **das politische** ~ (fig.) the political climate; **im Büro herrscht ein angenehmes** ~ (fig.) there's a pleasant atmosphere in the office

Klima-: ~**anlage** *die* air-conditioning *no indef. art.;* air-conditioning system; **mit** ~**anlage** air-conditioned; ~**technik** *die; o. Pl.* air-conditioning engineering *no art.*

Klimakterium /klimak'te:riʊm/ *das;* ~**s** (Med.) menopause; change of life

klimatisch /kli'ma:tɪʃ/ **1** *Adj.; nicht präd.* climatic. **2** *adv.* climatically

klimatisieren *tr. V.* air condition

Klimatologie /klimatolo'gi:/ *die;* ~**s:** climatology *no art.*

Klima·wechsel *der* change of climate

Klimax /'kli:maks/ *die;* ~**:** climax

Klima·zone *die* climatic zone

Klimbim /klɪm'bɪm/ *der;* ~**s** (ugs.) **(a)** (Kram) junk; odds and ends *pl.;* **(b)** (Wirbel) fuss; ~ **um etw. machen** make a fuss about sth.

Klimm·zug *der* (Turnen) pull-up

klimpern /'klɪmpɐn/ **1** *itr. V.* jingle; tinkle; ⟨*coins, keys*⟩ jingle; **mit den Schlüsseln** ~ jingle the keys; **mit den Wimpern** ~ (scherzh.) flutter one's eyelashes [seductively]; **auf dem Klavier** ~ (ugs.) plunk away on the piano. **2** *tr. V.* (ugs. abwertend) plunk out ⟨*tune etc.*⟩

Klinge *die;* ~, ~n (a) blade; (b) jmdn. über die ~ springen lassen (fig.) (ugs.: ruinieren) ruin sb.; (beruflich) put paid to sb.'s career (coll.)

Klingel /'klɪŋl/ *die;* ~, ~n bell

Klingel-: ~**beutel** *der* offertory bag; collection bag; ~**knopf** *der* bell button; bell push

klingeln *itr. V.* (a) ring; ⟨*alarm clock*⟩ go off; ring; **es klingelt** somebody is ringing the doorbell; there is a ring at the door; **es klingelte zur Pause** the bell went for the break; **es hat bei ihm/ihr** *usw.* **geklingelt** (ugs.) the penny's dropped (coll.); (b) (die Klingel betätigen) ring [the bell]; **nach jmdm.** ~: ring for sb.; (c) (Kfz-W.) ⟨*engine*⟩ pink

klingen *unr. itr. V.* (a) ⟨*bell*⟩ ring; ⟨*glass*⟩ clink; **aus dem Haus klangen fröhliche Stimmen** the sound of merry voices came from the house; **die Gläser** ~ **lassen** clink glasses [in a toast]; (b) (einen bestimmten Klang haben) sound; **es klang, als ob** ...: it sounded as if ...

klingend *Adj.* ~**e Münze** [hard] cash

Klinik /'kliːnɪk/ *die;* ~, ~**en** hospital; (spezialisiert) clinic

Klinikum /'kliːnikʊm/ *das;* ~**s**, **Klinika** *od.* **Kliniken** hospital complex

klinisch 1 *Adj.; nicht präd.* (Med.) clinical. 2 *adv.* ~ **tot** clinically dead

Klinke /'klɪŋkə/ *die;* ~, ~**n** doorhandle; **sich** (*Dat.*) **die** ~ **in die Hand geben** (ugs.) come and go in a continuous stream

Klinken·putzer *der* (ugs. abwertend) door-to-door salesman

Klinker *der;* ~**s**, ~: [Dutch] clinker

klipp /klɪp/ *in* ~ **und klar** (ugs.) quite plainly *or* clearly

Klippe *die;* ~, ~**n** rock; **alle** ~**n umschiffen** (fig.) negotiate every obstacle [successfully]

klirren /'klɪrən/ *itr. V.* ⟨*glasses, ice cubes*⟩ clink; ⟨*weapons in fight*⟩ clash; ⟨*window pane*⟩ rattle; ⟨*chains, spurs*⟩ clank, rattle; ⟨*harness*⟩ jingle; ~**der Frost** (fig.) sharp frost

Klischee /kli'ʃeː/ *das;* ~**s**, ~**s** (a) cliché; **das** ~ **vom braven Hausmütterchen** the conventional picture *or* stereotype of the good little housewife; (b) (Druckw.) block; plate

Klistier /klis'tiːɐ̯/ *das;* ~**s**, ~**e** (Med.) enema

Klitoris /'kliːtoris/ *die;* ~, ~ *od.* **Klitorides** /kli'toːride:s/ (Anat.) clitoris

Klitsche *die;* ~, ~**n** (ugs.) (a) (kleiner Betrieb) little shoestring outfit (coll.); (b) (Schmierentheater) third-rate little theatre

klitsch·nass, *****klitsch·naß** *Adj.* (ugs.) soaking *or* sopping wet; (tropfnass) dripping wet; **wir sind** ~ **geworden** we got soaked [to the skin] *or* drenched

klitze·klein /'klɪtsə-/ *Adj.* (ugs.) teeny[-weeny] (coll.)

Klo /klo:/ *das;* ~**s**, ~**s** (ugs.) loo (Brit. coll.); john (Amer. coll.); **aufs** ~ **müssen** have to go to the loo; **etw. ins** ~ **schütten** tip sth. down the loo

Kloake /klo'aːkə/ *die;* ~, ~**n** cesspit; (Kanal) sewer

Kloben /'kloːbn̩/ *der;* ~**s**, ~ log

klobig *Adj.* (a) (kantig) heavy and clumsy[-looking] ⟨*shoes, furniture*⟩; heavily-built, bulky ⟨*figure*⟩; (b) (plump) clumsy; boorish

Klo-: ~**bürste** *die* (ugs.) loo brush (Brit. coll.); toilet brush; ~**frau** *die* (ugs.) loo attendant (Brit. coll.); bathroom attendant (Amer.)

klomm /klɔm/ *1. u. 3. Pers. Sg. Prät. v.* **klimmen**

Klon /klo:n/ *der;* ~**s**, ~**e** (Biol.) clone

klonen *tr. V.* clone

Klo·papier *das* (ugs.) loo-paper (Brit. coll.); toilet paper

klopfen /'klɔpfn̩/ 1 *itr. V.* (a) (schlagen) knock; **an die Tür** ~: knock at the door; **es hat geklopft** there's somebody knocking at the door; **jmdm.** *od.* **jmdn. auf die Schulter** ~: slap sb. on the shoulder; „**bitte** ~!" 'please knock'; (b) (pulsieren) ⟨*heart*⟩ beat; ⟨*pulse*⟩ throb; **mit** ~**dem Herzen** with pounding *or* beating heart; **ein** ~**der Schmerz** a throbbing pain; (c) (Kfz-W.) ⟨*engine*⟩ knock. 2 *tr. V.* beat ⟨*carpet*⟩; **den Takt [zur Musik]** ~:

beat time [to the music]; **Staub vom Mantel** ~: beat dust from one's coat; **einen Nagel in die Wand** ~: knock *or* hammer a nail into the wall

Klopfer *der;* ~**s**, ~ (a) (Teppich~) carpet-beater; (b) (Tür~) [door-] knocker; (c) (Fleisch~) meat mallet

Klopf·zeichen *das* knock; (leiser) tap

Klöppel /'klœpl/ *der;* ~**s**, ~: clapper

Klöppel·arbeit *die* piece of pillow-lace *or* bobbin-lace

klöppeln *tr., itr. V.* **[etw.]** ~: make *or* work [sth. in] pillow-lace *or* bobbin-lace

Klöppel·spitze *die* pillow-lace; bobbin-lace

kloppen (nordd., md.) 1 *tr. V.* hit. 2 *refl. V.* fight; scrap (coll.)

Klöpplerin *die;* ~, ~**nen** pillow-lace *or* bobbin-lace maker

Klops /klɔps/ *der;* ~**es**, ~**e** (nordostd.) meat ball

Klosett /klo'zɛt/ *das;* ~**s**, ~**s** *od.* ~**e** lavatory; **etw. ins** ~ **schütten** tip sth. down the lavatory

Klosett-: ~**brille** *die* (ugs.) loo seat (Brit. coll.); toilet seat; ~**bürste** *die* lavatory brush; toilet brush; ~**deckel** *der* toilet lid; ~**papier** *das* toilet paper; lavatory paper

Kloß /klo:s/ *der;* ~**es**, **Klöße** /'kløːsə/ dumpling; (Fleisch~) meat ball; **einen** ~ **im Hals haben** (ugs.) have a lump in one's throat

Kloster /'kloːstɐ/ *das;* ~**s**, **Klöster** /'kløːstɐ/ (Mönchs~) monastery; (Nonnen~) convent; nunnery

Kloster·kirche *die* monastery/convent church

klösterlich *Adj.* monastic; monastic/convent ⟨*life*⟩

Kloster-: ~**regel** *die* rules *pl.* of the monastery/convent; ~**schule** *die* monastery-school/ convent-school; ~**schüler** *der* monastery-school/convent-school pupil

Klotz /klɔts/ *der;* ~**es**, **Klötze** /'klœtsə/ (a) block [of wood]; (Stück eines Baumstamms) log; **[jmdm.] ein** ~ **am Bein sein** (ugs.) be a millstone round sb.'s neck; **sich** (*Dat.*) **einen** ~ **ans Bein binden** (ugs.) tie a millstone round one's neck; (b) (salopp abwertend) (ungehobelter Mensch) clod; oaf; (roher Mensch) lout

Klötzchen /'klœtsçən/ *das;* ~**s**, ~: small block of wood

klotzen *itr. V.* (ugs.: großzügig vorgehen) lash out in a big way (coll.); *s. auch* **kleckern 1 c**

klotzig *Adj.* (abwertend) large and ugly[-looking] ⟨*building*⟩; large and clumsy[-looking] ⟨*furniture*⟩

Klub /klʊp/ *der;* ~**s**, ~**s** club

Klub-: ~**haus** *das* club-house; ~**jacke** *die* blazer; ~**mitglied** *das* club-member; ~**sessel** *der* club chair

Kluft¹ /klʊft/ *die;* ~, ~**en** (ugs.) rig-out (coll.); gear (coll.); (Uniform) uniform; garb

Kluft² /klʊft/ *die;* ~, **Klüfte** /'klʏftə/ (a) (veralt.) (Spalte) cleft; fissure; (im Gletscher) crevasse; (Abgrund) chasm; (b) (Gegensatz) gulf

klug /kluːk/; **klüger** /'klyːgɐ/, **klügst**... /'klyːkst.../ 1 *Adj.* (a) clever; intelligent; clever, bright ⟨*child, pupil*⟩; intelligent ⟨*eyes*⟩; **er ist ein** ~**er Kopf** he's clever *or* bright; he's got brains; (b) (gelehrt, weise) wise; **so** ~ **wie vorher** *od.* **zuvor sein** be none the wiser; **hinterher ist man immer klüger** it's easy to be wise after the event; **daraus werde ich nicht** ~, **daraus soll ein Mensch** ~ **werden** I can't make head or tail of it; **aus jmdm. nicht** ~ **werden** not know what to make of sb.; (c) (vernünftig) wise; wise, sound ⟨*advice*⟩; wise, prudent ⟨*remark, course of action*⟩; (geschickt) clever, shrewd ⟨*politician, negotiator, question*⟩; shrewd, astute ⟨*businessman*⟩; great ⟨*foresight*⟩; **der Klügere gibt nach** (Spr.) discretion is the better part of valour (prov.). 2 *adv.* (a) cleverly; intelligently; ~ **daherreden** talk as if one knows it all; (b) (vernünftig) wisely; (geschickt) cleverly; shrewdly

klüger ⇨ **klug**

klugerweise *Adv.* wisely

Klugheit *die;* ~ ⇨ **klug a, b, c:** cleverness; intelligence; brightness; wisdom; soundness; prudence; shrewdness; astuteness

Klug·scheißer *der* (salopp abwertend) know-it-all (coll.); smart aleck (coll.)

klügst... ⇨ **klug**

**alte Schreibung (vgl. Hinweise auf S. xvi–xvii)

klumpen /'klʊmpn̩/ *itr. V.* go lumpy
Klumpen *der;* ~s, ~ lump; **ein** ~ **Erde** a lump *or* clod of earth; **ein** ~ **Gold** a gold nugget
Klump·fuß *der* club foot
klumpig *Adj.* lumpy
Klüngel /'klyŋl̩/ *der;* ~s, ~ (abwertend) clique
Klunker /'klʊŋkɐ/ *die;* ~, ~n *od. der;* ~s, ~ (ugs.) rock (sl.)
km *Abk.* **Kilometer** km.
knabbern /'knabɐn/ **1** *tr. V.* nibble. **2** *itr. V.* **an etw.** (*Dat.*) ~: nibble *or* gnaw [at] sth.; **an etw.** (*Dat.*) [**noch lange**] **zu** ~ **haben** (ugs.) (sich anstrengen müssen) have sth. to think about *or* chew on; (leiden müssen) take a long time to get over sth.
Knabe /'kna:bə/ *der;* ~n, ~n (a) (geh. veralt./ südd., österr., schweiz.) boy; (b) (ugs.: Bursche) chap (coll.)
Knaben·chor *der* boys' choir
knabenhaft 1 *Adj.* boyish. **2** *adv.* boyishly
Knaben·kraut *das* orchis; wild orchid
Knäcke·brot /'knɛkə-/ *das* crispbread; (Scheibe) slice of crispbread
knacken 1 *itr. V.* ⟨*bed, floor, etc.*⟩ creak; **es knackte im Gebälk** the beams creaked. **2** *tr. V.* (a) crack ⟨*nut, shell*⟩; (salopp) squash ⟨*louse, bug*⟩; (b) (aufbrechen) crack ⟨*safe*⟩ [open]; break into ⟨*car, bank, etc.*⟩; crack, break ⟨*code*⟩
Knacker *der;* ~s, ~: **alter** ~ (salopp) old fogey
Knacki /'knaki/ *der;* ~s, ~s (salopp) con (coll.); jailbird
knackig *Adj.* (a) (knusprig) crisp; crisp, crunchy ⟨*apple*⟩; (b) (ugs.: attraktiv) luscious, delectable ⟨*girl*⟩
knacks *Interj.* crack
Knacks *der;* ~es, ~e (ugs.) (a) (Ton) crack; (b) (Sprung) crack; (c) (fig.: Defekt) **einen** ~ **bekommen** ⟨*person*⟩ have *or* suffer a breakdown; ⟨*health*⟩ suffer; **die Ehe hatte einen** ~: the marriage was in difficulties
Knall /knal/ *der;* ~[e]s, ~e bang; (fig.) big row; **einen** ~ **haben** (salopp) be barmy (coll.) *or* off one's rocker (fig. coll.); **auf** ~ **und Fall**, ~ **auf Fall** (ugs.) without warning
Knall-: ~**bonbon** *der od. das* cracker; ~**effekt** *der* (ugs.) (Überraschendes) astonishing part; (Sensation) sensational part
knallen 1 *itr. V.* (a) ⟨*shot*⟩ ring out; ⟨*firework*⟩ go bang; ⟨*cork*⟩ pop; ⟨*door*⟩ bang, slam; ⟨*whip, rifle*⟩ crack; **an der Kreuzung hat es geknallt** (ugs.) there was a crash at the crossroads; (b) (ugs.: schießen) shoot, fire (**auf** + *Akk.* at); (mehrere Male) blaze *or* (coll.) bang away (**auf** + *Akk.* at); (c) *mit sein* (ugs.: prallen) **die Tür knallte ins Schloss** the door slammed *or* banged shut; **sie knallte mit dem Fahrrad gegen einen Laternenpfahl** she crashed into a lamp-post on her bicycle; **der Ball knallte gegen die Latte** the ball slammed against the crossbar; (d) (ugs.: scheinen) ⟨*sun*⟩ blaze *or* beat down. **2** *tr. V.* (a) (ugs.) (hart aufsetzen) slam *or* bang down; (werfen) sling (coll.); (b) (ugs.: schlagen) **jmdm. eine** ~ (salopp) belt *or* clout sb. one (coll.); (c) (Ballspiele ugs.) belt (coll.) ⟨*ball*⟩
Knaller *der;* ~s, ~: banger
knall-, Knall-: ~**erbse** *die* ≈ cap-bomb; ~**frosch** *der* jumping jack; ~**gelb** *Adj.* (ugs.) bright *or* vivid yellow; ~**hart** (ugs.) **1** *Adj.* (a) very tough ⟨*job, demands, action, measures, etc.*⟩; ⟨*person*⟩ as hard as nails; (b) (kraftvoll) crashing ⟨*blow*⟩; **2** *adv.* (a) (rücksichtslos, brutal) brutally; **gegen etw.** ~**hart vorgehen** take very tough action against sth.; (b) (kraftvoll) ⟨*hit*⟩ really hard
Knallerei *die;* ~, ~en (ugs.) (von Korken) popping; (einer Peitsche) cracking; (von Gewehren) banging, shooting; (von Feuerwerk) banging
knallig *Adj.* (ugs.) loud; gaudy
knall-, Knall-: ~**kopf** *der*, ~**kopp** *der* (salopp) [stupid] berk (Brit. sl.) *or* (Amer. sl.) jerk; ~**rot** *Adj.* bright *or* vivid red; **sie bekam einen** ~**roten Kopf** she *or* her face turned [bright] scarlet *or* as red as a beetroot ~**tüte** *die* (ugs.) nitwit (coll.); clot (Brit. sl.)
knapp /knap/ **1** *Adj.* (a) meagre, low ⟨*pension, wage, salary*⟩; meagre ⟨*pocket money*⟩; ~ **sein** be scarce *or* in short supply; ~ **werden** ⟨*supplies*⟩ run short; ⟨*money*⟩ get tight; ~ **mit etw. sein** be short of sth.; ..., **und nicht zu**

~**!** ... and how!; **jmdn.** [**mit Geld**] ~ **halten** (ugs.) keep sb. short [of money]; (b) narrow ⟨*victory, lead*⟩; narrow, bare ⟨*majority*⟩; close ⟨*result*⟩; (c) **vor einer** ~**en Stunde** just under an hour ago; (d) (eng) tight-fitting ⟨*garment*⟩; **zu** ~ **sein** ⟨*garment*⟩ be too tight; (e) (kurz) terse ⟨*reply, greeting*⟩; concise, succinct ⟨*description, account, report*⟩. **2** *adv.* (a) ~ **bemessen sein** be meagre; ⟨*time*⟩ be limited; ~ **gerechnet** at the lowest estimate; (b) ~ **gewinnen** win narrowly *or* by a narrow margin; **eine Prüfung** ~ **bestehen** just pass an examination; (c) (sehr nahe) just; ~ **über dem Knie enden** come to just above the knee; (d) (nicht ganz) just under; **vor** ~ **einer Stunde** just under an hour ago; (e) (eng) ~ **sitzen** fit tightly; (f) (kurz) ⟨*reply*⟩ tersely; ⟨*describe*⟩ concisely, succinctly
*knapp|halten ⇒ **knapp 1 a**
Knappheit *die;* ~ (a) (Mangel) shortage, scarcity (**an** + *Dat.* of); (b) (Kürze) (einer Antwort) terseness; (einer Beschreibung) conciseness, succinctness
knapsen /'knapsn̩/ *itr. V.* (ugs.) skimp; scrimp
Knarre /'knarə/ *die;* ~, ~n (a) (Rassel) rattle; (b) (salopp: Gewehr) shooting-iron (sl.)
knarren *itr. V.* creak; **mit** ~**der Stimme** in a rasping *or* grating voice
Knast /knast/ *der;* ~[e]s, **Knäste** /'knɛstə/ *od.* ~**e** (ugs.) (a) *o. Pl.* (Strafe) bird (sl.); time (coll.); **er hat zwei Jahre** ~ **gekriegt** he got two years' bird (sl.); (b) (Gefängnis) clink (sl.); jug (sl.); prison; **im** ~: in clink *or* jug (sl.)
Knast·bruder *der* (a) jailbird; old lag (sl.); (b) (Mitgefangener) fellow jailbird
Knastologe /knasto'lo:gə/ *der;* ~n, ~n (ugs. scherzh.) jailbird; old lag (sl.)
Knatsch /kna:tʃ/ *der;* ~[e]s (ugs.: Ärger) trouble; **die beiden haben** ~: the two of them are rowing
knatschig *Adj.* (ugs.) grumpy; (weinerlich) fretful
knattern /'knatɐn/ *itr. V.* (a) ⟨*machine gun*⟩ rattle, clatter; ⟨*sail*⟩ flap; ⟨*motor vehicle, engine*⟩ clatter; (b) *mit sein* (~d fahren) clatter
Knäuel /'knɔyəl/ *der od. das;* ~s, ~ (a) ball; (wirres ~) tangle; (b) (fig.) (von Menschen) knot
Knauf /knauf/ *der;* ~[e]s, **Knäufe** /'knɔyfə/ knob; (eines Schwertes, Dolches) pommel
Knauser *der;* ~s, ~ (ugs. abwertend) Scrooge; skinflint; miser
Knauserei *die;* ~ (ugs. abwertend) stinginess; penny-pinching; miserliness
knaus[e]rig *Adj.* (ugs. abwertend) stingy; tight-fisted; close-fisted
Knauserigkeit *die;* ~, ~en ⇒ **Knauserei**
knausern /'knauzɐn/ *itr. V.* (ugs. abwertend) be stingy; scrimp
knautschen /'knautʃn̩/ (ugs.) **1** *tr. V.* crumple; crumple, crease ⟨*dress*⟩. **2** *itr. V.* ⟨*dress, material*⟩ crease, get creased
Knautsch·zone *die* (Kfz-W.) crumple zone
Knebel /'kne:bl̩/ *der;* ~s, ~ (a) gag; (b) (Griff) toggle
knebeln *tr. V.* gag; (fig.) gag, muzzle ⟨*the press, a people*⟩
Knecht /knɛçt/ *der;* ~[e]s, ~**e** farm-labourer; farm-hand; (fig.) slave; vassal
knechten *tr. V.* (geh.) reduce to servitude *or* slavery; enslave; (unterdrücken) oppress ⟨*people*⟩
Knechtschaft *die;* ~, ~**en** (geh.) bondage; servitude; slavery
kneifen /'knaifn̩/ **1** *unr. tr., itr. V.* pinch; **jmdn.** *od.* **jmdn. in den Arm** ~: pinch sb.'s arm. **2** *unr. itr. V.* (a) (drücken) ⟨*clothes*⟩ be too tight; (b) (ugs. abwertend: sich drücken) chicken (coll.) *or* back out (**vor** + *Dat.* of); **vor einer Prüfung/Verantwortung** ~: funk an examination (coll.)/(coll.) duck [out of] a responsibility
Kneifer *der;* ~s, ~: pince-nez
Kneif·zange *die* pincers *pl.;* **eine** ~: a pair of pincers
Kneipe /'knaipə/ *die;* ~, ~n (ugs.) pub (Brit.); bar (Amer.)
kneippen /'knaipn̩/ *itr. V.* (ugs.) take *or* undergo a Kneipp cure

Kneipp·kur *die* Kneipp cure

Knete *die;* ~ **(a)** (ugs.) ⇨ **Knetmasse; (b)** (salopp: Geld) dough (sl.)

kneten /'kne:tn̩/ *tr. V.* **(a)** knead ‹*dough, muscles*›; work ‹*clay*›; **(b)** (formen) model ‹*figure*›

Knet·masse *die* Plasticine (**P**); plastic modelling-material

Knick /knɪk/ *der;* ~[e]s, ~e **(a)** (Biegung) sharp bend; (in einem Draht) kink; **(b)** (Falz) crease

knicken **1** *tr. V.* **(a)** (brechen) snap; **(b)** (falten) crease ‹*page, paper, etc.*›; „Bitte nicht ~!" 'please do not bend'; (bitte nicht falten) 'please do not fold'. **2** *itr. V.; mit sein* snap

Knicker *der;* ~s, ~ **(a)** (ugs. abwertend) Scrooge; skinflint; miser; **(b)** (niederd.: Murmel) marble

Knickerbocker /-bɔkɐ/ *Pl.* knickerbockers; (länger und breiter) plus-fours

Knick[e]rigkeit *die;* ~ (ugs. abwertend) stinginess; tight-fistedness

knick[e]rig *Adj.* (ugs. abwertend) stingy; tight-fisted

Knicks /knɪks/ *der;* ~es, ~e curtsy; **einen** ~ **machen** make *or* drop a curtsy (**vor** + *Dat.* to)

Knie /kni:/ *das;* ~s, ~ /'kni:(ə)/ **(a)** ▶ 326┘ knee; **jmdm. auf [den]** ~n **danken** go down on one's knees and thank sb.; **jmdn. auf** ~n **bitten** beg sb. on bended knees; **vor jmdm. auf die** ~ **fallen** go down on one's knees before sb.; **er hatte/bekam weiche** ~ (ugs.) his knees trembled/started to tremble; **jmdn. auf** *od.* **in die** ~ **zwingen** (geh.) force sb. to his knees; **in die** ~ **gehen** sink to one's knees; (fig.) submit, bow (**vor** + *Dat.* to); **jmdn. übers** ~ **legen** (ugs.) put sb. across one's knee; **etw. übers** ~ **brechen** (ugs.) rush sth.; **(b)** (Biegung) sharp bend; (eines Rohres) elbow

knie-, Knie-: ~**beuge** *die* knee-bend; ~**bund·hose** *die* knee-breeches *pl.;* **eine** ~: a pair of knee-breeches; ~**fall** *der:* **einen** ~**fall tun** *od.* **machen** (auch fig.) go down on one's knees (**vor** + *Dat.* before); ~**gelenk** *das* knee joint; ~**hoch** *Adj.* knee-high; kneelength ‹*boots*›; ~**kehle** *die* hollow of the knee; ~**lang** *Adj.* knee-length

knien /'kni:(ə)n/ **1** *itr. V.* kneel; ~**d, im Knien** kneeling; on one's knees. **2** *refl. V.* kneel [down]; get down on one's knees; **sich in die Arbeit** ~ (fig. ugs.) get stuck into one's work (sl.)

Knies /kni:s/ *der;* ~es (ugs.) quarrel; **ständig** ~ **mit jmdm. haben** always be quarrelling with sb.

knie-, Knie-: ~**scheibe** *die* kneecap; ~**schützer** *der* (Sport) knee-pad; ~**strumpf** *der* knee-length sock; knee-sock; ~**tief** *Adj.* knee-deep

Kniff /knɪf/ *der;* ~[e]s, ~e **(a)** (Kunstgriff) trick; dodge; **den** ~ **[bei etw.] heraushaben** have got the knack [of sth.]; **(b)** (Falte) crease; (in Papier) crease; fold

kniff[e]lig *Adj.* tricky

Knilch /knɪlç/ *der;* ~s, ~e (salopp abwertend) bastard (coll.)

knipsen /'knɪpsn̩/ **1** *tr. V.* **(a)** (entwerten) clip; punch; **(b)** (fotografieren) snap; take a snap[shot] of. **2** *itr. V.* **(a)** (fotografieren) take snapshots

Knirps /knɪrps/ *der;* ~es, ~e **(a)** (Ⓦ *Taschenschirm*) telescopic umbrella; **(b)** (ugs.: Junge) nipper (coll.); **(c)** (ugs. abwertend: kleiner Mann) [little] squirt (coll.)

knirschen /'knɪrʃn̩/ *itr. V.* **(a)** crunch; **(b) mit den Zähnen** ~: grind one's teeth

knistern /'knɪstɐn/ *itr. V.* rustle; ‹*wood, fire*› crackle; **mit etw.** ~: rustle sth.; **eine** ~**de Atmosphäre** (fig.) a tense *or* charged atmosphere; *s. auch* **Gebälk**

knitter·frei *Adj.* non-crease

knittern *tr., itr. V.* crease; crumple

knobeln *itr. V.* **(a)** (mit Würfeln) play dice; (mit Streichhölzern) play spoof; (mit Handzeichen) play scissors, paper, stone; **(b)** (ugs.: nachdenken) puzzle (**an** + *Dat.* over)

Knob·lauch /'kno:p-/ *der* garlic

Knoblauch-: ~**butter** *die* garlic butter; ~**zehe** *die* clove of garlic

Knöchel /'knœçl̩/ *der;* ~s, ~ **(a)** ▶ 326┘ (am Fuß) ankle; **bis an/über die** ~: up to the *or* one's ankles/to above ankle level; **(b)** ▶ 326┘ (am Finger) knuckle

knöchel-: ~**lang** *Adj.* ankle-length; ~**tief** *Adj.* ankle-deep

Knochen /'knɔxn̩/ *der;* ~s, ~ ▶ 326┘ bone; **Fleisch mit/ohne** ~: meat on/off the bone; **mir tun sämtliche** ~ **weh** (ugs.) every bone in my body aches; **der Schreck fuhr ihm in die** ~ (ugs.) he was shaken to the core; **keinen Mumm in den** ~ **haben** (ugs.) be a weed; **nass/abgemagert bis auf die** ~ **sein** be soaked to the skin/just skin and bones (coll.); **jmdn. bis auf die** ~ **blamieren** (ugs.) make a complete fool of sb. (coll.); **seine** ~ **für etw. hinhalten [müssen]** (ugs.) [have to] risk one's neck fighting for sth.

knochen-, Knochen-: ~**arbeit** *die* (ugs.) back-breaking work; ~**bruch** *der* ▶ 329┘ fracture; ~**hart** *Adj.* (ugs.) rock-hard; ~**mark** *das* bone marrow; ~**mehl** *das* bonemeal; ~**trocken** *Adj.* (ugs.) bone dry

knochig **1** *Adj.* bony. **2** *adv.* **sehr** ~ **gebaut sein** be very bony

Knock-out, Knockout /nɔk|'aut/ *der;* ~[s], ~s (Boxen) knockout

Knödel /'kno:dl̩/ *der;* ~s, ~ (bes. südd., österr.) dumpling

Knolle /'knɔlə/ *die;* ~, ~n **(a)** (einer Pflanze) tuber; **(b)** (ugs.) (Auswuchs) large round lump; (Nase) big fat conk (sl.) *or* (Amer.) schnozzle

Knollen *der;* ~s, ~ (ugs.: Strafzettel) [parking-]ticket

Knollen-: ~**blätterpilz** *der* amanita; ~**nase** *die* large bulbous nose

Knopf /knɔpf/ *der;* ~[e]s, **Knöpfe** /'knœpfə/ **(a)** button; **(b)** (Knauf) knob; **(c)** (ugs.: Kind) little thing (coll.)

knöpfen /'knœpfn̩/ *tr. V.* button [up]; **hinten/vorn geknöpft werden** ‹*dress etc.*› button up at the back/in front

Knopf·loch *das* buttonhole

Knorpel /'knɔrpl̩/ *der;* ~s, ~ **(a)** (Anat.) cartilage; **(b)** (im Steak o. ä.) gristle

knorp[e]lig *Adj.* **(a)** (Anat.) cartilaginous; **(b)** gristly ‹*meat*›

knorrig *Adj.* **(a)** gnarled ‹*tree, branch*›; **(b)** gruff ‹*person*›

Knospe /'knɔspə/ *die;* ~, ~n bud; ~**n ansetzen** put forth buds; bud

knospen *itr. V.* bud

knoten /'kno:tn̩/ *tr. V.* knot; tie a knot in; do *or* tie up ‹*shoelace*›; **etw. um/an etw. (Akk.)** ~: tie sth. round/to sth.

Knoten *der;* ~s, ~ **(a)** knot; **(b)** (Haartracht) bun; knot; **(c)** (Maßeinheit) knot; **(d)** (Bot.) node; **(e)** (Med.) lump

Knoten·punkt *der* (Verkehrs~) junction; intersection

knotig *Adj.* **(a)** knobby; knobbly; gnarled; knobbly ‹*fabric*›; **(b)** (knotenförmig) nodular

Know-how /nou'hau/ *das;* ~[s] know-how

Knuff /knuf/ *der;* ~[e]s, **Knüffe** /'knyfə/ (ugs.) poke

knuffen /'knufn̩/ *tr. V.* poke

knüllen *tr. V.* crumple [up]

Knüller *der;* ~s, ~ (ugs.) sensation; (Film, Buch usw.) sensation; sensational success; (Angebot, Verkaufsartikel) sensational offer

knüpfen /'knypfn̩/ **1** *tr. V.* **(a)** tie (**an** + *Akk.* to); **(b)** (durch Knoten herstellen) knot; make ‹*net*›; **(c)** (fig.) **große Erwartungen an etw. (Akk.)** ~: have great expectations of sth.; **Bedingungen an etw. (Akk.)** ~: attach conditions to sth. **2** *refl. V.* **sich an etw. (Akk.)** ~: be connected with sth.

Knüppel /'knypl̩/ *der;* ~s, ~ **(a)** cudgel; club; (Polizei~) truncheon; *s. auch* **Bein; (b)** ⇨ **Steuerknüppel; (c)** ⇨ **Schaltknüppel**

knüppel·dick *Adv.* **es kam** ~ (ugs.) it was one disaster after the other

knüppeln **1** *tr. V.* cudgel; club; beat with a cudgel *or* club/(Polizeiknüppel) truncheon. **2** *itr. V.* use a/one's cudgel *or* club/truncheon

knurren /'knurən/ **1** *itr. V.* **(a)** ‹*animal*› growl; (wütend) snarl; (fig.) ‹*stomach*› rumble; **(b)** (murren) grumble (**über**

+ *Akk.* about); **(c)** (verärgert reden) growl. **2** *tr. V.* (verärgert sagen) growl

knuspern /'knʊspən/ *tr., itr. V.* nibble; (geräuschvoll) crunch; **an etw.** (*Dat.*) ∼: nibble [at] sth.

knusprig 1 *Adj.* **(a)** crisp; crisp, crusty ‹*roll*›; crusty ‹*bread*›; crunchy ‹*nuts, crisps*›; **etw.** ∼ **braten** roast/fry sth. crisp and brown; **(b)** (ugs.: frisch u. adrett) delightfully fresh and attractive. **2** *adv.* ∼**-frisch** crunchy fresh ‹*crisps, nuts*›; crispy fresh ‹*rolls*›

Knute /'knuːtə/ *die;* ∼, ∼**n** knout; **unter jmds.** ∼ **[stehen]** (fig.) [be] under sb.'s heel

knutschen /'knuːtʃn/ (ugs.) **1** *tr. V.* smooch with (coll.); neck with (coll.); (sexuell berühren) pet. **2** *itr. V.* smooch (coll.), neck (coll.) **(mit** with); (sich sexuell berühren) pet

Knutscherei *die;* ∼, ∼**en** (ugs.) smooching (coll.); necking (coll.); (sexuelle Berührung) petting

Knutsch·fleck *der* (ugs.) love bite

k. o. /kaː'|oː/ *Adj.; nicht attr.* **(a)** (Boxen) **jmdn.** ∼ **schlagen** knock sb. out; **(b)** (ugs.: übermüdet) all in (coll.); whacked (coll.)

K. o. *der;* ∼, ∼ (Boxen) knockout

Koala /ko'aːla/ *der;* ∼**s**, ∼**s** koala [bear]

koalieren /ko|a'liːrən/ *itr. V.* (Politik) form a coalition **(mit** with)

Koalition /ko|ali'tsi̯oːn/ *die;* ∼, ∼**en** coalition

Koalitions·regierung *die* coalition government

Koaxial·kabel /ko|a'ksi̯aːl-/ *das* (Technik) coaxial cable

Kobalt /'koːbalt/ *das;* ∼**s** (Chemie) cobalt

Kobold /'koːbɔlt/ *der;* ∼**[e]s**, ∼**e** goblin; kobold; (fig.) imp

Kobra /'koːbra/ *die;* ∼, ∼**s** cobra

Koch /kɔx/ *der;* ∼**[e]s**, **Köche** /'kœçə/ ▶ 85 | cook; (als Beruf, Küchenchef) chef; **viele Köche verderben den Brei** (Spr.) too many cooks spoil the broth (prov.)

Koch·buch *das* cookery book; cookbook

kochen 1 *tr. V.* **(a)** boil; (zubereiten) cook ‹*meal*›; make ‹*purée, jam*›; **Tee** ∼/**sich** (*Dat.*) **einen Tee** ∼ make some tea; **die Eier hart/weich** ∼: hard-/soft-boil the eggs; **etw. weich/gar** ∼: cook sth. until it is soft/ [properly] done; **(b)** (waschen) boil ‹*washing*›; **(c)** (verflüssigen) heat ‹*tar, glue, etc.*›. **2** *itr. V.* **(a)** (Speisen zubereiten) cook; (das Kochen übernehmen) do the cooking; **gerne/gut** ∼: like cooking/be a good cook; **fett/fettarm** ∼: use a lot of fat/little fat in cooking; **(b)** (sieden) boil ‹*water, milk, etc.*› boil; (fig.) ‹*sea*› boil, seethe; **etw. zum Kochen bringen** bring sth. to the boil; **(c)** (gekocht werden) ‹*meat, vegetables, washing, etc.*› be boiled; **(d)** (ugs.: wütend sein) **vor Wut/inner-lich** ∼: be boiling *or* seething with rage/inwardly

***kochend·heiß** ⇒ **heiß 1** a

Kocher *der;* ∼**s**, ∼ [small] stove

Köcher /'kœçɐ/ *der;* ∼**s**, ∼ **(a)** (für Pfeile) quiver; **(b)** (für Fernglas o. ä.) case

koch·fertig *Adj.* ready-to-cook *attrib.;* ready to cook *pred.*

Koch·gelegenheit *die* cooking facilities *pl.*

Köchin /'kœçɪn/ *die;* ∼, ∼**nen** ▶ 85 | cook

Koch-: ∼**kunst** *die* **(a)** culinary art; **(b)** (ugs.: Fertigkeit im Kochen) culinary skill[s *pl.*]; ∼**kurs[us]** *der* cookery course; ∼**löffel** *der* wooden spoon; ∼**nische** *die* kitchenette; ∼**platte** *die* **(a)** hotplate; **(b)** (Kocher) [small] stove; ∼**rezept** *das* recipe; ∼**salz** *das* common salt; sodium chloride (Chem.); ∼**topf** *der* [cooking] pot; ∼**wäsche** *die; o. Pl.* washing that is to be boiled

Kode /koːt/ *der;* ∼**s**, ∼**s** code

Köder /'køːdɐ/ *der;* ∼**s**, ∼**:** bait; (fig.) bait; lure; **einen/ mehrere** ∼ **auslegen** put out bait/a number of baits

ködern *tr. V.* lure; **sich von jmdm./etw. nicht** ∼ **lassen** (fig. ugs.) not be tempted by sb.'s offer/by sth.

kodieren *tr. V.* code; encode

Koeffizient /ko°ɛfi'tsi̯ɛnt/ *der;* ∼**en**, ∼**en** (bes. Math.) co-efficient

Koexistenz *die;* ∼**:** coexistence

Koffein /kɔfe'iːn/ *das;* ∼**s** caffeine

koffein·frei *Adj.* decaffeinated

Koffer /'kɔfɐ/ *der;* ∼**s**, ∼ [suit]case; **die** ∼ **packen** pack one's bags [and leave]

Koffer-: ∼**anhänger** *der* luggage tag *or* label; ∼**kuli** *der* luggage trolley; ∼**radio** *das* portable radio; ∼**raum** *der* boot (Brit.); trunk (Amer.)

Kognak /'kɔnjak/ *der;* ∼**s**, ∼**s** brandy; *s. auch* **Cognac**

Kohl /koːl/ *der;* ∼**[e]s** **(a)** cabbage; **das macht den** ∼ **[auch] nicht fett** (ugs.) that doesn't help a lot; **(b)** (ugs. abwertend: Unsinn) rubbish; rot (coll.); **red keinen** ∼**!** don't talk rot! (coll.)

Kohl·dampf *der;* ∼ **haben/schieben** (salopp) be ravenously hungry/go hungry

Kohle /'koːlə/ *die;* ∼, ∼**n (a)** coal; **wir haben keine** ∼**n mehr** we have run out of coal; **[wie] auf [glühenden]** ∼**n sitzen** be fidgeting on one's seat (fig.); **(b)** (salopp: Geld) dough (sl.); **Hauptsache, die** ∼ **stimmen!** as long as the money's right; **(c)** (Zeichen∼) charcoal

Kohle-: ∼**hydrat** ⇒ **Kohlenhydrat;** ∼**kraft-werk** *das* coal-fired power station

kohlen-, **Kohlen-:** ∼**berg·werk** *das* coal mine; colliery; ∼**dioxid** *das* (fachspr.), ∼**dioxyd** /--'---/ *das* (Chemie) carbon dioxide; ∼**grube** *die* coal mine; [coal-] pit; ∼**halde** *die* coal heap; ∼**hydrat** *das* (Chemie) carbohydrate; ∼**keller** *der* coal cellar; ∼**monoxid** (fachspr.), ∼**monoxyd** /--'---/ *das* (Chemie) carbon monoxide; ∼**ofen** *der* coal-burning stove; ∼**säure** *die* carbonic acid; ∼**schaufel** *die* coal-shovel; ∼**stoff** *der; o. Pl.* carbon; ∼**wasserstoff** /--'---/ *der* (Chemie) hydrocarbon

Kohle-: ∼**ofen** ⇒ **Kohlenofen;** ∼**papier** *das* carbon paper; ∼**tablette** *die* charcoal tablet; ∼**zeich-nung** *die* charcoal drawing

kohl-, **Kohl-:** ∼**kopf** *der* [head of] cabbage; ∼**meise** *die* great tit; ∼**rabenschwarz** *Adj.* ⇒ **rabenschwarz;** ∼**rabi** /'raːbi/ *der;* ∼**[s]**, ∼**[s]** kohl-rabi; ∼**roulade** *die* (Kochk.) stuffed cabbage; ∼**rübe** *die* swede; ∼**weißling** *der* cabbage white; cabbage butterfly

Koitus /'koːitʊs/ *der;* ∼, **Koitus** (geh.) sexual intercourse; coitus (formal)

Koje /'koːjə/ *die;* ∼, ∼**n (a)** (Seemannsspr.) bunk; berth; **(b)** (ugs. scherzh.: Bett) bed

Kokain /koka'iːn/ *das;* ∼**s** cocaine

kokain·süchtig *Adj.* addicted to cocaine *postpos.*

kokeln /'koːkl̩n/ *itr. V.* (ugs.) play with fire

kokett /ko'kɛt/ **1** *Adj.* coquettish. **2** *adv.* coquettishly

Koketterie /kokɛtə'riː/ *die;* ∼**:** coquetry; coquettishness

kokettieren *itr. V.* play the coquette; flirt; **mit etw.** ∼**:** make much play with sth.

Kokolores /koko'loːrəs/ *der;* ∼ (ugs.) rubbish; nonsense; rot (sl.)

Kokos- /'koːkɔs-/: ∼**flocken** *Pl.* coconut ice *sing.;* (als Füllung) desiccated coconut *sing.;* ∼**milch** *die* coconut milk; ∼**nuss**, *****nuß** *die* coconut; ∼**palme** *die* coconut palm; coconut tree

Koks[1] /koːks/ *der;* ∼**es** coke

Koks[2] *der;* ∼**es** (Drogenjargon: Kokain) coke (sl.); snow (sl.)

koksen *itr. V.* (Drogenjargon) take coke (sl.)

Kokser *der;* ∼**s**, ∼ (Drogenjargon) [cocaine] sniffer; snow-bird (Amer. sl.)

Kolben /'kɔlbn̩/ *der;* ∼**s**, ∼ **(a)** (Technik) piston; **(b)** (Chemie: Glasgefäß) flask; **(c)** (Teil des Gewehrs) butt; **(d)** (Bot.) spadix; (Mais∼) cob; **(e)** (salopp: dicke Nase) hooter (Brit. sl.); conk (sl.)

Kolben·fresser *der* (ugs.) piston seizeup; **einen** ∼**fresser haben** have piston seizure *or* a seized[-up] piston

Kolchose /kɔl'çoːzə/ *die;* ∼, ∼**n** kolkhoz; Soviet collective farm

Kolibri /'koːlibri/ *der;* ∼**s**, ∼**s** hummingbird

Kolik /'koːlɪk/ *die;* ∼, ∼**en** colic

kollabieren /kɔla'biːrən/ *itr. V.; mit sein* (Med., fig.) collapse

Kollaborateur /kɔlabora'tøːɐ̯/ *der;* ∼**s**, ∼**e** collaborator

Kollaboration /kɔlabora'tsi̯oːn/ *die;* ∼**:** collaboration

kollaborieren *itr. V.* collaborate **(mit** with)

Kollaps /'kɔlaps/ *der;* ∼**es**, ∼**e** (Med., fig.) collapse; **einen** ∼ **erleiden** collapse

Kolleg /kɔ'le:k/ *das;* ~s, ~s (Vorlesung) lecture; (Vorlesungsreihe) course of lectures

Kollege /kɔ'le:gə/ *der;* ~n, ~n ▶ 34 | colleague; (Arbeiter) workmate; **Herr** ~! Mr. Smith/Jones *etc.!;* **Herr** ~ **[Müller** *usw.*] (Abgeordneter) ≈ the Honourable Gentleman

kollegial /kɔle'gja:l/ **1** *Adj.* helpful and considerate. **2** *adv.* ‹*act etc.*› like a good colleague/good colleagues

Kollegialität /kɔlegjali'tɛ:t/ *die;* ~: helpfulness and consideration

Kollegin *die;* ~, ~nen ⇒ **Kollege**

Kollegium /kɔ'le:gjʊm/ *das;* ~s, **Kollegien** (Lehrkörper) [teaching] staff

Kollekte /kɔ'lɛktə/ *die;* ~, ~n collection

Kollektion /kɔlɛk'tsjo:n/ *die;* ~, ~en (a) (auch Mode) collection; (b) (Sortiment) range

kollektiv /kɔlɛk'ti:f/ **1** *Adj.* collective; joint ‹*collaboration*›. **2** *adv.* collectively

Kollektiv *das;* ~s, ~e *od.* ~s (a) group; (b) (bes. DDR: Arbeitsgruppe) collective

Kollektiv·schuld *die; o. Pl.* collective guilt

Koller /'kɔlə/ *der;* ~s, ~ (ugs.) rage; **einen** ~ **haben/ bekommen** be in/fly or get into a rage

kollidieren /kɔli'di:rən/ *itr. V.* (a) *mit sein* collide, be in collision (**mit** with); (b) (fig.) clash, conflict (**mit** with)

Kollier /kɔ'lje:/ *das;* ~s, ~s necklace

Kollision /kɔli'zjo:n/ *die;* ~, ~en (a) collision; (b) (fig.) conflict, clash (*Gen.* between)

Kollisions·kurs *der; o. Pl.* collision course; **auf** ~ **gehen** (fig.) be heading for a confrontation

Kolloquium /kɔ'lo:kvjʊm/ *das;* ~s, **Kolloquien** colloquium

Köln /kœln/ *(das);* ~s ▶ 490 | Cologne

Kölner ▶ 490 | **1** *indekl. Adj.; nicht präd.* Cologne *attrib.;* (in Köln) in Cologne *postpos., not pred;* ‹*suburb, archbishop, mayor, speciality*› of Cologne; ‹*car factory, river bank*› at Cologne; **der** ~ **Dom/Karneval** Cologne Cathedral/the Cologne carnival. **2** *der;* ~s, ~ (von Geburt) native of Cologne; **er ist** ~: he comes from Cologne; **die** ~: the people of Cologne

Kölnerin *die;* ~, ~nen ⇒ **Kölner 2**

kölnisch *Adj.* ▶ 490 | Cologne *attrib.;* of Cologne *postpos., not pred.;* **kölnisch Wasser** eau-de-Cologne

kolonial /kolo'nja:l/ *Adj.; nicht präd.* colonial

Kolonialismus *der;* ~: colonialism *no art.*

Kolonial-: ~**macht** *die* colonial power; ~**zeit** *die; o. Pl.* colonial era or period

Kolonie /kolo'ni:/ *die;* ~, ~n (a) (auch Biol.) colony; (b) (Siedlung) colony; settlement

kolonisieren *tr. V.* (a) (zur Kolonie machen) colonize; (b) (besiedeln, erschließen) settle and develop; (urbar machen) clear and cultivate ‹*land*›; reclaim ‹*swampland*›

Kolonne /ko'lɔnə/ *die;* ~, ~n (a) (Truppe, Gruppe von Menschen, Zahlenreihe) column; (b) (Fahrzeuge) column; (Konvoi) convoy; ~ **fahren** drive in a [long] line of traffic; (c) (Arbeits~) gang

kolorieren /kolo'ri:rən/ *tr. V.* colour

Kolorit /kolo'ri:t/ *das;* ~[e]s, ~e *od.* ~s (geh.) colour

Koloss, *Koloß /ko'lɔs/ *der;* **Kolosses, Kolosse** (fig.: riesiges Gebilde, ugs. scherzh.: große Person) colossus; giant

kolossal /kolo'sa:l/ **1** *Adj.* (a) (riesenhaft) colossal; gigantic; enormous; (b) (ugs.: sehr groß) tremendous (coll.); incredible (coll.) ‹*rubbish, nonsense*›; ~**es Glück haben** be incredibly lucky (coll.). **2** *adv.* (ugs.) tremendously (coll.); ~ **viel Geld** a tremendous or vast amount of money (coll.)

Kolossal·schinken *der* (salopp abwertend) (a) (Film) massive great epic (coll.); (b) (Gemälde) whacking great painting (sl.)

kolportieren /kɔlpɔr'ti:rən/ *tr. V.* (geh.) spread; circulate

Kolumbianer /kolʊm'bja:nɐ/ *der;* ~s, ~, **Kolumbianerin** *die;* ~, ~nen Colombian

kolumbianisch *Adj.* Colombian

Kolumbien /ko'lʊmbjən/ *(das);* ~s Colombia

Kolumbus /ko'lʊmbʊs/ *(der)* Columbus; *s. auch* **Ei a**

Kolumne /ko'lʊmnə/ *die;* ~, ~n (Druckw., Zeitungsw.) column

Koma /'ko:ma/ *das;* ~s, ~s *od.* ~ta (Med.) coma

Kombi /'kɔmbi/ *der;* ~[s], ~s ⇒ **Kombiwagen**

Kombinat /kɔmbi'na:t/ *das;* ~[e]s, ~e (Wirtsch., bes. DDR) combine

Kombination /kɔmbina'tsjo:n/ *die;* ~, ~en (a) (auch Schach) combination; (b) (gedankliche Verknüpfung) deduction; piece of reasoning; (c) (Kleidungsstücke) ensemble; suit; (Herren~) suit; (Flieger~) flying-suit; (d) (Ballspiele) combined move

Kombinations·gabe *die; o. Pl.* powers *pl.* of reasoning or deduction

kombinieren /kɔmbi'ni:rən/ **1** *tr. V.* combine (**zu** into). **2** *itr. V.* (a) (Zusammenhänge herstellen) deduce; reason; (b) (Ballspiele) combine

Kombi-: ~**wagen** *der* estate [car]; station wagon (Amer.); ~**zange** *die* combination pliers *pl.;* **eine** ~**zange** a pair of combination pliers

Komet /ko'me:t/ *der;* ~en, ~en comet

kometen·haft *Adj.* meteoric ‹*rise, career*›

Komfort /kɔm'fo:ɐ̯/ *der;* ~s comfort; **mit allem** ~ ‹*flat, house*› with all modern conveniences *pl.;* ‹*car*› with all the latest luxury features *pl.*

komfortabel /kɔmfɔr'ta:bl̩/ **1** *Adj.* comfortable. **2** *adv.* comfortably

Komik /'ko:mɪk/ *die;* ~: comic effect; (komisches Element) comic element or aspect; **Sinn für** ~ **haben** have a sense of the comic

Komiker *der;* ~s, ~ comedian; comic (coll.)

komisch /'ko:mɪʃ/ *Adj.* (a) (lustig) comical; funny; **ich finde das gar nicht** ~ (ugs.) I don't think that's at all funny; (b) (seltsam) funny; strange; odd; ~ **[zu jmdm.] sein** act or behave strangely [towards sb.]; **mir ist/wird so** ~: I'm feeling funny or peculiar; (c) (Literaturw., Theater) comic ‹*part*›

komischer·weise *Adv.* (ugs.) strangely enough

Komitee /komi'te:/ *das;* ~s, ~s committee

Komma /'kɔma/ *das;* ~s, ~s *od.* ~ta ▶ 600 | (a) (Satzzeichen) comma; (b) (Math.) decimal point; **zwei** ~ **acht** two point eight; **zwei Stellen hinter dem** ~: two decimal places

Kommandant /kɔman'dant/ *der;* ~en, ~en (einer Stadt, Festung) commandant; (eines Panzers, Raumschiffs) commander; (einer Militäreinheit) commander; commanding officer; (eines Flugzeugs, Schiffs) captain

Kommandeur /kɔman'dø:ɐ̯/ *der;* ~s, ~e (Milit.) commander; commanding officer

kommandieren **1** *tr. V.* (a) (befehligen) command; be in command of; (b) (abkommandieren) **jmdn. an die Front** ~: order sb. to the front; (c) (ugs.: herumkommandieren) **jmdn.** ~: order or (sl.) boss sb. about. **2** *itr. V.* (ugs.) order or (sl.) boss people about

Kommandit·gesellschaft /kɔman'di:t-/ *die* (Wirtsch.) limited partnership

Kommando /kɔ'mando/ *das;* ~s, ~s, österr. auch: **Kommanden** (a) (Befehl) command; **das** ~ **zum Schießen geben** give the command or order to shoot; **wie auf** ~: as if by command; (b) *o. Pl.* (Befehlsgewalt) command; **das** ~ **haben** *od.* **führen/übernehmen** be in/ assume or take command; (c) (Milit.) (Einheit) detachment; (Stoßtrupp) commando

Kommando-: ~**brücke** *die* bridge; ~**sache** *die in geheime* ~**sache** (Milit.) military secret

Kommata ⇒ **Komma**

kommen /'kɔmən/ *unr. itr. V.; mit sein* (a) come; (eintreffen) come; arrive; **ich komme schon!** I'm coming!; **der Kellner kommt sofort** the waiter will be with you directly; **angelaufen/angebraust** *usw.* ~: come running/roaring *etc.* along; (auf jmdn. zu) come running/roaring *etc.* up; **angekrochen** ~ (fig.) come crawling up; **zu spät**

∼: be late; **durch eine Gegend** ∼: pass through a region; **nach Hause** ∼: come or get home; **zu jmdm.** ∼ (jmdn. besuchen) come and see sb.; **ist für mich keine Post ge**∼? is/was there no post for me?; **etw.** ∼ **lassen** (etw. bestellen) order sth.; **jmdn.** ∼ **lassen** send for or call sb.; **da könnte ja jeder** ∼! (ugs.) who do you think you are?/ who does he think he is? etc.; **komm mir bloß nicht damit!** (ugs.) don't give me that!; [**bitte**] ∼! (im Funkverkehr) come in[, please]; **(b)** (gelangen) get; **ans Ufer/Ziel** ∼: reach the bank/finishing-line; **wie komme ich nach Paris?** how do I get to Paris?; (fig.) **auf etw.** (Akk.) **zu sprechen** ∼: turn to the discussion of sth.; **jmdm. auf die Spur/Schliche** ∼: get on sb.'s trail/get wise to sb.'s tricks; **wie kommst du darauf?** what gives you that idea?; **dazu** ∼, **etw. zu tun** get round to doing sth.; **zum Einkaufen/Waschen** ∼: get round to doing the shopping/washing; **(c)** (auftauchen) ‹seeds, plants› come up; ‹buds, flowers› come out; ‹peas, beans› form; ‹teeth› come through; **zur Welt** ∼: be born; **ihr ist ein Gedanke/ eine Idee ge**∼: she had a thought/an idea; a thought/an idea came to her; **jmdm.** ∼ **die Tränen** tears come to sb.'s eyes; **(d)** (aufgenommen werden) **zur Schule** ∼: go to or start school; **ins Krankenhaus/Gefängnis** ∼: go into hospital/to prison; **in den Himmel/in die Hölle** ∼ (fig.) go to heaven/hell; **(e)** (gehören) belong; **in die Schublade/ins Regal** ∼: go or belong in the drawer/on the shelf; **(f)** (gebracht, befördert werden) go; **in den Müll** ∼: be thrown out; **(g)** (geraten) get; **in Gefahr/Not/Verlegenheit** ∼: get into danger/serious difficulties/get or become embarrassed; **unter ein Auto/zu Tode** ∼: be knocked down by a car/be or get killed; **ins Schleudern** ∼: go into a skid; **neben jmdn. zu sitzen** ∼: get to sit next to sb.; s. auch **Schwung; Stimmung; (h)** (nahen) **ein Gewitter/die Flut kommt** a storm is approaching/ the tide's coming in; **der Tag/die Nacht kommt** (geh.) day is breaking/night is falling; **dieses Unglück habe ich schon lange** ∼ **sehen** I saw this disaster coming a long time ago; **im Kommen sein** ‹fashion etc.› be coming in; ‹person› be on the way up; **(i)** (sich ereignen) come about; happen; **was auch immer** ∼ **mag** come what may; **das durfte [jetzt] nicht** ∼ (ugs. spött.) that's hardly the thing to say now; **gelegen/ungelegen** ∼ ‹offer, opportunity› come/not come at the right moment; ‹visit› be/not be convenient; **überraschend [für jmdn.]** ∼: come as a surprise [to sb.]; **daher kommt es, dass** …: that's [the reason] why …; **das kommt davon, dass** …: that's because …; **vom vielen Rauchen/vom Vitaminmangel** ∼: be due to smoking/vitamin deficiency; **wie kommt es, dass** …: how is it that you/he etc. …; how come that … (coll.); **das kommt davon!** see what happens!; **(j)** unpers. **es kam zum Streit/Kampf** there was a quarrel/fight; **es kam alles ganz anders** it all or everything turned out quite differently; **so weit kommt es noch [, dass ich euern Dreck wieder wegräume]!** (ugs. iron.) that really is the limit[, expecting me to clear up your rubbish after you]!; **(k)** (ugs.: erreicht werden) **wann kommt der nächste Bahnhof?** when do we get to the next station? (coll.); **jetzt kommt gleich Mannheim** we'll be at Mannheim any moment; **da vorn kommt eine Tankstelle** there's a petrol station coming up (coll.); **(l)** **zu Geld** ∼: become wealthy; **zu Erfolg/Ruhm** usw. ∼: gain success/fame etc.; **nie zu etwas** ∼ (ugs.) never get anywhere; **wieder zu Kräften** ∼: regain one's strength; [**wieder**] **zu sich** ∼: regain consciousness; come round; **um etw.** ∼: lose sth.; **ums Leben** ∼: lose one's life; **(m)** (an der Reihe sein; folgen) **zuerst/zuletzt kam** …: first/last came …; **als erster/letzter** ∼ come first/last; **jetzt komme ich [an die Reihe]** it is my turn now; **(n)** (ugs.: sich verhalten) **jmdm. frech/unverschämt/grob** ∼: be cheeky/impertinent/ rude to sb.; **so lasse ich mir nicht** ∼! I don't stand for that sort of thing!; **(o)** **ich lasse auf ihn** usw. **nichts** ∼: I won't hear anything said against him etc.; **über jmdn.** ∼ (jmdn. erfassen) ‹feeling› come over sb.; **(p)** (entfallen) **auf hundert Berufstätige** ∼ **vier Arbeitslose** for every hundred people in employment, there are four people unemployed; **(q) woher** ∼ **diese Sachen?** where do these things come from?; **seine Eltern** ∼ **aus Sachsen** his parents come or are from Saxony; **(r)** (ugs.: kosten) **auf 100**

Mark ∼: cost 100 marks; **alles zusammen kam auf …:** altogether it came to …; **wie teuer kommt der Stoff?** how much or dear is that material?; **etw. kommt [jmdn.] teuer** sth. comes expensive [for sb.]; **(s)** (ugs.: anspringen) ‹engine› start; **(t)** (salopp: Orgasmus haben) come (sl.); **(u)** (ugs.: als Aufforderung, Ermahnung) **komm/kommt/kommen Sie** come on, now; **komm, komm** oh, come on; **(v)** (Sportjargon: gelingen) [**gut**] ∼/**nicht** ∼ ‹serve, backhand, forehand, etc.› be going/not be going well; **(w)** in festen Wendungen: ⇒ **Ausbruch b; Einsatz c; Entfaltung a; Fall**

kommend Adj. ; nicht präd. **(a)** ▶ 119 |, ▶ 595 | (nächst…) next; **das** ∼**e Wochenende/am** ∼**en Sonntag** next weekend/Sunday; **(b)** (zukünftig) ∼**e Generationen** generations to come; future generations; **(c)** (mit großer Zukunft) **der** ∼**e Mann** the coming man

Kommentar /kɔmɛnˈtaː̯ɐ̯/ der; ∼**s**, ∼**e (a)** (Erläuterung) commentary; **(b)** (Stellungnahme) commentary; comment; **kein** ∼! no comment!; **(c)** (oft abwertend: Anmerkung) comment

Kommentator /kɔmɛnˈtaːtɔr/ der; ∼**s**, ∼**en** /-ˈtaːto: rən/, **Kommentatorin** die; ∼, ∼**nen** commentator

kommentieren tr. V. comment on

Kommerz /kɔˈmɛrts/ der; ∼**es** (abwertend) business interests pl.

kommerzialisieren /kɔmɛrtsi̯aliˈziːrən/ tr. V. commercialize

kommerziell /kɔmɛrˈtsi̯ɛl/ **1** Adj. commercial. **2** adv. commercially

Kommilitone /kɔmiliˈtoːnə/ der; ∼**n**, ∼**n**, **Kommilitonin** die; ∼, ∼**nen** (Studentenspr.) fellow student

Kommiss, *****Kommiß** /kɔˈmɪs/ der; **Kommisses** (Soldatenspr.) army

Kommissar /kɔmɪˈsaːɐ̯/ der; ∼**s**, ∼**e (a)** commissioner; **(b)** ▶ 34 | (Polizist) detective superintendent

Kommissariat /kɔmɪsaˈri̯aːt/ das; ∼**s**, ∼**e (a)** ⇒ **Kommissar:** commissioner's office; detective superintendent's office; **(b)** (österr.) police station

kommissarisch 1 Adj.; nicht präd. acting. **2** adv. in an acting capacity

Kommission /kɔmɪˈsi̯oːn/ die; ∼, ∼**en (a)** (Gremium) committee; (Prüfungs∼) commission; **(b) etw. in** ∼ **nehmen/haben/geben** (Wirtsch.) take/have sth. on commission/give sth. to a dealer for sale on commission

Kommode /kɔˈmoːdə/ die; ∼, ∼**n** chest of drawers

kommunal /kɔmuˈnaːl/ **1** Adj. local; (städtisch) municipal; local. **2** adv. **etw. wird** ∼ **verwaltet** sth. comes under local government

Kommunal-: ∼**politik** die local politics sing., ∼**wahl** die local [government] elections pl.

Kommune /kɔˈmuːnə/ die; ∼, ∼**n** local authority; (städtische Gemeinde) municipality

Kommunikation /kɔmunikaˈtsi̯oːn/ die; ∼, ∼**en** communication

Kommunion /kɔmuˈni̯oːn/ die; ∼, ∼**en** (kath. Kirche) [Holy] Communion

Kommuniqué /kɔmyniˈkeː/ das; ∼**s**, ∼**s** communiqué

Kommunismus der; ∼: communism

Kommunist der; ∼**en**, ∼**en**, **Kommunistin** die; ∼, ∼**nen** communist

kommunistisch 1 Adj. communist; (die ∼e Partei betreffend) Communist. **2** adv. Communist-‹influenced, led, ruled, etc.›

kommunizieren /kɔmuniˈtsiːrən/ itr. V. **(a)** (geh.) communicate; **(b)** (kath. Kirche) receive [Holy] Communion

Komödiant /komøˈdi̯ant/ der; ∼**en**, ∼**en**, **Komödiantin** die; ∼, ∼**nen (a)** (veralt.) actor/actress; player; **(b)** (abwertend: Heuchler/∼in) play-actor

Komödie /koˈmøːdi̯ə/ die; ∼, ∼**n (a)** comedy; (fig.) farce; **(b)** (Theater) comedy theatre; **(c)** (Heuchelei) play-acting

Kompagnon /kɔmpanˈjõː/ der; ∼**s**, ∼**s** (Wirtsch.) partner; associate

kompakt /kɔmˈpakt/ Adj. **(a)** (massiv) solid; **(b)** (ugs.: gedrungen) stocky

Kompanie /kɔmpa'niː/ *die;* ~, ~n (Milit.) company

Komparativ /'kɔmparatiːf/ *der;* ~s, ~e (Sprachw.) comparative

Komparse /kɔm'parzə/ *der;* ~n, ~n (Theater) supernumerary; super (coll.); (Film) extra

Kompass, ***Kompaß** /'kɔmpas/ *der;* **Kompasses**, **Kompasse** compass

Kompass·nadel, ***Kompaß·nadel** *die* compass needle

Kompensation /kɔmpɛnza'tsi̯oːn/ *die;* ~, ~en (fachspr., geh.) compensation

kompensieren *tr. V.* etw. mit etw. *od.* durch etw. ~: compensate for *or* make up for sth. by sth.

kompetent /kɔmpe'tɛnt/ *Adj.* (a) (sachverständig) competent; (b) (bes. Rechtsw.: zuständig) competent, responsible ‹*authority*›

Kompetenz /kɔmpe'tɛnts/ *die;* ~, ~en (a) competence; (b) (bes. Rechtsw.: Zuständigkeit) authority; powers *pl.;* **in jmds.** ~ (*Dat.*) **liegen/in jmds.** ~ (*Akk.*) **fallen** be/come within sb.'s authority *or* powers; **das liegt außerhalb meiner** ~: that doesn't lie within my authority *or* powers

komplementär /kɔmplemɛn'tɛːɐ̯/ *Adj.* complementary

Komplementär·farbe *die* (Optik) complementary colour

komplett /kɔm'plɛt/ **1** *Adj.* (a) complete; **es kostet** ~ **1 500 Mark** it costs 1,500 marks complete; **heute sind wir** ~ (ugs.) today we are all here; (b) *nicht präd.* (ugs.: ganz und gar) complete; utter; (c) (österr.: voll) full ‹*hotel, tram, etc.*›. **2** *adv.* (a) fully ‹*furnished, equipped*›; (b) (ugs.: ganz und gar) completely; totally

komplettieren *tr. V.* complete

komplex /kɔm'plɛks/ *Adj.* (geh.) complex

Komplex *der;* ~es, ~e (auch Psych.) complex

Komplexität /kɔmplɛksi'tɛːt/ *die;* ~: complexity

Komplikation /kɔmplika'tsi̯oːn/ *die;* ~, ~en complication

Kompliment /kɔmpli'mɛnt/ *das;* ~[e]s, ~e compliment; **jmdm. ein** ~ **machen** pay sb. a compliment (**über** + *Akk.* on); **nicht gerade ein** ~ **für jmdn. sein** (fig.) not exactly do sb. credit

komplimentieren *tr. V.* (geh.) **jmdn. ins Haus** ~: usher *or* show sb. into the house; **jmdn. aus dem Zimmer** ~ (verhüll.) usher sb. out of the room

Komplize /kɔm'pliːtsə/ *der;* ~n, ~n (abwertend) accomplice

komplizieren *tr. V.* complicate

kompliziert 1 *Adj.* complicated; complicated, intricate ‹*device, piece of apparatus*›; complicated, involved ‹*problem, procedure*›; (Med.) compound ‹*fracture*›. **2** *adv.* **sich** ~ **ausdrücken** express oneself in a complicated *or* an involved way *or* manner

Komplizin *die;* ~, ~nen (abwertend) accomplice

Komplott /kɔm'plɔt/ *das;* ~[e]s, ~e plot; conspiracy; **ein** ~ **schmieden** hatch a plot

Komponente /kɔmpo'nɛntə/ *die;* ~, ~n component

komponieren *tr., itr. V.* (auch fig. geh.) compose

Komponist *der;* ~en, ~en, **Komponistin** *die;* ~, ~nen composer

Komposition /kɔmpozi'tsi̯oːn/ *die;* ~, ~en (auch fig. geh.) composition

Kompositum /kɔm'poːzitʊm/ *das;* ~s, **Komposita** (Sprachw.) compound [word]

Kompost /kɔm'pɔst/ *der;* ~[e]s, ~e compost

Kompost·haufen *der* compost heap

Kompott /kɔm'pɔt/ *das;* ~[e]s, ~e stewed fruit; compote

Kompresse /kɔm'prɛsə/ *die;* ~, ~n (Med.) (a) (Umschlag) [wet] compress; (b) (Mull) [gauze] pad

Kompression /kɔm'prɛsi̯oːn/ *die;* ~, ~en (fachspr.) compression

Kompressor /kɔm'prɛsɔr/ *der;* ~s, ~en /-'soːrən/ (Technik) compressor

komprimieren /kɔmpri'miːrən/ *tr. V.* (fachspr., geh.) compress

komprimiert *Adj.* (fig. geh.) condensed ‹*account, form, etc.*›

Kompromiss, ***Kompromiß** /kɔmpro'mɪs/ *der;* **Kompromisses**, **Kompromisse** compromise; **einen** ~ **schließen** make a compromise; compromise; **ein fauler** ~ (ugs.) a poor sort of compromise (coll.)

kompromiss-, ***kompromiß-**, **Kompromiss-**, ***Kompromiß-:** ~**bereit** *Adj.* ready *or* willing to compromise *pred.;* ~**bereitschaft** *die; o. Pl.* readiness *or* willingness to compromise; ~**los 1** *Adj.* uncompromising; **2** *adv.* uncompromisingly; ~**lösung** *die* compromise solution; ~**vorschlag** *der* compromise proposal *or* suggestion

kompromittieren /kɔmprɔmɪ'tiːrən/ *tr. V.* compromise; **sich** ~: compromise oneself

Kondensat /kɔɔdɛn'zaːt/ *das;* ~[e]s, ~e (Physik, Chemie) condensate

Kondensation /kɔndɛnza'tsi̯oːn/ *die;* ~, ~en (Physik, Chemie) condensation

Kondensator /kɔndɛn'zaːtɔr/ *der;* ~s, ~en /-zaːto:rən/ (a) (Elektrot.) capacitor; condenser; (b) (Technik) condenser

kondensieren *tr., itr. V.* (itr. auch mit sein) (Physik, Chemie) condense

Kondens-: ~**milch** *die* condensed milk; ~**streifen** *der* condensation trail; vapour trail; ~**wasser** *das* condensation

Kondition /kɔndi'tsi̯oːn/ *die;* ~, ~en (a) *meist Pl.* (bes. Kaufmannsspr., Finanzw.) condition; **zu günstigen** ~en on favourable terms *or* conditions; (b) *o. Pl.* (körperlich-seelische Verfassung) condition; **eine gute/schlechte** ~ **haben** be/not be in good condition *or* shape; **keine** ~ **haben** be out of condition; (fig.) have no stamina

konditional /kɔnditsi̯o'naːl/ *Adj.* (bes. Sprachw.) conditional

Konditional·satz *der* (Sprachw.) conditional clause

konditionieren *tr. V.* (Technik, Psych.) condition

Konditions-: ~**schwäche** *die* lack of condition *or* fitness; ~**training** *das* fitness training

Konditor /kɔn'diːtɔr/ *der;* ~s, ~en /-diːto:rən/ ▶ 85 | confectioner; pastry-cook; **beim** ~: at the cake-shop

Konditorei *die;* ~, ~en cake-shop; (Lokal) café

kondolieren /kɔndo'liːrən/ *itr. V.* offer one's condolences; **jmdm.** [**zu jmds. Tod**] ~: offer one's condolences to sb. *or* condole with sb. [on sb.'s death]

Kondom /kɔn'doːm/ *das od. der;* ~s, ~e condom; [contraceptive] sheath

Kondor /'kɔndɔr/ *der;* ~s, ~e condor

Kondukteur /kɔndʊk'tøːɐ̯/ *der;* ~s, ~e ▶ 85 | (schweiz.) ⇒ **Schaffner**

Konfekt /kɔn'fɛkt/ *das;* ~[e]s (a) confectionery; sweets *pl.* (Brit.); candies *pl.* (Amer.); (b) (bes. südd., österr., schweiz.: Teegebäck) [small] fancy biscuits *pl.* (Brit.) *or* (Amer.) cookies *pl.*

Konfektion /kɔnfɛk'tsi̯oːn/ *die;* ~, ~en ready-made *or* off-the-peg (Brit.) *or* (Amer.) off-the-rack clothes *pl. or* garments *pl.*

Konfektions-: ~**geschäft** *das* [ready-made *or* off-the-peg (Brit.) *or* (Amer.) off-the-rack] clothes shop; ~**größe** *die* size; ~**ware** *die* ⇒ **Konfektion**

Konferenz /kɔnfe'rɛnts/ *die;* ~, ~en conference; (Besprechung) meeting

Konferenz·schaltung *die* (Rundf., Ferns., Fernspr.) conference circuit

konferieren /kɔnfe'riːrən/ *itr. V.* confer (**über** + *Akk.* on, about)

Konfession /kɔnfɛ'si̯oːn/ *die;* ~, ~en denomination; religion; **welche** ~ **haben Sie?** what denomination *or* religion are you?

konfessionell /kɔnfɛsi̯oˈnɛl/ **1** *Adj.; nicht präd.* denominational. **2** *adv.* as regards denomination

konfessions·los *Adj.* not belonging to any denomination *or* religion *postpos., not pred.*

Konfessions·schule *die* denominational school

Konfetti /kɔnˈfɛti/ *das;* ~[s] confetti

Konfirmand /kɔnfɪrˈmant/ *der;* ~en, ~en, **Konfirmandin** *die;* ~, ~nen (ev. Rel.) confirmand

Konfirmation /kɔnfɪrmaˈtsi̯oːn/ *die;* ~, ~en (ev. Rel.) confirmation

konfiszieren /kɔnfɪsˈtsiːrən/ *tr. V.* (bes. Rechtsw.) confiscate

Konfitüre /kɔnfiˈtyːrə/ *die;* ~, ~n jam

Konflikt /kɔnˈflɪkt/ *der;* ~[e]s, ~e conflict; **mit etw. in** ~ **geraten** come into conflict with sth.

konflikt-, Konflikt-: ~**frei** *Adj.* conflict-free; ~**situation** *die* conflict situation; ~**stoff** *der* cause for conflict *or* dispute

Konföderation /kɔnføderaˈtsi̯oːn/ *die;* ~, ~en confederation

konform /kɔnˈfɔrm/ *Adj.* concurring *attrib.* ⟨views⟩; **mit jmdm./etw.** ~ **gehen** be in agreement with sb./sth.

Konformist *der;* ~en, ~en, **Konformistin** *die;* ~, ~nen conformist

konformistisch **1** *Adj.* conformist. **2** *adv.* in a conformist way

Konfrontation /kɔnfrɔntaˈtsi̯oːn/ *die;* ~, ~en confrontation

konfrontieren *tr. V.* confront

konfus /kɔnˈfuːs/ **1** *Adj.* confused; muddled; **jmdn.** ~ **machen** confuse *or* muddle sb. **2** *adv.* in a confused *or* muddled fashion; confusedly

kongenial /kɔngeˈni̯aːl/ *Adj.* congenial, kindred ⟨spirits⟩; ideally matched ⟨translation⟩

Konglomerat /kɔnglomeˈraːt/ *das;* ~[e]s, ~e (geh.) conglomeration

Kongo /ˈkɔŋgo/ *(das);* ~s *od. der;* ~[s] (Staat) the Congo

Kongress, ·Kongreß /kɔnˈgrɛs/ *der;* **Kongresses, Kongresse** (a) congress; conference; **(b) der** ~ (USA) Congress

Kongress-, Kongreß-: ~**halle** *die* conference hall; ~**mitglied** *das* (USA) Congressman/Congresswoman; ~**teilnehmer** *der* congress *or* conference participant

kongruent /kɔngruˈɛnt/ *Adj.* (Math.) congruent

Kongruenz /kɔngruˈɛnts/ *die;* ~, ~en (Math.) congruence

König /ˈkøːnɪç/ *der;* ~s, ~e (auch Schach, Kartenspiele, fig.) king; **der Kunde ist** ~: the customer is always right

Königin *die;* ~, ~nen (auch Bienen~) queen

Königin·mutter *die;* *Pl.* **Königinmütter** queen mother

königlich **1** *Adj.* (a) *nicht präd.* royal; **(b)** (vornehm) regal; **(c)** (reichlich) princely ⟨gift, salary, wage⟩; lavish ⟨hospitality⟩; **(d)** (ugs.: außerordentlich) tremendous (coll.) ⟨fun⟩. **2** *adv.* (a) (reichlich) ⟨entertain⟩ lavishly; ⟨pay⟩ handsomely; ~ **beschenkt werden** be showered with lavish presents; **(b)** (ugs.: außerordentlich) ⟨enjoy oneself⟩ immensely (coll.)

König·reich *das* kingdom

königs-, Königs-: ~**blau** *Adj.* royal blue; ~**haus** *das* royal house; ~**hof** *der* royal court; king's court; ~**paar** *das* royal couple; ~**sohn** *der* prince; king's son; ~**tochter** *die* princess; king's daughter; ~**treu** *Adj.* loyal to the king *postpos.;* (der Monarchie treu) royalist

konisch /ˈkoːnɪʃ/ *Adj.* conical

Konjugation /kɔnjugaˈtsi̯oːn/ *die;* ~, ~en (Sprachw.) conjugation

konjugieren *tr. V.* (Sprachw.) conjugate

Konjunktion /kɔnjʊŋkˈtsi̯oːn/ *die;* ~, ~en (Sprachw.) conjunction

Konjunktiv /ˈkɔnjʊŋktiːf/ *der;* ~s, ~e (Sprachw.) subjunctive

Konjunktur /kɔnjʊŋkˈtuːɐ̯/ *die;* ~, ~en (Wirtsch.) (a) (wirtschaftliche Lage) [level of] economic activity; economy;

(Tendenz) economic trend; **die** ~ **beleben/bremsen** stimulate/slow down the economy; **(b)** (Hoch~) boom; (Aufschwung) upturn [in the economy]; ~ **haben** (fig.) be in great demand

konjunktur·abhängig *Adj.* (Wirtsch.) dependent on economic trends *postpos.*

konjunkturell /kɔnjʊŋktuˈrɛl/ **1** *Adj.; nicht präd.* economic; **die** ~**e Entwicklung** the development of the economy. **2** *adv.* ~ **bedingt** due to economic trends *postpos.*

Konjunktur- (Wirtsch.): ~**politik** *die* stabilization policy; measures *pl.* aimed at avoiding violent fluctuations in the economy; ~**schwankung** *die* fluctuation in the level of economic activity

konkav /kɔnˈkaːf/ (Optik) **1** *Adj.* concave. **2** *adv.* concavely

Konkordanz /kɔnkɔrˈdants/ *die;* ~, ~en (Wissensch.) concordance

Konkordat /kɔnkɔrˈdaːt/ *das;* ~[e]s, ~e concordat

konkret /kɔnˈkreːt/ **1** *Adj.* concrete. **2** *adv.* in concrete terms; **kannst du mal** ~ **sagen, was du damit meinst?** could you tell me exactly what you mean by that?

konkretisieren *tr. V.* etw. ~: put sth. in concrete terms

Konkurrent /kɔnkʊˈrɛnt/ *der;* ~en, ~en, **Konkurrentin** *die;* ~, ~nen rival; (Sport, Wirtsch.) competitor

Konkurrenz /kɔnkʊˈrɛnts/ *die;* ~, ~en (a) o. Pl. (Rivalität) rivalry *no indef. art.;* (Sport, Wirtsch.) competition *no indef. art.;* **jmdm.** ~ **machen** compete with sb.; **mit jmdm. in** ~ **treten/stehen** enter into/be in competition with sb.; **außer** ~ **starten/teilnehmen** (bes. Sport) take part as an unofficial competitor; **(b)** o. Pl. (die Konkurrenten) competition

konkurrenz-, Konkurrenz-: ~**druck** *der;* o. Pl. pressure of competition; ~**fähig** *Adj.* competitive; ~**kampf** *der* competition; (zwischen zwei Menschen) rivalry; ~**los** *Adj.* ⟨product, firm, etc.⟩ that has no competition *or* competitors; (unvergleichlich) unrivalled

konkurrieren *itr. V.* compete; **mit jmdm./etw. [um etw.]** ~: compete with sb./sth. [for sth.]

Konkurs /kɔnˈkʊrs/ *der;* ~es, ~e (a) bankruptcy; ~ **machen** *od.* **in** ~ **gehen** go bankrupt; **[den]** ~ **anmelden** file for bankruptcy; have oneself declared bankrupt; **(b)** (~verfahren) bankruptcy proceedings *pl.*

Konkurs- (Wirtsch.): ~**masse** *die* bankrupt's assets *pl.;* ~**verfahren** *das* bankruptcy proceedings *pl.*

können /ˈkœnən/ **1** *unr. Modalverb; 2. Part.* ~ **(a)** be able to; **er hat/hätte es machen** ~; he was able to *or* he could do it/he could have done it; **er kann es machen/nicht machen** he can do it *or* is able to do it/cannot do it *or* (coll.) can't do it *or* is unable to do it; **er kann gut reden/tanzen** he can talk/dance well; he is a good talker/dancer; **ich kann nicht schlafen** I cannot *or* (coll.) can't sleep; **ich kann das nicht mehr hören/sehen** I can't stand *or* bear to hear it/can't stand *or* bear the sight of it any longer (coll.); **ich kann dir sagen!** (ugs.) I can tell you; **kann das explodieren?** could it explode?; **er kann jeden Moment kommen** he may come at any moment; **wer kann es sein/gewesen sein?** who can it be/could it have been?; **man kann nie wissen** you never know; one never knows; **es kann sein, dass ...:** it may be that ...; **das könnte [gut] sein** that could [well] be the case; **das kann nicht sein** that's not possible; **kann ich Ihnen helfen?** can I help you?; **können Sie mir sagen, ...?** can you tell me ...?; **kannst du nicht aufpassen?** can't you be more careful?; **kann sein** (ugs.) could be (coll.); **Kommst du morgen? — Kann sein** Are you coming tomorrow? — Might do; **(b)** (Grund haben) **du kannst ganz ruhig sein** you don't have to worry; **wir** ~ **uns/er kann sich freuen, dass ...:** we can/he should be glad that ...; **er kann einem Leid tun** (ugs.) you have to feel sorry for him; **das kann man wohl sagen!** you could well say that; **(c)** (dürfen) **kann ich gehen?** can I go?; ~ **wir mitkommen?** can we come too?; **du kannst mich [mal]!** (salopp verhüll.) you can get stuffed (sl.); you know what you can do

können

Es kommen hauptsächlich zwei Übersetzungen in Betracht: **to be able to** (die einzige Möglichkeit im Infinitiv und im Futur und den anderen zusammengesetzten Zeiten) und **can/could**. Im Präsens ist **can** fast immer möglich und in vielen Fällen vorzuziehen. In der Vergangenheit dagegen ist **was able to** manchmal vorzuziehen, da **could** auch konditional sein kann (= könnte).

Es ist wichtig, kochen zu können	= It is important to be able to cook
Wenn sie frei bekommt, wird sie hingehen können	= If she gets time off she will be able to go there
Er kann sie oft durch einen Freund bekommen	= He can often get them od. is often able to get them through a friend
Ich kann es nur mit einer Brille lesen	= I can only read it with spectacles
Er kann sie nicht leiden	= He can't stand her
Sie können (= dürfen) rauchen, wenn Sie wollen	= You can smoke if you wish
Ich konnte mit vier Jahren lesen	= I could od. was able to read at the age of four
Sie konnten nicht früher kommen	= They couldn't od. were unable to come any earlier

In den beiden letzten Beispielen ist keine Verwechslung möglich.

Er konnte sie durch einen Freund bekommen	= He was able to get them through a friend

Aber

Er könnte sie durch einen Freund bekommen	= He could get them through a friend

Im Perfekt, auch konditional:

Glücklicherweise habe ich umbuchen können	= Fortunately I was able/have been able to change the booking
Sie hätten uns Bescheid sagen können	= You could have let us know

Und schließlich im Plusquamperfekt:

Sie hatte das Buch nicht finden können	= She had been unable to find the book

Bitten und Vorschläge

Könntest du mir helfen?	= Could you help me?
Könnten Sie vielleicht Freitag kommen?	= Perhaps you could come on Friday?

Unpersönlicher Gebrauch: may, might

Es kann sein, dass er es vergessen hat	= It may be that he has forgotten it, He may have forgotten it
Es könnte sein, dass wir es noch brauchen	= We might still need it
Es könnte ratsam sein, sie anzurufen	= It might be advisable to telephone her
Das kann nicht sein	= That's not posssible, It can't be

(coll.). **2** *unr. tr. V.* (**a**) (beherrschen) know ‹*language*›; be able to play, know how to play ‹*game*›; **sie kann das [gut]** she can do that [well]; **sie kann Mathe/keine Mathe** she can/can't do maths; **er kann etwas auf seinem Gebiet** he has quite a lot of know-how in his field; **hast du die Hausaufgabe gekonnt?** could you do the homework?; (**b**) **etwas/nichts für etw. ~:** be/not be responsible for sth. **3** *unr. itr. V.* (**a**) (fähig sein) **er kann nicht anders** there's nothing else he can do; (es ist seine Art) he can't help it (coll.); (**b**) (Zeit haben) **ich kann heute nicht** I can't today (coll.); (**c**) (ugs.: Kraft haben) **kannst du noch?** can you go on?; (**d**) (ugs.: essen **~**) **ich kann nicht mehr** I couldn't manage any more; (**e**) (ugs.: umgehen **~**) **[gut] mit jmdm. ~:** get on *or* along [well] with sb.

Können *das;* ~s ability; (Kunstfertigkeit) skill

Könner *der;* ~s, ~ expert

konnte /ˈkɔntə/ *1. u. 3. Pers. Sg. Prät. v.* **können**

könnte /ˈkœntə/ *1. u. 3. Pers. Sg. Konjunktiv II v.* **können**

konsekutiv /kɔnzekuˈtiːf/ *Adj.* (Sprachw.) consecutive

konsequent /kɔnzeˈkvɛnt/ **1** *Adj.* (**a**) (folgerichtig) logical; (**b**) (unbeirrbar) consistent. **2** *adv.* (**a**) (folgerichtig) logically; (**b**) (unbeirrbar) consistently; **ein Ziel ~ verfolgen** resolutely and single-mindedly pursue a goal; **~ durchgreifen** take rigorous action

Konsequenz /kɔnzeˈkvɛnts/ *die;* ~, ~en (**a**) (Folge) consequence; **die ~en tragen** take the consequences; **[aus etw.] die ~en ziehen** draw the obvious conclusion [from sth.]; (gezwungenermaßen) accept the obvious consequences [of sth.]; (**b**) *o. Pl.* (Unbeirrbarkeit) resolution; determination; (**c**) *o. Pl.* (Folgerichtigkeit) logicality; (eines Gedankenganges) logical consistency; logicality

konservativ /kɔnzɛrvaˈtiːf/ **1** *Adj.* conservative. **2** *adv.* conservatively

Konservative *der/die; adj. Dekl.* conservative

Konservatorium /kɔnzɛrvaˈtoːriʊm/ *das;* ~s, **Konservatorien** conservatoire; conservatory (Amer.)

*alte Schreibung (vgl. Hinweise auf S. xvi–xvii)

Konserve /kɔnˈzɛrvə/ *die;* ~, ~n preserved food; (in Dosen) canned *or* (Brit.) tinned food; (ugs.: Dose) can; tin (Brit.); **von ~n leben** eat out of cans *or* (Brit.) tins; live on canned *or* (Brit.) tinned food; **Musik aus der ~** (fig. ugs.) canned music (coll.)

Konserven-: ~**büchse** *die,* ~**dose** *die* can; tin (Brit.)

konservieren *tr. V.* preserve; conserve, preserve ‹*building, work of art*›

Konservierung *die;* ~, ~en preservation

Konservierungs-: ~**mittel** *das,* ~**stoff** *der* preservative

konsistent /kɔnzɪsˈtɛnt/ *Adj.* consistent

Konsistenz /kɔnzɪsˈtɛnts/ *die;* ~, ~en consistency

Konsole /kɔnˈzoːlə/ *die;* ~, ~n (**a**) (Archit.) console; (**b**) (Brett) shelf; (Tischchen) console [table]

konsolidieren /kɔnzoliˈdiːrən/ **1** *tr. V.* consolidate. **2** *refl. V.* become consolidated

Konsolidierung *die;* ~, ~en consolidation

Konsonant /kɔnzoˈnant/ *der;* ~en, ~en consonant

Konsorten /kɔnˈzɔrtn̩/ *Pl.* (abwertend) **Meier und ~:** Meier and his lot *or* crowd (coll.); Meier and Co. (coll.)

Konsortium /kɔnˈzɔrtsiʊm/ *das;* ~s, **Konsortien** (Wirtsch.) consortium

Konspiration /kɔnspiraˈtsi̯oːn/ *die;* ~, ~en conspiracy

konspirativ /kɔnspiraˈtiːf/ *Adj.* conspiratorial

konspirieren *itr. V.* conspire, plot (**gegen** against)

konstant /kɔnˈstant/ **1** *Adj.* (**a**) constant; **eine ~e Leistung zeigen** maintain a consistent standard; (**b**) (beharrlich) consistent; persistent. **2** *adv.* (**a**) constantly; (**b**) (beharrlich) consistently; persistently

Konstante *die;* ~, ~n *od. adj. Dekl.* (Math., Physik) constant; (fig.) constant factor (+ *Gen.* in)

konstatieren /kɔnstaˈtiːrən/ *tr. V.* (**a**) establish ‹*facts*›; detect ‹*changes etc.*›; (**b**) (erklären) state

Konstellation /kɔnstɛlaˈtsi̯oːn/ *die;* ~, ~en (**a**) (von Parteien usw.) grouping; (von Umständen) combination; (**b**) (Astron., Astrol.) constellation

konsterniert *Adj.* filled with consternation *pred.*
konstituieren /kɔnstitu'i:rən/ **1** *tr. V.* constitute; set up; **die ∼de Versammlung** the constituent assembly. **2** *refl. V.* be constituted
Konstitution /kɔnstitu'tsi̯o:n/ *die;* ∼, ∼**en** constitution
konstitutionell /kɔnstitutsi̯o'nɛl/ *Adj.* constitutional
konstitutiv /kɔnstitu'ti:f/ *Adj.* (geh.) constitutive; **für etw.** ∼ **sein** be a[n essential] constitutive element of sth.
konstruieren /kɔnstru'i:rən/ *tr. V.* (a) (entwerfen) design; (entwerfen und zusammenbauen) design and construct; (b) (aufbauen, Geom., Sprachw.) construct; **dieses Verb wird mit dem Dativ konstruiert** this verb takes the dative *or* is construed with the dative; (c) (künstlich aufbauen) fabricate; **ein konstruierter Fall** a hypothetical *or* fictitious case; **die Handlung wirkt sehr konstruiert** the plot seems very contrived
Konstrukteur /kɔnstrʊk'tøːɐ̯/ *der;* ∼**s**, ∼**e**, **Konstrukteurin** *die;* ∼, ∼**nen** ▶ 85] designer; design engineer
Konstruktion /kɔnstrʊk'tsi̯o:n/ *die;* ∼, ∼**en** (a) (Aufbau, Geom., Sprachw.) construction; (das Entwerfen) designing; (das Entwerfen und Zusammenbauen) designing and construction; (b) (Entwurf) design; (Bau) construction; structure
Konstruktions·fehler *der* design fault
konstruktiv /kɔnstrʊk'ti:f/ **1** *Adj.* (a) constructive; (b) (Technik) constructional. **2** *adv.* (a) constructively; (b) (Technik) with regard to construction
Konsul /'kɔnzʊl/ *der;* ∼**s**, ∼**n** ▶ 34], ▶ 85] (Dipl., hist.) consul
Konsulat /kɔnzu'la:t/ *das;* ∼**[e]s**, ∼**e** (Dipl., hist.) consulate
Konsultation /kɔnzʊlta'tsi̯o:n/ *die;* ∼, ∼**en** consultation
konsultieren *tr. V.* (auch fig.) consult
Konsum /kɔn'zu:m/ *der;* ∼**s** consumption (**an** + *Dat.* of)
Konsum·artikel *der* (Wirtsch.) consumer item *or* article; ∼ *Pl.* consumer goods
Konsument /kɔnzu'mɛnt/ *der;* ∼**en**, ∼**en**, **Konsumentin** *die;* ∼, ∼**nen** consumer
Konsum·gesellschaft *die* consumer society
Konsum·gut *das; meist Pl.* (Wirtsch.) ⇒ **Konsumartikel**
Konsumgüter·industrie *die* (Wirtsch.) consumer goods industry
konsumieren *tr. V.* consume; (fig.) devour ‹ *book* ›
Konsum-: ∼**terror** *der* (abwertend), ∼**zwang**, *der; o. Pl.* pressure to buy
Kontakt /kɔn'takt/ *der;* ∼**[e]s**, ∼**e** (auch fachspr.) contact; **mit od. zu jmdm.** ∼ **haben, in** ∼ **mit jmdm. stehen** be in contact *or* touch with sb.; **[den]** ∼ **mit jmdm./etw. finden/suchen** establish/try to establish contact with sb./sth.; **den** ∼ **zu jmdm. abbrechen/verlieren** break off contact/lose contact *or* touch with sb.; **mit jmdm.** ∼ **aufnehmen** get into contact with sb.; contact sb.
kontakt-, Kontakt-: ∼**anzeige** *die* contact advertisement; ∼**freudig** *Adj.* sociable; ∼**freudig sein** make friends easily; ∼**linse** *die* contact lens; ∼**mann** *der; Pl.:* ∼**männer** *od.* ∼**leute** (Agent) contact; ∼**schale** *die* ⇒ ∼**linse**; ∼**schwierigkeiten** *Pl.* problems in mixing with others
Kontamination /kɔntamina'tsi̯o:n/ *die;* ∼, ∼**en** (fachspr.) contamination
kontaminieren *tr. V.* (fachspr.) contaminate
Konter /'kɔntɐ/ *der;* ∼**s**, ∼ (a) (Boxen) counter; (b) (Ballspiele, fig.) counter-attack
Konterfei /'kɔntɐfai̯/ *das;* ∼**s**, ∼**s** *od.* ∼**e** (veralt., scherzh.) likeness
kontern *tr., itr. V.* (Boxen) counter; (Ballspiele) counter-attack; (fig.) counter (**mit** with)
Konter-: ∼**revolution** *die* counter-revolution; ∼**schlag** *der* ⇒ **Konter**
Kontext /kɔn'tɛkst/ *der;* ∼**[e]s**, ∼**e** context
Kontinent /kɔnti'nɛnt/ *der;* ∼**[e]s**, ∼**e** continent
kontinental /kɔntinɛn'ta:l/ *Adj.* continental
Kontinental-: ∼**klima** *das* (Geogr.) continental climate; ∼**verschiebung** *die* (Geol.) continental drift

Kontingent /kɔntɪŋ'gɛnt/ *das;* ∼**[e]s**, ∼**e** contingent; (begrenzte Menge) quota
kontinuierlich /kɔntinu'i:ɐ̯lɪç/ **1** *Adj.* steady; continuous. **2** *adv.* steadily
Kontinuität /kɔntinui'tɛ:t/ *die;* ∼: continuity
Konto /'kɔnto/ *das;* ∼**s**, **Konten** *od.* **Konti** account; **ein laufendes** ∼: a current account; **etw. geht auf jmds.** ∼ (ugs.: jmd. ist schuld an etw.) sb. is to blame *or* is responsible for sth.
Konto-: ∼**auszug** *der* (Bankw.) [bank] statement; statement of account; ∼**auszugs·drucker** *der* (Bankw.) statement machine *or* printer; ∼**führungs·gebühr** *die* (Bankw.) bank charges *pl.;* ∼**nummer** *die* account number
Kontor /kɔn'to:ɐ̯/ *das;* ∼**s**, ∼**e** (veralt.) office; *s. auch* **Schlag a**
Konto·stand *der* (Bankw.) balance; state of an/one's account
kontra /'kɔntra/ **1** *Präp. mit Akk.* (Rechtsspr., auch fig.) versus. **2** *Adv.* against
Kontra *das;* ∼**s**, ∼**s** (Kartenspiele) double; ∼ **sagen** *od.* **geben** double; **jmdm.** ∼ **geben** (fig. ugs.) flatly contradict sb.
Kontra·bass, *****Kontra·baß** *der* double bass
Kontrahent /kɔntra'hɛnt/ *der;* ∼**en**, ∼**en** (a) (Gegner) adversary; opponent; (b) (Rechtsw., Kaufmannsspr.: Vertragspartner) contracting party
kontrahieren **1** *itr., refl. V.* (Biol., Med.) contract. **2** *tr. V.* (a) (Biol., Med.) contract; (b) (Rechtsw., Kaufmannsspr.) **Erdgaslieferungen** ∼: contract to supply natural gas
Kontrakt /kɔn'trakt/ *der;* ∼**[e]s**, ∼**e** contract
Kontra·punkt *der* (Musik, fig.) counterpoint
konträr /kɔn'trɛ:ɐ̯/ contrary; opposite
Kontrast /kɔn'trast/ *der;* ∼**[e]s**, ∼**e** contrast; **etw. steht im/in** ∼ **zu etw. anderem** sth. is in contrast with sth. else
kontrastieren *tr., itr. V.* contrast
Kontrast-: ∼**mittel** *das* (Med.) contrast medium ∼**programm** *das* (Rundf., Fernsehen) alternative programme
kontrast·reich *Adj.* rich in *or* full of contrasts *pred.*
Kontroll·abschnitt *der* stub
*****Kontrollampe** ⇒ **Kontrolllampe**
Kontrolle /kɔn'trɔlə/ *die;* ∼, ∼**n** (a) (Überwachung) surveillance; **unter** ∼ **stehen** be under surveillance; (b) (Überprüfung) check; (bei Waren) check; inspection; (bei Lebensmitteln) inspection; **jmdn./etw. einer** ∼ **unterziehen** check sb./sth.; **in eine** ∼ **kommen** be stopped at a police check; **zur** ∼; as a check, (c) (Herrschaft) control; **die** ∼ **über etw./sich** (*Akk.*) **verlieren** lose control of sth./oneself; **außer** ∼ **geraten** get out of control; **etw. unter** ∼ (*Akk.*) **bringen/halten** get *or* bring/keep sth. under control
Kontrolleur /kɔntrɔ'løːɐ̯/ *der;* ∼**s**, ∼**e** inspector
Kontroll-: ∼**gang** *der* tour of inspection; (eines Nachtwächters) round; (eines Polizisten) patrol; ∼**gruppe** *die* (Med. Psych., Soziol.) control group
kontrollieren **1** *tr. V.* (a) (überwachen) check; monitor; **die Regierung** ∼: scrutinize the actions of the government; **die Lebensmittelproduktion wird streng kontrolliert** strict checks are kept *or* made on the production of food; (b) (überprüfen) check; check, inspect ‹ *goods* ›; inspect ‹ *food* ›; **jmdn./etw. auf etw.** (*Akk.*) **[hin]** ∼: check sb./check *or* inspect sth. for sth.; (c) (beherrschen) control. **2** *itr. V.* carry out a check/checks
Kontroll-: *****∼**lampe** *die* pilot light; indicator light; (Warnleuchte) warning light; ∼**punkt** *der* checkpoint; (bei einer Rallye) control [point]; ∼**turm** *der* control tower; ∼**uhr** *die* time clock; (für Wächter) tell-tale clock
kontrovers /kɔntro'vɛrs/ *Adj.* conflicting; (strittig) controversial
Kontroverse *die;* ∼, ∼**n** controversy (**um, über** + *Akk.* about)
Kontur /kɔn'tu:ɐ̯/ *die;* ∼, ∼**en; meist Pl.** contour; outline; ∼ **gewinnen/an** ∼ **verlieren** (fig.) become clearer/fade

Konvention /kɔnvɛnˈtsi̯oːn/ *die;* ~, ~en convention
Konventional·strafe *die* (Rechtsw.) liquidated damages *pl.*
konventionell 1 *Adj.* (a) conventional; (b) (förmlich) formal. **2** *adv.* (a) conventionally; in a conventional way; (b) (förmlich) formally; **hier geht es sehr** ~ **zu** things are very formal here
Konversation /kɔnvɛrzaˈtsi̯oːn/ *die;* ~, ~en conversation; ~ **machen** make conversation
Konversations·lexikon *das* encyclopaedia
Konversion *die;* ~, ~en (fachspr.) conversion
konvertierbar *Adj.* (Wirtsch.) convertible ‹currency›
konvertieren *itr. V.; auch mit sein* (Rel.) be converted
konvex /kɔnˈvɛks/ (Optik) **1** *Adj.* convex. **2** *adv.* convexly
Konvoi /kɔnˈvɔy/ *der;* ~s, ~s (bes. Milit.) convoy; **im** ~ **fahren** travel in convoy
Konzentrat /kɔntsɛnˈtraːt/ *das;* ~[e]s, ~e concentrate
Konzentration /kɔntsɛntraˈtsi̯oːn/ *die;* ~, ~en concentration
Konzentrations-: ~**fähigkeit** *die; o. Pl.* ability to concentrate; powers *pl.* of concentration; ~**lager** *das* (bes. ns.) concentration camp; ~**schwäche** *die* poor powers *pl.* of concentration
konzentrieren 1 *refl. V.* (a) concentrate; **sich auf etw.** *(Akk.)* ~: concentrate on sth.; (b) (gerichtet sein) be concentrated. **2** *tr. V.* concentrate
konzentriert 1 *Adj.* concentrated. **2** *adv.* with concentration; **sehr** ~ **arbeiten** work with great concentration
konzentrisch (Math. fig.) **1** *Adj.* concentric. **2** *adv.* concentrically
Konzept /kɔnˈtsɛpt/ *das;* ~[e]s, ~e (a) (Rohfassung) [rough] draft; (b) **aus dem** ~ **kommen** *od.* **geraten** lose one's thread; **jmdn. aus dem** ~ **bringen** put sb. off his/her stroke; (c) (Programm) programme; (Plan) plan; **jmdm. das** ~ **verderben** (ugs.) ruin sb.'s plans; **jmdm. nicht ins** ~ **passen** (ugs.) not suit sb.'s plans
Konzeption /kɔntsɛpˈtsi̯oːn/ *die;* ~, ~en central idea; (Entwurf) conception
konzeptionslos 1 *Adj.* haphazard. **2** *adv.* haphazardly; with no clear plan
Konzept·papier *das; o. Pl.* rough paper
Konzern /kɔnˈtsɛrn/ *der;* ~[e]s, ~e (Wirtsch.) group [of companies]
Konzert /kɔnˈtsɛrt/ *das;* ~[e]s, ~e (a) (Komposition) concerto; (b) (Veranstaltung) concert; **ins** ~ **gehen** go to a concert
Konzert-: ~**abend** *der* concert evening; ~**agentur** *die* concert artists' agency; ~**flügel** *der* concert grand; ~**meister** *der*, ~**meisterin** *die* ▶ 85 ▮ leader [of a/the orchestra]; concert-master; ~**pianist** *der*, ~**pianistin** *die;* ▶ 85 ▮ concert pianist; ~**saal** *der* concert hall
Konzession /kɔntsɛˈsi̯oːn/ *die;* ~, ~en (a) (Amtsspr.) licence; (b) (Zugeständnis) concession; ~en [an jmdn./etw.] **machen** make concessions [to sb./sth.]
konzessionsbereit *Adj.* ready *or* willing *or* prepared to make concessions *pred.*
konzessiv /kɔntsɛˈsiːf/ *Adj.* (Sprachw.) concessive
Konzil /kɔnˈtsiːl/ *das;* ~s, ~e *od.* ~ien (kath. Kirche) council
konziliant /kɔntsiˈli̯ant/ (geh.) **1** *Adj.* accommodating, obliging. **2** *adv.* accommodatingly; obligingly
konzipieren /kɔntsiˈpiːrən/ *tr. V.* draft ‹speech, essay›; draw up, draft ‹plan, policy, etc.›; design ‹device, car, etc.›
konzis /kɔnˈtsiːs/ **1** *Adj.* concise. **2** *adv.* concisely
Kooperation *die;* ~, ~en cooperation *no indef. art.*
kooperations·bereit *Adj.* ready *or* willing *or* prepared to cooperate *pred.*
kooperativ 1 *Adj.* cooperative. **2** *adv.* cooperatively
kooperieren *tr. V.* cooperate
Koordinate *die;* ~, ~n coordinate
Koordinaten-: ~**achse** *die* coordinate axis; ~**kreuz** *das* coordinate axes *pl.;* ~**system** *das* system of coordinates

Koordination *die;* ~, ~en coordination
koordinieren *tr. V.* coordinate
Koordinierung *die;* ~, ~en coordination
Kopf /kɔpf/ *der;* ~[e]s, **Köpfe** /ˈkœpfə/ (a) ▶ 326 ▮ head; **jmdm. den** ~ **waschen** wash sb.'s hair; (fig. ugs.: jmdn. zurechtweisen) give sb. a good talking-to (sl.); give sb. what for (sl.); [um] **einen ganzen/halben** ~ **größer sein** be a good head/a few inches taller; **die Köpfe zusammenstecken** go into a huddle; **sie haben sich die Köpfe heiß geredet** the conversation/debate became heated; ~ **an** ~ (im Wettlauf) neck and neck; **den** ~ **einziehen** duck; (fig.: sich einschüchtern lassen) be intimidated; **und wenn du dich auf den** ~ **stellst** you can talk until you're blue in the face; **ich werde/er wird dir nicht gleich den** ~ **abreißen** (ugs.) I'm/he's not going to bite your head off; **jmdm. schwirrt/raucht der** ~: sb.'s head is spinning; **nicht wissen, wo einem der** ~ **steht** not know whether one is coming or going; **einen dicken** ~ **haben** (vom Alkohol) have a thick head (coll.) *or* a hangover; **jmdm.** *od.* **jmdn. den** ~ **kosten** cost sb. dearly; (jmdn. das Leben kosten) cost sb. his/her life; ~ **hoch!** chin up!; **den** ~ **hängen lassen** become disheartened; ~ **und Kragen riskieren** risk one's neck; **den** ~ **hinhalten [müssen]** (ugs.) [have to] face the music; [have to] take the blame *or* (coll.) rap; **den** ~ **aus der Schlinge ziehen** avoid any adverse consequences *or* (coll.) the rap; **den** ~ **in den Sand stecken** bury one's head in the sand; **den** ~ **hoch tragen** hold one's head high; **jmdm. den** ~ **zurechtrücken** (ugs.) bring sb. to his/her senses; **sich [gegenseitig] die Köpfe einschlagen** be at each other's throats; **sich** *(Dat.)* **an den** ~ **fassen** *od.* **greifen** (ugs.) throw up one's hands in despair; **jmdm. Beleidigungen an den** ~ **werfen** hurl insults at sb.; **sein Geld auf den** ~ **hauen** (ugs.) blow one's money (coll.); **etw. auf den** ~ **stellen** (ugs.) turn sth. upside down; **auf dem** ~ **stehen** (ugs.) be upside down; ~ **stehen** stand on one's head; (ugs.: überrascht sein) be bowled over; **den Ablauf der Ereignisse auf den** ~ **stellen** get the order of events completely *or* entirely wrong; **jmdm. auf dem** ~ **herumtanzen** (ugs.) treat sb. just as one likes; do what one likes with sb.; **jmdm. auf den** ~ **spucken können** (salopp scherzh.) be head and shoulders taller than sb.; **er ist nicht auf den** ~ **gefallen** (ugs.) there are no flies on him (fig. coll.); **jmdm. etw. auf den** ~ **zusagen** say sth. to sb.'s face; **jmdm. in den** *od.* **zu** ~**e steigen** go to sb.'s head; **mit dem** ~ **durch die Wand wollen** (ugs.) /sich *(Dat.)* **den** ~ **einrennen** beat *or* run one's head against a brick wall; **etw. über jmds.** ~ **[hin]weg entscheiden/über jmds.** ~ **hinwegreden** decide sth./talk over sb.'s head; **jmdm. über den** ~ **wachsen** (ugs.) outgrow sb.; (jmdn. überfordern) become too much for sb.; **bis über den** ~ **in etw.** *(Dat.)* **stecken** (ugs.) be up to one's ears in sth.; **es geht um** ~ **und Kragen** (ugs.) it's a matter of life and death; **sein um** ~ **und Kragen reden** (ugs.) risk one's neck with careless talk; **von** ~ **bis Fuß** from head to toe *or* foot; **jmdn. vor den** ~ **stoßen** (ugs.) offend sb.; *s. auch* **Hand c**; (b) (Person) person; **ein kluger/fähiger** ~ **sein** be a clever/able man/woman; **pro** ~: per head *or* person; (c) (geistige Leitung) **er ist der** ~ **der Firma** he's the brains of the firm; **die führenden Köpfe der Wirtschaft** the leading minds in the field of economics; (d) (Wille) **seinen** ~ **durchsetzen** make sb. do what one wants; **muss es immer nach deinem** ~ **gehen?** why must you always decide?; (e) (Verstand) mind; head; **er hat die Zahlen im** ~ (ugs.) he has the figures in his head; **er hat nur Autos im** ~ (ugs.) all he ever thinks about is cars; **was wohl in ihrem** ~ **vorgeht?** what's going on in her mind?; **sie ist nicht ganz richtig im** ~ (ugs.) she's not quite right in the head; **einen klaren/kühlen** ~ **bewahren** *od.* **behalten** keep a cool head; keep one's head; **ich habe den** ~ **voll mit anderen Dingen** I've got a lot of other things on my mind; **den** ~ **verlieren** lose one's head; **jmdm. den** ~ **verdrehen** (ugs.) steal sb.'s heart [away]; **sich** *(Dat.)* **den** ~ **zerbrechen** (ugs.) rack one's brains ‹über + *Akk.* over›; (sich Sorgen machen) worry ‹über + *Akk.* about›; **aus dem** ~ (aus dem Gedächtnis) off the top of one's head; **das geht** *od.* **will ihm nicht aus dem** ~: he can't get it out of his mind; **sich**

(*Dat.*) **etw. aus dem** ~ **schlagen** put sth. out of one's head; **sich** (*Dat.*) **etw. durch den** ~ **gehen lassen** think sth. over; **jmdm. im** ~ **herumgehen** (ugs.) go round and round in sb.'s mind; **jmdm./sich etw. in den** ~ **setzen** put sth. into sb.'s head/get sth. into one's head; **etw. im** ~ **[aus]rechnen** work sth. out in one's head; **was man nicht im** ~ **hat, muss man in den Beinen haben** a short memory makes work for the legs; **jmdm. geht** *od.* **will etw. nicht in den** ~ **[hinein]** (ugs.) sb. can't get sth. into his/her head; (**f**) (von Nadeln, Nägeln, Blumen) head; (von Pfeifen) bowl; (**g**) **ein** ~ **Salat/Blumenkohl/Rotkohl** a lettuce/cauliflower/red cabbage; (**h**) (oberer Teil) head; (**i**) (auf Münzen) ~ **[oder Zahl?]** heads [or tails?]

kopf-, Kopf-: ~**-an-Kopf-Rennen** *das* (Sport, auch fig.) neck-and-neck race (*Gen.* between); ~**arbeit** *die* brain-work; intellectual work; ~**bahnhof** *der* terminal station; ~**ball** *der* (Fußball) header; ~**ball·tor** *das* (Fußball) headed goal; ~**bedeckung** *die* head-covering; **ohne** ~**bedeckung** without anything on one's head; without a hat

Köpfchen /'kœpfçən/ *das;* ~**s**, ~ (**a**) little head; (**b**) (Findigkeit) brains *pl.;* ~ **muss man haben** you've got to have it up here (coll.); ~, ~**!** clever, eh? (coll.)

köpfen /'kœpfn/ *tr. V.* (**a**) decapitate; (hinrichten) behead; (fig.) break *or* crack open ‹*bottle*›; slice the top off ‹*egg*›; (**b**) (Fußball) head; **das 2:0** ~**:** head [in] the goal to make it 2–0

kopf-, Kopf-: ~**ende** *das* head end; ~**form** *die* head shape; shape of the head; ~**geld** *das* reward; bounty; ~**haut** *die* ▶ 326 | [skin of the] scalp; ~**höhe** *die:* **in** ~**höhe** at head height; ~**hörer** *der* headphones *pl.*

-köpfig *Adj.* (**a**) -headed; (**b**) **eine dreiköpfige/ fünfköpfige Familie** a family of three/five

kopf-, Kopf-: ~**jäger** *der* headhunter; ~**kissen** *das* pillow; ~**kissen·bezug** *der* pillow-case; ~**länge** *die:* **mit einer** ~**länge Vorsprung** by a head; ~**lastig** *Adj.* down by the head *pred.;* (fig.) top-heavy; ~**los** **1** *Adj.* (**a**) rash; (in Panik) panic-stricken; (**b**) (ohne Kopf) headless; **2** *adv.* rashly; ~**los davonrennen/ umherrennen** flee in panic/run round in a panic; ~**nicken** *das;* ~**s** nod [of the head]; ~**nuss,** ***~**nuß** *die* (ugs.) rap on the head with one's *or* the knuckles; ~**rechnen** *das* mental arithmetic; ~**salat** *der* cabbage *or* head lettuce; ~**schmerz** *der;* ▶ 329 | *meist Pl.* headache; ~**schmerzen haben** have a headache *sing.;* **sich** (*Dat.*) **über etw.** (*Akk.*) *od.* **wegen etw. keine** ~**schmerzen machen** (ugs.) not worry about *or* concern oneself about sth.; **etw. bereitet** *od.* **macht jmdm.** ~**schmerzen** (ugs.) sth. weighs on sb.'s mind; ~**schmuck** *der* headdress; ~**schuppen** *Pl.* dandruff *sing;* ~**schuss,** ***~**schuß** *der* bullet wound in the head; **durch einen** ~**schuss getötet werden** be killed by a bullet in the head; ~**schütteln** *das;* ~**s** shake of the head; **ein allgemeines** ~**schütteln auslösen** cause everyone to shake their heads; ~**schutz** *der* (Sport) protective headgear; ~**sprung** *der* header; **einen** ~**sprung machen** dive head first; ~**stand** *der* headstand;***~**stehen** ⇒ **Kopf a;** ~**steinpflaster** *das* cobblestones *pl.;* ~**stütze** *die* headrest; ~**tuch** *das* headscarf; ~**über** /-'--/ *Adv.* head first; (fig.: ohne Zögern) headlong; ~**verband** *der* head bandage; ~**verletzung** *die* head injury; ~**wäsche** *die* hair-wash; shampoo; ~**weh** *das; o. Pl.* (ugs.) headache; ~**weh haben** have a headache; ~**zerbrechen** *das;* ~**s: etw. bereitet** *od.* **macht jmdm.** ~**zerbrechen** sb. has to rack his/her brains about sth.; (etw. macht jmdm. Sorgen) sth. is a worry to sb.; **sich** (*Dat.*) **über etw.** (*Akk.*) **[kein]** ~**zerbrechen machen** [not] worry about sth.

Kopie /ko'pi:/ *die;* ~, ~**n** (**a**) copy; (Imitation) imitation; (**b**) (Durchschrift) carbon copy; (**c**) (Fotokopie) photocopy; (**d**) (Fot., Film) print

kopieren *tr. V.* (**a**) copy; (imitieren) imitate; (**b**) (fotokopieren) photocopy; (**c**) (Fot., Film) print

Kopierer *der;* ~**s**, ~ (ugs.) [photo]copier

Kopier-: ~**gerät** *das* photocopier; photocopying machine; ~**schutz** *der* (DV) copy protection; ~**stift** *der* indelible pencil

Kopilot *der;* ~**en**, ~**en, Kopilotin** *die;* ~, ~**nen** (Flugw.) co-pilot; (Motorsport) co-driver

Koppel *die;* ~, ~**n** (**a**) (Weide) paddock; **auf** *od.* **in der** ~**:** in the paddock; (**b**) (Hunde~) pack

koppeln *tr. V.* (**a**) dock ‹*spacecraft*›; couple [up] ‹*railway carriage, trailers, etc.*› (**an** + *Akk.* to); (**b**) (verbinden) link; couple ‹*circuits, systems, etc.*›; **etw. an etw.** (*Akk.*) ~**:** link sth. to sth.; **mit etw. gekoppelt sein** be associated with sth.

Kopplung *die;* ~, ~**en;** ⇒ **koppeln:** docking; coupling [up]; linking; coupling

Koproduktion *die;* ~, ~**en** co-production; joint production

Koproduzent *der;* ~**en**, ~**en** co-producer

Kopulation /kopula'tsio:n/ *die;* ~, ~**en** copulation

kopulieren *itr. V.* copulate

kor /ko:ɐ̯/ ⇒ **küren; kiesen**

Koralle /ko'ralə/ *die;* ~, ~**n** coral

korallen-, Korallen-: ~**bank** *die; Pl.* ~**bänke** coral reef; ~**fischer** *der* coral fisherman; ~**insel** *die* coral island; ~**riff** *das* coral reef; ~**rot** *Adj.* coral-red

Koran /ko'ra:n/ *der;* ~**s**, ~**e** Koran

Korb /kɔrp/ *der;* ~**es, Körbe** /'kœrbə/ (**a**) basket; (Last~ auf einem Tier) pannier; (Bienen~) hive; (Förder~) cage; **ein** ~ **Kartoffeln** a basket[ful] of potatoes; (**b**) (Gondel) basket; (**c**) (Korbball) net; (Basketball) basket; (Treffer) goal; (**d**) *o. Pl.* (Flechtwerk) wicker[work]; (**e**) **jmdm. einen** ~ **geben** turn sb. down; **einen** ~ **bekommen** be turned down

Korb·ball *der; o. Pl.* netball

Körbchen /'kœrpçən/ *das;* ~**s**, ~ (**a**) [little] basket; **husch, husch ins** ~ (fam.) time for bye-bye[s] *or* beddy-byes (child lang.); (**b**) (des Büstenhalters) cup

Korb-: ~**flasche** *die* wicker bottle; ~**macher** *der* ▶ 85 | basket-maker; ~**möbel** *das* piece of wicker[work] furniture; ~**möbel** *Pl.* wickerwork furniture *sing.*

Kord /kɔrt/ *der;* ~**[e]s** (**a**) corduroy; cord; (**b**) ⇒ **Kord·samt**

Kordel /'kɔrdl/ *die;* ~, ~**n** (**a**) cord; (**b**) (landsch.: Bindfaden) string

Kord·hose *die* corduroy *or* cord trousers *pl.*

Kordon /kɔr'dõ, österr.: -'do:n/ *der;* ~**s**, ~**s** *od.* österr.: ~**e** cordon

Kord·samt *der* cord velvet

Korea /ko're:a/ (*das*); ~**s** Korea

Koreaner /kore'a:nɐ/ *der;* ~**s**, ~, **Koreanerin** *die;* ~, ~**nen** ▶ 388 | Korean

koreanisch *Adj.* ▶ 388 |, ▶ 487 | Korean

Koriander /ko'riandɐ/ *der;* ~**s**, ~**:** coriander

Korinthe /ko'rɪntə/ *die;* ~, ~**n** currant

Kork /kɔrk/ *der;* ~**s**, ~**e** cork

Kork·eiche *die* cork-oak

Korken *der;* ~**s**, ~**:** cork

Korken·zieher *der* corkscrew

Kormoran /kɔrmo'ra:n/ *der;* ~**s**, ~**e** cormorant

Korn[1] *der;* /kɔrn/ *das;* ~**[e]s, Körner** /'kœrnɐ/ (**a**) (Frucht) seed; grain; (Getreide~) grain [of corn]; (Pfeffer~) corn; (**b**) *o. Pl.* (Getreide) corn; grain; **das** ~ **steht gut** the grain harvest looks promising; (**c**) (Salz~, Sand~) grain; (Hagel~) stone; (**d**) *Pl.* ~**e** (an Handfeuerwaffen) front sight; foresight; **etw./jmdn. aufs** ~ **nehmen** take aim at *or* draw a bead on sth./sb.; (fig. ugs.) attack sth./start to keep close tabs on sb. (coll.)

Korn[2] *der;* ~**[e]s**, ~ (ugs.) corn schnapps; corn liquor (Amer.)

korn-, Korn-: ~**ähre** *die* ear of corn; ~**blume** *die* cornflower; ~**blumen·blau** *Adj.* cornflower [blue]

Körnchen /'kœrnçən/ *das;* ~**s**, ~ (Frucht) tiny seed *or* grain; (von Sand usw.) [tiny] grain; granule; **ein** ~ **Wahrheit** (fig.) a grain of truth

körnen /'kœrnən/ *tr. V.* (**a**) granulate; **gekörnte Brühe** stock granules *pl.* (*for* soup); (**b**) (Handw.: markieren) punch

Körperteile

Im Englischen verwendet man ein Possessivum (**my, his, your** usw.) für Körperteile viel häufiger, auch zum Beispiel für die, die zum Subjekt des Satzes gehören:

Er hob die Hand = He raised his hand
Sie schloss die Augen = She closed her eyes

Ebenso in Fällen, wo man im Deutschen einen Dativ der Person (auch ein Reflexivum), gefolgt von einem Akkusativobjekt, verwendet:

Sie schloss ihm die Augen = She closed his eyes

Du hast ihm fast den Arm ausgerenkt = You nearly dislocated his arm

Kannst du mir den Rücken eincremen? = Can you put some cream on my back [for me]?

Ich habe mir das Bein gebrochen = I've broken my leg

Er hat sich den Arm ausgerenkt = He dislocated his arm

Sie hat sich den Kopf am Balken angestoßen = She hit her head on the beam

Sie fuhr mir/sich mit der Hand über die Stirn = She passed her hand over my/her forehead

Verwendet man diese Konstruktion mit einem Substantiv statt dem Personalpronomen im Dativ, so entspricht dem im Englischen Genitiv:

Sie massierte ihrem Sohn den Rücken = She massaged her son's back

Die deutsche unpersönliche Konstruktion hat keine direkte Entsprechung im Englischen. Auch hier verwendet man ein Possessivum:

Mir dreht sich der Kopf = My head is spinning
Es kribbelte mir in den Füßen = My feet were tingling

Siehe auch □ **Krankheiten und Schmerzen**

Körner ⇒ **Korn**
Korn·feld *das* cornfield
körnig /'kœrnɪç/ *Adj.* granular
Korn·kammer *die* granary
Korona /ko'ro:na/ *die;* ~, **Koronen** (**a**) (Astron.) corona; (**b**) (fig.) crowd (coll.)
Körper /'kœrpɐ/ *der;* ~s, ~ (**a**) body; ~ **und Geist** body and mind; **am ganzen** ~ **frieren/zittern** be [freezing] cold/shake all over; (**b**) (Rumpf) trunk; body; (**c**) (Physik, Chemie) body; (**d**) (Geom.) solid body; solid
körper-, Körper-: ~**bau** *der; o. Pl.* physique; ~**behaarung** *die* body hair *no indef. art.;* ~**beherrschung** *die* body control; ~**behindert** *Adj.* physically handicapped *or* disabled; ~**behinderte** *der/die* physically handicapped *or* disabled person; ~**fülle** *die* corpulence; ~**geruch** *der* body odour; BO (coll.); ~**gewicht** *das* ▶ 228 | body weight; ~**größe** *die* ▶ 277 | height; ~**haltung** *die* posture; ~**hygiene** *die* ⇒ ~**pflege;** ~**kontakt** *der* (Psych.) physical contact; ~**kraft** *die* physical strength
körperlich 1 *Adj.* physical. **2** *adv.* physically; ~ [**hart**] **arbeiten** do [hard] physical work
Körper-: ~**maße** *Pl.* measurements; ~**pflege** *die* body care *no art.;* (Reinigung) personal hygiene
Körperschaft *die;* ~, ~**en** (Rechtsw.) corporation; corporate body; ~ **des öffentlichen Rechts** public corporation
Körper-: ~**spray** *der od. das* aerosol deodorant; deodorant spray; ~**teil** *der* part of the/one's body; ~**temperatur** *die* body temperature; ~**verletzung** *die* (Rechtsw.) bodily harm *no indef. art.;* **schwere/leichte** ~**verletzung** grievous/actual bodily harm; ~**wärme** *die* body heat
Korpora ⇒ **Korpus²**
Korps /ko:ɐ̯/ *das;* ~ /ko:ɐ̯(s)/, ~ /ko:ɐ̯s/ (Milit.) corps
korpulent /kɔrpu'lɛnt/ *Adj.* corpulent
Korpulenz /kɔrpu'lɛnts/ *die;* ~: corpulence
Korpus¹ /'kɔrpʊs/ *der;* ~, ~**se** (usg. scherzh.) body
Korpus² *das;* ~, **Korpora** /'kɔrpora/ (**a**) (Sprachw.) corpus; (**b**) *o. Pl.* (Musik) body
korrekt /kɔ'rɛkt/ **1** *Adj.* correct; **es wäre** ~ **gewesen, ...:** the correct thing would have been ... **2** *adv.* correctly
korrekter·weise *Adv.* to be [strictly] correct
Korrektheit *die;* ~: correctness
Korrektor /kɔ'rɛktor/ *der;* ~s, ~**en** /-'to:rən/, **Korrektorin** *die;* ~, ~**nen** ▶ 85 | proof-reader
Korrektur /kɔrɛk'tu:ɐ̯/ *die;* ~, ~**en** (**a**) correction; (von Ansichten usw.) revision; (**b**) (Druckw.) proof-reading; (Verbesserung) proof-correction; ~ **lesen** read/correct the proofs
Korrektur-: ~**abzug** *der,* ~**fahne** *die* galley [proof]; ~**zeichen** *das* proof-correction mark

Korrespondent /kɔrɛspɔn'dɛnt/ *der;* ~**en**, ~**en**, **Korrespondentin** *die;* ~, ~**nen** (**a**) (Zeitungsw.) correspondent; (**b**) (Wirtsch.) correspondence clerk
Korrespondenz /kɔrɛspɔn'dɛnts/ *die;* ~, ~**en** correspondence; **die** ~ **erledigen** deal with the correspondence; **in** ~ **mit jmdm. stehen** correspond with sb.
korrespondieren *itr. V.* (**a**) correspond (**mit** with); (**b**) (fig. geh.) correspond (**mit** to, with)
Korridor /'kɔrido:ɐ̯/ *der;* ~**s**, ~**e** corridor
korrigierbar *Adj.* correctable
korrigieren /kɔri'gi:rən/ *tr. V.* correct; revise ⟨opinion, view⟩
Korrosion /kɔro'zio:n/ *die;* ~, ~**en** (fachspr.) corrosion
korrumpieren /kɔrʊm'pi:rən/ *tr. V.* corrupt
korrupt /kɔ'rʊpt/ *Adj.* corrupt
Korruption /kɔrʊp'tsio:n/ *die;* ~, ~**en** corruption
Korsett /kɔr'zɛt/ *das;* ~**s**, ~**s** *od.* ~**e** corset; (fig.) straitjacket
Korso /'kɔrzo/ *der;* ~**s**, ~**s** procession
Kortison /kɔrti'zo:n/ *das;* ~**s** (Med.) cortisone
Koryphäe /kory'fɛ:ə/ *die;* ~, ~**n** eminent authority; distinguished expert
koscher /'ko:ʃɐ/ *Adj.* (auch fig. ugs.) kosher
K.-o.-Schlag *der* (Boxen) knockout punch
Kose·form *die* familiar form
kosen /'ko:zn̩/ (dichter. veralt.) **1** *tr. V.* caress. **2** *itr. V.* **mit jmdm.** ~: caress sb.
Kose·name *der* pet name
K.-o.-Sieg *der* (Boxen) knockout victory; victory by a knockout
Kosinus /'ko:zinʊs/ *der;* ~, ~ *od.* ~**se** (Math.) cosine
Kosmetik /kɔs'me:tɪk/ *die;* ~ (**a**) beauty culture *no art.;* (**b**) (fig.) cosmetic procedures *pl.*
Kosmetika ⇒ **Kosmetikum**
Kosmetiker *der;* ~**s**, ~, **Kosmetikerin** *die;* ~, ~**nen** ▶ 85 | cosmetician; beautician
Kosmetik·salon *der* beauty salon
Kosmetikum /kɔs'me:tikʊm/ *das;* ~**s**, **Kosmetika** cosmetic
kosmetisch *Adj.* (auch fig.) cosmetic
kosmisch /'kɔsmɪʃ/ *Adj.* cosmic
Kosmologie /kɔsmolo'gi:/ *die;* ~, ~**n** cosmology
Kosmonaut /kɔsmo'naʊt/ *der;* ~**en**, ~**en**, **Kosmonautin** *die;* ~, ~**nen** cosmonaut
Kosmopolit /kɔsmopo'li:t/ *der;* ~**en**, ~**en**, **Kosmopolitin** *die;* ~, ~**nen** (geh.) cosmopolitan

kosmopolitisch *Adj.* cosmopolitan

Kosmos /'kɔsmɔs/ *der;* ~ cosmos

Kosovo·albaner /'kɔsɔvo.../ *der* Kosovo Albanian

Kost /kɔst/ *die;* ~ food; **geistige** ~ (fig.) intellectual nourishment; **leichte/schwere** ~ (fig.) easy/heavy going; ~ **und Logis** board and lodging

kostbar 1 *Adj.* valuable; precious ‹*time*›. 2 *adv.* expensively ‹*dressed*›; luxuriously ‹*decorated*›

Kostbarkeit *die;* ~, ~en (a) (Sache) treasure; precious object; (b) *o. Pl.* (Eigenschaft) value

kosten[1] 1 *tr. V.* (a) (probieren) taste; try; sample; (b) (geh.: empfinden) taste; (fig. iron.) have a taste of. 2 *itr. V.* (probieren) have a taste; **von etw.** ~: have a taste of *or* taste sth.

kosten[2] *tr. V.* (a) ▶216│ cost; **wieviel kostet .../was kostet ...?** how much/what does ... cost?; how much is ...?; **koste es od. es koste, was es wolle** whatever the cost; **sich etw. etwas** ~ **lassen** (ugs.) spend a fair bit of money on sth.; (b) (erfordern) take; cost ‹*lives*›; **viel Arbeit** ~: take a great deal of work; (c) (Verlust nach sich ziehen) **jmdn. od. jmdm. etw.** ~: cost sb. sth.

Kosten *Pl.* cost *sing.;* costs; (Auslagen) expenses; (Rechtsw.) costs; **die** ~ **tragen, für die** ~ **aufkommen** bear the cost[s]; **auf seine** ~ **kommen** cover one's costs; (fig.) get one's money's worth; **auf jmds.** ~: at sb.'s expense; **auf** ~ **einer Sache** (*Gen.*) at the expense of sth.

kosten-, Kosten-: ~**aufwand** *der* expense; cost; **mit einem** ~**aufwand von ...:** at a cost of ...; ~**deckend** *Adj.* that covers/cover [one's] costs *postpos., not pred.;* ~**ersparnis** *die* cost saving; ~**erstattung** *die* reimbursement of costs; ~**frage** *die* question of cost; ~**los** 1 *Adj.* free; 2 *adv.* free of charge; ~**pflichtig** 1 *Adj.* with costs *postpos.;* 2 *adv.* **eine Klage** ~**pflichtig abweisen** dismiss a case with costs; **ein Auto** ~**pflichtig abschleppen** tow a car away at the owner's expense; ~**punkt** *der:* ~**punkt?** (ugs.) how much is it/are they?; ~**sparend** *Adj.* (Wirtsch.) cost-saving; ~**voranschlag** *der* estimate

köstlich /'kœstlɪç/ 1 *Adj.* (a) delicious; (b) (unterhaltsam) delightful. 2 *adv.* (a) ‹*taste*› delicious; (b) **sich** ~ **amüsieren/unterhalten** enjoy oneself enormously (coll.)

Köstlichkeit *die;* ~, ~en (a) (Sache) delicacy; **eine literarische** ~: a literary gem; (b) *o. Pl.* (geh.: Eigenschaft) deliciousness

Kost·probe *die;* ~, ~n taste; (fig.) sample

kost·spielig /-ʃpiːlɪç/ 1 *Adj.* expensive; costly. 2 *adv.* expensively

Kostüm /kɔs'tyːm/ *das;* ~s, ~e (a) costume; (b) (Mode) suit

Kostüm-: ~**ball** *der* fancy-dress ball; ~**bildner** *der,* ~**bildnerin** *die* (Theater, Film) costume-designer

kostümieren *tr. V.* **jmdn./sich** ~: dress sb. up/dress [oneself] up; **wie hatte er sich kostümiert?** what was he dressed [up] as?

Kostüm-: ~**probe** *die* (Theater) dress rehearsal; ~**verleih** *der* [theatrical] costume agency

Kost·verächter *der* **in kein** ~ **sein** (scherzh.) be fond of one's food; (fig.) be one for the ladies

K.-o.-System *das* (Sport) knockout system

Kot /koːt/ *der;* ~[e]s, ~e excrement

Kotangens /'koːtangɛns/ *der;* ~, ~ (Math.) cotangent

Kotelett /kɔt'lɛt/ *das;* ~s, ~s chop; (vom Nacken) cutlet

Koteletten *Pl.* side-whiskers

koten /'koːtn̩/ *itr. V.* (Zool.) defecate

Köter /'køːtɐ/ *der;* ~s, ~ (abwertend) cur; tyke

Kot·flügel *der* (Kfz-W.) wing

Kotze /'kɔtsə/ *die;* ~ (derb) vomit; puke (coarse)

kotzen *itr. V.* (derb) puke (coarse); throw up (coll.); **das ist/ich finde ihn zum Kotzen** it/he makes me sick; it/he makes me want to puke (coarse)

kotzübel *Adj.* **mir ist** ~ (derb) I feel as if I'm going to throw up (coll.) *or* (coarse) puke

KP *Abk.* **Kommunistische Partei** CP

Krabbe /'krabə/ *die;* ~, ~n (a) (Zool.) crab; (b) (Garnele) shrimp; (größer) prawn

Krabbel·alter *das* (ugs.) crawling stage

krabbeln /'krabl̩n/ *itr. V.; mit sein* crawl

Krach /krax/ *der;* ~[e]s, **Kräche** /'krɛçə/ (a) *o. Pl.* (Lärm) noise; row; ~ **machen** make a noise *or* (coll.) a row; be noisy; (b) (lautes Geräusch) crash; bang; (c) (ugs.: Streit) row; **mit jmdm.** ~ **anfangen/kriegen** start/have a row with sb. (coll.); ~ **machen od. schlagen** (ugs.) kick up *or* make a fuss; (d) (ugs.: Börsen~) crash

krachen 1 *itr. V.* (a) ‹*thunder*› crash; ‹*shot*› ring out; ‹*floorboard*› creak; ~**de Kälte/**~**der Frost** (fig.) bitter cold/heavy frost; (b) *mit sein* (ugs.: bersten) ‹*ice*› crack; ‹*bed*› collapse; ‹*trousers, dress, etc.*› split; (c) *mit sein* (ugs.) krachend auftreffen) crash; **die Tür krachte ins Schloss** the door banged *or* slammed shut; (d) (ugs.: Bankrott machen) crash; (e) (*unpers.*) **an der Kreuzung kracht es dauernd** there are frequent crashes at that junction; **sonst krachts!** (fig. ugs.) or there'll be trouble. 2 *refl. V.* (ugs.) row (coll.); have a row (coll.)

Kracher *der;* ~s, ~ (ugs.: Knallkörper) banger

krächzen /'krɛçtsn̩/ *itr. V.* ‹*raven, crow*› caw; ‹*parrot*› squawk; ‹*person*› croak; (fig.) ‹*loudspeaker etc.*› crackle and splutter

Kräcker /'krɛkɐ/ *der;* ~s, ~: ⇒ **Cracker**

kraft /kraft/ *Präp.* + *Gen.* (Amtsspr.) ~ **[meines] Amtes** by virtue of my office; ~ **Gesetzes** by law; ~ **[des] Gesetzes hat der Richter ihn zum Tode verurteilt** as empowered by the law, the judge sentenced him to death

Kraft *die;* ~, **Kräfte** /'krɛftə/ (a) strength; **geistige/schöpferische Kräfte** mental/creative powers; **unter Aufbietung aller Kräfte** applying all one's energies; **jmds. Kräfte übersteigen** be too much for sb.; **wieder bei Kräften sein** have [got] one's strength back; **bei Kräften bleiben** keep one's strength up; **mit letzter** ~: with one's last ounce of strength; **mit frischer** ~: with renewed energy; **aus eigener** ~: by oneself *or* one's own efforts; **ich werde tun, was in meinen Kräften steht** I shall do everything [with]in my power; **mit vereinten Kräften sollte es gelingen** if we join forces *or* combine our efforts we should succeed; **nach [besten] Kräften** to the best of one's ability; (b) (Wirksamkeit) power; (c) (Arbeits~) employee; (in einer Fabrik) employee; worker; **Kräfte** employees/workers; personnel *pl.;* (Angestellte auch) staff *pl.;* (d) *Pl.* (Gruppe) forces; (e) (Physik) force; **die treibende** ~ (fig.) the driving force; (f) (Seemannsspr.) **volle/halbe** ~ **voraus!** full/half speed ahead!; (g) *in* **außer** ~ **setzen** repeal ‹*law*›; countermand ‹*order*›; **außer** ~ **sein/treten** no longer be/cease to be in force; **in** ~ **treten/sein/bleiben** come into/be in/remain in force

Kraft-: ~**akt** *der* feat of strength; (im Zirkus usw.) strongman act; ~**aufwand** *der* effort; ~**ausdruck** *der* swear word; ~**brühe** *die* strong meat broth

Kräfte·verhältnis *das* (bes. Politik) balance of power

Kraft·fahrer *der* ▶85│ (bes. Amtsspr.) driver; motorist

Kraft·fahrzeug *das;* ~[e]s, ~e (bes. Amtsspr.) motor vehicle

Kraftfahrzeug-: ~**brief** *der* vehicle registration document; logbook (Brit.); ~**mechaniker** *der* ▶85│ motor mechanic; ~**schein** *der* vehicle registration document; ~**steuer** *die* vehicle or road tax

Kraft·feld *das* (Physik) force field

kräftig /'krɛftɪç/ 1 *Adj.* (a) strong ‹*person*›; strong, powerful ‹*arms, voice*›; vigorous ‹*plant, shoot*›; (b) (fest) powerful, hefty, hard ‹*blow, kick, etc.*›; firm ‹*handshake*›; (c) (ausgeprägt) strong ‹*breeze, high-pressure area*›; considerable ‹*increase*›; **einen** ~**en Schluck nehmen** take a deep drink *or* (coll.) good swig; **eine** ~**e Tracht [Prügel]** a good hiding (coll.); a sound beating; (d) (intensiv) strong, powerful ‹*smell, taste, etc.*›; bold ‹*pattern*›; strong ‹*colour*›; (e) (gehaltvoll) nourishing ‹*soup, bread, meal, etc.*›; **etw. Kräftiges essen** eat a good nourishing meal; (f) (grob) strong ‹*language*›; coarse ‹*expression, oath, etc.*›. 2 *adv.* (a) strongly, powerfully ‹*built*›; ‹*hit, kick, press, push*› hard; ‹*sneeze*› loudly ‹*rain, snow*› heavily; ‹*eat*› heartily; ‹*sing*› lustily; **etw.** ~ **schütteln** shake sth. vigorously; give sth. a good shake; **die Preise sind** ~ **gestiegen** prices have risen steeply; **dem Alkohol** ~

zusprechen hit the bottle in a big way (coll.); **jmdm.** ∼ **die Meinung sagen** give sb. a piece of one's mind

kräftigen *tr. V.* ⟨*holiday, air, etc.*⟩ invigorate; ⟨*food etc.*⟩ fortify; **sich** ∼**:** build up one's strength

Kräftigung *die;* ∼, ∼**en** strengthening

Kräftigungs·mittel *das* tonic

kraft-, Kraft-: ∼**los** *Adj.* weak; feeble; (fig.) weak ⟨*sun*⟩; ∼**losigkeit** *die;* ∼**:** weakness; feebleness; ∼**mei·er** *der;* ∼**s,** ∼ (ugs.: abwertend) muscleman; ∼**meierei** *die;* ∼ (ugs. abwertend) playing the muscleman; ∼**probe** *die* trial of strength; ∼**protz** *der* (abwertend) ⇒ ∼**meier;** ∼**rad** *das* (Amtsspr.) motorcycle; ∼**reserven** *Pl.* reserves of strength; ∼**stoff** *der* (Kfz-W.) fuel; ∼**stoff·verbrauch** *der* fuel consumption; ∼**strotzend** *Adj.* vigorous; bursting with vigour *postpos.;* ∼**voll** 1 *Adj.* powerful; 2 *adv.* powerfully; ∼**wagen** *der* motor vehicle; ∼**werk** *das* power station

Kragen /ˈkraːgn̩/ *der;* ∼**s,** ∼, südd., österr. u. schweiz. auch: **Krägen** /ˈkrɛːgn̩/ (a) collar; **jmdn. am** *od.* **beim** ∼ **packen** *od.* **nehmen** (ugs.) collar sb.; (b) (fig.) **ihm platzte der** ∼ (salopp) he blew his top (coll.); **jetzt platzt mir aber der** ∼**!** (salopp) that's the last straw!; **es geht ihm an den** ∼ (ugs.) he's in for it now; **jmdm. an den** ∼ **wollen** (ugs.) get at *or* be after sb.; (jmdm. verantwortlich machen) try to hang sth. on sb. (coll.)

Kragen·weite *die* collar size; [**nicht**] **jmds.** ∼ **sein** (salopp) [not] be sb.'s cup of tea (coll.)

Krähe /ˈkrɛːə/ *die;* ∼, ∼**n** crow; **eine** ∼ **hackt der anderen kein Auge aus** (Spr.) dog does not eat dog (prov.)

krähen *itr. V.* (auch fig.) crow; *s. auch* **Hahn**

Krähen-: ∼**füße** *Pl.* (ugs.) (Hautfalten) crow's feet; ∼**nest** *das* (auch Seemannsspr.) crow's nest

Krake /ˈkraːkə/ *der;* ∼**n,** ∼**n** (a) (Tintenfisch) octopus; (b) (Meeresungeheuer) kraken

krakeelen 1 *itr. V.* (ugs. abwertend) kick up a row (coll.). 2 *tr. V.* scream

Krakel /ˈkraːkl̩/ *der;* ∼**s,** ∼ (ugs. abwertend) scrawl; scribble

krakeln *tr., itr. V.* (ugs. abwertend) scrawl; scribble

krak[e]lig *Adj.* (ugs. abwertend) scrawly

Kralle /ˈkralə/ *die;* ∼, ∼**n** claw

krallen 1 *refl. V.* **sich an etw.** (*Akk.*) ∼ ⟨*cat*⟩ dig its claws into sth.; ⟨*bird*⟩ dig its claws *or* talons into sth.; ⟨*person*⟩ clutch sth. [tightly]; **sich in/um etw.** (*Akk.*) ∼**:** dig into/clutch sth. 2 *tr. V.* (a) (fest greifen) **die Finger in/ um etw.** (*Akk.*) ∼**:** dig one's fingers into sth./clutch sth. [tightly] with one's fingers; (b) (salopp: stehlen) pinch (sl.); nick (Brit. coll.); (c) (salopp) (ergreifen) collar; (verhaften) nab (sl.)

Kram /kraːm/ *der;* ∼**[e]s** (ugs.) (a) stuff; (Gerümpel) junk; **den ganzen** ∼ **hinschmeißen** (fig. ugs.) chuck the whole thing in (coll.); (b) (Angelegenheit) business; affair; **mach deinen** ∼ **alleine!** do it yourself!; **jmdm. [genau] in den** ∼ **passen** suit sb. [down to the ground (coll.)]

kramen 1 *itr. V.* (ugs.: herumwühlen) **in etw.** (*Dat.*) ∼**:** rummage about in *or* rummage through sth.; **nach etw.** ∼**:** rummage about looking for sth. 2 *tr. V.* (ugs.) **etw. aus etw.** ∼**:** fish (coll.) *or* get sth. out of sth.

Krämer /ˈkrɛːmɐ/ *der;* ∼**s,** ∼ (a) (veralt.) grocer; (b) (geiziger Mensch) skinflint; stingy person; (engstirniger Mensch) petty-minded *or* small-minded person

Krämer·seele *die* (abwertend) ⇒ **Krämer b**

Kram·laden *der* (ugs. abwertend) junk shop

Krampe /ˈkrampə/ *die;* ∼, ∼**n** staple

Krampf /krampf/ *der;* ∼**[e]s,** **Krämpfe** /ˈkrɛmpfə/ (a) cramp; (Zuckung) spasm; (bei Anfällen) convulsion; **einen** ∼ **bekommen** *od.* (ugs.) **kriegen** get cramp; (b) (ugs.) *o. Pl.* (gequältes Tun) painful strain; (sinnloses Tun) senseless waste of effort

Krampf·ader *die* ▶329 varicose vein

krampf·artig 1 *Adj.* convulsive. 2 *adv.* convulsively

krampfen *tr. V.* be affected with cramp; (bei Anfällen) be convulsed. 2 *refl. V.* be affected with cramp; (bei Anfällen) be convulsed. 3 *tr. V.* **die Fäuste/Finger um/in etw.** (*Akk.*) ∼**:** clench sth./dig one's hands/fingers into sth.

krampfhaft 1 *Adj.* (a) convulsive; (b) (verbissen) desperate; forced ⟨*cheerfulness*⟩. 2 *adv.* (a) convulsively; (b) (verbissen) desperately

Kran /kraːn/ *der;* ∼**[e]s, Kräne** /ˈkrɛːnə/ (a) crane; (b) *Pl.:* **Kräne** *od.* ∼**en** (südwestd.: Wasserhahn) tap; faucet (Amer.)

Kran·führer *der* ▶85 crane-operator; (∼fahrer) crane-driver

Kranich /ˈkraːnɪç/ *der;* ∼**s,** ∼**e** crane

krank /kraŋk/; **kränker** /ˈkrɛŋkɐ/, **kränkst**... /ˈkrɛŋkst.../ *Adj.* (a) ▶329 ill *usu. pred.;* sick; bad ⟨*leg, tooth*⟩; diseased ⟨*plant, organ*⟩; (fig.) sick, ailing ⟨*economy, business*⟩; **ein** ∼**es Herz/eine** ∼**e Leber haben** have a bad heart/a liver complaint; [**schwer**] ∼ **werden** be taken *or* fall [seriously *or* very] ill; **er wurde immer kränker** he got steadily worse; **sie liegt** ∼ **zu/im Bett** she is ill in bed; **jmdn.** ∼ **machen** make sb. ill; (fig.) get on sb.'s nerves; **vor Heimweh/Liebe** ∼ **sein** be homesick/lovesick; (b) (Jägerspr.: angeschossen) wounded

Kranke /ˈkraŋkə/ *der/die; adj. Dekl.* sick man/woman; (Patient) patient; **die** ∼**n** the sick/the patients

kränkeln /ˈkrɛŋkl̩n/ *itr. V.* be in poor health; not be well; (fig.) be in poor shape; **er kränkelt leicht** he is always ailing

kranken *itr. V.* **an etw.** (*Dat.*) ∼ ⟨*firm, project, etc.*⟩ suffer from sth.

kränken /ˈkrɛŋkn̩/ *tr. V.* **jmdn.** ∼**:** hurt *or* wound sb. *or* sb.'s feelings; **jmdn. in seiner Ehre/seinem Stolz/ seiner Eitelkeit** ∼**:** wound sb.'s honour/injure *or* wound sb.'s pride/vanity; ∼**d sein** be hurtful; **tief/schwer gekränkt sein** be deeply hurt

Kranken-: ∼**besuch** *der* visit to a sick person; ∼**geld** *das* sickness benefit; ∼**geschichte** *die* case history; ∼**gymnastik** *die* remedial *or* medical gymnastics *sing.;* physiotherapy; ∼**gymnastin** *die* ▶85 remedial gymnast; physiotherapist; ∼**haus** *das* hospital; **jmdn. ins** ∼**haus einliefern/aus dem** ∼**haus entlassen** take sb. to hospital/discharge sb. from hospital; **im** ∼**haus liegen** be in hospital; **ins** ∼**haus müssen** have to go [in]to hospital; ∼**haus·aufenthalt** *der* stay in hospital; ∼**kasse** *die* health insurance institution; (privat) health insurance company; ∼**pflege** *die* nursing; ∼**pfleger** *der* ▶85 male nurse; ∼**schein** *der* health insurance certificate; ∼**schwester** *die* ▶85 nurse; ∼**versicherung** *die* health insurance; ∼**wagen** *der* ambulance

kränker ⇒ **krank**

krank|feiern *itr. V.* (ugs.) skive off work (Brit. coll.) [pretending to be ill]

krankhaft 1 *Adj.* (a) pathological ⟨*change etc.*⟩; morbid ⟨*growth, state, swelling, etc.*⟩; (abnorm gesteigert) pathological; pathological, morbid ⟨*fear, obsession*⟩. 2 *adv.* (a) pathologically; morbidly ⟨*swollen, grown*⟩; (b) (abnorm gesteigert) pathologically; pathologically, morbidly ⟨*obsessed, sensitive*⟩

Krankheit *die;* ∼, ∼**en** (a) ▶329 illness; (bestimmte Art, von Pflanzen, Organen) disease; **sich** (*Dat.*) **eine** ∼ **zuziehen** contract *or* catch an illness/a disease; **an einer** ∼ **leiden/ sterben** suffer from/die of an illness/a disease; **das ist doch kein Auto, das ist eine** ∼ (fig. ugs.) that's just an apology for a car; (b) *o. Pl.* (Zeit des Krankseins) illness; **nach langer/schwerer** ∼**:** after a long/serious illness

Krankheits-: ∼**erreger** *der* pathogen; disease-causing agent; ∼**fall** *der* case of illness; **im** ∼**fall** in the event of illness

krank|lachen *refl. V.* (ugs.) laugh one's head off; laugh oneself silly

kränklich /ˈkrɛŋklɪç/ *Adj.* sickly; ailing

krank-,, Krank-: ∼**|machen** *itr. V.* (ugs.) ⇒ ∼**feiern;** *s. auch* **krank a;** ∼**melden** *tr. V.* **jmdn./sich** ∼**melden** let the boss/office *etc.* know that sb./one is off sick; ∼**meldung** *die* notification of absence through illness; ∼**|schreiben** *unr. tr. V.* give ⟨*person*⟩ a medical certificate

kränkst... ⇒ **krank**

Krankheiten und Schmerzen

Verletzungen

Wo haben Sie Schmerzen?, Wo tut es weh?	= Where does it hurt?
Mir tut der Arm weh	= My arm is hurting
Sie hat sich am Fuß weh getan/verletzt	= She has hurt her foot
Ich habe mir den Fuß verstaucht/die Hand verbrannt	= I have sprained my ankle/burnt my hand
Er hat sich das Bein gebrochen	= He has broken his leg
ein Kieferbruch	= a fracture of the jaw
Sie hat einen Kieferbruch/Schädelbruch/Beckenbruch	= She has a fractured jaw/skull/pelvis

Man sieht, dass das Possessivum im Englischen verwendet wird, wo im Deutschen der bestimmte Artikel mit dem Dativ der Person steht.
Siehe auch □ **Körperteile**

Schmerzen

Ich habe Zahnschmerzen/ Kopfschmerzen/ Magenschmerzen od. Zahnweh/Kopfweh/ Magenweh	= I've got toothache/ a headache/ a stomach ache od. a pain in my stomach
Sie hat Schmerzen im Rücken	= *(allgemein)* She has back pain/*(dumpf)* backache; *(an verschiedenen Stellen)* She has pains in her back
Sie hat Schmerzen	= She is in pain
ein stechender/bohrender Schmerz	= a stab of pain/a gnawing pain

Ein starker Schmerz kann also nur **pain** sein, **ache** ist immer dumpf und anhaltend. Und *Schmerzen* sind auch meist **pain**; nur bei Schmerzen an verschiedenen Stellen sagt man **pains**.

Das Kranksein

Ich fühle mich krank/ elend	= I feel ill/wretched
Mir ist schlecht/sauschlecht (ugs.)	= I don't feel well/I feel awful *(ugs.)*
Ihnen war/wurde bei der Überfahrt übel	= They felt/were sick on the crossing
Sie ist schwer/unheilbar krank	= She is seriously/ terminally ill
Er ist an Grippe erkrankt	= He is ill with flu od. has [got] flu
Sie hat sich erkältet/ ist erkältet	= She has caught a cold/has a cold
Du holst dir eine Lungenentzündung	= You'll catch pneumonia
Sie leiden an Asthma/ Bronchitis	= They suffer from asthma/bronchitis

Mit Ausnahme von **cold** wird der unbestimmte Artikel bei Krankheiten nicht verwendet, auch dann nicht, wenn ein Adjektiv vor dem Substantiv steht:

Ich habe eine schlimme Gelenkarthrose	= I have bad arthritis
Er bekommt immer eine leichte Bronchitis	= He always gets slight bronchitis

Allerdings:

eine schlimme Grippe	= a nasty bout of flu
ein schwerer Fall von Kehlkopfkrebs	= a serious case of throat cancer

eine hartnäckige Halsinfektion	= a persistent throat infection
ein Asthmaanfall	= an attack of asthma

Leiden und Leidende

Er hat ein Herzleiden/ ein Magenleiden/eine Hautkrankheit	= He has a heart condition/a stomach complaint/a skin complaint
Sie hat Rückenprobleme od. hats mit dem Rücken	= She suffers from back trouble
Herzbeschwerden/ Magenbeschwerden	= heart/stomach trouble

In Zusammensetzungen wird *-kranke(r)* meist mit **sufferer** bzw. **patient** übersetzt:

ein Aidskranker	= an Aids sufferer
ein Asthmakranker	= an asthma sufferer
Krebskranke	= cancer patients

Aber:

ein Epileptiker	= an epileptic
ein Diabetiker	= a diabetic

Behandlung

Sie ist [bei einem Facharzt] in Behandlung	= She is having od. receiving treatment [from a specialist]
Er wird wegen Krebs/ eines Magengeschwürs behandelt	= He is being treated for cancer/a stomach ulcer
Sie haben ihn auf ein Magengeschwür behandelt, aber es stellte sich heraus, dass er Krebs hatte	= They treated him for a stomach ulcer, but it turned out he had cancer
Ich bin wegen Gallensteinen operiert worden	= I was operated on for gallstones
Ich bin viermal operiert worden	= I have had four operations
mit Vollnarkose/Lokalanästhesie	= under a general/local anaesthetic
Die Krankenschwester gab mir eine Spritze	= The nurse gave me an injection
Sind Sie gegen Cholera geimpft [worden]?	= Have you been vaccinated against cholera od. had a cholera vaccination?

Heilmittel

Haben Sie etwas gegen Verstopfung?	= Have you got anything for constipation?
Was kann ich gegen Heuschnupfen nehmen?	= What can I take for hay fever?
Dreimal täglich einzunehmen	= To be taken three times a day
Vor Gebrauch schütteln	= Shake the bottle
Es gibt kein Mittel gegen Aids	= There is no cure for Aids

Erholung

Er ist auf dem Wege der Besserung	= He is getting better od. is on the mend
Es geht ihr od. Sie fühlt sich viel besser	= She is [feeling] much better
Ich habe mich vollständig erholt	= I am fully recovered

Kränkung die; ~, ~en: eine ~: an injury to one's/ sb.'s feelings; etw. als ~ empfinden be hurt by sth.; take offence at sth.

Kranz /krants/ der; ~es, **Kränze** /'krɛntsə/ (a) wreath; garland; (auf einem Grab, Sarg, an einem Denkmal) wreath; (b) (Haar~) chaplet (of plaited hair); (c) (Kuchen) ring cake

Kränzchen /'krɛntsçən/ das; ~s, ~ (a) (Kaffee~) coffee circle; coffee klatch (Amer.); (b) (kleiner Kranz) small wreath or garland

Kranz-: ~**gefäß** das ⇒ **Herzkranzgefäß**; ~**kuchen** der ⇒ **Kranz** c; ~**niederlegung** die laying of a wreath

Krapfen /'krapfn̩/ der; ~s, ~ doughnut

krass, *****kraß** /kras/ **1** Adj. blatant (case); gross, flagrant (injustice); rank, complete (outsider); glaring, stark (contrast); complete (contradiction); sharp (difference); gross (discrepancy, imbalance); out-and-out (egoist). **2** adv. sich ~ ausdrücken put sth. bluntly; **sich von etw. ~ unterscheiden** be in stark contrast to sth.

Krater /'kra:tɐ/ der; ~s, ~: crater

Kratz·bürste die (ugs. scherzh.) stroppy (Brit. coll.) or prickly so-and-so

kratzbürstig Adj. (ugs. scherzh.) stroppy (Brit. coll.); prickly

Krätze /'krɛtsə/ die; ~: ▶ 329⌋ scabies sing.

kratzen /'kratsn̩/ **1** tr. V. (a) scratch; **jmdm./sich den Arm blutig ~:** scratch sb.'s/one's arm and make it bleed; **seinen Namen in die Wand ~:** scratch one's name on the wall; (b) **etw. aus/von etw. ~:** scrape sth. out of/off sth.; (c) (ugs.: stören) bother; **jmdn. wenig ~:** not bother sb. all that much. **2** itr. V. (a) scratch; **das Kratzen** scratching; (b) (jucken) itch; be scratchy or itchy; (c) (brennen) **im Hals ~** (wine) taste rough; (tobacco) be rough on the throat; (smoke) irritate the throat. **3** refl. V. scratch [oneself]; **sich hinter dem Ohr/am Kopf ~:** scratch oneself behind the ear/scratch one's head

Kratzer der; ~s, ~ (a) (ugs.) scratch; (b) (Schaber) scraper

kratz·fest Adj. scratch-proof; non-scratch

Kratz·fuß der (veralt.) leg (arch.); **einen ~machen** make a leg (arch.)

kratzig Adj. scratchy, itchy (material, pullover, etc.); scratchy, rough (voice)

krauchen /'krauxn̩/ itr. V.; mit sein (md.) ⇒ **kriechen**

Kraul /kraul/ das; ~s (Sport) crawl

kraulen¹ 1 itr. V.; mit Richtungsangabe mit sein do or swim the crawl; **über den See/ans Ufer ~:** swim across the lake/to the bank using the crawl. **2** tr. V.; auch mit sein **eine Strecke ~:** cover a distance using the crawl

kraulen² tr. V. **jmdm. das Kinn ~:** tickle sb. under the chin; **jmdn. in den Haaren ~:** run one's fingers through sb.'s hair

kraus /kraus/ Adj. (a) frizzy (hair, beard); creased (skirt etc.); wavy (sea); wrinkled (brow); **die Stirn ~ ziehen** wrinkle one's brow; (unmutig) frown; (b) (abwertend: verworren) muddled; confused

Krause die; ~, ~n (a) (Kragen) ruff; (am Ärmel) ruffle; frill; (b) (im Haar) frizziness

kräuseln /'krɔyzl̩n/ **1** tr. V. ruffle (water, surface); gather (material etc.); frizz (hair); pucker [up] (lips). **2** refl. V. (hair) go frizzy; (water) ripple; (smoke) curl up; (material) pucker up

krausen 1 tr. V. gather (material etc.); frizz (hair); wrinkle [up] (forehead, nose). **2** itr. V. (material, clothes) crease

kraus·haarig Adj. frizzy-haired (person); curly-coated (dog etc.)

Kraus·kopf der frizzy hair; **einen ~ haben** have frizzy hair; be frizzy-haired

Kraut /kraut/ das; ~[e]s, **Kräuter** /'krɔytɐ/ (a) herb; **dagegen ist kein ~ gewachsen** (ugs.) there's nothing anyone can do about it; (b) o. Pl. (Blätter) foliage; stems and leaves pl.; (von Kartoffeln, Bohnen usw.) haulm; **ins ~ schießen** put on too much foliage; bolt; (fig.) run wild; **wie**

~ **und Rüben** (ugs.) all over the place; in a complete muddle; (c) o. Pl. (bes. südd., österr.: Kohl) cabbage; (d) (ugs. abwertend: Tabak) tobacco

Kräuter-: ~**butter** die herb butter; ~**essig** der herb vinegar; ~**likör** der herb liqueur; ~**tee** der herb tea

Kraut·salat der coleslaw

Krawall /kra'val/ der; ~s, ~e (a) (Tumult) riot; (b) o. Pl. (ugs.: Lärm) row (coll.); racket; ~ **machen** kick up or make a row (coll.) or racket

Krawall·macher der rowdy

Krawatte /kra'vatə/ die; ~, ~n tie

Krawatten-: ~**nadel** die tiepin; ~**zwang** der: **hier herrscht [kein] ~zwang** you [do not] have to wear a tie here

kraxeln /'kraksl̩n/ itr. V.; mit sein (bes. südd., österr. ugs.) climb; (mit Mühe) clamber; **auf etw. (Akk.) ~:** climb [up] sth.; (mit Mühe) clamber up sth.

Kreation /krea'tsio:n/ die; ~, ~en (bes. Mode) creation

kreativ /krea'ti:f/ **1** Adj. creative. **2** adv. ~ **veranlagt sein** have a creative bent

Kreativität /kreativi'tɛ:t/ die; ~: creativity

Kreativ·urlaub der [arts and crafts] activity holiday

Kreatur /krea'tu:ɐ/ die; ~, ~en (a) (Geschöpf) creature; **Gott schuf alle ~:** God made all creatures pl.; (b) (willenloser Mensch) minion; creature

kreatürlich /krea'ty:ɐliç/ Adj. creaturely, natural (feeling, love, etc.); animal attrib. (fear)

Krebs /kre:ps/ der; ~es, ~e (a) crustacean; (Fluss~) crayfish; (Krabbe) crab; **rot wie ein ~:** as red as a lobster; (b) ▶ 329⌋ (Krankheit) cancer; (c) (Astrol.) Cancer; the Crab

krebs·artig 1 Adj. cancerous. **2** adv. cancerously; in the manner of a cancer

krebsen itr. V. (ugs.: sich abmühen) **mit etw. zu ~ haben** find sth. a real or uphill struggle

krebs-, **Krebs-:** ~**erregend**, ~**erzeugend** Adj. carcinogenic; cancer-producing usu. attrib.; ~**forschung** die cancer research; ~**gang** der o. Pl. retrogression; **im** ~**gang gehen** go backwards; ~**geschwulst** die cancerous growth or tumour; ~**geschwür** das (volkst.) cancerous ulcer; (fig. geh.) cancer; ~**krank** Adj. cancer attrib. (patient etc.); ~**krank** sein suffer from or have cancer; ~**kranke** der/die person suffering from cancer; (Patient) cancer patient; ~**leiden** das cancer no def. art.; ~**rot** Adj. as red as a lobster postpos.; (aus Verlegenheit) as red as a beetroot postpos. ~**vorsorge** die (bes. Amtsspr.) [Maßnahmen zur] ~**vorsorge** precautions pl. against cancer;

Kredit /kre'di:t/ der; ~[e]s, ~e (a) (Darlehen) loan; credit; **jmdm. einen** ~ **gewähren** od. **einräumen** give or grant sb. a loan or a credit; (b) o. Pl. (Zahlungsaufschub) credit; **er hat bei uns** ~**:** his credit is good with us; **auf** ~**:** on credit; (c) o. Pl. (Kaufmannsspr.: Vertrauenswürdigkeit) good reputation or name

kredit-, **Kredit-:** ~**abteilung** die credit department; ~**anstalt** die credit institution; ~**geber** der lender; ~**hai** der (ugs. abwertend) loan shark (coll.); ~**institut** das credit institution; ~**karte** die ▶ 216⌋ credit card; ~**nehmer** der borrower; ~**würdig** Adj. (Finanzw.) credit worthy

kreditieren tr. V. (Kaufmannsspr.) **jmdm. einen Betrag ~/jmdn. für einen Betrag ~:** advance sb. an amount or give sb. an amount on credit/credit sb. with an amount

Kredo /'kre:do/ das; ~s, ~s (a) (kath. Kirche) creed; credo; (b) (fig. geh.) credo

Kreide /'kraidə/ die; ~, ~n (a) o. Pl. (Kalkstein) chalk; (b) (zum Schreiben) chalk; **mit ~ zeichnen/schreiben** draw/ write in or with chalk; **bei jmdm. [tief] in der ~ stehen** be [deeply] in debt to sb.; owe sb. [a lot of] money; (c) o. Pl. (Geol.) Cretaceous [period]

kreide-, **Kreide-:** ~**bleich** Adj. as white as a sheet postpos.; ~**felsen** der chalk cliff; ~**weiß** Adj.: ⇒ ~**bleich**; ~**zeit** die ⇒ **Kreide** c

kreieren /kre'i:rən/ tr. V. create

Kreis /krais/ der; ~es, ~e (a) circle; **einen ~ schlagen** od. **beschreiben** describe a circle; **einen ~**

bilden *od.* **schließen** form *or* make a circle; **in einem** *od.* **im ~ sitzen** sit in a circle; **sich im ~ drehen** *od.* **bewegen** go *or* turn round in a circle; (fig.) go round in circles; **~e ziehen** (fig.) ⟨*court case*⟩ have [wide] repercussions; ⟨*movement*⟩ grow in size and influence; **(b)** (Gruppe) circle; **im ~e der Freunde/Familie** among *or* with friends/within the family; **im kleinen** *od.* **engsten ~:** with a few close friends [and relatives]; **der ~ seiner Leser/Anhänger** his readers *pl.*/followers *pl.*; **in seinen ~en** in the circles in which he moves/moved; **in weiten** *od.* **breiten ~en der Bevölkerung** amongst wide sections of the population; **die besseren/besten ~e** the best circles; **(c)** (von Problemen, Lösungen usw.) range; **(d)** (Verwaltungsbezirk) district; (Wahl~) ward; **der ~ Heidelberg** the Heidelberg district *or* district of Heidelberg; **(e)** (Elektrot.) circuit

Kreis-: ~bahn *die* orbit; **~bogen** *der* (Geom.) arc [of a/the circle]

kreischen /ˈkraiʃn̩/ *itr. V.* ⟨*person*⟩ screech, shriek; ⟨*bird*⟩ screech; ⟨*brakes*⟩ squeal, screech; ⟨*door*⟩ creak; ⟨*saw*⟩ screech; **mit ~den Bremsen** with a squeal *or* screech of brakes

Kreisel /ˈkraizl̩/ *der;* **~s, ~** **(a)** (Technik) gyroscope; **(b)** (Kinderspielzeug) top; **(c)** (ugs.: Kreisverkehr) roundabout

Kreisel·kompass, *Kreisel·kompaß *der* (Schifffahrt) gyro-compass

kreiseln *itr. V.* **(a)** *auch mit sein* (sich drehen) spin [round]; gyrate; **(b)** (mit einem Kreisel spielen) spin a top

kreisen *itr. V.* **(a)** *auch mit sein* ⟨*planet*⟩ revolve (**um** around); ⟨*satellite etc.*⟩ orbit; ⟨*aircraft, bird*⟩ circle; **die Flasche ~ lassen** (fig.) pass the bottle round; **seine Gedanken kreisten immer um dasselbe Thema** (fig.) his thoughts always revolved around the same subject; **(b)** (Sport) **die Arme ~ lassen** swing one's arms round [in a circle]

kreis-, Kreis-: ~förmig *Adj.* circular; **~lauf** *der* **(a)** (der Natur, der Wirtschaft, des Lebens usw.) cycle; (des Geldes; Technik) circulation; **(b)** (Physiol.) circulation; **~lauf·kollaps** *der* (Med.) circulatory collapse; **~lauf·mittel** *das* circulatory preparation; **~lauf·störungen** *Pl.* circulatory trouble *sing.;* **~rund** *Adj.* [perfectly] circular *or* round; **~säge** *die* circular saw

Kreiß·saal *der* (Med.) delivery room

Kreis-: ~stadt *die* chief town of a/the district; **~tag** *der* district assembly; **~verkehr** *der* roundabout

Krematorium /kremaˈtoːriʊm/ *das;* **~s, Kremato-rien** crematorium

Kreml /ˈkrɛml̩/ *der;* **~s** Kremlin

Krempe /ˈkrɛmpə/ *die;* **~, ~n** brim

Krempel /ˈkrɛmpl̩/ *der;* **~s** (ugs. abwertend) stuff; (Gerümpel) junk; **den ganzen ~ hinwerfen** (fig.) chuck the whole thing in (coll.)

Kren /kreːn/ *der;* **~[e]s** (südd., bes. österr.) ⇒ **Meerrettich**

krepieren /kreˈpiːrən/ *itr. V.; mit sein* **(a)** (zerplatzen) explode; go off; **(b)** ⟨salopp: sterben⟩ ⟨*animal*⟩ die; ⟨*person*⟩ snuff it (sl.)

Krepp /krɛp/ *der;* **~s, ~s** *od.* **~e** crêpe

***Kreppapier** ⇒ **Krepppapier**

Krepp-: ~papier *das* crêpe paper; **~sohle** *die* crêpe sole

Kresse /ˈkrɛsə/ *die;* **~, ~n** (Bot.) cress

Kretin /kreˈtɛ̃ː/ *der;* **~s, ~s** **(a)** (Med.) cretin; **(b)** (fig. abwertend) imbecile

kreucht /krɔyçt/ **alles, was da ~und fleucht** all living creatures *or* things

kreuz/Kreuz: ~ und quer durch die Stadt fahren drive all over/round the town; **in die Kreuz und [in die] Quere fahren** drive all over the place

Kreuz /krɔyts/ *das;* **~es, ~e** **(a)** (Symbol) cross; crucifix; **etw. über ~ legen/falten** lay sth. down/fold sth. crosswise; **zu ~e kriechen** humble oneself; **jmdn. ans ~ schlagen** *od.* nageln nail sb. to the cross; **das Kreuz/ ein ~ schlagen** make the sign of the cross; (sich bekreuzigen) cross oneself; **drei ~e machen** (ugs.) heave a sigh of relief; **(b)** *o. Pl.* (Leid) cross; **sein ~ auf sich nehmen/**

tragen take up/bear one's cross; **es ist ein ~ mit jmdm./etw.** (ugs.) sb. is a real strain *or* is really trying/ sth. is a real problem; **(c)** ▶326 | (Teil des Rückens) small of the back; **ein steifes ~ haben** have a stiff back; **Schmerzen im ~:** pain in the small of the back; **ich habs im ~** (ugs.) I've got back .trouble *or* a bad back; **jmdn. aufs ~ legen** (salopp) take sb. for a ride (fig. coll.); **(d)** (Kartenspiel) clubs *pl.;* (Karte) club; *s. auch* **Pik²; (e)** (Kreuzung) interchange; **(f)** (Musik) sharp

kreuz-, Kreuz-: *~ass, ~ass** *das* ace of clubs; **~brav** *Adj.* thoroughly good and honest ⟨*person*⟩; very good *or* well-behaved ⟨*child*⟩; **~bube** *der* jack of clubs; **~dame** *die* queen of clubs

kreuzen 1 *tr. V.* (auch Biol.) cross; **die Arme/Beine ~:** cross *or* fold one's arms/cross one's legs. **2** *refl. V.* **(a)** cross; intersect; **(b)** (zuwiderlaufen) clash (**mit** with). **3** *itr. V.* **(a)** *mit haben od. sein* (hin und her fahren) cruise; **(b)** (Seemannsspr.) tack

Kreuzer *der;* **~s, ~ (a)** (Milit.: Kriegsschiff) cruiser; **(b)** (Segelsport) cruising yacht; cruiser

kreuz-, Kreuz-: ~fahrer *der* (hist.) crusader; **~fahrt** *die* (Seereise) cruise; **eine ~fahrt machen** go on a cruise; **~feuer** *das* (Milit., auch fig.) crossfire; **im ~feuer stehen/ins ~ geraten** (fig.) be/come under fire from all sides; **~fidel** *Adj.* (ugs.) (sehr gut gelaunt) very cheerful; (sehr lustig) very jolly; **~förmig 1** *Adj.* cross-shaped; cruciform; **2** *adv.* ⟨*built, arranged, etc.*⟩ in the shape of a cross; **~gang** *der* cloister

kreuzigen /ˈkrɔytsɪɡn̩/ *tr. V.* crucify; **der Gekreuzigte** Christ crucified

Kreuzigung *die;* **~, ~en** crucifixion

Kreuz-: ~könig *der* king of clubs; **~otter** *die* adder; [common] viper; **~schlitzschraube** *die* Phillips screw **(P); ~schlüssel** *der* four-way wheel-brace; **~schmerzen** *Pl.* pain *sing.* in the small of the back; **~spinne** *die* cross *or* garden spider

Kreuzung *die;* **~, ~en (a)** ▶583 | junction; crossroads *sing.;* **(b)** (Biol.) crossing; cross-breeding; (Ergebnis) cross; cross-breed; **eine ~ aus … und …:** a cross between … and …

kreuz·unglücklich *Adj.* (ugs.) terribly miserable (coll.)

kreuz-, Kreuz-: ~verhör *das* cross-examination; **jmdn. ins ~verhör nehmen** (fig.) crossexamine sb.; **~weise** *Adv.* crosswise; crossways; **du kannst mich mal ~weise!** (derb) [you can] get stuffed! (sl.); **~wort-rätsel** *das* crossword [puzzle]; **~zeichen** *das* (bes. kath. Kirche) sign of the cross; **~zug** *der* (hist., fig.) crusade

kribbelig *Adj.* (ugs.) fidgety; (nervös) edgy

kribbeln /ˈkrɪbl̩n/ *itr. V.* tickle; (prickeln) tingle; **es kribbelt mir od. mich in der Nase/in den Füßen/unter der Haut** I've got a tickle in my nose/my feet are tingling *or* I've got pins and needles in my feet/my skin is itching *or* prickling; **es kribbelt mir in den Fingern, es zu tun** (fig.) I'm just itching to do it

Kricket /ˈkrɪkət/ *das;* **~s** cricket

kriechen /ˈkriːçn̩/ *unr. itr. V.* **(a)** *mit sein* ⟨*insect, baby*⟩ crawl; ⟨*plant*⟩ creep; ⟨*person, animal*⟩ creep, crawl; ⟨*car, train, etc.*⟩ crawl *or* creep [along]; **aus dem Ei/der Puppe ~:** hatch [out]/emerge from the chrysalis; **auf allen vieren/auf dem Bauch ~:** crawl on all fours/ crawl [along] on one's stomach; **die Zeit kriecht** (fig.) time creeps by; **kaum noch ~ können** hardly be able to get about *or* walk; *s. auch* **Kreuz a; (b)** *auch mit sein* (abwertend: sich unterwürfig verhalten) crawl, grovel (**vor** + *Dat.* to)

Kriecher *der;* **~s, ~** (abwertend) crawler; groveller

kriecherisch *Adj.* (abwertend) crawling; grovelling

Kriech-: ~spur *die* (Verkehrsw.) crawler lane; **~tier** *das* (Zool.) reptile

Krieg /kriːk/ *der;* **~[e]s, ~e** war; (~sführung) warfare; **~ führen** wage war (**gegen** on); **den ~ erklären** declare war (**Dat.** on); **in den ~ ziehen** go to war; **der kalte ~:** the cold war; **~ führend** warring; belligerent

kriegen (ugs.) **1** *tr. V.* **(a)** ⇒ **bekommen 1 a: am Ende des Films ~ sie sich** at the end of the film boy gets girl; **zu viel ~:** blow one's top (coll.); (bei jmds. Worten) see red; *s. auch* **genug; Motte a; (b)** ⇒ **bekommen 1 b; (c)** ⇒

bekommen 1 c; (d) (fangen, festnehmen) catch; **(e)** (bewältigen) **wir werden das schon ~:** we'll soon sort it out. **2** *zur Umschreibung des Passivs:* ⇒ **bekommen 2**

Krieger *der;* **~s, ~:** warrior; (indianischer ~) brave; **kalter ~** (Politik) cold warrior; **ein müder ~** (fig.) a tired old thing

kriegerisch *Adj.* **(a)** (kampflustig) warlike; **(b)** *nicht präd.* (militärisch) military; **eine ~e Auseinandersetzung** an armed conflict

krieg·führend ⇒ **Krieg**

kriegs-, Kriegs-: ~aus·bruch *der* outbreak of war; **~beil** *das* tomahawk; **das ~beil ausgraben/begraben** (fig. scherzh.) start fighting/bury the hatchet; **~bemalung** *die* (Völkerk., fig. scherzh.) warpaint; **~beschädigt** *Adj.* war-disabled; **~beschädigte** *der/die; adj. Dekl.* war-disabled person; war invalid; **~dienst** *der* **(a)** active service; **(b)** (Wehrdienst) military service; **~dienst·verweigerer** *der* conscientious objector; **~ende** *das* end of the war; **~erklärung** *die* declaration of war; **~fall** *der:* **im ~fall[e]** in the event of war; **~fuß** *der in* **mit jmdm. auf [dem] ~fuß stehen** *od.* **leben** (scherzh.) be at loggerheads with sb.; **mit etw. auf [dem] ~fuß stehen** be totally lost when it comes to sth.; **~gefangene** *der* prisoner of war; POW; **~gefangenschaft** *die* captivity; **in ~gefangenschaft sein/geraten** be a prisoner of war/be taken prisoner; **~gegner** *der* **(a)** (Gegner im Krieg) enemy; **(b)** (Gegner des Krieges) opponent of the/a war; (Pazifist) opponent of war; **~gericht** *das* court martial; **jmdn. vor ein ~gericht stellen** court-martial sb.; **~hetze** *die; o. Pl.* (abwertend) warmongering; **~hetze betreiben** stir up war; **~invalide** *der/die* ⇒ **~beschädigte; ~kamerad** *der* wartime comrade; **~list** *die* military stratagem; (fig. scherzh.) ruse; **~marine** *die* navy; **~maschinerie** *die* (abwertend) machinery of war; **~opfer** *das* war victim; **~pfad** *der* **auf dem ~pfad** (auch fig.) on the warpath; **~rat** *der* **rat [ab]halten** (scherzh.) have a pow-wow; **~recht** *das; o. Pl.* martial law; **~schau·platz** *der* theatre of war; **~schiff** *das* warship; **~verbrechen** *das* war crime; **~verbrecher** *der* war criminal; **~verbrecher·prozess, *~verbrecher·prozeß*** *der* war crimes trial; **~verletzung** *die* war wound *or* injury; **~zeit** *die* wartime; **in ~zeiten** *Pl.* in wartime

Krill /krɪl/*der;* **~[e]s** krill

Krim /krɪm/ *die;* **~: die ~:** the Crimea

Krimi /'kri:mi/ *der;* **~[s], ~[s]** (ugs.) (Film, Stück, Roman) crime thriller; whodunit (coll.); (Roman mit Detektiv als Held) detective story

Kriminal-: ~beamte *der* ▶ 85 ⌡ [plain-clothes] detective; **~fall** *der* criminal case; **~film** *der* crime film *or* thriller

kriminalisieren *tr. V.* **(a)** **jmdn./etw. ~:** make sb. into a criminal/make sth. a criminal offence; **jmdn. ~** (zu Straftaten treiben) make sb. turn to crime; **(b)** (als kriminell hinstellen) **jmdn./etw. ~:** present sb. as a criminal/sth. as [being] criminal *or* a criminal act

Kriminalistik *die;* **~:** criminalistics *sing., no art.*

kriminalistisch 1 *Adj.* ⟨methods, practice⟩ of criminalistics; ⟨abilities⟩ in the field of criminalistics. **2** *adv.* ⟨proceed etc.⟩ using the methods of criminalistics

Kriminalität /kriminali'tɛːt/ *die;* **~ (a)** crime *no art.;* **(b)** (Straffälligkeit) criminality

Kriminal-: ~kommissar *der* ▶ 85 ⌡ ≈ detective superintendent; **~polizei** *die* criminal investigation department; **~roman** *der* crime novel *or* thriller; (mit Detektiv als Held) detective novel

kriminell /krimi'nɛl/ **1** *Adj.* (auch ugs.: rücksichtslos) criminal; **~ werden/sein** become a criminal *or* turn to crime/ be a criminal. **2** *adv.* **(a)** **~ veranlagt sein** have criminal tendencies; **~ handeln** act illegally; break the law; **(b)** (ugs.: rücksichtslos) criminally; ⟨drive⟩ with criminal recklessness

*alte Schreibung (vgl. Hinweise auf S. xvi–xvii)

Kriminelle *der/die; adj. Dekl.* criminal

Krimskrams /'krɪmskrams/ *der;* **~[es]** (ugs.) stuff

Kringel /'krɪŋl/ *der;* **~s, ~ (a)** (Kreis) [small] ring; (Kritzelei) round squiggle; **(b)** (Gebäck) [ring-shaped] biscuit; ring

kringelig *Adj.* crinkly ⟨hair⟩; squiggly ⟨shape, line, etc.⟩; **sich ~ lachen** (ugs.) laugh one's head off; kill oneself [laughing] (coll.)

kringeln 1 *tr. V.* curl [up] ⟨tail⟩. **2** *refl. V.* curl [up]; ⟨hair⟩ go curly; **sich [vor Lachen] ~** (ugs.) laugh one's head off; kill oneself [laughing] (coll.)

Kripo /'kri:po/ *die;* **~** (ugs.) **die ~:** ≈ the CID

Krippe /'krɪpə/ *die;* **~, ~n (a)** (Futtertrog) manger; crib; **(b)** (Weihnachts~) model of a nativity scene; crib; **(c)** (Kinder~) crèche; day nursery

Krippen·spiel *das* nativity play

Krise /'kri:zə/ *die;* **~, ~n** crisis; **in eine ~ geraten** enter a state of crisis; **wenn sie das hört, kriegt sie die ~** (ugs.) she'll have a fit when she hears that (coll.)

kriseln /'kri:zl̩n/ *itr. V.; unpers.* **es kriselt in ihrer Ehe/ in der Partei** (eine Krise droht) their marriage is running into trouble/there is a crisis looming in the party; (eine Krise ist vorhanden) their marriage is in trouble/the party is in a state of crisis

krisen-, Krisen-: ~fest *Adj.* that is/are unaffected by crises *postpos., not pred.;* **~gebiet** *das* crisis area; **~herd** *der* trouble spot

Kristall¹ /krɪs'tal/ *der;* **~s, ~e** crystal

Kristall² *das;* **~s** crystal *no indef. art.*

Kristall- crystal ⟨glass, chandelier, etc.⟩

Kristallisation /krɪstaliza'tsi̯oːn/ *die;* **~, ~en** crystallization

kristallisieren *itr., refl. V.* (auch fig.) crystallize

kristall·klar *Adj.* (auch fig.) crystal clear

Kriterium /kri'te:ri̯ʊm/ *das;* **~s, Kriterien** criterion

Kritik /kri'ti:k/ *die;* **~, ~en (a)** criticism *no indef. art.* **(an + Dat. of); an jmdm./etw. ~ üben** criticize sb./ sth.; **unter aller ~ sein** (ugs.) be absolutely hopeless; **(b)** (Besprechung) review; notice; **eine gute/schlechte ~** *od.* **gute/schlechte ~en bekommen** get good/bad reviews *or* notices; **(c) die ~:** the critics *pl. or* reviewers *pl.*

Kritiker /'kri:tike/ *der;* **~s, ~, Kritikerin** *die;* **~, ~nen** ▶ 85 ⌡ critic

kritik·los 1 *Adj.* uncritical; **2** *adv.* uncritically; **etw. ~ hinnehmen** accept sth. without criticism

kritisch /'kri:tɪʃ/ **1** *Adj.* critical. **2** *adv.* critically; **sich mit etw. ~ auseinander setzen** make a critical study of sth.

kritisieren /kriti'zi:rən/ *tr. V.* criticize; review ⟨book, play, etc.⟩

Krittelei *die;* **~, ~en** (abwertend) fault-finding; carping

kritteln /'krɪtl̩n/ *itr. V.* (abwertend) find fault **(an + Dat., über + Akk.** with); carp **(an + Dat., über + Akk.** at)

Kritzelei *die;* **~, ~en (a)** *o. Pl.* (das Schreiben) scribbling; (das Zeichnen) doodling; **(b)** (Geschriebenes) scribble; (Zeichnung) doodle; (an Wänden) graffiti *sing. or pl.*

kritzeln /'krɪtsl̩n/ **1** *itr. V.* (schreiben) scribble; (zeichnen) doodle. **2** *tr. V.* scribble

kroch *1. u. 3. Pers. Sg. Prät. v.* **kriechen**

Krokant /kro'kant/ *der;* **~s** praline

Krokette /kro'kɛtə/ *die;* **~, ~n** (Kochk.) croquette

Kroko /'kro:ko/ *das;* **~[s]** crocodile [leather]

Krokodil /kroko'di:l/ *das;* **~s, ~e** crocodile

Krokodils·tränen *Pl.* (ugs.) crocodile tears

Kroko·tasche *die* crocodile[-skin] [hand]bag

Krokus /'kro:kʊs/ *der;* **~, ~ od. ~se** crocus

Krone /'kro:nə/ *die;* **~, ~n (a)** crown; (kleinere, eines Herzogs, eines Grafen) coronet; **die ~** (fig.: Herrscherhaus) the Crown; **einer Sache** (*Dat.*) **die ~ aufsetzen** cap sth.; **einen in der ~ haben** (ugs.) have had a drop too much (coll.); *o. Pl.* (das Beste) **die ~ der Schöpfung/meiner Sammlung** (fig.) the pride of creation/my collection; **(b)** (eines Baumes) top; crown; (einer Welle) crest; **(c)** (Zahnmed.) crown

krönen /'krø:nən/ *tr. V.* (auch fig.) crown; **jmdn. zum König** ∼: crown sb. king; **von Erfolg gekrönt sein** *od.* **werden** (fig.) be crowned with success; **der** ∼**de Abschluss** the culmination

Kronen·korken *der* crown cap *or* cork

Kron-: ∼**juwelen** *Pl.* crown jewels; ∼**kolonie** *die* crown colony; ∼**leuchter** *der* chandelier; ∼**prinz** *der* crown prince; ∼**prinzessin** *die* crown princess

Krönung *die;* ∼, ∼**en** (a) coronation; (b) (Höhepunkt) culmination

Kron·zeuge *der* (Rechtsw.) person who turns Queen's/King's evidence; **als** ∼ **auftreten** turn Queen's/King's evidence

Kropf /krɔpf/ *der;* ∼[e]s, **Kröpfe** /'krœpfə/ (a) crop; (b) (Med.) goitre

kross, *****kroß** /krɔs/ *Adj., adv.* (nordd.) ⇒ **knusprig**

Krösus /'krø:zʊs/ *der;* ∼ *od.* ∼**ses**, ∼**se** (oft scherzh.) Croesus; **ich bin doch kein** ∼: I'm not made of money

Kröte /'krø:tə/ *die;* ∼, ∼**n** (a) toad; (b) *Pl.* (salopp: Geld) **ein paar/eine ganze Menge** ∼**n verdienen** earn a few bob (Brit. sl.) /a fair old whack (coll.); **meine letzten paar** ∼**n** my last few bob (Brit. sl.) /bucks (Amer. sl.); **(c)** (ugs. abwertend: Mensch) creature

Krücke /'krʏkə/ *die;* ∼, ∼**n** (a) (Stock) crutch; **an** *od.* **auf** ∼**n** (*Dat.*) **gehen** walk on crutches; (b) (Griff) crook; handle; **(c)** (ugs. abwertend) (Versager) dead loss (coll.); washout (coll.); (Gegenstand) dead loss (coll.)

Krück·stock *der* walking stick; *s. auch* **Blinde**

Krug /kru:k/ *der;* ∼[e]s, **Krüge** /'kry:gə/ (Gefäß für Flüssigkeiten) jug; (größer) pitcher; (Bier∼) mug; (aus Ton) mug; stein

Krume /'kru:mə/ *die;* ∼, ∼**n** crumb

Krümel /'kry:ml̩/ *der;* ∼**s**, ∼ crumb

krümelig *Adj.* (a) crumbly

krümeln *itr. V.* (a) (zerfallen) crumble; be crumbly; (b) (Krümel machen) make crumbs

krumm /krʊm/ **1** *Adj.* (a) bent ‹ *nail etc.* ›; crooked ‹ *stick, branch, etc.* ›; bandy ‹ *legs* ›; bent ‹ *back* ›; **eine** ∼**e Nase** a crooked nose; (Hakennase) a hooked nose; ∼ **sein/werden** ‹ *person* › stoop/develop a stoop; **etw.** ∼ **biegen** bend sth.; **jmdn.** ∼ **und lahm schlagen** beat sb. black and blue; **sich** ∼ **und schief lachen** (ugs.) laugh oneself laughing; **laugh one's head off** (coll.); **sich** ∼ **legen** (ugs.) scrimp and scrape; pinch and scrape; **etw.** ∼ **nehmen** (ugs.) take offence at sth.; take sth. the wrong way; (b) **nicht präd.** (ugs.: unrechtmäßig) crooked; **ein** ∼**es Ding drehen** get up to sth. crooked. **2** *adv.* crookedly; ∼ **gewachsen** crooked ‹ *tree etc.* ›; ∼ **dasitzen/gehen** slouch/walk with a stoop; **steh/sitz nicht so** ∼ **da!** stand/sit up straight!; *s. auch* **Finger b**

krumm·beinig *Adj.* bandy[-legged]; bow legged

krümmen /'krʏmən/ **1** *tr. V.* bend; **gekrümmt** curved ‹ *line, surface* ›. **2** *refl. V.* writhe; **sich vor Schmerzen/in Krämpfen** ∼: double up with pain/cramp

krumm-: ∼**lachen** *refl. V.* (ugs.) ⇒ **schieflachen**; *****∼**legen** ⇒ **krumm 1 a;** *****∼**nehmen:** ⇒ **krumm 1 a**

Krümmung *die;* ∼, ∼**en** (a) (der Wirbelsäule) curvature; (der Nase usw.) curve; (b) (Geom.) curvature

Krüppel /'krʏpl̩/ *der;* ∼**s**, ∼: cripple; **zum** ∼ **werden** be crippled; **jmdn. zum** ∼ **schlagen** beat sb. and leave him/her a cripple

Kruste /'krʊstə/ *die;* ∼, ∼**n** (a) crust; (vom Braten) crisp; (b) (Überzug) coating

Kruzifix /'kru:tsifɪks/ *das;* ∼**es**, ∼**e** crucifix

Kübel /'ky:bl̩/ *der;* ∼**s**, ∼: (a) pail; (Pflanzen∼) tub; **es gießt wie aus** ∼**n** (ugs.) it's bucketing down; (b) (Toiletteneimer) [latrine] bucket

Kubik- /ku'bi:k-/ **▶426** | cubic ‹ *metre, foot, etc.* ›

kubisch /'ku:bɪʃ/ *Adj.* (a) cubical; cube-shaped; (b) (Math.) cubic ‹ *equation etc.* ›

Kubismus *der;* ∼ (Kunstw.) cubism *no art.*

Küche /'kʏçə/ *die;* ∼, ∼**n** (a) kitchen; (b) (Einrichtung) kitchen furniture *no indef. art.;* (c) (Kochk.) cooking; cuisine; **die chinesische** *usw.* ∼: Chinese *etc.* cooking; **kalte/**

warme ∼: cold/hot meals *pl. or* food; *s. auch* **gutbürgerlich**

Kuchen /'ku:xn̩/ *der;* ∼**s**, ∼: cake; (Obst∼) flan; (Torte) gateau; cake

Küchen·abfälle *Pl.* kitchen scraps

Küchen·blech *das* baking sheet *or* tray

Küchen·chef *der* chef

Küchen-: ∼**form** *die* cake-tin; ∼**gabel** *die* pastry fork

Küchen-: ∼**gerät** *das* kitchen utensil; (als Kollektivum) kitchen utensils *pl.;* ∼**messer** *das* kitchen knife; ∼**schabe** *die* cockroach; ∼**schrank** *der* kitchen cupboard

Kuchen-: ∼**teig** *der* cake mixture; ∼**teller** *der* cake-plate

Küchen-: ∼**tisch** *der* kitchen table; ∼**waage** *die* kitchen scales *pl.;* ∼**zettel** *der* menu

kuckuck /'kʊkʊk/ *Interj.* cuckoo

Kuckuck *der;* ∼**s**, ∼**e** (a) cuckoo; **[das] weiß der** ∼ **heaven [only] knows; it's anybody's guess; zum** ∼ **[nochmal]!** (salopp) for crying out loud! (coll.); **wo, zum** ∼**, hast du nur die Zeitung hingelegt?** (salopp) where the hell did you put the newspaper? (coll.); (b) (scherzh.: Siegel des Gerichtsvollziehers) bailiff's seal (*placed on distrained goods*)

Kuckucks-: ∼**ei** *das* (fig. ugs.) **sich als** ∼**ei erweisen** turn out to be more of a liability than an asset; **jmdm./sich ein** ∼**ei ins Nest legen** do sb./oneself a dubious service; ∼**uhr** *die* cuckoo clock

Kuddelmuddel /'kʊdl̩mʊdl̩/ *der od. das;* ∼**s** (ugs.) muddle; confusion

Kufe /'ku:fə/ *die;* ∼, ∼**n** (von Schlitten, Schlittschuh) runner; (von Flugzeug, Hubschrauber) skid

Kugel /'ku:gl̩/ *die;* ∼, ∼**n** (a) ball; (Geom.) sphere; (Kegeln) bowl; (beim Kugelstoßen) shot; (eines ∼lagers) ball[-bearing] (coll.); (b) (ugs.: Geschoss) bullet; (Kanonen∼) [cannon-] ball; (Luftgewehr∼) pellet; **sich** (*Dat.*) **eine** ∼ **durch den Kopf schießen** blow one's brains out

kugel-, **Kugel-:** ∼**blitz** *der* (Met.) ball lightning; ∼**förmig** *Adj.* spherical; ∼**gelenk** *das* (Anat., Technik) ball-and-socket joint; ∼**hagel** *der* hail of bullets; ∼**kopf** *der* golf ball; ∼**kopfmaschine** *die* golf-ball typewriter; ∼**lager** *das* (Technik) ball-bearing

kugeln **1** *tr. V.* roll. **2** *V.* roll [about]; **sich [vor Lachen]** ∼ (ugs.) double *or* roll up [laughing *or* with laughter]. **3** *itr. V.; mit sein* roll

kugel-, **Kugel-:** ∼**rund** /-'-'-/ *Adj.* (a) round as a ball *postpos.;* (b) (scherzh.: dick) rotund; plump; tubby; ∼**schreiber** *der* hallpoint [pen]; ball pen; Biro (**P**); ∼**sicher** *Adj.* bullet-proof; ∼**stoßen** *das;* ∼**s** shot[-put]; (Disziplin) shot-putting *no art.;* putting the shot *no art.;* ∼**stoßer** *der,* ∼**stoßerin** *die* shot-putter

Kuh /ku:/ *die;* ∼, **Kühe** /'ky:ə/ (a) cow; **heilige** ∼ (ugs.) sacred cow; (b) (Elefanten∼, Giraffen∼, Flusspferd∼) cow; (Hirsch∼) hind; (c) (salopp abwertend: Frau) cow (sl. derog.)

Kuh-: ∼**dorf** *das* (salopp abwertend) one-horse town (sl.); ∼**fladen** *der* cow-pat; ∼**glocke** *die* cow-bell; ∼**handel** *der* (ugs. abwertend) shady horse-trading *no indef. art.;* ∼**haut** *die* cowhide; **das geht auf keine** ∼**haut** (fig. salopp) it's absolutely staggering *or* beyond belief; ∼**herde** *die* herd of cows

kühl /ky:l/ **1** *Adj.* (a) cool; **mir ist/wird** ∼: I feel/I'm getting chilly; **etw.** ∼ **lagern/aufbewahren** store/keep sth. in a cool place; (b) (abweisend, nüchtern) cool; **ein** ∼**er Rechner** a cool, calculating person. **2** *adv.* (abweisend, nüchtern) coolly

Kühle /'ky:lə/ *die;* ∼ (auch fig.) coolness; **die** ∼ **der Nacht** the cool of the night

kühlen **1** *tr. V.* cool; chill, cool ‹ *drink* ›; refrigerate ‹ *food* ›; **seinen Zorn/seine Rache [an jmdm.]** ∼: vent one's rage/revenge oneself [on sb.]. **2** *itr. V.* ‹ *cold compress, ointment, breeze, etc.* › have a cooling effect

Kühler *der;* ∼**s**, ∼ (a) (am Auto) radiator; (∼haube) bonnet (Brit.); hood (Amer.); **jmdn. auf den** ∼ **nehmen** (ugs.) drive *or* run into *or* hit sb.; (b) (Sekt∼) ice-bucket

Kühler-: ~**figur** *die* radiator mascot; ~**haube** *die* bonnet (Brit.); hood (Amer.)

Kühl-: ~**haus** *das* cold store; ~**mittel** *das* (Technik) coolant; ~**raum** *der* cold store; cold-storage room; ~**schrank** *der* refrigerator; fridge (Brit. coll.); icebox (Amer.); ~**tasche** *die* cool bag; ~**theke** *die* cold shelves *pl.;* ~**truhe** *die* [chest] freezer; deep-freeze; (im Lebensmittelgeschäft) freezer [cabinet]; ~**turm** *der* (Technik) cooling tower

Kühlung *die;* ~, ~**en** (a) cooling; (b) (Vorrichtung) cooling system; (für Lebensmittel) refrigeration system; (c) *o. Pl.* (Frische) coolness; **sich** (*Dat.*) ~ **verschaffen** cool down *or* off

Kühl-: ~**wagen** *der* (a) (Eisenb.) refrigerated *or* refrigerator car *or* (Brit.) wagon; (b) (Lastwagen) refrigerated *or* refrigerator truck *or* (Brit.) lorry; ~**wasser** *das* cooling water

Kuh-: ~**milch** *die* cow's milk; ~**mist** *der* cow dung

kühn /kyːn/ **1** *Adj.* (a) bold; (gewagt) daring; brave, fearless ‹*warrior*›; **das übertraf meine** ~**sten Träume** that exceeded my wildest dreams; (b) (dreist) audacious; impudent. **2** *adv.* (a) boldly; (gewagt) daringly; (b) (dreist) audaciously; impudently

Kühnheit *die;* ~ (a) boldness; (Gewagtheit) daringness; (b) (Dreistigkeit) audacity; impudence

Kuh·stall *der* cowshed

Küken /'kyːkn̩/ *das;* ~**s**, ~**:** chick

kulant /ku'lant/ *Adj.* obliging; accommodating; fair ‹*terms*›

Kulanz /ku'lants/ *die;* ~**:** readiness *or* willingness to oblige; **aus** ~**:** out of good will

Kuli /'kuːli/ *der;* ~**s**, ~**s** (a) coolie; (b) (ugs.: Kugelschreiber) ballpoint; Biro (**P**)

kulinarisch /kuli'naːrɪʃ/ *Adj.* culinary

Kulisse /ku'lɪsə/ *die;* ~, ~**n** piece of scenery; flat; wing; (Hintergrund) backdrop; **die** ~**n** the scenery *sing.;* **die** ~ **für etw. bilden** (fig.) form the backdrop to sth.; **hinter den** ~**n** (fig.) behind the scenes

Kulissen·schieber *der* (ugs. scherzh.) scene-shifter

Kuller·augen *Pl.* (ugs. scherzh.) big, round eyes; **er machte** ~**:** his eyes nearly popped out of his head

kullern /'kʊlɐn/ (ugs.) **1** *itr. V.* (a) *mit sein* roll; (b) *mit* **den Augen** ~**:** roll one's eyes. **2** *tr. V.* roll

Kulmination /kʊlmina'tsi̯oːn/ *die;* ~, ~**en** (auch Astron.) culmination

Kulminations·punkt *der* (a) culmination; culminating point; (b) (Astron.) point of culmination

kulminieren /kʊlmi'niːrən/ *itr. V.* (auch Astron.) culminate (**in** + *Dat.* in)

Kult /kʊlt/ *der;* ~**[e]s**, ~**e** (auch fig.) cult; **mit jmdm./ etw. einen** ~ **treiben** make a cult out of sb./sth.

Kult-: ~**bild** *das* devotional image; ~**figur** *die* cult figure; ~**film** *der* cult film; ~**handlung** *die* ritual; ritualistic act

kultisch **1** *Adj.* cultic; ritual, cultic ‹*object*›. **2** *adv.* ‹*worship*› cultically

kultivieren /kʊlti'viːrən/ *tr. V.* (auch fig.) cultivate

kultiviert **1** *Adj.* (a) cultivated; cultured; (b) (fein) refined. **2** *adv.* in a cultivated *or* cultured manner; (fein) in a refined manner; with refinement

Kultivierung *die;* ~, ~**en** (auch fig.) cultivation; improvement

Kult·stätte *die* centre of cult worship

Kultur /kʊl'tuːɐ̯/ *die;* ~, ~**en** (a) *o. Pl.* (geistiger Überbau) culture; (b) (Zivilisation, Lebensform) civilization; (c) *o. Pl.* (Kultiviertheit, geistiges Niveau) **ein Mensch von** ~**:** a cultured person; **sie hat [keine]** ~**:** she is [un]cultured; (d) *o. Pl.* (kultivierte Lebensart) refinement; ~ **haben** be refined; (e) (Landw., Gartenbau) young crop; (Forstw.) young plantation; (f) (Biol., Med.) culture

Kultur-: ~**attaché** *der* cultural attaché; ~**austausch** *der* cultural exchange; ~**banause** *der* (abwertend, oft scherzh.) philistine; ~**beutel** *der* sponge bag (Brit.); toilet bag

kulturell /kʊltʊ'rɛl/ **1** *Adj.* cultural. **2** *adv.* culturally

kultur-, Kultur-: ~**epoche** *die* cultural epoch; ~**film** *der* documentary film; ~**geschichte** *die o. Pl.* history of civilization; (einer bestimmten Kultur) cultural history; ~**gut** *das* cultural possessions *pl.;* ~**haupt·stadt** *die* cultural capital; ~**hoheit** *die* autonomy *or* independence in cultural and educational matters; ~**kreis** *der* cultural area; ~**kanal** *der* (Ferns.) cultural channel; ~**los** *Adj.* uncultured; lacking in culture *post-pos.;* ~**magazin** *das* (Ferns.) arts magazine; ~**minister** *der* minister for the arts; ~**ministerium** *das* ministry for the arts; ~**politik** *die* cultural and educational policy; ~**revolution** *die* cultural revolution; ~**stufe** *die* level of civilization; ~**szene** *die; o. Pl.* (ugs.) cultural scene; ~**volk** *das* civilized people *sing.;* ~**zentrum** *das* (a) cultural centre; centre of cultural life; (b) (Anlage) arts centre

Kultus-: ~**minister** *der*, ~**ministerin** *die* minister for education and cultural affairs; ~**ministerium** *das* ministry of education and cultural affairs

Kümmel /'kyml̩/ *der;* ~**s**, ~ (a) caraway [seed]; (b) (Branntwein) kümmel

Kummer /'kʊmɐ/ *der;* ~**s** sorrow; grief; (Ärger, Sorgen) trouble; ~ **um** *od.* **über jmdn.** grief for *or* over sb.; **hast du** ~**?** is there a problem?; **jmdm.** ~ **machen** give sb. trouble *or* bother; **ich bin** ~ **gewohnt** (ugs.) it happens all the time; I'm used to it

kümmerlich **1** *Adj.* (a) puny; stunted ‹*vegetation, plants*›; (b) (ärmlich) wretched; miserable; (c) (abwertend: gering) miserable; meagre, scanty ‹*knowledge, leftovers*›; very poor ‹*effort*›. **2** *adv.* **sich** ~ **ernähren** live on a poor *or* meagre diet; **sich** ~ **durchschlagen** eke out a bare/miserable existence

kümmern /'kymɐn/ **1** *refl. V.* (a) **sich um jmdn./etw.** ~**:** take care of *or* look after sb./sth.; **sich darum** ~, **dass** …: see to it that …; (b) (sich befassen mit) **sich nicht um das Geschwätz** *usw.* ~**:** not worry *or* mind about the gossip *etc.;* **sich nicht um Politik** ~**:** not care about *or* be interested in politics; **kümmere dich um deine eigenen Angelegenheiten** mind your own business. **2** *tr. V.* concern; **was kümmert dich das?** what concern *or* business is it of yours?; what's it to you?; **Was kümmerts mich?** What do I care?

Kummer·speck *der* (ugs.) **sie hat** ~ **angesetzt** all the worrying has made her eat too much, and she's [really] put on weight

kummer·voll **1** *Adj.* sorrowful; sad. **2** *adv.* sorrowfully; sadly

Kumpan /kʊm'paːn/ *der;* ~**s**, ~**e**, **Kumpanin** *die;* ~, ~**nen** (ugs.) (a) pal (coll.); mate; buddy (coll.); (b) (abwertend: Mittäter) accomplice

Kumpel /'kʊmpl̩/ *der;* ~**s**, ~, *ugs. auch:* ~**s** (a) (Bergmannsspr.) miner; collier; (b) (salopp: Kamerad) pal; mate; buddy (coll.)

kumpelhaft **1** *Adj.* matey; chummy (coll.). **2** *adv.* matily; chummily (coll.)

Kumulation /kumula'tsi̯oːn/ *die;* ~, ~**en** cumulation; (von Ämtern) plurality‘

kumulativ /kumula'tiːf/ *Adj.* kumulativ

kumulieren /kumu'liːrən/ *tr. V.* cumulate; **eine** ~**de Bibliographie** a cumulative bibliography

Kumulierung *die;* ~, ~**en** cumulation

Kumulus /'kuːmʊls/ *der;* ~, **Kumuli** (Met.) cumulus [cloud]

Kumulus·wolke *die* (Met.) cumulus cloud

kündbar *Adj.* terminable ‹*contract*›; redeemable ‹*loan, mortgage*›; **Beamte sind nicht** ~**:** established civil servants cannot be dismissed *or* given their notice

Kündbarkeit *die;* ~ (von Verträgen) terminability; (von Anleihen, Hypotheken) redeemability

Kunde¹ /'kʊndə/ *der;* ~**n**, ~**n** (a) customer; (eines Architekten, einer Versicherung usw.) client; (b) (ugs.: Kerl) customer (coll.)

Kunde² *die;* ~ (geh.) tidings *pl.* (literary); **jmdm. von etw.** ~ **geben** (veralt.) bring sb. tidings of sth.

künden /'kyndn̩/ **1** *tr. V.* (geh.: ver~) proclaim; **diese Zeichen** ~ **Unglück** these omens herald misfortune. **2** *itr. V.* (geh.) **von etw.** ~**:** bear witness to *or* tell of sth.

Kunden-: ∼**dienst** der (a) o. Pl. service to customers; (Wartung) after-sales service; (b) (Abteilung) service department; ∼**kreis** der customers pl.; (eines Architekten-, Anwaltbüros, einer Versicherung usw.) clientele; ∼**stamm** der regular clientele or trade

kund|geben unr. tr. V. (geh.) declare; announce; express, make known ⟨opinion, feelings⟩

Kundgebung die; ∼, ∼en rally

kundig 1 Adj. knowledgeable; well-informed; (sachverständig) expert; **einer Sache** (Gen.) ∼/**nicht** ∼ **sein** (geh.) know about sth./have no knowledge of sth. 2 adv. expertly

kündigen /'kʏndɪgn/ 1 tr. V. call in, cancel ⟨loan⟩; foreclose ⟨mortgage⟩; cancel, discontinue ⟨magazine subscription, membership⟩; terminate ⟨contract, agreement⟩; denounce ⟨treaty⟩; **seine Stellung** ∼: give in or hand in one's notice (**bei** to); **ich bin gekündigt worden** (ugs.) I've been given my notice; **der Vermieter hat ihm die Wohnung gekündigt** the landlord gave him notice to quit the flat (Brit.) or (Amer.) apartment; **er hat seine Wohnung gekündigt** he's given notice that he's leaving his flat (Brit.) or (Amer.) apartment; **jmdm. die Freundschaft** ∼ (fig.) break off a friendship with sb. 2 unr. itr. V. (a) (ein Mietverhältnis beenden) ⟨tenant⟩ give notice [that one is leaving]; **jmdm.** ∼ ⟨landlord⟩ give sb. notice to quit; **zum 1. Juli** ∼: give notice for 1 July; (b) (ein Arbeitsverhältnis beenden) ⟨employee⟩ give in or hand in one's notice (**bei** to); **jmdm.** ∼ ⟨employer⟩ give sb. his/her notice

Kündigung die; ∼, ∼en (a) (eines Kredits) calling-in; cancellation; (einer Hypothek) foreclosure; (der Mitgliedschaft, eines Abonnements) cancellation; discontinuation; (eines Vertrags) termination; (b) (eines Arbeitsverhältnisses) **jmdm. die** ∼ **aussprechen** give sb. his/her notice; dismiss sb.; **mit** ∼ **drohen** ⟨employee⟩ threaten to give in or hand in one's notice or to quit; ⟨employer⟩ threaten dismissal; **fristlose** ∼: dismissal without notice; (c) (eines Mietverhältnisses) **sie musste mit** ∼ **rechnen** she had to reckon on being given notice to quit; (d) ⇒ **Kündigungsschreiben**; (e) (Kündigungsfrist) [period or term of] notice

Kündigungs-: ∼**frist** die period of notice; ∼**grund** der (Arbeitsrecht) grounds pl. for dismissal; grounds pl. for giving sb. his/her notice; (Mietrecht) grounds pl. for giving sb. notice to quit; ∼**schreiben** das written notice; notice in writing; ∼**schutz** der protection against wrongful dismissal

Kundin die; ∼, ∼nen ⇒ **Kunde¹ a:** customer; client

Kundschaft die; ∼, ∼en o. Pl.; ⇒ **Kunde¹ a:** customers pl.; clientele; ∼! service!

Kundschafter der; ∼s, ∼, **Kundschafterin** die; ∼, ∼nen scout

kund|tun (geh.) 1 unr. tr. V. announce; make known. 2 unr. refl. V. be revealed; show itself

künftig /'kʏnftɪç/ 1 Adj. future. 2 adv. in future

Kungelei die; ∼, ∼en (abwertend) wheeling and dealing; **eine Kungelei um etw.** bargaining over sth.; **große** ∼en a great deal opf wheeling and dealing

kungeln /'kʊŋln/ itr. V. [mit jmdm.] um etw. ∼: bargain [with sb.] over sth.; **dort wird viel gekungelt** there is a lot of wheeling and dealing there

Kunst /kʊnst/ die; ∼, **Künste** /'kʏnstə/ (a) art; **die Schwarze** ∼ (Magie) the black art; (Buchdruck) [the art of] printing; **die schönen Künste** [the] fine arts; fine art sing.; **was macht die** ∼? (ugs.) how are things?; how's tricks? (sl.); (b) (das Können) skill; **die ärztliche** ∼: medical skill; **die** ∼ **des Reitens/der Selbstverteidigung** the art of riding/selfdefence; **das ist keine** ∼! (ugs.) there's nothing 'to it; **mit seiner** ∼ **am Ende sein** be at a complete loss; s. auch **Regel a**

kunst-, Kunst-: ∼**akademie** die art college; college of art; ∼**ausstellung** die art exhibition; ∼**banause** der (abwertend) philistine; ∼**buch** das art book; ∼**denkmal** das artistic and cultural monument; ∼**druck** der [fine] art print; ∼**dünger** der chemical or artificial fertilizer; ∼**erzieher** der, ∼**erzieherin** die ▶85◀ art teacher; ∼**erziehung** die art education; (Schulfach) art; ∼**faser** die man-made or synthetic fibre; ∼**fehler** der professional error; **ein ärztlicher**

∼**fehler** a professional error on the part of a doctor; ∼**fertig** 1 Adj. skilful; 2 adv. skilfully; ∼**fertigkeit** die skill; skilfulness; ∼**flieger** der aerobatic pilot; stunt pilot (coll.); ∼**flug** der aerobatics sing.; stunt-flying (coll.); ∼**gegenstand** der work of art; ∼**gerecht** 1 Adj. expert; skilful; 2 adv. expertly; skilfully; ∼**geschichte** die (a) o. Pl. art history; history of art; (b) (Buch) art history book; book on the history of art; ∼**geschichtlich** 1 Adj. art historical ⟨studies, evidence, expertise, point of view, etc.⟩; 2 adv. ∼**geschichtlich interessiert/versiert** interested/well versed in art history or the history of art; ∼**gewerbe** das arts and crafts pl.; ∼**gewerblich** Adj. craft attrib. ⟨objects, skills, etc.⟩; ∼**gewerbliche Arbeiten** craftwork sing.; ∼**griff** der move; (fig.) trick; dodge; ∼**handel** der [fine-]art trade; ∼**händler** der [fine-]art dealer; ∼**handwerk** das craftwork; ∼**harz** das (Chemie) synthetic resin; ∼**historiker** der ▶85◀ art historian; ∼**historisch** ⇒ ∼**geschichtlich**; ∼**kenner** der art connoisseur or expert; ∼**kritik** die art criticism; die ∼: the art critics pl.; ∼**kritiker** der ▶85◀ art critic; ∼**leder** das artificial or imitation leather

Künstler /'kʏnstlɐ/ der; ∼s, ∼, **Künstlerin** die; ∼, ∼nen ▶85◀ (a) artist; (Zirkus∼, Varietee∼) artiste; **ein bildender** ∼: a visual artist; (b) (Könner) genius (**in** + Dat. at); **ein** ∼ **in seinem Fach** a genius in one's field/ at one's trade

künstlerisch 1 Adj. artistic. 2 adv. artistically; **ein** ∼ **wertvoller Film** a film of great artistic worth

Künstler-: ∼**name** der stage-name; ∼**pech** das (ugs. scherzh.) hard luck

künstlich /'kʏnstlɪç/ 1 Adj. (a) artificial; artificial, glass ⟨eye⟩; false ⟨teeth, eyelashes, hair⟩; synthetic, man-made ⟨fibre⟩; imitation, synthetic ⟨diamond⟩; (b) (gezwungen) forced ⟨laugh, cheerfulness, etc.⟩; enforced ⟨rest⟩. 2 adv. (a) artificially; (b) **sich** ∼ **aufregen** (ugs.) get worked up or excited about nothing

kunst-, Kunst-: ∼**liebhaber** der art lover; lover of the arts; ∼**los** 1 Adj. plain; 2 adv. plainly; ∼**maler** der ▶85◀ artist; painter; ∼**pause** die pause for effect; (iron.: Stockung) awkward pause; ∼**richtung** die trend in art; ∼**sammlung** die art collection; ∼**schatz** der art treasure; ∼**seide** die artificial silk; rayon; ∼**springen** das (Sport) springboard diving; ∼**stoff** der synthetic material; plastic; ∼**stück** das trick; **das ist kein** ∼**stück** (ugs.) it's no great feat or achievement; ∼**stück!** (ugs. iron.) that's no great achievement; (ist nicht verwunderlich) it's hardly surprising; ∼**turnen** das gymnastics sing.; ∼**verstand** der artistic sense; feeling for art; ∼**voll** 1 Adj. ornate or elaborate and artistic; (kompliziert) elaborate; 2 adv. (a) ornately or elaborately and artistically; (b) (geschickt) skilfully; ∼**werk** das work of art; ∼**wissenschaft** die aesthetics and art history

kunter·bunt /'kʊntɐ-/ 1 Adj. (a) (vielfarbig) multi-coloured; (b) (abwechslungsreich) varied; (c) (ungeordnet) jumbled ⟨confusion, muddle, rows, etc.⟩. 2 adv. (a) ⟨painted, printed⟩ in many colours; (b) (abwechslungsreich) **ein** ∼ **gestalteter Abend** an evening of varied entertainment; (c) (ungeordnet) ∼ **durcheinander sein** be higgledy-piggledy or all jumbled up; **es ging** ∼ **durcheinander** it was completely chaotic

Kunz /kʊnts/ ⇒ **Hinz**

Kupfer /'kʊpfɐ/ das; ∼s (a) copper; (b) (∼geschirr) copperware; (∼geld) coppers pl.

kupfer-, Kupfer-: ∼**geld** das coppers pl.; ∼**münze** die copper coin; copper; ∼**rot** Adj. copperred; copper-coloured; ∼**stich** der (a) o. Pl. copperplate engraving no art.; (b) (Blatt) copperplate print or engraving

Kupon ⇒ **Coupon**

Kuppe /'kʊpə/ die; ∼, ∼n (a) [rounded] hilltop; (b) (Finger∼) tip; end

Kuppel /'kʊpl/ die; ∼, ∼n dome; (kleiner) cupola

Kuppel-: ∼**bau** der; Pl. ∼**bauten** domed building; ∼**dach** das domed or dome-shaped roof

Kuppelei die; ∼, ∼en (a) (veralt. abwertend) match-making; (b) o. Pl. (Rechtsspr.) procuring; procuration

kuppeln 1 *itr. V.* (bei einem Kfz) operate the clutch. **2** *tr. V.* (**a**) (koppeln) couple (**an** + *Akk.*, **zu** [on] to); (**b**) (Technik) couple

Kuppler *der;* ~s, ~ (abwertend) procurer

Kupplerin *die;* ~, ~**nen** (abwertend) procuress

Kupplung *die;* ~, ~**en** (**a**) (Kfz-W.) clutch; (**b**) (Technik: Vorrichtung zum Verbinden) coupling

Kupplungs·pedal *das* clutch pedal

Kur /kuːɐ̯/ *die;* ~, ~**en ▶ 329** [health] cure; (ohne Aufenthalt im Badeort) course of treatment; **eine** ~ **machen** take a cure/a course of treatment; **in** ~ **gehen** go to a health resort *or* spa [to take a cure]

Kür /kyːɐ̯/ *die;* ~, ~**en** (Eiskunstlauf) free programme; (Turnen) optional exercises *pl.;* **eine** ~ **laufen/tanzen** skate/dance one's free programme; **eine** ~ **turnen** perform one's optional exercises

Kuratorium /kuraˈtoːri̯ʊm/ *das;* ~s, **Kuratorien** board of trustees

Kur-: ~**aufenthalt** *der* stay at a health resort *or* spa; ~**bad** *das* health resort; spa

Kurbel /ˈkʊrbl̩/ *die;* ~, ~**n** crank [handle]; (an Fenstern, Spieldosen, Grammophonen) winder

kurbeln 1 *tr. V.* etw. nach oben/unten ~: wind sth. up/down. **2** *itr. V.* turn *or* wind a/the handle

Kurbel·welle *die* (Technik) crankshaft

Kürbis /ˈkʏrbɪs/ *der;* ~ses, ~se (**a**) pumpkin; (**b**) (salopp: Kopf) nut (coll.); bonce (Brit. sl.)

küren *regelm.* (*veralt. auch unr.*) *tr. V.* choose (**zu** as)

Kur-: ~**fürst** *der* (hist.) Elector; ~**fürstentum** *das* (hist.) electorate; ~**gast** *der* visitor to a/the health resort *or* spa; (Patient) patient at a/the health resort *or* spa; ~**haus** *das* assembly rooms [at a health resort *or* spa]

Kurier /kuˈriːɐ̯/ *der;* ~s, ~e courier; messenger

Kurier·dienst *der* courier *or* messenger service

kurieren *tr. V.* (auch fig.) cure (**von** of)

kurios /kuˈri̯oːs/ **1** *Adj.* curious; strange; odd. **2** *adv.* curiously; strangely; oddly

Kuriosität /kuri̯oziˈtɛːt/ *die;* ~, ~**en** (**a**) o. Pl. strangeness; oddity; peculiarity; (**b**) (Gegenstand) curiosity; curio

Kuriositäten·kabinett *das* gallery of curios

Kur-: ~**klinik** *die* health clinic; ~**konzert** *das* concert [at a health resort or spa]; spa concert

Kür·lauf *der* (Eiskunstlauf) free programme

Kur-: ~**ort** *der* health resort; spa; ~**park** *der* gardens *pl.* [of a/the health resort *or* spa]; ~**pfuscher** *der* (ugs. abwertend) quack; doctor; ~**pfuscherei** *die* (ugs. abwertend) quackery

Kurs /kʊrs/ *der;* ~es, ~e (**a**) (Richtung) course; **auf** [**nördlichen**] ~ **gehen** set [a northerly] course; **ein harter/weicher** ~ (fig.) a hard/soft line; **den** ~ **ändern/halten** (auch fig.) change *or* alter/hold *or* maintain course; ~ **auf Hamburg** (*Akk.*) **nehmen** set course for *or* head for Hamburg; (**b**) (von Wertpapieren) price; (von Devisen) rate of exchange; exchange rate; **zum** ~ **von** …: at a rate of …; **der** ~ **des Dollars** the dollar rate; **hoch im** ~ **stehen** ‹securities› be high; (fig.) be very popular (**bei** with); (**c**) (Lehrgang) course; **ein** ~ **in Spanisch** (*Dat.*) a course in Spanish; a Spanish course; (**d**) (die Teilnehmer eines Kurses) class; (**e**) (Sport: Rennstrecke) course

Kurs-: ~**änderung** *die* (auch fig.) change of course; ~**anstieg** *der* (Börsenw.) rise in prices/price; price rise; (bei Devisen) rise in exchange rates/the exchange rate; ~**buch** *das* (Eisenb.) timetable

Kürschner /ˈkʏrʃnɐ/ *der;* ~s, ~, **Kürschnerin** *die;* ~, ~**nen ▶ 85** furrier

kursieren *itr. V.; auch mit sein* circulate

kursiv /kʊrˈziːf/ (Druckw.) **1** *Adj.* italic. **2** *adv.* **etw.** ~ **drucken** print sth. in italics; (zur Hervorhebung) italicize sth.

Kurs-: ~**korrektur** *die* (auch fig.) course correction; ~**leiter** *der* course-leader; ~**rück·gang** *der* (Börsenw.) fall in prices/price; price fall; (bei Devisen) fall in exchange rates/the exchange rate; ~**schwankung** *die* (Börsenw.)

fluctuation in prices/price; (bei Devisen) fluctuation in exchange rates/the exchange rate; ~**teilnehmer** *der* course participant

Kursus /ˈkʊrzʊs/ *der;* ~, **Kurse** ⇨ **Kurs** c, d

Kurs-: ~**wagen** *der* (Eisenb.) through carriage *or* coach; ~**wechsel** *der* (auch fig.) change of course

Kur·taxe *die* visitors' tax

Kurve /ˈkʊrvə/ *die;* ~, ~**n** (**a**) (einer Straße) bend; curve; **die Straße macht eine [scharfe]** ~: the road bends *or* curves [sharply]; **die** ~ **kratzen** (ugs.) quickly make oneself scarce (coll.); **die** ~ **kriegen** (ugs.) manage to do it; (etw. überwinden) manage to do something decisive about it; (**b**) (Geom.) curve; (**c**) (in der Statistik, Temperatur~ usw.) graph; curve; (**d**) (Bogenlinie) curve; **eine** ~ **fliegen** do a banking turn; (**e**) *Pl.* (ugs.: Körperformen) curves

kurven *itr. V.; mit sein* (ugs.: fahren) **durch die Gegend** ~: drive/ride around; **durch ganz Europa** ~: drive/ride around the whole of Europe

kurven·reich *Adj.* (**a**) winding; twisting; „~**reiche Strecke**" 'series of bends'; (**b**) (ugs. scherzh.) curvaceous

Kur·verwaltung *die* administrative office/offices of a/the health resort *or* spa

kurz /kʊrts/; **kürzer** /ˈkʏrtsɐ/, **kürzest**… /ˈkʏrtsəst…/ **1** *Adj.* (**a**) (räumlich) short; ~**e Hosen** short trousers; shorts; **etw. kürzer machen** make sth. shorter; shorten sth.; **jmdn. einen Kopf kürzer machen** (ugs.) chop sb.'s head off; **etw./alles** ~ **und klein schlagen** *od.* **hauen** (ugs.) smash sth./everything to bits *or* pieces; **den Kürzeren ziehen** come off worst *or* second-best; get the worst of it; **nicht zu** ~/**zu** ~ **kommen** get one's/less than one's fair share; (**b**) (zeitlich) short, brief ‹trip, journey, visit, reply›; short ‹life, break, time›; quick ‹look›; **nach einer** ~**en Weile** after a short *or* little while; ~ **machen** make *or* keep it short; be brief; (**c**) (knapp) short, brief ‹outline, note, report, summary, introduction›; ~ **und bündig** *od.* **knapp** brief and succinct; (**d**) **jmdn.** ~ **halten** (jmdm. wenig Geld geben) keep sb. short of money; (jmd. wenig erlauben) keep sb. on a tight rein. **2** *adv.* (**a**) (zeitlich) briefly; for a short time *or* while; **die Freude währte nur** ~ (geh.) his/her *etc.* joy was short-lived; **binnen** ~**em** shortly; soon; **über** ~ **oder lang** sooner *or* later; **vor** ~**em** a short time *or* while ago; recently; **sie lebt erst seit** ~**em in Bonn** she's only been living in Bonn [for] a short time *or* while; (**b**) (knapp) ~ **gesagt**/~ **und gut** in a word; ~ **angebunden sein** be curt *or* brusque (**mit** with); **sich** ~ **fassen** be brief; (**c**) (rasch) **ich muss mal** ~ **weg** I must leave you for a few minutes; **er schaute** ~ **herein** he looked *or* dropped in for a short while; **kann ich Sie** ~ **sprechen?** can I speak to you *or* have a word with you for a moment?; ~ **und schmerzlos** (ugs.) quickly and smoothly *or* without any hitches; *s. auch* **entschlossen 3**; (**d**) (wenig) just; ~ **vor/hinter der Kreuzung** just before/past the crossroads; ~ **vor/nach Pfingsten** just *or* shortly before/after Whitsun; ~ **bevor** …/**nachdem** …: just *or* shortly before …/after …; (**e**) ~ **treten** take things *or* it easy; (sparsam sein) retrench; cut back; **kürzer treten** take things *or* it easier; (sparsamer sein) cut back; spend less

kurz-, Kurz-: ~**arbeit** *die* short time; short-time working; ~**arbeiten** *itr. V.* work short time; ~**arbeiter** *der* short-time worker; worker on short time; ~**ärm[e]lig** /~ˀɛrm(ə)lɪç/ *Adj.* short-sleeved; ~**atmig** /~aːtmɪç/ *Adj.* (auch fig.) short-winded; ~**atmig sein** be short of breath; be short-winded

Kurze *der; adj. Dekl.* (ugs.) (**a**) (Kurzschluss) short (coll.); (**b**) (Schnaps) schnapps

Kürze /ˈkʏrtsə/ *die;* ~, ~**n** (**a**) o. Pl. shortness; (**b**) o. Pl. (geringe Dauer) shortness; short duration; brevity; **in** ~: shortly; soon; (**c**) o. Pl. (Knappheit) brevity; **in aller/gebotener** ~: very briefly/with due brevity; **in der** ~ **liegt die Würze** (Spr.) brevity is the soul of wit (prov.)

Kürzel /ˈkʏrtsl̩/ *das;* ~s, ~ (**a**) shorthand symbol; (**b**) (Abkürzung) abbreviation

kürzen *tr. V.* (**a**) shorten; shorten, take up ‹garment›; (**b**) (verringern) shorten ‹speech›; shorten, abridge ‹article, book›; reduce, cut ‹pension, budget, etc.›; (**c**) (Math.) cancel

---

*alte Schreibung (vgl. Hinweise auf S. xvi–xvii)

kürzer ⇨ **kurz**
kurzer·hand *Adv.* without more ado; **jmdn.** ~ **vor die Tür setzen** (ugs.) unceremoniously throw sb. out; **etw.** ~ **ablehnen** flatly reject sth.; reject sth. out of hand
***kürzer|treten** ⇨ **kurz** 2 e
kürzest… ⇨ **kurz**
kurz-, Kurz-: ~**fassung** *die* shortened *or* abridged version; ~**film** *der* short; short film; ~**fristig** 1 *Adj.* (a) (plötzlich) ⟨*refusal, resignation, etc.*⟩ at short notice; (b) (für kurze Zeit) short-term; 2 *adv.* (a) (plötzlich) at short notice; **sich** ~**fristig entschließen, etw. zu tun** make up one's mind within a short time to do sth.; (b) (für kurze Zeit) for a short time *or* period; (auf kurze Sicht) in the short term; (c) (in kurzer Zeit) without delay; ~**geschichte** *die* (Literaturw.) short story; ~**haarig** *Adj.* short-haired ⟨*dog, breed, etc.*⟩; ⟨*person*⟩ with short hair;*~**|halten** ⇨ **kurz** 1 d; ~**lebig** /~le:bɪç/ *Adj.* (auch fig.) short-lived; (wenig haltbar) non-durable ⟨*goods, materials*⟩; with a short life *postpos.*
kürzlich *Adv.* recently; not long ago; **erst** ~: just *or* only recently; only a short time ago
kurz-, Kurz-: ~**meldung** *die* brief report; (während einer anderen Sendung) news flash; ~**nachrichten** *Pl.* news *sing.* in brief; news summary *sing.;* ~**|schließen** *unr. tr. V.* short-circuit; ~**schluss**, *~**schluß** *der* (a) (Elektrot.) short-circuit; (b) (fig. ugs.) brainstorm; (c) (falscher Schluss) fallacy; ~**schluss·handlung**, *~**schluß·handlung** *die* sudden irrational act; ~**schrift** *die* shorthand; ~**sichtig** (auch fig.) 1 *Adj.* short-sighted; 2 *adv.* short-sightedly; ~**sichtigkeit** *die;* ~ (auch fig.) short-sightedness
Kurzstrecken-: ~**flug** *der* short-haul flight; ~**läufer** *der* (Sport) sprinter
kurz-: *~**|treten** ⇨ **kurz** 2 e; ~**um** /-'-/ *Adv.* in short; in a word
Kürzung *die;* ~, ~**en** (a) cut; reduction; **eine** ~ **des Gehaltes** a cut *or* reduction in salary; a salary cut; (b) (Streichung) cut; (das Streichen) abridgement
kurz-, Kurz-: ~**wahl** *die* (Fernspr.) abbreviated dialling; ~**waren** *Pl.* haberdashery *sing.* (Brit.); notions (Amer.); ~**weilig** *Adj.* entertaining; ~**welle** *die* (Physik, Rundf.) short wave; ~**wellen·sender** *der* (Funkt., Rundf.) short-wave transmitter; ~**zeitig** 1 *Adj.* brief; 2 *adv.* briefly; for a short time
kuschelig *Adj.* cosy
kuscheln /'kʊʃln̩/ *refl. V.* **sich an jmdn.** ~: snuggle up *or* cuddle up to sb.; ⟨*cat etc.*⟩ snuggle up to sb.; **sich in etw.** (*Akk.*) ~: snuggle up in sth.
kuschen /'kʊʃn̩/ *itr. V.* (a) ⟨*dog*⟩ lie down; (b) (fig.) knuckle under (**vor** + *Dat.* to)
Kusine /ku'zi:nə/ *die;* ~, ~**n** ⇨ **Cousine**
Kuss, *Kuß /kʊs/ *der;* **Kusses, Küsse** /'kʏsə/ kiss
Küsschen, *Küßchen /'kʏsçən/ *das;* ~**s**, ~: little kiss
kuss·echt, *kuß·echt *Adj.* kissproof
küssen /'kʏsn̩/ *tr., itr. V.* kiss; **jmdm. die Hand** ~: kiss sb.'s hand; **küss die Hand** (südd., österr.) (beim Kommen) how do you do?; good day; (beim Gehen) goodbye; **sich** *od.* (geh.) **einander** ~: kiss [each other]
Kuss·hand, *Kuß·hand *die:* **jmdm. eine** ~ **zuwerfen** blow sb. a kiss; **jmdm./etw. mit** ~ **nehmen** (ugs.) be only too glad *or* pleased to take sb./sth.
Küste /'kʏstə/ *die;* ~, ~**n** coast
Küsten-: ~**fischerei** *die* inshore fishing; *~**schiffahrt**, ~**schifffahrt** *die* coastal shipping *no art.;* ~**wache** *die* coastguard [service]
Küster /'kʏstɐ/ *der;* ~**s**, ~: ▶ 85⟩ sexton
Kutsche /'kʊtʃə/ *die;* ~, ~**n** (a) coach; carriage; (b) (salopp: Auto) jalopy (coll.)
Kutscher *der;* ~**s**, ~: coachman; coach driver
kutschieren 1 *itr. V.; mit sein* (a) drive, ride [in a coach *or* carriage]; (b) (ugs.) **durch die Gegend/durch Europa** ~: drive around/drive around Europe. 2 *tr. V.* (a) **jmdn.** ~: drive sb. [in a coach *or* carriage]; (b) (ugs.) **jmdn. nach Hause** ~: run sb. home
Kutte /'kʊtə/ *die;* ~, ~**n** (monk's/nun's) habit
Kutteln /'kʊtln̩/ *Pl.* (südd., österr., schweiz.) tripe *sing.*
Kutter /'kʊtɐ/ *der;* ~**s**, ~: cutter

Kuvert /ku've:ɐ̯/ *das;* ~**s**, ~**s** (landsch., veralt.) envelope
Kuvertüre /kuvɛr'ty:rə/ *die;* ~, ~**n** chocolate coating
kW /ka:'ve:/ *Abk.* (Physik) **Kilowatt** kW
KW *Abk.* **Kurzwelle** SW
kWh *Abk.* (Physik) **Kilowattstunde** kWh
Kybernetik /kybɐ'ne:tɪk/ *die;* ~: cybernetics *sing.*
kyrillisch /ky'rɪlɪʃ/ *Adj.* Cyrillic
KZ /ka:'tsɛt/ *das;* ~**[s]**, ~**[s]** *Abk.* **Konzentrationslager**

···

Ll

···

l, L /ɛl/ *das;* ~, ~: l/L; *s. auch* **a, A**
labb[e]rig /'labərɪç/ *Adj.* (ugs. abwertend) (a) (fade) wishy-washy; ~ **schmecken** taste of nothing; (b) (weich) floppy, limp ⟨*material*⟩; floppy ⟨*trousers, dress, etc.*⟩
laben /'la:bn̩/ (geh.) 1 *tr. V.* **jmdn.** ~: give sb. refreshment; **ein** ~**der Trunk** a refreshing drink. 2 *refl. V.* refresh oneself (**an** + *Dat.,* **mit** with)
labern /'la:bɐn/ (ugs. abwertend) 1 *tr. V.* talk; **was laberst du da?** what are you rabbiting (Brit. coll.) *or* babbling on about? 2 *itr. V.* rabbit (Brit. coll.) *or* babble on
labil /la'bi:l/ *Adj.* delicate, frail ⟨*constitution, health*⟩; poor ⟨*circulation*⟩; unstable ⟨*person, character, situation, equilibrium, etc.*⟩
Labilität /labili'tɛ:t/ *die;* ~, ~**en** ⇨ **labil:** delicateness; frailness; poorness; instability
Labor /la'bo:ɐ̯/ *das;* ~**s**, ~**s**, *auch:* ~**e** laboratory
Laborant /labo'rant/ *der;* ~**en**, ~**en**, **Laborantin** *die;* ~, ~**nen** ▶ 85⟩ laboratory *or* (coll.) lab assistant *or* technician
Laboratorium /labora'to:riʊm/ *das;* ~**s**, **Laborato·rien** laboratory
laborieren *itr. V.* (ugs.) (a) (leiden) suffer (**an** + *Dat.* from); **er laboriert schon seit Wochen an einer Grippe** he's been trying to shake off the flu for weeks (coll.); (b) (sich abmühen) **an etw.** (*Dat.*) ~: labour *or* toil away at sth.
Labyrinth /laby'rɪnt/ *das;* ~**[e]s**, ~**e** maze; labyrinth
Lach·anfall *der* laughing-fit; fit of laughing
Lache[1] /'laxə/ *die;* ~, ~**n** (ugs.) laugh
Lache[2] /'la(:)xə/ *die;* ~, ~**n** puddle, (von Blut, Öl) pool
lächeln /'lɛçln̩/ *itr. V.* smile (**über** + *Akk.* at); **freundlich/verlegen** ~: give a friendly/an embarrassed smile
Lächeln *das;* ~**s** smile
lachen *itr. V.* laugh (**über** + *Akk.* at); **da kann man** ~ **ich doch nur** ~: that's a laugh; **jmdn. zum Lachen bringen** make sb. laugh; **platzen/sterben vor Lachen** (fig.) split one's sides laughing/die laughing; **die Sonne** *od.* **der Himmel lacht** (fig.) the sun is shining brightly; **wer zuletzt lacht, lacht am besten** (Spr.) he who laughs last, laughs longest; **zum Lachen sein** (ugs. abwertend) be laughable *or* ridiculous; **dass ich nicht lache!** (ugs.) don't make me laugh (coll.); **was gibt es denn zu** ~? what's so funny?; **es wäre ja** *od.* **doch gelacht, wenn …** (ugs.) it would be ridiculous if …; **nichts zu** ~ **haben** (ugs.) have a hard time of it; *s. auch* **dritt…; Erbe[2]**
Lachen *das;* ~**s** laughter; **ein lautes** ~: a loud laugh; **sie konnte sich das** ~ **kaum verbeißen** she could hardly stop herself laughing; **ihm wird das** ~ **noch vergehen** he'll be laughing on the other side of his face
Lacher *der;* ~**s**, ~ (a) laugher; **die** ~: those who are/were laughing; **die** ~ **auf seiner Seite haben** score by making everybody laugh; (b) (ugs.: kurzes Lachen) laugh
lächerlich /'lɛçɐlɪç/ (abwertend) 1 *Adj.* (a) (komisch) ridiculous; **jmdn./sich [vor jmdm.]** ~ **machen** make a fool of sb./oneself *or* make sb./oneself look silly [in front of sb.]; **etw. ins Lächerliche ziehen** make a joke out of sth.;

(b) (töricht) ridiculous; ludicrous ‹*argument, statement*›; **(c)** (gering) derisory, ridiculously *or* ludicrously small ‹*sum, amount*›; ridiculously low ‹*price, payment*›; **(d)** (geringfügig) ridiculously trivial *or* trifling; ~**e Kleinigkeiten** ridiculous trivialities. **2** *adv.* ridiculously; ~ **wenig** ridiculously *or* ludicrously little

Lächerlichkeit *die;* ~, ~**en** (abwertend) **(a)** *o. Pl.* ridiculousness; (von Argumenten, Behauptungen usw.) ridiculousness; ludicrousness; **jmdn. der** ~ **preisgeben** make a laughing stock of sb.; make sb. look ridiculous; **(b)** *meist Pl.* ridiculous triviality

lach-, Lach-: ~**gas** *das* laughing gas; ~**haft** (abwertend) **1** *Adj.* ridiculous; laughable; **2** *adv.* ridiculously; ~**krampf** *der* paroxysm of laughter; violent fit of laughter; **einen** ~**krampf bekommen** go [off] into fits of laughter ~**möwe** *die* laughing gull; peewit gull; ~**nummer** *die* (ugs.) **eine** ~**nummer sein** be just a joke

Lachs *der;* ~**es**, ~**e** salmon

Lachs·ersatz *der* rock salmon

lachs·farben *Adj.* salmon pink; salmon-coloured

Lack /lak/ *der;* ~**[e]s**, ~**e** varnish; (für Metall, Lackarbeiten) lacquer; (Auto~) paint; (transparent) lacquer; (Nagel~) varnish

Lack·affe *der* (ugs. abwertend) dandy

lackieren *tr. V.* varnish ‹*wood*›; varnish, paint ‹*fingernails*›; spray ‹*car*›; (mit Emaillelack) paint ‹*metal*›; **einen Wagen neu** ~: respray a car

Lackierte *der/die:* **der/die** ~ **sein** (ugs.) have to carry the can (fig. coll.)

Lackierung *die;* ~, ~**en** (auf Holz) varnish; (auf Metall, Autos) paintwork; (auf Lackarbeiten) lacquer

Lack·leder *das* patent leather

Lackmus·papier /'lakmʊs-/ *das* (Chemie) litmus paper

Lack-: ~**schaden** *der* damage to the paintwork; ~**schuh** *der* patent-leather shoe

Lade /'la:də/ *die;* ~, ~**n** (landsch.) drawer

Lade·gerät *das* (Elektrot.) charger

laden[1] **1** *unr. tr. V.* **(a)** load; **etw. aus etw.** ~: unload sth. from sth.; **die Schiffe** ~ **Getreide** the ships are taking on *or* are being loaded with grain; **der LKW hat Sand ge**~: the truck is loaded up with sand; **der Tanker hat Flüssiggas ge**~: the tanker has a cargo of *or* is carrying liquid gas; **(b)** (legen) load; **sich** (*Dat.*) **einen Sack auf die Schultern** ~: load a sack on one's shoulders; **schwere Schuld auf sich** ~ (fig.) incur a heavy burden of guilt; **(c)** (Munition einlegen) load ‹*gun, pistol, etc.*›; **(d)** (Physik) charge; **er ist ge**~ (ugs.) he's livid (coll.); he's hopping mad (coll.). **2** *unr. itr. V.* load [up]; **der LKW hat schwer ge**~: the truck is heavily loaded

laden[2] *unr. tr. V.* **(a)** (Rechtsspr.) summon; **(b)** (geh.: ein~) invite

Laden *der;* ~**s**, **Läden** /'lɛ:dn̩/ **(a)** shop; store (Amer.); **(b)** (ugs.: Unternehmung) **der** ~ **läuft** business is good; **wie ich den** ~ **kenne** (fig.) if I know how things go in this outfit (coll.); **den** ~ **dichtmachen** shut up shop; **den** ~ **schmeißen** manage *or* handle everything with no problem; **(c)** *Pl. auch* ~ (Fenster~) shutter

Laden-: ~**dieb** *der* shoplifter; ~**diebstahl** *der* shoplifting; ~**hüter** *der* (abwertend) non-seller; article/line which isn't/wasn't selling; ~**preis** *der* shop price; ~**schluss**, ***~**schluß** *der* shop *or* (Amer.) store closing time; **kurz vor/nach** ~**schluss** shortly before/after the shops *or* (Amer.) stores close/closed; **um 14 Uhr ist** ~**schluss** the shops *or* (Amer.) stores close at two o'clock; ~**tisch** *der* [shop-]counter; **unterm** ~**tisch** (ugs.) under the counter

Lade-: ~**rampe** *die* loading ramp; ~**raum** *der* **(a)** (beim Auto) luggage-space; **(b)** (beim Flugzeug, Schiff) hold; **(c)** (bei LKWs) payload space

lädieren /lɛ'di:rən/ *tr. V.* damage; (fig.) damage, harm ‹*reputation etc.*›; undermine ‹*confidence*›; **lädiert aussehen** (ugs., scherzh.) look battered

---

lädst /lɛ:tst/ *2. Pers. Sg. Präsens v.* **laden**

lädt /lɛ:t/ *3. Pers. Sg. Präsens v.* **laden**

Ladung *die;* ~, ~**en** **(a)** (Schiffs~, Flugzeug~) cargo; (LKW~) load; **(b)** (beim Sprengen, Schießen) charge; **(c)** (ugs.: Menge) load (coll.); **(d)** (Physik) charge; **(e)** (Rechtsspr.: Vor~) summons *sing.*

lag /la:k/ *1. u. 3. Pers. Sg. Prät. v.* **liegen**

Lage /'la:gə/ *die;* ~, ~**n (a)** situation; location; **in ruhiger** ~: in a quiet location; **eine gute** ~ **haben** be peacefully/well situated; be in a good/peaceful location; **in höheren/tieferen** ~**n** (Met.) on high/low ground; **(b)** (Art des Liegens) position; **jetzt habe ich eine bequeme** ~: now I'm lying comfortably; now I'm [lying] in a comfortable position; **(c)** (Situation) situation; **er war nicht in der** ~, **das zu tun** he was not in a position to do that; **versetzen Sie sich in meine** ~: put yourself in my position *or* place; **nach** ~ **der Dinge** as matters stand/stood; **die** ~ **peilen** *od.* **spannen** (ugs.) see how the land lies; find out the lie of the land; *s. auch* **Herr**; **(d)** *meist Pl.* (Schwimmen) **die 400 m** ~**n** the 400 m. individual medley; **die 4 × 100 m** ~**n** the 4 × 100 m. medley relay; **(e)** (Schicht) layer; **(f)** (Stimm~) register; **(g)** (ugs.: Runde) round; **eine** ~ **ausgeben** (ugs.) *od.* schmeißen (salopp) get *or* stand a round

Lage-: ~**besprechung** *die* discussion of the situation; ~**plan** *der* map of the area

Lager /'la:gɐ/ *das;* ~**s**, ~ **(a)** camp; **ein** ~ **aufschlagen** set up *or* pitch camp; **(b)** (Gruppe, politischer Block) camp; **ins andere** ~ **überwechseln** change camps *or* sides; join the other side; **(c)** (Raum) storeroom; (in Geschäften, Betrieben) stockroom; **etw. auf** *od.* **am** ~ **haben** have sth. in stock; **etw. auf** ~ **haben** (fig. ugs.) be ready with sth.; **(d)** (Warenbestand) stock; **(e)** (geh.) bed; **an jmds.** ~ **treten** step up to sb.'s bedside

Lager-: ~**bestand** *der* (Wirtsch.) stock; **den** ~**bestand aufnehmen** do a stocktaking; ~**feuer** *das* campfire; ~**halle** *die*, ~**haus** *das* warehouse

Lagerist *der;* ~**en**, ~**en** ▶ 85 | storeman; storekeeper

Lageristin *die;* ~, ~**nen** ▶ 85 | storekeeper

Lager·koller *der:* **einen** ~ **bekommen** *od.* **kriegen** be driven to a frenzy by life in the camp

lagern 1 *tr. V.* **(a)** store; **etw. kühl/trocken** ~: keep *or* store sth. in a cool/dry place; **(b)** (hinlegen) lay down; **jmdn. flach/bequem** ~: lay sb. flat/in a comfortable position; **die Beine hoch** ~: rest one's legs in a raised position; **(c)** (Technik) support; mount ‹*machine-part, workpiece*›. **2** *itr. V.* **(a)** camp; be encamped; **(b)** (liegen) lie; ‹*foodstuffs, medicines, etc.*› be stored *or* kept; (sich ab~) have settled; **(c)** (Geol.) **hier** ~ **Ölvorräte** there are deposits of oil here; **(d)** ganz ähnlich/anders **gelagert sein** ‹*case*› be quite similar/different [in nature]. **3** *refl. V.* settle oneself/itself down

Lager-: ~**raum (a)** storeroom; (im Geschäft, Betrieb) stockroom; **(b)** *o. Pl.* (Kapazität) storage space; (in Lagerhallen) warehouse space; ~**stätte** *die* (Geol.) deposit

Lagerung *die;* ~, ~**en (a)** storage; **bei** ~ **im Tiefkühlfach** if *or* when stored in a deep-freeze; **(b)** bei richtiger/falscher ~ **des Verletzten** if the injured person is placed in the correct/wrong position

Lager·verwalter *der* storekeeper; stores supervisor

Lagune /la'gu:nə/ *die;* ~, ~**n** lagoon

lahm /la:m/ **1** *Adj.* **(a)** lame; crippled, useless ‹*wing*›; **ein** ~**es Bein haben** be lame in one leg; **den Verkehr/die Produktion lahm legen** bring traffic/the production to a standstill; **die Industrie** ~ **legen** bring the industry to a standstill; paralyse the industry; **(b)** (ugs.: unbeweglich) stiff; **ihm wurde der Arm** ~: his arm became *or* got stiff; **(c)** (ugs. abwertend: schwach) lame, feeble ‹*excuse, explanation, etc.*›; **(d)** (ugs. abwertend: matt) dreary; dull; feeble ‹*protest*›; dull, dreary, lifeless ‹*discussion*›; **ein** ~**er Typ** a dull, lethargic [sort of] bloke (Brit. coll.) *or* (coll.) guy; *s. auch* **Ente** *a.* **2** *adv.* **(a)** (kraftlos) feebly; **(b)** (ugs. abwertend) lethargically

Lahme *der/die; adj. Dekl.* cripple

lahmen *itr. V.* be lame

lahmen /'la:mən/ *tr. V.* **(a)** paralyse; **einseitig gelähmt sein** be paralysed down one side of one's body; **vor Angst**

wie gelähmt sein be paralysed with fear; **(b)** (fig.) cripple, paralyse ⟨*economy, industry*⟩; bring ⟨*traffic*⟩ to a standstill; deaden ⟨*enthusiasm*⟩; numb ⟨*will*⟩

*lahm|legen ⇒ lahm 1 a

Lähmung *die;* ~, ~en **(a)** paralysis; **(b)** (fig.) (der Wirtschaft, Industrie) paralysis; (der Begeisterung) deadening; (des Willens) numbing

Laib /laip/ *der;* ~[e]s, ~e loaf; **ein** ~ **Käse** a whole cheese

Laich /laiç/ *der;* ~[e]s, ~e spawn

laichen *itr. V.* spawn

Laie /'laiə/ *der;* ~n, ~n **(a)** layman/laywoman; **da staunt der** ~ **[und der Fachmann wundert sich]** it's incredible; **(b)** (Kirche) layman/laywoman; **die** ~n the laity *pl.*

laien-, Laien-: ~**haft 1** *Adj.* amateurish; unprofessional; inexpert. **2** *adv.* amateurishly; unprofessionally; inexpertly; ~**prediger** *der* (Rel.) lay preacher; ~**richter** *der* lay judge; ~**schau·spieler** *der* amateur actor; ~**spiel** *das; o. Pl.* amateur performance; ~**theater** *das* amateur theatre group

Lakai /la'kai/ *der;* ~en, ~en **(a)** lackey; liveried footman; **(b)** (fig. abwertend) lackey

Lake /'la:kə/ *die;* ~, ~n brine

Laken /'la:kn̩/ *das;* ~s, ~ (bes. nordd.) sheet

lakonisch /la'ko:nɪʃ/ **1** *Adj.* laconic. **2** *adv.* laconically

Lakritz /la'krɪts/ *der od. das;* ~es, ~e, **Lakritze** *die;* ~, ~n liquorice

la la /la'la/ *in* **so** ~ ~ (ugs.) so-so

lallen /'lalən/ *tr., itr. V.* ⟨*baby*⟩ babble; ⟨*drunk/drowsy person*⟩ mumble

Lama /'la:ma/ *das;* ~s, ~s llama

Lamelle /la'mɛlə/ *die;* ~, ~n **(a)** (einer Jalousie) slat; **(b)** (eines Pilzes) gill; lamella (Bot.)

lamentieren /lamɛn'tiːrən/ *itr. V.* (ugs.) moan, complain (**über** + *Akk.* about)

Lametta /la'mɛta/ *das;* ~s **(a)** lametta; **(b)** (ugs. iron.: Orden) gongs *pl.* (coll.)

Lamm /lam/ *das;* ~[e]s, **Lämmer** /'lɛmɐ/ lamb

lamm-, Lamm-: ~**braten** *der* roast lamb *no indef. art.;* (Gericht) roast of lamb; ~**fell** *das* lambskin; ~**fleisch** *das* lamb; ~**fromm 1** ⟨*horse*⟩ as gentle as a [little] lamb; ⟨*person*⟩ as meek as a [little] lamb; **2** *adv.* ~**fromm antworten** answer like a lamb; ~**kotelett** *das* lamb chop

Lampe /'lampə/ *die;* ~, ~n **(a)** light; (Tisch~, Öl~, Signal~) lamp; (Straßen~) lamp; light; **(b)** (bes. fachspr.: Glüh~) bulb; *s. auch* **Meister**

Lampen-: ~**fieber** *das* stage fright; ~**schirm** *der* [lamp]shade

Lampion /lam'piɔŋ/ *der;* ~s, ~s Chinese lantern

lancieren /lã'siːrən/ *tr. V.* **(a)** [deliberately] spread ⟨*report, rumour, etc.*⟩; **(b)** jmdn. in eine Stellung ~: get sb. into a position by pulling strings; **(c)** (bes. Wirtsch., Werbung) launch

Land /lant/ *das;* ~es, **Länder** /'lɛndɐ/ *od.* (veralt.) ~e **(a)** *o. Pl.* land *no indef. art.;* **an** ~: ashore; ~ **in Sicht!** (Seemannsspr.) land [ahead]!; „~" **melden** report that the land is flooded *or* under water; **[wieder]** ~ **sehen** (fig.) be able to see light at the end of the tunnel (fig.); **[sich** (*Dat.*)**] eine Millionärin/antike Truhe/einen fetten Auftrag an** ~ **ziehen** (ugs., oft scherzh.) hook a millionairess/get one's hands on an antique chest/land a fat contract; **(b)** *o. Pl.* (Grund und Boden) land; **ein Stück** ~: a plot *or* piece of land *or* ground; **das** ~ **bebauen/bestellen** farm/till the land; **(c)** *Pl.* ~**e** (veralt.) (Gegend) country; land; **Jahre waren ins** ~ **gegangen** years had passed *or* gone by; **(d)** *o. Pl.* (dörfliche Gegend) country *no indef. art.;* **auf dem** ~ **wohnen** live in the country; **aufs** ~ **ziehen** move into the country; **(e)** *Pl.* **Länder** (Staat) country; **andere Länder, andere Sitten** (Spr.) every nation has its own ways of behaving; ~ **und Leute kennen lernen** get to know the country and its people *or* inhabitants; **außer** ~**es gehen/sich außer** ~**es befinden** leave the country/be out of the country; **wieder im** ~**e sein** (ugs.) be

back again; **hier zu** ~**e** [here] in this country; **(f)** *Pl.* **Länder** (Bundesland) Land; state; (österr.) province

land-, Land-: ~**ab** /'-'-/ ⇒ ~**auf**; ~**adel** *der* (hist.) landed aristocracy; ~**arbeiter** *der* agricultural worker; farm worker; ~**auf** /'-'-/ *Adv. in* ~**auf**, ~**ab** (geh.) throughout the land; far and wide; ~**besitz** *der* ⇒ **Grundbesitz**; ~**bevölkerung** *die* rural population

Lande-: ~**anflug** *der* (Flugw.) [landing] approach; ~**bahn** *die* (Flugw.) [landing] runway

land·einwärts /'-'-/ *Adv.* inland

Lande·klappe *die* (Flugw.) landing flap

landen 1 *itr. V.; mit sein* **(a)** land; (ankommen) arrive; **weich** ~: make a soft landing; **bei jmdm. nicht** ~ **[können]** (fig. ugs.) not get anywhere *or* very far with sb.; **(b)** (ugs.: gelangen) land *or* end up; **im Krankenhaus/Zuchthaus/Papierkorb** ~: land up in hospital/end up in prison/the waste-paper basket. **2** *tr. V.* **(a)** land ⟨*aircraft, troops, passengers, fish, etc.*⟩; **(b)** (ugs.: zustande bringen) pull off ⟨*victory, coup*⟩; have ⟨*smash hit*⟩; **(c)** (Boxen) land ⟨*punch*⟩

Lande·platz *der* (Flugw.) landing-strip; airstrip; (Hubschrauber~) landing-pad

Ländereien /lɛndə'raiən/ *Pl.* estates

Länder-: ~**kampf** *der* (Sport) international match; ~**spiel** *das* (Sport) international [match]

landes-, Landes-: ~**grenze** *die* national border *or* frontier; ~**haupt·stadt** *die* capital; ~**innere** *das* interior [of the country]; ~**liste** *die* (Politik) regional list; ~**regierung** *die* government of a/the Land/province; ~**sprache** *die* language of the country; ~**tracht** *die* national costume *or* dress; ~**üblich** *Adj.* usual *or* customary in a/the country; ~**verrat** *der* (Rechtsw.) treason; ~**verteidigung** *die; o. Pl.* national defence; ~**währung** *die* currency of a/the country

land-, Land-: ~**flucht** *die* migration from the land *or* countryside [to the towns]; ~**frau** *die* countrywoman; ~**friedensbruch** *der* (Rechtsw.) breach of the peace; ~**funk** *der* (Sendefolge) farming programmes *pl.* [on the radio]; ~**gericht** *das* regional court; Land court; ~**haus** *das* country house; ~**karte** *die* map; ~**kreis** *der* district; ~**krieg** *der* land warfare; ~**läufig** *Adj.* widely held *or* accepted; (nicht fachlich) popular; ~**leben** *das; o. Pl.* country life; ~**leute** *Pl.* country folk *or* people

Land-: ~**luft** *die* country air; ~**maschine** *die* agricultural machine; farm machine; ~**plage** *die* plague [on the country]; (fig.) pest; nuisance; ~**ratte** *die* (ugs., oft scherzh.) landlubber; ~**regen** *der* steady rain

Landschaft *die;* ~, ~en **(a)** landscape; (ländliche Gegend) countryside; **(b)** (Gemälde) landscape; **(c)** (Gegend) region

landschaftlich 1 *Adj.* **(a) die** ~**e Schönheit** the scenic beauty; the beauty of the landscape; **(b)** regional ⟨*accent, speech, expression, custom, usage, etc.*⟩. **2** *adv.* ~ **herrlich gelegen sein** be in a glorious natural setting

Landschafts-: ~**bild** *das* (Gemälde) landscape [painting]; **(b)** (Aussehen) landscape; ~**maler** *der* landscape painter; ~**pflege** *die; o. Pl.* landscape conservation *no art.;* ~**schutzgebiet** *das* conservation area

Land·sitz *der* country seat

Lands·mann *der; Pl.* ~**leute** fellow-countryman; compatriot

Land-: ~**straße** *die* country road; (im Gegensatz zur Autobahn) ordinary road; ~**streicher** *der* tramp; vagrant; ~**streicherei** *die; o. Pl.* vagrancy *no art.;* ~**streitkräfte** *Pl.* land forces; ~**strich** *der* area; ~**tag** *der* Landtag; state parliament; (österr.) provincial parliament

Landung *die;* ~, ~en landing; **zur** ~ **ansetzen** begin one's/its landing approach

Landungs-: ~**boot** *das* landing craft; ~**brücke** *die* [floating] landing stage; ~**steg** *der* landing stage

Land-: ~**vermesser** *der* [land] surveyor; ~**weg** *der* overland route; **auf dem** ~**weg** overland; by the overland route; ~**wein** *der* ordinary local wine; vin du pays; ~**wirt** *der* farmer

Land·wirtschaft *die* **(a)** *o. Pl.* agriculture *no art.;* farming *no art.;* **(b)** (Betrieb) [small] farm

---

Länge und Breite

1 Millimeter = one millimetre* (1 mm) = 0.039 inch (in.)
1 Zentimeter = one centimetre* (1 cm) = 0.394 inch (in.)
1 Meter   = one metre* (1 m)   = 39.4 inches (ins), 3 feet (ft) 3.4 inches†
1 Kilometer = one kilometre* (1 km) = 1094 yards (yds) *od.* 0.6214 mile

*Die amerikanische Schreibweise hat **-er** am Ende (**millimeter, centimeter, meter, kilometer**).
†Kann auch so geschrieben werden: 3' 3.4". Vergessen Sie nicht, dass bei Dezimalbrüchen ein Punkt gesetzt wird, und kein Komma.

Wie breit/lang ist es?	= How wide/long is it?, What width/length is it?	*Sie sind nicht gleich breit od. sind verschieden breit*	= They are not the same width *od.* are different widths
Das Zimmer ist vier mal fünf Meter [groß]	= The room is four metres [wide] by five metres [long], ≈ The room is 12 feet [wide] by 15 feet [long]	*eine 100 Meter lange Einfahrt*	= a drive 100 metres long *od.* in length
		ein fünf Zentimeter breites Brett	= a plank five centimetres wide
A hat die gleiche Länge/ Breite wie B	= A is the same length/width as B	*Der Stoff wird meterweise verkauft*	= The material is sold by the metre
Sie haben die gleiche Länge od. sind gleich lang	= They are the same length *od.* are equal in length	*drei Meter Stoff zu 10 Mark das od. der Meter*	= three metres of material at 10 marks a *od.* the metre
		ein vier Meter langes Stück Seide	= a four-metre length of silk

---

la̱nd·wirtschaftlich 1 *Adj.; nicht präd.* agricultural; agricultural, farm *attrib.* ⟨*machinery*⟩. **2** *adv.* ~ **genutzt werden** be used for agricultural *or* farming purposes
La̱ndwirtschaftsministerium *das* ministry of agriculture
La̱nd·zunge *die* (Geogr.) tongue of land
lang¹ /laŋ/; **länger** /'lɛŋɐ/, **längst...** /'lɛŋst.../ **1** *Adj.* **(a)** ▶ **340**| (räumlich) long; **eine Bluse mit ~en Ärmeln** a long-sleeved blouse; **etw. länger machen** make sth. longer; lengthen sth.; **ein fünf Meter ~es Seil** a rope five metres long *or* in length; **(b)** (ugs.: groß) tall; *s. auch* **Latte a; Lulatsch; (c)** (ausführlich) long; **des Langen und Breiten** (geh.) at great length; in great detail; **(d)** (zeitlich) long; long, lengthy ⟨*speech, lecture, etc.*⟩; prolonged ⟨*thought*⟩; **seit ~er Zeit, seit ~em** for a long time. **2** *adv.* **(a)** (zeitlich) [for] a long time; **der ~ anhaltende Beifall** the lengthy *or* prolonged applause; **etw. nicht länger ertragen können** be unable to bear *or* stand sth. any longer; **~ und breit** at great length; in great detail; **(b)** **einen Augenblick/mehrere Stunden ~:** for a moment/several hours; **den ganzen Winter ~:** all through the winter; **sein Leben ~:** all one's life; *s. auch* **länger 2, 3**
lang² (bes. nordd.) **1** *Präp. mit Akk.:* ⇒ **entlang 1. 2** *Adv.* ⇒ **entlang 2;** [nicht] **wissen, wo es ~ geht** (fig.) [not] know what it's all about
lang-: ~ärm[e]lig /~ɛrm(ə)lɪç/ *Adj.* long-sleeved; **~atmig** /~|a:tmɪç/ **1** *Adj.* long-winded; **2** *adv.* long-windedly; **etw. ~atmig erzählen** relate sth. at great length
lange; länger, am längsten *Adv.* **(a)** a long time; **er ist schon ~ fertig** he finished a long time ago; **~ schlafen/arbeiten** sleep/work late; **bist du schon ~ hier?** have you been here long?; **es ist noch gar nicht ~ her, dass ich ihn gesehen habe** it's not long since I saw him; I saw him not long ago; **da kannst du ~ warten** you can wait for ever; **sie wird es nicht mehr ~ machen** (ugs.) she won't last much longer; *s. auch* **länger 3; (b)** (bei weitem) **das ist [noch] ~ nicht alles** that's not all by any means; that's not all, not by a long chalk *or* shot (coll.); **ich bin noch ~ nicht fertig** I'm nowhere near finished; **er ist noch ~ nicht soweit** he's got a long time to go till then; **hier ist es ~ nicht so schön** it isn't nearly as nice here
Länge /'lɛŋə/ *die;* ~, ~**n (a)** ▶ **340**| (auch zeitlich) (hoher Wuchs) tallness; length; **eine ~ von zwei Metern haben** be two metres in length; **auf einer ~ von zwei Kilometern** for two kilometres; **sich zu seiner ganzen ~ aufrichten** draw oneself up to one's full height; **ein Film von einer Stunde ~:** a film one hour in length; an hour-long film; **etw./sich in die ~ ziehen** drag sth. out/drag on; go on and on; **(b)** (Sport) length; **mit einer ~ [Vorsprung] siegen** win by a length; **(c)** *Pl.* (in einem Film, Theaterstück usw.) long drawn-out *or* tedious scene; (in einem Buch) long drawn-out *or* tedious passage; **(d)** (Geogr.) longitude
langen (ugs.) **1** *itr. V.* **(a)** ⇒ **reichen 1 a; (b)** (greifen) reach **(in** + *Akk.* into; **auf** + *Akk.* on to; **nach** for); **(c)** ⇒ **reichen 1 b. 2** *tr. V.* **(a)** (landsch.) ⇒ **reichen 2 a; (b)** **jmdm. eine ~:** give sb. a clout [around the ear] (coll.)
Längen-: ~grad *der* (Geogr.) degree of longitude; **~maß** *das* unit of length
länger /'lɛŋɐ/ **1** ⇒ **lang¹, lange. 2** *Adj.* **eine ~e Abwesenheit/Behandlung** a fairly long *or* prolonged absence/period of treatment; **seit ~er Zeit** for quite some time. **3** *adv.* for some time
Lange·weile *die;* ~ *od.* **Langenweile** boredom; ~ **haben** be bored
lang-, Lang-: ~finger *der* (oft scherzh.) (Dieb) thief; (Taschendieb) pickpocket; **~fristig** /~frɪstɪç/ **1** *Adj.* long-term; long-dated ⟨*loan*⟩; **2** *adv.* on a long-term basis; **~fristig gesehen** in the long term; **~haarig** *Adj.* long-haired; **~jährig** *Adj.; nicht präd.* ⟨*customer, friend*⟩ of many years' standing; long-standing ⟨*friendship*⟩; **~jährige Erfahrung** many years of experience; many years' experience; **~lauf** *der* (Skisport) cross-country; **~läufer** *der* cross-country skier; **~lebig** /~le:bɪç/ *Adj.* long-lived ⟨*animal, organism*⟩; durable ⟨*goods, materials*⟩; **~lebige Gebrauchsgüter** consumer durables; **~lebigkeit** *die;* ~ longevity; long-livedness; (von Gebrauchsgütern) durability; **~|legen** *refl. V.* (ugs.) **(a)** lie down; have a lie down; **(b)** (salopp: hinfallen) fall flat [on one's face/back]
länglich /'lɛŋlɪç/ *Adj.* oblong; long narrow ⟨*opening*⟩; long [narrow] ⟨*envelope*⟩
La̱ng·mut *die;* ~: forbearance
längs /lɛŋs/ **1** *Präp.* + *Gen. od.* (selten) *Dat.* along; ~ **des Flusses** *od.* **dem Fluss** along the river [bank]. **2** *Adv.* **(a)** lengthways; **stellt das Sofa hier ~ an die Wand** put the sofa along here against the wall; **(b)** (nordd.) ⇒ **entlang 2**
Längs·achse *die* longitudinal axis
langsam 1 *Adj.* **(a)** slow; low ⟨*speed*⟩; **(b)** (allmählich) gradual. **2** *adv.* **(a)** slowly; **geh [etwas] ~er!** go [a bit] more slowly; slow down [a bit]!; ~, **aber sicher** (ugs.) slowly but surely; **(b)** (allmählich) gradually; **es wird ~ Zeit, dass du gehst** it's about time you left *or* went

---

*alte Schreibung (vgl. Hinweise auf S. xvi–xvii)

Langsamkeit *die;* ~: slowness
Lang·schläfer *der* late riser
Langspiel·platte *die* long-playing record; LP
längs-, Längs-: ~**richtung** *die* longitudinal direction; **in** ~**richtung** lengthways; ~**schnitt** *der* longitudinal section; ~**selte** *die* long side; ~**seits** (Seemannsspr.) **1** *Präp.* + *Gen.* alongside; **2** *Adv.* alongside
längst /lɛŋst/ *Adv.* **(a)** (schon lange) long since; **er ist** [**schon**] ~ **fertig** he finished a long time ago; **ich wusste das** ~: I've known that for a long time; I knew that a long time ago; **(b)** ⇒ **lange b**
längstens /ˈlɛŋstn̩s/ *Adv.* (ugs.) at [the] most; ~ **eine Woche** a week at the most
Lang·strecke *die* **(a)** long haul *or* distance; **(b)** (Sport) long distance
Langstrecken-: ~**flug** *der* long-haul flight; ~**lauf** *der* (Sport) long-distance race; (Disziplin) long-distance running *no art.;* ~**läufer** *der* (Sport) long-distance runner
Languste /laŋˈgʊstə/ *die;* ~, ~**n** spiny lobster; langouste
lang-, Lang-: ~**weilen 1** *tr. V.* bore; **er sah gelangweilt aus dem Fenster** he gazed out of the window, feeling bored. **2** *refl. V.* be bored; **sich tödlich** *od.* **zu Tode** ~**weilen** be bored to death; ~**weiler** *der* (ugs. abwertend) **(a)** bore; **(b)** (schwerfälliger Mensch) slowcoach; ~**weilig 1** *Adj.* **(a)** boring; dull ‹*place*›; **(b)** (ugs.: schleppend) slow ‹*person*›; tedious ‹*business*›; **2** *adv.* boringly; ~**welle** *die* (Physik, Rundf.) long wave; ~**wierig** /~viːrɪç/ *Adj.* lengthy; prolonged ‹*search*›; protracted, lengthy, long ‹*negotiations, treatment*›
Lanze /ˈlantsə/ *die;* ~, ~**n** lance; (zum Werfen) spear; **für jmdn. eine** ~ **brechen** (fig.) take up the cudgels on sb.'s behalf
lapidar /lapiˈdaːɐ̯/ **1** *Adj.* (kurz, aber wirkungsvoll) succinct; (knapp) terse. **2** *adv.* succinctly/tersely
Lappalie /laˈpaːliə/ *die;* ~, ~**n** trifle
Lappe /ˈlapə/ *der;* ~**n**, ~**n** Lapp; Laplander
Lappen *der;* ~**s**, ~ **(a)** cloth; (Fetzen) rag; (Wasch~) flannel; **(b)** (salopp: Geldschein) [large] note; (ugs.) **jmdm. durch die** ~ **gehen** (ugs.) slip through sb.'s fingers
läppern /ˈlɛpɐn/ *refl. V.* **es läppert sich** (ugs.) it's mounting up
läppisch /ˈlɛpɪʃ/ *Adj.* silly
Lapp·land (*das*) Lapland
Laptop /ˈlɛptɔp/ *der;* ~**s**, ~**s** (DV) laptop
Lärche /ˈlɛrçə/ *die;* ~, ~**n** larch
Larifari *das;* ~**s** (ugs.) nonsense; rubbish
Lärm /lɛrm/ *der;* ~[**e**]**s** noise; (fig.) fuss (**um** about) to-do; ~ **schlagen** kick up *or* make a fuss
lärm-, Lärm-: ~**bekämpfung** *die; o. Pl.* noise abatement; ~**belästigung** *die* disturbance caused by noise; ~**empfindlich** *Adj.* sensitive to noise *postpos.*
lärmen *itr. V.* make a noise; ~**d** noisy
Lärm-: ~**pegel** *der* noise level; ~**quelle** *die* source of noise; ~**schutz** *der* **(a)** protection against noise; **(b)** (Vorrichtung) noise barrier; noise *or* sound insulation *no indef. art.*
Larve /ˈlarfə/ *die;* ~, ~**n** grub; larva
las /laːs/ *1. u. 3. Pers. Sg. Prät. v.* **lesen**
lasch /laʃ/ **1** *Adj.* limp ‹*handshake*›; feeble ‹*action, measure*›; listless ‹*movement, gait*›; lax ‹*upbringing*›. **2** *adv.: s. Adj.:* limply; feebly; listlessly; laxly; ~ **gewürzt sein** be insipid *or* tasteless
Lasche *die;* ~, ~**n** (Gürtel~) loop; (eines Briefumschlags) flap; (Schuh~) tongue
Laser /ˈleːzɐ/ *der;* ~**s**, ~ (Physik) laser
Laser·drucker *der* (DV) laser printer
Laser·strahl *der* (Physik) laser beam
lasieren /laˈziːrən/ *tr. V.* varnish
lass, *laß /las/ *Imperativ Sg. v.* **lassen**
lassen /ˈlasn̩/ **1** *unr. tr. V.* **(a)** mit *Inf.* (2. *Part.* ~) (veranlassen) **etw. tun** ~: have *or* get sth. done; **Wasser in die Wanne laufen** ~: run water into the bath; **das Licht über Nacht brennen** ~: keep the light on overnight;

jmdn. warten/erschießen ~: keep sb. waiting/have sb. shot; **jmdn. grüßen** ~: send one's regards to sb.; **jmdn. kommen/rufen** ~: send for sb.; **jmdn. etw. wissen** ~: let sb. know sth.; **(b)** *mit Inf.* (2. *Part.* ~) (erlauben) **jmdn. etw. tun** ~: let sb. do sth.; allow sb. to do sth., **jmdn. ausreden** ~: let sb. finish speaking; allow sb. to finish speaking; **er lässt sich** (*Dat.*) **nichts sagen** you can't tell him anything; **(c)** (zugestehen, belassen) **lass den Kindern den Spaß** let the children enjoy themselves; **jmdn. in Frieden** ~: leave sb. in peace; **lass ihn in seinem Glauben** don't disillusion him; **jmdn. unbeeindruckt** ~: leave sb. unimpressed; **das muss man ihm/ihr** ~: one must grant *or* give him/her that; **(d)** (hinein~/heraus~) **let** *or* allow (**in** + *Akk.* into, **aus** out of); **jmdn. ins Zimmer** ~: let *or* allow sb. into the room; **(e)** (unterlassen) stop; (Begonnenes) put aside; **lass das!** stop that *or* it!; **lass das Grübeln!** stop brooding!; **etw. nicht** ~ **können** be unable to stop sth.; **es nicht** ~ **können, etw. zu tun** be unable to stop doing sth.; **tu, was du nicht** ~ **kannst** go ahead and do what you want to do; **(f)** (zurück~; bleiben ~) leave; **jmdn. allein** ~: leave sb. alone *or* on his/her own; **(g)** (überlassen) **jmdm. etw.** ~: let sb. have sth.; **(h)** **lass/ lasst uns gehen/fahren!** let's go!; **(i)** (verlieren) lose; (ausgeben) spend; **sein Leben für eine Idee** ~: lay down one's life for an idea; **(j)** **lass sie nur erst einmal erwachsen sein** wait till she's grown up. **2** *unr. refl. V.* (2. *Part.* ~) **die Tür lässt sich leicht öffnen** the door opens easily; **das lässt sich nicht beweisen** it can't be proved; **das lässt sich machen** that can be done; **es lässt sich nicht leugnen/verschweigen, dass …:** it cannot be denied *or* there's no denying that …; **we/you** *etc.* cannot hide the fact that …; *s. auch* **hören 1 b, c**; **(b)** *impers.* **hier lässt es sich leben/wohl sein** it's a good life here. **3** *unr. itr. V.* **(a)** (ugs.) **Lass mal. Ich mache das schon** Leave it. I'll do it; **Lass doch od. nur! Du kannst mir das Geld später zurückgeben** That's all right. You can pay me back later; **(b)** (2. *Part.* ~) (veranlassen) **ich lasse bitten** would you ask him/her/them to come in; **ich habe mir sagen** ~, **dass …:** I've been told *or* informed that …; **(c)** (veralt.: aufgeben) **von jmdm./etw.** ~: part from sb./sth.
lässig /ˈlɛsɪç/ **1** *Adj.* casual. **2** *adv.* **(a)** (ungezwungen) casually; **(b)** (ugs.: leicht) easily; effortlessly
Lässigkeit *die;* ~ **(a)** casualness; **(b)** (ugs.: Leichtigkeit) effortlessness
Lasso /ˈlaso/ *das od. der;* ~**s**, ~**s** lasso
lässt, *läßt /lɛst/ *2. u. 3. Pers. Sg. Präsens v.* **lassen**
Last /last/ *die;* ~, ~**en (a)** load; (Trag~) load; burden; **(b)** (Gewicht) weight; **(c)** (Bürde) burden; **die** ~ **des Amtes/ der Verantwortung** the burden of office/responsibility; **jmdm. zur** ~ **fallen/werden** be/become a burden on sb.; **jmdm. etw. zur** ~ **legen** charge sb. with sth.; accuse sb. of sth.; **(d)** *Pl.* (Abgaben) charges; (Kosten) costs; **die steuerlichen** ~**en** the tax burden *sing.;* **die Verpackungskosten gehen zu** ~**en des Kunden** the cost of packaging will be charged to the customer
Last·auto *das* (ugs.) ⇒ ~**kraftwagen**
lasten *itr. V.* **(a)** be a burden; **auf jmdm./etw.** ~: weigh heavily [up]on sb./sth.; **das Amt lastet auf seinen Schultern** (fig.) the burden of office rests on his shoulders; **(b)** (belastet sein mit) **auf dem Haus** ~ **zwei Hypotheken** the house is encumbered with two mortgages
Lasten·auf·zug *der* goods lift (Brit.); freight elevator (Amer.)
Laster[1] *der;* ~**s**, ~ (ugs.: Lkw) truck; lorry (Brit.)
Laster[2] *das;* ~**s**, ~: vice
lasterhaft *Adj.* (abwertend) depraved
Laster·höhle *die* (ugs. abwertend) den of vice *or* iniquity
lästerlich 1 *Adj.* malicious ‹*remark*›; malevolent ‹*curse, oath*›. **2** *adv.* ‹*curse*› malevolently; ‹*speak*› maliciously
Läster·maul *das* (abwertend salopp) **ein** ~ **sein/haben** have a malicious tongue; be constantly making malicious remarks
lästern /ˈlɛstɐn/ *itr. V.* (abwertend) make malicious remarks (**über** + *Akk.* about)

Lästerung *die;* ~, ~**en** (gegen Gott) blasphemy
lästig /'lɛstɪç/ *Adj.* tiresome ‹*person*›; tiresome, irksome ‹*task, duty, etc.*›; troublesome ‹*illness, cough, etc.*›; **jmdm.** ~ **sein** *od.* **fallen/werden** be/become a nuisance to sb.
Last-: ~**kahn** *der* [cargo] barge; ~**kraftwagen** *der* heavy goods (Brit.) *or* (Amer.) freight vehicle; ~**schrift** *die* debit; ~**wagen** *der* truck; lorry (Brit.); ~**wagen··fahrer** *der* ▶ 85 | truck driver; lorry driver (Brit.)
Lasur /la'zuːɐ̯/ *die;* ~, ~**en** varnish; (farbig) glaze
Latein /la'tain/ *das;* ~**s** ▶ 487 | Latin; **mit seinem** ~ **am Ende sein** be at one's wit's end; *s. auch* **Deutsch**
Latein·amerika *(das)* Latin America
latein·amerikanisch *Adj.* Latin American
lateinisch *Adj.* ▶ 487 | Latin; *s. auch* **deutsch; Deutsche²**
latent /la'tɛnt/ **1** *Adj.* latent. **2** *adv.* ~ **vorhanden sein** be latent
Laterne /la'tɛrnə/ *die;* ~, ~**n** **(a)** (Leuchte) lamp; lantern (Naut.); **(b)** (Straßen~) street light; street lamp
Laternen·pfahl *der* lamppost
Latinum /la'tiːnʊm/ *das;* ~**s: das kleine/große** ~: ≈ GCSE/'A' level Latin [examination]
Latrine /la'triːnə/ *die;* ~, ~**n** latrine
latschen /'laːtʃn̩/ *itr. V.; mit sein* (salopp) trudge; (schlurfend) slouch
Latschen *der;* ~**s**, ~ (ugs.) old worn-out shoe; (Hausschuh) old worn-out slipper; **er ist bald aus den** ~ **gekippt, als er hörte, …** (salopp) he was flabbergasted when he heard …
Latte /'latə/ *die;* ~, ~**n** **(a)** lath; slat; (Zaun~) pale; **eine lange** ~ (ugs.) a beanpole; **(b)** (Sport: des Tores) [cross]bar; **(c)** (Leichtathletik) bar; **(d) eine [lange]** ~ **von Schulden/Vorstrafen** (ugs.) a [large] pile of debts/a [long] list *or* string of previous convictions
Latten-: ~**kreuz** *das* (Fuß-, Handball) angle of the [cross]bar and the post; ~**rost** *der* (auf dem Boden) duckboards *pl.;* (eines Bettes) slatted frame; ~**zaun** *der* paling fence
Latz /lats/ *der;* ~**es**, **Lätze** /'lɛtsə/ bib; **jmdm. eine[n] vor den** ~ **knallen** *od.* **ballern** (salopp) sock (sl.) *or* thump sb.
Lätzchen /'lɛtsçən/ *das;* ~**s**, ~: bib
Latz·hose *die* bib and brace; (für Kinder) dungarees *pl.*
lau /lau/ *Adj.* **(a)** tepid, lukewarm ‹*water etc.*›; (nicht mehr kalt) warm ‹*beer etc.*›; **(b)** (mild) mild ‹*wind, air, evening, etc.*›; mild and gentle ‹*rain*›; **(c)** (unentschlossen) lukewarm; half-hearted
Laub /laup/ *das;* ~**[e]s** leaves *pl.;* **dichtes/neues** ~: thick/new foliage
Laub·baum *der* broad-leaved tree
Laube *die;* ~, ~**n** summer house; (überdeckter Sitzplatz) bower; arbour; *s. auch* **fertig**
Laub-: ~**frosch** *der* tree frog; ~**säge** *die* fretsaw; ~**wald** *der* deciduous wood/forest
Lauch /laux/ *der;* ~**[e]s**, ~**e** (Bot.) allium; (Porree) leek
Lauer /'lauɐ/ *die;* ~ (ugs.) **auf der** ~ **liegen** *od.* **sein** (ugs.) lie in wait; **sich auf die** ~ **legen** settle down to lie in wait
lauern *itr. V.* **(a)** (auch fig.) lurk; **auf jmdn./etw.** ~: lie in wait for sb./sth.; **ein** ~**der Blick** a sly look; **(b)** (ugs.: ungeduldig warten) **auf jmdn./etw.** ~: wait [impatiently] for sb./sth.
Lauf /lauf/ *der;* ~**[e]s**, **Läufe** /'lɔyfə/ **(a)** *o. Pl.* running; **(b)** (Sport: Wettrennen) heat; **(c)** *o. Pl.* (Ver~, Entwicklung) course; **im** ~**[e] der Zeit** in the course of time; **im** ~**[e] der Jahre** over the years; as the years go/went by; **im** ~**[e] des Tages** during the day; **einer Sache** *(Dat.)* **ihren** *od.* **freien** ~ **lassen** give free rein to sth.; **der** ~ **der Geschichte/Welt** the course of history/the way of the world; **seinen** ~ **nehmen** take its course; **(d)** (von Schusswaffen) barrel; etw. **vor den** ~ **bekommen** get a shot at sth.; **(e)** *o. Pl.* (eines Flusses, einer Straße) course; **der**

obere/untere ~ **eines Flusses** the upper/lower reaches *pl.* of a river; **(f)** (Musik) run; **(g)** (Jägerspr.) leg
Lauf-: ~**bahn** *die* **(a)** (Werdegang) career; **eine wissenschaftliche/künstlerische** ~**bahn einschlagen** take up a career in the sciences/as an artist; **(b)** (Leichtathletik) running-track; ~**bursche** *der* errand boy; messenger boy
laufen 1 *unr. itr. V.; mit sein* **(a)** run; **ge**~ **kommen** come running up; **er lief, was er konnte** (ugs.) he ran as fast as he could; **jmdn.** ~ **lassen** (ugs.) let sb. go; **(b)** (gehen) (zu Fuß gehen) walk; **es sind noch/nur fünf Minuten zu** ~: it's another/only five minutes' walk; **in** *(Akk.)* /**gegen etw.** ~: walk into sth.; **dauernd zum Arzt/in die Kirche** ~ (ugs.) keep running to the doctor/be always going to church; **(c)** (im Wettkampf) run; (beim Eislauf) skate; (beim Ski~) ski; **ein Pferd** ~ **lassen** run a horse; **(d)** (im Gang sein) ‹*machine*› be running; ‹*radio, television, etc.*› be on; (funktionieren) ‹*machine*› run; ‹*radio, television, etc.*› work; **auf Hochtouren** ~: be running at full speed; **(e)** (sich bewegen, fließen; auch fig.) **auf Schienen/über Rollen** ~: run on rails/over pulleys; **von den Fließbändern** ~: come off the conveyor belts; **es lief mir eiskalt über den Rücken** a chill ran down my spine; **ihm lief der Schweiß über das Gesicht** the sweat ran down his face; **Wasser in die Wanne** ~ **lassen** run the bathwater; **deine Nase läuft** your nose is running; you've got a runny nose; **der Käse läuft** the cheese has gone runny (coll.); **(f)** (gelten) ‹*contract, agreement, engagement, etc.*› run; **(g)** ‹*programme, play*› be on; ‹*film*› be on *or* showing; ‹*show*› be on *or* playing; **der Hauptfilm läuft schon** the main film has already started; **(h)** (fahren) run; **auf Grund** ~: run aground; **(i)** (vonstatten gehen) **parallel mit etw.** ~: run in parallel with sth.; **der Laden läuft/die Geschäfte** ~ **gut/schlecht** (ugs.) the shop is doing well/badly/business is good/bad; **wie geplant/nach Wunsch** ~: go as planned *or* according to plan; **schief** ~ (ugs.) go wrong; **(j)** ‹*negotiations, investigations*› be in progress *or* under way; **(k)** (registriert sein) **auf jmds. Namen** *(Akk.)* ~: be in sb.'s name; **(l)** (ugs.: gut verkäuflich sein) go *or* sell well. **2** *unr. tr. u. itr. V.* **(a)** *mit sein* run; (zu Fuß gehen) walk; **(b)** *mit sein* **einen Rekord** ~: set up a record; **über die 100 m 9,9 Sekunden** ~: run the 100 m. in 9.9 seconds; **(c)** *mit haben od. sein* **Ski/Schlittschuh/Rollschuh** ~: ski/skate/roller skate; **(d) sich** *(Dat.)* **die Füße wund** ~: get sore feet from running/walking; **sich** *(Dat.)* **ein Loch in die Schuhsohle** ~: wear a hole in one's shoe *or* sole. **3** *unr. refl. V.* **(a) sich warm** ~: warm up; **(b)** *unpers.* **in diesen Schuhen läuft es sich sehr bequem** these shoes are very comfortable for running/walking in *or* to run/walk in
laufend 1 *Adj.; nicht präd.* **(a)** (ständig) regular ‹*interest, income*›; recurring ‹*costs*›; **die** ~**en Arbeiten** the day-to-day *or* routine work *sing.;* **(b)** (gegenwärtig) current ‹*issue, year, month, etc.*›; **(c)** (aufeinander folgend) **zehn Mark der** ~**e Meter** ten marks a *or* per metre; **(d) auf dem** ~**en sein/bleiben** be/keep *or* stay up-to-date *or* fully informed; **jmdn. auf dem** ~**en halten** keep sb. up-to-date *or* informed. **2** *adv.* constantly; continually; ‹*increase*› steadily
***laufen|lassen** ⇨ **laufen 1 a**
Läufer /'lɔyfɐ/ *der;* ~**s**, ~ **(a)** (Sport) runner; (Handball) half-back; **(b)** (Fußball veralt.) half-back; **(c)** (Teppich) (long, narrow) carpet; **(d)** (Schach) bishop
Lauferei *die;* ~, ~**en** (ugs.) running around *no pl.*
Läuferin *die;* ~, ~**nen** runner
Lauf·feuer *das* brush fire; **wie ein** ~: like wildfire
läufig /'lɔyfɪç/ *Adj.* on heat *postpos.;* in season *postpos.*
Lauf-: ~**kundschaft** *die* passing trade; ~**masche** *die* ladder; ~**pass**, ***~**paß** *der:* **jmdm. den** ~**pass geben** (ugs.) give sb. his/her marching orders (coll.); **er hat seiner Freundin den** ~**pass gegeben** (ugs.) he finished with his girlfriend (coll.); ~**rad** *das* (Fachspr.) wheel; ~**schritt** *der* **(a)** **wir haben die ganze Strecke im** ~**schritt zurückgelegt** we ran all the way; **im** ~**schritt, marsch, marsch!** at the double, quick march!; **(b)** (Leichtathletik) running step

läufst /lɔyfst/ 2. Pers. Sg. Präsens v. **laufen**

Lauf-: ～**stall** der playpen; ～**steg** der catwalk

läuft /lɔyft/ 3. Pers. Sg. Präsens v. **laufen**

Lauf·zeit die term; **ein Kredit mit befristeter** ～: a limited-term loan

Lauge /'laugə/ die; ～, ～**n** (a) soapy water; soapsuds pl.; (b) (Chemie) alkaline solution

Laune /'launə/ die; ～, ～**n** (a) mood; **schlechte/gute** ～ **haben** be in a bad/good mood or temper; **jmdn. bei** [**guter**] ～ **halten** keep sb. in a good mood; keep sb. happy (coll.); **bringt gute** ～ **mit!** come ready to enjoy yourselves; (b) meist Pl. (wechselnde Stimmung) mood; **die** ～**n des Wetters** (fig.) the vagaries of the weather; (c) (spontane Idee) whim; **aus einer** ～ **heraus** on a whim; on the spur of the moment

launenhaft, launisch Adj. temperamental; (unberechenbar) capricious

Laus /laus/ die; ～, **Läuse** /'lɔyzə/ louse; **ihm ist eine** ～ **über die Leber gelaufen** (ugs.) he has got out of bed on the wrong side; **jmdm./sich eine** ～ **in den Pelz setzen** (ugs.) let sb./oneself in for something

Laus·bub der little rascal or devil; scamp

Lausbuben·streich der prank

Lausch·aktion die, **Lausch·angriff** der bugging operation (coll.)

lauschen /'lauʃn/ itr. V. (a) (horchen) listen (so as to overhear sth.); (b) (zuhören) listen [attentively] (Dat. to)

Lauscher der; ～**s**, ～ (a) eavesdropper; (b) (Jägerspr.: Ohr) ear

Lause-: ～**bengel** der, ～**junge** der (salopp) ⇒ **Lausbub**

lausen tr. V. delouse; **ich denk, mich laust der Affe!** (salopp) well, I'll be damned or blowed!

lausig (ugs.) **1** Adj. (a) (abwertend) lousy (coll.); rotten (coll.); ～**e Zeiten** hard times; (b) perishing (Brit. sl.), freezing 〈cold〉; terrible (coll.), awful 〈heat〉. **2** adv. terribly (coll.); awfully; ～ **kalt** perishing cold (Brit. sl.)

laut¹ /laut/ **1** Adj. (a) loud; (fig.) loud, garish 〈colour〉; **der Motor ist zu** ～: the engine is too noisy; **spreche ich jetzt** ～ **genug?** can you hear me now?; **werden Sie bitte nicht** ～**!** there's no need to shout; ～ **werden** (fig.: bekannt werden) be made known; (b) (geräuschvoll) noisy. **2** adv. (a) loudly; ～**er sprechen** speak louder; speak up; ～ **lachen** laugh out loud; **etw.** [**nicht**] ～ **sagen** [**dürfen**] [not be allowed to] say sth. out loud; ～ **denken** think aloud; **das kannst du aber** ～ **sagen** (ugs.) you can say 'that again; (b) (geräuschvoll) noisily

laut² Präp. + Gen. od. Dat. (Amtsspr.) according to

Laut der; ～[**e**]**s**, ～**e** (auch Phon.) sound; **keinen** ～ **von sich geben** not make a sound; **fremde/heimatliche** ～**e** sounds of a foreign/familiar tongue

Laute die; ～, ～**n** lute

lauten itr. V. 〈answer, instruction, slogan〉 be, run; 〈letter, passage, etc.〉 read, go; 〈law〉 state; **die Anklage lautet auf ...**: the charge is ...; **auf jmds. Namen** (Akk.) ～: be in sb.'s name

läuten /'lɔytn/ **1** tr., itr. V. ring; 〈alarm clock〉 go off; **Mittag** ～: strike midday; **ich habe davon** ～ **gehört** od. **hören, dass ...** (fig. ugs.) I have heard rumours that ... **2** itr. V. (bes. südd.: klingeln) ring; **nach jmdm.** ～: ring for sb.; **es läutete** the bell rang or went

lauter¹ Adj. (geh.) honourable 〈person, intentions, etc.〉; honest 〈truth〉

lauter² indekl. Adj. nothing but; sheer, pure 〈nonsense, joy, etc.〉; **das sind** ～ **Lügen** that's nothing but lies; that's a pack of lies; **vor** ～ **Arbeit komme ich nicht ins Theater** I can't go to the theatre because of all the work I've got

läutern /'lɔytɐn/ tr. V. (geh.) reform 〈character〉; purify 〈soul〉

laut·hals Adv. 〈sing, shout, etc.〉 at the top of one's voice; ～ **lachen** roar with laughter

lautlich 1 Adj. phonetic. **2** adv. phonetically

laut·|los 1 Adj. silent; soundless; (wortlos) silent. **2** adv. silently; soundlessly

Laut·schrift die (Phon.) phonetic alphabet

Laut·sprecher der loudspeaker; loud hailer (esp. Naut.); (einer Stereoanlage usw.) speaker

Lautsprecher-: ～**anlage** die public address or PA system; loudspeaker system; ～**box** die speaker cabinet

laut·stark 1 Adj. loud; vociferous, loud 〈protest〉. **2** adv. loudly; 〈protest〉 vociferously, loudly

Laut·stärke die volume; **in/bei voller** ～: at full volume

lau·warm Adj. lukewarm 〈food〉; lukewarm, tepid 〈drink〉; (nicht mehr kalt) warm 〈beer etc.〉

Lava /'la:va/ die; ～, **Laven** (Geol.) lava

Lavabo /la'va:bo/ das; ～[**s**], ～**s** (schweiz.) ⇒ **Waschbecken**

Lavendel /la'vɛndl/ der; ～**s**, ～: lavender

lavieren /la'vi:rən/ tr. V., itr. V. manœuvre

Lawine /la'vi:nə/ die; ～, ～**n** (auch fig.) avalanche; **eine** ～ **von Protesten** (fig.) a storm of protest

Lawinen·gefahr die danger of avalanches

lax /laks/ **1** Adj. lax. **2** adv. laxly

Lazarett /latsa'rɛt/ das; ～[**e**]**s**, ～**e** military hospital

Leasing /'li:zɪŋ/ das; ～**s**, ～**s** (Wirtsch.) leasing

leben /'le:bn/ **1** itr. V. live; (lebendig sein) be alive; **für jmdn./etw.** ～ od. (geh.) **jmdm./einer Sache** ～: live for sb./sth.; **leb**[**e**] **wohl!** farewell!; **nicht mehr** ～ **wollen** not want to go on living; have lost the will to live; **von seiner Rente** ～: live on one's pension/salary; **von seiner Hände Arbeit** ～: live by the work of one's hands; **Wie geht es dir?** — **Man lebt!** (ugs.) How are you? — Oh, surviving (coll.); **fleischlos** ～: not eat meat; **von Kartoffeln** ～: live on potatoes. **2** tr. V. live; **ein glückliches Leben** ～: live a happy life

Leben das; ～**s**, ～ (a) life; **das** ～: life; **jmdm. das** ～ **retten** save sb.'s life; **sich** (Dat.) **das** ～ **nehmen** take one's [own] life; **am** ～ **sein/bleiben** be/stay alive; **seines** ～**s nicht** [**mehr**] **sicher sein** not be safe [any more]; **um sein** ～ **rennen** run for one's life; **ums** ～ **kommen** lose one's life; **auf Tod und** ～ **kämpfen** be engaged in a life-and-death struggle; **etw. für sein** ～ **gern essen/tun** love sth./doing sth.; **etw. ins** ～ **rufen** bring sth. into being; **mit dem** ～ **davonkommen/das nackte** ～ **retten** escape/barely escape with one's life; **jmdm. nach dem** ～ **trachten** try to kill sb.; **ein/sein** [**ganzes**] ～ **lang** one's whole life long; **noch nie im** ～**/zum ersten Mal im** ～**!** never in/for the first time in one's life; **mit beiden Beinen** od. **Füßen im** ～ **stehen** have one's feet firmly on the ground; **nie im** ～, **im** ～ **nicht!** (ugs.) not on your life! (coll.); never in your life! (coll.); **ein** ～ **in Wohlstand** a life of affluence; **wie das** ～ **so spielt** it's funny the way things turn out; **ins öffentliche** ～ **stehen** be in public life; **so ist das** ～**:** such is life; that's the way things go; **die Musik ist ihr** ～**:** music is her [whole] life; (b) (Betriebsamkeit) **auf dem Markt herrschte ein reges** ～: the market was bustling with activity; **das** ～ **auf der Straße** the comings and goings in the street; ～ **ins Haus bringen** bring some life into the house

lebend Adj. living; live 〈animal〉; **tot oder** ～: dead or alive

lebendig /le'bɛndɪç/ **1** Adj. (a) (auch fig.) living; **jmdn.** ～ od. **bei** ～**em Leibe verbrennen** burn sb. alive; **man fühlt sich hier wie** ～ **begraben** being stuck here is like being buried alive (coll.); **die Erinnerung daran wurde in ihm wieder** ～: the memory of it came back to him vividly; (b) (lebhaft) lively 〈account, imagination, child, etc.〉; gay, bright 〈colours〉. **2** adv. (lebhaft) in a lively fashion or way

Lebendigkeit die; ～: liveliness

Lebens-, Lebens-: ～**abend** der (geh.) evening or autumn of one's life (literary); ～**abschnitt** der stage of or chapter in one's life; ～**art** die o. Pl. manners pl.; ～**bedingungen** Pl. conditions of life; ～**bejahend** Adj. 〈person〉 with a positive attitude or approach to life; ～**bereich** der area of life; ～**dauer** die (a) life-span; (b) (von Maschinen) [useful] life; ～**echt 1** Adj. true-to-life; **2** adv. in a true-to-life way; ～**ende** das end [of one's life]; ～**erfahrung** die experience no indef. art. of life;

~**erinnerungen** *Pl.* (Memoiren) memoirs; ~**erwartung** *die* life expectancy; ~**fähig** *Adj.* (auch fig.) viable; ~**fremd** *Adj.* out of touch with *or* remote from everyday life *postpos.;* ~**freude** *die; o. Pl.* zest for life; joie de vivre; ~**froh** *Adj.* full of zest for life *or* joie de vivre *postpos.;* ~**führung** *die* lifestyle; ~**gefahr** *die* mortal danger; „Achtung, ~gefahr!" 'danger'; **sie schwebt in** ~**gefahr** she is in danger of dying; (von einer Kranken) her condition is critical; **außer** ~**gefahr sein** be out of danger; ~**gefährlich** 1 *Adj.* highly *or* extremely dangerous; critical 〈*injury*〉; 2 *adv.* critically 〈*injured, ill*〉; ~**gefährte** *der,* ~**gefährtin** *die* (geh.) companion through life (literary); ~**gemeinschaft** *die* (a) (von Menschen) long-term relationship; (b) (Biol.: von Tieren, Pflanzen) biocoenosis; ~**geschichte** *die* life-story; ~**groß** *Adj.* life-size; ~**größe** *die:* **eine Statue in** ~**größe** a life-size statue; ~**haltungs·kosten** *Pl.* cost of living *sing.;* ~**inhalt** *der* purpose in life; **ihre Familie ist ihr** ~**inhalt** her family is her whole life; ~**jahr** *das* year of [one's] life; **in seinem 12.** ~**jahr** in his twelfth year; **mit dem vollendeten 18.** ~**jahr** on reaching the age of eighteen; ~**kraft** *die* vitality; vital energy; ~**künstler** *der:* **ein [echter/wahrer]** ~**künstler** a person who always knows how to make the best of things; ~**lage** *die* situation [in life]; ~**lang** 1 *Adj.* lifelong; 2 *adv.* all one's life; ~**länglich** 1 *Adj.* ~**länglicher Freiheitsentzug** life imprisonment; „~**länglich" bekommen** get life imprisonment *or* (coll.) life; 2 *adv.* **jmdn.** ~**länglich gefangen halten** keep sb. imprisoned for life; ~**lauf** *der* curriculum vitae; c. v.; ~**lustig** *Adj.* 〈*person*〉 full of the joys of life

Lebens·mittel *das; meist Pl.* food[stuff]; ~ *Pl.* food *sing.;* foods (formal); foodstuffs (formal); (als Ware) food *sing.*

Lebensmittel-: ~**abteilung** *die* food department; ~**geschäft** *das* food shop

lebens-, Lebens-: ~**müde** *Adj.* weary of life *pred.;* **du bist wohl** ~**müde?** (scherzh.) you must be tired of living; ~**mut** *der* courage to go on living; ~**nah** 1 *Adj.* true-to-life 〈*film, description, etc.*〉; 〈*teaching*〉 closely related to life; 2 *adv.* **etw.** ~**nah schildern** describe sth. in a true-to-life way; ~**notwendig** *Adj.* essential 〈*foodstuff*〉; vital 〈*organ*〉; ~**plan** *der* life plan; **so etwas wie einen** ~**plan hat sie nie gehabt** she has never planned her life; ~**qualität** *die; o. Pl.* quality of life; ~**raum** *der* (a) (Umkreis) lebensraum; (b) (Biol.) ⇒ **Biotop;** ~**regel** *die* rule [of life]; maxim; ~**retter** *der* rescuer; **sein** ~**retter** the person who saved his life; ~**standard** *der* standard of living; ~**stellung** *die* permanent position *or* job; job for life; ~**stil** *der* lifestyle; ~**tüchtig** *Adj.* able to cope with life *postpos.;* ~**umstände** *Pl.* circumstances; ~**unfähig** *Adj.* non-viable; ~**unterhalt** *der:* **seinen** ~**unterhalt verdienen** earn one's living; **für jmds.** ~**unterhalt sorgen** support sb.; ~**untüchtig** *Adj.* unable to cope with life *postpos.;* ~**versicherung** *die* life insurance; life assurance; **eine** ~**versicherung abschließen** take out a life insurance *or* assurance policy; ~**wandel** *der* way of life; **einen zweifelhaften/einwandfreien** ~**wandel führen** lead a dubious/an irreproachable life; ~**weg** *der* [journey through] life; ~**weise** *die* way of life; ~**werk** *das* life's work; ~**wert** *Adj.* **ein** ~**wertes Leben** a life worth living; ~**wichtig** ⇒ ~**notwendig;** ~**wille** *der* will to live; ~**zeichen** *das* sign of life; **kein** ~**zeichen [von sich] geben** show no sign of life; ~**zeit** *die* life[-span]; **auf** ~**zeit** for life; **ein Beamter auf** ~**zeit** an established civil servant

Leber /'le:bɐ/ *die;* ~, ~**n** ▶ 326⌡ liver; **es an der** ~ **haben** (ugs.) have [got] liver trouble; **frisch** *od.* **frei von der** ~ **weg sprechen** *od.* **reden** (ugs.) speak one's mind; *s. auch* **Laus**

leber-, Leber-: ~**fleck** *der* liver spot; ~**käse** *der; o. Pl.:* meat loaf made with mincemeat, [minced liver,] eggs, and spices; ~**knödel** *der* (südd., österr.) meat ball made from minced liver, onions, eggs, and flour; ~**krank** *Adj.* 〈*patient etc.*〉 suffering from a liver complaint *or* disorder; ~**leiden** *das* ▶ 329⌡ (Med.) liver complaint *or* disorder;

~**pastete** *die* liver pâté; ~**tran** *der* fish-liver oil; (des Kabeljaus) cod-liver oil; ~**wurst** *die* liver sausage; **die gekränkte** *od.* **beleidigte** ~**wurst spielen** (ugs.) get all huffy (coll.)

Lebe-: ~**wesen** *das* living being *or* thing *or* creature; ~**wohl** /-'-'-/ *das;* [e]s, ~ *od.* ~**e** (geh.) farewell; **jmdm.** ~**wohl sagen** bid sb. farewell

lebhaft 1 *Adj.* (a) lively 〈*person, gesture, imagination, bustle, etc.*〉; lively, animated 〈*conversation, discussion*〉; lively, brisk 〈*activity*〉; busy 〈*traffic*〉; brisk 〈*business*〉; vivid 〈*idea, picture, etc.*〉; (b) (kräftig) lively 〈*interest*〉; lively, gay 〈*pattern*〉; bright, gay 〈*colour*〉; vigorous 〈*applause, opposition*〉. 2 *adv.* (a) in a lively way *or* fashion; 〈*remember sth.*〉 vividly; **sich** ~ **unterhalten** have a lively *or* animated conversation; **sich (Dat.) etw.** ~ **vorstellen können** have a vivid picture of sth.; (b) (kräftig) brightly, gaily 〈*coloured*〉; gaily 〈*patterned*〉

Leb·kuchen *der* ≈ gingerbread

leb-, Leb-: ~**los** *Adj.* lifeless 〈*body, eyes*〉; [wie] ~**los daliegen** lie there as if dead; ~**tag** *der:* [all] mein/dein *usw.* ~**tag** (ugs.) all my/your *etc.* life; **so was habe ich mein** ~**tag nicht erlebt** (ugs.) I've never seen anything like it in all my life *or* in all my born days; ~**zeiten** *Pl.* **zu jmds.** ~**zeiten** while sb. is/was still alive; during sb.'s lifetime

lechzen /'lɛçtsn̩/ *itr. V.* (geh.) **nach einem Trunk/nach Kühlung** ~: long for a drink/to be able to cool off; **nach Rache** *usw.* ~: thirst for revenge *etc.*

leck /lɛk/ *Adj.* leaky; ~ **sein** leak

Leck *das;* ~[e]s, ~s leak

lecken[1] 1 *tr. V.* lick; **sich (Dat.) die Lippen** *usw.* ~: lick one's lips *etc.;* **jmdm. die Hand** *usw.* ~: lick sb.'s hand *etc.;* **leck mich [doch]!** (derb) [why don't you] piss off! (coarse); *s. auch* **Arsch a; Finger b.** 2 *itr. V.* **an etw. (Dat.)** ~: lick sth.

lecken[2] *itr. V.* (leck sein) leak

lecker *Adj.* tasty 〈*meal*〉; delicious 〈*cake etc.*〉; good 〈*smell, taste*〉; (fig.) ansprechend) lovely 〈*girl*〉

Lecker·bissen *der* delicacy; **ein musikalischer** ~ (fig.) a musical treat

Leckerei *die;* ~, ~**en** (ugs.) dainty; (Süßigkeit) sweet [meat]

leck|schlagen *unr. itr V.; mit sein* (Seemannsspr.) be holed

led. *Abk.* **ledig**

Leder /'le:dɐ/ *das;* ~**s**, ~ (a) leather; **in** ~ **[gebunden]** leather-bound; **zäh wie** ~ **sein** 〈*person*〉 be as hard as nails; **jmdm. ans** ~ **gehen/wollen** (ugs.) go for sb./be out to get sb.; (b) (Fenster~) leather; chamois *or* chammy [leather]; (c) (Fußballjargon: Ball) ball; leather (dated sl.)

Leder-: ~**garnitur** *die* leather-upholstered suite; ~**hand·schuh** *der* leather glove; ~**hose** *die* leather shorts *pl.;* lederhosen *pl.;* (lang) leather trousers; ~**jacke** *die* leather jacket; ~**mantel** *der* leather [over]coat

ledern[1] *tr. V.* leather

ledern[2] *Adj.* (a) nicht präd. (aus Leder) leather; (b) (wie Leder) leathery

Leder-: ~**sessel** *der* leather[-upholstered] armchair; ~**sohle** *die* leather sole; ~**waren** *Pl.* leather goods

ledig /'le:dɪç/ *Adj.* (a) single; unmarried 〈*mother*〉; (b) **einer Sache (Gen.)** ~ **sein** (geh.) be free of sth.

Ledige *der/die; adj. Dekl.* single person

lediglich *Adj.* only; merely; simply

Lee /le:/ *die od. das;* ~ (Seemannsspr.) **nach** ~ **drehen/in** ~ **liegen** turn to/tie to leeward

leer /le:ɐ̯/ *Adj.* (a) empty; blank, clean 〈*sheet of paper*〉; **sein Glas** ~ **trinken** empty *or* drain one's glass; **seinen Teller** ~ **essen** clear one's plate; **die Schachtel** ~ **machen** (ugs.) finish the box; ~ **ausgehen** come away empty-handed; ~ **laufen** 〈*barrel etc.*〉 run dry; 〈*machine*〉 idle; **die Badewanne läuft** ~: the bathwater is running out; (b) (menschenleer) empty; empty 〈*streets*〉; **die Wohnung steht** ~: the house is standing empty *or* is unoccupied; ~ **stehend** empty, unoccupied 〈*house, flat*〉; ~ **gefegt** deserted 〈*street, town*〉; **wie** ~ **gefegt** deserted;

(c) (abwertend: oberflächlich) empty ‹*words, promise, talk, display*›; vacant ‹*expression*›; **mit ~en Augen/~em Blick starren** stare vacantly

Leere *die;* ~ (auch fig.) emptiness; **eine gähnende ~:** a gaping void; **eine innere ~** (fig.) a feeling of emptiness inside

leeren 1 *tr. V.* **(a)** empty; empty, clear ‹*postbox*›; **(b)** (österr.: gießen) pour ‹*water, milk, etc.*›. 2 *refl. V.* ‹*hall, theatre, etc.*› empty

leer-, Leer-: **~gefegt* ⇨ **leer b;** **~gewicht** *das* unladen weight; **~gut** *das* empties *pl.;* **~lauf** *der; o. Pl.* **(a)** **im ~lauf den Berg hinunterfahren** ‹*driver*› coast down the hill in neutral; ‹*cyclist*› freewheel *or* coast down the hill; **(b)** (fig.) **es gab [viel] ~lauf im Büro** there were [long] slack periods in the office;*~\|laufen* ⇨ **leer a;** **~stehend* ⇨ **leer b;** **~taste** *die* space bar

Leerung *die;* ~, **~en** emptying; **nächste ~ um 12 Uhr** (auf Briefkästen) next collection at 12.00

Lefze /ˈlɛftsə/ *die;* ~, **~n** lip

legal /leˈgaːl/ 1 *Adj.* legal. 2 *adv.* legally

legalisieren *tr. V.* legalize

Legalität /legaliˈtɛːt/ *die;* ~: legality; **außerhalb der ~:** outside the law

Legasthenie /legasteˈniː/ *die;* ~, **~n** (Psych., Med.) difficulty in learning to read and write

Legastheniker /legasˈteːnikɐ/ *der;* ~s, ~ (Psych., Med.) one who has difficulty with reading and writing

Lege-: **~batterie** *die* laying battery; **~henne** *die* laying hen

legen /ˈleːgn̩/ 1 *tr. V.* **(a)** lay [down]; **jmdm. auf den Rücken ~:** lay sb. on his/her back; **etw. auf den Tisch ~:** lay sth. on the table; **etw. aus der Hand/beiseite ~:** put sth. down/aside *or* down; **etw. in den Kühlschrank ~:** put sth. in the refrigerator; **die Füße auf den Tisch ~:** put one's feet on the table; **(b)** (verlegen) lay ‹*pipe, cable, railway track, carpet, tiles, etc.*›; **(c)** (in eine bestimmte Form bringen) **etw. in Falten ~:** fold sth.; **sich** (*Dat.*) **die Haare ~ lassen** have one's hair set; *s. auch* **Falte c;** **(d)** (schräg hinstellen) lean; **etw. an etw.** (*Akk.*) **~:** lean sth. [up] against sth. 2 *tr., itr. V.* ‹*hen*› lay. 3 *refl. V.* **(a)** lie down; **sich auf etw.** (*Akk.*) **~:** lie down on sth.; **das Schiff/Flugzeug legte sich auf die Seite** the ship keeled over/the aircraft banked steeply; **sich in die Kurve ~:** lean into the bend; *s. auch* **Bett a; Ohr b;** **(b)** (nachlassen) ‹*wind, storm*› die down, abate, subside; ‹*noise*› die down, abate; ‹*enthusiasm*› wear off, subside, fade; ‹*anger*› abate, subside; ‹*excitement*› die down, subside; **(c)** (sich herabsenken) **sich auf** *od.* **über etw.** (*Akk.*) **~** ‹*mist, fog*› descend *or* settle on sth., [come down and] blanket sth.

legendär /legɛnˈdɛːɐ̯/ *Adj.* legendary

Legende /leˈgɛndə/ *die;* ~, **~n** **(a)** legend; **zur ~ werden** (fig.) ‹*event, incident, etc.*› become legendary; ‹*person*› become a legend; **(b)** (Zeichenerklärung) legend; key

leger /leˈʒeːɐ̯/ 1 *Adj.* **(a)** casual; relaxed; **(b)** (bequem) casual ‹*jacket etc.*›. 2 *adv.* **(a)** casually; in a casual *or* relaxed manner; **(b)** (bequem) ‹*dress*› casually

Legierung *die;* ~, **~en** alloy

Legion /leˈgioːn/ *die;* ~, **~en** **(a)** (Milit.) legion; (Fremden~) Legion; **(b)** (Menge) horde **(von** of**)**

Legionär /legioˈnɛːɐ̯/ *der;* ~s, **~e** legionary

legislativ /legɪslaˈtiːf/ (Politik) 1 *Adj.* legislative. 2 *adv.* by legislation

Legislative /legɪslaˈtiːvə/ *die;* ~, **~n** (Politik) legislature

Legislatur·periode /legɪslaˈtuːɐ̯-/ *die* (Politik) parliamentary term; legislative period

legitim /legiˈtiːm/ 1 *Adj.* legitimate. 2 *adv.* legitimately

Legitimation /legitimaˈtsi̯oːn/ *die;* ~, **~en** **(a)** (auch Rechtsw.: Ehelicherklärung) legitimation; **(b)** (Ausweis) proof of identity; (Bevollmächtigung) authorization

legitimieren 1 *tr. V.* **(a)** (rechtfertigen) justify; **(b)** (bevollmächtigen) authorize; **(c)** (für legitim erklären) legitimize ‹*child, relationship*›. 2 *refl. V.* show proof of one's identity

Legitimität /legitimiˈtɛːt/ *die;* ~: legitimacy

Lehm /leːm/ *der;* ~s loam; (Ton) clay

Lehm-: **~boden** *der* loamy soil; (Tonerde) clay soil; **~hütte** *die* mud hut

lehmig *Adj.* loamy ‹*soil, earth*›; (tonartig) clayey ‹*soil, shoes, etc.*›

Lehm·ziegel *der* clay brick

Lehne /ˈleːnə/ *die;* ~, **~n** (Rücken~) back; (Arm~) arm

lehnen 1 *tr. V.* lean **(an** + *Akk.,* **gegen** against); **den Kopf an etw.** (*Akk.*) **~:** lean one's head on sth. 2 *refl. V.* lean **(an** + *Akk.,* **gegen** against; **über** + *Akk.* over); **sich aus dem Fenster ~:** lean out of the window. 3 *itr. V.* be leaning **(an** + *Dat.* against)

Lehn-: **~stuhl** *der* armchair; **~wort** *das* loanword

Lehr-: **~amt** *das* (Schulw.) teaching post; (Beruf) **das ~amt** the teaching profession; **~auftrag** *der* lectureship; **~beauftragte** *der/die* lecturer; **~buch** *das* textbook

Lehre /ˈleːrə/ *die;* ~, **~n** **(a)** (Berufsausbildung) apprenticeship; **eine ~ machen** serve an apprenticeship **(als** as**)**; **bei jmdm. in die ~ gegangen sein** (fig.) have learnt a lot from sb.; **(b)** (Weltanschauung) doctrine; **die christliche ~:** Christian doctrine; **die ~ Kants/Hegels/Buddhas** the teachings *pl.* of Kant/Hegel/Buddha; **(c)** (Theorie, Wissenschaft) theory; **die ~ vom Schall** the science of sound *or* acoustics; **(d)** (Erfahrung) lesson; **lass dir das eine ~ sein!** let that be a lesson to you; **jmdm. eine [heilsame] ~ erteilen** teach sb. a [salutary] lesson

lehren *tr., itr. V.* (auch fig.) teach; **jmdn. lesen** *usw.* **~:** teach sb. to read *etc.;* **ich werde dich ~, so bockig zu sein!** (ugs.) I'll teach you to be so contrary (coll.)

Lehrer *der;* ~s, ~ ▶85❘ **(a)** (auch fig.) teacher; **er ist ~ für Geschichte** he teaches history; he is a history teacher; **(b)** (Ausbilder) instructor

Lehrer·ausbildung *die* teacher training *no art.*

Lehrerin *die;* ~, **~nen** ▶85❘ teacher

Lehrer-: **~kollegium** *das* teaching staff; faculty (Amer.); **~mangel** *der* shortage of teachers

Lehrerschaft *die;* ~, **~en** teachers *pl.;* (einer Schule) teaching staff; faculty (Amer.)

Lehrer-: **~schwemme** *die* (ugs.) glut of teachers; **~zimmer** *das* staffroom

Lehr-: **~fach** *das* **(a)** subject; **(b)** (Beruf des Lehrens) teaching profession; **im ~fach tätig sein** be a teacher; **~gang** *der* course **(für, in** + *Dat.* in); **einen ~gang machen, an einem ~gang teilnehmen** take a course; **~geld** *das* (fig.) **du kannst dir dein ~geld zurückgeben lassen!** your education was wasted on you; **~geld geben** *od.* **[be]zahlen [müssen]** learn the hard way; **~herr** *der* (geh. veralt.) master (*of an apprentice*); **~jahr** *das* year as an apprentice; **~körper** *der* (Amtsspr.) teaching staff; faculty (Amer.); **~kraft** *die* teacher

Lehrling /ˈleːrlɪŋ/ *der;* ~s, **~e** ▶85❘ apprentice; (in kaufmännischen Berufen) trainee

Lehrlings·ausbildung *die* training of apprentices

lehr-, Lehr-: **~mädchen** *das* [girl] apprentice; (in kaufmännischen Berufen) [girl] trainee; **~meister** *der* teacher; (Vorbild) mentor; **~methode** *die* teaching method; **~mittel** *das* (Schulw.) teaching aid; **~mittel** *Pl.* teaching materials; **~reich** *Adj.* instructive, informative ‹*book, film, etc.*›; **es war eine ~reiche Erfahrung für ihn** the experience taught him a lot; **~stelle** *die* apprenticeship; (in kaufmännischen Berufen) trainee post; **~stoff** *der* (Schulw.) syllabus; **~stuhl** *der* (Hochschulw.) chair **(für** of); **~veranstaltung** *die* (Hochschulw.) class; (Vorlesung) lecture; **~zeit** *die* [period of] apprenticeship

Leib /laip/ *der;* ~[e]s, **~er** (geh.) **(a)** body; **am ganzen ~ zittern** shiver all over; **bleib mir vom ~[e]!** keep away from me!; **etw. am eigenen ~ erfahren** *od.* **erleben** experience sth. for oneself; **er hat sich mit ~ und Seele der Musik verschrieben** he dedicated himself heart and soul to music; **mit ~ und Seele dabei sein** put one's whole heart into it; **jmdm. auf den ~ ~e rücken** (ugs.) chivvy sb.; (mit Kritik) get at sb. (coll.); **sich** (*Dat.*) **jmdn. vom ~e halten** (ugs.) keep sb. at arm's length; **jmdm. mit einer Sache vom ~e bleiben** (ugs.) not pester sb. with sth.; **einer Sache** (*Dat.*) **zu ~e rücken** tackle sth.; set about sth.; **jmdm. auf den ~ geschnitten sein** be tailor-made for sb.; suit sb. down to the ground; **(b)** (geh., fachspr.: Bauch) belly; (Magen) stomach;

(c) **eine Gefahr für ～ und Leben** (veralt.) a danger to life and limb
Leib·eigenschaft *die; o. Pl.* (hist.) serfdom *no def. art.*
leiben *itr. V.* **wie er/sie** *usw.* **leibt und lebt** to a T
Leibes·erziehung *die* (Schulw.) physical education; PE
Leib·gericht *das* favourite dish
leibhaftig /laɪpˈhaftɪç/ **1** *Adj.* (a) (persönlich) in person *postpos.;* **da stand er ～ vor uns** there he was, as large as life; (b) (echt) real; **ein ～er Herzog** a real live duke; **der Leibhaftige** (scherzh.) the devil incarnate. **2** *adv.* (ugs.) actually; believe it or not
leiblich *Adj.* (a) physical ⟨*well-being*⟩; (b) (blutsverwandt) real ⟨*mother, parents, etc.*⟩
Leib-: **～rente** *die* life annuity; **～speise** *die* ⇒ **～gericht;** **～wache** *die,* **～wächter** *der* bodyguard; **～wäsche** *die* underwear; underclothes *pl.*
Leiche /ˈlaɪçə/ *die;* **～,** **～n** [dead] body; (bes. eines Unbekannten) corpse; **er sieht aus wie eine lebende** *od.* **wandelnde ～** (salopp) he looks like death warmed up (sl.); **nur über meine ～!** over my dead body!; **über ～n gehen** (abwertend) be utterly ruthless *or* unscrupulous
leichen-, Leichen-: **～blass,** **~*blaß *Adj.* deathly pale; white as a sheet *postpos.;* **～halle** *die* mortuary; **～hemd** *das* burial garment; **～schändung** *die* desecration of a corpse; (sexuell) necrophilia *no art.;* **～schau·haus** *das* morgue; **～starre** *die* rigor mortis; **～tuch** *das* (veralt.) winding-sheet; shroud; **～wagen** *der* hearse; **～zug** *der* (geh.) cortège; funeral procession
Leichnam /ˈlaɪçnaːm/ *der;* **～s,** **～e** (geh.) body; **jmds. ～:** sb.'s body *or* mortal remains *pl.*
leicht /laɪçt/ **1** *Adj.* (a) light; lightweight ⟨*suit, material*⟩; **～e Waffen** small-calibre arms; **～e Kleidung** thin clothes; (luftig) light *or* cool clothes; **gewogen und zu ～ befunden** tried and found wanting; **mit ～er Hand** with ease; **etw. auf die ～e Schulter nehmen** (ugs.) take sth. casually; make light of sth.; (b) (einfach) easy ⟨*task, question, job, etc.*⟩; (nicht anstrengend) light ⟨*work, duties, etc.*⟩; **ein ～es Leben haben** have an easy life; **es ～/nicht ～ haben** have/not have it easy *or* an easy time of it; **nichts ～er als das** nothing could be simpler *or* easier; **mit jmdm. [kein] ～es Spiel haben** find sb. is [not] easy meat; **jmdm./sich etw. ～ machen** make sth. easy for sb./oneself; **es sich** (*Dat.*) **～ machen** make it *or* things easy for oneself; take the easy way out; **～ fallen** (leicht sein) be easy; **das fällt mir ～:** it is easy for me; I find it easy; **sich mit etw. ～ tun/nicht ～ tun** (ugs.) manage sth. easily/have a hard time with sth.; (c) (schwach) slight ⟨*accent, illness, wound, doubt, etc.*⟩; light ⟨*wind, rain, sleep, perfume*⟩; **ein ～er Stoß [in die Rippen]** a gentle nudge [in the ribs]; (d) (bekömmlich) light ⟨*food, wine*⟩; mild ⟨*cigar, cigarette*⟩; (e) (heiter) light-hearted; **ihr wurde es etwas/viel ～er** she felt somewhat/much easier *or* relieved; **etw. ～ nehmen** make light of sth.; **seine Aufgabe nicht ～ nehmen** take one's task seriously; **nimms ～:** don't worry about it; (f) (unterhaltend) light ⟨*music, reading, etc.*⟩; (g) **ein ～es Mädchen** (veralt. abwertend) a loose-living girl. **2** *adv.* (a) lightly ⟨*built*⟩; **～ bekleidet** be lightly *or* thinly dressed; (b) (einfach, schnell, spielend) easily; **～ verdaulich** [easily] digestible; **～ verständlich** *od.* **zu verstehen sein** be easy to understand; be easily understood; **sie hat ～ reden** it's easy *or* all very well for her to talk; **das ist ～er gesagt als getan** that's easier said than done; **sie wird ～ böse** she has a quick temper; **das ist ～ möglich** that is perfectly possible; **ihr wird ～ schlecht** the slightest thing makes her sick; (c) (geringfügig) slightly; **～ gewürzt** lightly seasoned; **es regnete ～:** there was a light rain falling; **es hat ～ gefroren** there was a slight frost; **～ verletzt** slightly injured
leicht-, Leicht-: **～athlet** *der* [track/field] athlete; **～athletik** *die* [track and field] athletics *sing.;* **~*be·kleidet ⇒ **leicht 2 a;** **～benzin** *das* benzine; **~*entzündlich: ⇒ **entzündlich a;** **~*fallen ⇒ **leicht 1 b;** **～fertig 1** *Adj.* (a) careless ⟨*behaviour, person*⟩; rash ⟨*promise*⟩; ill-considered, slapdash ⟨*plan*⟩; (b) (veralt.: moralisch bedenkenlos) promiscuous; loose

⟨*woman*⟩; **2** *adv.* carelessly; **～fertigkeit** *die; o. Pl.* carelessness; **～gewicht** *das* (Schwerathletik) (a) *o. Pl.* lightweight; *s. auch* **Fliegengewicht;** (b) (ugs. scherzh.) (Mädchen) sylph; (Mann) featherweight; **～gläubig** *Adj.* gullible; credulous; **～gläubigkeit** *die* gullibility; credulity; **～hin** *Adv.* without [really] thinking; (lässig) casually; **etw. ～hin sagen** say sth. casually *or* unthinkingly
Leichtigkeit /ˈlaɪçtɪçkaɪt/ *die;* **～** (a) lightness; (b) (Mühelosigkeit) ease; **mit ～:** with ease; easily
leicht-, Leicht-: **～lebig** *Adj.* happy-go-lucky; **~*machen ⇒ **leicht 1 b;** **～matrose** *der* ordinary seaman; **～metall** *das* light metal; (Legierung) [light] alloy;**~*nehmen ⇒ **leicht 1 e;** **～sinn** *der; o. Pl.* carelessness *no indef. art.;* (mit Gefahr verbunden) recklessness *no indef. art.;* (Fahrlässigkeit) negligence *no indef. art.;* **～sinnig 1** *Adj.* careless; (sich, andere gefährdend) reckless; (fahrlässig) negligent; **2** *adv.* carelessly; (gefährlich) recklessly; ⟨*promise*⟩ rashly; **～sinnig mit seinem Geld umgehen** be careless with one's money; **~*tun ⇒ **leicht 1b;** **~*verdaulich ⇒ **leicht 2 b;** **~*verletzt ⇒ **leicht 2 c;** **～verletzte** *der/die* slightly injured man/woman/person
leid /laɪt/ *Adj.; nicht attr.* **etw./jmdn. ～ sein/werden** (ugs.) be/get fed up with (coll.) *or* tired of sth./sb.; *s. auch* **Leid c**
Leid *das;* **～[e]s** (a) (Schmerz) suffering; (Kummer) grief; sorrow; **großes** *od.* **schweres ～ erfahren** suffer greatly; (Kummer) suffer great sorrow; **geteiltes ～ ist halbes ～** (Spr.) a sorrow shared is a sorrow halved; **jmdm. sein ～ klagen** tell sb. all one's woes; (b) (Unrecht) wrong; (Böses) harm; **jmdm. ein ～ zufügen** wrong/harm sb.; do sb. wrong/harm; (c) ▶163 **es tut mir ～[, dass…]** I'm sorry [that…]; **so ～ es mir tut, aber…:** I'm very sorry, but…; **er tut mir ～/es tut mir ～ um ihn** I feel sorry for him; **es tut mir ～ darum** I feel sorry *or* (coll.) bad about it
leiden 1 *unr. itr. V.* ▶329 (a) suffer (**an, unter** + *Dat.* from); **unter jmdm. ～:** suffer because of sb.; (b) (Schaden nehmen) suffer (**durch, unter** + *Dat.* from). **2** *unr. tr. V.* (a) **jmdn. [gut] ～ können** *od.* **[gern] ～ mögen** like sb.; **ich kann sie/das nicht ～:** I can't stand her/it; (b) (geh.: ertragen müssen) suffer ⟨*hunger, thirst, want, torment, etc.*⟩; (c) (dulden) tolerate; **sie ist überall wohl gelitten** (geh.) she is liked by everybody
Leiden *das;* **～s,** **～** (a) ▶329 (Krankheit) illness; (Gebrechen) complaint; (b) (Qual) suffering; **Freud[en] und ～[en]** joy[s] and sorrow[s]
leidend *Adj.* (a) (krank) ailing; in poor health *postpos.;* **～ aussehen** look sickly *or* poorly; (b) (schmerzvoll) strained ⟨*voice*⟩; martyred ⟨*expression*⟩; ⟨*look*⟩ full of suffering
Leidenschaft *die;* **～,** **～en** passion; **mit ～:** fervently; passionately; **seine ～ für etw. entdecken** realize one's great love for sth.; **er ist Sammler aus ～:** he is a dedicated collector
leidenschaftlich 1 *Adj.* passionate; ardent, passionate ⟨*lover*⟩; passionate[ly keen] ⟨*skier, collector, etc.*⟩; violent, passionate ⟨*hatred, quarrel*⟩; vehement ⟨*protest*⟩. **2** *adv.* (a) passionately; (eifrig) dedicatedly; **～ diskutiert werden** be discussed heatedly; (b) **etw. ～ gern tun** adore doing sth.
Leidens-: **～gefährte** *der,* **～gefährtin** *die,* **～genosse** *der,* **～genossin** *die* fellow-sufferer; **～geschichte** *die; o. Pl.* (christl. Rel.) **die ～geschichte Christi** Christ's Passion; **seine ～geschichte** (fig.) his tale of woe; **～miene** *die* woeful *or* martyred expression
leider *Adv.* ▶163 unfortunately; **ich habe ～ keine Zeit** unfortunately *or* I'm afraid I haven't any time; **～ ja/nein** I'm afraid so/afraid not; **～ Gottes ist es nun einmal so** (ugs.) that's how it is, I'm afraid *or* worse luck; (in förmlichen Briefen) **wir müssen Ihnen ～ mitteilen …:** we regret to inform you …
leid·geprüft *Adj.* sorely tried; long-suffering
leidig *Adj.* tiresome; wretched
leidlich 1 *Adj.* reasonable; passable. **2** *adv.* reasonably; fairly; **es geht mir [ganz] ～** (ugs.) I'm quite well *or* not too bad; **sie kann ～ Klavier spielen** she can play the piano reasonably well

---

Leid-: ~**tragende** *der/die; adj. Dekl.* victim; **der/die** ~**tragende/die** ~**tragenden** [**dabei**] **sein** be the one/ones to suffer [in this]; ~**wesen** *das:* **zu jmds.** ~**wesen** to sb.'s regret

Leier /ˈlaiɐ/ *die;* ~, ~**n** lyre; [**es ist**] **immer die alte/dieselbe** ~ (ugs. abwertend) [it's] always the same old story

Leier·kasten *der* (ugs.) barrel organ; hurdy-gurdy (coll.)

leiern (ugs.) **1** *tr. V.* (**a**) (kurbeln) [**nach oben/unten**] ~: wind [up/down]; (**b**) (monoton aufsagen) drone through; (schnell) reel *or* rattle off. **2** *itr. V.* (**a**) **an etw.** (*Dat.*) ~: wind away at sth.; (**b**) (monoton sprechen) drone [on]

Leih-: ~**arbeit** *die; o. Pl.* (Wirtsch.) subcontracted labour; ~**arbeiter** *der* subcontracted worker; ~**bibliothek** *die,* ~**bücherei** *die* lending library

leihen /ˈlaiən/ *unr. tr. V.* (**a**) **jmdm. etw.** ~: lend sb. sth.; lend sth. to sb.; (**b**) (entleihen) borrow; [**sich** (*Dat.*)] [**von** *od.* **bei jmdm.**] **etw.** ~: borrow sth. [from sb.]; **ein geliehener Wagen** a borrowed car; (**c**) (geh.: gewähren) lend, give ‹*support*›; give ‹*attention*›

Leih-: ~**gabe** *die* loan (*Gen.* from); ~**gebühr** *die* hire *or* (Amer.) rental charge; (bei Büchern) lending charge; borrowing fee; ~**haus** *das* pawnbroker's; pawnshop; ~**mutter** *die* surrogate mother; ~**wagen** *der* hire *or* (Amer.) rental car; [**sich** (*Dat.*)] **einen** ~**wagen nehmen** hire *or* (Amer.) rent a car; ~**weise** *Adv.* on loan; **hier hast du das Buch, aber nur** ~**weise** I'll give you the book, but only to borrow; **jmdm. etw.** ~ **überlassen** lend sth. to sb.

Leim /laim/ *der;* ~[**e**]**s** glue; **aus dem** ~ **gehen** (ugs.) come apart; **jmdm. auf den** ~ **gehen** *od.* **kriechen** (ugs.) be taken in by sb.; fall for sb.'s trick/tricks; **jmdn. auf den** ~ **führen** (ugs.) take sb. in

leimen *tr. V.* (**a**) glue (**an** + *Akk.* to); (zusammen~) glue [together]; (**b**) **jmdn.** ~ (ugs.) take sb. in

Leine /ˈlainə/ *die;* ~, ~**n** (**a**) rope; (Zelt~) guy-rope; ~ **ziehen** (ugs.) clear off; (**b**) (Wäsche~, Angel~) line; (**c**) (Hunde~) lead (esp. Brit.); leash; **den Hund an die** ~ **nehmen** put the dog on the lead/leash; **jmdn. an der** [**kurzen**] ~ **haben** *od.* **halten** (ugs.) keep sb. on a tight rein; **jmdn. an die** ~ **legen** (ugs.) get sb. under one's thumb

leinen *Adj.* linen

Leinen *das;* ~**s** (**a**) (Gewebe) linen; (**b**) (Buchw.) cloth; **Ausgabe in** ~ **cloth** edition

Leinen-: ~**band** *der* cloth-bound volume; ~**einband** *der* cloth binding; ~**kleid** *das* linen dress; ~**tuch** *das* linen cloth

Lein-: ~**öl** *das* linseed oil; ~**samen** *der* linseed; ~**wand** *die* (**a**) *o. Pl.* linen; (grob) canvas; (**b**) (des Malers) canvas; (**c**) (für Filme und Dias) screen; **einen Roman** *usw.* **auf die** ~**wand bringen** (fig.) film a novel *etc.*

leise /ˈlaizə/ **1** *Adj.* (**a**) quiet; soft ‹*steps, music, etc.*›; faint ‹*noise*›; **sei** ~! be quiet!; **könnt ihr nicht** ~**r sein?** can't you make less noise?; **die Musik** ~[**r**] **stellen** turn the music down; (**b**) *nicht präd.* (leicht; kaum merklich) faint; slight; slight, gentle ‹*touch*›; light ‹*rain*›; **nicht die** ~**ste Ahnung haben, nicht im Leisesten ahnen** not have the faintest *or* slightest idea. **2** *adv.* (**a**) quietly; **sprich doch etwas** ~**r** lower your voice; ~ **weinen** cry softly; (**b**) (leicht; kaum merklich) slightly; ‹*touch, rain*› gently

Leise·treter *der* (abwertend) pussyfooter

Leiste /ˈlaistə/ *die;* ~, ~**n** (**a**) strip; (Holz~) batten; (profiliert) moulding; (halbrund) beading; (am Auto) trim; (Tapeten~) [picture-]rail; picture moulding (Amer.); **eine** ~: a piece *or* strip of moulding/beading/trim; (Holz~) a batten; (**b**) (Knopf~) facing; (**c**) ▶ **326**┘ (Anat.) groin; (**d**) (Weberei) selvage

leisten **1** *tr. V.* (**a**) do ‹*work*›; (schaffen) achieve ‹*a lot, nothing*›; **gute** *od.* **ganze Arbeit** ~: do good work *or* a good job; (gründlich arbeiten) do a thorough job; **der Motor leistet 80 PS** the engine develops *or* produces 80 b.h.p.; (**b**) (verblasst *od.* als Funktionsverb) **jmdm. Hilfe** ~: help sb.; **einen Eid** ~: swear *or* take an oath **2** *refl. V.* (ugs.) (**a**) **sich** (*Dat.*) **etw.** ~: treat oneself to sth.; (**b**) **sich** (*Dat.*) **etw.** [**nicht**] ~ **können** [not] be able to afford sth.; **er kann es sich** (*Dat.*) ~, **das zu tun** he can afford to do it; (etw. Riskantes) he can get away with doing it; (**c**) (wagen)

sich (*Dat.*) **etw.** ~: get up to sth.; **was der sich** (*Dat.*) **leistet!** the things he gets away with!; **wer hat sich** (*Dat.*) **diese Frechheit geleistet?** who was it who had the cheek to do/say *etc.* that?

Leisten *der;* ~**s,** ~: last; **alles/alle über einen** ~ **schlagen** (ugs.) lump everybody/everything together

Leisten·bruch *der* rupture

Leistung *die;* ~, ~**en** (**a**) *o. Pl.* (Qualität bzw. Quantität der Arbeit) performance; **Bezahlung nach** ~: payment according to performance *or* results; (in der Industrie) payment according to productivity; (**b**) (Errungenschaft) achievement; (im Sport) performance; **eine große sportliche/technische** ~: a great sporting/technical feat; (**c**) *o. Pl.* (Leistungsvermögen, Physik: Arbeits~) power; (Ausstoß) output; **die** ~ **einer Fabrik** the output *or* [production] capacity of a factory; (**d**) (Zahlung, Zuwendung) payment; (Versicherungsw.) benefit; **die sozialen** ~**en der Firma** the firm's fringe benefits; (**e**) (Dienst~) service; (**f**) *o. Pl.* (das Leisten) carrying out; (Eides~) swearing

leistungs-, Leistungs-: ~**druck** *der* (bei Arbeitnehmern) pressure to work harder; (bei Sportlern, Schülern) pressure to achieve *or* to do well; ~**fähig** *Adj.* capable ‹*person*›; (körperlich) able-bodied ‹*person*›; (gute Arbeit leistend) efficient ‹*worker, factory, industry, etc.*›; powerful ‹*engine, computer, etc.*›; (konkurrenzfähig) competitive ‹*firm, industry*›; ~**fähigkeit** *die* (eines Menschen) capability; (bei guter Arbeitsleistung) efficiency; (eines Betriebes, der Industrie) productivity; (Wirtschaftlichkeit) efficiency; (eines Motors, eines Computers usw.) power; performance; ~**gerecht 1** *Adj.* ‹*salary, income*› based on performance *or* results; (in der Industrie) based on productivity; **2** *adv.* ~**gerecht bezahlt werden** receive a performance-related salary; ~**gesellschaft** *die* [highly] competitive society; performance-oriented society; ~**kurs** *der* (Schulw.) extension course; ~**orientiert** *Adj.* achievement-oriented; [highly] competitive ‹*society*›; ~**prämie** *die* productivity bonus; ~**prinzip** *das; o. Pl.* achievement principle; competitive principle; ~**schau** *die* (Wirtsch., Landw.) [product] exhibition; ~**schwach** *Adj.* not performing well *pred.*; low-achieving *attrib.* ‹*worker, pupil*›; (minderbegabt) less able, lower-ability *attrib.* ‹*pupil*›; weak ‹*team*›; low-powered ‹*engine*›; ~**sport** *der* competitive sport *no art.*; ~**sportler** *der,* ~**sportlerin** *die* competitive sportsman/sportswoman; ~**stark** *Adj.* high-performing *attrib.* ‹*athlete*›; able ‹*pupil, athlete, etc.*›; high-performance *attrib.*, powerful ‹*engine, car*›; highly efficient ‹*business, power station*›; (sehr konkurrenzfähig) highly competitive ‹*business, athlete*›; ~**träger** *der,* ~**trägerin** *die* (Sport) key player; ~**vermögen** *das* ⇒ ~**fähigkeit;** ~**zentrum** *das* (Sport) intensive training centre; ~**zwang** *der* (Soziol.) (bei Arbeitnehmern) compulsion to work hard; (bei Sportlern/Schülern) compulsion to achieve *or* to do well

Leit-: ~**artikel** *der* (Zeitungsw.) leading article; leader; ~**bild** *das* model

leiten /ˈlaitn/ *tr. V.* (**a**) (anführen) lead, head ‹*expedition, team, discussion, etc.*›; be head of ‹*school*›; (verantwortlich sein für) be in charge of ‹*project, expedition, etc.*›; manage ‹*factory, enterprise*›; (den Vorsitz führen bei) chair ‹*meeting, discussion, etc.*›; (Musik: dirigieren) conduct ‹*orchestra, choir*›; direct ‹*small orchestra etc.*›; (Sport: als Schiedsrichter) referee ‹*game, match*›; ~**der Angestellter** executive; manager; ~**de Angestellte** senior *or* managerial staff; ~**der Beamter** senior civil servant; (**b**) (begleiten, führen) lead; **jmdn. auf die richtige Spur** ~: put sb. on the right track; **sich von etw.** ~ **lassen** [let oneself] be guided by sth.; (**c**) (lenken) direct; route ‹*traffic*›; (um~) divert ‹*traffic, stream*›; (**d**) *auch itr.* (Physik) conduct ‹*heat, current, sound*›; **etw. leitet gut/schlecht** sth. is a good/bad conductor

Leiter¹ *der;* ~**s,** ~ (**a**) (einer Gruppe) leader; head; (einer Abteilung) head; manager; (eines Instituts) director; (einer Schule) head teacher; headmaster (Brit.); principal (esp. Amer.); (einer Diskussion) leader; (Vorsitzender) chair[man]; (eines Chors) choirmaster; (Dirigent) conductor; **kaufmännischer** ~: marketing manager; (Verkaufs~) sales manager; (**b**) (Physik) conductor

Leiter² *die;* ∼, ∼n ladder; (Steh∼) stepladder

Leiterin *die;* ∼, ∼nen ⇒ **Leiter¹**; (einer Schule) head teacher; headmistress (Brit.); principal (esp. Amer.); (eines Chors) choirmistress

Leit-: ∼**faden** *der* (a) [basic] textbook; ∼**faden der Physik** basic course in physics; introduction to physics; (b) (Leitgedanke) main idea *or* theme; ∼**hammel** *der* (abwertend: Führer) leader [of the herd]; boss-figure; ∼**linie** *die* (a) (Richtlinie) guideline; (b) (Verkehrsw.) lane marking; ∼**motiv** *das* (Musik, Literaturw., fig.) (a) leitmotiv; (b) (Leit-gedanke) dominant *or* central theme; ∼**planke** *die* crash barrier; guardrail (Amer.); ∼**satz** *der* guiding principle; ∼**spruch** *der* motto

Leitung *die;* ∼, ∼en (a) *o. Pl.* ⇒ **leiten a:** leading; heading; (Schulw.) working as a/the head; being in charge; management; chairing; (Musik) conducting; directing; (Sport) refereeing; (b) *o. Pl.* (einer Expedition usw.) leadership; (Ver-antwortung) responsibility (*Gen.* for); (einer Firma) manage-ment; (einer Sitzung, Diskussion) chairmanship; (Schulw.) headship; (Musik) conductorship; (Sport) [task of] refereeing; **unter der** ∼ **eines Managers stehen** be headed by a manager; **die** ∼ **der Sendung/Diskussion hat X** the programme is presented/the discussion is chaired by X; (c) (leitende Personen) management; (einer Schule) head and senior staff; (d) (Rohr∼) pipe; (Haupt∼) main; **Wasser aus der** ∼ **trinken** drink tap water; (e) (Draht, Kabel) cable; (für ein Gerät) lead; (einzelne od. ohne Isolierung) wire; **die** ∼**en [im Haus** *usw.*] the wiring *sing.* [of the house *etc.*]; (f) (Tele-fon∼) line; **es ist jemand in der** ∼ (ugs.) there's some-body on the line; **gehen Sie aus der** ∼! get off the line!; **auf einer anderen** ∼ **sprechen** be [talking] on another line; (fig.) **eine lange** ∼ **haben** (ugs.) be slow on the up-take; **er steht od. sitzt auf der** ∼ (salopp) he's not really with it (coll.)

Leitungs-: ∼**mast** *der* (für Strom) pylon; (Telefonmast) telegraph-pole; ∼**rohr** *das* [water/gas] pipe; (Haupt∼) main; ∼**wasser** *das* tap water

Leit-: ∼**währung** *die* (Wirtsch.) base *or* key currency; ∼**werk** *das* (Flugw., Waffent.) control surfaces *pl.;* (am Heck) tail unit

Lektion /lɛkˈtsi̯oːn/ *die;* ∼, ∼en lesson; **jmdm. eine** ∼ **erteilen** (fig.) teach sb. a lesson

Lektor /ˈlɛktɔr/ *der;* ∼s, ∼en /lɛkˈtoːrən/ (a) ▶85| (Hoch-schulw.) *junior university teacher in charge of practical or supplementary classes etc.;* (b) ▶85| (Verlags∼) [pub-lisher's] editor

Lektorat /lɛktoˈraːt/ *das;* ∼[e]s, ∼e (a) (Hochschulw.) post of 'Lektor'; (b) (im Verlag) editorial department

Lektorin *die;* ∼, ∼nen ⇒ **Lektor**

Lektüre /lɛkˈtyːrə/ *die;* ∼, ∼n (a) *o. Pl.* reading; **bei der** ∼ **des Romans** when reading the novel; (b) (Lesestoff) reading [matter]; **etw. als** ∼ **empfehlen** recommend sth. as a good read

Lende /ˈlɛndə/ *die;* ∼, ∼n ▶326| loin

Lenden-: ∼**schurz** *der* loincloth; ∼**stück** *das* (Kochk.) piece of loin

Leninismus /leniˈnɪsmʊs/ *der;* ∼: Leninism *no art.*

lenkbar *Adj.* (a) **leicht/schwer** ∼ **sein** be easy/difficult to steer; (b) (von Menschen) acquiescent; obedient; man-ageable, controllable ⟨child⟩

lenken /ˈlɛŋkn̩/ *tr. V.* (a) *auch itr.* steer ⟨car, bicycle, etc.⟩; be at the controls of ⟨aircraft⟩; guide ⟨missile⟩; (fahren) drive ⟨car etc.⟩; **wenn du geschickt lenkst** if you do some crafty steering; (b) direct, guide ⟨thoughts etc.⟩ (**auf** + *Akk.* to); turn ⟨attention⟩ (**auf** + *Akk.* to); steer ⟨conversation⟩; **die Diskussion auf etw./jmdn.** ∼: steer *or* bring the discussion round to sth./sb.; **den Ver-dacht auf jmdn.** ∼: throw suspicion on sb.; (c) control ⟨person, press, economy⟩; rule, govern ⟨state⟩; **eine ge-lenkte Wirtschaft** a planned economy

Lenker *der;* ∼s, ∼ (a) (Lenkstange) handlebars *pl.;* (b) (Fahrer) driver

Lenker-: ∼**band** *das* handlebar tape; ∼**hörnchen** *das* bar end

---

Lenkerin *die;* ∼, ∼nen ⇒ **Lenker b**

Lenker·vorbau *der* stem

Lenk-: ∼**rad** *das* steering wheel; ∼**stange** *die* handlebars *pl.*

Lenkung *die;* ∼, ∼en (a) *o. Pl.* (Leitung) control; (eines Staates) ruling *no indef. art.;* governing *no indef. art.;* (b) (Kfz-W.) steering

Lenz /lɛnts/ *der;* ∼es, ∼e (dichter. veralt.) spring; **einen sonnigen od. ruhigen od. faulen** ∼ **haben** *od.* **schie-ben** (salopp) have an easy time of it; (eine leichte Arbeit haben) have a cushy job (coll.); **sich** (*Dat.*) **einen schönen** ∼ **machen** (salopp) take it easy

Leopard /leoˈpart/ *der;* ∼en, ∼en leopard

Lepra /ˈleːpra/ *die;* ∼: leprosy *no art.*

Lepra·kranke *der/die* leper

Lerche /ˈlɛrçə/ *die;* ∼, ∼n lark

lern-, Lern-: ∼**bar** *Adj.* learnable; **das ist [für jeden]** ∼: that can be learnt [by anybody]; ∼**begierig** *Adj.* eager to learn *postpos.;* ∼**behindert** *Adj.* (Päd.) educationally subnormal; with learning difficulties *post-pos., not pred.;* ∼**eifer** *der* eagerness to learn

lernen /ˈlɛrnən/ **1** *itr. V.* (a) study; **gut/schlecht** ∼: be a good/poor learner *or* pupil; (fleißig/nicht fleißig sein) work hard/not work hard [at school]; **leicht** ∼: find it easy to learn; find school work easy; **mit jmdm.** ∼ (ugs.) help sb. with his/her [school-]work; (b) (Lehrling sein) train. **2** *tr. V.* (a) learn; **schwimmen/Klavier** ∼: learn to swim/play the piano; **er/mancher lernt es nie** (ugs.) he/some people [will] never learn; **von ihm kann man noch was** ∼: you can learn a thing or two from him; **das will gelernt sein** that is something one has to learn; **gelernt ist ge-lernt** once learnt, never forgotten; **das Fürchten** ∼: find out what it is to be afraid; (b) (einen Beruf) ∼: learn a trade; **Bäcker** *usw.* ∼: train to be *or* as a baker *etc.*

Lern-: ∼**hilfe** *die* aid to learning; ∼**mittel** *das* learning aid; (Lehrmittel) teaching aid; ∼**mittel** *Pl.* teaching materials; ∼**prozess**, *∼**prozeß** *der* learning process

lesbar *Adj.* (a) legible; (b) (klar) lucid ⟨style⟩; (verständlich) comprehensible; **gut** ∼: easy to read; very readable

Lesbe /ˈlɛsbə/ *die;* ∼, ∼n (ugs.) Lesbian; dike (sl.)

Lesbierin /ˈlɛsbi̯ərɪn/ *die;* ∼, ∼nen Lesbian

lesbisch *Adj.* Lesbian; ∼ **sein** be a Lesbian/Lesbians

Lese /ˈleːzə/ *die;* ∼, ∼n grape-harvest

Lese-: ∼**brille** *die* reading glasses *pl.;* ∼**buch** *das* reader; ∼**gerät** *das* (DV) reader; ∼**lampe** *die* reading lamp

lesen¹ 1 *unr. tr., itr. V.* (a) read; **sie las in einem Buch** she was reading a book; **er liest aus seinem neuesten Werk** he is reading from his latest work; **ein Gesetz [zum ersten Mal]** ∼ (Parl.) give a bill a [first] reading; **die/eine Messe** ∼: say Mass/a Mass; (b) (fig.) Ge-**danken** ∼ **können** be a mind-reader; **jmds. Gedanken** ∼: read sb.'s mind *or* thoughts; **aus der Hand** ∼: read palms; (c) (Hochschulw.) lecture (**über** + *Akk.* on); **er liest neue Geschichte** he lectures on modern history. **2** *unr. refl. V.* read

lesen² *unr. tr. V.* (a) (sammeln, pflücken) pick ⟨grapes, berries, fruit⟩; gather ⟨firewood⟩; glean ⟨ears of corn⟩; (b) (aussondern) pick over

lesens·wert *Adj.* worth reading *postpos.*

Leser *der;* ∼s, ∼: reader

Lese·ratte *die* (ugs. scherzh.) bookworm; voracious reader

Leser·brief *der* reader's letter; ∼**e** readers' letters; „∼**e**" (Zeitungsrubrik) 'Letters to the editor'

Leserin *die;* ∼, ∼nen ⇒ **Leser**

leserlich 1 *Adj.* legible. **2** *adv.* legibly

Leserschaft *die;* ∼: readership

Leser·zuschrift *die* ⇒ **Leserbrief**

Lese-: ∼**saal** *der* reading room; ∼**stoff** *der* reading matter; ∼**zeichen** *das* bookmark

Lesung *die;* ∼, ∼en (a) (auch Parl.) reading; (b) (christl. Kirche) lesson

Lethargie /letarˈgiː/ *die;* ∼: lethargy

lethargisch 1 *Adj.* lethargic. **2** *adv.* lethargically

Lette /ˈlɛtə/ *der;* ∼n, ∼n, **Lettin** *die;* ∼, ∼nen ▶388| Latvian; Lett

lẹttisch *Adj.* ▶ 388 |, ▶ 487 | Latvian; Lettish ‹*language*›
Lẹtt·land (*das*)*; ~*s Latvia
Lẹtzt /'lɛtst/ **zu guter ~:** in the end; (endlich) at long last
letzt... *Adj.; nicht. präd.* ▶ 119 | (a) last; **die ~e Reihe** the back row; **auf dem ~en Platz sein** be [placed] last; (während des Rennens) be in last place; (in einer Tabelle) be in bottom place; **er war** *od.* **wurde Lẹtzter, er ging als Letzter durchs Ziel** he came last; **der/die Lẹtzte sein** be the last; **als Letzter aussteigen** be the last [one] to get off; **er ist der Lẹtzte, dem ich das sagen würde** he's the last person I would tell [about it]; **am Lẹtzten [des Monats]** on the last day of the month; **mein ~es Geld** the last of my money; **mit ~er Kraft** gathering all his/her remaining strength; **~en Endes** in the end; when all is said and done; **jmds./die ~e Rettung sein** (fig.) be sb.'s/the last hope; *s. auch* **Ölung; Wille;** (b) (äußerst...) ultimate; **jmdm. das Letzte an**... (*Dat.*) **abverlangen** demand of sb. the utmost *or* maximum...; **das Lẹtzte hergeben** give one's all; **bis aufs Letzte** totally; (finanziell) down to the last penny; **bis ins Letzte** down to the last detail; **bis zum Letzten** to the utmost; (c) ▶ 595 | (gerade vergangen) last; (neuest...) latest ‹*news*›; **in den ~en Wochen/Jahren** in the last few weeks/in recent years; **in der ~en Zeit** recently; *s. auch* **Schrei;** (d) (ugs. abwertend) (schlechtest...) worst; (entsetzlichst...) most dreadful; **er ist der ~e Mensch** he is the lowest of the low; **die Show war das Letzte** (ugs.) the show was the end (coll.) *or* the pits (coll.); **das ist doch das Letzte!** (ugs.) that really is the limit!
***lẹtzte·mal** ⇨ **Mal**¹
lẹtzt·ẹndlich *Adv.* in the end; (schließlich doch) ultimately
***lẹtzten·mal** ⇨ **Mal**¹
lẹtzter... *Adj.* ~er/~e/~es... *od.* **der/die/das ~e** ... the latter...
lẹtzt·genannt *Adj.; nicht präd.* last-mentioned; last-named ‹*person*›
lẹtztlich *Adv.* ultimately; in the end
lẹtzt·möglich *Adj.; nicht präd.* latest possible
Leucht·diode *die* light-emitting diode; LED
Leuchte /'lɔyçtə/ *die;* ~, ~n (a) light; (Tischlampe) lamp; (b) (fig. ugs.) **er ist eine ~ auf diesem Gebiet** he is a leading light in this field
leuchten *itr. V.* (a) ‹*moon, sun, star, etc.*› be shining; ‹*fire, face*› glow; **grell ~:** give a glaring light; glare; **in der Sonne ~:** ‹*hair, sea, snow*› gleam in the sun; ‹*mountains etc.*› glow in the sun; **golden ~:** have a golden glow; **seine Augen leuchteten vor Freude** (fig.) his eyes were shining *or* sparkling with joy; (b) shine a/the light; **jmdm. ~:** light the way for sb.; **mit etw. in etw.** (*Akk.*) **~:** shine sth. into sth.; **jmdm. mit etw. ins Gesicht ~:** shine sth. into sb.'s face
leuchtend *Adj.; nicht präd.* (a) shining ‹*eyes*›; brilliant; luminous ‹*colours*›; bright ‹*blue, red, etc.*›; **grell ~:** glaring; **etw. in den ~sten Farben schildern** (fig.) paint sth. in glowing colours; (b) (großartig) shining ‹*example*›
Leuchter *der;* ~s, ~ candelabrum; (für eine Kerze) candlestick; (Kron~) chandelier
Leucht-: ~**farbe** *die* luminous paint; ~**feuer** *das* (Seew.) beacon; light; (Flugw.) runway light; ~**käfer** *der* firefly; (Glühwürmchen) glow-worm; ~**kugel** *die* flare; ~**rakete** *die* rocket flare; ~**reklame** *die* neon [advertising] sign; ~**röhre** *die* neon tube; ~**schrift** *die* neon letters *pl.;* ~**stoff·röhre** *die* fluorescent tube; (für ~reklame) neon tube; ~**turm** *der* lighthouse; ~**ziffer** *die* luminous numeral
leugnen /'lɔygnən/ **1** *tr. V.* deny; **er leugnete die Tat/ das Verbrechen** he denied doing the deed/committing the crime; **es ist nicht zu ~:** it is undeniable; **2** *itr. V.* deny it; (alles ~) deny everything
Leukämie /lɔykɛ'mi:/ *die;* ~, ~n ▶ 329 | (Med.) leukaemia
Leukoplast Ⓦⓩ /lɔyko'plast/ *das* sticking plaster
Leumund /'lɔymʊnt/ *der;* ~[e]s (geh.) reputation; **jmdm. einen guten ~ bescheinigen** vouch for sb.'s good character

Leute /'lɔytə/ *Pl.* (a) people; **die reichen/alten ~:** the rich/the old; **wir sind hier bei feinen ~n** we are in a respectable household; **die kleinen ~:** the ordinary people; **the man** *sing.* in the street; **was werden die ~ sagen?** (ugs.) what will people say?; **wir sind geschiedene ~:** I will have no more to do with you/him *etc.;* **vor allen ~n** in front of everybody; **unter die ~ bringen** (ugs.) spread ‹*rumour*›; tell everybody about ‹*suspicions etc.*›; (b) (ugs.: als Anrede) **los, ~!** come on, everybody! (coll.); c'mon, folks! (Amer.); (c) (ugs.: Arbeiter) people; (Milit.: Soldaten) men; **die Hälfte der ~:** half the staff
Leutnant /'lɔytnant/ *der;* ~s, ~s ▶ 34 | *od. selten:* ~e second lieutenant (Milit.)
leut·selig **1** *Adj.* affable. **2** *adv.* affably
Leut·seligkeit *die; o. Pl.* affability
Leviten /le'vi:tn̩/ *Pl.* **in jmdm. die ~ lesen** (ugs.) read sb. the Riot Act (coll.)
Lexikon /'lɛksikɔn/ *das;* ~s, **Lexika** (a) encyclopaedia; (b) (veralt.: Wörterbuch) dictionary
Liaison /liɛ'zõ:/die/ ~, ~s (geh.) liaison; (fig.: zwischen Staaten, Firmen) link; tie-up; **eine ~ eingehen** enter into a liaison
Liane /'liːanə/ *die;* ~, ~n (Bot.) liana
Libanese /liba'neːzə/ *der;* ~n, ~n, **Libanesin** *die;* ~, ~nen ▶ 388 | Lebanese
Libanon /'liːbanɔn/ (*das*) *od. der;* ~s Lebanon
Libelle /li'bɛlə/ *die;* ~, ~n dragonfly
liberal /liba'raːl/ **1** *Adj.* liberal. **2** *adv.* liberally; **jmdn. ~ erziehen** give sb. a liberal education
Liberale *der/die; adj. Dekl.* liberal
liberalisieren *tr. V.* liberalize
Liberalisierung *die;* ~, ~en liberalization
Liberalismus /libəra'lɪsmʊs/ *der;* ~: liberalism
Libero /'liːbəro/ *der;* ~s, ~s (Fußball) sweeper
Libretto /li'brɛto/ *das;* ~s, ~s *od.* **Libretti** libretto
Libyen /'liːbjən/ (*das*)*;* ~s Libya
libysch /'liːbʏʃ/ *Adj.* ▶ 388 | Libyan
licht /lɪçt/ *Adj.* (a) (geh.) light; light, pale ‹*colour*›; **es war ~er Tag** it was broad daylight; **einen ~en Moment** *od.* **Augenblick/~e Momente haben** (fig.) have a lucid moment/lucid moments; (scherzh.) have a bright moment/ bright moments; (b) (dünn bewachsen) sparse; thin; ~**es Haar haben** be thin on top; **die Reihen der alten Kameraden/der Zuschauer werden ~er** (fig.) the ranks of old comrades are dwindling/the rows of spectators are emptying; (c) (bes. Technik) **die ~e Höhe/Weite** the [overall] internal height/width
Licht *das;* ~[e]s, ~er (a) *o. Pl.* light; **das ~ des Tages** the light of day; **etw. gegen das ~ halten** hold sth. up to the light; **bei ~ besehen** (fig.) seen in the light of day; **jmdm. im ~ stehen** stand in sb.'s light; **das ~ der Welt erblicken** (geh.) see the light of day; (fig.) **ein zweifelhaftes/ungünstiges ~ auf jmdn. werfen** throw a dubious/unfavourable light on sb.; **~ in etw.** (*Akk.*) **bringen** shed some light on sth.; **jmdm. hinters ~ führen** fool sb.; pull the wool over sb.'s eyes; **jmdm./etw./ sich ins rechte ~ rücken** *od.* **setzen** *od.* **stellen** show sb./sth. in the correct light/appear in the correct light; **in einem guten** *od.* **günstigen/schlechten ~ erscheinen** appear in a good *or* a favourable/a bad *or* an unfavourable light; **in ein falsches ~ geraten** give the wrong impression; **das ~ scheuen** shun the light; **ans ~ kommen** come to light; be revealed; (b) (elektrisches ~) light; **das ~ anmachen/ausmachen** switch *or* turn the light on/off; (c) *Pl. auch* ~e (Kerze) candle; (fig.) **kein** *od.* **nicht gerade ein großes ~ sein** (ugs.) be no genius; be not exactly brilliant; **mir ging ein ~ auf** (ugs.) it dawned on me; I realized what was going on; **sein ~ [nicht] unter den Scheffel stellen** [not] hide one's light under a bushel; (d) *o. Pl.* (ugs.: Strom) electricity
licht-, Licht-: ~**anlage** *die* lighting installation; ~**beständig** *Adj.* light-fast; ~**bild** *das* (a) [small] photograph (*for passport etc.*); (b) (veralt.) (Diapositiv) slide; (Fotografie) photograph; ~**bilder·vortrag** *der* slide lecture; ~**blick** *der* bright spot; ~**durchlässig** *Adj.*

translucent; **~empfindlich** *Adj.* sensitive to light; **~empfindlichkeit** *die* sensitivity to light

lichten[1] **1** *tr. V.* thin out ⟨*trees etc.*⟩; (fig.) reduce ⟨*number*⟩. **2** *refl. V.* ⟨*trees*⟩ thin out; ⟨*hair*⟩ grow thin; ⟨*fog, mist*⟩ clear, lift; **die Reihen ~ sich** (fig.) the numbers are dwindling; (im Theater usw.) the rows are emptying

lichten[2] *tr. V.* (Seemannsspr.) **den/die Anker ~:** weigh anchor

lichterloh /'lɪçtɐ'lo:/ **1** *Adj.; nicht präd.* blazing ⟨*fire*⟩; fierce, leaping ⟨*flames*⟩. **2** *adv.* **~ brennen** be blazing fiercely

licht-, Licht-: **~geschwindigkeit** *die* speed of light; **~hupe** *die* headlight flasher; **~jahr** *das* (Astron.) light year; **~kegel** *der* beam; **~maschine** *die* (Kfz-W.) (für Gleichstrom) dynamo; (für Wechselstrom) alternator; generator (esp. Amer.); **~mast** *der* lamp standard; **~pause** *die* photostat (*Brit.* P) (*of transparent original*); **~quelle** *die* light source; **~schacht** *der* light shaft; **~schalter** *der* light switch; **~schein** *der* gleam [of light]; (~strahl) beam of light; **~scheu** *Adj.* (a) shadeloving ⟨*plant*⟩; ⟨*animal*⟩ that shuns the light; (b) (fig.) shady ⟨*riff-raff*⟩; **~schranke** *die* photoelectric beam; **~schutz·faktor** *der* protection factor (*against sunburn*); **~seite** *die* bright or good side; **alles hat seine Licht- und Schattenseiten** everything has its good and bad sides; **~strahl** *der* beam [of light]; **~undurch·lässig** *Adj.* lightproof

Lichtung *die;* **~, ~en** clearing; **auf dieser ~:** in this clearing

Licht-: **~verhältnisse** *Pl.* light conditions; **~zeichen** *das* light signal

Lid /li:t/ *das;* **~[e]s, ~er ▶ 326]** eyelid

Lid·schatten *der* eyeshadow

lieb /li:p/ **1** *Adj.* (a) (liebevoll) kind ⟨*words, gesture*⟩; **viele ~e Grüße [an … (***Akk.***)]** much love [to …] (coll.); **das ist ~ von dir** it's sweet of you; (b) (liebenswert) likeable; nice; (stärker) lovable, sweet ⟨*child, girl, pet*⟩; **seine Frau/ihr Mann ist sehr ~:** his wife/her husband is a dear; (c) (artig) good, nice ⟨*child, dog*⟩; **sei schön ~!** be a good girl/ boy!; **sich bei jmdm. ~ Kind machen** (ugs. abwertend) get on the right side of sb.; (d) (geschätzt) dear; **sein liebstes Spielzeug** his favourite toy; **~e Karola, ~er Ernst!** (am Briefanfang) dear Karola and Ernst; **~er Gott** dear God; **der ~e Gott** the Good Lord; **wenn dir dein Leben ~ ist,** …: if you value your life …; **eine ~ gewordene Gewohnheit ablegen** give up a habit of which one has grown very fond; **das ~e Geld** (iron.) the wretched money; **den ~en langen Tag** (ugs.) all the livelong day; **meine Lieben** (Familie) my people; my nearest and dearest (joc.); (als Anrede) [you] good people; (an Familie usw.) my dears; **meine Liebe** my dear; (herablassend) my dear woman/girl; **mein Lieber** (Mann an Mann) my dear fellow; (Frau/Mann an Jungen) my dear boy; (Frau an Mann) my dear man; **~e Mit·bürgerinnen und Mitbürger!** fellow citizens; **~e Kinder/Freunde!** children/friends; **~ Gemeinde, ~e Schwestern und Brüder!** (christl. Kirche) dearly beloved; **[ach] du ~e Güte od. ~e Zeit od. ~er Himmel od. ~es bisschen!** (ugs.) (erstaunt) good grief!; good heavens!; [good] gracious!; (entsetzt) good heavens above!; **mit jmdm./etw. seine ~e Not haben** have no end of trouble with sb./sth.; (e) (angenehm) welcome; **es wäre mir ~/~er, wenn …:** I should be glad or should like it/ should prefer it if …; **am ~sten wäre mir, ich könnte heute noch abreisen** I should like it best if I could leave today; **wir hatten mehr Schnee, als mir ~ war** we had too much snow for my liking; (f) **jmdn./etw. ~ gewinnen** grow fond of sb./sth.; **jmdn. ~ haben** love sb.; (gern haben) be fond of sb. **2** *adv.* (a) (liebenswert) kindly; **das hast du aber ~ gesagt** you 'did put that nicely; (b) (artig) nicely

lieb·äugeln *itr. V.* **mit etw. ~:** have one's eye on sth.; fancy sth.

Liebchen /'li:pçən/ *das;* **~s, ~** (abwertend) lady-love

Liebe /'li:bə/ *die;* **~, ~n** (a) *o. Pl.* love; **~ zu jmdm.** love for sb.; **~ zu etw.** love of sth.; **~ zu Gott** love of

God; **aus ~ [zu jmdm.]** for love [of sb.]; **bei aller ~,** **aber das geht zu weit** much as I sympathize, that's going too far; (Briefschluss) **in ~ Dein Egon** [with] all my love, yours, Egon; **~ geht durch den Magen** (scherzh.) the way to a man's heart is through his stomach; **~ macht blind** (Spr.) love is blind (prov.); **~ auf den ersten Blick** love at first sight; **seine ganze ~ gehört dem Meer** he adores the sea; **mit ~** (liebevoll) lovingly; with loving care; (b) (ugs.: geliebter Mensch) love; **seine große ~:** his great love; the [great] love of his life; (c) **tu mir die ~ und … do me a favour and …**

liebe·bedürftig *Adj.* in need of love or affection *postpos.*

Liebelei /li:bə'lai/ *die;* **~, ~en** (abwertend) flirtation

lieben 1 *tr. V.* (a) **jmdn. ~:** love sb.; (verliebt sein) be in love with or love sb.; (sexuell) make love to sb.; **sich ~:** be in love; (sexuell) make love; **was sich liebt, das neckt sich** (Spr.) lovers always tease each other; (b) **etw. ~:** be fond of sth.; like sth.; (stärker) love sth.; **es ~, etw. zu tun** like or enjoy doing sth.; (stärker) love doing sth.; (c) **jmdn./ etw. ~ lernen** learn to love sb./sth. **2** *itr. V.* be in love; (sexuell) make love; **er ist unfähig zu ~:** he is incapable of love

liebend 1 *Adj.; nicht präd.* loving; **der/die Liebende** the lover. **2** *adv.* **etw. ~ gerne tun** [simply] love doing sth.

*****lieben|lernen** ⇒ **lieben 1 c**

liebens-, Liebens-: **~wert** *Adj.* likeable ⟨*person*⟩; (stärker) loveable ⟨*person*⟩; attractive, endearing ⟨*trait*⟩; **~würdig** *Adj.* kind; charming ⟨*smile*⟩; **~würdigerweise** *Adv.* kindly; **~würdigkeit** *die;* **~, ~en** kindness; **würden Sie die ~würdigkeit haben, das Fenster zu schließen?** would you be so kind as to shut the window?

lieber 1 *Adj.:* ⇒ **lieb. 2** *Adv.:* ⇒ **gern**

Liebes-: **~beziehung** *die* [love] affair (**zu, mit** with); **~brief** *der* love letter; **~dienst** *der* [act of] kindness; favour; **~erklärung** *die* declaration of love; **~film** *der* romantic film; **~geschichte** *die* (a) love story; (b) (~affäre) [love] affair; **~heirat** *die* love-match; **~kummer** *der* lovesickness; **~kummer haben** be lovesick; be unhappily in love; **sich aus ~kummer umbringen** kill oneself for love; **~leben** *das; o. Pl.* love life; **~lied** *das* love song; **~müh[e]** *die:* **das ist vergebliche od. verlorene ~müh[e]** that is a waste of effort; **~paar** *das* courting couple; [pair of] lovers; **~roman** *der* romantic novel; **~spiel** *das* love-play

liebestoll *Adj.* love-crazed

liebe·voll 1 *Adj.* loving *attrib.* ⟨*care*⟩; affectionate ⟨*embrace, person*⟩. **2** *adv.* (a) lovingly; affectionately; (b) (mit Sorgfalt) lovingly; with loving care

*****lieb|gewinnen** ⇒ **lieb 1 f**

*****lieb·geworden** ⇒ **lieb 1 d**

*****lieb|haben** ⇒ **lieb 1 f**

Liebhaber /'li:pha:bɐ/ *der;* **~s, ~** (a) lover; (b) (Interessierter, Anhänger) enthusiast (*Gen.* for); (Sammler) collector; **ein ~ von schönen Teppichen/Oldtimern** a lover of beautiful carpets/a vintage-car enthusiast

Liebhaber·ausgabe *die* collector's edition; bibliophile edition

Liebhaberei *die;* **~, ~en** hobby

Liebhaberin *die;* **~, ~nen** ⇒ **Liebhaber b**

Liebhaberstück *das* collector's item

lieb·kosen *tr. V.* (geh.) caress

Liebkosung *die;* **~, ~en** (geh.) caress

lieblich 1 *Adj.* (a) charming; appealing; gentle ⟨*landscape*⟩; sweet ⟨*scent, sound*⟩; fragrant ⟨*flower*⟩; melodious ⟨*sound*⟩; (b) mellow ⟨*red wine*⟩; [medium] sweet ⟨*white wine*⟩. **2** *adv.* charmingly; sweetly; (angenehm) pleasingly

Lieblichkeit *die;* **~** charm; sweetness; (einer Landschaft) gentleness

Liebling *der;* **~s, ~e** (a) (geliebte Person; bes. als Anrede) darling; (b) (bevorzugte Person) favourite; (des Publikums) darling; **der ~ des Lehrers** teacher's pet

Lieblings- favourite

lieb·los 1 *Adj.* loveless; heartless, unfeeling ‹*treatment, behaviour*›. **2** *adv.* **(a)** without affection; **(b)** (ohne Sorgfalt) carelessly; without proper care

Lieblosigkeit *die;* ~ unkindness; lack of feeling; (Mangel an Sorgfalt) lack of care

Liebschaft *die;* ~, ~en [casual] affair; (Flirt) flirtation

liebst... /liːpst.../ **1** *Adj.:* ⇒ **lieb. 2** *Adv.* **am** ~**en** ⇒ **gern**

Liebste *der/die; adj. Dekl.* (veralt.) loved one; sweetheart; **meine** ~: my dearest

Liebstöckel /ˈliːp-ʃtœkl/ *das od. der;* ~**s**, ~ (Bot.) lovage

Lied /liːt/ *das;* ~[e]s, ~er song; (Kirchen~) hymn; (deutsches Kunst~) lied; **das Hohe** ~ (bibl.) The Song of Songs; **es ist immer das alte** *od.* **das gleiche** *od.* **dasselbe** ~ (ugs.) it's always the same old story; **davon kann ich ein** ~ **singen** I can tell you a thing or two about that

Lieder-: ~**abend** *der* [evening] song recital; (mit deutschen Kunstliedern) [evening] lieder recital; ~**buch** *das* songbook

liederlich /ˈliːdɐlɪç/ **1** *Adj.* **(a)** (schlampig) slovenly; messy ‹*hairstyle, person*›; slipshod, slovenly ‹*work*›; **(b)** (verwerflich) dissolute. **2** *adv.* sloppily; messily; ~ **angezogen sein** be slovenly dressed

Liederlichkeit *die;* ~ **(a)** (Schlampigkeit) slovenliness; **(b)** (Verwerflichkeit) dissoluteness

Lieder-: ~**macher** *der,* ~**macherin** *die* singer-songwriter (writing satirical songs mainly on topical/political subjects); ~**zyklus** *der* song-cycle

lief /liːf/ *1. u. 3. Pers. Sg. Prät. v.* **laufen**

Lieferant /lifəˈrant/ *der;* ~**en**, ~**en** supplier

Lieferanten·eingang *der* goods entrance; (bei Wohnhäusern) tradesmen's entrance

lieferbar *Adj.* available; **sofort** ~: available for immediate delivery

Liefer-: ~**bedingungen** *Pl.* terms of delivery; ~**frist** *die* delivery time; **bei Möbeln besteht eine** ~**frist von 6–8 Wochen** there is 6–8 weeks delivery on furniture

liefern /ˈliːfɐn/ **1** *tr. V.* **(a)** deliver (**an** + *Akk.* to); (zur Verfügung stellen) supply; **jmdm. etw.** ~: supply sb. with sth.; deliver sth. to sb.; **(b)** (hervorbringen) produce; (geben) provide ‹*eggs, honey, examples, raw material, etc.*›; **(c)** **sich** (*Dat.*) **eine Schlacht** ~: fight a battle [with each other]; **(d) geliefert sein** (ugs.) be sunk (coll.); have had it (coll.). **2** *itr. V.* deliver; **wir** ~ **auch ins Ausland** we also supply our goods abroad *or* deliver to foreign destinations

Liefer-: ~**schein** *der* acknowledgement of delivery; delivery note; ~**termin** *der* delivery date; ~**umfang** *der* (Kaufmannspr.) scope of supply; **die Batterien gehören zum** ~**umfang** batteries are included [in the price]

Lieferung *die;* ~, ~**en (a)** *o. Pl.* delivery; **(b)** (Ware) consignment [of goods]; delivery; **(c)** (Buchw.) instalment; (eines Wörterbuchs usw.) fascicle

Liefer-: ~**wagen** *der* [delivery] van; (offen) pick-up; ~**zeit** *die* ⇒ ~**frist**

Liege /ˈliːgə/ *die;* ~, ~**n** day-bed; (zum Ausklappen) bed-settee; sofa bed; (als Gartenmöbel) sun-lounger

liegen *unr. itr. V.* **(a)** lie; ‹*person*› be lying down; **während der Krankheit musste er** ~: while he was ill he had to lie down all the time; **auf den Knien** ~: be prostrate on one's knees; **im Krankenhaus/auf Station 6** ~: be in hospital/in ward 6; **[krank] im Bett** ~: be [ill] in bed; **[im Bett]** ~ **bleiben** stay in bed; **bewusstlos/bewegungslos** ~ **bleiben** lie unconscious/motionless; **der Wagen liegt gut auf der Straße** the car holds the road well; **(b)** (vorhanden sein) lie; **es liegt Schnee auf den Bergen** there is snow [lying] on the hills; **der Schnee bleibt** ~: the snow lies; **der Stoff liegt 80 cm breit** the material is 80 cm wide; **(c)** (sich befinden) be; ‹*object*› be [lying]; ‹*town, house, etc.*› be [situated]; **die Preise** ~ **höher** prices are higher; **wie die Dinge** ~: as things are *or* stand [at the moment]; **die Stadt liegt an der Küste** the town is *or* lies on the coast; **das Dorf liegt sehr hoch**

the village is very high up; **das liegt auf meinem Weg** it is on my way; **etw. rechts/links** ~ **lassen** leave sth. on one's right/left; **das Fenster liegt nach vorn/nach Süden/zum Garten** the window is at the front/faces south/faces the garden; **es liegt nicht in meiner Absicht, das zu tun** it is not my intention to do that; **das Essen lag mir schwer im Magen** the food/meal lay heavy on my stomach; **(d)** (zeitlich) be; **das liegt noch vor mir/schon hinter mir** I still have that to come/that's all behind me now; **(e) das liegt an ihm** *od.* **bei ihm** it is up to him; (ist seine Schuld) it is his fault; **die Verantwortung/Schuld liegt bei ihm** it is his responsibility/fault; **an mir soll es nicht** ~: I won't stand in your way; (ich werde mich beteiligen) I'm easy (coll.); **ich weiß nicht, woran es liegt** I don't know what the reason is; **woran mag es nur** ~**, dass …?** why ever is it that …?; **(f)** (gemäß sein) **es liegt mir nicht** it doesn't suit me; it isn't right for me; (es spricht mich nicht an) it doesn't appeal to me; (ich mag es nicht) I don't like it *or* care for it; **es liegt ihm nicht, das zu tun** he does not like doing that; (so etwas tut er nicht) it is not his way to do that; **(g) daran liegt ihm viel/wenig/nichts** he sets great/little/no store by that; it means a lot/little/nothing to him; **an ihm liegt mir schon etwas** I do care about him [a bit]; **(h)** (bedeckt sein) **der Tisch liegt voller Bücher** the desk is covered with books; **(i)** (bes. Milit.: verweilen) be; ‹*troops*› be stationed; ‹*ship*› lie; **(j)** ~ **bleiben** ‹*things*› stay, be left; (vergessen werden) be left behind; (nicht verkauft werden) remain unsold; (nicht erledigt werden) be left undone; (eine Panne haben) break down; **diese Briefe können bis morgen** ~ **bleiben** these letters can wait until tomorrow; **etw.** ~ **lassen** (vergessen) leave sth. [behind]; (unerledigt lassen) leave sth. undone; **alles** ~ **und stehen lassen** drop everything; *s. auch* **Straße a; liegend**

*liegen|bleiben ⇒ **liegen a, b, j**

liegend reclining, recumbent ‹*figure, posture*›; prone ‹*position*›; horizontal ‹*position, engine*›

*liegen|lassen ⇒ **liegen j; links 1 a**

Liegenschaft *die;* ~, ~**en;** *meist Pl.* (bes. Rechtsspr.) land holding; (Gebäude) property

Liege-: ~**platz** *der* mooring; ~**sitz** *der* reclining seat; ~**stuhl** *der* deckchair; ~**stütz** *der* press-up; ~**wagen** *der* couchette car; ~**wiese** *die* sunbathing lawn

lieh /liː/ *1. u. 3. Pers. Sg. Prät. v.* **leihen**

lies /liːs/ *Imperativ Sg. v.* **lesen**

Lieschen /ˈliːsçen/ *das;* ~ **(a)** ~ **Müller** (ugs.) the average girl/woman (coll.); **(b) Fleißiges** ~ (Bot.) busy Lizzie

ließ /liːs/ *1. u. 3. Pers. Sg. Prät. v.* **lassen**

liest /liːst/ *3. Pers. Sg. Präsens v.* **lesen**

Lift /lɪft/ *der;* ~[e]s, ~e *od.* ~s **(a)** lift (Brit.); elevator (Amer.); **(b)** *Pl.:* ~e (Ski~, Sessel~) lift

liften *tr. V.* **sich** ~ **lassen** (ugs.) have a facelift

Liga /ˈliːga/ *die;* ~, **Ligen** league; (Sport) division

liieren /liˈiːrən/ *refl. V.* start an affair; **mit jmdm. liiert sein** be having an affair with sb.

Likör /liˈkøˈɐ̯/ *der;* ~**s**, ~**e** liqueur

lila /ˈliːla/ *indekl. Adj.* mauve; (dunkel~) purple

Lila *das;* ~**s** *od.* (ugs.) ~**s** mauve; (Dunkel~) purple

Lilie /ˈliːliə/ *die;* ~, ~**n** lily

Liliput- /ˈliːliput-/ miniature

Liliputaner /liliputˈtaːnɐ/ *der;* ~**s**, ~: dwarf; midget

Limerick /ˈlɪmərɪk/ *der;* ~[s], ~s limerick

Limit /ˈlɪmɪt/ *das;* ~**s**, ~**s** limit

limitieren *tr. V.* limit; restrict

Limo /ˈlɪmo/ *die, auch: das;* ~, ~[s] (ugs.), **Limonade** /limoˈnaːdə/ *die;* ~, ~**n** fizzy drink; mineral; (Zitronen~) lemonade

Limone /liˈmoːnə/ *die;* ~, ~**n** lime

Limousine /limuˈziːnə/ *die;* ~, ~**n** [large] saloon (Brit.) *or* (Amer.) sedan; (mit Trennwand) limousine

Linde /ˈlɪndə/ *die;* ~, ~**n (a)** (Baum) lime[-tree]; **(b)** *o. Pl.* (Holz) limewood

Lindenblüten-: ~**honig** *der* lime-blossom honey; ~**tee** *der* lime-blossom tea

lindern /'lɪndɐn/ tr. V. alleviate, relieve ⟨suffering⟩; ease, relieve ⟨pain⟩; quench, slake ⟨thirst⟩
Linderung die; ~ (der Not) relief; alleviation; (des Schmerzes) relief
lind·grün Adj. lime green
Lineal /line'aːl/ das; ~s, ~e ruler; **Striche mit einem ~ ziehen** rule lines
linear /line'aːɐ̯/ Adj. (fachspr., geh.) linear
Linguist /lɪŋˈɡu̯ɪst/ der; ~en, ~en linguist
Linguistik die; ~: linguistics sing., no art.
Linguistin die; ~, ~nen linguist
linguistisch 1 Adj. linguistic. 2 adv. linguistically
Linie /'liːni̯ə/ die; ~, ~n (a) line; **auf die [schlanke] ~ achten** (ugs. scherzh.) watch one's figure; **die feindliche[n] ~[n]** (Milit.) [the] enemy lines pl.; **in vorderster ~ stehen** (fig.) be in the front line; (b) ▶ 583 | (Verkehrsstrecke) route; (Eisenbahn~, Straßenbahn~) line; route; **fahren Sie mit der ~ 4** take a or the number 4; (c) (allgemeine Richtung) line; policy; **eine/keine klare ~ erkennen lassen** reveal a/ no clear policy; (d) (Verwandtschaftszweig) line; **in direkter ~ von jmdm. abstammen** be directly descended from or a direct descendant of sb.; (e) **in erster ~ geht es darum, dass das Projekt beschleunigt wird** the first priority is to speed up the project; **auf der ganzen ~:** all along the line
linien-, Linien-: ~**bus** der regular bus; ~**flug** der scheduled flight; ~**richter** der (Fußball usw.) linesman; (Tennis) line judge; (Rugby) touch judge; ~**treu** (abwertend) 1 Adj. loyal to the party line postpos.; 2 adv. ⟨act⟩ in accordance with the party line; ~**verkehr** der regular services pl.; (Flugw.) scheduled or regular services pl.
liniert /li'niːɐ̯t/ Adj. ruled; lined
link /lɪŋk/ (salopp) 1 Adj. underhand; shady, underhand ⟨deal⟩. 2 adv. in an underhand way
Link der; ~s, ~s (DV) link
link... Adj. (a) left; left[-hand] ⟨edge⟩; **die ~e Spur** the left-hand lane; ~**er Hand, auf der ~en Seite** on the left-hand side; **mit dem ~en Fuß od. Bein zuerst aufgestanden sein** (fig. ugs.) have got out of bed on the wrong side; (b) (innen, nicht sichtbar) wrong, reverse ⟨side⟩; ~**e Maschen** (Handarb.) purl stitches; (c) (in der Politik) left-wing; leftist (derog.); **der ~e Flügel einer Partei** the left wing of a party
Linke¹ der/die; adj. Dekl. left-winger; leftist (derog.); **die ~n** the left sing.
Linke² die; ~n, ~n (a) (Hand) left hand; **jmdm. zur ~n** on sb.'s left; to the left of sb.; **zur ~n** on the left; (b) (Politik) left
linkisch 1 Adj. awkward. 2 adv. awkwardly
links /lɪŋks/ 1 Adv. ▶ 583 | (auf der linken Seite) on the left; ~ **von jmdm/etw.** on sb.'s left or to the left of sb./ on or to the left of sth.; **von ~:** from the left; **nach ~:** to the left; **sich ~ halten** keep to the left; **er blickte weder nach ~ noch nach rechts, sondern rannte einfach über die Straße** he didn't look left or right, but just ran straight across the road; **sich ~ einordnen** move or get into the left-hand lane; ~ **außen** (Ballspiele) ⟨run, break through⟩ down the left wing; **jmdn./etw. ~ liegen lassen** (fig.) ignore sb./sth.; (b) (Politik) on the left wing; ~ **stehen** od. **sein** be left-wing or on the left; ~ **außen** (ugs.) on the extreme left [wing]; (c) (Handarb.) **zwei ~, zwei rechts** two purl, two plain; purl two, knit two; **ein ~ gestrickter Pullover** a purl[-knit] pullover. 2 Präp. mit Gen. ▶ 583 | ~ **des Rheins** on the left side or bank of the Rhine. 3 **mit ~** (fig. ugs.) easily; with no trouble
links-, Links-: ~**abbieger** der (Verkehrsw.) motorist/ cyclist/car etc. turning left; ~**außen** Adv. (a) (Ballspiele) ⟨run, break through⟩ down the left wing; (b) (Politik ugs.) on the extreme left [wing]; *~**außen** ⇒ **links** 1 a, b; ~**extremismus** der (Politik) left-wing extremism; ~**extremist** der (Politik) left-wing extremist; ~**ge-richtet** Adj. (Politik) left-wing orientated; ~**gewinde** das (Technik) left-hand thread; ~**händer** /~hɛndɐ/ der;

~**s**, ~, ~**händerin** die; ~, ~**nen** left-hander; ~**händer[in] sein** be left-handed; ~**händig** 1 Adj. left-handed; 2 adv. with one's left hand; ~**herum** Adv. [round] to the left; **etw. ~herum drehen** turn sth. anticlockwise or [round] to the left; ~**intellektuelle** der/ die left-wing intellectual; ~**kurve** die left-hand bend; ~**lastig** Adj. (Politik ugs.) leftist; ~**liberal** Adj. left-wing liberal; ~**radikal** Adj. (Politik) radical left-wing; ~**radikalismus** der left-wing radicalism; ~**ruck** der (Politik ugs.) shift to the left; ~**rum** Adv. (ugs.) ⇒ ~**herum**; ~**seitig** 1 Adj. ⟨paralysis⟩ of the left side; **die ~seitige Uferbefestigung** the reinforcement of the left bank; 2 adv. on the left [side]; ~**verkehr** der driving on the left; on the left; **in Irland ist ~verkehr** they drive on the left in Ireland
Linoleum /li'noːleʊm/ das; ~s linoleum; lino
Linol·schnitt der linocut
Linse /'lɪnzə/ die; ~, ~n (a) lentil; (b) (Med., Optik) lens
Linsen·suppe die lentil soup
Lippe /'lɪpə/ die; ~, ~n ▶ 326 | lip; **sie brachte es nicht über die ~n** she couldn't bring herself to say it; **an jmds. Lippen** (Dat.) **hängen** hang on sb.'s every word; **eine [dicke** od. **große] ~ riskieren** (salopp) shoot one's mouth off (sl.)
Lippen-: ~**bekenntnis** das (abwertend) empty talk no pl.; ~**bekenntnisse für etw. ablegen** pay lip-service to sth. ~**stift** der lipstick
liquid /li'kvɪt/ Adj. (Wirtsch.) liquid ⟨funds, resources⟩; solvent ⟨business⟩; **ich bin nicht ~:** I'm out of funds
Liquidation /likvida'tsi̯oːn/ die; ~, ~en (a) (verhüll.: Tötung) liquidation; (b) (Wirtsch.) liquidation no indef. art.
liquidieren /likvi'diːrən/ tr. V. (auch Wirtsch.) liquidate
Liquidität /likvidi'tɛːt/ die; ~, ~en (Wirtsch.) liquidity; solvency
lispeln /'lɪspl̩n/ itr. V. lisp; **er hat schon immer gelispelt** he's always had a lisp
List /lɪst/ die; ~, ~en (a) [cunning] trick or ruse; (b) o. Pl. (listige Art) cunning; **mit ~ und Tücke** (ugs.) by cunning and trickery
Liste die; ~, ~n list; **schwarze ~:** blacklist
Listen-: ~**platz** der (Politik) place on the [party] list; ~**preis** der list price; ~**wahl** die (Parl.) list system
listig 1 Adj. cunning; crafty. 2 adv. cunningly; craftily; **jmdn. ~ ansehen/angrinsen** look/grin at sb. slyly.
Litanei /lita'nai̯/ die; ~, ~en (Rel., auch fig. abwertend) litany
Litauen /'liːtau̯ən/ (das); ~s Lithuania
Litauer der; ~s, ~, **Litauerin** die; ~, ~nen ▶ 388 | Lithuanian
litauisch Adj. ▶ 388 | Lithuanian
Liter /'liːtɐ/ der, auch: das; ~s, ~: ▶ 427 | litre
literarisch /litəˈraːrɪʃ/ 1 Adj. literary. 2 adv. ~ interessiert/gebildet sein be interested in literature/be well-read
Literat /litəˈraːt/ der; ~en, ~en writer; literary figure
Literatur /litəraˈtuːɐ̯/ die; ~, ~en literature; **belletristische ~:** belles-lettres pl.
Literatur-: ~**angabe** die [bibliographical] reference; ~**gattung** die literary genre; ~**geschichte** die literary history; history of literature; ~**kritik** die literary criticism; ~**kritiker** der literary critic; ~**verzeichnis** das list of references; ~**wissenschaft** die literary studies pl., no art.; study of literature
Liter·flasche die litre bottle
liter·weise Adv. by the litre; in litres
Litfaß·säule /'lɪtfas-/ die advertising column or pillar
Lithografie, Lithographie /litograˈfiː/ die; ~, ~n (a) o. Pl. lithography no art.; (b) (Druck) lithograph
litt /lɪt/ 1. u. 3. Pers. Sg. Prät. v. **leiden**
Liturgie /litʊrˈɡiː/ die; ~, ~n (christl. Kirche) liturgy
liturgisch Adj. liturgical
Litze /'lɪtsə/ die; ~, ~n braid
live /lai̯f/ (Rundf., Ferns.) 1 Adj. live. 2 adv. live
Live·sendung die (Rundf., Ferns.) live programme; (Übertragung) live broadcast

---

*alte Schreibung (vgl. Hinweise auf S. xvi–xvii)

Lizenz /li'tsɛnts/ *die;* ~, ~**en** licence; **etw. in** ~ **herstellen** manufacture sth. under licence

Lizenz·ausgabe *die* (Buchw.) licensed edition

Lkw, LKW /ɛlka:'ve:/ *der;* ~[s], ~[s] *Abk.* **Lastkraftwagen**

Lkw-Fahrer *der* truck *or* (Brit.) lorry driver; trucker (Amer.)

Lob /lo:p/ *das;* ~[e]s, ~e praise *no indef. art.;* **ein** ~ **bekommen** receive praise; come in for praise; **ein** ~ **dem Küchenchef/der Hausfrau** my compliments to the chef/the hostess

Lobby /'lɔbi/ *die;* ~, ~s *od.* **Lobbies** lobby

Lobbyist *der;* ~en, ~en lobbyist

loben *tr. V.* praise; **jmdn./etw.** ~**d erwähnen** commend sb./sth.

lobens·wert *Adj.* praiseworthy; laudable; commendable

Lobes·hymne *die* (oft iron.) hymn of praise

Lob-: ~**gesang** *der* song *or* hymn of praise; ~**hudelei** *die* (abwertend) extravagant praise *no pl.* (**auf** + *Akk.* of)

löblich /'lø:plɪç/ *Adj.* laudable; commendable

lob-, Lob-: ~**lied** *das* song of praise; **ein** ~**lied auf jmdn./etw. anstimmen** (fig.) sing sb.'s praises/the praises of sth.; ~**rede** *die* eulogy; panegyric; **eine** ~**rede auf jmdn. halten** make a speech in praise of sb.; eulogize sb.

Loch /lɔx/ *das;* ~[e]s, **Löcher** /'lœçɐ/ **(a)** hole; **ein** ~ **im Zahn/Kopf haben** have a hole *or* cavity in one's tooth/gash on one's *or* the head; **jmdm. ein** ~ *od.* **Löcher in den Bauch fragen** (salopp) drive sb. up the wall with [all] one's questions (coll.); **Löcher in die Luft gucken** *od.* **starren** (ugs.) gaze into space; **auf dem letzten** ~ **pfeifen** be on one's/its last legs; **(b)** (salopp abwertend: Wohnraum) hole

lochen *tr. V.* punch holes/a hole in; punch, clip ⟨*ticket*⟩; punch [holes in] ⟨*invoice, copy, bill*⟩ (*for filing*); (perforieren) perforate

Locher *der;* ~s, ~ punch

löcherig *Adj.* holey; full of holes *pred.*

löchern *tr. V.* (ugs.) **jmdn.** ~: pester sb. to death

Loch-: ~**karte** *die* (Technik, DV) punch[ed] card; ~**streifen** *der* (Technik, DV) punch[ed] tape

Locke /'lɔkə/ *die;* ~, ~**n** curl; ~**n haben** have curly hair

locken *tr. V.* **(a)** lure; (fig.) entice (**aus** out of, **in** + *Akk.* into); **(b)** (reizen) tempt

Locken-: ~**kopf** *der* **(a)** curly hair; **(b)** (Mensch) curly head; ~**pracht** *die* (scherzh.) magnificent head of curls; ~**wickler** *der* [hair] curler *or* roller

locker 1 *Adj.* **(a)** loose ⟨*tooth, nail, chair-leg, etc.*⟩; *s. auch* **Schraube**; **(b)** (durchlässig, leicht) loose ⟨*soil, snow, fabric*⟩; light ⟨*mixture, cake*⟩; **(c)** (entspannt) relaxed ⟨*position, muscles*⟩; slack ⟨*rope, rein*⟩; (fig.: unverbindlich) loose ⟨*relationship, connection, etc.*⟩; **die Seil/die Zügel** ~ **lassen** slacken the rope [off]/slacken the reins; **(d)** (leichtfertig) loose ⟨*morals, life*⟩; frivolous ⟨*jokes, remarks*⟩; **sein** ~**es Mundwerk** (salopp) his big mouth (coll.); **ein** ~**er Vogel** (ugs.) a bit of a lad (coll.). 2 *adv.* **(a)** loosely; **(b)** (entspannt, ungezwungen) loosely; **dieses Gesetz wird** ~ **gehandhabt** this law is not strictly enforced

locker-: ~|**lassen** *unr. tr. V.* **nicht** ~**lassen** (ugs.) not give *or* let up; ~|**machen** *tr. V.* (ugs.) fork up *or* out (sl.); shell out (coll.)

lockern 1 *tr. V.* **(a)** loosen ⟨*screw, tie, collar, etc.*⟩; slacken [off] ⟨*rope, dog-leash, etc.*⟩; (fig.) relax ⟨*regulation, law, etc.*⟩; **(b)** (entspannen) loosen up, relax ⟨*muscles, limbs*⟩; **(c)** (auf~) loosen, break up ⟨*soil*⟩. 2 *refl. V.* **(a)** ⟨*brick, tooth, etc.*⟩ work itself loose; **(b)** (entspannen) ⟨*person*⟩ loosen up; (vor Spielbeginn) loosen *or* limber up; (fig.) ⟨*tenseness, tension*⟩ ease

Lockerung *die;* ~, ~**en (a)** loosening; (fig.: von Bestimmung, Gesetz usw.) relaxation; **(b)** (Entspannung) loosening up; relaxation

lockig *Adj.* curly

Lock·mittel *das* enticement

Lockung *die;* ~, ~**en** (geh.) temptation; **jmds.** ~**en** (*Dat.*) **widerstehen** resist sb.'s enticements

Lock·vogel *der* decoy

Loden /'lo:dn̩/ *der;* ~s, ~: loden

Loden·mantel *der* loden coat

lodern *itr. V.* (geh.) blaze

Löffel /'lœfl̩/ *der;* ~s, ~ **(a)** spoon; (als Maßangabe) spoonful; **(b)** (Jägerspr.) ear; **jmdm. eins** *od.* **ein paar hinter die** ~ **geben** (ugs.) give sb. a clout round the ear

löffeln *tr. V.* spoon [up]

löffel·weise *Adv.* by the spoonful

log /lo:k/ *1. u. 3. Pers. Sg. Prät. v.* **lügen**

Log /lɔk/ *das;* ~s, ~e (Seew.) log

Logarithmen ⇒ **Logarithmus**

Logarithmen·tafel *die* (Math.) log[arithmic] table

Logarithmus /loga'rɪtmʊs/ *der;* ~, **Logarithmen** (Math.) logarithm; log

Log·buch *das* (Seew.) log [book]

Loge /'lo:ʒə/ *die;* ~, ~**n (a)** box; **(b)** (Freimaurer~) lodge

Logen·platz *der* seat in a box

Loggia /'lɔdʒia/ *die;* ~, **Loggien** balcony

logieren *itr. V.* (veralt.) stay

Logik /'lo:gɪk/ *die;* ~: logic

Logis /lo'ʒi:/ *das;* ~ /lo'ʒi:(s)/, ~ /lo'ʒi:s/ lodgings *pl.;* room/rooms *pl.; s. auch* **Kost**

logisch /'lo:gɪʃ/ **1** *Adj.* logical; **[ist doch]** ~ (ugs.) yes, of course. **2** *adv.* logically

logischerweise *Adv.* logically; (ugs.: selbstverständlich) naturally

Logistik *die;* ~ (Milit., Wirtsch.) logistics, *pl.;* (als Fachbereich) logistics *sing.*

logistisch (Milit., Wirtsch.) **1** *Adj.* logistic[al]. **2** *adv.* logistically

logo /'lo:go/ *Adj.* (salopp) **[ist doch]** ~! you bet! (coll.); of course!

Logo *der od. das;* ~s, ~s logo

Lohn /lo:n/ *der;* ~[e]s, **Löhne** /'lø:nə/ **(a)** wage[s *pl.*]; pay *no indef. art., no pl.;* **(b)** *o. Pl.* (Belohnung, auch fig.) reward

Lohn-: ~**abhängige** *der/die* wage earner; ~**ausfall** *der* loss of earnings; ~**ausgleich** *der* making-up of wages; **[eine] kürzere Arbeitszeit bei vollem** ~**ausgleich** shorter working hours with no loss of pay; ~**buchhalter** *der* payroll clerk; ~**buchhaltung** *die* **(a)** *o. Pl.* payroll accounting; **(b)** (Abteilung) payroll office; ~**büro** *das* payroll office; ~**empfänger** *der* wage earner

lohnen 1 *refl., itr. V.* be worth it; be worthwhile; **die Anstrengung hat sich gelohnt** it was worth the effort; **das lohnt sich nicht für mich** it's not worth my while; **die Mühe hat [sich] gelohnt** it was worth the trouble *or* effort. **2** *tr. V.* be worth; **die Ausstellung lohnt einen Besuch** the exhibition is worth a visit *or* is worth visiting; **das lohnt die Mühe nicht** it is not worth the trouble

löhnen *tr., itr. V.* (salopp) pay; fork out *or* up (coll.)

lohnend *Adj.* rewarding ⟨*task*⟩; worthwhile, rewarding ⟨*occupation*⟩; worthwhile ⟨*aim*⟩; (einträglich) financially rewarding; lucrative

Lohn-: ~**erhöhung** *die* wage *or* pay increase *or* (Brit.) rise; ~**forderung** *die* wage demand *or* claim; ~**fortzahlung** *die* continued payment of wages; ~**kosten** *Pl.* wage costs; ~**neben·kosten** *Pl.* non-wage [labour] costs *pl.;* ~**runde** *die* wage *or* pay round

Lohn·steuer *die* income tax

Lohnsteuer-: ~**jahres·ausgleich** *der* annual adjustment of income tax; ~**karte** *die* income-tax card

Lohn·zettel *der* payslip

Loipe /'lɔypə/ *die;* ~, ~**n** (Skisport) [cross-country] course

Lok /lɔk/ *die;* ~, ~**s** engine; locomotive

lokal /lo'ka:l/ *Adj.* local; **Lokales** (Zeitungsw.) local news *sing.*

Lokal *das;* ~s, ~**e** pub (Brit.); bar (Amer.); (Speise~) restaurant

Lokal·blatt das (Zeitungsw.) local paper
lokalisieren tr. V. (geh., fachspr.) locate
Lokal-: ~**kolorit** das local colour; ~**patrio-tismus** der local patriotism; ~**redaktion** die (Rundf., Ferns., Zeitungsw.) local-news section; ~**runde** die round for everyone [in the pub (Brit.) or (Amer.) bar]; ~**teil** der (Zeitungsw.) local section; ~**termin** der (Rechtsspr.) visit to the scene [of the crime]; ~**verbot** das: [in einer Gaststätte] ~**verbot haben/bekommen** be/get banned [from a pub (Brit. coll.) or (Amer.) bar]; ~**zeitung** die local [news]paper
Lok·führer der ⇒ **Lokomotivführer**
Lokomotive /lokomo'ti:və/ die; ~, ~**n** locomotive; [railway] engine
Lokomotiv·führer der ▶ 85 engine driver (Brit.); engineer (Amer.)
Lokus /'lo:kʊs/ der; ~ od. ~**ses**, ~ od. ~**se** (salopp) loo (Brit. coll.); john (Amer. coll.)
Lokus·papier das (salopp) loo paper (Brit. coll.); toilet paper
London /'lɔndən/ (das); ~s ▶ 490 London
Londoner ▶ 490 1 indekl. Adj.; nicht präd. London. 2 der; ~s, ~: Londoner; s. auch **Kölner**
Lorbeer /'lɔrbe:ɐ̯/ der; ~s, ~**en** (a) laurel; (b) (Gewürz) bayleaf; (c) (~kranz) laurel wreath; [sich] **auf seinen** ~**en ausruhen** (fig. ugs.) rest on one's laurels
Lorbeer-: ~**blatt** das bayleaf; ~**kranz** der laurel wreath
Lore /'lo:rə/ die; ~, ~**n** car; (kleiner) tub
los /lo:s/ 1 Adj.; nicht attr. (a) **der Knopf ist** ~: the button has come off; **ich habe die Schraube/das Brett/das Rad** ~: I have got the screw out/the board/wheel off; (b) **jmdn./etw.** ~ **sein** (befreit sein von) be rid or (coll.) shot of sb./sth.; (verloren haben) have lost sth.; (c) **hier ist viel/wenig/immer etw.** ~: there is a lot/not much/always sth. going on here; **was ist hier** ~? (was geschieht?) what's going on here?; (was ist nicht in Ordnung?) what's the matter here?; what's up here? (coll.); **mit jmdm./etw. ist nichts/nicht viel** ~ (ugs.) sb./sth. isn't up to much (coll.); **was ist denn mit dir** ~? what's up or wrong or the matter with you? 2 Adv. (a) (als Aufforderung) come on!; (geh schon!) go on!; **auf die Plätze! Achtung, fertig,** ~! on your marks, get set, go; **nun aber** ~! [come on,] let's get moving or going!; (b) **er ist mit dem Wagen** ~ (ugs.: weggefahren) he's gone off in the car
Los das; ~**es**, ~**e** (a) lot; **das** ~ **soll entscheiden** it shall be decided by drawing lots; (b) (Lotterie~) ticket; **das Große** ~: [the] first prize; **mit jmdm./etw. das Große** ~ **ziehen** (fig.) hit the jackpot with sb./sth.; (c) (geh.: Schicksal) lot
-los Adj. -less
lösbar Adj. soluble, solvable ⟨problem, equation, etc.⟩
los-: ~|**bekommen** unr. tr. V. get ⟨string, tape, ribbon, etc.⟩ off; get ⟨screw, nail, etc.⟩ out; ~|**binden** unr. tr. V. untie; ~|**brechen** 1 unr. itr. V.; mit sein (a) (beginnen) ⟨storm⟩ break; ⟨cheering, laughter, etc.⟩ break out; (b) (abbrechen) break off. 2 unr. tr. V. break off
Lösch·blatt das piece of blotting paper
löschen[1] /'lœʃn̩/ tr. V. (a) put out, extinguish ⟨fire, candle, flames, etc.⟩; (b) close ⟨bank account⟩; delete, strike out ⟨entry⟩; erase, wipe out ⟨recording, memory, etc.⟩; (c) quench ⟨thirst⟩
löschen[2] tr. V. (Seemannsspr.) unload
Lösch-: ~**fahrzeug** das fire engine; ~**papier** das blotting paper; ~**zug** der set of fire-fighting appliances
lose 1 Adj. (a) (nicht fest, auch fig.) loose; (b) (nicht verpackt) loose ⟨sugar, cigarettes, sweets, sheets of paper, nails, etc.⟩; unbottled ⟨drink⟩; (c) (ugs.: leichtfertig) **er ist ein** ~**er Vogel** he is a bit of a lad; (d) (ugs.: vorlaut, frech) cheeky; impudent; **einen** ~**n Mund haben** be a cheeky or impudent so-and-so (coll.). 2 adv. (auch fig.) loosely; ~ **herunterhängen** hang down loosely or loose

Löse·geld das ransom; **das** ~ **wurde in einer Telefonzelle hinterlegt** the ransom money was left in a telephone kiosk
los|eisen tr. V. jmdn./sich ~ (ugs.) prise or get sb. away (von from)/get away (von from)
losen itr. V. draws lots (um for); ~, **wer anfangen soll** draw lots to decide who will start
lösen /'lø:zn̩/ 1 tr. V. (a) remove, take or get off ⟨stamp, wallpaper⟩; **etw. von etw.** ~: remove sth. from sth.; **das Fleisch von den Knochen** ~: take the meat off the bones; (b) (lockern) take or let ⟨handbrake⟩ off; release ⟨handbrake⟩; undo ⟨screw, belt, tie⟩; remove, untie ⟨string, rope, knot, bonds⟩; loosen ⟨phlegm⟩; ease ⟨cramp⟩; (fig.) ease, relieve ⟨mental⟩ pain, tension, etc.⟩; remove ⟨inhibitions⟩; **jmds. Zunge** ~ (fig.) loosen sb.'s tongue; (c) (klären) solve ⟨problem, puzzle, equation, etc.⟩; resolve ⟨contradiction, conflict⟩; solve, resolve ⟨difficulty⟩; (d) (annullieren) break off ⟨engagement⟩; cancel ⟨contract⟩; sever ⟨connection, relationship⟩; (e) (auflösen) **etw. in etw. (Dat.)** ~: dissolve sth. in sth.; (f) (kaufen) buy; obtain ⟨ticket⟩. 2 refl. V. (a) come off; ⟨avalanche⟩ start; ⟨wallpaper, plaster⟩ come off or away; ⟨packing, screw⟩ come loose or undone; ⟨paint, book cover⟩ come off; ⟨phlegm, cough⟩ get looser; ⟨cramp⟩ ease; **sich von etw.** ~: come off sth.; **sich von seinem Elternhaus** ~ (fig.) break away from one's parental home; (b) (sich klären, entwirren) ⟨puzzle, problem⟩ be solved; **sich von selbst** ~ ⟨problem⟩ solve or resolve itself; (c) (zergehen) **sich in etw. (Dat.)** ~: dissolve in sth.; (d) **aus seiner Pistole löste sich ein Schuss** (geh.) his pistol went off
Los·entscheid der: durch ~: by drawing lots; (bei einem Preisausschreiben) by [making or having] a draw
los-: ~|**fahren** unr. itr. V.; mit sein (a) (starten) set off; (wegfahren) move off; (b) (zufahren) **auf jmdn./etw.** ~**fahren** drive/ride towards sb./sth.; **direkt auf jmdn./etw.** ~**fahren** drive/ride straight at sb./sth.; ~|**gehen** unr. itr. V.; mit sein (a) (aufbrechen) set off; **auf ein Ziel** ~**gehen** (fig.) go straight for a goal; ~ **gehts** let's be off; (b) (ugs.: beginnen) start; **es geht** ~: it's starting; (fangen wir an) let's go; ~ **gehts** let's get started; (c) (ugs.: abgehen) ⟨button, handle, etc.⟩ come off; (d) (angreifen) **auf jmdn.** ~**gehen** go for sb.; (e) (abgefeuert werden) ⟨gun, mine, firework, etc.⟩ go off; ~|**kommen** unr. itr. V.; mit sein (ugs.) (a) get away; (b) (freikommen) get free; free oneself; (freigelassen werden) be freed; **von jmdm./etw.** ~**kommen** (fig.) get away from sb./get rid of sth.; **vom Alkohol** ~**kommen** (fig.) get off or give up alcohol; ~|**kriegen** tr. V. (ugs.) (a) get ⟨screw, nail, etc.⟩ out; get ⟨lid⟩ off; (b) (loswerden) get rid or (sl.) shot of; (c) (verkaufen können) get rid of; ~|**lassen** unr. tr. V. (a) let go of; **der Gedanke/das Bild ließ sie nicht mehr** ~ (fig.) she could not get the thought/image out of her mind; (b) (freilassen) let ⟨person, animal⟩ go; (c) **jmdn. auf jmdn.** ~**lassen** (ugs. abwertend) let sb. loose on sb./sth.; (d) (ugs.: äußern) come out with ⟨remark, joke, etc.⟩; (e) (abschicken) send off ⟨letter, telegram, etc.⟩; ~|**laufen** unr. itr. V.; mit sein start running; **lauf schnell los und hol Brot** run out and get some bread; ~|**legen** itr. V. (ugs.) get going or started
löslich Adj. soluble; **leicht/schwer** ~: readily/not readily or only slightly soluble
los-: ~|**machen** 1 tr. V. (ugs.) let ⟨animal⟩ loose; untie, undo ⟨string, line, rope⟩; take out ⟨plank⟩; unhitch ⟨trailer⟩; **das Boot** ~**machen** cast off; 2 refl. V. (ugs., auch fig.) free oneself (von from); ~|**müssen** unr. itr. V. (ugs.) have to be off; have to go; **ich muss** ~ I must be off
Los·nummer die [lottery] ticket number
los|reißen 1 unr. tr. V. tear off; (schneller, gewaltsamer) rip off; pull ⟨plank⟩ off; ⟨wind⟩ rip ⟨tile⟩ off; 2 unr. refl. V. break free or loose; **sich von etw. (Dat.)** ~**reißen** break free or loose from sth.; (fig.) tear oneself away from sth.
Löss, *Löß /lœs/ der; **Lösses, Lösse** (Geol.) loess
los|sagen refl. V. **sich von jmdm./etw.** ~**sagen** renounce sb./sth.; break with sb./sth.
Löss·boden, *Löß·boden der loess soil
los-: ~|**schicken** tr. V. (ugs.) send off ⟨letter, telegram, etc.⟩; **jmdn.** ~**schicken, um etw. zu holen** send sb. out to get sth.; ~|**schießen** unr. itr. V. (fig. ugs.) fire away;

∼|**schlagen** *unr. itr. V.* (bes. Milit.) attack; launch one's attack

Los·trommel *die* [lottery] drum

Losung *die;* ∼, ∼**en** (a) slogan; (b) (Milit.: Kennwort) password

Lösung *die;* ∼, ∼**en** (a) solution (*Gen.* to); (eines Konflikts, Widerspruchs) resolution; **des Rätsels** ∼**:** the answer to the mystery; (b) (einer Verlobung) breaking off; (eines Vertrags) cancellation; (einer Verbindung, eines Verhältnisses) severing; (eines Arbeitsverhältnisses) termination; (c) (Flüssigkeit) solution

Lösungs-: ∼**mittel** *das* (Physik, Chemie) solvent; ∼**vorschlag** *der* proposed solution (**für** to)

Los·verkäufer *der* [lottery-] ticket seller

los-: ∼|**werden** *unr. tr. V.; mit sein* (a) (sich befreien können von) get rid of; **ich werde den Gedanken/Verdacht nicht** ∼, **dass** …**:** I can't get the thought/suspicion/impression out of my mind that …; (b) (ugs.: aussprechen, mitteilen) tell; **er wollte etwas** ∼**werden** he wanted to tell me/us *etc.* something; (c) (ugs.: verkaufen) get rid of; flog (Brit. sl.); (d) (ugs.: verlieren) lose; ∼|**wollen** *unr. itr. V.* (ugs.) want to be off; ∼|**ziehen** *unr. itr. V.; mit sein* (ugs.) set off

Lot /loːt/ *das;* ∼[e]s, ∼**e** (a) (Senkblei) plumb[-bob]; (b) **im** ∼ **stehen** be plumb; **nicht im** ∼ **sein, außer** ∼ **sein** be out of plumb; **nicht im** ∼ **sein** (fig.) not be straightened *or* sorted out; [**wieder**] **ins** ∼ **kommen** (fig.) be all right [again]; (c) (Geom.) perpendicular

löten /ˈløːtn̩/ *tr. V.* solder

Lotion /loˈtsi̯oːn/ *die;* ∼, ∼**en** *od.* ∼**s** lotion

Löt-: ∼**kolben** *der* soldering iron; ∼**lampe** *die* blowlamp

Lotos /ˈloːtɔs/ *der;* ∼, ∼**:** lotus

lot·recht 1 *Adj.* perpendicular; vertical. **2** *adv.* perpendicularly; vertically

Lotse /ˈloːtsə/ *der;* ∼**n**, ∼**n** ▶ 85 | (Seew.) pilot; (fig.) guide

lotsen *tr. V.* (a) (Seew.) pilot; (Flugw.) guide; (b) (leiten) guide; (c) (ugs.: führen, leiten) drag

Lotterie /lɔtəˈriː/ *die;* ∼, ∼**n** lottery

Lotterie-: ∼**gewinn** *der* win in the lottery; (gewonnenes Geld) lottery winnings *pl.;* ∼**los** *das* lottery-ticket

Lotter·leben *das; o. Pl.* (abwertend) dissolute life

Lotto /ˈlɔto/ *das;* ∼**s**, ∼**s** (a) national lottery; (b) (Gesellschaftsspiel) lotto

Lotto-: ∼**gewinn** *der* win on the national lottery; (gewonnenes Geld) winnings *pl.* on the national lottery; ∼**schein** *der* national-lottery coupon; ∼**zahlen** *Pl.* winning national-lottery numbers

Lover /ˈlavɐ/ *der;* ∼**s**, ∼ (ugs.) boyfriend

Löwe /ˈløːvə/ *der;* ∼**n**, ∼**n** (a) lion; (b) (Astrol.) Leo; the Lion

Löwen-: ∼**anteil** *der* lion's share; ∼**maul**, ∼**mäulchen** *das; o. Pl.* (Bot.) snapdragon; antirrhinum; ∼**zahn** *der; o. Pl.* (Bot.) dandelion

Löwin /ˈløːvɪn/ *die;* ∼, ∼**nen** lioness

loyal /loaˈjaːl/ *1 Adj.* loyal (**gegenüber** to). **2** *adv.* loyally

Loyalität /loajaliˈtɛːt/ *die;* ∼**:** loyalty (**gegenüber** to)

LP /ɛlˈpeː/ *die;* ∼, ∼[**s**] *Abk.* **Langspielplatte** LP

lt. *Abk.* **laut²**

Luchs /lʊks/ *der;* ∼**es**, ∼**e** lynx; **wie ein** ∼ **aufpassen** watch like a hawk

Lücke /ˈlʏkə/ *die;* ∼, ∼**n** (a) gap; (Park∼, auf einem Formular, in einem Text) space; (b) (Mangel) gap; (in der Versorgung) break; (im Gesetz) loophole

Lücken·büßer *der* (ugs.) stopgap

lückenhaft 1 *Adj.* ⟨*teeth*⟩ full of gaps; gappy ⟨*teeth*⟩; sketchy ⟨*knowledge*⟩; sketchy, vague ⟨*memory*⟩; incomplete, sketchy ⟨*report, account, etc.*⟩; incomplete ⟨*statement*⟩; ⟨*alibi*⟩ full of holes; **sein Wissen/seine Erinnerung ist** ∼**:** there are gaps in his knowledge/memory. **2** *adv.* ⟨*remember*⟩ vaguely, sketchily

lücken·los 1 *Adj.* unbroken ⟨*line, row, etc.*⟩; complete ⟨*account, report, curriculum vitae*⟩; solid, cast-iron ⟨*alibi*⟩; comprehensive, perfect ⟨*knowledge*⟩; **sie hat ein strahlend weißes,** ∼**es Gebiss** she has gleaming white teeth without any gaps. **2** *adv.* without any gaps

lud /luːt/ *1. u. 3. Pers. Sg. Prät. v.* **laden**

Lude /ˈluːdə/ *der;* ∼**n**, ∼**n** (salopp) pimp; ponce (Brit. sl.)

Luder *das;* ∼**s**, ∼ (salopp) so-and-so (coll.)

Luft /lʊft/ *die;* ∼, **Lüfte** /ˈlʏftə/ (a) *o. Pl.* air; **an die frische** ∼ **gehen/in der frischen** ∼ **sein** get out in[to]/be out in the fresh air; **jmdn. an die** [**frische**] ∼ **setzen** *od.* **befördern** (ugs.: hinauswerfen) show sb. the door; **die** ∼ **anhalten** hold one's breath; **halt die** ∼ **an!** (ugs.) (hör auf zu reden!) pipe down (coll.); put a sock in it (Brit. sl.); (übertreib nicht so!) come off it! (coll.); **tief** ∼ **holen** take a deep breath; ∼ **schnappen** (ugs.) get some fresh air; **er kriegte keine/kaum** ∼**:** he couldn't breathe/ could hardly breathe; **die** ∼ **ist rein** (fig.) the coast is clear; **sich in** ∼ **auflösen** (ugs.) vanish into thin air; ⟨*plans*⟩ go up in smoke (fig.); **er ist** ∼ **für mich** I ignore him completely; **da bleibt einem die** ∼ **weg** (ugs.) it takes your breath away; **ihm/der Firma geht die** ∼ **aus** (fig. ugs.) he's/the firm's going broke (coll.); (b) (Himmelsraum) air; **Aufnahmen aus der** ∼ **machen** take pictures from the air; **etw. in die** ∼ **sprengen** *od.* **jagen** (ugs.) blow sth. up; **in die** ∼ **fliegen** *od.* **gehen** (ugs.: explodieren) go up; **in die** ∼ **gehen** (fig. ugs.) blow one's top (coll.); **aus der** ∼ **gegriffen sein** (fig.) ⟨*story, accusation*⟩ be pure invention; **in der** ∼ **liegen** (fig.) ⟨*crisis, ideas, etc.*⟩ be in the air; **in die** ∼ **gehen** (fig. ugs.) blow one's top (coll.); **etw. in der** ∼ **zerreißen** (fig. ugs.) tear sth. to pieces; (c) *o. Pl.* (fig.: Spielraum) space; room; (d) **sich** (*Dat.*) *od.* **seinem Herzen** ∼ **machen** get it off one's chest (coll.); **seinem Zorn/Ärger** *usw.* ∼ **machen** (ugs.) give vent to one's anger

Luft-: ∼**abwehr** *die* (Milit.) air defence; anti-aircraft defence; ∼**angriff** *der* (Milit.) air raid; ∼**ballon** *der* balloon; ∼**bild** *das* aerial photograph; ∼**blase** *die* air bubble; ∼**brücke** *die* airlift

Lüftchen /ˈlʏftçən/ *das;* ∼**s**, ∼**:** breeze

luft-, Luft-: ∼**dicht** *Adj.* airtight; ∼**druck** *der* air pressure; atmospheric pressure; ∼**durchlässig** *Adj.* pervious *or* permeable to air *postpos.;* well-ventilated ⟨*shoes*⟩

lüften 1 *tr. V.* (a) air; (b) (hochheben) raise, lift ⟨*hat, lid, veil, etc.*⟩; (c) (enthüllen) reveal; disclose ⟨*secret*⟩. **2** *itr. V.* air the room/house *etc.;* **wir müssen hier mal** ∼**:** we must let some [fresh] air in here

Lüfter *der;* ∼**s**, ∼**:** fan

Luft·fahrt *die; o. Pl.* aeronautics *sing., no art.;* (mit Flugzeugen) aviation *no art.*

Luftfahrt·gesellschaft *die* airline

luft-, Luft-: ∼**feuchtigkeit** *die* [atmospheric] humidity; ∼**filter** *der od. das* (Technik) air filter; ∼**fracht** *die* air freight; ∼**gekühlt** *Adj.* air-cooled; ∼**gewehr** *das* air rifle; airgun; ∼**hoheit** *die* air sovereignty

luftig *Adj.* airy ⟨*room, building, etc.*⟩; well ventilated ⟨*cellar, store*⟩; light, cool ⟨*clothes*⟩

Luftikus /ˈlʊftikʊs/ *der;* ∼[**ses**], ∼**se** (ugs. abwertend) careless and unreliable sort (coll.)

Luftkissen-: ∼**boot** *das* hovercraft; ∼**fahrzeug** *das* hovercraft

luft-, Luft-: ∼**krieg** *der* air warfare *no art.;* aerial warfare *no art.;* ∼**kur·ort** *der* climatic health resort; ∼**leer** *Adj.* **ein** ∼**leerer Raum** a vacuum; **im** ∼**leeren Raum** (fig.) in a vacuum; ∼**linie** *die;* **1 000 km** ∼**linie** 1,000 km. as the crow flies; ∼**loch** *das* air hole; ∼**matratze** *die* airbed; air mattress; Lilo (P); ∼**pirat** *der* [aircraft] hijacker; ∼**post** *die* airmail; **etw. per** *od.* **mit** ∼**post schicken** send sth. [by] airmail; ∼**post·brief** *der* airmail letter; ∼**pumpe** *die* air pump; (für Fahrrad) [bicycle] pump; ∼**raum** *der* airspace; ∼**röhre** *die* ▶ 326 | (Anat.) windpipe; trachea (Anat.); ∼**sack** *der* (Kfz-W.) airbag; ∼**schacht** *der* ventilation shaft; (einer Klimaanlage) ventilation duct; ∼**schadstoff** *der* air pollutant; atmospheric pollutant; ∼**schiff** *das* airship; ∼**schlacht** *die* air battle; aerial battle; ∼**schlange** *die meist Pl.* [paper] streamer; ∼**schloss**, *∼***schloß** *das; meist Pl.* castle in the air

Luftschutz-: ∼**bunker**, ∼**keller** *der* air-raid shelter

Luft-: ~**spiegelung** die mirage; ~**sprung** der jump in the air; ~**streitkräfte** Pl. (Milit.) air force sing.; ~**strom** der stream of air; ~**strömung** die (Met.) airstream; air current; ~**temperatur** die (Met.) air temperature

Lüftung die; ~, ~en (a) ventilation; (b) (Anlage) ventilation system

Lüftungs·klappe die ventilation flap

Luft-: ~**veränderung** die change of air; ~**verpestung** die (abwertend), ~**verschmutzung** die air pollution; ~**waffe** die air force; ~**weg** der (a) auf dem ~: by air; (b) Pl. (Anat.: Atemwege) airways; air passages; ~**widerstand** der (Physik) air resistance; ~**zufuhr** die air supply; ~**zug** der o. Pl. [gentle] breeze; (in Zimmern, Gebäuden) draught

Lug /luːk/ in ~ und Trug lies pl. and deception

Lüge /ˈlyːɡə/ die; ~, ~n lie; ~n haben kurze Beine (Spr.) [the] truth will out; jmdn./etw. ~n strafen prove sb. a liar/give the lie to sth.; s. auch **fromm 1 c**

lügen 1 itr. V. lie; ~ wie gedruckt lie like mad (coll.); be a terrible liar (coll.). 2 tr. V. das ist gelogen! that's a lie!

Lügen·detektor der lie detector

Lügner der; ~s, **Lügnerin** die; ~, ~nen liar

Lukas[1] /ˈluːkas/ (der) Luke

Lukas[2] der; ~, ~ try-your-strength machine; hau den ~! try your strength!

Luke /ˈluːkə/ die; ~, ~n (a) (Dach~) skylight; (b) (bei Schiffen) hatch; (Keller~) trap-door

lukrativ /lukraˈtiːf/ 1 Adj. lucrative. 2 adv. lucratively

Lulatsch /ˈluːl(a:)tʃ/ der; ~[e]s, ~e (ugs.) [long] lanky fellow; ein langer ~: a beanpole

Lümmel /ˈlʏml/ der; ~s, ~ (a) (abwertend: Flegel) lout; (b) (ugs., fam.: Bengel) rascal

lümmeln refl. V. (ugs. abwertend) ⇒ **flegeln**

Lump /lʊmp/ der; ~en, ~en scoundrel; rogue

lumpen tr. V. sich nicht ~ lassen (ugs.) splash out (coll.)

Lumpen der; ~s, ~: rag

Lumpen-: ~**gesindel** das (abwertend) rabble; riff-raff; ~**sammler** der rag-and-bone man

lumpig Adj. nicht präd. (abwertend) paltry, miserable ⟨pay etc.⟩

Lunge /ˈlʊŋə/ die; ~, ~n ▶326┃ lungs pl.; (Lungenflügel) lung; er hat es auf der ~ (ugs.) he has got lung trouble (coll.); auf ~ od. über die ~ rauchen inhale; sich (Dat.) die ~ aus dem Hals od. Leib schreien (ugs.) yell one's head off (coll.)

lungen-, Lungen-: ~**embolie** die ▶329┃ (Med.) pulmonary embolism; ~**entzündung** die ▶329┃ pneumonia no indef. art.; ~**flügel** der ▶329┃ lung; ~**krank** Adj. suffering from a lung disease postpos.; ~**kranke** der/die person with or suffering from a lung disease; ~**krebs** der ▶329┃ lung cancer; ~**zug** der inhalation

Lunte /ˈlʊntə/ die; ~, ~n fuse; match; ~ riechen (ugs.) smell a rat

Lupe /ˈluːpə/ die; ~, ~n magnifying glass; jmdn./etw. unter die ~ nehmen (ugs.) examine sb./sth. closely; take a close look at sb./sth.

lupenrein Adj. (a) flawless ⟨diamond, stone, etc.⟩; ⟨diamond⟩ of the first water; (b) (musterhaft) genuine ⟨amateur⟩; unimpeachable ⟨record, reputation⟩; perfect ⟨forgery, gentleman⟩

lupfen /ˈlʊpfn̩/ (südd., schweiz., österr.), **lüpfen** /ˈlʏpfn̩/ tr. V. raise; lift

Lurch /lʊrç/ der; ~[e]s, ~s amphibian

Lusche /ˈlʊʃə/ die; ~, ~n (Kartenspiele ugs.) low card

Lust /lʊst/ die; ~ (a) (Bedürfnis) ~ haben od. verspüren, etw. zu tun feel like doing sth.; große/keine ~ haben, etw. zu tun really/not feel like doing sth.; wir hatten nicht die geringste ~, das zu tun we didn't feel in the least or slightest like doing it; auf etw. (Akk.) ~ haben fancy sth.; (b) (Vergnügen) pleasure; joy; die ~ an etw. (Dat.) verlieren lose interest in or stop enjoying sth.; etw. mit ~ und Liebe tun love doing sth.

Lüster /ˈlʏstɐ/ der; ~s, ~ chandelier

lüstern 1 Adj. lecherous; lascivious. 2 adv. (a) lecherously; lasciviously; (b) (begierig) greedily

Lust-: ~**gefühl** das feeling of pleasure; ~**gewinn** der o. Pl. pleasure

lustig 1 Adj. (a) (vergnügt) merry; jolly; merry, jolly, jovial ⟨person⟩; happy, enjoyable ⟨time⟩; das kann ja ~ werden! (ugs. iron.) this/that is going to be fun! sich über jmdn./etw. ~ machen make fun of sb./sth.; (b) (komisch) funny; amusing. 2 adv. (a) (vergnügt) ⟨laugh, play⟩ merrily, happily; (b) (komisch) funnily; amusingly; sie kann so ~ erzählen she can tell such funny or amusing stories; (c) (unbekümmert) gaily

-lustig /ˈlʊstɪç/ adj. [sehr] tanz~/sanges~/lese~ sein be very fond of or keen on dancing/singing/reading

Lustigkeit die; ~ (a) merriness; jolliness; (Frohsinn auch) joviality; (b) (Komik) funniness

Lüstling /ˈlʏstlɪŋ/ der; ~s, ~e (veralt. abwertend, scherzh.) lecher

lust-, Lust-: ~**los** 1 Adj. listless; (ohne Begeisterung) unenthusiastic [and uninterested]; 2 adv. listlessly; (ohne Begeisterung) without enthusiasm [or interest]; ~**spiel** das comedy; ~**wandeln** itr. V.; mit sein od. haben (geh. veralt.) stroll; take a stroll

Lutheraner /lʊtəˈraːnɐ/ der; ~s, ~ Lutheran

Luther·bibel die Luther's Bible; Lutheran Bible

lutherisch Adj. Lutheran

lutschen /ˈlʊtʃn̩/ 1 tr. V. suck. 2 itr. V. suck; an etw. (Dat.) ~: suck sth.

Lutscher der; ~s, ~ (a) lollipop; (b) (Schnuller) dummy (Brit.); pacifier (Amer.)

Luv /luːf/ die od. das; ~ (Seemannsspr.) in/nach ~: to windward

Luxemburg /ˈlʊksm̩bʊrk/ (das); ~s ▶490┃ Luxembourg

luxuriös /lʊksuˈriø:s/ 1 Adj. luxurious. 2 adv. luxuriously

Luxus /ˈlʊksʊs/ der; ~ (auch fig.) luxury; etw. ist reiner ~: sth. is sheer extravagance

Luxus-: ~**artikel** der luxury article; ~**ausführung** die de luxe version; ~**hotel** das luxury hotel; ~**jacht** die luxury yacht; ~**klasse** die luxury class

Luzifer /ˈluːtsifɐ/ (der) Lucifer

LW Abk. Langwelle LW

Lymph·drüse die (veralt.), **Lymph·knoten** der lymph node or gland

lynchen /ˈlʏnçn̩/ tr. V. lynch; (scherzh.) lynch; kill

Lynch·justiz die lynch-law

Lyra /ˈlyːra/ die; ~, **Lyren** (Mus.) lyre

Lyrik /ˈlyːrɪk/ die; ~: lyric poetry

Lyriker der; ~s, ~, **Lyrikerin** die; ~, ~nen lyric poet; lyricist

lyrisch 1 Adj. (a) lyric ⟨poem, poetry, epic, drama⟩; lyrical ⟨passage, style, description, etc.⟩; (b) (gefühlvoll) lyrical; (c) nicht präd. (Mus.) lyric. 2 adv. lyrically

Lyzeum /lyˈtseːʊm/ das; ~s, **Lyzeen** /lyˈtseːən/ girls' high school

┈┈┈┈┈┈┈┈┈┈┈┈┈┈┈┈┈┈┈┈┈┈┈┈┈┈┈┈┈┈┈┈┈┈

Mm

┈┈┈┈┈┈┈┈┈┈┈┈┈┈┈┈┈┈┈┈┈┈┈┈┈┈┈┈┈┈┈┈┈┈

m, M /ɛm/ das; ~, ~: m/M; s. auch **a, A**

M Abk. **Mark**[1]

Maat /maːt/ der; ~[e]s, ~e[n] ▶34┃ (a) [ship's] mate; (b) (Dienstgrad) petty officer

Mach·art die style; (Schnitt) cut

machbar Adj. feasible

Mache die; ~ (ugs.) (a) (abwertend) sham; (b) etw. in der ~ haben have sth. on the stocks; be working on sth.

machen /'maxŋ/ **1** tr. V. **(a)** (herstellen) make; **aus diesen Äpfeln ~ wir Saft** we will make juice from these apples; **sich** (Dat.) **etw. ~ lassen** have sth. made; **Geld/ein Vermögen/einen Gewinn ~**: make money/a fortune/a profit; **dafür ist er einfach nicht gemacht** (fig.) he's just not cut out for it; **etw. aus jmdm. ~**: make sb. into sth.; (verwandeln) turn sb. into sth.; **jmdn. zum Präsidenten** usw. **~**: make sb. president etc.; **(b) jmdm. einen Kostenvoranschlag ~**: let sb. have or give sb. an estimate; **jmdm. einen guten Preis ~** (ugs.) name a good price; **(c)** (zubereiten) get, prepare ‹meal›; **jmdm./sich [einen] Kaffee ~**: make [some] coffee for sb./oneself; **jmdm. einen Cocktail ~**: get or mix sb. a cocktail; **(d)** (verursachen) **jmdm. Arbeit ~**: cause or make [extra] work for sb.; **jmdm. Sorgen ~**: cause sb. anxiety; worry sb.; **jmdm. Mut/Hoffnung ~**: give sb. courage/hope; **das macht Durst/Hunger** od. **Appetit** this makes one thirsty/hungry; **this gives one a thirst/an appetite; das macht das Wetter** that's [because of] the weather; **das macht das viele Rauchen** that comes from smoking a lot; **mach, dass du nach Hause kommst!** (ugs.) off home with you!; **ich muss ~, dass ich zum Bahnhof komme** (ugs.) I must see that I get to the station; **(e)** (ausführen) do ‹job, repair, etc.›; **seine Hausaufgaben ~**: do one's homework; **ein Foto** od. **eine Aufnahme ~** take a photograph; **ein Examen ~**: take an exam; **einen Spaziergang ~**: go for or take a walk; **eine Reise ~**: go on a journey or trip; **einen Besuch [bei jmdm.] ~**: pay [sb.] a visit; **wie mans macht, macht mans falsch** od. **verkehrt** (ugs.) [however you do it,] there's always something wrong; **er macht es nicht unter 100 DM** he won't do it for under or less than 100 marks; **(f) jmdn. glücklich/eifersüchtig** usw. **~**: make sb. happy/jealous etc.; **etw. größer/länger/kürzer ~**: make sth. bigger/longer/shorter; **mach es dir gemütlich** od. **bequem!** make yourself comfortable or at home; **das Kleid macht sie älter** the dress makes her look older; **(g)** (tun) do; **musst du noch viel ~?** do you still have a lot to do?; **mach ich, wird gemacht!** (ugs.) will do!; **was ~ Sie [beruflich]?** what do you do [for a living]?; **was soll ich nur ~?** what am I to do?; **so etwas macht man nicht** that [just] isn't done; **mit mir könnt ihr es ja ~** (ugs.) you can get away with it with me; **(h) was macht ...?** (wie ist es um ... bestellt?) how is ...?; **was macht die Arbeit?** how is the job [getting on]?; how are things at work?; **(i)** (ugs.) (beim Rechnen) be; (bei Geldbeträgen) come to; **zwei mal zwei macht vier** two times two is four; **was** od. **wieviel macht das [alles zusammen]?** how much does that come to?; **das macht 12 DM** that is or costs 12 marks; (Endsumme) that comes to 12 marks; **(j)** (schaden) **was macht das schon?** what does it matter?; **macht das was?** does it matter?; do you mind?; **macht nichts!** (ugs.) never mind!; it doesn't matter; **(k)** (teilnehmen an) **einen Kursus** od. **Lehrgang ~**: take a course; **(l)** (ugs.: veranstalten) organize, (coll.) do ‹trips, meals, bookings, etc.›; **ein Fest ~**: give a party; **(m) machs gut!** (ugs.) look after yourself!; (auf Wiedersehen) so long!; **(n)** (ugs.: ordnen, sauber machen, renovieren); do ‹room, stairs, washing, etc.›; **das Bett ~**: make the bed; **sich** (Dat.) **die Haare/Fingernägel ~**: do one's hair/nails; **(o)** (ugs.: verhüll. seine Notdurft verrichten) **sein Geschäft ~**: relieve oneself; **groß/klein ~**: do big jobs/small jobs (child language). **2** refl. V. **(a)** mit Adj. **sich hübsch ~**: smarten [oneself] up; **sich schmutzig ~**: get [oneself] dirty; **sich verständlich ~**: make oneself clear; **das macht sich bezahlt!** it's worth it!; **(b)** (beginnen) **sich an etw.** (Akk.) **~**: get down to sth.; **(c)** (ugs.: sich entwickeln) do well; get on; **du hast dich aber gemacht!** you've made great strides!; **(d)** (passen) **das macht sich gut hier** this fits in well; this looks good here; **(e) mach dir nichts daraus!** (ugs.) don't let it bother you; **ich mache mir nichts daraus** it doesn't bother me; **sich** (Dat.) **nichts/wenig aus jmdm./etw. ~** (ugs.) not care at all/much for sb./sth.; **(f) wir wollen uns** (Dat.) **einen schönen Abend ~**: we want to have an enjoyable evening; **(g) sich** (Dat.) **Feinde ~**: make enemies; **sich** (Dat.) **jmdn. zum Freund/Feind ~**: make a friend/an enemy of sb.; **(h) wenn es sich [irgendwie] ~ lässt** if it can [somehow] be done; if it is [at all] possible. **3** itr. V. **(a)** (ugs.: sich beeilen) **mach schon!** get a move on! (coll.); look snappy! (coll.); **mach schneller!** hurry up!; **(b) das macht müde** it makes you tired; it is tiring; **das macht hungrig/durstig** it makes you hungry/thirsty; **das Kleid macht dick** the dress makes one look fat; **(c)** (tun) **lass mich nur ~** (ugs.) leave it to me; **(d)** (ugs. verhüll.) ‹child, pet› perform (coll.); **ins Bett/in die Hose ~**: wet one's bed/pants; **(e)** (ugs.) **auf naiv** usw. **~**: pretend to be naïve; **auf feine Dame** usw. **~**: act the fine lady; **(f)** (landsch. ugs.: sich begeben) go

Machenschaften Pl. (abwertend) machinations; wheeling and dealing sing.

Macher der; **~s**, **~** (ugs.) doer; **der Typ des ~s** the dynamic type who just gets on with things

Machete /ma'xe:tə/ die; **~**, **~n** machete

Macho /'matʃo/der; **~s**, **~s** (abwertend) macho

Macht /maxt/ die; **~**, **Mächte** /'mɛxtə/ **(a)** o. Pl. power; (Stärke) strength; (Befugnis) authority; power; **mit aller ~**: with all one's might; **alles, was in seiner ~ steht**, tun do everything in one's power; **seine ~ ausspielen** show one's authority or power; **das liegt nicht in ihrer ~**: that is not within her power; that is outside her authority; **die ~ der Gewohnheit/der Verhältnisse** the force of habit/circumstances; **(b)** o. Pl. (Herrschaft) power no art.; **die ~ ergreifen** od. **an sich reißen** seize power; **an die ~ kommen** come to power; **an der ~ sein** be in power; **(c)** (Staat) power; **(d) die Mächte der Finsternis** the powers of darkness; **böse Mächte** evil forces

Macht-: **~anspruch** der claim or pretension to power; **~befugnis** die authority no pl., no art.; power no art.; **~bereich** der sphere of influence; **~ergreifung** die (Politik) seizure of power (Gen. by); **~gier** die (abwertend) craving for power; **~haber** der; **~s**, **~**: ruler; **~hunger** der hunger for power

mächtig /'mɛçtɪç/ **1** Adj. **(a)** powerful; **die Mächtigen dieser Welt** the high and mighty; the wielders of power; **(b)** (beeindruckend groß) mighty; powerful, mighty ‹voice, blow›; tremendous, powerful ‹effect›; (ugs.) terrific (coll.) ‹luck›; terrible (coll.) ‹fright›; **~en Hunger/~e Angst haben** be terribly hungry/afraid; **(c)** (landsch.: schwer) heavy ‹food›. **2** adv. (ugs.) terribly (coll.); extremely; **er ist ~ gewachsen** he has grown a lot; **ihr müsst euch ~ beeilen** you'll really have to step on it (coll.)

macht-, Macht-: **~kampf** der (bes. Politik) power struggle; **~los** Adj. powerless; impotent; **gegen etw. ~los sein, einer Sache** (Dat.) **~los gegenüberstehen** be powerless in the face of sth.; **~losigkeit** die impotence (**gegen**, **gegenüber** in the face of); **~politik** die power politics sing., no art.; **~probe** die trial of strength; **~streben** das ambition for power; **~voll 1** Adj. powerful; (imponierend) impressive ‹demonstration, appearance›; **2** adv. powerfully; (imponierend) impressively; **~wechsel** der (Politik) change of government; **~wort** das word of command; decree; **ein ~wort sprechen** put one's foot down; lay down the law

Mach·werk das (abwertend) shoddy effort

Macke /'makə/ die; **~**, **~n** **(a)** (salopp: Tick) fad; **'ne ~ haben** have a fad; (verrückt sein) be off one's rocker (fig. coll.); **(b)** (ugs.: Defekt) defect; (optisch) mark; blemish

Macker der; **~s**, **~** **(a)** (Jugendspr.: Freund, Kerl) guy (coll.); bloke (Brit. sl.); **(b)** (abwertend) macho

Mädchen /'mɛ:tçən/ das; **~s**, **~** **(a)** girl; **(b)** (Haus~) maid; **~ für alles** (ugs.) maid of all work; (im Büro usw.) girl Friday; (Mann) man Friday

mädchenhaft Adj. girlish

Mädchen-: **~handel** der; o. Pl. white-slave traffic; **~händler** der white-slave trader; **~klasse** die girls' class; **~kleidung** die girls' clothes pl.; **~name** der **(a)** (Vorname) girl's name; **(b)** (Geburtsname) maiden name; **~schule** die girls' school; school for girls

Made /'ma:də/ die; **~**, **~n** maggot; (Larve) larva; **leben wie die ~ im Speck** be living in the lap of luxury or off the fat of the land

madig Adj. maggoty; **jmdn./etw. ~ machen** (ugs.) run sb./sth. down

Madonna /ma'dɔna/ *die;* ∼, **Madonnen** (a) (christl. Rel.) *die* ∼: Our Lady; the Virgin Mary; (b) (Kunst) madonna

Madrigal /madri'gaːl/ *das;* ∼s, ∼e (Literaturw., Musik) madrigal

Maf[f]ia /'mafi̯a/ *die;* ∼, ∼s (a) *o. Pl.* Mafia; (b) (fig.) mafia

mag /maːk/ *1. u. 3. Pers. Sg. Präsens v.* **mögen**

Magazin /maga'tsiːn/ *das;* ∼s, ∼e (a) (Lager) store; (für Waren) stockroom; (für Waffen u. Munition) magazine; (b) (für Patronen, Dias, Film usw.) magazine; (c) (Zeitschrift) magazine; (Rundf., Fems.) magazine programme

Magd /maːkt/ *die;* ∼, **Mägde** /'mɛːkdə/ (veralt.) [female] farmhand; (Vieh∼) milkmaid; (Dienst∼) maidservant

Magen /'maːgn̩/ *der;* ∼s, **Mägen** /'mɛːgn̩/ ▶ 326 *od.* ∼: stomach; **mir knurrt der** ∼ (ugs.) my tummy is rumbling (coll.); **sich** (*Dat.*) **den** ∼ **verderben** get an upset stomach; **etw. auf nüchternen** ∼ **essen/trinken** eat/ drink sth. on an empty stomach; **jmdm. auf den** ∼ **schlagen** upset sb.'s stomach; **jmdm. schwer im** ∼ **liegen** lie heavy on sb.'s stomach; **diese Sache liegt mir schwer auf dem** ∼ (fig. ugs.) this business is preying on my mind; **da dreht sich einem/mir der** ∼ **um** (ugs.) it's enough to make *or* it makes one's/my stomach turn; (fig.) it makes you/me sick; *s. auch* **Liebe** a

magen-, Magen-: ∼**beschwerden** *Pl.* stomach trouble *sing.;* ∼**bitter** *der;* ∼s, ∼: bitters *pl.;* ∼**gegend** *die* region of the stomach; ∼**geschwür** *das* ▶ 329 stomach ulcer; ∼**grube** *die* pit of the stomach; ∼**knurren** *das* (ugs.) tummy rumbles *pl.* (coll.); ∼**krampf** *der* stomach cramp; ∼**krank** *Adj.* ∼ **sein** have a stomach complaint; ∼**krebs** *der* ▶ 329 cancer of the stomach; ∼**saft** *der* gastric juice; ∼**säure** *die* gastric acid; ∼**schmerzen** *Pl.* ▶ 329 stomach ache *sing.*

mager /'maːgɐ/ **1** *Adj.* (a) (dünn) thin; (b) (fettarm) low-fat; low in fat *pred.;* lean ‹*meat*›; (c) (nicht ertragreich) poor ‹*soil, harvest*›; infertile ‹*field*›; lean ‹*years*›; (fig.: dürftig) meagre ‹*profit, increase, success, report, etc.*›; thin ‹*programme*›. **2** *adv.* ∼ **essen** follow a low-fat diet; eat low-fat foods

Mager·käse *der* low-fat cheese

Magerkeit *die;* ∼ (a) thinness; (b) (fig.: Dürftigkeit) meagreness

Mager-: ∼**milch** *die* skim[med] milk; ∼**quark** *der* low-fat curd cheese; ∼**sucht** *die* ▶ 329 anorexia

Magie /ma'giː/ *die;* ∼: magic; **Schwarze/Weiße** ∼: black/white magic

Magier /'maːgi̯ɐ/ *der;* ∼s, ∼ (auch fig.) magician

magisch 1 *Adj.* magic ‹*powers*›; (geheimnisvoll) magical ‹*attraction, light, force, etc.*›; (unwirklich) eerie ‹*light, half-light*›. **2** *adv.* (durch Zauber) by magic; (wie durch Zauber) as if by magic; magically; (unwirklich) eerily

Magistrat /magɪs'traːt/ *der;* ∼[e]s, ∼e City Council

Magma /'magma/ *das;* ∼s, **Magmen** (Geol.) magma

Magnat /ma'gnaːt/ *der;* ∼en, ∼en magnate

Magnesium /ma'gneːzi̯ʊm/ *das;* ∼s (Chemie) magnesium

Magnet /ma'gneːt/ *der;* ∼en *od.* ∼[e]s, ∼e (auch fig.) magnet

Magnet-: ∼**band** *das Pl.:* ∼**bänder** magnetic tape; ∼**feld** *das* (Physik) magnetic field

magnetisch (auch fig.) **1** *Adj.* magnetic. **2** *adv.* magnetically

magnetisieren *tr. V.* (Physik) magnetize

Magnetismus *der;* ∼ (Physik) magnetism

Magnolie /ma'gnoːli̯ə/ *die;* ∼, ∼n magnolia

mäh /mɛː/ *Interj.* baa

Mahagoni /maha'goːni/ *das;* ∼s mahogany

Mäh·drescher *der* combine harvester

mähen /'mɛːən/ **1** *tr. V.* mow ‹*grass, lawn, meadow*›; cut, reap ‹*corn*›. **2** *itr. V.* mow; (Getreide ∼) reap

Mahl /maːl/ *das;* ∼[e]s, **Mähler** /'mɛːlɐ/ (geh.) meal; repast (formal)

mahlen *unr. tr., itr. V.* grind; **etw. fein/grob** ∼: grind sth. fine/ coarsely

Mahl·zeit meal; ∼! (ugs.) have a good lunch; bon appetit; [na dann] **prost** ∼! (ugs.) what a delightful prospect! (iron.)

Mäh·maschine *die* [power] mower; (für Getreide) reaper

Mahn-: ∼**bescheid** *der* writ for payment; ∼**brief** *der* ⇒ ∼**schreiben**

Mähne /'mɛːnə/ *die;* ∼, ∼n mane; (scherzh.: Haarschopf) mane [of hair]

mahnen /'maːnən/ *tr., itr. V.* (a) urge; **zur Eile/Vorsicht** ∼: urge haste/caution; **jmdn. zur Eile/Vorsicht** ∼: urge sb. to hurry/to be careful; **jmdn. eindringlich** ∼: give sb. an urgent warning; (b) (erinnern) remind (**an** + *Akk.* of); **einen Schuldner [schriftlich]** ∼: send a debtor a [written] demand for payment *or* a reminder

Mahn-: ∼**gebühr** *die* reminder fee; ∼**mal** *das* memorial (*erected as a warning to future generations*); ∼**schreiben** *das* reminder

Mahnung *die;* ∼, ∼en (a) exhortation; (Warnung) admonition; (b) ([Zahlungs]erinnerung) reminder

Mähre /'mɛːrə/ *die;* ∼, ∼n (veralt. abwertend) jade (dated)

Mai /mai̯/ *der;* ∼[e]s *od.* ∼, ∼e ▶ 119 May; **der Erste** ∼: the first of May; May Day

Mai-: ∼**baum** *der* maypole; ∼**bowle** *die* cup made of white wine and champagne with fresh woodruff; ∼**glöckchen** *das* lily of the valley; ∼**käfer** *der* May-bug; ∼**kundgebung** *die* May Day rally

Mais /mai̯s/ *der;* ∼es maize; corn (esp. Amer.); (als Gericht) sweetcorn

Maische /'mai̯ʃə/ *die;* ∼, ∼n mash

Mais-: ∼**kolben** *der* corn cob; (als Gericht) corn on the cob; ∼**korn** *das* grain of maize *or* (Amer.) corn; ∼**mehl** *das* maize *or* (Amer.) corn flour

Majestät /majɛs'tɛːt/ *die;* ∼, ∼en (a) ▶ 34 (Titel) Majesty; **Seine/Ihre/Eure** *od.* **Euer** ∼: His/Her/Your Majesty; (b) *o. Pl.* (geh.) majesty

majestätisch 1 *Adj.* majestic. **2** *adv.* majestically

Majestäts·beleidigung *die* lèse-majesté

Majonäse /majo'nɛːzə/ *die;* ∼, ∼n mayonnaise

Major /ma'joːɐ̯/ *der;* ∼s, ∼e ▶ 34 (Milit.) major; (Luftwaffe) squadron leader (Brit.); major (Amer.)

Majoran /'maːjoran/ *der;* ∼s, ∼e marjoram

majorisieren *tr. V.* (geh.) outvote

Majorität /majori'tɛːt/ *die;* ∼, ∼en majority

makaber /ma'kaːbɐ/ *Adj.* macabre

Makel /'maːkl̩/ *der;* ∼s, ∼ (geh.) (a) (Schmach) stigma; taint; **an ihm haftet ein** ∼: a stain *or* taint clings to him; (b) (Fehler) blemish; flaw

makel·los 1 *Adj.* flawless, perfect ‹*skin, teeth, figure, stone*›; spotless, immaculate ‹*white, cleanness, clothes*›; (fig.) spotless, unblemished ‹*reputation, character*›. **2** *adv.* immaculately; spotlessly ‹*clean*›; (fehlerfrei) flawlessly

Makellosigkeit *die;* ∼ ⇒ **makellos:** flawlessness; perfection; spotlessness; immaculateness

mäkeln /'mɛːkl̩n/ *itr. V.* (abwertend) carp

Make-up /meːk'ʔap/ *das;* ∼s, ∼s make-up

Makkaroni /maka'roːni/ *Pl.* macaroni *sing.*

Makler /'maːklɐ/ *der;* ∼s, ∼ (a) ▶ 85 estate agent (Brit.); realtor (Amer.); (b) ▶ 85 (Börsen∼) broker

Makler-: ∼**gebühr** *die*, ∼**provision** *die* agent's fee *or* commission; (eines Börsenmaklers) brokerage charges *pl.*

Makrele /ma'kreːlə/ *die;* ∼, ∼n mackerel

Makro *der od. das;* ∼s, ∼s (DV) macro

makro-, Makro-/makro-/: ∼**biotisch 1** *Adj.* macrobiotic; **2** *adv.* on macrobiotic principles; ∼**kosmos** *der* macrocosm; ∼**molekül** *das* macromolecule

Makrone /ma'kroːnə/ *die;* ∼, ∼n macaroon

Makulatur /makula'tuːɐ̯/ *die;* ∼, ∼en (a) (Druckw.) spoilt sheets *pl.;* spoilage *no pl.;* (b) (Altpapier) waste paper; (c) ∼ **reden** (ugs.) talk rubbish

mal /maːl/ **1** *Adv.* times; (bei Flächen) by; **zwei** ∼ **zwei** twice two; two times two; **der Raum ist 5** ∼ **6 Meter groß** the room is five metres by six. **2** *Partikel* (ugs.) **komm** ∼ **her!** come here!; **hör** ∼ **zu!** listen!; *s. auch* **einmal** 2

Mal¹ *das;* ∼[e]s, ∼e time; **nur dies eine** ∼: just this once; **kein einziges** ∼: not once; not a single time; **das letzte** ∼: [the] last time; **das erste/zweite** ∼: for the first/second time; **jedes** ~, **wenn das Telefon klingelt,** … every time the telephone rings, …; **beim ersten/ letzten** ~: the first/last time; **zum ersten/zweiten/ x-ten** ~: for the first/ second/n-th time; **von** ~ **zu** ~ **heftiger werden/nachlassen** become more and more violent/decrease more and more [each time]; **mit einem** ~[e] (plötzlich) all at once; all of a sudden

Mal[2] *das;* ~[e]s, ~e *od.* **Mäler** /'mɛːlɐ/ mark; (Muttermal) birthmark; (braun) mole

Malachit /mala'xiːt/ *der;* ~s, ~e malachite

Malaie /ma'lajə/ *der;* ~n, ~n ▶ 388 | Malay

malaiisch *Adj.* ▶ 388 |, ▶ 487 | Malayan

Malaria /ma'laːrja/ *die;* ~: ▶ 329 | malaria

Mal·buch *das* colouring-book

malen *tr., itr. V.* paint ‹*picture, portrait, person, etc.*›; (mit Farbstiften) draw with crayons; (ausmalen) colour; **sich** ~ **lassen** have one's portrait painted; **etw. in düsteren Farben** ~ (fig.) paint *or* portray sth. in gloomy colours; **etw. allzu rosig/schwarz** ~ (fig.) paint far too rosy/black a picture of sth.

Maler /'maːlɐ/ *der;* ~s, ~ ▶ 85 | painter

Malerei *die;* ~, ~en (a) *o. Pl.* painting *no art.;* (b) (Gemälde) painting

Malerin *die;* ~, ~nen ▶ 85 | [woman] painter

malerisch 1 *Adj.* (a) (pittoresk) picturesque; (b) (zur Malerei gehörend) artistic ‹*skill, talent*›; ‹*skill, talent*› as a painter. **2** *adv.* (pittoresk) picturesquely ‹*situated*›

Maler·meister *der* master painter [and decorator]

Malheur /ma'løːɐ̯/ *das;* ~s, ~e *od.* ~s mishap

Mal·kasten *der* paintbox

mal|nehmen *unr. tr., itr. V.* multiply (**mit** by)

Mal-: ~**pinsel** *der* paintbrush; ~**technik** *die* painting technique

Malteser- /mal'teːzɐ-/: ~**hilfsdienst** *der* ≈ St John Ambulance Brigade; ~**kreuz** *das* (auch Technik) Maltese cross; ~**orden** *der o. Pl.* Order of the Knights of St John

malträtieren /maltrɛ'tiːrən/ *tr. V.* maltreat; ill-treat

Malve /'malvə/ *die;* ~, ~n mallow

Malz /malts/ *das;* ~es malt

Malz-: ~**bier** *das* malt beer; ~**bonbon** *das* malted cough lozenge

Mal·zeichen *das* multiplication sign

Malz·kaffee *der: coffee substitute made from germinated, dried, and roasted barley*

Mama /'mama, *geh. veralt.:* ma'ma:/ *die;* ~, ~s (fam.) mamma

Mami /'mami/ *die;* ~, ~s (fam.) mummy (Brit. coll.); mommy (Amer. coll.)

Mammographie /mamogra'fiː/ *die;* ~, ~n (Med.) mammography *no art.*

Mammut /'mamʊt/ *das;* ~s, ~e *od.* ~s mammoth

Mammut- mammoth ‹*project, undertaking, etc.*›; (lange dauernd) marathon ‹*trial*›

mampfen /'mampfn̩/ *tr., itr. V.* (salopp) munch; nosh (Brit. sl.)

man /man/ *Indefinitpron. im Nom.* (a) one; you; ~ **kann nie wissen** one *or* you never can tell; ~ **versteht sein eigenes Wort nicht** you can't hear yourself speak; ~ **nehme 250 g Butter** take 250 grams of butter; (b) (irgendjemand) somebody; (die Behörden; die Leute dort) they; **hat** ~ **dir das nicht mitgeteilt?** didn't anybody/they tell you that?; ~ **vermutet/hat herausgefunden, dass** …: it is thought/has been discovered that …; (c) (die Menschen im Allgemeinen) people *pl.;* **das trägt** ~ **heute** that's what people wear *or* what is worn nowadays; **so etwas tut** ~ **nicht** that's not done

Management /'mænɪdʒmənt/ *das;* ~s, ~s management

managen /'mɛnɪdʒn̩/ *tr. V.* (a) (ugs.) fix; organize; **ich manage das schon** I'll fix it; (durch Tricks) I'll fiddle it (coll.); (b) (betreuen) manage, act as manager for ‹*singer, artist, player*›; **von jmdm. gemanagt werden** have sb. as one's manager

Manager /'mɛnɪdʒɐ/ *der;* ~s, ~, **Managerin** *die;* ~, ~nen ▶ 85 | manager; (eines Fußballvereins) club secretary

Manager·krankheit *die* ▶ 329 | stress disease *no def. art.*

manch /manç/ *Indefinitpron.* (a) *attr.* many a; [so] ~**er Beamte**, ~ **ein Beamter** many an official; **in** ~**er Beziehung** in many respects; ~ **einer** many a person/man; ~ **eine** many a woman; (b) (*allein stehend*) ~**er** many a person/man; ~**e** (~ eine) many a woman; (~ Leute) some; [so] ~**es** a number of things; (allerhand Verschiedenes) all kinds of things; [so] ~**es von dem, was wir lernten** much of what we learnt

mancherlei *indekl. unbest. Gattungsz.: attr.* various; a number of; (*allein stehend*) various things; a number of things

manch·mal *Adv.* sometimes

Mandant /man'dant/ *der;* ~en, ~en, **Mandantin** *die;* ~, ~nen (Rechtsw.) client

Mandarine /manda'riːnə/ *die;* ~, ~n mandarin [orange]; tangerine

Mandat /man'daːt/ *das;* ~[e]s, ~e (a) (Parlamentssitz) [parliamentary] seat; (b) (Auftrag) (eines Abgeordneten) mandate; (eines Anwalts) brief

Mandats-: ~**gebiet** *das* mandated territory; mandate; ~**träger** *der* (Politik) member of parliament; deputy

Mandel /'mandl̩/ *die;* ~, ~n (a) almond; (b) (Anat.) tonsil

Mandel-: ~**baum** *der* almond[-tree]; ~**entzündung** *die* ▶ 329 | tonsillitis *no indef. art.;* ~**operation** *die* tonsillectomy

Mandoline /mando'liːnə/ *die;* ~, ~n mandolin

Manege /ma'neːʒə/ *die;* ~, ~n (im Zirkus) ring; (in der Reitschule) arena

Mangan /maŋ'gaːn/ *das;* ~s (Chemie) manganese

Mangel[1] /'maŋl̩/ *der;* ~s, **Mängel** /'mɛŋl̩/ (a) *o. Pl.* (Fehlen) lack (**an** + *Dat.* of); (Knappheit) shortage, lack (**an** + *Dat.* of); ~ **an Vitaminen** vitamin deficiency; **wegen** ~**s an Beweisen** for lack of evidence; **aus** ~ **an Erfahrung** from *or* owing to lack of experience; (b) (Fehler) defect; **geringfügige Mängel** minor flaws *or* imperfections

Mangel[2] *die;* ~, ~n (Wäsche~) [large] mangle; **jmdn. durch die** ~ **drehen** *od.* **in die** ~ **nehmen** (fig. salopp) put sb. through the hoop

Mangel-: ~**beruf** *der* understaffed profession; ~**erscheinung** *die* (Med.) deficiency symptom

mangelhaft 1 *Adj.* (fehlerhaft) defective ‹*goods, memory*›; faulty ‹*goods, German, English, etc.*›; (schlecht) poor ‹*memory, lighting*›; (unzulänglich) inadequate ‹*knowledge, lighting*›; incomplete ‹*reports*›; (Schulw.) **die Note „**~**"** the mark 'unsatisfactory'; (bei Prüfungen) the fail mark. **2** *adv.* (fehlerhaft) defectively; faultily; (schlecht) poorly; (unzulänglich) inadequately

Mangel·krankheit *die* (Med.) deficiency disease

mangeln[1] *itr. V.* **es mangelt an etw.** (*Dat.*) (ist nicht vorhanden) there is a lack of sth.; (ist unzureichend vorhanden) there is a shortage of sth.; sth. is in short supply; **jmdm./einer Sache mangelt es an etw.** (*Dat.*) sb./sth. lacks sth.; **seine** ~**de Menschenkenntnis** his inadequate understanding of people

mangeln[2] **1** *tr. V.* mangle. **2** *itr. V.* do the mangling

mangels /'maŋls/ *Präp. mit Gen.* in the absence of

Mangel·ware *die;* ~ **sein** be scarce *or* in short supply; ‹*article*› be a scarce commodity; **erfahrene Fachkräfte sind** ~ (fig. ugs.) experienced skilled workers are thin on the ground (coll.)

Mango /'maŋgo/ *die;* ~, ~s mango

Mangrove /maŋ'groːvə/ *die;* ~, ~n mangrove forest

Manie /ma'niː/ *die;* ~, ~n mania; **bei jmdm. zur** ~ **werden** become an obsession with sb.

Manier /ma'niːɐ̯/ *die;* ~, ~en (a) manner; **in gewohnter** ~: in his/her usual way *or* manner; (b) *Pl.* (Umgangsformen) manners

Manierismus *der;* ~ (Kunstwiss., Literaturw.) mannerism

manierlich 1 *Adj.* (a) (fam.) well-mannered; well-behaved ‹*child*›; (b) (ugs.: einigermaßen gut) reasonable; decent. **2** *adv.* (a) (fam.) properly; nicely; (b) (ugs.: einigermaßen gut) **ganz/recht** ~: quite/really nicely *or* decently

Manifest *das;* ~[e]s, ~e manifesto

manifestieren *refl. V.* (geh.) be manifested; manifest itself

Maniküre /mani'ky:rə/ *die;* ~, ~n (a) *o. Pl.* manicure; ~ **machen** manicure oneself; (b) (Person) manicurist

maniküren *tr. V.* manicure

Manipulation /manipula'tsi̯o:n/ *die;* ~, ~en manipulation

manipulierbar *Adj.* leicht ~: easy to manipulate

manipulieren /manipu'li:rən/ *tr. V.* manipulate; rig ‹*election result, composition of a committee*›

manisch /'ma:nɪʃ/ (geh., Psych.) **1** *Adj.* manic. **2** *adv.* maniacally

manisch-depressiv *Adj.* (Psych., Med.) manic-depressive

Manko /'maŋko/ *das;* ~s, ~s (Mangel) shortcoming; deficiency; (Nachteil) handicap

Mann /man/ *der;* ~[e]s, **Männer** /'mɛnɐ/; *s. auch* **Mannen** (a) man; **ein** ~, **ein Wort** a man's word is his bond; **ein** ~ **der Tat** a man of action; **ein** ~ **aus dem Volk** a man of humble origins; **ein** ~ **des Volkes** a man of the people; **der geeignete** *od.* **richtige** ~ **sein** be the right man; **der böse** *od.* **schwarze** ~: the bogy man; **der** ~ **auf der Straße** the man in the street; **auf den** ~ **dressiert sein** ‹*dog*› be trained to attack people; **der** ~ **im Mond** the man in the moon; [**mein lieber**] ~! (ugs.) (überrascht, bewundernd) my goodness!; (verärgert) for goodness sake!; **seinen** ~ **stehen** do one's duty; **du hast wohl einen kleinen** ~ **im Ohr** (salopp) you must be out of your tiny mind (sl.); **etw. an den** ~ **bringen** (ugs.: verkaufen) flog sth. (Brit. sl.); push sth. (Amer.); find a taker/takers for sth.; **Kämpfe** *od.* **der Kampf** ~ **gegen** ~: hand-to-hand fighting; **von** ~ **zu** ~: [from] man to man; (b) (Besatzungsmitglied) man; **mit 1 000** ~ **Besatzung** with a crew of 1,000 [men]; **alle** ~ **an Deck!** (Seemannsspr.) all hands on deck!; ~ **über Bord!** (Seemannsspr.) man overboard!; (c) (Teilnehmer) **uns fehlt der dritte/vierte** ~ **zum Skatspielen** we need a third/fourth person *or* player for a game of skat; (d) (Ehemann) husband

Männchen /'mɛnçən/ *das;* ~s, ~ (a) little man; ~ **malen** draw matchstick men; (b) (Tier~) male; ~ **machen** ‹*animal*› sit up and beg

Mannen *Pl.* (scherzh.: Team, Mannschaft usw.) troops

Mannequin /'manəkɛ̃/ *das;* ~s, ~s mannequin; [fashion] model

Männer-: ~**arbeit** *die* a man's work; work for a man; ~**bekanntschaft** *die* male *or* gentleman friend; ~**beruf** *der* all-male profession; (überwiegend von Männern ausgeübt) male-dominated profession; ~**chor** *der* male voice choir; ~**sache** *die:* **das ist** ~**sache** that's men's business; ~**stimme** *die* man's voice; male voice

Mannes-: ~**alter** *das* manhood *no art.;* **im besten** ~**alter sein** be in the prime of life *or* in one's prime; ~**kraft** *die* (geh.) virility

Mannig·faltigkeit *die;* ~: [great] diversity

Männlein /'mɛnlaɪn/ *das;* ~s, ~ (a) [kleines] ~: little man; (b) (ugs. scherzh.) ~ **und/oder Weiblein** men and/or women; (bei jüngeren) boys and/or girls

männlich 1 *Adj.* (a) male ‹*sex, line, descendant, flower, etc.*›; ~**er Vorname** boy's *or* man's name; (b) (für den Mann typisch) masculine ‹*behaviour, characteristic, etc.*›; male ‹*vanity*›; (c) (Sprachw.) masculine. **2** *adv.* in a masculine way

Männlichkeit *die;* ~ (a) masculinity; manliness; (b) (Potenz) virility

Manns·bild *das* (ugs., bes. südd., österr.) man

Mannschaft *die;* ~, ~en (a) (Sport, auch fig.) team; **die erste/zweite** ~ (Fußball) the first/second eleven; (b) (Schiffs-, Flugzeugbesatzung) crew; (c) (Milit.: Einheit) unit; **vor versammelter** ~ (fig.) in front of everybody

Mannschafts-: ~**aufstellung** *die* (Sport) (a) [composition of the] team; team line-up; (b) (das Aufstellen) selection of the team; ~**geist** *der; o. Pl.* (Sport) team spirit;

~**kapitän** *der* (Sport) team captain; ~**spiel** *das* (Sport) team game; ~**wagen** *der* personnel carrier

manns-: ~**hoch** *Adj.* as tall as a man *postpos.;* six-foot-high; ~**toll** *Adj.* (ugs. abwertend) man-mad (coll.); nymphomaniac

Mann·weib *das* (abwertend) amazon

Manöver /ma'nø:vɐ/ *das;* ~s, ~ (a) (Milit.) exercise; ~ *Pl.* manœuvres; **ins** ~ **gehen** *od.* **ziehen** go on manœuvres; (b) (Bewegung; fig. abwertend: Trick) manœuvre

Manöver·kritik *die* (fig.) postmortem (coll.)

manövrieren *tr., itr. V.* manœuvre

manövrier-: ~**fähig** *Adj.* manœuvrable; ~**unfähig** *Adj.* unmanœuvrable

Mansarde /man'zardə/ *die;* ~, ~n attic; (Zimmer) attic room

Manschette /man'ʃɛtə/ *die;* ~, ~n (a) cuff; [vor etw. (*Dat.*)] ~n **haben** (fig. ugs.) have got the willies (coll.) *or* have got the wind up (Brit. coll.) [about sth.]; (b) (Umhüllung) paper frill

Manschetten·knopf *der* cuff link

Mantel /'mantl/ *der;* ~s, **Mäntel** /'mɛntl/ (a) coat; (schwerer) overcoat; **den** ~ **des Schweigens über etw.** (*Akk.*) **breiten** (fig. geh.) observe a strict silence about sth.; (b) (Technik) (Isolier~, Kühl~) jacket; (Rohr~) sleeve; (Kabel~) sheath; (Geschoss~) [bullet-]casing; (einer Granate) [shell-]case; (Reifen~) [outer] cover; casing; (c) (Geom.: Zylinder~, Kegel~) curved surface

Mäntelchen /'mɛntlçən/ *das;* ~s, ~: little coat; (für Kinder) [child's] coat; *s. auch* **Wind**

Mantel-: ~**tarif** *der* (Arbeitswelt) terms of the *Manteltarifvertrag;* ~**tarifvertrag** *der* (Wirtsch.) framework collective agreement [on working conditions]

Manual /ma'nu̯a:l/ *das;* ~s, ~e, **Manuale** *das;* ~[s], ~[n] (Musik) keyboard; manual

manuell /ma'nu̯ɛl/ **1** *Adj.* manual. **2** *adv.* manually; by hand

Manufaktur /manufak'tu:ɐ/ *die;* ~, ~en [small] factory (*where goods are produced largely by hand*)

Manuskript /manu'skrɪpt/ *das;* ~[e]s, ~e (a) (auch hist.) manuscript; (Typoskript) typescript; (zu einem Film/Fernsehspiel/Hörspiel) script; (b) (Notizen eines Redners usw.) notes *pl.*

Maoismus /mao'ɪsmʊs/ *der;* ~: Maoism *no art.*

maoistisch 1 *Adj.* Maoist. **2** *adv.* on Maoist lines

Mäppchen /'mɛpçən/ *das;* ~s, ~: pencil case

Mappe /'mapə/ *die;* ~, ~n (a) folder; (größer, für Zeichnungen usw.) portfolio; (b) (Aktentasche) briefcase; (Schul~) school-bag

Marathon- /'ma(:)raton/**:** ~**lauf** *der* marathon; ~**läufer** *der* marathon runner; ~**sitzung** *die* marathon session

Märchen /~mɛ:ɐçən/ *das;* ~s, ~ (a) fairy story; fairy tale; (b) (ugs.: Lüge) [tall] story (coll.); **erzähl doch keine** ~! don't give me that story! (coll.)

Märchen-: ~**buch** *das* book of fairy stories; ~**erzähler** *der* teller of fairy stories; ~**figur** *die* fairy-tale figure; ~**film** *der* film of a fairy story

märchenhaft 1 *Adj.* (a) fairy-story *attrib.;* (wie ein Märchen) fairy-story-like; as in a fairy story *postpos.;* (b) (zauberhaft) magical; (feenhaft) fairy-like; ~ **sein** be sheer magic; be like a dream; (c) (ugs.) (großartig) fabulous; (sehr groß) fantastic (coll.), incredible (coll.) ‹*speed, wealth*›. **2** *adv. s. Adj.:* (a) as in a fairy story; (b) magically; ~ **schön** bewitchingly beautiful; (c) (ugs.) fantastically (coll.); incredibly (coll.)

Märchen-: ~**land** *das:* **das** ~**land** the world of fairy tale; fairyland; ~**prinz** *der* fairy-tale prince; (fig.) Prince Charming; ~**schloss** *das* fairy-tale castle

Marder /'mardɐ/ *der;* ~s, ~: marten

Margarine /marga'ri:nə/ *die;* ~: margarine

Marge /'marʒə/ *die;* ~, ~n (Wirtsch.) margin

Margerite /margə'ri:tə/ *die;* ~, ~n ox-eye daisy; (als Zierpflanze) marguerite

Maria /ma'ri:a/ (*die*) ~s *od.* **Mariens** *od.* (Rel.) **Mariä** Mary

Marien·käfer *der* ladybird
Marihuana /mariˈhuːaːna/ *das;* ~s marijuana
Marinade /mariˈnaːdə/ *die;* ~, ~n (a) (Beize) marinade; **(b)** (Salatsauce) [marinade] dressing
Marine /maˈriːnə/ *die;* ~, ~n (a) (Flotte) fleet; **(b)** (Kriegs~) navy
Marine-: ~**soldat** *der* marine; ~**stütz·punkt** *der* naval base; ~**uniform** *die* naval uniform
marinieren *tr. V.* marinade; **marinierte Heringe** soused herrings
Marionette /marioˈnɛtə/ *die;* ~, ~n puppet; marionette; (fig. abwertend) puppet
Marionetten-: ~**regierung** *die* (abwertend) puppet government; ~**spieler** *der* puppet-master; puppeteer; ~**theater** *das* puppet theatre
Mark¹ /mark/ *die;* ~, ~ ▶ 216◀ mark; **Deutsche** ~: Deutschmark; German mark; ~ **der DDR** GDR mark; **zwei** ~ **fünfzig** two marks fifty; **keine müde** ~ (ugs.) not a penny; not a cent (Amer.)
Mark² *das;* ~[e]s (a) (Knochen~) marrow; medulla (Anat.); **das ging mir durch** ~ **und Bein** (a) it put my teeth on edge; it went right through me; **(b)** (Bot.) (Frucht~) pulp
markant /marˈkant/ *Adj.* striking; distinctive; prominent ⟨figure, nose, chin⟩
Marke *die;* ~, ~n (a) (Waren~) brand; (Fabrikat) make; **(b)** (Brief~, Rabatt~, Beitrags~) stamp; **(c)** (Garderoben~) [cloak-room or (Amer.) checkroom] counter or tag; (Zettel) [cloak-room or (Amer.) checkroom] ticket; (Essen~) meal ticket; **(d)** (Erkennungs~) [identification] disc; (Dienst~) [police] identi-fication badge; ≈ warrant card (Brit.) or (Amer.) ID card; **(e)** (Lebensmittel~) coupon; **(f)** (Markierung) mark; (Sport: Rekord) record [height/distance]; **(g)** (salopp) **du bist mir viel-leicht eine** ~! you are a fine one! (iron.)
Marken-: ~**artikel** *der* proprietary or (Brit.) branded article; ~**artikel** *Pl.* proprietary or (Brit.) branded goods; ~**erzeugnis** *das,* ~**fabrikat** *das* proprietary or (Brit.) branded product; ~**name** *der* brand name; ~**zeichen** *das* trade mark
Marketing /ˈmarkətɪŋ/ *das;* ~s (Wirtsch.) marketing
markieren 1 *tr. V.* (a) (auch fig.) mark; (Sport) mark out ⟨course⟩; **(b)** (ugs.) sham ⟨illness, breakdown, etc.⟩; **(c)** (Sport) mark ⟨player⟩. 2 *itr. V.* (ugs.) sham; put it on (coll.)
Markierung *die;* ~, ~en (a) (Zeichen) marking; **(b)** o. *Pl.* (das Markieren) marking [out]
markig 1 *Adj.* (kernig) pithy ⟨saying, style⟩; (kraftvoll) vig-orous, breezy ⟨commands, manner⟩; ~**e Worte** strong words; (iron.: große Reden) big words. 2 *adv.* pithily
Markise /marˈkiːzə/ *die;* ~, ~n awning
Mark-: ~**klößchen** *das* (Kochk.) bone-marrow dump-ling; ~**knochen** *der* marrowbone; ~**stück** *das* ▶ 216◀ one-mark piece
Markt /markt/ *der;* ~[e]s, **Märkte** /ˈmɛrktə/ (a) market; **heute/freitags ist** ~: today/Friday is market-day; **auf dem** ~: at the market; **(b)** ⇒ ~**platz;** **(c)** (Super~) super-market; **(d)** (Warenverkehr, Absatzgebiet) market; **eine Ware auf den** ~ **bringen** od. **werfen** market a product; **auf dem** ~ **sein** ⟨article⟩ be on the market
markt-, Markt-: ~**anteil** *der* share of the market; ~**beherrschend** *Adj.* market-dominating *attrib.;* ~**forschung** *die* market research no def. art.; ~**frau** *die* market-woman; ~**halle** *die* covered market; ~**lei-ter** *der* supermarket manager; ~**lücke** *die* gap in the market; ~**platz** *der* market place or -square; ~**schreier** *der* barker; stall-holder who cries his wares; ~**stand** *der* market stall; ~**tag** *der* market-day; ~**wert** *der* market value; ~**wirtschaft** *die* market economy; ~**wirtschaftlich** 1 *Adj.; nicht präd.* mar-ket-economy; free-market; 2 *adv.* on market-economy lines
Markus /ˈmarkʊs/ ⟨der⟩: **Markus'** Mark
Marmelade /marməˈlaːdə/ *die;* ~, ~n jam; (Orangen~) marmalade
Marmelade[n]·glas *das* jam jar
Marmor /ˈmarmɔr/ *der;* ~s marble
marmoriert *Adj.* marbled
Marmor·kuchen *der* marble cake
marmorn *Adj.* marble
marode *Adj.* (ugs. abwertend) clapped-out (Brit. coll.)
Marokko /maˈrɔko/ ⟨das⟩; ~s Morocco

Marone /maˈroːnə/ *die;* ~, ~n [sweet] chestnut
Marotte /maˈrɔtə/ *die;* ~, ~n fad
Mars /mars/ *der;* ~ (Astron.) Mars no def. art.
Mars·bewohner *der* Martian
marsch /marʃ/ *Interj.* (a) (Milit.) [forward] march; **(b)** (ugs.) ~ ~! off with you!; (beeil dich!) move it! (coll.); look snappy! (coll.); ~ **ins Bett!** off to bed [with you]!
Marsch¹ *der;* ~[e]s, **Märsche** /ˈmɛrʃə/ (a) (Milit.) march; (Wanderung) [long] walk; hike; **jmdn. in** ~ **setzen** (Milit.) march sb. off; (fig.) mobilize sb.; **sich in** ~ **setzen** make a move; get moving; (Milit.) march off; **(b)** (Musikstück) march
Marsch² *die;* ~, ~en fertile marshland
Marschall /ˈmarʃal/ *der;* ~s, **Marschälle** /ˈmarʃɛlə/ (hist.) marshal
Marsch-: ~**flugkörper** *der* cruise missile; ~**ge-päck** *das* (Milit.) marching pack
marschieren *itr. V.; mit sein* (a) march; **(b)** (ugs.: mit großen Schritten gehen) march; stalk; (wandern) walk; hike
Marsch-: ~**musik** *die* march music; ~**route** *die* (Milit.) route; (fig.) line [of approach]; ~**verpflegung** *die* (Milit.) marching rations *pl.;* (fig. ugs.) rations *pl.* [for the jour-ney]
Mars-: ~**mensch** *der* Martian; ~**sonde** *die* Mars probe
Marter /ˈmartɐ/ *die;* ~, ~n (geh.) (Folter) torture; (fig.: see-lisch) torment
martern *tr. V.* (geh.) torture; (fig.: seelisch) torment
Marter·pfahl *der* stake
martialisch /marˈtsiaːlɪʃ/ (geh.) **1** *Adj.* warlike ⟨appearance, figure, etc.⟩; martial ⟨music⟩. **2** *adv.* in a war-like manner; (drohend) threateningly; aggressively
Martins·horn *das* (volkst.) siren (of emergency vehicle)
Märtyrer /ˈmɛrtyrɐ/ *der;* ~s, ~, **Märtyrerin** *die;* ~, ~nen martyr
Martyrium /marˈtyːriʊm/ *das;* ~s, **Martyrien** martyr-dom; **ein** ~ (fig.) sheer martyrdom
Marxismus /marˈksɪsmʊs/ *der;* ~: Marxism no art.
Marxist *der;* ~en, ~en, **Marxistin** *die;* ~, ~nen Marxist
marxistisch 1 *Adj.* Marxist. 2 *adv.* ⟨view, interpret⟩ from a Marxist point of view; ⟨think, act⟩ in line with Marxism
März /mɛrts/ *der;* ~[es], *dichter.:* ~en ▶ 119◀ March; s. auch **April**
Marzipan /martsiˈpaːn, österr. '---/ *das;* ~s marzipan
Marzipan·schwein *das* marzipan pig
Masche /ˈmaʃə/ *die;* ~, ~n (a) stitch; (Lauf~) run; lad-der (Brit.); (beim Netz) mesh; **durch die** ~n **des Gesetzes schlüpfen** (fig.) slip through a loophole in the law; **(b)** (ugs.: Trick) trick; **das ist die** ~: that's the way or trick; **(c)** (ugs.: Mode, Gag) **die neueste** ~: the latest fad or craze
Maschen·draht *der* wire netting
Maschine /maˈʃiːnə/ *die;* ~, ~n (a) machine; **(b)** (ugs.: Automotor) engine; **(c)** (Flugzeug) [aero]plane; **(d)** (ugs.: Motor-rad) machine; **(e)** (Schreib~) typewriter; ~ **schreiben** type
maschine·geschrieben *Adj.* typed; typewritten
maschinell /maʃiˈnɛl/ **1** *Adj.* machine *attrib.;* by machine *postpos.* **2** *adv.* by machine; ~ **hergestellt** machine-made
maschinen-, Maschinen-: ~**bau** *der; o. Pl.* (a) machine construction no art.; mechanical engineering no art.; **(b)** (Lehrfach) mechanical engineering no art.; ~**bau·ingenieur** *der* mechanical engineer; ~**ge-schrieben** *Adj.* ⇒ **maschinegeschrieben;** ~**gewehr** *das* machine gun; ~**park** *der* plant; ~**pis-tole** *die* sub-machine gun; ~**schlosser** *der* ▶ 85◀ fitter; ~**schreiben** *das* typing; ~**schrift** *die* typing; (Schriftart) typeface; type
Maschinerie /maʃinəˈriː/ *die;* ~, ~n machinery
***Maschine·schreiben** ⇒ **Maschine** e
Maschinist *der;* ~en, ~en ▶ 85◀ (a) machinist; **(b)** (Schiffs~) engineer

Masern *Pl.* ▶329┃ measles *sing. or pl.*

Maserung *die;* ~, ~**en** (in Holz, Leder) [wavy] grain; (in Marmor) vein; (in Fell) patterning

Maske /'maskə/ *die;* ~, ~**n** (a) (auch fig.) mask; (b) (Theater) make-up

Masken·ball *der* masked ball; masquerade

Maskerade /maskə'ra:də/ *die;* ~, ~**n** [fancy-dress] costume; ~ **sein** (fig.) be a masquerade

maskieren 1 *tr. V.* (a) mask; (b) (verkleiden) dress up. 2 *refl. V.* (a) put on a mask/masks; (b) (sich verkleiden) dress up

Maskierung *die;* ~, ~**en** (a) (das Verkleiden) dressing up; (b) (Verkleidung) disguise; (c) (Tarnung) masking; disguising

Maskottchen /mas'kɔtçən/ *das;* ~s, ~: [lucky] mascot

maskulin /masku'li:n, *auch* '---/ 1 *Adj.* (auch Sprachw.) masculine. 2 *adv.* in a masculine way

Maskulinum /'maskuli:nʊm/ *das;* ~s, **Maskulina** (Sprachw.) masculine noun

Masochismus /mazɔ'xɪsmʊs/ *der;* ~ (Psych.) masochism *no art.*

Masochist /mazɔ'xɪst/ *der;* ~**en**, ~**en** (Psych.) masochist

masochistisch (Psych.) 1 *Adj.* masochistic. 2 *adv.* masochistically

maß 1. u. 3. *Pers. Sg. Prät. v.* **messen**

Maß¹ /ma:s/ *das;* ~**es**, ~**e** (a) measure (**für** of); ~**e und Gewichte** weights and measures; (b) (fig.) **ein gerüttelt** ~ **[an** (*Dat.*) *od.* **von etw.]** (geh.) a good measure [of sth.]; **das** ~ **ist voll** enough is enough; **das** ~ **voll machen** go too far; **mit zweierlei** ~ **messen** apply different [sets of] standards; ~ **halten** exercise moderation; (c) (Größe) measurement; (von Räumen, Möbeln) dimension; measurement; **[bei] jmdm.** ~ **nehmen** take sb.'s measurements; measure sb. [up]; (d) (Grad) measure, degree (**an** + *Dat.* of); **im höchsten** ~**[e]** extremely; exceedingly; (e) **über die** *od.* **alle** ~**en** (geh.) beyond [all] measure

Maß² *die;* ~, ~**[e]** (bayr., österr.) litre [of beer]

Massage /ma'sa:ʒə/ *die;* ~, ~**n** massage

Massage·gerät *das* massager

Massaker /ma'sa:kɐ/ *das;* ~s, ~: massacre

massakrieren *tr. V.* massacre

Maß-: ~**an·zug** *der* made-to-measure suit; tailor-made suit; ~**arbeit** *die* (a) (von Kleidungsstücken) **[eine]** ~**arbeit sein** be made-to-measure; (b) (genaue Arbeit) neat work

Masse /'masə/ *die;* ~, ~**n** (a) mass; (Kochk.) mixture; (b) (Menge) mass; **die** ~ **macht's** (ugs.) it's quantity that's important; **sie kamen in** ~**n** they came in their masses *or* in droves; **das ist eine ganze** ~ (ugs.) that's a lot (coll.) *or* a great deal; (c) (Menschen~) **die breite** ~: the bulk *or* broad mass of the population; (d) (Physik) mass

Maß·einheit *die* unit of measurement

Massen-: ~**an·drang** *der* crush; ~**arbeitslosigkeit** *die* mass unemployment; ~**aufgebot** *das* large body *or* contingent; ~**bewegung** *die* mass movement; ~**blatt** *das* mass-circulation paper; ~**entlassungen** *Pl.* mass redundancies *pl.;* ~**fabrikation** *die* mass production; ~**grab** *das* mass grave

massenhaft 1 *Adj.; nicht präd.* in huge numbers *postpos.;* **das** ~**e Auftreten dieser Schädlinge** the appearance of huge numbers of these pests. 2 *adv.* on a huge *or* massive scale; ~ **Geld haben** (ugs.) have pots of money (coll.)

massen-, Massen-: ~**hysterie** *die* mass hysteria; ~**karambolage** *die* multiple crash; [multiple] pile-up; ~**kundgebung** *die* mass rally; ~**medium** *das* mass medium; ~**mord** *der* mass murder; ~**mörder** *der* mass murderer; ~**produktion** *die* mass production; ~**schlägerei** *die* [grand] free-for-all; pitched battle (fig.); ~**sport** *der* mass sport; ~**tourismus** *der* mass tourism *no art.;* ~**weise** *Adv.* in huge quantities; (in großer Zahl) in huge numbers

Masseur /ma'søːɐ/ *der;* ~s, ~**e** ▶85┃ masseur

Masseurin *die;* ~, ~**nen** ▶85┃ masseuse

Masseuse /ma'søːzə/ *die;* ~, ~**n** ▶85┃ (auch verhüll.) masseuse

Maß·gabe *die:* **nach** ~ (+ *Gen.*) (geh.) in accordance with

maß·gearbeitet *Adj.* custom-made; made-to-measure ⟨*clothes*⟩

maß·gebend, maß·geblich 1 *Adj.* authoritative ⟨*book, expert, opinion*⟩; definitive ⟨*text*⟩; important, influential ⟨*person, circles, etc.*⟩; decisive ⟨*factor, influence, etc.*⟩; (zuständig) competent ⟨*authority, person, etc.*⟩; **sein Urteil ist nicht** ~: his opinion carries no weight. 2 *adv.* ⟨*influence*⟩ considerably, to a considerable extent; (entscheidend) decisively; ~ **an etw.** (*Dat.*) **beteiligt sein** play a leading role in sth.

maß-: ~**geschneidert** *Adj.* made-to-measure; (fig.) tailor-made;*~*|**halten** ⇒ **Maß¹** b

massieren *tr. V.* massage

massig 1 *Adj.* massive; bulky; massive ⟨*figure*⟩. 2 *adv.* (ugs.) ~ **Geld verdienen** earn pots of money (coll.)

mäßig /'mɛːsɪç/ 1 *Adj.* (a) moderate; (b) (gering) moderate, modest ⟨*interest, income, talent, attendance*⟩; (c) (mittel~) mediocre; indifferent; indifferent ⟨*health*⟩. 2 *adv.* (a) in moderation; ~, **aber regelmäßig** (scherzh.) in moderation but regularly; (b) (gering) moderately ⟨*gifted, talented*⟩; (c) (mittel~) indifferently

mäßigen *refl. V.* (geh.) (a) practise *or* exercise moderation (**bei** in); (b) (sich beherrschen) control *or* restrain oneself

Mäßigung *die;* ~: moderation; restraint

massiv /ma'si:f/ 1 *Adj.* (a) solid; ~ **bauen** build solidly; (b) (heftig) massive ⟨*demand*⟩; crude ⟨*accusation, threat*⟩; heavy, strong ⟨*attack, criticism, pressure*⟩. 2 *adv.* ⟨*attack*⟩ heavily, strongly; ⟨*accuse, threaten*⟩ crudely

Massiv *das;* ~s, ~**e** massif

Maß·krug *der* (südd., österr.) litre tankard *or* beer mug; (aus Steingut) stein

maß·los 1 *Adj.* (äußerst) extreme; (übermäßig) inordinate; gross ⟨*exaggeration, insult*⟩; excessive ⟨*demand, claim*⟩; (grenzenlos) boundless ⟨*ambition, greed, sorrow, joy*⟩; extravagant ⟨*spendthrift*⟩. 2 *adv.* (äußerst) extremely; (übermäßig) inordinately; ⟨*exaggerate*⟩ grossly

Maßlosigkeit *die;* ~ ⇒ **maßlos:** extremeness; inordinateness; grossness; excessiveness; boundlessness

Maßnahme *die;* ~, ~**n** measure; ~**n ergreifen** take measures

Maß·regel *die* regulation; (Maßnahme) measure

maßregeln *tr. V.* (zurechtweisen) reprimand; (bestrafen) discipline

Maß·reg[e]lung *die* (Zurechtweisung) reprimand; (Bestrafung) disciplinary measure

Maß·stab *der* (a) standard; **einen hohen** ~ **anlegen/setzen** apply/set a high standard; (b) (Geogr.) scale; **diese Karte hat einen großen/kleinen** ~: this is a large-/small-scale map; **im** ~ **1:100** to a scale of 1:100

maßstab[s]gerecht, maßstab[s]getreu 1 *Adj.* scale *attrib.* ⟨*model, drawing, etc.*⟩; [true] to scale *pred.;* 2 *adv.* to scale

maß·voll 1 *Adj.* moderate; 2 *adv.* in moderation

Mast¹ /mast/ *der;* ~**[e]s**, ~**en**, *auch:* ~**e** (Schiffs~, Antennen~) mast; (Stange, Fahnen~) pole; (Hochspannungs~) pylon

Mast² *die;* ~, ~**en** (Landw.) fattening

Mast·darm *der* (Anat.) rectum

mästen /'mɛstn̩/ *tr. V.* fatten; (fig. ugs.) overfeed

Mast·schwein *das* fattening pig; (gemästet) fattened pig

Mästung *die;* ~: fattening

Masturbation /mastʊrba'tsio:n/ *die;* ~, ~**en** masturbation

masturbieren /mastʊr'bi:rən/ *itr., tr. V.* masturbate

Matador /mata'do:ɐ/ *der;* ~s, ~**e** (a) matador; (b) (fig.) star

---

Match /mɛtʃ/ *das od. der;* ∼[e]s, ∼s *od.* ∼e match

Match·ball *der* ([Tisch]tennis) match point

Material /mate'riːaːl/ *das;* ∼s, ∼ien (a) material; (Bau∼) materials *pl.;* (b) (Hilfsmittel, Utensilien) materials *pl.;* (für den Bau) equipment; (c) (Beweis∼) evidence

Material·fehler *der* material defect

Materialismus *der;* ∼ (auch abwertend) materialism

Materialist *der;* ∼en, ∼en, **Materialistin** *die;* ∼, ∼en (auch abwertend) materialist

materialistisch (auch abwertend) **1** *Adj.* materialistic. **2** *adv.* materialistically

Material-: ∼kosten *Pl.* cost *sing.* of materials; ∼sammlung *die* collection *or* gathering of material; ∼schlacht *die* (Milit.) battle of matériel

Materie /ma'teːriə/ *die;* ∼, ∼n (a) matter; (b) (geh.: Thema, Gegenstand) subject

materiell /mate'riɛl/ **1** *Adj.* (a) (stofflich) material; physical; (b) (wirtschaftlich) material ⟨*value, damage*⟩; (finanziell) financial. **2** *adv.* (wirtschaftlich) materially; (finanziell) financially

Mathe /'matə/ *o. Art.* (Schülerspr.) maths *sing.* (Brit. coll.); math (Amer. coll.)

Mathe·arbeit *die* (Schülerspr.) maths test (coll.)

Mathematik /matəma'tiːk/ *die;* ∼: mathematics *sing.,* no *art.*

Mathematiker *der;* ∼s, ∼, **Mathematikerin** *die;* ∼, ∼nen mathematician

Mathematik·unterricht *der* mathematics teaching/ lesson; *s. auch* **Englischunterricht**

mathematisch **1** *Adj.* mathematical. **2** *adv.* mathematically

Matinee /mati'neː/ *die;* ∼, ∼n matinée

Matjes /'matjəs/ *der;* ∼, ∼: matie [herring]

Matjes-: ∼filet *das* filleted matie [herring]; ∼hering *der* salted matie [herring]

Matratze /ma'tratsə/ *die;* ∼, ∼n mattress

Matriarchat /matriar'çaːt/ *das;* ∼[e]s, ∼e matriarchy

Matrize /ma'triːtsə/ *die;* ∼, ∼n (Druckw.) (a) matrix; (b) (Folie) stencil

Matrone /ma'troːnə/ *die;* ∼, ∼n matron

Matrose /ma'troːzə/ *der;* ∼n, ∼n ▶85◀ (a) sailor; seaman; (b) (Dienstgrad) ordinary seaman

Matrosen-: ∼an·zug *der* sailor suit; ∼mütze *die* sailor's cap

Matsch *der;* ∼[e]s (ugs.) (a) (aufgeweichter Boden) mud; (breiiger Schmutz) sludge; (Schnee∼) slush; (b) (Brei) mush

matschig *Adj.* (ugs.) (a) muddy; slushy ⟨*snow*⟩; (b) (weich) mushy; squashy ⟨*fruit*⟩

matt /mat/ **1** *Adj.* (a) weak; weary ⟨*limbs, spirit, etc.*⟩; weak, faint ⟨*voice, smile, pulse*⟩; feeble ⟨*applause, reaction*⟩; limp, feeble ⟨*handshake*⟩; faint ⟨*echo*⟩; (b) (glanzlos) matt ⟨*paper, polish, etc.*⟩; dull ⟨*metal, mirror, etc.*⟩; dull, lustreless ⟨*eyes, look*⟩; (c) (undurchsichtig) frosted ⟨*glass*⟩; pearl ⟨*lightbulb*⟩; (d) (gedämpft) soft, subdued ⟨*light*⟩; soft, pale ⟨*colour*⟩; (e) (beim Schachspiel) [**Schach und**] ∼! checkmate!; ∼ **sein** be checkmated; **jmdn.** ∼ **setzen** (auch fig.) checkmate sb. **2** *adv.* (a) (kraftlos) weakly; ⟨*smile*⟩ weakly, faintly; ⟨*applaud, react*⟩ feebly; (b) (gedämpft) softly ⟨*lit*⟩; (c) (mäßig) ⟨*protest, contradict*⟩ feebly, weakly

Matt *das;* ∼s (Schach) [check]mate

matt·blau *Adj.* pale blue

Matte /'matə/ *die;* ∼, ∼n mat

Matthäus /ma'tɛːʊs/ (*der*); **Matthäus'** Matthew

Mattigkeit *die;* ∼: weakness; (Erschöpfung) weariness

Matt·scheibe *die* (ugs.) telly (Brit. coll.); box (coll.)

Matura *die;* ∼ (österr., schweiz.) ⇒ **Abitur**

Matz /mats/ *der;* ∼es, ∼e *od.* **Mätze** /'mɛtsə/ (fam.) kleiner ∼: little man

Mätzchen /'mɛtsçən/ *Pl.* (ugs.) **lasst die** ∼: stop fooling about *or* around; stop your antics; ∼ **machen** fool about *or* around

mau /mau/ (ugs.) **1** *Adj.; nicht attr.* (flau) queasy; (unwohl) poorly. **2** *adv.* badly; **die Geschäfte gehen** ∼: business is bad

Mauer /'mauɐ/ *die;* ∼, ∼n (auch fig., Sport) wall; **die [Berliner]** ∼ (hist.) the [Berlin] Wall; **die Chinesische** ∼: the Great Wall of China

Mauer·blümchen *das* (ugs.) (beim Tanz) wallflower (coll.); (unscheinbares Mädchen, auch fig.) Cinderella

mauern 1 *tr. V.* build; **gemauert** (aus Ziegeln) brick ⟨*chimney, wall, etc.*⟩. **2** *itr. V.* (a) lay bricks; (b) (Ballspiele) play defensively; (c) (Kartenspiele) hold back one's good cards

Mauer-: ∼segler *der* swift; ∼vorsprung *der* projecting section of a/the wall; ∼werk *das* (a) (aus Stein) stonework; masonry; (aus Ziegeln) brickwork; (b) (Mauern) walls *pl.*

Maul /maul/ *das;* ∼[e]s, **Mäuler** /'mɔylɐ/ (a) (von Tieren) mouth; (b) (derb: Mund) gob (sl.); **er hat fünf hungrige Mäuler zu stopfen** (fig.) he's got five hungry mouths to feed; **das** *od.* **sein** ∼ **aufmachen** (fig.) say something; **ein großes** ∼ **haben** (fig.) shoot one's mouth off (fig. sl.); **halts** ∼ *od.* **halt dein** ∼: shut your trap (sl.); shut up (coll.); *s. auch* **stopfen 1 d; verbrennen 2 b**

Maul·beer·baum *der* mulberry tree

maulen *itr. V.* (salopp) grouse (coll.); moan; grumble

maul-, Maul-: ∼esel *der* mule; (Zool.) hinny; ∼faul *Adj.* (ugs. abwertend) uncommunicative; taciturn; ∼held *der* (ugs. abwertend) loudmouth; braggart; ∼korb *der* (auch fig.) muzzle; **einem Hund**/(fig.) **jmdm. einen** ∼ **anlegen** muzzle a dog/sb.; ∼sperre *die* (salopp) **die** ∼sperre **kriegen** (fig.) gape in surprise; ∼tasche *die* (Kochk.) filled pasta case [*served in soup*]; ∼tier *das* mule; ∼-**und Klauen·seuche** *die* (Tiermed.) foot-and-mouth disease

Maul·wurf *der* mole

Maulwurfs-: ∼haufen *der,* ∼hügel *der* molehill

maunzen /'mauntsn/ *itr. V.* (ugs.) ⟨*cat*⟩ miaow plaintively

Maurer /'maurɐ/ *der;* ∼s, ∼: ▶85◀ bricklayer

Maurer-: ∼kelle *die* brick [-layer's] trowel; ∼meister *der* master bricklayer

Maus /maus/ *die;* ∼, **Mäuse** /'mɔyzə/ (a) mouse; **weiße Mäuse sehen** (fig. ugs.) see pink elephants; **eine graue** ∼ (fig. ugs. abwertend) a colourless nondescript sort of [a] person; *s. auch* **Katz, Katze;** (b) *Pl.* (salopp: Geld) bread *sing.* (sl.); dough *sing.* (sl.)

Mauschelei *die;* ∼, ∼en (ugs. abwertend) shady wheeling and dealing *no indef. art.*

mauscheln /'mauʃln/ *itr. V.* (ugs. abwertend) engage in shady wheeling and dealing

Mäuschen /'mɔysçən/ *das;* ∼s, ∼ (a) little mouse; ∼ **sein** *od.* **spielen** (fig. ugs.) be a fly on the wall (coll.); (b) (fig. ugs.) **mein** ∼: my sweet

mäuschen·still *Adj., adv.* ⇒ **mucksmäuschenstill**

Mause-: ∼falle *die* mousetrap; (fig.) trap; ∼loch *das* mouse-hole

Mauser *die;* ∼: moult; **in der** ∼ **sein** be moulting

mausern *refl. V.* moult; **sich zur Dame** ∼ (fig. ugs.) blossom into a lady

mause·tot *Adj.* (ugs.) [as] dead as a doornail *pred.;* stone-dead

maus-: ∼grau *Adj.* mouse-grey; ∼klick *der;* ∼s, ∼s (DV) mouse click; ∼taste *die* (DV) mouse button; ∼zeiger *der* (DV) mouse pointer

Mausoleum /mauzo'leːʊm/ *das;* ∼s, **Mausoleen** mausoleum

Maut /maut/ *die;* ∼, ∼en toll

Max /maks/: **strammer Max** fried egg on ham and bread

Maxi- /'maksi-/ maxi-⟨*coat, skirt, etc., single*⟩

maximal /maksi'maːl/ **1** *Adj.* maximum. **2** *adv.* **bis zu** ∼ 85 °C/20 t up to a maximum of 85 °C/20 t

Maximal·forderung *die* maximum demand

Maxime /ma'ksiːmə/ *die;* ∼, ∼n maxim

maximieren *tr. V.* maximize

Maximierung *die;* ∼, ∼en maximization

Maximum /'maksimʊm/ *das;* ∼s, **Maxima** maximum (an + *Dat.* of)

Mayonnaise /majɔ'nɛːzə/ *die;* ~, ~n mayonnaise

MAZ /mats/ *die;* ~ (Ferns.) VTR

Mäzen /mɛ'tseːn/ *der;* ~s, ~e (geh.) patron

MdB, M.d.B. *Abk.* **Mitglied des Bundestages** Member of the Bundestag

MdL, M.d.L. *Abk.* **Mitglied des Landtages** Member of the Landtag

MdNR *Abk.* **Mitglied des Nationalrates** (Österreich) Member of the Nationalrat

m.E. *Abk.* **meines Erachtens** in my opinion *or* view

Mechanik /me'çaːnɪk/ *die;* ~ (a) (Physik) mechanics *sing., no art.;* (b) (Mechanismus) mechanism; (c) (Funktion) mechanics *sing. or pl.*

Mechaniker *der;* ~s, ~, **Mechanikerin** *die;* ~, ~nen ▶ 85 ◀ mechanic

mechanisch 1 *Adj.* mechanical; power *attrib.* ⟨loom, press⟩. 2 *adv.* mechanically

Mechanismus *der;* ~, **Mechanismen** (auch fig.) mechanism

Meckerei *die;* ~, ~en (ugs. abwertend) moaning; grousing (sl.); grumbling

Meckerer *der;* ~s, ~ (ugs. abwertend) moaner; grouser (sl.); grumbler

meckern /'mɛkɐn/ *itr. V.* (a) (auch fig.) bleat; (b) (ugs. abwertend: nörgeln) grumble; moan; grouse (sl.); **etw. zu** ~ **haben** have sth. to grumble *etc.* about

Mecklenburg-Vorpommer *der;* ~n, ~n Mecklenburg-West Pomeranian

mecklenburg-vorpommerisch *Adj.* Mecklenburg-West Pomeranian

Mecklenburg-Vorpommern (*das*); ~s Mecklenburg-West Pomerania

Medaille /me'daljə/ *die;* ~, ~n medal; *s. auch* **Kehrseite** a

Medaillen·gewinner *der* medallist; medal winner

Medaillon /medal'jõ/ *das;* ~s, ~s (a) locket; (b) (Kochk., bild. Kunst) medallion

Medien ⇨ **Medium**

Medien- media ⟨concern, policy, syndicate, etc.⟩

Medikament /medika'mɛnt/ *das;* ~[e]s, ~e medicine; (Droge) drug; **ein** ~ **gegen Kopfschmerzen** a remedy for headaches

medikamentös /medikamɛn'tøːs/ 1 *Adj.* ⟨treatment⟩ with drugs. 2 *adv.* ⟨treat, cure⟩ with drugs

Meditation /medita'tsi̯oːn/ *die;* ~, ~en meditation

meditieren /medi'tiːrən/ *itr. V.* meditate (**über** + *Akk.* [up]on)

Medium /'meːdi̯ʊm/ *das;* ~s, **Medien** medium

Medizin /medi'tsiːn/ *die;* ~, ~en (a) *o. Pl.* medicine *no art.;* (b) (Heilmittel) medicine (**gegen** for)

Mediziner /medi'tsiːnɐ/ *der;* ~s, ~, **Medizinerin** *die;* ~, ~nen ▶ 85 ◀ doctor; (Student) medical student

medizinisch 1 *Adj.* (a) medical ⟨journal, problem, etc.⟩; ~e **Fakultät** faculty of medicine; (b) (heilend) medicinal ⟨bath etc.⟩; medicated ⟨toothpaste, soap, etc.⟩. 2 *adv.* medically

Medizin-: ~**mann** *der; Pl.* ~**männer** medicine man; ~**student** *der,* ~**studentin** *die* medical student

Meer /meːɐ̯/ *das;* ~[e]s, ~e (auch fig.) sea; (Welt~) ocean; **ans** ~ **fahren** go to the seaside; **am** ~: by the sea; **aufs** ~ **hinausfahren** go out to sea; **übers** ~ **fahren** cross the sea; **1 000 m über dem** ~: 1 000 m above sealevel

Meer-: ~**busen** *der* gulf; ~**enge** *die* straits *pl.;* strait

Meeres-: ~**biologie** *die* marine biology *no art.;* ~**boden** *der* sea bed *or* bottom *or* floor; ~**bucht** *die* bay; ~**fauna** *die* marine fauna; ~**früchte** *Pl.* (Kochk.) seafood *sing.;* ~**klima** *das* maritime climate; ~**luft** *die* (Met.) maritime air; ~**spiegel** *der* sealevel; **20 m über/unter dem** ~**spiegel** 20 m above/below sealevel; ~**strömung** *die* current; (im Weltmeer) ocean current

meer-, Meer-: ~**jungfrau** *die* mermaid; ~**katze** *die* guenon; ~**rettich** *der* horse-radish; ~**salz** *das* sea salt; ~**schaum** *der* meerschaum; ~**schweinchen** *das* guinea pig; ~**wasser** *das* sea water

Mega- /'mɛga-/ mega⟨watt, -ton, -hertz, etc.⟩

Megaphon *das;* ~s, ~e megaphone; loud hailer

Mehl /meːl/ *das;* ~[e]s (a) flour; (gröber) meal; (b) (Pulver) powder; (Knochen~, Fisch~) meal

mehlig *Adj.* (a) floury; (b) (wie Mehl) powdery ⟨sand etc.⟩; (c) mealy ⟨potato, apple, etc.⟩

Mehl-: ~**schwitze** *die* (Kochk.) roux; ~**speise** *die* (österr.) sweet; dessert; ~**tau** *der* mildew

mehr /meːɐ̯/ 1 *Indefinitpron.* more; **ein Grund** ~, **es zu tun** one more *or* an additional reason for doing it; **das war** ~ **als unverschämt** that was impertinent, to say the very least; **das schmeckt nach** ~ (ugs.) it's very moreish (coll.); ~ **nicht?** is that all?; ~ **oder minder** *od.* **weniger** more or less. 2 *adv.* (a) (in größerem Maße) more; (b) (eher) ~ **schlecht als recht** after a fashion; **er ist** ~ **Künstler als Gelehrter** he is more of an artist than a scholar; (c) **nicht** ~: not ... any more; no longer; **es war niemand** ~ **da** there was no one left; **es hat sich keiner** ~ **gemeldet** there was not another word from anyone; **ich erinnere mich nicht** ~: I no longer remember; **das wird nie** ~ **vorkommen** it will never happen again; **davon will ich nichts** ~ **hören** I don't want to hear any more about it; **da ist nichts** ~ **zu machen** there is nothing more to be done; **ich habe keine Lust/kein Interesse** ~: I have lost all desire/interest; **du bist doch kein Kind** ~: you're no longer a child; you're not a child any more; **sie hat ihren Großvater nicht** ~ **gekannt** she never hat the chance to know her grandfather; (d) **ich habe nur** ~ **5 Mark** (südd., österr., schweiz.) I've only 5 marks left

Mehr *das;* ~s: **ein** ~ **an Zeit** (*Dat.*) *usw.* more time *etc.*

mehr-, Mehr-: ~**aufwand** *der* additional expenditure *no pl.;* ~**bändig** *Adj.* in several volumes *postpos.;* ~**belastung** *die* extra *or* additional burden (*Gen.* on); ~**deutig** 1 *Adj.* ambiguous; 2 *adv.* ambiguously; ~**deutigkeit** *die;* ~, ~en ambiguity; ~**einnahme** *die* additional revenue

mehren (geh.) 1 *tr. V.* increase. 2 *refl. V.* increase

mehrer... *Indefinitpron.* (a) *attr.* several; a number of; (verschieden) various; several; ~**e hundert Bücher** several hundred[s of] books; (b) *allein stehend* ~**e** several people; **sie kamen zu** ~**en** several of them came

Mehr·erlös *der* extra *or* additional proceeds *pl.*

mehr·fach 1 *Adj.; nicht präd.* multiple; (wiederholt) repeated; **ein Bericht in** ~**er Ausfertigung** several copies *pl.* of a report; **der** ~**e deutsche Meister** the player/sprinter *etc.* who has been German champion several times; **ein** ~**er Millionär** a multimillionaire. 2 *adv.* several times; (wiederholt) repeatedly; ~ **vorbestraft sein** have several previous convictions

mehr-, Mehr-: ~**familienhaus** *das* multiple dwelling (formal); large house with several flats (Brit.) *or* (Amer.) apartments; ~**farbig** *Adj.* multi-coloured; [multi-]colour *attrib.;* ~**geschossig** *Adj.* ⇨ **stöckig**

Mehrheit *die;* ~, ~en majority; **in der** ~ **sein** be in the majority; **die** ~ **haben/erringen** have/win a majority; **die** ~ **verlieren** lose one's majority; **er wurde mit großer** ~ **gewählt** he was elected by a large majority; **die einfache/relative/absolute** ~ (Politik) a simple/a relative/an absolute majority

mehrheitlich 1 *Adj.; nicht präd.* majority; of the majority *postpos.* 2 *adv.* by a majority

Mehrheits-: ~**entscheidung** *die* majority decision; ~**fähig** *Adj.* ~**fähig sein** ⟨law⟩ be capable of securing a majority; ⟨party⟩ be capable of forming a majority; ~**wahlrecht** *das* first-past-the-post electoral system

mehr-, Mehr-: ~**jährig** *Adj.; nicht präd.* lasting several years *postpos.;* **eine** ~**jährige Erfahrung** several years' experience; several years of experience; ~**kampf** *der* (Sport) multi-discipline event; ~**kosten** *Pl.* additional *or* extra costs; ~**malig** *Adj.; nicht präd.* repeated; ~**mals** *Adv.* several times; (wiederholt) repeatedly; ~**parteien·system** *das* multi-party system; ~**seitig** *Adj.* consisting of several pages *postpos., not pred.;* several pages long *postpos.;* ~**silbig** *Adj.* polysyllabic; ~**spra-chig** *Adj.* multilingual; ~**sprachigkeit** *die* multilingualism; ~**stimmig** (Musik) **1** *Adj.* for several voices *postpos.;* **ein** ~**stimmiges Lied** a part-song; **2** *adv.* ~**stimmig singen** sing in harmony; ~**stöckig** *Adj.* several storeys high *postpos.;* (vielstöckig) multi-storey; ~**stufig** *Adj.* consisting of several steps *postpos., not pred.;* multi-stage 〈*rocket*〉; ~**stündig** *Adj.; nicht präd.* lasting several hours *postpos., not pred.;* 〈*delay*〉 of several hours; ~**stündige Verhandlungen** several hours of negotiations; ~**tägig** *Adj.; nicht präd.* lasting several days *postpos., not pred.;* ~**teilig** *Adj.* in several parts *postpos.;* ~**weg·flasche** *die* returnable *or* reusable bottle; ~**weg·verpackung** *die* reusable packaging; ~**wert·steuer** *die* (Wirtsch.) value added tax (Brit.); VAT (Brit.); sales tax (Amer.); ~**wöchig** *Adj.; nicht präd.* lasting several weeks *postpos., not pred.;* 〈*absence*〉 of several weeks; ~**zahl** *die; o. Pl.* (a) (Sprachw.) plural; (b) (Mehrheit) majority

Mehr·zweck-: multi-purpose

meiden /'maidn̩/ *unr. tr. V.* (geh.) avoid

Meile /'mailə/ *die;* ~, ~**n** ▶ **224**▎, ▶ **340**▎ mile; **das riecht man drei** ~**n gegen den Wind** (abwertend) you can smell it a mile off; (fig.) you can tell that a mile off; it stands out a mile

Meilen·stein *der* (auch fig.) milestone

meilen·weit 1 *Adj.* 〈*distance*〉 of many miles. **2** *adv.* for miles; ~ **entfernt** (auch fig.) miles away (**von** from)

Meiler *der;* ~**s**, ~ (a) charcoal kiln; (b) (Atom~) [atomic] pile

mein /main/ *Possessivpron.* my; ~**e Damen und Herren** ladies and gentlemen; **das Buch dort, ist das** ~**[e]s?** that book over there, is it mine?; **was** ~ **ist, ist auch dein** what's mine is yours; **das Meine** *od.* ~**e** (geh.: Eigentum) my possessions *pl. or* property; **ich habe das Meine** *od.* ~**e getan** (was ich konnte) I have done what I could; (meinen Teil) I have done my share; **sie kann Mein und Dein nicht unterscheiden** (scherzh.) she doesn't understand that some things don't belong to her; **die Meinen** (geh.) my family

Mein·eid *der* perjury *no indef. art.;* **einen** ~ **schwören** perjure oneself; commit perjury

meinen 1 *itr. V.* think; **[ganz] wie Sie** ~**!** whatever you think; (wie Sie möchten) [just] as you wish; ~ **Sie?** do you think so?; **ich meine ja nur [so]** (ugs.) it was just an idea *or* a thought. **2** *tr. V.* (a) (denken, glauben) think; **man sollte** ~, ...: one would think *or* would have thought ...; **das meine ich auch** I think so too; (b) (sagen wollen, im Sinn haben) mean; **was meint er damit?** what does he mean by that?; **das habe ich nicht gemeint** that's not what I meant; (c) (beabsichtigen) mean; intend; **er meint es gut/ehrlich** he means well *or* his intentions are good/his intentions are honest; **es gut mit jmdm.** ~**:** mean well by sb.; **er hat es nicht so gemeint** (ugs.) he didn't mean it like that; (d) (sagen) say

meiner *Gen. von* **ich** (geh.) **gedenke** ~**:** remember me; **erbarme dich** ~**:** have mercy upon me

meinerseits *Adv.* (von meiner Seite) on my part; (auf meiner Seite) for my part; **ganz** ~**:** the pleasure is [all] mine

meinesgleichen *indekl. Pron.* people *pl.* like me *or* myself; (abwertend) the likes *pl.* of me; my sort *or* kind

meinetwegen *Adv.* (a) because of me; on my account; (für mich) on my behalf; (mir zuliebe) for my sake; (um mich) about me; (b) /*auch* -'--/ (ugs.) as far as I'm concerned; ~**!** if you like; **also gut,** ~**!** fair enough!; (c) (zum Beispiel) for instance

meinetwillen *Adv. in* **um** ~**:** for my sake

Meinung *die;* ~, ~**en** opinion (**zu** on, **über** + *Akk.* about); **eine vorgefasste/gegenteilige** ~ **haben** have preconceived ideas *pl.*/hold an opposite opinion; **anderer/geteilter** ~ **sein** be of a different opinion/differing opinions *pl.;* hold a different view/differing views *pl.;* **nach meiner** ~, **meiner** ~ **nach** in my opinion *or* view; **ganz meine** ~**:** I agree entirely; **einer** ~ **sein** be of *or* share the same opinion; **die öffentliche** ~**:** public opinion; **jmdm. [gehörig] die** ~ **sagen** give sb. a [good] piece of one's mind

meinungs-, Meinungs-: ~**äußerung** *die* [expression of] opinion; **das Recht auf freie** ~**äußerung** the right of free speech; ~**austausch** *der* exchange of views; ~**forscher** *der* opinion pollster *or* researcher; ~**forschung** *die* opinion research; ~**forschungs·institut** *das* opinion research institute; ~**freiheit** *die* freedom to form and express one's own opinions; (Redefreiheit) freedom of speech; ~**umfrage** *die* [public] opinion poll; ~**umschwung** *der* swing of opinion; ~**verschiedenheit** *die* (auch verhüll.: Streit) difference of opinion

Meise /'maizə/ *die;* ~, ~**n** tit[mouse]; **eine** ~ **haben** (salopp) be nuts (sl.); be off one's head (coll.)

Meißel /'maisl̩/ *der;* ~**s**, ~**:** chisel

meißeln 1 *tr. V.* chisel; carve 〈*statue, sculpture*〉 with a chisel. **2** *itr. V.* chisel; work with a chisel; carve

meist /maist/ *Adv.* mostly; usually; (zum größten Teil) mostly; for the most part; **er hat** ~ **keine Zeit** he doesn't usually have any time

meist... 1 *Indefinitpron. u. unbest. Zahlw.* most; **das** ~**e Geld haben** have [the] most money; **die** ~**en Leute haben ...:** most people have ...; **die** ~**en Leute, die da waren** most of the people who were there; **die** ~**e Zeit des Jahres** most of the year; **er hat das** ~**e vergessen** he has forgotten most of it. **2** *Adv.* **am** ~**en** most; **die am** ~**en befahrene Straße** the most used road; **darüber habe ich mich am** ~**en gefreut** that pleased me [the] most

meist·bietend *adv.* etw. ~**bietend versteigern/ver-kaufen** auction sth. off/sell sth. to the highest bidder

meistens /'maistn̩s/ *Adv.* ⇒ **meist**

meistenteils *Adv.* for the most part

Meister /'maistɐ/ *der;* ~**s**, ~ (a) master craftsman; **seinen** ~ **machen** (ugs.) get one's master craftsman's diploma *or* certificate; (b) (Vorgesetzter) (in der Fabrik, auf der Baustelle) foreman; (in anderen Betrieben) boss (coll.); (c) (geh.: Könner) master; **es ist noch kein** ~ **vom Himmel gefallen** (Spr.) you can't always expect to get it right first time; [**in jmdm.**] **seinen** ~ **gefunden haben** have met one's match [in sb.]; (d) (Künstler, geh.: Lehrer) master; (e) (Sport) champion; (Mannschaft) champions *pl.;* (f) (salopp: Anrede) chief (coll.); guv (Brit. sl.); (g) ~ **Lampe** Master Hare; ~ **Petz** Bruin the Bear

Meister·brief *der* master craftsman's diploma *or* certificate

meisterhaft 1 *Adj.* masterly. **2** *adv.* in a masterly manner; **es** ~ **verstehen, etw. zu tun** be a [past]master *or* an expert at doing sth.

Meister·hand *die* master-hand; **von** ~**:** by a master-hand

Meisterin *die;* ~, ~**nen** (a) master craftswoman; (b) (geh.: Könnerin) master; (c) (Sport) [women's] champion

Meister·leistung *die* masterly performance; (Meisterstück) masterpiece; (geniale Tat) master-stroke

meistern *tr. V.* master; master, overcome 〈*problem, difficulty*〉; control 〈*anger, excitement, etc.*〉; **sein Schicksal/Leben** ~**:** cope with one's fate/with life

Meister·prüfung *die* examination for the/one's master craftsman's diploma *or* certificate

Meisterschaft *die;* ~, ~**en** (a) *o. Pl.* mastery; (b) (Sport) championship; (Veranstaltung) championships *pl.;* **die** ~ **erringen** take the championship

Meisterschafts·spiel *das* (Sport) championship match *or* game

Meister-: ~**singer** *der* Meistersinger; mastersinger; ~**stück** *das* (a) piece of work executed to qualify as a master craftsman; (b) (Meisterleistung) masterpiece (**an** + *Dat.* of); (geniale Tat) master-stroke; ~**titel** *der* (a) (Sport) championship [title]; (b) (im Handwerksberuf) title of master craftsman; ~**werk** *das* masterpiece (**an** + *Dat.* of)

Mekka /'mɛka/ *(das);* ~**s** ▶ **490**▎ Mecca

Melancholie /melaŋko'li:/ *die;* ~, ~**n** melancholy; (Psych.) melancholia

Melancholiker /melaŋ'ko:likɐ/ *der;* ~**s**, ~, **Melancholikerin** *die;* ~, ~**nen** melancholic

melancholisch 1 *Adj.* melancholy; melancholy, melancholic ‹*person, temperament*›. 2 *adv.* melancholically
Melange /me'lã:ʒ(ə)/ *die;* ~, ~n (österr.) ⇒ **Milchkaffee**
melden /'mɛldn̩/ 1 *tr. V.* (a) report; (registrieren lassen) register ‹*birth, death, etc.*› (*Dat.* with); **wie soeben gemeldet wird** (Fernseh., Rundf.) according to reports just coming in; **jmdn. als vermisst** ~: report sb. missing; **nichts/nicht viel zu** ~ **haben** (ugs.) have no/little say; (b) (ankündigen) announce; (c) (Schülerspr.) **jmdn.** ~: tell on sb. 2 *refl. V.* (a) report; **sich freiwillig** ~: volunteer (**zu** for); **sich auf eine Anzeige** ~: reply to *or* answer an advertisement; **sich zu einer Prüfung** ~: enter for an examination; **polizeilich gemeldet sein** be registered with the police; (b) (am Telefon) answer; **es meldet sich niemand** there is no answer *or* reply; (c) (ums Wort bitten) put one's hand up; (d) (von sich hören lassen) get in touch (**bei** with); **wenn du etwas brauchst, melde dich** if you need anything let me/us know; **Otto 2, bitte** ~! Otto 2, come in please!
Melde·pflicht *die* (Verwaltung) obligation to register with the authorities; **polizeiliche** ~ obligation to register with the police
melde·pflichtig *Adj.* (Gesundheitsw.) notifiable ‹*disease*›
Meldung *die;* ~, ~en (a) report; (Nachricht) piece of news; (Ankündigung) announcement; ~**en vom Sport** sports news *sing.;* (b) ~ **machen** *od.* **erstatten** (Milit.) report; make a report; (c) (Anmeldung) (bei einem Wettbewerb, Examen) entry; (bei einem Kurs) enrolment; **wir bitten um freiwillige** ~**en** we are asking *or* calling for volunteers; (d) (Wort~) request to speak; **gibt es noch weitere** ~**en?** does anyone else wish to speak?
meliert /mɛ'li:ɐt/ *Adj.* mottled; **braun** ~: mottled brown; [**grau**] ~**es Haar** hair streaked with grey
Melisse /me'lɪsə/ *die;* ~, ~n melissa; balm
melken /'mɛlkn̩/ *regelm., unr. tr. V.* milk
Melk·maschine *die* milking machine
Melodie /melo'di:/ *die;* ~, ~n melody; (Weise) tune; melody; **nach einer** ~: to a melody/tune
Melodik /me'lo:dɪk/ *die;* ~ (Musik) melodic characteristics *pl.;* (Lehre) theory of melody
melodisch 1 *Adj.* melodic; melodious. 2 *adv.* melodically; melodiously; ~ **sprechen** speak in a melodic *or* melodious voice
melodramatisch *Adj.* melodramatic
Melone /me'lo:nə/ *die;* ~, ~n (a) melon; (b) (ugs. scherzh.) bowler [hat]
Membran /mɛm'bra:n/ *die;* ~, ~en, **Membrane** *die;* ~, ~n (a) (Technik) diaphragm; (b) (Biol., Chemie) membrane
Memoiren /me'moa:rən/ *Pl.* memoirs
Memorandum /memo'randʊm/ *das;* ~s, **Memoranden** *od.* **Memoranda** memorandum
Menge /'mɛŋə/ *die;* ~, ~n (a) (Quantum) quantity; amount; **die dreifache** ~: three times *or* triple the amount; (b) (große Anzahl) large number; lot (coll.); **eine** ~ **Leute** a lot *or* lots *pl.* of people (coll.); **er weiß eine** [**ganze**] ~ (ugs.) he knows [quite] a lot (coll.) *or* a great deal; **sie bildet sich eine** ~ **ein** (ugs.) she is very conceited; **jede** ~ **Arbeit/Alkohol** *usw.* (ugs.) masses *pl.* or loads *pl.* of work/alcohol *etc.* (coll.); *s. auch* **rau 1 h;** (c) (Menschen~) crowd; throng; (d) (Math.) set
mengen *tr. V.* (veralt.) mix
mengen-, Mengen-: ~**lehre** *die; o. Pl.* set theory *no art.;* ~**mäßig** 1 *Adj.* quantitative; 2 *adv.* quantitatively; ~**rabatt** *der* (Wirtsch.) bulk discount
Meningitis /meniŋ'gi:tɪs/ *die;* ~, **Meningitiden** ▶ 329 (Med.) meningitis
Meniskus /me'nɪskʊs/ *der;* ~, **Menisken** ▶ 326 (Anat., Optik) meniscus
Mennige /'mɛnɪgə/ *die;* ~: red lead
Mensa /'mɛnza/ *die;* ~, ~s *od.* **Mensen** refectory, canteen (*of university, college*)
Mensch /mɛnʃ/ *der;* ~en, ~en (a) (Gattung) **der** ~: man; **die** ~**en** man *sing.;* human beings; mankind *sing. no art.;* **nur noch ein halber** ~ **sein** be just about all

in; **wieder ein** ~ **sein** (ugs.) feel like a human being again; (b) (Person) person; man/woman; ~**en** people; **kein** ~: no one; **unter die** ~**en gehen** mix with people; **wie der erste** ~/**die ersten** ~**en:** extremely awkwardly; **von** ~ **zu** ~: man to man/woman to woman; ~, **ärgere dich nicht** (Gesellschaftsspiel) ludo; (c) (salopp: Anrede) (bewundernd) wow; (erstaunt) wow; good grief; (vorwurfsvoll) for heaven's sake; ~, **war das ein Glück!** boy, that was a piece of luck!; ~ **Meier!** good grief!
menschen-, Menschen-: ~**affe** *der* anthropoid [ape]; ~**auflauf** *der* crowd [of people]; ~**feindlich** 1 *Adj.* (a) misanthropic; (b) (unmenschlich) inhuman ‹*system, policy etc.*›; ‹*environment*› hostile to man; 2 *adv.* (a) misanthropically; (b) (unmenschlich) inhumanly; ~**fresser** *der* (ugs.) cannibal; (Mythol.) maneater; ~**freundlichkeit** *die; o. Pl.* philanthropy; **aus reiner** ~**freundlichkeit** out of the sheer goodness of one's heart; ~**führung** *die* leadership; ~**gedenken** *das:* **das wird seit** ~**gedenken so gemacht** it has been done that way for as long as anyone can remember; **der heißeste Sommer seit** ~**gedenken** the hottest summer in living memory; ~**gestalt** *die* human form; **ein Engel/Teufel** *od.* **Satan in** ~**gestalt sein** be an angel in human form/the devil incarnate; ~**hand** *die:* **von** ~**hand** (geh.) ‹*created*› by the hand of man, by human hand; ~**handel** *der* trade *or* traffic in human beings; (Sklavenhandel) slave trade; ~**händler** *der* trafficker [in human beings]; (Sklavenhändler) slave trader; ~**kenntnis** *die; o. Pl.* ability to judge character *or* human nature; ~**kette** *die* human chain; ~**leben** *das* life; **der Unfall forderte vier** ~**leben** (geh.) the accident claimed four lives; ~**leer** *Adj.* deserted; ~**menge** *die* crowd [of people]; ~**möglich** *Adj.; nicht attr.* humanly possible; **das Menschenmögliche tun** do all that is/was humanly possible; ~**opfer** *das* human sacrifice; ~**raub** *der* kidnapping; abduction; ~**recht** *das* human right; ~**rechts·verletzung** *die* human rights violation; ~**rechts·konvention** *die* Human Rights Convention; ~**schlag** *der* race *or* breed [of people]; ~**seele** *die:* **keine** ~**seele** not a [living] soul
Menschens·kind: ~! (salopp) (erstaunt) good heavens; good grief; (vorwurfsvoll) for heaven's sake
menschen-, Menschen-: ~**unwürdig** 1 *Adj.* ‹*accommodation*› unfit for human habitation; ‹*conditions*› unfit for human beings; ‹*behaviour*› unworthy of a human being; 2 *adv.* ‹*treat*› in a degrading and inhumane way; ‹*live, be housed*› in conditions unfit for human beings; ~**verachtung** *die* contempt for humanity *or* mankind; ~**verstand** *der* human intelligence *or* intellect; *s. auch* **gesund;** ~**würde** *die* human dignity *no art.;* ~**würdig** 1 *Adj.* humane ‹*treatment*›; ‹*accommodation*› fit for human habitation; ‹*conditions*› fit for human beings; 2 *adv.* ‹*treat*› humanely; ‹*live, be housed*› in conditions fit for human beings
Menschheit *die;* ~: mankind *no art.;* humanity *no art.*
Menschheits-: ~**entwicklung** *die* evolution of man; ~**traum** *der* dream of mankind
menschlich 1 *Adj.* (a) human; ~**es Versagen** human error; *s. auch* **irren a;** (b) (annehmbar) civilized; (c) (human) humane ‹*person, treatment, etc.*›; human ‹*trait, emotion, etc.*›. 2 *adv.* (a) **er ist** ~ **sympathisch** I like him as a person; **sich** ~ **näherkommen** get on closer [personal] terms [with one another]; (b) (human) humanely; in a humane manner
Menschlichkeit *die* humanity *no art.;* **etw. aus reiner** ~ **tun** do sth. for purely humanitarian reasons
Mensen ⇒ **Mensa**
Menstruation /mɛnstrua'tsio:n/ *die;* ~, ~en menstruation; (Periode) [menstrual] period
mental /mɛn'ta:l/ (geh.) 1 *Adj.* mental. 2 *adv.* mentally
Mentalität /mɛntali'tɛ:t/ *die;* ~, ~en mentality
Menthol /mɛn'to:l/ *das;* ~s menthol
Menü /me'ny:/ *das;* ~s, ~s (auch DV) menu; (im Restaurant) set meal *or* menu
Menü·leiste *die* (DV) menu bar

Meridian /meri'dia:n/ *der;* ~s, ~e (Geogr., Astron.) meridian

Merino /me'ri:no/ *der;* ~s, ~s (Stoff) merino

Merino-: ~**schaf** *das* merino [sheep]; ~**wolle** *die* merino wool

merkbar 1 *Adj.* perceptible; noticeable; (deutlich) noticeable. **2** *adv.* perceptibly; noticeably; (deutlich) noticeably

Merk·blatt leaflet; (mit Anweisungen) instruction leaflet

merken /'mɛrkn̩/ **1** *tr. V.* notice; **deutlich zu** ~ **sein** be plain to see; be obvious; **an seinem Benehmen merkt man, dass** … you can tell by his behaviour that …; **das merkt doch jeder/keiner** everybody/nobody will notice; **jmdn. etw.** ~ **lassen** let sb. see sth.; **du merkst aber auch alles!** (ugs. iron.) how very observant of you!; **merkst du was?** (ugs.) have you noticed something?. **2** *refl., auch tr. V.* **sich** (*Dat.*) **etw.** ~: remember sth.; (sich einprägen) memorize; **hast du dir die Adresse gemerkt?** have you made a mental note of the address?; **diesen Mann muss man sich** (*Dat.*) ~: this is a man to take note of; **ich werd mirs** *od.* **werds mir** ~ (ugs.) I won't forget that; I'll remember that; **merk dir das** just remember that

merklich 1 *Adj.* perceptible; noticeable; (deutlich) noticeable. **2** *adv.* perceptibly; noticeably; (deutlich) noticeably

Merkmal *das;* ~s, ~e feature; characteristic

Merkur /mɛr'ku:ɐ̯/ *der;* ~s (Astron.) Mercury

merkwürdig 1 *Adj.* strange; odd; peculiar. **2** *adv.* strangely; oddly; peculiarly

merkwürdiger·weise *Adv.* strangely *or* oddly *or* curiously enough

meschugge /me'ʃʊgə/ *Adj.; nicht attrib.* (salopp) barmy (Brit. coll.); nuts *pred.* (sl.); off one's rocker *pred.* (fig. coll.)

messbar, *meßbar /'mɛsba:ɐ̯/ *Adj.* measurable

Mess-, *Meß-: ~**becher** *der* measuring jug; ~**diener** *der* (kath. Kirche) server

Messe¹ /'mɛsə/ *die;* ~, ~n (Gottesdienst, Musik) mass; **die** ~ **halten** *od.* (geh.) zelebrieren say *or* celebrate mass; **für jmdn. eine** ~ **lesen** say a mass for sb.

Messe² *die;* ~, ~n **(a)** (Ausstellung) [trade] fair; **auf der** ~: at the [trade] fair; **(b)** (landsch.: Jahrmarkt, Volksfest) fair

Messe³ *die;* ~, ~n (Seew., Milit.) mess; (Raum) mess-room

Messe-: ~**gelände** *das* site of a/the [trade] fair; (mit festen ~hallen) exhibition centre; ~**halle** *die* exhibition hall

messen 1 *unr. tr. V.* **(a)** measure; take ⟨*pulse, blood, pressure, temperature*⟩; **(b)** (beurteilen) judge (**nach, an** + *Dat.* by); **jmdn. an jmdm.** ~: judge sb. by comparison with sb.; **ge**~ **an** (+ *Dat.*) having regard to. **2** *unr. itr. V.* measure; **er misst 1,85 m** he's 1.85 m [tall]; **genau** ~: make an exact measurement/exact measurements. **3** *unr. refl. V.* (geh.) compete (**mit** with); **sich mit jmdm./etw. [in etw.** (*Dat.*)] **[nicht]** ~ **können** [not] be as good as sb./sth. [in sth.]

Messer *das;* ~s, ~ **(a)** knife; (Hack~) chopper; (Rasier~) [cut-throat] razor; **jmdm. das** ~ **an die Kehle setzen** (fig. ugs.) hold sb. at gunpoint; **auf des** ~s **Schneide stehen** (fig.) hang in the balance; be balanced on a knife-edge; **jmdn. ans** ~ **liefern** (fig. ugs.) inform on sb.; **bis aufs** ~ (fig. ugs.) ⟨*fight etc.*⟩ to the bitter end; **jmdm. ins [offene]** ~ **laufen** (fig. ugs.) play right into sb.'s hands; **(b)** (ugs.: Skalpell) **unters** ~ **müssen** have to go under the knife (coll.)

messer-, Messer-: ~**scharf 1** *Adj.* razor-sharp; (fig.) trenchant ⟨*criticism*⟩; incisive ⟨*logic*⟩; razor-sharp ⟨*wit, intellect*⟩; **2** *adv.* (fig. ugs.) ⟨*think*⟩ with penetrating insight; ⟨*argue*⟩ incisively; ~**spitze** *die* **(a)** point of a/ the knife; **(b)** (Mengenangabe) **eine** ~**spitze** just a trace; **eine** ~**spitze Salz** a large pinch of salt; ~**stecherei** /-ʃtɛçə'rai/ *die;* ~, ~en knife-fight; fight with knives; ~**stich** *der* knife-thrust; (Wunde) knife-wound; stab wound

Mess·gerät, *Meß·gerät *das* measuring device *or* instrument

Messias /mɛ'si:as/ *der;* ~: Messiah

Messing /'mɛsɪŋ/ *das;* ~s brass

Messing·waren *Pl.* brassware *sing.*

Mess-, *Meß-: ~**instrument** *das* measuring instrument; ~**technik** *die* technology of measurement

Messung *die;* ~, ~en measurement

Mess·wert, *Meß·wert *der* measured value; (Ableseergebnis) reading

Mestize /mɛs'ti:tsə/ *der;* ~n, ~n mestizo

Met /me:t/ *der;* ~[e]s mead

Metall /me'tal/ *das;* ~s, ~e metal; ~ **verarbeitend** metalworking

Metall·arbeiter *der* metalworker

metallen *Adj. nicht präd.* metal

Metaller *der;* ~s, ~, **Metallerin** *die;* ~, ~nen (ugs.) metalworker

metall·haltig *Adj.* metalliferous

metallic /me'talɪk/ *indekl. Adj.* metallic [grey/blue/*etc.*]

Metall·industrie *die* metal-processing and metal-working industries *pl.*

metallisch *Adj.* metallic; metal *attrib.*, metallic ⟨*conductor*⟩

Metallurgie /metalʊr'gi:/ *die;* ~: [extractive] metallurgy *no art.*

*metall·verarbeitend ⇒ **Metall**

Metamorphose /metamɔr'fo:zə/ *die;* ~, ~n metamorphosis

Metapher /me'tafɐ/ *die;* ~, ~n (Stilk.) metaphor

Metaphorik /meta'fo:rɪk/ *die;* ~ (Stilk.) imagery; metaphors *pl.*

metaphorisch *Adj.* (Stilk.) metaphorical

meta·physisch 1 *Adj.* metaphysical; **2** *adv.* metaphysically

Meteor /mete'o:ɐ̯/ *der;* ~s, ~e (Astron.) meteor

Meteorit /meteo'ri:t/ *der;* ~en *od.* ~s, ~e[n] (Astron.) meteorite

Meteorologe /meteoro'lo:gə/ *der;* ~n, ~n meteorologist

Meteorologie *die;* ~: meteorology *no art.*

meteorologisch 1 *Adj.* meteorological. **2** *adv.* meteorologically

Meter /'me:tɐ/ *der od. das;* ~s, ~: ▶ 160 |, ▶ 189 |, ▶ 277 |, ▶ 340 | metre; **drei** ~ **lang** three metres long; **in 100** ~ **Höhe** at a height of 100 metres; **auf den letzten** ~**n** in the last few metres

meter-, Meter-: ~**dick** *Adj.* metres thick *postpos.;* ~**hoch** *Adj.* metres high *postpos.;* ⟨*snow*⟩ metres deep; **der Schnee lag** ~**hoch** the snow was metres deep; ~**lang** *Adj.* metres long *postpos.;* ~**maß** *das* tape measure; (Stab) [metre] rule; ~**ware** *die* fabric/material *etc.* sold by the metre; ~**weise** *Adv.* by the metre; ~**weit** *Adj.* metres long *postpos.*

Methan /me'ta:n/ *das;* ~s methane

Methanol /meta'no:l/ *das;* ~s (Chemie) methanol

Methode /me'to:də/ *die;* ~, ~n method

Methodik /me'to:dɪk/ *die;* ~, ~en methodology

methodisch 1 *Adj.* methodological; (nach einer Methode vorgehend) methodical. **2** *adv.* methodologically; (nach einer Methode) methodically

Methodist /meto'dɪst/ *der;* ~en, ~en Methodist

Metier /me'tie:/ *das;* ~s, ~s profession; **sein** ~ **beherrschen** know one's job

Metrik /'me:trɪk/ *die;* ~, ~en metrics

metrisch 1 *Adj.* **(a)** (Verslehre, Musik) metrical; **(b)** metric ⟨*ton, system, etc.*⟩. **2** *adv.* metrically

Metronom /metro'no:m/ *das;* ~s, ~e (Musik) metronome

Metropole /metro'po:lə/ *die;* ~, ~n metropolis

Mett /mɛt/ *das;* ~[e]s (landsch.) minced meat, mince (pork)

Mett·wurst *die soft smoked sausage made of minced pork and beef*

Metzelei /mɛtsə'lai/ *die;* ~, ~en (abwertend) slaughter; butchery

Metzger /'mɛtsgɐ/ *der;* ~s, ~ ▶ 85 | (bes. westmd., südd., schweiz.) butcher; (im Schlachthof) slaughterman

Metzger- ⇨ Fleischer-

Metzgerei *die;* ∼, ∼**en** (bes. westmd., südd., schweiz.) butcher's [shop]

Meute /ˈmɔytə/ *die;* ∼, ∼**n** (a) (Jägerspr.) pack; (b) (ugs. abwertend: Menschengruppe) mob

Meuterei /mɔytəˈraɪ/ *die;* ∼, ∼**en** mutiny; (fig.) revolt; mutiny

Meuterer /ˈmɔytərɐ/ *der;* ∼**s**, ∼: mutineer; (fig.) rebel

meutern *itr. V.* (a) mutiny; ⟨*prisoners*⟩ riot; (b) (fig. ugs.) rebel; (murren) moan

Mexikaner /mɛksiˈkaːnɐ/ *der;* ∼**s**, ∼, **Mexikanerin** *die;* ∼, ∼**nen** ▶388⟩ Mexican

mexikanisch *Adj.* ▶388⟩ Mexican

Mexiko /ˈmɛksiko/ *(das);* ∼**s** ▶490⟩ Mexico

MEZ *Abk.* **mitteleuropäische Zeit** CET

mg *Abk.* **Milligramm** mg

MG /ɛmˈgeː/ *das;* ∼**s**, ∼**s** *Abk.* **Maschinengewehr**

Mi. *Abk.* **Mittwoch** Wed.

miau /miˈaʊ/ *Interj.* miaow

miauen *itr. V.* miaow

mich /mɪç/ **1** *Akk.* **von ich** me. **2** *Akk. des Reflexivpron. der 1. Pers.* myself

mick[e]rig /ˈmɪk(ə)rɪç/ *Adj.* (ugs.) miserable; measly (sl.); puny ⟨*person*⟩; puny, stunted ⟨*plant, tree*⟩

Midi- /ˈmiːdi-/ midi⟨-skirt, dress, coat⟩

mied /miːt/ *1. u. 3. Pers. Sg. Prät. v.* **meiden**

Mieder /ˈmiːdɐ/ *das;* ∼**s**, ∼ (a) (*Korsage*) girdle; (b) (*Leibchen*) bodice

Mieder·waren *Pl.* corsetry *sing.*

Mief /miːf/ *der;* ∼**[e]s** (salopp abwertend) fug (coll.)

miefen *itr. V.* (ugs. abwertend) pong (coll.); stink

Miene /ˈmiːnə/ *die;* ∼, ∼**n** expression; face; **mit unbewegter** ∼: with an impassive expression; impassively; **gute** ∼ **zum bösen Spiel machen** grin and bear it

Mienen·spiel *das* facial expressions *pl.*

mies /miːs/ (ugs.) **1** *Adj.* (abwertend) terrible (coll.); lousy (coll.); rotten (coll.); lousy (coll.), foul (coll.) ⟨*mood*⟩; **jmdn./ etw.** ∼ **machen** (ugs. abwertend) run sb.sth. down. **2** *adv.* (a) (abwertend: schlecht) terribly badly (coll.); lousily (coll.); rottenly (coll.); (b) (unwohl) **ihm geht es** ∼: he's in a terrible state (coll.)

Miese /ˈmiːzə/ *Pl.; adj. Dekl.* (salopp) **2 000** ∼ **auf dem Konto haben** be 2,000 marks in the red at the bank; **in den** ∼**n sein** be in the red; (beim Kartenspiel) be down on points

mies-, Mies-: *∗∼|machen* ⇨ mies 1; ∼**macher** *der* (ugs. abwertend) carping critic; (Spielverderber) killjoy; ∼**muschel** *die* [common] mussel

Miete /ˈmiːtə/ *die;* ∼, ∼**n** (a) rent; (für ein Auto, Boot) hire charge; (für Fernsehgeräte usw.) rental; (b) *o. Pl.* (das Mieten) renting; **zur** ∼ **wohnen** live in rented accommodation; rent a house/flat (Brit.) *or* (Amer.) apartment/room/rooms; **bei jmdm. zur** ∼ **wohnen** lodge with sb.

Miet·einnahmen *Pl.* income *sing.* from rents

mieten *tr. V.* rent; (für kürzere Zeit) hire

Mieter /ˈmiːtɐ/ *der;* ∼**s**, ∼: tenant

Miet·erhöhung *die* rent increase

Mieterin *die;* ∼, ∼**nen** tenant

miet-, Miet-: ∼**frei** *Adj., adv.* rent-free; ∼**kauf** *der* (Wirtsch.) ≈ hire purchase (Brit.) *or* (Amer.) installment plan *(with option to buy outright or terminate the agreement at a specified date)*; ∼**partei** *die* tenant

Miets-: ∼**haus** *das* block of rented flats (Brit.) *or* (Amer.) apartments; ∼**kaserne** *die* (abwertend) tenement block

Miet-: ∼**vertrag** *der* tenancy agreement; ∼**wagen** *der* hire car; ∼**wohnung** *die* rented flat (Brit.) *or* (Amer.) apartment; ∼**wucher** *der* charging of exorbitant rents; ∼**zins** *der; Pl.* ∼**e** (südd., österr., schweiz., Amtsspr.) rent

Mieze /ˈmiːtsə/ *die;* ∼, ∼**n** (a) (fam.: Katze) puss; pussy (child lang.); (b) (salopp: Mädchen) chick (sl.); (als Anrede) sweetie

∗alte Schreibung (vgl. Hinweise auf S. xvi–xxii)

Migräne /miˈgrɛːnə/ *die;* ∼, ∼**n** ▶329⟩ migraine

Mikado /miˈkaːdo/ *das;* ∼**s** spillikins *sing.;* jack-straws *sing.*

Mikro /ˈmiːkro/ *das;* ∼**s**, ∼**s** (ugs.) mike (coll.)

mikro-, Mikro- micro-

Mikrobe /miˈkroːbə/ *die;* ∼, ∼**n** microbe

mikro-, Mikro-: ∼**elektronik** *die* microelectronics *sing., no art.;* ∼**faser** *die* microfibre; ∼**fon** /-ˈ-/ *das;* ∼**s**, ∼**e** microphone; ∼**organismus** *der* (Biol.) microorganism; ∼**phon** ⇨ ∼**fon;** ∼**prozessor** /∼pro ˈtsɛsɔr/ *der;* ∼**s**, ∼**en** /...ˈsoːrən/ microprocessor; ∼**skop** /∼ˈskoːp/ *das;* ∼**s**, ∼**e** microscope; ∼**skopisch** **1** *Adj.* microscopic; **2** *adv.* microscopically; ∼**welle** *die* (ugs.) microwave [oven]; ∼**wellen·herd** *der* microwave oven

Milbe /ˈmɪlbə/ *die;* ∼, ∼**n** mite; (Zecke) tick

Milch /mɪlç/ *die;* ∼ milk; ∼ **geben** give *or* yield milk

Milch-: ∼**bar** *die* milk bar; ∼**brötchen** *das* milk roll; ∼**drüse** *die* ▶326⟩ mammary gland; ∼**flasche** *die* (a) milk bottle; (b) (für Säuglinge) feeding bottle; baby's bottle; ∼**gebiss,** ∗∼**gebiß** *das* ▶326⟩ milk teeth *pl.*

milchig **1** *Adj.* milky. **2** *adv.* ∼ **weiß** milky-white

Milch-: ∼**kaffee** *der* coffee with plenty of milk; ∼**kännchen** *das* milk jug; ∼**kanne** *die* milk-can; (zum Transportieren von ∼) [milk-]churn; ∼**kuh** *die* dairy or milk *or* milch cow; ∼**mädchen·rechnung** *die* (ugs.) naïve miscalculation; ∼**mix·getränk** *das* milk shake; ∼**reis** *der* rice pudding; ∼**schokolade** *die* milk chocolate; ∼**straße** *die* Milky Way; Galaxy; ∼**vieh** *das* dairy cattle; ∼**wirtschaft** *die* dairying *no art.;* ∼**zahn** *der* milk tooth

mild /mɪlt/, **milde** **1** *Adj.* (a) (gütig) lenient ⟨*judge, judgement*⟩; benevolent ⟨*ruler*⟩; mild, lenient, light ⟨*punishment*⟩; mild ⟨*words, accusation*⟩; mild, gentle ⟨*reproach*⟩; gentle ⟨*smile, voice*⟩; **jmdn.** ∼ **stimmen** induce sb. to take a lenient attitude; (b) (nicht rauh) mild ⟨*climate, air, winter, etc.*⟩; (c) (nicht scharf) mild ⟨*spice, coffee, tobacco, cheese, etc.*⟩; ∼ **schmecken** be mild; (d) (schonend) mild ⟨*soap, shampoo, detergent*⟩; (e) *nicht präd.* (veralt.: mildtätig) charitable; **eine** ∼**e Gabe** alms *pl.* **2** *adv.* (a) (gütig) leniently ⟨*smile, say*⟩ gently; (b) (gelinde) mildly; ∼ **ausgedrückt** to put it mildly; putting it mildly

Milde *die;* ∼ (a) (Gnade, Güte) leniency; [jmdm. gegenüber] ∼ **walten lassen** be lenient [with sb.]; (b) (des Klimas usw.) mildness; (c) (milder Geschmack) mildness

mildern **1** *tr. V.* moderate ⟨*criticism, judgement*⟩; mitigate ⟨*punishment*⟩; soothe ⟨*anger*⟩; reduce ⟨*intensity, strength, effect*⟩; modify ⟨*impression*⟩; ease, soothe, relieve ⟨*pain*⟩; alleviate ⟨*poverty, need*⟩; ∼**de Umstände** (Rechtsw.) mitigating circumstances. **2** *refl. V.* ⟨*anger, rage, agitation*⟩ abate

Milderung *die;* ∼ (eines Tadels, Urteils) moderation; (einer Strafe) mitigation; (von Schmerz) easing; soothing; relief; (von Armut, Not) alleviation

mild·tätig *Adj.* charitable

Mild·tätigkeit *die; o. Pl.* charity

Milieu /miˈliø:/ *das;* ∼**s**, ∼**s** milieu; environment; (fig.: Prostitution usw.) world of pimps and prostitutes; **er stammt aus kleinbürgerlichem** ∼: his background is petit bourgeois

militant /miliˈtant/ *Adj.* militant

Militär[1] /miliˈtɛːɐ̯/ *das;* ∼**s** (a) armed forces *pl.;* military; **beim** ∼ **sein/vom** ∼ **entlassen werden** be in/be discharged from the forces; (b) (Soldaten) soldiers *pl.;* army

Militär[2] *der;* ∼**s**, ∼**s** [high-ranking military] officer

Militär-: ∼**arzt** *der* medical officer; ∼**dienst** *der* military service; **seinen** ∼**dienst ableisten** do one's military *or* national service; ∼**diktatur** *die* military dictatorship; ∼**fahrzeug** *das* military vehicle; ∼**flugzeug** *das* military aircraft; ∼**geistliche** *der* army chaplain; ∼**gericht** *das* military court; court martial; **vor ein** ∼**gericht gestellt werden** be brought before *or* tried by a military court; be courtmartialled

militärisch **1** *Adj.* military. **2** *adv.* **jmdn.** ∼ **grüßen** salute sb.

Militarisierung *die;* ~**:** militarization

Militarist *der;* ~**en,** ~**en** (abwertend) militarist

militaristisch *Adj.* (abwertend) militarist; militaristic

Militär-: ~**junta** *die* military junta; ~**parade** *die* military parade; ~**putsch** *der* military putsch

Military /'mɪlɪtərɪ/ *die;* ~, ~**s** (Reiten) three-day event

Miliz /miˈliːts/ *die;* ~, ~**en** militia; (Polizei) police

milk /mɪlk/, **milkst, milkt** (veralt.) *Imperativ Sg.,* 2. *u.* 3. *Pers. Sg. Präsens v.* **melken**

Mill. *Abk.* **Million** m.

Mille /'mɪlə/ *die;* ~, ~ (salopp) grand (sl.); thousand marks/ pounds *etc.*

Milliardär /mɪliarˈdɛːɐ̯/ *der;* ~**s,** ~**e, Milliardärin** *die;* ~, ~**nen** multi-millionaire (possessing at least a thousand million marks etc.); billionaire (Amer.)

Milliarde /mɪrˈliardə/ *die;* ~, ~**n** ▶ 600 ⏐ thousand million; billion; *s. auch* **Million**

Milliardenhöhe *die in* in ~**:** of the order of a billion *or* a thousand million

Milli-: ~**bar** *das* (Met.) millibar; ~**gramm** *das* milligram

Millimeter *der* ▶ 340 ⏐ *od. das* millimetre

Millimeter-: ~**arbeit** *die; o. Pl.* (ugs.) (am Steuer) delicate piece of manœuvring; (bei Ballspielen) [neat] piece of precision play; ~**papier** *das* [graph] paper ruled in millimetre squares

Million /mɪˈljoːn/ *die;* ~, ~**en** ▶ 600 ⏐ million; eine/zwei ~**en** a/two million; ~**en** [von …] millions [of …]

Millionär /mɪljoˈnɛːɐ̯/ *der;* ~**s,** ~**e, Millionärin** *die;* ~, ~**nen** millionaire

millionen-, Millionen-: ~**auflage** *die* (Buchw.) dieses Buch erschien in ~**auflage** [over] a million copies of this book were printed; ~**fach** 1 *Adj.* millionfold ⟨ *increase etc.*⟩; **2** *adv.* a million times; ~**gewinn** *der* (a) (Ertrag) profit of a million/of millions; (b) (Lotteriegewinn) prize of a million/of millions; ~**schaden** *der* damage *no pl., no indef. art.* running into millions; ~**schwer** *Adj.* (ugs.) worth millions *pred.;* ~**stadt** *die* town with over a million inhabitants

millionst... *Ordinalz.* ▶ 600 ⏐ millionth; *s. auch* **hundertst...**

million[s]tel *Bruchz.* ▶ 600 ⏐ millionth; *s. auch* **hundertstel**

Million[s]tel *das od.* (schweiz.) der; ~**s,** ~**:** ▶ 600 ⏐ millionth

Milz /mɪlts/ *die;* ~ ▶ 326 ⏐ (Anat.) spleen

Mime /'miːmə/ *der;* ~**n,** ~**n** (geh.) Thespian

mimen *tr. V.* put on a show of ⟨ *admiration, efficiency*⟩; **den Kranken/Unschuldigen** ~**:** pretend to be ill/act the innocent

Mimik /'miːmɪk/ *die;* ~**:** gestures and facial expressions *pl.*

Mimikry /'mɪmikri/ *die;* ~ (Zool.) mimicry; (fig.) camouflage

mimisch 1 *Adj.; nicht präd.* mimic. **2** *adv.* ⟨ *show*⟩ by means of gestures and facial expressions

Mimose /miˈmoːzə/ *die;* ~, ~**n** (a) mimosa; (b) (fig.) oversensitive person; **die reinste** ~ **sein** be extraordinarily sensitive

mimosenhaft (fig.) 1 *Adj.* oversensitive. **2** *adv.* oversensitively

Min. *Abk.* **Minute[n]** min.

Minarett /mina'rɛt/ *das;* ~**s,** ~**e** *od.* ~**s** minaret

minder /'mɪndɐ/ *Adv.* (geh.) less; [**nicht**] ~ **angenehm sein** be [no] less pleasant; *s. auch* **mehr 1**

minder... *Adj.; nicht präd.* inferior, lower ⟨ *quality*⟩; **von** ~**er Bedeutung sein** be of less importance

minder-, Minder-: ~**begabt** *Adj.* less gifted *or* able; ~**bemittelt** *Adj.* without much money *postpos., not pred.;* ~**bemittelt sein** not have much money; **er ist doch geistig** ~**bemittelt** (fig. salopp abwertend) he isn't all that bright (coll.); ~**bemittelte** *Pl.* needy persons

Minderheit *die;* ~, ~**en** minority

Minderheitsregierung *die* minority government

minder-, Minder-: ~**jährig** *Adj.* (Rechtsw.) ⟨ *child etc.*⟩ who is/was a minor *or* under age; ~**jährig sein** be a minor *or* under age; ~**jährige** *der/die; adj. Dekl.* (Rechtsw.) minor; person under age; ~**jährigkeit** *die;* ~ (Rechtsw.) minority

mindern *tr. V.* (geh.) reduce ⟨ *income, price, number of staff, tension, etc.*⟩; impair ⟨ *performance, abilities*⟩; diminish, reduce ⟨ *value, quality, dignity, pleasure, influence*⟩; detract from ⟨ *reputation*⟩

Minderung *die;* ~, ~**en** ⇨ **mindern:** reduction (*Gen.* in); impairment (*Gen.* of); diminution (*Gen.* of); detraction (*Gen.* from)

minderwertig *Adj.* (abwertend) inferior, low-quality ⟨ *goods, material*⟩; low-quality, low-grade ⟨ *meat*⟩; (fig.) inferior

Minderwertigkeit *die; o. Pl.* ⇨ **minderwertig:** inferiority; low quality; low grade; (fig.) inferiority

Minderwertigkeits-: ~**gefühl** *das* (Psych.) feeling of inferiority; ~**komplex** *der* (Psych.) inferiority complex

Minderzahl *die; o. Pl.* minority

mindest... /'mɪndəst…/ *Adj.; nicht präd.* slightest; least; **das ist das Mindeste, was du tun kannst** it is the least you can do; **nicht im Mindesten** not in the least

Mindest-: ~**alter** *das* minimum age; ~**anforderung** *die* minimum requirement

mindestens /'mɪndəstn̩s/ *Adv.* at least

Mindest-: ~**gebot** *das* reserve price; ~**haltbarkeitsdatum** *das* best-before date; ~**lohn** *der* minimum wage; ~**maß** *das* minimum (**an** + *Dat.,* von of)

Mine /'miːnə/ *die;* ~, ~**n** (a) (Erzbergwerk) mine; (b) (Sprengkörper) mine; **auf eine** ~ **laufen** strike a mine; (c) (Bleistift~) lead; (Kugelschreiber~, Filzschreiber~) refill

Minensuchboot *das* (Milit.) minesweeper

Mineral /mineˈraːl/ *das;* ~**s,** ~**e** *od.* **Mineralien** mineral

Mineralogie *die;* ~**:** mineralogy *no art.*

Mineralöl *das* mineral oil

Mineralöl-: ~**gesellschaft** *die* oil company; ~**steuer** *die* tax on oil

Mineral-: ~**quelle** *die* mineral spring; ~**wasser** *das* mineral water

Mini /'mɪni/ *das;* ~**s,** ~**s** (Mode) mini (coll.)

Mini- mini-

Miniatur /miniaˈtuːɐ̯/ *die;* ~, ~**en** miniature

Miniaturausgabe *die* (Buchw.) abridged edition

Minigolf *das* minigolf; crazy golf

minimal /miniˈmaːl/ 1 *Adj.* minimal; marginal ⟨ *advantage, lead*⟩; very slight ⟨ *benefit, profit*⟩. **2** *adv.* minimally

Minimalforderung *die* minimum demand

Minimum /'miːnimʊm/ *das;* ~**s, Minima** minimum (**an** + *Dat.* of)

Minirock *der* miniskirt

Minister /miˈnɪstɐ/ *der;* ~**s,** ~**:** ▶ 34 ⏐ minister (**für** for); (eines britischen Hauptministeriums) Secretary of State (**für** for); (eines amerikanischen Hauptministeriums) Secretary (**für** of)

ministeriell /minɪsteˈriɛl/ 1 *Adj.* ministerial. **2** *adv.* by the minister

Ministerin *die;* ~, ~**nen** ⇨ **Minister**

Ministerium /minɪsˈteːriʊm/ *das;* ~**s, Ministerien** Ministry; Department (Amer.)

Ministerpräsident *der* ▶ 34 ⏐ (a) (eines deutschen Bundeslandes) minister-president; prime minister (Brit.); governor (Amer.); (b) (Premierminister) Prime Minister

Ministrant /minɪsˈtrant/ *der;* ~**en,** ~**en** (kath. Kirche) server

Minna /'mɪna/ *die;* ~, ~**s** (ugs. veralt.) maid; **jmdn. zur** ~ **machen** (ugs.) tear sb. off a strip (Brit. coll.); bawl out (coll.); **eine grüne** ~ (ugs.) a Black Maria; a patrol wagon (Amer.)

Minorität /minoriˈtɛːt/ *die;* ~, ~**en** ⇒ **Minderheit**

minus /ˈmiːnʊs/ ▶600┃ 1 *Konj.* minus. 2 *Adv.* (a) ▶511┃ minus; ~ **fünf Grad, fünf Grad** ~: minus five degrees; five degrees below [zero]; (b) (Elektrot.) negative. 3 *Präp. mit Gen.* (Kaufmannsspr.) less; minus

Minus *das;* ~ (a) (Fehlbetrag) deficit; (auf einem Konto) overdraft; ~ **machen** make a loss; **im** ~ **sein** be in debit; be in the red; (b) (Nachteil) minus; drawback; (im Beruf) disadvantage

Minus-: ~**pol** *der* negative pole; (einer Batterie) negative terminal; ~**punkt** *der* (a) minus *or* penalty point; (b) (Nachteil) disadvantage; ~**zeichen** *das* minus sign

Minute /miˈnuːtə/ *die;* ~, ~**n** ▶530┃ minute; **es ist neun Uhr [und] sieben** ~**n** it is seven minutes past nine *or* nine seven; **hast du ein paar** ~**n Zeit für mich?** can you spare me a few minutes *or* moments?; **in letzter** ~: at the last minute *or* moment; **auf die** ~ **pünktlich** punctual to the minute

minuten·lang 1 *Adj.; nicht präd.* ⟨*applause, silence, etc.*⟩ lasting [for] several minutes. 2 *adv.* for several minutes

Minuten·zeiger *der* minute hand

-minütig *Adj.* **ein fünf**~**er Heulton** a wail lasting five minutes; **eine fünfzehn**~**e Verspätung** a fifteen-minute delay

minuziös /minuˈtsi̯øːs/ (geh.) 1 *Adj.* minutely *or* meticulously precise *or* detailed ⟨*account, description*⟩; minute ⟨*detail*⟩; ⟨*manœuvre*⟩ requiring minute precision. 2 *adv.* meticulously

Minze /ˈmɪntsə/ *die;* ~, ~**n** mint

Mio. *Abk.* **Million[en]** m.

mir /miːɐ̯/ 1 *Dat. Sg. von ich* (a) to me; (nach Präpositionen) me; **gib es** ~: give it to me; give me it; **Freunde von** ~: friends of mine; **gehen wir zu** ~: let's got to my place; ~ **nichts, dir nichts** (ugs.) just like that; without so much as a 'by your leave'; **von** ~ **aus** as far as I'm concerned; **(b)** **geht** ~ **nicht an meinen Schreibtisch!** keep away from my desk!; **und grüß** ~ **alle Verwandten!** and give my regards to all the relatives!; **du bist** ~ **vielleicht einer!** (ugs.) a fine one you are!. 2 *Dat. des Reflexivpron. der 1. Pers. Sg.* myself; **ich habe** ~ **gedacht, dass ...:** I thought that ...; **ich will** ~ **ein neues Kleid kaufen** I want to buy myself a new dress

Mirabelle /miraˈbɛlə/ *die;* ~, ~**n** mirabelle

Misanthrop /mizanˈtroːp/ *der;* ~**en**, ~**en** (geh.) misanthrope

Misch-: ~**brot** *das* bread made from wheat and rye flour; ~**ehe** *die* mixed marriage

mischen /ˈmɪʃn̩/ 1 *tr. V.* mix; **etw. in etw.** (*Akk.*) ~: put sth. into sth.; **Wasser und Wein** ~: mix water with wine; **die Karten** ~: shuffle the cards. 2 *refl. V.* (a) (sich ver~) mix (**mit** with); ⟨*smell, scent*⟩ blend (**mit** with); **in meine Freude mischte sich Angst** my joy was mingled with fear; (b) (sich ein~) **sich in etw.** (*Akk.*) ~: interfere *or* meddle in sth.; (c) (sich begeben) **sich unters Publikum** *usw.* ~: mingle with the audience *etc.* 3 *itr. V.* (Kartenspiel) shuffle; *s. auch* **gemischt**

Mischer *der;* ~**s**, ~ (Bauw.) [cement-]mixer

Misch-: ~**farbe** *die* non-primary colour; ~**form** *die* mixture; ~**gewebe** *das* mixture

Mischling /ˈmɪʃlɪŋ/ *der;* ~**s**, ~**e** half-caste; half-breed

Mischmasch /ˈmɪʃmaʃ/ *der;* ~**[e]s**, ~**e** (ugs., meist abwertend) hotchpotch; mishmash

Misch-: ~**maschine** *die* (Bauw.) cement-mixer; ~**pult** *das* (Film, Rundf., Ferns.) mixing desk *or* console

Mischung *die;* ~, ~**en** (auch fig.) mixture; (Tee~, Kaffee~, Tabak~) blend; (Pralinen~) assortment

Mischungs·verhältnis *das* proportion in the mixture

Misch·wald *der* mixed [deciduous and coniferous] forest

miserabel /mizəˈraːbl̩/ (ugs.) 1 *Adj.* (a) (schlecht) dreadful (coll.), atrocious ⟨*film, food*⟩; pathetic, miserable ⟨*achievement*⟩; miserable, dreadful (coll.), atrocious ⟨*weather*⟩; (b) (elend) miserable; wretched; **ich fühle**

mich ~: I feel dreadful; **(c)** (niederträchtig) abominable ⟨*behaviour*⟩. 2 *adv.* (a) (schlecht) dreadfully (coll.); atrociously; ⟨*sleep*⟩ dreadfully badly (coll.); ~ **bezahlt werden** be very badly *or* poorly paid; **(b)** (elend) **ihm geht es gesundheitlich** ~: he's in a bad way; **(c)** (niederträchtig) abominably

Misere /miˈzeːrə/ *die;* ~, ~**n** (geh.) wretched *or* dreadful state

Mispel /ˈmɪspl̩/ *die;* ~, ~**n** medlar

miss, *Imperativ Sg. v.* **messen**

miss·achten, *Imperativ Sg. v.* **messen**

miss·achten, ***miß·achten** *tr. V.* disregard; ignore

Miss·achtung[1], ***Miß·achtung** *die* disregard

Miss·achtung[2], ***Miß·achtung** *die* (Geringschätzung) disdain; contempt

Miss·behagen, ***Miß·behagen** *das* [feeling of] unease; uncomfortable feeling

Miss·bildung, ***Miß·bildung** *die* deformity

missbilligen, ***mißbilligen** *tr. V.* disapprove of

Miss·billigung, ***Miß·billigung** *die* disapproval

Miss·brauch, ***Miß·brauch** *der* abuse; misuse; (falsche Anwendung) misuse; (von Feuerlöscher, Notbremse) improper use

missbrauchen, ***mißbrauchen** *tr. V.* abuse; misuse; abuse ⟨*trust*⟩; **jmdn. für** *od.* **zu etw.** ~: use sb. for sth.

missbräuchlich, ***mißbräuchlich** /-brɔʏçlɪç/ 1 *Adj.* ~**e Verwendung/Anwendung** misuse. 2 *adv.* **etw.** ~ **verwenden/handhaben** misuse sth.

missdeuten, ***mißdeuten** *tr. V.* misinterpret

missen *tr. V.* (geh.) do *or* go without; do without ⟨*person*⟩; **jmdn./etw. nicht** ~ **mögen** not want to be without sb./sth.

Miss·erfolg, ***Miß·erfolg** *der* failure

Miss·ernte, ***Miß·ernte** *die* crop failure

Misse·tat /ˈmɪsə-/ *die* (geh. veralt.) misdeed

Misse·täter *der,* **Misse·täterin** *die* (geh. veralt.) malefactor

missfallen, ***mißfallen** *unr. itr. V.* **etw. missfällt jmdm.** sb. dislikes *or* does not like sth.

Missfallen, ***Mißfallen** *das;* ~**s** displeasure (**über** + *Akk.* at); (Missbilligung) disapproval (**über** + *Akk.* of); **jmds.** ~ **erregen** incur sb.'s displeasure/disapproval

Missfallens·äußerung, ***Mißfallens·äußerung** *die* expression of displeasure/disapproval

miss·gebildet, ***miß·gebildet** *Adj.* deformed

Miss·geburt, ***Miß·geburt** *die* (Med.) monster; monstrosity

Miss·geschick, ***Miß·geschick** *das* mishap; (Pech) bad luck; (Unglück) misfortune; **jmdm. passiert ein** ~: sb. has a mishap/a piece *or* stroke of bad luck/a misfortune

miss·gestaltet, ***miß·gestaltet** *Adj.* misshapen; deformed ⟨*person, child*⟩

miss·glücken, ***miß·glücken** *itr. V.; mit sein:* ⇒ **misslingen**

missgönnen, ***mißgönnen** *tr. V.* **jmdm. etw.** ~: begrudge sb. sth.

Miss·griff, ***Miß·griff** *der* error of judgement

Miss·gunst, ***Miß·gunst** *die* [envy and] resentment (**gegenüber** of)

miss·günstig, ***miß·günstig** 1 *Adj.* resentful. 2 *adv.* resentfully

misshandeln, ***mißhandeln** *tr. V.* maltreat; ill-treat

Miss·handlung, ***Miß·handlung** *die* maltreatment; ill-treatment; ~**en** maltreatment *sing.*; ill-treatment *sing.*

Mission /mɪˈsi̯oːn/ *die;* ~, ~**en** (a) (geh.: Auftrag) mission; **in geheimer** ~: on a secret mission; **(b)** *o. Pl.* (Rel.) mission; **in der [äußeren/inneren]** ~ **tätig sein** do missionary work [abroad/in one's own country]; **(c)** (geh.: diplomatische Vertretung) mission

Missionar /mɪsi̯oˈnaːɐ̯/ *der;* ~**s**, ~**e**, **Missionarin** *die;* ~, ~**nen** missionary

missionarisch *Adj.* missionary

missionieren 1 *itr. V.* do missionary work. 2 *tr. V.* convert by missionary work; (fig.) convert to one's own ideas

Missionierung *die;* ~: **die** ~ **eines Landes/eines Volkes** missionary work in a country/among a people;

(Bekehrung) the conversion of a country/people [by missionary work]

Miss·kredit, *****Miß·kredit** der in jmdn./etw. in ~ **bringen** bring sb./sth. into discredit; bring discredit on sb./sth.

misslang, *****mißlang** 1. u. 3. Pers. Sg. Prät. v. **misslingen**

misslich, *****mißlich** Adj. (geh.) awkward, difficult ‹situation›; difficult ‹conditions›; unfortunate ‹incident›

missliebig, *****mißliebig** /'mɪsli:bɪç/ Adj. unpopular; ~e Ausländer unwanted foreigners

misslingen, *****mißlingen** /mɪs'lɪŋən/ unr. itr. V.; mit sein fail; be unsuccessful; be a failure; **ein misslungener Versuch** a failed or unsuccessful attempt

misslungen, *****mißlungen** /mɪs'lʊŋən/ 2. Part. v. **misslingen**

miss·mutig, *****miß·mutig** 1 Adj. bad-tempered; sullen ‹face›; **warum bist du heute so ~?** why are you in such a bad mood today? 2 adv. bad-temperedly

missraten, *****mißraten** unr. itr. V.; mit sein ‹cake, photo, etc.› turn out badly; **ein ~es Kind** a child who has turned out badly

Miss·stand, *****Miß·stand** der deplorable state of affairs no. pl.; (Übel) evil; (üble Praktiken) abuse; **die Missstände im Bildungswesen** the deplorable state of education

misst, *****mißt** 2. u. 3. Pers. Sg. Präsens v. **messen**

Miss·ton, *****Miß·ton** der discordant note; (fig.) note of discord; discordant note

misstrauen, *****mißtrauen** itr. V. jmdm./einer Sache ~: mistrust or distrust sb./sth.

Miss·trauen, *****Miß·trauen** das; ~s mistrust, distrust (**gegen** of); **voll[er] ~:** extremely mistrustful or distrustful (**gegen** of)

Miss·trauens-, *****Miß·trauens-:** ~**antrag** der motion of no confidence; ~**votum** das vote of no confidence

miss·trauisch, *****miß·trauisch** /'mɪstrauɪʃ/ 1 Adj. mistrustful; distrustful; (argwöhnisch) suspicious. 2 adv. mistrustfully; distrustfully; (argwöhnisch) suspiciously

Miss·verhältnis, *****Miß·verhältnis** das disparity; (an Größe) disproportion

miss·verständlich, *****miß·verständlich** 1 Adj. unclear; ‹formulation, concept, etc.› that could be misunderstood; ~ **sein** be liable to be misunderstood. 2 adv. ‹express oneself, describe› in a way that could be misunderstood

Miss·verständnis, *****Miß·verständnis** das misunderstanding

miss|verstehen, *****miß|verstehen; ich missverstehe, missverstanden, misszuverstehen** unr. tr. V. misunderstand

Miss·wahl, *****Miß·wahl** die: contest for the title of ‘Miss Europe’, ‘Miss World’ etc.

Miss·wirtschaft, *****Miß·wirtschaft** die mismanagement

Mist /mɪst/ der; ~[e]s (a) dung; (Dünger) manure; (mit Stroh usw. gemischt) muck; (~haufen) dung/manure/muck heap; **das ist nicht auf ihrem ~ gewachsen** (fig. ugs.) that didn't come out of her own head; (b) (ugs. abwertend) (Schund) rubbish, junk, trash all no indef. art.; (Unsinn) rubbish, nonsense, (sl.) rot all no indef. art.; (lästige, dumme Angelegenheit) nonsense; ~ **bauen** make a mess of things; mess things up; **mach bloß keinen ~!** just don't do anything stupid

Mistel /'mɪstl̩/ die; ~, ~n mistletoe

Mistel·zweig der piece of mistletoe

Mist-: ~**forke** die (nordd.), ~**gabel** die dung-fork; ~**haufen** der dung/manure/muck heap

mistig (salopp) 1 Adj. rotten (sl.). 2 adv. in a rotten way (sl.)

Mist-: ~**käfer** der dung-beetle; ~**stück** das (derb) lousy good-for-nothing bastard (sl.); (Frau) lousy good-for-nothing bitch (sl.); ~**wetter** das (salopp) lousy weather (coll.)

mit /mɪt/ 1 Präp. mit Dat. (a) (Gemeinsamkeit, Beteiligung) with; (b) (Zugehörigkeit) with; **ein Haus ~ Garten** a house with a garden; **Herr Müller ~ Frau** Herr Müller and

his wife; (c) (einschließlich) with; including; **ein Zimmer ~ Frühstück** a room with breakfast included; (d) (Inhalt) **ein Sack ~ Kartoffeln/Glas ~ Marmelade** a sack of potatoes/pot of jam; (e) (Begleitumstände) with; **etw. ~ Absicht tun/~ Nachdruck fordern** do sth. deliberately/demand sth. forcefully; ~ **50 [km/h] fahren** drive at 50 [k.p.h]; (f) (Hilfsmittel) with; ~ **der Bahn/dem Auto fahren** go by train/car; ~ **der Fähre/„Hamburg“** on the ferry/the 'Hamburg'; (g) (allgemeiner Bezug) with; ~ **der Arbeit ging es recht langsam voran** the work went very slowly; ~ **einer Tätigkeit beginnen/aufhören** take up/give up an occupation; **raus/fort ~ dir!** out/off you go!; (h) (zeitlich) ~ **Einbruch der Dunkelheit/Nacht** when darkness/night falls/fell; ~ **20 [Jahren]** at [the age of] twenty; ~ **der Zeit/den Jahren** in time/as the years go/went by; (i) (gleichlaufende Bewegung) with; ~ **dem Strom/Wind** with the tide/wind. 2 Adv. (a) (auch) too; as well; ~ **dabei sein** be there too; **er ist beim letzten Ausflug nicht ~ gewesen** he didn't come [with us] on our last trip; **waren eure Kinder im Urlaub ~?** did your children go on holiday with you?; **warst du auch ~ im Konzert?** were you at the concert too?; s. auch **Partie** f; (b) (neben anderen) also; too; as well; **es lag ~ an ihm** it was partly his doing; (c) (ugs.) ~ **das wichtigste der Bücher** one of the most important of the books; **seine Arbeit war ~ am besten** his work was among the best; (d) (vorübergehende Beteiligung) **ihr könntet ruhig einmal ~ anfassen** it wouldn't hurt you to lend a hand just for once; (e) s. auch **damit** 1 c; **womit** b

Mit·angeklagte der/die co-defendant; (mit geringerer Strafandrohung) defendant to a lesser charge

Mit·arbeit die; o. Pl. (a) (das Tätigsein) collaboration (**bei, an** + Dat. on); **die ~ in der Praxis ihres Mannes** working in her husband's practice; (b) (Mithilfe) assistance (**bei, in** + Dat. in); **seine zwanzigjährige ~ in der Organisation** his twenty years of service to the organization; (c) (Beteiligung) participation (**in** + Dat. in)

mit|arbeiten itr. V. (a) **bei einem Projekt/an einem Buch** ~: collaborate on a project/book; **im elterlichen Geschäft** ~: work in one's parents' shop; (b) (sich beteiligen) participate (**in** + Dat. in); **im Unterricht besser** ~: take a more active part in lessons

Mit·arbeiter der (a) (Betriebsangehörige[r]) employee; (b) (bei einem Projekt, an einem Buch) collaborator; **ein freier ~:** a freelance; a freelance worker

mit|bekommen unr. tr. V. (a) **etw.** ~: be given or get sth. to take with one; (fig.) inherit sth.; (b) (wahrnehmen) be aware of; (durch Hören/Sehen) hear/see; **es war so laut, dass ich nur die Hälfte mitbekam** it was so noisy that I only caught half of it; (c) (verstehen) **ich war so müde, dass ich nicht viel ~ habe** I was so tired that I did not grasp very much

mit|benutzen tr. V. share; have the use of

Mit·besitzer der joint owner; co-owner

mit|bestimmen 1 itr. V. have a say (**in** + Dat. in). 2 tr. V. have an influence on

Mit·bestimmung die; o. Pl. participation (**bei** in); (der Arbeitnehmer) co-determination

Mit·bestimmungs·recht das right of co-determination

Mit·bewerber der fellow applicant; (Wirtsch.) competitor; **ich hatte nur einen ~ um diese Stelle** there was only one other applicant for the job [besides me]

Mit·bewohner der fellow resident; (in Wohnung) flatmate

mit|bringen unr. tr. V. (a) **etw.** ~: bring sth. with one; **etw. aus der Stadt/aus dem Urlaub/vom Markt/von der Reise** ~: bring sth. back from town/holiday/the market/one's trip; **jmdm./sich etw.** ~: bring sth. with one for sb./bring sth. back for oneself; **Gäste** ~: bring guests home; (b) (fig.: haben) have, possess ‹ability, gift, etc.› (**für** for); **genügend Zeit** ~: come with enough time at one's disposal; s. auch **Laune** a

Mitbringsel /-brɪŋzl̩/ das; ~s, ~: [small] present; (Andenken) [small] souvenir

Mit·bürger der fellow citizen; **ältere** ~ (Amtsspr.) senior citizens

mịt|denken *unr. itr. V.* follow [the argument/explanation/what is being said *etc.*]

mịt|dürfen *unr. itr. V.* (ugs.) (mitkommen dürfen) be allowed to come along *or* too; (mitgehen, mitfahren dürfen) be allowed to go along *or* too

mit·einander *Adv.* (a) with each other *or* one another; ~ **sprechen/kämpfen** talk to each other *or* one another/ fight with each other *or* one another; (b) (gemeinsam) together; **ihr seid Gauner, alle ~!** you are all a pack of rogues!; you're all rogues, the lot of you!

Mịt·einander *das;* ~[s] living and working together *no art.*

mịt|erleben *tr. V.* (a) witness ‹*events etc.*›; (b) **er hat den Krieg noch miterlebt** he was still alive during the war

mịt|essen *unr. tr. V.* eat ‹*skin etc.*› as well

Mịt·esser *der* (Pickel) blackhead

mịt|fahren *unr. itr. V.; mit sein* **bei jmdm. [im Auto] ~:** go with sb. [in his/her car]; (auf einer Reise) travel with sb. [in his/her car]; (mitgenommen werden) get *or* have a lift with sb. [in his/her car]

Mịt·fahrer *der* fellow passenger; (vom Fahrer aus gesehen) passenger

Mịtfahr·gelegenheit *die* lift

mịt·fühlend 1 *Adj.* sympathetic. 2 *adv.* sympathetically

mịt|führen *tr. V.* (a) (Amtsspr.: bei sich tragen) **etw. ~:** carry sth. [with one]; (b) (transportieren) ‹*river, stream*› carry along

mịt|geben *unr. tr. V.* **jmdm. etw. ~:** give sb. sth. to take with him/her; **jmdm. eine gute Erziehung ~geben** (fig.) provide sb. with a good education

Mịt·gefangene *der/die* fellow prisoner

Mịt·gefühl *das; o. Pl.* sympathy

mịt|gehen *unr. itr. V.; mit sein* (a) go too; **mit jmdm. ~:** go with sb.; **etw. ~ lassen** (fig. ugs.) walk off with sth. (coll.); pinch sth. (sl.); (b) (sich mitreißen lassen) **begeistert/ enthusiastisch ~:** respond enthusiastically (**bei, mit** to)

mịt·genommen *Adj.* worn-out ‹*furniture, carpet*›; ~ **sein/aussehen** ‹*look etc.*› be/look to be in a sorry state; (fig.) ‹*person*› be/look worn out

Mịt·gift *die;* ~, ~en (veralt.) dowry

Mịt·glied *das* member (*Gen.,* **in** + *Dat.* of); ~ **im Ausschuss sein** be a member of *or* sit on the committee; „**Zutritt nur für ~er**" 'members only'

Mịtglieder·versammlung *die* general meeting

Mịtglieds-: ~**ausweis** *der* membership card; ~**beitrag** *der* membership subscription; ~**staat** *der* member state *or* country

mịt|haben *unr. tr. V.* (ugs.) **etw. ~:** have got sth. with one

mịt|halten *unr. itr. V.* keep up (**bei** in, **mit** with)

mịt|helfen *unr. itr. V.* help (**bei, in** + *Dat.* with); **beim Bau der Garage ~:** help to build the garage

mịt·hilfe 1 *Präp. mit Gen.* with the help *or* aid of. 2 *Adv.* ~ **von** with the help *or* aid of

Mịt·hilfe *die; o. Pl.* help; assistance

mịt|hören 1 *tr. V.* listen to; (zufällig) overhear ‹*conversation, argument, etc.*›; (abhören) listen in on. 2 *itr. V.* listen; (zufällig) overhear; (jmdn. abhören) listen in

Mịt·inhaber *der* joint owner; co-owner; (einer Firma, eines Restaurants auch) joint proprietor

mịt|kommen *unr. itr. V.; mit sein* (a) come too; **kommst du mit?** are you coming [with me/us]?; **ich kann nicht ~:** I can't come; **bis zur Tür ~:** come with sb. to the door; (b) (Schritt halten) keep up; **in der Schule/ im Unterricht gut/schlecht ~:** get on well/badly at school/with one's lessons; **da komme ich nicht mehr mit!** (fig. ugs.) I can't understand it at all

mịt|kriegen *tr. V.* (ugs.) ⇒ **mitbekommen**

mịt|laufen *unr. itr. V.; mit sein* (a) **mit jmdm. ~:** run with sb.; (b) (Sport) **beim 100-m-Lauf** *usw.* ~: run in the 100 m. *etc.*; (c) **ein Tonband ~ lassen** have a tape recorder running

Mịt·läufer *der* (abwertend) [mere] supporter

Mịt·laut *der* consonant

Mịt·leid *das* pity, compassion (**mit** for); (Mitgefühl) sympathy (**mit** for); **mit jmdm. ~ haben** *od.* **empfinden** feel pity *or* compassion/have *or* feel sympathy for sb.; ~ **erregend** pitiful

Mịt·leidenschaft *die:* **jmdn./etw. in ~ ziehen** affect sb./sth.

mịtleid·erregend *Adj.* pitiful

mịt·leidig 1 *Adj.* compassionate; (mitfühlend) sympathetic. 2 *adv.* compassionately; (mitfühlend) sympathetically; (iron.) pityingly

mịt|machen 1 *tr. V.* (a) go on ‹*trip*›; join in ‹*joke*›; follow ‹*fashion*›; fight in ‹*war*›; do ‹*course, seminar*›; (b) (ugs.: billigen) **das mache ich nicht mit** I can't go along with it; **ich mache das nicht länger mit!** I'm not standing for it any longer; (c) (ugs.: zusätzlich erledigen) **jmds. Arbeit ~:** do sb.'s work as well as one's own; (d) (ugs.: erleiden) **zwei Weltkriege/viele Bombenangriffe mitgemacht haben** have been through two world wars/ many bomb attacks. 2 *itr. V.* (a) (sich beteiligen) take part (**bei** in); **willst du ~?** do you want to join in?; (b) (ugs.) **meine Beine machen nicht mehr mit** my legs are giving up on me (coll.)

Mịt·mensch *der* fellow man; fellow human being

mịt|mischen *itr. V.* (ugs.) be involved (**bei** in); **er will auch ~:** he wants to get involved, too

Mịtnahme·preis *der* (Kaufmannsspr.) takeaway price

mịt|nehmen *unr. tr. V.* (a) **jmdn. ~:** take sb. with one; **etw. ~:** take sth. with one; (verhüll.: stehlen) walk off with sth. (coll.); (kaufen) take sth.; **etw. wieder ~:** take sth. away [with one] again; **das Frachtschiff nimmt auch Passagiere mit** the cargo ship also carries passengers; **Essen/ Getränke zum Mitnehmen** food/drinks to take away *or* (Amer.) to go; **jmdn. im Auto ~:** give sb. a lift [in one's car]; (b) (ugs.: streifen) **der LKW hat die Hecke mitgenommen** the truck *or* (Brit.) lorry took the hedge with it; (c) (fig. ugs.: nicht verzichten auf) do (coll.) ‹*sights etc.*›; **auch Soho ~:** take in Soho as well; (d) (in Mitleidenschaft ziehen) **jmdn. ~:** take it out of sb.; **von etw. mitgenommen sein** be worn out by sth.; (traurig gemacht) be grieved by sth.

mịt|rechnen 1 *itr. V.* work the sum out at the same time. 2 *tr. V.* **etw. ~:** include sth. [in the calculation]

mịt|reden *itr. V.* (a) join in the conversation; (b) (mitbestimmen) have a say

Mịt·reisende *der/die* fellow passenger

mịt|reißen *unr. tr. V.* (a) ‹*avalanche, flood*› sweep away; (b) (begeistern) **seine Rede hat alle Zuhörer mitgerissen** the audience was carried away by his speech; **die ~de Musik** the rousing music

mịt·samt *Präp. mit Dat.* together with; **die ganze Familie ~ Hund und Katze** the whole family, complete with cat and dog

mịt|schleppen *tr. V.* (ugs.) (tragen) **etw. ~:** lug *or* (sl.) cart sth. with one

mịt|schneiden *unr. tr. V.* record [live]

Mịt·schnitt *der* (Rundf., Ferns.) [live] recording

mịt|schreiben 1 *unr. tr. V.* **etw. ~:** take sth. down. 2 *unr. itr. V.* write *or* take down what is/was said; (in Vorlesungen usw.) take notes

Mịt·schuld *die* share of the blame *or* responsibility (**an** + *Dat.* for); (an Verbrechen) complicity (**an** + *Dat.* in)

mịt·schuldig *Adj.* **an etw.** (*Dat.*) ~ **sein/werden** be/ become partly to blame *or* partly responsible for sth.; (an Verbrechen) be/become guilty of complicity in sth.; **sich ~ machen** put oneself in the position of being partly to blame *or* partly responsible for sth.; (an Verbrechen) become guilty of complicity as a result of one's own actions

Mịt·schüler *der,* **Mịt·schülerin** *die* schoolfellow

mịt|schwingen *unr. itr. V.* **in seinen Worten/seiner Stimme schwang Triumph/Freude mit** there was a note of triumph/joy in his words/voice

*mit|sein ⇒ **mit 2 a**

mit|singen 1 *unr. tr. V.* join in ‹*song etc.*›. **2** *unr. itr. V.* join in [the singing]; sing along

mit|spielen *itr. V.* **(a)** join in the game; **wenn das Wetter mitspielt** (fig.) if the weather is kind; **(b)** (mitwirken) **in einem Film/bei einem Theaterstück ∼:** be *or* act in a film/play; **in einem Orchester ∼:** play in an orchestra; **(c)** (sich auswirken) play a part (**bei** in); **(d)** (zusetzen) **jmdm. übel** *od.* **böse ∼:** ‹*authorities*› treat sb. badly; ‹*opponent*› give sb. a rough time

Mit·spieler *der,* **Mit·spielerin** *die* player; (in derselben Mannschaft) team-mate

Mitsprache·recht *das; o. Pl.* **ein/kein ∼ bei etw. haben** have a say/no say in sth.

mit|sprechen 1 *unr. tr. V.* join in [saying]. **2** *unr. itr. V.:* ⇒ **mitreden**

*mittag ⇒ **Mittag¹**

Mittag¹ /'mɪtaːk/ *der;* ∼s, ∼e **(a)** midday *no art.;* **gegen ∼:** around midday *or* noon; **über ∼:** at midday *or* lunchtime; **zu ∼ essen** have lunch; **heute/morgen/gestern ∼:** at midday *or* lunchtime today/tomorrow/yesterday; **was gibt es heute ∼ zu essen?** what's for lunch today?; **(b) ∼ machen** (ugs.) take one's lunch hour *or* lunch break

Mittag² *das;* ∼s (ugs.) lunch; **∼ essen** have lunch

Mittag·essen *das* lunch; midday meal; **beim ∼ sitzen** be having [one's] lunch *or* one's midday meal

mittäglich /'mɪtɛːklɪç/ **1** *Adj.; nicht präd.* midday; lunchtime ‹*invitation*›. **2** *adv.* at midday *or* lunchtime

mittags /'mɪtaːks/ *Adv.* ▶ 530 ⏐ at midday *or* lunchtime; **12 Uhr ∼:** 12 noon; 12 o'clock midday; **Dienstag ∼** *od.* **dienstags ∼:** Tuesday lunchtime

Mittags-: **∼glut** *die,* **∼hitze** *die* midday *or* noonday heat; heat of midday; **∼pause** *die* lunch hour; lunch break; **∼ruhe** *die* period of quiet after lunch; **∼schlaf** *der* after-lunch sleep; **∼sonne** *die* midday *or* noonday sun; **∼tisch** *der:* **am ∼tisch sitzen** be sitting at the table having lunch; **∼zeit** *die o. Pl.* (Zeit gegen 12 Uhr) lunchtime *no art.;* midday *no art.*

Mit·täter *der* accomplice

Mitte /'mɪtə/ *die;* ∼, ∼n **(a)** middle; (Punkt) middle; centre; (eines Kreises, einer Kugel, Stadt) centre; **wir nahmen sie in die ∼:** we had her between us; **die goldene ∼** (fig.) the golden mean; **ab durch die ∼!** (fig. ugs.) off you go; **(b)** ▶ 119 ⏐, ▶ 22 ⏐ (Zeitpunkt) middle; **∼ des Monats/Jahres** in the middle of the month/year; **∼ Februar** in mid-February; in the middle of February; **er ist ∼ [der] Dreißig** he's in his mid-thirties; **(c)** (Politik) centre; **(d) wir haben sie wieder in unserer ∼ begrüßt** we welcomed her back into our midst *or* amongst us

mit|teilen *tr. V.* **jmdm. etw. ∼:** tell sb. sth.; (informieren) inform sb. of *or* about sth.; communicate sth. to sb. (formal); (amtlich) notify *or* inform sb. of sth.; **er teilte mit, dass ...** (gab bekannt) he announced that ...

mitteilsam *Adj.* communicative; (gesprächig) talkative

Mit·teilung *die* communication; (Bekanntgabe) announcement; **jmdm. eine vertrauliche ∼ machen** give sb. confidential information; **ich muss dir eine traurige ∼ machen** I have some sad news for you

Mitteilungs·bedürfnis *das* need to talk [to others]

Mittel /'mɪtl/ *das;* ∼s, ∼ **(a)** means *sing.;* (Methode) way; method; (Werbe∼, Propaganda∼, zur Verkehrskontrolle) device (+ *Gen.* for); **mit allen ∼n versuchen, etw. zu tun** try by every means to do sth.; **[nur] ∼ zum Zweck sein** be [just] a means to an end; **∼ und Wege suchen/finden** look for/find ways and means; **(b)** (Arznei) **ein ∼ gegen Husten/Schuppen** *usw.* a remedy *or* cure for coughs *pl./* dandruff *sing. etc.;* **(c)** (Substanz) **ein ∼ gegen Ungeziefer/Insekten** a pesticide/an insect repellent; **(d)** *Pl.* (Geld∼) funds; [financial] resources; (Privat∼) means; resources; **mit öffentlichen ∼n** from public funds

mittel-, Mittel-: **∼alter** *das; o. Pl.* Middle Ages *pl.;* **das sind Zustände wie im ∼alter** (ugs.) it's positively medieval; **∼alterlich** *Adj.* medieval; **∼amerika** (*das*) Central America [and the West Indies]

mittelbar 1 *Adj.* indirect. **2** *adv.* indirectly

mittel-, Mittel-: **∼ding** *das; o. Pl.* **ein ∼ding zwischen Moped und Fahrrad** something between a moped and a bicycle; **∼europa** (*das*) Central Europe; **∼feld** *das* **(a)** (Fußball) midfield; **(b)** (Sport: im Wettbewerb) **im ∼feld sein** be in the pack; (in der Tabelle) be in midtable; **∼feld·spieler** *der* (Fußball) midfield player; **∼finger** *der* middle finger; **∼fristig** /-frɪstɪç/ **1** *Adj.* medium-term ‹*solution, financial planning*›; **2** *adv.* [etw.] **∼fristig planen** plan [sth.] on a medium-term basis; **∼gebirge** *das* low-mountain region; low mountains *pl.;* **∼groß** *Adj.* medium-sized; ‹*person*› of medium height; **∼klasse** *die* middle range; (Größenklasse) middle [size-]range; **∼klasse·wagen** *der* car in the middle range; (hinsichtlich der Größe) medium-sized car; **∼kreis** *der* (Ballspiele) centre circle; **∼linie** *die* centre line; (Fußball) halfway line; **∼los** *Adj.* without means·*postpos.;* penniless; (arm) poor; (verarmt) impoverished; **∼maß** *das:* **gutes ∼maß sein** be a good average; **∼mäßig** (oft abwertend) **1** *Adj.* mediocre; indifferent; indifferent ‹*weather*›; **2** *adv.* indifferently; **∼mäßigkeit** *die* (oft abwertend) mediocrity; **∼meer** *das* Mediterranean [Sea]

Mittelmeer-: **∼länder** *Pl.* Mediterranean countries; **∼raum** *der* Mediterranean [area]

mittel-, Mittel-: **∼ohr·entzündung** *die* (Med.) inflammation of the middle ear; **∼prächtig** *Adj.* (ugs. scherzh.) **[nur] ∼prächtig** not particularly marvellous; **∼punkt** *der* **(a)** centre; (einer Strecke) midpoint; **(b)** (Mensch/Sache im Zentrum) centre *or* focus of attention; **ein kultureller ∼punkt** a cultural centre; **etw. in den ∼punkt stellen** focus on sth.

mittels *Präp. mit Gen.* (Papierdt.) by means of

Mittel·scheitel *der* centre parting

Mittels-: **∼mann** *der Pl.* **∼männer** *od.* **∼leute**, **∼person** *die* intermediary; go-between

mittel-, Mittel-: **∼stand** *der; o. Pl.* middle class; **∼ständisch** *Adj.* middle-class; medium-sized ‹*firm*› (in private ownership); **∼streifen** *der* central reservation; median strip (Amer.); **∼stürmer** *der* (Sport) centre forward; **∼weg** *der* middle course; **der goldene ∼weg** the happy medium; **∼welle** *die* (Physik, Rundf.) medium wave; **∼wert** *der* mean [value]

mitten *Adv.* **∼ an/auf etw.** (*Akk./Dat.*) in the middle of sth.; **der Teller brach ∼ durch** the plate broke in half; **∼ in etw.** (*Akk./Dat.*) into/in the middle of sth.; **∼ durch die Stadt** right through the town; **∼ unter uns** (*Dat.*) in our midst; **der Schuss traf ihn ∼ ins Herz** the shot hit him right in the heart; **∼ im Pazifik** in mid-Pacific; **∼ in der Aufregung** in the midst of the excitement

mitten-: **∼drin** *Adv.* [right] in the middle; **∼durch** *Adv.* [right] through the middle

Mitter·nacht /'mɪtɐ-/ *die;* ▶ 530 ⏐ *o. Pl.* midnight *no art.*

mitter·nächtlich *Adj.; nicht präd.* midnight; **zu ∼er Stunde** at midnight

Mitt·fünfziger *der* man in his mid-fifties

mittler... /'mɪtlər.../ *Adj.; nicht präd.* **(a)** middle; **der/die/das Mittlere** the middle one; **die ∼e Reife** (Schulw.) *standard of achievement for school-leaving certificate at a Realschule or for entry to the sixth form in a Gymnasium; s. auch* **Osten** c; **(b)** (einen Mittelwert darstellend) average ‹*temperature*›; moderate ‹*speed*›; medium-sized ‹*company, town*›; medium ‹*quality, size*›; **ein Mann ∼en Alters** a middle-aged man

Mittler /'mɪtlɐ/ *der;* ∼s, ∼: mediator

Mittler·rolle *die* mediating role

mittler·weile /'mɪtlɐ'vaɪlə/ *Adv.* **(a)** (seitdem, allmählich) since then; (bis jetzt) by now; **(b)** (unterdessen) in the mean time

mit|tragen *unr. tr. V.* bear part of, share ‹*responsibility, cost*›; take part of, share ‹*blame*›

mit|trinken *unr. tr. V.* **etw. ∼:** drink sth. with me/us *etc.;* **trinkst du einen mit?** are you going to have a drink with me/us *etc.?*

Mitt·sommernacht *die* midsummer's night; (zur Sommersonnenwende) Midsummer Night

Mittwoch /'mɪtvɔx/ *der;* ~[e]s, ~e ▶ 119 , ▶ 595 Wednesday; *s. auch* **Dienstag; Dienstag-**

mittwochs *Adv.* ▶ 595 on Wednesday[s]; *s. auch* **dienstags**

mit·unter *Adv.* now and then; from time to time; sometimes

mit·verantwortlich *Adj.* partly responsible *pred.;* (beide/alle zusammen) jointly responsible *pred.*

Mit·verantwortung *die* share of the responsibility

mit|verdienen *itr. V.* go out to work as well

mit|versichern *tr. V.* include in one's insurance

mit·wirken *itr. V.* **an etw.** (*Dat.*) /**bei etw.** ~: collaborate on/be involved in sth.

Mitwirkende *der/die adj. Dekl.* (an einer Sendung) participant; (in einer Show) performer; (in einem Theaterstück) actor

Mit·wirkung *die; o. Pl.* ⇒ **mitwirken:** collaboration; involvement

Mit·wisser *der;* ~s ~, **Mit·wisserin** *die;* ~, ~nen: **er hatte zu viele** ~: there were too many people who knew about what he'd done

Mitwisserschaft *die;* ~: knowledge of the matter/ crime

mit|wollen *unr. itr. V.* (ugs.) (mitkommen wollen) want to come with sb.; (mitgehen, mitfahren wollen) want to go with sb.

mit|zählen 1 *itr. V.* count; **die Sonntage zählen bei den Urlaubstagen nicht mit** Sundays don't count as holidays. **2** *tr. V.* count in; include

mit|ziehen *unr. itr. V.; mit sein* (**a**) (mitgehen) go with him/ them *etc.;* (**b**) (ugs.: mitmachen) go along with it; (bei einer Klage, Initiative) give it one's backing

Mix·becher /'mɪks-/ *der* [cocktail-]shaker

mixen /'mɪksn̩/ *tr. V.* (auch Rundf., Ferns., Film) mix

Mixer *der;* ~s, ~ (**a**) (Bar~) barman; bartender (Amer.); (**b**) (Gerät) blender and liquidizer

Mix·getränk *das* mixed drink; cocktail

Mixtur /mɪks'tuːɐ̯/ *die;* ~, ~en (Pharm., fig.) mixture

mm *Abk.* **Millimeter** mm.

Mo. *Abk.* **Montag** Mon.

Mob /mɔp/ *der;* ~s (abwertend) mob

mobben /'mɔbn̩/ *tr. V.* (ugs.) harass and bully

Mobbing /'mɔbɪŋ/ *das;* ~s (ugs.) harassing and bullying

Möbel /'møːbl̩/ *das;* ~s, ~ (**a**) *Pl.* furniture *sing., no indef. art.;* (**b**) piece of furniture

Möbel-: ~**haus** *das* furniture store; ~**packer** *der* removal man; ~**spedition** *die* furniture-removal firm; ~**stück** *das* piece of furniture; ~**wagen** *der* furniture van; removal van

mobil /mo'biːl/ *Adj.* (auch Milit.) mobile; (einsatzbereit) mobilized; ~ **machen** mobilize

Mobile /'moːbilə/ *das;* ~s, ~s mobile

Mobil·funk *der* mobile telephony

Mobiliar /mobi'li̯aːɐ̯/ *das;* ~s furnishings *pl.*

mobilisieren *tr. V.* (Milit., fig.) mobilize; **die Massen** ~ (fig.) stir the masses into action

Mobilisierung *die;* ~, ~en (Milit., fig.) mobilization

Mobilität /mobili'tɛːt/ *die;* ~ (Soziol.) mobility

Mobilmachung *die;* ~, ~en mobilization

Mobil·telefon *das* cellular phone

möblieren *tr. V.* furnish

Mocca /'mɔka/ *der;* ⇒ **Mokka**

mochte /'mɔxtə/ *1. u. 3. Pers. Sg. Prät. v.* **mögen**

möchte /'mœçtə/ *1. u. 3. Pers. Sg. Konjunktiv II v.* **mögen**

Möchte·gern- would-be ‹*poet, Casanova, etc.*›

modal /mo'daːl/ *Adj.* (Sprachw.) modal

Modalität /modali'tɛːt/ *die;* ~, ~en (geh.) provision; condition

Modal·verb *das* (Sprachw.) modal verb

Mode /'moːdə/ *die;* ~, ~n (**a**) fashion; **jede** ~ **mitmachen** follow fashion's every whim; **mit der** ~ **gehen**

follow the fashion; **nach der neuesten** ~: in the latest style; **in** ~ (*Akk.*)/ **aus der** ~ **kommen** come into/go out of fashion; (**b**) *Pl.* (~kleidung) fashions

mode-, Mode-: ~**bewusst**, **~**bewußt** *Adj.* fashion-conscious; ~**farbe** *die* fashionable colour; ~**journal** *das* fashion magazine

Modell /mo'dɛl/ *das;* ~s, ~e (auch fig.) model; (Technik: Entwurf) [design] model; pattern; (in Originalgröße) mock-up; jmdm. ~ **sitzen** *od.* **stehen** model *or* sit for sb.

Modell-: ~**eisen·bahn** *die* model railway; ~**flugzeug** *das* model aircraft

modellhaft *Adj.* exemplary; model *attrib.;* pilot ‹*scheme*›

modellieren *tr. V.* model, mould ‹*figures*›; mould ‹*clay, wax*›

Modellier·masse *die* modelling material (esp. clay or wax)

Modell-: ~**projekt** *das* pilot scheme; ~**versuch** *der* pilot scheme

Modem /'moːdem/ *der od. das;* ~s, ~s (DV) modem

Moden·schau *die* fashion show *or* parade

Mode-: ~**püppchen** *das,* ~**puppe** *die* fashion-crazy bird (Brit. sl.) *or* (Amer. coll.) dame

Moder /'moːdɐ/ *der;* ~s mould; (~geruch) mustiness; (Verwesung, auch fig.) decay

Moderation /modera'tsi̯oːn/ *die;* ~, ~en (Rundf., Ferns.) presentation

Moderator /mode'raːtɔr/ *der;* ~s, ~en /-'toːrən/, **Moderatorin** *die;* ~, ~nen ▶ 85 (Rundf., Ferns.) presenter

moderieren /mode'riːrən/ **1** *tr. V.* (Rundf., Ferns.) present ‹*programme*›. **2** *itr. V.* be the presenter

moderig *Adj.* musty

modern[1] /'moːdɐn/ *itr. V.; auch mit sein* go mouldy; (verwesen) decay

modern[2] /mo'dɛrn/ **1** *Adj.* modern; (modisch) fashionable. **2** *adv.* in a modern manner *or* style; (modisch) fashionably; (aufgeschlossen) progressively

Moderne *die;* ~ (**a**) modern age; modern times *pl.;* (**b**) (Kunstrichtung) modern arts *pl., no art.*

modernisieren 1 *tr. V.* modernize. **2** *itr. V.* introduce modern methods

Modernisierung *die;* ~, ~en modernization

Modernität *die;* ~: modernity

Mode-: ~**schau** *die* ⇒ **Modenschau;** ~**schmuck** *der* costume jewellery; ~**schöpfer** *der* couturier; ~**schöpferin** *die* couturière; ~**tanz** *der* dance [briefly] in vogue; ~**wort** *das; Pl.* ~**wörter** vogue-word; 'in' expression (coll.); ~**zeit·schrift** *die* fashion magazine

Modi ⇒ **Modus**

modifizieren /modifi'tsiːrən/ *tr. V.* (geh.) modify

modisch /'moːdɪʃ/ **1** *Adj.* fashionable. **2** *adv.* fashionably

Modul /mo'duːl/ *das;* ~s, ~e (DV, Elektronik) module

Modus /'moːdʊs/ *der;* ~, **Modi** (Sprachw.) mood

Mofa /'moːfa/ *das;* ~s, ~s [low-powered] moped

Mogelei *die;* ~, ~en (ugs.) cheating *no pl.*

mogeln (ugs.) **1** *itr. V.* cheat. **2** *tr. V.* **etw. in etw.** (*Akk.*) ~: slip sth. into sth.

mögen /'møːgn̩/ **1** *unr. Modalverb; 2. Part.* ~: (**a**) (wollen) want to; **das hätte ich sehen** ~: I would have liked to see that; (**b**) (geh.: sollen) **das mag genügen** that should be *or* ought to be enough; (**c**) (geh.: Wunschform) **möge er bald kommen!** I do hope he'll come soon!; (**d**) (Vermutung, Möglichkeit) **sie mag/mochte vierzig sein** she must be/ must have been [about] forty; **Meier, Müller, Koch — und wie sie alle heißen** ~: Meier, Müller, Koch and [the rest,] whatever they're called; **wie viele Personen** ~ **das sein?** how many people would you say there are?; **was mag sie damit gemeint haben?** what can she have meant by that?; [**das**] **mag sein** maybe; (**e**) (geh.: Einräumung) **es mag kommen, was will** come what may; (**f**) *Konjunktiv II* (den Wunsch haben) **ich/sie möchte gern wissen** ...: I would *or* should/she would like to know ...; **ich möchte nicht stören, aber** ...: I don't want to interrupt, but ...; **ich möchte zu gerne wissen** I'd love to know ...; **man möchte meinen, er sei der Chef** one

---

would [really] think he was the boss. **2** *unr. tr. V.* **(a)** **[gern]** ∼**:** like; **sie mag keine Rosen** she does not like roses; **sie mag ihn sehr [gern]** she likes him very much; (hat ihn sehr gern) she is very fond of him; **ich mag lieber/am liebsten Bier** I like beer better/best [of all]; **(b)** *Konjunktiv II* (haben wollen) **möchten Sie ein Glas Wein?** would you like a glass of wine?; **ich möchte lieber Tee** I would prefer tea *or* rather have tea. **3** *unr. itr. V.* **(a)** (es wollen) like to; **ich mag nicht** I don't want to; **magst du?** do you want to?; (bei einem Angebot) would you like one/some?; **(b)** *Konjunktiv II* (fahren, gehen usw. wollen) **ich möchte nach Hause/in die Stadt/auf die Schaukel** I want *or* I'd like to go home/into town/on the swing; **er möchte zu Herrn A** he would like to see Mr A

möglich /ˈmøːklɪç/ *Adj.* possible; **es war ihm nicht** ∼ **[zu kommen]** he was unable [to come]; it was not possible for him [to come]; **sobald/so gut es mir** ∼ **ist** as soon/as well as I can; **das** *od.* **alles Mögliche tun, sein Möglichstes tun** do everything possible; do one's utmost; **dort kann man alles Mögliche kaufen** (ugs.) you can get all sorts of things there; **sie hatte alles Mögliche zu kritisieren** she criticized everything; **alle** ∼**en Leute** (ugs.) all sorts of people; **das ist gut/leicht/durchaus** ∼**:** that is very/wholly/entirely possible; **man sollte es nicht für** ∼ **halten** one would not believe it possible; **[das ist doch] nicht** ∼**!** impossible!; I don't believe it!

möglicherweise *Adv.* possibly

Möglichkeit *die;* ∼**,** ∼**en** possibility; (Gelegenheit) opportunity; chance; (möglicher Weg) way; **nach** ∼**:** if possible; **es besteht die** ∼**, dass** …**:** there is a chance *or* possibility that …**; ist es die** *od.* **ist [denn] das die** ∼**!** (ugs.) well, I'll be damned! (coll.); whatever next!; **die** ∼ **haben, etw. zu tun** have an opportunity of doing sth. *or* to do sth.; **das übersteigt meine [finanziellen]** ∼**en** that is beyond my [financial] means

möglichst *Adv.* **(a)** (so weit wie möglich) as much *or* far as possible; (wenn möglich) if [at all] possible; **macht** ∼ **keinen Lärm** don't make any noise if you can possibly help it; **(b)** (so … wie möglich) ∼ **groß/schnell/oft** as big/fast/often as possible; **mit** ∼ **großer Sorgfalt** with the greatest possible care; *s. auch* **möglich**

Mohair /moˈhɛːɐ̯/ *der;* ∼**s** mohair

Mohammed /moːhamɛt/ *(der)* Muhammad

Mohammedaner *der;* ∼**s,** ∼**, Mohammedanerin,** *die;* ∼**,** ∼**nen** Muslim; Muhammadan

mohammedanisch *Adj.* Muslim, Muhammadan

Mohikaner /mohiˈkaːnɐ/ *der;* ∼**s,** ∼**:** Mohican; **der letzte** ∼**, der Letzte der** ∼ (ugs. scherzh.) the last one; the last survivor (joc.)

Mohn /moːn/ *der;* ∼**s (a)** poppy; **(b)** (Samen) poppy seed; (auf Brot, Kuchen) poppy seeds *pl.*

Mohn-: ∼**blume** *die* poppy; ∼**brötchen** *das* poppy-seed roll; ∼**kuchen** *der* poppy-seed cake

Mohr /moːɐ̯/ *der;* ∼**en,** ∼**en** (veralt.) Moor

Möhre /ˈmøːrə/ *die;* ∼**,** ∼**n** carrot

Mohren·kopf *der* chocolate marshmallow

Möhren·saft *der* carrot juice

Mohr·rübe *die* carrot

Mokassin /ˈmɔkaˈsiːn/ *der;* ∼**s,** ∼**s** moccasin

mokieren /moˈkiːrən/ *refl. V.* (geh.) **sich über etw.** *(Akk.)* ∼**:** mock *or* scoff at sth.; **sich über jmdn.** ∼**:** mock sb.

Mokka /ˈmɔka/ *der;* ∼**s (a)** mocha [coffee]; **(b)** (Getränk) strong black coffee

Mokka-: ∼**löffel** *der* [small] coffee-spoon; ∼**tasse** *die* small coffee cup

Molch /mɔlç/ *der;* ∼**[e]s,** ∼**e** newt

Mole /ˈmoːlə/ *die;* ∼**,** ∼**n** [harbour] mole

Molekül /moleˈkyːl/ *das;* ∼**s,** ∼**e** (Chemie) molecule

Molekular- molecular

molk /mɔlk/ *1. u. 3. Pers. Sg. Prät. v.* **melken**

Molkerei *die;* ∼**,** ∼**en** dairy

Molkerei·produkt *das* dairy product

Moll /mɔl/ *das;* ∼ (Musik) minor [key]; **a-Moll** A minor

mollig /ˈmɔlɪç/ **1** *Adj.* **(a)** (rundlich) plump; **(b)** (warm) cosy; snug. **2** *adv.* cosily; snugly; ∼ **warm** warm and cosy

Moloch /ˈmoːlɔx/ *der;* ∼**s,** ∼**e** (geh.) Moloch; voracious giant

Molotow·cocktail /ˈmɔlotɔf-/ *der* Molotov cocktail

Moment[1] /moˈmɛnt/ *der;* ∼**[e]s,** ∼**e** moment; **einen** ∼ **bitte!** just a moment, please!; ∼ **[mal]!** [hey!] just a moment!; wait a mo! (coll.); **im nächsten/selben** ∼**:** the next/at the same moment; **jeden** ∼ (ugs.) [at] any moment; **im** ∼**:** at the moment

Moment[2] *das;* ∼**[e]s,** ∼**e** factor, element **(für** in); **das auslösende** ∼ **für etw. sein** be the trigger for sth.

momentan /momɛnˈtaːn/ **1** *Adj.* **(a)** *nicht präd.* present; current; **(b)** (vorübergehend) temporary; (flüchtig) momentary. **2** *adv.* **(a)** at the moment; at present; **(b)** (vorübergehend) temporarily; (flüchtig) momentarily; for a moment

Monarch /moˈnarç/ *der;* ∼**en,** ∼**en** monarch

Monarchie *die;* ∼**,** ∼**n** monarchy

Monarchin *die;* ∼**,** ∼**nen** monarch

monarchisch **1** *Adj.* monarchical. **2** *adv.* monarchically

Monarchist *der;* ∼**en,** ∼**en** monarchist

monarchistisch **1** *Adj.* monarchist ‹*party, group*›; monarchistic ‹*tendency, views*›. **2** *adv.* monarchistically

Monat /ˈmoːnat/ *der;* ∼**s,** ∼**e** month; **im** ∼ **April** in the month of April; **Ihr Schreiben vom 22.** ∼**s** your letter of the 22nd [inst.]; **sie ist im vierten** ∼ **[schwanger]** she is four months pregnant; **was verdienst du im** ∼**?** how much do you earn per month?

monatelang **1** *Adj.; nicht präd.* lasting for months *postpos., not pred.;* **die** ∼**en Verhandlungen** the negotiations, which lasted for several months; **nach** ∼**er Krankheit** after months of illness. **2** *adv.* for months [on end]

-monatig (a) (… Monate alt) …-month-old; **(b)** (… Monate dauernd) … month's/months'; …-month; **eine viermonatige Kur** a four-month course of treatment; **mit dreimonatiger Verspätung** three months late

monatlich **1** *Adj.* monthly. **2** *adv.* monthly; every month; (je Monat) per month

Monats-: ∼**anfang** *der,* ∼**beginn** *der* beginning of the month; ∼**binde** *die* sanitary towel (Brit.); sanitary napkin (Amer.); ∼**blutung** *die* [monthly] period; ∼**einkommen** *das* monthly income; ∼**ende** *das* end of the month; ∼**erste** *der* first [day] of the month; ∼**frist** *o. Art.; o. Pl.* **in** *od.* **innerhalb** *od.* **binnen** ∼**frist** within [a period of] a *or* one month; ∼**gehalt** *das* month's salary; **vier** ∼**gehälter** four months' salary *sing.;* **ein dreizehntes** ∼**gehalt** an extra month's salary; ∼**karte** *die* monthly season ticket; ∼**letzte** *der* last day of the month; ∼**lohn** *der* month's wages; **vier** ∼**löhne** four months' wages *pl.;* ∼**miete** *die* month's rent; **zwei** ∼**mieten** two months' rent; **eine** ∼**miete von 1 000 DM** a monthly rent of 1,000 marks; ∼**mitte** *die* middle of the month; ∼**rate** *die* monthly instalment

Mönch /mœnç/ *der;* ∼**[e]s,** ∼**e** monk

Mönchs-: ∼**kloster** *das* monastery; ∼**kutte** *die* monk's habit *or* cowl

Mönch[s]tum *das;* ∼**s** monasticism

Mond /moːnt/ *der;* ∼**[e]s,** ∼**e** moon; **ich könnte ihn auf den** ∼ **schießen** (salopp) I wish he'd get lost (sl.); **hinter dem** ∼ **leben** (fig. ugs.) be a bit behind the times *or* not quite with it (coll.); **nach dem** ∼ **gehen** (ugs.) ‹*clock, watch*› be hopelessly wrong

mondän /mɔnˈdɛːn/ **1** *Adj.* [highly] fashionable; smart. **2** *adv.* fashionably; in a fashionable style

mond-, Mond-: ∼**auf·gang** *der* moonrise; ∼**fähre** *die* (Raumf.) lunar module; ∼**finsternis** *die* (Astron.) lunar eclipse; eclipse of the moon; ∼**gesicht** *das* moon-face; ∼**hell** *Adj.* (geh.) moonlit; ∼**kalb** *das* (salopp) dimwit (coll.); dope (coll.); ∼**lande·fähre** *die* (Raumf.) lunar module; ∼**landschaft** *die* (auch fig.) lunar landscape; ∼**landung** *die* moon landing; ∼**licht** *das; o. Pl.* moonlight; ∼**los** *Adj.* moonless; ∼**oberfläche** *die* lunar surface; ∼**phase** *die* moon's phase; ∼**schein** *der; o. Pl.* moonlight; **der kann mir mal im** ∼**schein begegnen** (salopp) he can get lost (sl.); ∼**sichel** *die* crescent moon; ∼**süchtig** *Adj.* sleepwalking *attrib.*

(esp. by moonlight); **~umlaufbahn** *die* lunar orbit; **~untergang** *der* moonset

Monetarismus /moneta'rɪsmʊs/ *der;* ~ (Wirtsch.) monetarism *no art.*

Moneten /mo'ne:tn̩/ *Pl.* (ugs.) cash *sing.;* dough *sing.* (sl.)

Mongole /mɔŋ'go:lə/ *der;* **~n**, **~n** (a) Mongol; (b) ▶ 388 | (Bewohner der Mongolei) Mongolian

Mongolei /mɔŋgo'lai̯/ *die;* ~: Mongolia *no art.*

mongolid /mɔŋgo'li:t/ *Adj.* (Anthrop.) Mongoloid

mongolisch *Adj.* ▶ 388 | Mongolian

Mongolismus *der;* ~ (Med.) mongolism *no art.*

mongoloid *Adj.* (Med.) mongoloid

monieren /mo'ni:rən/ *tr. V.* criticize; (beanstanden) find fault with

Monitor /'mo:nitɔr/ *der;* **~s**, **~en** /-'to:rən/ monitor

mono /'mo:no/ *Adv.* (ugs.) ‹*hear, play, etc.*› in mono (coll.)

mono-, **Mono-** mono-

monogam /mono'ga:m/ **1** *Adj.* monogamous. **2** *adv.* monogamously

Monogamie *die;* ~: monogamy

Monogramm *das;* **~s**, **~e** monogram

Monokel /mo'nɔkl̩/ *das;* **~s**, ~: monocle

Monokultur *die* (Landw.) monoculture

Monolog /mono'lo:k/ *der;* **~s**, **~e** monologue

Monopol /mono'po:l/ *das;* **~s**, **~e** monopoly (**auf** + *Akk.*, **für** in, of)

Monopolstellung *die* [position of] monopoly

monotheistisch /monote'ɪstɪʃ/ monotheistic

monoton /mono'to:n/ **1** *Adj.* monotonous. **2** *adv.* monotonously

Monotonie *die;* ~, **~n** monotony

Monster /'mɔnstɐ/ *das;* **~s**, ~: monster; (hässlich) [hideous] brute

Monster- ⇨ **Mammut-**

Monstranz /mɔn'strants/ *die;* ~, **~en** (kath. Kirche) monstrance

Monstren ⇨ **Monstrum**

monströs /mɔn'strøːs/ *Adj.* (geh., auch fig.) monstrous; [huge and] hideous

Monstrum /'mɔnstrʊm/ *das;* **~s**, **Monstren** (a) (auch fig.: Mensch) monster; (b) (Ungetüm) hulking great thing (coll.)

Monsun /mɔn'zu:n/ *der;* **~s**, **~e** (Geogr.) monsoon

Montag /'mo:nta:k/ *der* ▶ 119 |, ▶ 595 | Monday; *s. auch* **blau; Dienstag; Dienstag-**

Montage /mɔn'ta:ʒə/ *die;* ~, **~n** (a) (Bauw., Technik) (Zusammenbau) assembly; (Einbau) installation; (Aufstellen) erection; (Anbringen) fitting (**an** + *Akk. od. Dat.* to); mounting (**auf** + *Akk. od. Dat.* on); **auf ~:** (ugs.) away on a job; (b) (Film, Fot., bild. Kunst, Literaturw.) montage

Montage-: **~band** *das* assembly line; **~halle** *die* assembly shop

montags *Adv.* ▶ 595 | on Monday[s]; *s. auch* **dienstags**

Montanindustrie *die* coal and steel industry

Monteur /mɔn'tøːɐ̯/ *der;* **~s**, **~e** mechanic; (Installateur) fitter; (Elektro~) electrician

montieren /mɔn'ti:rən/ *tr. V.* (a) (zusammenbauen) assemble (**aus** from); erect ‹*building*›; (b) (anbringen) fit (**an** + *Akk. od. Dat.* to; **auf** + *Akk. od. Dat.* on); (einbauen) install (**in** + *Akk.* in); (befestigen) fix (**an** + *Akk. od. Dat.* to); **eine Lampe an die** *od.* **der Decke ~:** put up *or* fix a light on the ceiling

Montur /mɔn'tu:ɐ̯/ *die;* ~, **~en** (ugs.) outfit (coll.); gear *no pl.* (coll.)

Monument /monu'mɛnt/ *das;* **~[e]s**, **~e** (auch fig.) monument

monumental *Adj.* (auch fig.) monumental; (massiv) massive

Monumental- monumental

Moor /mo:ɐ̯/ *das;* **~[e]s**, **~e** bog; (Bruch) marsh; (Flach~) fen; (Hoch~) high moor

---

*alte Schreibung (vgl. Hinweise auf S. xvi–xxii)

Moorbad *das* mudbath

Moos /mo:s/ *das;* **~es**, **~e** (a) moss; ~ **ansetzen** gather moss; (b) *o. Pl.* (salopp) cash; dough (sl.)

moos-: **~bedeckt**, **~bewachsen** *Adj.* moss-covered; **~grün** *Adj.* moss-green

***Mop** ⇨ **Mopp**

Moped /'mo:pɛt/ *das;* **~s**, **~s** moped

Mopedfahrer *der* moped-rider

Mopp *der;* **~s**, **~s** mop

Mops /mɔps/ *der;* **~es**, **Möpse** /'mœpsə/ (a) (Hund) pug [dog]; (b) (salopp: dicke Person) podge (coll.); fatty (derog.)

mopsen *tr. V.* (fam.) pinch (sl.)

Moral /mo'ra:l/ *die;* ~ (a) (Norm) morality; **gegen die ~ verstoßen** offend against morality *or* the code of conduct; **die herrschende ~:** [currently] accepted standards *pl.;* **doppelte ~:** double standards *pl.;* (b) (Sittlichkeit) morals *pl.;* **keine ~ haben** have no sense of morals; (c) (Selbstvertrauen) morale; **die ~ ist gut/schlecht** morale is high/low; (d) (Lehre) moral; (e) (Philos.) ethics *sing.*

Moralapostel *der* (abwertend) upholder of moral standards

moralisch /mo'ra:lɪʃ/ **1** *Adj.* (a) *nicht präd.* moral; (b) (sittlich einwandfrei) moral; morally upright; (tugendhaft) virtuous. **2** *adv.* morally; (tugendhaft) morally; virtuously

Moralist *der;* **~en**, **~en** moralist

Moral-: **~philosophie** *die* moral philosophy; **~prediger** *der* (abwertend) moralizing prig; **~predigt** *die* (abwertend) [moralizing] lecture; homily; **[jmdm.] eine ~predigt halten** deliver a homily [to sb.]

Morast /mo'rast/ *der;* **~[e]s**, **~e** *od.* **Moräste** /mo'rɛstə/ (a) bog; swamp; (b) *o. Pl.* (Schlamm) mud; (auch fig.) mire

morastig *Adj.* muddy

Moratorium /mora'to:rɪʊm/ *das;* ~, **Moratorien** (Wirtsch., Politik) moratorium (**für** on)

morbid /mɔr'bi:t/ *Adj.* (geh.) (kränklich) sickly; (todgeweiht) deathly pale; (fig.) moribund, degenerate ‹*society, institution, etc.*›

Morchel /'mɔrçl̩/ *die;* ~, **~n** morel

Mord /mɔrt/ *der;* **~[e]s**, **~e** murder (**an** + *Dat.* of); (durch ein Attentat) assassination; **einen ~ begehen** commit murder; **versuchter ~:** attempted murder; ~ **aus Eifersucht** (Schlagzeile) jealousy killing; **dann gibt es ~ und Totschlag** (fig. ugs.) all hell is/will be let loose

Mord-: **~anklage** *die* charge of murder; **~anschlag** *der* attempted murder (**auf** + *Akk.* of); (Attentat) assassination attempt (**auf** + *Akk.* on); **~drohung** *die* murder threat

morden *tr., itr. V.* murder; **das sinnlose Morden** the senseless killing

Mörder /'mœrdɐ/ *der;* **~s**, ~: murderer (esp. Law); killer; (politischer ~) assassin

Mörderin *die;* ~, **~nen** murderer; murderess; (politische ~) assassin

mörderisch **1** *Adj.* (a) (ugs.) murderous; fiendish ‹*cold*›; dreadful (coll.) ‹*clamour, weather, storm*›; (b) (todbringend) murderous. **2** *adv.* (ugs.) dreadfully (coll.); frightfully (coll.)

mord-, **Mord-:** **~fall** *der* murder case; **~instrument** *das* (fig. scherzh.) murderous[-looking] weapon *or* device; **~kommission** *die* murder *or* (Amer.) homicide squad; **~prozess**, ***~prozeß** *der* murder trial

mords-, **Mords-** (ugs.) terrific (coll.); tremendous (coll.)

mords-, **Mords-:** **~ding** *das* (ugs.) whopper (coll.); **~hunger** *der* (ugs.) terrific hunger (coll.); **einen ~hunger haben** be ravenous *or* famished; **~krach** *der* (ugs.) (a) terrible din *or* racket (coll.); (b) (Streit) terrific row (coll.); **~mäßig 1** *Adj.; nicht präd.* terrific (coll.); tremendous (coll.); (entsetzlich) terrible (coll.); infernal (coll.) ‹*din, racket*›; **2** *adv.* tremendously (coll.); incredibly (coll.); (entsetzlich) terribly (coll.); **~stimmung** *die* (ugs.) terrific atmosphere (coll.)

Mord-: **~verdacht** *der* suspicion of murder; **~versuch** *der* attempted murder; (Attentat) assassination attempt; **~waffe** *die* murder weapon

morgen /'mɔrgn̩/ *Adv.* tomorrow; ~ **früh/Mittag/ Abend** tomorrow morning/lunchtime/evening; ~ **in einer Woche/in vierzehn Tagen** tomorrow week/ fortnight; a week/fortnight tomorrow; ~ **um diese** *od.* **die gleiche Zeit** this time tomorrow; **bis ~!** until tomorrow!; see you tomorrow!; ~ **ist auch [noch] ein Tag** tomorrow is another day; **die Mode/Technik von ~** (fig.) tomorrow's fashions *pl.*/technology

Morgen *der;* ~**s,** ~ ▶ 530| (a) morning; **am ~** in the morning; **am folgenden** *od.* **nächsten ~:** next *or* the following morning; **früh am ~, am frühen ~:** early in the morning; **eines [schönen] ~s** one [fine] morning; **gegen ~:** towards morning; ~ **für ~:** every single morning; morning after morning; **den ganzen ~** all morning; **guten ~!** good morning!; ~**!** (ugs.) morning! (coll.); **[jmdm.] guten ~ sagen** *od.* **wünschen** say good morning [to sb.]; wish [sb.] good morning; (grüßen) say hello [to sb.]; **heute/gestern ~:** this/yesterday morning; **(b)** ▶ 189| (veralt.: Feldmaß) ≈ acre; **fünf ~ Land** five acres of land

Morgen-: ~**ausgabe** *die* morning edition; ~**dämmerung** *die* dawn; daybreak

morgendlich *Adj.; nicht präd.* morning; **die ~e Kühle/Stille** the cool/peace of [early] morning

Morgen-: ~**grauen** *das* daybreak; **im** *od.* **beim ~grauen** in the first light of day; ~**gymnastik** *die* morning exercises *pl.;* daily dozen (coll.); ~**land** *das; o. Pl.* (veralt.) East; Orient; ~**luft** *die* morning air; ~**luft wittern** (fig. scherzh.) see one's chance; ~**mantel** *der* dressing gown; ~**muffel** *der* (ugs.) **ein ~muffel sein** be grumpy in the mornings; ~**rock** *der* dressing gown; ~**rot** *das* rosy/red dawn

morgens *Adv.* ▶ 530| in the morning; (jeden Morgen) every morning; ~ **um 7 Uhr, um 7 Uhr ~:** at 7 in the morning/every morning; **dienstags ~:** on Tuesday morning[s]; **von ~ bis abends** all day long; from morning to evening

Morgen-: ~**sonne** *die* morning sun; ~**spaziergang** *der* (esp. early) morning walk; ~**stern** *der* morning star; ~**stunde** *die* hour of the morning; ~**stunde hat Gold im Munde** (Spr.) the early bird catches the worm (prov.); ~**zeitung** *die* morning paper

morgig *Adj.; nicht präd.* tomorrow's; **der ~e Tag** tomorrow

Mormone /mɔr'moːnə/ *der;* ~**n,** ~**n, Mormonin** *die;* ~, ~**nen** Mormon

Morphing /'mɔrfɪŋ/ *das;* ~**s** (DV) morphing

Morphium /'mɔrfiʊm/ *das;* ~**s** morphine

morphium·süchtig *Adj.* addicted to morphine *pred.*

morsch /mɔrʃ/ *Adj.* (auch fig.) rotten; brittle ‹*bones*›; crumbling ‹*rock, masonry*›

Morse·alphabet /'mɔrzə-/ *das* Morse code *or* alphabet

morsen /'mɔrzn̩/ **1** *itr. V.* send a message/messages in Morse. **2** *tr. V.* send ‹*signal, message*› in Morse

Mörser /'mœrzɐ/ *der;* ~**s,** ~ (auch Milit.) mortar

Morse·zeichen *das* Morse symbol

Mortadella /mɔrta'dɛla/ *die;* ~, ~**s** mortadella

Mortalität /mɔrtali'tɛːt/ *die;* ~**:** mortality [rate]

Mörtel /'mœrtl̩/ *der;* ~**s** mortar

Mosaik /moza'iːk/ *das;* ~**s,** ~**en** *od.* ~**e** (auch fig.) mosaic

Mosambik /mozam'biːk/ *(das);* ~**s** Mozambique

Moschee /mɔ'ʃeː/ *die;* ~, ~**n** mosque

Moschus /'mɔʃʊs/ *der;* ~**:** musk

Mose /'moːzə/ *(der)* Moses; **das erste/zweite/dritte/ vierte/fünfte Buch ~:** Genesis/Exodus/Levithicus/ Numbers/Deuteronomy; *s. auch* **Buch a**

Mosel /'moːzl̩/ *die;* ~**:** Moselle

mosern /'moːzɐn/ *itr. V.* (ugs.) gripe (coll.) (**über** + *Akk.* about)

Moses *(der)* Moses

Moskau /'mɔskaʊ/ *(das);* ~**s** ▶ 490| Moscow

Moskauer ▶ 490| **1** *indekl. Adj.* Moscow *attrib.* **2** *der;* ~**s,** ~**:** Muscovite; *s. auch* **Kölner**

Moskito /mɔs'kiːto/ *der;* ~**s,** ~**s** mosquito

Moslem /'mɔslɛm/ *der;* ~**s,** ~**s** Muslim

moslemisch *Adj.* Muslim

Most /mɔst/ *der;* ~**[e]s,** ~**e (a)** (südd.: junger Wein) new wine; **(b)** (südd.: Obstsaft) [cloudy fermented] fruit juice; **(c)** (südd., schweiz., österr.: Obstwein) fruit-wine; (Apfel~) [rough] cider

Mostrich /'mɔstrɪç/ *der;* ~**s** (nordostd.) mustard

Motel /'moːtl̩/ *das;* ~**s,** ~**s** motel

Motiv /mo'tiːf/ *das;* ~**s,** ~**e (a)** motive; **(b)** (Literaturw., Musik usw.: Thema) motif; theme; **(c)** (bild. Kunst, Fot., Film: Gegenstand) subject

Motivation /motiva'tsi̯oːn/ *die;* ~, ~**en** (Psych., Päd.) motivation

motivieren *tr. V.* (geh.) motivate

Motivierung *die;* ~, ~**en** (geh.) motivation

Motodrom /moto'droːm/ *das;* ~**s,** ~**e** autodrome; speedway (Amer.)

Motor /'moːtɔr/ *der;* ~**s,** ~**en** (Verbrennungs~) engine; (Elektro~) motor; (fig.) driving force (*Gen.* behind)

Motor·boot *das* motor boat; (Rennboot) power boat

Motoren-: ~**geräusch** *das* sound of the engine/engines; ~**lärm** *der* engine noise

Motor·haube *die* (Kfz-W.) bonnet (Brit.); hood (Amer.)

-motorig *adj.* -engined; **ein~/zwei~:** single-engined/ twin-engined

Motorik /mo'toːrɪk/ *die;* ~ (bes. Med.) motor functions *pl.*

motorisch *Adj.* (Psych.) motor *attrib.*

motorisieren *tr. V.* motorize

Motorisierung *die;* ~**:** motorization

Motor-: ~**öl** *das* (Kfz-W.) engine oil; ~**rad** *das* motorcycle

Motorrad-: ~**fahrer** *der* motorcyclist; ~**rennen** *das* motorcycle race; (Sport) motorcycle racing; ~**sport** *der* motor-cycling

Motor-: ~**roller** *der* motor scooter; ~**säge** *die* power saw; ~**schaden** *der* engine trouble *no indef. art.;* (Panne) mechanical breakdown; ~**sport** *der* motor sport *no art.;* ~**wäsche** *die* engine wash-down

Motte /'mɔtə/ *die;* ~, ~**n** moth; **von etw. angezogen werden wie die ~n vom Licht** be attracted by sth. as moths to the light; **[ach,] du kriegst die ~n!** (ugs.) my godfathers!

Motten-: ~**kiste** *die* **(a)** (fig.) **Filme/Geschichten/ Gags aus der ~kiste** ancient films/stories/gags; ~**kugel** *die* mothball

Motto /'mɔto/ *das;* ~**s,** ~**s** motto; (Schlagwort) slogan; **nach dem ~: ... leben** live according to the maxim: ...

motzen /'mɔtsn̩/ *itr. V.* (ugs.) grouch (coll.), bellyache (sl.) (**über** + *Akk.* about)

Mountain·bike /'maʊntnbaɪk/ *das* mountain bike

moussieren /mu'siːrən/ *itr. V.* sparkle; (als Eigenschaft) be sparkling

Möwe /'møːvə/ *die;* ~, ~**n** gull

MP /ɛm'piː/ *die;* ~, ~**s** *Abk.* **(a) Maschinenpistole** sub-machinegun; **(b) Militärpolizei** MPs *pl.;* military police *pl.*

Mrd. *Abk.* **Milliarde** bn.

Ms., MS *Abk.* **Manuskript** MS

MTA /ɛmteː'|aː/ *die;* ~, ~**[s]** *Abk.* **medizinisch-technische Assistentin** medical-laboratory assistant

MTB *Abk.* **Mountainbike** MTB

mtl. *Abk.* **monatlich** mthly.

Mücke /'mykə/ *die;* ~, ~**n** midge; gnat; (größer) mosquito; **aus einer ~ einen Elefanten machen** (ugs.) make a mountain out of a molehill

mucken /'mʊkn̩/ *itr. V.* (ugs.) grumble; mutter; **ohne zu ~:** without a murmur

Mucken *Pl.* (ugs.) whims; (Eigenarten) little ways *or* peculiarities; (Launen) moods; **[seine] ~ haben** ‹*person*› have one's little ways/one's moods; ‹*car, machine*› be a little unpredictable *or* temperamental

Mücken·stich *der* midge/mosquito bite

Mucks /mʊks/ *der;* ~**es,** ~**e** (ugs.) murmur [of protest]; slight[est] sound; **keinen** ~ **sagen** not utter a [single] word *or* sound

mucksen *refl. V.* (ugs.) make a sound

Muckser *der;* ~**s,** ~ (ugs.) ⇒ **Mucks**

mucks·mäuschen·still (ugs.) **1** *Adj.; nicht attr.* utterly silent; ⟨*person*⟩ as quiet as a mouse *postpos..* **2** *adv.* in total silence; without making a sound

müde /'myːdə/ **1** *Adj.* tired; (ermattet) weary; (schläfrig) sleepy; **Bier macht** ~: beer makes you feel sleepy; **ein** ~**s Lächeln** (auch fig.) a weary smile; **etw.** ~ **sein** (geh.) be tired of sth.; **einer Sache** (*Gen.*) ~ **werden** (geh.) tire *or* grow tired of sth.; **nicht** ~ **werden, etw. zu tun** never tire of doing sth.; *s. auch* **Mark**[1]. **2** *adv.* wearily; (schläfrig) sleepily

-müde *adj.* tired of ...; **amts**~: tired of [holding] office

Müdigkeit *die;* ~: tiredness; **ich könnte vor** ~ **umfallen** I'm so tired I can hardly stand; **[nur] keine** ~ **vorschützen!** (ugs.) it's no use saying you're tired!

-müdigkeit *die* weariness of ...; **Zivilisations**~: weariness of civilized living; culture fatigue

Muff[1] /mʊf/ *der;* ~**[e]s** (nordd.) musty smell; (Gestank) fug

Muff[2] *der;* ~**[e]s,** ~**e** muff

Muffe *die;* ~, ~**n** (a) (Technik) sleeve; (Verbindungsstück) sleeve [coupling]; (b) (fig.) **jmdm. geht die** ~ (salopp) sb. is shaking in his/her shoes; ~ **haben** (salopp) be in a funk (sl.) (**vor** + *Dat.* about)

Muffel /'mʊfl/ *der;* ~**s,** ~ (ugs.) sourpuss (coll.); grouch (coll.)

-muffel *der;* ~**s,** ~ (ugs.) person who is not into ... at all (coll.); **er ist ein Fußball**~: he isn't into football at all (ugs.)

muffelig (ugs.) **1** *Adj.* grumpy; surly **2** *adv.* grumpily

Muffen·sausen *das* (salopp) ~ **haben/kriegen** be/get in a funk (sl.) (**vor** + *Dat.* about)

muffig[1] *Adj.* (modrig riechend) musty; (stickig; auch fig.) stuffy

muffig[2] (ugs.) ⇒ **muffelig**

Mufflon /'mʊflɔn/ *der;* ~**s,** ~**s** (Zool.) moufflon

muh /mu:/ *Interj.* moo

Müh /my:/: **mit** ~ **und Not** with great difficulty; only just

Mühe /'my:ə/ *die;* ~, ~**n** trouble; **alle** ~ **haben, etw. zu tun** be hard put to do sth.; **mit jmdm./etw. seine** ~ **haben** have a lot of trouble *or* a hard time with sb./sth.; **keine** ~ **scheuen** spare no pains *or* effort; **sich** (*Dat.*) **viel** ~ **machen** go to *or* take a lot of trouble (**mit** over); **machen Sie sich [bitte] keine** ~! [please] don't put yourself out!; [please] don't bother!; **es hat viel** ~ **gekostet** it took much time and effort; **sich** (*Dat.*) ~ **geben** make an effort *or* take pains; **sich** (*Dat.*) **mit jmdm./etw.** ~ **geben** take [great] pains *or* trouble over sb./sth.; **gib dir keine** ~! you needn't bother

mühelos 1 *Adj.* effortless. **2** *adv.* effortlessly; without the slightest difficulty

Mühelosigkeit *die;* ~: effortlessness

muhen *itr. V.* moo

mühen *refl. V.* (geh.) strive; **sich mit etw.** ~: take pains over sth.

mühe·voll *Adj.* laborious; painstaking ⟨*work*⟩; **ein** ~**er Weg** an arduous path

Mühle /'my:lə/ *die;* ~, ~**n (a)** mill; **in die** ~ **der Justiz geraten** (fig.) become enmeshed in the wheels *or* machinery of justice; **das ist Wasser auf seine** ~ (ugs.) it's [all] grist to his mill; it just confirms what he has always thought; **(b)** (Kaffee~) [coffee-] grinder; **(c)** (Spiel) *o. Art., o. Pl.* nine men's morris; **(d)** (Konstellation beim ~spiel) mill; **(e)** (ugs. abwertend) (Auto, Motorrad) heap (coll.); (Auto, Flugzeug) crate (coll.); (Fahrrad) rattletrap; boneshaker

Mühle·spiel *das* nine men's morris

Mühl-: ~**rad** *das* mill-wheel; ~**stein** *der* millstone

Mühsal /'my:za:l/ *die;* ~, ~**e** (geh.) tribulation; (Strapaze) hardship; (Arbeit) toil *no pl.*

mühsam 1 *Adj.* laborious; **ein** ~**es Lächeln** a forced smile. **2** *adv.* laboriously; (schwierig) with difficulty

müh·selig (geh.) **1** *Adj.* laborious; arduous ⟨*journey, life*⟩. **2** *adv.* with [great] difficulty

Mulatte /mu'latə/ *der;* ~**n,** ~**n, Mulattin** *die;* ~, ~**nen** mulatto

Mulde /'mʊldə/ *die;* ~, ~**n** hollow

Muli /'mu:li/ *das;* ~**s,** ~**s** mule

Mull /mʊl/ *der;* ~**[e]s** (Stoff) mull; (Verband~) gauze

Müll /mʏl/ *der;* ~**s** refuse; rubbish; garbage (Amer.); trash (Amer.); (Industrie~) [industrial] waste; **etw. in den** ~ **werfen** throw sth. in the dustbin (Brit.) *or* (Amer.) garbage can; „~ **abladen verboten"** 'no dumping'; 'no tipping' (Brit.)

Müll-: ~**abfuhr** *die* **(a)** refuse *or* (Amer.) garbage collection; **(b)** (Unternehmen) refuse *or* (Amer.) garbage collection [service]; ~**beutel** *der* dustbin (Brit.) *or* (Amer.) garbage can liner

Müll·binde *die* gauze bandage

Müll-: ~**deponie** *die* (Amtsspr.) refuse disposal site; ~**eimer** *der* rubbish *or* waste bin

Müller /'mʏlɐ/ *der;* ~**s,** ~: **▶ 85** miller

Müll-: ~**halde** *die* refuse dump; ~**haufen** *der* heap of rubbish *or* (Amer.) garbage; ~**kippe** *die* [refuse] dump *or* (Brit.) tip; ~**mann** *der; Pl.* ~**männer** (ugs.) dustman (Brit.); garbage man (Amer.); ~**sack** *der* refuse bag; ~**schlucker** *der* rubbish *or* (Amer.) garbage chute; ~**tonne** *die* dustbin (Brit.); garbage *or* trash can (Amer.); ~**tüte** *die* bin bag; ~**verbrennung** *die* refuse *or* (Amer.) garbage incineration; ~**verbrennungs·anlage** *die* refuse *or* (Amer.) garbage incinerator; ~**wagen** *der* dustcart (Brit.); garbage truck (Amer.)

mulmig /'mʊlmɪç/ *Adj.* (ugs.: unbehaglich) uneasy; **ein** ~**es Gefühl haben** feel uneasy

multi-, Multi-: **multi**⟨*lateral, -lingual, -millionaire, -national*⟩

Multi /'mʊlti/ *der;* ~**s,** ~**s** (ugs.) multinational

Multi·halle *die* multi-purpose hall

multikulturell *Adj.* multicultural

multi·medial 1 *Adj.* multimedia *attrib.;* ~**er Unterricht** teaching with multimedia material. **2** *adv.* on a multimedia basis

Multimedia-Show /-'me:dia-/: *die* multimedia presentation

multipel /mʊl'ti:pl/ *Adj.; nicht präd.* (fachspr.) multiple

Multiple|choice·verfahren /'mʌltɪpl'tʃɔɪs-/ *das* (fachspr.) multiple-choice method

Multiplikation /mʊltiplika'tsi̯o:n/ *die;* ~, ~**en** multiplication

multiplizieren /mʊltipli'tsi:rən/ *tr., itr. V.* (auch fig.) multiply (**mit** by)

Mumie /'mu:mi̯ə/ *die;* ~, ~**n** mummy

mumienhaft 1 *Adj.* mummy-like. **2** *adv.* like a mummy; as though mummified

mumifizieren /mumifi'tsi:rən/ *tr. V.* mummify

Mumifizierung *die;* ~, ~**en** mummification

Mumm /mʊm/ *der;* ~**s** (ugs.) (Mut) guts *pl.* (coll.); spunk (coll.); (Tatkraft) drive; zap (coll.); (Kraft) muscle-power

mummeln (nordd.), **mümmeln** *tr., itr. V.* (fam.) (kauen) chew; (knabbern) nibble

Mumpitz /'mʊmpɪts/ *der;* ~**es** (ugs. abwertend) rubbish; tripe (coll.)

Mumps /mʊmps/ *der od. die;* ~: **▶ 329** mumps *sing.*

München /'mʏnçn̩/ *(das);* ~**s ▶ 490** Munich

Münch[e]ner /'mʏnçnɐ/ **▶ 490** **1** *indekl. Adj.* Munich *attrib.* **2** *der;* ~**s,** ~: inhabitant/native of Munich; *s. auch* **Kölner**

Mund /mʊnt/ *der;* ~**[e]s, Münder** /'mʏndɐ/ **▶ 326** mouth; **vor Staunen blieb ihm der** ~ **offen stehen** he gaped in astonishment; **er küsste ihren** ~ **od. küsste sie auf den** ~: he kissed her on the lips; **von** ~ **zu** ~ **beatmet werden** be given mouth-to-mouth resuscitation *or* the kiss of life; **mit vollem** ~ **sprechen** speak with one's mouth full; **etw. aus jmds.** ~ **hören** hear *or* have sth. from sb.'s [own] lips; **sein** ∼ **steht nicht** od. **nie still** (ugs.) he never stops talking; **den** ∼ **nicht aufkriegen** (fig. ugs.) not open one's mouth; have nothing to say for oneself; **den** ∼ **aufmachen/nicht aufmachen** (fig. ugs.) say something/not say anything; **den** ∼ **voll nehmen** (fig. ugs.) talk big (coll.); **nimm doch den** ∼ **nicht so voll!** (fig. ugs.) don't be such a bighead!; **einen großen** ∼ **haben** (fig. ugs.) talk big (coll.); **den** od. **seinen** ∼ **halten** (ugs.) (schweigen) shut up (coll.); (nichts sagen) not say anything; (nichts verraten) keep quiet (**über** + Akk. about); **jmdm. den** ∼ **verbieten** silence sb.; **jmdm. den** ∼ **[ganz] wässrig machen** (fig. ugs.) [really] make sb.'s mouth water; **er/sie ist nicht auf den** ∼ **gefallen** (fig. ugs.) he's/she's never at a loss for words; … **ist in aller** ∼**e** (fig.) everybody's talking about …; **etw./ein Wort in den** ∼ **nehmen** utter sth./use a word; **jmdm. nach dem** ∼ **reden** (fig.) echo what sb. says; (schmeichelnd) butter sb. up; tell sb. what he/she wants to hear; **jmdm. über den** ∼ **fahren** (fig. ugs.) cut sb. short

Mund·art die dialect

Mundart·dichter der dialect author; (Lyriker) dialect poet

mundartlich **1** Adj. dialectal ⟨forms, expressions, words⟩; ⟨texts, poems, etc.⟩ in dialect. **2** adv.; **stark** ∼ **gefärbt** strongly coloured by dialect

Mundart·sprecher der dialect speaker

Mund·dusche die water pick

Mündel /ˈmʏndl̩/ das; ∼s, ∼: ward

munden itr. V. (geh.) taste good; **es mundete ihm nicht** he did not enjoy it; he did not like the taste of it; **das wird dir** ∼: this will tickle your palate

münden /ˈmʏndn̩/ itr. V. ▶ 193 ; mit sein ⟨river⟩ flow (**in** + Akk. into); ⟨corridor, street, road⟩ lead (**in** + Akk. od. Dat., **auf** + Akk. od. Dat. into)

mund-, Mund-: ∼**faul** (ugs.) **1** Adj. uncommunicative; **2** adv. uncommunicatively; ∼**gerecht** Adj. bitesized; (fig.) easily digestible ⟨information⟩; ∼**geruch** der bad breath no indef. art.; ∼**harmonika** die mouth organ

mündig Adj. **(a)** (of age pred.; ∼ **werden** come of age; **(b)** (urteilsfähig) responsible adult attrib.; ∼ **werden** become capable of mature judgement

mündlich **1** Adj. oral; ∼**e Vereinbarung** verbal agreement; ∼**e Verhandlung** (Rechtsw.) hearing. **2** adv. orally; ⟨agree⟩ verbally; **alles weitere** ∼! (im Brief) I'll tell you the rest when we meet

Mund-: ∼**raub** der petty theft [of food/consumables]; ∼**schutz** der **(a)** (Med.) face-mask; **(b)** (Boxen) gum-shield

M-und-S-Reifen /ˈɛm ʊnt ˈɛs-/ der snow tyre

Mund·stück das **(a)** (bei Instrumenten, Pfeifen usw.) mouthpiece; **(b)** (bei Zigaretten) tip

mund·tot Adj. **jmdn.** ∼ **machen** silence sb.

Mündung die; ∼, ∼**en** **(a)** ▶ 193 mouth; (größere Trichter∼) estuary; **(b)** (bei Feuerwaffen) muzzle

Mund-: ∼**werk** das; o. Pl. (ugs.) **ein loses** ∼**werk** [**haben**] [have] a loose tongue; ∼**winkel** der corner of one's mouth; ∼**-zu-Mund-Beatmung** die mouth-to-mouth resuscitation; kiss of life

Munition /muniˈtsi̯oːn/ die; ∼ (auch fig.) ammunition

Munitions-: ∼**fabrik** die munitions factory; ∼**lager** das ammunition dump

munkeln /ˈmʊŋkl̩n/ tr., itr. V. (ugs.) **man munkelt, dass** …: there is a rumour that …

Münster /ˈmʏnstɐ/ das; ∼s, ∼: minster; (Dom) cathedral

munter /ˈmʊntɐ/ **1** Adj. **(a)** cheerful; merry; (lebhaft) lively ⟨eyes, game⟩; ∼ **werden** cheer up; liven up; [**gesund und**] ∼ **sein** be as fit as a fiddle; ⟨elderly person⟩ be hale and hearty; **(b)** (wach) awake; ∼ **werden** wake up; come round (joc.). **2** adv. **(a)** merrily; cheerfully; **(b)** (unbekümmert) gaily; cheerfully

Munterkeit die; ∼: cheerfulness; gaiety

Münz·automat der slot machine; (Telefon) payphone; pay station (Amer.)

Münze /ˈmʏntsə/ die; ∼, ∼**n** ▶ 216 **(a)** coin; **klingende** od. **bare** ∼ (geh.) cash; **etw. für bare** ∼ **nehmen** (fig.)

take sth. literally; **jmdm. [etw.] mit gleicher** ∼ **heimzahlen** pay sb. back in the same coin [for sth.]; **(b)** (Münzanstalt) mint

münzen tr. V. coin; **auf jmdn./etw. gemünzt sein** (fig.) ⟨remark etc.⟩ be aimed at sb./sth.

Münz-: ∼**fernsprecher** der coin-box telephone; payphone; pay station (Amer.); ∼**kunde** die numismatics sing.; ∼**sammlung** die coin collection; ∼**tankstelle** die coin-in-the-slot petrol (Brit.) or (Amer.) gas station

Muräne /muˈrɛːnə/ die moray eel

mürb /mʏrp/ (südd., österr.), **mürbe** /ˈmʏrbə/ Adj. **(a)** crumbly ⟨biscuit, cake, etc.⟩; tender ⟨meat⟩; soft ⟨fruit⟩; mealy ⟨apple⟩; **das Fleisch** ∼ **machen** tenderize the meat; **(b)** (brüchig) crumbling; (morsch) rotten; ⟨leather⟩ worn soft; ∼ **werden/sein** (fig.: zermürbt) get/be worn out; **jmdn.** ∼ **machen** (fig.) wear sb. down

Mürbe·teig, (südd., österr.) **Mürb·teig** der short pastry

Murks /mʊrks/ der; ∼**es** (salopp abwertend) botch; mess; ∼ **machen** make a botch or mess [of it]

Murmel /ˈmʊrml̩/ die; ∼, ∼**n** marble

murmeln tr., itr. V. mumble; mutter; (sehr leise) murmur; **etw. vor sich hin** ∼: mutter or mumble/murmur sth. to oneself

Murmel·tier das marmot; s. auch **schlafen** 1 a

murren /ˈmʊrən/ itr. V. grumble (**über** + Akk. about); **ohne zu** ∼: without a murmur

mürrisch /ˈmʏrɪʃ/ **1** Adj. grumpy; surly, sullen ⟨expression⟩. **2** adv. grumpily

Mus /muːs/ das od. der; ∼**es**, ∼**e** purée; **zu** ∼ **kochen** cook to a pulp

Muschel /ˈmʊʃl̩/ die; ∼, ∼**n** **(a)** mussel; **(b)** (Schale) [mussel-]shell; **(c)** (am Telefon) (Hör∼) ear-piece; (Sprech∼) mouthpiece

Muse /ˈmuːzə/ die; ∼, ∼**n** muse; **die leichte** ∼: light [musical] entertainment; **von der** ∼ **geküsst werden** (scherzh.) get some inspiration

Museen ⇨ **Museum**

Musen·tempel der (veralt., noch scherzh.) temple of the Muses

Museum /muˈzeːʊm/ das; ∼s, **Museen** museum

museums-, Museums-: ∼**führer** der museum guide; ∼**reif** Adj. (ugs. iron.) fit for a museum postpos.; ∼**stück** das (auch fig. ugs. iron.) museum piece; ∼**wärter** der ▶ 85 museum attendant

Musical /ˈmjuːzikl̩/ das; ∼s, ∼s musical

Musik /muˈziːk/ die; ∼, ∼**en** **(a)** o. Pl. music; ∼ **im Blut haben** have music in one's blood; ∼ **in jmds. Ohren** (Dat.) **sein** (fig. ugs.) be music to sb.'s ears; **(b)** (Werk) piece [of music]; (Partitur) score (**zu** for); **die** ∼ **zu diesem Stück** the [incidental] music for this play; s. auch **Handkäse**

musikalisch /muziˈkaːlɪʃ/ **1** Adj. musical; ∼**e Leitung:** …: conducted by … **2** adv. musically; **er ist** ∼ **veranlagt** he is musical

Musikalität /muzikaliˈtɛːt/ die; ∼: musicality

Musikant /muziˈkant/ der; ∼**en**, ∼**en** musician

Musikanten·knochen der funny bone

Musik·box die jukebox

Musik-: Musik-CD die audio CD; music CD; ∼**video** das music video

Musiker der; ∼s, ∼, **Musikerin** die; ∼, ∼**nen** ▶ 85 musician

Musik-: ∼**geschichte** die history of music; ∼**hochschule** die academy or college of music; ∼**instrument** das musical instrument; ∼**lehrer** der, ∼**lehrerin** die music-teacher; ∼**schule** die school of music; ∼**stück** das piece of music; ∼**stunde** die music lesson; ∼**unterricht** der **(a)** o. Pl. (das Unterrichten) music-teaching; **(b)** (Stunde) music lesson; (Stunden) music lessons pl.; **(c)** (als Schulfach) music

Musik-: ∼**wissenschaft** die o. Pl. musicology; ∼**wissenschaftler** der ▶ 85 musicologist

musisch /ˈmuːzɪʃ/ **1** Adj. artistic ⟨talent, person, family, etc.⟩; ⟨talent⟩ for the arts; ⟨education⟩ in the arts. **2** adv. artistically; ∼ **veranlagt sein** have an artistic disposition

musizieren /muzi'tsiːrən/ *itr. V.* play music; (bes. unter Laien) make music

Muskat /mʊs'kaːt/ *der;* ~[e]s, ~e nutmeg

Muskateller /mʊska'tɛlɐ/ *der;* ~s, ~: muscatel [wine]

Muskat·nuss, *Muskat·nuß *die* nutmeg

Muskel /'mʊskl̩/ *der;* ~s, ~n muscle

Muskel-: ~**faser** *die* muscle fibre; ~**kater** *der* stiff muscles *pl.;* ~**kraft** *die* muscle-power; ~**krampf** *der* cramp; ~**paket** *das* (ugs.) **(a)** bulging muscles *pl.* **(b)** (ugs.) ⇒ ~**protz**; ~**protz** *der* (ugs.) muscleman; Tarzan (joc.); ~**riss**, *~**riß** *der* ▶ 329 | torn muscle; ~**schwund** *der* ▶ 329 | (Med.) muscular atrophy; ~**zerrung** *die* ▶ 329 | (Med.) pulled muscle

Muskulatur /mʊskula'tuːɐ̯/ *die;* ~, ~en musculature; muscular system

muskulös /mʊsku'løːs/ *Adj.* muscular

Müsli /'mʏsli/ *das;* ~s, ~s muesli

Muslim /'mʊslɪm/ *der;* ~s, ~e Muslim

muslimisch *Adj.* Muslim

muss, *muß /mʊs/ *1. u. 3. Pers. Sg. Präsens v.* **müssen**

Muss, *Muß *das;* ~: necessity; must (coll.)

Muße /'muːsə/ *die;* ~: leisure; **etw. in** *od.* **mit** ~ **tun** do sth. at one's leisure; take one's time over sth.

Muss·ehe, *Muß·ehe *die* (ugs.) shotgun marriage

müssen /'mʏsn̩/ **1** *unr. Modalverb;* 2. Part. ~ **(a)** (gezwungen, verpflichtet sein) have to; **er muss es tun** he must do it; he has to *or* (coll.) has got to do it; **er muss es nicht tun** he does not have to do it; he has not got to do it (coll.); **er musste es tun** *od.* **hat es tun** ~: he had to do it; **muss er es tun?** must he do it?; does he have to *or* (coll.) has he got to do it?; **wir werden zurückkommen** ~: we shall have to come back; **muss das jetzt sein?** does it have to be now?; **muss das sein?** it is really necessary?; **es muss nicht sein** it is not essential; **so musste es ja kommen** it was inevitable that it should come to this; **wir** ~ **Ihnen leider mitteilen, dass ...:** we regret to have to inform you that ...; **das muss 1968 gewesen sein** it must have been in 1968; **er muss gleich hier sein** he will be here *or* he is bound to be here at any moment; **(b)** *Konjunktiv II* **es müsste doch möglich sein** it ought to be possible; **reich müsste man sein!** how nice it would be to be rich!; **man müsste nochmals zwanzig sein** oh to be twenty again!. **2** *unr. itr. V.* **(a)** (gehen, fahren, gebracht werden usw. müssen) have to go; **ich muss zur Arbeit/ nach Hause** I have to *or* must go to work/go home; **(b)** **ich muss mal** (fam.) I've got to *or* need to spend a penny (Brit. coll.) *or* (Amer. coll.) go to the john; **(c)** (gezwungen, verpflichtet sein) **muss er?** does he have to?; has he got to? (coll.); **er muss nicht** he doesn't have to *or* (coll.) hasn't got to

Muße·stunde *die* free hour; hour of leisure

müßig /'mʏːsɪç/ **1** *Adj.* **(a)** (idle ⟨person⟩; ⟨hours, weeks, life⟩ of leisure; **(b)** (zwecklos) pointless. **2** *adv.* idly

Müßig-: ~**gang** *der o. Pl.* leisure; (Untätigkeit) idleness; ~**gänger** *der* idler

musste, *mußte /'mʊstə/ *1. u. 3. Pers. Sg. Prät. v.* **müssen**

Mustang /'mʊstaŋ/ *der;* ~s, ~s mustang

Muster /'mʊstɐ/ *das;* ~s, ~ **(a)** (Vorlage) pattern; **(b)** (Vorbild) model (**an** + *Dat.* of); **er ist ein** ~ **an Fleiß** he is a model of industry; **er ist ein** ~ **von einem Ehemann** (ugs.) he is a model husband; **(c)** (Verzierung) pattern; **(d)** (Probe) specimen; (Warenprobe) sample

muster-, Muster-: ~**beispiel** *das* perfect example; (Vorbild) model; ~**exemplar** *das* **(a)** (oft iron.: Vorbild) perfect specimen; **(b)** (Probeexemplar) specimen copy; ~**gültig** **1** *Adj.* exemplary; perfect, impeccable ⟨order⟩; **2** *adv.* in an exemplary fashion

musterhaft **1** *Adj.* exemplary; perfect, impeccable ⟨order, condition⟩; model ⟨pupil⟩. **2** *adv.* in an exemplary fashion

Muster-: ~**knabe** *der* (oft abwertend) model child; ~**koffer** *der* case of samples

---

mustern *tr. V.* **(a)** eye; (gründlich) scrutinize; **(b)** (Milit.) **jmdn.** ~: give sb. his medical

Muster-: ~**schüler** *der*, ~**schülerin** *die* model pupil

Musterung *die;* ~, ~en (Milit.) medical examination; medical

Musterungs·bescheid *der* summons to attend one's medical examination

Mut /muːt/ *der;* ~[e]s **(a)** courage; **allen** *od.* **all seinen** ~ **zusammennehmen** take one's courage in both hands; screw up one's courage; **das gab** *od.* **machte ihr neuen** ~: that gave her new heart; **nur** ~! don't lose heart!; (trau dich) be brave!; **(b)** (veralt.) **in guten** *od.* **frohen** ~**es sein** be in good spirits

Mutation /muta'tsi̯oːn/ *die;* ~, ~en (Biol.) mutation

Mütchen /'mʏːtçən/ **sein** ~ **[an jmdm.] kühlen** (ugs. [scherzh.]) vent one's wrath [on sb.]

mutieren *itr. V.* (Biol.) mutate

mutig **1** *Adj.* brave; courageous, brave ⟨words, decision, speech⟩. **2** *adv.* bravely; courageously

mut·los *Adj.* (niedergeschlagen) dejected; despondent; (entmutigt) disheartened; dispirited

Mut·losigkeit *die;* ~: dejection; despondency

mutmaßen /'muːtmaːsn̩/ *tr., itr. V.* conjecture

mutmaßlich *Adj.; nicht präd.* supposed; presumed; suspected ⟨terrorist etc.⟩

Mutmaßung *die;* ~, ~en conjecture

Mut·probe *die* test of courage

Mutter¹ /'mʊtɐ/ *die;* ~, **Mütter** /'mʏtɐ/ mother; **sie wird** ~ (ist schwanger) she is expecting a baby; **eine** ~ **von drei Kindern** a mother of three

Mutter² *die;* ~, ~n (Schrauben~) nut

Mutter-: ~**boden** *der* topsoil; ~**brust** *die* mother's breast

Mütterchen /'mʏtɐçən/ *das;* ~s, ~: [altes] ~: little old lady

Mutter·freuden *Pl.:* ~ **entgegensehen** (geh.) be expecting a child

Mutter-: ~**land** *das Pl.* ~**länder** **(a)** (Kolonialstaat) mother country; **(b)** (Heimat) original home; motherland; ~**leib** *der* womb

mütterlich **1** *Adj.* **(a)** *nicht präd.* the/his/her *etc.* mother's; maternal ⟨line, love, instincts, etc.⟩; **(b)** (fürsorglich) motherly ⟨woman, care⟩. **2** *adv.* in a motherly way

mütterlicher·seits *Adv.* on the/his/her *etc.* mother's side; **sein Großvater** ~: his maternal grandfather; his grandfather on his mother's side

Mutter-: ~**liebe** *die* motherly love *no art.;* ~**mal** *das; Pl.* ~**male** birthmark; ~**milch** *die* mother's milk; ~**mund** *der* ▶ 326 | neck of the womb; cervix; ~**schaf** *das* mother ewe

Mutterschaft *die;* ~: motherhood

mutter-, Mutter-: ~**schutz** *der* laws *pl.* protecting *working pregnant women and mothers of newborn babies;* ~**seelen·allein** *Adj.; nicht attr.* all alone; all on my *etc.* own; ~**söhnchen** *das* (abwertend) mummy's *or* (Amer.) mama's boy; ~**sprache** *die* native language; mother tongue; ~**tag** *der; o. Pl.* Mother's Day *no def. art.;* ~**tier** *das* mother [animal]; dam; ~**witz** *der o. Pl.* **(a)** (Humor) natural wit; **(b)** (Schläue) native cunning

Mutti /'mʊti/ *die;* ~, ~s mummy (Brit. coll.); mum (Brit. coll.); mommy (Amer. coll.); mom (Amer. coll.)

mut-, Mut-: ~**wille** *der; o. Pl.* wilfulness; (Übermut) devilment; **aus [bloßem]** ~**n** from [sheer] devilment; ~**willig** **1** *Adj.* wilful; wanton ⟨destruction⟩; (übermütig) high-spirited; **2** *adv.* wilfully; wantonly; (aus Übermut) from devilment; ~**willigkeit** *die;* ~: ⇒ **Mutwille**

Mütze /'mʏtsə/ *die;* ~, ~n cap; **was** *od.* **eins auf die** ~ **kriegen** (fig. ugs.) get told off; get a telling off

MW *Abk.* (Rundf.) **Mittelwelle** MW

Mw.-St., MwSt. *Abk.* **Mehrwertsteuer** VAT

Myrte /'mʏrtə/ *die;* ~, ~n myrtle

Myrten·kranz *der* myrtle wreath

mysteriös /mʏste'ri̯øːs/ **1** *Adj.* mysterious. **2** *adv.* mysteriously

mystifizieren /mʏstifiˈtsiːrən/ *tr. V.* shroud in mystery
Mystik /ˈmʏstɪk/ *die;* ~**:** mysticism
mystisch 1 *Adj.* mystical. **2** *adv.* mystically
Mythologie /mytoloˈgiː/ *die;* ~, ~**n** mythology
mythologisch *Adj.* mythological
Mythos /ˈmyːtɔs/ *der;* ~, **Mythen** (a) myth; (b) (glorifizierte Person od. Sache) legend

....

Nn

....

n, N /ɛn/ *das;* ~, ~**:** n/N; *s. auch* **a, A**
N *Abk.* **Nord[en]** N
na /na/ *Interj.* (ugs.) (a) (als Frage, Anrede, Aufforderung) well;
na, du? oh, it's you?; **na los!** come on then!; **na, wird's
bald?** come on, aren't you ready yet?; **na und?** (wennschon)
so what?; (b) (beschwichtigend) **na, na, na!** now, now, come
along; (c) ([zögernd] zustimmend) **na schön!, na gut!** oh, OK
(coll.); well, all right; **na, dann bis später** right, see you
later then; (d) (bekräftigend) **na und ob!** and how! (coll.); I'll
say! (coll.); **na und wie!** and how! (coll.); **na eben!** exactly!;
na endlich! at last!; (e) (triumphierend) **Na also! Ich hatte
doch recht!** There you are! I was right!; (f) (zweifelnd, besorgt) **na, wenn das mal gutgeht** *od.* **klappt** well, let's
hope it'll be OK (coll.); **na, wenn das dein Vater merkt!**
oh dear, what if your father notices?; **na, ich weiß nicht**
hmm, I'm not sure; (g) (staunend) **na so [et]was!** well I
never!; (h) (drohend) **na warte!** just [you] wait!; (auf einen
nicht Anwesenden bezogen) just let him wait!
Nabe /ˈnaːbə/ *die;* ~, ~**n** hub
Nabel /ˈnaːbl̩/ *der;* ~**s,** ~**:** ▶ 326 ⏐ navel
Nabel-, nabel-: ~**frei** *Adj.* **ein** ~**es Top** a crop top;
~ **gehen** wear a crop top; ~**schau** *die* (salopp) ~**schau
halten** bare one's soul; ~**schnur** *die Pl.* ~**schnüre**
umbilical cord
Naben-: ~**dynamo** *der* hub dynamo; ~**schaltung** *die* hub gear
nach /naːx/ **1** *Präp. mit Dat.* ▶ 382 ⏐ (a) (räumlich) to; **ist
das der Zug** ~ **Köln?** is that the train for Cologne *or*
the Cologne train?; ~ **Hause gehen** go home; **sich** ~
vorn/hinten beugen bend forwards/backwards; **komm
ganz** ~ **vorn** come right to the front; ~ **links/rechts** to
the left/right; ~ **allen Richtungen** in all directions; ~
Osten [zu] eastwards; [towards the] east; ~ **außen/in-
nen** outwards/inwards; **ich bringe den Abfall** ~
draußen I am taking the rubbish outside; (b) ▶ 530 ⏐ (zeitlich) after; **zehn [Minuten]** ~ **zwei** ten [minutes] past
two; (c) ~ **fünf Minuten** after five minutes; five minutes
later; (d) (bei bestimmten Verben, bezeichnet das Ziel der Handlung)
for; (e) (bezeichnet [räumliche und zeitliche] Reihenfolge) after; (f)
(gemäß) according to; ~ **meiner Ansicht** *od.* **Meinung,
meiner Ansicht** *od.* **Meinung** ~**:** in my view *or*
opinion; **aller Wahrscheinlichkeit** ~**:** in all probability;
[frei] ~ **Goethe** [freely] adapted from Goethe; ~ **der
neuesten Mode gekleidet** dressed in [accordance with]
the latest fashion; ~ **etw. schmecken/riechen** taste/
smell of sth.; **sie kommt eher** ~ **dem Vater** (ugs.) she
takes more after her father; **jmdn. nur dem Namen** ~
kennen know sb. by name only; **dem Gesetz** ~**:** in accordance with the law; by law. **2** *Adv.* (a) (räumlich) **[alle]
mir** ~**!** [everybody] follow me!; (b) (zeitlich) ~ **und** ~**:**
little by little; gradually; ~ **wie vor** still; as always
nach|äffen /-ʔɛfn̩/ *tr. V.* (abwertend) mimic
Nachäfferei *die;* ~ (abwertend) mimicry; mimicking
nach|ahmen /-ʔaːmən/ *tr. V.* imitate
nachahmens·wert *Adj.* worthy of imitation *postpos.;*
exemplary
Nachahmung *die;* ~, ~**en** imitation
nach|arbeiten *tr. V.* (a) (nachholen) **eine Stunde** ~**:**
work an extra hour to make up; **sie muss die ver-
säumten Stunden** ~**:** she has to make up for the hours

she missed; (b) (überarbeiten) go over, finish off ‹*workpiece*›
Nachbar /ˈnaxbaːɐ̯/ *der;* ~**n** *od. selten* ~**s,** ~**n** neighbour; ~**s Hund** the neighbours'/neighbour's dog
Nachbar-: ~**dorf** *das* neighbouring village; ~**haus**
das house next door
Nachbarin *die;* ~, ~**nen** neighbour
Nachbar·land *das; Pl.* ...**länder** neighbouring country
nachbarlich *Adj.* (a) *nicht präd.* (dem Nachbarn/den Nachbarn gehörend) neighbour's/neighbours'; (b) (unter Nachbarn
üblich) neighbourly
Nachbarschaft *die;* ~ (a) (die Nachbarn) **die [ganze]**
~**:** all the neighbours *pl.;* the whole neighbourhood; (b)
(Beziehungen) **gute** ~**:** good neighbourliness; (c) (Gegend)
neighbourhood; (Nähe) vicinity
nachbarschaftlich *Adj.* neighbourly
Nachbar·tisch *der* next *or* neighbouring table
nach|behandeln *tr. V.* (a) treat again; (b) (nach
ärztlicher Behandlung) **jmdn./etw.** ~**:** give sb./sth. follow-up
treatment
Nach·behandlung *die* follow-up treatment; aftercare
nach|bestellen *tr. V.* **[noch] etw.** ~**:** order more of
sth.; ‹*shop*› order further stock of sth., reorder sth.
nach|beten *tr. V.* (ugs. abwertend) repeat parrot-fashion;
regurgitate
nach|bilden *tr. V.* reproduce, copy (+ *Dat.* from)
Nach·bildung *die* (a) *o. Pl.* copy- z ing; (b) (Kopie) copy;
replica
nach|bringen *unr. tr. V.* bring along ‹*sth. left behind*›
nach·dem 1 *Konj.* after; **ich ging erst,** ~ **ich mich
vergewissert hatte** I only left when I had made sure. **2**
Adv.: ⇒ **je¹ 3 b**
nach|denken *unr. itr. V.* think (**über** + *Akk.* about);
(lange u. erwägend) reflect (**über** + *Akk.* on); **denk mal
[scharf] nach** have a [good] think; think carefully; **ohne
nachzudenken** without stopping to think
Nach·denken *das* thought; **Zeit zum** ~**:** time to
think; **nach langem** ~**:** after thinking about it for a long
time
nachdenklich 1 *Adj.* thoughtful; pensive. **2** *adv.*
thoughtfully; pensively
nach|drängen *itr. V.; mit sein* push from behind
Nach·druck *der; Pl.* ~**e** (a) *o. Pl.* **mit** ~**:** emphatically;
auf etw. (*Akk.*) **[besonderen]** ~ **legen** place [particu-
lar] emphasis on sth.; stress sth. [particularly]; (b) (Druckw.)
reprint
nach|drucken *tr. V.* reprint ‹*book*›; print more
‹*letterheads etc.*›
nachdrücklich 1 *Adj.; nicht präd.* emphatic ‹*warning,
confirmation, advice*›; insistent ‹*demand*›; urgent ‹*request,
appeal*›. **2** *adv.* emphatically; ~ **darauf hinweisen,
dass** ...**:** emphasize that ...:
Nach·durst *der* morning-after thirst
nach|eifern *itr. V.* **jmdm.** ~**:** emulate sb.
nach·einander *Adv.* (a) one after the other; **kurz/un-
mittelbar** ~**:** one shortly/immediately after the other;
(b) ~ **sehen** keep an eye on each other; **sich** ~ **richten**
coordinate with one another
nach|empfinden *unr. tr. V.* (a) empathize with
‹*feeling*›; share ‹*delight, sorrow*›; **ich kann [dir] deinen
Ärger gut** ~**:** I can well understand *or* appreciate your
feeling of anger; (b) (nachmachen) recreate ‹*expression, atmosphere, event*›; **einer Sache** (*Dat.*) **nachempfunden
sein** take its inspiration from sth.; be modelled on sth.
nach|erzählen *tr. V.* retell
Nach·erzählung *die* retelling [of a story]; (Schulw.) reproduction
Nachfahr /-faːɐ̯/ *der;* ~**en,** ~**en** (geh.) descendant
nach|fahren *unr. itr. V.; mit sein* follow [on]; **jmdm.** ~**:**
follow sb.
nach|feiern *tr. V.* celebrate ‹*birthday, Christmas*› at a
later date
Nach·folge *die* succession; **die** ~ **B.s regeln** settle
who is to be B's successor; **jmds.** ~ **antreten** succeed sb.

nach

Wohin? = to

Ich fuhr mit dem Zug nach Wien	= I went to Vienna by train, I took the train to Vienna

Aber:

Der Zug nach Wien hält nicht in Wels	= The train for *od.* to Vienna does not stop in Wels
Passagiere nach Zürich	= passengers [bound] for Zurich
Das Schiff ist unterwegs od. auf dem Wege nach Bombay	= The ship is on its way to *od.* is bound for Bombay
Sie sind nach Australien abgereist	= They have left for Australia
Die Maschine flog nach Osten	= The aircraft flew east[wards] *od.* towards the east
nach dem Meer zu	= towards the sea
nach allen Richtungen	= in all directions

Wann? = after

Nach dem Rennen gab er ein Interview	= He gave an interview after the race
nach Erhalt der Rechnung	= after receiving the invoice
Nach fünf Minuten trafen die ersten Läufer ein	= After five minutes *od.* Five minutes later the first runners arrived
Nach 22.00 Uhr verkehren die Züge stündlich	= After 10 p.m. trains run every hour

Aber bei Uhrzeitangaben:

um Viertel/fünfundzwanzig nach sieben	= at a quarter/twenty-five past seven

Auch in der Reihenfolge:

Nach Ihnen!	= After you
eins nach dem andern	= one thing after another
Nach „für" steht der Akkusativ	= 'Für' is followed by the accusative
B kommt nach A in der Weltrangliste	= B comes after *od.* below A in the world rankings

Gemäß = according to, in accordance with

Diesem Bericht nach soll sie ein Kind bekommen	= According to this report she is expecting a child
nach deutschem Recht	= in accordance with German law
nach der neuesten Mode gekleidet	= dressed in [accordance with] the latest fashion
nach italienischer Art	= in the Italian manner
meiner Ansicht od. Meinung nach	= in my opinion
aller Wahrscheinlichkeit nach	= in all probability
nach etwas urteilen	= to judge by sth.
Seiner Sprache nach ist er Norddeutscher	= Going *od.* Judging by the way he speaks, he's North German

---

nach·folgend *Adj.; nicht präd.* following; subsequent ‹*chapter, issue*›

Nachfolger *der;* ~s, ~, **Nachfolgerin** *die;* ~, ~nen successor

Nach·forderung *die* additional demand (*Gen.*, von for)

nach|forschen *itr. V.* make inquiries; investigate [the matter]

Nach·forschung *die* investigation; inquiry; ~en [nach etw.] anstellen make inquiries [into sth.]

Nach·frage *die* (a) (Wirtsch.) demand (**nach** for); (b) danke der [gütigen] ~ (meist scherzh.) how kind of you to inquire

nach|fragen *itr. V.* ask; inquire; **bei jmdm.** ~: ask sb.

nach|fühlen *tr. V.* empathize with; **das kann ich dir** ~! I know how you feel!

nach|füllen *tr. V.* refill ‹*glass, vessel, etc.*›; (wenn nicht leer) fill up; top up; **Salz/Wein** ~: put [some] more salt/wine in

nach|geben *unr. itr. V.* (a) give way; (aus Schwäche) give in; (b) (sich dehnen) stretch; **das Material gibt ein wenig nach** there is some give in the material; (c) (Bankw., Wirtsch.: sinken) ‹*prices, currency*› weaken

Nach·gebühr *die* excess postage

Nach·geburt *die* afterbirth

nach|gehen *unr. itr. V.; mit sein* (a) (folgen) **jmdm./ einer Sache** ~: follow sb./sth.; **einer Sache/einer Frage/einem Problem** *usw.* ~ (fig.) look into a matter/ question/problem *etc.;* (b) (nicht aus dem Kopf gehen) **jmdm.** ~: remain on sb.'s mind; occupy sb.'s thoughts; (c) **seinen Geschäften** *od.* **Beschäftigungen/seinem Tagewerk** ~: go about one's business/daily work; **einem Beruf** ~: practise a profession; (d) ‹*clock, watch*› be slow; **[um] eine Stunde** ~: be an hour slow; **eine Stunde am Tag** ~: lose an hour a day

---

nach·gemacht *Adj.* imitation ‹*leather, gold*›

Nach·geschmack *der* after-taste

nach·giebig /-giːbɪç/ *Adj.* indulgent; yielding; (weich) soft

Nachgiebigkeit *die;* ~: indulgence; (Weichheit) softness

nach|gießen 1 *unr. tr. V.* pour [in] some more; **jmdm. Wein** ~: top up sb.'s wine. 2 *unr. itr. V.* **jmdm.** ~: pour sb. some more; top sb. up

nach|grübeln *itr. V.* ponder (**über** + *Akk.* over)

nach|gucken *tr., itr. V.* (ugs.) ⇒ **nachsehen** 1 a, b, c, 2 a, b

Nach·hall *der;* ~[e]s, ~e reverberation; (fig.) reverberations *pl.*

nach|hallen *itr. V.* reverberate

nach·haltig 1 *Adj.* (a) lasting; (b) (Ökologie) sustainable. 2 *adv.* (a) (auf längere Zeit) for a long time; (nachdrücklich) persistently; (b) (Ökologie) sustainably

Nach·hause·weg *der* way home

nach|helfen *unr. itr. V.* help

nach·her /*auch:* '--/ *Adv.* (a) afterwards; (später) later [on]; **bis** ~! see you later!; (b) (ugs.: womöglich) then perhaps; (sonst) otherwise

Nach·hilfe *die* coaching

Nachhilfe-: ~**lehrer** *der* coach; ~**stunde** *die* private lesson; ~**unterricht** *der* coaching

***nach·hinein, Nach·hinein:** **im** ~ (nachträglich) afterwards; later; (zurückblickend) with hindsight

Nach·hol·bedarf *der* need to catch up; **ein** ~ **an etw.** (*Dat.*) a need to make up for the shortage of sth.

nach|holen *tr. V.* (a) catch up on ‹*work, sleep*›; make up for ‹*working hours missed*›; **den Schulabschluss** ~: take one's final school examination as a mature student; (b) **seine Familie** ~: bring one's family to join one

Nach·hut *die;* ~, ~en (Milit.; auch fig.) rearguard

nach|jagen *itr. V.; mit sein* **jmdm./einer Sache** ~: chase after sb./sth.; **dem Erfolg/Geld** ~ (fig.) devote oneself to the pursuit of success/money

---

*alte Schreibung (vgl. Hinweise auf S. xvi–vxii)

Nachkomme *der;* ∼**n**, ∼**n** descendant; (eines Tieres) offspring

nach|kommen *unr. itr. V.; mit sein* (a) follow [later]; come [on] later; **seine Familie wird [später]** ∼: his family will join him later; (b) **seinen Verpflichtungen** ∼: meet one's commitments; **einem Wunsch/Befehl/ einer Bitte** ∼: comply with a wish/an order/grant a request; (c) (Schritt halten können) be able to keep up

Nachkommenschaft *die;* ∼: descendants *pl.;* (eines Tieres) offspring

Nachkömmling /-kœmliŋ/ *der;* ∼**s**, ∼**e** much younger child (than the rest)

Nach·kriegs-: ∼**generation** *die* post-war generation; ∼**zeit** *die* post-war period

nach|laden *unr. tr., itr. V.* reload

Nach·lass, ***Nachlaß** *der;* **Nachlasses**, **Nachlasse** *od.* **Nachlässe** (a) estate; (hinterlassene Gegenstände) personal effects *pl.* (left by the deceased); (b) (Kaufmannsspr.: Rabatt) discount; reduction

nach|lassen 1 *unr. itr. V.* let up; ⟨*rain, wind*⟩ ease, let up; ⟨*storm, heat*⟩ abate, die down; ⟨*anger*⟩ subside, die down; ⟨*pain, stress, pressure*⟩ ease, lessen; ⟨*noise*⟩ lessen; ⟨*fever*⟩ go down; ⟨*effect*⟩ wear off; ⟨*interest, enthusiasm, strength, courage*⟩ flag, wane; ⟨*resistance*⟩ weaken; ⟨*health, hearing, eyesight, memory*⟩ get worse, deteriorate; ⟨*performance*⟩ deteriorate, fall off; ⟨*business*⟩ drop off, fall off. **2** *unr. tr. V.* (Kaufmannsspr.) give *or* allow a discount of

nach·lässig 1 *Adj.* careless; untidy ⟨*dress*⟩. **2** *adv.* carelessly

nachlässigerweise *Adv.* carelessly

Nach·lässigkeit *die;* ∼, ∼**en** ⇒ **nachlässig 1**: carelessness; untidiness

nach|laufen *unr. itr. V.; mit sein* (a) jmdm./einer Sache ∼: run *or* chase after sb./sth.; (b) (fig.) chase after, pursue ⟨*illusion*⟩

nach|legen *tr., itr. V.* [Holz/Kohlen] ∼: put some more wood/coal on

nach|lesen *unr. tr. V.* look up; (überprüfen) check; **in den Statistiken ist nachzulesen, dass** ...: the statistics show that ...

nach|liefern *tr. V.* (später liefern) supply later; (zusätzlich liefern) supply additionally; **der Rest wird nächste Woche nachgeliefert** the rest of the delivery will follow next week

nach|lösen 1 *tr. V.* **eine Fahrkarte** ∼: buy a ticket [on the train/tram (Brit.) *or* (Amer.) streetcar]. **2** *itr. V.* pay the excess [fare]

nach|machen *tr. V.* (a) copy; (imitieren) imitate; do an impersonation of ⟨*politician etc.*⟩; forge ⟨*signature*⟩; forge, counterfeit ⟨*money*⟩; **jmdm. alles** ∼: copy everything sb. does; **das soll mir einer** ∼! follow that!; *s. auch* **nachgemacht**; (b) (ugs.: später machen) do later

nach|messen 1 *unr. tr. V.* check the measurements of; check ⟨*distance, length, etc.*⟩. **2** *itr. V.* check the measurements

***nach·mittag** ⇒ **Nachmittag**

Nach·mittag *der* afternoon; **am** ∼: in the afternoon; (heute) this afternoon; **am frühen/späten** ∼: early/late in the afternoon; **am selben** ∼: the same afternoon; **am** ∼ **des 8. März** on the afternoon of 8 March; **heute/ morgen/gestern** ∼: this/tomorrow/yesterday afternoon

nach·mittags *Adv.* ▶530⟩ in the afternoon; (heute) this afternoon; **dienstags** ∼: on Tuesday afternoons; **um vier Uhr** ∼: at four in the afternoon; at 4 p.m.

Nach·mittags·vor·stellung *die* afternoon performance; [afternoon] matinée

Nachnahme *die;* ∼, ∼**n: per** ∼: cash on delivery; COD

Nach·name *der* surname; **wie heißt du mit** ∼**n?** what is your surname?

nach|plappern *tr. V.* repeat parrot-fashion; **jmdm. alles** ∼: repeat everything sb. says

Nach·porto *das* excess postage

nachprüfbar *Adj.* verifiable

nach|prüfen *tr. V.* check ⟨*document, statement, weight, alibi*⟩; verify ⟨*correctness*⟩

Nach·prüfung *die* checking

nach|rechnen 1 *tr. V.* check ⟨*figures*⟩. **2** *itr. V.* (zur Kontrolle) check [the figures]

Nach·rede *die:* **üble** ∼: malicious gossip; (Rechtsw.) defamation [of character]

nach|reichen *tr. V.* hand in subsequently

nach|rennen *unr. itr. V.:* ⇒ **nachlaufen**

Nachricht /'naːxrɪçt/ *die:* ∼, ∼**en** (a) news *no pl.;* **das ist eine gute** ∼: that is [a piece of] good news; **eine** ∼ **hinterlassen** leave a message; **ich habe keine** ∼ **von ihm** [Brief usw.) I haven't heard *or* had any word from him; **jmdm.** ∼ **geben** inform sb.; (b) *Pl.* (Ferns., Rundf.) news *sing.;* ∼**en hören** listen to the news; **Sie hören** ∼**en** here is the news

Nachrichten-: ∼**agentur** *die* news agency; ∼**dienst** *der* intelligence service; ∼**sendung** *die* news broadcast; ∼**sprecher** *der,* ∼**sprecherin** *die* newsreader; ∼**technik** *die* telecommunications [technology] *no art.*

nach|rücken *itr. V.; mit sein* move up; **[auf den Posten]** ∼: be promoted [to the post]; take over [the post]

Nach·ruf *der;* ∼**[e]s**, ∼**e** obituary (**auf** + *Akk.* of)

nach|rufen *unr. tr., itr. V.* **jmdm. [etw.]** ∼: call [sth.] after sb.

nach|rüsten *itr. V.* (Milit.) counter-arm

Nach·rüstung *die;* ∼ (Milit.) counter-arming

nach|sagen *tr. V.* (a) (wiederholen) repeat; (b) **jmdm. Schlechtes** ∼: speak ill of sb.; **man sagt ihm nach, er verstehe etwas davon** he is said to know something about it; **du darfst dir nicht** ∼ **lassen, dass** ...: you mustn't let it be said of you that ...

Nach·saison *die* late season

nach|salzen *unr., auch regelm. tr., itr. V.* **[etw.]** ∼: put more salt in/on [sth.]

Nach·satz *der* postscript; (gesprochen) final remark

nach|schauen (bes. südd., österr., schweiz.) ⇒ **nach·sehen 1 a, b, c, 2 a, b**

nach|schenken 1 *tr. V.* **jmdm. Wein/Tee** ∼: top up sb.'s glass with wine/cup with tea. **2** *itr. V.* **jmdm.** ∼: top up sb.'s glass/cup *etc.*

nach|schicken *tr. V.* (a) (durch die Post o. ä.) forward; send on; (b) (folgen lassen) **jmdm. jmdn.** ∼: send sb. after sb.

Nach·schlag *der* (ugs.: zusätzliche Portion) second helping; seconds *pl.*

nach|schlagen 1 *unr. tr. V.* look up ⟨*word, reference, text*⟩. **2** *unr. itr. V.* **im Lexikon/Wörterbuch** ∼: consult the encyclopaedia/dictionary

Nachschlage·werk *das* work of reference

nach|schleichen *unr. itr. V.; mit sein* **jmdm.** ∼: creep *or* steal after sb.

nach|schleifen *tr. V.* (ugs.) drag [along] behind one/it

Nach·schlüssel *der* duplicate key

nach|schmeißen *unr. tr. V.* (ugs.) (a) (billig o. ä. geben) give away; **man kriegt sie nachgeschmissen** you get them for next to nothing; (b) ⇒ **nachwerfen**

Nach·schub *der* (Milit.) (a) supply (**an** + *Dat.* of); (fig.) [provision of] further *or* fresh supplies *pl.* (**an** + *Dat.* of); (b) (∼**material**) supplies *pl.* (**an** + *Dat.* of); (fig.) further supplies *pl.*

nach|schütten *tr. V.* put on more ⟨*coal, coke, etc.*⟩; pour in more ⟨*water*⟩

nach|sehen 1 *unr. itr. V.* (a) jmdm./einer Sache ∼: look *or* gaze after sb./sth.; (b) (kontrollieren) check *or* have a look [to see]; (c) (nachschlagen) look it up; have a look. **2** *unr. tr. V.* (a) (nachlesen) look up ⟨*word, passage*⟩; (b) (überprüfen) check [over]; look over; (c) (nicht verübeln) overlook, let pass ⟨*remark*⟩

Nach·sehen *das:* **das** ∼ **haben** not get a look-in; (nichts abbekommen) be left with nothing

nach|senden *unr. od. regelm. tr. V.:* ⇒ **nachschicken** a

Nach·sicht *die* leniency; **mit jmdm.** ∼ **haben** *od.* **üben** be lenient with sb.; make allowances for sb.

nachsichtig 1 *Adj.* lenient, forbearing (**gegen, mit** towards). **2** *adv.* leniently

Nach·silbe *die* (Sprachw.) suffix

nach|sitzen *unr. itr. V.* (Schulw.) be in detention; [**eine Stunde**] ~ **müssen** have [an hour's] detention

Nach·speise *die* dessert; sweet

Nach·spiel *das:* **die Sache wird noch ein ~ haben!** this affair will have repercussions; **ein gerichtliches ~ haben** result in court proceedings

nach|spielen *itr. V.* (Ballspiele, bes. Fußball) [**einige Minuten**] ~**:** play [a few minutes of] time added on; ~ **lassen** ‹*referee*› add on time

nach|spionieren *itr. V.* jmdm. ~**:** spy on sb.

nach|sprechen *unr. tr. V.* [jmdm.] etw. ~**:** repeat sth. [after sb.]

nächst... 1 *Sup. zu* **nahe. 2** *Adj.* (**a**) ▶ 583 |, ▶ 595 | (räumliche od. zeitliche Reihenfolge) next *attrib.;* **die ~e Straße links** the next street on the left; **am ~en Tag** the next day; **am ~en Ersten** on the first of next month; **bei ~er Gelegenheit** at the next opportunity; **beim ~en Mal, das ~e Mal** the next time; **der Nächste bitte!** next [one], please; **wer kommt als Nächster dran?** whose turn is it next?; (**b**) ▶ 583 | (kürzest) **der ~e Weg zum Bahnhof** the shortest way to the station. **3** *adv.* **am ~en** nearest; *s. auch* **best... b**

nächst·best ... *Adj.* ⇒ **erstbest** ...

Nächste *der;* ~**n,** ~**n** (geh.) neighbour

nach|stehen *unr. itr. V.* jmdm./einer Sache in nichts ~**:** be in no way inferior to sb./sth.

nach·stehend *Adj.* following

nach|steigen *unr. itr. V.;* mit sein (ugs.) **einem Mädchen** ~**:** try to get off with (Brit. coll.) *or* (Amer. coll.) make it with a girl

nach|stellen 1 *tr. V.* (**a**) (Sprachw.) **A wird B** (*Dat.*) **nachgestellt** A is placed after B; **nachgestellte Präposition** postpositive preposition; (**b**) (zurückstellen) put back ‹*clock, watch*›; (**c**) (neu/genauer einstellen) [re]adjust; take up the adjustment on ‹*brakes, clutch*›. **2** *itr. V.* (geh.) **einem Tier/einem Flüchtling** ~**:** hunt an animal/hunt *or* pursue a fugitive; **einem Mädchen** ~ (ugs.) chase a girl

Nach·stellung *die* (**a**) (Sprachw.) postposition; (**b**) *Pl.* (Verfolgung) pursuit *sing.*

Nächsten·liebe *die* charity [to one's neighbour]; brotherly love

nächstens /ˈnɛːçstn̩s/ *Adv.* (**a**) (demnächst) shortly; in the near future; **passen Sie ~ besser auf!** be more careful next time; (**b**) (ugs.: wenn es so weitergeht) if it goes on like this

nächst-: ~**gelegen** *Adj.; nicht präd.* nearest; ~**höher** ... *Adj.* next higher; **die ~höhere Klasse** the next class [up]; ~**liegend** *Adj.; nicht präd.* first, immediate ‹*problem*›; [most] obvious ‹*explanation etc.*›; **das Nächstliegende** the [most] obvious thing; ~**möglich** *Adj.; nicht präd.* earliest possible

nach|suchen *itr. V.* um etw. ~ (geh.) request sth.; (bes. schriftlich) apply for sth.

*Nacht ⇒ Nacht

Nacht /naxt/ *die;* ~**, Nächte** /ˈnɛçtə/ night; **es wird/ist ~:** it is getting dark/it is dark; night is falling/has fallen; **bei ~, in der ~** at night[-time]; **heute ~:** tonight; (letzte Nacht) last night; **gestern/morgen ~:** last night/tomorrow night; **eines ~s** one night; **letzte ~:** last night; **die halbe ~:** half the night; **die ganze ~** [**hindurch**] all night long; **diese ~:** tonight; **mitten in der ~:** in the middle of the night; **bis tief in die ~ hinein, bis spät in der ~:** until late at night; (bis in die Morgenstunden) into the small hours; **in der ~ vom 12. auf den 13. Mai** on the night of 12 May; **in der ~ auf Montag** on Sunday night; **über ~ bleiben** stay overnight; **über ~ berühmt werden** (fig.) become famous overnight; **sich** (*Dat.*) **die ~ um die Ohren schlagen** (ugs.) stay up all night; **zu[r] ~ essen** (südd., österr.) have one's evening meal; **gute ~!** good night!; [**na,**] **dann gute ~!** (iron.)

[well,] that's that; **bei ~ und Nebel** under cover of darkness; (heimlich) furtively; like a thief in the night; *s. auch* **heilig b; schwarz 1 a**

nacht·aktiv *Adj.* (Zool.) nocturnal

nacht-, Nacht-: ~**arbeit** *die; o. Pl.* night work *no art.;* ~**bar** *die* night-spot (coll.); ~**blind** *Adj.* night-blind; ~**dienst** *der* night duty; ~**dienst haben** be on night duty; ‹*chemist's shop*› be open late

Nach·teil *der* disadvantage; **im ~ sein, sich im ~ befinden** be at a disadvantage; **sich zu seinem ~ verändern** change for the worse

nachteilig 1 *Adj.* detrimental; harmful; **über sie ist nichts Nachteiliges bekannt** nothing to her disadvantage is known about her. **2** *adv.* detrimentally; harmfully; **sich ~ auswirken** have a detrimental *or* harmful effect

nächte·lang 1 *Adj.; nicht präd.* lasting several nights *postpos.;* (ganze Nächte dauernd) all-night. **2** *adv.* night after night

Nacht-: ~**essen** *das* (bes. südd., schweiz.) ⇒ **Abendessen;** ~**eule** *die* (ugs. scherzh.) night owl (coll.); ~**falter** *der* moth; ~**frost** *der* night frost; ~**gespenst** *das* [nocturnal] ghost; ~**hemd** *das* nightshirt; ~**himmel** *der; o. Pl.* night sky

Nachtigall /ˈnaxtɪɡal/ *die;* ~**, ~en** nightingale

Nach·tisch *der; o. Pl.* dessert; sweet; **zum** *od.* **als ~:** as a *or* for dessert; **was gibt's zum ~?** what's for pudding *or* (coll.) afters?

Nacht·leben *das* nightlife

nächtlich /ˈnɛçtlɪç/ *Adj.; nicht präd.* nocturnal; night ‹*sky*›; ‹*darkness, stillness*› of the night

Nacht-: ~**lokal** *das* night-spot (coll.); ~**mensch** *der* night owl (coll.); ~**portier** *der* night porter

nach|tragen *unr. tr. V.* (**a**) (schriftlich ergänzen) insert, add; (noch sagen) add; (**b**) jmdm. etw. ~**:** follow sb. carrying sth.; (**c**) jmdm. etw. ~ (fig.) hold sth. against sb.

nach·tragend *Adj.* unforgiving; (rachsüchtig) vindictive; **ich bin nicht ~:** I don't bear grudges

nachträglich /-trɛːklɪç/ **1** *Adj.; nicht präd.* later; subsequent ‹*apology*›; (verspätet) belated ‹*greetings, apology*›; (zusätzlich) additional. **2** *adv.* afterwards; subsequently; (verspätet) belatedly

nach|trauern *itr. V.* jmdm./einer Sache ~**:** bemoan *or* lament the passing of sb./sth.; (sich sehnen nach) pine for sb./sth.

Nacht·ruhe *die* night's sleep; **angenehme ~!** sleep well!

nachts *Adv.* ▶ 530 | at night; **Montag** *od.* **montags ~:** on Monday nights; **um 3 Uhr ~, ~ um 3** [**Uhr**] at 3 o'clock in the morning

Nacht-: ~**schicht** *die* night shift; ~**schicht haben** be on night shift; work nights; ~**schwester** *die* night nurse; ~**tisch** *der* bedside table; ~**tisch·lampe** *die* bedside light; ~**tresor** *der* night safe; ~**wache** *die* (**a**) (Wachdienst) night-watch; (im Krankenhaus) night-duty; (eines Soldaten) night guard-duty; (**b**) (Person) night-guard; (für Fabrik, Büro) nightwatchman; ~**wächter** *der* nightwatchman; ~**wanderung** *die* nocturnal ramble

Nach·untersuchung *die* follow-up examination; check-up

nachvollziehbar *Adj.* comprehensible; **leicht/schwer ~:** easy/difficult to comprehend

nach|vollziehen *unr. tr. V.* reconstruct ‹*train of thought*›; (begreifen) comprehend

nach|wachsen *unr. itr. V.; mit sein* [**wieder**] ~**:** grow again

Nach·wahl *die* by-election

Nach·wehen *Pl.* (Med.) afterpains; (fig. geh.) unpleasant after-effects

nach|weinen *itr. V.* jmdm./einer Sache ~**:** bemoan the loss of sb./sth.; *s. auch* **Träne**

Nachweis /-vais/ *der;* ~**es,** ~**e** proof *no indef. art.* (*Gen.,* **über** + *Akk.* of); (Zeugnis) certificate (**über** + *Akk.* of)

nachweisbar 1 *Adj.* demonstrable ‹*fact, truth, error, defect, guilt*›; provable ‹*fact, guilt*›; detectable ‹*substance, chemical*›. **2** *adv.* demonstrably

---

nach|weisen *unr. tr. V.* prove; **jmdm. einen Fehler/ Diebstahl** ∼: prove sb. made a mistake/committed a theft; **man konnte ihm nichts** ∼: they could not prove anything against him

nachweislich 1 *Adj.; nicht präd.* demonstrable. **2** *adv.* demonstrably; as can be proved

Nach·welt *die; o. Pl.* posterity *no art.;* future generations *pl., no art.*

nach|werfen *unr. tr. V.* **jmdm. etw.** ∼: throw sth. after sb.; **eine Münze** ∼: put in another coin

nach|winken *itr. V.* **jmdm./einer Sache** ∼: wave after sb./sth.

nach|wirken *itr. V.* have a lasting effect (**bei** on); ‹*medicine*› continue to have an effect; ‹*literary work*› continue to have an influence

Nach·wirkung *die* after-effect; (fig.: Einfluss) influence

Nach·wort *das; Pl.* ∼**worte** afterword, postface (**zu** to)

Nach·wuchs *der; o. Pl* **(a)** (fam.: Kind[er]) offspring; **sie erwartet** ∼: she's expecting [a baby]; (junge Kräfte) new blood; (für eine Branche usw.) new recruits *pl.*

nach|zahlen *tr., itr. V.* **(a)** pay later; **1 000 DM Steuern** ∼: pay 1,000 marks back tax; **(b)** (zusätzlich zahlen) 25 **DM** ∼: pay another 25 marks

nach|zählen *tr., itr. V.* [re]count; check

Nach·zahlung *die* additional payment; (spätere Zahlung) deferred payment; (Steuerzahlung) back tax

nach|ziehen 1 *unr. itr. V.* **(a)** (ugs.: ebenso handeln) do likewise; follow suit; **(b)** *mit sein* (hinterhergehen) **jmdm./ einer Sache** ∼: follow sb./sth. **2** *unr. tr. V.* **(a)** (hinter sich herziehen) drag ‹*foot, leg*›; **(b)** (verstärkend) retrace, go over ‹*line*›; pencil ‹*eyebrows*›; **(c)** (festziehen) tighten [up] ‹*nut, bolt*›

Nachzügler /-tsyːklɐ/ *der* straggler; (spät Ankommender) latecomer

Nackedei /ˈnakədai̯/ *der;* ∼**s,** ∼**s (a)** (fam. scherzh.: Kind) [kleiner] ∼: naked little thing *or* monkey; little bare-bum (Brit. sl.); **(b)** (ugs. scherzh.: Person) person in the buff

Nacken /ˈnakn̩/ *der;* ∼**s,** ∼: ▶**326**⟩ back *or* nape of the neck; (Hals) neck; **den Kopf in den** ∼ **werfen** throw one's head right back; **jmdm. im** ∼ **sitzen** (fig.) be breathing down sb.'s neck; **die Furcht/Angst sitzt ihm im** ∼: he is gripped by fear

nackend (veralt., landsch.) ⇒ **nackt a**

Nacken·haar *das* hair on the back of one's neck; neck hair

nackert /ˈnakɐt/ (südd., österr.), **nackig** (bes. md.) ⇒ **nackt a**

nackt /nakt/ *Adj.* **(a)** (unbekleidet) naked; bare ‹*feet, legs, arms, skin, fists*›; **sich** ∼ **ausziehen** strip naked; strip off completely; ∼ **baden** bathe in the nude; **(b)** (kahl) bald ‹*head*›; hairless ‹*chin*›; featherless ‹*bird*›; bare ‹*rocks, island, tree, branch, walls, bulb*›; **auf dem** ∼**en Boden schlafen** sleep on the bare floor; **(c)** (unverhüllt) stark ‹*poverty, misery, horror*›; naked ‹*greed*›; plain ‹*fact, words*›; plain, unvarnished ‹*truth*›; ∼**e Angst** sheer *or* stark terror; **(d)** bare ‹*existence*›; **das** ∼**e Leben retten** barely manage to escape with one's life; save one's skin [and nothing more]

Nackt-: ∼**baden** *das;* ∼**s** nude bathing; ∼**bade-strand** *der* nudist beach

Nackte *der/die; adj. Dekl.* naked man/woman

Nackt·foto *das* nude photo

Nacktheit *die;* ∼: nakedness; nudity; (fig.: der Landschaft usw.) bareness

Nadel /ˈnaːdl̩/ *die;* ∼, ∼**n** needle; (Steck∼, Hut∼, Haar∼) pin; (Häkel∼) hook; (für Tonabnehmer) stylus

Nadel-: ∼**baum** *der* conifer; coniferous tree; ∼**holz** *das; Pl.* ∼**hölzer** softwood; pine-wood; ∼**kissen** *das* pincushion

nadeln *itr. V.* ‹*tree*› shed its needles

Nadel-: ∼**öhr** *das* eye of a/the needle; ∼**stich** *der* **(a)** needle-prick; (einer Stecknadel usw.) pinprick; (fig.: Bosheit) barbed *or* (coll.) snide remark; **(b)** (Nähstich) stitch; ∼**streifen·anzug** *der* pinstripe suit; ∼**wald** *der* coniferous forest

Nagel /ˈnaːgl̩/ *der;* ∼**s, Nägel** /ˈnɛːgl̩/ **(a)** nail; **(b)** (fig.) **den** ∼ **auf den Kopf treffen** (ugs.) hit the nail on the head (coll.); **Nägel mit Köpfen machen** (ugs.) do things properly; make a real job of it; **den Sport** *usw.* /**den Beruf an den** ∼ **hängen** (ugs.) give up sport *etc.*/(coll.) chuck in one's job; **(c)** (Finger∼, Zehen∼) nail; **das brennt mir auf** *od.* **unter den Nägeln** (fig. ugs.) it's so urgent I just have to get on with it *or* it just won't wait; **sich** (*Dat.*) **etw. unter den** ∼ **reißen** (fig. salopp) make off with sth.

Nagel-: ∼**bürste** *die* nail brush; ∼**feile** *die* nail file; ∼**lack** *der* nail varnish (Brit.); nail polish

nageln *tr. V.* nail (**an** + *Akk.* to, **auf** + *Akk.* on); (Med.) pin ‹*bone, leg, etc.*›

nagel-, Nagel-: ∼**neu** *Adj.* (ugs.) brand-new; ∼**reiniger** *der* nail-cleaner; ∼**schere** *die* nail scissors *pl.*

nagen /ˈnaːgn̩/ **1** *itr. V.* gnaw; **an etw.** (*Dat.*) ∼: gnaw [at] sth. **2** *tr. V.* gnaw off; **ein Loch ins Holz** ∼: gnaw a hole in the wood

nagend *Adj.* gnawing ‹*pain, hunger, fear*›; nagging ‹*pain, doubts, uncertainty, etc.*›

Nage·tier *das* rodent

nah /naː/ ⇒ **nahe**

Näh·arbeit *die* [piece of] sewing; ∼**en** sewing jobs; sewing *sing.*

Näh·aufnahme *die* close-up [photograph]

nahe /ˈnaːə/ **1** *Adj.* **näher** /ˈnɛːçst/.../ **(a)** ▶**160**⟩ (räumlich) near *pred.;* close *pred.;* nearby *attrib.;* **in der näheren Umgebung** in the neighbourhood; around here/there; *s. auch* **Osten c; (b)** (zeitlich) imminent; near *pred.;* **in** ∼**r Zukunft** in the near future; **(c)** (eng) close ‹*relationship, relative, friend*›. **2** *adv.* **näher, am nächsten (a)** ▶**160**⟩ (räumlich) ∼ **an** (+ *Dat./Akk.*), close to; ∼ **bei** close to; ∼ **gelegen** nearby; **komm mir nicht zu** ∼! don't come too close!; keep your distance!; ∼ **beieinander** close together; **von** ∼**m** from close up; at close quarters; **aus** *od.* **von nah und fern** (geh.) from near and far; **jmdm. zu** ∼ **treten** (fig.) offend sb.; **jmdm. die moderne Kunst** *usw.* ∼ **bringen** make modern art *etc.* accessible to sb.; **jmdm. etw. näher bringen** (fig.) make sth. more real *or* more accessible to sb.; **jmdm.** ∼ **gehen** (fig.) affect sb. deeply; **einer Sache** (*Dat.*) ∼ **kommen** (fig.) come close to sth.; ‹*amount*› approximate to sth.; **jmdm. [menschlich] näher kommen** get on closer terms with sb.; **sich** (*Dat.*) **näher kommen** (fig.) become closer; **jmdm. etw.** ∼ **legen** (fig.) suggest sth. to sb.; **einen Verdacht/einen Gedanken** *usw.* ∼ **legen** give rise to a suspicion/thought *etc.;* ∼ **liegen** (fig.) ‹*thought*› suggest itself; ‹*suspicion, question*› arise; ∼ **liegend** ‹*question, idea*› which [immediately] suggests itself; natural ‹*suspicion*›; obvious ‹*reason, solution*›; **jmdm.** ∼ **stehen** (fig.) be on close *or* intimate terms with sb.; **einer Partei** ∼ **stehen** sympathize with a party; **eine der Witwe** ∼ **stehende Cousine** (fig.) a cousin who is/was on close terms with the widow; **(b)** (zeitlich) ∼ **daran sein, etw. zu tun** be on the point of doing sth.; **(c)** (eng) closely; *s. auch* **näher. 3** *Präp. mit Dat.* (geh.) near; close to; **den Tränen/dem Wahnsinn** ∼ **sein** be on the brink of tears/on the verge of madness

Nähe /ˈnɛːə/ *die;* ∼: ▶**583**⟩ **(a)** closeness; proximity; (Nachbarschaft) vicinity; **in der** ∼ **der Stadt** near the town; **in meiner** ∼: near me; **er wohnt in der** ∼/**ganz in der** ∼: he lives in the vicinity *or* nearby/very near; **etw. aus der** ∼ **betrachten** take a closer look at sth.; **aus der** ∼ **betrachtet** (auch fig.) viewed more closely; *s. auch* **greifbar 1**

nahe-: ∼**bei** *Adv.* nearby; close by;*∼*|**bringen** *usw.:* ⇒ **nahe 2 a**; *∼*|**liegend** ⇒ **nahe 2 a**

nahen *itr. V.; mit sein* (geh.) draw near; **sein/ihr Ende nahte** the end was near; **eine** ∼**de Katastrophe** imminent disaster

nähen 1 *itr. V.* sew; (Kleider machen) make clothes. **2** *tr. V.* **(a)** sew ‹*seam, hem*›; (mit der Maschine) machine ‹*seam, hem*›; (herstellen) make ‹*dress, coat, curtains, etc.*›; **(b)** (Med.) stitch ‹*wound etc.*›; *s. auch* **doppelt 2 a**

näher 1 *Komp. zu* **nahe. 2** *Adj.; nicht präd.* **(a)** ▶**583**⟩ (kürzer) shorter ‹*way, road*›; **(b)** (genauer) further, more precise ‹*information*›; closer ‹*investigation, inspection*›; **die**

~en **Umstände** the precise circumstances; **bei ~em Hinsehen** on closer examination; **wissen Sie Näheres [darüber]?** do you know any more [about it]?; do you know any details?; **Näheres hierzu siehe unten** for further information on this see below. **3** *adv.* **(a) bitte treten Sie ~!** please come in/nearer/this way; **(b)** (genauer) more closely; (im einzelnen) in [more] detail; **jmdn./ etw. ~ kennen lernen** get to know sb./sth. better; **ich kenne ihn nicht ~:** I don't know him well

****näher|bringen** ⇒ **nahe 2 a**

Nah·erholungs·gebiet *das* nearby recreational area

Näherin *die; ~, ~nen* needlewoman

****näher|kommen** ⇒ **nahe 2 a**

nähern *refl. V.* approach; **die Tiere näherten sich bis auf wenige Meter** the animals came up to within a few metres; **sich jmdm./einer Sache** (*Dat.*) **~:** approach sb./sth.; draw nearer to sb./sth.; **sich dem Ziel der Reise ~:** near one's destination

nahe-: ***~**|stehen**, ***~**stehend** ⇒ **nahe 2 a**; ~**zu** *Adv.* (mit Adjektiven) almost; nearly; well-nigh ⟨*impossible*⟩; all but ⟨*exhausted, impossible*⟩; (mit Zahlenangabe) close on

Näh·garn *das* [sewing] cotton

Nah·kampf *der* (Milit.) close combat

Näh-: ~**kästchen** *das* **(a)** ⇒ ~**kasten**; **(b) aus dem** ~**kästchen plaudern** (ugs. scherzh.) tell all; (als Kenner, Fachmann) tell the inside story; ~**kasten** *der* sewing-box; workbox

nahm /naːm/ *1. u. 3. Pers. Sg. Prät. v.* **nehmen**

Näh-: ~**maschine** *die* sewing machine; ~**nadel** *die* sewing-needle

Nähr·boden *der* culture medium; (fig.) breeding ground

nähren /ˈnɛːrən/ *tr. V.* **(a)** (ernähren) feed ⟨*animal, child*⟩ **(mit** on); **gut/schlecht genährt** well-fed/underfed; **(b)** (geh.: entstehen lassen) nurture ⟨*hope, suspicion, hatred*⟩; cherish ⟨*desire, hope*⟩; foster ⟨*plan, hatred*⟩

nahrhaft *Adj.* nourishing; nutritious; **ein ~es Essen** *od.* (geh.) **Mahl** a square meal

Nahrung /ˈnaːrʊŋ/ *die; ~:* food; **dem Verdacht/den Gerüchten** *usw.* ~ **geben** *od.* **bieten** (fig.) help to nurture *or* foster the suspicion/the rumours *etc.*

Nahrungs-: ~**aufnahme** *die* intake of food; **die** ~**aufnahme verweigern** refuse food; ~**mittel** *das* food [item]; ~**mittel** *Pl.* foodstuffs; ~**suche** *die* search for food

Nähr·wert *der* nutritional value

Näh·seide *die* sewing silk

Naht /naːt/ *die; ~, Nähte* /ˈnɛːtə/ **(a)** seam; **aus den** *od.* **allen Nähten platzen** (fig. ugs.) ⟨*person, fig.: institution etc.*⟩ be bursting at the seams; **(b)** (Med., Anat.) suture

naht·los 1 *Adj.* seamless; (fig.) perfectly smooth ⟨*transition*⟩. **2** *adv.* **Studium und Beruf gehen nicht** ~ **ineinander über** there is not a perfectly smooth transition from study to work

Naht·stelle *die* **(a)** (Schweißnaht) seam; **(b)** (Berührungsstelle) point of contact, interface (**von** between); (Grenzlinie) borderline

Nah-: ~**verkehr** *der* local traffic; ~**verkehrsmittel** *das* form of local transport; ~**verkehrszug** *der* local train

Näh·zeug *das* sewing things *pl.*

Nah·ziel *das* short-term *or* immediate aim

naiv /naˈiːf/ **1** *Adj.* naïve; ingenuous ⟨*look; child*⟩; unaffected ⟨*pleasure*⟩. **2** *adv.* naïvely

Naivität /naivitɛːt/ *die; ~:* naïvety; (eines Blickes, Kindes) ingenuousness; (von Vergnügen) unaffectedness

Naivling *der; ~s, ~e* (ugs. abwertend) [naïve] simpleton

Name /ˈnaːmə/ *der; ~ns, ~n* name; **wie war gleich Ihr** ~? what was your name again?; **ich kenne ihn/es nur dem** ~**n nach** I know him/it only by name; **unter jmds.** ~**n** (*Dat.*) under sb.'s name; **das Konto/das Auto läuft auf meinen** ~**n** the account is in/the car is registered in

my name; **ein Mann mit** ~**n Emil** a man by the name of Emil; **in jmds./einer Sache** ~**n, im** ~**n von jmdm./etw.** on behalf of sb./sth.; **in Gottes** ~**n!** (ugs.) for God's sake; *s. auch* **Hase a**; **Kind a**

namen-, Namen-: ~**gedächtnis** *das* memory for names; ~**liste** *die* list of names; ~**los** *Adj.* nameless; (unbekannt) unknown; anonymous ⟨*author, poet*⟩

namens 1 *Adv.* by the name of; called. **2** *Präp. mit Gen.* (Amtsspr.) on behalf of

Namens-: ~**änderung** *die* change of name; ~**schild** *das* **(a)** (an Türen usw.) nameplate; **(b)** (zum Anstecken) name-badge; ~**tag** *der* name-day; **sie hat am …** ~**tag** it is her name-day on the …; ~**vetter** *der* namesake

namentlich /ˈnaːməntlɪç/ **1** *Adj.* by name *postpos.;* **eine** ~**e Abstimmung** a roll-call vote. **2** *adv.* by name; **jmdn.** ~ **nennen** mention sb. by name; name sb.; **3** *Adv.* (besonders) particularly; especially

namhaft *Adj.* **(a)** *nicht präd.* (berühmt) noted; of note *postpos.;* **(b)** (ansehnlich) noteworthy ⟨*sum, difference*⟩; notable ⟨*contribution, opportunity*⟩

nämlich /ˈnɛːmlɪç/ *Adv.* **(a) er kann nicht kommen, er ist** ~ **krank** he cannot come, as he is ill; he can't come — he's ill[, you see] (coll.); **(b)** (und zwar) namely; (als Füllwort) **das war** ~ **ganz anders** it was quite different in fact *or* actually

nannte /ˈnantə/ *1. u. 3. Pers. Sg. Prät. v.* **nennen**

Nano·technologie /ˈnano…/ *die* nanotechnology

nanu /naˈnuː/ *Interj.* ~**, was machst du denn hier?** hello, what are you doing here?; ~**, wo ist denn der ganze Käse geblieben?** that's funny, what's happened to all that cheese?; ~**, Sie gehen schon?** what, you're going already?

Napalm /ˈnaːpalm/ *das;* ~**s** napalm

Napalm·bombe *die* napalm bomb

Napf /napf/ *der;* ~**[e]s, Näpfe** /ˈnɛpfə/ bowl

Napf·kuchen *der* gugelhupf; ring cake

Nappa /ˈnapa/ *das;* ~**[s]** ~**s, Nappa·leder** *das* nappa [leather]

Narbe /ˈnarbə/ *die;* ~**, **~**n** **(a)** scar; **(b)** (Bot.) stigma

narbig *Adj.* scarred; (von Pocken o. ä.) pitted; pock-marked

Narkose /narˈkoːzə/ *die;* ~**, **~**n** (Med.) narcosis; **aus der** ~ **aufwachen** come round from the anaesthetic

Narkose·arzt *der* anaesthetist

Narkotikum /narˈkoːtikʊm/ *das;* ~**s, Narkotika** (Med.) narcotic

narkotisieren *tr. V.* (Med.) anaesthetize ⟨*patient*⟩; put ⟨*patient*⟩ under a general anaesthetic

Narr /nar/ *der;* ~**en, **~**en** fool; (Hof~) jester; fool; (Fastnachts~) carnival jester *or* reveller; **sich zum** ~**en machen** let oneself be fooled; **jmdn. zum** ~**en haben** *od.* **halten** play tricks on sb.; (täuschen) pull the wool over sb.'s eyes; **einen** ~**en an jmdm. gefressen haben** (ugs.) be dotty about sb. (coll.)

narren /ˈnarən/ *tr. V.* (geh.) **jmdn.** ~**:** make a fool of sb.; (täuschen) deceive sb.

Narren·freiheit *die* freedom to do as one pleases

narren·sicher (ugs.) **1** *Adj.* foolproof; **2** *adv.* in a foolproof way

Närrin /ˈnɛrɪn/ *die;* ~**, **~**nen** fool

närrisch /ˈnɛrɪʃ/ **1** *Adj.* **(a)** (verrückt) crazy; (wirr im Kopf) scatterbrained; dotty (coll.); **[ein]** ~**es Zeug reden** talk gibberish; **auf etw.** (*Akk.*) *od.* **nach etw. ganz** ~ **sein** be mad keen on sth. (coll.); **(b)** *nicht präd.* (karnevalistisch) carnival-crazy ⟨*season*⟩; **das** ~**e Treiben [beim Karneval** *od.* **Fasching]** the mad *or* crazy carnival antics *pl.* **2** *adv.* (verrückt) crazily terrifically (coll.)

Narzisse /narˈtsɪsə/ *die;* ~**, **~**n** narcissus; **gelbe** ~**:** daffodil

narzisstisch, ***narzißtisch** *Adj.* narcissistic

nasal /naˈzaːl/ **1** *Adj.* nasal. **2** *adv.* nasally

Nasal *der;* ~**s, **~**e** (Sprachw.) nasal

naschen /ˈnaʃn/ **1** *itr. V.* **(a)** eat sweet things; (Bonbons essen) eat sweets (Brit.) *or* (Amer.) candy; **gern** ~**:** have a sweet tooth; **(b)** (heimlich essen) have a nibble. **2** *tr. V.* eat ⟨*sweets, chocolate, etc.*⟩; **er/sie hat Milch genascht** he/ she has been at the milk

---

**alte Schreibung (vgl. Hinweise auf S. xvi–vxii)

Nascherei *die;* ~, ~**en (a)** *o. Pl.* [continually] eating sweet things; **(b)** (Süßigkeit) ~**en** sweets

naschhaft *Adj.* fond of sweet things *postpos.;* sweet-toothed; ~ **sein** have a sweet tooth

Nasch·katze *die* (fam.) compulsive nibbler; (Süßigkeiten naschend) compulsive sweet- (Brit.) *or* (Amer.) candy-eater

Nase /'naːzə/ *die;* ~, ~**n (a)** ▶ **326** ∣ nose; **mir blutet die** ~: my nose is bleeding; I've got a nosebleed; **mir läuft die** ~, **meine** ~ **läuft** I've got a runny nose; **(b)** (fig.) **der Bus ist mir vor der** ~ **weggefahren** (ugs.) I missed the bus by a whisker; **jmdm. die Tür vor der** ~ **zuschlagen** (ugs.) shut the door in sb.'s face; **die** ~ **voll haben** (ugs.) have had enough; **von jmdm./etw. die** ~ **[gestrichen] voll haben** (ugs.) be sick [to death] of sb./sth.; **seine** ~ **in etw./alles stecken** (ugs.) stick one's nose into sth./everything (coll.); **jmdm. eine lange** ~ **machen** *od.* **eine** ~ **drehen** (ugs.) cock a snook at sb.; **immer der** ~ **nach** (ugs.) just follow your nose; **jmdm. an der** ~ **herumführen** (ugs.) pull the wool over sb.'s eyes; **auf die** ~ **fallen** (ugs.) come a cropper (sl.); **jmdm. etw. auf die** ~ **binden** (ugs.) let sb. in on sth.; **jmdm. auf der** ~ **herumtanzen** (ugs.) play sb. up; **jmdm. eins** *od.* **was auf die** ~ **geben** (ugs.) put sb. in his/her place; **jmdm. etw. aus der** ~ **ziehen** (ugs.) worm sth. out of sb.; **das sticht mir schon lange in die** ~ (ugs.) I've had my eye on that for a long time; **jmdm. mit der** ~ **auf etw.** (*Akk.*) **stoßen** (ugs.) spell sth. out to sb.; **pro** ~ (ugs.) per head; **jmdm. unter die** ~ **reiben, dass …** (ugs.) rub it in that …; **(c)** (Geruchssinn, Gespür) nose; **eine gute** ~ **für etw. haben** have a good nose for sth.; (etw. intuitiv wissen) have a sixth sense for sth.

näseln /'nɛːzl̩n/ *itr. V.* talk through one's nose

Nasen-: ~**bein** *das* nasal bone; ~**bluten** *das;* ~**s** bleeding from the nose; ~**bluten haben/bekommen** have/get a nosebleed; ~**flügel** *der* side of the nose; (einschl. ~loch) nostril; ~**länge** *die:* **mit einer** ~**länge** (Pferdesport), **um eine** ~**länge** (fig.) by a head; ~**loch** *das* nostril; ~**pflaster** *das* nose plaster; ~**rücken** *der* ridge of the/one's nose; ~**spitze** *die* tip of the/one's nose; **jmdm. etw. an der** ~**spitze ansehen** (fig. ugs.) tell sth. by sb.'s face; ~**stüber** *der* swat on the nose; ~**tropfen** *Pl.* nose-drops

nase-, Nase-: ~**rümpfend 1** *Adj.* disapproving; **2** *adv.* disdainfully; ~**weis 1** *Adj.* precocious; pert ⟨*remark, reply*⟩; **sei nicht so** ~**weis!** don't be such a little know-all!; **2** *adv.* precociously; ~**weis** *der;* ~**es,** ~**e** (fam.) [little] know-all; [little] clever Dick (coll.)

nas-, Nas-: ~**führen** *tr. V.* lead up the garden path; ~**horn** *das* rhinoceros; ~**lang** *in* **alle** ~**lang** constantly; all the time

nass, *naß /nas/ **nasser** *od.* **nässer** /'nɛsɐ/, **nassest…** *od.* **nässest…** /'nɛsəst…/ **1** *Adj.* wet; ~ **machen** make wet; sprinkle ⟨*washing*⟩; **sich/das Bett** ~ **machen** wet oneself/one's bed; **durch und durch** *od.* **bis auf die Haut** ~: wet through; soaked to the skin. **2** *adv.* **sich** ~ **rasieren** have a wet shave; (immer) use a razor and shaving cream

Nässe /'nɛsə/ *die;* ~: wetness; (an Wänden usw.) dampness; **bei** ~: in the wet; in wet weather

nässen 1 *itr. V.* ⟨*wound, eczema*⟩ suppurate. **2** *tr. V.* (geh.) make wet; wet ⟨*bed, feet, etc.*⟩

nass-, *naß-, Nass-, *Naß-: ~**forsch 1** *Adj.* brash. **2** *adv.* brashly; ~**kalt** *Adj.* cold and wet; raw; ~**rasur** *die* wet shaving *no art.*

Nation /na'tsi̯oːn/ *die;* ~, ~**en** nation

national /natsi̯o'naːl/ **1** *Adj.* **(a)** national; **(b)** (patriotisch) nationalist. **2** *adv.* **(a)** at a national level; nationally; **(b)** (patriotisch) ⟨*think, feel*⟩ nationalistically

national-, National-: ~**bewusst, *~bewußt** *Adj.* nationally conscious; ~**bewusst sein** be conscious of one's nationality; have a sense of national identity; ~**bewusstsein, *~bewußtsein** *das* [sense of] national consciousness; sense of national identity; ~**elf** *die* (Fußball) national team *or* side; ~**feier·tag** *der* national holiday; ~**flagge** *die* national flag; ~**gericht** *das* national dish; ~**hymne** *die* national anthem

Nationalismus *der;* ~: nationalism *usu. no art.*

nationalistisch 1 *Adj.* nationalist; nationalistic. **2** *adv.* nationalistically

Nationalität /natsi̯onaliˈtɛːt/ *die;* ~, ~**en** nationality

National-: ~**mannschaft** *die* national team; ~**sozialismus** *der* National Socialism; ~**sozialist** *der* National Socialist; ~**spieler** *der* (Sport) national player; international; ~**straße** *die* (schweiz.) national highway; ~**versammlung** *die* National Assembly

nativ *Adj.* virgin ⟨*olive oil*⟩

NATO, Nato /'naːto/ *die;* ~: NATO; Nato *no art.*

Natrium /'naːtri̯ʊm/ *das;* ~**s** (Chemie) sodium

Natron /'naːtrɔn/ *das;* ~**s [doppeltkohlensaures]** ~: sodium bicarbonate; bicarbonate of soda; bicarb (coll.); **[kohlensaures]** ~: sodium carbonate; soda

Natter /'natɐ/ *die;* ~, ~**n** colubrid

Natur /na'tuːɐ̯/ *die;* ~, ~**en (a)** *o. Pl.* nature *no art.;* **wider die** ~: unnatural; **die freie** ~: [the] open countryside; **Tiere in freier** ~ **sehen** see animals in the wild; **zurück zur** ~: back to nature; **(b)** (Art, Eigentümlichkeit) nature; **eine gesunde/eiserne/labile** ~ **haben** (ugs.) have a healthy/cast-iron/delicate constitution; **das widerspricht ihrer** ~: it is not in her nature; **jmdm. zur zweiten** ~ **werden** become second nature to sb.; **in der** ~ **der Sache/der Dinge liegen** be in the nature of things; **(c)** (Mensch) sort *or* type of person; sort (coll.); type (coll.); **(d)** *o. Pl.* (natürlicher Zustand) **Möbel in Kiefer** ~: natural pine furniture; **sie ist von** ~ **aus blond/gutmütig** she is naturally fair/good-natured

Naturalien /natuˈraːli̯ən/ *Pl.* natural produce *sing.* (used as payment); **in** ~ (*Dat.*) **bezahlen** pay in kind

Naturalismus *der;* ~: naturalism

naturalistisch 1 *Adj.* **(a)** naturalistic; **(b)** (den Naturalismus betreffend) naturalist. **2** *adv.* **(a)** naturalistically; **(b)** (den Naturalismus betreffend) ⟨*influenced*⟩ by naturalism

natur-, Natur-: ~**belassen** *Adj.* natural ⟨*oils, foods, etc.*⟩; ~**blond** *Adj.* naturally fair *or* blond; ~**bursche** *der* child of nature; ~**denkmal** *das* natural monument

Naturell *das;* ~**s,** ~**e** disposition; temperament; **das widerspricht seinem** ~: it's not in his nature

natur-, Natur-: ~**ereignis** *das,* ~**erscheinung** *die* natural phenomenon; ~**faser** *die* natural fibre; ~**forscher** *der* naturalist; ~**forschung** *die* natural-history research; ~**freund** *der* nature lover; ~**gegeben** *Adj.* natural and inevitable ⟨*state of affairs*⟩; **etw. als** ~**gegeben ansehen** regard sth. as part of the natural order [of things]; ~**gemäß** *Adv.* naturally; ~**geschichte** *die; o. Pl.* natural history; ~**gesetz** *das* law of nature; ~**getreu 1** *Adj.;* lifelike ⟨*portrait, imitation*⟩; faithful ⟨*reproduction*⟩; **2** *adv.* ⟨*draw*⟩ true to life; ⟨*reproduce*⟩ faithfully; ~**gewalt** *die* force of nature; ~**heilkunde** *die* naturopathy *no art.;* ~**identisch** *Adj.* nature-identical; ~**katastrophe** *die* natural disaster; ~**kunde** *die; o. Pl.* (veralt.) nature study *no art.*

natürlich /na'tyːɐ̯lɪç/ **1** *Adj.* natural; **eines** ~**en Todes sterben** die a natural death; die of natural causes; **ein Bild in** ~**er Größe** a life-size portrait; **das ist die** ~**ste Sache der Welt** it is the most natural thing in the world. **2** *adv.* ⟨*laugh, behave*⟩ naturally. **3** *Adv.* **(a)** (wie erwartet) naturally; of course; **(b)** (zwar) of course

natürlicher·weise *Adv.* naturally; of course

Natürlichkeit *die;* ~: naturalness

natur-, Natur-: ~**nah** *Adj.* semi-natural; ~**produkt** *das* natural product; ~**produkte** natural produce *sing.;* ~**rein** *Adj.* pure ⟨*honey, jam, fruit, juice, etc.*⟩; ⟨*wine*⟩ free of additives; ~**schauspiel** *das* natural spectacle; ~**schutz** *der* [nature] conservation; **unter** ~**schutz** (*Dat.*) **stehen** be protected by law; be a protected species/variety/area *etc.;* ~**schutz·gebiet** *das* nature reserve; ~**talent** *das* [great] natural talent *or* gift; (begabter Mensch) naturally talented *or* gifted person; **ein** ~**talent sein** have a [great] natural gift *or* talent; ~**verbunden** *Adj.* ⟨*person*⟩ in tune with nature;

Nationalität

1. Adjektive

Alle Nationalitätsbezeichnungen im Englischen werden groß geschrieben:

die italienische Sprache	= the Italian language
ein indischer Brauch	= an Indian custom
Diese Haltung ist typisch deutsch	= This attitude is typically German

Wenn man bloß die Nationalität einer Person angeben will, verwendet man im Englischen oft das prädikative Adjektiv, wo man im Deutschen das Substantiv verwendet:

Seine Frau ist Schottin	= His wife is Scottish
Der Lehrer ist Franzose	= The teacher is French

Diese Adjektive werden von den Ländernamen abgeleitet. Bei Ländernamen, die auf **-a** enden, werden sie durch Hinzufügen eines **-n** gebildet, und bei denen, die auf **-y** enden, wird das **-y** durch **-ian** ersetzt. (Ausnahmen: China→Chinese; Germany→German; Canada→Canadian).

America→American	Austria→Austrian
Australia→Australian	Russia→Russian
Roumania→Roumanian	India→Indian
Italy→Italian	Burgundy→Burgundian
usw.	

Andere Ableitungen sind nicht regelmäßig gebildet. Mehrere enden auf **-ish,** den deutschen Formen entsprechend:

England→English	Britain→British
Scotland→Scottish	Spain→Spanish
Turkey→Turkish	Denmark→Danish
Finland→Finnish	

Sonstige Beispiele:

France→French	Greece→Greek
Iceland→Icelandic	

2. Substantive

Die Bezeichnungen der Einwohner haben die gleiche Form wie das Adjektiv, sofern dieses auf **-an** oder **-ese** endet. Die substantivierte Einwohnerbezeichnung erfordert im Singular einen Artikel:

ein reicher Amerikaner	= a rich American
die Inder	= the Indians
Sie heiratet einen Italiener	= She is marrying an Italian
Als Japanerin fühlt sie sich benachteiligt	= As a Japanese she feels disadvantaged

Die Substantive, die auf **-ese** und **-ss** enden, lauten im Singular und Plural gleich:

die Chinesen	= the Chinese
die Schweizer	= the Swiss

In den Fällen, wo das entsprechende Adjektiv auf **-[i]sh** oder **-ch** endet, wird oft **-man** bzw. **-woman** angefügt (im Plural **-men** bzw. **-women**). Nur wenn das Volk gemeint ist, verwendet man oft die Form des Adjektivs. Andere Formen sind unregelmäßig, aber meist ihren deutschen Entsprechungen sehr ähnlich:

English→Englishman/Englishwoman→Englishmen/ Englishwomen; the English

Scottish, Scots→Scot, Scotsman/Scotswoman→ Scotsmen/Scotswomen; the Scots

Welsh→Welshman/Welshwoman→Welshmen/ Welshwomen; the Welsh

Irish→Irishman/Irishwoman→Irishmen/Irishwomen; the Irish

French→Frenchman/Frenchwoman→Frenchmen/ Frenchwomen; the French

Dutch→Dutchman/Dutchwoman→Dutchmen/ Dutchwomen; the Dutch

British→Briton→Britons; the British

Swedish→Swede→Swedes; the Swedish

Finnish→Finn→Finns; the Finnish

Danish→Dane→Danes; the Danish

Spanish→Spaniard→Spaniards; the Spanish

Polish→Pole→Poles; the Polish

Turkish→Turk→Turks; the Turkish

eine Britin/Schwedin/Finnin/Dänin/Spanierin/Polin/ Türkin kann nur als 'a British/Swedish/Finnish/ Danish/Spanish/Polish/Turkish woman/girl' übersetzt werden.

Sonstige Ausdrücke

Sie ist von Geburt Spanierin	= She is Spanish by birth
Er ist deutscher Abstammung	= He is of German extraction
Ich stamme aus Norddeutschland	= I come from North Germany
Er ist belgischer Staatsbürger	= He is a Belgian national
ein eingebürgerter Schweizer	= a naturalized Swiss [citizen]

∼wissenschaft *die* natural science *no art.;* **∼wissenschaftler** *der* [natural] scientist; **∼wissenschaftlich** **1** *Adj.* scientific; **2** *adv.* scientifically; **∼wunder** *das* miracle *or* wonder of nature

nautisch /'nautɪʃ/ *Adj.* (Seew.) naval ‹*officer*›; navigational ‹*instrument, calculation*›

Navigation /naviga'tsi̯oːn/ *die;* ∼ (Seew., Flugw.) navigation *no art.*

Navigations·fehler *der* (Seew., Flugw.) navigational error

Nazi /'naːtsi/ *der;* ∼s, ∼s Nazi

Nazismus *der;* ∼: Nazi[i]sm *no art.*

nazistisch *Adj.* Nazi

Nazi·zeit *die* Nazi period

n. Chr. *Abk.* ▶ 119 | nach Christus AD

Neandertaler /ne'andɐtaːlɐ/ *der;* ∼s, ∼ (Anthrop.) Neanderthal man

Neapel /ne'aːpl̩/ *(das);* ∼s ▶ 490 | Naples

Nebel /'neːbl̩/ *der;* ∼s, ∼ fog; (weniger dicht) mist; **bei** ∼:

in fog/mist; when it is foggy/misty; **ausfallen wegen** ∼[s] (ugs. scherzh.) be cancelled; *s. auch* **Nacht**

Nebel-: ∼**bank** *die; Pl.:* ∼**bänke** (über dem Meer) fogbank; (über dem Land) large patch of fog; ∼**feld** *das* mist/fog patch; patch of mist/fog

nebelhaft *Adj.* hazy ‹*idea, recollection, etc.*›

Nebel·horn *das Pl.:* ∼**hörner** foghorn

nebelig ⇒ **neblig**

Nebel-: ∼**scheinwerfer** *der* fog lamp; ∼**schlussleuchte,** *∗*∼**schlußleuchte** *die* rear fog lamp; ∼**wand** *die* wall of fog

neben /'neːbn̩/ **1** *Präp. mit Dat.* **(a)** (Lage) next to; beside; **dicht** ∼ **jmdm./etw. sitzen** sit close *or* right beside sb./sth.; **(b)** (außer) apart from; aside from (Amer.). **2** *Präp. mit Akk.* **(a)** (Richtung) next to; beside; **(b)** (verglichen mit) beside; compared to *or* with

neben·an *Adv.* next door

Neben-: ∼**anschluss,** *∗*∼**anschluß** *der* extension; ∼**bedeutung** *die* secondary meaning

neben·bei *Adv.* **(a)** ‹*work*› on the side, as a sideline; (zusätzlich) as well; in addition; **für Geologie interessiert er sich nur** ∼: his interest in geology is only secondary;

(b) (beiläufig) ‹remark› incidentally, by the way; ‹ask› by the way; ‹inform› by the by; ‹mention› in passing; ~ gesagt od. bemerkt incidentally; by the way

neben-, Neben-: ~**beruf** der second job; sideline; **er ist im** ~**beruf Fotograf** he has a second job or sideline as a photographer; ~**beruflich** 1 Adj. eine ~**berufliche Tätigkeit** a second job; 2 adv. on the side; **er arbeitet** ~**beruflich als Übersetzer** he translates as a sideline; ~**beschäftigung** die second job; sideline; ~**buhler** der, ~**buhlerin** die rival

neben·einander Adv. (a) next to one another or each other; (fig.: zusammen) ‹live, exist› side by side; ~ **wohnen** live next door to one another or each other; **sich zu zweit** ~ **aufstellen** line up two abreast; (b) (gleichzeitig) together

nebeneinander·her Adv. alongside each other or one another; ‹walk› side by side

*****nebeneinander|legen** usw.: ⇨ nebeneinander a

Neben-: ~**eingang** der side entrance; ~**einkünfte** Pl., ~**einnahme**, die, ~**einnahmen** Pl. additional or supplementary income sing.; ~**erwerb** der second job; secondary occupation; ~**fach** das subsidiary subject; minor (Amer.); **etw. im** ~**fach studieren** study sth. as a subsidiary subject; minor in sth. (Amer.); ~**fluss**, *~**fluß** der ▶193┃ tributary; ~**frage** die side issue; secondary issue; ~**gebäude** das (a) annexe; outbuilding; (b) (Nachbargebäude) adjacent or neighbouring building; ~**geräusch** das background noise; ~**geräusche** (Funkw., Fernspr.) interference sing.; noise sing.; (bei Tonband, Plattenspieler) [background] noise sing.; ~**handlung** die sub-plot; ~**haus** das house next door; neighbouring house

neben·her Adv. ⇨ nebenbei

nebenher-: ~|**fahren** unr. itr. V.; mit sein drive alongside; (mit dem Rad, Motorrad) ride alongside; ~|**laufen** unr. itr. V.; mit sein (a) run alongside; (b) (zugleich ablaufen) proceed at the same time

neben-, Neben-: ~**höhle** die (Anat.) ▶326┃ paranasal sinus ~**kosten** Pl. (a) additional costs; (b) (bei Mieten) heating, lighting, and services; ~**mann** der; Pl.: ~**männer** od. ~**leute** neighbour; **sein** ~**mann** the person sitting/standing/walking next to him; his neighbour; ~**produkt** das (auch fig.) by-product; ~**raum** der next or adjoining room; room next door; (kleiner, unwichtiger) sideroom; ~**rolle** die supporting role; **eine** ~**rolle [in etw. (Dat.)] spielen** (fig.) play a secondary or minor role [in sth.]; ~**sache** die minor or inessential matter; **das ist** ~**sache** (ugs.) that's beside the point; ~**sächlich** Adj. of minor importance postpos.; unimportant; minor, trivial ‹detail›; **etw. als** ~**sächlich abtun** reject sth. as irrelevant or beside the point; ~**sächlichkeit** die; ~, ~**en** (a) o. Pl. unimportance; (fehlender Bezug zur Sache) irrelevance; (b) (Unwichtiges) matter of minor importance; unimportant matter; (nicht zur Sache Gehörendes) irrelevancy; ~**satz** der (Sprachw.) subordinate clause; ~**stelle** die (a) extension; (b) (Filiale) branch; ~**straße** die side street; (außerhalb der Stadt) minor road; ~**tätigkeit** die second job; sideline; ~**tisch** der next or neighbouring table; ~**verdienst** der additional earnings pl. or income; ~**wirkung** die side effect; ~**zimmer** das next room; **sie gingen in ein** ~**zimmer** they went into an adjoining room

neblig Adj. foggy; (weniger dicht) misty

Necessaire /nesɛˈsɛːɐ̯/ das; ~s, ~s sponge bag (Brit.); toilet bag (Amer.)

necken /ˈnɛkn̩/ tr. V. tease; **jmdn. mit jmdm./etw.** ~: tease sb. about sth./sth.; **sich** ~: tease each other or one another

Neckerei die; ~: teasing

neckisch 1 Adj. (a) teasing; (verspielt) playful; (schelmisch) mischievous; (b) (kess) jaunty, saucy ‹cap›; saucy, provocative ‹dress, blouse, etc.›. 2 adv. ‹smile, say› saucily, cheekily

nee /neː/ (ugs.) no; nope (Amer. coll.)

Neffe /ˈnɛfə/ der; ~n, ~n nephew

Negation /negaˈtsi̯oːn/ die; ~, ~**en** negation

negativ /ˈneːgatiːf/ 1 Adj. negative. 2 adv. ‹answer› in the negative; **etw.** ~ **beeinflussen** have a negative influence on sth.; **etw.** ~ **bewerten** judge sth. unfavourably; **sich** ~ **äußern** comment negatively (zu on); **der**

Test/die Testbohrung verlief ~: the test proved unsuccessful/the test well yielded nothing

Negativ das; ~s, ~e (Fot.) negative

Neger /ˈneːgɐ/ der; ~s, ~ Negro

Negerin die; ~, ~**nen** Negress

negieren tr. V. deny ‹fact, assertion, guilt, etc.›

Negligé, Negligee /negliˈʒeː/ das; ~s, ~s négligé, negligee

nehmen /ˈneːmən/ unr. tr. V. (a) take; **etw. in die Hand/unter den Arm** ~: take sth. in one's hand/take or put sth. under one's arm; **etw. an sich** (Akk.) ~: pick sth. up; (und aufbewahren) take charge of sth.; **sich** (Dat.) **etw.** ~: take sth.; (sich bedienen) help oneself to sth.; **zu sich** ~: take in ‹orphan›; **sie nahm ihren Vater zu sich** she had her father come and live with her; **auf sich** (Akk.) ~: take on ‹responsibility, burden›; take ‹blame›; **die Dinge** ~, **wie sie kommen** take things as they come; (b) (wegnehmen) **jmdm./einer Sache etw.** ~: deprive sb. of sth.; **jmdm. die Sicht/den Ausblick** ~: block sb.'s view; **die Angst von jmdm.** ~: relieve sb. of his/her fear; **es sich** (Dat.) **nicht** ~ **lassen, etw. zu tun** not let anything stop one from doing sth.; (c) (benutzen) use ‹ingredients, washing powder, wool, brush, knitting needles, etc.›; **man nehme** … (in Rezepten) take …; **den Zug/ein Taxi** usw. ~: take the train/a taxi etc.; [sich (Dat.)] **einen Anwalt** usw. ~: get a lawyer etc.; (d) (aussuchen) take; **ich nehme die Pastete** I'll have the pâté; (e) (in Anspruch nehmen) take ‹lessons, holiday, etc.›; (f) (verlangen) charge; (g) (einnehmen, essen) take ‹medicines, tablets, etc.›; **etwas [Richtiges] zu sich** ~: have something [decent] to eat; **sie nimmt die Pille** she's taking or she's on the pill (coll.); (h) (auffassen) take (**als** as); **etw./jmdn. ernst/etw. leicht** ~: take sth./sb. seriously/take sth. lightly; **jmdn. nicht für voll** ~ (ugs.) not take sb. seriously; (i) (behandeln) treat ‹person›; (j) (überwinden, militärisch einnehmen) take ‹obstacle, bend, incline, village, bridgehead, etc.›; (fig.) take ‹woman›; (k) (Sport) take ‹ball, punch›; **einen Spieler hart** ~: foul a player blatantly

Nehrung /ˈneːrʊŋ/ die; ~, ~**en** sand bar

Neid /naɪt/ der; ~[e]s envy; jealousy; **vor** ~ **platzen** (ugs.) die of envy (coll.); **gelb od. grün vor** ~ **werden, vor** ~ **erblassen** turn or go green with envy; **das muss der** ~ **ihr lassen** (ugs.) you've got to give her that; you've got to say that much for her

neiden tr. V. (geh.) **jmdm. etw.** ~: envy sb. [for] sth.

Neider der; ~s, ~: envious person

Neid·hammel der (salopp abwertend) envious sod (sl.)

neidisch 1 Adj. envious; **auf jmdn./etw.** ~ **sein** be envious of sb./sth. 2 adv. enviously

neid-: ~**los** 1 Adj. ungrudging ‹admiration›; ‹joy› without envy; 2 adv. ‹acknowledge, admire› without envy; ~**voll** 1 Adj. envious ‹glance›; ‹person› filled with or full of envy ‹admiration› mixed with envy; 2 adv. ‹watch› full of envy

Neige /ˈnaɪgə/ die; ~ (geh.) dregs pl.; lees pl.; **ein Glas bis zur** ~ **leeren** drain a glass to the dregs; **zur** ~ **gehen** (aufgebraucht sein) ‹money, supplies, etc.› run low; (zu Ende gehen) ‹year, day, holiday› draw to its close

neigen 1 tr. V. tip, tilt ‹bottle, glass, barrel, etc.›; incline ‹head, upper part of body›. 2 refl. V. (a) ‹person› lean, bend; ‹ship› heel over, list; ‹scales› tip; (b) (schräg abfallen) ‹meadows› slope down; (c) (geh.: zu Ende gehen) ‹day, year, holiday› draw to its close. 3 itr. V. (a) **zu Erkältungen** ~: be susceptible or prone to colds; **zur Korpulenz/Schwermut** ~: have a tendency to put on weight/tend to be melancholy; (b) (tendieren) tend; **zu der Ansicht** ~, **dass** …: tend towards the view that …

Neigung die; ~, ~**en** (a) o. Pl. (des Kopfes) nod; (b) o. Pl. (Geneigtsein) inclination; (eines Geländes) slope; (c) (Vorliebe) inclination; **seine politischen/künstlerischen** ~**en** his political/artistic leanings; **eine** ~ **für etw.** a penchant or fondness for sth.; (d) o. Pl. (Anfälligsein) tendency; (e) o. Pl. (Lust) inclination; (f) (Liebe) affection; fondness; liking

Neigungs·winkel der angle of inclination

nein /naɪn/ Interj. no; ~ **danke** no, thank you; **man muss auch** ~ od. **Nein sagen können** one must be able to say no; ~, **nicht!** no, don't!; ~ **und abermals** ~! no, and that's final!

Nein *das;* ~[s], ~[s] no; **mit** ~ **stimmen** vote no

Nein·stimme *die* no-vote; vote against

Nektar /'nɛktar/ *der;* ~s, ~e (Bot.) nectar

Nektarine /nɛkta'riːnə/ *die;* ~, ~n nectarine

Nelke /'nɛlkə/ *die;* ~, ~n (a) pink; (Dianthus caryophyllus) carnation; (b) (Gewürz) clove

nennen /'nɛnən/ **1** *unr. tr. V.* (a) call; **jmdn. nach jmdm.** ~: call *or* name sb. after sb.; **jmdn. beim Vornamen** ~: call sb. by his/her first *or* Christian name; **das nenne ich Mut/eine Überraschung** that's what I call courage/well, that 'is a surprise; (b) (mitteilen) give ⟨*name, date of birth, address, reason, price, etc.*⟩; (c) (anführen) give, cite ⟨*example*⟩; (erwähnen) mention ⟨*person, name*⟩. **2** *unr. refl. V.* ⟨*person, thing*⟩ be called; **er nennt sich Maler** *usw.* (behauptet Maler usw. zu sein) he calls himself a painter *etc.;* **und so was nennt sich nun ein Freund** (ugs.) and he/she has the nerve to call himself/herself a friend

nennens·wert *Adj.* considerable ⟨*influence, changes, delays, damage*⟩; **nichts Nennenswertes** nothing worth mentioning *or* nothing of note

Nenner *der;* ~s, ~ (Math.) denominator; **etw. auf einen** ~ **bringen** (fig.) reduce sth. to a common denominator

Nennung *die;* ~, ~en ⇒ **nennen** 1 b, c: giving; citing; mentioning

neo-, Neo-: neo-

Neon /'neːɔn/ *das;* ~s (Chemie) neon

Neon-: ~**licht** *das* neon light; ~**reklame** *die* neon sign; ~**röhre** *die* neon tube; [neon] strip light

Nepp /nɛp/ *der;* ~s (ugs. abwertend) daylight robbery *no art.;* rip-off (coll.)

neppen *tr. V.* (ugs. abwertend) rook; rip ⟨*tourist, customer, etc.*⟩ off (sl.)

Nepp·lokal *das* (ugs. abwertend) clip joint (sl. derog.)

Neptun¹ /nɛp'tuːn/ *der;* ~s (Astron.), **Neptun²** (*der*); ~s (Myth.) Neptune

Nerv /nɛrf/ *der;* ~s, ~en (a) nerve; **jmdm. den** ~ **töten** (fig. ugs.) drive sb. up the wall (coll.); (b) *Pl.* (nervliche Konstitution) nerves; **gute/schwache** ~**en haben** have strong/bad nerves; **die** ~**en [dazu] haben, etw. zu tun** have the nerve to do sth.; **die** ~**en bewahren** *od.* **behalten** keep calm; **die** ~**en verlieren** lose control [of oneself]; lose one's cool (sl.); **ich bin mit den** ~**en am Ende** my nerves cannot take any more; **du hast vielleicht** ~**en!** (ugs.) you've got a nerve!; **jmdm. auf die** ~**en gehen** *od.* **fallen** get on sb.'s nerves

nerven (salopp) **1** *tr. V.* **jmdn.** ~: get on sb.'s nerves. **2** *itr. V.* be wearing on the nerves

nerven-, Nerven-: ~**anspannung** *die* nervous strain; nervous tension *no indef. art.;* ~**arzt** *der* neurologist; ~**aufreibend** *Adj.* nerve-racking; ~**belastung** *die* strain on the nerves; ~**bündel** *das* (ugs.) bundle of nerves (coll.); ~**gift** *das* neurotoxin; ~**heilanstalt** *die* (veralt.) mental *or* psychiatric hospital; ~**kitzel** *der* (ugs.) kick (coll.); ~**krank** *Adj.* (a) ⟨*person*⟩ suffering from a nervous disease *or* disorder; (b) (psychisch krank) mentally ill; ~**krankheit** *die* ▶ 329┃ (a) nervous disease *or* disorder; (b) (psychische Krankheit) mental illness; ~**krieg** *der* (ugs.) war of nerves; ~**leiden** *das* ▶ 329┃ nervous complaint *or* disorder; ~**sache** *die in* **das ist reine** ~**sache** (ugs.) it's a matter *or* question of nerves; ~**säge** *die* (salopp) pain in the neck (coll.); ~**zusammenbruch** *der* ▶ 329┃ nervous breakdown

nervlich 1 *Adj.* nervous ⟨*strain*⟩. **2** *adv.* **dieser ständigen Spannung war er** ~ **nicht gewachsen** his nerves were not up to this constant tension

nervös /nɛr'vøːs/ **1** *Adj.* (a) nervy, jittery ⟨*person*⟩; nervous ⟨*haste, movement*⟩; ~ **sein** be jittery (coll.) *or* on edge; **das macht mich ganz** ~: it really gets on my nerves; (das beunruhigt mich) it makes me really nervous; (b) (Med.) nervous ⟨*twitch, gastric disorder, etc.*⟩. **2** *adv.* nervously

Nervosität /nɛrvozi'tɛːt/ *die;* ~: nervousness

nerv·tötend *Adj.* nerve-racking ⟨*wait*⟩; nerve-shattering ⟨*sound, noise*⟩; soul-destroying ⟨*activity, work*⟩

Nerz /nɛrts/ *der;* ~es, ~e mink

Nerz·mantel *der* mink coat

Nessel¹ /'nɛsl/ *die;* ~, ~n nettle; **sich in die** ~**n setzen** (fig. ugs.) get [oneself] into hot water (coll.)

Nessel² *der;* ~s, ~ (Stoff) coarse, untreated cotton cloth

Nessel·sucht *die;* ~: nettle-rash; hives

Nest /nɛst/ *das;* ~[e]s, ~er (a) nest; **das eigene** ~ **beschmutzen** (fig.) foul one's own nest; **er hat sich ins warme** *od.* **gemachte** ~ **gesetzt** (fig. ugs.) he had his future made for him; (b) (fam.: Bett) bed; (c) (ugs. abwertend: kleiner Ort) little place; **ein gottverlassenes** ~: a God-forsaken hole (sl.); (d) (Schlupfwinkel) hideout; den

Nest·beschmutzer *der;* ~s, ~ (abwertend) person who is/was guilty of fouling his/her own nest

nesteln /'nɛstln/ *itr. V.* fiddle, (ungeschickt) fumble (**an** + *Dat.* with)

Nest-: ~**häkchen** *das* (fam.) [spoilt] baby of the family; ~**wärme** *die* warmth of a [happy] family upbringing *or* of [happy] family life

nett /nɛt/ **1** *Adj.* (a) nice; (freundlich) nice; kind; **sei so** ~ **und hilf mir!** would you be so good *or* kind as to help me?; ~, **dass du anrufst** it's nice *or* kind of you to ring; **etwas Nettes erleben/sagen** have a pleasant experience/say something nice; (b) (hübsch) pretty ⟨*girl, town, dress, etc.*⟩; nice, pleasant ⟨*pub, house, town, etc.*⟩; (c) *nicht präd.* (ugs.: beträchtlich) nice little (coll.) ⟨*profit, extra earnings, income*⟩; **eine** ~**e Summe/eine** ~**e Stange Geld** a tidy sum (coll.); (d) (ugs. iron.: unerfreulich) nice (coll.) ⟨*affair*⟩; nice (coll.), fine ⟨*state of affairs, mess*⟩; **das kann ja** ~ **werden!** that'll be fun (coll.). **2** *adv.* (angenehm) nicely; (freundlich) nicely; kindly; **sich** ~ **mit jmdm. unterhalten** have a pleasant conversation with sb.

netter·weise *Adv.* (ugs.) kindly

Nettigkeit *die;* ~, ~en (a) *o. Pl.* kindness; goodness; (b) (Äußerung) **jmdm. ein paar** ~**en sagen** say a few nice *or* kind things to sb.

netto /'nɛto/ *Adv.* ⟨*weigh, earn, etc.*⟩ net

Netto- net ⟨*income, salary, etc*⟩

Netz /nɛts/ *das;* ~es, ~e (a) (auch Fischer~, Tennis~, Ballspiele) net; (Einkaufs~) string bag; (Gepäck~) [luggage-]rack; **ein** ~ **von Lügen** (fig.) a web of lies; **jmdm. ins** ~ **gehen** (fig.) fall into sb.'s trap; (b) (Spinnen~) web; (c) (Verteiler~, Verkehrs~, System von Einrichtungen) network; (für Strom, Wasser, Gas) mains *pl.*

Netz-: ~**anschluss**, ***~**anschluß** *der* mains connection; ~**ball** *der* (Tennis, Volleyball) net ball; ~**gerät** *das* (Elektrot.) power pack; ~**haut** *die* ▶ 326┃ (Anat.) retina; ~**hemd** *das* string vest; ~**karte** *die* area season ticket; (Eisenb.) unlimited travel ticket; ~**roller** *der* (Tennis) net-cord [stroke]; ~**spannung** *die* (Elektrot.) mains voltage; ~**stecker** *der* mains plug; ~**strumpf** *der* net stocking; ~**werk** *das* (auch Elektrot.) network

neu /nɔy/ **1** *Adj.* (a) ▶ 240┃ new; **ein ganz** ~**es Fahrrad** a brand new bicycle; **die Neue Welt** the New World; **das Neue Testament** the New Testament; **die** ~**este Mode** the latest fashion; **die** ~**esten Nachrichten/Ereignisse** the latest news/most recent events; **viel Glück im** ~**en Jahr** best wishes for the New Year; Happy New Year; **das ist mir** ~: that is news to me; **das Neue daran ist …:** what's new about it is …; **das Neueste auf dem Markt** the latest thing on the market; **der/die Neue** the new man/woman/boy/girl; **was gibt es Neues?** what's new?; **weißt du schon das Neueste?** (ugs.) have you heard the latest?; **aufs Neue** anew; afresh; again; **auf ein Neues!** let's try again!; **von** ~**em** all over again; (noch einmal) [once] again; **seit** ~**estem werden dort keine Kreditkarten mehr akzeptiert** just recently they've started refusing to accept credit cards; **in** ~**erer**/~**ester Zeit** quite/just *or* very recently; **das ist** ~**eren Datums** that is of a more recent date; **die** ~**en** *od.* ~**eren Sprachen** modern languages; (b) *nicht präd.* (kürzlich geerntet) new ⟨*wine, potatoes*⟩; (c) (sauber) clean ⟨*shirt, socks, underwear,* *etc.*⟩. **2** *adv.* (a) ~ **tapeziert/gespritzt/gestrichen/ möbliert** repapered/resprayed/repainted/refurnished; **ein Geschäft** ~ **eröffnen** reopen a shop; ~ **eröffnet** newly opened; (wieder eröffnet) reopened; **sich** ~ **einkleiden** provide oneself with a new set of clothes; **noch einmal** ~ **beginnen** start again from scratch; (b) (gerade erst) **diese Ware ist** ~ **eingetroffen** this item has just come in *or* arrived; ~ **erschienene Bücher** newly published books; books that have just come out *or* appeared; **3 000 Wörter sind** ~ **hinzugekommen** 3,000 new words have been added; ~ **vermählt** (geh.) newly wed *or* married

neu-, Neu-: ~**ankömmling** *der* new arrival; ~**anschaffung** *die:* **die** ~**anschaffung von Produktionsanlagen** the acquisition of new production plant; ~**anschaffungen machen** buy new items; ~**artig** *Adj.* new; **ein** ~**er Staubsauger** a new type of vacuum cleaner; ~**auflage** *die* new edition; ~**ausgabe** *die* new edition

Neu·bau *der; Pl.* **Neubauten** new house/building

Neubau-: ~**viertel** *das* new district; ~**wohnung** *die* flat (Brit.) *or* (Amer.) apartment in a new block/house; new flat (Brit.) *or* (Amer.) apartment

Neu-: ~**bearbeitung** *die* (a) (eines Buches, Textes) revision; (eines Theaterstücks) adaptation; (b) (neue Fassung) new version; ~**beginn** *der* new beginning; ~**druck** *der* reprint [with corrections]; ~**einstellung** *die:* **eine** ~**einstellung vornehmen** take on a new employee; (von Angestellten) make a new appointment; ~**entdeckung** *die* (a) (auch fig.) new discovery; (b) (Wiederentdeckung) rediscovery; ~**entwicklung** *die* (a) **die** ~**entwicklung von Heilmitteln** the development of new medicines; (b) (neu Entwickeltes) new development

neuerdings /'nɔyɐ'dɪŋs/ *Adv.* recently; **Fahrkarten gibt es** ~ **nur noch am Automaten** as of a short while ago one can only get tickets from a machine; **er trägt** ~ **eine Perücke** he has recently started wearing a wig

Neuerer *der;* ~**s,** ~ innovator

neu-, Neu-: ***~**eröffnet** ⇒ **neu 2 a;** ~**eröffnung** *die* (a) opening; (b) (Wiedereröffnung) reopening; ~**erscheinung** *die* new publication; (Schallplatte) new release

Neuerung *die;* ~**,** ~**en** innovation

neu-, Neu-: ~**erwerbung** *die* (a) **die** ~ **von Büchern** *usw.* the acquisition of new books *etc.*; (b) (Gegenstand) new acquisition; ~**fassung** *die* revised version; (eines Films) remake; ~**fundland** *(das);* ~**s** Newfoundland; ~**fundländer** *der;* ~**s,** ~ (Hunderasse) Newfoundland [dog]; ~**geboren** *Adj.* newborn; **sich wie** ~**geboren fühlen** feel a new man/woman; ~**geborene** *das; adj. Dekl.* newborn child

Neu·gier, Neugierde /-giːɐdə/ *die;* ~**:** curiosity; (Wissbegierde) inquisitiveness; **aus [reiner]** ~**:** out of [sheer] curiosity

neu·gierig 1 *Adj.* curious; inquisitive; prying (derog.), nosy (coll. derog.) ⟨*person*⟩; **da bin ich aber** ~**!** (iron.) I'll believe it when I see it; I can hardly wait! (iron.); **auf etw.** (*Akk.*) ~ **sein** be curious about sth.; **viele Neugierige** many inquisitive people *or* spectators; **ich bin** ~**, was er dazu sagt** I'm curious to know what he'll say about it; **ich bin** ~**, ob er kommt** I wonder whether he'll come. **2** *adv.* ⟨*ask*⟩ inquisitively; ⟨*peer*⟩ nosily (coll. derog.); **jmdn.** ~ **mustern** eye sb. curiously

Neu·gründung *die* (a) **die** ~ **eines Vereins** *usw.* the founding *or* establishment of a new club *etc.;* (b) (neu Gegründetes) **eine** ~ **sein** have recently been founded *or* established; (c) (erneute Gründung) refoundation; re-establishment

Neuheit *die;* ~**,** ~**en** (a) *o. Pl.* novelty; (b) (Neues) new product/gadget/article *etc.*

Neuigkeit *die;* ~**,** ~**en** piece of news; ~**en** news *sing.*

Neu·jahr *das* ▶240▎ New Year's Day; ~ **feiern** celebrate New Year; *s. auch* **prosit**

Neujahrs-: ~**nacht** *die* New Year's night; ~**tag** *der* New Year's Day

Neu·land *das* (a) newly reclaimed *or* new land; (b) (unerforschtes Land) new *or* virgin territory; **wissenschaftliches** ~ **betreten** (fig.) break new ground in science

neulich *Adv.* recently; the other day

Neuling /'nɔylɪŋ/ *der;* ~**s,** ~**e** newcomer (**in** + *Dat.* to); new man/woman/girl/boy; (auf einem Gebiet) novice

neu·modisch (abwertend) **1** *Adj.* newfangled (derog.). **2** *adv.* ⟨*dress*⟩ in a newfangled way

Neu·mond *der* new moon; **heute ist/haben wir** ~**:** there's a new moon today

neun /nɔyn/ *Kardinalz.* ▶22▎, ▶530▎, ▶600▎ nine; **alle** ~**[e]** (Kegeln) a floorer; *s. auch* **acht**

Neun *die;* ~**,** ~**en** nine; **ach, du grüne** ~**e** (ugs.) oh, my goodness!; good grief!; *s. auch* **Acht**[1]

neun-, Neun- (*s. auch* **acht-, Acht-**)**:** ~**fach** *Vervielfältigungsz.* ninefold; *s. auch* **achtfach;** ~**fache** *das;* ~**n: das** ~**fache von 4 ist 36** nine fours are *or* nine times four makes thirty-six; *s. auch* **Achtfache;** ~**hundert** *Kardinalz.* ▶600▎ nine hundred; ~**jährig** *Adj.* (9 Jahre alt) nine-year-old *attrib.;* (9 Jahre dauernd) nine-year *attrib.;* ~**mal** *Adv.* nine times; *s. auch* **achtmal;** ~**malklug 1** *Adj.* smart-aleck *attrib.* (coll.); **2** *adv.* in a smart-aleck way (coll.)

neunt /nɔynt/ *in* **wir waren zu** ~**:** there were nine of us; *s. auch* **acht**[2]

neun·tausend *Kardinalz.* ▶600▎ nine thousand

Neuntel *das* (schweiz. meist der) ▶600▎; ~**s,** ~**:** ninth

neuntens *Adv.* ninthly

neun·zehn *Kardinalz.* ▶22▎, ▶530▎, ▶600▎ nineteen; *s. auch* **achtzehn**

neunzig /'nɔyntsɪç/ *Kardinalz.* ▶22▎, ▶600▎ ninety; *s. auch* **achtzig**

neunziger *indekl. Adj.; nicht präd.* **die** ~ **Jahre** the nineties; *s. auch* **achtziger**

Neunziger *der;* ~**s,** ~**:** ninety-year-old

Neunziger·jahre *Pl.* ▶22▎, ▶119▎ nineties *pl.*

neu-, Neu-: ~**ordnung** *die* reorganization; ~**reg[e]lung** *die* (a) *o. Pl.* **die** ~**regelung der Arbeitszeit** *usw.* the revision of regulations governing working hours *etc.;* (b) (Bestimmung) new regulation; ~**reich** *Adj.* (abwertend) nouveau riche; ~**reiche** *der/die* nouveau riche

Neurodermitis *die;* ~**, Neurodermitiden** (Med.) neurodermatitis

Neurologe *der;* ~**n,** ~**n** neurologist

Neurologie *die;* ~ neurology

Neurologin *die;* ~**,** ~**nen** neurologist

Neurose /nɔy'roːzə/ *die;* ~**,** ~**n** ▶329▎ (Med., Psych.) neurosis

Neurotiker /nɔy'roːtikɐ/ *der;* ~**s,** ~**, Neurotikerin** *die;* ~**,** ~**nen** (Med., Psych., auch ugs.) neurotic

neurotisch *Adj.* (Med., Psych., auch ugs.) neurotic

Neu·schnee *der* fresh snow

Neu·see·land *(das);* ~**s** New Zealand

Neuseeländer *der;* ~**s,** ~ ▶388▎ New Zealander

neuseeländisch *Adj.* ▶388▎ New Zealand

neu·sprachlich *Adj.* modern languages *attrib.* ⟨*teaching*⟩; **ein** ~**sprachliches Gymnasium** a grammar school with emphasis on modern languages

neutral /nɔy'traːl/ *Adj.* (auch Völkerr., Phys., Chem.) neutral

neutralisieren *tr. V.* (auch Völkerr., Chem., Elektrot.) neutralize

Neutralität /nɔytrali'tɛːt/ *die;* ~**,** ~**en** (auch Völkerr., Chem., Elektrot.) neutrality

Neutron /'nɔytrɔn/ *das;* ~**s,** ~**en** /-'troːnən/ (Kernphysik) neutron

Neutronen·bombe *die* neutron bomb

Neutrum /'nɔytrʊm/ *das;* ~**s, Neutra** (österr. nur so) *od.* **Neutren** (Sprachw.) neuter

neu-, Neu-: ***~**vermählt** ⇒ **neu 2 b;** ~**vermählten** *Pl.* (geh.) **die** ~**vermählten** the newly-weds; ~**wahl** *die* new election; **die** ~**wahl des Bundespräsidenten** the election of a new Federal President; ~**wert** *der* value when new; original value; (Versicherungsw.) replacement value; ~**wertig** *Adj.* as new; ~**zeit** *die; o, Pl.* (Zeit nach 1500) modern era *or* age; (Gegenwart) modern times *pl.;* modern age; ~**zeitlich 1** *Adj.* modern; since the Middle Ages *postpos., not pred.;* (modern)

modern ⟨*device, equipment, methods, etc.*⟩; **2** *adv.* (modern) ⟨*equip, fit*⟩ with all modern conveniences; **~zugang** *der* (im Krankenhaus) new admission; (in der Bibliothek) new accession; **~zulassung** *die:* **die ~zulassung von Kraftfahrzeugen** the registration of new vehicles

nicht /nɪçt/ *Adv.* **(a)** not; **sie raucht ~** (im Moment) she is not smoking; (gewöhnlich) she does not *or* doesn't smoke; **~ rostend** non-rusting ⟨*blade*⟩; stainless ⟨*steel*⟩; **alle klatschten, nur sie ~:** they all applauded except for her; **Wer hat das getan? — Sie ~!** Who did that? — It wasn't her; **Gehst du hin? — Nein, ich gehe ~!** Are you going? — No, I'm not; **Ich mag ihn ~. — Ich auch ~:** I don't like him. — Neither do I; **ich kann das ~ mehr** *od.* **länger sehen** I can't stand the sight of it any more *or* longer; **~ einmal** *od.* (ugs.) mal not even; **~ mehr als** no more than; **(b)** (Bitte, Verbot o. Ä. ausdrückend) **~!** [no,] don't!; **„~ hinauslehnen!"** (im Zug) 'do not lean out of the window'; **bitte ~!** please don't!; **(c)** (Zustimmung erwartend) **er ist dein Bruder, ~?** he's your brother, isn't he?; **du magst das, ~ [wahr]?** you like that, don't you?; **kommst du [etwa] ~?** aren't you coming[, then]?; **willst du ~ mitkommen?** won't you come too?; **(d)** (verwundert) **was du ~ sagst!** you don't say!; **(e)** ([bedingte] Anerkennung ausdrückend) **~ übel!** not bad!

nicht-, Nicht-: non-
Nicht-: ~achtung *die* **(a)** in jmdn. mit **~achtung strafen** punish sb. by ignoring him/her; send sb. to Coventry; **(b)** (Geringschätzung) lack of regard *or* respect; **~angriffs·pakt** *der* non-aggression pact; **~beachtung** *die* non-observance; **~beachtung einer roten Ampel** failure to observe a red light; **~befolgung** *die:* **~befolgung der Vorschriften** non-compliance *or* failure to comply with the regulations
Nichte *die;* **~, ~n** niece
Nicht-: ~einmischung *die* (Politik) non-intervention; non-interference; **~gefallen** *das* in **bei ~gefallen** (Kaufmannsspr.) if not satisfied
nichtig *Adj.* **(a)** (geh.: wertlos, belanglos) vain ⟨*things, pleasures, etc.*⟩; trivial ⟨*reason*⟩; petty ⟨*quarrel*⟩; idle ⟨*thoughts, chatter*⟩; empty ⟨*pretext*⟩; **(b)** (Rechtsspr.) ungültig) invalid, void ⟨*contract, will, etc.*⟩
nicht-, Nicht-: ~mitglied *das* non-member; **~öffentlich** *Adj.* not open to the public *pred.;* closed, private ⟨*meeting*⟩; **~raucher** *der* non-smoker; **ich bin ~raucher** I don't smoke; I'm a non-smoker; **~raucher·abteil** *das* non-smoking *or* no-smoking compartment;**~rostend** ⇒ **nicht a**
nichts /nɪçts/ *Indefinitpron.* nothing; **er sieht ~:** he sees nothing; he doesn't see anything; **hast du ~ gegessen?** haven't you eaten anything?; **für ~ und wieder ~** (ugs.) for nothing at all; **~ zu machen!/~ da!** (ugs.) nothing doing (coll.); **von mir bekommst du ~ mehr** you'll get nothing more from me; you won't get anything more from me; **~ anderes** nothing else; **jetzt interessiert er sich für ~ anderes mehr** he's now no longer interested in anything else; **~ als** nothing but; **~ wie ins Bett/weg!** quick into bed/let's go!; **~ wie hinterher!** put your skates on, after him/her/them! (sl.); **~ ahnend** unsuspecting; **~ sagend** (fig.) meaningless, empty ⟨*talk, phrases, etc.*⟩; vacant ⟨*smile*⟩; expressionless ⟨*face*⟩; **~ sagend formuliert** (fig.) meaninglessly formulated; **~ sagend lächeln** (fig.) smile vacantly; *s. auch* **danken 2 a**
Nichts *das;* **~, ~e (a)** o. Pl. (Philos.: das Nicht-Sein) nothingness *no art.;* **(b)** o. Pl. (leerer Raum) void; **er war wie aus dem ~ aufgetaucht** he appeared from nowhere; **(c)** o. Pl. (wenig von etw.) **etw. aus dem ~ aufbauen** built sth. up from nothing; **vor dem ~ stehen** be left with nothing; be faced with ruin; **(d)** (abwertend: Mensch) nobody; nonentity
***nichts·ahnend** ⇒ **nichts**
Nicht-: ~schwimmer *der* non-swimmer; **er war ~schwimmer** he could not swim; **~schwimmer·becken** *das* non-swimmers' *or* learners' pool
nichts·desto·weniger *Adv.* nevertheless; none the less

Nicht·sesshafte, *****Nicht·seßhafte** *der/die; adj. Dekl.* (Amtsspr.) person of no fixed abode (Admin. Lang.)
nichts-, Nichts-: ~könner *der* (abwertend) incompetent; bungler; **~nutz** *der;* **~es, ~e** (veralt. abwertend) good-for-nothing; **~nutzig** *Adj.* (veralt. abwertend) good-for-nothing *attrib.;* worthless ⟨*existence*⟩;*****~sagend** ⇒ **nichts; ~tuer** *der;* **~tu:ɐ/ *der;* ~s, ~** (abwertend) layabout; loafer; **~tun** *das* **(a)** inactivity; doing nothing *no art.;* **(b)** (Müßiggang) idleness *no art.;* lazing about *no art.*
Nicht·zutreffende *das; adj. Dekl.* **~s streichen** delete as applicable
Nickel /'nɪkl/ *das;* **~s** nickel
Nickel·brille *die* metal-rimmed glasses *or* spectacles
nicken /'nɪkn̩/ *itr. V.* **(a)** nod; **zustimmend ~:** nod one's agreement; **mit dem Kopf ~:** nod one's head; **(b)** (fam.: schlafen) doze; snooze (coll.)
Nickerchen *das;* **~s, ~** (fam.) nap; snooze (coll.); **ein ~ machen** take *or* have forty winks *or* a nap
Nicki /'nɪki/ *der;* **~[s], ~s** velour pullover *or* sweater
nie /niː/ *Adv.* never; **mich besucht ~ jemand** nobody ever visits me; **~ mehr!** never again!; **~ und nimmer!** never!; **~ im Leben!** not on your life!; **das werde ich ~ im Leben vergessen** I shall never forget it as long as I live
nieder /'niːdɐ/ **1** *Adj.; nicht präd.* **(a)** lower ⟨*class, intelligence*⟩; petty, minor ⟨*official*⟩; lowly ⟨*family, origins, birth*⟩; menial ⟨*task*⟩; **(b)** (Biol.: nicht hoch entwickelt) lower ⟨*plant, animal, organism*⟩. **2** *Adv.* (hinunter) down
nieder-, Nieder-: ~brennen **1** *unr. itr. V.; mit sein* (herunterbrennen) ⟨*fire*⟩ burn low; ⟨*building*⟩ burn down; **2** *unr. tr. V.* burn down ⟨*building, village, etc.*⟩; **~brüllen** *tr. V.* (ugs.) jmdn. **~brüllen** shout sb. down; **~deutsch** *Adj.* Low German ⟨*dialect*⟩; **~gang** *der* fall; decline; **~gehen** *unr. itr. V.; mit sein* **(a)** (landen) ⟨*plane, spacecraft, balloonist*⟩ come down; ⟨*parachutist*⟩ drop; ⟨*birds*⟩ land; **(b)** (fallen) ⟨*rain, satellite, avalanche*⟩ come down; **(c)** (Boxen: zu Boden fallen) go down; **~geschlagen** *Adj.* despondent; dejected; **~geschlagenheit** *die:* **~:** despondency; dejection; **~halten** *unr. tr. V.* oppress ⟨*nation, people, class*⟩; keep ⟨*nation, people, class*⟩ in subjection; keep ⟨*person*⟩ down; **~knien** *itr. V.* (auch mit sein), *refl. V.* kneel down; (unterwürfig, demütig) go down on one's knees; **~lage** *die* defeat; jmdm. **eine ~lage beibringen** inflict a defeat on sb.
Nieder·lande *Pl.:* **die ~:** the Netherlands
Niederländer *der;* **~s, ~:** ▶ 388 Dutchman; Netherlander
Niederländerin *die;* **~, ~nen** Dutchwoman; Netherlander; *s. auch* **-in**
niederländisch *Adj.* ▶ 388, ▶ 487 Dutch; Netherlands *attrib.* ⟨*government, embassy, etc.*⟩
nieder-, Nieder-: ~lassen *unr. refl. V.* **(a)** (ein Geschäft, eine Praxis eröffnen) set up *or* establish oneself in business; ⟨*doctor, lawyer*⟩ set up a practice *or* in practice; **(b)** (seinen Wohnsitz nehmen) settle; **(c)** (geh.: sich setzen) sit down; seat oneself; ⟨*bird*⟩ settle, alight; **~lassung** *die:* **~, ~en (a)** o. Pl. ⇒ **~lassen a:** setting up in business; setting up of a practice *or* in practice; **(b)** (Ort) settlement; **(c)** (Wirtsch.: Zweigstelle) branch; **~legen** *tr. V.* **(a)** (geh.: hinlegen) lay *or* put *or* set down; lay ⟨*wreath*⟩; lay down ⟨*one's arms*⟩; **(b)** (nicht weitermachen) lay down, resign [from] ⟨*office*⟩; relinquish ⟨*command*⟩; **(c)** (geh.: aufschreiben) set down; **~legung** *die:* **~, ~en (a)** (geh.: eines Kranzes) laying; **(b)** (eines Amtes) resignation (*Gen.* from); (eines Kommandos) relinquishing; **(c)** (geh.: Niederschrift) setting down; **~machen** (ugs.), **~metzeln** *tr. V.* butcher; **~prasseln** *itr. V.; mit sein* ⟨*rain, hail*⟩ beat down; ⟨*blows, rebukes, questions, etc.*⟩ rain down; **~reißen** *unr. tr. V.* **(a)** (abreißen) pull down ⟨*building, wall*⟩; **(b)** (zu Boden reißen) jmdn. **~reißen** knock sb. over
Nieder·sachse *der;* **~n, ~n** inhabitant of Lower Saxony; (von Geburt) native of Lower Saxony; *s. auch* **Kölner 2**
Nieder·sachsen *(das)* **~s** Lower Saxony
niedersächsisch *Adj.* Lower Saxon
nieder-, Nieder-: ~schießen *unr. tr. V.* gun down; **~schlag** *der* **(a)** (Met.) precipitation; **(b)** (Boxen)

knock-down; **(c)** (Ausdruck) **[seinen]** ∼**schlag in etw.** (*Dat.*) **finden** find expression in sth.; ∼|**schlagen 1** *unr. tr. V.* **(a)** (zu Boden schlagen) **jmdn.** ∼**schlagen** knock sb. down; **(b)** (umschlagen) turn down ‹*hat-brim, collar*›; **(c)** (beenden) suppress, put down ‹*revolt, uprising, etc.*›; put an end to ‹*strike*›; **(d)** (senken) lower ‹*eyes, eyelids*›, *s. auch* **niedergeschlagen; 2** *unr. refl. V.* **sich in etw.** (*Dat.*) ∼**schlagen** ‹*experience, emotion*› find expression in sth.; ‹*performance, hard work*› be reflected in sth.; ∼**schlags·frei** *Adj.* ‹*period*› without [any] precipitation *not pred.;* ∼**schlagung** *die* suppression; putting down; ∼|**strecken** (geh.) **1** *tr. V.* **jmdn.** ∼**strecken** knock sb. down; (mit einem Schuss) shoot sb. down; **einen Tiger/Hirsch** ∼**strecken** bring down a tiger/stag; **2** *refl. V.* (sich hinlegen) lie down; **auf das** *od.* **dem Sofa** ∼**ge·streckt** stretched out on the sofa; ∼**tracht** *die;* ∼ (geh.) malice; (als Charaktereigenschaft) vileness; despicableness; ∼**trächtig 1** *Adj.* malicious ‹*person, slander, lie, etc.*›; (verachtenswert) vile, despicable ‹*person*›; base, vile ‹*misrepresentation, slander, lie*›; **2** *adv.* ‹*betray, lie, treat*› in a vile *or* despicable way; ‹*smile*› maliciously; ∼**träch·tigkeit** *die;* ∼, ∼**en** (a) *o. Pl.* ⇒ ∼**trächtig 1:** maliciousness; vileness; despicableness; baseness; **(b)** (gemeine Handlung) vile *or* despicable act, ∼|**treten** *unr. tr. V.* tread ‹*grass, flowers, carpet-pile, etc.*›; (fig.) trample ‹*person*› underfoot

Niederung *die;* ∼, ∼**en** low-lying area; (an Flussläufen, Küsten) flats *pl.;* (Tal) valley

nieder|werfen *unr. tr. V.* **(a)** (geh.: besiegen) overcome, defeat ‹*enemy, rebels, etc.*›; **(b)** (geh.: beenden) ⇒ **niederschlagen 1 c; (c)** (geh.: schwächen) ‹*illness, fever*› lay ‹*person*› low

niedlich /'niːtlɪç/ **1** *Adj.* sweet; cute (Amer. coll.); sweet little *attrib.;* dear little *attrib.* **2** *adv.* ‹*dance, nibble*› sweetly, prettily; ‹*babble, play*› sweetly, cutely (Amer. coll.)

niedrig 1 *Adj.* **(a)** ▸ **277** low; short ‹*grass*›; **(b)** (von geringem Rang) lowly ‹*origins, birth*›; low ‹*rank, status, intellectual level*›; **(c)** (sittlich tief stehend) base ‹*instinct, desire, emotion, person*›; vile ‹*motive*›. **2** *adv.* ‹*hang, fly*› low

niemals /'niːmaːls/ *Adv.* never

niemand /'niːmant/ *Indefinitpron.* nobody; no one; ∼ **war im Büro** there was nobody *or* no one in the office; there wasn't anybody *or* any one in the office; ∼ **anders** *od.* **anderer** nobody *or* no one else; **es kann** ∼ **anders** *od.* **anderer als du gewesen sein** it can't have been anybody *or* any one [else] but you; **das darfst du** ∼[**em**] **sagen!** you mustn't tell anybody that!; **lass** ∼ **Fremdes herein** don't let anybody *or* anyone in you don't know; don't let any strangers in

Niemands·land *das; o. Pl.* (auch fig.) no man's land

Niere /'niːrə/ *die;* ∼, ∼**n** ▸ **326** kidney; **jmdm. an die** ∼**n gehen** (fig. ugs.) get to sb. (coll.)

nieren, Nieren-: ∼**förmig** *Adj.* kidney-shaped; ∼**leiden** *das* ▸ **329** kidney disease; ∼**stein** *der* kidney stone; renal calculus (Med.)

nieseln /'niːzl̩n/ *unpers. V.* drizzle

Niesel·regen *der* drizzle

niesen /'niːzn̩/ *itr. V.* sneeze

Nies·pulver *das* sneezing-powder

Niete¹ /'niːtə/ *die;* ∼, ∼**n** (a) (Los) blank; **(b)** (ugs.: Mensch) dead loss (coll.) **(in** + *Dat.* at)

Niete² *die;* ∼, ∼**n** rivet

nieten /'niːtn̩/ *tr. V.* rivet

Nieten·hose *die* [pair of] studded jeans

niet- und nagelfest *in* [**alles**] **was nicht** ∼ ∼ ∼ **ist** (ugs.) [everything] that's not nailed *or* screwed down

Nihilismus /nihiˈlɪsmʊs/ *der;* ∼: nihilism

Nihilist *der;* ∼**en**, ∼**en** nihilist

nihilistisch *Adj.* nihilistic

Nikolaus /'nɪkolaʊs/ *der;* ∼, ∼**e** St Nicholas

Nikolaus·tag *der* St Nicholas' Day

Nikotin /niko'tiːn/ *das;* ∼**s** nicotine

nikotin-, Nikotin-: ∼**arm** *Adj.* low-nicotine *attrib.;* low in nicotine *pred.;* ∼**gehalt** *der* nicotine content; ∼**vergiftung** *die* nicotine poisoning

Nil /niːl/ *der;* ∼[**s**] Nile

Nil·pferd *das* hippopotamus; hippo (coll.)

nimmer-, Nimmer-: ∼**mehr** *Adv.* **(a)** (veralt.: nie) never; **(b)** (südd., österr.: nie wieder) never again; ∼**satt** *Adj.; nicht präd.* (fam.) insatiable, ∼**wieder·sehen** *in* **auf** ∼**wiedersehen verschwinden** (ugs., oft scherzh.) vanish never to be seen again

Nippel /'nɪpl̩/ *der;* ∼**s**, ∼ **(a)** (Technik; ugs.: Brustwarze) nipple; **(b)** (am Wasserball) valve

nippen /'nɪpn̩/ *itr. V.* (trinken) sip; take a sip/sips; (essen) nibble **(von** at); **am Glas** ∼: sip from *or* take a sip/sips from the glass

Nippes /'nɪpəs/, **Nipp·sachen** *Pl.* [porcelain] knickknacks; small [porcelain] ornaments

nirgends /'nɪrɡn̩ts/, **nirgendwo** *Adv.* nowhere; **er war** ∼ **zu finden** he was nowhere *or* wasn't anywhere to be found

nirgend-: ∼**woher** *Adv.* from nowhere; **sie konnten die Medikamente** ∼**woher bekommen** they couldn't get the medicines from anywhere; ∼**wohin** *Adv.* **wir gehen** ∼**wohin** we're not going anywhere

Nische /'niːʃə/ *die;* ∼, ∼**n (a)** (Einbuchtung) niche; **(b)** (Erweiterung eines Raumes) recess

nisten /'nɪstn̩/ *itr. V.* nest

Nist·kasten *der* nest-box; nesting-box

Nitrat /ni'traːt/ *das;* ∼[**e**]**s**, ∼**e** (Chemie) nitrate

Nitro·glyzerin /nitro-/ *das; o. Pl.* nitro-glycerine

Niveau /ni'voː/ *das;* ∼**s**, ∼**s** (a) level; **eine Zeitung mit** ∼: a quality newspaper; **er hat wenig** ∼: he is not very cultured *or* knowledgeable; **(b)** (Qualitäts∼) standard

niveau·voll *Adj.* cultured and intelligent ‹*person*›; ‹*entertainment, programme*› of quality *postpos., not pred.*

nix /nɪks/ *Indefinitpron.* (ugs.) ⇒ **nichts**

Nixe *die;* ∼, ∼**n** (germ. Myth.) nixie; (mit Fischschwanz) mermaid

NO *Abk.* **Nordost[en]** NE

nobel /'noːbl̩/ **1** *Adj.* **(a)** (geh.: edel) noble; noble[-minded] ‹*person*›; **(b)** ‹*oft spött.: luxuriös*› elegant, (coll.) posh ‹*boutique, house, hotel*›; fine ‹*cigar*›; **(c)** (ugs.: freigebig) lavish, generous ‹*tip, present*›; generous ‹*person*›. **2** *adv.* **(a)** (geh.: edel) nobly; **(b)** (oft spött.: luxuriös) ‹*dress, live, eat*› in the grand style

Nobel-: ∼**herberge die** (salopp) posh *or* swish hotel; ∼**kutsche** *die* (salopp) posh *or* swish car (coll.)

Nobel- /'noːbɛl-/: ∼**preis** *der* Nobel prize; ∼**preis·träger** *der* Nobel prizewinner

noch /nɔx/ **1** *Adv.* **(a)** ([wie] bisher, derzeit) still; ∼ **nicht** not yet; **sie sind immer** ∼ **nicht da** they're still not here; **ich sehe ihn kaum** ∼: I hardly ever see him any more; ∼ **nach Jahren** even years later; **(b)** (als Rest einer Menge) **ich habe [nur]** ∼ **zehn Mark** I've [only] ten marks left; **es dauert** ∼ **fünf Minuten** it'll be another five minutes; **es fehlt [mir/dir** *usw.*] ∼ **eine Mark** I/you *etc.* need another mark; **(c)** (bevor etw. anderes geschieht) just; **ich mache das [jetzt/dann]** ∼ **fertig** I'll just get this finished; **(d)** (irgendwann einmal) some time; one day; **du wirst ihn [schon]** ∼ **kennen lernen** you'll get to know him yet; **er wird** ∼ **kommen** he will still come; **(e)** (womöglich) if you're/he's *etc.* not careful; **du kommst** ∼ **zu spät!** you'll be late if you're not careful; **(f)** (drückt eine geringe zeitliche Distanz aus) only; **sie war eben** *od.* **gerade** ∼ **hier** she was here only a moment ago; **es ist** ∼ **keine Woche her, dass …:** it was less than a week ago that …; **(g)** (nicht später als) ∼ **am selben Abend** the [very] same evening; **(h)** (drückt aus, dass etw. unwiederholbar ist) **ich habe** ∼ **Großvater** ∼ **gekannt** I'm old enough to have known grandfather; **(i)** (drückt aus, dass sich etw. im Rahmen hält) **Er hat** ∼ **Glück gehabt. Es hätte weit schlimmer kommen können** He was lucky. It could have been much worse; **das geht** ∼: that's [still] all right *or* (coll.) OK; **das ist** ∼ **lange kein Grund** that still isn't any sort of reason; **das ist ja** ∼ [**ein**]**mal gut gegangen** (ugs.) it was just about all right; **(j)** (außerdem, zusätzlich) **wer war** ∼ **da?** who else was there?; **er hat [auch/außerdem]** ∼ **ein Fahrrad** he has a bicycle as well; ∼ **etwas Kaffee?** [would you like] some more coffee?; ∼ **ein/zwei Bier,**

bitte! another beer/two more beers, please!; **ich habe das ~ einmal/~ einige Male gemacht** I did it again/several times more; **er ist frech und ~ dazu dumm** *od.* **dumm dazu** he's cheeky and stupid with it; **Geld/ Kleider** *usw.* **~ und ~:** heaps and heaps of money/ clothes *etc.* (coll.); **(k)** (bei Vergleichen) **er ist ~ größer [als Karl]** he is even taller [than Karl]; **er will ~ mehr haben** he wants even *or* still more; **das ist ~ besser** that's even better *or* better still; **und wenn er auch ~ so bittet** however much he pleads; **(l)** (nach etw. Vergessenem fragend) **wie heißt/hieß sie [doch] ~?** [now] what's/what was her name again? **2** *Partikel* **das ist ~ Qualität!** that's what I call quality; **du wirst es ~ bereuen!** you'll regret it!; **der wird sich ~ wundern** (ugs.) he's in for a surprise; **er kann ~ nicht einmal lesen** he can't even read. **3** *Konj.* (und auch nicht) nor; **weder ... noch** neither ... nor

nochmalig /'nɔxmaːlɪç/ *Adj.; nicht präd.* further

noch·mals *Adv.* again

NOK /ɛn|oː'kaː/ *das;* ~[s] *Abk.* **Nationales Olympisches Komitee** NOC

Nomade /no'maːdə/ *der;* ~n, ~n, **Nomadin** *die;* ~, ~nen nomad

Nomen /'noːmən/ *das;* ~s, **Nomina** noun; substantive

Nominativ /'noːminatiːf/ *der;* ~s, ~e (Sprachw.) nominative [case]

nominell /nomi'nɛl/ *Adj.; nicht präd.* nominal ⟨member, leader⟩; ⟨Christian⟩ in name only

nominieren /nomi'niːrən/ *tr. V.* **(a)** nominate; **(b)** (Sport: aufstellen) name ⟨player, team⟩

Nonkonformismus /nɔnkɔnfɔr'mɪsmʊs/ *der;* ~: nonconformism

nonkonformistisch 1 *Adj.* nonconformist; unconventional ⟨dress⟩. **2** *adv.* ⟨think, behave, etc.⟩ in an unconventional way

Nonne /'nɔnə/ *die;* ~, ~n nun

Nonnen·kloster *das* convent; nunnery

Nonsens /'nɔnzɛns/ *der;* ~[es] nonsense

nonstop /nɔn'stɔp/ *adv.* non-stop

Non-Stop-: ~**Flug** *der* non-stop flight; ~**Kino** *das* 24-hour cinema

Noppe /'nɔpə/ *die;* ~, ~n **(a)** (in einem Faden, Gewebe) knop; nub; **(b)** (auf einer Oberfläche) bump; (auf einem Tischtennisschläger) pimple

Nord /nɔrt/ *o. Art.; o. Pl.* ▶ 266⌋ **(a)** (bes. Seemannsspr., Met.: Richtung) north; **nach ~:** northwards; **(b)** (Gebiet) North; **(c)** (Politik) North; **(d)** *einem Subst. nachgestellt* (nördlicher Teil, nördliche Lage) North; **Autobahnkreuz Köln ~:** motorway intersection Cologne North

nord-, Nord-: ~**amerika** *(das)* North America; ~**amerikaner** *der* North American; ~**deutsch 1** *Adj.* North German; **2** *adv.* **etw. ~deutsch aussprechen** pronounce sth. with a North German accent; ~**deutschland** *(das)* North Germany

Norden *der;* ~s ▶ 266⌋ **(a)** (Richtung) north; **nach ~:** northwards; to the north; **im/aus dem** *od.* **von** *od.* **vom ~:** in/from the north; **die Grenze nach ~:** the northern border; **(b)** (Gegend) Northern part; **(c)** (Geogr., Politik) North; **der hohe/höchste ~:** the far North

Nord-: ~**england** *(das)* the North of England; ~**europa** *(das)* Northern Europe; ~**irland** *(das)* Northern Ireland

nordisch *Adj.* (auch Völkerk.) Nordic; ~**e Kombination** (Skisport) Nordic combined

Nord-: ~**kap** *das* North Cape; ~**korea** *(das)* North Korea; ~**küste** *die* north *or* northern coast

nördlich /'nœrtlɪç/ ▶ 266⌋ **1** *Adj.* **(a)** (im Norden) northern; **15 Grad ~er Breite** 15 degrees north [latitude]; **(b)** (nach, aus dem Norden) northerly; **(c)** (des Nordens) Northern. **2** *adv.* northwards; ~ **von ...:** [to the] north of ...; **sehr [weit] ~ sein** be a long way north. **3** *Präp. mit Gen.* [to the] north of

nord-, Nord-: ~**licht** /'--/ *das* northern lights *pl.;* aurora borealis; ~**osten** *der* ▶ 266⌋ (Richtung, Gegend) north-east; *s. auch* **Norden**; ~**östlich** ▶ 266⌋ **1** *Adj.* **(a)** (im ~osten gelegen) north-eastern; **(b)** (nach ~osten gerichtet, aus ~osten kommend) north-easterly; **2** *adv.* north-eastwards; ~**östlich von ...:** [to the] north-east of ...; *s. auch* **nördlich 2**; **3** *Präp. mit Gen.* [to the] north-east of; ~**pol** /'--/ *der* North Pole

Nordrhein-Westfale *der;* ~n, ~n North Rhine-Westphalian

Nord·rhein-Westfalen *(das)* North Rhine-Westphalia

nordrhein-westfälisch *Adj.* North Rhine-Westphalian

Nord·see *die;* ~ North Sea

nord-, Nord-: ~**seite** /'---/ *die* northern side; ~**südlich** *Adj.* ▶ 266⌋ **in ~südlicher Richtung** from north to south; ~**wärts** /'--/ *Adv.* ▶ 266⌋ (nach Norden) northwards; ~**westen** *der* ▶ 266⌋ (Richtung, Gegend) north-west; *s. auch* **Norden** a; ~**westlich** ▶ 266⌋ **1** *Adj.* **(a)** (im ~westen gelegen) north-western; **(b)** (nach ~westen gerichtet, aus ~westen kommend) north-westerly; **2** *adv.* (nach ~westen) north-westwards; ~**westlich von ...:** [to the] north-west of ...; *s. auch* **nördlich 2**; **3** *Präp. mit Gen.* [to the] north-west of; ~**wind** /'--/ *der* north *or* northerly wind

Nörgelei *die;* ~, ~en (abwertend) **(a)** *o. Pl.* (das Nörgeln) moaning; grumbling; (das Kritteln) carping; **(b)** (Äußerung) moan; grumble

nörgeln /'nœrgln/ *itr. V.* (abwertend) moan, grumble (**an** + *Dat.* about); (kritteln) carp (**an** + *Dat.* about)

Nörgler *der;* ~s, ~ (abwertend) moaner; grumbler; (Krittler) carper; fault-finder

Norm /nɔrm/ *die;* ~, ~en **(a)** norm; **als ~ gelten** count as the norm; **(b)** (geforderte Arbeitsleistung) quota; target; **die ~ erfüllen** fulfil one's/its quota; meet *or* achieve one's/its target; **(c)** (Sport) qualifying standard; **(d)** (technische, industrielle ~) standard; standard specifications *pl.*

normal /nɔr'maːl/ **1** *Adj.* **(a)** normal; **du bist doch nicht ~!** (ugs.) there must be something wrong with you!; **(b)** (ugs.: gewöhnlich) ordinary. **2** *adv.* **(a)** normally; **(b)** (ugs.: gewöhnlich) in the normal *or* ordinary way

Normal·benzin *das* ≈ two-star petrol (Brit.); regular (Amer.)

normalerweise *Adv.* normally; usually

Normal-: ~**fall** *der* normal case; **im ~fall** normally, usually; ~**gewicht** *das* normal weight

normalisieren 1 *tr. V.* normalize. **2** *refl. V.* return to normal

Normalität /nɔrmali'tɛːt/ *die;* ~: normality *no def. art.*

Normal-: ~**maß** *das* **(a)** (normales Maß) normal size; **(b)** (Messwesen) standard measure; ~**verbraucher** *der* **(a)** average consumer; **(b)** (ugs.: Durchschnittsmensch) **Otto ~verbraucher** (scherzh.) the average punter (coll.); ~**zustand** *der* normal state

Normandie /nɔrman'diː/ *die;* ~: Normandy

normativ /nɔrma'tiːf/ *Adj.* normative

normen, normieren *tr. V.* standardize

Normung *die;* ~, ~en standardization

Norwegen /'nɔrveːgn/ *(das);* ~s Norway

Norweger *der;* ~s, ~, **Norwegerin** *die;* ~, ~nen ▶ 388⌋ Norwegian

norwegisch *Adj.* ▶ 388⌋, ▶ 487⌋ Norwegian

Nostalgie /nɔstal'giː/ *die;* ~: nostalgia

*not → **Not e**

Not *die;* ~, **Nöte** /'nøːtə/ **(a)** (Bedrohung, Gefahr) **Rettung in** *od.* **aus höchster ~:** rescue from extreme difficulties; **in ~ sein** be in desperate straits; **(b)** *o. Pl.* (Mangel, Armut) need; poverty [and hardship]; ~ **leiden** suffer poverty *or* want [and hardship]; **in ~ geraten** encounter hard times; ~ **macht erfinderisch** necessity is the mother of invention (prov.); **in der ~ frisst der Teufel Fliegen** beggars can't be choosers (prov.); **(c)** *o. Pl.* (Verzweiflung) anguish; distress; **(d)** (Sorge, Mühe) trouble; **in Nöten sein** have many troubles; **seine [liebe] ~ mit jmdm./etw. haben** have a lot of trouble *or* a lot of problems with sb./sth.; **mit**

knapper ～: by the skin of one's teeth; **(e)** *o. Pl.* (veralt.: Notwendigkeit) necessity; **zur** ～: if need be; if necessary; **wenn** ～ **am Mann ist** when the need arises; **aus der** ～ **eine Tugend machen** make a virtue of necessity; ～ **tun** *or* **sein** (geh., landsch.) be necessary

Notar /no'taːɐ̯/ *der;* ～s, ～e notary

Notariat /notar'jaːt/ *das;* ～[e]s, ～e **(a)** (Amt) notaryship; **(b)** (Kanzlei) notary's office

notariell /nota'riɛl/ **1** *Adj.* notarial. **2** *adv.* ～ **beglaubigt** attested by a notary

Not-: ～**arzt** *der* doctor on [emergency] call; emergency doctor; ～**arzt·wagen** *der* doctor's car for emergency calls; ～**ausgang** *der* emergency exit; ～**behelf** *der* makeshift; ～**bremse** *die* emergency brake; ～**dienst** *der* ⇒ **Bereitschaftsdienst**

Notdurft /-dʊrft/ *die;* ～ (geh.) **seine [große/kleine]** ～ **verrichten** relieve oneself

not·dürftig **1** *Adj.* meagre ⟨*payment, pension*⟩; rough and ready, makeshift ⟨*shelter, repair*⟩; scanty ⟨*cover, clothing*⟩. **2** *adv.* scantily ⟨*clothed*⟩; **etw.** ～ **reparieren** repair sth. in a rough and ready *or* makeshift way

Note /'noːtə/ *die;* ～, ～n **(a)** (Zeichen) note; **eine ganze/ halbe** ～: a crotchet/quaver (Brit.); **a whole note/half note** (Amer.); **(b)** *Pl.* (Text) music *sing.;* **nach/ohne** ～**n spielen** play from/without music; **(c)** (Schul～) mark; **(d)** (Eislauf, Turnen) score; **(e)** (Dipl.) note; **(f)** *o. Pl.* (Flair) touch

Notebook /'noʊtbʊk/ *das;* ～s, ～s (DV) notebook [computer]

Noten-: ～**blatt** *das* sheet of music; ～**heft** *das* **(a)** (Publikation) book of music; **(b)** (Heft mit ～papier) manuscript book; ～**papier** *das* music-paper; ～**schlüssel** *der* clef; ～**schrift** *die* [musical] notation; ～**ständer** *der* music stand

not-, Not-: ～**fall** *der* **(a)** (Gefahr) emergency; **für den** ～**fall** in case of emergency; **(b)** (Schwierigkeiten) case of need; **im** ～**fall** if need be; ～**falls** *Adv.* if need be; if necessary; ～**gedrungen** *Adv.* of necessity; **ich habe** ～**gedrungen eine neue gekauft** I had no choice but to *or* I was forced to buy a new one; ～**groschen** *der* nest egg

notieren /no'tiːrən/ **1** *tr. V.* **(a)** [sich (*Dat.*)] **etw.** ～: note sth. down; make a note of sth.; **(b)** (Börsenw., Wirtsch.) quote (**mit** at). **2** *itr. V.* (Börsenw., Wirtsch.) be quoted (**mit** at); **die meisten Rohstoffe** ～ **unverändert** most commodity prices are unchanged

nötig /'nøːtɪç/ **1** *Adj.* necessary; **dafür** *od.* **dazu fehlt mir die** ～**e Geduld/das** ～**e Geld** I don't have the patience/money necessary *or* needed for that; **etw./jmdn.** ～ **haben** need sth./sb.; **etw. zu tun** ～ **haben** need to do sth.; **sich zu entschuldigen, hat er natürlich nicht** ～ (iron.) of course he does not feel the need to apologize; **du hast/er hat** *usw.* **es gerade** ～ (ugs.) you're/he's a fine one to talk (coll.); **das wäre [doch] nicht** ～ **gewesen!** (ugs.) you shouldn't have!; **das Nötigste** the bare essentials *pl.* **2** *adv.* **er braucht** ～ **Hilfe** he is in urgent need of *or* urgently needs help; **was er am** ～**sten braucht, ist …:** what he most urgently needs is …

nötigen *tr. V.* **(a)** (zwingen) compel; force; (Rechtsspr.) intimidate; coerce; **jmdn. zur Unterschrift** ～: compel *or* force sb. to sign; **sich genötigt sehen, etw. zu tun** feel compelled to do sth.; **(b)** (geh.: auffordern) press; urge

Nötigung *die;* ～, ～**en** (bes. Rechtsspr.) intimidation; coercion

Notiz /no'tiːts/ *die;* ～, ～**en** **(a)** note; **sich** (*Dat.*) **eine** ～ **machen** make a note; **(b)** (Zeitungs～) **eine [kurze]** ～: a brief report; **(c)** *in* **von jmdm./etw. [keine]** ～ **nehmen** take [no] notice of sb./sth.

Notiz-: ～**block** *der; Pl.* ～**blocks, schweiz.:** ～**blöcke** notepad; ～**buch** *das* notebook; ～**zettel** *der* note

not-, Not-: ～**lage** *die* serious difficulties *pl.;* ～**landen; ich notlande, notgelandet, notzulanden** *itr. V.; mit sein* do an emergency landing; ～**landung** *die* emergency landing; ～**leidend** *Adj.* needy; impoverished; (fig.) ailing ⟨*industry*⟩; **die Notleidenden** the [poor and] needy; ～**lösung** *die* stopgap; ～**lüge** *die* evasive lie; (aus Rücksichtnahme) white lie

notorisch /no'toːrɪʃ/ **1** *Adj.* notorious. **2** *adv.* notoriously

not-, Not-: ～**ruf** *der* **(a)** (Hilferuf) emergency call; (eines Schiffes) Mayday call; distress call; **(b)** (Nummer) emergency number; ～**ruf·säule** *die* emergency telephone (mounted in a pillar); ～**schlachten; ich notschlachte, notgeschlachtet, notzuschlachten** *tr., itr. V.* slaughter ⟨*sick or injured animal*⟩; ～**sitz** *der* extra seat; (ausklappbar) tip-up seat; fold-away seat; ～**stand** *der* **(a)** (Krise, Übelstand) crisis; **(b)** (Staatsrecht) state of emergency; ～**stands·gebiet** *das* **(a)** (auch fig.) disaster area; **(b)** (Wirtsch.) depressed area; ～**stands·gesetz** *das* emergency law; ～**unterkunft** *die* emergency accommodation *no pl., no indef. art.;* ～**unterkünfte** emergency accommodation *sing.;* ～**vorrat** *der* emergency supply; ～**wehr** *die* (Rechtsw.) self-defence; **in** *od.* **aus** ～**wehr in** self-defence

not·wendig **1** *Adj.* necessary; (unvermeidlich) inevitable; **es ist** ～, **dass wir etwas tun** we must do something; **das Notwendigste** the bare essentials *pl.* **2** *adv.* **(a)** ⇒ **nötig 2; (b)** (zwangsläufig, unbedingt) necessarily

notwendiger·weise *Adv.* necessarily

Notwendigkeit *die;* ～, ～**en** necessity

Not-: ～**zeit** *die* time of emergency; (Zeit des Mangels) time of need; ～**zucht** *die* (Rechtsw. veralt.) rape

Nougat /'nuːgat/ *der; auch das;* ～s nougat

Novelle /no'vɛlə/ *die;* ～, ～n **(a)** (Literaturw.) novella; **(b)** (Gesetzes～) amendment

novellieren *tr. V.* (Politik, Rechtsw.) amend

November /no'vɛmbɐ/ *der;* ～[s], ～: ▶ 119 November; *s. auch* **April**

Novität /novi'tɛːt/ *die;* ～, ～**en** novelty; (neue Erfindung) innovation; (neue Schallplatte) new release; (neues Buch) new publication

Novize /no'viːtsə/ *der;* ～n, ～n, **Novizin** *die;* ～, ～**nen** novice

Nr. *Abk.* **Nummer** No

N. T. *Abk.* **Neues Testament** NT

Nu *der in* **im Nu, in einem Nu** in no time

Nuance /'nʏãːsə/ *die;* ～, ～n **(a)** (Unterschied, Feinheit) nuance; **(b)** (Grad) shade; **eine** ～ **dunkler/schneller** a shade darker/faster

nüchtern /'nʏçtɐn/ **1** *Adj.* **(a)** (nicht betrunken) sober; **wieder** ～ **werden** sober up; **(b)** (mit leerem Magen) **der Patient muss** ～ **sein** the patient's stomach must be empty; **auf** ～**en Magen rauchen** smoke on an empty stomach; **(c)** (realistisch) sober; sober, matter-of-fact ⟨*account, assessment, question, etc.*⟩; bare ⟨*figures*⟩; **(d)** (schmucklos, streng) austere; bare ⟨*room*⟩; unadorned, bare ⟨*walls*⟩; (ungeschminkt) bare, plain ⟨*fact*⟩. **2** *adv.* **(a)** (realistisch) soberly; **(b)** (schmucklos, streng) austerely

nuckeln *itr. V.* (ugs.) suck (**an** + *Dat.* at); **am Daumen/ Schnuller** ～: suck one's thumb/a *or* one's dummy

Nudel /'nuːdl̩/ *die;* ～, ～n **(a)** piece of spaghetti/vermicelli/tortellini *etc.;* (als Suppeneinlage) noodle; ～n (Teigwaren) pasta *sing.;* (als Suppeneinlage, Reisnudel) noodles; **(b)** (ugs.) **eine komische** ～: a real character

Nudel-: ～**salat** *der* pasta salad; ～**suppe** *die* soup with noodles

Nudist /nu'dɪst/ *der;* ～**en**, ～**en** nudist; naturist

Nugat ⇒ **Nougat**

nuklear /nukle'aːɐ̯/ **1** *Adj.* nuclear. **2** *adv.* ～ **angetrieben** nuclear-powered

Nuklear·krieg *der* nuclear war

null /nʊl/ ▶ 511 , ▶ 600 **1** *Kardinalz.* nought; ～ **Komma sechs** [nought] point six; **sieben,** ～, ～, **sechs,** ～, **vier** (Fernspr.) seven double-O, six O four (Brit.); seven zero zero, six zero four (Amer.); ～ **Grad Celsius** nought *or* zero degrees Celsius; **bei** ～ **Fehlern** if there are no mistakes; **fünf zu** ～: five–nil; **das Spiel endete** ～ **zu** ～: the game was a goalless draw; **fünfzehn** ～ (Tennis) fifteen-love; **gegen** ～ **Uhr** around twelve midnight; **es ist** ～ **Uhr dreißig** it is twelve-thirty a.m.; **auf** ～ **stehen** ⟨*indicator, needle, etc.*⟩ be at zero; **fünf Grad unter/über** ～: five degrees below/above *or* freezing; **etw. für** ～ **und**

nichtig erklären declare sth. null and void; **gleich ~ sein** (fig.) be practically zero; **in ~ Komma nichts** (ugs.) in less than no time. **2** *indekl. Adj.* (ugs.) **~ Ahnung** no idea at all

Null *die;* **~, ~en (a)** (Ziffer) nought; zero; *s. auch* **null 1;** (abwertend) (Versager) failure; dead loss (coll.); (unbedeutender Mensch) nonentity

null·acht·fünfzehn, null·acht·fuffzehn (ugs. abwertend) **1** *indekl. Adj.; nicht attr.* run-of-the-mill. **2** *adv.* ⟨dressed, furnished⟩ in a run-of-the-mill way

Null-: **~punkt** *der* zero; **die Temperatur ist auf den ~punkt abgesunken** the temperature has dropped to zero or to freezing point; **~tarif** *der:* **zum ~tarif** free of charge

*numerieren ⇒ **nummerieren**

numerisch /nu'me:rɪʃ/ **1** *Adj.* numerical. **2** *adv.* numerically

Numerus /'nʊmərʊs/ *der;* **~, Numeri** (Sprachw.) number

Numerus clausus /~ 'klauzʊs/ *der;* **~ ~:** *fixed number of students admissible to a university to study a particular subject;* numerus clausus

Nummer /'nʊmɐ/ *die;* **~, ~n (a)** number; **ein Wagen mit Münchner ~:** a car with a Munich registration; **ich bin unter der ~ 24 26 79 zu erreichen** I can be reached on 24 26 79; **bloß eine ~ sein** (fig.) be just a or nothing but a number; **[die] ~ eins** [the] number one; **auf ~ sicher** od. **Sicher gehen** (ugs.) play safe; not take any chances; **(b)** (Ausgabe) number; issue; **(c)** (Größe) size; **(d)** (Darbietung) turn; **(e)** (ugs.: Musikstück) number; **(f)** (ugs.: Person) character

nummerieren /nʊmə'ri:rən/ *tr. V.* number

Nummern·schild *das* number plate; license plate (Amer.)

nun /nu:n/ **1** *Adv.* now; **von ~ an** from now on; **~, wo sie krank ist** now [that] she's ill; **~ erst** only now. **2** *Partikel* now; **so wichtig ist es ~ auch wieder nicht** it's not all 'that important; **das hast du ~ davon!** it serves you right!; **~ gib schon her!** now hand it over!; **kommst du ~ mit oder nicht?** now are you coming or not?; **so ist das ~ [einmal/mal]** that's just the way it is or things are; **~ gut** od. **schön** [well,] all right; **~, ~!** now, come on; **ja ~!** oh, well!; **~? ** well?; **~ ja ...:** well, yes ...; **~ denn!** (also gut) well, all right!; (also los) well then

nun·mehr *Adv.* (geh.) **(a)** now; **(b)** (von ~ an) from now on; henceforth

nur /nu:ɐ̯/ **1** *Adv.* **(a)** (nicht mehr als) only; just; **ich habe ~ eine Stunde Zeit** I only have an hour; **er hat ~ einen einzigen Fehler gemacht** he made just a single mistake; **das ist ~ recht und billig** it is only right and proper; **(b)** (ausschließlich) only; **alle durften mitfahren, ~ ich nicht** everyone was allowed to go, all except me; **er tut das mit Absicht, ~ um dich zu provozieren** he does it deliberately, just to provoke you; **nicht ~ ..., sondern auch ...:** not only ..., but also ...; **nicht ~, dass ...:** it's not just that ...; **ich male ~ so zum Spaß** I paint just for fun; **Warum fragst du? — Ach, ~ so** Why do you ask? — Oh, no particular reason; **~ dass ...:** except that ...; **das ist ~ zu wahr!** it's only too true! **2** *Partikel* **(a)** (in Wünschen) **wenn das ~ gut geht!** let's [just] hope it goes well; **wenn er ~ käme/hier wäre** if only he would come/he were here; **(b)** (ermunternd, tadelnd) **~ keine Hemmungen!** don't be inhibited!; **~ zu!** go ahead; **(c)** (warnend) **lass dich ~ nicht erwischen** just don't let me/him/her/them catch you; **~ Geduld/vorsichtig/langsam** just be patient/careful/take it easy; **~ nicht!** don't, for goodness' sake!; **(d)** (fragend) just; **wie soll ich ihm das ~ erklären?** just how am I supposed to explain it to him?; **was sollen wir ~ tun?** what on earth are we going to do?; **was hat er ~?** whatever's the matter with him?; **(e)** (verallgemeinernd) just; **er lief, so schnell er ~ konnte** he ran just as fast as he could; **(f)** (sogar) only; just; **(g)** es **wimmelte ~ so von Insekten** it was just teeming with insects; **er schlug auf den Tisch, dass es ~ so krachte** he crashed his fist [down] on the table. **3** *Konj.* but

---

Nürnberg /'nʏrnbɛrk/ (das); **~s ▶ 490** Nuremberg

nuscheln /'nʊʃln/ *tr., itr. V.* (ugs.) mumble

Nuss, *Nuß /nʊs/ *die;* **~, Nüsse** /'nʏsə/ **(a)** nut; **eine harte ~ [für jmdn.]** (fig.) a hard or tough nut [for sb. to crack]; **(b)** (salopp abwertend: Mensch) so-and-so (coll.)

Nuss-, *Nuß-: **~baum** *der* **(a)** walnut-tree; **(b)** o. Pl. (Holz) walnut; **~knacker** *der* nutcrackers *pl.;* **~schale** *die* nutshell; (fig.: Boot) cockleshell; **~schokolade** *die* nut chocolate

Nüster /'nʏstɐ/ *die;* **~, ~n** nostril

Nutte /'nʊtə/ *die;* **~, ~n** (derb abwertend) tart (sl.); pro (Brit. coll.); hooker (Amer. sl.)

nutz-: **~bar** *Adj.* usable; exploitable, utilizable ⟨mineral resources, invention⟩; cultivatable ⟨land, soil⟩; **etw. praktisch ~bar machen** turn sth. to practical use; **die Sonnenenergie ~bar machen** harness solar energy (für for); **~bringend 1** *Adj.* (nützlich) useful; (gewinnbringend) profitable. **2** *adv.* profitably

nütze /'nʏtsə/ *in* **zu etw. ~ sein** be good for sth.; **[jmdm.] zu nichts ~ sein** be no use or good [to sb.]

nutzen /'nʊtsn̩/ **1** *tr. V.* **(a)** use; exploit, utilize ⟨natural resources⟩; cultivate ⟨land, soil⟩; use, harness ⟨energy source⟩; exploit ⟨advantage⟩; **eine Fläche landwirtschaftlich ~:** use an area for agriculture; **(b)** (be~, aus~) use; make use of; **eine Gelegenheit ~, etw. zu tun** take [advantage of] an opportunity to do sth.; **seine Chance ~:** take one's chance. **2** *itr. V.* ⇒ **nützen 1**

Nutzen *der;* **~s (a)** benefit; **den ~ [von etw.] haben** benefit or gain [from sth.]; **~ aus etw. ziehen** benefit from sth.; exploit sth.; **[jmdm.] von ~ sein** be of use or useful [to sb.]; **(b)** (Profit) profit

nützen /'nʏtsn̩/ **1** *itr. V.* be of use (Dat. to); **nichts ~:** be useless or no use; **jmdm. sehr ~:** be very useful or of great use to sb.; **was hat ihm das genützt?** what good did it do him?; **es würde nichts/wenig ~:** it wouldn't be any/much use or wouldn't do any/much good; **da nützt alles nichts** there's nothing to be done. **2** *tr. V.* ⇒ **nutzen 1**

Nutz-: **~fahrzeug** *das* (Lastwagen, Lieferwagen usw.) commercial vehicle; goods vehicle; (Bus, Straßenbahn usw.) public-service vehicle; **~fläche** *die* **(a)** (von Gebäuden) usable floor space; **(b)** (Landw.) **landwirtschaftliche ~flächen** land *sing.* available for agriculture

nützlich /'nʏtslɪç/ *Adj.* useful; **sich ~ machen** make oneself useful

Nützlichkeit *die;* **~:** usefulness

nutzlos 1 *Adj.* useless; (vergeblich) futile; vain *attrib.;* in vain *pred.;* **es wäre ~, das zu tun** it would be useless or pointless or futile doing that. **2** *adv.* uselessly; (vergeblich) futilely; in vain; **er hat das Geld ~ vergeudet** he squandered the money on useless items

Nutz·losigkeit *die;* **~:** uselessness; (Vergeblichkeit) futility; vainness

Nutznießer *der;* **~s, ~, Nutznießerin** *die;* **~, ~nen (a)** beneficiary; **(b)** (Rechtsw.) usufructuary

Nutzung *die;* **~, ~en** use; (des Landes, des Bodens) cultivation; (von Bodenschätzen) exploitation; utilization; (einer Energiequelle) use; harnessing; **die wirtschaftliche ~ einer Fläche** the use of an area for financial benefit; **jmdm. etw. zur ~ überlassen** give sb. the use of sth.

NVA *Abk.* **Nationale Volksarmee** (ehem. DDR) National People's Army

NW *Abk.* **Nordwest[en]** NW

Nylon ⓌⓏ /'naɪlɔn/ *das;* **~s** nylon

Nylon·strumpf *der* nylon stocking

Nymphe /'nʏmfə/ *die;* **~, ~n** (Myth., Zool.) nymph

Nymphomanin *die;* **~, ~nen** (Psych.) nymphomaniac

Oo

o, O /oː/ *das;* ~, (ugs.:) ~s, ~, (ugs.:) ~s o/O; *s. auch* **a**, **A**
O *Abk.* **Ost[en]** E

ö, Ö /øː/ *das;* ~, (ugs.:) ~s, ~, (ugs.:) ~s o/O umlaut; *s. auch* **a**, **A**

Oase /oˈaːzə/ *die;* ~, ~n (auch fig.) oasis

ob /ɔp/ *Konj.* **(a)** whether; **ob wir es schaffen?** will we manage it?; **ob er will oder nicht** whether he wants to or not; **ob arm, ob reich** whether rich or poor; **(b)** *in* **und ob!** of course!; you bet! (coll.)

OB *Abk.* **Oberbürgermeister/Oberbürgermeisterin**

Obacht /ˈoːbaxt/ *die;* ~ (bes. südd.) caution; ~, **da kommt ein Auto!** watch out! *or* look out! *or* careful!, there's a car coming; ~ **auf jmdn./etw. geben** look after *or* take care of sb./sth.; (aufmerksam sein) pay attention to sb./sth.; ~ **geben, dass** … take care that …

Obdach /ˈɔpdax/ *das;* ~[e]s (geh.) shelter

obdach·los *Adj.* homeless; ~ **werden** be made homeless

Obdachlose *der/die; adj. Dekl.* homeless person/man/woman; **die** ~**n** the homeless

Obdachlosen·asyl *das* hostel for the homeless

Obduktion /ɔpdukˈtsi̯oːn/ *die;* ~, ~en (Med., Rechtsw.) postmortem [examination]; autopsy

O-Beine *Pl.* bandy legs; bow-legs

oben /ˈoːbn̩/ *Adv.* **(a)** (an hoch/höher gelegenem Ort) **hier/dort** ~: up here/there; [hoch] ~ **am Himmel** [high] up in the sky; ~ **bleiben** stay up; **weiter** ~: further up; **nach** ~: upwards; **der Weg nach** ~: the way up; **warme Luft steigt nach** ~: warm air rises; ~ **auf dem Dach** up on the roof; **von** ~: from above; **von** ~ **herab** (fig.) condescendingly; **(b)** (im Gebäude) upstairs; **nach** ~: upstairs; **der Aufzug fährt nach** ~: the lift (Brit.) *or* (Amer.) elevator is going up; **(c)** (am oberen Ende, zum oberen Ende hin) at the top; ~ **im/auf dem Schrank** at the/up on top of the cupboard; **nach** ~ [hin] towards the top; **weiter** ~ [im Tal] further *or* higher up [the valley]; **von** ~: from the top; ~ **links/rechts** at the top on the left/right; ~ [links/rechts] (in Bildunterschriften) above [left/right]; **auf Seite 25** ~: at the top of page 25; **die fünfte Zeile von** ~: the fifth line from the top; the fifth line down; **nach** ~ **kommen** (an die Oberfläche) come up; „~" 'this side up'; **wo** *od.* **was ist [bei dem Bild]** ~: which is the right way up [on the picture]?; which is the top [of the picture]?; **bis** ~ **hin voll sein** (ugs.) be full to the top; **von** ~ **bis unten** from top to bottom; **er musterte sie von** ~ **bis unten** he looked her up and down(coll.); ~ **ohne** topless; ~ **an der Tafel** at the head of the table; **(d)** (an der Oberseite) on top; **(e)** (in einer Hierarchie, Rangfolge) at the top; **weit/ganz** ~: near the top/right at the top; **der Befehl kam von** ~: the order came from above; **die da** ~ (ugs.) the high-ups (coll.); **(f)** ([weiter] vorn im Text) above; ~ **erwähnt/genannt/stehend** above-mentioned; **(g)** (im Norden) up north; **hier/dort** ~: up here/there [in the north]

oben-: ~**an** *Adv.* at the top; ~**drauf** *Adv.* (ugs.) on top; *~**erwähnt**, *~**genannt**, *~**stehend** ⇨ oben f

ober… /ˈoːbɐ/ *Adj.* **(a)** upper *attrib.;* top *attrib.;* (ganz oben liegend) top *attrib.;* **die** ~ **rechte Ecke** the top right-hand corner; **am** ~**en Ende der Straße** at the top [end] of the street; **das Oberste zuunterst kehren** turn everything upside down; **das** ~**ste Stockwerk** the top[most] storey; **(b)** (der Quelle näher gelegen) upper; **(c) die** ~**en Klassen der Schule** the senior classes *or* forms of the school; **das** ~**ste Gericht des Landes** the highest court in the land; **der Oberste Sowjet** the Supreme Soviet

Ober *der;* ~**s**, ~ waiter; **Herr** ~**!** waiter!

Ober-: ~**arm** *der* ▶ 326 | upper arm; ~**arzt** *der* (Vertreter des Chefarztes) assistant medical director; (Leiter einer Spezialabteilung) consultant; ~**befehlshaber** *der*,

~**befehlshaberin** *die* (Milit.) supreme commander; commander-in-chief; ~**begriff** *der* generic term; ~**bekleidung** *die* outer clothing; ~**bett** *das* duvet (Brit.); stuffed quilt (Amer.); ~**bürger·meister** *der*, ~ **bürgermeisterin** *die* ▶ 34 | mayor; ~**deck** *der* upper deck; (eines Busses) upper *or* top deck

Ober·fläche *die* surface; (Flächeninhalt) surface area; **die Diskussion blieb zu sehr an der** ~ (fig.) the discussion remained far too superficial

oberflächlich **1** *Adj.* superficial; **eine erste,** ~ **Schätzung** a first, rough estimate. **2** *adv.* superficially; **etw. nur** ~ **kennen** have only a superficial knowledge of sth.; **etw.** ~ **lesen** read sth. cursorily; **er arbeitet zu** ~ he is too superficial in the way he works

Oberflächlichkeit *die;* ~: superficiality

Ober·geschoss, *****Ober·geschoß** *das* upper storey

ober·halb **1** *Adv.* above; **weiter** ~: further up; ~ **von** above. **2** *Präp. mit Gen.* above

Ober-: ~**hand** **die** in **die** ~**hand** [über jmdn./etw.] **haben/gewinnen** *od.* **bekommen** have/gain *or* get the upper hand [over sb./sth.]; ~**haupt** *das* head; (einer Verschwörung) leader; ~**haus** *das* (Parl.) upper house *or* chamber; (in Großbritannien) House of Lords; Upper House; ~**hemd** *das* shirt; ~**herrschaft** *die o. Pl.* sovereignty; supreme power; ~**kellner** *der* head waiter; ~**kiefer** *der* upper jaw; ~**klasse** *die* **(a)** (Soziol.) upper class; **(b)** (Schulw.) senior class *or* form; ~**kommandierende** *der/die; adj. Dekl.* (Milit.) ⇨ **befehlshaber;** ~**körper** *der* upper part of the body; **den** ~**körper frei machen** strip to the waist; ~**leder** *das* upper; ~**leitung** *die* (elektrische Leitung) overhead cable; ~**leutnant** *der* ▶ 34 | (beim Heer) lieutenant (Brit.); (bei der Luftwaffe) flying officer (Brit.); first lieutenant (Amer.); ~**leutnant zur See** sub-lieutenant (Brit.); lieutenant junior grade (Amer.); ~**licht** *das* high window; (über einer Tür) fanlight; ~**lippe** *die* ▶ 326 | upper lip; ~**schenkel** *der* ▶ 326 | thigh; ~**schicht** *die* upper class; ~**schule** *die* secondary school; ~**seite** *die* top[side]; upper side; (eines Stoffes) right side

oberst… ⇨ **ober…**

Oberst *der;* ~**en**, *od.* ~**s**, ~**en** *od.* ~**e** ▶ 34 | colonel

Ober·staats·anwalt *der* ▶ 34 | senior public prosecutor (*at a regional court*)

Oberst·leutnant *der* ▶ 34 | (beim Heer) lieutenant-colonel; (bei der Luftwaffe) wing commander; lieutenant-colonel (Amer.)

Ober-: ~**stübchen** *das* ⇨ **richtig 1 b;** ~**studien·direktor** *der* **(a)** ▶ 34 | headmaster (Brit.); principal; **(b)** ▶ 34 | (DDR) highest honorary title for a teacher; ~**studien·rat** *der* **(a)** ▶ 34 | senior teacher; **(b)** ▶ 34 | (DDR) honorary title for a teacher; ~**stufe** *die* (Schulw.) upper school; ~**teil** *das od. der* top [part]; (eines Bikinis, Anzugs, Kleids usw.) top [half]; *o. Pl.* headwater; (fig.) ~**wasser haben** feel in a strong position; ~**wasser bekommen** have one's hand strengthened

ob·gleich *Konj.* ⇨ **obwohl**

Ob·hut *die;* ~: (geh.) care; **jmdn./etw. jmds.** ~ (*Dat.*) **anvertrauen** entrust sb./sth. to sb.'s care

obig /ˈoːbɪç/ *Adj.; nicht präd.* above

Objekt /ɔpˈjɛkt/ *das;* ~**s**, ~**e (a)** (auch Sprachw., Kunstwiss.) object; (Fot., bei einem Experiment) subject; **(b)** (Kaufmannsspr.: Immobilie) property

objektiv /ɔpjɛkˈtiːf/ **1** *Adj.* objective; real, actual ⟨*cause, danger*⟩. **2** *adv.* objectively

Objektiv *das;* ~**s**, ~**e (a)** (Optik) objective; **(b)** (Fot.) lens

Objektivität /ɔpjɛktiviˈtɛːt/ *die;* ~: objectivity

Objekt·satz *der* (Sprachw.) object clause

obligatorisch /ɔbligaˈtoːrɪʃ/ **1** *Adj.* **(a)** obligatory; compulsory ⟨*subject, lecture, etc.*⟩; necessary ⟨*qualification*⟩; **(b)** (iron.: unvermeidlich) obligatory. **2** *adv.* obligatorily; compulsorily

Oboe /o'bo:ə/ *die;* ~, ~n oboe

Obrigkeit /'o:brɪçkai̯t/ *die;* ~, ~en authorities *pl.*

Obrigkeits·staat *der* authoritarian state

ob·schon *Konj.* (geh.) ⇒ **obwohl**

observieren *tr. V.* (a) jmdn./etw. ~: keep sb./sth. under surveillance; (b) (wissenschaftlich) observe

obskur /ɔps'ku:ɐ̯/ *Adj.* (geh.) (a) (unbekannt, unklar) obscure; (b) (dubios) dubious

Obst /o:pst/ *das;* ~[e]s fruit

Obst-: ~**baum** *der* fruit tree; ~**garten** *der* orchard; ~**händler** *der* fruiterer; ~**kuchen** *der* fruit flan

Obstler /'o:pstlɐ/ *der;* ~s, ~ (bes. südd.) fruit brandy

Obst-: ~**saft** *der* fruit juice; ~**salat** *der* fruit salad; ~**torte** *die* fruit flan

obszön /ɔps'tsø:n/ **1** *Adj.* obscene. **2** *adv.* obscenely

Obszönität /ɔpstsøni'tɛ:t/ *die;* ~, ~en obscenity

O·bus *der* trolley bus (Brit.)

ob·wohl *Konj.* although; though

Ochs /ɔks/ *der;* ~en, ~en (südd., österr., schweiz., ugs.), **Ochse** /'ɔksə/ *der;* ~n, ~n (a) ox; bullock; ~ am Spieß roast ox; (b) (salopp) numskull (coll.); **ich** ~! what a numskull I am!

Ochsen-: ~**brust** *die* (Kochk.) brisket of beef; ~**schwanzsuppe** *die* (Kochk.) oxtail soup; ~**zunge** *die* (Kochk.) ox-tongue

öd /ø:t/ (geh.) ⇒ **öde**

od. *Abk.* **oder**

Ode /'o:də/ *die;* ~, ~n ode (an + *Akk.* to, auf + *Akk.* on)

öde /'ø:də/ *Adj.* (a) (verlassen) deserted ⟨*beach, village, house, street, etc.*⟩; (unbewohnt) desolate ⟨*area, landscape*⟩; (b) (unfruchtbar) barren; (c) (langweilig) tedious; dreary

Öde *die;* ~, ~n (a) *o. Pl.* ⇒ **öde a–b:** desertedness; desolateness; barrenness; (b) (öde Gegend) wasteland; waste; (c) (Langeweile) tediousness; dreariness

oder /'o:dɐ/ *Konj.* (a) or; ~ aber or else; *s. auch* **entweder;** (b) (in Fragen) du kommst doch mit, ~? you will come, won't you?; er ist doch hier, ~? he is here, isn't he? (zweifelnd) he is here — or isn't he?; das ist doch erlaubt, ~ [etwa nicht]? that is allowed, isn't it?

Oder-Neiße-Linie *die* Oder-Neisse Line

Ofen /'o:fn̩/ *der;* ~s, **Öfen** (a) heater; (Kohle~) stove; (Öl~, Petroleum~) stove; heater; (elektrischer ~) heater; fire; wenn sie uns erwischen, ist der ~ aus (ugs.) if they catch us, it's all over; (b) (Back~) oven; (c) (Brenn~, Trocken~) kiln; (d) (landsch.: Herd) cooker

Ofen-: ~**heizung** *die; o. Pl.* heating *no art.* by stoves; ~**rohr** *das* [stove] flue

offen /'ɔfn̩/ **1** *Adj.* (a) open; unsealed ⟨*envelope*⟩; ulcerated ⟨*legs*⟩; mit ~em Mund with one's mouth open; der Knopf/Schlitz ist ~: the button is/one's flies are undone; ein ~es Hemd a shirt with the collar unfastened; sie trägt ihr Haar ~: she wears her hair loose; ~ haben od. sein be open; die Tür ist ~ (nicht abgeschlossen) the door is unlocked; etw. ~ lassen leave sth. open; ~ bleiben remain or stay open; jmdm. ~ stehen (fig.) be open to sb.; es steht dir ~, es zu tun you are free to do it; mit ~en Karten spielen play with the cards face up on the table; (fig.) put one's cards on the table; ~es Licht/ Feuer a naked light/an open fire; das ~e Meer, die ~e See the open sea; ~e Türen einrennen (fig.) fight a battle that's/battles that are already won; mit ~en Augen od. Sinnen durch die Welt od. durchs Leben gehen go about/go through life with one's eyes open; für neue Ideen od. gegenüber neuen Ideen ~ sein be receptive or open to new ideas; (b) (lose) loose ⟨*sugar, flour, oats, etc.*⟩; ~er Wein wine on tap or draught; (c) (frei) vacant ⟨*job, post*⟩; ~e Stellen vacancies; (als Rubrik) 'Situations Vacant'; (d) (ungewiss, ungeklärt) open, unsettled ⟨*question*⟩; uncertain ⟨*result*⟩; der Ausgang des Spiels ist noch völlig ~: the result of the match is still wide open; ~ bleiben ⟨*decision*⟩ be left open; ~ lassen, ob …: leave it open whether …; etw. ~ halten keep sth. open; (e) (noch

nicht bezahlt) outstanding ⟨*bill*⟩; ~ stehen be oustanding; (f) (freimütig, aufrichtig) frank [and open] ⟨*person*⟩; frank, candid ⟨*look, opinion, reply*⟩; honest ⟨*character, face*⟩; ~ zu jmdm. sein be open or frank with sb.; (g) *nicht präd.* (unverhohlen) open ⟨*threat, mutiny, hostility, opponent, etc.*⟩; (h) (Sprachw.) open ⟨*vowel, syllable*⟩. **2** *adv.* (a) (frei zugänglich, sichtbar, unverhohlen) openly; (b) (freimütig, aufrichtig) openly; frankly; ~ gesagt frankly; to be frank or honest; ~ gestanden to tell you the truth

offen·bar 1 *Adj.* obvious. **2** *adv.* (a) (offensichtlich) obviously; clearly; (b) (anscheinend) evidently

offenbaren (geh.) **1** *tr. V.* reveal. **2** *refl. V.* (a) (sich erweisen) sich als etw. ~: ⟨*person*⟩ show or reveal oneself to be sth.; (b) (sich mitteilen) sich jmdm. ~: confide in sb.

Offenbarung *die;* ~, ~en revelation

Offenbarungs·eid *der* oath of disclosure

***offen|bleiben, *offen|halten** ⇒ **offen 1 a, 1 d**

Offen·heit *die;* ~: ⇒ **offen f:** frankness [and openness]; candidness; honesty

offen-, Offen-: ~**herzig 1** *Adj.* frank, candid ⟨*conversation, remark*⟩; frank and open ⟨*person*⟩; **2** *adv.* frankly; openly; ~**herzigkeit** *die;* ~: frankness; candidness; candour; ~**kundig 1** *Adj.* obvious, evident (für to); obvious, patent, manifest ⟨*lie, betrayal, misuse*⟩; **2** *adv.* obviously; clearly;*~|lassen* ⇒ **offen 1 a, 1 d;** ~**sichtlich 1** *Adj.* obvious; evident; **2** *adv.* obviously; (anscheinend) evidently

offensiv /ɔfɛn'zi:f/ **1** *Adj.* (a) offensive; (b) (Sport) attacking. **2** *adv.* (a) offensively; (b) (Sport) ~ spielen play an attacking game

Offensive *die;* ~, ~n (auch Sport) offensive; in der ~: on the offensive; die ~ ergreifen, in die ~ gehen go on to the offensive

***offen|stehen** ⇒ **offen 1 a, 1 e**

öffentlich /'œfn̩tlɪç/ **1** *Adj.* public; state *attrib.,* [state-] maintained ⟨*school*⟩; die ~e Meinung public opinion; Erregung ~en Ärgernisses (Rechtsw.) creating a public nuisance; der ~e Dienst the civil service; die Ausgaben der ~en Hand public spending *sing.;* eine Persönlichkeit des ~en Lebens a public figure. **2** *adv.* (a) publicly; ⟨*perform, appear*⟩ in public; ~ tagen meet in open session; etw. ~ versteigern sell sth. by public auction; (b) (vom Staat usw.) publicly ⟨*funded etc.*⟩

Öffentlichkeit *die;* ~: (a) public; unter Ausschluss der ~: in private or secret; (Rechtsw.) in camera; etw. an die ~ bringen bring sth. to public attention; make sth. public; vor die ~ treten appear in public; in aller ~: [quite openly] in public; (b) (das Öffentlichsein) das Prinzip der ~ in der Rechtsprechung the principle that justice be administered in open court

Öffentlichkeits·arbeit *die; o. Pl.* public relations work *no art.*

öffentlich-rechtlich *Adj.* under public law *postpos., not pred.;* ~es Fernsehen state-owned television

offerieren /ɔfə'ri:rən/ *tr. V.* (bes. Kaufmannsspr.) offer

Offerte /ɔ'fɛrtə/ *die;* ~, ~n (Kaufmannsspr.) offer

offiziell /ɔfi'tsi̯ɛl/ **1** *Adj.* official. **2** *adv.* officially

Offizier /ɔfi'tsi:ɐ̯/ *der;* ~s, ~e ▶ 85◀ officer

Offiziers·lauf·bahn *die* officer's career

öffnen /'œfnən/ **1** *tr. V.* (*auch fig.*) open; turn on ⟨*tap*⟩; undo ⟨*coat, blouse, button, zip*⟩; die Bank ist od. hat über Mittag geöffnet the bank is open at lunchtime; „hier ~" 'open here'; jmdm. den Blick für etw. ~: open sb.'s eyes to sth. **2** *itr. V.* (a) [jmdm.] ~: open the door [to sb.]; wenn es klingelt, musst du ~: if there's a ring at the door, you must go and answer it; (b) (geöffnet werden) ⟨*shop, bank, etc.*⟩ open; (c) (sich ~) ⟨*door*⟩ open. **3** *refl. V.* (a) open; die Erde öffnete sich the ground opened up; (b) (sich erweitern) ⟨*valley, lane, forest, etc.*⟩ open out (auf + *Akk.,* zu on to); ⟨*view*⟩ open up

Öffner *der;* ~s, ~: opener

Öffnung *die;* ~, ~en (a) (offene Stelle) opening; (Fot., Optik) aperture; (b) *o. Pl.* (das Öffnen) opening; eine ~ der Leiche a postmortem on the body; (c) *o. Pl.* (das Aufgeschlossensein) openness (für to); eine ~ der Partei nach links

anstreben (Pol.) strive to open the party up to left-wing ideas

Öffnungs·zeiten Pl. (eines Geschäfts, einer Bank) opening times; hours of business; (eines Museums, Zoos usw.) opening times

Offsetdruck /'ɔfzɛt-/ der; -[e]s offset printing

oft /ɔft/ Adv. öfter /'œftɐ/; (selten) am öftesten /'œftəst/ often; **wie oft soll ich dir noch sagen, dass …?** how many [more] times do I have to tell you that …?

öfter /'œftɐ/ Adv. now and then; [every] once in a while; **des ~en** (geh.) on many occasions

oftmals Adv. often; frequently

OG Abk. **Obergeschoss**

oh /o:/ Interj. oh

OHG Abk. **Offene Handelsgesellschaft** general partnership

ohne /'o:nə/ 1 Präp. mit Akk. (a) without; **~ mich!** [you can] count me out!; **der Versuch blieb ~ Erfolg** the attempt was unsuccessful; **ein Mann ~ jeglichen Humor** a man totally lacking in humour or without any sense of humour; (b) (mit Auslassung des Akkusativs) **ich rauche nur ~:** I only smoke untipped or filterless cigarettes; **wir baden am liebsten ~:** we prefer to bathe in the nude; **er/sie ist [gar] nicht [so] ~** (ugs.) he's/she's quite something; s. auch **oben c; (c) ~ weiteres** (leicht, einfach) easily; (ohne Einwand) readily; **das traue ich ihm ~ weiteres zu** I can quite or easily believe he's capable of that; (d) excluding. 2 Konj. **er nahm Platz, ~ dass er gefragt hätte** he sat down without asking; **~ zu zögern** without hesitating; without hesitation

ohne-: **~dies** Adv. (geh.) in any case; **~einander** Adv. without each other; **~gleichen** Adj.; attr. nachgestellt unparalleled; **eine Frechheit ~gleichen** an unprecedented impertinence; **~hin** Adv. anyway; **er war ~hin schon überlastet** he was already overburdened as it was

Ohnmacht /'o:nmaxt/ die; ~, ~en (a) faint; swoon (literary); **in ~ fallen** od. (geh.) sinken faint or pass out/swoon; (b) (Machtlosigkeit) powerlessness; impotence

ohnmächtig Adj. (a) unconscious; **~ werden** faint; pass out; **~ sein** have fainted or passed out; be in a dead faint; (b) (machtlos) powerless; impotent; impotent, helpless ⟨fury, rage⟩; helpless ⟨bitterness, despair⟩. 2 adv. impotently; **~ zusehen** watch powerless or helplessly

Ohnmachts·anfall der fainting fit

oho /o'ho:/ 1 Interj. oho; (protestierend) oh no. 2 ⇒ **klein 1 a**

Ohr /o:ɐ̯/ das; ~[e]s, ~en (a) ▶ 326¦ ear; **auf dem linken ~ taub sein** be deaf in one's left ear; **gute/ schlechte ~en haben** have good/poor hearing sing.; **er hört nur auf einem ~:** he only has one good ear; **ich habe seine Worte/die Melodie noch im ~:** his words are still ringing in my ears/the tune is still going around my head; (b) (fig.) **die ~en aufmachen** od. **aufsperren/ spitzen** (ugs.) pin back/prick up one's ears; **die Wände haben ~en** the walls have ears; **ein offenes ~ für jmdn./etw. haben** be ready to listen to sb./be open to or ready to listen to sth.; **auf dem ~ hört er schlecht/ nicht** (ugs.) he doesn't want to hear anything about that; **sich aufs ~ legen** od. (ugs.) hauen get one's head down (coll.); **noch feucht/nicht [ganz] trocken hinter den ~en sein** (ugs.) be still wet behind the ears; **schreib dir das mal hinter die ~en!** (ugs.) just you remember that!; **eine** od. **eins/ein paar hinter die ~en kriegen** (ugs.) get a thick ear (Brit. coll.); **jmdm. [mit etw.] in den ~en liegen** (ugs.) pester sb. the whole time [with sth.]; **bis über beide ~en verliebt [in jmdn.]** (ugs.) head over heels in love [with sb.]; **bis über beide** od. **die ~en in etw. stecken** be up to one's ears in sth. (coll.); **jmdn. übers ~ hauen** (ugs.) take sb. for a ride (fig. coll.); put one over on sb. (coll.); **viel** od. **eine Menge um die ~en haben** (ugs.) have a lot on one's plate (coll.); **zum einen ~ rein- und zum anderen wieder rausgehen** (ugs.) go in one ear and out the other (coll.); s. auch **faustdick 2; Fell a; Floh a**

Öhr /ø:ɐ̯/ das; ~[e]s, ~e eye

ohren-, Ohren-: **~arzt** der otologist; ear specialist; **~betäubend** 1 Adj. ear-splitting; deafening; deafening ⟨applause⟩; 2 adv. deafeningly; **~ sausen** das ringing in the or one's ears; **~schmalz** das ear-wax; **~schmaus** der (ugs.) in ein **~schmaus sein** be a joy to hear; **~schmerz** der earache; **~schmerzen haben** have [an] earache sing.; **~schützer** der ear-muff; **~sessel** der wing-chair

ohr-, Ohr-: **~feige** die box on the ears; **jmdm. eine ~feige geben** od. (ugs.) verpassen box sb.'s ears; give sb. a box on the ears; **~feigen** /-faign/ tr. V. **jmdn. ~feigen** box sb.'s ears; **ich könnte mich [selbst] ~feigen!** (ugs.) I could kick myself!; **~läppchen** das earlobe; **~muschel** die external ear; auricle; **~ring** der earring; **~stecker** der ear-stud; **~wurm der** (a) earwig; (b) (ugs.: Melodie) catchy tune; **ein ~wurm sein** be really catchy

oje /o'je:/ Interj. (veralt.), **ojemine** /o'je:mine/Interj. (veralt.) oh dear; dear me

okay /o'ke/ Interj., Adj., adv. (ugs.) OK (coll.); okay (coll.)

okkupieren tr. V. occupy

öko-, Öko- /øko-/ eco-

Ökoaudit /'ø:koɔ:dɪt/ das; ~s, ~s eco-audit; environmental audit

Ökologe /øko'lo:gə/ der; ~n, ~n ecologist

Ökologie die; ~: ecology

ökologisch 1 Adj. ecological. 2 adv. ecologically

Ökonomie die; ~, ~n economics sing.; **politische ~:** political economy

ökonomisch 1 Adj. (a) economic; (b) (sparsam) economical. 2 adv. economically

Öko·steuer die; ~, ~n eco-tax

Öko·system das ecosystem

Oktave /ɔk'ta:və/ die; ~, ~n octave

Oktober /ɔk'to:bɐ/ der; ~[s], ~: ▶ 119¦ October; s. auch **April**

Öl /ø:l/ das; ~[e]s, ~e oil; **auf ~ stoßen** strike oil; **in ~ malen** paint in oils; **~ ins Feuer gießen** (fig.) add fuel to the flames

Öl-: **~baum** der olive-tree; **~bild** das oil painting

Oldtimer /'ouldtaɪmɐ/ der; ~s, ~: vintage car; (vor 1905 gebaut) veteran car

Oleander /ole'andɐ/ der; ~s, ~: (Bot.) oleander

ölen tr. V. oil; lubricate ⟨shaft, engine, etc.⟩; **wie geölt** (fig. ugs.) like clockwork; s. auch **Blitz a**

Öl-: **~farbe** die (a) oil-based paint; (b) (zum Malen) oil-paint; **mit ~farben malen** paint in oils; **~gemälde** das oil painting; **~götze** der in **wie ein ~götze/wie die ~götzen** (ugs.) like a zombie/zombies; **~heizung** die oil-fired heating no indef. art.

ölig 1 Adj. oily. 2 adv. **~ glänzen** have an oily sheen

Oligarchie /oligar'çi:/ die; ~, ~n oligarchy

oliv /o'li:f/ Adj. olive[-green]

Olive /o'li:və/ die; ~, ~n olive

Oliven-: **~baum** der olive-tree; **~öl** das olive oil

oliv·grün Adj. olive-green

Öl-: **~kanister** der, **~kanne** die oilcan; **~krise** die oil crisis

oll /ɔl/ Adj. (ugs., bes. nordd.) old; **je ~er, je doller** (ugs. scherzh.) the older they get, the more they want to live it up

Öl-: **~lampe** die oil lamp; **~leitung** die oil-pipe; (größer) oil pipeline; **~malerei** die oil painting no art.; **~mess·stab**, *~**meß·stab** der (bes. Kfz-W.) dipstick; **~ofen** der oil heater; **~pest** das oil pollution no indef. art.; **~sardine** die sardine in oil; **eine Dose ~n** a tin of sardines; **~scheich** der (ugs.) oil sheikh; **~stand** der oil level; **~tank** der oil tank; **~tanker** der oil tanker; **~teppich** der oil slick

Ölung die; ~, ~en oiling; lubrication; **Letzte Ölung** (kath. u. orthodoxe Kirche) extreme unction

Öl-: **~wanne** die (bes. Kfz-W.) sump; **~wechsel** der (bes. Kfz-W.) oil-change

Olymp /o'lʏmp/ der; ~s Mount Olympus

Olympiade /olʏm'pia:də/ die; ~, ~n (a) Olympic Games pl.; Olympics pl.; (b) (Wettbewerb) Olympiad

Olympia-: ∼**mannschaft** *die* Olympic team *or* squad; ∼**sieger** *der;* ∼**siegerin** *die;* Olympic champion; ∼**stadion** *das* Olympic stadium

olympisch *Adj.* Olympic; **die Olympischen Spiele** the Olympic Games; the Olympics

Öl·zeug *das* oilskins *pl.*

Oma /'o:ma/ *die;* ∼, ∼**s** (fam.) gran[ny] (coll./child lang.); grandma (coll./child lang.)

Omelett *das;* ∼[e]**s**, ∼**e** *od.* ∼**s**, (Kochk.) omelette

Omen /'o:mən/ *das;* ∼**s**, ∼ *od.* **Omina** /'o:mina/ omen

ominös /omi'nø:s/ **1** *Adj.* (a) ominous; (b) (bedenklich, zweifelhaft) sinister. **2** *adv.* ominously

Omnibus /'ɔmnibʊs/ *der;* ∼**ses**, ∼**se** omnibus (formal); (Privat- und Reisebus auch) coach

Omnibus- ⇨ **Bus-**

Onanie /ona'ni:/ *die;* ∼: onanism *no art.;* masturbation *no art.*

onanieren *itr. V.* masturbate

ondulieren /ɔndu'li:rən/ *tr. V.* (veralt.) crimp; wave

Onkel /'ɔnkl/ *der;* ∼**s**, ∼ *od.* (ugs.) ∼**s** (a) uncle; (b) (Kinderspr.: Mann) **sag dem** ∼ **guten Tag!** say hello to the nice man; **der** ∼ **Doktor** the nice doctor

online /'ɔnlaɪn/ **1** *Adj.* on-line; ∼ **gehen** go on-line. **2** *Adv.* on-line

Online-: ∼**betrieb** *der* (DV) on-line operation; ∼**dienst** *der* (DV) on-line service; ∼**zeit** *die* (DV) connection *or* usage time

OP /o:'pe:/ *der;* ∼[**s**], ∼[**s**] *Abk.* **Operationssaal**

Opa /'o:pa/ *der;* ∼**s**, ∼**s** (fam.) grandad (coll./child lang.); grandpa (coll./child lang.)

Opal /o'pa:l/ *der;* ∼**s**, ∼**e** opal

Oper /'o:pɐ/ *die;* ∼, ∼**n** opera; (Institution, Ensemble) Opera; **in die** ∼ **gehen** go to the opera; **an die/zur** ∼ **gehen** (als Sänger) become an opera singer; **quatsch keine** ∼**n!** (salopp) don't talk rot! (sl.)

Operation /opəra'tsjo:n/ *die;* ∼, ∼**en** ▶ 329 ◀ operation

Operations-: ∼**saal** *der* operating theatre (Brit.) *or* -room; ∼**schwester** *die* theatre sister (Brit.); operating-room nurse (Amer.); ∼**tisch** *der* operating-table

operativ /opəra'ti:f/ **1** *Adj.; nicht präd.* (Med.) operative. **2** *adv.* (Med.) by operative surgery

Operette /opə'rɛtə/ *die;* ∼, ∼**n** operetta

operieren 1 *tr. V.* ▶ 329 ◀ operate on ⟨*patient*⟩; **sich** ∼ **lassen** have an operation. **2** *itr. V.* operate; **vorsichtig** ∼ (vorgehen) proceed carefully

Opern-: ∼**arie** *die* [operatic] aria; ∼**glas** *das* opera glass[es *pl.*]; ∼**haus** *das* opera house; ∼**sänger** *der,* ∼**sängerin** *die* ▶ 85 ◀ opera singer

Opfer /'ɔpfɐ/ *das;* ∼**s**, ∼ (a) (Verzicht) sacrifice; **ein** ∼ [**für etw.**] **bringen** make a sacrifice [for sth.]; **kein** ∼ **scheuen** consider no sacrifice too great; (b) (Geschädigter) victim; **jmdm./einer Sache** ∼ **fallen** fall victim to sb./sth.; be the victim of sb./sth.; (c) (∼gabe) sacrifice; **jmdm./einer Sache etw. zum** ∼ **bringen** sacrifice sth. to sb./sth.

opfer-, Opfer-: ∼**bereit** *Adj.* ⟨*person*⟩ who is ready *or* willing to make sacrifices; ∼**bereitschaft** *die* readiness *or* willingness to make sacrifices; ∼**gabe** *die* [sacrificial] offering; ∼**lamm** *das* sacrificial lamb; **wie ein** ∼**lamm** (fig. ugs.) like a lamb to the slaughter

opfern 1 *tr. V.* (a) (darbringen) sacrifice; make a sacrifice of; offer up ⟨*fruit, produce, etc.*⟩; (b) (fig.: hingeben) sacrifice, give up ⟨*time, holiday, money, life*⟩. **2** *itr. V.* [**den Göttern**] ∼: offer sacrifice [to the gods]. **3** *refl. V.* (a) **sich für jmdn./etw.** ∼: sacrifice oneself for sb./sth.; (b) (ugs. scherzh.) be the martyr; **wer opfert sich denn und isst den Nachtisch auf?** who's going to volunteer to finish off the dessert?

Opfer·stock *der; Pl.* ...**stöcke** offertory box

Opiat /o'pja:t/ *das;* ∼[e]**s**, ∼**e** opiate

Opium /'o:pjʊm/ *das;* ∼**s** (auch fig.) opium

ÖPNV *Abk.* **öffentlicher Personennahverkehr** local public transport

opponieren *itr. V.* take the opposite side; **gegen jmdn./etw.** ∼: oppose sb./sth.

opportun /ɔpɔr'tu:n/ *Adj.* (geh.) appropriate; (günstig) advantageous

Opportunismus *der;* ∼: opportunism

Opportunist *der;* ∼**en**, ∼**en** opportunist

opportunistisch 1 *Adj.* opportunist; opportunistic. **2** *adv.* opportunistically

Opposition /ɔpozi'tsjo:n/ *die;* ∼, ∼**en** (auch Politik, Sprachw., Astron., Schach, Fechten) opposition; **etw. aus** [**reiner** *od.* **lauter**] ∼ **tun** do sth. just to be contrary

oppositionell /ɔpozitsjo'nɛl/ **1** *Adj.* opposition *attrib.* ⟨*group, movement, circle, etc.*⟩; ⟨*newspaper, writer, artist, etc.*⟩ opposed to the government. **2** *adv.* ∼ **eingestellt sein** hold opposing views

Oppositions-: ∼**führer** *der* opposition leader; (in Großbritannien) Leader of the Opposition; ∼**partei** *die* opposition party

Optik *die;* ∼, ∼**en** (a) *o. Pl.* (Wissenschaft) optics *sing., no art.;* (b) (Fot. ugs.) (Linse) lens; (Linsen) optics *pl.;* lens system; **das ist eine Frage der** ∼ (fig.) it depends on your point of view; (c) *o. Pl.* (Erscheinungsbild) appearance; **der** ∼ **wegen** for visual effect

Optiker *der;* ∼**s**, ∼, **Optikerin** *die;* ∼, ∼**nen** ▶ 85 ◀ optician

optimal /ɔpti'ma:l/ **1** *Adj.* optimal; optimum *attrib.* **2** *adv.* **jmdn.** ∼ **beraten** give sb. the best possible advice

Optimismus *der;* ∼: optimism

Optimist *der;* ∼**en**, ∼**en**, **Optimistin** *die;* ∼, ∼**nen** optimist

optimistisch 1 *Adj.* optimistic. **2** *adv.* optimistically

optisch 1 *Adj.* optical; visual ⟨*impression*⟩; **aus** ∼**en Gründen** for [the sake of] optical *or* visual effect; (fig.) for [the sake of] effect. **2** *adv.* optically; visually ⟨*impressive, successful, effective*⟩; ∼ **wahrnehmbar sein** be perceivable with the eye

Orakel /o'ra:kl/ *das;* ∼**s**, ∼ oracle

orakeln 1 *tr. V.* ∼, **dass ...:** make mysterious prophecies that ... **2** *itr. V.* make mysterious prophecies

oral /o'ra:l/ **1** *Adj.* oral. **2** *adv.* orally

orange /o'rã:ʒ(ə)/ *indekl. Adj.* orange

Orange *die;* ∼, ∼**n** orange

orange·farben, orange·farbig *Adj.* orange[-coloured]

orangen /o'rã:ʒn/ *Adj.* orange

Orangen-: ∼**baum** *der* orange-tree; ∼**marmelade** *die* orange marmalade; ∼**saft** *der* orange juice; ∼**schale** *die* orange peel *no pl.*

Orang-Utan /'o:raŋ'|u:tan/ *der;* ∼**s**, ∼**s** orang-utan

Oratorium /ora'to:rjʊm/ *das;* ∼**s**, **Oratorien** oratorio

Orchester /ɔr'kɛstɐ/ *das;* ∼**s**, ∼: orchestra

Orchidee /ɔrçi'de:(ə)/ *die;* ∼, ∼**n** orchid

Orden /'ɔrdn/ *der;* ∼**s**, ∼ (a) (Gemeinschaft) order; **in einen** ∼ **eintreten, einem** ∼ **beitreten** join an order; become a member of an order; (b) (Ehrenzeichen, Milit.) decoration; (in runder Form) medal; **jmdm. einen** ∼ [**für etw.**] **verleihen** decorate sb. [for sth.]

ordentlich /'ɔrdntlɪç/ **1** *Adj.* (a) (ordnungsliebend) [neat and] tidy; (methodisch) orderly; (b) (geordnet) [neat and] tidy ⟨*room, house, desk, etc.*⟩; neat ⟨*handwriting, clothes*⟩; (c) (anständig) respectable; proper ⟨*manners*⟩; **etwas Ordentliches lernen** learn a proper trade; (d) *nicht präd.* (planmäßig) regular, ordinary ⟨*meeting*⟩; full ⟨*member*⟩; ∼**es Gericht** court exercising civil and criminal jurisdiction; *s. auch* **Professor a**; (e) (ugs.: richtig) proper; real; **etwas Ordentliches essen** have some proper food; **eine** ∼**e Tracht Prügel** a real good hiding (coll.); (f) (ugs.: tüchtig) **ein** ∼**es Stück Kuchen** a nice big piece of cake; **ein** ∼**es Stück Arbeit** a fair old bit of work (coll.); (g) (ugs.: recht gut) decent ⟨*wine, flat, marks, etc.*⟩. **2** *adv.* (a) (geordnet) tidily; neatly; ⟨*write*⟩ neatly; ∼ **aufgeräumt** neatly tidied; (b) (anständig) properly; (c) (ugs.: gehörig) ∼ **feiern** have a real good celebration (coll.); **greift** ∼ **zu!** tuck in!; (d) (ugs.: recht gut) ⟨*ski, speak, etc.*⟩ really well

Ordentlichkeit *die;* ∼: [neatness and] tidiness; (der Schrift, Kleidung) neatness; (methodische Veranlagung) orderliness

Order /ˈɔrdɐ/ *die;* ~, ~s *od.* ~n **(a)** (Befehl) order; ~ **haben, etw. zu tun** have orders to do sth.; **(b)** *Pl.* ~s (Kaufmannsspr.: Auftrag) order; **einer Firma eine** ~ **erteilen** place an order with a firm

Order·papier *das* (Bankw.) instrument made out to order *(and transferable by endorsement)*

ordinär /ɔrdiˈnɛːɐ̯/ **1** *Adj.* **(a)** (abwertend) vulgar; common; vulgar ⟨*joke, song, expression, language*⟩; cheap and obtrusive ⟨*perfume*⟩; **(b)** *nicht präd.* (alltäglich) ordinary. **2** *adv.* vulgarly; in a vulgar manner

Ordinarius /ɔrdiˈnaːriʊs/ *der;* ~, **Ordinarien** [full] professor **(für** of)

ordnen /ˈɔrdnən/ **1** *tr. V.* **(a)** arrange; **(b)** (regeln) regulate ⟨*traffic*⟩; settle ⟨*one's affairs*⟩; **sein Leben/seine Finanzen** ~: straighten out one's life/put one's finances in order. **2** *refl. V.* form up

Ordner *der;* ~s, ~ **(a)** (Hefter) file; **(b)** (Aufsichtsperson) steward; **(c)** (DV) folder

Ordnung *die;* ~, ~en *o. Pl.* (ordentlicher Zustand) order; tidiness; ~ **halten** keep things tidy; **hier herrscht** ~: everything is neat and tidy here; ~ **schaffen, für** ~ **sorgen** sort things out; **etw. in** ~ **bringen** sort sth. out; **ist dein Pass in** ~? is your passport in order?; **hier ist etw. nicht in** ~: there's something wrong here; **mit ihr ist etwas nicht in** ~, **sie ist nicht in** ~ (ugs.) there's something wrong *or* the matter with her; **sie ist in** ~ (ugs.: ist nett, verlässlich o. ä.) she's OK (coll.); **alles [ist] in schönster** *od.* **bester** ~: everything's [just] fine; [things] couldn't be better; **[das] geht [schon] in** ~ (ugs.) that'll be OK (coll.) *or* all right; **(b)** *o. Pl.* (geregelter Ablauf) routine; **(c)** *o. Pl.* (System [von Normen]) order; (Struktur) structure; **(d)** *o. Pl.* (Disziplin) order; **hier herrscht** ~: we have some discipline here; ~ **halten** ⟨*teacher etc.*⟩ keep order; **(e)** (Formation) formation; **(f)** (Biol.) order; **(g)** *o. Pl.* (Rang) **eine Straße zweiter** ~: a second-class road; **ein Reinfall erster** ~ (fig. ugs.) a disaster of the first order *or* water; **(h)** *o. Pl.* (Math.) order; **(i)** (Mengenlehre) ordered set

ordnungs-, Ordnungs-: ~**gemäß 1** *Adj.* ⟨*conduct etc.*⟩ in accordance with the regulations; **2** *adv.* in accordance with the regulations; ~**halber** *Adv.* as a matter of form; ~**liebe** *die* liking for neatness and tidiness; ~**liebend** *Adj.* ⟨*person*⟩ who likes to see things neat and tidy; ~**ruf** *der* call to order; ~**strafe** *die* (Rechtsw.) penalty for contempt of court; ~**widrig** (Rechtsw.) **1** *Adj.* ⟨*actions, behaviour, etc.*⟩ contravening the regulations; illegal ⟨*parking*⟩; **2** *adv.* ~**widrig handeln** act in contravention of the regulations; contravene *or* infringe the regulations; ~**widrigkeit** *die* (Rechtsw.) infringement of the regulations

Organ /ɔrˈgaːn/ *das;* ~s, ~e **(a)** (Anat., Biol.) organ; **(b)** (ugs.: Stimme) voice; **(c)** (Zeitung) organ (formal); **(d)** (Institution) organ; (Mensch) agent

Organisation /ɔrɡaniҡaˈtsi̯oːn/ *die;* ~, ~en organization

Organisations·talent *das* **(a)** (Fähigkeit) talent for organization; **(b)** (Mensch) person with a talent for organization

Organisator /ɔrɡaniˈzaːtɔr/ *der;* ~s, ~en /-ˈtoːrən/ organizer

organisatorisch 1 *Adj.* organizational. **2** *adv.* organizationally

organisch 1 *Adj.* **(a)** (auch Chemie) organic; **(b)** (Med.) organic; physical. **2** *adv.* **(a)** organically; **sich** ~ **in etw.** (*Akk.*) **einfügen** form an organic part of sth.; **(b)** (Med.) organically; physically

organisieren 1 *tr. V.* **(a)** (vorbereiten, aufbauen) organize; **(b)** (ugs.: beschaffen) get [hold of]. **2** *itr. V.* **gut** ~ **können** be a good organizer. **3** *refl. V.* organize **(zu** into); **er will sich** ~: he wants to join the union *etc.*

Organismus *der;* **Organismen** organism

Organist *der;* ~en, ~en, **Organistin** *die;* ~, ~nen ▶ 85 ◀ organist

Organ-: ~**spender** *der* organ donor; ~**verpflanzung** *die* organ transplantation

Organ·verpflanzung *die* organ transplantation

Orgasmus /ɔrˈɡasmʊs/ *der;* ~, **Orgasmen** orgasm

Orgel /ˈɔrɡl̩/ *die;* ~, ~n organ

Orgel-: ~**konzert** *das* organ concerto; (Solo) organ recital; ~**pfeife** *die* organ-pipe; **[dastehen] wie die** ~**pfeifen** (scherzh.) [stand in a row] from the tallest to the shortest

Orgie /ˈɔrɡi̯ə/ *die;* ~, ~n (auch fig.) orgy; **eine** ~ **feiern** have an orgy

Orient /ˈoːri̯ɛnt/ *der;* ~s **(a)** (Vorder- u. Mittelasien) Middle East and south-western Asia (including Afghanistan and Nepal); **der Vordere** ~: the Middle East; **(b)** (veralt.: Osten) Orient

Orientale /ɔri̯ɛnˈtaːlə/ *der;* ~n, ~n, **Orientalin** *die;* ~, ~nen ⇒ **Orient a:** man/woman from the Middle East [*or south-western Asia*]

orientalisch *Adj.* oriental

orientieren 1 *refl. V.* **(a)** (sich zurechtfinden) get one's bearings; **sich an etw.** (*Dat.*) /**nach einer Karte** ~: get one's bearings by sth./using a map; **(b)** (sich unterrichten) **sich über etw.** (*Akk.*) ~: inform oneself about sth.; **(c)** (sich ausrichten) **sich an etw.** (*Dat.*) ~: be oriented towards sth.; ⟨*policy, advertising*⟩ be geared towards sth.; **politisch links/rechts orientiert sein** lean towards the left/right politically. **2** *tr. V.* **(a)** (unterrichten) inform **(über** + *Akk.* about); **(b)** (ausrichten) **seine Ziele nach etw.** ~: base one's aims on sth. **3** *itr. V.* **über etw.** (*Akk.*) ~: report on sth.

Orientierung *die;* ~ **(a)** (Orientierungssinn, -möglichkeit) **hier ist die** ~ **schwer** it's difficult to get your bearings here; **die** ~ **verlieren** lose one's bearings; **(b)** (Unterrichtung) **zu Ihrer** ~: for your information; **(c)** (das Sichausrichten) orientation **(auf** + *Akk.* towards, **an** + *Dat.* according to)

orientierungs-, Orientierungs-: ~**hilfe** *die* aid to orientation; ~**los** *Adj.* (auch fig.) disoriented; ~**sinn** *der* sense of direction

Orient·teppich *der* oriental carpet; (Läufer) oriental rug

original /oriɡiˈnaːl/ **1** *Adj.* original; (echt) genuine; authentic. **2** *adv.* ~ **indische Seide** genuine Indian silk; **etw.** ~ **übertragen** broadcast sth. live

Original *das;* ~s, ~e **(a)** (Urschrift o. ä.) original; **(b)** (eigenwilliger Mensch) character

Original·fassung *die* original version

original·getreu 1 *Adj.* faithful *or* true [to the original] *postpos.* **2** *adv.* in a manner faithful *or* true to the original

Originalität /oriɡinaliˈtɛːt/ *die;* ~ **(a)** (Echtheit) genuineness; authenticity; **(b)** (Einmaligkeit) originality

Original·ton *der* (Film, Ferns.) direct sound; original sound; **Reportageausschnitte im** ~ **von 1936** excerpts from news reports with the original 1936 soundtrack; „~**ton UdSSR-Fernsehen"** 'USSR television commentary';

originell /oriɡiˈnɛl/ **1** *Adj.* (ursprünglich) original; (neu) novel; (ugs.: witzig) witty, funny, comical ⟨*story*⟩; comical, funny ⟨*costume*⟩. **2** *adv.* (ursprünglich) ⟨*write, argue*⟩ with originality; (ugs.: witzig) ⟨*write, argue*⟩ wittily

Orkan /ɔrˈkaːn/ *der;* ~[e]s, ~e hurricane; (fig.) thunderous storm

orkan·artig *Adj.* ⟨*winds, gusts*⟩ of almost hurricane force

Ornament /ɔrnaˈmɛnt/ *das;* ~[e]s, ~e (Kunstw.) ornament

Ornithologie *die;* ~: ornithology *no art.*

Ort¹ /ɔrt/ *der;* ~[e]s, ~e **(a)** (Platz) place; **etw. an seinem** ~ **lassen** leave sth. where it is/was; ~ **der Handlung: ...:** the scene of the action is ...; **an den** ~ **des Verbrechens zurückkehren** return to the scene of the crime; **an** ~ **und Stelle** there and then; **an** ~ **und Stelle sein/ankommen** an der gewünschten Stelle) be/arrive there; **(b)** (~schaft) (Dorf) village; (Stadt) town; **von** ~ **zu** ~: from place to place; **das beste Hotel am** ~: the best hotel in the place

Ort² *in* **vor** ~: on the spot; (Bergmannsspr.) at the [coal-]face

Örtchen /ˈœrtçən/ *das;* ~s, ~ (ugs. verhüll.) **das** ~: the smallest room (coll. euphem.); **aufs** ~ **müssen** have to pay a visit (coll. euphem.)

orten *tr. V.* find the position of

orthodox /ɔrto'dɔks/ *Adj.* (a) (Rel.) orthodox; (b) (starr) rigid; (c) (strenggläubig) strict

Orthographie *die;* ~; ~n orthography

orthographisch *Adj.* orthographic; ~e Fehler spelling mistakes

Orthopäde /ɔrto'pɛːdə/ *der;* ~n, ~n ▶ 85 orthopaedist; orthopaedic specialist

Orthopädie /ɔrtopɛ'diː/ *die;* ~, ~n (a) *o. Pl.* orthopaedics *sing., no art.;* (b) (ugs.: Abteilung) orthopaedic department

Orthopädin *die;* ~, ~nen ▶ 85 ⇒ **Orthopäde**

orthopädisch 1 *Adj.* orthopaedic. 2 *adv.* orthopaedically

örtlich /'œrtlɪç/ 1 *Adj.* local. 2 *adv.* locally; ~ betäubt werden be given a local anaesthetic; ~ begrenzte Kampfhandlungen [limited] local encounters

Örtlichkeit *die;* ~, ~en (a) (Gebiet) locality; (b) (Stelle) place; (c) ⇒ **Örtchen**

orts-, Orts-: ~angabe *die* indication of place; ~ansässig *Adj.* local; die ~ansässigen the local residents; ~ausgang *der* end of the village/town

Ortschaft *die;* ~, ~en (Dorf) village; (Stadt) town; geschlossene ~: built-up area

orts-, Orts-: ~eingang *der* entrance to the village/town; ~fremd *Adj.* (a) (nicht ~ansässig) ~fremde Personen visitors to the village/town; (b) (nicht ~kundig) ~fremd sein be a stranger [to the village/town]; ~gespräch *das* (Fernspr.) local call; ~kenntnis *die* knowledge of the place; [gute] ~kenntnisse haben know the place [well]; ~kundig *Adj.* ein ~kundiger Führer/ ein Ortskundiger a guide/someone who knows the place well; ~name *der* place name; ~netz *das* (Fernspr.) local exchange network; ~netz·kennzahl *die* (Fernspr.) dialling code; area code (Amer.); ~sinn *der* sense of direction; ~verkehr *der* (a) (Straßenverkehr) local traffic; (b) (Telefon) local telephone service; ~zeit *die* local time

Öse /'øːzə/ *die;* ~, ~n eye; (an Schuh, Stiefel) eyelet

Ossi /'ɔsi/ *der;* ~s, ~s (salopp) East German

Ost /ɔst/ *o. Art.; o. Pl.* ▶ 266 (a) (bes. Seemannsspr., Met.: Richtung) east; *s. auch* **Osten a;** (b) (östliches Gebiet, Politik) East; (c) *einem Substantiv nachgestellt* (östlicher Teil, östliche Lage) East; **Autobahnausfahrt Köln ~:** motorway exit Cologne East

ost-, Ost-: ~asien *(das)* East *or* Eastern Asia; ~block *der; o. Pl.* Eastern bloc; ~block·staat *der* Eastern-bloc state; ~deutsch *Adj.* Eastern German; (hist.: auf die DDR bezogen) East German; ~deutsche *der/die* Eastern German; (hist.: DDR-Bürger[in]) East German; ~deutschland *(das)* Eastern Germany; (hist.: DDR) East Germany

Osten *der;* ~s ▶ 266 (a) (Richtung) east; nach ~: eastwards; im/aus dem *od.* von ~: in/from the east; (b) (Gegend) eastern part; (c) (Geogr.) der Ferne ~: the Far East; der Mittlere ~: south-western Asia (including Afghanistan and Nepal); der Nahe ~: the Middle East; (d) (Politik) der ~ (der Ostblock) the East

ostentativ /ɔstɛnta'tiːf/ (geh.) 1 *Adj.* pointed ‹absence, silence›; overt ‹hostility›; exaggerated ‹heartiness›; ostentatious ‹gesture›. 2 *adv.* pointedly; ‹embrace› ostentatiously

Oster-: ~ei *das* Easter egg; ~fest *das* Easter [holiday]; ~glocke *die* daffodil; ~hase *der* Easter hare; ~lamm *das* Paschal lamb

österlich /'øːstɐlɪç/ 1 *Adj.* Easter *attrib.* 2 *adv.* ~ geschmückt decorated for Easter

Oster-: ~marsch *der* Easter march (against war and nuclear weapons); ~montag *der* Easter Monday *no. def. art.; s. auch* **Dienstag**

Ostern /'oːstɐn/ *das;* ~, ~: ▶ 240 Easter; Frohe *od.* Fröhliche ~! Happy Easter!; zu *od.* (bes. südd.) an ~: at Easter; wenn ~ und Pfingsten auf einen Tag fallen (ugs.) not this side of doomsday (coll.)

Österreich /'øːstəraɪç/ *(das);* ~s Austria

Österreicher *der;* ~s, ~, **Österreicherin** *die;* ~, ~nen ▶ 388 Austrian

österreichisch *Adj.* ▶ 388 Austrian; *s. auch* **deutsch; Deutsch**

Oster-: ~sonntag *der* Easter Sunday *no def. art.;* ~woche *die* week before Easter

ost-, Ost-: ~europa *(das)* Eastern Europe; ~europäisch *Adj.* East[ern] European

Ost·friesland *(das);* ~s East Friesland; Ostfriesland

Ost·küste *die* east[ern] coast

östlich /'œstlɪç/ ▶ 266 1 *Adj.* (a) (im Osten) eastern; 15 Grad ~er Länge 15 degrees east [longitude]; (b) (nach, aus dem Osten) easterly; (c) (des Ostens, auch Politik) Eastern. 2 *adv.* eastwards; ~ von …: [to the] east of …; sehr [weit] ~ sein be a long way east. 3 *Präp. mit Gen.* [to the] east of

Ost·politik *die* Ostpolitik (*German policy towards Eastern Europe*)

Östrogen /œstro'geːn/ *das;* ~s, ~e (Physiol.) oestrogen

Ost·see *die; o. Pl.* Baltic [Sea]

ost·wärts *Adv.* ▶ 266 eastwards

Ost·wind *der* east[erly] wind

O-Ton *der* (Film, Ferns.) ⇒ **Originalton**

Otter[1] /'ɔtɐ/ *der;* ~s, ~ (Fisch~) otter

Otter[2] *die;* ~, ~n (Viper) adder; viper

Otto /'ɔto/ *der;* ~s, ~s (salopp) whopper (sl.); *s. auch* **Normalverbraucher**

Otto·motor *der* Otto engine

Ouvertüre /uvɛr'tyːrə/ *die;* ~, ~n (auch fig.) overture (*Gen.* to)

oval /o'vaːl/ *Adj.* oval

Oval *das;* ~s, ~e oval

Ovation /ova'tsĭoːn/ *die;* ~, ~en ovation; jmdm. ~en darbringen give sb. an ovation

Overall /'ɔʊvərɔːl/ *der;* ~s, ~s overalls *pl.*

Oxid /ɔ'ksiːt/ *das;* ~[e]s, ~e (Chemie) oxide

Oxidation /ɔksida'tsĭoːn/ *die;* ~, ~en (Chemie, Physik) oxidation

oxidieren 1 *itr. V.; auch mit sein* (Chemie, Physik) oxidize. 2 *tr. V.* (Chemie) oxidize

oxyd …, Oxyd … ⇒ **oxid …, Oxid …**

Ozean /'oːtseaːn/ *der;* ~s, ~e (auch fig.) ocean

Ozean·dampfer *der* ocean-going steamer; (für Passagiere) ocean liner

Ozon /o'tsoːn/ *der od. das;* ~s ozone

Ozon·loch *das* (ugs.) hole in the ozone layer

Pp

p, P /peː/ *das;* ~, ~: p/P; *s. auch* **a, A**

paar /paːɐ̯/ *indekl. Indefinitpron.* ein ~ …: a few …; (zwei *od.* drei) a couple of …; a few …; ein ~ waren dagegen a few [people]/a couple [of people] were against [it]; deine ~ Mark the few marks/couple of marks you've got; alle ~ Minuten every few minutes/every couple of minutes; du kriegst gleich ein ~ [gelangt] (ugs.) I'll stick one on you (sl.); ein ~ Mal a few times; (zwei oder drei Mal) a couple of *or* a few times

Paar *das;* ~[e]s, ~e pair; (Mann und Frau, Tanz~) couple; ein ~ Würstchen two sausages; a couple of sausages; zwei ~ Socken two pairs of socks; ein ~ Hosen (ugs.) a pair of trousers

paaren 1 *refl. V.* (a) (sich begatten) ‹animals› mate; ‹people› couple, copulate; (b) (sich verbinden) sich mit etw. ~: be combined with sth. 2 *tr. V.* (a) (kreuzen) mate; (b) (zusammenstellen) pair; (c) (verbinden) combine (mit with)

paar-, Paar-: ∼**hufer** *der;* ∼**s,** ∼ (Zool.) even-toed ungulate (fachspr.); cloven-hoofed animal; ∼**lauf** *der,* ∼**laufen** *das* pair-skating; pairs *pl.;**∼**mal** ⇒ **paar**

Paarung *die;* ∼, ∼**en** (a) (Zool.) mating; (b) (das Zusammenstellen) pairing; (c) (das Verbinden) combination

paar·weise 1 *Adv.* in pairs. **2** *adj.* ⟨*arrangement etc.*⟩ in pairs

Pacht /paxt/ *die;* ∼, ∼**en** (a) (Nutzung) etw. in ∼ nehmen/geben lease sth.; take/let sth. on lease; etw. in ∼ haben have sth. on lease; (b) (Vertrag) lease; (c) (Miete) rent

pachten *tr. V.* lease; take a lease on; jmdn./etw. [für sich] gepachtet haben (fig. ugs.) have got a monopoly on sb./sth. (coll.)

Pächter /'pɛçtɐ/ *der;* ∼**s,** ∼, **Pächterin** *die;* ∼, ∼**nen** leaseholder; lessee; (eines Hofes) tenant

Pack[1] /pak/ *der;* ∼**[e]s,** ∼**e** *od.* **Päcke** /'pɛkə/ pile; (zusammengeschnürt) bundle; (Packung) pack

Pack[2] *das;* ∼**[e]s** (ugs. abwertend) rabble; riff-raff

Päckchen /'pɛkçən/ *das;* ∼**s,** ∼ (a) (kleines Paket) package; small parcel; (Postw.) small parcel (below a specified weight); (Bündel) packet; bundle; (b) ⇒ **Packung a**

Pack·eis *das* pack-ice

packen 1 *tr. V.* (a) pack; etw. in einen Koffer/ein Paket ∼: pack or put sth. in[to] a suitcase/put sth. in[to] a parcel; etw. aus etw. ∼: unpack sth. from sth.; sich/jmdn. ins Bett ∼ (ugs.) go to bed/put sb. to bed; (b) (fassen) grab [hold of]; seize; jmdn. am *od.* beim Kragen ∼: grab [hold of] or seize sb. by the collar; (c) (überkommen) Furcht/Angst *usw.* packte ihn he was seized with fear *etc.;* (d) (fesseln) enthral; ⟨*thriller, crime story, etc.*⟩ grip; ein ∼des Rennen a thrilling race; (e) (ugs.: schaffen) ein Examen ∼: manage to get through an exam (coll.); es ∼: make a go of it; ∼ wirs noch? are we going to make it?; einen Gegner ∼ (Sportjargon: besiegen) get the better of an opponent; (f) (ugs.: begreifen) get (coll.); (g) (salopp: weggehen) ∼ wir's? shall we push off? (coll.). **2** *itr. V.* (Koffer usw. ∼) pack. **3** *refl. V.* (ugs. veralt.) beat it (sl.); clear off (coll.)

Packen *der;* ∼**s,** ∼: pile; (zusammengeschnürt) bundle; (von Geldscheinen) wad

Pack-: ∼**esel** *der* (ugs.) pack-donkey; (fig.) pack-horse; ∼**papier** *das* [stout] wrapping paper

Packung *die;* ∼, ∼**en** (a) packet; pack (esp. Amer.); eine ∼ Zigaretten a packet or (Amer.) pack of cigarettes; (b) (Med., Kosmetik) pack

Pädagoge /pɛda'go:gə/ *der;* ∼**n,** ∼**n ▶ 85** (a) (Erzieher, Lehrer) teacher; (b) (Wissenschaftler) educationalist; educational theorist

Pädagogik *die;* ∼: [theory and methodology of] education

Pädagogin *die;* ∼, ∼**nen ▶ 85** ⇒ **Pädagoge**

pädagogisch 1 *Adj.* educational; ⟨*lecture, dissertation, etc.*⟩ on education; ⟨*training*⟩ in education; **Pädagogische Hochschule** College of Education. **2** *adv.* educationally ⟨*sound, wrong*⟩

Paddel /'padl/ *das;* ∼**s,** ∼: paddle

Paddel·boot *das* canoe

paddeln *itr. V.; mit sein; ohne Richtungsangabe auch mit haben* (a) (Paddelboot fahren) paddle; canoe; (als Sport) canoe; (b) (ugs.: schlecht schwimmen) dog-paddle

paffen 1 *tr. V.* puff at ⟨*pipe etc.*⟩; puff out ⟨*smoke*⟩. **2** *itr. V.* puff away

Page /'pa:ʒə/ *der;* ∼**n,** ∼**n ▶ 85** (Hotel∼) page; bellboy

Pagen·kopf *der* pageboy cut *or* style

Pager /'peɪdʒɐ/ *der;* ∼**s,** ∼: pager

Paket /pa'ke:t/ *das;* ∼**[e]s,** ∼**e** (a) pile; (zusammengeschnürt) bundle; (Eingepacktes, Post∼, Schachtel) parcel; (Packung) packet; pack (esp. Amer.); (b) (fig.: Gesamtheit) package

Paket-: ∼**annahme** *die* (a) *o. Pl.* acceptance of parcels; (b) (Stelle) parcels office; (Schalter) parcels counter; ∼**ausgabe** *die* (a) *o. Pl.* issue of parcels; (b) ⇒ ∼**annahme b;** ∼**dienst** *der* parcel service; ∼**karte** *die* parcel dispatch form; ∼**sendung** *die* parcel

Pakistan /'pa:kɪsta:n/ (*das);* ∼**s** Pakistan

Pakistaner *der;* ∼**s,** ∼, **Pakistani** /pakɪs'ta:ni/ *der;* ∼**[s],** ∼**[s]/die;** ∼, ∼**[s] ▶ 388]** Pakistani

Pakt /pakt/ *der;* ∼**[e]s,** ∼**e** pact; einen ∼ [ab]schließen make *or* conclude a pact

Palast /pa'last/ *der;* ∼**[e]s,** **Paläste** /pa'lɛstə/ palace

Palästina /palɛ'sti:na/ (*das);* ∼**s** Palestine

Palästinenser *der;* ∼**s,** ∼, **Palästinenserin** *die;* ∼, ∼**nen ▶ 388]** Palestinian

Palaver /pa'la:vɐ/ *das;* ∼**s,** ∼ (ugs. abwertend) palaver

palavern *itr. V.* (ugs. abwertend) palaver

Palette /pa'lɛtə/ *die;* ∼, ∼**n** (a) (Malerei) palette; (b) (bes. Werbespr.: Vielfalt) diverse range

paletti in alles ∼ (ugs.) everything's OK (coll.) *or* all right

Palme /'palmə/ *die;* ∼, ∼**n** palm[-tree]; jmdn. auf die ∼ bringen (ugs.) ⟨*person*⟩ rile sb. (coll.); ⟨*situation*⟩ make sb. wild

Palmen·wedel *der* palm frond

Palm-: ∼**kätzchen** *das* [willow] catkin ∼**sonntag** /*auch: ·'--*/ *der* (christl. Kirche) Palm Sunday; ∼**wedel** *der* palm frond

Pampe /'pampə/ *die;* ∼ (bes. nordd. u. md.) (a) (Matsch) mud; mire; (b) (Brei) mush

Pampelmuse /'pampl̩mu:ze/ *die;* ∼, ∼**n** grapefruit

Pamphlet /pam'fle:t/ *das;* ∼**[e]s,** ∼**e** (Streitschrift) polemical pamphlet; (Schmähschrift) defamatory pamphlet

pampig 1 *Adj.* (a) (ugs. abwertend: frech) insolent; (b) (bes. nordd., ostd.: breiig) mushy. **2** *adv.* (ugs. abwertend: frech) insolently

Panama /'panama/ (*das);* ∼**s** Panama

Panama·kanal *der; o. Pl.* Panama Canal

panieren *tr. V.* (Kochk.) etw. ∼: bread sth.; coat sth. with breadcrumbs

Panier·mehl *das* breadcrumbs *pl.*

Panik /'pa:nɪk/ *die;* ∼, ∼**en** panic; [eine] ∼ brach aus panic broke out; jmdn. in ∼ (*Akk.*) versetzen throw sb. into a state of panic; nur keine ∼! don't panic!

Panik·mache *die; o. Pl.* (abwertend) panic-mongering

panisch *Adj.* panic *attrib.* ⟨*fear, terror*⟩; panic-stricken ⟨*voice, flight*⟩; ∼**e** Angst vor etw. (*Dat.*) haben have a panic fear of sth.

Panne /'panə/ *die;* ∼, ∼**n** (a) (Auto∼) breakdown; (Reifen∼) puncture; flat [tyre]; ich hatte eine ∼ my car broke down/my car or I had a puncture; (b) (Betriebsstörung) breakdown; (c) (Missgeschick) slip-up; mishap; bei der Organisation gab es viele ∼**n** there were many organizational hitches

Pannen·dienst *der* breakdown service

Panorama /pano'ra:ma/ *das;* ∼**s, Panoramen** panorama

panschen /'panʃn̩/ **1** *tr. V.* (ugs. abwertend) water down; adulterate. **2** *itr. V.* (a) (ugs. abwertend: mischen) water down *or* adulterate the wine/beer *etc.;* (b) (ugs.: planschen) splash about

Panter, *Panther /'pantɐ/ *der;* ∼**s,** ∼: panther

Pantoffel /pan'tɔfl̩/ *der;* ∼**s,** ∼**n** (a) backless slipper; (b) (mit Absatz) mule; (c) (fig.) unterm ∼ stehen (ugs.) be henpecked

Pantoffel-: ∼**held** *der* (ugs. abwertend) henpecked husband; ∼**kino** *das* (ugs.) telly (coll.); ∼**tierchen** *das* (Biol.) slipper animalcule

Pantomime /panto'mi:mə/ *die;* ∼, ∼**n** mime

pantschen *usw.* /'pantʃn̩/ ⇒ **panschen** *usw.*

Panzer /'pantsɐ/ *der;* ∼**s,** ∼ (a) (Milit.) tank; (b) (Zool.) amour *no indef. art.;* (von Schildkröten, Krebsen) shell; (c) (hist.: Rüstung) armour *no indef. art.;* ein ∼: a suit of armour; (d) (Panzerung) armour-plating *or* -plate *no indef. art.;* (eines Reaktors) shielding

Panzer-: ∼**faust** *die* (Milit.) anti-tank rocket launcher; bazooka; ∼**glas** *das* bullet-proof glass; ∼**kreuzer** *der* (Marine hist.) armoured cruiser

panzern *tr. V.* armour[-plate]

Panzer-: ~**schrank** *der* safe; ~**wagen** *der* (Milit.) (a) ⇨ **Panzer a;** (b) (Waggon) armoured wagon

Papa /'papa, *geh.*, *veralt.* pa'pa:/ *der;* ~**s**, ~**s** (ugs.) daddy (coll.)

Papagei /papa'gai/ *der;* ~**en** *od.* ~**s**, ~**e[n]** parrot

Papeterie /papɛtə'ri:/ *die;* ~, ~**n** (schweiz.) stationer's

Papi /'papi/ *der;* ~**s**, ~**s** (ugs.) ⇨ **Papa**

Papier /pa'pi:ɐ̯/ *das;* ~**s**, ~**e** (a) paper; **ein Blatt** ~: a sheet of paper; **[nur] auf dem** ~ (fig.) [only] on paper; **etw. zu** ~ **bringen** get *or* put sth. down on paper; (b) *Pl.* (Ausweis[e]) [identity] papers; (c) (Finanzw.: Wert~) security

Papier-: ~**deutsch** *das* (abwertend) officialese; ~**fabrik** *die* paper mill; ~**geld** *das* paper money; ~**handtuch** *das* paper towel; ~**korb** *der* waste-paper basket; ~**kram** *der* (ugs. abwertend) [tedious] paperwork; ~**krieg** *der* (ugs. abwertend) tedious form-filling; (Korrespondenz) tiresome exchange of letters; ~**schlange** *die* [paper] streamer; ~**taschentuch** *das* paper handkerchief; ~**waren** *Pl.* stationery *sing.*

papp /pap/ *in* **ich kann nicht mehr** ~ **sagen** (ugs.) I'm full to bursting-point (coll.)

Papp-: ~**becher** *der* paper cup; ~**deckel** *der* cardboard

Pappe /'papə/ *die;* ~, ~**n** (a) (Karton) cardboard; (b) (ugs.: Brei) mush; **5 000 Mark sind nicht von** *od.* **aus** ~ (ugs.) 5,000 marks isn't chicken feed (coll.)

Pappel /'papl̩/ *die;* ~, ~**n** poplar

pappen (ugs.) **1** *tr. V.* stick (**an, auf** + *Akk.* on). **2** *itr. V.* (haften bleiben) stick (**an** + *Dat.* to); (klebrig sein) be sticky

Pappen-: ~**deckel** *der* cardboard; ~**stiel** *in* **das ist kein** ~**stiel** (ugs.) it's not chicken feed (coll.); **etw. für einen** ~**stiel kaufen/kriegen** (ugs.) buy/get sth. for a song *or* for next to nothing

papperlapapp /papɐla'pap/ *Interj.* rubbish

pappig *Adj.* (a) sticky; (b) (breiig) mushy

Papp-: ~**karton** *der* cardboard box; ~**teller** *der* paper *or* cardboard plate

Paprika /'paprika/ *der;* ~**s**, ~**[s]** (a) pepper; (b) *o. Pl.* (Gewürz) paprika

Paprika·schnitzel *das* cutlet with paprika sauce

Paps /paps/ *der;* ~, ~**e** (ugs.) dad (coll.)

Papst /pa:pst/ *der;* ~**[e]s**, **Päpste** /'pɛ:pstə/ pope; (fig. iron.) high priest

päpstlich /'pɛ:pstlɪç/ *Adj.* papal; (fig. abwertend) pontifical

Parabel /pa'ra:bl̩/ *die;* ~, ~**n** (a) (bes. Literaturw.) parable; (b) (Math.) parabola

Parabol-: ~**antenne** *die* parabolic antenna; ~**spiegel** *der* (Technik) parabolic mirror

Parade /pa'ra:də/ *die;* ~, ~**n** (a) parade; (b) (Ballspiele) save

Parade-: ~**beispiel** *das* perfect example; ~**marsch** *der* (Milit.) marching in parade-step; (Stechschritt) goose-stepping; ~**stück** *das* showpiece

Paradies /para'di:s/ *das;* ~**es**, ~**e** (auch fig.) paradise

paradiesisch /para'di:zɪʃ/ **1** *Adj.* (a) (Rel.) paradisiacal; (b) (herrlich) heavenly; magnificent ‹*view*›. **2** *adv.* (herrlich) ~ **ruhig gelegen** in a wonderfully peaceful situation; **dort ist es** ~ **schön** it's beautiful there, a real paradise

paradox /para'dɔks/ *Adj.* (a) paradoxical; (b) (ugs.: merkwürdig) odd; strange

Paradox *das;* ~**es**, ~**e** (bes. Philos., Rhet.) paradox

paradoxer·weise *Adv.* (a) paradoxically; (b) (ugs.: merkwürdigerweise) strangely *or* oddly enough

Paragraph /para'gra:f/ *der;* ~**en**, ~**en** section; (im Vertrag) clause

Paragraphen·reiter *der* (abwertend) (a) (Jurist) lawyer; (b) (Pedant) stickler for the rules

parallel /para'le:l/ **1** *Adj.* (auch fig.) parallel. **2** *adv.* ~ **verlaufen** (auch fig.) run parallel (**mit, zu** to); ~ **zu etw.** (fig.) in parallel with sth.

Parallele *die;* ~, ~**n** (a) (Math.) parallel [line]; **eine** ~ **zu etw. ziehen** draw a line parallel to sth.; (b) (fig.) parallel

Parallel·klasse *die* (Schulw.) parallel class

Parallelogramm /paralelo'gram/ *das;* ~**s**, ~**e** (Math.) parallelogram

Parallel-: ~**schaltung** *die* (Elektrot.) parallel connection; ~**schwung** *der* (Skisport) parallel swing; ~**straße** *die* street running parallel (**von** to)

Paranoia /para'nɔya/ *die;* ~ (Med.) paranoia

paranoid /parano'i:t/ *Adj.* (Med.) paranoid

Para·nuss, ***Para**nuß** *die* Brazil nut

Parasit /para'zi:t/ *der;* ~**en**, ~**en** (Biol., fig. abwertend) parasite

parasitär /parazi'tɛ:ɐ̯/ *Adj.* (Biol., fig. abwertend) parasitic

parat /pa'ra:t/ *Adj.* ready; **eine Ausrede/Antwort** ~ **haben** be ready with an excuse/answer; **ich habe kein passendes Beispiel** ~: I can't think of a suitable example

Pärchen /'pɛ:ɐ̯çən/ *das;* ~**s**, ~: pair; (Liebespaar) couple

Parcours /par'ku:ɐ̯/ *der;* ~ /...ɐ̯(s)/, ~ /...ɐ̯s/ course

Parfum /par'fœ:/, **Parfüm** /par'fy:m/ *das;* ~**s**, ~**s** perfume; scent

Parfümerie /parfymə'ri:/ *die;* ~, ~**en** perfumery

parfümieren *tr. V.* perfume; scent; **sich [viel zu stark]** ~: put [too much] perfume *or* scent on

parieren /pa'ri:rən/ *itr. V.* (ugs.) do what one is told; **aufs Wort** ~: jump to it (coll.)

Pariser /pa'ri:zɐ/ [▶490] **1** *indekl. Adj.* Parisian; Paris *attrib.;* **die** ~ **Metro** the Paris Metro. **2** *der;* ~**s**, ~ (a) (Einwohner) Parisian; (b) (ugs.: Kondom) French letter (coll.)

Pariserin *die;* ~, ~**nen** Parisian

Parität /pari'tɛ:t/ *die;* ~, ~**en** parity; equality

paritätisch **1** *Adj.* equal; ~**e Mitbestimmung** co-determination based on equal representation. **2** *adv.* equally

Park /park/ *der;* ~**s**, ~**s** park; (Schloss~ usw.) grounds *pl.*

Parka *der;* ~**s**, ~**s** parka

Park·anlage *die* park; (bei Schlössern usw.) grounds *pl.*

parken **1** *tr. V.* park. **2** *itr. V.* (a) park; (b) (stehen) be parked

Parkett /par'kɛt/ *das;* ~**[e]s**, ~**e** (a) (Bodenbelag) parquet floor; ~ **legen** lay parquet flooring; **sich auf jedem** ~ **bewegen können** (fig.) be able to move in any circles; (b) (Theater) [front] stalls *pl.;* parquet (Amer.); (c) *in* **etw. aufs** ~ **legen** (ugs.) dance sth.; *s. auch* **Sohle a**

Parkett·platz *der* seat in the [front] stalls

Park-: ~**gebühr** *die* parking-fee; ~**haus** *das* multistorey car park; ~**kralle** *die* wheel clamp; ~**landschaft** *die* parkland; ~**leitsystem** *das* (Verkehrsw.) traffic-control system providing information on the location of available parking spaces; ~**lücke** *die* parking space; ~**platz** *der* (a) car park; parking lot (Amer.); (b) (für ein einzelnes Fahrzeug) parking space; place to park; ~**scheibe** *die* parking-disc; ~**schein** *der* car park ticket; ~**uhr** *die* parking meter; ~**verbot** *das* ban on parking; **hier ist** ~**verbot** you are not allowed to park here; **im** ~**verbot stehen** be parked illegally

Parlament /parla'mɛnt/ *das;* ~**[e]s**, ~**e** parliament; (ein bestimmtes) Parliament *no def. art.*

Parlamentarier /parlamɛn'ta:riɐ/ *der;* ~**s**, ~, **Parlamentarierin** *die;* ~, ~**nen** member of parliament; (in Großbritannien) Member of Parliament; MP; (in den Vereinigten Staaten) Congressman/Congresswoman

parlamentarisch *Adj.; nicht präd.* parliamentary

Parlaments-: ~**ausschuss**, ***~**ausschuß** *der* parliamentary committee; ~**gebäude** *das* parliament building[s *pl.*]; ~**sitzung** *die* sitting [of parliament]; ~**wahl** *die* parliamentary election

Parmesan /parme'za:n/ *der;* ~**[s]** Parmesan

Parodie /paro'di:/ *die;* ~, ~**n** parody; **eine** ~ **auf etw./jmdn.** a parody of sth./take-off of sb.

parodieren *tr. V.* parody ‹*literary work, manner*›; take off ‹*person*›; satirize ‹*event*›

Parole /pa'ro:lə/ *die;* ~, ~n (a) (Wahlspruch) motto; (Schlagwort) slogan; (b) (bes. Milit.: Kennwort) password

Paroli /pa'ro:li/ *in:* **jmdm./einer Sache** ~ **bieten** give sb. as good as one gets/pit oneself against sth.

Part /part/ *der;* ~s, ~s *od.* ~e (a) (Musik: Stimme, Partie) part; (b) (Theater, Film; Rolle) part; role; **den [entscheidenden]** ~ **bei etw.** (*Dat.*) **spielen** (auch fig.) play the [crucial] part *or* role in sth.

Partei /par'tai/ *die;* ~, ~en (a) (Politik) party; **in** *od.* **bei der** ~ **sein** be a party member; **die** ~ **wechseln** change parties; (b) (Rechtsw.) party; (c) (Gruppe, Mannschaft) side; **es mit beiden** ~**en halten** run with the hare and hunt with the hounds (fig.); **jmds.** *od.* **für jmdn./für etw.** ~ **ergreifen** *od.* **nehmen** side with sb./take a stand for sth.; (d) (Miets~) tenant; (mehrere Personen) tenants *pl.*

partei-, Partei-: ~**buch** *das* party membership book; ~**chef** *der* party leader; ~**führung** *die* party leadership; ~**genosse** *der* (hist.: Mitglied der NSDAP) party member; (einer Arbeiterpartei) ~**genosse X** Comrade X; ~**intern** 1 *Adj.; nicht präd.* internal [party] ⟨*conflict, matters, material, etc.*⟩; 2 *adv.* within the party

parteiisch 1 *Adj.* biased. 2 *adv.* in a biased manner

partei-, Partei-: ~**linie** *die* party line; ~**los** *Adj.* (Politik) independent ⟨*MP*⟩; **er ist** ~**los** he is not attached to *or* aligned with any party; ~**lose** *der/die; adj. Dekl.* (Politik) independent; person not attached to a party; ~**mitglied** *das* party member; ~**nahme** *die;* ~, ~n partisanship; taking sides *no art.;* ~**politik** *die* party politics *sing.;* ~**politisch** 1 *Adj.* party political; 2 *adv.* from a party political point of view; ~**programm** *das* party manifesto *or* programme; ~**tag** *der* party conference *or* (Amer.) convention; ~**vorsitzende** *der/die* party leader; ~**vorstand** *der* party executive

Parterre *das;* ~s, ~s (a) (Erdgeschoss) ground floor; first floor (Amer.); **im** ~: on the ground *or* (Amer.) first floor; (b) (Theater veralt.) stalls *pl.* (Brit.); parterre (Amer.); parquet (Amer.)

Partie /par'ti:/ *die;* ~, ~n (a) (Teil) part; (b) (Spiel, Sport: Runde) game; (Golf) round; **eine** ~ **Schach spielen** play a game of chess; (c) (Musik) part; (d) (Ehepartner) **eine gute** ~ [**für jmdn.**] **sein** be a good match [for sb.]; **sie hat eine gute/glänzende** ~ **gemacht** she has married well/extremely well; (e) **mit von der** ~ **sein** join in; (bei einer Reise usw.) go along too; (f) (Kaufmannsspr.) batch

partiell /par'tsiɛl/ 1 *Adj.* partial. 2 *adv.* partially

Partikel[1] /par'ti:kl/ *die;* ~, ~n (Sprachw.) particle

Partikel[2] *das;* ~s, ~ *od. die;* ~, ~n (bes. Physik, Chemie, Technik) particle

Partisan /parti'za:n/ *der;* ~s *od.* ~en, ~en guerrilla; (gegen Besatzungstruppen im Krieg) partisan

Partisanen·krieg *der* guerrilla war; (Kriegführung) guerrilla warfare

Partisanin *die;* ~, ~nen ⇒ **Partisan**

Partitur /parti'tu:ɐ/ *die;* ~, ~en (Musik) score

Partizip /parti'tsi:p/ *das;* ~s, ~ien /-'tsi:pjən/ (Sprachw.) participle; **das 1.** ~ *od.* ~ **Präsens/das 2.** ~ *od.* ~ **Perfekt** the present/past participle

Partner /'partnɐ/ *der;* ~s, ~, **Partnerin** *die;* ~, ~nen partner; (Bündnis~) ally; (im Film/Theater) co-star

Partnerschaft *die;* ~, ~en partnership

partnerschaftlich 1 *Adj.* ⟨*cooperation etc.*⟩ on a partnership basis. 2 *adv.* in a spirit of partnership; (als Partnerschaft) as a partnership

Partner·stadt *die* twin town (Brit.); sister city *or* town (Amer.)

partout /par'tu:/ *Adv.* (ugs.) at all costs

Party /'pa:ɐti/ *die;* ~, ~s *od.* **Parties** party; **eine** ~ [**zu ihrem bestandenen Examen/zu seinem Geburtstag**] **geben** give a party [to celebrate her passing the exam/for his birthday]; **auf** *od.* **bei** ~**s** at parties

Pascal /pas'kal/ *das;* ~s, ~: pascal

Pasch /paʃ/ *der;* ~[e]s, ~e *u.* **Päsche** (a) (beim Würfelspiel) **einen** ~ **werfen** (bei zwei Würfeln) throw doubles *pl.;* (bei drei Würfeln) throw triplets; (b) (beim Domino) double

Pascha /'paʃa/ *der;* ~s, ~s (a) (hist.) pasha; (b) (fig. abwertend) male chauvinist; **den** ~ **spielen** act the lord and master

Pass, *Paß /pas/ *der;* **Passes, Pässe** /'pɛsə/ (a) (Reise~) passport; (b) (Gebirgs~) pass; (c) (Ballspiele) pass

passabel /pa'sa:bl/ 1 *Adj.* reasonable; tolerable; fair ⟨*report*⟩; presentable ⟨*appearance*⟩. 2 *adv.* reasonably *or* tolerably well

Passage /pa'sa:ʒə/ *die;* ~, ~n (a) (Ladenstraße) [shopping] arcade; (b) (Abschnitt) (im Text) passage; (im Film) sequence; (Musik) [virtuoso] passage

Passagier /pasa'ʒi:ɐ/ *der;* ~s, ~e passenger; **blinder** ~: stowaway

Passagier-: ~**dampfer** *der* passenger steamer; ~**flugzeug** *das* passenger aircraft

Pass·amt, *Paß·amt *das* passport office

Passant /pa'sant/ *der;* ~en, ~en, **Passantin** *die;* ~, ~nen passer-by

Pass·bild, *Paß·bild *das* passport photograph

*passé, passee /pa'se:/ *Adj.; nicht attr.* (ugs.) passé; out of date

passen 1 *itr. V.* (a) (die richtige Größe/Form haben) fit; **etw. passt [jmdm.] gut/nicht** sth. fits [sb.] well/does not fit [sb.]; **der Schlüssel passt nicht ins Schloss** the key does not fit the lock; (b) (geeignet sein) be suitable, be appropriate (**auf** + *Akk.,* **zu** for); (harmonieren) ⟨*colour etc.*⟩ match; **dieses Bild passt besser in die Diele** this picture goes better in the hall; **zu etw./jmdm.** ~: go well with sth./be well suited to sb.; **zueinander** ~: ⟨*things*⟩ go well together; ⟨*two people*⟩ be suited to each other; **dieses Benehmen passt zu ihm/passt nicht zu ihm** (ugs.) that's just like him (coll.) /that's not like him; **diese Beschreibung passt [genau] auf sie** this description fits her [exactly]; (c) (genehm sein) **jmdm.** ~ ⟨*time*⟩ be convenient for sb., suit sb.; **jmdm. passt etw. nicht** sth. is inconvenient for sb.; **das könnte dir so** ~! (ugs.) you'd just love that, wouldn't you?; (d) (Kartenspiel) pass; **bei dieser Frage muss ich** ~ (fig.) I'll have to pass on that question. 2 *tr.* (*auch itr.*) *V.* (Ballspiele) pass ⟨*ball*⟩

passend *Adj.* (a) (geeignet) suitable ⟨*dress, present, etc.*⟩; appropriate, right ⟨*words, expression*⟩; right ⟨*moment*⟩; **bei einer** ~**en Gelegenheit** at an opportune moment; (b) (harmonierend) matching ⟨*shoes etc.*⟩; **die zum Kleid** ~**en Schuhe** the shoes to go with *or* match the dress

Pass·foto, *Paß·foto *das* ⇒ ~**bild**

passierbar *Adj.* passable ⟨*road*⟩; navigable ⟨*river*⟩

passieren 1 *tr. V.* pass; **die Grenze** ~: cross the border; **die Zensur** ~ (fig.) be passed by the censor; get past the censor. 2 *itr. V.; mit sein* happen; **es ist ein Unglück/etwas Schreckliches passiert** there has been an accident/something dreadful has happened; **jmdm. ist etwas/nichts passiert** something/nothing happened to sb.; (jmd. ist verletzt/nicht verletzt) sb. was/was not hurt

Passier·schein *der* pass; permit

Passion /pa'sio:n/ *die;* ~, ~en (a) passion; (b) *o. Pl.* (christl. Rel., Kunst, Musik) Passion

passioniert *Adj.; nicht präd.* ardent, passionate ⟨*collector, card-player, huntsman*⟩

passiv /'pasi:f/ 1 *Adj.* passive; non-active ⟨*member*⟩; ~**e Handelsbilanz** balance of trade deficit; *s. auch* **Bestechung.** 2 *adv.* passively; **sich [bei** *od.* **in etw.** (*Dat.*)] ~ **verhalten** take a passive stance [in sth.]; take no active part [in sth.]

Passiv *das;* ~s, ~e (Sprachw.) passive

Passiva /pa'si:va/ *Pl.* (Wirtsch.) liabilities

Passivität /pasivi'tɛ:t/ *die;* ~: passivity

Passiv-: ~**posten** *der* (Kaufmannsspr.) liability; ~**saldo** *der* (Kaufmannsspr.) debit balance; ~**seite** *die* (Kaufmannsspr.) liabilities side

Pass-, *Paß-: ~**kontrolle** *die* (a) (das Kontrollieren) passport inspection *or* check; (b) (Stelle) passport control; ~**straße** *die* [mountain] pass road; ~**wort** *das* (DV) password

Paste /'pastə/ *die;* ~, ~n (auch Pharm.) paste

Pastell /pas'tɛl/ *das;* ~[e]s, ~e (a) (Farbton) pastel shade; (b) *o. Pl.* (Maltechnik) pastel *no art.*

pastell-, Pastell-: ~**farbe** *die* pastel colour; ~**farben** *Adj.* pastel-coloured; ~**ton** *der* pastel shade

Pastete /pas'te:tə/ *die;* ~, ~**n** (a) (gefüllte ~) vol-au-vent; (b) (in einer Schüssel o. ä. gegart) pâté; (in einer Hülle aus Teig gebacken) pie

pasteurisieren /pastøri'zi:rən/ *tr. V.* pasteurize

Pastille /pas'tɪlə/ *die;* ~, ~**n** pastille

Pastor /'pastɔr/ *der;* ~**s**, ~**en** ▶ 34 pastor

pastoral /pasto'ra:l/ *Adj.* (a) (seelsorgerlich) pastoral; (b) (salbungsvoll) unctuous; (c) (idyllisch) pastoral ⟨*literature*⟩

Pastorin *die;* ~, ~**nen** pastor

Pate /'pa:tə/ *der;* ~**n**, ~**n** (Taufzeuge) godparent; (Patenonkel) godfather; (Patin) godmother; **bei jmdm.** ~ **stehen** act as *or* be godfather/godmother to sb.; **bei etw.** ~ **stehen** (fig.) be [the influence/influences] behind sth.; (Vorbild sein) act as the model for sth.

Paten-: ~**kind** *das* godchild; ~**onkel** *der* godfather

Patenschaft *die;* ~, ~**en** (christl. Rel.) godparenthood

Paten·stadt *die* ⇒ **Partnerstadt**

patent /pa'tɛnt/ (ugs.) **1** *Adj.* (a) (tüchtig) capable; (b) (zweckmäßig) ingenious ⟨*device, method, idea*⟩; clever ⟨*slogan etc.*⟩. **2** *adv.* ingeniously; cleverly

Patent *das;* ~[e]s, ~e (a) (Schutz) patent; **ein** ~ **auf etw.** (Akk.) **haben**/**etw. zum** *od.* **als** ~ **anmelden** have/apply for a patent for sth.; (b) (Erfindung) [patented] invention; (c) (Ernennungsurkunde) certificate [of appointment]; (eines Kapitäns) master's certificate; (eines Offiziers) commission

Paten·tante *die* ⇒ **Patin**

patentieren *tr. V.* patent; **jmdm. etw.** ~: grant sb. a patent for sth.; **sich** (Dat.) **eine Erfindung** ~ **lassen** have an invention patented

Patent-: ~**inhaber** *der* patentee; ~**lösung** *die* patent remedy (**für, zu** for); ~**schutz** *der* patent protection

Pater /'pa:tə/ *der;* ~**s**, ~ *od.* **Patres** /'pa:tre:s/ (kath. Kirche) Father

Paternoster /pa:tə'nɔstə/ *der;* ~**s**, ~ (Aufzug) paternoster [lift]

pathetisch /pa'te:tɪʃ/ **1** *Adj.* emotional, impassioned ⟨*speech, manner*⟩; melodramatic ⟨*gesture*⟩; emotive ⟨*style*⟩; pompous ⟨*voice*⟩. **2** *adv.* emotionally; with much emotion; (dramatisch) [melo]dramatically

pathologisch **1** *Adj.* (Med.; auch fig.) pathological. **2** *adv.* pathologically

Pathos /'pa:tɔs/ *das;* ~ emotionalism; **ein unechtes/hohles** ~: false/empty pathos; **etw. mit** ~ **vortragen** recite sth. with much feeling

Patient /pa'tsi̯ɛnt/ *der;* ~**en**, ~**en**, **Patientin** *die;* ~, ~**nen** ▶ 329 patient

Patin *die;* ~, ~**nen** godmother

Patriarch /patri'arç/ *der;* ~**en**, ~**en** patriarch

patriarchalisch **1** *Adj.* patriarchal; (fig.: autoritär) authoritarian. **2** *adv.* in a patriarchal *or* (fig.) authoritarian manner

Patriot /patri'o:t/ *der;* ~**en**, ~**en**, **Patriotin** *die;* ~, ~**nen** patriot

patriotisch **1** *Adj.* patriotic. **2** *adv.* patriotically

Patriotismus *der;* ~: patriotism *usu. no def. art.*

Patron /pa'tro:n/ *der;* ~**s**, ~**e** (a) (Heiliger) patron saint; (b) (Stifter einer Kirche) patron; founder; (c) (ugs.: Kerl) type (coll.)

Patrone /pa'tro:nə/ *die;* ~, ~**n** cartridge

Patronen-: ~**gurt** *der*, ~**gürtel** *der* cartridge belt; (über der Schulter getragen) bandoleer; ~**hülse** *die* cartridge case

Patronin *die;* ~, ~**nen** (Schutzheilige) patron saint

Patrouille /pa'trʊljə/ *die;* ~, ~**n** patrol

patrouillieren /patrʊl'ji:rən/ *itr. V.; auch mit sein* be on patrol; **durch die Straßen** ~: patrol the streets

Patsche /'patʃə/ *die;* ~, ~**n** (a) (ugs.) ⇒ **Klemme** b; (b) (ugs.: Hand) paw (coll.)

patschen *itr. V.* (ugs.) (a) (klatschen) slap; **sich** (Dat.) **auf die Schenkel** ~: slap one's thighs; (b) *mit sein* (~d gehen/fallen) splash

---

**alte Schreibung (vgl. Hinweise auf S. xvi–xvii)

patsch-, Patsch-: ~**hand** *die;* ~**händchen** *das* (fam.) [little] hand; handy-pandy (child lang.); ~**nass**, ***~**naß** *Adj.* (ugs.) sopping wet; ~**nass geschwitzt** soaked in sweat

Patt *das;* ~**s**, ~**s** (Schach; auch fig.) stalemate

patzen /'patsn/ *itr. V.* (ugs.) slip up (coll.); boob (Brit. sl.)

Patzer *der;* ~**s**, ~ (ugs.) slip (coll.); boob (Brit. sl.)

patzig (ugs. abwertend) **1** *Adj.* snotty (coll.); (frech) cheeky. **2** *adv.* snottily (coll.); (frech) cheekily

Pauke /'paukə/ *die;* ~, ~**n** kettledrum; **die** ~ **schlagen** beat the drum/drums; **auf die** ~ **hauen** (ugs.) (feiern) paint the town red (fig. coll.); (großtun) blow one's own trumpet; **mit** ~**n und Trompeten durchfallen** (ugs.) ⟨*candidate*⟩ fail resoundingly; ⟨*broadcast, film, etc.*⟩ be a resounding failure

pauken **1** *tr. V.* (ugs.) swot up (Brit. sl.), bone up on (Amer. coll.) ⟨*facts, figures, etc.*⟩. **2** *itr. V.* (ugs.) swot (Brit. sl.); (fürs Examen) cram (coll.)

Pauken·schlag *der* (a) drumbeat; (b) (fig. Eklat) sensation; bombshell

Pauker *der;* ~**s**, ~ (Schülerspr.) teacher; teach (school sl.)

Paukerei *die;* ~: (ugs. abwertend) swotting (Brit. sl.); boning up (Amer. coll.); (fürs Examen) cramming

Paus·backen *Pl.* (fam.) chubby cheeks

pausbäckig /'pausbɛkɪç/ *Adj.* chubby-cheeked; chubbyfaced; chubby ⟨*face*⟩

pauschal /pau'ʃa:l/ **1** *Adj.* (a) all-inclusive ⟨*price, settlement*⟩; (b) (verallgemeinernd) sweeping ⟨*judgement, criticism, statement*⟩; indiscriminate ⟨*prejudice*⟩; wholesale ⟨*discrimination*⟩. **2** *adv.* (a) ⟨*cost*⟩ overall, all in all; ⟨*pay*⟩ in a lump sum; (b) (verallgemeinernd) wholesale

Pauschale *die;* ~, ~**n** *od. das;* ~**s**, **Pauschalien** /-'ʃa:li̯ən/ flat-rate payment

Pauschal-: ~**gebühr** *die* flat-rate [charge]; ~**preis** *der* (Einheitspreis) flat rate; (Inklusivpreis) inclusive *or* all-in price; ~**reise** *die* package holiday; (mit mehreren Reisezielen) package tour; ~**summe** *die* lump sum

Pause¹ /'pauzə/ *die;* ~, ~**n** (a) (Unterbrechung) break; (Ruhe~) rest; (Theater) interval (Brit.); intermission (Amer.); (Kino) intermission; (Sport) half-time interval; **kleine/große** ~: (Schule) short/[long] break; **[eine]** ~ **machen**/**eine** ~ **einlegen** take *or* have a break; (zum Ausruhen) have a rest; (b) (in der Unterhaltung o. ä.) pause; (verlegenes Schweigen) silence; (c) (Musik) rest

Pause² *die;* ~, ~**n** (Kopie) tracing; (Licht~) Photostat (Brit. ℗)

pausen *tr. V.* trace; (eine Lichtpause machen) Photostat (Brit. ℗)

Pausen·brot *das* sandwich (eaten during break)

pausen·los 1 *Adj.; nicht präd.;* incessant ⟨*noise, moaning, questioning*⟩; continous, uninterrupted ⟨*work, operation*⟩. **2** *adv.* incessantly; ceaselessly; ⟨*work*⟩ nonstop

pausieren *itr. V.* (a) (innehalten) pause; (b) (aussetzen) have *or* take a rest

Paus·papier *das* tracing paper; (Kohlepapier) carbon paper

Pavian /'pa:vi̯a:n/ *der;* ~**s**, ~**e** baboon

Pavillon /'pavɪljɔn/ *der;* ~**s**, ~**s** (Archit.) pavilion

Paycard /'peɪka:d/ *die;* ~, ~**s** [charge] card

Pazifik /pa'tsi:fɪk/ *der;* ~**s** Pacific

pazifisch *Adj.* Pacific ⟨*area*⟩; **der Pazifische Ozean** the Pacific Ocean

Pazifismus *der;* ~: pacifism *no art.*

Pazifist *der;* ~**en**, ~**en**, **Pazifistin** *die;* ~, ~**nen** pacifist

pazifistisch **1** *Adj.* pacifist. **2** *adv.* in a pacifist way

PDS /pe:de:'|ɛs/ *die;* ~ *Abk.* **Partei des Demokratischen Sozialismus** Party of Democratic Socialism

Pech /pɛç/ *das;* ~[e]s, ~e (a) pitch; **zusammenhalten wie** ~ **und Schwefel** (ugs.) be inseparable; ⟨*friends*⟩ be as thick as thieves (coll.); (b) *o. Pl.* (Missgeschick) bad luck; **großes/unerhörtes** ~: rotten (coll.) / (coll.) terrible luck; **bei** *od.* **mit etw./ mit jmdm.** ~ **haben** have bad luck with sth./sb.; be unlucky with sth./sb.; **dein** ∼, **wenn du nicht aufpasst** (ugs.) that's just your hard luck (coll.) if you don't pay attention

pẹch-, Pẹch-: ∼**schwarz** *Adj.* (ugs.) ⇒ **raben-schwarz;** ∼**strähne** *die* run of bad luck; ∼**vogel** *der* unlucky devil (coll.); (Opfer vieler Unfälle) walking disaster area (coll.)

Pedal /pe'daːl/ *das;* ∼**s,** ∼**e** pedal; [**kräftig**] **in die** ∼**e treten** (beim Fahrrad) pedal [really] hard

Pedale *die;* ∼, ∼**n** (landsch.) ⇒ **Pedal**

Pedant /pe'dant/ *der;* ∼**en,** ∼**en, Pedạntin,** *die;* ∼, ∼**nen** pedant

pedạntisch 1 *Adj.* pedantic. **2** *adv.* pedantically

Pediküre /pedi'kyːrə/ *die;* ∼, ∼**n** (a) *o. Pl.;* ⇒ **Fuß-pflege;** (b) (Berufsbez.) chiropodist

pediküren *tr. V.* pedicure ⟨*feet, nails*⟩

Pegel /'peːgl̩/ *der;* ∼**s,** ∼ (a) (Gerät) water-level indicator; (für die Gezeiten am Meer) tide-gauge; (b) (Wasserstand) waterlevel

Pegel·stand *der* water level

peilen /'pailən/ *tr. V.* (a) take a bearing on ⟨*transmitter, fixed point*⟩; (b) (Wassertiefe messen) sound ⟨*depth*⟩; take soundings in ⟨*bay etc.*⟩

Pein /pain/ *die;* ∼ (geh.) torment; **jmdm.** [**viel** *od.* **große**] ∼ **bereiten** cause sb. [much] anguish

peinigen /'painign̩/ *tr. V.* (geh.) torment; (foltern) torture; **von Durst/Kälte gepeinigt werden** suffer agonies from thirst/cold

peinlich 1 *Adj.* (a) embarrassing; awkward ⟨*question, position, pause*⟩; **es ist mir sehr** ∼: I feel very bad (coll.) *or* embarrassed about it; (b) *nicht präd.* (äußerst genau) meticulous; scrupulous. **2** *adv.* (a) unpleasantly ⟨*surprised*⟩; [**von etw.**] ∼ **berührt sein** be painfully embarrassed [by sth.]; (b) (überaus [genau]) scrupulously; meticulously

Peinlichkeit *die;* ∼ (a) embarrassment; **die** ∼ **der Situation** the awkwardness of the situation; (b) (Genauigkeit) scrupulousness; meticulousness

Peitsche /'paitʃə/ *die;* ∼, ∼**n** whip; **er knallte mit der** ∼: he cracked the whip

peitschen 1 *tr. V.* whip; (fig.) ⟨*storm, waves, rain*⟩ lash. **2** *itr. V.; mit sein* ⟨*rain*⟩ lash (**an, gegen** + *Akk.* against, **in** + *Akk.* into); ⟨*shot*⟩ ring out

Pekinese /peki'neːzə/ *der;* ∼**n,** ∼**n** Pekinese

Pelikan /'peːlikaːn/ *der;* ∼**s,** ∼**e** pelican

Pelle /'pɛlə/ *die;* ∼, ∼**n** (bes. nordd.) skin; (abgeschält) peel; *s. auch* **rücken 2 a; sitzen a**

pẹllen (bes. nordd.) **1** *tr. V.* peel ⟨*potato, egg, etc.*⟩. **2** *refl. V.* ⟨*person, skin*⟩ peel

Pẹll·kartoffel *die* potato boiled in its skin

Pelz /pɛlts/ *der;* ∼**es,** ∼**e** (a) fur; coat; (des toten Tieres) skin; pelt; (b) *o. Pl.* (gegerbt; als Material) fur; **mit** ∼ **gefüttert** fur-lined; (c) fur; (∼mantel) fur coat; (d) (ugs.: Haut) **sich** (*Dat.*) **die Sonne auf den** ∼ **brennen lassen** soak up the sun; *s. auch* **rücken 2 a; sitzen a**

pẹlzig *Adj.* (a) furry; downy ⟨*peach*⟩; (b) (bes. westd.: mehlig) mealy ⟨*apple*⟩; (holzig) woody ⟨*radish*⟩; (c) (belegt) furred, coated ⟨*tongue, mouth*⟩

Pẹlz-: ∼**jacke** *die* fur jacket; ∼**kragen** *der* fur collar; ∼**mantel** *der* fur coat; ∼**mütze** *die* fur hat

Pendel /'pɛndl̩/ *das;* ∼**s,** ∼ pendulum

pẹndeln *itr. V.* (a) (hin u. her schwingen) swing [to and fro] (**an** + *Dat.* by); (mit weniger Bewegung) dangle; (b) *mit sein* (hin- u. herfahren) **zwischen X und Y** ∼ ⟨*bus, ferry, etc.*⟩ operate a shuttle service between X and Y; ⟨*person*⟩ commute between X and Y

Pẹndel-: ∼**tür** *die* swing-door; ∼**uhr** *die* pendulum clock; ∼**verkehr** *der* (a) (Berufsverkehr) commuter traffic; (b) (mit Pendelzug o. ä.) shuttle service

penetrant /pene'trant/ (abwertend) **1** *Adj.* (a) (durchdringend) penetrating, pungent ⟨*smell, taste*⟩; overpowering ⟨*stink, perfume*⟩; (b) (aufdringlich) pushing, (coll.) pushy ⟨*person*⟩; overbearing ⟨*tone, manner*⟩; aggressive, pointed ⟨*question*⟩. **2** *adv.* (a) (durchdringend) overpoweringly; **es riecht** ∼ **nach** …: there is an overpowering smell of …; (b) (aufdringlich) overbearingly; in an overbearing manner

peng /pɛŋ/ *Interj.* bang

penibel /pe'niːbl̩/ **1** *Adj.* over-meticulous ⟨*person*⟩; (pedantisch) pedantic. **2** *adv.* painstakingly; over-meticulously ⟨*dressed*⟩

Penis /'peːnɪs/ *der;* ∼, ∼**se** *od.* **Penes** /'peːneːs/ ▶ 326 | penis

Penizillin /penitsɪ'liːn/ *das;* ∼**s,** ∼**e** penicillin

Pennäler /pɛ'nɛːlɐ/ *der;* ∼**s,** ∼**s** (ugs.) [secondary] schoolboy

Pennälerin *die;* ∼, ∼**nen** (ugs.) [secondary] schoolgirl

Penn·bruder *der* (ugs. abwertend) tramp (Brit.); hobo (Amer.)

Penne /'pɛnə/ *die;* ∼, ∼**n** [secondary] school; swot-shop (Brit. sl.)

pẹnnen *itr. V.* (salopp) (a) (schlafen) kip (Brit. coll.); (b) (fig.: nicht aufpassen) be half asleep; (c) (koitieren) **mit jmdm.** ∼: sleep with sb.

Pẹnner *der;* ∼**s,** ∼, **Pẹnnerin** *die;* ∼, ∼**nen** (salopp abwertend) (Stadtstreicher) tramp (Brit.) hobo (Amer.)

Pension /pãˈzi̯oːn/ *die;* ∼, ∼**en** (a) *o. Pl.* (Ruhestand) [**vor-zeitig**] **in** ∼ **gehen** retire [early]; **in** ∼ **sein** be retired *or* in retirement; (b) (Ruhegehalt) [retirement] pension; (c) (Haus für [Ferien]gäste) guest house; (auf dem Kontinent) pension; (d) *o. Pl.* (Unterkunft u. Verpflegung) board

Pensionär /pãˈzi̯oːnɛːɐ̯/ *der;* ∼**s,** ∼**e, Pensionärin** *die;* ∼, ∼**nen** retired civil servant; (ugs.: Rentner) [old-age] pensioner

Pensionat /pãˈzi̯oˈnaːt/ *das;* ∼[**e**]**s,** ∼**e** (veralt.) boarding school (esp. for girls)

pensionieren *tr. V.* pension off; retire; **sich** [**vorzeitig**] ∼ **lassen** retire [early]; take [early] retirement

Pensionierung *die;* ∼, ∼**en** retirement

pensions-, Pensions-: ∼**alter** *das* retirement age; ∼**anspruch** *der* pension entitlement; ∼**berechtigt** *Adj.* entitled to a pension *postpos.;* ∼**reif** *Adj.* (ugs.) ripe for retirement *pred.*

Pensum /'pɛnzʊm/ *das;* ∼**s, Pẹnsen** (a) (Arbeit) amount of work; work quota; (b) (Päd. veralt.: Lehrstoff) syllabus

Pep /pɛp/ *der;* ∼[**s**] (ugs.) pep (sl.); zip; ∼ **haben** be dynamic *or* full of zip

Peperoni /pepeˈroːni/ *die;* ∼, ∼: chilli

per /pɛr/ *Präp. mit Akk.* (a) (mittels) by; ∼ **Adresse X** care of X; c/o X; (b) (Kaufmannsspr.: [bis] zum) by; (am) on; ∼ **sofort** immediately; as of now; (c) (Kaufmannsspr.: pro) per; **etw.** ∼ **Stück verkaufen** sell sth. by the piece *or* separately

perfekt /pɛr'fɛkt/ **1** *Adj.* (a) (hervorragend) outstanding; first-rate; (vollkommen) perfect ⟨*crime, host*⟩; faultless ⟨*English, French, etc.*⟩; (b) *nicht attr.* (ugs.: abgeschlossen) finalized; concluded; ∼ **sein/werden** ⟨*contract, deal*⟩ be concluded *or* finalized; ⟨*scandal, defeat*⟩ be complete. **2** *adv.* (a) (hervorragend) outstandingly well; (vollkommen) ⟨*fit, work, etc.*⟩ perfectly; (b) (ugs.: vollständig) good and proper (coll.)

Perfekt /'pɛrfɛkt/ *das;* ∼**s,** ∼**e** (Sprachw.) perfect [tense]

Perfektion /pɛrfɛk'tsi̯oːn/ *die;* ∼: perfection; **hand-werkliche/technische** ∼: mastery of a technical/technical mastery

Perfektionismus *der;* ∼: perfectionism

perforieren *tr. V.* (Technik, Med.) perforate

Pergament /pɛrga'mɛnt/ *das;* ∼[**e**]**s,** ∼**e** parchment

Pergamẹnt·papier *das* greaseproof paper

Periode /pe'ri̯oːdə/ *die;* ∼, ∼**n** (a) (auch Chemie, Physik, Technik, Astron., Met., Sprachw., Musik) period; (Geol.) era; (b) (Math.) repetend; period; **3,3** ∼: 3.3 recurring

periodisch 1 *Adj.* regular; ⟨*meeting, statement of account*⟩ at regular intervals; (Chemie) periodic ⟨*system*⟩. **2** *adv.* regularly; at regular intervals

peripher /peri'feːɐ̯/ **1** *Adj.* peripheral. **2** *adv.* peripherally

Peripherie /perife'riː/ *die;* ∼, ∼**n** periphery; (einer Stadt) outskirts *pl.;* fringe; (Geom.: Begrenzungslinie) circumference

Perle /'pɛrlə/ *die;* ∼, ∼**n** (a) (auch fig.) pearl; ∼**n vor die Säue werfen** (fig. ugs.) cast pearls before swine (b) (aus Holz, Glas o. ä.) bead; (Bläschen beim Sekt usw.) bubble; (c) (ugs. scherzh.: Hausgehilfin) [invaluable] home help

perlen *itr. V.* (a) *auch mit sein* **auf etw.** (*Dat.*) ~: form pearls on sth.; (b) *mit sein* **von etw.** ~: ‹dew, sweat› trickle *or* drip from sth.; (c) (Bläschen bilden) ‹champagne *etc.*› sparkle, bubble

Perlen-: ~**fischer** *der* pearl-fisher; ~**kette** *die* string of pearls; pearl necklace; (mit Holzperlen usw.) string of beads; bead necklace

Perl-: ~**huhn** *das* guinea-fowl; ~**mutt** /~mʊt/ *das;* ~s, ~**mutter** *die;* ~ *od. das;* ~s mother-of-pearl

Perlon Ⓦ *das;* ~s ≈ nylon

Perl-: ~**wein** *der* sparkling wine; ~**zwiebel** *die* pearl *or* cocktail onion

permanent /pɛrma'nɛnt/ **1** *Adj.* permanent ‹institution, deficit, crisis›; constant ‹danger, threat, squabble›. **2** *adv.* constantly

perplex /pɛr'plɛks/ *Adj.* (ugs.) baffled, puzzled (**über** + *Akk.* by); (verwirrt) bewildered

per saldo /-'saldo/ (Kaufmannsspr.) net; (fig.: im Endeffekt) on balance; ~ ~ **rund 4 Millionen Verlust/Gewinn** a net loss/gain of about four million

Perser /'pɛrzɐ/ *der;* ~s, ~ ▶ 388 | (a) Persian; (b) ⇒ **Perserteppich**

Perserin *die;* ~, ~**nen** Persian

Perser·teppich *der* Persian carpet; (kleiner) Persian rug

Persianer /pɛr'zia:nɐ/ *der;* ~s, ~: Persian lamb; (~mantel) Persian lamb coat

Persien /'pɛrziən/ (*das*); ~s Persia

Persiflage /pɛrzi'fla:ʒə/ *die;* ~, ~**n** [gentle] mocking *no indef. art.; eine* ~ **auf jmdn./etw.** a [gentle] satire of sb./sth.

persisch *Adj.* ▶ 388 |, ▶ 487 | Persian; *s. auch* **deutsch; Deutsch**

Person /pɛr'zo:n/ *die;* ~, ~**en** (a) person; **eine männliche/weibliche** ~: a male/female; ~**en** (als Gruppe) people; **die Familie besteht aus fünf** ~**en** it is a family of five; **ich für meine** ~ ...: I for my part ...; **der Minister in [eigener]** ~: the minister in person; **sie ist die Güte/Geduld in** ~: she is kindness/patience personified *or* itself; **Angaben zur** ~ **machen** give one's personal details; (b) (in der Dichtung, im Film) character; (c) (emotional: Frau) female (derog./joc.); (d) *o. Pl.* (Sprachw.) person

Personal /pɛrzo'na:l/ *das;* ~s (a) (in einem Betrieb o. Ä.) staff; (b) (im Haushalt) servants *pl.;* [domestic] staff *pl.*

Personal-: ~**abbau** *der* reduction in staff; (in mehreren Abteilungen/Betrieben) staff cuts *pl.;* ~**abteilung** *die* personnel department; ~**ausweis** *der* identity card; ~**büro** *das* personnel office; ~**chef** *der* personnel manager

Personalien /pɛrzo'na:liən/ *Pl.* personal details *or* particulars

Personal-: ~**kosten** *Pl.* (Wirtsch., Verwaltung) staff costs; ~**mangel** *der* staff shortage; ~**pronomen** *das* (Sprachw.) personal pronoun

personell /pɛrzo'nɛl/ **1** *Adj.; nicht präd.* staff ‹changes, difficulties›; ‹savings› in staff; ‹questions, decisions› regarding staff *or* personnel. **2** *adv.* with regard to staff *or* personnel

Personen-: ~**aufzug** *der* passenger lift (Brit.) *or* (Amer.) elevator; ~**beschreibung** *die* personal description; ~**gedächtnis** *das* memory for faces; ~**kraftwagen** *der* (bes. Amtsspr.) private car *or* (Amer.) automobile; ~**kreis** *der* group [of people]; ~**kult** *der* (abwertend) personality cult; ~**nah·verkehr** *der* local public transport; ~**schaden** *der* (Versicherungsw.) physical *or* personal injury; **Unfälle mit** ~**schaden** accidents in which injuries are/were sustained; ~**wagen** *der* (a) (Auto) [private] car; automobile (Amer.); (im Unterschied zum Lastwagen) passenger car *or* (Amer.) automobile; (b) (bei Zügen) passenger coach; ~**zug** *der* slow *or* stopping train; (im Unterschied zum Güterzug) passenger train

persönlich /pɛr'zøːnlɪç/ **1** *Adj.* personal. ~ **werden** get personal. **2** *adv.* personally; (auf Briefen) 'private [and confidential]'; **nimm doch nicht gleich alles [so]** ~! don't take everything so personally!

Persönlichkeit *die;* ~, ~**en** personality; (Mensch) person of character; **eine** ~ **sein** have a strong personality; ~**en des öffentlichen Lebens** public figures

Perspektive /pɛrspɛk'ti:və/ *die;* ~, ~**n** (Optik, bild. Kunst, auch fig.) perspective; (Blickwinkel) angle; viewpoint; (Zukunftsaussicht) prospect; **aus soziologischer** ~/**aus der** ~ **des Soziologen** (fig.) from a sociological viewpoint/the viewpoint of a sociologist

perspektivisch 1 *Adj.* ‹drawing *etc.*› in perspective; ‹effect, narrowing, *etc.*› of perspective. **2** *adv.* in perspective; ~ **verkürzen** foreshorten

Peru /pe'ru:/ (*das*); ~s Peru

Peruaner /pe'rua:nɐ/ *der;* ~s, ~ ▶ 388 | Peruvian

Perücke /pe'rʏkə/ *die;* ~, ~**n** wig

pervers /pɛr'vɛrs/ (abwertend) **1** *Adj.* perverted; (fig.: gegen jede Vernunft) perverse. **2** *adv.* ~ **veranlagt sein** be of a perverted disposition

Pessimismus /pɛsi'mɪsmʊs/ *der;* ~: pessimism

Pessimist *der;* ~**en**, ~**en**, **Pessimistin** *die;* ~, ~**nen** pessimist

pessimistisch 1 *Adj.* pessimistic. **2** *adv.* pessimistically; **etw.** ~ **sehen** *od.* **betrachten** take a pessimistic view of sth.

Pest /pɛst/ *die;* ~: ▶ 329 | plague; (fig.: Mensch, Ungeziefer) pest; menace; **ich hasse ihn/es wie die** ~ (ugs.) I hate his guts/can't stand it (coll.); **wie die** ~ **stinken** (salopp) stink to high heaven (coll.)

Peter /'pe:tɐ/ *der;* ~s, ~: (ugs.) fellow; **schwarzer** ~ (Kartenspiel) ≈ old maid (*with a black cat card instead of an old maid*); **jmdm. den schwarzen** ~ **zuschieben** (fig.) pass the buck to sb. (coll.)

Petersilie /pe:tɐ'zi:liə/ *die;* ~: parsley; **ihm ist die** ~ **verhagelt** (ugs.) he's down in the dumps

Petition /peti'tsio:n/ *die;* ~, ~**en** (Amtsspr.) petition

Petri Heil /'pe:tri-/ good fishing!; make a good catch!

Petroleum /pe'tro:leʊm/ *das;* ~s paraffin (Brit.); kerosene (Amer.)

Petrus /'pe:trʊs/ (*der*); **Petrus'** *od.* **Petri** (a) (christl. Rel.: Apostel) St Peter; (b) (Patron des Wetters) the clerk of the weather

Petting /'pɛtɪŋ/ *das;* ~s, ~s petting

Petze *die;* ~, ~**n** (Schülerspr. abwertend) tell-tale; sneak (Brit. school sl.); tattle-tale (Amer. school sl.)

petzen (Schülerspr.) **1** *itr. V.* tell tales; sneak (Brit. school sl.). **2** *tr. V.* ~, **dass** ...: tell teacher/sb.'s parents that ...

Petzer *der;* ~s, ~ ⇒ **Petze**

Pf *Abk.* **Pfennig**

Pfad /pfa:t/ *der;* ~[**e**]**s**, ~**e** (a) path; **vom** ~ **der Tugend abweichen** (fig. geh.) stray from the path of virtue; (b) (DV) path

Pfad-: ~**finder** *der;* ~s, ~ Scout; **er ist bei den** ~**n** he is in the Scouts; ~**finderin** *die;* ~, ~**nen** Guide (Brit.); girl scout (Amer.); **sie ist bei den** ~**nen** she is in the Guides (Brit.) *or* (Amer.) girl scouts

Pfaffe /'pfafə/ *der;* ~**n**, ~**n** (abwertend) cleric; Holy Joe (derog.)

Pfahl /pfa:l/ *der;* ~[**e**]**s**, **Pfähle** /'pfɛːlə/ post; stake; (Bauw.: Stütze für Gebäude) pile; [**jmdm.**] **ein** ~ **im Fleisch[e] sein** be a thorn in sb.'s flesh

Pfahl·bau *der;* ~[**e**]**s**, ~**ten** pile-dwelling

Pfand /pfant/ *das;* ~[**e**]**s**, **Pfänder** /'pfɛndɐ/ (a) security; pledge (esp. fig.); **etw. als** ~ *od.* **in** ~ **nehmen/etw. als** *od.* **zum** *od.* **in** ~ **geben** take/give sth. as [a] security; (b) (für Mehrwegflaschen usw.) deposit (**auf** + *Dat.* on); (c) (beim Pfänderspiel) forfeit

pfänden /'pfɛndn̩/ *tr.* (auch *itr.*) *V.* impound, seize [under distress] (Law) ‹goods, chattels›; attach ‹wages *etc.*› (Law); **er ist gepfändet worden** the bailiffs have been on to him; execution was levied against him (Law.)

Pfänder·spiel *das* [game of] forfeits

Pfand-: ~**flasche** *die* returnable bottle (*on which a deposit is payable*); ~**leiher** *der* ▶ 85 | pawnbroker

Pfändung /'pfɛndʊŋ/ *die;* ~, ~**en** seizure; distraint (Law); (von Geldsummen, Vermögensrechten) attachment (Law)

Pfanne /'pfanə/ *die;* ~, ~**n** [frying-]pan; **sich** (*Dat.*) **ein paar Eier in die** ~ **schlagen** fry [up] some eggs; **jmdn.**

in die ~ **hauen** (ugs.) (kritisieren) take sb. to pieces; (vernichtend schlagen) beat sb. hollow (coll.)

Pfann·kuchen der (a) (bes. südd.: Eierkuchen) pancake; (b) (Berliner ~) doughnut

Pfarr·amt das (a) parish office; (b) (Stellung) pastorate

Pfarrei /pfaˈraɪ/ die; ~, ~en (a) (Bezirk) parish; (b) (Dienststelle) parish office

Pfarrer /ˈpfarɐ/ der; ~s, ~ ▶ 34⌉ (katholisch) parish priest; (evangelisch) pastor; (anglikanisch) vicar; (von Freikirchen) minister; (Militär~) chaplain; padre

Pfarrerin die; ~, ~nen [woman] pastor; (in Freikirchen) [woman] minister

Pfarr·haus das vicarage; (katholisch) presbytery; (in Schottland) manse

Pfau /pfaʊ/ der; ~[e]s, ~en (österr. auch:) ~en, ~e peacock

Pfauen·auge das peacock butterfly

Pfeffer /ˈpfɛfɐ/ der; ~s, ~ pepper; **hingehen** od. **bleiben, wo der ~ wächst** (ugs.) go to hell (coll.); get lost (sl.); s. auch **Hase** a

Pfeffer-: ~**korn** das peppercorn; ~**kuchen** der ≈ gingerbread

Pfefferminz /ˈpfɛfɛmɪnts/ o. Art., indekl. peppermint

Pfefferminz·bonbon der od. das peppermint [sweet]

Pfeffer·minze die; o. Pl. peppermint [plant]

Pfefferminz·tee der peppermint tea

Pfeffer·mühle die pepper mill

pfeffern tr. V. (a) (würzen) season with pepper; (b) (ugs.: werfen) chuck (coll.); (mit Wucht) fling; hurl; **jmdm. eine ~** (salopp) sock or biff sb. one (coll.); s. auch **gepfeffert**

Pfeffer-: ~**nuss**, *~**nuß** die [small round] gingerbread biscuit; ~**steak** das steak au poivre; pepper steak; ~**streuer** der pepper pot

pfeffrig /ˈpfɛfrɪç/ Adj. peppery

Pfeife /ˈpfaɪfə/ die; ~, ~n (a) (Tabak~) pipe; ~ **rauchen** smoke a pipe; be a pipe-smoker; (b) (Musikinstrument) pipe; (der Militärkapelle) fife; (Triller~, an einer Maschine usw.) whistle; (Orgel~) [organ-]pipe; **nach jmds. ~ tanzen** (fig.) dance to sb.'s tune; (c) (salopp abwertend: Versager) wash-out (coll.)

pfeifen 1 unr. itr. V. (a) whistle; ⟨bird⟩ sing; pipe; **dreimal kurz ~:** give three short whistles; **es pfeift in seiner Brust** he wheezes in his chest; s. auch **Loch** a; (b) mit sein **die Kugeln pfiffen ihm um die Ohren** the bullets whistled around him; (c) (auf einer Trillerpfeife o. Ä.) ⟨policeman, referee, etc.⟩ blow one's whistle; (Sport: als Schiedsrichter fungieren) act as referee; (d) (salopp) **auf jmdn./etw. ~:** not give a damn about sb./sth.; **ich pfeife auf dein Geld** you can keep your money (coll.); (e) (salopp: geständig sein) squeal (sl.). 2 unr. tr. V. (a) whistle ⟨tune etc.⟩; ⟨bird⟩ pipe, sing ⟨song⟩; (b) **sich** (Dat.) **eins ~** (ugs.) whistle [nonchalantly] to oneself; (auf einer Pfeife) pipe, play ⟨tune etc.⟩; (auf einer Trillerpfeife o. Ä.) blow ⟨signal etc.⟩ on one's whistle; **einen Elfmeter ~** (Sport) blow [the whistle] for a penalty; (c) (salopp spött.) **ich pfeif dir was** go and get knotted (coll.); (d) (Sport: als Schiedsrichter leiten) referee ⟨match⟩; (e) (salopp: verraten) let out ⟨secret⟩

Pfeifen-: ~**reiniger** der pipe-cleaner; ~**tabak** der pipe tobacco

Pfeifer der; ~s, ~ (a) (Musik) (bes. hist.) piper; (in einer Militärkapelle) fife-player; (b) (jmd., der pfeift) whistler

Pfeil /pfaɪl/ der; ~[e]s, ~e arrow; ~ **und Bogen** bow and arrow; **schnell wie ein ~:** as quick as lightning

Pfeiler der; ~s, ~: pillar; (Brücken~) pier

pfeil, Pfeil-: ~**gerade** 1 Adj. [as] straight as an arrow postpos.; dead straight; 2 adv. [as] straight as an arrow; ~**gift** das arrow-poison; ~**schnell** 1 Adj. lightning-swift; 2 adv. like a shot; ~**spitze** die arrowhead

Pfennig /ˈpfɛnɪç/ der; ~s, ~e ▶ 216⌉ pfennig; **eine Briefmarke zu 60 ~:** a 60-pfennig stamp; **er hat keinen ~ [Geld]** he hasn't a penny or (Amer.) cent; **auf den ~ sehen** (ugs.) watch or count every penny or (Amer.) cent; **nicht für fünf ~ Verstand/Humor haben** (ugs.) have not an ounce of common sense/have no sense of humour whatsoever; **wer den ~ nicht ehrt, ist des Talers**

nicht wert (Spr.) take care of the pennies and the pounds will look after themselves (prov.); s. auch **Heller**

Pfennig·fuchser /-fʊksɐ/ der; ~s, ~ (ugs.) pennypincher

Pferch /pfɛrç/ der; ~[e]s, ~e pen

pferchen tr. V. cram; pack

Pferd /pfeːɐ̯t/ das; ~[e]s, ~e (a) horse; **aufs/vom ~ steigen** mount/dismount; **zu ~:** by horse; on horseback; **das hält ja kein ~ aus** (ugs.) that's more than flesh and blood can stand; **ich denk, mich tritt ein ~** (salopp) I'm absolutely flabbergasted; **man hat schon ~e kotzen sehen** (salopp) [you never know,] anything can happen; **wie ein ~ arbeiten** (ugs.) work like a Trojan; **ihm gehen die ~e durch** (ugs.) he flies off the handle (coll.); **auf das falsche ~ setzen** (fig.) back the wrong horse; **die ~e scheu machen** (ugs.) put people off; **das ~ am** od. **beim Schwanze aufzäumen** (ugs.) put the cart before the horse; **mit ihr kann man ~e stehlen** (ugs.) she's game for anything; (b) (Turngerät) horse; (c) (Schachfigur) knight

Pferde-: ~**äpfel** Pl. (ugs.) horse droppings; horse dung; ~**fuß** der (fig.: Mangel, Nachteil) snag; drawback; ~**gebiss**, *~**gebiß** das (fig. ugs.) **er hat ein ~gebiss** he has teeth pl. like a horse; ~**gesicht** das (ugs.) horsy face; ~**koppel** die paddock; ~**pfleger** der groom; ~**rasse** die breed of horse; ~**rennbahn** die racecourse; ~**rennen** das horse race; (Sportart) horse racing; **beim ~rennen sein** be at the races pl.; ~**schwanz** der horse's tail; (fig.: Frisur) ponytail; ~**sport** der equestrian sport no art.; (~rennen) horse racing no art.; ~**stall** der stable; ~**stärke** die horsepower; ~**wagen** der (für Güter) cart; (für Personen) carriage; (der amerikanischen Pioniere usw.) wagon

pfiff /pfɪf/ 1. u. 3. Pers. Sg. Prät. v. **pfeifen**

Pfiff der; ~[e]s, ~e (a) whistle; (b) (ugs.: besonderer Reiz) style; **mit ~:** stylish; with style; (adverbiell) stylishly; ⟨cook⟩ with flair

Pfifferling /ˈpfɪfɐlɪŋ/ der; ~s, ~e chanterelle; **keinen ~ wert sein** (ugs.) be not worth a bean (sl.)

pfiffig 1 Adj. smart; bright, clever ⟨idea⟩; artful, knowing ⟨smile, expression⟩. 2 adv. artfully; cleverly; **jmdn. ~ ansehen** look knowingly or artfully at sb.

Pfingsten /ˈpfɪŋstn/ das; ~, ~: Whitsun

Pfingst-: ~**montag** der Whit Monday no def. art.; ~**ochse** der in **herausgeputzt wie ein ~ochse** (ugs.) dressed up like a dog's dinner (coll.); ~**rose** die peony; ~**sonntag** der Whit Sunday no def. art.; ~**woche** die week before Whitsun

Pfirsich /ˈpfɪrzɪç/ der; ~s, ~e peach

Pflänzchen /ˈpflɛntsçən/ das; ~s, ~ (a) little plant; (b) (fig.: Mensch) **ein [zartes] ~:** a delicate creature

Pflanze /ˈpflantsə/ die; ~, ~n plant

pflanzen 1 tr. V. plant (**in** + Akk. in). 2 refl. V. (ugs.) plant oneself

Pflanzen-: ~**fresser** der herbivore; ~**kunde** die botany no def. art.; ~**öl** das vegetable oil; ~**reich** das; o. Pl. plant kingdom; ~**schutz·mittel** das [crop] pesticide; (für den Garten) garden pesticide

pflanzlich Adj. plant attrib. ⟨life, motif⟩; vegetable ⟨dye, fat⟩; (vegetarisch) vegetarian

Pflaster /ˈpflastɐ/ das; ~s, ~ (a) (Straßen~) road surface; (auf dem Gehsteig) pavement; (b) (ugs.: Ort) **ein teures/gefährliches** od. **heißes ~:** an expensive/dangerous place or spot to be; (c) (Wund~) sticking plaster

Pflaster·maler der pavement artist

pflastern tr. (auch itr.) V. surface ⟨road, path⟩; (mit Kopfsteinpflaster, Steinplatten) pave ⟨street, path⟩

Pflaster·stein der paving stone; (Kopfstein) cobblestone

Pflaume /ˈpflaʊmə/ die; ~, ~n (a) plum; **getrocknete ~n** [dried] prunes; (b) (ugs. abwertend: Versager) dead loss (coll.)

Pflaumen-: ~**baum** der plum-tree; ~**kuchen** der plum flan; ~**mus** das plum purée

Pflege /ˈpfleːɡə/ die; ~: care; (Maschinen~, Fahrzeug~) maintenance; (fig.: von Beziehungen, Kunst, Sprache) cultivation; fostering; **jmdn./etw. in ~ nehmen** look after sb./sth.; **jmdm. etw.** od. **etw. bei jmdm. in ~ geben** give sb. sth. to look after; entrust sth. to sb.'s care; **ein Kind in ~** (Akk.) **nehmen** look after a child; (als

Pflegeeltern) foster a child; **ein Kind bei jmdm. in** ∼ (*Akk.*) **geben** give sb. a child to look after; (bei Pflegeeltern) have a child fostered by sb.

pflege-, Pflege-: ∼**bedürftig** *Adj.* needing care *or* attention *postpos.; ⟨person⟩* in need of care; ∼**eltern** *Pl.* foster-parents; ∼**kind** *das* foster-child; ∼**leicht** *Adj.* easy-care *attrib. ⟨textiles, flooring⟩*; minimum-care *attrib. ⟨plant, pan⟩*

pflegen 1 *tr. V.* look after; care for, nurse *⟨sick person⟩*; care for, take care of *⟨skin, teeth, floor⟩*; look after, maintain *⟨bicycle, car, machine⟩*; cultivate *⟨relations, arts, interests⟩*; foster *⟨contacts, cooperation⟩*; keep up, pursue *⟨hobby⟩*; **jmdn./ein Tier gesund** ∼: nurse sb./an animal back to health. **2** *itr. V.; mit Inf. + zu* **etw. zu tun** ∼: be in the habit of doing sth.; usually do sth.; …, **wie er zu sagen pflegt/pflegte** …, as he is wont to say/as he used to say. **3** *refl. V.* take care of oneself; (gesundheitlich) look after oneself; *s. auch* **gepflegt**

Pfleger *der;* ∼**s,** ∼ **(a)** ▶ 85 (Kranken∼) [male] nurse; **(b)** ▶ 85 (Tier∼) keeper

Pflegerin *die;* ∼, ∼**nen (a)** ▶ 85 (Kranken∼) nurse; **(b)** ▶ 85 (Tier∼) keeper

Pflege-: ∼**sohn** *der* foster-son; ∼**tochter** *die* foster-daughter

pfleglich 1 *Adj.* careful. **2** *adv.* carefully; with care

Pflicht /pflɪçt/ *die;* ∼, ∼**en (a)** duty; ∼ **sein** be obligatory; **es ist seine** ∼ **und Schuldigkeit** it's his bounden duty; **(b)** (Sport) compulsory exercises *pl.*

pflicht-, Pflicht-: ∼**bewusst,** ***∼**bewußt 1** *Adj.* conscientious; ∼**bewusst sein** have a sense of duty; **2** *adv.* conscientiously; with a sense of duty; ∼**bewusstsein,** ***∼**bewußtsein** *das* sense of duty; ∼**eifrig 1** *Adj.* zealous; **2** *adv.* zealously; full of zeal; ∼**fach** *das* compulsory subject; ∼**gefühl** *das; o. Pl.* sense of duty; ∼**gemäß 1** *Adj.* in accordance with one's duty *postpos.;* **2** *adv.* in accordance with one's duty; ∼**lektüre** *die* required reading; (Schulw.) set books *pl.;* ∼**übung** *die* **(a)** (Sport) compulsory exercise; **(b)** (fig.) ritual exercise; (Buch, Film usw.) obligatory effort; ∼**versicherung** *die* compulsory insurance

Pflock /pflɔk/ *der;* ∼**[e]s,** **Pflöcke** /'pflœkə/ peg; (für Tiere) stake

pflücken /'pflʏkn̩/ *tr. V.* pick *⟨flowers, fruit, hops⟩*

Pflücker *der;* ∼**s,** ∼, **Pflückerin** *die;* ∼, ∼**nen** ▶ 85 picker

Pflug /pfluːk/ *der;* ∼**[e]s,** **Pflüge** /'pflyːgə/ plough

pflügen /'pflyːgn̩/ *tr., itr. V.* plough

Pflug·schar *die* ploughshare

Pforte /'pfɔrtə/ *die;* ∼, ∼**n** (Tor) gate; (Tür) door; (Eingang) entrance

Pförtner /'pfœrtnɐ/ *der;* ∼**s,** ∼ porter; (eines Wohnblocks, Büros) doorkeeper; (am Tor) gatekeeper

Pförtner·haus *das* gatehouse; porter's lodge

Pfosten /'pfɔstn̩/ *der;* ∼**s,** ∼ **(a)** post; (Tür∼) jamb; **(b)** (Sport: Tor∼) [goal-]post

Pfötchen /'pføːtçən/ *das;* ∼**s,** ∼: [little] paw; **[gib]** ∼**!** [give us a] paw!

Pfote /'pfoːtə/ *die;* ∼, ∼**n (a)** paw; **(b)** (ugs.: Hand) paw (coll.); mitt (sl.); **sich** (*Dat.*) **die** ∼**n verbrennen** (fig.) burn one's fingers (fig.)

Pfriem /pfriːm/ *der;* ∼**[e]s,** ∼**e** awl

Pfropf /pfrɔpf/ *der;* ∼**[e]s,** ∼**e** blockage; (in der Vene) clot

pfropfen *tr. V.* (ugs.) cram; stuff; **gepfropft voll** crammed [full]; packed

Pfropfen *der* (für Flaschen) stopper; (Korken) cork; (für Fässer) bung

Pfründe /'pfrʏndə/ *die;* ∼, ∼**n (a)** (kath. Kirche) living; benefice; **(b)** (fig.) sinecure

pfui /pfʊi/ *Interj.* **(a)** (Ekel ausdrückend) ugh; yuck (sl.); (zu Kindern, Hunden) [ugh,] you mucky pup; ∼ **Teufel** *od.* **Deibel** *od.* **Spinne!** (ugs.) ugh *or* (sl.) yuck, how disgusting!; **(b)** (Missbilligung, Empörung ausdrückend) ugh; really; (Ruf) boo; ∼, **schäm dich!** shame on you!; ∼ **rufen** boo

Pfui·ruf *der* boo

Pfund /pfʊnt/ *das;* ∼**[e]s,** ∼**e** (bei Maßangaben ungebeugt) **(a)** ▶ 228 (Gewicht) pound (= 500 grams in German-speaking countries); **zwei** ∼ **Kartoffeln** two pounds of potatoes; **(b)** ▶ 216 (Währungseinheit) pound; **100** ∼: £100; **one hundred pounds**

pfundig (ugs.) **1** *Adj.* great (coll.); fantastic (coll.). **2** *adv.* fantastically (coll.)

Pfunds·kerl *der* (ugs.) great bloke (Brit. coll.); great guy (coll.)

pfund·weise *Adv.* by the pound

Pfusch /pfʊʃ/ *der;* ∼**[e]s** *o. Art.* (ugs. abwertend) a botch-up; ∼ **machen** botch it

pfuschen *itr. V.* (ugs. abwertend) botch it; do a botched-up job

Pfuscher *der;* ∼**s,** ∼, **Pfuscherin** *die;* ∼, ∼**nen** (ugs. abwertend) botcher; bungler

Pfütze /'pfʏtsə/ *die;* ∼, ∼**n** puddle

PH /peː'haː/ *die;* ∼, ∼**s** *Abk.* **Pädagogische Hochschule**

Phänomen /fɛno'meːn/ *das;* ∼**s,** ∼**e** phenomenon

phänomenal /fɛnome'naːl/ **1** *Adj.* phenomenal. **2** *adv.* phenomenally

Phantasie *usw.:* ⇒ **Fantasie** *usw.*

Phantom /fan'toːm/ *das;* ∼**s,** ∼**e** phantom; illusion; **einem** ∼ **nachjagen** (fig.) chase [after] an illusion *or* a shadow

Pharisäer /fari'zɛːɐ/ *der;* ∼**s,** ∼ (auch fig.) Pharisee

Pharmakologie /farmakolo'giː/ *die;* ∼**:** pharmacology *no art.*

pharmazeutisch 1 *Adj.* pharmaceutical. **2** *adv.* pharmaceutically

Pharmazie /farma'tsiː/ *die;* ∼**:** pharmaceutics *sing., no art.;* pharmaceutical chemistry *no art.*

Phase /'faːzə/ *die;* ∼, ∼**n** phase

Philanthrop /filan'troːp/ *der;* ∼**en,** ∼**en** (geh.) philanthropist

Philharmonie /fɪlharmo'niː/ *die;* ∼, ∼**n (a)** (Orchester) philharmonic [orchestra]; **(b)** (Gebäude, Saal) philharmonic hall

Philharmoniker /fɪlhar'moːnikɐ/ *der;* ∼**s,** ∼**:** member of a/the philharmonic orchestra; **die Wiener** ∼**:** the Vienna Philharmonic Orchestra

Philippinen /fɪlɪ'piːnən/ *Pl.* Philippines

Philologe /filo'loːgə/ *der;* ∼**n,** ∼**n** teacher/student of language and literature; philologist (Amer.)

Philologie *die;* ∼, ∼**n** study of language and literature; philology *no art.* (Amer.)

Philologin *die;* ∼, ∼**nen** ⇒ **Philologe**

Philosoph /filo'zoːf/ *der;* ∼**en,** ∼**en** philosopher

Philosophie *die;* ∼, ∼**n** philosophy

philosophieren *itr. V.* (auch tr.) V. philosophize

Philosophin *die;* ∼, ∼**nen** philosopher

philosophisch 1 *Adj.* philosophical; *⟨dictionary⟩* of philosophy. **2** *adv.* philosophically

phlegmatisch /flɛ'maːtɪʃ/ **1** *Adj.* phlegmatic. **2** *adv.* phlegmatically

Phobie /fo'biː/ *die;* ∼, ∼**n** (Psych.) phobia

Phonetik /fo'neːtɪk/ *die;* ∼**:** phonetics *sing.*

phonetisch 1 *Adj.* phonetic. **2** *adv.* phonetically

Phono- /'foːno-/ phono *⟨socket, input⟩*

Phono·typistin /-ty'pɪstɪn/ *die;* ∼, ∼**nen** audio typist

Phosphat /fɔs'faːt/ *das;* ∼**[e]s,** ∼**e** (Chemie) phosphate

Phosphor /'fɔsfɔr/ *der;* ∼**s** phosphorus

Photo /'foːto/*das;* ∼**s,** ∼**s** ⇒ **Foto**

photo-, Photo- *s. auch* **foto-, Foto-**

Photo-: ∼**synthese** *die* photosynthesis; ∼**zelle** *die* phot[electric] cell

Phrase /'fraːzə/ *die;* ∼, ∼**n (a)** (abwertend) [empty] phrase; cliché; ∼**n dreschen** (ugs.) spout clichés; dole out catchphrases; **(b)** (Musik, Sprachw.) phrase

phrasen-, Phrasen-: ∼**drescher** *der;* ∼**s,** ∼ (ugs. abwertend) phrase-monger; cliché-monger; ∼**drescherei**

/~drɛʃə'raɪ/ die; ~, ~en (ugs. abwertend) phrase-mongering; cliché-mongering; ~haft (abwertend) 1 Adj. empty; trite; (voller Klischees) cliché-ridden; 2 adv. in an empty or trite manner

pH-Wert /pe:'ha:-/ der (Chemie) pH[-value]

Physik /fy'zi:k/ die; ~: physics sing., no art.

physikalisch /fyzi'ka:lɪʃ/ 1 Adj. physics attrib. ‹experiment, formula, research, institute›; physical ‹map, chemistry, therapy, process›. 2 adv. in terms of physics

Physiker der; ~s, ~, **Physikerin** die; ~, ~nen physicist

Physik·saal der (Schulw.) physics laboratory

Physiologie /fyziolo'gi:/ die; ~: physiology

physiologisch 1 Adj. physiological. 2 adv. physiologically

physisch 1 Adj. physical. 2 adv. physically

Pianist /pia'nɪst/ der; ~en, ~en, **Pianistin** die; ~, ~nen pianist

Piano /'pia:no/ das; ~s, ~s piano

Pickel /'pɪkl̩/ der; ~s, ~ (a) (auf der Haut) pimple; (b) (Spitzhacke) pickaxe; (Eis~) ice-axe

Pickel·haube die spiked helmet

pickelig Adj. pimply

picken /'pɪkn̩/ 1 itr. V. peck (**nach** at; **an** + Akk., **gegen** on, against). 2 tr. V. ‹bird› peck; (ugs.) ‹person› pick; (aufheben) pick up

picklig ⇒ pickelig

Picknick /'pɪknɪk/ das; ~s, ~e od. ~s picnic; ~ **machen** od. **halten** have a picnic

picknicken itr. V. picnic

Piefke /'pi:fkə/ der; ~s, ~[s] (a) (bes. nordd. abwertend) bumptious lout; (b) (österr. abwertend: Deutscher) bloody (Brit. sl.) or damn German

pieken ⇒ piken

piek·fein /'pi:k'faɪn/ (ugs.) 1 Adj. posh (coll.). 2 adv. poshly (coll.); ~ **angezogen** wearing posh clothes (coll.); dressed to the nines

piep /pi:p/ Interj. cheep

Piep der; ~s, ~e (ugs.) (a) (Ton) peep; **keinen ~ [davon] sagen** not say a thing [about it]

piepe /'pi:pə/, **piep·egal** Adj. in [jmdm.] ~ **sein** (ugs.) not matter at all [to sb.]; **es ist mir ~** (ugs.) I don't give a damn

piepen itr. V. (ugs.) squeak; ‹small bird› cheep; chirp; **bei dir piepts wohl** (salopp) you must be off your rocker (fig. coll.); **zum Piepen sein** be a hoot or a scream (coll.)

Piep·matz der (Kinderspr.) dicky bird (coll.)

piepsen (ugs.) 1 itr. V. ⇒ **piepen**. 2 itr., tr. V. (mit hoher Stimme sprechen) pipe; (aufgeregt) squeal

piepsig Adj. (ugs.) squeaky

Piercing /'pi:ɐsɪŋ/ das; ~s [body] piercing

piesacken /'pi:zakn̩/ tr. V. (ugs.) pester

Pietät /pie'tɛ:t/ die; ~, ~en (a) o. Pl. respect; (Ehrfurcht) reverence; (b) (Bestattungsinstitut) [firm of] funeral directors or (Amer.) morticians

pietät·los 1 Adj. irreverent; (gefühllos) unfeeling; (respektlos) disrespectful; lacking in respect postpos. 2 adv. irreverently

Pigment /pɪ'gmɛnt/ das; ~[e]s, ~e pigment

Pik¹ /pi:k/ der in **einen ~ auf jmdn. haben** (ugs.) have it in for sb.

Pik² das; ~[s], ~[s] (Kartenspiel) (a) (Farbe) spades pl.; ~ **ziehen/ausspielen** draw/play spades; (b) (Karte) spade

pikant /pi'kant/ 1 Adj. (a) piquant; (würzig) spicy; well-seasoned; (appetitanregend) appetizing; (b) (fig.: witzig) piquant; ironical; (c) (verhüll.: schlüpfrig) racy ‹joke, story›. 2 adv. ~ **gewürzt** piquantly or appetizingly seasoned

Pikanterie /pikantə'ri:/ die; ~, ~n (a) o. Pl. (fig.) piquancy; (Witzigkeit) irony; (b) (verhüll.: schlüpfrige Geschichte) racy story

pikanter·weise Adv.(geh.) ironically [enough]

***Pik·as**, **Pik·ass** das ace of spades

Pike /'pi:kə/ die; ~, ~n pike; **etw. von der ~ auf [er]-lernen** learn sth. by working one's way up from the bottom

piken tr., itr. V. (ugs.) prick; **jmdm. mit einer Nadel in den Arm ~**: poke a needle into sb.'s arm

pikiert /pi'ki:ɐt/ 1 Adj. piqued; nettled. 2 adv. ‹reply, say› in an aggrieved tone or voice

Pikkolo·flöte die piccolo

piksen /'pi:ksn̩/ tr., itr. V. (ugs.) ⇒ **piken**

Pik·sieben die (Kartenspiel) seven of spades; **dastehen wie ~** (ugs.) stand there looking stupid

Pilger /'pɪlgɐ/ der; ~s, ~: pilgrim

Pilger·fahrt die pilgrimage

pilgern itr. V. (a) (auch fig.) go on or make a pilgrimage; (b) (ugs.: gehen) traipse (coll.)

Pille /'pɪlə/ die; ~, ~n pill; **sie nimmt die ~:** she's on the pill (coll.); **eine bittere ~ [für jmdn.] sein** (fig.) be a bitter pill [for sb.] to swallow

Pilot /pi'lo:t/ der; ~en, ~en (a) ▶ 85| pilot; (b) (Motorsport) [racing] driver

Pils /pɪls/ das; ~, ~: Pils; Pils[e]ner [beer]

Pilz /pɪlts/ der; ~es, ~e (a) fungus; (Speise~, auch fig.) mushroom; **giftige ~e** poisonous fungi; **wie ~e aus dem Boden** od. **der Erde schießen** be springing up like mushrooms; (b) o. Pl. (ugs.) ~infektion) fungus [infection]

Pilz-: ~**krankheit** die ▶ 329| (a) (Mykose) mycosis; (b) (bei Pflanzen) fungus [disease]; ~**vergiftung** die ▶ 329| fungus poisoning no art.; (durch verdorbene Pilze) mushroom poisoning no art.

Pilzling /'pɪltslɪŋ/ der; ~s, ~e (österr.) ⇒ **Steinpilz**

Piment /pi'mɛnt/ der od. das; ~[e]s, ~e pimento; allspice

Pimmel /'pɪml̩/ der; ~s, ~ (salopp) willy (sl.)

pingelig /'pɪŋəlɪç/ (ugs.) 1 finicky; pernickety (coll.); (wählerisch) fussy; choosy (coll.). 2 adv. in a pernickety way (coll.); (pedantisch) pedantically

Pingpong /'pɪŋpɔŋ/ das; ~s (ugs.) ping-pong

Pinguin /'pɪŋguiːn/ der; ~s, ~e penguin

Pinie /'pi:niə/ die; ~, ~n [stone- or umbrella] pine

Pinke /'pɪŋkə/ die; ~ (ugs. veralt.) dough (sl.); lolly (Brit. sl.)

Pinkel /'pɪŋkl̩/ der; ~s, ~ (ugs. abwertend) **ein [feiner] ~:** a stuck-up prig

pinkeln itr. (auch tr.) V. (salopp) pee (coll.); ‹esp. child› wee (sl.)

Pinkel·pause die (ugs.) stop for a pee (coll.); rest stop (Amer.)

Pinn·wand die pin-board

Pinscher /'pɪnʃɐ/ der; ~s, ~ pinscher

Pinsel /'pɪnzl̩/ der; ~s, ~ (a) brush; (Mal~) paintbrush; (b) (ugs. abwertend: Dummkopf) nitwit (coll.); idiot (coll.)

pinseln tr. V. (a) (ugs.: anstreichen) paint ‹room, house, etc.›; (b) (malen) paint ‹landscape, picture›; daub ‹slogans›; (c) (Med.: ein~) paint ‹wound, gums, throat, etc.›

Pinte /'pɪntə/ die; ~, ~n (ugs.) ⇒ **Kneipe** a

Pinzette /pɪn'tsɛtə/ die; ~, ~n tweezers pl.

Pionier /pio'ni:ɐ/ der; ~s, ~e (a) (Milit.) sapper; engineer; (b) (fig.: Wegbereiter) pioneer; (c) (bes. DDR) **[Junger] ~:** [Young] Pioneer

Pipapo /pipa'po:/ das; ~s (salopp) **mit allem ~:** with all the frills

Pipeline /'paiplain/ die; ~, ~s pipeline

Pipi /pi'pi:/ das; ~s (Kinderspr.) ~ **machen** do wee-wees (sl.)

Pirat /pi'ra:t/ der; ~en, ~en pirate

Piraten·sender der pirate radio station

Piraterie /piratə'ri:/ die; ~, ~n piracy no art.

Pirouette /pi'ruɛtə/ die; ~, ~n pirouette

Pirsch /pɪrʃ/ die; ~ (Jägerspr.) [deer-] stalking; **auf die ~ gehen** go [deer-]stalking

pirschen 1 itr. V. (a) (Jägerspr.) stalk; go stalking; (b) (ugs.: schleichen) creep [silently]; steal. 2 refl. V. (ugs.) creep [silently]; steal

Pisse /'pɪsə/ die; ~ (derb) piss (coarse)

pissen itr. (auch tr.) V. (derb) piss (coarse)

Pistazie /pɪs'ta:tsiə/ die; ~, ~n pistachio

Piste /'pɪstə/ die; ~, ~n (a) (Skisport) piste; ski run; (Renn~) course; (b) (Rennstrecke) track; (c) (Flugw.) runway

Pistole /pɪs'toːlə/ *die;* ~, ~n pistol; **wie aus der** ~ **geschossen** like a shot *or* a flash; **jmdm. die** ~ **auf die Brust setzen** (fig.) hold a pistol to sb.'s head

pitsch·nass, *pitsch·naß /'pɪtʃ'nas/ *Adj.* (ugs.) dripping wet; wet through

Pizza /'pɪtsa/ *die;* ~, ~s *od.* **Pizzen** pizza

Pizzeria /pɪtse'riːa/ *die;* ~, ~s *od.* **Pizzerien** pizzeria

Pkw, PKW /'peːkaːveː/ *der;* ~[s], ~[s] [private] car; automobile (Amer.)

placken /'plakn̩/ *refl. V.* (ugs.) slave away

plädieren /plɛ'diːrən/ *itr. V.* (Rechtsw.) plead (**auf** + *Akk.*, **für** for); (fig.) argue (**für** for, in favour of)

Plädoyer /plɛdoa'jeː/ *das;* ~s, ~s (Rechtsw.) final speech, summing up (*for the defence/prosecution*); (fig.) plea

Plage /'plaːgə/ *die;* ~, ~n (a) [cursed *or* (coll.) pestilential] nuisance; (b) (ugs.: Mühe) bother; trouble; **seine** ~ **mit jmdm./etw. haben** find sb./sth. a real handful

plagen 1 *tr. V.* (a) torment; plague; (b) (ugs.: bedrängen) harass; (mit Bitten, Fragen) pester. 2 *refl. V.* (a) (sich abmühen) slave away; (b) (leiden) **sich mit etw.** ~: be troubled *or* bothered by sth.

Plagiat /pla'giaːt/ *das;* ~[e]s, ~e plagiarism *no art.*

Plakat /pla'kaːt/ *das;* ~[e]s, ~e poster; „~e ankleben verboten" 'post no bills'

plakatieren 1 *tr. V.* announce by poster. 2 *itr. V.* put up posters

Plakat·wand *die* [poster] hoarding; billboard

Plakette /pla'kɛtə/ *die;* ~, ~n badge; (Scheibe) disc

plan /plaːn/ (Technik) *Adj.* flat; plane (*surface*); ~ **liegen** lie flat

Plan¹ *der;* ~[e]s, **Pläne** /'plɛːnə/ (a) plan; **nach** ~ **verlaufen** go according to plan; (b) (Karte) map; plan; (Stadt~) [street] plan

Plan² *der* in **auf den** ~ **treten** appear on the scene; **auf den** ~ **rufen** bring (*person*) on to the scene; bring (*opponent*) into the arena; arouse (*curiosity*)

Plane *die;* ~, ~n tarpaulin

planen *tr., itr. V.* plan

Planet /pla'neːt/ *der;* ~en, ~en planet

planieren *tr. V.* level; grade (as tech. term)

Planier·raupe *die* bulldozer

Planke /'plaŋkə/ *die;* ~, ~n plank; board

Plänkelei *die;* ~, ~en ⇒ **Geplänkel a**

Plankton /'plaŋktɔn/ *das;* ~s (Biol.) plankton

plan-, Plan-: ~**los** 1 *Adj.* aimless; (ohne System) unsystematic; 2 *adv.* ⇒ **1:** aimlessly; unsystematically; ~**mäßig** 1 *Adj.* (a) regular, scheduled (*service, steamer*); ~**mäßige Ankunft/Abfahrt** scheduled time of arrival/departure; (b) (systematisch) systematic. 2 *adv.* (a) (wie geplant) according to plan; as planned; (pünktlich) on schedule; (b) (systematisch) systematically; ~**quadrat** *das* grid square

Plansch·becken /'planʃ-/ *das* paddling pool

planschen *itr. V.* splash [about]

Plantage /plan'taːʒə/ *die;* ~, ~n plantation

Planung *die;* ~, ~en (a) (das Planen) planning; **bei der** ~: at the planning stage; (b) (Plan) plan

Plan-: ~**wagen** *der* covered wagon; ~**wirtschaft** *die* planned economy

plappern /'plapɐn/ (ugs.) 1 *itr. V.* chatter. 2 *tr. V.* babble (*nonsense*)

plärren /'plɛrən/ 1 *tr. V.* bawl [out] (*song*); (*radio etc.*) blare out. 2 *itr. V.* (a) bawl; yell; (*radio etc.*) blare; (b) (ugs.: weinen) wail

Plasma /'plasma/ *das;* ~s, **Plasmen** (Med., Physik) plasma; (Proto~) protoplasm

Plast /plast/ *der;* ~[e]s, ~e (regional) plastic

Plastik¹ /'plastɪk/ *die;* ~, ~en sculpture

Plastik² *das;* ~s (ugs.) plastic

Plastik-: ~**beutel** *der* plastic bag; ~**geld** *das* (ugs.) plastic money (coll.); ~**tüte** *die* plastic bag

plastisch 1 *Adj.* (a) (knetbar) plastic; workable; (b) *nicht präd.* (bildhauerisch) sculptural; (*ability*) as a sculptor; (c) (dreidimensional) three-dimensional (*effect, formation, vision*); sculptural (*decoration*); (d) (fig.: anschaulich) vivid (*description, picture*); (e) (Med.) plastic (*surgery, surgeon*). 2 *adv.* (a) (bildhauerisch) sculpturally; (b) (dreidimensional) three-dimensionally; (c) (fig.: anschaulich) vividly; **sich** (*Dat.*) **etw.** ~ **vorstellen können** have a clear picture of sth. [in one's mind]

Platane /pla'taːnə/ *die;* ~, ~n plane tree

Platin /'plaːtiːn/ *das;* ~s platinum

*Platitüde: ⇒ **Plattitüde**

Platon /'plaːtɔn/ (*der*) Plato

platonisch /pla'toːnɪʃ/ 1 *Adj.* (a) Platonic (*philosophy, state*); (b) (nicht sinnlich) platonic (*love, relationship*). 2 *adv.* platonically

platsch /platʃ/ *Interj.* splash

platschen *itr. V.* (a) splash; (b) **mit sein** (~d schlagen) splash (**an** + *Akk.*, **gegen** against); (c) (planschen) splash about

plätschern /'plɛtʃɐn/ *itr. V.* (a) splash; (*rain*) patter; (*stream*) burble; (b) (planschen) splash about; (c) **mit sein** (*stream*) burble along

platt /plat/ *Adj.* (a) (flach) flat; **ein Platter** (ugs.) a flat (coll.); a flat tyre; (mit Loch) a puncture; **sie ist** ~ **wie ein [Bügel]brett** (salopp) she is flat-chested; (b) (geistlos) dull, vapid (*conversation, book*); vacuous, feeble (*poem, joke*); shallow, empty (*materialism, argument, imitation*); (c) *nicht präd.* (ausgesprochen) downright (*lie, swindle, slander*); sheer (*cynicism*); (d) *nicht attr.* (ugs., bes. nordd.: erstaunt) dumbfounded; flabbergasted

Platt *das;* ~[s] [local] Low German dialect; (allgemein: Niederdeutsch) Low German

platt·deutsch *Adj.:* ⇒ **niederdeutsch**

Platte *die;* ~, ~n (a) (Stein~) slab; (Metall~) plate; sheet; (Mikroskopie usw.: Glas~) slide; (Paneel) panel; (Span~, Hartfaser~ usw.) board; (Styropor~ usw.) sheet; (Tisch~) [table-] top; (Grab~) [memorial] slab; (fotografische ~) [photographic] plate; (Druck~) [pressure] plate; (Kachel, Fliese) tile; (zum Pflastern) flagstone; paving stone; (b) (Koch~) hotplate; (c) (Schall~) [gramophone] record; **etw. auf** ~ (*Akk.*) **aufnehmen** make a record of sth.; **die** ~ **kenne ich [schon]** (fig. ugs.) I've heard that one before; (d) (Teller) plate; (zum Servieren, aus Metall) dish; (e) (Speise) dish; **kalte** ~: selection of cold meats [and cheese]

Platten-: ~**cover** *das* record sleeve; ~**firma** *die* record company; ~**hülle** *die* record sleeve; ~**sammlung** *die* record collection; ~**spieler** *der* (als Baustein) record deck; (komplettes Gerät) record player; ~**teller** *der* turntable

Platt-: ~**form** *die* (a) platform; (b) (fig.: Basis) basic programme; ~**fuß** *der* (a) flat foot; (b) (ugs.: Reifenpanne) flat (coll.); flat tyre

Plattheit *die;* ~, ~en (a) *o. Pl.* flatness; (b) *o. Pl.* (fig.) dullness; (c) (Plattitüde) platitude

Plattitüde /plati'tyːdə/ *die;* ~, ~n (geh.) platitude

Platz /plats/ *der;* ~es, **Plätze** /'plɛtsə/ (a) (freie Fläche) space; area; (Bau~, Ausstellungsgelände usw.) site; (umbaute Fläche) square; (b) (Park~) car park; [parking] lot (Amer.); (c) (Sport~) (ganze Anlage) ground; (Spielfeld) field; (Tennis~, Volleyball~ usw.) court; (Golf~) course; **einen Spieler vom** ~ **stellen/tragen** send/carry a player off [the field]; (d) (Stelle) place; spot; (Position) location; position; (wo jmd., etw. hingehört) place; **auf die Plätze, fertig, los!** on your marks, get set, go!; **nicht** *od.* **fehl am** ~[e] **sein** (fig.) be out of place; be inappropriate; **am** ~[e] **sein** (fig.) be appropriate; be called for; (e) (Sitz~) seat; (am Tisch, Steh usw.; fig.: im Kurs, Krankenhaus, Kindergarten usw.) place; ~ **nehmen** sit down; **nehmen Sie** ~! take a seat; ~ **behalten** (geh.) remain seated; (f) (bes. Sport: Platzierung) place; **den dritten** ~ **belegen** come third; (g) (Ort) place; locality; **am** ~: in the town/village; **das größte Hotel am** ~: the largest hotel in the place; (h) *o. Pl.* (Raum) space; room; **er/es hat [noch]** ~/**keinen** ~: there is enough space *or* room [left] for him/it/no room for him/it; **der Saal bietet** ~ *od.* **hat** ~ **für 3 000 Personen** the hall takes *or* holds

3,000 people; **im Viktoriasee hätte ganz Irland** ∼: the whole of Ireland could fit into Lake Victoria; **[jmdm./ einer Sache]** ∼ **machen** make room [for sb./sth.]; ∼ **da!** make way!; out of the way!

Platz-: ∼**angst** *die* (volkst.) claustrophobia; agoraphobia; ∼**anweiser** *der;* ∼**s,** ∼: usher; ∼**anweiserin** *die;* ∼, ∼**nen** usherette

Plätzchen /'plɛtsçən/ *das;* ∼**s,** ∼ **(a)** little place *or* spot; (kleiner Raum) little space; **(b)** (Keks) biscuit (Brit.); cookie (Amer.); (Schokoladen∼) [chocolate] pastille

platzen *itr. V.; mit sein* **(a)** burst; (explodieren) explode; **ihm war eine Augenbraue geplatzt** one of his eyebrows had split open; **vor Wut** *(Dat.)* ∼ (fig.) be bursting with rage; **(b)** (ugs.: scheitern) fall through; **geplatzt sein** ⟨*concert, meeting, performance, holiday, engagement*⟩ be off; **der Wechsel ist geplatzt** the bill has bounced (sl.); **etw.** ∼ **lassen** put the kibosh on sth. (sl.); **(c)** (ugs.: hinein∼) **in eine Versammlung** ∼: burst into a meeting

Platz·hirsch *der* **(a)** (Jägerspr.) dominant stag; **(b)** (fig. ugs.) boss-type (coll.); **er ist hier der** ∼**hirsch** he's the big noise around here (coll.)

platzieren /pla'tsiːrən/ **1** *tr. V.* **(a)** place; position ⟨*loudspeakers*⟩; **(b)** (Sport: gezielt werfen, schlagen usw.) place ⟨*shot, ball*⟩; (Boxen, Fechten) land ⟨*blow, hit*⟩. **2** *refl. V.* **(a)** (sich setzen) place *or* seat oneself **(auf** + *Akk. od. Dat.* on); (sich stellen) take up position **(an** + *Akk. od. Dat.* at, by); **(b)** (Sport) be placed; **er konnte sich nicht** ∼: he was unplaced

Platzierung *die;* ∼, ∼**en** (Sport) placing; place

platz, Platz-: ∼**karte** *die* reserved-seat ticket; ∼**konzert** *das* open-air concert; ∼**mangel** *der* lack of space; ∼**patrone** *die* blank [cartridge]; ∼**regen** *der* downpour; cloudburst; ∼**sparend 1** *Adj.* space-saving; **2** *adv.* economically; in a space-saving manner; ∼**verweis** *der* (Sport) sending-off; ∼**vorteil** *der; o. Pl.* (Sport) home advantage; ∼**wart** *der* (Sport) groundsman; ∼**wunde** *die* lacerated wound

Plauderei *die;* ∼, ∼**en** chat

plaudern /'plaudɐn/ *itr. V.* **(a)** chat **(über** + *Akk.,* **von** about); **(b)** (etw. aus∼) let on (coll.)

Plausch /plauʃ/ *der;* ∼**[e]s,** ∼**e** (bes. südd., österr.) cosy chat

plauschen *itr. V.* (bes. südd., österr.) chat; **miteinander** ∼: have a chat

plausibel /plau'ziːbl̩/ **1** *Adj.* plausible; **jmdm. etw.** ∼ **machen** make sth. seem convincing to sb. **2** *adv.* plausibly

Play-back, Playback /'pleɪbæk/ *das;* ∼**s,** ∼**s** pre-recorded version; recording; (Begleitung) [pre-recorded] backing; (im Fernsehen) miming to a recording

Play·boy /'pleɪbɔɪ/ *der* playboy

Plazenta /pla'tsɛnta/*die;* ∼, ∼**s** *od.* **Plazenten** (Med.) placenta

Plazet /'plaːtsɛt/ *das;* ∼**s,** ∼**s** (geh.) approval

*∗**plazieren** ⇨ **platzieren***

*∗**Plazierung** ⇨ **Platzierung***

pleite /'plaɪtə/ (ugs.) *in* ∼ **sein** ⟨*person*⟩ be broke (coll.); ⟨*company*⟩ have gone bust (coll.); *s. auch* **Pleite a**

Pleite *die;* ∼, ∼**n** (ugs.) **(a)** bankruptcy *no def. art.;* **vor der** ∼ **stehen** be faced with bankruptcy; ∼ **gehen/ machen** go bust (coll.); **(b)** (Misserfolg) flop (sl.); wash-out (coll.)

Plektrum /'plɛktrʊm/ *das;* ∼**s,** **Plektren** plectrum

Plenum /'pleːnʊm/ *das;* ∼**s** (Versammlung) plenary meeting; (Sitzung) plenary session

Pleuel·stange /'plɔɪəl-/ *die* (Technik) connecting-rod

Plexi·glas ⓦ /'plɛksiɡlaːs/ *das; o. Pl.* ≈ Perspex (P)

Plissee /plɪ'seː/ *das;* ∼**s,** ∼**s (a)** (Falten) accordion pleats *pl.;* **(b)** (Stoff) accordion-pleated material

Plissee·rock *der* accordion-pleated skirt

Plombe /'plɔmbə/ *die;* ∼, ∼**n (a)** (Siegel) [lead] seal; **(b)** (veralt.: Zahnfüllung) filling

plombieren *tr. V.* **(a)** (versiegeln) seal; **(b)** (veralt.) fill ⟨*tooth*⟩

plötzlich /'plœtslɪç/ **1** *Adj.* sudden. **2** *adv.* suddenly; …, **aber etwas** *od.* **ein bisschen** ∼ (salopp) …, and jump to it; …, and make it snappy (coll.)

Pluder·hose /'pluːdɐ-/ *die* pantaloons *pl.;* (orientalischer Art) Turkish trousers *pl.*

plump /plʊmp/ **1** *Adj.* **(a)** (dick) plump; podgy; massive ⟨*stone, lump*⟩; (unförmig) ungainly, clumsy ⟨*shape*⟩; (rundlich) bulbous; **(b)** (schwerfällig) awkward, clumsy ⟨*movements, style*⟩; **(c)** (abwertend: dreist) crude, blatant ⟨*lie, deception, trick*⟩; (leicht durchschaubar) blatantly obvious; (unbeholfen) clumsy ⟨*excuse, advances*⟩; crude ⟨*joke, forgery*⟩. **2** *adv.* **(a)** (schwerfällig) clumsily; awkwardly; **(b)** (abwertend: dreist) in a blatantly obvious manner

Plumpheit *die;* ∼, ∼**en (a)** *o. Pl.* (Dicke) plumpness; podginess; (Unförmigkeit) ungainliness; clumsiness; (Rundlichkeit) bulbousness; **(b)** *o. Pl.* (Schwerfälligkeit) clumsiness; awkwardness; (eines dicken Menschen) ponderousness; **(c)** *o. Pl.* (abwertend: Dreistigkeit) blatant nature; (primitive Art) crudity; clumsiness

plumps *Interj.* bump; thud; (ins Wasser) splash

Plumps *der;* ∼**es,** ∼**e** (ugs.) bump; thud; (ins Wasser) splash

plumpsen *itr. V.* fall with a bump; thud; (ins Wasser) splash

Plumps·klo *das* (ugs.) earth-closet

plump·vertraulich, *plump-vertraulich* 1 *Adj.* over-familiar. **2** *adv.* with excessive familiarity

Plunder /'plʊndɐ/ *der;* ∼**s** (ugs. abwertend) junk; rubbish

plündern /'plʏndɐn/ *itr., tr. V.* **(a)** loot; plunder, pillage ⟨*town*⟩; **(b)** (scherzh.: [fast] leeren) raid ⟨*larder, fridge, account*⟩; ⟨*bird, animal*⟩ strip ⟨*tree, border*⟩

Plünderung *die;* ∼, ∼**en** looting; (einer Stadt) plundering; ∼**en** cases of looting/plundering

Plural /'pluːraːl/ *der;* ∼**s,** ∼**e (a)** *o. Pl.* plural; **(b)** (Wort) word in the plural; plural form; **im** ∼ **stehen** be [in the] plural

plus /plʊs/ **▶ 600** **1** *Konj.* (Math.) plus. **2** *Adv.* **(a)** **▶ 511** plus; **(b)** (Elektrot.) positive. **3** *Präp. mit Dat.* (Kaufmannsspr.) plus

Plus *das;* ∼ **(a)** (Überschuss) surplus; (auf einem Konto) credit balance; (Gewinn) profit; **im** ∼ **sein** be in credit; **(b)** (Vorteil) advantage; (Aktiva) asset; **das ist ein** ∼ **für dich** it's a point in your favour

Plüsch /plyːʃ/ *der;* ∼**[e]s,** ∼**e** plush

Plüsch·tier *das* cuddly toy

Plus·pol *der* positive pole; (einer Batterie) positive terminal

Plusquam·perfekt /'plʊskvampɛrfɛkt/ *das* pluperfect [tense]

Plus·zeichen *das* plus sign

pneumatisch (Technik) **1** *Adj.* pneumatic. **2** *adv.* pneumatically

Po /poː/ *der;* ∼**s,** ∼**s** (ugs.) bottom

Pöbel /'pøːbl̩/ *der;* ∼**s** (abwertend) rabble

pöbelhaft (abwertend) **1** *Adj.* loutish; uncouth. **2** *adv.* in a loutish manner

pochen /'pɔxn̩/ *itr. V.* **(a)** (meist geh.: klopfen) knock **(gegen** at, on); (kräftig) rap; thump; **es pocht** somebody is knocking at *or* on the door; **(b)** (geh.: sich berufen) **auf etw.** *(Akk.)* ∼: insist on sth.; **(c)** (geh.: pulsieren) ⟨*heart*⟩ pound, thump; ⟨*blood*⟩ pound, throb

Pocken /'pɔkn̩/ *Pl.* **▶ 329** smallpox *sing.*

Pocken·schutz·impfung *die* smallpox vaccination

pockig *Adj.* pock-marked ⟨*face, surface*⟩; pimpled ⟨*leather*⟩

Podest /po'dɛst/ *das od. der;* ∼**[e]s,** ∼**e** rostrum

Podium /'poːdjʊm/ *das;* ∼**s,** **Podien (a)** (Plattform) platform; (Bühne) stage; **(b)** (trittartige Erhöhung) rostrum; podium

Podiums·diskussion *die* panel discussion

Poesie /poe'ziː/ *die;* ∼, ∼**n (a)** *o. Pl.* poetry; **(b)** (Gedicht) poem

Poesie·album *das* autograph album (*with verses or sayings contributed by friends*)

Poet /poˈeːt/ der; ~en, ~en (veralt.) poet; bard (literary)

poetisch 1 Adj. poetic[al]. 2 adv. poetically

Pogrom /poˈgroːm/ das od. der; ~s, ~e pogrom

Pointe /ˈpo̯ɛ̃ːtə/ die; ~, ~n (eines Witzes) punch line; (einer Geschichte) point; (eines Sketches) curtain line

pointiert /po̯ɛ̃ˈtiːɐ̯t/ 1 Adj. pointed ‹remark›. 2 adv. pointedly

Pokal /poˈkaːl/ der; ~s, ~e (a) (Trinkgefäß) goblet; (b) (Siegestrophäe, ~wettbewerb) cup

Pokal-: ~**sieger** der (Sport) cup-winners pl.; ~**spiel** das (Sport) cup-tie

Pökel·fleisch das salt meat

pökeln /ˈpøːkl̩n/ tr. V. salt

Poker /ˈpoːkɐ/ das od. der; ~s poker; (fig.) manoeuvrings pl.

Poker·gesicht das poker-face

pokern itr. V. play poker; (fig.) um etw. ~: bid for sth.

Pol /poːl/ der; ~s, ~e pole; der ruhende ~ (fig.) the calming influence

polar /poˈlaːɐ̯/ Adj. polar

Polar-: ~**kreis** der polar circle; nördlicher/südlicher ~**kreis** Arctic/Antarctic Circle; ~**licht** das; Pl. ~**lichter** aurora; polar lights pl.; ~**stern** der polar star; pole star

Polaroid·kamera Ⓦ /polaroˈiːt-/ die Polaroid camera (P)

Pole der; ~n, ~n ▶ 388 | Pole

Polemik /poˈleːmɪk/ die; ~, ~en polemic

polemisch 1 Adj. polemic[al]. 2 adv. polemically

polemisieren itr. V. polemize

Polen (das); ~s Poland

Polente /poˈlɛntə/ die; ~ (salopp) cops pl. (coll.)

Police /poˈliːsə/ die; ~, ~n (Versicherungsw.) policy

Polier /poˈliːɐ̯/ der; ~s, ~e [site] foreman

polieren tr. V. polish; jmdm. die Fresse ~ (derb) smash sb.'s face in

Poli·klinik die outpatients' department or clinic

Polin die; ~, ~nen Pole

Politesse /poliˈtɛsə/ die; ~, ~n [woman] traffic warden

Politik /poliˈtiːk/ die; ~, ~en (a) o. Pl. politics sing., no art.; (b) (eine spezielle ~) policy

Politiker /poˈliːtikɐ/ der; ~s, ~, **Politikerin** die; ~, ~nen politician

politisch 1 Adj. (a) political; (b) (klug u. berechnend) politic. 2 adv. (a) politically; (b) (klug u. berechnend) politicly; judiciously

politisieren 1 itr. V. talk politics; politicize. 2 tr. V. politicize; (politisch aktivieren) make politically active

Politisierung die; ~: politicization

Politologe /politoˈloːgə/ der; ~n, ~n, **Politologin** die; ~, ~nen political scientist

Politur /poliˈtuːɐ̯/ die; ~, ~en polish

Polizei /poliˈtsai/ die; ~, ~en (a) police pl.; er ist od. arbeitet bei der ~: he is in the police force; (b) o. Pl. (Dienststelle) police station

Polizei-: ~**auto** das police car; ~**beamte** der ▶ 85 | police officer; ~**chef** der chief of police; chief constable (Brit.); ~**einsatz** der police operation; ~**funk** der police radio; ~**hund** der police dog; ~**kontrolle** die police check

polizeilich 1 Adj., nicht präd. police; ~e Meldepflicht obligation to register with the police. 2 adv. by the police

Polizei-: ~**präsident** der ⇒ ~chef; ~**präsidium** das police headquarters sing. or pl.; ~**revier** das police station; ~**schutz** der police protection; ~**spitzel** der police informer; ~**staat** der police state; ~**streife** die police patrol; ~**stunde** die closing time; ~**wache** die police station

Polizist /poliˈtsɪst/ der; ~en, ~en, **Polizistin** die; ~, ~nen ▶ 85 | policeman/policewoman

---

*alte Schreibung (vgl. Hinweise auf S. xvi–xvii)

Pollen /ˈpɔlən/ der; ~s, ~ (Bot.) pollen

polnisch /ˈpɔlnɪʃ/ Adj. ▶ 388 |, ▶ 487 | Polish; s. auch deutsch; Deutsch

Polo·hemd das short-sleeved shirt

Polster /ˈpɔlstɐ/ das; ~s, ~: (a) upholstery no pl., no indef. art.; (b) (Rücklage) reserves pl.

Polster·möbel Pl. upholstered furniture sing.

polstern tr. V. upholster ‹furniture›; pad ‹door›; sie ist gut gepolstert (fig. ugs. scherzh.) she is well-upholstered (joc.)

Polster-: ~**sessel** der [upholstered] armchair; easy chair; ~**stuhl** der upholstered chair

Polter·geist der poltergeist

poltern /ˈpɔltɐn/ itr. V. (a) (lärmen) crash or thump about; es poltert there is a bang or crash; (b) mit sein der Karren polterte über das Pflaster the cart clattered over the cobblestones; (c) (schimpfen) rant [and rave]

Poly-: ~**ester** /~ˈ|ɛstɐ/ der; ~s, ~ (Chemie) polyester; ~**gamie** /~gaˈmiː/ die; ~: polygamy

Polyp /poˈlyːp/ der; ~en, ~en (a) (Zool., Med.) polyp; (b) (salopp: Polizist) cop (coll.); copper (Brit. sl.)

poly·technisch 1 Adj. polytechnic. 2 adv. er war ~ ausgebildet he had a polytechnic training

Pomade /poˈmaːdə/ die; ~, ~n pomade; hair-cream

Pommern (das); ~s Pomerania

Pommes frites /pɔmˈfrit/ Pl. chips pl. (Brit.); French fries pl. (Amer.)

Pomp /pɔmp/ der; ~[e]s pomp

pompös /pɔmˈpøːs/ 1 Adj. grandiose; ostentatious. 2 adv. grandiosely; ostentatiously

Pontius /ˈpɔntsi̯ʊs/ in von ~ zu Pilatus laufen (ugs.) rush from pillar to post

Pony¹ /ˈpɔni/ das; ~s, ~s pony

Pony² der; ~s, ~s (Frisur) fringe

Pony·frisur die [hairstyle with a] fringe

Pop /pɔp/ der; ~[s] pop

Popanz der; ~es, ~e (abwertend) bogey; bugbear

Popcorn /ˈpɔpkɔrn/ das; ~s popcorn

popelig (ugs. abwertend) 1 Adj. crummy (coll.); lousy (coll.); (durchschnittlich) second-rate. 2 adv. crummily (sl.)

Popeline·mantel der poplin coat

popeln itr. V. (ugs.) [in der Nase] ~: pick one's nose

Pop-: ~**festival** das pop festival; ~**gruppe** die pop group; ~**musik** die pop music

Popper /ˈpɔpɐ/ der; ~s, ~: fashion-conscious, apolitical young person

poppig /ˈpɔpɪç/ 1 Adj. trendy. 2 adv. trendily

populär /popuˈlɛːɐ̯/ 1 Adj. popular (bei with). 2 adv. popularly

Popularität die; ~: popularity

Pore /ˈpoːrə/ die; ~, ~n pore

Porno /ˈpɔrno/ der; ~s, ~s (ugs.) porn[o] (coll.)

Porno·graphie /-graˈfiː/ die; ~, ~n pornography

porno·graphisch 1 Adj. pornographic. 2 adv. pornographically

porös /poˈrøːs/ porous

Porree /ˈpɔre/ der; ~s, ~s leek; ich mag ~: I like leeks

Portal /pɔrˈtaːl/ das; ~s, ~e portal

Portemonnaie /pɔrtmɔˈneː/ das; ~s, ~s purse

Porti Pl. ⇒ Porto

Portier /pɔrˈti̯eː/ der; ~s, ~s porter

Portion /pɔrˈtsi̯oːn/ die; ~, ~en (a) portion; helping; eine halbe ~ (fig. ugs. spött.) a feeble little titch (coll.); eine ~ Eis one icecream; (b) (ugs.: Anteil) amount

Porto /ˈpɔrto/ das; ~s, ~s od. **Porti** postage (für on, for); „~ zahlt Empfänger" 'postage will be paid by licensee'

porträtieren /pɔrtrɛˈtiːrən/ tr. V. paint a portrait of/take a portrait [photograph] of; (fig.) portray

Portugal /ˈpɔrtugal/ (das); ~s Portugal

Portugiese /pɔrtuˈgiːzə/ der; ~n, ~n, **Portugiesin** die; ~, ~nen ▶ 388 | Portuguese

portugiesisch *Adj.* ▶388⌐, ▶487⌐ Portuguese
Port·wein /'pɔrtvain/ *der* port
Porzellan /pɔrtsɛ'laːn/ *das;* ~s porcelain; china
Posaune /po'zaunə/ *die;* ~, ~n trombone
posaunen 1 *itr. V.* (musizieren) play the trombone. **2** *tr. V.* (ugs.) **etw. in die** *od.* **alle Welt** ~**:** tell the whole world about sth.
Posaunist *der;* ~en, ~en trombonist
Pose /'poːzə/ *die;* ~, ~n pose
posieren *itr. V.* pose
Position /pozi'tsioːn/ *die;* ~, ~en position
positiv /'poːzitiːf/ **1** *Adj.* positive. **2** *adv.* positively; **etw.** ~ **bewerten** judge sth. favourably; **der Test verlief** ~**:** the test proved successful
Positiv *das;* ~s, ~e (Fot.) positive
Positur /pozi'tuːɐ̯/ *die;* ~, ~en pose; posture; **sich in** ~ **setzen** *od.* **stellen** *od.* **werfen** (ugs. leicht spött.) strike a pose; take up a posture
Posse /'pɔsə/ *die;* ~, ~n farce
Possen *der;* ~s, ~ *Pl.* (veralt.) pranks; tricks; ~ **reißen** play tricks
possessiv /'pɔsɛsiːf/ *Adj.* (Sprachw.) possessive
Possessiv·pronomen *das* (Sprachw.) possessive pronoun
possierlich /pɔ'siːɐ̯lɪç/ **1** *Adj.* sweet; cute (Amer.). **2** *adv.* sweetly; cutely (Amer.)
Post /pɔst/ *die;* ~, ~en **(a)** post (Brit.); mail; **er ist** *od.* **arbeitet bei der** ~**:** he works for the Post Office; **etw. mit der** *od.* **per** ~ **schicken** send sth. by post or mail; **mit gleicher/getrennter** ~**:** by the same post/under separate cover; **(b)** (~amt) post office; **auf die** *od.* **zur** ~ **gehen** go to the post office
Post-: ~**amt** *das* post office; ~**anweisung** *die* **(a)** (Geldsendung) remittance paid in at a post office and delivered to the addressee by a postman; **(b)** (Formular) postal remittance form; ~**auto** *das* post-office or mail van; ~**beamte** *der* ▶85⌐ post-office official; ~**bote** *der* (ugs.) postman (Brit.); mailman (Amer.)
Posten /'pɔstn/ *der;* ~s, ~ **(a)** (bes. Milit.: Wach~) post; **auf dem** ~ **sein** (ugs.) (in guter körperlicher Verfassung sein) be in good form; (wachsam sein) be on one's guard; **auf verlorenem** ~ **stehen** *od.* **kämpfen** be fighting a losing battle; **(b)** (bes. Milit.: Wachmann) sentry; guard; ~ **stehen** stand guard or sentry; **(c)** (Anstellung) post; position; job; **(d)** (Funktion) position; **(e)** (bes. Kaufmannsspr.: Rechnungs~) item **(f)** (bes. Kaufmannsspr.: Waren~) quantity
Poster /'poːstɐ/ *das od. der;* ~s, ~ poster
Post-: ~**fach** *das* **(a)** ▶107⌐ (im ~amt) post-office or PO box; **(b)** (im Büro, Hotel o. Ä.) pigeon-hole; ~**geheimnis** *das* secrecy of the post; ~**giro·amt** *das* post-office giro office; ≈ national giro[bank] centre (Brit.); ~**girokonto** *das* post-office giro account; ≈ national giro[bank] account (Brit.); ~**horn** *das* post-horn
postieren *tr. V.* **(a)** (aufstellen) post; station; **sich** ~**:** station or position oneself; **(b)** (stellen) position
post-, Post-: ~**karte** *die* postcard; ~**kutsche** *die* mail coach; ~**lagernd** *Adj., adv.* poste restante; general delivery (Amer.); ~**leit·zahl** *die* ▶107⌐ postcode; postal code; Zip code (Amer.); ~**minister** *der* Postmaster General; ~**modern** **1** *Adj.* postmodern[ist] ⟨architecture, style⟩; **2** *adv.* **etw.** ~ **stylen/bauen** design/build sth. in the postmodern[ist] style; ~**moderne** *die* **(a)** (Stil) postmodernism; **(b)** (Epoche) postmodern age; ~**scheck** *der* post-office giro cheque; ≈ national giro[bank] cheque (Brit.); ~**spar·buch** *das* post-office savings book (Brit.); ~**spar·kasse** *die* post-office savings bank (Brit.); ~**stempel** *der* **(a)** (Gerät) stamp [for cancelling mail]; **(b)** (Abdruck) postmark
postum /pɔs'tuːm/ **1** *Adj.; nicht präd.* posthumous. **2** *adv.* posthumously
post-, Post-: ~**wendend** *Adv.* by return [of post]; (fig.) immediately; ~**wurf·sendung** *die* direct-mail item; ~**zustellung** *die* postal delivery *no def. art.*
potemkinsch /po'tɛmkiːnʃ/ *Adj.; in* ~**e Dörfer** façade *sing.;* sham *sing.*

potent /po'tɛnt/ *Adj.* **(a)** potent; **(b)** (finanzstark) [financially] strong
***Potential** ⇒ **Potenzial**
***potentiell** ⇒ **potenziell**
Potenz /po'tɛnts/ *die;* ~, ~en ▶600⌐ **(a)** o. *Pl.* potency; **(b)** (Stärke) power; **(c)** (Math.) power
Potenzial /potɛn'tsiaːl/ *das;* ~s, ~e potenzial
potenziell /potɛn'tsiɛl/ **1** *Adj.* potential. **2** *adv.* potentially
potenzieren 1 *tr. V.* **(a)** (verstärken) increase; **(b)** (Math.) **mit 5** ~**:** raise to the power [of] 5. **2** *refl. V.* (sich steigern) increase
Potpourri /'pɔtpʊri/ *das;* ~s, ~s potpourri, medley (aus, von of)
Präambel /prɛ'ambl̩/ *die;* ~, ~n preamble
Pracht /praxt/ *die;* ~**:** splendour; magnificence; **eine [wahre]** ~ **sein** (ugs.) be [really] marvellous or (coll.) great
Pracht·exemplar *das* (ugs.) magnificent specimen; beauty
prächtig /'prɛçtɪç/ **1** *Adj.* **(a)** (prunkvoll) splendid; magnificent; **(b)** (großartig) splendid; marvellous. **2** *adv.* **(a)** (prunkvoll) splendidly; magnificently; **(b)** (großartig) splendidly; marvellously
Pracht-: ~**kerl** *der* (ugs.) great chap or (Brit. coll.) bloke or (coll.) guy; ~**stück** *das* ⇒ ~**exemplar**
prädestinieren *tr. V.* predestine
Prädikat /prɛdi'kaːt/ *das;* ~[e]s, ~e **(a)** (Auszeichnung) rating; **(b)** (Sprachw.) predicate
prädikativ /prɛdika'tiːf/ (Sprachw.) **1** *Adj.* predicative. **2** *adv.* predicatively
Prag /praːk/ *(das);* ~s ▶490⌐ Prague
prägen /'prɛːgn/ *tr. V.* **(a)** emboss ⟨metal, paper, leather⟩; mint, strike ⟨coin⟩; **(b)** (auf~) (vertieft) impress; (erhaben) emboss; **(c)** (fig.: beeinflussen) shape; mould; **(d)** (fig.: erfinden) coin ⟨word, expression, concept⟩
Pragmatiker *der;* ~s, ~**:** pragmatist
pragmatisch 1 *Adj.* pragmatic. **2** *adv.* pragmatically
Pragmatismus *der;* ~**:** pragmatism
prägnant /prɛ'gnant/ **1** *Adj.* concise; succinct. **2** *adv.* concisely; succinctly
Prägnanz /prɛ'gnants/ *die;* ~**:** conciseness; succinctness
Prägung *die;* ~, ~en **(a)** (von Papier, Leder, Metall) embossing; (von Münzen) minting; striking; **(b)** (auf Metall, Papier) (vertieft) impression; (erhaben) embossing; **(c)** (Eigenart) character; **(d)** (eines sprachlichen Ausdrucks) coining; (geprägter Ausdruck) coinage
prahlen /'praːlən/ *itr. V.* boast, brag (**mit** about)
Prahlerei *die;* ~, ~en (abwertend) boasting; bragging
Praktik /'praktɪk/ *die;* ~, ~en practice
Praktika ⇨ **Praktikum**
praktikabel /prakti'kaːbl̩/ *Adj.* practicable; practical
Praktikant /prakti'kant/ *der;* ~en, ~en, **Praktikantin** *die;* ~, ~nen **(a)** (in einem Betrieb) student trainee; trainee student; **(b)** (an der Hochschule) physics/chemistry student ⟨doing a period of practical training⟩
Praktiker *der;* ~s, ~ practical person
Praktikum /'praktikʊm/ *das;* ~s, **Praktika** period of practical instruction or training
praktisch /'praktɪʃ/ **1** *Adj.* **(a)** (auf die Praxis bezogen) practical; ~**er Arzt** general practitioner; **(b)** (wirklich) practical ⟨result, problem, matter, etc.⟩; concrete ⟨example⟩; **(c)** (nützlich) practical ⟨furniture, clothes, etc.⟩; useful ⟨present⟩; **(d)** (geschickt, realistisch) practical. **2** *adv.* **(a)** (auf die Praxis bezogen) in practice; ~ **arbeiten** do practical work; **(b)** (wirklich) in practice; **(c)** (nützlich) practically; **(d)** (geschickt, realistisch) practically; **(e)** (ugs.: so gut wie) practically; virtually
praktizieren /prakti'tsiːrən/ *tr. V.* **(a)** (anwenden) practise; **(b)** (ugs.: irgendwohin bringen) conjure; **jmdm. etw. ins Essen** ~**:** slip sth. into sb.'s food
Praline /pra'liːnə/ *die;* ~, ~n [filled] chocolate
prall /pral/ **1** *Adj.* **(a)** (fest und straff) hard ⟨ball⟩, firm ⟨tomato, grape⟩; bulging ⟨sack, wallet, bag⟩; big strong *attrib.* ⟨thighs, muscles, calves⟩; full, well-rounded

⟨*breasts*⟩; full, chubby ⟨*cheeks*⟩; taut, full ⟨*sail*⟩; (fig.) intense ⟨*life*⟩; vivid ⟨*picture*⟩; fully inflated ⟨*balloon*⟩; **(b)** (intensiv) blazing ⟨*sun*⟩; strong ⟨*light*⟩. **2** *adv.* fully ⟨*inflated*⟩; **eine ~ gefüllte Brieftasche** a wallet bulging with banknotes

prallen *itr. V.* **(a)** *mit sein* (hart auftreffen) crash **(gegen/ auf/an** + *Akk.* into); collide **(gegen/auf/an** + *Akk.* with); **der Ball prallte an den Pfosten** the ball hit the post; **(b)** (scheinen) blaze

prall·voll *Adj.* (ugs.) ⟨*suitcase, rucksack*⟩ full to bursting; packed ⟨*room*⟩

Prämie /ˈprɛːmi̯ə/ *die; ~, ~n* **(a)** (Leistungs~) bonus; (Belohnung) reward; (Spar~, Versicherungs~) premium; **(b)** (einer Lotterie) [extra] prize

prämieren /prɛˈmiːrən/, **prämiieren** /prɛmiˈiːrən/ *tr. V.* award a prize to ⟨*person, film*⟩; give an award for ⟨*best essay etc.*⟩

Prämierung, **Prämiierung** *die; ~, ~en* **(a)** (Auszeichnung) **er/der Film wurde zur ~ vorgeschlagen** it was proposed that he should be given a prize/that a prize should be given for the film; **(b)** (Preisverleihung) **die ~ der besten Schüler/Filme** the presentation of prizes to the best pupils/for the best films

Prämisse /prɛˈmɪsə/ *die; ~, ~n* premiss

prangen /ˈpraŋən/ *itr. V.* be prominently displayed

Pranger /ˈpraŋɐ/ *der; ~s, ~* (hist.) pillory; **jmdn./etw. an den ~ stellen** (fig.) pillory sb./sth.

Pranke /ˈpraŋkə/ *die; ~, ~n* **(a)** (Pfote) paw; **(b)** (salopp: große Hand) paw (coll.)

Präparat /prɛpaˈraːt/ *das; ~[e]s, ~e* preparation

präparieren *tr. V.* **(a)** (Biol., Med.: konservieren) preserve; **(b)** (Biol., Anat.: zerlegen) dissect

Präposition /prɛpoziˈtsi̯oːn/ *die; ~, ~en* (Sprachw.) preposition

Prärie /prɛˈriː/ *die; ~, ~n* prairie

Präsens /ˈprɛːzɛns/ *das; ~,* **Präsentia** /prɛˈzɛntsi̯a/ *od.* **Präsenzien** /prɛˈzɛntsi̯ən/ (Sprachw.) present [tense]

präsent /prɛˈzɛnt/ *Adj.* present

präsentieren *tr. V.* **(a)** (anbieten; überreichen) offer; **(b)** (vorlegen) present; **jmdm. die Rechnung [für etw.] ~:** present sb. with the bill [for sth.]

Präservativ /prɛzɛrvaˈtiːf/ *das; ~s, ~e* condom

Präsident /prɛziˈdɛnt/ *der; ~en, ~en* ▶ 34⏐ president

Präsidenten·wahl *die* presidential election

Präsidentin *die; ~, ~nen* president

Präsidentschaft *die; ~, ~en* presidency

Präsidien *Pl.* ⇒ **Präsidium**

Präsidium /prɛˈziːdi̯ʊm/ *das; ~s,* **Präsidien** **(a)** (Führungsgruppe) committee; **(b)** (Vorsitz) chairmanship; **(c)** (Polizei~) police headquarters *sing. or pl.*

prasseln /ˈprasl̩n/ *itr. V.* ⟨*rain, hail*⟩ pelt down; ⟨*shots*⟩ clatter; ⟨*fire*⟩ crackle

prassen /ˈprasn̩/ *itr. V.* live extravagantly; (schlemmen) feast

Präteritum /prɛˈteːritʊm/ *das; ~s,* **Präterita** (Sprachw.) preterite [tense]

präventiv /prɛvɛnˈtiːf/ *Adj.* preventive

Praxis /ˈpraksɪs/ *die; ~,* **Praxen (a)** *o. Pl.* (im Unterschied zur Theorie) practice *no art.;* **in der ~:** in practice; **etw. in die ~ umsetzen** put sth. into practice; **(b)** *o. Pl.* (Erfahrung) [practical] experience; **(c)** (eines Arztes, Anwalts, Psychologen usw.) practice; **(d)** (~räume) (eines Arztes) surgery (Brit.); office (Amer.); (eines Anwalts, Psychologen usw.) office; **(e)** (Handhabung) procedure

Präzedenz·fall /prɛtseˈdɛnts-/ *der* precedent

präzise /prɛˈtsiːzə/ **1** *Adj.* precise ⟨*definition, answer*⟩; specific ⟨*wishes, suspicion*⟩. **2** *adv.* precisely

präzisieren *tr. V.* make more precise; state more precisely

Präzision /prɛtsiˈzi̯oːn/ *die; ~:* precision

Präzisions·arbeit *die* precision work; (genau nach Zeitplan) precise timing

---

*alte Schreibung (vgl. Hinweise auf S. xvi–xvii)

predigen /ˈpreːdɪɡn̩/ **1** *itr. V.* (Predigt halten) deliver *or* give a/the sermon. **2** *tr. V.* **(a)** (verkündigen) preach; **(b)** (ugs.: auffordern zu) preach; **(c)** (ugs.: belehrend sagen) **wie oft habe ich dir das schon gepredigt!** how often have I told you that!

Prediger *der; ~s, ~,* **Predigerin** *die; ~, ~nen* preacher

Predigt /ˈpreːdɪçt/ *die; ~, ~en* **(a)** sermon; **(b)** (ugs.: Ermahnung) lecture; **jmdm. eine ~ halten** lecture sb.

Preis /praɪs/ *der; ~es, ~e* **(a)** (Kauf~) price **(für** of); **etw. zum halben ~ erwerben** buy sth. at half-price; **um jeden ~** (fig.) at all costs; **(b)** (Belohnung) prize; **der Große ~ von Frankreich** (Rennsport) the French Grand Prix

preis-, **Preis-:** **~ab·schlag** *der* (Kaufmannsspr.) ⇒ **~nachlass**; **~anstieg** *der* rise *or* increase in prices; **~auf·schlag** *der* (Kaufmannsspr.) additional *or* extra charge; **~ausschreiben** *das* [prize] competition; **~bewusst**, ***~bewußt 1** *Adj.* price-conscious; **2** *adv.* price-consciously; **~bindung** *die* (Wirtsch.) price-fixing

Preisel·beere /ˈpraɪzl̩beːrə/ *die* cowberry; cranberry (Gastr.)

Preis·empfehlung *die* (Kaufmannsspr.) recommended price

preisen *unr. tr. V.* (geh.) praise; **sich glücklich ~:** count *or* consider oneself lucky

Preis-: **~erhöhung** *die* price increase *or* rise; **~frage** *die* **(a)** (bei einem ~ausschreiben) [prize] question; **(b)** (Geldfrage) question of price; **~gabe** *die* (geh.) **(a)** (Verzicht) abandonment; **(b)** (von Geheimnissen) revelation; giving away; **~geben** *unr. tr. V.* (geh.) **(a)** (ausliefern) **jmdn. einer Sache** (*Dat.*) **~geben** expose sb. to *or* leave sb. to be the victim of sth.; **(b)** (aufgeben) relinquish ⟨*ideal, independence*⟩; surrender ⟨*territory*⟩; **(c)** (verraten) betray; give away; **~gekrönt** *Adj.* prize- *or* awardwinning; **~gericht** *das* jury; panel of judges; **~günstig 1** *Adj.* ⟨*goods*⟩ available at unusually low prices; ⟨*purchases*⟩ at favourable prices. **2** *adv.* **etw. ~günstig verkaufen/bekommen** sell/get sth. at a low price; **hier kann man ~günstig einkaufen** their prices are very reasonable here; **~lage** *die* price range

preislich *Adj.; nicht präd.* price; in price *postpos.*

preis-, **Preis-:** **~nachlass**, ***~nachlaß** *der* price reduction; discount; **~rätsel** *das* [prize] competition; **~schild** *das* price tag; **~schlager** *der* (ugs.) bargain [offer]; **~senkung** *die* price reduction *or* cut; **~steigerung** *die* rise *or* increase in prices; **~träger** *der*, **~trägerin** *die* prizewinner; **~treiberei** *die* (abwertend) forcing up of prices; **~vergleich** *der* price comparison; **~vergleiche anstellen** compare prices; **~verleihung** *die* presentation [of prizes/awards]; award ceremony; **~wert 1** *Adj.* good value *pred.* **2** *adv.* **dort kann man ~wert einkaufen** you get good value for money there; **hier kann man ~wert essen** you can eat at a reasonable price here

prekär /preˈkɛːɐ̯/ *Adj.* precarious

Prell·bock *der* (Eisenb.) buffer

prellen /ˈprɛlən/ **1** *tr. V.* **(a)** (betrügen) cheat **(um** out of); **die Zeche ~:** avoid paying the bill; **(b)** (verletzen) bash; bruise; **(c)** (Ballsport) bounce. **2** *refl. V.* (sich verletzen) bruise oneself

Prellung *die; ~, ~en* bruise

Premiere /prəˈmi̯eːrə/ *die; ~, ~n* opening night; first night; (Uraufführung) première; (fig.) first appearance

Premier- /prəˈmi̯eː-/: **~minister** *der*, **~ministerin** *die* ▶ 34⏐ prime minister

preschen /ˈprɛʃn̩/ *itr. V.; mit sein* tear

Presse /ˈprɛsə/ *die; ~, ~n* **(a)** press; (für Zitronen) squeezer; **(b)** *o. Pl.* (Zeitungen, ~kritik) press

Presse-: **~agentur** *die* press agency; news agency; **~bericht** *der* press report; **~empfang** *der* press reception; **~erklärung** *die* press statement; **~freiheit** *die* freedom of the press; **~konferenz** *die* press conference; **~meldung** *die* press report

pressen *tr. V.* **(a)** (zusammendrücken) press; **(b)** (auspressen) press ⟨*fruit, garlic*⟩; squeeze ⟨*lemon*⟩; **(c)** (drücken) press; **(d)** (herstellen) press ⟨*record*⟩; mould ⟨*plastic object*⟩

Presse-: ~**sprecher** der ▶85⌋ spokesman; press officer; ~**stimmen** Pl. press commentaries or reviews

pressieren itr. V. (bes. südd.) ⟨matter⟩ be urgent; **mir pressiert sehr** I am in a great hurry

Press·luft, ***Preß·luft** die; o. Pl. compressed air

Press·luft-, ***Preß·luft-:** ~**bohrer** der pneumatic drill; ~**hammer** der pneumatic or air hammer

Prestige /prɛsˈtiːʒə/ das; ~s prestige

preußisch /ˈprɔ̯ʏsɪʃ/ Adj. Prussian

prickeln /ˈprɪkln̩/ itr. V. (a) (kribbeln, kitzeln) tingle; (b) (perlen) sparkle; (c) (reizen) **eine** ~**de Spannung** a tingling atmosphere

Priel /priːl/ der; ~[e]s, ~e narrow channel (in mudflats)

Priem /priːm/ der; ~[e]s, ~e (Kautabak) chewing-tobacco

pries /priːs/ 1. u. 3. Pers. Sg. Prät. v. **preisen**

Priester /ˈpriːstɐ/ der; ~s, ~: priest; **Hoher** ~ (bibl.) high priest

Priesterin die; ~, ~nen priestess

Priester·seminar das seminary

prima /ˈpriːma/ 1 indekl. Adj. (a) (ugs.) great (coll.); fantastic (coll.); (b) nicht präd. (Kaufmannsspr. veralt.) first-class; top-quality. 2 adv. (ugs.) ⟨taste⟩ great (coll.), fantastic (coll.); ⟨sleep⟩ fantastically (coll.) or really well; **es geht mir** ~: I feel great (coll.)

Prima die; ~, **Primen** (Schulw.) (veralt.() eighth and ninth years (of a Gymnasium)

primär /priˈmɛːɐ̯/ 1 Adj. primary. 2 adv. primarily

Primat[1] /priˈmaːt/ der od. das; ~[e]s, ~e (a) (Vorrang) primacy, priority (**vor** + Dat., **über** + Akk. over); (b) (kath. Kirche) primacy

Primat[2] der; ~en, ~en (Zool.) primate

Primel /ˈpriːml̩/ die; ~, ~n primula; primrose; (Schlüsselblume) cowslip

primitiv /primiˈtiːf/ 1 Adj. (a) primitive; (b) (schlicht) simple; crude (derog.). 2 adv. (a) primitively; (b) (schlicht) in a simple manner; crudely (derog.)

Primus /ˈpriːmʊs/ der; ~, **Primi** od. ~se (veralt.) top of the class

Prim·zahl die prime [number]

Prinz /prɪnts/ der; ~en, ~en prince

Prinzessin die; ~, ~nen princess

Prinzip /prɪnˈtsiːp/ das; ~s, ~ien /-ˈtsiːpi̯ən/ principle; **aus/im** ~: on/in principle; **ein Mensch von** ~ien a man/woman of principle

prinzipiell /prɪntsiˈpi̯ɛl/ 1 Adj.; nicht präd. in principle postpos., not pred.; ⟨rejection⟩ on principle; **eine** ~**e Frage/Frage von** ~**er Bedeutung** a question of principle/of fundamental importance. 2 adv. (a) (im Prinzip) in principle; (b) (aus Prinzip) on principle; as a matter of principle

Priorität /prioriˈtɛːt/ die; ~, ~en (a) o. Pl. (Vorrang) priority; precedence; ~ **vor etw.** (Dat.) **haben** have or take precedence over sth.; (b) Pl. (Rangfolge) priorities; ~**en setzen** establish priorities

Prise /ˈpriːzə/ die; ~, ~n pinch; **eine** ~ **Sarkasmus/Ironie** (fig.) a hint or touch of sarcasm/irony

Prisma /ˈprɪsma/ das; ~s, **Prismen** (Math., Optik) prism

Pritsche /ˈprɪtʃə/ die; ~, ~n plank bed

privat /priˈvaːt/ 1 Adj. private; personal ⟨opinion, happiness, etc.⟩; **an/von Privat** to/from private individuals pl. 2 adv. privately; **jmdn.** ~ **sprechen** speak to sb. in private or privately

Privat-: ~**adresse** die private or home address; ~**angelegenheit** die private affair or matter; **das ist seine** ~**angelegenheit** that's his own business or his own private affair; ~**besitz** der private property; **sich im** ~**besitz befinden** be privately owned or in private ownership; ~**eigentum** das private property; ~**fernsehen** das privately operated television; ≈ commercial television; ~**gespräch** das private conversation; (Telefongespräch) private call

privatisieren tr. V. privatize; transfer into private ownership

Privat-: ~**klinik** die private clinic or hospital; ~**leben** das; o. Pl. private life; ~**patient** der private patient; ~**person** die private individual; ~**sache** die ⇨ ~**angelegenheit;** ~**schule** die private school; (Eliteschule in Großbritannien) public school; ~**unterricht** der private tuition; private lessons pl.; ~**wirtschaft** die private sector

Privileg /priviˈleːk/ das; ~[e]s, ~ien /-ˈleːgi̯ən/ privilege

privilegieren tr. V. grant privileges to

privilegiert Adj. privileged

pro /proː/ Präp. mit Akk. per; ~ **Jahr** per year or annum; ~ **Kopf** per head; ~ **Stück** each; apiece; ~ **Nase** (ugs.) each; a head

Pro das in [das] ~ **und** [das] **Kontra** the pros and cons pl.

pro-: pro-; ~**westlich** pro-western

Probe /ˈproːbə/ die; ~, ~n (a) (Prüfung) test; **die** ~ **aufs Exempel machen** put it to the test; **auf** ~: on probation; **jmdn./etw. auf die** ~ **stellen** put sb./sth. to the test; (b) (Muster, Teststück) sample; **eine** ~ **seines Könnens zeigen** od. **geben** (fig.) show what one can do; (c) (Theater~, Orchester~) rehearsal

Probe-: ~**alarm** der practice alarm; (Feueralarm) fire drill or -practice; ~**exemplar** das specimen copy; ~**fahrt** die trial run; (vor dem Kauf, nach einer Reparatur) test drive; ~**lauf** der (Technik) test run

proben tr., itr. V. rehearse

probe·weise Adv. ⟨employ⟩ on a trial basis; **den Motor** ~ **laufen lassen** test[-run] the engine

Probe·zeit die probationary or trial period

probieren 1 tr. V. (a) (versuchen) try; have a go or try at; (b) (kosten) taste; try; sample; (c) (aus~) try out; (an~) try on ⟨clothes, shoes⟩. 2 itr. V. (a) (versuchen) try; have a go or try; **Probieren geht über Studieren** the proof of the pudding is in the eating (prov.); (b) (kosten) have a taste

Problem /proˈbleːm/ das; ~s, ~e problem

Problematik /probleˈmaːtɪk/ die; ~ (Schwierigkeit) problematic nature; (Probleme) problems pl.

problematisch Adj. problematic[al]

problem·los 1 Adj. problem-free. 2 adv. without any problems

Produkt /proˈdʊkt/ das; ~[e]s, ~e product

Produktenhandel der (Kaufmannsspr.) trade in agricultural commodities

Produktion /prodʊkˈtsi̯oːn/ die; ~, ~en production

Produktions-: ~**abteilung** die production department; ~**anlage** die; meist Pl. production unit; ~**anlagen** production plant sing.; ~**leiter** der production manager; ~**mittel** Pl. (marx.) means of production; ~**prozess,** *~**prozeß** der, ~**verfahren** das production process

produktiv /prodʊkˈtiːf/ 1 Adj. productive; prolific ⟨writer, artist, etc.⟩. 2 adv. ⟨cooperate, work⟩ productively

Produktivität /prodʊktiviˈtɛːt/ die; ~: productivity

Produzent /produˈtsɛnt/ der; ~en, ~en, **Produzentin** die; ~, ~nen producer

produzieren 1 tr. V. (a) auch itr. (herstellen) produce; (b) (ugs.: hervorbringen) make ⟨bow, noise⟩; come up with ⟨excuse, report⟩. 2 refl. V. (ugs.: großtun) show off

Prof. Abk. **Professor** Prof.

profan /proˈfaːn/ Adj. nicht präd. profane; secular

professionell /profɛsi̯oˈnɛl/ 1 Adj. professional. 2 adv. professionally

Professor /proˈfɛsɔr/ der; ~s, ~en /-ˈsoːrən/ ▶34⌋, ▶85⌋ (a) (Hochschul~) professor; **ordentlicher** ~: [full] professor (holding a chair); **außerordentlicher** ~: extraordinary professor (not holding a chair); (b) (österr., sonst veralt.: Gymnasial~) [grammar school] teacher

Professorin /profɛˈsoːrɪn/ die; ~, ~nen (a) (Hochschul~) professor; (b) (österr.: Studienrätin) mistress

Professur /profɛˈsuːɐ̯/ die; ~, ~en professorship, chair (**für** in)

Profi der; ~s, ~s (ugs.) pro (coll.)

Profil /proˈfiːl/ das; ~s, ~e (a) (Seitenansicht) profile; **im** ~: in profile; (b) (von Reifen, Schuhsohlen) tread; (c) (ausgeprägte Eigenart) image

profilieren *refl. V.* make one's name *or* mark; (sich unterscheiden) give oneself a clearer image

profiliert *Adj.* prominent

Profi-: ~**spieler** *der* professional player; ~**sport** *der* professional sport

Profit /proˈfiːt/ *der;* ~[e]s, ~e profit; **aus etw.** ~ **ziehen** *od.* **herausschlagen** turn sth. to one's profit *or* advantage; ~ **machen** make a profit; **mit/ohne** ~ **arbeiten** run/not run at a profit

Profit·gier *die* (abwertend) greed for profit

profitieren *itr. V.* profit (**von, bei** *by*); **ich kann dabei nur** ~: I can't lose

Profit·streben *das* (abwertend) profit-seeking

pro forma /proː ˈfɔrma/ *Adv.* (a) (der Form halber) as a matter of form; (b) (zum Schein) for the sake of appearances

Prognose /proˈgnoːzə/ *die;* ~, ~n (auch Med.) prognosis; (Wetter~, Wirtschafts~) forecast

prognostizieren /prognɔstiˈtsiːrən/ *tr. V* (geh.) forecast; predict

Programm /proˈgram/ *das;* ~s, ~e (a) programme; program (Amer., Computing); (Verlags~) list; (Ferns.: Sender) channel; (Ferns., Rundfunk: Sendefolge) programmes *pl. or* (Amer.) programs *pl.;* (Tagesordnung) agenda; **etw. passt jmdm. nicht ins** *od.* **in sein** ~: sth. doesn't fit in with sb.'s plans; **auf dem** ~ **stehen** (fig.) be on the programme *or* agenda; (bei einer Sitzung) be on the agenda; (b) (Kaufmannsspr.: Sortiment) range

programm-, Programm-: ~**gemäß** *adv.* according to programme *or* plan; ~**heft** *das* programme; ~**hinweis** *der* programme announcement

programmieren *tr. V.* (a) (DV) program; (b) (auf etw. festlegen) programme; condition

Programmierer *der;* ~s, ~, **Programmiererin** *die;* ~, ~**nen** ▶ 85 | (DV) programmer

Programm-: ~**vorschau** *die* (im Fernsehen) preview [of the week's/evening's *etc.* viewing]; (im Kino) trailers *pl.;* ~**zeitschrift** *die* radio and television magazine

progressiv /progrɛˈsiːf/ 1 *Adj.* progressive. 2 *adv.* progressively

Projekt /proˈjɛkt/ *das;* ~[e]s, ~e project

Projektil /projɛkˈtiːl/ *das;* ~s, ~e projectile

Projektor /proˈjɛktɔr/ *der;* ~s, ~en /-ˈtoːrən/ projector

projizieren /projiˈtsiːrən/ *tr. V.* (Optik, Math.) project

Proklamation /proklamaˈtsioːn/ *die;* ~, ~en proclamation

proklamieren *tr. V.* proclaim

Pro-Kopf- per head *or* capita *postpos.*

Prokura /proˈkuːra/ *die;* ~, **Prokuren** (Kaufmannsspr.) [full] power of attorney; procuration (formal)

Prolet /proˈleːt/ *der;* ~en, ~en (abwertend) peasant; boor

Proletariat /proletaˈriaːt/ *das;* ~[e]s proletariat

Proletarier /proleˈtaːriɐ/ *der;* ~s, ~: proletarian

proletarisch *Adj.* proletarian

proletenhaft (abwertend) 1 *Adj.* boorish. 2 *adv.* boorishly

Prolog /proˈloːk/ *der;* ~[e]s, ~e prologue

Promenade /promeˈnaːdə/ *die;* ~, ~n promenade

Promenaden-: ~**deck** *das* promenade deck; ~**mischung** *die* (scherzh.) mongrel

Promille /proˈmilə/ *das;* ~s, ~ (a) (Tausendstel) **ein Blutalkoholgehalt von zwei** ~: a blood alcohol level of two parts per thousand; **bei 0,4/unter einem** ~ **liegen** be 0.4/less than one in a *or* per thousand; (b) (ugs.: Blutalkohol) alcohol level

Promille·grenze *die* legal [alcohol] limit

prominent /promiˈnɛnt/ *Adj.* prominent

Prominente *der/die; adj. Dekl.* prominent figure

Prominenz /promiˈnɛnts/ *die;* ~: prominent figures *pl.;* (das Prominentsein) prominence

Promotion /promoˈtsioːn/ *die;* ~, ~en gaining of a/ one's doctorate; **er schloss sein Studium mit der** ~

ab he completed his studies by gaining *or* obtaining his doctorate

promovieren /promoˈviːrən/ *itr. V.* (a) (die Doktorwürde erlangen) gain *or* obtain a/one's doctorate; (b) (eine Dissertation schreiben) do a doctorate (**über** + *Akk.* on)

prompt /prɔmpt/ 1 *Adj.* prompt. 2 *adv.* (a) (umgehend) promptly; (b) (ugs., meist iron.: wie erwartet) [and] sure enough

Pronomen /proˈnoːmən/ *das;* ~s, ~ *od.* **Pronomina** /proˈnoːmina/ (Sprachw.) pronoun

Propaganda /propaˈganda/ *die;* ~: (auch fig. ugs.) propaganda

Propagandist *der;* ~en, ~en, **Propagandistin** *die;* ~, ~**nen** (a) propagandist; (b) (Wirtsch.: Werbefachmann/-frau) demonstrator

propagieren *tr. V.* (geh.) propagate ⟨idea, view, belief, etc.⟩

Propan /proˈpaːn/ *das;* ~s, **Propan·gas** *das; o. Pl.* propane

Propeller /proˈpɛlɐ/ *der;* ~s, ~: propeller; airscrew; prop (coll.)

proper /ˈprɔpɐ/ 1 *Adj.* (a) (adrett) smart; (b) (ordentlich und sauber) neat and tidy; (c) (sorgfältig, genau) meticulous. 2 *adv.* (a) (ordentlich und sauber) neatly and tidily; (b) (sorgfältig, genau) meticulously

Prophet /proˈfeːt/ *der;* ~en, ~en prophet

Prophetin *die;* ~, ~**nen** prophetess

prophetisch 1 *Adj.* prophetic. 2 *adv.* prophetically

prophezeien /profeˈtsaiən/ *tr. V.* prophesy (*Dat.* for); predict ⟨result, weather⟩

Prophezeiung *die;* ~, ~**en** ⇒ **prophezeien:** prophecy; prediction

Proportion /proporˈtsioːn/ *die;* ~, ~**en** proportion

proportional /proporˈtsioˈnaːl/ (auch Math.) 1 *Adj.* proportional. 2 *adv.* proportionally; in proportion

Proporz /proˈpɔrts/ *der;* ~**es**, ~**e** (Politik) proportional representation *no art.*

proppen·voll *Adj.* (ugs.) jam-packed (coll.)

Prosa /ˈproːza/ *die;* ~: prose

prosaisch 1 *Adj.* prosaic. 2 *adv.* prosaically

prosit /ˈproːzɪt/ *Interj.* ▶ 240 | your [very good] health; ~ **Neujahr!** happy New Year!

Prosit *das;* ~**s**, ~**s** ▶ 240 | toast; **ein** ~ **dem Geburtstagskind!** here's to the birthday boy/girl!

Prospekt /proˈspɛkt/ *der od.* (bes. österr.) *das;* ~[e]s, ~e (Werbeschrift) brochure; (Werbezettel) leaflet; (Verlags~) illustrated catalogue; (nur mit Neuerscheinungen) seasonal list

prost /proːst/ *Interj.* (ugs.) cheers (Brit. coll.); **na denn** *od.* **dann** ~! (ugs. iron.) that's brilliant! (coll. iron.); *s. auch* **Mahlzeit**

Prost *das;* ~[e]s, ~e (ugs.) ⇒ **Prosit**

Prostituierte *die/der;* ▶ 85 | *adj. Dekl.* prostitute

Prostitution /prostituˈtsioːn/ *die;* ~: prostitution *no art.*

Protagonist /protagoˈnɪst/ *der;* ~en, ~en, **Protagonistin** *die;* ~, ~**nen** (geh.) protagonist

protegieren /proteˈʒiːrən/ *tr. V.* (geh.) sponsor; patronize ⟨artist, composer, etc.⟩

Protektorat /protɛktoˈraːt/ *das;* ~[e]s, ~e (a) (geh.: Schirmherrschaft) patronage; (b) (Völkerr.: Schutzherrschaft, Schutzgebiet) protectorate

Protest /proˈtɛst/ *der;* ~[e]s, ~e protest; [**bei jmdm.**] ~ **gegen jmdn./etw. einlegen** make a protest [to sb.] against sb./sth.; **etw. aus** ~ **tun** do sth. as a *or* in protest

Protestant /protɛsˈtant/ *der;* ~en, ~en, **Protestantin** *die;* ~, ~**nen** Protestant

protestantisch *Adj.* Protestant

Protest-: ~**bewegung** *die* protest movement; ~**demonstration** *die* protest demonstration

protestieren *itr. V.* protest, make a protest (**gegen** against, about)

Protest-: ~**kundgebung** *die* protest rally; ~**marsch** *der* protest march; ~**welle** *die* wave of protest

---

Prothese /pro'te:zə/ *die;* ∼, ∼**n (a)** artificial limb; prosthesis (Med.); **(b)** (Zahn∼) set of dentures; dentures *pl.;* prosthesis (Med.)

Protokoll /proto'kɔl/ *das;* ∼**s,** ∼**e (a)** (wörtlich) transcript; (Ergebnis∼) minutes *pl.;* (bei Gericht) record; records *pl.;* **[das]** ∼ **führen** make a transcript [of the proceedings]; (bei einer Sitzung Notizen machen) take *or* keep the minutes; **etw. zu** ∼ **geben/zu** ∼ **geben, dass ...:** make a statement about sth./to the effect that ...; **zu** ∼ **nehmen** take down ⟨*statement etc.*⟩; (bei Gericht) enter ⟨*objection, statement*⟩ in the record; **(b)** (diplomatisches Zeremoniell) protocol; **(c)** (Strafzettel) ticket

Protokollant /protokɔ'lant/ *der;* ∼**en,** ∼**en, Protokollantin** *die;* ∼, ∼**nen** transcript writer; (eines Ergebnisprotokolls) keeper of the minutes; (bei Gericht) court reporter

protokollieren 1 *tr. V.* take down; minute, take the minutes of ⟨*meeting*⟩; minute, record in the minutes ⟨*remark*⟩. **2** *itr. V.* (bei einer Sitzung) take *or* keep the minutes; (bei Gericht) keep the record; (bei polizeilicher Vernehmung) keep a record

Proto·plasma /proto'plasma/ *das; o. Pl.* (Biol.) protoplasm

Proto·typ /'pro:toty:p/ *der* **(a)** (geh.: Inbegriff) archetype; epitome; **(b)** (Urform, erste Ausführung; Motorsport) prototype

protzen *itr. V.* (ugs.) swank (coll.); show off; **mit etw.** ∼**:** show sth. off

protzig (ugs. abwertend) **1** *Adj.* swanky (coll.); showy. **2** *adv.* swankily (coll.)

Proviant /pro'vi̯ant/ *der;* ∼**s,** ∼**e** provisions *pl.*

Provider /pro'vai̯də/ *der;* ∼**s,** ∼ (DV) [service] provider

Provinz /pro'vɪnts/ *die;* ∼, ∼**en (a)** (Verwaltungsbezirk) province; **(b)** *o. Pl.* (abwertend: kulturell rückständige Gegend) provinces *pl.*

provinziell /provɪn'tsi̯el/ (meist abwertend) **1** *Adj.* provincial; parochial ⟨*views*⟩. **2** *adv.* provincially

Provinzler /pro'vɪntslɐ/ *der;* ∼**s,** ∼ (ugs. abwertend) [narrow-minded] provincial

Provinz·nest *das* (ugs. abwertend) [tiny] provincial backwater

Provision /provi'zi̯o:n/ *die;* ∼, ∼**en** (Kaufmannsspr.) commission

provisorisch /provi'zo:rɪʃ/ **1** *Adj.* temporary ⟨*accommodation, filling, bridge, etc.*⟩; provisional ⟨*status, capital, etc.*⟩; provisional, caretaker *attrib.* ⟨*government*⟩; provisional, temporary ⟨*measure, regulation, etc.*⟩. **2** *adv.* temporarily; **etw.** ∼ **reparieren** do *or* effect a temporary repair on sth.

Provokation /provoka'tsi̯o:n/ *die;* ∼, ∼**en** provocation

provokativ /provoka'ti:f/ **1** *Adj.* provocative. **2** *adv.* provocatively

provozieren /provo'tsi:rən/ *tr. V.* **(a)** (herausfordern) provoke; **(b)** (auslösen) provoke; cause ⟨*accident, fight*⟩

Prozedur /protse'du:ɐ/ *die;* ∼, ∼**en** procedure

Prozent /pro'tsɛnt/ *das;* ∼**[e]s,** ∼ **(a)** *nach Zahlenangaben Pl. ungebeugt* (Hundertstel) per cent *sing.;* **ich bin mir zu 90** ∼ **sicher** I'm 90 per cent certain; **der Plan wurde zu 90** ∼ **erfüllt** 90 per cent of the plan was fulfilled; **etw. in** ∼**en ausdrücken** express sth. as a percentage; **(b)** *Pl.* (ugs.: Gewinnanteil) share *sing.* of the profits; (Rabatt) discount *sing.;* **auf etw.** *(Akk.)* ∼**e bekommen** get a discount on sth.

Prozent-: ∼**rechnung** *die* percentage calculation; ∼**satz** *der* percentage

prozentual /protsɛn'tua:l/ **1** *Adj.; nicht präd.* percentage. **2** *adv.* ∼ **am Gewinn beteiligt sein** have a percentage share in the profits

Prozess, ***Prozeß** /pro'tsɛs/ *der;* **Prozesses, Prozesse (a)** trial; (Fall) [court] case; **jmdm. den** ∼ **machen** take sb. to court; **einen** ∼ **gewinnen/verlieren** win/lose a case *or* lawsuit; **(b)** (Entwicklung, Ablauf) process; **(c)** (fig.) **mit jmdm./etw. kurzen** ∼ **machen** (ugs.) make short work of sb./sth.

prozessieren *itr. V.* go to court; **gegen jmdn.** ∼**:** bring an action *or* a lawsuit against sb.; (seit längerer Zeit) be engaged in an action *or* a lawsuit against sb.

Prozession /protsɛ'si̯o:n/ *die;* ∼, ∼**en** processi

Prozess·kosten, ***Prozeß·kosten** *Pl.* legal

prüde /'pry:də/ (abwertend) **1** *Adj.* prudish. **2** prudis

Prüderie /pry:də'ri:/ *die;* ∼ (abwertend) prudery; pruc ness

prüfen /'pry:fṇ/ **1** *tr. V.* **(a)** *auch itr.* test ⟨*pupil*⟩ (in *Dat.* in); (beim Examen) examine ⟨*pupil, student, etc.*⟩ (in + *Dat.* in); **mündlich/schriftlich geprüft werden** have an oral/a written test/examination; **(b)** (untersuchen) examine **(auf** + *Akk.* for); check, examine ⟨*device, machine, calculation*⟩ **(auf** + *Akk.* for); investigate, look into ⟨*complaint*⟩; (testen) test **(auf** + *Akk.* for); **(c)** (kontrollieren) check ⟨*papers, passport, application, calculation, information, correctness, etc.*⟩; audit, check, examine ⟨*accounts, books*⟩; **(d)** (vor einer Entscheidung) check ⟨*price*⟩; examine ⟨*offer*⟩; consider ⟨*application*⟩; **drum prüfe, wer sich ewig bindet** (Spr.) marry in haste, repent at leisure (prov.); **(e)** (geh.: großen Belastungen aussetzen) try; **sie ist vom Leben schwer geprüft worden** her life has been a hard trial. **2** *refl. V.* search one's heart

Prüfer *der;* ∼**s,** ∼, **Prüferin** *die;* ∼, ∼**nen (a)** tester; inspector; (Buch∼) auditor; **(b)** (im Examen) examiner

Prüfling /'pry:flɪŋ/ *der;* ∼**s,** ∼**e** examinee; [examination] candidate

Prüf-: ∼**stand** *der* (Technik) test bed; test stand; ∼**stein** *der* touchstone **(für** for, of); measure **(für** of)

Prüfung *die;* ∼, ∼**en (a)** ▶ 240 (Examen) examination; exam (coll.); **eine** ∼ **machen** *od.* **ablegen** take *or* do an examination; **(b)** (das [Über]prüfen) ⇒ **prüfen b–d:** examination; investigation; (Kontrolle) check; (das Kontrollieren) checking *no indef. art.;* (Test) test; (das Testen) testing *no indef. art.;* **nach/bei** ∼ **Ihrer Beschwerde** after/on examining *or* investigating your complaint; **(c)** (geh.: schicksalhafte Belastung) trial

Prüfungs-: ∼**angst** *die* examination phobia; (im Einzelfall) examination nerves *pl.;* ∼**ordnung** *die* examination regulations *pl.*

Prügel /'pry:gḷ/ *der;* ∼**s,** ∼ **(a)** stick; cudgel; **(b)** *Pl.* (Schläge) beating *sing.;* (als Strafe für Kinder) hiding (coll.); ∼ **beziehen** get a hiding (coll.) *or* beating

Prügelei *die;* ∼, ∼**en** (ugs.) punch-up (coll.); fight

Prügel·knabe *der* whipping-boy

prügeln 1 *tr.* (*auch itr.*) *V.* beat **2** *refl. V.* **sich** ∼**:** fight; **sich mit jmdm. [um etw.]** ∼**:** fight sb. [over *or* for sth.]

Prügel·strafe *die* corporal punishment *no art.*

Prunk /prʊŋk/ *der;* ∼**[e]s** splendour; magnificence

Prunk·stück *das* showpiece

prunk·voll 1 *Adj.* magnificent; splendid. **2** *adv.* magnificently; splendidly; magnificently, splendidly, sumptuously ⟨*furnished, decorated*⟩

prusten /'pru:stṇ/ *itr. V.* (ugs.) (schnauben) snort; **vor Lachen** ∼**:** snort with laughter

PS /pe:'|ɛs/ *das;* ∼, ∼ *Abk.* **(a) Pferdestärke** h.p.; **(b) Postskript[um]** PS

Psalm /psalm/ *der;* ∼**s,** ∼**en** psalm

pseudo-, Pseudo- /psɔydo-/ (abwertend) pseudo-

Pseudonym /psɔydo'ny:m/ *das;* ∼**s,** ∼**e** pseudonym; (eines Schriftstellers) pseudonym; nom de plume; pen-name

Psyche /'psy:çə/ *die;* ∼, ∼**n** psyche

Psychiater /psy'çi̯a:tɐ/ *der;* ∼**s,** ∼**:** ▶ 85 psychiatrist

Psychiatrie /psy̩çi̯a'tri:/ *die;* ∼ psychiatry *no art.*

psychiatrisch 1 *Adj.; nicht präd.* psychiatric. **2** *adv.* jmdn. ∼ **behandeln** give sb. a psychiatric treatment

psychisch 1 *Adj.* psychological; psychological, mental ⟨*strain, disturbance, process*⟩; mental ⟨*illness*⟩. **2** *adv.* psychologically; ∼ **gesund/krank sein** be mentally fit/ ill; **ein** ∼ **bedingtes Leiden** an illness of psychological origin

psycho-, Psycho- /psy̩ço-/: ∼**analyse** *die* psychoanalysis *no art.;* ∼**analytiker** *der,* ∼**analytikerin** *die* psychoanalyst; ∼**analytisch 1** *Adj.* psychoanalytical; **2** *adv.* psychoanalytically; ∼**krimi** /'----/ *der* (ugs.) psychological thriller; ∼**loge** /∼'lo:gə/ *der;* ∼**n,** ∼**n** ▶ 85 psychologist; ∼**logie** /∼lo'gi:/ *die;* ∼**:** psychology; ∼**login** *die* ⇒ ∼**loge;** ∼**logisch 1** *Adj.* psychological;

psychologically; ~path /~'pa:t/ der; ~en, ~en, ~hin die; ~, ~nen psychopath; ~terror /'----/ der ...logical intimidation; ~therapeut der, ~thera...tin die ▶85┘ psychotherapist; ~therapeutisch 1 ...j. psychotherapeutic; 2 adv. jmdn. ~therapeutisch be...andeln give sb. psychotherapeutic treatment; ~thera...pie die psychotherapy no art.; ~thriller /'----/ der ⇒ ~krimi

PTA /pe:te:'|a:/ die; ~, ~[s] Abk. **pharmazeutisch-technische Assistentin** pharmaceutical-laboratory assistant

pubertär /pubɐr'tɛ:ɐ̯/ **1** Adj. pubertal. **2** adv. ~ **bedingt** caused by puberty postpos.

Pubertät /pubɐr'tɛ:t/ die; ~: puberty

Publicity /pʌ'blɪsɪti/ die; ~: publicity

publik /pu'bli:k/ Adj. in ~ **sein/werden** be/become public knowledge; **etw.** ~ **machen** make sth. public

Publikation /publika'tsi̯o:n/ die; ~, ~en publication

Publikum /'pu:blikʊm/ das; ~s (a) (Zuschauer, Zuhörer) audience; (beim Sport) crowd; (b) (Kreis von Interessierten) public; (c) (Besucher) clientele

publikums-, Publikums-: ~**erfolg** der success with the public; ~**liebling** der idol of the public; ~**wirksam** Adj. with public appeal postpos., not pred.; punchy ‹headline›; ‹headline› with a strong appeal; effective, compelling ‹broadcast›

publizieren /publi'tsi:rən/ tr. (auch itr.) V. publish

Publizist der; ~en, ~en, **Publizistin** die; ~, ~nen commentator on politics and current affairs; publicist

Puck /pʊk/ der; ~s, ~s (Eishockey) puck

Pudding /'pʊdɪŋ/ der; ~s, ~e od. ~s ≈ blancmange

Pudding·pulver das ≈ blancmange powder

Pudel /'pu:dl̩/ der; ~s, ~ poodle; **das war also des** ~s **Kern** (fig.) so 'that's what was behind it; **wie ein begossener** ~ **dastehen** (ugs.) stand there sheepishly

Pudel·mütze die bobble or pom-pom hat

pudel·wohl Adv. (ugs.) **sich** ~**wohl fühlen** feel on top of the world

Puder /'pu:dɐ/ der; ~s, ~: powder

Puder·dose die powder compact

pudern tr. V. powder; **sich** (Dat.) **die Nase** ~: powder one's nose

Puder-: ~**quaste** die powder-puff; ~**zucker** der icing sugar (Brit.); confectioners' sugar (Amer.)

Puff¹ der; ~[e]s, **Püffe** /'pʏfə/ (ugs.) (Stoß) thump; (leichter/ kräftiger Stoß mit dem Ellenbogen) nudge/dig

Puff² der od. das; ~s, ~s (salopp: Bordell) knocking-shop (sl.); brothel

puffen (ugs.) **1** tr. V. (a) (stoßen) thump; (mit dem Ellenbogen) nudge; dig; (b) (irgendwohin befördern) push; shove; (mit dem Ellenbogen) elbow. **2** itr. V. ‹locomotive› puff

Puffer der; ~s, ~ (Vorrichtung) buffer

Puff·mutter die (salopp) madam

puh /pu:/ Interj. ugh; (erleichtert) phew

Pulk /pʊlk/ der; ~[e]s, ~s od. ~e (a) (Milit.: Verband) group; (b) (Menge) crowd

Pulle /'pʊlə/ die; ~, ~n (salopp) bottle; **volle** ~ (fig. salopp) flat out

Pulli /'pʊli/ der; ~s, ~s (ugs.), **Pullover** /pʊ'lo:vɐ/ der; ~s, ~: pullover; sweater

Pullunder /pʊ'lʊndɐ/ der; ~s, ~: slipover

Puls /pʊls/ der; ~es, ~e pulse; jmds. ~ **fühlen/messen** feel/take sb.'s pulse

Puls·ader die artery; **sich** (Dat.) **die** ~n **aufschneiden** slash one's wrists

pulsieren itr. V. (auch fig.) pulsate; ‹blood› pulse

Puls-: ~**schlag** der (auch fig.) pulse; (einzelner ~schlag) beat; ~**wärmer** der wristlet

Pult /pʊlt/ das; ~[e]s, ~e (a) desk; (Lese~) lectern; desk; (b) (Schalt~) control desk; console

Pulver /'pʊlfɐ/ das; ~s, ~ (a) powder; (b) (Schieß~) [gun]powder; **das** ~ **hat er [auch] nicht [gerade] erfunden** (ugs.) he'll never set the world or (Brit.) the Thames

on fire; **sein** ~ **verschossen haben** (fig. ugs.) have shot one's bolt

Pulver·fass, *Pulver·faß das barrel of gunpowder; (kleiner) powder keg; **auf einem** od. **dem** ~ **sitzen** (fig.) be sitting on a powder keg or on top of a volcano

pulverisieren tr. V. pulverize; powder

Pulver-: ~**kaffee** der instant coffee; ~**schnee** der powder snow

Puma /'pu:ma/ der; ~s, ~s puma

Pummel /'pʊml̩/ der; ~s, ~ (ugs.), **Pummelchen** das; ~s, ~ (ugs.) podge

pumm[e]lig /'pʊm(ə)lɪç/ Adj. (ugs.) chubby

Pump /pʊmp/ der; ~s (salopp) **auf** ~: on tick (coll.)

Pumpe /'pʊmpə/ die; ~, ~n pump

pumpen tr., itr. V. (a) (auch fig.) pump; (b) (ugs.: verleihen) lend; (c) (ugs. entleihen) borrow

Pumper·nickel der pumpernickel

Pumps /pœmps/ der; ~, ~: court shoe

Punk /paŋk/ der; ~[s], ~s punk

Punker /'paŋkɐ/ der; ~s, ~ (a) (Musiker) punk rocker; (b) (Anhänger) punk

Punkt /pʊŋkt/ der; ~[e]s, ~e (a) (Tupfen) dot; (größer) spot; **das ist [nicht] der springende** ~ (fig.) that's [not] the point; **ein dunkler** ~ [in jmds. Vergangenheit] a dark chapter [in sb.'s past]; (b) (Satzzeichen) full stop; period; **nun mach [aber] mal einen** ~! (fig. ugs.) come off it! (coll.); **ohne** ~ **und Komma reden** (ugs.) talk nineteen to the dozen (Brit.); rabbit (Brit. coll.) or talk on and on; (c) (I-Punkt) dot; (d) (Stelle) point; **ein schwacher/wunder** ~ (fig.) a weak/sore point; **die Verhandlungen waren an einem toten** ~ **angelangt** the talks had reached deadlock or an impasse; (e) (Gegenstand, Thema, Abschnitt) point; (einer Tagesordnung) item; point; (f) (Bewertungs~) point; (bei einer Prüfung) mark; **nach** ~**en siegen** win on points; (g) (Musik) dot; (h) (Math.) point; (i) (Zeit~) point; ~ **12 Uhr** at 12 o'clock on the dot

punkt·gleich Adj. (Sport) level on points pred.

Punkt·gleichheit die (Sport) **bei** ~: if the same number of points have been scored

punktieren tr. V. (a) dot ‹line etc.›; (b) (Med.) puncture; (c) (Musik) dot ‹note›

pünktlich /'pʏŋktlɪç/ **1** Adj. punctual; **der Zug ist** ~/ **nicht** ~: the train is on time/is late. **2** adv. punctually; on time; ~ **um 20 Uhr** at 8 o'clock sharp

Pünktlichkeit die; ~: punctuality

Punkt-: ~**niederlage** die (Sport) defeat on points; ~**richter** der (Sport) judge; ~**sieg** der (Sport) win on points; points win

punktuell /pʊŋk'tu̯ɛl/ **1** Adj. isolated ‹interventions, checks, approaches, initiatives, etc.›. **2** adv. **sich mit einem Thema nur** ~ **befassen** deal only with certain or particular points relating to a topic

Punkt·zahl die score; number of points

Punsch /pʊnʃ/ der; ~[e]s, ~e od. **Pünsche** /'pʏnʃə/ punch

Pupille /pu'pɪlə/ die; ~, ~n pupil

Puppe /'pʊpə/ die; ~, ~n (a) doll[y]; (b) (Marionette) puppet; marionette; (fig.) puppet; **die** ~n **tanzen lassen** (fig. ugs.) pull the strings; (es hoch hergehen lassen) paint the town red (fig. coll.); (c) (salopp: Mädchen) bird (sl.); (d) (Zool.) pupa; (e) **bis in die** ~n (ugs.) till all hours

Puppen-: ~**haus** das ⇒ ~**stube**; ~**spiel** das (Stück) puppet show; ~**spieler** der puppeteer; ~**stube** die doll's house; dollhouse (Amer.); ~**theater** das puppet theatre; ~**wagen** der doll's pram

pur /pu:ɐ̯/ Adj. (a) (rein) pure; (b) (unvermischt) neat; straight; **bitte einen Whisky** ~! a neat whisky, please; (c) (bloß) sheer; pure

Püree /py're:/ das; ~s, ~s (a) purée; (b) ⇒ **Kartoffel-brei**

Puritaner /puri'ta:nɐ/ der; ~s, ~ (a) Puritan; (b) (fig.) puritan

puritanisch *Adj.* (a) Puritan; (b) (fig.) puritanical

Purpur /'pʊrpʊr/ *der;* ~s crimson

Purpur·mantel *der* crimson *or* purple robe

purpur·rot *Adj.* crimson

Purzel·baum *der* (ugs.) somersault; **einen** ~ **machen** *od.* **schlagen** do *or* turn a somersault

purzeln /'pʊrts̩ln/ *itr. V.; mit sein* (fam.) tumble

pushen /'pʊʃn̩/ **1** *tr. V* (a) (Drogenjargon) push; (b) (Journalistenjargon) push. **2** *itr. V.* (Drogenjargon) be a pusher

Pusher *der* ~s, ~ (Drogenjargon) pusher

Puste /'puːstə/ *die;* ~ (salopp) puff; breath; **ganz aus der** *od.* **außer** ~ **sein** be out of puff; be puffed [out]; *s. auch* **ausgehen 1 b**

Pustel /'pʊstl̩/ *die;* ~, ~n pimple; spot; pustule (Med.)

pusten (ugs.) **1** *itr. V.* (a) ⟨person, wind⟩ blow; (b) (keuchen) puff [and pant *or* blow]. **2** *tr. V.* blow

Pute /'puːtə/ *die;* ~, ~n (a) turkey hen; (als Braten) turkey; (b) (salopp abwertend: Mädchen, Frau) **eine dumme** ~: a silly goose *or* creature; **eine eingebildete** ~: a stuck-up little madam

Puter *der;* ~s, ~: turkeycock; (als Braten) turkey

puter·rot *Adj.* scarlet; bright red

Putsch /pʊtʃ/ *der;* ~[e]s, ~e putsch; coup [d'état]

putschen *itr. V.* organize a putsch *or* coup

Putschist *der;* ~en, ~en putschist; rebel

Putsch·versuch *der* attempted putsch *or* coup

Putte /'pʊtə/ *die;* ~, ~n (Kunstwiss.) putto

Putz /pʊts/ *der;* ~es plaster; (Rau~) roughcast; (für Außenmauern) rendering; **auf den** ~ **hauen** (fig. salopp) (angeben) boast; brag; (ausgelassen feiern) have a rave-up (Brit. sl.); ~ **machen** (fig. salopp) cause aggro (Brit. sl.)

Putze *die;* ~, ~n (salopp) char (Brit. coll.); cleaner

putzen *tr. V.* (a) (blank reiben) polish; (b) (säubern) clean; groom ⟨horse⟩; **sich** (*Dat.*) **die Zähne/die Nase** ~: clean *or* brush one's teeth/blow one's nose; ⟨*cat*⟩ wash itself; ⟨*bird*⟩ preen itself; (c) *auch itr.* (bes. rhein., südd., schweiz.: sauber machen) clean ⟨room, shop, etc.⟩; ~ **gehen** work as a cleaner *or* (Brit.) char[woman]; (d) (zum Kochen vorbereiten) wash and prepare ⟨vegetables⟩

Putz-: ~**fimmel** *der; o. Pl.* (ugs. abwertend) mania for cleaning; ~**frau** *die* ▸ 85 ┃ cleaner; char[lady] (Brit.)

putzig (ugs.) **1** *Adj.* (entzückend) sweet; cute (Amer.); (possierlich) funny; comical. **2** *adv.* (entzückend) sweetly; cutely (Amer.); (possierlich) comically

putz-, Putz-: ~**lappen** *der* [cleaning-]rag; cloth; ~**munter** (ugs.) **1** *Adj.* chirpy (coll.); perky; ~**munter sein** be as bright as a button; **2** *adv.* chirpily (coll.); perkily; ~**tuch** *das* ⇒ ~**lappen**

Puzzle /'pazl̩/ *das;* ~s, ~s, **Puzzle·spiel** *das* jigsaw [puzzle]

PVC /pe:fau'tse:/ *das;* ~[s] *Abk.* **Polyvinylchlorid** PVC

Pygmäe /py'gmɛːə/ *der;* ~n, ~n pygmy

Pyjama /py'dʒaːma/ *der* (österr., schweiz. auch: das); ~s, ~s pyjamas *pl.*

Pyramide /pyra'miːdə/ *die;* ~, ~n pyramid

pyramiden·förmig *Adj.* pyramidal; pyramid-shaped

Pyrenäen /pyre'nɛːən/ *Pl.* **die** ~: the Pyrenees

Pyromane /pyro'maːnə/ *der;* ~n, ~n (Psych.) pyromaniac

Pyrrhus·sieg /'pyrʊs-/ *der* (geh.) Pyrrhic victory

---

q, Q /ku:/ *das;* ~, ~: q, Q; *s. auch* **a, A**

qm *Abk.* ▸ 189 ┃ **Quadratmeter** sq. m.

Quacksalber /'kvakzalbɐ/ *der;* ~s, ~ (abwertend) quack [doctor]

Quaddel /'kvadl̩/ *die;* ~, ~n [irritating] spot

Quader /'kvaːdɐ/ *der;* ~s, ~ *od.* (österr.:) ~n (a) ashlar block; [rectangular] block of stone; (b) (Geom.) cuboid

Quadrat /kva'draːt/ *das;* ~[e]s, ~e (a) (Geom., Math.) square; **6 cm im** ~: 6 cm. square; **drei im** *od.* **zum** ~: three squared; (b) (bebaute Fläche) block [of houses]

Quadrat- ▸ 189 ┃ square ⟨*kilometre etc.*⟩

quadratisch *Adj.* (a) square; (b) (Math.) quadratic

Quadrat·meter *der od. das* ▸ 189 ┃ square metre

Quadratur /kvadra'tuːɐ/ *die;* ~, ~en (Math., Astron.) quadrature; **die** ~ **des Kreises** (geh.) the achievement of the impossible

Quadrat-: ~**wurzel** *die* (Math.) square root (**aus** of); ~**zahl** *die* square number

quadrieren (Math.) **1** *tr. V.* square. **2** *itr. V.* square numbers

Quadriga /kva'driːga/ *die;* ~, **Quadrigen** quadriga

quadro-, Quadro- /'kvaːdro-/ quadraphonic ⟨*system, effect*⟩

quaken /'kvaːkn̩/ *itr. V.* ⟨*duck*⟩ quack; ⟨*frog*⟩ croak

quäken /'kvɛːkn̩/ **1** *tr. V.* squawk; bawl out ⟨*song*⟩. **2** *itr. V.* (a) ⟨*voice*⟩ squawk; (kreischen) screech; ⟨*radio*⟩ blare; (b) (klagen) ⟨*child*⟩ whine, whinge

Qual /kvaːl/ *die;* ~, ~en (a) *o. Pl.* torment; agony *no indef. art.;* [für jmdn.] **eine** ~ **sein** be agony *or* torment for sb.; **er macht uns** (*Dat.*) **das Leben zur** ~: he's making our lives pl. a misery; **er hat die** ~ **der Wahl** (scherzh.) he is spoilt for choice; (b) *meist Pl.* (Schmerzen) agony; ~**en** pain *sing.;* agony *sing.;* (seelisch) torment *sing.;* **jmdn. von seinen** ~**en erlösen** put sb. out of his/her agony

quälen /'kvɛːlən/ **1** *tr. V.* (a) (körperlich, seelisch) torment ⟨*person, animal*⟩; maltreat, be cruel to ⟨*animal*⟩; (foltern) torture; ~**de Ungewissheit** agonizing uncertainty; (b) (plagen) ⟨*cough etc.*⟩ plague; (belästigen) pester. **2** *refl. V.* (a) (leiden) suffer; (b) (sich abmühen) struggle

Quälerei *die;* ~, ~en (a) torment; (Folter) torture; (Grausamkeit) cruelty; **Tierversuche sind [eine] reine** ~: animal experiments are simply cruel; (b) (das Belästigen) pestering; (c) *o. Pl.* (ugs.: große Anstrengung) struggle

Quäl·geist *der; Pl.* ~**er** (fam.) pest

Qualifikation /kvalifika'tsi̯oːn/ *die;* ~, ~en (a) (Ausbildung) qualifications *pl.;* (b) (Befähigung) capability; (c) (Sport) qualification; (Wettkampf) qualifier; qualifying round

Qualifikations·spiel *das* (Sport) qualifier, qualifying match

qualifizieren /kvalifi'tsiːrən/ *refl. V.* (a) gain qualifications; **sich zum Facharbeiter** ~: gain the qualifications needed to be a skilled worker; (b) (Sport) qualify

qualifiziert **1** *Adj.* (a) ⟨*work, post*⟩ requiring particular qualifications; (b) (sachkundig) competent; skilled ⟨*work*⟩. **2** *adv.* (sachkundig) competently

Qualität /kvali'tɛːt/ *die;* ~, ~en quality

qualitativ /kvalita'tiːf/ **1** *Adj.* qualitative; ⟨*difference, change*⟩ in quality. **2** *adv.* with regard to quality

Qualitäts-: ~**arbeit** *die* high-quality workmanship; ~**erzeugnis** *das* quality product

Qualle /'kvalə/ *die;* ~, ~n jellyfish

Qualm /kvalm/ *der;* ~[e]s [thick] smoke

qualmen **1** *itr. V.* (a) give off clouds of [thick] smoke; **aus dem Kamin qualmt es** clouds of [thick] smoke are coming from the fireplace; (b) (ugs.: rauchen) puff away. **2** *tr. V.* (ugs.: rauchen) puff away at ⟨*cigarette etc.*⟩

1 *Adj.* agonizing. **2** *adv.* agonizingly; ~
...e in great pain

...**en** /'kvɛntçən/ *das;* ~**s**, ~ (veralt.) scrap; **ein** ~
...ng. geh.) a little bit of luck

...**en** *Pl.* (salopp) dirty great feet (sl.)

...**ntität** /kvanti'tɛːt/ *die;* ~, ~**en** quantity; (Zahl) num-

...**antitativ** /kvantita'tiːf/ **1** *Adj.* quantitative. **2** *adv.*
...uantitatively

Quantum /'kvantʊm/ *das;* ~**s**, **Quanten** quota (an +
Dat. of); (Dosis) dose

Quarantäne /karan'tɛːnə/ *die;* ~, ~**n** quarantine

Quark /kvark/ *der;* ~**s** (a) quark; [sour skim milk] curd
cheese; (b) (ugs. abwertend) ⇒ **Käse b**

Quart /kvart/ *die;* ~, ~**en** (Musik) ⇒ **Quarte**

Quarta /'kvarta/ *die;* ~, **Quarten** (Schulw.) (a) (veralt.)
third year (*of a Gymnasium*); (b) (österr.) fourth year (*of a
Gymnasium*)

Quartal /kvar'taːl/ *das;* ~**s**, ~**e** quarter [of the year]

Quarte *die;* ~, ~**n** (Musik) fourth

Quarten ⇒ **Quarta**

Quartett /kvar'tɛt/ *das;* ~**[e]s**, ~**e** (a) (Musik, fig.) quartet; (b) *o. Pl.* (Spiel) *card game in which one tries to get sets
of four;* ≈ Happy Families; (c) (Spielkarten) pack (Brit.) *or*
(Amer.) deck of cards for *Quartett;* (Satz von vier Karten) set of
four *Quartett* cards

Quartier /kvar'tiːɐ̯/ *das;* ~**s**, ~**e** accommodation *no indef. art.;* accommodations *pl.* (Amer.); place to stay; (Mil.)
quarters *pl.;* **bei jmdm.** ~ **beziehen** put up *or* move in
with sb.

Quarz /kvaːɐ̯ts/ *der;* ~**es**, ~**e** quartz

Quarz·uhr *die* quartz clock; (Armbanduhr) quartz watch

quasi /'kvaːzi/ *Adv.* [so] ~: more or less; (so gut wie) as
good as

quasi-, **Quasi-** quasi-

quasseln /'kvasl̩n/ (ugs.) **1** *itr. V.* chatter; rabbit on (Brit.
sl.) (**von** about). **2** *tr. V.* spout, babble ⟨*nonsense*⟩

Quassel·strippe *die* (ugs. abwertend) chatterbox

Quaste *die;* ~, ~**n** tassel

Quatsch /kvatʃ/ *der;* ~**[e]s** (a) (ugs. abwertend) (Äußerung)
rubbish; (Handlung) nonsense; **so ein** ~! what rubbish!; (b)
(ugs.: Unfug) messing about; **lass den** ~: stop messing
about; **mach keinen** ~: don't do anything stupid; (c)
(ugs.: Jux) lark (coll.); ~ **machen** fool around; lark about
(coll.); **aus** ~: for a laugh

quatschen **1** *itr. V.* (a) (ugs.) (dumm reden) rabbit on (Brit.
coll.); blather; (viel reden) chatter; natter (Brit. coll.); (b) (ugs.:
klatschen) gossip; (c) (ugs.: Geheimes ausplaudern) blab; open
one's mouth; (d) (ugs.: sich unterhalten) [have a] chat *or* (coll.)
natter (**mit** with). **2** *tr. V.* spout ⟨*nonsense, rubbish*⟩

Quatsch·kopf *der* (salopp) stupid chatterbox; (Schwätzer,
Schwafler) windbag

Queck·silber /'kvɛk-/ *das* mercury; (fig.) quicksilver

Quelle /'kvɛlə/ *die;* ~, ~**n** (a) spring; (eines Baches, eines
Flusses) source; (b) (fig.) source; **an der** ~ **sitzen** (ugs.) (für
Informationen) have access to inside information; (für günstigen
Erwerb) be at the source of supply

quellen *unr. itr. V.; mit sein* (a) ⟨*liquid*⟩ gush, stream;
(aus der Erde) well up; ⟨*smoke*⟩ billow; ⟨*crowd*⟩ stream, pour;
(fig.) ⟨*tears*⟩ well up; (b) (sich ausdehnen) swell [up]

Quell·wasser *das; Pl.* ~**wasser** spring water

quengelig (ugs.) **1** *Adj.* whining; fretful. **2** *adv.* in a
whining voice; fretfully

quengeln /'kvɛŋl̩n/ *itr. V.* (ugs.) (a) ⟨*baby*⟩ whimper,
(coll.) grizzle; (b) (nörgeln) carp

*Quentchen ⇒ **Quäntchen**

quer /kveːɐ̯/ *Adv.* sideways; crosswise; (schräg) diagonally;
at an angle; ~ **zu etw.** at an angle to sth.; (rechtwinklig) at
right angles to sth.; **der Wagen steht** ~ **auf der
Fahrbahn** the car is standing sideways across the road;
sich ~ **legen** (fig. ugs.) make difficulties; ~ **durch/über**
(+ *Akk.*) straight through/across

---

*alte Schreibung (vgl. Hinweise auf S. xvi–xvii)

Quer-: ~**achse** *die* transverse axis; ~**balken** *der*
(a) cross-beam; (b) (Musik) stroke; ~**denker** *der* lateral
thinker

Quere *die in* jmdm. **in die** ~ **kommen** *od.* **geraten**
(fig.) get in sb.'s way (coll.)

quer·feld·ein *Adv.* across country

quer-, **Quer-:** ~**flöte** *die* transverse flute; ~**format** *das* landscape format; ~**kopf** *der* (ugs.) awkward
cuss (coll.);*~**legen** ⇒ **quer;** ~**pass**, *~**paß** *der*
(Sport) crossfield pass; cross; lateral pass (Amer.); ~**schiff**
das (Archit.) transept; (auch fig.) cross-sec-
tion; ~**schnitt[s]·gelähmt** *Adj.* ▶329 (Med.) paraplegic; ~**schnitt[s]·lähmung** *die;* ▶329 *o. Pl.* (Med.)
paraplegia *no indef. art.;* paraplegic condition; ~**straße**
die intersecting road; ~**summe** *die* (Math.) sum of the
digits (**von**, **aus** of); ~**treiber** *der* (ugs. abwertend)
troublemaker; ~**verbindung** *die* link; (Straße) link
[road]

quetschen **1** *tr. V.* (a) crush ⟨*person, limb, thorax*⟩;
sich (*Dat.*) **den Arm/die Hand** ~: get one's arm/hand
caught; **sich** (*Dat.*) **den Finger/die Zehe** ~: pinch one's
finger/toe; (b) (drücken, pressen) squeeze, squash (**gegen**, **an**
+ *Akk.* against, **in** + *Akk.* into). **2** *refl. V.* **sich in/durch
etw.** (*Akk.*) ~ (ugs.) squeeze into/through sth.

Quetschung *die;* ~, ~**en** bruise; contusion (Med.)

quick·lebendig *Adj.* [very] lively; active; (bes. im Alter)
sprightly; spry; frisky ⟨*small animal*⟩

quiek[s]en /'kviːk(s)n̩/ squeak; ⟨*piglet*⟩ squeal

quietschen /'kviːtʃn̩/ *itr. V.* squeak; ⟨*brakes, tyres,
crane*⟩ squeal, screech; (ugs.) ⟨*person*⟩ squeal; shriek

quietsch-: ~**fidel** *Adj.* (ugs.) (a) [really] chirpy (coll.)
or (esp. Amer.) chipper; (b) (gesund und munter) bright-eyed
and bushy-tailed *pred.* (coll.); ~**vergnügt** *Adj.* (ugs.) ⇒
~**fidel a**

Quint /kvɪnt/ *die;* ~, ~**en** (Musik) ⇒ **Quinte**

Quinta /'kvɪnta/ *die;* ~, **Quinten** (Schulw.) (a) (veralt.)
second year (*of a Gymnasium*); (b) (österr.) fifth year (*of a
Gymnasium*)

Quinte /'kvɪntə/ *die;* ~, ~**n** (Musik) fifth

Quint·essenz *die* (geh.) essential point; essence

Quintett /kvɪn'tɛt/ *das;* ~**[e]s**, ~**e** (Musik, fig.) quintet

Quirl /kvɪrl/ *der;* ~**[e]s**, ~**e** *long-handled blender with a
star-shaped head*

quirlen *tr. V.* ≈ whisk

quirlig *Adj.* lively

quitt /kvɪt/ *Adj.; nicht attr.* (ugs.) quits; **damit sind wir
~:** that makes us quits

Quitte /'kvɪtə/ *die;* ~, ~**n** quince

quittieren *tr. V.* (a) acknowledge, confirm ⟨*receipt,
condition*⟩; receipt, give a receipt for ⟨*sum, invoice*⟩; (b)
etw. mit etw. ~ (fig.) react *or* respond to sth. with sth.;
etw. mit Pfiffen ~: greet sth. with catcalls

Quittung *die;* ~, ~**en** (a) receipt (**für**, **über** + *Akk.*
for); (b) (fig.) come-uppance (coll.); deserts *pl.;* **nun hast du
die ~:** you've got what you deserve

Quiz /kvɪs/ *das;* ~, ~: quiz

quoll /kvɔl/ *1. u. 3. Pers. Sg. Prät. v.* **quellen**

Quote /'kvoːtə/ *die;* ~, ~**n** (Anteil) proportion; (Zahl) number

Quoten·regelung *die: requirement that women should
be adequately represented*

Quotient /kvo'tsi̯ɛnt/ *der;* ~**en**, ~**en** (Math.) quotient
(**aus** of)

R r

r, R /ɛr/ *das;* ~, ~: r, R; **er rollt das R̄** he rolls his r's; *s. auch* **a, A**

Rabatt /ra'bat/ *der;* ~[e]s, ~e discount

Rabatte /ra'batə/ *die;* ~, ~n border

rabattieren *tr. V.* (Kaufmannsspr.) [**jmdm.**] **einen Auftrag mit 30 Prozent** ~: give [sb.] a discount of 30 per cent on an order

Rabatz /ra'bats/ *der;* ~es (ugs.) (**a**) (Lärm) racket; din; (**b**) (Protest) ~ **machen** kick up a fuss, (coll.) raise a stink (**bei** with)

Rabauke /ra'baukə/ *der;* ~n, ~n (ugs.) roughneck (coll.); (Rowdy) hooligan

Rabbi /'rabi/ *der;* ~[s], ~nen /ra'bi:nən/*od.* ~s ▶34| rabbi; (Titel) Rabbi

Rabbiner /ra'bi:nɐ/ *der;* ~s, ~: rabbi

Rabe /'ra:bə/ *der;* ~n, ~n raven; **schwarz wie ein** ~ (ugs.) (schmutzig) as black as soot; **stehlen wie ein** ~ (ugs.) pinch everything one can lay one's hands on (coll.)

Raben·mutter *die* (abwertend) uncaring [brute of a] mother

raben·schwarz *Adj.* jet-black; raven-black ⟨*beard, hair*⟩; pitch-black ⟨*night*⟩

rabiat /ra'bia:t/ **1** *Adj.* violent; brutal; savage ⟨*kick*⟩; ruthless ⟨*methods*⟩. **2** *adv.* violently; brutally

Rache /'raxə/ *die;* ~: revenge; [**an jmdm.**] ~ **nehmen** take revenge [on sb.]; **aus** ~: in revenge

Rachen /'raxn̩/ *der;* ~s, ~ (**a**) ▶326| (Schlund) pharynx (Anat.); (**b**) (Maul) mouth; maw (literary); (fig.) jaws *pl.*

rächen /'rɛçn̩/ **1** *tr. V.* avenge ⟨*person, crime*⟩; take revenge for ⟨*insult, crime*⟩. **2** *refl. V.* (**a**) take one's revenge; **sich an jmdm.** [**für etw.**] ~: take one's revenge on sb. [for sth.]; get even with sb. [for sth.]; (**b**) (fig.) ⟨*mistake[s], bad behaviour*⟩ take its/their toll

Rachitis /ra'xi:tɪs/ *die;* ~ ▶329| (Med.) rickets *sing.*

Rach·sucht *die; o. Pl.* (geh.) lust for revenge

rach·süchtig *Adj.* (geh.) vengeful; ~ **sein** be out for revenge

rackern /'rakɐn/ *itr. V.* (ugs.) drudge; toil

Rad /ra:t/ *das;* ~es, **Räder** /'rɛ:dɐ/ (**a**) wheel; **fünftes** *od.* **das fünfte** ~ **am Wagen sein** (fig. ugs.) be superfluous; (die Harmonie stören) be in the way; **unter die Räder kommen** (fig. ugs.) fall into bad ways; (**b**) **nur ein** ~ **im Getriebe sein** be just a small cog in the machine; (**c**) (Fahr~) bicycle; bike (coll.); **mit dem** ~ **fahren** go by bicycle *or* (coll.) bike; ~ **fahren** cycle; ride a bicycle *or* (coll.) bike; (fig. ugs. abwertend: unterwürfig sein) suck up to people; (**d**) (Turnen) cartwheel; **ein** ~ **schlagen** do a cartwheel; ~ **schlagen** do cartwheels

Radar /ra'da:ɐ/ *der od. das;* ~s (Technik) radar

Radar-: ~**falle** *die* (ugs.) [radar] speed trap; ~**kontrolle** *die* [radar] speed check; ~**schirm** *der* radar screen

Radau /ra'dau/ *der;* ~s (ugs.) row (coll.); racket

Rädchen /'rɛ:tçən/ *das;* ~s, ~ [little] wheel; (Zahnrad) [small] cog

Rad·dampfer *der* paddle steamer

radebrechen 1 *tr. V.* **Französisch/Deutsch** *usw.* ~: speak broken French/German *etc.* **2** *itr. V.* speak pidgin

radeln /'ra:dl̩n/ *itr. V.; mit sein* (ugs., bes. südd.) cycle

Rädels·führer /'rɛ:dls-/ *der* (abwertend) ringleader

rädern /'rɛ:dɐn/ *tr. V.* **jmdn.** ~ (hist.) break sb. on the wheel; *s. auch* **gerädert**

rad-, Rad-: *~|**fahren** ⇒ **Rad c;** ~**fahrer** *der,* ~**fahrerin** *die* (**a**) cyclist; (**b**) (ugs. abwertend: Schmeichler) toady; crawler (coll.)

Radi /'ra:di/ *der;* ~s, ~s (bayr., österr. ugs.) [large white] radish

Radiator /ra'dia:tɔr/ *der;* ~s, ~en /-'to:rən/ radiator

Radien ⇒ **Radius**

radieren /ra'di:rən/ *tr.* (*auch itr.*) *V.* erase

Radier·gummi *der* rubber [eraser]

Radierung *die;* ~, ~en (Grafik) etching

Radieschen /ra'di:sçən/ *das;* ~s, ~: radish

radikal /radi'ka:l/ **1** *Adj.* radical; drastic ⟨*measure, method, cure*⟩. **2** *adv.* radically; (vollständig) totally, completely

Radikale *der/die; adj. Dekl.* radical

radikalisieren 1 *tr. V.* make [more] radical. **2** *refl. V.* become more radical

Radikalismus *der;* ~ radicalism; (Haltung) radical attitude

Radikalität /radikali'tɛ:t/ *die;* ~: radicalness; radical nature

Radio /'ra:dio/ *das* (südd., schweiz. auch: der); ~s, ~s radio; **im** ~: on the radio; ~ **hören** listen to the radio

radio-, Radio-: ~**aktiv** **1** *Adj.* radioactive; **2** *adv.* radioactively; ~**aktiv verseucht** contaminated by radioactivity *postpos.;* ~**aktivität** *die; o. Pl.* radioactivity; ~**sender** /'----/ *der* radio station; ~**wecker** /'----/ *der* radio alarm clock

Radius /'ra:dius/ *der;* ~, **Radien** /'ra:diən/ (Math.) radius

Rad-: ~**kappe** *die* hubcap; ~**lager** *das* wheel bearing

Radler *der;* ~s, ~, **Radlerin** *die;* ~, ~nen cyclist

Radon /'ra:dɔn/ *das;* ~s (Chemie) radon

Rad-: ~**renn·bahn** *die* cycle-racing track; (Stadion) velodrome; ~**rennen** *das* cycle race; (Sport) cycle-racing; ~**rennfahrer** *der* racing cyclist

-rädrig /-rɛ:drɪç/ *Adj.* -wheeled

rad-, Rad-: *~|**schlagen** ⇒ **Rad d;** ~**sport** *der* cycling *no def. art.;* ~**tour** *die* cycling tour; ~**weg** *der* cycle path *or* track

raffen /'rafn̩/ *tr. V.* (**a**) snatch; grab; rake in (coll.) ⟨*money*⟩; **etw. [an sich]** ~ (abwertend) seize sth.; (eilig) snatch *or* grab sth.; (**b**) (zusammenhalten) gather ⟨*material, curtain*⟩; (**c**) (gekürzt wiedergeben) condense ⟨*text*⟩

Raffinerie /rafinə'ri:/ *die;* ~, ~n refinery

Raffinesse /rafi'nɛsə/ *die;* ~, ~n (**a**) *o. Pl.* (Schlauheit) guile; ingenuity; (**b**) *meist Pl.* (Finesse) refinement

raffinieren /rafi'ni:rən/ *tr. V.* (bes. Chemie, Geol.) refine

raffiniert 1 *Adj.* (**a**) ingenious ⟨*plan, design*⟩; (verfeinert) refined, subtle ⟨*colour, scheme, effect*⟩; sophisticated ⟨*dish, cut (of clothes)*⟩; (**b**) (gerissen) cunning, artful ⟨*person, trick*⟩. **2** *adv.* (**a**) ingeniously; cleverly; (verfeinert) with great refinement/ sophistication; **eine** ~ **geschnittene Bluse** a blouse with a sophisticated cut; (**b**) (gerissen) cunningly; artfully

Rage /'ra:ʒə/ *die;* ~ (ugs.) fury; rage; **in** ~ **sein** be livid (Brit. coll.) *or* furious; **jmdn. in** ~ **bringen** make sb. hopping mad (coll.) *or* absolutely furious; **in** ~ **kommen** fly into a rage

ragen /'ra:gn̩/ *itr. V.* (**a**) (vertikal) rise [up] ⟨*mountains*⟩ tower up; **aus dem Wasser** ~: stick *or* jut right out of the water; **in den Himmel** ~: tower *or* soar into the sky; (**b**) (horizontal) project, stick out (**in** + *Akk.* into; **über** + *Akk.* over)

Ragout /ra'gu:/ *das;* ~s, ~s (Kochk.) ragout

Rahm /ra:m/ *der;* ~[e]s (bes. südd., österr., schweiz.) cream; *s. auch* **abschöpfen**

rahmen *tr. V.* frame

Rahmen *der;* ~s, ~ (**a**) frame; (Kfz-W.: Fahrgestell) chassis; (**b**) (fig.: Bereich) framework; (szenischer Hintergrund) setting; (Zusammenhang) context; (Grenzen) bounds *pl.;* limits *pl.;* **aus dem** ~ **fallen** be out of place; stick out; ⟨*behaviour*⟩ be unsuited to the occasion; **im** ~ **einer Sache** (*Gen.*) (in den Grenzen) within the bounds of sth.; (im Zusammenhang) within the context of sth.; (im Verlauf) in the course of sth.; **den** ~ **sprengen** be out of proportion

Rain /rain/ *der;* ~[e]s, ~e margin of a/the field

Rakete /ra'ke:tə/ *die;* ~, ~n rocket; (Lenkflugkörper) missile

allye /'rali/ *die;* ~, ~s (Motorsport) rally

ammen *tr. V.* ram

Rampe /'rampə/ *die;* ~, ~n (a) (Lade~) [loading] platform; (b) (schiefe Fläche) ramp; (Auffahrt) [sloping] drive; (c) ⇒ **Startrampe;** (d) (Theater) apron; forestage

Rampen·licht *das:* im ~ [der Öffentlichkeit] stehen be in the limelight

ramponieren /rampo'niːrən/ *tr. V.* (ugs.) batter; **ramponiert** battered, knocked-about ⟨furniture, phone-box⟩; run-down, down-at-heel ⟨dwelling, room⟩; shabby ⟨suit⟩; dented ⟨confidence⟩

Ramsch /ramʃ/ *der;* ~[e]s, ~e (ugs. abwertend) (a) (Ware) trashy goods *pl.;* (b) (Kram) junk

Ramsch·laden *der* (ugs. abwertend) shop selling trashy goods

ran /ran/ *Adv.* (ugs.) (a) ⇒ **heran;** (b) ~! (fang an) off you go; (fangen wir an) let's go; **los,** ~ **an die Arbeit!** come on, get down to work!; (c) ~! (greif[t] an) go at him/them!

Ranch /rɛntʃ/ *die;* ~, ~[e]s ranch

Rand /rant/ *der;* ~[e]s, **Ränder** /'rɛndɐ/ (a) edge; (Einfassung) border; (Hut~) brim; (Brillen~, Gefäß~, Krater~) rim; (eines Abgrunds) brink; (auf einem Schriftstück) margin; (Weg~) verge; (Stadt~) edge; outskirts *pl.;* (fig.) **etw. am** ~**e erwähnen** mention sth. in passing; **außer** ~ **und Band geraten/sein** (ugs.) go/be wild (**vor** with); (rasen) go/be berserk (**vor** with); **mit etw. [nicht] zu** ~**e kommen** (ugs.) [not] be able to cope with sth.; *s. auch* **Grab;** (b) (Schmutz~) mark; (rund) ring; (in der Wanne) tidemark (coll.); **dunkle Ränder unter den Augen haben** have dark lines under one's eyes; (c) **den** ~ **halten** (salopp) shut one's gob (sl.) *or* trap (sl.)

Randale /ran'daːlə/ *die;* ~ (salopp) riot; ~ **machen** riot

randalieren *itr. V.* riot; rampage; (Radau machen) create an uproar; ~**de Halbstarke** young hooligans on the rampage

Randalierer *der;* ~s, ~: hooligan

rand-, Rand-: ~**bemerkung** *die* marginal note *or* comment; ~**erscheinung** *die* peripheral phenomenon; ~**gebiet** *das* outlying district; (fig.) fringe area; **die** ~**gebiete einer Stadt** the outskirts of a town; ~**gruppe** *die* (Soziol.) fringe *or* marginal group; ~**streifen** *der* verge; ~**voll** *Adj.* ⟨glass etc.⟩ full to the brim (**mit** with); brim-full ⟨glass, cup, bowl⟩ (**mit** of)

rang /raŋ/ *1. u. 3. Pers. Sg. Prät. v.* **ringen**

Rang *der;* ~[e]s, **Ränge** /'rɛŋə/ (a) rank; (in der Gesellschaft) status; (in Bezug auf Bedeutung, Qualität) standing; **jmdm./einer Sache den** ~ **ablaufen** leave sb./sth. far behind; **alles, was** ~ **und Namen hat** everybody who is anybody; **ein Physiker von** ~: an eminent physicist; **ersten** ~**es** of the first order; (b) (im Theater) circle; **erster** ~: dress circle; **zweiter** ~: upper circle; **dritter** ~: gallery; (c) (Sport) ⇒ **Platz f**

Range /'raŋə/ *die;* ~, ~n (bes. md.) [young] tearaway

ran|gehen *unr. itr. V.* (ugs.) ⇒ **herangehen**

Rangelei *die;* ~, ~en (ugs.) ⇒ **Gerangel**

rangeln /'raŋln/ *itr. V.* (ugs.) wrestle; struggle; (kämpfen) ⟨children⟩ scrap; **um etw.** ~: scramble *or* tussle for sth.; (fig.: argumentieren) wrangle over sth.

Rang·folge *die* order of precedence

Rangier·bahn·hof *der* marshalling yard

rangieren /raŋ'ʒiːrən/ *1 tr., itr. V.* shunt ⟨trucks, coaches⟩; switch ⟨cars⟩ (Amer.). *2 itr. V.* be placed; **an letzter Stelle/auf Platz zwei** ~: be placed last/second

Rangierer *der;* ~s, ~: shunter (Brit.); switchman (Amer.)

Rang-: ~**liste** *die* (Sport) ranking list; ~**ordnung** *die* order of precedence; (Verhaltensf.) pecking order

ran|halten *unr. refl. V.* (ugs.) get a move on (coll.); (bei der Arbeit) get stuck in (coll.)

Ranke /'raŋkə/ *die;* ~, ~n (Bot.) tendril

Ränke /'rɛŋkə/ *Pl.* (geh. veralt.) intrigues; ~ **schmieden** (geh.) scheme; hatch plots

ranken *itr., refl. V.* climb; grow; **sich um etw.** ~: entwine itself around sth.; (fig. geh.) ⟨legends, mysteries⟩ be woven around sth.

Ranken·gewächs *das* creeper

ran-: ~**|klotzen** *itr. V.* (salopp) get stuck in (coll.); ~**|kommen** *unr. itr. V.; mit sein* (ugs.) ⇒ **herankommen a, c;** ~**|lassen** *unr. tr. V.* (ugs.); **jmdn. an etw.** (*Akk.*) **nicht** ~**lassen** not let sb. anywhere near sth.; **lass mich mal** ~! let me have a go!; ~**|machen** *refl. V.* (ugs.) ⇒ **heranmachen a, b**

rann /ran/ *1. u. 3. Pers. Sg. Prät. v.* **rinnen**

rannte /'rantə/ *1. u. 3. Pers. Sg. Prät. v.* **rennen**

ran|schmeißen *unr. refl. V.* **sich an jmdn.** ~ (ugs.) throw oneself at sb.

Ranzen /'rantsn̩/ *der;* ~s, ~ (a) satchel; (b) (salopp: Bauch) [fat] belly

ranzig *Adj.* rancid

rapid /ra'piːt/ (südd., österr., schweiz.), **rapide** *1 Adj.* rapid. *2 adv.* rapidly

Rappe /'rapə/ *der;* ~n, ~n black horse

Rappel /'rapl/ *der;* ~s, ~ (ugs.) crazy turn (coll.); **du hast wohl einen** ~? are you crazy?

rappeln *itr. V.* (ugs.) rattle (**an** + *Dat.* at); ⟨alarm, telephone⟩ jangle

Rappen *der;* ~s, ~: [Swiss] centime

Rapport /ra'pɔrt/ *der;* ~s, ~e (veralt.) report

Raps /raps/ *der;* ~es rape

rar /raːɐ̯/ *Adj.* (knapp) scarce; (selten) rare; **sich** ~ **machen** (ugs.) not be around much (coll.)

Rarität /rari'tɛːt/ *die;* ~, ~en rarity

rasant /ra'zant/ *1 Adj.* (a) (ugs.) (schnell) tremendously fast (coll.) ⟨car, horse, runner, etc.⟩; tremendous (coll.), lightning *attrib.* ⟨speed, acceleration, development, progress, growth⟩; hairy (sl.) ⟨driving⟩; (schnittig) racy ⟨car, styling⟩; (b) (ugs.) (schwungvoll) dynamic, lively ⟨show⟩; action-packed, exciting ⟨film, story⟩; (rassig) classy (sl.) ⟨woman⟩; dashing ⟨style, dress⟩. *2 adv.* (a) (ugs.) (schnell) at terrific speed (coll.); ⟨increase⟩ by leaps and bounds; (b) (ugs.) (schwungvoll) dashingly; (rassig) stylishly

rasch /raʃ/ *1 Adj.* quick; quick, rapid ⟨step, progress, decision, action⟩; speedy, swift ⟨end, action, decision, progress⟩; fast, quick ⟨service, work, pace, tempo, progress⟩; **in** ~**er Folge** in rapid *or* swift succession. *2 adv.* quickly; ⟨drive, act⟩ quickly, fast; ⟨decide, end, proceed⟩ swiftly, rapidly

rascheln /'raʃln̩/ *itr. V.* rustle; **es raschelte im Stroh** there was a rustling in the straw

rasen /'raːzn̩/ *itr. V.* (a) *mit sein* (ugs.: eilen) dash *or* rush [along]; (fahren) tear *or* race along; (fig.) ⟨pulse⟩ race; **gegen einen Baum** ~: crash [at full speed] into a tree; (b) (toben) ⟨person⟩ rage; (wie wahnsinnig) rave; (fig.) ⟨storm, sea, war⟩ rage

Rasen *der;* ~s, ~: grass *no indef. art.;* (gepflegte ~fläche) lawn; (eines Spielfeldes usw.) turf

rasend *1 Adj.* (a) **in** ~**er Fahrt** at breakneck speed; (b) (tobend) raging; (wie wahnsinnig) raving; (verrückt) mad; **[vor Wut usw.]** ~ **werden** be beside oneself [with rage etc.]; **die Schmerzen machen mich** ~: the pain is driving me mad; (c) (heftig) violent ⟨jealousy, rage, pain⟩; tumultuous ⟨applause⟩; ~**e Kopfschmerzen haben** have a splitting headache. *2 adv.* (ugs.) incredibly (coll.) ⟨fast, funny, expensive⟩; insanely ⟨jealous⟩

Rasen-: ~**mäher** /~mɛːɐ̯/ *der;* ~s, ~: lawnmower; ~**platz** (Fußball usw.) pitch; (Tennis) grass court

Raser *der;* ~s, ~ (ugs. abwertend) speed merchant (coll.); (rücksichtslos) road hog

Raserei *die;* ~, ~en (a) (ugs.: schnelles Fahren) tearing along *no art.;* (b) *o. Pl.* (das Toben) [insane] frenzy; (Wut) rage

Rasier·apparat *der* [safety] razor; (elektrisch) electric shaver *or* razor

rasieren /ra'ziːrən/ *tr. V.* shave; **sich** ~: shave; **sich nass/trocken/elektrisch** ~: have a wet/dry shave/use an electric shaver; **sich** (*Dat.*) **die Beine** usw. ~: shave one's legs

Rasierer *der;* ~s, ~ (ugs.) [electric] shaver

Rasier-: ~**klinge** *die* razor blade; ~**messer** *das* cutthroat razor; ~**wasser** *das* (nach der Rasur) aftershave; (vor der Rasur) pre-shave lotion; ~**zeug** *das* shaving things *pl.*

Räson /rɛ'zɔn/ *die; ~ in zur ~ kommen* come to one's senses; **jmdn. zur ~ bringen** make sb. see reason

Raspel /'raspl̩/ *die;* ~, ~**n** (a) rasp; (b) (Küchengerät) grater

raspeln *tr. V.* (a) *auch itr.* rasp; **an etw.** (*Dat.*) ~: work away at sth. with a rasp; (b) (Kochk.) grate

Rasse /'rasə/ *die;* ~, ~**n** (a) breed; (Menschen~) race; (b) ~ **haben** (ugs.) be terrific (coll.); (Temperament haben) have plenty of spirit *or* mettle

Rasse·hund *der* pedigree dog

Rassel /'rasl̩/ *die;* ~, ~**n** rattle

rasseln *itr. V.* (a) rattle; **mit seinem Schlüsselbund** ~: jangle one's bunch of keys; **der Wecker rasselt** the alarm goes off with a jangling sound; (b) *mit sein* (sich ~d fortbewegen) clatter; (c) *mit sein* **durch eine Prüfung** ~ (salopp) come unstuck in *or* (Amer.) flunk an exam (coll.)

Rassen- racial ⟨*discrimination, hatred, segregation, etc.*⟩

Rasse·pferd *das* thoroughbred [horse]

rassig *Adj.* spirited, mettlesome ⟨*horse*⟩; spirited, vivacious ⟨*woman*⟩; sporty ⟨*car*⟩; tangy ⟨*wine, perfume*⟩; (markant) striking ⟨*face, features, beauty*⟩

Rassismus *der;* ~: racism; racialism

Rassist *der;* ~**en**, ~**en**, **Rassistin** *die;* ~, ~**nen** racist; racialist

rassistisch 1 *Adj.* racist; racialist. 2 *adv.* racialistically

Rast /rast/ *die;* ~, ~**en** rest; ~ **machen** stop for a break

rasten *itr. V.* rest; take a rest *or* break

Raster *der;* ~s, ~ (a) (Druckw.) screen; (b) (fig.) [conceptual] framework

Raster·fahndung *die* (Kriminologie) *pinpointing of suspects by means of computer analysis of data on many people*

Raster·schaltung *die* ⇒ **Indexschaltung**

rast-, Rast-: ~**haus** *das* roadside café; (an der Autobahn) motorway restaurant; ~**hof** *der* [motorway] motel [and service area]; ~**los** 1 *Adj.* restless ⟨*person, spirit, life*⟩; unremitting, ceaseless ⟨*work, search*⟩; 2 *adv. s. Adj.:* restlessly; unremittingly; ceaselessly; ~**platz** *der* (a) place to rest; (b) (an Autobahnen) parking place (*with benches and WCs*); picnic area; ~**stätte** *die* service area

Rasur /ra'zuːɐ̯/ *die;* ~, ~**en** shave

Rat /raːt/ *der;* ~**[e]s, Räte** /'rɛːtə/ (a) *o. Pl.* (Empfehlung) advice; **ein** ~: a piece *or* word of advice; **da ist guter ~ teuer** I/we *etc.* hardly know which way to turn; **ich gab ihm den** ~ **zu** ...: I advised him to ...; **bei jmdm.** ~ **suchen** seek sb.'s advice; **jmdm. mit** ~ **und Tat beistehen** stand by sb. with moral and practical support; **jmdn./etw. zu** ~[e] **ziehen** consult sb./sth.; **ich wusste [mir] keinen** ~ **mehr** I was at my wit's end *or* completely at a loss; (b) (Gremium) council; (Sowjet) soviet; **der** ~ **der Stadt** the town council; (c) (Ratsmitglied) councillor; council member

rät /rɛːt/ *3. Pers. Sg. Präsens v.* **raten**

Rate /'raːtə/ *die;* ~, ~**n** (a) (Teilbetrag) instalment; **etw. auf** ~**n kaufen** buy sth. by instalments *or* (Brit.) on hire purchase *or* (Amer.) on the installment plan; (b) (Statistik) rate

raten 1 *unr. itr. V.* (a) (einen Rat, Ratschläge geben) **jmdm.** ~: advise sb.; **wozu rätst du mir?** what do you advise me to do?; (b) (schätzen) guess; **richtig/falsch** ~: guess right/wrong; **dreimal darfst du** ~ (ugs. iron.) I'll give you three guesses. 2 *tr. V.* (a) (an~) **jmdm.** ~, **etw. zu tun** advise sb. to do sth.; **lass dir das** ~ **sein!** you better had [do that]!; (tu das nicht) don't you dare do that!; (b) (er~) guess

Raten·zahlung *die* payment by instalments

Rate·spiel *das* guessing-game

Rat-: ~**geber** *der* adviser; (Buch) guide; ~**haus** *das* town hall

ratifizieren /ratifi'tsiːrən/ *tr. V.* ratify

Rätin /'rɛːtɪn/ *die;* ~, ~**nen** councillor

Ration /ra'tsi̯oːn/ *die;* ~, ~**en** ration; *s. auch* **eisern** 1 d

rational /ratsi̯o'naːl/ 1 *Adj.* rational. 2 *adv.* rationally

rationalisieren *tr., itr. V.* rationalize

rationell /ratsi̯o'nɛl/ 1 *Adj.* efficient; (wirtschaftlich) economic. 2 *adv.* efficiently; (wirtschaftlich, kräftesparend) economically

rationieren *tr. V.* ration

Rationierung *die;* ~, ~**en** rationing *no indef. art.*

rat·los 1 *Adj.* baffled; at a loss *pred.*; helpless ⟨*look*⟩. 2 *adv.* helplessly; in a baffled way

Ratlosigkeit *die;* ~: perplexity; helplessness

ratsam /'raːtzaːm/ *Adj.; nicht attr.* advisable; (weise) prudent

ratsch /ratʃ/ *Interj.* zip; (beim Zerreißen) rip

Rat·schlag *der* [piece of] advice; (Hinweis) tip; ~**schläge** advice *sing.*/tips

Rätsel /'rɛːtsl̩/ *das;* ~s, ~ (a) riddle; (Bilder~, Kreuzwort~ usw.) puzzle; (b) (Geheimnis) mystery; enigma

rätselhaft 1 *Adj.* mysterious; (unergründlich) enigmatic ⟨*smile, expression, person*⟩; baffling ⟨*problem*⟩. 2 *adv.* mysteriously; (unergründlich) enigmatically

rätseln *itr. V.* puzzle, rack one's brains (**über** + *Akk.* over)

Rätsel·raten *das* (a) ⇒ **Rätsel** a: solving puzzles/riddles *no art.*; (b) (das Rätseln) puzzling; (das Raten) guessing; (fig.) guessing-game

Ratte /'ratə/ *die;* ~, ~**n** (auch fig.) rat

Ratten·fänger *der* (a) rat-catcher; **der** ~ **von Hameln** (Lit.) the Pied Piper of Hamelin; (b) (fig. abwertend) pied piper

rattern /'ratɐn/ *itr. V.* (a) clatter; ⟨*sewing machine, machine gun*⟩ chatter; ⟨*engine*⟩ rattle; (b) *mit sein* (~d fahren) clatter [along]

rau /rau̯/ 1 *Adj.* (a) (nicht glatt) rough; **in einer** ~**en Schale steckt oft ein weicher Kern** (Spr.) behind a rough exterior there often beats a heart of gold; (b) (nicht mild) harsh, raw ⟨*climate, winter*⟩; raw ⟨*wind*⟩; (c) (unwirtlich) bleak, inhospitable ⟨*region, mountains, etc.*⟩; rough ⟨*weather*⟩; (d) (kratzig) husky, hoarse ⟨*voice*⟩; (e) (entzündet) sore ⟨*throat*⟩; (f) (grob, nicht feinfühlig) rough; harsh ⟨*words, tone*⟩; **er ist** ~, **aber herzlich** he is a rough diamond; (g) **in** ~**en Mengen** (ugs.) in huge *or* vast quantities. 2 *adv.* (a) (kratzig) ⟨*speak etc.*⟩ huskily, hoarsely; (b) (grob, nicht feinfühlig) roughly

Raub /rau̯p/ *der;* ~[e]s (a) robbery; (Entführung) kidnapping; (b) (Beute) [robber's] loot; stolen goods *pl.*

Raub·bau *der;* ~s over-exploitation (**an** + *Dat.* of); (*beim Fischfang*) overfishing; (*beim Bergbau*) overworking; ~**bau an etw.** (*Dat.*) **treiben** over-exploit sth.; ~**bau mit seiner Gesundheit treiben** (fig.) ruin one's health by overdoing things

rau·beinig *Adj.* (ugs.) gruff; rough and ready

rauben 1 *tr. V.* steal; kidnap ⟨*person*⟩; **jmdm. etw.** ~: rob sb. of sth.; (geh.: wegnehmen) deprive sb. of sth.; **jmdm. den Atem/die Sprache** ~: take sb.'s breath away/render sb. speechless. 2 *itr. V.* rob; (plündern) plunder

Räuber /'rɔy̯bɐ/ *der;* ~s, ~ (a) robber; (b) (Zool.: Tier) predator

Raub-: ~**fisch** *der* predatory fish; ~**katze** *die* wild cat; ~**mord** *der* (Rechtsw.) murder (**an** + *Dat.* of) in the course of a robbery *or* with robbery as motive; ~**tier** *das* predator; beast of prey; ~**überfall** *der* robbery (**auf** + *Akk.* of); ~**vogel** *der* bird of prey; ~**zug** *der* plundering raid

Rauch /rau̯x/ *der;* ~[e]s smoke; **sich in** ~ **auflösen, in** ~ **aufgehen** (fig.) go up in smoke

Rauch·abzug *der* smoke outlet; (Rohr, Schacht) flue

rauchen 1 *itr. V.* smoke; **es rauchte in der Küche** there was smoke in the kitchen; **sonst raucht es!** (ugs.) or there'll be trouble. 2 *tr.* (*auch itr.*) *V.* smoke ⟨*cigarette, pipe, etc.*⟩; **eine** ~ (ugs.) have a smoke; **stark** *od.* **viel** ~: be a heavy smoker; „**Rauchen verboten**" 'No smoking'

Raucher der; ~s, ~: smoker; **er ist [starker] ~**: he smokes [heavily]; he is a [heavy] smoker; **möchten Sie ~ oder Nichtraucher [fliegen]?** would you like smoking or no smoking?

Räucher·aal der smoked eel

Raucher·abteil das smoking compartment; smoker

Räucher·hering der smoked herring

Raucher·husten der smoker's cough

Raucherin die; ~, ~nen smoker

räuchern /'rɔʏçɐn/ **1** tr. V. smoke ‹meat, fish›. **2** itr. V. burn incense/joss sticks etc.

Räucher-: ~**schinken** der smoked ham; ~**stäbchen** das joss stick

rauchig Adj. smoky; husky ‹voice›

Rauch-: ~**pilz** der mushroom cloud; ~**schwaden** der cloud of smoke; ~**verbot** das ban on smoking; **es herrscht** ~**verbot** smoking is prohibited; ~**vergiftung** die poisoning no art. by smoke inhalation; ~**wolke** die cloud of smoke; ~**zeichen** das smoke signal

räudig Adj. mangy; **du** ~**er Hund!** (derb) you dirty rat! (sl.)

rauf /rauf/ Adv. (ugs.) up; ~ **mit euch!** up you go!; s. auch **herauf; hinauf**

Raufaser·tapete die woodchip wallpaper

Raufbold /-bɔlt/ der; ~[e]s, ~e (veralt.) ruffian

rauf|bringen unr. tr. V. (ugs.) (her) bring up; (hin) take up

raufen 1 itr., refl. V. fight; **[sich] wegen** od. **um etw.** ~: fight [each other] over sth. **2** tr. V. **sich** (Dat.) **die Haare/den Bart** ~: tear one's hair/at one's beard

Rauferei die; ~, ~en fight

rauf-: ~**|gehen** unr. itr. V.; mit sein (ugs.) go up; ~**|kommen** unr. itr. V.; mit sein (ugs.) come up

***rauh** usw.: ⇒ **rau** usw.

Rauhaar·dackel der wire-haired dachshund

Raum der; ~[e]s, **Räume** /'rɔʏmə/ (a) (Wohn~, Nutz~) room; **im** ~ **stehen** (fig.) be in the air; (b) (Gebiet) area; region; (c) o. Pl. (Platz) room; space; (d) (Math., Philos., Astron.) space

räumen /'rɔʏmən/ tr. V. (a) clear [away]; clear ‹snow›; **Minen** ~: clear mines; **etw. aus dem Weg** ~: clear sth. out [of] the way; **seine Sachen auf die Seite** ~: clear or move one's things to one side; **etw. in Schubfächer** (Akk.) ~: put sth. away in drawers; (b) (frei machen) clear ‹street, building, warehouse, stocks, etc.›; (c) (verlassen) vacate ‹hotel room, cinema, house, flat, military position, area›

Raum-: ~**fahrer** der astronaut; (Kosmonaut) cosmonaut; ~**fahrt** die o. Pl. space flight; space travel; ~**fahrzeug** das spacecraft; ~**flug** der space flight; ~**gleiter** der; ~s, ~: space shuttle; ~**inhalt** der ▶427| (Math.) volume; ~**kapsel** die space capsule

räumlich 1 Adj. (a) (den Raum betreffend) spatial; **aus** ~**en Gründen** for reasons of space; (b) (dreidimensional) three-dimensional; stereophonic ‹sound›; stereoscopic ‹vision›. **2** adv. (a) spatially; (b) (dreidimensional) three-dimensionally

Räumlichkeit die; ~, ~en meist Pl. rooms

raum-, Raum-: ~**pflegerin** die cleaning lady; cleaner; ~**schiff** das spaceship; ~**sparend** Adj. ⇒ **platzsparend**; ~**station** die space station

Räumung die; ~, ~en (a) clearing; (b) (das Verlassen) vacation; vacating; (c) (Evakuierung) evacuation; (d) (eines Lagers) clearance

Räumungsverkauf der (Kaufmannsspr.) clearance sale

raunen /'raunən/ tr., itr. V. (geh.) whisper; **ein Raunen ging durch die Reihen** a murmur went through the ranks

Raupe /'raupə/ die; ~, ~n caterpillar

Rau·reif der hoar frost

raus /raus/ Adv. (ugs.) out; ~ **mit euch!** out you go!

Rausch /rauʃ/ der; ~[e]s, **Räusche** /'rɔʏʃə/ (a) (durch Alkohol) state of drunkenness; **sich** (Dat.) **einen** ~ **antrinken** get drunk; **einen** ~ **haben** be drunk; **etw. im**

~ **tun** do sth. while drunk; (b) (durch Drogen) drugged state; **einen** ~ **haben** be drugged; be high (coll.) [on drugs]; **etw. im** ~ **tun** do sth. while drugged; (c) (starkes Gefühl) transport; **ein wilder/blinder** ~: a wild/blind frenzy; **der** ~ **der Geschwindigkeit** the exhilaration or thrill of speed

rauschen itr. V. (a) ‹water, wind, torrent› rush; ‹trees, leaves› rustle; ‹skirt, curtains, silk› swish; ‹waterfall, surf, sea, strong wind› roar; ‹rain› pour down; ~**der Beifall** (fig.) resounding applause; (b) mit sein (sich bewegen) ‹water, river, etc.› rush; **sie rauschte aus dem Zimmer** she swept out of the room

Rausch·gift das drug; narcotic; ~ **nehmen** take drugs; **be on drugs**

rauschgift-, Rauschgift-: ~**handel** der drug-trafficking; ~**händler** der drug-trafficker; ~**süchtig** Adj. drug-addicted; addicted to drugs postpos.; ~**süchtige** der/die; adj. Dekl. drug addict

rausch·haft Adj. ecstatic

Rausch·mittel das ⇒ **Rauschgift**

raus-: ~**|ekeln** tr. V. (ugs.) ⇒ **hinausekeln**; ~**|fahren** unr. tr. V.; mit sein (ugs.) ⇒ **hinaus-|-**; ~**|feuern** tr. V. (ugs.) chuck out (coll.); ~**|fliegen** unr. itr. V.; mit sein (ugs.) ⇒ **heraus-, hinausfliegen**; ~**|gehen** unr. itr. V.; mit sein (ugs.) ⇒ **heraus-, hinausgehen**; ~**|kommen** unr. itr. V.; mit sein (ugs.) ⇒ **heraus-, hinauskommen**; ~**|kriegen** tr. V. (ugs.) get out (aus of); **ich habe das Rätsel/die Aufgabe nicht** ~**gekriegt** I couldn't do the puzzle/exercise; ~**|nehmen** unr. tr. V. (ugs.) ⇒ **herausnehmen**; ~**|pauken** tr. V. jmdn. ~**pauken** (ugs.) get sb. off the hook (fig. coll.)

räuspern /'rɔʏspɐn/ refl. V. clear one's throat

raus-, Raus-: ~**|schmeißen** unr. tr. V. (ugs.) chuck (coll.) or sling (coll.) ‹objects› out or away; give ‹employee› the push (Brit. coll.) or sack (coll.) or boot (sl.); chuck (coll.) or throw ‹customer, drunk, tenant› out (aus of); **das ist** ~**geschmissenes Geld** that's money down the drain (coll.); ~**schmeißer** der; ~s, ~ (ugs.) chucker-out (coll.); bouncer (coll.); ~**schmiss**, *~**schmiß** der (ugs.) chucking out; throwing out; (Entlassung) sacking

Raute /'rautə/ die; ~, ~n (Geom.) rhombus

rauten·förmig Adj. rhombic; diamond-shaped

Rave /'reɪv/ der; ~s, ~s rave

raven /'reɪvn̩/ itr. V. rave

Raver /'reɪvɐ/ der; ~s, ~ raver

Razzia /'ratsi̯a/ die; ~, **Razzien** raid

Re das; ~s, ~s (Skat) redouble

Reagenz·glas das test tube

reagieren itr. V. react (**auf** + Akk. to)

Reaktion /reak'tsi̯oːn/ die; ~, ~en reaction (**auf** + Akk. to)

reaktionär /reaktsi̯o'nɛːr/ Adj. (Politik abwertend) reactionary

Reaktionär der; ~s, ~e, **Reaktionärin** die; ~, ~nen (Politik abwertend) reactionary

reaktions-, Reaktions-: ~**fähigkeit** die; o. Pl. ability to react; **jmds.** ~**fähigkeit überprüfen** test sb.'s reactions; ~**schnell** Adj. ‹person› with quick reactions; ~**schnell sein** have quick reactions; ~**vermögen** das ⇒ **fähigkeit**

Reaktor /re'aktɔr/ der; ~s, ~en /-'toːrən/ reactor

real /re'aːl/ Adj. real

realisierbar Adj. ⇒ **realisieren a:** realizable; implementable

Realisierbarkeit die; ~: practicability; feasibility

realisieren /reali'ziːrən/ tr. V. (geh.) realize ‹plan, idea, aim, proposals, project, wish›; implement ‹plan, programme, decision›

Realismus der; ~ realism

Realist der; ~en, ~en realist

realistisch 1 Adj. realistic. **2** adv. realistically

Realität die; ~, ~en reality

Realitäts·sinn der; o. Pl. sense of reality

Real-: ~**schule** die ≈ secondary modern school (Brit. Hist.); ~**schüler** der ≈ secondary modern school pupil (Brit. Hist.)

---

*alte Schreibung (vgl. Hinweise auf S. xvi–xvii)

Rauminhalt

Raummaße

1 Kubikzentimeter = one cubic centimetre (cc) = 0.06 cubic inch (cu. in.)
1 Kubikmeter = one cubic metre (cu. m) = 35.714 cubic feet (cu. ft) *od.* 1.307 cubic yards (cu. yds)

Hohlmaße

1 Zentiliter = one centilitre (cl) = 0.0176 pints *(brit.)*, 0.021 pints *(amerik.)*
1 Liter = one litre (l) = 1.76 pints *(brit.)*, 2.1 pints *(amerik.) od.* 0.22 gallons *(brit.)*,
0.264 gallons *(amerik.)*

Wie viel od. Welches Volumen hat es?	= What is its volume?
Es hat ein Volumen von 6 m³	= Its volume is 6 cubic metres, ≈ the volume is 200 cubic feet
Wie viel fasst der Tank?	= How much does the tank hold? What is the capacity of the tank?
Der Tank fasst 45 Liter	= The tank holds 45 litres, ≈ the tank holds 10 gallons *(brit.)/* 12 gallons *(amerik.)*
Die beiden Tanks haben das gleiche Fassungs- vermögen	= The two tanks have the same capacity *od.* hold the same amount
Mein Wagen verbraucht 10 Liter auf 100 Kilometer	≈ My car does 28 *(UK) od.* 23 *(USA)* miles per gallon (m.p.g.).

[Um Liter auf 100 Kilometer in miles per gallon umzurechnen (oder auch umgekehrt), dividiert man 280 (bei britischen *gallons*) bzw. 230 (bei *US gallons*) durch die bekannte Zahl].

Benzin wird literweise verkauft	= Petrol is sold by the litre

Der Hubraum eines Motors wird im britischen Einflussbereich in Kubikzentimeter (cc) bzw. Liter angegeben, dagegen in den USA und Kanada in cubic inches (cu. in.):

Wie viel Hubraum hat der Motor?	= What is the capacity of the engine *od.* *(amerik.)* motor?
Der Motor hat 1 600 cm³ = od. 1,6 Liter Hubraum	It's a 1600 cc *od.* 1.6 litre engine *(brit.) od.* a 96 cu. in. motor *(amerik.)*

Rebe /ˈreːbə/ *die;* ~, ~n (a) vine shoot; (b) (geh.: Weinstock) [grape] vine
Rebell /reˈbɛl/ *der;* ~en, ~en rebel
rebellieren *itr. V.* rebel (**gegen** against)
Rebellin *die;* ~, ~nen ⇒ **Rebell**
Rebellion /rebɛˈli̯oːn/ *die;* ~, ~en rebellion
rebellisch 1 *Adj.* rebellious. 2 *adv.* rebelliously
Reb-: ~**huhn** *das* partridge; ~**stock** *der* vine
rechen /ˈrɛçn̩/ *tr. V.* (bes. südd.) rake
Rechen *der;* ~s, ~ (bes. südd.) rake
Rechen-: ~**art** *die* type of arithmetical operation; ~**aufgabe** *die* arithmetical problem; ~**fehler** *der* arithmetical error; ~**maschine** *die* calculator
Rechenschaft *die;* ~: account; **jmdm. über etw.** (*Akk.*) ~ **geben** *od.* **ablegen** account to sb. for sth.; **jmdm. über etw.** (*Akk.*) ~ **schuldig sein** have to account to sb. for sth.; **ich bin Ihnen keine** ~ **schuldig** I am not answerable to you; I owe you no explanation; **jmdn. für etw. zur** ~ **ziehen** call *or* bring sb. to account for sth.
Rechenschafts·bericht *der* report
Rechen-: ~**schieber** *der*, ~**stab** *der* slide-rule; ~**stunde** *die* arithmetic lesson; ~**unterricht** *der* teaching of arithmetic; (Fach) arithmetic *no art.*
recherchieren *itr., tr. V.* (geh.) investigate
rechnen /ˈrɛçnən/ 1 *tr. V.* (a) **eine Aufgabe** ~: work out a problem; (b) (veranschlagen) reckon; estimate; **wir müssen zwei Stunden** ~: we must reckon on two hours; **gut/rund gerechnet** at a generous/rough estimate; (c) (berücksichtigen) take into account; (d) (einbeziehen) count; **jmdn. zu seinen Freunden** ~: count sb. among *or* as one of one's friends. 2 *itr. V.* (a) do *or* make a calculation/calculations; **gut/schlecht** ~ **können** be good/bad at figures *or* arithmetic; (b) (zählen) reckon; **vom 1. April an gerechnet** reckoning from 1 April; **in Schillingen** ~: reckon in shillings; (c) (ugs.: berechnen) calculate; estimate; **er ist ein klug** ~**der Kopf** he is a shrewdly calculating person; (d) (wirtschaften) budget carefully; **mit jeder Mark** *od.* **jedem Pfennig** ~ **müssen** have to count *or* watch every penny; (e) **auf jmdn./etw.** *od.* **mit jmdm./ etw.** ~: reckon *or* count on sb./sth.; (f) **mit etw.** ~ (etw. einkalkulieren) reckon with sth.; (etw. erwarten) expect sth.; **mit dem Schlimmsten** ~: be prepared for the worst. 3 *refl. V.* pay

Rechnen *das;* ~s arithmetic
Rechner *der;* ~s, ~ (a) **ein guter/schlechter** ~ **sein** be good/bad at figures *or* arithmetic; **ein nüchterner** ~ **sein** (fig.) be shrewdly calculating; (b) (Gerät) calculator; (Computer) computer
rechnerisch 1 *Adj.* arithmetical; ⟨*value*⟩ in figures. 2 *adv.* ⟨*determine*⟩ by calculation, mathematically
Rechnung *die;* ~, ~en (a) calculation; [jmdm.] **eine** ~ **aufmachen** work it out [for sb.]; **nach meiner** ~ (auch fig.) according to my calculations; **seine** ~ **geht [nicht] auf** (fig.) his plans [do not] work out; (b) (schriftliche Kosten~) bill; invoice (Commerc.); **eine hohe/niedrige** ~: a large/small bill; **eine** ~ **über 500 Mark** a bill for 500 marks; **das geht auf meine** ~: I'm paying for that; **diese Runde geht auf meine** ~: this round's on me; **auf eigene** ~: on one's own account; (auf eigenes Risiko) at one's own risk; [jmdm.] **etw. in** ~ **stellen** charge [sb.] for sth.; (c) **einer Sache** (*Dat.*) ~ **tragen** take sth. into account, *s. auch* **begleichen**
recht /rɛçt/ 1 *Adj.* (a) (geeignet) right; (b) (richtig) right; **ganz** ~! quite right!; **das ist** ~, **so ist es** ~, (ugs.) ~ **so** that's fine; (c) (gesetzmäßig, anständig) right; proper; **alles, was** ~ **ist** (das geht zu weit) there is a limit; (d) (wunschgemäß) **jmdm.** ~ **sein** be all right with sb.; (e) (wirklich, echt) real; **keine** ~**e Lust haben, etw. zu tun** not particularly *or* really feel like doing sth. 2 *adv.* (a) (geeignet) **du kommst gerade** ~, **um zu** …: you are just in time to …; **du kommst mir gerade** ~ (auch iron.) you're just the person I needed; (b) (richtig) correctly; **wenn ich es mir** ~ **überlege, dann** …: if I really stop and think about it; **verstehen Sie mich bitte** ~: please don't misunderstand me; **gehe ich** ~ **in der Annahme, dass** …? am I right in assuming that …?; (c) (gesetzmäßig, anständig) ~ **handeln/leben** act/live properly; (d) (wunschgemäß) **man kann ihm nichts** ~ **machen** there's no pleasing him; **man kann es nicht allen** ~ **machen** you can't please everyone; (e) (wirklich, echt) really; rightly; (f) (ziemlich) quite; rather; *s. auch* **erst 2**; **Recht d**
Recht *das;* ~[e]s, ~e (a) (Rechtsordnung) law; **das** ~ **brechen/beugen** break/bend the law; ~ **sprechen** administer the law; administer justice; **von** ~**s wegen** by law; (ugs.: eigentlich) by rights; (b) (Rechtsanspruch) right; **das** ~ **des Stärkeren** the law of the jungle; **das ist sein gutes** ~: that is his right; **alle** ~**e vorbehalten** all

rights reserved; **sein ~ fordern** *od.* **verlangen** demand one's rights; **zu seinem ~ kommen** (fig.) be given due attention; **(c)** *o. Pl.* (Berechtigung) right **(auf** + *Akk.* to); **gleiches ~ für alle!** equal rights for all!; **im ~ sein** be in the right; **zu ~:** rightly; with justification; **(d) ~ haben** be right; **~ behalten** be proved right; **jmdm. ~ geben** concede *or* admit that sb. is right

Rechte¹ *der/die; adj. Dekl.* right-winger; rightist (derog.); **die ~n** the right *sing.*

Rechte² *die; adj. Dekl.* **(a)** (Hand) right hand; **jmdm. zur ~n** to the right of sb.; **zur ~n** on the right; **(b)** (Politik) right

Recht·eck *das* rectangle

recht·eckig *Adj.* rectangular

recht·fertigen 1 *tr. V.* justify **(vor** + *Dat.* to). **2** *refl. V.* justify oneself **(vor** + *Dat.* to)

Recht·fertigung *die* justification

recht-, Recht-: **~haber** *der; ~s, ~* (abwertend) self-opinionated person; **~haberei** *die; ~* (abwertend) self-opinionatedness; **~haberisch** *Adj.* (abwertend) self-opinionated

rechtlich 1 *Adj.* legal. **2** *adv.* legally

recht·los *Adj.* without rights *postpos.*

Rechtlosigkeit *die; ~:* lack of rights

rechtmäßig 1 *Adj.* lawful; rightful; legitimate ‹claim›. **2** *adv.* lawfully; rightfully; **das steht ihm ~ zu** that is his by right *or* rightfully his

Rechtmäßigkeit *die; ~:* legality; lawfulness; (eines Anspruchs) legitimacy

rechts 1 *Adv.* **(a)** ▶ 583 | (auf der rechten Seite) on the right; **~ von jmdm./etw.** on sb.'s right *or* the right of sb./on *or* to the right of sth.; **von ~:** from the right; **nach ~:** to the right; **sich ~ halten** keep to the right; **sich ~ einordnen** move *or* get into the right-hand lane; **~ außen** (Ballspiele) ‹run, break through› down the right wing; *s. auch* **links 1 a; (b)** (Politik) on the right wing; **~ stehen** *od.* **sein** be right-wing *or* on the right; **~ außen** (ugs.) on the extreme right [wing]; **(c)** (Handarb.) **ein glatt ~ gestrickter Pullover** a pullover in stocking stitch; *s. auch* **links 1 c. 2** *Präp. mit Gen.* ▶ 583 | **~ des Rheins** on the right side *or* bank of the Rhine

Rechts-: **~abbieger** *der* (Verkehrsw.) motorist/cyclist/ car *etc.* turning right; **~an·spruch** *der* legal right *or* entitlement; **einen ~anspruch auf etw.** (*Akk.*) **haben** have a legal right to *or* be legally entitled to sth.; **~an·walt** *der,* **~anwältin** *die* ▶ 85 | lawyer; solicitor (Brit.); attorney (Amer.); (vor Gericht) barrister (Brit.); attorney[-at-law] (Amer.); advocate (Scot.)

rechts-, Rechts-: *****~außen** ⇒ **rechts 1 a, b;** **~außen** *der; ~, ~* (Ballspiele) right wing; outside right; **~beistand** *der* ▶ 85 | legal adviser; **~beratung** *die* legal advice

recht-, Recht-: **~schaffen 1** *Adj.* honest; upright; honest, decent ‹work›; **2** *adv.* **(a)** honestly; uprightly; **(b)** (intensivierend) really ‹tired, full, etc.›; **~schaffenheit** *die; ~:* honesty, uprightness; **~schreib[e]·buch** *das* spelling-book; speller; (Wörterbuch) spelling dictionary; **~schreibfehler** *der* spelling mistake; **~schreibung** *die* orthography; **er ist in ~schreibung schwach** he's poor at spelling

rechts-, Rechts-: **~empfinden** *das* sense of [what is] right and wrong; **~extremismus** *der* (Politik) right-wing extremism; **~extremist** *der* (Politik) right-wing extremist; **~frage** *die* (Rechtsw.) legal question *or* issue; **~gelehrte** *der/die* jurist; **~gerichtet** *Adj.* (Politik) right-wing orientated; **~grundsatz** *der* (Rechtsw.) legal principle; **~gültig** *Adj.* (Rechtsw.) legally valid; **~händer** /~hɛndɐ/ *der; ~s, ~,* **~händerin** *die; ~, ~nen** right-hander; **~händer[in] sein** be right-handed; **~händig 1** *Adj.* right-handed; **2** *adv.* right-handed; with one's right hand; **~herum** *Adv.* [round] to the right; **etw. ~herum drehen** turn sth. clockwise *or* [round] to the right; **~kräftig** (Rechtsw.) **1** *Adj.* final [and absolute] ‹decision, verdict›; **~kräftig sein/werden** ‹contract,

agreement› be/come into force; **2** *adv.* **jmdn. ~kräftig verurteilen** pass a final sentence on sb.; **~kurve** *die* right-hand bend; **~lage** *die* (Rechtsw.) legal situation; **~lastig** *Adj.* (Politik ugs.) rightist; **~liberal** *Adj.* right-wing liberal; **~mittel** *das* (Rechtsw.) appeal; **~mittel einlegen** lodge an appeal; appeal; **~ordnung** *die* legal system; **~pflege** *die* (Rechtsw.) administration of justice

Rechtsprechung *die; ~,* **~en** administration of justice; (eines Gerichts) jurisdiction

rechts-, Rechts-: **~radikal** *Adj.* (Politik) radical right-wing; **~radikalismus** *der* right-wing radicalism; **~ruck** *der* (Politik ugs.) shift to the right; **~rum** *Adv.* (ugs.) **~herum;** **~seitig 1** ‹paralysis› of the right side; **die ~seitige Uferbefestigung** the reinforcement of the right bank; **2** *adv.* on the right [side]; **~staat** *der* [constitutional] state founded on the rule of law; **~staatlich** *Adj.* founded on the rule of law *postpos.;* **~staatlichkeit** *die; ~:* rule of law; **~verkehr** *der* driving *no art.* on the right; **in Frankreich ist ~verkehr** they drive on the right in France; **~weg** *der* (Rechtsw.) recourse to legal action *or* the courts *or* the law; **~widrig 1** *Adj.* unlawful; illegal; **2** *adv.* unlawfully; illegally; **~widrigkeit** *die o. Pl.* unlawfulness; illegality; **~wissenschaft** *die* jurisprudence

recht-: **~wink[e]lig** *Adj.* right-angled; **~zeitig 1** *Adj.* timely; (pünktlich) punctual. **2** *adv.* in time; (pünktlich) on time; **~zeitig zu/zum/zur** in [good] time for

Reck /rɛk/ *das;* **~[e]s,** **~e** *od.* **~s** horizontal bar; high bar

recken 1 *tr. V.* stretch; **den Hals/Kopf ~:** crane one's neck. **2** *refl. V.* stretch oneself; **sich ~ und strecken** have a good stretch

Reckturnen *das* horizontal-bar exercises *pl.*

Recorder /re'kɔrdɐ/ *der; ~s, ~:* recorder

Redakteur /redak'tøːɐ̯/ *der; ~s, ~e,* **Redakteurin** *die; ~, ~nen** ▶ 85 | editor; **~ für Politik/Wirtschaft** political/economics editor

Redaktion /redak'tsi̯oːn/ *die; ~, ~en* **(a)** (Redakteure) editorial staff; **(b)** (Büro) editorial department *or* office/ offices *pl.;* **(c)** *o. Pl.* (das Redigieren) editing

redaktionell /redaktsi̯o'nɛl/ **1** *Adj.* editorial. **2** *adv.* editorially

Redaktions·schluss, *Redaktions·schluß *der* time of going to press

Rede /'reːdə/ *die; ~, ~n* **(a)** (Ansprache) address; speech; **eine ~ halten** give *or* make a speech; **(b)** *o. Pl.* (Vortrag) rhetoric; **die Kunst der ~:** the art of rhetoric; **(c)** (Äußerung) **der langen ~ kurzer Sinn ist, dass …:** the long and the short of it is that …; **es ist die ~ davon, dass …:** it is being said *or* people are saying that …; **davon kann keine ~ sein** it's out of the question; **nicht der ~ wert sein** be not worth mentioning; **jmdm. ~ und Antwort stehen** give a full explanation [of one's actions] to sb.; **jmdn. zur ~ stellen** make someone explain himself/herself; **(d)** *o. Pl.* (Sprachw.) **direkte** *od.* **wörtliche/indirekte ~:** direct/indirect speech

rede-, Rede-: **~freiheit** *die; o. Pl.* freedom of speech; **~gewandt** *Adj.* eloquent; **~gewandtheit** *die* eloquence

reden 1 *tr. V.* talk; **Unsinn ~:** talk nonsense; **kein Wort ~:** not say *or* speak a word. **2** *itr. V.* **(a)** (sprechen) talk; speak; **viel/wenig ~:** talk a lot (coll.) /not talk much; **(b)** (sich äußern, eine Rede halten) speak; **er lässt mich nicht zu Ende ~:** he doesn't let me finish what I'm saying; *s. auch* **gut 2 b; (c)** (sich unterhalten) talk; **mit jmdm./über jmdn. ~:** talk to/about sb.; **miteinander ~:** have a talk [with one another]; **sie ~ nicht mehr miteinander** they are no longer on speaking terms; **mit sich ~ lassen** (bei Geschäften) be open to offers; (bei Meinungsverschiedenheiten) be willing to discuss the matter. **3** *refl. V.* **sich heiser/in Wut ~:** talk oneself hoarse/into a rage

Redens·art *die* **(a)** expression; (Sprichwort) saying; **(b)** *Pl.* (Phrase) empty *or* meaningless words; **allgemeine ~en** empty generalizations

Rede-: **~schwall** *der* (abwertend) torrent of words; **~wendung** *die* (Sprachw.) idiom; idiomatic expression

---

redlich 1 *Adj.* honest; honest, upright ‹*person*›. **2** *adv.* (**a**) honestly; **sich ~ durchs Leben schlagen** make an honest living; (**b**) (intensivierend) really

Redlichkeit *die;* ~: honesty

Redner *der;* ~s, ~ (**a**) speaker; (**b**) (Rhetoriker) orator

Rednerin *die;* ~, ~**nen** ⇨ **Redner**

Redner·pult *das* lectern

red·selig *Adj.* talkative

Red·seligkeit *die* talkativeness

Reduktion /redʊk'tsioːn/ *die;* ~, ~**en** reduction

reduzieren /redu'tsiːrən/ **1** *tr. V.* reduce (**auf** + *Akk.* to). **2** *refl. V.* decrease; diminish

Reeder *der;* ~s, ~: shipowner

Reederei *die;* ~, ~**en** shipping firm *or* company

reell /re'ɛl/ **1** *Adj.* honest, straight ‹*person, deal, etc.*›; sound, solid ‹*business, firm, etc.*›; straight ‹*offer*›; decent; realistic ‹*price*›. **2** *adv.* honestly; **~ einschenken** pour [out] a decent measure

Reet /reːt/ *das;* ~s (nordd.) reeds *pl.*

reet·gedeckt *adj.* thatched

Referat /refe'raːt/ *das;* ~[**e**]**s**, ~**e** (**a**) paper; **ein ~ halten** give *or* present a paper; (**b**) (kurzer schriftlicher Bericht) report (*Gen.* on); (**c**) (Abteilung) department

Referendar /referɛn'daːɐ̯/ *der;* ~s, ~**e**, **Referendarin** *die;* ~, ~**nen** *candidate for a higher civil-service post who has passed the first state examination and is undergoing in-service training*

Referent /refe'rɛnt/ *der;* ~**en**, ~**en**, **Referentin** *die;* ~, ~**nen** person presenting a/the paper; (Redner) speaker

Referenz /refe'rɛnts/ *die;* ~, ~**en** (**a**) (Empfehlung) reference; (**b**) (Person, Stelle) referee

referieren /refe'riːrən/ **1** *itr. V.* **über etw.** (*Akk.*) ~: give *or* present a paper on sth.; (zusammenfassend) give a report on sth. **2** *tr. V.* **etw.** ~: give *or* present a paper on sth.; (zusammenfassend) give a report on sth.

reflektieren /reflɛk'tiːrən/ **1** *tr. V.* (**a**) *auch itr.* (zurückstrahlen) reflect; (**b**) (geh.: nachdenken über) reflect or ponder [up]on. **2** *itr. V.* (geh.: nachdenken) reflect, ponder (**über** + *Akk.* [up]on)

Reflex /re'flɛks/ *der;* ~**es**, ~**e** (**a**) (Physiol.) reflex; **bedingter** ~: conditioned reflex; (**b**) (Licht~) reflection

Reflexion /reflɛ'ksioːn/ *die;* ~, ~**en** reflection

reflexiv /reflɛ'ksiːf/ *Adj.* (Sprachw.) reflexive

Reflexiv·pronomen *das* (Sprachw.) reflexive pronoun

Reform /re'fɔrm/ *die;* ~, ~**en** reform

Reformation *die;* ~ (hist.) Reformation

Reformator /refɔr'maːtɔr/ *der;* ~s, ~**en** /-ma'toːrən/ reformer

reform·bedürftlg *Adj.* in need of reform *postpos.*

Reformer *der;* ~s, ~: reformer

Reform·haus *das* health-food shop

reformieren *tr. V.* reform

Refrain /rə'frɛː/ *der;* ~s, ~s chorus; refrain

Regal /re'gaːl/ *das;* ~s, ~**e** [set *sing.* of] shelves *pl.;* **ein Buch aus dem ~ nehmen** take a book from the shelf

Regatta /re'gata/ *die;* ~, **Regatten** (Sport) regatta

rege /'reːgə/ **1** *Adj.* (**a**) (betriebsam) busy ‹*traffic*›; brisk ‹*demand, trade, business, etc.*›; good ‹*participation; attendance*›; lively ‹*correspondence*›; (**b**) (lebhaft) lively; lively, animated ‹*discussion, conversation*›; keen ‹*interest*›; **geistig** ~: mentally alert *or* active. **2** *adv.* (**a**) (betriebsam) actively; **~ an etw.** (*Akk.*) **teilnehmen** take an active part in sth.; (**b**) (lebhaft) actively

Regel /'reːgl̩/ *die;* ~, ~**n** (**a**) rule; **die ~n eines Spiels/ des Anstands** the rules of a game/of decency; **nach allen ~n der Kunst** (fig.) well and truly; (**b**) **die ~ sein** be the rule; **in der** *od.* **aller** ~: as a rule; (**c**) (Menstruation) period

regelbar *Adj.* adjustable

regel-, Regel-: ~**los 1** *Adj.* disorderly; **2** *adv.* in a disorderly manner; ~**mäßig 1** *Adj.* regular; **2** *adv.* regularly; ~**mäßigkeit** *die* regularity

regeln 1 *tr. V.* (**a**) settle ‹*matter, question, etc.*›; put ‹*finances, affairs, etc.*› in order; **etw. durch Gesetz** ~:

regulate sth. by law; **wir haben die Sache so geregelt, dass ...:** we've arranged .things so that ...; (**b**) (einstellen, regulieren) regulate; (steuern) control; *s. auch* **Verkehr a. 2** *refl. V.* take care of itself; **die Sache hat sich [von selbst] geregelt** the matter has sorted itself out *or* resolved itself

regel·recht (ugs.) **1** *Adj.; nicht präd.* proper (coll.); real; real ‹*shock*›; real, absolute ‹*scandal*›; complete, utter ‹*flop, disaster*›; real, downright ‹*impertinence, insult*›. **2** *adv.* really

Regelung *die;* ~, ~**en** (**a**) *o. Pl.* ⇨ **regeln 1 a, b:** settlement; putting in order; regulation; control; (**b**) (Vorschriften) regulation

regel·widrig 1 *Adj.* that is against the rules *postpos.;* ~ **sein** be against the rules. **2** *adv.* **sich ~ verhalten** break the rules; **den Stürmer ~ attackieren** (Ballspiele) foul the forward

regen /'reːgn̩/ **1** *tr. V.* (geh.) move. **2** *refl. V.* (**a**) (sich bewegen) move; **kein Lüftchen regte sich** not a breath of air stirred; (**b**) (geh.: sich bemerkbar machen) ‹*hope, doubt, desire, conscience*› stir

Regen *der;* ~s, ~ (**a**) rain; **bei strömendem ~: in** pouring rain; **es wird ~ geben** it will rain; it is going to rain; **ein warmer** ~ (fig.) a windfall; **vom ~ in die Traufe kommen** (fig.) jump out of the frying pan into the fire; **jmdn. im ~ stehen lassen** (fig. ugs.) leave sb. in the lurch; (**b**) (fig.) shower

regen·arm *Adj.* ‹*period, region, etc.*› with little rain[fall], with low rainfall

Regen·bogen *der* rainbow

Regen·bogen-: ~**haut** *die* ▶ 326⦘ (Anat.) iris; ~**presse** *die* (abwertend) gossip magazines *pl.*

Regen-: ~**cape** *das* rain cape; ~**dach** *das* rain-canopy

Regeneration *die* regeneration

regenerieren /regene'riːrən/ (fachspr.) **1** *refl. V.* regenerate; (geh.: sich erholen) recuperate. **2** *tr. V.* regenerate

regen-, Regen-: ~**guss**, ***~**guß** *der* downpour; ~**haut** *die* [light] plastic mackintosh *or* (coll.) mac; ~**mantel** *der* raincoat; mackintosh; mac (coll.); ~**reich** *Adj.* ‹*period, region, etc.*› with high rainfall; ~**rinne** *die* gutter; ~**schauer** *der* shower [of rain]; rain-shower; ~**schirm** *der* umbrella

Regent /re'gɛnt/ *der;* ~**en**, ~**en** (**a**) (Herrscher) ruler; (Monarch) monarch; (**b**) (Stellvertreter) regent

Regen·tag *der* rainy day

Regentin *die;* ~, ~**nen** ⇨ **Regent**

Regen·tonne *die* water butt

Regentschaft *die;* ~, ~**en** regency

Regen-: ~**wasser** *das; o. Pl.* rainwater; ~**wetter** *das; o. Pl.* rainy *or* wet weather; ~**wolke** *die* rain cloud; ~**wurm** *der* earthworm; ~**zeit** *die* rainy season

Regie /re'ʒiː/ *die;* ~ (**a**) (Theater, Film, Ferns., Rundf.) direction; **bei etw.** ~ **führen** direct sth.; **unter der** ~ **von ...:** directed by ...; (**b**) (Leitung, Verwaltung) management; **unter staatlicher** ~: under state control

regieren /re'giːrən/ **1** *itr. V.* rule (**über** + *Akk.* over); ‹*monarch*› reign, rule (**über** + *Akk.* over); ‹*party, administration*› govern. **2** *tr. V.* (**a**) rule; govern; ‹*monarch*› reign over, rule; (**b**) (Sprachw.) govern, take ‹*case*›

Regierung *die;* ~, ~**en** (**a**) *o. Pl.* (Herrschaft) rule; (eines Monarchen) reign; **die** ~ **übernehmen** *od.* **antreten** take over; come to power; (**b**) (Kabinett) government

regierungs-, Regierungs-: ~**bildung** *die* formation of a/the government; ~**chef** *der* head of government; ~**erklärung** *die* government statement; ~**feindlich** *Adj.* anti-government; ~**freundlich** *Adj.* pro-government; ~**gewalt** *die* government power *no art.;* ~**krise** *die* government crisis; ~**rat** *der* senior civil servant; ~**sitz** *der* seat of government; ~**sprecher** *der* government spokesman; ~**umbildung** *die* government reshuffle; ~**wechsel** *der* change of government

Regime /re'ʒi:m/ *das;* ~s, ~ /re'ʒi:mə/ (abwertend) regime
Regime-: ~**gegner** *der* opponent of a/the regime; ~**kritiker** *der* critic of a/the regime
Regiment /regi'mɛnt/ *das;* ~[e]s, ~e *od.* ~er (a) *Pl.* ~e (Herrschaft) rule; **das** ~ **führen** (fig.) give the orders; **ein strenges** ~ **führen** (fig.) be strict; (b) *Pl.* ~er (Milit.) regiment
Region /re'gio:n/ *die;* ~, ~en region
regional /regio'na:l/ **1** *Adj.* regional. **2** *adv.* regionally; ~ **verschieden sein** differ from region to region
Regisseur /reʒɪ'sø:ɐ/ *der;* ~s, ~e, **Regisseurin** *die;* ~, ~nen (Theater, Film) director; (Ferns., Rundf.) director; producer
Register /re'gɪstɐ/ *das;* ~s, ~ (a) index; (b) (amtliche Liste) register; (c) (Musik) (bei Instrumenten) register; (Orgel~) stop; **alle** ~ **ziehen** (fig.) pull out all the stops
registrieren /regɪs'tri:rən/ *tr. V.* (a) register; (b) (bewusst wahrnehmen) note; register
Registrierung *die;* ~, ~en registration
reglementieren *tr. V.* regulate; regiment ‹*people, life*›
Reglementierung *die;* ~, ~en regulation; (Bevormundung) regimentation
Regler *der;* ~s, ~ (Technik) regulator; (Kybernetik) control
reg·los *Adj.* motionless
Reglosigkeit *die;* ~: motionlessness
regnen /'re:gnən/ **1** *itr., tr. V.* (unpers.) rain; **es regnet** it is raining; **es regnete Steine** (fig.) stones rained down. **2** *itr. V.; mit sein* (fig.) rain down
regnerisch *Adj.* rainy
regulär /regu'lɛ:ɐ/ *Adj.* (a) proper; regular ‹*troops*›; normal, regular ‹*working hours, flight*›; (b) (ugs.: regelrecht) proper (coll.); regular (coll.)
regulierbar *Adj.* regulable; adjustable ‹*backrest*›
regulieren /regu'li:rən/ *tr. V.* regulate
Regulierung *die;* ~, ~en regulation
Regung *die;* ~, ~en (geh.: Gefühl) stirring; **seine erste** ~ **war Unmut** his first emotion was displeasure; **sie folgte einer** ~ **ihres Herzens** she followed the promptings of her heart
regungs·los *Adj.* motionless
Regungslosigkeit *die;* ~: motionlessness
Reh /re:/ *das;* ~[e]s, ~e roe-deer
reh-, Reh-: ~**bock** *der* roebuck; ~**braun** *Adj.* light reddish brown; ~**kitz** *das* fawn *or* kid [of a/the roe-deer]
Reibach /'raibax/ *der;* ~s (ugs.) profits *pl.;* **einen [kräftigen]** ~ **machen** make a killing (coll.)
Reibe /'raibə/ *die;* ~, ~n grater
Reib·eisen *das* grater; **eine Stimme wie ein** ~: a voice like a rasp
Reibe·kuchen *der* (landsch.) ⇒ **Kartoffelpuffer**
reiben 1 *unr. tr. V.* (a) rub; **etw. blank** ~ rub sth. until it shines; **sich** (*Dat.*) **den Schlaf aus den Augen** ~: rub the sleep from one's eyes; (b) (zerkleinern) grate. **2** *unr. itr. V.* rub (**an** + *Dat.* on). **3** *unr. refl. V.* rub oneself/itself (**an** + *Dat.* against); **sie** ~ **sich ständig aneinander** (fig.) there is constant friction between them
Reiberei *die;* ~, ~en friction *no pl.;* **es gab ständig** ~**en mit seinem Sohn** there was constant friction between him and his son
Reibung *die;* ~, ~en (Physik, fig.) friction
reibungs·los 1 *Adj.* smooth; **2** *adv.* smoothly
reich /raiç/ **1** *Adj.* (a) (vermögend) rich; ~ **heiraten** marry [into] money; **die Reichen** the rich; (b) (prächtig) costly ‹*goods, gifts*›; rich ‹*décor, ornamentation, finery, furnishings*›; (c) (üppig) rich; rich, abundant ‹*harvest*›; lavish, sumptuous ‹*meal*›; abundant ‹*mineral resources*›; ~ **an etw.** (*Dat.*) **sein** be rich in sth.; (d) (vielfältig) rich ‹*collection, possibilities, field of activity*›; wide, large, extensive ‹*selection, choice*›; wide ‹*knowledge, experience*›. **2** *adv.* richly
-reich rich in …; **kontrast**~: rich in contrast; **wasser**~ **sein** have abundant water

---

*alte Schreibung (vgl. Hinweise auf S. xvi–xvii)

Reich *das;* ~[e]s, ~e (a) empire; (König~) kingdom; realm; **das [Deutsche]** ~ (hist.) the German Reich *or* Empire; **das Dritte** ~ (hist.) the Third Reich; (b) (fig.) realm; **ins** ~ **der Fabel gehören** belong to the realm[s] of fantasy; **das** ~ **der Pflanzen/Tiere** the plant/animal kingdom; **Dein** ~ **komme** (bibl.) thy Kingdom come
reichen 1 *itr. V.* (a) (aus~) be enough; **das Geld reicht nicht** I/we *etc.* haven't got enough money; **das Brot muss noch bis Montag** ~: the bread must last till Monday; **die Farbe hat gerade gereicht** there was just enough paint; **das Seil reicht nicht** the rope's not long enough; **jetzt reicht's mir aber!** now I've had enough!; **danke, das reicht** that's enough, thank you; (b) (sich erstrecken) reach; ‹*forest, fields, etc.*› extend; **bis zu etw.** ~: extend as far as sth.; **sein Einfluss reicht sehr weit** his influence extends a long way; **jmdm. bis an die Schultern** ~: come up to sb.'s shoulder; (c) (ugs.) ⇒ **auskommen** a. **2** *tr. V.* (geh.) (a) pass; hand; **jmdm. die Hand** ~: hold out one's hand to sb.; **sich** (*Dat.*) **die Hand** ~: shake hands; (b) (servieren) serve ‹*food, drink*›
reich·haltig *Adj.* extensive; varied ‹*programme*›; substantial ‹*meal*›
reichlich 1 *Adj.* large; substantial; ample ‹*space, time, reward*›; good ‹*hour, litre, etc.*›; generous ‹*tip*›. **2** *adv.* (a) amply; (b) (in großer Menge) ~ **Trinkgeld geben** tip generously; **Fleisch ist noch** ~ **vorhanden** there is still plenty of meat left; ~ **Zeit/Platz/Gelegenheit haben** have plenty of *or* ample time/room/opportunity; (c) (mehr als) over; more than; ~ **5 000 Mark** a good 5,000 marks. **3** *Adv.* (ugs.: ziemlich, sehr) ~ **frech** a bit too cheeky
Reichs·tag *der o. Pl.* (hist.) Reichstag; (des Heiligen Römischen Reichs) Imperial Diet
Reichtum *der;* ~s, **Reichtümer** /'raiçty:mɐ/ (a) *o. Pl.* (auch fig.) wealth (**an** + *Dat.* of); **der** ~ **an Vögeln** the abundance of birds; (b) *Pl.* (auch fig.) riches
Reich·weite *die* reach; (eines Geschützes, Senders, Flugzeugs) range; **in** ~ **sein** be within reach/range; **Geschütze mit großer** ~: long-range guns
reif /raif/ *Adj.* (a) ripe ‹*fruit, grain, cheese*›; mature ‹*brandy, cheese*›; ~ **für etw. sein** (ugs.) be ready for sth.; **die Zeit ist noch nicht** ~: the time is not yet ripe; (b) (erwachsen, erfahren) mature; **die** ~**eren Jahrgänge** those of mature age; (c) (ausgewogen, durchdacht) mature; **eine** ~**e Leistung** (ugs.) a solid achievement
-reif ready for …; **test-/olympia**~: ready for testing/for the Olympics; **aufführungs**~: ready to be performed
Reif¹ *der;* ~[e]s hoar frost
Reif² *der;* ~[e]s, ~e (geh.) ring; (Arm~) bracelet; (Diadem) circlet
Reife *die;* ~ (a) ripeness; (von Menschen, Gedanken, Produkten) maturity; **Zeugnis der** ~: Abitur certificate; **mittlere** ~ (Schulw.) *school-leaving certificate usually taken after the fifth year of secondary school;* (b) (Reifung) ripening; **während der** ~: during ripening
reifen 1 *itr. V.; mit sein* (a) ‹*fruit, cereal, cheese*› ripen; ‹*ovum, embryo, cheese*› mature; (b) (geh.: älter, reifer werden) mature (**zu** into); **ein gereifter Mann** (geh.) a mature man; (c) ‹*idea, plan, decision*› mature. **2** *tr. V.* ripen ‹*fruit, cereal*›
Reifen *der;* ~s, ~ (a) (Metallband, Sportgerät) hoop; (b) (Gummi~) tyre; (c) ⇒ **Reif²**
Reifen-: ~**druck** *der* tyre pressure; ~**panne** *die* flat tyre; puncture; ~**profil** *das* [tyre] tread; ~**wechsel** *der* tyre change
Reife-: ~**prüfung** *die* school-leaving examination for university entrance qualification; ~**zeugnis** *das* Abitur certificate
Reif·glätte *die* ice on the roads
reiflich 1 *Adj.* [very] careful; **bei/nach** ~**er Überlegung** on mature consideration/after [very] careful consideration. **2** *adv.* [very] carefully
Reifung *die;* ~ ⇒ **reifen 1**: ripening; maturing; maturation
Reigen /'raign/ *der;* ~s, ~ round dance; **den** ~ **eröffnen** (fig.) start off; **ein bunter** ~ **von Melodien** a medley of tunes

Reihe /'raiə/ *die;* ~, ~n **(a)** row; **in** ~n (*Dat.*) **antreten** line up; (Milit.) fall in; **sich in fünf** ~n **aufstellen** line up in five rows; form five lines; **in Reih und Glied** (Milit.) in rank and file; **aus der** ~ **tanzen** (fig. ugs.) be different; **etw. in die** ~ **bringen** (fig. ugs.) put sth. straight *or* in order; **(b)** *o. Pl.* (Reihenfolge) series; **die** ~ **ist an ihm/ihr** *usw.*, **er/sie** *usw.* **ist an der** ~: it's his/her *etc.* turn; **der** ~ **nach, nach der** ~: in turn; one after the other; **(c)** (größere Anzahl) number; **(d)** (Gruppe) ranks *pl.;* **aus den eigenen** ~n from one's/its own ranks; **(e)** (Math., Musik) series

reihen (geh.) **1** *tr. V.* (auf~) string; thread; **Perlen auf eine Schnur** ~: string pearls [on a thread]. **2** *refl. V.* **sich an etw.** (*Akk.*) ~: follow sth.

reihen-, Reihen-: ~**folge** *die* order; ~**haus** *das* terraced house; ~**untersuchung** *die* (Med.) mass screening; ~**weise** *Adv.* (ugs.) by the dozen

Reiher *der;* ~s, ~ heron

reihern *itr. V.* (salopp) puke (coarse)

reih·um *Adv.* **etw.** ~ **gehen lassen** pass sth. round

Reim /raim/ *der;* ~[e]s, ~e rhyme; **sich** (*Dat.*) **keinen** ~ **auf etw.** (*Akk.*) **machen [können]** (fig.) not [be able] to see rhyme or reason in sth.

reimen 1 *itr. V.* make up rhymes. **2** *tr. V.* rhyme; **ein Wort auf ein anderes** ~: rhyme one word with another. **3** *refl. V.* rhyme (**auf** + *Akk.* with); **das reimt sich nicht** (fig.) that makes no sense

reim·los *Adj.* unrhymed; rhymeless

rein[1] /rain/ *Adv.* (ugs.) ~ **mit dir!** in you go/come!

rein[2] **1** *Adj.* **(a)** (unvermischt) pure; **(b)** (nichts anderes als) pure; sheer; **etw. aus** ~**em Trotz tun** do sth. out of sheer *or* pure contrariness; **die** ~**e Theorie** pure theory; **die** ~**e Wahrheit sagen** tell the plain *or* unvarnished truth; **es war eine** ~**e Männersache** it was exclusively a men's affair; **eine** ~**e Arbeitergegend** a purely *or* entirely working-class district; **der** ~**ste Quatsch** (ugs.) pure *or* sheer *or* absolute nonsense; **dein Zimmer ist der** ~**ste Saustall** (derb) your room is a real pigsty; **(c)** (meist geh.: frisch, sauber) clean; fresh ‹*clothes, sheet of paper, etc.*›; pure, clean ‹*water, air*›; clear ‹*complexion*›; (fig.) **jmdn./jmds. Namen** ~ **waschen** (ugs.) clear sb./sb.'s name; **sich** ~ **waschen** (ugs.) clear oneself *or* one's name; **ein** ~**es Gewissen haben** have a clear conscience; **etw. ins Reine schreiben** make a fair copy of sth.; **etw. ins Reine bringen** clear sth. up; put sth. straight; **mit jmdm./etw. ins Reine kommen** get things straightened out with sb./ get sth. sorted *or* straightened out. **2** *Adv.* purely; ~ **zufällig** purely *or* quite by chance; ~ **gar nichts** (ugs.) absolutely nothing

Reine·machen *das;* ~s (bes. nordd.) cleaning session

Rein·fall *der* (ugs.) let-down; **das Stück war ein absoluter** *od.* **totaler** ~: the play was a complete flop (coll.)

rein|fallen *unr. itr. V.; mit sein* (ugs.) ⇒ **hereinfallen a**

rein|gehen *unr. itr. V.; mit sein* (ugs.) ⇒ **hineingehen**

Rein-: ~**gewinn** *der* net profit; ~**haltung** *die:* **die** ~ **der Seen/der Luft** keeping the lakes/air clean *or* pure

rein|hauen 1 *unr. tr. V.* **jmdm. eine** ~ (salopp) thump sb. [one] (coll.). **2** *unr. itr. V.* (essen) tuck in (coll.)

Reinheit *die;* ~ **(a)** purity; (Sauberkeit) cleanness; (des Wassers, der Luft) purity; (der Haut) clearness

reinigen /'rainɪgn/ *tr. V.* clean; clean, cleanse ‹*wound, skin*›; purify ‹*effluents, air, water, etc.*›; **Kleider [chemisch]** ~ **lassen** have clothes [dry-]cleaned

Reinigung *die;* ~, ~en **(a)** ⇒ **reinigen:** cleaning; cleansing; purification; dry-cleaning; **(b)** (Betrieb) [dry-]cleaner's

rein-: ~|**knien** *refl. V.* (ugs.) ⇒ **hineinknien;** ~|**kommen** *unr. itr. V.; mit sein* (ugs.) ⇒ **hereinkommen;** ~**kriechen** crawl into sth.; ~|**kriegen** *tr. V.* (ugs.) ⇒ **hereinbekommen; hinein|-;** ~|**legen** *tr. V.* (ugs.) ⇒ **hereinlegen**

reinlich *Adj.* cleanly

Reinlichkeit *die;* ~: cleanliness

rein-, Rein-: ~**rassig** *Adj.* purebred, thoroughbred ‹*animal*›; ~|**reden** *itr. V.* **jmdm.** ~ (ugs.) interfere in sb.'s affairs; ~|**reißen** *unr. tr. V.* (ugs.) **jmdn.** ~**reißen**

drag sb. in (fig.); ~|**reiten** *unr. tr. V.* (ugs.) **jmdn.** ~**reiten** drag sb. in (fig.); ~|**schlagen** *unr. tr. V.* **(a)** (ugs.) knock in; **etw. in etw.** (*Akk.*) ~**schlagen** knock sth. into sth.; **(b) jmdm. eine** ~**schlagen** (salopp) thump sb. [one] (coll.); ~**schrift** *die* fair copy; ~|**steigern** *refl. V.* (ugs.) work oneself up; become worked up; ~|**treten** (ugs.) **1** *unr. itr. V.; mit sein* **in etw.** (*Akk.*) ~**treten** step in[to] sth.; **2** *unr. tr., itr. V.* **jmdm.** *od.* **jmdn. hinten** ~**treten** kick sb. up the backside;*~|**waschen** ⇒ **rein 1 c;** ~|**wollen** *unr. itr. V.* (ugs.) want to come/go in; ~|**würgen** *tr. V.* (ugs.) **jmdm. eine** *od.* **eins** ~**würgen** come down on sb. like a ton of bricks (coll.)

Reis /rais/ *der;* ~**es** rice

Reise /'raizə/ *die;* ~, ~n journey; (kürzere Fahrt, Geschäfts~) trip; (Ausflug) outing; excursion; trip; (Schiffs~) voyage; **eine** ~ **mit dem Auto/der Eisenbahn** a journey by car/train; a car/train journey; **eine** ~ **zur See** a sea voyage; (Kreuzfahrt) a cruise; **eine** ~ **machen** make a journey/go on a trip/an outing; **auf** ~**n sein** travel; (nicht zu Hause sein) be away; **glückliche** *od.* **gute** ~! have a good journey

reise-, Reise-: ~**andenken** *das* souvenir; ~**begleiter** *der* (~gefährte) travelling companion; (~leiter) courier; (für Kinder) chaperon; ~**büro** *das* travel agency; travel agency; ~**bus** *der* coach; ~**fieber** *das* (ugs.) nervous excitement about the journey; ~**führer** *der* (Buch) guidebook; ~**gepäck** *das* luggage (Brit.); baggage (Amer.); (am Flughafen) baggage; ~**gesellschaft** *die,* ~**gruppe,** *die* party of tourists; ~**kosten** *Pl.* travel expenses; ~**leiter** *der,* ~**leiterin** *die* ▶ 85◀ courier; ~**lektüre** *die* reading matter for the journey; ~**lustig** *Adj.* ~**lustig sein** be a keen traveller

reisen *itr. V.; mit sein* **(a)** travel; **er reist für einige Tage nach Paris** he's going to Paris for a few days; **(b)** (ab~) leave; set off

Reisende *der/die; adj. Dekl.* traveller; (Fahrgast) passenger

Reise-: ~**pass,** *~**paß** *der* passport; ~**rad** *das* touring bicycle; tourer; ~**ruf** *der* SOS message for travellers; ~**scheck** *der* ▶ 216◀ traveller's cheque; ~**tasche** *die* holdall; ~**verkehr** *der* holiday traffic; ~**wecker** *der* travel alarm; ~**welle** *die* surge of holiday traffic; ~**wetter·bericht** *der* holiday weather forecast; ~**ziel** *das* destination

Reis·feld *das* paddy field

Reisig *das;* ~**s** brushwood

Reisig·besen *der* besom

Reis·korn *das* grain of rice

Reiß-: ~**aus** *der:* ~**aus nehmen** (ugs.) scram (coll.); scarper (Brit. sl.); ~**brett** *das* drawing board

reißen /'raisn/ **1** *unr. tr. V.* **(a)** tear; **sich** (*Dat.*) **ein Loch in die Hose** ~: tear *or* rip a hole in one's trousers; **jmdm. etw. aus den Händen/Armen** ~: snatch *or* tear sth. from sb.'s hands/arms; **sich** (*Dat.*) **die Kleider vom Leibe** ~: tear one's clothes off; **jmdn. aus seinen Gedanken** ~ (fig.) awaken sb. rudely from his/her thoughts; **(b)** (ziehen an) pull; (heftig) yank (coll.); **(c)** (werfen, ziehen) **eine Welle riss ihn zu Boden** a wave knocked him to the ground; **jmdn. in die Tiefe** ~: drag sb. down into the depths; **[innerlich] hin und her gerissen sein** *od.* **werden** (fig.) be torn [two ways]; **(d)** (töten) ‹*wolf, lion, etc.*› kill, take ‹*prey*›; **etw. an sich** ~ (fig.) seize sth.; **(f)** (ugs.: machen) crack ‹*joke*›; make ‹*remark*›; **(g)** (Leichtathletik) **die Latte/eine Hürde** ~: knock the bar down/ knock a hurdle out of the way. **2** *unr. itr. V.* **(a)** *mit sein* ‹*paper, fabric*› tear, rip; ‹*rope, thread*› break, snap; ‹*film*› break; ‹*muscle*› tear; **wenn alle Stricke** *od.* **Stränge** ~ (fig.) if all else fails; **(b)** (ziehen) **an etw.** (*Dat.*) ~: pull at sth.; **(c)** (Leichtathletik) bring the bar down/knock the hurdle over. **3** *unr. refl. V.* **(a)** tear oneself/itself (**aus, von** from); **(b)** (ugs.: sich bemühen um) **ich reiße mich nicht um diese Arbeit** I'm not all that keen on this work (coll.); **sie** ~ **sich um die Eintrittskarten** they are scrambling to *or* fighting each other to get tickets

reißend *Adj.* rapacious ‹*animal*›; stabbing ‹*pain*›; ~**en Absatz finden** sell like hot cakes; **ein** ~**er Fluss** a raging torrent

Reißer *der;* ~s, ~ (ugs., oft abwertend) thriller

reißerisch (abwertend) **1** *Adj.* sensational; lurid ‹*headline*›. **2** *adv.* sensationally

Reiß-: ~**leine** *die* (Flugw.) ripcord; ~**nagel** *der* ⇒ ~**zwecke;** ~**verschluss,** ***~**verschluß** *der* zip [fastener]; ~**wolf** *der* shredder; ~**zwecke** *die* drawing pin (Brit.); thumbtack (Amer.)

Reit·bahn *die* riding arena

reiten /'raɪtn̩/ **1** *unr. itr. V.; meist mit* sein ride. **2** *unr. tr. V.; auch mit* sein ride; **Schritt/Trab/Galopp** ~: ride at a walk/trot/gallop; **ein Turnier** ~: ride in a tournament

Reiten *das;* ~s riding *no art.*

Reiter *der;* ~s, ~, **Reiterin** *die;* ~, ~nen rider

Reit-: ~**hose** *die* riding breeches *pl.;* ~**peitsche** *die* riding whip; ~**pferd** *das* saddle-horse; ~**sport** *der* [horse-] riding; ~**stall** *der* riding stable; ~**stiefel** *der* riding boot; ~**turnier** *das* riding event

Reiz /raɪts/ *der;* ~es, ~e **(a)** (Physiol.) stimulus; **(b)** (Attraktion) attraction; appeal *no pl.;* (des Verbotenen, Fremdartigen, der Ferne usw.) lure; **ich kann dem keinen** ~ **abgewinnen** this has no appeal for me; **(c)** (Zauber) charm; **weibliche** ~e female charms

reizbar *Adj.* irritable; **leicht** ~ **sein** be very irritable

Reizbarkeit *die;* ~: irritability

reizen 1 *tr. V.* **(a)** annoy; tease ‹*animal*›; (herausfordern, provozieren) provoke; (zum Zorn treiben) anger; *s. auch* **gereizt; (b)** (Physiol.) irritate; **(c)** (Interesse erregen bei) **jmdn.** ~: attract sb.; appeal to sb.; **es würde mich sehr** ~, **das zu tun** I'd love to do that; **das Angebot reizt mich** I find the offer tempting; **(d)** (Kartenspiele) bid. **2** *itr. V.* **(a) das reizt zum Lachen** it makes people laugh; **(b)** (Kartenspiele) bid; **hoch** ~ (fig.) play for high stakes

reizend 1 *Adj.* charming; delightful, lovely ‹*child*›; **das ist ja** ~**!** (iron.) [that's] charming! (iron.). **2** *adv.* charmingly; **wir haben uns** ~ **unterhalten** we had a delightful chat

Reiz·husten *der* (Med.) dry cough

reizlos *Adj.* unattractive; ‹*landscape, scenery*› lacking in charm

Reizung *die;* ~, ~en (Physiol., Med.) irritation

reiz·voll *Adj.* **(a)** (hübsch) charming; delightful; **(b)** (interessant) attractive; **die Aussicht ist nicht gerade** ~**:** the prospect isn't exactly enticing

Reiz·wort *das* emotive word

rekapitulieren *tr. V.* recapitulate

rekeln /'re:kl̩n/ *refl. V.* (ugs.) stretch; **sich in der Sonne** ~: stretch out in the sun

Reklamation /reklama'tsi̯o:n/ *die;* ~, ~en complaint (wegen about); **spätere** ~**[en] ausgeschlossen** money cannot be refunded after purchase

Reklame /re'kla:mə/ *die;* ~, ~n **(a)** *o. Pl.* (Werbung) advertising *no indef. art.;* (Ergebnis) publicity *no indef. art;* ~ **für jmdn./etw. machen** promote sb./advertise *or* promote sth.; **(b)** (ugs.: Werbemittel) advert (Brit. coll.); ad (coll.); advertisement; (im Fernsehen, Radio auch) commercial

Reklame·trommel *die:* **für jmdn./etw. die** ~ **rühren** promote sb./sth. in a big way

reklamieren 1 *itr. V.* complain; make a complaint. **2** *tr. V.* **(a)** (beanstanden) complain about, make a complaint about (**bei** to, **wegen** on account of); **(b)** (beanspruchen) claim

rekonstruieren *tr. V.* reconstruct

Rekonstruktion *die;* ~, ~en reconstruction

Rekord /re'kɔrt/ *der;* ~**[e]s,** ~**e** record; **einen** ~ **aufstellen/innehaben** set up/hold a record

Rekord- record ‹*harvest, temperature, fee*›

Rekorder /re'kɔrdɐ/ *der;* ~**s,** ~**:** recorder

Rekord-: ~**lauf** *der* record-breaking run; ~**leistung** *die* record; ~**zeit** *die* record time

Rekrut /re'kru:t/ *der;* ~**en,** ~**en** (Milit.) recruit

Rektor /'rɛktor/ *der;* ~**s,** ~**en** /-'to:rən/ **(a)** (einer Schule) head[master]; **(b)** (Universitäts~) Rector; ≈ Vice-Chancellor (Brit.); (einer Fachhochschule) principal

---

**alte Schreibung (vgl. Hinweise auf S. xvi–xvii)

Rektorin *die;* ~, ~nen **(a)** (einer Schule) head[mistress]; **(b)** ⇒ **Rektor b**

Relais /rə'lɛ:/ *das;* ~ /rə'lɛ:(s)/, ~ /rə'lɛ:s/ (Elektrot.) relay

Relation /rela'tsi̯o:n/ *die;* ~, ~en relation; **in einer/keiner** ~ **zu etw. stehen** bear a/no relation to sth.

relativ /rela'ti:f/ **1** *Adj.* relative. **2** *adv.* relatively; ~ **zu** relative to

relativieren *tr. V.* relativize

Relativität /relativi'tɛ:t/ *die;* ~, ~en relativity

Relativitäts·theorie *die; o. Pl.* (Physik) theory of relativity

Relativ-: ~**pronomen** *das* (Sprachw.) relative pronoun; ~**satz** *der* (Sprachw.) relative clause

relaxed /ri'lɛkst/ *Adj.; nicht attr.* (salopp) laid-back (coll.)

relevant /rele'vant/ *Adj.* relevant (**für** to)

Relief /re'li̯ɛf/ *das;* ~s, ~s *od.* ~e (bild. Kunst) relief

Religion /reli'gi̯o:n/ *die;* ~, ~en **(a)** (auch fig.) religion; **(b)** *o. Pl.; o. Art.* (Unterrichtsfach) religious instruction *or* education; RI; RE

Religions-: ~**freiheit** *die; o. Pl.* religious freedom; ~**krieg** *der* religious war; ~**unterricht** *der* ⇒ **Religion b;** ~**zugehörigkeit** *die* religion; religious confession

religiös /reli'gi̯ø:s/ **1** *Adj.* religious. **2** *adv.* in a religious manner; ~ **erzogen werden** have *or* receive a religious upbringing

Religiosität /religiozi'tɛ:t/ *die;* ~: religiousness

Relikt /re'lɪkt/ *das;* ~**[e],** ~**e** relic

Reling /'re:lɪŋ/ *die;* ~, ~s *od.* ~e (Seew.) [deck-]rail

Reliquie /re'li:kvi̯ə/ *die;* ~, ~n (Rel., bes. kath. Kirche) relic

remis /rə'mi:/ (bes. Schach) **1** *indekl. Adj.; nicht attr.* drawn; ~ **enden/ausgehen** end in a draw. **2** *adv.* ~ **spielen** draw

Remis *das;* ~ /rə'mi:(s)/, ~ /rə'mi:s/ *od.* ~en (bes. Schach) draw; ~ **anbieten** offer a draw

Remmidemmi /rɛmi'dɛmi/ *das;* ~ (ugs.) row (coll.); racket

Rempelei *die;* ~, ~en (ugs.) pushing and shoving; jostling; (Sport) pushing

rempeln /'rɛmpl̩n/ (ugs.) push; shove; jostle; (Sport) push

Ren /rɛn/ *das;* ~s, ~s *od.* ~e reindeer

Renaissance /rəne'sã:s/ *die;* ~, ~n **(a)** *o. Pl.* Renaissance; **(b)** (fig.) revival; **eine** ~ **erleben** enjoy a renaissance

Rendezvous /rãde'vu:/ *das;* ~ /-'vu:(s)/, ~ /-'vu:s/ rendezvous

Reneklode /re:nə'klo:də/ *die;* ~, ~n greengage

renitent /reni'tɛnt/ **1** *Adj.* refractory. **2** *adv.* refractorily

Renitenz /reni'tɛnts/ *die;* ~ refractoriness

Renn-: ~**auto** *das* racing car; ~**bahn** *die* (Sport) racetrack; (für Pferde) racecourse; racetrack; ~**boot** *das* (Motorboot) power boat; (Segelboot) racing yacht

rennen /'rɛnən/ **1** *unr. itr. V.; mit* sein run; **um die Wette** ~: have a race; race each other; **in sein Verderben** ~ (fig.) rush headlong to one's doom; **dauernd zur Polizei** ~ (ugs.) be always running to the police; **an/gegen jmdn./etw.** ~: run *or* bang into sb./sth. **2** *unr. tr. V.* **(a) sich** (*Dat.*) **an etw.** (*Dat.*) **ein Loch in den Kopf** ~: run *or* bang into sth. and hurt one's head; **(b)** (ugs.: stoßen) **jmdm. etw. in die Rippen** ~: run sth. into sb.'s ribs

Rennen *das;* ~s, ~ running; (Pferde~, Auto~) racing; (einzelner Wettbewerb) race; **zum** ~ **gehen** (Pferde~) go to the races; (Auto~) go to the racing; **das** ~ **machen** (ugs.) win

Renner *der;* ~s, ~ (ugs.) big seller

Rennerei *die;* ~, ~en (ugs.) running around; chasing around

Renn-: ~**fahrer** *der* ▶ 85| racing driver/cyclist/motorcyclist; ~**lenker** *der* drop[ped] handlebars *pl.;* ~**maschine** *die* (Jargon) racing bike; ~**pferd** *das* racehorse; ~**platz** *der* ⇒ ~**bahn;** ~**rad** *das* racing cycle; ~**sport** *der* racing *no art.;* ~**strecke** *die* racetrack; ~**wagen** *der* racing car

Renommee /renɔ'me:/ *das;* ~s, ~s (geh.) reputation

renommieren /renɔ'mi:rən/ *itr. V.* show off; **mit etw.** ~: brag about sth.

renommiert *Adj.* renowned (**wegen** for)

renovieren /reno'vi:rən/ *tr. V.* renovate; redecorate ⟨*room, flat*⟩

Renovierung *die;* ~, ~en renovation; (eines Zimmers, einer Wohnung) redecoration

rentabel /rɛn'ta:bl̩/ **1** *Adj.* profitable. **2** *adv.* profitably

Rente /'rɛntə/ *die;* ~, ~n (a) pension; **auf** *od.* **in** ~ **gehen** (ugs.) retire; **auf** *od.* **in** ~ **sein** (ugs.) be retired; (b) (Kapitalertrag) annuity

Renten·alter *das* pensionable age *no art.*

Ren·tier *das* reindeer

rentieren /rɛn'ti:rən/ *refl. V.* be profitable; ⟨*machinery, equipment*⟩ pay its way; ⟨*effort, visit, etc.*⟩ be worth while

Rentner /'rɛntnɐ/ *der;* ~s, ~, **Rentnerin** *die;* ~, ~nen pensioner

reparabel /repa'ra:bl̩/ *Adj.* repairable; **nicht mehr** ~ **sein** be beyond repair

Reparationen /repara'tsi̯o:nən/ *Pl.* (Politik) reparations; ~ **leisten/zahlen** make/pay reparations

Reparatur /repara'tu:ɐ̯/ *die;* ~, ~en repair (**an** + *Dat.* to); **in** ~ **sein** be being repaired

reparatur-, Reparatur-: ~**anfällig** *Adj.* prone to break down *postpos.;* ~**arbeit** *die* repair work; ~**en** repair work *sing.;* repairs; ~**bedürftig** *Adj.* ⟨*device, appliance, vehicle, etc.*⟩ [which is] in need of repair; ~**werkstatt** *die* repair [work]shop; (für Autos) garage

reparieren /repa'ri:rən/ *tr. V.* repair; mend

Repertoire /repɛ'to̯a:ɐ̯/ *das;* ~s, ~s (auch fig.) repertoire

Report /re'pɔrt/ *der;* ~[e]s, ~e report

Reportage /repɔr'ta:ʒə/ *die;* ~, ~n report

Reporter /re'pɔrtɐ/ *der;* ~s, ~, **Reporterin** *die;* ~, ~nen reporter

Repräsentant /reprɛzɛn'tant/ *der;* ~en, ~en, **Repräsentantin** *die;* ~, ~nen representative

repräsentativ /reprɛzɛnta'ti:f/ *Adj.* (a) (auch Politik) representative (**für** of); (b) (ansehnlich) imposing; (mit hohem Prestigewert) prestigious

Repräsentativ·umfrage *die* (Statistik) representative survey

repräsentieren /reprɛzɛn'ti:rən/ **1** *tr. V.* represent. **2** *itr. V.* attend official and social functions

Repressalie /reprɛ'sa:li̯ə/ *die;* ~, ~n repressive measure

Repression /reprɛ'si̯o:n/ *die;* ~, ~en repression

repressiv /reprɛ'si:f/ **1** *Adj.* repressive. **2** *adv.* repressively

Reproduktion *die* reproduction

reproduzieren *tr. V.* (fachspr., geh.) reproduce

Reptil /rɛp'ti:l/ *das;* ~s, ~ien /rɛp'ti:li̯ən/ reptile

Republik /repu'bli:k/ *die;* ~, ~en republic

Republikaner /republi'ka:nɐ/ *der;* ~s, ~ (a) republican; (b) (Parteimitglied) Republican

republikanisch *Adj.* republican

Requiem /'re:kvi̯ɛm/ *das;* ~, ~s requiem

Requisit /rekvi'zi:t/ *das;* ~[e]s, ~en (a) (Theater) prop (coll.); property; (b) (fig.) requisite

Reservat /rezɛr'va:t/ *das;* ~[e]s, ~e (a) reservation; (b) (Naturschutzgebiet) reserve

Reserve /re'zɛrvə/ *die;* ~, ~n (a) reserve (**an** + *Dat.* of); **etw. in** ~ **haben** have sth. in reserve; *s. auch* **eisern 1 d; still 1 f;** (b) (Milit., Sport) reserves *pl.;* (c) *o. Pl.* (Zurückhaltung) reserve; **jmdn. aus der** ~ **locken** (ugs.) bring sb. out of his/her shell

Reserve-: ~**bank** *die Pl.* ~**bänke** (Sport) substitutes' bench; ~**kanister** *der* spare [petrol (Brit.) *or* (Amer.) gasoline] can; ~**offizier** *der* reserve officer; ~**rad** *das* spare wheel; ~**reifen** *der* spare tyre; ~**spieler** *der* (Sport) substitute; reserve; ~**tank** *der* reserve [fuel] tank

reservieren *tr. V.* reserve

reserviert 1 *Adj.* reserved. **2** *adv.* in a reserved way

Reservierung *die;* ~, ~en reservation

Reservist *der;* ~en, ~en (Milit.) reservist

Reservoir /rezɛr'vo̯a:ɐ̯/ *das;* ~s, ~e (auch fig.) reservoir (**an** + *Dat.* of)

Residenz /rezi'dɛnts/ *die;* ~, ~en (a) residence; (b) (Stadt) [royal] capital

residieren /rezi'di:rən/ *itr. V.* reside

Resignation /rezigna'tsi̯o:n/ *die;* ~, ~en resignation

resignieren /rezi'gni:rən/ *itr. V.* give up

resigniert 1 *Adj.* resigned. **2** *adv.* resignedly

resistent /rezis'tɛnt/ *Adj.* (Biol., Med.) resistant (**gegen** to)

resolut /rezo'lu:t/ **1** *Adj.* resolute. **2** *adv.* resolutely

Resolution /rezolu'tsi̯o:n/ *die;* ~, ~en resolution

Resonanz /rezo'nants/ *die;* ~, ~en (a) (Physik, Musik) resonance; (b) (Reaktion) response (**auf** + *Akk.* to); ~/ **keine** ~ **finden** meet with a/no response

Resopal Ⓦ /rezo'pa:l/ *das;* ~s ≈ melamine

resozialisieren *tr. V.* reintegrate into society

Resozialisierung *die;* ~, ~en reintegration into society

Respekt /re'spɛkt/ *der;* ~[e]s (a) respect; ~ **vor jmdm./etw. haben** have respect for sb./sth.; **jmdm.** ~ **abnötigen** command sb.'s respect; **bei allem** ~**!** with all due respect (**vor** + *Dat.* to); **allen** ~**!, ~, ~!** good for you!; well done!; (b) (Furcht) **jmdm.** ~ **einflößen** intimidate sb.; **vor jmdm./etw. [größten]** ~ **haben** be [much] in awe of sb./sth.

respektabel /respɛk'ta:bl̩/ **1** *Adj.* respectable. **2** *adv.* respectably

respektieren *tr. V.* respect

respekt·los 1 *Adj.* disrespectful. **2** *adv.* disrespectfully

Respektlosigkeit *die;* ~, ~en (a) *o. Pl.* disrespectfulness; lack of respect; (b) (Äußerung) disrespectful remark; (Handlung) impertinence

respekt·voll 1 *Adj.* respectful. **2** *adv.* respectfully

Ressentiment /rɛsãti'mã:/ *das;* ~s, ~s antipathy (**gegen** towards)

Ressort /rɛ'so:ɐ̯/ *das;* ~s, ~s area of responsibility; (Abteilung) department

Rest /rɛst/ *der;* ~[e]s, ~e (a) rest; ~e (historische ~e, Ruinen) remains; (einer Kultur) relics; **jmdm./einer Sache den** ~ **geben** (ugs.) finish sb./sth. off; **ein** ~ **Wein ist noch da** there's still a little bit *or* a drop of wine left; **morgen gibt es** ~**e** tomorrow we're having leftovers; **das ist der** ~ **vom Schützenfest** (ugs.) that's all there is left; (b) (Endstück, Stoff~ usw.) remnant; (c) (Math.) remainder; **20 durch 6 ist 3,** ~ **2** 20 divided by 6 is 3 with *or* and 2 left over

Restaurant /rɛsto'rã:/ *das;* ~s, ~s restaurant

Restauration /rɛstaura'tsi̯o:n/ *die;* ~, ~en (auch Politik) restoration

restaurieren /rɛstau'ri:rən/ *tr. V.* restore

restlich *Adj.; nicht präd.* remaining; **die** ~**e Butter** the rest of the butter

rest·los 1 *Adj.; nicht präd.* complete; total. **2** *adv.* completely; totally

Rest·posten *der* (Kaufmannsspr.) remaining stock *no indef. art.*

Resultat /rezʊl'ta:t/ *das;* ~[e]s, ~e result; **zu dem** ~ **kommen, dass …:** come to the conclusion that …

resultieren /rezʊl'ti:rən/ *itr. V.* result (**aus** from); **daraus resultiert, dass …:** the result *or* upshot of this is that …

Resümee /rezy'me:/ *das;* ~s, ~s résumé

resümieren /rezy'mi:rən/ **1** *tr. V.* summarize; give a résumé of. **2** *itr. V.* sum up

Retorte /re'tɔrtə/ *die;* ~, ~n (Chemie) retort

retour /re'tu:ɐ̯/ *Adv.* (bes. südd., österr., schweiz.) back

Retrospektive /retrospɛk'ti:və/ *die;* ~, ~n (a) (geh.) retrospective view; **in der** ~: in retrospect; (b) (Ausstellung) retrospective

retten /'rɛtn̩/ **1** *tr. V.* save; (vor Gefahr) save; rescue; (befreien) rescue; **jmdm. das Leben** ~: save sb.'s life; **jmdn. vor jmdm./etw.** ~: save sb. from sb./sth.; **ist er noch zu** ~? (ugs. fig.) has he gone [completely] round the bend? (coll.); **das alte Haus/der Patient ist nicht mehr zu** ~: the old house is past saving/the patient is beyond help. **2** *refl. V.* (fliehen) escape (**aus** from); **sich vor etw.** (*Dat.*) ~: escape [from] sth.; **sich vor jmdm./etw. nicht** *od.* **kaum [noch]** ~ **können** be besieged by sb./be swamped with sth.. **3** *itr. V.* (Ballspiele) save

Retter *der;* ~**s**, ~, **Retterin** *die;* ~, ~**nen** rescuer; (eines Landes, einer Bewegung o. ä.) saviour; **Christ der** ~: Christ the Saviour

Rettich /'rɛtɪç/ *der;* ~**s**, ~**e** radish

Rettung *die* (a) rescue; (Rel., eines Landes usw.) salvation; (vor Zerstörung) saving; **auf** ~ **warten/hoffen** wait for rescue/hope to be rescued; **es war jmds.** ~, **dass** ...: sb. was saved by the fact that ...; **das war meine** ~: that was my salvation

rettungs-, Rettungs-: ~**aktion** *die* rescue operation; ~**boot** *das* lifeboat; ~**dienst** *der* ambulance service; (Bergwacht, Seerettungsdienst, bei Katastrophen) rescue service; ~**hubschrauber** *der* rescue helicopter; ~**insel** *die* (Seew.) inflatable life raft; ~**los 1** *Adj.* hopeless; **2** *adv.* hopelessly; ~**ring** *der* lifebelt; ~**schwimmer** *der,* ~**schwimmerin** *die* lifesaver; (am Strand, im Schwimmbad) lifeguard; ~**wagen** *der* ambulance ~**weste** *die* (Seew.) life jacket

Retusche /re'tʊʃə/ *die;* ~, ~**n** (bes. Fot., Druckw.) retouching; (Stelle) retouch; **eine** ~/~**n vornehmen** retouch

retuschieren *tr. V.* (Fot., Druckw.) retouch; (fig.) gloss over

Reue /'rɔʏə/ *die;* ~: remorse (**über** + *Akk.* for); (Rel.) repentance

reuen *tr. V.* (meist geh.) **etw. reut jmdn.** sb. regrets sth.

reu·mütig 1 *Adj.; nicht präd.* remorseful; repentant, penitent ⟨*sinner*⟩. **2** *adv.* remorsefully; **du wirst** ~ **zurückkehren** you'll be back, saying you're sorry

Reuse /:rɔʏzə/ *die;* ~, ~**n** fish-trap

Revanche /re'vã:ʃ(ə)/ *die;* ~, ~**n** revenge; (Sport: Rückkampf, ~spiel) return match/fight/game

revanchieren *refl. V.* (a) get one's revenge, (coll.) get one's own back (**bei** on); (b) (ugs.: sich erkenntlich zeigen) **sich bei jmdm. für eine Einladung/seine Gastfreundschaft** ~: return sb.'s invitation/repay sb.'s hospitality

Revers /rə've:ɐ̯/ *das od.* (österr.) der; ~ /rə've:ɐ̯(s)/, ~ /rə've:ɐ̯s/ lapel

reversibel /rever'zi:bl̩/ *Adj.* (Technik, Med.) reversible

revidieren /revi'di:rən/ *tr. V.* revise; amend ⟨*law, contract*⟩

Revier /re'vi:ɐ̯/ *das;* ~**s**, ~**e** (a) (Aufgabenbereich) province; (b) (Zool.) territory; (c) (Polizei~) (Dienststelle) [police] station; (Bereich) district; (des einzelnen Polizisten) beat; (d) (Forst~) district; (e) (Jagd~) preserve; shoot; (f) (Bergbau) coalfield; **das** ~: the Ruhr/Saar coalfields *pl.*

Revision /revi'zjo:n/ *die;* ~, ~**en** (a) revision; (Änderung) amendment; (b) (Rechtsw.) appeal [on a point/points of law]; ~ **einlegen, in die** ~ **gehen** lodge an appeal [on a point/points of law]

Revolte /re'vɔltə/ *die;* ~, ~**n** revolt

revoltieren *itr. V.* revolt, rebel (**gegen** against); (fig.) ⟨*stomach*⟩ rebel

Revolution /revolu'tsjo:n/ *die;* ~, ~**en** (auch fig.) revolution

revolutionär /revolutsjo'nɛ:ɐ̯/ **1** *Adj.* revolutionary. **2** *adv.* in a revolutionary way

Revolutionär *der;* ~**s**, ~**e**, **Revolutionärin** *die;* ~, ~**nen** revolutionary

revolutionieren *tr. V.* revolutionize

Revoluzzer /revo'lʊtsɐ/ *der;* ~**s**, ~ (abwertend) phoney revolutionary

Revolver /re'vɔlvɐ/ *der;* ~**s**, ~ revolver

Revolver·held *der* (abwertend) gun-slinger

Rezensent /retsɛn'zɛnt/ *der;* ~**en**, ~**en** reviewer

rezensieren *tr. V.* review

Rezension *die;* ~, ~**en** review

Rezept /re'tsɛpt/ *das;* ~[**e**]**s**, ~**e** (a) (Med.) prescription; (fig.) remedy (**gegen** for); (b) (Anleitung) recipe; (fig.) formula

rezept·frei 1 *Adj.* ⟨*medicine, drug, etc.*⟩ obtainable without a prescription. **2** *adv.* **etw.** ~ **verkaufen** sell sth. without a prescription *or* over the counter

Rezeption /retsɛp'tsjo:n/ *die;* ~, ~**en** reception *no art.*

rezept·pflichtig *Adj.* ⟨*medicine, drug, etc.*⟩ obtainable only on prescription

rezessiv /retsɛ'si:f/ (Biol.) **1** *Adj.* recessive. **2** *adv.* recessively

reziprok /retsi'pro:k/ *Adj.* (bes. Math., Sprachw.) reciprocal

Rezitativ /retsita'ti:f/ *das;* ~**s**, ~**e** (Musik) recitative

rezitieren /retsi'ti:rən/ *tr., itr. V.* recite

R-Gespräch /'ɛr-/ *das* (Fernspr.) reverse-charge call (Brit.); collect call (Amer.)

Rhabarber /ra'barbɐ/ *der;* ~**s** rhubarb

Rhapsodie /rapso'di:/ *die;* ~, ~**n** (Musik, Literaturw.) rhapsody

Rhein /raɪn/ *der;* ~[**e**]**s** Rhine

Rhein·fall *der* Rhine Falls

rheinisch *Adj.* Rhenish; **eine** ~**e Spezialität** a speciality of the Rhine region

Rhein·land *das;* ~[**e**]**s** Rhineland

Rheinland-Pfalz *(das);* **Rheinland-Pfalz'** the Rhineland-Palatinate; **in/aus** ~ in/from the Rhineland-Palatinate

rheinland-pfälzisch *Adj.* ⟨*capital, citizen, etc.*⟩ of the Rhineland-Palatinate

Rhesus- /'re:zʊs/**:** ~**affe** *der* rhesus monkey; ~**faktor** *der; o. Pl.* (Med.) rhesus factor; Rh factor

Rhetorik /re'to:rɪk/ *die;* ~, ~**en** rhetoric

Rhetoriker *der;* ~**s**, ~ rhetorician

rhetorisch 1 *Adj.* rhetorical. **2** *adv.* rhetorically

Rheuma /'rɔʏma/ *das;* ~**s** ▶329❘ (ugs.) rheumatism; rheumatics *pl.* (coll.)

Rheumatiker /rɔʏ'ma:tikɐ/ *der;* ~**s**, ~ (Med.) rheumatic

rheumatisch (Med.) **1** *Adj.* rheumatic. **2** *adv.* rheumatically

Rheumatismus /rɔʏma'tɪsmʊs/ *der;* ~ ▶329❘ (Med.) rheumatism

Rhinozeros /ri'no:tseros/ *das;* ~[**ses**], ~**se** rhinoceros; rhino (coll.)

Rhododendron /rodo'dɛndrɔn/ *der od. das;* ~**s**, **Rhododendren** rhododendron

Rhomben ⇨ **Rhombus**

rhombisch *Adj.* (bes. Math.) rhombic

Rhombus /'rɔmbʊs/ *der;* ~, **Rhomben** /'rɔmbn̩/ rhombus

Rhythmen ⇨ **Rhythmus**

rhythmisch 1 *Adj.* rhythmical; rhythmic. **2** *adv.* rhythmically

Rhythmus /'rʏtmʊs/ *der;* ~, **Rhythmen** /'rʏtmən/ rhythm; **aus dem** ~ **kommen** lose the rhythm

Rhythmus-: rhythm ⟨*guitar, section, etc.*⟩

richten /'rɪçtn̩/ **1** *tr. V.* (a) direct ⟨*gaze*⟩ (**auf** + *Akk.* at, towards); turn ⟨*eyes, gaze*⟩ (**auf** + *Akk.* towards); point ⟨*torch, telescope, gun*⟩ (**auf** + *Akk.* at); aim, train ⟨*gun, missile, telescope, searchlight*⟩ (**auf** + *Akk.* on); (fig.) direct ⟨*activity, attention*⟩ (**auf** + *Akk.* towards); address ⟨*letter, remarks, words*⟩ (**an** + *Akk.* to); direct, level ⟨*criticism*⟩ (**an** + *Akk.* at); send ⟨*letter of thanks, message of greeting*⟩ (**an** + *Akk.* to); (b) (gerade~) straighten; set ⟨*fracture*⟩; (c) (einstellen) aim ⟨*cannon, missile*⟩; direct ⟨*aerial*⟩; (d) (aburteilen) judge; (verurteilen) condemn; *s. auch* **zugrunde a. 2** *refl. V.* (a) (sich hinwenden) **sich auf jmdn./etw.** ~ (auch fig.) be directed towards sb./sth.; (**b**) **sich an jmdm./etw.** ∼ ⟨*person*⟩ turn on sb./sth.; ⟨*appeal, explanation*⟩ be directed at sb./sth.; **sich gegen jmdn./etw.** ∼ ⟨*person*⟩ criticize sb./sth.; ⟨*criticism, accusations, etc.*⟩ be aimed *or* levelled *or* directed at sb./sth.; (**c**) (sich orientieren) **sich nach jmdm./jmds. Wünschen** ∼: fit in with sb./sb.'s wishes; **sich nach den Vorschriften** ∼: keep to the rules; (**d**) (abhängen) **sich nach jmdm./etw.** ∼: depend on sb./sth. **3** *itr. V.* (urteilen) judge; pass judgement; **über jmdn.** ∼: judge sb.; pass judgement on sb.; (zu Gericht sitzen) sit in judgement over sb.

Richter *der;* ∼**s,** ∼ ▸ 85 | judge; **jmdn. vor den** ∼ **bringen** take sb. to court

Richterin *die;* ∼, ∼**nen** ▸ 85 | judge

richterlich *Adj.; nicht präd.* judicial

Richt-: ∼**fest** *das* topping-out ceremony; ∼**geschwindigkeit** *die* (Verkehrsw.) recommended maximum speed

richtig 1 *Adj.* (**a**) right; (zutreffend) right; correct; correct ⟨*realization*⟩; accurate ⟨*prophecy, premonition*⟩; **bin ich hier** ∼ **bei Schulzes?** is this the Schulzes' home?; **das ist genau das Richtige für mich** that's just right for me; **ja** ∼! yes, that's right; **etw.** ∼ **stellen** correct sth.; (**b**) (ordentlich) proper; **nicht ganz** ∼ **[im Kopf** *od.* (ugs.) **im Oberstübchen] sein** be not quite right in the head (coll.) *or* not quite all there (coll.); (**c**) (wirklich, echt) real; **du bist ein** ∼**er Esel** you're a right *or* proper idiot (coll.). **2** *adv.* (**a**) right; correctly; ∼ **sitzen** *od.* **passen** ⟨*clothes*⟩ fit properly; **meine Uhr geht** ∼: my watch is right; ∼ **liegen** (ugs.) be right; (**b**) (ordentlich) properly; ∼ **ausschlafen** have a good sleep; (**c**) (richtiggehend) really

Richtige[1] *der/die; adj. Dekl.* right man/ woman/person; **sie sucht noch den** ∼**n** she's still looking for Mr Right

Richtige[2] *der; adj. Dekl.* **drei/sechs** ∼ **im Lotto** three/ six right in the lottery

Richtige[3] *das; adj. Dekl.* right thing

richtig·gehend *Adj.; nicht präd., adv.* ⇨ **regelrecht**

Richtigkeit *die;* ∼: correctness; **etw. hat seine** ∼, **mit etw. hat es seine** ∼: sth. is right

richtig-, Richtig-: *∼*∼**|liegen** ⇨ **richtig 2 a**, *∼*∼**|stellen** ⇨ **richtig 1 a**; ∼**stellung** *die* correction

Richt-: ∼**linie** *die* guideline; ∼**platz** *der* place of execution; ∼**schnur** *die; Pl.* ∼**schnuren** (fig.) guiding principle

Richtung *die;* ∼, ∼**en** (**a**) ▸ 583 | direction; **die** ∼ **ändern** *od.* **wechseln** change direction; ⟨*ship, aircraft*⟩ change course; **nach/aus allen** ∼**en** in/from all directions; **der Zug/die Autobahn** ∼ **Ulm** the train to Ulm/ the motorway in the direction of Ulm; **wir gehen in diese** ∼: we're going this way; (**b**) (fig.: Tendenz) movement; trend; (die Vertreter einer ∼) (in der Kunst, Literatur) movement; (in einer Partei) faction; (Denk∼) school of thought

Richtungs·kämpfe *Pl.* factional struggles

richtung·weisend *Adj.* ⟨*idea, resolution, paper, speech*⟩ that points the way ahead; (in der Mode) trend-setting

rieb /riːp/ *1. u. 3. Pers. Sg. Prät. v.* **reiben**

riechen /ˈriːçn̩/ **1** *unr. tr. V.* (**a**) smell; **jmdn./etw. nicht** ∼ **können** (fig. salopp) not be able to stand sb./sth.; (**b**) (wittern) ⟨*dog etc.*⟩ scent, pick up the scent of ⟨*animal*⟩; **ich konnte ja nicht** ∼, **dass** … (fig.) [I'm not psychic,] I couldn't know that … **2** *unr. itr. V.* (**a**) smell; **Hunde können sehr gut** ∼: dogs have a very good sense of smell; **an jmdm./etw.** ∼: smell sb./sth.; **lass mich mal [daran]** ∼: let me have a sniff; (**b**) (einen Geruch haben) smell (**nach** of); **gut/schlecht** ∼: smell good/bad; **er roch aus dem Mund** he had bad breath; his breath smelt

Riecher *der;* ∼**s,** ∼ (salopp) (**a**) (Nase) conk (sl.); (**b**) (fig.: Gespür) nose; **einen guten** ∼ **für etw. haben** have a sixth sense for sth.

Ried /riːt/ *das;* ∼**[e]s,** ∼**e** (**a**) *o. Pl.* (Schilf) reeds *pl.;* (**b**) (Gebiet) reedy marsh

rief /riːf/ *1. u. 3. Pers. Sg. Prät. v.* **rufen**

Riege /ˈriːɡə/ *die;* ∼, ∼**n** (Turnen) squad

Riegel /ˈriːɡl̩/ *der;* ∼**s,** ∼: (**a**) bolt; **einer Sache** (*Dat.*) **einen** ∼ **vorschieben** (fig.) put a stop to sth.; (etw. verhindern) not let sth. happen; (**b**) **ein** ∼ **Schokolade** a bar of chocolate

Riegel·haus *das* (schweiz.) half-timbered house

Riemchen *das;* ∼**s,** ∼: [small] strap *or* belt

Riemen /ˈriːmən/ *der;* ∼**s,** ∼ (**a**) strap; (Treib∼, Gürtel) belt; **sich am** ∼ **reißen** (ugs.) pull oneself together; **den** ∼ **enger schnallen** (fig. ugs.) tighten one's belt; (**b**) (Ruder) [long] oar

Riese /ˈriːzə/ *der;* ∼**n,** ∼**n** giant

rieseln /ˈriːzln̩/ *itr. V.; mit Richtungsangabe mit sein* trickle; ⟨*sand, lime*⟩ trickle [down]; ⟨*snow*⟩ fall gently *or* lightly

Riesen- giant ⟨*building, tree, salamander, tortoise, etc.*⟩; enormous ⟨*task, selection, profit, sum, portion*⟩; tremendous (coll.) ⟨*effort, rejoicing, success, hit*⟩; (abwertend: schrecklich) terrific (coll.), terrible (coll.) ⟨*stupidity, mess, scandal, fuss*⟩

riesen-, Riesen-: ∼**groß** *Adj.* enormous; huge; gigantic; terrific (coll.) ⟨*surprise*⟩; ∼**rad** *das* big wheel; Ferris wheel; ∼**schritt** *der* giant stride; ∼**slalom** *der* (Skisport) giant slalom

riesig 1 *Adj.* (**a**) enormous; huge; gigantic; vast ⟨*country*⟩; tremendous ⟨*joy, enthusiasm, effort, progress, strength*⟩; terrific (coll.), terrible (coll.) ⟨*hunger, thirst*⟩; (**b**) (ugs.: großartig) fabulous (coll.), tremendous (coll.) ⟨*party, film, etc.*⟩. **2** *adv.* (ugs.) tremendously (coll.); terribly (coll.)

Riesling /ˈriːslɪŋ/ *der;* ∼**s,** ∼**e** Riesling

riet /riːt/ *1. u. 3. Pers. Sg. Prät. v.* **raten**

Riff /rɪf/ *das;* ∼**[e]s,** ∼**e** reef

rigoros /riɡoˈroːs/ **1** *Adj.* rigorous. **2** *adv.* rigorously

Rille /ˈrɪlə/ *die;* ∼, ∼**n** groove

Rind /rɪnt/ *das;* ∼**[e]s,** ∼**er** (**a**) (Kuh) cow; (Bulle) bull; ∼**er** cattle *pl.;* **20** ∼**er** twenty head of cattle; **Hackfleisch/ein Steak vom** ∼: minced *or* (Amer.) ground beef/a beef steak; (**b**) (∼fleisch) beef; (**c**) (Zool.) bovine

Rinde *die;* ∼, ∼**n** (**a**) (Baum∼) bark; (**b**) (Brot∼) crust; (Käse∼) rind

Rinder-: ∼**braten** *der* roast beef *no indef. art.;* (roh) roasting beef *no indef. art.;* **ein** ∼**braten** a joint of roast beef; (roh) a joint of [roasting] beef; ∼**leber** *die* ox liver; ∼**seuche** *die* cattle disease; ∼**wahn·sinn** *der* ▸ 329 | mad cow disease; ∼**zucht** *die* cattle-breeding *or* -rearing *no art.*

Rind·fleisch *das* beef

Rinds-: ∼**braten** *der* (bes. südd., österr.) ⇨ **Rinderbraten;** ∼**leder** *das* cowhide; oxhide

Rind·vieh *das; Pl.* **Rindviecher** (**a**) *o. Pl.* cattle *pl.;* (**b**) (ugs. abwertend) ass; [stupid] fool

Ring /rɪŋ/ *der;* ∼**[e]s,** ∼**e** (**a**) ring; (**b**) (Box∼) ring; ∼ **frei zur zweiten Runde** seconds out for the second round

Ring·buch *das* ring binder

Ringel·blume *die* marigold

ringeln 1 *tr. V.* curl; coil ⟨*tail*⟩. **2** *refl. V.* curl

Ringel-: ∼**natter** *die* ring-snake; ∼**reihen** *der* ring-a-ring-o'-roses; ∼**schwanz** *der* curly tail

ringen 1 *unr. tr. V.* (Sport, fig.) wrestle; (fig.: kämpfen) struggle, fight (**um** for); (fig.) **mit den Tränen** ∼: fight back one's tears; **die Ärzte** ∼ **um sein Leben** the doctors are struggling *or* fighting to save his life; **nach Atem** ∼: struggle for breath. **2** *unr. tr. V.* (**a**) **den Gegner zu Boden** ∼ (auch fig.) bring one's opponent down; (**b**) **jmdm. etw. aus den Händen** ∼: wrest sth. from sb.'s hands; (**c**) **die Hände** ∼: wring one's hands

Ringen *das;* ∼**s** (Sport) wrestling *no art.*

Ringer *der;* ∼**s,** ∼: wrestler

ring-, Ring-: ∼**finger** *der* ring finger; ∼**förmig 1** *Adj.* in the shape of a ring *postpos.;* circular; **2** *adv.* ⟨*arrange*⟩ in a ring *or* circle; ∼**kampf** *der* (**a**) (stand-up) fight; (**b**) (Sport) wrestling bout; ∼**kämpfer** *der* wrestler; ∼**richter** *der* (Boxen) referee

rings /rɪŋs/ *Adv.* all around

Ring·schlüssel *der* ring spanner

rings·herum *Adv.* all around [it/them *etc.*]

Ring·straße *die* ring road

rings-: **~um, ~umher** *Adv.* all around

Rinne /'rɪnə/ *die;* ~, ~n channel; (Dach~, Rinnstein) gutter; (Rille) groove

rinnen *unr. itr. V.* (a) *mit sein* run; (b) (südd.: undicht sein) leak

Rinnsal /'rɪnzaːl/ *das;* ~[e]s, ~e (geh.) rivulet

Rinn·stein *der* gutter; **im ~ landen** (fig.) end up in the gutter

Rippchen *das;* ~s, ~ (Kochk. südd.) rib [of pork]

Rippe /'rɪpə/ *die;* ~, ~n ▶ 326] (auch Bot., Technik, Textilw., fig.) rib; **sie hat nichts auf den ~n** (ugs.) she is only skin and bone

Risiko /'riːziko/ *das;* ~s, **Risiken** *od.* österr. **Risken** risk; **ein/kein ~ eingehen** take a risk/not take any risks; **auf dein ~:** at your own risk

risiko-: **~freudig** 1 *Adj.* risky ⟨driving⟩; ⟨player, speculator⟩ who likes taking risks; 2 *adv.* **er fährt/spielt sehr ~freudig** he likes to take [a lot of] risks when he drives/plays; **~los** 1 *Adj.* safe; without risk *postpos.;* 2 *adv.* safely; without taking risks

riskant /rɪs'kant/ 1 *Adj.* risky. 2 *adv.* riskily

riskieren /rɪs'kiːrən/ *tr. V.* risk; venture ⟨smile, remark⟩; run the risk of ⟨accident, thrashing, etc.⟩; put ⟨reputation, job⟩ at risk; **etwas/nichts ~:** take a risk/not take any risks

riss, *riß /rɪs/ *1. u. 3. Pers. Sg. Prät. v.* **reißen**

Riss, *Riß /rɪs/ *der;* **Risses, Risse** (a) (in Stoff, Papier usw.) tear; (b) (Spalt, Sprung) crack; (fig.: Kluft) rift; split

rissig *Adj.* cracked; chapped ⟨lips⟩

Riten ⇒ **Ritus**

ritsch *Interj.* rip; zip; ~, **ratsch** rip, rip

ritt *1. u. 3. Pers. Sg. Prät. v.* **reiten**

Ritt *der;* ~[e]s, ~e ride

Ritter *der;* ~s, ~ knight; **jmdn. zum ~ schlagen** (hist.) knight sb.; dub sb. [a] knight

ritterlich *Adj.* chivalrous

Ritter-: **~schlag** *der* (hist.) knightly accolade; **~sporn** *der* (Bot.) larkspur; (Gartenrittersporn) delphinium

rittlings /'rɪtlɪŋs/ *Adv.* astride

Ritual /ri'tuaːl/ *das;* ~s, ~e *od.* **Ritualien** /-li̯ən/ (Rel., fig.) ritual

rituell /ri'tuɛl/ (Rel., fig.) 1 *Adj.* ritual. 2 *adv.* ritually

Ritus /'riːtʊs/ *der;* ~, **Riten** (Rel., fig.) rite

Ritz /rɪts/ *der;* ~es, ~e, **Ritze** *die;* ~, ~n crack; [narrow] gap

Ritzel /'rɪtsl̩/ *das;* ~s, ~ (Technik) pinion

ritzen *tr. V.* (a) scratch; (tiefer) cut; (b) (einritzen) carve ⟨name etc.⟩ (**in** + Akk. in)

Rivale /ri'vaːlə/ *der;* ~n, ~n, **Rivalin** *die;* ~, ~nen rival

rivalisieren *itr. V.* mit jmdm. um etw. ~: compete with sb. for sth.; **~de Gruppen** rival groups

Rivalität /rivali'tɛːt/ *die;* ~, ~en rivalry *no indef. art.*

Roastbeef /'roːstbiːf/ *das;* ~s, ~s roast [sirloin (Brit.) of] beef

Robbe /'rɔbə/ *die;* ~, ~n seal

robben *itr. V.; mit sein* crawl

Robe /'roːbə/ *die;* ~, ~n robe; (schwarz) gown

Roboter /'rɔbɔtɐ/ *der;* ~s, ~: robot

robust /ro'bʊst/ *Adj.* robust

Robustheit *die;* ~: robustness; (Gesundheit) robust constitution

roch /rɔx/ *1. u. 3. Pers. Sg. Prät. v.* **riechen**

Rochade /rɔ'xaːdə/ *die;* ~, ~n (Schach) castling; **kleine/große ~:** short/long castling; **eine ~ ausführen** castle

röcheln /'rœçl̩n/ *itr. V.* breathe stertorously; ⟨dying person⟩ give the death-rattle

Rochen /'rɔxn̩/ *der;* ~s, ~ (Zool.) ray

rochieren /rɔ'xiːrən/ *itr. V.* (a) (Schach) castle; (b) *mit Richtungsangabe mit sein* (Sport) change over; switch positions

Rock¹ /rɔk/ *der;* ~[e]s, **Röcke** /'rœkə/ (a) skirt; (b) (landsch.: Jacke) jacket

Rock² *der;* ~[s] rock [music]

Rocker *der;* ~s, ~: rocker

rockig *Adj.* rock-like ⟨jazz etc.⟩

Rock·musik *die* rock music

Rodel /'roːdl̩/ *der;* ~s, ~ (südd.) ⇒ **Rodelschlitten**

Rodel·bahn *die* toboggan-run; (Sport) luge-run

rodeln /'roːdl̩n/ *itr. V.; mit sein* sledge; toboggan; (Sport) luge

Rodeln *das;* ~s sledging *no art.;* tobogganing *no art.;* (Sport) luge

Rodel·schlitten *der* sledge; toboggan; (Sport) luge

roden /'roːdn̩/ 1 *tr. V.* (a) clear ⟨wood, land⟩; (ausgraben) grub up ⟨tree⟩; (b) (landsch.) lift ⟨potatoes etc.⟩. 2 *itr. V.* clear the land

Rogen /'roːgn̩/ *der;* ~s, ~: roe

Roggen /'rɔgn̩/ *der;* ~s rye

Roggen-: **~brot** *das* rye bread; **ein ~brot** a loaf of rye bread; **~brötchen** *das* rye-bread roll

roh /roː/ 1 *Adj.* (a) raw ⟨food⟩; **jmdn./etw. wie ein ~es Ei behandeln** handle sb./sth. with kid gloves; (b) (nicht bearbeitet) rough, unfinished ⟨wood⟩; rough, uncut ⟨diamond⟩; rough-hewn, undressed ⟨stone⟩; crude ⟨ore, metal⟩; untreated ⟨skin⟩; raw ⟨silk, sugar⟩; (c) (brutal) brutish ⟨person, treatment, etc.⟩; (grausam) callous ⟨person, treatment⟩; (grob) coarse, uncouth ⟨manners, words, joke⟩; brute *attrib.* ⟨force⟩. 2 *adv.* (brutal) brutishly; (grausam) callously; (grob) coarsely; in an uncouth manner

Roh·bau *der* shell [of a/the building]

*Roheit, Rohheit /'roːhait/ *die;* ~, ~en (a) o. Pl. (Brutalität) brutishness; (Grausamkeit) callousness; (Grobheit) coarseness; uncouthness; (b) (Handlung) brutish/callous deed

Roh·kost *die* raw fruit and vegetables *pl.*

Rohling /'roːlɪŋ/ *der;* ~s, ~e (abwertend: Mensch) brute

Roh-: **~material** *das* raw material; **~öl** *das* crude oil

Rohr /roːɐ̯/ *das;* ~[e]s, ~e (a) (Leitungs~) pipe; (als Bauteil) tube; (Geschütz~) barrel; (b) o. Pl. (Röhricht) reeds *pl.;* (c) o. Pl. (Schilf usw. als Werkstoff) reed

Rohr·bruch *der* burst pipe

Röhrchen /'røːɐ̯çən/ *das;* ~s, ~: small pipe; (Behälter) small tube; **ins ~ blasen** (ugs.) take the breathalyser test

Röhre /'røːrə/ *die;* ~, ~n (a) (auch Neon~, Bild~, Tabletten~) tube; (Elektronen~) valve (Brit.); tube (Amer.); **vor der ~ sitzen** (ugs.) sit in front of the box (coll.); (b) (Leitungs~) pipe; (c) (eines Ofens) oven; **in die ~ gucken** (fig. ugs.) be left out [in the cold]

röhren *itr. V.* ⟨stag etc.⟩ bell; (fig.) roar

röhren·förmig *Adj.* tubular

Röhren·hose *die* drainpipe trousers

Rohr-: **~flöte** *die* reed-pipe; **~post** *die* pneumatic dispatch; **etw. mit ~post befördern** convey sth. by pneumatic tube; **~spatz** *der in* **schimpfen wie ein ~spatz** (ugs.) really create (coll.); **~stock** *der* cane [walking stick]; **~zucker** *der* cane sugar

Roh·stoff *der* raw material

Rokoko /'rɔkoko/ *das;* ~[s] rococo; (Zeit) rococo period

*Rolladen ⇒ **Rollladen**

Roll·bahn *die* (Flugw.) taxiway

Rolle /'rɔlə/ *die;* ~, ~n (a) (Spule) reel; spool; (b) (zylindrischer [Hohl]körper; Zusammengerolltes) roll; (Schrift~) scroll; **eine ~ Bindfaden/Markstücke/Kekse** a reel of string/roll of one-mark pieces/[round] packet of biscuits; (c) (Walze) roller; (Teig~) rolling pin; (d) (Rad) [small] wheel; (an Möbeln usw.) castor; (für Gardine, Schiebetür usw.) runner; (e) (Turnen, Kunstflug) roll; (f) (Theater, Film usw., fig.) role; part; (Soziol.) role; **[bei jmdm./einer Sache] eine entscheidende ~ spielen** be of crucial importance [to sb./for sth.]; **es spielt keine ~:** it is of no importance; (es macht nichts aus) it doesn't matter; **aus der ~ fallen** forget oneself

---

*alte Schreibung (vgl. Hinweise auf S. xvi–xvii)

rollen 1 *tr. V.* roll; **das R** ~: roll one's r's; **sich** (*Dat.*) **eine Zigarette** ~: roll oneself a cigarette. **2** *itr. V.* **(a)** *mit sein* ‹*ball, wheel, etc.*› roll; ‹*vehicle*› move; ‹*aircraft*› taxi; **etw. ins Rollen bringen** set sth. in motion; get sth. going (lit. or fig.); (unbeabsichtigt) set sth. moving; **(b)** *mit Richtungsangabe mit sein* ‹*thunder, guns, echo*› rumble. **3** *refl. V.* **(a)** roll; **(b)** ‹*paper, carpet*› curl [up]

Rollen·spiel *das* (Sozialpsych.) role-playing *no pl., no art.;* role-play *no pl., no art.*

Roller *der;* ~s, ~ scooter

Rollerblade Ⓦ /'rɔʊləbleɪd/ *der;* ~s, ~s Rollerblade (P)

Rollerskate /'rɔʊləskeɪt/ *der;* ~s, ~s roller skate

Roll-: ~**feld** *das* [operational] airfield; landing-field; ~**kommando** *das* party of bully-boys; ~**kragen** *der* polo neck; ~**laden** *der* [roller] shutter; ~**mops** *der* rollmops

Rollo /'rɔlo/ *das;* ~s, ~s [roller] blind

Roll·schuh *der* roller skate; ~**laufen** roller skate

Rollschuh·bahn *die* roller skating rink

Roll-: ~**splitt** *der* loose chippings *pl.;* ~**stuhl** *der* wheelchair; ~**stuhl·fahrer** *der* person in a wheelchair; ~**treppe** *die* escalator

Rom /roːm/ ▶ 490 (das); ~s Rome; **Zustände wie im alten** ~ (fig.) everything in chaos

Roman /ro'maːn/ *der;* ~s, ~e novel

Roman·figur *die* character from *or* in a novel

Romanik /ro'maːnɪk/ *die;* ~: Romanesque; (Zeit) Romanesque period

romanisch *Adj.* **(a)** Romance ‹*language, literature*›; Latin ‹*people, country, charm*›; **(b)** (der Romanik) Romanesque

Romanistik /roma'nɪstɪk/ *die;* ~: Romance studies *pl., no art.;* (Sprache und Literatur) Romance languages and literature *no art.*

Romantik /ro'mantɪk/ *die;* ~ **(a)** romanticism; romantic nature; **(b)** (Literaturw., Musik usw.) Romanticism *no art.;* (Epoche) Romantic period

romantisch 1 *Adj.* **(a)** romantic; **(b)** (Literaturw., Musik usw.) Romantic. **2** *adv.* romantically

Romanze /ro'mantsə/ *die;* ~, ~n (auch fig.) romance

Römer /'røːmɐ/ *der;* ~s, ~, **Römerin** *die;* ~, ~nen ▶ 388 |, ▶ 490 | Roman

römisch *Adj.* ▶ 388 |, ▶ 490 | Roman

römisch-katholisch 1 *Adj.* Roman Catholic. **2** *adv.* ~ **getauft** baptized into the Roman Catholic church

röm.-kath. *Abk.* **römisch-katholisch** RC

Rommé /'rɔme/ *das;* ~s, ~s (Kartenspiele) rummy *no art.*

Rondo /'rɔndo/ *das;* ~s, ~s (Musik) rondo

röntgen /'rœntgn̩/ *tr. V.* X-ray; **sich** (*Akk.*)/**sich** (*Dat.*) **den Magen** ~ **lassen** have an X-ray/have one's stomach X-rayed

Röntgen- X-ray ‹*picture, screen, apparatus, etc.*›

Röntgen·strahlen *Pl.* X-rays

rosa /'roːza/ *indekl. Adj., adv.* pink

Rosa *das;* ~s, ~ *od.* ~s pink

rosa-: ~**farben**, ~**farbig** *Adj.* pink; ~**rot** *Adj.* [deep] pink

Röschen /'røːsçən/ *das;* ~s, ~ [little] rose

Rose /'roːzə/ *die;* ~, ~n rose

rosé /ro'ze:/ *indekl. Adj., adv.* pale pink

Rosé *der;* ~s, ~s rosé [wine]

rosen-, Rosen-: ~**beet** *das* rose bed; ~**duft** *der* scent of roses; ~**garten** *der* rose-garden; ~**kohl** *der; o. Pl.* [Brussels] sprouts *pl.;* ~**kranz** *der* (kath. Kirche) rosary; **einen** ~**kranz beten** say a rosary; ~**montag** *der* the day before Shrove Tuesday; ~**montags·zug** *der* carnival procession on the day before Shrove Tuesday; ~**stock** *der* rose-tree; standard rose

Rosette /ro'zɛtə/ *die;* ~, ~n **(a)** (Archit.) rose-window; **(b)** (Verzierung, Bot.) rosette

rosig 1 *Adj.* **(a)** rosy ‹*face, complexion, etc.*›; pink ‹*piglet etc.*›; **(b)** (fig.) rosy; optimistic ‹*mood*›. **2** *adv.* **ihm geht es nicht gerade** ~: things aren't too good with him

Rosine /ro'ziːnə/ *die;* ~, ~n raisin; (Korinthe) currant; **[große]** ~**n im Kopf haben** (fig. ugs.) have big ideas

Rosmarin /'roːsmariːn/ *der;* ~s rosemary

Ross, *Roß /rɔs/ *das;* **Rosses, Rosse** *od.* **Rösser** /'rœsɐ/ (geh., südd., österr., schweiz.) horse; steed (poet./joc.); **hoch zu** ~: on horseback; **auf dem hohen** ~ **sitzen** be on one's high horse; **von seinem** *od.* **vom hohen** ~ **herunterkommen** *od.* **-steigen** get down off one's high horse

Roß-, *Ross-: ~**haar** *das* horsehair; ~**kastanie** *die* horse chestnut; ~**kur** *die* **(a)** (ugs.) drastic cure *or* remedy; **(b)** (Bett~) base; frame

Rost¹ /rɔst/ *der;* ~[e]s, ~e **(a)** (Gitter) grating; grid; (eines Ofens, einer Feuerstelle) grate; (Brat~) grill; **(b)** (Bett~) base; frame

Rost² *der;* -[e]s rust

rost-, Rost-: ~**beständig** *Adj.* rust-resistant; (absolut) rustproof; ~**braten** *der* grilled steak; (österr.: Entrecote) entrecôte; rib steak; ~**braun** *Adj.* reddish-brown; russet; auburn ‹*hair*›

rosten *itr. V.; auch mit sein* rust; (auch fig.) get rusty

rösten /'rœstn̩, 'røːstn̩/ *tr. V.* **(a)** roast; toast ‹*bread*›; **sich [in der Sonne]** ~ **lassen** roast oneself in the sun; **(b)** (bes. südd., österr., schweiz.) ⇒ **braten 1**

rost-, Rost-: ~**farben**, ~**farbig** *Adj.* rust-coloured; russet; ~**fleck** *der* rust stain; ~**frei** *Adj.* **(a)** (nicht rostend) stainless ‹*steel*›; **(b)** (ohne Rost) rust-free

Rösti /'rœsti/ *die;* ~ (schweiz. Kochk.) thinly sliced fried potatoes *pl.*

rostig *Adj.* rusty

rost·rot *Adj.* rust-coloured; russet

Rost·stelle *die* patch of rust; (kleiner) rust spot

rot /roːt/ **1** *Adj.* red; **ein Roter** (ugs.) (Wein) a red [wine]; (Rothaariger) a redhead; (Sozialist) a red (coll.); a leftie (coll.); ~ **werden** turn red; ‹*person*› go red; blush; ‹*traffic light*› change to red. **2** *adv.* **etw.** ~ **anstreichen** mark sth. in red; **[im Gesicht]** ~ **anlaufen** go red in the face; blush; ~ **glühend** red-hot

Rot *das;* ~s, ~ *od.* ~s red; (Schminke) rouge; **die Ampel zeigt** ~: the traffic lights are red; **bei** ~ **über die Kreuzung fahren** cross the junction on the red

Rotation /rota'tsioːn/ *die;* ~, ~en rotation

rot-, Rot-: ~**backig**, ~**bäckig** *Adj.* rosy-cheeked ‹*child, girl*›; ruddy-cheeked ‹*old man, farmer, etc.*›; ~**barsch** *der* rose-fish; ~**blond** *Adj.* sandy ‹*hair*›; sandy-haired ‹*person*›; ~**braun** *Adj.* reddish-brown; russet; ~**buche** *die* [European] beech

Röte /'røːtə/ *die;* ~: red[ness]

Röteln /'røːtl̩n/ *Pl.* **[die]** ~: ▶ 329 | German measles *sing.*

röten *refl. V.* go *or* turn red

rot-, Rot-: ~**fuchs** *der* **(a)** (Tier, Pelz) red fox; **(b)** (Pferd) chestnut; (heller) sorrel;*~**glühend** ⇒ **rot 2**; ~**haarig** *Adj.* red-haired; ~**haut** *die* (ugs. scherzh.) redskin; ~**hirsch** *der* red deer

rotieren /ro'tiːrən/ *itr. V.* **(a)** rotate; **(b)** (ugs.: hektisch sein) flap (coll.); get into a flap (coll.)

Rot-: ~**käppchen** (*das*) Little Red Riding Hood; ~**kehlchen** *das;* ~s, ~: robin [redbreast]; ~**kohl** *der*, (bes. südd., österr.) ~**kraut** *das* red cabbage

rötlich /'røːtlɪç/ *Adj.* reddish

rot-, Rot-: ~**licht** *das; o. Pl.* red light; **bei** ~**licht** under a red light; ~**schwanz** *der*, ~**schwänzchen** *das* redstart; ~|**sehen** *unr. itr. V.* (ugs.) see red; ~**stift** *der* red pencil; **dem** ~**stift zum Opfer fallen** (aufgegeben werden) be scrapped; (gestrichen werden) be deleted

Rotte /'rɔtə/ *die;* ~, ~n gang; mob (sl.)

Rötung *die;* ~, ~en reddening

Rot-: ~**wein** *der* red wine; ~**wild** *das* (Jägerspr.) red deer

Rotz /rɔts/ *der;* ~es (salopp) snot (sl.); **frech wie** ~ (salopp) cheeky as anything; ~ **und Wasser heulen** (salopp) cry one's eyes out

rọtzen itr. V. (derb) (**a**) blow one's nose loudly; (**b**) (Schleim in den Mund ziehen) sniff back one's snot (sl.); (**c**) (ausspucken) gob (coarse)

rọtz·frẹch (salopp) **1** Adj. insolent; snotty (coll.). **2** adv. insolently; snottily (coll.)

rọtzig Adj. (derb) snotty (coll.)

Rọtz·nase die (**a**) (derb) snotty nose (sl.); (**b**) (salopp abwertend: Bengel) snotty little brat (sl.)

Rouge /ruːʒ/ das; ~s, ~s rouge

Roulade /ruːlaːdə/ die; ~, ~n (Kochk.) [beef/veal/pork] olive

Route /ˈruːtə/ die; ~, ~n route

Routine /ruˈtiːnə/ die; ~ (**a**) (Erfahrung) experience; (Übung) practice; (Fertigkeit) proficiency; expertise; (**b**) (gewohnheitsmäßiger Ablauf) routine no def. art.

routịne·mäßig **1** Adj. routine; **2** adv. as a matter of routine

routiniert /rutiˈniːɐt/ **1** Adj. (gewandt) expert; skilled; (erfahren) experienced. **2** adv. expertly; skilfully

Rowdy /ˈraʊdi/ der; ~s, ~s (abwertend) hooligan

rubbeln /ˈrʊbl̩n/ tr., itr. V. (bes. nordd.) rub [vigorously]

Rübe /ˈryːbə/ die; ~, ~n (**a**) turnip; **rote** ~: beetroot; **gelbe** ~ (südd.) carrot; (**b**) (salopp: Kopf) nut (coll.); **eins auf die** ~ **kriegen** get a bonk or bash on the nut (coll.)

Rubel /ˈruːbl̩/ der; ~s, ~: rouble; **der** ~ **rollt** (fig. ugs.) the money keeps rolling in

Rüben·zucker der beet sugar

rüber /ˈryːbɐ/ Adv. (ugs.) over

rüber-: ~|**gehen** unr. itr. V.; mit sein go over; (über die Straße) cross over; ~|**kommen** unr. itr. V.; mit sein (**a**) come over; (**b**) (~können) manage to get over/across; ~|**schicken** tr. V. send over; ~|**wollen** unr. itr. V. want to get over or across

Rubin /ruˈbiːn/ der; ~s, ~e ruby

Rubrik /ruˈbriːk/ die; ~, ~en (Spalte) column; (Zeitungs~) column; section; (fig.: Kategorie) category; **unter der** ~ ...: under the heading [of] ...

Ruch /ruːx/ der; ~[e]s [bad] reputation; **im** ~ **der Korruption stehen** have the reputation of being corrupt

rụch·bar Adj. **in** ~ **werden** (geh.) become known

rụch·los (geh.) **1** Adj. dastardly; heinous ⟨crime⟩. **2** adv. in a dastardly fashion

Ruck /rʊk/ der; ~[e]s, ~e jerk; **sich** (Dat.) **einen** ~ **geben** (fig.) pull oneself together

rụck·artig **1** Adj. jerky. **2** adv. with a jerk

rück-, Rück-: ~**bezüglich** (Sprachw.) **1** Adj. reflexive; **2** adv. reflexively; ~**blende** die flashback; ~**blick** der look back (**auf** + Akk. at); retrospective view (**auf** + Akk. of); **im** ~**blick** in retrospect; ~**blickend** **1** Adj. retrospective; **2** adv. retrospectively; in retrospect

rücken /ˈrʏkn̩/ **1** tr. V. move; **den Tisch an die Wand** ~: move or push the table against the wall. **2** itr. V.; mit sein move; **mit seinem Stuhl näher an den Tisch** ~: move one's chair closer to the table; **jmdm. auf den Pelz od. die Pelle** ~ (ugs.) squeeze right up to sb; **kannst du ein bisschen** ~? could you move up/over a bit?; **hört auf, mit den Stühlen zu** ~: stop shifting your chairs

Rücken /ˈrʏkn̩/ der; ~s, ~: (**a**) ▶326 back; **ein Stück vom** ~ (Rindfleisch) a piece of chine; (Hammel, Reh) a piece of saddle; **auf dem** ~ **liegen** lie on one's back; **es lief mir [heiß und kalt] über den** ~: [hot and cold] shivers ran down my spine; **den Wind im** ~ **haben** have the wind behind one; **verlängerter** ~ (scherzh.) backside; posterior (joc.); **jmdm./einer Sache den** ~ **kehren** (fig.) turn one's back on sb./sth.; **jmdm. den** ~ **stärken** (fig.) give sb. moral support; **jmdm. den** ~ **freihalten** (fig.) ensure sb. is not troubled with other problems; **hinter jmds.** ~ (Dat.) (fig.) behind sb.'s back; **jmdm. in den** ~ **fallen** (fig.) stab sb. in the back; **mit dem** ~ **an der od. zur Wand** (fig.) with one's back to the wall; (**b**) (Rückseite) back; (Buch~) spine; (des Berges) ridge

rücken-, Rücken-: ~**deckung** die (**a**) (bes. Milit.) rear cover; (**b**) (fig.) backing; **jmdm.** ~**deckung geben** give sb. one's backing; ~**flosse** die dorsal fin; ~**frei** Adj. backless ⟨dress⟩; ~**lehne** die [chair/seat] back; ~**mark** das ▶326 (Anat.) spinal marrow or cord; ~**schmerzen** Pl. backache sing.; ~**schwimmen** das backstroke; ~**stärkung** die [moral] support; ~**wind** der tail or following wind; ~**wind haben** have a tail or following wind

rück-, Rück-: ~|**erstatten** tr. V.; nur im Inf. u. 2. Part. repay; ~**erstattung** die repayment; reimbursement; ~**fahrkarte** die, ~**fahrschein** der return [ticket]; ~**fahr·scheinwerfer** der (Kfz-W.) reversing light; ~**fahrt** die return journey; **auf der** ~**fahrt** on the return journey or way back; ~**fall** der (Med., auch fig.) relapse; ~**fällig** (**a**) (Med., auch fig.) relapsed ⟨patient, alcoholic, etc.⟩; ~**fällig werden** have a relapse; ⟨alcoholic etc.⟩ go back to one's old ways; (**b**) (Rechtsspr.); ~**fällig werden** commit a second offence; ~**flug** der return flight; ~**frage** die query; ~|**fragen** itr. V.; nur im Inf. u. 2. Part. query it; ~**führung** die return; (in die Heimat) repatriation; ~**gabe** die (**a**) return; (**b**) (Ballspiele) back pass; ~**gang** der drop, fall (Gen. in); ~**gängig** adj. ~**gängig machen** cancel ⟨agreement, decision, etc.⟩; break off ⟨engagement⟩; **einen Kauf** ~**gängig machen** return what one has bought; ~**grat** das ▶326 spine; (bes. fig.) backbone; ~**grat haben/kein** ~**grat haben** have guts (coll.) /be spineless; **jmdm. das** ~**grat brechen** (fig.) break sb.'s resistance; ~**halt** der support; backing; ~**halt·los** **1** Adj. unreserved, unqualified ⟨support⟩; complete, absolute ⟨frankness⟩; **2** adv. unreservedly; without reservation; ⟨trust⟩ completely, absolutely; ⟨confess⟩ with complete frankness; ~**hand** die (Sport) backhand; **mit [der]** ~**hand** on one's backhand

Rückkehr /ˈrʏkkeːɐ/ die; ~: return

rück-, Rück-: ~**lage** die savings pl.; **eine kleine** ~**lage haben** have a small sum saved up; have a small nest egg; ~**lauf** der (**a**) (~fluss) return flow; (**b**) (beim Tonbandgerät) rewind; ~**läufig** Adj. decreasing ⟨number⟩; declining ⟨economic growth etc.⟩; falling ⟨rate, production, etc.⟩; ~**licht** das rear- or tail light

rücklings Adv. on one's back

Rück-: ~**porto** das return postage; ~**reise** die return journey; ~**ruf** der (**a**) (Fernspr.) return call; (**b**) (das Zurückbeordern) recall

Rụck·sack der rucksack; (Touren~) back-pack

rück-, Rück-: ~**schau** die review (**auf** + Akk. of); ~**schau halten** look back; ~**schlag** der (**a**) setback; (**b**) (Tennis, Tischtennis usw.) return; ~**schluss**, *~**schluß** der conclusion (**auf** + Akk. about); **aus etw.** ~**schlüsse auf etw.** (Akk.) **ziehen** draw conclusions from sth. about sth.; ~**schritt** der backward step; ~**seite** die back; (eines Gebäudes usw.) back; rear; (einer Münze usw.) reverse; (des Mondes) far side; **siehe** ~**seite** see over[leaf]; ~**sicht** die consideration; **mit** ~**sicht auf etw.** (Akk.) taking sth. into consideration; in view of sth.; ~**sicht auf jmdn. nehmen** show consideration for or towards sb.; (Verständnis haben) make allowances for sb.; **ohne** ~**sicht auf etw.** (Akk.) with no regard for or regardless of sth.; **ohne** ~**sicht auf Verluste** (ugs.) regardless; ~**sicht·nahme** die; ~: consideration

rücksichts-, Rücksichts-: ~**los** **1** Adj. (**a**) inconsiderate; thoughtless; **ein** ~**loser Autofahrer** an inconsiderate driver; (verantwortungslos) a reckless driver; (**b**) (schonungslos) ruthless; **2** adv. (**a**) inconsiderately; thoughtlessly; (verantwortungslos) recklessly; (**b**) (schonungslos) ruthlessly; ~**losigkeit** die; ~, ~en (**a**) lack of consideration; thoughtlessness; (Verantwortungslosigkeit) recklessness; **so eine** ~**losigkeit!** how inconsiderate or thoughtless; (**b**) (Schonungslosigkeit) ruthlessness; ~**voll** **1** Adj. considerate; thoughtful; **2** adv. considerately; thoughtfully

rück-, Rück-: ~**sitz** der back seat; ~**spiegel** der rear-view mirror; ~**spiel** das (Sport) second or return leg; ~**sprache** die consultation; **[mit jmdm.]** ~**sprache nehmen** (Papierdt.) consult [sb.]; ~**stand** der (**a**) (Übriggebliebenes, Rest) residue; (**b**) (offener Rechnungsbetrag) ~**stände/ein** ~**stand** arrears pl.; ~**stände eintreiben**

---

*alte Schreibung (vgl. Hinweise auf S. xvi–xvii)

collect outstanding debts; **(c)** (Zurückbleiben hinter dem gesetzten Ziel, Soll usw.) backlog; (bes. Sport: hinter dem Gegner) deficit; [**mit etw.**] **im ~stand sein/in ~stand** (*Akk.*) **geraten** be/get behind [with sth.]; **die Mannschaft lag mit 0:3 im ~stand** (Sport) the team was trailing by three to nil; **~ständig** *Adj.* **(a)** backward; **~ständig sein** be behind the times; **(b)** (schon länger fällig) outstanding ⟨*payment, amount*⟩; ⟨*wages*⟩ still owing; **~stau** *der* (von Wasser) backing up; backwater; (von Fahrzeugen) tailback; **~stellung** *die* postponement (**um** by); **eine ~stellung vom Wehrdienst** a temporary exemption from military service; **~strahler** *der* reflector; **~taste** *die* backspacer; backspace key; **~tritt** *der* **(a)** resignation (**von** from); (von einer Kandidatur, von einem Vertrag usw.) withdrawal (**von** from); **(b)** (ugs.) ⇒ **~trittbremse; ~tritt·bremse** *die* back-pedal brake; **~vergütung** *die* refund; **~|versichern** *refl. V.; nur im Inf. u. 2. Part.* cover oneself [two ways]; hedge one's bets; **~versicherung** *die* (fig.) safeguard; protection

rückwärtig /-vɛrtɪç/ *Adj.* back; rear; **die ~e Seite** the back or rear

rückwärts /-vɛrts/ *Adv.* backwards; **ein Blick [nach] ~:** a look back; a backward look; **ein Salto/eine Rolle ~:** a back somersault/backward roll; **~ einparken** reverse into a parking space

Rückwärts·gang *der* reverse [gear]; **den ~ einlegen** (auch fig.) go into reverse; **im ~:** in reverse

Rückweg *der* way back; **jmdm. den ~ abschneiden** cut off sb.'s line of retreat

ruck·weise 1 *Adv.* in [a series of] jerks. 2 *adj.* jerky

rück-, Rück-: ~wirkend 1 *Adj.* retrospective; backdated ⟨*pay increase*⟩; 2 retrospectively; **~wirkung** *die* **(a)** (zeitlich) retrospective force; **mit ~wirkung vom …:** [retrospectively] as from …; **(b)** (Auswirkung) repercussion (**auf** + *Akk.* on); **~zahlung** *die* repayment; **~zieher** *der;* **~s, ~ (a)** (Fußball) overhead kick; **(b)** (fig. ugs.) backing out *no art.;* **einen ~zieher machen** back out; **~zug** *der* retreat; **auf dem ~zug sein** be retreating

rüde /'ry:də/ 1 *Adj.* uncouth; coarse ⟨*language*⟩. 2 *adv.* in an uncouth manner

Rüde *der;* **~n, ~n** [male] dog

Rudel /'ru:dl/ *das;* **~s, ~** (von Hirschen, Gämsen) herd; (von Wölfen, Hunden) pack

Ruder /'ru:dɐ/ *das;* **~s, ~ (a)** (Riemen) oar; **(b)** (Steuer~) rudder; (Steuerrad) helm; **am ~ sein** (fig.) be at the helm; **das ~ herumwerfen** (fig.) change course or tack; **ans ~ kommen** (fig.) ⟨*party, leader*⟩ come to power; **aus dem ~ laufen** (fig.) go off course

Ruder·boot *das* rowboat; rowing boat (Brit.)

Ruderer *der;* **~s, ~:** oarsman; rower

Ruderin *die;* **~, ~nen** oarswoman; rower

rudern 1 *itr. V.; mit sein* row; **mit den Armen ~** (fig.) swing one's arms [about]. 2 *tr. V.* row

Ruder·regatta *die* rowing regatta

rudimentär /rudimɛn'tɛ:ɐ/ (Biol., geh.) 1 *Adj.* rudimentary. 2 *adv.* in a rudimentary form

Ruf /ru:f/ *der;* **~[e]s, ~e (a)** call; (Schrei) shout; cry; (Tierlaut) call; **(b)** *o. Pl.* (fig.: Aufforderung, Forderung) call (**nach** for); **(c)** (Leumund) reputation; **ein Mann von gutem/schlechtem ~:** a man with a good/bad reputation; **jmdn./etw. in schlechten ~ bringen** give sb./sth. a bad name; **er/es ist besser als sein ~:** he/it is not as bad as he/it is made out to be

rufen 1 *unr. itr. V.* call (**nach** for); (schreien) shout (**nach** for); ⟨*animal*⟩ call; **die Pflicht/die Arbeit ruft** (fig.) duty calls 2 *unr. tr. V.* **(a)** call; (schreien) shout; **(b)** (herbei-) call; **jmdn. zu Hilfe ~:** call to sb. to help; **jmdn./sich** (*Dat.*) **etw. ins Gedächtnis** *od.* **in Erinnerung ~:** remind sb. of sth./recall sth.; [**jmdm.**] **wie gerufen kommen** (ugs.) come at just the right moment; **(c)** (telefonisch) call; **~ Sie 88 86 66** ring 888 666; **(d)** (nennen) **jmdn. etw. ~:** call sb. sth.

Rüffel /'ryfl/ *der;* **~s, ~** (ugs.) ticking-off (coll.)

Ruf-: ~mord *der* character assassination **~name** *der* first name (*by which one is generally known*); **~nummer** *die* telephone number **~zeichen** *das* **(a)**

o. Pl. (Fernspr.) ringing tone; **(b)** (österr.: Ausrufezeichen) exclamation mark

Rugby /'rakbi/ *das;* **~[s]** rugby [football]

Rüge /'ry:gə/ *die;* **~, ~n** reprimand; **eine ~ erhalten** be reprimanded

rügen *tr. V.* reprimand ⟨*person*⟩ (**wegen** for); censure ⟨*carelessness etc.*⟩

Ruhe /'ru:ə/ *die;* **~ (a)** (Stille) silence; **~ [bitte]!** quiet or silence [please]!; **jmdn. um ~ bitten** ask sb. to be quiet; **~ geben** be quiet; **(b)** (Ungestörtheit) peace; **in ~ [und Frieden]** in peace [and quiet]; **die [öffentliche] ~ wiederherstellen** restore [law and] order; **jmdn. in ~ lassen** leave sb. in peace; **jmdn. mit etw. in ~ lassen** stop bothering sb. with sth.; **keine ~ geben** not stop pestering; (nicht nachgeben) not give up; (weiter protestieren) go on protesting; **(c)** (Unbewegtheit) rest; **zur ~ kommen** come to rest; **(d)** (Erholung, das Sichausruhen) rest *no def. art.;* **angenehme ~** (geh.) sleep well; **sich zur ~ begeben** (geh.) retire [to bed]; **sich zur ~ setzen** (in den Ruhestand treten) take one's retirement; retire (**in** + *Dat.* to); **(e)** (Gelassenheit) calm[ness]; composure; **er ist die ~ selbst** (ugs.) he is calmness itself; **[die] ~ bewahren/die ~ verlieren** keep calm/lose one's composure; keep/lose one's cool (coll.); **in [aller] ~:** [really] calmly; **die ~ weghaben** (ugs.) be completely unflappable (coll.); **immer mit der ~!** (nur keine Panik) don't panic!; (nichts überstürzen) no need to rush

ruhe-, Ruhe-: ~bedürfnis *das; o. Pl.* need of rest; **~bedürftig** *Adj.* in need of rest *postpos.;* **~los** 1 *Adj.* restless; 2 *adv.* restlessly; **~losigkeit** *die;* **~:** restlessness

ruhen *itr. V.* **(a)** (aus~) rest; **(b)** (geh.: schlafen) sleep; **(c)** **im Grabe ~:** lie in one's grave; „**Ruhe sanft** *od.* **in Frieden!**" 'Rest in Peace'; „**Hier ruht …**" 'Here lies …'; **(d)** (stillstehen) ⟨*work, business*⟩ have stopped; ⟨*production, firm*⟩ be at a standstill; ⟨*employment, insurance*⟩ be suspended; **der Verkehr ruht fast völlig** there is hardly any traffic; **nicht ~, bis …:** not rest until …; **(e)** (liegen) rest; **in sich** (*Dat.*) [**selbst**] **~:** be a well-balanced [and harmonious] person

Ruhe-: ~pause *die* break; **eine ~pause einlegen** take a break; **~stand** *der; o. Pl.* retirement; **in den ~stand gehen/versetzt werden** go into retirement/be retired; **Versetzung in den ~stand** retirement; **~störung** *die* disturbance; (Rechtsw.) disturbance of the peace; **~tag** *der* closing day; „**Dienstag ~tag**" 'closed on Tuesdays'

ruhig /'ru:ɪç/ 1 *Adj.* **(a)** (still, leise) quiet; **seid doch mal ~!** do be quiet!; **(b)** (friedlich, ungestört) peaceful ⟨*times, life, scene, valley, spot, etc.*⟩; quiet ⟨*talk, reflection, life, spot*⟩; **er hat keine ~e Minute** he doesn't have a moment's peace; **(c)** (unbewegt) calm ⟨*sea, weather*⟩; still ⟨*air*⟩; (fig.) peaceful ⟨*melody*⟩; quiet ⟨*pattern*⟩; (gleichmäßig) steady ⟨*breathing, hand, flame, steps*⟩; smooth ⟨*flight, crossing*⟩; **(d)** (gelassen) calm ⟨*voice etc.*⟩; quiet, calm ⟨*person*⟩; **~ bleiben** keep calm; keep one's cool (coll.). 2 *adv.* **(a)** (still, leise) quietly; **wir wohnen sehr ~:** we live in a very quiet area; **sich ~ verhalten** keep quiet; **(b)** (friedlich, ohne Störungen) ⟨*sleep*⟩ peacefully; ⟨*go off*⟩ smoothly, peacefully; (ohne Zwischenfälle) uneventfully; ⟨*work, think*⟩ in peace; **(c)** (unbewegt) ⟨*sit, lie, stand*⟩ still; (gleichmäßig) ⟨*burn, breathe*⟩ steadily; ⟨*run, fly*⟩ smoothly; **(d)** (gelassen) ⟨*speak, watch, sit*⟩ calmly. 3 *Adv.* by all means; **du kannst ~ mitkommen** by all means come along; you're welcome to come along; **lach mich ~ aus** all right or go ahead, laugh at me[, I don't care]; **soll er ~ meckern** (ugs.) let him moan[, I don't care]

Ruhm /ru:m/ *der;* **~[e]s** fame; **sich mit ~ bedecken** (geh.) cover oneself with glory

rühmen /'ry:mən/ 1 *tr. V.* praise. 2 *refl. V.* **sich einer Sache** (*Gen.*) **~:** boast about sth.

Ruhmes·blatt *das:* **das war kein ~ für ihn** it did not reflect any credit on him; it did him no credit

rühmlich *Adj.* laudable; praiseworthy; notable ⟨*exception*⟩

ruhm·reich 1 *Adj.* glorious ‹*victory, history*›; celebrated ‹*general, army, victory*›. **2** *adv.* ~ **siegen** win a glorious victory

Ruhr /ruːɐ̯/ *die;* ~, ~**en** ► 329 | dysentery *no art.*

Rühr·ei *das* scrambled egg[s *pl.*]

rühren /'ryːrən/ **1** *tr. V.* **(a)** (um~) stir ‹*sauce, dough, etc.*›; (ein~) stir ‹*egg, powder, etc.*› (**an, in** + *Akk.* into); **(b)** (bewegen) move ‹*limb, fingers, etc.*›; *s. auch* **Finger** b; **(c)** (fig.) move; touch; **jmdn. zu Tränen** ~: move sb. to tears; **es rührte ihn überhaupt nicht, dass** ...: it didn't bother him at all that ... **2** *itr. V.* **(a)** (um~) stir; **in etw.** (*Dat.*) ~: stir sth. **(b)** (geh.: her~) **das rührt daher, dass** ...: that stems from the fact that ... **3** *refl. V.* **(a)** (sich bewegen) move; **niemand rührte sich** nobody moved *or* stirred; (fig.: unternahm etwas) nobody did anything; **(b)** (Milit.) **rührt euch!** at ease!

rührend 1 *Adj.* touching; **das ist** ~ **von Ihnen** (ugs.) that is terribly sweet *or* kind of you (coll.) **2** *adv.* touchingly; **sie sorgt** ~ **für ihn** it is touching the way she looks after him

Ruhr·gebiet *das;* ~[e]s Ruhr [district]

rührig 1 *Adj.* active; (mit Unternehmungsgeist) enterprising; go-ahead; (emsig) busy; industrious. **2** *adv.* actively; (mit Unternehmungsgeist) enterprisingly; (emsig) busily; industriously

rühr·selig *Adj.* **(a)** emotional ‹*person*›; **(b)** (allzu gefühlvoll) over-sentimental ‹*manner, mood, etc.*›; maudlin, (coll.) tear-jerking ‹*play, song, etc.*›

Rührung *die;* ~: emotion; **von tiefer** ~ **ergriffen** deeply moved

Ruin /ru'iːn/ *der;* ~s ruin

Ruine *die;* ~, ~**n** ruin

ruinieren *tr. V.* ruin; **sich finanziell** ~: ruin oneself [financially]

rülpsen /'rʏlpsn̩/ *itr. V.* (ugs.) belch

Rülpser *der;* ~s, ~ (ugs.) belch

rum /rʊm/ *Adv.* (ugs.) ⇒ **herum**

rum|- (ugs.) ⇒ **herum|-**

Rum /rʊm/ *der;* ~s, ~s rum

Rumäne /ru'mɛːnə/ *der;* ~**n**, ~**n** ► 388 | Romanian

Rumänien (*das*); ~s Romania

Rumänin *die;* ~, ~**nen** Romanian

rumänisch *Adj.* ► 388 |, ► 490 | Romanian

rum-: ~|**ballern** *itr. V.* (ugs.) blast away; ~|**fliegen** (ugs.: herumliegen) lie about *or* around; ~|**gammeln** *itr. V.* (ugs.) ⇒ **gammeln** b; ~|**hampeln** *itr. V.* (ugs.) hop *or* jig about; ~|**hängen** *unr. itr. V.* (ugs. abwertend: nichts Sinnvolles tun) hang about *or* around; ~|**kriegen** *tr. V.* (ugs.) ⇒ **herumkriegen**; ~|**labern** *itr. V.* (salopp abwertend) natter (Brit. coll.) *or* chatter away (coll.); rabbit on (Brit. sl.); ~|**machen** *itr. V.* (salopp) **(a)** ⇒ **herummachen**; **(b)** ⇒ **herumfummeln** a; **(c)** (sich [sexuell] einlassen) play around; (schmusen) neck (coll.)

Rummel /'rʊml̩/ *der;* ~s (ugs.) **(a)** (laute Betriebsamkeit) commotion; (Aufhebens) fuss, to-do (**um** about); **(b)** (bes. nordd.: Jahrmarkt) fair

Rummel·platz *der* (bes. nordd.) fairground

rumoren /ru'moːrən/ *itr. V.* (ugs.) make a noise; (poltern) ‹*person*› bang about; **es rumorte in seinem Bauch** (fig.) his stomach rumbled

Rumpel·kammer *die* (ugs.) boxroom (Brit.); junk-room

rumpeln /'rʊmpl̩n/ *itr. V.* (ugs.) **(a)** (poltern) bump and bang about; **(b)** *mit sein* (sich rumpelnd fortbewegen) rumble; bump and bang

Rumpf /rʊmpf̩/ *der;* ~[e]s, **Rümpfe** /'rʏmpfə/ **(a)** trunk [of the body]; **den** ~ **drehen/beugen** turn one's body/ bend from the hips; **(b)** (beim Schiff) hull; **(c)** (beim Flugzeug) fuselage

rümpfen /'rʏmpfn̩/ *tr. V.* **die Nase [bei etw.]** ~: wrinkle one's nose at sth.; **über jmdn./etw. die Nase rümpfen** (fig.) look down one's nose at sb./turn up one's nose at sth.

Rump·steak /'rʊmp-/ *das* rump steak

rums /rʊms/ *Interj.* bump; (lauter, heller) bang; (beim Zusammenstoß) crash

rum|toben *itr. V.* (ugs.) **(a)** *auch mit sein* ‹*child*› charge *or* romp [noisily] about; ‹*students etc.*› rag; **(b)** (wüten) rant and rave

Run /rʌn/ *der;* ~**s**, ~**s** [big] rush; **ein [starker]** ~ **auf etw.** (*Akk.*) a [big] run on sth.

rund /rʊnt/ **1** *Adj.* **(a)** round; **ein Gespräch am** ~**en Tisch** (fig.) a round-table conference; **(b)** (dicklich) plump ‹*arms etc.*›; chubby ‹*cheeks*›; fat ‹*stomach*›; **(c)** (ugs.: ganz) round ‹*dozen, number, etc.*›; ~**e drei Jahre** three years *or* as near as makes no difference. **2** *Adv.* **(a)** (ugs.: etwa) about; approximately; **(b)** ~ **um jmdn./etw.** [all] around sb./sth.; *s. auch* **Uhr**

Rund-: ~**blick** *der* panorama; view in all directions; ~**brief** *der* circular [letter]

Runde /'rʊndə/ *die;* ~, ~**n (a)** (Sport: Strecke) lap; **die schnellste** ~ **fahren** do the fastest lap; **seine** ~**n ziehen** *od.* **drehen** do one's laps; **(b)** (Sport: Durchgang, Partie; Boxen: Abschnitt) round; **eine** ~ **Golf/Skat** a round of golf/skat; **über die** ~**n kommen** (fig. ugs.) get by; manage; **(c)** (Personenkreis) circle; (Gesellschaft) company; **(d)** (Rundgang) round; **die** ~ **machen** (ugs.) ‹*drink, rumour*› go the rounds *pl.*; circulate; **(e)** (Lage) round; **eine** ~ **Bier schmeißen** (ugs.) buy *or* stand a round of beer

runden **1** *tr. V.* **(a)** (rund machen) round; **(b)** (fig.: abrunden) round off, fill out ‹*picture, impression*›. **2** *refl. V.* become round

rund-, Rund-: ~**erneuern** *tr. V.* (Kfz-W.) remould; retread; ~**erneuerte Reifen** remoulds; retreads; ~**fahrt** *die* (auch Sport) tour (**durch** of); ~**flug** *der* [short] circular flight; circuit

Rund·funk *der* **(a)** radio; **im** ~: on the radio; **(b)** ⇒ **Rundfunkanstalt**

Rundfunk-: ~**anstalt** *die* broadcasting corporation; (Sender) radio station; ~**gebühren** *Pl.* radio licence fees; ~**gerät** *das* radio set; ~**programm** *das* **(a)** (Sendefolge) [schedule *sing.* of] radio programmes *pl.*; **(b)** (Programmheft) radio programme guide; ~**reporter** *der* radio reporter; ~**sender** *der* radio station; (technische Anlage) radio transmitter; ~**sendung** *die* radio programme; ~**sprecher** *der* radio announcer; ~**übertragung** *die* radio broadcast

rund-, Rund-: ~**gang** *der* (des Wachmanns, Chefarztes usw.) round (**durch** of); ~|**gehen** *unr. itr. V.; mit sein* **(a)** *unpers.* (ugs.) **es geht rund** (es ist viel Betrieb) it's all go (coll.); (es geht flott zu) things are going with a swing; **(b)** (herumgereicht werden) be passed round; (fig.) ‹*story, rumours*› go *or* do the rounds; ~**heraus** *Adv.* straight out; ‹*say, ask*› bluntly; ‹*refuse*› flatly; ~**herum** *Adv.* **(a)** (ringsum) all around; (darum herum) all round it; **(b)** (völlig) completely; (fig.) entirely ‹*satisfied*›

rundlich *Adj.* **(a)** roundish; **(b)** (mollig) plump; chubby

rund-, Rund-: ~**reise** *die* [circular] tour (**durch** of); **eine** ~**reise durch den Schwarzwald machen** tour the Black Forest; ~**schreiben** *das* ⇒ ~**brief**; ~**um** *Adv.* ⇒ ~**herum**

Rundung *die;* ~, ~**en** curve; (hervortretend) bulge

rund·weg *Adv.* ‹*refuse, deny*› flatly, point-blank

Rund·weg *der* circular path *or* walk

Rune /'ruːnə/ *die;* ~, ~**n** rune

runter /'rʊntɐ/ *Adv.* (ugs.) ~ **[da, das ist mein Platz]!** get off [there, that's my seat]; ~ **mit den Klamotten** off with your clothes; get those clothes off; **Kopf** ~**!** head/ heads down; *s. auch* **herunter; hinunter**

runter- ⇒ **herunter-, hinunter-**

runter-: ~|**dürfen** *unr. itr. V.* (ugs.) be allowed to come down; (hinausgehen dürfen) be allowed out; ~|**fallen** *unr. itr. V.; mit sein* (ugs.) fall down; (von der Leiter usw.) fall off; **die Leiter/von der Leiter** ~**fallen** fall off the ladder; **die Kreide fiel ihm** ~: he dropped the chalk; ~|**gehen** *unr. itr. V.; mit sein* (ugs.) **(a)** (nach unten gehen) go down; **(b)** (niedriger werden) ‹*price, temperature, pressure, etc.*› go down, drop; **(c)** (die Höhe senken) go down (**auf** + *Akk.* to); **wir müssen mit den Preisen** ~**gehen** we must reduce our prices; ~|**hauen** *unr. tr. V.* **jmdm. eine/ein paar** ~**hauen** (salopp) give sb. a clip/a couple of clips round the ear; ~|**rutschen** *itr. V.; mit sein* (ugs.) ⇒ **herunterrutschen**; *s. auch* **Buckel** a

---

*alte Schreibung (vgl. Hinweise auf S. xvi–xvii)

Runzel /'rʊntsl̩/ *die;* ~, ~n wrinkle
runz[e]lig *Adj.* wrinkled
runzeln *tr. V.* **die Stirn/die Brauen** ~: wrinkle one's
brow/knit one's brows; (ärgerlich) frown; **mit gerunzelter
Stirn** with wrinkled brow; (ärgerlich) frowning
Rüpel /'ryːpl̩/ *der;* ~s, ~ (abwertend) lout
rüpelhaft (abwertend) **1** *Adj.* loutish. **2** *adv.* in a loutish
manner
rupfen /'rʊpfn̩/ *tr. V.* **(a)** pluck ⟨*goose, hen, etc.*⟩; *s. auch*
Hühnchen; (b) (abreißen) pull up ⟨*weeds, grass*⟩; pull off
⟨*leaves etc.*⟩; **(c)** (ugs.: übervorteilen) fleece ⟨*person*⟩ [of his/
her money]
ruppig /'rʊpɪç/ **1** *Adj.* (abwertend) gruff ⟨*person,
behaviour*⟩; sharp ⟨*tone*⟩. **2** *adv.* (abwertend) gruffly
Rüsche /'ryːʃə/ *die;* ~, ~n ruche; frill
Ruß /ruːs/ *der;* ~es soot
Russe /'rʊsə/ *der;* ~n, ~n ▶ 388 ⌋ Russian
Rüssel /'rʏsl̩/ *der;* ~s, ~ **(a)** (des Elefanten) trunk; (des
Schweins) snout; (bei Insekten u. ä.) proboscis; **(b)** (salopp: Nase)
conk (sl.)
rußen *itr. V.* give off sooty smoke
Russen·mafia *die* Russian Mafia
rußig *Adj.* sooty
Russin *die;* ~, ~nen Russian
russisch ▶ 388 ⌋, ▶ 487 ⌋ **1** *Adj.* Russian; *s. auch* **Ei** a. **2**
adv. **(a)** ~ **verwaltet/besetzt** administered/occupied by
Russia; **(b)** (auf Russisch) in Russian
Russisch *das;* ~[s] ▶ 487 ⌋ Russian
Russ·land, ***Ruß·land** (*das*); ~s Russia
rüsten /'rʏstn̩/ **1** *itr. V.* (sich bewaffnen) arm; **zum Krieg**
~: arm for war. **2** *itr., refl. V.* (geh.: sich bereit machen, auch
fig.) get ready; prepare
Rüster *die;* ~, ~n **(a)** elm [tree]; **(b)** (Holz) elm[wood]
rüstig *Adj.* sprightly; active; **er ist noch** ~: he is still
hale and hearty
rustikal /rʊstiˈkaːl/ **1** *Adj.* country-style ⟨*food, inn,
clothes, etc.*⟩; farmhouse *attrib.* ⟨*food*⟩; rustic ⟨*pattern*⟩;
rustic, farmhouse *attrib.* ⟨*furniture*⟩; (als Nachahmung) rus-
tic-style ⟨*furniture etc.*⟩. **2** *adv.* in [a] country style
Rüstung *die;* ~, ~en **(a)** (Bewaffnung) armament *no art.;*
(Waffen) arms *pl.;* weapons *pl.;* **(b)** (hist.: Schutzbekleidung) suit
of armour; **in voller** ~: in full armour
Rüstungs-: ~**betrieb** *der* armaments factory;
~**industrie** *die* armaments *or* arms industry; ~**kontrolle** *die* arms control; ~**stopp** *der* arms freeze;
~**wettlauf** *der* arms race
Rüst·zeug *das* **(a)** (Wissen) requisite know-how; **(b)** (Ausrüstung) equipment [for the job *or* task]
Rute /'ruːtə/ *die;* ~, ~n (Stock) switch; (Birken~, Angel~,
Wünschel~) rod; (zum Züchtigen) cane; (Ründel) birch
Rutsch /rʊtʃ/ *der;* ~[e]s, ~e slide; **in einem** *od.* **auf
einen** ~ (fig. ugs.) in one go; **guten** ~ **[ins neue Jahr]!**
happy New Year!
Rutsch·bahn *die* slide
Rutsche *die;* ~, ~n chute
rutschen *itr. V.; mit sein* slide; ⟨*clutch, carpet*⟩ slip;
(aus~) ⟨*person*⟩ slip; ⟨*car etc.*⟩ skid; (nach unten) slip [down];
rutsch mal zur Seite! (ugs.) move up a bit (coll.)
rutschig *Adj.* slippery
rütteln /'rʏtl̩n/ **1** *tr. V.* shake; **jmdn. aus dem Schlaf**
od. **wach** ~: shake sb. out of his/her sleep. **2** *itr. V.* shake;
an der Tür ~: shake the door; ⟨*wind*⟩ make the door
rattle; **daran ist nicht** *od.* **gibt es nichts zu** ~ (fig.)
there's nothing you can do about that

S s

s, S /ɛs/ *das;* ~, ~: s, S; *s. auch* **a, A**
S *Abk.* **(a)** Süd, Süden S.; **(b)** (österr.) Schilling Sch.
s. *Abk.* **siehe**
S. *Abk.* **Seite** p.
s. a. *Abk.* **siehe auch**
Sa. *Abk.* **Samstag** Sat.
Saal /zaːl/ *der;* ~[e]s, **Säle** /'zɛːlə/ **(a)** hall; (Ball~) ballroom; **(b)** (Publikum) audience
Saal·ordner *der* steward
Saar·land /'zaːɐ̯lant/ *das;* ~[e]s Saarland
Saar·länder /-lɛndɐ/ *der;* ~s, ~, **Saarländerin** *die;*
~, ~nen Saarlander
saar·ländisch *Adj.* Saarland *attrib.* ⟨*government, population, etc.*⟩; Saar *attrib.* ⟨*industry, miners, etc.*⟩; ⟨*history*⟩
of the Saar
Saat /zaːt/ *die;* ~, ~en **(a)** (das Gesäte) [young] crops *pl.;*
(b) *o. Pl.* (das Säen) sowing; **mit der** ~ **beginnen** start
sowing; **(c)** (Samenkörner) seed[s *pl.*]
Saat-: ~**gut** *das; o. Pl.* seed[s *pl.*]; ~**kartoffel** *die*
seed-potato
sabbern *itr. V.* ⟨*dog, person*⟩ slaver, slobber; ⟨*baby*⟩ dribble
Säbel /'zɛːbl̩/ *der;* ~s, ~: sabre
Säbel·rasseln *das;* ~s (abwertend) sabre-rattling
Sabotage /zaboˈtaːʒə/ *die;* ~, ~n sabotage *no art.*
Sabotage·akt *der* act of sabotage
Saboteur /zaboˈtøːɐ̯/ *der;* ~s, ~e, **Saboteurin** *die;*
~, ~nen saboteur
sabotieren *tr. V.* sabotage
sach-, ~Sach-: ~**bearbeiter** *der* person responsible (**für** for); ~**bezogen 1** *Adj.* relevant; pertinent
⟨*remark*⟩; **2** *adv.* to the point; ~**buch** *das* [popular] non-
fiction *or* informative book; ~**dienlich** *Adj.* (Papierdt.)
useful; helpful
Sache /'zaxə/ *die;* ~, ~n **(a)** *Pl.* things; **scharfe** ~n
trinken drink the hard stuff (coll.); **(b)** (Angelegenheit) matter; business (esp. derog.); **es ist beschlossene** ~, **dass
…**: it's [all] arranged *or* settled that …; **es ist die einfachste** ~ **[von] der Welt** it's the simplest thing in the world;
das ist so eine ~: it's a bit tricky; **[mit jmdm.]** ge-
meinsame ~ **machen** join forces [with sb.]; [**sich**
(*Dat.*)] **seiner** ~ **sicher** *od.* **gewiss sein** be sure one is
right; **bei der** ~ **sein** concentrate on it; **zur** ~ **kommen**
come to the point; **das tut nichts zur** ~: that's irrelevant; that's got nothing to do with it; **(c)** (Rechts~) case;
Fragen zur ~: questions about the case; **(d)** *o. Pl.* (Anliegen) cause; **(e)** *Pl.* (ugs.: Stundenkilometer) kilometres per
hour
sach-, Sach-: ~**gebiet** *das* subject [area]; field;
~**gemäß**, ~**gerecht 1** *Adj.* proper; correct; **2** *adv.*
properly; correctly; ~**kenntnis** *die* expertise; knowledge of the subject; ~**kunde** *die* **(a)** ⇒ ~**kenntnis**;
(b) (Schulw.) ≈ general subjects *pl.;* ~**kundig 1** *Adj.* with
a knowledge of the subject *postpos., not pred.;* **sich** ~**kundig machen** acquaint oneself with the subject; **2** *adv.* expertly; ~**lage** *die; o. Pl.* situation
sachlich 1 *Adj.* **(a)** (objektiv) objective; (nüchtern) functional ⟨*building, style, etc.*⟩; matter-of-fact, down-to-earth
⟨*letter etc.*⟩; **(b)** *nicht präd.* (sachbezogen) factual ⟨*error*⟩;
material ⟨*consideration*⟩; **aus** ~**en Gründen** for practical reasons. **2** *adv.* **(a)** (objektiv) objectively; ⟨*state*⟩ as a
matter of fact; (nüchtern) ⟨*furnished*⟩ in a functional style;
⟨*written*⟩ in a matter-of-fact way; **(b)** (sachbezogen) factually
⟨*wrong*⟩
sächlich /'zɛçlɪç/ *Adj.* (Sprachw.) neuter
Sachlichkeit *die;* ~: objectivity; (Nüchternheit) functionalism

Sach·schaden *der* damage [to property] *no indef. art.*

Sachse /'zaksə/ *der;* ~n, ~n Saxon

Sachsen *(das);* ~s Saxony

Sachsen-Anhalt *(das);* ~s Saxony-Anhalt

Sachsen-Anhalter, Sachsen-Anhaltiner *der;* ~s, ~: native of Saxony-Anhalt; (Einwohner) inhabitant of Saxony-Anhalt

sachsen-anhaltinisch, sachsen-anhaltisch *Adj.* Saxony-Anhalt *attrib.*

sächsisch /'zɛksɪʃ/ *Adj.* Saxon

sacht /zaxt/ **1** *Adj.* gentle. **2** *adv.* gently

sachte *Adv.* (ugs.) ~[, ~] take it easy; (nicht so hastig) not so fast

sach-, Sach-: ~**verhalt** *der;* ~[e]s, ~e facts *pl.* [of the matter]; ~**verstand** *der* expertise; grasp of the subject; ~**verständig 1** *Adj.* expert ‹*opinion etc.*›; knowledgeable ‹*person*›; **2** *adv.* expertly; knowledgeably; ~**wissen** *das* specialist knowledge; ~**zwang** *der* [factual *or* material] constraint

Sack /zak/ *der;* ~[e]s, **Säcke** /'zɛkə/ **(a)** sack; (aus Papier, Kunststoff) bag; **drei ~ Zement/Kartoffeln** three bags of cement/sacks of potatoes; **jmdn. in den ~ stecken** (ugs.) put sb. in the shade; **mit ~ und Pack** with bag and baggage; **(b)** (Hautfalte) **Säcke unter den Augen haben** have bags under one's eyes; **(c)** (derb: Hoden~) balls *pl.* (coarse); **(d)** (derb abwertend: Mensch) sod (Brit. sl.)

sacken *itr. V.; mit sein* ‹*person*› slump; ‹*ship etc.*› sink; ‹*plane*› drop rapidly, plummet

Sack-: ~**gasse** *die* cul-de-sac; (fig.) impasse; ~**hüpfen** *das;* ~s sack race

Sadismus /za'dɪsmʊs/ *der;* ~: sadism *no art.*

Sadist *der;* ~en, ~en, **Sadistin** *die;* ~, ~nen sadist

sadistisch 1 *Adj.* sadistic. **2** *adv.* sadistically; ~ **veranlagt sein** have sadistic tendencies

säen /'zɛːən/ *tr.* (*auch itr.*) *V.* (auch fig.) sow; **dünn gesät sein** (fig.) be thin on the ground

Safari /za'faːri/ *die;* ~, ~s safari

Safe /seɪf/ *der od. das;* ~s, ~s **(a)** safe; **(b)** (Schließfach) safe-deposit box

Safran /'zafran/ *der;* ~s, ~e saffron

Saft /zaft/ *der;* ~[e]s, **Säfte** /'zɛftə/ **(a)** juice; **(b)** (in Pflanzen) sap; **ohne ~ und Kraft** (abwertend) weak and lifeless; **(c)** (salopp: Elektrizität) juice (sl.)

saftig *Adj.* **(a)** juicy; sappy ‹*stem*›; lush ‹*meadow, green*›; (fig.: lebensvoll) lusty; **(b)** (ugs.) hefty ‹*slap, blow*›; steep (coll.) ‹*prices, bill*›; terrific, big ‹*surprise, punch-up*›; crude, coarse ‹*joke, song, etc.*›; strongly-worded ‹*letter etc.*›; strong, juicy ‹*curse*›

Saft·laden *der* (salopp abwertend) lousy outfit (coll.)

saft·los *Adj.* (fig.) feeble, anodyne ‹*language*›; **saft- und kraftlos** feeble; wishy-washy

Saft-: ~**presse** *die* juice extractor; ~**sack** *der* (derb abwertend) bastard (coll.)

Sage /'zaːɡə/ *die;* ~, ~n legend; (bes. nordische) saga; **es geht die ~, dass …** (fig.: es heißt, dass …) there's a rumour going round that …

Säge /'zɛːɡə/ *die;* ~, ~n saw

Säge-: ~**blatt** *das* saw-blade; ~**mehl** *das* sawdust

sagen 1 *tr. V.* **(a)** say; **das kann jeder** *V.* anybody can claim that; it's easy to talk; **sag das nicht!** (ugs.) don't [just] assume that; not necessarily; **dann will ich nichts gesagt haben** in that case forget I said anything; **was ich noch ~ wollte** [oh] by the way; before I forget; **unter uns gesagt** between you and me; **wie gesagt** as I've said *or* mentioned; **das kann man wohl ~:** you can say 'that again; **heute Abend, ~ wir, um acht** tonight, say, eight o'clock; **sage und schreibe** (ugs.) believe it or not; would you believe; **(b)** (meinen) say; **was ~ Sie dazu?** what do you think about that?; **(c)** (mitteilen) **jmdm. etw. ~:** say sth. to sb.; (zur Information) tell sb. sth.; **[jmdm.] seinen Namen/seine Gründe ~:** give [sb.] one's name/reasons; **[jmdm.] die Wahrheit ~:** tell [sb.] the truth; **das sag ich dir** (ugs.) I'm telling *or* warning you; **ich habs [dir] ja gleich gesagt!** (ugs.) I told you so!; (habe dich gewarnt) I

warned you!; **ich will dir mal was ~:** let me tell you something; **lass dir das gesagt sein** (ugs.) make a note of *or* remember what I'm saying; **wem ~ Sie das!** (ugs.) you don't need to tell me [that]!; **was Sie nicht ~!** (ugs., oft iron.) you don't say!; **das ist zu viel gesagt** that's going too far; that's an exaggeration; **er lässt sich** (*Dat.*) **nichts ~:** he won't be told; you can't tell him anything; **(d)** (nennen) **zu jmdm./etw. X ~:** call sb./sth. X; **(e)** (formulieren, ausdrücken) say; **so kann man es auch ~:** you could put it like that; **etw. in aller Deutlichkeit ~:** make sth. perfectly clear; **du sagst es!** very true!; **willst du damit ~, dass …?** are you trying to say *or* do you mean [to say] that …?; **(f)** (bedeuten) mean; **hat das etwas zu ~?** does that mean anything?; **(g)** (anordnen, befehlen) tell; **du hast mir gar nichts zu ~:** you've no right to order me about; **etwas/nichts zu ~ haben** ‹*person*› have a/no say. **2** *refl. V.* **sich** (*Dat.*) **etw. ~:** say sth. to oneself. **3** *itr. V.* **wie sagt man [da]?** what does one say?; what's the [right] word?; **sag bloß!** (ugs.) you don't say!

sägen /'zɛːɡn̩/ **1** *itr. V.* **(a)** saw; **(b)** (ugs. scherzh.: schnarchen) snore loudly. **2** *tr. V.* saw; (zersägen) saw up ‹*tree etc.*›

sagenhaft (ugs.) **1** *Adj.* incredible (coll.); fabulous (coll.) ‹*party, wealth*›. **2** *adv.* incredibly (coll.)

Säge-: ~**späne** *Pl.* wood shavings; ~**werk** *das* sawmill

sah /zaː/ *1. u. 3. Pers. Sg. Prät. v.* **sehen**

Sahne /'zaːnə/ *die;* ~: cream

Saison /zɛ'zõː/ *die;* ~, ~s season; **während/außerhalb der ~:** during the season/out of season *or* in the off-season; ~ **haben** have one's busy time *or* season

saison-, Saison-: ~**arbeit** *die* seasonal work; ~**arbeiter** *der* seasonal worker; ~**bedingt 1** *Adj.* seasonal; **2** *adv.* due to seasonal influences

Saite /'zaɪtə/ *die;* ~, ~n string; **andere** *od.* **strengere ~n aufziehen** (fig.) take stronger measures; get tough (coll.)

Saiten·instrument *das* stringed instrument

Sakko /'zako/ *der od. das;* ~s, ~s jacket

Sakrament /zakra'mɛnt/ *das;* ~[e]s, ~e **(a)** (bes. kath. Kirche) sacrament; **(b)** ~ **[noch mal]!** (salopp) for Heaven's sake!

Sakristei /zakrɪs'taɪ/ *die;* ~, ~en sacristy

Salamander /zala'mandɐ/ *der;* ~s, ~: salamander

Salami /za'laːmi/ *die;* ~, ~[s] salami

Salat /za'laːt/ *der;* ~[e]s, ~e **(a)** salad; **(b)** *o. Pl.* [grüner] ~: lettuce; **ein Kopf ~:** a [head of] lettuce; **(c)** *o. Pl.* (ugs.: Wirrwarr) muddle; mess; **jetzt haben wir den ~!** (ugs. iron.) now we're in a right mess

Salat-: ~**besteck** *das* salad servers *pl.;* ~**soße** *die* salad dressing

Salbe /'zalbə/ *die;* ~, ~n ointment

Salbei /'zalbaɪ/ *der od. die;* ~: sage

salben *tr. V.* **(a)** put ointment on ‹*part of body*›; **(b)** (kath. Kirche) anoint ‹*sick or dying person,* (Hist.) *king, emperor, etc.*›

Saldo /'zaldo/ *der;* ~s, ~s *od.* **Saldi** (Buchf., Finanzw.) balance

Säle ⇨ **Saal**

Saline /za'liːnə/ *die;* ~, ~n salt-works *sing. or pl.*

Salm /zalm/ *der;* ~[e]s, ~e (bes. rhein.) salmon

Salmiak /zal'mjak/ *der od. das;* ~: sal ammoniac

Salmiak-: ~**geist** *der* [liquid] ammonia; ammonia water; ~**pastille** *die* sal ammoniac pastille

Salmonelle /zalmo'nɛlə/ *die;* ~, ~n; *meist Pl.* salmonella *sing.*

salomonisch (geh.) **1** *Adj.* Solomon-like; **ein ~es Urteil** a judgment of Solomon. **2** *adv.* with the wisdom of Solomon

Salon /za'lõː/ *der;* ~s, ~s **(a)** (Raum) drawing room; salon; **(b)** (Geschäft) [hair- *etc.*] salon

salon·fähig *Adj.* socially acceptable

salopp /za'lɔp/ **1** *Adj.* casual ‹*clothes*›; free and easy, informal ‹*behaviour*›; very colloquial, slangy ‹*saying, expression, etc.*›. **2** *adv.* ‹*dress*› casually; informally; ~ **reden** use slangy *or* [very] colloquial language

Salpeter /zal'peːtɐ/ *der;* ∼s saltpetre

Salto /'zalto/ *der;* ∼s, ∼s *od.* **Sạlti** somersault; (beim Turnen auch) salto

Salut /za'luːt/ *der;* ∼[e]s, ∼e (Milit.) salute; ∼ **schießen** fire a salute

salutieren *itr. V.* (bes. Milit.) salute; **vor jmdm.** ∼: salute sb.

Salve /'zalvə/ *die;* ∼, ∼n (Milit.) salvo; (aus Gewehren) volley

Salz /zalts/ *das;* ∼es, ∼e salt

sạlz·arm 1 *Adj.* low in salt *postpos.;* low-salt. **2** *adv.* ∼ **essen** eat food containing little salt

Sạlz·brezel *die* [salted] pretzel

salzen *unr., auch regelm. tr. V.* salt; **die Suppe ist stark gesalzen** the soup has a lot of salt in it

sạlzig *Adj.* salty

salz-, Salz-: ∼**kartoffel** *die; meist Pl.* boiled potato; ∼**los 1** *Adj.* salt-free; (nicht gesalzen) unsalted; **2** *adv.* ⟨*cook*⟩ without any salt; ∼**los essen** eat unsalted food; ∼**lösung** *die* saline solution; ∼**säure** *die; o. Pl.* (Chemie) hydrochloric acid; ∼**stange** *die* salt stick; ∼**streuer** *der;* ∼s, ∼: salt-sprinkler; salt-shaker (Amer.); ∼**wasser** *das; Pl.* ∼**wässer** (a) *o. Pl.* (zum Kochen) salted water; (b) (Meerwasser) salt water

Samariter /zama'riːtɐ/ *der;* ∼s, ∼ [**barmherziger**] ∼: good Samaritan

Sambia /'zambĭa/ *(das);* ∼s Zambia

Samen /'zaːmən/ *der;* ∼s, ∼ (a) (∼korn) seed; (b) *o. Pl.* (∼körner) seed[s. *pl.*]; (c) *o. Pl.* (Sperma) sperm; semen

Sạmmel-: ∼**band** *der; Pl.* ∼**bände** anthology; ∼**becken** *das* collecting basin; reservoir; (fig.) gathering-point *or* -place; ∼**bestellung** *die* joint order; ∼**büchse** *die* collecting-box; ∼**fahrschein** *der* group ticket

sammeln /'zamln̩/ **1** *tr.* (*auch itr.*) *V.* collect; gather ⟨*honey, firewood, material, experiences, impressions, etc.*⟩; gather, pick ⟨*berries, herbs, mushrooms, etc.*⟩; gather ⟨*people*⟩ [together]; assemble ⟨*people*⟩; cause ⟨*light rays*⟩ to converge; **gesammelte Werke** collected works. **2** *refl. V.* (a) gather [together]; ⟨*light rays*⟩ converge; **sich um jmdn./etw.** ∼: gather round sb./sth.; (b) (sich konzentrieren) collect oneself; gather oneself together

Sạmmel·platz *der* collection *or* collecting point; (für Menschen) assembly point

Sammelsurium /zaml'zuːrĭom/ *das;* ∼s, **Sammelsurien** (abwertend) hotchpotch

Sammler /'zamlɐ/ *der;* ∼s, ∼, **Sammlerin** *die;* ∼, ∼nen collector; (von Pilzen, Kräutern, Beeren usw.) gatherer; picker

Sammlung *die;* ∼, ∼en (a) collection; (b) [**innere**] ∼: composure

Samstag /'zamstaːk/ *der;* ∼[e]s, ∼e ▶ 119 |, ▶ 595 | Saturday; **langer** ∼: Saturday on which the shops stay open late; *s. auch* **Dienstag; Dienstag-**

samstags *Adv.* ▶ 595 | on Saturdays

samt /zamt/ **1** *Präp. mit Dat.* together with. **2** *Adv.* ∼ **und sonders** without exception

Samt *der;* ∼[e]s, ∼e velvet

samten *Adj.; nicht präd.* (a) velvet; (b) (wie Samt) velvety

Sạmt·hand·schuh *der* velvet glove; **jmdn. mit** ∼**en anfassen** (fig.) handle sb. with kid gloves

sạmtig *Adj.* velvety

sämtlich /'zɛmtlɪç/ *Indefinitpron. u. unbest. Zahlwort* (a) *attr.* all the; ∼**e Werke** complete works; (b) *allein stehend* all

samt·weich *Adj.* velvety[-soft]; soft as velvet *postpos.*

Sanatorium /zana'toːrĭom/ *das;* ∼s, **Sanatorien** sanatorium

Sand /zant/ *der;* ∼[e]s sand; ... **gibt es wie** ∼ **am Meer** (ugs.) there are countless ...; ... are pretty thick on the ground (coll.); **da ist** ∼ **im Getriebe** (fig. ugs.) there's something gumming up the works (coll.); **jmdm.** ∼ **in die Augen streuen** (fig.) pull the wool over sb.'s eyes; **im** ∼[e] **verlaufen** (fig. ugs.) come to nothing; **etw. [total] in den** ∼ **setzen** (fig. ugs.) make a [complete] mess of sth.

Sandale /zan'daːlə/ *die;* ∼, ∼n sandal

Sandalette /zanda'lɛtə/ *die;* ∼, ∼n [high-heeled] sandal

Sand-: ∼**bank** *die; Pl.* ∼**bänke** sandbank; ∼**burg** *die* sandcastle

sạndig *Adj.* sandy

Sand-: ∼**kasten** *der* [child's] sandpit; sandbox (Amer.); ∼**korn** *das; Pl.* ∼**körner** grain of sand; ∼**kuchen** *der* Madeira cake; ∼**männchen** *das; o. Pl.* sandman; ∼**papier** *das* sandpaper; ∼**sack** *der* (a) sandbag; (b) (Boxen) punching bag; ∼**stein** *der* sandstone; ∼**strahlen** *tr. V.* (Technik) sandblast; ∼**strand** *der* sandy beach; ∼**sturm** *der* sandstorm

sandte /'zantə/ *1. u. 3. Pers. Sg. Prät. v.* **senden**

Sand·uhr *die* sand-glass

Sandwich /'zɛntvɪtʃ/ *der od. das;* ∼s, ∼[e]s sandwich

sanft /zanft/ **1** *Adj.* gentle; (leise, nicht intensiv) soft ⟨*music, colour, light*⟩; (friedlich) peaceful; **es auf die** ∼**e Tour versuchen** (ugs.) try the gentle approach. **2** *adv.* gently; (leise) ⟨*speak, play*⟩ softly; (friedlich) peacefully; **ruhe** ∼ (auf Grabsteinen) rest in peace

Sänfte /'zɛnftə/ *die;* ∼, ∼n litter; (geschlossen) sedan chair

Sạnftheit *die;* ∼: gentleness; (von Klängen, Licht, Farben) softness

sang /zaŋ/ *1. u. 3. Pers. Sg. Prät. v.* **singen**

Sänger /'zɛŋɐ/ *der;* ∼s, ∼: ▶ 85 | singer

Sängerin *die;* ∼, ∼nen singer

sạng·los *Adv. in* **sang- und klanglos** (ugs.) simply; without any ado *or* fuss

sanieren /za'niːrən/ **1** *tr. V.* (a) redevelop ⟨*area*⟩; rehabilitate ⟨*building*⟩; (renovieren) renovate [and improve] ⟨*flat etc.*⟩; (b) (Wirtsch.) restore ⟨*firm*⟩ to profitability; rehabilitate ⟨*agriculture, coal mining, etc.*⟩. **2** *refl. V.* ⟨*company etc.*⟩ restore itself to profitability, get back on its feet again; ⟨*person*⟩ get oneself out of the red

Sanierung *die;* ∼, ∼en ⇒ **sanieren:** (a) redevelopment; rehabilitation; renovation; (b) restoration to profitability

sanitär /zani'tɛːɐ/ *Adj.; nicht präd.* sanitary ⟨*installations*⟩

Sanitäter /zani'tɛːtɐ/ *der;* ∼s, ∼ first-aid man; (im Krankenwagen) ambulance man

Sanitäts·wagen *der* ambulance

sank /zaŋk/ *1. u. 3. Pers. Sg. Prät. v.* **sinken**

Sanktion /zaŋk'tsĭoːn/ *die;* ∼, ∼en sanction

sanktionieren *tr. V.* sanction

sann /zan/ *1. u. 3. Pers. Sg. Prät. v.* **sinnen**

Saphir /'zaːfɪr/ *der;* ∼s, ∼e sapphire

Sardelle /zar'dɛlə/ *die;* ∼, ∼n anchovy

Sardine /zar'diːnə/ *die;* ∼, ∼n sardine

Sarg /zark/ *der;* ∼[e]s, **Särge** /'zɛrgə/ coffin

Sarkasmus /zar'kasmʊs/ *der;* ∼: sarcasm

sarkạstisch 1 *Adj.* sarcastic. **2** *adv.* sarcastically

saß /zaːs/ *1. u. 3. Pers. Sg. Prät. v.* **sitzen**

Satan /'zaːtan/ *der;* ∼s, ∼e (a) *o. Pl.* (bibl.) Satan *no def. art.;* (b) (ugs. abwertend: Mensch) fiend

Satellit /zatɛ'liːt/ *der;* ∼en, ∼en (auch fig.) satellite

Satelliten-: ∼**anlage** *die* satellite receiver; ∼**schüssel** *die* (ugs.) satellite dish; ∼**staat** *der* (abwertend) satellite [state]

Satire /za'tiːrə/ *die;* ∼, ∼n satire

Satiriker *der;* ∼s, ∼: satirist

satịrisch 1 *Adj.* satirical. **2** *adv.* satirically; with a satirical touch

satt /zat/ **1** *Adj.* (a) full [up] *pred.;* well-fed; ∼ **sein** be full [up]; have had enough [to eat]; **sich** ∼ **essen** eat as much as one wants; **etw. macht** ∼: sth. is filling; (b) (selbstgefällig) smug, self-satisfied ⟨*person, smile, expression, etc.*⟩; (c) **jmdn./etw.** ∼ **haben/kriegen** (ugs.) be/get fed up with sb./sth. (coll.); (d) (intensiv) rich, deep ⟨*colour*⟩; rich, pure ⟨*sound*⟩. **2** *adv.* (a) (selbstgefällig) smugly; complacently; (b) (reichlich) **nicht** ∼ **zu essen haben** not have enough to eat; **Tennis** ∼ (fig.) as much tennis as one could possibly want

Sattel /'zatl/ *der;* ~s, **Sättel** /'zɛtl/ saddle

sattel·fest *Adj.* experienced; **in etw.** (*Dat.*) ~ **sein** be au fait with sth.; be well up in sth.

satteln *tr. V.* saddle

Sattel-: ~**stütze** *die* seatpost; seat pillar; ~**tasche** *die* saddlebag

sättigen /'zɛtɪɡn̩/ **1** *itr. V.* be filling. **2** *tr. V.* (a) (geh.) fill; (b) (fig.) saturate

sättigend *Adj.* filling

Sättigung *die;* ~, ~**en** (fig.) saturation

Sattler /'zatlɐ/ *der;* ~s, ~; ▶85⌋ saddler

sattsam *Adv.* ad nauseam; ~ **bekannt** only too well known; notorious

Saturn /za'tʊrn/ *der;* ~s Saturn *no def. art.*

Satz /zats/ *der;* ~es, **Sätze** /'zɛtsə/ (a) (sprachliche Einheit) sentence; (Teil~) clause; **in od. mit einem** ~: in one sentence; briefly; (b) (Musik) movement; (c) (Tennis, Volleyball) set; (Tischtennis, Badminton) game; (d) (Sprung) leap; jump; **einen** ~ **über etw.** (*Akk.*) **machen** jump *or* leap across sth.; (e) (Amtsspr.: Tarif) rate; (f) (Set) set; (g) (Boden~) sediment; (Kaffee~) grounds *pl.;* (h) *o. Pl.* (Druckw.) (das Setzen) setting; (Gesetztes) type matter

Satz-: ~**aussage** *die* (Sprachw.) predicate; ~**ergänzung** *die* (Sprachw.) complement; ~**gefüge** *das* (Sprachw.) complex sentence; ~**gegen·stand** *der* (Sprachw.) subject [of a/the sentence]; ~**glied** *das* (Sprachw.) component part [of a/the sentence]; ~**teil** *der* (Sprachw.) ⇒ ~**glied**

Satzung /'zatsʊŋ/ *die;* ~, ~**en** articles of association *pl.;* statutes *pl.*

satzungs·gemäß *Adj., adv.* in accordance with the articles of association *or* the statutes

Satz·zeichen *das* (Sprachw.) punctuation mark

Sau /zau/ *die;* ~, **Säue** /'zɔyə/ (a) (weibliches Schwein) sow; (b) (bes. südd.: Schwein) pig; **jmdn. zur** ~ **machen** (derb) tear a strip off sb. (Brit. coll.); **wie eine gesengte Sau fahren** (derb) drive like a madman; (c) (derb abwertend: schmutziger Mensch) (Mann) dirty pig; (Frau) dirty cow (sl. derog.); (d) (derb abwertend: gemeiner Mensch) swine

Sau·bande *die* (salopp) wretched swine (derog.) *pl.;* (mehr scherzh.) bunch of good-for-nothings (sl.)

sauber /'zaubɐ/ **1** *Adj.* (a) clean; **etw.** ~ **machen** clean sth.; ~ **machen** (putzen) clean; do the cleaning; (b) (sorgfältig) neat ‹*handwriting, division, work, etc.*›; (c) (einwandfrei) perfect, faultless ‹*accent, technique, etc.*›; (d) (anständig) upstanding ‹*attitude, person*›; fair ‹*solution*›; unsullied ‹*character*›; ~ **bleiben** (ugs.) keep one's hands clean (coll.); (e) *nicht präd.* (iron.: unanständig) nice, fine (iron.). **2** *adv.* (a) (sorgfältig) neatly ‹*written, dressed, mended, etc.*›; (b) (fehlerlos) [**sehr**] ~: [quite] perfectly *or* faultlessly; (c) (anständig) conscientiously; (gerecht) ‹*judge etc.*› fairly; (d) (iron.) nicely (iron.); **das hast du** ~ **hingekriegt** a fine job you made of that

sauber|halten *unr. tr. V.* keep ‹*room, floor, etc.*› clean

Sauberkeit *die;* ~: cleanness; (bes. der Person) cleanliness

säuberlich /'zɔybɐlɪç/ **1** *Adj.* neat. **2** *adv.* [**fein**] ~: neatly

*****sauber|machen** ⇒ **sauber 1 a**

säubern /'zɔybɐn/ *tr. V.* (a) clean; **die Schuhe vom Lehm** ~: clean the mud off the shoes; (b) (fig.) clear, rid (von of); purge ‹*party, government, etc.*› (von of)

Säuberung *die;* ~, ~**en** (a) cleaning; (b) (fig.) purging; (c) (Politik) ~**saktion**) purge; **ethnische** ~ (verhüll.) ethnic cleansing

sau·blöd[e] (salopp abwertend) **1** *Adj.* bloody silly *or* stupid (sl.). **2** *adv.* in an bloody silly *or* stupid manner (sl.)

Sauce ⇒ **Soße a**

Saudi /zaudi/ *der;* ~s, ~s, **Saudi·araber** *der* ▶388⌋ Saudi

Saudi-Arabien (*das);* ~s Saudi Arabia

saudiarabisch, **saudisch** *Adj.* ▶388⌋ Saudi Arabian; Saudi

---

sau·dumm ⇒ **saublöd**

sauer /'zauɐ/ **1** *Adj.* (a) sour; sour, tart ‹*fruit*›; pickled ‹*herring, gherkin, etc.*›; acid[ic] ‹*wine, vinegar*›; **saurer Regen** acid rain; *s. auch* **Apfel a;** (b) *nicht attr.* (ugs.) (verärgert) cross, annoyed (**auf** + *Akk.* with); (verdrossen) sour; (c) (mühselig) hard; difficult; **gib ihm Saures!** (ugs.) let him have it! (coll.). **2** *adv.* (a) (in Essig) in vinegar; (b) crossly; ~ **reagieren** (ugs.) get annoyed *or* cross (**auf** + *Akk.* with)

Sauer-: ~**ampfer** /~ampfɐ/ *der* sorrel; ~**braten** *der* braised beef marinated in vinegar and herbs; sauerbraten (Amer.)

Sauerei *die;* ~, ~**en** (salopp abwertend) (a) (Unflätigkeit) obscenity; (b) (Gemeinheit) bloody (Brit. sl.) *or* (coll.) damn scandal (sl.)

Sauer-: ~**kirsche** *die* sour cherry; ~**kraut** *das o. Pl.* sauerkraut; pickled cabbage

säuerlich **1** *Adj.* [**leicht**] ~: slightly sour. **2** *adv.* (missvergnügt) somewhat sourly

Sauer-: ~**milch** *die* sour milk; ~**stoff** *der o. Pl.* oxygen

Sauerstoff- oxygen ‹*cylinder, apparatus, mask, etc.*›

Sauer·teig *der* leaven

saufen /'zaufn̩/ **1** *unr. itr. V.* (a) ‹*animal*› drink; (b) (salopp) (trinken) drink; swig (coll.); (Alkohol trinken) drink; booze (coll.); ~ **wie ein Loch** drink like a fish. **2** *unr. tr. V.* (a) ‹*animal*› drink; (b) (salopp: trinken) drink; **einen** ~ **gehen** go for a drink

Säufer /'zɔyfɐ/ *der;* ~s, ~ (salopp, oft abwertend) boozer (coll.); piss artist (sl.)

Sauferei *die;* ~, ~**en** (salopp) booze-up (coll.)

Säuferin *die;* ~, ~**nen** (salopp, oft abwertend) boozer (coll.); drunkard

säufst /zɔyfst/ *2. Pers. Sg. Präsens v.* **saufen**

säuft /zɔyft/ *3. Pers. Sg. Präsens v.* **saufen**

saugen /'zaugn̩/ **1** *tr. V.* (a) *auch unr.* suck; *s. auch* **Finger b;** (b) *auch itr.* (staub~) vacuum; hoover (coll.). **2** *regelm.* (*auch unr.*) *itr. V.* **an etw.** (*Dat.*) ~: suck [at] sth.. **3** *unr.* (*auch regelm.*) *refl. V.* **sich voll etw.** ~: become soaked with sth.

säugen /'zɔygn̩/ *tr. V.* suckle

Sauger *der;* ~s, ~ (a) (auf Flaschen) teat; (b) (Saugheber) siphon

Säuger /'zɔygɐ/ *der;* ~s, ~, **Säuge·tier** *das* (Zool.) mammal

saug·fähig *Adj.* absorbent

Säugling /'zɔyklɪŋ/ *der;* ~s, ~**e** baby; infant

Säuglings-: ~**alter** *das; o. Pl.* infancy; babyhood; ~**pflege** *die* baby care; ~**schwester** *die* infant *or* baby nurse

Saug·napf *der* (Zool.) sucker

Sau·haufen *der* (salopp abwertend) bunch of layabouts (sl.)

säuisch /'zɔyɪʃ/ (salopp) **1** *Adj.* (a) (abwertend: unanständig) obscene ‹*phone call*›; (b) (stark, groß) hellish (coll.). **2** *adv.* (sehr) hellishly (coll.)

sau·kalt *Adj.* (salopp) bloody cold (Brit. sl.); damn cold (coll.)

Sau·laden *der* (salopp abwertend) dump (coll.)

Säule /'zɔylə/ *die;* ~, ~**n** column; (nur als Stütze, auch fig.) pillar

Säulen-: ~**gang** *der* colonnade; ~**halle** *die* columned hall

Saum /zaum/ *der;* ~[e]s, **Säume** /'zɔymə/ hem

Sau·magen *der* (Kochk.) stuffed pig's stomach

sau·mäßig (salopp) **1** *Adj.* (a) (sehr groß) **das ist eine** ~**e Arbeit/Hitze** that's a hell of a job/temperature (coll.); ~**es Glück haben** be damned lucky (coll.); (b) (abwertend: schlecht) lousy (coll.). **2** *adv.* (a) (sehr) damned (coll.); (b) (abwertend: schlecht) lousily (coll.)

säumen /'zɔymən/ *tr. V.* hem; (fig. geh.) line

säumig *Adj.* (geh.) tardy; dilatory

Sauna /'zauna/ *die;* ~, ~s *od.* **Saunen** sauna

Säure /'zɔyrə/ *die;* ~, ~**n** (a) *o. Pl.* (von Früchten) sourness; tartness; (von Wein, Essig) acidity; (von Soßen) sharpness; (b) (Chemie) acid

säure-: ~**arm** *Adj.* low in acid *postpos.;* ~**beständig** *Adj.* acid-resistant; ~**frei** *Adj.* acid-free

*Saure·gurken·zeit, Saure-Gurken-Zeit *die* (ugs.) silly season (Brit.)

säure·haltig *Adj.* acid[ic]

Saurier /'zaʊriɐ̯/ *der;* ~s, ~: large prehistoric reptile

Saus /zaʊs/ *in* **in ~ und Braus leben** live the high life

säuseln /'zɔyzln̩/ **1** *itr. V.* ⟨*leaves etc.*⟩ rustle; ⟨*wind*⟩ murmur. **2** *tr. V.* (iron.: sagen) whisper

sausen *itr. V.* (a) ⟨*wind*⟩ whistle; ⟨*storm*⟩ roar; ⟨*head, ears*⟩ buzz; ⟨*propeller, engine, etc.*⟩ whirr; (b) *mit sein* (fahren, gehen) ⟨*person*⟩ rush; ⟨*vehicle*⟩ roar; ⟨*whip, bullet, etc.*⟩ whistle; **einen Plan ~ lassen** (salopp) not bother to follow up a plan; **ein Geschäft ~ lassen** (salopp) let a business deal go; **ein Konzert ~ lassen** (salopp) give a concert a miss

*sausen|lassen ⇨ sausen b

Sau·wetter *das* (salopp abwertend) lousy weather (coll.)

sau·wohl *Adj.* **sich ~ fühlen** (salopp) feel bloody (Brit. sl.) or (coll.) damn good or great

Savanne /za'vanə/ *die;* ~, ~n savannah

Saxophon /zakso'foːn/ *das;* ~s, ~e saxophone

S-Bahn /'ɛs-/ *die* city and suburban railway; S-bahn

S-Bahn-: **~hof** *der,* **~-Station** *die* S-bahn station; **~-Zug** *der* city and suburban train; S-bahn train

SB- /ɛs'beː-/: **~-Laden** *der* self-service shop; **~-Tank-stelle** *die* self-service petrol (Brit.) or (Amer.) gasoline station

sch /ʃ/ *Interj.* (a) (ruhig) sh[h]; hush; (b) (weg da) shoo

Schabe /'ʃaːbə/ *die;* ~, ~n cockroach

Schabe·fleisch *das* minced beef

schaben **1** *tr. V.* (a) (schälen) scrape ⟨*carrots, potatoes, etc.*⟩; (glätten) shave ⟨*leather, hide, etc.*⟩; plane ⟨*wood, surface, etc.*⟩; (b) (scheuern) rub; (c) (entfernen) scrape. **2** *itr. V.* scrape; **an/auf etw.** (*Dat.*) ~: scrape against sth./scrape sth.

Schaber *der;* ~s, ~: scraper

Schabernack /'ʃaːbɐnak/ *der;* ~[e]s, ~e (a) (Streich) prank; **jmdm. einen ~ spielen, mit jmdm. seinen ~ treiben** play a prank on sb.; (b) *o. Pl.* (Scherz, Spaß) **aus ~ etw. tun** do sth. for a joke

schäbig /'ʃɛːbɪç/ **1** *Adj.* (a) (abgenutzt) shabby; (b) (jämmerlich, gering) pathetic; miserable; **~e Gehälter** paltry wages; (c) (gemein) shabby; mean. **2** *adv.* (a) (abgenutzt) shabbily; (b) (jämmerlich) miserably; **~ bezahlen** pay poorly; (c) (gemein) meanly

Schäbigkeit *die;* ~ shabbiness; (des Gehalts) paltriness

Schablone /ʃa'bloːnə/ *die;* ~, ~n (a) pattern; (b) **in ~n denken** (fig. abwertend) think in stereotypes

schablonen·haft **1** *Adj.* stereotyped ⟨*thinking*⟩. **2** *adv.* ⟨*think, argue, etc.*⟩ in a stereotyped manner

Schach /ʃax/ *das;* ~s, ~s (a) *o. Pl.* (Spiel) chess; (b) (Stellung) check; **~ bieten** give check; **dem Gegner ~ bieten** check the opponent; **jmdn./etw. in ~ halten** (fig. ugs.) keep sb./sth. in check; *s. auch* matt **1** e

Schach·brett *das* chessboard

schachern *itr. V.* haggle (**um** over)

schach-, Schach-: **~figur** *die* chess piece; chessman; **~matt** *Adj.* (a) (Schachspiel) **~matt!** checkmate; **~matt sein** be checkmated; **jmdn. ~matt setzen** checkmate sb.; (fig.) render sb. powerless; (b) (ugs.: erschöpft) exhausted; **~spiel** *das* (a) *o. Pl.* (Spiel) chess; (das Spielen) chess-playing; (b) (Brett und Figuren) chess set

Schacht /ʃaxt/ *der;* ~[e]s, **Schächte** /'ʃɛçtə/ shaft

Schachtel /'ʃaxtl̩/ *die;* ~, ~n (a) box; **eine ~ Zigaretten** a packet or (Amer.) pack of cigarettes; (b) **alte ~** (salopp abwertend) old bag (sl. derog.)

Schachtel·halm *der* (Bot.) horsetail

Schach·zug *der* move [in chess]; (fig.) move

schade /'ʃaːdə/ *Adj.; nicht attr.* **[wie] ~!** [what a] pity or shame; **das ist [sehr] ~!** that's a [terrible] pity or shame; **[es ist] ~ um jmdn./etw.** it's a pity or shame about sb./ sth.; **für jmdn./für** *od.* **zu etw. zu ~ sein** be too good for sb./sth.

Schädel /'ʃɛːdl̩/ *der;* ~s, ~ (a) ▶ 326 | skull; (Kopf) head; **jmdm. eins auf** *od.* **über den ~ geben** (ugs.) hit or

knock sb. over the head; **mir brummt der ~** (ugs.) my head is throbbing; **einen dicken** *od.* **harten ~ haben** (fig.) be stubborn or pigheaded; (b) (fig.: Verstand) **streng deinen ~ mal an!** tax your brains a bit; **es geht** *od.* **will nicht in seinen ~ [hinein], dass** ... (ugs.) he can't get it into his head that ...

Schädel-: **~basis·bruch** *der* ▶ 329 | (Med.) basal skull fracture; **~bruch** *der* ▶ 329 | (Med.) skull fracture

schaden *itr. V.* **jmdm./einer Sache ~:** damage or harm sb./sth.; **Rauchen schadet der Gesundheit/dir** smoking damages your health/is bad for you; **jmds. Ansehen [sehr] ~:** do [great] damage to sb.'s reputation; **das schadet nichts** (ugs.) that doesn't matter; (ist ganz gut) that won't do any harm

Schaden *der;* ~s, **Schäden** /'ʃɛːdn̩/ (a) damage *no pl., no indef. art.;* **ein kleiner/großer ~:** little/major damage; **jmdm.** [einen] **~ zufügen** harm sb.; **das Haus weist einige Schäden auf** the house has some defects; **zu ~ kommen** (verletzt werden) be hurt or injured; (b) (Nachteil) disadvantage; **zu ~ kommen** suffer; be adversely affected

schaden-, Schaden-: **~ersatz** *der* damages *pl.;* **~freude** *die o. Pl.* malicious pleasure; ..., **sagte er voller ~freude** ... he said gloatingly; **~froh 1** *Adj.* gloating; **~froh sein** gloat; **2** *adv.* with malicious pleasure

schadhaft /'ʃaːthaft/ *Adj.* defective

schädigen /'ʃɛːdɪɡn̩/ *tr. V.* damage ⟨*health, reputation, interests*⟩; harm, hurt ⟨*person*⟩; cause losses to ⟨*firm, industry, etc.*⟩

Schädigung *die;* ~: damage *no pl., no indef. art.* (Gen. to)

schädlich /'ʃɛːtlɪç/ *Adj.* harmful; **~e Folgen** damaging or detrimental consequences

Schädlichkeit *die;* ~: harmfulness

Schädling /'ʃɛːtlɪŋ/ *der;* ~s, ~e pest

Schädlings-: **~bekämpfung** *die* pest control; **~bekämpfungsmittel** *das* pesticide

schadlos *Adj.* **in sich an jmdm./etw. ~ halten** take advantage of sb./sth.

Schad·stoff *der* harmful chemical

schadstoff·arm *Adj.* (bes. Kfz-W.) low in harmful substances *postpos.;* clean-exhaust ⟨*vehicle*⟩; (mit Katalysator) ⟨*vehicle*⟩ with exhaust emission control

Schaf /ʃaːf/ *das;* ~[e]s, ~e (a) sheep; *s. auch* **schwarz b;** (b) (ugs.: Dummkopf) twit (Brit. coll.); idiot (coll.)

Schaf·bock *der* ram

Schäfchen /'ʃɛːfçən/ *das;* ~s, ~ (a) [little] sheep; (Lamm) lamb; **sein[e] ~ ins Trockene bringen** (ugs.) take care of number one (coll.); (b) *Pl.* (ugs.: Schutzbefohlene) flock *sing. or pl.*

Schäfer *der;* ~s, ~: ▶ 85 | shepherd

Schäfer·hund *der* sheepdog; **[deutscher] ~:** Alsatian (Brit.); German shepherd

Schäfer·stündchen *das* lovers' tryst

Schaf·fell *das* sheepskin

schaffen /'ʃafn̩/ **1** *unr. tr. V.* (a) (er~) create; **für jmdn./ etw.** *od.* **zu jmdm./etw. wie geschaffen sein** be made or perfect for sb./sth.; (b) *auch regelm.* (herstellen) create ⟨*conditions, jobs, situation, etc.*⟩; make ⟨*room, space, fortune*⟩; **klare Verhältnisse ~:** clear things up; straighten things out. **2** *tr. V.* (a) (bewältigen) manage; **es ~, etw. zu tun** manage to do sth.; **wenn wir uns beeilen, ~ wir es vielleicht noch** we might still make it if we hurry; **er hat die Prüfung nicht geschafft** (ugs.) he didn't pass the exam; (b) (ugs.: erschöpfen) wear out; **die Hitze/Arbeit hat mich geschafft** the heat/work took it out of me; (c) **etw. aus etw./in etw.** (*Akk.*) **~:** get sth. out of/into sth.. **3** *itr. V.* (a) (südd.: arbeiten) work; (b) **sich** (*Dat.*) **zu ~ machen** busy oneself; **mit ihm will ich nichts zu ~ haben** I don't want to have anything to do with him; **jmdm. zu ~ machen** cause sb. trouble

Schaffen *das;* ~s (geh.) work; **im Zenit seines ~s** at the peak of his creative work

Schaffens·kraft *die o. Pl.* (geh.) energy for work; (eines Künstlers) creativity; creative power

Schaffner /ˈʃafnɐ/ *der;* ~s ~ (im Bus) conductor; (im Zug) guard (Brit.); conductor (Amer.)
Schaffnerin *die;* ~, ~nen (im Bus) conductress (Brit.); (im Zug) guard (Brit.); conductress (Amer.)
Schaffung *die;* ~: creation
Schaf-: ~**garbe** *die* yarrow; ~**herde** *die* flock of sheep; ~**hirt** *der* shepherd
Schafott /ʃaˈfɔt/ *das;* ~[e]s, ~e scaffold
Schafs-: ~**käse** *der* sheep's milk cheese; ~**kopf** **der** (a) *o. Pl.* (Kartenspiel) sheep's head; (b) (ugs.: Trottel) dope (coll.); idiot (coll.)
Schaf·stall *der* sheep-fold
Schaft /ʃaft/ *der;* ~[e]s, **Schäfte** /ˈʃɛftə/ (a) shaft; (eines Gewehrs usw.) stock; (b) (am Stiefel) leg
Schaft·stiefel *der* high boot
Schakal /ʃaˈkaːl/ *der;* ~s, ~e jackal
schäkern *itr. V.* (veralt.) (a) (spaßen) fool about; (b) (flirten) flirt
schal /ʃaːl/ *Adj.* stale ⟨*drink, taste, joke*⟩; empty ⟨*words, feeling*⟩
Schal *der;* ~s, ~s *od.* ~e scarf
Schale /ˈʃaːlə/ *die;* ~, ~n (a) (Obst~) skin; (abgeschält) peel *no pl.;* (b) (Nuss~, Eier~, Muschel~ usw.) shell; (c) (Schüssel) bowl; (flacher) dish; (Waag~) pan; scale; (d) **sich in** ~ **werfen** *od.* **schmeißen** (ugs.) get dressed [up] to the nines
schälen /ˈʃɛːlən/ **1** *tr. V.* peel ⟨*fruit, vegetable*⟩; shell ⟨*egg, nut, pea*⟩; skin ⟨*tomato, almond*⟩; **einen Baumstamm** ~: remove the bark from a tree trunk; **etw. aus etw.** ~: get sth. out of sth. **2** *refl. V.* ⟨*person, skin, nose, etc.*⟩ peel; **du schälst dich am Rücken** your back is peeling
Schalk /ʃalk/ *der;* ~[e]s, ~e *od.* **Schälke** /ˈʃɛlkə/ rogue; prankster; **jmdm. sitzt der** ~ **im Nacken** (fig.) sb. is really roguish or mischievous
schalkhaft (geh.) **1** *Adj.* roguish; mischievous. **2** *adv.* roguishly; mischievously
Schall /ʃal/ *der;* ~[e]s, ~e *od.* **Schälle** /ˈʃɛlə/ (a) (geh.) sound; **mit lautem** ~: loudly; **Name ist** ~ **und Rauch** names mean nothing; (b) **der** ~ (Physik) sound
schall-, Schall-: ~**dämmend** *Adj.* sound-deadening; sound-absorbing; ~**dämpfer** *der* (a) silencer; (b) (Musik) mute; ~**dicht** *Adj.* soundproof
schallen regelm., auch unr. *itr. V.* ring out; (nachhallen) resound; echo; ~**des Gelächter** ringing laughter; ~**d lachen** roar with laughter
Schall-: ~**geschwindigkeit** *die* speed or velocity of sound; ~**mauer** *die* sound or sonic barrier; ~**platte** *die* record
Schallplatten-: ⇒ **Platten-**
Schall·welle *die* (Physik) sound wave
Schalotte /ʃaˈlɔtə/ *die;* ~, ~n shallot
schalt /ʃalt/ *1. u. 3. Pers. Sg. Prät. v.* **schelten**
schalten /ˈʃaltn̩/ **1** *tr. V.* (a) switch; (b) (Elektrot.: verbinden) connect; (c) (Zeitungsw.) place ⟨*advertisement*⟩. **2** *itr. V.* (a) (Schalter betätigen) switch, turn (**auf** + Akk. to); (b) ⟨*machine*⟩ switch (**auf** + Akk. to); ⟨*traffic light*⟩ change (**auf** + Akk. to); (c) (im Auto) change [gear]; **in den 4. Gang** ~: change into fourth gear; (d) **sie kann** ~ **und walten, wie sie will, sie kann frei** ~ **und walten** she can manage things as she pleases; (e) (ugs.: begreifen) twig (coll.); catch on (coll.)
Schalter /ˈʃaltɐ/ *der;* ~s, ~ (a) (Strom~) switch; (b) (Post~, Bank~ usw.) counter; (c) (am Fahrrad) gear lever
Schalter-: ~**beamte** *der* counter clerk; (im Bahnhof) ticket clerk; ~**halle** *die* hall; (im Bahnhof) booking-hall (Brit.); ticket office
Schalt-: ~**fläche** *die* (DV) button; ~**getriebe** *das* (Kfz-W.) [manual] gearbox; ~**hebel** *der* gear[shift] lever; ~**jahr** *das* leap year; **alle** ~**jahre** **[ein]mal** (ugs.) once in a blue moon; ~**knüppel** *der* [floor-mounted] gear lever
Schaltung *die;* ~, ~en (a) (Rundfunk: Verbindung) link-up; (b) (Gang~) manual gear change; (c) (Elektrot.) circuit; wiring system

Schalt-: ~**werk** *das* changer; derailleur; ~**zug** *der* gear cable
Scham /ʃaːm/ *die;* ~ shame; **nur keine falsche** ~! no need for any false modesty
schämen /ˈʃɛːmən/ *refl. V.* be ashamed (*Gen.,* **für, wegen** of); **du solltest dich [was** (ugs.)] ~! you [really] should be ashamed of yourself; **schäm dich** shame on you
Scham·gefühl *das; o. Pl.* sense of shame
schamhaft 1 *Adj.* bashful. **2** *adv.* bashfully
scham·los 1 *Adj.* (a) (skrupellos, dreist) shameless; barefaced, shameless ⟨*lie, slander*⟩; (b) (unanständig) indecent ⟨*gesture, remark, etc.*⟩; shameless ⟨*person*⟩. **2** *adv.* (a) (skrupellos, dreist) shamelessly; (b) (unanständig) indecently
Scham·losigkeit *die;* ~, ~en: ⇒ **schamlos 1 a, b:** shamelessness; indecency
Schampon /ˈʃampɔn/ ⇒ **Shampoo**
schamponieren /ʃampoˈniːrən/ *tr. V.* shampoo
scham·rot *Adj.* red with shame *postpos.*
Scham·röte *die:* **ihm stieg die** ~ **ins Gesicht** he blushed with shame
Schande /ˈʃandə/ *die;* ~: disgrace; shame; **es ist eine [wahre]** ~: it is a[n absolute] disgrace; **jmdm./einer Sache [keine]** ~ **machen** [not] disgrace sb./sth.; bring [no] disgrace or shame on sb./sth.
schänden /ˈʃɛndn̩/ *tr. V.* defile ⟨*memorial, work of art, etc.*⟩; desecrate, defile ⟨*holy place, grave, relic*⟩; violate ⟨*corpse*⟩
schändlich 1 *Adj.* shameful; disgraceful. **2** *adv.* shamefully; disgracefully
Schändlichkeit *die;* ~, ~en (a) *o. Pl.* shamefulness; disgracefulness; (b) (Tat) shameful action
Schand·tat *die* disgraceful or abominable deed; **zu jeder** ~ *od.* **allen** ~**en bereit sein** (ugs. scherzh.) be game for anything
Schändung *die;* ~, ~en ⇒ **schänden:** desecration; defilement
Schank·wirtschaft *die* public house (Brit.); bar (Amer.)
Schar /ʃaːɐ/ *die;* ~, ~en crowd; horde; (von Vögeln) flock; **in [hellen]** ~**en** in swarms or droves
Schäre /ˈʃɛːrə/ *die;* ~, ~n skerry
scharen *tr., refl. V.* gather (**um** around)
scharen·weise *Adv.* in swarms or hordes
scharf /ʃarf/; **schärfer** /ˈʃɛrfɐ/, **schärfst...** /ˈʃɛrfst.../ **1** *Adj.* (a) sharp; (b) (stark gewürzt, brennend, stechend) hot; strong ⟨*drink, vinegar, etc.*⟩; caustic ⟨*chemical*⟩; pungent, acrid ⟨*smell*⟩; (c) (durchdringend) shrill; (hell) harsh; biting ⟨*wind, air, etc.*⟩; sharp ⟨*frost*⟩; (d) (deutlich wahrnehmbar) keen; sharp; (e) (deutlich hervortretend) sharp ⟨*contours, features, nose, photograph*⟩; (f) (schonungslos) tough, fierce ⟨*resistance, competition, etc.*⟩; sharp ⟨*criticism, remark, words, etc.*⟩; strong, fierce ⟨*opponent, protest, etc.*⟩; severe, harsh ⟨*censure, law, measure, etc.*⟩; fierce ⟨*dog*⟩; **eine** ~**e Zunge haben** have a sharp tongue; (g) (schnell) fast; hard ⟨*ride, gallop, etc.*⟩; (h) (explosiv) live; (Ballspiele) powerful ⟨*shot*⟩; ~**e Schüsse abgeben** fire live bullets; (i) **das** ~**e S** (bes. österr.) the German letter 'ß'; (j) (ugs.: geil) sexy ⟨*girl, clothes, pictures, etc.*⟩; randy ⟨*fellow, thoughts, etc.*⟩; (k) ~ **auf jmdn./etw. sein** (ugs.) really fancy sb. (coll.) /be really keen on sth. **2** *adv.* (a) ~ **würzen/abschmecken** season/flavour highly; ~ **riechen** smell pungent or strong; (b) (durchdringend) shrilly; (hell) harshly; (kalt) bitingly; (c) (deutlich wahrnehmbar) ⟨*listen, watch, etc.*⟩ closely, intently; ⟨*think, consider, etc.*⟩ hard; ~ **aufpassen** pay close attention; (d) (deutlich hervortretend) sharply; (e) (schonungslos) ⟨*attack, criticize, etc.*⟩ sharply, strongly; ⟨*contradict, oppose, etc.*⟩ strongly, fiercely; ⟨*watch, observe, etc.*⟩ closely; (f) (schnell) fast; ~ **bremsen** brake hard or sharply; (g) ~ **schießen** shoot with live ammunition
Scharf·blick *der; o. Pl.* perspicacity
Schärfe /ˈʃɛrfə/ *die;* ~, ~n (a) *o. Pl.* sharpness; (b) *o. Pl.* (von Geschmack) hotness; (von Chemikalien) causticity; (von Geruch) pungency; (c) *o. Pl.* (Intensität) shrillness; (von Licht, Farbe usw.) harshness; (des Windes) bitterness; (des Frostes) sharpness; (d) *o. Pl.* ⇒ **scharf 1 d:** sharpness; keenness; (e) *o. Pl.* (Klarheit) clarity; sharpness; (f) *o. Pl.* ⇒ **scharf 1**

---

*alte Schreibung (vgl. Hinweise auf S. xvi–xvii)

f: toughness; ferocity; sharpness; strength; **(g)** (Heftigkeit) harshness

schärfen 1 *tr. V.* (auch fig.) sharpen. **2** *refl. V.* become sharper *or* keener

schärfer ⇨ **scharf**

scharf-, Scharf-: ∼**kantig** *Adj.* sharp-edged; ∼|**machen** *tr. V.* (ugs.) stir up; **einen Hund** ∼**machen** urge a dog on; ∼**schütze** *der* marksman; ∼**sichtig** /∼zɪçtɪç/ *Adj.* sharp-sighted; perspicacious; ∼**sinn** *der o. Pl.* astuteness; acumen; ∼**sinnig 1** *Adj.* astute; **2** *adv.* astutely

schärfst... ⇨ **scharf**

scharfzüngig /-tsʏnɪç/ **1** *Adj.* sharp-tongued. **2** *adv.* sharply

Scharlach /'ʃarlax/ *der;* ∼**s** ▶ 329 | (Med.) scarlet fever

Scharlatan /'ʃarlatan/ *der;* ∼**s**, ∼**e** (abwertend) charla-tan

Scharnier /ʃar'niːɐ̯/ *das;* ∼**s**, ∼**e** hinge

Schärpe /'ʃɛrpə/ *die;* ∼, ∼**n** sash

scharren /'ʃarən/ **1** *itr. V.* **(a)** scrape; **mit den Füßen** ∼: scrape one's feet; **(b)** (wühlen) scratch. **2** *tr. V.* scrape, scratch out ⟨*hole, hollow, etc.*⟩

Scharte /'ʃartə/ *die;* ∼, ∼**n** nick

schartig *Adj.* nicked; jagged

Schaschlik /'ʃaʃlɪk/ *der od. das;* ∼**s**, ∼**s** (Kochk.) shash-lik

Schatten /'ʃatn/ *der;* ∼**s**, ∼ **(a)** shadow; **man kann nicht über seinen [eigenen]** ∼ **springen** a leopard cannot change its spots (prov.); **(b)** *o. Pl.* (schattige Stelle) shade; **in jmds.** ∼ **stehen** (fig.) be in sb.'s shadow; **jmdn./ etw. in den** ∼ **stellen** (fig.) put sb./sth. in the shade; **(c)** (dunkle Stelle, fig.) shadow

schattenhaft *Adj.* shadowy

Schatten-: ∼**morelle** /∼morɛlə/ *die;* ∼, ∼**n** mor-ello cherry; ∼**seite** *die* shady side; **die** ∼**seiten des Lebens kennen lernen** (fig.) get to know the dark side of life

schattig *Adj.* shady

Schatulle /ʃa'tʊlə/ *die;* ∼, ∼**n** casket

Schatz /ʃats/ *der;* ∼**es**, **Schätze** /'ʃɛtsə/ **(a)** treasure *no indef. art.;* **(b)** (ugs.: Liebling) love (coll.); darling; **(c)** (ugs.: hilfsbereiter Mensch) treasure (coll.)

schätzen /'ʃɛtsn̩/ **1** *tr. V.* **(a)** estimate; **wie alt schätzt du ihn?** how old do you think he is?; **sich glücklich** ∼: deem oneself lucky; **grob geschätzt** at a rough estimate; **ein Haus** ∼: value a house; **(b)** (ugs.: annehmen) reckon; think; *or* (würdigen, hoch achten) **jmdn.** ∼: hold sb. in high regard *or* esteem; **etw. zu** ∼ **wissen** appreciate sth.; **ich weiß es zu** ∼, **dass** ...: I appreciate the fact that ...; **etw.** ∼ **lernen** come to appreciate *or* value **2** *itr. V.* guess; **schätz mal** guess; have a guess

*schätzen|lernen ⇨ **schätzen 1 c**

Schatz·meister *der* treasurer

Schätzung *die;* ∼, ∼**en** estimate; **nach grober/vor-sichtiger** ∼: at a rough/cautious estimate

Schau /ʃau/ *die;* ∼, ∼**en (a)** (Ausstellung) exhibition; **(b)** (Vorführung) show; **eine** ∼ **machen** *od.* **abziehen** (ugs.) (sich in Szene setzen) put on a show; (sich aufspielen) show off; (sich lautstark ereifern) make a scene *or* fuss; **jmdm. die** ∼ **stehlen** steal the show from sb.; **(c) jmdm./etw. zur** ∼ **stellen** exhibit *or* display sb./sth.; (fig.) display sb./sth.; **etw. zur** ∼ **tragen** make a show of sth.

Schau·bild *das* chart

Schauder /'ʃaudɐ/ *der;* ∼**s**, ∼ (vor Kälte, Angst) shiver; (vor Angst) shudder; **mir lief ein** ∼ **den Rücken hinunter** a shiver/shudder ran down my spine

schauderhaft 1 *Adj.* terrible; dreadful; awful. **2** *adv.* terribly; dreadfully

schaudern *itr. V.* (vor Kälte) shiver; (vor Angst) shudder; *unpers.* **es schauderte ihn** he shivered/shuddered

schauen (bes. südd., österr., schweiz.) **1** *itr. V.* **(a)** look; **auf jmdn./etw.** ∼: look at sb./sth.; (fig.) look to sb./sth.; **um sich** ∼: look around [one]; **schau, schau!** well, well; **schau [mal], ich finde, du solltest** ...: look, I think you should ...; **(b)** (sich kümmern um) **nach jmdm./etw.** ∼:

take *or* have a look at sb./sth.; **(c)** (achten) **auf etw.** (*Akk.*) ∼: set store by sth.; **er schaut darauf, dass alle pünktlich sind** he sets store by everybody being punctual; **(d)** (ugs.: sich bemühen) **schau, dass du** ...: see *or* mind that you ...; **(e)** (nachsehen) have a look. **2** *tr. V.* **Fernsehen** ∼: watch television

Schauer *der;* ∼**s**, ∼ shower

Schauer·geschichte *die* horror story

schauerlich 1 *Adj.* **(a)** horrifying; ghastly; **(b)** (ugs.: fürchterlich) terrible (coll.); dreadful (coll.). **2** *adv.* (ugs.: fürchter-lich) dreadfully (coll.), terribly (coll.)

Schaufel /'ʃaufl/ *die;* ∼, ∼**n** shovel; (für Mehl usw.) scoop; (Kehr∼) dustpan; **zwei** ∼**n Erde** two shovelfuls of soil

schaufeln /'ʃaufl̩n/ *tr. V.* shovel; (graben) dig

Schau·fenster *das* shop window

Schaufenster-: ∼**aus·lage** *die* window display; ∼**bummel** *der* window-shopping expedition; **einen** ∼**bummel machen** go window-shopping; ∼**puppe** *die* mannequin

Schau-: ∼**kampf** *der* (Boxen) exhibition fight; ∼**kasten** *der* display case; showcase

Schaukel /'ʃaukl/ *die;* ∼, ∼**n (a)** swing; **(b)** (Wippe) see-saw

schaukeln 1 *itr. V.* **(a)** swing; (im Schaukelstuhl) rock; **auf einem Stuhl** ∼: rock one's chair backwards and for-wards; **(b)** (sich hin und her bewegen) sway [to and fro]; (sich auf und ab bewegen) ⟨*ship, boat*⟩ pitch and toss; ⟨*vehicle*⟩ bump [up and down]; *unpers.* **es hat ganz schön ge-schaukelt** (auf dem Boot) the boat pitched and tossed quite a bit. **2** *tr. V.* **(a)** rock; **ein Kind auf den Knien** ∼: dandle a child on one's knee; **(b)** (ugs.: fahren) take; **jmdn. durch die Gegend** ∼: drive sb. round the area; **(c)** (ugs.: bewerkstelligen) manage

Schaukel-: ∼**pferd** *das* rocking horse; ∼**stuhl** *der* rocking chair

schau·lustig *Adj.* curious

Schau·lustige *der/die; adj. Dekl.* curious onlooker

Schaum /ʃaum/ *der;* ∼**s**, **Schäume** /'ʃɔymə/ **(a)** foam; (von Seife usw.) lather; (von Getränken, Suppen usw.) froth; **etw. zu** ∼ **schlagen** (Kochk.) beat sth. until frothy; **(b)** (Geifer) foam; froth; ∼ **vor dem Mund haben** (auch fig.) foam *or* froth at the mouth

Schaum·bad *das* bubble bath

schäumen /'ʃɔymən/ *itr. V.* foam; froth; ⟨*soap etc.*⟩ lather; ⟨*beer, fizzy drink, etc.*⟩ froth [up]

Schaum·gummi *der* foam rubber

schaumig *Adj.* frothy ⟨*drink, dessert, etc.*⟩; sudsy, la-thery ⟨*water*⟩

Schaum-: ∼**krone** *die* **(a)** (auf Wellen) white crest; **(b)** (auf Bier) head [of froth]; ∼**stoff** *der* [plastic] foam; ∼**wein** *der* sparkling wine

Schau·platz *der* scene

schaurig /'ʃaurɪç/ **1** *Adj.* **(a)** dreadful; frightful; (unheim-lich) eerie; **(b)** (ugs.: grässlich, geschmacklos) hideous; dreadful (coll.). **2** *adv.* **(a)** (fürchterlich) dreadfully; (unheimlich) eerily; **(b)** (ugs.: grässlich, geschmacklos) hideously; horribly (coll.); **(c)** (ugs.: überaus) dreadfully (coll.)

Schau-: ∼**spiel** *das* **(a)** *o. Pl.* (Drama) drama *no art.;* **(b)** (ernstes Stück) play; **(c)** (geh.: Anblick) spectacle; ∼**spie-ler** *der* ▶ 85 | (auch fig.) actor; ∼**spielerin** *die* (auch fig.) actress

schauspielern *itr. V.* (ugs.) **(a)** (als Schauspieler) act; **(b)** (fig.) play-act

Schau-: ∼**steller** /-ʃtɛlɐ/ *der;* ∼**s**, ∼: ▶ 85 | show-man; ∼**tafel** *die* illustrated chart

Scheck /ʃɛk/ *der;* ∼**s**, ∼**s** ▶ 216 | cheque

Scheckheft *das* chequebook

scheckig *Adj.* ⇨ **gescheckt**

Scheck·karte *die* ▶ 216 | cheque card

scheel /ʃeːl/ (ugs.) **1** *Adj.* disapproving; (misstrauisch) suspi-cious; (neidisch) envious; jealous. **2** *adv.* disapprovingly; (misstrauisch) suspiciously; (neidisch) enviously; jealously

scheffeln *tr. V.* (ugs.) rake in (coll.) ⟨*money etc.*⟩; pile up, accumulate ⟨*medals, awards, etc.*⟩

Scheibe /'ʃaibə/ *die;* ~, ~**n** (a) disc; (Sportjargon: Puck) puck; (Schieß~) target; (b) (abgeschnittene ~) slice; **etw. in** ~**n schneiden** slice sth. up; cut sth. [up] into slices; **sich** (*Dat.*) **von jmdm./etw. eine** ~ **abschneiden können** (fig.) be able to learn a thing or two from sb./sth.; (c) (Glas~) pane; (Fenster~) [window-] pane; (Windschutz~) windscreen (Brit.); windshield (Amer.)

Scheiben-: ~**bremse** *die* (Kfz-W.) disc brake; ~**kleister** *der* (ugs. verhüll.) ~**kleister!** blast [it]! (coll.); damn it! (coll.); ~**wischer** *der* windscreen-wiper

Scheich /ʃaiç/ *der;* ~[e]s, ~**s** *od.* ~**e** sheikh

Scheide /'ʃaidə/ *die;* ~, ~**n** (a) sheath; (b) ▶326◀ (Anat.) vagina

scheiden 1 *unr. tr. V.* (a) dissolve ⟨*marriage*⟩; divorce ⟨*married couple*⟩; **sich** ~ **lassen** get divorced or get a divorce; (b) (geh.: trennen) divide; separate; (c) (geh.: unterscheiden) distinguish. 2 *unr. itr. V.; mit sein* (geh.) (a) (auseinander gehen) part; (b) (sich entfernen) depart; leave; **von jmdm.** ~: part from sb.; **aus dem Dienst/Amt** ~: retire from service/one's post or office; **aus dem Leben** ~: depart this life

Scheide·weg *der in* **am** *od.* **an einem** ~ **stehen** face a crucial decision

Scheidung *die;* ~, ~**en** divorce; **die** ~ **einreichen** file [a petition] for divorce; **in** ~ **leben** be in the process of getting a divorce

Schein /ʃain/ *der;* ~[e]s, ~**e** (a) *o. Pl.* (Licht~) light; **der** ~ **des brennenden Hauses/der sinkenden Sonne** the glow of the burning house/setting sun; (b) *o. Pl.* (An~) appearances *pl., no art.;* (Täuschung) pretence; **den** ~ **wahren** keep up appearances; **der** ~ **trügt** appearances are deceptive; **etw. nur zum** ~ **tun** [only] pretend to do sth.; make a show of doing sth.; (c) (Bescheinigung) certificate; (Gepäck~) ticket; (Tipp~) coupon; (d) ▶216◀ (Geld~) note

scheinbar 1 *Adj.* apparent; seeming. 2 *adv.* seemingly

scheinen 1 *unr. itr. V.* (a) shine; (b) (den Eindruck erwecken) seem; appear; **mir scheint, [dass]** ...: it seems or appears to me that ...; **wie es scheint** ...: apparently. 2 *unr. mod. V.* seem; appear; **jmd. scheint etw. nicht tun zu können** sb. doesn't seem or appear to be able to do sth.; sb. can't seem to do sth. (coll.)

schein-, Schein-: ~**heilig** 1 *Adj.* (heuchlerisch) hypocritical; (Nichtwissen vortäuschend) innocent; 2 *adv.* (heuchlerisch) hypocritically; (Nichtwissen vortäuschend) innocently; ~**heiligkeit** *die* hypocrisy; ~**werfer** *der* floodlight; (am Auto) headlight; (im Theater, Museum usw.) spotlight; ~**werfer·licht** *das* floodlight; (des Autos) headlights *pl.;* (im Theater, Museum usw.) spotlight [beam]

scheiß-, Scheiß- (derb) bloody (Brit. sl.)

Scheiße /'ʃaisə/ *die;* ~ (derb, auch fig.) shit (coarse); crap (coarse); **[bis zum Hals] in der** ~ **sitzen** *od.* **stecken** (fig.) be in the shit (coarse); be up shit creek (coarse)

scheißen *unr. itr. V.* (derb) [have or (Amer.) take a] shit (coarse); **auf jmdn./etw.** ~ (fig.) not give a shit (coarse) or (sl.) damn about sb./sth.

Scheit /ʃait/ *der;* ~[e]s, ~**e** *od.* ~**er** ⇒ **Holzscheit**

Scheitel /'ʃaitl/ *der;* ~**s**, ~ (a) parting; **einen** ~ **ziehen** make a parting; **vom** ~ **bis zur Sohle** from head to toe; (b) (höchster Punkt, Math.) vertex; (eines Winkels) apex; vertex

scheiteln *tr. V.* part ⟨*hair*⟩

Scheiter·haufen *der:* **auf dem** ~ **sterben/verbrannt werden** die/be burned at the stake

scheitern /'ʃaitɐn/ *itr. V.; mit sein* fail; ⟨*talks, marriage*⟩ break down; ⟨*plan, project*⟩ fail, fall through; **eine gescheiterte Existenz sein** be a failure

Schelf /ʃɛlf/ *der od. das;* ~**s**, ~**e** (Geogr.) continental shelf

Schellack /'ʃɛlak/ *der;* ~**s**, ~**e** shellac

Schelle /'ʃɛlə/ *die;* ~, ~**n** bell

schellen *itr. V.* (westd.) ⇒ **klingeln** a, b

Schellen·baum *der* Turkish crescent; pavillon chinois

Schell·fisch *der* haddock

Schelm /ʃɛlm/ *der;* ~[e]s, ~**e** rascal; rogue

schelmisch 1 *Adj.* roguish; mischievous. 2 *adv.* roguishly; mischievously

Schelte /'ʃɛltə/ *die;* ~, ~**n** (geh.) scolding; ~ **bekommen** be given or get a scolding

schelten (südd., geh.) 1 *unr. itr. V.* **auf** *od.* **über jmdn./etw.** ~: moan about sb./sth.; **[mit jmdm.]** ~: scold [sb.]. 2 *unr. tr. V.* (a) (tadeln) scold; (b) (geh.: nennen) call

Schema /'ʃe:ma/ *das;* ~**s**, ~**s** *od.* ~**ta** *od.* **Schemen** (a) (Muster) pattern; *s. auch* **F;** (b) (Skizze) diagram

schematisch 1 *Adj.* (a) diagrammatic; (b) (mechanisch) mechanical. 2 *adv.* (a) in diagram form; (b) (mechanisch) mechanically

Schemel /'ʃe:ml/ *der;* ~**s**, ~: stool; (südd.: Fußbank) footstool

Schemen¹ ⇒ **Schema**

Schemen² /'ʃe:mən/ *der od. das;* ~**s**, ~: shadowy figure

schemenhaft 1 *Adj.* shadowy. 2 *adv.* **etw.** ~ **sehen** see only the outline or silhouette of sth.

Schenkel /'ʃɛŋkl/ *der;* ~**s**, ~ (a) ▶326◀ thigh; (b) (Math.) side; (c) (von einer Zange, Schere) shank; (vom Zirkel) leg

schenken 1 *tr. V.* (a) give; **jmdm. etw. [zum Geburtstag]** ~: give sb. sth. or sth. to sb. [as a birthday present or for his/her birthday]; **das ist ja geschenkt!** (ugs.) it's a gift!; **jmdm./einer Sache Beachtung/Aufmerksamkeit** ~: give sb./sth. one's attention; **jmdm. das Leben** ~: spare sb.'s life; *s. auch* **Gaul;** (b) (ugs.: erlassen) **jmdm. etw.** ~: spare sb. sth.; **ihr ist im Leben nichts geschenkt worden** she has never had it easy in life. 2 *refl. V.* **sich** (*Dat.*) **etw.** ~ (ugs.) give sth. a miss

scheppern /'ʃɛpɐn/ *itr. V.* (ugs.) clank; ⟨*bell*⟩ clang; **es hat gescheppert** (hat einen Autounfall gegeben) there was a smash or crash

Scherbe /'ʃɛrbə/ *die;* ~, ~**n** fragment; **die** ~**n zusammenkehren** sweep up the [broken] pieces; **in tausend** ~**n zerspringen** be smashed to smithereens; ~**n bringen Glück** (Spr.) break a thing, mend your luck

Schere /'ʃe:rə/ *die;* ~, ~**n** (a) scissors *pl.;* **eine** ~: a pair of scissors; (b) (Zool.) claw

scheren¹ *unr. tr. V.* (kürzen) crop; (von Haar befreien) shear, clip ⟨*sheep*⟩; clip ⟨*dog*⟩

scheren² *tr., refl. V.* **sich um jmdn./etw. nicht** ~: not care about sb./sth.

scheren³ *refl. V.* **scher dich in dein Zimmer** go or get [off] to your room

Scheren·schnitt *der* silhouette

Scherereien *Pl.* (ugs.) trouble *no pl.*

Scherz /ʃɛrts/ *der;* ~**es**, ~**e** joke; **seine** ~**e mit jmdm. treiben** play jokes on sb.; **etw. aus** *od.* **zum** ~ **sagen** say sth. as a joke or in jest; ~ **beiseite** joking aside or apart

scherzen *itr. V.* joke; **über etw.** (*Akk.*) ~: joke about sth.; **mit jmdm./etw. ist nicht zu** ~ (fig.) sb./sth. is not to be trifled with

Scherz·frage *die* riddle

scherzhaft 1 *Adj.* jocular; joking *attrib.* 2 *adv.* jocularly; jokingly

scheu /ʃɔy/ 1 *Adj.* shy; timid ⟨*animal*⟩; (ehrfürchtig) awed; ~ **machen** frighten ⟨*animal*⟩; *s. auch* **Pferd.** 2 *adv.* shyly; (von Tieren) timidly

Scheu *die;* ~ (a) shyness; (von Tieren) timidity; (Ehrfurcht) awe; **ohne jede** ~: without any inhibitions

scheuchen *tr. V.* (a) (treiben) shoo; drive; (b) (fig. ugs.) force; **jmdn. zum Arzt/an die Arbeit** ~: make sb. go or urge sb. to go to the doctor/to work

scheuen 1 *tr. V.* shrink from; shun ⟨*people, light, company, etc.*⟩; **weder Kosten noch Mühe** ~: spare neither expense nor effort. 2 *refl. V.* **sich** ~, **etw. zu tun** shrink from doing sth. 3 *itr. V.* ⟨*horse*⟩ shy (**vor** + *Dat.* at)

scheuern 1 *tr., itr. V.* (a) (reinigen) scour; scrub; (b) (reiben) rub; chafe. 2 *tr. V.* (reiben an) rub. 3 *refl. V.* (reiben) **sich** (*Akk.*) **wund** ~: rub oneself raw; chafe oneself; **sich** (*Dat.*) **das Knie [wund]** ~: rub one's knee raw; chafe one's knee

Scheuer-: ~**pulver** *das* scouring powder; ~**tuch** *das; Pl.* ~**tücher** scouring cloth

---

Scheune /'ʃɔynə/ *die;* ~, ~n barn

Scheusal /'ʃɔyzal/ *das;* ~s, ~e (abwertend) monster

scheußlich /'ʃɔyslɪç/ **1** *Adj.* (a) dreadful; (b) (ugs.: äußerst unangenehm) terrible (coll.); dreadful (coll.); dreadful (coll.), ghastly (coll.) ‹*weather, taste, smell*›. **2** *adv.* (a) dreadfully; (b) (ugs.: sehr) terribly (coll.); dreadfully (coll.)

Scheußlichkeit *die;* ~, ~en (a) *o. Pl.* dreadfulness; (b) *meist Pl.* (etw. Scheußliches) dreadful thing; (Grausamkeit) atrocity

Schi /ʃiː/ *usw.* ⇒ **Ski** *usw.*

Schicht /ʃɪçt/ *die;* ~, ~en (a) layer; (Geol.) stratum; (von Farbe) coat; (sehr dünn) film; (b) (Gesellschafts~) stratum; **breite ~en [der Bevölkerung]** broad sections of the population; **in allen ~en** at all levels of society; (c) (Abschnitt eines Arbeitstages, Arbeitsgruppe) shift; **~ arbeiten** work shifts; be on shift work

Schicht·arbeiter *der* shift worker

schichten *tr. V.* stack

Schicht·wechsel *der* change of shifts; **~ ist um 6** we/they *etc.* change shifts at 6

schicht·weise *Adv.* (a) in layers; layer by layer; (b) (in Gruppen) in shifts

schick /ʃɪk/ **1** *Adj.* (a) stylish; stylish, chic ‹*clothes, fashions*›; smart ‹*woman, girl, man*›; (b) (ugs.: großartig, toll) great (coll.); fantastic (coll.). **2** *adv.* stylishly; stylishly, smartly ‹*furnished, decorated*›

Schick *der;* ~[e]s style

schicken **1** *tr. V.* send; **jmdm. etw. ~, etw. an jmdn. ~:** send sth. to sb.; send sb. sth.; **jmdn. nach Hause/in den Krieg ~:** send sb. home/to war; **jmdn. einkaufen ~:** send sb. to do the shopping. **2** *itr. V.* **nach jmdm. ~:** send for sth. **3** *refl. V.* (a) (veralt.: sich ziemen) be proper or fitting; (b) **sich in etw.** (*Akk.*) **~:** resign or reconcile oneself to sth.

Schickeria /ʃɪkə'riːa/ *die;* ~ (ugs.) smart set

Schicki[micki] /'ʃɪkɪ('mɪkɪ)/ *der;* ~s, ~s (ugs.) trendy (coll.)

schicklich (veralt.) **1** *Adj.* proper; fitting; (dezent) seemly. **2** *adv.* fittingly; (dezent) in a seemly way

Schicksal /'ʃɪkzaːl/ *das;* ~s, ~e fate; destiny; (schweres Los) fate; **das ~:** fate; destiny; **[das ist] ~** (ugs.) it's just fate; **das ~ hat es mit ihm gut gemeint** fortune smiled on him; **~ spielen** play the role of fate or destiny

schicksalhaft **1** *Adj.* fateful. **2** *adv.* **~ verbunden** linked by fate

Schicksals·schlag *der* stroke of fate

Schiebe·dach *das* sliding roof; sunroof

schieben /'ʃiːbn̩/ **1** *unr. tr. V.* (a) push; push, wheel ‹*bicycle, pram, shopping trolley*›; (drängen) push; shove; (b) (stecken) put; (gleiten lassen) slip; **den Riegel vor die Tür ~:** slip the bolt across; (c) **etw. auf jmdn./etw. ~:** blame sb./sth. for sth.; **die Schuld/die Verantwortung auf jmdn. ~:** put the blame on sb. or lay the blame at sb.'s door/lay the responsibility at sb.'s door; (d) (salopp: handeln mit) traffic in; push ‹*drugs*›. **2** *unr. refl. V.* (a) **sich zwängen) sich durch die Menge ~:** push one's way through the crowd; (b) (sich bewegen) move; **ihr Rock schob sich nach oben** her skirt slid up. **3** *unr. itr. V.* (a) push; (heftig) push; shove; (b) *mit sein* (salopp: gehen) mooch (sl.); (c) (ugs.: mit etw. handeln) **mit etw. ~:** traffic in sth.; (d) (Skat) shove

Schieber *der;* ~s, ~ (ugs.: Schwarzhändler) black market-eer

Schiebe·tür *die* sliding door

Schieb·lehre *die* (Technik) vernier [calliper] gauge

Schiebung *die;* ~, ~en (ugs.) (a) (betrügerisches Geschäft) shady deal; (b) *o. Pl.* (Begünstigung) pulling strings; (bei einer Wahl, einem Wettbewerb) rigging; (bei einem Wettlauf, -rennen) fixing; „~!‟ 'it's a] fix!'

schied /ʃiːt/ *1. u. 3. Pers. Sg. Prät. v.* **scheiden**

Schieds-: **~gericht** *das* (a) (Rechtsw.) arbitration tribunal; (b) (Sport) panel of judges; **~richter** *der* (Sport) referee; (Tennis, Tischtennis, Hockey, Kricket, Federball) umpire; (Eislauf, Ski, Schwimmen) judge; **~richter·ball** *der* (Fußball) drop ball; (Basketball) jump ball

schief /ʃiːf/ **1** *Adj.* (a) (schräg) leaning ‹*wall, fence, post*›; (nicht parallel) crooked; not straight *pred.*; crooked ‹*nose*›; sloping, inclined ‹*surface*›; worn[-down] ‹*heels*›; **er hält den Kopf ~:** he holds his head to one side; **der Schiefe Turm von Pisa** the Leaning Tower of Pisa; **eine ~e Ebene** (Phys.) an inclined plane; (b) (fig.: verzerrt) distorted ‹*picture, presentation, view, impression*›; false ‹*comparison*›. **2** *adv.* (a) (schräg) **das Bild hängt/der Teppich liegt ~:** the picture/carpet is crooked; **der Tisch steht ~:** the table isn't level; **jmdn. ~ ansehen** (ugs.) look at sb. askance; **~ gewickelt sein** (fig. ugs.) be very much mistaken; **~ liegen** (fig. ugs.) be on the wrong track; *s. auch* **Haussegen;** (b) (fig.: verzerrt) etw. **~ darstellen** give a distorted account of sth.

Schiefer /'ʃiːfɐ/ *der;* ~s (Gestein) slate

schief-: **~***|gehen** ⇒ **gehen 1;****~***|gewickelt** ⇒ **schief 2 a;** **~|lachen** *refl. V.* (ugs.) kill oneself laughing (coll.); laugh one's head off;**~***|laufen** ⇒ **laufen 1 i;** **~***|liegen** ⇒ **schief 2 a**

schielen /'ʃiːlən/ *itr. V.* (a) squint; have a squint; **leicht/stark ~:** have a slight/pronounced squint; **auf dem rechten Auge ~:** have a squint in one's right eye; (b) (ugs.: blicken) look out of the corner of one's eye; **nach etw. ~:** steal a glance at sth.; (fig.) have one's eye on sth.; (c) (ugs.: spähen) peep

schien /ʃiːn/ *1. u. 3. Pers. Sg. Prät. v.* **scheinen**

Schien·bein *das* shinbone; **sich am ~ stoßen** bang one's shin

Schiene /'ʃiːnə/ *die;* ~, ~n (a) rail; (b) (Gleit~) runner; (c) (Med.) Stütze) splint

schienen *tr. V.* **jmds. Arm ~:** put sb.'s arm in a splint

Schienen-: **~bus** *der* railbus; **~fahrzeug** *das* track vehicle

schier /ʃiːɐ/ *Adv.* well-nigh; almost

Schieß-: **~bude** *die* shooting gallery; **~eisen** *das* (ugs.) shooting-iron (sl.)

schießen /'ʃiːsn̩/ **1** *unr. itr. V.* (a) shoot; ‹*pistol, rifle*› shoot, fire; **auf jmdn./etw. ~:** shoot/fire at sb./sth.; **gut/schlecht ~** ‹*person*› be a good/bad shot; (b) (Fußball) shoot; (c) *mit sein* (ugs.: schnellen) shoot; **ein Gedanke schoß ihr durch den Kopf** (fig.) a thought flashed through her mind; **zum Schießen sein** (ugs.) be a scream (coll.); (d) *mit sein* (fließen, heraus~) gush; (spritzen) spurt; **ich spürte, wie mir das Blut in den Kopf schoß** I felt the blood rush to my head; (e) *mit sein* (schnell wachsen) shoot up; **die Preise ~ in die Höhe** prices are shooting up or rocketing. **2** *unr. tr. V.* (a) shoot; fire ‹*bullet, missile, rocket*›; **jmdn. zum Krüppel ~:** shoot and maim sb.; (b) (Fußball) score ‹*goal*›; **den Ball ins Netz ~:** put the ball in the net; **das 3:2 ~:** make it 3–2; (c) (ugs.: fotografieren) **einige Aufnahmen ~:** take a few snaps

Schießerei *die;* ~, ~en (a) shooting *no indef. art., no pl.;* (b) (Schusswechsel) gun battle; **die ~ am Ende des Films** the shoot-out at the end of the film

Schieß-: **~pulver** *das* gunpowder; **er hat das ~pulver [auch] nicht erfunden** (ugs.) he's not exactly a genius; **~scharte** *die* crenel; **~scheibe** *die* target; **~sport** *der* shooting *no art.;* **~stand** *der* shooting range

Schiff /ʃɪf/ *das;* ~[e]s, ~e (a) ship; **mit dem ~:** by ship or sea; (b) (Archit.: Kirchen~) (Mittel~) nave; (Quer~) transept; (Seiten~) aisle

***Schiffahrt** *usw.* ⇒ **Schifffahrt** *usw.*

schiffbar *Adj.* ▶ **193** navigable

schiff-, Schiff-: **~bau** *der; o. Pl.* shipbuilding *no art.;* **~bruch** *der* (veralt.) shipwreck; **~bruch erleiden** ‹*ship*› be wrecked; ‹*person*› be shipwrecked; [mit etw.] **~bruch erleiden** (fig.) fail [in sth.]; **~brüchig** *Adj.* shipwrecked; **ein Schiffbrüchiger** a shipwrecked man

Schiffchen *das;* ~s, ~ (a) [little] boat; (b) (ugs.: Kopfbedeckung) forage cap; (c) (Weberei, Handarbeit, Nähen) shuttle

Schiffer *der;* ~s, ~: boatman; (eines Lastkahns) bargee; (Kapitän) skipper

Schiffer·klavier *das* accordion

Schiff·fahrt *die; o. Pl.* (Schiffsverkehr) shipping *no indef. art.;* (Schifffahrtskunde) navigation; **die ~ einstellen** suspend all shipping movements

Schifffahrts-: ~**linie** *die* shipping route; ~**weg** *der* [navigable] waterway

Schiffs-: ~**arzt** *der* ship's doctor; ~**brücke** *die* pontoon bridge

Schiff·schaukel *die* swingboat

Schiffs-: ~**fahrt** *die* boat trip; (länger) cruise; ~**junge** *der* ▶ 85 ⌋ ship's boy; ~**modell** *das* model ship; ~**reise** *die* voyage; (Vergnügungsreise) cruise; ~**schraube** *die* ship's propeller *or* screw; ~**verkehr** *der* shipping traffic

Schiit /ʃi'iːt/ *der;* ~**en**, ~**en** Shiite

schiitisch *Adj.* Shiite

Schikane /ʃi'kaːnə/ *die;* ~, ~**n** (a) harassment *no indef. art.;* **das ist eine** ~: that amounts to *or* is harassment; **aus reiner** ~: purely in order to harass him/her *etc.;* (b) **mit allen** ~**n** (ugs.) ‹*kitchen, house*› with all mod cons (Brit. coll.); ‹*car, bicycle, stereo*› with all the extras

schikanieren *tr. V.* jmdn. ~: harass sb.; mess sb. about (coll.); **Rekruten** ~: bully recruits

Schild[1] /ʃɪlt/ *der;* ~[e]s, ~e (a) shield; **etw./nichts im** ~**e führen** be up to something/not be up to anything; **etwas gegen jmdn./etw. im** ~**e führen** be plotting sth. against sb./sth.; (b) (Wappen~) shield; escutcheon; (c) ⇒ **Schirm** c

Schild[2] *das;* ~[e]s, ~**er** (Verkehrs~) sign; (Nummern~) number plate; (Namens~) nameplate; (Plakat) placard; (an einer Mütze) badge; (auf Denkmälern, Gebäuden, Gräbern) plaque; (Etikett) label

Schild·drüse *die* (Med.) thyroid [gland]

schildern /'ʃɪldɐn/ *tr. V.* describe

Schilderung *die;* ~, ~**en** description; (von Ereignissen) account; description

Schild·kröte *die* tortoise; (Seeschildkröte) turtle

Schilf /ʃɪlf/ *das;* ~[e]s (a) reed; (Röhricht) reeds *pl.*

schillern /'ʃɪlɐn/ *itr. V.* shimmer

Schilling /'ʃɪlɪŋ/ *der;* ~s, ~e ▶ 216 ⌋ schilling

schilt /ʃɪlt/ *3. Pers. Sg. Präsens v.* **schelten**

Schimäre /ʃi'mɛːrə/ *die;* ~, ~**n** chimera

Schimmel /'ʃɪml/ *der;* ~s, ~ (a) *o. Pl.* mould; (auf Leder, Papier) mildew; (b) (Pferd) white horse

schimmelig *Adj.* mouldy; mildewy ‹*paper, leather*›

schimmeln *itr. V.; auch mit sein* go mouldy; ‹*leather, paper*› get covered with mildew

Schimmel·pilz *der* mould

Schimmer /'ʃɪmɐ/ *der;* ~s (Schein) gleam; (von Perlmutt) lustre; shimmer; (von Seide) shimmer; sheen; (von Haar) sheen; **keinen** [**blassen**] *od.* **nicht den leisesten** ~ [**von etw.**] **haben** (ugs.) not have the faintest *or* foggiest idea [about sth.] (coll.)

schimmern *itr. V.* (a) gleam; ‹*water, sea*› glisten, shimmer; ‹*metal*› glint, gleam; ‹*mother-of-pearl, silk*› shimmer; **der Stoff/die Seide schimmert rötlich** the material has a reddish tinge/the silk has a reddish sheen; (b) (durch~) show (**durch** through)

schimmlig ⇒ **schimmelig**

Schimpanse /ʃɪm'panzə/ *der;* ~**n**, ~**n** chimpanzee

schimpfen **1** *itr. V.* (a) carry on (coll.) (**auf, über** + *Akk.* about); (meckern) grumble, moan (**auf, über** + *Akk.* at); (b) **mit jmdm.** ~: tell sb. off; scold sb. **2** *tr. V.* **jmdn. dumm/faul** ~: call sb. stupid/lazy

Schimpf·wort *das* (Beleidigung) insult; (derbes Wort) swear word

Schindel /'ʃɪndl/ *die;* ~, ~**n** shingle

schinden /'ʃɪndn̩/ **1** *unr. tr. V.* (a) maltreat; ill-treat; (ausbeuten) slave-drive; **jmdn./ein Tier zu Tode** ~: work sb./an animal to death; (b) (ugs.: herausschlagen) [**bei jmdn.**] **Eindruck** ~: make an impression [on sb.]; **Zeit** ~: play for time. **2** *unr. refl. V.* (ugs.: sich abplagen) slave away

Schinderei *die;* ~, ~**en** (a) ill-treatment *no pl.;* (Ausbeutung) slave-driving *no pl.;* (b) (Strapaze, Qual) struggle; (Arbeit) toil

Schind·luder *das;* **mit etw.** ~ **treiben** (ugs.) (ausbeuten) take advantage of *or* abuse sth.; (vergeuden) squander sth.

Schinken /'ʃɪŋkn̩/ *der;* ~s, ~ (a) ham; (b) (ugs.) (Buch) great tome; (Gemälde) enormous painting; (Film, Theaterstück) epic

Schinken·speck *der* bacon

Schippe /'ʃɪpə/ *die;* ~, ~**n** (a) (nordd., md.: Schaufel) shovel; ~ **und Handfeger** dustpan and brush; **jmdn. auf die** ~ **nehmen** (fam.) kid sb. (sl.); pull sb.'s leg; (b) (Kartenspiel) ⇒ **Pik**[2]

schippen *tr. V.* (nordd., md.) shovel; (graben) dig

schippern (ugs.) **1** *itr. V.; mit sein* cruise. **2** *tr. V.* ship ‹*goods, materials*›; skipper ‹*ship*›

Schirm /ʃɪrm/ *der;* ~[e]s, ~e (a) umbrella; brolly (Brit. coll.); (Sonnen~) sunshade; parasol; (b) (Lampen~) shade; (c) (Mützen~) peak

Schirm-: ~**herr** *der* patron; ~**herrin** *die* patroness; ~**herrschaft** *die* patronage; ~**mütze** *die* peaked cap; ~**ständer** *der* umbrella stand

schiss, *schiß /ʃɪs/ *1. u. 3. Pers. Sg. Prät. v.* **scheißen**

Schiss, *Schiß *der;* **Schisses** (salopp: Angst) [**vor etw.**] ~ **haben** be shit-scared [of sth.] (coarse); ~ **kriegen** get the shits (coarse)

schlabberig *Adj.* (ugs.) baggy ‹*clothes*›; loose, limp ‹*material*›

schlabbern /'ʃlabɐn/ **1** *tr. V.* (ugs.) (schlürfen) ‹*person*› slurp; ‹*animal*› lap up. **2** *itr. V.* (a) (abwertend) slobber; (b) (schlenkern) ‹*dress*› flap; ‹*trousers*› be baggy

Schlacht /ʃlaxt/ *die;* ~, ~**en** battle; **die** ~ **bei** *od.* **von/um X** the battle of/for X; **in die** ~ **ziehen** go into battle; **sich eine** ~ **liefern** do battle; **sich eine erbitterte** ~ **liefern** (fig.) fight fiercely

schlachten *tr.* (*auch itr.*) *V.* slaughter; kill ‹*rabbit, chicken, etc.*›

Schlachtenbummler /-bʊmlɐ/ *der* (Sportjargon) away supporter

Schlachter *der;* ~s, ~, **Schlächter** *der;* ~s, ~ ▶ 85 ⌋ (nordd.) butcher

Schlachterei *die;* ~, ~**en**, **Schlächterei** *die;* ~, ~**en** (nordd.: Fleischerei) butcher's [shop]

Schlacht-: ~**feld** *das* battlefield; ~**haus** *das* slaughterhouse; ~**hof** *der* slaughterhouse; abattoir; ~**plan** *der* (fig.) plan of action; ~**platte** *die* dish with assorted cooked meats, sausages, and sauerkraut; ~**schiff** *das* (Milit.) battleship; ~**vieh** *das* animals *pl.* kept for meat; (kurz vor der Schlachtung) animals *pl.* for slaughter

Schlacke /'ʃlakə/ *die;* ~, ~**n** (a) cinders *pl.;* (größere Stücke) clinker; (b) (Hochofen~) slag

schlackern /'ʃlakɐn/ *itr. V.* (nordd., westmd.) (a) ‹*dress*› flap; ‹*bag*› dangle; ‹*trousers*› be baggy; (b) (wackeln, zittern) shake; tremble; **mit den Armen** ~: flap one's arms about

Schlaf /ʃlaːf/ *der;* ~[e]s sleep; **einen leichten/festen/ gesunden** ~ **haben** be a light/heavy/good sleeper; **jmdn. um den** ~ *od.* **seinen** ~ **bringen** ‹*worry etc.*› give sb. sleepless nights/a sleepless night; ‹*noise*› stop sb. from sleeping; **jmdn. in den** ~ **singen/wiegen** sing/rock sb. to sleep; **das kann** *od.* **mache ich im** ~ (fig.) I can do that with my eyes closed *or* shut; **halb im** ~: half asleep

Schlaf·anzug *der* pyjamas *pl.;* **ein** ~: a pair of pyjamas

Schläfchen /'ʃlɛːfçən/ *das;* ~s, ~: nap; snooze (coll.); **ein** ~ **halten** have a nap *or* (coll.) snooze

Schlaf·couch *die* bed-settee; sofa-bed

Schläfe /'ʃlɛːfə/ *die;* ~, ~**n** ▶ 326 ⌋ temple; **er hat graue** ~**n** his hair has gone grey at the temples

schlafen *unr. itr. V.* (a) (auch fig.) sleep; **tief** *od.* **fest** ~ (zur Zeit) be sound asleep; (gewöhnlich) sleep soundly; be a sound sleeper; **lange** ~: sleep for a long time; (am Morgen) sleep in; ~ **wie ein Murmeltier** (ugs.) sleep like a log *or* top; ~ **gehen** go to bed; **im Hotel/bei Bekannten** ~: stay in a hotel/with friends; **darüber muss ich noch** ~: I'd like to sleep on it; **bei jmdn.** ~: sleep at sb.'s house/ in sb.'s room *etc.;* **mit jmdm.** ~ (verhüll.) sleep with sb. (euphem.); (b) (ugs.: nicht aufpassen) be asleep

Schlafens·zeit *die* bedtime

Schläfer /ˈʃlɛːfɐ/ *der;* ~s, ~, **Schläferin** *die;* ~, ~nen sleeper

schlaff /ʃlaf/ **1** *Adj.* **(a)** (nicht straff, nicht fest) slack ‹*cable, rope, sail*›; flaccid, limp ‹*penis*›; loose, slack ‹*skin*›; sagging ‹*breasts*›; flabby ‹*stomach, muscles*›; **(b)** (schlapp, matt) limp ‹*body, hand, handshake*›; shaky ‹*knees*›; feeble ‹*blow*›; **(c)** (abwertend: träge) lethargic. **2** *adv.* **(a)** (locker, nicht straff) slackly; **das Segel hing** ~: the sail hung limply; **(b)** (schlapp, matt) limply

schlaf-, Schlaf-: ~**gast** *der* overnight guest; ~**gelegenheit** *die* place to sleep; ~**lied** *das* lullaby; ~**los** *Adj.* sleepless ‹*night*›; ~**losigkeit** *die;* ~: sleeplessness; insomnia; ~**mittel** *das* sleep-inducing drug; soporific [drug]; ~**mütze** *die* (ugs.) sleepyhead; (jmd., der unaufmerksam ist) daydreamer

Schlaffittchen /ʃlaˈfɪtçən/ *das in* **jmdn. am** *od* **beim** ~ **kriegen** *od.* **fassen** (ugs.) collar *or* (sl.) nab. sb.

schläfrig /ˈʃlɛːfrɪç/ **1** *Adj.* sleepy; ~ **sein/werden** ‹*person*› be/become sleepy *or* drowsy. **2** *adv.* sleepily

Schlaf-: ~**saal** *der* dormitory; ~**sack** *der* sleeping bag

schläfst /ʃlɛːfst/ *2. Pers. Sg. Präsens v.* **schlafen**

schläft /ʃlɛːft/ *3. Pers. Sg. Präsens v.* **schlafen**

schlaf-, Schlaf-: ~**tablette** *die* sleeping pill *or* tablet; ~**wagen** *der* sleeping car; sleeper; ~**wandeln** *itr. V.; auch mit sein* sleepwalk; ~**wandler** *der;* ~s, ~, ~**wandlerin** *die;* ~, ~**nen** sleepwalker; ~**zimmer** *das* bedroom; (Einrichtung) bedroom suite

Schlag /ʃlaːk/ *der;* ~[e]s, **Schläge** /ˈʃlɛːɡə/ **(a)** blow; (Faust~) punch; blow; (Klaps) slap; (leichter) pat; (als Strafe für ein Kind) smack; (Peitschenhieb) lash; (Tennis, Golf) stroke; shot; **Schläge kriegen** (ugs.) get *or* be given a thrashing *or* beating; **alles ging** ~ **auf** ~: everything went quickly; **keinen** ~ **tun** (ugs.) not do a stroke [of work]; **jmdm. einen** ~ **versetzen** deal sb. a blow; (fig.) be a blow to sb.; **auf einen** ~ (ugs.) at one go; all at once; (plötzlich) (Auf~, Aufprall) bang; (dumpf) (thud) (Klopfen) knock; **(c)** *o. Pl.* (des Herzens, Pulses, der Wellen) beating; (eines Pendels) swinging; **(d)** (einzelne rhythmische Bewegung) (Herz~, Puls~, Takt~) beat; (eines Pendels) swing; (Ruder~, Kolben~) stroke; **(e)** *o. Pl.* (Töne) (einer Uhr) striking; (einer Glocke) ringing; (einer Trommel) beating; (eines Gongs) clanging; **(f)** (einzelner Ton) (Stunden~) stroke; (Glocken~) ring; (Trommel~) beat; (Gong~) clang; ~ **acht Uhr** on the dot *or* stroke of eight; **(g)** *o. Pl.* (Vogelsang) song; **(h)** (Blitz~) flash [of lightning]; **(i)** (Stromstoß) shock; **(j)** (ugs.: ~anfall) stroke; **jmdn. trifft** *od.* **rührt der** ~ (ugs.) sb. is flabbergasted; **wie vom** ~ **getroffen** *od.* **gerührt** (ugs.) as if thunderstruck; **(k)** (Schicksals~) blow; **(l)** (Tauben~) cote; **(m)** (ugs.: Portion) helping; **(n)** *o. Pl.* (österr.: ~sahne) whipped cream

schlag-, Schlag-: ~**ader** *die* ▶ **326** artery; ~**anfall** *der* stroke; **einen** ~**anfall bekommen** [**haben**] have [had] a stroke; ~**artig 1** *Adj.; nicht präd.* very sudden; (sofortig) instantaneous; **2** *adv.* quite suddenly; (sofort) instantly; ~**baum** *der* barrier; ~**bohrer** *der* percussion drill; hammer drill

Schlägel /ˈʃlɛːɡl̩/ *der;* ~s, ~ **(a)** mallet; **(b)** (Trommelstock) stick

schlagen 1 *unr. tr. V.* **(a)** hit; beat; strike; (mit der Faust) punch; hit; (mit der flachen Hand) slap; (mit der Peitsche) lash; **ein Kind** ~: smack a child; (aufs Hinterteil) spank a child; **jmdn. bewusstlos/zu Boden** ~: beat sb. senseless/to the ground; (mit einem Schlag) knock sb. senseless/to the ground; **die Hände vors Gesicht** ~: cover one's face with one's hands; **ein Loch ins Eis** ~: break *or* smash a hole in the ice; *s. auch* **grün a**; **(b)** (mit Richtungsangabe) knock ‹*nail*›; hit ‹*ball*›; (mit dem Fuß) kick; **etw. durch ein Sieb** ~: press sth. through a sieve; **(c)** (rühren) beat ‹*mixture*›; whip ‹*cream*›; (mit einem Schneebesen) whisk; **die Sahne steif** ~: beat the cream till stiff; **(d)** (läuten) ‹*clock*› strike; ‹*bell*› ring; **die Uhr schlägt acht** the clock strikes eight; **eine geschlagene Stunde** (ugs.) a whole hour; *s. auch* **dreizehn**; **Stunde a**; **(e)** (legen) throw; **die Decke zur Seite** ~: throw aside the blanket; **(f)** (einwickeln) wrap (**in** + *Akk.* in); **(g)** (besiegen, übertreffen) beat; **jmdn. in etw.** (*Dat.*) ~: beat sb. at sth.; **eine Mannschaft [mit**

2:0 ~: beat a team [by] 2–0; **(h)** *auch itr.* (bes. Schach) take ‹*chessman*›; **(i)** (fällen) fell ‹*tree*›; **(j)** (spielen) beat ‹*drum*›; (geh.) play ‹*lute, zither, harp*›; **den Takt/Rhythmus** ~: beat time; **(k)** etw. in etw./auf etw. (*Akk.*) ~: add sth. to sth. **2** *unr. itr. V.* **(a)** (hauen) **er schlug mit der Faust auf den Tisch** he beat the table with his fist; **jmdm. auf die Hand/ins Gesicht** ~: slap sb.'s hand/hit sb. in the face; **um sich** ~: lash *or* hit out; **(b)** **mit den Flügeln** ~ ‹*bird*› beat *or* flap its wings; **(c)** *mit sein* (prallen) bang; **mit dem Kopf auf etw.** (*Akk.*) /**gegen etw.** ~: bang one's head on/against sth.; **auf den Boden** ~: land with a thud on the floor; **(d)** *mit sein* **jmdm. auf den Magen** ~: affect sb.'s stomach; **(e)** (pulsieren) ‹*heart, pulse*› beat; (heftig) ‹*heart*› pound; ‹*pulse*› throb; **(f)** (läuten) ‹*clock*› strike; ‹*bell*› ring; ‹*funeral bell*› toll; **(g)** *auch mit sein* (auftreffen) **gegen/an etw.** (*Akk.*) ~: ‹*rain, waves*› beat against sth.; **(h)** *meist mit sein* (einschlagen) **in etw.** (*Akk.*) ~ ‹*lightning, bullet, etc.*› strike *or* hit sth.; **(i)** *mit sein* **nach dem Onkel** *usw.* ~: take after one's uncle *etc.*. **3** *unr. refl. V.* **(a)** (sich prügeln) fight; **sich mit jmdm.** ~: fight with sb.; **sich um etw.** ~ (auch fig.) fight over sth.; **(b)** (ugs.: sich behaupten) hold one's own; **sich tapfer** ~: hold one's own well; put up a good showing; **(c)** (sich schädlich auswirken) **sich auf die Leber** ~: affect the liver

schlagend 1 *Adj.* cogent, compelling ‹*argument, reason*›; cogent ‹*comparison*›; conclusive ‹*proof, evidence*›; *s. auch* **Wetter c. 2** *adv.* ‹*prove, disprove*› conclusively; ‹*formulate*› cogently

Schlager *der;* ~s, ~ **(a)** (Lied) pop song; (Hit) hit; **(b)** (Erfolg) (Buch) best seller; (Ware) best-selling line; (Film, Stück) hit

Schläger /ˈʃlɛːɡɐ/ *der;* ~s, ~ **(a)** (abwertend: Raufbold) tough; thug; **(b)** (Tennis~, Federball~, Squash~) racket; (Tischtennis~, Kricket~) bat; ([Eis]hockey~, Polo~) stick; (Golf~) club

Schlägerei *die;* ~, ~**en** brawl; fight

Schlager-: ~**musik** *die;* o. Pl. popular music; pop music; ~**sänger** *der* pop singer

schlag-, Schlag-: ~**fertig 1** *Adj.* quick-witted ‹*reply*›; ‹*person*› who is quick at repartee; **er ist** ~**fertig** he is quick at repartee; **2** *adv.* ~**fertig antworten/parieren** give a quick-witted reply/riposte; ~**fertigkeit** *die; o. Pl.* quickness at repartee; ~**instrument** *das* percussion instrument; ~**kräftig 1** *Adj.* **(a)** (Milit.) powerful; **(b)** (überzeugend) compelling ‹*argument*›; convincing ‹*example*›; **(c)** (effektiv) strong, effective ‹*support, back-up, team*›; **2** *adv.* (überzeugend) ‹*argue*› compellingly; ~**loch** *das* pothole; ~**obers** /~|oːbɐs/ *das;* ~ (österr.); ~**rahm** *der* (bes. südd., österr., schweiz.); ~**sahne** *die* whipping cream; (geschlagen) whipped cream; ~**seite** *die* list; **[starke od. schwere]** ~**seite haben/bekommen** be listing [heavily] *or* have a [heavy] list/develop a [heavy] list; ~**seite haben** (ugs. scherzh.) be rolling drunk; ~**stock** *der* cudgel; (für Polizei) truncheon; ~**wort** *das; Pl. meist* ~**worte (a)** (Parole) slogan; catchphrase; **(b)** (abwertend: Redensart) cliché; ~**zeile** *die* (Zeitungsw.) headline; ~**zeug** *das* drums *pl.;* ~**zeuger** *der;* ~s, ~, ~**zeugerin** *die;* ~, ~**nen** drummer

schlaksig /ˈʃlaːksɪç/ *Adj.* (ugs.) gangling; lanky

Schlamassel /ʃlaˈmasl̩/ *der od. das;* ~s (ugs.) mess; **da haben wir den** ~! a right *or* fine mess we're in now!

Schlamm /ʃlam/ *der;* ~[e]s, ~**e** *od.* **Schlämme** /ˈʃlɛmə/ **(a)** mud; **(b)** (Schlick) sludge; silt

schlammig *Adj.* **(a)** muddy; **(b)** (schlickig) sludgy; muddy

Schlampe /ˈʃlampə/ *die;* ~, ~**n** (ugs. abwertend) slut

schlampen *itr. V.* (ugs. abwertend) be sloppy; **bei etw.** ~: do sth. sloppily

Schlamperei *die;* ~, ~**en** (ugs. abwertend) sloppiness

schlampig (ugs. abwertend) **1** *Adj.* **(a)** (liederlich) slovenly; **(b)** (nachlässig) sloppy, slipshod ‹*work*›. **2** *adv.* **(a)** (liederlich) in a slovenly way; **(b)** (nachlässig) sloppily; in a sloppy *or* slipshod way

schlang /ʃlaŋ/ *1. u. 3. Pers. Sg. Prät. v.* **schlingen**

Schlange *die;* ~, ~**n (a)** snake; **(b)** (Menschen~) queue; line (Amer.); ~ **stehen** queue; stand in line (Amer.); **(c)** (Auto~) tailback (Brit.); backup (Amer.)

schlänge /ˈʃlɛŋə/ *1. u. 3. Pers. Sg. Konjunktiv II v.* **schlingen**

schlängeln /ˈʃlɛŋln̩/ *refl. V.* (a) ⟨*snake*⟩ wind [its way]; ⟨*road*⟩ wind, snake [its way]; **eine geschlängelte Linie** a wavy line; (b) (sich irgendwo hindurch bewegen) wind one's way

Schlangen-: ∼**beschwörer** *der;* ∼**s,** ∼: snake charmer; ∼**biss,** ***∼**biß** *der* snakebite; ∼**gift** *das* snake venom *or* poison; ∼**linie** *die* wavy line; ∼**linien** **fahren** ⟨*cyclist*⟩ weave along

schlank /ʃlaŋk/ *Adj.* slim ⟨*person*⟩; slim, slender ⟨*build, figure*⟩; slender ⟨*column, tree, limbs*⟩; ∼ **werden** get slimmer; slim down; **dieser Rock macht [dich]** ∼: this skirt makes you look slim; *s. auch* **Linie a**

Schlankheit *die;* ∼ ⇨ **schlank:** slimness; slenderness

Schlankheits·kur *die* slimming diet; **eine** ∼ **machen/beginnen** be/go on a slimming diet

schlank·weg *Adv.* (ugs.) ⟨*refuse*⟩ flatly, point-blank; ⟨*accept*⟩ straight away

schlapp /ʃlap/ *Adj.* (a) worn out; tired out; (wegen Schwüle) listless; (wegen Krankheit) run-down; listless; (b) (ugs.: ohne Schwung) wet (coll.); feeble; (c) slack ⟨*rope, cable*⟩; loose, slack ⟨*skin*⟩; flabby ⟨*stomach, muscles*⟩

Schlappe *die;* ∼, ∼**n** setback; **eine [schwere]** ∼ **erlei·den** suffer a [severe] setback

schlappen *itr. V.; mit sein* (schlurfend gehen) shuffle

schlapp|machen *itr. V.* (ugs.) flag; (zusammenbrechen) flake out (coll.); (aufgeben) give up

Schlapp·schwanz *der* (salopp abwertend) weed; wet (coll.)

Schlaraffen·land /ʃlaˈrafn̩-/ *das; o. Pl.* Cockaigne

schlau /ʃlaʊ/ **1** *Adj.* (a) shrewd; astute; (gerissen) wily; crafty; cunning, (b) (ugs.: gescheit) clever; bright; smart; **aus etw. nicht** ∼ **werden** (ugs.) not be able to make head or tail of sth.; **aus jmdm. nicht** ∼ **werden** (ugs.) not be able to make sb. out; *s. auch* **Buch a**. **2** *adv.* shrewdly; astutely; (gerissen) craftily; cunningly

Schlauberger /ˈʃlaʊbɛrɡɐ/ *der;* ∼**s,** ∼ (ugs. scherzh.) wily *or* crafty customer (coll.)

Schlauch /ʃlaʊx/ *der;* ∼[e]**s,** **Schläuche** /ˈʃlɔʏçə/ (a) hose; **das war ein [ganz schöner]** ∼! (fig. ugs.) it was a [real] slog; (b) (Fahrrad∼, Auto∼) tube

Schlauch·boot *das* rubber dinghy; inflatable [dinghy]

schlauchen *tr., auch itr. V.* (ugs.) **jmdn.** ∼: take it out of sb.

schlauch·los *Adj.* tubeless ⟨*tyre*⟩

Schläue /ˈʃlɔʏə/ *die;* ∼: shrewdness; astuteness; (Gerissenheit) wiliness; craftiness; cunning

Schlaufe /ˈʃlaʊfə/ *die;* ∼, ∼**n** loop; (zum Festhalten) strap

Schlaukopf, *der* (ugs.), ∼**meier** *der;* ∼**s,** ∼ (ugs. scherzh.) ⇨ ∼**berger**

Schlawiner /ʃlaˈviːnɐ/ *der;* ∼**s,** ∼ (ugs.) trickster; (scherzh.: Schlingel) rogue; rascal

schlecht /ʃlɛçt/ **1** *Adj.* (a) bad; poor, bad ⟨*food, quality, style, harvest, health, circulation*⟩; poor ⟨*salary, eater, appetite*⟩; poor-quality ⟨*goods*⟩; bad, weak ⟨*eyes*⟩; **in Mathematik** ∼ **sein** be bad at mathematics; **das wäre nicht** ∼ that wouldn't be a bad idea; **mit jmdm.** *od.* **um jmdn./mit etw. steht es** ∼: sb./sth. is in a bad way; **jmdn.** ∼ **machen** (herabsetzen) run sb. down; disparage sb.; (b) (böse) bad; wicked; **das Schlechte im Menschen** the evil in man; **sie ist nicht die Schlechteste** she's not too bad; (c) *nicht attr.* (ungenießbar) off; **das Fleisch ist** ∼ **geworden** the meat has gone off. **2** *adv.* (a) badly; **sie spricht** ∼ **Englisch** she speaks poor English; **er sieht/hört** ∼: his sight is poor/he has poor hearing; **die Geschäfte gehen im Moment** ∼: business is bad at the moment; **über jmdn.** *od.* **von jmdm.** ∼ **sprechen** speak ill of sb.; ∼ **bezahlt** badly *or* poorly paid; (b) (schwer) **heute geht es** ∼: today is difficult; **das kann ich** ∼ **sagen** I can't really say; **das wird sich** ∼ **vermeiden lassen** it can hardly be avoided; (c) *in* ∼ **und recht, mehr** ∼ **als recht** after a fashion; **sie hat sich** ∼ **und recht durchs Leben geschlagen** she got by in life as best she could

---

**alte Schreibung (vgl. Hinweise auf S. xvi–xvii)

schlecht-: ***∼**bezahlt** ⇨ **schlecht 2 a;** ***∼|**gehen** ⇨ **gehen k;** ***∼**gelaunt** ⇨ **gelaunt;** ∼**hin** *Adv.* (a) einem *Subst.* nachgestellt **er war der Romantiker** ∼**hin** he was the quintessential Romantic *or* the epitome of the Romantic; (b) (ganz einfach) quite simply

Schlechtigkeit *die;* ∼ badness; wickedness

*****schlecht|machen** ⇨ **schlecht 1 a**

schlecken /ˈʃlɛkn̩/ (bes. südd., österr.) **1** *tr. V.* lap up. **2** *itr. V.* **an etw.** (*Dat.*) ∼: lick sth.

Schlegel /ˈʃleːɡl̩/ *der;* ∼**s,** ∼ (südd., österr.) ⇨ **Keule c;** *s. auch* **Schlägel**

Schlehe /ˈʃleːə/ *die;* ∼, ∼**n** sloe

schleichen /ˈʃlaɪçn̩/ **1** *unr. itr. V.; mit sein* creep; (heimlich) creep; steal; sneak; ⟨*cat*⟩ slink, creep; (langsam fahren) crawl along; **die Zeit schlich** time crept by. **2** *unr. refl. V.* creep; steal; sneak; ⟨*cat*⟩ slink, creep; **schleich dich!** (ugs., bes. österr.) get lost! (sl.); buzz off! (coll.)

schleichend *Adj.* insidious ⟨*disease*⟩; slow[-acting], insidious ⟨*poison*⟩; creeping ⟨*inflation*⟩; gradual ⟨*crisis*⟩

Schleicher *der;* ∼**s,** ∼ (abwertend) toadying hypocrite

Schleich·weg *der* secret path

Schleie /ˈʃlaɪə/ *die;* ∼, ∼**n** (Zool.) tench

Schleier /ˈʃlaɪɐ/ *der;* ∼**s,** ∼ (a) veil; (b) (von Dunst) veil of mist

schleier-, Schleier-: ∼**eule** *die* barn owl; ∼**haft** *Adj.* jmdm. [völlig *od.* vollkommen] ∼ **sein/bleiben** be/remain a [total *or* complete] mystery to sb.; ∼**tanz** *der* dance of the veils

Schleife /ˈʃlaɪfə/ *die;* ∼, ∼**n** (a) bow; (Fliege) bow tie; (b) (starke Biegung) loop; (eines Flusses) loop; horseshoe bend

schleifen[1] *unr. tr. V.* (a) (schärfen) sharpen; grind, sharpen ⟨*axe*⟩; (b) (glätten) grind; cut ⟨*diamond, glass*⟩; (mit Sand-/Schmirgelpapier) sand; (c) (bes. Soldatenspr.: drillen) **jmdn.** ∼: drill sb. hard

schleifen[2] **1** *tr. V.* (a) (auch fig.) drag; (b) (niederreißen) **etw.** ∼: raze sth. [to the ground]. **2** *itr. V.; auch mit sein* drag; **die Kette schleift am Schutzblech** the chain scrapes the guard; **die Kupplung** ∼ **lassen** (Kfz-W.) slip the clutch; **etw.** ∼ **lassen** (fig.) let sth. slide; *s. auch* **Zügel**

Schleif·stein *der* grindstone

Schleim /ʃlaɪm/ *der;* ∼[e]**s,** ∼**e** (a) mucus; (im Hals) phlegm; (von Schnecken, Aalen) slime; (b) (sämiger Brei) gruel

Schleim·haut *die* mucous membrane

schleimig *Adj.* (auch fig.) slimy; (Physiol., Zool.) mucous

schlemmen /ˈʃlɛmən/ **1** *itr. V.* (prassen) have a feast. **2** *tr. V.* (verzehren) feast on

Schlemmer *der;* ∼**s,** ∼: gourmet

Schlemmer·lokal *das* gourmet restaurant

schlendern /ˈʃlɛndɐn/ *itr. V.; mit sein* stroll

Schlendrian /ˈʃlɛndriaːn/ *der;* ∼[e]**s** (ugs. abwertend) slackness

Schlenker /ˈʃlɛŋkɐ/ *der;* ∼**s,** ∼ (ugs.) swerve; **einen** ∼ **machen** swerve

schlenkern **1** *itr. V.* swing; dangle; **mit den Armen/ mit den Beinen** ∼: swing *or* dangle one's arms/legs. **2** *tr. V.* swing, dangle ⟨*arms, legs*⟩

schlenzen /ˈʃlɛntsn̩/ *tr. V.* (Sport, bes. [Eis]hockey, Fußball) flick

Schlepp /ʃlɛp/ *der in* **ein Fahrzeug in** ∼ **nehmen** take a vehicle in tow

Schlepp·bügel *der* (Skisport) T-bar

Schleppe *die;* ∼, ∼**n** train

schleppen **1** *tr. V.* (a) (ziehen) tow ⟨*vehicle, ship*⟩; (b) (tragen) carry; lug; (c) (ugs.: mitnehmen) drag. **2** *refl. V.* drag *or* haul oneself

schleppend **1** *Adj.* (a) (schwerfällig) shuffling, dragging ⟨*walk, steps*⟩; (b) (gedehnt) dragging ⟨*speech*⟩; slow ⟨*song, melody*⟩; (c) (nicht zügig) slow ⟨*service*⟩. **2** *adv.* (a) (schwerfällig) ∼ **gehen** shuffle along; (b) (gedehnt) ⟨*speak*⟩ in a dragging voice; ⟨*sing, play*⟩ slowly; (c) (nicht zügig) **die Arbeiten gehen nur** ∼ **voran** the work is progressing slowly

Schlepper *der;* ∼**s,** ∼ (a) (Schiff) tug; (b) (Traktor) tractor; (c) (ugs.: jmd., der Kunden zuführt) tout

Schlepp-: ∼**lift** *der* T-bar [lift]; ∼**tau** *das* tow-line; row-rope; (aus Draht) tow-line; tow-cable; **etw. ins** ∼**tau nehmen** take sth. in tow; **in jmds.** ∼**tau** (fig.) in sb.'s wake

Schlesien /'ʃleːzi̯ən/ *(das);* ∼**s** Silesia

Schlesier /'ʃleːzi̯ɐ/ *der;* ∼**s,** ∼**, Schlesierin** *die;* ∼, ∼**nen** Silesian

Schleswig-Holstein *(das)*; ∼**s** Schleswig-Holstein

Schleswig-Holsteiner 1 *indekl. Adj.; nicht präd.* Schleswig-Holstein. 2 *der;* ∼**s,** ∼**:** native of Schleswig-Holstein; (Einwohner) inhabitant of Schleswig-Holstein

schleswig-holsteinisch *Adj.* Schleswig-Holstein *attrib.*

Schleuder /'ʃlɔy̯dɐ/ *die;* ∼, ∼**n** sling; (mit Gummiband) catapult (Brit.); slingshot (Amer.)

schleudern 1 *tr. V.* (a) (werfen) hurl; fling; **der Wagen wurde aus der Kurve geschleudert** the car was sent skidding off the bend; (b) (rotieren lassen) centrifuge; spin 〈*washing*〉. 2 *itr. V. mit sein* (rutschen) skid; (fig. ugs.) run into trouble

Schleuder-: ∼**preis** *der* (ugs.) knock-down price; ∼**sitz** *der* ejector seat

schleunigst *Adv.* (a) (auf der Stelle) at once; immediately; straight away; (b) (eilends) hastily; with all haste

Schleuse /'ʃlɔy̯zə/ *die;* ∼, ∼**n** (a) sluice[-gate]; (b) (Schiffs∼) lock

schleusen *tr. V.* (a) **ein Schiff** ∼**:** pass a ship through a/the lock; (b) (geleiten) shepherd; (c) (schmuggeln) smuggle 〈*secrets*〉; infiltrate 〈*spy, agent, etc.*〉 **(in** + *Akk.* into)

schlich /ʃlɪç/ 1. u. 3. Pers. Sg. Prät. v. **schleichen**

Schlich *der;* ∼**[e]s,** ∼**e** trick; **jmdm. auf die** ∼**e** *od.* **hinter jmds.** ∼**e kommen** get on to sb.

schlicht /ʃlɪçt/ 1 *Adj.* (a) simple; plain, simple 〈*pattern, furniture*〉; (b) (unkompliziert) simple, unsophisticated 〈*person, view, etc.*〉; **ein** ∼**es Ja oder Nein** a simple yes or no. 2 *adv.* simply; simply, plainly 〈*dressed, furnished*〉; ∼ **und einfach** (ugs.) quite *or* just simply

schlichten 1 *tr. V.* settle 〈*argument, difference of opinion*〉; settle 〈*industrial dispute etc.*〉 by mediation. 2 *itr. V.* mediate **(in** + *Dat.* in, **zwischen** between)

Schlichtheit *die;* ∼ ⇒ **schlicht a, b:** simplicity; plainness; unsophisticatedness

Schlick /ʃlɪk/ *der;* ∼**[e]s,** ∼**e** silt

schlief /ʃliːf/ 1. u. 3. Pers. Sg. Prät. v. **schlafen**

Schließe /'ʃliːsə/ *die;* ∼, ∼**n** clasp; (Schnalle) buckle

schließen 1 *unr. tr. V.* (a) (zumachen) close; shut; put the top on 〈*bottle*〉; turn off 〈*tap*〉; fasten 〈*belt, bracelet*〉; do up 〈*button, zip*〉; close 〈*street, route, electrical circuit*〉; close off 〈*pipe*〉; (fig.) close 〈*border*〉; fill, close 〈*gap*〉; (b) (unzugänglich machen) close, shut 〈*shop, factory*〉, (außer Betrieb setzen) close [down] 〈*shop, school*〉; (c) (ein∼) **etw./jmdn./sich in etw.** *(Akk.)* ∼**:** lock sth./sb./oneself in sth.; (d) (beenden) close 〈*meeting, proceedings, debate*〉; end, conclude 〈*letter, speech, lecture*〉; (e) (befestigen) **etw. an etw.** *(Akk.)* ∼**:** connect sth. to sth.; (mit Schloss) lock sth. to sth.; (f) (eingehen, vereinbaren) conclude 〈*treaty, pact, ceasefire, agreement*〉; reach 〈*settlement, compromise*〉; enter into 〈*contract*〉; **wann wurde Ihre Ehe geschlossen?** when did you get married?; **Freundschaft mit jmdm.** ∼**:** make friends with sb.; (g) (umfassen) **jmdn. in die Arme** ∼**:** take sb. in one's arms; embrace sb.; (h) (folgern) **etw. aus etw.** ∼**:** infer *or* conclude sth. from sth. 2 *unr. itr. V.* (a) close; shut; **der Schlüssel/das Schloss schließt schlecht** the key won't turn properly/the lock doesn't work properly; (b) 〈*shop*〉 close, shut; 〈*stock exchange*〉 close; (den Betrieb einstellen) close [down]; (c) (enden) end; conclude; (d) (urteilen) **[aus etw.] auf etw.** *(Akk.)* ∼**:** infer *or* conclude sth. [from sth.]; **die Symptome lassen auf Hepatitis** ∼**:** the symptoms indicate hepatitis; **von sich auf andere** ∼**:** judge others by one's own standards. 3 *unr. refl. V.* 〈*door, window*〉 close, shut; 〈*wound, circle*〉 close; 〈*flower*〉 close [up]

Schließ·fach *das* locker; (bei der Post) post-office box; PO box; (bei der Bank) safe-deposit box

schließlich *Adv.* (a) finally; in the end; (bei Erwünschtem auch) at last; ∼ **und endlich** (ugs.) in the end; finally; (b)

(immerhin, doch) after all; **er ist** ∼ **mein Freund** he is my friend, after all

Schließ·muskel *der* (Anat.) sphincter

Schließung *die;* ∼, ∼**en** (a) (der Geschäfte, Büros usw.) closing; shutting, (Stilllegung, Einstellung) closure; closing; (fig.: einer Grenze) closing; (b) (Beendigung) **vor/nach** ∼ **der Versammlung** before/after the meeting was closed; before/after the conclusion of the meeting; (c) ⇒ **schließen** 1 f: conclusion; reaching

schliff /ʃlɪf/ 1. u. 3. Pers. Sg. Prät. v. **schleifen**

Schliff *der;* ∼**[e]s,** ∼**e** (a) *o. Pl.* (das Schleifen) cutting; (von Messern, Sensen usw.) sharpening; (b) (Art, wie etw. geschliffen wird) cut; (von Messern, Scheren, Schneiden) edge; (c) *o. Pl.* (Lebensart) refinement; polish; (d) *o. Pl.* (Vollkommenheit) **einem Text** *usw.* **den letzten** ∼ **geben** put the finishing touches *pl.* to a text *etc.*

schlimm /ʃlɪm/ 1 *Adj.* (a) grave, serious 〈*error, mistake, accusation, offence*〉; bad, serious 〈*error, mistake*〉; **das ist** ∼ **für ihn** that's serious for him; (b) (übel) bad; nasty, bad 〈*experience*〉; **[das ist alles] halb so** ∼**:** it's not as bad as all that; **es ist nichts Schlimmes** it's nothing serious; **ist nicht** ∼**!** [it] doesn't matter; **es gibt Schlimmeres** there are worse things; (c) (schlecht, böse) wicked; (ungezogen) naughty 〈*child*〉; (d) (fam.: schmerzend) bad; sore; bad, nasty 〈*wound*〉. 2 *adv.* ∼ **d[a]ran sein** (körperlich, geistig) be in a bad way; (in einer ∼en Situation) be in dire straits; **es hätte** ∼**er ausgehen können** things could have turned out worse

schlimmsten·falls *Adv.* if the worst comes to the worst; ∼ **kriegt man eine Verwarnung** at worst you'll get a caution

Schlinge /'ʃlɪŋə/ *die;* ∼, ∼**n** (a) (Schlaufe) loop; (für den gebrochenen Arm o. Ä.) sling; (zum Aufhängen) noose; (b) (Fanggerät) snare; **sich in der eigenen** ∼ **fangen** (fig.) be hoist with one's own petard

Schlingel /'ʃlɪŋl̩/ *der;* ∼**s,** ∼**:** rascal; rogue

schlingen 1 *unr. tr. V.* (a) (winden) **etw. um etw.** ∼**:** loop sth. round sth.; (und zusammenbinden) tie sth. round sth.; **die Arme um jmdn./etw.** ∼**:** wrap one's arms round sb./sth.; (b) (binden) tie 〈*knot*〉; **etw. zu einem Knoten** ∼**:** tie sth. up in a knot. 2 *unr. refl. V.* (sich winden) **sich um etw.** ∼ 〈*snake*〉 wind *or* coil itself round sth.; 〈*plant*〉 wind *or* twine itself round sth. 3 *unr. itr. V.* bolt one's food; wolf one's food [down]

schlingern /'ʃlɪŋɐn/ *itr. V.; mit sein* 〈*ship, boat*〉 roll; 〈*train, vehicle*〉 lurch from side to side

Schling·pflanze *die* creeper

Schlips /ʃlɪps/ *der;* ∼**es,** ∼**e** tie; **jmdm. auf den** ∼ **treten** (fig. ugs.) tread on sb.'s toes

Schlitten /'ʃlɪtn̩/ *der;* ∼**s,** ∼ (a) sledge; sled; (Pferde∼) sleigh; (Rodel∼) toboggan; ∼ **fahren** go tobogganing; **die Kinder fuhren mit dem** ∼ **den Hang hinunter** the children tobogganed down the slope; **mit jmdm.** ∼ **fahren** (fig. ugs.) bawl sb. out (coll.); (b) (salopp: Auto) car; motor (Brit.)

Schlitten-: ∼**fahrt** *die* sleigh ride; ∼**hund** *der* sled dog

schlittern /'ʃlɪtɐn/ *itr. V.* (a) auch mit sein (rutschen) slide; (b) *mit sein* (ins Rutschen kommen) slip; slide; 〈*vehicle*〉 skid; 〈*wheel*〉 slip; (c) *mit sein* (fig.) **in die Pleite** ∼**:** slide into bankruptcy

Schlitt-: ∼**schuh** *der* [ice-]skate; ∼**schuh laufen** *od.* **fahren** [ice-] skate; ∼**schuh·laufen** *das* [ice-] skating *no art.;* ∼**schuh·läufer** *der* [ice-]skater

Schlitz /ʃlɪts/ *der;* ∼**es,** ∼**e** (a) slit; (Briefkasten∼, Automaten∼) slot; (b) (Hosen∼) flies *pl.;* fly

Schlitz-: ∼**auge** *das; meist Pl.* slit eye; ∼**ohr** *das* (ugs.) wily *or* crafty devil

schloss, *schloß /ʃlɔs/ 1. u. 3. Pers. Sg. Prät. v. **schließen**

Schloss, *Schloß *das;* **Schlosses, Schlösser** /'ʃlœsɐ/ (a) (Tür∼, Gewehr∼) lock; (b) (Vorhänge∼) padlock; **hinter** ∼ **und Riegel** (ugs.) behind bars; (c) (Verschluss) clasp; (d) (Wohngebäude) castle; (Palast) palace; (Herrschaftshaus) mansion

Schlosser *der;* ~s, ~: ▶ 85⌋ metalworker; (Maschinen~) fitter; (für Schlösser) locksmith; (Auto~) mechanic

Schlosserei *die;* ~, ~en **(a)** (Werkstatt) metalworking shop; (für Schlösser) locksmith's workshop; **(b)** *o. Pl.;* ⇒ ~handwerk

Schlosser-: ~**handwerk** *das; o. Pl.;* ⇒ **Schlosser:** metalworking; fitter's trade; locksmithery; mechanic's trade; ~**werkstatt** *die* ⇒ **Schlosserei a**

Schloss-, *Schloß-: ~**park** *der* castle *etc.* grounds *pl.;* ~**ruine** *die* ruined castle *etc.*

Schlot /ʃloːt/ *der;* ~[e]s, ~e *od.* **Schlöte** /ˈʃløːtə/ (bes. md.: Schornstein) chimney[-stack]; (eines Schiffes) funnel; **rauchen** *od.* **qualmen wie ein** ~ (ugs.) smoke like a chimney

schlottern /ˈʃlɔtɐn/ *itr. V.* **(a)** shake; tremble; **jmdm.** ~ **die Knie** sb.'s knees are shaking *or* trembling; **(b)** 〈*clothes*〉 hang loose

Schlucht /ʃlʊxt/ *die;* ~, ~en ravine; gorge

schluchzen /ˈʃlʊxtsn̩/ *itr. V.* sob; **in heftiges Schluchzen ausbrechen** burst into heavy sobbing

Schluchzer *der;* ~s, ~: sob

Schluck /ʃlʊk/ *der;* ~[e]s, ~e *od.* **Schlücke** /ˈʃlʏkə/ swallow; mouthful; (großer ~) gulp; (kleiner ~) sip; **einen tüchtigen** ~ **[Bier] trinken** take a good *or* long swig [of beer] (coll.); **hast du einen** ~ **zu trinken für uns?** have you got a drop of something for us to drink?

Schluck·auf *der;* ~s hiccups *pl.;* hiccoughs *pl.*

Schlückchen /ˈʃlʏkçən/ *das;* ~s, ~: sip

schlucken 1 *tr. V.* **(a)** (auch fig. ugs.) swallow; **etw. hastig** ~: gulp sth. down; **(b)** (ugs.: einatmen) swallow 〈*dust*〉; breathe in 〈*gas*〉. 2 *itr. V.* (auch fig.) swallow

Schlucker *der;* ~s, ~: **in armer** ~ (ugs.) poor devil *or* (Brit. coll.) blighter

Schluck·impfung *die* oral vaccination

schluderig ⇒ **schludrig**

schludern /ˈʃluːdɐn/ *itr. V.* (ugs. abwertend) work sloppily

schludrig (ugs. abwertend) 1 *Adj.* **(a)** (nachlässig) slipshod 〈*work, examination*〉; botched 〈*job*〉; slapdash 〈*person, work*〉; **(b)** (schlampig [aussehend]) scruffy. 2 *adv.* **(a)** (nachlässig) in a slipshod *or* slapdash way; **(b)** (schlampig [aussehend]) scruffily

schlug /ʃluːk/ *1. u. 3. Pers. Sg. Prät. v.* **schlagen**

Schlummer /ˈʃlʊmɐ/ *der;* ~s (geh.) slumber (poet./rhet.); (Nickerchen) doze

schlummern *itr. V.* (geh.) slumber (poet./rhet.); (dösen) doze

Schlund /ʃlʊnt/ *der;* ~[e]s, **Schlünde** /ˈʃlʏndə/ [back of the] throat; pharynx (Anat.); (eines Tieres) maw

schlüpfen /ˈʃlʏpfn̩/ *itr. V.; mit sein* slip; **in ein/aus einem Kleid** *usw.* ~: slip into *or* slip on/slip out of *or* slip off a dress *etc.;* **[aus dem Ei]** ~: 〈*chick*〉 hatch out

Schlüpfer *der;* ~s, ~ (für Damen) knickers *pl.* (Brit.); panties *pl.;* (für Herren) [under]pants *pl. or* trunks *pl.;* **ein** ~: a pair of knickers/underpants

Schlupf·loch /ˈʃlʊpf-/ *das* **(a)** (Schlupfwinkel) hiding place; **(b)** (Durchschlupf) hole; (Lücke im Gesetz usw.) loophole

schlüpfrig /ˈʃlʏpfrɪç/ *Adj.* **(a)** (feucht u. glatt) slippery; **(b)** (abwertend: anstößig) lewd

Schlupf·winkel *der* hiding place; (von Banditen, Flüchtlingen usw.) hideout

schlurfen /ˈʃlʊrfn̩/ *itr. V.; mit sein* shuffle

schlürfen /ˈʃlʏrfn̩/ *tr. V.* (geräuschvoll) slurp [up] (coll.); drink noisily; (genussvoll) savour; (in kleinen Schlucken) sip

Schluss, *Schluß /ʃlʊs/ *der;* **Schlusses, Schlüsse** /ˈʃlʏsə/ **(a)** *o. Pl.* (Endzeitpunkt) end; (eines Vortrags *o. Ä.*) conclusion; (Dienst~) knocking-off time; **nach/gegen** ~ **der Aufführung** after/towards the end of the performance; **mit etw. ist** ~: sth. is at an end *or* over; (ugs.: etw. ist ruiniert) sth. has had it (coll.); **mit dem Rauchen ist jetzt** ~: there's to be no more smoking; you must stop smoking; (auf sich bezogen) I've given up smoking; ~ **jetzt!**, ~ **damit!** stop it!; that'll do!; ~ **für heute!** that's it *or* that'll do for today; **am** *od.* **zum** ~: at the end; (schließlich) in the end; finally; ~ **machen** (ugs.) stop; (Feierabend machen)

knock off; (seine Stellung aufgeben) pack in one's job (coll.); (eine Freundschaft usw. lösen) break it off; (sich das Leben nehmen) end it all (coll.); **ich mache** ~ **für heute** I'm calling it a day; **mit etw.** ~ **machen** stop sth.; **mit jmdm.** ~ **machen** finish with sb.; break it off with sb.; **(b)** (letzter Abschnitt) end; (eines Zuges) back; (eines Buchs, Schauspiels usw.) ending; **(c)** (Folgerung) conclusion (**auf** + *Akk.* regarding); (Logik) deduction; **Schlüsse aus etw. ziehen** draw conclusions from sth.

Schluss-, *Schluß-: ~**abstimmung** *die* (Parl.) final vote; ~**akkord** *der* (Musik) final chord; ~**akte** *die* (Dipl.) final communiqué; ~**bilanz** *die* (Kaufmannsspr.) annual balance sheet; (nach Abwicklung eines Unternehmens) final balance [sheet]

Schlüssel /ˈʃlʏsl̩/ *der;* ~s, ~ **(a)** key; **der** ~ **zur Wohnungstür** the front door key; **(b)** (Schrauben~) spanner; **(c)** (Lösungsweg, Lösungsheft) key; (Kode) code; cipher; **(d)** (Musik) clef

Schlüssel-: ~**bart** *der* bit [of a/the key]; ~**anhänger** *der* key-fob; ~**bein** *das* collar bone; ~**blume** *die* cowslip; (Primel) primula; ~**bund** *der od. das* bunch of keys; ~**kind** *das* (ugs.) latchkey child; ~**loch** *das* keyhole; ~**ring** *der* key-ring; ~**roman** *der* (Literaturw.) roman à clef

schluss-, *schluß-: ~**endlich** *Adv.* (bes. schweiz.) finally; ~**folgern** *tr. V.* conclude (**aus** from)

schlüssig /ˈʃlʏsɪç/ 1 *Adj.* **(a)** conclusive 〈*proof, evidence*〉; convincing, logical 〈*argument, conclusion, statement*〉; **(b) sich** (*Dat.*) **[darüber]** ~ **werden** make up one's mind. 2 *adv.* conclusively

Schluss-, *Schluß-: ~**kapitel** *das* (auch fig.) final *or* closing chapter; ~**läufer** *der* (Leichtathletik) last runner, anchor man (in a relay team); ~**licht** *das; Pl.* ~**lichter (a)** (an Fahrzeugen) tail- *or* rear light; **(b)** (ugs.: letzter einer Kolonne) **das** ~**licht machen/sein** bring up the rear; **(c)** (ugs.: Letzter, Schlechtester) **das** ~**licht der Klasse sein** be bottom of the class; ~**mann** *der; Pl.* ~**männer** (Ballspiele) goalie (coll.); ~**pfiff** *der* (Ballspiele) final whistle; ~**punkt** *der* **(a)** (Satzzeichen) full stop; **(b)** (Abschluss) conclusion; (einer Feier) finale; ~**runde** *die* (Sport: eines Rennens) final *or* last lap; (Boxen, Ringen, fig.: des Wahlkampfes usw.) final *or* last round; ~**strich** *der* [bottom] line; **einen** ~**strich ziehen/unter etw.** (*Akk.*) **ziehen** (fig.) make a clean break/draw a line under sth.; ~**verkauf** *der* [end-of-season] sale[s *pl.*]

Schmach /ʃmaːx/ *die;* ~ (geh.) ignominy; shame; (Demütigung) humiliation; **[mit]** ~ **und Schande** [in] deep disgrace

schmachten /ˈʃmaxtn̩/ *itr. V.* (geh.) **(a)** (leiden) languish; **(b)** (spött.: sich sehnen) **nach jmdm./etw.** ~: pine *or* yearn for sb./sth.

schmachtend *Adj.* (spött.) soulful (coll.) 〈*look, song*〉; schmaltzy (coll.) 〈*song, music*〉

schmächtig *Adj.* slight; weedy (coll. derog.)

schmach·voll *Adj.* (geh.) ignominious; (erniedrigend) humiliating

schmackhaft /ˈʃmakhaft/ 1 *Adj.* tasty; **jmdm. etw.** ~ **machen** (fig. ugs.) make sth. palatable to sb. 2 *adv.* in a tasty way; **etw.** ~ **zubereiten** make sth. tasty

schmähen /ˈʃmɛːən/ *tr. V.* (geh.) revile

schmählich 1 *Adj.* shameful; (verächtlich) despicable. 2 *adv.* shamefully; (in verächtlicher Weise) despicably

Schmäh·wort *das; Pl.* ~**worte** term of abuse

schmal /ʃmaːl/; **schmaler** *od.* **schmäler** /ˈʃmɛːlɐ/; **schmalst...** *od.* **schmälst...:** *Adj.* narrow; slim, slender 〈*hips, hands, figure, etc.*〉; thin 〈*lips, face, nose, etc.*〉

schmälern *tr. V.* diminish; reduce; restrict, curtail 〈*rights*〉; (herabsetzen) belittle

Schmal-: ~**film** *der* 8 mm/16 mm cine film; ~**hans** *in* **bei ihnen ist** ~**hans Küchenmeister** (ugs. verait.) they are on short commons; ~**film·kamera** *die* 8 mm/16 mm cine camera; ~**seite** *die* short side; (eines Korridors usw.) end

Schmalspur- (ugs.) small-time (coll.) 〈*politician, academic*〉; (dilettantisch) lightweight 〈*academic*〉; amateur 〈*engineer*〉

---

*alte Schreibung (vgl. Hinweise auf S. xvi–xvii)

Schmalz¹ /ʃmalts/ *das;* ∼es (Schweine∼) lard

Schmalz² *der;* ∼es (abwertend) schmaltz (coll.); **mit viel** ∼: with plenty of slushy *or* soppy sentimentality (coll.)

Schmalz·brot *das* slice of bread and dripping

schmalzig (abwertend) **1** *Adj.* schmaltzy (coll.); slushy[-sentimental]. **2** *adv.* with schmaltzy (coll.) *or* slushy sentimentality

Schmankerl /ˈʃmaŋkɐl/ *das;* ∼s, ∼n (bayr., österr.) delicacy; (fig.) treat

schmarotzen /ʃmaˈrɔtsn̩/ *itr. V.* **(a)** (abwertend) sponge; free-load (sl.); **bei jmdm.** ∼: sponge on sb.; **(b)** (Biol.) live as a parasite (**in/auf** + *Dat.* in/on)

Schmarotzer *der;* ∼s, ∼ **(a)** (abwertend) sponger; free-loader (sl.); **(b)** (Biol.) parasite

Schmarren /ˈʃmarən/ *der;* ∼s, ∼ **(a)** (österr., auch südd.) *pancake broken up with a fork after frying;* **(b)** (ugs. abwertend: Unsinn) trash; rubbish

schmatzen *itr. V.* smack one's lips; (geräuschvoll essen) eat noisily

Schmaus /ˈʃmaus/ *der;* ∼es, **Schmäuse** /ˈʃmɔyzə/ (veralt., noch scherzh.) [good] spread (coll.); (reichhaltig) feast

schmausen (veralt.) **1** *itr. V.* eat with relish. **2** *tr. V.* eat ⟨*food*⟩ with relish

schmecken /ˈʃmɛkn̩/ **1** *itr. V.* taste (**nach** of); [**gut**] ∼: taste good; **das hat geschmeckt** that was good; (war köstlich) that was delicious; **schmeckt es [dir]?** are you enjoying it *or* your meal?; [how] do you like it?; **lasst es euch** ∼! enjoy your food!; tuck in! (coll.) **2** *tr. V.* taste; (kosten) sample

Schmeichelei *die;* ∼, ∼en flattering remark; blandishment

schmeichelhaft **1** *Adj.* flattering; complimentary ⟨*words, speech*⟩; **wenig** ∼: not very flattering. **2** *adv.* flatteringly

schmeicheln /ˈʃmaiçln̩/ *itr. V.* jmdm. ∼: flatter sb.

Schmeichler /ˈʃmaiçlɐ/ *der;* ∼s, ∼, **Schmeichlerin** *die;* ∼, ∼nen flatterer

schmeichlerisch *Adj.* flattering; honeyed ⟨*words, tone*⟩

schmeißen /ˈʃmaisn̩/ (ugs.) **1** *unr. tr. V.* **(a)** (werfen) chuck (coll.); sling (coll.); (schleudern) fling; hurl; **etw. nach jmdm.** ∼: throw *or* (coll.) chuck sth. at sb.; **(b)** (abbrechen, aufgeben) chuck in (coll.) ⟨*job, studies, etc.*⟩; **(c)** (spendieren) stand ⟨*drink*⟩; [**für jmdn.**] **eine Party** ∼: throw a party [for sb.] (coll.); **(d)** (bewältigen) handle; deal with; **wir werden den Laden schon** ∼: we'll manage OK (coll.). **2** *unr. refl. V.* **(a)** (sich werfen) throw oneself; (mit Wucht) hurl oneself; **(b) sich in seinen Smoking** *usw.* ∼: get togged up (sl.) in one's dinner jacket *etc.* **3** *unr. itr. V.* **mit Steinen/Tomaten** *usw.* [**nach jmdm.**] ∼: chuck stones/tomatoes *etc.* [at sb.] (coll.); **mit Geld um sich** ∼ (fig.) throw one's money around; lash out (coll.)

Schmeiß·fliege *die* blowfly; (blaue ∼) bluebottle

Schmelze *die;* ∼, ∼n [process of] melting

schmelzen /ˈʃmɛltsn̩/ **1** *unr. itr. V.; mit sein* melt; (fig.) ⟨*doubts, apprehension, etc.*⟩ dissolve, fade away. **2** *unr. tr. V.* smelt ⟨*ore*⟩; render ⟨*fat*⟩

Schmelz-: ∼käse *der* processed cheese; ∼punkt *der* melting point; ∼tiegel *der* crucible; melting pot (esp. fig.)

Schmer·bauch /ˈʃmeːɐ̯-/ *der* (ugs.) potbelly

Schmerle /ˈʃmɛrlə/ *die;* ∼, ∼n (Zool.) loach

Schmerz /ʃmɛrts/ *der;* ∼es, ∼en **(a)** ▶329 (physisch) pain; (dumpf u. anhaltend) ache; **wo haben Sie** ∼en? where does it hurt?; ∼en **im Arm** pain in one's arm; (an verschiedenen Stellen) pains in one's arm; ∼en **haben** be in pain; **vor** ∼[**en**] **weinen/sich vor** ∼en **winden** cry with/writhe in pain *or* agony; **(b)** ▶329 (psychisch) pain; (Kummer) grief; **ein seelischer** ∼: mental anguish *or* suffering; **jmdm.** ∼en **bereiten** cause sb. pain/grief

schmerz·empfindlich *Adj.* sensitive to pain *pred.;* ∼ **sein** have a low pain threshold

schmerzen ▶329 **1** *tr. V.* jmdm. ∼: hurt sb.; (Kummer bereiten) grieve sb.; cause sb. sorrow; **es schmerzt mich,**

dass …: it grieves *or* pains me that … **2** *itr. V.* hurt; **heftig** ∼: be intensely painful

Schmerzens-: ∼geld *das* compensation (*for pain and suffering caused*); exemplary damages (Law); ∼schrei *der* cry of pain; (laut) scream [of pain]

schmerz·frei *Adj.* free of pain *pred.;* painless ⟨*operation*⟩

Schmerz·grenze *die* (fig.) **jetzt/dann ist die** ∼ **erreicht** this/that is the absolute limit

schmerzhaft *Adj.* painful; (wund) sore

schmerzlich **1** *Adj.* painful; distressing; **die** ∼e **Gewissheit haben, dass** …: be painfully aware that … **2** *adv.* painfully

schmerz-, Schmerz-: ∼lindernd **1** *Adj.* pain-relieving; **2** *adv.* ∼lindernd wirken relieve pain; ∼los **1** *Adj.* painless; **2** *adv.* painlessly; *s. auch* kurz **2** c; ∼stillend **1** *Adj.* pain-killing; analgesic (Med.); ∼stillendes Mittel painkiller; analgesic; **2** *adv.* ∼stillend wirken have a painkilling *or* analgesic effect; ∼tablette *die* pain-killing *or* (Med.) analgesic tablet; ∼verzerrt *Adj.* ⟨*face, smile*⟩ distorted *or* twisted with pain

Schmerz·schwelle *die* (Physiol.) pain threshold

Schmetter·ball *der* (Tennis usw.) smash

Schmetterling *der;* ∼s, ∼e butterfly; (Nachtfalter) moth

Schmetterlings·stil *der; o. Pl.* (Schwimmen) butterfly [stroke]

schmettern /ˈʃmɛtɐn/ **1** *tr. V.* **(a)** (schleudern) hurl (**an** + *Akk.* at, **gegen** against); **jmdn./etw. zu Boden** ∼: send sb./sth. crashing to the ground; **(b)** (laut spielen, singen usw.) blare out ⟨*march, music*⟩; ⟨*person*⟩ sing lustily ⟨*song*⟩; bellow ⟨*order*⟩; **einen Tusch** ∼: unleash a loud flourish; **(c)** (Tennis usw.) smash ⟨*ball*⟩. **2** *itr. V.* **(a)** *mit sein* (aufprallen) crash; smash; **(b)** (schallen) ⟨*trumpet, music, etc.*⟩ blare out

Schmetter·schlag *der* (bes. Faustball, Volleyball) smash

Schmied /ʃmiːt/ *der;* ∼[e]s, ∼e ▶85 blacksmith; *s. auch* Glück b

Schmiede *die;* ∼, ∼n smithy; forge

schmiede·eisern *Adj.* wrought-iron

schmieden *tr. V.* (auch fig.) forge (**zu** into, **aus** from, out of); **Pläne/ein Komplott** ∼ (fig.) hatch plans/a plot

schmiegen /ˈʃmiːgn̩/ **1** *refl. V.* snuggle, nestle (**in** + *Akk.* in); **sich an jmdn.** ∼: snuggle [close] up to sb.; **sie schmiegte sich eng an seine Seite** she pressed *or* nestled close to his side. **2** *tr. V.* press (**an** + *Akk.* against)

schmiegsam *Adj.* supple ⟨*leather, material*⟩

Schmiere¹ *die;* ∼, ∼n **(a)** (Schmierfett) grease; **(b)** (schwieriger Schmutz) greasy *or* slimy mess; **(c)** (ugs. abwertend: Provinztheater) flea-pit (sl.) of a provincial theatre

Schmiere² *die;* ∼: *in* [**bei etw.**] ∼ **stehen** (ugs.) act as lookout [while sth. takes place]

schmieren /ˈʃmiːrən/ **1** *tr. V.* **(a)** (mit Schmiermitteln) lubricate; (mit Schmierfett) grease; [**gehen** *od.* **laufen**] **wie geschmiert** (ugs.) [go] like clockwork *or* without a hitch; **(b)** (streichen, auftragen) spread ⟨*butter, jam, etc.*⟩ (**auf** + *Akk.* on); **Salbe auf eine Wunde** ∼: apply ointment to a wound; **sich** (*Dat.*) **Creme ins Gesicht** ∼: rub cream into one's face; **(c)** (mit Aufstrich) **Brote** ∼: spread slices of bread; **(d)** (abwertend: unsauber schreiben) scrawl ⟨*essay, school work*⟩; (schnell und nachlässig schreiben) scribble, dash off ⟨*article, play, etc.*⟩; **(e) jmdm. eine** ∼ (salopp) give sb. a clout (coll.). **2** *itr. V.* **(a)** ⟨*oil, grease*⟩ lubricate; **(b)** (ugs. unsauber schreiben) ⟨*person*⟩ scrawl, scribble; ⟨*pen, ink*⟩ smudge, make smudges

Schmieren·komödiant *der* (abwertend) cheapjack play-actor

Schmiererei *die;* ∼, ∼en (ugs. abwertend) **(a)** *o. Pl.* (unsauberes Schreiben) scrawling; scribbling; **(b)** (unsauber Geschriebenes) scrawl; scribble

Schmier-: ∼fett *das* grease; ∼fink *der* (ugs. abwertend) (im Schreiben) messy writer; (jmd., der Wände beschmiert) graffiti-writer; (jmd., der Diffamierendes schreibt) muck-raker; ∼heft *das* rough-book

schmierig *Adj.* **(a)** greasy ⟨*surface, clothes, hands, step, etc.*⟩; slimy ⟨*earth, surface*⟩; **(b)** (abwertend: widerlich freundlich) slimy, (coll.) smarmy ⟨*person*⟩

Schmier-: ~**mittel** *das* lubricant; ~**papier** *das* scrap paper; ~**seife** *die* soft soap

Schmier·papier *das* scrap paper

schmilzt /ʃmɪltst/ *2. u. 3. Pers. Sg. Präsens v.* **schmelzen**

Schminke /'ʃmɪŋkə/ *die;* ~, ~n make-up

schminken 1 *tr. V.* make up ‹*face, eyes*›; **die Lippen** ~: put lipstick on. 2 *refl. V.* make oneself up; put on make-up

schmirgeln /'ʃmɪrgl̩n/ *tr. V.* rub down; (bes. mit Sandpapier) sand; remove ‹*paint, rust*› with emery paper/sandpaper

Schmirgel·papier *das* emery paper; (Sandpapier) sandpaper

schmiss, *schmiß /ʃmɪs/ *1. u. 3. Pers. Sg. Prät. v.* **schmeißen**

Schmöker /'ʃmøːkɐ/ *der;* ~s, ~ (ugs.) lightweight adventure story/romance; **ein dicker** ~: a thick tome of light reading

schmökern (ugs.) 1 *itr. V.* bury oneself in a book. 2 *tr. V.* bury oneself in ‹*book*›

schmollen /'ʃmɔlən/ *itr. V.* sulk; **mit jmdm.** ~: be in a huff and refuse to speak to sb.

Schmoll·mund *der* pouting mouth; **einen** ~**mund machen** *od.* **ziehen** pout

schmolz /ʃmɔlts/ *1. u. 3. Pers. Sg. Prät. v.* **schmelzen**

Schmonzes /'ʃmɔntsəs/ *der;* ~ (ugs. abwertend) idle chatter; silly talk

Schmor·braten *der* pot roast; braised beef

schmoren /'ʃmoːrən/ 1 *tr. V.* braise; **jmdn. [im eigenen Saft]** ~ **lassen** (ugs.) leave sb. to stew in his/her own juice. 2 *itr. V.* (a) (garen) braise; (b) (ugs.: schwitzen) swelter

Schmu /ʃmuː/ *der;* ~s (ugs.) *in* ~ **machen** cheat; work a fiddle (coll.)

schmuck /ʃmʊk/ *Adj.* attractive; pretty; (schick) smart ‹*clothes, house, ship, etc.*›

Schmuck *der;* ~[e]s (a) (~stücke) jewelry; jewellery (esp. Brit.); (b) (~stück) piece of jewelry/jewellery; (c) (Zierde) decoration

schmücken /'ʃmʏkn̩/ *tr. V.* decorate; embellish ‹*writings, speech*›

schmuck-, Schmuck-: ~**kästchen** *das*, ~**kasten** *der* jewelry *or* (esp. Brit.) jewellery box; ~**los** *Adj.* plain; bare ‹*room*›

Schmucklosigkeit *die;* ~: plainness; (eines Zimmers) bareness

Schmuck·stück *das* piece of jewelry *or* (esp. Brit.) jewellery; **das** ~ **seiner Sammlung** (fig.) the jewel of his collection

schmuddelig /'ʃmʊdəlɪç/ *Adj.* (ugs. abwertend) grubby; mucky (coll.); (schmutzig u. unordentlich) messy; grotty (Brit. coll.)

Schmuggel /'ʃmʊgl̩/ *der;* ~s smuggling *no art.;* ~ **treiben** smuggle

schmuggeln *tr., itr. V.* smuggle (**in** + *Akk.* into; **aus** out of)

Schmuggel·ware *die* smuggled goods *pl.;* contraband *no pl.*

Schmuggler *der;* ~s, ~, **Schmugglerin** *die;* ~, ~**nen** smuggler

schmunzeln /'ʃmʊntsl̩n/ *itr. V.* smile to oneself

Schmus /ʃmuːs/ *der;* ~es (ugs.) waffle; (Schmeichelei) soft soap

schmusen /'ʃmuːzn̩/ *itr. V.* (ugs.) cuddle; ‹*couple*› kiss and cuddle; **mit jmdm.** ~: cuddle sb.; ‹*lover*› kiss and cuddle *or* (coll.) neck with sb.

Schmuser *der;* ~s, ~ (ugs.) affectionate type; cuddly sort (coll.)

Schmutz /ʃmʊts/ *der;* ~es (a) dirt; (Schlamm) mud; **etw. macht viel/keinen** ~: sth. makes a great deal of/leaves no mess; **jmdn./etw. durch den** ~ **ziehen** (fig.) drag sb./sth. through the mud (fig.); (b) (abwertend: Literatur usw.) filth; ~ **und Schund** trash and filth

schmutzen *itr. V.* get dirty

Schmutz-: ~**fänger** *der* (a) (etw., das Schmutz anzieht) dirt-trap; (b) (bei Fahrzeugen) mudflap; ~**fink** *der;* ~en *od.* ~s, ~en (ugs.) (a) (unsauberer Mensch) [dirty] pig (coll.); (Kind) dirty brat; (b) (unmoralischer Mensch) depraved type (coll.); ~**fleck** *der* dirty mark (**in** + *Dat.* on); (in der Landschaft usw.) blot

schmutzig 1 *Adj.* (a) (unsauber) dirty; (ungepflegt) dirty, slovenly ‹*person, restaurant, etc.*›; **sich** ~ **machen** get [oneself] dirty; (b) (abwertend) cocky ‹*remarks*›; smutty ‹*joke, song, story*›; dirty ‹*thoughts, business, war*›; crooked, shady ‹*practices, deal*›. 2 *adv.* (abwertend) ~ **grinsen** smirk

Schmutzigkeit *die;* ~: dirtiness

Schmutz-: ~**titel** *der* (Druckw.) half-title; ~**wäsche** *die* dirty washing

Schnabel /'ʃnaːbl̩/ *der;* ~s, **Schnäbel** /'ʃnɛːbl̩/ (a) beak; (bei ‹: Mund) gob (sl.); **reden, wie einem der** ~ **gewachsen ist** say just what one thinks

schnäbeln /'ʃnɛːbl̩n/ *itr. V.* (a) ‹*birds*› bill; (b) (ugs. scherzh.: sich küssen) bill and coo

Schnabel·tier *das* duck-billed platypus

schnabulieren /ʃnabuˈliːrən/ *tr., itr. V.* (fam.) eat with great enjoyment

Schnack /ʃnak/ *der;* ~[e]s, ~s *od.* **Schnäcke** /'ʃnɛkə/ (nordd.) (a) (Unterhaltung) chat; (b) (abwertend: Gerede) [idle] chatter; gossip; (c) (witziger Spruch) witty saying; bon mot

schnacken *itr. V.* (nordd.) chat; **Platt** ~: speak Low German dialect

Schnake /'ʃnaːkə/ *die;* ~, ~n (a) daddy-long-legs; crane-fly; (b) (bes. südd.: Stechmücke) mosquito

Schnaken·stich *der* (bes. südd.) mosquito bite

Schnalle /'ʃnalə/ *die;* ~, ~n (a) (Gürtel~) buckle; (b) (österr.: Türklinke) door handle

schnallen *tr. V.* (a) (mit einer Schnalle festziehen) buckle ‹*shoe, belt*›; fasten ‹*strap*›; **den Gürtel enger/weiter** ~: tighten/loosen one's belt; (b) (mit Riemen/Gurten befestigen) strap (**auf** + *Akk.* on to); (c) (los~) **etw. von etw.** ~: unstrap sth. from sth.; (d) (salopp: begreifen) twig (coll.)

schnalzen *itr. V.* [**mit der Zunge/den Fingern**] ~: click one's tongue/snap one's fingers; **mit der Peitsche** ~: crack the whip

Schnäppchen /'ʃnɛpçən/ *das;* ~s, ~ (ugs.) snip (Brit. coll.); [real] bargain; **ein** ~ **machen** get a [real] bargain

Schnäppchen·jäger *der* (ugs.) bargain hunter

schnappen /'ʃnapn̩/ 1 *itr. V.* (a) **nach jmdm./etw.** ~ ‹*animal*› snap *or* take a snap at sb./sth.; **nach Luft** ~ (fig.) gasp for breath *or* air; (b) *mit sein* **ins Schloss** ~ ‹*door*› click shut; ‹*bolt*› snap home. 2 *tr. V.* (a) ‹*dog, bird, etc.*› snatch; [**sich** (*Dat.*)] **jmdn./etw.** ~ (ugs.) ‹*person*› grab sb./sth.; (mit raschem Zugriff) snatch sb./sth.; (b) (ugs.: festnehmen) catch, (coll.) nab ‹*thief etc.*›

Schnapp-: ~**messer** *das* (a) clasp-knife; (b) (Stichwaffe) flick knife; ~**schloss, *~schloß** *das* spring lock; ~**schuss, *~schuß** *der* snapshot

Schnaps /ʃnaps/ *der;* ~es, **Schnäpse** /'ʃnɛpsə/ (a) spirit; (Klarer) schnapps; **zwei Schnäpse** two glasses of spirit/schnapps; (b) *o. Pl.* (Spirituosen) spirits *pl.*

Schnaps·idee *die* (ugs.) hare-brained idea

schnarchen /'ʃnarçn̩/ *itr. V.* snore

Schnarcher *der;* ~s, ~ (ugs.) snorer

schnarren /'ʃnarən/ *itr. V.* ‹*alarm clock, telephone, doorbell*› buzz [shrilly]

schnattern /'ʃnatɐn/ *itr. V.* (a) ‹*goose etc.*› cackle, gaggle; (b) (ugs.: eifrig schwatzen) jabber [away]; chatter

schnauben /'ʃnaubn̩/ *regelm.* (*auch unr.*) *itr. V.* ‹*person, horse*› snort (**vor** with); (fig.) ‹*steam locomotive*› puff, chuff

schnaufen /'ʃnaufn̩/ *itr. V.* puff, pant (**vor** with); (fig.) ‹*steam locomotive*› puff, chuff

Schnaufer *der;* ~s, ~ (ugs.) breath; **den letzten** ~ **tun** (verhüll.) breathe one's last

Schnauz·bart /'ʃnauts-/ *der* large moustache; mustachio (arch.); (an den Seiten herabhängend) walrus moustache

Schnauze *die;* ~, ~n (a) (von Tieren) muzzle; (der Maus usw.) snout; (Maul) mouth; **eine kalte** ~: a cold nose; (b)

(derb: Mund) gob (sl.); **jmdm. in die ～ hauen** smack sb. in the gob (sl.); **die ～ voll haben** (salopp) be fed up to the back teeth (coll.); **eine große ～ haben** shoot one's mouth off (sl.); **[halt die] ～!** shut your trap! (sl.); **frei [nach] ～, nach ～** (salopp) as one thinks fit; as the mood takes one; **(c)** (ugs.) (eines Flugzeugs) nose; (eines Fahrzeugs) front

schnauzen *tr., itr. V.* (ugs.) bark; (ärgerlich) snap; snarl

schnäuzen /'ʃnɔytsn̩/ **1** *tr. V.* **einem Kind die Nase ～:** blow a child's nose; **sich** (*Dat.*) **die Nase ～:** blow one's nose. **2** *refl. V.* (geh.) blow one's nose

Schnauzer *der;* **～s, ～** **(a)** (Hund) schnauzer; **(b)** (ugs.) ⇒ **Schnauzbart**

Schnecke /'ʃnɛkə/ *die* **(a)** (Tier) snail; (Nackt～) slug; **jmdn. [so] zur ～ machen** (ugs.) give sb. [such] a good carpeting (coll.); **(b)** (ugs.: Gebäck) Belgian bun

Schnecken-: ～haus *das* snail-shell; **～tempo** *das* (ugs.) snail's pace

Schnee /ʃneː/ *der;* **～s** **(a)** snow; **in tiefem ～ liegen** lie under deep snow; **(b)** (Eier～) beaten egg white; **das Eiweiß zu ～ schlagen** beat the egg white until stiff; **(c)** (Jargon: Kokain) snow (sl.)

Schnee·ball *der* **(a)** snowball; **(b)** (Strauch) snowball-tree; guelder rose

Schneeball·schlacht *die* snowball fight

schnee-, Schnee-: ～bedeckt *Adj.* snow-covered; **～besen** *der* whisk; **～blind** *Adj.* snow-blind; **～brille** *die* snow goggles *pl.;* **～fall** *der* snowfall; fall of snow; **～flocke** *die* snowflake; **～frei** *Adj.* free of snow *postpos.;* **～gestöber** *das* snow flurry; **～glätte** *die* [slippery surface due to] packed snow; **～glöckchen** *das* snowdrop; **～grenze** *die* ▶ 277 | snow-line; (beweglich) snow limit; **～kette** *die* snow-chain; **～könig** *der* **in sich freuen wie ein ～könig** (ugs.) be as pleased as Punch; **～mann** *der* snowman; **～matsch** *der* slush; **～pflug** *der* (auch Ski) snowplough; **～schmelze** *die* melting of the snow; thaw; **～sturm** *der* snowstorm; **～treiben** *das* driving snow; **～verhältnisse** *Pl.* snow conditions; **～verwehungen** *Pl.* snowdrifts *pl.*

Schneewittchen /-'vɪtçən/ *das;* **～s** Snow White

Schneid *der;* **～[e]s,** südd., österr.: *die;* **～** (ugs.) guts *pl.* (coll.)

Schneid·brenner *der* (Technik) cutting torch; oxyacetylene cutter

Schneide /'ʃnaɪdə/ *die;* **～, ～n** [cutting] edge; (Klinge) blade

schneiden 1 *unr. itr. V.* **(a)** cut (**in** + *Akk.* into); **(b)** (Medizinerjargon) operate; **(c) ～d** biting ‹*wind, cold, voice, sarcasm*›. **2** *unr. tr. V.* **(a)** cut; cut, reap ‹*corn etc.*›; cut, mow ‹*grass*›; (in Scheiben) slice ‹*bread, sausage, etc.*›; (klein ～·) cut up, chop ‹*wood, vegetables*›; (zu～) cut out ‹*dress*›; (stutzen) prune ‹*tree, bush*›; trim ‹*beard*›; **sich** (*Dat.*) **jmdm. die Haare ～ lassen** have one's hair cut by sb.; **hier ist eine Luft zum Schneiden** (fig.) there's a terrible fug in here (coll.); **ein eng/weit/gut geschnittenes Kleid** a tight-fitting/loose-fitting/well-cut dress; **(b)** (Medizinerjargon: auf～) operate on ‹*patient*›; cut [open] ‹*tumour, ulcer, etc.*›; lance ‹*boil, abscess*›; **(c)** (Film, Rundf., Ferns.: cutten) cut, edit ‹*film, tape*›; **(d)** (beim Fahren) **eine Kurve ～:** cut a corner; **jmdn./einen anderen Wagen ～:** cut in on sb./another car; **(e)** (kreuzen) ‹*line, railway, etc.*› intersect, cross; **die Linien/Straßen ～ sich** the lines/roads intersect; **(f)** (Tennis usw.) slice, put spin on ‹*ball*›; (Fußball) curve ‹*ball, free kick*›; (Billard) put side on ‹*ball*›; **(g) eine Grimasse ～:** grimace; **(h)** (ignorieren) **jmdn. ～:** cut sb. dead; send sb. to Coventry (Brit.). **3** *refl. V.* **ich habe mir** *od.* **mich in den Finger geschnitten** I've cut my finger

Schneider *der;* **～s, ～** ▶ 85 | **(a)** tailor; (Damen～) dressmaker; **frieren wie ein ～** (ugs.) be frozen stiff; **(b)** (ugs.: Schneidegerät) cutter; (für Scheiben) slicer; **(c)** (Skat) schneider; **aus dem ～ sein** (fig.) be in the clear; be clear of trouble

Schneiderei *die;* **～, ～en** **(a)** tailor's shop; (Damen～) dressmaker's shop; **(b)** *o. Pl.* (das Schneidern) tailoring; (von Damenkleidern) dressmaking

Schneiderin *die;* **～, ～nen** ▶ 85 | tailor; (Damen～) dressmaker

schneidern 1 *tr. V.* make ‹*dress, clothes*›; make, tailor ‹*suit*›. **2** *itr. V.* make clothes/dresses; (beruflich) work as a tailor; (als Damenschneider) work as a dressmaker

Schneider-: ～puppe *die* tailor's dummy; **～sitz** *der* cross-legged position; **im ～sitz** cross-legged

Schneide·zahn *der* ▶ 326 | incisor

schneidig 1 *Adj.* **(a)** (forsch, zackig) dashing; (waghalsig) daring; bold; rousing, brisk ‹*music*›; **(b)** (flott, sportlich) dashing ‹*appearance, fellow*›; trim ‹*figure*›. **2** *adv.* briskly

schneien /'ʃnaɪən/ *itr. V.* **(a)** (unpers.) **es schneit** it is snowing; **es schneit jeden Tag** it snows every day; **(b)** *mit sein* (fig.) ‹*blossom, confetti, etc.*› rain down, fall like snow

Schneise /'ʃnaɪzə/ *die;* **～, ～n** **(a)** (Wald～) aisle; (als Feuerschutz) firebreak; **(b)** (Flug～) [air] corridor

schnell /ʃnɛl/ **1** *Adj.* ▶ 224 | quick ‹*journey, decision, service, etc.*›; fast ‹*car, skis, road, track, etc.*›; quick, rapid, swift ‹*progress*›; quick, swift ‹*movement, blow, action*›; **ein ～es Tempo** a high speed; a fast pace; **auf die Schnelle** (ugs.) in a trice; (übereilt) in [too much of] a hurry; in a rush; (kurzfristig) at short notice; quickly. **2** *adv.* ▶ 224 | quickly; ‹*drive, move, etc.*› fast, quickly; ‹*spread*› quickly, rapidly; (bald) soon ‹*sold, past, etc.*›; **nicht so ～!** not so fast!; **mach ～!** (ugs.) move it! (coll.); **wie heißt er noch ～?** (ugs.) what's his name again?

Schnell·bahn *die* (Verkehrsw.) municipal railway

Schnelle *die;* **～, ～n** **(a)** *o. Pl.* rapidity; **(b)** (Geogr.: Strom～) rapids *pl.*

***schnellebig** ⇒ **schnelllebig**

schnellen 1 *itr. V.; mit sein* shoot (**aus** + *Dat.* out of; **in** + *Akk.* into); **in die Höhe ～:** ‹*person*› leap to one's feet *or* up; ‹*rocket, fig.: prices etc.*› shoot up. **2** *tr. V.* send ‹*ball, stone, etc.*› flying; hurl ‹*ball, stone, etc.*›; whip ‹*fishing-line*›

Schnell·hefter *der* loose-leaf binder; quick-release file

Schnelligkeit *die;* **～, ～en** speed

schnell-, Schnell-: ～imbiss, *～imbiß *der* snackbar; **～koch·topf** *der* pressure cooker; **～kurs** *der* crash course; **～lebig** /-leːbɪç/ *Adj.* fast-moving ‹*age*›; **～reinigung** *die* express cleaner's; **～spanner** *der* quick-release; **～spann·nabe** *die* quick-release hub; **～straße** *die* expressway (on which slow-moving vehicles are prohibited); **～zug** *der* express [train]

schnellstens *Adv.* as quickly as possible; (möglichst bald) as soon as possible

schnellst·möglich 1 *Adj.* quickest possible; **auf ～e Erledigung der Arbeit drängen** press for the earliest possible completion of the work. **2** *adv.* ⇒ **schnellstens**

Schnell·verfahren *das* **(a)** (bes. Technik) high speed process; **im ～verfahren** (fig.) at high speed; in a crash programme; **(b)** (Rechtsw.) summary trial; summary proceedings *pl.;* **im ～verfahren** in summary proceedings

Schnepfe /'ʃnɛpfə/ **(a)** *die;* **～, ～n** snipe; (Wald～) woodcock **(b)** (salopp abwertend: weibliche Person) [blöde] **～:** [silly] cow (sl. derog.)

schnetzeln /'ʃnɛtsln̩/ (bes. südd.) cut ‹*meat*› into thin strips

***schneuzen** ⇒ **schnäuzen**

Schnick·schnack *der* (ugs.) **(a)** (wertloses Zeug) trinkets *pl.;* (Zierrat) frills *pl.* (fig.); **(b)** (Geschwätz) waffle; (Unsinn) drivel

schniefen /'ʃniːfn̩/ *itr. V.* sniffle; (bes. beim Weinen) snivel

schniegeln /'ʃniːgln̩/ *refl. V.* spruce oneself up

schnieke /'ʃniːkə/ **1** *Adj.* (berlin.) **(a)** (schick, elegant) snazzy (sl.) ‹*clothes, fashion, etc.*›; **(b)** (großartig) super (Brit. coll.). **2** *adv.* snazzily (sl.)

schnipp *Interj.* snip; **～, schnapp!** snip, snip

Schnippchen *das;* **～s** trick; **jmdm. ein ～ schlagen** (ugs.) outsmart sb. (coll.); put one over on sb. (sl.)

Schnippel *der od. das;* **～s, ～** (ugs.) ⇒ **Schnipsel**

schnippeln (ugs.) **1** *itr. V.* (mit der Schere) snip [away] (**an** + *Dat.* at); **an der Wurst ～** (mit dem Messer) cut little snippets of sausage. **2** *tr. V.* **(a)** (ausschneiden) snip [out]; **(b)** (zerkleinern) shred ‹*vegetables*›; chop ‹*beans etc.*› [finely]

schnippen /'ʃnɪpn/ **1** *itr. V.* (mit den Fingern) snap one's fingers (**nach** at). **2** *tr. V.* (**a**) (wegschleudern) flick (**von** off, from); **die Asche von der Zigarette** ~: flick the ash off one's cigarette; (**b**) (herausschleudern) tap ‹*cigarette, card, etc.*› (**aus** out of)

schnippisch 1 *Adj.* pert ‹*reply, tone, etc.*›; (anmaßend) cocky ‹*girl, tone, expression*›. **2** *adv.* pertly; (anmaßend) cockily

Schnipsel /'ʃnɪpsl̩/ *der od. das;* ~**s,** ~: scrap; (Papier~, Stoff~) snippet; shred

schnipseln ⇨ **schnippeln**

schnitt /ʃnɪt/ *1. u. 3. Pers. Sg. Prät. v.* **schneiden**

Schnitt *der;* ~**[e]s,** ~**e** (**a**) cut; (**b**) (das Mähen) (von Gras) mowing; cut; (von Getreide) harvest; **einen** *od.* **seinen** ~ **[bei etw.] machen** (fig. ugs.) make a profit [from sth.]; (**c**) (Film, Ferns.) editing; cutting; (**d**) (~muster) [dressmaking] pattern; (**e**) (Längs~, Quer~, Schräg~) section; (**f**) (ugs.: Durch~) average; **er fährt einen** ~ **von 200 km/h** he is driving at *or* doing an average [speed] of 125 m.p.h.; **im** ~: on average; (**g**) (Math.) ⇨ **golden 1c;** (**h**) (Geom.: ~fläche) intersection; (**i**) (Ballspiele: Drall) spin

Schnitt-: ~**blume** *die* cut flower; ~**bohne** *die* French bean; ~**brot** *das* cut *or* sliced bread

Schnittchen *das;* ~**s,** ~: canapé; [small] open sandwich

Schnitte *die;* ~, ~**n** (**a**) (bes. nordd.: Scheibe) slice; **eine** ~ **[Brot]** a slice of bread; **eine [belegte]** ~: an open sandwich; (**b**) *meist Pl.* (österr.: Waffel) wafer

schnitt-, Schnitt-: ~**fest** *Adj.* firm ‹*tomato, sausage, etc.*›; ~**fläche** *die* cut surface

Schnitt·fläche *die* cut surface

schnittig 1 *Adj.* stylish, smart ‹*suit, appearance, etc.*›; (sportlich) racy ‹*car, yacht, etc.*›. **2** *adv.* stylishly; (sportlich) racily

Schnitt-: ~**käse** *der* cheese suitable for slicing; hard cheese; (in Scheiben) cheese slices *pl.;* ~**lauch** *der* chives *pl.;* ~**menge** *die* (Math.) **die** ~**menge A ∩ B** the intersection of the sets A and B; ~**muster** *das* [dressmaking] pattern; ~**muster·bogen** *der* pattern chart; ~**punkt** *der* intersection; (Geom.) point of intersection; ~**stelle** *die* (DV) interface; ~**wunde** *die* cut; (lang und tief) gash

Schnitzel /'ʃnɪtsl̩/ *das;* ~**s,** ~ (**a**) (Fleisch) [veal/pork] escalope; (**b**) (Stückchen) (von Papier) scrap; snippet; (von Holz) shaving

Schnitzel·jagd *die* paperchase

schnitzeln *tr. V.* chop up ‹*vegetables etc.*› [into small pieces]; shred ‹*cabbage*›

schnitzen *tr., itr. V.* carve; **an etw.** (*Dat.*) ~: carve away at sth.

Schnitzer *der;* ~**s,** ~ (**a**) (Handwerker) carver; (**b**) (ugs.: Fehler) boob (Brit. sl.); goof (sl.); **sich** (*Dat.*) **einen groben** ~ **leisten** make an awful boob (Brit. sl.) *or* (sl.) goof; (mit einer Bemerkung) drop an awful clanger (Brit. sl.)

Schnitzerei *die;* ~, ~**en** carving

Schnitz·messer *das* wood-carving knife

schnob /ʃnoːp/ *1. u. 3. Pers. Sg. Prät. v.* **schnauben**

schnodderig /'ʃnɔdərɪç/ (ugs.) **1** *Adj.* brash. **2** *adv.* brashly

Schnodderigkeit *die;* ~, ~**en** (ugs.) (**a**) *o. Pl.* (Art, Wesen) brashness; (**b**) (Äußerung/Handlung) brash remark/action

schnöde (geh. abwertend) **1** *Adj.* (**a**) (verachtenswert) despicable; contemptible; base ‹*cowardice*›; (**b**) (gemein) contemptuous, scornful ‹*glance, reply, etc.*›; harsh ‹*reprimand*›. **2** *adv.* (gemein) contemptuously; ‹*reprimand*› harshly; ‹*exploit, misuse*› flagrantly, blatantly

Schnorchel /'ʃnɔrçl̩/ *der;* ~**s,** ~: snorkel

Schnörkel /'ʃnœrkl̩/ *der;* ~**s,** ~: scroll; curlicue; (der Handschrift, in der Rede) flourish

schnorren /'ʃnɔrən/ *tr., itr. V.* (ugs.) scrounge (coll.); **etw. bei** *od.* **von jmdm.** ~: scrounge (coll.) *or* cadge sth. off sb.

Schnorrer *der;* ~**s,** ~ (ugs.) scrounger (coll.); sponger

Schnösel /'ʃnøːzl̩/ *der;* ~**s,** ~ (ugs. abwertend) young whippersnapper

schnuckelig *Adj.* (ugs.) sweet; cute (Amer. coll.)

schnüffeln /'ʃnʏfl̩n/ **1** *itr. V.* (**a**) (riechen) sniff; **an etw.** (*Dat.*) ~: sniff sth.; (**b**) (ugs. abwertend: heimlich suchen; spionieren) snoop [about] (coll.); **in etw.** (*Akk.*) ~: pry into sth.; stick one's nose into sth. (coll.); **in jmds. Papieren** ~: nose about in sb.'s papers; (**c**) (Drogenjargon: Dämpfe ~) sniff [glue/paint *etc.*]; (**d**) (ugs.: die Nase hochziehen) sniff. **2** *tr. V.* (Drogenjargon) sniff ‹*glue etc.*›

Schnüffler *der;* ~**s,** ~ (**a**) (ugs. abwertend) Nosey Parker; (Spion) snooper (coll.); (**b**) (Drogenjargon) [glue-, paint-, *etc.*]sniffer

Schnuller /'ʃnʊlɐ/ *der;* ~**s,** ~: dummy (Brit.); pacifier (Amer.)

Schnulze /'ʃnʊltsə/ *die;* ~, ~**n** (ugs. abwertend) (Lied/Melodie) slushy song/tune; (Theaterstück, Film, Fernsehspiel) tearjerker (coll.); slushy play

schnupfen /'ʃnʊpfn̩/ **1** *itr. V.* (**a**) (Tabak ~) take snuff; (**b**) (bei Tränen, Nasenschleim) sniff. **2** *tr. V.* take a sniff of ‹*cocaine etc.*›; (gewohnheitsmäßig) sniff ‹*cocaine etc.*›; **Tabak** ~: take snuff

Schnupfen *der;* ~**s,** ~: [head] cold; [**den** *od.* **einen**] ~ **haben** have a [head] cold

Schnupf·tabak *der* snuff

schnuppe /'ʃnʊpə/ *das/er ist mir* ~**/ist mir völlig** ~ (ugs.) I don't care/I couldn't care less about it/him (coll.)

schnuppern /'ʃnʊpɐn/ **1** *itr. V.* sniff; **an etw.** (*Dat.*) ~: sniff sth.. **2** *tr. V.* sniff

Schnur /ʃnuːɐ/ *die;* ~, **Schnüre** /'ʃnyːrə/ *od.* **Schnuren** (**a**) (Bindfaden) piece of string; (Kordel) piece of cord; (Zelt~) guy[-rope]; (**b**) (ugs.: Kabel) flex (Brit.); lead; cord (Amer.)

Schnürchen *das;* ~**s,** ~: *in* **wie am** ~**[gehen** *od.* **klappen]** (ugs.) [go] like clockwork *or* without a hitch; **ein Gedicht wie am** ~ **aufsagen** (ugs.) say a poem off pat

schnüren /'ʃnyːrən/ **1** *tr. V.* (**a**) tie ‹*bundle, string, sb.'s hands, etc.*›; tie [up] ‹*parcel, person*›; tie, lace up ‹*shoe, corset, etc.*›; **etw. zu Bündeln** ~: tie sth. up in bundles; (**b**) **Angst schnürte ihm die Kehle** (fig.) fear constricted his throat. **2** *refl. V.* **sich in das Fleisch** *usw.* ~: cut into the flesh *etc.*

schnur·gerade *Adj., adv.* dead straight

schnur·los *Adj.* cordless

Schnürl·regen *der* (österr.) persistent rain

Schnurr·bart *der* moustache

schnurr·bärtig *Adj.* with a moustache *postpos.;* ~ **sein** have a moustache

schnurren /'ʃnʊrən/ *itr. V.* ‹*cat*› purr; ‹*machine*› hum; ‹*camera, spinning wheel, etc.*› whirr

Schnurr·haar *das* (Zool.) whiskers *pl.*

Schnür-: ~**schuh** *der* lace-up shoe; ~**senkel** /~zɛŋkl̩/ *der* (bes. nordd.) [shoe-]lace; (für Stiefel) bootlace; **sich** (*Dat.*) **die** ~**senkel binden** tie one's shoe-laces; ~**stiefel** *der* lace-up boot

schnur·stracks *Adv.* (ugs.) straight

schnurz /ʃnʊrts/ *Adj.* (ugs.) ⇨ **schnuppe**

Schnute /'ʃnuːtə/ *die;* ~, ~**n** (fam., bes. nordd.: Mund) mouth; gob (sl.); **eine** ~ **ziehen** *od.* **machen** make *or* pull a [sulky] face

schob /ʃoːp/ *1. u. 3. Pers. Prät. v.* **schieben**

Schober /'ʃoːbɐ/ *der;* ~**s,** ~ (**a**) open-sided barn; (**b**) (Heuhaufen) [hay-]stack; (Getreide) [hay-]rick

Schock *der;* ~**[e]s,** ~**s** (auch Med.) shock; **jmdm. einen [schweren/leichten]** ~ **versetzen** *od.* **geben** give sb. a [nasty/slight] shock *or* a [nasty/bit of a] fright; **unter** ~ **stehen** be in [a state of] shock; be suffering from shock

schocken *tr. V.* (ugs.) shock

Schocker *der;* ~**s,** ~ (ugs.) (Roman/Film) sensational book/film; shocker (coll.)

schockieren *tr. V.* shock; **über etw.** (*Akk.*) **schockiert sein** be shocked at sth.

schofel /'ʃoːfl̩/, **schofelig** (ugs. abwertend) **1** *Adj.* horrid (coll.); beastly (coll.); (schändlich) disgusting. **2** *adv.* horridly

Schöffe /'ʃœfə/ *der;* ~n, ~n lay judge (*acting together with another lay judge and a professional judge*)

Schöffen·gericht *das; court presided over by a professional judge and two lay judges*

Schöffin *die;* ~, ~nen ⇨ Schöffe

Schokolade /ʃoko'laːdə/ *die;* ~, ~n (a) (Süßigkeit) chocolate; (b) (Getränk) [drinking] chocolate

schokolade[n]-, Schokolade[n]-: ~**braun** *Adj.* chocolate[-brown]; ~**eis** *das* chocolate ice cream; ~**guss**, ***~**guß** *der* chocolate icing

Schokoladen-: ~**pudding** *der* chocolate blancmange; ~**seite** *die* (ugs.) best side; ~**torte** *die* chocolate cake *or* gateau

scholl /ʃɔl/ *1. u. 3. Pers. Sg. Prät. v.* **schallen**

Scholle /'ʃɔlə/ *die;* ~, ~n (a) (Erd~) clod [of earth]; **die heimatliche** ~ (fig.) one's native soil; (b) (Eis~) [ice-]floe; (c) (Fisch) plaice; **die** ~**n** the plaice

Scholli /'ʃɔli/ *in* **mein lieber** ~! (ugs.) my goodness!; good heavens!

schon /ʃoːn/ **1** *Adv.* (a) (bereits) (oft nicht übersetzt) already; (in Fragen) yet; **er kommt** ~ **heute/ist** ~ **gestern gekommen** he's coming today/he came yesterday; **er ist** ~ **da/[an]gekommen** he is already here/has already arrived; **er ist** ~ **gestern angekommen** he arrived as early as yesterday; **wie lange bist du** ~ **hier?** how long have you been here?; ~ **damals/jetzt** even at that time *or* in those days/even now; ~ **[im Jahre] 1926** as early as 1926; back in 1926; (b) (fast gleichzeitig) there and then; **er schwang sich auf das Fahrrad, und** ~ **war er weg** he jumped on the bicycle and was away [in a flash]; (c) (jetzt) ~ **[mal]** now; (inzwischen) meanwhile; (d) (selbst, sogar) even; (nur) only; **das bekommt man** ~ **für 150 Mark** you can get it for as little as 150 marks; (e) (ohne Ergänzung, ohne weiteren Zusatz) on its own; **[allein]** ~ **der Gedanke daran ist schrecklich** the mere thought *or* just the thought of it is dreadful; ~ **der Name ist bezeichnend** the very name is significant; ~ **darum** *od.* **aus diesem Grund** for this reason alone. **2** *Partikel* (a) (verstärkend) really; (gewiss) certainly; **du wirst** ~ **sehen!** you'll see!; (b) (ugs. ungeduldig: endlich) **nun komm** ~! come on!; hurry up!; **und wenn** ~! so what; what if he/she/it does/did/was *etc.;* (c) (beruhigend: wahrscheinlich) all right; **er wird sich** ~ **wieder erholen** he'll recover all right; he's sure to recover; (d) (zustimmend, aber etwas einschränkend) ~ **gut** OK (coll.); **Lust hätte ich** ~, **nur keine Zeit** I'd certainly like to, but I've no time; **das ist** ~ **möglich, nur …:** that is quite possible, only …; (e) (betont: andererseits) **er ist nicht besonders intelligent, aber sein Bruder** ~: he's not particularly intelligent, but his brother is; (f) (einschränkend, abwertend) **was weiß der** ~! what does 'he know [about it]!; **was soll das** ~ **heißen?** what's 'that supposed to mean?

schön /ʃøːn/ **1** *Adj.* (a) (anziehend, reizvoll) beautiful; handsome ⟨*youth, man*⟩; **die** ~**en Künste** the fine arts; ~**e Literatur** belles-lettres *pl.;* **ich finde das Buch** ~: the book appeals to me; (b) (angenehm, erfreulich) pleasant, nice ⟨*day, holiday, dream, relaxation, etc.*⟩; fine ⟨*weather*⟩; (nett) nice; **das war eine** ~**e Zeit** those were wonderful days; **einen** ~**en Tod haben** die peacefully; **das ist** ~ **von dir** it's nice of you; **das Schöne daran/an ihm** the nice thing about it/him; **das ist zu** ~, **um wahr zu sein** that is too good to be true; (c) (gut) good ⟨*wine, beer, piece of work, etc.*⟩; (d) (in Höflichkeitsformeln) ~**e Grüße** best wishes; **recht** ~**en Dank für …:** thank you very much for …; many thanks for …; (e) (ugs.: einverstanden) OK (coll.); all right; **also** ~: right then; ~ **und gut** (ugs.) all well and good; (f) (iron.: leer) ~**e Worte** fine[-sounding] words; (schmeichlerisch) honeyed words; (g) (ugs.: beträchtlich) handsome, (coll.) tidy ⟨*sum, fortune, profit*⟩; considerable ⟨*quantity, distance*⟩; pretty good ⟨*pension*⟩; **das hat ein ganz** ~**es Gewicht** it's quite a weight; (h) (iron.: unerfreulich) nice (coll. iron.); **das sind ja** ~**e Aussichten!** this is a fine lookout *sing.* (iron.); what a delightful prospect! *sing.* (iron.); **eine** ~**e Bescherung** a nice *or* fine mess (coll. iron.). **2** *adv.* (a) (anziehend, reizvoll) beautifully; **sich** ~ **zurechtmachen** make oneself look nice; (b) (angenehm, erfreulich) nicely; ~ **warm/weich/langsam** nice and warm/soft/slow; **wir haben es** ~ **hier** we're very well off here; (c)

(gut, ausgezeichnet) well; (d) (in Höflichkeitsformeln) **bitte** ~, **können Sie mir sagen, …:** excuse me, could you tell me …; **grüß deine Mutter** ~ **von mir** give your mother my kind regards; (e) (iron.) **wie es so** ~ **heißt, wie man so** ~ **sagt** as they say; (f) (ugs.: beträchtlich) really, (vor einem Adjektiv) pretty; **ganz** ~ **arbeiten müssen** have to work jolly hard (Brit. coll.); **[ganz]** ~ **dämlich** damned stupid. **3** *Partikel* (ugs. verstärkend) ~ **ruhig bleiben/**~ **langsam fahren** be nice and quiet/drive nice and slowly; **bleib** ~ **liegen!** lie there and be good; **sei** ~ **brav** be a good boy/girl

schonen **1** *tr. V.* treat ⟨*clothes, books, furniture, etc.*⟩ with care; (schützen) protect ⟨*hands, furniture*⟩; (nicht strapazieren) spare ⟨*voice, eyes, etc.*⟩; conserve ⟨*strength*⟩; (nachsichtig behandeln) go easy on, spare ⟨*person*⟩; **jmdm. eine Nachricht** ~**d beibringen** break news gently to sb.; **eine** ~**de Behandlung** gentle treatment. **2** *refl. V.* take care of oneself; (sich nicht überanstrengen) take things easy; **sich mehr** ~: take things easier

Schoner *der;* ~s, ~ (Seemannsspr.) schooner

Schön·färberei *die;* ~, ~en embellishment; **ohne jede** ~: without any whitewashing

Schon-: ~**frist** *die* period of grace; (nach einer Operation) period of convalescence; ~**gang** *der* (a) (Kfz-W.) high gear; (Overdrive) overdrive; (b) (bei Waschmaschinen) programme for delicate fabrics

schön·geistig *Adj.* aesthetic; **die** ~**e Literatur** belletristic literature

Schönheit *die;* ~, ~en beauty

Schönheits-: ~**chirurgie** *die* cosmetic surgery *no art.;* ~**farm** *die* health farm; ~**fehler** *der* blemish; (fig.) minor defect; (Nachteil) slight drawback; ~**königin** *die* beauty queen; ~**pflege** *die* beauty care *no art.;* ~**reparatur** *die* cosmetic repair; (in einem Haus/einer Wohnung) redecorating *no pl.;* ~**wettbewerb** *der* beauty contest

Schon·kost *die* light food

schön|machen (ugs.) **1** *tr. V.* smarten ⟨*person, thing*⟩ up; make ⟨*person, thing*⟩ look nice. **2** *refl. V.* smarten oneself up; make oneself look smart

schön-, Schön-: ~|**reden** *itr. V.* (abwertend) turn on the smooth talk; sweet-talk (Amer.); ~**redner** *der* (abwertend) smooth *or* (Amer.) sweet talker; ~**schrift** *die* (a) (Zierschrift) calligraphy; (sorgfältige Schrift) neat handwriting; **etw. in** ~**schrift abschreiben** copy sth. out neatly *or* in one's best handwriting; (b) (ugs.: Reinschrift) neat *or* clean copy; ~|**tun** *unr. itr. V.* (ugs.) **jmdm.** ~**tun** soft-soap sb.; butter sb. up

Schonung *die;* ~, ~en (a) *o. Pl.* (Nachsicht) consideration; (nachsichtige Behandlung) considerate treatment; (nach Krankheit/Operation) [period of] rest; (von Gegenständen) careful treatment; (b) (Jungwald) [young] plantation

schonungs·los **1** *Adj.* unsparing, ruthless ⟨*criticism etc.*⟩; blunt ⟨*frankness*⟩. **2** *adv.* unsparingly; ⟨*say*⟩ without mincing one's words

Schön·wetter·periode *die* spell of fine weather; fine spell

Schon·zeit *die* (Jagdw.) close season

Schopf /ʃɔpf/ *der;* ~[e]s, **Schöpfe** /'ʃœpfə/ shock of hair; **die Gelegenheit beim** ~[e] **packen** *od.* **ergreifen** (ugs.) seize *or* grasp the opportunity with both hands

schöpfen /'ʃœpfn/ *tr. V.* (a) scoop [up] ⟨*water, liquid*⟩; (mit einer Kelle) ladle ⟨*soup*⟩; **Wasser aus einem Brunnen** ~: draw water from a well; (b) (geh.: einatmen) draw, take ⟨*breath*⟩; **frische Luft** ~: take a breath of fresh air; (c) (geh.: für sich gewinnen) draw ⟨*wisdom, strength, knowledge*⟩ (aus from); **neuen Mut/neue Hoffnung** ~: take fresh heart/find fresh hope

Schöpfer[1] *der;* ~s, ~: creator; (Gott) Creator

Schöpfer[2] *der;* ~s, ~ (Kelle) ladle

Schöpferin *die;* ~, ~nen creator

schöpferisch **1** *Adj.* creative; **eine** ~**e Pause** a pause for inspiration. **2** *adv.* creative; ~ **tätig sein** be creative

Schöpferkraft *die* creative powers *pl.;* creativity

Schöpf-: ~**kelle** *die,* ~**löffel** *der* ladle

Schöpfung *die;* ~, ~en (a) *o. Pl.* (geh.: Erschaffung) creation; (Erfindung) invention; (b) (geh.: ~ der Welt) **die** ~: the

Creation; (von Gott Erschaffenes) Creation; (c) (geh.: Kunstwerk, ~ der Mode usw.) creation; (Werk) work

Schöpfungs·geschichte *die* Creation story

Schöppchen /ˈʃœpçən/ *das;* ~s, ~: small glass of wine/beer

Schoppen /ˈʃɔpn̩/ *der;* ~s, ~ (a) [quarter-litre/half-litre] glass of wine/beer; (b) (veralt.: Hohlmaß) **ein** ~: ≈ half a litre

Schoppen·wein *der* wine by the glass

Schöps /ʃœps/*der;* ~es, ~e (österr) ⇒ **Hammel a, b**

Schöpserne /ˈʃœpsɛnə/ *das; adj. Dekl., o. Pl.* (österr.) mutton

schor /ʃoːɐ̯/ *1. u. 3. Pers. Sg. Prät. v.* **scheren**[1]

Schorf /ʃɔrf/ *der;* ~[e]s, ~e ▶ 329 | scab

Schorle /ˈʃɔrlə/ *die;* ~, ~n wine with mineral water; ≈ spritzer; (mit Apfelsaft) apple juice with mineral water

Schorn·stein /ˈʃɔrn-/ *der* chimney; (Schiffs~, Lokomotiv~) funnel; **der** ~ **raucht** (fig.) things are ticking over nicely; business is good; **Geld in den** ~ **schreiben** (fig. ugs.) write off money

Schornstein·feger *der;* ~s, ~: ▶ 85 | chimney sweep

schoss, *schoß /ʃɔs/ *1. u. 3. Pers. Sg. Prät. v.* **schießen**

Schoß /ʃoːs/ *der;* ~es, **Schöße** /ˈʃøːsə/ (a) lap; **ein Kind auf den** ~ **nehmen** take *or* sit a child on one's lap; **die Hände in den** ~ **legen** (fig.) sit back and do nothing; **jmdm. in den** ~ **fallen** (fig.) just fall into sb.'s lap; **im** ~ **der Familie/der Kirche** (fig.) in the bosom of the family/of Mother Church; *s. auch* **Hand f**; (b) (geh.: Mutterleib) womb

Schoß·hund *der,* **Schoßhündchen** *das* lap-dog

Schössling, *Schößling /ˈʃœslɪŋ/ *der;* ~s, ~e (a) (Trieb) shoot; (b) (Ableger zum Pflanzen) cutting

Schote /ˈʃoːtə/ *die;* ~, ~n pod; siliqua (as tech. term); **fünf** ~n **Paprika** five peppers

Schott /ʃɔt/ *das;* ~[e]s, ~en (Seemannsspr.) bulkhead

Schotte /ˈʃɔtə/ *der;* ~n, ~n ▶ 388 | Scot; Scotsman; **er ist** ~: he's a Scot; he's Scottish; **die** ~n the Scots; the Scottish

Schotten·rock *der* tartan skirt; (Kilt) kilt

Schotter /ˈʃɔtɐ/ *der;* ~s, ~ (a) (für Straßen) [road-]metal; gravel; (für Schienen) ballast; (b) (Geol.) gravel

Schotter·straße *die* road with [loose] gravel surface

Schottin *die;* ~, ~nen Scot; Scotswoman

schottisch ▶ 388 | 1 *Adj.* Scottish; Scots, Scottish ‹dialect, accent, voice, etc.›; ~er **Whisky** Scotch whisky. 2 *adv.* ‹speak› with a Scots *or* Scottish accent

Schottland (*das*); ~s Scotland

schraffieren /ʃraˈfiːrən/ *tr. V.* hatch; (feiner) shade ‹drawing›

schräg /ʃrɛːk/ 1 *Adj.* (a) diagonal ‹line, beam, cut, etc.›; sloping ‹surface, roof, wall, side, etc.›; slanting, slanted ‹writing, eyes, etc.›; tilted ‹position of the head etc., axis›; (b) (ugs.: unseriös) offbeat; (c) (ugs.: zweifelhaft) shady, (coll.) dodgy ‹type, firm, etc.›. 2 *adv.* at an angle; (diagonal) diagonally; **den Kopf** ~ **halten** hold one's head to one side; tilt one's head; ~ **stehende Augen** slanting eyes; ~ **gegenüber** diagonally opposite; **er saß** ~ **vor/hinter mir** he was sitting in front of/behind me and to one side; ~ **gedruckt** [printed] in italics *postpos.;* **jmdn.** ~ **angucken** (fig. ugs.) look askance at sb.

Schräge *die;* ~, ~n (a) (schräge Fläche) sloping surface; (Hang) slope; **das Zimmer hat eine** ~: the room has a sloping wall; (b) (Neigung) slope

Schräg-: ~**lage** *die* angle; (eines Schiffes) list; (eines Flugzeugs) bank; **das Schiff hat** ~**lage** the ship is listing *or* is at an angle; ~**streifen** *der* diagonal stripe; ~**strich** *der* oblique stroke

*alte Schreibung (vgl. Hinweise auf S. xvi–xvii)

schrak /ʃraːk/ *1. u. 3. Pers. Sg. Prät. v.* **schrecken**

Schramme /ˈʃramə/ *die;* ~, ~n scratch

Schrammel·musik /ˈʃraml-/ *die Viennese popular music played on violins, guitar, and accordion;* Schrammeln ensemble music

schrammen *tr. V.* scratch (**an** + *Dat.* on)

Schrank /ʃraŋk/ *der;* ~[e]s, **Schränke** /ˈʃrɛŋkə/ cupboard; closet (Amer.); (Glas~, kleiner Wand~) cabinet; (Kleider~) wardrobe; (Bücher~) bookcase; (im Schwimmbad, am Arbeitsplatz usw.) locker

Schränkchen /ˈʃrɛŋkçən/ *das;* ~s, ~: cabinet

Schranke /ˈʃraŋkə/ *die;* ~, ~n (a) (auch fig.) barrier; **jmdn. in die** ~ **fordern** (geh.) throw down the gauntlet to sb.; (b) (fig.: Grenze) limit

schrankenlos 1 *Adj.* boundless, unbounded ‹admiration, confidence, loyalty, etc.›; unlimited, limitless ‹power, freedom, etc.›. 2 *adv.* boundlessly

Schranken·wärter *der* level-crossing (Brit.) *or* (Amer.) grade-crossing attendant; crossing-keeper

Schrank-: ~**koffer** *der* wardrobe trunk; ~**wand** *die* shelf *or* wall unit

Schraub·deckel *der* screw top

Schraube /ˈʃraubə/ *die;* ~, ~n (a) (Schlitz~) screw; (Bolzen) bolt; **bei ihm ist eine** ~ **locker** *od.* **los** (fig. salopp) he has [got] a screw loose (coll.); (b) (Schiffs~) propeller; screw; (c) (Turnen) twist; (Kunstspringen) twist dive; (d) (Kunstflug) vertical spin

schrauben 1 *tr. V.* (a) (befestigen) screw (**an, auf** + *Akk.* on to); (mit Schraubenbolzen) bolt (**an, auf** + *Akk.* [on] to); (entfernen) unscrew/ unbolt (**von** from); (b) (drehen) screw ‹nut, hook, lightbulb, etc.› (**auf** + *Akk.* on to; **in** + *Akk.* into); (lösen) unscrew ‹cap etc.› (**von** from); (c) **die Preise/Erwartungen in die Höhe** ~: push prices up *or* make prices spiral/raise expectations. 2 *refl. V.* **sich [in die Höhe]** ~: spiral upwards

Schrauben-: ~**schlüssel** *der* spanner; ~**zieher** *der;* ~s, ~: screwdriver

Schrauber *der* (ugs.) (a) [power] screwdriver; (b) (salopp scherzh.) mechanic

Schraub·glas *das* screw-top jar

Schraub-: ~**stock** *der* vice; ~**verschluss, *verschluß** *der* screw top

Schreber- /ˈʃreːbɐ-/: ~**garten** *der* ≈ allotment (cultivated primarily as a garden); ~**gärtner** *der* ≈ allotment-holder

Schreck /ʃrɛk/ *der;* ~[e]s, ~e fright; scare; (Schock) shock; **jmdm. einen** ~ **einjagen** give sb. a fright *or* scare/shock; **vor** ~: with fright; ‹run away› in one's fright; **ach du** ~! (ugs.) oh my God!; [oh] ~, **lass nach!** (scherzh.) God help us!; oh no, not that!

schrecken 1 *tr. V.* (a) (geh.) frighten; scare; (b) (auf~) startle (**aus** out of); make ‹person› jump. 2 *regelm.* (auch unr.) *itr. V.* start [up]; **aus dem Schlaf** ~: awake with a start; start from one's sleep

Schrecken *der;* ~s, ~ (a) (Schreck) fright; scare; (Entsetzen) horror; (große Angst) terror; **jmdn. in Angst und** ~ **versetzen** terrify sb.; **mit dem [bloßen]** ~ **davonkommen** escape with no more than a scare *or* fright; (b) (Schrecklichkeit, Schreckns) horror; **ein Bild des** ~s a terrible *or* terrifying picture; (c) (fig.: gefürchtete Sache, Person) **der** ~ **des Volkes**/(scherzh.) **der Schule** usw. the terror of the nation/(joc.) the school *etc.*

schrecken·erregend 1 *Adj.* terrifying. 2 *adv.* terrifyingly

schreckens-, Schreckens-: ~**bleich** *Adj.* (geh.) pale with terror *postpos.*; as white as a sheet *postpos.*; ~**herrschaft** *die* reign of terror; ~**nachricht** *die* terrible piece of news; **die** ~**nachricht von…:** the terrible news of…

Schreck·gespenst *das* spectre; (gegenwärtig) nightmare

schreckhaft *Adj.* easily scared

Schreckhaftigkeit *die;* ~: easily scared nature; tendency to take fright

schrecklich 1 *Adj.* (a) terrible; (b) (ugs.: unerträglich) terrible (coll.); (c) (ugs.: sehr groß) **es hat ihm ~en Spaß gemacht** he found it terrific fun (coll.). 2 *adv.* (a) terribly; horribly; (b) (ugs. abwertend: unerträglich) terribly (coll.); dreadfully (coll.); (c) (ugs.: sehr, äußerst) terribly (coll.).

Schreck-: **~schraube** *die* (ugs. abwertend) battleaxe; **~schuss**, **~schuß* *der* (auch fig.) warning shot; **~schuss·pistole**, **~schuß·pistole* *die* blank [cartridge] gun *or* pistol; **~sekunde** *die* moment of terror/shock; (Reaktionszeit) reaction time

Schredder *der;* ~s, ~: shredder

Schredder-: **~anlage** *die* shredding plant; shredder; **~müll** *der* shredded waste

schreddern *tr. V.* shred

Schrei /ʃrai/ *der;* ~[e]s, ~e cry; (lauter Ruf) shout; (durchdringend) yell; (gellend) scream; (kreischend) shriek; (des Hahns) crow; **der letzte ~** (fig. ugs.) the latest thing

Schreib-: **~automat** *der* word processor; **~block** *der; Pl.* **~blocks** *od.* **~blöcke** writing pad

Schreibe *die;* ~ (ugs.: Schreibstil) style [of writing]

schreiben /ˈʃraibn̩/ 1 *unr. itr. V.* write; ⟨*typewriter*⟩ type; **orthographisch richtig ~:** spell correctly; **auf** *od.* **mit der Maschine ~:** type; **hast du mal was zum Schreiben?** have you got anything to write with?; **er hat großes Talent zum Schreiben** he has great talent as a writer; **an einem Roman** *usw.* **~:** be writing a novel *etc.; jmdm. od.* **an jmdn. ~:** write to sb. 2 *unr. tr. V.* (a) write; **etw. mit der Hand/Maschine ~:** write sth. by hand *or* in longhand/type sth.; **wie schreibt man dieses Wort?** how is this word spelt?; **eine Klausur/Klassenarbeit ~:** do an exam/a class test; **die Zeitungen ~ viel Unsinn** the newspapers print a lot of nonsense; **Karl hat geschrieben. — So, was schreibt er denn?** I've had a letter from Karl. — Oh, what does he say?; (b) (veralt.) **wir ~ heute den 21. September** today is 21 September; **man schreibt das Jahr 1925** the year is 1925. 3 *unr. refl. V.* be spelt

Schreiben *das;* ~s, ~ (a) *o. Pl.* writing *no def. art.;* (b) (Brief) letter

Schreiber *der;* ~s, ~ (a) writer; (Verfasser) author; (b) (veralt.: Sekretär, Schriftführer) secretary; clerk

Schreiberin *die;* ~, ~en writer; (Verfasserin) authoress

Schreiberling /ˈʃraibɐlɪŋ/ *der;* ~s, ~e (abwertend) hack [writer]; scribbler

schreib-, Schreib-: **~faul** *Adj.* lazy about [letter]writing *postpos.;* **~fehler** *der* spelling mistake; (Versehen) slip [of the pen]; **~gerät** *das* writing implement; **~heft** *das* (usu. lined) exercise book; **~maschine** *die* typewriter; **etw. mit [der]** *od.* **auf der ~maschine schreiben** type sth.; **mit [der] ~maschine geschrieben** (typewritten) typed; **~maschinen·papier** *das* typing paper; **~papier** *das* writing paper; **~schrift** *die* cursive writing; (gedruckt) [cursive] script; **~stube** *die* (Milit.) orderly room; **~tisch** *der* desk; **~tisch·täter** *der* mastermind behind the scenes; (Beamter) deskbound director of operations

Schreibung *die;* ~, ~en spelling

Schreib-: **~verbot** *das* writing ban; **~waren** *Pl.* stationery *sing.;* writing materials; **~waren·geschäft** *das* stationer's; stationery shop *or* (Amer.) store; **~weise** *die* spelling; **~zeug** *das* writing things *pl.*

schreien 1 *unr. itr. V.* ⟨*person*⟩ cry [out]; (laut rufen/sprechen) shout; (durchdringend) yell; (gellend) scream; ⟨*baby*⟩ yell, bawl; ⟨*animal*⟩ scream; ⟨*owl, gull, etc.*⟩ screech; ⟨*cock*⟩ crow; ⟨*donkey*⟩ bray; ⟨*crow*⟩ caw; ⟨*monkey*⟩ shriek; **zum Schreien sein** (ugs.) be a scream (coll.); **nach etw. ~:** yell for sth.; (fig.) cry out for sth.; (fordern) demand sth. 2 *unr. tr. V.* shout

schreiend *Adj.* (fig.) (a) (grell) garish ⟨*colour, poster, etc.*⟩; loud ⟨*pattern*⟩; (b) (empörend) glaring, flagrant ⟨*injustice, anomaly*⟩; blatant ⟨*wrong*⟩

Schrei·hals *der* (ugs.) (Kind) bawler

Schrein /ʃrain/ *der;* ~[e]s, ~e (geh.) shrine

Schreiner *der;* ~s, ~ ▶ 85⫼ (bes. südd.) ⇒ **Tischler**

Schreinerei *die;* ~, ~en (bes. südd.) ⇒ **Tischlerei**

schreinern (bes. südd.) 1 *itr. V.* do joinery. 2 *tr. V.* make ⟨*furniture etc.*⟩

schreiten /ˈʃraitn̩/ *unr. itr. V.; mit sein* (geh.) (a) walk; (mit großen Schritten) stride; (marschieren) march; **auf und ab ~:** pace up and down; (b) **zu etw. ~** (fig.) proceed to sth.; **zur Tat ~:** go into action/get down to work

schrickt /ʃrɪkt/ *3. Pers. Sg. Präsens v.* **schrecken**

schrie /ʃriː/ *1. u. 3. Pers. Sg. Prät. v.* **schreien**

schrieb /ʃriːp/ *1. u. 3. Pers. Sg. Prät. v.* **schreiben**

Schrieb *der;* ~[e]s, ~e (ugs.) missive (coll.)

Schrift /ʃrɪft/ *die;* ~, ~en (a) (System) script; (Alphabet) alphabet; (b) (Hand~) [hand]writing; (c) (Druckw.: ~art) [type-]face; (d) (Text) text; (wissenschaftliche Abhandlung) paper; (Werk) work; **die [Heilige] ~:** the Scriptures *pl.*

Schrift·bild *das* (bei Druckschrift) [appearance of the] type; (bei Handschrift) [appearance of one's] writing;

schrift·deutsch *Adj.* (a) written German; (b) ⇒ **hochdeutsch**

Schrift·führer *der,* **Schriftführerin** *die;* ~, ~en secretary

schriftlich 1 *Adj.* written; **das Schriftliche** written work; (ugs.: die ~e Prüfung) the written exam; **ich habe [darüber] leider nichts Schriftliches** I'm afraid I haven't got anything in writing. 2 *adv.* in writing; **jmdn. ~ einladen** send sb. a written invitation; **das lasse ich mir ~ geben** I'll get that in writing

schrift-, Schrift-: **~satz** *der* (Druckw.) type matter; **~setzer** *der* ▶ 85⫼ typesetter; **~sprache** *die* written language; **~sprachlich** 1 *Adj.* used in the written language *postpos.;* 2 *adv.* in the written language; **~steller** *der* ▶ 85⫼ writer; **~stellerei** *die;* ~: writing *no def. art.;* **~stellerin** *die;* ~, ~nen ▶ 85⫼ writer; **~stellerisch** *Adj.* literary ⟨*work, activity*⟩; ⟨*talent*⟩ as a writer; **~stellerisch begabt sein** be talented as a writer; **~stück** *das* [official] document

Schrifttum *das;* ~s literature; **das ~ zu diesem Thema** the literature on this subject

Schrift-: **~verkehr** *der; o. Pl.* correspondence; **~wechsel** *der* correspondence; **~zeichen** *das* character; **~zug** *der* (a) *Pl.* lettering *sing.;* (Handschrift) handwriting *sing;* (b) (Namenszug) lettering; (als Firmenzeichen) logo

schrill /ʃrɪl/ 1 *Adj.* shrill; (fig.) strident ⟨*propaganda, colours, etc.*⟩. 2 *adv.* shrilly

schrillen *itr. V.* shrill; sound shrilly

Schrippe /ˈʃrɪpə/ *die;* ~, ~n (bes. berlin.) long [bread] roll

schritt /ʃrɪt/ *1. u. 3. Pers. Sg. Prät. v.* **schreiten**

Schritt *der;* ~[e]s, ~e (a) step; **einen ~ zur Seite machen** *od.* **tun** take a step sideways; **~ für ~** (auch fig.) step by step; **den ersten ~ machen** *od.* **tun** (fig.) (den Anfang machen) take the first step; (als erster handeln) make the first move; **auf ~ und Tritt** wherever one goes; at every step; (b) *Pl.* (Geräusch) footsteps; (c) (Entfernung) pace; **nur ein paar ~e von uns entfernt** only a few yards away from us; (d) (Gleich~) **aus dem ~ kommen** *od.* **geraten** get out of step; **im ~ gehen** walk in step; (e) *o. Pl.* (des Pferdes) walk; **im ~:** at a walk; (f) *o. Pl.* (Gangart) walk; **seinen ~ verlangsamen/beschleunigen** slow/quicken one's pace; **[mit jmdm./etw.] ~ halten** (auch fig.) keep up *or* keep pace [with sb./sth.]; (g) (~geschwindigkeit) walking pace; **[im] ~ fahren** go at walking pace *or* a crawl; **„~ fahren"** 'dead slow'; (h) (fig.: Maßnahme) step; measure; (i) (Teil der Hose, Genitalbereich) crotch

*Schrittempo ⇒ **Schritttempo**

schritt-, Schritt-: **~geschwindigkeit** *die* walking pace; **[mit] ~geschwindigkeit fahren** go at walking pace *or* crawl; **~macher** *der* (Sport, Med.: auch fig.) pacemaker; **~tempo** *das;* walking pace; **[im] ~ fahren** go at walking pace *or* a crawl; **~weise** 1 *Adv.* step by step; gradually; 2 *adj.; nicht präd.* step by step; gradual

schroff /ʃrɔf/ 1 *Adj.* (a) precipitous, sheer ⟨*rock etc.*⟩; (b) (plötzlich) sudden, abrupt ⟨*transition, change*⟩; (krass) stark ⟨*contrast*⟩; (c) (barsch) abrupt, curt ⟨*refusal, manner*⟩; brusque ⟨*manner, behaviour, tone*⟩. 2 *adv.* (a) ⟨*rise, drop*⟩ sheer; ⟨*fall away*⟩ precipitously; (b) (plötzlich, unvermittelt) suddenly; abruptly; (c) (barsch) curtly; ⟨*interrupt*⟩ abruptly; ⟨*treat*⟩ brusquely

Schroffheit *die;* ~, ~**en** (a) *o. Pl.* precipitousness; (b) *o. Pl.* (Plötzlichkeit) suddenness; abruptness; (Krassheit) starkness; (c) *o. Pl.* (Barschheit) curtness; abruptness; brusqueness; **mit** ~: curtly

schröpfen /'ʃrœpfn/ *tr. V.* (ugs.) fleece

Schrot /ʃroːt/ *der od. das;* ~[e]s, ~e (a) coarse meal; (aus Getreide) whole meal (Brit.); whole grain; (b) (aus Blei) shot; (c) *in* **ein Mann von echtem/bestem** ~ **und Korn** a man of sterling qualities

schroten *tr. V.* grind ‹grain etc.› [coarsely]; crush ‹malt› [coarsely]

Schrot-: ~**flinte** *die* shotgun; ~**kugel** *die* pellet; ~**ladung** *die* round of shot; small-shot charge

Schrott /ʃrɔt/ *der;* ~[e]s, ~e (a) scrap [-metal]; **ein Auto zu** ~ **fahren** (ugs.) write a car off; (b) *o. Pl.* (salopp fig.) rubbish; junk

schrott-, Schrott-: ~**händler** *der* scrap-dealer; scrap-merchant; ~**platz** *der* scrapyard; ~**reif** *Adj.* ready for the scrap heap *postpos.;* fit for scrap *postpos.;* ~**wert** *der* scrap value

schrubben /'ʃrʊbn̩/ *tr.* (*auch itr.*) *V.* scrub

Schrubber *der;* ~s, ~: [long-handled] scrubbing-brush

Schrulle /'ʃrʊlə/ *die;* ~, ~**n** cranky idea; (Marotte) quirk

schrullig *Adj.* cranky ‹person, idea›; zany (coll.) ‹story etc.›

schrumpelig *Adj.* (ugs.) wrinkly; wrinkled

schrumpeln /'ʃrʊmpl̩n/ *itr. V.; mit sein* (ugs.) ‹skin› go wrinkled; ‹apple etc.› shrivel

schrumpfen /'ʃrʊmpfn̩/ *itr. V.; mit sein* shrink; ‹metal, rock› contract; ‹apple etc.› shrivel; ‹skin› go wrinkled; (abnehmen) decrease; ‹supplies, capital, hopes› dwindle

Schrumpf·kopf *der* (Völkerk.) shrunken head

Schrunde /'ʃrʊndə/ *die;* ~, ~**n** crack; (von Kälte) chap

schrundig *Adj.* cracked, chapped ‹skin, hands, etc.›

Schub /ʃuːp/ *der;* ~[e]s, **Schübe** /'ʃyːbə/ (a) (Physik: ~kraft) thrust; (b) (Med.: Phase) phase; stage; (c) (Gruppe, Anzahl) batch; (d) (bes. ostmd.: ~lade) drawer

Schuber /'ʃuːbɐ/ *der;* ~s, ~ slip case

Schub·fach *das* ⇒ **Schublade**

Schub-: ~**karre** *die,* ~**karren** *der* wheelbarrow; ~**kasten** *der* drawer; ~**kraft** *die* thrust; ~**lade** *die* drawer; (fig.: Kategorie) pigeon-hole

Schubs /ʃʊps/ *der;* ~es, ~e (ugs.) shove; (fig.: Ermunterung) prod

Schub·schiff *das* push boat; pusher

schubsen *tr.* (*auch itr.*) *V.* (ugs.) push; shove

schüchtern /'ʃʏçtɐn/ **1** *Adj.* (a) shy ‹person, smile, etc.›; shy, timid ‹voice, knock, etc.›; (b) (fig.: zaghaft) tentative, cautious ‹attempt, beginnings, etc.›; cautious ‹hope›. **2** *adv.* (a) shyly; ‹knock, ask, etc.› timidly; (b) (fig.: zaghaft) tentatively; cautiously

Schüchternheit *die;* ~: shyness

Schuft /ʃʊft/ *der;* ~[e]s, ~e (abwertend) scoundrel; swine

schuften *itr. V.* (ugs.) slave *or* slog away; **er schuftet für zwei** he does the work of two [people]

schuftig **1** *Adj.* mean; despicable. **2** *adv.* meanly; despicably

Schuh /ʃuː/ *der;* ~[e]s, ~e shoe; (hoher ~, Stiefel) boot; **umgekehrt wird ein** ~ **draus** (fig. ugs.) the reverse *or* opposite is true; **wissen, wo jmdn. der** ~ **drückt** (fig. ugs.) know where sb.'s problems lie; **jmdm. etw. in die** ~**e schieben** (fig. ugs.) pin the blame for sth. on sb.

Schuh-: ~**bürste** *die* shoe-brush; ~**creme** *die* shoe polish; ~**größe** *die* shoe size; **welche** ~**größe hast du?** what size shoe[s] do you take?; ~**löffel** *der* shoehorn; ~**macher** *der;* ~s, ~ ▶85 | shoemaker; *s. auch* **Bäcker;** ~**macherei** *die;* ~, ~**en** (a) shoemaker's; (b) *o. Pl.* (Handwerk) shoemaking *no art.;* ~**plattler** /~platlɐ/ *der;* ~s, ~: folk dance in Tirol, Bavaria and Carinthia, involving the slapping of the thighs, knees, and shoe soles; ~**sohle** *die* sole [of a/one's shoe]

Schuko·stecker /'ʃuːko-/ *der* two-pin earthed (Brit.) or (Amer.) grounded plug

---

*alte Schreibung (vgl. Hinweise auf S. xvi–xvii)

Schul-: ~**abgänger** *der;* ~**s,** ~: school leaver; ~**abschluss,** *~**abschluß** *der* school-leaving qualification; ~**alter** *das; o. Pl.* school age; ~**amt** *das* education authority; ~**anfang** *der* first day at school; **um 8 Uhr ist** ~**anfang** school starts at 8 o'clock; ~**anfänger** *der* child [just] starting school; ~**arbeit** *die* (a) ⇒ ~**aufgabe;** (b) (österr.: Klassenarbeit) [written] class test; ~**aufgabe** *die* item of homework; ~**aufgaben** homework *sing.;* ~**aufsatz** *der* school essay; ~**ausflug** *der* school outing; **die** ~**bank drücken** (ugs.) go to or be at school; ~**beginn** *der* ⇒ ~**anfang;** ~**beispiel** *das* textbook example (**für** of); ~**besuch** *der* school attendance; ~**bildung** *die; o. Pl.* [school] education; schooling; ~**brot** *das* sandwich (*eaten during break*); ~**buch** *das* school book; ~**bus** *der* school bus

schuld ⇒ **Schuld b**

Schuld /ʃʊlt/ *die;* ~, ~**en** (a) *o. Pl.* (das Schuldigsein) guilt; **er ist sich** (*Dat.*) **keiner** ~ **bewußt** he is not conscious of having done any wrong; ~ **und Sühne** crime and punishment; (b) *o. Pl.* (Verantwortlichkeit) blame; **es ist [nicht] seine** ~: it is [not] his fault; **jetzt hat er durch deine** ~ **seinen Zug verpasst** now he has missed his train because of you; **[an etw.** (*Dat.*)**] Schuld haben** *od.* **schuld sein** be to blame [for sth.]; **sie ist an allem schuld:** it's all her fault; (Verpflichtung zur Rückzahlung) debt; (Hypothek) mortgage; **in** ~**en geraten/sich in** ~**en stürzen** get into debt/into serious debt; (d) *in* **[tief] in jmds.** ~ **stehen** *od.* **sein** (geh.) be [deeply] indebted to sb.

Schuld·bekenntnis *das* confession [of guilt]

schuld·bewusst, *****schuldbewußt** *Adj.* guilty ‹look, face, etc.›; **jmdn.** ~ **ansehen** give sb. a guilty look

schulden *tr. V.* owe ‹money, respect, explanation›; **was schulde ich Ihnen?** how much do I owe you?

schulden·frei *Adj.* debt-free ‹person etc.›; unmortgaged ‹house etc.›; **ich bin/das Haus ist** ~: I am free of debt/ the house is free of mortgage

Schuld·gefühl *das* feeling of guilt; guilty feeling; ~**e haben/bekommen** feel/start to feel guilty

Schul·dienst *der; o. Pl.* [school-]teaching *no art.;* **in den** ~ **gehen** go into teaching

schuldig *Adj.* (a) guilty; **jmdn.** ~ **sprechen** *od.* **für** ~ **erklären** find sb. guilty; **er bekennt sich** ~: he admits his guilt; **auf** ~ **plädieren** ‹public prosecutor› ask for a verdict of guilty; **der [an dem Unfall]** ~**e Autofahrer** the driver to blame *or* responsible [for the accident]; (b) **jmdm. etw.** ~ **sein/bleiben** owe sb. sth.; **was bin ich Ihnen** ~? what *or* how much do I owe you?; (c) *nicht präd.* (gebührend) due; proper

Schuldige *der/die; adj. Dekl.* guilty person; (im Strafprozess) guilty party; **einer muss ja der** ~ **sein** 'someone must have done it

Schuldigkeit *die;* ~, ~**en** duty; **meine [verdammte] Pflicht und** ~: my bounden duty

schuld·los *Adj.* innocent (**an** + *Dat.* of)

Schuldner *der;* ~s, ~ debtor

Schuld-: ~**schein** *der* IOU; promissory note (Commerc.); (formell) bond; **Schuld·spruch** *der* verdict of guilty; ~**zu·weisung** *die* recrimination

Schule /'ʃuːlə/ *die;* ~, ~**n** (a) school; **zur** *od.* **in die** ~ **gehen, die** ~ **besuchen** go to school; **zur** *od.* **in die** ~ **kommen** come to school; (als Schulanfänger) start school; **auf** *od.* **in der** ~: at school; **aus der** ~ **plaudern** (fig.) reveal [confidential] information; spill the beans (coll.); ~ **machen** (fig.) become the accepted thing; form a precedent; (b) *o. Pl.* (Ausbildung) training; **hohe** ~ (Reiten) haute école; (c) (Lehr-, Übungsbuch) manual; handbook

schulen *tr. V.* train; **ein geschultes Auge** a practised *or* expert eye

Schul·englisch *das* school English

Schüler /'ʃyːlɐ/ *der;* ~s, ~ (a) pupil; (Schuljunge) schoolboy; **er ist noch** ~: he is still at school; (b) (fig.: eines Meisters) pupil; (Jünger) disciple

Schüler-: ~**austausch** *der* school exchange; ~**ausweis** *der* schoolchild's pass

Schülerin *die;* ~, ~**nen** pupil; schoolgirl

Schüler-: ~**karte** *die* schoolchild's season ticket; ~**lotse** *der pupil trained to help other schoolchildren to cross the road;* ~**mitverwaltung** *die* pupil participation *no art.* in school administration; ~**sprache** *die* school slang; ~**zeitung** *die* school magazine

schul-, Schul-: ~**fach** *das* school subject; ~**te-rien** *Pl.* school holidays *or* (Amer.) vacation *sing.;* ~**fest** *das* school open day; ~**frei** *Adj.* ‹*day*› off school; **morgen ist/haben wir** ~**frei** there is/we have no school tomorrow; ~**freund** *der* school friend; ~**funk** *der* schools broadcasting *no art.;* (Sendungen) [radio] programmes *pl.* for schools; ~**gelände** *das* school grounds *pl. or* premises *pl.;* ~**geld** *das* school fees *pl.;* **lass dir dein** ~**geld wiedergeben!** (ugs.) they can't have taught you a thing at school; ~**heft** *das* exercise book; ~**hof** *der* school yard

schulisch *Adj.; nicht präd.* ‹*conflicts, problems, etc.*› at school; school ‹*work etc.*›; **seine** ~**en Leistungen** [the standard of] his school work *sing.*

schul-, Schul-: ~**jahr** *das* (a) school year; (b) (Klasse) year; **ein zehntes** ~**jahr** a tenth-year class; ~**jugend** *die* schoolchildren *pl.;* ~**junge** *der* schoolboy; ~**kind** *das* schoolchild; ~**klasse** *die* [school] class; ~**landheim** *das* [school's] country hostel (*visited by school classes*); ~**leiter** *der* headmaster; head teacher; ~**lektüre** *die* school reading [material]; (einzelner Text) school text; ~**mädchen** *das* schoolgirl; ~**medizin** *die; o. Pl.* orthodox *or* traditional medicine *no art.;* ~**meister** *der* (veralt., scherzh.) schoolmaster; ~**ordnung** *die* school rules *pl.;* ~**pflichtig** *Adj.* required to attend school *postpos.;* **im** ~**pflichtigen Alter** of school age; ~**ranzen** *der* [school] satchel; ~**rat** *der* schools inspector; ~**reif** *Adj.* ready for school *postpos.;* ~**schiff** *das* training ship; ~**schluss**, ***~**schluß** *der; o. Pl.* end of school; **nach** ~**schluss** after school; ~**schwänzer** *der* (ugs.) truant; ~**sprecher** *der* pupils' representative; ≈ head boy; ~**stunde** *die* [school] period; lesson; ~**tag** *der* school day; **der erste/letzte** ~**tag** the first/last day of school; ~**tasche** *die* school-bag; (Ranzen) [school] satchel

Schulter /ˈʃʊltɐ/ *die;* ~, ~**n** ▸ 326⟩ shoulder; ~ **an** ~ (auch fig.) shoulder to shoulder; **jmdm. auf die** ~ **klopfen** pat sb. on the shoulder *or* (fig.) back; *s. auch* **kalt 1; leicht a**

schulter-, Schulter-: ~**blatt** *das* (Anat.) shoulder blade; ~**frei** *Adj.* off-the-shoulder ‹*dress*›; ~**klappe** *die* shoulder strap; epaulette; ~**lang** *Adj.* shoulder-length

schultern *tr. V.* shoulder; **das Gewehr** ~: shoulder arms

Schul·tüte *die: cardboard cone of sweets given to a child on its first day at school*

Schulung *die,* ~, ~**en** training; (Veranstaltung) training course; **politische** ~: political schooling

Schul-: ~**unterricht** *der* school lessons *pl., no art.;* ~**weg** *der* way to school; ~**zeit** *die* schooldays *pl.;* ~**zeugnis** *das* school report

schummeln *itr., tr., refl. V.* (ugs.) ⇨ **mogeln**

schummerig /ˈʃʊmərɪç/ **1** *Adj.* dim ‹*light etc.*›; dimly lit ‹*room etc.*›. **2** *adv.* dimly

Schund *der;* ~[e]s (abwertend) trash

Schund·roman *der* (abwertend) trashy novel

schunkeln /ˈʃʊŋkln̩/ *itr. V.* rock to and fro together (in time to music, with linked arms)

schupfen /ˈʃʊpfn̩/ *tr. V.* (österr., schweiz., südd.) (a) (stoßen) give sb. a shove *or* push; (b) (werfen) throw; chuck (coll.)

Schupfen *der;* ~**s**, ~ (österr., südd.) shed; (Wetterdach) [wooden] shelter

Schuppe /ˈʃʊpə/ *die;* ~, ~**n** (a) scale; **es fiel ihm wie** ~**n von den Augen** he had a sudden, blinding realization; the scales fell from his eyes; (b) *Pl.* (auf dem Kopf) dandruff *sing.;* (auf der Haut) flaking skin *sing.*

schuppen 1 *tr. V.* scale ‹*fish*›. **2** *refl. V.* ‹*skin*› flake; ‹*person*› have flaking skin

Schuppen *der;* ~**s**, ~ (a) shed; (b) (ugs.: Lokal) joint (sl.)

Schur /ʃuːɐ̯/ *die;* ~, ~**en** (a) (das Scheren) shearing; (b) (Landw.: das Mähen, Schneiden) cut

Schür·eisen *das* poker

schüren /ˈʃyːrən/ *tr. V.* (a) poke ‹*fire*›; (gründlich) rake ‹*fire, stove, etc.*›; (b) (fig.) stir up ‹*hatred, envy, etc.*›; fan the flames of ‹*passion*›; **jmds. Hoffnung** ~: raise sb.'s hopes

schürfen /ˈʃʏrfn̩/ **1** *itr. V.* (a) scrape; (b) (Bergbau) dig [experimentally] (**nach** for); **nach Gold** *usw.* ~: prospect for gold *etc.*. **2** *tr. V.* (a) **sich** (*Dat.*) **das Knie** *usw.* [**wund/blutig**] ~: graze one's knee *etc.* [and make it sore/bleed]; (b) (Bergbau) mine ‹*ore etc.*› open-cast *or* (Amer.) opencut. **3** *refl. V.* graze oneself

Schürf·wunde *die* graze; abrasion

Schür·haken *der* poker (*with hooked end*); (für den Ofen) rake

Schurke /ˈʃʊrkə/ *der;* ~**n**, ~**n** (abwertend) rogue; villain

Schur·wolle *die:* [**reine**] ~: pure new wool

Schurz /ʃʊrts/ *der;* ~**es**, ~**e** (a) apron; (b) (Lenden~) loincloth

Schürze /ˈʃʏrtsə/ *die;* ~, ~**n** apron; (Frauen~, Latz~) pinafore; **jmdm. an der** ~ **hängen** (fig.) be tied to sb.'s apron-strings

schürzen *tr. V.* (a) gather up; (b) (aufwerfen) purse ‹*lips, mouth*›; (c) (geh.: binden) tie ‹*knot*›

Schürzen-: ~**band** ⇨ **Schürzenzipfel**; ~**zipfel** *der* apron-string; **jmdm. am** ~**zipfel hängen** (fig. ugs.) be tied to sb.'s apron-strings

Schuss, ***Schuß */ʃʊs/ der;* **Schusses, Schüsse** /ˈʃʏsə/ (bei Maßangaben ungebeugt) (a) shot (**auf** + *Akk.* at); **21** ~ **Salut** a 21-gun salute; **weit** *od.* **weitab vom** ~ (fig. ugs.) well away from the action; at a safe distance; (abseits) far off the beaten track; **der** ~ **kann nach hinten losgehen** (fig. ugs.) it could backfire *or* turn out to be an own goal; **ein** ~ **in den Ofen** (fig.) a complete waste of effort; (b) (Menge Munition/Schießpulver) round; **drei** ~ **Munition** three rounds of ammunition; **keinen** ~ **Pulver wert sein** (fig. ugs.) be worthless *or* not worth a thing; (c) (~wunde) gunshot wound; (d) (mit einem Ball, Puck usw.) shot (**auf** + *Akk.* at); (e) (kleine Menge) dash; **Cola** *usw.* **mit** ~: Coke (**P**) *etc.* with something strong; brandy/rum *etc.* and Coke (**P**) *etc.*; (f) (Drogenjargon) shot; fix (sl.); (g) (Skisport) ~ **fahren** schuss; (h) (ugs.) **in etw. in** ~ **bringen/halten** get sth. into/keep sth. in[good] shape

Schussel /ˈʃʊsl̩/ *der;* ~**s**, ~ (ugs.) scatterbrain; woolgatherer

Schüssel /ˈʃʏsl̩/ *die;* ~, ~**n** bowl; (flacher) dish

schusselig (ugs.) **1** *Adj.* scatterbrained; (fahrig) dithery. **2** *adv.* in a scatterbrained way

Schusseligkeit *die;* ~ (ugs.) wool-gathering; muddle-headedness; (schusselige Art) scatterbrained way

Schuss-, ***Schuß-: ~**fahrt** *die* (Ski) schuss; ~**linie** *die* line of fire; **in die/jmds.** ~**linie geraten** (auch fig.) come under fire/come under fire from sb.; ~**verletzung** *die* gunshot wound; ~**waffe** *die* weapon (*firing a projectile*); (Gewehr usw.) firearm; ~**wechsel** *der* exchange of shots

Schuster /ˈʃuːstɐ/ *der;* ~**s**, ~ ▸ 85⟩ (ugs.) shoemaker; (Flick~) shoe-repairer; cobbler (dated); **auf** ~**s Rappen** (scherzh.) on Shanks's pony

Schutt /ʃʊt/ *der;* ~[e]s (a) rubble; „~ **abladen verboten**" 'no tipping'; 'no dumping'; **in** ~ **und Asche liegen/sinken** (geh.) lie in ruins/be reduced to rubble; (b) (Geol.) debris; detritus

Schutt·ablade·platz *der* rubbish dump *or* (Brit.) tip; garbage dump (Amer.)

Schütte /ˈʃʏtə/ *die;* ~, ~**n** (a) (Behälter) [kitchen] drawer-container (*for flour etc.*); (b) (Rutsche) chute

Schüttel·frost *der* ▸ 329⟩ [violent] shivering fit; ~ **haben** have violent shivers

schütteln /ˈʃʏtln̩/ **1** *tr.* (*auch itr.*) *V.* (a) shake; **den Kopf [über etw.** (*Akk.*)]/**die Faust [gegen jmdn.]** ~: shake one's head [over sth.]/one's fist [at sb.]; **jmdm. die Hand** ~: shake sb.'s hand; shake sb. by the hand; **das Fieber/die Angst/das Grauen schüttelte ihn** he was shivering *or* shaking with fever/fear/gripped with horror; **(b)** *(unpers.)* **es schüttelte ihn [vor Kälte]** he was shaking [with *or* from cold]. **2** *refl. V.* shake oneself/itself. **3** *itr. V.* **mit dem Kopf ~:** shake one's head

schütten /'ʃʏtn̩/ **1** *tr. V.* pour ⟨ *liquid, flour, grain, etc.* ⟩; (unabsichtlich) spill ⟨ *liquid, flour, etc.* ⟩; tip ⟨ *rubbish, coal, etc.* ⟩; **jmdm./sich Wein über den Anzug ~:** spill wine on sb.'s/one's suit. **2** *itr. V.* *(unpers.)* (ugs.: regnen) pour [down]

schütter /'ʃʏtɐ/ *Adj.* sparse; thin

Schutt-: **~halde** *die* pile *or* heap of rubble; **~haufen** *der* pile of rubble; (Abfallhaufen) rubbish heap; **~platz** *der* [rubbish] dump *or* (Brit.) tip; garbage dump (Amer.)

Schutz /ʃʊts/ *der;* **~es** protection (**vor** + *Dat.,* **gegen** against); (Feuer**~**) cover; (Zuflucht) refuge; **im ~ der Dunkelheit/Nacht** under cover of darkness/night; **unter einem Baum ~** [vor dem Regen *usw.*] **suchen/finden** seek/find shelter *or* take refuge [from the rain *etc.*] under a tree; **~ suchend** seeking protection *postpos.*; **jmdn.** [vor **jmdm./gegen etw.**] **in ~ nehmen** defend sb. *or* take sb.'s side [against sb./sth.]

schutz-, Schutz-: **~bedürftig** *Adj.* in need of protection *postpos.;* **~blech** *das* mudguard; **~brief** *der* (Kfz-W.) travel insurance; (Dokument) travel insurance certificate; **~brille** *die* [protective] goggles *pl.*

Schütze /'ʃʏtsə/ *der;* **~n,** **~n** **(a)** marksman; **(b)** (Fußball *usw.*: Tor**~**) scorer; **(c)** (Milit.: einfacher Soldat) private; **(d)** (Astrol., Astron.) Sagittarius; **er/sie ist [ein] ~:** he/she is a Sagittarian

schützen **1** *tr. V.* protect (**vor** + *Dat.* from, **gegen** against); safeguard ⟨ *interest, property, etc.* ⟩ (**vor** + *Dat.* from); **sich ~d vor jmdn./etw. stellen** stand protectively in front of sb./sth.; **gesetzlich geschützt** registered [as a trade mark]; „**vor Wärme/Kälte/Licht ~**": 'keep away from heat/cold/light'. **2** *itr. V.* provide *or* give protection (**vor** + *Dat.* from, **gegen** against); (vor Wind, Regen) provide *or* give shelter (**vor** + *Dat.* from)

Schützen·fest *das* shooting competition with fair

Schutz·engel *der* guardian angel

Schützen-: **~graben** *der* (Milit.) trench; **~hilfe** *die* (ugs.) support; **~panzer** *der* armoured personnel carrier; **~verein** *der* shooting *or* rifle club

Schutz-: **~film** *der* protective film; **~gebühr** *die* **(a)** token *or* nominal charge; **(b)** (verhüll.: erpresste Zahlung) protection money *no pl., no indef. art.;* **~heilige** *der/ die* (kath. Rel.) patron saint; **~helm** *der* helmet; (bei Renn-, Motorradfahrern) crash helmet; (bei Bauarbeitern usw.) safety helmet; **~hülle** *die* [protective] cover; (für Dokumente usw.) folder; **~hütte** *die* **(a)** (Unterstand) shelter; **(b)** (Berghütte) mountain hut; **~impfung** *die* vaccination; inoculation; **~kleidung** *die* protective clothing; **~leute** ⇨ **~mann**

Schützling /'ʃʏtslɪŋ/ *der;* **~s,** **~e** protégé; (Anvertrauter) charge

schutz-, Schutz-: **~los** *Adj.* defenceless; unprotected; **~mann** *der; Pl.* **~männer** *od.* **~leute** (ugs. veralt.) [police] constable; copper (Brit. sl.); **~patron** *der* patron saint; **~schicht** *die* protective layer (**aus** of); (flüssig aufgetragen) protective coating;*~**~suchend** ⇨ **Schutz; ~umschlag** *der* dust jacket; (für Papiere) cover

schwabbelig /'ʃvabəlɪç/ *Adj.* flabby ⟨ *stomach, person, etc.* ⟩; wobbly ⟨ *jelly etc.* ⟩

schwabbeln *itr. V.* (ugs.) wobble

Schwabe /'ʃvaːbə/ *der;* **~n,** **~n** Swabian

Schwaben *(das);* **~s** Swabia

Schwaben·streich *der* (scherzh.) piece of folly

Schwäbin /'ʃvɛːbɪn/ *die;* **~,** **~nen** Swabian

schwäbisch **1** *Adj.* Swabian. **2** *adv.* in Swabian dialect

schwach /ʃvax/; **schwächer** /'ʃvɛçɐ/, **schwächst...** /'ʃvɛçst.../ **1** *Adj.* **(a)** (kraftlos) weak; weak, delicate ⟨ *child, woman* ⟩; frail ⟨ *invalid, old person* ⟩; low-powered ⟨ *engine, car, bulb, amplifier, etc.* ⟩; weak, poor ⟨ *eyesight, memory, etc.* ⟩; poor ⟨ *hearing* ⟩; delicate ⟨ *health,*

constitution ⟩; **~ werden** grow weak; (fig.: schwanken) weaken; waver; (nachgeben) give in; **mir wird [ganz] ~:** I feel [quite] faint; **in einer ~en Stunde** in a weak moment; **(b)** (nicht gut) poor ⟨ *pupil, player, runner, performance, result, effort, etc.* ⟩; weak ⟨ *candidate, argument, opponent, play, film, etc.* ⟩; **er ist in Latein sehr ~:** he is very bad at Latin; **das ist aber ein ~es Bild!** (fig. ugs.) that's a poor show (coll.); **(c)** (gering, niedrig, klein) poor, low ⟨ *attendance etc.* ⟩; sparse ⟨ *population* ⟩; slight ⟨ *effect, resistance, gradient, etc.* ⟩; light ⟨ *wind, rain, current* ⟩; faint ⟨ *groan, voice, pressure, hope, smile, smell* ⟩; weak, faint ⟨ *pulse* ⟩; lukewarm ⟨ *applause, praise* ⟩; faint, dim ⟨ *light* ⟩; pale ⟨ *colour* ⟩; **das Licht wird schwächer** the light is fading; **(d)** (wenig konzentriert) weak ⟨ *solution, acid, tea, coffee, beer, poison, etc.* ⟩; **(e)** (Sprachw.) weak ⟨ *conjugation, verb, noun, etc.* ⟩. **2** *adv.* **(a)** (kraftlos) weakly; **(b)** (nicht gut) poorly; **(c)** (in geringem Maße) poorly ⟨ *attended, developed* ⟩; sparsely ⟨ *populated* ⟩; slightly ⟨ *poisonous, acid, alcoholic, sweetened, salted, inclined, etc.* ⟩; ⟨ *rain* ⟩ slightly; ⟨ *remember, glow, smile, groan* ⟩ faintly; lightly ⟨ *accented* ⟩; ⟨ *beat* ⟩ weakly; **(d)** (Sprachw.) **~ gebeugt/konjugiert** weak

schwach-: **~besiedelt,** **~bevölkert** ⇨ **schwach 2 c**

Schwäche /'ʃvɛçə/ *die;* **~,** **~n** weakness; **eine ~ für jmdn./etw. haben** have a soft spot for sb./a weakness for sth.

Schwäche·anfall *der* sudden feeling of faintness

schwächen *tr. V.* weaken

schwächer ⇨ **schwach**

Schwachheit *die;* **~:** weakness; **die ~ des Greises/ des Alters** the frailty of the old man/of old age

Schwach·kopf *der* (salopp) bonehead (sl.); dimwit (coll.)

schwächlich *Adj.* weakly, delicate ⟨ *person* ⟩; frail ⟨ *old person, constitution* ⟩; delicate ⟨ *nerves, stomach, constitution* ⟩

Schwächling /'ʃvɛçlɪŋ/ *der;* **~s,** **~e** weakling

schwach-, Schwach-: **~punkt** *der* weak point; **~sichtig** *Adj.* (Med.) weak-sighted; **~sinn** *der; o. Pl.* **(a)** (Med.) mental deficiency; **(b)** (ugs. abwertend: Unsinn) [idiotic (coll.)] rubbish *or* nonsense; **~sinnig 1** *Adj.* **(a)** (Med.) mentally deficient; **(b)** (ugs.: unsinnig) idiotic (coll.), nonsensical ⟨ *measure, policy, etc.* ⟩; rubbishy ⟨ *film etc.* ⟩; **2** *adv.* (ugs.) idiotically (coll.); stupidly

schwächst... ⇨ **schwach**

Schwach-: **~stelle** *die* weak spot *or* point; **~strom** *der* (Elektrot.) current of low amperage

Schwächung *die;* **~,** **~en** weakening

Schwaden /'ʃvaːdn̩/ *der;* **~s,** **~:** [thick] cloud

Schwadron /ʃva'droːn/ *die;* **~,** **~en** (Milit. hist.) squadron

schwadronieren *itr. V.* (abwertend) bluster

Schwafelei *die;* **~,** **~en** (ugs. abwertend) **(a)** *o. Pl.* rabbiting on (Brit. sl.); **(b)** (Bemerkung) rubbishy remark; **~en** blether *sing.*

schwafeln /'ʃvaːfln̩/ (ugs. abwertend) **1** *itr. V.* rabbit on (Brit. sl.), waffle (**von** about). **2** *tr. V.* blether ⟨ *nonsense* ⟩

Schwager /'ʃvaːgɐ/ *der;* **~s,** **Schwäger** /'ʃvɛːgɐ/ brother-in-law

Schwägerin /'ʃvɛːgərɪn/ *die;* **~,** **~nen** sister-in-law

Schwalbe /'ʃvalbə/ *die;* **~,** **~n** (a) swallow; **eine ~ macht noch keinen Sommer** (Spr.) one swallow does not make a summer (prov.); **(b)** (ugs.: Papierflieger) paper aeroplane

Schwalben·schwanz *der* **(a)** swallow's tail; **(b)** (Schmetterling) swallowtail; **(c)** (scherzh. veralt.: Frack) [swallow]tails *pl.*; **(d)** (Tischlerei) dovetail [joint]

Schwall /ʃval/ *der;* **~[e]s,** **~e** torrent; flood

schwamm /ʃvam/ *1. u. 3. Pers. Sg. Prät. v.* **schwimmen**

Schwamm *der;* **~[e]s,** **Schwämme** /'ʃvɛmə/ **(a)** sponge; **~ drüber!** (ugs.) [let's] forget it; **(b)** (südd., österr.: Pilz) mushroom

Schwammerl /'ʃvamɐl/ *das;* **~s,** **~[n]** (bayr., österr.) mushroom

---

*alte Schreibung (vgl. Hinweise auf S. xvi–xvii)

schwammig 1 *Adj.* (a) spongy; (b) (aufgedunsen) flabby, bloated ⟨*face, body, etc.*⟩; (c) (unpräzise) woolly ⟨*concept, manner of expression, etc.*⟩. **2** *adv.* (unpräzise) vaguely

Schwammigkeit *die;* ∼ (a) sponginess; (b) (Aufgedunsenheit) flabbiness; bloated appearence; (c) (Vagheit) woolliness

Schwan /ʃvaːn/ *der;* ∼[e]s, **Schwäne** /ˈʃvɛːnə/ swan; **mein lieber** ∼! (ugs.) my goodness!; good heavens!

schwand /ʃvant/ *1. u. 3. Pers. Sg. Prät. v.* **schwinden**

schwanen *itr. V.* (ugs.) **jmdm. schwant etw.** sb. senses sth.

Schwanen·hals *der* (a) swan's neck; (b) (oft. scherzh.: langer Hals) swanlike neck; (c) (Technik) swan-neck

schwang /ʃvaŋ/ *1. u. 3. Pers. Sg. Prät. v.* **schwingen**

schwanger /ˈʃvaŋɐ/ *Adj.* pregnant (**von** by); **sie ist im vierten Monat** ∼: she is in her fourth month [of pregnancy]

Schwangere *die; adj. Dekl.* expectant mother; pregnant woman

schwängern /ˈʃvɛŋɐn/ *tr. V.* make ⟨*woman*⟩ pregnant; **sich von jmdm.** ∼ **lassen** get [oneself] pregnant by sb.

Schwangerschaft *die;* ∼, ∼en pregnancy

Schwangerschafts·abbruch *der* termination of pregnancy; abortion

Schwank /ʃvaŋk/ *der;* ∼[e]s, **Schwänke** /ˈʃvɛŋkə/ (a) (Literaturw.: Erzählung) comic tale; (auf der Bühne) farce; (b) (komische Episode) comic event

schwanken *itr. V.* (mit Richtungsangabe mit sein) (a) sway; ⟨*boat*⟩ rock; (heftiger) roll; ⟨*ground, floor*⟩ shake; (b) (fig.: unbeständig sein) ⟨*prices, temperature, etc.*⟩ fluctuate; ⟨*number, usage, etc.*⟩ vary; (c) (fig.: unentschieden sein) waver; (zögern) hesitate; **er schwankt noch, ob...** he is still undecided [as to] whether...

Schwankung *die;* ∼, ∼en variation; (der Kurse usw.) fluctuation

Schwanz /ʃvants/ *der;* ∼es, **Schwänze** /ˈʃvɛntsə/ (a) tail; **kein** ∼ (fig. salopp) not a bloody (Brit. sl.) or (coll.) damn soul; **den** ∼ **einklemmen** (fig. salopp) draw in one's horns; (b) (salopp) prick (coarse); cock (coarse)

schwänzeln /ˈʃvɛntsl̩n/ *itr. V.* wag its tail/their tails

schwänzen /ˈʃvɛntsn̩/ *tr., itr. V.* (ugs.) skip, cut ⟨*lesson etc.*⟩; **[die Schule]** ∼: play truant or (Amer.) hookey; **den Dienst** ∼: skive [off] (Brit. coll.)

schwanz-, Schwanz-: ∼**feder** *die* tail feather; ∼**flosse** *die* (Zool., Flugw.) tail fin; (des Wals) tail flukes *pl.*

schwappen /ˈʃvapn̩/ *itr. V.* (a) **[hin und her]** ∼: slosh [around]; **an die Bordwand** ∼: splash or slap against the side of the boat; (b) *mit Richtungsangabe mit sein* splash, slosh (**über** + *Akk.* over, **aus** out of)

Schwäre /ˈʃvɛːrə/ *die;* ∼, ∼n (geh.) [festering] ulcer

Schwarm /ʃvarm/ *der;* ∼[e]s, **Schwärme** /ˈʃvɛrmə/ (a) swarm; **ein** ∼ **Krähen/Heringe** a flock of crows/shoal of herrings; (b) (fam.: Angebetete[r]) idol; heart-throb

schwärmen /ˈʃvɛrmən/ *itr. V.* (a) *mit Richtungsangabe mit sein* swarm; (b) (begeistert sein) **für jmdn./etw.** ∼: be mad about or really keen on sb./sth.; **sie schwärmt für ihren Skilehrer** she has a crush on her skiing instructor (coll.); **von etw.** ∼: go into raptures about sth.

Schwärmer *der;* ∼s, ∼ (a) (Fantast) dreamer; (Begeisterter) [passionate] enthusiast; (b) (Zool.) hawk-moth

schwärmerisch 1 *Adj.* rapturous ⟨*enthusiasm, admiration, letter, etc.*⟩; effusive ⟨*person, language*⟩; (begeistert) wildly enthusiastic. **2** *adv.* rapturously; ⟨*speak*⟩ effusively

Schwarte /ˈʃvartə/ *die;* ∼, ∼n (a) (Speck∼) rind; (Haut∼) skin; (b) (ugs.: dickes Buch) **[dicke]** ∼: thick or weighty tome

Schwarten·magen *der* brawn

schwarz /ʃvarts/; **schwärzer** /ˈʃvɛrtsɐ/, **schwärzest...** /ˈʃvɛrtsəst.../ **1** *Adj.* (a) black; Black ⟨*person*⟩; filthy[-black] ⟨*hands, fingernails, etc.*⟩; ∼ **wie die Nacht/wie Ebenholz** as black as pitch/jet-black; **mir wurde** ∼ **vor den Augen** everything went black; (b) (fig.) **der** ∼**e Erdteil** *od.* **Kontinent** the Dark Continent; **die** ∼**e Rasse** the Blacks *pl.*; **das** ∼**e Schaf sein** be the black sheep; ∼**e Liste** blacklist; **das habe ich** ∼ **auf weiß**

(fig.) I've got it in black and white *or* in writing; **er kann warten, bis er** ∼ **wird** (ugs.) he can wait till the cows come home (coll.); ∼ **sehen** look on the black side; be pessimistic (**für** about); **das Schwarze Meer** the Black Sea; *s. auch* **Mann a;** (c) (illegal) illicit, shady ⟨*deal, exchange, etc.*⟩; **der** ∼**e Markt** the black market; (d) (ugs.: katholisch) Catholic; (e) (ugs.: christdemokratisch) Christian Democrat. **2** *adv.* (a) ⟨*write, underline, etc.*⟩ in black; ∼ **gestreift** with black stripes; (b) (illegal) illegally; illicitly; **etw.** ∼ **kaufen** buy sth. illegally *or* on the black market; ∼ **Bus fahren** travel on the bus without paying

Schwarz *das;* ∼[es], ∼: black; **in** ∼ **gehen,** ∼ **tragen** wear black

schwarz-, Schwarz-: ∼**afrika** (*das*) Black Africa; ∼**arbeit** *die; o. Pl.* work done on the side (*and not declared for tax*); (abends) moonlighting (coll.); ∼**arbeiten** *itr. V.* do work on the side (not declared for tax); (abends) moonlight (coll.); ∼**arbeiter** *der* person who does work on the side; (abends) moonlighter (coll.); ∼**bär** *der* black bear; ∼**brot** *das* black bread

Schwarze[1] *der; adj. Dekl.* (a) (Neger) Black; (Dunkelhaariger) dark-haired man/boy; (b) (österr.: Kaffee) black coffee

Schwarze[2] *die; adj. Dekl.* (Negerin) Black [woman/girl]; (Dunkelhaarige) dark haired woman/girl

Schwarze[3] *das; adj. Dekl.* (der Zielscheibe) bull's eye; **ins** ∼ **treffen** hit the bull's eye; (fig.) hit the nail on the head

schwärzen *tr. V.* blacken; black out ⟨*words*⟩

schwarz-, Schwarz-: ∼|**fahren** *unr. itr. V.; mit sein* travel without a ticket or without paying; dodge paying the fare; ∼**fahrer** *der* fare-dodger; ∼**haarig** *Adj.* black-haired; ∼**handel** *der* black market (**mit** in); (Tätigkeit) black marketeering (**mit** in); ∼**händler** *der* black marketeer; ∼**hörer** *der* radio user without a licence; radio licence dodger; ∼**markt** *der* black market; ∼|**sehen** *unr. itr. V.* watch television without a licence; *s. auch* **schwarz 1 b;** ∼**seher** *der* (a) (ugs.) pessimist; (b) (Ferns.) [television] licence dodger

Schwarz·wald *der;* ∼[e]s Black Forest

Schwarzwälder /-ˈvɛldɐ/ *die;* ∼, ∼ (Torte) Black Forest gateau

schwarz·weiß *Adj.* black and white; ∼ **malen** (fig.) paint *or* put things in [crude] black-and-white terms

schwarzweiß-, Schwarzweiß-: ∼**fernseher** *der,* ∼**fernseh·gerät** *das* black and white television [set]; ∼**foto** *das* black and white photo; *∼|**malen** ⇒ **schwarzweiß**

Schwarz·wurzel *die* black salsify

Schwatz /ʃvats/ *der;* ∼es, ∼e (fam.) chat; natter (coll.); **einen** ∼ **halten** have a chat *or* (coll.) natter

Schwätzchen /ˈʃvɛtsçən/ *das;* ∼s, ∼ (fam.) [little] chat; [little] natter (coll.)

schwatzen, (bes. südd.) **schwätzen** /ˈʃvɛtsn̩/ **1** *itr. V.* (a) chat; (b) (über belanglose Dinge) chatter; natter (coll.); (c) (etw. ausplaudern) talk; blab; (d) (in der Schule) talk. **2** *tr. V.* say; talk ⟨*nonsense, rubbish*⟩

Schwätzer *der;* ∼s, ∼, **Schwätzerin** *die;* ∼, ∼nen (abwertend) chatterbox; (klatschhafter Mensch) gossip

schwatzhaft *Adj.* (abwertend) talkative; garrulous; (klatschhaft) gossipy

Schwebe /ˈʃveːbə/ *die* **in der** ∼ **sein/bleiben** (fig.) be/remain in the balance

Schwebe-: ∼**bahn** *die* (Seilbahn) cableway; (Hängebahn) [overhead] monorail; (Magnetschwebebahn) levitation railway; ∼**balken** *der* (Turnen) [balance] beam

schweben *itr. V.* (a) ⟨*bird, balloon, etc.*⟩ hover; ⟨*cloud, balloon, mist*⟩ hang; (im Wasser) float; **in Gefahr** ∼ (fig.) be in danger; (b) *mit sein* (durch die Luft) float; (herab∼) float [down]; (mit dem Fahrstuhl) glide; (wie schwerelos gehen) ⟨*dancer etc.*⟩ glide; (c) (unentschieden sein) be in the balance; **alle** ∼**den Fragen** all outstanding questions

Schwede /ˈʃveːdə/ *der;* ∼n, ∼n ▶388⟩ Swede

Schweden /ˈʃveːdn̩/ (*das*) ∼s Sweden

Schwedin *die;* ∼, ∼nen Swede

schwedisch /ˈʃveːdɪʃ/ ▶388⟩, ▶487⟩ *Adj.* (a) Swedish; *s. auch* **deutsch; Deutsch;** (b) *in* **hinter** ∼**en Gardinen** (ugs.) behind bars (coll.)

Schwefel /'ʃveːfl̩/ *der;* ~s sulphur

schwefel·haltig *Adj.* containing sulphur *postpos., not pred.;* sulphurous ⟨*Quelle, Boden*⟩; **schwach** ~ **sein** have a low sulphur content

schwefelig ⇨ schweflig

schwefeln *tr. V.* sulphurize

Schwefel-: ~**säure** *die* (Chemie) sulphuric acid; ~**wasserstoff** *der* (Chemie) hydrogen sulphide

schweflig *Adj.* sulphurous ⟨*acid*⟩

Schweif /ʃvaɪf/ *der;* ~[e]s, ~e (auch fig.: eines Kometen) tail; (eines Fuchses) brush

schweifen *itr. V.; mit sein* (geh.; auch fig.) wander; roam

Schweige-: ~**geld** *das* hush money; ~**marsch** *der* silent [protest-]march; ~**minute** *die* minute's silence

schweigen *unr. itr. V.* (a) (nicht sprechen) remain or stay or keep silent; say nothing; **kannst du** ~? can you keep a secret?; ~ **Sie!** be silent or quiet! hold your tongue!; **ganz zu** ~ **von** …: not to mention …; let alone …; **die** ~**de Mehrheit** the silent majority; (b) (aufhören zu tönen usw.) ⟨*music, noise, etc.*⟩ stop

Schweigen *das;* ~s silence; **sich in** ~ **hüllen** maintain one's silence; **jmdn. zum** ~ **bringen** (auch verhüll.) silence sb.

Schweige·pflicht *die* (eines Priesters) obligation of secrecy; (eines Arztes, Anwalts) duty to maintain confidentiality

schweigsam *Adj.* silent; quiet; (verschwiegen) discreet

Schweigsamkeit *die;* ~: silence; quietness; (Verschwiegenheit) discretion

Schwein /ʃvaɪn/ *das;* ~[e]s, ~e (a) pig; Hackfleisch **vom** ~: pork mince; (b) *o. Pl.* (Fleisch) pork; (c) (salopp abwertend) (gemeiner Mensch) swine; (Schmutzfink) dirty or mucky devil (coll.); mucky pig (coll.); (d) (salopp: Mensch) **ein armes** ~: a poor devil; **kein** ~ **war da** there wasn't a bloody (Brit. sl.) or (coll.) damn soul there; (e) (ugs.: Glück) [**großes**] ~ **haben** have a [big] stroke of luck; (davonkommen) get away with it (coll.)

Schweine-: ~**bauch** *der* (Kochk.) belly pork; ~**braten** *der* (Kochk.) roast pork *no indef. art.;* **ein** ~**braten** a joint of pork; ~**fleisch** *das* pork; ~**fraß** *der* (derb abwertend) pigswill (coll.); ~**hund** *der* (derb abwertend) bastard (sl.); swine; **der innere** ~**hund** lack of willpower; ~**lende** *die* (Kochk.) loin of pork; ~**pest** *die* swine fever

Schweinerei *die;* ~, ~en (ugs. abwertend) (a) (Schmutz) mess; (b) (Gemeinheit) mean or dirty trick; **es ist eine** ~, **dass das nicht erlaubt ist** it's disgusting that that's not allowed; (c) (Zote) dirty or smutty joke; (Handlung) obscene act

Schweine-: ~**schmalz** *das* lard; (zum Streichen) dripping; ~**schnitzel** *das* (Kochk.) escalope of pork; ~**stall** *der* (auch fig.) pigsty; pigpen (Amer.)

Schwein·igel *der* (ugs. abwertend) (a) (Schmutzfink) dirty or mucky devil (coll.); mucky pig (coll.); (b) (unanständiger Mensch) dirty so-and-so (coll.)

Schweinigelei *die;* ~, ~en (ugs. abwertend) (a) *o. Pl.* making *no art.* [filthy] mess; (Schmutz) [filthy] mess; (b) (Zote) dirty or smutty story

schweinigeln *itr. V.* (ugs. abwertend) (a) (Schmutz machen) make a [filthy] mess; (b) (Zoten reißen) tell dirty or smutty stories

schweinisch (ugs. abwertend) **1** *Adj.* (a) (schmutzig) filthy; (b) (unanständig) dirty; smutty. **2** *adv.* (unanständig) ⟨*behave*⟩ obscenely, disgustingly

schweins-, Schweins-: ~**hachse** *die,* (bes. südd.) ~**haxe** *die* (Kochk.) knuckle of pork; ~**leder** *das* pigskin; ~**ledern** *Adj.* pigskin

Schweiß /ʃvaɪs/ *der;* ~es sweat; (Transpiration) perspiration; **mir brach der** ~ **aus** I broke out in a sweat; **ihm brach der kalte** ~ **aus** he came out in a cold sweat

schweiß-, Schweiß-: ~**ausbruch** *der* sweat; **einen** ~**ausbruch bekommen** start to sweat;

~**bedeckt** *Adj.* covered in or with sweat *postpos.;* ~**brenner** *der* (Technik) welding torch

schweißen *tr., itr. V.* weld

Schweißer *der;* ~s, ~, **Schweißerin** *die;* ~, ~**nen** ▶ 85 welder

schweiß-, Schweiß-: ~**fuß** *der* sweaty foot; ~**gebadet** *Adj.* bathed in sweat *postpos.;* ~**naht** *die* (Technik) weld; ~**nass,** *~**naß** *Adj.* sweaty; damp with sweat *pred.;* ~**perle** *die* bead of sweat

Schweiz /ʃvaɪts/ *die;* ~: Switzerland *no art.;* **in die** ~ **reisen** travel to Switzerland; **aus der** ~ **stammen** come from Switzerland

Schweizer *der;* ~s, ~ ▶ 388 Swiss

schweizer·deutsch *Adj.* Swiss German; *s. auch* deutsch; Deutsch

Schweizerin *die;* ~, ~**nen** Swiss

schweizerisch *Adj.* ▶ 388 Swiss

Schweizer Käse *der* Swiss cheese

Schwel·brand *der* smouldering fire

schwelen /'ʃveːlən/ (auch fig.) smoulder

schwelgen /'ʃvɛlɡn̩/ *itr. V.* (a) (essen u. trinken) feast; **in etw.** (*Dat.*) ~: feast on sth.; (b) **in Erinnerungen** *usw.* ~: wallow in memories *etc.;* **in Farben** ~ (geh.) revel in colours

schwelgerisch *Adj.* sumptuous, opulent ⟨*meal, grandeur*⟩; luxuriant ⟨*blossom*⟩

Schwelle /'ʃvɛlə/ *die;* ~, ~n (a) (auch Physiol., Psych., fig.) threshold; **ich werde keinen Fuß mehr über seine** ~ **setzen** (fig. geh.) I shall not set foot in his house/flat *etc.* again; (b) (Eisenbahn~) sleeper (Brit.); [cross-]tie (Amer.); (c) (Geogr.) swell

schwellen *unr. itr. V.; mit sein* swell; ⟨*limb, face, cheek, etc.*⟩ swell [up], become swollen; ⟨*river*⟩ become swollen, rise

Schwellen-: ~**angst** *die; o. Pl.* fear of entering a place; ~**land** *das:* country at the stage of economic take-off

Schwellung *die;* ~, ~en (Med.) swelling

Schwemme /'ʃvɛmə/ *die;* ~, ~n (a) (Wirtsch.) glut (**an** + *Dat.* of); (b) (für Tiere) watering-place

schwemmen *tr. V.* wash

Schwemm·land *das; o. Pl.* alluvial land

Schwengel /'ʃvɛŋl̩/ *der;* ~s, ~ (a) (Glocken~) clapper; (b) (Pumpen~) handle

Schwenk /ʃvɛŋk/ *der;* ~s, ~s (a) (Drehung) swing; (b) (Film, Ferns.) pan; **die Kamera machte einen** ~ **auf den Helden** the camera panned to the hero

schwenken 1 *tr. V.* (a) (schwingen) swing; wave ⟨*flag, handkerchief*⟩; (b) (spülen) rinse; (c) (drehen) swing round; swivel; pan ⟨*camera*⟩; swing, traverse ⟨*gun*⟩. **2** *itr. V.; mit sein* ⟨*marching column*⟩ swing, wheel; ⟨*camera*⟩ pan; ⟨*road, car*⟩ swing; **rechts schwenkt!** (Milit.) right wheel!

schwer /ʃveːɐ̯/ **1** *Adj.* (a) ▶ 228 heavy; heavy[-weight] ⟨*fabric*⟩; (massiv) solid ⟨*gold*⟩; **2 Kilo** ~ **sein** weigh two kilos; **wie** ~ **bist du?** how much do you weigh?; (b) (anstrengend, mühevoll) heavy ⟨*work*⟩; hard, tough ⟨*job*⟩; hard ⟨*day*⟩; difficult ⟨*birth*⟩; **es** ~/**nicht** ~ **haben** have it hard/easy; **Schweres durchmachen** go through hard times; **jmdm./sich etw.** ~ **machen** make sth. difficult for sb./oneself; **jmdm. fällt etw. schwer** sb. finds sth. difficult; **auch wenns** ~ **fällt** whether you like it or not; **sich** (*Akk. od. Dat.*) **mit od. bei etw.** ~ **tun** have trouble with sth.; **sich** (*Akk. od. Dat.*) **mit jmdm.** ~ **tun** not get along with sb.; (c) (schlimm) severe ⟨*shock, disappointment, strain, storm*⟩; serious, grave ⟨*wrong, injustice, error, illness, blow, reservation*⟩; serious ⟨*accident, injury*⟩; heavy ⟨*punishment, strain, loss, blow*⟩; grave ⟨*suspicion*⟩; **etw.** ~ **nehmen** take sth. seriously; **ein** ~**er Junge** (ugs.) a crook with a record (coll.). **2** *adv.* (a) ▶ 228 heavily ⟨*built, laden, armed*⟩; ~ **wiegen** be heavy; ~ **tragen** be carrying sth. heavy [with difficulty]; ~ **heben** lift heavy weights; ~ **auf jmdn./etw. liegen** *od.* **lasten** (auch fig.) weigh heavily on sb./sth.; (b) (anstrengend, mühevoll) ⟨*work*⟩ hard; ⟨*breathe*⟩ heavily; ~ **erziehbare Kinder** difficult children; ~ **verdaulich** hard to digest; ~ **erkämpft sein** be hard won; ~ **erkauft** dearly bought; bought at great cost *postpos.;* ~ **hören** be hard of hearing; (c) (sehr) seriously ‹*injured, wounded, ill*›; greatly, deeply ‹*disappointed*›; ‹*punish*› severely, heavily severely ‹*disabled, handicapped*›; badly ‹*damaged*›; ~ **aufpassen** (ugs.) take great care; ~ **verunglücken** have a serious accident; ~ **im Irrtum sein** (ugs.) be very much mistaken; **das will ich** ~ **hoffen** (ugs.) I should jolly well think so (Brit. coll.); **er ist** ~ **in Ordnung** (ugs.) he's a good bloke (Brit. coll.) *or* (coll.) guy

schwer-, Schwer-: ~**arbeit** *die; o. Pl.* heavy work; ~**arbeiter** *der* worker engaged in heavy physical work; ~**athletik** *die* weightlifting *no art.*/combat sports *no art.*/shot-putting *no art.*/discus-throwing *no art.;* *~**behindert** ⇨ **schwer 2 c**; ~**behinderte** *der*/ *die* severely handicapped person; (körperlich auch) severely disabled person; **die** ~**behinderten** the severely handicapped/disabled; ~**behinderten-ausweis** *der* disabled person's pass;*~**beschädigt** ⇨ **schwer 2 c**; *~**bewaffnet** ⇨ **schwer 2 a**

Schwere *die;* ~: (a) weight; (b) (Physik: Schwerkraft) gravity; (c) ⇨ **schwer 1 c**: severity; seriousness; gravity; heaviness; (d) (Schwierigkeitsgrad) difficulty

schwere·los 1 *Adj.* weightless. **2** *adv.* weightlessly

Schwerelosigkeit *die;* ~: weightlessness

Schwerenöter /ˈʃveːrənøːtɐ/ *der;* ~**s**, ~ (ugs. scherzh.) ladykiller (coll.)

schwer-, Schwer-: *~**erziehbar** ⇨ **schwer 2 b**;*~**|fallen** ⇨ **schwer 1 b**; ~**fällig 1** *Adj.* ponderous, heavy ‹*movement, steps*›; (fig.) cumbersome ‹*bureaucracy, procedure*›; ponderous ‹*style, thinking*›; **2** *adv.* ponderously; ~**fälligkeit** *die; o. Pl.* ⇨ ~**fällig:** ponderousness; heaviness; (fig.) cumbersomeness; ponderousness; ~**gewicht** *das* (a) *o. Pl.* heavyweight; **die Meisterschaften im** ~**gewicht** the heavyweight championships; (b) (Sportler) heavyweight; (c) *o. Pl.* (Schwerpunkt) main focus; emphasis; ~**gewichtig** *Adj.* heavyweight *attrib.*; ~**gewichtler** /ˈɡəvɪçtlɐ/ *der;* ~**s**, ~ (Schwerathletik) heavyweight; ~**hörig** *Adj.* hard of hearing *pred.*; ~**hörigkeit** *die;* ~: hardness of hearing; ~**indust-rie** *die* heavy industry; ~**kraft** *die; o. Pl.* (Physik, Astron.) gravity;*~**krank** ⇨ **schwer 2 c**

schwerlich *Adv.* hardly

schwer-, Schwer-: *~**|machen** ⇨ **schwer 1 b**; ~**metall** *das* heavy metal; ~**mut** *die* melancholy; ~**mütig 1** *Adj.* melancholic; **2** *adv.* melancholically; *~**|nehmen** ⇨ **schwer 1 c**; ~**punkt** *der* (Physik) centre of gravity; (fig.) main focus; (Hauptgewicht) main stress

Schwert /ʃveːɐt/ *das;* ~**[e]s**, ~**er** sword; **das** ~ **ziehen** *od.* **zücken** draw one's sword

Schwert-: ~**fisch** *der* swordfish; ~**lilie** *die* iris

*schwer|tun** ⇨ **schwer 1 b**

schwer-, Schwer-: ~**verbrecher** *der* serious offender; *~**verdaulich** ⇨ **schwer 2 c**; *~**verletzt** ⇨ **schwer 2 c**; ~**verletzte** *der*/*die* seriously injured person; serious casualty; *~**verwundet** ⇨ **schwer 2 c**; ~**wiegend** *Adj.* serious, grave ‹*reservation, consequence, objection, accusation, etc.*›; momentous ‹*decision*›; serious ‹*case, problem*›

Schwester /ˈʃvɛstɐ/ *die;* ~, ~**n** (a) sister; (b) (Nonne) nun; (als Anrede) Sister; ~ **Petra** Sister Petra; (c) (Kranken~) nurse; (als Anrede) Nurse; (zur Oberschwester) Sister

schwesterlich 1 *Adj.* sisterly. **2** *adv.* ~ **handeln** act in a sisterly way

Schwestern-: ~**helferin** *die* nursing auxiliary; auxiliary nurse; ~**schülerin** *die* probationer

Schwester·partei *die* sister party

schwieg /ʃviːk/ *1. u. 3. Pers. Prät. v.* **schweigen**

Schwieger- /ˈʃviːgɐ-/: ~**eltern** *Pl.* parents-in-law; ~**mutter** *die* mother-in-law; ~**sohn** *der* son-in-law; ~**tochter** *die* daughter-in-law; ~**vater** *der* father-in-law

Schwiele /ˈʃviːlə/ *die;* ~, ~**n** callus

schwielig *Adj.* callused; ~**e Hände** horny hands

schwierig /ˈʃviːrɪç/ *Adj.* difficult

Schwierigkeit *die;* ~, ~**en** difficulty; **in** ~**en** (*Akk.*) **geraten** get into difficulties; ~**en bekommen** have problems *or* trouble; **jmdn./sich in** ~**en** (*Akk.*) **bringen** get sb./oneself into trouble; **ohne** ~**en** without difficulty

Schwierigkeits·grad *der* degree of difficulty; (von Lehrmaterial usw.) level of difficulty

Schwimm-: ~**bad** *das* swimming baths *pl.* (Brit.); swimming pool; ~**becken** *das* swimming pool; ~**dock** *das* floating dock

schwimmen 1 *unr. itr. V.* (a) *meist mit sein* swim; ~ **gehen** go swimming; (b) *meist mit sein* (treiben, nicht untergehen) float; (c) (ugs.: unsicher sein) be all at sea; **ins Schwimmen geraten** start to flounder; (d) (überschwemmt sein) be awash; (e) *mit sein* (triefen von) **in etw.** (*Dat.*) ~: be swimming in sth.; **im Geld** ~ (fig.) be rolling in money *or* in it (coll.); (f) *mit sein* (ver~) swim. **2** *unr. tr. V.; auch mit sein* swim

Schwimmen *das;* ~**s:** swimming *no art.*

Schwimmer *der;* ~**s**, ~: (a) swimmer; (b) (der Angel, Technik) float

Schwimmer·becken *das* swimmers' pool

Schwimm-: ~**flosse** *die* flipper; ~**fuß** *der* webbed foot; ~**gürtel** *der* swimming-belt; ~**kran** *der* floating crane; ~**lehrer** *der* swimming instructor; ~**vogel** *der* web-footed bird; ~**weste** *die* life jacket

Schwindel /ˈʃvɪndl̩/ *der;* ~**s** (a) (Gleichgewichtsstörung) dizziness; giddiness; vertigo; (b) (Anfall) dizzy *or* giddy spell; attack of dizziness *or* giddiness *or* vertigo; (c) (abwertend) (Betrug) swindle; fraud; (Lüge) lie; **den** ~ **kenne ich** (ugs.) that's an old trick; I know that trick

Schwindelei *die;* ~, ~**en** (ugs.) (a) *o. Pl.* fibbing; (b) (Lüge) fib

schwindel-: ~**erregend** *Adj.* vertiginous ‹*height, speed, depths*›; (fig.) meteoric ‹*career, success*›; ~**frei** *Adj.* ~**frei sein** have a head for heights; not suffer from vertigo

schwindelig ⇨ **schwindlig**

schwindeln *itr. V.* (a) **mich** *od.* **mir schwindelt** I feel dizzy *or* giddy; **in** ~**der Höhe** at a dizzy height; (b) (lügen) tell fibs

schwinden /ˈʃvɪndn̩/ *unr. itr. V.; mit sein* fade; ‹*supplies, money*› run out, dwindle; ‹*effect*› wear off; ‹*interest*› wane, fall off; ‹*fear, mistrust*› lessen, diminish; ‹*powers, influence*› wane, decline; ‹*courage, strength*› fail; **ihm schwand der Mut** his courage failed him

Schwindler *der;* ~**s**, ~ (Lügner) liar; (Betrüger) swindler; (Hochstapler) confidence trickster; con man (coll.)

schwindlig *Adj.* dizzy; giddy; **jmdm. wird es** ~: sb. gets dizzy *or* giddy

Schwind·sucht *die* (veralt.) consumption; tuberculosis

schwind·süchtig *Adj.* (veralt.) consumptive; tubercular

Schwinge /ˈʃvɪŋə/ *die;* ~, ~**n** (geh.; auch fig.) wing

schwingen 1 *unr. itr. V.* (a) *mit sein* (sich hin- u. herbewegen) swing; (b) (vibrieren) vibrate; (c) (Physik) ‹*wave*› oscillate. **2** *unr. tr. V.* (hin- u. herbewegen) swing; wave ‹*flag, wand*›; (fuchteln mit) brandish ‹*sword, axe, etc.*›; **große Reden** ~ (ugs.) talk big; *s. auch* **Tanzbein. 3** *unr. refl. V.* (sich schnell bewegen) **sich aufs Pferd/Fahrrad** ~: swing oneself *or* leap on to one's horse/bicycle; **der Vogel schwang sich in die Luft** (fig.) the bird soared [up] into the air

Schwinger *der;* ~**s**, ~ (Boxen) swing

Schwing·tür *die* swing-door

Schwingung *die;* ~, ~**en** (a) swinging; (Vibration) vibration; **etw. in** ~ **versetzen** set sth. swinging/vibrating; (b) (Physik) oscillation

Schwips /ʃvɪps/ *der;* ~**es**, ~**e** (ugs.) **einen [kleinen]** ~ **haben** be [a bit] tipsy *or* (coll.) merry

schwirren /ˈʃvɪrən/ *itr. V.* (a) (tönen) ‹*insect*› buzz; ‹*bowstring*› twang; (b) *mit sein* ‹*arrow, bullet, etc.*› whiz; ‹*bird*› whirr; ‹*insect*› buzz; **allerlei schwirrte mir durch den Kopf** (fig.) all sorts of things buzzed through my head

schwitzen 1 *itr. V.* (a) (auch fig.) sweat; **ins Schwitzen kommen** (auch fig.) start to sweat; (b) (beschlagen) steam up. **2** *refl. V.* **sich bei der Arbeit klatschnass** ~: get soaked with sweat from working

schwitzig *Adj.* (ugs.) sweaty

schwofen /ˈʃvoːfn̩/ *itr. V.* (ugs.) shake a leg (coll.); ~ **gehen** go and shake a leg

schwor /ʃvoːɐ̯/ *1. u. 3. Pers. Sg. Prät. v.* **schwören**

schwören /ˈʃvøːrən/ **1** *unr. tr., itr. V.* swear ⟨*fidelity, allegiance, friendship*⟩; swear, take ⟨*oath*⟩; **ich schwöre es[, so wahr mir Gott helfe]** I swear it[, so help me God]; **jmdm./sich etw. ~:** swear sth. to sb./oneself. **2** *unr. itr. V.* swear an/the oath; **auf die Bibel ~:** swear on the Bible

Schwuchtel /ˈʃvʊxtl̩/ *die;* ~, ~**n** (salopp) queen (sl.)

schwul /ʃvuːl/ *Adj.* (ugs.) gay (coll.)

schwül /ʃvyːl/ *Adj.* **(a)** (feuchtwarm) sultry; close; **(b)** (beklemmend) oppressive

Schwule *der; adj. Dekl.* (ugs.) gay (coll.); (abwertend) queer (sl. derog.)

Schwüle *die;* ~: sultriness

schwülstig /ˈʃvʏlstɪç/ **1** *Adj.* bombastic, pompous; overornate ⟨*art, architecture*⟩. **2** *adv.* bombastically; pompously

schwumm[e]rig /ˈʃvʊmərɪç/ *Adj.* (ugs.) **(a)** (unwohl) queasy; funny (coll.); **(b)** (bang) jittery (coll.); nervous; apprehensive

Schwund /ʃvʊnt/ *der;* ~**[e]s (a)** decrease, drop (*Gen.* in); (an Interesse) waning; falling off; **(b)** (Kaufmannsspr.) shrinkage

Schwung /ʃvʊŋ/ *der;* ~**[e]s, Schwünge** /ˈʃvʏŋə/ **(a)** (Bewegung) swing; **(b)** (Linie) sweep; **der elegante ~ ihrer Brauen/ihrer Nase** the elegant arch of her eyebrows/curve of her nose; **(c)** *o. Pl.* (Geschwindigkeit) momentum; ~ **holen** build *or* get up momentum; (auf einer Schaukel usw.) work up a swing; **etw. in ~ bringen** (fig. ugs.) get sth. going; **in ~ sein** (fig. ugs.) (in guter Stimmung) have livened up; (wütend) be worked up; (gut laufen) ⟨*business, practice*⟩ do a lively trade; (gut vorankommen) be getting on well; be right in the swing [of it]; **in ~ kommen** (fig. ugs.) (in gute Stimmung kommen) get going; liven up; (wütend werden) get worked up; (gut vorankommen) get right in the swing [of it]; ⟨*business*⟩ pick up; **(d)** *o. Pl.* (Antrieb) drive; energy; **(e)** *o. Pl.* (mitreißende Wirkung) sparkle; vitality; **(f)** *o. Pl.* (ugs.: größere Menge) stack (coll.); (von Menschen) crowd; bunch (sl.)

schwung·haft *Adj.* thriving; brisk, flourishing ⟨*trade, business*⟩

schwung-: ~**los 1** *Adj.* **(a)** (antriebsschwach) lacking in energy *or* drive *postpos.;* listless; **(b)** (langweilig) lack-lustre ⟨*speech, performance, etc.*⟩; **2** *adv.* ⟨*sing, dance, etc.*⟩ in a lack-lustre way; ~**voll 1** *Adj.* **(a)** (mitreißend) lively; spirited; spirited ⟨*words*⟩; lively, (coll.) snappy ⟨*tune*⟩; **(b)** (kraftvoll) vigorous; **ein** ~**voller Handel** a roaring trade; **(c)** (elegant) sweeping ⟨*movement, gesture*⟩; bold ⟨*handwriting, line, stroke*⟩; **2** *adv.* **(a)** (mitreißend) spiritedly; with verve; ⟨*speak*⟩ spiritedly; **(b)** (kraftvoll) with great vigour

Schwur /ʃvuːɐ̯/ *der;* ~**[e]s, Schwüre** /ˈʃvyːrə/ **(a)** (Gelöbnis) vow; **(b)** (Eid) oath; **die Hand zum ~ erheben** raise one's hand to take the oath

Schwur·gericht *das* court with a jury

Sciencefiction, ⁺Science-fiction /ˈsaɪəns'fɪkʃən/ *die;* ~: science fiction

sechs /zɛks/ *Kardinalz.* ▶ 22 |, ▶ 530 |, ▶ 600 | six; *s. auch* **acht**

Sechs *die;* ~, ~**en** six; **eine ~ schreiben/bekommen** (Schulw.) get a 'fail' mark; *s. auch* **Acht¹** a, b, d, e; **Zwei** b

Sechs·eck *das* hexagon

sechs·eckig *Adj.* hexagonal

Sechser *der;* ~**s,** ~ (ugs.) (Ziffer, beim Würfeln) six; (Bahn, Bus) [number] six; (im Lotto) six winning numbers

sechs-, Sechs-: ~**fach** *Vervielfältigungsz.* sixfold; *s. auch* **achtfach**; ~**fache** *das; adj. Dekl.* **etw. um ein** ~**faches/um das** ~**fache erhöhen** increase sth. by a factor of six; *s. auch* **Achtfache**; ~**hundert** *Kardinalz.* ▶ 600 | six hundred; ~**jährig** *Adj.* (6 Jahre alt) six-year-old *attrib.;* six years old *postpos.;* (6 Jahre dauernd) six-year *attrib.;* ~**kant·mutter** *die* hexagon nut; ~**köpfig** *Adj.* six-headed ⟨*monster*⟩; ⟨*family, committee*⟩ of six

sechs·mal *Adv.* six times; *s. auch* **achtmal**

sechst /zɛkst/ *in* **wir waren zu ~:** there were six of us; *s. auch* **acht²**

sechst... *Ordinalz.* ▶ 119 |, ▶ 600 | sixth; *s. auch* **acht...**

sechs-, Sechs-: ~**tage·rennen** *das* (Radsport) six-day race; ~**tägig** *Adj.* (6 Tage alt) six-day-old *attrib.;* (6 Tage dauernd) six-day[-long] *attrib.;* ~**tausend** *Kardinalz.* ▶ 600 | six thousand

sechs·teilig *Adj.* six-piece ⟨*tool set etc.*⟩; six-part ⟨*serial*⟩

sechstel *Bruchz.* ▶ 600 | sixth

Sechstel *das, schweiz. meist der;* ~**s,** ~: ▶ 600 | sixth; *s. auch* **Achtel**

sechstens *Adv.* sixthly

Sechs-: ~**und·sechzig** *das;* ~: ▶ 600 | sixty-six; ~**zylinder·motor** *der* six-cylinder engine

sechzehn /ˈzɛçtseːn/ *Kardinalz.* ▶ 22 |, ▶ 530 |, ▶ 600 | sixteen; *s. auch* **achtzehn**

Sechzehn·meter·raum *der* (Fußball) penalty area

sechzig /ˈzɛçtsɪç/ *Kardinalz.* ▶ 22 |, ▶ 600 | sixty; *s. auch* **achtzig**

sechziger *indekl. Adj.; nicht präd.* **die ~ Jahre** the sixties; **zwei ~ Briefmarken/Zigarren** two sixty-pfennig stamps/cigars; **eine ~ Glühbirne** a 60-watt bulb

Sechziger¹ *der;* ~**s,** ~ sixty-year-old

Sechziger² *die;* ~, ~ **(a)** (Briefmarke) sixty-pfennig/schilling *etc.* stamp; **(b)** (Zigarre) sixty-pfennig cigar; (Glühbirne) 60-watt bulb

Sechziger·jahre ▶ 22 |, ▶ 119 | *Pl.* sixties *pl.*

sechzigst... /ˈzɛçtsɪçst/ *Ordinalz.* ▶ 600 | sixtieth; *s. auch* **achtzigst...**

SED /ɛsʔeˈdeː/ *die;* ~: *Abk.* (ehem. DDR) **Sozialistische Einheitspartei Deutschlands** Socialist Unity Party of Germany

Sediment /zediˈmɛnt/ *das;* ~**[e]s,** ~**e** (Geol., Chemie) sediment

See¹ /zeː/ *der;* ~**s,** ~**n** lake; **der Genfer ~** Lake Geneva; **der Obere ~:** Lake Superior

See² *die;* ~, ~**n (a)** *o. Pl.* (Meer) sea; **an die ~ fahren** go to the seaside; **an der ~:** by the sea[side]; **auf ~:** at sea; **er ist auf ~:** he is away at sea; **auf hoher ~:** on the high seas; **in ~ gehen** *od.* **stechen** put to sea; **Leutnant/Kapitän zur ~** (Marine) sub-lieutenant/[naval] captain; **zur ~ fahren** be a seaman; **(b)** *o. Pl.* (Seemannsspr.: ~**gang**) **ruhige/raue** *od.* **schwere ~:** calm/rough *or* heavy sea

see-, See-: ~**adler** *der* sea eagle; white-tailed [sea] eagle; ~**bad** *das* seaside health resort; ~**beben** *das* seaquake; ~**fahrt** *die* **(a)** *o. Pl.* seafaring *no art.;* sea travel *no art.;* (~**fahrtskunde**) navigation; **(b)** (~reise) voyage; (Kreuzfahrt) cruise; ~**fisch** *der* sea fish; salt-water fish; ~**gang** *der; o. Pl.* **leichter/starker** *od.* **hoher** *od.* **schwerer** ~**gang** light/heavy *or* rough sea; ~**gefecht** *das* naval engagement; sea battle; naval battle; ~**hafen** *der* **(a)** (Hafenanlagen) harbour; **(b)** (Stadt) seaport; ~**handel** *der* maritime trade; ~**herrschaft** *die; o. Pl.* maritime supremacy; ~**hund** *der* **(a)** common seal; **(b)** (Pelz) seal[skin]; ~**igel** *der* sea urchin; ~**karte** *die* sea chart; ~**klima** *das* (Geogr.) maritime climate; ~**krank** *Adj.* seasick; ~**krankheit** *die; o. Pl.* seasickness; ~**krieg** *der* naval war; (Kriegsführung) naval warfare; ~**lachs** *der* pollack

Seele /ˈzeːlə/ *die;* ~, ~**n** (auch Rel., fig.) soul; (Psyche) mind; **sich** (*Dat.*) **die ~ aus dem Leib schreien** (ugs.) shout/scream one's head off (coll.); **jmdm. auf der ~ liegen** (geh.) weigh on sb.['s mind]; **jmdm. aus der ~ sprechen** (ugs.) take the words out of sb.'s mouth; **aus tiefster ~:** with all one's heart; ⟨*thank*⟩ from the bottom of one's heart; **sich** (*Dat.*) **etw. von der ~ reden** unburden oneself about sth.; **die ~ von etw. sein** be the heart of sth.; **eine ~ von Mensch sein** be a good [-hearted] soul

seelen-, Seelen-: ~**friede[n]** *der* peace of mind; ~**heil** *das* (christl. Rel.) salvation of one's/sb.'s soul; ~**leben** *das; o. Pl.* (geh.) inner life; ~**ruhe** *die* calmness; **in aller** ~**ruhe** calmly; ~**ruhig 1** *Adj.* calm; unruffled; **2** *adv.* calmly

---

seelisch 1 *Adj.* psychological ⟨*cause, damage, tension*⟩; mental ⟨*equilibrium, breakdown, illness, health*⟩. **2** *adv.* ∼ **bedingt sein** have psychological causes; ∼ **krank** mentally ill

See·löwe *der* sea lion

Seel·sorge *die; o. Pl.* pastoral care

Seelsorger *der;* ∼**s,** ∼**:** pastoral worker; (Geistlicher) pastor

See-: ∼**macht** *die* maritime *or* naval power; sea power; ∼**mann** *der; Pl.* ∼**leute** ▶ 85 ⏐ seaman; sailor

seemännisch /'ze:mɛnɪʃ/ *Adj.* nautical

Seemanns·garn *das; o. Pl.* seaman's yarn

See-: ∼**meile** *die* nautical mile; ∼**not** *die; o. Pl.* distress [at sea]; **jmdn. aus** ∼ **retten** rescue sb. in distress; ∼**pferd[chen]** *das* sea horse; ∼**räuber** *der* pirate; ∼**recht** *das; o. Pl.* maritime law; ∼**reise** *die* voyage; (Kreuzfahrt) cruise; ∼**rose** *die* waterlily; ∼**sack** *der* kitbag; *∼**schiffahrt,** ∼**schifffahrt** *die* maritime shipping *no art.;* sea shipping *no art.;* ∼**schlacht** *die* sea battle; naval battle; ∼**stern** *der* starfish; ∼**streitkräfte** *Pl.* naval forces; ∼**tang** *der* seaweed; ∼**tüchtig** *Adj.* seaworthy; ∼**ufer** *das* lake shore; shore of a/ the lake; ∼**vogel** *der* seabird; ∼**weg** *der* sea route; **auf dem** ∼**weg** by sea; ∼**zunge** *die* sole

Segel /'ze:gl̩/ *das;* ∼**s,** ∼**:** sail; **die** ∼ **streichen** strike sail; (fig.) throw in the towel (**vor** + *Dat.* in the face of)

Segel-: ∼**boot** *das* sailing-boat; ∼**fliegen** *das;* ∼**s** gliding *no art.;* ∼**flieger** *der* glider pilot; ∼**flugzeug** *das* glider; ∼**jacht** *die* sailing-yacht

segeln *itr. V. mit sein* sail; ∼ **gehen** go sailing; go for a sail

Segel-: ∼**regatta** *die* sailing regatta; ∼**schiff** *das* sailing ship; ∼**törn** *der* (Seemannsspr.) sailing trip; ∼**tuch** *das* sailcloth

Segen /'ze:gn̩/ *der;* ∼**s,** ∼ (**a**) blessing; (Gebet in der Messe) benediction; **über jmdn./etw. den** ∼ **sprechen** bless sb./sth.; **[jmdm.] seinen** ∼ **[zu etw.] geben** (ugs.) give [sb.] one's blessing [on sth.]; **meinen** ∼ **hat er!** (ugs.) I have no objection [to his doing that]; (iron.) the best of luck to him!; (**b**) *o. Pl.* (Wohltat) blessing; **etw. zum** ∼ **der Menschheit nutzen** exploit sth. to the benefit of mankind

Segens·wünsche *Pl.* good wishes

Segler *der;* ∼**s,** ∼ (**a**) (Schiff) sailing-ship *or* -vessel; (**b**) (Sportler) yachtsman; (**c**) (Zool.) swift

Seglerin *die;* ∼, ∼**nen** yachtswoman

Segment /zɛ'gmɛnt/ *das;* ∼**[e]s,** ∼**e** segment

segnen /'ze:gnən/ *tr. V.* (**a**) bless; (**b**) (ausstatten mit) **mit jmdm./etw. gesegnet sein** (auch iron.) be blessed with sb./ sth.; **im gesegneten Alter von 88 Jahren** at the venerable age of 88 years

Segnung *die;* ∼, ∼**en** blessing; (iron.) dubious blessing

sehen /'ze:ən/ **1** *unr. itr. V.* (**a**) see; **schlecht/gut** ∼**:** have bad *or* poor/good eyesight; **hast du ge**∼**?** did you see?; **mal** ∼**, wir wollen** *od.* **werden** ∼ (ugs.) we'll see; **siehste!** (ugs.), **siehst du wohl!** there, you see!; **lass mal** ∼**:** let me *or* let's see; let me *or* let's have a look; **siehe oben/unten/Seite 80** see above/below/page 80; **da kann man** *od.* (ugs.) **kannste mal** ∼**, …:** that just goes to show …; (**b**) (hin∼) look; **auf etw.** (*Akk.*) ∼**:** look at sth.; **nach der Uhr** ∼**:** look at one's watch; **sieh mal** *od.* **doch!** look!; **siehe da!** lo and behold!; **alle Welt sieht auf Washington** (fig.) all eyes are turned on Washington; (**c**) (zeigen, liegen) **nach Süden/Norden** ∼**:** face south/north; (**d**) (nach∼) have a look; see; (**e**) **nach jmdm.** ∼ (betreuen) keep an eye on sb.; (besuchen) drop by to see sb.; **nach**∼ look in on sb.; **nach etw.** ∼ (betreuen) keep an eye on sth.; (nach∼) take a look at sth.. **2** *unr. tr. V.* (**a**) (erblicken) see; **jmdn./etw. [nicht] zu** ∼ **bekommen** [not] get to see sb./sth.; **von ihm/davon ist nichts zu** ∼**:** he/it is nowhere to be seen; **ich habe ihn kommen [ge]**∼**:** I saw him coming; **da sieht man** you can see that; **sieht man das?** does it show?; **hat man so was schon ge**∼**!** did you ever see anything like it!; [**überall**] **gern ge**∼ **sein** be welcome [everywhere]; **jmdn. vom Sehen kennen** know sb. by sight; **etw. gern** ∼**:** approve of sth.; **jmdn./**

etw. nicht mehr ∼ **können** (fig. ugs.) not be able to stand the sight of sb./sth. any more; **kein Blut** ∼ **können** (ugs.) not be able to stand the sight of blood; **er kann sich in dieser Gegend nicht mehr** ∼ **lassen** he can't show his face around here any more; (**b**) (an∼, betrachten) watch ⟨*television, performance*⟩; look at ⟨*photograph, object*⟩; (**c**) (treffen) see; **wir** ∼ **uns morgen!** see you tomorrow!; (**d**) (sich vorstellen) see; (**e**) (feststellen, erkennen) see; **ich möchte doch einmal** ∼**, ob er es wagt** I'd just like to see whether he dares [to]; **das sieht man an der Farbe** you can tell by the colour; **wir sahen, dass wir nicht mehr helfen konnten** we saw that we could not help any more; **etw. in jmdm.** ∼**:** see sth. in sb.; **das wollen wir [doch] erst mal** ∼**!** we'll 'see about that; **man wird** ∼ [**müssen**] we'll [just have to] see; **da sieht man es [mal] wieder** it's the same old story; (**f**) (beurteilen) see; **das sehe ich anders** I see it differently; **so darf man das nicht** ∼**:** you mustn't look at it that way *or* like that; **so ge**∼**:** looked at that way *or* in that light; **rechtlich ge**∼**:** seen from a legal point of view; **ich werde** ∼**, was ich für Sie tun kann** I'll see what I can do for you. **3** *unr. refl. V.* (**a**) **er kann sich nicht satt** ∼**:** he can't see enough (**an** + *Dat.* of); (**b**) (sich betrachten als) **sich genötigt/veranlasst** ∼**, … zu …:** feel compelled to …; **sich in der Lage** ∼**, … zu …:** feel able to …; think one is able to …

sehens·wert *Adj.* worth seeing *postpos.*

Sehens·würdigkeit *die* sight; **die** ∼**en [der Stadt] besichtigen** go sightseeing [in the town]; see the sights [of the town]

Seher *der;* ∼**s,** ∼**:** seer; prophet

Seherin *die;* ∼, ∼**nen** seer; prophetess

Seh-: ∼**fehler** *der* sight defect; defect of vision; ∼**kraft** *die; o. Pl.* sight

Sehne /'ze:nə/ *die;* ∼, ∼**n** (**a**) (Anat.) tendon; sinew; (**b**) (Bogen∼) string; (**c**) (Geom.) chord

sehnen *refl. V.* **sich nach jmdm./etw.** ∼**:** long *or* yearn for sb./sth.; **sich [danach]** ∼**, etw. zu tun** long *or* yearn to do sth.; **er sehnt sich nach Hause** he longs to go home

Seh·nerv *der* (Anat.) optic nerve

sehnig *Adj.* (**a**) stringy ⟨*meat*⟩; (**b**) (kräftig) sinewy ⟨*figure, legs, arms, etc.*⟩

sehnlichst 1 *Adj.; nicht präd.* **das ist mein** ∼**es Verlangen/mein** ∼**er Wunsch** what's what I long for most/ that's my dearest wish. **2** *adv.* **sich** (*Dat.*) **etw.** ∼ **wünschen** long *or* yearn for sth.

Sehn·sucht *die* longing; yearning; ∼ **nach jmdm. haben** long *or* yearn to see sb.

sehn·süchtig 1 *Adj.* longing *attrib.*, yearning *attrib.* ⟨*desire, look, gaze, etc.*⟩; (wehmütig verlangend) wistful ⟨*gaze, sigh, etc.*⟩. **2** *adv.* longingly; (wehmütig verlangend) wistfully; **jmdn./etw.** ∼ **erwarten** look forward longingly to seeing sb./to sth.; long for sb. to come/for sth.

sehnsuchts·voll (geh.) ⇒ **sehnsüchtig**

sehr /ze:ɐ̯/ *Adv.* (**a**) *mit Adj. u. Adv.* very; ∼ **viel** a great deal; **ich bin** ∼ **dafür/dagegen** I'm very much in favour/against [it]; **ich bin Ihnen** ∼ **dankbar** I'm most grateful to you; **jmdn.** ∼ **gern haben** like sb. a lot (coll.) *or* a great deal; (**b**) *mit Verben* very much; greatly; **er hat** ∼ **geweint** he cried a great deal *or* (coll.) a lot; **danke** ∼**!** thank you *or* thanks [very much]; **bitte** ∼**, Ihr Schnitzel!** here's your steak, sir/madam; **Danke** ∼**! — Bitte** ∼**!** Thank you — You're welcome; **ja,** ∼**!** yes, very much!; **nein, nicht** ∼**!** no, not much!; **zu** ∼**:** too much

Seh-: ∼**schwäche** *die* weak vision *or* sight *no indef. art.;* ∼**test** *der* eye test

sei /zai̯/ *1. u. 3. Pers. Sg. Präsens Konjunktiv u. Imperativ Sg. v.* **sein**

seicht /zai̯çt/ **1** *Adj.* ▶ 277 ⏐ shallow; (fig.) shallow; superficial. **2** *adv.* (fig.) shallowly; superficially

seid /zai̯t/ *2. Pers. Pl. Präsens u. Imperativ Pl. v.* **sein**

Seide /'zai̯də/ *die;* ∼, ∼**n** silk

Seidel /'zai̯dl̩/ *das;* ∼**s,** ∼ ⟨*half-litre*⟩ beer mug

Seidel·bast *der* daphne

seiden 1 *Adj.* (**a**) *nicht präd.* (aus Seide) silk; (**b**) (wie Seide) silky. **2** *adv.* silkily

Seiden-: ~**papier** *das* tissue paper; ~**raupe** *die* silkworm; ~**strumpf** *der* silk stocking

seidig 1 *Adj.* silky. 2 *adv.* silkily

Seife /'zaifə/ *die;* ~, ~**n** soap

Seifen-: ~**blase** *die* soap bubble; (fig.) bubble; ~**blasen machen** blow bubbles; ~**lauge** *die* [soap]-suds *pl.;* ~**pulver** *das* soap powder; ~**schale** *die* soap-dish; ~**schaum** *der; o. Pl.* lather

seifig *Adj.* soapy

seihen /'zaiən/ *tr. V.* strain

Seil /zail/ *das;* ~**s,** ~**e** rope; (Draht~) cable; **auf dem** ~ **tanzen** dance on the high wire

Seil·bahn *die* cableway

Seiler *der;* ~**s,** ~: rope maker

Seilschaft *die;* ~, ~**en** (Bergsteigen) rope; (fig.) followers *pl.*

seil-, Seil-: ~**springen** *unr. itr. V.; nur im Inf. u. im 2. Part.; mit sein* skip; ~**tänzer** *der,* ~**tänzerin** *die* tightrope-walker; ~**winde** *die* cable winch

sein¹ /zain/ 1 *unr. itr. V.* **(a)** be; **wie ist das Wetter?** what is the weather like?; **wie wäre es mit einem Schnaps?** how about a schnaps?; **ist das kalt heute!** it's so cold today; **wie dem auch sei** be that as it may; **seien Sie bitte so freundlich und geben Sie mir …:** [would you] be so kind as to give me …; **das Buch ist meins** *od.* (ugs.) **mir** the book is mine; **das wärs** that's that; (beim Einkaufen) that's all; that's it (coll.); **er ist Schwede/Lehrer** he is Swedish *or* a Swede/a teacher; **was ist er [von Beruf]?** what does he do [for a living]?; **wo warst du so lange?** where have you been all this time?; **bist du es?** is that you?; **Karl wars** (ist verantwortlich) it was Karl [who did/ said *etc.* it]; **(b)** (unpers.) **mir ist kalt/besser** I am *or* feel cold/better; **mir ist schlecht** I feel sick; **jmdm. ist, als [ob]** …: sb. feels as if …; (jmd. hat den Eindruck [als]) sb. has a feeling that …; **jmdm. ist nach etw.** (ugs.) sb. feels like *or* fancies sth.; **(c)** (ergeben) be; make; **drei und vier ist** *od.* (ugs.) **sind sieben** three and four is *or* makes seven; **(d)** (unpers.) (bei Zeitangabe) be; **es ist drei Uhr/Mai/Winter** it is three o'clock/May/winter; **(e)** (sich befinden) be; **sind noch Tomaten da?** are there any tomatoes left?; **bist du schon mal bei Eva gewesen?** have you ever been to Eva's?; **(f)** (stammen) be; come; **er ist aus Berlin** he is *or* comes from Berlin; **(g)** (stattfinden) be; (sich ereignen) be; happen; **es war an einem Sonntag im April** it was on a Sunday in April; **muss das** ~? is that really necessary?; **was darf es** ~? (im Geschäft) what can I get you?; **das kann doch nicht** ~! that's just not possible!; **(h)** (existieren) be; exist; **ist was?** (ugs.) is anything wrong *or* the matter?; **das war einmal** that's all past now; **es war einmal ein Prinz** once upon a time there was a prince; **wenn du nicht gewesen wärst** if it hadn't been for you; **(i)** etw. ~ **lassen** (ugs.) stop sth.; **lass das** ~! stop it! 2 *Hilfsverb* **(a)** (… werden können) **es ist niemand zu sehen** there's no one to be seen; **das war zu erwarten** that was to be expected; **die Schmerzen sind kaum zu ertragen** the pain is hardly bearable; **es ist zu verkaufen** it is for sale; **(b)** (… werden müssen) **die Richtlinien sind strengstens zu beachten** the guide-lines are to be strictly followed; **(c)** (zur Perfektumschreibung) have; **er ist gestorben** he has died; **sie sind gerade mit dem Wagen in die Stadt** (ugs.) they've just driven off into town; **(d)** (zur Bildung des Zustandspassivs) be; **wir waren gerettet** we were saved

sein² *Possessivpron.* **(a)** (vor Substantiven) (bei Männern) his; (bei Mädchen) her; (bei Dingen, Abstrakta) its; (bei Tieren) its; (bei Männchen auch) his; (bei Weibchen auch) her; (bei Ländern) its; her; (bei Städten) its; (bei Schiffen) her; its; (nach „man") one's; his (Amer.); **(b)** *o. Subst.* his; **er hat das Seine** *od.* ~**e getan** (was er konnte) he has done what *or* all he could; (sein Teil) he has done his part *or* (coll.) bit

Sein *das;* ~**s** (Philos.) being; (Dasein) existence; ~ **und Schein** appearance and reality

seiner (geh.) 1 *Gen. von* **er: sich** ~ **erbarmen** have pity on him; ~ **gedenken** remember him. 2 *Gen. von* **es: das**

Tier lag dort, bis sich jemand ~ **annahm** the animal lay there until somebody came and looked after it

seiner-: ~**seits** *Adv.* for his part; (von ihm) on his part; ~**zeit** *Adv.* at that time; in those days

seines·gleichen *indekl. Pron.* **(a)** (nach er) his own kind; people *pl.* like himself; **er verkehrt am liebsten mit** ~: he prefers to associate with his own kind; **der König hat mich wie** ~ **behandelt** the King treated me as an equal; **(b)** (nach man) one's own kind; **(c)** (nach es) **das Kind soll mit** ~ **spielen** the child should play with others its own age; **das sucht** ~: it is without equal *or* is unequalled

seinet-: ~**wegen** *Adv.* **(a)** because of him; on his account; **(b)** (ihm zuliebe, für ihn) for his sake; for him; **(c)** (von ihm aus) **er sagte,** ~**wegen sollten wir ruhig gehen** he said as far as he was concerned we could go; ~**willen** *Adv. in* **um** ~**willen** for his sake; for him

*****sein|lassen** ⇨ **sein¹** 1 i

Seismograph /zaismo'gra:f/ *der;* ~**en,** ~**en** seismograph

seit /zait/ 1 *Präp. mit Dat.* (Zeitpunkt) since; (Zeitspanne) for; ~ 1955/**dem Unfall** since 1955/the accident; ~ **Wochen/einiger Zeit** for weeks/some time [past]; **ich bin** ~ **zwei Wochen hier** I've been here [for] two weeks; **er geht** ~ **vier Wochen zur Schule** he has been going to school for four weeks; ~ **damals,** ~ **der Zeit** since then; ~ **wann hast du ihn nicht mehr gesehen?** when was the last time you saw him?. 2 *Konj.* since; ~ **du hier wohnst** since you have been living here

seit·dem 1 *Adv.* since then; **das Haus steht** ~ **leer** since then the house has stood empty. 2 *Konj.* ⇨ **seit** 2

Seite /'zaitə/ *die;* ~, ~**n** **(a)** side; **auf** *od.* **zu beiden** ~**n der Straße/des Tores** on both sides of the road/gate; **die hintere/vordere** ~: the back/front; **zur** *od.* **auf die** ~ **gehen** *od.* **treten** move aside *or* to one side; move out of the way; **zur** ~**! make way!; jmdn. zur** ~ **nehmen** take sb. aside; **etw. auf die** ~ **schaffen** (ugs.) help oneself to sth.; **etw. auf die** ~ **legen** (ugs.: sparen) put sth. away *or* aside; **alles** *od.* **jedes Ding hat seine zwei** ~**n** (fig.) there are two sides to everything; ~ **an** ~: side by side; **jmdm. zur** ~ **stehen** stand by sb.; **(b)** (Richtung) side; **von allen** ~**n** (auch fig.) from all sides; **nach allen** ~**n** in all directions; (fig.) on all sides; **(c)** (Buch~, Zeitungs~) page; **(d)** (Eigenschaft, Aspekt) side; **auf der einen** ~, … **auf der anderen** ~ …: on the one hand … on the other hand …; **etw. ist jmds. schwache** ~ (ugs.) sth. is not exactly sb.'s forte; (ist jmds. Schwäche) sth. has a weakness for sth.; **jmds. starke** ~ **sein** be sb.'s forte *or* strong point; **sich von der besten** ~ **zeigen** show one's best side; **(e)** (Partei) side; **sich auf jmds.** ~ (Akk.) **schlagen** take sb.'s side; **auf jmds.** ~ **stehen** *od.* **sein** be on sb.'s side; **jmdn. auf seine** ~ **bringen** *od.* **ziehen** win sb. over; **auf/von** ~**n der Direktion** on/from the management side; **von anderer** ~ **verlautete, dass …:** it was learned from other sources that …; **(f)** (Familie) side

*****seiten** *in* **auf/von** ~: ⇨ **Seite e, aufseiten, von·seiten**

Seiten-: ~**airbag** *der* (Kfz.-W.) side airbag; ~**ausgang** *der* side exit; ~**blick** *der* sidelong look; (kurzer Blick) sidelong glance; ~**eingang** *der* side entrance; ~**flügel** *der* **(a)** (eines Gebäudes) wing; **(b)** (eines Flügelaltars) side panel; ~**gebäude** *das* annex; ~**hieb** *der* (fig.) sideswipe (**auf** + *Akk.* at); ~**linie** *die* **(a)** (Geneal.) offset; offshoot; **(b)** (Fußball, Rugby) touchline; (Tennis, Hockey, Federball) sideline; ~**ruder** *das* (Flugw.) rudder

seitens *Präp. mit Gen.* (Papierdt.) on the part of

seiten-, Seiten-: ~**schiff** *das* [side] aisle; ~**sprung** *der* infidelity; **einen** ~**sprung machen** have an affair; ~**stechen** *das;* ~**s:** ~**stechen haben/bekommen** have/get a stitch; ~**straße** *die* side street; **eine** ~**straße der Schillerstraße** a side street off the Schillerstrasse; ~**streifen** *der* verge; (einer Autobahn) hard shoulder; „~**streifen nicht befahrbar"** 'Soft Verges'; ~**verkehrt** *Adj.* reversed; ~**wand** *die* side wall; ~**wechsel** *der* (Ballspiele) change of ends; ~**wind** *der; o. Pl.* side wind; crosswind; ~**zahl** *die* **(a)** page number; **(b)** (Anzahl der Seiten) number of pages

---

*alte Schreibung (vgl. Hinweise auf S. xvi–xvii)

seit

1. Als Präposition

Mit einem Zeitpunkt	= since
Wir wohnen seit 1995 hier	= We have been living here since 1995
Seit damals leidet er an Depressionen	= Since then he has suffered from fits of depression
Mit einer Zeitspanne	= for
Wir wohnen seit zwei Jahren hier	= We have been living here for two years
Er ist seit 20 Jahren bei der Firma	= He has been with the firm for 20 years
Ich kenne ihn schon seit einiger Zeit	= I have known him for some time

Die Übersetzungen von *seit* sind also nicht problematisch, aber die Zeiten des Verbs sind in den beiden Sprachen meist unterschiedlich: im Deutschen steht durchweg das Präsens, während man im Englischen das Perfekt oder – bei einem ununterbrochenen Vorgang – vor allem seine Verlaufsform, das *Perfect Continuous*, verwendet (mit *know* und *love* z.B. kann man aber das *Perfect Continuous* nicht verwenden). Ähnlich wird ein Verb im Imperfekt durch ein Verb im Plusquamperfekt übersetzt:

Ich wartete seit 8 Uhr/ zwei Stunden	= I had been waiting since 8 o'clock/for two hours

Negative und andere Beispiele, bei denen kein ununterbrochener Vorgang vorliegt, weisen aber in beiden Sprachen die gleichen Zeiten auf:

Wir haben sie seit der Hochzeit nicht gesehen/nur einmal gesehen	= We haven't seen her/have only seen her once since the wedding
Ich war seit 1980 nicht dort gewesen	= I hadn't been there since 1980

2. Als Konjunktion

Auch hier wird das englische *Perfect Continuous* bzw. das Perfekt bei einem ununterbrochenen Vorgang verwendet, wo im Deutschen das Präsens steht:

Seit sie in Deutschland lebt, haben wir keinen Kontakt mehr	= Since she has been living in Germany we are no longer in touch
Seit er dieses Mittel nimmt, hat er keine Schmerzen mehr	= Since he has been taking this medication, he no longer has any pain
Seit ich sie kenne, hat sie nie gelacht	= Since I have known her, she has never laughed

Und in der Vergangenheit (etwa in der Erzählform):

Seit sie in Deutschland lebte, hatten wir keinen Kontakt mehr	= Since she had been living in Germany, we were no longer in touch
Seit ich sie kannte, hatte sie nie gelacht	= Since I had known her, she had never laughed

Aber bei einem Geschehen, das nicht andauert, wird das deutsche Perfekt mit dem englischen *Simple Past* übersetzt:

Seit er das gehört hat, ist er wie verwandelt	= Since he heard that, he's a changed man

---

seit·her *Adv.* since then

seitlich 1 *Adj.* side-‹door›; **ein ~er Wind** a side wind, a cross-wind. 2 *adv.* (an der Seite) at the side; (von der Seite) from the side; (nach der Seite) to the side; **~ von jmdm. stehen** stand to the side of sb.

seit·wärts *Adv.* sideways

sek., Sek. *Abk.* Sekunde sec.

Sekret /ze'kre:t/ *das;* ~[e]s, ~e (Med., Biol.) secretion

Sekretär /zekre'tɛːɐ̯/ *der;* ~s, ~e (a) ▶85┃ secretary; (b) ▶85┃ (Beamter) middle-ranking civil servant; (c) (Schreibschrank) secretaire; secretary; bureau (Brit.)

Sekretariat /zekreta'rịa:t/ *das;* ~[e]s, ~e [secretary's/secretaries'] office

Sekretärin *die;* ~, ~nen ▶85┃ secretary

Sekt /zɛkt/ *der;* ~[e]s, ~e high-quality sparkling wine; ≈ champagne

Sekte /'zɛktə/ *die;* ~, ~n sect

Sektion /zɛk'tsịo:n/ *die;* ~, ~en (Abteilung) section; (im Ministerium) department

Sektor /'zɛktɔr/ *der;* ~s, ~en /-'to:rən/ (a) (Fachgebiet) field; sphere; **industrieller/wirtschaftlicher ~:** industrial/economic sector; (b) (Geom.) sector

Sekunda /ze'kʊnda/ *die;* ~, Sekunden (Schulw.) (a) (veralt.) sixth and seventh years (*of a Gymnasium*); (b) (österr.) second year (*of a Gymnasium*)

Sekundant /zekʊn'dant/ *der;* ~en, ~en second (in a duel or match)

sekundär /zekʊn'dɛːɐ̯/ 1 *Adj.* secondary. 2 *adv.* secondarily

Sekundär·literatur *die* secondary literature

Sekundar-: ~schule *die* (schweiz.) secondary school; ~stufe *die* secondary stage (*of education*)

Sekunde /ze'kʊndə/ *die;* ~, ~n ▶530┃ (a) (auch Math., Musik) second; **es ist auf die ~ 12 Uhr** it is twelve o'clock precisely; (b) (ugs.: Augenblick) second; moment

sekundenlang 1 *Adj.* momentary. 2 *adv.* for a moment; momentarily

Sekunden-: ~schnelle *die; o. Pl.* **in ~schnelle** in a matter of seconds ~zeiger *der* second hand

sekundieren *itr. V.* (geh.) jmdm. [bei etw.] ~: support sb., back sb. up [in sth.]; jmdm. [bei einem Duell] ~: act as sb.'s second [in a duel]

selber /'zɛlbɐ/ *indekl. Demonstrativpron.* ⇒ **selbst 1**

Selber·machen *das;* ~s (ugs.) do-it-yourself *no art.*

selbst /zɛlpst/ 1 *indekl. Demonstrativpron.* **ich/du/er ~:** I myself/you yourself/he himself; **wir/ihr ~:** we ourselves/you yourselves; **sie ~:** she herself; (*Pl.*) they themselves; **Sie ~:** you yourself; (*Pl.*) you yourselves; **das Haus ~:** the house itself; **du hast es ~ gesagt** you said so yourself; (betonter) you yourself said so; **Wie gehts dir? — Gut! Und ~?** (ugs.) How are you? — Fine! And how about you?; **von ~:** automatically; **es versteht sich von ~:** it goes without saying; **die Ruhe ~ sein** (ugs.) be calmness itself; **~ gemacht** home-made ‹jam, liqueur, sausage, basket, etc.›; self-made ‹dress, pullover, etc.›; ‹dress, pullover, etc.› one has made oneself; **~ gebacken** home-made; home-baked; **~gestrickt** home-made; hand-knitted; **~ gedrehte Zigaretten** [one's own] rolled cigarettes. 2 *adv.* even

Selbst-: ~abholer *der;* ~s, ~ (a) (Kaufmannsspr.) *buyer who collects the goods himself/herself;* **ein Möbelmarkt für ~abholer** a cash-and-carry furniture store; (b) (Postw.) *person who collects his post himself/herself;* ~abholer sein collect the post oneself; ~achtung *die* self-respect; self-esteem

selb·ständig 1 *Adj.* ▶85┃ independent; **ein ~er Unternehmer** a self-employed business man; **sich ~**

machen set up on one's own. **2** *adv.* independently; ∼ **denken** think for oneself

Selbständige *der/die;* ▶85 *adj. Dekl.* self-employed [business] person

Selbständigkeit *die;* ∼: independence

selbst-, Selbst-: ∼**auslöser** *der* (Fot.) delayed-action shutter release; ∼**bedienungs·laden** *der* self-service shop; ∼**befriedigung** *die* masturbation *no art.;* ∼**beherrschung** *die* self-control *no art.;* ∼**be·stätigung** *die* (Psych.) selfaffirmation *no art.;* ∼**bestimmungs·recht** *das; o. Pl.* right of self-determination; ∼**beteiligung** *die* (Versicherungsw.) [personal] excess; ∼**betrug** *der* self-deception *no art.;* ∼**bewusst**, *∼**bewußt** **1** *Adj.* self-confident; self-possessed; **2** *adv.* self-confidently; ∼**bewusstsein**, *∼**bewußtsein** *das* self-confidence *no art.;* (einer sozialen Schicht o. Ä.) self-assurance; ∼**bildnis** *das* self-portrait; ∼**disziplin** *die; o. Pl.* self-discipline *no art.;* ∼**erhaltungs·trieb** *der* instinct for self-preservation; survival instinct; ∼**erkenntnis** *die; o. Pl.* self-knowledge *no art.;* *∼**gebacken** ⇒ **selbst 1**; *∼**gedreht** ⇒ **selbst 1**; ∼**gefällig** (abwertend) **1** *Adj.* self-satisfied; smug; **2** *adv.* smugly; in a self-satisfied way; ∼**gefälligkeit** *die; o. Pl.* self-satisfaction; smugness; *∼**gemacht** ⇒ **selbst 1**; ∼**gerecht** (abwertend) **1** *Adj.* self-righteous; **2** *adv.* self-righteously; ∼**gespräch** *das* conversation with oneself; ∼**gespräche führen** talk to oneself; *∼**gestrickt** ⇒ **selbst 1**; ∼**herrlich 1** *Adj.* high-handed; **2** *adv.* high-handedly; in a highhanded manner; ∼**hilfe** *die; o. Pl.* self-help *no art.;* ∼**justiz** *die* self-administered justice; ∼**justiz üben** take the law into one's own hands; ∼**klebe·folie** *die* self-adhesive plastic sheeting; ∼**klebend** *Adj.* self-adhesive; ∼**kosten·preis** *der* (Wirtsch.) cost price; **zum [reinen]** ∼**kostenpreis** at [no more than] cost; ∼**kritik** *die; o. Pl.* self-criticism; ∼**kritisch 1** *Adj.* self-critical; **2** *adv.* self-critically; ∼**laut** *der* vowel; ∼**los 1** *Adj.* selfless; **2** *adv.* selflessly; unselfishly; ∼**mord** *der* suicide *no art.;* ∼**mord begehen** commit suicide; ∼**mörder** *der* suicide; ∼**mörderisch** *Adj.* suicidal

selbstmord·gefährdet *Adj.* potentially suicidal

Selbstmord·versuch *der* suicide attempt

selbst-, Selbst-: ∼**redend** *Adv.* naturally; of course; ∼**sicher 1** *Adj.* self-confident; **2** *adv.* in a self-confident manner; full of self-confidence; ∼**ständig** *usw.:* ⇒ **selbständig** usw.; ∼**sucht** *die; o. Pl.* selfishness; self-interest; ∼**süchtig 1** *Adj.* selfish; **2** *adv.* selfishly; unselfishly; ∼**tätig 1** *Adj.* automatic; **2** *adv.* automatically; ∼**verständlich 1** *Adj.* natural; **etw. für** ∼**verständlich halten** regard sth. as a matter of course; (für gegeben hinnehmen) take sth. for granted; **das ist doch** ∼**verständlich** that goes without saying; **2** *adv.* naturally; of course; ∼**verständlich nicht!** of course not!; ∼**verständlichkeit** *die* matter of course; **etw. mit der größten** ∼**verständlichkeit tun** do sth. as if it were the most natural thing in the world; ∼**verteidigung** *die* self-defence *no art.;* ∼**vertrauen** *das* self-confidence; ∼**verwaltung** *die* self-government *no art.;* ∼**wähl·ferndienst** *der* (Postw.) direct dialling; STD; ∼**zerstörung** *die* self-destruction; ∼**zweck** *der; o. Pl.* end in itself; ∼**zweck sein/zum** ∼**zweck werden** be/become an end in itself

Selen /ze'le:n/ *das;* ∼s (Chemie) selenium

selig /'ze:lıç/ **1** *Adj.* (a) (Rel.) blessed; **Gott hab ihn** ∼: God rest his soul; *s. auch* **geben a; glauben b;** (b) (tot) late [lamented]; (c) (kath. Kirche: selig gesprochen) **die** ∼**e Dorothea** the blessed Dorothy; (d) (glücklich) blissful ⟨idleness, slumber, etc.⟩; blissfully happy ⟨person⟩; ∼ **[über etw.** (*Akk.*)**] sein** be overjoyed *or* (coll.) over the moon [about sth.]. **2** *adv.* blissfully

Seligkeit *die;* ∼, ∼**en** (a) *o. Pl.* (Rel.) [state of] blessedness; beatitude; **die ewige** ∼ eternal bliss; (b) (Glücksgefühl) bliss *no pl.;* [blissful] happiness *no pl.*

Selig·sprechung *die;* ∼, ∼**en** (kath. Kirche) beatification

---
*alte Schreibung (vgl. Hinweise auf S. xvi–xvii)

Sellerie /'zɛləri/ *der;* ∼s, ∼[s] *od. die;* ∼, ∼ (Stauden∼) celeriac; (Stangen∼) celery

selten /'zɛltn̩/ **1** *Adj.* rare; infrequent ⟨visit, visitor⟩; **in den** ∼**sten Fällen** very rarely. **2** *adv.* (a) rarely; **wir sehen uns nur noch** ∼: we seldom *or* hardly ever see each other now; (b) (sehr) exceptionally; uncommonly

Seltenheit *die;* ∼, ∼**en** rarity; **es ist eine** ∼, **dass ...:** it is rare that ...

Seltenheits·wert *der;* ∼[e]s rarity value

Selters·wasser /'zɛltɐs-/ *das* seltzer [water]

seltsam 1 *Adj.* strange; peculiar; odd. **2** *adv.* strangely; peculiarly

seltsamerweise *Adv.* strangely enough

Semantik /ze'mantık/ *die;* ∼ (Sprachw.) semantics *sing., no art.*

semantisch (Sprachw.) **1** *Adj.* semantic. **2** *adv.* semantically

Semester /ze'mɛstɐ/ *das;* ∼s, ∼ semester; **er hat 14** ∼ **Jura studiert** he studied law for seven years

Semikolon /zemi'ko:lɔn/ *das;* ∼s, ∼s *od.* **Semikola** semicolon

Seminar /zemi'na:ɐ̯/ *das;* ∼s, ∼e (a) (Lehrveranstaltung) seminar (**über** + *Akk.* on); (b) (Institut) department; **das juristische** ∼/∼ **für Alte Geschichte** the Law Department/Department of Ancient History; (c) (Priester∼) seminary; (d) (für Referendare) course for student teachers prior to their second state examination

Seminar-: ∼**arbeit** *die* seminar paper; ∼**schein** *der* certificate of attendance [at a seminar]

Semit /ze'mi:t/ *der;* ∼**en**, ∼**en**, **Semitin** *die;* ∼, ∼**nen** Semite

semitisch *Adj.* Semitic

Semmel /'zɛml/ *die;* ∼, ∼**n** (bes. österr., bayr., ostmd.) [bread] roll; **weggehen wie warme** ∼**n** (ugs.) sell like hot cakes

Semmel-: ∼**brösel** *der; meist Pl.* breadcrumb; ∼**knödel** *der* (bayr., österr.) bread dumpling

sen. *Abk.* **senior** sen.

Senat /ze'na:t/ *der;* ∼[e]s, ∼e (Hist., Politik, Hochschulw.) senate; **der US-**∼: the US Senate

Senator *der;* ∼s, ∼**en**, **Senatorin** *die;* ∼, ∼**nen** senator

Sende- /'zɛndə-/: ∼**bereich** *der,* ∼**gebiet** *das* (Rundf., Ferns.) transmitting area

senden[1] *unr.* (*auch regelm.*) *tr. V.* (geh.) send; **jmdm. etw.** ∼: send sb. sth.; **etw. an jmdn.** ∼: send sth. to sb.

senden[2] *regelm.* (*schweiz. unr.*) *tr., itr. V.* broadcast ⟨programme, play, etc.⟩; transmit ⟨concert, signals, Morse, etc.⟩; **Hilferufe** ∼: send out distress signals

Sender *der;* ∼s, ∼: [broadcasting] station; (Anlage) transmitter

Sende·reihe *die* (Rundf., Ferns.) series [of programmes]

Sender·such·lauf *der* (Rundf., Ferns.) [automatic] station search

Sende-: ∼**schluss**, *∼**schluß** *der* (Rundf., Ferns.) close-down; end of broadcasting; **zum** ∼**schluss noch ein Krimi** now as our last programme, a thriller; ∼**station** *die* (Funk, Rundf., Ferns.) broadcasting station; ∼**zeit** *die* (Rundf., Ferns.) broadcasting time; **die** ∼**zeit um zehn Minuten überschreiten** overrun by ten minutes

Sendung *die;* ∼, ∼**en** (a) consignment; (b) *o. Pl.* (geh.: Aufgabe) mission; (c) (Rundf., Ferns.: Darbietung) programme; broadcast; (d) (Rundfunkt., Ferns.: Ausstrahlung) transmission; broadcast[ing]

Senf /zɛnf/ *der;* ∼[e]s, ∼e mustard

Senf-: ∼**gas** *das* mustard gas; ∼**gurke** *die* gherkin pickled with mustard seeds

sengen 1 *tr. V.* singe. **2** *itr. V.* (a) (brennen) singe; (b) (heiß sein) be scorching; **eine** ∼**de Hitze** a scorching heat

senil /ze'ni:l/ **1** *Adj.* senile. **2** *adv.* in a senile manner

Senilität *die;* ∼: senility

senior /'ze:niɐ/ *indekl. Adj.; nach Personennamen* senior

Senior *der;* ∼s, ∼**en** /ze'nio:rən/ (a) (Kaufmannsspr.) senior partner; (b) (Sport) senior [player]; (c) (Rentner) senior citizen; (d) (Ältester) oldest member

Senior·chef *der* (Kaufmannsspr.) boss (coll.) (*in a family firm*)

Senioren·heim *das* home for the elderly

Seniorin /ze'nio:rin/ *die;* ~, ~nen ⇒ Senior

Senk·blei *das* (Bauw.) plumb[-bob]

Senke /'zɛŋkə/ *die;* ~, ~n hollow

Senkel /'zɛŋkl̩/ *der;* ~s, ~ (a) (Schnürsenkel) shoelace; (b) jmdn. in den ~ stellen (ugs.) put sb. in his/her place

senken 1 *tr. V.* (a) lower; (Bergbau) sink ⟨*shaft*⟩; lower ⟨*flag*⟩; drop ⟨*starting flag*⟩; **den Kopf** ~: bow one's head; **die Augen** *od.* **den Blick/die Stimme** ~: lower one's eyes *or* glance/voice; (b) (herabsetzen) reduce ⟨*fever, pressure, prices, etc.*⟩. 2 *refl. V.* ⟨*curtain, barrier, etc.*⟩ fall, come down; ⟨*ground, building, road*⟩ subside, sink; ⟨*water level*⟩ fall, sink

senk-, Senk-: ~fuß *der* (Anat.) flat foot; ~grube *die* (Bauw.) cesspit; ~recht 1 *Adj.* vertical; in ~rechter Stellung in an upright position; 2 *adv.* vertically; ~rechte *die; adj. Dekl.* (a) (Geom.) perpendicular; (b) vertical line; vertical; upright; ~recht·starter *der;* ~s, ~ (a) (Flugzeug) vertical take-off aircraft; (b) (ugs.) (Aufsteiger) whizz-kid (coll.); (Sache) instant success

Senkung *die;* ~, ~en (a) *o. Pl.* lowering; (b) *o. Pl.* (Reduzierung) reduction; lowering

Senner *der;* ~s, ~ (bayr., österr.) Alpine herdsman and dairyman

Sennerin *die;* ~, ~nen (bayr., österr.) Alpine herdswoman and dairywoman

Senn·hütte *die* (bayr., österr.) Alpine hut

Sensation /zɛnza'tsi̯o:n/ *die;* ~, ~en sensation; (Darbietung) sensational performance

sensationell 1 *Adj.* sensational. 2 *adv.* in a sensational manner; sensationally; **eine** ~ **aufgemachte Story** a sensationalized story

Sense /'zɛnzə/ *die;* ~, ~n (a) scythe; (b) (salopp) **jetzt ist** ~: this really is [the end of] it (coll.)

sensibel /zɛn'zi:bl̩/ 1 *Adj.* sensitive. 2 *adv.* sensitively

sensibilisieren *tr. V.* (a) (geh.) make ⟨*person*⟩ more sensitive (**für** to); (b) (Physiol.) sensitize

Sensibilität *die;* ~: sensitivity

Sensor /'zɛnzɔr/ *der;* ~s, ~en /-'zo:rən/ (Technik) sensor

Sensor·taste *die* (Technik) touch key

sentimental /zɛntimɛn'ta:l/ 1 *Adj.* sentimental. 2 *adv.* sentimentally

Sentimentalität *die;* ~, ~en sentimentality; **das sind bloße** ~en that is mere sentimentality

separat /zepa'ra:t/ 1 *Adj.* separate; ~e Wohnung self-contained flat (Brit.) *or* (Amer.) apartment. 2 *adv.* separately; **er wohnt** ~: he has self-contained accommodation

Separatismus *der;* ~: separatism *no art.*

September /zɛp'tɛmbɐ/ *der;* ~[s], ~: ▶ 119 September; *s. auch* April

Septime /zɛp'ti:mə/ *die;* ~, ~n (Musik) seventh

Serbe /'zɛrbə/ *der;* ~n, ~n Serb; Serbian

Serbien /'zɛrbi̯ən/ (*das*); ~s Serbia

Serbin *die;* ~, ~nen ⇒ Serbe

serbisch *Adj.* ▶ 487 | Serbian; *s. auch* deutsch; Deutsch

serbo·kroatisch /zɛrbokro'a:tɪʃ/ *Adj.* ▶ 487 | Serbo-Croat; *s. auch* deutsch; Deutsch

Serenade /zere'na:də/ *die;* ~, ~n (Musik) serenade

Sergeant /'zɛrdʒant/ *der;* ~en, ~en *od.* (bei engl. Ausspr.:) /'sa:dʒənt/ ~s, ~s (Milit.) sergeant

Serie /'ze:ri̯ə/ *die;* ~, ~n series; **eine** ~ **Briefmarken** a set of stamps

serien·mäßig 1 *Adj.* standard ⟨*product, model, etc.*⟩; (immer eingebaut) ⟨*feature, accessory*⟩ fitted as standard. 2 *adv.* (a) ~ **gefertigt** *od.* **gebaut** produced in series; (b) (nicht als Sonderausstattung) ⟨*fitted, supplied, etc.*⟩ as standard; ~ **mit etw. ausgerüstet sein** have sth. as a standard fitting

Serien·produktion *die* series production

seriös /ze'ri̯ø:s/ 1 *Adj.* (a) (solide) respectable ⟨*person, hotel, etc.*⟩; (vertrauenswürdig) reliable, trustworthy ⟨*firm,*

partner, etc.⟩; (b) (ernst gemeint) serious ⟨*offer, applicant, artist, etc.*⟩. 2 *adv.* (solide) respectably; (vertrauenswürdig) in a trustworthy manner

Seriosität /zeri̯ozi'tɛ:t/ *die;* ~ (geh.) respectability; (Vertrauenswürdigkeit) reliability; trustworthiness; (eines Geschäftsmanns, einer Firma) probity

Serpentine /zɛrpɛn'ti:nə/ *die;* ~, ~n (a) (Weg) zigzag mountain road (*with numerous hairpin bends*); (b) (Kehre) hairpin bend

Serum /'ze:rʊm/ *das;* ~s, **Seren** *od.* **Sera** (Med., Physiol.) serum

Service¹ /zɛr'vi:s/ *das;* ~[s] /...'vi:s[əs]/, ~ /...'vi:sə/ [dinner *etc.*] service

Service² /'zø:ɐvɪs/ *der od. das;* ~s /'zø:ɐvɪsɪs/ (a) *o. Pl.* service; (Abteilung) service department; (b) (Tennis: Aufschlag) serve; service

servieren /zɛr'vi:rən/ 1 *tr. V.* (a) (auftragen) serve ⟨*food, drink*⟩; (fig.) serve up ⟨*information*⟩; deliver ⟨*line, punchline, etc.*⟩; **jmdm. etw.** ~: serve sb. sth.; (b) (Ballspiele) **jmdm. den Ball** ~: feed/(Tennis) serve the ball to sb. 2 *itr. V.* (a) serve [at table]; (b) (Fußball) pass; make a pass; (Tennis) serve

Serviererin *die;* ~, ~nen waitress

Servier·wagen *der* [serving-] trolley

Serviette /zɛr'vi̯ɛtə/ *die;* ~, ~n napkin; serviette (Brit.)

Servietten·ring *der* napkin *or* (Brit.) serviette ring

servil /zɛr'vi:l/ (geh. abwertend) 1 *Adj.* obsequious; servile. 2 *adv.* obsequiously; in a servile manner

Servilität *die;* ~ (geh. abwertend) servility; obsequiousness

Servo- /'zɛrvo-/: ~bremse *die* servo [-assisted] brake; ~lenkung *die* power [-assisted] steering *no indef. art.*

Servus /'zɛrvʊs/ *Interj.* (bes. südd., österr.) (beim Abschied) goodbye; so long (coll.); (zur Begrüßung) hello

Sesam /'ze:zam/ *der;* ~s, ~s (a) (Pflanze) sesame; (Samen) sesame seeds *pl.*; (b) ~, **öffne dich!** open sesame!

Sessel /'zɛsl̩/ *der;* ~s, ~ (a) easy chair; (mit Armlehne) armchair; (b) (österr.: Stuhl) chair

Sessel·lift *der* chairlift

sesshaft, *seßhaft /'zɛshaft/ *Adj.* settled ⟨*tribe, way of life*⟩; ~ **werden** settle [down]

Set /zɛt/ *das od. der;* ~s, ~s (a) (Satz) set, combination (aus of); (b) (Deckchen) table- *or* place mat

setzen /'zɛtsn̩/ 1 *refl. V.* (a) (hin~) sit [down]; **setz dich/setzt euch/setzen Sie sich** sit down; take a seat; **sich aufs Sofa** *usw.* ~: sit on the sofa *etc.*; **sich zu jmdm.** ~: [go and] sit with sb.; join sb.; (b) (sinken) ⟨*coffee, solution, froth, etc.*⟩ settle; ⟨*sediment*⟩ sink to the bottom; (c) (in präp. Verbindungen) **sich mit jmdm. ins Einvernehmen** ~: come to an agreement with sb.; (d) (dringen) **der Staub setzt sich in die Kleider** the dust gets into one's clothes. 2 *tr. V.* (a) (platzieren) put; **eine Figur/einen Stein** ~: move a piece/man; (b) (einpflanzen) plant ⟨*tomatoes, potatoes, etc.*⟩; (c) (aufziehen) hoist ⟨*flag etc.*⟩; set ⟨*sails, navigation lights*⟩; (d) (Druckw.) set ⟨*manuscript etc.*⟩; (e) (schreiben) put ⟨*name, address, comma, etc.*⟩; **seinen Namen unter etw.** (*Akk.*) ~: put one's signature to sth.; sign sth.; (f) (in präp. Verbindungen) **in/außer Betrieb** ~: start up/stop ⟨*machine etc.*⟩; put ⟨*lift etc.*⟩ into operation/take ⟨*lift etc.*⟩ out of service; (ein-/ausschalten) switch on/off; (g) (aufstellen) put up, build ⟨*stove*⟩; stack ⟨*logs, bricks*⟩; (h) **sein Geld auf etw.** (*Akk.*) ~: put one's money on sth.; *s. auch* **Akzente; Ende;** (i) (ugs.) **es setzt was** *od.* **Prügel** *od.* **Hiebe** he/she *etc.* gets a hiding (coll.) *or* thrashing. 3 *itr. V.* (a) *meist mit sein* (im Sprung) leap, jump (**über** + *Akk.* over); **über einen Fluss** ~ (mit einer Fähre *o. ä.*) cross a river; (b) (beim Wetten) bet; **auf ein Pferd/auf Rot** ~: back a horse/put one's money on red

Setzer *der;* ~s, ~, **Setzerin** *die;* ~, ~nen (Druckw.) [type]setter

Setz·kasten *der* (Druckw.) [type-]case

Setzling /'zɛtslɪŋ/ *der;* ~s, ~e seedling

Setz·maschine *die* composing *or* typesetting machine

Seuche /'zɔɪçə/ *die;* ~, ~n epidemic

Seuchen-: ~bekämpfung *die* epidemic control *no art.;* ~gefahr *die; o. Pl.* danger of an epidemic

seufzen /'zɔyftsn̩/ *itr.*, *tr. V.* sigh; **schwer/erleichtert** ∼: give *or* heave a deep sigh/a sigh of relief

Seufzer *der;* ∼s, ∼: sigh

Sex /zɛks/ *der;* ∼[es] sex *no art.*

Sex-: ∼**appeal** /∼ ə'pi:l/ *der;* ∼s sex appeal; ∼**bombe** *die* (salopp) sex-bomb (coll.); sexpot (coll.); ∼**film** *der* sex film

Sexismus *der;* ∼: sexism *no art.*

sexistisch 1 *Adj.* sexist. **2** *adv.* ‹*behave, think, etc.*› in a sexist manner

Sex·shop *der;* ∼s, ∼s sex shop

Sexta /'zɛksta/ *die;* ∼, **Sexten** (Schulw.) **(a)** (veralt.) first year (*of a Gymnasium*); **(b)** (österr.) sixth year (*of a Gymnasium*)

Sextaner *der;* ∼s, ∼ (Schulw.) **(a)** (veralt.) pupil in the first year (*of a Gymnasium*); **(b)** (österr.) pupil in the sixth year (*of a Gymnasium*)

Sextant /zɛks'tant/ *der;* ∼en, ∼en sextant

Sexte /'zɛkstə/ *die;* ∼, ∼n (Musik) sixth

Sextett /zɛks'tɛt/ *das;* ∼[e]s, ∼e (Musik) sextet

Sexual- /zɛ'ksu̯a:l-/: ∼**erziehung** *die* sex education; ∼**hormon** *das* sex hormone

Sexualität /zɛksu̯ali'tɛ:t/ *die;* ∼: sexuality *no art.*

Sexual-: ∼**kunde** *die; o. Pl.* (Schulw.) sex education *no art.;* ∼**leben** *das; o. Pl.* sex life; ∼**verbrechen** *das* sex crime; ∼**verbrecher** *der* sex offender

sexuell 1 *Adj.* sexual. **2** *adv.* sexually

sexy /'zɛksi/ (ugs.) **1** *indekl. Adj.* sexy. **2** *adv.* sexily

Sezessions·krieg *der; o. Pl.* [American] Civil War

sezieren /ze'tsi:rən/ *tr. V.* dissect ‹*corpse*›

sfr., (schweiz. nur:) **sFr.** *Abk.* **Schweizer Franken**

Shampoo /ʃam'pu:/, **Shampoon** /ʃam'po:n/ *das;* ∼s, ∼s shampoo

shampoonieren /ʃampo'ni:rən/ *tr. V.* shampoo

Sheriff /'ʃɛrɪf/ *der;* ∼s, ∼s sheriff

Sherry /'ʃɛri/ *der;* ∼s, ∼s sherry

Shooting·star /'ʃu:tɪŋsta:/ *der;* ∼s, ∼s whizz-kid (coll.)

Shorts /ʃɔrts/ *Pl.* shorts

Show /ʃoʊ/ *die;* ∼, ∼s show

Show·master /'-ma:stə/ *der;* ∼s, ∼: compère

Siam /zi:am/ (*das*); ∼s (hist.) Siam

Siamese /zi̯a'me:zə/ *der;* ∼n, ∼n, **Siamesin** *die;* ∼, ∼**nen** Siamese

siamesisch *Adj.* Siamese

Siam·katze *die* Siamese cat

Sibirien /zi'bi:ri̯ən/ (*das*); ∼s Siberia

sibirisch *Adj.* Siberian; ∼**e Kälte** Arctic temperatures *pl.*

sich /zɪç/ *Reflexivpron. der 3. Pers. Sg. und Pl. Akk. und Dat.* **(a)** himself / herself / itself / themselves; (*auf man bezogen*) oneself; (*auf das Anredepron.* Sie *bezogen*) yourself/yourselves; (mit reflexiven Verben) ∼ **freuen/wundern/schämen/täuschen** be pleased/surprised/ashamed/mistaken; ∼ **sorgen/verspäten/öffnen** worry/be late/open; *s. auch* **an 1 d**; **kommen** I; **(b)** (*reziprok*) one another; each other

Sichel /'zɪçl̩/ *die;* ∼, ∼n sickle

sicher /'zɪçɐ/ **1** *Adj.* **(a)** (ungefährdet) safe ‹*road, procedure, etc.*›; secure ‹*job, investment, etc.*›; **vor jmdm./etw.** ∼ **sein** be safe from sb./sth.; ∼ **ist** ∼: it's better to be on the safe side; better safe than sorry; **(b)** (zuverlässig) reliable ‹*evidence, source*›; secure ‹*income*›; certain, undeniable ‹*proof*›; (vertrauenswürdig) reliable, sure ‹*judgment, taste, etc.*›; **(c)** (selbstbewusst) [self-]assured, [self-]confident ‹*person, manner*›; **(d)** (gewiss) certain; sure; **der** ∼**e Sieg/Tod** certain victory/ death. **2** *adv.* **(a)** (ungefährdet) safely; **um ganz** ∼ **zu gehen** to be quite sure; **(b)** (zuverlässig) reliably; ∼ **[Auto] fahren** be a safe driver; **(c)** (selbstbewusst) [self-]confidently; ∼ **auftreten** behave in a self-assured *or* self-confident manner. **3** *Adv.* certainly; (plädierend) surely; ∼ **kommt er bald** he is sure to come soon

―――――――
*alte Schreibung (vgl. Hinweise auf S. xvi–xvii)

sicher|gehen *unr. itr. V.; mit sein* play safe; **um sicherzugehen** to be on the safe side

Sicherheit *die;* ∼, ∼**en (a)** *o. Pl.* safety; (der Öffentlichkeit) security; **die** ∼ **der Arbeitsplätze** job security; **in** ∼ **sein** be safe; **jmdn./etw. in** ∼ [**vor etw.** (*Dat.*)] **bringen** save *or* rescue sb./sth. [from sth.]; **sich vor etw.** (*Dat.*) **in** ∼ **bringen** escape from sth.; **(b)** *o. Pl.* (Gewissheit) certainty; **mit an** ∼ (*Akk.*) **grenzender Wahrscheinlichkeit** with almost complete certainty; almost certainly; **(c)** (Wirtsch.: Bürgschaft) security; **(d)** *o. Pl.* (Zuverlässigkeit, Vertrauenswürdigkeit) reliability; soundness; **(e)** *o. Pl.* (Selbstbewusstsein) [self-] confidence; [self-]assurance; ∼ **im Auftreten** [self-]confidence of manner

sicherheits-, Sicherheits-: ∼**abstand** *der* (Verkehrsw.) safe distance between vehicles; ∼**bindung** *die* (Ski) safety binding; ∼**glas** *das* safety glass; ∼**gurt** *der* **(a)** (im Auto, Flugzeug) seat belt; **(b)** (für Bauarbeiter, Segler) safety harness; ∼**halber** *Adv.* to be on the safe side; for safety's sake; ∼**kette** *die* safety *or* door chain; ∼**nadel** *die* safety pin; ∼**rat** *der* (der UN) Security Council; ∼**schloss**, *∗*∼**schloß** *das* safety lock; ∼**vorkehrung** *die* [safety] precaution; safety measure; ∼**vorschrift** *die* safety regulation

sicherlich *Adv.* certainly

sichern *tr. V.* **(a)** make ‹*door etc.*› secure; (garantieren) safeguard ‹*rights, peace*›; (schützen) protect ‹*rights etc.*›; **(b)** (verschaffen; polizeilich ermitteln) secure ‹*ticket, clue, etc.*›; **sich** (*Dat.*) **etw.** ∼: secure sth.

sicher|stellen *tr. V.* **(a)** (beschlagnahmen) impound ‹*goods, vehicle*›; seize ‹*stolen goods*›; confiscate ‹*licence etc.*›; **(b)** (gewährleisten) guarantee ‹*supply, freedom, etc.*›

Sicherung *die;* ∼, ∼**en (a)** *o. Pl.* (das Sichern) safeguarding (**vor** + *Dat.*, **gegen** from, against); (das Schützen) protection (**vor** + *Dat.*, **gegen** from, against); **(b)** (Elektrot.) fuse; **(c)** (techn. Vorrichtung) safety catch

Sicherungs·kasten *der* fuse box

Sicht /zɪçt/ *die;* ∼, ∼**en (a)** *o. Pl.* (∼weite) visibility *no art.;* (Ausblick) view (**auf** + *Akk.*, **in** + *Akk.* of); **gute** *od.* **klare/schlechte** ∼: good/poor visibility; **außer** ∼ **sein** be out of sight; **Land in** ∼! land ahoy!; **(b)** *o. Pl.* (Kaufmannsspr.) **Wechsel auf** ∼: bill payable on demand *or* at sight; **(c) auf lange/kurze** ∼: in the long/short term; **auf lange** *od.* **weite** ∼ **planen** plan on a long-term basis; **(d)** (Betrachtungsweise) point of view; **aus meiner** ∼: as I see it

sichtbar 1 *Adj.* visible; (fig.) apparent ‹*reason*›. **2** *adv.* visibly

sichten *tr. V.* **(a)** (erspähen) sight; **(b)** (durchsehen) sift [through]; (prüfen) examine

sichtlich 1 *Adj.* obvious; evident. **2** *adv.* obviously; evidently; visibly ‹*impressed*›

Sicht-: ∼**verhältnisse** *Pl.* visibility *sing.;* ∼**vermerk** *der* visa; ∼**weite** *die* visibility *no art.;* **außer/in** ∼**weite sein** be out of/in sight

sickern /'zɪkɐn/ *itr. V.; mit sein* seep; (spärlich fließen) trickle; (fig.) ‹*money*› leak away

sie /zi:/ **1** *Personalpron.; 3. Pers. Sg. Nom. Fem.* (bei weiblichen Personen und Tieren) she; (bei Dingen, Tieren) it; (bei Behörden) they *pl.;* **Wer hat es gemacht? — Sie war es/ Sie** Who did it? — It was her/She did; *s. auch* **ihr**[1]; **ihrer a. 2** *Personalpron.; 3. Pers. Pl. Nom.* **(a)** they; **Wer hat es gemacht? — Sie waren es/Sie** Who did it? — It was them/They did; *s. auch* **ihnen**; **ihrer b**; **(b)** (ugs.: man) **hier wollen** ∼ **das neue Rathaus bauen** here's where they are going to build the new town hall. **3** *Akk. des Personalpron.* **sie 1** (bei weiblichen Personen und Tieren) her; (bei Dingen und Tieren) it; (bei Behörden) them *pl.* **4** *Akk. des Personalpron.* **sie 2 a** them

Sie *Personalpron.* you; **jmdn. mit** ∼ **anreden** address sb. as 'Sie'; use the polite form of address to sb.

Sieb /zi:p/ *das;* ∼[e]s, ∼e sieve; (Kaffee∼, Tee∼) strainer; (für Sand, Kies usw.) riddle

sieben[1] **1** *tr. V.* **(a)** (durch∼) sieve ‹*flour etc.*›; riddle ‹*sand, gravel, etc.*›; **(b)** (auswählen) screen ‹*candidates, visitors, etc.*›. **2** *itr. V.* **(a)** use a sieve/strainer/riddle; **(b)** (auswählen) pick and choose

sieben² *Kardinalz.* ▶22❘, ▶530❘, ▶600❘ seven; *s. auch* **acht**

Sieben *die;* ∼, ∼**en** (a) seven; (b) (ugs.: Bus-, Bahnlinie) number seven

Siebener *der;* ∼s, ∼ (ugs.) ⇒ **Sieben**

sieben-, Sieben-: ∼**fach** *Vervielfältigungsz.* seven-fold; *s. auch* **achtfach;** ∼**fache** *das; adj. Dekl.* das ∼**fache** seven times as much; *s. auch* **Achtfache;** ∼**hundert** *Kardinalz.* ▶600❘ seven hundred; ∼**jährig** *Adj.* (a) (7 Jahre alt) seven-year-old *attrib.;* seven years old *pred.;* (b) (7 Jahre dauernd) seven-year *attrib.;* **der Siebenjährige Krieg** the Seven Years War; ∼**köpfig** *Adj.* seven-headed ⟨*monster*⟩; ⟨*family, committee*⟩ of seven; ∼**mal** *Adj.* seven times; *s. auch* **achtmal;** ∼**meilenstiefel** *Pl.* (scherzh.) seven-league boots; ∼**meter** *der* (Hockey) penalty [shot]; (Hallenhandball) penalty [throw]; ∼**sachen** *Pl.* (ugs.) **meine/deine** *usw.* ∼**sachen** my/your *etc.* belongings *or* (coll.) bits and pieces; ∼**schläfer** *der* dormouse

siebent… *Ordinalz.* ▶600❘ ⇒ **siebt…**

sieben·tausend *Kardinalz.* ▶600❘ seven thousand

sieben·teilig *Adj.* seven-piece ⟨*tool-set etc.*⟩; seven-part ⟨*serial*⟩

siebentel /ˈziːbn̩tl̩/ ▶600❘, ⇒ **siebtel**

Siebentel *das;* ∼s, ∼ ▶600❘ ⇒ **Siebtel**

siebentens *Adv.* ⇒ **siebtens**

siebt /ziːpt/ *in* **wir waren zu** ∼: there were seven of us; *s. auch* **acht²**

siebt… /ziːpt…/ *Ordinalz.* ▶119❘, ▶600❘ seventh; *s. auch* **acht…**

siebtel /ˈziːpt̩/ *Bruchz.* ▶600❘ seventh

Siebtel *das* (schweiz. meist *der*) ▶600❘, ∼s, ∼: seventh

siebtens *Adv.* seventhly

sieb·zehn *Kardinalz.* ▶22❘, ▶530❘, ▶600❘ seventeen

siebzig /ˈziːptsɪç/ *Kardinalz.* ▶22❘, ▶600❘ seventy; *s. auch* **achtzig**

Siebziger¹ *der;* ∼s, ∼: seventy-year-old

Siebziger² *die;* ∼, ∼ (ugs.) (a) (Briefmarke) seventy-pfennig/ centimes *etc.* stamp; (b) (Zigarre) seventy-pfennig cigar; (c) *Pl.* (ugs.: 70er-Jahre) seventies

siebzigst… *Ordinalz.* ▶600❘ seventieth

siedeln /ˈziːdl̩n/ *itr. V.* settle

sieden /ˈziːdn̩/ *unr. od. regelm. itr. V.* boil

*siedend·heiß ⇒ **heiß 1 a**

Siede·punkt *der* ▶511❘ (Physik; auch fig.) boiling point

Siedler *der;* ∼s, ∼, **Siedlerin** *die;* ∼, ∼**nen** settler

Siedlung *die;* ∼, ∼**en** (a) (Wohngebiet) [housing] estate; (b) (Niederlassung) settlement

Siedlungs·haus *das* house on an estate; estate house

Sieg /ziːk/ *der;* ∼[e]s, ∼**e** victory, (bes. Sport) win (**über** + *Akk.* over); **den** ∼ **davontragen** *od.* **erringen** (geh.) be victorious; (Sport) be the winner/winners; **ein** ∼ **der Vernunft** (fig.) a victory for common sense

Siegel /ˈziːgl̩/ *das;* ∼s, ∼: seal; (von Behörden) stamp; **unter dem** ∼ **der Verschwiegenheit** (fig.) under the seal of secrecy

siegeln *tr. V.* seal

Siegel·ring *der* signet ring

siegen *itr. V.* win; **über jmdn.** ∼: gain *or* win a victory over sb.; (bes. Sport) win against sb.; beat sb.; **mit 2:0** ∼ (Sport) win 2–0 *or* by two goals to nil

Sieger *der;* ∼s, ∼: winner; (Mannschaft) winners *pl.;* (einer Schlacht) victor; **zweiter** ∼ **sein** (ugs.) be runner-up/runners-up

Sieger·ehrung *die* presentation ceremony; awards ceremony

Siegerin *die;* ∼, ∼**nen** ⇒ **Sieger**

Siege·macht *die* victorious power

sieges·sicher **1** *Adj.* certain *or* confident of victory *pred.;* (erfolgssicher) certain *or* confident of success *pred.;* **2** *adv.* confident of victory; ⟨*say, smile*⟩ confidently

sieg·reich *Adj.* victorious; winning ⟨*team*⟩; successful ⟨*campaign*⟩; **nach einer** ∼**en Schlacht** after winning a battle

sieh /ziː/, **siehe** *Imperativ Sg. v.* **sehen**

siehst /ziːst/ *2. Pers. Sg. Präsens v.* **sehen**

sieht /ziːt/ *3. Pers. Sg. Präsens v.* **sehen**

Siel /ziːl/ *der od. das;* ∼[e]s, ∼**e** (nordd.) dike sluice *or* floodgate

siezen /ˈziːtsn̩/ *tr. V.* call 'Sie' (*the polite form of address*)

Siff *der;* ∼s (ugs.) filth; muck

siffig *Adj.* (ugs.) filthy

Sigel /ˈziːgl̩/ *das;* ∼s, ∼ (Zeichen) logogram; (in der Stenographie) grammalogue; (Kürzel) abbreviation

Signal /zɪˈgnaːl/ *das;* ∼s, ∼**e** signal; **das** ∼ **steht auf „Halt"** the signal is at 'stop'

Signal-: ∼**anlage** *die* (Verkehrsw.) signals *pl.;* ∼**flagge** *die* (Seew.) signal flag

signalisieren *tr. V.* indicate ⟨*danger, change, etc.*⟩; (fig.: übermitteln) signal ⟨*message, warning, order*⟩ (+ *Dat.* to)

Signal-: ∼**lampe** *die* indicator light; ∼**mast** *der* (a) (Seew.) signalling mast; (b) (Eisenb.) signal post *or* mast

Signatur /zɪgnaˈtuːɐ̯/ *die;* ∼, ∼**en** (a) initials *pl.;* (Kürzel) abbreviated signature; (des Künstlers) autograph; (b) (veralt.: Unterschrift) signature; (c) (in einer Bibliothek) shelf-mark; (d) (auf Landkarten) [map] symbol

Signet /zɪnˈjeː/ *das;* ∼s, ∼s (Buchw.) [publisher's] imprint

signieren *tr. V.* sign; autograph ⟨*one's own work*⟩

signifikant /zɪgnifiˈkant/ (geh.) **1** *Adj.* (a) (wesentlich) significant; (b) (typisch) characteristic, typical (**für** of). **2** *adv.* significantly

Silbe /ˈzɪlbə/ *die;* ∼, ∼**n** syllable; **etw. mit keiner** ∼ **erwähnen** not say a word about sth.

Silben-: ∼**rätsel** *das:* puzzle in which syllables must be combined to form words; ∼**trennung** *die* word-division (*by syllables*)

Silber /ˈzɪlbɐ/ *das;* ∼s (a) (Edelmetall, Farbe) silver; (b) (silbernes Gerät) silver[ware]

silber-, Silber-: ∼**besteck** *das* silver cutlery; ∼**blond** *Adj.* silver-blond; ∼**fischchen** *das* silver-fish; ∼**geld** *das; o. Pl.* silver; ∼**geschirr** *das* silver plate; silverware; ∼**grau** *Adj.* silver-grey; ∼**haltig** *Adj.* silverbearing; argentiferous; ∼**hochzeit** *die* silver wedding; ∼**medaille** *die* silver medal; ∼**mine** *die* silver mine; ∼**münze** *die* silver coin

silbern **1** *Adj.* silver; silvery ⟨*moonlight, shade, gleam, etc.*⟩. **2** *adv.* ⟨*ornament, coat, etc.*⟩ with silver; ⟨*shine, shimmer, etc.*⟩ with a silvery lustre

Silber-: ∼**papier** *das* silver paper; ∼**streif** *der,* ∼**streifen** *der in* **ein** ∼**streifen am Horizont** (fig.) a ray of hope on the horizon

Silhouette /zɪˈlu̯ɛtə/ *die;* ∼, ∼**n** (a) silhouette; (b) (Mode) line

Silicium /zɪˈliːtsi̯ʊm/ *das;* ∼s silicon

Silikat /zɪliˈkaːt/ *das;* ∼[e]s, ∼**e** (Chemie) silicate

Silikon /zɪliˈkoːn/ *das;* ∼s, ∼**e** (Chemie) silicone

Silizium ⇒ **Silicium**

Silo /ˈziːlo/ *der od. das;* ∼s, ∼s silo

Silvester /zɪlˈvɛstɐ/ *der od. das;* ∼s, ∼: New Year's Eve; ∼ **feiern** see the New Year in

Silvester·nacht *die* night of New Year's Eve

Simbabwe /zɪmˈbaːbvə/ (*das*); ∼s Zimbabwe

Simmer·ring ⓌⓏ /ˈzɪmɐ-/ *der* (Technik) ring-type oil seal

simpel /ˈzɪmpl̩/ **1** *Adj.* (a) simple ⟨*question, task*⟩; (b) (abwertend: beschränkt) simple-minded ⟨*person*⟩; simple ⟨*mind*⟩; (c) (oft abwertend: schlicht) basic ⟨*toy, dress, etc.*⟩. **2** *adv.* (a) simply; (b) (abwertend: beschränkt) in a simple-minded manner

Simpel *der;* ∼s, ∼ (bes. südd. ugs.) simpleton; fool

Simplex /ˈzɪmplɛks/ *das;* ∼, ∼**e** *od.* **Simplizia** /zɪmˈpliːtsi̯ɐ/ (Sprachw.) simplex

Sims /zɪms/ *der od. das;* ∼**es**, ∼**e** ledge; sill; (Kamin∼) mantelpiece

Simulant /zimuˈlant/ *der;* ∼**en**, ∼**en**, **Simulantin** *die;* ∼, ∼**nen** malingerer

Simulator /zimuˈlaːtɔr/ *der;* ∼s, ∼**en** /-ˈtoːrən/ (Technik) simulator

simulieren 1 *tr. V.* feign, sham ⟨*illness, emotion, etc.*⟩; simulate ⟨*situation, condition, etc.*⟩. **2** *itr. V.* (Krankheit vortäuschen) feign illness; pretend to be ill; **er simuliert nur** he's just putting it on
simultan /zimʊl'taːn/ **1** *Adj.* simultaneous. **2** *adv.* simultaneously
Simultan·dolmetscher *der* simultaneous interpreter
Sinai·halb·insel /'ziː̯naị-/ *die* Sinai Peninsula
sind /zɪnt/ *1. u. 3. Pers. Pl. Präsens v.* **sein**
Sinfonie /zɪnfo'niː/ *die;* ~, ~n symphony
Sinfonie·orchester *das* symphony orchestra
sinfonisch *Adj.* symphonic
Singapur /'zɪŋɡapuːɐ̯/ *(das);* ~s Singapore
singen /'zɪŋən/ **1** *unr. itr. V.* **(a)** sing; **einen** ~**den Tonfall haben** have a lilting cadence; **(b)** (salopp: vor der Polizei aussagen) squeal (sl.). **2** *unr. tr. V.* **(a)** sing ⟨*song, aria, contralto, tenor, etc.*⟩; **(b)** jmdn. **in den Schlaf** ~: sing sb. to sleep
Single[1] /'zɪŋl/ *die;* ~, ~s (Schallplatte) single
Single[2] *der;* ~s, ~s single person; ~s single people *no art.*
Sing·spiel *das* (Musik) Singspiel
singulär (geh.) **1** *Adj.* rare. **2** *adv.* rarely
Singular /'zɪŋɡulaːɐ̯/ *der;* ~s, ~e singular
Sing·vogel *der* songbird
sinken /'zɪŋkn̩/ *unr. itr. V.; mit sein* **(a)** ⟨*ship, sun*⟩ sink, go down; ⟨*plane, balloon*⟩ descend, go down; (geh.) ⟨*leaves, snowflakes*⟩ fall; **(b)** (nieder~) fall; **den Kopf** ~ **lassen** let one's head drop; **auf** *od.* (geh.) **in die Knie** ~: sink or fall to one's knees; (niedriger werden) ⟨*temperature, level*⟩ fall, drop; **das Thermometer/Barometer sinkt** the temperature is falling/the barometer is going back; **(d)** (an Wert verlieren) ⟨*price, value*⟩ fall, go down; **(e)** (nachlassen, abnehmen) fall; go down; ⟨*excitement, interest*⟩ diminish, decline; **jmds. Mut sinkt** sb. loses courage
Sinn /zɪn/ *der;* ~[e]s, ~e **(a)** sense; **den** *od.* **einen sechsten** ~ **[für etw.] haben** have a sixth sense [for sth.]; **seine fünf** ~**e nicht beisammen haben** (ugs.) be not quite right in the head; **(b)** *Pl.* (geh.: Bewusstsein) senses; mind *sing.;* **nicht bei** ~**en sein** be out of one's senses *or* mind; **wie von** ~**en** as if he/she had gone out of his/her mind; **(c)** *o. Pl.* (Gefühl, Verständnis) feeling; **einen** ~ **für Gerechtigkeit/Humor** *usw.* **haben** have a sense of justice/humour *etc.;* **(d)** *o. Pl.* (geh.: Gedanken, Denken) mind; **er hat ganz in meinem** ~ **gehandelt** he acted correctly to my mind *or* my way of thinking; **mir steht der** ~ **[nicht] danach/nach etw.** I [don't] feel like it/sth.; **sich** *(Dat.)* **etw. aus dem** ~ **schlagen** put [all thoughts of] sth. out of one's mind; **etw. im** ~ **haben** have sth. in mind; **jmdm. in den** ~ **kommen** come to sb.'s mind; **(e)** *o. Pl.* (~gehalt, Bedeutung) meaning; **im strengen/wörtlichen** ~: in the strict/literal sense; **(f)** (Ziel u. Zweck) point; **der** ~ **des Lebens** the meaning of life
Sinn·bild *das* symbol
sinnen *unr. itr. V.* (geh.) think; ponder; **auf Rache** ~: be out for revenge
sinn·entstellend 1 *Adj.* which distorts/distorted the meaning *postpos., not pred.* **2** *adv.* ⟨*translate, shorten*⟩ so that the *or* its meaning is distorted
Sinnes-: ~**eindruck** *der* sense impression; sensation; ~**organ** *das* sense-organ; sensory organ; ~**täuschung** *die* trick of the senses; ~**wandel** *der* change of mind *or* heart
Sinn·gedicht *das* epigram
sinn·gemäß 1 *Adj.* **eine** ~**e Übersetzung** a translation which conveys the general sense; **2** *adv.* **etw.** ~ **übersetzen/wiedergeben** translate the general sense of sth./give the gist of sth.
sinnieren *itr. V.* ponder (**über** + *Akk.* over); muse (**über** + *Akk.* [up]on)
sinnig *Adj.* (meist spött. *od.* iron.) clever; sensible (iron.)
sinnlich *Adj.* sensory ⟨*impression, perception, stimulus*⟩; sensual ⟨*love, mouth*⟩; sensuous ⟨*pleasure, passion*⟩

Sinnlichkeit *die;* ~ sensuality
sinn·los 1 *Adj.* **(a)** (unsinnig) senseless; **(b)** (zwecklos) pointless; **(c)** (abwertend: übermäßig) mad; wild. **2** *adv.* **(a)** (unsinnig) senselessly; **(b)** (zwecklos) pointlessly; **(c)** (abwertend: übermäßig) like mad (coll.); ~ **betrunken** blind drunk
Sinnlosigkeit *die* **(a)** senselessness; **(b)** (Zwecklosigkeit) pointlessness
sinn-, Sinn-: ~**spruch** *der* saying; ~**verwandt** *Adj.* (Sprachw.) synonymous ⟨*words*⟩; ~**voll 1** *Adj.* **(a)** (vernünftig) sensible; **(b)** (einen Sinn ergebend) meaningful; **2** *adv.* **(a)** (vernünftig) sensibly; **(b)** (einen Sinn ergebend) meaningfully; ~**widrig** *Adj.* (geh.) nonsensical
Sinologe /zino'loːɡə/ *der;* ~n, ~n sinologist
Sinologie *die;* ~: sinology *no art.*
Sint·flut /'zɪnt-/ *die* Flood; Deluge; **nach mir/uns die** ~: I/we don't care what happens after I've/we've gone
sintflut·artig 1 *Adj.* torrential. **2** *adv.* in torrents
Sinus /'ziːnʊs/ *der;* ~, ~ /...nuːs/ *od.* ~**se** (Math.) sine
Siphon /'ziːfõ/ *der;* ~s, ~s **(a)** siphon; **(b)** (Geruchsverschluss) [anti-siphon] trap
Sippe /'zɪpə/ *die;* ~, ~n **(a)** (Völkerk.) sib; **(b)** (meist scherzh. *od.* abwertend: Verwandtschaft) clan
Sippschaft *die;* ~, ~en **(a)** (meist abwertend: Sippe) clan; **(b)** (abwertend: Gesindel) bunch (coll.); crowd (coll.)
Sirene /zi're:nə/ *die;* ~, ~n siren
Sirenen·geheul *das* wail of a/the siren/of sirens
sirren /'zɪrən/ *itr. V.* buzz
Sirup /'ziːrʊp/ *der;* ~s, ~e syrup; (streichfähig auch) treacle (Brit.); molasses *sing.* (Amer.)
Sisyphus·arbeit /'ziːzyfʊs-/ *die* Sisyphean task; never-ending task
Sitte /'zɪtə/ *die;* ~, ~n **(a)** (Brauch) custom; tradition; **(b)** (moralische Norm) common decency; **(c)** *Pl.* (Benehmen) manners; **das sind ja feine** ~**n!** (iron.) that's a nice way to behave! (iron.)
sitten-, Sitten-: ~**dezernat** *das* vice squad; ~**geschichte** *die* history of life and customs; ~**lehre** *die* ethics *sing.;* moral philosophy; ~**los 1** *Adj.* immoral; **2** *adv.* immorally; ~**polizei** *die* (volkst.) vice squad; ~**strolch** *der* (Pressejargon) [sexual] molester; ~**verfall** *der* moral decline; decline in moral standards; ~**widrig 1** *Adj.* **(a)** (Rechtsw.) illegal ⟨*methods, advertising, etc.*⟩; **(b)** (unmoralisch) immoral ⟨*behaviour*⟩; **2** *adv.* ⇒ **1:** illegally; immorally
Sittich /'zɪtɪç/ *der;* ~s, ~e parakeet
sittlich 1 *Adj.* moral. **2** *adv.* morally
Sittlichkeit *die; o. Pl.* morality; morals *pl.*
Sittlichkeits-: ~**verbrechen** *das* sexual crime; ~**verbrecher** *der* sex offender
sittsam (veralt.) **1** *Adj.* **(a)** well-behaved ⟨*child etc.*⟩; decorous ⟨*behaviour*⟩; **(b)** (keusch) demure. **2** *adv.* **(a)** in a well-behaved way; **(b)** (keusch) demurely
Situation /zitu̯a'tsi̯oːn/ *die;* ~, ~en situation
situiert *Adj.* gut/schlechter *usw.* ~ **sein** be well off/worse off *etc.*
Sitz /zɪts/ *der;* ~es, ~e **(a)** seat; **(b)** (mit Stimmrecht) seat; ~ **und Stimme haben** have a seat and a vote; **(c)** (Regierungs~) seat; (Verwaltungs~) headquarters *sing. or pl.;* **(d)** (sitzende Haltung) sitting position; (beim Reiten) seat; **(e)** (von Kleidungsstücken) fit; **(f) auf einen** ~ (ugs.) in *or* at one go
Sitz-: ~**bad** *das* sitz-bath; hip-bath; ~**ecke** *die* sitting area
sitzen *unr. itr. V.; südd., österr., schweiz. mit sein* **(a)** sit; **bleiben Sie bitte** ~: please don't get up; please remain seated; **er saß den ganzen Tag in der Kneipe** he spent the whole day in the pub (Brit.) *or* (Amer.) bar; **im Sattel** ~: be in the saddle; **jmdm. auf der Pelle** *od.* **dem Pelz** ~ (salopp) keep bothering sb.; keep on at sb. (coll.); **(b)** (sein) be; **die Firma sitzt in Berlin** the firm is based in Berlin; **einen** ~ **haben** (salopp) have had one too many; **(c)** ([gut] passen) fit; **die Krawatte sitzt nicht** the tie isn't straight; **(d)** (ugs.: gut eingeübt sein) **Lektionen so oft wiederholen, bis sie** ~: keep on repeating lessons till they stick (coll.); **(e)** (ugs.: wirksam treffen) hit home; **(f)** (Mitglied sein) be, sit (**in** + *Dat.* on); **(g)** (ugs.: eingesperrt sein) be in prison *or* (sl.)

inside; **(h)** ~ **bleiben** (ugs.) (*nicht versetzt werden*) stay down [a year]; have to repeat a year; (abwertend: als Frau unverheiratet bleiben) be left on the shelf; **auf etw.** (*Dat.*) ~ **bleiben** (etw. nicht loswerden) be left *or* (coll.) stuck with sth.; **jmdn.** ~ **lassen** (ugs.: nicht heiraten) jilt sb.; (ugs.: im Stich lassen) leave sb. in the lurch; **er hat Frau und Kinder** ~ **lassen** *od.* (*seltener:*) ~ **gelassen** he left his wife and children; **etw. nicht auf sich** (*Dat.*) ~ **lassen** not take sth.; not stand for sth.

sitzen-: *~|**bleiben** ⇒ sitzen h;*~|**lassen** ⇒ sitzen h

Sitz-: ~**erhöhung** die booster cushion; booster seat; ~**fleisch** das (ugs. scherzh.) **kein** ~**fleisch haben** not have the staying power; not be able to stick at it; (nicht stillsitzen können) not be able to sit still; ~**gruppe** die group of seats; ~**kissen** das (im Sessel, Sofa) [seat] cushion; (auf dem Fußboden) [floor] cushion; ~**ordnung** die seating plan *or* arrangement; ~**platz** der seat; ~**rohr** das seat tube; saddle tube; ~**streik** der sit-down strike

Sitzung die; ~, ~en meeting; (Parlaments~) sitting; session

Sitzungs-: ~**periode** die session; ~**saal** der conference hall; (eines Gerichts) court-room

Sizilianer /zitsi'lia:nɐ/ der; ~s, ~, **Sizilianerin** die; ~, ~nen Sicilian

Sizilien /zi'tsi:liən/ (das) ; ~s Sicily

Skala /'ska:la/ die; ~, **Skalen** (a) scale; (b) (Reihe) range

Skalp /skalp/ der; ~s, ~e scalp

Skalpell /skal'pɛl/ das; ~s, ~e scalpel

skalpieren tr. V. scalp

Skandal /skan'da:l/ der; ~s, ~e scandal

skandalös Adj. scandalous

skandieren /skan'di:rən/ tr. V. **(a)** chant; **(b)** (Verslehre) scan

Skandinavien /skandi'na:viən/ (das) ; ~s Scandinavia

Skandinavier /skandi'na:viɐ/ der; ~s, ~, **Skandinavierin** die; ~, ~nen Scandinavian

skandinavisch Adj. Scandinavian

Skat /ska:t/ der; ~[e]s, ~e *od.* ~s skat; ~ **dreschen** ~ *od.* **kloppen** (salopp) play skat

Skateboard /'skeɪtbɔːd/ das; ~s, ~s skateboard

skateboarden /'skeɪtbɔːdn̩/ itr. V.; mit sein skateboard

Skateboarder /'skeɪtbɔːdɐ/ der; ~s, ~: skateboarder

skaten /'skeɪtn̩/ itr. V.; mit sein skate

Skater /'skeɪtɐ/ der; ~s, ~: skater

Skelett /ske'lɛt/ das; ~[e]s, ~e skeleton

Skepsis /'skɛpsɪs/ die; ~: scepticism

Skeptiker der; ~s, ~: sceptic

skeptisch **1** Adj. sceptical. **2** adv. sceptically

Sketch /skɛtʃ/ der; ~es, ~e sketch

Ski /ʃiː/ der; ~s, ~er *od.* ~: ski; ~ **laufen** *od.* **fahren** ski

Ski-: ~**bindung** die ski binding; ~**lauf** der, ~**laufen** das skiing no art.; ~**läufer** der skier; ~**lehrer** der ski-instructor; ~**lift** der ski lift; ~**springen** das; ~s, ~: ski jumping no art.; ~**stiefel** der ski boot; ~**stock** der ski stick; ski pole

Skizze /'skɪtsə/ die; ~, ~n (a) (Zeichnung) sketch; (b) (Konzept) outline; (c) (kurze Aufzeichnung) [brief] account

Skizzen·block der sketch pad; sketch-block

skizzieren tr. V. **(a)** (zeichnen) sketch; **(b)** (aufzeichnen) outline; **(c)** (entwerfen) draft

Sklave /'skla:və/ der; ~n, ~n slave

Sklaven-: ~**halter** der slave-owner; ~**händler** der (auch fig. abwertend) slave-trader

Sklaverei die; ~: slavery no art.

Sklavin die; ~, ~nen slave

sklavisch /'skla:vɪʃ/ (abwertend) **1** Adj. slavish. **2** adv. slavishly

Sklerose /skle'ro:zə/ die; ~, ~n (Med.) sclerosis no art.; **multiple** ~: multiple sclerosis

skontieren /skɔn'ti:rən/ tr. V. (Kaufmannsspr.) **eine Rechnung** ~: allow a [cash] discount on a bill

Skonto /'skɔnto/ der od. das; ~s, ~s (Kaufmannsspr.) [cash] discount

Skorbut /skɔr'buːt/ der; ~[e]s ▶329| (Med.) scurvy no art.

Skorpion /skɔr'pio:n/ der; ~s, ~e **(a)** (Tier) scorpion; **(b)** (Astrol.) Scorpio

Skrupel /'skruːpl̩/ der; ~s, ~: scruple

skrupel·los (abwertend) **1** Adj. unscrupulous. **2** adv. unscrupulously

Skrupellosigkeit die; ~ (abwertend) unscrupulousness

Skulptur /skolp'tuːɐ/ die; ~, ~en sculpture

skurril /sko'riːl/ **1** Adj. absurd; droll ⟨person⟩. **2** adv. absurdly

S-Kurve /ɛs-/ die S-bend; double bend

Slalom /'sla:lɔm/ der; ~s, ~s (Ski-, Kanusport) slalom; **im** ~ **fahren** (fig.) zigzag

Slawe /'sla:və/ der; ~n, ~n, **Slawin** die; ~, ~nen Slav

slawisch Adj. Slav[ic]; Slavonic

Slip /slɪp/ der; ~s, ~s briefs pl.

Slogan /'slo:gn̩/ der; ~s, ~s slogan

Slowake /slo'va:kə/ der; ~n, ~n ▶388| Slovak

Slowakei die; ~: Slovakia no art.

Slowakin die; ~, ~nen Slovak

slowakisch Adj. ▶388|, ▶487| Slovak; Slovakian

Slowene /slo've:nə/ der; ~n, ~n ▶388| Slovene; Slovenian

Slowenien (das) ; ~s Slovenia

Slowenin die; ~, ~nen Slovene; Slovenian

slowenisch Adj. ▶388| Slovene; Slovenian

Slum /slam/ der; ~s, ~s slum

Smaragd /sma'rakt/ der; ~[e]s, ~e emerald

Smog /smɔk/ der; ~[s], ~s smog

Smog·alarm der smog warning; **bei** ~: if there is a smog warning

Smoking /'smo:kɪŋ/ der; ~s, ~s dinner jacket or (Amer.) tuxedo and dark trousers

Snob /snɔp/ der; ~s, ~s snob

Snobismus der; ~: snobbery; snobbishness

Snowboard /'snoʊbɔːd/ das; ~s, ~s snowboard

snowboarden /'snoʊbɔːdn̩/ itr. V.; mit sein snowboard

Snowboarder /'snoʊbɔːdɐ/ der; ~s, ~: snowboarder

so /zo/ **1** Adv. **(a)** meist betont (auf diese Weise; in, von dieser Art) like this/that; this/that way; **so ist sie nun mal** that's the way she is; **wenn dem so ist** if that's the case; **so ist es!** that's correct or right!; **recht so!, gut so!** right!; that's fine!; **so oder so gerät der Minister unter Druck** either way the minister will come under pressure; **weiter so!** carry on in the same way!; **so genannt** so-called; **(b)** (in solchem Maße) so; **er ist nicht so dumm, das zu tun** he is not so stupid as to do that; **(c)** (genauso) as; **so gut ich konnte** as best I could; **er ist [nicht] so groß wie du** he is [not] as tall as you [are]; **so viel wie** as much as; **halb/doppelt so viel** half/twice as much; **so weit wie möglich** as far as possible; **so weit sein** (ugs.) be ready; **es ist so weit** the time has come; **so wenig wie möglich** as little as possible; **ich kann es so wenig wie du** I can't do it any more than you can; **so weit** (im großen Ganzen) by and large; on the whole; (bis jetzt) up to now; **(d)** meist betont (ugs.: solch) such; **so ein Kind** such a child; a child like that; **so ein Pech/eine Frechheit!** what bad luck/a cheek!; **so ein Idiot!** what an idiot!; **ist sie nicht Kontoristin oder so was?** isn't she a clerk or something?; **[na od. nein od. also] so was!** (überrascht/empört) well, I never!; **so einer/eine/eins** one like that; one of those; **(e)** betont (eine Zäsur ausdrückend) right; OK (coll.); **(f)** (ugs.: schätzungsweise) about; **(g)** unbetont (bei Zitaten od. Quellenangaben) **die Religion, so Marx, ist** …: religion, according to Marx is …; **(h)** unbetont (ugs.: und/oder Ähnliches) **ich spiele ein bisschen Tischtennis, Billard und so** I play a bit of table tennis, billiards and that sort of thing; **(i)** betont (erstaunt, zweifelnd) **so?** really?; **so, so** (meist iron.) oh, I see; **(j)** betont (ohne Hilfsmittel) **ich brauche keine Leiter, da komme ich auch so dran** (ugs.) I don't need a ladder, I can reach it [without one]; **(k)** *betont* (ohne Zutaten) just as it is; **(l)** *betont* (ugs.: umsonst) for nothing. **2** *Konj.* **(a)** so dass ⇒ **sodass; (b)** (konzessiv) however; ∼ **Leid es mir tut,**... much as I regret it,... **3** *Partikel* **(a)** just; **ich weiß nicht so recht, ob ich gehen soll** I'm not really sure if I should go; **Warum fragst du?** — Ach, nur so Why do you ask? — Oh, no particular reason; **(b)** (in Aufforderungssätzen verstärkend) **so komm doch** come on now

So. *Abk.* **Sonntag** Sun.

s. o. *Abk.* **siehe oben**

SO *Abk.* **Südost[en]** SE

sobald *Konj.* as soon as

Socke /'zɔkə/ *die;* ∼, ∼**n** sock; **sich auf die** ∼**n machen** (ugs.) get going; **von den** ∼**n sein** (ugs.) be flabbergasted

Sockel /'zɔkl/ *der;* ∼**s,** ∼ **(a)** (einer Säule, Statue) plinth; **(b)** (unterer Teil eines Hauses, Schranks) base; **(c)** (Elektrot.) base

Sockel·betrag *der* (Wirtsch.) basic sum

Soda /'zo:da/ *die;* ∼ *od. das;* ∼**s** soda

so·dann *Adv.* **(a)** (danach) then; thereupon; **(b)** (außerdem) and furthermore

so·dass, *so·daß *Konj.* **(a)** (damit) so that; **(b)** (und deshalb) and so

Soda·wasser *das; Pl.* **Sodawässer** soda; soda water

Sod·brennen *das;* ∼**s** heartburn; pyrosis

so·eben *Adv.* just; **die Nachricht kam** ∼**:** the news came just now

Sofa /'zo:fa/ *das;* ∼**s,** ∼**s** sofa; settee

Sofa·kissen *das* [sofa] cushion; scatter cushion

so·fern *Konj.* provided [that]

soff /zɔf/ *1. u. 3. Pers. Sg. Prät. v.* **saufen**

so·fort *Adv.* immediately; at once; **ich bin** ∼ **fertig** I'll be ready/(mit einer Arbeit) finished in a moment

Sofort·bild·kamera *die* (Fot.) instant-picture camera

Sofort·hilfe *die* emergency relief *or* aid

sofortig *Adj.* (unmittelbar) immediate

Sofort·maßnahme *die* immediate measure

Soft-Eis /'zɔft|ais/ *das* soft ice cream

Software /'zɔftvɛːɐ̯/ *die;* ∼, ∼**s** (DV) software

sog /zo:k/ *1. u. 3. Pers. Sg. Prät. v.* **saugen**

Sog *der;* ∼**[e]s,** ∼**e** suction; (bei Schiffen) wake; (bei Fahr-, Flugzeugen) slipstream; (von Wasser, auch fig.) current

sog. *Abk.* **so genannt**

so·gar *Adv.* even; **sie ist krank,** ∼ **schwer krank** she is ill, in fact *or* indeed seriously ill

***so·genannt** ⇒ **so 1 a**

so·gleich *Adv.* immediately; at once

Sohle /'zo:lə/ *die;* ∼, ∼**n (a)** (Schuh∼) sole; **eine kesse** *od.* **heiße** ∼ **aufs Parkett legen** (ugs.) put up a good show on the dance-floor; **auf leisen** ∼**n** softly; noiselessly; **(b)** (Fuß∼) sole [of the foot]; **(c)** (Tal∼) bottom; (eines Flusses) bottom; bed; **(d)** (Einlege∼) insole

sohlen *tr. V.* sole

Sohn /zo:n/ *der;* ∼**es,** **Söhne** /'zø:nə/ **(a)** (männlicher Nachkomme) son; **der** ∼ **Gottes** the Son of God; **der verlorene** ∼**:** the prodigal son; **(b)** *o. Pl.* (fam.: Anrede an einen Jüngeren) son; boy

Soja- /'zo:ja-/**:** ∼**bohne** *die* soy[a] bean; ∼**soße** *die* soy[a] sauce

Sokrates /'zo:kratɛs/ *(der);* **Sokrates'** Socrates

so·lang[e] *Konj.* so *or* as long as; ∼ **du nicht aufgegessen hast** unless *or* until you have eaten everything up

solar /zo'la:ɐ̯/ *Adj.* solar

Solarium /zo'la:riʊm/ *das;* ∼**s,** **Solarien** /...iən/ solarium

Solar-: ∼**technik** *die* solar technology *no art.;* ∼**zelle** *die* (Physik, Elektrot.) solar cell

solch /zɔlç/ *Demonstrativpron.* **(a)** *attr.* such; **ich habe** ∼**en Hunger** I am so hungry; **ich habe** ∼**e Kopfschmerzen** I've got such a headache; **das macht** ∼**en Spaß!** it's so much fun!; **(b)** *selbstständig* ∼**e wie die**

---

people like that; **die Sache als** ∼**e** the thing as such; **es gibt** ∼**e und** ∼**e** (ugs.) it takes all sorts *or* kinds [to make a world]; **(c)** *ungebeugt* (geh.: so [ein]) such; **bei** ∼ **einem herrlichen Wetter** when the weather is so beautiful

Sold /zɔlt/ *der;* ∼**[e]s,** ∼**e** [military] pay

Soldat /zɔl'da:t/ *der;* ∼**en,** ∼**en** ▶ 85◀ soldier; ∼ **auf Zeit** soldier serving for a fixed period

Soldaten·fried·hof *der* military *or* war cemetery

Soldatin *die;* ∼, ∼**nen** [female *or* woman] soldier; **sie ist** ∼**:** she is a soldier

soldatisch 1 *Adj.* military ‹discipline, expression, etc.›; soldierly ‹figure, virtue›. **2** *adv.* in a military *or* soldierly manner

Söldner /'zœldnɐ/ *der;* ∼**s,** ∼**:** mercenary

Sole /'zo:lə/ *die;* ∼, ∼**n** salt water; brine

Sol·ei *das* pickled egg

solid /zo'li:t/ ⇒ **solide**

solidarisch 1 *Adj.* ∼**es Verhalten zeigen** show one's solidarity **2** *adv.* ∼ **handeln/sich** ∼ **verhalten** act in/ show solidarity

solidarisieren *refl. V.* show [one's] solidarity

Solidarität *die;* ∼**:** solidarity

Solidaritäts·streik *der* solidarity strike

solide 1 *Adj.* **(a)** solid ‹rock, wood, house›; sturdy ‹shoes, shed, material, fabric›; solid, sturdy ‹furniture›; [good]quality ‹goods›; **(b)** (gut fundiert) sound ‹work, workmanship, education, knowledge›; solid ‹firm, business›; **(c)** (anständig) respectable ‹person, life, occupation, profession›. **2** *adv.* **(a)** solidly ‹built›; sturdily ‹made›; **(b)** (gut fundiert) soundly ‹educated, constructed›; **(c)** (anständig) ‹live› respectably, steadily

Solidität *die;* ∼ ⇒ **solide 1 a–c:** solidness; sturdiness; soundness; respectability

Solist /zo'lɪst/ *der;* ∼**en,** ∼**en** soloist

soll *1. u. 3. Pers. Sg. Präsens v.* **sollen**

Soll /zɔl/ *das;* ∼**[s],** ∼**[s] (a)** (Kaufmannsspr., Bankw.: Schulden) debit; ∼ **und Haben** debit and credit; **im** ∼**:** in debit; **(b)** (Kaufmannsspr.: linke Buchführungsseite) debit side; **(c)** (Wirtsch.: Arbeits∼) quota; **sein** ∼ **erfüllen** achieve *or* meet one's target; **(d)** (Wirtsch.: Plan∼) quota; target

sollen 1 *unr. Modalverb; 2. Part.* ∼ **(a)** (bei Aufforderung, Anweisung, Auftrag) **solltest du nicht bei ihm anrufen?** were you not supposed to ring him?; **was soll ich als Nächstes tun?** what shall I do next?; **what do you want me to do next?; [sagen Sie ihm,] er soll hereinkommen** tell him to come in; **ich soll dir schöne Grüße von Herrn Meier bestellen** Herr Meier asked me to give you *or* sends his best wishes; **(b)** (bei Wunsch, Absicht, Vorhaben) **du sollst alles haben, was du brauchst** you shall have everything you require; **das sollte ein Witz sein** that was meant to be a joke; **was soll denn das heißen?** what is that supposed to mean?; **(c)** (bei Ratlosigkeit) **was soll ich nur machen?** what am I to do?; **was soll nur aus ihm werden?** what is to become of him?; **(d)** (Notwendigkeit ausdrückend) **man soll so etwas nicht unterschätzen** it's not to be taken *or* it shouldn't be taken so lightly; **(e)** *häufig im Konjunktiv II* (Erwartung, Wünschenswertes ausdrückend) **du solltest dich schämen** you ought to be ashamed of yourself; **das hättest du besser nicht tun** ∼**:** it would have been better if you hadn't done that; **(f)** (jmdm. beschieden sein) **er sollte seine Heimat nicht wieder sehen** he was never to see his homeland again; **es hat nicht sein** ∼ *od.* **nicht** ∼ **sein** it was not to be; **(g)** *im Konjunktiv II* (eine Möglichkeit ausdrückend) **wenn du ihn sehen solltest, sage ihm bitte ...:** if you should see him, please tell him ...; **(h)** *im Präsens* (sich für die Wahrheit nicht verbürgend) **das Restaurant soll sehr teuer sein** the restaurant is supposed *or* said to be very expensive; **(i)** *im Konjunktiv II* (Zweifel ausdrückend) **sollte das sein Ernst sein?** is he really being serious?; **(j)** (können) **mir soll es gleich sein** it's all the same to me; it doesn't matter to me; **man sollte glauben, dass ...:** you would think that ... **2** *tr., itr. V.* **was soll das?** what's the idea?; **was soll ich dort?** what would I do there?

solo /'zo:lo/ *indekl. Adj.; nicht attr.* **(a)** (bes. Musik: als Solist) solo; **(b)** (ugs., oft scherzh.: ohne Begleitung) on one's own *postpos.*

---

sollen

1. Verpflichtung

Im Präsens:

soll, sollst, sollt, sollen	= am/is/are to; (vor allem bei Nichterfüllung) = am/is/are supposed to
Er soll morgen zum Arzt	= He is to go to the doctor tomorrow
Er soll morgen zum Arzt, aber er hat keine Möglichkeit hinzukommen	= He's supposed to go to the doctor tomorrow, but he has no way of getting there

Bei Dingen wird ausgesagt, wie etwas gewünscht wird:

Die beiden Flächen sollen fluchten	= The two surfaces are meant to be od. should be in alignment

Besonders in der 2. Person wirkt es oft als Befehl:

Du sollst sofort damit aufhören!	= You're to stop that at once!
Sie sollen die Pillen jeden Tag einnehmen	= You're to od. You must take the pills every day; (wenn man es nicht tut) You're supposed to take the pills every day
Er soll hereinkommen	= He is to come in; (sagen Sie es ihm) Tell him to come in

In der Vergangenheit:

Er sollte gestern zum Arzt	= He was [supposed] to go to the doctor yesterday
Sie sollte die Hauptrolle spielen	= She was [meant] to play the lead
Du solltest ihn anrufen od. hättest ihn anrufen sollen	= You were meant to phone him od. should have phoned him

Im Konjunktiv:

sollte, solltest, solltet, sollten	= should, ought to
Wir sollten früher aufstehen	= We ought to od. should get up earlier
Du solltest dich schämen!	= You ought to be ashamed!

In der Vergangenheit:

hätte/hättest/hätten ... sollen	= should have
Das hätte er nicht tun/ sagen sollen	= He shouldn't have done/said that
Du hättest dort hingehen sollen	= You should have gone there

2. Zukunft

soll, sollst, sollt, sollen	= am/is/are to;
sollte, solltest, solltet, sollten	= was/were to

Hier wird vor allem das Geplante ausgedrückt:

Ich soll die Abteilung übernehmen	= I am to take over the department
Er sagte mir, ich sollte die Abteilung übernehmen	= He told me I was to take over the department
Hier soll ein Bürogebäude gebaut werden	= An office block is to be built here
Du sollst dein Geld zurückbekommen	= You shall get your money back
Es soll nicht wieder vorkommen	= It won't happen again

Vor allem in Fragen kommt Ratlosigkeit zum Ausdruck:

Was soll man da machen?	= What is one to do?, What shall I/we do?
Ich weiß nicht, was ich machen soll	= I don't know what I should do od. what to do

Die Vergangenheit sollte, solltest, solltet, sollten kann auch von einem Zeitpunkt in der Vergangenheit auf damals noch zukünftige Ereignisse bezogen sein:

Sie sollten ihr Reiseziel nie erreichen	= They were never to reach their destination
Es sollte ganz anders kommen	= Things were to turn out quite differently

3. Allgemein verbreitete Meinung, Bericht

soll/sollte usw.	= is/was supposed to
Er soll sehr reich sein (= Es heißt, dass er sehr reich ist)	= He is supposed od. is said to be very rich
Sie soll geheiratet haben	= They say od. I gather she has got married
Seine Worte sollten als Warnung aufgefasst werden	= His words were meant od. supposed to be taken as a warning
Was soll dieses Bild darstellen?	= What is this picture supposed od. meant to represent?
Was soll das heißen?	= What is that supposed to mean?

Die drei letzten Beispiele beziehen sich auf die Absicht des Sprechenden bzw. des Urhebers.

4. Konditional

sollte usw. in Bedingungssätzen	= should
Sollte er anrufen od. Falls er anrufen sollte, ...	= Should he od. If he should telephone, ...

Solo /'zo:lo/ das; ~s, ~s od. **Soli** /'zo:li/ (bes. Musik) solo

solvent /zɔl'vɛnt/ Adj. (bes. Wirtsch.) solvent

Solvenz /zɔl'vɛnts/ die; ~, ~en (bes. Wirtsch.) solvency

Sombrero /zɔm'bre:ro/ der; ~s, ~s sombrero

so·mit /auch: '--/ Adv. consequently; therefore

Sommer /'zɔmɐ/ der; ~s, ~: ▸ 293 | summer; s. auch Frühling

Sommer-: ~anfang der beginning of summer; ~ferien Pl. summer holidays; ~frische die (veralt.) (a) summer holiday; (b) (Ort) summer [holiday] resort

sommerlich ▸ 293 | 1 Adj. summer; summery ⟨warmth, weather⟩; summer's attrib. ⟨day, evening⟩. 2 adv.

es war oft schon ~ warm it was often as warm as summer

sommer-, Sommer-: ~loch (ugs.) summer recess; ~reifen der standard tyre; ~saison die summer season; ~schluss·verkauf, *~schluß·verkauf der summer sale/sales; ~semester das summer semester; ~sprosse die freckle; ~sprossig Adj. freckled; ~zeit die (a) (Jahreszeit) summertime; (b) (Uhrzeit) summer time

Sonate /zo'na:tə/ die; ~, ~n (Musik) sonata

Sonde /'zɔndə/ die; ~, ~n (a) (Med.) (zur Untersuchung) probe; (zur Ernährung) tube; (b) (Raum~) [space] probe

Sonder·angebot *das* special offer; **etw. im** ~**ange-bot haben** have a special offer on sth.
sonderbar 1 *Adj.* strange; odd. **2** *adv.* strangely; oddly
Sonderbarkeit *die;* ~: strangeness; oddness
Sonder·fall *der* special case; exception
sonder·gleichen *Adv., nachgestellt* **eine Frechheit/Unverschämtheit** ~: the height of cheek/impudence
sonderlich 1 *Adj.* **(a)** particular; [e]special; **(b)** (sonderbar) strange; peculiar; odd. **2** *adv.* **(a)** particularly; especially; **(b)** (sonderbar) strangely
Sonderling *der;* ~**s,** ~**e** strange *or* odd person
Sonder-: ~**marke** *die* special issue [stamp]; ~**müll** *der* hazardous waste
sondern[1] *tr. V.* (geh.) separate (**von** from)
sondern[2] *Konj.* but; **nicht er hat es getan,** ~ **sie** 'he didn't do it, 'she did; **nicht nur ...,** ~ **[auch] ...:** not only ... but also ...
Sonder·nummer *die* special edition *or* issue
sonders ⇨ **samt 2**
Sonder-: ~**schule** *die* special school; ~**urlaub** *der* **(a)** (Milit.) special leave; **(b)** (zusätzlicher Urlaub) special *or* extra holiday; ~**zug** *der* special train
sondieren /zɔnˈdiːrən/ *tr. V.* sound out; **das Terrain** ~: see *or* find out how the land lies
Sonett /zoˈnɛt/ *das;* ~**[e]s,** ~**e** (Dichtk.) sonnet
Sonn·abend /ˈzɔn|aːbn̩t/ *der* ▶ 119 , ▶ 595 (bes. nordd.) Saturday
sonn·abends *Adv.* ▶ 595 on Saturday[s]
Sonne *die;* ~, ~**n** sun; (Licht der ~) sun[light]
sonnen *refl. V.* sun oneself; **sich in etw.** (*Dat.*) ~ (fig.) bask in sth.
sonnen-, Sonnen-: ~**aufgang** *der* sunrise; ~**bad** *das* sunbathing *no pl., no indef. art.;* ~**baden** *itr. V.* sunbathe; ~**blende** *die* **(a)** (Fot.) lens-hood; **(b)** (im Auto) sun visor; ~**blume** *die* sunflower; ~**brand** *der* sunburn *no indef. art.;* ~**bräune** *die* suntan; ~**brille** *die* sunglasses *pl.;* ~**energie** *die* solar energy; ~**finsternis** *die* solar eclipse; eclipse of the sun; ~**fleck** *der* (Astron.) sunspot; ~**gebräunt** *Adj.* suntanned; ~**hut** *der* sunhat; ~**klar** *Adj.* (ugs.) crystal clear; ~**kollektor** *der* (Technik) solar collector; ~**licht** *das* sunlight; ~**öl** *das* suntan oil; sun-oil; ~**schein** *der; o. Pl.* sunshine; **bei** ~**schein** in sunshine; ~**schutz·creme** *die* suntan lotion; ~**schirm** *der* sunshade; ~**stich** *der* (Med.) sunstroke *no indef. art.;* **du hast wohl einen** ~**stich** (fig. salopp) you must be mad; ~**strahl** *der* ray of sun[shine]; ~**system** *das* (Astron.) solar system; ~**uhr** *die* sundial; ~**untergang** *der* sunset; ~**zelle** *die* (Physik, Elektrot.) solar cell
sonnig *Adj.* **(a)** sunny; (fig.) happy ⟨*youth, childhood, time*⟩; cheerful ⟨*sense of humour, ways*⟩; **(b)** (iron.: naiv) naive
Sonn·tag *der* ▶ 119 , ▶ 595 Sunday; *s. auch* **Dienstag, Dienstag-**
sonn·täglich ▶ 595 **1** *Adj.* Sunday *attrib.* **2** *adv.* ~ **gekleidet sein** be dressed in one's Sunday best
sonntags *Adv.* ▶ 595 on Sunday[s]
Sonntags-: ~**arbeit** *die; o. Pl.* Sunday working *no art.;* ~**dienst** *der* Sunday duty; ~**fahrer** *der* (abwertend) Sunday driver; ~**kind** *das:* **er ist ein** ~**kind** (fig.) he was born lucky *or* under a lucky star; ~**predigt** *die* Sunday sermon; ~**staat** *der; o. Pl.* (scherzh.) Sunday best; **im** ~**staat** in one's Sunday best
sonst /zɔnst/ *Adv.* **(a)** **der** ~ **so freundliche Mann ...:** the man, who is/was usually so friendly, ...; **er hat es besser als** ~ **gemacht** he did it better than usual; **alles war wie** ~: everything was [the same] as usual; **haben Sie** ~ **noch Fragen?** have you any other questions?; **hat er** ~ **nichts erzählt?** [apart from that,] he didn't say anything else?; ~ **noch was?** (ugs., auch iron.) anything else?; ~ **nichts, nichts** ~: nothing else; **wer/was/wie/wo [denn]** ~**?** who/what/how/where else?; **(b)** (andernfalls) otherwise; or
sonstig... *Adj.; nicht präd.* other; further; „**Sonstiges**" 'miscellaneous'

sonst-: ~**was** *Indefinitpron.* (ugs.) anything else; **er hat** ~**was unternommen** he has tried all sorts of things; ~**wer** *Indefinitpron.* (ugs.) somebody else; (fragend, verneinend) anybody else; **er meint, er ist** ~**wer** he thinks he's really something (coll.); he thinks he's the bee's knees (coll.); ~**wie** *Adv.* (ugs.) in some other way; (fragend, verneinend) in any other way; ~**wo** *Adv.* (ugs.) somewhere else; (fragend, verneinend) anywhere else
so·oft *Konj.* whenever
Sopran /zoˈpraːn/ *der;* ~**s,** ~**e** (Musik) **(a)** (Stimmlage) soprano [voice]; **(b)** *o. Pl.* (im Chor) sopranos *pl.;* **(c)** (Sängerin) soprano
Sopranist *der;* ~**en,** ~**en** sopranist
Sopranistin *die;* ~, ~**nen** soprano
Sorge /ˈzɔrɡə/ *die;* ~, ~**n** **(a)** *o. Pl.* (Unruhe, Angst) worry; **keine** ~: don't [you] worry; **in** ~ **um jmdn./etw. sein** be worried about sb./sth.; **(b)** (sorgenvoller Gedanke) worry; **ich mache mir** ~**n um dich** I am worried about you; **lassen Sie das meine** ~ **sein** let 'me worry about that; **(c)** *o. Pl.* (Mühe, Fürsorge) care; **die** ~ **um das tägliche Brot** the worry of providing one's daily bread; **ich werde dafür** ~ **tragen, dass ...:** I will see to it *or* make sure that ...
sorgen 1 *refl. V.* worry, be worried (**um** about). **2** *itr. V.* **(a)** **für jmdn./etw.** ~: take care of *or* look after sb./sth.; **für die Zukunft der Kinder ist gesorgt** the children's future is provided for; **(b)** (bewirken) **für etw.** ~: cause sth.
sorgen-, Sorgen-: ~**frei 1** *Adj.* carefree ⟨*person, future, existence, etc.*⟩; **2** *adv.* ~**frei leben** live in a carefree manner; ~**kind** *das* (auch fig.) problem child; ~**voll 1** *Adj.* worried; anxious; **2** *adv.* worriedly; anxiously
Sorge·recht *das; o. Pl.* (Rechtsw.) custody (**für** of)
Sorg·falt /ˈzɔrkfalt/ *die;* ~: care; **große** ~ **auf etw.** (*Akk.*) **verwenden** *od.* **legen** take great *or* a great deal of care over sth.
sorg·fältig 1 *Adj.* careful. **2** *adv.* carefully
Sorgfältigkeit *die;* ~: carefulness
sorg·los 1 *Adj.* **(a)** (ohne Sorgfalt) careless; **(b)** (unbekümmert) carefree. **2** *adv.* ~ **mit etw. umgehen** treat sth. carelessly
Sorglosigkeit *die;* ~ **(a)** (Mangel an Sorgfalt) carelessness; **(b)** (Unbekümmertheit) carefreeness
sorgsam 1 *Adj.* careful. **2** *adv.* carefully
Sorte /ˈzɔrtə/ *die;* ~, ~**n** **(a)** sort; type; kind; (Marke) brand; **bitte ein Pfund von der besten** ~: a pound of the best quality, please; **(b)** *Pl.* (Devisen) foreign currency *sing.*
sortieren *tr. V.* sort [out] ⟨*pictures, letters, washing, etc.*⟩; grade ⟨*goods etc.*⟩; (fig.) arrange ⟨*thoughts*⟩
Sortiment /zɔrtiˈmɛnt/ *das;* ~**[e]s,** ~**e** range (**an** + *Dat.* of)
Sortiments·buch·handel *der* retail book trade
so·sehr *Konj.* however much
Soße /ˈzoːsə/ *die;* ~, ~**n** sauce; (Braten~) gravy; sauce; (Salat~) dressing
sott /zɔt/ *1. u. 3. Pers. Sg. Prät. v.* **sieden**
Souffleur /zuˈfløːɐ̯/ *der;* ~**s,** ~**e,** **Souffleuse** /zuˈfløːzə/ *die;* ~, ~**n** ▶ 85 (Theater) prompter
soufflieren /zuˈfliːrən/ *tr. V.* prompt
Sound·karte /ˈsaʊnd.../ *die* (DV) sound card
Souterrain /ˈzuːtɛrɛ̃/ *das;* ~**s,** ~**s** basement
Souvenir /zuvəˈniːɐ̯/ *das;* ~**s,** ~**s** souvenir
souverän /zuvəˈrɛːn/ **1** *Adj.* **(a)** sovereign; **(b)** (überlegen) superior. **2** *adv.* **er siegte ganz** ~: he won in a very impressive way
Souverän *der;* ~**s,** ~**e** sovereign
Souveränität *die;* ~ sovereignty
so·viel *Konj.* **(a)** (nach dem, was) as *or* so far as; ~ **mir bekannt ist** so far as I know; **(b)** (in wie großem Maße auch immer) however much; *s. auch* **so 1 c**
so·weit *Konj.* **(a)** (nach dem, was) as *or* so far as; ~ **mir bekannt ist** so far as I know; **(b)** (in dem Maße, wie) [in] so far as.; *s. auch* **so 1 c**

so·we̲nig Konj. however little; s. auch **so 1 c**

so·wie̲ Konj. (a) (und auch) as well as; (b) (sobald) as soon as

so·wie̲·so̲ Adv. anyway; das ∼! (ugs.) that goes without saying!; of course!

Sowjet /zɔ'vjɛt/ der; ∼s, ∼s (a) (Gremium) soviet; der Oberste ∼: the Supreme Soviet; (b) die ∼s the Soviets

Sowjet·bürger der Soviet citizen

sowjetisch Adj. Soviet

Sowjet·union die Soviet Union

so·wo̲hl ∼ ... als od. wie [auch] ...: both ... and ...; ... as well as ...

sozial /zo'tsi̲a:l/ **1** Adj. social; ∼e Marktwirtschaft social market economy. **2** adv. socially; ∼ handeln act in a socially conscious or public-spirited way

sozial-, Sozial-: ∼abgaben Pl. social welfare contributions; ∼amt das social welfare office; ∼arbeit die; o. Pl. social work; ∼arbeiter der, ∼arbeiterin die ▶ 85 | social worker; ∼demokrat der Social Democrat; ∼demokratie die social democracy no art.; ∼demokratisch Adj. social democratic; Sozialdemokratische Partei [Deutschlands] [German] Social Democratic Party; ∼hilfe die social welfare

Sozialisation die; ∼ (Soziol., Psych.) socialization

sozialisieren tr. V. (a) (Wirtsch.: vergesellschaften) nationalize; (b) (Soziol., Psych.: zum Gemeinschaftsleben befähigen) socialize

Sozialismus der; ∼: socialism no art.

Sozialist der; ∼en, ∼en, **Sozialistin** die; ∼, ∼nen socialist

sozialistisch 1 Adj. socialist. **2** adv. ∼ regierte Länder countries with socialist governments

sozial-, Sozial-: ∼kunde die; o. Pl. social studies sing., no art.; ∼leistungen Pl. social welfare benefits; ∼liberal Adj. liberal socialist ⟨politician etc.⟩; (aus SPD und FDP) liberal-social democrat ⟨coalition etc.⟩; ∼politik die social policy; ∼prestige das social status; ∼produkt das (Wirtsch.) national product; ∼staat der welfare state; ∼versicherung die social security; ∼wohnung die ≈ council flat (Brit.); municipal housing unit (Amer.)

Soziologe /zotsio'lo:gə/ der; ∼n, ∼n sociologist

Soziologie die; ∼: sociology

Soziologin die; ∼, ∼nen sociologist

soziologisch 1 Adj. sociological. **2** adv. sociologically

Sozius /'zo:tsius/ der; ∼, ∼se (a) Pl. auch: Sozii /'zo:tsii/ (Wirtsch.: Teilhaber) partner; (b) (beim Motorrad) pillion

so·zu·sagen Adv. so to speak; as it were

Spachtel /'ʃpaxtl/ der; ∼s, ∼ od. die; ∼, ∼n (a) (für Kitt) putty-knife; (zum Abkratzen von Farbe) paint-scraper; (zum Malen) palette-knife; spatula; (b) (∼masse) filler

Spachtel·masse die filler

spachteln tr. V. (a) stop, fill ⟨hole, crack, etc.⟩; smooth over ⟨wall, panel, surface, etc.⟩; (b) (ugs.: essen) put away (coll.) ⟨food, meal⟩

Spagat¹ /ʃpa'ga:t/ der od. das; ∼[e]s, ∼e splits pl.; [einen] ∼ machen do the splits

Spagat² der; ∼[e]s, ∼e (südd., österr.) string

Spaghetti /ʃpa'gɛti/ Pl. spaghetti sing.

spähen /'ʃpɛ:ən/ itr. V. peer; (durch eine Ritze usw.) peep

Späher der; ∼s, ∼ (Milit.) scout; (Posten) lookout; (Spitzel) informer

Spalier /ʃpa'li:ɐ̯/ das; ∼s, ∼e (a) trellis; (b) (aus Menschen) double line; (Ehren∼) guard of honour; ∼ stehen line the route; ⟨soldiers⟩ form a guard of honour

Spalt /ʃpalt/ der; ∼[e]s, ∼e opening; (im Fels) fissure; crevice; (zwischen Vorhängen) chink; gap; (langer Riß) crack; die Tür einen ∼ [weit] öffnen open the door a crack or slightly

Spalte die; ∼, ∼n (a) crack; (Fels∼) crevice; cleft; (b) (Druckw.: Druck∼) column; (c) (österr.: Scheibe) slice

spalten 1 unr. (auch regelm.) tr. V. (auch Physik, fig.) split; Holz ∼: chop wood. **2** unr. (auch regelm.) refl. V. (a) (auch Physik, fig.) split; (b) (Chemie) split; break down

Span /ʃpa:n/ der; ∼[e]s, **Späne** /'ʃpɛ:nə/ (Hobel∼) shaving; (Feil∼) filing usu. in pl.; (beim Bohren) boring usu. in pl.; (beim Drehen) turning usu. in pl.; feine [Metall]späne swarf sing.; wo gehobelt wird, [da] fallen Späne (Spr.) you cannot make an omelette without breaking eggs (prov.)

Span·ferkel das sucking pig

Spange /'ʃpaŋə/ die; ∼, ∼n clasp; (Haar∼) hairslide (Brit.); barrette (Amer.); (Arm∼) bracelet; bangle

Spaniel /'ʃpa:niəl/ der; ∼s, ∼s spaniel

Spanien /'ʃpa:niən/ (das); ∼s Spain

Spanier /'ʃpa:niɐ̯/ der; ∼s, ∼: ▶ 388 | Spaniard; die ∼: the Spanish or Spaniards

spanisch Adj. ▶ 388 |, ▶ 487 | Spanish; das kommt mir ∼ vor (ugs.) that strikes me as odd; s. auch **deutsch; Deutsch**

Span·korb der chip basket; chip

spann /ʃpan/ 1. u. 3. P. Sing. Prät. v. **spinnen**

Spann der; ∼[e]s, ∼e instep

Spann·beton der (Bauw.) pre-stressed concrete

Spanne die; ∼, ∼n (a) (Zeit∼) span of time; (b) (veralt.: Längenmaß) span

spannen 1 tr. V. (a) tighten, tauten ⟨violin string, violin bow, etc.⟩; draw ⟨bow⟩; tension ⟨spring, tennis net, drumhead, saw-blade⟩; stretch ⟨fabric, shoe, etc.⟩; draw or pull ⟨line⟩ tight or taut; tense, flex ⟨muscle⟩; cock ⟨gun, camera shutter⟩; (b) (befestigen) put up ⟨washing-line⟩; stretch ⟨net, wire, tarpaulin, etc.⟩ (über + Akk. over); einen Bogen Papier in die Schreibmaschine ∼: insert or put a sheet of paper in the typewriter; etw. in einen Schraubstock ∼: clamp sth. in a vice; (c) (schirren) hitch up, harness (vor, an + Akk. to); (d) (bes. südd., österr.: merken) notice. **2** refl. V. (a) become or go taut; ⟨muscles⟩ tense; (b) (geh.: sich wölben) sich über etw. (Akk.) ∼ ⟨bridge, rainbow⟩ span sth. **3** itr. V. (zu eng sein) ⟨clothing⟩ be [too] tight; ⟨skin⟩ be taut

spannend 1 Adj. exciting; (stärker) thrilling; machs nicht so ∼! (ugs.) don't keep me/us in suspense. **2** adv. excitingly; (stärker) thrillingly

Spanner der; ∼s, ∼ (a) (Schuh∼) shoe-tree; (Stiefel∼) boot-tree; (Hosen∼) [trouser-] hanger; (b) (Zool.) geometer; (c) (ugs.: Voyeur) peeping Tom

Spann·kraft die; o. Pl. vigour

Spannung die; ∼, ∼en (a) o. Pl. excitement; (Neugier) suspense; tension; jmdn. mit ∼ erwarten await sb. eagerly; (b) o. Pl. (eines Romans, Films usw.) suspense; (c) (Zwistigkeit, Nervosität) tension; (d) (das Straffsein) tension; tautness; (e) (elektrische ∼) tension; (Voltzahl) voltage; unter ∼ stehen be live; (f) (Mechanik) stress

Spannungs·gebiet das (Politik) area of tension

spannungs·geladen Adj. (a) (gespannt) ⟨atmosphere etc.⟩ charged with tension; (b) (spannend) ⟨novel, film, etc.⟩ full of suspense

Spann·weite die (Zool.: Flügel∼) [wing]span; wingspread; (eines Flugzeugs) [wing]span

Span·platte die chipboard

Spant /ʃpant/ das od. der; ∼[e]s, ∼en (eines Schiffs) rib; (eines Flugzeugs) frame; former

Spar-: ∼brief der (Bankw.) savings certificate; ∼buch das (Bankw.) savings book; passbook; ∼büchse die money box; ∼einlage die (Bankw.) savings deposit

sparen /'ʃpa:rən/ **1** tr. V. save; deine Ratschläge kannst du dir ∼: you can keep your advice. **2** itr. V. (a) für od. auf etw. (Akk.) ∼: save up for sth.; (b) (sparsam wirtschaften) economize (mit on); er sparte nicht mit Lob (fig.) he was unstinting or generous in his praise; an etw. (Dat.) ∼: be sparing with sth.; (Billigeres nehmen) economize on sth.

Sparer der; ∼s, ∼, **Sparerin** die; ∼, ∼nen saver

Spar·flamme die; o. Pl. low flame or heat; auf ∼: on a low flame or heat

Spargel /'ʃpargl̩/ der; ∼s, ∼, schweiz. auch die; ∼, ∼n asparagus no pl., no indef. art.; ein ∼: an asparagus stalk

Spar-: ∼groschen der (ugs.) nest egg; savings pl.; ∼guthaben das credit balance (in a savings account);

~**kasse** *die* savings bank; ~**kassen·buch** *das* savings book; passbook; ~**konto** *das* savings *or* deposit account

spärlich /ˈʃpɛːɐlɪç/ **1** *Adj.* sparse ⟨*vegetation, beard, growth*⟩; thin ⟨*hair, applause*⟩; scanty ⟨*leftovers, knowledge, news, evidence*⟩; scanty, skimpy ⟨*clothing*⟩; slack ⟨*demand*⟩; scattered ⟨*remains, remnants*⟩; poor ⟨*lighting, harvest, result, source*⟩; meagre ⟨*income, salary*⟩. **2** *adv.* sparsely, thinly ⟨*populated, covered*⟩; poorly ⟨*lit, attended*⟩; scantily, skimpily ⟨*dressed*⟩

Spar-: ~**maßnahme** *die* economy measure; ~**paket** *das* austerity package

Sparren /ˈʃparən/ *der;* ~**s**, ~ (Dach~) rafter

sparsam 1 *Adj.* **(a)** thrifty ⟨*person*⟩; (wirtschaftlich) economical; **mit etw.** ~ **sein** be economical with sth.; **er ist mit Worten/Lob immer sehr** ~ (fig.) he is a man of few words/he is very sparing in his praise; **(b)** (fig.: gering, wenig, klein) sparse ⟨*detail, decoration, interior, etc.*⟩; economical ⟨*movement, manner of expression, etc.*⟩. **2** *adv.* **(a)** ~ **mit dem Papier umgehen** use paper sparingly; economize on paper; ~ **leben** live frugally; ~ **mit seinen Kräften umgehen** conserve one's energy; **(b)** (wirtschaftlich) economically; **(c)** (fig.: in geringem Maße) ⟨*use*⟩ sparingly; sparsely ⟨*decorated, furnished*⟩

Sparsamkeit *die;* ~ **(a)** thrift[iness]; **aus** ~**:** for the sake of economizing; **(b)** (Wirtschaftlichkeit) economicalness; **(c)** (fig.: geringes Maß) economy

Spar·schwein *das* piggy bank

Spartakiade /ʃpartaˈkiaːdə/ *die;* ~, ~**n** Spartakiad

spartanisch 1 *Adj.* (auch fig.). Spartan. **2** *adv.* ~ **leben** lead a Spartan life

Sparte /ˈʃpartə/ *die;* ~, ~**n (a)** (Teilbereich) area; branch; (eines Geschäfts) line [of business]; (des Wissens) branch; field; speciality; **(b)** (Rubrik) section

Sparten-: ~**kanal** *der* special-interest channel; ~**sender** *der* special-interest station

Spaß /ʃpaːs/ *der;* ~**es**, **Späße** /ˈʃpɛːsə/ **(a)** *o. Pl.* (Vergnügen) fun; **wir hatten alle viel** ~**:** we all had a lot of fun *or* a really good time; we all really enjoyed ourselves; ~ **an etw.** (*Dat.*) **haben** enjoy sth.; **[jmdm.]** ~**/keinen** ~ **machen** be fun/no fun [for sb.]; **ein teurer** ~ (ugs.) an expensive business; **was kostet der** ~**?** (ugs.) how much will that little lot cost? (coll.); **viel** ~**!** have a good time!; **(b)** (Scherz) joke; (Streich) prank; antic; **er macht nur** ~**:** he's only joking *or* (sl.) kidding; ~ **beiseite!** joking aside *or* apart; ~ **muss sein!** there's no harm in a joke; **da hört [für mich] der** ~ **auf** that's getting beyond a joke; ~**/keinen** ~ **verstehen** be able to/not be able to take a joke; have a/have no sense of humour; **in Gelddingen versteht er keinen** ~**:** he won't stand for any nonsense where money is concerned; **er ist immer zu Späßen aufgelegt** he's always ready for a laugh; **im** *od.* **zum** *od.* **aus** ~**:** as a joke; for fun; **sich** (*Dat.*) **einen** ~ **mit jmdm. erlauben** play a joke on sb.

spaßen /ˈʃpaːsn̩/ *itr. V.* joke; kid (coll.); **er lässt nicht mit sich** ~**:** he won't stand for any nonsense; **mit ihm/damit ist nicht zu** ~**:** he/it is not to be trifled with

spaßes·halber *Adv.* for the fun of it; for fun

spaßig *Adj.* funny; comical; amusing

Spaß-: ~**macher** *der* joker; ~**vogel** *der* joker

spastisch (Med.) **1** *Adj.* spastic. **2** *adv.* ~ **gelähmt sein** suffer from spastic paralysis

spät /ʃpɛːt/ **1** *Adj.* ▶530 late; belated ⟨*fame, repentance*⟩; **am** ~**en Abend** in the late evening; **bis in die** ~**e Nacht** until late into the night; **wie** ~ **ist es?** what time is it? **2** *adv.* late; ~ **am Abend** late in the evening; **du kommst aber** ~**!** you're very late; **wenn ich jetzt nicht losfahre, komme ich zu** ~**:** if I don't leave now I'll be late; **wir sind [schon ziemlich]** ~ **dran** (ugs.) we're late [enough already]

Spat /ʃpaːt/ *der;* ~**[e]s**, ~**e** *od.* **Späte** /ˈʃpɛːtə/ (Mineral.) spar

Spät·dienst *der* late duty; (im Betrieb) late shift

Spatel /ˈʃpaːtl̩/ *der;* ~**s**, ~ **(a)** spatula; **(b)** ⇨ **Spachtel a**

---

*alte Schreibung (vgl. Hinweise auf S. xvi–xvii)

Spaten /ˈʃpaːtn̩/ *der;* ~**s**, ~**:** spade

später 1 *Adj.; nicht präd.* **(a)** (nachfolgend, kommend) later ⟨*years, generations, etc.*⟩; **(b)** (zukünftig) future ⟨*owner, wife, etc.*⟩. **2** *Adv.* later; **was willst du denn** ~ **[einmal] werden?** what do you want to do when you grow up?; **[also dann] bis** ~**!** see you later!

spätestens *Adv.* at the latest; ~ **[am] Freitag** [by] Friday at the latest

Spät-: ~**folge** *die* long-term consequence; (Med.) late sequela; ~**lese** *die* late vintage; ~**schaden** *der* long-term damage *no pl.*, *no indef. art.*; ~**schicht** *die* late shift

Spatz /ʃpats/ *der;* ~**en**, ~**en (a)** sparrow; **er isst wie ein** ~**:** he eats like a bird; **die** ~**en pfeifen es von den** *od.* **allen Dächern** it's common knowledge; **(b)** (fam.: Liebling) pet; **(c)** (fam.: kleines Kind) mite; tot (coll.)

Spätzle /ˈʃpɛtslə/ *Pl.* spaetzle; spätzle; *kind of noodles*

spazieren /ʃpaˈtsiːrən/ *itr. V.; mit sein* **(a)** stroll; ~ **fahren** (im Auto) go for a drive *or* ride *or* spin; (im Bus usw., mit dem Fahrrad usw.) go for a ride; **jmdn.** ~ **fahren** (im Auto) take sb. for a drive *or* ride *or* spin; **ein Kind [im Kinderwagen]** ~ **fahren** take a baby for a walk [in a pram]; ~ **gehen** go for a walk *or* stroll; **ein Stück** ~ **gehen** go for a little walk *or* stroll; **(b)** (veralt.: spazieren gehen) go for a walk *or* a stroll

spazieren-: ***~**\|fahren** ⇨ **spazieren;** ***~**\|gehen** ⇨ **spazieren**

Spazier-: ~**fahrt** *die* (mit dem Auto) drive; ride; spin; (mit dem Bus usw., mit dem Fahrrad *od.* Motorrad) ride; ~**gang** *der* walk; stroll; ~**gänger** *der;* ~**s**, ~, ~**gängerin** *die;* ~, ~**nen** person out for a walk *or* stroll; ~**weg** *der* footpath

SPD /ɛspeːˈdeː/ *die;* ~ *Abk.* **Sozialdemokratische Partei Deutschlands** SPD

Specht /ʃpɛçt/ *der;* ~**[e]s**, ~**e** woodpecker

Speck /ʃpɛk/ *der;* ~**[e]s**, ~**e (a)** bacon fat; (Schinken~) bacon; **(b)** (von Walen, Robben) blubber; **(c)** (ugs. scherzh.: Fettpolster) fat; flab (sl.); **er hat ganz schön** ~ **auf den Rippen** he's well padded

speckig *Adj.* greasy

Speck-: ~**scheibe** *die* rasher *or* slice of bacon; ~**schwarte** *die* bacon rind; ~**seite** *die* side of bacon; ~**stein** *der* (Mineral.) lard stone; soapstone; steatite

Spediteur /ʃpediˈtøːɐ/ *der;* ~**s**, ~**e** carrier; haulier; haulage contractor; (per Schiff) carrier; (Möbel~) furniture-remover

Spedition /ʃpediˈtsioːn/ *die;* ~, ~**en (a)** (Beförderung) carriage; transport; **(b)** ⇨ **Speditionsfirma**

Speditions·firma *die* forwarding agency; (per Schiff) shipping agency; (Transportunternehmen) haulage firm; firm of hauliers; (per Schiff) firm of carriers; (Möbelspedition) removal firm

Speer /ʃpeːɐ/ *der;* ~**[e]s**, ~**e (a)** spear; **(b)** (Sportgerät) javelin

Speer-: ~**spitze** *die* (auch fig.) spearhead; ~**werfen** *das;* ~**s** ⇨ ~**wurf a;** ~**werfer** *der* (Sport) javelin-thrower; ~**wurf** *der* **(a)** *o. Pl.* (Disziplin) javelin-throwing; **(b)** (Wurf) javelin-throw

Speiche /ˈʃpaiçə/ *die;* ~, ~**n (a)** spoke; **(b)** (Anat.) radius

Speichel /ˈʃpaiçl̩/ *der;* ~**s** saliva; spittle

Speichen·reflektor *der* wheel reflector

Speicher /ˈʃpaiçɐ/ *der;* ~**s**, ~ **(a)** storehouse; (Lagerhaus) warehouse; (~becken) reservoir; (fig.) store; **(b)** (südd.: Dachboden) loft; attic; **auf dem** ~**:** in the loft *or* attic; **(c)** (Elektronik) memory; store

speichern *tr. V.* store

Speicherung *die;* ~, ~**en** storing; storage

speien /ˈʃpaiən/ *unr. tr., itr. V.* (geh.) **(a)** spit; spew [forth] ⟨*lava, fire, etc.*⟩; belch ⟨*smoke*⟩; spout ⟨*water*⟩; **(b)** (erbrechen) vomit

Speise /ˈʃpaizə/ *die;* ~, ~**n (a)** (Gericht) dish; **(b)** *o. Pl.* (geh.: Nahrung) food

Speise-: ~**gaststätte** *die* restaurant; ~**kammer** *die* larder; pantry; ~**karte** *die* menu; ~**lokal** *das* restaurant

speisen 1 *itr. V.* (geh.) eat; (dinieren) dine; **zu Mittag/ Abend** ~: lunch *or* have lunch/dine *or* have dinner. **2** *tr. V.* **(a)** (geh.: verzehren) eat; (dinieren) dine on; **(b)** (geh.) feed; **(c)** (Technik) **etw. mit Strom/Wasser** ~: supply sth. with electricity/water

Speise-: ~**öl** *das* edible oil; ~**reste** *Pl.* leftovers; (zwischen den Zähnen) food particles; ~**röhre** *die* ▶ 326| (Anat.) gullet; oesophagus (Anat.); ~**saal** *der* dining hall; (im Hotel, in einer Villa usw.) dining room; ~**schrank** *der* food-cupboard; ~**wagen** *der* dining car; restaurant car (Brit.); ~**zettel** *der* menu

spei·übel *Adj.; nicht attr.* **mir ist** ~: I think I'm going to be violently sick

Spektakel /ʃpɛkˈtaːkl̩/ *der;* ~**s,** ~ (ugs.) **(a)** (Lärm) row (coll.); rumpus (coll.); racket; **(b)** (laute Auseinandersetzung) fuss; **einen** ~ **machen** kick up *or* make a fuss

spektakulär /ʃpɛktakuˈlɛːɐ̯/ **1** *Adj.* spectacular. **2** *adv.* spectacularly

Spektral-: ~**analyse** *die* (Technik) spectral analysis; ~**farbe** *die* colour of the spectrum

Spektrum /ˈʃpɛktrʊm/ *das;* ~**s, Spektren** (auch fig.) spectrum

Spekulant /ʃpekuˈlant/ *der;* ~**en,** ~**en** speculator

Spekulation /ʃpekulaˈtsi̯oːn/ *die;* ~, ~**en (a)** (Mutmaßung, Erwartung; auch Philos.) speculation; **(b)** (Wirtsch.) speculation (**mit** in)

Spekulatius /ʃpekuˈlaːtsi̯ʊs/ *der;* ~, ~: spiced biscuit *in the shape of a human or other figure, eaten at Christmas*

spekulativ /ʃpekulaˈtiːf/ **1** *Adj.* speculative. **2** *adv.* speculatively

spekulieren /ʃpekuˈliːrən/ *itr. V.* **(a)** (ugs.) **darauf** ~, **etw. tun zu können** count on being able to do sth.; **er spekuliert auf den Laden** he's counting on getting the shop; **(b)** (mutmaßen) speculate; **(c)** (Wirtsch.) speculate (**mit** in)

Spelunke /ʃpeˈlʊŋkə/ *die;* ~, ~**n** (ugs. abwertend) dive (coll.)

Spelze /ˈʃpɛltsə/ *die;* ~, ~**n** (des Getreidekorns) husk

spendabel /ʃpɛnˈdaːbl̩/ *Adj.* generous; open-handed

Spende /ˈʃpɛndə/ *die;* ~, ~**n** donation; contribution; **eine kleine** ~ **bitte!** would you like to make a small donation?

spenden *tr., itr. V.* **(a)** donate; give; contribute; **[etw.] fürs Rote Kreuz** ~: contribute [sth.] to *or* for the Red Cross; **Blut/eine Niere** ~: give blood/donate a kidney; **(b)** (fig. geh.) give ‹*light, applause, comfort*›; afford, give ‹*shade*›; give off ‹*heat*›; provide ‹*water*›; administer ‹*communion, baptism*›; give, bestow ‹*blessing*›; confer ‹*holy orders*›

Spenden-: ~**aktion** *die* campaign for donations; ~**aufruf** *der* appeal for donations

Spender *der;* ~**s,** ~, **Spenderin** *die;* ~, ~**nen** donor; donator; contributor

Spender-: ~**herz** *das* donor heart; ~**niere** *die* donor kidney; ~**organ** *das* donor organ

spendieren *tr. V.* (ugs.) get, buy ‹*drink, meal, etc.*›; stand ‹*round*›

Spendier·hosen *Pl.* **in die/seine** ~ **anhaben** be in a generous mood; be feeling generous

Spengler /ˈʃpɛŋlɐ/ *der;* ~**s,** ~ (südd., österr., schweiz.) ⇨ **Klempner**

Spenzer /ˈʃpɛntsɐ/ *der;* ~**s,** ~ **(a)** (Jacke) spencer; **(b)** (Unterhemd) tight-fitting short-sleeved vest

Sperber /ˈʃpɛrbɐ/ *der;* ~**s,** ~: sparrow-hawk

Sperenzchen /ʃpeˈrɛntsçən/ *Pl.* (ugs.) ~ **machen** give trouble; **mach keine** ~! don't be difficult!

Sperling /ˈʃpɛrlɪŋ/ *der;* ~**s,** ~**e** sparrow

Sperma /ˈʃpɛrma/ *das;* ~**s, Spermen** *od.* **Spermata** sperm; semen

sperr·angel·weit *Adv.* (ugs.) ~ **offen** *od.* **geöffnet** wide open

Sperr·bezirk *der* restricted *or* prohibited area

Sperre /ˈʃpɛrə/ *die;* ~, ~**n (a)** (Barriere) barrier; (Straßen~) roadblock; **(b)** (Milit.) obstacle; **(c)** (Eisenb.) barrier; **(d)** (fig.: Verbot, auch Sport) ban; (Handels~) embargo; (Import~, Export~)

blockade; (Nachrichten~) [news] blackout; **(e)** (Psych.: Blockierung, Hemmung) block; **(f)** (Technik) locking device

sperren 1 *tr. V.* **(a)** close ‹*road, tunnel, bridge, entrance, border, etc.*›; close off ‹*area*›; **etw. für jmdn./etw.** ~: close sth. to sb./ sth.; **(b)** (blockieren) block ‹*access, entrance, etc.*›; **(c)** (Technik) lock ‹*mechanism etc.*›; **(d)** cut off, disconnect ‹*water, gas, electricity, etc.*›; **jmdm. den Strom/das Telefon** ~: cut off *or* disconnect sb.'s electricity/telephone; **(e)** (Bankw.) stop ‹*cheque, overdraft facility*›; freeze ‹*bank account*›; **(f)** (ein~) **ein Tier/jmdn. in etw.** (*Akk.*) ~: shut *or* lock an animal/sb. in sth.; **jmdn. ins Gefängnis** ~: put sb. in prison; lock sb. up [in prison]; **(g)** (Sport: behindern) obstruct; **(h)** (Sport: von der Teilnahme ausschließen) ban; **(i)** (Druckw.: spationieren) print ‹*word, text*› with the letters spaced. **2** *refl. V.* **sich [gegen etw.]** ~: balk *or* jib [at sth.]. **3** *itr. V.* (Sport) obstruct

Sperr·holz *das* plywood

sperrig *Adj.* unwieldy

Sperr-: ~**konto** *das* (Bankw.) blocked account; ~**müll** *der* bulky refuse (*for which there is a separate collection service*); ~**sitz** *der* (im Kino) seat in the back stalls; (im Zirkus) front seat; (im Theater) seat in the front stalls; ~**stunde** *die* closing time

Sperrung *die;* ~, ~**en** ⇨ **sperren** 1 a–e, i: closing; closing off; blocking; locking; cutting off; disconnection; stopping; freezing; banning

Sperr·vermerk *der* restriction note (*regarding sale of property, withdrawal of investment, disclosure of information, etc.*)

Spesen /ˈʃpeːzn̩/ *Pl.* expenses; **auf** ~: on expenses; **außer** ~ **nichts gewesen** (scherzh.) [it was] a waste of time and effort

Spezi /ˈʃpeːtsi/ *der;* ~**s,** ~**s (a)** (südd., österr., schweiz. ugs.) [bosom] pal (coll.); chum (coll.); **(b)** (ugs.: Getränk) lemonade and cola

Spezial-: ~**gebiet** *das* special *or* specialist field; ~**geschäft** *das* specialist shop

spezialisieren *refl. V.* specialize (**auf** + *Akk.* in)

Spezialist *der;* ~**en,** ~**en, Spezialistin** *die;* ~, ~**nen** specialist

Spezialität /ʃpetsi̯aliˈtɛːt/ *die;* ~, ~**en** speciality; specialty

Spezial·slalom *der* (Ski) special slalom

speziell /ʃpeˈtsi̯ɛl/ **1** *Adj.* special; specific ‹*question, problem, etc.*›; specialized ‹*book, knowledge, etc.*›. **2** *Adv.* (besonders, gerade) especially; (eigens) specially

spezifisch 1 *Adj.* specific; characteristic ‹*smell, style*›; ~**es Gewicht/**~**e Wärme** (Phys.) specific gravity/heat. **2** *adv.* specifically

spezifizieren *tr. V.* specify; (einzeln aufführen) itemize ‹*bill, expenses, etc.*›

Sphäre /ˈsfɛːrə/ *die;* ~, ~**n** (auch fig.) sphere; **in höheren** ~**n schweben** (scherzh.) have one's head in the clouds

sphärisch *Adj.* **(a)** spherical; **(b)** (fig.: himmlisch) heavenly

Sphinx /sfɪŋks/ *die od. der;* ~, ~**e** *od.* **Sphingen** /ˈsfɪŋən/ (Ägyptologie, Kunstwiss.) sphinx

Spick·aal *der* (bes. nordd.) smoked eel

spicken /ˈʃpɪkn̩/ *tr. V.* **(a)** (Kochk.) lard; **(b)** (fig. ugs.: reichlich versehen) **eine Rede mit Zitaten** ~: lard a speech with quotations

Spick·zettel *der* (ugs.) crib (coll.)

spie /ʃpiː/ *1. u. 3. Pers. Sg. Prät. v.* **speien**

Spiegel /ˈʃpiːgl̩/ *der;* ~**s,** ~ **(a)** mirror; **im** ~ **der Presse** (fig.) as mirrored *or* reflected in the press; **(b)** (Wasserstand, Blutzucker~, Alkohol~ usw.) level; (Wasseroberfläche) surface

spiegel-, Spiegel-: ~**bild** *das* (auch fig., Math.) reflection; ~**bildlich 1** *Adj.* **eine** ~**bildliche Abbildung** a mirror image; **2** *adv.* ~**bildlich abgebildet** reproduced as a *or* in mirror image; ~**blank** *Adj.* shining; ~**ei** *das* fried egg; ~**glas** *das* mirror glass; ~**glatt** *Adj.* like glass *postpos.;* as smooth as glass *postpos.*

spiegeln 1 *itr. V.* **(a)** (glänzen) shine; gleam; **(b)** (als Spiegel wirken) reflect the light. **2** *tr. V.* reflect; mirror. **3** *refl. V.* (auch fig.) be mirrored *or* reflected

Spiegel-: ∼**reflex·kamera** *die* reflex camera; ∼**schrift** *die* mirror writing

Spiegelung *die;* ∼, ∼**en** (a) (auch fig., Math.) reflection; (b) (Med.) speculum examination

spiegel·verkehrt ⇨ **spiegelbildlich**

Spiel /ʃpiːl/ *das;* ∼[e]s, ∼**e** (a) (das Spielen, Spielerei) play; **für ihn ist alles nur ein** ∼: everything's just a game to him; **ein** ∼ **mit dem Feuer** (fig.) playing with fire; (b) (Glücks∼; Gesellschafts∼) game; (Wett∼) game; match; **gewonnenes** ∼ **haben** be home and dry; **auf dem** ∼ **stehen** be at stake; **etw. aufs** ∼ **setzen** put sth. at stake; risk sth.; **jmdn./etw. aus dem** ∼ **lassen** (fig.) leave sb./ sth. out of it; **ins** ∼ **kommen** (fig.) ⟨*factor*⟩ come into play; ⟨*person, authorities, etc.*⟩ become involved; ⟨*matter, subject, etc.*⟩ come into it; **im** ∼ **sein** (fig.) be involved; (c) (Utensilien) game; (d) *o. Pl.* (eines Schauspielers) performance; (e) (eines Musikers) performance; playing; (f) (Sport: ∼weise) game; (g) (Schau∼) play; (h) (Technik: Bewegungsfreiheit) [free] play

Spiel-: ∼**art** *die* variety; ∼**automat** *der* gaming machine; (Geschicklichkeitsspiel) amusement machine; ∼**ball** *der* (a) (Sport) (Tennis) game point; (Volleyball) match ball; (b) (Billard) red [ball]; (c) (fig.) plaything; **sie ist der** ∼**ball ihrer Leidenschaften** she allows herself to be torn hither and thither by her passions; ∼**bank** *die* casino

spielen 1 *itr. V.* (a) play; **um die Meisterschaft** ∼: play for the championship; **sie haben 1:0 gespielt** the match ended 1–0; **auf der Gitarre** ∼: play the guitar; **er kann vom Blatt/nach Noten** ∼: he can sight-read/play from music; (b) (um Geld) play; **er begann zu trinken und zu** ∼: he began to drink and to gamble; **um Geld** ∼: play for money; (c) (als Schauspieler) act; perform; (d) (sich abspielen) **der Film spielt in Berlin** the film is set in Berlin; (e) (fig.: sich bewegen) ⟨*wind, water, etc.*⟩ play; **seine Muskeln** ∼ **lassen** flex one's muscles; **seinen Charme/ seine Beziehungen** ∼ **lassen** (fig.) bring one's charm/ connections to bear; (f) (fig.: übergehen) **das Blau spielt ins Violette** the blue is tinged with purple. 2 *tr. V.* (a) play; **Räuber und Gendarm** ∼: play cops and robbers; **Cowboy** ∼: play at being a cowboy; **Geige** *usw.* ∼: play the violin *etc.;* **Trumpf/Pik/ein Ass** ∼: play a trump/ spades/an ace; (b) (aufführen, vorführen) put on ⟨*play*⟩; show ⟨*film*⟩; perform ⟨*piece of music*⟩; play ⟨*record*⟩; **was wird hier gespielt?** (fig. ugs.) what's going on here?; (c) (schauspielerisch darstellen) play ⟨*role*⟩; **den Beleidigten/Unschuldigen** ∼ (fig.) act offended/play the innocent; **sein Interesse war [nur] gespielt** he [only] pretended to be interested; his interest was [merely] feigned; (d) (Sport: werfen, treten, schlagen) play; **einen Ball mit Rückhand** ∼: play a ball backhand. 3 *refl. V.* **sich warm** ∼: warm up

spielend 1 *Adj.; nicht präd.* **mit** ∼**er Leichtigkeit** with consummate *or* effortless ease. 2 *adv.* easily; **etw.** ∼ **beherrschen** master sth. effortlessly

Spieler *der;* ∼**s,** ∼ player; (Glücks∼) gambler

Spielerei *die;* ∼, ∼**en** (a) *o. Pl.* playing *no art.;* (im Glücksspiel) gambling *no art.;* (das Herumspielen) playing *or* fiddling about*or* around (**an** + *Dat.* with); (b) (müßiges Tun, Spiel) **eine** ∼ **mit Zahlen** playing [around] with numbers; (c) (Kinderspiel, Leichtigkeit) child's play *no art.;* (d) (Tand) gadget

Spielerin *die;* ∼, ∼**nen** ⇨ **Spieler**

spielerisch 1 *Adj.* (a) (voll Spiellust) playful; **mit** ∼**er Leichtigkeit** with consummate *or* effortless ease; (b) *nicht präd.* (Sport) **sein** ∼**es Können** his skill as a player. 2 *adv.* (a) playfully; (b) (Sport) in playing terms

Spiel-: ∼**feld** *das* (Fußball, Hockey, Rugby usw.) field; pitch (Brit.); (Tennis, Squash, Federball, Volleyball usw.) court; ∼**figur** *die* piece; ∼**film** *der* feature film; ∼**führer** *der* (Sport) [team] captain; ∼**geld** *das* play *or* toy money; ∼**hölle** *die* (ugs. abwertend) gambling-den; ∼**kamerad** *der* playmate; playfellow; ∼**karte** *die* playing card; ∼**kasino** *das* casino; ∼**leiter** *der* (a) (im Fernsehen) quizmaster; (im Roulett) tourneur; (b) ⇨ **Regisseur**; ∼**macher** *der* (Sportjargon) key player; ∼**marke** *die* chip; jetton; ∼**plan** *der* programme; ∼**platz** *der* playground;

∼**raum** *der* (a) room to move (fig.); scope; latitude; (bei Ausgaben, Budget) leeway; (b) (Technik) clearance; ∼**regel** *die* (auch fig.) rule of the game; **gegen die** ∼**regeln verstoßen** (auch fig.) break the rules; ∼**sachen** *Pl.* toys; ∼**stein** *der* piece; (beim Damespiel, Schach) piece; man; ∼**straße** *die* play street; ∼**uhr** *die* (a) musical clock; (b) musical box (Brit.); music box (Amer.); ∼**verderber** *der;* ∼**s,** ∼, ∼**verderberin** *die;* ∼, ∼**nen** spoilsport; ∼**waren** *Pl.* toys; ∼**waren·geschäft** *das* toyshop; ∼**zeit** *die* (a) (Theater: Saison) season; (b) (Aufführungsdauer) run; (c) (Sport) playing time; ∼**zeug** *das* (a) toy; (fig.) toy; plaything; (b) *o. Pl.* (∼sachen, ∼waren) toys *pl.;* ∼**zug** *der* (Sport, in einem Brettspiel) move

Spieß /ʃpiːs/ *der;* ∼**es,** ∼**e** (a) (Waffe) spear; **den** ∼ **umdrehen** (ugs.) turn the tables; **wie am** ∼ **brüllen** (ugs.) scream one's head off; scream blue murder (sl.); (b) (Brat∼) spit; (Schaschlik∼) skewer; **ein am** ∼ **gebratener Ochse** an ox roasted on the spit; a spit-roasted ox; (c) (Fleisch∼) kebab; (d) (Soldatenspr.) [company] sergeant major

Spieß·bürger *der* (abwertend) [petit] bourgeois

spieß·bürgerlich ⇨ **spießig**

Spießchen *das;* ∼**s,** ∼ (a) (Cocktailspieß) cocktail stick; (b) (Schaschlikspieß) skewer; (c) (Fleischspieß) kebab

spießen *tr. V.* (a) **eine Olive auf einen Cocktailspieß** ∼: spear an olive with a cocktail stick; **etw. in etw.** (*Akk.*) ∼: stick sth. in sth.

Spießer *der;* ∼**s,** ∼ (abwertend) [petit] bourgeois

Spieß·geselle *der* (abwertend: Komplize) accomplice

spießig (abwertend) 1 *Adj.* [petit] bourgeois. 2 *adv.* ⟨*think, behave, etc.*⟩ in a [petit] bourgeois way

Spießigkeit *die;* ∼ (abwertend) [petit] bourgeois narrow-mindedness

Spieß·rute *die* **in** ∼**n laufen** (auch fig.) run the gauntlet

Spike /ʃpaik/ *der;* ∼**s,** ∼**s** (a) spike; (b) (eines Reifens) stud

Spike[s]·reifen *der* studded tyre

Spinat /ʃpiˈnaːt/ *der;* ∼[e]s, ∼**e** spinach

Spind /ʃpɪnt/ *der od. das;* ∼[e]s, ∼**e** locker

Spindel /ˈʃpɪndl̩/ *die;* ∼, ∼**n** spindle

spindel·dürr *Adj.* skinny

Spinett /ʃpiˈnɛt/ *das;* ∼[e]s, ∼**e** spinet

Spinne /ˈʃpɪnə/ *die;* ∼, ∼**n** spider

*****spinne·feind, Spinne·feind** (ugs.) **in jmdm.** ∼ **sein** hate sb.'s guts (coll.)

spinnen /ˈʃpɪnən/ 1 *unr. tr. V.* spin (fig.); plot ⟨*intrigue*⟩; think up ⟨*idea*⟩; hatch ⟨*plot*⟩. 2 *unr. itr. V.* (a) spin; (b) (ugs.: verrückt sein) be crazy *or* (sl.) nuts *or* (sl.) crackers; **Ich soll bezahlen? Du spinnst wohl!** [What,] me pay? You must be joking *or* (sl.) kidding

Spinnen·netz *das* spider's web

Spinner *der;* ∼**s,** ∼ (a) ▸85] (Beruf) spinner; (b) (ugs. abwertend) nutcase (coll.); idiot

Spinnerei *die;* ∼, ∼**en** (a) *o. Pl.* spinning *no art.;* (b) (Werkstatt) spinning mill; (c) (ugs. abwertend) crazy idea

Spinnerin *die;* ∼, ∼**nen** (Beruf) spinner

spinnert /ˈʃpɪnɐt/ *Adj.* (ugs., bes. südd.) slightly potty (Brit. coll.)

spinnig *Adj.* (ugs.) slightly potty (Brit. coll.)

Spinn-: ∼**rad** *das* spinning wheel; ∼**webe** *die;* ∼, ∼**n** cobweb

spintisieren /ʃpɪntiˈziːrən/ *itr. V.* (ugs.) get weird *or* crazy ideas (coll.)

Spion /ʃpiˈoːn/ *der;* ∼**s,** ∼**e** (a) spy; (b) (Guckloch) spyhole; (c) (Spiegel am Fenster) tell-tale mirror

Spionage /ʃpioˈnaːʒə/ *die;* ∼: spying; espionage

Spionage·abwehr *die* (a) counter-espionage; counter-intelligence; (b) (Dienst) counterespionage *or* counter-intelligence service

spionieren *itr. V.* (a) spy (**gegen** against); (b) (fig. abwertend) spy; snoop [about] (coll.)

Spioniererei *die;* ∼, ∼**en** (fig. abwertend) snooping [about] *no pl.* (coll.)

Spionin *die;* ∼, ∼**nen** spy

Spiral·bohrer *der* twist drill *or* bit

Spirale /ʃpiˈraːlə/ *die;* ∼, ∼**n** (a) (auch Geom., fig.) spiral; (b) (zur Empfängnisverhütung) coil

Spiral·feder *die* coil spring

spiral·förmig 1 *Adj.* spiral[-shaped]. 2 *adv.* spirally

Spiral·nebel *der* (Astron.) spiral nebula

Spiritismus /ʃpiri'tɪsmʊs/ *der;* ~: spiritualism; spiritism

SpiritĮst *der;* ~en, ~en spiritualist; spiritist

spiritistisch *Adj.* spiritualist[ic]; spiritistic

Spiritual /'spɪrɪtjʊəl/ *das od. der;* ~s, ~s [negro] spiritual

Spirituose /spiri'tuo:zə/ *die;* ~, ~n spirit *usu. in pl.*

Spiritus /'ʃpi:ritʊs/ *der;* ~, ~se spirit; ethyl alcohol; **mit** ~ **kochen** cook on a spirit stove

Spiritus·kocher *der* spirit stove

Spital /ʃpi'ta:l/ *das;* ~s, **Spitäler** /ʃpi'tɛ:lɐ/ (bes. österr., schweiz.) hospital

spitz /ʃpɪts/ 1 *Adj.* (a) (nicht stumpf) pointed 〈*tower, arch, shoes, nose, beard, etc.*〉; sharp 〈*pencil, needle, stone, etc.*〉; fine 〈*pen nib*〉; (Geom.) acute 〈*angle*〉; (b) (schrill) shrill 〈*cry etc.*〉; (c) (ugs.: abgezehrt) haggard; (d) (boshaft) cutting 〈*remark, etc.*〉. 2 *adv.* (a) ~ **zulaufen** taper to a point; ~ **zulaufend** pointed; (b) (boshaft) cuttingly

Spitz *der;* ~es, ~e (Hund) spitz

spitz-, Spitz-: ~**bart** *der* (a) goatee; pointed beard; (b) (Mann) man with a/the goatee or pointed beard; ~**bube** *der* (scherzh.: Schlingel) rascal; scallywag; scamp; ~**bübisch** 1 *Adj.* roguish; mischievous; 2 *adv.* roguishly; mischievously

spitze *indekl. Adj.* (ugs.) ⇨ **klasse**

Spitze *die;* ~, ~n (a) (Nadel~, Bleistift~ usw.) point; (Pfeil~, Horn~ usw.) tip; (b) (Turm~, Baum~, Mast~ usw.) top; (eines Dreiecks, Kegels, einer Pyramide) top; apex; vertex (Math.); (eines Berges) summit; top; (c) (Zigarren~, Haar~, Zweig~) end; (Schuh~) toe; (Finger~, Nasen~, Schwanz~, Flügel~, Spargel~) tip; (d) (vorderes Ende) front; **an der** ~ **liegen** (Sport) be in the lead or in front; (e) (führende Position) top; **an der** ~ [**der Tabelle**] **stehen** *od.* **liegen** (Sport) be [at the] top [of the table]; **sich an die** ~ [**einer Bewegung**] **setzen** put oneself at the head [of a movement]; (f) (einer Firma, Organisation usw.) head; (einer Hierarchie) top; (leitende Gruppe) management; **die** ~**n der Gesellschaft** the leading figures of society; (g) ▶ **224|** (Höchstwert) maximum; peak; (ugs.: Spitzenzeit) peak period; **das Auto fährt 160 km** ~: the car has or does a top speed of 160 km. per hour; (h) [**absolute/einsame**] ~ **sein** (ugs.) be [absolutely] great (coll.); (i) (fig.: Angriff) dig 〈**gegen** at〉; ~**n austeilen** make pointed remarks; (j) (Textilwesen) lace

Spitzel *der;* ~s, ~ (abwertend) informer

spitzeln *itr. V.* (abwertend) act as an informer

spitzen *tr. V.* sharpen 〈*pencil*〉; purse 〈*lips, mouth*〉; **die Ohren** ~ 〈*dog*〉 prick up its ears; (fig.) 〈*person*〉 prick up one's ears

Spitzen-: ~**bluse** *die* lace blouse; ~**erzeugnis** *das* top-quality product; ~**geschwindigkeit** *die* ▶ **224|** top speed; ~**kandidat** *der* leading or top candidate; ~**klasse** *die* (a) top class; **ein Hotel der** ~**klasse** a top-class hotel; (b) ~**klasse sein** (ugs.) be really great (coll.); ~**kraft** *die* top-class or top-flight professional; ~**leistung** *die* top-class performance; ~**politiker** *der* top or leading politician; ~**qualität** *die* top quality; ~**reiter** *der* top rider; (fig.) leader; (Ware) top or best seller; (Mannschaft) top team; ~**sportler** *der* top sportsman; ~**stellung** *die* top position; ~**technologie** *die* state-of-the-art technology; ~**wert** *der* peak; maximum [value]

Spitzer *der;* ~s, ~: (pencil-) sharpener

spitz-, Spitz-: ~**findig** 1 *Adj.;* hair-splitting, over-subtle; quibbling 〈*distinction*〉; pettifogging 〈*quibble*〉; 2 *adv.* in an over-subtle way; ~**findigkeit** *die;* ~, ~en (a) *o. Pl.* over-subtlety; (Haarspalterei) hair-splitting; (b) (etwas Spitzfindiges) nicety; (Äußerung) hair-splitting remark; ~**hacke** *die* pick; pickaxe

spitz-, Spitz-: ~|**kriegen** *tr. V.* (ugs.) tumble to (coll.); get wise to (sl.); ~**maus** *die* (a) shrew; ~**name** *der* nickname; ~**wegerich** /~ve:gərɪç/ *der* (Bot.) ribwort; ~**winklig** 1 *Adj.* acute-angled 〈*triangle*〉; 2 *adv.* at an

acute angle; ~**züngig** 1 *Adj.* sharp-tongued; 2 *adv.* 〈*reply*〉 sharply

Spleen /ʃpli:n/ *der;* ~s, ~e *od.* ~s strange or peculiar habit; eccentricity; **du hast ja einen** ~! there must be something the matter with you'; you must be dotty (coll.)

spleenig *Adj.* eccentric; dotty (coll.)

Splitt /ʃplɪt/ *der;* ~[e]s, ~e [stone] chippings *pl.;* (zum Streuen) grit

splitten *tr. V.* (Wirtsch.) (a) split 〈*shares*〉; (b) (Politik) **die Stimmen** ~: give one's first vote to a particular candidate and one's second to a party other than that of the chosen candidate

Splitter *der;* ~s, ~: splinter; (Granat~, Bomben~) splinter; fragment

Splitter·gruppe *die* splinter group

splittern *itr. V.* (a) (Splitter bilden) splinter; (b) *mit sein* (in Splitter zerbrechen) 〈*glass, windscreen, etc.*〉 shatter

splitter·nackt *Adj.* (ugs.) stark naked; starkers *pred.* (Brit. sl.)

Splitter·partei *die* splinter party

splittrig ⇨ **splitterig**

SPÖ /ɛspe:'ø:/ *die;* ~: *Abk.:* **Sozialistische Partei Österreichs** Austrian Socialist Party

Spoiler /'ʃpɔylɐ/ *der;* ~s, ~ (Kfz-W.) spoiler

sponsern /'ʃpɔnzɐn/ *tr. V.* sponsor

Sponsor /'ʃpɔnze/ *der;* ~s, ~s *od.* ~en /-'zo:rən/ sponsor

spontan /ʃpɔn'ta:n/ 1 *Adj.* spontaneous. 2 *adv.* spontaneously

sporadisch /ʃpo'ra:dɪʃ/ 1 *Adj.* sporadic. 2 *adv.* sporadically

Spore /'ʃpo:rə/ *die;* ~, ~n (Biol.) spore

Sporen ⇨ **Spore, Sporn**

Sporen-: ~**pflanze** *die* (Bot.) cryptogam; ~**tierchen** *das* (Zool.) sporozoan

Sporn /ʃpɔrn/ *der;* ~[e]s, **Sporen** /'ʃpo:rən/ spur; **einem Pferd die Sporen geben** spur a horse; **sich die [ersten] Sporen verdienen** (fig.) win one's spurs

spornen *tr. V.* spur 〈*horse*〉

Sport /ʃpɔrt/ *der;* ~[e]s (a) sport; (als Unterrichtsfach) PE; physical education; PE; ~ **treiben** do sport; **beim** ~: while doing sport; (b) (~art) sport; (c) (Hobby, Zeitvertreib) hobby; pastime

Sport-: ~**abzeichen** *das* sports badge; ~**anlage** *die* sports complex; ~**art** *die* [form of] sport; ~**artikel** *der* piece of sports equipment; ~**artikel** *Pl.* sports equipment *sing.;* ~**fest** *das* sports festival; (einer Schule) sports day; ~**flieger** *der* sports pilot; ~**flugzeug** *das* sports plane; ~**freund** *der* (a) sports fan; (b) (Kamerad) sporting friend; ~**funktionär** *der* sports official; ~**geist** *der; o. Pl.* sportsmanship; sporting spirit; ~**hochschule** *die* college of physical education; ~**journalist** *der* sports journalist; ~**kleidung** *die* sportswear; sports clothes *pl.;* ~**lehrer** *der* sports instructor; (in einer Schule) PE or physical education teacher; games teacher

Sportler /'ʃpɔrtlɐ/ *der;* ~s, ~: sportsman

Sportlerin *die;* ~, ~nen sportswoman

sportlich 1 *Adj.* (a) sporting *attrib.* 〈*success, performance, interests, etc.*〉; ~**e Veranstaltungen** sports events; sporting events; **auf** ~**em Gebiet** in the field of sport; (b) (fair) sportsmanlike; sporting; (c) (fig.: flott, rasant) sporty 〈*car, driving, etc.*〉; (d) (zu sportlicher Leistung fähig) sporty, athletic 〈*person*〉; (e) (jugendlich wirkend) sporty, smart but casual 〈*clothes*〉; smart but practical 〈*hairstyle*〉. 2 *adv.* (a) as far as sport is concerned; ~ **aktiv sein** be an active sportsman/sportswoman; (b) (fair) sportingly; (c) (fig.: flott, rasant) in a sporty manner

sportlich-elegant 1 *Adj.* casually elegant. 2 *adv.* casually but elegantly 〈*dressed*〉

Sport-: ~**platz** *der* sports field; (einer Schule) playing field/fields *pl.;* ~**rad** *das* sports bike; ~**schuh** *der* (a) sports shoe; (b) (sportlicher Schuh) casual shoe; ~**sendung** *die* sports programme

Sports·freund *der* sports enthusiast; **Hallo,** ~**freund! Wie geht's?** (ugs.) hello, mate (coll.)

Sport-: ∼**stadion** das [sports] stadium; ∼**student** der sports student; ∼**taucher** der skin diver; ∼**un·· fall** der sporting or sports accident; ∼**verein** der sports club; ∼**verletzung** die sports injury; ∼**wagen** der **(a)** (Auto) sports car; **(b)** (Kinderwagen) pushchair (Brit.); stroller (Amer.)

Spot /spɔt/ der; ∼s, ∼s **(a)** (Werbespot) commercial; advertisement; ad (coll.); **(b)** (Leuchte) spotlight; spotlamp; **(c)** (Theat., Film, Fernsehen) spot[light]

Spott /ʃpɔt/ der; ∼[e]s mockery; (höhnischer) ridicule; derision; ∼ **und Hohn** scorn and derision

spott·billig (ugs.) **1** Adj. dirt cheap; **2** adv. **da kann man** ∼ **einkaufen** you can get or buy things dirt cheap there

spötteln /'ʃpœtl̩n/ itr. V. mock [gently]; poke or make [gentle] fun

spotten /'ʃpɔtn̩/ itr. V. **(a)** mock; poke or make fun; (höhnischer) ridicule; be derisive; **über jmdn./etw.** ∼: mock sb./sth.; make fun of sb./sth.; (höhnischer) ridicule sb./sth.; be derisive about sb./sth.; **(b)** (fig.) be contemptuous of; scorn; **er spottete der Gefahr** (Gen.) (geh.) he was contemptuous of or scorned the danger

Spötter /'ʃpœtɐ/ der; ∼s, ∼: mocker

spöttisch /'ʃpœtɪʃ/ **1** Adj. mocking ⟨smile, remark, speech, etc.⟩; (höhnischer) derisive, ridiculing ⟨remark, speech, etc.⟩; **ein** ∼**er Mensch** a person who likes poking fun. **2** adv. mockingly; ∼ **lächeln** give a mocking smile

Spott-: ∼**lust** die; o. Pl. love of or delight in mockery or poking fun; ∼**preis** der (ugs.) ridiculously low price; **etw. für einen** od. **zu einem** ∼**preis bekommen** get sth. dirt cheap or for a song

sprach /ʃpra:x/ 1. u. 3. Pers. Sg. Prät. v. **sprechen**

Sprach·begabung die; o. Pl. talent or gift for languages

Sprache /'ʃpra:xə/ die; ∼, ∼n **(a)** language; **in englischer** ∼: in English; **hast du die** ∼ **verloren?** (ugs.) haven't you got a tongue in your head?; **(b)** (Sprechweise) way of speaking; speech; (Stil) style; **(c)** (Rede) **die** ∼ **auf jmdn./etw. bringen** bring the conversation round to sb./ sth.; **etw. zur** ∼ **bringen** bring sth. up; raise sth.; **heraus mit der** ∼! come on, out with it!

spräche /'ʃprɛːçə/ 1. u. 3. Pers. Sg. Konjunktiv II v. **sprechen**

Sprachen-: ∼**schule** die language school; ∼**studium** das language studies pl., no art.

sprach-, Sprach-: ∼**fehler** der speech impediment or defect; ∼**führer** der phrase book; ∼**gebrauch** der [linguistic] usage; ∼**kenntnisse** Pl. knowledge sing. of a language/languages; **seine französischen** ∼**kenntnisse** his knowledge of French; ∼**kundig** Adj. proficient in or conversant with the language postpos.; ∼**kurs** der language course; ∼**labor** das language laboratory or (coll.) lab; ∼**lehre** die **(a)** grammar; **(b)** (Buch) grammar [book]

sprachlich 1 Adj. linguistic; ∼**e Feinheiten** subtleties of language. **2** adv. linguistically

sprach-, Sprach-: ∼**los** Adj. (überrascht) speechless; dumbfounded; ∼**philosophie** die philosophy of language; ∼**regelung** die instructions pl. as to the wording to be used; **nach der offiziellen** ∼**regelung ist er „aus gesundheitlichen Gründen" zurückgetreten** according to the official version or as the official version has it, he resigned 'for reasons of health'; ∼**rohr** das (Repräsentant) spokesman; (Propagandist) mouthpiece; ∼**übung** die language exercise; linguistic exercise; ∼**unterricht** der language teaching or instruction; ∼**wissenschaft** die linguistics sing., no art.; ∼**wissenschaftlich 1** Adj. linguistic; **eine** ∼**wissenschaftliche Abhandlung** a linguistics dissertation; **2** adv. linguistically

sprang /ʃpraŋ/ 1. u. 3. Pers. Sg. Prät. v. **springen**

spränge /'ʃprɛŋə/ 1. u. 3. Pers. Sg. Konjunktiv II v. **springen**

Spray /ʃpre:/ das od. der; ∼s, ∼s spray

Spray·dose die aerosol [can]

sprayen tr., itr. V. spray

Sprayer /'ʃpre:ɐ/ der; ∼s, ∼: graffiti artist;

Sprech-: ∼**an·lage** die intercom (coll.); ∼**blase** die balloon (coll.); ∼**chor** der chorus

sprechen /'ʃprɛçn̩/ **1** unr. itr. V. speak (über + Akk. about; von about, of); (sich unterhalten, sich besprechen auch) talk (über + Akk., von about); ⟨parrot etc.⟩ talk; **deutsch/flüsternd** ∼: speak German/in a whisper or whispers; **er spricht wenig** he doesn't say or talk much; **es spricht Pfarrer N.** the speaker is the Revd. N.; **für/ gegen etw.** ∼: speak in favour of/against sth.; **mit jmdm.** ∼: speak or talk with or to sb.; **ich muss mit dir** ∼: I must talk or speak with you; **er spricht mit sich selbst** he talks to himself; **mit wem spreche ich?** who is speaking please?; to whom am I speaking, please?; ∼ **Sie noch?** (am Telefon) are you still there?; **gut/ schlecht von jmdm.** od. **über jmdn.** ∼: speak well/ill of sb.; **für jmdn.** ∼: speak for sb.; speak on or (Amer.) in behalf of sb.; **vor der Betriebsversammlung** ∼: speak to or address a meeting of the work-force; **zu einem** od. **über ein Thema** ∼: speak on or about a subject; **frei** ∼: extemporize; speak without notes; **aus seinen Worten/ seinem Blick sprach Angst** usw. his words/the look in his eyes expressed fear etc.; **auf jmdn./etw. zu** ∼ **kommen** get to talking about sb./sth.; **für/gegen jmdn./etw.** ∼ (in günstigem/ungünstigem Licht erscheinen lassen) be a point in sb.'s/sth.'s favour/against sb./sth.; **was spricht denn dafür/dagegen?** what is there to be said for/against it? **2** unr. tr. V. **(a)** speak ⟨language, dialect⟩; say ⟨word, sentence⟩; ∼ **Sie Französisch?** do you speak French?; „**Hier spricht man Deutsch**" 'German spoken'; 'we speak German'; **(b)** (rezitieren) say, recite ⟨poem, text⟩; say ⟨prayer⟩; recite ⟨spell⟩; pronounce ⟨blessing, oath⟩; s. auch **Recht a**; **(c)** jmdn. ∼: speak to sb.; **Sie haben mich** ∼ **wollen?** you wanted to see me or speak to me?; **ich bin heute für niemanden mehr zu** ∼: I can't see anyone else today; **(d)** (aus∼) pronounce ⟨name, word, etc.⟩

Sprecher der; ∼s, ∼ **(a)** spokesman; **(b)** (Ansager) announcer; (Nachrichten∼) newscaster; news-reader; **(c)** (Kommentator, Erzähler) narrator; **(d)** (Sprachw.) speaker

Sprecherin die; ∼, ∼nen **(a)** spokeswoman; **(b)** ⇒ **Sprecher b, c, d**

sprech-, Sprech-: ∼**funk** der radio-telephone system; ∼**funkgerät** das radio-telephone; (Walkie-talkie) walkie-talkie; ∼**stunde** die consultation hours pl.; (eines Arztes) surgery; consulting hours pl.; (eines Rechtsanwalts usw.) office hours pl.; **wann haben Sie** ∼**stunde?** when are your consultation hours/when is your surgery or what are your surgery hours?; ∼**stunden·hilfe** die (eines Arztes) receptionist; (eines Zahnarztes) assistant; ∼**übung** die elocution or speech exercise; (zu therapeutischen Zwecken) speech exercise; ∼**weise** die manner of speaking; ∼**zeit** die visiting time; ∼**zimmer** das consulting-room

Spreißel /'ʃpraisl̩/ der, (österr.) das; ∼s, ∼ **(a)** (bes. südd.: Splitter) splinter; **(b)** (bes. österr.: Span) splint

Spreiz·dübel der expanding anchor

spreizen 1 tr. V. spread ⟨fingers, toes, etc.⟩; **die Beine** ∼: spread one's legs apart; open one's legs; **mit gespreizten Beinen stehen/sitzen** stand/sit with one's legs apart. **2** refl. V. (geh.) (sich zieren) **sie spreizte sich erst dagegen, dann stimmte sie zu** she made a fuss at first, [but] then agreed

Spreiz·fuß der (Med.) spread foot

Sprengel /'ʃprɛŋl̩/ der; ∼s, ∼ **(a)** (Kirchen∼) parish; (Diözese) diocese; **(b)** (österr.) administrative district

sprengen /'ʃprɛŋn̩/ tr. V. **(a)** blow up; blast ⟨rock⟩; **etw. in die Luft** ∼: blow sth. up; **(b)** (gewaltsam öffnen, aufbrechen) force [open] ⟨door⟩; force ⟨lock⟩; break open ⟨burial chamber etc.⟩; burst, break ⟨bonds, chains⟩; (fig.) break up ⟨meeting, demonstration⟩; s. auch **Rahmen b**; **(c)** (be∼) water ⟨flower bed, lawn⟩; sprinkle ⟨street, washing⟩ with water; (verspritzen) sprinkle; (mit dem Schlauch) spray

Spreng-: ∼**kraft** die explosive power; ∼**ladung** die explosive charge; ∼**satz** der explosive charge; ∼**stoff** der explosive

Sprengstoff·anschlag der bomb attack

Sprengung die; ∼, ∼en **(a)** blowing-up; (im Steinbruch) blasting; **(b)** ⇒ **sprengen 1b**: forcing [open]; forcing; breaking open; bursting; breaking; (fig.) breaking up; **(c)** (das Besprengen) sprinkling; (mit dem Schlauch) spraying

Sprachen

Wie die Nationalitätsbezeichnungen, werden die
englischen Bezeichnungen der Sprachen (auch die
Adjektive) groß geschrieben:

französische Verben	= French verbs
Das Buch ist deutsch geschrieben	= The book is written in German
In Finnland spricht man Finnisch	= In Finland they speak Finnish
Die Belgier sprechen meist entweder Flämisch oder Französisch	= The Belgians mostly speak either Flemish or French
Hindi, die Amtssprache Indiens, wird von den Hindus gesprochen	= Hindi, India's official language, is spoken by the Hindus

auf/in/zu Deutsch usw.

Die verschiedenen Kombinationen von Präposition
und Sprache, sowie in den meisten Fällen das
deutsche Adverb, werden durch **in** +
Sprachbezeichnung übersetzt:

Die Rede wurde auf Englisch gehalten od. englisch gehalten	= The speech was given in English
Sagen Sie es auf Deutsch	= Say it in German
Der Brief ist in Suaheli geschrieben	= The letter is written in Swahili
„Aquaplaning", zu Deutsch das Gleiten eines Kfzs auf einer Wasserschicht	= 'Aquaplaning', in plain English the skidding of a vehicle on a film of water
Dort war ein Engländer, der italienisch sprach	= There was an Englishman there who was speaking [in] Italian

Das substantivierte Adjektiv

Das Englische, das Deutsche usw. = **English,
German** usw.., also ohne Artikel. Vergleichen Sie:

Das Englische hat od. Im Englischen gibt es eine Verlaufsform	= English has *od.* In English there is a continuous form
Es wurde aus dem od. vom Italienischen ins Deutsche übersetzt	= It was translated from Italian into German

Das Substantiv

Das englische Substantiv zur Bezeichnung einer
Sprache wird selten mit einem bestimmten Artikel
verwendet, und zwar nur dann (wie im Deutschen),
wenn es sich um eine näher bezeichnete Form der
Sprache handelt:

das Latein der Mönche des Mittelalters	= the Latin of the medieval monks

Der unbestimmte Artikel **a, an** wird meist vermieden.

Sie schreibt ein fehlerfreies/gepflegtes Englisch	= She writes [a] faultless/cultivated English
Er spricht ein fließendes, akzentfreies Spanisch	= He speaks fluent Spanish without an accent
Die Quäker sprachen ein altmodisches Englisch	= The Quakers spoke an old-fashioned form of English

Das Adjektiv

Das englische Adjektiv übersetzt auch den ersten Teil
von Zusammensetzungen wie

Deutschstunde, Französischunterricht, Englischlehrer	= German lesson, French teaching, English teacher

Letzteres kann natürlich auch "englischer Lehrer"
heißen, diese Bedeutung wird aber in der
gesprochenen Sprache durch stärkere Betonung des
Substantivs gekennzeichnet (English 'teacher),
wohingegen, wenn ein Englischlehrer gemeint ist, das
Adjektiv betont wird ('English teacher). Um
Verwechslungen in der Schriftsprache zu vermeiden,
kann man im letzteren Fall 'teacher of English'
schreiben.

Die Adjektive, die mit **-sprachig** enden, haben
zweierlei Bedeutungen (eine bestimmte Sprache
sprechend oder in dieser Sprache verfasst bzw.
gehalten) und Übersetzungen:

Die deutschsprachige Bevölkerung	= the German-speaking population

Aber:

eine englischsprachige Zeitung	= an English-language newspaper
französischsprachiger Unterricht	= teaching in French

Sprenkel /ˈʃprɛŋkl/ *der;* ~s, ~: spot; dot; speckle
sprenkeln *tr. V.* sprinkle spots of ⟨*colour*⟩; sprinkle
⟨*water*⟩
Spreu /ʃprɔy/ *die;* ~: chaff; **die ~ vom Weizen
trennen** (fig.) separate the wheat from the chaff
sprich /ʃpriç/ *Imperativ Sg. v.* **sprechen**
sprichst /ʃpriçst/ *2. Pers. Sg. Präsens v.* **sprechen**
spricht /ʃpriçt/ *3. Pers. Sg. Präsens v.* **sprechen**
Sprich·wort *das; Pl.* **Sprichwörter** proverb
sprich·wörtlich **1** *Adj.* proverbial. **2** *adv.* proverbially
sprießen /ˈʃpriːsn̩/ *unr. itr. V.; mit sein* ⟨*leaf, bud*⟩ shoot,
sprout; ⟨*seedlings*⟩ come *or* spring up; ⟨*beard*⟩ sprout; (fig.)
⟨*club, organization, etc.*⟩ spring up
Spriet /ʃpriːt/ *das;* ~[e]s, ~e (Seemannsspr.) sprit
Spring·brunnen *der* fountain
springen /ˈʃprɪŋən/ **1** *unr. itr. V.* **(a)** *mit sein* jump; (mit
Schwung) leap; spring; jump; ⟨*frog, flea*⟩ hop, jump; **vom
Fünfmeterbrett ~:** dive from the five-metre board;
jmdm. an die Kehle ~: leap at sb.'s throat; **auf die
Beine** *od.* **Füße ~:** jump to one's feet; **(b)** *meist mit sein*
(Sport) jump; (beim Stabhochsprung, beim Kasten, Pferd) vault;
(beim Turm~, Kunst~) dive; **(c)** *mit sein* (sich in Sprüngen
fortbewegen) bound; **(d)** (ugs.) *in* **eine Runde Bier ~**

lassen stand a round of beer; **er könnte ruhig mal was
~ lassen** he could easily fork out something just once in a
while (coll.); **(e)** *mit sein* (fig.: schnellen, hüpfen, fliegen) ⟨*pointer,
milometer, etc.*⟩ jump (**auf** + *Akk.* to); ⟨*traffic lights*⟩
change (**auf** + *Akk.* to); ⟨*spark*⟩ leap; ⟨*ball*⟩ bounce;
⟨*spring*⟩ jump out; [**von etw.**] ~ ⟨*fan belt, bicycle-chain,
button, tyre, etc.*⟩ come off [sth.]; **(f)** *mit sein* ⟨*string, glass,
porcelain, etc.*⟩ break; (Risse, Sprünge bekommen) crack; **ge-
sprungene Lippen** cracked *or* chapped lips. **2** *unr. tr. V.;
auch mit sein* (Sport) perform ⟨*somersault, twist dive, etc.*⟩;
5,20 m/einen neuen Rekord ~: jump 5.20m/make a record jump

Springer *der;* ~s, ~ **(a)** (Weit~, Hoch~, Ski~) jumper;
(Stabhoch~) [pole-]vaulter; (Kunst~, Turm~) diver;
(Fallschirm~) parachutist; **(b)** (Schachfigur) knight

Springerin *die;* ~, ~nen ⇒ **Springer a**

spring-, Spring-: ~**flut** *die* spring tide; ~**kraut**
das impatience; ~**lebendig** *Adj.* extremely lively; full
of beans *pred.* (coll.); ~**pferd** *das* jumper; ~**reiten** *das*
showjumping *no art.;* ~**seil** *das* skipping rope (Brit.);
jump-rope (Amer.); ~**turnier** *das* (Reiten) showjumping
competition

Sprint /ʃprɪnt/ *der;* ~s, ~s (auch Sport) sprint

sprinten *itr.* (*auch tr.*) *V.; mit sein* (Sport; ugs.: schnell laufen) sprint

Sprinter *der;* ~s, ~, **Sprinterin** *die;* ~, ~nen (Sport) sprinter

Sprit /ʃprɪt/ *der;* ~[e]s, ~e (a) (ugs.: Treibstoff) gas (Amer. coll.); juice (sl.); petrol (Brit.); (b) (ugs.: Schnaps) shorts *pl.*

Spritze /'ʃprɪtsə/ *die;* ~, ~n (a) (zum Vernichten von Ungeziefer) spray; (Teig~, Torten~, Injektions~) syringe; (b) (Injektion) injection; jab (coll.); **eine** ~ **bekommen** have an injection *or* (coll.) jab; (c) (Feuer~) hose; (Löschfahrzeug) fire engine

spritzen /'ʃprɪtsn̩/ **1** *tr. V.* (a) (versprühen) spray; (ver~) splash ⟨*water, ink, etc.*⟩; spatter ⟨*ink etc.*⟩; (in Form eines Strahls) spray, squirt ⟨*water, foam, etc.*⟩; pipe ⟨*cream etc.*⟩; (b) (be~, besprühen) water ⟨*lawn, tennis court*⟩; water, spray ⟨*street, yard*⟩; spray ⟨*plants, crops, etc.*⟩; pump ⟨*concrete*⟩; (mit Lack) spray ⟨*car etc.*⟩; **jmdn. nass** ~: splash sb.; (mit Wasserpistole, Schlauch) spray sb.; (c) (injizieren) inject ⟨*drug etc.*⟩; (d) (~d herstellen) create ⟨*ice rink*⟩ by spraying; pipe ⟨*cake-decoration etc.*⟩; produce ⟨*plastic article*⟩ by injection moulding; (e) (ugs.: einer Injektion unterziehen) **jmdn./sich** ~: give sb. an injection/inject oneself; **jmdm. ein Schmerzmittel** ~: give sb. a pain-killing injection; (f) (verdünnen) dilute ⟨*wine etc.*⟩ with soda water/lemonade *etc.* **2** *itr. V.* (a) **die Kinder planschten und spritzten** the children splashed and threw water about; (b) *mit Richtungsangabe mit sein* ⟨*hot fat*⟩ spit; ⟨*mud etc.*⟩ spatter, splash; ⟨*blood, water*⟩ spurt; **das Wasser spritzte ihm ins Gesicht** the water splashed up into his face; (c) *mit sein* (ugs.: rennen) dash

Spritzer *der;* ~s, ~ (kleiner Tropfen) splash; (von Farbe) splash; spot; (Schuss) dash; splash

spritzig 1 *Adj.* (a) sparkling ⟨*wine*⟩; tangy ⟨*fragrance, perfume*⟩; (b) (lebendig) lively ⟨*show, music, article*⟩; sparkling ⟨*production, performance*⟩; racy ⟨*style*⟩; (c) (temperamentvoll) nippy (coll.); zippy ⟨*car, engine*⟩; (d) (flink) agile, nimble ⟨*person*⟩. **2** *adv.* sparklingly ⟨*produced, performed, etc.*⟩; racily ⟨*written*⟩; **die Mannschaft spielte sehr** ~: the team played with great speed and agility

Spritz·tour *die* (ugs.) spin

spröd, spröde /ʃprøːt/ *Adj.* (a) brittle ⟨*glass, plastic, etc.*⟩; dry ⟨*hair, lips, etc.*⟩; (rissig) chapped ⟨*lips, skin*⟩; (rauh) rough ⟨*skin*⟩; (b) (fig.: rau klingend) harsh, rough ⟨*voice*⟩; (c) (fig.: abweisend) aloof ⟨*person, manner, nature*⟩

Sprödheit, Sprödigkeit *die;* ~ (a) ⇒ **spröde a**: brittleness; dryness; roughness; (b) (fig.: rauer Klang) harshness; roughness; (c) (fig.: abweisendes Wesen) aloofness

spross, *sproß /ʃprɔs/ *1. u. 3. Pers. Sg. Prät. v.* **sprießen**

Spross, *Sproß *der;* **Sprosses, Sprosse** *od.* **Sprossen** (Bot.) shoot

Sprosse *die;* ~, ~n (a) (auch fig.) rung; (b) (eines Fensters) glazing bar; sash bar

Sprossen-: ~**fenster** *das* window with glazing bars; ~**kohl** *der* (österr.) ⇒ **Rosenkohl;** ~**wand** *die* wall bars *pl.*

Sprössling, *Sprößling /'ʃprœslɪŋ/ *der;* ~s, ~e (ugs. scherzh.) offspring; **seine** ~e his offspring *pl.*

Sprotte /'ʃprɔtə/ *die;* ~, ~n sprat; **Kieler** ~n smoked [Kiel] sprats

Spruch /ʃprʊx/ *der;* ~[e]s, **Sprüche** /'ʃprʏçə/ (a) (Wahl~) motto; (Sinn~) maxim; adage; (Aus~) saying; aphorism; (Zitat) quotation; quote; (Parole) slogan; (Bibel~) quotation; saying; (b) *Pl.* (ugs. abwertend: Phrase) **das sind doch alles nur Sprüche** that's just talk *or* empty words *pl.;* **Sprüche machen** *od.* **klopfen** talk big (coll.)

Spruch·band *das; Pl.* ~**bänder** banner

Sprüche·klopfer *der;* ~s, ~ (ugs. abwertend) big mouth (coll.)

spruch·reif *Adj.* **das ist noch nicht** ~: that's not definite, so people mustn't start talking about it yet

Sprudel /'ʃpruːdl̩/ *der;* ~s, ~ (a) (Selterswasser) sparkling mineral water; (b) (österr.: Erfrischungsgetränk) fizzy drink

sprudeln *itr. V.* (a) *mit sein* ⟨*spring, champagne, etc.*⟩ bubble (**aus** out of); (b) (beim Kochen) bubble; (c) (beim Entweichen von Gas) ⟨*lemonade, champagne, etc.*⟩ fizz, effervesce

Sprudel·wasser *das; Pl.* -**wässer** sparkling mineral water

Sprüh·dose *die* aerosol [can]

sprühen /'ʃpryːən/ **1** *tr. V.* spray; **Wasser auf die Blätter** ~: spray the leaves with water; **seine Augen sprühten Hass** (fig.) his eyes flashed hatred. **2** *itr. V. mit Richtungsangabe mit sein* ⟨*sparks, spray*⟩ fly; ⟨*flames*⟩ spit; ⟨*waterfall*⟩ send out a fine spray; (fig.) ⟨*eyes*⟩ sparkle (**vor** + *Dat.* with); ⟨*intellect, wit*⟩ sparkle; ~**der Witz** sparkling wit

Sprüh·regen *der* drizzle; fine rain

Sprung /ʃprʊŋ/ *der;* ~[e]s, **Sprünge** /'ʃprʏŋə/ (a) (auch Sport) jump; (schwungvoll) leap; (Satz) bound; (Sprung über das Pferd) vault; (Wassersport) dive; (fig.) leap; **sein Herz machte vor Freude einen** ~ (fig.) his heart leapt for joy; **ein [großer]** ~ **nach vorn** (fig.) a [great] leap forward; **keine großen Sprünge machen können** (fig. ugs.) not be able to afford many luxuries; **auf einen** ~ (fig. ugs.) for a few minutes; **auf dem** ~[**e**] **sein** (fig. ugs.) be in a rush; (b) (ugs.: kurze Entfernung) stone's throw; (c) (Riß) crack; **einen** ~ **haben/bekommen** be cracked/crack; (d) *in* **jmdm. auf die Sprünge helfen** (ugs.) help sb. on his/her way

Sprung-: ~**brett** *das* (auch fig.) springboard; ~**feder** *die* [spiral] spring

sprunghaft 1 *Adj.* (a) erratic ⟨*person, character, manner*⟩; disjointed ⟨*conversation, thoughts*⟩; (b) (unvermittelt) sudden; abrupt; (c) (ruckartig) rapid ⟨*change*⟩; sharp ⟨*increase*⟩. **2** *adv.;* ⇒ **1 b–c:** disjointedly; suddenly; abruptly; rapidly; sharply

Sprung-: ~**lauf** *der* (Ski) ski jumping *no art.;* ~**rahmen** *der* spring bed-frame; ~**schanze** *die* (Ski) ski jumping hill; ~**seil** *das* skipping rope (Brit.); jump-rope (Amer.); ~**tuch** *das; Pl.* ~**tücher** safety blanket; ~**turm** *der* (Sport) diving-platform

Spucke *die;* ~: spit; **mir blieb die** ~ **weg** (ugs.) it took my breath away; I was speechless

spucken /'ʃpʊkn̩/ **1** *itr. V.* (a) spit; **in die Hände** ~ (fig.: an die Arbeit gehen) go to work with a will; (b) (ugs.: erbrechen) throw up (coll.); be sick (Brit.). **2** *tr. V.* spit; spit [up], cough up ⟨*blood, phlegm*⟩; **Feuer** ~: breathe fire; ⟨*volcano*⟩ belch fire; *s. auch* **Ton²d**

Spuk /ʃpuːk/ *der;* ~[e]s, ~e (a) [ghostly *or* supernatural] manifestation; (b) (schreckliches Geschehen) horrific episode

spuken *itr. V., auch unpers.* **hier/in dem Haus spukt es** this place/the house is haunted; **dieser Aberglaube spukt noch immer in den Köpfen vieler Menschen** (fig.) this superstition still lurks in many people's minds

Spül·becken *das* sink

Spule /'ʃpuːlə/ *die;* ~, ~n (a) spool; bobbin; (für Tonband, Film) spool; reel; (b) (Elektrot.) coil

Spüle *die;* ~, ~n sink unit; (Becken) sink

spulen *tr., itr. V.* spool; (am Tonbandgerät) wind

spülen /'ʃpyːlən/ **1** *tr. V.* (a) rinse; bathe ⟨*wound*⟩; (b) (landsch.: abwaschen) wash up ⟨*dishes, glasses, etc.*⟩; **Geschirr** ~: wash up; (c) (schwemmen) wash. **2** *itr. V.* (a) (beim WC) flush [the toilet]; (b) (den Mund ausspülen) rinse out [one's mouth]; (c) (landsch.) ⇒ **abwaschen 2**

Spül-: ~**maschine** *die* dishwasher; ~**mittel** *das* washing-up liquid

Spülung *die;* ~, ~en (a) (Med.) irrigation; (der Vagina) douche; (b) (beim WC) flush

Spund /ʃpʊnt/ *der;* ~[e]s, ~e/**Spünde** /'ʃpʏndə/ (a) *Pl.* **Spünde** (Zapfen) bung; (b) *Pl.* ~e (ugs.) **junger** ~: young greenhorn *or* tiro

Spund·loch *das* bung-hole

Spur /ʃpuːɐ̯/ *die;* ~, ~en (a) (Abdruck im Boden) track; (Folge von Abdrücken) tracks *pl.;* (Blut~, Schleim~ usw.) trail; **von dem Vermissten fehlt jede** ~: there is no trace of the missing person; **eine heiße** ~ (fig.) a hot trail; **jmdm./einer Sache auf der** ~ **sein** be on the track *or* trail of sb./sth.; (b) (Anzeichen) trace; (eines Verbrechens) clue (*Gen.* to); (c) (sehr kleine Menge; auch fig.) trace; **da fehlt noch eine** ~ **Paprika** it needs just a touch of paprika; **von**

Reue keine ~: not a trace *or* sign of penitence; **keine** *od.* **nicht die ~** (ugs.: als Antwort) not in the slightest; **(d)** (Verkehrsw.: Fahr~) lane; **die ~ wechseln** change lanes; **in** *od.* **auf der linken ~ fahren** drive in the left-hand lane; **(e)** (Fahrlinie) **[die] ~ halten** stay on its line; **(f)** (Elektrot., DV) track

spürbar 1 *Adj.* noticeable; perceptible; distinct, perceptible ‹*improvement*›; evident ‹*relief, embarrassment*›. **2** *adv.* noticeably; perceptibly; (sichtlich) clearly ‹*relieved, on edge*›

spuren *itr. V.* (ugs.) toe the line (coll.); do as one's told

spüren /ˈʃpyːrən/ *tr. V.* feel; (instinktiv) sense; (merken) notice; **die Peitsche zu ~ bekommen** get a taste of the whip

Spür·hund *der* tracker dog; (fig.: Spitzel) bloodhound; snooper (coll.)

spur·los 1 *Adj.; nicht präd.* total, complete ‹*disappearance*›. **2** *adv.* ‹*disappear*› completely *or* without trace; **es ist nicht ~ an ihm vorübergegangen** it has not failed to leave its mark on him

Spür-: **~nase** *die* (ugs.) **(a)** (Geruchssinn, fig.) nose; **(b)** (Person) bloodhound; snooper (coll.) **~sinn** *der; o. Pl.* (feiner Instinkt) intuition

Spurt /ʃpʊrt/ *der;* ~[e]s, ~s *od.* ~e **(a)** spurt; **(b)** *o. Pl.* (Sport.: ~vermögen) turn of speed

spurten *itr. V.* **(a)** mit Richtungsangabe *mit sein* spurt; **(b)** *mit sein* (ugs.: schnell laufen) sprint

Spur·wechsel *der* change of lane

sputen /ˈʃpuːtn̩/ *refl. V.* (veralt.) make haste

Squaw /skwɔː/ *die;* ~, ~s squaw

St. *Abk.* **(a)** Sankt St.; **(b)** Stück

Staat /ʃtaːt/ *der;* ~[e]s, ~en **(a)** state; **die ~en** (die USA) the States; **von ~s wegen** on the part of the [state] authorities; **(b)** *o. Pl.* (ugs.: Festkleidung, Pracht) finery; **in vollem ~:** in all one's finery; **mit diesem Mantel ist kein ~ mehr zu machen** (fig. ugs.) this coat is past it (coll.)

staaten-, Staaten-: **~bund** *der* confederation; **~los** *Adj.* stateless; **~lose** *der/die; adj. Dekl.* stateless person *or* subject

staatlich 1 *Adj.* state *attrib.* ‹*sovereignty, institutions, authorities, control, etc.*›; ‹*power, unity, etc.*› of the state; state-owned ‹*factory etc.*›; **~e Mittel** government *or* public money *sing.* **2** *adv.* by the state; **~ anerkannt/geprüft/finanziert** state-approved/-certified/-financed; **~ subventioniert werden** receive a state subsidy

staats-, Staats-: **~akt** *der* (Festakt) state ceremony; **~amt** *das* public office; **~angehörige** *der/die* national; **~angehörigkeit** *die* nationality; **~anwalt** *der* ▶85 I, ▶314 I public prosecutor; **~anwaltschaft** *die* public prosecutor's office; **~bank** *die* national bank; **~beamte** *der* ▶85 I civil servant; **~besuch** *der* state visit; **~bürger** *der* ▶388 I citizen; **er ist deutscher ~bürger** he is a German citizen *or* national; **~bürgerkunde** *die* (DDR) school subject involving ideological education of socialist citizens; ≈ civics *sing. no art.;* **~bürgerlich** *Adj.; nicht präd.* civil ‹*rights*›; civic ‹*duties, loyalty*›; ‹*education, attitude*› as a citizen; **~bürgerschaft** *die* ⇒ **~angehörigkeit;** **~chef** *der* head of state; **~dienst** *der* civil service; **~examen** *das* final university examination; **~examen machen** ≈ take one's finals; **~form** *die* type of state; state system; **~gebiet** *das* territory [of a/the state]; **~geheimnis** *das* (auch fig.) state secret; **~gewalt** *die* authority of the state; (Exekutive) executive power; **~grenze** *die* state frontier *or* border; **~kanzlei** *die* (BRD) Minister-President's Office; (Schweiz) Cantonal Chancellery; **~kirche** *die* state *or* established church; **~mann** *der; Pl.* -männer statesman; **~männisch** /~mɛnɪʃ/ **1** *Adj.* statesmanlike ‹*wisdom, far-sightedness, etc.*›; ‹*abilities, skill*› of a statesman; **2** *adv.* in a statesmanlike manner; **~minister** *der* minister of state; (Minister ohne Ressort) minister without portfolio; (BRD: Staatssekretär) secretary of state; **~oberhaupt** *das* head of state; **~präsident** *der* [state] president; **~raison** *die,* **~räson** *die* reasons *pl.* of State *no def. art.;* **~sekretär** *der* ▶314 I permanent secretary; **~streich** *der* coup d'état; **~trauer** *die* national mourning *no indef. art.*

Stab /ʃtaːp/ *der;* ~[e]s, Stäbe /ˈʃtɛːbə/ **(a)** rod; (länger, für ~hochsprung o. ä.) pole; (eines Käfigs, Gitters, Geländers) bar; (Staffel~; geh.: Taktstock) baton; (Bischofs~) crosier; (Hirten~) crook; **den ~ über jmdn./etw. brechen** (geh.) condemn sb./sth. out of hand; **(b)** (Milit.) staff; **(c)** (Team) team

Stäbchen /ˈʃtɛːpçən/ *das;* ~s, ~ **(a)** (kleiner Stab) little rod; [small] stick; **(b)** (Eß~) chopstick

Stab-: **~hoch·springer** *der* pole-vaulter; **~hoch·sprung** *der* **(a)** *o. Pl.* (Disziplin) pole-vaulting *no art.;* **im ~hochsprung** in the pole vault; **(b)** (Sprung) pole vault

stabil /ʃtaˈbiːl/ **1** *Adj.* sturdy ‹*chair, cupboard*›; robust, sound ‹*health*›; stable ‹*prices, government, economy, etc.*›. **2** *adv.* **~ gebaut** solidly built

stabilisieren 1 *tr. V.* stabilize. **2** *refl. V.* **(a)** stabilize; become more stable; **(b)** ‹*health, circulation, etc.*› become stronger

Stabilität /ʃtabiliˈtɛːt/ *die;* ~ sturdiness; (von Gesundheit, Konstitution usw.) robustness; soundness; (das Beständigsein) stability

Stab·lampe *die* torch (Brit.); flashlight (Amer.)

Stabs-: **~arzt** *der* (Milit.) medical officer, MO (*with the rank of captain*); **~feldwebel** *der* (Milit.) warrant-officer 2nd class; **~offizier** *der* (Milit.) staff officer

stach /ʃtax/ *1. u. 3. Pers. Sg. Prät. v.* **stechen**

Stachel /ˈʃtaχl̩/ *der;* ~s, ~n **(a)** spine; (Dorn) thorn; **(b)** (Gift~) sting; **(c)** (spitzes Metallstück) spike; (von ~draht) barb

Stachel-: **~beere** *die* gooseberry; **~draht** *der* barbed wire

stachelig *Adj.* prickly

Stachel·schwein *das* porcupine

stachlig ⇒ **stachelig**

Stadel /ˈʃtaːdl̩/ *der;* ~s, ~ *od.* (Schweiz.) **Städel** /ˈʃtɛːdl̩/ *od.* (österr.) ~n (südd., österr., schweiz.) barn

Stadion /ˈʃtaːdi̯ɔn/ *das;* ~s, **Stadien** stadium

Stadium /ˈʃtaːdi̯ʊm/ *das;* ~s, **Stadien** stage

Stadt /ʃtat/ *die;* ~, **Städte** /ˈʃtɛ(ː)tə/ **(a)** town; (Groß~) city; **die ~ Basel** the city of Basel; **in die ~ gehen** go into town; go downtown (Amer.); **(b)** (Verwaltung) town council; (in der Großstadt) city council; city hall *no art.* (Amer.); **bei der ~ [angestellt] sein/arbeiten** work for the council *or* (Amer.) for city hall

stadt-, Stadt-: **~auswärts** *Adv.* out of town; **~auto·bahn** *die* urban motorway (Brit.) *or* (Amer.) freeway; **~bahn** *die* urban railway; **~bibliothek** *die* municipal library; **~bummel** *der* (ugs.) **einen ~bummel machen** take a stroll through the town/city centre; **~einwärts** *Adv.* into town; downtown (Amer.)

Städte·partnerschaft *die* twinning (Brit.) *or* (Amer.) sister-city arrangement ‹*between towns/cities*›

Städter *der;* ~s, ~, **Städterin** *die;* ~, ~nen **(a)** town-dweller; (Großstädter, -städterin) city-dweller; **(b)** (Stadtmensch) townie (coll.)

Stadt-: **~führer** *der* town/city guidebook; **~gespräch** *das* **(a)** (Telefongespräch) local call; **(b)** *in* **~gespräch sein** be the talk of the town; **~halle** *die* civic *or* municipal hall

städtisch 1 *Adj.* **(a)** (kommunal) municipal; **(b)** (urban) urban ‹*life, way of life, etc.*›; town ‹*clothes*›; ‹*manners, clothes*› of a town-dweller. **2** *adv.* **(a)** (kommunal) municipally; **~ verwaltet** run by the town/city council; **(b)** (urban) ausgesprochen **~ gekleidet** wearing clothes with a decidedly town style

Stadt-: **~kasse** *die* **(a)** (Geldmittel) municipal funds *pl.,* *no art.;* **(b)** (Stelle) town/city treasurer's office; **~kern** *der* ⇒ **~mitte;** **~mauer** *die* town/city wall; **~mensch** *der* townie (coll.); **~mitte** *die* town centre; (einer Großstadt) city centre; downtown area (Amer.); **~park** *der* municipal park; **~plan** *der* [town/city] street plan *or* map; **~rand** *der* outskirts *pl.* of the town/city; **am ~:** on the outskirts of the town/city; **~rat** *der* **(a)** town/city council; **(b)** (Mitglied) town/city councillor; **~rundfahrt** *die* sightseeing tour round a/the town/city; **~staat** *der* city-state; **~streicher** *der* town/city tramp; **~teil** *der* district; part [of a/the town]; **~theater** *das* municipal theatre; **~tor** *das* town/city gate; **~verkehr** *der* town/city traffic; **~verwaltung** *die* municipal authority; town/

Städte

Nur für wenige deutsche Städte gibt es besondere englische Namensformen: Am bekanntesten sind *Köln* = Cologne, *München* = Munich und *Hannover* = Hanover. In Österreich *Wien* = Vienna, in der Schweiz *Genf* = Geneva, *Basel* = Basle und *Luzern* = Lucerne. Unter den europäischen Hauptstädten fallen auf: *Brüssel* = Brussels, *den Haag* = the Hague, *Rom* = Rome, *Athen* = Athens, *Prag* = Prague, *Warschau* = Warsaw und *Moskau* = Moscow. Überhaupt gibt es viele Unterschiede in der Transliteration von slawischen, griechischen, indischen und anderen fremdländischen Ortsnamen. Am besten schlägt man im Hauptteil dieses Wörterbuchs nach, der die wichtigsten geographischen Namen aufführt, oder auf einer englischsprachigen Landkarte.

Einwohnerbezeichnungen und Adjektive

Die von den Städtenamen abgeleiteten Einwohnerbezeichnungen und Adjektive haben im Englischen verschiedene Formen, aber es gibt sie nur für bestimmte größere Städte. Einige Substantive haben die gleiche Form wie die deutschen, die auf **-er** enden (Londoner, New Yorker usw.).

Für britische Städte gibt es einige ganz ausgefallene Ableitungen:

Glasgow→Glaswegian	Aberdeen→Aberdonian
Bath→Bathonian	Liverpool→Liverpudlian
Manchester→ Mancunian	Oxford→Oxonian

Die Endung **-ian** kommt recht häufig vor (z.B. Bristol →Bristolian, Lancaster→Lancastrian), aber für die meisten britischen Städte gibt es keine Einwohnerbezeichnungen. Die hier angegebenen werden sowohl als Adjektive wie auch als Substantive verwendet; die Adjektive beziehen sich meist auf Charaktereigenschaften (*Liverpooler Humor* = Liverpudlian humour).

Weitere Beispiele im europäischen Ausland:

Paris→Parisian	Rome→Roman
Vienna→Viennese	Milan →Milanese
Venice→Venetian	Athens→Athenian
Florence→Florentine	Moscow → Muscovite

In Deutschland gibt es lediglich *Hannoveraner* = Hanoverian (das sich hauptsächlich auf das englische Königshaus und die Pferderasse bezieht). Man kann aber in vielen Fällen die deutsche Form mit der Endung auf **-er** verwenden (Berliner, Frankfurter usw.), die sich aber nur als Einwohnerbezeichnung eignet. Sonst muss man auf die Formel 'inhabitant of …' bzw. bei einer Großstadt, die als city gilt, 'citizen of …' zurückgreifen:

ein Dinkelsbühler/ *eine Dinkelsbühlerin*	= an inhabitant of Dinkelsbühl, a Dinkelsbühler
die Münchener	= the citizens *od*. people of Munich

Das gleiche gilt natürlich für Städte in anderen Ländern. Wenn man das Geschlecht hervorheben will, kann man 'a man/woman from …' oder sogar den landessprachlichen Ausdruck verwenden:

ein alter Bremer	= an old man from Bremen, an old Bremen man
eine schöne Madriderin	= a beautiful woman/girl from Madrid, a beautiful madrileña
eine junge Römerin	= a young Roman girl
viele Wiener/ *Wienerinnen*	= many Viennese men/ women

An Stelle eines fehlenden abgeleiteten Adjektivs verwendet man einfach den Namen attributiv vor dem Substantiv (ohne Artikel bei Gebäuden und Einrichtungen), oder nachgestellt mit of bzw. in:

der Aachener Dom	= Aachen Cathedral
der Ravensburger *Stadtrat*	= Ravensburg Town Council, the Town Council of Ravensburg
der Berliner Dialekt	= Berlin dialect
die New Yorker Gegend	= the New York area
die Pariser Straßen	= the streets of Paris
der Londoner Verkehr	= the London traffic, the traffic in London

Der attributive Gebrauch von Städtenamen erstreckt sich auch auf Straßen:

die Straße nach *Portsmouth*	= the road to Portsmouth, the Portsmouth road

Die Adjektive, die auf **-isch** enden, werden auf ähnliche Weise übersetzt.

hamburgischer Humor	= Hamburg humour
hannoverischer *Gleichmut*	= Hanoverian equanimity

Die Dialekte, die auf **-erisch** enden, kann man nur als '… dialect' wiedergeben:

Wienerisch = Viennese [dialect]
Berlinerisch = Berlin dialect

---

city council; **~viertel** *das* district; **~zentrum** *das* town/city centre; downtown area (Amer.)

Staffel /'ʃtafl/ *die;* ~, ~n (a) (Sport: Mannschaft) team; (für den ~lauf) relay team; (b) (Sport: ~lauf) relay race; (c) (Luftwaffe: Einheit) flight; (d) (Formation von Schiffen, begleitenden Polizisten, usw.) escort formation

Staffelei *die;* ~, ~en easel

Staffel-: **~lauf** *der* (Sport) relay race; **~läufer** *der*, **~läuferin** *die* (Sport) relay runner/skier

staffeln *tr. V.* (a) (aufstellen) arrange in a stagger *or* in an echelon; (b) (abstufen) grade ‹*salaries, fees, prices*›; stagger ‹*times, arrivals, starting places*›

Staffelung *die;* ~, ~en (a) (Anordnung) staggered arrangement; (b) (Abstufung) (von Gebühren, Gehältern, Preisen) grad[u]ation; (von Vorgängen) staggering

Stagnation /ʃtagnaˈtsi̯oːn/ *die;* ~, ~en stagnation

stagnieren *itr. V.* stagnate

stahl /ʃtaːl/ *1. u. 3. Pers. Sg. Prät. v.* **stehlen**

Stahl *der;* ~[e]s, **Stähle** /'ʃtɛːlə/ *od.* ~e steel; **Nerven wie** *od.* **aus ~ haben** have nerves of steel

Stahl-: **~bau** *der; Pl.* **~bauten** (a) *o. Pl.* (Bautechnik) steel construction *no art.;* (b) (Gebäude) steel-frame building; **~beton** *der* (Bauw.) reinforced concrete; ferro-concrete; **~beton·bau** *der; o. Pl.* reinforced concrete construction; **~blech** *das* sheet steel

stählen *tr. V.* (geh.) toughen; harden

stählern *Adj.* (a) *nicht präd.* (aus Stahl) steel; (b) (fig. geh.) ‹*muscles, nerves*› of steel; ‹*will*› of iron

stahl-, Stahl-: **~grau** *Adj.* steel-grey; **~hart** *Adj.* as hard as steel *postpos.;* **~helm** *der* (Milit.) steel helmet; **~ross**, ***~roß *das* (ugs. scherzh.) bike (coll.); trusty steed (coll. joc.); **~wolle** *die* steel wool

stak /ʃtaːk/ *1. u. 3. Pers. Sg. Prät. v.* **stecken**

Stakkato /ʃtaˈkaːto/ *das;* ~s, ~s *od.* **Stakati** (Musik; auch fig.) staccato

staksen /'ʃtaːksn̩/ *itr. V.; mit sein* (ugs.) stalk; (taumelnd) teeter

staksig (ugs.) **1** *Adj.* spindly, shaky-legged ‹*foal etc.*›; teetering ‹steps›. **2** adv. ~ **gehen** walk as though on stilts; (unsicher) walk with teetering steps

Stalagmit /ʃtalak'miːt/ der; ~s od. ~en, ~e[n] (Geol.) stalagmite

Stalaktit /ʃtalak'tiːt/ der; ~s od. ~en, ~e[n] (Geol.) stalactite

Stalinismus /stalɪnɪsmʊs/ der; ~: Stalinism no art.

stalinistisch 1 Adj. Stalinist. **2** adv. in a Stalinist way; along Stalinist lines

Stall /ʃtal/ der; ~[e]s, **Ställe** /'ʃtɛlə/ (Pferde~, Renn~) stable; (Kuh~) cowshed; (Hühner~) [chicken-]coop; (Schweine~) [pig]sty; (für Kaninchen, Kleintiere) hutch; (für Schafe) pen

***Stallaterne** ⇨ Stalllaterne

Stall-: ~**bursche** der ▶85| stable lad; ~**dung** der (von Kühen/Schweinen/Schafen) cow/pig/sheep dung; (von Pferden) horse manure; ~**hase** der (ugs.) domestic rabbit; ~**knecht** der ▶85| (veralt.) stable lad; (für Kühe) cowhand; ~**laterne** die stable lamp; ~**meister** der ▶85| head groom; ~**mist** der ⇨ ~**dung**

Stallung die; ~, ~**en** (Pferdestall) stable; (Kuhstall) cowshed; (Schweinestall) [pig]sty

Stamm /ʃtam/ der; ~[e]s, **Stämme** (a) (Baum~) trunk; **eine Hütte aus rohen Stämmen** a hut of rough-hewn boles; (b) (Volks~, Geschlecht) tribe; **der ~ Davids** the house of David; (c) o. Pl. (fester Bestand) core; (von Fachkräften, Personal) permanent staff; **zum ~ gehören** be one of the regulars (coll.); (der Belegschaft einer Firma) be a permanent member of staff; (d) (Sprachw.) stem

Stamm-: ~**baum** der family tree; (eines Tieres) pedigree; (Biol.) phylogenetic tree; ~**buch** das family album ‹recording births, marriages, deaths, etc.›

stammeln /'ʃtamln/ tr., itr. V. stammer

stammen itr. V. ▶388| come (**aus, von** from); (datieren) date (**aus, von** from); **die Idee stammt nicht von ihm** the idea isn't his

Stammes-: ~**geschichte** die; o. Pl. (Biol.) phylogenesis no art.; ~**häuptling** der tribal chief

Stamm-: ~**essen** das set meal; ~**form** die; meist Pl. (Sprachw.) principal part; ~**gast** der (im Lokal/Hotel) regular customer/visitor; regular (coll.); ~**gericht** das set dish; ~**halter** der (oft scherzh.) son and heir (esp. joc.); ~**kneipe** die (ugs.) favourite or usual pub (Brit.) or (Amer.) bar; ~**kunde** der regular customer; ~**lokal** das favourite or usual restaurant/pub (Brit.) or bar (Amer.)/café; ~**platz** der (auch fig.) regular place; (Sitz) regular or usual seat; (für Wohnwagen, Zelt usw.) regular site; ~**silbe** die (Sprachw.) stem syllable; ~**tisch** der (a) (Tisch) regulars' table (coll.); (b) (~tischrunde) group of regulars (coll.); (c) (Treffen) gettogether with the regulars (coll.) ~**würze** die (Brauerei) original wort; (Gehalt) original gravity

stampfen /'ʃtampfn/ **1** itr. V. (a) (laut auftreten) stamp; **mit den Füßen/den Hufen ~:** stamp one's feet/its hoofs; (b) mit sein (sich fortbewegen) tramp; (mit schweren Schritten) trudge; (c) (mit wuchtigen Stößen sich bewegen) ‹machine, engine, etc.› pound. **2** tr. V. (a) **mit den Füßen den Rhythmus ~:** tap the rhythm with one's feet; (b) (fest~) compress; (rammen) drive ‹pile› (**in** + Akk. into); (c) (zerkleinern) mash ‹potatoes›; pulp ‹fruit›; crush ‹sugar›; pound ‹millet, flour›

Stampfer der; ~s, ~ (a) (für Erde usw.) tamper; (Stößel) pestle; (b) (Küchengerät) masher

Stampf·kartoffeln Pl. (nordd.) mashed potatoes

stand /ʃtant/ 1. u. 3. Pers. Sg. Prät. v. **stehen**

Stand der; ~[e]s, **Stände** (a) o. Pl. (das Stehen) standing position; **keinen sicheren ~ haben** not have a secure footing; **ein Sprung/Start aus dem ~:** a standing jump/start; **bei jmdm. od. gegen jmdm.] einen schweren ~ haben** (fig.) have a tough time [of it] [with sb.]; **etw. aus dem ~ [heraus] beantworten** (ugs.) answer sth. off the top of one's head (coll.); (b) (~ort) position; (c) (Verkaufs~; Box für ein Pferd) stall; (Messe~, Informations~) stand; (Zeitungs~) [newspaper] kiosk; (d) o. Pl. (erreichte Stufe; Zustand) state; **etw. auf den neu[e]sten ~ bringen** bring sth. up to date or update sth.; **außer ~[e]** ⇨ **außerstande; im ~[e]** ⇨ **imstande;** (e) (des Wassers, Flusses)

level; (des Thermometers, Zählers, Barometers) reading; (der Kasse, Finanzen) state; (eines Himmelskörpers) position; **den ~ des Thermometers ablesen** take the thermometer reading; (f) o. Pl. (Familien~) status; (g) (Gesellschaftsschicht) class; (Berufs~) trade; (Ärzte, Rechtsanwälte) [professional] group; **der geistliche ~:** the clergy

Standard /'ʃtandart/ der; ~s, ~s standard

Standard-: standard ‹equipment, example, letter, form, solution, model, work, language›

Standard·situation die (Sport) set piece

Standarte /ʃtan'dartə/ die; ~, ~n standard

Stand·bild das statue

Ständchen /'ʃtɛntçən/ das; ~s, ~: serenade; jmdm. **ein ~ bringen** serenade sb.

Stander /'ʃtandɐ/ der; ~s, ~: pennant

Ständer /'ʃtɛndɐ/ der; ~s, ~ (a) (Gestell, Vorrichtung) stand; (Kleider~) coat-stand; (Wäsche~) clothes horse; (Kerzen~) candle-holder; (b) (Elektrot.) stator; (c) (salopp: erigierter Penis) hard-on (sl.)

standes-, Standes-: ~**amt** das registry office; ~**amtlich 1** Adj.; nicht präd. registry office ‹wedding, document›; **2** adv. ~**amtlich heiraten** get married in a registry office; ~**beamte** der registrar; ~**bewusst,** *~**bewußt** Adj. conscious of one's social standing or rank postpos.; ~**bewusstsein** das, *~**bewußtsein** das consciousness of one's social standing or rank; ~**dünkel** der (abwertend) snobbery; ~**gemäß 1** Adj. befitting sb.'s station or social standing postpos.; ~**gemäß sein** befit sb.'s station or social standing; **2** adv. as befits one's station or social standing; ~**unterschied** der difference of rank; class difference

stand-, Stand-: ~**fest** Adj. (a) (fest stehend) steady; stable; strong ‹stalk, stem›; (b) (standhaft) steadfast; ~**festigkeit** die (a) stability; (eines Gebäudes) structural strength; (b) (Standhaftigkeit) steadfastness; ~**haft** 1 Adj. steadfast; **2** adv. steadfastly; ~**haftigkeit** die; ~: steadfastness; ~**|halten** unr. itr. V. stand firm; **einer Sache** (Dat.) ~**halten** withstand or stand up to sth.; **einer näheren Überprüfung nicht ~halten** not stand [up to] or bear closer scrutiny

ständig 1 Adj.; nicht präd. (a) (andauernd) constant ‹noise, worry, pressure, etc.›; (b) (fest) permanent ‹residence, correspondent, staff, member, etc.›; standing ‹committee›; regular ‹income›. **2** adv. constantly; **musst du sie ~ unterbrechen?** do you have to keep [on] interrupting her?; **sie kommt ~ zu spät** she's forever coming late

ständisch Adj. corporative

stand-, Stand-: ~**licht** das; Pl. ~**lichter** (Kfz-W.) (Beleuchtung) sidelights pl.; (Leuchte, Lampe) sidelight; ~**ort** der; Pl. ~**orte** (a) position; (eines Betriebes o. ä.) location; site; (b) (Milit.: Garnison) garrison; base; (c) (Wirtsch.) industrial location; **der ~ort Deutschland** Germany as an industrial location or as a place for industrial investment; ~**ort·vorteil** der (Wirtsch.) **um des ~ortvorteils willen ins Ausland gehen** more go abroad for the better location; **sich** (Dat.) **einen ~ortvorteil verschaffen** move to a better location; ~**punkt** der (fig.) point of view; viewpoint; **den ~punkt vertreten/auf dem ~punkt stehen, dass …:** take the view that …; ~**quartier** das base; ~**rechtlich 1** Adj.; nicht präd. summary ‹execution, shooting›; **2** adv. jmdn. ~**rechtlich erschießen** shoot sb. summarily; ~**spur** die (Verkehrsw.) hard shoulder; ~**uhr** die grandfather clock

Stange /'ʃtaŋə/ die; ~, ~**n** (a) (aus Holz) pole; (aus Metall) bar; (dünner) rod; (Kleider~) rail; (Vogel~) perch; **Kleider/Anzüge von der ~** (ugs.) off-the-peg dresses/suits; **von der ~ kaufen** (ugs.) buy off-the-peg clothes; **bei der ~ bleiben** (ugs.) keep at it (coll.); **eine ~ Zimt/Vanille/Lakritze** usw. a stick of cinnamon/vanilla/liquorice etc.; **eine ~ Zigaretten** a carton containing ten packets of cigarettes; **eine [schöne] ~ Geld** (ugs.) a small fortune (coll.); (b) (bes. md.: zylindrisches Trinkglas) [straight] glass

Stängel /'ʃtɛŋl/ der; ~s, ~: stem; stalk

Stangen-: ~**brot** das French bread; ~**spargel** der asparagus spears pl. or stalks pl.

stank /ʃtaŋk/ *1. u. 3. Pers. Sg. Prät. v.* **stinken**

Stänkerer *der;* ~s, ~ (ugs. abwertend) grouser (coll.); stirrer

stänkern /'ʃtɛŋkɐn/ *itr. V.* (ugs. abwertend) stir (coll.); **gegen jmdn./etw.** ~: go on about sb./sth.

Stanniol /ʃta'njoːl/ *das;* ~s, ~e tin foil; (Silberpapier) silver paper

Stanniol·papier *das* silver paper

stanzen *tr. V.* press; (prägen) stamp; (ausstanzen) punch ‹numbers, holes, punch-cards, etc.›

Stapel /'ʃtaːpl̩/ *der;* ~s, ~ (a) pile; **ein** ~ **Holz** a pile *or* stack of wood; (b) (Schiffbau) stocks *pl.;* **vom** ~ **laufen** be launched; **vom** ~ **lassen** launch ‹ship›

Stapel·lauf *der* launch[ing]

stapeln **1** *tr. V.* (schichten) pile up; stack; (fig.: ansammeln) accumulate. **2** *refl. V.* pile up; (gestapelt sein) be piled up

stapfen *itr. V.; mit sein* tramp

Star¹ /ʃtaːɐ̯/ *der;* ~[e]s, ~e *od.* (schweiz.) ~en (Vogel) starling

Star² *der;* ~s, ~s (berühmte Persönlichkeit) star

Star³ *der;* ~[e]s, ~e ▶ 329 | **grauer** ~: cataract; **grüner** ~: glaucoma

Star-: star ‹conductor, guest singer, etc.›; top ‹lawyer, model, agent›

starb /ʃtarp/ *1. u. 3. Pers. Sg. Prät. v.* **sterben**

stark /ʃtark/; **stärker** /'ʃtɛrkɐ/, **stärkst...** /'ʃtɛrkst.../ **1** *Adj.* (a) strong ‹man, current, structure, team, drink, verb, pressure, wind, etc.›; potent ‹drink, medicine, etc.›; powerful ‹engine, lens, voice, etc.›; (ausgezeichnet) excellent ‹runner, player, performance›; **sich für jmdn./etw.** ~ **machen** (ugs.) throw one's weight behind sb./sth.; *s. auch* **Seite d; Stück c;** (b) (dick) thick; stout ‹rope, string›; (verhüll.: korpulent) well-built (euphem.); (c) (zahlenmäßig groß, umfangreich) sizeable, large ‹army, police›; big ‹demand›; **eine 100 Mann** ~e **Truppe** a 100-strong unit; (d) (heftig, intensiv) heavy ‹rain, snow, traffic, smoke, heat, cold, drinker, smoker, demand, pressure›; severe ‹frost, pain›; strong ‹impression, influence, current, resistance, dislike›; grave ‹doubt, reservations›; great ‹exaggeration, interest›; hearty ‹eater, appetite›; loud ‹applause›; (e) (Jugendspr.: großartig) great (coll.); fantastic (coll.). **2** *adv.* (a) (sehr, überaus, intensiv) (mit Adj.) very; heavily ‹indebted, stressed›; greatly ‹increased, reduced, enlarged›; strongly ‹emphasized, characterized›; badly ‹damaged, worn, affected›; (mit Verb) ‹rain, snow, drink, smoke, bleed› heavily; ‹exaggerate, impress› greatly; ‹enlarge, reduce, increase› considerably; ‹support, oppose, suspect› strongly; ‹remind› very much; ~ **wirkend** with a powerful effect *postpos.;* ~ **riechen/duften** have a strong smell/scent; ~ **gewürzt** strongly seasoned; **es ist** ~/**zu** ~ **gesalzen** it is very/too salty; ~ **erkältet sein** have a heavy *or* bad cold; **er geht** ~ **auf die Sechzig zu** (ugs.) he's pushing sixty (coll.); (b) (Jugendspr.: großartig) fantastically (coll.); (c) (Sprachw.) ~ **flektieren** *od.* **flektiert werden** be a strong noun/verb

Stark·bier *das* strong beer

Stärke /'ʃtɛrkə/ *die;* ~, ~n (a) *o. Pl.* strength; (eines Motors) power; (einer Glühbirne) wattage; (b) (Dicke) thickness; (Technik) gauge; (c) *o. Pl.* (zahlenmäßige Größe) strength; size; (d) (besondere Fähigkeit, Vorteil) strength; **jmds.** ~/**nicht jmds.** ~ **sein** be sb.'s forte/not be sb.'s strong point; (e) (von Wind, Strömung, Einfluss, Empfindung, Widerstand usw.) strength; (von Hitze, Kälte, Druck, Regenfall, Sturm, Schmerzen, Abneigung) intensity; (von Frost) severity; (von Lärm, Verkehr) volume; (f) (organischer Stoff) starch

stärken **1** *tr. V.* (a) (kräftigen, festigen; auch fig.) strengthen; boost ‹power, prestige›; ‹drink, food, etc.› fortify ‹person›; **jmds. Selbstbewusstsein** ~ (fig.) give sb.'s self-confidence a boost; (b) (steif machen) starch ‹washing etc.›. **2** *refl. V.* (sich erfrischen) fortify *or* refresh oneself. **3** *itr. V.* **ein** ~**des Mittel** a tonic

stärker, stärkst... ⇒ **stark**

Stark·strom *der* (Elektrot.) heavy current

Star·kult *der* (abwertend) star worship

---

*alte Schreibung (vgl. Hinweise auf S. xvi–xvii)

Stärkung *die;* ~, ~en (a) *o. Pl.* strengthening; **zur** ~ **trank er erst mal einen Whisky** he drank a whisky to fortify himself; (b) (Erfrischung) refreshment

Stärkungs·mittel *das* tonic

starr /ʃtar/ **1** *Adj.* (a) rigid; (steif) stiff (**vor** + *Dat.* with); fixed ‹expression, smile, stare›; ~ **vor Schreck** paralysed with terror; (b) (nicht abwandelbar) inflexible, rigid ‹law, rule, principle›; (c) (unnachgiebig) inflexible, obdurate ‹person, attitude, etc.›. **2** *adv.* (a) rigidly; (steif) stiffly; **jmdn.** ~ **ansehen** look at sb. with a fixed stare; (b) (unnachgiebig) obdurately

starren *itr. V.* (a) (starr blicken) stare (**in** + *Akk.* into, **auf, an, gegen** + *Akk.* at); **jmdm. ins Gesicht** ~: stare sb. in the face; (b) (ganz bedeckt sein) **vor/von Schmutz** *od.* **Dreck** ~: be filthy; be covered in filth; **vor Waffen** ~: be bristling with weapons

Starrheit *die;* ~: ⇒ **starr 1:** (a) rigidity; stiffness; fixity; (b) inflexibility; rigidity; (c) inflexibility; obduracy

starr-, Starr-: ~**köpfig** *Adj.* (abwertend) pig-headed; ~**sinn** *der; o. Pl.* pig-headedness; ~**sinnig** *Adj.* (abwertend) pig-headed

Start /ʃtart/ *der;* ~[e]s, ~s (a) (Sport; auch fig.) start; **einen guten** ~ **haben** get off to *or* make a good start; (b) (Sport: ~platz) start; **an den** ~ **gehen/am** ~ **sein** (fig.: teilnehmen) start; (c) (Sport: Teilnahme) participation; (d) (eines Flugzeugs) take-off; (einer Rakete) launch

start-, Start-: ~**bahn** *die* [take-off] runway; ~**bereit** *Adj.* ready to start *postpos.;* ‹aircraft› ready for take-off; (zum Aufbruch bereit) ready to set off *postpos.;* ~**block** *der; Pl.* ~**blöcke** (Sport) starting block

starten **1** *itr. V.; mit sein* (a) start; ‹aircraft› take off; ‹rocket› blast off, be launched; (b) (an einem Wettkampf teilnehmen) compete; (bei einem Rennen) start (**bei, in** + *Dat.* in); (c) (den Motor anlassen) start the engine; (d) (aufbrechen) set off; set out; (e) (beginnen) start; begin. **2** *tr. V.* start ‹race, campaign, tour, production, etc.›; launch ‹missile, rocket, satellite, attack›; start [up] ‹engine, machine, car›

Starter *der;* ~s, ~ (Sport, Kfz-W.) starter

start-, Start-: ~**erlaubnis** *die* (a) (Sport) authorization to compete; (b) (Flugw.) clearance [for take-off]; ~**hilfe** *die* (a) (Unterstützung) financial help, backing (to get a project off the ground); (b) **ich brauche** ~**hilfe** I need help to get my car started; ~**hilfe·kabel** *das* jump leads *pl.;* ~**klar** *Adj.* ready to start *postpos.;* ‹aircraft› clear *or* ready for take-off; ~**linie** *die* (Sport) starting line; ~**nummer** *die* (Sport) [start] number; ~**rampe** *die* launching pad; ~**schuss, *****schuß** *der* (Sport) **der den** ~**schuss zum 100-m-Lauf geben** fire the gun for the start of the 100 metres; **den** ~**schuss zu** *od.* **für etw. geben** (fig.) give sth. the go-ahead *or* the green light

Statement /'steitmənt/ *das;* ~s, ~s statement

Statik /'ʃtaːtɪk/ *die;* ~ (a) (Physik) statics *sing., no art.;* (b) (Bauw.) static equilibrium

Statiker *der;* ~s, ~: structural engineer [concerned with statics]

Station /ʃta'tsi̯oːn/ *die;* ~, ~en (a) (Haltestelle) stop; (b) (Bahnhof, Sender, Forschungs~, Raum~) station; (c) (Zwischen~, Aufenthalt) stopover; ~ **machen** stop over *or* off; make a stopover; (d) (Kranken~) ward; (e) (einer Entwicklung, Karriere usw.) stage

stationär /ʃtatsi̯o'nɛːɐ̯/ **1** *Adj.* (Med.) ‹admission, examination, treatment› in hospital, as an in-patient. **2** *adv.* (Med.) in hospital; **jmdn.** ~ **behandeln/aufnehmen** treat/admit sb. as an in-patient

stationieren *tr. V.* station ‹troops›; deploy ‹weapons, bombers, etc.›

Stationierung *die;* ~, ~en stationing; (von Waffen, Raketen usw.) deployment

Stations-: ~**arzt** *der* ward doctor; ~**schwester** *die* ward sister; ~**taste** *die* (Rundf.) preset [tuning] button; preset; ~**vorsteher** *der* (Eisenb.) stationmaster

statisch /'ʃtaːtɪʃ/ *Adj.* static; ‹laws› of statics; ~e **Berechnungen** (Bauw.) calculations relating to static equilibrium

Statist /ʃta'tɪst/ *der;* ~en, ~en (Theater, Film) extra; (fig.) bystander; supernumerary

Statistik /ʃtaˈtɪstɪk/ *die;* ~, ~**en** (a) *o. Pl.* (Wissenschaft) statistics *sing., no art.;* (b) (Zusammenstellung) statistics *pl.;* **eine** ~: a set of statistics

statistisch 1 *Adj.* statistical. 2 *adv.* statistically

Stativ /ʃtaˈtiːf/ *das;* ~**s**, ~**e** tripod

statt[1] /ʃtat/ 1 *Konj.* ⇨ **anstatt** 1. 2 *Präp. mit Gen.* instead of; *s. auch* **stattdessen**

statt[2] *in* an jmds./einer Sache ~: in sb.'s place/in place of sth.; instead of sb./sth.; ⇨ **auch Eid**

***Statt** ⇨ statt[2]

statt·dessen *Adv.* instead [of this]

Stätte /ˈʃtɛtə/ *die;* ~, ~**n** (geh.) place; **eine heilige/historische** ~: a holy/historic site

statt-, Statt-: ~**|finden** *unr. itr. V.* take place; ⟨*process, development*⟩ occur; ~**|geben** *unr. itr. V.* (Amtsspr.) **einer Sache** (*Dat.*) ~**geben** accede to sth.; **einer Klage** ~**geben** uphold a complaint; ~**haft** *Adj.;* *nicht attr.* permissible; ~**halter** *der* (hist.) governor

stattlich 1 *Adj.* (a) well-built; strapping ⟨*lad*⟩; (beeindruckend) imposing ⟨*figure, stature, building, etc.*⟩; impressive ⟨*trousseau, collection*⟩; (b) (beträchtlich) considerable; sizeable ⟨*part*⟩; considerable, appreciable ⟨*sum, number*⟩. 2 *adv.* impressively; splendidly

Statue /ˈʃtaːtuə/ *die;* ~, ~**n** statue

statuieren *tr. V.* (geh.) establish ⟨*principle, purpose*⟩; lay down ⟨*right, principle*⟩; *s. auch* **Exempel**

Statur /ʃtaˈtuːɐ̯/ *die;* ~, ~**en** build; **kräftig von** ~ *od.* **von kräftiger** ~ **sein** have a powerful build

Status /ˈʃtaːtʊs/ *der;* ~, ~ /ˈʃtaːtuːs/ (a) (geh.: Stand) state; (b) ([rechtliche] Stellung) status

Statut /ʃtaˈtuːt/ *das;* ~**[e]s**, ~**en** statute

Stau *der;* ~**[e]s**, ~**s** *od.* ~**e** (a) (von Wasser, Blut usw.) build-up; (b) (von Fahrzeugen) tailback (Brit.); backup (Amer.); **im** ~ **stehen** sit *or* be stuck in a jam

Staub /ʃtaup/ *der;* ~**[e]s** dust; **[im ganzen Haus]** ~ **wischen** dust [the whole house]; **[im Wohnzimmer]** ~ **saugen** vacuum *or* (Brit. coll.) hoover [the sitting room]; **[viel]** ~ **aufwirbeln** (fig. ugs.) stir things up [quite a bit] (coll.); cause [a lot of] aggro (Brit. sl.); **sich aus dem** ~**[e] machen** (fig. ugs.) make oneself scarce (coll.)

Stäubchen /ˈʃtɔypçən/ *das;* ~**s**, ~: speck of dust

stauben *itr. V.* cause dust; ⟨*person*⟩ cause *or* raise dust; **es staubt sehr** there is a lot of dust

stäuben /ˈʃtɔybn̩/ *tr. V.* etw. auf/über etw. (*Akk.*) ~: sprinkle sth. on/over sth.

staubig *Adj.* dusty

staub-, Staub-: ~**lappen** *der* duster; ~**saugen** *tr. V.* vacuum, (Brit. coll.) hoover ⟨*room, carpet, etc.*⟩; ~**sauger** *der* vacuum cleaner; Hoover (*Brit.* P); ~**tuch** *das; Pl.* ~**tücher** duster; ~**wedel** *der* feather duster; ~**wolke** *die* cloud of dust

Stau·damm *der* dam

Staude /ˈʃtaudə/ *die;* ~, ~**n** (Bot.) herbaceous perennial

stauen /ˈʃtauən/ 1 *tr. V.* dam [up] ⟨*stream, river*⟩; staunch *or* stem flow of ⟨*blood*⟩. 2 *refl. V.* ⟨*water, blood, etc.*⟩ accumulate, build up; ⟨*people*⟩ form a crowd; ⟨*traffic*⟩ form a tailback/tailbacks (Brit.) *or* (Amer.) backup/backups; (fig.) ⟨*anger*⟩ build up

Stau·mauer *die* dam [wall]

staunen /ˈʃtaunən/ *itr. V.* be amazed *or* astonished (**über** + *Akk.* at); (beeindruckt sein) marvel (**über** + *Akk.* at); **er staunte nicht schlecht, als er das hörte** (ugs.) he was flabbergasted when he heard it; **da staunst du, was?** (ugs.) quite a shock, isn't it?; shattered, eh? (coll.); ~**d** with *or* in amazement; *s. auch* **Bauklotz**

Staunen *das;* ~**s** amazement, astonishment (**über** + *Akk.* at); (staunende Bewunderung) wonderment; **jmdn. in** ~ **[ver]setzen** astonish *or* amaze sb.; **er kam aus dem** ~ **nicht mehr heraus** he couldn't get over it

Stau·see *der* reservoir

Stauung *die;* ~, ~**en** (a) (eines Bachs, Flusses) damming; (des Blutes, Wassers) stemming the flow; (das Sichstauen) build-up; (b) (Verkehrsstau) tailback (Brit.); backup (Amer.); jam

Std. *Abk.* **Stunde** hr.

Steak /steːk/ *das;* ~**s**, ~**s** steak

stechen /ˈʃtɛçn̩/ 1 *unr. itr. V.* (a) ⟨*thorn, thistle, spine, needle*⟩ prick; ⟨*wasp, bee*⟩ sting; ⟨*mosquito*⟩ bite; ⟨*fig.: sun*⟩ be scorching; **sich** (*Dat.*) **in den Finger** ~: prick one's finger; (b) (hinein~) **mit etw. in etw.** (*Akk.*) ~: stick *or* jab sth. into sth.; (c) (die Stechuhr betätigen) (bei Arbeitsbeginn) clock on; (bei Arbeitsende) clock off; (d) (Kartenspiel) ⟨*suit*⟩ be trumps; (e) (Sport) jump-off. 2 *unr. tr. V.* (a) (mit dem Messer, Schwert) stab; (mit der Nadel, mit einem Dorn usw.) prick; ⟨*bee, wasp*⟩ sting; ⟨*mosquito*⟩ bite; (Fischereiw.: fangen) spear ⟨*eel, pike*⟩; (ab~) stick ⟨*pig, calf*⟩; **sich an etw.** (*Dat.*) ~: prick oneself on sth.; (b) (hervorbringen) make ⟨*hole, pattern*⟩; (c) (unpers.) **es sticht mich in der Seite** I've got a stabbing pain in my side; (d) (herauslösen) cut ⟨*peat, turf, asparagus, etc.*⟩; pick ⟨*lettuce, mushrooms*⟩; (e) (gravieren) engrave ⟨*design etc.*⟩; (f) (Kartenspiel) take ⟨*card*⟩

Stechen *das;* ~**s**, ~ (Sport) jump-off

stechend *Adj.* penetrating, pungent ⟨*smell*⟩; penetrating ⟨*glance, eyes*⟩

Stech-: ~**karte** *die* clocking-on card; ~**mücke** *die* mosquito; gnat; ~**uhr** *die* time clock

steck-, Steck-: ~**brief** *der* description [of a/the wanted person]; (Plakat) 'wanted' poster; ~**brieflich** *Adv.* **der** ~**brieflich Gesuchte** the wanted man; **der Mörder wird** ~**brieflich gesucht** descriptions/'wanted' posters of the murderer have been circulated; ~**dose** *die* socket; power point

stecken /ˈʃtɛkn̩/ 1 *tr. V.* (a) put; **etw. in die Tasche** ~: put *or* (coll.) stick sth. in one's pocket; (b) (mit Nadeln) pin ⟨*hem, lining, etc.*⟩; pin [on] ⟨*badge*⟩; pin up ⟨*hair*⟩. 2 *regelm.* (geh. auch *unr.*) *itr. V.* be; **der Schlüssel steckt [im Schloss]** the key is in the lock; **den Schlüssel [im Schloss]** ~ **lassen** leave the key in the lock; **wo hast du denn so lange gesteckt?** (ugs.) where did you get to *or* have you been all this time?; **er steckt in Schwierigkeiten** (ugs.) he's having problems; **hinter etw.** (*Dat.*) ~ (fig. ugs.) be behind sth.; ~ **bleiben** get stuck; (fig.) ⟨*negotiations etc.*⟩ get bogged down; **es blieb in den Anfängen** ~ (fig.) it never got beyond the early stages; **das Wort blieb ihm vor Angst im Halse** *od.* **in der Kehle** ~: he was speechless with fear

stecken-, Stecken-: *~**|bleiben,***~**|lassen** ⇨ **stecken 2;** ~**pferd** *das* (a) (Spielzeug) hobby horse; (b) (Liebhaberei) hobby

Stecker *der;* ~**s**, ~: plug

Steckling /ˈʃtɛklɪŋ/ *der;* ~**s**, ~**e** cutting

Steck-: ~**nadel** *die* pin; **jmdn./etw. suchen wie eine** ~**nadel** (ugs.) search high and low for sb./sth.; ~**rübe** *die* (bes. nordd.) swede; ~**schlüssel** *der* socket spanner

Steg /ʃteːk/ *der;* ~**[e]s**, ~**e** (schmale Brücke) [narrow] bridge; (Fußgänger~) foot bridge; (Laufbrett) gangplank; (Boots~) landing stage

Steg·reif *der:* **aus dem** ~: impromptu; **er hielt aus dem** ~ **eine kleine Rede** he gave a short speech extempore *or* off the cuff

Stegreif·rede *die* impromptu *or* extempore speech

Steh·auf·männchen *das* tumbling figure; tumbler

stehen /ˈʃteːən/ 1 *unr. itr. V.; südd., österr., schweiz. mit sein* (a) stand; **er arbeitet** ~**d** *od.* **im Stehen** he works standing up; **mit jmdm./etw.** ~ **und fallen** (fig.) stand *or* fall with sb./sth.; **das Haus steht noch** the house is still standing; (b) (sich befinden) be; ⟨*upright object, building*⟩ stand; **das Verb steht am Satzende** the verb comes at the end of the sentence; **wo steht dein Auto?** where is your car [parked]?; **Schweißperlen standen auf seiner Stirn** beads of sweat stood out on his brow; **ich tue alles, was in meinen Kräften** *od.* **meiner Macht steht** I'll do everything in my power; **vor dem Bankrott** ~: be faced with bankruptcy; (c) (einen bestimmten Stand haben) **auf etw.** (*Dat.*) ~ ⟨*needle, hand*⟩ point to sth.; **das Barometer steht tief/auf Regen** the barometer is reading low/indicating rain; **die Ampel steht auf Rot** the traffic lights are [on] red; **es steht mir bis zum Hals[e]** *od.* **bis oben** *od.* **bis hier[hin]** I'm fed up to the back teeth with it (coll.); I'm sick to death of it (coll.);

der Wind steht günstig/nach Norden the wind stands fair/is from the south; **wie steht es/das Spiel?** (Sport) what's the score?; **die Chancen ~ fifty-fifty** the chances are fifty-fifty; **die Sache steht gut** things are going well; **wie steht es mit deiner Gesundheit?** how is your health?; **der Weizen steht gut** the wheat is growing well; **(d)** (einen bestimmten Kurs, Wert haben) ⟨currency⟩ stand (**bei** at); **wie steht das Pfund?** what is the rate for the pound?; how is the pound doing? (coll.); **die Aktie steht gut** the share price is high; **(e)** (nicht in Bewegung sein) be stationary; ⟨machine etc.⟩ be at a standstill; **meine Uhr steht** my watch has stopped; **~ bleiben** (anhalten) stop; ⟨traffic⟩ come to a standstill; (fig.) ⟨time⟩ stand still; (unverändert gelassen werden) stay; be left; (zurückgelassen werden) be left behind; (der Zerstörung entgehen) ⟨building⟩ be left standing; **wo sind wir ~ geblieben?** (fig.) where had we got to?; where were we?; **etw. ~ lassen** (belassen, nicht entfernen) leave sth.; (zurücklassen, vergessen) leave sth. [behind]; **alles ~ und liegen lassen** drop everything; **sich** (Dat.) **einen Bart ~ lassen** (ugs.) grow a beard; (vergessen) leave [behind]; (sich abwenden von) **jmdn. ~ lassen** (sich von jmdm. abwenden) walk off and leave sb. standing there; **(f)** (geschrieben, gedruckt sein) be; **was steht in dem Brief?** what does it say in the letter?; **in der Zeitung steht, dass …:** it says in the paper that …; **(g)** (Sprachw.: gebraucht werden) ⟨subjunctive etc.⟩ occur; be found; **mit dem Dativ ~:** be followed by or take the dative; **(h) zu jmdm./etw. ~:** stand by sb./sth.; **wie stehst du dazu?** what's your view on this?; **hinter jmdm./etw. ~** (jmdn. unterstützen) be [right] behind sb./sth.; support sb./sth.; **(i) jmdm. [gut] ~** ⟨dress etc.⟩ suit sb. [well]; **Lächeln steht dir gut** (fig.) it suits you or you look nice when you smile; **(j)** (sich verstehen) **mit jmdm. gut/schlecht ~:** be on good/bad terms or get on well/badly with sb.; **(k) auf etw.** (Akk.) **steht Gefängnis** sth. is punishable by imprisonment. **2** unr. refl. V.; südd., österr., schweiz. mit sein (ugs.) **(a)** (in bestimmten Verhältnissen leben) **sich gut/schlecht ~:** be comfortably/badly off; **(b)** (sich verstehen) **sich gut/schlecht mit jmdm. ~:** be on good/bad terms or get on well/badly with sb.

***stehen|bleiben**, ***stehen|lassen** ⇒ **stehen 1 e**
Steh-: **~kneipe** die stand-up bar; **~lampe** die standard lamp (Brit.); floor lamp (Amer.); **~leiter** die stepladder

stehlen /'ʃteːlən/ **1** unr. tr., itr. V. steal; **jmdm. etw. ~:** steal sth. from sb.; **jmdm. das Portemonnaie ~:** steal sb.'s purse. **2** unr. refl. V. steal; creep
Steh-: **~platz** der (im Theater/Stadion) standing place; (im Bus) space to stand; **es gab nur noch ~plätze** there was standing room only; **~vermögen** das; o. Pl. stamina; staying power

steif /ʃtaif/ **1** Adj. **(a)** stiff; (ugs.: erigiert) erect ⟨penis⟩; **(b)** (förmlich) stiff, formal ⟨person, greeting, style⟩; formal ⟨reception⟩; **(c)** (Seemannsspr.: stark) stiff ⟨wind, breeze⟩; **(d)** (ugs.: stark) strong ⟨coffee⟩; stiff, strong ⟨alcoholic drink⟩. **2** adv. **(a)** stiffly; **(b)** (Seemannsspr.: stark) **der Wind steht od. weht ~ aus Südost** there's a stiff wind blowing from the south-east; **(c) ~ und fest behaupten/glauben, dass …** (ugs.) swear blind/be completely convinced that …
Steig·bügel der (auch Anat.) stirrup

steigen /'ʃtaiɡn/ **1** unr. itr. V.; mit sein **(a)** ⟨person, animal, aircraft, etc.⟩ climb; ⟨mist, smoke, sun, object⟩ rise; ⟨balloon⟩ climb, rise; **Drachen ~ lassen** fly kites; **auf eine Leiter/die Leiter ~:** climb a ladder/get on to the ladder; **aus der Wanne/in die Wanne ~:** get out of/into the bath; **in den/aus dem Zug ~:** board or get on/get off or out of the train; **ins/aus dem Flugzeug ~:** board/leave the aircraft; **der Duft steigt mir in die Nase** the scent gets up my nose; s. auch **Kopf a**; **(b)** (ansteigen, zunehmen) rise (**auf** + Akk.) ⟨price, cost, salary, output⟩ increase, rise; ⟨debts, tension⟩ increase, mount; ⟨chances⟩ improve; **in jmds. Achtung ~** (fig.) go up or rise in sb.'s estimation; **(c)** (ugs.: stattfinden) be on; **morgen soll ein Fest ~:** there's to be a party tomorrow. **2** unr. tr. V.; mit sein climb ⟨stairs, steps⟩

Steiger der; ~s, ~ ▶ 85 ⌋ (Bergbau) overman
steigern 1 tr. V. **(a)** increase ⟨speed, value, sales, consumption, etc.⟩ (**auf** + Akk. to); step up ⟨demands, production, pace, etc.⟩; raise ⟨standards, requirements⟩; (verstärken) intensify ⟨fear, tension⟩; heighten, intensify ⟨effect⟩; exacerbate ⟨anger⟩; **(b)** (Sprachw.) compare ⟨adjective⟩. **2** refl. V. **(a)** ⟨confusion, speed, profit, etc.⟩ increase; ⟨pain, excitement, tension⟩ become more intense; ⟨excitement, tension⟩ mount; ⟨hate, anger⟩ grow, become more intense; ⟨costs⟩ escalate; ⟨effect⟩ be heightened or intensified; **sich od. seine Leistung[en] ~:** improve one's performance; **(b)** (hineinsteigern) **sich [mehr und mehr] in einen Erregungszustand ~:** work oneself up into [more and more of] a state [of excitement]
Steigerung die; ~, ~en **(a)** increase (Gen. in); (Verstärkung) intensification; (einer Wirkung) heightening; (des Zorns) exacerbation; (Verbesserung) improvement (Gen. in); (bes. Sport: Leistungs~) improvement [in performance]; **(b)** (Sprachw.) comparison
Steigung die; ~, ~en gradient

steil /ʃtail/ **1** Adj. **(a)** steep; upright, straight ⟨handwriting, flame⟩; meteoric ⟨career⟩; rapid ⟨rise⟩; **(b)** nicht präd. (Jugendspr. veralt.: beeindruckend) fabulous (coll.); super (coll.). **2** adv. steeply
Steil-: **~hang** der steep escarpment; **~küste** die (Geogr.) cliffs pl.; **~pass, *~paß** der (Fußball) deep [forward] pass; **~wand** die rock wall

Stein /ʃtain/ der; ~[e]s, ~e **(a)** o. Pl. stone; (Fels) rock; **ihr Gesicht war zu ~ geworden** (fig.) her face had hardened; **(b)** (losgelöstes Stück, Kern, Med., Edel~, Schmuck~) stone; (Kiesel~) pebble; **eine Uhr mit 12 ~en** a 12-jewel watch; **der ~ der Weisen** (geh.) the philosophers' stone; **ein ~ des Anstoßes** (geh.) a bone of contention; **mir fällt ein ~ vom Herzen** that's a weight off my mind; **es friert ~ und Bein** (ugs.) it's freezing hard; **~ und Bein schwören** (ugs.) swear blind; **den ~ ins Rollen bringen** (fig.) set the ball rolling; **jmdm. [die od. alle] ~e aus dem Weg räumen** (fig.) smooth sb.'s path; make things easy for sb.; **jmdm. ~e in den Weg legen** (fig.) create obstacles or make things difficult for sb.; **(c)** (Bau~) [stone] block; (Ziegel~) brick; **keinen ~ auf dem anderen lassen** not leave one stone upon another; **(d)** (Spiel~) piece; (rund, flach) counter; **bei jmdm. einen ~ im Brett haben** (fig.) be in sb.'s good books
stein-, Stein-: **~alt** Adj. aged; ancient; **~alt werden** live to a great age; **~bock** der **(a)** (Tier) ibex; **(b)** (Astrol.) Capricorn; the Goat; s. auch **Fisch c**; **~bruch** der quarry
steinern Adj. **(a)** nicht präd. stone ⟨floor, bench, etc.⟩; **(b)** (wie versteinert) stony ⟨face, features⟩
stein-, Stein-: **~fuß·boden** der stone floor; **~gut** das earthenware; **~hart** Adj. rock-hard
steinig Adj. stony
steinigen tr. V. stone ⟨person⟩
stein-, Stein-: **~kohle** die [hard] coal; **~metz** /~mɛts/ der stonemason; **~obst** das stone-fruit; **~pilz** der cep; **~reich** Adj. (ugs.) filthy rich; **~schlag** der (Fachspr.) rock fall; „Achtung **~schlag**" 'beware falling rocks'; **~topf** der earthenware pot; **~wurf** der: jmdn. mit **~würfen wegjagen** chase sb. away by throwing stones [at him/her]; **~zeit** die Stone Age; (fig.) stone age
Steiß /ʃtais/ der; ~es, ~e **(a)** (Anat.: ~bein) coccyx; **(b)** (ugs.: Gesäß) backside; behind (coll.)
Steiß·bein das ⇒ **Steiß a**
Stellage /ʃtɛ'laːʒə/ die; ~, ~n rack
Stell·dich·ein das; ~[s], ~[s] (veralt.) rendezvous; tryst (arch./literary); **sich** (Dat.) **ein ~ geben** (fig.) gather; assemble
Stelle /'ʃtɛlə/ die; ~, ~n **(a)** place; **eine schöne ~ zum Campen** a nice spot for camping; **die Truhe ließ sich nicht von der ~ rücken** the chest could not be shifted or would not budge; **an jmds. ~ treten** take sb.'s place; **ich an deiner ~ würde das nicht machen** I wouldn't do it if I were you; **ich möchte nicht an deiner ~ sein** I shouldn't like to be in your place; **auf der ~:** immediately; **er war auf der ~ tot** he died instantly; **auf der ~ treten** (ugs.), **nicht von der ~ kommen** (fig.) make

no headway; **not get anywhere; zur ~ sein** be there or on the spot; **(b)** (begrenzter Bereich) patch; (am Körper) spot; **eine kahle ~:** a bare patch; (am Kopf) a bald patch; **seine empfindliche ~** (fig.) his sensitive or sore spot; **(c)** (Passage) passage; **an anderer ~:** elsewhere; in another passage; (d) (Punkt im Ablauf einer Rede usw.) point; **an dieser/ früherer ~:** at this point or here/earlier; **eine schwache ~ in der Argumentation** (fig.) a weak point in the argument; **(e)** (in einer Rangordnung, Reihenfolge) place; **an achter ~ liegen** be in eighth place; **an erster ~ geht es hier um …:** here it is primarily a question of …; **(f)** (Math.) figure; **die erste ~ hinter** od. **nach dem Komma** the first decimal place; **(g)** (Arbeits~) job; (formeller) position; (bes. als Beamter) post; **ohne ~ sein** be unemployed; **eine freie ~:** a vacancy; **(h)** (Dienst~) office; (Behörde) authority

stellen 1 tr. V. **(a)** put; (mit Sorgfalt, ordentlich) place; (aufrecht hin~) stand; **jmdn. wieder auf die Füße ~** (fig.) put sb. back on his/her feet; **jmdn. vor eine Entscheidung ~** (fig.) confront sb. with a decision; **auf sich [selbst] gestellt sein** (fig.) be thrown back on one's own resources; **(b)** (ein~, regulieren) set ‹points, clock, scales›; set ‹clock› to the right time; **den Wecker auf 6 Uhr ~:** set the alarm for 6 o'clock; **das Radio lauter/leiser ~:** turn the radio up/down; **(c)** (bereit~) provide; produce ‹witness›; **(d)** jmdn. besser ~: ‹firm› improve sb.'s pay; **gut/schlecht gestellt** comfortably/badly off; **(e)** (auf~) set ‹trap›; lay ‹net›; **(f) kalt ~:** put ‹food, drink› in a cold place; leave ‹champagne etc.› to chill; **warm ~:** put ‹plant› in a warm place; keep ‹food› warm or hot; **(g)** (fassen, festhalten) catch ‹game›; apprehend ‹criminal›; **(h)** (aufrichten) ‹dog, horse, etc.› prick up ‹ears›; stick up ‹tail›; **(i)** (erstellen) prepare ‹horoscope, bill›; make ‹diagnosis, prognosis›; **(j)** (verblasst) put ‹question›; set ‹task, essay, topic, condition›; make ‹application, demand, request›; **jmdm. eine Frage ~:** ask sb. a question. **2** refl. V. **(a)** place oneself; **stell dich neben mich/ans Ende der Schlange/in die Reihe** come and stand by me/go to the back of the queue (Brit.) or (Amer.) line/get into line; **sich auf die Zehenspitzen ~:** stand on tiptoe; **sich gegen jmdn./etw. ~** (fig.) oppose sb./sth.; **sich hinter jmdn./etw. ~** (fig.) give sb./sth. one's backing; **(b)** sich schlafend/taub usw. ~: feign sleep/deafness etc.; pretend to be asleep/deaf etc.; **(c)** (sich ausliefern) **sich [der Polizei] ~:** give oneself up [to the police]; **(d)** (nicht ausweichen) **sich einem Herausforderer/der Presse ~:** face a challenger/the press; **sich einer Diskussion ~:** consent to take part in a discussion; **(e)** (Stellung beziehen) **sich positiv/negativ zu jmdm./etw. ~:** take a positive/negative view of sb./sth.; **sich mit jmdm. gut ~:** try to get on good terms with sb.

stellen-, Stellen-: **~angebot** das offer of a job; (Inserat) job advertisement; **~angebote** ‘situations vacant’; **~anzeige** die job advertisement; **~gesuch** das ‘situation wanted’ advertisement; **„~gesuche“** ‘situations wanted’; **~suche** die job-hunting no art.; search for a job; **auf ~suche sein** be looking for a job; be jobhunting; **~weise** Adv. in places; **~wert** der **(a)** (Math.) place value; **(b)** (fig.: Bedeutung) standing; status

Stell·platz der space; (auf einem Campingplatz) pitch; site

Stellung die; ~, ~en **(a)** position; **in gebückter ~:** in a bent posture; **die ~ der Frau in der Gesellschaft** the position or standing of women in society; **in ~ gehen** (Milit.) take up [one's] position; **[zu/gegen etw.] ~ beziehen** (fig.) take a stand [on/against sth.]; **(b)** (Posten) job; (formeller) position; (bes. als Beamter) post; **(c)** o. Pl. (Einstellung) attitude (zu to, towards); **zu etw. ~ nehmen** express one's opinion or make known one's view on sth.; **er hat zu dem Vorschlag offiziell ~ genommen** he made an official statement on the proposal

Stellungnahme die; ~, ~n opinion; (kurze Äußerung) statement; **eine ~ zu etw. abgeben** give one's opinion or views on sth.; (sich kurz zu etw. äußern) make a statement on sth.

stellungs·los Adj. unemployed; jobless

stell-, Stell-: **~vertretend 1** Adj.; nicht präd. acting; (von Amts wegen) deputy ‹minister, director, etc.›; **2** adv.

as a deputy; **~vertretend für jmdn.** deputizing for sb.; on sb.'s behalf; **~vertreter** der deputy; **der ~vertreter Christi** (kath. Rel.) the Vicar of Christ; **~werk** das (Eisenb.) signal box (Brit.); switch-tower (Amer.); (Anlage) control gear for signals and points (Brit.) or (Amer.) switches

Stelze die; ~, ~n meist Pl. stilt

stelzen itr. V.; mit sein strut; stalk

stemmen /ˈʃtɛmən/ **1** tr. V. **(a)** (hoch~) lift [above one's head]; (Gewichtheben) lift ‹weight›; **(b)** (drücken) brace ‹feet, knees› (gegen against); **die Arme in die Hüften/Seiten ~:** place one's arms akimbo; put one's hands on one's hips; **(c)** (meißeln) chisel ‹hole etc.›. **2** refl. V. **sich in die Höhe ~:** haul oneself to one's feet; **sich gegen etw. ~:** brace oneself against sth.; (fig.) resist sth. **3** itr. V. (Skisport) stem

Stempel /ˈʃtɛmpl/ der; ~s, ~ **(a)** stamp; (Post~) postmark; **einer Sache** (Dat.) **seinen ~ aufdrücken** (fig.) leave one's mark on sth.; **(b)** (Punze) hallmark; **(c)** (Bot.: Teil der Blüte) pistil

stempeln tr. V. **(a)** stamp ‹passport, form›; postmark ‹letter›; cancel ‹postage stamp›; **(b)** hallmark ‹gold, silver, ring, etc.›

***Stengel** ⇒ **Stängel**

Steno¹ /ˈʃteːno/ die; ~; meist o. Art. (ugs.) shorthand

Steno² das; ~s, ~s (ugs.) ⇒ **Stenogramm**

steno-, Steno-: **~block** /'---/ der shorthand pad; **~graf** der; ~en, ~en stenographer; **~grafie** die; ~en, ~n stenography no art.; **~grafieren** itr. V. do shorthand; **~gramm** das shorthand text; **ein ~gramm aufnehmen** take a dictation in shorthand; **~graph** usw.: ⇒ **~graf** usw.; **~typistin** die shorthand typist

Stepp·decke die quilt

Steppe /ˈʃtɛpə/ die; ~, ~n steppe

steppen¹ tr. (auch itr.) V. (nähen) backstitch

steppen² itr. V. (tanzen) tap-dance

Stepp·jacke die quilted jacket

Stepp-, *Step-: **~tanz** der tap-dance; **~tänzer** der, **~tänzerin** die tap-dancer

Sterbe-: **~bett** das death-bed; **~fall** der ⇒ **Todesfall**

sterben /ˈʃtɛrbn̩/ **1** unr. itr. V.; mit sein die; **im Sterben liegen** lie dying; **und wenn sie nicht gestorben sind, dann leben sie noch heute** and they lived happily ever after; **er ist für mich gestorben** (fig.) he's finished or he doesn't exist as far as I'm concerned; **vor Angst/Neugier ~** (ugs.) die of fright/be dying of curiosity. **2** unr. tr. V.; mit sein **den Hungertod ~:** die of starvation; starve to death; **den Heldentod ~:** die a hero's death

sterbens-, Sterbens-: **~angst** die terrible fear; **~elend** Adj. wretched; **~krank** Adj. **(a)** ⇒ **elend**; **(b)** (sehr krank) mortally ill; **~langweilig** Adj. deadly boring; **~wort, ~wörtchen** das in kein od. nicht ein ~wort od. ~wörtchen not a [single] word

Sterbe-: **~sakramente** Pl. (kath. Kirche) last rites; **~urkunde** die death certificate

sterblich Adj. mortal; s. auch **Überrest**

Sterbliche der/die; adj. Dekl. **(a)** (dichter.) mortal; **(b)** ein gewöhnlicher ~ an ordinary mortal or person

Sterblichkeit die; ~; mortality

stereo /ˈʃteːreo/ Adv. in stereo

Stereo das; ~s stereo

stereo-, Stereo-: **~anlage** die stereo [system]; **~aufnahme** die stereo recording; **~phonie** /-foˈniː/ die; ~ stereophony no art.; **~ton** der stereo sound; **~typ** /---'-/ **1** Adj. stereotyped ‹discussion, pattern, etc.›; stereotyped, stock ‹question, reply, phrase, utterance›; mechanical ‹smile›; **2** adv. in a stereotyped way

steril /ʃteˈriːl/ **1** Adj. (auch fig. abwertend) sterile. **2** adv. **(a)** (keimfrei) **~ verpackt sein** be in a sterile pack/sterile packs; **(b)** (fig. abwertend: unschöpferisch, nüchtern) sterilely

sterilisieren tr. V. sterilize

Sterling /ˈʃtɛːlɪŋ/ der; ~s, ~e: **2 Pfund ~:** £2 sterling; **einen Betrag in Pfund ~ tauschen** change a sum into sterling

Stern /ʃtɛrn/ der; ~[e]s, ~e **(a)** star; **~e sehen** (ugs.) see stars; **in den ~en stehen** (fig.) be in the lap of the gods; **(b)** (Orden, Auszeichnung) star; **ein Hotel mit fünf ∼en** a five-star hotel

Stern·bild das constellation

Sternchen das; ∼s, ∼ **(a)** [little] star; **(b)** (als Zeichen, Symbol) asterisk

Sternen·banner das Star-spangled Banner; Stars and Stripes pl.

sternen·klar Adj. starlit, starry ⟨sky, night⟩

stern-, Stern-: ∼**fahrt** die rally; ∼**förmig** Adj. star-shaped; ∼**hagel·voll** Adj. (salopp) paralytic (Brit. sl.); blotto (sl.); ∼**himmel** der starry sky; ∼**klar** Adj. ⇒ **sternenklar;** ∼**kunde** die; o. Pl. astronomy no art.; ∼**marsch** der [protest] march; ∼**schnuppe** die; ∼, ∼**n** shooting star; ∼**stunde** die (geh.) great moment; ∼**warte** die observatory; ∼**zeichen** das ⇒ **Tierkreiszeichen**

stet /ʃteːt/ Adj. (geh.) **(a)** constant ⟨goodwill, devotion, companion⟩; steady ⟨rhythm⟩; **(b)** (ständig) constant; continuous

Stethoskop /ʃtetoˈskoːp/ das; ∼s, ∼e (Med.) stethoscope

stetig /ˈʃteːtɪç/ **1** Adj. steady ⟨growth, increase, decline⟩; constant, continuous ⟨movement, vibration⟩. **2** adv. ⟨grow, increase, drop⟩ steadily; ⟨move, vibrate⟩ constantly, continuously

stets /ʃteːts/ Adv. always

Steuer¹ /ˈʃtɔʏɐ/ das; ∼s, ∼ (von Fahrzeugen) [steering-]wheel; (von Schiffen) helm; **sich ans od. hinters ∼ setzen** get behind the wheel; **das ∼ übernehmen** take over the wheel or the driving; (bei Schiffen, fig.) take over the helm; **Trunkenheit am ∼:** drunken driving; being drunk at the wheel

Steuer² die; ∼, ∼**n (a)** tax; ∼**n zahlen** (Lohn-/Einkommensteuer) pay tax; **etw. von der ∼ absetzen** set sth. off against tax; **(b)** o. Pl. (ugs.: Behörde) tax authorities pl.

steuer-, Steuer-: ∼**berater** der ▶ 85⌋ tax consultant or adviser; ∼**bord** das od. österr. der; o. Pl. (Seew., Flugw.) starboard; ∼**bord[s]** Adv. (Seew., Flugw.) to starboard; ∼**erhöhung** die tax increase; ∼**erklärung** die tax return; ∼**ermäßigung** die tax relief; ∼**frei** Adj. tax-free; free of tax pred.; ∼**freibetrag** der tax allowance; ∼**gelder** Pl. taxes; ∼**gerät** das **(a)** (Rundfunkt.) receiver; **(b)** (Elektrot.) control device or unit; ∼**gesetz** das; meist Pl. tax law; ∼**klasse** die tax category; ∼**knüppel** der control column; joystick (coll.)

steuerlich 1 Adj.; nicht präd. tax ⟨advantages, benefits, etc.⟩. **2** adv. ∼ **absetzbar** tax-deductible

steuer-, Steuer-: ∼**los** Adj. out of control; ∼**mann** der; Pl. ∼**leute** od. ∼**männer (a)** (Seew. veralt.) helmsman; steersman; **(b)** (Rudersport) cox; **Vierer mit/ohne ∼mann** coxed/coxless fours; ∼**marke** die revenue stamp; (für Hunde) licence disc

steuern 1 tr. V. **(a)** (fahren) steer; (fliegen) pilot, fly ⟨aircraft⟩; fly ⟨course⟩; **(b)** (Technik) control; **(c)** (beeinflussen) control, regulate ⟨process, activity, price, etc.⟩; steer ⟨discussion etc.⟩; influence ⟨opinion etc.⟩. **2** itr. V. **(a)** (im Fahrzeug) be at the wheel; (auf dem Schiff) be at the helm; **(b)** mit sein (Kurs nehmen, ugs.: sich hinbewegen; auch fig.) head

steuer-, Steuer-: ∼**pflicht** die; o. Pl. (Steuerw.) liability to [pay] tax; ∼**pflichtig** Adj. (Steuerw.) ⟨person⟩ liable to [pay] tax; taxable ⟨goods, assets, income, profits, etc.⟩; ∼**rad** das **(a)** steering wheel; **(b)** (Seew.) [ship's] wheel; helm; ∼**recht** das tax law; ∼**schuld** die (Steuerw.) tax[es] owing no indef. art.; (Verpflichtung) tax liability; ∼**senkung** die (Steuerw.) tax cut

Steuerung die; ∼, ∼**en (a)** (System) controls pl.; **(b)** o. Pl. ⇒ **steuern 1 a, c, d:** steering; piloting; flying; control; regulation; steering; influencing

Steven /ˈʃteːvn̩/ der; ∼s, ∼ (Vorder∼) stem; (Achter∼) stern-post

Steward /ˈstjuːɐt/ der; ∼s, ∼s ▶ 85⌋ steward

Stewardess, ⁺Stewardeß /ˈstjuːɐdɛs/ die; ∼, Stewardessen ▶ 85⌋ stewardess

---

*⁺alte Schreibung (vgl. Hinweise auf S. xvi–xvii)

StGB Abk. **Strafgesetzbuch**

stibitzen /ʃtiˈbɪtsn̩/ tr. V. (fam.) pinch (sl.); swipe (coll.)

Stich der; ∼**[e]s,** ∼**e (a)** (mit einer Waffe) stab; (fig.: böse Bemerkung) dig; gibe; **(b)** (Dornen∼, Nadel∼) prick; (von Wespe, Biene, Skorpion usw.) sting; (Mücken∼ usw.) bite; **(c)** (∼wunde) stab wound; **(d)** (beim Nähen) stitch; **(e)** (Schmerz) stabbing or shooting or sharp pain; **es gab mir einen ∼** [ins **Herz]** (fig.) I was cut to the quick; **(f)** (Kartenspiel) trick; **(g) jmdn./etw. im ∼ lassen** leave sb. in the lurch/abandon sth.; **mein Gedächtnis hat mich im ∼ gelassen** my memory has failed me; **(h)** (Fechten) hit; **(i)** (bild. Kunst) engraving; **(j)** o. Pl. (Farbschimmer) tinge; **ein ∼ ins Blaue** a tinge of blue; **(k) einen [leichten] ∼ haben** (ugs.) ⟨food, drink⟩ be off, have gone off; (salopp) ⟨person⟩ be nuts (sl.); be round the bend (coll.)

Stichel der; ∼s, ∼: graver; burin

Stichelei die; ∼, ∼**en** (ugs. abwertend) **(a)** (Bemerkung) dig; gibe; **(b)** o. Pl. **hör auf mit deiner ∼:** stop getting at me/him etc. (coll.)

sticheln itr. V. make snide remarks (coll.) **(gegen** about)

stich-, Stich-: ∼**fest** ⇒ **hiebfest;** ∼**flamme** die tongue or jet of flame; ∼**haltig,** (österr.) ∼**hältig 1** Adj. sound, valid ⟨argument, reason⟩; valid ⟨assertion, reply⟩; conclusive ⟨evidence⟩. **2** adv. **etw.** ∼**haltig begründen** back sth. with sound or valid reasons; ∼**haltigkeit,** (österr.) ∼**hältigkeit** die; ∼ ⇒ ∼**haltig:** soundness; validity; conclusiveness

Stichling /ˈʃtɪçlɪŋ/ der; ∼s, ∼e stickleback

Stich-: ∼**probe** die [random] sample; (bei Kontrollen) spot check; ∼**säge** die compass saw

stichst /ʃtɪçst/ 2. Pers. Sg. Präsens v. **stechen**

sticht /ʃtɪçt/ 3. Pers. Sg. Präsens v. **stechen**

Stich-: ∼**tag** der set date; (letzter Termin) deadline; ∼**wahl** die final or deciding ballot; run-off; ∼**wort** das **(a)** Pl. ∼**wörter** headword; (in Registern) entry; **(b)** Pl. ∼**worte** (Theater) cue; ∼**wunde** die stab wound

sticken /ˈʃtɪkn̩/ **1** tr. V. do embroidery. **2** tr. V. embroider

Stickerei die; ∼, ∼**en** (Handarb.) **(a)** (Verzierung) embroidery no pl.; embroidered pattern; **(b)** (gestickte Arbeit) piece of embroidery

stickig Adj. stuffy; stale ⟨air⟩

Stick·stoff der nitrogen

stieben /ˈʃtiːbn̩/ unr. (auch regelm.) itr. V. (geh., veralt.) **(a)** auch mit sein (auseinander wirbeln) ⟨dust, snow⟩ be thrown up in a cloud; ⟨sparks⟩ fly; ⟨water⟩ spray; **(b)** mit sein **Schnee stiebt durch die Ritzen** snow blows through the cracks; **(c)** mit sein (davoneilen) dash; **nach allen Seiten ∼:** scatter in all directions

Stief·bruder /ˈʃtiːf-/ der stepbrother; (ugs.: Halbbruder) half-brother

Stiefel /ˈʃtiːfl̩/ der; ∼s, ∼ boot

Stiefel·knecht der bootjack

stiefeln itr. V.; mit sein (ugs.) stride

stief-, Stief-: ∼**kind** das stepchild; (fig.) poor relation (fig.); ∼**mutter** die stepmother; ∼**mütterchen** das (Bot.) pansy; ∼**mütterlich 1** Adj. poor, shabby ⟨treatment⟩; **2** adv. ∼**mütterlich behandeln** treat ⟨person⟩ poorly or shabbily; neglect ⟨pet, flowers, doll, problem⟩; ∼**schwester** die stepsister; (ugs.: Halbschwester) half-sister; ∼**sohn** der stepson; ∼**tochter** die step-daughter; ∼**vater** der stepfather

stieg /ʃtiːk/ 1. u. 3. Pers. Sg. Prät. v. **steigen**

Stiege die; ∼, ∼**n (a)** (Holztreppe) [wooden] staircase; [wooden] stairs pl.; **(b)** (südd., österr.: Treppe) stairs pl.; steps pl.

Stieglitz /ˈʃtiːɡlɪts/ der; ∼es, ∼e goldfinch

stiehlst /ʃtiːlst/ 2. u. 3. Pers. Sg. Präsens v. **stehlen**

Stiel /ʃtiːl/ der; ∼**[e]s,** ∼**e (a)** (Griff) handle; (Besen∼) [broom-]stick; (für Süßigkeiten) stick; **ein Eis am ∼:** an ice-lolly (Brit.); a Popsicle (Amer. P); **(b)** (bei Gläsern) stem; **(c)** (bei Blumen) stem; stalk; (an Obst, Obstblüten usw.) stalk

Stiel·kamm der tail comb

stier 1 Adj. vacant. **2** adv. vacantly

Stier /ʃtiːɐ/ der; ∼**[e]s,** ∼**e (a)** bull; **(b)** (Astrol.) Taurus; the Bull

stieren *itr. V.* stare [vacantly] (**auf** + *Akk.* at); **vor sich hin** ~: stare [vacantly] into space

Stier-: ~**kampf** *der* bullfight; ~**kämpfer** *der* bullfighter

stieß /ʃti:s/ *1. u. 3. Pers. Sg. Prät. v.* **stoßen**

Stift¹ /ʃtɪft/ *der;* ~[**e]s,** ~**e** (a) (aus Metall) pin; (aus Holz) peg; (b) (Blei~, Bunt~, Zeichen~) pencil; (Mal~) crayon; (Schreib~) pen; (c) (ugs.: Lehrling) apprentice

Stift² *das;* ~[**e]s,** ~**e** (a) (christl. Kirche: Institution) foundation; (b) (österr.: Kloster) monastery

stiften¹ *tr. V.* (a) found, establish ⟨*monastery, hospital, prize, etc.*⟩; endow ⟨*prize, professorship, scholarship*⟩; (als Spende) donate, give (**für** to); (b) (herbeiführen) cause, create ⟨*unrest, confusion, strife, etc.*⟩; bring about ⟨*peace, order, etc.*⟩; arrange ⟨*marriage*⟩

stiften² *in* ~ **gehen** (ugs.) disappear; hop it (Brit. coll.)

***stiften|gehen** ⇒ **stiften²**

Stifter *der;* ~**s,** ~: founder; (Spender) donor

Stiftung *die;* ~, ~**en** (a) (Rechtsspr.) foundation; endowment; (b) (Anstalt) foundation; (c) (Spende) donation (*Gen.* by)

Stift·zahn *der* (Zahnmed.) post crown

Stigma /'stɪgma/ *das;* ~**s, Stigmen** *od.* ~**ta** (auch fig., kath. Kirche) stigma

Stigmatisation /stɪgmatizaˈtsi̯o:n/ *die;* ~, ~**en** stigmatization

stigmatisieren *tr. V.* stigmatize

Stigmen ⇒ **Stigma**

Stil /ʃti:l/ *der;* ~[**e]s,** ~**e** style; **in dem** ~ **ging es weiter** (ugs.) it went on in that vein

Stil·blüte *die* howler (coll.)

stilisieren *tr. V.* stylize

stilistisch 1 *Adj.* stylistic. 2 *adv.* stylistically

still /ʃtɪl/ 1 *Adj.* (a) (ruhig, leise) quiet; (ganz ohne Geräusche) silent; still; quiet, peaceful ⟨*valley, area, etc.*⟩; **sei** ~! be quiet!; **im Saal wurde es** ~: the hall went quiet; (b) (reglos) still; ~**es** [**Mineral]wasser** still [mineral] water; (c) (ohne Aufregung, Hektik) quiet ⟨*day, life*⟩; quiet, calm ⟨*manner*⟩; (d) (nicht gesprächig) quiet; (e) (wortlos) silent ⟨*reproach, grief, etc.*⟩; (f) (heimlich) secret; ~**e Reserven** (Wirtsch.) secret *or* hidden reserves; (ugs.) [secret] savings; (g) **der Stille Ozean** the Pacific [Ocean]. 2 *adv.* (a) (ruhig, leise) quietly; (geräuschlos) silently; (b) (zurückhaltend) quietly; (c) (wortlos) in silence

Stille *die;* ~ (a) (Ruhe) quiet; (Geräuschlosigkeit) silence; stillness; **in der** ~ **der Nacht** in the still of the night; (b) (Regungslosigkeit) (des Meeres) calm[ness]; (der Luft) stillness; (c) **in aller** ~ **heiraten** have a quiet wedding; **die Beerdigung fand in aller** ~ **statt** it was a quiet funeral

***Stilleben** ⇒ **Stillleben**

***stillegen** ⇒ **stilllegen**

***Stillegung** ⇒ **Stilllegung**

stillen 1 *tr. V.* (a) **ein Kind** ~: breastfeed a baby; **ich muss das Baby jetzt** ~: I must feed the baby *or* give the baby a feed now; (b) (befriedigen) satisfy ⟨*hunger, desire, curiosity*⟩; quench ⟨*thirst*⟩; still (literary) ⟨*hunger, thirst, desire*⟩; (c) (eindämmen) stop ⟨*bleeding, tears, pain*⟩; stanch ⟨*blood*⟩. 2 *itr. V.* breastfeed

still-, Still-: ~|**halten** *unr. itr. V.* (a) (sich nicht bewegen) keep *or* stay still; (b) (nicht reagieren) keep quiet; ~**leben** *das* still life; ~|**legen** *tr. V.* close *or* shut down; close ⟨*railway line*⟩; lay up ⟨*ship, vehicle, fleet*⟩; ~**legung** *die;* ~, ~**en** closure; shutdown; (von Schiff, Fahrzeug, Flotte) laying up; (einer Eisenbahnstrecke) closure; ~**schweigen** *das* (a) (Schweigen) silence; **mit** ~**schweigen** in silence; (b) (Diskretion) ~**schweigen bewahren** maintain silence; keep silent; ~**schweigend** 1 *Adj.; nicht präd.* (a) (wortlos) silent; (b) (ohne Abmachung) tacit ⟨*assumption, agreement*⟩; 2 *adv.* (a) (wortlos) in silence; (b) (ohne Abmachung) tacitly; ~|**sitzen** *unr. itr. V.* sit still; ~**stand** *der; o. Pl.* standstill; **die Entzündung/den Verkehr zum** ~**stand bringen** stop the inflammation/bring the traffic to a standstill; **die Blutung ist zum** ~**stand gekommen** the bleeding has stopped; ~|**stehen** *unr. itr. V.* (a) ⟨*factory, machine*⟩ be *or* stand idle; ⟨*traffic*⟩ be at a

standstill; ⟨*heart etc.*⟩ stop; (b) (Milit.) stand at *or* to attention; ~**gestanden!** attention!

still·vergnügt 1 *Adj.* inwardly contented. 2 *adv.* ⟨*listen, smile, etc.*⟩ with inner contentment

Still·zeit *die* lactation period

Stil·mittel *das* stylistic device

stil·voll 1 *Adj.* stylish. 2 *adv.* stylishly

Stimm-: ~**band** *das; meist Pl.* vocal cord; ~**bruch** *der:* **er ist im** ~**bruch** his voice is breaking

Stimme /'ʃtɪmə/ *die;* ~, ~**n** (a) voice; **der** ~ **der Vernunft folgen** (fig.) listen to the voice of reason; **der** ~ **des Herzens/Gewissens folgen** (fig. geh.) follow [the dictates of] one's heart/conscience; **mit stockender** ~: in a faltering voice; (b) (Meinung) voice; **die** ~**n in der Presse waren kritisch** press opinion was critical; (c) (bei Wahlen, auch Stimmrecht) vote

stimmen 1 *itr. V.* (a) (zutreffen) be right *or* correct; **stimmt es, dass ...?** is it true that ...?; **das kann unmöglich** ~: that can't possibly be right; (b) (in Ordnung sein) ⟨*bill, invoice, etc.*⟩ be right *or* correct; **stimmt so** that's all right; keep the change; **hier stimmt etwas nicht** there's something wrong here; **bei ihm stimmt es od. was nicht** (salopp) there must be something wrong with him; (c) (seine Stimme geben) vote; **mit Ja** ~: vote yes *or* in favour. 2 *tr. V.* (a) (in eine Stimmung versetzen) make; **das stimmt mich traurig** that makes me [feel] sad; (b) (Musik) tune ⟨*instrument*⟩; **eine Gitarre höher/tiefer** ~: raise/lower the pitch of a guitar

Stimmen·gewirr *das* babble of voices

Stimm·enthaltung *die* abstention

stimm·gewaltig 1 *Adj.* ⟨*singer etc.*⟩ with strong *or* powerful voice; strong, powerful ⟨*bass, contralto, etc.*⟩. 2 *adv.* ⟨*sing, speak*⟩ with *or* in a strong *or* powerful voice

stimmhaft (Sprachw.) 1 *Adj.* voiced. 2 *adv.* ~ **gesprochen werden** be voiced

stimmig *Adj.* harmonious; **die Argumentation ist [in sich (*Dat.*)]** ~: the argument is consistent

Stimm·lage *die* (a) voice; (b) (Musik) voice; register

stimm·los (Sprachw.) 1 *Adj.* voiceless; unvoiced; 2 *adv.* ~ **ausgesprochen werden** not be voiced

Stimm·recht *das* right to vote

Stimmung *die;* ~, ~**en** (a) mood; **in** ~ **sein** be in a good mood; **in** ~ **kommen** get in the mood; liven up; **jmdn. in** ~ **bringen** liven sb. up; (b) (Atmosphäre) atmosphere; (c) (öffentliche Meinung) opinion; ~ **für/gegen jmdn./etw. machen** stir up [public] opinion in favour of/against sb./sth.

stimmungs-, Stimmungs-: ~**kanone** *die* (ugs. scherzh.) entertainer who is always the life and soul of the party; ~**umschwung** *der* change of mood; ~**voll** 1 *Adj.* atmospheric; 2 *adv.* ⟨*describe, light*⟩ atmospherically; ⟨*sing, recite*⟩ with great feeling

Stimm·zettel *der* ballot paper

Stimulans /'sti:mulans/ *das;* ~, **Stimulanzien** *od.* **Stimulantia** /stimuˈlantsi̯a/ (auch fig.) stimulant

Stimuli ⇒ **Stimulus**

stimulieren *tr. V.* stimulate

Stimulus /'sti:mulʊs/ *der;* ~, **Stimuli** (Psych., fig.) stimulus (**für** to)

stink-, Stink- (salopp) stinking (sl.) ⟨*drunk, mood*⟩; terribly (coll.) ⟨*bourgeois, posh*⟩

Stink·bombe *die* stink bomb

Stinke·finger *der* (ugs.) *middle finger pointing up as a gesture of abuse, contempt, etc.;* **jmdm. den** ~ **zeigen** give sb. a one-finger salute (coll.)

stinken /'ʃtɪŋkn̩/ *unr. itr. V.* (a) (abwertend) stink; pong (coll.); **nach etw.** ~: stink *or* reek of (b), (c) (ugs.: Schlechtes vermuten lassen) **die Sache/es stinkt** it smells; it's fishy (coll.); (c) (salopp: missfallen) **die Hausarbeit stinkt mir** I'm fed up to the back teeth with housework (coll.); **mir stinkts** I'm fed up to the back teeth (coll.)

stink-, Stink-: ~**faul** *Adj.* (salopp abwertend) bone idle (coll.); ~**langweilig** (ugs.) 1 *Adj.* deadly boring; 2 *adv.* in a deadly boring way; ~**normal** (salopp) 1 *Adj.* dead (coll.) *or* boringly ordinary; 2 *adv.* in a dead ordinary way (coll.); ~**reich** *Adj.* (salopp) stinking rich (sl.); ~**tier** *das* skunk; ~**wut** *die* (salopp) towering rage; **eine** ~**wut [auf jmdn.] haben** be livid (Brit. coll.) *or* furious [with sb.]

Stipendium /ʃtipɛndjʊm/ *das;* ~**s, Stipendien** (als Auszeichnung) scholarship; (als finanzielle Unterstützung) grant

stirbst /ʃtɪːrbst/, **stirbt** *2. u. 3. Pers. Sg. Präsens v.* **sterben**

Stirn /ˈʃtɪrn/ *die;* ~, ~**en** ▶ 326⌋ forehead; brow; **jmdm./ einer Sache die ~ bieten** (fig.) stand *or* face up to sb./ sth.; **die ~ haben, etw. zu tun** (fig.) have the nerve *or* (coll.) gall to do sth.

Stirn-: ~**band** *das; Pl.* ~**bänder** headband; ~**runzeln** *das;* ~**s** frown

stob /ʃtoːp/ *1. u. 3. Pers. Sg. Prät. v.* **stieben**

stöbern /ˈʃtøːbɐn/ *itr. V.* (ugs.) rummage

stochern /ˈʃtɔxɐn/ *itr. V.* poke; **mit dem Feuerhaken im Feuer ~:** poke the fire; **im Essen ~:** pick at one's food

Stock¹ /ʃtɔk/ *der;* ~**[e]s, Stöcke** /ˈʃtœkə/ **(a)** (Ast, Spazier~) stick; (Zeige~) pointer; stick; (Takt~) baton; **steif wie ein ~:** as stiff as a poker; **am ~ gehen** walk with a stick; (ugs.: erschöpft sein) be whacked (Brit. coll.) *or* dead beat; **(b)** (Ski~) pole; stick; **(c)** (Pflanze) (Rosen~) [rose-]bush; (Reb~) vine; **(d)** (Eishockey, Hockey, Rollhockey) stick

Stock² *der;* ~**[e]s,** ~ (Etage) floor; storey; **das Haus hat vier ~:** the house is four storeys high; **im fünften ~:** on the fifth (Brit.) *or* (Amer.) sixth floor

stock-: ~**besoffen** *Adj.* (derb) pissed as a newt/as newts *pred.* (coarse); blind drunk; ~**blind** *Adj.* (ugs.) as blind as a bat *pred.* (coll.); totally blind; ~**dunkel** *Adj.* (ugs.) pitch-dark

Stöckel·schuh *der* high- *or* stiletto-heeled shoe; ~**e** high heels; high- *or* stiletto-heeled shoes

stocken *itr. V.* **(a) ihm stockte das Herz/der Atem** his heart missed *or* skipped a beat/he caught his breath; **(b)** (unterbrochen sein) ⟨*traffic*⟩ be held up, come to a halt; ⟨*conversation, production*⟩ stop; ⟨*talks negotiations, etc.*⟩ grind to a halt; ⟨*business*⟩ slacken *or* drop off; ⟨*journey*⟩ be interrupted; **die Antwort kam ~d** he/she gave a hesitant reply; **(c)** (innehalten) falter

stock-, Stock-: ~**finster** *Adj.* (ugs.) ⇒ **stockdunkel;** ~**fisch** *der* (a) stockfish; **(b)** (ugs. abwertend: Mensch) boring *or* dull old stick; ~**nüchtern** *Adj.* (ugs.) stonecold sober; ~**sauer** *Adj.; nicht attr.* (salopp) pissed off (Brit. sl.) **(auf** + *Akk.* with); ~**schirm** *der* walking-length umbrella; ~**steif** *Adj.* **1** *Adj.* extremely stiff *or* ⟨*gait*⟩; **2** *adv.* extremely stiffly; as stiff as a poker; ~**taub** *Adj.* (ugs.) stone-deaf; as deaf as a post

Stockung *die;* ~, ~**en** hold-up (Gen. in)

Stockwerk *das* ⇒ **Stock²**

Stoff /ʃtɔf/ *der;* ~**[e]s,** ~**e** **(a)** (für Textilien) material; fabric; **(b)** (Materie) substance; **(c)** *o. Pl.* (Philos.) matter; **(d)** (Thema) subject[-matter]; ~ **für einen Roman sammeln** collect material for a novel; **(e)** (Gesprächsthema) topic; **(f)** *o. Pl.* (salopp: Alkohol) booze (coll.); **(g)** *o. Pl.* (salopp: Rauschgift) stuff (sl.); dope (sl.)

Stoffel /ˈʃtɔfl/ *der;* ~**s,** ~ (ugs. abwertend) boor; churl

Stoff-: ~**wechsel** *der* metabolism; ~**wechselkrankheit** *die* ▶ 329⌋ metabolic disease

stöhnen /ˈʃtøːnən/ *itr. V.* moan; (vor Schmerz) groan

stoisch **1** *Adj.* (Philos.) Stoic; (fig.) stoic. **2** *adv.* stoically

Stola /ˈʃtoːla/ *die;* ~, **Stolen** shawl; (Pelz~) stole

Stollen /ˈʃtɔlən/ *der;* ~**s,** ~ **(a)** (Kuchen) Stollen; **(b)** (unterirdischer Gang) gallery; tunnel; **(c)** (Bergbau) gallery; **(d)** (bei Sportschuhen) stud

stolpern /ˈʃtɔlpɐn/ *itr. V.; mit sein* **(a)** stumble; trip; **ins Stolpern kommen** stumble; trip; (fig.) lose one's thread; **über jmdn. ~** (fig. ugs.) bump *or* run into sb.; **ich bin über dieses Wort gestolpert** (fig.) I was puzzled by that word; **(b)** (fig.: straucheln) come to grief, (coll.) come unstuck **(über** + *Akk.* over)

Stolper·stein *der* stumbling block; **jmdm.** ~**e in den Weg legen** put obstacles in sb.'s way

---

stolz /ʃtɔlts/ **1** *Adj.* **(a)** proud **(auf** + *Akk.* of); **(b)** (überheblich) proud[-hearted]; **(c)** (imposant) proud ⟨*building, castle, ship, etc.*⟩; **(d)** (ugs.: beträchtlich) steep (coll.), hefty (coll.) ⟨*price*⟩; tidy (coll.) ⟨*sum*⟩; ~ **wie ein Spanier** as proud as can be. **2** *adv.* proudly

Stolz *der;* ~**es** pride **(auf** + *Akk.* in); **die Rosen sind sein ganzer ~:** his roses are his pride and joy

stolzieren *itr. V.; mit sein* strut

stop /stɔp/ *Interj.* stop; (Verkehrsw.) halt

stopfen /ˈʃtɔpfn/ **1** *tr. V.* **(a)** darn ⟨*socks, coat, etc., hole*⟩; **(b)** (hineintun) stuff; **jmdm./sich etwas in den Mund ~:** stuff sth. into sb.'s/one's mouth; **(c)** (füllen) stuff ⟨*cushion, quilt, etc.*⟩; fill ⟨*pipe*⟩; **(d)** (ausfüllen, verschließen) plug, stop [up] ⟨*hole, leak*⟩; **jmdm. das Maul ~** (salopp) shut sb. up. **2** *itr. V.* **(a)** (den Stuhlgang hemmen) cause constipation; **(b)** (ugs.: sehr sättigen) be very filling

Stopf-: ~**garn** *das* darning-cotton *or* -thread; ~**nadel** *die* darning needle

Stopp *der;* ~**s,** ~ **(a)** (das Anhalten) stop; **(b)** (Einstellung) freeze (Gen. on)

Stopp·ball *der* (Badminton, [Tisch]tennis) drop shot

Stoppel /ˈʃtɔpl/ *die;* ~, ~**n;** *meist Pl.* (auch Bart~) stubble *no pl.*

Stoppel-: ~**bart** *der* (ugs.) stubble; ~**feld** *das* stubble-field

stoppelig *Adj.* stubbly

stoppen **1** *tr. V.* **(a)** stop; **den Ball ~** (Fußball) trap *or* stop the ball; **(b)** time ⟨*athlete, run*⟩. **2** *itr. V.* stop; **der Angriff stoppte** (fig.) the attack got no further *or* fizzled out

Stopper *der;* ~**s,** ~ (Fußball) centre half; stopper

Stopp·licht *das; Pl.* ~**er** stop light

stopplig *Adj.* ⇒ **stoppelig**

Stopp-: ~**schild** *das* stop sign; ~**straße** *die* side road; road with a stop sign/stop signs; ~**uhr** *die* stopwatch

Stöpsel /ˈʃtœpsl/ *der;* ~**s,** ~ **(a)** plug; (einer Karaffe usw.) stopper; **(b)** (Elektrot.) [jack-]plug

Stör /ʃtøːɐ̯/ *der;* ~**s,** ~**e** sturgeon

Storch /ʃtɔrç/ *der;* ~**[e]s, Störche** /ˈʃtœrçə/ stork; **wie ein ~ im Salat gehen** walk clumsily and stiff-leggedly

Store /ʃtoːɐ̯/ *der;* ~**s,** ~**s** net curtain

stören **1** *tr. V.* **(a)** (behindern) disturb; disrupt ⟨*court proceedings, lecture, church service, etc.*⟩; **bitte lassen Sie sich nicht ~:** please don't let me disturb you; **(b)** (stark beeinträchtigen) disturb ⟨*relation, security, law and order, peaceful atmosphere, etc.*⟩; interfere with ⟨*transmitter, reception*⟩; (absichtlich) jam ⟨*transmitter*⟩; **hier ist der Empfang oft gestört** there is often interference [with reception] here; **(c)** (missfallen) bother; **das stört mich nicht** I don't mind; that doesn't bother me; **das stört mich an ihr** that's what I don't like about her. **2** *itr. V.* **(a)** **darf ich reinkommen, oder störe ich?** may I come in, or am I disturbing you?; **entschuldigen Sie bitte, dass** *od.* **wenn ich störe** I'm sorry to bother you; **bitte nicht ~!** [please] do not disturb; **(b)** (als Mangel empfunden werden) spoil the effect; **(c)** (Unruhe stiften) make *or* cause trouble. **3** *refl. V.* **sich an jmdm./etw. ~:** take exception to sb./sth.

Störenfried /ˈʃtøːrənfriːt/ *der;* ~**[e]s,** ~**e Störer** *der;* ~**s,** ~ (abwertend) troublemaker

stornieren *tr. V.* **(a)** (Finanzw., Kaufmannsspr.) reverse ⟨*wrong entry*⟩; **(b)** (Kaufmannsspr.) cancel ⟨*order, contract*⟩

Storno /ˈʃtɔrno/ *der od. das;* ~**s, Storni** (Finanzw., Kaufmannsspr.) reversal

störrisch /ˈʃtœrɪʃ/ **1** *Adj.* stubborn; obstinate; refractory ⟨*child, horse*⟩; unmanageable ⟨*hair*⟩. **2** *adv.* stubbornly; obstinately

Stör·sender *der* jammer

Störung *die;* ~, ~**en** **(a)** disturbance; (einer Gerichtsverhandlung, Vorlesung, eines Gottesdienstes) disruption; **(b)** (Beeinträchtigung) disturbance; disruption; **eine technische ~:** a technical fault; **atmosphärische ~** (Met.) atmospheric disturbance; (Rundf.) atmospherics *pl.*

---

*alte Schreibung (vgl. Hinweise auf S. xvi–xvii)

Story /ˈstɔrɪ/ *die;* ∼, ∼s *od.* **Stories** story

Stoß /ʃtoːs/ *der;* ∼**es**, **Stöße** /ˈʃtøːsə/ **(a)** (mit der Faust) punch; (mit dem Fuß) kick; (mit dem Kopf, den Hörnern) butt; (mit dem Ellbogen) dig; **jmdm. einen kleinen** ∼ **mit dem Ellenbogen geben** nudge sb.; give sb. a nudge; **(b)** (mit einer Waffe) (Stich) thrust; (Schlag) blow; **(c)** (beim Schwimmen, Rudern) stroke; **(d)** (Stapel) pile; stack; **(e)** (beim Kugelstoßen) put; throw; **(f)** (stoßartige Bewegung) thrust; (Atem∼) gasp; **(g)** (Erd∼) tremor

Stoß·dämpfer *der* (Kfz-W.) shock absorber

Stößel /ˈʃtøːsl̩/ *der;* ∼**s**, ∼: pestle

stoß·empfindlich *Adj.* sensitive to shock *postpos.*

stoßen 1 *unr. tr. V.* **(a)** *auch itr.* (mit der Faust) punch; (mit dem Fuß) kick; (mit dem Kopf, den Hörnern) butt; (mit dem Ellbogen) dig; **jmdm.** *od.* **jmdm. in die Seite** ∼: dig sb. in the ribs; (leicht) nudge sb. in the ribs; **(b)** (hineintreiben) plunge, thrust ⟨*dagger, knife*⟩; push ⟨*stick, pole*⟩; **(c)** (stoßend hervorbringen) knock, bang ⟨*hole*⟩; **(d)** (schleudern) push; **die Kugel** ∼: (beim Kugelstoßen) put the shot; (beim Billard) strike the ball; **(e)** (zer∼) pound ⟨*sugar, cinnamon, pepper*⟩. 2 *unr. itr. V.* **(a)** *mit sein* (auftreffen) bump ⟨**gegen** into⟩; **(b)** *mit sein* (begegnen) **auf jmdn.** ∼: bump or run into sb.; **(c)** *mit sein* (entdecken) **auf etw.** (*Akk.*) ∼: come upon or across sth.; **auf Erdöl** ∼: strike oil; **auf Ablehnung** ∼ (fig.) meet with disapproval; **(d)** *mit sein* **zu jmdm.** ∼ (jmdn. treffen) meet up with sb.; (sich jmdm. anschließen) join sb.; **(e)** *mit sein* (zuführen) **auf etw.** (*Akk.*) ∼: ⟨*path, road*⟩ lead [in]to sth.; **(f)** (grenzen) **an etw.** (*Akk.*) ∼ ⟨*room, property, etc.*⟩ be [right] next to sth. 3 *unr. refl. V.* bump or knock oneself; **ich habe mich am Kopf gestoßen** I bumped or banged my head; **sich** (*Dat.*) **den Kopf blutig** ∼: bang one's head and cut it; **sich an etw.** (*Dat.*) ∼ (fig.) object to or take exception to sth.

Stoß-: ∼**gebet** *das* quick prayer; ∼**seufzer** *der* heartfelt groan; ∼**stange** *die* bumper

stößt /ʃtøːst/ *2. od. 3. Pers. Sg. Präsens v.* **stoßen**

stoß-, Stoß-: ∼**verkehr** *der; o. Pl.* rush hour traffic; ∼**waffe** *die* thrust weapon; ∼**weise** *Adv.* **(a)** (ruckartig) spasmodically; ⟨*breathe*⟩ spasmodically, jerkily; **(b)** (in Stapeln) by the pile; in piles; ∼**zahn** *der* tusk

stottern /ˈʃtɔtɐn/ 1 *itr. V.* stutter; stammer; **sie stottert stark** she has a strong or bad stutter or stammer; **ins Stottern kommen** *od.* **geraten** start stuttering or stammering. 2 *tr. V.* stutter [out]; stammer [out]

Stövchen /ˈʃtøːfçən/ *das;* ∼**s**, ∼: [teapot *etc.*] warmer

Str. *Abk.* **Straße** St./Rd.

stracks /ʃtraks/ *Adv.* **(a)** (direkt) straight; **(b)** (sofort) straight away

straf-, Straf-: ∼**anstalt** *die* penal institution; prison; ∼**arbeit** *die* imposition (Brit.); ∼**bank** *die; Pl.* ∼**bänke** (Eishockey, Handball) penalty bench; ∼**bar** *Adj.* punishable; **das ist** ∼**bar** that is a punishable offence; **sich** ∼**bar machen** make oneself liable to prosecution

Strafe /ˈʃtraːfə/ *die;* ∼, ∼**n** punishment; (Rechtsspr.) penalty; (Freiheits∼) sentence; (Geld∼) fine; **sie empfand die Arbeit als** ∼: she found the work a real drag or (coll.) bind; **etw. unter** ∼ **stellen** make sth. punishable; **zur** ∼: as a punishment

strafen *tr. V.* punish; **jmdn.** ∼**d ansehen** give sb. a reproachful look; **jmdn. mit Verachtung** ∼: treat sb. with contempt as a punishment; **mit ihm sind wir gestraft** he is a real pain; *s. auch* **Lüge**

Straf-: ∼**entlassene** *der/die; adj. Dekl.* ex-convict; ex-prisoner; ∼**erlass**, ***∼**erlaß** *der* (Rechtsw.) remission [of a/the sentence]

straff /ʃtraf/ 1 *Adj.* **(a)** (fest, gespannt) tight, taut ⟨*rope, lines, etc.*⟩; firm ⟨*breasts, skin*⟩; erect ⟨*posture, figure*⟩; tight ⟨*rein[s]*⟩; **(b)** (energisch) tight ⟨*organization, planning, etc.*⟩; strict ⟨*discipline, leadership, etc.*⟩. 2 *adv.* **(a)** (fest, gespannt) **[zu]** ∼ **sitzen** ⟨*clothes*⟩ be [too] tight; ∼ **zurückgekämmtes Haar** hair combed back tightly; **(b)** (energisch) tightly, strictly ⟨*organized, planned, etc.*⟩

straf·fällig *Adj.* ∼ **werden** commit a criminal offence; **die Zahl der Straffälligen** the number of offenders

straffen 1 *tr. V.* **(a)** (spannen) tighten; **diese Creme strafft die Haut** this cream firms the skin; **(b)** (raffen)

tighten up ⟨*text, procedure, organization, etc.*⟩. 2 *refl. V.* ⟨*person*⟩ straighten oneself, draw oneself up; ⟨*rope etc.*⟩ tighten; ⟨*body, back*⟩ stiffen; ⟨*posture, bearing*⟩ straighten

straf-, Straf-: ∼**frei** *Adj.* ∼**frei ausgehen** go unpunished; **get off** [scot-]free (coll.); ∼**freiheit** *die; o. Pl.* exemption from punishment; ∼**gefangene** *der/die* prisoner; ∼**gericht** *das* (fig.) judgement; **ein** ∼**gericht des Himmels** divine judgement; ∼**gesetz** *das* criminal or penal law; ∼**gesetz·buch** *das* criminal or penal code; ∼**kolonie** *die* penal colony

sträflich /ˈʃtrɛːflɪç/ 1 *Adj.* criminal. 2 *adv.* criminally

Sträfling /ˈʃtrɛːflɪŋ/ *der;* ∼**s**, ∼**e** prisoner

straf-, Straf-: ∼**mandat** *das* [parking, speeding, *etc.*] ticket; ∼**maß** *das* sentence; ∼**minute** *die* **(a)** (bes. Eishockey, Handball) minute of penalty time; **(b)** (Rennsport, Springreiten, Biathlon, usw.) penalty minute; ∼**porto** *das* surcharge; ∼**predigt** *die* (ugs.) lecture; ∼**punkt** *der* (Sport) penalty point; ∼**raum** *der* (bes. Fußball) penalty area; ∼**register** *das* criminal records *pl.;* ∼**richter** *der* (Rechtsw.) criminal judge; ∼**stoß** *der* (Fußball) ⇒ **Elfmeter;** ∼**tat** *die* criminal offence; ∼**täter** *der* offender; ∼**verfahren** *das* criminal proceedings *pl.;* ∼**versetzen** *tr. V.* transfer for disciplinary reasons; ∼**würdig** *Adj.* (Rechtsw.) punishable; ∼**zettel** *der* (ugs.) ⇒ ∼**mandat**

Strahl /ʃtraːl/ *der;* ∼**[e]s**, ∼**en** **(a)** (Licht, fig.) ray; (von Scheinwerfern, Taschenlampen) beam; **(b)** (Flüssigkeit) jet; **(c)** (Math., Phys.) ray

strahlen *itr. V.* **(a)** shine; **bei** ∼**dem Wetter** in glorious sunny weather; ∼**d weiß** sparkling white; **(b)** (glänzen) sparkle; **(c)** (lächeln) beam ⟨**vor** + *Dat.* with⟩; **er strahlte über das ganze Gesicht** he was beaming all over his face; **(d)** (Physik) radiate; emit rays

strahlen-, Strahlen-: ∼**belastung** *die* radioactive contamination; ∼**förmig** 1 *Adj.* radial; 2 *adv.* radially; ∼**schutz** *der* radiation protection; ∼**unfall** *der* radiation accident

Strahl·triebwerk *das* jet engine

Strahlung *die;* ∼, ∼**en** radiation

Strähne /ˈʃtrɛːnə/ *die;* ∼, ∼**n** **(a)** (Haare) strand; **eine graue** ∼: a grey streak; **(b)** (fig.: Zeitspanne) streak

strähnig 1 *Adj.* straggly ⟨*hair*⟩. 2 *adv.* in strands

stramm /ʃtram/ 1 *Adj.* **(a)** (straff) tight, taut ⟨*rope, line, etc.*⟩; tight ⟨*clothes*⟩; **(b)** (kräftig) strapping ⟨*girl, boy*⟩; sturdy ⟨*legs, body*⟩; **(c)** (gerade) upright, erect ⟨*posture, etc.*⟩; **(d)** (energisch) strict ⟨*discipline*⟩; strict, staunch ⟨*Marxist, Catholic, etc.*⟩; brisk ⟨*step*⟩. 2 *adv.* **(a)** (straff) tightly; **die Hose saß ziemlich** ∼: the trousers were rather tight; **(b)** (kräftig) sturdily ⟨*built*⟩; **(c)** (energisch) strictly; strictly, staunchly ⟨*Marxist, Catholic, etc.*⟩; ⟨*bring up*⟩ strictly; ⟨*hold out*⟩ resolutely, (d) (ugs.: zügig) ⟨*work*⟩ hard; ⟨*walk, march*⟩ briskly; ⟨*drive*⟩ fast, hard

stramm|stehen *unr. itr. V.* stand to or at attention

Strampel·höschen *das,* **Strampel·hose** *die* rompers *pl.;* romper suit; playsuit

strampeln /ˈʃtrampl̩n/ *itr. V.* **(a)** ⟨*baby*⟩ kick [his/her feet] (coll.) wave his/her arms about]; **(b)** *mit sein* (ugs.: mit dem Rad) pedal; **(c)** (ugs.: sich sehr anstrengen) sweat; struggle

Strampler *der;* ∼**s**, ∼: ⇒ **Strampelhöschen**

Strand /ʃtrant/ *der;* ∼**[e]s**, **Strände** /ˈʃtrɛndə/ beach; (geh. veralt.: Meeresufer) shore; strand; **am** ∼: on the beach

Strand·bad *das* bathing beach (*on river, lake*)

stranden *itr. V.; mit sein* **(a)** (festsitzen) ⟨*ship*⟩ run aground, (fig.) be stranded; **(b)** (geh.: scheitern) fail

Strand-: ∼**gut** *das; o. Pl.* flotsam and jetsam; ∼**hotel** *das* beach hotel; ∼**kleid** *das* beach dress; ∼**korb** *der* basket chair; ∼**promenade** *die* promenade

Strang /ʃtraŋ/ *der;* ∼**[e]s**, **Stränge** /ˈʃtrɛŋə/ **(a)** (Seil) rope; **jmdn. zum Tod durch den** ∼ **verurteilen** (geh.) sentence sb. to be hanged; **(b)** (von Wolle, Garn usw.) hank; skein; **(c)** (Nerven∼, Muskel∼, Sehnen∼) cord; **(d)** (Leine) trace; **über die Stränge schlagen** (ugs.) kick over the traces; *s. auch* **ziehen** 2 a

strangulieren /ʃtraŋguˈliːrən/ *tr. V.* strangle

Strapaze /ʃtraˈpaːtsə/ *die;* ∼, ∼**n** strain *no pl.*

strapazieren 1 *tr. V.* be a strain on ⟨*person, nerves*⟩; **die tägliche Rasur strapaziert die Haut** shaving daily is hard on the skin; **die Reise würde ihn zu sehr ~:** the journey would be too much [of a strain] for him; **jmds. Geduld ~** (fig.) tax sb.'s patience. **2** refl. V. strain or tax oneself

strapazier·fähig Adj. hard-wearing ‹clothes, shoes›; hard-wearing, durable ‹material›

strapaziös /ʃtrapa'tsiøːs/ Adj. wearing

Straps /ʃtraps/ der; ~es, ~e suspender

Straße /'ʃtraːsə/ die; ~, ~n ▶583| **(a)** (in Ortschaften) street; road; (außerhalb) road; **auf offener ~:** in [the middle of] the street; **Verkauf über die ~:** take away sales pl.; (von alkoholischen Getränken) off-licence sales pl.; **mit Prostituierten kann man hier die ~n pflastern** (ugs.) the place is full of prostitutes (coll.); **jmdn. auf die ~ setzen** od. **werfen** (ugs.) (aus einer Stellung) sack sb. (coll.); give sb. the sack (coll.); (aus einer Wohnung) turn sb. out on to the street; **auf der ~ liegen** od. **sitzen** od. **stehen** (ugs.) (arbeitslos sein) be out of work; (ohne Wohnung sein) be on the streets; **auf die ~ gehen** (ugs.) (demonstrieren) take to the streets; (der Prostitution nachgehen) go on or walk the streets; **(b)** (Meerenge) strait[s pl.]

Straßen·bahn die tram (Brit.); streetcar (Amer.)

Straßen·bahn-: ~**halte·stelle** die tram stop (Brit.); ~**linie** die tram route (Brit.); ~**schaffner** der tram conductor (Brit.)

Straßen-: ~**bau** der; o. Pl. road building no art.; road construction no art.; ~**ecke** die street corner; ~**glätte** die slippery road surface; ~**graben** der ditch [at the side of the road]; ~**händler** der street trader; ~**kampf** der **(a)** street fight; street battle; **(b)** o. Pl. (Taktik, Strategie) streetfighting; ~**karte** die road map; ~**kreuzung** die crossroads sing.; ~**laterne** die street lamp; ~**musikant** der street musician; busker; ~**rennen** das (Rennsport) road race; ~**sammlung** die street collection; ~**schild** das street-name sign; ~**schlacht** die street battle; ~**schuh** der walking-shoe; ~**seite** die side of the street/road; (eines Gebäudes) street side; ~**sperre** die roadblock; ~**überführung** die (für Fußgänger) footbridge; (für Fahrzeuge) road bridge; ~**unterführung** die (für Fußgänger) subway; (für Fahrzeuge) underpass; ~**verkäufer** der street vendor; ~**verkehr** der traffic

Strategie /ʃtrate'giː/ die; ~, ~n strategy

strategisch 1 Adj. strategic. **2** adv. strategically

Strato·sphäre /ʃtrato-/ die stratosphere

sträuben /'ʃtrɔybn̩/ **1** tr. V. ruffle [up] ‹feathers›; bristle ‹fur, hair›. **2** refl. V. **(a)** ‹hair, fur› bristle, stand on end; ‹feathers› become ruffled; **(b)** (sich widersetzen) resist; **sich ~, etw. zu tun** resist doing sth.; **sie hat sich mit Händen und Füßen gegen die Versetzung gesträubt** she resisted the transfer with all her might

Strauch /ʃtraux/ der; ~[e]s, **Sträucher** /'ʃtrɔyçɐ/ shrub

straucheln /'ʃtrauxl̩n/ itr. V.; mit sein (geh.) **(a)** (stolpern) stumble; **(b)** (scheitern) fail; **(c)** (straffällig werden) go astray

Strauß[1] /ʃtraus/ der; ~es, **Sträuße** /'ʃtrɔysə/ bunch of flowers; (bes. als Geschenk) bouquet [of flowers]; (von kleinen Blumen) posy

Strauß[2] der; ~es, ~e (Vogel) ostrich

Strebe /'ʃtreːbə/ die; ~, ~n brace; strut

streben itr. V. **(a)** mit sein (hinwollen) make one's way briskly; **er strebte zur Tür** he made briskly for the door; **die Partei strebt an die Macht** the party is reaching out for power; **(b)** (trachten) strive (nach for); **danach ~, etw. zu tun** strive to do sth.

Strebe·pfeiler der buttress

Streber der; ~s, ~, **Streberin** die; ~, ~nen (abwertend) over-ambitious or pushing or (coll.) pushy person; (in der Schule) swot (Brit. sl.); grind (Amer. sl.)

strebsam Adj. ambitious and industrious

Strebsamkeit die; ~: ambition and industriousness

Strecke /'ʃtrɛkə/ die; ~, ~n **(a)** (Weg~) distance; **auf der ~ bleiben** (ugs.) fall by the wayside; **(b)** (Abschnitt, Route) route; (Eisenbahn~) line; **der Zug hielt auf freier** od. **offener ~:** the train stopped between stations; **(c)**

(Sport) distance; **die Läufer gehen auf die ~:** the runners are setting off; **(d)** (Geom.) line segment; **(e)** (Jägerspr.) **ein Tier zur ~ bringen** bag or kill an animal; **jmdn. zur ~ bringen** (fig.) hunt sb. down

strecken 1 tr. V. **(a)** (gerade machen) stretch ‹arms, legs›; **(b)** (dehnen) stretch [out] ‹arms, legs, etc.›; **(c)** (lehnen) stick (coll.); **den Kopf aus dem Fenster ~:** stick one's head out of the window (coll.); **(d)** (größer, länger, breiter machen) stretch; hammer/roll out ‹metal›; **(e)** (verdünnen) thin down; **(f)** (rationieren) eke out ‹provisions, fuel, etc.›. **2** refl. V. stretch out

Strecken·netz das route network; (Eisenbahnw.) rail network

strecken·weise Adv. in places; (fig.: zeitweise) at times

Streetball /'striːtbɔːl/ der; ~s streetball

Streich /ʃtraiç/ der; ~[e]s, ~e **(a)** (geh.: Hieb) blow; **auf einen ~** (veralt.) at one blow; (fig.) at one fell swoop; at one go; **(b)** (Schabernack) trick; prank; **jmdm. einen ~ spielen** play a trick on sb.; **mein Gedächtnis hat mir wieder einen ~ gespielt** my memory has been playing tricks on me again

streicheln /'ʃtraiçl̩n/ tr. (auch itr.) V. stroke; (liebkosen) stroke; caress

streichen 1 unr. tr. V. **(a)** stroke; **(b)** (an~) paint; „**frisch gestrichen**" 'wet paint'; **(c)** (wegstreifen) sweep ‹crumbs etc.›; **sich** (Dat.) **das Haar aus der Stirn ~:** push or smooth the hair back from one's forehead; **(d)** (drücken) **Kitt in die Fugen ~:** press putty into the joints; **Tomaten durch ein Sieb ~:** rub or press tomatoes through a sieve; **(e)** (auftragen) spread ‹butter, jam, ointment, etc.›; **(f)** (be~) **ein Brötchen [mit Butter]/mit Honig ~:** butter a roll/spread honey on a roll; **(g)** (aus~, tilgen) delete; cross out; cancel ‹train, flight›; **jmdn. von der Liste ~:** cross sb. off the list; **Nichtzutreffendes bitte ~!** please delete as appropriate or applicable; **(h)** (Rudern) **die Riemen ~:** back water. **2** unr. itr. V. **(a)** stroke; **jmdm. durch die Haare/über den Kopf ~:** run one's fingers through sb.'s hair/stroke sb.'s head; **(b)** (an~) paint; **(c)** mit sein (umhergehen) wander

Streicher der; ~s, ~ (Musik) string-player; **die ~:** the strings

Streich·holz das match; (als Spielzeug) matchstick

Streichholz·schachtel die matchbox

Streich-: ~**instrument** das string[ed] instrument; ~**käse** der cheese spread; ~**orchester** das string orchestra; ~**quartett** das string quartet

Streichung die; ~, ~en **(a)** (Tilgung) deletion; (Kürzung) cutting no indef. art.; **(b)** (gestrichene Stelle) deletion; (Kürzung) cut

Streife die; ~, ~n patrol; **auf ~ gehen/sein** go/be on patrol

streifen 1 tr. V. **(a)** touch; brush [against]; ‹shot› graze; **jmdn. am Arm/an der Schulter ~:** touch sb. on the arm or brush against sb.'s arm/touch sb. on the shoulder; **mit dem Auto eine Mauer ~:** scrape a wall with the car; **jmdn. mit einem Blick ~** (fig.) glance fleetingly at sb.; (fig.) touch [up]on ‹problem, subject, etc.›; **(c)** **den Ring auf den/vom Finger ~:** slip the ring on/off one's finger; **die Ärmel nach oben ~:** pull/push up one's sleeves; **die Butter vom Messer ~:** wipe the butter off the knife; **sich** (Dat.) **die Kapuze/den Pullover über den Kopf ~:** pull the hood/slip the pullover over one's head. **2** itr. V. mit sein **durch die Wälder ~:** roam the forests

Streifen der; ~s, ~ **(a)** (Linie) stripe; (auf der Fahrbahn) line; **ein heller ~ am Horizont** a streak of light on the horizon; **(b)** (Stück, Abschnitt) strip; (Speck~) rasher; **(c)** (ugs.: Film) film

Streifen-: ~**dienst** der patrol duty; ~**wagen** der patrol car

streifig Adj. streaky

Streif-: ~**licht** das; Pl. ~**lichter** streak of light; **ein ~licht auf etw.** (Akk.) **werfen** (fig.) highlight sth.; ~**schuss, ***~**schuß** der grazing shot; (Wunde) graze; ~**zug** der expedition; (fig.) expedition; journey; (eines Tieres) prowl

---

Streik /ʃtraik/ *der;* ~[e]s, ~s strike; **in den ~ treten** come out *or* go on strike; **mit ~ drohen** threaten to strike; threaten strike action; *s. auch* **wild 1 b**

Streik·brecher *der* strike-breaker; blackleg (derog.); scab (derog.)

streiken *itr. V.* (a) strike; be on strike; (in den Streik treten) come out *or* go on strike; strike; (b) (ugs.: nicht mitmachen) go on strike; strike; (c) (ugs.: nicht funktionieren) pack up (coll.); **der Kühlschrank streikt** the fridge has packed up (coll.)

Streikende *der/die; adj. Dekl.* striker

Streik-: ~**posten** *der* picket; ~**recht** *das* right to strike

Streit /ʃtrait/ *der;* ~[e]s; (Zank) squabble; quarrel; (Auseinandersetzung) dispute; argument; ~ **anfangen** start a quarrel *or* an argument; **mit jmdm.** ~ **bekommen** get into an argument *or* a quarrel with sb.

Streit·axt *die* battleaxe

streit·bar *Adj.* (geh.) (a) pugnacious; (b) (veralt.: tapfer) brave; valiant

streiten *unr. itr., refl. V.* quarrel; argue; (sich zanken) squabble; quarrel; (sich auseinander setzen) argue; have an argument; **die Erben stritten [sich] um den Nachlass** the heirs argued *or* fought over *or* disputed the estate; **darüber lässt sich ~:** one can argue about that; that's a debatable point

Streit-: ~**frage** *die* disputed question *or* issue; ~**gespräch** *das* debate; disputation

streitig *Adj.* disputed ‹question, issue›; **jmdm. jmdn./ etw. ~ machen** dispute sb.'s right to sth./sth.

Streitigkeit *die;* ~, ~**en** *meist Pl.* (a) quarrel; argument; (b) (Streitfall) dispute

streit-, Streit-: ~**kräfte** *Pl.* armed forces; ~**macht** *die; o. Pl.* (veralt.) forces *pl.;* ~**süchtig** *Adj.* quarrelsome

streng /ʃtrɛŋ/ **1** *Adj.* (a) (hart) strict ‹*teacher, parents, upbringing, principle*›; severe ‹*punishment*›; stringent, strict ‹*rule, regulation, etc.*›; stringent ‹*measure*›; rigorous ‹*examination, check, test, etc.*›; stern ‹*reprimand, look*›; (b) *nicht präd.* (strikt) strict ‹*order, punctuality, diet, instruction, Catholic*›; absolute ‹*discretion*›; complete ‹*rest*›; (c) *nicht präd.* (schnörkellos) austere, severe ‹*cut, collar, style, etc.*›; severe ‹*hairstyle*›; (d) (herb) severe ‹*face, features, etc.*›; (e) (durchdringend) pungent, sharp ‹*taste, smell*›; (f) (rauh) severe ‹*winter*›; sharp, severe ‹*frost*›. **2** *adv.* (a) (hart) ‹*mark, judge, etc.*› strictly, severely; ‹*punish*› severely; ‹*look, reprimand*› sternly; ~ **durchgreifen** take rigorous action; (b) (strikt) strictly; ~ **verboten** strictly prohibited; ~ **genommen** strictly speaking; (c) (schnörkellos) **ein ~ geschnittenes Kostüm** a severe suit; (d) (durchdringend) ‹*smell*› strongly

Strenge *die;* ~ (a) ⇒ **streng a:** strictness; severity; stringency; rigour; sternness; (b) (Striktheit) strictness; (c) (von [Gesichts]zügen) severity; (d) (von Geruch, Geschmack) pungency; sharpness; (e) ⇒ **streng f:** severity; sharpness; (f) (Schnörkellosigkeit) austerity; severity

streng-: ***~**genommen** ⇒ **streng 2 b;** ~**gläubig** *Adj.* strict

strengstens /ʃtrɛŋstn̩s/ *Adv.* [most] strictly

Stress, *Streß /ʃtrɛs/ *der;* **Stresses, Stresse** stress; **im ~ sein** (ugs.) be under stress

stressen *tr. V.* (ugs.) **jmdn.** ~**:** put sb. under stress; **vollkommen gestresst sein** be under an enormous amount of stress

stressig *Adj.* (ugs.) stressful

Stretch /ʃtrɛtʃ/ *der;* ~[e]s, ~**es** stretch fabric *or* material

Streu /ʃtrɔy/ *die;* ~, ~**en** straw

streuen *tr. V.* (a) spread ‹*manure, sand, grit*›; sprinkle ‹*salt, herbs, etc.*›; strew, scatter ‹*flowers*›; (fig.) spread ‹*rumour*›; **weit gestreut** (fig.) scattered *or* spread over a wide area; (b) (auch itr.) (mit Streugut) **die Straßen [mit Sand/Salz]** ~**:** grit/salt the roads; put grit/salt down on the roads

streunen *itr. V.; meist mit sein* (oft abwertend) wander *or* roam about *or* around; ~**de Hunde** stray dogs; **durch die Straßen** ~**:** roam *or* wander the streets

Streusel *der od. das;* ~**s,** ~ streusel

Streusel·kuchen *der* streusel cake

strich /ʃtrɪç/ *1. u. 3. Pers. Sg. Prät. v.* **streichen**

Strich *der;* ~[e]s, ~**e** (a) (Linie) line; (Gedanken~) dash; (Schräg~) diagonal; slash; (Binde~, Trennungs~) hyphen; (Markierung) mark; **keinen ~ tun** *od.* **machen** *od.* **arbeiten** not do a stroke *or* a thing; **jmdm. einen ~ durch die Rechnung/durch etw.** (*Akk.*) **machen** (ugs.) mess up *or* wreck sb.'s plans/mess up sb.'s plans for sth.; **unter dem ~:** at the end of the day; all things considered; **unter dem ~ sein** (ugs.) not be up to scratch; be below par; (b) *o. Pl.* **der ~** (salopp) (Prostitution) [street] prostitution; street-walking; (Gegend) the red-light district; **auf den ~ gehen** walk the streets; (c) (streichende Bewegung) stroke; (d) *o. Pl.* (Pinselführung) strokes *pl.;* (e) *o. Pl.* (Bogen~) bowing *no indef. art.;* (f) *o. Pl.* (Haar~, Fell~) lie; (eines Teppichs) pile; (von Samt *o.* ä.) nap; **gegen den/mit dem ~ bürsten** brush ‹*hair, fur*› the wrong/right way; **jmdm. gegen den ~ gehen** (ugs.) go against the grain [with sb.]; **nach ~ und Faden** (ugs.) good and proper (coll.); well and truly

stricheln /ʃtrɪçln̩/ *tr. V.* (a) (zeichnen) sketch in [with short lines]; **eine gestrichelte Linie** a broken line; (b) (schraffieren) hatch

strich-, Strich-: ~**junge** *der* (salopp) [young] male prostitute; ~**mädchen** *das* (salopp) street-walker; hooker (Amer. sl.); ~**punkt** *der* semicolon; ~**weise** (bes. Met.) **1** *Adv.* ‹*rain etc.*› in places; **2** *adj.; nicht präd.* in places *postpos.;* local

Strick /ʃtrɪk/ *der;* ~[e]s, ~**e** (a) cord; (Seil) rope; **jmdm. aus etw. einen ~ drehen** (fig.) use sth. against sb.; **da kann ich mir ja gleich einen ~ nehmen** *od.* **kaufen!** I might as well end it all now; *s. auch* **reißen 2 a; ziehen 2 a;** (b) (fam.: Schlingel) rascal

stricken *tr., itr. V.* knit

Strickerei *die;* ~, ~**en** (a) *o. Pl.* (Tätigkeit) knitting; (b) (Produkt) piece of knitting

Strick-: ~**jacke** *die* cardigan; ~**leiter** *die* rope ladder; ~**muster** *das* knitting pattern; (fig.) formula; ~**nadel** *die* knitting needle; ~**waren** *Pl.* knitwear *sing.;* ~**zeug** *das* knitting

Striegel /ʃtriːgl̩/ *der;* ~**s,** ~**:** curry-comb

striegeln *tr. V.* groom ‹*horse*›; **gestriegelt und gebügelt** (fig.) all spruced up

Strieme /ʃtriːmə/ *die;* ~, ~**n, Striemen** *der;* ~**s,** ~**:** weal

strikt /ʃtrɪkt/ **1** *Adj.* strict; exact ‹*opposite*›. **2** *adv.* strictly; **ich bin ~ dagegen** I am totally opposed to it

Strippe /ʃtrɪpə/ *die;* ~, ~**n** (ugs.) string; **an der ~ hängen** (fig.) be on the phone (coll.); (dauernd) hog the phone (coll.); **jmdn. an der ~ haben/an die ~ kriegen** (fig.) have sb./get sb. on the phone (coll.) *or* line

strippen *itr. V.* (ugs.) do striptease; strip

Stripperin *die;* ~, ~**nen** ▸ 85◂ (ugs.) stripper

Striptease /ʃtrɪptiːs/ *der od. das;* ~**:** striptease

Striptease·tänzerin *die* ▸ 85◂ striptease dancer

stritt /ʃtrɪt/ *1. u. 3. Pers. Sg. Prät. v.* **streiten**

strittig *Adj.* contentious ‹*point, problem*›; disputed ‹*territory*›; ‹*question*› in dispute, at issue; ~ **ist nur, ob …:** the only point at issue is whether …

Stroh /ʃtroː/ *das;* ~[e]s straw; **mit ~ gedeckt** ‹*roof, cottage*› thatched with straw

stroh-, Stroh-: ~**blume** *die* (a) (Immortelle) immortelle; everlasting [flower]; (b) (Korbblütler) straw-flower; ~**dumm** *Adj.* (ugs.) witless (coll.); thick-headed; ~**feuer** *das:* **wie ein ~feuer aufflammen** flare up briefly; **das war nur ein ~feuer** (fig.) it was just a flash in the pan; ~**halm** *der* straw; **sich [wie ein Ertrinkender] an einen ~halm klammern** (fig.) grasp at a straw [like a drowning man]; ~**hut** *der* straw hat; ~**kopf** *der* (ugs. abwertend) thickhead; ~**sack** *der* palliasse; **[ach du] heiliger ~sack!** (ugs.) jeepers creepers! (coll.); goodness gracious [me]!; ~**witwe** *die* (ugs. scherzh.) grass widow; ~**witwer** *der* (ugs. scherzh.) grass widower

Strolch /ʃtrɔlç/ *der;* ~[e]s, ~**e** (a) (veralt.) ruffian; (b) (fam. scherzh.: Junge) rascal

strolchen *itr. V.; mit sein* roam *or* wander [aimlessly] about; **durch die Straßen ~:** roam the streets

Strom /ʃtroːm/ *der;* ~[e]s, **Ströme** /ʃtrøːmə/ **(a) ▶ 193 |** river; (von Blut, Schweiß, Wasser, fig.: Erinnerungen, Menschen, Autos usw.) stream; **ein reißender ~:** a raging torrent; **in Strömen regnen** *od.* (ugs.) gießen pour with rain; **in Strömen fließen** (fig.) flow freely; **das Blut floss in Strömen** (fig.) there was heavy bloodshed; **(b)** (Strömung) current; **mit dem/gegen den ~ schwimmen** (fig.) swim with/against the tide (fig.); **(c)** (Elektrizität) current; (~versorgung) electricity; **das Kabel führt** *od.* **steht unter ~:** the cable is live; **der ~ ist ausgefallen** there has been a power failure

strom-: ~**ab,** ~**abwärts** *Adv.* downstream; ~**auf,** ~**aufwärts** *Adv.* upstream

strömen /ˈʃtrøːmən/ *itr. V.; mit sein* stream; (intensiv) pour; ~**der Regen** pouring rain

strömen /ˈʃtrøːmən/ *itr. V.; mit sein* stream; (intensiv) pour; (fließen) flow; ~**der Regen** pouring rain

Stromer *der;* ~**s,** ~ (ugs.) vagabond; roamer

stromern *itr. V.; mit Richtungsangabe mit sein* (ugs.) roam *or* wander around; **durch die Gegend/Stadt ~:** roam *or* wander around the place/through the town

strom-, Strom-: ~**kreis** *der* [electric] circuit; ~**leitung** *die* power line *or* cable; ~**linien·förmig** *Adj.* streamlined; ~**schnelle** *die* rapids *pl.*

Strömung *die;* ~, ~**en (a)** current; (Met.) airstream; **(b)** (fig.) (Bewegung) movement; (Tendenz) trend

Strom·verbrauch *der* electricity consumption

Strophe /ˈʃtroːfə/ *die;* ~, ~**n** verse; (einer Ode) strophe

strotzen /ˈʃtrɔtsn̩/ *itr. V.* **von** *od.* **vor etw.** (*Dat.*) ~**:** be full of sth.; **von** *od.* **vor Kraft/Gesundheit ~:** be bursting with strength/health

strubb[e]lig /ˈʃtrʊb(ə)lɪç/ *Adj.* tousled; **du bist ja so ~!** your hair is in such a mess

Strudel /ˈʃtruːdl̩/ *der;* ~**s,** ~ **(a)** whirlpool; (kleiner) eddy; **(b)** (bes. südd., österr.: Gebäck) strudel

strudeln *itr. V.* ‹*water*› eddy, swirl

Struktur /ʃtrʊkˈtuːɐ̯/ *die;* ~, ~**en** structure

strukturell /ʃtrʊktuˈrɛl/ **1** *Adj.* structural. **2** *adv.* structurally

strukturieren *tr. V.* structure

Strumpf /ʃtrʊmpf/ *der;* ~**[e]s, Strümpfe** /ˈʃtrʏmpfə/ stocking; (Socke, Knie~) sock; **auf Strümpfen** in stockinged feet/in one's socks

Strumpf·band *das; Pl.* ~**bänder** garter; (Straps) suspender (Brit.); garter (Amer.)

Strumpf-: ~**halter** *der* suspender (Brit.); garter (Amer.); ~**hose** *die* tights *pl.* (Brit.); pantyhose (esp. Amer.); **eine ~hose** a pair of tights (Brit.)

Strunk /ʃtrʊŋk/ *der;* ~**[e]s, Strünke** /ˈʃtrʏŋkə/ stem; stalk; (Baum~) stump

struppig /ˈʃtrʊpɪç/ *Adj.* shaggy ‹*coat, dog, beard*›; tangled, tousled ‹*hair*›

Struwwel·peter /ˈʃtrʊvl̩-/ *der* tousle-head

Strychnin /ʃtrʏçˈniːn/ *das;* ~**s** strychnine

Stube /ˈʃtuːbə/ *die;* ~, ~**n** (veralt.: Wohnraum) [living-]room; parlour (dated); **die gute ~:** the front room *or* (dated) parlour; **immer rein in die gute ~!** (ugs.) come on in!

stuben-, Stuben-: ~**arrest** *der* (ugs.) detention (in one's room); **[zwei Tage] ~arrest bekommen** be kept in [for two days]; ~**fliege** *die* [common] house-fly; ~**hocker** *der* (ugs. abwertend) stay-at-home; ~**rein** *Adj.* **(a)** house-trained; **(b)** (scherzh.: nicht zotig) clean ‹*joke etc.*›

Stuck /ʃtʊk/ *der;* ~**[e]s** stucco

Stück /ʃtʏk/ *das;* ~**[e]s, Stücke (a)** piece; (kleines) bit; (Teil, Abschnitt) part; **ein ~ Kuchen/Zucker/Seife** a piece *or* slice of cake/a piece *or* lump of sugar/ a piece *or* bar of soap; **ein [gutes] ~ weiterkommen** get a [good] bit further; **ein hartes ~ Arbeit** a really tough job; **alles in ~e schlagen** smash everything [to pieces]; **im** *od.* **am ~:** unsliced ‹*sausage, cheese, etc.*›; **in einem ~** (ugs.)

‹*talk, rain*› non-stop; **(b)** (Einzel~) item; article; (Exemplar) specimen; (Möbel~) piece [of furniture]; **zwanzig ~ Vieh** twenty head of cattle; **ich nehme 5 ~/5 ~ von den Rosen** I'll take five [of them]/five of the roses; **30 Pfennig das ~, das ~ 30 Pfennig** thirty pfennigs each; ~ **für ~:** piece by piece; (eins nach dem andern) one by one; **das gute ~** (oft iron.) the precious thing; **(c) das ist [ja] ein starkes** *od.* **tolles ~** (ugs.) that's a bit much *or* a bit thick (coll.); **(d)** (salopp abwertend: Person) **ein faules/freches ~:** a lazy/cheeky thing *or* devil; **(e)** (Bühnen~) play; **(f)** (Musik~) piece

Stuckateur /ʃtʊkaˈtøːɐ̯/ *der;* ~**s,** ~**e** [stucco] plasterer

Stuck·decke *die* stucco[ed] ceiling

stückeln 1 *tr. V.* put together ‹*sleeve, curtain*› with patches. **2** *itr. V.* sew on patches

Stücke·schreiber *der* playwright

stück-, Stück-: ~**lohn** *der* (Wirtsch.) piecework pay; (Akkordsatz) piece-rate; ~**preis** *der* unit price; ~**weise** *Adv.* piece by piece; (einzeln) ‹*sell*› separately; ~**werk** *das:* ~**werk sein/bleiben** be/remain incomplete; ‹*book, work of art*› remain a torso

Student /ʃtuˈdɛnt/ *der;* ~**en,** ~**en** student

Studenten-: ~**ausweis** *der* student card; ~**bude** *die* (ugs.) student's room; ~**heim** *das* student hostel; students' [hall of] residence

Studentin *die;* ~, ~**nen** student

studentisch *Adj.; nicht präd.* student

Studie /ˈʃtuːdi̯ə/ *die;* ~, ~**n** study

Studien-: ~**aufenthalt** *der* study visit (**in** + *Dat.* to); ~**fach** *das* subject [of study]; ~**gang** *der* course of study; ~**gebühr** *die* tuition fee; ~**kolleg** *das* (Hochschulw.) preparatory course (*esp. for foreign students*); ~**platz** *der* university/college place; ~**rat** *der,* ~**rätin** *die* **▶ 34 |** established graduate secondary-school teacher (Brit.); graduate high-school teacher with tenure (Amer.); ~**referendar** *der* probationary graduate teacher; ~**reise** *die* study trip

studieren /ʃtuˈdiːrən/ **1** *itr. V.* study; **er studiert noch** he is still a student. **2** *tr. V.* study

Studierende *der/die; adj. Dekl.* student

studiert *Adj.* (ugs.) ‹*person*› who has been to university; ‹*painter etc.*› with an academic training

Studio /ˈʃtuːdi̯o/ *das;* ~**s,** ~**s** studio

Studio·bühne *die* studio theatre

Studium /ˈʃtuːdi̯ʊm/ *das;* ~**s, Studien (a)** *o. Pl.* study; (Studiengang) course of study; **während seines ~s** (als er Student war) in his student days; **(b)** (Erforschung) study; **Studien über etw.** (*Akk.*) **betreiben** carry out studies into sth.; **(c)** *o. Pl.* (genaues Lesen) study; **beim ~ der Akten** while studying the files

Stufe /ˈʃtuːfə/ *die;* ~, ~**n (a)** step; (einer Treppe) stair; „**Achtung** *od.* **Vorsicht, ~!**" 'mind the step'; **(b)** (Raketen~, Geol., fig.: Stadium) stage; (Niveau) level; (Steigerungs~, Grad) degree; (Rang) grade; **auf der gleichen ~ stehen [wie ...]** be of the same standard [as ...]; have the same status [as ...]; (gleichwertig sein) be equivalent [to ...]; **sich mit jmdm./etw. auf eine** *od.* **auf die gleiche ~ stellen** put oneself on a level with sb./sth.

stufen-, Stufen-: ~**barren** *der* (Turnen) asymmetric bars *pl.*; ~**heck** *das* (Kfz-W.) booted rear; ~**los 1** *Adj.* continuously variable; **2** *adv.* ~**los verstellbar** continuously adjustable; ~**weise 1** *Adv.* in stages *or* phases; **2** *adj.; nicht präd.* phased

stufig 1 *Adj.* layered ‹*hair [style]*›; terraced ‹*terrain*›. **2** *adv.* ~ **geschnittenes Haar** layered hair; hair cut in layers

Stuhl /ʃtuːl/ *der;* ~**[e]s, Stühle** /ˈʃtyːlə/ **(a)** chair; **(b)** (fig.) **sein ~ wackelt** his position is threatened *or* no longer secure; **jmdm. den ~ vor die Tür setzen** kick sb. out; show sb. the door; **jmdn. vom ~ reißen** *od.* **jagen/hauen** (ugs.) get sb. excited/take sb.'s breath away; **das hat mich fast** *od.* **bald vom ~ gehauen** (ugs.) you could have knocked me down with a feather; *s. auch* **elektrisch 1;** **(c)** (kath. Kirche) see; **der ~ Petri** the Holy See *or* See of Rome; **(d)** (Med.) stool; **(e) ⇒ Stuhlgang a**

Stuhl-: ~**bein** das chair-leg; ~**gang** der; o. Pl. **(a)** bowel movement[s]; **(b)** (Kot) stool; ~**lehne** die **(a)** (Rückenlehne) chair back; **(b)** (Armlehne) chair-arm

***Stukkateur** ⇒ **Stuccateur**

stülpen /'ʃtʏlpn̩/ tr. V. etw. auf od. über etw. (Akk.) ~: pull/put sth. on to or over sth.

stumm /ʃtʊm/ Adj. dumb ‹person›; (schweigsam) silent ‹person, reproach, greeting, prayer, etc.›; (wortlos) wordless ‹greeting, complaint, prayer, gesture, dialogue›; mute ‹glance, gesture›; (Theater) non-speaking ‹part, character›; ~ **vor Schreck** speechless with fear; **sie sahen sich** ~ **an** they looked at one another without speaking or in silence

Stumme der/die; adj. Dekl. mute; **die** ~**n** the dumb

Stummel /'ʃtʊml̩/ der; ~**s**, ~: stump; (Bleistift~) stub; (Zigaretten~/Zigarren~) [cigarette-/cigar-]butt

Stumm·film der silent film

Stummheit die dumbness; (Schweigsamkeit) silence

Stumpen /'ʃtʊmpn̩/ der; ~**s**, ~: stumpy cigar

Stümper /'ʃtʏmpɐ/ der; ~**s**, ~ (abwertend) botcher; bungler

Stümperei die; ~, ~**en** (abwertend) **(a)** o. Pl. botching; incompetence; **(b)** (Ergebnis) botched job; piece of incompetence

stümperhaft (abwertend) **1** Adj. incompetent; botched ‹job›; (laienhaft) amateurish ‹attempt, drawing›. **2** adv. incompetently; (laienhaft) amateurishly

stümpern itr. V. (abwertend) work incompetently; (pfuschen) bungle

stumpf /ʃtʊmpf/ **1** Adj. **(a)** blunt ‹pin, needle, knife, etc.›; snub ‹nose›; flat-topped ‹tower›; **(b)** (Math.) truncated ‹cone, pyramid›; obtuse ‹angle›; **(c)** (glanzlos, matt) dull ‹paint, hair, metal, colour, etc.›; (rauh) rough ‹stone, wood›; **(d)** (abgestumpft, teilnahmslos) impassive, lifeless ‹person, glance›; impassive, apathetic ‹indifference, resignation›; dulled ‹senses›; blank ‹look, despair›. **2** adv. (abgestumpft) ‹sit, stare› impassively

Stumpf der; ~**[e]s**, **Stümpfe** /'ʃtʏmpfə/ stump; **etw. mit** ~ **und Stiel ausrotten** eradicate sth. root and branch

Stumpf·sinn der; o. Pl. **(a)** apathy; **(b)** (Monotonie) monotony; tedium

stumpf·sinnig 1 Adj. **(a)** apathetic; vacant ‹look›; **(b)** (monoton) tedious; dreary; soul-destroying ‹job, work›. **2** adv. **(a)** apathetically; ‹stare› vacantly; **(b)** (monoton) tediously

Stündchen /'ʃtʏntçən/ das; ~**s**, ~ (fam.) **[für** od. **auf] ein** ~: for an hour or so; **jmds. letztes** ~ **ist gekommen** od. **hat geschlagen** sb.'s last hour has come

Stunde /'ʃtʊndə/ die; ~, ~**n (a** ▶224▎, ▶530▎) hour; **eine** ~ **Pause** an hour's break; a break of an hour; **drei** ~**n zu Fuß/mit dem Auto** three hours' walk/drive; **120 km in der** ~ **fahren** do 120 kilometres per hour; **jede** ~: once an hour; ~ **um** ~: [for] hours; [for] hour after hour; **jmds. letzte** ~ **hat geschlagen** od. **ist gekommen** sb.'s last hour has come; **(b)** (geh.) (Zeitpunkt) hour; (Zeit) time; (Augenblick) moment; **in** ~**n der Not** in times of need; **zu vorgerückter** od. **später** ~: at a late hour; **zur** ~: at the present time; **(c)** (Unterrichts~) lesson; **in der dritten** ~: in the third period

stunden tr. V. **jmdm. einen Betrag** usw. ~: give sb. [extra] time to pay or allow sb. to defer payment of a sum etc.

stunden-, Stunden-: ~**geschwindigkeit** die: ▶224▎ bei/mit einer ~**geschwindigkeit von 60 km** at a speed of 60 k.p.h.; ~**kilometer** der ▶224▎ (ugs.) kilometre per hour; k.p.h.; **er fuhr 120** ~**kilometer** he was driving at or doing 120 k.p.h.; ~**lang 1** Adj.; nicht präd. lasting hours postpos.; **2** adv. for hours; ~**lohn** der hourly wage; **sie bekommt 12 Mark** ~**lohn** she gets paid 12 marks an hour or per hour; ~**plan** der timetable; ~**weise 1** Adv. for an hour or two [at a time]; **er wird** ~**weise bezahlt** he is paid by the hour; **2** adj.; nicht präd. ‹hiring, payment› by the hour; ~**zeiger** der hour hand

stündlich ▶530▎ **1** Adj. hourly. **2** adv. **(a)** hourly; once an hour; **(b)** (jeden Augenblick) at any moment

Stundung die; ~, ~**en** deferment of payment

Stunk /ʃtʊŋk/ der; ~**s** (ugs.) trouble; ~**machen/anfangen** cause/start trouble

stupid[e] /ʃtu'piːdə/ (abwertend) **1** Adj. **(a)** moronic, empty-headed ‹person›; moronic, vacuous ‹expression›; **(b)** (monoton) soul-destroying. **2** adv. moronically

Stups /ʃtʊps/ der; ~**es**, ~**e** (ugs.) push; shove; (leicht) nudge

stupsen tr. V. (ugs.) push; shove; (leicht) nudge

Stups·nase die snub nose

stur (ugs.) **1** Adj. **(a)** (abwertend) (eigensinnig, unnachgiebig) obstinate; pig-headed; obstinate, dogged ‹insistence›; (phlegmatisch) stolid; dour; **ein** ~**er Bock** a pig-headed so-and-so (coll.); **auf** ~ **schalten** dig one's heels in; **(b)** (unbeirrbar) dogged; persistent; **(c)** (abwertend: stumpfsinnig) tedious. **2** adv. **(a)** (abwertend: eigensinnig, unnachgiebig) obstinately; **(b)** (unbeirrbar) doggedly; **sie las/redete** ~ **weiter** she carried on reading/kept on talking regardless; **(c)** (abwertend: stumpfsinnig) tediously; ‹learn, copy› mechanically

Sturheit die; ~ (ugs. abwertend) **(a)** (Eigensinnigkeit, Unnachgiebigkeit) obstinacy; pig-headedness; (phlegmatisches Wesen) stolidity; dourness; **(b)** (Stumpfsinnigkeit) deadly monotony

Sturm /-/ der; ~**[e]s**, **Stürme** /'ʃtʏrmə/ **(a)** storm; (heftiger Wind) gale; **bei** od. **in** ~ **und Regen** in the wind and rain; **ein** ~ **im Wasserglas** a storm in a teacup; **(b)** (Milit.: Angriff) assault (**auf** + Akk. on); **etw. im** ~ **erobern** od. **nehmen** (auch fig.) take sth. by storm; **gegen etw.** ~ **laufen** (fig.) be up in arms against sth.; ~ **klingeln** ring the [door]bell like mad (coll.); lean on the [door]bell; **(c)** (Sport: die Stürmer) forward line

stürmen /'ʃtʏrmən/ **1** itr. V. **(a)** unpers. **es stürmt [heftig]** it's blowing a gale; **(b)** mit sein (rennen) rush; (verärgert) storm; **(c)** (Sport: als Stürmer spielen) play up front or as a striker; **(d)** (Sport, Milit.: angreifen) attack. **2** tr. V. (Milit.) storm ‹town, position, etc.›; (fig.) besiege ‹booking office, shop, etc.›

Stürmer /'ʃtʏrmɐ/ der; ~**s**, ~ (Sport) striker; forward

Sturm·flut die storm tide

stürmisch /'ʃtʏrmɪʃ/ **1** Adj. **(a)** stormy; (fig.) tempestuous, turbulent ‹days, life, times, years›; **(b)** (ungestüm) tempestuous ‹nature, outburst, welcome›; tumultuous ‹applause, welcome, reception›; wild ‹enthusiasm›; passionate ‹lover, embrace, temperament›; vehement ‹protest›; **nicht so** ~! calm down!; take it easy!; **(c)** (rasant) meteoric ‹development, growth›; lightning, breakneck ‹speed›. **2** adv. **(a)** ‹protest› vehemently; ‹embrace› impetuously, passionately; ‹demand› clamorously; ‹applaud› wildly; **(b)** (rasant) at a tremendous rate or speed; at lightning speed

Sturm·schritt der: **im** ~**schritt** at the double

Sturz /ʃtʊrts/ der; -es, **Stürze** /'ʃtʏrtsə/ **(a)** fall (**aus, von** from); (Unfall) accident; **ein** ~ **in die Tiefe** a plunge into the depths; **bei einem** ~ **vom Pferd** falling off a horse; **(b)** (fig.: von Preis, Temperatur usw.) [sharp] fall, drop (Gen. in); **(c)** (Verlust des Amtes, der Macht) fall; (Absetzung) overthrow; (Amtsenthebung) removal from office

Sturz·bach der [mountain] torrent; (fig.: von Fragen usw.) torrent

stürzen /'ʃtʏrtsn̩/ **1** itr. V.; mit sein **(a)** fall (**aus, von** from); (in die Tiefe) plunge; plummet; **(b)** (fig.) ‹temperature, exchange rate, etc.› drop [sharply]; ‹prices› tumble; ‹government› fall, collapse; **(c)** (laufen) rush; dash; **er stürzte ins Zimmer** he burst into the room; **(d)** (fließen) stream; pour. **2** refl. V. **sich auf jmdn./etw.** ~ (auch fig.) pounce on sb./sth.; **sich aus dem Fenster** ~: hurl oneself or leap out of the window; **sich in etw.** ~ (Akk.) ~: throw oneself or plunge into sth.; **sich ins Vergnügen** ~: abandon oneself to pleasure. **3** tr. V. **(a)** throw; (mit Wucht) hurl; **jmdn. ins Unglück** ~: plunge sb. into misfortune; **(b)** (umdrehen) upturn, turn upside-down ‹mould, pot, box, glass, cup›; turn out ‹pudding, cake, etc.›; **(c)** (des Amtes entheben) oust ‹person› [from office]; (gewaltsam) overthrow, topple ‹leader, government›

Sturz-: ~**flug** der (Flugw.) [nose-]dive; ~**helm** der crash helmet

Stuss, *****Stuß** /ʃtʊs/ der; **Stusses** (ugs. abwertend) rubbish; twaddle (coll.)

Stute /'ʃtuːtə/ *die;* ~, ~n mare
Stütze *die;* ~, ~n (auch fig.) support; (für die Wäscheleine) prop; ~n für Kopf, Arme und Füße head-, arm-, and footrests
stutzen¹ /'ʃtʊtsn̩/ *itr. V.* stop short
stutzen² *tr. V.* trim; dock ‹*tail*›; clip ‹*ear, hedge, wing*›; prune ‹*tree, bush*›
stützen /'ʃtʏtsn̩/ **1** *tr. V.* support; (mit Pfosten o. ä.) prop up; (aufstützen) rest ‹*head, hands, arms, etc.*› (auf + *Akk.* on); **die Hände in die Seiten/den Kopf in die Hände gestützt** hands on hips/head in hands; **wo sind die Beweise, auf die Sie Ihre Anschuldigungen** ~? where is the evidence to support your accusations *or* on which your accusations are based?. **2** *refl. V.* **sich auf jmdn./ etw.** ~: lean *or* support oneself on sb./sth.; **sich auf Fakten** (*Akk.*) ~ (fig.) ‹*theory, statement etc.*› be based on facts
stutzig *Adj.* ~ werden begin to wonder; get suspicious; **jmdn.** ~ machen make sb. wonder *or* suspicious
Stütz·punkt *der* (bes. Milit.) base
stylen /'staɪlən/*tr. V.* (ugs.) style ‹*car etc.*›; do up ‹*person*›; **ein hervorragend gestyltes Modell** a model with outstanding lines
Styling /'staɪlɪŋ/ *das;* ~s, ~s styling
s.u. *Abk.* **siehe unten** see below
subaltern /zʊp|al'tɛrn/ (geh.) **1** *Adj.* **(a)** (untergeordnet) subordinate; **(b)** (abwertend) (unselbständig) unoriginal ‹*mind, literature*›; (unterwürfig) servile. **2** *adv.* (abwertend: unterwürfig) in a servile manner
Sub·dominante /'zʊp-/ *die* (Musik) subdominant
Subjekt /zʊp'jɛkt/ *das;* ~[e]s, ~e **(a)** subject; **(b)** (abwertend: Mensch) creature; type (coll.)
subjektiv /zʊpjɛk'tiːf/ **1** *Adj.* subjective. **2** *adv.* subjectively
Subjektivität /zʊpjɛktivi'tɛːt/ *die;* ~: subjectivity
Subjekt·satz *der* (Sprachw.) subject clause
Sub-: ~kontinent *der* (Geogr.) subcontinent; ~kultur *die* (Soziol.) subculture
sublim /zu'bliːm/ (geh.) **1** *Adj.* subtle; (erhaben) sublime. **2** *adv.* subtly
sublimieren *tr., itr. V.* sublimate
subskribieren /zʊpskri'biːrən/ (Buchw.) **1** *tr. V.* subscribe to. **2** *itr. V.* take out a subscription
Subskription /zʊpskrɪp'tsi̯oːn/ *die;* ~, ~en (Buchw.) subscription
***substantiell** ⇨ substanziell
Substantiv /'zʊpstantiːf/ *das;* ~s, ~e (Sprachw.) noun
Substanz /zʊp'stants/ *die;* ~, ~en **(a)** (auch fig.) substance; **(b)** (Grundbestand) **die** ~: the reserves *pl.;* **etw. geht an die** ~ (fig. ugs.) (seelisch, nervlich) sth. gets you down; (körperlich) sth. takes it out of you
substanziell /zʊpstan'tsi̯ɛl/ (geh.) **1** *Adj.* substantial. **2** *adv.* substantially
subsumieren /zʊpzu'miːrən/ *tr. V.* (geh.) subsume (**unter** + *Dat. od. Akk.* under)
subtil /zʊp'tiːl/ (geh.) **1** *Adj.* subtle. **2** *adv.* subtly
subtrahieren *tr., itr. V.* (Math.) subtract
Subtraktion /zʊptrak'tsi̯oːn/ *die;* ~, ~en (Math.) subtraction
Sub·tropen *Pl.* (Geogr.) subtropics
sub·tropisch *Adj.* subtropical
Subvention /zʊpvɛn'tsi̯oːn/ *die;* ~, ~en (Wirtsch.) subsidy
subventionieren *tr. V.* (Wirtsch.) subsidize
subversiv /zʊpvɛr'ziːf/ (Politik) **1** *Adj.* subversive. **2** *adv.* subversively
Such·anzeige *die* **(a)** missing-person report; **(b)** (in der Zeitung) 'lost' advertisement
Suche /'zuːxə/ *die;* ~, ~n search (nach for); **auf der** ~ [nach jmdm./etw.] sein be looking/(intensiver) searching [for sb./sth.]; **sich [nach jmdm./etw.] auf die** ~ machen start searching *or* start a search [for sb./sth.]
suchen 1 *tr. V.* **(a)** look for; (intensiver) search for; „**Kellner gesucht**" 'waiter wanted'; **jemanden wie ihn**

kann man ~ (ugs.) you don't come across someone like him every day; **seinesgleichen** ~: be without equal *or* unequalled; **(b)** (bedacht sein auf, sich wünschen) seek ‹*protection, advice, company, warmth, etc.*›; look for ‹*adventure*›; **Kontakt** *od.* **Anschluss** ~: try to get to know people; **Streit** ~: seek a quarrel; **er hat hier nichts zu** ~ (ugs.) he has no business [to be] here; **(c)** (geh.: trachten) ~, **etw. zu tun** seek *or* endeavour to do sth. **2** *itr. V.* search; **nach jmdm./etw.** ~: look/search for sb./ sth.; **sich** ~d **umsehen** look around
Sucher *der;* ~s, ~ (Fot.) viewfinder
Such-: ~hund *der* tracker dog; ~maschine *die* (DV) search engine; ~meldung *die* announcement about a missing or wanted person; ~roboter *der* (DV) ⇨ **Suchmaschine**
Sucht /zʊxt/ *die;* ~, **Süchte** /zʏçtə/ *od.* ~en **(a)** addiction (nach to); [bei jmdm.] zur ~ werden (auch fig.) become addictive [in sb.'s case]; **(b)** *Pl.* **Süchte** (übermäßiges Verlangen) craving, obsessive desire (nach for)
süchtig /'zʏçtɪç/ *Adj.* **(a)** addicted; ~ machen (auch fig.) be addictive; ~ [nach etw.] sein be an addict *or* addicted [to sth.]; **(b)** (versessen, begierig) obsessive; **nach etw.** ~ sein be obsessed with sth.
Süchtige *der/die; adj. Dekl.,* **Suchtkranke** *der/die* addict
Süd /zyːt/ *o. Art.; o. Pl.* ▶266⁆ **(a)** (Seemannsspr., Met.: Richtung) south; **(b)** (Gebiet) South; **(c)** (Politik) South; **(d)** *einem Subst. nachgestellt* (südlicher Teil, südliche Lage) South
Süd-: ~afrika (*das*) South Africa; ~amerika (*das*) South America
Sudan /zu'daːn/ (*das*); ~s *od. der;* ~s Sudan
süd·deutsch *Adj.* South German
Süd·deutschland (*das*) South Germany
sudeln /'zuːdl̩n/ *itr. V.* (ugs. abwertend) make a [disgusting] mess; (pfuschen) make a mess of it; botch it
Süden *der;* ~s ▶266⁆ **(a)** (Richtung) south; *s. auch* **Norden** a; **(b)** (Gegend) South; **(c)** (Geogr.) South; **der tiefe/tiefste** ~: the far South
Süd-: ~england (*das*) Southern England; the South of England; ~europa (*das*) Southern Europe; ~frucht *die* tropical [or sub-tropical] fruit; ~hang *der* southern slope; ~korea (*das*) South Korea; ~küste *die* south coast
Südländer /'zyːtlɛndɐ/ *der;* ~s, ~: Southern European; Mediterranean type
südländisch *Adj.* Southern [European]; Mediterranean; Latin ‹*temperament*›; ~ aussehen have Latin looks; look like a Southern European
südlich ▶266⁆ **1** *Adj.* **(a)** (im Süden) southern; *s. auch* **Eismeer; nördlich 1 a; Polarkreis; Wendekreis a;** **(b)** (nach, aus dem Süden) southerly; **(c)** (des Südens) Southern. **2** *adv.* southwards; *s. auch* **nördlich 2. 3** *Präp. mit Gen.* [to the] south of
süd-, Süd-: ~osten *der* ▶266⁆ south-east; *s. auch* **Norden;** ~östlich ▶266⁆ **1** *Adj.* south-eastern; southeasterly ‹*direction, wind, course*›; **2** *adv.* ~östlich [von X] liegen be to the south-east [of X]; **3** *Präp. mit Gen.* [to the] south-east of; ~pol /'--/ *der* South Pole; ~polar·gebiet *das* Antarctic [Region]; ~see /'--/ *die;* ~: **die** ~: the South Seas *pl.;* ~seite /'---/ *die* south side; ~wärts /'--/ *Adv.* ▶266⁆ southwards; ~westen *der* ▶266⁆ south-west; *s. auch* **Norden** a; ~westlich ▶266⁆ **1** *Adj.* south-western; south-westerly ‹*direction, wind, course*›; **2** *adv.* ~ [von X] liegen be to the south-west [of X]; **3** *Präp. mit Gen.* [to the] south-west of; ~wind /'--/ *der* south *or* southerly wind
Sues·kanal /'zuːɛs-/ *der;* ~s Suez Canal
Suff /zʊf/ *der;* ~[e]s (salopp) **(a)** **im** ~: while under the influence (coll.); **(b)** (Trunksucht) boozing (coll.); **sich dem** ~ ergeben become a victim of the demon drink; take to the bottle (coll.)
süffeln /'zʏfl̩n/ *tr., itr. V.* (ugs.) tipple (coll.)
süffig *Adj.* (ugs.) [very] drinkable
süffisant /zʏfi'zant/ (geh. abwertend) **1** *Adj.* smug. **2** *adv.* smugly

---

Süffisanz /sʏfi'zants/ *die;* ~ (geh. abwertend) smugness

Suffix /zʊ'fɪks/ *das;* ~es, ~e (Sprachw.) suffix

suggerieren /zʊgɛ'riːrən/ *tr. V.* (a) (geh., Psych.) suggest; (b) (geh.: den Eindruck erwecken) suggest; give the *or* an impression of

Suggestion /zʊgɛs'tioːn/ *die;* ~, ~en (a) (geh., Psych.) suggestion; (b) *o. Pl.* (geh.: suggestive Wirkung) suggestive effect *or* power

suggestiv /zʊgɛs'tiːf/ (geh., Psych.) **1** *Adj.* suggestive. **2** *adv.* suggestively

Suggestiv·frage *die* leading question

suhlen *refl. V.* wallow

Sühne /'zyːnə/ *die;* ~, ~n (geh.) atonement; expiation; ~ [für etw.] leisten make atonement *or* atone [for sth.]

sühnen *tr., itr. V.* [für] etw. ~: atone for *or* pay the penalty for sth.

Sühne·termin *der* (Rechtsw.) conciliation hearing

Suite /'sviːt(ə)/ *die;* ~, ~n suite

Suizid /zui'tsiːt/ *der od. das;* ~[e]s, ~e (bes. Med., Psych.) suicide

Sujet /zʏ'ʒeː/ *das;* ~s, ~s (bes. Literaturw., bild. Kunst) subject

sukzessiv /zʊktsɛ'siːf/ **1** *Adj.* gradual. **2** *adv.* gradually

Sulfat /zʊl'faːt/ *das;* ~[e]s, ~e (Chemie) sulphate

Sulfonamid /zʊlfona'miːt/ *das;* ~[e]s, ~e (Pharm.) sulphonamide

Sultan /'zʊltaːn/ *der;* ~s, ~e sultan

Sultanine /zʊlta'niːnə/ *die;* ~, ~n sultana

Sülze /'zʏltsə/ *die;* ~, ~n (a) diced meat/fish in aspic; (vom Schweinskopf) brawn; (b) (Aspik) aspic

sülzen *tr., itr. V.* (salopp) ⇒ **quatschen** 1a, 2

summarisch /zʊ'maːrɪʃ/ (geh.) **1** *Adj.* summary; brief ‹summary›. **2** *adv.* summarily; briefly

Sümmchen /'zʏmçən/ *das;* ~s, ~ (ugs.) **ein hübsches** *od.* **nettes** ~: a tidy little sum (coll.)

Summe /'zʊmə/ *die;* ~, ~n sum

summen 1 *itr. V.* hum; (lauter, heller) buzz; **es summt** there's a hum/buzzing. **2** *tr., auch itr. V.* hum ‹tune, song, etc.›

Summer *der;* ~s, ~: buzzer

summieren *refl. V.* add up (auf + *Akk.* to)

Summ·ton *der* buzzing [tone]; (leiser) hum

Sumpf /zʊmpf/ *der;* ~[e]s, **Sümpfe** /'zʏmpfə/ marsh; (bes. in den Tropen) swamp; (fig.) morass; quagmire

sumpfig *Adj.* marshy

Sund /zʊnt/ *der;* ~[e]s, ~e (Geogr.) sound

Sünde /'zʏndə/ *die;* ~, ~n sin; (fig.) misdeed; transgression; **eine ~ wert sein** (scherzh.) be worth a little transgression; ‹food› be naughty but nice

Sünden-: ~bekenntnis *das* confession of one's sins; ~bock *der* (ugs.) scapegoat

Sünder *der;* ~s, ~, **Sünderin** *die;* ~, ~nen sinner

sündhaft 1 *Adj.* (a) sinful; (b) (ugs.) **ein ~er Preis** an outrageous price. **2** *adv.* (a) sinfully; (b) (ugs.: sehr) outrageously ‹expensive›; stunningly ‹beautiful›

sündig 1 *Adj.* sinful; (lasterhaft) wicked. **2** *adv.* sinfully

sündigen *itr. V.* sin

super (salopp) **1** *indekl. Adj.* super (coll.); fantastic (coll.); ~ aussehen/sich ~ fühlen look/feel great (coll.). **2** *adv.* fantastically (coll.)

Super /'zuːpɐ/ *das;* ~s, ~: four star (Brit.); premium (Amer.)

super- ultra-‹long, high, fast, modern, masculine, etc.›

Super- super-‹hero, figure, car, group, etc.›; terrific (coll.), tremendous (coll.) ‹success, offer, chance, idea, etc.›

Super-8-Film *der* super 8 film

super·klug (iron.) **1** *Adj.* extra clever; smart-aleck (coll. derog.). **2** *adv.* in a smart-aleck way (coll. derog.)

Superlativ /'zuːpɐlatiːf/ *der;* ~s, ~e (Sprachw.) superlative

super-, Super-: ~markt *der* supermarket; ~schlau *Adj.* (iron.) ⇒ ~klug; ~schnell (ugs.) **1** *Adj.* ultra-fast; **2** *adv.* at tremendous speed

Suppe /'zʊpə/ *die;* ~; ~n soup; **jmdm. die ~ versalzen** (ugs.) put a spoke in sb.'s wheel; put a spanner in sb.'s works; **jmdm. in die ~ spucken** (salopp) mess things up for sb.; *s. auch* **auslöffeln** a

Suppen-: ~fleisch *das* beef for making soup; ~grün *das* green vegetables for making soup; ~huhn *das* boiling fowl; ~löffel *der* soup spoon; ~schüssel *die* soup-tureen; ~tasse *die* soup-bowl; ~teller *der* soup plate; ~terrine *die* soup-tureen; ~würfel *der* stock cube

Surf·brett /'səːf-/ *das* surf-board

surfen /'səːfn̩/ *itr. V.* surf

Surfer /'səːfɐ/ *der;* ~s, ~: surfer

Sur·realismus /zʊrea'lɪsmʊs/ *der;* ~: surrealism *no art.*

surrealistisch 1 *Adj.* surrealist ‹movement, painting, literature›; surrealistic ‹image, story, scene›. **2** *adv.* surrealistically; ‹paint› in a surrealistic style; ‹influenced› by surrealism

surren /'zʊrən/ *itr. V.* (a) (summen) hum; ‹camera, fan› whirr; (b) *mit sein* (schwirren) whirr

suspekt /zʊs'pɛkt/ **1** *Adj.* suspicious; **jmdm. ~ sein** seem suspicious to sb.; arouse sb.'s suspicions. **2** *adv.* suspiciously

suspendieren /zʊspɛn'diːrən/ *tr. V.* suspend; (entlassen) dismiss; **jmdn. vom Dienst/von seinem Amt ~:** suspend/dismiss sb. from his/her post

süß /zyːs/ **1** *Adj.* sweet; **er isst gern Süßes** he likes sweet things; he has a sweet tooth; **na, mein Süßer/meine Süße?** well, sweetheart? **2** *adv.* sweetly; **träum ~!** sweet dreams!

süßen 1 *tr. V.* sweeten. **2** *itr. V.* sweeten things; **mit Saccharin** *usw.* ~: use saccharine *etc.* as a sweetener

Süß·holz *das; o. Pl.* liquorice [plant]; ~ **raspeln** (fig. ugs.) ooze charm

Süßigkeit *die;* ~, ~en *meist Pl.* sweet (Brit.); candy (Amer.); ~en sweets (Brit.); candy *sing.* (Amer.); (als Ware) confectionery *sing.*

süßlich 1 *Adj.* (a) [slightly] sweet; on the sweet side *pred.;* **ein widerlich ~er Geschmack** an unpleasantly sickly *or* cloying taste; (b) (abwertend) (sentimental) sickly mawkish ‹film›; (heuchlerisch freundlich) sugary ‹smile etc.›; smarmy (coll.) ‹expression, manners›; honeyed ‹words›. **2** *adv.* (abwertend) ‹write, paint› mawkishly *or* in a sickly-sentimental style; ‹smile› smarmily (coll.)

süß-, Süß-: ~most *der* unfermented fruit juice; ~rahm·butter *die* sweet cream butter; ~sauer **1** *Adj.* sweet-and-sour; (fig.) wry ‹smile, face›; **2** *adv.* etw. ~ zubereiten give sth. a sweet-and-sour flavour; (fig.) ‹smile› wryly; ~speise *die* sweet; dessert; ~stoff *der* sweetener; ~waren *Pl.* confectionery *sing.;* candy *sing.* (Amer.); ~wasser *das; Pl.* ~wasser fresh water

svw. *Abk.* soviel wie

SW *Abk.* Südwest[en] SW

Sweatshirt /'swɛtʃəːt/ *das;* ~s, ~s sweatshirt

Swing /svɪŋ/ *der;* ~s (a) (Musik) swing *no art.;* (b) (Wirtsch.) swing

swingen *itr. V.* (a) (Musik) ‹player› swing [it]; ‹music› have a swing [to it]; (b) (tanzen) swing

Symbol /zʏm'boːl/ *das;* ~s, ~e symbol

symbolhaft 1 *Adj.* symbolic (für of). **2** *adv.* symbolically

Symbolik /zʏm'boːlɪk/ *die;* ~: symbolism

symbolisch 1 *Adj.* symbolic. **2** *adv.* symbolically

symbolisieren *tr. V.* symbolize

Symbolismus *der;* ~: symbolism; (Kunstrichtung) Symbolism *no art.*

Symmetrie /zʏme'triː/ *die;* ~, ~n symmetry

symmetrisch 1 *Adj.* symmetrical. **2** *adv.* symmetrically

Sympathie /zʏmpa'tiː/ *die;* ~, ~n sympathy; ~ **für jmdn. haben** sympathize with *or* have sympathy with sb.; **sich** (*Dat.*) **jmds./alle ~n verscherzen** forfeit sb.'s/ everybody's sympathy; **bei aller ~:** with the best will in the world

Sympathisant /zʏmpati'zant/ *der;* ~en, ~en, **Sympathisantin** *die;* ~, ~nen sympathizer (*Gen.* with)

sympathisch 1 *Adj.* congenial, likeable ⟨*person, manner*⟩; appealing, agreeable ⟨*voice, appearance, material*⟩; **er war mir gleich ~:** I took to him at once; I took an immediate liking to him. 2 *adv.* in a likeable *or* appealing way; (angenehm) agreeably

sympathisieren *itr. V.* sympathize (**mit** with); **mit einer Partei ~:** be sympathetic towards a party

Symphonie /zʏmfo'ni:/ *usw.* ⇒ **Sinfonie** *usw.*

Symptom /zʏmp'to:m/ *das;* ~s, ~e (Med., geh.) symptom (*Gen.*, **für, von** of)

symptomatisch (Med., geh.) 1 *Adj.* symptomatic (**für** of). 2 *adv.* symptomatically

Synagoge /zyna'go:gə/ *die;* ~, ~n synagogue

Synchronisation /zʏnkroniza'tso:n/*die;* ~, ~en ⇒ **Synchronisierung**

synchronisieren *tr. V.* (a) (Film) dub ⟨*film*⟩; (b) (Technik, fig.) synchronize ⟨*watches, operations, etc.*⟩; **synchronisiertes Getriebe** synchromesh gearbox

Synchronisierung *die;* ~, ~en (a) (Film) dubbing; (b) (Technik, fig.) synchronization; (Kfz-W.) fitting of synchromesh (*Gen.* to)

Syndikus /'zʏndikʊs/ *der;* ~s, ~e *od.* **Syndizi** /'zʏn ditsi/ (Rechtsanwalt einer Firma) company lawyer *or* (Amer.) attorney

Syndrom /zʏn'dro:m/ *das;* ~s, ~e (Med.) syndrome

Synkope *die;* ~, ~n /zʏn'ko:pə/; (Musik) syncopation

Synonomie /zynony'mi:/*die;* ~, ~n (Sprachw.) synonymity

synonym /zyno'ny:m/ (Sprachw.) 1 *Adj.* synonymous. 2 *adv.* synonymously

Synonym /zyno'ny:m/ *das;* ~s, ~e (Sprachw.) synonym

Synonym·wörterbuch *das* dictionary of synonyms

syntaktisch /zʏn'taktɪʃ/ (Sprachw.) 1 *Adj.* syntactic. 2 *adv.* syntactically

Syntax /'zʏntaks/ *die;* ~, ~en (Sprachw.) syntax

Synthese /zʏn'te:zə/ *die;* ~, ~n synthesis (*Gen.*, **von, aus** of)

Synthesizer /'sɪntəsaɪzɐ/*der;* ~s, ~ (Musik) synthesizer

synthetisch 1 *Adj.* synthetic. 2 *adv.* synthetically

Syphilis /'zy:filɪs/ *die;* ~ ▶329❘ (Med.) syphilis

Syrer /'zy:rɐ/ *der;* ~s, ~, **Syrerin** *die;* ~, ~nen ▶388❘ Syrian

Syrien /'zy:riən/ *(das);* ~s Syria

syrisch /'zy:rɪʃ/ *Adj.* ▶388❘ Syrian

System /zys'te:m/ *das;* ~, ~e system; ~ **in etw.** (*Akk.*) **bringen** introduce some system into sth.; **etw. hat ~:** there's method in sth.

Systematik /zyste'ma:tɪk/ *die;* ~, ~en systematics *sing.*

systematisch /zyste'ma:tɪʃ/ 1 *Adj.* systematic. 2 *adv.* systematically

systematisieren *tr. V.* systematize

System·zwang *der* pressure imposed by the system

Szenario /stse'na:rio/ *das;* ~s, ~s, **Szenarium** /stse'na:riʊm/ *das;* ~s, **Szenarien** (Theater, Film) scenario

Szene /'stse:nə/ *die;* ~, ~n scene; **hinter der ~:** backstage; behind the scenes; **er erhielt Beifall auf offener ~:** he was applauded during the scene; **sich in ~ setzen** (fig.) put oneself in the limelight; (b) (Auseinandersetzung) scene; **[jmdm.] eine ~ machen** make a scene [in front of sb.]; (c) (ugs.: bestimmtes Milieu) scene (coll.)

Szenen·wechsel *der* (Theater) scene-change

Szenerie /stsenə'ri:/ *die;* ~, ~n (a) (Bühnendekoration) set (*Gen.* for); (b) (Schauplatz) scene

szenisch *Adj.* dramatic; ~**e Gestaltung/Effekte** staging/stage effects

Szepter /'stsɛptɐ/ *das;* ~s, ~ ⇒ **Zepter**

*alte Schreibung (vgl. Hinweise auf S. xvi–xvii)

t, T /te:/ *das;* ~, ~, (ugs.) ~s, ~s t/T; *s. auch* **a, A**

Tabak /'ta(:)bak/ *der;* ~s, ~e tobacco

Tabaks-: ~**beutel** *der* tobacco-pouch; ~**dose** *die* tobacco-tin; ~**pfeife** *die* [tobacco-]pipe

tabellarisch /tabɛ'la:rɪʃ/ 1 *Adj.* tabular; **ein ~er Lebenslauf** a curriculum vitae in tabular form. 2 *adv.* in tabular form

Tabelle /ta'bɛlə/ *die;* ~, ~n (a) (Übersicht) table; (b) (Sport) [league/championship] table

Tabellen·führer *der* (Sport) top team/player in the [league/championship] table

Tablett /ta'blɛt/ *das;* ~[e]s, ~s *od.* ~e tray; **jmdm. etw. auf einem silbernen ~ servieren** (fig.) hand sth. to sb. on a silver platter

Tablette *die;* ~, ~n tablet

tabu /ta'bu:/ *Adj.* taboo

Tabu *das;* ~s, ~s taboo

tabuieren, tabuisieren *tr. V.* (geh.) **etw. ~:** taboo sth; make sth. taboo

Tacheles /'taxələs/ *in* [**mit jmdm.**] ~ **reden** (ugs.) do some straight talking [to sb.]

Tacho /'taxo/ *der;* ~s, ~s (ugs.) speedo (coll.)

Tacho·meter *der od. das* speedometer

Tadel /'ta:dl/ *der;* ~s, ~ (a) censure; (b) (im Klassenbuch) black mark; (c) (geh.: Mangel, Makel) blemish; flaw; **ohne ~:** ⇒ **tadellos 1 a**

tadel·los 1 *Adj.* (a) (makellos) impeccable; immaculate ⟨*hair, clothing, suit, etc.*⟩; perfect ⟨*condition, teeth, pronunciation, German, etc.*⟩; (b) (ugs.: sehr gut) excellent; (c) /'--'-/ (ugs.: als Ausruf der Zustimmung) splendid (coll.). 2 *adv.* (a) (makellos) ⟨*dress*⟩ impeccably, immaculately; ⟨*fit, speak, etc.*⟩ perfectly; ⟨*live, behave, etc.*⟩ irreproachably; (b) (ugs.: sehr gut) **hier wird man ~ bedient** the service is excellent here

tadeln *tr. V.* jmdn. [**für sein Verhalten** *od.* **wegen seines Verhaltens**] ~: rebuke sb. [for his/her behaviour]; **jmds. Arbeit ~:** criticize sb.'s work; ~**der Blick** reproachful look

tadelns·wert *Adj.* reprehensible

Tafel /'ta:fl/ *die;* ~, ~n (a) (Schiefer~) slate; (Wand~) blackboard; (b) (plattenförmiges Stück) slab; **eine ~ Schokolade** a bar of chocolate; (c) (Gedenk~) plaque; (d) (geh.: festlicher Tisch) table; **die ~ aufheben** (fig.) rise from the table; (e) (Druckw.) plate

tafel-, Tafel-: ~**apfel** *der* (Kaufmannsspr.) dessert apple; ~**fertig** *Adj.* (Kochk.) ready to serve *postpos.;* ~**lappen** *der* blackboard cloth

tafeln *itr. V.* (geh.) feast

täfeln /'tɛ:fl̩n/ *tr. V.* panel

Tafel-: ~**obst** *das* [dessert] fruit; ~**salz** *das* table salt

Täfelung *die;* ~, ~en (a) (das Täfeln) panelling; (b) (Paneel) [wooden] panelling

Tafel-: ~**wasser** *das; Pl.* ~**wässer** [bottled] mineral water; ~**wein** *der* table wine

Taft /taft/ *der;* ~[e]s, ~e taffeta

Tag /ta:k/ *der;* ~[e]s, ~e ▶240❘ (a) day; **es wird/ist ~:** it's getting/it is light; **der ~ bricht an** *od.* **erwacht/ neigt sich** (geh.) the day breaks/draws to an end *or* a close; **am ~[e]** during the day[time]; **am helllichten ~:** in broad daylight; **er redet viel, wenn der ~ lang ist** (ugs.) you can't put any trust in what he says; **man soll den ~ nicht vor dem Abend loben** (Spr.) don't count your chickens before they're hatched (prov.); **es ist noch nicht aller ~e Abend** we haven't yet seen the end of the matter; **guten ~!** hello; (nachmittags auch) good afternoon; (bei Vorstellung) how do you do?; **etw. an den ~ legen** display sth.; **etw. an den** ∼ **bringen** *od.* (geh.) **ziehen** bring sth. to light; reveal sth.; **an den** ∼ **kommen** come to light; **über/unter** ∼[e] (Bergmannsspr.) above ground/underground; (**b**) ▶595 (Zeitraum von 24 Stunden) day; **welchen** ∼ **haben wir heute?** (Wochentag) what day is it today? what's today?; (Datum) what date is it today?; **heute in/vor drei** ∼**en** three days from today/three days ago today; **den** ∼ **über** during the day; **an diesem** ∼: on this day; **dreimal am** ∼: three times a day; **am** ∼**e vorher** on the previous day; the day before; ∼ **für** ∼: every [single] day; **von** ∼ **zu** ∼: day by day; **in den nächsten** ∼**en** in the next few days; **der** ∼ **X** the great day; **am folgenden** ∼: the next day; **er hatte heute einen schlechten** ∼: today was one of his bad days; **sich** (*Dat.*) **einen schönen/faulen** ∼ **machen** (ugs.) have a nice/lazy day; **den lieben langen** ∼: all day long; ∼ **der offenen Tür** Open Day; **eines** ∼**es** one day; some day; **eines schönen** ∼**es** one of these days; **von einem** ∼ **auf den anderen** from one day to the next; overnight; (**c**) (Ehren∼, Gedenk∼) ∼ **der Deutschen Einheit** Day of German Unity; (**d**) *Pl.* ([Lebens]zeit) days; **seine** ∼**e sind gezählt** his days are numbered; **auf meine/deine** *usw.* **alten** ∼**e** in my/your *etc.* old age; (**e**) *Pl.* (ugs.: verhüll.: Menstruation) period *sing.*

tag·aus *Adv.* ∼, **tagein** day in, day out; day after day

tage-, Tage-: ∼**bau** *der; Pl.* ∼**e** (Bergbau) (**a**) *o. Pl.* (Bergbau über Tage) opencast mining *no art.;* (**b**) (Anlage) opencast mine; ∼**buch** *das* diary; [**über etw.** (*Akk.*)] ∼**buch führen** keep a diary [about sth.]; ∼**dieb** *der* (abwertend) idler; lazybones *sing.;* ∼**lang** 1 *Adj.; nicht präd.* lasting for days *postpos.;* **das** ∼**lange Warten** the days of waiting; **nach** ∼**langem Regen** after days of rain; 2 *adv.* for days [on end]; ∼**löhner** /∼løːnɐ/ *der;* ∼**s,** ∼: day-labourer

tagen *itr. V.* (**a**) (konferieren) meet; **das Gericht tagt** the court is in session; (**b**) (geh.: dämmern) **es tagt** day is breaking *or* dawning

Tage·reise *die* day's journey; **nach Passau sind es zchn** ∼**n** it's a ten-day journey to Passau

Tages-: ∼**ablauf** *der* day; daily routine; ∼**anbruch** *der* daybreak; dawn; ∼**arbeit** *die* day's work; ∼**ausflug** *der* day's outing; ∼**bedarf** *der* daily requirement; ∼**creme** *die* (Kosmetik) day cream; ∼**fahrt** *die* day trip; day excursion; ∼**gespräch** *das* topic of the day; ∼**karte** *die* (**a**) (Gastron.) menu of the day; (**b**) (Fahr-, Eintrittskarte) day ticket; ∼**kasse** *die* (**a**) box office (*open during the day*); (**b**) (∼einnahme) day's takings *pl.;* ∼**licht** *das; o. Pl.* daylight; **etw. ans** ∼**licht bringen** *od.* ∼**ziehen** (fig.) /**ans** ∼**licht kommen** (fig.) bring sth./come to light; ∼**marsch** *der* (**a**) (Fußmarsch) day's hike; (**b**) (Strecke eines ∼marsches) day's march; ∼**mutter** *die; Pl.* ∼**mütter** childminder; ∼**ordnung** *die* agenda; **an der** ∼**ordnung sein** (fig.) be the order of the day; ∼**ration** *die* daily ration; ∼**tour** *die* ⇒ ∼**fahrt;** ∼**zeit** *die* time of day; **um diese** ∼**zeit** at this time; **zu jeder** ∼**- und Nachtzeit** at any time of the day or night; ∼**zeitung** *die* daily newspaper; daily

tage·weise *Adv.* on some days

tag·hell 1 *Adj.; nicht attr.* (**a**) (durch Tageslicht) [day]light; (**b**) (wie am Tag) bright as daylight *postpos.* 2 *adv.* **etw. ist** ∼ **erleuchtet** sth. is very brightly lit [up]

täglich /ˈtɛːklɪç/ 1 *Adj.; nicht präd.* daily. 2 *adv.* every day; **zweimal** ∼: twice a day; ∼ **zwei Stunden** for two hours a day

tags *Adv.* (**a**) by day; in the daytime; (**b**) ∼ **zuvor** the day before; ∼ **darauf** the next *or* following day; the day after

Tag·schicht *die* day shift; ∼ **haben** be on [the] day shift

tags·über *Adv.* during the day

tag·täglich 1 *Adj.* day-to-day; daily. 2 *adv.* every single day

Tag-: ∼**träumer** *der* daydreamer; ∼**und·nacht·gleiche** *die;* ∼, ∼**n** equinox

Tagung *die;* ∼, ∼**en** conference

Tagungs·ort *der; Pl.* ∼**orte** venue [for a/the conference]

Taifun /taɪˈfuːn/ *der;* ∼**s,** ∼**e** typhoon

Taiga *die;* ∼: taiga

Taille /ˈtaljə/ *die;* ∼, ∼**n** waist; **in der** ∼: at the waist

Taillen·weite *die* waist measurement

taillieren /taˈjiːrən/ *tr. V.* fit [at the waist]; **ein tailliertes Kostüm** a suit with the jacket fitted at the waist

Takelage /takəˈlaːʒə/ *die;* ∼, ∼**n** (Seew.) masts and rigging

Takt /takt/ *der;* ∼[**e**]**s,** ∼**e** (**a**) (Musik) time; (Einheit) bar; measure (Amer.); **den** ∼ [**ein**]**halten** keep in time; **aus dem** ∼ **kommen/sich nicht aus dem** ∼ **bringen lassen** lose/not lose the beat; **mit ihm muss ich mal ein paar** ∼**e reden** (fig. ugs.) I need to have a serious talk with him; (**b**) *o. Pl.* (rhythmischer Bewegungsablauf) rhythm; **im/gegen den** ∼: in/out of rhythm; (**c**) *o. Pl.* (Feingefühl) tact; (**d**) (Verslehre) foot

Takt·gefühl *das; o. Pl.* sense of tact

taktieren *itr. V.* proceed tactically; **vorsichtig/klug** ∼: use caution/clever tactics

Taktik /ˈtaktɪk/ *die;* ∼, ∼**en:** [**eine**] ∼: tactics *pl.*

Taktiker *der;* ∼**s,** ∼, **Taktikerin** *die;* ∼, ∼**nen** tactician

taktisch 1 *Adj.* tactical. 2 *adv.* tactically; ∼ **klug vorgehen** use clever *or* good tactics

takt·los 1 *Adj.* tactless. 2 *adv.* tactlessly

Taktlosigkeit *die;* ∼, ∼**en** (**a**) *o. Pl.* tactlessness; (**b**) (taktlose Handlung) piece of tactlessness

Takt·stock *der* baton

takt·voll 1 *Adj.* tactful. 2 *adv.* tactfully

Tal /taːl/ *das;* ∼[**e**]**s,** **Täler** /ˈtɛːlɐ/ valley

tal·abwärts *Adv.* down the valley

Talar /taˈlaːɐ̯/ *der;* ∼**s,** ∼**e** robe

tal·aufwärts *Adv.* up the valley

Talent /taˈlɛnt/ *das;* ∼[**e**]**s,** ∼**e** (**a**) (Befähigung) talent (**zu,** **für** for); (**b**) (Mensch) talented person; **junge** ∼**e fördern** promote young talent

talentiert /talɛnˈtiːɐ̯t/ *Adj.* talented

Talg /talk/ *der;* ∼[**e**]**s,** ∼**e** (**a**) (Speisefett) suet; (zur Herstellung von Seife, Kerzen usw.) tallow; (**b**) (Haut∼) sebum

Talisman /ˈtaːlɪsman/ *der;* ∼**s,** ∼**e** talisman

Talk·show, *✶***Talk-Show** /ˈtɔːkʃoʊ/ *die* (Ferns.) talk show; chat show

Talmi /ˈtalmi/ *das;* ∼**s** (**a**) (wertloser Schmuck) imitation *or* cheap jewellery; (fig.) tinsel; (**b**) (vergoldete Legierung) pinchbeck

Tal-: ∼**sohle** *die* valley floor *or* bottom; (fig.) depression; ∼**sperre** *die* dam (*with associated reservoir and power station*); ∼**station** *die* valley station

Tambour /ˈtambuːɐ̯/ *der;* ∼**s,** ∼**e** *od.* (schweiz.) ∼**en** (veralt.) drummer

Tamburin /tambuˈriːn/ *das;* ∼**s,** ∼**e** tambourine

Tampon /ˈtampɔn/ *der;* ∼**s,** ∼**s** (**a**) (Med.: Wattebausch) tampon; plug; (**b**) (Menstruations∼) tampon

Tamtam /tamˈtam/ *das;* ∼**s** (ugs. abwertend) [**großes**] ∼: [a big] fuss; ∼ **machen** make a fuss

Tand /tant/ *der;* ∼[**e**]**s** trumpery

tändeln /ˈtɛndln/ *itr. V.* dally

Tandem /ˈtandɛm/ *das;* ∼**s,** ∼**s** tandem; (fig.) pair

Tang /taŋ/ *der;* ∼[**e**]**s,** ∼**e** seaweed

Tanga /ˈtaŋa/ *der;* ∼**s,** ∼**s** tanga

Tangens /ˈtaŋgɛns/ *der;* ∼, ∼ (Math.) tangent

Tangente /taŋˈgɛntə/ *die;* ∼, ∼**n** (**a**) (Math.) tangent; (**b**) (Straße) ring road; bypass

tangieren /taŋˈgiːrən/ *tr. V.* (**a**) affect; (**b**) (Math.) be tangent to

Tango /ˈtaŋgo/ *der;* ∼**s,** ∼**s** tango

Tank /taŋk/ *der;* ∼**s,** ∼**s,** (seltener) ∼**e** tank

Tanke *die;* ∼, ∼**n** (salopp) filling station

tanken *tr., itr. V.* fill up; **Öl** ∼: fill up with oil; **er tankte dreißig Liter** [**Super**] he put in thirty litres [of four-star]

Tanker *der;* ∼**s,** ∼: tanker

Tank-: ∼**säule** *die* petrol pump (Brit.); gasoline pump (Amer.); ∼**stelle** *die* petrol station (Brit.); gas station

(Amer.); ~**wagen** der tanker; ~**wart** /~vart/ der; ~**s**, ~**e ▶ 85** petrol pump attendant (Brit.)

Tanne /'tanə/ die; ~, ~**n** (a) fir[-tree]; **schlank wie eine** ~: slender as a reed; (b) (Holz) fir

Tannen-: ~**baum** der (a) (ugs.: Tanne a) fir-tree; (b) (Weihnachtsbaum) Christmas tree; ~**nadel** die fir-needle; ~**wald** der fir forest; ~**zapfen** der fir cone

Tante /'tantə/ die; ~, ~**n** (a) aunt; (b) (Kinderspr.: Frau) lady; (c) (ugs.: Frau) woman

tantenhaft 1 Adj. old-maidish; (belehrend) nannyish. 2 adv. like an old maid; (belehrend) nannyishly

Tantieme /tã'tiɛ:mə/ die; ~, ~**n** (a) (Gewinnbeteiligung) percentage of the profits; (b) (von Künstlern) royalty

Tanz /tants/ der; ~**es**, **Tänze** /'tɛntsə/ (a) dance; jmdn. **zum** ~ **auffordern** ask sb. to dance or for a dance; **heute Abend ist** ~: there is dancing this evening; (b) (Zank, Auftritt) song and dance (fig. coll.)

Tanz-: ~**abend** der evening dance; ~**bar** die nightspot (coll.) with dancing; ~**bär** der dancing bear; ~**bein** das in **das** ~**bein schwingen** (ugs. scherzh.) shake a leg (coll.); ~**boden** der dance-floor; ~**café** das coffeehouse with dancing

tänzeln /'tɛntsl̩n/ itr. V. (a) prance; (b) mit sein **sie tänzelte ins Zimmer** she skipped into the room

tanzen 1 itr. V. (a) dance; ~ **gehen** go dancing; **auf dem Seil** ~: walk the tightrope; (b) mit sein (sich ~d fortbewegen) dance; skip. 2 tr. V. **Walzer** ~: dance a waltz; waltz

Tänzer /'tɛntsə/ der; ~**s**, ~, **Tänzerin** die; ~, ~**nen** ▶ **85** (a) dancer; (b) (Partner[in]) dancing partner

tänzerisch 1 Adj. dance-like ‹movement, rhythm, step›; ~**e Begabung** talent for dancing. 2 adv. ~ **begabt sein** have a talent for dancing

Tanz-: ~**fläche** die dance-floor; ~**kapelle** die dance band; ~**lehrer** der dancing-teacher; ~**lokal** das café/restaurant with dancing; ~**musik** die dance music; ~**orchester** das ⇒ ~**kapelle**; ~**saal** der dance hall; (in hotel, castle, etc.) ballroom; ~**sport** der ballroom or competition dancing no art.; ~**stunde** die (a) (~kurs) dancing-class; ~**stunde nehmen, in die** ~**stunde gehen** take dancing lessons; go to dancing-class; (b) (einzelne Stunde) dancing lesson; ~**tee** der tea dance; thé dansant

Tapet das in **aufs** ~ **kommen** (ugs.) be brought up; come up [for discussion]; **etw. aufs** ~ **bringen** (ugs.) bring sth. up; broach sth.

Tapete /ta'pe:tə/ die; ~, ~**n** wallpaper

Tapeten-: ~**rolle** die roll of wallpaper; ~**wechsel** der (ugs.) change of scene

tapezieren /tape'tsi:rən/ tr. V. [wall]paper

Tapezierer der; ~**s**, ~: ▶ **85** paper-hanger

tapfer /'tapfə/ 1 Adj. brave; courageous. 2 adv. (a) bravely; courageously; **sich** ~ **halten** be brave; (b) (kräftig) ‹eat, drink› heartily

Tapferkeit die; ~: courage; bravery

tappen itr. V. (a) mit sein patter; **in eine Falle** ~ (fig.) stumble into a trap; (b) (tastend greifen) grope (**nach** for)

täppisch /'tɛpɪʃ/ 1 Adj. awkward; clumsy. 2 adv. awkwardly; clumsily

tapsig /'tapsɪç/ (ugs.) 1 Adj. awkward; clumsy. 2 adv. awkwardly; clumsily

Tarif /ta'ri:f/ der; ~**s**, ~**e** (a) (Preis, Gebühr) charge; (Post~, Wasser~) rate; (Verkehrs~) fares pl.; (Zoll~) tariff; (b) (~verzeichnis) list of charges/rates/fares; tariff; (c) (Lohn~) [wage] rate; (Gehalts~) [salary] scale; **weit über/unter** ~ **verdienen** earn well above/far below the agreed rate

Tarif·gruppe die (Lohngruppe) wage group; (Gehaltsgruppe) salary group

tariflich 1 Adj.; nicht präd. wage ‹demand, dispute, etc.›. 2 adv. **Löhne und Gehälter sind** ~ **festgelegt** there are fixed rates for wages and salaries

Tarif·lohn der wage under the collective agreement

tarnen /'tarnən/ 1 tr., itr. V. camouflage. 2 refl. V. camouflage oneself

Tarn·farbe die camouflage [colour]

Tarnung die; ~, ~**en** (auch fig.) camouflage

Tartan·bahn /'tartan-/ die Tartan track (P)

Tasche /'taʃə/ die; ~, ~**n** (a) bag; (b) (in Kleidung, Koffer, Rucksack usw.) pocket; (c) (fig.) **sich** (Dat.) **die eigenen** ~**n füllen** (ugs.) line one's own pockets or purse; **jmdm. auf der** ~ **liegen** (ugs.) live off sb.; **etw. aus eigener** od. **der eigenen** ~ **bezahlen** pay for sth. out of one's own pocket; **jmdm. etw. aus der** ~ **ziehen** (ugs.) wangle money out of sb. (coll.); [**für etw.**] **tief in die** ~ **greifen [müssen]** (ugs.) [have to] dig deep in or into one's pocket [for sth.]; **jmdn. in die** ~ **stecken** (ugs.) put sb. in the shade; **sich** (Dat.) **in die eigene** ~ **lügen** (ugs.) fool oneself

Taschen-: ~**buch** das paperback; ~**dieb** der pickpocket; ~**geld** das pocket money; ~**lampe** die [pocket] torch (Brit.) or (Amer.) flashlight; ~**messer** das pocket-knife; penknife; ~**rechner** der pocket calculator; ~**tuch** das; Pl. ~**tücher** handkerchief; ~**uhr** die pocket-watch

Tässchen, *****Täßchen** /'tɛsçən/ das; ~**s**, ~: [small] cup

Tasse /'tasə/ die; ~, ~**n** (a) cup; **eine** ~ **Tee** a cup of tea; **trübe** ~ (ugs. abwertend) drip (coll.); (b) (~ mit Untertasse) cup and saucer; **nicht alle** ~**n im Schrank haben** (ugs.) not be right in the head (coll.)

Taste /'tastə/ die; ~, ~**n** (a) key; (b) (am Telefon, Radio, Fernsehgerät, Taschenrechner usw.) button

tasten 1 itr. V. grope, feel (**nach** for); ~**de Fragen** (fig.) tentative questions. 2 refl. V. grope or feel one's way

Tasten-: ~**instrument** das keyboard instrument; ~**telefon** das push-button telephone

tat /ta:t/ 1. u. 3. Pers. Sg. Prät. v. **tun**

Tat die; ~, ~**en** (a) (Handlung) act; (das Tun) action; **zur** ~ **schreiten** proceed to action; **jmdn. auf frischer** ~ **ertappen** catch sb. red-handed or in the act; **etw. in die** ~ **umsetzen** put sth. into action or effect; **eine gute** ~ **vollbringen** do a good deed; (b) **in der** ~ (verstärkend) actually; (zustimmend) indeed

Tat·bestand der (a) facts pl. [of the matter or case]; (b) (Rechtsw.) elements pl. of an offence; **der** ~**bestand der vorsätzlichen Tötung** the offence of premedidated murder

Taten·drang der desire or thirst for action

taten·los 1 Adj. idle. 2 adv. idly; **einer Sache** (Dat.) ~**los zusehen** watch sth. without taking any action

Täter /'tɛ:tə/ der; ~**s**, ~: culprit; **wer ist der** ~? who did it?; **der** ~ **hat sich der Polizei gestellt** the person who committed the crime gave himself/herself up to the police; **nach dem** ~ **fahnden** search or look for the person responsible [for the crime]

Täterin die; ~, ~**nen** ⇒ **Täter**

tätig /'tɛ:tɪç/ Adj. (a) ~ **sein** work; ~ **werden** (bes. Amtsspr.) take action; (b) (rührig, aktiv) active

tätigen /'tɛ:tɪgn̩/ tr. V. (Kaufmannsspr., Papierdt.) transact ‹business, deal, etc.›; (Einkäufe) effect purchases

Tätigkeit die; ~, ~**en** (a) activity; (Arbeit) job; **eine** ~ **ausüben** do work; do a job; (b) o. Pl. (das In-Betrieb-Sein) operation

Tat·kraft die energy; drive

tat·kräftig 1 Adj. energetic, active ‹person›; active ‹help, support›. 2 adv. energetically; actively

tätlich /'tɛ:tlɪç/ 1 Adj. physical ‹clash, attack, resistance, etc.›; **gegen jmdn.** ~ **werden** become violent towards sb. 2 adv. physically

Tat·ort der; Pl. ~**e** scene of a/the crime

tätowieren /tɛto'vi:rən/ tr. V. tattoo; **sich** (Dat.) **etw.** ~ **lassen** have oneself tattooed with sth.

Tätowierung die; ~, ~**en** (a) tattoo; (b) (das Tätowieren) tattooing

Tat·sache die fact; ~? (ugs.) really?; is that true?; **nackte** ~**n** hard facts; (scherzh.) naked bodies; **vollendete** ~**n schaffen** create a fait accompli; s. auch **Vorspiegelung**

Tatsachen·bericht *der* factual report

tatsächlich /'ta:tzɛçlɪç/ **1** *Adj.* actual; real. **2** *adv.* actually; really; **ist das ∼ wahr?** is that really true?; **ich habe mich ∼ geirrt** I was indeed mistaken

tätscheln /'tɛtʃln/ *tr. V.* pat

tatschen /'tatʃn/ *itr. V.* (ugs.) **an/auf etw.** (*Akk.*) **∼:** paw sth.

tatt[e]rig *Adj.* (ugs.) shaky ⟨*hands, movements, etc.*⟩; doddery ⟨*person*⟩

tat·verdächtig *Adj.* suspected

Tatze /'tatsə/ *die;* ∼, ∼n paw

Tau¹ /tau/ *der;* ∼[e]s dew

Tau² *das;* ∼[e]s, ∼e (Seil) rope

taub /taup/ *Adj.* **(a)** deaf; **(b)** (wie abgestorben) numb; **(c)** (leer, unbefruchtet usw.) empty ⟨*nut*⟩; unfruitful ⟨*ear of corn*⟩; dead ⟨*rock*⟩

Taube¹ *die;* ∼, ∼n pigeon; (Turtel∼; auch Politik fig.) dove

Taube² *der/die; adj. Dekl.* deaf person; deaf man/woman; **die ∼n** the deaf

Tauben·schlag *der* pigeon-loft; (für Turteltauben) dovecot; **hier geht es zu wie in einem** *od.* **im ∼** (ugs.) it's like Piccadilly Circus here (Brit. coll.); it's like being in the middle of Times Square (Amer.)

Taubheit *die;* ∼: deafness

taub·stumm *Adj.* deaf and dumb

Taub·stumme *der/die; adj. Dekl.* deaf mute

tauchen 1 *itr. V.* **(a)** auch mit sein dive (**nach** for); **er kann zwei Minuten [lang] ∼:** he can stay under water for two minutes; **(b)** *mit sein* dive; (auf∼) rise; emerge. **2** *tr. V.* **(a)** (ein∼) dip; **(b)** (unter∼) duck

Taucher *der;* ∼s, ∼: diver; (mit Flossen und Atemgerät) skin diver

Taucher-: ∼**anzug** *der* diving suit; ∼**brille** *die* diving-goggles *pl.*

Taucherin *die;* ∼, ∼nen ⇒ Taucher

Tauch-: ∼**sieder** *der;* ∼s, ∼: portable immersion heater; ∼**station** *die:* **auf ∼station gehen** (*auf dem U-Boot*) go to one's diving station; (fig. ugs.) go to ground

tauen 1 *itr. V.* **(a)** (unpers.) **es taut** it's thawing; **(b)** *mit sein* (schmelzen) melt. **2** *tr. V.* melt; thaw

Tauf·becken *das* font

Taufe *die;* ∼, ∼n **(a)** *o. Pl.* (christl. Rel.: Sakrament) baptism; **(b)** (christl. Rel.: Zeremonie) christening; baptism; **etw. aus der ∼ heben** (fig. ugs.) launch sth.

taufen *tr. V.* **(a)** (die Taufe vollziehen an) baptize; **katholisch getauft sein** be baptized a Catholic; (einen Namen geben) christen ⟨*child, ship, animal, etc.*⟩; **ein Kind auf den Namen Peter ∼:** christen a child Peter

Täufling /'tɔyflɪŋ/ *der;* ∼s, ∼e child to be baptized; (Erwachsener) person to be baptized

Tauf-: ∼**pate** *der* godparent; (männlicher ∼pate) godfather; ∼**patin** *die* godmother; ∼**schein** *der* certificate of baptism; baptismal certificate

taugen /'taugn/ *itr. V.* **nichts/wenig** *od.* **nicht viel/ etwas ∼:** be no/not much/some good *or* use; **zu** *od.* **für etw. ∼** ⟨*person*⟩ be suited to sth.; ⟨*thing*⟩ be suitable for sth.; **nicht wissen, was etw. wirklich taugt** not know how useful sth. really is

Taugenichts *der;* ∼[es], ∼e (veralt. abwertend) good-for-nothing

tauglich *Adj.* **(a)** [**nicht**] ∼: [un]suitable; **(b)** (für Militärdienst) fit [for service]

Taumel *der;* ∼s **(a)** (Schwindel, Benommenheit) [feeling of] dizziness *or* giddiness; **(b)** (Begeisterung, Rausch) frenzy; fever; **ein ∼ der Begeisterung** a fever of excitement

taumeln /'taumln/ *itr. V.* **(a)** auch mit sein reel, sway; **(b)** *mit sein* (sich ∼d bewegen) stagger

Tausch *der;* ∼[e]s, ∼e exchange; **ein guter/ schlechter ∼:** a good/bad deal; **im ∼ gegen** *od.* **für etw.** in exchange for sth.

tauschen 1 *tr. V.* exchange (**gegen** for); **Briefmarken ∼:** exchange *or* swap stamps; **sie tauschten die Partner/Plätze** they changed *or* swapped partners/places. **2** *itr. V.* **mit jmdm. ∼** (fig.) change *or* swap places with sb.

täuschen /'tɔyʃn/ **1** *tr. V.* deceive; **der Schein täuscht uns oft** appearances are often deceiving; **wenn mich nicht alles täuscht** unless I'm completely mistaken. **2** *itr. V.* **(a)** (irreführen) be deceptive; **(b)** (bes. Sport: ablenken) make a feint. **3** *refl. V.* be wrong *or* mistaken (**in** + *Dat.* about); **ich habe mich in ihm getäuscht** I was wrong about him; he disappointed me; **da täuschst du dich aber [gewaltig]** but that's where you're [very much] mistaken

täuschend 1 *Adj.* remarkable, striking ⟨*similarity, imitation*⟩. **2** *adv.* remarkably

Tausch-: ∼**geschäft** *das* exchange [deal]; ∼**handel** *der* **(a)** bartering; **(b)** (Wirtsch.) trade by barter

Täuschung *die;* ∼, ∼en **(a)** (das Täuschen) deception; **(b)** (Selbst∼) delusion; illusion; **optische ∼:** optical illusion

tausend /'tauznt/ *Kardinalz.* ▶600 **(a)** a *or* one thousand; **(b)** (ugs.: sehr viele) thousands of; **∼ Dank** a thousand thanks

Tausend *das;* ∼s, ∼e *od.* ∼ **(a)** *nicht in Verbindung mit Kardinalzahlen; Pl.:* ∼ (Einheit von tausend Stück) thousand; **vom ∼:** per thousand; **(b)** *Pl.* (eine unbestimmte große Zahl) thousands; **∼e Zuschauer** thousands of spectators; **die Tiere starben zu ∼en** the animals died in [their] thousands

Tausender *der;* ∼s, ∼ **(a)** (ugs.) (Tausendmarkschein usw.) thousand-mark/-dollar *etc.* note; (Betrag) thousand marks/ dollars *etc.*; **(b)** (Math.) thousand

tausenderlei *Gattungsz.; indekl.* (ugs.) **(a)** (von verschiedener Art) a thousand and one different ⟨*answers, kinds, etc.*⟩; **(b)** (viele) a thousand and one

Tausend·jahr·feier *die* millenary; millennial

tausend·jährig *Adj.; nicht präd.* **(a)** (tausend Jahre alt) [one-]thousand-year-old; **(b)** (tausend Jahre dauernd) thousand-year[-long]

tausend·mal *Adv.* a thousand times

tausendst... *Ordinalz.* ▶600 thousandth

tausendstel /'tauzntstl/ *Bruchz.* ▶600 thousandth

Tau-: ∼**tropfen** *der* dew-drop; ∼**wetter** *das* thaw

Taxa·meter /taxa-/ *der* [taxi]meter

Taxe /'taksə/ *die;* ∼, ∼n **(a)** taxi; **(b)** (Gebühr) charge; **(c)** (taxierter Preis) valuation

Taxi /'taksi/ *das;* ∼s, ∼s taxi; **mit dem ∼:** by taxi *or* in a taxi

taxieren *tr. V.* **(a)** (ugs.: schätzen) estimate (**auf** + *Akk.* at); **etw. zu hoch/niedrig ∼:** overestimate/underestimate sth.; **(b)** (den Wert ermitteln von) value (**auf** + *Akk.* at); **etw. zu hoch/niedrig ∼:** overvalue/undervalue sth.; **(c)** (ugs.: mustern, prüfen) size up (coll.); **(d)** (einschätzen) assess

Taxi-: ∼**fahrer** *der* ▶85 taxi driver; ∼**fahrt** *die* taxi ride; ∼**stand** *der* taxi rank (Brit.); taxi stand

Tb, Tbc /te:'be:, te:be:'tse:/ *die;* ∼ *Abk.* **Tuberkulose** TB

Tb-Kranke /te:'be:-/ *der/die; adj. Dekl.* TB patient; patient with TB

Team /ti:m/ *das;* ∼s, ∼s team

Teamwork /'ti:mwə:k/ *das;* ∼s teamwork

Technik /'tɛçnɪk/ *die;* ∼, ∼en (a) *o. Pl.* technology; (Studienfach) engineering *no art.*; **auf dem neuesten Stand der ∼:** incorporating the latest technical advances; **(b)** *o. Pl.* (Ausrüstung) equipment; machinery; **(c)** (Arbeitsweise, Verfahren) technique; **(d)** *o. Pl.* (eines Gerätes) workings *pl.*

Techniker *der;* ∼s, ∼, **Technikerin** *die;* ∼, ∼nen **(a)** technical expert; **(b)** (im Sport, in der Kunst) technician

technisch /'tɛçnɪʃ/ **1** *Adj.* technical ⟨*fault*⟩; technological ⟨*progress, age*⟩. **2** *adv.* technically; technologically ⟨*advanced*⟩; **∼ begabt sein** have a technical flair

Techno¹ /'tɛkno/ *das od. der;* ∼s techno

Techno² /'tɛkno/ *der;* ∼s, ∼s techno fan

Technologie /tɛçnoloˈgi:/ *die;* ∼, ∼n technology

Technologie·park *der* science park

technologisch **1** *Adj.* technological. **2** *adv.* technologically

Techno·party *die* techno party

Techtelmechtel /tɛçtl'mɛçtl/*das;* ~s, ~: affair

Teddy·bär /'tɛdi-/ *der* teddy bear

Tee /te:/ *der;* ~s, ~s tea; [einen] ~ **machen** make some tea

Tee-: ~**beutel** *der* tea bag; ~**glas** *das; Pl.* ~**gläser** tea-glass; ~**kanne** *die* teapot; ~**löffel** *der* teaspoon

Teenager /'ti:ne:dʒɐ/ *der;* ~s, ~: ▶ 22 ⌐ teenager

Teer /te:ɐ/ *der;* ~[e]s, (Arten:) ~e tar

teeren *tr. V.* tar; jmdn. ~ **und federn** tar and feather sb.

Tee-: ~**rose** *die* tea rose; ~**service** *das* tea service; teaset; ~**sieb** *das* tea-strainer; ~**stube** *die* tearoom; ~**tasse** *die* teacup

Teich /taiç/ *der;* ~[e]s, ~e pond

Teig /taik/ *der;* ~[e]s, ~e dough; (Kuchen~, Biskuit~) pastry; (Pfannkuchen~, Waffel~) batter; (in Rezepten auch) mixture

teigig *Adj.* **(a)** (wie Teig) doughy; **(b)** (blass u. schwammig) pasty ⟨face, skin, complexion⟩

Teig·waren *Pl.* pasta *sing.*

Teil /tail/ **(a)** *der;* ~[e]s, ~e (etw. von einem Ganzen) part; **achter** ~ (Achtel) eighth; **weite** ~**e des Landes** wide areas of the country; **ein [großer** *od.* **guter]** ~ **der Bevölkerung** a [large] section of the population; **zum** ~: partly; **den größten** ~ **des Weges hat er zu Fuß zurückgelegt** he walked most of the way; **(b)** *der od. das;* ~[e]s, ~e (Anteil) share; **(c)** *der od. das;* ~[e]s, ~e (Beitrag) share; **ich will gerne mein[en]** ~ **dazu beisteuern** I should like to do my share *or* bit; **(d)** *der;* ~[e]s, ~e (beteiligte Person[en]; Rechtsw.: Partei) party; **(e)** *das;* ~[e]s, ~e (Einzel~) part; **etw. in seine** ~**e zerlegen** take sth. apart *or* to pieces

teil·bar *Adj.* divisible (**durch** by)

Teilchen *das;* ~s, ~ **(a)** (kleines Stück) [small] part; **(b)** (Partikel) particle

teilen 1 *tr. V.* **(a)** (zerlegen, trennen) divide [up]; **(b)** (dividieren) divide (**durch** by); **(c)** (auf~) share (**unter** + *Dat.* among); **(d)** (teilweise überlassen, gemeinsam nutzen, teilhaben an) share; **(e)** (in zwei Teile ~) divide. 2 *refl. V.* **(a)** sich (*Dat.*) etw. [mit jmdm.] ~: share sth. [with sb.]; **(b)** (auseinander gehen) **der Weg teilt sich** the road forks; **geteilter Meinung sein** have different views *or* opinions. 3 *itr. V.* share

teil|haben *unr. itr. V.* share (**an** + *Dat.* in)

Teilhaber *der;* ~s, ~, **Teilhaberin** *die;* ~, ~**nen** partner

Teil·kasko·versicherung *die* insurance giving limited cover

Teilnahme /'tailna:mə/ *die;* ~, ~**n (a)** (das Mitmachen) participation (**an** + *Dat.* in); ~ **an einem Kurs** attendance at a course; **(b)** (Interesse) interest (**an** + *Dat.* in); **(c)** (geh.: Mitgefühl) sympathy

teilnahms-: ~**los** *Adj.* (gleichgültig) indifferent; (apathisch) apathetic; ~**voll** 1 *Adj.* compassionate; 2 *adv.* compassionately; **jmdn.** ~ **ansehen** look at sb. with compassion

teil|nehmen /'tailne:mən/ *unr. itr. V.* **(a)** (dabei sein bei) [an etw. (*Dat.*)] ~: attend [sth.]; **(b)** (beteiligt sein) [an etw. (*Dat.*)] ~: take part [in sth.]; **am Krieg** ~: fight in the war; **(c)** (als Lernender) [an einem Lehrgang/am Unterricht ~: attend [a course]/lessons; **(d)** (Teilnahme zeigen) **an jmds. Schmerz/Glück** ~: share sb.'s pain/happiness

Teilnehmer *der;* ~s, ~ **(a)** participant (*Gen.*, **an** + *Dat.* in); (bei Wettbewerb auch) competitor, contestant (**an** + *Dat.* in); **(b)** (Fernspr.) subscriber

teils /tails/ *Adv.* partly; **Wie hat es dir gestern gefallen? — Teils,** ~ (ugs.) How did you like it yesterday? — So so

Teil-: ~**strecke** *die* (einer Straße) stretch; (einer Buslinie usw.) stage; (Rennsport) stage; ~**stück** *das* piece; part

Teilung *die;* ~, ~**en** division

teil·weise 1 *Adv.* partly. 2 *adj.* partial

Teil-: ~**zahlung** *die* instalment; ~**zeit·arbeit** *die* part-time work *no indef. art.;* (Stelle) part-time job

---

Teint /tɛ̃:/ *der;* ~s, ~s complexion

tele-, Tele- /'te:le-/ tele-

Tele-: ~**arbeit** *die* (salopp) teleworking; telecommuting; ~**arbeiter** *der* teleworker; telecommuter

Telefon /'te:lefo:n, *auch* tele'fo:n/ *das;* ~s, ~e telephone; phone (coll.); **ans** ~ **gehen** answer the [tele]phone

Telefon-: ~**anruf** *der* [tele]phone call; ~**anschluss, *** ~**anschluß** *der* telephone; line; ~**apparat** *der* telephone

Telefonat /telefo'na:t/ *das;* ~[e]s, ~e telephone call

Telefon-: ~**buch** *das* [tele]phone book *or* directory; ~**gebühr** *die* telephone charge; ~**gespräch** *das* telephone conversation

telefonieren /telefo'ni:rən/ *itr. V.* make a [tele]phone call; **mit jmdm.** ~: talk to sb. [on the telephone]/be on the telephone to sb.; **nach Hause/England** ~: phone home/make a [tele]phone call to England; **er telefoniert gerade** he is on the phone at the moment

telefonisch 1 *Adj.* telephone; **die** ~**e Zeitansage** the speaking clock (Brit. coll.); the telephone time service. 2 *adv.* by telephone; **jmdm. etw.** ~ **mitteilen** inform sb. of sth. over the *or* by telephone; **ich bin** ~ **zu erreichen** I can be contacted by telephone

Telefonist /telefo'nɪst/ *der;* ~en, ~en, **Telefonistin** *die;* ~, ~**nen** ▶ 85 ⌐ telephonist; (in einer Firma) switchboard operator

Telefon-: ~**karte** *die* phonecard; ~**nummer** *die* [tele]phone number; ~**rechnung** *die* [tele]phone bill; ~**verbindung** *die* telephone line; ~**verzeichnis** *das* telephone list; ~**zelle** *die* [tele]phone booth *or* (Brit.) box; call box (Brit.)

Telegraf /tele'gra:f/ *der;* ~en, ~en telegraph

Telegrafie *die;* ~: telegraphy *no art.*

telegrafieren /telegra'fi:rən/ *itr., tr. V.* telegraph; **jmdm.** ~: send a telegram to sb.

telegrafisch 1 *Adj.* telegraphic. 2 *adv.* by telegraph *or* telegram; ~ **überwiesenes Geld** money sent by telegram *or* cable

Telegramm *das* telegram

Tele-: ~**kolleg** *das* ≈ Open University (Brit.); ~**objektiv** *das* (Fot.) telephoto lens

Telepathie /telepa'ti:/ *die;* ~: telepathy *no art.*

Tele·shopping *das* teleshopping

Tele·skop /tele'sko:p/ *das;* ~s, ~e telescope

Telex /'te:lɛks/ *das;* ~, ~[e] telex

Teller /'tɛlɐ/ *der;* ~s, ~ plate; **ein** ~ **Suppe** a plate of soup

Teller·wäscher *der* dishwasher; **vom** ~ **zum Millionär [werden]** [go] from rags to riches

Tempel /'tɛmpl/ *der;* ~s, ~ temple

Temperament /tɛmpəra'mɛnt/ *das;* ~[e]s, ~e **(a)** (Wesensart) temperament; **(b)** *o. Pl.* **eine Frau mit** ~: a lively *or* vivacious woman; a woman with spirit; **sein** ~ **reißt alle mit** his vivacity infects everyone; **das** ~ **geht oft mit mir durch** I often lose my temper

temperament-: ~**los** *Adj.* spiritless; lifeless; ~**voll** *Adj.* spirited ⟨person, speech, dance, etc.⟩; lively ⟨start etc.⟩

Temperatur /tɛmpəra'tu:ɐ/ *die;* ~, ~**en** ▶ 511 ⌐ temperature; **die richtige** ~ **haben** be [at] the right temperature; **[erhöhte]** ~ **haben** ⟨person⟩ have *or* be running a temperature; **jmds.** ~ **messen** take sb.'s temperature

Temperatur-: ~**anstieg** *der* rise in temperature; ~**rückgang** *der* drop *or* fall in temperature; ~**sturz** *der* [sudden] fall *or* drop in temperature

temperieren /tɛmpə'ri:rən/ *tr. V.* bring to the right temperature; **das Wasser ist gut temperiert** the water is [at] the right temperature

Tempo /'tɛmpo/ *das;* ~s, ~s *od.* **Tempi (a)** *Pl.* ~s speed; **das** ~ **erhöhen** speed up; accelerate; **in** *od.* **mit hohem** ~: at high speed; **hier gilt** ~ **100** there is a 100 k.p.h. speed limit here; ~ **[~]!** (ugs.), **mach mal ein bisschen** ~ (ugs.) get a move on; **(b)** (Musik) tempo; time

Tempo·limit *das* ▶ 224 ⌐ (Verkehrsw.) speed limit

Tendenz /tɛn'dɛnts/ *die;* ~, ~**en (a)** trend; **es herrscht die** ~/**die** ~ **geht dahin, … zu …:** there is a tendency

---

*alte Schreibung (vgl. Hinweise auf S. xvi–xvii)

Temperaturen

Temperaturen werden in Großbritannien zum Teil noch in Fahrenheit angegeben, obwohl alle Wetterberichte, Schulprüfungen und andere amtliche Quellen die Celsiusskala gebrauchen. In den USA dagegen sind Temperaturen in Fahrenheit noch gang und gäbe.

Um Celsius in Fahrenheit umzurechnen, benutzt man die folgende Formel: Grad in Celsius mal 9 dividiert durch 5 plus 32 (°C × 9 ÷ 5 + 32 = °F).

	Celsius (°C)	Fahrenheit (°F)	
Siedepunkt	100	212	Boiling point
	90	194	
	80	176	
	70	158	
	60	140	
	50	122	
	40	104	
Körpertemperatur	37	98.4	Body temperature
	30	86	
	20	68	
	10	50	
Gefrierpunkt	0	32	Freezing point
	– 10	14	
	– 17,8	0	
absoluter Nullpunkt	– 273,15	– 459.67	Absolute zero

Das Wetter

Wie viel Grad sind es? = What's the temperature?

Die Außentemperatur beträgt 20 Grad [Celsius] = The outside temperature is 20 degrees [centigrade] *od. (bes. amerik.)* 68 degrees Fahrenheit

Höchsttemperaturen um 27 Grad = Maximum temperatures around 27 degrees, *(bes. amerik.)* Highs around 80 degrees

Tiefsttemperaturen um 10 Grad = Temperatures falling to 10 degrees, *(bes. amerik.)* Lows around 50 degrees

Temperaturen um den Gefrierpunkt = temperatures around freezing

zehn Grad unter Null = ten degrees below freezing

– 15°C (minus fünfzehn Grad Celsius) = – 15°C (minus fifteen degrees centigrade)

Die Temperatur liegt über/unter dem Gefrierpunkt = The temperature is above/below freezing

In Berlin herrscht die gleiche Temperatur = It's the same temperature *od.* The temperature is the same in Berlin

Bei Personen

Sie hat erhöhte Temperatur = She has a [slight] temperature, Her temperature is above normal

Er hat [hohes] Fieber/40 Grad Fieber = He has a high temperature/ a temperature of 40 [centigrade] *od.* 104 [Fahrenheit]

Wie hoch ist od. Was ist Ihre Temperatur? = What is your temperature?

Ich habe kein Fieber = I haven't got a temperature, My temperature is normal

Sie hat bei ihm Fieber gemessen = She took his temperature

Bei Dingen

Bei welcher Temperatur kocht Wasser? = What temperature does water boil at?

Wasser kocht bei 100°C = Water boils at 100° *od.* 212°F

Welche Temperatur hat der Wein? = What is the temperature of the wine?

Der Wein muss die richtige Temperatur haben = The wine must be the right temperature

A hat die gleiche Temperatur wie B = A is the same temperature as B

---

to ...; the trend is to ...; (**b**) (Hang, Neigung) tendency; (**c**) (oft abwertend: Darstellungsweise) slant; bias

tendenziös /...'tsiø:s/ *Adj.* tendentious

tendieren /tɛn'diːrən/ *itr. V.* tend (**zu** towards); **der nach links ～de Flügel dieser Partei** the branch of the party with left-wing leanings

Tennis /'tɛnɪs/ *das; ～:* tennis *no art.*

Tennis-: **～ball** *der* tennis ball; **～platz** *der* tennis court; **～schläger** *der* tennis racket; **～spiel** *das* (**a**) *o. Pl.* (Tennis) tennis *no art.;* (**b**) (Einzelspiel) game of tennis; **～spieler** *der* tennis player

Tenor¹ /te'noːɐ̯/ *der;* ～**s**, **Tenöre** /te'nøːrə/, (österr. auch:) ～**e** (Musik) (**a**) (Stimmlage, Sänger) tenor; (**b**) *o. Pl.* (im Chor) tenors *pl.;* tenor voices *pl.*

Tenor² /'teːnɔr/ *der;* ～**s** tenor

Teppich /'tɛpɪç/ *der;* ～**s**, ～**e** carpet; (kleiner) rug; **auf dem ～ bleiben** (fig. ugs.) keep one's feet on the ground; **etw. unter den ～ kehren** (fig. ugs.) sweep sth. under the carpet

Teppich-: **～boden** *der* fitted carpet; **～kehrer** *der* carpet sweeper; **～klopfer** *der* carpet-beater

Term /tɛrm/ *der;* ～**s**, ～**e** (Math., Logik, Physik) term

Termin /tɛr'miːn/ *der;* ～**s**, ～**e** (**a**) (festgelegter Zeitpunkt) date; (Anmeldung) appointment; (Verabredung) engagement; **sich** (*Dat.*) **einen ～ geben lassen** make an appointment; (**b**) (Rechtsw.) hearing

Terminal /'tø:ɐ̯mɪnəl/ *das;* ～**s**, ～**s** terminal

termin·gemäß **1** *Adj.* on time *postpos.* **2** *adv.* on time; on schedule

Termini ⇒ **Terminus**

Termin·kalender *der* appointments book; (für gesellschaftliche Termine) engagements diary

Terminus /'tɛrminʊs/ *der;* ～, **Termini** term

Termite /tɛr'miːtə/ *die;* ～, ～**n** termite

Terpentin /tɛrpɛn'tiːn/ *das,* (österr. meist:) *der;* ～**s** (**a**) (Harz) turpentine; (**b**) (ugs.: Terpentinöl) turps *sing.* (coll.)

Terrain /tɛ'rɛ̃:/ *das;* ～**s**, ～**s** (**a**) (Gelände) terrain; **es ist für ihn ein unbekanntes ～** (fig.) it is unknown territory to him; **das ～ sondieren** (fig. geh.) sound out the situation; (**b**) (Baugelände) building land

Terrarium /tɛ'raːri̯ʊm/ *das;* ～**s**, **Terrarien** terrarium

Terrasse /tɛ'rasə/ *die;* ～, ～**n** terrace

terrassen·förmig **1** *Adj.* terraced. **2** *adv.* in terraces

terrestrisch /tɛ'rɛstrɪʃ/ **1** *Adj.* terrestrial. **2** *adv.* terrestrially

Terrier /'tɛri̯ɐ̯/ *der;* ～**s**, ～: terrier

Terrine /tɛ'riːnə/ *die;* ～, ～**n** tureen

territorial /tɛrito'ri̯aːl/ *Adj.* territorial

Territorium /tɛri'toːri̯ʊm/ *das;* ～**s**, **Territorien** (**a**) (Gebiet, Land) land; territory; (**b**) (Hoheitsgebiet) territory

Terror /'tɛrɔr/ *der;* ～**s** (**a**) terrorism *no art.;* **blutiger ～:** terror and bloodshed; (**b**) (ugs.: Zank u. Streit) trouble;

(c) (ugs.: großes Aufheben) big row (coll.) *or* fuss; ~ **machen** raise hell (coll.)

Terror·anschlag *der* terrorist attack

terrorisieren *tr. V.* (a) (durch Terror unterdrücken) terrorize; (b) (ugs.: belästigen) pester

Terrorismus *der;* ~: terrorism *no art.*

Terrorist *der;* ~en, ~en, **Terroristin** *die;* ~, ~nen terrorist

terroristisch *Adj.; nicht präd* terrorist

Tertia /'tɛrtsi̯a/ *die;* ~, **Tertien** (Schulw.) (veralt.) fourth and fifth year (*of a Gymnasium*)

Terz /tɛrts/ *die;* ~, ~en (Musik) third

Tesa·film ⓦ /'te:za-/ *der;* ~[e]s Sellotape (Brit.) (P); Scotch tape (Amer.) (P)

Test /tɛst/ *der;* ~[e]s, ~s *od.* ~e test

Testament /tɛsta'mɛnt/ *das;* ~[e]s, ~e (a) will; **das ~ eröffnen** read the will; **er kann sein ~ machen** (fig. ugs.) he is [in] for it (coll.); (b) (christl. Rel.) Testament; **das Alte/Neue ~:** the Old/New Testament

testamentarisch /tɛstamɛn'ta:rɪʃ/ 1 *Adj.; nicht präd.* testamentary. 2 *adv.* **etw. ~ verfügen** write sth. in one's will

testen *tr. V.* test (**auf** + *Akk.* for)

Test-: ~**fall** *der* test case; ~**frage** *die* test question

Tetanus /'te:tanʊs/ *der;* ~ ▶ 329| (Med.) tetanus *no art.*

teuer /'tɔy̯ɐ/ 1 *Adj.* (a) expensive; dear *usu. pred.;* **wie ~ war das?** how much did that cost?; **Kaffee soll wieder teurer werden** coffee is supposed to be going up again; *s. auch* **Rat** a; (b) (veralt.: geschätzt) dear; **teurer Freund!** [my] dear friend!; [**mein**] **Teuerster!** [my] dearest; (von Mann zu Mann) [my] dearest friend. 2 *adv.* expensively; dearly; **etw. ~ kaufen/verkaufen** pay a great deal for sth./sell sth. at a high price; **sie haben ihren Sieg ~ erkauft** they paid a high price for their victory

Teuerung *die;* ~, ~en rise in prices

Teufel /'tɔy̯fl̩/ *der;* ~s, ~: devil; **der ~:** the Devil; **wie der ~ fahren** drive in daredevil fashion; **der ~ ist los** all hell's let loose (coll.); **dich reitet wohl der ~!** what's got into you?; **hol dich/ihn** *usw.* **der ~!/der ~ soll dich/ihn** *usw.* **holen!** (salopp) sod (Brit. sl.) *or* (coll.) damn you/him *etc.;* **das weiß der ~!** (salopp) God [only] knows; **hinter etw. her sein wie der ~** hinter der armen Seele (ugs.) be greedy for sth.; **den ~ werde ich [tun]!** (salopp) like hell [I will]! (coll.); **mal bloß nicht den ~ an die Wand!** (ugs.) don't invite trouble/(stärker) disaster by talking like that!; **des ~s sein** (ugs.) be mad; have taken leave of one's senses; **in ~s Küche kommen/jmdn. in ~s Küche bringen** (ugs.) get into/put sb. in a hell of a mess (coll.); **warum musst du den jetzt auf ~ komm raus überholen?** (ugs.) why are you so hell-bent on overtaking him now? (coll.); **zum ~ gehen** (ugs.: kaputtgehen) be ruined; **er soll sich zum ~ scheren!** (salopp) he can go to hell (coll.) *or* blazes (coll.); **wer/wo** *usw.* **zum ~ ...** (salopp) who/where *etc.* the hell ... (coll.); **wenn man vom ~ spricht[, dann ist er nicht weit]** (scherzh.) speak *or* talk of the devil [and he will appear]

Teufels-: ~**kerl** *der* (ugs.) amazing fellow; ~**werk** *das* devil's work *no indef. art.*

teuflisch 1 *Adj.* (a) devilish, fiendish ‹plan, trick, *etc.*›; fiendish, diabolical ‹laughter, pleasure, *etc.*›; (b) (ugs.: groß, intensiv) terrible (coll.); dreadful (coll.). 2 *adv.* (a) fiendishly; diabolically; (b) (ugs.) terribly (coll.); dreadfully (coll.)

Text /tɛkst/ *der;* ~[e]s, ~e (a) text; (eines Gesetzes, auf einem Plakat) wording; (eines Theaterstücks) script; (einer Oper) libretto; **weiter im ~!** (ugs.) [let's] carry on!; (b) (eines Liedes, Chansons usw.) words *pl.;* (eines Schlagers) words *pl.;* lyrics *pl.;* (c) (zu einer Abbildung) caption

Text-: ~**aufgabe** *die* (Schule) problem; ~**buch** *das* libretto

texten *tr. V.* write ‹song, advertisement, *etc.*›

Texter *der;* ~s, ~: writer; (in der Werbung) copy-writer

Textil-: ~**branche** *die*, ~**gewerbe** *das* textile trade *or* industry

Textilien *Pl.* (a) textiles; (b) (Fertigwaren) textile goods

Textil-: ~**industrie** *die* textile industry ~**strand** *der* (ugs. scherzh.) beach where there is no nude bathing; ~**waren** *Pl.* textile goods

Text-: ~**stelle** *die* passage [in a/the text]; ~**verarbeitung** *die* text processing; word processing

Thailand (*das*); ~s Thailand

Thailänder *der;* ~s, ~, **Thailänderin** *die;* ~, ~nen ▶ 388| Thai

Theater /te'a:tɐ/ *das;* ~s, ~ (a) theatre; **ins ~ gehen** go to the theatre; **zum ~ gehen** (ugs.) go into the theatre; tread the boards; **beim** *od.* **am ~ sein** be *or* work in the theatre; ~ **spielen** act; (fig.) play-act; pretend; (put on an act; (b) *o. Pl.* (fig. ugs.) fuss; **mach [mir] kein ~!** don't make a fuss; **das ist doch alles nur ~:** that's all just play-acting

Theater-: ~**besucher** *der* theatre goer; ~**karte** *die* theatre ticket; ~**stück** *das* [stage] play

theatralisch /tea'tra:lɪʃ/ (auch fig.) 1 *Adj.* theatrical. 2 *adv.* theatrically

Theke /'te:kə/ *die;* ~, ~n (a) (Schanktisch) bar; (b) (Ladentisch) counter; **unter der ~** (fig.) under the counter

Thema /'te:ma/ *das;* ~s, **Themen** *od.* ~ta subject; topic; (einer Abhandlung) subject; theme; (Leitgedanke) theme; **das ~ wechseln** change the subject; **vom ~ abkommen** *od.* **abschweifen** wander off the subject *or* point

Thematik /te'ma:tɪk/ *die;* ~, ~en theme; (Themenkreis) themes *pl.;* (Themenkomplex) complex of themes

thematisch 1 *Adj.* thematic; **etw. nach ~en Gesichtspunkten ordnen** arrange sth. according to subject. 2 *adv.* thematically; (was das Thema betrifft) as regards subject matter

Theologe /teo'lo:gə/ *der;* ~n, ~n theologian

Theologie /teolo'gi:/ *die;* ~, ~n theology *no art.*

Theologin *die;* ~, ~nen theologian

theologisch 1 *Adj.* theological. 2 *adv.* theologically

Theoretiker /teo're:tikɐ/ *der;* ~s, ~: theoretician; theorist

theoretisch /teo're:tɪʃ/ 1 *Adj.* theoretical. 2 *adv.* theoretically

Theorie /teo'ri:/ *die;* ~, ~n theory

Therapeut /tera'pɔy̯t/ *der;* ~en, ~en, **Therapeutin** *die;* ~, ~nen therapist; therapeutist

therapeutisch 1 *Adj.* therapeutic. 2 *adv.* therapeutically

Therapie /tera'pi:/ *die;* ~, ~n therapy (**gegen** for); **eine ~ machen** (ugs.) undergo *or* have therapy *or* treatment

therapieren *tr. V.* treat

Thermal·bad *das* (a) (Ort) thermal spa; (b) (Bad) thermal bath

Thermik /'tɛrmɪk/ *die;* ~ (Met.) thermal

Thermo·meter /tɛrmo-/ *das* thermometer

Thermos·flasche ⓦ /'tɛrmɔs-/ *die* Thermos flask (P); vacuum flask

Thermostat /tɛrmo'sta:t/ *der;* ~[e]s *od.* ~en, ~e *od.* ~en thermostat

These /'te:zə/ *die;* ~, ~n thesis

Thomas /'to:mas/ *der;* ~, ~se **in ungläubiger ~:** doubting Thomas

Thriller /'θrɪlɐ/ *der;* ~s, ~: thriller

Thrombose /trɔm'bo:zə/ *die;* ~, ~n thrombosis

Thron /tro:n/ *der;* ~[e]s, ~e throne; **sein ~ wackelt** (fig.) his position is becoming very shaky

thronen *itr. V.* sit enthroned; (fig.: erhöht liegen) tower

Thron·folger *der;* ~s, ~, **Thron·folgerin** *die;* ~, ~nen heir to the throne

Thun·fisch /'tu:n-/ *der* tuna

Thüringen /'ty:rŋən/ (*das*); ~s Thuringia

Thüringer 1 *indekl. Adj.; nicht präd.* Thuringian. 2 *der;* ~s, ~: Thuringian

---

*alte Schreibung (vgl. Hinweise auf S. xvi–xvii)

thüringisch *Adj.* Thuringian; *s. auch* **badisch**
Thymian /'ty:mia:n/ *der;* ~s, ~e thyme
Tibet /'ti:bɛt/ *(das);* ~s Tibet
tibetisch *Adj.* Tibetan
Tick *der;* ~[e]s, ~s (a) (ugs.: Schrulle) quirk; thing (coll.); **du hast wohl einen kleinen** ~: you must be round the bend (coll.); (b) (Med.) tic
ticken *itr. V.* tick; **du tickst wohl nicht richtig** (salopp) you must be off your rocker (fig. coll.)
Ticker *der;* ~s, ~ (bes. Pressejargon) teleprinter; telex
Ticket /'tɪkət/ *das;* ~s, ~s ticket
ticktack /'tɪk'tak/ *Interj.* tick-tock
Tide /'ti:də/ *die;* ~, ~n (nordd., bes. Seemannsspr.) tide
tief /ti:f/ **1** *Adj.* (a) ▶ 277 ⏐ (auch fig.) deep; low ‹*neckline, bow*›; long ‹*fall*›; (b) ▶ 277 ⏐ (niedrig) low ‹*table, chair, temperature, tide, level, cloud*›; **den Sattel etwas** ~**er stellen** lower the saddle a bit; (c) (intensiv, stark) deep; intense ‹*pain, suffering*›; utter ‹*misery*›; great ‹*need, want*›; (d) (weit im Innern gelegen) **im** ~**en/**~**sten Afrika** in the depths of/in darkest Africa; **es freut mich aus** ~**stem Herzen/**~**ster Seele** I really am delighted; **in** ~**er/** ~**ster Nacht** in the *or* at dead of night; **im** ~**en/**~**sten Winter** in the depths of winter. **2** *adv.* (a) (weit unten) deep; **100 m** ~ **in/unter der Erde** 100 metres [down] under the earth; ~ **verschneit** deep in snow *postpos.;* **er war** ~ **in Gedanken** he was deep in thought; (b) (weit nach unten) ‹*dig, drill*› deep; ‹*fall, sink*› a long way; ‹*stoop, bow*› low; ~**er graben** dig deeper *or* more deeply; ~ **schürfend** (fig.) profound; (c) (in nur geringer Höhe) ‹*fly, hover, etc.*› low; ~ **liegen** be at a lower level; ~ **liegend** low-lying ‹*area*›; deep-set ‹*eyes*›; (d) (nach unten) ‹*hang etc.*› low; ~**er gehen** ‹*pilot*› go lower; (e) (weit innen) deep; ~ **im Dschungel** deep in the jungle; (f) (weit nach innen) deep; ‹*breathe, inhale*› deeply; **er sah ihr** ~ **in die Augen** he looked deep into her eyes; ~**er ins All vorstoßen** push deeper into space; **bis** ~ **in die Nacht/in den Winter** (fig.) until deep *or* late into the night/well into winter; ~ **greifend** (fig.) profound; (weit reichend) far-reaching; (g) **er sprach ganz** ~: he spoke in a deep voice; **zu** ~ **singen** sing flat; (h) (intensiv, stark) ‹*feel etc.*› deeply; ‹*sleep*› deeply, soundly; ~ **betrübt** deeply distressed *or* saddened
Tief *das;* ~s, ~s (Met.) low; depression; (fig.) low
tief-, Tief-: ~**bau** *der; o. Pl.* civil engineering *no art.* (at or below ground level);*~**betrübt** ⇒ **tief** 2 h; ~**druck** *der;* (a) *o. Pl.* (Met.) low pressure; (b) *der; Pl.* ~**drucke** intaglio *or* gravure [printing]; (Erzeugnis) intaglio *or* gravure [print]; ~**druck·gebiet** *das* (Met.) area of low pressure; depression
Tiefe *die;* ~, ~n (a) ▶ 277 ⏐ (Ausdehnung, Entfernung nach unten) depth; (b) (weit unten, im Innern gelegener Bereich; auch fig.) depths *pl.;* **in die** ~ **stürzen** plunge into the depths; **in der** ~ **ihres Herzens** (fig.) deep down in her heart; *s. auch* **Höhe** f; (c) (Ausdehnung nach hinten) depth; (d) *o. Pl.* ⇒ **tief** 1 c: depth; intensity; greatness; (e) (von Tönen, Klängen, Stimmen) deepness; (f) *o. Pl.* (fig.: Tiefgründigkeit) depth; profundity
Tief·ebene *die* (Georgr.) lowland plain
Tiefen·psychologie *die* depth psychology *no art.*
tief-, Tief-: ~**flug** *der* low-altitude flight *no art.;* flying *no art.* at low altitude; ~**gang** *der* (Schiffbau) draught; (fig.) depth; ~**garage** *die* underground car park;*~**greifend** ⇒ **tief** 2 f; ~**gründig** /~gryndɪç/ **1** *Adj.* profound; **2** *adv.* ‹*discuss, examine*› in depth; ~**kühlen** *tr. V.* [deep-]freeze
Tief·kühl-: ~**fach** *das* freezer [compartment]; ~**kost** *die* frozen food; ~**truhe** *die* [chest] freezer *or* deep-freeze
tief-, Tief-: ~**land** *das; Pl.* ~**länder** *od.* ~**lande** lowlands *pl.;**~**liegend** ⇒ **tief** 2 c; ~**punkt** *der* low [point]; ~**schlaf** *der* deep sleep; ~**schlag** *der* (Boxen) low punch; punch below the belt (lit. *or* fig.); *~**schürfend** ⇒ **tief** 2 b; ~**see** *die* (Geogr.) deep sea; ~**sinn** *der; o. Pl.* profundity; ~**sinnig** **1** *Adj.* profound; **2** *adv.* profoundly; ~**stand** *der* (auch fig.) (tiefer Stand) low level; (tiefster Stand) lowest level; ~**stapeln** /~ʃta:pəln/ *itr. V.*

understate the case; (aus Bescheidenheit) be modest; *~**verschneit** ⇒ **tief** 2 a
Tiegel /'ti:gl/ *der;* ~s, ~ (zum Kochen) pan; (Schmelz~) crucible; (Behälter) pot
Tier /ti:ɐ̯/ *das;* ~[e]s, ~e animal; (in der Wohnung gehaltenes) pet; **ein hohes** *od.* **großes** ~ (ugs.) a big noise (coll.) *or* shot (sl.)
Tier-: ~**art** *die* animal species; species of animal; ~**arzt** *der* ▶ 85 ⏐ veterinary surgeon; vet
Tierchen *das;* ~s, ~: [little] animal; **jedem** ~ **sein Pläsierchen** (ugs.) each to his own; if that's what he/she wants
Tier-: ~**freund** *der* animal-lover; ~**garten** *der* zoo; zoological garden; ~**handlung** *die* pet shop; ~**heim** *das* animal home
tierisch **1** *Adj.* (a) animal *attrib.;* bestial, savage ‹*cruelty, crime*›; (b) (ugs.: unerträglich groß) terrible (coll.); ~**er Ernst** deadly seriousness. **2** *adv.* (a) ‹*roar*› like an animal; savagely ‹*cruel*›; (b) (ugs.: unerträglich) terribly (coll.); deadly ‹*serious*›; baking ‹*hot*›; perishing (coll.) ‹*cold*›
tier-, Tier-: ~**kreis** *der; o. Pl.* (Astron., Astrol.) zodiac; ~**kreis·zeichen** *das* (Astron., Astrol.) sign of the zodiac; ~**lieb** *Adj.* animal-loving *attrib.;* fond of animals *postpos.;* ~**liebe** *die; o. Pl.* love of animals; ~**liebend** *Adj.* ⇒ ~**lieb;** ~**medizin** *die; o. Pl.* veterinary medicine; ~**mehl** *das* animal meal; ~**park** *der* zoo; ~**pfleger** *der* ▶ 85 ⏐ animal keeper; ~**quälerei** /---'-/ *die* cruelty to animals; ~**reich** *das; o. Pl.* animal kingdom; ~**welt** *die* fauna
Tiger /'ti:gɐ̯/ *der;* ~s, ~: tiger
Tigerin *die;* ~, ~**nen** tigress
Tiger·staat *der* tiger [economy]
Tilde /'tɪldə/ *die;* ~, ~**n** tilde
tilgen /'tɪlgn̩/ *tr. V.* (a) (geh.) delete ‹*word, letter, error*›; erase ‹*record, endorsement*›; (fig.) wipe out ‹*shame, guilt, traces*›; (b) (Wirtsch., Bankw.) repay; pay off
Tilgung *die;* ~, ~**en** (a) (geh.) ⇒ **tilgen** a: deletion; erasure; wiping out; (b) (Wirtsch., Bankw.) repayment
Till /tɪl/ *(der) in* ~ **Eulenspiegel** Till Eulenspiegel; (fig.) practical joker
timen /'taɪmən/ *tr. V.* time
Timing /'taɪmɪŋ/ *das;* ~s, ~s timing
Tingeltangel /'tɪŋltaŋl/ *das od. der;* ~s, ~ (veralt. abwertend: Lokal) cheap nightclub/dance hall; honky-tonk (coll.)
Tinnef /'tɪnɛf/ *der;* ~s (ugs. abwertend) rubbish; junk
Tinte /'tɪntə/ *die;* ~, ~**n** ink; **in der** ~ **sitzen** (ugs.) be in the soup (fig. coll.)
Tinten-: ~**fass,** *~**faß** *das* ink·pot; ~**fisch** *der* cuttlefish; (Kalmar) squid; (Krake) octopus
Tintenstrahl·drucker *der* (DV) ink-jet printer
***Tip, Tipp** /tɪp/ *der;* ~s, ~s (a) (ugs.: Fingerzeig) tip; (b) (bei Toto, Lotto usw.) [row of] numbers
tippen /'tɪpn̩/ **1** *itr. V.* (a) **an/gegen etw.** (*Akk.*) ~: tap sth.; **an seine Mütze** ~: touch one's cap; **sich** (*Dat.*) **an die Stirn** ~: tap one's forehead; (b) (ugs.: Maschine schreiben) type; (c) (ugs.: vermuten) reckon; **auf jmds. Sieg** ~: tip sb. to win; **du hast gut/richtig getippt** you were right; (d) (wetten) do the pools/lottery etc.; **im Lotto** ~: do the lottery. **2** *tr. V.* (a) tap; **jmdn. auf die Schulter** ~: tap sb. on the shoulder; (b) (ugs.: mit der Maschine schreiben) type; (c) (bei der Registrierkasse) ring up; (d) (setzen auf) choose; **sechs Richtige** ~: make six correct selections
Tipp·schein *der* [pools/lottery etc.] coupon
tipp·topp (ugs.) **1** *Adj.* (tadellos) immaculate; (erstklassig) tip-top. **2** *adv.* immaculately
Tipp·zettel *der* (ugs.) ⇒ **Tippschein**
Tirol /ti'ro:l/ *(das);* ~s [the] Tyrol
Tiroler *der;* ~s, ~, **Tirolerin** *die;* ~, ~**nen** Tyrolese; Tyrolean
Tisch /tɪʃ/ *der;* ~[e]s, ~e (a) table; (Schreib~) desk; **vor/nach** ~: before/after lunch/dinner/the meal *etc.;* **bei** ~ **sein** *od.* **sitzen** be at table; **zu** ~ **sein** be having one's lunch/dinner *etc.;* **vom** ~ **aufstehen** get up from the table; ‹*child*› get down [from the table]; **bitte zu** ~**:** please

take your places for lunch/dinner; **es wird gegessen, was auf den ∼ kommt!** [you'll] eat what's put on the table!; **(b)** (fig.) **reinen ∼ machen** (ugs.) clear things up; sort things out; **jmdn. über den ∼ ziehen** (ugs.) outmanœuvre sb.; **unter den ∼ fallen** (ugs.) go by the board

Tisch-: ∼**bein** das table-leg; leg of the table; ∼**dame** die dinner partner; ∼**decke** die tablecloth; ∼**gebet** das grace; ∼**herr** der dinner partner

Tischler der; ∼s, ∼: ▶ 85 | joiner; (bes. Kunst∼) cabinetmaker

Tischlerei die; ∼, ∼**en (a)** (Werkstatt) joiner's/cabinetmaker's [workshop]; **(b)** o. Pl. (Handwerk) joinery/cabinet-making

tischlern 1 itr. V. do woodwork. 2 tr. V. make ⟨shelves, cupboard, etc.⟩

Tisch-: ∼**manieren** Pl. table manners; ∼**nachbar** der person next to one [at table]; ∼**platte** die table-top; ∼**rede** die after-dinner speech; ∼**tennis** das table tennis; ∼**tuch** das; Pl. ∼**tücher** tablecloth; ∼**wein** der table wine

Titan das; ∼s (Chemie) titanium

Titel /'ti:tl/ der; ∼s, ∼ **(a)** ▶ 33 | title; **(b)** (ugs.: Musikstück, Song usw.) number

Titel-: ∼**anwärter** der (Sport) title contender; contender for the title; ∼**bild** das cover picture; ∼**blatt** das title-page; ∼**kampf** der (Sport) title final; (Boxen) title fight; ∼**rolle** die title role; ∼**seite** die **(a)** (einer Zeitung, Zeitschrift) [front] cover; **(b)** (eines Buchs) title-page; ∼**verteidiger** der (Sport) title-holder; (Mannschaft) title-holders pl.

Titte /'tɪtə/ die; ∼, ∼**n** (derb) tit (coarse)

titulieren /titu'li:rən/ tr. V. **(a)** (bezeichnen) call; **jmdn. als** od. **mit „Flasche" ∼:** call sb. a dead loss (coll.); **(b)** (veralt.: mit dem Titel anreden) address; **jmdn.** [**als** od. **mit**] **Herr Doktor ∼:** address sb. as Doctor

tja /tja(:)/ Interj. [yes] well; (Resignation ausdrückend) oh, well

Toast /to:st/ der; ∼[e]s, ∼**e** od. ∼**s (a)** toast; (Scheibe ∼) piece of toast; **(b)** (Trinkspruch) toast

toasten tr. V. toast

Toaster der; ∼s, ∼: toaster

toben /'to:bņ/ itr. V. **(a)** go wild (**vor** + Dat. with); (fig.) ⟨storm, sea, battle⟩ rage; **(b)** (tollen) romp or charge about; **(c)** mit sein (laufen) charge

Tob·sucht die; o. Pl. frenzied or mad rage; [mad] frenzy

tob·süchtig Adj. frenzied; raving mad

Tochter /'tɔxtɐ/ die; ∼, **Töchter** /'tœçtɐ/ daughter; **die ∼ des Hauses** the daughter or young lady of the house; **höhere ∼:** young lady

Tod /to:t/ der; ∼[e]s, ∼**e** (auch fig.) death; **eines natürlichen/gewaltsamen ∼es sterben** die a natural/violent death; **jmdn. zum ∼ durch den Strang/zum ∼ durch Erschießen verurteilen** sentence sb. to death by hanging/by firing squad; **bis in den ∼:** till death; **für jmdn./etw. in den ∼ gehen** die for sb./sth.; **sich zu ∼e stürzen/trinken** fall to one's death/drink oneself to death; **jmdn./etw. auf den ∼ nicht leiden/ausstehen können** (ugs.) not be able to stand or abide sb./sth.; **sich zu ∼e schämen/langweilen** be utterly ashamed/bored to death; **zu ∼e betrübt** extremely distressed; **sich** (Dat.) **den ∼ holen** (ugs.) catch one's death [of cold]

tod-: ∼**bringend** Adj. fatal ⟨illness, disease, etc.⟩; deadly, lethal ⟨poison etc.⟩; ∼**elend** Adj. utterly miserable; ∼**ernst** 1 Adj. deadly serious; 2 adv. deadly seriously

todes-, Todes-: ∼**angst** die **(a)** fear of death; **(b)** (große Angst) extreme fear; ∼**ängste ausstehen** be scared to death; ∼**anzeige** die **(a)** (in einer Zeitung) death notice; **(b)** (Karte) card announcing a person's death; ∼**fall** der death; (in der Familie) bereavement; ∼**jahr** das year of death; ∼**mutig** 1 Adj. utterly fearless; 2 adv. utterly fearlessly; ∼**opfer** das death; fatality; **der Unfall forderte drei ∼opfer** the accident claimed three lives; ∼**spirale** die (Eis-, Rollkunstlauf) death spiral; ∼**stoß** der death-blow; ∼**strafe** die death penalty; ∼**stunde** die

hour of death; ∼**tag** der: **sein ∼tag** the date of his death; **Mozarts 200. ∼tag** the 200th anniversary of Mozart's death; ∼**ursache** die cause of death; ∼**urteil** das death sentence; ∼**verachtung** die [utter] fearlessness in the face of death

Tod·feind der deadly enemy

tod·krank Adj. critically ill

tödlich /'tø:tlɪç/ 1 Adj. **(a)** fatal ⟨accident, illness, outcome, etc.⟩; lethal, deadly ⟨poison, bite, shot, trap, etc.⟩; lethal ⟨dose⟩; deadly, mortal ⟨danger⟩; **(b)** (sehr groß, ausgeprägt) deadly ⟨hatred, seriousness, certainty, boredom⟩. 2 adv. **(a)** fatally; **er ist ∼ verunglückt/abgestürzt** he was killed in an accident/he fell to his death; **(b)** (sehr) terribly (coll.)

tod-, Tod-: ∼**müde** Adj. dead tired (coll.); ∼**schick** (ugs.) 1 Adj. dead smart (coll.); 2 adv. dead smartly (coll.); ∼**sicher** (ugs.) 1 Adj. sure-fire (coll.) ⟨system, method, tip, etc.⟩; **eine ∼sichere Sache** a (coll.) dead certainty or (coll.) cert; 2 adv. for certain or sure; ∼**sünde** die (auch fig.) deadly or mortal sin; ∼**unglücklich** Adj. (ugs.) extremely or desperately unhappy

Tohuwabohu /'to:huva'bo:hu/ das; ∼s, ∼s chaos

Toilette /toa'lɛta/ die; ∼, ∼**n (a)** toilet; lavatory; **auf die** od. **zur ∼ gehen** go to the toilet or lavatory; **eine öffentliche ∼:** a public lavatory or convenience; **(b)** o. Pl. (geh.: das Sichankleiden) toilet

Toiletten-: ∼**artikel** der toiletry; ∼**becken** das lavatory or toilet bowl or pan; ∼**frau** die, ∼**mann** der lavatory attendant; ∼**papier** das toilet paper

toi, toi, toi /'tɔy 'tɔy 'tɔy:/ Interj. **(a)** (gutes Gelingen!) good luck!; **(b)** (unberufen!) touch wood!

tolerant /tole'rant/ 1 Adj. tolerant (**gegen** of). 2 adv. tolerantly

Toleranz die; ∼, ∼**en** tolerance

tolerieren /tole'ri:rən/ tr. V. tolerate

toll /tɔl/ 1 Adj. **(a)** (ugs.) (großartig) great (coll.); fantastic (coll.); (erstaunlich) amazing; (heftig, groß) enormous ⟨respect⟩; terrific (coll.) ⟨noise, storm⟩; **(b)** (wild, ausgelassen, übermütig) wild; wild, mad ⟨tricks, antics⟩; **(c)** (ugs.: schlimm, übel) terrible (coll.); **(d)** (veralt.) ⇒ **verrückt** 1 a. 2 adv. **(a)** (ugs.: großartig) terrifically well (coll.); (ugs.: heftig, sehr) ⟨rain, snow⟩ like billy-o (coll.); **∼ hast du das gemacht** you've made a great job of that (coll.); **(b)** (wild, übermütig) **bei dem Fest ging es ∼ zu** it was a wild party; **(c)** (ugs.: schlimm, übel) **treibt es nicht zu ∼:** don't go too mad

tollen itr. V. **(a)** romp about; **(b)** mit sein romp

toll-, Toll-: ∼**kühn** 1 Adj. daredevil attrib.; daring; 2 adv. daringly; ∼**patsch** /'tɔlpatʃ/ der; ∼[e]s, ∼**e** (ugs.) clumsy or awkward creature; ∼**patschig** (ugs.) 1 Adj. clumsy; awkward. 2 adv. clumsily; awkwardly; ∼**wut** die ▶ 329 | rabies sing.; ∼**wütig** Adj. rabid

*Tolpatsch ⇒ **Tollpatsch**

*tolpatschig ⇒ **tollpatschig**

Tölpel /'tœlpl/ der; ∼s, ∼ (abwertend; einfältiger Mensch) fool

tölpelhaft (abwertend) 1 Adj. foolish. 2 adv. foolishly

Tomahawk /'tɔmahaːk/ der; ∼s, ∼s tomahawk

Tomate /to'ma:tə/ die; ∼, ∼**n** tomato; **du hast wohl ∼n auf den Augen!** (salopp) you must be blind!

Tomaten- tomato ⟨juice, purée, salad, sauce, soup, etc.⟩

tomaten·rot Adj. brilliant red

Tombola /'tɔmbola/ die; ∼, ∼**s** od. **Tombolen** raffle

Tomographie /tomogra'fi:/ die; ∼ (Med.) tomography no art.

Ton¹ /to:n/ der; ∼[e]s, ∼**e** clay

Ton² der; ∼[e]s, **Töne** /'tø:nə/ **(a)** (auch Physik, Musik; beim Telefon) tone; (Klang) note; **(b)** (Film, Ferns. usw., ∼wiedergabe) sound; **(c)** (Sprechweise, Umgangs∼) tone; **den richtigen ∼ finden** strike the right note; **ich verbitte mir diesen ∼!** I will not be spoken to like that!; **der gute ∼:** good form; **(d)** (ugs.: Äußerung) word; **er konnte keinen ∼ herausbringen** he couldn't say a word; **hast du/hat der Mensch [da noch] Töne?** that's just unbelievable; **große Töne reden** od. **spucken** (ugs.) talk big; **(e)** (Farb∼) shade; tone; **∼ in ∼ gehalten** colour coordinated; **(f)** (Akzent) stress

---

ton-, Ton-: ~**abnehmer** *der;* ~**s,** ~: pick-up; ~**angebend** *Adj.* predominant; ~**angebend sein** (in der Mode, Kunst usw.) set the tone; (in einer Gruppe o. Ä.) have the most *or* greatest say; ~**arm** *der* pick-up arm; ~**art** *die* (a) (Musik) key; (b) (fig.) tone; ~**band** *das; Pl.* ~**bänder** (a) tape; (b) (ugs.: Gerät) tape recorder

Ton·band-: ~**aufnahme** *die* tape recording; ~**gerät** *das* tape recorder

Ton·blende *die* (Rundf., Ferns.) tone control

tönen /'tøːnən/ **1** *itr. V.* (a) (geh.) sound; ‹*bell*› sound, ring; (schallen, widerhallen) resound; (b) (ugs. abwertend) boast. **2** *tr. V.* (färben) tint

Ton·erde *die* ⇒ **essigsauer**

tönern /'tøːnɐn/ *Adj.; nicht präd.* clay

Ton-: ~**fall** *der* tone; (Intonation) intonation; ~**folge** *die* sequence of notes; ~**gefäß** *das* earthen[ware] vessel; ~**höhe** *die* pitch

Tonika /'toːnika/ *die;* ~, **Toniken** (Musik) tonic

ton-, Ton-: ~**ingenieur** *der* sound engineer; ~**kopf** *der* head; ~**leiter** *die* (Musik) scale; ~**los 1** *Adj.* toneless; **2** *adv.* tonelessly

Tonnage /tɔ'naːʒə/ *die;* ~, ~**n** (Seew.) tonnage

Tonne /'tɔnə/ *die;* ~, ~**n** (a) (Behälter) drum; (Müll~) bin; (Regen~) water-butt; (b) ▸ **228**] (Gewicht) tonne; metric ton; (c) (ugs.: dicker Mensch) fatty (coll.)

Ton-: ~**spur** *die* soundtrack; ~**störung** *die* interference *no def. art.* on sound; ~**system** *das* (Musik) tone *or* tonic system; ~**tauben·schießen** *das* clay-pigeon shooting *no art.;* ~**techniker** *der* sound technician

Tönung *die;* ~, ~**en** (a) tinting; (b) (Farbton) tint; shade

Ton·ware *die* earthenware *no pl.*

Top /tɔp/ *das;* ~**s,** ~**s** (Mode) top

top- ultra ‹*modern, topical*›

Top- top; outstanding ‹*location, performance, time*›

Topas /to'paːs/ *der;* ~**es,** ~**e** topaz

Topf /tɔpf/ *der;* ~**es, Töpfe** /'tœpfə/ (a) pot; (Braten~, Schmor~) casserole; (Stielkasserolle) saucepan; **alles in einen** ~ **werfen** (fig. ugs.) lump everything together; (b) (zur Aufbewahrung) pot; jar; (c) (Krug) jug; (d) (Nacht~) chamber pot; po (coll.); (für Kinder) potty (Brit. coll.); (e) (Blumen~) [flower]pot; (f) (salopp: Toilette) loo (Brit. coll.); john (Amer. coll.)

Topf·blume *die* [flowering] pot plant

Töpfer /'tœpfɐ/ *der;* ~**s,** ~: ▸ **85**] potter

Töpferei *die;* ~, ~**en** (a) o. Pl. pottery *no art.;* (b) (Werkstatt) pottery; potter's workshop; (c) (Erzeugnis) piece of pottery

Töpferin *die;* ~, ~**nen** ▸ **85**] potter

töpfern 1 *itr. V.* do pottery. **2** *tr. V.* make ‹*vase, jug, etc.*›; **getöpferte Teller** hand-made pottery plates

Töpfer-: ~**scheibe** *die* potter's wheel; ~**waren** *Pl.* pottery *sing.*

top·fit *Adj.* in *or* on top form *postpos.;* (gesundheitlich) in fine fettle; as fit as a fiddle

Topf-: ~**lappen** *der* oven cloth; ~**pflanze** *die* pot plant

Topographie /topogra'fiː/ *die;* ~, ~**n** (Geogr.) topography *no art.*

Topspin /'tɔpspɪn/ *der;* ~**s,** ~**s** (bes. Golf, Tennis, Tischtennis) top spin

Tor /toːɐ̯/ *das;* ~**[e]s,** ~**e** (a) gate; (einer Garage, Scheune) door; (fig.) gateway; (b) (Ballspiele) goal; (c) (Ski) gate

Torero /to're:ro/ *der;* ~**[s],** ~**s** torero

Tores·schluss, ***Tores·schluß** *der in* **kurz vor** ~ (ugs.) at the last minute *or* the eleventh hour

Torf /tɔrf/ *der;* ~**[e]s,** ~**e** peat

Torf-: ~**ballen** *der* bale of peat; ~**moor** *das* peat bog; ~**stecher** *der* peat-cutter

Torheit *die;* ~, ~**en** (geh.) (a) o. Pl. foolishness; (b) (Handlung) foolish act; **eine [große]** ~ **begehen** do something [extremely] foolish

Tor·hüter *der* (Ballspiele) goalkeeper

töricht /'tøːrɪçt/ (geh.) **1** *Adj.* foolish ‹*behaviour, action, hope*›; stupid ‹*person, question, smile, face*›. **2** *adv.* ‹*behave, act*› foolishly; ‹*smile, ask*› stupidly

Tor·jäger *der* (Ballspiele) goal-scorer

torkeln /'tɔrkl̩n/ *itr. V.; mit sein* stagger; reel

Tor·mann *der; Pl.* ~**männer** *od.* ~**leute** (Ballspiele) goalkeeper

Törn /tœrn/ *der;* ~**s,** ~**s** (Seemannsspr.) trip

Tornado /tɔr'naːdo/ *der;* ~**s,** ~**s** tornado

Tornister /tɔr'nɪstɐ/ *der;* ~**s,** ~ (a) knapsack; (b) (Schulranzen) satchel

torpedieren /tɔrpe'diːrən/ *tr. V.* (Milit., fig.) torpedo

Torpedo /tɔr'pe:do/ *der;* ~**s,** ~**s** torpedo

Tor-: ~**pfosten** *der* (Ballspiele) [goal-] post; ~**schluss,** *~**schluß** ⇒ **Toresschluss;** ~**schluss·panik,** *~**schluß·panik** *die* last-minute panic; (Furcht, keinen Partner mehr zu finden) fear of being left on the shelf; ~**schütze** *der* (Ballspiele) [goal-]-scorer

Törtchen /'tœrtçən/ *das;* ~**s,** ~: tartlet

Torte /'tɔrtə/ *die;* ~, ~**n** gateau; (Obst~) [fruit] flan

Torten-: ~**boden** *der* flan case; (ohne Rand) flan base; ~**guss,** *~**guß** *der* glaze; ~**heber** *der* cake-slice; ~**platte** *die* cake-plate

Tortur /tɔr'tuːɐ̯/ *die;* ~, ~**en** (a) ordeal; (b) (veralt.: Folter) torture

Tor-: ~**verhältnis** *das* (Ballspiele) goal average ~**wart** *der;* ~**[e]s,** ~**e** (Ballspiele) goalkeeper

tosen /'toːzn̩/ *itr. V.* ‹*sea, surf*› roar, rage; ‹*storm*› rage; ‹*torrent, waterfall*› roar, thunder; ‹*wind*› roar; ~**der Beifall** (fig.) thunderous applause

tot /toːt/ *Adj.* (a) dead; **das Kind wurde** ~ **geboren** the baby was stillborn; ~ **geboren** stillborn; **er war auf der Stelle** ~: he died instantly; ~ **zusammenbrechen** collapse and die; **sich** ~ **stellen** pretend to be dead; play dead; ~ **umfallen** drop dead; **er ist politisch ein** ~**er Mann** (fig.) he is finished as a politician; **ein** ~ **gebore-nes Kind sein** (fig.) ‹*Projekt*› be stillborn; **halb** ~ **vor Angst** *usw.* (ugs.) paralysed with fear *etc.;* **den** ~**en Mann machen** (ugs.) float on one's back; (b) (abgestorben) dead ‹*tree, branch, leaves, etc.*›; (c) (fig.) dull ‹*colour*›; bleak ‹*region etc.*›; dead ‹*town, telephone line, socket, language*›; disused ‹*railway line*›; extinct ‹*volcano*›; dead, quiet ‹*time, period*›; useless ‹*knowledge*›; s. *auch* **Punkt** d; **Winkel** a

total /to'taːl/ **1** *Adj.* total. **2** *adv.* totally

totalitär /totali'tɛːɐ̯/ (Politik) **1** *Adj.* totalitarian. **2** *adv.* in a totalitarian way; ‹*organized, run*› along totalitarian lines

Total·schaden *der* (Versicherungsw.) **an beiden Fahrzeugen entstand** ~: both vehicles were a write-off

tot-: ~**arbeiten** *refl. V.* (ugs.) work oneself to death; ~**ärgern** *refl. V.* (ugs.) get livid (coll.); **ich könnte mich** ~**ärgern** I'm livid (coll.) *or* really furious

Tote /'toːtə/ *der/die; adj. Dekl.* dead person; dead man/ woman; **die** ~**n** the dead; **es gab zwei** ~: two people died *or* were killed; there were two fatalities

töten /'tøːtn̩/ *tr., itr. V.* kill; s. *auch* **Nerv** a

toten-, Toten-: ~**amt** *das* (kath. Kirche) ⇒ **messe;** ~**blass,** *~**blaß,** ~**bleich** *Adj.* deathly pale; pale as death *postpos.;* ~**gräber** *der* gravedigger; ~**hemd** *das* shroud; ~**klage** *die* lamentation *or* bewailing of the dead; ~**kopf** *der* (a) skull; (b) (als Symbol) death's head; (mit gekreuzten Knochen) skull and crossbones; ~**messe** *die* (kath. Kirche) requiem [mass]; ~**schein** *der* death certificate; ~**still** *Adj.* deathly quiet *or* silent; ~**wache** *die* vigil by the body

tot-, Tot-: ~**fahren 1** *unr. tr. V.* [run over and] kill; **2** *unr. V.* kill oneself; *~**geboren** ⇒ **tot a;** ~**ge-burt** *die* (a) stillbirth; (b) (Kind) stillbirth; stillborn baby; ~**gesagte** *der/die; adj. Dekl.* person declared dead; ~**lachen** *refl. V.* (ugs.) kill oneself laughing; **zum Tot-lachen sein** be killing (coll.); be killingly funny (coll.); ~**laufen** *unr. refl. V.* (ugs.) ‹*movement, trend, fashion*› peter *or* die out; ‹*talks, discussions*› peter out

Toto /'toːto/ *das od. der;* ~**s,** ~**s** (a) (Pferde~) tote (sl.); (b) (Fußball~) [football] pools *pl.;* **[im]** ~ **spielen** do the pools

Toto-: ~**gewinn** *der* win on the pools/(sl.) tote; ~**schein** *der* pools coupon/(sl.) tote ticket

tot-, Tot-: ~|**sagen** tr. V. declare ⟨person⟩ dead; ~|**schießen** unr. tr. V. (ugs.) jmdn. ~schießen shoot sb. dead; ~**schlag** der (Rechtsw.) manslaughter no indef. art.; ~|**schlagen** unr. tr. V. beat to death; **die Zeit** ~schlagen kill time; ~**schläger** der (a) (Mensch) manslaughterer; (b) (Waffe) cosh (Brit. coll.); blackjack (Amer.); ~|**schweigen** unr. tr. V. hush up; jmdn. ~schweigen keep quiet about sb.;*~|**stellen** ⇒ tot a; ~|**treten** unr. tr. V. trample ⟨person⟩ to death; step on and kill ⟨insect⟩

Tötung die; ~, ~en killing; **fahrlässige** ~ (Rechtsspr.) manslaughter by culpable negligence

Touch /tatʃ/ der; ~s, ~s (ugs.) touch

Toupet /tu'pe:/ das; ~s, ~s toupee

toupieren /tu'pi:rən/ tr. V. backcomb

Tour /tu:ɐ̯/ die; ~, ~en (a) tour (**durch** of); (Kletter~) [climbing] trip; (kürzere Fahrt, Ausflug) trip; (mit dem Auto) drive; (mit dem Fahrrad) ride; **eine** ~ **machen** go on a tour/ trip or outing; (Zech~) go on a pub crawl (Brit. coll.); bar-hop (Amer.); (b) (feste Strecke) route; (c) (Tournee) tour; **auf** ~ **gehen** go on tour; (d) (ugs.: Methode) ploy; **die** ~ **zieht bei mir nicht** that [one] won't work with me; **etw. auf die sanfte** ~ **erreichen** get sth. by soft-soaping; (e) **jmdm. die** ~ **vermasseln** (ugs.) put paid to sb.'s [little] plans; (f) Pl. (Technik: Umdrehungen) revolutions; revs (coll.); **jmdn. auf** ~**en bringen** (ugs.) really get sb. going; **auf vollen/ höchsten** ~**en laufen** (ugs.) ⟨preparations, work, etc.⟩ be in full swing; (g) **in** ei**ner** ~ (ugs.) the whole time

Touren-: ~**rad** das roadster; ~**wagen** der (Motorsport) touring car

Tourismus /tu'rɪsmʊs/ der; ~: tourism no art.

Tourist der; ~en, ~en tourist

Touristik die; ~: tourism no art.; tourist industry or business

Touristin die; ~, ~nen tourist

Tournee /tʊr'ne:/ die; ~, ~s od. ~n /tʊr'ne:ən/ ⇒ **Tour** c

Tower /'taʊə/ der; ~s, ~s (Flugw.) [control] tower

Trab /tra:p/ der; ~[e]s trot; **im** ~: at a trot; **im** ~ **reiten** trot; **jmdn. auf** ~ **bringen** (ugs.) make sb. get a move on; **jmdn. in** ~ **halten** (ugs.) keep sb. on the go (coll.)

Trabant /tra'bant/ der; ~en, ~en (Astron.) satellite

Trabanten·stadt die satellite town

traben itr. V.; mit sein (auch ugs.: laufen) trot

Trab·rennen das trotting; (einzelne Veranstaltung) trotting race

Tracht /traxt/ die; ~, ~en (a) (Volks~) traditional or national costume; (Berufs~) uniform; **die** ~ **der Nonnen** the nuns' dress or habit; (b) in **eine** ~ **Prügel** a beating or thrashing; (als Strafe für ein Kind) a hiding

trachten itr. V. (geh.) strive (**nach** for, after); **all sein Trachten** all his striving or endeavours

Trachten·anzug der suit in the style of a traditional or national costume

trächtig /'trɛçtɪç/ pregnant

Tradition /tradi'tsi̯o:n/ die; ~, ~en tradition

traditionell /traditsi̯o'nɛl/ 1 Adj. traditional. 2 adv. traditionally

traf /tra:f/ 1. u. 3. Pers. Sg. Prät. v. **treffen**

Trafik /tra'fɪk/ die; ~, ~en (österr.) tobacconist's [shop]

Trafo /'tra:fo/ der; ~s, ~s transformer

Trag·bahre die stretcher

tragbar Adj. (a) portable; (b) wearable ⟨clothes⟩; (c) (finanziell) supportable ⟨cost, debt, etc.⟩; (d) (erträglich) bearable; tolerable

Trage die; ~, ~n (a) (Bahre) stretcher; (b) (Traggestell) pannier

träge /'trɛ:gə/ 1 Adj. (a) sluggish; (geistig) lethargic; (b) (Physik) inert. 2 adv. sluggishly; (geistig) lethargically

tragen /tra:gn/ 1 unr. tr. V. (a) carry; **das Auto wurde aus der Kurve getragen** (fig.) the car went off the bend; (b) (bringen) take; **vom Wind getragen** (fig.) carried by

[the] wind; (c) (ertragen) bear ⟨fate, destiny⟩; bear, endure ⟨suffering⟩; (d) (halten) hold; **einen Arm in der Schlinge** ~: have one's arm in a sling; (e) (von unten stützen) support; **zum Tragen kommen** ⟨advantage, improvement, quality⟩ become noticeable; s. auch **tragend a–c**; (f) (belastbar sein durch) be able to carry or take ⟨weight⟩; **der Ast trägt dich nicht** the branch won't take your weight; (g) (übernehmen, aufkommen für) bear, carry ⟨costs etc.⟩; take ⟨blame, responsibility, consequences⟩; (unterhalten, finanzieren) support; (h) (am Körper) wear ⟨clothes, wig, glasses, jewellery, etc.⟩; have ⟨false teeth, beard, etc.⟩; **getragene Kleider** second-hand clothes; (i) (fig.: haben) have ⟨label etc.⟩; have, bear ⟨title⟩; bear, carry ⟨signature, inscription, seal⟩; (j) (hervorbringen) ⟨tree⟩ bear ⟨fruit⟩; ⟨field⟩ produce ⟨crops⟩; (fig.) yield ⟨interest⟩; **gut/wenig** ~ ⟨tree⟩ produce a good/ poor crop; ⟨field⟩ produce a good/poor yield; (k) (geh.: schwanger sein mit) be carrying. 2 unr. itr. V. (a) carry; **wir hatten schwer zu** ~: we were heavily laden; **schwer an etw.** (Dat.) **zu** ~ **haben** have difficulty carrying sth.; find sth. very heavy to carry; (fig.) find sth. hard to bear; **das Eis trägt noch nicht** the ice is not yet thick enough to skate/walk etc. on; (b) (am Körper) **man trägt [wieder] kurz/lang** short/long skirts are in fashion [again]; (c) **eine** ~ **Sau/Kuh** a pregnant sow/cow; s. auch **tragend** d. 3 unr. refl. V. (a) **sich gut/schlecht** usw. ~ ⟨load⟩ be easy/difficult or hard etc. to carry; (b) **der Mantel/Stoff trägt sich angenehm** the coat/material is pleasant to wear; (c) **in sich mit etw.** ~: be contemplating sth.; (d) (sich kleiden) dress

tragend Adj. (a) (Stabilität gebend) load-bearing; supporting ⟨wall, column, function, etc.⟩; (b) (fig.: grundlegend) basic, main ⟨idea, motif⟩; (c) (fig.: wichtig, zentral) leading, major ⟨role, figure⟩; (d) (weithin hörbar) ⟨voice⟩ that carries [a long way]

Träger /'trɛ:gɐ/ der; ~s, ~ (a) porter; (Sänften~, Sarg~) bearer; (b) (Zeitungs~) paper boy/girl; delivery boy/girl; (c) (Bauw.) girder; [supporting] beam; (d) (an Kleidung) strap; (Hosen~) braces pl.; (e) (Inhaber) (eines Amts) holder; (eines Namens, Titels) bearer; (eines Preises) winner; (f) (fig.: Urheber, treibende Kraft) moving force; (g) (fig.: Unterhalter) ~ **der Arbeitslosenversicherung ist der Staat** unemployment insurance is financed or funded by the state; (h) (fig.: einer Substanz, eines Erregers usw.) carrier; (i) (Flugzeug~) carrier; (j) (jmd., der etw. als Kleidung, Schmuck usw. trägt) wearer

Trägerin die; ~, ~nen ⇒ **Träger** a, b, e, f, g, h, j

Träger-: ~**kleid** das pinafore dress; ~**rakete** die carrier vehicle or rocket; ~**rock** der skirt with straps

Trage-: ~**tasche** die carrier bag

trag-, Trag-: ~**fähig** Adj. able to take a load or weight postpos.; **eine** ~**fähige Mehrheit** (fig.) a workable majority; ~**fläche** die wing; (eines Boots) hydrofoil; ~**flächen·boot**, ~**flügelboot** das hydrofoil

Trägheit die; ~, ~en (a) o. Pl. ⇒ **träge** 1 a: sluggishness; lethargy; (b) (Physik) inertia

Tragik /'tra:gɪk/ die; ~ tragedy

Tragi·komödie /tra:gi-/ die tragicomedy

tragisch /'tra:gɪʃ/ 1 Adj. tragic; **das ist nicht [so]** ~ (ugs.) it's not the end of the world (coll.); **etw.** ~ **nehmen** take sth. to heart (coll.). 2 adv. tragically; **der Film/die Tour endete** ~: the film had a tragic ending/the trip ended in tragedy

Tragödie /tra'gø:di̯ə/ die; ~, ~n tragedy

Trag·weite die; o. Pl. consequences pl.; **ein Ereignis von weltpolitischer** ~: an event of moment in world politics

Trainer /'trɛ:nɐ/ der; ~s, ~, **Trainerin** die; ~, ~nen (a) coach; trainer; (eines Schwimmers, Tennisspielers) coach; (einer Fußballmannschaft) manager; (b) (Pferdesport) trainer

trainieren 1 tr. V. (a) train; coach; ⟨swimmer, tennis player⟩; manage ⟨football team⟩; train ⟨horse⟩; exercise ⟨muscles etc.⟩; **jmdn./ein Tier darauf** ~, **etw. zu tun** train sb./an animal to do sth.; **ein trainierter Schwimmer/Radfahrer** usw. a swimmer/cyclist etc. [who is] in training; (b) (üben, einüben) practise ⟨exercise, jump, etc.⟩; (c) (zu Trainingszwecken ausüben) **Fußball**/

Tennis ~: do football/tennis training. **2** *itr. V.* train; (Motorsport) practise; **mit jmdm.** ~: ‹*trainer*› coach sb.; ‹*player*› train with sb.

Training /'trɛːnɪŋ/ *das;* ~s, ~s (Fitness~, auch *fig.*: Ausbildung) training *no indef. art.*; (Motorsport, *fig.*) practice; **Radfahren ist ein gutes** ~: cycling is a good form of training *or* exercise

Trainings-: ~**anzug** *der* track suit; ~**hose** *die* track-suit bottoms *pl.;* ~**jacke** *die* track-suit top; ~**schuh** *der* training-shoe; trainer

Trakt /trakt/ *der;* ~[e]s, ~e section; (Flügel) wing

Traktat /trak'taːt/ *der od. das;* ~[e]s, ~e **(a)** (Abhandlung) treatise; **(b)** (religiöse Flugschrift) tract

traktieren *tr. V.* set about ‹*person, thing*›; **jmdn. mit Ohrfeigen/Faustschlägen** ~: slap sb. round the face/punch sb.

Traktor /'traktor/ *der;* ~s, ~en /-'toːrən/ tractor

trällern /'trɛlɐn/ *tr., itr. V.* warble

Tramp /trɛmp/ *der;* ~s, ~s tramp; hobo (Amer.)

Trampel /'trampl̩/ *der;* ~s, ~ (ugs. abwertend) ⇒ **Trampeltier** b

trampeln 1 *itr. V.* **(a)** [mit den Füßen] ~: stamp one's feet; **(b)** *mit sein* (abwertend: treten) trample. **2** *tr. V.* trample

Trampel-: ~**pfad** *der* [beaten] path; ~**tier** *das* **(a)** (Kamel) Bactrian camel; **(b)** (salopp abwertend) clumsy clot (Brit. coll.) *or* oaf

trampen /'trɛmpn̩/ *itr. V.; mit sein* hitch-hike

Tramper *der;* ~s, ~, **Tramperin** *die;* ~, ~**nen** hitch-hiker

Trampolin /'trampoliːn/ *das;* ~s, ~e trampoline

Tran /traːn/ *der;* ~[e]s **(a)** (train-oil; **(b) im** ~ (ugs.) befuddled; in a daze; (im Rausch) stoned (coll.)

Trance /'trãːs(ə)/ *die;* ~, ~**n** trance; **in** ~: in a trance; **in** ~ **fallen** go into a trance

tranchieren *tr. V.* (Kochk.) carve

Tranchiermesser *das* carving knife

Träne /'trɛːnə/ *die;* ~, ~**n** tear; **seine** ~**n trocknen** dry one's eyes; ~**n lachen** laugh till one cries *or* till the tears run down one's cheeks; **in** ~**n aufgelöst sein** be in floods of tears; **jmdm./einer Sache keine** ~ **nachweinen** not shed any tears over sb./sth.

tränen *itr. V.* ‹*eyes*› water

Tränen-: ~**drüse** *die* (Anat.) tear-gland; **auf die** ~**drüsen drücken** (fig.) lay on the agony; ~**gas** *das* tear gas

Tran·funzel *die* (ugs. abwertend) **(a)** (trübe Lampe) miserable lamp; **(b)** (langweiliger Mensch) ponderous dimwit (coll.); (langsamer Mensch) slowcoach; slowpoke (Amer.)

tranig *Adj.* **(a)** ‹*meat, fish*› full of train-oil; ~ **schmecken** taste like *or* of train-oil; **(b)** (ugs.: langsam) sluggish; slow

trank /traŋk/ *1. u. 3. Pers. Sg. Prät. v.* **trinken**

Tränke /'trɛŋkə/ *die;* ~, ~**n** watering-place

tränken *tr. V.* **(a)** (auch fig.) water; **(b)** (sich voll saugen lassen) soak

Trans·aktion /trans-/ *die* transaction

trans·atlantisch *Adj.* transatlantic; across the Atlantic *postpos.*

Transfer /trans'feːɐ̯/ *der;* ~s, ~s (bes. Wirtsch., Sport) transfer

trans-, Trans-: ~**formator** /~fɔr'maːtor/ *der;* ~s, ~**en** /-'toːrən/ transformer; ~**formieren** *tr. V.* transform (**in** + *Akk.* into, **auf** + *Akk.* to); ~**fusion** *die* (Med.) transfusion

transgen *Adj.* transgenic

Transistor /tran'zɪstor/ *der;* ~s, ~**en** /-'toːrən/ transistor

Transit¹ /*auch:* '--/ *der;* ~s, ~e transit

Transit² /tran'ziːt, *auch:* 'tranzɪt/ *das;* ~s, ~s transit visa

transitiv /'tranzitiːf/ (Sprachw.) **1** *Adj.* transitive. **2** *adv.* transitively

Transit·verkehr *der* transit traffic

transparent /transpa'rɛnt/ *Adj.* **(a)** transparent; (Licht durchlassend) translucent, diaphanous ‹*curtain, fabric, etc.*›; **(b)** (fig.: verständlich) intelligible

Transparent *das;* ~[e]s, ~e **(a)** (Spruchband) banner; **(b)** (Bild) transparency

Transparenz *die;* ~ **(a)** transparency; (von Gewebe, Porzellan usw.) translucence; **(b)** (fig.: Verständlichkeit) intelligibility

transpirieren /transpiːˈriːrən/ *itr. V.* (bes. Med.) perspire

Transplantation /transplantaˈtsi̯oːn/ *die;* ~, ~**en** (Med.) transplant; (von Haut) graft

transplantieren /transplanˈtiːrən/ *tr. V.* (Med.) transplant; graft ‹*skin*›

Transport /transˈpɔrt/ *der;* ~[e]s, ~e **(a)** transportation; **beim od. auf dem** ~: during carriage; **(b)** (beförderte Lebewesen od. Sachen) (mit dem Zug) train-load; (mit mehreren Fahrzeugen) convoy; (Fracht) consignment; shipment

transportabel /transpɔrˈtaːbl̩/ *Adj.* transportable

Transporter *der;* ~s, ~ (Flugzeug) transport aircraft; (Schiff) cargo ship

Transporteur /...ˈtøːɐ̯/ *der;* ~s, ~e carrier

transportfähig *Adj.* moveable

transportieren *tr. V.* transport ‹*goods, people*›; move ‹*patient*›

Transport-: ~**kosten** *Pl.* carriage *sing.;* transport costs; ~**unter·nehmen** *das* haulage firm *or* contractor

Tran·suse *die;* ~, ~**n** (ugs. abwertend) ⇒ **Tranfunzel** b

Transvestit /transvɛsˈtiːt/ *der;* ~en, ~en transvestite

transzendental /transtsɛndɛnˈtaːl/ *Adj.* (Philos.) transcendental

Transzendenz /transtsɛnˈdɛnts/ *die;* ~ **(a)** transcendency; transcendent nature; **(b)** (Philos.) transcendence

Trapez /traˈpeːts/ *das;* ~es, ~e **(a)** (Geom.) trapezium (Brit.); trapezoid (Amer.); **(b)** (im Zirkus o. ä.) trapeze

trappeln /'trapl̩n/ *itr. V.; mit sein* patter [along]; ‹*feet*› patter; ‹*hoofs*› go clip-clop

trara /traˈraː/ *Interj.* tantara

Trara /traˈraː/ *das;* ~s (ugs. abwertend) razzmatazz (coll.); **viel** ~ **um etw.** (*Akk.*) **machen** make a great song and dance about sth. (coll.)

Trasse /'trasə/ *die;* ~, ~**n (a)** (Verkehrsweg) [marked-out] route *or* line; **(b)** (Damm) [railway/road] embankment

trat /traːt/ *1. u. 3. Pers. Sg. Prät. v.* **treten**

Tratsch /traːtʃ/ *der;* ~[e]s (ugs. abwertend) gossip; tittle-tattle

tratschen *itr. V.* (ugs. abwertend) gossip; (schwatzen) chatter [with sb.]

Trau·altar *der:* [mit jmdm.] **vor den** ~ **treten** (geh.) enter into matrimony [with sb.]

Traube /'traubə/ *die;* ~, ~**n (a)** (Beeren) bunch; (von Johannisbeeren o. ä.) cluster; **(b)** (Wein~) grape; **(c)** (Menschenmenge) bunch; cluster

Trauben-: ~**lese** *die* grape harvest; ~**saft** *der* grape-juice; ~**zucker** *der* glucose

trauen /'trauən/ **1** *itr. V.* **jmdm./einer Sache** ~: trust sb./sth.; *s. auch* **Auge a. 2** *refl. V.* dare; **du traust dich ja nicht!** you haven't the courage *or* nerve; **sich irgendwohin** ~: dare [to] go somewhere. **3** *tr. V.* (verheiraten) ‹*vicar, registrar, etc.*› marry

Trauer /'trauɐ/ *die;* ~ **(a)** grief (**über** + *Akk.* over); (um einen Toten) mourning (**um** + *Akk.* for); ~ **haben, in** ~ **sein** be in mourning; **(b)** (~kleidung) mourning

Trauer-: ~**fall** *der* bereavement; ~**feier** *die* memorial ceremony; (beim Begräbnis) funeral ceremony; ~**flor** *der* mourning-band; black [crape] ribbon; ~**karte** *die* [pre-printed] card of condolence; ~**kleidung** *die* mourning clothes *pl.;* mourning; ~**kloß** *der* (ugs. scherzh.) wet blanket; ~**marsch** *der* (Musik) funeral march

trauern *itr. V.* **(a)** mourn; **um jmdn.** ~: mourn for sb.; **die** ~**den Hinterbliebenen** the bereaved; **(b)** (Trauer tragen) be in mourning

Trauer-: ~**rand** *der* black border *or* edging; ~**spiel** *das* tragedy; (fig. ugs.) deplorable business; **es ist doch ein** ~ **spiel, dass** …: it's quite pathetic that …; ~**weide** *die* weeping willow; ~**zug** *der* funeral procession

Traufe /'traʊfə/ *die;* ~, ~n eaves *pl.*

träufeln /'trɔyfl̩n/ *tr. V.* [let] trickle (**in** + *Akk.* into); drip ‹*ear-drops etc.*›

traulich /'traʊlɪç/ **1** *Adj.* cosy; **in** ~**er Runde** in a friendly *or* an intimate circle. **2** *adv.* cosily; (vertraut) intimately

Traum /traʊm/ *der;* ~[e]s, **Träume** /'trɔymə/ dream; **nicht im** ~ **habe ich mit der Möglichkeit gerechnet, zu gewinnen** I didn't imagine in my wildest dreams that I could win

Trauma /'traʊma/ *das;* ~s, **Traumen** *od.* ~**ta** (Psych., Med.) trauma

träumen /'trɔymən/ **1** *itr. V.* dream (**von** of, about); (unaufmerksam sein) [day-]dream. **2** *tr. V.* dream; **etwas Schreckliches** ~: have a terrible dream; **ich hätte mir nie** ~ **lassen, dass** ...: I should never have imagined it possible that ...; I never imagined that ...

Träumer *der;* ~s, ~, **Träumerin** *die;* ~, ~**nen** dreamer

träumerisch 1 *Adj.* dreamy; (sehnsüchtig) wistful. **2** *adv.* dreamily; (sehnsüchtig) wistfully

traumhaft 1 *Adj.* (a) dreamlike; (b) (ugs.: schön) marvellous; fabulous (coll.). **2** *adv.* (a) as if in a dream; (b) (ugs.: schön) fabulously (coll.)

Traum·tänzer *der* (abwertend) wooly-headed idealist; fantasizer

traurig /'traʊrɪç/ **1** *Adj.* (a) sad; sad, sorrowful ‹*eyes, expression*›; unhappy ‹*childhood, youth*›; unhappy, painful ‹*duty*›; (b) (kümmerlich) sorry, pathetic ‹*state etc.*›; miserable ‹*result*›; **eine** ~**e Rolle** an unfortunate role. **2** *adv.* sadly

Traurigkeit *die;* ~: sadness; sorrow

Trau-: ~**ring** *der* wedding ring; ~**schein** *der* marriage certificate

Trauung *die;* ~, ~**en** wedding [ceremony]

Trau·zeuge *der* witness (*at wedding ceremony*)

Traveller·scheck /'trɛvəlɐʃɛk/ *der* traveller's cheque

Travestie /travɛs'tiː/ *die;* ~, ~n travesty

Treck /trɛk/ *der;* ~s, ~s train, column (*of refugees etc.*)

Treff /trɛf/ *der;* ~s, ~s (ugs.) (a) (Treffen) rendezvous; (bes. von mehreren Personen) get-together (coll.); (b) (Ort) meeting place

treffen 1 *unr. tr. V.* (a) (erreichen [und verletzen/schädigen]) hit; ‹*punch, blow, object*› strike; **jmdn. am Kopf/ins Gesicht** ~: hit *or* strike sb. on the head/in the face; **vom Blitz getroffen** struck by lightning; **ihn trifft keine Schuld** (fig.) he is in no way to blame; (b) (erraten) hit on; hit ‹*right tone*›; **auf dem Foto ist er gut getroffen** the photo is a good likeness of him; that's a good photo of him; (c) (erschüttern) affect [deeply]; (verletzen) hurt; **es hat ihn in seinem Stolz getroffen** it hurt his pride; (d) (schaden) hit; damage; **warum muss es immer mich** ~**?** why does it always have to be me [who is affected *or* gets it]?; (e) (begegnen) meet; (f) (vorfinden) come upon, find ‹*anomalies etc.*›; **es gut/schlecht** ~: be *or* strike lucky/ be unlucky; (g) *als Funktionsverb* make ‹*arrangements, choice, preparations, decision, etc.*›; **eine Vereinbarung** *od.* **Absprache** ~: conclude an agreement. **2** *unr. itr. V.* (a) ‹*person, shot, etc.*› hit the target; **nicht** ~: miss [the target]; (b) *mit sein* **auf etw.** (*Akk.*) ~: come upon sth.; **auf Widerstand/Ablehnung** ~: meet with *or* encounter resistance/rejection; **auf jmdn./eine Mannschaft** ~ (Sport) come up against sb./a team. **3** *unr. refl. V.* (a) **sich mit jmdm.** ~: meet sb.; (b) (*unpers.*) **es trifft sich gut/schlecht** it is convenient/inconvenient

Treffen *das;* ~s, ~ (a) meeting; (b) (Sport) encounter

treffend 1 *Adj.* apt. **2** *adv.* aptly

Treffer *der;* ~s, ~ (a) (Milit., Boxen, Fechten usw.) hit; (Schlag) blow; (Ballspiele) goal; (b) (Gewinn) win; (Los) winner

trefflich (geh.) **1** *Adj.* excellent; splendid ‹*person*›; firstrate ‹*scholar*›. **2** *adv.* excellently; splendidly

Treff·punkt *der* (a) (Stelle, Ort) meeting place; rendezvous; (b) (Geom.) point of incidence

treff·sicher 1 *Adj.* with a sure aim *postpos., not pred.;* accurate ‹*marksman*›; (fig.) accurate ‹*language, mode of*

expression›; unerring ‹*judgement*›; **2** *adv.* (auch fig.) accurately; with unerring accuracy

Treib·eis *das* drift-ice

treiben /'traɪbn̩/ **1** *unr. tr. V.* (a) drive ‹*animals, people, leaves, etc.*›; **er ließ sich von der Strömung** ~: he let himself be carried along by the current; **die Preise in die Höhe** ~: push *or* force up prices; **jmdn. zur Raserei/zur Verzweiflung/in den Tod** ~: drive sb. mad/to despair/to his/her death; (b) (an~) drive ‹*wheels etc.*›; **jmdn. zur Eile** ~: make sb. hurry up; (c) (einschlagen) drive ‹*nail, wedge, stake, etc.*› (**in** + *Akk.* into); (d) (durch Bohrung schaffen) drive, cut ‹*tunnel, gallery*› (**in** + *Akk.* into; **durch** through); sink ‹*shaft*› (**in** + *Akk.* into); (e) (durchpressen) force; press; (f) (sich beschäftigen mit) go in for ‹*farming, cattle-breeding, etc.*›; study ‹*French etc.*›; carry on, pursue ‹*studies, trade, craft*›; **viel Sport** ~: do a lot of sport; go in for sport in a big way; **Handel** ~: trade; **was treibt ihr denn hier?** (ugs.) what are you up to *or* doing here?; (g) (ugs. abwertend) **es wüst/übel/toll** ~: lead a dissolute/bad life/live it up; **es zu toll** ~: overdo it; take things too far; **er hat es zu weit getrieben** he overstepped the mark; he went too far; **es [mit jmdm.]** ~ (ugs. verhüll.: koitieren) have it off [with sb.] (sl.); (h) (formen) beat ‹*metal, object*›; chase ‹*silver, gold*›; (i) (Gartenbau) force ‹*plants*›. **2** *unr. itr. V.* (a) meist, mit Richtungsangabe nur, mit sein drift; (b) (ugs.) (harntreibend sein) get the bladder going; (schweißtreibend sein) make you sweat; (c) (ausschlagen) ‹*tree, plant*› sprout

Treiben *das;* ~s, ~ (a) *o. Pl.* bustle; **in der Fußgängerzone herrscht ein lebhaftes** ~: the pedestrian precinct is full of bustling activity; (b) *o. Pl.* (Tun) activities *pl.;* doings *pl.;* (Machenschaften) wheelings and dealings *pl.*

Treiber *der;* ~s, ~ (Jägerspr.) beater

Treib-: ~**gas** *das* (a) (für Motoren) liquefied petroleum gas; LPG; (b) (in Spraydosen) propellant; ~**haus** *das* hothouse; ~**haus·effekt** *der* greenhouse effect; ~**jagd** *die* (Jägerspr.) battue; shoot (in which game is sent up by beaters); (fig.) witch-hunt; ~**mittel** *das* (Kochk.) raising agent; ~**sand** *der* quicksand; ~**stoff** *der* fuel

Tremolo /'treːmolo/ *das;* ~s, ~s *od.* **Tremoli** (Musik) tremolo

Trend /trɛnt/ *der;* ~s, ~s trend (**zu** + *Dat.* towards); (Mode) vogue

trennen /'trɛnən/ **1** *tr. V.* (a) separate (**von** from); (abschneiden) cut off; sever ‹*head, arm*›; (b) (auf~) unpick ‹*dress, seam*›; (c) (teilen) divide ‹*word, parts of a room etc., fig.: people*›; **uns** ~ **Welten** (fig.) we are worlds apart; (d) (beim Telefon) **wir wurden getrennt** we were cut off; (e) (zerlegen) separate ‹*mixture*›; (f) (auseinander halten) differentiate *or* distinguish between; make a distinction between ‹*terms*›. **2** *refl. V.* (a) (voneinander weggehen) part [company]; (fig.) **die Mannschaften trennten sich 0:0** the game ended in a goalless draw; the two teams drew 0:0; **die Firma hat sich von ihm getrennt** the company has dispensed with his services; (b) (eine Partnerschaft auflösen) ‹*couple, partners*› split up; **sich in Güte** ~: part on good terms; (c) (hergeben) **sich von etw.** ~: part with sth.

Trenn·scheibe *die* (a) glass partition; (b) (Schleifscheibe) cutting disc

Trennung *die;* ~, ~**en** (a) (von Menschen) separation (**von** from); **in** ~ **leben** have separated; (b) (von Gegenständen) parting (**von** with); (c) (von Wörtern) division; (d) (von Begriffen) distinction (**von** between)

Trennungs-: ~**linie** *die* (auch fig.) dividing line; ~**strich** *der* (a) hyphen; (b) (fig.) **einen** ~**strich ziehen** *od.* **machen** make a [clear] distinction; draw a [clear] line

trepp- /trɛp'-/**:** ~**ab** *Adv.* down the stairs; ~**auf** *Adv.* up the stairs

Treppe /'trɛpə/ *die;* ~, ~n staircase; [flight *sing.* of] stairs *pl.;* (im Freien, auf der Bühne) [flight *sing.* of] steps *pl.;* ~**n steigen** climb stairs; **eine** ~ **höher/tiefer** one floor *or* flight up/down

Treppen-: ~**absatz** *der* half-landing; ~**geländer** *das* banisters *pl.;* ~**haus** *das* stairwell; **das Licht im** ~**haus** the light on the staircase; ~**stufe** *die* stair; (im Freien) step

Tresen /'tre:zn̩/ *der;* ~s, ~ (bes. nordd.) (a) (Theke) bar; (b) (Ladentisch) counter

Tresor /tre'zo:ɐ̯/ *der;* ~s, ~e safe

Tret·boot *das* pedalo

treten /'tre:tn̩/ 1 *unr. itr. V.* (a) *mit sein* (einen Schritt, Schritte machen) step (**in** + *Akk.* into, **auf** + *Akk.* on to); **ins Zimmer** ~: enter the room; **ans Fenster** ~: go to the window; **von einem Fuß auf den anderen** ~: shift from one foot to the other; **der Schweiß ist ihm auf die Stirn getreten** (fig.) the sweat came to his brow; **der Fluss ist über die Ufer getreten** (fig.) the river has overflowed its banks; (b) (seinen Fuß setzen) **auf etw.** (*Akk.*) ~ (absichtlich) tread on sth.; (unabsichtlich; meist mit sein) step *or* tread on sth.; **jmdm. auf den Fuß** ~: step/tread on sb.'s foot *or* toes; **aufs Gas[pedal]** ~: step on the accelerator; (c) *mit sein* **in jmds. Dienste** ~: enter sb.'s service; (d) (ausschlagen) kick; **jmdm. an** *od.* **gegen das Schienbein** ~: kick sb. on the shin; **gegen die Tür** ~: kick the door. 2 *unr. tr. V.* (a) kick ⟨*person, ball, etc.*⟩; (b) (trampeln) trample, tread ⟨*path*⟩; (c) (mit dem Fuß niederdrücken) step on ⟨*brake, pedal*⟩; operate ⟨*clutch*⟩

Tret-: ~**kurbel** *die* crank arm; crank; ~**lager** *das* bottom bracket [bearing]; crank bearing; ~**mine** *die* anti-personnel mine; ~**mühle** *die* (fig. ugs. abwertend) treadmill

treu /trɔɪ̯/ 1 *Adj.* (a) faithful, loyal ⟨*friend, dog, customer, servant, etc.*⟩; faithful ⟨*husband, wife*⟩; loyal ⟨*ally, subject*⟩; staunch, loyal ⟨*supporter*⟩; **jmdm.** ~ **sein/bleiben** be/remain true to sb.; (b) (fig.) **sich selbst** (*Dat.*) ~ **bleiben** be true to oneself; **seinen Grundsätzen** ~ **bleiben** stick to one's principles; **das Glück/der Erfolg ist ihm** ~ **geblieben** his luck has held out/success keeps coming his way; (c) (ugs.: ~herzig) ingenuous, trusting ⟨*eyes, look*⟩. 2 *adv.* (a) faithfully; loyally; (b) (ugs.: ~herzig) trustingly

Treue *die;* ~ (a) loyalty; (von [Ehe]partnern) fidelity; (b) (Genauigkeit) accuracy

Treue·gelöbnis *das* pledge of loyalty; (von Ehepartnern) pledge of fidelity

treu-, Treu-: ~**herzig** 1 *Adj.* ingenuous; (naiv) naïve; (unschuldig) innocent; 2 *adv.* ingenuously; (naiv) naïvely; (unschuldig) innocently; ~**los** 1 *Adj.* disloyal, faithless ⟨*friend, person*⟩; unfaithful ⟨*husband, wife, lover*⟩; 2 *adv.* faithlessly; ~**losigkeit** *die;* ~: disloyalty; faithlessness; (von [Ehe]partnern) infidelity

Triangel /'triːaŋl̩/ *der;* österr. *das;* ~s, ~ (Mus.) triangle

Triathlon /'triːatlɔn/ *das od. der;* ~s, ~s triathlon

Tribunal /tribu'na:l/̩ *das;* ~s, ~e tribunal

Tribüne /tri'by:nə/ *die;* ~, ~n [grand]stand

Tribut /tri'buːt/ *der;* ~[e]s, ~e (a) (hist.) tribute *no indef. art.;* (b) (fig.) due

Trichter /'trɪçtɐ/ *der;* ~s, ~ (a) funnel; (b) (Bomben~, Geogr.) crater

Trick /trɪk/ *der;* ~s, ~s trick; (fig.: List) ploy; **technische** ~s cunning techniques

Trick·film *der* animated cartoon [film]

tricksen /'trɪksn̩/ (ugs., bes. Sportjargon) 1 *itr. V.* use tricks; work a fiddle (coll.); ⟨*footballer*⟩ play trickily. 2 *tr. V.* fiddle (coll.)

trieb /tri:p/ *1. u. 3. Pers. Sg. Prät. v.* **treiben**

Trieb *der;* ~[e]s, ~e (a) (innerer Antrieb) impulse; (Drang) urge; (Verlangen) [compulsive] desire; (b) (Spross) shoot

trieb-, Trieb-: ~**feder** *die* mainspring; (fig.) driving *or* motivating force; ~**haft** 1 *Adj.* compulsive ⟨*need, behaviour, action, etc.*⟩; carnal ⟨*sensuality*⟩; 2 *adv.* compulsively; ~**wagen** *der* (Eisenb.) railcar; ~**werk** *das* engine

triefen /'tri:fn̩/ *unr. od. regelm. itr. V.* (a) *mit sein* (fließen) (in Tropfen) drip; (in kleinen Rinnsalen) trickle; (b) (nass sein) be dripping wet; ⟨*nose*⟩ run; ~**d nass** dripping wet; (durchnässt) wet through; **von Fett** ~: be dripping with fat

triezen /'tri:tsn̩/ *tr. V.* (ugs.) torment; (plagen) pester; plague

trifft *3. Pers. Sg. Präsens v.* **treffen**

triftig *Adj.* good ⟨*reason, excuse*⟩; valid, convincing ⟨*motive, argument*⟩

Trigonometrie /trigonome'tri:/ *die;* ~: trigonometry *no art.*

Trikot¹ /tri'ko/ *der od. das;* ~s, ~s (Stoff) cotton jersey

Trikot² *das;* ~s, ~ (ärmellos) singlet; (eines Tänzers) leotard; (eines Fußballspielers) shirt; **das gelbe** ~ (Radsport) the yellow jersey

Triller /'trɪlɐ/ *der;* ~s, ~: trill

trillern 1 *itr. V.* (Musik) trill; (mit Trillern singen) ⟨*bird, person*⟩ warble. 2 *tr. V.* warble ⟨*song*⟩

Triller·pfeife *die* police/referee's whistle

Trillion /trɪ'lio:n/ *die;* ~, ~en quintillion

Trilogie /trilo'gi:/ *die;* ~, ~n trilogy

Trimester /tri'mɛstɐ/ *das;* ~s, ~ (Hochschulw.) term

Trimm-dich-Pfad *der* keep-fit *or* trim trail

trimmen /'trɪmən/ *tr. V.* (a) (durch Sport) get ⟨*person*⟩ into shape; **trimm dich durch Sport** keep fit with sport; (b) etw. auf alt *usw.* ~: do sth. up to look old *etc.;* (c) (durch Scheren) clip ⟨*dog*⟩; (durch Bürsten) groom ⟨*dog*⟩

trinken /'trɪŋkn̩/ 1 *unr. itr. V.* drink; **jmdm. etw. zu geben** give sb. sth. to drink; **was** ~ **Sie?** what are you drinking?; (was möchten Sie ~?) what would you like to drink?; **auf jmdn./etw.** ~: drink to sb./sth. 2 *unr. tr. V.* drink; **einen Kaffee** *usw.* ~: have a coffee *etc.;* **einen Schluck Wasser** ~: have a drink of water; **einen** ~: have a drink; **einen** ~ **gehen** (ugs.) go for a drink. 3 *refl. V.* **sich satt** ~: drink one's fill

Trinker *der;* ~s, ~, **Trinkerin** *die;* ~, ~nen alcoholic; **ein heimlicher/starker** ~: a secret/heavy drinker

trink-, Trink-: ~**fest** *Adj.* ~**fest sein** be able to hold one's drink; ~**flasche** *die* [drinking] bottle; ~**gelage** *das* (oft scherzh.) drinking spree; ~**geld** *das* tip; **wie viel** ~**geld gibst du ihm?** how much do you tip him?; ~**halle** *die* (a) (in einem Heilbad) pump room; (b) (Kiosk) refreshment kiosk; (größer) refreshment stall; ~**halm** *der* [drinking-]straw; ~**milch** *die* low-fat pasteurized milk; ~**wasser** *das; Pl.* ~**wässer** drinking water; „**kein** ~**wasser**" 'not for drinking'

Trio /'tri:o/ *das;* ~s, ~s (Musik, fig.) trio

Triole /tri'o:lə/ *die;* ~, ~n (Musik) triplet

Trip /trɪp/ *der;* ~s, ~s (a) (ugs.: Ausflug) trip; jaunt; (b) (Drogenjargon: Rausch) trip (coll.); **auf dem** ~ **sein** be tripping (coll.)

trippeln /'trɪpl̩n/ *itr. V.; mit sein* trip; ⟨*child*⟩ patter; (affektiert) mince

Tripper /'trɪpɐ/ *der;* ~s, ~: ▶ 329 | gonorrhoea

trist /trɪst/ *Adj.* dreary; dismal

tritt /trɪt/ *Imperativ Sg. u. 3. Pers. Sg. Präsens v.* **treten**

Tritt *der;* ~[e]s, ~e (a) (Aufsetzen des Fußes) step; (einmalig) [foot]step; (b) (Gleichschritt) **im** ~ **marschieren/aus dem** ~ **geraten** *od.* **kommen** march in/get out of step; **im** ~ **fassen** fall in step; (fig.: sich fangen) recover oneself; (c) (Fuß~) kick; **jmdm. einen** ~ **versetzen** give sb. a kick; kick sb.; (d) (~brett) step; (e) (Bergsteigen) (Halt für Füße) foothold; (im Eis) step; (f) (Gestell) small stepladder

Tritt-: ~**brett** *das* step; (an älterem Auto) running-board; ~**leiter** *die* stepladder

Triumph /tri'ʊmf/ *der;* ~[e]s, ~e triumph; **einen großen** ~ **feiern** have a great triumph *or* success; be huge success

triumphieren *itr. V.* (a) (Genugtuung empfinden) exult; (b) (siegen) be triumphant *or* victorious; triumph (lit. or fig.) (**über** + *Akk.* over)

Triumph·zug *der* (hist.) triumph; **im** ~ (fig.) in a triumphal procession

trivial /tri'via:l/ 1 *Adj.* (a) (platt) banal; trite; (unbedeutend) trivial; (b) (alltäglich) humdrum ⟨*life, career*⟩. 2 *adv.* (platt) banally; ⟨*say etc.*⟩ tritely; ⟨*written*⟩ in a banal style

Trivialität *die;* ~, ~en (a) *o. Pl.* (Plattheit, Alltäglichkeit) banality; triteness; (b) (platte Äußerung) banality; (Gemeinplatz) commonplace [remark]

trocken /'trɔkn̩/ 1 *Adj.* (a) dry; **etw.** ~ **bügeln/reinigen** dry-iron/dry-clean sth.; **sich** ~ **rasieren** use an electric razor; **auf dem Trock[e]nen sitzen** *od.* **sein** (ugs.) be completely stuck (coll.); (pleite sein) be skint (Brit. sl.); (b) (ohne Zutat) ~**es** *od.* (ugs.) ~ **Brot essen** eat dry bread; (c) (sachlich-langweilig) dry, factual ⟨*account, report, treatise*⟩; bare ⟨*words, figures*⟩; dull, dry ⟨*person*⟩; (d) (unverblümt) dry

⟨*humour, remark, etc.*⟩; **(e)** (dem Klang nach) dry ⟨*laugh, cough, sound*⟩; sharp ⟨*crack*⟩. **2** *adv.* **(a)** (sachlich-langweilig) ⟨*speak, write*⟩ drily, in a matter-of-fact way; **(b)** (unverblümt) drily

Trocken-: ~**blume** *die; meist Pl.* dried flower; ~**ge-biet** *das* (Geogr.) arid region; ~**haube** *die* [hood-type] hairdrier

Trockenheit *die;* ~, ~**en** **(a)** *o. Pl.* (auch fig.) dryness; **(b)** (Dürreperiode) drought

trocken-, Trocken-: ~**kurs** *der* dry-skiing course; ~**|legen** *tr. V.* **(a)** ein Baby ~**legen** change a baby's nappies (Brit.) *or* (Amer.) diapers; **(b)** (entwässern) drain ⟨*marsh, pond, etc.*⟩; ~**milch** *die* dried milk; ~**|reiben** *unr. tr. V.* rub ⟨*hair, child, etc.*⟩ dry; wipe ⟨*crockery, window, etc.*⟩ dry; ~**schwimmen** *das* preparatory swimming exercises *pl.* [on land]; ~**zeit** *die* dry season

trocknen **1** *itr. V.; meist mit sein* dry. **2** *tr. V.* dry

Troddel /'trɔdl̩/ *die;* ~, ~**n** tassel

Trödel /'trøːdl̩/ *der;* ~**s** (ugs., oft abwertend) junk; (für den Flohmarkt) jumble

trödeln *itr. V.* **(a)** (ugs., oft abwertend) dawdle (**mit** over); **(b)** *mit sein* (ugs.: schlendern) saunter

Trödler *der;* ~**s**, ~, **Trödlerin** *die;* ~, ~**nen** **(a)** (ugs. abwertend) dawdler; slowcoach; slowpoke (Amer.); **(b)** (ugs.: Händler[in]) junk-dealer

troff /trɔf/ *1. u. 3. Pers. Sg. Prät. v.* **triefen**

trog /troːk/ *1. u. 3. Pers. Sg. Prät. v.* **trügen**

Trog *der;* ~**[e]s**, **Tröge** /'trøːgə/ trough

Troika /'trɔyka/ *die;* ~, ~**s** troika; (fig.: Führungsgruppe) triumvirate

trollen /'trɔlən/ *refl. V.* (ugs.) push off (coll.); **der Junge trollte sich in sein Zimmer** the boy took himself off to his room

Trommel /'trɔml̩/ *die;* ~, ~**n** **(a)** (Schlaginstrument) drum; **(b)** (Behälter; Kabel~, Seil~) drum

Trommel-: ~**bremse** *die* (Kfz-W.) drum brake; ~**fell** *das* **(a)** (bei Trommeln) drumhead; **(b)** (im Ohr) eardrum; ~**feuer** *das* (Milit.; auch fig.) [constant] barrage

trommeln **1** *itr. V.* **(a)** beat the drum; (als Beruf, Hobby usw.) play the drums; **(b)** ([auf etw.] schlagen, auftreffen) drum (**auf** + *Akk.* on, **an** + *Akk.* against); **sie trommelte mit den Fäusten gegen die Tür** she hammered the door with her fists. **2** *tr. V.* beat [out] ⟨*march, rhythm, etc.*⟩

Trommel-: ~**schlag** *der* drumbeat; ~**schlägel**, ***~**schlegel** *der*, ~**stock** *der* drumstick; ~**wirbel** *der* drum roll

Trommler *der;* ~**s**, ~, **Trommlerin** *die;* ~, ~**nen** drummer

Trompete /trɔm'peːtə/ *die;* ~, ~**n** trumpet

trompeten **1** *itr. V.* play the trumpet; (fig.) ⟨*elephant*⟩ trumpet. **2** *tr. V.* play ⟨*piece*⟩ on the trumpet

Trompeter *der;* ~**s**, ~, **Trompeterin** *die;* ~, ~**nen** trumpeter

Tropen *Pl.* tropics

Tropen- tropical

Tropen·helm *der* sun-helmet

Tropf[1] /trɔpf/ *der;* ~**[e]s**, **Tröpfe** /'trœpfə/ (abwertend) twit (Brit. coll.); moron (coll.)

Tropf[2] *der;* ~**[e]s**, ~**e** (Med.) drip; **am** ~ **hängen** be on a drip

Tröpfchen·infektion *die* (Med.) droplet infection

tröpfeln /'trœpfl̩n/ **1** *itr. V.* **(a)** *mit sein* drip (**auf** + *Akk.* on to, **aus, von** from); **(b)** (unpers.) (ugs.: leicht regnen) **es tröpfelt** it's spitting [with rain]. **2** *tr. V.* let ⟨*sth.*⟩ drip (**in** + *Akk.* into, **auf** + *Akk.* on to)

tropfen **1** *itr. V.; mit Richtungsangabe mit sein* drip; ⟨*tears*⟩ fall; **seine Nase tropft** his nose is running; (unpers.) **es tropft [vom Dach** usw.**]** water is or it's dripping from the roof etc.. **2** *tr. V.* let ⟨*sth.*⟩ drip (**in** + *Akk.* into, **auf** + *Akk.* on to); **jmdm. eine Tinktur auf die Wunde** ~: pour drops of a tincture into sb.'s wound

Tropfen *der;* ~**s**, ~ **(a)** drop; **es regnet dicke** ~: the rain is falling in large drops *or* spots; **er hat keinen** ~

[Alkohol] **getrunken** he hasn't touched a drop; **ein** ~ **auf den heißen Stein sein** (fig. ugs.) be a drop in the ocean; **(b)** ein guter/edler ~: a good/fine vintage

Tropfen·form *die; o. Pl.* tear shape; **in** ~: tear-shaped *attrib.*

tropf·nass, *tropf·naß *Adj.* dripping *or* soaking wet

Tropf·stein·höhle *die* limestone cave with stalactites and/or stalagmites

Trophäe /tro'fɛːə/ *die;* ~, ~**n** (hist., Jagd, Sport) trophy

tropisch *Adj.* tropical

Tropo·sphäre /tropo'sfɛːrə/ *die;* ~ (Meteor.) troposphere

Trosse /'trɔsə/ *die;* ~, ~**n** hawser (Naut.)

Trost /troːst/ *der;* ~**[e]s** consolation; (bes. geistlich) comfort; **jmdm.** ~ **zusprechen** *od.* **spenden** comfort *or* console sb.; **nicht [ganz** *od.* **recht] bei** ~ **sein** (ugs.) be out of one's mind; have taken leave of one's senses

trösten /'trøːstn̩/ **1** *tr. V.* comfort, console (**mit** with); ~**de Worte** words of comfort; comforting words; **etw. tröstet jmdn.** sth. is a comfort to sb.. **2** *refl. V.* console oneself; **sich mit einer anderen Frau** ~: find consolation with another woman

tröstlich *Adj.* comforting

trost-, Trost-: ~**los** *Adj.* **(a)** (ohne Trost) hopeless; without hope *postpos.;* (verzweifelt) in despair *postpos.;* **(b)** (deprimierend, öde) miserable, dreary ⟨*time, weather, area, food, etc.*⟩; hopeless ⟨*situation*⟩; ~**pflaster** *das* (scherzh.) consolation; ~**preis** *der* consolation prize

Trott /trɔt/ *der;* ~**[e]s**, ~**e** (Gangart) trot; **(b)** (leicht abwertend: Ablauf) routine; **in den alten** ~ **verfallen** fall back into the same old rut

Trottel *der;* ~**s**, ~ (ugs. abwertend) fool; wally (Brit. coll.)

trotten *itr. V.; mit sein* trot [along]; (freudlos) trudge

Trottoir /trɔ'toaːɐ̯/ *das;* ~**s**, ~**e** *od.* ~**s** pavement

trotz /trɔts/ *Präp. mit Gen., seltener mit Dat.* in spite of; despite; ~ **allem** in spite of everything

Trotz *der;* ~**es** defiance; (Oppositionsgeist) cussedness (coll.); contrariness; **jmdm./einer Sache zum** ~: in defiance of sb./sth.

Trotz·alter *das* difficult age

trotz·dem /auch: '-'-/ *Adv.* nevertheless; **er tat es** ~: he did it all *or* just the same

trotzen /'trɔtsn̩/ *itr. V.* **(a)** (geh.: widerstehen) **jmdm./einer Sache** ~ (auch fig.) defy sb./sth.; **Gefahren/der Kälte** ~: brave dangers/the cold; **(b)** (trotzig sein) be contrary

trotzig **1** *Adj.* defiant; (widerspenstig) contrary; bolshie (coll.); difficult ⟨*child*⟩. **2** *adv.* defiantly

trüb[e] /'tryːb(ə)/ **1** *Adj.* **(a)** (nicht klar) murky ⟨*stream, water*⟩; cloudy ⟨*liquid, wine, juice*⟩; (schlammig) muddy ⟨*puddle*⟩; (schmutzig) dirty ⟨*glass, window pane*⟩; dull ⟨*eyes*⟩; **im Trüben fischen** (ugs.) fish in troubled waters; **(b)** (nicht hell) dim ⟨*light*⟩; dull, dismal ⟨*day, weather*⟩; grey, overcast ⟨*sky*⟩; dull, dingy ⟨*red, yellow*⟩; **(c)** (gedrückt) gloomy ⟨*mood, voice, etc.*⟩; dreary ⟨*time*⟩; *s. auch* **Tasse a**; **(d)** (unerfreulich) unfortunate, bad ⟨*experience etc.*⟩. **2** *adv.* **(a)** (nicht hell) ⟨*shine, light*⟩ dimly; **(b)** (gedrückt) ⟨*smile, look*⟩ gloomily; **(c)** (unerfreulich) ~ **laufen** go badly

Trubel /'truːbl̩/ *der;* ~**s** [hustle and] bustle; **im** ~ **der Ereignisse** (fig.) in the excitement of the moment; in the rush of events

trüben **1** *tr. V.* **(a)** make ⟨*liquid*⟩ cloudy; cloud ⟨*liquid*⟩; **(b)** (beeinträchtigen) dampen, cast a cloud over ⟨*mood*⟩; mar ⟨*relationship*⟩; cloud ⟨*judgement*⟩; **jmds. Blick [für etw.]** ~: blind sb. [to sth.]. **2** *refl. V.* **(a)** ⟨*liquid*⟩ become cloudy; ⟨*eyes*⟩ become dull; ⟨*sky*⟩ darken; **(b)** (sich verschlechtern) ⟨*relationship*⟩ deteriorate; ⟨*awareness, memory, etc.*⟩ become dulled *or* dim

Trübsal /'tryːpzaːl/ *die;* ~, ~**e** (geh.) **(a)** (Leiden) affliction; **(b)** *o. Pl.* (Kummer) grief; ~ **blasen** (ugs.) mope (**wegen** over, about)

trüb·selig **1** *Adj.* **(a)** (öde) dreary, depressing ⟨*place, area, colour*⟩; dismal ⟨*house*⟩; **(b)** (traurig) gloomy, melancholy ⟨*thoughts, mood*⟩; gloomy, miserable ⟨*face*⟩. **2** *adv.* (traurig) gloomily

Trüb·sinn *der; o. Pl.* melancholy; gloom

Trübung *die;* ~, ~**en** (a) clouding; (*des Auges*) dimming; (b) (Beeinträchtigung) deterioration; (der Stimmung) dampening

trudeln /'tru:dḷn/ *itr. V. mit sein* (rollen) roll; **das Flugzeug geriet ins Trudeln** the plane went into a spin

Trüffel /'tryfḷ/ *die;* ~, ~**n** *od.* (ugs.) *der;* ~**s**, ~: truffle

trug /tru:k/ *1. u. 3. Pers. Prät. v.* **tragen**

Trug·bild *das* hallucination; illusion; (Bild der Fantasie) figment of the imagination

trügen 1 *unr. tr. V.* deceive; **wenn mich nicht alles trügt** unless I am very much mistaken. 2 *unr. itr. V.* be deceptive; ⟨*feeling, deception*⟩ be a delusion; *s. auch* **Schein b**

trügerisch 1 *Adj.* (a) deceptive; false ⟨*hope, sign, etc.*⟩; treacherous ⟨*ice*⟩; (b) (veralt.: auf Betrug zielend) deceitful; **in** ~**er Absicht** with intent to deceive. 2 *adv.* (a) deceptively; (b) (veralt.: auf Betrug zielend) deceitfully

Trug·schluss, *Trug·schluß *der* wrong conclusion; (Irrtum) fallacy

Truhe /'tru:ə/ *die;* ~, ~**n** chest

Trümmer /'trymɐ/ *Pl.* (eines Gebäudes) rubble *sing.;* (Ruinen) ruins; (eines Flugzeugs usw.) wreckage *sing.;* (kleinere Teile) debris *sing.;* **die Stadt lag in** ~**n** the town lay in ruins; **eine Stadt in** ~ **legen** reduce a town to rubble; flatten a town [completely]

Trümmer-: ~**feld** *das* expanse of rubble; ~**haufen** *der* pile *or* heap of rubble

Trumpf /trʊmpf/ *der;* ~[e]s, **Trümpfe** /'trympfə/ (auch fig.) trump [card]; (Farbe) trumps *pl.;* **was ist** ~? what are trumps?; **alle Trümpfe in der Hand haben** (fig.) hold all the [trump] cards; ~ **sein** (fig.) (das Nötigste sein) be what matters; be the order of the day; (Mode sein) be the in thing

trumpfen *itr. V.* play a trump

Trumpf·karte *die* (auch fig.) trump card

Trunk /trʊŋk/ *der;* ~[e]s, **Trünke** /'tryŋkə/ (geh.) (a) (Getränk) drink; beverage (formal); (b) (das Trinken) **sich dem** ~ **ergeben** take to drink

Trunkenbold /-bɔlt/ *der;* ~[e]s, ~**e** (abwertend) drunkard

Trunkenheit *die;* ~ (a) drunkenness; ~ **am Steuer** drunken driving; (b) (geh.: Begeisterung) [state of] intoxication

Trunk·sucht *die; o. Pl.* alcoholism *no art.*

trunk·süchtig *Adj.* alcoholic; ~ **sein** be an alcoholic

Trupp /trʊp/ *der;* ~**s**, ~**s** troop; (von Arbeitern, Gefangenen) gang; (von Soldaten, Polizisten) detachment; squad

Truppe *die;* ~, ~**n** (a) (Einheit der Streitkräfte) unit; (b) *Pl.* (Soldaten) troops; (c) *o. Pl.* (Streitkräfte) [armed] forces *pl.;* (d) (Gruppe von Schauspielern, Artisten) troupe; company; (von Sportlern) squad; (Mannschaft) team

Truppen-: ~**gattung** *die* arm [of the service]; corps; ~**parade** *die* military parade; ~**übungsplatz** *der* military training area

Trut- /'tru:t-/: ~**hahn** *der* turkey [cock]; (als Braten) turkey; ~**henne** *die* turkey [hen]

Tschad /tʃat/ (das); ~**s**, *od. der;* ~**s** Chad

Tscheche /'tʃɛçə/ *der;* ~**n**, ~**n** ▶388 Czech

Tschechien (das); ~**s** Czech Republic

tschechisch ▶388, ▶487 1 *Adj.* Czech. 2 *adv.* **Tschechisch sprechen** Czech-speaking; *s. auch* **deutsch; Deutsch; Deutsche²**

Tschechoslowakei /tʃɛçoslova'kai/ *die;* ~: Czechoslovakia *no art.*

Tschetschene /tʃɛ'tʃɛnə/ *der;* ~**n**, ~**n** Chechen; **die** ~**n** the Chechen[s]

Tschetschenien /tʃɛ'tʃɛniən/ (das); ~**s** Chechenia; Chechnya

tschetschenisch *Adj.* ▶388 Chechen

tschilpen /'tʃɪlpn/ *itr. V.* chirp

tschüs /tʃy:s/ *Interj.* (ugs.) bye (coll.); so long (coll.)

T-Shirt /'ti:ʃø:t/ *das;* ~**s**, ~**s** T-shirt

Tuba /'tu:ba/ *die;* ~, **Tuben** tuba

Tube /'tu:bə/ *die;* ~, ~**n** tube; **auf die** ~ **drücken** (fig. ugs.) step on it (coll.); put one's foot down

tuberkulös /tubɛrku'lø:s/ *Adj.* (Med.) tubercular

Tuberkulose /tubɛrku'lo:zə/ *die;* ~, ~**n** ▶329 (Med.) tuberculosis *no art.*

Tuch /tu:x/ *das;* ~[e]s, **Tücher** /'ty:çɐ/ *od.* ~**e** (a) *Pl.* **Tücher** cloth; (Bade~) [bath-]towel; (Kopf~, Hals~) scarf; (b) *Pl.* ~**e** (Gewebe) cloth

Tuch·fühlung *die* (scherzh.) physical contact; (fig.: Kontakte) [close] contact; **auf** *od.* **mit** ~: close together

tüchtig /'tyçtɪç/ 1 *Adj.* (a) efficient ⟨*secretary, assistant, worker, etc.*⟩; (fähig) capable, competent (**in** + *Dat.* at); **freie Bahn dem Tüchtigen!** let ability win through; (b) (von guter Qualität) excellent ⟨*performance, piece of work, etc.*⟩; ~, ~! (auch iron.) well done!; (c) *nicht präd.* (ugs.: beträchtlich) sizeable ⟨*piece, portion*⟩; big ⟨*gulp*⟩; hearty ⟨*eater, appetite*⟩. 2 *adv.* (a) efficiently; (fähig) competently; ~ **arbeiten** work hard; (b) (ugs.: sehr) really ⟨*cold, warm*⟩; ⟨*snow, rain*⟩ good and proper (coll.); ⟨*eat*⟩ heartily

Tüchtigkeit *die;* ~ (a) efficiency; (Fähigkeit) ability; competence; (Fleiß) industry; (b) **körperliche** ~: physical fitness

Tücke /'tykə/ *die;* ~, ~**n** (a) *o. Pl.* (Hinterhältigkeit) deceit[-fulness]; (List) guile; scheming *no indef. art.;* **die** ~ **des Objekts** the perversity *or* (coll.) cussedness of inanimate objects; *s. auch* **List b**; (b) *meist Pl.* (hinterhältige Handlung) wile; ruse; (c) *meist Pl.* ([verborgene] Gefahr/Schwierigkeit) [hidden] danger/difficulty; (unberechenbare Eigenschaft) vagary

tuckern /'tukɐn/ *itr. V.; mit Richtungsangabe mit sein* chug

tückisch 1 *Adj.* (a) (hinterhältig) wily; (betrügerisch) deceitful; (b) (gefährlich) treacherous ⟨*bend, slope, spot, etc.*⟩; (Gefahr signalisierend) menacing ⟨*look, eyes*⟩. 2 *adv.* (a) (hinterhältig) craftily; (b) (Gefahr signalisierend) menacingly

Tüftelei *die;* ~, ~**en** (ugs.) (a) *o. Pl.* fiddling [about]; (geistig) racking one's brains; (b) (tüftelige Arbeit) fiddly job (coll.)

tüfteln /'tyftḷn/ *itr. V.* (ugs.) fiddle (**an** + *Dat.* with); do finicky work (**an** | *Dat.* on); (geistig) rack one's brains, puzzle (**an** + *Dat.* over)

Tüftler *der;* ~**s**, ~ (ugs.) *person who likes finicky jobs/ niggling problems;* (jmd., der gern Rätselspiele macht) puzzle freak (coll.)

Tugend /'tu:gṇt/ *die;* ~, ~**en** virtue

tugendhaft 1 *Adj.* virtuous. 2 *adv.* virtuously; ~ **leben** live a life of virtue

Tüll /tyl/ *der;* ~**s**, ~**e** tulle

Tulpe /'tʊlpə/ *die;* ~, ~**n** (a) (Pflanze) tulip; (b) (Glas) tulip glas

Tulpen·zwiebel *die* tulip-bulb

tummeln /'tʊmḷn/ *refl. V.* (a) (umhertollen) romp [about]; (im Wasser) splash about; (b) (bes. westmd., österr., sich beeilen) stir one's stumps (coll.); get a move on (coll.)

Tummel·platz *der* (auch fig.) playground

Tümmler /'tʏmlɐ/ *der;* ~**s**, ~ (Delphin) bottle-nosed dolphin

Tumor /'tu:mɔr/ *der;* ~**s**, ~**en** /tu'mo:rən/, *ugs. auch* ~**e** /tu'mo:rə/ (Med.) tumour

Tümpel /'tʏmpḷ/ *der;* ~**s**, ~: pond

Tumult /tu'mʊlt/ *der;* ~[e]s, ~**e** tumult; commotion; (Protest) uproar

tun /tu:n/ 1 *unr. tr. V.* (a) (machen) do; **ich weiß nicht, was ich** ~ **soll** I don't know what to do; **so etwas tut man nicht** that is just not done; **er hat sein Möglichstes getan** he did his [level] best; **was** ~? what is to be done?; **man tut, was man kann** one does what one can; one tries one's best; (b) (erledigen) do ⟨*work, duty, etc.*⟩; **ich muss noch etwas [für die Schule]** ~: I've still got some [school-]work to do; **nach getaner Arbeit** when the work is/was done; **mit Geld/einer Entschuldigung** *usw.* **ist es nicht getan** money/an apology *etc.* is not enough; **es** ~ (ugs. verhüll.: koitieren) do it (sl.); (c) [etwas] **zu** ~ **haben** have something to do; **ich hatte dort zu** ~/**dort geschäftlich zu** ~: I had things/business to do there; [es] **mit jmdm. zu** ~ **bekommen** *od.* (ugs.) **kriegen** get into trouble with sb./sth.; **mit sich [selbst]**

zu ~ haben have problems [of one's own]; **[etwas] mit etw./jmdm. zu ~ haben** be concerned with sth./have dealings with sb.; **er hat noch nie [etwas] mit der Polizei zu ~ gehabt** he has never been involved with the police; **mit etw. nichts zu ~ haben** have nothing to do with sth.; not be concerned with sth.; **mit jmdm./etw. nichts zu ~ haben wollen** not want [to have] anything to do with sb./sth.; **(d)** *nimmt die Aussage eines vorher gebrauchten Verbs auf* **es sollte am nächsten Tag regnen, und das tat es dann auch** it was expected to rain the next day, and it did [so]; **(e)** *als Funktionsverb* make ⟨*remark, catch, etc.*⟩; take ⟨*step, jump*⟩; do ⟨*deed*⟩; *(unpers.)* **plötzlich tat es einen furchtbaren Knall** suddenly there was a dreadful bang; **(f)** (bewirken) work, perform ⟨*miracle*⟩; **seine Wirkung ~:** have its effect; **(g)** (an~) **jmdm. etw. ~:** do sth. to sb.; **er tut dir nichts** he won't hurt *or* harm you; **(h) es ~** (ugs.: genügen) be good enough; **(i)** (ugs.: irgendwohin bringen) put. **2** *unr. itr. V.* **(a)** (ugs.: funktionieren) work; **(b) freundlich/geheimnisvoll ~:** pretend to be *or* (coll.) act friendly/act mysteriously; **er tut [so], als ob** *od.* **als wenn** *od.* **wie wenn er nichts wüsste** he pretends not to know anything. **3** *unr. refl. V. (unpers.)* (geschehen) **es tut sich einiges getan** quite a bit has happened; **es tut sich nichts** there's nothing happening. **4** *Hilfsverb zur Umschreibung des Konjunktivs* (ugs.) **das täte mich interessieren/freuen** I'd be interested in/pleased about that

Tun *das;* ~s action; activity

Tünche /ˈtʏnçə/ *die;* ~, ~n **(a)** (Farbe) distemper; wash; **[weiße] ~:** whitewash; **(b)** *o. Pl.,* (abwertend: Oberfläche) veneer (fig.)

tünchen *tr. V. (auch itr.)* V. distemper; **weiß ~:** whitewash

Tunesien /tuˈneːzi̯ən/ *(das);* ~s Tunisia

Tu·nicht·gut *der;* ~ *od.* ~[e]s, ~e good-for-nothing; ne'er-do-well

Tunke /ˈtʊŋkə/ *die;* ~, ~n (bes. ostmd.) sauce; (Bratensoße) gravy

tunken *tr. V.* (bes. ostmd.) dip; dip, dunk ⟨*biscuit, piece of bread, etc.*⟩

tunlichst /ˈtuːnlɪçst/ *Adv.* (geh.) **(a)** (möglichst) as far as possible; **(b)** (unbedingt) at all costs

Tunnel /ˈtʊnl̩/ *der;* ~s, ~ *od.* ~s tunnel

Tunte /ˈtʊntə/ *die;* ~, ~n **(a)** (ugs. abwertend: Frau) female; **(b)** (salopp, auch abwertend: Homosexueller) queen (sl.)

Tüpfelchen /ˈtʏpflçən/ *das;* ~s, ~: dot; **das ~ auf dem i** the final touch

tupfen /ˈtʊpfn̩/ *tr. V.* **(a)** dab; **sich** *(Dat.)* **den Schweiß von der Stirn ~:** dab the sweat from one's brow; **etw. auf etw.** *(Akk.)* **~:** dab sth. on to sth.; **(b)** (mit Tupfen versehen) dot; **ein getupftes Kleid** a spotted dress

Tupfen *der;* ~s, ~: dot; (größer) spot

Tupfer *der;* ~s, ~ **(a)** (ugs.) ⇒ **Tupfen**; **(b)** (Med.) swab

Tür /tyːɐ̯/ *die;* ~, ~en door; (Garten~) gate; **an die ~ gehen** (öffnen) [go and] answer the door; **in der ~ stehen** stand in the doorway; **den Kopf zur ~ hereinstecken** put one's head round the door; **jmdm. die ~ einlaufen** *od.* **einrennen** (fig. ugs.) keep badgering sb.; **jmdm. die ~ vor der Nase zuschlagen** (fig.) slam the door in sb.'s face; **einer Sache** *(Dat.)* **~ und Tor öffnen** (fig.) open the door *or* way to sth.; **mit der ~ ins Haus fallen** (fig. ugs.) blurt out what one is after; **vor verschlossener ~ stehen** be locked out; **zwischen ~ und Angel** (fig. ugs.) in passing; **jmdm. die ~ weisen** (fig. geh.) show sb. the door; **jmdm. vor die ~ setzen** (fig. ugs.) chuck (coll.) *or* throw sb. out; **vor seiner eigenen ~ kehren** (fig. ugs.) set one's own house in order

Tür·angel *die* door-hinge

Turban /ˈtʊrbaːn/ *der;* ~s, ~e turban

Turbine /tʊrˈbiːnə/ *die;* ~, ~n (Technik) turbine

Turbinen·flugzeug *das* turbo-jet aircraft

turbinen·getrieben *Adj.* turbine-propelled ⟨*ship, aircraft*⟩; turbine-driven ⟨*generator*⟩

Turbo- /ˈtʊrbo-/: (Technik) turbo-

turbulent /tʊrbuˈlɛnt/ **1** *Adj.* (auch Physik, Astron., Met.) turbulent. **2** *adv.* (auch Physik, Astron., Met.) turbulently

Turbulenz /tʊrbuˈlɛnts/ *die;* ~, ~en (auch Physik, Astron., Met.) turbulence *no pl.*

Tür-: **~drücker** *der;* ~s, ~ **(a)** doorknob; **(b)** (Türöffner) [automatic] door-opener; **~griff** *der* door handle

Türke /ˈtʏrkə/ *der;* ~n, ~n ▶ 388 | Turk

Türkei *die;* ~: Turkey *no art.*

türkis /tʏrˈkiːs/ *indekl. Adj.* turquoise

Türkis *der;* ~es, ~e (Mineral.) turquoise

türkisch *Adj.* ▶ 388 |, ▶ 487 | Turkish; *s. auch* **deutsch; Deutsch; Deutsche²**

Tür-: **~klinke** *die* door handle; **~klopfer** *der* door knocker

Turm /tʊrm/ *der;* ~[e]s, **Türme** /ˈtʏrmə/ **(a)** tower; (spitzer Kirch~) spire; steeple; **(b)** (Schach) rook; castle; **(c)** ⇒ **Sprung~**

türmen¹ **1** *tr. V.* (stapeln) stack up; (häufen) pile up. **2** *refl. V.* be piled up; ⟨*clouds*⟩ gather

türmen² *itr. V.; mit sein* (salopp) scarper (Brit. sl.); do a bunk (Brit. sl.)

Turm-: **~falke** *der* kestrel; **~springen** *das; o. Pl.* high diving *no art.;* **~uhr** *die* tower clock

turnen /ˈtʊrnən/ **1** *itr. V.* **(a)** (Sport) do gymnastics; (Schulw.) do gym *or* PE; **sie turnt gut** she's a good gymnast; (Schulw.) she's good at gym *or* PE; **er turnte am Reck** he was doing *or* performing exercises *or* was working on the horizontal bar; **(b)** *mit sein* (ugs.: klettern) clamber; **(c)** (ugs.: herumklettern) clamber about. **2** *tr. V.* (Sport) do, perform ⟨*exercise, routine*⟩

Turnen *das;* ~s gymnastics *sing., no art.;* (Schulw.) gym *no art.;* PE *no art.*

Turner *der;* ~s, ~, **Turnerin** *die;* ~, ~nen gymnast

Turn-: **~halle** *die* gymnasium; **~hemd** *das* [gym] singlet; (für Turnunterricht) gym *or* PE vest; **~hose** *die* (mit langem Bein) gym trousers *pl.;* (mit kurzem Bein) gym shorts *pl.;* (für Turnunterricht) gym *or* PE shorts *pl.*

Turnier /tʊrˈniːɐ̯/ *das;* ~s, ~e (auch hist.) tournament; (Reit~) show; (Tanz~) competition

Turn-: **~lehrer** *der* gym *or* PE teacher; **~schuh** *der* gym shoe; (Trainingsschuh) training shoe; trainer (coll.); **~unterricht** *der* gym *no art.;* PE *no art.*

Turnus /ˈtʊrnʊs/ *der;* ~, ~se regular cycle; **er führt das Amt im ~ mit seinen Kollegen** he and his colleagues hold the office in rotation

Turn-: **~verein** *der* gymnastics club; **~zeug** *das* gym *or* PE kit

Tür-: **~öffner** *der* door-opener; **~rahmen** *der* doorframe; **~schild** *das* sign on a/the door; (Namensschild) nameplate; door plate; **~schloss, *~schloß** *das* door lock; **~schwelle** *die* threshold

turteln *itr. V.* (scherzh.: zärtlich sein) bill and coo

Turtel·taube /ˈtʊrtl̩-/ *die* turtle-dove; (fig.) love-bird

Tür·vorleger *der* doormat

Tusch /tʊʃ/ *der;* ~[e]s, ~e fanfare

Tusche /ˈtʊʃə/ *die;* ~, ~n Indian (Brit.) *or* (Amer.) India ink

tuscheln /ˈtʊʃl̩n/ *itr., tr. V.* whisper

tuschen *tr. V.* **sich** *(Dat.)* **die Wimpern ~:** put one's mascara on

Tusch·zeichnung *die* pen-and-ink drawing

Tussi /ˈtʊsi/ *die;* ~, ~s (salopp) female (derog.); (Mädchen) bird (sl.); chick (sl.)

Tüte /ˈtyːtə/ *die;* ~, ~n **(a)** bag; **~n kleben** *od.* **drehen** (fig. ugs.) be doing time; **das kommt nicht in die ~!** (fig. ugs.) not on your life! (coll.); no way!; **(b)** (Eis~) cone; cornet; **(c)** (ugs.: beim Alkoholtest) bag; **in die ~ blasen müssen** be breathalysed

tuten /ˈtuːtn̩/ *itr. V.* hoot; ⟨*siren,* [*fog-*]*horn*⟩ sound; **er tutete auf seiner Spielzeugtrompete** he tooted on his toy trumpet

Twen /tvɛn/ *der;* ~s, ~s twenty-to-thirty-year-old

Typ /typ/ *der;* ~s, ~en **(a)** type; **sie ist genau mein ~** (ugs.) she's just my type; **dein ~ wird verlangt** (salopp)

you're wanted; **er ist ein dunkler/blonder ∼**: he's dark/fair; **(b)** *Gen. auch* **∼en** (ugs.: Mann) bloke (Brit. sl.); guy (coll.); **(c)** (Technik: Modell) (Auto) model; (Flugzeug) type

Type /'ty:pə/ *die;* ∼, **∼n (a)** (Druck∼, Schreibmaschinen∼) type; **(b)** (ugs.) (Person) type; sort; character

Typhus /'ty:fʊs/ *der;* ∼ ▶ 329 ◀ typhoid [fever]

typisch 1 *Adj.* typical **(für** of). **2** *adv.* typically; **das ist ∼ Mann** that's just typical of a man; **∼ Gisela!** that's Gisela all over!

Typographie /typogra'fi:/ *die;* ∼, **∼n** (Druckw.) typography

Tyrann /ty'ran/ *der;* **∼en**, **∼en** (auch fig.) tyrant

Tyrannei *die;* ∼, **∼en** (auch fig.) tyranny

tyrannisch 1 *Adj.* tyrannical. **2** *adv.* tyrannically

tyrannisieren *tr. V.* tyrannize

....

Uu

....

u, U /u:/ *das;* ∼, ∼: u, U; *s. auch* **a**, **A**; **X**

ü, Ü /y:/ *das;* ∼, ∼: u umlaut; *s. auch* **a**, **A**

u. *Abk.* **und**

u. a. *Abk.* **unter anderem**

U-Bahn *die* underground (Brit.); subway (Amer.); (bes. in London) tube

U-Bahnhof *der*, **U-Bahn-Station** *die* underground station (Brit.); subway station (Amer.); (bes. in London) tube station

übel /'y:bl̩/ **1** *Adj.* **(a)** foul, nasty ⟨*smell, weather*⟩; bad, nasty ⟨*headache, cold, taste*⟩; nasty ⟨*situation, consequences*⟩; sorry ⟨*state, affair*⟩; foul, (coll.) filthy ⟨*mood*⟩; **nicht ∼** (ugs.) not bad at all; **(b)** ▶ 329 ◀ (unwohl) **jmdm. ist/wird ∼**: sb. feels sick; **(c)** (verwerflich) bad; wicked; nasty, dirty ⟨*trick*⟩; **ein übler Bursche** a bad sort (coll.) *or* lot. **2** *adv.* **(a)** **∼ riechend** foul-smelling; evil-smelling; **er spielt nicht ∼**: he plays pretty well; **(b)** (nachteilig, schlimm) badly; **er ist ∼ dran** he's in a bad way; **etw. ∼ vermerken** take sth. amiss; **jmdn. ∼ zurichten** give sb. a working over (coll.); **jmdm. ∼ wollen** wish sb. ill; **jmdm. etw. ∼ nehmen** hold sth. against sb.; **etw. ∼ nehmen** take offence at sth.; take sth. amiss

Übel *das;* ∼s, ∼ **(a)** (Missstand, Ärgernis) evil; **zu allem ∼**: on top of everything else; to make matters [even] worse; **das kleinere ∼**: the lesser evil; **(b)** (meist geh.: Krankheit) illness; malady; **(c)** (geh., veralt.: das Böse) evil *no art.;* **von** *od.* **vom ∼ sein** be an evil

*übel·gelaunt: ⇒ **gelaunt**

Übelkeit *die;* ∼, **∼en** ▶ 329 ◀ nausea

übel-, Übel-: ***∼|nehmen:** ⇒ **übel 2 b**; **∼riechend:** ⇒ **übel 2 a**; **∼täter** *der* wrongdoer; (Verbrecher) criminal; (Verantwortlicher) culprit;***∼|wollen:** ⇒ **übel 2 b**

üben /'y:bn̩/ **1** *tr. V.* **(a)** (auch itr.) practise; rehearse ⟨*scene, play*⟩; practise on ⟨*musical instrument*⟩; **(b)** (trainieren, schulen) exercise ⟨*fingers*⟩; train ⟨*memory*⟩; **mit geübten Händen** with practised hands; **(c)** (geh.: bekunden, tun) exercise ⟨*patience, restraint, etc.*⟩; commit ⟨*treason*⟩; take ⟨*revenge, retaliation*⟩; **Kritik an etw.** (*Dat.*) **∼**: criticize sth. **2** *refl. V.* **sich in etw.** (*Dat.*) **∼**: practise sth.

über /'y:bɐ/ **1** *Präp. mit Dat.* **(a)** (Lage, Standort) over; above; (in einer Rangfolge) above; ∼ **jmdm. wohnen** live above sb.; **zehn Grad ∼ Null** ten degrees above zero; ∼ **jmdm. stehen** (fig.) be above sb.; **(b)** (während) during; ∼ **dem Lesen einschlafen** fall asleep over one's book/ magazine *etc.;* **(c)** (infolge) because of; as a result of; ∼ **der Aufregung vergaß ich, dass …:** in all the excitement I forgot that … **2** *Präp. mit Akk.* **(a)** (Richtung) over; (quer hinüber) across; ∼ **die Straße gehen** go across the road;

cross the road; ∼ **Karlsruhe nach Stuttgart** via Karlsruhe to Stuttgart; **Tränen liefen ihr** ∼ **die Wangen** tears ran down her cheeks; **er zog sich** (*Dat.*) **die Mütze** ∼ **die Ohren** he pulled the cap down over his ears; **bis** ∼ **die Knöchel im Schlamm versinken** sink up past one's ankles in mud; **seine Tochter geht ihm** ∼ **alles** his daughter means more to him than anything; **(b)** (während) over; ∼ **Mittag** over lunchtime; ∼ **Wochen/Monate** for weeks/months; ∼ **Weihnachten** over Christmas; **die ganze Zeit** ∼: the whole time; **die Woche/den Sommer** ∼: during the week/summer; **den ganzen Winter/Tag** ∼: all winter/day long; **(c)** (betreffend) about; ∼ **etw. reden/schreiben** talk/write about sth.; **ein Buch** ∼ **die byzantinische Kunst** a book about *or* on Byzantine art; **(d)** (in Höhe von) **ein Scheck/ eine Rechnung** ∼ **1 000 Mark** a cheque/bill for 1,000 marks; **(e)** (von mehr als) **Kinder** ∼ **10 Jahre** children over ten [years of age]; **(f)** Gewalt ∼ **jmdn. haben** have power over sb.; **Wellingtons Sieg** ∼ **Napoleon** Wellington's victory over Napoleon; **(g)** **das geht** ∼ **meine Kraft** that's too much for me; **(h)** **sie macht Fehler** ∼ **Fehler** she makes mistake after mistake; **(i)** (mittels, durch) through ⟨*person*⟩; by ⟨*post, telex, etc.*⟩; over ⟨*radio, loudspeaker*⟩; **ich bin** ∼ **die Autobahn gekommen** I came along the motorway; **etw.** ∼ **alle Sender bringen/ ausstrahlen** broadcast sth. on all stations **3** *Adv.* **(a)** (mehr als) over; ⟨*c*⟩ **und** ∼: all over. **4** *Adj.; nicht attr.* (ugs.) **jmdm.** ∼ **sein** have the edge on sb. (coll.)

über·all /od. --ˈ-/ *Adv.* **(a)** everywhere; **sie weiß** ∼ **Bescheid** (fig.) she knows about everything; **(b)** (bei jeder Gelegenheit) always

überall-: **∼her** *Adv.* from all over the place; **∼hin** *Adv.* everywhere

Über·angebot *das* surplus **(an +** *Dat.* of); (Schwemme) glut **(an +** *Dat.* of)

über·ängstlich 1 *Adj.* over-anxious. **2** *adv.* over-anxiously

über·anstrengen *tr. V.* overtax ⟨*person, energy*⟩; strain ⟨*eyes, nerves, heart*⟩; **sich** ∼: overstrain *or* overexert oneself

Über·anstrengung *die* over-exertion; ∼ **der Augen/ des Herzens** strain on the eyes/heart

über·arbeiten 1 *tr. V.* rework; revise ⟨*text, edition*⟩. **2** *refl. V.* overwork

Über·arbeitung *die;* ∼, **∼en** reworking; (von Text, Manuskript, Ausgabe usw.) revision; (überarbeitete Fassung) revised version

über·aus *Adv.* (geh.) extremely

über·backen *unr. tr. V.* **etw. mit Käse** *usw.* ∼: top sth. with cheese *etc.* and brown it lightly [under the grill/in a hot oven]; **ein mit Käse ∼er Auflauf** a soufflé au gratin

Über·bau *der; Pl.* **∼e** (marx.) superstructure

überbeanspruchen; **ich überbeanspruche**, **überbeansprucht**, **überzubeanspruchen** *tr. V.* put too great a strain on ⟨*heart, circulation, etc.*⟩; strain ⟨*nerves*⟩; overstrain, overstress ⟨*material*⟩; overburden, overstretch ⟨*facilities, services*⟩; overload ⟨*machine*⟩; make excessive use of ⟨*right, privilege*⟩; overtax ⟨*person, body, strength*⟩

überbelichten; **ich überbelichte**, **überbelichtet**, **überzubelichten** *tr. V.* (Fot.) overexpose

Über·beschäftigung *die; o. Pl.* (Wirtsch.) over-employment

überbetonen; **ich überbetone**, **überbetont**, **überzubetonen** *tr. V.* overstress

überbewerten; **ich überbewerte**, **überbewertet**, **überzubewerten** *tr. V.* overvalue; (überschätzen) overvalue; overrate; mark ⟨*pupil, piece of work, gymnast, skater, etc.*⟩ too high

über·bieten *unr. tr. V.* **(a)** outbid **(um** by); **(b)** (übertreffen) surpass; outdo ⟨*rival*⟩; break ⟨*record*⟩ **(um** by); exceed ⟨*target*⟩ **(um** by); **das ist kaum noch zu** ∼: that takes some beating

über|bleiben *unr. itr. V.; mit sein* (ugs.) ⇒ **übrigbleiben**

Überbleibsel /-blaɪpsl̩/ *das;* ∼s, ∼: remnant; (einer Kultur) relic

Über·blick der (a) view; **einen guten ~ über etw.** (Akk.) **haben** have a good view over sth.; (b) (Abriss) survey; (c) o. Pl. (Einblick) overall view or perspective; **den ~ über etw.** (Akk.) **verlieren** lose track of sth.

über·blicken tr. V. ⇨ **übersehen a, b**

über·bringen unr. tr. V. deliver; convey ⟨greetings, congratulations⟩

Über·bringer der; ~s, ~: bearer

über·brücken tr. V. bridge ⟨gap, gulf⟩; reconcile ⟨difference⟩

Überbrückungs·kredit der (Finanzw.) bridging loan

über·dachen tr. V. roof over; **überdacht** covered ⟨terrace, station platform, etc.⟩

über·dauern tr. V. survive ⟨war, separation, hardship⟩

über·decken tr. V. (a) (bedecken) cover; (b) (verdecken) cover up

über·denken unr. tr. V. **etw. ~:** think sth. over

über·dies Adv. moreover; what is more

über·dimensional 1 Adj. inordinately large ⟨spectacles, table, statue, etc.⟩; inordinate ⟨love, influence⟩. 2 adv. enormously ⟨enlarged⟩

Über·dosis die overdose

über·drehen tr. V. (a) overwind ⟨watch⟩; over-tighten ⟨screw, nut⟩; (b) (Technik) over-rev (coll.) ⟨engine⟩

überdreht Adj. (ugs.) wound up; (verrückt) crazy

Über·druck der; Pl. ~drücke excess pressure

Überdruss, *Überdruß /-drus/ der; **Überdrusses** surfeit (an + Dat. of); **etw. bis zum ~ tun** do sth. until one has wearied of it

überdrüssig /-drysıç/ Adj. **jmds./einer Sache ~ sein/werden** be/grow tired of sb./sth.

über·durchschnittlich 1 Adj. above average. 2 adv. **sie ist ~ begabt** she is more than averagely gifted or talented; **er verdient ~ gut** he earns more than the average

über·eifrig 1 Adj. overeager; (zu emsig) overzealous. 2 adv. overeagerly; (zu emsig) overzealously

über·eignen tr. V. **jmdm. etw. ~:** transfer sth. or make sth. over to sb.

über·eilen tr. V. rush; **übereilt** overhasty

über·einander Adv. (a) (räumlich) one on top of the other; **~ legen** lay (things) one on top of the other; **sie wohnen ~:** they live one above the other; **die Enden des Tuches ~ schlagen** fold the cloth in the middle so that it is edge to edge; **die Arme/Beine ~ schlagen** fold one's arms/cross one's legs; (b) (fig.: voneinander) about each other; about one another

*übereinander|legen usw.: ⇨ **übereinander a**

überein|kommen unr. itr. V.; mit sein agree; come to an agreement

Überein·kommen das; ~s, ~, **Übereinkunft** /-'ainkʊnft/ die; ~, **Übereinkünfte** agreement; **ein Übereinkommen** od. **eine Übereinkunft treffen** enter into or make an agreement

überein|stimmen itr. V. (a) (einer Meinung sein) agree; **mit jmdm. in etw.** (Dat.) **~:** agree with sb. on sth.; (b) (sich gleichen) ⟨colours, styles⟩ match; ⟨figures, statements, reports, results⟩ tally, agree; ⟨views, opinions⟩ coincide

übereinstimmend 1 Adj.; nicht präd. concurrent ⟨views, opinions, statements, reports⟩. 2 adv. **sie stellten ~ fest, dass ...:** they agreed in stating that ...; **wir sind ~ der Meinung, dass ...:** we share the view that ...

Überein·stimmung die (a) (von Meinungen) agreement (in + Dat. on); (b) (Gleichheit) agreement (Gen. between); **etw. mit etw. in ~ bringen** reconcile sth. with sth.

über·empfindlich Adj. oversensitive (**gegen** to); (Med.) hypersensitive (**gegen** to)

über|essen unr. tr. V. **sich** (Dat.) **Hamburger/Nougat ~:** eat too many hamburgers/too much nougat

über|fahren¹ 1 unr. tr. V. **jmdn. ~:** ferry or take sb. over. 2 unr. itr. V.; mit sein cross over

über·fahren² unr. tr. V. (a) run over; (b) (übersehen u. weiterfahren) go through ⟨red light, stop signal, etc.⟩; (c)

(hinwegfahren über) cross; go over ⟨crossroads⟩; (d) (ugs.: überrumpeln) **jmdn. ~:** catch or take sb. unawares

Über·fahrt die crossing (**über** + Akk. of)

Über·fall der attack (**auf** + Akk. on); (aus dem Hinterhalt) ambush (**auf** + Akk. on); (mit vorgehaltener Waffe) hold-up; (auf eine Bank o. ä.) raid (**auf** + Akk. on); (fig. ugs.) surprise visit

über·fallen unr. tr. V. (a) attack; raid ⟨bank, enemy position, village, etc.⟩; (hinterrücks) ambush; (mit vorgehaltener Waffe) hold up; (fig.: besuchen) descend on; **jmdn. mit Fragen ~** (fig.) bombard sb. with questions; (b) (überkommen) ⟨tiredness, homesickness, fear⟩ come over

über·fällig Adj. overdue

Überfall·kommando das flying squad

über·fischen tr. V. overfish

über·fliegen unr. tr. V. (a) (hinwegfliegen über) fly over; overfly (formal); (b) (flüchtig lesen) skim [through]

über|fließen unr. itr. V.; mit sein ⇨ **überlaufen¹ a, b**

über·flügeln tr. V. outshine; outstrip

Über·fluss, *Über·fluß der; o. Pl. abundance (**an** + Dat. of); (Wohlstand) affluence; **etw. im ~ haben** have sth. in abundance; **im ~ vorhanden sein** be in abundant or plentiful supply; **zu allem ~:** to cap or crown it all

über·flüssig Adj. superfluous; unnecessary ⟨purchase, words, work⟩; (zwecklos) pointless

über·fluten tr. V. (auch fig.) flood

über·fordern tr. V. **jmdn.** [**mit etw.**] **~:** overtax sb. [with sth.]; ask or demand too much of sb. [with sth.]

über·fragen tr. V. **da bin ich überfragt** I don't know the answer to that

über·fremden tr. V. **überfremdet werden/sein** ⟨language, culture, etc.⟩ be swamped [by foreign influences]; ⟨economy⟩ be dominated [by foreign firms/capital]; ⟨country⟩ be dominated [by foreign influences]

über·fressen unr. refl. V. overeat; **der Hund/(salopp) sie hat sich an Schokolade ~:** the dog gorged itself/she gorged herself on chocolate

über·frieren unr. itr. V.; mit sein freeze over; **~de Nässe** black ice

über|führen¹ tr. V. transfer; **der Tote wurde in seine Heimat übergeführt** the body of the dead man was brought back to his home town/country

über·führen² tr. V. (a) ⇨ **überführen¹**; (b) **jmdn.** [**eines Verbrechens**] **~:** find sb. guilty [of a crime]; convict sb. [of a crime]

Über·führung die (a) transfer; (b) (eines Verdächtigen) conviction; (c) (Brücke) bridge; (Hochstraße) overpass; (Fußgänger~) [foot-] bridge

über·füllt Adj. crammed full, chock-full (**von** with); (mit Menschen) overcrowded, packed (**von** with); over-subscribed ⟨course⟩

Über·gabe die (a) handing over (**an** + Akk. to); (einer Straße, eines Gebäudes) opening; (von Macht) handing over; transfer; (b) (Auslieferung an den Gegner) surrender (**an** + Akk. to)

Über·gang der (a) crossing; (Bahn~) level crossing (Brit.); grade crossing (Amer.); (Fußgängerbrücke) foot bridge; (an der Grenze, eines Flusses) crossing-point; (b) (Wechsel, Überleitung) transition (**zu, auf** + Akk. to)

übergangs-, Übergangs-: ~erscheinung die transitional phenomenon; **~los** 1 Adj.; nicht präd. without any transition postpos.; 2 adv. without any transition; **~lösung** die interim or temporary solution; **~zeit** die (a) transitional period; (b) (Frühling) spring; (Herbst) autumn; (Frühling und Herbst) spring and autumn

über·geben 1 unr. tr. V. (a) hand over; pass ⟨baton⟩; (b) (übereignen) transfer, make over (Dat. to); (c) (ausliefern) surrender (Dat., **an** + Akk. to); (d) **eine Straße dem Verkehr ~:** open a road to traffic; (e) (abgeben, überlassen) **er hat sein Amt ~:** he has handed over his position; **jmdm. etw. ~:** entrust sb. with sth.. 2 unr. refl. V. (sich erbrechen) vomit

über|gehen¹ unr. itr. V.; mit sein (a) pass; **an jmdn./in jmds. Besitz ~:** become sb.'s property; (b) **zu etw. ~/dazu ~, etw. zu tun** go over to sth./to doing sth.;

(c) **in etw.** (*Akk.*) ~ (zu etw. werden) turn into sth.; **in Gärung/Verwesung ~:** begin to ferment/decompose; **einander ~** (sich vermischen) merge; (d) **uns gingen die Augen über** we were overwhelmed by the sight

über·gehen² *unr. tr. V.* (a) (nicht beachten) ignore; (nicht eingehen auf) **etw. [mit Stillschweigen] ~:** pass sth. over in silence; (b) (auslassen, überspringen) skip [over]; (c) (nicht berücksichtigen) pass over; **jmdn. bei der Beförderung ~:** pass sb. over for promotion

über·genau 1 *Adj.* over-meticulous. 2 *adv.* over-meticulously

über·geordnet *Adj.* higher ‹*authority, position, court*›; greater ‹*significance*›; superordinate ‹*concept*›

Über·gepäck *das* (Flugw.) excess baggage

Über·gewicht *das* ▶228], ▶329] (a) excess weight; (von Person) overweight; [5 kg] **~ haben** ‹*person*› be [5 kilos] overweight; (b) (fig.) predominance; **das ~ [über jmdn./etw.] haben/gewinnen** be/become predominant [over sb./sth.]; (c) **das ~ bekommen** *od.* **kriegen** (ugs.) ‹*person*› overbalance

über·gießen *unr. tr. V.* **etw. mit Wasser/Soße ~:** pour water/sauce over sth.

über·glücklich *Adj.* blissfully happy; (hoch erfreut) overjoyed

über|greifen *unr. itr. V.* (a) (bes. beim Klavierspiel, Turnen) cross one's hands over; (b) (sich ausdehnen) **auf etw.** (*Akk.*) **~:** spread to sth.

übergreifend *Adj.* predominant; (allumfassend) all-embracing

Über·griff *der* (unrechtmäßiger Eingriff) encroachment (**auf** + *Akk.* on); infringement (**auf** + *Akk.* of); (Angriff) attack (**auf** + *Akk.* on)

Über·größe *die* outsize

über|haben *unr. tr. V.* (ugs.) be fed up with (coll.)

überhand *in* **~ nehmen** get out of hand; ‹*attacks, muggings, etc.*› increase alarmingly; ‹*weeds*› run riot

über|hängen¹ *unr. itr. V.; südd., österr., schweiz. mit sein* ‹*part of building*› overhang; ‹*branch*› hang over; ‹*rock face*› form an overhang

über|hängen² *tr. V.* **sich** (*Dat.*) **eine Jacke/eine Tasche ~:** put a jacket round one's shoulders/hang or sling a bag over one's shoulder

über·häufen *tr. V.* **jmdn. mit etw. ~:** heap *or* shower sth. on sb.; **jmdn. mit Ratschlägen/Vorwürfen ~:** bombard sb. with advice/pour reproaches on sb.

überhaupt 1 *Adv.* (a) (insgesamt, im Allgemeinen) in general; **soweit es ~ Zweck hat** as far as there's any point in it at all; (b) (meist bei Verneinungen: gar) **~ nicht** not at all; **das ist ~ nicht wahr** that's not true at all; **~ keine Zeit haben** have no time at all; not have any time at all; **das kommt ~ nicht in Frage** it's quite *or* completely out of the question; **~ nichts** nothing at all; nothing what[so]ever; **wenn ~:** if at all; (c) (überdies, außerdem) besides. 2 *Partikel* anyway; **was willst du hier ~?** what ar you doing here anyway?; **wie konnte das ~ passieren?** how could it happen in the first place?; **wissen Sie ~, mit wem Sie reden?** do you realize who you're talking to?

überheblich /-'he:plɪç/ 1 *Adj.* arrogant; supercilious ‹*grin*›. 2 *adv.* arrogantly ‹*grin*› superciliously

Überheblichkeit *die;* **~:** arrogance

über·hitzen *tr. V.* (auch fig.) overheat

überhöht /y:bɐ'hø:t/ *Adj.* (zu hoch) excessive

über·holen *tr. V.* (a) overtake (esp. Brit.); pass (esp. Amer.); (b) (übertreffen) outstrip; (c) (wieder instand setzen) overhaul. 2 *itr. V.* overtake (esp. Brit.); pass (esp. Amer.)

Überhol-: **~manöver** *das* overtaking (esp. Brit.) *or* (esp. Amer.) passing manœuvre; **~spur** *die* overtaking lane (esp. Brit.); pass lane (esp. Amer.); **~verbot** *das* prohibition of overtaking

über·hören *tr. V.* not hear; **das möchte ich überhört haben** I'll pretend I didn't hear that

über·irdisch 1 *Adj.* celestial; heavenly; (übernatürlich) supernatural; ethereal ‹*beauty*›. 2 *adv.* celestially; (übernatürlich) supernaturally; ethereally ‹*beautiful*›

über·kandidelt /-kandi:d]t/ *Adj.* (ugs.) affected

über·kleben *tr. V.* **die alten Plakate mit neuen ~:** stick new posters over the old ones; **wir überklebten die Anschrift** we stuck something over the address; we covered the address by sticking something over it

über|kochen *itr. V.; mit sein* (auch fig. ugs.) boil over

über·kommen¹ *unr. tr. V.* **Ekel/Furcht überkam mich** I was overcome by revulsion/fear

überkommen² *Adj.* (geh.) traditional

über|kriegen *tr. V.* (ugs.) **jmdn./etw. ~:** get fed up with sb./sth. (coll.)

über·laden¹ *unr. tr. V.* (auch fig.) overload

überladen² *Adj.* over-ornate ‹*façade, style, etc.*›; overcrowded ‹*shop window*›

über·lagern *tr. V.* (a) overlie; (fig.) combine with; **sich ~:** combine; (b) (Physik) ‹*wave*› interfere with; ‹*force, field*› be superimposed on; **sich ~** ‹*waves*› interfere; ‹*forces, fields*› be superimposed

über·lappen *tr. V.* (auch fig.) overlap

über|lassen¹ *unr. tr. V.* (ugs.) **etw. ~:** leave sth. over

über·lassen² 1 *unr. tr. V.* (a) (geben) **jmdm. etw. ~:** let sb. have sth.; (b) **jmdn. jmds. Fürsorge ~:** leave sb. in sb.'s care; **jmdn. sich** (*Dat.*) **selbst ~ sein** be left to one's own devices; (c) **etw. jmdm. ~** (etw. jmdn. entscheiden/tun lassen) leave sth. to sb.; **das bleibt [ganz] dir ~:** that's [entirely] up to you; **überlass das bitte mir** let that be my concern; let me worry about that; **etw. dem Zufall ~:** leave sth. to chance. 2 *unr. refl. V.* **sich der Leidenschaft/den Träumen** *usw.* **~:** abandon oneself to one's passions/dreams *etc.*

über·lasten *tr. V.* overload; overburden, overstretch ‹*facilities, authorities*›; put too great a strain on ‹*heart, circulation, etc.*›; overstress ‹*structure, material*›; overtax ‹*person*›; (mit Arbeit) overwork ‹*person*›; (psychisch) put too great a strain *or* much on ‹*person*›

über|laufen¹ *unr. itr. V.; mit sein* (a) ‹*liquid, container*› overflow; (b) (auf die gegnerische Seite überwechseln) defect; ‹*partisan*› go over to the other side

über·laufen² *unr. tr. V.* seize; **ein Frösteln/Schauer überlief mich, es überlief mich [eis]kalt** a cold shiver ran down my spine; **es überlief sie heiß** a hot flush came over her

überlaufen³ *Adj.* overcrowded; over-subscribed ‹*course, subject*›

Über·läufer *der* (auch fig.) defector

über·leben 1 *tr., auch itr. V.* survive; **das überleb ich nicht!** I'll never get over it!; **jmdn. ~:** survive *or* outlive sb. (**um** by). 2 *refl. V.* become outdated *or* outmoded; **sich überlebt haben** have become outdated; have had its day

Über·lebende *der/die; adj. Dekl.* survivor

über·lebens·groß *Adj.* larger than life-size

über|legen¹ *tr. V.* **jmdm. etw. ~:** put sth. over sb.

über·legen² 1 *tr. V.* consider; think over *or* about; **etw. noch einmal ~:** reconsider sth.; **es sich anders ~:** change one's mind; **wenn ich es mir recht überlege, …:** now I come to think of it, … 2 *itr. V.* think; reflect; **ohne zu ~** (unbedacht) without thinking; (spontan) without a moment's thought; **ohne lange zu ~:** without much reflection; **lass mich mal ~:** let me think

überlegen³ 1 *Adj.* (a) superior; clear, convincing ‹*win, victory*›; **jmdm. ~ sein** be superior to sb. (**an** + *Dat.* in); (b) (herablassend) supercilious; superior. 2 *adv.* (a) in a superior manner; ‹*play*› much the better: ‹*win, argue*› convincingly; (b) (herablassend) superciliously; superiorly

Überlegenheit *die;* **~:** superiority

überlegt /y:bɐ'le:kt/ 1 *Adj.* carefully considered. 2 *adv.* in a carefully considered way

Überlegung *die;* **~, ~en** (a) *o. Pl.* thought; reflection; **nach reiflicher ~:** on careful consideration; (b) (Gedanke) idea; **~en** (Gedankengang) thoughts; reflections

über|leiten *itr. V.* **zum nächsten/zu einem neuen Thema ~** ‹*speaker*› move on to the next topic; **in etw.** (*Akk.*) **~:** lead into sth.

Über·leitung *die* transition

über·lesen *unr. tr. V.* overlook; miss

über·liefern *tr. V.* hand down

Über·lieferung *die* (a) (etw. Überliefertes) tradition; schriftliche ∼nen written records; (b) (Brauch) tradition; custom

überlisten *tr. V.* outwit

überm *Präp. + Art.* = **über dem**

Über·macht *die; o. Pl.* superior strength; (zahlenmäßig) superior numbers *pl.*; **in der** ∼ **sein** be superior in strength/numbers

über·mächtig *Adj.* (a) superior; (b) (nicht mehr bezähmbar) overpowering ‹desire, hatred, urge, etc.›

über·malen *tr. V.* etw. ∼: paint sth. over

Über·maß *das; o. Pl.* excessive amount, excess (**an** + *Dat.* of); **ein** ∼ **an Arbeit** *od.* **Arbeit im** ∼ **haben** have an excessive amount of work *or* more than enough work

über·mäßig 1 *Adj.* excessive. 2 *adv.* excessively; ∼ **viel essen** eat to excess *or* excessively; **nicht** ∼ **attraktiv** not especially attractive

Über·mensch *der* superman

über·menschlich *Adj.* superhuman

über·mitteln *tr. V.* send; (als Mittler weitergeben) pass on, convey ‹greetings, regards, etc.›

über·morgen *Adv.* the day after tomorrow

über·müden *tr. V.* overtire

Übermüdung *die;* ∼: overtiredness; exhaustion

Über·mut *der* high spirits *pl.;* etw. aus [lauter] *od.* im ∼ **tun** do sth. out of [pure] high spirits

übermütig /'y:bɐmy:tɪç/ 1 *Adj.* high-spirited; in high spirits *pred.* 2 *adv.* high-spiritedly

über·nächst... *Adj.* ▶595] *; nicht präd.* im ∼en Jahr, ∼es Jahr the year after next; am ∼en Tag two days later; the next day but one; ∼en Montag a week on Monday; Monday week; er wohnt im ∼en Haus he lives in the next house but one *or* lives two doors away

über·nachten *itr. V.* stay overnight; bei jmdm. ∼: stay *or* spend the night at sb.'s house/flat (Brit.) *or* (Amer.) apartment *etc.;* im Hotel ∼: stay the night at the hotel; im Freien ∼: sleep in the open air

übernächtigt /y:bɐ'nɛçtɪçt/ *Adj.* ‹person› tired *or* worn out [through lack of sleep]; tired ‹face, look, etc.›

Übernachtung *die;* ∼, ∼en overnight stay; ∼ und Frühstück bed and breakfast

Übernahme /'y:bɐna:mə/ *die;* ∼, ∼n (a) *o. Pl.* (von Waren, einer Sendung) taking delivery *no art.;* (einer Idee, eines Themas, von Methoden) adoption, taking over *no indef. art.;* (einer Praxis, eines Geschäfts, der Macht) takeover; (von Wörtern, Ausdrücken) borrowing (**von** from); (b) (etw. Übernommenes) borrowing

über·natürlich *Adj.* supernatural

über·nehmen 1 *unr. tr. V.* (a) take delivery of ‹goods, consignment›; receive ‹relay baton›; take over ‹power, practice, business, building, school class›; take on ‹job, position, task, role, case, leadership›; undertake to pay ‹costs›; **das lass mich** ∼: let me do that; (b) (bei sich einstellen) take on ‹staff›; (c) (sich zu Eigen machen) adopt, take over ‹ideas, methods, subject, etc.›; (**von** from); borrow ‹word, phrase› (**von** from). 2 *unr. refl. V.* overdo things *or* it; **sich mit etw.** ∼: take on too much with sth.; **übernimm dich nur nicht** (iron.) don't strain yourself!

über|ordnen *tr. V.* (a) etw. einer Sache (*Dat.*) ∼: give sth. precedence over sth.; (b) jmdn. jmdm. ∼: place sb. above sb.; *s. auch* **übergeordnet**

über·prüfen *tr. V.* (a) check (**auf** + *Akk.* for); check [over], inspect, examine ‹machine, device›; (b) (kontrollieren) check, inspect, examine ‹papers, luggage›; review ‹issue, situation, results›; (Finanzw.) examine, inspect ‹accounts, books›

Über·prüfung *die* (a) *o. Pl.* ⇒ **überprüfen a:** checking *no indef. art.* (**auf** + *Akk.* for); checking [over] *no indef.*

art.; inspection; examination; (**b**) (Kontrolle) check; (des Ausweises, der Geschäftsbücher) examination; inspection; (einer Lage, Frage, der Ergebnisse) review

über|quellen *unr. itr. V.; mit sein* (a) spill over; (**b**) (zu voll sein) be brimming

über·queren *tr. V.* cross

über·ragen *tr. V.* (a) (hinausragen über) jmdn./etw. ∼: tower above sb./sth.; **der Berg überragt die Ebene** the mountain towers over the plain; (**b**) (übertreffen) jmdn. an etw. (*Dat.*) ∼: be head and shoulders above sb. in sth.

überragend 1 *Adj.* outstanding. 2 *adv.* outstandingly

überraschen *tr. V.* surprise; ‹storm, earthquake› take by surprise; (durch einen Angriff) take by surprise; catch unawares; **jmdn. beim Rauchen/Stehlen** ∼: catch sb. smoking/stealing; **jmdn. überrascht ansehen** look at sb. in surprise

überraschend 1 *Adj.* surprising; surprise *attrib.* ‹attack, visit›; (unerwartet) unexpected. 2 *adv.* surprisingly; (unerwartet) unexpectedly; **die Nachricht kam** ∼: the news came as a surprise

Überraschung *die;* ∼, ∼en surprise; **zu meiner [großen]** ∼: to my [great] surprise

über·reden *tr. V.* persuade; jmdn. ∼, etw. zu tun persuade sb. to do sth.; talk sb. into doing sth.

Überredung *die;* ∼: persuasion

über·regional 1 *Adj.* national ‹newspaper, radio station›; ∼e Veranstaltungen events involving several regions. 2 *adv.* nationally; ∼ bekannt werden become known outside one's/its own region

über·reich 1 *Adj.* lavish ‹meal, decoration›; abundant, very rich ‹harvest›. 2 *adv.* jmdn. ∼ beschenken/belohnen lavish gifts on sb./reward sb. lavishly

über·reichen *tr. V.* [jmdm.] etw. ∼: present sth. [to sb.]

über·reichlich 1 *Adj.* over-ample 2 *adv.* over-amply

über·reif *Adj.* over-ripe

über·reizen *tr. V.* overtax ‹person›; overstrain ‹eyes, nerves, etc.›

über·rennen *unr. tr. V.* (Milit.) overrun

Über·rest *der; meist Pl.* remnant; ∼e (eines Gebäudes) remains; ruins; (einer Mahlzeit) leftovers; **die sterblichen** ∼e (geh. verhüll.) the mortal remains

über·rollen *tr. V.* (a) (Milit.) overrun; (fig.) overwhelm ‹person›; ‹fashion, craze› sweep through ‹country›; (**b**) (hinwegrollen über) run down

über·rumpeln *tr. V.* jmdn. ∼: take sb. by surprise; (bei einem Angriff) catch sb. unawares; take sb. by surprise; jmdn. mit etw. ∼: take sb. by surprise with sth.

über·runden *tr. V.* (a) (Sport) lap; (**b**) (übertreffen) outstrip

übers *Präp. + Art.* (a) = **über das**; (**b**) ∼ Jahr one year later

übersät /y:bɐ'zɛ:t/ *Adj.* mit *od.* von etw. ∼ sein be covered with sth.

über·sättigen *tr. V.* supersaturate ‹solution›; glut ‹market›; satiate ‹public›

Überschall-: supersonic

über·schätzen *tr. V.* overestimate; overrate ‹writer, performer, book, performance, talent, ability›

überschaubar *Adj.* eine ∼e Menge/Zahl a manageable quantity/number; ein ∼er Zeitraum/∼es Gebiet a reasonably short period/small area

über·schauen *tr. V.* ⇒ **übersehen a, b**

über|schäumen *itr. V.; mit sein* froth over; ∼de Begeisterung bubbling enthusiasm

über·schlafen *unr. tr. V.* sleep on ‹matter, problem, etc.›

Über·schlag *der* (a) rough calculation *or* estimate; (**b**) (Turnen) handspring

über|schlagen[1] 1 *unr. tr. V.* die Beine ∼: cross one's legs. 2 *unr. itr. V.; mit sein* ‹wave› break; ‹spark› jump

über·schlagen[2] 1 *unr. tr. V.* (a) (auslassen) skip ‹chapter, page, etc.›; (**b**) (ungefähr berechnen) calculate *or* estimate roughly; make a rough calculation *or* estimate of. 2 *unr. refl. V.* (a) go head over heels; ‹car› turn over; (**b**) ‹voice› crack

überschlagen[3] *Adj.* (bes. md.) lukewarm ⟨*liquid*⟩; moderately warm ⟨*room*⟩

über|schnappen *itr. V.; mit sein* (a) (ugs.: den Verstand verlieren) go crazy; go round the bend (coll.); (b) (ugs.: sich überschlagen) ⟨*voice*⟩ crack

über·schneiden *unr. refl. V.* cross; intersect; (fig.) ⟨*problems, events, etc.*⟩ overlap

über·schreiben *unr. tr. V.* (a) entitle; head ⟨*chapter, section*⟩; (b) (übertragen) etw. jmdm. *od.* auf jmdn. ∼: transfer sth. to sb.; make sth. over to sb.

über·schreiten *unr. itr. V.* (a) cross; (fig.) pass; (b) (hinausgehen über) exceed ⟨*authority, powers, budget, speed, limit, deadline, etc.*⟩

Über·schrift *die* heading; (in einer Zeitung) headline; (Titel) title

Über·schuss, *·*Über·schuß *der* surplus (an + *Dat.* of)

überschüssig /ˈyːbɐʃʏsɪç/ *Adj.* surplus

über·schütten *tr. V.* cover; jmdn./etw. mit Wasser ∼: throw water over sb./sth.; jmdn. mit Vorwürfen/ Lob ∼ (fig.) heap reproach/praise on sb.

Überschwang *der;* ∼[e]s exuberance

über·schwänglich /-ʃvɛŋlɪç/ 1 *Adj.* effusive ⟨*words, manner, etc.*⟩; wild ⟨*joy, enthusiasm*⟩. 2 *adv.* effusively

über|schwappen *itr. V.; mit sein* ⟨*liquid, container*⟩ slop over

über·schwemmen *tr. V.* (auch fig.) flood; den Markt mit Waren ∼ (fig.) flood *or* swamp the market with goods

Überschwemmung *die;* ∼, ∼en flood; (das Überschwemmen) flooding *no pl.*

Überschwemmungs·katastrophe *die* disastrous floods *pl.*

*∗***überschwenglich** ⇒ überschwänglich

Über·see *o. Art.* aus *od.* von ∼: from overseas; nach ∼ auswandern emigrate overseas; Exporte nach ∼: overseas exports

Übersee-: ∼dampfer *der* ocean-going steamer; ∼hafen *der* international port; ∼handel *der* overseas trade

überseeisch /ˈyːbzeːɪʃ/ *Adj.; nicht präd.* overseas

übersehbar *Adj.* (abschätzbar) assessable; der Schaden ist noch nicht ∼: the damage cannot yet be assessed

über·sehen *unr. tr. V.* (a) look out over; (fig.) survey ⟨*subject*⟩; (b) (abschätzen) assess ⟨*damage, situation, consequences, etc.*⟩; (c) (nicht sehen) overlook; miss ⟨*turning, signpost*⟩; (d) (ignorieren) ignore

über·senden *unr. (auch regelm.) tr. V.* send; remit, send ⟨*money*⟩

über|setzen[1] 1 *tr. V.* ferry over. 2 *itr. V.; auch mit sein* cross [over]

über·setzen[2] *tr., itr. V.* (auch fig.) translate; etw. ins Deutsche/aus dem Deutschen ∼: translate sth. into/ from German

Über·setzer *der*, **Übersetzerin** *die;* ∼, ∼nen translator

Übersetzung *die;* ∼, ∼en (a) translation; (b) (Technik) transmission ratio

Übersetzungs·büro *das* translation agency

Über·sicht *die* (a) *o. Pl.* overall view, overview (über + *Akk.* of); die ∼ [über etw. (*Akk.*)] verlieren lose track [of sth.]; (b) (Darstellung) survey; (Tabelle) summary

über·sichtlich 1 *Adj.* clear; ⟨*crossroads*⟩ which allows a clear view. 2 *adv.* clearly

über|siedeln[1], **über·siedeln**[2] *itr. V.; mit sein* move (nach to)

über·sinnlich *Adj.* supersensory; (übernatürlich) supernatural

über·spannen *tr. V.* (a) (bespannen) cover; (b) (zu stark spannen) over-tension, over-tighten ⟨*string, cable*⟩; overdraw ⟨*bow*⟩; over-tension ⟨*spring*⟩; *s. auch* Bogen c

überspannt *Adj.* exaggerated ⟨*ideas, behaviour, gestures*⟩; extreme ⟨*views*⟩; inflated ⟨*demands, expectations*⟩

über·spielen *tr. V.* (a) (hinweggehen über) cover up; cover up, gloss over ⟨*mistake*⟩; smooth over ⟨*difficult situation*⟩; (b) [auf ein Tonband] ∼: transfer ⟨*record*⟩ to tape; put ⟨*record*⟩ on tape; [auf ein anderes Tonband] ∼: transfer to another tape; (c) (Funkw., Ferns.) transfer

über·spitzen *tr. V.* etw. ∼: push *or* carry sth. too far; überspitzt ausgedrückt, könnte man sagen, dass …: to exaggerate, one might say that …

über|springen[1] *unr. itr. V.; mit sein* (a) ⟨*spark, fire*⟩ jump across; seine Begeisterung sprang auf uns alle über (fig.) his enthusiasm communicated itself to all of us; (b) (unvermittelt übergehen zu) auf etw. (*Akk.*) ∼: switch abruptly to sth.

über·springen[2] *unr. tr. V.* (a) jump ⟨*obstacle*⟩; (b) (auslassen) miss out; skip; eine Klasse ∼: jump a class

über·stehen *unr. tr. V.* come through ⟨*danger, war, operation*⟩; get over ⟨*illness*⟩; withstand ⟨*heat, strain*⟩; ⟨*boat*⟩ weather, ride out ⟨*storm*⟩; (überleben) survive

über·steigen *unr. tr. V.* (a) climb over; (b) (fig.: hinausgehen über) exceed; jmds. Fähigkeiten/Kräfte ∼: be beyond sb.'s abilities/strength

über·steuern 1 *tr. V.* (Elektrot.) overdrive. 2 *itr. V.* (Kfz-W.) ⟨*vehicle*⟩ oversteer

über·stimmen *tr. V.* outvote

über·streichen *unr. tr. V.* paint over

über|streifen *tr. V.* [sich (*Dat.*)] etw. ∼: slip sth. on

über|strömen[1] *itr. V.; mit sein* overflow

über·strömen[2] *tr. V.* flood; von Blut überströmt [sein] [be] streaming with blood; eine Welle des Glücks überströmte ihn (fig.) a wave of happiness flooded over him

über|stülpen *tr. V.* pull on ⟨*hat etc.*⟩

Über·stunde *die:* er hat eine ∼/drei ∼n gearbeitet he did one hour's/three hours' overtime; ∼n machen *od.* leisten *od.* (salopp) schieben do overtime

über·stürzen 1 *tr. V.* rush; nur nichts ∼: don't rush things; take it easy. 2 *refl. V.* rush; (rasch aufeinander folgen) ⟨*events, news, etc.*⟩ come thick and fast

überstürzt 1 *Adj.* hurried ⟨*escape, departure*⟩; overhasty ⟨*decision*⟩. 2 *adv.* ⟨*decide, act*⟩ overhastily; ⟨*depart*⟩ hurriedly

über·tariflich 1 *Adj.* ∼e Bezahlung/Zulagen payment/bonuses above agreed rates. 2 *adv.* jmdn. ∼ bezahlen pay sb. above agreed rates

über·teuert *Adj.* over-expensive

übertölpeln *tr. V.* dupe; con (coll.)

über·tönen *tr. V.* drown out

Übertrag /ˈyːbɐtraːk/ *der;* ∼[e]s, Überträge /-trɛːgə/ (bes. Buchf.) carry-over

über·tragbar *Adj.* transferable (auf + *Akk.* to); (auf etw. anderes anwendbar) applicable (auf + *Akk.* to); (übersetzbar) translatable; (ansteckend) communicable, infectious ⟨*disease*⟩

über·tragen 1 *unr. tr. V.* (a) transfer (auf + *Akk.* to); transmit ⟨*power, torque, etc.*⟩ (auf + *Akk.* to); communicate ⟨*disease, illness*⟩ (auf + *Akk.* to); carry over ⟨*subtotal*⟩; (auf etw. anderes anwenden) apply (auf + *Akk.* to); (übersetzen) translate; render; etw. ins Reine *od.* in die Reinschrift ∼: make a fair copy of sth.; in ∼er Bedeutung, im ∼en Sinne in a transferred sense; (b) (senden) broadcast ⟨*concert, event, match, etc.*⟩; (im Fernsehen) televise; (c) (geben) jmdm. Aufgaben/Pflichten *usw.* ∼: hand over tasks/duties *etc.* to sb.; (anvertrauen) entrust sb. with tasks/duties *etc.;* jmdm. ein Recht ∼: confer a right on sb. 2 *refl. V.* sich auf jmdn. ∼ ⟨*disease, illness*⟩ be communicated *or* be passed on to sb.; (fig.) ⟨*enthusiasm, nervousness, etc.*⟩ communicate itself to sb.

Übertragung *die;* ∼, ∼en (a) ⇒ übertragen 1 a: transference; transmission; communication; carrying over; application; translation; rendering; (b) (das Senden) broadcasting; (Programm, Sendung) broadcast; (im Fernsehen) televising/television broadcast; (c) (von Aufgaben, Pflichten *usw.*) entrusting; (von Rechten) conferral

Übertragungs·wagen *der* outside broadcast vehicle; OB vehicle

über·treffen *unr. tr. V.* (a) surpass, outdo (an + *Dat.* in); break ⟨*record*⟩; **jmdn. an Ausdauer** ∿: be superior to sb. in stamina; **jmdn. an Fleiß/Intelligenz** ∿: be more diligent/intelligent than sb.; **jmdn. in einem Fach** ∿: be better than sb. at a subject; **sich selbst** ∿: excel oneself; **(b)** (übersteigen) exceed

über·treiben *unr. tr. V.* (a) *auch itr.* exaggerate; **(b)** (zu weit treiben) overdo; take *or* carry too far; **man kann es auch** ∿: you can take things *or* go too far

Übertreibung *die;* ∿, ∿en exaggeration

über|treten¹ *unr. itr. V.; mit sein* (a) *auch mit haben* (Sport) step over the line/step out of the circle; **(b)** (überwechseln) change sides; **zu einer anderen Partei** ∿: join another party; switch parties; **zum Katholizismus** ∿: convert to Catholicism

über·treten² *unr. tr. V.* break, contravene ⟨*law*⟩; infringe, violate ⟨*regulation, prohibition*⟩

Übertretung *die;* ∿, ∿en (a) ⇨ **übertreten²**: breaking; contravention; infringement; violation; **(b)** (Vergehen) misdemeanour

übertrieben /-tri:bn/ **1** *Adj.* exaggerated; (übermäßig) excessive ⟨*care, thrift, etc.*⟩. **2** *adv.* excessively

Über·tritt *der* change of allegiance, switch (**zu** to); (Rel.) conversion (**zu** to)

über·trumpfen *tr. V.* outdo

über·tünchen *tr. V.* cover with whitewash; (fig.) cover up

Übervölkerung *die;* ∿: over-population

über·voll *Adj.* overfull; overcrowded, packed ⟨*room, train, tram, etc.*⟩; packed ⟨*theatre, cinema*⟩

über·vorsichtig 1 *Adj.* overcautious. **2** *adv.* overcautiously

über·vorteilen *tr. V.* cheat

über·wachen *tr. V.* watch, keep under surveillance ⟨*suspect, agent, area, etc.*⟩; supervise ⟨*factory, workers, process*⟩; control ⟨*traffic*⟩; monitor ⟨*progress, production process, experiment, patient*⟩

überwältigen /-'vɛltɪɡn̩/ *tr. V.* (a) overpower; **(b)** (fig.) ⟨*sleep, emotion, fear, etc.*⟩ overcome; ⟨*sight, impressions, beauty, etc.*⟩ overwhelm

überwältigend 1 *Adj.* overwhelming ⟨*sight, impression, victory, majority, etc.*⟩; overpowering ⟨*smell*⟩; stunning ⟨*beauty*⟩. **2** *adv.* stunningly ⟨*beautiful*⟩

über|wechseln *itr. V.; mit sein* (a) cross over (**auf** + *Akk.* to); **auf eine andere Spur** ∿: change lanes; move to another lane; **(b)** (übertreten) change sides; **ins feindliche Lager**∿: go over to the enemy; **(c)** (mit etw. anderem beginnen) **zu etw.** ∿: change over to sth.; **zu einem anderen Thema** ∿: turn to another topic

über·weisen *unr. tr. V.* (a) transfer ⟨*money*⟩ (**an, auf** + *Akk.* to); **(b)** (zu einem anderen Arzt schicken) refer (**an** + *Akk.* to); **(c)** (zuleiten) refer ⟨*proposal*⟩ (**an** + *Akk.* to); pass on ⟨*file, application*⟩ (**an** + *Akk.* to)

Über·weisung *die* (a) *o. Pl.* transfer (**an, auf** + *Akk.* to); **(b)** (Summe) remittance; **(c)** (eines Patienten) referral (**an** + *Akk.* to); **(d)** ⇨ **Überweisungsschein**

Überweisungs-: ∿**formular** *das* (Bankw.) [credit] transfer form; ∿**schein** *der* (Med.) certificate of referral

über|werfen¹ *unr. tr. V.* throw on ⟨*clothes*⟩

über·werfen² *unr. refl. V.* **sich mit jmdm.** ∿: fall out with sb.

über·wiegen 1 *unr. itr. V.* predominate. **2** *unr. tr. V.* ⟨*advantages, disadvantages, etc.*⟩ outweigh; ⟨*emotion, argument*⟩ prevail over

überwiegend /*auch* --'--/ *Adj.* overwhelming; **der** ∿**e Teil der Bevölkerung** the majority of the population. **2** *adv.* mainly

über·winden 1 *unr. tr. V.* (a) overcome ⟨*resistance*⟩; overcome, surmount ⟨*difficulty, obstacle, gradient*⟩; conquer ⟨*capitalism, apartheid, etc.*⟩; overcome, get over ⟨*fear, inhibitions, disappointment, grief*⟩; get past ⟨*stage*⟩; **(b)** (aufgeben) overcome ⟨*doubt, misgivings, reservations*⟩; give

up ⟨*way of thinking, point of view*⟩; **(c)** (geh.: besiegen) overcome; vanquish (literary). **2** *unr. refl. V.* overcome one's reluctance; **sich [dazu]** ∿, **etw. zu tun** bring oneself to do sth.

Über·windung *die* (a) ⇨ **überwinden 1 a:** overcoming; surmounting; conquest; getting over/past; **(b)** (Besiegung) overcoming; vanquishing (literary); **(c)** (das Sichüberwinden) **es war eine große** ∿ **für ihn** it cost him a great effort; **das hat mich viel** ∿ **gekostet** that was a real effort of will for me

über·wintern 1 *itr. V.* [over]winter; spend the winter. **2** *tr. V.* overwinter ⟨*plant*⟩

über·wuchern *tr. V.* overgrow

Über·zahl *die; o. Pl.* majority; **in der** ∿ **sein** be in the majority; ⟨*army, enemy*⟩ be superior in numbers

überzählig /-tsɛlɪç/ *Adj.* surplus; spare

Über·zeit *die* (schweiz.) overtime

überzeugen 1 *tr. V.* convince; **jmdn. von etw.** ∿: convince/persuade sb. of sth. **2** *itr. V.* be convincing. **3** *refl. V.* convince *or* satisfy oneself; **sich persönlich** *od.* **mit eigenen Augen [von etw.]** ∿: see [sth.] for oneself

überzeugend 1 *Adj.* convincing; convincing, persuasive ⟨*arguments, proof, words, speech*⟩. **2** *adv.* convincingly; ⟨*argue, speak*⟩ convincingly, persuasively

überzeugt *Adj.* (a) *nicht präd.* convinced; **(b) von etw.** ∿ **sein** (etw. hoch einschätzen) be convinced by sth.; **er ist sehr von sich [selbst]** ∿: he's very sure of himself

Über·zeugung *die* (a) *o. Pl.* convincing; (das Umstimmen) persuasion; **(b)** (feste Meinung) conviction; **zu der** ∿ **kommen** *od.* **gelangen, dass …:** become convinced that …; **meiner** ∿ **nach …:** I am convinced that …

Überzeugungs·kraft *die; o. Pl.* power[s] of persuasion; persuasiveness

über|ziehen¹ *unr. tr. V.* (a) pull on ⟨*clothes*⟩; **(b) jmdm. eins** *od.* **ein paar** ∿ (ugs.) give sb. a clout

über·ziehen² *unr. tr. V.* (a) etw. **mit etw.** ∿: cover sth. with sth.; **die Betten frisch** ∿: put clean sheets on the beds; change the sheets on the beds; **(b)** overdraw ⟨*account*⟩ (**um** by); **sie hat ihr Konto [um 300 Mark]** **überzogen** she is [300 marks] overdrawn; **die vorgesehene Sendezeit** ∿: overrun the programme time. **2** *unr. itr. V.* (a) overdraw one's account; go overdrawn; **(b)** (bei einer Sendung, einem Vortrag) overrun. **3** *unr. refl. V.* ⟨*sky*⟩ cloud over, become overcast

Überzieher *der;* ∿**s**, ∿ (a) (veralt.: Herrenmantel) [light] overcoat; **(b)** (salopp: Kondom) johnny (Brit. sl.); rubber (sl.)

Überziehungs·kredit *der* (Finanzw.) overdraft facility

überzüchtet /y:bɐ'tsʏçtət/ *Adj.* overbred; over-sophisticated ⟨*engines, systems*⟩

über·zuckern *tr. V.* sugar

Überzug *der* (a) (Beschichtung) coating; **(b)** (Bezug) cover

üblich /'y:plɪç/ *Adj.* usual; (normal) normal; (gebräuchlich) customary; **das ist hier so** ∿: that's the accepted *or* (coll.) done thing here; **wie** ∿: as usual

U-Boot *das* submarine; sub (coll.)

übrig /'y:brɪç/ *Adj.* remaining *attrib.;* (ander…) other; **das/alles Übrige erzähle ich dir später** I'll tell you the rest/all the rest later; **die/alle Übrigen** the/all the rest *or* others; **im Übrigen** besides; ∿ **bleiben** be left; remain; ⟨*food, drink*⟩ be left over; **ihm bleibt nichts [anderes** *od.* **weiter]** ∿, **als zu …:** he has no [other] choice but to …; there is nothing he can do but to …; **etw.** ∿ **lassen** leave sth.; **Essen/Trinken** ∿ **lassen** leave food/drink over; **sehr** *od.* **viel/nichts zu wünschen** ∿ **lassen** leave much *or* (coll.) a lot/nothing to be desired; **ich habe noch Geld** ∿ I [still] have some money left; (ich habe mehr Geld, als ich brauche) I [still] have some money to spare; **für jmdn./etw. wenig/nichts** ∿ **haben** have little/no time for sb./sth. (fig.)

***übrig|bleiben** ⇨ **übrig**

übrigens /'y:brɪɡn̩s/ *Adv.* by the way; incidentally

***übrig|lassen** ⇨ **übrig**

Übung /'y:bʊŋ/ *die;* ∿, ∿en (a) exercise; **(b)** *o. Pl.* (das Üben, Geübtsein) practice; **aus der** ∿ **kommen/außer** ∿ **sein** get/be out of practice; ∿ **macht den Meister** (Spr.)

---

practice makes perfect (prov.); (**c**) (Lehrveranstaltung) class; seminar

Übungs·buch *das* book of exercises; (Lehrbuch) textbook with exercises

UdSSR /uːdeːˈɛsˈɛsˈɛr/ *Abk. die;* ∼**: Union der Sozialistischen Sowjetrepubliken** USSR

UEFA /uˈeːfaː/ *Abk. die;* ∼ (Fußball) UEFA

Ufer /ˈuːfɐ/ *das;* ∼**s,** ∼**:** bank; (des Meeres) shore; **ans** ∼ **gespült werden** be washed ashore; **der Fluss trat über die** ∼**:** the river burst its banks

ufer-, Ufer-: ∼**befestigung** *die* bank reinforcement; ∼**böschung** *die* [river/canal] embankment; ∼**los** *Adj.* limitless; boundless ⟨*love, indulgence, etc.*⟩; endless ⟨*discussions, talks, quarrel, subject*⟩; **ins Uferlose gehen** ⟨*plans, ambitions, etc.*⟩ know no bounds; ∼**promenade** *die* riverside walk; (am Meer) promenade

UFO, Ufo /ˈuːfo/ *das;* ∼**[s],** ∼**s** UFO

UG *Abk.* **Untergeschoß**

Uganda /uˈɡanda/ (*das*); ∼**s** Uganda

Ugander /uˈɡandɐ/ *der;* ∼**s,** ∼, **Uganderin** *die;* ∼, ∼**nen ▶388|** Ugandan

Uhr /uːɐ̯/ *die;* ∼, ∼**en ▶530|** (**a**) clock; (Armband∼, Taschen∼) watch; (Wasser∼, Gas∼) meter; (an Messinstrumenten) dial; gauge; **auf die** *od.* **nach der** ∼ **sehen** look at the time; **nach meiner** ∼**:** by *or* according to my clock/watch; **jmds.** ∼ **ist abgelaufen** (fig.) the sands of time have run out for sb.; **wissen, was die** ∼ **geschlagen hat** (fig.) know what's what; know how things stand; **rund um die** ∼ (ugs.) round the clock; (**b**) (bei Uhrzeitangaben) **acht** ∼**:** eight o'clock; **acht** ∼ **dreißig** half past eight; 8.30 /ɛɪ̯tˈθɛːtɪ/; **wie viel** ∼ **ist es?** what's the time?; what time is it?; **um wie viel** ∼ **treffen wir uns?** [at] what time shall we meet?; when shall we meet?

Uhr-: ∼**armband** *das* watch strap; ∼**kette** *die* watch-chain; ∼**macher** *der ▶85|* watchmaker/clockmaker; ∼**werk** *das* clock/watch mechanism; ∼**zeiger** *der* clock-/watch-hand; ∼**zeigersinn** *der:* **im** ∼**zeigersinn** clockwise; **entgegen dem** ∼**zeigersinn** anticlockwise; ∼**zeit** *die ▶530|* time

Uhu /ˈuːhu/ *der;* ∼**s,** ∼**s** eagle owl

Ukraine /ukraˈinə/ *die;* ∼**:** Ukraine

Ukrainer *der;* ∼**s,** ∼, **Ukrainerin** *die;* ∼, ∼**nen ▶388|** Ukrainian

UKW-Sender /uːkaːˈveː-/ *der* VHF station; ≈ FM station

Ulk /ʊlk/ *der;* ∼**s,** ∼**e** lark (coll.); (Streich) trick; [practical] joke

ulkig (ugs.) **1** *Adj.* funny. **2** *adv.* in a funny way

Ulme /ˈʊlmə/ *die;* ∼, ∼**n** (**a**) elm [tree]; (**b**) (Holz) elm[wood]

Ultima ratio /ˈʊltima ˈraːtsi̯o/ *die;* ∼ ∼ (geh.) last resort

ultimativ /ʊltimaˈtiːf/ **1** *Adj.* (**a**) ⟨*demand*⟩ made as an ultimatum (**b**) ultimate; **der** ∼**e Videorekorder** the ultimate video recorder *or* ultimate in video recorders. **2** *adv.* **etw.** ∼ **fordern** demand sth. in [the form of] an ultimatum

Ultimatum /ʊltiˈmaːtʊm/ *das;* ∼**s, Ultimaten** ultimatum; [**jmdm.**] **ein** ∼ **stellen** give *or* set [sb.] an ultimatum

Ultimo /ˈʊltimo/ *der;* ∼**s,** ∼**s** last day of the month

Ultra·kurz·welle /ʊltraˈkʊrt͡svɛlə/ *die* (**a**) (Phys., Funkw., Rundf.) ultra-short wave; (**b**) (Rundf.: Wellenbereich) very high frequency; VHF

Ultra·schall /ˈ---/ *der* (Physik, Med.) ultrasound

ultra·violett *Adj.* (Physik) ultraviolet

um /ʊm/ **1** *Präp. mit Akk.* (**a**) (räumlich) [a]round; **um etw. herum** [a]round sth.; **das Rad dreht sich um seine Achse** the wheel turns on its axle; **um die Ecke** round the corner; **um sich schlagen** lash *or* hit out; (**b**) (zeitlich) (genau) at; (etwa) around [about]; **um acht [Uhr]** at eight [o'clock]; **um den 20. August [herum]** around [about] 20 August; (**c**) **Stunde um Stunde** hour after hour; **Meter um Meter/Schritt um Schritt** metre by metre/step by step; (**d**) (bei Maß- u. Mengenangaben) by; **die Temperatur stieg um 5 Grad** the temperature rose [by] five degrees; **um nichts/einiges/vieles besser sein** be no/

somewhat/a lot better. **2** *Adv.* (**a**) around; about; **um [die] 50 Personen [herum]** around *or* about *or* round about 50 people; (**b**) (ugs.: vorüber) ⇒ **herum e. 3** *Konj.* (**a**) (final) **um ... zu** [in order] to; (**b**) (konsekutiv) **er ist groß genug, um ... zu ...:** he is big enough to ...

um|ändern *tr. V.* change; alter; revise ⟨*text, novel*⟩; alter ⟨*garment*⟩

um|arbeiten *tr. V.* alter ⟨*garment*⟩; revise, rework ⟨*text, novel, music*⟩

umarmen *tr. V.* embrace; put one's arms around; (an sich drücken) hug; **sie umarmten sich** they embraced/hugged

Um·bau *der;* ∼**[e]s,** ∼**ten** rebuilding; reconstruction; (kleinere Änderung) alteration; (zu etw. anderem) conversion; (fig.: eines Systems, einer Verwaltung) reorganization

um|bauen¹ *tr., auch itr. V.* rebuild; reconstruct; (leicht ändern) alter; (zu etw. anderem) convert (**zu** into); (fig.) reorganize ⟨*system, administration, etc.*⟩; **das Bühnenbild** ∼**:** change the set

um·bauen² *tr. V.* surround; **umbauter Raum** interior space

um|behalten *unr. tr. V.* keep ⟨*apron, scarf, etc.*⟩ on

um|benennen *unr. tr. V.* change the name of, rename ⟨*street, square, etc.*⟩; **etw. in etw. (Akk.)** ∼**:** change the name of sth. to sth.; rename sth. sth.

um|besetzen *tr., auch itr. V.* change ⟨*team*⟩; recast ⟨*role, play*⟩; reallocate ⟨*post, position*⟩

um|biegen 1 *unr. tr. V.* bend. **2** *unr. itr. V.; mit sein* turn; ⟨*path*⟩ bend, turn

um|bilden *tr. V.* reorganize, reconstruct ⟨*department etc.*⟩; reshuffle ⟨*government, cabinet*⟩

um|binden *unr. tr. V.* put on ⟨*tie, apron, scarf, etc.*⟩

um|blasen *unr. tr. V.* blow over

um|blättern 1 *tr. V.* turn [over] ⟨*page*⟩. **2** *itr. V.* turn the page/pages

um|blicken *refl. V.* (**a**) look around; (**b**) (zurückblicken) [turn to] look back (**nach** at)

um|brechen¹ 1 *unr. tr. V* (**a**) bring down ⟨*telephone pole, tree, etc.*⟩; (**b**) (umpflügen) break up, turn over ⟨*land*⟩; plough up ⟨*field*⟩. **2** *unr. itr. V.; mit sein* collapse; fall down

um·brechen² *unr. tr. V.* (Druckw.) make up

um|bringen *unr. tr. V.* kill; **diese Packerei bringt mich fast um** (fig. ugs.) all this packing's nearly killing me (coll.)

Um·bruch *der* (**a**) radical change; (Umwälzung) upheaval; (**b**) *o. Pl.* (Druckw.) make-up; (Ergebnis) page proofs *pl.*

um|buchen 1 *tr. V.* (**a**) change ⟨*flight, journey route*⟩ (**auf** + *Akk.* to); (**b**) (Finanzw.) transfer (**auf** + *Akk.* to). **2** *itr. V.* change one's booking (**auf** + *Akk.* to)

Um·buchung *die* (**a**) change of booking; **eine** ∼ **Ihres Fluges ist jederzeit möglich** you can change your flight at any time; (**b**) (Finanzw.) transfer (**auf** +*Akk.* to)

um|datieren *tr. V.* change the date of; redate ⟨*contract, letter, etc.*⟩

um|denken *unr. itr. V.* revise one's thinking; rethink

um|disponieren *itr. V.* change one's arrangements; make new arrangements

um|drehen 1 *tr. V.* turn round; turn over ⟨*coin, hand, etc.*⟩; turn ⟨*key*⟩; **jeden Pfennig [dreimal]** ∼ (ugs.) watch every penny. **2** *refl. V.* turn round; (den Kopf wenden) turn one's head; **sich nach jmdm.** ∼**:** turn/turn one's head to look at sb. **3** *itr. V.; auch mit sein* (ugs.: umkehren) turn back; (ugs.: wenden) turn round

Um·drehung *die* turn; (eines Motors usw.) revolution; rev (coll.); (eines Planeten) rotation

um·einander *Adv.* **sich** ∼ **kümmern/sorgen** take care of/worry about each other *or* one another; **sich** ∼ **drehen** revolve around each other

um|fahren¹ *unr. tr. V.* knock over *or* down

um·fahren² *unr. tr. V.* go round; make a detour round ⟨*obstruction, busy area*⟩; (in Auto) drive *or* go round; (in Schiff) sail *or* go round; (auf einer Umgehungsstraße) bypass ⟨*town, village, etc.*⟩

um|fallen *unr. itr. V.; mit sein* (**a**) (umstürzen) fall over; (**b**) (zusammenbrechen) collapse; **tot** ∼**:** fall down dead; **vor**

Uhrzeit

Wie viel Uhr ist es?, Wie spät ist es?	= What time is it?, What's the time?
Könnten Sie mir sagen, wie spät es ist?	= Could you tell me the time?
Wie viel Uhr hast du?	= What time do you make it?
Nach meiner Uhr ist es fünf vor/zehn nach neun	= By my watch it's five to/ten past nine
Meine Uhr geht vor/nach	= My watch is fast/slow
Es war soeben zehn Uhr	= It's just after od. just gone ten [o'clock]
Es ist elf Uhr vorbei	= It's gone eleven [o'clock]
Es ist gleich sieben	= It's coming up to seven

Im englischsprachigen Raum wird hauptsächlich die 12-Stunden-Uhr verwendet, mit den Zusätzen **a.m.** = ante meridiem = vor Mittag, also morgens, und **p.m.** = post meridiem = nach Mittag, also nachmittags oder abends. Der Ausdruck **o'clock** wird nur bei Uhrzeitangaben verwendet, die sich auf die volle Stunde beziehen. Danach steht statt a.m. bzw. p.m. **in the morning** bzw. **in the afternoon/evening**. Die 24-Stunden-Uhr wird meist nur beim Militär, in der Luftfahrt und für Fahrpläne benutzt. In der folgenden Aufstellung werden Beispiele ihrer hauptsächlich militärischen Form gegeben (jeweils nach dem Schrägstrich).

GESCHRIEBEN	GESPROCHEN
1 Uhr	ein Uhr, eins
= 1.00 a.m./0100	one [a.m. od. in the morning]/one hundred hours
13 Uhr	dreizehn Uhr, ein Uhr mittags
= 1.00 p.m./1300	one [p.m. od. in the afternoon]/thirteen hundred hours
2.05 Uhr	fünf [Minuten] nach zwei, zwei Uhr fünf
= 2.05 a.m./0205	five past two [in the morning]/[o] two o five
14.05 Uhr	vierzehn Uhr fünf
= 2.05 p.m./1405	five past two [in the afternoon]/fourteen o five
4.15 Uhr	Viertel od. fünfzehn Minuten nach vier, vier Uhr fünfzehn
= 4.15 a.m./0415	four fifteen [a.m.], a quarter past four [in the morning]/[o] four fifteen
16.15 Uhr	sechzehn Uhr fünfzehn
= 4.15 p.m./1615	four fifteen [p.m.], a quarter past four [in the afternoon]
5.30 Uhr	halb sechs, fünf Uhr dreißig
= 5.30 a.m./0530	five thirty [a.m.], half past five [in the morning]/[o] five thirty
17.30 Uhr	siebzehn Uhr dreißig
= 5.30 p.m./1730	five thirty [p.m.], half past five [in the afternoon]/seventeen thirty
7.45 Uhr	Viertel od. fünfzehn Minuten vor acht, sieben Uhr fünfundvierzig
= 7.45 a.m./0745	seven forty-five [a.m.], a quarter to eight [in the morning]/[o] seven forty-five
19.45 Uhr	neunzehn Uhr fünfundvierzig
= 7.45 p.m./1945	seven forty-five p.m., a quarter to eight [in the evening]/nineteen forty-five
0 Uhr, 24 Uhr	null Uhr, vierundzwanzig Uhr
= 12.00 [midnight]/0000, 2400*	twelve [o'clock], [twelve] midnight/oo double o, twenty-four hundred hours*
12 Uhr	zwölf Uhr
= 12 [noon]/1200	twelve [o'clock], [twelve] noon/twelve hundred hours

*Beim 24-Stunden-System zeigt 0000 = null Uhr den Tagesbeginn an, 2400 = vierundzwanzig Uhr das Tagesende.

Wann?

um + Uhrzeit	= **at** + Uhrzeit
Er kam um acht Uhr	= He came at eight o'clock
Um wie viel Uhr wollen Sie frühstücken?	= [At] what time do you want breakfast?
um halb	= at half past
um halb neun	= at half past eight od. (ugs.) half eight
Punkt sechs, genau um sechs	= at six exactly, on the dot of six
gegen zehn	= at about ten
spätestens um zwölf	= at twelve at the latest
Es muss bis elf fertig sein	= It must be ready by eleven
Ich bin heute bis achtzehn Uhr hier	= I'll be here until six this evening
Ich bin erst um sechs dort	= I won't be there until six
von 13 bis 14 Uhr geschlossen	= closed from 1 to 2 p.m.
stündlich zur vollen Stunde	= every hour on the hour

Hunger fast ∼: be faint with hunger; **(c)** (ugs. abwertend: seine Meinung ändern) do an about-face; do a U-turn
Um·fang der **(a)** circumference; (eines Quadrats usw.) perimeter; (eines Baums, Menschen usw.) girth; circumference; **(b)** (Größe) size; **der Band hat einen ∼ von 250 Seiten** the volume contains 250 pages or is 250 pages thick; **(c)** (Ausmaß) extent; (von Wissen) range; extent; (einer Stimme) range; (einer Arbeit, Untersuchung) scope; **in vollem** ∼: fully; completely; **in großem** ∼: on a large scale
umfänglich /ˈʊmfɛŋlɪç/ Adj. extensive; ⟨case, parcel, etc.⟩ of considerable size; voluminous, extensive ⟨correspondence⟩
umfang·reich Adj. extensive; substantial ⟨book⟩
um·fassen tr. V. **(a)** grasp; (umarmen) embrace; **(b)** (ent-

halten) contain; (einschließen) include; take in; span, cover ⟨*period*⟩; (**c**) (umgeben) enclose; surround; (**d**) (Milit.: umzingeln) surround; encircle

umfassend 1 *Adj.* full ⟨*reply, information, survey, confession*⟩; extensive, wide, comprehensive ⟨*knowledge, powers*⟩; broad ⟨*education*⟩; extensive ⟨*preparations, measures*⟩. **2** *adv.* ⟨*inform*⟩ fully

Um·feld *das* (**a**) (Psych., Soziol.) milieu; (**b**) ⇒ **Umgebung a**

um|fliegen[1] *unr. itr. V.; mit sein* (salopp) go flying (coll.)

um·fliegen[2] *unr. tr. V.* fly around

um·fließen *unr. tr. V.* flow round

um|formen *tr. V.* (**a**) reshape; remodel; recast, revise, ⟨*poem, novel*⟩; transform ⟨*person*⟩; (**b**) (Elektrot.) convert

Um·frage *die* survey; (Politik) opinion poll; **eine ~ machen** *od.* **veranstalten** carry out a survey/conduct an opinion poll

um|füllen *tr. V.* **etw. in etw.** (*Akk.*) **~:** transfer sth. into sth.

um|funktionieren *tr. V.* change the function of; **etw. zu etw. ~:** turn sth. into sth.

Um·gang *der* (**a**) *o. Pl.* (gesellschaftlicher Verkehr) contact; dealings *pl.*; **jmd. hat guten/schlechten ~:** sb. keeps good/bad company; **mit jmdm. ~ haben/pflegen** associate with sb.; **mit jmdm. keinen ~ haben** have nothing to do with sb.; **er ist kein ~ für dich!** he is not suitable *or* fit company for you; (**b**) *o. Pl.* (das Umgehen) **den ~ mit Pferden lernen** learn how to handle horses; **im ~ mit Kindern erfahren sein** be experienced in dealing with children

umgänglich /ˈʊmgɛŋlɪç/ *Adj.* (verträglich) affable; friendly; (gesellig) sociable

umgangs-, Umgangs-: **~form** *die; meist Pl.* **gute/ schlechte/keine ~formen haben** have good/bad/no manners; **~sprache** *die* colloquial language; **~sprachlich 1** *Adj.* colloquial; **2** *adv.* colloquially

um·geben *unr. tr. V.* (**a**) surround ⟨*hedge, fence, wall, etc.*⟩ enclose; ⟨*darkness, mist, etc.*⟩ envelop; (**b**) **etw. mit etw. ~:** surround sth. with sth.; (einfrieden) enclose sth. with sth.; **sich mit jmdm./etw. ~:** surround oneself with sb./sth.

Umgebung *die; ~, ~en* (**a**) surroundings *pl.*; (Nachbarschaft) neighbourhood; (eines Ortes) surrounding area; **die nähere/weitere ~ Mannheims** the immediate/broader environs *pl.* of Mannheim; (**b**) (fig.) milieu; **jmds. nähere ~:** those *pl.* close to sb.

um|gehen[1] *unr. itr. V.; mit sein* (**a**) (im Umlauf sein) ⟨*list, rumour, etc.*⟩ go round, circulate, ⟨*illness, infection*⟩ go round; **Angst geht in der Bevölkerung um** fear is spreading in the population; (**b**) (spuken) **im Schloss geht ein Gespenst um** a ghost haunts this castle; the castle is haunted; (**c**) (behandeln) **mit jmdm. freundlich** *usw.* **~:** treat sb. kindly *etc.*; **mit etw. sorgfältig** *usw.* **~:** treat sth. carefully *etc.*; **er kann mit Geld nicht ~:** he can't handle money

um·gehen[2] *unr. tr. V.* (**a**) (herumgehen, -fahren um) go round; make a detour round ⟨*obstruction, busy area*⟩; (auf einer Umgehungsstraße) bypass ⟨*town, village, etc.*⟩; (**b**) (vermeiden) avoid; avoid, get round ⟨*problem, difficulty*⟩; evade ⟨*question, issue*⟩; (**c**) (nicht befolgen) get round, circumvent ⟨*law, restriction, etc.*⟩; evade ⟨*obligation, duty*⟩

umgehend 1 *Adj.; nicht präd.* immediate. **2** *adv.* immediately

Umgehungs·straße *die* bypass

umgekehrt 1 *Adj.* inverse ⟨*ratio, proportion*⟩; reverse ⟨*order*⟩; opposite ⟨*sign*⟩; **es verhält sich** *od.* **ist genau ~:** the very opposite *or* reverse is true *or* the case. **2** *adv.* inversely ⟨*proportional*⟩; **vom Englischen ins Deutsche und ~ übersetzen** translate from English into German and vice versa

um|gestalten *tr. V.* reshape; remodel; redesign ⟨*square, park, room, etc.*⟩; rework ⟨*text, music, etc.*⟩; (reorganisieren) reorganize; (verändern) change

um|gießen *unr. tr. V.* (**a**) **etw. ~:** pour sth. into another container/into bottles *etc.*; **etw. in etw.** (*Akk.*) **~:** pour sth. into sth.; (**b**) (in eine andere Form gießen) recast

um|graben *unr. tr. V.* dig over

um|gruppieren *tr. V.* rearrange

um|haben *unr. tr. V.* **etw. ~:** have sth. on

Um·hang *der* cape

um|hängen *tr. V.* (**a**) **etw. ~:** hang sth. somewhere else; (**b**) **jmdm./sich einen Mantel ~:** drape a coat round sb.'s/one's shoulders; **jmdm. eine Medaille ~:** hang a medal round sb.'s neck

Umhänge·tasche *die* shoulder bag

um|hauen *unr. tr. V.* (**a**) (fällen) fell; (**b**) (ugs.: niederwerfen) knock down; floor; **es hat mich fast umgehauen, als ich davon hörte** (salopp) I was flabbergasted when I heard

um·her *Adv.* around; **weit ~:** all around

umher-: ⇒ **herum-**

umhin|können *unr. itr. V.* **sie konnte nicht/kaum umhin, das zu tun** she had no/scarcely had any choice but to do it; (einem inneren Zwang folgend) she couldn't help/ could scarcely help but do it

um|hören *refl. V.* keep one's ears open; (direkt fragen) ask around

um·hüllen *tr. V.* wrap; (fig.) ⟨*mist, fog, etc.*⟩ shroud; **jmdn./etw. mit etw. ~:** wrap sb./sth. in sth.

um·jubeln *tr. V.* cheer

Umkehr /ˈʊmkeːɐ̯/ *die; ~* (auch fig.) turning back; **zur ~ gezwungen werden** be forced to turn back

um|kehren 1 *itr. V.; mit sein* turn back; (fig. geh.: sich wandeln) change one's ways; **auf halbem Wege ~** (fig.) stop halfway. **2** *tr. V.* (**a**) turn upside down; turn over ⟨*sheet of paper*⟩; (nach links drehen) turn ⟨*garment etc.*⟩ inside out; (nach rechts drehen) turn ⟨*garment etc.*⟩ right side out; **das ganze Haus [nach etw.] ~** (fig. ugs.) turn the whole house upside down [looking for sth.]; (**b**) (ins Gegenteil verkehren) reverse; invert ⟨*ratio, proportion*⟩

Umkehr·film *der* (Fot.) reversal film

um|kippen 1 *itr. V.; mit sein* (**a**) fall over; ⟨*boat*⟩ capsize, turn over; ⟨*vehicle*⟩ overturn; (**b**) (ugs.: ohnmächtig werden) keel over; (**c**) (ugs. abwertend) ⇒ **umfallen c;** (**d**) (ugs.: umschlagen) ⟨*wine*⟩ go off; (**e**) (Ökologie) ⟨*river, lake*⟩ reach the stage of biological collapse. **2** *tr. V.* tip over; knock over ⟨*lamp, vase, glass, cup*⟩; capsize ⟨*boat*⟩; turn ⟨*boat*⟩ over; overturn ⟨*vehicle*⟩

um|klammern *tr. V.* clutch; clasp; **etw./jmdn. fest umklammert halten** keep a firm grip on sth./clutch sb. tightly

um|klappen *tr. V.* fold down

Umkleide·kabine *die* changing-cubicle

um|kleiden (geh.) **1** *refl. V.* change; change one's clothes. **2** *tr. V.* **jmdn. ~:** change sb.; change sb.'s clothes

Umkleide·raum *der* changing room (Brit.); (im Theater) green-room

um|knicken 1 *itr. V.; mit sein* (**a**) [**mit dem Fuß**] **~:** go over on one's ankle; (**b**) ⟨*tree, stalk, blade of grass, etc.*⟩ bend; ⟨*branch*⟩ bend and snap. **2** *tr. V.* (**a**) (falten) fold ⟨*page, sheet of paper*⟩ over; (**b**) (abknicken) bend over; break ⟨*flower, stalk*⟩

um|kommen *unr. itr. V.; mit sein* die; (bei einem Unglück, durch Gewalt) get killed; die; **ich komme um vor Hitze/ Hunger** (fig. ugs.) I'm dying in this heat/of hunger (coll.); **vor Langeweile ~** (fig. ugs.) be bored to death (coll.); die of boredom (coll.)

Um·kreis *der o. Pl.* surrounding area; **im ~ von 5 km** within a radius of 5 km.; **im [näheren] ~ der Stadt** in the [immediate] vicinity of the town

um·kreisen *tr. V.* circle; ⟨*spacecraft, satellite*⟩ orbit; ⟨*planet*⟩ revolve [a]round; **seine Gedanken umkreisten das Thema** (fig.) he kept turning the matter over in his mind

um|krempeln *tr. V.* (**a**) (aufkrempeln) turn up ⟨*cuff*⟩; roll up ⟨*sleeve, trouser leg*⟩; (**b**) (ugs.: von Grund auf ändern) **etw. ~:** give sth. a shake-up; **jmdn. ~:** [completely] change sb.

um|laden *unr. tr. V.* transfer ⟨*goods etc.*⟩

Um·lage *die; ~[n]* share of the cost[s]; (bei einer Wohnung) share of the bill[s]; **die ~ beträgt 30 Mark pro Person** the cost is 30 marks per person

um·lagern *tr. V.* besiege

Um·land *das; o. Pl.* surrounding area; **das ~ von Köln** the area around Cologne

um|lassen *unr. tr. V.* (ugs.) leave ⟨*garment, watch, etc.*⟩ on

Um·lauf *der* **(a)** rotation; **ein ~ [der Erde um die Sonne] dauert ein Jahr** one revolution [of the earth around the sun] takes a year; **(b)** *o. Pl.* (Zirkulation) circulation; **in od. im ~ sein** ⟨*magazine, report, etc.*⟩ be circulating; ⟨*coin, banknote*⟩ be in circulation; **in ~ bringen** *od.* **setzen** circulate ⟨*report, magazine, etc.*⟩; circulate, put about, start ⟨*rumour*⟩; bring ⟨*coin, banknote*⟩ into circulation; **(c)** (Rundschreiben) circular

Umlauf·bahn *die* (Astron., Raumf.) orbit

um|laufen¹ **1** *unr. tr. V.* knock over. **2** *unr. itr. V.; mit sein* **(a)** (rotieren) rotate; revolve; ⟨*planet, satellite, etc.*⟩ orbit; **(b)** **~d** (ringsherum verlaufend) surrounding; **(c)** (kursieren, zirkulieren) circulate

um·laufen² *unr. tr. V.* run around; ⟨*planet, satellite, etc.*⟩ orbit

Um·laut *der* (Sprachw.) umlaut

um|legen *tr. V.* **(a)** (um einen Körperteil) put on; **(b)** (auf den Boden, die Seite legen) lay down; flatten ⟨*corn, stalks, etc.*⟩; (fällen) fell; **(c)** (umklappen) fold down; turn down ⟨*collar*⟩; throw ⟨*lever*⟩; turn over ⟨*calendar-page*⟩; **(d)** (ugs.: zu Boden werfen) floor, knock down ⟨*person*⟩; **(e)** (salopp: ermorden) **jmdn. ~:** do sb. in (sl.); bump sb. off (sl.); **(f)** (verlegen) transfer ⟨*patient, telephone call*⟩; **den Termin ~:** change the date **(auf** + *Akk.* to); **(g)** (anteilmäßig verteilen) split, share ⟨*costs*⟩ **(auf** + *Akk.* between)

um|leiten divert; re-route; divert ⟨*river, stream*⟩

Um·leitung *die* diversion; re-routing

um|lernen *itr. V.* **(a)** (beruflich) retrain; **(b)** (seine Anschauungen ändern) learn to think differently

umliegend *Adj.* surrounding ⟨*area, district*⟩; (nahe) nearby ⟨*building*⟩

Um·luft *die; o. Pl.* (Technik) recirculated air

um|modeln *tr. V.* (ugs.) change ⟨*house, flat*⟩ round; re-fashion, alter ⟨*jacket etc.*⟩

um·nachtet *Adj.* (geh.) **[geistig] ~ sein** be [mentally] deranged

Umnachtung *die; ~, ~en* (geh.) derangement

um|packen **1** *itr. V.* repack. **2** *tr. V.* repack; **seine Sachen aus der Reisetasche in einen Koffer ~:** take one's things out of the holdall and pack them into a suitcase

um|pflanzen *tr. V.* transplant

um|pflügen *tr. V.* plough up

um|quartieren *tr. V.* re-accommodate ⟨*person*⟩ **(in** + *Akk.* in); re-quarter, re-billet ⟨*troops*⟩ **(in** + *Akk.* in); move ⟨*patient*⟩

um|rahmen *tr. V.* frame ⟨*face etc.*⟩; **eine Feier mit Musik od. musikalisch ~** (fig.) begin and end a ceremony with music; give a ceremony a musical framework

Um|rahmung *die; ~, ~en* **(a)** (das Umrahmen) bordering; **musikalische ~** (fig.) musical framework; music before and after; **(b)** (Umrahmendes) border; (fig.) setting

umrändert /ʊmˈrɛndɐt/ *Adj.* **schwarz ~:** with a black border; **rot ~e Augen** red-rimmed eyes

um|räumen **1** *tr. V.* rearrange. **2** *tr. V.* rearrange things

um|rechnen *tr. V.* convert **(in** + *Akk.* into)

Um·rechnung *die* conversion **(in** + *Akk.* into)

Umrechnungs·kurs *der* exchange rate

um|reißen¹ *unr. tr. V.* pull ⟨*mast, tree*⟩ down; knock ⟨*person*⟩ down; ⟨*wind*⟩ tear ⟨*tent etc.*⟩ down

um·reißen² *unr. tr. V.* outline; summarize ⟨*subject, problem, situation*⟩; **fest od. klar od. scharf umrissen** clearly defined ⟨*programme*⟩; clear-cut ⟨*ideas, views*⟩

um|rennen *unr. tr. V.* [run into and] knock down

um·ringen *tr. V.* surround; (in großer Zahl) crowd round

Um·riss, *Um·riß *der* (auch fig.) outline

um|rühren *tr. V.* (auch itr.) *V.* stir

um·runden *tr. V.* go round ⟨*lake, town*⟩; (Raumf.) orbit; (Seew.) round ⟨*cape*⟩

---

*alte Schreibung (vgl. Hinweise auf S. xvi–xvii)

um|rüsten *tr. V.* **(a)** (Technik) convert **(auf** + *Akk.* to, **zu** into); **(b)** (Milit.) **eine Armee [auf Atomwaffen] ~:** re-equip an army [with nuclear weapons]

ums /ʊms/ *Präp.* + *Art.* **(a)** = **um das**; **(b)** **~ Leben kommen** lose one's life

um|satteln *itr. V.* (ugs.) change jobs; ⟨*student*⟩ change courses

Um·satz *der* turnover; (Verkauf) sales *pl.* **(an** + *Dat.* of); **1 000 Mark ~ machen** turn over 1,000 marks

Umsatz·steuer *die* turnover or (Amer.) sales tax

um|säumen¹ *tr. V.* hem

um·säumen² *tr. V.* (fig.) surround

um|schalten **1** *tr. V.* (auch fig.) switch [over] (auf + *Akk.* to); move ⟨*lever*⟩. **2** *itr. V.* **(a)** (auch fig.) switch or change over (auf + *Akk.* to); **in den zweiten Gang ~:** change into second gear; **wir schalten jetzt ins Stadion um** now we're going over to the stadium; **(b)** (umgeschaltet werden) **die Ampel schaltet [auf Grün] um** the traffic lights are changing [to green]

um|schauen *refl. V.* (bes. südd., österr., schweiz.) ⇒ **umsehen**

um·schiffen *tr. V.* round ⟨*headland, cape*⟩; steer clear of ⟨*rocks, fig.: obstacle*⟩

Um·schlag *der* **(a)** cover; **(b)** (Brief~) envelope; **(c)** (Schutz~) jacket; (einer Broschüre, eines Heftes) cover; **(d)** (Med.: Wickel) compress; (warm) poultice; **(e)** (Hosen~) turn-up; (Ärmel~) cuff; **(f)** (Veränderung) [sudden] change (*Gen.* in); **(g)** (Wirtsch.: Güter~) transfer; trans-shipment

um|schlagen **1** *unr. tr. V.* **(a)** (umklappen) turn up ⟨*sleeve, collar, trousers*⟩; turn over ⟨*page*⟩; **(b)** (umladen, verladen) turn round, trans-ship ⟨*goods*⟩. **2** *unr. itr. V.; mit sein* ⟨*weather, mood*⟩ change **(in** + *Akk.* into); ⟨*wind*⟩ veer [round]; ⟨*voice*⟩ break; **ins Gegenteil ~:** change completely; become the opposite

Umschlag-: **~hafen** *der* port of trans-shipment; **~platz** *der* trans-shipment centre

um·schließen *unr. tr. V.* **(a)** ⟨*river, wall*⟩ surround; ⟨*shell, husk, etc.*⟩ enclose; ⟨*hand, fingers, tentacles*⟩ clasp, hold; **(b)** (einschließen, umzingeln) surround, encircle ⟨*position, enemy*⟩

um·schlingen *unr. tr. V.* **jmdn./etw. [mit den Armen] ~:** put one's arms around sb./sth.; embrace sb./sth.

um·schmeicheln *tr. V.* heap flattery on; (fig.) caress ⟨*part of body*⟩

um|schmeißen *unr. tr. V.* (ugs.) ⇒ **umwerfen a, b**

um|schreiben¹ *unr. tr. V.* **(a)** rewrite; **(b)** (übertragen) transfer ⟨*money, property*⟩ **(auf** + *Akk.* to); **(c)** (transkribieren) transcribe

um·schreiben² *unr. tr. V.* **(a)** (in Worte fassen) describe; (definieren) define ⟨*meaning, sb.'s task, etc.*⟩; (paraphrasieren) paraphrase ⟨*word, expression*⟩; **(b)** (mit einer Linie umgeben) outline; (andeuten) indicate

Um·schreibung *die* description; (Definition) definition; (Verhüllung) circumlocution (*Gen.* for)

um|schulden *tr. (auch itr.) V.* (Finanzw.) convert ⟨*loan*⟩; (mit längerer Laufzeit) reschedule ⟨*loan, debt*⟩

Umschuldung *die; ~, ~en* (Finanzw.) loan conversion; (mit längerer Laufzeit) extension of credit; rescheduling [of a/ the loan/loans]

um|schulen **1** *tr. V.* **(a)** **ein Kind [auf eine andere Schule] ~:** transfer a child [to another school]; **(b)** (beruflich) retrain. **2** *itr. V.* retrain **(auf** + *Akk.* as)

Umschulung *die* (beruflich) retraining *no pl.* **(auf** + *Akk.* as)

um|schütten *tr. V.* **(a)** pour [into another container]; decant ⟨*liquid*⟩; **(b)** (verschütten) spill

um·schwärmen *tr. V.* **(a)** swarm around; **von Moskitos umschwärmt werden** be besieged by mosquitoes; **(b)** (fig.) flock around; **sie war sehr od. von vielen umschwärmt** she had many admirers

Um·schweif *der* circumlocution; **ohne ~e** without beating about the bush

Um·schwung *der* complete change; (in der Politik usw.) U-turn; volte-face

um·segeln *tr. V.* sail round ‹*world, island, etc.*›; circumnavigate ‹*world*›; (fig.) negotiate ‹*obstacle etc.*›

um|sehen *unr. refl. V.* **(a)** look (**nach** for); **sich im Zimmer** ∼: look [a]round the room; **sehen Sie sich ruhig um** (im Geschäft usw.) by all means have a look round; **du wirst dich noch** ∼! (ugs.) you're in for a [nasty] shock; **(b)** (zurücksehen) look round *or* back

*um|sein ⇒ **um 2 b**

umseitig 1 *Adj.* ‹*text, illustration, etc.*› overleaf. **2** *adv.* overleaf

um|setzen 1 *tr. V.* **(a)** move; (auf anderen Sitzplatz) move to another seat/other seats; (auf anderen Posten, Arbeitsplatz usw.) move, transfer (**in** + *Akk.* to); (umpflanzen) transplant ‹*bush etc.*›; (in anderen Topf) repot ‹*plant*›; **(b)** (verwirklichen) implement ‹*plan*›; translate ‹*plan, intention, etc.*› into action *or* reality; realize ‹*ideas*›; **(c)** (Wirtsch.) turn over, have a turnover of ‹*x marks etc.*›; sell ‹*goods*›. **2** *refl. V.* (den Sitzplatz wechseln) move to another seat/other seats; change seats; (den Tisch wechseln) move to another table; change tables

Um·sicht *die; o. Pl.* circumspection; prudence

um·sichtig 1 *Adj.* circumspect; prudent. **2** *adv.* circumspectly; prudently

um|siedeln 1 *tr. V.* resettle; **nach X umgesiedelt werden** be moved to X. **2** *itr. V.; mit sein* move (**in** + *Akk.*, **nach** to)

Um·siedler *der*, **Um·siedlerin** *die* resettled person; (freiwillig) resettler

Um·siedlung *die* resettlement

um|sinken *unr. itr. V.; mit sein* sink *or* fall to the ground

um·so *Konj.* **(c) je länger** ..., ∼ **besser** ...: the longer ..., the better ...; ∼ **besser/schlimmer!** all the better/worse!; ∼ **mehr, als** ... (zumal, da ...) all the more so, as *or* since ...

um·sonst *Adv.* **(a)** (unentgeltlich) free; for nothing; **für** ∼ (ugs.) free, gratis, and for nothing (joc.); **(b)** (vergebens) in vain; **(c) nicht** ∼ **hat er davor gewarnt** not for nothing did he warn of that

um·sorgen *tr. V.* care for; look after

um·spannen *tr. V.* clasp ‹*hand, wrist, ankle, etc.*›; put one's hands round ‹*neck etc.*›

um|springen *unr. itr. V.; mit sein* **(a)** ‹*wind*› veer round (**auf** + *Akk.* to); ‹*traffic light*› change; **(b)** (ugs. abwertend) **mit jmdm. grob** usw. ∼: treat sb. roughly *etc.*

um|spulen *tr. V.* rewind ‹*tape, film*›

um·spülen *tr. V.* wash round; **ein von den Wellen umspültes Riff** a reef washed by the waves

Um·stand *der* **(a)** (Gegebenheit) circumstance; (Tatsache) fact; **die näheren Umstände** the particular circumstances; (Einzelheiten) the details; **ein glücklicher** ∼: a lucky *or* happy chance; **unter allen Umständen** whatever happens; **unter Umständen** possibly; **in anderen Umständen sein** (ugs.) be expecting; be in the family way (coll.); **(b)** (Aufwand) business; hassle (coll.); **macht keine [großen] Umstände** please don't go to any bother *or* trouble

umstände·halber *Adv.* owing to circumstances; „umständehalber zu verkaufen" 'forced to sell'; 'genuine reason for sale'

umständlich /ˈʊmʃtɛntlɪç/ **1** *Adj.* involved, elaborate ‹*procedure, method, description, explanation, etc.*›; awkward, difficult ‹*journey, job*›; (kompliziert) involved; complicated; (weitschweifig) long-winded; (Umstände machend) awkward, (coll.) pernickety ‹*person*›. **2** *adv.* in an involved *or* roundabout way; (weitschweifig) ‹*explain etc.*› at great length *or* in a long-winded way; **warum einfach, wenns auch** ∼ **geht?** (iron.) why do things the easy way if you can make them difficult? (iron.)

Umstands-: ∼**kleid** *das* maternity dress; ∼**wort** *das* (Sprachw.) adverb

umstehend *Adj.; nicht präd.* standing round *postpos.*; **die Umstehenden** the bystanders

um|steigen *unr. itr. V.* **(a)** change (**in** + *Akk.* [on] to); **nach Frankfurt** ∼ (ugs.) change for Frankfurt; **(b)** (fig. ugs.) change over, switch (**auf** + *Akk.* to)

um|stellen¹ 1 *tr. V.* **(a)** (anders stellen) rearrange, change round ‹*furniture, books, etc.*›; reshuffle ‹*team*›; **(b)** (anders einstellen) reset ‹*lever, switch, points, clock*›; **(c)** (ändern) change *or* switch over (**auf** + *Akk.* to). **2** *refl. V.* **(a)** adjust; **(b)** ⇒ **umsteigen b**

um·stellen² *tr. V.* surround

Um·stellung *die* ⇒ **umstellen¹ 1, 2**; **(a)** rearrangement; reshuffle; **(b)** resetting; **(c)** changeover, switch (**auf** + *Akk.* to); **(d)** (das Sichumstellen) change; [re]adjustment

um|stimmen *tr. V.* win ‹*person*› round; **er ließ sich nicht** ∼: he was not to be persuaded; he refused to change his mind

um|stoßen *unr. tr. V.* **(a)** knock over; **(b)** (fig.) reverse ‹*judgement, decision*›; change ‹*plan, decision*›

umstritten *Adj.* disputed; controversial ‹*bill, book, author, etc.*›

um|strukturieren *tr. V.* restructure

um|stülpen *tr. V.* turn inside out

Um·sturz *der* coup

um|stürzen 1 *tr. V.* overturn; knock over; (fig.) topple, overthrow ‹*political system, government*›. **2** *itr. V.* overturn; ‹*wall, building, chimney*› fall down

Umstürzler /ˈʊmʃtʏrtslɐ/ *der;* ∼**s,** ∼ (abwertend) subversive agent

umstürzlerisch (abwertend) **1** *Adj.* subversive. **2** *adv.* **sich** ∼ **betätigen** engage in subversive activities

Umsturz·versuch *der* attempted coup

Um·tausch *der* exchange; **reduzierte Ware ist vom** ∼ **ausgeschlossen** sale goods cannot be exchanged

um|tauschen *tr. V.* exchange ‹*goods, article*› (**gegen** for); change ‹*dollars, pounds, etc.*› (**in** + *Akk.* into)

Um|triebe *Pl.* (abwertend) [subversive] intrigues; subversion *sing.*

Um·trunk *der* communal drink

um|tun *unr. refl. V.* (ugs.) look [a]round; **sich nach etw.** ∼: be on the lookout *or* looking for sth.

U-Musik *die; o. Pl.* light music

um|verteilen *tr. V.* redistribute

um|wälzen *tr. V.* **(a)** roll over; ∼**d** (fig.) revolutionary ‹*ideas, effect*›; epoch-making ‹*events*›; **(b)** circulate ‹*water, air*›

Umwälzung *die;* ∼, ∼**en** (fig.) revolution

um|wandeln *tr. V.* convert ‹*substance, building, etc.*› (**in** + *Akk.* into); commute ‹*sentence*› (**in** + *Akk.* to); (ändern) change; alter; **er ist wie umgewandelt** he is a changed man

Um·wandlung *die* conversion (**in** + *Akk.* into), (einer Strafe) commutation (**in** + *Akk.* to); (der Gesellschaft usw.) transformation

um|wechseln *tr. V.* change ‹*money*› (**in** + *Akk.* into)

Um·weg *der* detour; **auf** ∼**en** by a circuitous *or* roundabout route; (fig.) in a roundabout way; **auf dem** ∼ **über** (+ *Akk.*) (fig.) [indirectly] via

Um·welt *die* **(a)** environment; **(b)** (Menschen) people *pl.* around sb.

umwelt-, Umwelt-: ∼**bedingt** *Adj.* caused by the *or* one's environment *postpos.;* ∼**belastung** *die* environmental pollution *no indef. art.;* ∼**bewusst,** *∼**bewußt** *Adj.* environmentally conscious *or* aware; ∼**feindlich 1** *Adj.* inimical to the environment *postpos.;* ecologically undesirable; **2** *adv.* in an ecologically undesirable way; ∼**forschung** *die; o. Pl.* ecology; ∼**freundlich 1** *Adj.* environment-friendly; ecologically desirable; **2** *adv.* in an ecologically desirable way; ∼**politik** *die* ecological policy; ∼**schäden** *Pl.* environmental damage *sing.* damage *sing.* to the environment; ∼**schädlich** *Adj.* harmful to the environment *postpos.;* ecologically harmful; ∼**schutz** *der* environmental protection *no art.;* conservation of the environment; ∼**schützer** *der* environmentalist; conservationist; ∼**sünder** *der* (ugs.) deliberate polluter of the environment; ∼**verschmutzung** *die* pollution [of the environment]

um·werben *unr. tr. V.* court; woo

um|werfen *unr. tr. V.* **(a)** knock over; (fig. ugs.: aus der Fassung bringen) bowl ⟨*person*⟩ over; stun ⟨*person*⟩; **(b)** (fig. ugs.; umstoßen) knock ⟨*plan*⟩ on the head (coll.)

umwerfend (ugs.) **1** *Adj.* fantastic (coll.); stunning (coll.). **2** *adv.* fantastically [well] (coll.); brilliantly; ~ **komisch** hilariously funny

Um·werfer *der* derailleur

um·wickeln *tr. V.* wrap; bind; (mit einem Verband) bandage; etw. **mit Draht** ~: wind wire round sth.

um·wittern *tr. V.* (geh.) **von Gefahren/einem Geheimnis umwittert sein** be beset *or* fraught with danger/shrouded in mystery

Umzäunung *die;* ~, ~en fence, fencing (*Gen.* round)

um|ziehen 1 *unr. itr. V.; mit sein* move **(an** + *Akk.,* **in** + *Akk.,* **nach** to). **2** *unr. tr. V.* **jmdn.** ~: change sb.; get sb. changed; **sich** ~: change; get changed

um·zingeln /ʊmˈt͡sɪŋ̩ln/ *tr. V.* surround; encircle

Um·zug *der* **(a)** move; (von Möbeln) removal; **(b)** (Festzug) procession

UN /uːˈɛn/ *Pl.* UN *sing.*

unabänderlich /ʊnˈapˈ|ɛndɐlɪç/ **1** *Adj.* unalterable; irrevocable ⟨*decision*⟩. **2** *adv.* irrevocably; **das steht** ~ **fest** that is absolutely certain

unabdingbar /ʊnˈapˈdɪŋbaːɐ̯/ *Adj.* (geh.) indispensable

unabhängig 1 *Adj.* independent **(von** of). **2** *adv.* independently **(von** of); ~ **davon, ob** … *usw.* irrespective *or* regardless of whether … *etc.*

Unabhängigkeit *die* independence

unabkömmlich /ʊnˈapˈkœmlɪç/ *Adj.* indispensable; **sie ist im Moment** ~: she is otherwise engaged

unablässig /ˈʊnˈaplɛsɪç/ **1** *Adj.* incessant; constant ⟨*repetition*⟩; unremitting ⟨*effort*⟩. **2** *adv.* incessantly; constantly

unabsehbar 1 *Adj.* **(a)** (fig.) incalculable, immeasurable ⟨*extent, damage, etc.*⟩; **(b)** (noch nicht vorauszusehen) unforeseeable ⟨*consequences*⟩. **2** *adv.* **(a)** incalculably; immeasurably; **(b)** (in einem noch nicht erkennbaren Ausmaß) to an unforeseeable extent

unabsichtlich 1 *Adj.* unintentional. **2** *adv.* unintentionally

unabweisbar 1 *Adj.* irrefutable; absolute ⟨*necessity*⟩. **2** *adv.* irrefutably; undeniably

unabwendbar *Adj.* inevitable

unachtsam 1 *Adj.* **(a)** inattentive; **einen Augenblick** ~ **sein** let one's attention wander for a moment; **(b)** (nicht sorgfältig) careless. **2** *adv.* (ohne Sorgfalt) carelessly

Unachtsamkeit *die;* ~ **(a)** inattentiveness; **(b)** (mangelnde Sorgfalt) carelessness

unangebracht *Adj.* inappropriate; misplaced

unangefochten *Adj.* unchallenged ⟨*victor, leadership, etc.*⟩; (unbestritten) undisputed, unchallenged ⟨*assertion, thesis*⟩

unangemeldet *Adj.* unexpected ⟨*visit, guest*⟩; unauthorized ⟨*demonstration*⟩

unangemessen 1 *Adj.* unsuitable; inappropriate; unreasonable, disproportionate ⟨*demand, claim, sentence, etc.*⟩. **2** *adv.* unsuitably; inappropriately; disproportionately ⟨*high, low*⟩

unangenehm 1 *Adj.* unpleasant (*Dat.* for); (peinlich) embarrassing, awkward ⟨*question, situation*⟩; **es ist mir sehr** ~, **dass ich mich verspätet habe** I am most upset about being late; ~ **werden** ⟨*person*⟩ get *or* turn nasty. **2** *adv.* unpleasantly; ~ **auffallen** make a bad impression

unangetastet *Adj.* untouched

unangreifbar *Adj.* (auch fig.) unassailable; impregnable ⟨*fortress*⟩; (unanfechtbar) irrefutable ⟨*argument, thesis*⟩; incontestable ⟨*judgement etc.*⟩

unannehmbar *Adj.* unacceptable

Unannehmlichkeit *die* trouble; **jmdm.** ~**en bereiten** cause sb. [a lot of (coll.)] problems *or* difficulties

---

*alte Schreibung (vgl. Hinweise auf S. xvi–xvii)

unansehnlich *Adj.* unprepossessing; plain ⟨*girl*⟩

unanständig 1 *Adj.* **(a)** improper; (anstößig) indecent ⟨*behaviour, remark*⟩; dirty ⟨*joke*⟩; rude ⟨*word, song*⟩; **(b)** (verwerflich) immoral. **2** *adv.* **(a)** improperly; indecently; **(b)** (verwerflich) immorally

Unanständigkeit *die o. Pl.* impropriety; indecency; (Obszönität) obscenity

unantastbar *Adj.* inviolable

unappetitlich 1 *Adj.* unappetizing; (fig.) unsavoury ⟨*joke*⟩; unsavoury-looking ⟨*person*⟩; disgusting ⟨*washbasin, nails, etc.*⟩. **2** *adv.* unappetizingly

Unart *die* bad habit

unartig *Adj.* naughty

unästhetisch *Adj.* unpleasant, unsavoury ⟨*sight etc.*⟩; ugly ⟨*building etc.*⟩; (abstoßend) disgusting

unauffällig 1 *Adj.* inconspicuous; unobtrusive ⟨*scar, defect, skill, behaviour, surveillance, etc.*⟩; discreet ⟨*signal, elegance*⟩. **2** *adv.* inconspicuously; unobtrusively ⟨*behave, follow, observe, disappear, leave*⟩ unobtrusively, discreetly

unauffindbar *Adj.* untraceable; ~ **sein** be nowhere to be found

unaufgefordert *Adv.* without being asked; ~ **eingesandte Manuskripte** unsolicited manuscripts

unaufhaltsam 1 *Adj.* inexorable. **2** *adv.* inexorably

unaufhörlich 1 *Adj.; nicht präd.* constant; incessant; continuous ⟨*rain*⟩. **2** *adv.* constantly; ⟨*rain, snow*⟩ continuously

unauflöslich *Adj.* irreconcilable ⟨*contradiction etc.*⟩; indissoluble ⟨*marriage, link*⟩

unaufmerksam *Adj.* inattentive

Unaufmerksamkeit *die* inattentiveness

unaufrichtig *Adj.* insincere; **jmdm. gegenüber** ~ **sein** not be honest with sb.

Unaufrichtigkeit *die o. Pl.* insincerity

unaufschiebbar *Adj.* **es war** ~: it could not be put off *or* postponed

unausbleiblich *Adj.* inevitable; unavoidable

unausgefüllt *Adj.* uncompleted, blank ⟨*form*⟩; (fig.) unfulfilled ⟨*person*⟩; unfilled ⟨*time*⟩; empty ⟨*life*⟩

unausgeglichen *Adj.* **(a)** [emotionally] unstable ⟨*person, behaviour*⟩; **(b)** (Wirtsch.) ⟨*balance of payments*⟩ not in balance; unsettled ⟨*account, debt*⟩

unausgegoren *Adj.* (abwertend) immature

unaussprechlich 1 *Adj.* **(a)** inexpressible; **(b)** (geh.: unbeschreiblich) indescribable ⟨*misery, joy*⟩; unutterable ⟨*misery, sorrow*⟩. **2** *adv.* (geh.) unutterably; indescribably ⟨*suffer, love*⟩ beyond expression

unausstehlich 1 *Adj.* unbearable ⟨*person, noise, smell, etc.*⟩; insufferable ⟨*person*⟩; intolerable ⟨*noise, smell*⟩. **2** *adv.* unbearably; intolerably

unausweichlich *Adj.* unavoidable; inevitable

unbändig /ˈʊnbɛndɪç/ **1** *Adj.* **(a)** boisterous ⟨*person, horse, temperament*⟩; **(b)** unbridled, unrestrained ⟨*desire, longing, joy, merriment*⟩; unbridled, uncontrollable ⟨*fury, hate, anger*⟩. **2** *adv.* **(a)** wildly; **(b)** (sehr) unrestrainedly; tremendously (coll.); **sich** ~ **freuen** jump for joy

unbarmherzig 1 *Adj.* (auch fig.) merciless; remorseless, unsparing ⟨*severity*⟩; (fig.) very severe ⟨*winter, cold*⟩. **2** *adv.* mercilessly; without mercy

unbeabsichtigt 1 *Adj.* unintentional. **2** *adv.* unintentionally

unbeachtet *Adj.* unnoticed; obscure ⟨*existence*⟩; **jmdn./etw.** ~ **lassen** not take any notice of sb./sth.

unbeanstandet 1 *Adj.* **etw.** ~ **lassen** let sth. pass. **2** *adv.* without objection

unbeantwortet *Adj.* unanswered

unbearbeitet *Adj.* **(a)** undealt with *pred.*; which has/have not been dealt with *postpos.*; **(b)** (roh) untreated ⟨*wood, leather, metal*⟩

unbebaut *Adj.* **(a)** undeveloped ⟨*site, land*⟩; **(b)** (unbestellt) uncultivated ⟨*land, area*⟩

unbedacht 1 *Adj.* rash; thoughtless. **2** *adv.* rashly; thoughtlessly

unbedarft *Adj.* (ugs.) **(a)** inexpert; lay; **(b)** (naiv) naïve; (dümmlich) gormless (coll.)

unbedenklich *Adj.* harmless, safe ‹*substance, drug*›; unobjectionable ‹*joke, reading matter*›

unbedeutend **1** *Adj.* insignificant; minor ‹*artist, poet*›; slight, minor ‹*improvement, change, error*›. **2** *adv.* slightly

unbedingt **1** *Adj.* absolute ‹*trust, faith, reliability, secrecy, etc.*›; complete ‹*rest*›. **2** *Adv.* absolutely; (auf jeden Fall) whatever happens; **nicht ~:** not necessarily

unbeeindruckt *Adj.* unimpressed

unbeeinflusst, *****unbeeinflußt** *Adj.* uninfluenced

unbefangen **1** *Adj.* **(a)** (ungehemmt) uninhibited; natural, uninhibited ‹*behaviour*›; **(b)** (unvoreingenommen) impartial. **2** *adv.* **(a)** freely; without inhibition; ‹*behave*› naturally; **(b)** (unvoreingenommen) **jmdm./einer Sache ~ gegenübertreten** approach sb./sth. with an open mind

Unbefangenheit *die* ⇒ **unbefangen 1 a, b:** uninhibitedness; naturalness; impartiality

unbefriedigend *Adj.* unsatisfactory

unbefriedigt *Adj.* dissatisfied **(von** with); unsatisfied ‹*need, curiosity, desire, etc.*›; (unausgefüllt) unfulfilled **(von** by); (sexuell) [sexually] frustrated

unbefristet **1** *Adj.* for an indefinite *or* unlimited period *postpos.;* indefinite ‹*strike*›; unlimited ‹*visa*›. **2** *adv.* for an indefinite *or* unlimited period

unbefugt **1** *Adj.* unauthorized. **2** *adv.* without authorization

unbegabt *Adj.* ungifted; untalented

unbegreiflich *Adj.* incomprehensible (*Dat.*, **für** to); incredible ‹*love, goodness, stupidity, carelessness, etc.*›

unbegreiflicherweise *Adv.* inexplicably

unbegrenzt **1** *Adj.* unlimited. **2** *adv.* ‹*stay, keep, etc.*› indefinitely; **ich habe nicht ~ Zeit** I don't have unlimited time

unbegründet *Adj.* unfounded; groundless

Unbehagen *das* uneasiness, disquiet; **ein körperliches ~:** a physical discomfort; **es bereitet mir ~:** it makes me feel uneasy

unbehaglich **1** *Adj.* uneasy, uncomfortable ‹*feeling, atmosphere*›; uncomfortable ‹*thought, room*›; **mir war ~ zumute** I was *or* felt uneasy. **2** *adv.* uneasily; uncomfortably

unbehelligt *Adj.* unmolested

unbeherrscht **1** *Adj.* uncontrolled; intemperate, wild ‹*reaction, behaviour, remark*›. **2** *adv.* without any self-control

Unbeherrschtheit *die; ~:* lack of self-control

unbeholfen **1** *Adj.* clumsy; awkward. **2** *adv.* clumsily; awkwardly

unbeirrbar **1** *Adj.* unwavering. **2** *adv.* unwaveringly

unbeirrt **1** *Adj.* unwavering. **2** *adv.* without wavering

unbekannt **1** *Adj.* **(a)** unknown; unidentified ‹*caller, donor, flying object*›; (nicht vertraut) unfamiliar; **sie ist hier ~:** she is not known here; **~e Täter** unknown *or* unidentified culprits; **[Straf]anzeige gegen Unbekannt** (Rechtsw.) charge against person *or* persons unknown; **(b)** (nicht vielen bekannt) little known; obscure ‹*poet, painter, etc.*›; **(c)** jmd./etw. ist jmdm. **~:** sb. does not know sb./sth.; „Empfänger **~**" 'not known at this address'. **2** *adv.* „Empfänger **~** verzogen" 'moved'; 'address unknown'

Unbekannte[1] *der/die; adj. Dekl.* unknown *or* unidentified man/woman; (Fremde[r]) stranger; **der große ~** (scherzh.) the mystery man *or* person

Unbekannte[2] *die; adj. Dekl.* (Math.; auch fig.) unknown

unbekannter·weise *Adv.* grüßen Sie ihn/sie **~ [von mir]** give him/her my regards, although we haven't met

unbekleidet *Adj.* without any clothes on *postpos.;* bare ‹*torso etc.*›; naked ‹*corpse*›

unbekümmert **1** *Adj.* carefree; (ohne Bedenken, lässig) casual; **sie ist [ziemlich] ~:** she doesn't worry [much]; she is [pretty] unconcerned. **2** *adv.* **(a)** in a carefree way; without a care in the world; **(b)** (ohne Bedenken) without caring *or* worrying

Unbekümmertheit *die; ~* **(a)** carefree manner *or* attitude; carefreeness; **(b)** (Bedenkenlosigkeit) lack of concern

unbelastet *Adj.* **(a)** not under load *postpos.;* **(b)** (sorgenfrei) free from care *or* worries *postpos.;* **(c)** (ohne Schuld) **~ sein** have a clean record; **(d)** (schuldenfrei) unmortgaged ‹*property, land*›

unbelebt *Adj.* **(a)** inanimate ‹*nature*›; (anorganisch) inorganic ‹*matter*›; **(b)** (ohne Lebewesen) uninhabited; deserted; empty ‹*streets*›

unbeleckt *Adj.* (salopp) **von etw. ~ sein** not have a clue about sth. (coll.); **sie sind von jeder Kultur ~:** they are complete savages

unbelehrbar *Adj.* incorrigible; not accessible to reason *postpos.;* **er ist ~:** he will not learn

unbeleuchtet *Adj.* unlit ‹*vehicle*› without [any] lights

unbeliebt *Adj.* unpopular **(bei** with)

Unbeliebtheit *die* unpopularity

unbemannt *Adj.* unmanned

unbemerkt *Adj.* unnoticed

unbenommen *Adj.* es ist/bleibt jmdm. **~, zu ...:** sb. is/remains free *or* at liberty to ...

unbenutzt *Adj.* unused

unbeobachtet *Adj.* unobserved; **in einem ~en Augenblick** when no one is/was watching

unbequem **1** *Adj.* **(a)** uncomfortable; **(b)** (lästig) awkward, embarrassing ‹*question, opinion*›; awkward, troublesome ‹*politician etc.*›; unpleasant ‹*criticism, truth, etc.*›; **er wurde ihnen ~:** he became a nuisance *or* an embarrassment to them. **2** *adv.* uncomfortably

Unbequemlichkeit *die; ~* **(a)** lack of comfort; **(b)** (Lästigkeit) awkwardness

unberechenbar **1** *Adj.* unpredictable. **2** *adv.* unpredictably

unberechtigt **1** *Adj.* **(a)** (ungerechtfertigt) unjustified; **(b)** (unbefugt) unauthorized. **2** *adv.* (unbefugt) without authorization

unberücksichtigt *Adj.* unconsidered; **etw. ~ lassen** leave sth. out of consideration; ignore sth.

unberührt *Adj.* **(a)** untouched; virgin ‹*snow, forest, wilderness*›; **ein Stück ~er Natur** a stretch of unspoilt countryside; **(b)** (geh.: jungfräulich) in the virgin state *postpos.;* **sie ist noch ~:** she is still a virgin; **(c)** (unbeeindruckt) unmoved **(von** by)

Unberührtheit *die; ~* **(a)** unspoiled state; **(b)** (geh.: Jungfräulichkeit) virginity; **(c)** (das Unbeeindrucktsein) lack of emotion; impassivity

unbeschadet *Präp. mit Gen.* regardless of; notwithstanding

unbeschädigt *Adj.* undamaged

unbescheiden *Adj.* presumptuous

unbescholten *Adj.* respectable; **~ sein** (Rechtsspr.) have no [previous] convictions

unbeschrankt *Adj.* ‹*crossing*› without gates, with no gates

unbeschränkt **1** *Adj.* unlimited; limitless ‹*possibilities, power*›. **2** *adv.* **für etw. ~ haften** have unlimited liability for sth.

unbeschreiblich **1** *Adj.* indescribable; unimaginable ‹*fear, beauty*›; ‹*fear, beauty*› beyond description. **2** *adv.* indescribably ‹*beautiful*›; unbelievably ‹*busy*›

unbeschrieben *Adj.* blank, empty ‹*piece of paper, page*›; s. auch **Blatt b**

unbeschwert **1** *Adj.* carefree. **2** *adv.* free from care; ‹*dance, play*› with a light heart

unbesehen **1** *Adj.* unquestioning ‹*acceptance*›. **2** *adv.* without hesitation

unbesiegbar *Adj.* invincible

unbesiegt *Adj.* undefeated ‹*army*›; unbeaten ‹*team, player*›

unbesonnen **1** *Adj.* impulsive ‹*person, nature*›; unthinking ‹*remark*›; (übereilt) ill-considered, rash ‹*decision, action*›. **2** *adv.* ‹*act*› without thinking; (übereilt) rashly

unbesorgt *Adj.* unconcerned; **seien Sie ~!** don't [you] worry; you can set your mind at rest

unbespielt *Adj.* blank ⟨*tape, cassette*⟩

unbeständig *Adj.* changeable, unsettled ⟨*weather*⟩; erratic, inconsistent ⟨*performance, person*⟩

unbestätigt *Adj.* unconfirmed

unbestechlich *Adj.* (**a**) incorruptible; (**b**) (fig.) uncompromising ⟨*critic*⟩; incorruptible ⟨*character*⟩; unerring ⟨*judgement*⟩

unbestimmt **1** *Adj.* (**a**) indefinite; indeterminate ⟨*age, number*⟩; (ungewiss) uncertain; (**b**) (ungenau) vague; (**c**) (Sprachw.) indefinite ⟨*article, pronoun*⟩. **2** *adv.* (ungenau) vaguely

unbestreitbar **1** *Adj.* indisputable; unquestionable. **2** *adv.* indisputably; unquestionably

unbestritten **1** *Adj.* undisputed. **2** *adv.* indisputably

unbeteiligt **1** *Adj.* (**a**) uninvolved; **ein Unbeteiligter** someone who is/was not involved; an outsider; (ein Unschuldiger) an innocent party; (**b**) (gleichgültig) indifferent; detached ⟨*manner, expression*⟩. **2** *adv.* with a detached *or* indifferent air

unbetont *Adj.* unstressed

unbeugsam *Adj.* uncompromising; tenacious; indomitable, unshakeable ⟨*will, pride*⟩; unwavering, resolute ⟨*character*⟩

unbewacht *Adj.* unsupervised ⟨*prisoners etc.*⟩; unattended ⟨*car park*⟩

unbewaffnet *Adj.* unarmed

unbewältigt *Adj.* unmastered, uncompleted ⟨*task*⟩; unresolved ⟨*conflict, problem*⟩

unbeweglich *Adj.* (**a**) (bewegungslos) motionless; still ⟨*air, water*⟩; fixed ⟨*gaze, expression*⟩; (**b**) (starr) immovable, fixed ⟨*part, joint, etc.*⟩; (**c**) (nicht mobil) immobile; (**d**) (schwerfällig) (geistig) ponderous; (körperlich) slow-moving; slow on one's feet *pred.*

unbewiesen *Adj.* unproved

unbewohnbar *Adj.* uninhabitable; **ein Gebäude für** ∼ **erklären** declare a building unfit for human habitation

unbewohnt *Adj.* uninhabited ⟨*area*⟩; unoccupied ⟨*house, flat*⟩

unbewusst, *unbewußt **1** *Adj.* unconscious. **2** *adv.* unconsciously

unbezahlbar *Adj.* prohibitively expensive; priceless ⟨*painting, china*⟩; **meine Sekretärin ist einfach** ∼ (ugs.) my secretary is worth her weight in gold

unbezahlt *Adj.* unpaid; ⟨*goods etc.*⟩ not [yet] paid for

Unbilden /'ʊnbɪldn̩/ *Pl.* (geh.) rigours

unblutig **1** *Adj.* bloodless. **2** *adv.* without bloodshed

unbrauchbar *Adj.* unusable; (untauglich) useless ⟨*method, person*⟩

unbürokratisch **1** *Adj.* unbureaucratic; **auf möglichst** ∼**e Weise** with as little red tape as possible. **2** *adv.* unbureaucratically; without a great deal of red tape

und /ʊnt/ *Konj.* (**a**) (nebenordnend) and; (folglich) [and] so; **das deutsche** ∼ **das französische Volk** the German and French peoples; **zwei** ∼ **drei ist fünf** two and *or* plus three makes five; **es wollte** ∼ **wollte nicht gelingen** it simply *or* just wouldn't work; **hoch** ∼ **höher** higher and higher; ∼ **ich?** [and] what about me?; **der** ∼ **der** so-and-so; **zu der** ∼ **der Zeit** at such-and-such a time; **so** ∼ **so ist es gewesen** it was like this; *s. auch* **na a; ob b; wie 1 c;** (**b**) (unterordnend) (konsekutiv) **sei so gut** ∼ **mach das Fenster zu** be so good as to shut the window; **es fehlte nicht viel,** ∼ **der Deich wäre gebrochen** it wouldn't have taken much to breach the dike; (konzessiv) **du musst es tun,** ∼ **fällt es dir noch so schwer** you must do it however difficult you may find it

Undank *der* ingratitude; ∼ **ist der Welt Lohn** (Spr.) that's all the thanks you get

undankbar **1** *Adj.* (**a**) ungrateful ⟨*person, behaviour*⟩; (**b**) thankless ⟨*task*⟩; unrewarding ⟨*role, job, etc.*⟩. **2** *adv.* ungratefully

undefinierbar *Adj.* (**a**) indefinable; (**b**) (nicht bestimmbar) unidentifiable; indeterminable ⟨*feeling*⟩; indeterminate ⟨*colour*⟩

undenkbar *Adj.* unthinkable; inconceivable

undenklich *Adj. in* **vor** ∼**er Zeit** *od.* ∼**en Zeiten** an eternity ago; **seit** ∼**er Zeit** *od.* ∼**en Zeiten** since time immemorial

undeutlich **1** *Adj.* unclear; indistinct; (ungenau) vague ⟨*idea, memory, etc.*⟩. **2** *adv.* indistinctly; (ungenau) vaguely

undicht *Adj.* leaky; leaking; ∼ **werden** start to leak; develop a leak; **eine** ∼**e Stelle** (auch fig.) a leak; ∼**e Fenster** windows which do not fit tightly

Unding *das in* **ein** ∼ **sein** be preposterous *or* ridiculous

undiszipliniert **1** *Adj.* undisciplined; ⟨*pupils, class*⟩ lacking in discipline. **2** *adv.* in an undisciplined way

undogmatisch **1** *Adj.* undogmatic. **2** *adv.* undogmatically

unduldsam **1** *Adj.* intolerant. **2** *adv.*intolerantly

undurchdringlich *Adj.* impenetrable; pitch-dark ⟨*night*⟩

undurchlässig *Adj.* impermeable; (wasserdicht) watertight; waterproof; (luftdicht) airtight

undurchschaubar *Adj.* inscrutable ⟨*person, plan, etc.*⟩; unfathomable ⟨*cause, etc.*⟩; **für jmdn.** ∼ **sein** be baffling to sb.

undurchsichtig *Adj.* (**a**) opaque ⟨*glass*⟩; non-transparent ⟨*fabric etc.*⟩; (**b**) (fig.) unfathomable, inscrutable ⟨*plan, intention, role*⟩; shady ⟨*character, business*⟩

uneben *Adj.* uneven; (holprig) bumpy ⟨*road, track*⟩

unecht *Adj.* artificial ⟨*fur, hair*⟩; false ⟨*teeth*⟩; imitation ⟨*jewellery, marble, etc.*⟩; (gefälscht) counterfeit ⟨*notes*⟩; bogus, fake ⟨*painting*⟩; false, insincere ⟨*friendliness, sympathy, smile, etc.*⟩

unehelich *Adj.* illegitimate ⟨*child*⟩; ∼ **geboren sein** be born out of wedlock

unehrenhaft **1** *Adj.* dishonourable. **2** *adv.* dishonourably

unehrlich **1** *Adj.* dishonest. **2** *adv.* dishonestly; by dishonest means

Unehrlichkeit *die* dishonesty

uneigennützig **1** *Adj.* unselfish; selfless. **2** *adv.* unselfishly; selflessly

Uneigennützigkeit *die* unselfishness; selflessness

uneinig *Adj.* ⟨*party*⟩ divided by disagreement; [**sich** (*Dat.*)] ∼ **sein** disagree; be in disagreement

Uneinigkeit *die* disagreement (**in** + *Dat.* on)

uneins *Adj.; nicht attr.* ∼ **sein** be divided (**in** + *Dat.* on); ⟨*persons, bodies*⟩ be at variance *or* at cross purposes (**in** + *Dat.* over); **mit jmdm.** ∼ **sein[, wie ...]** be unable to agree with sb. [how ...]

unempfänglich *Adj.* unreceptive (**für** to)

unempfindlich *Adj.* (**a**) insensitive (**gegen** to); (**b**) (nicht anfällig, immun) immune (**gegen** to, against); (**c**) (strapazierfähig) hard-wearing; (pflegeleicht) easy-care *attrib.*

unendlich **1** *Adj.* infinite, boundless ⟨*space, sea, expanse, fig.*: *love, care, patience, etc.*⟩; (zeitlich) endless; never-ending; **das Unendliche** the infinite (Philos.); infinity (Math.); **auf „**∼**" stellen** (Fot.) focus ⟨*lens*⟩ on infinity. **2** *adv.* infinitely ⟨*lovable, sad*⟩; immeasurably ⟨*happy*⟩; **sich** ∼ **freuen** be tremendously pleased

Unendlichkeit *die;* ∼ (**a**) infinity *no def. art.;* (**b**) (geh.: Ewigkeit) eternity *no def. art.*

unentbehrlich *Adj.* indispensable (*Dat.,* **für** to)

unentgeltlich /*od.* '—-/ **1** *Adj.* free. **2** *adv.* free of charge; ⟨*work*⟩ for nothing, without pay

unentschieden **1** *Adj.* (**a**) unsettled ⟨*case, matter*⟩; undecided ⟨*question*⟩; (**b**) (Sport, Schach) drawn ⟨*game, match*⟩; (**c**) (unentschlossen) indecisive ⟨*person*⟩. **2** *adv.* (Sport, Schach) ∼ **spielen** draw; ∼ **enden** end in a draw; **das Spiel steht 0:0** ∼: the game is a goalless draw [so far]

Unentschieden *das;* ∼**s,** ∼ (Sport, Schach) draw

unentschlossen *Adj.* (**a**) undecided; (**b**) (entschlussunfähig) indecisive

unentschuldbar **1** *Adj.* inexcusable. **2** *adv.* inexcusably

---

unentschuldigt 1 *Adj.* without giving any reason *postpos., not pred.;* ~**es Fernbleiben vom Unterricht** absence from school. **2** *adv.* without giving any reason

unentwegt */od.* -ˈ-/ **1** *Adj.* **(a)** persistent ⟨*fighter, champion, efforts*⟩; **ein paar Unentwegte** a few stalwarts; **(b)** (unaufhörlich) constant; incessant. **2** *adv.* **(a)** persistently; **(b)** (unaufhörlich) constantly; incessantly

unerbittlich (auch fig.) **1** *Adj.* inexorable; unsparing, unrelenting ⟨*critic*⟩; relentless ⟨*battle, struggle*⟩; implacable ⟨*hate, enemy*⟩; **gegen jmdn.** ~ **sein** be completely unyielding towards sb. **2** *adv.* inexorably; relentlessly; ~ **durchgreifen** take uncompromising action

unerfahren *Adj.* inexperienced

unerfindlich *Adj.* (geh.) unfathomable; inexplicable

unerfreulich 1 *Adj.* unpleasant; bad ⟨*news*⟩. **2** *adv.* unpleasantly

unerfüllbar *Adj.* unrealizable

unergiebig *Adj.* (auch fig.) unproductive; (fig.: nicht lohnend) unrewarding ⟨*work, subject*⟩

unergründlich *Adj.* unfathomable, inscrutable ⟨*motive, mystery, etc.*⟩; inscrutable ⟨*expression, smile*⟩

unerheblich 1 *Adj.* insignificant. **2** *adv.* insignificantly; [very] slightly

unerhört 1 *Adj.* **(a)** enormous, tremendous ⟨*sum, quantity, etc.*⟩; incredible (coll.), phenomenal ⟨*speed, effort, performance, increase*⟩; incredible (coll.), fantastic (coll.) ⟨*splendour, luck*⟩; **(b)** (empörend) outrageous; scandalous. **2** *adv.* **(a)** (überaus) incredibly (coll.); **(b)** (empörend) outrageously

unerkannt *Adj.* unrecognized; (nicht identifiziert) unidentified

unerklärlich *Adj.* inexplicable

unerlässlich, *unerläßlich /ʊn|ɛpˈlɛslɪç/ *Adj.* indispensable; essential

unerlaubt 1 *Adj.* ⟨*entry, parking, absenteeism*⟩ without permission; unauthorized ⟨*parking, entry*⟩; (illegal) illegal. **2** *adv.* without authorization *or* permission; (illegal) illegally

unerledigt *Adj.* not dealt with *postpos.;* ⟨*work*⟩ not done; unanswered ⟨*mail, letters*⟩; unprocessed ⟨*application*⟩

unermesslich, *unermeßlich 1 *Adj.* (geh.) immeasurable ⟨*expanse, distance*⟩; boundless ⟨*spaces*⟩; immeasurable, immense ⟨*wealth, fortune*⟩; untold ⟨*suffering, misery, damage*⟩; inestimable ⟨*value, importance*⟩. **2** *adv.* immeasurably ⟨*rich*⟩ beyond measure

unermüdlich 1 *Adj.* tireless; untiring. **2** *adv.* tirelessly

unerreichbar 1 *Adj.* **(a)** inaccessible; **in** ~**er Ferne** *od.* **Entfernung** so distant as to be beyond reach; **sie ist für ihn** ~ (fig.) she is beyond his reach; **(b)** (nicht kontaktierbar) unobtainable; **(c)** (fig.) unattainable ⟨*aim, ideal, accuracy, etc.*⟩. **2** *adv.* **(a)** (räumlich) inaccessibly; **(b)** (fig.) unattainably

unerreicht *Adj.* unequalled ⟨*record, achievement*⟩; ~ **bleiben** remain unequalled; ⟨*goal*⟩ not be attained

unersättlich *Adj.* insatiable

unerschöpflich *Adj.* inexhaustible

unerschrocken 1 *Adj.* intrepid; fearless. **2** *adv.* intrepidly; fearlessly

unerschütterlich 1 *Adj.* unshakeable; imperturbable ⟨*calm, equanimity*⟩. **2** *adv.* unshakeably

unerschwinglich *Adj.* prohibitively expensive

unersetzlich *Adj.* irreplaceable; irretrievable, irrecoverable ⟨*loss*⟩; irreparable ⟨*harm, damage, loss of person*⟩

unersprießlich *Adj.* (geh.) unprofitable; unproductive

unerträglich */od.* -ˈ--ˈ-/ **1** *Adj.* unbearable ⟨*pain, heat, person, etc.*⟩; intolerable ⟨*situation, conditions, moods, etc.*⟩. **2** *adv.* unbearably

unerwartet 1 *Adj.* unexpected; **es kam für alle** ~: it came as a surprise to everybody. **2** *adv.* unexpectedly

unerwünscht *Adj.* unwanted; unwelcome ⟨*interruption, visit, visitor*⟩; undesirable ⟨*side effects*⟩; **Sie sind hier** ~: you are not wanted *or* welcome here

unfähig *Adj.* **(a)** ~ **sein, etw. zu tun** (ständig) be incapable of doing sth.; (momentan) be unable to do sth.; **(b)** (abwertend) incompetent

Unfähigkeit *die* **(a)** inability; **(b)** (abwertend) incompetence

unfair 1 *Adj.* unfair ⟨**gegen** to⟩. **2** *adv.* unfairly

Unfall *der* accident; **bei einem** ~: in an accident

unfall-, Unfall-: ~**arzt** *der* casualty doctor; ~**flucht** *die* (Rechtsspr.) ~**flucht begehen** fail to stop after [being involved in] an accident; ~**folge** *die* consequence *or* effect of an/the accident; **er starb an den** ~**folgen** he died as a result of the accident; ~**frei 1** *Adj.* accident-free; free from accidents *postpos.;* **2** *adv.* without an accident; ~**station** *die* accident *or* casualty department; ~**stelle** *die* scene of an/the accident; ~**versicherung** *die* accident insurance; ~**wagen** *der* **(a)** (Krankenwagen) ambulance; **(b)** (beschädigter Wagen) car [that has been] damaged in an/the accident

unfassbar, *unfaßbar 1 *Adj.* incomprehensible; (unglaublich) incredible, unimaginable ⟨*poverty, cruelty, etc.*⟩. **2** *adv.* incomprehensibly; (unglaublich) incredibly; unimaginably

unfehlbar *Adj.* infallible

Unfehlbarkeit *die;* ~: infallibility

unfein 1 *Adj.* ill-mannered, unrefined ⟨*behaviour etc.*⟩; unrefined, coarse ⟨*manner, word*⟩; bad ⟨*manners*⟩. **2** *adv.* ⟨*behave*⟩ badly, in an ill-mannered way

unfertig *Adj.* **(a)** unfinished ⟨*manuscript, article, etc.*⟩; **(b)** (fig.: unreif) immature

unflätig /ˈʊnflɛ:tɪç/ (geh. abwertend) **1** *Adj.* coarse ⟨*behaviour, manners, speech, etc.*⟩; obscene ⟨*expression, word, curse*⟩; dirty ⟨*song*⟩. **2** *adv.* coarsely; obscenely

unförmig *Adj.* shapeless ⟨*lump, shadow, etc.*⟩; huge ⟨*legs, hands, body*⟩; bulky, ungainly ⟨*shape, shoes, etc.*⟩

unfrei *Adj.* not free *pred.;* subject, dependent ⟨*people*⟩

Unfreiheit *die; o. Pl.* slavery *no art.;* bondage (esp. Hist./literary) *no art.;* **ein Leben in** ~: a life of bondage *or* without freedom

unfreiwillig 1 *Adj.* involuntary; (erzwungen) enforced ⟨*stay*⟩; (nicht beabsichtigt) unintended ⟨*joke, humour*⟩. **2** *adv.* involuntarily; without wanting to; (unbeabsichtigt) unintentionally

unfreundlich 1 *Adj.* **(a)** unfriendly ⟨**zu, gegen** to⟩; unkind ⟨*words, remark*⟩; **(b)** (fig.) unpleasant; cheerless ⟨*room*⟩. **2** *adv.* in an unfriendly way

Unfreundlichkeit *die* **(a)** *o. Pl.* unfriendliness; **(b)** (Handlung) unfriendly act; (Äußerung) unkind remark

Unfriede[n] *der* discord; **in** ~ **leben/auseinander gehen** live in a state of strife/part in hostility

unfrisiert *Adj.* ungroomed ⟨*hair*⟩; **sie war** ~: she had not done her hair

unfruchtbar *Adj.* **(a)** infertile ⟨*soil, field, land*⟩; **(b)** (Biol.) infertile; sterile

Unfruchtbarkeit *die* **(a)** infertility; **(b)** (Biol.) infertility; sterility

Unfug /ˈʊnfu:k/ *der;* ~**[e]s (a)** [piece of] mischief; **allerlei** ~ **anstellen** get up to all kinds of mischief *or* (coll.) monkey business; **grober** ~: public nuisance; **(b)** (Unsinn) nonsense

Ungar /ˈʊngar/ *der;* ~**n**, ~**n, Ungarin** *die;* ~, ~**nen** ▶388▎ Hungarian

ungarisch ▶388▎, ▶487▎ **1** *Adj.* Hungarian. **2** *adv.* in Hungarian

Ungarisch *das;* ~**[s]** ▶487▎ Hungarian

Ungarn *(das);* ~**s** Hungary

ungastlich 1 *Adj.* inhospitable. **2** *adv.* inhospitably

ungeachtet *Präp. mit Gen.* (geh.) notwithstanding; despite; ~ **dessen** nevertheless; notwithstanding [this]

ungeahnt 1 *Adj.* unsuspected; (stärker) undreamt-of *attrib.* **2** *adv.* unexpectedly

ungebeten *Adj.* uninvited

ungebildet *Adj.* uneducated

ungeboren *Adj.* unborn

ungebräuchlich *Adj.* uncommon; rare; rarely used ⟨*method*⟩

ungebührlich (geh.) **1** *Adj.* improper, unseemly ⟨*behaviour*⟩; unreasonable ⟨*demand*⟩. **2** *adv.* ⟨*behave*⟩ improperly; unreasonably ⟨*high, long, etc.*⟩

ungedeckt *Adj.* **(a)** uncovered ⟨*cheque, bill of exchange, etc.*⟩; **(b)** unlaid ⟨*table*⟩; **(c)** (ungeschützt) unprotected; **(d)** (Ballspiele) unmarked ⟨*player*⟩

Ungeduld *die* impatience

ungeduldig 1 *Adj.* impatient. **2** *adv.* impatiently

ungeeignet *Adj.* unsuitable; (für eine Aufgabe, Stellung) unsuited

ungefähr /'ʊngəfɛːɐ̯/ **1** *Adj.; nicht präd.* approximate; rough ⟨*idea, outline*⟩. **2** *Adv.* **(a)** approximately; roughly; ∼ 100 about *or* roughly 100; **so** ∼ (ugs.) more or less; **wo** ∼ ...? whereabouts ...?; **(b)** [**wie**] **von** ∼: [as if] by chance; **es kommt nicht von** ∼[, **dass** ...] it's no accident [that ...]

ungefährlich 1 *Adj.* safe; harmless ⟨*animal, person, illness, etc.*⟩; **nicht** ∼ **sein** be not without danger. **2** *adv.* safely

ungefragt *Adj.; nicht attr.* unasked

ungehalten (geh.) **1** *Adj.* annoyed (**über** + *Akk.*, **wegen** about); (entrüstet) indignant. **2** *adv.* indignantly; ⟨*reply, say*⟩ in an aggrieved tone

ungeheizt *Adj.* unheated

ungeheuer 1 *Adj.* enormous; immense; tremendous ⟨*strength, energy, effort, enthusiasm, fear, success, pressure, etc.*⟩; vast, immense ⟨*fortune, knowledge*⟩; terrible (coll.), terrific (coll.) ⟨*pain, rage*⟩. **2** *adv.* tremendously; terribly (coll.) ⟨*difficult, clever*⟩

Ungeheuer *das;* ∼**s,** ∼ (auch fig.) monster

ungeheuerlich 1 *Adj.* monstrous; outrageous. **2** *adv.* (ugs.) terribly (coll.)

Ungeheuerlichkeit *die;* ∼, ∼**en (a)** *o. Pl.* monstrous nature; outrageousness; **(b)** (Vorgang) monstrous *or* outrageous thing

ungehindert *Adj.* unimpeded

ungehobelt *Adj.* (fig.) uncouth

ungehörig 1 *Adj.* improper ⟨*behaviour*⟩; (frech) impertinent ⟨*tone, answer*⟩. **2** *adv.* improperly; (frech) impertinently

ungehorsam *Adj.* disobedient

Ungehorsam *der* disobedience

ungekämmt *Adj.* uncombed

ungeklärt *Adj.* unsolved ⟨*question, problem*⟩; unknown ⟨*cause*⟩

ungekrönt *Adj.* (auch fig.) uncrowned

ungekündigt *Adj.* **in** ∼**er Stellung** not under notice *postpos.*

ungekünstelt 1 *Adj.* natural; unaffected. **2** *adv.* naturally; unaffectedly

ungekürzt *Adj.* unabridged ⟨*edition, book*⟩; uncut ⟨*film, speech*⟩

ungeladen *Adj.* **(a)** unloaded ⟨*gun, camera*⟩; **(b)** uninvited ⟨*guest*⟩

ungelegen *Adj.* inconvenient, awkward ⟨*time*⟩; **das kommt mir sehr** ∼/**nicht** ∼: that is very inconvenient *or* awkward/quite convenient for me

Ungelegenheit *die* inconvenience; **jmdm. große** ∼**en machen** *od.* **bereiten** inconvenience sb. greatly

ungelernt *Adj.* unskilled

ungeliebt *Adj.* unloved; (verhüll.: verhasst) hateful, odious ⟨*task*⟩; odious ⟨*school etc.*⟩

ungelogen *Adv.* (ugs.) honestly

ungemein 1 *Adj.; nicht präd.* exceptional ⟨*progress, popularity*⟩; tremendous ⟨*advantage, pleasure*⟩. **2** *adv.* exceptionally; **das freut mich** ∼: that pleases me no end (coll.)

ungemütlich 1 *Adj.* **(a)** uninviting, cheerless ⟨*room, flat*⟩; uncomfortable, unfriendly ⟨*atmosphere*⟩; **(b)** (unangenehm) unpleasant ⟨*situation*⟩; **es wird jetzt** ∼: things are getting nasty. **2** *adv.* uncomfortably ⟨*furnished*⟩

*alte Schreibung (vgl. Hinweise auf S. xvi–xvii)

ungenannt *Adj.* anonymous; **ein Ungenannter** an anonymous person

ungenau 1 *Adj.* inaccurate ⟨*measurement, estimate, thermometer, translation, etc.*⟩; imprecise, inexact ⟨*definition, formulation, etc.*⟩; (undeutlich) vague ⟨*memory, idea, impression*⟩. **2** *adv.* **(a)** inaccurately; ⟨*define*⟩ imprecisely, inexactly; ⟨*remember*⟩ vaguely; **(b)** (nicht sorgfältig) ⟨*work*⟩ carelessly

Ungenauigkeit *die* inaccuracy; (einer Definition) imprecision; inexactness

ungeniert /'ʊnʒeniːɐ̯t/ **1** *Adj.* free and easy; uninhibited; **er war ganz** ∼: he was not at all embarrassed *or* concerned. **2** *adv.* openly; ⟨*yawn*⟩ unconcernedly; (ohne Scham) ⟨*undress etc.*⟩ without any embarrassment

ungenießbar *Adj.* **(a)** (nicht essbar) inedible; (nicht trinkbar) undrinkable; **(b)** (fig. ugs.) unbearable ⟨*person*⟩; **er ist heute** ∼: he's in a foul mood today (coll.)

ungenügend 1 *Adj.* inadequate; **die Note „**∼**"** (Schulw.) the 'unsatisfactory' [mark]. **2** *adv.* inadequately

ungepflegt *Adj.* neglected ⟨*garden, park, car, etc.*⟩; unkempt ⟨*person, appearance, hair*⟩; uncared-for ⟨*hands*⟩

ungerade *Adj.* odd ⟨*number*⟩

ungerecht 1 *Adj.* unjust, unfair. **2** *adv.* unjustly; unfairly

ungerechtfertigt *Adj.* unjustified; unwarranted

Ungerechtigkeit *die;* ∼, ∼**en** injustice

ungeregelt *Adj.* irregular; disorganized

ungereimt *Adj.* (fig.) inconsistent; illogical; (ugs. abwertend: verworren) muddled

Ungereimtheit *die;* ∼, ∼**en** (Unstimmigkeit) inconsistency; (ugs. abwertend: Unsinnigkeit, Verworrenheit) muddle

ungern *Adv.* reluctantly; **etw.** ∼ **tun** not like *or* dislike doing sth.

ungerührt *Adj.* unmoved

ungesättigt *Adj.* (Chemie) unsaturated; **mehrfach** ∼: polyunsaturated

ungeschält *Adj.* unpeeled ⟨*fruit*⟩; ∼**er Reis** paddy rice

ungeschehen *Adj.* **in etw.** ∼ **machen** undo sth.

Ungeschicklichkeit *die* clumsiness; ineptitude

ungeschickt 1 *Adj.* clumsy; awkward ⟨*movement, formulation, etc.*⟩. **2** *adv.* clumsily; ⟨*bow, express oneself, etc.*⟩ awkwardly; **sich** ∼ **anstellen** show a lack of skill; show oneself to be inept

ungeschminkt *Adj.* **(a)** not made-up *pred.;* without make-up *postpos.;* **(b)** (fig.) unvarnished ⟨*truth*⟩; uncoloured ⟨*account*⟩

ungeschoren *Adj.* **(a)** unshorn; **(b)** ∼ **bleiben** (fig.) be left in peace; be spared

ungeschützt *Adj.* unprotected; (Wind und Wetter ausgesetzt) exposed

ungesehen *Adj.; nicht attr.* unseen

ungesetzlich 1 *Adj.* unlawful; illegal. **2** *adv.* unlawfully; illegally

ungestalt *Adj.* **(a)** (geh.) shapeless; **(b)** (veralt.: missgestaltet) misshapen

ungestempelt *Adj.* unstamped ⟨*licence etc.*⟩; uncancelled ⟨*stamp*⟩

ungestört *Adj.* undisturbed; uninterrupted ⟨*development*⟩; ∼ **arbeiten** work in peace *or* without interruption

ungestraft 1 *Adj.; nicht attr.* unpunished. **2** *adv.* with impunity

ungestüm /'ʊngəʃtyːm/ (geh.) **1** *Adj.* impetuous, tempestuous ⟨*person, embrace, nature, etc.*⟩. **2** *adv.* impetuously

ungesund 1 *Adj.* (auch fig.) unhealthy; (fig.: übermäßig) excessive ⟨*ambition, activity*⟩; **Rauchen ist** ∼: smoking is bad for you *or* for your health. **2** *adv.* unhealthily; ∼ **leben** lead an unhealthy life

ungesüßt /'ʊngəzyːst/ *Adj.* unsweetened

ungetan *Adj.* still to be done *postpos.;* **etw.** ∼ **lassen** leave sth. undone

ungeteilt *Adj.* **(a)** undivided; **(b)** (fig.) unrestricted, absolute ‹*power*›; undivided ‹*attention, interest*›; (einmütig) unanimous; universal ‹*approval, agreement, etc.*›

ungetrübt *Adj.* unclouded, perfect ‹*happiness*›; unalloyed ‹*pleasure*›; unspoilt, perfect ‹*days, relationship*›

Ungetüm /'ʊngəty:m/ *das;* ~s, ~e monster

ungeübt *Adj.* unpractised ‹*hand*›; **in etw.** ~ **sein** lack practice in sth.

ungewiss, *ungewiß *Adj.* uncertain; **jmdn. [über etw. (***Akk.***)] im Ungewissen lassen** leave sb. in the dark *or* keep sb. guessing [about sth.]

Ungewissheit, *Ungewißheit *die* uncertainty

ungewöhnlich 1 *Adj.* **(a)** unusual; **(b)** (enorm) exceptional ‹*strength, beauty, ability, etc.*›; outstanding ‹*achievement, success*›. **2** *adv.* **(a)** (unüblich) ‹*behave*› abnormally, strangely; **(b)** (enorm) exceptionally

ungewohnt 1 *Adj.* unaccustomed; unfamiliar ‹*method, work, surroundings, etc.*›. **2** *adv.* unusually

ungewollt 1 *Adj.* unwanted; (unbeabsichtigt) unintentional; inadvertent. **2** *adv.* unintentionally; inadvertently

Ungeziefer /'ʊngətsi:fɐ/ *das;* ~s vermin *pl.*

ungezogen 1 *Adj.* naughty; badly behaved; bad ‹*behaviour*›; (frech) cheeky. **2** *adv.* naughtily; ‹*behave*› badly

ungezwungen 1 *Adj.* natural, unaffected ‹*person, behaviour, cheerfulness*›; informal, free and easy ‹*tone, conversation, etc.*›. **2** *adv.* ‹*behave*› naturally, unaffectedly; ‹*talk*› freely

Ungezwungenheit *die;* ~ ⇒ **ungezwungen 1**: naturalness; unaffectedness; informality

ungiftig *Adj.* non-poisonous; non-toxic ‹*gas, substance*›

Unglaube[n] *der* **(a)** disbelief; incredulity; **(b)** (Rel.) unbelief

ungläubig 1 *Adj.* **(a)** disbelieving; incredulous; **(b)** (Rel.) unbelieving. **2** *adv.* incredulously; in disbelief

Ungläubige *der/die* (Rel.) unbeliever

unglaublich 1 *Adj.* **(a)** incredible; **(b)** (ugs.: sehr groß) incredible (coll.), fantastic (coll.) ‹*speed, amount, luck, etc.*›. **2** *adv.* (ugs.: äußerst) incredibly (coll.)

unglaubwürdig *Adj.* implausible; untrustworthy, unreliable ‹*witness etc.*›

ungleich 1 *Adj.* unequal; odd, unmatching ‹*socks, gloves, etc.*›; odd ‹*couple*›. **2** *adv.* **(a)** unequally; **(b)** (ungleichmäßig) unevenly. **3** *Adv.* far ‹*larger, more difficult, etc.*›

Ungleichgewicht *das* imbalance

ungleichmäßig 1 *Adj.* uneven. **2** *adv.* unevenly

Unglück *das;* ~[e]s, ~e **(a)** (Unfall) accident; (Flugzeug~, Zug~) crash; accident, (Missgeschick) mishap; **das ist [doch] kein** ~**!** that's not a disaster; it doesn't really matter; **(b)** *o. Pl.* (Not) misfortune; (Leid) suffering; distress; **sich ins** ~ **stürzen, in sein** ~ **rennen** rush headlong into disaster *or* to one's ruin; **(c)** (Pech) bad luck; misfortune; **das bringt** ~**:** that's unlucky; **zu allem** ~**:** to make matters worse; **ein** ~ **kommt selten allein** (ugs.) it never rains but it pours

unglücklich 1 *Adj.* **(a)** unhappy; **mach dich nicht** ~**!** don't do it!; **(b)** (nicht vom Glück begünstigt) unfortunate ‹*person*›; (bedauernswert) hapless ‹*person, animal*›; **(c)** (ungünstig) unfortunate ‹*moment, combination, meeting, etc.*›; unhappy ‹*end, choice*›; unfortunate, unhappy ‹*coincidence, formulation*›. **2** *adv.* **(a)** unhappily; ~ **verliebt sein** be unhappy in love; **(b)** (ungünstig) unfortunately; (ungeschickt) unhappily, clumsily ‹*translated, expressed*›

unglücklicherweise *Adv.* unfortunately

Unglücks-: ~**fall** *der* accident; ~**zahl** *die* unlucky number

Ungnade *die* **in [bei jmdm.] in** ~ (*Akk.*) **fallen/in** ~ (*Dat.*) **sein** fall/be out of favour [with sb.]

ungnädig 1 *Adj.* bad-tempered; grumpy. **2** *adv.* in a bad-tempered way; grumpily

ungültig *Adj.* invalid; void (esp. Law); spoilt ‹*vote, ballot paper*›

ungünstig 1 *Adj.* **(a)** unfavourable; unfavourable, poor ‹*climate, weather*›; (unglücklich) unfortunate ‹*consequence*›;

unfortunate, bad ‹*shape, layout*›; (unvorteilhaft) unfavourable, unflattering ‹*light, perspective, impression*›; unflattering ‹*cut of dress*›; inconvenient ‹*position*›; (schädlich) harmful ‹*effect*›; **(b)** (unpassend) inconvenient ‹*time*›; (ungeeignet) inappropriate, inconvenient ‹*time, place*›; unsuitable ‹*colour etc.*›. **2** *adv.* **(a)** unfavourably; badly ‹*designed, laid out*›; (unvorteilhaft) unflatteringly ‹*cut*›; **sich** ~ **auswirken** have a harmful effect; **(b)** (unpassend, ungeeignet) inconveniently

ungut *Adj.* **(a)** uneasy ‹*feeling, premonition*›; unpleasant ‹*after-taste, recollection, memories*›; **(b) nichts für** ~**!** no offence [meant]! (coll.)

unhaltbar *Adj.* **(a)** untenable ‹*thesis, statement, etc.*›; **(b)** (unerträglich) unbearable, intolerable ‹*conditions, situation*›; **(c)** (Ballspiele) unstoppable

unhandlich *Adj.* unwieldy

Unheil *das* disaster; ~ **anrichten** *od.* **stiften** wreak havoc

unheilbar 1 *Adj.* incurable. **2** *adv.* incurably

unheil·voll *Adj.* disastrous; (verhängnisvoll) fateful; ominous ‹*development*›

unheimlich 1 *Adj.* **(a)** eerie ‹*story, figure, place, sound*›; eerie, uncanny ‹*feeling*›; **jmdm.** ~ **sein** give sb. an eerie feeling *or* (coll.) the creeps; **mir ist/wird [es]** ~**:** I have an eerie *or* uncanny feeling; **(b)** (ugs.) (schrecklich) terrible (coll.) ‹*coward, idiot, hunger, headache, etc.*›; terrific (coll.) ‹*fun, sum, etc.*›. **2** *adv.* **(a)** eerily; uncannily; **(b)** (ugs.) terribly (coll.) ‹*fat, nice, etc.*›; terrifically (coll.) ‹*important, large*›; incredibly (coll.) ‹*quick, long*›

unhöflich 1 *Adj.* impolite. **2** *adv.* impolitely

Unhöflichkeit *die* impoliteness

Unhold *der;* ~[e]s, ~e **(a)** fiend; demon; **(b)** (abwertend: böser Mensch) monster

unhygienisch 1 *Adj.* unhygienic. **2** *adv.* unhygienically

uni /y'ni:, 'yni/ *indekl. Adj.* plain, single-colour ‹*material etc.*›; plain ‹*tie*›

Uni /'ʊni/ *die;* ~, ~s (ugs.) university

Uniform /'ʊnifɔrm/ *die;* ~, ~en uniform

Unikum /'u:nikʊm/ *das;* ~s, **Unika** *od.* ~s (ugs.: Original) [real] character

uninteressant *Adj.* **(a)** uninteresting; (nicht von Belang) of no interest *postpos.;* unimportant; **nicht** ~**:** quite interesting; **(b)** (nicht lohnend, nicht attraktiv) untempting, unattractive ‹*offer*›

uninteressiert *Adj.* uninterested; not interested (an + *Dat.* in)

Union /u'nio:n/ *die;* ~, ~en union

universell /univɛr'zɛl/ **1** *Adj.* universal. **2** *adv.* universally

Universität /univɛrzi'tɛ:t/ *die;* ~, ~en university

Universitäts-: ~**klinik** *die* university hospital; ~**stadt** *die* university town; ~**studium** *das* study *no art.* at university

Universum /uni'vɛrzʊm/ *das;* ~s universe

Unke /'ʊŋkə/ *die;* ~, ~n **(a)** fire-bellied toad; **(b)** (ugs. abwertend: Schwarzseher[in]) Jeremiah; prophet of doom

unken /'ʊŋkn̩/ *itr. V.* (ugs.) prophesy doom [and destruction] (joc.)

unkenntlich *Adj.* unrecognizable ‹*person, face*›; indecipherable ‹*writing, stamp*›

Unkenntnis *die; o. Pl.* ignorance

unkeusch (geh.) **1** *Adj.* unchaste. **2** *adv.* unchastely

Unkeuschheit *die* unchastity *no art.*

unklar *Adj.* **(a)** (undeutlich) unclear; indistinct; (fig.: unbestimmt) vague ‹*feeling, recollection, idea*›; **(b)** (nicht klar verständlich) unclear; **(c)** (nicht durchschaubar) unclear ‹*origin, situation, etc.*›; (ungewiss) uncertain ‹*outcome*›; **sich** (*Dat.*) **über etw.** (*Akk.*) **im Unklaren sein** be unclear *or* unsure about sth.; **jmdn. über etw.** (*Akk.*) **im Unklaren lassen** keep sb. guessing about sth.

Unklarheit *die* **(a)** *o. Pl.* (Undeutlichkeit) lack of clarity; indistinctness; (Unverständlichkeit) lack of clarity (*Gen.* in); (Ungewissheit) uncertainty; **(b)** (unklarer Punkt) unclear point

unklug 1 *Adj.* unwise. **2** *adv.* unwisely

unkollegial *Adj.* inconsiderate *or* unhelpful [to one's colleagues]

unkompliziert 1 *Adj.* uncomplicated, straightforward ⟨*person, mechanism, etc.*⟩. **2** *adv.* ⟨*express*⟩ straightforwardly, simply

unkontrollierbar *Adj.* impossible to check *or* supervise *postpos.;* (nicht zu beherrschen) uncontrollable

unkontrolliert *Adj.* **(a)** unsupervised; **(b)** (unbeherrscht) uncontrolled ⟨*emotions, outburst*⟩

unkonventionell 1 *Adj.* unconventional. **2** *adv.* unconventionally

unkonzentriert *Adj.* lacking in concentration *postpos.*

Unkosten *Pl.* **(a)** [extra] expense *sing.;* expenses; **sich in ∼ stürzen** dig deep into one's pocket; **(b)** (Kosten) costs; expenditure *sing.*

Unkraut *das o. Pl.* weeds *pl.;* **∼ vergeht nicht** (ugs. scherzh.) it would take a great deal to finish off his/her/our sort (coll.)

unkritisch 1 *Adj.* uncritical. **2** *adv.* uncritically

unkultiviert *Adj.* uncultivated

unkündbar *Adj.* permanent; **er ist ∼:** he cannot be given notice

unkundig *Adj.* (geh.) ignorant; **des Lesens/Schreibens/Deutschen ∼:** unable to read/to write/to speak German

unlängst *Adv.* (geh.) not long ago; recently

unlauter *Adj.* (geh.) dishonest; **∼er Wettbewerb** (Rechtsspr.) unfair competition

unleidlich 1 *Adj.* tetchy. **2** *adv.* tetchily

unleserlich 1 *Adj.* illegible. **2** *adv.* illegibly

unleugbar 1 *Adj.* undeniable; indisputable. **2** *adv.* undeniably; indisputably

unliebsam 1 *Adj.* unpleasant. **2** *adv.* **er ist ∼ aufgefallen** he made a bad impression

unlogisch 1 *Adj.* illogical. **2** *adv.* illogically

Unlust *die* (Widerwille) reluctance; (Lustlosigkeit) lack of enthusiasm

unmaßgeblich *Adj.* of no consequence *postpos.;* inconsequenzial

unmäßig 1 *Adj.* **(a)** immoderate; excessive; **(b)** (enorm) tremendous ⟨*desire, thirst, fear, etc.*⟩. **2** *adv.* **(a)** excessively; ⟨*eat, drink*⟩ to excess; **(b)** (sehr) tremendously (coll.)

Unmenge *die* mass; enormous number/amount

Unmensch *der* brute; **man ist ja kein ∼** (ugs.) I'm not inhuman

unmenschlich 1 *Adj.* **(a)** inhuman; brutal; subhuman, appalling ⟨*conditions*⟩; **(b)** (entsetzlich) terrible (coll.), appalling ⟨*pain, heat, suffering, etc.*⟩. **2** *adv.* **(a)** in an inhuman way; **(b)** (entsetzlich) appallingly (coll.)

unmerklich 1 *Adj.* imperceptible. **2** *adv.* imperceptibly

unmissverständlich, *unmißverständlich 1 *Adj.* **(a)** (eindeutig) unambiguous; **(b)** (offen, direkt) blunt ⟨*answer, refusal*⟩; unequivocal ⟨*language*⟩. **2** *adv.* **(a)** (eindeutig) unambiguously; **(b)** (offen, direkt) bluntly; unequivocally

unmittelbar 1 *Adj.* **(a)** *nicht präd.* immediate ⟨*vicinity, past, future*⟩; **aus ∼er Nähe schießen** shoot at close quarters *or* from point-blank range; **(b)** (direkt) direct ⟨*contact, connection, influence, etc.*⟩; immediate ⟨*cause, consequence, predecessor, successor*⟩. **2** *adv.* **(a)** immediately; right ⟨*behind, next to*⟩; **∼ bevorstehen** be imminent; be almost upon us *etc.;* **(b)** (direkt) directly

unmöbliert *Adj.* unfurnished

unmodern 1 *Adj.* old-fashioned; (nicht modisch) unfashionable. **2** *adv.* in an old-fashioned way; (nicht modisch) unfashionably

unmöglich 1 *Adj.* **(a)** impossible; **ich verlange ja nichts Unmögliches [von dir]** I'm not asking [you] for the impossible; **(b)** (ugs.: nicht akzeptabel, unangebracht) impossible ⟨*person, behaviour, colour, ideas, place, etc.*⟩; **sich ∼ machen** make a fool of oneself; make oneself look ridiculous; **(c)** (ugs.: erstaunlich, seltsam) incredible. **2** *adv.* (ugs.)

*alte Schreibung (vgl. Hinweise auf S. xvi–xvii)

⟨*behave*⟩ impossibly; ⟨*dress*⟩ ridiculously. **3** *Adv.* (ugs.: unter keinen Umständen) **ich/es** *usw.* **kann ∼ …:** I/it *etc.* can't possibly …

Unmoral *die* immorality *no art.*

unmoralisch 1 *Adj.* immoral. **2** *adv.* immorally

unmotiviert 1 *Adj.* unmotivated. **2** *adv.* without reason; for no reason

unmündig *Adj.* **(a)** under-age; **∼ sein** be under age *or* a minor; **(b)** (fig.) dependent

unmusikalisch *Adj.* unmusical

Unmut *der* (geh.) displeasure; annoyance; **seinen ∼ an jmdm. auslassen** take it out on sb.

unnachahmlich 1 *Adj.* inimitable. **2** *adv.* inimitably

unnachgiebig *Adj.* intransigent

unnachsichtig 1 *Adj.* merciless; unmerciful; unrelenting ⟨*severity*⟩. **2** *adv.* mercilessly; ⟨*punish*⟩ unmercifully

unnahbar *Adj.* unapproachable

unnatürlich 1 *Adj.* unnatural; forced ⟨*laugh*⟩. **2** *adv.* unnaturally; ⟨*laugh*⟩ in a forced way; ⟨*speak*⟩ affectedly

unnormal 1 *Adj.* abnormal. **2** *adv.* abnormally

unnötig 1 *Adj.* unnecessary; needless, pointless ⟨*heroism*⟩. **2** *adv.* unnecessarily

unnütz 1 *Adj.* useless ⟨*stuff, person, etc.*⟩; pointless ⟨*talk*⟩; wasted ⟨*words*⟩; pointless, wasted ⟨*expense, effort*⟩; vain ⟨*attempt*⟩. **2** *adv.* needlessly

UNO /ˈuːno/ *die:* **die ∼:** the UN

unordentlich 1 *Adj.* untidy. **2** *adv.* untidily; ⟨*tie, treat, etc.*⟩ carelessly

Unordnung *die* disorder; mess

unorthodox 1 *Adj.* unorthodox. **2** *adv.* in an unorthodox way

unparteiisch 1 *Adj.* impartial. **2** *adv.* impartially

Unparteiische *der/die; adj. Dekl.* (Sport) ⇒ **Schiedsrichter a**

unpassend 1 *Adj.* inappropriate; unsuitable ⟨*dress etc.*⟩. **2** *adv.* inappropriately; unsuitably ⟨*dressed etc.*⟩

unpassierbar *Adj.* impassable

unpässlich, *unpäßlich /ˈʊnpɛslɪç/ *Adj.* indisposed

Unpässlichkeit, *Unpäßlichkeit *die; ∼, ∼en* indisposition

Unperson *die* unperson

unpersönlich 1 *Adj.* impersonal; distant, aloof ⟨*person*⟩. **2** *adv.* impersonally; ⟨*answer, write*⟩ in impersonal terms

Unpersönlichkeit *die; o. Pl.* impersonal nature

unpolitisch *Adj.* unpolitical; apolitical

unpopulär *Adj.* unpopular

unpraktisch 1 *Adj.* unpractical. **2** *adv.* in an unpractical way

unproblematisch 1 *Adj.* unproblematic; straightforward; **nicht ganz ∼:** not without its problems. **2** *adv.* without any problems

unpünktlich 1 *Adj.* **(a)** unpunctual ⟨*person*⟩; **(b)** (verspätet) late, unpunctual ⟨*payment*⟩. **2** *adv.* late

Unpünktlichkeit *die* lack of punctuality

unrasiert *Adj.* unshaven

Unrast *die; o. Pl.* (geh.) restlessness

Unrat *der; ∼[e]s* (geh.) garbage (lit. or fig.); refuse (Brit.); **∼ wittern** smell a rat (fig.)

unrealistisch 1 *Adj.* unrealistic. **2** *adv.* unrealistically

unrecht 1 *Adj.* wrong; **auf ∼e Gedanken kommen** get wicked ideas. **2** *adv.* wrongly; **∼ tun** do wrong: *s. auch* **Unrecht a**

Unrecht *das; o. Pl.* **(a)** **∼ haben** be wrong; **jmdm. [ein] ∼ tun** do sb. an injustice; do wrong by sb.; **(b)** wrong; **im ∼ sein** be [in the] wrong

unrechtmäßig 1 *Adj.* unlawful; illegal. **2** *adv.* unlawfully; illegally

unredlich (geh.) **1** *Adj.* dishonest. **2** *adv.* dishonestly

unregelmäßig 1 *Adj.* irregular. **2** *adv.* irregularly

Unregelmäßigkeit *die* irregularity

unreif *Adj.* **(a)** unripe; **(b)** (nicht erwachsen) immature

Unreife *die* ⇒ **unreif a, b:** unripeness; immaturity

unrein *Adj.* **(a)** (auch fig.) impure; bad ⟨*breath, skin*⟩; (nicht sauber) dirty, polluted ⟨*water, air*⟩; **(b)** etw. ins **Unreine**

schreiben make a rough copy of sth.; write sth. [out] in rough

Unreinheit *die* (a) *o. Pl.* ⇨ **unrein a**: impurity; badness; dirtiness; polluted state; lack of clarity; (b) ∼**en der Haut** skin disorders

unrentabel 1 *Adj.* unprofitable. 2 *adv.* unprofitably

unrichtig 1 *Adj.* incorrect; inaccurate. 2 *adv.* incorrectly

Unruhe *die* (a) (auch fig.) unrest; (Lärm) noise; commotion; (Unrast) restlessness; agitation; (Besorgnis) anxiety; disquiet; (b) (Unfrieden) unrest; ∼ **stiften** stir up trouble; (c) *Pl.* (Tumulte) disturbances; unrest *sing.*

unruhig 1 *Adj.* (a) restless; (besorgt) anxious; (nervös) agitated; jittery; (fig.) choppy ⟨*sea*⟩; busy ⟨*pattern*⟩; busy, eventful ⟨*life*⟩; unsettled, troubled ⟨*time*⟩; (b) (ungleichmäßig) uneven ⟨*breathing, pulse, running, etc.*⟩; fitful ⟨*sleep, motion*⟩; disturbed ⟨*night*⟩; unsettled ⟨*life*⟩. 2 *adv.* (a) restlessly; (besorgt) anxiously; (b) (ungleichmäßig) ⟨*breathe, run*⟩ unevenly; ⟨*sleep*⟩ fitfully

uns /ʊns/ 1 *Dat. u. Akk. von* **wir** us; **gib es** ∼: give it to us; **gib** ∼ **das Geld** give us the money; **Freunde von** ∼: friends of ours; **bei** ∼: at our home *or* (coll.) place; (in der Helmat) where I/we live *or* come from; **bei** ∼ **gegenüber** opposite us *or* our house. 2 *Dat. u. Akk. des Reflexivpron. der 1. Pers. Pl. refl.* ourselves; **wir schämen** ∼: we are ashamed [of ourselves]; **von** ∼ **aus** (aus eigenem Antrieb) on our own initiative; (b) *reziprok* one another; **wir haben** ∼ **gestritten** we had an argument *or* quarrel

unsachgemäß 1 *Adj.* improper. 2 *adv.* improperly

unsachlich 1 *Adj.* unobjective; ∼ **werden** lose one's objectivity. 2 *adv.* without objectivity

unsagbar, unsäglich /ʊnˈzɛːklɪç/ (geh.) 1 *Adj.* indescribable; unutterable. 2 *adv.* indescribably; unutterably

unsanft 1 *Adj.* rough; hard ⟨*push, impact*⟩. 2 *adv.* roughly; ∼ **geweckt werden** be rudely awoken

unsauber 1 *Adj.* (a) (schmutzig) dirty; (b) (nachlässig) untidy, sloppy ⟨*work, writing, etc.*⟩; (c) (unlauter) shady ⟨*practice, deal, character, etc.*⟩; underhand, dishonest ⟨*method, means, intention*⟩; (Sport: unfair) unsporting, unfair ⟨*play*⟩. 2 *adv.* (a) (nachlässig) untidily; carelessly; (b) (unklar) ⟨*sing, play*⟩ inaccurately; (c) (Sport: unfair) unsportingly; unfairly

unschädlich *Adj.* harmless; ∼ **machen** render harmless, neutralize ⟨*toxic substance, germ, etc.*⟩; put ⟨*weapon, person*⟩ out of action; render ⟨*bomb etc.*⟩ safe; (verhüll.: töten) eliminate ⟨*person*⟩

unscharf *Adj.* blurred, fuzzy ⟨*photo, picture*⟩

unschätzbar *Adj.* inestimable ⟨*value etc.*⟩; invaluable ⟨*service*⟩; priceless ⟨*riches etc.*⟩

unscheinbar *Adj.* inconspicuous; nondescript; unspectacular ⟨*plumage, blossom*⟩

unschicklich (geh.) 1 *Adj.* unseemly; improper. 2 *adv.* improperly

unschlagbar *Adj.* unbeatable ⟨*opponent, prices, etc.*⟩

unschlüssig *Adj.* undecided *pred.;* undecisive ⟨*gesture, attitude*⟩

unschön *Adj.* 1 (a) ugly; unattractive ⟨*colour, voice*⟩; (b) (unerfreulich, unfair) unpleasant, nasty ⟨*business, incident, weather, conduct, etc.*⟩; ugly ⟨*scene*⟩. 2 *adv.* (a) unattractively; (b) (unfreundlich, unfair) badly

Unschuld *die; o. Pl.* (a) innocence; **seine Hände in** ∼ **waschen** (fig.) wash one's hands in innocence; (b) (Jungfräulichkeit) virginity

unschuldig 1 *Adj.* innocent; **an etw.** (*Dat.*) ∼ **sein** be not guilty of sth.; (b) **er/sie ist noch** ∼: he/she is still a virgin. 2 *adv.* innocently

Unschulds-: ∼**lamm** *das* (spött.) little innocent; ∼**miene** *die* innocent expression

unselbständig, unselbst·ständig *Adj.* dependent [on other people]; **sei doch nicht immer so** ∼! try to be a bit more independent!

Unselbständigkeit, Unselbstständigkeit *die* (a) lack of independence; (b) (Abhängigkeit) dependence

unselig *Adj.* (geh.) wretched ⟨*fate, person, etc.*⟩; [extremely] unfortunate ⟨*situation*⟩; ill-starred ⟨*inheritance*⟩; (verhängnisvoll) disastrous ⟨*journey, decision, etc.*⟩

unser[1] /ˈʊnzɐ/ *Possessivpron. der 1. Pers. Pl.* our; **das ist** ∼**s** *od.* (geh.) ∼**es** *od.* (geh.) das ∼**e** that is ours; **sein Wagen stand neben** ∼**[e]m** *od.* **unsrem** his car was next to ours; **die Unseren** our family; **wir müssen das Uns[e]re/**∼**e/unsre dazu tun** we must do our share

unser[2] *Gen. von* **wir** (geh.) of us; **in** ∼ **aller Interesse** in the interest of all of us

unser·einer, unser·eins *Indefinitpron.* (ugs.) the likes of us *pl.;* our sort (coll.)

unserer·seits *Adv.* for our part

unseres·gleichen *indekl. Indefinitpron.* people *pl.* like us

unseret-: ∼**halben,** ∼**wegen** *Adv.* ⇨ **unsertwegen;** ∼**willen** *Adv.* ⇨ **unsertwillen**

unseriös (abwertend) 1 *Adj.* (unlauter) shady, dubious ⟨*practice, deal*⟩; (unredlich) questionable, dishonest ⟨*method etc.*⟩; (nicht reell) dubious ⟨*firm, pseudoscientist, faith healer*⟩; dishonest, shady ⟨*business man*⟩. 2 *adv.* (unlauter, unredlich) dishonestly; unfairly

unsert-: ∼**wegen** *Adv.* (a) because of us; on our account; (für uns) on our behalf; (uns zuliebe) for our sake; (b) (was uns angeht) as far as we are concerned; ∼**willen** *Adv.* **um** ∼**willen** for our sake[s]

unsicher 1 *Adj.* (a) (gefährlich) unsafe; dangerous; (gefährdet) at risk *pred.;* insecure ⟨*job*⟩; **einen Ort** ∼ **machen** (scherzh.) honour a place with one's presence (joc.); (sich vergnügen) have a good time in a place; (sein Unwesen treiben) get up to one's tricks in a place; (b) (unzuverlässig) uncertain, unreliable ⟨*method*⟩; unreliable ⟨*source, person*⟩; (c) (zögernd) uncertain, hesitant ⟨*step*⟩; (zitternd) unsteady, shaky ⟨*hand*⟩; (nicht selbstsicher) insecure; diffident; unsure of oneself *pred.;* **jmdn.** ∼ **machen** put sb. off his/her stroke; (d) (keine Gewissheit habend) unsure; uncertain; (e) (ungewiss) uncertain. 2 *adv.* (a) ⟨*walk, stand, etc.*⟩ unsteadily; ⟨*drive*⟩ without [much] confidence; (b) (nicht selbstsicher) ⟨*smile, look*⟩ diffidently

Unsicherheit *die* (a) *o. Pl.* (Gefährlichkeit) dangerousness; (Gefahren) dangers *pl.;* (b) *o. Pl.* (Unzuverlässigkeit) uncertainty; unreliability; (c) *o. Pl.* (Zaghaftigkeit) unsureness; (der Schritte o. Ä.) unsteadiness; (d) *o. Pl.* (fehlende Selbstsicherheit) insecurity; lack of [self-]confidence; (e) *o. Pl.* (Ungewissheit) uncertainty; (f) *o. Pl.* (der Arbeitsplätze) insecurity; (des Friedens) instability

Unsicherheits·faktor *der* element of uncertainty

unsichtbar *Adj.* invisible (**für** to)

Unsinn *der; o. Pl.* (a) nonsense; (b) (Unfug) tomfoolery; fooling about *no art.;* **mach [ja] keinen** ∼: don't do anything silly; no messing about

unsinnig *Adj.* nonsensical ⟨*statement, talk, etc.*⟩; absurd, ridiculous ⟨*demand etc.*⟩

Unsitte *die* bad habit; (allgemein verbreitet) bad practice

unsittlich 1 *Adj.* indecent. 2 *adv.* indecently

unsozial 1 *Adj.* unsocial ⟨*policy, measure, rent, etc.*⟩; antisocial ⟨*behaviour*⟩. 2 *adv.* unsocially; ⟨*behave*⟩ antisocially

unsportlich 1 *Adj.* (a) unathletic ⟨*person*⟩; (b) (unfair) unsporting; unsportsmanlike. 2 *adv.* (unfair) in an unsporting way

unsr... ⇨ **unser**[1]

unsrer·seits ⇨ **unsererseits**

unsres·gleichen ⇨ **unseresgleichen**

unstatthaft *Adj.* inadmissible

unsterblich 1 *Adj.* immortal; (fig.) undying ⟨*love*⟩. 2 *adv.* (ugs.: außerordentlich) incredibly (coll.)

unstet (geh.) 1 *Adj.* (a) (ruhelos) restless ⟨*person, glance, thoughts, etc.*⟩; unsettled ⟨*life*⟩; (b) (unbeständig) vacillating ⟨*person, nature*⟩; (labil) unstable ⟨*person, character*⟩. 2 *adv.* (ruhelos) restlessly

Unstimmigkeit *die;* ∼, ∼**en** (a) *o. Pl.* inconsistency; (b) (etw. Unstimmiges) discrepancy; (c) (Meinungsverschiedenheit) difference [of opinion]

Unsumme *die* vast *or* huge sum

unsympathisch *Adj.* uncongenial, disagreeable ⟨*person*⟩; unpleasant ⟨*characteristic, nature, voice*⟩; **er ist mir** ∼**/nicht** ∼: I find him disagreeable/quite likeable

Untat *die* misdeed; evil deed
untätig *Adj.* idle
untauglich *Adj.* (a) unsuitable ⟨*applicant*⟩; (b) (für Militärdienst) unfit [for service] *postpos.*
unteilbar *Adj.* indivisible
unten /'ʊntn̩/ *Adv.* (a) down; **hier/da** ∼: down here/ there; **nach** ∼ (auch fig.) downward; **mit dem Gesicht nach** ∼: face downwards; **von** ∼: from below; ∼ **liegen** be down below; (darunter) lie underneath; (b) (in Gebäuden) downstairs; **nach** ∼: downstairs; **der Aufzug fährt nach** ∼/**kommt von** ∼: the lift (Brit.) *or* (Amer.) elevator is going down/coming up; (c) (am unteren Ende, zum unteren Ende hin) at the bottom; **nach** ∼ [**hin**] towards the bottom; (als Bildunterschrift) „∼ [**rechts**]" 'below [right]'; (auf einem Karton o. Ä.) „∼" 'other side up'; ∼ **erwähnt/genannt** undermentioned; mentioned below *postpos.*; ∼ **stehend** following; given below *postpos.*; (d) (an der Unterseite) underneath; (e) (in einer Hierarchie, Rangfolge) at the bottom; **ziemlich weit** ∼ **auf der Liste** rather a long way down/ right at the bottom of the list; (f) ([weiter] hinten im Text) below; **weiter** ∼: further on; below; (g) (im Süden) down south; **hier/dort** ∼: down here/there [in the south]
unten drunter *Adv.* (ugs.) underneath [it/them]
unten-: ∼**durch** *Adv.* through underneath; **∼**erwähnt**, **∼**genannt** ⇒ **unten** c; ∼**herum**, ∼**rum** *Adv.* (ugs.) down below;**∼**stehend** ⇒ **unten** c
unter /'ʊntɐ/ **1** *Präp. mit Dat.* (a) (Lage, Standort, Abhängigkeit, Unterordnung) under; ∼ **jmdm. wohnen** live below sb.; (b) (weniger, niedriger usw. als) **Mengen** ∼ **100 Stück** quantities of less than 100; (c) during; (modal) ∼ **Angst/Tränen** in *or* out of fear/in tears; ∼ **dem Beifall der Menge** applauded by the crowd; (d) (aus einer Gruppe) among[st]; ∼ **anderem** among[st] other things; (e) (zwischen) among[st]; ∼ **sich** by themselves; ∼ **uns gesagt** between ourselves *or* you and me; (f) (Zustand) under; ∼ **Strom stehen** be live; *s. auch* **Tag** a, **Woche. 2** *Präp. mit Akk.* (a) (Richtung, Ziel, Abhängigkeit, Unterordnung) under; (b) (niedriger als) ∼ **Null sinken** drop below zero; (c) (zwischen) among[st]; ∼ **Strom/Dampf setzen** switch on/put under steam. **3** *Adv.* less than
unter... *Adj.* (a) lower; bottom; (ganz unten) bottom; **das** ∼**e**/∼**ste Stockwerk** the lower/bottom storey; **das Unterste zuoberst kehren** (ugs.) turn everything upside down; (b) (unterer ⟨*Rhine, Nile, etc.*⟩; (c) (in der Rangfolge o. Ä.) lower; lesser ⟨*authority*⟩; **die** ∼**en Klassen der Schule** the junior classes *or* forms of the school
unter-, Unter-: ∼**abteilung** *die* department; ∼**arm** *der* ▶ 326┃ forearm; ∼**belichten** *tr. V.* (Fot.) underexpose; ∼**bewerten** *tr. V.* undervalue; underrate; mark ⟨*gymnast, skater*⟩ too low
unter-, Unter-: ∼**bieten** *unr. tr. V.* (a) (weniger fordern) undercut (**um** by); (b) (bes. Sport) beat ⟨*record*⟩; ∼**binden** *unr. tr. V.* stop; ∼**bleiben** *unr. itr. V.; mit sein* **etw.** ∼**bleibt** sth. does not occur *or* happen; **das hat zu** ∼**bleiben!** this must stop; ∼**brechen** *unr. tr. V.* interrupt; break ⟨*journey, silence*⟩; terminate ⟨*pregnancy*⟩; **wir sind unterbrochen worden** (im Telefongespräch) we've been cut off; ∼**brechung** *die* ⇒ ∼**brechen**: interruption; break (*Gen.* in); termination; ∼**breiten** *tr. V.* (geh.) present
unter-, Unter-: ∼|**bringen** *unr. tr. V.* (a) put; (b) (beherbergen) put up; (c) **jmdn. bei einer Firma** ∼**bringen** (ugs.) get sb. a job in a company; ∼**bringung** *die;* ∼, ∼**en** accommodation *no indef. art.;* ∼|**buttern** *tr. V.* (ugs.: unterdrücken) push aside (fig.); ∼**deck** *das* lower deck
****unter der hand** ⇒ **Hand** c
unter-, Unter-: ∼**dessen** ⇒ **inzwischen**; ∼**drücken** *tr. V.* (a) suppress; hold back ⟨*comment, question, answer, criticism, etc.*⟩; (b) (niederhalten) suppress ⟨*revolution etc.*⟩; oppress ⟨*minority etc.*⟩; ∼**drücker** *der* (abwertend) oppressor; ∼**drückung** *die;* ∼, ∼**en** (a) suppression; (b) (das Unterdrücktwerden, -sein) oppression

unter durchschnittlich 1 *Adj.* below average. **2** *adv.* below the average
unter einander *Adv.* (a) (räumlich) one below the other; ∼ **liegen** lie *or* be one below *or* underneath the other; (b) (miteinander) among[st] ourselves/themselves *etc.*
****untereinander|liegen** *usw.:* ⇒ **untereinander** a
unter-, Unter-: ∼**entwickelt** *Adj.* underdeveloped; ∼**ernährt** *Adj.* undernourished; suffering from malnutrition *postpos.;* ∼**ernährung** *die* malnutrition
Unter fangen *das;* ∼**s** (geh.) venture; undertaking
unter|fassen *tr. V.* (ugs.) (a) **jmdn.** ∼: take sb.'s arm; (b) (stützen) support
Unter führung *die* underpass; (für Fußgänger) subway (Brit.); [pedestrian] underpass (Amer.)
Unter gang *der* (a) (Sonnen∼, Mond∼ usw.) setting; (b) (von Schiffen) sinking; (c) (das Zugrundegehen) decline; (plötzlich) destruction; (von Personen) downfall; (der Welt) end
unter geben *Adj.* subordinate
Untergebene *der/die; adj. Dekl.* subordinate
unter-, Unter-: ∼|**gehen** *unr. itr. V.; mit sein* (a) ⟨*sun, star, etc.*⟩ set; ⟨*ship*⟩ sink, go down; ⟨*person*⟩ drown, go under; **seine Worte gingen in dem Lärm** ∼: his words were drowned by *or* lost in the noise; (b) (zugrunde gehen) come to an end; ∼**geordnet** *Adj.* (a) secondary ⟨*role, importance, etc.*⟩; subordinate ⟨*position, post, etc.*⟩; (b) (Sprachw.) subordinate; ∼**geschoss**, **∼**geschoß** *das* basement; ∼**gewicht** *das;* ▶ 228┃ *o. Pl.* underweight; ∼**gewichtig** *Adj.* underweight
unter-: ∼**gliedern** *tr. V.* subdivide; ∼**graben**[1] *unr. tr. V.* undermine (fig.)
unter-, Unter-: ∼**graben**[2] *unr. tr. V.* dig in; ∼**grenze** *die* lower limit; ∼**grund** *der* (a) (bes. Landw.) subsoil; (b) (Bauw.: Baugrund) foundation; (c) (Farbschicht) background; (d) *o. Pl.* (bes. Politik) underground
Untergrund bahn *die* underground [railway] (Brit.); subway (Amer.)
unter-, Unter-: ∼|**haken** *tr. V.* (ugs.) **jmdn.** ∼**haken** take sb.'s arm; ∼**gehakt gehen** walk arm in arm; ∼**halb 1** *Adv.* below; weiter ∼**halb** further down; ∼**halb von** below; **2** *Präp. mit Gen.* below; ∼**halt** *der; o. Pl.* (a) living; (b) (∼haltszahlung) maintenance; (c) (Instandhaltung[skosten]) upkeep
unter halten 1 *unr. tr. V.* (a) (versorgen) support; (b) (instand halten) maintain ⟨*building*⟩; (c) (betreiben) run, keep ⟨*car, hotel*⟩; (d) (pflegen) maintain, keep up ⟨*contact, correspondence*⟩; (e) entertain ⟨*guest, audience*⟩. **2** *unr. refl. V.* (a) talk; converse; (b) (sich vergnügen) enjoy oneself; **habt ihr euch gut** ∼? did you have a good time?
unterhaltsam *Adj.* entertaining
Unterhalts-: ∼**anspruch** *der* maintenance claim; claim for maintenance; ∼**kosten** *Pl.* maintenance *sing.;* ∼**pflicht** *die* obligation to pay maintenance
Unterhaltung *die* (a) *o. Pl.* (Versorgung) support; (b) *o. Pl.* (Instandhaltung) maintenance; upkeep; (c) *o. Pl.* (Aufrechterhaltung) maintenance; (d) (Gespräch) conversation; (e) (Zeitvertreib) entertainment; **ich wünsche gute** ∼: enjoy yourself/yourselves
Unterhaltungs-: ∼**lektüre** *die* light reading *no art.;* ∼**musik** *die* light music
Unter-: ∼**händler** *der* (bes. Politik) negotiator; ∼**haus** *das* (Parl.) lower house *or* chamber; (in Großbritannien) House of Commons; Lower House; ∼**hemd** *das* vest (Brit.); undershirt (Amer.)
unter höhlen *tr. V.* hollow out; erode
unter-, Unter-: ∼**holz** *das; o. Pl.* underwood; undergrowth; ∼**hose** *die* (für Männer) [under]pants *pl.;* (für Frauen) panties; knickers (Brit.); briefs *pl.;* ∼**irdisch 1** *Adj.* underground; **2** *adv.* underground
unter jochen *tr. V.* subjugate
unter-, Unter-: ∼|**jubeln** *tr. V.* **jmdm. etw.** ∼**jubeln** (ugs.) palm sth. off on sb.; ∼**kiefer** *der* lower jaw; ∼|**kommen** *unr. itr. V.; mit sein* (a) (Unterkunft finden) find accommodation; (b) (ugs.: eine Stelle finden) find *or* get a job; (c) (bes. südd., österr.: begegnen) **so etwas ist mir noch nicht** ∼**gekommen** I've never come across 'anything

like it; **~körper** *der* lower part of the body; **~|krie-gen** *tr. V.* sich nicht **~kriegen lassen** (ugs.) not let things get one down

unterkühlt *Adj.* (a) ~ **sein** be suffering from hypothermia *or* exposure; (b) (fig.) dry, factual ‹*style*›; cool ‹*person*›; icy ‹*tone*›

Unter·kühlung *die* reduction of body temperature

Unterkunft /'ʊntɐkʊnft/ *die;* ~, **Unterkünfte** /...kʏnftə/ accommodation *no indef. art.;* lodging *no indef. art.;* ~ **und Frühstück** bed and breakfast; ~ **und Verpflegung** board and lodging; **die Unterkünfte der Soldaten** the soldiers' quarters

Unter·lage *die* (a) (Schreib~, Matte o. Ä.) pad; (für eine Schreibmaschine usw.) mat; (unter einer Matratze, einem Teppich) underlay; (zum Schlafen usw.) base; (b) *Pl.* (Akten, Papiere) documents; papers

Unter·lass, *Unterlaß *der;* ohne ~: incessantly

unter·lassen *unr. tr. V.* refrain from [doing]; (versäumen) omit, fail to [do]

Unterlassung *die;* ~, ~**en** omission; failure

unter·laufen 1 *unr. tr. V.; mit sein* occur; **jmdm. ist ein Fehler/Irrtum ~:** sb. made a mistake. **2** *unr. tr. V.* evade; get round

unter|legen[1] *tr. V.* (a) put under[neath]; (b) **einem Text einen anderen Sinn ~:** read another meaning into a text

unter·legen[2] *tr. V.* (a) underlay (**mit** with); (b) **einem Film Musik ~:** put music to a film

unter·legen[3] *Adj.* inferior; **jmdm. zahlenmäßig ~ sein** be outnumbered by sb.

Unterlegene *der/die; adj. Dekl.* loser

Unter·leib *der* lower abdomen

unter·liegen *unr. itr. V.* (a) *mit sein* lose; be beaten *or* defeated; **in einem Kampf ~:** lose a fight; (b) **einer Sache** (*Dat.*) ~: be subject to sth.

Unter·lippe *die* ▶ 326⟩ lower lip

unterm *Präp. + Art.* = **unter dem**

Unter·malung *die;* ~, ~**en** accompaniment (*Gen.* to)

unter·mauern *tr. V.* (fig.) back up; support

unter-, Unter-: ~|**mengen** *tr. V.* mix in; ~**miete** *die; o. Pl.* subtenancy; sublease; **bei jmdm. zur ~miete wohnen** be sb.'s subtenant; lodge with sb.; ~**mieter** *der* subtenant; lodger

unterminieren /ʊntɐmi'niːrən/ *tr. V.* undermine

untern *Präp. + Art.* (ugs.) = **unter den**

unter·nehmen *unr. tr. V.* (a) undertake; make; make ‹*attempt*›; take ‹*steps*›; (b) **etwas ~:** do something

Unter·nehmen *das;* ~**s**, ~ (a) enterprise; venture; undertaking; (b) (Firma) enterprise; concern

unternehmend *Adj.* enterprising; active

Unternehmer *der;* ~**s**, ~: employer; (in der Industrie) industrialist

unternehmerisch 1 *Adj.* entrepreneurial. **2** *adv.* ‹*think*› in an entrepreneurial *or* businesslike way

Unternehmung *die;* ~, ~**en** ⇨ **Unternehmen**

Unternehmungs·geist *der; o. Pl.* spirit of enterprise; **er war voller ~:** he was full of initiative

unternehmungs·lustig *Adj.* active

unter-, Unter-: ~**offizier** *der* (a) non-commissioned officer; (b) ▶ 34⟩ (Dienstgrad) corporal; ~|**ordnen 1** *tr. V.* subordinate; **2** *refl. V.* accept a subordinate role; ~**ordnung** *die* subordination; ~**prima** *die* (Schulw. veralt.) eighth year (*of a Gymnasium*); ~**privilegiert** *Adj.* (geh.) underprivileged; ~**privilegierte** *der/die; adj. Dekl.* (geh.) underprivileged person; ~**punkt** *der* subsidiary point

Unter·redung *die;* ~, ~**en** discussion; **er bat ihn um eine ~:** he asked to see him to discuss something [with him]

Unterricht /'ʊntɐrɪçt/ *der;* ~**[e]s**, ~**e** instruction; (Schul~) teaching; (Schulstunden) classes *pl.;* lessons *pl.;* **jmdm. ~ [in Musik** *usw.***] geben** give sb. [music *etc.*] lessons; teach sb. [music]

unterrichten 1 *tr. V.* (a) (lehren) teach; (b) (informieren) inform (**über** + *Akk.* of, about). **2** *itr. V.* (Unterricht geben)

teach. **3** *refl. V.* (sich informieren) inform oneself (**über** + *Akk.* about)

Unterrichts-: ~**fach** *das* subject; ~**stoff** *der* subject matter; ~**stunde** *die* lesson; period

Unterrichtung *die;* ~, ~**en** instruction; (Information) information

Unter·rock *der* [half] slip

unter|rühren *tr. V.* stir in

unters *Präp. + Art.* = **unter das**

unter·sagen *tr. V.* forbid; prohibit

Unter·satz *der* ⇨ **Untersetzer**

unter-, Unter-: ~**schätzen** *tr. V.* underestimate ‹*amount, effect, meaning, distance, etc.*›; underrate ‹*writer, performer, book, performance, talent, ability*›; ~**scheiden 1** *unr. tr. V.* distinguish; **die Zwillinge sind kaum zu ~scheiden** you can hardly tell the twins apart; **2** *unr. itr. V.* distinguish; differentiate; **zwischen Richtigem und Falschem ~scheiden** tell the difference between right and wrong; **3** *unr. refl. V.* differ (**durch** in, **von** from); ~**scheidung** *die* (Vorgang) differentiation; (Resultat) distinction

unter-, Unter-: ~**schenkel** *der* ▶ 326⟩ shank; lower leg; ~**schicht** *die* (Soziol.) lower class; ~|**schieben**[1] *tr. V.* push under[neath]

unter·schieben[2] *unr. tr. V.* **jmdm. etw. ~** (fig.) attribute sth. falsely to sb.

Unter·schied *der;* ~**[e]s**, ~**e** difference; **es ist [schon] ein [großer] ~, ob ...:** it makes a [big] difference whether ...; **ohne ~ der Rasse/des Geschlechts** without regard to *or* discrimination against race/sex; **im ~ zu ihm/zum ~ von ihm** in contrast to him

unter·schieden *Adj.* different

unterschiedlich 1 *Adj.* different; (uneinheitlich) variable; varying. **2** *adv.* in different ways

Unterschiedlichkeit *die;* ~, ~**en** difference (*Gen.* between); (Uneinheitlichkeit) variability

unterschieds·los 1 *Adj.* uniform; equal ‹*treatment*›. **2** *adv.* ‹*treat*› equally; (ohne Benachteiligung) without discrimination

unter·schlagen 1 *unr. tr. V.* embezzle, misappropriate ‹*money, funds, etc.*›; (unterdrücken) intercept ‹*letter*›; withhold, suppress ‹*fact, news, information, etc.*›. **2** *unr. itr. V.* **er hat ~:** he embezzled money

Unterschlagung *die;* ~, ~**en** ⇨ **unterschlagen:** embezzlement; misappropriation; withholding; suppression

Unter·schlupf *der;* ~**[e]s**, ~**e** shelter; (Versteck) hiding place; hideout

unter|schlüpfen *itr. V.; mit sein* (ugs.) hide out; (Obdach finden) take shelter (**vor** + *Dat.* from)

unter·schreiben 1 *unr. itr. V.* sign. **2** *unr. tr. V.* sign; (fig.) approve; subscribe to

unter·schreiten *unr. tr. V.* fall below

Unter·schrift *die* (a) signature; **seine ~ unter etw.** (*Akk.*) **setzen** put one's signature to sth.; sign sth.; (b) (Bild~) caption

unterschwellig /-ʃvɛlɪç/ **1** *Adj.* subliminal. **2** *adv.* subliminally

unter-, Unter-: ~**see·boot** *das* submarine; ~**seite** *die* under-side; (eines Stoffes) wrong side; ~**sekunda** *die* (Schulw. veralt.) sixth year (*of a Gymnasium*); ~|**setzen** *tr. V.* put underneath; ~**setzer** *der* mat; (für Gläser) coaster

untersetzt *Adj.* stocky

unter·spülen *tr. V.* undermine and wash away

unterst... ⇨ **unter...**

Unter·stand *der* (a) (Bunker) dugout; (b) (Unterschlupf) shelter

unter·stehen 1 *unr. itr. V.* **jmdm. ~:** be subordinate *or* answerable to sb.; **jmdm. untersteht eine Abteilung** sb. is responsible for a department. **2** *unr. refl. V.* dare; **untersteh dich!** [don't] you dare!

unter|stellen[1] **1** *tr. V.* (a) (zur Aufbewahrung) keep; store ‹*furniture*›; (b) (unter etw.) put underneath. **2** *refl. V.* take shelter

unter·stellen² *tr. V.* **(a)** (jmdm. unterordnen, übertragen) **jmdm. eine Abteilung ~:** put sb. in charge of a department; **die Behörde ist dem Ministerium unterstellt** the office is under the ministry; **(b)** (annehmen) assume; **(c)** (unterschieben) **jmdm. böse Absichten ~:** insinuate *or* imply that sb.'s intentions are bad

Unter·stellung *die* **(a)** subordination (**unter** + *Akk.* to); **(b)** (falsche Behauptung) insinuation

unter·streichen *unr. tr. V.* **(a)** underline; **(b)** (fig.: hervorheben) emphasize

Unter·streichung *die;* **~, ~en (a)** underlining; **(b)** (fig.) emphasizing

Unter·stufe *die* (Schulw.) lower school

unter·stützen *tr. V.* support

Unter·stützung *die* **(a)** support; **(b)** (finanzielle Hilfe) allowance; (für Arbeitslose) [unemployment] benefit *no art.;* **staatliche ~:** state aid

unter·suchen *tr. V.* **(a)** examine; **etw. auf etw.** (*Akk.*) **~:** test sth. for sth.; **sich ärztlich ~ lassen** have a medical examination *or* check-up; **(b)** (aufzuklären suchen) investigate

Untersuchung *die;* **~, ~en (a)** ⇒ **untersuchen:** examination; test; investigation; **(b)** (wissenschaftliche Arbeit) study

Untersuchungs-: **~gefängnis** *das* prison (*for people awaiting trial*); **~haft** *die* imprisonment *or* detention while awaiting trial; **jmdn. in ~haft nehmen** commit sb. for trial

untertan /-taːn/ *Adj.* sich (*Dat.*) **jmdn./etw. ~ machen** (geh.) subjugate sb./dominate sth.

Untertan *der;* **~s** *od.* **~en, ~en** subject

untertänig /-tɛːnɪç/ **1** *Adj.* subservient; **Ihr ~ster Diener** (veralt.) your most obedient *or* humble servant. **2** *adv.* subserviently

unter-, Unter-: **~tasse** *die* saucer; **fliegende ~tasse** (fig.) flying saucer; **~tauchen 1** *itr. V.; mit sein* **(a)** dive [under]; **(b)** (fig.) go underground; **2** *tr. V.* duck; **~teil** *das od. der* bottom part

unter·teilen *tr. V.* subdivide; (aufteilen) divide

Unter·teilung *die;* **~, ~en** [sub]division

Unter-: **~tertia** *die* (Schulw. veralt.) fourth year (*of a Gymnasium*); **~titel** *der* subtitle

unter·treiben *unr. itr. V.* play things down

Untertreibung *die;* **~, ~en** understatement

unter-, Unter-: **~vermieten** *tr., itr. V.* sublet; **~vermietung** *die* subletting; **~versorgung** *die* under-supply (**mit** of)

unter·wandern *tr. V.* infiltrate

Unter·wanderung *die* infiltration *no indef. art.*

Unter·wäsche *die; o. Pl.* underwear

unterwegs *Adv.* on the way; **~ sein** be on the *or* one's/its way (**nach** to); (nicht zu Hause sein) be out [and about]; **sie waren vier Wochen ~:** they travelled for four weeks

unter·weisen *unr. tr. V.* (geh.) instruct (**in** + *Dat.* in)

Unter·weisung *die* instruction

Unter·welt *die; o. Pl.* underworld

unter·werfen 1 *unr. tr. V.* **(a)** subjugate 〈*people, country*〉; **(b)** (unterziehen) subject (*Dat.* to); **(c) einer Sache** (*Dat.*) **unterworfen sein** be subject to sth. **2** *unr. refl. V.* **sich** [**jmdm./einer Sache**] **~:** submit [to sb./sth.]

Unterwerfung *die;* **~, ~en (a)** (das Unterwerfen) subjugation (**unter** + *Akk.* to); **(b)** (das Sichunterwerfen) submission (**unter** + *Akk.* to)

unterwürfig /-vyrfɪç/ (abwertend) **1** *Adj.* obsequious. **2** *adv.* obsequiously

Unterwürfigkeit *die;* **~** (abwertend) obsequiousness

unter·zeichnen *tr. V.* sign

Unterzeichnung *die* signing

unter|ziehen¹ *unr. tr. V.* [**sich** (*Dat.*)] **etw. ~:** put sth. on underneath

---

*alte Schreibung (vgl. Hinweise auf S. xvi–xvii)

unter·ziehen² 1 *unr. refl. V.* **sich einer Sache** (*Dat.*) **~:** undertake sth.; **sich einer Operation** (*Dat.*) **~:** undergo *or* have an operation. **2** *unr. tr. V.* **etw. einer Untersuchung/Überprüfung** (*Dat.*) **~:** examine/check sth.

Untiefe *die;* **~, ~en** shallow

Untier *das* monster

untragbar *Adj.* unbearable; intolerable

untrennbar *Adj.* inseparable

untreu *Adj.* **(a)** disloyal; **jmdm. ~ werden** be disloyal to sb.; **seinen Grundsätzen ~ werden** abandon one's principles; **(b)** (in der Ehe, Liebe) unfaithful

Untreue *die* **(a)** disloyalty; **(b)** (in der Ehe, Liebe) unfaithfulness

untröstlich *Adj.* inconsolable; **ich bin ~, dass ...:** I am extremely sorry that ...

untrüglich *Adj.* unmistakable

Untugend *die* bad habit

unüberlegt 1 *Adj.* rash. **2** *adv.* rashly

unübersehbar *Adj.* **(a)** (offenkundig) conspicuous; obvious; **(b)** (sehr groß) enormous; immense

unübersichtlich 1 *Adj.* unclear; confusing 〈*arrangement*〉; blind 〈*bend*〉. **2** *adv.* unclearly; confusingly 〈*arranged*〉

unübertrefflich 1 *Adj.* superb. **2** *adv.* superbly

unübertroffen *Adj.* unsurpassed

unüblich *Adj.* not usual *or* customary *pred.;* unusual

unumgänglich *Adj.* [absolutely] necessary

unumschränkt /'ʊn|ʊmʃrɛŋkt/ *Adj.* absolute

unumwunden /'ʊn|ʊmvʊndn/ **1** *Adj.* frank. **2** *adv.* frankly; openly

ununterbrochen 1 *Adj.* incessant. **2** *adv.* incessantly

unveränderlich *Adj.* unchangeable, unchanging 〈*law, principle*〉; constant 〈*quantity etc.*〉; permanent 〈*mark*〉

Unveränderlichkeit *die;* **~:** ⇒ **unveränderlich:** unchangeableness; unchangingness; constancy; permanence

unverändert *Adj.* unchanged 〈*appearance, weather, condition*〉; unaltered, unrevised 〈*edition etc.*〉

unverantwortlich. 1 *Adj.* irresponsible. **2** *adv.* irresponsibly

unveräußerlich *Adj.* (geh.) inalienable 〈*rights, principles*〉

unverbesserlich *Adj.* incorrigible

unverbindlich 1 *Adj.* not binding *pred.;* without obligation *postpos;* non-committal 〈*answer, words*〉; detached, impersonal 〈*attitude, person*〉. **2** *adv.* 〈*send, reserve*〉 without obligation

Unverbindlichkeit *die;* **~, ~en (a)** *o. Pl.* freedom from obligation; (einer Person) detached *or* impersonal manner; **(b)** (Äußerung) non-committal remark

unverblümt /ʊnfɛɐ̯'blyːmt/ **1** *Adj.* blunt. **2** *adv.* bluntly

unverdächtig 1 *Adj.* free from suspicion *postpos.* **2** *adv.* in a way that does/did not arouse suspicion

unverdaulich *Adj.* indigestible

unverdient 1 *Adj.* undeserved. **2** *adv.* undeservedly

unverdorben *Adj.* unspoilt

unverdrossen *Adj.* undeterred; (unverzagt) undaunted

unverdünnt *Adj.* undiluted

unvereinbar *Adj.* incompatible

unverfälscht 1 *Adj.* genuine; unadulterated 〈*wine etc.*〉; pure 〈*dialect*〉; unaltered 〈*custom, text*〉. **2** *adv.* in pure/unaltered form

unverfänglich *Adj.* harmless

unverfroren 1 *Adj.* insolent; impudent. **2** *adv.* insolently; impudently

Unverfrorenheit *die;* **~, ~en (a)** *o. Pl.* insolence; impudence; **(b)** (Äußerung) insolent remark; impertinence

unvergänglich *Adj.* immortal 〈*fame*〉; unchanging 〈*beauty*〉; abiding 〈*recollection*〉

Unvergänglichkeit *die* ⇒ **unvergänglich:** immortality; unchangingness; abidingness

unvergesslich, *unvergeßlich *Adj.* unforgettable; **dieses Erlebnis wird mir ∼ bleiben** *od.* **sein** I shall never forget this experience

unvergleichlich 1 *Adj.* incomparable. **2** *adv.* incomparably

unverhältnismäßig *Adv.* unusually

unverheiratet *Adj.* unmarried

unverhofft /'ʊnfɛɐ̯hɔft/ **1** *Adj.* unexpected. **2** *adv.* unexpectedly

unverhohlen 1 *Adj.* unconcealed. **2** *adv.* openly

unverkäuflich *Adj.* **(a)** (nicht zum Verkauf bestimmt) **diese Vase ist ∼:** this vase is not for sale; **∼es Muster** free sample; **(b)** (nicht absetzbar) unsaleable

unverkennbar 1 *Adj.* unmistakable. **2** *adv.* unmistakably

unvermeidlich *Adj.* **(a)** (nicht vermeidbar) unavoidable; **(b)** (sich als Folge ergebend) inevitable

unvermindert *Adj., adv.* undiminished

unvermittelt 1 *Adj.* sudden; abrupt. **2** *adv.* suddenly; abruptly

Unvermögen *das* lack of ability; inability

unvermutet 1 *Adj.* unexpected. **2** *adv.* unexpectedly

Unvernunft *die* stupidity

unvernünftig 1 *Adj.* stupid; foolish. **2** *adv.* **er raucht/trinkt ∼ viel** he smokes/drinks more than is good for him

unverrichtet *Adj.* **∼er Dinge** without having achieved anything

unverschämt 1 *Adj.* **(a)** impertinent, impudent 〈*person, manner, words, etc.*〉; barefaced, blatant 〈*lie*〉; **(b)** (ugs.: sehr groß) outrageous 〈*price, luck, etc.*〉. **2** *adv.* **(a)** impertinently; impudently; 〈*lie*〉 barefacedly; blatantly; **(b)** (ugs.: sehr) outrageously 〈*expensive*〉

Unverschämtheit *die;* **∼, ∼en (a)** *o. Pl.* impertinence; impudence; (einer Lüge) barefacedness, blatancy; **(b)** (Äußerung o. Ä.) [piece of] impertinence; **das ist eine ∼!** that's outrageous!

unversehens *Adv.* suddenly

unversehrt *Adj.* unscathed; unhurt; (unbeschädigt) undamaged

Unversehrtheit *die;* **∼:** intactness

unversöhnlich *Adj.* irreconcilable

unverständlich *Adj.* incomprehensible; (undeutlich) unclear 〈*pronunciation, presentation, etc.*〉; **es ist [mir] ∼, warum …:** I cannot *or* do not understand why …

Unverständnis *das* lack of understanding

unversucht *Adj.* **nichts ∼ lassen** try everything; leave no stone unturned

unverträglich *Adj.* **(a)** (unbekömmlich) indigestible; unsuitable 〈*medicine*〉; **(b)** (streitsüchtig) quarrelsome; **(c)** (nicht harmonierend) incompatible 〈*blood groups, medicines, transplant tissue*〉

Unverträglichkeit *die* ⇒ **unverträglich:** indigestibility; unsuitability; quarrelsomeness; incompatibility

unvertretbar *Adj.* unjustifiable

unverwechselbar *Adj.* unmistakable; distinctive

unverwundbar *Adj.* invulnerable

unverwüstlich *Adj.* indestructible; (fig.) irrepressible 〈*nature, humour*〉; robust 〈*health*〉

unverzeihlich *Adj.* unforgivable; inexcusable

unverzüglich 1 *Adj.* prompt; immediate. **2** *adv.* promptly; immediately

unvollkommen 1 *Adj.* **(a)** imperfect; **(b)** (unvollständig) incomplete 〈*collection, account, etc.*〉. **2** *adv.* **(a)** imperfectly; **(b)** (unvollständig) incompletely

unvollständig *Adj.* incomplete

unvorbereitet *Adj.* unprepared

unvorhergesehen 1 *Adj.* unforeseen 〈*difficulty, event, expenditure*〉; unexpected 〈*visit*〉. **2** *adv.* unexpectedly

unvorhersehbar *Adj.* unforeseeable

unvorsichtig 1 *Adj.* careless; (unüberlegt) rash. **2** *adv.* carelessly; (unüberlegt) rashly

unvorsichtigerweise *Adv.* carelessly; (unüberlegt) without thinking

Unvorsichtigkeit *die* ⇒ **unvorsichtig 1: (a)** *o. Pl.* (Art) carelessness; rashness; **(b)** (Handlung usw.) **eine ∼ begehen** do sth. careless/rash

unvorstellbar 1 *Adj.* inconceivable; unimaginable. **2** *adv.* unimaginably; **∼ leiden** suffer terribly

unvorteilhaft *Adj.* **(a)** (nicht attraktiv) unattractive 〈*figure, appearance*〉; **(b)** (ohne Vorteil) unfavourable, poor 〈*purchase, exchange*〉; unprofitable 〈*business*〉

unwägbar *Adj.* imponderable; incalculable 〈*quantity, behaviour*〉

Unwägbarkeit *die;* **∼, ∼en (a)** *o. Pl.* imponderability; (eines Verhaltens) incalculability; **(b)** (etw. Unwägbares) uncertainty; imponderability

unwahr *Adj.* untrue

Unwahrheit *die* **(a)** *o. Pl.* untruthfulness; **(b)** (Äußerung) untruth

unwahrscheinlich 1 *Adj.* **(a)** improbable; unlikely; **(b)** (ugs.: sehr viel) incredible (coll.). **2** *adv.* (ugs.: sehr) incredibly (coll.)

Unwahrscheinlichkeit *die* improbability

unweigerlich /ʊn'vaɪgɐlɪç/ **1** *Adj.* inevitable. **2** *adv.* inevitably

unweit 1 *Präp. mit Gen.* not far from. **2** *Adv.* not far (**von** from)

Unwesen *das; o. Pl.* dreadful state of affairs; **sein ∼ treiben** (abwertend) be up to one's mischief *or* one's tricks

unwesentlich 1 *Adj.* unimportant; insignificant. **2** *adv.* slightly; marginally

Unwetter *das* [thunder]storm

unwichtig *Adj.* unimportant

unwiderlegbar 1 *Adj.* irrefutable. **2** *adv.* irrefutably

unwiderruflich 1 *Adj.* irrevocable. **2** *adv.* irrevocably

unwidersprochen *Adj.* unchallenged

unwiderstehlich *Adj.* irresistible

Unwiderstehlichkeit *die;* **∼:** irresistibility

unwiederbringlich (geh.) **1** *Adj.* irretrievable. **2** *adv.* irretrievably

Unwille[n] *der; o. Pl.* displeasure; indignation

unwillig 1 *Adj.* indignant; angry; (widerwillig) unwilling; reluctant. **2** *adv.* indignantly; angrily; (widerwillig) unwillingly; reluctantly

unwillkommen *Adj.* unwelcome

unwillkürlich 1 *Adj.* **(a)** spontaneous 〈*cry, sigh*〉; instinctive 〈*reaction, movement, etc.*〉; **(b)** (Physiol.) involuntary 〈*movement etc.*〉. **2** *adv.* **(a)** 〈*shout etc.*〉 spontaneously; 〈*react, move, etc.*〉 instinctively; **(b)** (Physiol.) 〈*move etc.*〉 involuntarily

unwirklich *Adj.* (geh.) unreal

unwirksam *Adj.* ineffective

Unwirksamkeit *die* ineffectiveness

unwirsch 1 *Adj.* surly; ill-natured. **2** *adv.* ill-naturedly

unwirtlich *Adj.* inhospitable; rough 〈*weather*〉

Unwirtlichkeit *die;* **∼:** inhospitableness; inhospitality; (des Wetters) roughness

Unwissen *das* ignorance

unwissend *Adj.* **(a)** (unerfahren) ignorant; innocent 〈*child*〉; **(b)** (unbewusst) unwitting; unknowing

Unwissenheit *die;* **∼** ignorance; **∼ schützt nicht vor Strafe** ignorance is no defence

unwissenschaftlich *Adj.* unscientific

unwissentlich 1 *Adj.* unconscious. **2** *adv.* unknowingly; unwittingly

unwohl *Adv.* **(a)** ▶329┃ unwell; **mir ist ∼:** I don't feel well; **(b)** (unbehaglich) uneasy

Unwohlsein *das; ∼* ▶329┃ indisposition; **ein heftiges ∼ überkam ihn** he suddenly felt very unwell

Unwucht *die;* ~, ~**en** (Technik) imbalance

unwürdig *Adj.* **(a)** undignified ⟨*person, behaviour*⟩; degrading ⟨*treatment*⟩; **(b)** (unangemessen) unworthy

Unzahl *die; o. Pl.* huge *or* enormous number

unzählbar *Adj.* uncountable

unzählig *Adj.* innumerable; countless

unzähmbar *Adj.* untameable

Unze /'ʊntsə/ *die;* ~, ~**n** ounce

Unzeit *die:* **zur** ~ (geh.) at an inopportune moment

unzeitgemäß *Adj.* anachronistic

unzensiert *Adj.* **(a)** uncensored; **(b)** (unbenotet) unmarked; ungraded (Amer.)

unzerbrechlich *Adj.* unbreakable

unzerstörbar *Adj.* indestructible

unzertrennlich *Adj.* inseparable

unzivilisiert *Adj.* (abwertend) uncivilized

Unzucht *die; o. Pl.* (veralt.) ~ **mit Abhängigen** illicit sexual relations *pl.* with dependants; **widernatürliche** ~: unnatural sexual act[s]; **gewerbsmäßige** ~: prostitution

unzüchtig **1** *Adj.* obscene ⟨*letter, gesture*⟩. **2** *adv.* ⟨*touch, approach, etc.*⟩ indecently; ⟨*speak*⟩ obscenely

unzufrieden *Adj.* dissatisfied; (stärker) unhappy

Unzufriedenheit *die* dissatisfaction; (stärker) unhappiness

unzugänglich *Adj.* inaccessible; (fig.) unapproachable ⟨*character, person, etc.*⟩

Unzugänglichkeit *die;* ~: ⇒ **unzugänglich:** inaccessibility; unaproachability

unzulänglich (geh.) **1** *Adj.* insufficient; inadequate. **2** *adv.* insufficiently; inadequately

Unzulänglichkeit *die;* ~, ~**en** **(a)** *o. Pl.* insufficiency; inadequacy; **(b)** (etw. Unzulängliches) inadequacy; shortcoming

unzulässig *Adj.* inadmissible; undue ⟨*influence, interference, delay*⟩; improper ⟨*method, use, etc.*⟩

Unzulässigkeit *die* inadmissibility

unzumutbar *Adj.* unreasonable

Unzumutbarkeit *die;* ~ unreasonableness

unzurechnungsfähig *Adj.* not responsible for one's actions *pred.;* (geistesgestört) of unsound mind *postpos;* **für** ~ **erklärt werden** be certified insane

Unzurechnungs·fähigkeit *die; o. Pl.* (Geistesgestörheit) unsoundness of mind

unzureichend *Adj.* insufficient; inadequate

unzustellbar *Adj.* (Postw.) undeliverable ⟨*mail*⟩; „**falls** ~**, bitte zurück an Absender**" 'if undelivered, please return to sender'

unzutreffend *Adj.* inappropriate; inapplicable; (falsch) incorrect; „**Unzutreffendes bitte streichen**" 'please delete as appropriate'

unzuverlässig *Adj.* unreliable

Unzuverlässigkeit *die* unreliability

unzweckmäßig **1** *Adj.* unsuitable; (unpraktisch) impractical. **2** *adv.* unsuitably; (unpraktisch) impractically

unzweifelhaft **1** *Adj.* unquestionable; undoubted. **2** *adv.* unquestionably; undoubtedly

üppig **1** *Adj.* lush, luxuriant ⟨*vegetation*⟩; thick ⟨*hair, beard*⟩; sumptuous, opulent ⟨*meal*⟩; full ⟨*bosom*⟩; voluptuous ⟨*figure, woman*⟩. **2** *adv.* luxuriantly; ⟨*dine, eat*⟩ sumptuously

Üppigkeit *die;* ~ ⇒ **üppig 1:** lushness; luxuriance; thickness; sumptuousness; opulence; fullness; voluptuousness

up to date /'ʌp tə 'deɪt/ up to date; **er ist modisch** ~: he wears fashionable clothes; he is fashionably dressed

Ur·abstimmung *die* [esp. strike] ballot

Ur·ahn[e] *der* oldest known ancestor

ur·alt *Adj.* very old; ancient

Uran /u'raːn/ *das;* ~**s** (Chemie) uranium

ur·auf·führen *tr. V.* première, give the first performance of ⟨*play, concerto, etc.*⟩; première ⟨*film*⟩

Ur·auf·führung *die* première; first night *or* performance; (eines Films) première; first showing

urban /ʊr'baːn/ *Adj.* (geh.) **(a)** (weltmännisch) urbane; **(b)** (städtisch) urban

Urbanisation /ʊrbaniza'tsi̯oːn/ *die;* ~, ~**en** urbanization

urbanisieren *tr. V.* urbanize

Urbanität /ʊrbani'tɛːt/ *die;* ~: urbanity

urbar *Adj.* ~ **machen** cultivate ⟨*land*⟩; reclaim ⟨*swamp, desert*⟩

Urbarmachung *die;* ~ ⇒ **urbar:** cultivation; reclamation

Ur·bevölkerung *die* native population; native inhabitants *pl.*

Ur·bild *das* **(a)** (Vorbild) archetype; prototype; **(b)** (Inbegriff, Ideal) perfect example; epitome

ur·eigen *Adj.; nicht präd.* very own; **seine** ~**en Interessen** his own best interests

Ur·einwohner *der* native inhabitant; **die australischen** ~: the Australian Aborigines

Ur·enkel *der* great-grandson

Ur·enkelin *die* great-granddaughter

ur·gemütlich (ugs.) **1** *Adj.* extremely cosy; (bequem) extremely comfortable. **2** *adv.* extremely cosily/comfortably

Urgroß-: ~**eltern** *Pl.* great-grandparents; ~**mutter** *die* great-grandmother; ~**vater** *der* great-grandfather

Ur·heber *der;* ~**s**, ~ **(a)** originator; initiator; **(b)** (bes. Rechtsspr.: Verfasser, Autor) author

urig /'uːrɪç/ *Adj.* natural ⟨*person*⟩; real ⟨*beer*⟩; cosy ⟨*pub*⟩

Urin /u'riːn/ *der;* ~**s**, ~**e** urine

urinieren *itr. V.* urinate

ur·komisch *Adj.* extremely funny; hilarious

Ur·kunde *die;* ~, ~**n** document; (Bescheinigung, Sieger~, Diplom~ usw.) certificate

Urlaub *der;* ~[**e**]**s**, ~**e** holiday[s] (Brit.); vacation; (bes. Milit.) leave; ~ **haben** have a holiday/have leave; **auf** *od.* **in** *od.* **im** ~ **sein** be on holiday/leave; **in** ~ **gehen/fahren** go on holiday

Urlauber *der;* ~**s**, ~, **Urlauberin** *die;* ~, ~**nen** holiday-maker

Urlaubs-: ~**ort** *der; Pl.* ~**orte** holiday resort; ~**reise** *die* holiday [trip]; **eine** ~**reise ans Meer/ins Gebirge machen** go on holiday to the seaside/go for a holiday in the mountains; ~**sperre** *die* **(a)** (Milit.) ban on leave; **(b)** (österr.) holiday closure; ~**tag** *der* day of holiday; ~**zeit** *die* holiday period *or* season

Urne /'ʊrnə/ *die;* ~, ~**n** **(a)** urn; **(b)** (Wahl~) [ballot-]box; **(c)** (Verlosungs~) box; (Lostrommel) drum

Urologe /uro'loːɡə/ *der;* ~**n**, ~**n**, **Urologin** *die;* ~, ~**nen** ▶ 85 urologist

Ur·oma *die* (fam.) great-granny (coll./child lang.)

Ur·opa *der* (fam.) great-grandpa (coll./child lang.)

ur·plötzlich **1** *Adj.* extremely sudden. **2** *adv.* quite suddenly

Ur·sache *die* cause (**für** of); **keine** ~! don't mention it; you're welcome

ur·sächlich *Adj.* causal; **in** ~**em Zusammenhang stehen** be causally related (**mit** to)

Ur·schrei *der* (Psych.) primal scream

Ur·sprung *der* origin; **seinen** ~ **in etw.** (Dat.) **haben** originate from sth.

ur·sprünglich **1** *Adj.* **(a)** original ⟨*plan, price, form, material, etc.*⟩; initial ⟨*reaction, trust, mistrust, etc.*⟩; **(b)** (natürlich) natural. **2** *adv.* **(a)** originally; initially; **(b)** (natürlich) naturally

Ursprünglichkeit *die;* ~: naturalness

Ur·suppe *die* (Biol.) primordial soup

Urteil *das;* ~**s**, ~**e** judgement; (Meinung) opinion; (Strafe) sentence; (Gerichts~) verdict; **das** ~ **lautete auf 10 Jahre Freiheitsstrafe** the sentence was ten years' imprisonment

urteilen *itr. V.* form an opinion; judge; **über etw./jmdn.** ~: judge sth./sb.; give one's opinion on sth./sb.; **fachmännisch** ~: give an expert opinion

urteils-, Urteils-: ∼**fähig** *Adj.* competent *or* able to judge *postpos.;* ∼**fähigkeit** *die; o. Pl.* competence *or* ability to judge; ∼**kraft** *die; o. Pl.* [power of] judgement; ∼**vermögen** *das; o. Pl.* competence *or* ability to judge
Ur·text *der* original
urtümlich /'u:ɐ̯ty:mlɪç/ *Adj.* natural ‹ *landscape etc.* ›; primitive ‹ *culture etc.* ›
Ur·ur-: ∼**enkel** *der* great-great-grandson; ∼**enkelin** *die* great-great-granddaughter; ∼**großmutter** *die* great-great-grandmother; ∼**groß·vater** *der* great-great-grandfather
Ur·wald *der* primeval forest; **tropischer** ∼: tropical forest; jungle
ur·wüchsig /'u:ɐ̯vy:ksɪç/ *Adj.* natural ‹ *landscape, power* ›; earthy ‹ *language, humour* ›
Urwüchsigkeit *die;* ∼ ⇒ urwüchsig: naturalness; earthiness
Ur·zeit *die* primeval times *pl.;* **vor** ∼**en** in ages past; **seit** ∼**en** since primeval times; (ugs.: seit längerer Zeit) since the year dot (coll.)
USA /u:|ɛs'|a:/ *Pl.* USA
Usance /y'zã:s/ *die;* ∼, ∼**n**, (schweiz.), **Usanz** /u'zants/ *die;* ∼, ∼**en** (bes. Kaufmannsspr.) practice
Usurpator /uzʊr'pa:tɔr/ *der;* ∼**s**, ∼**en** /...pa'to:rən/ usurper
usurpieren *tr. V.* usurp
Usus /'u:zʊs/ *der;* ∼ (ugs.) custom; **das ist hier so** ∼: that's the custom here
usw. *Abk.* **und so weiter** etc.
Utensil /utɛn'zi:l/ *das;* ∼**s**, ∼**ien** /... ịən/ piece of equipment; ∼**ien** equipment *sing.*
Utopie /uto'pi:/ *die;* ∼, ∼**n** Utopia; (Idealvorstellung) Utopian dream
utopisch *Adj.* Utopian
UV *Abk.* **Ultraviolett** UV
UV-Strahlen *Pl.* UV rays; ultraviolet rays
Ü-Wagen *der* (Rundf., Ferns.) OB van or vehicle
u. Z. *Abk.* (bes. DDR) **unserer Zeitrechnung** AD

v, V /vaʊ/ *das;* ∼, ∼**:** v, V
v. *Abk.* **von** (in Familiennamen) von
V *Abk.* **Volt** V
Vagabund /vaga'bʊnt/ *der;* ∼**en**, ∼**en** (veralt.) vagabond
vagabundieren *itr. V.* (a) live as a vagabond/as vagabonds; (b) *mit sein* (umherziehen) wander *or* travel around
vage 1 *Adj.* vague. 2 *adv.* vaguely
Vagheit *die;* ∼: vagueness
Vagina /va'gi:na/ *die;* ∼, **Vaginen** ▶ 326 | (Anat.) vagina
vaginal *Adj.* (Anat.) vaginal
vakant /va'kant/ *Adj.* vacant
Vakanz /va'kants/ *die;* ∼, ∼**en** (geh.) vacancy
Vakuum /'va:kuʊm/ *das;* ∼**s**, **Vakuen** /... kuən/ (auch fig.) vacuum
vakuum·verpackt *Adj.* vacuum-packed
Valentins·tag /'va:lɛnti:ns-/ *der* [St] Valentine's Day
Valuta /va'lu:ta/ *die;* ∼, **Valuten** (Finanzw.) foreign currency
Vamp /vɛmp/ *der;* ∼**s**, ∼**s** vamp
Vampir /'vampi:ɐ̯/ *der;* ∼**s**, ∼**e** vampire
Vanille /va'nɪljə/ *die;* ∼**:** vanilla
Vanille-: ∼**eis** *das* vanilla ice cream; ∼**pudding** *der* vanilla pudding; ∼**zucker** *der* vanilla sugar

variabel /va'rịa:bl̩/ **1** *Adj.* variable. **2** *adv.* variably
Variable /va'rịa:blə/ *die; adj. Dekl.* (Math., Physik) variable
Variante /va'rịantə/ *die;* ∼, ∼**n** (geh.) variant; variation
Variation /varia'tsịo:n/ *die;* ∼, ∼**en** (auch Musik) variation (*Gen.*, **über, zu** on)
Varieté, Varietee /varie'te:/ *das;* ∼**s**, ∼**s** variety theatre; (Aufführung) variety show
variieren *tr., itr. V.* vary
Vase /'va:zə/ *die;* ∼, ∼**n** vase
Vater /'fa:tɐ/ *der;* ∼**s**, **Väter** /'fɛ:tɐ/ **(a)** father; **er ist** ∼ **von drei Kindern** he is the father of three children; **er ist der [geistige]** ∼ **dieser Idee** (fig.) he thought up this idea; this idea is his; ∼ **Staat** (scherzh.) the State; **Heiliger** ∼ (kath. Kirche) Holy Father; **(b)** (Tier) sire; **(c)** *o. Pl.* (Rel.) Father; **Gott** ∼: God the Father
Vater-: ∼**freuden** *Pl.* ∼**freuden entgegensehen** (meist scherzh.) be expecting a happy event; be going to be a father; ∼**haus** *das* (geh.) parental home; ∼**land** *das; Pl.* ∼**länder** fatherland
väterlich /'fɛ:tɐlɪç/ **1** *Adj.* **(a)** *nicht präd.* the/one's father's; paternal ‹ *line, love, instincts, etc.* ›; **(b)** (fürsorglich) fatherly. **2** *adv.* in a fatherly way
väterlicherseits *Adv.* on the/ one's father's side; **meine Großeltern** ∼: my paternal grandparents; my grandparents on my father's side
vater-, Vater-: ∼**schaft** *die;* ∼, ∼**en** fatherhood; (bes. Rechtsw.) paternity; ∼**schafts·klage** *die* paternity suit; ∼**stadt** *die* (geh.) home town; ∼**stelle** *die:* **bei jmdm.** ∼**stelle vertreten** take the place of a father to sb.; ∼**tag** *der* Father's Day *no def. art.;* ∼**unser** *das;* ∼**s**, ∼**:** Lord's Prayer
Vati /'fa:ti/ *der;* ∼**s**, ∼**s** (fam.) dad[dy] (coll.)
Vatikan /vati'ka:n/ *der;* ∼**s** Vatican
vatikanisch *Adj.; nicht präd.* Vatican
Vatikan·stadt *die;* ▶ 490 | *o. Pl.* Vatican City
V-Ausschnitt /'faʊ-/ *der* V-neck
v. Chr. *Abk.* ▶ 119 | **vor Christus** BC
VEB /faʊ|e:'be:/ *Abk.* **Volkseigener Betrieb**
Vegetarier /vege'ta:rịɐ/ *der;* ∼**s**, ∼**:** vegetarian
vegetarisch **1** *Adj.* vegetarian. **2** *adv.* **er lebt** *od.* **ernährt sich** ∼: he is a vegetarian; he lives on a vegetarian diet
Vegetation /...'tsịo:n/ *die;* ∼, ∼**en** vegetation *no indef. art.*
vegetieren *itr. V.* vegetate
vehement /vehe'mɛnt/ (geh.) **1** *Adj.* vehement. **2** *adv.* vehemently
Vehemenz /...'mɛnts/ *die;* ∼ (geh.) vehemence
Vehikel /ve'hi:kl̩/ *das;* ∼**s**, ∼ (oft abwertend, auch fig. geh.) vehicle; **ein altes/klappriges** ∼: an old crock (sl.)
Veilchen /'faɪlçən/ *das;* ∼**s**, ∼**:** violet
veilchen·blau *Adj.* violet
Vektor /'vɛktɔr/ *der;* ∼**s**, ∼**en** /-'to:rən/ (Math., Physik) vector
Velo /'ve:lo/ *das;* ∼**s**, ∼**s** (schweiz.) bicycle; bike (coll.)
Velours¹ /vɛ'lu:ɐ̯/ *der;* ∼ /və'lu:ɐ̯s/, ∼ /ve'lu:ɐ̯s/ (Stoff) velour[s]
Velours² *das;* ∼ /və'lu:ɐ̯s/, ∼ /ve'lu:ɐ̯s/, **Velours·leder** *das* suede
Vene /'ve:nə/ *die;* ∼, ∼**n** ▶ 326 | (Anat.) vein
Venedig /ve'ne:dɪç/ *(das);* ∼**s** ▶ 490 | Venice
Venezianer /vene'tsịa:nɐ/ *der;* ∼**s**, ∼**:** ▶ 490 | Venetian
venezianisch *Adj.* Venetian
Venezolaner /venetso'la:nɐ/ *der;* ∼**s**, ∼, **Venezolanerin** *die;* ∼, ∼**nen** ▶ 388 | Venezuelan
venezolanisch *Adj.* ▶ 388 | Venezuelan
Venezuela /vene'tsue:la/ *(das);* ∼**s** Venezuela
venös *Adj.* (Med.) venous
Ventil /vɛn'ti:l/ *das;* ∼**s**, ∼**e** **(a)** valve; (fig.) outlet; **(b)** (der Orgel) pallet
Ventilation /vɛntila'tsịo:n/ *die;* ∼, ∼**en** ventilation
Ventilator /vɛnti'la:tɔr/ *der;* ∼**s**, ∼**en** /...la'to:rən/ ventilator

Venus /'ve:nʊs/ *die;* ~**:** Venus *no def. art.*

verabreden 1 *tr. V.* arrange; **am verabredeten Ort** at the agreed place. **2** *refl. V.* **sich im Park/zum Tennis** ~**:** arrange to meet in the park/for tennis; **sich mit jmdm.** ~**:** arrange to meet sb.; **ich bin mit ihm verabredet** I am meeting him

Verabredung *die;* ~, ~**en** (a) (Absprache) arrangement; **eine** ~ **treffen** arrange to meet *or* a meeting; (b) (verabredete Zusammenkunft) appointment; **eine** ~ **absagen** call off a meeting *or* an engagement; **ich habe eine** ~**:** I am meeting somebody; (formell) I have an appointment; (mit meinem Freund/meiner Freundin) I have a date (coll.)

verabreichen *tr. V.* administer ⟨*medicine*⟩; give ⟨*injection, thrashing*⟩

Verabreichung *die;* ~, ~**en** administration; administering

verabsäumen *tr. V.* (Papierdt.) neglect; omit

verabscheuen *tr. V.* detest; loathe

verabscheuenswürdig *Adj.* (geh.) detestable; loathsome

verabschieden 1 *tr. V.* (a) say goodbye to; (b) (aus dem Dienst) retire; (c) (annehmen) adopt ⟨*plan, budget*⟩; pass ⟨*law*⟩. **2** *refl. V.* **sich [von jmdm.]** ~**:** say goodbye [to sb.]; (formell) take one's leave [of sb.]

Verabschiedung *die;* ~, ~**en** (a) leave-taking; (b) (aus dem Dienst) retirement; (c) (eines Plans, Etats) adoption; (eines Gesetzes) passing

verachten *tr. V.* despise

Verächter /fɛɐ̯'|ɛçtɐ/ *der;* ~**s**, ~**:** opponent; critic

verächtlich /fɛɐ̯'|ɛçtlɪç/ **1** *Adj.* (a) (abschätzig) contemptuous; (b) (verachtenswürdig) contemptible; despicable; **jmdn./etw.** ~ **machen** disparage sb./sth.; run sb./sth. down. **2** *adv.* contemptuously

Verächtlichkeit *die;* ~**:** contempt; contemptuousness

Verachtung *die;* ~**:** contempt; **jmdn. mit** ~ **strafen** treat sb. with contempt

veralbern *tr. V.* make fun of

verallgemeinern *tr., itr. V.* generalize

Verallgemeinerung *die;* ~, ~**en** generalization

veralten *itr. V.; mit sein* become obsolete; **veraltete Methoden** obsolete *or* antiquated methods

Veranda /ve'randa/ *die;* ~, **Veranden** veranda; porch

veränderlich *Adj.* (a) changeable ⟨*weather*⟩; variable ⟨*character, star*⟩; (b) (veränderbar) variable

Veränderlichkeit *die;* ~, ~**en** ⇒ **veränderlich:** changeability; variability

verändern 1 *tr. V.* change; **der Bart verändert ihn stark** the beard makes him look very different. **2** *refl. V.* (a) change; **sich zu seinem Vorteil/Nachteil** ~**:** change for the better/worse; (b) (die Stellung wechseln) **sich [beruflich]** ~**:** change one's job

Veränderung *die* change ⟨*Gen.* in⟩; **an etw.** (*Dat.*) **eine** ~ **vornehmen** change sth.

verängstigen *tr. V.* frighten; scare

verankern *tr. V.* fix ⟨*tent, mast, pole, etc.*⟩; (mit einem Anker) anchor; (fig.) embody ⟨*right etc.*⟩

Verankerung *die;* ~, ~**en** (a) fixing; (mit einem Anker) anchoring; (fig.) embodiment; (b) (Halterung) anchorage; fixture

veranlagen *tr. V.* (Steuerw.) assess (**mit** at)

veranlagt *Adj.* **künstlerisch/praktisch/romantisch** ~ **sein** have an artistic bent/be practically minded/have a romantic disposition; **ein homosexuell** ~**er Mann** a man with homosexual tendencies

Veranlagung *die;* ~, ~**en** (a) [pre]disposition; **seine homosexuelle / künstlerische / praktische / romantische** ~**:** his homosexual tendencies *pl.*/artistic bent/ practical nature/romantic disposition; (b) (Steuerw.) assessment

veranlassen *tr. V.* (a) cause; induce; (b) (erledigen lassen) **etw.** ~**:** see to it that sth. is done *or* carried out; **ich werde alles Weitere/das Nötige** ~**:** I will take care of

or see to everything else/I will see [to it] that the necessary steps are taken

Veranlassung *die;* ~, ~**en** (a) reason, cause (**zu** for); (b) **auf jmds.** ~ **[hin]** on sb.'s orders

veranschaulichen *tr. V.* illustrate

Veranschaulichung *die;* ~, ~**en** illustration

veranschlagen *tr. V.* estimate (**mit** at); **etw. zu hoch/ niedrig** ~**:** overestimate/underestimate sth.

Veranschlagung *die;* ~, ~**en** estimate

veranstalten *tr. V.* (a) organize; hold, give ⟨*party*⟩; (b) (ugs.) make ⟨*noise, fuss*⟩

Veranstalter *der;* ~**s**, ~, **Veranstalterin** *die;* ~, ~**nen** organizer

Veranstaltung *die;* ~, ~**en** (a) (das Veranstalten) organizing; organization; (b) (Ereignis) event

verantworten 1 *tr. V.* take responsibility for; **ich kann das vor Gott/mir selbst/meinem Gewissen nicht** ~**:** I cannot be responsible for that before God/I cannot justify it to myself/I cannot square that with my conscience. **2** *refl. V.* **sich für etw.** ~**:** answer for sth.; **sich vor jmdm.** ~**:** answer to sb.; **sich vor Gericht** ~**:** answer to the courts

verantwortlich *Adj.* responsible; **jmdn. für etw.** ~ **machen** hold sb. responsible for sth.

Verantwortlichkeit *die;* ~, ~**en** responsibility

Verantwortung *die;* ~, ~**en** responsibility (**für** for); **die** ~ **für etw. übernehmen** take *or* accept [the] responsibility for sth.; **ich tue es auf deine** ~**:** you must take responsibility; on your own head be it; **jmdn. [für etw.] zur** ~ **ziehen** call sb. to account [for sth.]

verantwortungs-, **Verantwortungs-:** ~**bewusst**, **~**bewußt** *Adj.* responsible; ~**bewusstsein**, **~**bewußtsein** *das; o. Pl.,* ~**gefühl** *das; o. Pl.* sense of responsibility; ~**los** *Adj.* irresponsible; ~**losigkeit** *die;* ~**:** irresponsibility; ~**voll** *Adj.* responsible

veräppeln /fɛɐ̯'|ɛpl̩n/ *tr. V.* **jmdn** ~ (ugs.) have (Brit. coll.) *or* (Amer. coll.) put sb. on

verarbeiten *tr. V.* (a) use; **etw. zu etw.** ~**:** make sth. into sth.; use sth. to make sth.; (b) (verdauen) digest ⟨*food*⟩; (c) (geistig bewältigen) digest, assimilate ⟨*film, experience, impressions*⟩; come to terms with ⟨*disappointment*⟩

verarbeitet *Adj.* **gut/schlecht** *usw.* ~**:** well/badly *etc.* finished ⟨*suit, dress, car, etc.*⟩

Verarbeitung *die;* ~, ~**en** (a) use; (b) (Art der Fertigung) finish

verärgern *tr. V.* annoy

Verärgerung *die;* ~, ~**en** annoyance

verarmen *itr. V.; mit sein* become poor *or* impoverished

verarschen *tr. V.* **jmdn.** ~ (derb) take the piss (coarse) *or* (Brit. coll.) mickey out of sb.

verarzten *tr. V.* (ugs.) patch up (coll.) ⟨*person*⟩; fix (coll.) ⟨*wound, injury, etc.*⟩

verästeln /fɛɐ̯'|ɛstl̩n/ *refl. V.* branch out

Veräst[e]lung *die;* ~, ~**en** ramification

verätzen *tr. V.* corrode ⟨*metal etc.*⟩; burn ⟨*skin, face, etc.*⟩

Verätzung *die* corrosion; (der Haut) burn

verausgaben 1 *tr. V.* (Papierdt.) spend. **2** *refl. V.* wear oneself out

veräußern *tr. V.* dispose of, sell ⟨*property*⟩

Verb /vɛrp/ *das;* ~**s**, ~**en** verb

verbal /vɛr'ba:l/ *Adj.* **1** (auch Sprachw.) verbal. **2** *adv.* verbally

Verband *der* (a) (Binde) bandage; dressing; (b) (Vereinigung) association

Verband-: ~**kasten** *der* first-aid box; ~**material** *das* dressing materials *pl.;* ~**päckchen** *das* packet of dressings; ~**zeug** *das* first-aid things *pl.*

verbannen *tr. V.* (auch fig.) banish

Verbannung *die;* ~, ~**en** banishment; exile

verbarrikadieren 1 *tr. V.* barricade. **2** *refl. V.* barricade oneself

---

**alte Schreibung (vgl. Hinweise auf S. xvi–xvii)

verbauen *tr. V.* **(a)** (versperren) obstruct; block; **sich die Zukunft** ∼ (fig.) spoil one's prospects for the future; **(b)** (zum Bauen verwenden) use

verbeißen *unr. tr. V.* suppress; hold back ‹ *tears etc.* ›

verbergen *unr. tr. V.* **(a)** (auch fig.) hide; conceal; **sich** ∼: hide; **(b)** (verheimlichen) hide; **jmdm. etw.** ∼, **etw. vor jmdm.** ∼: keep sth. from sb.

verbessern 1 *tr. V.* **(a)** improve ‹ *machine, method, quality* ›; improve [up]on, better ‹ *achievement* ›; beat ‹ *record* ›; reform ‹ *schooling, world* ›; **(b)** (korrigieren) correct. 2 *refl. V.* **(a)** improve; **(b)** ([beruflich] aufsteigen) better oneself

Verbesserung *die* **(a)** improvement; **eine** ∼ **der Lage** an improvement in the situation; **(b)** (Korrektur) correction

verbeugen *refl. V.* bow **(vor** + *Dat.* to)

Verbeugung *die;* ∼, ∼**en** bow; **eine** ∼ **vor jmdm. machen** bow to sb.

verbeulen *tr. V.* dent

verbiegen 1 *unr. tr. V.* bend. 2 *unr. refl. V.* bend; buckle

verbieten 1 *unr. tr. V.* **(a)** forbid; **jmdm. etw.**∼: forbid sb. sth.; **sie hat ihm das Haus verboten** she forbade him to enter the house; **„Betreten des Rasens/ Rauchen verboten**"! 'keep off the grass'/'no smoking'; **(b)** (für unzulässig erklären) ban. 2 *unr. refl. V.* **sich [von selbst]** ∼: be out of the question

verbilligen 1 *tr. V.* bring down *or* reduce the cost of; bring down *or* reduce the price of, reduce ‹ *goods* ›. 2 *refl. V.* become *or* get cheaper; ‹ *goods* › come down in price, become *or* get cheaper

verbinden 1 *unr. tr. V.* **(a)** (bandagieren) bandage; dress; **jmdm./sich den Fuß** ∼: bandage *or* dress sb.'s/one's foot; **jmdm./sich** ∼: dress sb.'s/one's wounds; **(b)** (zubinden) bind; **jmdm. die Augen** ∼: blindfold sb.; **mit verbundenen Augen** blindfold[ed]; **(c)** (zusammenfügen) join ‹ *wires, lengths of wood, etc.* ›; join up ‹ *dots* ›; **(d)** (zusammenhalten) hold ‹ *parts* › together; **(e)** (in Beziehung bringen) connect **(durch** by); link ‹ *towns, lakes, etc.* › **(durch** by); **(f)** (verknüpfen) combine ‹ *abilities, qualities, etc.* ›; **die damit verbundenen Anstrengungen/Kosten** *usw.* the effort/ cost *etc.* involved; **(g)** *auch itr.* (telefonisch) **jmdn. [mit jmdm.]** ∼: put sb. through [to sb.]; **Moment, ich verbinde** one moment, I'll put you through; **falsch verbunden sein** have got the wrong number; **(h)** *auch itr.* **er war ihr freundschaftlich verbunden** he was bound to her by ties of friendship; **uns verbindet nichts mehr** nothing holds us together any longer; **(i)** (assoziieren) associate **(mit** with). 2 *unr. refl. V.* **(a)** (auch Chemie) combine **(mit** with); **(b)** (sich zusammentun) join [together]; join forces; **(c)** (in Gedanken) be associated **(mit** with)

verbindlich 1 *Adj.* **(a)** (freundlich) friendly; (entgegenkommend) forthcoming; ∼**sten Dank!** (geh.) a thousand thanks; **(b)** (bindend) obligatory; compulsory; binding ‹ *agreement, decision, etc.* ›. 2 *adv.* **(a)** (freundlich) in a friendly manner; (entgegenkommend) in a forthcoming manner; **(b)** ∼ **zusagen** definitely agree; **jmdm. etw.** ∼ **anbieten** make sb. a firm offer of sth.

Verbindlichkeit *die;* ∼, ∼**en** **(a)** *o. Pl.* ⇒ **verbindlich 1 a**: friendliness; forthcomingness; **(b)** *o. Pl.;* ⇒ **verbindlich 1 b**: obligatory *or* compulsory nature; **(c)** *Pl.* (Kaufmannsspr.: Schulden) liabilities **(gegen** to)

Verbindung *die* **(a)** (das Verknüpfen) linking; **(b)** (Zusammenhalt) join; connection; **(c)** (verknüpfende Strecke) link; **(d)** (durch Telefon, Funk) connection; **keine** ∼ **mit jmdm. bekommen** not be able to get through to sb.; **(e)** (Verkehrs∼) connection **(nach** to); **die** ∼ **zur Außenwelt** connections *pl.* with the outside world; **(f)** (Kombination) combination; **in** ∼ **mit etw.** in conjunction with sth.; **(g)** (Bündnis) association; **eheliche** ∼ (geh.) marriage; **(h)** (Kontakt) contact; **sich mit jmdm. in** ∼ **setzen,** ∼ **mit jmdm. aufnehmen** get in touch *or* contact with sb.; contact sb.; **in** ∼ **bleiben** keep in touch; **seine** ∼**en spielen lassen** pull a few strings (coll.); **(i)** (Zusammenhang) connection; **jmdm. mit etw. in** ∼ **bringen** connect sb. with sth.; **(j)** (Studenten∼) society; **(k)** (Chemie) compound

Verbindungs-: ∼**mann** *der; Pl.* ∼**männer** *od.* ∼**leute** intermediary; (Agent) contact [man] **(zu** with); ∼**tür** *die* connecting door

Verbiss, *****Verbiß** *der* (Jägerspr.) damage caused by browsing animals

verbissen 1 *Adj.* **(a)** (hartnäckig) dogged; doggedly determined; **(b)** (verkrampft) grim. 2 *adv.* **(a)** (hartnäckig) doggedly; with dogged determination; **(b)** (verkrampft) grimly

Verbissenheit *die;* ∼: doggedness; dogged determination

verbitten *unr. refl. V.* **sich** *(Dat.)* **etw.** ∼: refuse to tolerate sth.; **ich verbitte mir diesen Ton** I will not be spoken to in that tone of voice

verbittern *tr. V.* embitter; make bitter; **verbittert** embittered; bitter

Verbitterung *die;* ∼, ∼**en** bitterness; embitterment

verblassen *itr. V.; mit sein* (auch fig. geh.) fade

Verbleib *der;* ∼[e]s (geh.) **(a)** (Ort) whereabouts *pl.;* **(b)** (das Verbleiben) staying; **ein weiterer** ∼: a longer stay

verbleiben *unr. itr. V.; mit sein* **(a)** (sich einigen) **wie seid ihr denn nun verblieben?** what did you arrange?; **wir sind so verblieben, dass er sich bei mir meldet** we left it that he would contact me; **(b)** (geh.: bleiben) remain; stay; **(c)** (im Briefschluss) remain; **ich verbleibe mit freundlichen Grüßen Ihr** ...: I remain, Yours sincerely, ...; **(d)** (übrig bleiben) remain; **etw. verbleibt jmdm.** sb. has sth. left

verbleichen *unr. od. regelm. itr. V.; mit sein* (auch fig.) fade

verblendet *Adj.* blind

Verblendung *die;* ∼, ∼**en** blindness

verblöden *itr. V.; mit sein* (ugs.) become a zombie (coll.)

verblüffen /fɛɐ̯'blʏfn̩/ *tr., auch itr. V.* astonish; amaze; astound; (verwirren) baffle

verblüffend 1 *Adj.* astonishing; amazing; astounding. 2 *adv.* astonishingly; amazingly; astoundingly

Verblüffung *die;* ∼, ∼**en** astonishment; amazement

verblühen *itr. V.; mit sein* (auch fig.) fade

verbluten *itr., auch refl. V.; mit sein* bleed to death

verbocken *tr. V.* (ugs.) botch; bungle; make a botch-up of

verbohren *refl. V.* (ugs.) become obsessed **(in** + *Akk.* with)

verbohrt *Adj.* (abwertend) pigheaded; stubborn; obstinate; (unbeugsam) inflexible

Verbohrtheit *die;* ∼ (abwertend) pigheadedness; stubbornness; obstinacy; (Unbeugsamkeit) inflexibility

verborgen *Adj.* hidden; **es wird ihm nicht** ∼ **bleiben** he shall hear of it; (nicht entgehen) it will not escape his notice; **im Verborgenen** out of the public eye

Verbot *das;* ∼[e]s, ∼**e** ban (Gen., **von**, **von** on); **trotz ärztlichen** ∼**s** against doctor's orders

Verbots·schild *das* (Verkehrsw.) prohibitive sign

verbrämen /fɛɐ̯'brɛːmən/ *tr. V.* **(a)** (einfassen) trim **(mit** with); **(b)** (verschleiern) dress up (fig.); **wissenschaftlich verbrämter Unsinn** nonsense dressed up as scientific fact

verbraten *unr. tr. V.* (salopp) blow (sl.) ‹ *money* › **(für** on)

Verbrauch *der;* ∼[e]s consumption **(von, an** + *Dat.* of); **zum alsbaldigen** ∼ **bestimmt** for immediate consumption

verbrauchen *tr. V.* **(a)** use; consume ‹ *food, drink* ›; use up ‹ *provisions* ›; spend ‹ *money* ›; consume, use ‹ *fuel* ›; (fig.) use up ‹ *strength, energy* ›; **das Auto verbraucht 10 Liter [auf 100 Kilometer]** the car does 10 kilometres to the litre; ▶ **427** **(b)** (verschleißen) wear out ‹ *clothing, shoes, etc.* ›; **die Luft in den Räumen ist verbraucht** the air in the rooms is stale

Verbraucher *der;* ∼s, ∼, **Verbraucherin** *die;* ∼, ∼**nen** consumer

verbrechen *unr. tr. V.* (scherzh.) **ich habe nichts verbrochen!** I haven't been up to *or* haven't done anything!; **wer hat denn dieses Gedicht verbrochen?** who's responsible for *or* who's the perpetrator of this poem?

Verbrechen *das;* ∼s, ∼ crime **(an** + *Dat.,* **gegen** against)

Verbrecher *der;* ~s, ~: criminal
Verbrecher·bande *die* gang *or* band of criminals
Verbrecherin *die;* ~, ~nen criminal
verbrecherisch *Adj.* criminal
verbreiten 1 *tr. V.* (a) (bekannt machen) spread ‹*rumour, lies, etc.*›; **etw. über den Rundfunk** ~: broadcast sth. on the radio; (b) (weitertragen) spread ‹*disease, illness, etc.*›; (c) (erwecken) radiate ‹*optimism, happiness, calm, etc.*›; spread ‹*fear*›. 2 *refl. V.* (a) (bekannt werden) ‹*rumour*› spread; (b) (sich ausbreiten) ‹*smell, illness, religion, etc.*› spread
verbreitern 1 *tr. V.* widen; (fig.) broaden ‹*basis*›. 2 *refl. V.* widen out; get wider
Verbreitung *die;* ~, ~en (a) ⇒ **verbreiten** 1 a, b, c: spreading; broadcasting; radiation; (b) (Ausbreitung) spread
verbrennen 1 *unr. itr. V.; mit sein* burn; ‹*person*› burn to death; **die Dokumente sind verbrannt** the documents were destroyed by fire; **es riecht verbrannt** (ugs.) there's a smell of burning; **der Kuchen ist verbrannt** the cake got burnt. 2 *tr. V.* (a) burn; burn, incinerate ‹*rubbish*›; cremate ‹*dead person*›; (b) ▶ 329 ⏐ (verletzen) burn; **sich** (*Dat.*) **an der heißen Suppe die Zunge** ~: burn *or* scald one's tongue on the hot soup; **sich** (*Dat.*) **den Mund** *od.* (derb) **das Maul** ~ (fig.) say too much; *s. auch* **Finger** b
Verbrennung *die;* ~, ~en (a) ⇒ **verbrennen** 2 a: burning; incineration; cremation; (b) (Kfz-W.) combustion; (c) ▶ 329⏐ (Wunde) burn
Verbrennungs·motor *der* internal-combustion engine
verbringen *unr. tr. V.* spend ‹*time, holiday, etc.*›
verbrüdern *refl. V.* avow friendship and brotherhood
Verbrüderung *die;* ~, ~en avowal of friendship and brotherhood
verbrühen *tr. V.* ▶ 329⏐ scald; **sich** (*Dat.*) **den Arm** ~: scald one's arm
verbuchen *tr. V.* enter; (fig.) notch up ‹*success, score, etc.*›; **etw. auf einem Konto** ~: credit sth. to an account
verbuddeln *tr. V.* (ugs.) bury
verbummeln *tr. V.* (ugs., oft abwertend) (a) (verbringen) waste, fritter away ‹*time, day, afternoon, etc.*›; (b) (vergessen) forget [all] about; clean forget; (c) (verlieren) lose; (verlegen) mislay
verbünden /fɛɐ̯ˈbʏndn̩/ *refl. V.* form an alliance
verbündet *Adj.* [miteinander] ~: in alliance *postpos.*
Verbündete *der/die; adj. Dekl.* ally
verbüßen *tr. V.* serve ‹*sentence*›
Verbüßung *die;* ~: serving
Verdacht /fɛɐ̯ˈdaxt/ *der;* ~[e]s, ~e *od.* **Verdächte** /fɛɐ̯ˈdɛçtə/ suspicion; ~ **schöpfen** become suspicious; **wen hast du in** ~? who do you suspect?; **ich geriet in** [den] ~, **das Geld gestohlen zu haben** I was suspected of having stolen the money
verdächtig /fɛɐ̯ˈdɛçtɪç/ 1 *Adj.* suspicious; **sich** ~ **machen** arouse suspicion. 2 *adv.* suspiciously
Verdächtige *der/die; adj. Dekl.* suspect
verdächtigen *tr. V.* suspect (*Gen.* of)
Verdächtigung *die;* ~, ~en suspicion
verdammen *tr. V.* (a) condemn; (Rel.) damn ‹*sinner*›; (b) **dazu verdammt sein, etw. zu tun** (fig.) be condemned to do sth.
verdammt 1 *Adj.; nicht präd.* (a) (salopp abwertend) bloody (Brit. sl.); damned (coll.); ~ [noch mal *od.* noch eins]! damn [it all] (coll.); bloody hell (Brit. sl.); ~ und zugenäht! damn and blast [it]! (coll.); (b) (ugs.: sehr groß) [ein] ~es Glück haben be damn[ed] lucky (coll.). 2 *adv.* (ugs.: sehr) damn[ed] (coll.) ‹*cold, heavy, beautiful, etc.*›; **ich musste mich** ~ **beherrschen** I had to keep a bloody good grip on myself (Brit. sl.)
Verdammung *die;* ~, ~en condemnation; damnation
verdampfen 1 *itr. V.; mit sein* evaporate; vaporize. 2 *tr. V.* evaporate; vaporize

verdanken *tr. V.* jmdm./einer Sache etw. ~: owe sth. to sb./sth.
verdarb /fɛɐ̯ˈdarp/ *1. u. 3. Pers. Sg. Prät. v.* **verderben**
verdauen /fɛɐ̯ˈdaʊ̯ən/ *tr., itr. V.* (auch fig.) digest; (fig.) get over ‹*bad experience, shock, etc.*›
verdaulich /fɛɐ̯ˈdaʊ̯lɪç/ *Adj.* digestible
Verdauung *die;* ~: digestion
Verdauungs-: ~**beschwerden** *Pl.* digestive trouble *sing.;* ~**störung** *die* poor digestion *no pl.*
Verdeck *das;* ~[e]s, ~e top; hood (Brit.); (bei Kinderwagen) hood
verdecken *tr. V.* (a) (nicht sichtbar sein lassen) hide; cover; **jmdm. die Sicht** ~: block sb.'s view; (b) (verbergen) cover; conceal; (fig.) conceal ‹*intentions etc.*›
verdenken *unr. tr. V.* jmdm. etw. nicht ~ [können] not [be able to] hold sth. against sb.
Verderb ⇒ **Gedeih**
verderben 1 *unr. itr. V.; mit sein* ‹*food, harvest*› go bad *or* off, spoil. 2 *unr. tr. V.* (a) spoil; (stärker) ruin; (fig.) ruin ‹*evening*›; spoil ‹*appetite, enjoyment, fun, good mood, etc.*›; (b) (geh.: negativ beeinflussen) corrupt; deprave; **er will es mit niemandem** ~: he tries to please everybody. 3 *unr. refl. V.* **sich** (*Dat.*) **den Magen/die Augen** ~: give oneself an upset stomach/ruin one's eyesight
Verderben *das;* ~s undoing; ruin; **in sein** *od.* **ins** ~ **rennen** rush headlong towards ruin
verderblich *Adj.* (a) perishable ‹*food*›; **leicht** ~: highly perishable; (b) (unheilvoll) pernicious; (moralisch schädlich) corrupting; pernicious ‹*influence, effect, etc.*›
Verderblichkeit *die;* ~ ⇒ **verderblich**: perishableness; perniciousness; corrupting effect
verdeutlichen *tr. V.* etw. ~: make sth. clear; (erklären) explain sth.
verdichten 1 *refl. V.* ‹*fog, smoke*› thicken, become thicker; (fig.) ‹*suspicion, rumour*› grow; ‹*feeling*› intensify. 2 *tr. V.* (fig.) condense ‹*events etc.*› (zu into)
Verdickung *die;* ~, ~en thickened section; (Schwellung) swelling
verdienen 1 *tr. V.* (a) earn; (b) (wert sein) deserve; **er verdient kein Vertrauen** he doesn't deserve to be trusted; **womit habe ich das verdient?** what have I done to deserve that? 2 *itr. V.* **beide Eheleute** ~: husband and wife are both wage earners *or* are both earning; **gut** ~: have a good income
Verdiener *der;* ~s, ~: wage earner
Verdienst[1] *der* income; earnings *pl.*
Verdienst[2] *das;* ~[e]s, ~e merit
verdienst·voll 1 *Adj.* commendable. 2 *adv.* commendably
verdient 1 *Adj.* (a) ‹*person*› of outstanding merit; **sich um etw.** ~ **machen** render outstanding services to sth.; (b) (gerecht, zustehend) well-deserved. 2 *adv.* deservedly
verdientermaßen *Adv.* deservedly
verdonnern *tr. V.* (salopp) sentence; jmdn. dazu ~, etw. zu tun order *or* make sb. do sth. [as a punishment]
verdoppeln 1 *tr. V.* double; (fig.) double, redouble ‹*efforts etc.*›. 2 *refl. V.* double
Verdoppelung *die;* ~, ~en doubling
verdorben /fɛɐ̯ˈdɔrbn̩/ *2. Part. v.* **verderben**
Verdorbenheit *die;* ~: depravity
verdorren /fɛɐ̯ˈdɔrən/ *itr. V.; mit sein* wither [and die]; ‹*meadow*› scorch
verdrängen *tr. V.* (a) drive out ‹*inhabitants*›; (fig.: ersetzen) displace; jmdn. aus seiner Stellung ~: oust sb. from his/her job; (b) (Psych.) repress/(bewusst) suppress ‹*experience, desire, etc.*›
Verdrängung *die;* ~, ~en (a) ⇒ **verdrängen** a: driving out; displacement; ousting; (b) (Psych.) repression; (bewusst) suppression
Verdrängungs·wettbewerb *der* (Kaufmannsspr.) competition for markets
verdrecken (ugs. abwertend) 1 *tr. V.* make filthy dirty. 2 *itr. V.; mit sein* get *or* become filthy dirty

---

*alte Schreibung (vgl. Hinweise auf S. xvi–xvii)

verdrehen *tr. V.* (a) twist ⟨*joint*⟩; roll ⟨*eyes*⟩; **den Hals** ∼**:** twist one's head round; **sich** (*Dat.*) **den Hals** ∼**:** crick one's neck; (b) (ugs. abwertend: entstellen) twist ⟨*words, facts, etc.*⟩; distort ⟨*sense*⟩

verdreifachen *refl., tr. V.* treble; triple

verdreschen *unr. tr. V.* (ugs.) thrash

verdrießen /fɛɐ̯'driːsn̩/ *unr. tr. V.* (geh.) irritate; annoy

verdrießlich 1 *Adj.* morose. 2 *adv.* morosely

Verdrießlichkeit *die;* ∼**:** moroseness

verdross, *verdroß /fɛɐ̯'drɔs/ *1. u. 3. Pers. Sg. Prät. v.* **verdrießen**

verdrossen 1 *2. Part. v.* **verdrießen.** 2 *Adj.* morose; (missmutig und lustlos) sullen. 3 *adv.* morosely; (missmutig und lustlos) sullenly

Verdrossenheit *die;* ∼ ⇒ **verdrossen** 2: moroseness; sullenness

verdrücken (ugs.) 1 *tr. V.* (a) (essen) polish off (coll.); (b) (verknautschen) crumple ⟨*clothes*⟩. 2 *refl. V.* slip away

Verdruss, *Verdruß /fɛɐ̯'drʊs/ *der;* **Verdrusses, Verdrusse** annoyance; (Unzufriedenheit) dissatisfaction; discontentment; **jmdm.** ∼ **bereiten** annoy sb.

verduften *itr. V.; mit sein* (salopp: sich entfernen) hop it (Brit. coll.); clear off (coll.)

Verdummung *die;* ∼ (a) **die** ∼ **der Massen zum Ziel haben** be aimed at dulling the mind of the masses; (b) (das Dummwerden) stultification

verdunkeln 1 *tr. V.* (a) darken; (vollständig) black out ⟨*room, house, etc.*⟩; (b) (verdecken) darken; (fig.) cast a shadow on ⟨*happiness etc.*⟩. 2 *refl. V.* darken; grow darker; (fig.) ⟨*expression etc.*⟩ darken

Verdunk[e]lung *die;* ∼, ∼**en** darkening; (vollständig) blackout

verdünnen *tr. V.* (a) dilute; (mit Wasser) water down; dilute; thin [down] ⟨*paint etc.*⟩

Verdünnung *die;* ∼, ∼**en** dilution

verdunsten 1 *itr. V.; mit sein* evaporate. 2 *tr. V.* evaporate; ⟨*plant*⟩ transpire ⟨*water*⟩

Verdunstung *die;* ∼**:** evaporation

verdursten *itr. V.; mit sein* die of thirst

verdüstern 1 *tr. V.* darken; (fig. geh.) cast a shadow across. 2 *refl. V.* darken; grow dark; (fig.) darken

verdutzt /fɛɐ̯'dʊtst/ *Adj.* taken aback *pred.;* nonplussed; (verwirrt) baffled

veredeln *tr. V.* (a) (geh.) ennoble; improve ⟨*taste*⟩; (b) (Technik) refine

Vered[e]lung *die;* ∼, ∼**en** (a) (geh.) ennoblement; (b) (Technik) refinement

verehren *tr. V.* (a) (vergöttern) venerate; revere; **verehrte Frau Müller!** Dear Frau Müller; (b) (geh.: bewundern) admire; (ehrerbietig lieben) worship; adore; (c) (scherzh.: schenken) give

Verehrer *der;* ∼**s,** ∼, **Verehrerin** *die;* ∼, ∼**en** admirer

Verehrung *die; o. Pl.* (a) veneration; reverence; (b) (Bewunderung) admiration

vereidigen /fɛɐ̯'|aidɪɡn̩/ *tr. V.* swear in; **jmdn. auf etw.** (*Akk.*) ∼**:** make sb. swear to sth.; **ein vereidigter Sachverständiger** a sworn expert

Vereidigung *die;* ∼, ∼**en** swearing in

Verein organization; (zur Förderung der Denkmalspflege usw.) society; (der Kunstfreunde usw.) association; society; (Sport∼) club

vereinbar *Adj.; nicht attr.* compatible (**mit** with)

vereinbaren *tr. V.* (a) (festlegen) agree; arrange ⟨*meeting etc.*⟩; (b) (in Einklang bringen) reconcile; [**nicht**] **zu** ∼ **sein** be [in]compatible *or* [ir]reconcilable

Vereinbarung *die;* ∼, ∼**en** agreement; **eine** ∼ **treffen** come to an agreement

vereinfachen *tr. V.* simplify

Vereinfachung *die;* ∼, ∼**en** simplification

vereinheitlichen *tr. V.* standardize

vereinigen 1 *tr. V.* unite; merge ⟨*businesses*⟩; (zusammenfassen) bring together; **die Mehrheit der Stimmen auf**

sich ∼**:** receive the majority of the votes. 2 *refl. V.* unite; ⟨*organizations, firms*⟩ merge; (fig.) be combined

vereinigt *Adj.* united; **Vereinigtes Königreich [Großbritannien und Nordirland]** United Kingdom [of Great Britain and Northern Ireland]; **Vereinigte Staaten [von Amerika]** United States *sing.* [of America]

Vereinigung *die* (a) (Rechtsw.) organization; (b) (Zusammenschluss) uniting; (von Unternehmen) merging

vereinnahmen *tr. V.* (Kaufmannsspr.) take; collect ⟨*dividend*⟩; (fig.) monpolize

vereinsamen *itr. V.; mit sein* become [increasingly] lonely *or* isolated

Vereinsamung *die;* ∼**:** loneliness; isolation

vereinzelt 1 *Adj.; nicht präd.* occasional; isolated, occasional ⟨*shower, outbreak of rain, etc.*⟩. 2 *adv.* (zeitlich) occasionally; now and then; (örtlich) here and there

vereisen *itr. V.; mit sein* freeze *or* ice over; ⟨*wing*⟩ ice up; ⟨*lock*⟩ freeze up; **eine vereiste Fahrbahn** an icy carriageway

vereiteln *tr. V.* thwart; prevent; thwart, foil ⟨*attempt, plan, etc.*⟩; thwart, frustrate ⟨*efforts, intentions, etc.*⟩

Vereitelung *die;* ∼ ⇒ **vereiteln:** thwarting; prevention; foiling; frustrating

vereitern *itr. V.; mit sein* go septic; **vereitert sein** be septic

verenden *itr. V.; mit sein* perish; die

verengen 1 *refl. V.* narrow; become narrow; ⟨*pupils*⟩ contract; ⟨*blood vessel*⟩ constrict, become constricted. 2 *tr. V.* make narrower; narrow; restrict, narrow ⟨*field of vision etc.*⟩; make ⟨*circle, loop*⟩ smaller

vererben 1 *tr. V.* (a) leave, bequeath ⟨*property*⟩ (*Dat.,* **an** + *Akk.* to); (b) (Biol.) transmit, pass on ⟨*characteristic, disease*⟩; pass on ⟨*talent*⟩ (*Dat.,* **auf** + *Akk.* to). 2 *refl. V.* (Biol.) ⟨*disease, tendency*⟩ be passed on *or* transmitted (**auf** + *Akk.* to)

Vererbung *die;* ∼, ∼**en** (Biol.) heredity *no art.;* **das ist** ∼**:** it runs in the family

verewigen *refl. V.* (ugs.) leave one's mark

verfahren[1] 1 *unr. refl. V.* lose one's way. 2 *unr. tr. V.* use up ⟨*petrol*⟩. 3 *unr. itr. V.; mit sein* proceed; **mit jmdm./ etw.** ∼**:** deal with sb./sth.

verfahren[2] *Adj.* dead-end ⟨*situation*⟩

Verfahren *das;* ∼**s,** ∼ (a) procedure; (Technik) process; (Methode) method; (b) (Rechtsw.) proceedings *pl.*

Verfall *der; o. Pl.* (a) decay; dilapidation; (b) (Auflösung) decline; (c) (das Ungültigwerden) expiry

verfallen *unr. itr. V.; mit sein* (a) (baufällig werden) fall into disrepair; become dilapidated; (b) (körperlich) ⟨*strength*⟩ decline; (c) (untergehen) ⟨*empire*⟩ decline; ⟨*morals, morale*⟩ deteriorate; (d) (ungültig werden) expire; (e) **jmdm.** ∼**:** become a slave; **dem Alkohol** ∼**:** become addicted to alcohol; (f) (übergehen) **in seinen Dialekt** ∼**:** lapse into one's dialect; **das Pferd verfiel in [einen] Trab** the horse broke into a trot; (g) **auf jmdn./etw.** ∼**:** think of sb./sth.; **auf einen sonderbaren Gedanken** ∼**:** hit upon a strange idea

verfälschen *tr. V.* distort, misrepresent ⟨*statement, message*⟩; falsify, misrepresent ⟨*facts, history, truth*⟩; falsify ⟨*painting, banknote*⟩; adulterate ⟨*wine, milk, etc.*⟩

verfänglich /fɛɐ̯'fɛŋlɪç/ *Adj.* awkward, embarrassing ⟨*situation, question, etc.*⟩; incriminating ⟨*evidence, letter, etc.*⟩

verfärben 1 *refl. V.* change colour; ⟨*washing*⟩ become discoloured; ⟨*leaves*⟩ turn. 2 *tr. V.* discolour

Verfärbung *die* (a) change of colour; (b) (verfärbte Stelle) discoloration; discoloured patch

verfassen *tr. V.* write, compose ⟨*poetry*⟩; write, draw up ⟨*document, law*⟩

Verfasser *der;* ∼**s,** ∼, **Verfasserin** *die;* ∼, ∼**nen** author; writer

Verfassung *die* (a) (Politik) constitution; (b) *o. Pl.* (Zustand) state [of health/mind]; **in guter/schlechter** ∼ **sein** be in good/poor shape; **in bester** ∼**:** on top form

verfaulen *itr. V.; mit sein* rot; (fig.) ⟨*system, social order*⟩ decay; (fig.: moralisch) degenerate

verfechten *unr. tr. V.* (eintreten für) advocate, champion ‹*theory, hypothesis, etc.*›; uphold ‹*view*›; (verteidigen) defend

Verfechter *der,* **Verfechterin** *die;* ∼, ∼**nen** advocate; champion

verfehlen *tr. V.* **(a)** miss ‹*train, person, etc.*›; **(b)** miss ‹*target etc.*›

Verfehlung *die;* ∼, ∼**en** misdemeanour; (Rel.) transgression

verfeinden *refl. V.* **sich** ∼ **mit** make an enemy of; **verfeindet sein** be enemies

verfeinern /fɛɐ̯'fainɐn/ **1** *tr. V.* improve; refine ‹*method, procedure, sense*›. **2** *refl. V.* improve; ‹*method, procedure, sense*› be refined

Verfeinerung *die;* ∼, ∼**en** ⇒ **verfeinern** 1, 2: improvement; refinement

verfestigen 1 *tr. V.* harden. **2** *refl. V.* harden

verfeuern *tr. V.* **(a)** burn; **alles Holz verfeuert haben** have used up all the wood; **(b)** (verschießen) fire

verfilmen *tr. V.* film; make a film of; **der Roman wird jetzt verfilmt** the novel is now being made into a film

Verfilmung *die;* ∼, ∼**en (a)** filming; **(b)** (Film) film [version]

verfilzen *itr. V.; mit sein* ‹*fabric, garment*› felt; become felted; ‹*hair*› become matted

verfinstern 1 *tr. V.* obscure ‹*sun etc.*›. **2** *refl. V.* (auch fig.) darken

verflachen 1 *itr. V.; mit sein* ‹*ground*› flatten *or* level out, become flatter; ‹*water*› become shallow; (fig.) ‹*discussion*› become superficial *or* trivial. **2** *refl. V.* ‹*ground*› flatten *or* level out. **3** *tr. V.* flatten; level

verflechten *unr. tr. V.* interweave; intertwine; interlace; (verwickeln) involve; **miteinander verflochten sein** (fig.) be interlinked

Verflechtung *die;* ∼, ∼**en** interconnection; (Verwicklung) involvement

verfliegen 1 *unr. refl. V.* ‹*pilot*› lose one's way; ‹*aircraft*› get off course. **2** *unr. itr. V.; mit sein* **(a)** ‹*smoke*› disperse, vanish; ‹*scent, smell*› fade, disappear; ‹*mood, tiredness, alcohol etc.*› evaporate; **(b)** ‹*time*› fly by; ‹*anger*› pass

verflixt /fɛɐ̯'flɪkst/ (ugs.) **1** *Adj.* **(a)** (ärgerlich) awkward, unpleasant ‹*situation, business, etc.*›; **(b)** (abwertend: verdammt) blasted (Brit.); blessed; confounded; ∼ **[noch mal]!**, ∼ **noch eins!**, ∼ **und zugenäht!** [damn and] blast (Brit. coll.); **(c)** ⇒ **verdammt 1** b. **2** *adv.* (sehr) damned (coll.)

verflossen *Adj.* (ugs.) former; **seine** ∼**e Freundin** his ex-girlfriend; **ihr Verflossener** her ex

verfluchen *tr. V.* curse

verflucht 1 *Adj.* (salopp) **(a)** damned (coll.); bloody (Brit. sl.); ∼ **[noch mal]!**, ∼ **und zugenäht!** (derb) damn [it] (coll.); **(b)** *nicht präd.* (sehr groß) **wir hatten** ∼**es Glück** we were damned lucky (coll.). **2** *adv.* (sehr) damned (coll.)

verflüchtigen *refl. V.* ‹*alcohol etc.*› evaporate; ‹*smoke*› disperse; ‹*smell*› disappear; (fig.) ‹*fear, astonishment*› subside; ‹*cheerfulness, mockery*› vanish; ‹*time of youth*› be dissipated

verfolgen *tr. V.* **(a)** pursue; hunt, track ‹*animal*›; **jmdm. auf Schritt und Tritt** ∼: follow sb. wherever he/she goes; **der Gedanke daran verfolgte ihn** (fig.) the thought of it haunted him; **vom Pech verfolgt sein** (fig.) be dogged by bad luck; **(b)** (bedrängen) plague; **(c)** (bedrohen) persecute; **(d)** (zu verwirklichen suchen) pursue ‹*policy, plan, career, idea, purpose, etc.*›; **(e)** (beobachten) follow ‹*conversation, events, trial, developments, etc.*›; **(f)** etw. [strafrechtlich] ∼: prosecute sth.

Verfolger *der;* ∼**s**, ∼, **Verfolgerin** *die;* ∼, ∼**nen** pursuer; (Häscher) persecutor

Verfolgte *der/die; adj. Dekl.* victim of persecution

Verfolgung *die;* ∼, ∼**en (a)** pursuit; **die** ∼ **aufnehmen** take up the chase; **(b)** (Bedrohung) persecution; **(c)** ⇒ **verfolgen d:** pursuance; **(d)** [strafrechtliche] ∼: prosecution

Verfolgungs-: ∼**jagd** *die* pursuit; chase; ∼**wahn** *der* persecution mania

---

verfressen *Adj.* (salopp abwertend) piggish (coll.); greedy

verfroren *Adj.* sensitive to the cold

verfügen 1 *tr. V.* (anordnen) order; (dekretieren) decree. **2** *itr. V.* **(a)** (bestimmen) **über etw.** (*Akk.*) **[frei]** ∼ **können** be free to decide what to do with sth.; **über jmdn.** ∼**:** tell sb. what to do; **(b)** (haben) **über etw.** (*Akk.*) ∼**:** have sth. at one's disposal; have ‹*good connections, great experience*›

Verfügung *die;* ∼, ∼**en (a)** order; (Dekret) decree; **(b)** *o. Pl.* **etw. zur** ∼ **haben** have sth. at one's disposal; **jmdm. etw. zur** ∼ **stellen** put sth. at sb.'s disposal; **sein Amt zur** ∼ **stellen** offer to give up one's post *or* office; **jmdm. zur** ∼ **stehen** be at sb.'s disposal

verführen 1 *tr. V.* **(a)** tempt; **jmdn. zum Trinken** ∼**:** encourage sb. to take up drinking; **(b)** (sexuell) seduce. **2** *itr. V.* **zu etw.** ∼**:** be a temptation to sth.

Verführer *der* seducer

Verführerin *die* seductress

verführerisch 1 *Adj.* **(a)** tempting; **(b)** (aufreizend) seductive. **2** *adv.* **(a)** temptingly; **(b)** (aufreizend) seductively

Verführung *die* temptation; (sexuell) seduction

verfüttern *tr. V.* **(a)** (zu fressen geben) feed (*Dat.* to); **(b)** (verbrauchen) use [up] as animal/bird food

vergällen /fɛɐ̯'gɛlən/ *tr. V.* spoil ‹*enjoyment etc.*›; sour ‹*life*›

vergammeln (ugs.) **1** *itr. V.; mit sein* ‹*food*› go bad. **2** *tr. V.* waste ‹*time*›

vergammelt *Adj.* (ugs. abwertend) scruffy (coll.); tatty (coll.); tatty (coll.), decrepit ‹*vehicle*›

vergangen /fɛɐ̯'gaŋən/ *Adj.; nicht präd.* **(a)** (vorüber, vorbei) bygone, former ‹*times, years, etc.*›; **(b)** (letzt...) last ‹*year, Sunday, week, etc.*›

Vergangenheit *die;* ∼, ∼**en (a)** past; **die jüngste** ∼**:** the recent past; **etw. gehört der** ∼ **an** sth. is a thing of the past; **(b)** (Grammatik) past tense

vergänglich /fɛɐ̯'gɛnlɪç/ *Adj.* transient; transitory; ephemeral

Vergänglichkeit *die;* ∼**:** transience; transitoriness

vergasen *tr. V.* **(a)** (bes. Physik) gasify; **(b)** (töten) gas

Vergaser *der;* ∼**s**, ∼ (Kfz-W.) carburettor

vergaß /fɛɐ̯'ga:s/ *1. u. 3. Pers. Sg. Prät. v.* **vergessen**

Vergasung *die;* ∼, ∼**en (a)** (von Kohle) gasification; **(b)** (Tötung) gassing; **(c) bis zur** ∼ (ugs.) ad nauseam

vergattern *tr. V.* **jmdn. zu etw.** ∼**:** swear sb. to sth.; **jmdn. dazu** ∼**, etw. zu tun** enjoin sb. to do sth.

vergeben *unr. tr. V.* **(a)** ▶163 | *auch itr.* (geh.: verzeihen) forgive; **jmdm. etw.** ∼**:** forgive sb. [for] sth.; **(b)** throw away ‹*chance, goal, etc.*›; **einen Elfmeter** ∼**:** waste a penalty; **(c)** (geben) place ‹*order*› (**an** + *Akk.* with); award ‹*grant, prize*› (**an** + *Akk.* to); **(d) sich** (*Dat.*) **etwas/ nichts** ∼**:** lose/not lose face

vergebens 1 *Adv.* in vain; vainly. **2** *adj.* **es war** ∼**:** it was of *or* to no avail

vergeblich 1 *Adj.* futile; vain, futile ‹*attempt, efforts*›; ∼ **sein** be of *or* to no avail. **2** *adv.* in vain; vainly

Vergeblichkeit *die;* ∼**:** futility

Vergebung *die;* ∼, ∼**en** ▶163 | (geh.) forgiveness

vergegenwärtigen /*od.* ---'--/ *refl. V.* **sich** (*Dat.*) **etw.** ∼**:** imagine sth.; (erinnern) recall sth.

vergehen 1 *unr. itr. V.; mit sein* **(a)** ‹*time*› pass [by], go by; **es vergeht kein Tag, an dem er nicht anruft** not a day passes by without him ringing up (Brit.) *or* (coll.) phoning; **(b)** ‹*pain*› wear off, pass; ‹*pleasure*› fade; **ihr verging der Appetit** she lost her appetite; **(c)** ‹*cloud, scent*› disappear; ‹*fog*› lift. **2** *unr. refl. V.* **(a) sich gegen das Gesetz** ∼**:** violate the law; **(b) sich an jmdm.** ∼**:** commit indecent assault on sb.; indecently assault sb.

Vergehen *das;* ∼**s**, ∼**:** crime; (Rechtsspr.) offence

vergelten *unr. tr. V.* repay (**durch** with); **jmdm. etw.** ∼**:** repay sb. for sth.

Vergeltung *die* **(a)** repayment; **(b)** (Rache) revenge; ∼ **an jmdm. üben** take revenge on sb.

vergessen /fɛɐ̯'gɛsn̩/ **1** *unr. tr.* (*auch itr.*) *V.* forget; (liegen lassen) forget; leave behind; **das kannst du** ∼**!** (ugs.) forget it!; you can forget about that! **2** *refl. V.* forget oneself

---

*alte Schreibung (vgl. Hinweise auf S. xvi–xvii)

Vergessenheit *die;* ∼: oblivion; **in** ∼ **geraten** fall into oblivion

vergesslich, **vergeßlich* /fɛɐ̯'ɡɛslɪç/ *Adj.* forgetful

Vergesslichkeit, **Vergeßlichkeit die;* ∼: forgetfulness

vergeuden /fɛɐ̯'ɡɔydn̩/ *tr. V.* waste; squander, waste ⟨*money*⟩

Vergeudung *die;* ∼, ∼en waste; squandering

vergewaltigen *tr. V.* (a) rape; (b) (fig.) oppress ⟨*nation, people*⟩; violate ⟨*truth, conscience, law, language, etc.*⟩

Vergewaltigung *die;* ∼, ∼en (a) rape; (b) ⇒ **vergewaltigen b:** oppression; violation

vergewissern /fɛɐ̯ɡə'vɪsɐn/ *refl. V.* make sure (Gen of)

vergießen *unr. tr. V.* (a) spill; (b) **Tränen** ∼: shed tears; **viel Schweiß** ∼: sweat blood (fig.); *s. auch* **Blut**

vergiften *tr. V.* ▶329 | (auch fig.) poison

Vergiftung *die;* ∼, ∼en ▶329 poisoning

vergiss, **vergiß* /fɛɐ̯'ɡɪs/ *Imperativ Sg. v.* **vergessen**

Vergiss·mein·nicht, **Vergiß·mein·nicht das;* ∼[e]s, ∼[e] forget-me-not

vergisst, **vergißt* *2. u. 3. Pers. Sg. Präs. v.* **vergessen**

vergittert *Adj.* barred

Vergleich *der;* ∼[e]s, ∼e (a) comparison; **dieser** ∼ **hinkt** this is a poor comparison; **das ist doch kein** ∼! there is no comparison; **im** ∼ **zu** *od.* **mit etw.** in comparison with sth.; compared with *or* to sth.; (b) (Sprachw.) simile; (c) (Rechtsw.) settlement

vergleichbar *Adj.* comparable

vergleichen **1** *tr. V.* compare (**mit** with, to); **die Uhrzeit** ∼: check that one has the correct time; **das ist [doch gar] nicht zu** ∼: that [really] doesn't stand comparison *or* compare. **2** *refl. V.* (a) **sich mit jmdm.** ∼: compete with sb.; (b) (Rechtsw.) reach a settlement; settle

vergleichs-, **Vergleichs-:** ∼**form** *die* (Sprachw.) comparative/superlative form; ∼**möglichkeit** *die* opportunity for comparison; ∼**weise** *Adv.* comparatively

verglühen *itr. V.; mit sein* ⟨*log, wick, fire, etc.*⟩ smoulder and go out; ⟨*glow of sunset*⟩ fade; ⟨*satellite, rocket, wire, etc.*⟩ burn out

vergnügen /fɛɐ̯'ɡny:ɡn̩/ *refl. V.* enjoy oneself; have a good time

Vergnügen *das;* ∼s, ∼: pleasure; (Spaß) fun; **ein teueres** ∼ (ugs.) an expensive bit of fun (coll.); **es ist mir ein** ∼: it's a pleasure; **mit wem habe ich das** ∼? with whom do I have the pleasure of speaking?; **etw. macht jmdm. [großes]** ∼: sth. gives sb. [great] pleasure; sb. enjoys sth. [very much], **viel** ∼! (auch iron.) have fun!; **mit [dem größten]** ∼: with [the greatest of] pleasure

vergnüglich **1** *Adj.* amusing, entertaining ⟨*play, programme*⟩. **2** *adv.* amusingly; entertainingly

vergnügt **1** *Adj.* (a) cheerful; happy ⟨*smile*⟩; merry ⟨*group of people*⟩; (b) (unterhaltsam) enjoyable. **2** *adv.* cheerfully; ⟨*smile*⟩ happily

Vergnügung *die;* ∼, ∼en pleasure

Vergnügungs-: ∼**lokal** *das* bar providing entertainment; (Nachtlokal) nightclub; ∼**reise** *die* pleasure-trip; ∼**viertel** *das* pleasure district

vergolden *tr. V.* gold-plate ⟨*jewellery etc.*⟩; (mit Blattgold) gild ⟨*statue, dome, etc.*⟩; (mit Gold bemalen) paint ⟨*statue, dome, etc.*⟩ gold; (fig.) ⟨*evening sun*⟩ bathe ⟨*rooftops etc.*⟩ in gold

vergönnen *tr. V.* grant

vergöttern /fɛɐ̯'ɡœtɐn/ *tr. V.* idolize

vergraben **1** *unr. tr. V.* (auch fig.) bury. **2** *unr. refl. V.* ⟨*animal*⟩ bury itself (**in** + Akk. od. Dat. in); (fig.) withdraw from the world; hide oneself away

vergrämt *Adj.* care-worn

vergraulen *tr. V.* (ugs.) put off

vergreifen *unr. refl. V.* (a) **sich im Ton/Ausdruck** ∼: adopt the wrong tone/use the wrong expression; (b) **sich an etw.** (Dat.) ∼ (an fremdem Eigentum) misappropriate sth.; (c) **sich an jmdm.** ∼: assault sb.

vergriffen *Adj.* out of print *pred.*

vergrößern /fɛɐ̯'ɡrøːsɐn/ **1** *tr. V.* (a) extend ⟨*room, area, building, etc.*⟩; increase ⟨*distance*⟩; **sein Repertoire** ∼: extend *or* increase *or* enlarge one's repertoire; (b) (vermehren) increase, (c) (größer reproduzieren) enlarge ⟨*photograph etc.*⟩. **2** *refl. V.* (a) ⟨*firm, business, etc.*⟩ expand; **eine krankhaft vergrößerte Leber** a pathologically enlarged liver; (b) (zunehmen) increase. **3** *itr. V.* ⟨*lens etc.*⟩ magnify

Vergrößerung *die;* ∼, ∼en (a) ⇒ **vergrößern 1, 2:** extension; increase; enlargement; expansion; (b) (Foto) enlargement; **in 100facher** ∼: enlarged 100fold

Vergrößerungs·glas *das* magnifying glass

vergucken *refl. V.* (ugs.) (a) **sich in jmdn./etw.** ∼: fall for sb./sth. (coll.); (b) (falsch sehen) be mistaken [about what one saw]

Vergünstigung *die;* ∼, ∼en privilege

vergüten *tr. V.* (a) **jmdm. etw.** ∼: reimburse sb. for sth.; (b) (bes. Papierdt.: bezahlen) remunerate, pay for ⟨*work, services*⟩

Vergütung *die;* ∼, ∼en (a) (Rückerstattung) reimbursement; (b) (Geldsumme) remuneration

verhaften *tr. V.* arrest

Verhaftete *der/die; adj. Dekl.* person under arrest; man/woman under arrest; arrested man/woman

Verhaftung *die;* ∼, ∼en arrest

verhaken *refl. V.* ⟨*person*⟩ get hooked (coll.) *or* caught up; ⟨*zip*⟩ get caught

verhallen *itr. V.; mit sein* ⟨*sound*⟩ die away; [ungehört] ∼ (fig.) ⟨*call, words, etc.*⟩ go unheard *or* unheeded

verhalten[1] *unr. refl. V.* (a) behave; (reagieren) react; **sich still** *od.* **ruhig** ∼: keep quiet; **ich verhielt mich abwartend** I decided to wait and see; (b) (beschaffen sein) be; **die Sache verhält sich nämlich so** this is how things stand *or* the matter stands; (c) (im Verhältnis stehen) **a verhält sich zu b wie x zu y** a is to b as x is to y

verhalten[2] **1** *Adj.* (a) (unterdrückt) restrained; **mit** ∼**em Tempo** at a measured pace; (b) (dezent) restrained, subdued, muted ⟨*colours*⟩; muted, soft ⟨*notes, voice, etc.*⟩; (c) (zurückhaltend) reserved; **eine** ∼**e Fahrweise** a cautious way of driving. **2** *adv.* (a) (unterdrückt) in a restrained manner; (b) (zurückhaltend) in a reserved manner; ⟨*drive*⟩ cautiously; (c) (dezent) ⟨*speak, play, etc.*⟩ softly

Verhalten *das;* ∼s behaviour; (Vorgehen) conduct

Verhaltens-: ∼**maß·regel** *die; meist Pl.* rule of conduct; ∼**weise** *die* behaviour; ∼**weisen** behaviour patterns; patterns of behaviour

Verhältnis /fɛɐ̯'hɛltnɪs/ *das;* ∼ses, ∼se (a) **ein** ∼ **von drei zu eins** a ratio of three to one; **im** ∼ **zu früher** in comparison with *or* compared to earlier times; (b) (persönliche Beziehung) relationship (**zu** with); **ein gutes** ∼ **zu jmdm. haben** get on well with sb.; (c) (ugs.: intime Beziehung) affair; relationship; (d) (ugs.) (Geliebte) lady-friend; (Geliebter) man; (e) *Pl.* (Umstände) conditions; **in bescheidenen** *od.* **einfachen/gesicherten** ∼**sen leben** live in modest circumstances/be financially secure; **aus einfachen** ∼**sen kommen** come from a humble background; **über seine** ∼**se leben** live beyond one's means

verhältnis-, **Verhältnis-:** ∼**gleichung** *die* (Math.) proportion; ∼**mäßig** *Adv.* relatively; comparatively; ∼**wort** *das; Pl.* ∼**wörter** (Sprachw.) preposition

verhandeln **1** *itr. V.* (a) negotiate (**über** + Akk. about); (b) (strafrechtlich) try a case; (zivilrechtlich) hear a case. **2** *tr. V.* (a) **etw.** ∼: negotiate over sth.; (b) (strafrechtlich) try ⟨*case*⟩; (zivilrechtlich) hear ⟨*case*⟩

Verhandlung *die* (a) ∼en negotiations; **mit jmdm. in** ∼ **stehen** be negotiating with sb.; be [involved *or* engaged] in negotiations *pl.* with sb.; **zu** ∼**en bereit sein** be open to negotiation *sing.;* (b) (strafrechtlich) trial (**gegen** of); (zivilrechtlich) hearing

verhandlungs-, **Verhandlungs-:** ∼**bereit** *Adj.* ready *or* willing to negotiate *pred.;* ∼**grundlage** *die* basis for negotiation[s]; ∼**tisch** *der* negotiating table

verhangen *Adj.* overcast

verhängen *tr. V.* (**a**) cover (**mit** with); (**b**) impose ⟨*fine, punishment*⟩ (**über** + *Akk.* on); declare ⟨*state of emergency, state of siege*⟩; (Sport) award, give ⟨*penalty etc.*⟩

Verhängnis /fɛɐ̯ˈhɛŋnɪs/ *das;* ~**ses,** ~**se** undoing; **jmdm. zum** ~ **werden** be sb.'s undoing

verhängnis·voll *Adj.* disastrous; fatal, disastrous ⟨*mistake, weakness, hesitation, etc.*⟩

Verhängung *die;* ~ ⇒ **verhängen b:** imposition; declaration

verharmlosen *tr. V.* play down

verhärmt /fɛɐ̯ˈhɛrmt/ *Adj.* careworn

verharren *itr. V.* (geh.) remain; (plötzlich, kurz) pause; **in Resignation** ~: remain resigned

verhärten /fɛɐ̯ˈhɛrtn̩/ **1** *tr. V.* (**a**) harden ⟨*material etc.*⟩; (**b**) (unbarmherzig machen) harden; make ⟨*person*⟩ hard. **2** *refl. V.* (**a**) (hart werden) ⟨*tissue*⟩ become hardened; ⟨*tumour*⟩ become scirrhous; (**b**) (gefühllos werden) harden one's heart (**gegen** against); **die Fronten haben sich verhärtet** the positions of the opposing parties have become entrenched

verhaspeln *refl. V.* (ugs.) stumble over one's words

verhasst, *verhaßt *Adj.* hated; detested; **es war ihm** ~: he hated *or* detested it; **nichts ist mir so** ~ **wie** ...: there is nothing I detest so much as ...

verhätscheln *tr. V.* (ugs.) pamper

verhauen (ugs.) **1** *unr. tr. V.* (**a**) beat up; (als Strafe) beat; (**b**) (falsch machen) make a mess of; muck up (Brit. sl.). **2** *unr. refl. V.* make a mistake *or* slip

verheben *unr. refl. V.* do oneself an injury [while lifting sth.]

verheddern /fɛɐ̯ˈhɛdɐn/ *refl. V.* **sich in etw.** (*Dat.*) ~: get tangled up in sth.

verheerend *Adj.* (**a**) devastating; disastrous; (**b**) (ugs.: scheußlich) ghastly (coll.); dreadful (coll.)

verhehlen *tr. V.* (geh.) conceal, hide (*Dat.* from); **ich kann/will [es] nicht** ~**, dass** ...: there is no denying/I have no wish to deny that ...

verheilen *itr. V.; mit sein* ⟨*wound*⟩ heal [up]

verheimlichen *tr. V.* [**jmdm.**] **etw.** ~: keep sth. secret [from sb.]; conceal *or* hide sth. [from sb.]

verheiraten 1 *refl. V.* get married (**mit** to). **2** *tr. V.* (veralt.) marry (**mit, an** + *Akk.* to)

Verheiratete *der/die; adj. Dekl.* married person; married man/woman; ~ *Pl.* married people; married men/women

verheißen *unr. tr. V.* (geh.; auch fig.) promise; **nichts Gutes** ~: not bode *or* augur well

verheißungs·voll 1 *Adj.* promising. **2** *adv.* full of promise

verheizen *tr. V.* burn; use as fuel

verhelfen *unr. itr. V.* **jmdm. zu etw.** ~: help sb. to get/achieve sth.; **jmdm. zur Flucht/zum Sieg** ~: help sb. to escape/win

verherrlichen *tr. V.* glorify ⟨*war, violence, deed, etc.*⟩; extol ⟨*virtues, leader, etc.*⟩; celebrate ⟨*nature, freedom, peace, etc.*⟩

verhetzen *tr. V.* incite; stir up

verheult /fɛɐ̯ˈhɔʏlt/ *Adj.* (ugs.) ⟨*eyes*⟩ red from crying; ⟨*face*⟩ puffy *or* swollen from crying

verhexen *tr. V.* ⇒ **verzaubern a**

verhindern *tr. V.* prevent; prevent, avert ⟨*war, disaster, etc.*⟩; **er ist verhindert** he is prevented from coming; **ein verhinderter Künstler** (ugs.) a would-be artist

Verhinderung *die;* ~**,** ~**en** ⇒ **verhindern:** prevention; averting

verhohlen /fɛɐ̯ˈhoːlən/ *Adj.* concealed; **kaum** ~**e Neugier** ill-concealed curiosity

verhöhnen /vɛrˈhøːnən/ *tr. V.* mock; deride; ridicule

verhökern /fɛɐ̯ˈhøːkɐn/ *tr. V.* (salopp) flog (Brit. sl.)

Verhör /fɛɐ̯ˈhøːɐ̯/ *das;* ~**[e]s,** ~**e** interrogation; questioning; (bei Gericht) examination; **jmdn. ins** ~ **nehmen** interrogate *or* question sb.; (fig.) grill *or* quiz sb.

---

*alte Schreibung (vgl. Hinweise auf S. xvi–xvii)

verhören 1 *tr. V.* interrogate; question; (bei Gericht) examine. **2** *refl. V.* mishear; hear wrongly

verhüllen *tr. V.* cover; (fig.) disguise; mask; **eine verhüllte Drohung** (fig.) a veiled threat

verhüllend *Adj.* (Literaturw.) euphemistic

verhungern *itr. V.; mit sein* die of starvation; starve [to death]; **ich bin am Verhungern** (ugs.) I'm starving (fig. coll.)

verhüten *tr. V.* prevent; prevent, avert ⟨*disaster*⟩; **der Himmel verhüte, dass** ...: heaven forbid that ...

Verhütung *die;* ~**,** ~**en** prevention; (Empfängnis~) contraception

Verhütungs·mittel *das* contraceptive

verhutzelt /fɛɐ̯ˈhʊtsl̩t/ *Adj.* (ugs.) wizened ⟨*person, face*⟩; shrivelled ⟨*fruit, plant*⟩

verinnerlichen *tr. V.* (Soziol., Psych.) internalize

Verinnerlichung *die;* ~**,** ~**en** (Soziol., Psych.) internalization

verirren *refl. V.* (**a**) get lost; lose one's way; ⟨*animal*⟩ stray; (**b**) (gelangen) stray (**in, an** + *Akk.* into)

Verirrung *die;* ~**,** ~**en** aberration

verjagen *tr. V.* chase away

verjähren /fɛɐ̯ˈjɛːrən/ *itr. V.; mit sein* come under the statute of limitations

Verjährung *die;* ~**,** ~**en** limitation

verjubeln *tr. V.* (ugs.) blow (coll.) ⟨*money*⟩

verjüngen /fɛɐ̯ˈjʏŋən/ **1** *tr. V.* rejuvenate ⟨*person, skin, etc.*⟩; (jünger aussehen lassen) make ⟨*person*⟩ look younger; recruit younger blood into ⟨*team, company, etc.*⟩. **2** *refl. V.* (schmaler werden) taper; become narrower; narrow

verkabeln *tr. V.* connect up [by cable]

verkalken *itr. V.; mit sein* (**a**) ⟨*tissue*⟩ calcify, become calcified; ⟨*arteries*⟩ become hardened; ⟨*bone*⟩ thicken; ⟨*pipe, kettle, coffee-machine, etc.*⟩ fur up; (**b**) (ugs.: senil werden) become senile; **er ist schon ziemlich verkalkt** he is already pretty gaga (coll.)

verkalkulieren *refl. V.* miscalculate

Verkalkung *die;* ~**,** ~**en** (**a**) ⇒ **verkalken a:** calcification; hardening; thickening; furring-up; (**b**) (ugs.: Senilität) senility

verkannt /fɛɐ̯ˈkant/ *2. Part. v.* **verkennen**

verkappt *Adj.* disguised

verkatert /fɛɐ̯ˈkaːtɐt/ *Adj.* (ugs.) hung-over (coll.)

Verkauf *der* (**a**) sale; (das Verkaufen) sale; selling; **zum** ~ **stehen** be [up] for sale; (**b**) *o. Pl.* (Abteilung) sales *sing. or pl., no art.*

verkaufen 1 *tr. V.* (auch fig.) sell (*Dat.,* **an** + *Akk.* to); **„zu verkaufen"** 'for sale'. **2** *refl. V.* (**a**) ⟨*goods*⟩ sell; (**b**) (ugs.: falsch kaufen) make a bad buy

Verkäufer *der,* **Verkäuferin** *die* ▶85⟋ (**a**) seller; vendor (formal); (**b**) (Berufsbez.) sales *or* shop assistant; salesperson; (im Außendienst) salesman/saleswoman; salesperson

verkäuflich *Adj.* saleable; marketable; **schwer/leicht** ~ **sein** be hard/easy to sell

verkaufs-, Verkaufs-: ~**offen** *Adj.* **der** ~**offene Samstag** *od.* **Sonnabend** Saturday on which *or* when the shops are open all day; ~**personal** *das* sales staff; ~**preis** *der* retail price

Verkehr *der;* ~**s** (**a**) traffic; **den** ~ **regeln** regulate *or* control the [flow of] traffic; **aus dem** ~ **ziehen** take ⟨*coin, banknote*⟩ out of circulation; take ⟨*product*⟩ off the market; **jmdn. aus dem** ~ **ziehen** (ugs. scherzh.) put sb. out of circulation (joc.); (**b**) (Umgang) contact; communication; (**c**) (Sexual~) intercourse

verkehren 1 *itr. V.* (**a**) auch mit sein (fahren) run; ⟨*aircraft*⟩ fly; **der Dampfer verkehrt zwischen Hamburg und Helgoland** the steamer plies *or* operates *or* goes between Hamburg and Heligoland; (**b**) mit jmdm. ~: associate with sb.; **bei jmdm.** ~: visit sb. regularly; **in einem Lokal** ~: frequent a pub (Brit.); **in den besten Kreisen** ~: move in the best circles. **2** *tr. V.* turn (**in** + *Akk.* into); **den Sinn einer Aussage ins Gegenteil** ~: twist the meaning of a statement right round. **3** *refl. V.* turn (**in** + *Akk.* into); **sich ins Gegenteil** ~: change to the opposite

verkehrs-, Verkehrs-: ~**ampel** *die* traffic lights *pl.;* ~**amt** *das* tourist information office; ~**aufkommen** *das* volume of traffic; ~**büro** *das* tourist office; ~**gefährdung** *die* constituting *no art.* a hazard to other traffic; **eine** ~**gefährdung darstellen** be *or* constitute a hazard to other traffic; ~**hindernis** *das* obstruction to traffic; ~**knotenpunkt** *der* [traffic] junction; ~**kontrolle** *die* traffic check; ~**ministerium** *das* ministry of transport; ~**mittel** *das* means of transport; **die öffentlichen** ~**mittel** public transport *sing.;* ~**regel** *die; meist Pl.* traffic regulation; ~**schild** *das; Pl.* ~**schilder** traffic sign; road sign; ~**sicherheit** *die; o. Pl.* road safety; (eines Fahrzeugs) roadworthiness; ~**teilnehmer** *der* road user; ~**unfall** *der* road accident; ~**widrig 1** *Adj.* contrary to road traffic regulations *postpos.;* **2** *adv.* contrary to road traffic regulations; ~**zeichen** *das* traffic sign; road sign

verkehrt 1 *Adj.* wrong; **das ist gar nicht so** ~: that's not such a bad idea; **an den Verkehrten geraten** (ugs.) come to the wrong person. **2** *adv.* wrongly; **alles** ~ **machen** do everything wrong; *s. auch* **herum a**

verkeilen 1 *tr. V.* wedge. **2** *refl. V.* become wedged (**in** + *Akk.* in); **sich ineinander** ~: become wedged together

verkennen *unr. tr. V.* fail to recognize; misjudge ⟨*situation*⟩; fail to appreciate ⟨*efforts, achievement, etc.*⟩; **es ist nicht zu** ~, **dass ...:** it cannot be denied *or* is undeniable that ...; **ein verkanntes Genie** an unrecognized genius

Verkettung *die;* ~, ~**en** (von Zufällen usw.) chain

verklagen *tr. V.* sue (**auf** + *Akk.* for); take proceedings against; take to court

verklappen *tr. V.* dump ⟨*waste*⟩ [at sea]

Verklappung *die;* ~, ~**en** dumping [at sea]

verklären 1 *tr. V.* (auch Rel.) transfigure. **2** *refl. V.* (auch fig.) be transfigured; ⟨*eyes*⟩ shine blissfully

verklausulieren /fɛɐ̯klauˈzuːliːrən/ *tr. V.* (a) (mit Klauseln versehen) hedge ⟨*contract etc.*⟩ with qualifying clauses; (b) (verbergen) hedge ⟨*admission of guilt etc.*⟩ round with qualifications

verkleben 1 *itr. V.; mit sein* stick together. **2** *tr. V.* (a) (zusammenkleben) stick together; **verklebte Hände** sticky hands; (b) (zukleben) seal up ⟨*hole*⟩; (c) (festkleben) stick [down] ⟨*floor-covering etc.*⟩

verkleiden *tr. V.* (a) disguise; (kostümieren) dress up; **sich** ~: disguise oneself/dress [oneself] up; (b) (verdecken) cover; (auskleiden) line; face ⟨*façade*⟩

Verkleidung *die* (a) *o. Pl.* disguising; (das Kostümieren) dressing up; (b) (Kostüm) (als Tarnung) disguise; (bei einer Party usw.) fancy dress; (c) ⇒ **verkleiden b:** covering; lining; facing; (d) (Umhüllung) cover

verkleinern /fɛɐ̯ˈklainɐn/ **1** *tr. V.* (a) make smaller; reduce the size of; reduce ⟨*size, number, etc.*⟩; (b) (kleiner reproduzieren) reduce ⟨*photograph etc.*⟩. **2** *refl. V.* become smaller; ⟨*number*⟩ decrease, grow smaller. **3** *itr. V.* ⟨*lens etc.*⟩ make things look *or* appear smaller

Verkleinerung *die;* ~, ~**en** reduction in size; making smaller; (des Formats, der Anzahl, durch eine Linse) reduction

Verkleinerungs·form *die* (Sprachw.) diminutive form

verklemmen *refl. V.* get *or* become stuck; ⟨*door, window*⟩ jam, get *or* become jammed

verklemmt (fig. ugs.) **1** *Adj.* inhibited. **2** *adv.* in an inhibited manner

Verklemmtheit *die;* ~: inhibitedness

verklickern *tr. V.* (salopp) **jmdm. etw.** ~: make sth. clear to sb.; spell sth. out to sb.; (erklären) explain sth. to sb. in every detail

verklingen *unr. itr. V.; mit sein* ⟨*sound, voice, song, etc.*⟩ fade away; (fig.) ⟨*mood*⟩ wear off

verknacken *tr. V.* (salopp) **jmdn. zu Gefängnis/einer Geldstrafe** ~: put sb. inside (sl.)/slap a fine on sb. (coll.); **er wurde zu 18 Monaten verknackt** he got 18 months

verknacksen /fɛɐ̯ˈknaksn̩/ *refl. V.* (ugs.) twist, sprain ⟨*ankle, wrist*⟩; **sich** (*Dat.*) **den Fuß** twist *or* sprain one's ankle

verknallen *refl. V.* (ugs.: sich verlieben) fall head over heels in love (**in** + *Akk.* with); **in jmdn. verknallt sein** be crazy about sb. (coll.)

verknappen 1 *tr. V.* cut back [on] ⟨*imports*⟩. **2** *refl. V.* run short

Verknappung *die;* ~, ~**en** cutting back (*Gen.* on); (der Liquidität) loss

verkneifen *unr. refl. V.* (ugs.) (a) **sich** (*Dat.*) **eine Frage/Bemerkung** ~: bite back a question/remark; **ich konnte mir das Lachen kaum** ~: I could hardly keep a straight face; I could hardly stop myself laughing; (b) (verzichten) manage *or* do without; **es sich** (*Dat.*) ~, **etw. zu tun** stop oneself doing sth.

verkniffen *Adj.* strained ⟨*expression*⟩; pinched ⟨*mouth, lips*⟩

verknittern *tr. V.* crumple

verknoten 1 *tr. V.* (a) (verknüpfen) tie; knot; **miteinander** ~: tie together; (b) (festbinden) tie (**an** + *Akk.* to). **2** *refl. V.* become knotted

verknüpfen *tr. V.* (a) (knoten) tie; knot; **die beiden Fäden miteinander** ~: tie *or* knot the two threads together; (b) (zugleich tun) combine; (c) (in Beziehung setzen) link; (unwillkürlich) associate

Verknüpfung *die;* ~, ~**en** (a) ⇒ **verknüpfen 1:** tying; knotting; combination; linking; association; (b) (Knoten) knots *pl.*

verkochen *itr. V.; mit sein* (a) (verdampfen) boil away; (b) (breiig werden) boil down to a pulp

verkohlen *itr. V.* char; become charred

verkommen¹ *unr. itr. V.; mit sein* (a) (verwahrlosen) go to the dogs; (moralisch, sittlich) go to the bad; ⟨*child*⟩ go wild; (b) (verfallen) ⟨*building etc.*⟩ go to rack and ruin, fall into disrepair, become dilapidated; ⟨*garden*⟩ run wild; ⟨*area*⟩ become run down; (c) (herabsinken) degenerate (**zu** into); (d) (verderben) ⟨*food*⟩ go bad

verkommen² *Adj.* depraved; **ein** ~**es Subjekt** a dissolute character

verkomplizieren *tr. V.* complicate

verkonsumieren *tr. V.* (ugs.) get through; consume

verkorken *tr. V.* cork [up]

verkörpern *tr. V.* (a) (als Schauspieler) play [the part of]; (b) (bilden) ⟨*person*⟩ embody, personify

Verkörperung *die;* ~, ~**en** embodiment; personification

verköstigen /fɛɐ̯ˈkœstɪɡn̩/ *tr. V.* feed; provide with meals

Verköstigung *die;* ~, ~**en** (a) *o. Pl.* feeding; (b) (Kost) foods; meals *pl.*

verkraften *tr. V.* cope with

verkrampfen *refl. V.* ⟨*muscle*⟩ become cramped; ⟨*person*⟩ go tense, tense up; **verkrampft lächeln** smile tensely

verkriechen *unr. refl. V.* ⟨*animal*⟩ creep [away]; ⟨*person*⟩ hide [oneself away]; **am liebsten hätte ich mich [in den hintersten Winkel] verkrochen** I'd have liked to crawl away and hide in a corner; I wished the ground would open and swallow me up

verkrümeln *refl. V.* (ugs.: sich entfernen) slip off *or* away

verkrümmt *Adj.* bent ⟨*person*⟩; crooked ⟨*finger*⟩; curved ⟨*spine*⟩

Verkrümmung *die* crookedness; ~ **der Wirbelsäule** curvature of the spine

verkrüppeln 1 *itr. V.; mit sein* ⟨*tree*⟩ become stunted; **verkrüppelt** stunted. **2** *tr. V.* cripple ⟨*person*⟩; **verkrüppelte Arme/Füße** deformed arms/crippled feet

Verkrüppelung *die;* ~, ~**en** deformity

verkrusten *itr. V.; mit sein* form a crust; ⟨*wound*⟩ form a scab

verkümmern *itr. V.; mit sein* (a) ⟨*person, animal*⟩ go into a decline; ⟨*plant etc.*⟩ become stunted; ⟨*muscle, limb*⟩ waste away, atrophy; (b) ⟨*talent, emotional life, etc.*⟩ wither away; ⟨*strength*⟩ decline, fade; ⟨*relationship*⟩ become less close; ⟨*trade, initiative*⟩ dwindle

Verkümmerung *die;* ~, ~en ⇒ **verkümmern b:** withering away; declining; fading; becoming less close; dwindling

verkünden *tr. V.* announce; pronounce ⟨*judgement*⟩; promulgate ⟨*law, decree*⟩; ⟨*omen*⟩ presage

verkündigen *tr. V.* (geh.) **(a)** (predigen) preach; **(b)** (bekannt machen) announce; proclaim

Verkündigung *die* **(a)** (das Predigen) preaching; **(b)** (Bekanntmachung) announcement; proclamation

Verkündung *die;* ~, ~en announcement; (von Urteilen) pronouncement; (von Gesetzen, Verordnungen) promulgation

verkuppeln *tr. V.* pair off

verkürzen **1** *tr. V.* **(a)** (verringern) reduce; (abkürzen) shorten; **(b)** (abbrechen) cut short ⟨*stay, life*⟩; put an end to, end ⟨*suffering*⟩; **verkürzte Arbeitszeit** reduced *or* shorter working hours *pl.;* **(c) sich** (*Dat.*) **die Zeit** ~**:** while away the time; make the time pass more quickly. **2** *refl. V.* (kürzer werden) become shorter; shorten; ⟨*perspective*⟩ become foreshortened. **3** *itr. V.* (Ballspiele) close the gap (**auf** + *Akk.* to)

Verkürzung *die* ⇒ **verkürzen 1 a, b:** reduction; shortening; cutting short; ending

verlachen *tr. V.* laugh at

verladen *unr. tr. V.* **(a)** (laden) load; **(b)** (ugs.: betrügen) **jmdn.** ~**:** take sb. for a ride (fig. coll.); con sb. (sl.); (Ballspiele) out-trick sb.

Verlade·rampe *die* loading platform

Verladung *die* loading

Verlag /fɛɐ̯'laːk/ *der;* ~[e]s, ~e publishing house *or* firm; publisher's

verlagern **1** *tr. V.* shift ⟨*weight, centre of gravity*⟩; (an einen anderen Ort) move; (fig.) transfer; shift ⟨*emphasis*⟩. **2** *refl. V.* (auch fig.) shift; ⟨*area of high/low pressure etc.*⟩ move

Verlagerung *die* moving; **eine** ~ **des Schwergewichts** (fig.) a shift in emphasis

Verlags-: ~**haus** *das* publishing house *or* firm; ~**programm** *das* [publisher's] list

verlanden *itr. V.; mit sein* silt up

Verlandung *die* silting up

verlangen **1** *tr. V.* **(a)** (fordern) demand; (wollen) want; **das ist zu viel verlangt** that's asking too much; that's too much to expect; **von jedem wird Pünktlichkeit verlangt** everyone is required *or* expected to be punctual; **(b)** (nötig haben) ⟨*task etc.*⟩ require, call for ⟨*patience, knowledge, experience, skill, etc.*⟩; **(c)** (berechnen) charge; **sie verlangte 200 Mark von ihm** she charged him 200 marks; **(d)** (sehen wollen) ask for, ask to see ⟨*passport, driving licence, etc.*⟩; **(e)** (am Telefon) ask for; ask to speak to; **du wirst am Telefon verlangt** you're wanted on the phone (coll.). **2** *itr. V.* (geh.) **(a)** (bitten) **nach einem Arzt/Priester** *usw.* ~**:** ask for a doctor/priest *etc.;* **nach einem Glas Wasser** ~**:** ask for a glass of water; **(b)** (sich sehnen) **nach jmdm./etw.** ~**:** long for sb./sth.

Verlangen *das;* ~s, ~ **(a)** (Bedürfnis) desire (**nach** for); **(b)** (Forderung) demand; **auf** ~**:** on request; **auf jmds.** ~**:** at sb.'s request

verlängern /fɛɐ̯'lɛŋɐn/ **1** *tr. V.* **(a)** lengthen, make longer ⟨*skirt, sleeve, etc.*⟩; extend ⟨*flex, cable, road, etc.*⟩; **(b)** (länger gültig sein lassen) renew ⟨*passport, driving licence, etc.*⟩; extend, renew ⟨*contract*⟩; **(c)** (länger dauern lassen) extend, prolong ⟨*stay, life, suffering, etc.*⟩ (**um** by); **ein verlängertes Wochenende** a long weekend; **(d)** (verdünnen) add water *etc.* to ⟨*sauce, gravy, etc.*⟩ ⟨*to make it go further*⟩. **2** *refl. V.* (länger werden) become longer; ⟨*stay, life, suffering, etc.*⟩ be prolonged (**um** by); (länger gültig bleiben) ⟨*contract etc.*⟩ be extended

Verlängerung *die;* ~, ~en **(a)** ⇒ **verlängern 1 a–c:** lengthening; renewal; extension; prolongation; **(b)** (Ballspiele) extra time *no indef. art.;* (nachgespielte Zeit) injury time *no indef. art.;* **(c)** (Teilstück) extension

Verlängerungs·schnur *die* extension lead *or* (Amer.) cord

---

verlangsamen **1** *tr. V.* das Tempo/seine Schritte ~**:** reduce speed/slacken one's pace; slow down. **2** *refl. V.* slow down; ⟨*pace*⟩ slacken

Verlass, *Verlaß *der in* **auf jmdn./etw. ist [kein]** ~**:** sb./sth. can[not] be relied *or* depended [up]on

verlassen¹ **1** *unr. refl. V.* (vertrauen) rely, depend (**auf** + *Akk.* on); **er verlässt sich darauf, dass du kommst** he's relying on you to come; **worauf du dich** ~ **kannst** you can depend on *or* be sure of that. **2** *unr. tr. V.* leave; **Großvater hat uns für immer** ~ (verhüll.) grandfather has been taken from us (euphem.)

verlassen² *Adj.* deserted ⟨*street, square, village, etc.*⟩; empty ⟨*house*⟩; (öd) desolate ⟨*region etc.*⟩; **einsam und** ~**:** all alone

verlässlich, *verläßlich /fɛɐ̯'lɛslɪç/ **1** *Adj.* reliable, dependable ⟨*person*⟩. **2** *adv.* reliably

Verlässlichkeit, *Verläßlichkeit *die;* ~**:** reliability

Verlaub /fɛɐ̯'laup/ *der:* **mit** ~ (geh.) with your permission

Verlauf *der;* ~[e]s, **Verläufe** course; **der glückliche** ~ **der Revolution** the fortunate outcome of the revolution

verlaufen **1** *unr. itr. V.; mit sein* **(a)** (sich erstrecken) run; **(b)** (ablaufen) ⟨*test, rehearsal, etc.*⟩ go; ⟨*party etc.*⟩ go off; **(c)** ⟨*butter, chocolate, etc.*⟩ melt; ⟨*make-up, ink*⟩ run. **2** *unr. itr.* (auch refl.) *V.; mit sein* (sich verlieren) ⟨*track, path*⟩ disappear (**in** + *Dat.* in). **3** *unr. refl. V.* **(a)** (sich verirren) get lost; lose one's way; **(b)** (auseinander gehen) ⟨*crowd etc.*⟩ disperse; **(c)** (abfließen) ⟨*floods*⟩ subside

Verlaufs·form *die* (Sprachw.) progressive *or* continuous form

verlausen *itr. V.;* become infested with lice; **verlaust** louse-ridden; infested with lice *postpos.*

verlautbaren **1** *tr. V.* announce [officially]. **2** *itr. V.; mit sein* (geh.) become known

Verlautbarung *die;* ~, ~en announcement; (inoffizielle Meldung) [unofficial] report

verlauten **1** *tr. V.* announce. **2** *itr. V.; mit sein* be reported; **aus amtlicher Quelle verlautet, dass …:** official reports say that …

verleben *tr. V.* **(a)** (verbringen) spend; **(b)** (ugs.: verbrauchen) spend ⟨*money*⟩ on everyday needs

verlebt *Adj.* dissipated

verlegen¹ **1** *tr. V.* **(a)** (nicht wieder finden) mislay; **(b)** (verschieben) postpone (**auf** + *Akk.* until); (vor~) bring forward (**auf** + *Akk.* to); **(c)** (umlegen) move; transfer ⟨*patient*⟩; **(d)** (legen) lay ⟨*cable, pipe, carpet, etc.*⟩; **(e)** (veröffentlichen) publish. **2** *refl. V.* (sich ausrichten) take up ⟨*subject, activity, occupation, etc.*⟩; resort to ⟨*guesswork, flattery, silence, lying, etc.*⟩

verlegen² **1** *Adj.* **(a)** embarrassed; **(b) um etw.** ~ **sein** (etw. nicht zur Verfügung haben) be short of sth.; (etw. benötigen) be in need of sth. **2** *adv.* in embarrassment

Verlegenheit *die;* ~, ~en *o. Pl.* (Befangenheit) embarrassment; **in** ~ **geraten** get *or* become embarrassed; **jmdn. in** ~ **bringen** embarrass sb.; **(b)** (Unannehmlichkeit) embarrassing situation

Verleger *der;* ~s, ~, **Verlegerin** *die;* ~, ~nen ▶85| publisher

Verlegung *die;* ~, ~en **(a)** (Verschiebung) postponement; (Vorverlegung) bringing forward *no art.;* **um eine** ~ **des Termins bitten** ask to change the appointment; **(b)** ⇒ **verlegen¹ 1 c:** moving; transfer; **(c)** (von Kabeln, Rohren, Teppichen usw.) laying

verleiden *tr. V.* **jmdm. etw.** ~**:** spoil sth. for sb.

Verleih *der;* ~[e]s, ~e *o. Pl.* (das Verleihen) hiring out; (von Autos) renting *or* hiring out; **(b)** (Unternehmen) hire firm *or* company; (Film~) distribution company

verleihen *unr. tr. V.* **(a)** hire out; rent *or* hire out ⟨*car*⟩; (umsonst) lend [out]; **(b)** (überreichen) award; bestow, confer ⟨*award, honour*⟩; **jmdm. einen Orden** ~**:** decorate sb.; **(c)** (verschaffen) give; lend

Verleiher *der;* ~s, ~**:** hirer; (Film~) distributor

Verleihung *die;* ~, ~en **(a)** ⇒ **verleihen a:** hiring out; renting out; lending [out]; **(b)** ⇒ **verleihen b:** awarding; bestowing; conferring; (Zeremonie) award; conferment; bestowal

verleiten tr. V. **jmdn. dazu** ~, **etw. zu tun** lead or induce sb. to do sth.; (verlocken) tempt or entice sb. to do sth.; **jmdn. zum Stehlen** ~: lead sb. into stealing

verlernen tr. V. forget; **das Kochen** ~: forget how to cook

verlesen 1 unr. tr. V. read out. 2 unr. refl. V. (falsch lesen) make a mistake/mistakes in reading; **er hat sich wohl** ~: he must have read it wrongly

verletzen /fɛɐ'lɛtsn̩/ tr. V. (a) ▶329│ (beschädigen) injure; (durch Schuss, Stich) wound; (b) (kränken) hurt, wound ⟨person, feelings⟩; (c) (verstoßen gegen) violate; infringe ⟨regulation⟩; break ⟨agreement, law⟩; (d) (eindringen in) violate ⟨frontier, airspace, etc.⟩

verletzlich Adj. vulnerable

Verletzlichkeit die; ~: vulnerability

Verletzte der/die; adj. Dekl. injured person; casualty; (durch Schuss, Stich) wounded person

Verletzung die; ~, ~en (a) ▶329│ (Wunde) injury; **eine** ~ **am Knie haben** have an injury to one's knee or an injured knee; (b) (Kränkung) hurting; wounding; (c) ⇒ **verletzen** c: violation; infringement; breaking; (d) (Grenz~, Luftraum~ usw.) violation

verleugnen tr. V. deny; disown ⟨friend, relation⟩; **er kann seine Herkunft nicht** ~: it is obvious where he comes from; **sich selbst** ~: go against or betray one's principles

Verleugnung die denial; (eines Freundes, Verwandten) disownment

verleumden /fɛɐ'lɔymdn̩/ tr. V. slander; (schriftlich) libel

Verleumder der; ~, ~: slanderer; (schriftlich) libeller

verleumderisch Adj. slanderous; (in Schriftform) libellous

Verleumdung die; ~, ~en (a) o. Pl. slander; (in Schriftform) libelling

verlieben refl. V. fall in love (**in** + Akk. with); **ein verliebtes Pärchen** a pair of lovers

Verliebte der/die; adj. Dekl. lover

Verliebtheit die; ~: being no art. in love

verlieren /fɛɐ'liːrən/ 1 unr. tr. V. lose; ⟨plant, tree⟩ lose, shed ⟨leaves⟩; **die Katze verliert Haare** the cat is moulting. 2 unr. itr. V. lose; **an etw.** (Dat.) ~: lose sth. 3 unr. refl. V. (a) (weniger werden) ⟨enthusiasm⟩ subside; ⟨reserve etc.⟩ disappear; (b) (entschwinden) vanish; ⟨sound⟩ die away

Verlierer der; ~s, ~, **Verliererin** die; ~, ~nen loser

Verlies /fɛɐ'liːs/ das; ~es, ~e dungeon

verlischt /fɛɐ'lɪʃt/ 3. Pers. Sg. Präsens v. **verlöschen**

verloben refl. V. become or get engaged, (arch.) become betrothed (**mit** to)

Verlobte der/die; adj. Dekl. fiance/fiancée

Verlobung die; ~, ~en engagement; betrothal (arch.); (Feier) engagement party

verlocken tr. V. (geh.) tempt; entice

verlockend Adj. tempting; enticing

Verlockung die; ~, ~en temptation; enticement

verlogen /fɛɐ'loːgn̩/ 1 Adj. lying, mendacious ⟨person⟩; false ⟨morality, phrases, romanticism, etc.⟩; insincere ⟨compliment⟩. 2 adv. mendaciously; falsely

Verlogenheit die; ~, ~en (eines Menschen) mendacity; (einer Moral, von Phrasen usw.) falseness; (von Komplimenten) insincerity

verlor /fɛɐ'loːɐ/ 1. u. 3. Pers. Sg. Prät. v. **verlieren**

verloren 1 2. Part. v. **verlieren**. 2 Adj. lost; [**eine**] ~**e Mühe** a wasted effort; **die Sache ist** ~: it's hopeless; **er ist** ~: that's the end of him now; ⟨war, battle, etc.⟩ be lost; **durch diesen Umweg ging uns/ ging viel Zeit** ~: we lost a lot of time/a lot of time was lost by this detour

***verloren|gehen** ⇒ **verloren** 2

verlosch /fɛɐ'lɔʃ/ 1. u. 3. Pers. Sg. Prät. v. **verlöschen**

verloschen 2.Part. v. **verlöschen**

verlöschen unr. itr. V.; mit sein ⟨light, fire, etc.⟩ go out

verlosen tr. V. raffle

Verlosung die; ~, ~en raffle; draw; (Ziehung) draw; (Vorgang) raffling

verlottern /fɛɐ'lɔtɐn/ itr. V.; mit sein (abwertend) ⟨building, town, area, etc.⟩ become run-down; ⟨person⟩ go to seed; ⟨firm, business⟩ go downhill, go to the dogs

Verlust der; ~[e]s, ~e loss (**an** + Dat. of); **etw. mit** ~ **verkaufen** sell sth. at a loss

verlustieren refl. V. (scherzh.) amuse oneself; **wir haben uns auf der Party verlustiert** we had fun or enjoyed ourselves at the party; **sich mit jmdm. im Bett** ~: have a good time in bed with sb.

verlustig Adj. in **einer Sache** (Gen.) ~ **gehen** (Papierdt.) lose sth.; (verwirken) forfeit or lose sth.

Verlust·meldung die casualty report

verlust·reich Adj. (a) (mit vielen Toten) ⟨battle etc.⟩ involving heavy losses; (b) (finanziell) heavily loss-making ⟨product, project, etc.⟩

vermachen tr. V. **jmdm. etw.** ~: leave or bequeath sth. to sb.; (fig.: schenken, überlassen) give sth. to sb.; let sb. have sth.

vermählen /fɛɐ'mɛːlən/ refl. V. (geh.) **sich [jmdm.** od. **mit jmdm.]** ~: marry or wed [sb.]

Vermählung die; ~, ~en (geh.) (a) marriage; wedding; (b) (Fest) wedding ceremony

vermasseln /fɛɐ'masln̩/ tr. V. (salopp) (a) (verderben) muck up (Brit. sl.); mess up; ruin; (b) (verhauen) make a cock-up (Brit. sl.) or mess of ⟨exam etc.⟩

vermehren 1 tr. V. increase (**um** by). 2 refl. V. (a) increase; (b) (sich fortpflanzen) reproduce

vermehrt 1 Adj. increased. 2 adv. increasingly; ~ **auftreten** occur with increasing frequency

Vermehrung die; ~, ~en (a) increase (Gen. in); (b) (Fortpflanzung) reproduction

vermeidbar Adj. avoidable; **die Niederlage wäre** ~ **gewesen** the defeat could have been avoided

vermeiden unr. tr. V. avoid; **es lässt sich nicht** ~: it is unavoidable; **es** ~, **etw. zu tun** avoid doing sth.

Vermeidung die; ~, ~en avoidance

vermeintlich /fɛɐ'maintlɪç/ adv. supposedly

vermengen 1 tr. V. (mischen) mix (**miteinander** together). 2 refl. V. (sich mischen) mingle

Vermerk /fɛɐ'mɛrk/ der; ~[e]s, ~e note; (amtlich) remark; (Stempel) stamp; (im Kalender) entry

vermerken tr. V. (a) (notieren) make a note of; note [down]; (in Akten, Wachbuch usw.) record; **das sei aber nur am Rande vermerkt** but that is only by the way; (b) (feststellen) note

vermessen¹ unr. tr. V. measure; survey ⟨land, site⟩

vermessen² Adj. (geh.) presumptuous

Vermessenheit die; ~, ~en (geh.) presumption; presumptuousness

Vermessung die measurement; (Land~) surveying

vermiesen tr. V. (ugs.) **jmdm. etw.** ~: spoil sth. for sb.

vermieten tr. (auch itr.) V. rent [out], let [out] ⟨flat, room, etc.⟩ (**an** + Akk. to); hire [out] ⟨boat, car, etc.⟩; „**Zimmer zu** ~" 'room to let'

Vermieter der landlord

Vermieterin die landlady

Vermietung die; ~, ~en ⇒ **vermieten**: renting [out]; letting [out]; hiring [out]

vermindern 1 tr. V. reduce; decrease; reduce, lessen ⟨danger, stress⟩; lessen ⟨admiration, ability⟩; reduce ⟨debt⟩. 2 refl. V. decrease; ⟨influence, danger⟩ decrease, diminish

vermindert Adj. ~**e Zurechnungsfähigkeit** (Rechtsw.) diminished responsibility

Verminderung die ⇒ **vermindern** 1: reduction; decreasing; lessening

verminen tr. V. mine

vermischen 1 tr. V. mix (**miteinander** together); blend ⟨teas, tobaccos, etc.⟩; **Wahres und Erdachtes miteinander** ~: mingle truth and fiction. 2 refl. V. mix; (fig.) mingle

vermissen tr. V. (a) (sich sehnen nach) miss; (b) (nicht haben) **ich vermisse meinen Ausweis** my identity card is missing; **er gilt als** *od.* **ist vermisst** (fig.) he is listed as a missing person

Vermisste, •Vermißte *der/die; adj. Dekl.* missing person

vermitteln 1 *itr. V.* mediate, act as [a] mediator (**in** + *Dat.* in). **2** *tr. V.* **(a)** (herbeiführen) arrange; negotiate ‹*transaction, ceasefire, compromise*›; **(b)** (besorgen) **jmdm. eine Stelle ~:** find sb. a job; find a job for sb.; **(c)** (weitergeben) impart ‹*knowledge, insight, values, etc.*›; communicate, pass on ‹*message, information, etc.*›; convey, give ‹*feeling*›; pass on ‹*experience*›

Vermittler *der; ~s, ~* **(a)** ⇒ **vermitteln 1:** mediator; **(b)** ⇒ **vermitteln 2 c:** imparter; communicator; conveyer; **(c)** (von Berufs wegen) agent

Vermittler·rolle *die* role of mediator

Vermittlung *die; ~, ~en* **(a)** ⇒ **vermitteln 1:** mediation; **(b)** ⇒ **vermitteln 2 a:** arrangement; negotiation; **durch die ~ eines Beamten** through the good offices of an official; **(c)** (das Besorgen) **die ~ einer Stelle** finding a job for sb.; **(d)** ⇒ **vermitteln 2 c:** imparting; communicating; passing on; conveying; **(e)** (Telefonzentrale) exchange; (in einer Firma) switchboard; (Telefonist) operator

vermöbeln *tr. V.* (ugs.) beat up; (als Strafe) thrash

vermodern *itr. V.; mit sein* decay; rot

vermögen *unr. tr. V.* (geh.) **etw. zu tun ~:** be able to do sth.; be capable of doing sth.

Vermögen *das; ~s, ~* **(a)** *o. Pl.* (geh.: Fähigkeit) ability; **(b)** (Besitz) fortune; **er hat ~:** he has money; he is a man of means; **sein ganzes ~:** all his money

vermögend *Adj.* wealthy; well-off

Vermögens-: **~steuer** *die* wealth tax; **~verhältnisse** *Pl.* financial circumstances

vermummen /fɛɐ̯'mʊmən/ *tr. V.* **(a)** (einhüllen) wrap up [warmly]; **(b)** (verbergen) disguise

Vermummungs·verbot, *das* ban on wearing masks [during demonstrations]

vermurksen /fɛɐ̯'mʊrksn̩/ *tr. V.* (ugs.) mess up; muck up (Brit. sl.)

vermuten *tr. V.* suspect; **das ist zu ~:** that is what one would suppose *or* expect; we may assume that; **ich vermutete ihn in der Bibliothek** I supposed *or* presumed he was in the library

vermutlich 1 *Adj.* probable, likely ‹*result*›. **2** *Adv.* presumably; (wahrscheinlich) probably

Vermutung *die; ~, ~en* supposition; (Verdacht) suspicion

vernachlässigen *tr. V.* neglect; (unberücksichtigt lassen) ignore; disregard

Vernachlässigung *die; ~, ~en* neglect; (das Nichtberücksichtigen) disregard

vernageln *tr. V.* nail up, cover ‹*hole etc.*›; **mit Brettern vernagelt** boarded up

vernarben *itr. V.; mit sein* [form a] scar; heal (lit. *or* fig.)

vernarren *refl. V.* **in jmdn./etw. vernarrt sein** be infatuated with *or* (coll.) crazy about sb./be crazy (coll.) about sth.

vernaschen *tr. V.* **(a)** spend on sweets (Brit.) *or* (Amer.) candy; **(b)** (salopp) lay ‹*girl*› (sl.)

vernebeln *tr. V.* shroud ‹*area*› in fog; (mit Rauch) cover ‹*area*› with a smokescreen

vernehmbar *Adj.* (geh.) audible

vernehmen *unr. tr. V.* **(a)** (geh.: hören, erfahren) hear; **(b)** (verhören) question; (vor Gericht) examine

Vernehmen *das;* **dem/allem ~ nach** from what/all that one hears

vernehmlich 1 *Adj.* [clearly] audible. **2** *adv.* audibly; **laut und ~:** loud and clear

Vernehmung *die; ~, ~en* questioning; (vor Gericht) examination

vernehmungsfähig *Adj.* in a condition *or* fit to be questioned/examined *postpos.*

verneigen *refl. V.* (geh.) bow (**vor** + *Dat.* to, (literary) before)

Verneigung *die; ~, ~en* (geh.) bow

verneinen *tr.* (auch itr.) *V.* **(a)** say 'no' to ‹*question*›; answer ‹*question*› in the negative; **er schüttelte ~d den Kopf** he shook his head to say 'no'; **(b)** (Sprachw.) negate

Verneinung *die; ~, ~en* **(a)** ~ **einer Frage** negative answer to a question; **(b)** (Sprachw.) negation

vernetzen *tr. V.* (Chemie, Technik) interlink

vernichten *tr. V.* destroy; exterminate ‹*pests, vermin*›

vernichtend 1 *Adj.* crushing ‹*defeat*›; shattering ‹*blow*›; (fig.) devastating ‹*criticism*›. **2** *adv.* **den Feind ~ schlagen** inflict a crushing defeat on the enemy

Vernichtung *die; ~, ~en* destruction; (von Schädlingen) extermination

verniedlichen *tr. V.* trivialize ‹*matter, situation, etc.*›; play down ‹*guilt, error*›

Verniedlichung *die; ~, ~en* trivialization

Vernissage /vɛrnɪ'saːʒə/ *die; ~, ~n* (geh.) private view (of contemporary artist's exhibition)

Vernunft /fɛɐ̯'nʊnft/ *die; ~:* reason; **~ annehmen** see reason; come to one's senses; **jmdn. zur ~ bringen** make sb. see reason

vernunft·begabt *Adj.* rational

vernünftig /fɛɐ̯'nʏnftɪç/ **1** *Adj.* **(a)** sensible; **(b)** (ugs.: ordentlich, richtig) decent. **2** *adv.* **(a)** sensibly; **(b)** (ugs.: ordentlich, richtig) ‹*talk, eat*› properly; ‹*dress*› sensibly

veröden 1 *itr. V.; mit sein* become deserted. **2** *tr. V.* (Med.) treat ‹*varicose veins*› by injection

veröffentlichen *tr. V.* publish

Veröffentlichung *die; ~, ~en* publication

verordnen *tr. V.* [jmdm. etw.] ~: prescribe [sth. for sb.]

Verordnung *die* prescribing; prescription

verpachten *tr. V.* lease

Verpachtung *die; ~, ~en* leasing

verpacken *tr. V.* pack; wrap up ‹*present, parcel*›; **etw. als Geschenk ~:** gift-wrap sth.

Verpackung *die* **(a)** *o.Pl.* packing; **(b)** (Umhüllung) packaging *no pl.;* wrapping

verpassen *tr. V.* **(a)** miss ‹*train, person, entry* (Mus.), *chance, etc.*›; **(b)** (ugs.) **jmdm. eins ~:** clout sb. one (coll.)

verpatzen *tr. V.* (ugs.) make a mess of; muck up (Brit. sl.); botch ‹*job*›

verpennen (salopp) **1** *itr. V.* oversleep. **2** *tr. V.* **(a)** (versgessen) forget; **(b)** (verschlafen) sleep through ‹*morning etc.*›

verpesten *tr. V.* (abwertend) pollute

Verpestung *die; ~, ~en* (abwertend) pollution

verpetzen *tr. V.* **jmdn.** [beim Lehrer *usw.*] ~: tell *or* (coll.) split on sb. [to the teacher *etc.*]

verpfänden *tr. V.* pawn ‹*article*›; mortgage ‹*house*›; (fig.) pledge ‹*word, honour*›

Verpfändung *die* pawning; (von Hausbesitz) mortgaging; mortgage

verpfeifen *unr. tr. V.* (ugs. abwertend) grass (Brit. coll.) *or* (coll.) split on ‹*person*› (**bei** to)

verpflanzen *tr. V.* **(a)** transplant ‹*tree, bush*›; **(b)** (Med.) transplant ‹*heart etc.*›; graft ‹*skin*›

Verpflanzung *die; ~, ~en* **(a)** transplanting; **(b)** (Med.) transplant[ing]; (von Haut) graft

verpflegen *tr. V.* cater for; feed

Verpflegung *die; ~, ~en* **(a)** *o.Pl.* catering *no indef. art.* (Gen. for); **(b)** (Nahrung) food; **Unterkunft und ~:** board and lodging

Verpflegungs·kosten *Pl.* cost *sing.* of food *or* meals

verpflichten 1 *tr. V.* **(a)** oblige; commit; (festlegen, binden) bind; **zur Verschwiegenheit verpflichtet** sworn to secrecy; **jmdm. verpflichtet sein** be indebted to sb.; **(b)** (einstellen, engagieren) engage ‹*actor, manager, etc.*›; (Sport) sign ‹*player*›. **2** *refl. V.* undertake; promise; **sich zu einer Zahlung ~:** commit oneself to making a payment; **sich vertraglich ~:** sign a contract; bind oneself by contract

Verpflichtung *die; ~, ~en* **(a)** obligation; commitment; [finanzielle] ~en [financial] commitments; liabilities; **(b)** (Engagement) engaging; engagement; (Sport: eines Spielers) signing

---

verpfuschen *tr. V.* (ugs.) make a mess of; muck up (Brit. sl.)

verpissen *refl. V.* (salopp) piss off (Brit. sl.); beat it (sl.)

verplanen *tr. V.* (a) get the plans wrong for; (b) (festlegen, einteilen) book ⟨*person, time*⟩ up; commit ⟨*money, reprint*⟩

verplappern *refl. V.* (ugs.) blab (coll.); let the cat out of the bag

verplaudern 1 *tr. V.* chat away ⟨*time*⟩; spend ⟨*time*⟩ chatting. 2 *refl. V.* go on chatting too long

verplempern /fɛɐˈplɛmpɐn/ *tr. V.* (ugs.) fritter away

verplomben *tr. V.* seal

verpönt /fɛɐˈpøːnt/ *Adj.* scorned; (tabu) taboo

verprassen *tr. V.* squander, (coll.) blow ⟨*money, fortune*⟩

verprügeln *tr. V.* beat up; (zur Strafe) thrash

verpuffen *itr. V.; mit sein* go phut; (fig.) fizzle out

verpulvern *tr. V.* (ugs.) blow (coll.) ⟨*money*⟩; (allmählich) fritter away ⟨*money*⟩

verpuppen *refl. V.* (Zool.) pupate

Verputz *der* plaster; (auf Außenwänden) rendering

verputzen *tr. V.* (a) (mit Putz versehen) plaster; render ⟨*outside wall*⟩; (b) (ugs.: aufessen) polish off (coll.) ⟨*food*⟩

Verputzer *der; ~s, ~:* plasterer

verqualmen 1 *itr. V.; mit sein* ⟨*cigar, cigarette*⟩ go out. 2 *tr. V.* (ugs. abwertend) fill ⟨*room*⟩ with smoke; **verqualmt** smoke-filled

verquer 1 *Adj.* (a) (schief) angled, crooked ⟨*position*⟩; (b) (absonderlich) weird, outlandish ⟨*idea*⟩. 2 *adv.* (a) (schief) at an angle; crookedly; (b) (absonderlich) ⟨*behave*⟩ weirdly

verquicken /fɛɐˈkvɪkn̩/ *tr. V.* combine

Verquickung *die; ~, ~en* combination

verquirlen *tr. V.* mix [with a whisk]; whisk

verquollen /fɛɐˈkvɔlən/ *Adj.* swollen

verrammeln *tr. V.* barricade

verramschen /fɛɐˈramʃn̩/ ⇒ **verschleudern a**

verrannt /fɛɐˈrant/ *Adj.* obsessed

Verrat *der; ~[e]s* betrayal (**an** + *Dat.* of); ~ **begehen** (Politik) commit [an act of] treason

verraten 1 *unr. tr. V.* (a) betray ⟨*person, cause*⟩; betray, give away ⟨*secret, plan, etc.*⟩ (**an** + *Akk.* to); ~ **und verkauft sein** be well and truly in the soup (fig. coll.) or (coll.) sunk; (b) (ugs.: mitteilen) **jmdm. den Grund** *usw.* ~: tell sb. the reason *etc.;* (c) (erkennen lassen) show, betray ⟨*feelings, surprise, fear, etc.*⟩; show ⟨*influence, talent*⟩; (d) (zu erkennen geben) give ⟨*person*⟩ away. 2 *unr. refl. V.* (a) ⟨*person*⟩ give oneself away; (b) (sich zeigen) show itself; be revealed

Verräter /fɛɐˈrɛːtɐ/ *der; ~s, ~:* traitor

Verräterei *die; ~, ~en* treachery

Verräterin *die; ~, ~nen* traitress

verräterisch *Adj.* (a) treacherous ⟨*plan, purpose, act, etc.*⟩; (b) (erkennen lassend) tell-tale, give-away ⟨*look, gesture*⟩

verräuchern *tr. V.* fill with smoke

verraucht *Adj.* smoke-filled; smoky

verrechnen 1 *tr. V.* include, take into account ⟨*amount etc.*⟩; (gutschreiben) credit ⟨*cheque etc.*⟩ to another account. 2 *refl. V.* (auch fig.) miscalculate; make a mistake/mistakes

Verrechnung *die* settlement (**mit** + *Dat.* of); „**nur zur** ~" (Bankw.) 'not negotiable'; 'a/c payee [only]'

Verrechnungs·scheck *der* crossed cheque

verrecken *itr. V.; mit sein* (salopp) die [a miserable death]

verregnen *itr. V.; mit sein* be spoilt or ruined by rain; **verregnet** rainy, wet ⟨*spring, summer, holiday, etc.*⟩

verreiben *unr. tr. V.* rub in

verreisen *itr. V.; mit sein* go away; **verreist sein** be away

verreißen *unr. tr. V.* (ugs.) tear ⟨*book, play, etc.*⟩ to pieces

verrenken /fɛɐˈrɛŋkn̩/ *tr. V.* (a) (verletzen) dislocate; **sich** (*Dat.*) **den Fuß** ~: twist one's ankle; (b) (biegen) **sich** *od.* **seine Glieder** ~: go into or perform contortions

Verrenkung *die; ~, ~en* (a) (Verletzung) dislocation; (b) (Biegung des Körpers) contortion

verrennen *unr. refl. V.* get on the wrong track or off course; **sich in etw.** (*Akk.*) ~: become obsessed with sth.

verrichten *tr. V.* perform ⟨*work, duty, etc.*⟩

Verrichtung *die* carrying out; performance

verriegeln *tr. V.* bolt

Verriegelung *die; ~, ~en* (a) (das Verriegeln) bolting; (b) (Vorrichtung) bolt mechanism

verringern /fɛɐˈrɪŋɐn/ 1 *tr. V.* reduce. 2 *refl. V.* decrease

Verringerung *die; ~:* reduction; decrease (*Gen.,* **von** in)

Verriss, *Verriß *der* (ugs.) damning review or criticism (**über** + *Akk.* of)

verrohen 1 *tr. V.* brutalize. 2 *itr. V.; mit sein* become brutal

Verrohung *die; ~, ~en* brutalization

verrosten *itr. V.; mit sein* rust

verrotten *itr. V.; mit sein* rot; ⟨*building etc.*⟩ decay

verrücken *tr. V.* move; shift

verrückt (ugs.) 1 *Adj.* (a) mad; ~ **werden** go mad or insane; **jmdn.** ~ **machen** drive sb. mad; **du bist wohl** ~! you must be mad or crazy!; **wie** ~: like mad or crazy (coll.); **ich werde** ~! I'll be blowed (coll.) or (coll.) damned; ~ **spielen** (salopp) ⟨*person*⟩ act crazy (coll.); ⟨*car, machine, etc.*⟩ play up (coll); ⟨*watch, weather*⟩ go crazy; (b) (überspannt, ausgefallen) crazy ⟨*idea, fashion, prank, day, etc.*⟩; **so was Verrücktes!** what a crazy idea!; (c) (begierig) crazy; **auf jmdn.** *od.* **nach jmdm./auf etw.** (*Akk.*) ~ **sein** be crazy (coll.) or mad about sb./sth. 2 *adv.* crazily; ⟨*behave*⟩ crazily or like a madman; ⟨*paint, dress, etc.*⟩ in a mad or crazy way

Verrückte *der/die; adj. Dekl.* (ugs.) madman/madwoman; lunatic

Verrücktheit *die; ~, ~en* (a) *o.Pl.* madness; insanity; (Überspanntheit) craziness; (b) (überspannte Idee) crazy idea

Verruf *der in* **in** ~ **kommen** *od.* **geraten** fall into disrepute

verrufen *Adj.* disreputable

verrühren *tr. V.* stir together; mix

verrutschen *itr. V.* slip

Vers /fɛrs/ *der; ~es, ~e* verse; (Zeile) line; ~**e schreiben** *od.* (ugs.) **schmieden** write verse or poetry; **sich** (*Dat.*) **einen** ~ **auf etw.** (*Akk.*) /**darauf machen** (fig.) make sense of sth./put two and two together

versagen 1 *itr. V.* fail; ⟨*machine, engine*⟩ stop [working], break down; **menschliches Versagen** human error; **ihre Stimme versagte** her voice failed. 2 *tr. V.* (geh.) (nicht gewähren) **jmdm. etw.** ~: deny or refuse sb. sth.; **ein Kind blieb ihr versagt** a child was denied her; **ich konnte es mir nicht** ~, **darauf zu antworten** I could not refrain from answering. 3 *refl. V.* **sich jmdm.** ~: refuse to give oneself or surrender to sb.

Versager *der; ~s, ~:* failure

versalzen *unr. tr. V.* (a) put too much salt in/on; **die Suppe ist versalzen** there is too much salt in the soup; the soup is too salty; (b) (fig. ugs.) spoil (*Dat.* for)

versammeln 1 *tr. V.* assemble; gather [together]; **seine Leute um sich** ~: gather one's people around one. 2 *refl. V.* assemble; (weniger formell) gather

Versammlung *die* (a) meeting; (Partei~) assembly; (unter freiem Himmel, bes. politisch) rally; **auf einer** ~ **sprechen** speak at a meeting/rally; (b) (Gremium) assembly

Versand *der; ~[e]s* (a) dispatch; (b) (Abteilung) dispatch department

versanden *itr. V.; mit sein* fill with sand; ⟨*harbour etc.*⟩ silt up; (mit Sand bedeckt werden) be covered with sand

Versand·haus *das* mail-order firm

versauern *itr. V.; mit sein* (ugs.) waste away; stagnate

versaufen *unr. tr. V.* (salopp) drink one's way through

versäumen *tr. V.* (a) (verpassen) miss; lose ⟨*time, sleep*⟩; (b) (vernachlässigen, unterlassen) neglect ⟨*duty, task*⟩; **das Versäumte/Versäumtes nachholen** make up for or catch up on what one has neglected or failed to do

Versäumnis *das;* ~ses, ~se omission

verschaffen *tr. V.* jmdm. Arbeit/Geld/Unterkunft *usw.* ~: provide sb. with work/money/accommodation *etc.;* get sb. work/money/accommodation *etc.;* sich (*Dat.*) etw. ~: get hold of sth.; obtain sth.; sich (*Dat.*) Respekt ~: gain respect; was verschafft mir die Ehre? (iron.) to what do I owe this honour?

verschämt /fɛɐ̯ˈʃɛːmt/ 1 *Adj.* bashful. 2 *adv.* bashfully

verschandeln *tr. V.* (ugs.) spoil; ruin

Verschandelung *die;* ~, ~en (ugs.) ruination *no indef. art.*

verschanzen *refl. V.* (Milit.) take up a [fortified] position; (in einem Graben) entrench oneself; dig [oneself] in; sich hinter einer Zeitung ~ (fig.) take cover *or* hide behind a newspaper

verschärfen 1 *tr. V.* (a) intensify ⟨*conflict, difference, desire, etc.*⟩; increase, step up ⟨*pace, pressure*⟩; tighten ⟨*law, control, restriction, etc*⟩; make ⟨*penalty*⟩ more severe; (b) make ⟨*unemployment etc.*⟩ worse; aggravate ⟨*situation, crisis, etc.*⟩. 2 *refl. V.* (a) ⟨*pace, pressure, etc.*⟩ increase; ⟨*pain, tension, conflict, difference*⟩ intensify; (b) (sich verschlimmern) get worse

verschärft 1 *Adj.; nicht präd.* (a) increased ⟨*pressure*⟩; intensified ⟨*conflict*⟩; more intense ⟨*training*⟩; tighter, stricter ⟨*control, check, restriction*⟩; more severe ⟨*reprimand, punishment*⟩; (b) (schlimmer geworden) aggravated. 2 *adv.* (strenger) more strictly

verscharren *tr. V.* bury (just below the surface)

verschätzen *refl. V.* sich in etw. (*Dat.*) ~: misjudge sth.

verscheiden *unr. itr. V.; mit sein* (geh.) pass away

verscheißern *tr. V.* (derb) jmdm. ~: have (Brit. coll.) *or* (Amer. coll.) put sb. on; du willst mich wohl ~! pull the 'other one[, it's got bells on] (sl.)

verschenken *tr. V.* (a) give away; etw. an jmdn. ~: give sth. to sb.; (b) (ungewollt vergeben) waste ⟨*space*⟩; give away ⟨*points*⟩

verscherbeln /fɛɐ̯ˈʃɛrbl̩n/ *tr. V.* (ugs.) flog (Brit. sl.) (*Dat.*, an + *Akk.* to)

verscherzen *refl. V.* sich (*Dat.*) etw. ~: lose *or* forfeit sth. [through one's own folly]

verscheuchen *tr. V.* chase away (lit. or fig.); (durch Erschrecken) frighten *or* scare away

verscheuern *tr. V.* (ugs.) flog (Brit. sl.) (*Dat.*, an + *Akk.* to)

verschicken *tr. V.* ⇨ versenden

verschieben 1 *unr. tr. V.* (a) shift; move; (b) (aufschieben) put off, postpone (auf + *Akk.* till); etw. auf unbestimmte Zeit ~: postpone sth. indefinitely; (c) (ugs.: illegal verkaufen) traffic in ⟨*goods*⟩. 2 *unr. refl. V.* (a) get out of place; (rutschen) slip; (b) (erst später stattfinden) be postponed (um for)

Verschiebung *die* (a) movement; (fig.: Änderung) alteration, shift (*Gen.* in); (b) (zeitlich) postponement

verschieden 1 *Adj.* (a) (nicht gleich) different (von from); er hat zwei ~e Socken an he is wearing two odd socks *or* two socks that don't match; das ist von Fall zu Fall ~: that varies from one case to another; (b) *nicht präd.* (vielfältig) various; auf ~e Weise in various ways; die ~sten ...: all sorts of ...; in den ~sten Farben in the most varied colours; in a whole variety of colours; Verschiedenes various things *pl.;* „Verschiedenes" 'miscellaneous'; (Tagesordnungspunkt) 'any other business'. 2 *adv.* differently; ~ groß of different sizes *postpos.;* different-sized; ⟨*people*⟩ of different heights

verschieden·artig 1 *Adj.* different in kind *pred.;* (mehr als zwei) diverse. 2 *adv.* diversely; (auf verschiedene Weise) in various different ways

Verschiedenartigkeit *die;* ~: difference in nature; (unter mehreren) diversity

Verschiedenheit *die;* ~, ~en difference; dissimilarity; (unter mehreren) diversity

*alte Schreibung (vgl. Hinweise auf S. xvi–xvii)

verschiedentlich *Adv.* on various occasions

verschießen *unr. tr. V.* (a) (als Geschoss verwenden) fire ⟨*shell, cartridge, etc.*⟩; (b) (verbrauchen) use up ⟨*ammunition*⟩; *s. auch* Pulver b; (c) einen Strafstoß ~ (Fußball) miss with a penalty

verschiffen *tr. V.* ship ⟨*goods, coal*⟩; transport ⟨*troops, emigrants, etc.*⟩ by ship

verschimmeln *itr. V.; mit sein* go mouldy; verschimmelt mouldy

verschlafen¹ 1 *unr. itr. V.* (auch refl. V.) oversleep. 2 *unr. tr. V.* (a) (schlafend verbringen) sleep through ⟨*morning, journey, concert, etc.*⟩; (b) (versäumen) not wake up in time to catch ⟨*train, bus*⟩; (c) (ugs.: vergessen) forget about ⟨*appointment etc.*⟩

verschlafen² *Adj.* (a) half-asleep; (b) (fig.: ruhig, langweilig) sleepy ⟨*town, village*⟩

Verschlag *der* shed; (für Kaninchen) hutch

verschlagen¹ *unr. tr. V.* (a) [jmdm.] die Seite ~: lose sb.'s place *or* page; die Seite ~ (im eigenen Buch) lose one's place *or* page; (b) jmdm. die Sprache *od.* Rede/den Atem ~: leave sb. speechless/take sb.'s breath away; (c) (Ballspiele) mishit ⟨*ball*⟩; (d) das Leben hat ihn nach X ~: the vagaries of life caused him to end up in X

verschlagen² 1 *Adj.* (abwertend: gerissen) sly; shifty. 2 *adv.* (abwertend: gerissen) slyly; shiftily

Verschlagenheit *die;* ~ (abwertend) slyness; shiftiness

verschlampen *tr. V.* (ugs., bes. südd.) succeed in losing (iron.)

verschlechtern 1 *tr. V.* make worse. 2 *refl. V.* get worse; deteriorate; sich [finanziell/wirtschaftlich *usw.*] ~: be worse off [financially/economically *etc.*]

Verschlechterung *die;* ~, ~en worsening, deterioration (*Gen.* in)

verschleiern *tr. V.* (a) veil; (b) (fig.: verbergen) draw a veil over, cover up ⟨*deception, facts, scandal, etc.*⟩; hide ⟨*intentions*⟩

verschleiert 1 *Adj.* veiled; misty ⟨*vision etc.*⟩; fogged ⟨*photograph*⟩. 2 *adv.* ohne Brille sieht er alles nur ~: without [his] glasses he sees everything as in a mist

Verschleierung *die;* ~, ~en (a) *o. Pl.* veiling; (b) (fig.: von Sachverhalten, Motiven) covering up

verschleimt *Adj.* congested with phlegm *postpos.*

Verschleimung *die;* ~, ~en mucous congestion

Verschleiß /fɛɐ̯ˈʃlaɪs/ *der;* ~es, ~e (a) (Abnutzung) wear *no indef. art.;* wear and tear *sing., no indef. art;* einen höheren ~ haben wear more rapidly; have a higher rate of wear; (b) (Verbrauch) consumption (an + *Dat.* of)

verschleißen 1 *unr. itr. V.; mit sein* wear out. 2 *unr. tr. V.* wear out; (fig.) run down, ruin ⟨*one's nerves, one's health*⟩; use up ⟨*energy, ability, etc.*⟩; verschlissen worn ⟨*material, suit, etc.*⟩; worn out ⟨*machine parts etc.*⟩

verschleppen *tr. V.* (a) carry off ⟨*valuables, animals*⟩; take away ⟨*person*⟩; (bes. nach Übersee) transport ⟨*convicts, slaves, etc.*⟩; (b) (weiterverbreiten) carry, spread ⟨*disease, bacteria, mud, etc.*⟩; (c) (verzögern) delay; (in die Länge ziehen) draw out; (d) (unbehandelt lassen) let ⟨*illness*⟩ drag on [and get worse]; verschleppte Krankheit illness aggravated by neglect

Verschleppung *die;* ~, ~en ⇨ verschleppen: (a) carrying off; transportation; (b) carrying; spreading; (c) delaying; drawing out; (d) aggravation by neglect

verschleudern *tr. V.* (a) (billig verkaufen) sell dirt cheap; (mit Verlust) sell at a loss; (b) (abwertend: verschwenden) squander

verschließbar *Adj.* (a) closable; [luftdicht] ~: sealable ⟨*container etc.*⟩; (b) (abschließbar) lockable

verschließen 1 *unr. tr. V.* (a) close ⟨*package, tin, pores, mouth, etc*⟩; close up ⟨*blood vessel, aperture, etc.*⟩; stop ⟨*bottle*⟩; (mit einem Korken) cork ⟨*bottle*⟩; etw. luftdicht ~: make sth. airtight; put an airtight seal on sth.; die Augen/Ohren [vor etw. (*Dat.*)] ~ (fig.) close one's eyes *or* be blind/turn a deaf ear *or* be deaf [to sth.]; (b) (abschließen) lock ⟨*door, cupboard, drawer, etc.*⟩; lock up ⟨*house etc.*⟩; *s. auch* Tür; (c) (wegschließen) lock away (in + *Dat. od. Akk.* in); (d) (versperren) bar ⟨*way etc.*⟩. 2 *unr. refl. V.* (a) sich

jmdm. ∼: be closed to sb.; ⟨*person*⟩ shut oneself off from sb.; (**b**) *in* **sich einer Sache** (*Dat.*) ∼: close one's mind to sth.; (ignorieren) ignore sth.

verschlimmbessern *tr. V.* (ugs. scherzh.) make worse with so-called corrections

verschlimmern 1 *tr. V.* make worse; aggravate ⟨*state of health*⟩. 2 *refl. V.* get worse; worsen; ⟨*position, conditions*⟩ deteriorate, worsen

Verschlimmerung *die;* ∼, ∼en worsening

verschlingen 1 *unr. tr. V.* (**a**) [inter]twine ⟨*threads, string, etc.*⟩ (**zu** into); (**b**) (essen, fressen) devour ⟨*food*⟩; (fig.) devour, consume ⟨*novel, money, etc.*⟩. 2 *unr. refl. V.* **sich ineinander** ∼: become entwined *or* intertwined

verschlissen 2. *Part. v.* **verschleißen**

verschlossen *Adj.* (wortkarg) taciturn, tight-lipped; (zurückhaltend) reserved

Verschlossenheit *die;* ∼ (Wortkargheit) taciturnity; (Zurückhaltung) reserve

verschlucken 1 *tr. V.* swallow ⟨*food, bone, word, etc.*⟩; (fig.) absorb, deaden ⟨*sound*⟩; absorb, eliminate ⟨*rays*⟩. 2 *refl. V.* choke (**an** + *Dat.* over)

verschlungen *Adj.* entwined ⟨*ornamentation*⟩; winding ⟨*path etc.*⟩; **er saß mit** ∼**en Armen da** he sat there with arms folded

Verschluss, *****Verschluß** *der* (**a**) (am BH, an Schmuck usw.) fastener; fastening; (an Taschen, Schmuck) clasp; (an Schuhen, Gürteln) buckle; (am Schrank, Fenster, Koffer usw.) catch; (an Flaschen) top; (Stöpsel) stopper; (Schraub∼) [screw-]top; [screw-] cap; (Tank∼) cap; (**b**) **unter** ∼: under lock and key

verschlüsseln *tr. V.* [en]code

Verschlüsselung *die;* ∼, ∼en [en]coding

Verschluss·sache, *****Verschluß·sache** *die* [item of] confidential information

verschmachten *itr. V.; mit sein* (geh.) fade away (**vor** + *Dat.* from); (vor Sehnsucht) pine away

verschmähen *tr. V.* (geh.) spurn; **verschmähte Liebe** unrequited love

verschmerzen *tr. V.* get over ⟨*defeat, disappointment*⟩

verschmieren *tr. V.* (**a**) smear ⟨*window etc.*⟩; (beim Schreiben) mess up ⟨*paper*⟩; scrawl all over ⟨*page*⟩; (**b**) (verteilen) spread ⟨*butter etc.*⟩; smudge ⟨*ink*⟩

verschmitzt /fɛɐ̯ˈʃmɪtst/ 1 *Adj.* mischievous, roguish. 2 *adv.* mischievously; roguishly

verschmoren *itr. V.; mit sein* (ugs.) burn

verschmust /fɛɐ̯ˈʃmuːst/ *Adj.* (ugs.) ⟨*child, cat, etc.*⟩ that always wants to be cuddled

verschmutzen 1 *itr. V.; mit sein* ⟨*material*⟩ get dirty; ⟨*river etc.*⟩ become polluted. 2 *tr. V.* dirty, soil ⟨*carpet, clothes*⟩; pollute ⟨*air, water, etc.*⟩

Verschmutzung *die;* ∼, ∼en (**a**) (der Umwelt) pollution; (**b**) (von Stoffen, Teppichen usw.) soiling; (**c**) (Schmutz) dirt *no. pl.;* ∼en [cases *pl.* of] soiling *sing.*

verschnaufen *itr. V.* (*auch refl.*) *V.* have *or* take a breather

Verschnauf·pause *die* rest; breather

verschneit *Adj.* snow-covered *attrib.;* covered with snow *postpos.*

verschnörkelt *Adj.* ornate

verschnupft /fɛɐ̯ˈʃnʊpft/ *Adj.* suffering from a cold *postpos.*

verschnüren *tr. V.* tie up (**zu** into)

verschollen /fɛɐ̯ˈʃɔlən/ *Adj.* missing; **er ist** ∼: he has disappeared; (wird vermisst) he is missing; **er galt seit langem als** ∼: for a long time it had been thought he had disappeared

verschonen *tr. V.* spare; **von etw. verschont bleiben** be spared by sth.; escape sth.; **jmdn. mit etw.** ∼: spare sb. sth.

verschönern /fɛɐ̯ˈʃøːnɐn/ *tr. V.* brighten up

verschränken /fɛɐ̯ˈʃrɛŋkn̩/ *tr. V.* fold ⟨*arms*⟩; cross ⟨*legs*⟩; clasp ⟨*hands*⟩

verschrauben *tr. V.* screw on; [miteinander] ∼: screw together

verschrecken *tr. V.* frighten *or* scare [off *or* away]

verschreiben 1 *unr. tr. V.* (**a**) (verbrauchen) use up ⟨*paper, ink, pencils, etc.*⟩; (**b**) (Med.: verordnen) prescribe ⟨*medicine, treatment, etc.*⟩; **jmdm. ein Medikament** ∼: prescribe a medication for sb.; (**c**) (falsch schreiben) write incorrectly *or* wrongly. 2 *unr. refl. V.* (**a**) (einen Fehler machen) make a slip of the pen; (**b**) (sich widmen) **sich einer Sache** (*Dat.*) ∼: devote oneself to sth.

Verschreibung *die;* ∼, ∼en prescription

verschreibungs·pflichtig *Adj.* available only on prescription *postpos.*

*****verschrieen, verschrien** /fɛɐ̯ˈʃriː[ə]n/ *Adj.* notorious (**wegen** for)

verschroben /fɛɐ̯ˈʃroːbn̩/ 1 *Adj.* eccentric, cranky ⟨*person*⟩; cranky, weird ⟨*ideas*⟩. 2 *adv.* eccentrically; weirdly

verschrotten *tr. V.* scrap

verschrumpeln *itr. V.; mit sein* (ugs.) go shrivelled; **verschrumpelt** shrivelled

verschüchtern *tr. V.* intimidate; **verschüchtert** timid; (adverbial) timidly

verschulden 1 *tr. V.* be to blame for ⟨*accident, death, etc.*⟩; (Fußball usw.) give away ⟨*goal, corner*⟩. 2 *refl. V.* get into debt; **er hat sich dafür hoch** ∼ **müssen** he had to borrow heavily to do that

Verschulden *das;* ∼s guilt; **durch eigenes/fremdes** ∼: through one's own/someone else's fault

verschuldet *Adj.* (**a**) in debt *postpos.* (**bei** to); **hoch** ∼: deeply in debt; (**b**) (belastet) mortgaged; **hoch** ∼: heavily mortgaged

Verschuldung *die;* ∼, ∼en indebtedness *no. pl.*

verschütt *in* ∼ **gehen** (ugs.) do a vanishing trick *or* disappearing act (coll.); (salopp: umkommen) go for a burton (Brit. sl.)

verschütten *tr. V.* (**a**) spill; (**b**) (begraben) bury ⟨*person*⟩ [alive]; submerge, bury ⟨*road etc.*⟩; (fig.) submerge

*****verschütt|gehen** ⇒ **verschütt**

verschwägert /fɛɐ̯ˈʃvɛːɡɐt/ *Adj.* related by marriage *postpos.*

verschweigen *unr. tr. V.* conceal ⟨*truth etc.*⟩; (verheimlichen) keep quiet about; **jmdm. etw.** ∼: hide *or* conceal sth. from sb.; **du verschweigst mir doch etwas** you're keeping something from me; *s. auch* **verschwiegen** 2

verschweißen *tr. V.* weld [together]; **etw. mit etw.** ∼: weld sth. to sth.

verschwenden *tr. V.* waste (**an** + *Akk.* on)

Verschwender *der;* ∼s, ∼ (von Geld) spendthrift; (von Dingen) wasteful person

verschwenderisch 1 *Adj.* (**a**) wasteful, extravagant ⟨*person*⟩; ⟨*life*⟩ of extravagance; (**b**) (üppig) lavish; sumptuous. 2 *adv.* (**a**) wastefully, extravagantly; (**b**) (üppig) lavishly; sumptuously

Verschwendung *die;* ∼, ∼en wastefulness; extravagance; **so eine** ∼! what a waste!

verschwiegen 1 2. *Part. v.* **verschweigen**. 2 *Adj.* (**a**) (diskret) discreet; (**b**) (still, einsam) secluded ⟨*place, bay*⟩; quiet ⟨*restaurant etc.*⟩

Verschwiegenheit *die;* ∼: secrecy; (Diskretion) discretion

verschwimmen *unr. itr. V.; mit sein* blur; become blurred; **die Zeilen/Buchstaben verschwammen mir vor den Augen** the lines/letters swam in front of my eyes

verschwinden *unr. itr. V.; mit sein* (**a**) disappear; vanish; ⟨*pain, spot, etc.*⟩ go [away]; **es ist besser, wir** ∼**/lass uns hier** ∼: we'd better/let's make ourselves scarce (coll.); **verschwinde [hier]!** off with you!; go away!; hop it! (Brit. coll.); **ich muss mal** ∼ (ugs. verhüll.) I have to pay a visit (coll.) *or* (Brit. coll.) spend a penny; **jmdn.** ∼ **lassen** take sb. away; (ermorden) eliminate sb.; do away with sb.; ∼ **lassen** (wegzaubern) ⟨*conjurer*⟩ make sth. disappear *or* vanish; (stehlen) help oneself to sth. (coll.); (unterschlagen, beiseite schaffen) dispose of sth.; (**b**) **neben jmdm./etw.** ∼ (sehr klein wirken) be dwarfed by sb./sth.; (unbedeutend wirken) pale into insignificance beside sb./sth.

verschwindend 1 *Adj.* tiny. **2** *adv.* ~ **klein** tiny; minute

verschwistert /fɛɐ̯ˈʃvɪstɐt/ *Adj.* [**miteinander**] ~ **sein** (Bruder u. Schwester sein) be brother and sister; (Brüder u. Schwestern sein) be brothers and sisters; (Brüder/Schwestern sein) be brothers/sisters

verschwitzen *tr. V.* (a) make ‹*shirt, dress, etc.*› sweaty; **verschwitzt** sweaty; (b) (ugs.: vergessen) forget

verschwollen /fɛɐ̯ˈʃvɔlən/ *Adj.* swollen

verschwommen 1 *2. Part. v.* **verschwimmen. 2** *Adj.* blurred ‹*photograph, vision*›; blurred, hazy ‹*outline*›; vague, woolly ‹*idea, concept, formulation, etc.*›; vague ‹*hope*›. **3** *adv.* ‹*express, formulate, refer*› vaguely; ‹*remember*› hazily; **ich sehe alles ganz ~:** everything looks blurred to me

verschwören *unr. refl. V.* conspire, plot (**gegen** against)

Verschwörer *der;* ~**s**, ~, **Verschwörerin** *die;* ~, ~**nen** conspirator

Verschwörung *die;* ~, ~**en** conspiracy; plot

versehen 1 *unr. tr. V.* (a) (ausstatten) provide; equip ‹*car, factory, machine, etc.*›; (b) (ausüben, besorgen) perform ‹*duty etc.*›; **bei jmdm. den Haushalt ~:** keep house for sb.; (c) (innehaben) hold ‹*post, job*›. **2** *unr. refl. V.* (a) (einen Fehler machen) make a slip; slip up; (b) *in* **ehe man sichs versieht** before you know where you are

Versehen *das;* ~**s**, ~: oversight; slip; **aus ~:** by mistake; inadvertently

versehentlich 1 *Adv.* by mistake; inadvertently. **2** *adj.; nicht präd.* inadvertent

versehrt /fɛɐ̯ˈzeːɐt/ *Adj.* disabled

Versehrte *der/die; adj. Dekl.* disabled person

verselbständigen, verselbstständigen *refl. V.* become independent

versenden *unr.* (*auch regelm.*) *tr. V.* send ‹*letter, parcel*›; send out ‹*invitations*›; dispatch ‹*goods*›

Versendung *die* ⇒ **versenden:** sending; sending out; dispatch

versengen *tr. V.* scorch; singe ‹*hair*›

versenken *tr. V.* (a) sink ‹*ship*›; lower ‹*body, coffin*›; (b) (verschwinden lassen) lower, retract ‹*aerial, rostrum, etc.*›

Versenkung *die* (a) ⇒ **versenken a, b:** sinking; lowering; retraction; (b) **in der ~ verschwinden** (fig. ugs.) vanish from the scene; sink into oblivion

versessen /fɛɐ̯ˈzɛsn̩/ *Adj.* **auf jmdn./etw. ~ sein** be dead keen on *or* crazy about sb./sth. (coll.); **darauf ~ sein, etw. zu tun** be dying to do sth.

versetzen 1 *tr. V.* (a) move; transfer, move ‹*employee*›; (in die nächsthöhere Klasse) move ‹*pupil*› up, (Amer.) promote ‹*pupil*› (**in** + *Akk.* to); (fig.) transport (**in** + *Akk.* to); (b) (nicht geradlinig anordnen) stagger; (c) (verpfänden) pawn; (d) (verkaufen) sell; (e) (ugs.: vergeblich warten lassen) stand ‹*person*› up (coll.); (f) (vermischen) mix; (g) (erwidern) retort; (h) **etw. in Bewegung ~:** set sth. in motion; **jmdn. in Erstaunen/Unruhe/Angst/Begeisterung ~:** astonish sb./make sb. uneasy/frighten sb./fill sb. with enthusiasm; **jmdn. in die Lage ~, etw. zu tun** put sb. in a position to do sth.; **jmdm. einen Stoß/Fußtritt/Schlag** *usw.* **~:** give sb. a push/kick/deal sb. a blow *etc.* **2** *refl. V.* **sich an jmds. Stelle** (*Akk.*) *od.* **in jmds. Lage** (*Akk.*) **~:** put oneself in sb.'s position *or* place

Versetzung *die;* ~, ~**en** (a) moving; (einer Pflanze) transplanting; (eines Schülers) moving up, (Amer.) promotion (**in** + *Akk.* to); (eines Angestellten) transfer; move; (b) (Verpfändung) pawning; (c) (Verkauf) selling; sale; (d) (das Mischen) mixing; *s. auch* **Ruhestand**

Versetzungs·zeugnis *das* (Schulw.) end-of-year report (*confirming pupil's move to a higher class*)

verseuchen *tr. V.* (auch fig.) contaminate

Verseuchung (auch fig.) *die;* ~, ~**en** contamination

Versicherer *der;* ~**s**, ~: insurer

versichern 1 *tr. V.* (a) (als wahr hinstellen) assert, affirm ‹*sth.*›; **etw. hoch und heilig/eidesstattlich ~:** swear blind to sth./attest sth. in a statutory declaration; (b) (vertraglich schützen) insure (**bei** with); **sein Leben ist hoch**

versichert his life is assured *or* insured for a large sum. **2** *refl. V.* (geh.) **sich einer Sache** (*Gen.*) ~: make sure *or* certain of sth.

Versicherte *der/die; adj. Dekl.* insured [person]

Versicherung *die* (a) (Beteuerung) assurance; **eine eidesstattliche ~:** a statutory declaration; (b) (Schutz durch Vertrag) insurance; (Vertrag) insurance [policy] (**über** + *Akk.* for); **eine ~ abschließen** take out an insurance [policy]; (c) (Gesellschaft) insurance [company]

versicherungs-, Versicherungs-: ~**beitrag** *der* insurance premium; ~**fall** *der* event giving rise to a claim; ~**gesellschaft** *die* insurance company; ~**karte** *die* (a) (Sozialversicherung) insurance *or* contribution card; (b) (Kfz.-Versicherung) **die grüne ~karte** the green card; ~**nehmer** *der;* ~**s**, ~: policy holder; ~**pflichtig** *Adj.* (a) subject to compulsory insurance *postpos.;* (b) (Sozialversicherung) ‹*person*› liable for [insurance] contributions; ‹*earnings*› subject to [insurance] contributions; ~**police** *die* ⇒ ~**schein;** ~**prämie** *die* ⇒ ~**beitrag;** ~**schein** *der* insurance policy ~**summe** *die* sum insured

versickern *itr. V.; mit sein* ‹*river etc.*› drain *or* seep away

versieben *tr. V.* (ugs.) (a) (verlegen) mislay; (b) (verderben) ruin; waste ‹*chance*›

versiegeln *tr. V.* seal

Versiegelung *die;* ~, ~**en** (a) seal; (b) *o. Pl.* (das Versiegeln) sealing

versiegen *itr. V.; mit sein* (geh.) dry up; run dry; ‹*tears*› cease [to flow]; (fig.) peter out; ‹*energy*› run out

versiert /vɛrˈziːɐt/ *Adj.* experienced [and knowledgeable]; **in etw.** (*Dat.*) ~ **sein** be well versed in sth.

versifft *Adj.* (ugs.) filthy

versilbern *tr. V.* (a) silver-plate; (b) (ugs.: verkaufen) turn into cash; flog (Brit. sl.)

versinken *unr. itr. V.; mit sein* (a) sink; **im Schlamm/Schnee ~:** sink into the mud/snow; **im Moor ~:** be sucked into the bog; **ich wäre am liebsten im Erdboden versunken** I wished the ground would [open and] swallow me up; (b) (fig.) ~ **in** (+ *Akk.*) become immersed in *or* wrapped up in ‹*memories, thoughts*›; subside, lapse into ‹*melancholy, silence, etc.*›

versinnbildlichen *tr. V.* symbolize

Version /vɛrˈzjoːn/ *die;* ~, ~**en** version

versklaven *tr. V.* enslave

versnoben *itr. V.; mit sein* (abwertend) become snobbish; turn into a snob

versohlen *tr. V.* (ugs.) belt (coll.) ‹*person, backside, etc.*›

versöhnen /fɛɐ̯ˈzøːnən/ **1** *refl. V.* **sich [miteinander] ~:** become reconciled; make it up. **2** *tr. V.* reconcile; **jmdn. mit seinem Schicksal ~:** reconcile sb. to his/her fate

versöhnlich 1 *Adj.* (a) conciliatory; (b) (erfreulich) positive; optimistic. **2** *adv.* (a) in a conciliatory way; ‹*say*› in a conciliatory tone; (b) (erfreulich) ‹*end*› positively, optimistically

Versöhnung *die;* ~, ~**en** reconciliation

versonnen 1 *Adj.* dreamy; (in Gedanken versunken) lost in thought *postpos.* **2** *adv.* dreamily; (in Gedanken) lost in thought

versorgen *tr. V.* (a) supply; **hast du den Hund/die Blumen schon versorgt?** have you fed the dog/watered the flowers?; (b) (unterhalten, ernähren) provide for ‹*children, family*›; (c) (sorgen für) look after; attend to, see to ‹*heating, garden, etc.*›; **jmdn. ärztlich ~:** give sb. medical care; (kurzzeitig) give sb. medical attention

Versorger *der;* ~**s**, ~, **Versorgerin** *die;* ~, ~**nen** breadwinner; provider

Versorgung *die;* ~, ~**en** (a) *o. Pl.* supply[ing]; **die ~ einer Stadt mit etw.** the supply of sth. to a town; (b) (Unterhaltung, Ernährung) support[ing]; (c) (Bedienung, Pflege) care; **ärztliche ~:** medical care *or* treatment; (kurzzeitig) medical attention; (d) (Bezüge) maintenance

verspannen *refl. V.* ‹*muscle*› tense up; **verspannt** taut ‹*muscle*›; (verkrampft) seized-up ‹*back*›

Verspannung *die* (Med.: der Muskulatur) tension
verspäten *refl. V.* be late
verspätet *Adj.* late ⟨*arrival, rose, butterfly*⟩; belated ⟨*greetings, thanks*⟩
Verspätung *die;* ~, ~**en** lateness; (verspätetes Eintreffen) late arrival; [**fünf Minuten**] ~ **haben** be [five minutes] late; **eine fünfminütige** ~: a five-minute delay; **seine** *od.* **die** ~ **aufholen** make up the lost time; **mit dreimonatiger** ~: three months late
verspeisen *tr. V.* (geh.) consume; partake of
versperren *tr. V.* block ⟨*road, entrance*⟩; obstruct ⟨*view*⟩; **jmdm. den Weg/die Sicht** ~: block sb.'s path/ block *or* obstruct sb.'s view
verspielen 1 *tr. V.* gamble away; (fig.: verwirken) squander, throw away ⟨*opportunity, chance*⟩; forfeit ⟨*right, credibility, sb.'s trust, etc.*⟩. 2 *itr. V. in* [**bei jmdm.**] **verspielt haben** (ugs.) have had it [so far as sb. is concerned] (coll.). 3 *refl. V.* play a wrong note/wrong notes
verspielt 1 *Adj.* (auch fig.) playful; fanciful, fantastic ⟨*form, design, etc.*⟩. 2 *adv.* playfully (lit. or fig.); ⟨*dress, designed*⟩ fancifully, fantastically
verspinnen *unr. tr. V.* spin ⟨*wool*⟩ (**zu** into)
versponnen 1 2. *Part. v.* **verspinnen.** 2 *Adj.* eccentric, odd ⟨*person*⟩; odd, weird ⟨*idea*⟩
verspotten *tr. V.* mock; ridicule
Verspottung *die;* ~, ~**en** mocking; ridiculing
versprechen 1 *unr. tr. V.* (a) promise; **was er verspricht, hält er auch** he keeps his promises; **sein Blick versprach nichts Gutes** his glance was ominous; (b) **sich** (*Dat.*) **etw. von etw./jmdm.** ~: hope for sth. *or* to get sth. from sth./sb. 2 *unr. refl. V.* make a slip/slips of the tongue
Versprechen *das;* ~**s,** ~: promise
Versprecher *der;* ~**s,** ~: slip of the tongue
Versprechung *die;* ~, ~**en** promise
versprengen *tr. V.* (a) (bes. Milit.) disperse; scatter; (b) (verspritzen) sprinkle ⟨*water*⟩
verspritzen *tr. V.* (a) spray; (b) (bespritzen) spatter ⟨*windscreen, coat, etc.*⟩
versprühen *tr. V.* spray; **Geist** *od.* **Witz** ~ (fig.) show sparkling wit; scintillate
verspüren *tr. V.* feel
verstaatlichen *tr. V.* nationalize
Verstaatlichung *die;* ~, ~**en** nationalization
verstädtern /fɛɐ̯ˈʃtɛːtɐn/ *itr. V.; mit sein* become urbanized
Verstädterung *die;* ~, ~**en** urbanization
Verstand *der;* ~**[e]s** (Fähigkeit zu denken) reason *no art.;* (Fähigkeit, Begriffe zu bilden) mind; (Vernunft) [common] sense *no art.;* **Tiere haben keinen** ~: animals do not have the power *or* faculty of reason; **der menschliche** ~: the human mind; **wenn du deinen** ~ **gebraucht hättest** if you had used your brain *or* had been thinking; **ich hätte ihm mehr** ~ **zugetraut** I thought he would have had more sense; **manchmal zweifle ich an seinem** ~: I sometimes doubt his sanity; **hast du denn den** ~ **verloren?** (ugs.) have you taken leave of your senses?; are you out of your mind?; **das geht über meinen** ~: that's beyond me
verstandes·mäßig 1 *Adj.* rational; intellectual ⟨*inferiority, superiority*⟩. 2 *adv.* rationally; intellectually ⟨*inferior, superior*⟩
verständig /fɛɐ̯ˈʃtɛndɪç/ 1 *Adj.* sensible; intelligent. 2 *adv.* sensibly; intelligently
verständigen /fɛɐ̯ˈʃtɛndɪɡn̩/ 1 *tr. V.* notify, inform (**von, über** + *Akk.* of). 2 *refl. V.* (a) make oneself understood; **sich mit jmdm.** ~: communicate with sb.; (b) (sich einigen) **sich** [**mit jmdm.**] **über/auf etw.** (*Akk.*) ~: come to an understanding *or* reach agreement [with sb.] about *or.* on sth.
Verständigkeit *die;* ~: understanding; intelligence
Verständigung *die;* ~, ~**en** (a) notification; (b) (das Sichverständlichmachen) communication *no art.;* (c) (Einigung) understanding

Verständigungs·schwierigkeit *die* difficulty of communication
verständlich 1 *Adj.* (a) comprehensible; (deutlich) clear ⟨*pronunciation, presentation, etc.*⟩; [**leicht**] ~: easily understood; **schwer** ~: difficult to understand; **sich** ~ **machen** make oneself understood; **jmdm. etw.** ~ **machen** make sth. clear to sb.; (b) (begreiflich, verzeihlich) understandable. 2 *adv.* comprehensibly; in a comprehensible way; (deutlich) ⟨*speak, express oneself, present*⟩ clearly
verständlicher·weise *Adv.* understandably
Verständnis *das;* ~**ses,** ~**se** understanding; **ein** ~ **für Kunst/Musik** an appreciation of *or* feeling for art/music; **ich habe volles** ~ **dafür, dass** ...: I fully understand that ...; **für so etwas habe ich kein** ~: I have no time for that kind of thing; **für die Unannehmlichkeiten bitten wir um** [**Ihr**] ~: we ask for your forbearance *or* we apologize for the inconvenience caused
verständnis-, Verständnis-: ~**los** 1 *Adj.* uncomprehending; 2 *adv.* uncomprehendingly; ~**losigkeit** *die* incomprehension; **voller** ~**losigkeit** uncomprehendingly; with a complete lack of understanding; ~**voll** 1 *Adj.* understanding; 2 *adv.* understandingly
verstärken 1 *tr. V.* (a) strengthen; (b) (zahlenmäßig) reinforce ⟨*troops, garrison, etc.*⟩ (**um** by); enlarge, augment ⟨*orchestra, choir*⟩ (**um** by); (c) (intensiver machen) intensify, increase ⟨*effort, contrast, impression, suspicion*⟩; (lauter machen) amplify ⟨*signal, sound, guitar, etc.*⟩. 2 *refl. V.* increase
Verstärker *der;* ~**s,** ~: amplifier
verstärkt 1 *Adj.; nicht präd.* (a) increased; (größer) greater ⟨*efforts, vigilance, etc.*⟩; **in** ~**em Maße** to a greater *or* increased extent; (b) (zahlenmäßig) enlarged, augmented ⟨*orchestra, choir, etc.*⟩; reinforced (Mil.) ⟨*unit*⟩. 2 *adv.* to an increased extent
Verstärkung *die;* ~, ~**en** (a) strengthening; (b) (zahlenmäßig) reinforcement (esp. Mil.); (eines Orchesters usw.) enlargement; (c) (Intensivierung, Zunahme) increase (*Gen.* in); (der Lautstärke) amplification; (d) (zusätzliche Person[en]) reinforcements *pl.*
verstauben *itr. V.; mit sein* get dusty; gather dust (lit. or fig.)
verstaubt *Adj.* dusty; covered in dust *postpos.;* (fig. abwertend) old-fashioned; outmoded
verstauchen *tr. V.* ▶329| sprain; **sich** (*Dat.*) **den Fuß/die Hand** ~: sprain one's ankle/wrist
Verstauchung *die;* ~, ~**en** ▶329| sprain
verstauen *tr. V.* pack (**in** + *Dat. od. Akk.* in[to]); (bes. im Boot/Auto) stow (**in** + *Dat. od. Akk.* in); **etw. in einem Schrank** ~: put *or* (coll.) stash sth. away in a cupboard
Versteck *das;* ~**[e]s,** ~**e** hiding place; (eines Flüchtlings, Räubers usw.) hideout: ~ **spielen** play hide-and-seek; [**mit jmdm./miteinander**] ~ **spielen** (fig.) hide *or* keep things [from sb./one another]
verstecken 1 *tr. V.* hide (**vor** + *Dat.* from). 2 *refl. V.* **sich** [**vor jmdm./etw.**] ~: hide [from sb./sth.]; **sich versteckt halten** be [in] hiding; (versteckt bleiben) remain in hiding; **sich vor** *od.* **neben jmdm. nicht zu** ~ **brauchen** (fig.) not need to fear comparison with sb.; **sich hinter seinen Vorschriften** ~ (fig.) use one's rules and regulations to hide behind
versteckt *Adj.* hidden; concealed ⟨*polemics*⟩; veiled ⟨*threat*⟩; (heimlich) secret ⟨*malice, activity, etc.*⟩; disguised ⟨*foul*⟩; (verstohlen) furtive ⟨*glance, smile*⟩
verstehen 1 *unr. tr. V.* (a) (wahrnehmen) understand; make out; **er war am Telefon gut/schlecht/kaum zu** ~: it was easy/difficult/barely possible to understand *or* make out what he was saying on the telephone; (b) *auch itr.* (begreifen, interpretieren) understand; **ich verstehe** I understand; I see; **wir** ~ **uns schon** we understand each other; we see eye to eye; **du bleibst hier, verstehst du!** you stay here, understand!; **jmdm. etw. zu** ~ **geben** give sb. to understand sth.; **das ist in dem Sinne** *od.* **so zu** ~, **dass** ...: it is supposed to mean that ...; **wie soll ich das** ~? how am I to interpret that?; what am I supposed to make of that?; **jmdn./etw. falsch** ~: misunderstand sb./sth.; **versteh mich bitte richtig** *od.* **nicht**

falsch please don't misunderstand me *or* get me wrong; **etw. unter etw.** (*Dat.*) ∼: understand sth. by sth.; **jmdn./sich als etw.** ∼: see sb./oneself as sth.; consider sb./oneself to be sth.; *s. auch* **Spaß b**; **(c)** (beherrschen, wissen) **es** ∼, **die. zu tun** know how to do sth.; **er versteht eine Menge von Autos** he knows a lot about cars. **2** *unr. refl. V.* **(a) sich mit jmdm.** ∼: get on with sb.; **sie** ∼ **sich** they get on well together; **(b)** (selbstverständlich sein) **das versteht sich [von selbst]** that goes without saying; **(c)** (Kaufmannsspr.: gemeint sein) **der Preis versteht sich einschließlich Mehrwertsteuer** the price is inclusive of VAT; **(d) sich auf Pferde/Autos** *usw.* ∼: know what one is doing with horses/cars; know all about horses/cars

versteifen 1 *tr. V.* stiffen ⟨*collar, part of body, etc.*⟩. **2** *itr. V.; mit sein* stiffen [up]; become stiff. **3** *refl. V.* **(a)** stiffen [up]; become stiff; **(b)** *in* **sich auf etw.** (*Akk.*) ∼: insist on sth.

versteigen *unr. refl. V.* **(a)** (sich verirren) get lost [while climbing]; (nicht mehr herunterkönnen) get stuck; get into difficulties; **(b) sich zu einer Behauptung/zu Angriffen gegen jmdn.** *usw.* ∼: have the presumption to make an assertion/attacks on sb. *etc.*

versteigern *tr. V.* auction; **etw.** ∼ **lassen** put sth. up for auction

Versteigerung *die* auction *no indef. art.; zur* ∼ **kommen** *od.* **gelangen** (Amtsspr.) be auctioned

versteinern 1 *itr. V.; mit sein* ⟨*plant, animal*⟩ fossilize, become fossilized; ⟨*wood etc.*⟩ petrify, become petrified; (fig. geh.) ⟨*person*⟩ go rigid; ⟨*expression, face*⟩ harden, become stony. **2** *refl. V.* (geh.) ⟨*face, features*⟩ harden

Versteinerung *die;* ∼, ∼**en** **(a)** (das Versteinern) fossilization; (von Holz) petrification; **(b)** (Fossil) fossil

verstellbar *Adj.* adjustable

verstellen 1 *tr. V.* **(a)** (falsch platzieren) misplace; put [back] in the wrong place; **(b)** (anders einstellen) adjust ⟨*seat etc.*⟩; alter [the adjustment of] ⟨*mirror etc.*⟩; reset ⟨*alarm clock, points, etc.*⟩; **der Sitz lässt sich in der Höhe** ∼: the seat can be adjusted for height; **(c)** (versperren) block, obstruct ⟨*entrance, exit, view, etc.*⟩; **(d)** (zur Täuschung verändern) disguise, alter ⟨*voice, handwriting*⟩. **2** *refl. V.* **(a)** (seine Einstellung, Position verändern) alter; (sodass es falsch eingestellt ist) get out of adjustment; **(b)** (sich anders geben als man ist) pretend; play-act; **sich vor jmdm.** ∼: pretend to sb.

Verstellung *die* play-acting; pretence; (der Stimme, Schrift) disguising; alteration

versterben *unr. itr. V.; mit sein* (geh.) die; pass away; **mein verstorbener Mann** my late husband

verstiegen *Adj.* whimsical ⟨*person*⟩; extravagant, fantastic ⟨*idea, expectation, etc.*⟩

verstimmen *tr. V.* **(a)** (Musik) put ⟨*instrument*⟩ out of tune; **(b)** (schlecht gelaunt machen) put ⟨*person*⟩ in a bad mood; (verärgern) annoy

verstimmt *Adj.* **(a)** (Musik) out of tune *pred.;* **(b)** (verärgert) put out, peeved, disgruntled (**über** + *Akk.* by, about); **ein** ∼**er Magen** an upset stomach

Verstimmung *die* disgruntled *or* bad mood; (Verärgerung) annoyance

verstockt 1 *Adj.* obdurate; stubborn. **2** *adv.* obdurately; stubbornly

Verstocktheit *die;* ∼: obduracy; stubbornness

verstohlen /fɛɐ̯'ʃtoːlən/ **1** *Adj.* furtive; surreptitious. **2** *adv.* furtively; surreptitiously

verstopfen 1 *tr. V.* block. **2** *itr. V.; mit sein* become blocked

Verstopfung *die;* ∼, ∼**en** (Med.: Stuhl∼) constipation

Verstorbene /fɛɐ̯'ʃtɔrbənə/ *der/die; adj. Dekl.* (geh.) deceased

verstört *Adj.* distraught

Verstörtheit *die;* ∼: distressed *or* distraught state; distress

Verstoß *der* violation, infringement (**gegen** of)

verstoßen 1 *unr. tr. V.* disown; **aus dem Elternhaus** ∼ **werden** be turned out of one's parents' house; **ein Verstoßener** an outcast. **2** *unr. itr. V.* **gegen etw.** ∼: infringe

or contravene sth.; **gegen die Etikette** ∼: commit a breach of etiquette

verstrahlen *tr. V.* **(a)** radiate; **(b)** (radioaktiv verseuchen) contaminate with radiation

verstreichen 1 *unr. tr. V.* **(a)** (verteilen) apply, put on ⟨*paint*⟩; spread ⟨*butter etc.*⟩; **(b)** (verbrauchen) use [up] ⟨*paint*⟩. **2** *unr. itr. V.; mit sein* (geh.) ⟨*time*⟩ pass [by]

verstreuen *tr. V.* **(a)** (verteilen) scatter; put down ⟨*bird food, salt*⟩; (unordentlich) strew; **(b)** (versehentlich) spill

verstricken 1 *tr. V.* **jmdn. in etw.** (*Akk.*) ∼: involve sb. in sth.; draw sb. into sth. **2** *refl. V.* **sich in etw.** (*Akk.*) ∼: become entangled *or* caught up in sth.

Verstrickung *die;* ∼, ∼**en** involvement (**in** + *Akk.* in)

verströmen *tr. V.* exude

verstrubbeln *tr. V.* (ugs.) tousle

verstümmeln *tr. V.* mutilate; (fig.) garble ⟨*report*⟩; chop, mutilate ⟨*text*⟩; mutilate, do violence to ⟨*name*⟩; **sich selbst** ∼: maim oneself

Verstümmelung *die;* ∼, ∼**en** mutilation; (fig.: einer Meldung usw.) garbling

verstummen *itr. V.; mit sein* (geh.) fall silent; ⟨*music, noise, conversation*⟩ cease; (allmählich) die *or* fade away; (fig.) ⟨*rumour, question*⟩ go away

Versuch *der;* ∼**[e]s**, ∼**e** **(a)** attempt; **beim** ∼, **etw. zu tun** in attempting to do sth.; **das käme auf einen** ∼ **an** we'll have to try it and see; **(b)** (Experiment) experiment (**an** + *Dat.* on); (Probe) test

versuchen 1 *tr. V.* **(a)** try; attempt; **versuchs doch!** (drohend) just you try!; (ermunternd) just try it!; **es mit jmdm./etw.** ∼: give sb./sth. a try; **es bei jmdm.** ∼: try sb.; **versuchter Mord** (Rechtsspr.) attempted murder; *s. auch* **Glück a**; **(b)** (auch bibl.: in Versuchung führen) tempt. **2** *tr., itr. V.* (probieren) **den Kuchen/von dem Kuchen** ∼: try the cake/some of the cake. **3** *refl. V.* **sich in/an etw.** (*Dat.*) ∼: try one's hand at sth.

versuchs-, Versuchs-: ∼**anordnung** *die* set-up for an/ the experiment/for experiments; ∼**kaninchen** *das* (fig.) guinea pig; ∼**person** *die* (bes. Med., Psych.) test *or* experimental subject; ∼**weise 1** *Adv.* on a trial basis; as an experiment; **2** *adj.; nicht präd.* experimental

Versuchung *die;* ∼, ∼**en** temptation; **in** ∼ (*Akk.*) **kommen** *od.* **geraten[, etw. zu tun]** be *or* feel tempted [to do sth.]

versündigen *refl. V.* **sich an jmdm./etw.** ∼: sin against sb./sth.

Versunkenheit *die;* ∼ (geh.) [state of] contemplation; deep meditation

versüßen *tr. V.* **jmdm./sich etw.** ∼ (fig.) make sth. more pleasant for sb./oneself

vertagen 1 *tr. V.* adjourn ⟨*meeting, debate, etc.*⟩ (**auf** + *Akk.* until); postpone ⟨*decision, verdict*⟩ (**auf** + *Akk.* until). **2** *refl. V.* ⟨*court*⟩ adjourn; ⟨*meeting*⟩ be adjourned

vertauschen *tr. V.* **(a)** exchange; switch; reverse, switch ⟨*roles*⟩; reverse, transpose ⟨*poles*⟩; **etw. mit etw.** ∼: exchange sth. for sth.; **(b)** (verwechseln) mix up

Vertauschung *die;* ∼, ∼**en** **(a)** exchange; (von Buchstaben, Polen usw.) transposition; (von Rollen) reversal; switching; **(b)** (Verwechslung) mixing up

verteidigen /fɛɐ̯'taidɪɡn̩/ **1** *tr. V.* defend. **2** *itr. V.* (Ballspiele) defend

Verteidiger *der;* ∼**s**, ∼, **Verteidigerin,** *die;* ∼, ∼**nen** **(a)** (auch Sport) defender; **(b)** (Rechtsw.) defence counsel

Verteidigung *die;* ∼, ∼**en** (auch Sport, Rechtsw.) defence

Verteidigungs-: ∼**minister** *der* minister of defence; ∼**ministerium** *das* ministry of defence

verteilen 1 *tr. V.* **(a)** (austeilen) distribute, hand out ⟨*exercise books, leaflets, prizes, etc.*⟩ (**an** + *Akk.* to, **unter** + *Akk.* among); share [out], distribute ⟨*money, food*⟩ (**an** + *Akk.* to, **unter** + *Akk.* among); allocate ⟨*work*⟩; **(b)** (an verschiedene Plätze bringen) distribute ⟨*weight etc.*⟩ (**auf** + *Akk.* over); spread ⟨*cost*⟩ (**auf** + *Akk.* among); **(c)** (verstreichen, verstreuen, verrühren usw.) distribute, spread ⟨*butter, seed, dirt, etc.*⟩. **2** *refl. V.* **(a)** spread out; **(b)** (sich ausbreiten, verteilt sein) be distributed (**auf** + *Akk.* over)

Verteiler *der;* ~s, ~ **(a)** (Person) distributor; **(b)** (Technik: Zündverteiler) distributor; **(c)** (Bürow.) distribution list; „~" 'copies to'

Verteilung *die* distribution; (der Rollen, der Arbeit) allocation

vertelefonieren *tr. V.* (ugs.) spend ⟨*time*⟩ telephoning *or* on the phone; spend ⟨*money*⟩ on telephoning

verteuern **1** *tr. V.* make ⟨*goods*⟩ more expensive. **2** *refl. V.* become more expensive

Verteuerung *die* increase *or* rise in price

verteufeln *tr. V.* condemn; denigrate

Verteufelung *die;* ~, ~en condemnation; denigration

vertiefen **1** *tr. V.* **(a)** deepen (**um** by); make deeper; **(b)** (intensivieren) deepen ⟨*knowledge, understanding, love*⟩; deepen, strengthen ⟨*dislike, friendship, collaboration, etc.*⟩. **2** *refl. V.* **(a)** deepen; become deeper; **(b)** (sich konzentrieren) **sich** ~ **in** (+ *Akk.*) bury oneself in ⟨*book, work, etc.*⟩; become deeply involved in ⟨*conversation*⟩; **in Gedanken vertieft** deep in thought; **(c)** (intensiver werden) ⟨*friendship*⟩ deepen; ⟨*relations*⟩ become closer

Vertiefung *die;* ~, ~en **(a)** deepening; (von Zusammenarbeit, Beziehungen) strengthening; (von Wissen) consolidation; reinforcement; **(b)** (in Gedanken) absorption (**in** + *Akk.* in); **(c)** (Mulde) depression; hollow

vertikal /vɛrti'kaːl/ **1** *Adj.* vertical. **2** *adv.* vertically

Vertikale *die;* ~, ~n **(a)** (Linie) vertical line; **(b)** *o. Pl.* (Lage) **die** ~: the vertical *or* perpendicular

vertilgen *tr. V.* **(a)** (vernichten) exterminate ⟨*vermin*⟩; kill off ⟨*weeds*⟩; **(b)** (ugs.: verzehren) devour, (joc.) demolish ⟨*food*⟩

vertippen **1** *refl. V.* **(a)** make a typing mistake/typing mistakes; (auf der Rechenmaschine, dem Tastentelefon usw.) press the wrong number; **(b)** (im Lotto, Toto, bei Vorhersagen) get it wrong. **2** *tr. V.* mistype ⟨*word*⟩; type ⟨*word, letter*⟩ wrongly

vertonen *tr. V.* set ⟨*text, poem*⟩ to music; set, write the music to ⟨*libretto*⟩

Vertonung *die;* ~, ~en setting [to music]; **die** ~ **eines Librettos** writing the music to a libretto

vertrackt /fɛɐ'trakt/ *Adj.* (ugs.) **(a)** complicated, involved ⟨*situation, business, etc.*⟩; tricky, intricate ⟨*job*⟩; **(b)** (ärgerlich) confounded; infuriating; **das** ~**e Gefühl haben, dass…:** have a nasty feeling that…

Vertrag *der;* ~[e]s, **Verträge** /…'trɛːɡə/ contract; (zwischen Staaten) treaty; **mündlicher** ~: verbal agreement; **[bei jmdm.] unter** ~ **stehen** be under contract [to sb.]

vertragen **1** *unr. tr. V.* endure; tolerate (esp. Med.); (aushalten, leiden können) stand; bear; take ⟨*joke, criticism, climate, etc.*⟩; **sie verträgt dieses Medikament nicht** this medicine does not agree with her at all; **ich könnte jetzt einen Whisky** ~ (ugs.) I could do with *or* wouldn't say no to a whisky. **2** *unr. refl. V.* **(a)** **sich mit jmdm.** ~: get on *or* along with sb.; **sich gut [miteinander]** ~**:** get on well together; **sie** ~ **sich wieder** they are friends again; they have made it up; **(b)** (passen) **sich mit etw.** ~**:** go with sth.

vertraglich **1** *Adj.* contractual. **2** *adv.* contractually; by contract

verträglich /fɛɐ'trɛːklɪç/ *Adj.* **(a)** digestible ⟨*food*⟩; **leicht/schwer** ~**:** easily digestible/indigestible; **ein gut** ~**es Medikament** a drug which has no side effects; **(b)** (umgänglich) good-natured; easy to get on with *pred.*

Verträglichkeit *die;* ~, ~en **(a)** digestibility; **(b)** (Umgänglichkeit) good nature

Vertrags-: ~**entwurf** *der* draft contract/treaty; ~**händler** *der* authorized *or* appointed dealer; ~**partner** *der* party to a/the contract; **unser** ~**partner** our contractual partner

vertrauen *itr. V.* **jmdm./einer Sache** ~**:** trust sb./sth.; **auf etw.** (*Akk.*) ~**:** [put one's] trust in sth.; **auf sein Glück** ~ trust to luck

Vertrauen *das;* ~s trust; confidence; ~ **zu jmdm./etw. haben/fassen** have/come to have confidence in sb./sth.; trust/come to trust sb./sth.; **jmdm. [sein]** ~ **schenken** put one's trust in sb.; **sein** ~ **in jmdn./etw.**

setzen put *or* place one's trust in sb./sth.; **im** ~ **[gesagt]** [strictly] in confidence; between you and me; **im** ~ **auf etw.** (*Akk.*) trusting to *or* in sth.; **jmdn. ins** ~ **ziehen** take sb. into one's confidence

vertrauen·erweckend *Adj.* inspiring *or* that inspires confidence *postpos.*

vertrauens-, Vertrauens-: ~**arzt** *der,* ~**ärztin** *die* independent examining doctor (*working for health service, health insurance, etc.*); ~**bruch** *der* breach of trust; (wenn man Vertrauliches weitersagt) breach of confidence; ~**frage** *die* (Parl.) question of confidence; **die** ~**frage stellen** ask for a vote of confidence; ~**frau** *die* **(a)** spokeswoman (*Gen.* for); representative; **(b)** ⇒ ~**mann;** ~**mann** *der* **(a)** *Pl.* ~**männer** *od.* ~**leute** spokesman (*Gen.* for); representative; **(b)** *Pl.* ~**leute** (in der Gewerkschaft) [union] representative; (in einer Fabrik o. Ä.) shop steward; ~**person** *die* person in a position of trust; ~**sache** *die* matter *or* question of trust; ~**selig** *Adj.* all too trustful *or* trusting; ~**stellung** *die* position of trust; ~**verhältnis** *das* relationship based on trust; ~**voll** **1** *Adj.* trusting ⟨*relationship*⟩; ⟨*collaboration, cooperation*⟩ based on trust; (zuversichtlich) confident; **2** *adv.* trustingly; (zuversichtlich) confidently; **sich** ~**voll an jmdn. wenden** turn to sb. with complete confidence; ~**würdig** *Adj.* trustworthy; ~**würdigkeit** *die* trustworthiness

vertraulich **1** *Adj.* **(a)** confidential; **(b)** (freundschaftlich, intim) familiar ⟨*manner, tone, etc.*⟩; intimate ⟨*mood, conversation, whisper*⟩. **2** *adv.* **(a)** confidentially; in confidence; **(b)** (freundschaftlich, intim) in a familiar way; familiarly

Vertraulichkeit *die;* ~, ~en **(a)** *o. Pl.* confidentiality; **(b)** (vertrauliche Information) confidence; **(c)** *o. Pl.* (distanzloses Verhalten) familiarity; (Intimität) intimacy

verträumen *tr. V.* [day-]dream away ⟨*time*⟩

verträumt **1** *Adj.* dreamy. **2** *adv.* dreamily

vertraut /fɛɐ'traut/ *Adj.* **(a)** close ⟨*friend etc.*⟩; intimate ⟨*circle, conversation, etc.*⟩; **mit jmdm.** ~ **werden** become very friendly *or* close friends with sb.; **(b)** (bekannt) familiar; **mit etw. gut/wenig** ~ **sein** be well acquainted with sth./have little knowledge of sth.; **sich mit etw.** ~ **machen** familiarize oneself with sth.

Vertraute *der/die; adj. Dekl.* close friend; **enger** ~**r** intimate friend

Vertrautheit *die;* ~ ⇒ **vertraut:** closeness; intimacy; familiarity

vertreiben *unr. tr. V.* **(a)** drive out **(aus** of); (wegjagen) drive away ⟨*animal, smoke, clouds, etc.*⟩ **(aus** from); **die vertriebenen Juden** the exiled *or* expelled Jews; **die Müdigkeit/Sorgen** ~ (fig.) fight off tiredness/drive troubles away; **(b)** (verkaufen) sell

Vertreibung *die;* ~, ~en driving out; (das Wegjagen) driving away; (aus der Heimat) expulsion

vertretbar *Adj.* defensible ⟨*risk etc.*⟩; tenable, defensible ⟨*standpoint*⟩; justifiable ⟨*costs*⟩

vertreten **1** *unr. tr. V.* **(a)** stand in *or* deputize for ⟨*colleague etc.*⟩; ⟨*teacher*⟩ cover for ⟨*colleague*⟩; **(b)** (repräsentieren) represent ⟨*person, firm, interests, constituency, country, etc.*⟩; (Rechtsw.) act for ⟨*person, prosecution, etc.*⟩; **schwach/stark** ~ **sein** be poorly/well represented; **(c)** (einstehen für, verfechten) support ⟨*point of view, principle*⟩; hold ⟨*opinion*⟩; advocate ⟨*thesis etc.*⟩; pursue ⟨*policy*⟩; **etw. zu** ~ **haben** be responsible for sth. **2** *unr. refl. V.* **sich** (*Dat.*) **die Füße** *od.* **Beine** ~ (ugs.: sich Bewegung verschaffen) stretch one's legs

Vertreter *der;* ~s, ~, **Vertreterin** *die;* ~, ~nen **(a)** (Stell~) deputy; stand-in; (eines Arztes) locum (coll.); **(b)** (Interessen~, Repräsentant) representative; (Handels~) sales representative; commercial traveller; **ein** ~ **für Staubsauger** a traveller in vacuum cleaners; **(c)** (Verfechter, Anhänger) supporter; advocate

Vertretung *die;* ~, ~en **(a)** deputizing; **jmds.** ~ **übernehmen** stand in *or* deputize for sb.; ⟨*doctor*⟩ act as locum for sb. (coll.); **in** ~ **von Herrn N.** in place of *or* standing in for Mr. N.; **(b)** (Vertreter[in]) deputy; stand-in; (eines Arztes) locum (coll.); **(c)** (Delegierte[r]) representative;

(Delegation) delegation; **eine diplomatische ~:** a diplomatic mission; (**d**) (Handels~) [sales] agency; (Niederlassung) agency; branch; (**e**) (Interessen~) representation; (**f**) (Verfechtung) advocacy

Vertr<u>e</u>tungs·stunde *die* (Schulw.) cover lesson

vertr<u>e</u>tungs·weise *Adv.* as a [temporary] replacement *or* stand-in

Vertr<u>ie</u>bene *der/die; adj. Dekl.* expellee [from his/her homeland]

vertr<u>i</u>nken *unr. tr. V.* spend ⟨*money*⟩ on drink

vertr<u>o</u>cknen *itr. V.; mit sein* dry up

vertr<u>ö</u>deln *tr. V.* (ugs. abwertend) dawdle away, waste ⟨*time*⟩

vertr<u>ö</u>sten *tr. V.* put ⟨*person*⟩ off (**auf** + *Akk.* until)

vertr<u>o</u>tteln *itr. V.; mit sein* go gaga (sl.); **vetrottelt** gaga

vert<u>u</u>n 1 *unr. tr. V.* waste; **die Mühe war vertan** it was a waste of effort. **2** *unr. refl. V.* (ugs.) make a slip

vert<u>u</u>schen *tr. V.* hush up ⟨*scandal etc.*⟩; keep ⟨*truth etc.*⟩ secret

ver<u>ü</u>beln *tr. V.* jmdm. eine Äußerung *usw.* ~: take sb.'s remark *etc.* amiss; **das kann man ihm kaum ~:** one can hardly blame him for that

ver<u>ü</u>ben *tr. V.* commit ⟨*crime etc.*⟩

ver<u>u</u>lken *tr. V.* (ugs.) make fun of; take the mickey out of (Brit. coll.)

ver<u>u</u>nfallen *itr. V.; mit sein* (Amtsspr., bes. schweiz.) have an accident

ver<u>u</u>nglimpfen /fɛɐ̯'|ʊnglɪmpfn̩/ *tr. V.* (geh.) denigrate ⟨*person, etc.*⟩; sully ⟨*name, memory*⟩

ver<u>u</u>nglücken *itr. V.; mit sein* (**a**) have an accident; ⟨*car etc.*⟩ be involved in an accident; **mit dem Auto/ Flugzeug ~:** be in a car/an air accident *or* crash; (**b**) (scherzh.: misslingen) go wrong; ⟨*attempt*⟩ fail; ⟨*cake, sauce, etc.*⟩ be a disaster

Ver<u>u</u>nglückte *der/die; adj. Dekl.* accident victim; casualty

ver<u>u</u>nreinigen *tr. V.* (**a**) pollute; contaminate ⟨*water, milk, flour, oil*⟩; **~de Stoffe** pollutants/contaminants; (**b**) (geh.: beschmutzen) dirty, soil ⟨*clothes, floor, etc.*⟩; (durch Fäkalien) foul ⟨*pavement etc.*⟩

Ver<u>u</u>nreinigung *die* (**a**) *o. Pl.* pollution; (von Wasser, Milch, Mehl, Öl) contamination; (**b**) *o. Pl.* (von Kleidern, Fußböden usw.) soiling; (von Straßen usw.) fouling

ver<u>u</u>nsichern *tr. V.* jmdn. ~: make sb. feel unsure *or* uncertain; (so dass er sich gefährdet fühlt) undermine sb.'s sense of security; **verunsichert** insecure; (nicht selbstsicher) unsure of oneself

Ver<u>u</u>nsicherung *die* (Unsicherheit) [feeling of] insecurity

ver<u>u</u>nstalten /fɛɐ̯'|ʊnʃtaltn̩/ *tr. V.* disfigure

ver<u>u</u>ntreuen *tr. V.* embezzle

Ver<u>u</u>ntreuung *die;* ~, ~**en** embezzlement

ver<u>u</u>nzieren *tr. V.* spoil the look of

ver<u>u</u>rsachen *tr. V.* cause

Ver<u>u</u>rsacher *der;* ~**s**, ~: cause; person responsible; **der ~ des Unfalls** the person responsible for the accident

ver<u>u</u>rteilen *tr. V.* (**a**) pass sentence on; sentence; **jmdn. zu Gefängnis** *od.* **einer Haftstrafe ~:** sentence sb. to imprisonment; **jmdn. zu einer Geldstrafe ~:** impose a fine on sb.; **jmdn. zum Tode ~:** sentence *or* condemn sb. to death; **der zum Tode Verurteilte** the condemned man; **zum Scheitern verurteilt sein** (fig.) be condemned to failure *or* bound to fail; (**b**) (fig.: negativ bewerten) condemn ⟨*behaviour, action*⟩

Ver<u>u</u>rteilte *der/die; adj. Dekl.* convicted man/woman

Ver<u>u</u>rteilung *die;* ~, ~**en** (**a**) sentencing; (**b**) (fig.) condemnation

verv<u>ie</u>lfachen 1 *tr. V.* greatly increase; (multiplizieren) multiply ⟨*number*⟩. **2** *refl. V.* multiply [several times]

verv<u>ie</u>lfältigen *tr. V.* duplicate, make copies of ⟨*document etc.*⟩

Verv<u>ie</u>lfältigung *die;* ~, ~**en** (**a**) duplicating; copying; (**b**) (Kopie) copy

vervollk<u>o</u>mmnen /fɛɐ̯'fɔlkɔmnən/ **1** *tr. V.* perfect. **2** *refl. V.* become perfected

Vervollk<u>o</u>mmnung *die;* ~, ~**en** perfecting; (Zustand) perfection

vervollst<u>ä</u>ndigen *tr. V.* complete; (vollständiger machen) make ⟨*library etc.*⟩ more complete

Vervollst<u>ä</u>ndigung *die;* ~, ~**en** completion/making more complete

verw<u>a</u>chsen *Adj.* deformed

verw<u>a</u>ckeln (ugs.) **1** *tr. V.* make ⟨*picture*⟩ blurred; **verwackelt** blurred; shaky. **2** *itr. V.; mit sein* turn out blurred

verw<u>ä</u>hlen *refl. V.* misdial; dial the wrong number

verw<u>a</u>hren 1 *tr. V.* keep [safe]; (verstauen) put away [safely]. **2** *refl. V.* protest

verw<u>a</u>hrlosen *itr. V.; mit sein* (**a**) get in a bad state; ⟨*house, building*⟩ fall into disrepair, become dilapidated; ⟨*garden, hedge*⟩ grow wild, become overgrown; ⟨*person*⟩ let oneself go, (coll.) go to pot; **etw. ~ lassen** neglect sth.; allow sth. to get in a bad state; (**b**) (sittlich ~) fall into bad ways; [**sittlich**] **verwahrlost** depraved

Verw<u>a</u>hrlosung *die;* ~ (eines Gebäudes) dilapidation; (einer Person) advancing decrepitude; (sittliche ~) decline into depravity

Verw<u>a</u>hrung *die* keeping [in a safe place]; **etw. in ~ nehmen/haben** take sth. into safe keeping/hold sth. in safe keeping

verw<u>ai</u>st *Adj.* orphaned ⟨*child*⟩; (fig.) lonely, deserted ⟨*person, place*⟩; unoccupied ⟨*house*⟩

verw<u>a</u>lten *tr. V.* (**a**) (betreuen) administer, manage ⟨*estate, property, etc.*⟩; run, look after ⟨*house*⟩; hold ⟨*money*⟩ in trust; (**b**) (leiten) run, manage ⟨*hostel, kindergarten, etc.*⟩; (regieren) administer ⟨*area, colony, etc.*⟩; govern ⟨*country*⟩

Verw<u>a</u>lter *der;* ~**s**, ~, **Verw<u>a</u>lterin** *die;* ~, ~**nen** administrator; (eines Amts usw.) manager; (eines Nachlasses) trustee

Verw<u>a</u>ltung *die;* ~, ~**en** (**a**) (Betreuung, Leitung) administration; management; **die öffentliche/staatliche ~:** the public/state authority; (**b**) (eines Gebiets) administration; (eines Landes) government

Verw<u>a</u>ltungs-: ~**beamte** *der* administrative official; administrator; ~**bezirk** *der* administrative district; ~**gebühr** *die* administrative charge *or* fee

verw<u>a</u>ndelbar *Adj.* convertible

verw<u>a</u>ndeln 1 *tr. V.* (**a**) convert (**in** + *Akk.*, **zu** into); (völlig verändern) transform (**in** + *Akk.*, **zu** into); **ich fühlte mich wie verwandelt** I felt a different person *or* transformed; (**b**) (Ballspiele) score from ⟨*corner, free kick*⟩; convert ⟨*penalty*⟩. **2** *refl. V.* **sich in etw.** (*Akk.*) *od.* **zu etw. ~:** turn *or* change into sth.; (bei chemischen Vorgängen usw.) be converted into sth. **3** *itr. V.* (Ballspiele) **er verwandelte** [**zum 2:0**] he scored [to make it 2–0]

Verw<u>a</u>ndlung *die;* ~, ~**en** (das Verwandeln) conversion (**in** + *Akk.*, **zu** into); (völlige Veränderung) transformation (**in** + *Akk.*, **zu** into)

verw<u>a</u>ndt[1] /fɛɐ̯'vant/ *2. Part. v.* **verwenden**

verw<u>a</u>ndt[2] *Adj.* (**a**) related (**mit** to); (**b**) (fig.: ähnlich) similar ⟨*views, ideas, forms*⟩

Verw<u>a</u>ndte *der/die; adj. Dekl.* relative; relation

Verw<u>a</u>ndtschaft *die;* ~, ~**en** (**a**) relationship (**mit** to); (fig.: Ähnlichkeit) affinity; **zwischen ihnen besteht keine ~:** they are not related [to one another]; (**b**) *o. Pl.* (Verwandte) relatives *pl.;* relations *pl.;* **die ganze ~:** all one's relatives

verw<u>a</u>ndtschaftlich 1 *Adj.* family ⟨*ties, relationships, etc.*⟩. **2** *adv.* ~ **miteinander verbunden sein** be related [to each other]

Verw<u>a</u>ndtschafts·verhältnis *das* family relationship

verw<u>a</u>nzen 1 *itr. V.; mit sein* **verwanzt** bug-ridden. **2** *tr. V.* (fig.) bug

verw<u>a</u>rnen *tr. V.* warn, caution (**wegen** for)

Verw<u>a</u>rnung *die;* ~, ~**en** warning; caution; **eine gebührenpflichtige ~:** a fine and a caution

verwaschen *Adj.* **(a)** washed out, faded ⟨*jeans, material, inscription, etc.*⟩; **(b)** (blass) washy, watery ⟨*colour*⟩; blurred ⟨*lines, contours*⟩

verweben *tr. V.* **(a)** weave with; use [for weaving]; **(b)** *auch unr.* [miteinander] ∼: interweave ⟨*threads*⟩; **etw. in etw.** (*Akk.*) ∼ (auch fig.) weave sth. into sth.

verwechselbar *Adj.* mistakable (**mit** for)

verwechseln *tr. V.* **(a)** [miteinander] ∼: confuse ⟨*two things/people*⟩; **er verwechselt immer rechts und links** he always gets mixed up between *or* mixes up right and left; **etw. mit etw./jmdn. mit jmdm.** ∼: mistake sth. for sth./sb. for sb.; confuse sth. with sth./sb. with sb.; **Entschuldigung, ich habe Sie [mit jemandem] verwechselt/ich habe die Tür[en] verwechselt** sorry, I thought you were *or* I mistook you for somebody else/I've got the wrong door; **jmdm. zum Verwechseln ähnlich sehen** be the spitting image of sb.; **(b)** (vertauschen) mix up; **jemand hat meinen Regenschirm verwechselt** somebody has taken my umbrella by mistake

Verwechslung *die;* ∼, ∼**en (a)** [case of] confusion; mistake; **(b)** (Vertauschung) mixing up

verwegen 1 *Adj.* daring; (auch fig.) audacious. **2** *adv.* (auch fig.) audaciously

Verwegenheit *die;* ∼: daring; (auch fig.) audacity

verwehen *tr. V.* **(a)** (zudecken) cover [over] ⟨*track, path*⟩; **(b)** (wegwehen) blow away; scatter; **vom Winde verweht** (fig.) gone with the wind

verwehren *tr. V.* **jmdm. etw.** ∼: refuse *or* deny sb. sth.

Verwehung *die;* ∼, ∼**en** [snow]drift

verweichlichen 1 *itr. V.; mit sein* grow soft. **2** *tr. V.* make soft; **ein verweichlichter Junge** a mollycoddled boy

Verweichlichung *die;* ∼, ∼**en (a)** (Vorgang) **die** ∼ **der Jugendlichen verhindern** prevent young people from becoming soft; **(b)** (Zustand) softness

verweigern 1 *tr. V.* refuse; **die Aussage/einen Befehl/die Nahrungsaufnahme** ∼: refuse to make a statement/to obey an order/to take food; **den Kriegsdienst** ∼: refuse to do military service; be a conscientious objector. **2** *refl. V.* object; refuse to cooperate; **sich jmdm./einer Sache** ∼: refuse to accept sb./sth. **3** *itr. V.* **(a)** (ugs.: den Kriegsdienst ∼) refuse [to do military service]; be a conscientious objector; **(b)** (Pferdesport) refuse

Verweigerung *die;* ∼, ∼**en** refusal; (Protest) protest

verweilen *itr. V.* (geh.) stay; (länger als nötig) linger

verweint /fɛɐ̯'vai̯nt/ *Adj.* tear-stained ⟨*face*⟩; ⟨*eyes*⟩ red with tears *or* from crying; ⟨*person*⟩ with a tear-stained face

Verweis *der;* ∼**es**, ∼**e (a)** reference (**auf** + *Akk.* to); (Quer∼) cross-reference; **(b)** (Tadel) reprimand; rebuke; **jmdm. einen** ∼ **erteilen** reprimand *or* rebuke sb.

verweisen *unr. tr. V.* **(a)** **jmdn./einen Fall** *usw.* **an jmdn./etw.** ∼ (auch Rechtsspr.) refer sb./a case *etc.* to sb./sth.; **(b)** (wegschicken) **jmdn. von der Schule/aus dem Saal** ∼: expel sb. from the school/send sb. out of the room; **jmdn. des Landes** ∼: exile *or* (Hist.) banish sb.; **(c)** **jmdn. auf den zweiten Platz** ∼ (Sport) relegate sb. to *or* push sb. into second place; **(d)** *auch itr.* (hinweisen) **[jmdn.] auf etw.** (*Akk.*) ∼: refer [sb.] to sth.; (durch Querverweis) cross-refer [sb.] to sth.

verwelken *itr. V.; mit sein* wilt; (fig.) ⟨*fame*⟩ fade

verweltlichen 1 *tr. V.* secularize. **2** *itr. V.; mit sein* (geh.) become worldly *or* secularized

Verweltlichung *die;* ∼, ∼**en** secularization

verwendbar *Adj.* usable (**zu, für** for)

Verwendbarkeit *die;* ∼: usability

verwenden 1 *unr. od. regelm. tr. V.* **(a)** use (**zu, für** for); **(b)** (aufwenden) spend ⟨*time*⟩ (**auf** + *Akk.* on); **viel Energie/Mühe auf etw.** (*Akk.*) ∼: put a lot of energy/effort into sth. **2** *unr. od. regelm. refl. V.* (geh.) **sich [bei jmdm.] für jmdn./etw.** ∼: intercede [with sb.] for sb./use one's influence [with sb.] on behalf of sth.

Verwendung *die;* ∼, ∼**en** use; ∼ **finden** be used; **unter** ∼ **einer Sache** (*Gen.*) *od.* **von etw.** using sth.

Verwendungs-: ∼**möglichkeit** *die* [possible] application *or* use; ∼**zweck** *der* application; purpose; „∼zweck" (auf Zahlkarten usw.) 'as payment for'

verwerfen *unr. tr. V.* **(a)** reject; dismiss ⟨*thought*⟩; **etw. als unsittlich** ∼: condemn sth. as [being] immoral; **(b)** (Rechtsw.) dismiss ⟨*appeal, action*⟩; overturn, quash ⟨*judgement*⟩

verwerflich (geh.) **1** *Adj.* reprehensible. **2** *adv.* reprehensibly

Verwerflichkeit *die;* ∼ (geh.) reprehensibility; reprehensible *or* despicable nature

verwertbar *Adj.* utilizable; usable

Verwertbarkeit *die;* ∼: usability

verwerten *tr. V.* utilize, use (**zu** for); make use of, exploit ⟨*suggestion, experience, knowledge*⟩

Verwertung *die* utilization; use; (bes. kommerziell) exploitation

verwesen *itr. V.; mit sein* decompose

verweslich *Adj.* decomposable

Verwesung *die;* ∼: decomposition; **in** ∼ **übergehen** start to decompose

verwetten *tr. V.* spend ⟨*money*⟩ on betting

verwickeln 1 *refl. V.* **(a)** get tangled up *or* entangled; **(b)** (sich verfangen) **sich in etw.** (*Akk. od. Dat.*) ∼: get caught [up] in sth.; **sich in Widersprüche** ∼ (fig.) tie oneself up in contradictions. **2** *tr. V.* involve; **sich in etw.** (*Akk.*) **verwickelt werden/sein** get/be mixed up *or* involved in sth.

verwickelt *Adj.* involved; complicated

Verwicklung *die;* ∼, ∼**en** complication

verwildern *itr. V.* ⟨*garden*⟩ become overgrown, go wild; ⟨*domestic animal*⟩ go wild, return to the wild

verwildert *Adj.* overgrown ⟨*garden*⟩; ⟨*animal*⟩ which has gone wild

Verwilderung *die;* ∼, ∼**en (a)** return to the wild [state]; **(b)** (geh.: von Menschen) reversion to a primitive state

verwirken *tr. V.* (geh.) forfeit

verwirklichen 1 *tr. V.* realize ⟨*dream*⟩; realize, put into practice ⟨*plan, proposal, idea, etc.*⟩; carry out ⟨*project, intention*⟩. **2** *refl. V.* **(a)** ⟨*hope, dream*⟩ be realized *or* fulfilled; **(b)** (sich voll entfalten) **sich [selbst]** ∼: realize one's [full] potential; fulfil oneself

Verwirklichung *die;* ∼, ∼**en** realization; (eines Wunsches, einer Hoffnung) fulfilment

verwirren 1 *tr. V.* entangle, tangle up ⟨*thread etc.*⟩; tousle, ruffle ⟨*hair*⟩. **2** *tr.* (*auch itr.*) *V.* confuse; bewilder; ∼**d viele Möglichkeiten** a bewildering number of possibilities. **3** *refl. V.* ⟨*thread etc.*⟩ become entangled; ⟨*hair*⟩ become tousled *or* ruffled; ⟨*person, mind*⟩ become confused

Verwirrung *die;* ∼, ∼**en** confusion; **jmdn. in** ∼ **bringen** make sb. confused *or* bewildered; **in** ∼ **geraten** become confused *or* bewildered; **im Zustand geistiger** ∼: in a disturbed *or* confused mental state

verwirtschaften *tr. V.* squander ⟨*money*⟩ by mismanagement

verwischen 1 *tr. V.* smudge ⟨*signature, writing, etc.*⟩; smear ⟨*paint*⟩; **alle Spuren** ∼ (fig.) cover up all [one's] tracks. **2** *refl. V.* become blurred

verwittern *itr. V.; mit sein* weather

verwitwet /fɛɐ̯'vɪtvət/ *Adj.* widowed

verwohnen *tr. V.* ruin, make a mess of ⟨*house, flat*⟩; **das Zimmer sieht verwohnt aus** the room looks badly knocked about

verwöhnen /fɛɐ̯'vøːnən/ *tr. V.* spoil; **das Schicksal hat ihn nicht gerade verwöhnt** (fig.) fate has not exactly smiled upon him

verwöhnt *Adj.* spoilt; (anspruchsvoll) discriminating; ⟨*taste, palate*⟩ of a gourmet

verworren /fɛɐ̯'vɔrən/ *Adj.* confused, muddled ⟨*ideas, situation, etc.*⟩

verwundbar *Adj.* open to injury *pred.;* (fig.) vulnerable

Verwundbarkeit *die* vulnerability

verwunden *tr. V.* ▶329❘ wound; injure

verwunderlich *Adj.* surprising

verwundern 1 *tr. V.* surprise; (erstaunen) astonish; **verwundert** surprised/astonished (**über** + *Akk.* at). **2** *refl.*

V. be surprised (**über** + *Akk.* at); (erstaunt sein) be astonished (**über** + *Akk.* at)

Verwunderung *die;* ~**:** surprise; (Staunen) astonishment

Verwundete *der/die; adj. Dekl.* wounded person; casualty

Verwundung *die;* ~, ~**en** ▶ 329 | (a) wounding; (b) (Wunde, Verletzung) wound

verwunschen *Adj.* enchanted; bewitched

verwünschen *tr. V.* curse

Verwünschung *die;* ~, ~**en** (a) (das Verfluchen) cursing; (b) (Fluch) curse; oath

verwurschteln /fɛɐ̯'vʊrʃtl̩n/, **verwursteln** (ugs.) 1 *tr. V.* get ⟨*thing*⟩ in a muddle *or* a tangle. 2 *refl. V.* get in a muddle *or* a tangle

verwüsten *tr. V.* devastate

Verwüstung *die;* ~, ~**en** devastation

verzählen *refl. V.* miscount; **ich verzähle mich dauernd** I keep losing count

verzapfen *tr. V.* (ugs. abwertend) **Blödsinn** *od.* **Mist** ~**:** come out with *or* produce rubbish

verzärteln /fɛɐ̯'tsɛːɐ̯tl̩n/ *tr. V.* mollycoddle

verzaubern *tr. V.* (a) cast a spell on; bewitch; **jmdn. in etw.** (*Akk.*) ~**:** transform sb. into sth.; (b) (fig.) enchant

Verzauberung *die;* ~, ~**en** (a) casting of a/the spell (*Gen.* on); (b) (fig.) enchantment

verzehnfachen *tr., refl. V.* increase tenfold

Verzehr /fɛɐ̯'tseːɐ̯/ *der;* ~**[e]s** consumption; **zum alsbaldigen** ~ **bestimmt** for immediate consumption

verzehren *tr. V.* consume

verzeichnen *tr. V.* (a) (falsch zeichnen) draw wrongly; (b) (aufführen) list; (eintragen) enter; (registrieren) record; **der Ort ist auf der Karte nicht verzeichnet** the place is not [marked] on the map; **große Erfolge/Verluste zu** ~ **haben** have scored great successes/suffered great losses

Verzeichnis /fɛɐ̯'tsaiçnɪs/ *das;* ~**ses,** ~**se** list; (Register) index

verzeihen *unr. tr., itr. V.* ▶ 163 | forgive; (entschuldigen) excuse ⟨*behaviour, remark, etc.*⟩; **jmdm.** [**etw.**] ~**:** forgive sb. [sth. *or* for sth.]; ~ **Sie** [**bitte**] **die Störung** pardon the intrusion; [please] excuse me for disturbing you

verzeihlich *Adj.* forgivable; excusable; **kaum** ~**:** almost unforgivable

Verzeihung *die;* ~**:** ▶ 163 | forgiveness; ~, **können Sie mir sagen,** ...**?** excuse me, could you tell me ...?; ~**!** sorry!; **jmdn. um** ~ **bitten** apologize to sb.; **ich bitte vielmals um** ~**:** I do apologize *or* [do] beg your pardon

verzerren 1 *tr. V.* (a) contort ⟨*face etc.*⟩ (**zu** into); (b) (akustisch, optisch) distort ⟨*sound, image*⟩. 2 *itr. V.* ⟨*loudspeaker, mirror, etc.*⟩ distort. 3 *refl. V.* ⟨*face, features*⟩ become contorted (**zu** into)

Verzerrung *die;* ~, ~**en** (a) (des Gesichts usw.) contortion; (b) (des Klangs, eines Bildes, der Realität usw.) distortion

verzetteln *refl. V.* dissipate one's energies; try to do too many things at once

Verzicht /fɛɐ̯'tsɪçt/ *der;* ~**[e]s,** ~**e** (a) renunciation (**auf** + *Akk.* of); **auf etw.** (*Akk.*) ~ **leisten** (geh.) renounce sth.; (b) (auf Reichtum, ein Amt usw.) relinquishment (**auf** + *Akk.* of)

verzichten *itr. V.* do without; ~ **auf** (+ *Akk.*) (sich enthalten) refrain *or* abstain from; (aufgeben) give up ⟨*share, smoking, job, etc.*⟩; renounce ⟨*inheritance*⟩; renounce, relinquish ⟨*right, privilege*⟩; (opfern) sacrifice ⟨*holiday, salary*⟩; **ich verzichte auf deine Hilfe/Ratschläge** I can do without *or* you can keep your help/advice; **darauf kann ich** ~ (iron.) I can do without that; **auf eine Strafanzeige** ~**:** not bring a charge

verziehen[1] 2. *Part. v.* **verzeihen**

verziehen[2] 1 *unr. tr. V.* (a) screw up ⟨*face, mouth, etc.*⟩; (b) (schlecht erziehen) spoil. 2 *unr. refl. V.* (a) twist; be contorted; (b) (aus der Form geraten) go out of shape; ⟨*wood*⟩ warp; **ein verzogener Rahmen** a distorted frame; (c)

(wegziehen) ⟨*clouds, storm*⟩ move away, pass over: ⟨*fog, mist*⟩ disperse; (**d**) (ugs.: weggehen) take oneself off; **verzieh dich!** (salopp) clear (coll.) *or* (coll.) push off. 3 *unr. itr. V.; mit sein* move [away]; „**Empfänger** [**unbekannt**] **verzogen**" 'no longer at this address'

verzieren *tr. V.* decorate

Verzierung *die;* ~, ~**en** decoration

verzögern 1 *tr. V.* (a) delay (**um** by); (b) (verlangsamen) slow down. 2 *refl. V.* be delayed (**um** by)

Verzögerung *die;* ~, ~**en** (a) delaying; delay (*Gen.* in); (b) (Verlangsamung) slowing down; (Technik) deceleration; (c) (Verspätung) delay; hold-up

verzollen *tr. V.* pay duty on

Verzug *der;* ~**[e]s** (a) delay; [**mit etw.**] **im** ~ **sein/in** ~ **kommen** *od.* **geraten** be/fall behind [with sth.]; **jmdn./etw. in** ~ **bringen** delay sb./sth.; hold sb. up/put sth. back; (b) **es ist Gefahr im** ~ (ugs.) danger is imminent

verzweifeln *itr. V.; meist mit sein* despair; **über etw./ jmdn.** ~**:** despair at sth./of sb.; **am Leben/an den Menschen** ~**:** despair of life/humanity; **es ist zum Verzweifeln!** it's enough to drive you to despair

verzweifelt 1 *Adj.* (a) despairing ⟨*person, animal*⟩; ~ **sein** be in despair *or* full of despair; (b) desperate ⟨*situation, attempt, effort, struggle, etc*⟩. 2 *adv.* (a) (entmutigt) despairingly; (b) (sehr angestrengt) desperately

Verzweiflung *die;* ~**:** despair; **etw. aus** ~ **tun** do sth. out of despair; **jmdn. zur** ~ **treiben/bringen** drive sb. to despair

verzweigen *refl. V.* branch [out]; **das Unternehmen ist stark verzweigt** (fig.) the firm is very diversified

verzwickt /fɛɐ̯'tsvɪkt/ *Adj.* (ugs.) tricky; complicated

Veteran /vete'raːn/ *der;* ~**en,** ~**en** (auch fig.) veteran

Veterinär /veteri'nɛːɐ̯/ *der;* ~**s,** ~**e** veterinary surgeon

Veto /'veːto/ *das;* ~**s,** ~**s** veto; **ein** ~ **gegen etw. einlegen** veto sth.

Veto·recht *das* right of veto

Vetter /'fɛtɐ/ *der;* ~**s,** ~**n** cousin

Vettern·wirtschaft *die; o. Pl.* (abwertend) nepotism

vgl. *Abk.* **vergleiche** cf.

v. H. *Abk.* **vom Hundert** per cent

via /'viːa/ *Präp.* via

Viadukt /via'dʊkt/ *das od. der;* ~**[e]s,** ~**e** viaduct

Vibration /vibra'tsi̯oːn/ *die;* ~, ~**en** vibration

vibrieren /vi'briːrən/ *itr. V.* vibrate; ⟨*voice*⟩ quiver, tremble

Video *das;* ~**s,** ~**s** (ugs.) video

Video-: ~**auf·zeichnung** *die* video recording; ~**clip** /~klɪp/ *der;* ~**s,** ~**s** video; ~**film** *der* video [film]; ~**kamera** *die* video camera; ~**kassette** *die* video cassette; ~**konferenz** *die* videoconference; ~**rekorder** *der* video recorder; ~**text** *der* videotex[t]

Vieh /fiː/ *das;* ~**[e]s** (a) (Nutztiere) livestock *sing. or pl.*; **jmdn. wie ein Stück** ~ **behandeln** treat sb. like an animal; (b) (Rind~) cattle *pl.*; (c) (derb abwertend: Mensch) bastard

Vieh-: ~**bestand** *der* stocks *pl.* of animals/cattle; ~**futter** *das* animal/cattle feed *or* fodder; ~**händler** *der* livestock/cattle dealer

viehisch 1 *Adj.* terrible (coll.) ⟨*fear, stupidity, pain*⟩. 2 *adv.* (ugs.) ⟨*hurt*⟩ like hell (coll.)

Vieh-: ~**stall** *der* cowshed; ~**zucht** *die; o. Pl.* [live]-stock/cattle breeding *no art.;* ~**züchter** *der* [live]stock/cattle breeder

viel /fiːl/ 1 *Indefinitpron. u. unbest. Zahlw.* (a) *Sg.* a great deal of; a lot of (coll.); **so/wie/nicht/zu** ~**:** that/how/not/too much; ~**[es]** (viele Dinge, vielerlei) much; **ich kann mich an** ~**es nicht mehr erinnern** there's much I can't remember; **der** ~**e Regen** all the rain; **gleich** ~ **Geld** the same amount of money; **um** ~**es jünger** a great deal younger; ~ **Erfreuliches** a great many pleasant things; **er hat in** ~**em Recht** he is right on many points; ~ **sagend** (fig.) meaningful; ~ **sagend lächeln** smile meaningfully; ~ **versprechend** [very] promising; (b) *Pl.* many; **gleich** ~**[e]** the same number of; **wie** ~**[e]** how many; **zu** ∼[e] too many; ∼**e hundert** many hundreds of; **die** ∼**en Menschen** all the people; **seine** ∼**en Kinder** all his children. **2** *Adv.* (**a**) (oft, lange) a great deal; a lot (coll.); ∼ **beschäftigt** very busy; (**b**) (wesentlich) much; a great deal; a lot (coll.); ∼ **mehr/weniger** much more/less; ∼ **zu viel** far *or* much too much; ∼ **zu wenig** far too little; ∼ **zu klein** much too small; **er ist nicht** ∼ **über fünfzig** he is not much more than *or* much over fifty

viel-: *∼**beschäftigt** ⇒ viel 2 a; ∼**deutig** /∼dɔytɪç/ **1** *Adj.* ambiguous; **2** *adv.* ambiguously

vielerlei *indekl. unbest. Gattungsz.* (**a**) *attr.* many different; all kinds *or* sorts of; (**b**) *subst.* all kinds *or* sorts of things

viel-, Viel-: ∼**fach 1** *Adj.* (**a**) multiple; **die** ∼**fache Menge** many times the amount; **auf** ∼**fachen Wunsch unserer Zuschauer** at the request of many of our viewers; (**b**) (vielfältig) manifold; many kinds of; **2** *adv.* many times; ∼**fache** *das; adj. Dekl.* (**a**) **ein** ∼**faches** many times the amount/number; **um ein** ∼**faches** many times over; **um ein** ∼**faches schneller/teurer** many times faster/more expensive; ∼**falt** *die;* ∼: diversity; wide variety; ∼**fältig** /∼fɛltɪç/ **1** *Adj.* many and diverse; **2** *adv.* in many different ways; ∼**fraß** *der* (**a**) (ugs.: Mensch) glutton; [greedy-]guts *sing.* (sl.); (**b**) (Tier) wolverine

vielleicht /fiˈlaiçt/ **1** *Adv.* (**a**) perhaps; maybe; **hast du den Schirm** ∼ **im Büro liegen lassen?** could it be that you left your umbrella in the office?; (**b**) (ungefähr) perhaps; about. **2** *Partikel* (**a**) **kannst du mir** ∼ **sagen, …?** could you possibly tell me …?; **hast du** ∼ **meinen Bruder gesehen?** have you seen my brother by any chance? (**b**) (wirklich) really; **ich war** ∼ **aufgeregt** I was terribly excited *or* as excited as anything (coll.); **du bist** ∼ **ein Blödmann!** what a stupid idiot you are! (coll.)

viel-, Viel-: ∼**mals** *Adv.* ich bitte ∼**mals um Entschuldigung** I'm very sorry; I do apologize; **sie lässt** ∼**mals grüßen** she sends her best regards *or* wishes; **danke** ∼**mals** thank you very much; many thanks; ∼**mehr** /od. -ˈ-/ *Konj. u. Adv.* rather; (im Gegenteil) on the contrary;*∼**sagend** ⇒ viel 1 a; ∼**seitig 1** *Adj.* versatile ⟨*person*⟩: varied ⟨*work, programme, etc.*⟩; **auf** ∼ **seitigen Wunsch** by popular request; **diese Küchenmaschine ist sehr** ∼**seitig** this food processor has many uses; **2** *adv.* ∼**seitig begabt sein** be versatile; *∼**versprechend:** ⇒ viel 1 a; ∼**zahl** *die; o. Pl.* large number; multitude

vier /fiːɐ̯/ *Kardinalz.* ▶22|, ▶511|, ▶600| four; **alle** ∼**e von sich strecken** (ugs.) put one's feet up; **auf allen** ∼**en** (ugs.) on all fours; *s. auch* **acht**

Vier *die;* ∼, ∼**en** four; **eine** ∼ **schreiben/bekommen** (Schulw.) get a D; *s. auch* **Acht¹; Zwei**

vier-, Vier- (*s. auch* **acht-, Acht-**)*:* ∼**beiner** *der;* ∼**s,** ∼ (ugs.) four-legged friend; ∼**eck** *das* quadrilateral; (Rechteck) rectangle; (Quadrat) square; ∼**eckig** *Adj.* quadrilateral; (rechteckig) rectangular; (quadratisch) square

Vierer *der;* ∼**s** ∼ (**a**) (Rudern) four; (**b**) (ugs.: im Lotto) four winning numbers *pl.;* (**c**) (ugs.: Ziffer, beim Würfeln) four; (**d**) (landsch.: Schulnote) D; (**e**) (ugs.: Autobus) [number] four

vier·fach *Vervielfältigungsz.* fourfold; quadruple

Vier·fache *das; adj. Dekl.* **um das** ∼ fourfold; by four times the amount; **die Preise sind um das** ∼ **gestiegen** the prices have quadrupled *or* increased four times

vier-: ∼**hundert** *Kardinalz.* ▶600| four hundred; ∼**jährig** *Adj.* (4 Jahre alt) four-year-old *attrib.;* four years old *pred.;* (4 Jahre dauernd) four-year *attrib.;* ∼**köpfig** *Adj.* four-headed ⟨*monster*⟩; ⟨*family, staff*⟩ of four

Vierling *der;* ∼**s,** ∼**e** quadruplet

vier-, Vier-: ∼**mal** *Adv.* four times; *s. auch* **achtmal;** ∼**radantrieb** *der* fourwheel drive; ∼**räd[e]rig** /∼rɛːd[ə]rɪç/ *Adj.* four-wheeled; ∼**spurig 1** *Adj.* four-lane ⟨*road, motorway*⟩; ∼**spurig sein** have four lanes; **2** *adv.* ∼**spurig befahrbar sein** have all four lanes open; **eine Straße** ∼**spurig ausbauen** widen a road into four lanes; ∼**stellig** *Adj.* four-figure *attrib.; s. auch* **acht·stellig;** ∼**sterne·hotel** /-ˈ----/ *das* four-star hotel; ∼**stöckig** *Adj.* four-storey; *s. auch* **acht·stöckig**

viert /fiːɐ̯t/ *in* **wir waren zu** ∼: there were four of us; *s. auch* **acht²**

viert… *Ordinalz.* ▶119|, ▶600| fourth; *s. auch* **acht…**

vier-, Vier-: ∼**tägig** *Adj.* four-day *attrib.; s. auch* **achttägig;** ∼**takter** *der;* ∼**s,** ∼ (Auto) car with a four-stroke engine; (Motor) four-stroke engine; ∼**tausend** *Kardinalz.* ▶600| four thousand; ∼**teilen** *tr. V.* quarter

viertel /ˈfɪrtl/ *Bruchz.* ▶600| quarter; **ein** ∼ **Pfund/eine** ∼ **Million** a quarter of a pound/million; **drei** ∼ **Liter** three quarters of a litre

Viertel /ˈfɪrtl/ *das* (*schweiz. meist der;*) ∼**s,** ∼ (**a**) ▶530|, ▶600| quarter; **ein** ∼ **Wein** (ugs.) a quarter-litre of wine; ∼ **vor/nach eins** [a] quarter to/past one; **drei** ∼: three-quarters; (**b**) (Stadtteil) quarter; district

viertel-, Viertel-: ∼**finale** *das* (Sport) quarter-final; **sich für das** ∼**finale qualifizieren** qualify for the quarter-finals; ∼**jahr** *das* three months *pl.;* ∼**jährlich 1** *Adj.* quarterly; **2** *adv.* quarterly; every three months; ∼**liter** *der* quarter of a litre; ∼**note** *die* (Musik) crotchet (Brit.); quarter note (Amer.); ∼**pfund** *das* quarter [of a] pound; ∼**stunde** *die* quarter of an hour; ∼**stündlich 1** *Adj.* quarter-hourly; every quarter of an hour *postpos.;* **2** *adv.* every quarter of an hour

viertens /ˈfiːɐ̯tns/ *Adv.* fourthly; *s. auch* **zweitens**

viertürig /-ty·rɪç/ *Adj.* four-door *attrib.;* ∼ **sein** have four doors

Vierwaldstätter See, (schweiz.:) **Vierwaldstätter·see** *der* Lake Lucerne

vier-: ∼**wöchig** *Adj.* four-week [-long]; ∼**zehn** /ˈfɪr-/ *Kardinalz.* ▶22|, ▶530|, ▶600| fourteen; *s. auch* **achtzehn;** ∼**zehnjährig** *Adj.* (14 Jahre alt) fourteen-year-old *attrib.;* fourteen years old *pred.;* (14 Jahre dauernd) fourteen-year *attrib.;* ∼**zehn·tägig** *Adj.; nicht präd.* two-week; ∼**zehn·täglich 1** *Adj.; nicht präd.* fortnightly; **2** *adv.* fortnightly; every two weeks

vierzig /ˈfɪrtsɪç/ *Kardinalz.* ▶22|, ▶600| forty; *s. auch* **achtzig**

vierziger /ˈfɪrtsɪɡɐ/ *indekl. Adj.; nicht präd.* **die** ∼ **Jahre** the forties; *s. auch* **achtziger**

Vierziger /ˈfɪrtsɪɡɐ/ *der;* ∼**s,** ∼: forty-year-old

vierzig·jährig /ˈfɪrtsɪç-/ *Adj.* (40 Jahre alt) forty-year-old *attrib.;* forty years old *pred.;* (40 Jahre dauernd) forty-year *attrib.*

vierzigst… /ˈfɪrtsɪçst…/ *Ordinalz.* ▶600| fortieth; *s. auch* **acht…**

Vierzig·stunden·woche *die* forty-hour week

Vier-: ∼**zimmer·wohnung** *die* four-room flat (Brit.) *or* (Amer.) apartment; ∼**zylinder** *der* (ugs.) four-cylinder

Vietnam /viɛtˈnam/ (*das*)*;* ∼**s** Vietnam

Vietnamese /viɛtnaˈmeːzə/ *der;* ∼**n,** ∼**n, Vietnamesin,** *die;* ∼, ∼**nen** ▶388| Vietnamese

vietnamesisch ▶388| **1** *Adj.* Vietnamese. **2** *adv.* **wir waren** ∼ **essen** we went to a Vietnamese restaurant *or* for a Vietnamese meal

Vietnam·krieg *der; o. Pl.* Vietnam War

vif /viːf/ (veralt.) **1** *Adj.* lively; brisk. **2** *adv.* briskly

Vignette /vɪnˈjɛtə/ *die;* ∼, ∼**n** vignette

Vikar /viˈkaːɐ̯/ *der;* ∼**s,** ∼**e** (**a**) (kath. Kirche) locum tenens; (**b**) (ev. Kirche) ≈ [trainee] curate

Viktoria /vɪkˈtoːria/ (*die*) Victoria

viktorianisch *Adj.* Victorian

Villa /ˈvɪla/ *die;* ∼, **Villen** villa

Villen·viertel *das* exclusive residential district

violett /vioˈlɛt/ *Adj.* purple; violet

Violett *das;* ∼**s,** ∼**e** *od.* ugs. ∼**s** purple; violet; (im Spektrum) violet

Violine /vioˈliːnə/ *die;* ∼, ∼**n** (Musik) violin

Violin-: ∼**konzert** *das* violin concerto; ∼**schlüssel** *der* treble clef

Violon·cello /violɔnˈtʃɛlo/ *das* violoncello

Viper /ˈviːpɐ/ *die;* ∼, ∼**n** viper; adder

Viren ⇒ **Virus**

virtuell /vɪrtuˈɛl/ *Adj.* (bes. fachspr.) virtual; ∼**e Wirk·lichkeit** virtual reality

virtuos /vɪr'tŭoːs/ **1** *Adj.* virtuoso ‹*performance etc.*›. **2** *adv.* in a virtuoso manner

Virtuose /vɪr'tŭoːzə/ *der;* ∼**n**, ∼**n** virtuoso

Virtuosität *die;* ∼: virtuosity

virulent /viru'lɛnt/ *Adj.* (Med., geh.) virulent

Virus /'viːrʊs/ *das;* ∼, **Viren** /'viːrən/ virus

Virus·infektion *die* ▶ 329 | virus infection

Visa ⇒ **Visum**

vis-à-vis /viza'viː/ **1** *Präp mit Dat.* opposite. **2** *Adv.* opposite; ∼ **von etw./jmdm.** opposite sth./sb.

Visavis /viza'viː/ *das;* ∼ /viza'viː(s)/, ∼ /viza'viːs/ **mein** ∼: the person opposite me

Visen ⇒ **Visum**

Visier /vi'ziːɐ̯/ *das;* ∼**s**, ∼**e** (a) (am Helm) visor; (b) (an der Waffe) backsight

Vision /vi'zi̯oːn/ *die;* ∼, ∼**en** vision

Visite /vi'ziːtə/ *die;* ∼, ∼**n** round; **um 10 Uhr war** ∼: at 10 o'clock, the doctor did his round

Visiten·karte *die* visiting card

Visit·karte *die* (österr.) ⇒ **Visitenkarte**

Viskose /vɪs'koːzə/ *die;* ∼ (Chemie) viscose

visuell /vi'zŭɛl/ (geh.) **1** *Adj.* visual. **2** *adv.* visually

Visum /'viːzʊm/ *das;* ∼**s**, **Visa** /'viːza/ *od.* **Visen** /'viːzn̩/ visa

vital /vi'taːl/ **1** *Adj.* (a) (voller Energie) vital; energetic; vigorous; ∼ **sein** be full of life *or* vigour; (b) (wichtig) vital. **2** *adv.* (voller Energie) energetically

Vitalität *die;* ∼: vitality

Vitamin /vita'miːn/ *das;* ∼**s**, ∼**e** vitamin

vitamin-, Vitamin-: ∼**arm** *Adj.* ‹*food, diet, etc.*› low in vitamins; ∼**mangel** *der; o. Pl.* vitamin deficiency; ∼**reich** *Adj.* rich in vitamins *postpos.;* vitamin-rich

Vitrine /vi'triːnə/ *die;* ∼, ∼**n** display case; showcase; (Möbel) display cabinet

Vize /'fiːtsə/ *der;* ∼**s**, ∼**s** (ugs.) number two (coll.)

Vize- /'viːtsə/ ∼**kanzler** *der* vice-chancellor; ∼**könig** *der* viceroy; ∼**präsident** *der* vice-president

Vlies /fliːs/ *das;* ∼**es**, ∼**e** fleece

V-Mann /'fau̯-/ *der;* ∼[e]s, **V-Männer** *od.* **V-Leute** contact [man]; (Informant) informer

Vogel /'foːgl̩/ *der;* ∼**s**, **Vögel** /'føːgl̩/ (a) bird; [mit etw.] **den** ∼ **abschießen** (ugs.) take the biscuit [with sth.] (coll.); **einen** ∼ **haben** (salopp) be off one's rocker (fig. coll.) *or* (sl.) head; **jmdm. den** ∼ **zeigen** tap one's forehead at sb. (*as a sign that one thinks he/she is stupid*); (b) (salopp, oft scherzh.: Mensch) character; **ein komischer** ∼: an odd bird *or* character

vogel-, Vogel-: ∼**beere** *die* rowan-berry; ∼**ei** *das* bird's egg; ∼**frei** *Adj.* (hist.) outlawed; **jmdn./etw. für** ∼**frei erklären** outlaw sb./sth.; ∼**futter** *das* bird food; ∼**käfig** *der* birdcage; ∼**kunde** *die; o. Pl.* ornithology *no art.*

vögeln /'føːgl̩n/ *tr., itr. V.* (derb) screw (coarse)

Vogel-: ∼**nest** *das* bird's nest; ∼**perspektive** *die* bird's eye view; ∼**scheuche** /-ʃɔy̯çə/ *die;* ∼, ∼**n** scarecrow

Vogesen /vo'geːzn̩/ *Pl.* Vosges [Mountains]

Vokabel /vo'kaːbl̩/ *die;* ∼, ∼**n** *od.* österr. auch *das;* ∼**s**, ∼: word; vocabulary item; ∼**n** vocabulary *sing.;* vocab *sing.* (Sch. coll.)

Vokabel·heft *das* vocabulary *or* (coll.) vocab book

Vokabular *das;* ∼**s**, ∼**e** vocabulary

Vokal /vo'kaːl/ *der;* ∼**s**, ∼**e** (Sprachw.) vowel

Voliere /vo'li̯ɛːrə/ *die;* ∼, ∼**n** aviary

Volk /fɔlk/ *das;* ∼[e]**s**, **Völker** /'fœlkɐ/ (a) people; **das** ∼ **der Kurden** the Kurdish people; **das irische und das deutsche** ∼: the Irish and German peoples; (b) *o. Pl.* (Bevölkerung) people *pl.;* (Nation) people *pl.;* nation; **im** ∼**e** among the people; **das arbeitende/unwissende** ∼: the working people/the ignorant masses *pl.;* (c) *o. Pl.* (einfache Leute) people *pl.;* **ein Mann aus dem** ∼: a man of the

---

people; (d) *o. Pl.* (ugs.: Leute) people *pl.;* **viel junges** ∼: many young people

völker-, Völker-: ∼**bund** *der; o. Pl.* League of Nations; ∼**kunde** *die; o. Pl.* ethnology *no art.;* ∼**mord** *der* genocide; ∼**recht** *das; o. Pl.* international law *no art.;* ∼**rechtlich 1** *Adj.; nicht präd.* ‹*issue, problem, etc.*› of international law; ∼**rechtliche Verträge** agreements in *or* under international law; **2** *adv.* ‹*settle*› in accordance with international law; ‹*control, regulate*› by international law; ‹*recognize*› under international law; ∼**verständigung** *die* international understanding; understanding between nations; ∼**wanderung** *die* (a) (hist.) migration of peoples; (b) (ugs.) mass migration; (Zug) mass progression

volks-, Volks-: ∼**ab·stimmung** *die* plebiscite; ∼**armee** *die* People's Army; ∼**befragung** *die* (Politik) referendum; ∼**begehren** *das* (Politik) petition for a referendum; ∼**eigen** *Adj.* (DDR) publicly *or* nationally owned; ∼**er Betrieb** publicly *or* nationally owned company; ∼**eigentum** *das* (DDR) national[ly owned] property; ∼**entscheid** *der* (Politik) referendum; ∼**fest** *das* public festival; (Jahrmarkt) fair; ∼**held** *der* folk hero; ∼**hoch·schule** *die* adult education centre; **ein Kurs an der** ∼**hochschule** an adult education class; ∼**kammer** *die* (DDR) **die** ∼**kammer** the Volkskammer; the People's Chamber; ∼**kunde** *die* folklore; ∼**lied** *das* folk song; ∼**märchen** *das* folk tale; ∼**mund** *der; o. Pl.* **im** ∼**mund wird das ... genannt** in the vernacular it is called ...; ∼**musik** *die* folk music; ∼**polizei** *die; o. Pl.* (DDR) People's Police; ∼**polizist** *der* (DDR) People's Policeman; member of the People's Police; ∼**republik** *die* People's Republic; **die** ∼**republik China** the People's Republic of China; ∼**schule** *die* (a) (Bundesrepublik Deutschland und Schweiz veralt.) *school providing basic primary and secondary education;* (b) (österr.) primary school; ∼**stamm** *der* tribe; ∼**stück** *das* (Theater) folk play; ∼**tanz** *der* folk dance; ∼**tracht** *die* traditional costume; (eines Landes) national costume; ∼**trauer·tag** *der* (Bundesrepublik Deutschland) national remembrance day

volkstümlich /'fɔlkstyːmlɪç/ **1** *Adj.* popular; **ein** ∼**er Politiker** a politician of the people *or* with the common touch; **der** ∼**e Name einer Pflanze** the vernacular name of a plant; ∼**e Preise** popular prices. **2** *adv.* ∼ **schreiben** write in terms readily comprehensible to the layman

volks-, Volks-: ∼**verdummung** *die* (ugs. abwertend) deliberate deception of the public; ∼**verhetzung** *die* incitement of the people; ∼**vertreter** *der* representative of the people; ∼**vertretung** *die* representative body of the people; ∼**wirt** *der* economist; ∼**wirtschaft** *die* national economy; (Fach) economics *sing., no art.;* ∼**wirtschaftler** *der;* ∼**s**, ∼: economist; ∼**wirtschaftlich 1** *Adj.* economic; **2** *adv.* economically; ∼**zählung** *die* [national] census; ∼**zorn** *der* public anger

voll /fɔl/ **1** *Adj.* (a) full; **der Saal ist** ∼ **Menschen** the room is full of people; ∼ **von** *od.* **mit etw. sein** be full of sth.; **das Glas ist halb** ∼: the glass is half full; **jmdn./etw.** ∼ **spritzen** splash water *etc.* all over sb./sth.; (mit Schlauch usw.) spray water *etc.* all over sb./sth.; **etw.** ∼ **füllen** fill sth. up; **etw.** ∼ **gießen** fill sth. [up]; **etw.** ∼ **laden** load sth. up completely; ∼ **geladen** fully laden; **etw.** ∼ **laufen lassen** fill sth. [up]; **sich** ∼ **laufen lassen** (salopp) get completely paralytic *or* canned (Brit. sl.); **etw.** ∼ **packen** pack sth. full; **etw.** ∼ **stopfen** (ugs.) stuff *or* cram sth. full; **einen Reifen** ∼ **pumpen** pump up a tyre; **einen Behälter** ∼ **pumpen** fill up a reservoir; **etw.** ∼ **tanken** fill sth. up; **bitte** ∼ **tanken** fill it up, please; **sich** ∼ **saugen** ‹*leech*› suck itself full; ‹*sponge*› become saturated (**mit** with); **etw.** ∼ **machen** (ugs.: füllen) fill sth. up; (ugs.: beschmutzen) get *or* make sth. dirty; **sich** (*Dat.*) **die Hosen/Windeln** ∼**machen** mess one's pants/ nappy; **um das Maß** ∼ **zu machen** (fig.) to crown *or* cap it all; **etw.** ∼ **schmieren** (ugs.: beschmutzen) smear sth.; (ugs. abwertend: beschreiben, bemalen) scrawl/draw all over sth.; **etw.** ∼ **schreiben** fill sth. [with writing]; **jeder bekam einen Korb** ∼ everybody received a basketful; **mit** ∼**en Backen kauen** eat with bulging cheeks; **aus dem Vollen schöpfen** draw on abundant *or* plentiful resources; ∼**e**

Pulle od. ∼[es] **Rohr** (salopp) ⟨drive⟩ flat out; s. auch **Mund; (b)** (salopp: betrunken) plastered (sl.); canned (Brit. sl.); **(c)** (üppig) full ⟨figure, face, lip⟩; thick ⟨hair⟩; ample ⟨bosom⟩; **(d)** (ganz, vollständig) full; complete ⟨seriousness, success⟩; etw. mit ∼em **Recht tun** have every right to do sth.; **in** ∼er **Fahrt** at full speed; **in** ∼em **Gange sein** be in full swing; **die** ∼e **Wahrheit** the full or whole truth; **mit dem** ∼en **Namen unterschreiben** sign one's full name or one's name in full; **das Dutzend ist** ∼: it's a round dozen; **jmdn. nicht für** ∼ **nehmen** not take sb. seriously; etw. ∼ **machen** (komplettieren) complete sth.; **s. auch Hals b; (e)** (kräftig) full, rich ⟨taste, aroma⟩; rich ⟨voice⟩. **2** adv. fully; ∼ **und ganz** completely; etw. ∼ **auslasten** make full use of sth.; ∼ **verantwortlich für** etw. **sein** be wholly responsible or bear full responsibility for sth.

*volladen ⇒ **voll 1 a**

voll·auf /od. '--/ Adv. completely; fully; ∼ **genügen/reichen** be quite enough

*vollaufen ⇒ **voll 1 a**

voll-, Voll-: ∼**automatisch 1** Adj. fully automatic; **2** adv. fully automatically; ∼**bad** das bath; ∼**bart** der full beard; ∼**beschäftigung** die; o. Pl. (Wirtsch.) full employment no art.; ∼**blut** das thoroughbred; ∼**bremsung** die: eine ∼**bremsung machen** put the brakes full on; ∼**bringen** /-'--/ unr. tr. V. (geh.) accomplish; achieve; ∼**dampf** der; o. Pl. (Seemannsspr.) full steam; **mit** ∼**dampf** at full steam or speed; (fig. ugs.) flat out

Völle·gefühl /'fœlə-/ das; o. Pl. feeling of fullness

voll·enden tr. V. complete; finish; **mit vollendetem** od. **dem vollendeten 16. Lebensjahr** on reaching the age of 16 or completing one's sixteenth year

vollendet 1 Adj. accomplished ⟨performance⟩; perfect ⟨gentleman, host, manners, reproduction⟩. **2** adv. ⟨play⟩ in an accomplished manner; perfectly

vollends /'fɔlɛnts/ Adv. completely

Voll·endung die completion; **kurz vor der** ∼ **stehen** be nearing completion; **mit/nach** ∼ **des 65. Lebensjahres** on reaching the age of 65 or completing one's sixty-fifth year

voller indekl. Adj. full of; filled with; **sein Anzug war** ∼ **Flecken** his suit was covered with stains

Völlerei /fœlə'rai/ die; ∼, ∼**en** (abwertend) gluttony no pl., no art.

Volley·ball der volleyball

voll-, Voll-: ∼**führen** /-'--/ tr. V. perform, execute ⟨somersault, movement⟩; perform ⟨dance, deed⟩; ***∼|füllen** ⇒ **voll 1 a**; ∼**gas** das; o. Pl. ∼**gas geben** put one's foot down; ∼**gas fahren** drive flat out; ***∼|gießen** ⇒ **voll 1 a**

völlig /'fœlɪç/ **1** Adj.; nicht präd. complete; total. **2** adv. completely; totally; **du hast** ∼ **recht** you are absolutely right; **das ist** ∼ **unmöglich** that is absolutely impossible; **mit etw.** ∼ **einverstanden sein** be in complete agreement with sth.

voll-, Voll-: ∼**jährig** Adj. of age pred.; ∼**jährig werden** come of age; attain one's majority; **sie hat zwei** ∼**jährige Kinder** she has two children who are of age; ∼**jährigkeit** die; ∼: majority no art.; ∼**kasko·versicherung** die fully comprehensive insurance; ∼**klimatisiert** Adj. fully air-conditioned

voll·kommen 1 Adj. **(a)** /-'-- od. '---/ (vollendet) perfect; **(b)** /'---/ (vollständig) complete; total. **2** /'---/ adv. completely; totally

Vollkommenheit die; ∼: perfection

voll-, Voll-: ∼**korn·brot** das wholemeal (Brit.) or (Amer.) wholewheat bread;***∼|machen** ⇒ **voll 1 a, d;** ∼**macht** die; ∼, ∼**en (a)** authority; jmdm. [die] ∼**macht geben/erteilen** give/grant sb. power of attorney; **in** ∼**macht** per procurationem; **(b)** (Urkunde) power of attorney; ∼**milch** die full-cream milk; ∼**mond** der; o. Pl. full moon;***∼|packen** ⇒ **voll 1 a;** ∼**pension** die; meist o. Art.; o. Pl. full board no art.;***∼|pumpen** ⇒ **voll 1 a;*∼|saugen** ⇒ **voll 1 a;** ∼**schlank** Adj. with a fuller figure postpos., not pred.; ∼**schlank sein** have a fuller figure;***∼|schmieren** ⇒ **voll 1 a;**

*∼|schreiben ⇒ **voll 1 a;** ∼**sperrung** die (Verkehrsw.) complete closure;***∼|spritzen** ⇒ **voll 1 a;** ∼**ständig 1** Adj. complete; full ⟨text, address, etc.⟩; **2** adv. completely; ⟨list⟩ in full; ∼**ständigkeit** die; ∼: completeness;***∼|stopfen** ⇒ **voll 1 a;** ∼**strecken** /-'--/ tr. V. enforce ⟨penalty, fine, law⟩; carry out ⟨sentence⟩ **(an** + Dat. on); **ein Testament** ∼**strecken** execute a will; ∼**strecker** /-'--/ der; ∼**s,** ∼ (des Gesetzes) enforcer; (eines Testaments) executor; ∼**streckung** /-'--/ die; ∼, ∼**en** ⇒ **vollstrecken:** enforcement; carrying out; execution

Vollstreckungs·befehl der (Rechtsw.) enforcement order; writ of execution

voll-, Voll-: ***∼|tanken** ⇒ **voll 1 a;** ∼**treffer** der direct hit; **ein** ∼**treffer sein** (fig.) hit the bull's eye; ∼**trunken** Adj. completely or blind drunk; **in** ∼**trunkenem Zustand** in a state of total inebriation; ∼**trunkenheit** die total inebriation or intoxication; ∼**verb** das (Sprachw.) full verb; ∼**versammlung** die general meeting; ∼**waise** die orphan; ∼**wertig** Adj. full ⟨job, member⟩; [fully] adequate ⟨replacement, substitute, nourishment, diet⟩; ∼**zählig** /∼tsɛ:lɪç/ Adj. complete; **als wir** ∼**zählig [versammelt] waren** when everyone was present

voll·ziehen 1 unr. tr. V. carry out; perform ⟨sacrifice, ceremony, sexual intercourse⟩; **die Ehe** ∼: consummate the marriage; **die** ∼**de Gewalt** the executive [power]. **2** unr. refl. V. take place

Voll·zug der ⇒ **vollziehen 1:** carrying out; performance

Vollzugs-: ∼**anstalt** die penal institution; ∼**beamte** der [prison] warder

Volontär /volɔn'tɛ:ɐ/ der; ∼**s,** ∼**e** trainee (receiving a low salary in return for training)

Volontariat /volɔnta'ria:t/ das; ∼[e]**s,** ∼**e (a)** (Zeit) period of training; **(b)** (Stelle) traineeship

Volontärin die; ∼, ∼**nen** ⇒ **Volontär**

volontieren itr. V. work as a trainee (bei with)

Volt /vɔlt/ das; ∼ od. ∼[e]**s,** ∼ (Physik, Elektrot.) volt

voltigieren /vɔlti'ʒi:rən/ itr. V. perform acrobatics on horseback

Volt·meter das; ∼**s,** ∼ (Elektrot.) voltmeter

Volumen /vo'lu:mən/ das; ∼**s,** ∼: ▶ 427 | volume

vom /fɔm/ Präp. + Art. **(a)** = **von dem; (b)** (räumlich, zeitlich) from the; **links/rechts** ∼ **Eingang** to the left/right of the entrance; ∼ **Stuhl aufspringen** jump up out of one's chair; ∼ **ersten Januar an** [as] from the first of January; **(c)** (zur Angabe der Ursache) **das kommt** ∼ **Rauchen/Alkohol** that comes from smoking/drinking alcohol; jmdn. ∼ **Sehen kennen** know sb. by sight

Vom·hundert·satz der percentage

von /fɔn/ Präp. mit Dat. **(a)** (räumlich) from; **nördlich/südlich** ∼ **Mannheim** to the north/south of Mannheim; **rechts/links** ∼ **mir** on my right/left; ∼ **hier an** od. (ugs.) **ab** from here on[ward]; ∼ **Mannheim aus** from Mannheim; etw. ∼ **etw.** ∼ **etw. [ab]wischen/[ab]brechen/ [ab]reißen** wipe/break/tear sth. off sth.; s. auch **aus 2 c; her a; vorn¹; (b)** (zeitlich) from; ∼ **jetzt an** od. (ugs.) **ab** from now on; ∼ **heute/morgen an** [as] from today/tomorrow; etw. **steht today/tomorrow;** ∼ **Kindheit an** from or since childhood; **in der Nacht** ∼ **Freitag auf** od. **zu Samstag** during Friday night or the night of Friday to Saturday; **das Brot ist** ∼ **gestern** it's yesterday's bread; s. auch **her b; (c)** (anstelle eines Genitivs) of; **ein Stück** ∼ **dem Kuchen** a slice of the cake; **acht** ∼ **zehn** eight out of ten; **(d)** (zur Angabe des Urhebers, der Ursache, beim Passiv) by; **müde** ∼ **der Arbeit sein** be tired from work[ing]; etw. ∼ **seinem Taschengeld kaufen** buy sth. with one's pocket money; **sie hat ein Kind** ∼ **ihm** she has a child by him; s. auch **wegen 2; (e)** (zur Angabe von Eigenschaften) of; **eine Fahrt** ∼ **drei Stunden** a three-hour drive; **Kinder [im Alter]** ∼ **vier Jahren** children aged four; ∼ **bester Qualität** of the best quality; **(f)** (bestehend aus) of; **(g)** (als Adelsprädikat) von; **(h)** (in Bezug auf) **er ist** ∼ **Beruf Lehrer** he is a teacher by profession; **(i)** (über) about; ∼ **diesen Dingen spricht man besser nicht** it's better not to speak of such things

von·ein·ander *Adv.* from each other *or* one another; ‹*disappointed*› in each other *or* one another

vonnöten /fɔn'nøːtn̩/ *Adj.* ~ **sein** be necessary

von·seiten *Präp. mit Gen.* ~ **der Direktion** from the management side

vonstatten /fɔn'ʃtatn̩/ *Adv.* ~ **gehen** proceed

Vopo /'foːpo/ *der;* ~**s**, ~**s** (ugs.) ⇒ **Volkspolizist**

vor /foːɐ̯/ **1** *Präp. mit Dat.* **(a)** (räumlich) in front of; (weiter vorn als) ahead of; in front of; (nicht ganz so weit wie) before; (außerhalb) outside; ~ **einem Hintergrund** against a background; **200 m** ~ **der Abzweigung** 200 m. before the turn-off; ~ **der Stadt** outside the town; **etw.** ~ **sich haben** (fig.) have sth. before one; **(b)** ▶ **530 |** (zeitlich) before; **es ist fünf [Minuten]** ~ **sieben** it is five [minutes] to seven; **(c)** (bei Reihenfolge, Rangordnung) before; **knapp** ~ **jmdm. siegen** win just ahead *or* in front of sb.; **(d)** (in Gegenwart von) before; in front of; ~ **Zeugen** before *or* in the presence of witnesses; **(e)** (aufgrund von) with; ~ **Kälte zittern** shiver with cold; ~ **Hunger/Durst umkommen** die of hunger/thirst; ~ **Arbeit/Schulden nicht mehr aus und ein wissen** not know which way to turn for work/debts; ~ **fünf Minuten/Jahren** five minutes/years ago; **heute/gestern/morgen** ~ **einer Woche** a week ago today/yesterday/tomorrow. **2** *Präp. mit Akk.* in front of; **keinen Schritt** ~ **die Tür setzen** not set foot outside the door; **er fuhr bis** ~ **die Haustür** he drove right up to the front door; ~ **sich hin** to oneself; **still** ~ **sich hin arbeiten** work away quietly. **3** *Adv.* forward; **Freiwillige** ~**!** volunteers to the front!; ~ **und zurück** backwards and forwards

vor·ab *Adv.* beforehand

Vor·abend *der* evening before; (fig.) eve

Vor·ahnung *die* premonition; presentiment; **dunkle/ schlimme** ~**en** dark forebodings

vor·an /fo'ran/ *Adv.* forward[s] ahead; first

voran-: ~**|gehen** *unr. itr. V.; mit sein* **(a)** go first *or* ahead; **jmdm.** ~**gehen** go ahead of sb.; **[jmdm.] mit gutem Beispiel** ~**gehen** (fig.) set [sb.] a good example; **(b)** (Fortschritte machen) make progress; **rasch/nur schleppend** ~**gehen** make rapid/only slow progress; **es geht mit der Arbeit nicht [so recht]** ~**:** the work is not making [much] progress; **(c)** ⇒ **vorausgehen b;** ~**|kommen** *unr. itr. V.; mit sein* **(a)** make headway; **gut** ~**kommen** make good headway *or* progress; **(b)** (fig.) make progress; **die Arbeit kommt gut/nicht** ~**:** the work is making good progress *or* coming along well/not making any progress; **beruflich** ~**kommen** get on in one's job

Vor·ankündigung *die* advance announcement; **ohne** ~**:** without any advance *or* prior notice

Vor·arbeit *die* preliminary work *no pl.*

vor|arbeiten *refl. V.* work one's way forward

Vor·arbeiter *der* foreman

voraus *Präp. mit Dat., nachgestellt* in front; **jmdm./ seiner Zeit** ~ **sein** (fig.) be ahead of sb./one's time; *s. auch* **Voraus**

Voraus: im ~**:** in advance

voraus-, Voraus-: ~**|berechnen** *tr. V.* (auch fig.) calculate in advance; ~**|gehen** *unr. itr. V.; mit sein* **(a)** go [on] ahead; **ihm geht der Ruf** ~, **sehr streng zu sein** (fig.) he has the reputation of being very strict; **(b)** (zeitlich) **einem Ereignis** ~**gehen** precede an event; **dem Entschluss gingen lange Überlegungen** ~**:** the decision was preceded by *or* followed lengthy deliberations; ~**|haben** *unr. tr. V.* **jmdm./einer Sache etw.** ~**haben** have the advantage of sth. over sb./sth.; **er hat ihm viel/nichts** ~**:** he has a great/no advantage over him; ~**sage** *die* ⇒ **Vorhersage;** ~**|sagen** *tr. V.* predict; **jmdm. die Zukunft** ~**sagen** foretell *or* predict sb.'s future; ~**|schauen** *itr. V.* look ahead; ~**schauende Planung/Politik** foresighted planning/ policy; ~**|schicken** *tr. V.* **(a)** send [on] ahead; **(b)** (einleitend) say first; **ich muss folgendes** ~**schicken I** must start *or* begin by saying the following; ~**sehbar**

Adj. foreseeable; ~**|sehen** *unr. tr. V.* foresee; **das war/ war nicht** ~**zusehen** that was foreseeable/unforeseeable; ~**|setzen** *tr. V.* **(a)** assume; **etw. als bekannt** ~**setzen** assume sth. is known; **er setzte stillschweigend** ~, **dass ...:** he took it for granted that ...; **Ihr Einverständnis** ~ **gesetzt** provided that you agree; ~**gesetzt, [dass]** ...: provided [that] ...; **(b)** (erfordern) require ‹*skill, experience, etc.*›; presuppose ‹*good organization, planning, etc.*›; ~**setzung** *die;* ~, ~**en (a)** (Annahme) assumption; (Prämisse) premiss; **(b)** (Vorbedingung) prerequisite; **unter der** ~**setzung, dass ...:** on condition *or* on the precondition that ...; **er hat die besten** ~**setzungen für den Job** he has the best qualifications for the job; ~**sicht** *die* foresight; **aller** ~**sicht nach** in all probability; **in weiser** ~**sicht** (scherzh.) with great foresight; ~**sichtlich 1** *Adj.; nicht präd.* anticipated; expected; **2** *adv.* probably; **der Abflug wird sich** ~**sichtlich verzögern** the departure is expected to be delayed

Vor·bau *der; Pl.* ~**ten (a)** porch; **(b)** ⇒ **Lenkervorbau**

vor|bauen *itr. V.* make provision

Vor·bedacht *der:* **mit** ~**:** intentionally; deliberately

Vor·bedingung *die* [pre]condition

Vorbehalt /'foːɐ̯bəhalt/ *der;* ~**[e]s**, ~**e** reservation; **unter** ~**:** with reservations; **unter dem** ~, **dass ...:** with the reservation that ...; **ohne** ~**:** unreservedly; without reservation

vor|behalten *unr. tr. V.* **sich** (*Dat.*) **etw.** ~**:** reserve oneself sth.; reserve sth. [for oneself]; „**Änderungen** ~“ 'subject to alterations'; **alle Rechte** ~ (Druckw.) all rights reserved; **jmdm.** ~ **sein/bleiben** be left to sb.; ‹*decision*› be left [up] to sb.

vorbehaltlich *Präp. mit Gen.* (Papierdt.) subject to

vorbehalt·los 1 *Adj.* unreserved. **2** *adv.* unreservedly; without reservation[s]

vor·bei *Adv.* **(a)** (räumlich) past; by; **der Wagen war schon [an uns]** ~**:** the car was already past [us] *or* had already gone past *or* by [us]; **an etw.** (*Dat.*) ~**:** past sth.; **[wieder]** ~**!** missed [again]; **(b)** ▶ **530 |** (zeitlich) past; over; (beendet) finished; over; **es ist acht Uhr** ~ (ugs.) it is past *or* gone eight o'clock; *s. auch* **aus 2 a**

vorbei-: ~**|fahren** *1 unr. itr. V.; mit sein* **(a)** drive/ ride past; pass; **an jmdm.** ~**fahren** drive/ride past sb.; pass sb.; **(b)** [**bei jmdm./der Post**] ~**fahren** (ugs.) drop in (coll.) [at sb.'s/at the post office]; **2** *tr. V.* (ugs.) **kannst du mich schnell beim Bahnhof** ~**fahren?** can you just run me to the station?; ~**|gehen** *unr. itr. V.; mit sein* **(a)** pass; go past; **an jmdm./etw.** ~**gehen** pass sb./sth. go past sb./sth.; **im Vorbeigehen** in passing; **(b)** [**bei jmdm./der Post**] ~**gehen** (ugs.) drop in (coll.) [at sb.'s/at the post office]; **(c)** (nicht treffen) miss; **am Ziel** ~**gehen** miss its mark *or* target; **(d)** (vergehen) pass; ~**|kommen** *unr. itr. V.; mit sein* **(a)** pass; **an etw.** (*Dat.*) ~**kommen** pass sth.; **(b)** [**bei jmdm.**] ~**kommen** (ugs.) drop in (coll.) [at sb.'s]; **(c)** (vorbeigehen, -fahren können) get past *or* by; **daran kommt man nicht** ~ (fig.) there's no getting around *or* away from that; ~**|lassen** *unr. tr. V.* (ugs.) let past *or* by; ~**|reden** *itr. V.* **an etw.** (*Dat.*) ~**reden** miss sth.; **aneinander** ~**reden** talk at cross purposes; ~**|schießen** *unr. itr. V.* **(a)** miss; **am Ziel** ~**schießen** miss the target; **(b)** **am Tor** ~**schießen** shoot wide of the goal

vor·belastet *Adj.* handicapped (**durch** by); **erblich** ~ **sein** have an inherited defect

Vor·bemerkung *die* preliminary remark

vor|bereiten *tr. V.* **(a)** prepare (**auf** + *Akk.*, **für** for); **(b)** prepare for ‹*trip, party, etc.*›

Vor·bereitung *die;* ~, ~**en** preparation; ~**en für etw. treffen** make preparations for sth.

Vor·besitzer *der* previous owner

Vor·besprechung *die* preliminary discussion[s *pl.*]

vor|bestellen *tr. V.* order in advance

Vor·bestellung *die* advance order

vor·bestraft *Adj.* (Amtsspr.) with a previous conviction/ previous convictions *postpos., not pred.;* [mehrfach] ~ **sein** have [several] previous convictions

---

vor|beugen 1 *tr. V.* bend ‹*head, upper body*› forward. **2** *refl. V.* lean *or* bend forward. **3** *itr. V.* **einer Sache** (*Dat.*) *od.* **gegen etw. ∼:** prevent sth.; **∼de Maßnahmen** preventive measures; **Vorbeugen ist besser als Heilen** (Spr.) prevention is better than cure (prov.)

Vor·beugung *die* prevention (**gegen** of); **zur ∼:** as a preventive

Vor·bild *das* model; **jmdm. ein gutes ∼ sein** be a good example to sb.; set sb. a good example; **sich** (*Dat.*) **jmdn./ etw. zum ∼ nehmen** take sb. as a model *or* model oneself on sb./take sth. as a model

vor·bildlich 1 *Adj.* exemplary. **2** *adv.* in an exemplary way *or* manner

Vor·bote *der* harbinger

vor|bringen *unr. tr. V.* say; **eine Frage/Forderung/ ein Anliegen ∼:** ask a question/make a demand/express a desire; **Argumente ∼:** present *or* state arguments; **Beweise ∼:** produce evidence

Vor·dach *das* canopy

Vor·denker *der* (Politikjargon) guiding intellectual force

vorder... /'fɔrdɐ.../ *Adj.; nicht präd.* front; **die ∼sten Reihen** the rows at the very front; **der Vordere Orient** the Middle East

vorder-, Vorder-: **∼achse** *die* front axle; **∼ansicht** *die* front view; **∼bein** *das* foreleg; **∼gebäude** *das* front building; **∼grund** *der* foreground; **im ∼grund stehen** (fig.) be prominent *or* to the fore; **etw. in den ∼grund stellen** *od.* **rücken** (fig.) give priority to sth.; place special emphasis on sth.; **in den ∼grund treten** *od.* **rücken** (fig.) come to the fore; **sich in den ∼grund drängen** (fig.) push oneself forward; **∼gründig** /∼gryndɪç/ **1** *Adj.* superficial; **2** *adv.* superficially

Vorder-: **∼mann** *der; Pl.* **∼männer** person in front; **ihr/sein ∼mann** the person in front of her/him; **jmdn. auf ∼mann bringen** (ugs.) lick sb. into shape (coll.); **den Garten auf ∼mann bringen** (ugs.) get the garden shipshape; **∼pfote** *die* front paw; **∼rad** *das* front wheel; **∼rad·antrieb** *der* front-wheel drive; **∼seite** *die* front; (einer Münze, Medaille) obverse; **∼sitz** *der* front seat

vorderst... ⇒ **vorder...**

vor|drängen *refl. V.* push [one's way] forward *or* to the front; (fig.) push oneself forward

vor|dringen *unr. itr. V.; mit sein* push forward; advance; **bis zu jmdm. ∼** (fig.) reach sb.; get as far as sb.

vor·dringlich 1 *Adj.* (a) priority *attrib.* ‹*treatment*›; **∼ sein** be a matter of priority; (b) (dringlich) urgent; **unser ∼stes Anliegen** our main *or* overriding concern. **2** *adv.* (a) as a matter of priority; (b) as a matter of urgency

Vor·druck *der; Pl.* **Vordrucke** form

vor·ehelich *Adj.* premarital

vor·eilig 1 *Adj.* rash. **2** *adv.* rashly; **∼ schließen, dass ...:** jump to the conclusion that ...

vor·einander *Adv.* (a) one in front of the other; (b) **Geheimnisse ∼ haben** have secrets from each other; **Hochachtung/Furcht ∼ haben** have great respect for each other/be afraid of each other

vor·eingenommen *Adj.* biased; prejudiced (**für** in favour of, **gegen** against, **gegenüber** towards)

Voreingenommenheit *die;* **∼:** prejudice; bias

vorenthalten; ich enthalte vor (*od. seltener:* **vorenthalte**), **vorenthalten, vorzuenthalten** *unr. tr. V.* **jmdm. etw. ∼:** withhold sth. from sb.

Vor·entscheidung *die* preliminary decision

vor·erst /*od.* -'-/ *Adv.* for the present; for the time being

Vorfahr /-faːɐ̯/ *der;* **∼en** *od. selten* **∼s, ∼en** forefather; ancestor

vor|fahren *unr. itr. V.; mit sein* (a) [vor dem Hotel/ Haus] **∼:** drive/ride up [outside the hotel/house]; (b) (nach vorn fahren) ‹*person*› drive *or* move forward; ‹*car*› move forward; (c) (vorausfahren) drive *or* go on ahead

Vor·fahrt *die; o. Pl.* right of way; **„∼ beachten/gewähren!"** 'give way'; **die ∼ nicht beachten** fail to give way; **jmdm. die ∼ nehmen** fail to give way to sb.

Vorfahrt[s]-: **∼schild** *das* right-of-way sign; **∼straße** *die* main road

Vor·fall *der* incident; occurrence

vor|fallen *unr. itr. V.; mit sein* (a) happen; occur; **ist etwas [Besonderes] vorgefallen?** has anything [special] happened?; (b) (nach vorn fallen) fall forward

vor|finden *unr. tr. V.* find

Vor·freude *die* anticipation

Vor·frühling *der* early spring

vor|fühlen *itr. V.* **bei jmdm. ∼:** sound sb. out

vor|führen *tr. V.* (a) bring forward; **jmdn. dem Richter ∼:** bring sb. before the judge; (b) (zeigen) show; **wann führst du uns deinen Freund vor?** when are you going to introduce your boyfriend to us?; (c) (demonstrieren) demonstrate; **jmdm. etw. ∼:** demonstrate sth. to sb.; (d) (darbieten) show ‹*film, slides, etc.*›; present ‹*circus act, programme*›; perform ‹*play, trick, routine*›

Vor·führung *die* (a) bringing forward; **der Richter ordnete ihre ∼ an** the judge ordered her to be brought forward; (b) (das Zeigen) showing; exhibiting; (c) (das Demonstrieren) demonstration; (d) (das Darbieten) ⇒ **vorführen d:** showing; presentation; performance; (e) (Veranstaltung) ⇒ **vorführen d:** show; presentation; performance

Vorführ·wagen *der* demonstration car *or* model

Vor·gabe *die* (a) (Sport) handicap; (b) (Richtlinie) guideline

Vor·gang *der* (a) occurrence; event; (Prozess) process; (b) (Amtsspr.) file; **der ∼ XY** the file on XY

Vorgänger /-gɛŋɐ/ *der;* **∼s, ∼, Vorgängerin** *die;* **∼, ∼nen** (auch fig.) predecessor

Vor·garten *der* front garden

vor|gaukeln *tr. V.* **jmdm. ∼, dass ...:** lead sb. to believe that ...; **jmdm. eine heile Welt ∼:** lead sb. to believe in a perfect world

vor|geben *unr. tr. V.* (a) (vortäuschen) pretend; (b) (Sport) **jmdm. eine Runde/50 m/15 Punkte ∼:** give sb. a lap [start]/[a start of] 50 m/[a lead of] 15 points; (c) (im Voraus festlegen) set in advance

Vor·gebirge *das* promontory

vor·gedruckt *Adj.* pre-printed

vor·gefasst, *vor·gefaßt *Adj.; nicht präd.* preconceived

vorgefertigt *Adj.* pre-fabricated

Vor·gefühl *das* presentiment

vor|gehen *unr. itr. V.; mit sein* (a) (ugs.: nach vorn gehen) go forward; **zum Altar ∼:** go up to the altar; (b) (vorausgehen) go on ahead; **jmdn. ∼ lassen** let sb. go first; (c) ‹*clock*› be fast; (d) (einschreiten) **gegen jmdn./etw. ∼:** take action against sb./sth.; (e) (verfahren) proceed; (f) (sich abspielen) happen; go on; **in jmdm. ∼:** go on inside sb.; **mit ihm war eine Veränderung vorgegangen** there had been a change in him; a change had taken place in him; (g) (Vorrang haben) have priority; come first

Vor·geschichte *die* (a) *o. Pl.* prehistory *no art.;* (b) (eines Vorgangs) history

vor·geschichtlich *Adj.* prehistoric

Vor·geschmack *der; o. Pl.* foretaste

Vor·gesetzte *der/die; adj. Dekl.* superior

vor·gestern *Adv.* the day before yesterday; **∼ Mittag/ ∼ Abend/∼ Morgen** *od.* **früh** the day before yesterday at midday/the evening before last/the morning of the day before yesterday; **er ist von ∼** (ugs.) he is old-fashioned *or* behind the times; **Ansichten von ∼** (ugs.) old-fashioned *or* outdated views

vor·gestrig *Adj.; nicht präd.* of the day before yesterday *postpos.*

vor|greifen *unr. itr. V.* **jmdm. ∼:** anticipate sb.; jump in ahead of sb.; **einer Sache** (*Dat.*) **∼:** anticipate sth.

Vor·griff *der* anticipation (**auf** + *Akk.* of); (bei einer Erzählung) jump *or* leap ahead (**auf** + *Akk.* to)

vor|haben *unr. tr. V.* intend; plan; **er hat eine Reise vor** *od.* **er hat vor, eine Reise zu machen** he intends going on a journey/plans to go on a journey; **hast du heute Abend etwas vor?** have you anything planned *or* any plans for this evening?; are you doing anything this evening?; **er hat Großes mit seinem Sohn vor** he has great plans for his son

Vor·haben *das;* ~s, ~ (Plan) plan; (Projekt) project

Vor·halle *die* entrance hall

vor|halten 1 *unr. tr. V.* **(a)** hold up; **sich** (*Dat.*) **etw.** ~: hold sth. [up] in front of oneself; **mit vorgehaltener Waffe** at gunpoint; *s. auch* **Hand c**; **(b)** jmdm. etw. ~ (fig.) reproach sb. for sth. **2** *unr. itr. V.* (ugs., auch fig.) last

Vor·haltungen *Pl.* **jmdm.** ~ **machen** reproach sb. (wegen for)

Vor·hand *die* **(a)** (Sport, bes. Tennis) forehand; **mit** [der] ~: on one's forehand; **(b)** (beim Pferd) forehand

vorhanden /-'handn̩/ *Adj.* existing; (verfügbar) available; ~ **sein** exist *or* be in existence/be available

Vorhanden·sein *das;* ~s existence

Vor·hang *der* curtain

Vorhänge·schloss, *****Vorhänge·schloß** *das* padlock

Vor·haut *die* ▶ 326 foreskin; prepuce

vor·her /*od.* -'-/ beforehand; (davor) before; **eine Woche** ~: a week earlier *or* before

vorher|gehen *unr. itr. V.; mit sein* **in den** ~**den Wochen** in the preceding weeks; in the weeks before; **wie im Vorhergehenden erläutert** as explained above

vorherig /*od.* '---/ *Adj.; nicht präd.* prior ⟨*notice, announcement, warning*⟩; previous ⟨*discussion, agreement*⟩; ~**e Bezahlung** payment in advance

Vor·herrschaft *die; o. Pl.* supremacy; dominance

vor|herrschen *itr. V.* predominate; ~**d** predominant

vorher-, Vorher-: ~**sage** *die* prediction; (des Wetters) forecast; ~|**sagen** *tr. V.* predict; forecast ⟨*weather*⟩; ~**sehbar** *Adj.* foreseeable; ~|**sehen** *unr. tr. V.* foresee

vor|heucheln *tr. V.* feign (*Dat.* to); **er heuchelte ihr Liebe vor** he pretended to love her

vor·hin /*od.* -'-/ *Adv.* a short time *or* while ago; **der Junge von** ~ (ugs.) the boy who we saw a short time ago *or* just now

Vor·hut *die;* ~, ~**en** advance guard; (fig.) vanguard

vorig... *Adj.* ▶ 119, ▶ 595; *nicht präd.* last

Vor·jahr *das* previous year

Vor·kämpfer *der* pioneer; **ein** ~ **der Freiheit** a pioneering champion of freedom

Vorkehrungen *Pl.* precautions; ~ **treffen** take precautions

Vor·kenntnis *die* background knowledge

vor|knöpfen *tr. V.* **sich** (*Dat.*) **jmdn.** [**ordentlich**] ~ (ugs.) give sb. a [proper] talking-to (coll.)

vor|kommen *unr. itr. V.; mit sein* **(a)** happen; **dass mir so etwas nicht wieder vorkommt!** I hope I never experience anything like that again; **(b)** (vorhanden sein) occur; **die Pflanze kommt nur im Gebirge vor** the plant is found only in the mountains; **in einer Erzählung** ~ ⟨*character, figure*⟩ appear in a story; **(c)** (erscheinen) seem; **das Lied kommt mir bekannt vor** I seem to know the song; **es kam mir [so] vor, als ob …:** I felt *or* it seemed as if …; **du kommst dir wohl schlau vor** I suppose you think you're clever; **ich komme mir überflüssig vor** I feel [as if I am] superfluous; **(d)** (ugs.: nach vorne kommen) come forward; **(e)** (hervorkommen) come out; **hinter/unter etw.** (*Dat.*) ~: come out from behind/under sth.

Vorkommen *das;* ~s, ~ **(a)** *o. Pl.* occurrence; **(b)** (Geol.) deposit

Vorkommnis /-kɔmnɪs/ *das;* ~**ses**, ~**se** incident; occurence

Vor·kriegszeit *die* pre-war period

vor|laden *unr. tr. V.* summon

Vor·ladung *die* summons

Vor·lage *die* **(a)** *o. Pl.;* ⇒ **vorlegen a:** presentation; showing; production; submission; tabling; introduction; **gegen** ~ **einer Sache** (*Gen.*) on production *or* presentation of sth.; **(b)** (Gesetzentwurf) bill; **(c)** (Muster) pattern; (Modell) model; **nach einer/ohne** ~ **zeichnen** draw from/ without a model; **(d)** (Ballspiele, bes. Fußball) forward pass; **(e)** (Kaufmannsspr.) advance; **[für etw.] in** ~ **treten** advance the money [for sth.]

vor|lassen *unr. tr. V.* **(a)** jmdn. ~ (ugs.) let sb. go first *or* in front; **(b)** (empfangen) admit; let in

Vor·läufer *der* precursor; forerunner

vor·läufig 1 *Adj.* temporary; provisional ⟨*diagnosis, settlement, result, successor*⟩; interim ⟨*order, agreement*⟩. **2** *adv.* for the time being; for the present

vor·laut 1 *Adj.* forward. **2** *adv.* forwardly

Vor·leben *das; o. Pl.* past life; past

Vorlege- serving ⟨*cutlery, fork, spoon*⟩

vor|legen *tr. V.* **(a)** present; show, produce ⟨*certificate, identity card, etc.*⟩; show ⟨*sample*⟩; submit ⟨*evidence*⟩; table, introduce ⟨*parliamentary bill*⟩; **(b)** (anbringen vor) **eine Kette/einen Riegel** ~: put a chain on *or* across/a bolt across; **(c)** (geh.: aufgeben) serve ⟨*food*⟩; **jmdm. etw.** ~: serve sb. with sth.; serve sth. to sb.

Vorleger *der;* ~s, ~ mat; (Bett~) rug

Vor·leistung *die* advance concession

vor|lesen *unr. tr., itr. V.* read aloud *or* out; read ⟨*story, poem, etc.*⟩ aloud; **jmdm.** [**etw.**] ~: read [sth.] to sb.; **lies schon vor!** read it out!; read out what it says!

Vor·lesung *die* lecture; (~sreihe) series *or* course of lectures

Vorlesungs·verzeichnis *das* lecture timetable

vor·letzt... *Adj.* ▶ 595; *nicht präd.* last but one; next to last; penultimate ⟨*page, episode, etc.*⟩; **mein** ~**es Exemplar** my last copy but one; my next to last copy; ~**e Woche** the week before last

vor·lieb *in* **mit jmdm./etw.** ~ **nehmen** make do with sb./sth.

Vor·liebe *die* preference; [special] fondness *or* liking; **eine** ~ **für etw. haben** be fond of *or* partial to sth.; **etw. mit** ~ **tun** particularly like doing sth.

*****vorlieb|nehmen** ⇒ **vorlieb**

vor|liegen *unr. itr. V.* **(a)** jmdm. ~ ⟨*application, complaint, plans, etc.*⟩ be with sb.; **das Beweismaterial liegt dem Gericht vor** the evidence is before or has been submitted to the court; **die Ergebnisse liegen uns noch nicht vor** we do not have the results yet; **die mir** ~**de Ausgabe/**~**den Ergebnisse** the edition/results in front of me; **im** ~**den Fall** in the present case; **(b)** (bestehen) be [present]; exist; ⟨*symptom*⟩ be present; ⟨*book*⟩ be available; **gegen ihn liegt nichts vor** there is nothing against him; **hier liegt ein Irrtum vor** there is a mistake here; **ein Verschulden des Fahrers liegt nicht vor** the driver is/was not to blame

vorm /fo:ɐ̯m/ *Präp. + Art.* **(a)** = **vor dem**; **(b)** (räumlich) in front of the; **(c)** (zeitlich, bei Reihenfolge, Rangordnung) before the

vor|machen *tr. V.* (ugs.) **(a)** jmdm. etw. ~: show sb. sth.; **ihm macht niemand was vor** there is no one better than him; no one can teach him anything; **(b)** (vortäuschen) **jmdm./sich etwas** ~: kid (coll.) *or* fool sb./oneself; **der lässt sich nichts** ~: he's nobody's fool

Vormacht·stellung *die; o. Pl.* [position of] supremacy *no art.*

Vor·marsch *der* (auch fig.) advance; **auf dem** *od.* **im** ~ **sein** be advancing *or* on the advance; (fig.) be gaining ground

vor|merken *tr. V.* make a note of; **ich habe Sie für den Kurs vorgemerkt** I've put you down for the course

*****vor·mittag** ⇒ **Vormittag**

Vor·mittag *der* morning; **heute/morgen/gestern** ~: this/tomorrow/yesterday morning

vor·mittags *Adv.* ▶ 530 in the morning

Vor·monat *der* previous *or* preceding month

Vor·mund *der; Pl.* **Vormunde** *od.* **Vormünder** guardian; **ich brauche keinen** ~ (fig.) I don't need anyone telling me what to do

Vormundschaft *die;* ~, ~**en** guardianship

vorn /fɔrn/ *Adv.* at the front; **das Zimmer liegt nach** ~ [**raus**] (ugs.) the room faces the front; ~ **am Haus** at the front of the house; ~ **im Bild** in the foreground of the picture; **nach** ~ **sehen** look in front *or* to the front; **nach** ~ **gehen** go to the front; **da** ~: over there; **der Wind**

kam von ~: the wind came from the front; **noch einmal von ~ anfangen** start afresh; start from the beginning again; **von ~ bis hinten** (ugs.) from beginning to end

Vor·name *der* first *or* Christian name

vorne *Adv.* ⇒ **vorn**

vornehm /'fo'ɐnem/ **1** *Adj.* **(a)** noble ⟨*character, behaviour, gesture, etc.*⟩; **~e Gesinnung** noble-mindedness; **(b)** (der Oberschicht angehörend, kultiviert) distinguished; **die ~e Welt/die ~en Kreise** high society; **(c)** (adlig) noble; **(d)** (elegant) exclusive, (coll.) posh ⟨*district, hotel, resort*⟩; elegant, (coll.) posh ⟨*villa, clothes*⟩. **2** *adv.* **(a)** nobly; **(b)** (elegant) elegantly

vor|nehmen 1 *unr. refl. V.* **sich** (*Dat.*) **etw. ~:** plan sth.; **sich** (*Dat.*) **~, etw. zu tun** plan to do sth.; **sich** (*Dat.*) **~, mit dem Rauchen aufzuhören** resolve to give up smoking. **2** *unr. tr. V.* **(a)** carry out, make ⟨*examination, search, test*⟩; perform ⟨*action, ceremony*⟩; make ⟨*correction, change, division, choice, selection*⟩; take ⟨*measurements*⟩; **(b)** [**sich** (*Dat.*)] **ein Buch/eine Arbeit ~** (ugs.) get down to reading a book/to a piece of work; **(c) sich** (*Dat.*) **jmdn. ~** (ugs.) give sb. a talking-to (coll.)

Vornehmheit *die;* **~:** ⇒ **vornehm 1 a–d:** nobility; exclusivity; elegance; **seine ~ beeindruckte sie** she was impressed by his distinguished manner

vornehmlich *Adv.* (geh.) above all; primarily

vor|neigen *tr., refl. V.* lean forward

vorn-: ~herein: von ~herein from the start *or* outset *or* beginning; **~über** *Adv.* forwards

Vor·ort *der* suburb

Vor·platz *der* forecourt

Vor·posten *der* (Milit., fig.) outpost

vor|preschen *itr. V.; mit sein* (fig.) rush ahead

Vor·programm *das* supporting programme

vor|programmieren *tr. V.* (auch fig.) pre-programme

vor|ragen *itr. V.* project; jut out

Vor·rang *der; o. Pl.* **(a)** [**den**] **~** [**vor jmdm./etw.**] **haben** have priority *or* take precedence [over sb./sth.]; **jmdm./einer Sache den ~ geben** give sb./sth. priority; **(b)** (bes. österr.: Vorfahrt) right of way

vorrangig /-raŋɪç/ **1** *Adj.* priority *attrib.* ⟨*treatment*⟩; **~ sein** be a matter of priority *or* of prime importance; **unser ~es Anliegen** our primary concern. **2** *adv.* as a matter of priority; **jmdn. ~ behandeln** give sb. priority treatment

Vor·rat *der* supply, stock (**an** + *Dat.* of); **solange der ~ reicht** while stocks last

vorrätig /-rɛːtɪç/ *Adj.* in stock *postpos.;* **etw. nicht mehr ~ haben** be out of [stock of] sth.

Vorrats-: ~kammer *die* pantry; larder; **~keller** *der* cellar storeroom; **~raum** *der* storeroom

Vor·raum *der* anteroom

vor|rechnen *tr. V.* **jmdm. etw. ~:** work sth. out *or* calculate sth. for sb.; **jmdm. seine Fehler ~** (fig.) enumerate sb.'s mistakes

Vor·recht *das* privilege

Vor·rede *die* **(a)** introductory remarks *pl.;* **sich nicht lange mit der ~ aufhalten** not take long over the introductions; **(b)** (Vorwort) preface; foreword

Vor·redner *der* previous speaker; **mein ~:** the previous speaker

Vor·richtung *die* device

vor|rücken 1 *tr. V.* move forward; advance ⟨*chess piece*⟩. **2** *itr. V.; mit sein* move forward; (Milit.) advance; **mit dem Turm ~** (Schach) advance the rook; **auf den 5. Platz ~:** move up to fifth place; **zu vorgerückter Stunde** (geh.) at a late hour

Vor·ruhestand *der* early retirement

Vor·runde *die* (Sport) preliminary *or* qualifying round

vors *Präp.* + *Art.* **(a)** = **vor das; (b)** in front of the; **jmdm. ~ Auto laufen** run in front of sb.'s car

vor|sagen *tr. V.* **(a)** *auch itr.* **jmdm.** [**die Antwort**] **~:** tell sb. the answer; (flüsternd) whisper the answer to sb.; **(b)** (aufsagen) recite (*Dat.* to)

Vor·saison *die* start of the season; early [part of the] season

Vor·satz *der* intention; **den ~ fassen, etw. zu tun** resolve to do sth.; make a resolution to do sth.; **den ~ haben, etw. zu tun** intend to do sth.; have the intention of doing sth.; **mit ~:** with intent

vorsätzlich /-zɛtslɪç/ **1** *Adj.* intentional; deliberate; wilful ⟨*murder, arson, etc.*⟩. **2** *adv.* intentionally; deliberately

Vor·schau *die* preview

Vor·schein *der:* **etw. zum ~ bringen** reveal sth.; bring sth. to light; **zum ~ kommen** appear; (entdeckt werden) come to light; **wieder zum ~ kommen** reappear

vor|schieben 1 *unr. tr. V.* **(a)** push ⟨*bolt*⟩ across; *s. auch* **Riegel a; (b)** (nach vorn schieben) push forward. **2** *unr. refl. V.* push forward

vor|schießen *unr. tr. V.* **jmdm. Geld ~:** advance sb. money

Vor·schlag *der* suggestion; proposal

vor|schlagen *unr. tr. V.* suggest, propose (*Dat.* to)

Vorschlag·hammer *der* sledgehammer

vor·schnell *Adj., adv.:* ⇒ **voreilig**

vor·schreiben *unr. tr. V.* stipulate, lay down, set ⟨*conditions*⟩; lay down ⟨*rules*⟩; prescribe ⟨*dose*⟩; **er wollte uns ~, was wir zu tun hätten** he wanted to tell us *or* dictate to us what to do; **die vorgeschriebene Geschwindigkeit/Dosis** the prescribed speed/dose

Vor·schrift *die* instruction; order; (gesetzliche od. amtliche Bestimmung) regulation; **ich lasse mir von dir keine ~en machen** I won't be told what to do by you; I won't be dictated to by you; **das ist ~:** that's/those are the regulations; **das ist gegen die ~:** it's against the rules *or* regulations; **die Medizin nach ~ einnehmen** take the medicine as directed

vorschrifts·mäßig 1 *Adj.* correct; proper. **2** *adv.* correctly; properly

Vor·schub *der:* **jmdm./einer Sache ~ leisten** encourage sb./encourage *or* promote *or* foster sth.

Vorschul- preschool ⟨*age, education*⟩

Vor·schule *die* nursery school

Vor·schuss, *Vor·schuß *der* advance; **50 Mark ~:** an advance of 50 marks

vor|schützen *tr. V.* plead as an excuse; **wichtige Geschäfte/Krankheit ~:** pretend one has important business/feign illness; *s. auch* **Müdigkeit**

vor|schweben *itr. V.* **jmdm. schwebt etw. vor** sb. has sth. in mind

vor|sehen 1 *unr. tr. V.* **(a)** plan; **etw. für/als etw. ~:** intend sth. for/as sth.; **jmdn. für/als etw. ~:** designate sb. for/as sth.; **(b)** ⟨*law, plan, contract, etc.*⟩ provide for. **2** *unr. refl. V.* **sich** [**vor jmdm./etw.**] **~:** be careful [of sb./sth.]; **sieh dich vor dem Hund vor** be careful of *or* mind the dog; **sieh dich vor, dass du nicht krank wirst** be careful *or* take care you don't become ill

Vorsehung *die;* **~:** Providence *no art.*

vor|setzen *tr. V.* **(a)** move forward; **den rechten/ linken Fuß ~:** put one's right/left foot forward; **(b) jmdm. etw. ~:** serve sb. sth.

Vor·sicht *die; o. Pl.* care; (bei Risiko, Gefahr) caution; care; (Umsicht) circumspection; caution; **zur ~:** as a precaution; to be on the safe side; **~!** be careful!; watch *or* look out!; **„~, Glas"** 'glass — handle with care'; **„~, bissiger Hund"** 'beware of the dog'; **~ an der Bahnsteigkante** stand back from the edge of the platform; **„~, Stufe!"** 'mind the step!'; **„~, Steinschlag"** 'danger, falling rocks'; **„~, frisch gestrichen"** 'wet paint'

vorsichtig /-zɪçtɪç/ **1** *Adj.* careful; (bei Risiko, Gefahr) cautious; careful; (umsichtig) circumspect; cautious; guarded ⟨*remark, hint, question, optimism*⟩; cautious, conservative ⟨*estimate*⟩; **sei ~!** be careful!; take care! **2** *adv.* carefully; with care; **~ optimistisch** guardedly *or* cautiously optimistic; **etw. ~ andeuten** hint at sth. cautiously; **~ geschätzt** at a conservative estimate

vorsichts·halber *Adv.* as a precaution; to be on the safe side

Vorsichts·maßnahme *die* precautionary measure; precaution

Vor·silbe *die* (Präfix) prefix

vor|singen 1 *unr. tr. V.* sing (*Dat.* to). 2 *unr. itr. V.* (a) sing (*Dat.* to); **wenn er ∼ soll** when he has to sing in public *or* in front of people; (b) (zur Prüfung) have *or* take a singing test; **bei der Oper ∼:** audition for *or* have an audition with the opera company

vor·sintflutlich *Adj.* (ugs.) antiquated

Vor·sitz *der* chairmanship; **den ∼ haben** be the chairman; be in the chair; (im Gericht) preside over the trial

Vorsitzende *der/die; adj. Dekl.* chair[person]; (bes. Mann) chairman; (Frau auch) chairwoman

Vor·sorge *die; o. Pl.* precautions *pl.;* (für den Todesfall, Krankheit, Alter) provisions *pl.;* (Vorbeugung) prevention; **∼ treffen** take precautions (**gegen** against)/make provisions (**für** for)

vor|sorgen *itr. V.* make provisions

Vorsorge·untersuchung *die* (Med.) medical check-up

vorsorglich 1 *Adj.* precautionary ⟨*measure, check-up, etc.*⟩. 2 *adv.* as a precaution

Vor·spann *der* (Film, Ferns.) opening credits *pl.*

Vor·speise *die* starter; hors d'œuvre

Vor·spiegelung *die:* **unter ∼ falscher Tatsachen** under false pretences

Vor·spiel *das* (a) (Theater) prologue; (Musik) prelude; (b) (vorm Geschlechtsakt) foreplay

vor|spielen 1 *tr. V.* (a) play ⟨*piece of music*⟩ (*Dat.* to, for); act out, perform ⟨*scene*⟩ (*Dat.* for, in front of); (b) (vorspiegeln) feign (*Dat.* to); **spiel uns doch nichts vor!** don't try and fool us!; **jmdm. Theater/eine Komödie ∼:** put on an act for sb. 2 *itr. V.* (a) play (*Dat.* to, for); (b) (bei einer Bewerbung) audition, have an audition (**bei** for)

Vor·sprache *die* (österr.) visit (**bei** to)

vor|sprechen 1 *unr. tr. V.* (a) **jmdm. etw. ∼:** pronounce *or* say sth. first for sb.; (b) (zur Prüfung) recite. 2 *unr. itr. V.* (a) (zur Prüfung) recite one's examination piece; (bei Bewerbungen) audition; **am Theater ∼:** audition for the Theatre; **jmdm. ∼ lassen** audition sb.; (b) (einen Besuch machen) **bei jmdm. [in einer Angelegenheit] ∼:** call on sb. about a matter; **bei** *od.* **auf einer Behörde ∼:** call at an office

vor|springen *unr. itr. V.; mit sein* (a) (ugs.) jump out (**hinter** + *Dat.* from behind); (b) (vorstehen) jut out; project; **ein ∼des Kinn** a prominent chin

Vor·sprung *der* (a) lead; **einen ∼ [vor jmdm.] haben** have a lead [over sb.]; be ahead [of sb.]; **jmdm. zehn Schritte/Minuten ∼ geben** give sb. ten paces'/minutes' start; (b) (vorspringender Teil) projection; (Fels∼) ledge

Vor·stadt *die* suburb; **in der ∼ wohnen** live in the suburbs

vor·städtisch *Adj.* suburban

Vor·stand *der* (a) (einer Firma) board [of directors]; (eines Vereins) executive committee; (einer Partei) executive; **im ∼ sein** be on the board/executive committee/executive; (b) ⇒ **Vorstandsmitglied**

Vorstands·mitglied *das* ⇒ **Vorstand a:** member of the board; board member; member of the executive committee; member of the executive

vor|stehen *unr. itr. V.* (a) ⟨*house, roof, etc.*⟩ project, jut out; ⟨*teeth, chin*⟩ stick out; ⟨*cheek-bones*⟩ be prominent; **∼de Zähne** buck-teeth; projecting teeth; (b) (geh.) **einer Institution/dem Haushalt ∼:** be the head of an institution/the household; **einer Abteilung ∼:** be in charge of *or* run a department

vorstehend *Adj.* above *attrib;* **im Vorstehenden** above; **das Vorstehende** the above

Vorsteher *der;* **∼s, ∼:** head; (einer Gemeinde) chairman; (eines Klosters) abbot

Vorsteher·drüse *die* ▶ 326 | prostate [gland]

Vorsteherin *die;* **∼, ∼nen** head; (eines Klosters) abbess

vorstell·bar *Adj.* conceivable; imaginable

vor|stellen 1 *tr. V.* (a) put ⟨*leg, foot, etc.*⟩ out *or* forward; **die Uhr ∼:** put the clock forward; (b) (bekannt machen;

auch fig.) introduce; **jmdn./sich jmdm. ∼:** introduce sb./oneself to sb.; (c) **sich ∼** (bei Bewerbung) come/go for [an] interview (**bei** with); (d) (darstellen) represent; **er stellt etwas vor** (ugs.) (sieht gut aus) he looks good; (gilt als Persönlichkeit) he is somebody. 2 *refl. V.* (a) **sich** (*Dat.*) **etw. ∼:** imagine sth.; **ich habe mir das Wochenende ganz anders vorgestellt** the weekend was not at all what I had imagined; **ich kann ihn mir gut als Lehrer ∼:** I can easily imagine *or* see him as a teacher; **man stelle sich** (*Dat.*) **bitte einmal vor, dass …:** just imagine that …; (b) **sich** (*Dat.*) **unter etw.** (*Dat.*) **etw. ∼:** understand sth. by sth.; **darunter kann ich mir nichts ∼:** it doesn't mean anything to me

Vor·stellung *die* (a) (Begriff) idea; **er macht sich** (*Dat.*) **keine ∼ [davon], welche Mühe das kostet** he has no idea how much effort that costs; **das entspricht ganz/nicht meinen ∼en** that is exactly/not what I had in mind; (b) *o. Pl.* (Fantasie) imagination; **das geht über alle ∼ hinaus** it is unimaginable; (c) (Aufführung) performance; (im Kino) showing; **eine schwache ∼ geben** (fig.) perform badly; (d) (das Bekanntmachen) introduction; (e) (Präsentation) presentation; (f) (bei Bewerbung) interview

Vorstellungs-: **∼gespräch** *das* interview; **∼kraft** *die; o. Pl.,* **∼vermögen** *das; o. Pl.* [powers *pl.* of] imagination

Vor·stopper *der* (Fußball) central defender

Vor·stoß *der* advance; **einen ∼ unternehmen** push forward; advance

vor|stoßen *unr. itr. V.; mit sein* advance; push forward

Vor·strafe *die* (Rechtsw.) previous conviction

Vorstrafen·register *das* criminal records *pl.*

vor|strecken *tr. V.* (a) stretch ⟨*arm, hand*⟩ out; stick out ⟨*stomach*⟩; **den Kopf/Hals ∼:** crane one's neck forward; (b) (auslegen) advance ⟨*money, sum*⟩

Vor·stufe *die* preliminary stage

Vor·tag *der* day before; previous day; **am ∼ der Prüfung** the day before *or* on the eve of the examination

vor|tanzen 1 *tr. V.* **er tanzte ihnen den Foxtrott vor** he showed them *or* demonstrated how to dance the foxtrot. 2 *itr. V.* demonstrate one's dancing ability

vor|tasten *refl. V.* (auch fig.) feel one's way forward

vor|täuschen *tr. V.* feign ⟨*interest, illness, etc.*⟩; simulate ⟨*reality etc.*⟩; fake ⟨*crime*⟩

Vor·täuschung *die* ⇒ **vortäuschen:** feigning; simulation; faking

Vor·teil *der* 'fortail/ *der* advantage; **jmdm. gegenüber im ∼ sein** have an advantage over sb.; **[für jmdn.] von ∼ sein** be advantageous [to sb.]; **sich zu seinem ∼ verändern** change for the better

vorteilhaft 1 *Adj.* advantageous. 2 *adv.* advantageously; **sich ∼ auswirken** have a favourable *or* beneficial effect; **sich ∼ kleiden** wear clothes that suit one

Vortrag /-traːk/ *der;* **∼[e]s, Vorträge** /-trɛːgə/ (a) (Rede) talk; (wissenschaftlich) lecture; **einen ∼ halten** give a talk/lecture; (b) (Darbietung) presentation; performance; (eines Gedichts) recitation; rendering

vor|tragen *unr. tr. V.* (a) perform ⟨*gymnastic routine etc.*⟩; sing ⟨*song*⟩; perform, play ⟨*piece of music*⟩; recite ⟨*poem*⟩; (b) present ⟨*case, matter, request, demands*⟩; lodge, make ⟨*complaint*⟩; express ⟨*wish, desire*⟩

Vortragende *der/die; adj. Dekl.:* ⇒ **Vortrag a:** speaker; lecturer

Vortrags-: **∼reihe** *die* series of lectures/talks; **∼reise** *die* lecture tour

vor·trefflich 1 *Adj.* excellent; splendid; superb ⟨*singer, swimmer, etc.*⟩. 2 *adv.* excellently; splendidly; ⟨*sing, swim, etc.*⟩ superbly

vor|treiben *unr. tr. V.* drive ⟨*tunnel, shaft*⟩

vor|treten *unr. itr. V.; mit sein* step forward

Vor·tritt *der:* **jmdm. den ∼ lassen** (auch fig.) let sb. go first

vorüber *Adv.* (a) (zeitlich) over; **∼ sein** be over; ⟨*pain*⟩ be gone; ⟨*danger*⟩ be past; **das ist aus und ∼** (ugs.) that is [all] over and done with; (b) (räumlich) past; **an etw.** (*Dat.*) **∼:** past sth.

vorüber|gehen *unr. itr. V.; mit sein* **(a)** go *or* walk past; pass by; **an jmdm./etw. ~:** go past sb./sth.; pass sb./sth.; (achtlos) pass sb./sth. by; (fig.) ignore sb./sth.; **im Vorübergehen** in passing; (fig.: nebenbei) in a trice; **(b)** (vergehen) pass; ‹*pain*› go; ‹*storm*› pass, blow over; **das geht vorüber** (ugs.) (tröstend) it'll pass; (scherzh. iron.) that won't last long

vorübergehend 1 *Adj.* temporary; passing ‹*interest etc.*›; brief ‹*illness*›. **2** *adv.* temporarily; (kurz) for a short time; briefly

Vor·urteil *das* bias; (voreilige Schlussfolgerung) prejudice (**gegen** against, towards); **gegen etw. ~e haben** be biased/prejudiced against *or* towards sth.

Vor·väter *Pl.* forefathers

Vor·vergangenheit *die* (Sprachw.) pluperfect

Vor·verkauf *der* advance sale of tickets; advance booking

vor|verlegen *tr. V.* (zeitlich) bring forward (**um** by)

Vor·verurteilung *die* condemnation in advance of trial

vor·vor·gestern *Adv.* (ugs.) three days ago; the day before the day before yesterday

Vorwahl *die* **(a)** (Politik) preliminary election; (in den USA) primary; **(b)** (Fernspr.) dialling code

Vorwand *der;* ~**[e]s, Vorwände** pretext; (Ausrede) excuse; **etw. zum ~ nehmen** use sth. as a pretext/an excuse

vor|warnen *tr. V.* jmdn. ~: give sb. advance warning; warn sb. [in advance]; **vorgewarnt sein** be forewarned

vor·wärts *Adv.* forwards; (weiter) onwards; (mit der Vorderseite voran) facing forwards; **ein Schritt ~** (auch fig.) a step forwards; **ein Salto ~:** a forward somersault; **~ kommen** make progress; (im Beruf, Leben) get on; get ahead

*vorwärts|kommen ⇨ **vorwärts**

Vor·wäsche *die* prewash

vor·weg *Adv.* **(a)** (vorher) beforehand; **(b)** (voraus) in front; ahead

vorweg|nehmen *unr. tr. V.* anticipate; **um das Ergebnis vorwegzunehmen, ...:** to come straight to the result ...

vor|weisen *unr. tr. V.* produce; **etw. ~ können, etw. vorzuweisen haben** (fig.) possess sth.

vor|werfen *unr. tr. V.* **(a)** jmdm. etw. ~: reproach sb. with sth.; (beschuldigen) accuse sb. of sth.; **jmdm. ~, etw. getan zu haben** reproach sb. with *or* accuse sb. of doing *or* having done sth.; **jmdm. Parteilichkeit ~:** accuse sb. of being biased; **ich habe mir nichts vorzuwerfen** I've nothing to reproach myself for; **(b)** etw. den Tieren ~ (hinwerfen) throw sth. to the animals

vor·wiegend *Adv.* mainly

Vor·wissen *das* previous *or* existing knowledge

vor·witzig *Adj.* bumptious; pert ‹*child*›; (neugierig) curious

Vor·wort *das; Pl.* ~e foreword; preface

Vor·wurf *der* reproach; (Beschuldigung) accusation; **jmdm. etw. zum ~ machen** reproach sb. with sth.; **jmdm. [wegen etw.] einen ~/Vorwürfe machen** reproach sb. [for sth.]; **sich** *(Dat.)* **[wegen etw.] Vorwürfe machen** reproach *or* blame oneself [for sth.]

vorwurfs·voll 1 *Adj.* reproachful. **2** *adv.* reproachfully

Vor·zeichen *das* **(a)** (Omen) omen; **(b)** (Math.) [algebraic] sign; (Musik) sharp/flat [sign]; (für Tonart) key signature

vor|zeigen *tr. V.* show; produce, show ‹*passport, ticket, etc.*›

Vor·zeit *die* prehistory; **in grauer ~:** in the dim and distant past

vorzeitig 1 *Adj.* premature; early ‹*retirement*›. **2** *adv.* prematurely; ‹*be retired*› early

vor|ziehen *unr. tr. V.* **(a)** (lieber mögen) prefer (*Dat.* to); (bevorzugen) favour, give preference to ‹*person*›; **(b)** (zuziehen) draw ‹*curtain*›; **(c)** (vorverlegen) bring forward ‹*date*› (**um** by); **(d)** (nach vorn ziehen) pull forward

Vor·zimmer *das* outer office; ante-room

Vor·zug *der* **(a)** o. Pl. preference (**gegenüber** over); **jmdm./einer Sache den ~ geben** prefer sb./sth.; **(b)**

(gute Eigenschaft) good quality; merit; (Vorteil) advantage; **(c)** (österr. Schulw.) distinction

vorzüglich /foˈɐ̯ʦyːklɪç/ **1** *Adj.* excellent; first-rate. **2** *adv.* excellently; **~ speisen** have an excellent meal

vorzugs·weise *Adv.* preferably

Voten ⇨ **Votum**

Votum /ˈvoːtʊm/ *das;* ~s, **Voten** vote

vulgär /vʊlˈɡɛːɐ̯/ **1** *Adj.* vulgar. **2** *adv.* in a vulgar way; **sich ~ ausdrücken** use vulgar language

Vulkan /vʊlˈkaːn/ *der;* ~s, ~e volcano

vulkanisch *Adj.* volcanic

vulkanisieren *tr. V.* vulcanize

v. u. Z. *Abk.* **vor unserer Zeit[rechnung]** BC

w, W /veː/ *das;* ~s, ~: w, W

W *Abk.* **(a)** West, Westen W.; **(b)** Watt W.

WAA /veːaːˈaː/ *die;* ~, ~s *Abk.* **Wiederaufbereitungsanlage**

Waage /ˈvaːɡə/ *die;* ~, ~n **(a)** [pair *sing.* of] scales *pl.;* (Gold~, Apotheker~ usw.) balance; **er bringt 80 kg auf die ~** (ugs.) he tips the scales at 80 kilos; **sich** *(Dat.)* **die ~ halten** balance out; balance one another; **(b)** (Astrol., Astron.) Libra

waage·recht 1 *Adj.* horizontal. **2** *adv.* horizontally

Waage·rechte *die; adj. Dekl.:* ⇨ **Horizontale**

Waag·schale *die* scale pan; **etw. in die ~ werfen** (fig.) bring sth. to bear

wabb[e]lig /ˈvab(ə)lɪç/ *Adj.* (ugs.) wobbly; flabby ‹*muscles*›

Wabe /ˈvaːbə/ *die;* ~, ~n honeycomb

Waben·honig *der* comb honey

wabern *itr. V.* (geh.) **(a)** ‹*smoke, mist, cloud*› swirl, drift; ‹*steam*› billow; (fig.) fluctuate; **(b)** (flackern, lodern) ‹*flames etc.*› flicker

wach /vax/ **1** *Adj.* **(a)** awake; **in ~em Zustand** in a state of wakefulness; **jmdn. ~ machen** wake sb. up; **~werden** wake up; **das Interesse/die Erinnerung usw. ~ halten** (fig.) keep the interest/memory etc. alive; **(b)** (aufmerksam, rege) alert ‹*mind, eyes, etc.*›; attentive ‹*audience*›; lively, keen ‹*interest*›. **2** *adv.* alertly; attentively

Wach·ablösung *die* changing of the guard/watch

Wache /ˈvaxə/ *die;* ~, ~n **(a)** (Wachdienst) (Milit.) guard *or* sentry duty; (Seew.) watch; **~ haben** *od.* **halten** (Milit.) be on guard *or* sentry duty; (Seew.) be on watch; have the watch; **~ stehen** (Milit.) stand on guard; **(b)** (Wächter) guard; (Milit.: Posten) sentry; **(c)** (Mannschaft) (Milit.) guard; (Seew.) watch; **(d)** (Polizei~) police station

wachen *itr. V.* **(a)** (geh.) be awake; **(b)** bei jmdm. ~: stay up at sb.'s bedside; sit up with sb.; **(c)** über etw. *(Akk.)* ~: watch over *or* keep an eye on sth.; **er wachte darüber, dass ...:** he watched carefully to ensure that ...

wach-, Wach-: ~|**halten:** ⇨ **wach 1 a;** ~**hund** *der* guard dog; watchdog; ~**lokal** *das* (Milit.) guardroom; ~**mann** *der; Pl.* ~**männer** *od.* ~**leute** **(a)** watchman; **(b)** (österr.: Polizist) policeman; ~**mannschaft** *die* (Milit.) guard detachment

Wacholder /vaˈxɔldɐ/ *der;* ~s, ~ **(a)** juniper; **(b)** (Schnaps) *spirit from juniper berries;* ≈ gin

wach-, Wach-: ~**posten** *der* (Milit.) guard; sentry; ~|**rufen** *unr. tr. V.* awaken, rouse ‹*enthusiasm, ambition, etc.*›; evoke, bring back ‹*memory, past*›; ~|**rütteln** *tr. V.* rouse *or* shake ‹*sb.*› out of his/her apathy; stir ‹*conscience*›

Wachs /vaks/ *das;* ~es, ~e wax

wachsam /ˈvaxzaːm/ **1** *Adj.* watchful; vigilant; **sei ~!** be on your guard!. **2** *adv.* vigilantly

Wạchsamkeit *die;* ~: vigilance

wachsen[1] /'vaksn̩/ *unr. itr. V.; mit sein* **(a)** (auch fig.) grow; ‹*building*› rise; **sich** (*Dat.*) **einen Bart** ~ **lassen** grow a beard; **sich** (*Dat.*) **die Haare** ~ **lassen** let one's hair grow long; **(b)** (fig.: allmählich entstehen) evolve [naturally]; **eine gewachsene Ordnung** an organic order

wachsen[2] *tr. V.* wax

wächsern /'vɛksɐn/ *Adj.* (geh.: bleich) waxen

Wạchs-: ~**figur** *die* waxwork; wax figure; ~**figuren·kabinett** *das* waxworks *sing. or pl.;* waxworks museum

wächst /vɛkst/ *2. u. 3. Pers. Sg. Präsens v.* **wachsen**

Wạch·stube *die* (Milit.) guardroom; (Polizeiwache) duty room

Wạchstum /'vakstu:m/ *das;* ~s growth

wạchstums-, Wạchstums-: ~**fördernd** *Adj.* promoting growth *postpos.;* ~**hemmend** *Adj.* inhibiting growth *postpos.;* ~**hormon** *das* growth hormone

Wạchtel /'vaxtl̩/ *die;* ~, ~n quail

Wächter /'vɛçtɐ/ *der;* ~s, ~: guard; (Leib~) bodyguard; (Nacht~, Turm~) watchman; (Park~) [park-]keeper

Wạcht-: ~**meister** *der* ▶34◀ constable (Brit.); patrolman (Amer.); **Herr** ~**meister** (Anrede) officer; ~**posten** *der* ⇨ **Wachposten**

Wạch·traum *der* daydream; waking dream

Wạch[t]·turm *der* watchtower

wạckelig **1** *Adj.* **(a)** (nicht stabil) wobbly ‹*chair, table, etc.*›; loose ‹*tooth*›; shaky, rickety ‹*structure*›; rickety ‹*car, furniture*›; **(b)** (ugs.: kraftlos, schwach) frail ‹*person*›; frail, doddery ‹*old person*›; ~ **auf den Beinen sein** be a bit shaky on one's feet; **(c)** (fig. ugs.: gefährdet, bedroht) dodgy (Brit. coll.) ‹*business*›; insecure, shaky ‹*job*›; **er steht in der Schule/in Latein ziemlich** ~: things are dodgy for him at school (Brit. coll.) /his Latin is somewhat shaky. **2** *adv.* ~ **stehen** be wobbly

Wạckel·kontakt *der* (Elektrot.) loose connection

wạckeln /'vakl̩n/ *itr. V.* **(a)** wobble; ‹*post etc.*› move about; ‹*tooth etc.*› be loose; ‹*house, window, etc.*› shake; **mit dem Kopf/den Hüften** ~: waggle *or* wag one's head/wiggle one's hips; **mit dem Schwanz** ~: wag its tail; **(b)** *mit sein* (ugs.: gehen) ‹*person*› totter; **(c)** (ugs.: gefährdet, bedroht sein) ‹*job, government*› be insecure; ‹*firm*› be in a dodgy (Brit. coll.) *or* shaky state

Wạckel·peter *der;* ~s, ~ (ugs.) wobbly jelly

wạcker /'vakɐ/ (veralt.) **1** *Adj.* **(a)** (rechtschaffen) upright; decent; (iron.) trusty; worthy; **(b)** (tapfer) valiant; **(c)** (tüchtig) hearty ‹*drinker, eater*›. **2** *adv.* **(a)** (tapfer) valiantly; **sich** ~ **schlagen** put up a good show; **(b)** (tüchtig) ‹*eat, drink, etc.*› heartily

wạcklig /'vaklɪç/ ⇨ **wackelig**

Wade /'va:də/ *die;* ~, ~n ▶326◀ calf

Wạffe /'vafə/ *die;* ~, ~n (auch fig.) weapon; (Feuer~) firearm; ~**n tragen** bear arms; **Kriegsdienst mit der** ~: service under arms; **unter** ~**n** under arms; **die** ~**n strecken** lay down one's arms; (fig.) give up the struggle

Wạffel /'vafl̩/ *die;* ~, ~n **(a)** waffle; (dünne ~, Eis~) wafer; **(b)** (Eistüte) cone

Wạffel·eisen *das* waffle-iron

Wạffen-: ~**gewalt** *die;* **mit** ~**gewalt** by force of arms; ~**handel** *der* arms trade; arms trading; ~**lager** *das* arsenal; ~**ruhe** *die* ceasefire; ~**schein** *der* firearms licence; ~**still·stand** *der* armistice; [permanent] cease-fire

Wạge·mut *der* daring; audacity

wạge·mutig *Adj.* daring; audacious

wagen /'va:gn̩/ **1** *tr. V.* risk; **[es]** ~, **etw. zu tun** dare to do sth.; **einen Versuch** ~: dare to make an attempt; risk an attempt; *s. auch* **gewagt 2**. **2** *refl. V.* **sich irgendwohin/nicht irgendwohin** ~: venture somewhere/not dare to go somewhere

Wagen *der;* ~s, ~: **(a)** (PKW) car; (Omnibus) bus; (LKW) truck; lorry (Brit.); (Liefer~) van; **(b)** (Pferde~) cart; (Kutsche) coach; carriage; (Plan~) wagon; (Zirkus~, Wohn~) caravan

(Brit.); trailer (esp. Amer.); **der Große** ~ (Astron.) the Plough; the Big Dipper (Amer.); **jmdm. an den** ~ **fahren** (fig. ugs.) give sb. what for (sl.); pitch into sb. (coll.); **(c)** (Eisenbahn~) (Personen~) coach; carriage; (Güter~) truck; wagon; car (Amer.); (Straßenbahn~) car; **(d)** (Kinder~, Puppen~) pram (Brit.); baby carriage (Amer.); (Sport~) pushchair (Brit.); stroller (Amer.); **(e)** (Hand~) handcart; **(f)** (Einkaufs~) [shopping] trolley

Wagen-: ~**burg** *die* **(a)** (hist.) [defensive] circle of wagons; **(b)** *urban, gypsy-style encampment;* ~**heber** *der* jack; ~**park** *der* vehicle pool; ~**rad** *das* cartwheel

Waggon /va'gɔŋ, *südd., österr.:* va'goːn/ *der;* ~s, ~s, *südd., österr.:* ~s, ~e wagon; truck (Brit.); car (Amer.)

waghalsig **1** *Adj.* daring; risky ‹*speculation*›; (leichtsinnig) reckless ‹*driver, rider*›. **2** *adv.* daringly; ‹*speculate*› riskily; (leichtsinnig) recklessly

Wagnis /'va:knɪs/ *das;* ~ses, ~se daring exploit *or* feat; (Risiko) risk

Wahl /va:l/ *die;* ~, ~en **(a)** *o. Pl.* choice; **eine/seine** ~ **treffen** make a/one's choice; **jmdm. die** ~ **lassen** let sb. choose; **mir bleibt** *od.* **ich habe keine [andere]** ~: I have no choice *or* alternative; **es stehen drei Menüs zur Wahl** there are three set meals to choose from; **die** ~ **fiel auf ihn** the choice fell on him; **in die engere** ~ **kommen** be short-listed *or* put on the shortlist (Brit.); **(b)** (in ein Gremium, Amt) election; **in Hessen ist** ~ *od.* **sind** ~**en** there are elections in Hessen; **sich zur** ~ **stellen** stand *or* (Amer.) run for election; **geheime** ~: secret ballot; **(c)** (Güteklasse) quality; **die Socken sind zweite** ~: the socks are seconds

wählbar *Adj.* eligible for election *postpos.*

wahl-, Wahl-: ~**berechtigt** *Adj.* eligible *or* entitled to vote *postpos.;* ~**berechtigte** *der/die; adj. Dekl.* person entitled to vote; ~**beteiligung** *die* turnout; ~**bezirk** *der* ward

wählen /'vɛːlən/ **1** *tr. V.* **(a)** choose; select ‹*station, programme, etc.*›; **seine Worte [sorgfältig]** ~: choose one's words [carefully]; **(b)** (Fernspr.) dial ‹*number*›; **(c)** (durch Stimmabgabe) elect **(in** + *Akk.* to); **jmdn. zum Vorsitzenden** ~: elect sb. as chairman; **(d)** (stimmen für) vote for ‹*party, candidate*›. **2** *itr. V.* **(a)** choose **(zwischen** + *Dat.* between); **haben Sie schon gewählt?** (im Lokal) are you ready to order?; **(b)** (Fernspr.) dial; **(c)** (stimmen) vote; **wann wird gewählt?** when are the elections?

Wähler *der;* ~s, ~: voter

Wahl·ergebnis *das* election result

Wählerin *die;* ~, ~nen voter

wählerisch *Adj.* choosy; particular **(in** + *Dat.* about)

Wählerschaft *die;* ~, ~en electorate

wahl-, Wahl-: ~**fach** *das* (Schulw.) optional subject; ~**gang** *der* ballot; ~**geheimnis** *das* secrecy *or* confidentiality of the ballot; ~**geschenk** *das* pre-election bonus; ~**heimat** *die* adopted country/place of residence; ~**kabine** *die* polling booth; ~**kampf** *der* election campaign; ~**kreis** *der* constituency; ~**lokal** *das* polling station; ~**los** **1** *Adj.* indiscriminate; random; **2** *adv.* indiscriminately; at random; ~**programm** *das* election manifesto; ~**propaganda** *die* election propaganda; ~**recht** *das* **(a)** *o.Pl.* [aktives] ~**recht** right to vote; (innere Gruppe) franchise; **passives** ~**recht** right to stand [as a candidate] for election; **(b)** (Rechtsvorschriften) electoral law; ~**rede** *die* election speech

Wạhl·scheibe *die* (Fernspr.) dial

wahl-, Wahl-: ~**schein** *der* voting permit (esp. for postal voter); ~**sieg** *der* election victory; ~**spruch** *der* motto; ~**urne** *die* ballot box; ~**weise** *Adv.* as desired; to choice; ~**weise ... oder ...:** either ... or ... [as desired]; ~**wieder·holung** *die* (Fernspr.) redial

Wahn /va:n/ *der;* ~[e]s **(a)** mania; **(b)** (Täuschung) delusion; **er lebt in dem** ~, **dass ...:** he is labouring under the delusion that ...

wähnen /'vɛːnən/ *tr. V.* (geh.) think [mistakenly]; imagine; **jmdn. in Sicherheit** *od.* **sicher** ~: imagine *or* think sb. is safe

wahn-, Wahn-: ~**sinn** *der; o. Pl.* **(a)** insanity; madness; **(b)** (ugs.: Unvernunft) madness; lunacy; **das ist ja**

∼**sinn!** that's just crazy!; (c) ∼**sinn!** (salopp) incredible! (coll.); ∼**sinnig** 1 *Adj.* (a) insane; mad; ∼**sinnig werden** go insane; **wie** ∼**sinnig** (ugs.) like mad *or* crazy (coll.); **ich werde** ∼**sinnig!** (ugs.) fantastic! (coll.); (b) (ugs.: ganz unvernünftig) mad; crazy; (c) (ugs.: groß, heftig, intensiv) terrific (coll.) ⟨*effort, speed, etc.*⟩; terrible (coll.) ⟨*fright, job, pain*⟩. 2 *adv.* (ugs.) incredibly (coll.); terribly (coll.)

Wahnsinnige *der/die; adj. Dekl.* maniac; madman/madwoman

wahr /vaːɐ̯/ *Adj.* (a) true; [**das**] **ist ja gar nicht** ∼! that's just not true!; **du hast Hunger, nicht** ∼? you're hungry, aren't you?; **nicht** ∼**, er weiß es doch?** he does know, doesn't he?; **das darf [doch] nicht** ∼ **sein!** I don't believe it!; **etw.** ∼ **machen** carry sth. out; (b) *nicht präd.* (wirklich) real ⟨*reason, motive, feelings, joy, etc.*⟩; actual ⟨*culprit*⟩; true, real ⟨*friend, friendship, love, art*⟩; veritable ⟨*miracle*⟩; **im** ∼**sten Sinne des Wortes** in the truest sense of the word; **das ist das einzig Wahre** (ugs.) that's just what the doctor ordered (coll.)

wahren *tr. V.* (geh.) preserve, maintain ⟨*balance, equality, neutrality, etc.*⟩; maintain, assert ⟨*authority, right*⟩; keep ⟨*secret*⟩; defend, safeguard ⟨*interests, rights, reputation*⟩; *s. auch* **Distanz b; Form e**

während /ˈvɛːrən/ *itr. V.* (geh.) last; **ein lange** ∼**der Prozess** a process of long duration; **was lange währt, wird endlich gut** (Spr.) it will be/was worth it in the end

während /ˈvɛːrənt/ 1 *Konj.* (a) (zeitlich) while; (b) (adversativ) whereas. 2 *Präp. mit Gen.* during; (über einen Zeitraum von) for; ∼ **des ganzen Tages/Abends** all day [long]/throughout the [entire] evening

wahr|haben *unr. tr. V.* **etw. nicht** ∼ **wollen** not want to admit sth.

wahrhaftig 1 *Adj.* (geh.) truthful ⟨*person*⟩; **der** ∼**e Gott** the true God. 2 *adv.* really; genuinely

Wahrheit *die;* ∼, ∼**en** truth

wahrheits-, Wahrheits-: ∼**gemäß** 1 *Adj.* truthful; accurate ⟨*information*⟩; 2 *adv.* truthfully; ∼**getreu** 1 *Adj.* truthful; 2 *adv.* truthfully; ∼**liebe** *die* love of truth

wahrnehmbar *Adj.* perceptible

wahr|nehmen *unr. tr. V.* (a) perceive, discern; (spüren) feel; detect ⟨*sound, smell*⟩; (bemerken) notice; be aware of; (erkennen, ausmachen) make out; discern; detect, discern ⟨*atmosphere, undertone*⟩; (b) (nutzen) take advantage of ⟨*opportunity*⟩; exploit ⟨*advantage*⟩; exercise ⟨*right*⟩; (c) (vertreten) look after ⟨*sb.'s interests, affairs*⟩; (d) (erfüllen, ausführen) carry out, perform ⟨*function, task, duty*⟩; fulfil ⟨*responsibility*⟩

Wahrnehmung *die;* ∼, ∼**en** (a) perception; (eines Sachverhalts) awareness; (eines Geruchs, eines Tons) detection; (b) (Nutzung) (eines Rechts) exercise; (einer Gelegenheit, eines Vorteils) exploitation; (c) (Vertretung) representation; (d) (einer Funktion, Aufgabe, Pflicht) performance; execution; (einer Verantwortung) fulfilment

wahr|sagen; ich wahrsage/sage wahr, gewahrsagt/wahrsagt/wahrgesagt, zu wahrsagen/wahrzusagen 1 *itr. V.* tell fortunes; **aus den Karten/den Handlinien** ∼: read the cards/palms. 2 *tr. V.* predict, foretell ⟨*future*⟩; **sie hat ihm gewahrsagt, dass er …:** she predicted that he …

Wahrsager *der;* ∼**s**, ∼, **Wahrsagerin** *die;* ∼, ∼**nen** fortune-teller

wahrscheinlich 1 *Adj.* probable; likely; ∼ **klingen** sound plausible; **wenig** ∼: not very likely. 2 *adv.* probably

Wahrscheinlichkeit *die;* ∼, ∼**en** probability (also Math.); likelihood; **mit einiger/hoher** *od.* **großer** ∼: quite/very probably; **aller** ∼ **nach** in all probability

Wahrung *die;* ∼: preservation; maintenance; (eines Geheimnisses) keeping; (von Interessen, Rechten, Ruf) defence; safeguarding

Währung *die;* ∼, ∼**en** currency

Währungs-: ∼**einheit** *die* currency unit; monetary unit; ∼**reform** *die* currency reform; ∼**union** *die* currency union

Wahr·zeichen *das* symbol; (einer Stadt) [most famous] landmark

Waise /ˈvaɪzə/ *die;* ∼, ∼**n** orphan; **er/sie ist** ∼: he/she is an orphan

Waisen-: ∼**haus** *das* orphanage; ∼**kind** *das* orphan; ∼**rente** *die* orphan's [social] benefit

Wal /vaːl/ *der;* ∼**[e]s**, ∼**e** whale

Wald /valt/ *der;* ∼**[e]s, Wälder** /ˈvɛldɐ/ wood; (größer) forest; **viel** ∼: a great deal of woodland; **den** ∼ **vor [lauter] Bäumen nicht sehen** (fig.) not see the wood for the trees

Wald-: ∼**arbeiter** *der* forestry worker; ∼**brand** *der* forest fire

Wäldchen /ˈvɛltçən/ *das* copse; spinney

Wald-: ∼**frevel** *der* ⇒ **Forstfrevel**; ∼**gebiet** *das* forest area

waldig *Adj.* wooded

wald-, Wald-: ∼**lauf** *der:* [einen] ∼**lauf machen** go jogging through the woods; ∼**meister** *der; o. pl.* (Bot.) woodruff; ∼**reich** *Adj.* densely wooded; ∼**sterben** *das* death of the forest [as a result of pollution]; ∼**stück** *das* piece of woodland; ∼**weg** *der* forest path; (für Fahrzeuge) forest track

Wal-: ∼**fang** *der; o. Pl.* whaling *no def. art.;* ∼**fänger** *der* whaler; ∼**fisch** *der* (ugs.) whale

Waliser /vaˈliːzɐ/ *der;* ∼**s**, ∼: ▶ 388 | Welshman

Waliserin *die;* ∼, ∼**nen** Welshwoman

walisisch /vaˈliːzɪʃ/ *Adj.* ▶ 388 |, ▶ 487 | Welsh; **das Walisische** Welsh

Wall /val/ *der;* ∼**[e]s, Wälle** /ˈvɛlə/ earthwork; embankment; rampart (esp. Mil.)

Wallach /ˈvalax/ *der;* ∼**[e]s**, ∼**e** gelding

wallen *itr. V.* (a) boil; (b) ∼**des Haar/**∼**de Gewänder** (geh.) flowing hair/robes

wall-, Wall-: ∼**fahren** *itr. V.; mit sein* make a pilgrimage; ∼**fahrer** *der* pilgrim; ∼**fahrt** *die* pilgrimage

Wall·fahrts-: ∼**kirche** *die* pilgrimage church; ∼**ort** *der* place of pilgrimage

Wal·nuss, *Wal·nuß /ˈvalnʊs/ *die* walnut

Wal·ross, *Wal·roß /ˈvalrɔs/ *das; Pl.* ∼**rosse** walrus

walten /ˈvaltn̩/ *itr. V.* (geh.) ⟨*good sense, good spirit*⟩ prevail; ⟨*peace, silence, harmony, etc.*⟩ reign; **Vorsicht/ Gnade** *usw.* ∼ **lassen** exercise caution/mercy *etc.;* **Vernunft** ∼ **lassen** be reasonable; *s. auch* **Amt b, schalten 2 d**

Walze /ˈvaltsə/ *die;* ∼, ∼**n** (a) roller; (Schreib∼) platen; (b) (eines mechanischen Musikinstruments) barrel

walzen *tr. V.* roll ⟨*field, road, steel, etc.*⟩

wälzen /ˈvɛltsn̩/ 1 *tr. V.* (a) roll ⟨*round object*⟩; heave ⟨*heavy object*⟩; (drehen) roll ⟨*person etc.*⟩ over; **etw. in Mehl** ∼ (Kochk.) toss sth. in flour; (b) (fig. ugs.) **Bücher** ∼: pore over books; **Probleme** ∼: mull over problems. 2 *refl. V.* roll; (auf der Stelle) roll about *or* around; (im Krampf, vor Schmerzen) writhe around; **sich schlaflos im Bett** ∼: toss and turn in bed, unable to sleep

Walzen·dynamo *der* tread-driven dynamo

Walzer *der;* ∼**s**, ∼: waltz; **kannst du** ∼ **tanzen?** can you waltz?

Wälzer *der;* ∼**s**, ∼ (ugs.) hefty tome

Wampe /ˈvampə/ *die;* ∼, ∼**n** (ugs. abwertend) pot belly

wand *1. u. 3. Pers. Sg. Prät. v.* **winden**

Wand /vant/ *die;* ∼, **Wände** /ˈvɛndə/ (a) wall; (Trenn∼) partition; **die eigenen vier Wände** one's own four walls; **jmdn. an die** ∼ **stellen** (verhüll. ugs.) put sb. up against a wall (euphem.); ∼ **an** ∼ **wohnen** live next door to one another; be neighbours; (b) **spanische** ∼: folding screen; (c) (eines Behälters, Schiffs) side; (eines Zeltes) wall; side; (d) (Fels∼) face; wall

Wandalismus /vandaˈlɪsmʊs/ *der;* ∼: vandalism

Wand·behang *der* wall hanging

Wandel /ˈvandl̩/ *der;* ∼**s** change; **im** ∼ **der Zeiten** through the ages

wandeln 1 *refl. V.* change (**in** + *Akk.* into). 2 *tr. V.* change. 3 *itr. V.; mit sein* (geh.) stroll

Wander-: ~**ausstellung** *die* touring exhibition; ~**bühne** *die* touring company; ~**düne** *die* wandering dune

Wanderer *der;* ~**s,** ~: walker; (der weite Wege zurücklegt) rambler; hiker

Wander-: ~**falke** *der* peregrine falcon; ~**gewerbe** *das* itinerant trade; ~**heuschrecke** *die* migratory locust; ~**karte** *die* rambler's [path] map

wandern /'vandɐn/ *itr. V.; mit sein* (a) hike; ramble; (ohne Angabe des Ziels) go hiking *or* rambling; (b) (ugs.: gehen) wander (lit. *or* fig.); (fig.) ⟨*glance, eyes, thoughts*⟩ roam, wander; (c) (ziehen, reisen) travel; (ziellos) roam; ⟨*exhibition, circus, theatre*⟩ tour, travel; ⟨*animal, people, tribe*⟩ migrate; (fig.) ⟨*cloud, star*⟩ drift; ~**de Stämme** nomadic tribes; (d) ⟨*glacier, dune, island*⟩ move, shift; ⟨*kidney etc.*⟩ be displaced; (e) (ugs.: befördert werden) land; **in den Papierkorb** ~: land *or* be thrown in the waste-paper basket

Wander-: ~**pokal** *der* challenge cup; ~**ratte** *die* brown rat

Wanderschaft *die;* ~: travels *pl.*

Wanderung *die;* ~, ~**en** (a) hike; walking tour; (sehr lang) trek; **eine** ~ **machen** go on a hike/tour/trek; (b) (Zool., Soziol.) migration

Wander·weg *der* footpath (*for ramblers*)

Wandlung *die;* ~, ~**en** change; (Ver~) transformation

Wand·malerei *die* mural painting; wall painting; (Bild) mural; wall painting

Wand-: ~**schrank** *der* ⇒ **Einbauschrank;** ~**tafel** *die* [wall] blackboard

wandte /'vantə/ *1. u. 3. Pers. Prät. v.* **wenden**

Wand-: ~**teppich** *der* wall hanging; tapestry; ~**zeitung** *die* wall newspaper

Wange /'vaŋə/ *die;* ~, ~**n ▶ 326 |** (geh.) cheek; ~ **an** ~: cheek to cheek

Wankel·motor *der* Wankel engine

Wankel·mut *der* (geh.) vacillation

wankelmütig /-my:tɪç/ *Adj.* (geh.) vacillating

wanken /'vaŋkn̩/ *itr. V.* (a) sway; ⟨*person*⟩ totter; (unter einer Last) stagger; (b) *mit sein* (unsicher gehen) stagger; totter; (c) (geh.: bedroht sein) ⟨*government, empire, etc.*⟩ totter; **ins Wanken geraten** begin to totter; ⟨*theory, faith, etc.*⟩ become shaky; **ins Wanken bringen** make ⟨*monarchy, government, etc.*⟩ totter; shake ⟨*resolve, faith*⟩

wann /van/ *Adv.* when; ~ **kommst du morgen?** when *or* [at] what time are you coming tomorrow?; ~ **ist dieses Jahr Ostern?** when *or* on what date does Easter fall this year?; **seit** ~ **wohnst du dort?** how long have you been living there?; **bis** ~ **kann ich noch anrufen?** until when *or* how late can I still phone?; **von** ~ **an?** from when?; **von** ~ **bis** ~ **gilt es?** for what period is it valid?; **bis** ~ **ist das Essen fertig?** [by] when will the food be ready?; **ich weiß nicht,** ~: I don't know when; **du kannst kommen,** ~ **du willst** you can come when[ever] you like; ~ **[auch] immer** (geh.) whenever

Wanne *die;* ~, ~**n** bath[tub]

Wanst /vanst/ *der;* ~**[e]s, Wänste** /'vɛnstə/ (ugs. abwertend) belly; **sich den** ~ **vollschlagen** stuff oneself (sl.)

Wanze /'vantsə/ *die;* ~, ~**n** bug; (ugs.: Abhör~) bug (coll.)

Wappen /'vapn̩/ *das;* ~**s,** ~: coat of arms

Wappen-: ~**kunde** *die; o. Pl.* heraldry *no art.;* ~**spruch** *der* motto; ~**tier** *das* heraldic beast

wappnen *refl. V.* (geh.) forearm oneself

war /va:ɐ̯/ *1. u. 3. Pers. Sg. Prät. v.* **sein**

warb /varp/ *1. u. 3. Pers. Sg. Prät. v.* **werben**

ward /vart/ (geh.) *1. u. 3. Pers. Sg. Prät. v.* **werden**

Ware /'va:rə/ *die;* ~, ~**n** (a) ~**[n]** goods *pl.;* wares *pl.;* (einzelne ~) article; commodity (Econ., fig.); (Erzeugnis) product; **heiße** ~ (ugs.) hot goods (sl.); (b) (Kaufmannsspr.: Stoff) material

Waren-: ~**angebot** *das* range of goods; ~**annahme** *die;* „~**annahme**" 'goods in'; ~**haus** *das* department store; ~**lager** *das* (einer Fabrik o. Ä.) stores *pl.;* (eines Geschäftes) stockroom; (größer) warehouse; (Bestand)

stocks *pl.;* ~**muster** *das* sample; ~**zeichen** *das* trade mark

warf /varf/ *1. u. 3. Pers. Sg. Prät. v.* **werfen**

warm /varm/; **wärmer** /'vɛrmɐ/, **wärmst** ... /'vɛrmst .../ **1** *Adj.* (a) warm; hot ⟨*meal, food, bath, spring*⟩; hot, warm ⟨*climate, country, season, etc.*⟩; ~**e Küche** hot food; **das Essen** ~ **machen/stellen** heat up the food/keep the food warm *or* hot; **im Warmen sitzen** sit in the warm; ~ **halten** ⟨*coat, blanket, etc.*⟩ keep one warm; **etw.** ~ **halten** keep sth. warm; **sich** (*Dat.*) **jmdn.** ~ **halten** (fig. ugs.) keep on the right side of sb.; **mir ist/wird** ~: I feel warm/I'm getting warm; (**zu** ~) I feel hot/I'm getting hot; **sich** ~ **laufen** warm up; (b) (herzlich) warm ⟨*sympathy, appreciation, words, etc.*⟩; [**mit jmdm./etw.**] ~ **werden** (ugs.) warm [to sb./sth.]. **2** *adv.* warmly; ~ **essen/duschen** have a hot meal/shower

Wärme /'vɛrmə/ *die;* ~: warmth; (Hitze; Physik) heat

Wärme-: ~**isolation** *die* thermal insulation; ~**kraftwerk** *das* thermal power station; ~**lehre** *die* (Physik) theory of heat; (Thermodynamik) thermodynamics *sing., no art.*

wärmen **1** *tr. V.* warm; (aufwärmen) warm up ⟨*food, drink*⟩; **jmdn./sich** ~: warm sb./oneself up. **2** *itr. V.* be warm; (warm halten) keep one warm; **die Sonne wärmt kaum** the sun has hardly any warmth

Wärme-: ~**pumpe** *die* (Technik) heat pump; ~**strahlung** *die* thermal radiation

Wärm·flasche *die* hot-water bottle

warm-, Warm-: ~**front** *die* (Met.) warm front; *~**|halten** ⇒ **warm 1 a;** ~**herzig 1** *Adj.* warmhearted; **2** *adv.* warm-heartedly; ~**luft** *die; o. Pl.* warm air; ~**miete** *die* (ugs.) rent inclusive of heating

wärmstens /'vɛrmstn̩s/ *Adv.* warmly ⟨*recommend sth.*⟩

Warm·wasser *das; o. Pl.* hot water

Warm·wasser-: ~**heizung** *die* hot-water heating; ~**versorgung** *die* hot-water supply

Warn-: ~**blink·anlage** *die,* (ugs.) ~**blinker** *der* (Kfz-W.) hazard warning lights *pl.;* ~**dreieck** *das* (Kfz-W.) hazard warning triangle

warnen /'varnən/ *tr.* (*auch itr.*) *V.* warn (**vor** + *Dat.* of, about); **jmdn.** [**davor**] ~, **etw. zu tun** warn sb. against doing sth.; **die Polizei warnt vor Nebel/vor Taschendieben** the police have issued a fog warning/a warning against pickpockets; **ein** ~**des Beispiel** a cautionary example

Warn-: ~**schild** *das* warning sign; ~**schuss,** *~**schuß** *der* warning shot; ~**signal** *das* warning signal; ~**streik** *der* token strike

Warnung *die;* ~, ~**en** warning (**vor** + *Dat.* of, about); **das ist meine letzte** ~: that's the last warning I shall give you; I shan't warn you again

Warn·zeichen *das* warning sign

Warschau /'varʃau/ (*das*); ~**s ▶ 490 |** Warsaw

Warschauer ▶ 490 | 1 *der;* ~**s,** ~: citizen of Warsaw. **2** *indekl. Adj.* Warsaw

Warte /'vartə/ *die;* ~, ~**n** (geh.) vantage-point; **von jmds.** ~ **aus** [**gesehen**] (fig.) [seen] from sb.'s standpoint

Warte-: ~**halle** *die* waiting room; (Flugw.) departure lounge; ~**liste** *die* waiting list; **auf** ~**liste** (Flugw.) on standby

warten /'vartn̩/ **1** *itr. V.* wait (**auf** + *Akk.* for); **warte mal!** wait a moment!; just a moment!; **na warte!** (ugs.) just you wait!; „**bitte warten!**" 'wait'; (am Telefon) 'hold the line please'; **da kannst du lange** ~! (iron.) you'll have a long wait; you'll be lucky (iron.); **nicht lange auf sich** ~ **lassen** not be long in coming; **sie wollen mit dem Heiraten noch [etwas]** ~: they want to wait a little before getting married; **darauf habe ich schon lange gewartet** (iron.) I've seen that coming [for a long time]. **2** *tr. V.* service ⟨*car, machine, etc.*⟩

Wärter /'vɛrtɐ/ *der;* ~**s,** ~: attendant; (Tier~, Zoo~, Leuchtturm~) keeper; (Kranken~) orderly; (Gefängnis~) warder

Warte·raum *der* waiting room

Wärterin *die;* ~, ~**nen** ⇒ **Wärter**

Warte-: ~**saal** *der* waiting room; ~**zeit** *die* (a) wait; **nach einer** ~**zeit von einer Stunde** after waiting for

---

an hour; **(b)** (festgesetzte Frist) waiting period; **∿zimmer** *das* waiting room

-wärts /-vɛrts/ *adv.* ‹*north-, south-, up-, down-, etc.*›wards; **seit∿:** sideways

Wartung *die;* **∿, ∿en** service; (das Warten) servicing; (Instandhaltung) maintenance

warum /vaˈrʊm/ *Adv.* why; **∿ nicht gleich so?** why not do that in the first place?

Warze /ˈvartsə/ *die;* **∿, ∿n (a)** wart; **(b)** (Brust∿) nipple

was /vas/ **1** *Interrogativpron. Nom. u. Akk. u. (nach Präp.) Dat. Neutr.; s. auch (Gen.)* **wessen 1 b** *what;* **∿ kostet das?** what *or* how much does that cost?; **∿ ist er [von Beruf]?** what's his job?; **[das ist] gut, ∿?** (ugs.: nicht?) not bad, eh?; **∿ ist?, ∿ denn?** (was ist denn los?) what is it?; what's up?; **∿!** (ugs.) oh, come on!; of course not!; **für** *od.* **zu ∿ brauchst du es?** (ugs.) what do you need it for?; **∿ der alles weiß!** what a lot he knows!; **∿ es [nicht] alles gibt!** (Ding) what will they think of next?; (Ereignis) the things people will do!; **und ∿ nicht alles** (ugs.) and so on ad infinitum; **∿ [auch] immer** whatever; **∿ für [ein] …:** what sort *or* kind of … **2** *Relativpron. Nom. u. Akk. u. (nach Präp.) Dat. Neutr.; s. auch (Gen.)* **wessen 2 b: (a)** [das] **∿:** what; **alles, was …:** everything *or* all that …; **alles, ∿ ich weiß** all [that] I know; **das Beste, was du tun kannst** the best thing that you can do; **vieles/manches/nichts/dasselbe/etwas, ∿ …:** much/many things/nothing/the same one/something that …; **∿ mich betrifft/das anbelangt, [so] …:** as far as I'm/that's concerned, …; **(b)** *weiterführend* which; **er hat zugesagt, ∿ mich gefreut hat** he agreed, which pleased me; **es hat geregnet, ∿ uns aber nicht gestört hat** it rained, but that didn't bother us. **3** *Indefinitpron. Nom. u. Akk. u. (nach Präp.) Dat. Neutr.* (ugs.) **(a)** (etwas) something; (in Fragen, Verneinungen) anything; **er hat kaum ∿ gesagt** he hardly said anything *or* a thing; **ist ∿?** is anything wrong?; **so ∿:** such a thing; something like that; **nein, so ∿!** you don't say!; **so ∿ könnte mir nicht passieren** nothing like that could happen to me; **so ∿ Dummes!** how stupid!; **gibt es ∿ Neues?** Is there any news?; **aus ihm wird mal/wird nie ∿:** he'll make something of himself/he'll never come to anything; **(b)** (ein Teil) some. **4** *Adv.* (ugs.) **(a)** (warum, wozu) why; what … for; **∿ stehst du hier herum?** what are you standing around here for?; **(b)** (wie) how; **∿ hast du dich verändert!** how you've changed!

wasch-, Wasch-: **∿anlage** *die;* (Autowaschanlage) car-wash; **∿anleitung** *die* washing instructions *pl.;* **∿automat** *der* washing machine; **∿bar** *Adj.* washable; **∿bär** *der* racoon; **∿becken** *das* washbasin

Wäsche /ˈvɛʃə/ *die;* **∿, ∿n (a)** *o. Pl.* (zu waschende Textilien) washing; (für die Wäscherei) laundry; **schmutzige ∿ waschen** (fig.) wash [one's] dirty linen in public; **(b)** *o. Pl.* (Unter∿) underwear; **dumm/verdutzt aus der ∿ gucken** (ugs.) look stupid/flabbergasted; **(c)** (das Waschen) washing *no pl.;* **bei/nach der ersten ∿:** when washed for the first time/after the first wash; **in der ∿ sein** be in the wash; **große ∿ haben** be doing a big wash

wasch·echt *Adj.* **(a)** colour-fast ‹*textile, clothes*›; fast ‹*colour*›; **(b)** (fig.: echt) genuine; pukka (coll.)

Wäsche-: **∿klammer** *die* clothes-peg (Brit.); clothespin (Amer.); **∿korb** *der* laundry-basket; (für nasse Wäsche) clothes-basket; **∿leine** *die* clothes line

waschen 1 *unr. tr. V.* wash; **sich ∿:** wash [oneself]; have a wash; **jmdm./sich die Hände/das Gesicht** *usw.* **∿:** wash sb.'s/one's hands/face *etc.;* **Wäsche ∿:** do the/ some washing; **sich ge∿ haben** (fig. ugs.) be quite something. **2** *unr. itr. V.* do the washing

Wäscherei *die;* **∿, ∿en** laundry

Wäsche-: **∿schleuder** *die* spin-drier; **∿ständer** *der* clothes-airer; **∿trockner** *der* **(a)** (Maschine) tumble-drier; **(b)** (Gestell) clothes-airer

Wasch-: **∿gelegenheit** *die* washing facilities *pl.;* **∿küche** *die* **(a)** laundry-room; **(b)** (ugs.: Nebel) peasouper; **∿lappen** *der* **(a)** [face] flannel; washcloth (Amer.); **(b)** (ugs. abwertend) (Weichling) softie (coll.); (Feigling) sissy; **∿maschine** *die* washing machine; **∿mittel** *das* detergent; **∿muschel** *die* (österr.) washbasin;

∿pulver *das* washing powder; **∿raum** *der* washing-room; **∿salon** *der* launderette; laundromat (Amer.); **∿straße** *die* [automatic] car-wash

wäscht /vɛʃt/ *3. Pers. Sg. Präsens v.* **waschen**

Wasch-: **∿wasser** *das; o. Pl.* washing water; **∿zeug** *das; o. Pl.* washing things *pl.*

Wasser /ˈvasɐ/ *das;* **∿s, ∿/Wässer** /ˈvɛsɐ/ **(a)** *o. Pl.* water; **ins ∿ gehen** (zum Schwimmen) go for a swim; (verhüll.: sich ertränken) drown oneself; **direkt am ∿:** right by the water; (am Meer) right by the sea; **ein Boot zu ∿ lassen** put out *or* launch a boat; **unter ∿ stehen** be under water; be flooded; **etw. unter ∿ setzen** flood sth.; **zu ∿:** by sea; **(b)** *Pl.* **∿** (fig.) **sich über ∿** (*Dat.*) **halten** keep one's head above water; **ins ∿ fallen** fall through; **bis dahin fließt noch viel ∿ den Fluss** *od.* **Rhein** *usw.* **hinunter** a lot of water will have flowed under the bridge by then; **mit allen ∿n gewaschen sein** know all the tricks; **jmdm. das ∿ abgraben** pull the carpet from under sb.'s feet; **jmdn. nicht das ∿ reichen können** not be able to hold a candle to sb.; not be a patch on sb. (coll.); **(c)** *Pl.* **Wässer** (Mineral∿, Tafel∿) mineral water; (Heil∿) water; **(d)** *o. Pl.* (Gewässer) **ein fließendes/ stehendes ∿:** a moving/stagnant stretch of water; **(e)** *o. Pl.* (Schweiß) sweat; (Urin) water; urine; (Speichel) saliva; (Gewebsflüssigkeit) fluid; **∿ lassen** pass water; **ihm lief das ∿ im Munde zusammen** his mouth watered; **∿ in den Beinen haben** have fluid in one's legs; *s. auch* **Blut; Rotz** a; **(f)** *Pl.* **Wässer** (Lösung, Lotion usw.) lotion; (Duft∿) scent

wasser-, Wasser-: **∿arm** *Adj.* ‹*area*› suffering from a water shortage; **∿bad** *das* (Kochk.) bain-marie; **∿ball** *der* **(a)** beachball; **(b)** *o. Pl.* (Spiel) water polo; **∿becken** *das* pool; (∿tank) water-tank

Wässerchen /ˈvɛsɐçən/ *das;* **∿s, ∿ (a) er sieht aus, als könnte er kein ∿ trüben** (fig.) he looks as though butter wouldn't melt in his mouth; **(b)** ⇒ **Wasser f**

wasser-, Wasser-: **∿dampf** *der* steam; **∿dicht** *Adj.* **(a)** waterproof ‹*clothing, watch, etc.*›; watertight ‹*container, seal, etc.*›; **(b)** (fig. ugs.) watertight ‹*alibi, contract*›; **∿fahrzeug** *das* vessel; water-craft; **∿fall** *der* waterfall; **reden wie ein ∿** (ugs.) talk non-stop; **∿farbe** *die* watercolour; **∿floh** *der* water-flea; **∿flugzeug** *das* seaplane; **∿gekühlt** *Adj.* water-cooled; **∿glas** *das* (Gefäß) glass; tumbler; *s. auch* **Sturm** a; **∿graben** *der* **(a)** ditch; (um eine Burg) moat; **(b)** (Sport) water-jump; **∿hahn** *der* water-tap; faucet (Amer.)

wässerig /ˈvɛsərɪç/ ⇒ **wässrig**

Wasser-: **∿kessel** *der* kettle; **∿kraft** *die* water-power; **∿kraftwerk** *das* hydroelectric power station; **∿lache** *die* puddle [of water]; **∿leiche** *die* (ugs.) body of a drowned person; **∿leitung** *die* **(a)** water pipe; (Hauptleitung) water main; **(b)** (Aquädukt) aqueduct; **∿mann** *der; Pl.* **∿männer** (Astron., Astrol.) Aquarius; (Astrol.: Mensch) Aquarian; **∿melone** *die* watermelon

wassern *itr. V.; mit sein* land [on the water]

wässern /ˈvɛsən/ *tr. V.* **(a)** (einweichen) soak; (Phot.) wash ‹*negative, print*›; **(b)** (bewässern) water

wasser-, Wasser-: **∿ober·fläche** *die* surface of the water; **∿pfeife** *die* hookah; water pipe; **∿pflanze** *die* aquatic plant; **∿pistole** *die* water pistol; **∿rad** *das* waterwheel; **∿ratte** *die* **(a)** water-rat; **(b)** (ugs. scherzh.) keen swimmer; (Kind) water-baby; **∿rohr** *das* water pipe; **∿scheide** *die* (Geogr.) watershed; **∿scheu** *Adj.* scared of water; **∿schlauch** *der* [water-]hose; **∿schutz·polizei** *die* river/lake police; **∿ski¹** *der* water-ski; **∿ski fahren** water-ski; **∿ski²** *das;* **∿s** water-skiing *no art.;* **∿spiegel** *der* waterlevel; **∿sport** *der* water-sport *no art.;* **∿sportler** *der* water-sports enthusiast; **∿spülung** *die* flush; flushing system; **∿stand** *der* waterlevel; **∿stelle** *die* watering-place; **∿stoff** *der; o. Pl.* hydrogen; **∿stoff·bombe** *die* hydrogen bomb; **∿strahl** *der* jet of water; **∿straße** *die* waterway; **∿tank** *der* water-tank; **∿tropfen** *der* drop of water; **∿turm** *der* water tower; **∿uhr** *die* (volkst.) ⇒ **∿zähler; ∿verschmutzung** *die* water-pollution; **∿versorgung** *die* water supply; **∿vogel** *der* waterbird; aquatic bird; **∿vorrat** *der* water-reserves *pl.;* water supply; ~**waage** *die* water level; ~**weg** *der* water-route; **auf dem** ~**weg** by water; ~**werfer** *der* water cannon; ~**werk** *das* waterworks *sing.;* ~**zähler** *der* water meter; ~**zeichen** *das* watermark

wässrig, *wäßrig /'vɛs(ə)rıç/ *Adj.* (a) watery; (b) (Chemie) aqueous ‹*solution*›

waten /'va:tn/ *itr. V.; mit sein* wade

watscheln /'vatʃln/ *itr. V.; mit sein* waddle

Watt¹ /vat/ *das;* ~[e]s, ~en mudflats *pl.*

Watt² *das;* ~s, ~ (Technik, Physik) watt

Watte /'vatə/ *die;* ~, ~n cotton wool

Watte·bausch *der* wad of cotton wool

Watten·meer *das* tidal shallows *pl.* (covering mudflats)

wattieren *tr. V.* wad; (gesteppt) quilt ‹*garment*›; pad ‹*shoulder etc.*›

WC /ve:'tse:/ *das;* ~[s], ~[s] toilet; WC

weben /'ve:bn/ *regelm.,* (*geh., fig.*) *auch unr. tr., itr. V.* weave

Weber *der;* ~s, ~: weaver

Weberei *die;* ~, ~en (a) *o. Pl.* weaving *no art.;* (b) (Betrieb) weaving-mill

Web·stuhl *der* loom

Wechsel /'vɛksl/ *der;* ~s, ~ (a) change; (Geld~) exchange; (Spieler~) substitution; (b) (das Sichabwechseln) alternation; **der** ~ **der Jahreszeiten** the rotation *or* succession of the seasons; **im** ~: alternately; (bei mehr als zwei) in rotation; (c) (das Überwechseln) move; (Sport) transfer; (d) (Bankw.) bill of exchange (**über** + *Akk.* for)

wechsel-, Wechsel-: ~**beziehung** *die* interrelation; **in** [**einer**] ~**beziehung zueinander stehen** be interrelated; ~**fälle** *Pl.* vicissitudes; ups and downs (coll.); ~**geld** *das; o. Pl.* change; ~**haft** *Adj.* changeable; ~**jahre** *Pl.* change of life *sing.;* menopause *sing.;* **in die** ~**jahre kommen** reach the menopause; ~**kurs** *der* exchange rate

wechseln 1 *tr. V.* (a) change; **die Wohnung** ~: move home; **ein Hemd zum Wechseln** a spare shirt; *s. auch* **Besitzer a;** (b) ([aus]tauschen) exchange ‹*letters, words, glances, etc.*›; (c) ▶216| (um~) change ‹*money, note, etc.*› (**in** + *Akk.* into); **kannst du mir 100 Mark** ~? can you change 100 marks for me? **2** *itr. V.* (a) (sich ändern) change; **mit** ~**dem Erfolg** with varying success; ~**de Bewölkung,** ~**d wolkig** (bei Wettervorhersagen) variable cloud; (b) *mit sein* (über~) move

wechsel-, Wechsel-: ~**objektiv** *das* (Fot.) interchangeable lens; ~**seitig 1** *Adj.* mutual; ~**seitige Abhängigkeit** interdependence; **2** *adv.* mutually; ~**spiel** *das* interplay; ~**strom** *der* (Elektrot.) alternating current; ~**stube** *die* bureau de change; ~**weise** *Adv.* alternately; ~**wirkung** *die* interaction

wecken /'vɛkn/ *tr. V.* (a) jmdn. [aus dem Schlaf] ~: wake sb. [up]; (b) (fig.) arouse, awaken ‹*interest, curiosity*›; arouse ‹*anger*›; awaken ‹*desire, misgiving*›

Wecker *der;* ~s, ~ alarm clock; **jmdm. auf den** ~ **gehen** *od.* **fallen** (ugs.) get on sb.'s nerves

Weck·ruf *der* morning call

Wedel *der;* ~s, ~ (a) (Staub~) feather-duster; (b) (Palm~, Farn~) [palm/fern] frond

wedeln *itr. V.* (a) ‹*tail*› wag; [mit dem Schwanz] ~ ‹*dog*› wag its tail; (winken) **mit der Hand/einem Tuch** ~: wave one's hand/a handkerchief; (b) *mit Richtungsangabe mit sein* (Ski) wedel

weder /'ve:dɐ/ *Konj.:* ~ ... **noch** ...: neither ... nor ...

weg /vɛk/ *Adv.* (a) away; (verschwunden, ~gegangen) gone; **er ist schon seit einer Stunde** ~: he left an hour ago; **sie ist schon** ~: she has already gone or left; ~ **sein** (fig. ugs.) (eingeschlafen sein) have dropped off; (bewusstlos sein) be out [cold] (coll.); [**immer**] ~ **damit!** [let's] chuck it away! (coll.); ~ **mit dir!** away *or* off with you!; **da** ~! get away from there!; **Hände** ~ [**von meiner Kamera**]! hands off [my camera]!; **Kopf** ~! move your head!; [**nur**] ~ **von hier!, nichts wie** ~! let's hop it [Brit. coll.]; let's make ourselves scarce (coll.); **weit** ~: far away; a long way away;

(b) **von** ... ~ (ugs.: unmittelbar von) straight off *or* from; **von der Schule** ~ **eingezogen werden** be conscripted straight from school; (c) **über einen Schock/ Schrecken** *usw.* ~ **sein** (ugs.) have got over a shock/fright *etc.*

Weg /ve:k/ *der;* ~[e]s, ~e (a) (Fuß~) path; (Feld~) track; „**kein öffentlicher** ~" 'no public right of way'; **am** ~[e] by the wayside; (b) (Zugang) way; (Passage, Durchgang) passage; **sich** (*Dat.*) **einen** ~ **durch etw. bahnen** clear a path *or* way through sth.; **geh** [**mir**] **aus dem** ~[e]: get out of the *or* my way; **jmdm. den** ~ **abschneiden** head sb. off; **jmdm. im** ~[e] **stehen** *od.* (auch fig.) sein be in sb.'s way; (fig.) **einer Sache** (*Dat.*) **im** ~[e] **stehen** stand in the way of sth.; **jmdm. aus dem** ~[e] **gehen** keep out of sb's way; avoid sb.; **einer Diskussion aus dem** ~[e] **gehen** avoid a discussion; **jmdn./etw. aus dem** ~[e] **räumen** get rid of sb./sth.; (c) ▶583| (Route, Verbindung) way; route; [jmdn.] **nach dem** ~ **fragen** ask [sb.] the way; **wir haben denselben** ~: we're going the same way; **das liegt auf dem/meinem** ~: that's on the/my way; (fig.) **er ist mir über den** ~ **gelaufen** (ugs.) I ran *or* bumped into him; **jmdm. nicht über den** ~ **trauen** not trust sb. an inch; **den** ~ **des geringsten Widerstands gehen** take the line of least resistance; **seinen** ~ **machen** make one's way [in the world]; (d) ▶159| (Strecke, Entfernung) distance; (Gang) walk; (Reise) journey; **es sind 2 km/10 Minuten** ~: it is a distance of two kilometres/it is ten minutes' walk; **er hat noch einen weiten** ~ **vor sich** (*Dat.*) he still has a long way to go; **auf dem kürzesten** ~: by the shortest route; **auf halbem** ~[e] (auch fig.) halfway; **sich auf den** ~ **machen** set off; (fig.) **jmdm. einen guten Ratschlag mit auf den** ~ **geben** give sb. some good advice for his/her future life; **etw. in die** ~e **leiten** get sth. under way; **auf dem besten** ~ **sein, etw. zu tun** (meist iron.) be well on the way towards doing sth.; **er ist auf dem** ~[e] **der Besserung** he's on the road to recovery; (e) (ugs.: Besorgung) errand; **einen** ~ **machen** do *or* run an errand; **jmdm. einen** ~ **abnehmen** run an errand for sb.; (f) (Methode) way; (Mittel) means; **ich sehe keinen anderen** ~: I can't see any alternative; **auf schnellstem** ~[e] as speedily as possible; **auf schriftlichem** ~[e] by letter

Weg·bereiter *der;* ~s, ~: forerunner

weg-: ~|**blasen** *unr. tr. V.* blow away; **wie weggeblasen sein** have vanished; ~|**bleiben** *unr. itr. V.; mit sein* (a) stay away; (von zu Hause) stay out; (b) (ugs.: aussetzen) ‹*engine*› stop; ‹*electricity*› go off; **mir blieb die Luft** ~: I was left gasping; (c) (ugs.: weggelassen werden) be left out; ~|**brechen** *unr. itr. V.; mit sein* disappear; **es ist uns ein wichtiger Markt weggebrochen** we have lost an important market; ~|**bringen** *unr. tr. V.* (a) take away; (zur Reparatur, Wartung usw.) take in; (b) (ugs., bes. südd.) ⇒ ~|**kriegen;** ~|**denken** *unr. tr. V.* **sich** (*Dat.*) etw. ~**denken** imagine sth. is not there; **er ist aus unserem Team nicht** ~**zudenken** I/we can't imagine our team without him

Wegelagerer *der;* ~s, ~: highwayman

wegen 1 *Präp. mit Gen., in bestimmten Fällen auch mit Dat./mit endungslosem Nomen* (a) (zur Angabe einer Ursache, eines Grundes) because of; owing to; ~ **des schlechten Wetters** because of the bad weather; [**nur**] ~ **Peter/**(ugs.) euch all because of Peter/you; ~ **Hochwasser[s]** owing to flooding; **von Berufs** ~: for professional reasons; ~ **mir** (ugs., bes. südd.) because of me; (was mich betrifft) as far as I'm concerned; ~ **Umbau[s] geschlossen** closed for alterations; ~ **Mangel[s] an Beweisen** owing to lack of evidence; (b) (zur Angabe eines Zwecks, Ziels) for [the sake of]; **er ist** ~ **dringender Geschäfte verreist** he's away on urgent business; (c) (um ... willen) for the sake of; ~ **der Kinder/**(ugs.) dir for the children's/your sake; (d) (bezüglich) about; regarding. **2** (ugs.) **von** ~! you must be joking!; **von** ~ **billig!** cheap? not on your life!

Wegerich /'ve:gǝrıç/ *der;* ~s, ~e (Bot.) plantain

weg-: ~|**fahren 1** *unr. itr. V.; mit sein* (a) leave; (im Auto) drive off; **wann seid ihr in Kiel** ~**gefahren?** when did you leave Kiel?; (b) (irgendwohin fahren) go away. **2** *unr. tr. V.* take away; (mit dem Auto) drive away; ~|**fallen** *unr.*

Wegbeschreibung

Die Fragen

1.	*Wie komme ich zum Bahnhof?*	= How do I get to the station?
2.	*Wie kommt man am besten zum Museum?*	= Which is the best way to the museum?
3.	*Geht es hier zum White Hart Hotel?*	= Am I right for the White Hart Hotel ?
4.	*Wo ist hier die nächste Bank?*	= Where is the nearest bank?
5.	*Gibt es hier in der Nähe eine Apotheke?*	= Is there a chemist's near here?
6.	*Wie weit ist es zum Krankenhaus?*	= How far is it to the hospital?
7.	*Können Sie mir sagen, wo es hier ein gutes Restaurant gibt?*	= Can you direct me to a good restaurant?

Die Antworten

1.	*Gehen Sie die erste Straße rechts, dann die zweite links, dann immer nur geradeaus bis zur Kreuzung. Biegen Sie rechts ein und dann sehen Sie den Bahnhof vor sich*	= Take the first turning on the right, then the second on the left, then go straight on as far as the junction. Turn right and you will see the station in front of you
2.	*Am besten, Sie gehen hier an der Ampel über die Straße, dann die Gasse entlang, die links am Theater vorbeiführt. Sie kommen dann gegenüber vom Museum heraus*	= The best way is to cross over here at the lights and go down the alleyway along the left side of the theatre. You will come out opposite the museum
3.	*Nein, Sie sind zu weit gegangen/ gefahren. Gehen/ Fahren Sie zurück zur Kreuzung und biegen Sie links ab. Das Hotel liegt etwa hundert Meter weiter auf der rechten Seite*	= No, you've come too far. Go back to the crossroads and turn left, you'll find the hotel about a hundred yards further on on the right
4.	*Am Marktplatz ist eine Filiale von Barclays. Biegen Sie dort drüben rechts ein, Sie kommen dann nach ein paar hundert Metern zum Marktplatz*	= There is a branch of Barclays on the market place, which is a couple of hundred yards along that turning over there on the right
5.	*In der nächsten Straße links ist eine, allerdings nur eine kleine. Falls Sie eine größere brauchen, müssen Sie mit der Linie 11 ins Zentrum fahren*	= There's one in the next street on the left, but it's only small. If you want a bigger one you'll have to take the number 11 bus into the centre
6.	*Es liegt etwa zwei Kilometer von hier an der Hauptstraße nach Cardiff. Am besten nehmen Sie ein Taxi, die Busse fahren nämlich nicht sehr oft*	= It's about a mile and a half from here on the main Cardiff road. You'd best take a taxi as the buses aren't very frequent
7.	*Tut mir Leid, ich bin auch fremd hier*	= Sorry, I'm a stranger here myself

itr. V.; mit sein be discontinued; (nicht mehr zutreffen) ⟨*reason*⟩ no longer apply; (entfallen) be omitted; **~|fegen** *tr. V.* (auch fig.) sweep away; **~|fliegen** *unr. itr. V.; mit sein* fly away; (~geschleudert werden) fly off; **~|führen** *tr., itr. V.* lead away; **das führt vom Thema weg** this takes us away from the subject

Wegfahr·sperre *die* (Kfz.-W.) immobilizer

Weg·gang *der* departure

weg-: **~|geben** *unr. tr. V.* **(a)** **ich gebe meine Wäsche weg** I send my washing to the laundry; **(b)** (verschenken) give away; **~|gehen** *unr. itr. V.* **(a)** leave; (ugs.: ausgehen) go out; (ugs.: ~ziehen) move away; **von jmdm. ~gehen** leave sb.; **geh ~!** go away!; **geh mir [bloß] ~ damit!** (ugs.) you can keep that!; **(b)** (verschwinden) ⟨*spot, fog, etc.*⟩ go away; **(c)** (sich entfernen lassen) ⟨*stain*⟩ come out; **(d)** (ugs.: verkauft werden) sell; **~|gießen** *unr. tr. V.* pour away; **~|haben** *unr. tr. V.* (ugs.) have got rid of ⟨*dirt, stain, etc.*⟩; **etw. ~haben wollen** want to get rid of sth.; **~|holen** *tr. V.* (ugs.) take away; **~|jagen** *tr. V.* chase away; **~|kommen** *unr. itr. V.; mit sein* **(a)** get away; (~gehen können) manage to go out; **mach, dass du [hier] ~kommst!** (ugs.) come on, hop it! (Brit. coll.); make yourself scarce! (coll.); **(b)** (abhanden kommen) go missing; **(c) gut/ schlecht** *usw.* **[bei etw.] ~kommen** (ugs.) come off well/ badly *etc.* [in sth.]; **~|können** *unr. itr. V.* **(a)** be able to leave *or* get away; (ausgehen können) be able to go out; **(b) die Zeitung kann weg** the paper can be thrown away; **~|kriegen** *tr. V.* get rid of ⟨*cold, pain, etc.*⟩; get out, get rid of ⟨*stain*⟩; shift, move ⟨*stone, tree trunk*⟩; **~|lassen** *unr. tr. V.* **(a) jmdn. ~lassen** let sb. go; **(b)** (auslassen) leave out; omit; **~|laufen** *unr. itr. V.; mit sein* run away **(von, vor** + *Dat.* from); **von zu Hause ~laufen** run away from home; **seine Frau ist ihm ~gelaufen** (ugs.) his wife has gone *or* run off and left him (coll.); **die Arbeit läuft [dir] nicht ~** (ugs.) the work will keep; **~|legen** *tr. V.* put away; (aus der Hand legen) put down; **~|machen** *tr. V.* (ugs.) remove; **~|müssen** *unr. itr. V.* **(a)** have to

leave; (loskommen müssen) have to get away; **(b)** (entfernt werden müssen) have to be removed; (~gebracht werden müssen) ⟨*letter etc.*⟩ have to go; **du musst da ~:** you'll have to move; **der Diktator muss ~:** the dictator must go; **~|nehmen** *unr. tr. V.* **(a)** take away; remove; move ⟨*head, arm*⟩; **nimm die Finger da ~!** [keep your] fingers off!; **(b) jmdm. etw. ~nehmen** take sth. away from sb.; **jmdm. die Freundin ~nehmen** pinch sb.'s girlfriend (coll.); **jmdm. die Dame** *usw.* **~nehmen** (Schach) take sb.'s queen *etc.*; **~|räumen** *tr. V.* clear away; (an seinen Platz tun) tidy *or* put away; **~|schaffen** *tr. V.* take away; **~|scheren** *refl. V.* clear off (coll.); **~|schicken** *tr. V.* **(a)** send off ⟨*letter, parcel*⟩; **(b)** send ⟨*person*⟩ away; **~|schieben** *unr. tr. V.* push away; **~|schleichen** *unr. itr., refl. V.; itr. mit sein* creep away; **~|schleppen** *tr. V.* **(a)** carry *or* lug off *or* away; **(b)** tow ⟨*car, rig, etc.*⟩ away; **~|schmeißen** *unr. tr. V.* (ugs.) chuck away (coll.); **~|schnappen** *tr. V.* (ugs.) snatch away (*Dat.* from); **jmdm. die Freundin ~schnappen** pinch sb.'s girlfriend (coll.); **~|schütten** *tr. V.* pour away; **~|sehen** *unr. itr. V.* **(a)** look away; **(b)** (ugs.) ⇒ **hinwegsehen**; **~|spülen** *tr. V.* wash away; **~|stecken** *tr. V.* **(a)** put away; **(b)** (fig. ugs.: hinnehmen) take, accept ⟨*blow*⟩; swallow ⟨*insult*⟩; **~|stellen** *tr. V.* put away; **~|stoßen** *unr. tr. V.* push *or* shove away

Weg·strecke *die* stretch [of road]; (Entfernung) distance

weg-: **~|tragen** *unr. tr. V.* carry away; **~|treten 1** *unr. tr. V.* kick away; **2** *unr. tr. V.; mit sein* step away; (Milit.) dismiss; **[etwas] ~getreten sein** (fig. ugs.) be [somewhat] distracted; **~|tun** *tr. V.* (ugs.) **(a)** put away; **(b)** (wegwerfen) throw away

Wegweiser *der;* **~s,** **~** signpost

Weg·werf- disposable ⟨*nappy, towel, cup, lighter, etc.*⟩

weg-: **~|werfen** *unr. tr. V.* (auch fig.) throw away; **~werfend** *Adj.* dismissive ⟨*gesture, remark*⟩

Wegwerf·gesellschaft *die* (abwertend) throwaway society

weg-: ~|**wischen** *tr. V.* wipe away; (fig.) erase ⟨*memory*⟩; dispel ⟨*fear, doubt*⟩; dismiss ⟨*objection*⟩; ~|**wollen** *unr. itr. V.* want to go *or* leave; (loskommen wollen) want to get away; (ausgehen wollen) want to go out; ~|**zerren** *tr. V.* drag away; ~|**ziehen 1** *unr. tr. V.* pull away; pull off ⟨*blanket*⟩; **2** *unr. itr. V.; mit sein* (umziehen) move away; **aus X** ~**ziehen** leave X; move from X

weh /veː/*Adj.* (a) *nicht präd.* (ugs.: schmerzend) sore; **einen** ~**en Finger haben** have a sore *or* bad finger; (b) (geh.: schmerzlich) painful; **ein** ~**es Lächeln/Gefühl** a sad smile/an aching feeling; **ihr ist** ~ **ums-Herz** her heart aches; she is sore at heart; *s. auch* **wehtun**

Weh *das;* ~[e]s (geh.) sorrow; grief

wehe *Interj.* woe betide you/him *etc.;* ~ **[dir]**, **wenn du** ...: woe betide you if you ...

Wehe¹ /ˈveːə/ *die;* ~, ~**n** contraction; **die** ~**n setzten ein** the contractions started; she went into labour; ~**n haben** have contractions; **in den** ~**n liegen** be in labour

Wehe² *die;* ~, ~**n** drift

wehen 1 *itr. V.* (a) blow; (b) (flattern) flutter; **ihre Haare wehten im Wind** her hair was blowing about in the wind; (c) *mit sein* ⟨*leaves, snowflakes, scent*⟩ waft. **2** *tr. V.* blow

weh-, Weh-: ~**klage** *die* (geh.) lamentation; ~**klagen** *itr. V.* (geh.) lament; **über etw.** (*Akk.*) ~**klagen** lament *or* bewail sth.; ~**leidig** (abwertend) **1** *Adj.* soft; (weinerlich) whining *attrib.;* **sei nicht so** ~**leidig!** don't be so soft *or* such a sissy; **2** *adv.* self-pityingly; (weinerlich) whiningly; ~**mut** *die;* ~ (geh.) melancholy *or* wistful nostalgia; ~**mütig 1** *Adj.* melancholically *or* wistfully nostalgic; **2** *adv.* with melancholy *or* wistful nostalgia

Wehr¹ *die;* ~, ~**en** (a) **sich [gegen jmdn./etw.] zur** ~ **setzen** make a stand [against sb./sth.]; resist [sb./sth.]; (b) ⇒ **Feuerwehr**

Wehr² *das;* ~[e]s, ~**e** weir

Wehr-dienst *der; o. Pl.* military service *no art.;* **zum** ~ **einberufen werden** be called up; **seinen** ~ **ableisten** do one's military service

Wehr-dienst-: ~**verweigerer** *der;* ~s, ~: conscientious objector; ~**verweigerung** *die* conscientious objection

wehren 1 *refl. V.* (a) defend oneself; put up a fight; **sich tapfer** ~: defend oneself *or* resist bravely; **sich gegen etw.** ~: fight against sth.; (b) **sich [dagegen]** ~, **etw. zu tun** resist having to do sth. **2** *itr. V.* (geh.) **jmdm./einer Sache** ~: fight sb./fight [against] sth.

wehr-, Wehr-: ~**haft** *Adj.* (a) able to defend oneself *postpos.;* (b) (befestigt) fortified; ~**los** *Adj.* defenceless; **jmdm./einer Sache** ~**los ausgeliefert sein** be defenceless against sb./sth.; ~**losigkeit** *die* defencelessness; ~**pass** *der* service record [book]; ~**pflicht** *die; o. Pl.* military service; conscription; **die allgemeine** ~**pflicht** compulsory military service; ~**pflichtig** *Adj.* liable for military service *postpos;* ~**pflichtige** *der/die; adj. Dekl.* person liable for military service; ~**sold** *der* military pay; ~**übung** *die* reserve duty [re]training exercise

weh|tun *unr. itr. V.* ▶329 (ugs.) hurt; **mir tut der Kopf** ~: my head is aching *or* hurts; **jmdm./sich** ~: hurt sb./ oneself

Wehwehchen *das;* ~s, ~: little complaint

Weib /vaɪp/ *das;* ~[e]s, ~**er** (a) (veralt., ugs.: Frau) woman; female (derog.); **sie ist ein tolles** ~: she's a bit of all right (coll.); (b) (veralt., scherzh.: Ehefrau) wife

Weibchen *das;* ~s, ~: female

Weiber-held *der* (ugs.) ladykiller

weibisch (abwertend) **1** *Adj.* womanish; effeminate. **2** *adv.* womanishly; effeminately

weiblich 1 *Adj.* (a) female; (b) (für die Frau typisch) feminine; (c) (Sprachw.) feminine. **2** *adv.* femininely

Weiblichkeit *die;* ~: femininity

Weibs-: ~**bild** *das* (ugs.) woman; (abwertend) female; ~**stück** *das* (abwertend) bitch (sl.)

---

weich /vaɪç/ **1** *Adj.* (auch fig.) soft; soft, mellow ⟨*sound, voice*⟩; soft, gentle ⟨*features*⟩; gentle ⟨*mouth, face*⟩; **ein Ei** ~ **kochen** soft-boil an egg; ~ **gekochte Eier** soft-boiled eggs; **ein** ~**es Herz haben** be soft-hearted; ~ **werden** (ugs.) soften; weaken; **jmdn.** ~ **machen** (ugs.) soften sb. up. **2** *adv.* softly; ⟨*brake*⟩ gently; ~ **landen** *od.* **aufsetzen** make a soft landing

Weiche¹ *die;* ~, ~**n** (Flanke) flank

Weiche² *die;* ~, ~**n** points *pl.* (Brit.); switch (Amer.); **die** ~**n [für etw.] stellen** (fig.) set the course [for sth.]

weichen¹ *itr. V.; mit sein* soak

weichen² *unr. itr. V.; mit sein* move; **nicht von jmds. Seite** ~: not move from *or* leave sb.'s side; **dem Feind** ~: retreat from the enemy; **vor jmdm./etw. zur Seite** ~: step *or* move out of the way of sb./sth.; **die Angst wich von ihm** (fig. geh.) the fear left him

*****weich-gekocht** ⇒ **weich 1**

weich-, Weich-: ~**herzig 1** *Adj.* soft-hearted; **2** *adv.* soft-heartedly; ~**herzigkeit** *die;* ~: soft-heartedness; ~**käse** *der* soft cheese

weichlich 1 *Adj.* soft. **2** *adv.* softly

Weichling *der;* ~s, ~**e** (abwertend) weakling

*****weich|machen** ⇒ **weich 1**

Weich-teile *Pl.* (a) ▶326 (Anat.) soft parts; (b) ▶326 (ugs.: Genitalien) privates

Weide¹ /ˈvaɪdə/ *die;* ~, ~**n** (Wiese) pasture; **die Kühe auf die** ~ **treiben** drive the cows to pasture

Weide² *die;* ~, ~**n** (Baum) willow

Weide-land *das* pasture[land]; grazing land

weiden 1 *itr., tr. V.* graze. **2** *refl. V.* (a) (geh.) **er** *od.* **sein Auge weidete sich an dem Anblick** he feasted his eyes on the sight; (b) **sich an jmds. Schmerz** (*Dat.*) ~: gloat over sb.'s pain

Weiden-: ~**gerte** *die* willow rod; (zum Korbflechten) osier; (kleiner) wicker; ~**kätzchen** *das* willow catkin

weidlich *Adv.* **etw.** ~ **ausnutzen** make full use of sth.

Weid-mann *der; Pl.* ~**männer** (geh.) huntsman; hunter

weid-männisch 1 *Adj.* hunting, huntsman's *attrib.* **2** *adv.* in the manner of a huntsman; like a huntsman

weigern /ˈvaɪgɐn/ *refl. V.* refuse

Weigerung *die;* ~, ~**en** refusal

Weihe¹ *die;* ~, ~**n** (a) (Rel.: Einweihung) consecration; dedication; (b) (kath. Kirche: Priester~, Bischofs~) ordination; **die niederen/höheren** ~**n** (hist.) the minor/major orders

Weihe² *die;* ~, ~**n** (Zool.) harrier

weihen *tr. V.* (a) (Rel.) consecrate; (b) (kath. Kirche: ordinieren) ordain; **jmdn. zum Priester/Bischof** ~: ordain sb. priest/consecrate sb. bishop; (c) (Rel.: durch Weihe zueignen) dedicate (*Dat.* to); (d) **dem Tod[e]/dem Untergang geweiht sein** (geh.) be doomed to die/to fall

Weiher *der;* ~s, ~ (bes. südd.) [small] pond

Weihnachten *das;* ~, ~: ▶240 Christmas; **frohe** *od.* **fröhliche** ~! Merry *or* Happy Christmas!; **grüne** ~: Christmas without snow; **zu** *od.* (bes. südd.) **an/über** ~: at *or* for/over Christmas

weihnachtlich 1 *Adj.* Christmassy. **2** *adv.* ~ **geschmückt** decorated for Christmas

Weihnachts-: ~**abend** *der* Christmas Eve; ~**baum** *der* Christmas tree; ~**feiertag** *der:* **der erste/zweite** ~**feiertag** Christmas Day/Boxing Day; ~**fest** *das* ▶240 Christmas; ~**geld** *das* Christmas bonus; ~**geschenk** *das* Christmas present *or* gift; ~**lied** *das* Christmas carol; ~**mann** *der; Pl.* ~**männer** (a) Father Christmas; Santa Claus; (b) (ugs.: Dummkopf) silly idiot (coll.); ~**stern** *der* (a) Christmas star; (b) (Pflanze) poinsettia; ~**tag** *der* ⇒ ~**feiertag**; ~**zeit** *die* Christmas time; **in der** ~**zeit** at Christmas time

Weih-: ~**rauch** *der* incense; ~**wasser** *das* (kath. Kirche) holy water; ~**wasser-becken** *das* (kath. Kirche) stoup

---

*alte Schreibung (vgl. Hinweise auf S. xvi–xvii)

weil /vail/ *Konj.* because

Weile *die;* ~: while; **eine ganze** ~: a good while

weilen *itr. V.* (geh.) stay; (sein) be

Weiler *der;* ~s, ~: hamlet

Wein /vain/ *der;* ~[e]s, ~e (a) wine; **jmdm. reinen** ~ **einschenken** (fig.) tell sb. the truth; (b) *o. Pl.* (Reben) vines *pl.;* (Trauben) grapes *pl.;* (c) **wilder** ~: Virginia creeper

Wein-: ~[an]**bau** *der; o. Pl.* wine-growing *no art.;* ~**bauer** *der* wine-grower; ~**beere** *die* grape; ~**berg** *der* vineyard; ~**berg·schnecke** *die* [edible] snail; ~**brand** *der* brandy

weinen 1 *itr. V.* cry; **um jmdn.** ~: cry *or* weep for sb.; **über jmdn./etw.** ~: cry over *or* about sb./sth.; **vor Freude** ~: cry *or* weep for *or* with joy; **es ist zum Weinen** it's enough to make you weep; **leise** ~**d abziehen** (fig. ugs.) leave with one's tail between one's legs. 2 *tr. V.* shed ‹tears›. 3 *refl. V.* **sich in den Schlaf** ~: cry oneself to sleep

weinerlich 1 *Adj.* tearful; weepy. 2 *adv.* tearfully

wein-, Wein-: ~**essig** *der* wine vinegar; ~**flasche** *die* wine bottle; ~**garten** *der* vineyard; ~**geist** *der; o. Pl.* ethyl alcohol; ethanol; ~**glas** *das* wineglass; ~**gut** *das* vineyard; ~**handlung** *die* wine-merchant's; ~**karte** *die* wine-list; ~**keller** *der* wine cellar; ~**krampf** *der* crying fit; fit of crying; ~**lese** *die* grape harvest; ~**lokal** *das* wine bar; ~**probe** *die* wine tasting [session]; ~**rebe** *die* (a) grapevine; (b) (Ranke) [grapevine] shoot; ~**rot** *Adj.* wine-red; wine-coloured; ~**schaum·creme** *die* (Kochk.) zabaglione; ~**stock** *der; Pl.* ~**stöcke** [grape]vine; ~**stube** *die* wine bar; ~**traube** *die* grape

weise /vaizə/ 1 *Adj.* wise; **ein Weiser** a wise man. 2 *adv.* wisely

Weise *die;* ~, ~n (a) way; **auf diese/andere** ~: this way/ [in] another way; **auf meine** ~: in my own way; **auf geheimnisvolle** ~: in a mysterious manner; mysteriously; **in gewisser** ~: in certain respects; (b) (Melodie) tune; melody

weisen 1 *unr. tr. V.* (a) (geh.) show; **jmdm. etw.** ~: show sb. sth.; *s. auch* **Tür;** (b) **jmdn. aus dem Zimmer** ~: send sb. out of the room; **etw. von sich** ~ (fig.) reject sth.. 2 *unr. itr. V.* point

Weisheit *die;* ~, ~en (a) *o. Pl.* wisdom; **er hat die** ~ [**auch**] **nicht mit Löffeln gefressen** (ugs.) he is not all that bright; **mit seiner** ~ **am Ende sein** be at one's wit's end; (b) (Erkenntnis) wise insight; (Spruch) wise saying

Weisheits·zahn *der* ▶ 326 | wisdom tooth

weis|machen *tr. V.* (ugs.) **das kannst du mir nicht** ~! you can't expect me to swallow that!; **das kannst du anderen** ~! tell that to the marines (coll.)

weiß[1] /vais/ *1. u. 3. Pers. Sg. Präsens v.* **wissen**

weiß[2] *Adj.* (a) white (b) (Kaufmannsspr.) unbranded ‹product›

Weiß *das;* ~[e]s, ~: white

weis-, Weis-: ~**sagen** *tr. V., auch itr. V.* prophesy; foretell; ~**sager** *der* prophet; ~**sagerin** *die* prophetess; ~**sagung** *die;* ~, ~en prophecy

weiß-, Weiß-: ~**bier** *das* light, highly effervescent, top-fermented beer made from wheat and barley; weiss beer; ~**blond** *Adj.* ash-blond/-blonde; ~**brot** *das* white bread; **ein** ~**brot** a white loaf; ~**burgunder** *der;* ~s, ~: white burgundy; ~**dorn** *der* hawthorn

Weiße[1] *die;* ~, ~n ⇒ **Berliner**[1] 1

Weiße[2] *der/die; adj. Dekl.* white; white man/woman

weißeln (südd., österr., schweiz.), **weißen** *tr. V.* paint white; (tünchen) whitewash

weiß-, Weiß-: ~**glut** *die* white heat; **jmdn. zur** ~**glut bringen** (ugs.) make sb. livid (Brit. coll.); ~**haarig** *Adj.* white-haired; ~**herbst** *der* rosé wine; ~**kohl** *der,* (bes. südd., österr.) ~**kraut** *das* white cabbage

weißlich *Adj.* whitish

weißt *2. Pers. Sg. Präsens v.* **wissen**

weiß-, Weiß-: ~|**waschen** *unr. V.* **jmdn./sich** ~**waschen** (ugs.) clear sb.'s/one's name; ~**wein** *der* white wine; ~**wurst** *die* veal sausage

Weisung *die;* ~, ~en (geh., Amtsspr.) instruction; (Direktive) directive; **auf [jmds.]** ~ ‹Akk.› on [sb.'s] instructions; ~ **haben, etw. zu tun** have instructions to do sth.

weit /vait/ 1 *Adj.* (a) ▶ 160 |, ▶ 583 | wide; long ‹way, journey, etc.›; (fig.) broad ‹concept›; **die** ~**e Welt** the big wide world; **im** ~**eren Sinn** (fig.) in the broader sense; **das Weite suchen** (fig.) take to one's heels; (b) (locker sitzend) wide; **jmdm. zu** ~ **sein** ‹clothes› be too loose on sb.; **einen Rock** ~**er machen** let out a skirt; *s. auch* **weiter...** 2 *adv.* (a) ~ **geöffnet** wide open; ~ **verbreitet** widespread; common; common ‹plant, animal›; ~ **verzweigt** extensive ‹network›; ‹firm› with many [different] branches; ~ **gereist** widely travelled; ~ **herumgekommen sein** have got around a good deal; have travelled widely; ~ **und breit war niemand zu sehen** there was no one to be seen anywhere; (b) ▶ 160 |, ▶ 583 | (eine große Strecke) far; ~ [**entfernt** *od. weg*] **wohnen** live a long way away *or* off; live far away; ~ **reichend** long-range; (fig.) far-reaching ‹importance, consequences›; sweeping ‹changes, powers›; extensive ‹relations, influence›; **15 km** ~: 15 km. away; **von** ~**em** from a distance; **von** ~**her** from far away; (fig.) **es würde zu** ~ **führen, das alles jetzt zu analysieren** it would be too much to analyse it all now; **das geht zu** ~: that is going too far; **etw. zu** ~ **treiben, es mit etw. zu** ~ **treiben** overdo sth.; carry sth. too far; **so** ~, **so gut** so far, so good; *s. auch* **entfernt a; her e;** (c) (lange) ~ **nach Mitternacht** well past midnight; ~ **zurückliegen** be a long way back *or* a long time ago; (d) (in der Entwicklung) far; **sehr** ~ **mit etw. sein** have got a long way with sth.; **wie weit seid ihr?** how far have you got?; **wir wollen es gar nicht erst so** ~ **kommen lassen** we do not want to let it come to that; (e) (weitaus) far; **jmdn.** ~ **übertreffen** surpass sb. by far *or* by a long way; **bei** ~**em** by far; by a long way; **bei** ~**em nicht so gut wie** …: nowhere near as good as …; *s. auch* **gefehlt 2; weiter**

weit-, Weit-: ~**ab** *Adv.* far away; ~**aus** *Adv.* far ‹better, worse, etc.›; **der** ~**aus beste Reiter** by far *or* far and away the best rider; ~**blick** *der; o. Pl.* far-sightedness; **politischen** ~**blick haben** be politically far-sighted; ~**blickend** *Adj.* far-sighted

Weite *die;* ~, ~n (a) expanse; (b) (bes. Sport: Entfernung) distance; (eines Kleidungsstückes, einer Öffnung usw.) width

weiten 1 *tr. V.* widen. 2 *refl. V.* widen; ‹pupil› dilate

weiter *Adv.* (a) farther; further; **zwei Häuser** ~ **wohnen** live two houses further *or* farther on; **halt, nicht** ~! stop, don't go any further!; ~! go on!; **nur immer** ~ **so!** keep it up!; **und so** ~: and so on; **und so** ~ **und so fort** and so on and so forth; **was geschah** ~? what happened then *or* next?; (b) (außerdem, sonst) ~ **nichts, nichts** ~: nothing more *or* else; **ich brauche** ~ **nichts** I don't need anything else; there's nothing else I need; **das ist nicht** ~ **schlimm** it isn't that important; it doesn't really matter

weiter... *Adj.; nicht präd.* further; **ohne** ~**e Umstände** without any fuss; **bis auf** ~**es** for the time being; **des Weiteren** (geh.) furthermore; *s. auch* **ohne 1 c**

weiter-, Weiter-: ~|**arbeiten** *itr. V.* (fortbestehen) continue *or* carry on working; ~|**bestehen** *unr. itr. V.* continue to exist; ~|**bilden** *tr. V.* ⇒ **fortbilden;** ~**bildung** *die; o. Pl.* ⇒ **Fortbildung;** ~|**bringen** *unr. tr. V.* **das bringt uns nicht** ~: that does not get us any further *or* anywhere; ~|**entwickeln** *tr., refl. V.* develop [further]; ~|**erzählen** *tr. V.* (a) continue telling; *itr.* **erzähl doch** ~: do carry *or* go on; (b) (~sagen) pass on; **erzähl das nicht** ~: don't tell anyone; ~|**fahren** *unr. itr. V.; mit sein* continue [on one's way]; (~ reisen) travel on; ~|**führen** *tr., itr. V.* continue; ~**führende Schulen** secondary schools; ~|**geben** *unr. tr. V.* (a) pass on; (b) (Sport) pass; ~|**gehen** *unr. itr. V.; mit sein* (a) go on; **bitte** ~**gehen!** please move along *or* keep moving!; (b) (sich fortsetzen) continue; go on; **das Leben geht** ~: life goes on; **so kann es mit uns nicht** ~**gehen** we cannot go on like this; **wie soll es denn nun** ~**gehen?** what is going to happen now?; ~|**helfen** *unr. itr. V.* **jmdm.** [**mit etw.**] ~**helfen** help sb. [with sth.]; ~**hin** *Adv.* (a) (immer noch) still; (b) (künftig) in future; **etw. auch** ~**hin tun** continue to do sth. [in future]; ∼|**kommen** *unr. itr. V.; mit sein* (a) get further; **mach, dass du** ∼**kommst** (ugs.) clear off (coll.); (b) (Fortschritte machen) make progress *or* headway; (Erfolg haben) get on; ∼|**laufen** *unr. itr. V.; mit sein* (a) (in Betrieb bleiben, auch fig.) keep going; (b) (fortgeführt werden) continue; ∼|**leben** *itr. V.* (a) continue *or* carry on one's life; (b) (am Leben bleiben) go on living; (c) (fig.) live on; ∼|**leiten** *tr. V.* pass on ⟨*news, information, etc.*⟩; forward ⟨*letter, parcel, etc.*⟩; ∼|**machen** 1 *itr. V.* carry on; go on; 2 *tr. V.* carry on with; ∼|**reden** *itr. V.* go on *or* carry on talking; ∼|**reichen** *tr. V.* pass on; ∼|**sagen** *tr. V.* pass on; **sag es nicht weiter** don't tell anyone; ∼|**schicken** *tr. V.* forward; send on; send ⟨*person*⟩ on; ∼|**sehen** *unr. itr. V.* see; **morgen werden wir** ∼**sehen** we'll see what we can do tomorrow; ∼|**spielen** *tr., itr. V.* go on *or* carry on playing; **der Schiedsrichter ließ** ∼**spielen** the referee allowed play to continue; ∼|**sprechen** *unr. itr. V.* go on *or* carry on speaking *or* talking; ∼|**verarbeiten** *tr. V.* process; ∼|**verfolgen** *tr. V.* follow up ⟨*clue, case, etc.*⟩; continue to follow ⟨*developments, events, etc.*⟩; pursue further ⟨*idea, line of thought, etc.*⟩; ∼|**wissen** *unr. itr. V.* **nicht [mehr]** ∼**wissen** be at one's wit's end; ∼|**ziehen** *unr. itr. V., mit sein* move on

weit-, Weit-: ∼**gehend** 1 *Adj.* extensive, wide, sweeping ⟨*powers*⟩; far-reaching ⟨*support, concessions, etc.*⟩; wide ⟨*support, agreement, etc.*⟩; general ⟨*renunciation*⟩; 2 *adv.* to a large *or* great extent;*∼**gereist** ⇒ **weit 2 a;** ∼**her** *Adv.* (geh.) from afar; ∼**herzig** *Adj.* generous; liberal ⟨*interpretation*⟩; ∼**hin** *Adv.* for miles around; ∼**läufig** 1 *Adj.* (a) (ausgedehnt) extensive; (geräumig) spacious; (b) (entfernt) distant; (c) (ausführlich) lengthy; long-winded; 2 *adv.* (a) (ausgedehnt) spaciously; (b) (entfernt) distantly; (c) (ausführlich) at length; long-windedly; ∼**maschig** *Adj.* wide-meshed; ∼**räumig** 1 *Adj.* spacious ⟨*room, area, etc.*⟩; wide ⟨*gap, space*⟩; 2 *adv.* spaciously; **etw.** ∼**räumig umfahren** give sth. a wide berth; *∼**reichend** ⇒ **weit 2 b;** ∼**schweifig** 1 *Adj.* long-winded; 2 *adv.* long-windedly; ∼**sichtig** 1 *Adj.* long-sighted; (fig.) far sighted; 2 *adv.* (fig.) far-sightedly; ∼**sichtigkeit** *die;* ∼ long-sightedness; (fig.) far-sightedness; ∼**sprung** *der* (Sport) long jump (Brit.); broad jump (Amer.);*∼**verbreitet** ⇒ **weit 2 a;***∼**verzweigt** ⇒ **weit 2 a;** ∼**winkel·objektiv** *das* wide-angle lens

Weizen /'vaɪtsn̩/ *der;* ∼**s** wheat

Weizen-: ∼**bier** *das* ⇒ **Weißbier;** ∼**mehl** *das* wheat flour

welch /vɛlç/ 1 *Interrogativpron.* (a) (bei Wahl aus einer unbegrenzten Menge) what; **aus** ∼**em Grund?** for what reason?; **um** ∼**e Zeit?** [at] what time?; (b) (bei Wahl aus einer begrenzten Menge) *attr.* which; *allein stehend* which one; **an** ∼**em Tag/in** ∼**em Jahr?** on which day/in which year?; ∼**er/**∼**e/**∼**es auch immer** whichever one; ∼**er/** ∼**e/**∼**es von [den] beiden** which of the two; (c) (geh.: was für ein) what a; *oft unflektiert* ∼ **reizendes Geschöpf!** what a charming creature!; ∼ **ein Zufall/Glück!** what a coincidence/how fortunate! 2 *Relativpron.* (bei Menschen) who; (bei Sachen) which. 3 *Indefinitpron.* some; (in Fragen) any

welk /vɛlk/ *Adj.* withered ⟨*skin, hands, etc.*⟩; wilted ⟨*leaves, flower*⟩; limp ⟨*lettuce*⟩

welken *itr. V.; mit sein* wilt

Well·blech *das* corrugated iron

Welle /'vɛlə/ *die;* ∼, ∼**n** (a) (auch Haar∼, Physik, fig.) wave; **grüne** ∼ (Verkehrsw.) linked *or* synchronised traffic lights; **die weiche** ∼ (fig. ugs.) the soft approach *or* line; (b) (Rundf.: ∼nlänge) wavelength; (c) (Technik) shaft; (d) (Boden∼) undulation

wellen 1 *tr. V.* wave ⟨*hair*⟩; corrugate ⟨*iron, metal*⟩. 2 *refl. V.* ⟨*hair*⟩ be wavy; ⟨*ground, carpet*⟩ undulate

wellen-, Wellen-: ∼**bad** *das* artificial wave pool; ∼**bereich** *der* (Rundf.) waveband; ∼**brecher** *der* breakwater; ∼**förmig** 1 *Adj.* wavy ⟨*line, outline, seam, etc.*⟩; wavelike ⟨*motion, movement, etc.*⟩; 2 *adv.* ⟨*be propagated*⟩ in the form of waves *or* as waves; ∼**gang**

der; o. Pl. swell; **bei starkem** ∼**gang** in heavy seas; ∼**länge** *die* (Physik) wavelength; [**mit jmdm.**] **auf der gleichen** ∼**länge liegen** (fig. ugs.) be on the same wavelength [as sb.]; ∼**linie** *die* wavy line; ∼**reiten** *das* surfing *no art.;* ∼**sittich** *der* budgerigar

Well·fleisch *das* boiled belly pork

wellig *Adj.* wavy ⟨*hair*⟩; undulating ⟨*scenery, hills, etc.*⟩; uneven ⟨*surface, track, etc.*⟩

Well·pappe *die* corrugated cardboard

Welpe /'vɛlpə/ *der;* ∼**n,** ∼**n** (Hund) whelp; pup; (Wolf, Fuchs) whelp; cub

Wels /vɛls/ *der;* ∼**es,** ∼**e** catfish

Welt /vɛlt/ *die;* ∼, ∼**en** (a) *o. Pl.* world; **auf der** ∼**:** in the world; **in der ganzen** ∼ **bekannt sein** be known worldwide *or* all over the world; **die schönste Frau der Welt** the most beautiful woman in the world; **nicht die** ∼ **kosten** (ugs.) not cost the earth (coll.); **davon geht die** ∼ **nicht unter** (ugs.) it's not the end of the world; **auf die** *od.* **zur** ∼ **kommen** be born; **auf der** ∼ **sein** have been born; **aus aller** ∼**:** from all over the world; **in aller** ∼**:** throughout the world; all over the world; **in alle** ∼**:** all over the world; **um nichts in der** ∼, **nicht um alles in der** ∼**:** not for anything in the world *or* on earth; **um alles in der** ∼ (ugs.) for heaven's sake; **die ganze** ∼ (fig.) the whole world; **alle** ∼ (fig. ugs.) the whole world; everybody; **eine verkehrte** ∼**:** a topsy-turvy world; **Kinder in die** ∼ **setzen** (ugs.) have children; **zur** ∼ **bringen** bring into the world; give birth to; **eine Dame/ ein Mann von** ∼**:** a woman/man of the world; (b) (∼all) universe; **uns trennen** ∼**en** (fig.) we are worlds apart

welt-, Welt-: ∼**all** *das* universe; cosmos; ∼**anschauung** *die* world-view; Weltanschauung; ∼**atlas** *der* atlas of the world; ∼**ausstellung** *die* world fair; ∼**bekannt** *Adj.* known all over the world *pred.;* world-famous ⟨*artist, author, etc.*⟩; ∼**berühmt** *Adj.* world-famous; ∼**bewegend** *Adj.* world-shaking; **nicht** ∼**bewegend sein** (ugs. spött.) be nothing to write home about (coll.); ∼**bild** *das* world view; conception of the world

Welten·bummler *der;* ∼**s,** ∼**:** globe-trotter

Welt·erfolg *der* worldwide success

Welter·gewicht *das* welterweight

welt-, Welt-: ∼**fremd** 1 *Adj.* unworldly; 2 *adv.* unrealistically; ∼**frieden** *der* world peace; ∼**geltung** *die* international standing; ∼**geschichte** *die; o. Pl.* world history *no art.;* ∼**karte** *die* map of the world; ∼**klasse** *die* world class; ∼**krieg** *der* world war; **der Zweite** ∼**krieg** the Second World War; World War II

weltlich *Adj.* worldly; (nicht geistlich) secular

welt-, Welt-: ∼**literatur** *die* world literature *no art.;* ∼**macht** *die* world power; ∼**männisch** /∼mɛnɪʃ/ 1 *Adj.* sophisticated; 2 *adv.* in a sophisticated manner; ∼**markt** *der* (Wirtsch.) world market; ∼**meer** *das* ocean; ∼**meister** *der* world champion; ∼**meisterschaft** *die* world championship; ∼**musik** *die* world music; ∼**politik** *die* world politics *pl.;* ∼**politisch** *Adj.* **das** ∼**politische Klima** the climate in world politics; ∼**raum** *der* space *no art.;* ∼**reich** *das* empire; ∼**reise** *die* world tour; ∼**rekord** *der* world record; ∼**religion** *die* world religion; ∼**sprache** *die* world language; ∼**stadt** *die* cosmopolitan city; ∼**umspannend** *Adj.* global; ∼**untergang** *der* end of the world; ∼**verbesserer** *der;* ∼**s,** ∼ (iron.) **ein** ∼**verbesserer** someone who thinks he/she can set the world to rights; ∼**weit** 1 *Adj.; nicht präd.* worldwide; 2 *adv.* throughout *or* all over the world; ∼**wirtschaft** *die* world economy; ∼**wunder** *das:* **die sieben** ∼**wunder** the Seven Wonders of the World; ∼**zeit·uhr** *die* clock showing times around the world

wem /veːm/ *Dat. von* **wer** 1 *Interrogativpron.* to whom; who ... to; (nach Präp.) whom; who ...; **wem hast du das Buch geliehen?** to whom did you lend the book?; who did you lend the book to? 2 *Relativpron.* (derjenige, dem/diejenige, der) the person to whom ...; the person who ... to; (jeder, dem) anyone to whom. 3 *Indefinitpron.* (ugs.) to somebody *or* someone; (nach Präp.) somebody; someone; (fragend, verneint) to anybody *or* anyone; (nach Präp.) anybody; anyone

Wem·fall *der* dative [case]

wen /veːn/ *Akk. von* **wer 1** *Interrogativpron.* whom; who (coll.); **an/für ~:** to/for whom ...; who ... to/for; **an ~ schreibst du?** to whom are you writing? who are you writing to?; **~ von ihnen kennst du?** which [one] of these do you know? **2** *Relativpron.* (derjenige, den/diejenige, die) the person whom; (jeder, den) anyone whom. **3** *Indefinitpron.* (ugs.) somebody; someone; (fragend, verneint) anybody; anyone

Wende *die;* **~, ~n (a)** change; **eine ~ zum Besseren/Schlechteren** a change for the better/worse; **(b) um die ~ des Jahrhunderts** at the turn of the century; **(c)** (Turnen) front vault

Wende·kreis *der* **(a)** (Geogr.) tropic; **der nördliche ~, der ~ des Krebses** the Tropic of Cancer; **der südliche ~, der ~ des Steinbocks** the Tropic of Capricorn; **(b)** (Kfz-W.) turning circle

Wendel·treppe *die* spiral staircase

wenden¹ 1 *tr., auch itr. V.* (auf die andere Seite) turn [over]; toss ⟨*pancake, cutlet, etc.*⟩; (in die entgegengesetzte Richtung) turn [round]; **bitte ~!** please turn over. **2** *itr. V.* turn [round]. **3** *refl. V.* **sich zum Besseren/Schlechteren ~:** take a turn for the better/worse

wenden² 1 *unr., auch regelm. tr. V.* turn; **den Kopf ~:** turn one's head; **keinen Blick von jmdm. ~:** not take one's eyes off sb. **2** *unr., auch regelm. refl. V.* **(a)** ⟨*person*⟩ turn; **(b)** (sich richten) **sich an jmdn. ~:** turn to sb.; **sich mit einer Bitte an jmdn. ~:** ask a favour of sb.; **an wen soll ich mich ~?** whom should I approach?; **das Buch wendet sich an junge Leser** (fig.) the book is addressed to *or* intended for young readers

Wende·punkt *der* turning point

wendig 1 *Adj.* **(a)** agile; nimble; manœuvrable ⟨*vehicle, boat, etc.*⟩; **(b)** (gewandt) astute. **2** *adv.* **(a)** agilely; nimbly; **(b)** (gewandt) astutely

Wendigkeit *die;* **~:** ⇒ **wendig 1:** agility; nimbleness; manœuvrability; astuteness

Wendung *die;* **~, ~en (a)** turn; **eine ~ um 180°** a 180° turn; **(b)** (Veränderung) change; **eine ~ zum Besseren/Schlechteren** a turn for the better/worse; **(c)** (Rede~) expression

Wen·fall *der* accusative [case]

wenig /ˈveːnɪç/ **1** *Indefinitpron. u. unbest. Zahlw.* **(a)** *Sing.* little; **das ~e Geld reicht nicht aus** this small amount of money is not enough; **~ Zeit/Geld haben** not have much *or* have little time/money; **das ist ~:** that isn't much; **dazu kann ich ~ sagen** I can't say much about that; **zu ~ Zeit/Geld haben** not have enough time/money; **ein Exemplar/50 Mark zu ~:** one copy too few/ 50 marks too little; **nur ~es** only a little; **(b)** *Pl.* a few; **nur ~ Leute waren unterwegs** only a few people were about; **sie hatte ~ Bücher/Freunde** she had few books/ friends; **die ~en, die davon wussten** the few who knew about it; **nur ~e haben teilgenommen** only a few took part. **2** *Adv.* little; **nur ~ besser** only a little better; **wir waren nicht ~ erstaunt** we were more than a little astonished; **~ mehr** not much more; **ein ~:** a little; (eine Weile) for a little while

weniger 1 *Komp. von* **wenig 1: (a)** *Sing.* less; **(b)** *Pl.* fewer. **2** *Komp. von* **wenig 2:** less; **es kommt ~ auf Quantität als auf Qualität an** quantity is less important than quality; **das ist ~ angenehm** that is not very pleasant; *s. auch* **mehr 1. 3** *Konj.* less; **fünf ~ drei** five, take away three

wenigst... 1 *Sup. von* **wenig 1:** least; **am ~en** least; **in den ~en Fällen/für die ~en Menschen** in very few cases/for very few people; **nur die ~en** only very few; **das ~e, was wir tun können** the least we can do. **2** *Sup. von* **wenig 2:** am ~en the least; **das hätte ich am ~en erwartet** that's the last thing I should have expected

wenigstens *Adv.* at least

wenn /vɛn/ *Konj.* **(a)** (konditional) if; **außer ~:** unless; **und [selbst] ~:** even if; **~ es sein muss, komme ich mit** If I have to, I'll come along; **~ es nicht anders geht** if there's no other way; **~ du schon rauchen musst** if you 'must smoke; **(b)** (temporal) when; **jedes Mal** *od.* **immer,**

~: whenever; **(c)** (konzessiv) **wenn ... auch** even though; **und ~ es [auch] noch so spät ist ...:** no matter how late it is ...; however late it is ...; **[und] ~ auch!** (ugs.) even so; all the same; **(d)** (in Wunschsätzen) if only; **~ ich doch** *od.* **nur** *od.* **bloß wüsste, ob ...:** if only I knew whether ...

Wenn *das;* **~s,** *od.* (ugs.) **~s: das ~ und Aber, die ~[s] und Aber[s]** the ifs and buts

wenn·gleich *Konj.* (geh.) even though; although

wenn·schon *Adv.* **~ [nicht] ..., dann ...:** even if [not] ..., then ...; **[na** *od.* **und] ~!** (ugs.) so what?; **~, denn-schon** (ugs.) if you're going to do something, you may as well do it properly; no half measures!

wer /veːɐ̯/ *Nom.:* **1** *Interrogativpron.* who; **~ alles ist dabei gewesen?** which people were there?; who was there?; **~ von ...:** which of; **was glaubt sie eigentlich, ~ sie ist?** who does she think she is? **2** *Relativpron.* (derjenige, der/diejenige, die) the person who; (jeder, der) anyone *or* anybody who; **~ es auch [immer]** *od.* **~ immer es getan hat** (geh.) whoever did it. **3** *Indefinitpron.* (ugs.) someone; somebody; (fragend, verneint) anyone; anybody; *s. auch* **wem, wen, wessen**

Werbe-: **~abteilung** *die* advertising *or* publicity department; **~agentur** *die* advertising agency; **~fernsehen** *das* television commercials *pl.;* **~film** *der* advertising *or* promotional *or* publicity film; **~funk** *der* radio commercials *pl.;* **~geschenk** *das* [promotional] free gift

werben /ˈvɛrbn̩/ **1** *unr. itr. V.* **(a)** advertise; **für etw. ~:** advertise sth.; **für eine Partei ~:** canvass for a party; **(b)** (geh.: sich bemühen) **um Wählerstimmen ~:** seek to attract votes; **um jmds. Gunst/Freundschaft ~:** court sb.'s favour/friendship. **2** *unr. tr. V.* attract ⟨*customers etc.*⟩; recruit ⟨*soldiers, members, staff, etc.*⟩

Werbe-: **~slogan** *der* advertising slogan; **~spot** *der* commercial; advertisement; ad (coll.); **~trommel** *die:* **[für jmdn./etw.] die ~ rühren** *od.* **schlagen** beat *or* thump the drum [for sb./sth.]

Werbung *die;* **~, ~en (a)** *o. Pl.* advertising; **für etw. ~ machen** advertise sth.; **(b)** *o. Pl.:* ⇒ **Werbeabteilung**

Werde·gang *der* **(a)** development; **(b)** (Laufbahn) career

werden /ˈveːɐ̯dn̩/ **1** *unr. itr. V.; mit sein; 2. Part.* **geworden (a)** become; get; **älter ~:** get *or* grow old[er]; **du bist aber groß/schlank geworden!** you've grown so tall/slim; **wahnsinnig** *od.* **verrückt ~:** go mad; **gut ~:** turn out well; **das muss anders ~:** things have to change; **wach ~:** wake up; **rot ~:** go *or* turn red; **er ist 70 [Jahre alt] geworden** he has had his 70th birthday *or* has turned 70; **heute soll es/wird es heiß ~:** it's supposed to get/it's going to be hot today; **mir wird übel/ heiß/schwindelig** I feel sick/I'm getting hot/dizzy; **Arzt/ Vater ~:** become a doctor/a father; **was willst du einmal ~?** what do you want to be when you grow up?; **Erster/Letzter ~:** be *or* come first/last; **was soll das ~?** what is that going to be?; **eine ~de Mutter** a mother-to-be; an expectant mother; **(b)** (sich entwickeln) **zu etw. ~:** become sth.; **das Wasser wurde zu Eis** the water turned into ice; **was soll aus dir ~?** what is to become of you?; **aus ihm ist nichts/etwas geworden** he hasn't got anywhere/has got somewhere in life; **daraus wird nichts ~:** nothing will come of it/that!; **(c)** *unpers.* **es wird [höchste] Zeit** it is [high] time; **es wird 10 Uhr** it is nearly 10 o'clock; **es wird Tag/Nacht/Herbst** day is dawning/ night is falling/autumn is coming; **(d)** (entstehen) come into existence; **es werde Licht** (bibl.) let there be light; **(e)** (ugs.) **sind die Fotos [was] geworden?** have the photos turned out [well]?; **wirds bald?** (ugs.) hurry up!; **was soll nur ~?** what's going to happen now? **2** *Hilfsverb; 2. Part.* **worden (a)** (zur Bildung des Futurs) **wir ~ uns um ihn kümmern** we will take care of him; **dir werd ich helfen!** (ugs.) I'll give you what for (sl.); **es wird gleich regnen** it is going to rain any minute; **wir ~ nächste Woche in Urlaub fahren** we are going on holiday next week; (als Ausdruck der Vermutung) **es wird um die 80 Mark kosten** it will cost around 80 marks; **sie ~ [wohl] im Garten sein** they are probably in the garden; **er wird doch nicht [etwa] krank sein?** he wouldn't be ill, would he?; **sie wird schon wissen, was sie tut** she must know what she's doing; **(b)** (zur Bildung des Passivs) be; **du wirst gerufen** you are being called; **er wurde gebeten/ist gebeten worden** he was asked; **ihm wurde gesagt** he was told; **es wurde gelacht/gesungen/getanzt** there was laughter/singing/dancing; **unser Haus wird renoviert** our house is being renovated; **(c)** (zur Umschreibung des Konjunktivs) **was würdest du tun?** what would you do?; **würden Sie bitte …?** would you please …?

Wer·fall der nominative [case]

werfen /ˈvɛrfn̩/ **1** unr. tr. V. **(a)** throw; drop ‹bombs›; **die Tür ins Schloss ~:** slam the door shut; **jmdn. aus dem Saal ~** (fig. ugs.) throw sb. out of the hall; **(b)** (ruckartig bewegen) throw; **den Kopf in den Nacken ~:** throw or toss one's head back; **die Arme in die Höhe ~:** throw one's arms up; **(c)** (erzielen) throw; **eine Sechs ~:** throw a six; **ein Tor ~:** shoot or throw a goal; **(d)** (bilden) **Falten ~:** wrinkle; crease; **einen Schatten ~:** cast a shadow; **(e)** (gebären) give birth to. **2** unr. itr. V. **(a)** throw; **mit etw. [nach jmdm.] ~:** throw sth. [at sb.]; **mit Geld/Fremdwörtern um sich ~** (fig.) throw [one's] money around/bandy foreign words about; **(b)** (Junge kriegen) give birth; ‹dog, cat› litter. **3** unr. refl. V. **(a)** (auch fig.) throw oneself; **sich auf eine neue Aufgabe ~** (fig.) throw oneself into a new task; **sich in die Kleider ~** (fig.) throw on one's clothes; **(b)** (sich verziehen) buckle; ‹wood› warp

Werfer der; ~s, ~: thrower; (Baseball) pitcher; (Cricket) bowler

Werft /vɛrft/ die; ~, ~en shipyard; dockyard

Werk /vɛrk/ das; ~[e]s, ~e **(a)** o. Pl. (Arbeit) work; **am ~[e] sein** be at work; **sich ans ~ machen, ans ~ gehen** set to or go to work; **(b)** (Tat) work; **das ist dein ~!** that is your doing or handiwork; **(c)** (geistiges, künstlerisches Erzeugnis) work; **(d)** (Betrieb, Fabrik) factory; plant; works sing. or pl.; **ab ~:** ex works; **(e)** (Mechanismus) mechanism; **das ~ einer Uhr/Orgel** the works pl. of a clock/organ

werk-, Werk- (betriebs-, Betriebs-) ⇒ **werk[s]-, Werk[s]-**

Werk·bank die; Pl. **~bänke** workbench

werkeln itr. V. potter around or about

Werken das; ~s (Schulw.) handicraft

Werk[s]-: ~angehörige der/die factory or works employee; **~arzt** der factory or works doctor

Werk·schutz der **(a)** factory or works security; **(b)** (Personen) factory or works security service

Werk[s]-: ~gelände das factory or works premises pl.; **~halle** die workshop; **~spionage** die industrial espionage

werk-, Werk-: ~statt die; **~statt, ~stätten, ~stätte** die workshop; (Kfz-W.) garage; **~stoff** der material; **~stück** das workpiece; **~tag** der working day; workday; **~tags** Adv. on weekdays; **~tätig** Adj. working; **~tätige** der/die; adj. Dekl. worker; **~unterricht** der [handi]craft instruction no art.; (Unterrichtsstunde) [handi]craft lesson; **~zeug** das **(a)** (auch fig.) tool; **(b)** o. Pl. (Gesamtheit) tools pl.

Werkzeug·kasten der toolbox

Wermut /ˈveːrmuːt/ der; ~[e]s, ~s **(a)** (Pflanze) wormwood; **(b)** (Wein) vermouth

wert /veːɐt/ Adj. **(a)** (geh.) esteemed; (als Anrede) **~e Genossen!** my dear comrades; **wie ist Ihr ~er Name, bitte?** (geh.) may I have your name, please?; **(b)** etw. **sein** be worth sth.; **das ist nichts ~:** this is worth nothing or worthless; **der Teppich ist sein Geld nicht ~:** the carpet is not worth the money; **das ist nicht der Erwähnung** (Gen.) **~:** this is not worth mentioning; s. auch **Rede** c

Wert der; ~[e]s, ~e **(a)** value; **im ~ steigen/fallen** increase/decrease in value; **an ~ gewinnen/verlieren** gain/lose in value; **im ~[e] von** … worth …; etw. **unter [seinem] ~ verkaufen** sell sth. for less than its value; **einer Sache** (Dat.) **großen ~ beimessen** attach great value to sth.; **sich** (Dat.) **seines [eigenen] ~es bewusst sein** be conscious of one's own importance; **das hat [doch] keinen ~!** (ugs.: ist sinnlos) there's no point; **~ auf etw.** (Akk.) **legen** set great store by or on sth.; **(b)** Pl. objects of value; **(c)** (Briefmarke) denomination

Wert·arbeit die high-quality workmanship

wert·beständig Adj. of lasting value postpos.; stable ‹currency, investment, etc.›; **~beständig sein** retain its value

werten tr., itr. V. **(a)** judge; assess; **etw. als besondere Leistung ~:** rate sth. as a special achievement; **etw. als Erfolg ~:** regard sth. as or consider sth. a success; **(b)** (Sport) **etw. hoch/niedrig ~:** award high/low points to sth.

wert·frei 1 Adj. detached; impartial; neutral ‹term›. **2** adv. with detachment; impartially

Wert·gegenstand der valuable object; object of value; **Wertgegenstände** valuables

-wertig (Chemie, Sprachw.) -valent

Wertigkeit die; ~, ~en (Chemie, Sprachw.) valency (Brit.); valence (Amer.)

wert-, Wert-: ~los Adj. worthless; valueless; **~maßstab** der standard [of value]; **~paket** das (Postw.) registered parcel; **~papier** das (Wirtsch.) security; **~sache** die; meist Pl. valuable item or object; **~sachen** valuables; **~schätzung** die (geh.) esteem; high regard; **~steigerung** die appreciation; increase in value

Wertung die; ~, ~en judgement

Wert·urteil das value judgement

wert·voll Adj. valuable; (schätzenswert) estimable

Wesen /ˈveːzn̩/ das; **~s, ~ (a)** o. Pl. (Natur) nature; (Art, Charakter) character; nature; **ein freundliches/kindliches ~ haben** have a friendly/childlike nature or manner; **(b)** (Mensch) creature; soul; **ein weibliches/männliches ~:** a woman or female/a man or male; **(c)** (Lebe~) being; creature

Wesens-: ~art die nature; character; **~zug** der trait; characteristic

wesentlich 1 Adj. fundamental (**für** to); **von ~er Bedeutung** of considerable importance; **im Wesentlichen** essentially. **2** adv. (erheblich) considerably; much; **es wäre mir ~ lieber, wenn wir …:** I would much rather we …

Wes·fall der genitive [case]

wes·halb Adv. ⇒ **warum**

Wespe /ˈvɛspə/ die; ~, ~n wasp

Wespen-: ~nest das wasp's nest; **in ein ~nest stechen** (fig. ugs.) stir up a hornets' nest; **~stich** der wasp sting

wessen Interrogativpron. **(a)** (Gen. von **wer**) whose; **(b)** (Gen. von **was**) **~ wird er beschuldigt?** what is he accused of?

Wessi /ˈvɛsi/ der; ~s, ~s (salopp) West German

West /vɛst/ o. Art.; o. Pl. ▶ 266 **(a)** (bes. Seemannsspr., Met.) west; **(b)** (Gebiet) West; **(c)** (Politik) West; **(d)** einem Subst. nachgestellt (westlicher Teil, westliche Lage) West; s. auch **Ost[1]; Nord[1]**

West·Berlin (das) (hist.) West Berlin

west-, West-: ~deutsch Adj. Western German; (hist.: auf die alte BRD bezogen) West German; **~deutsche** der/die Western German; (hist.: Bürger der alten BRD) West German; **~deutschland** (das) Western Germany; (hist.: alte BRD) West Germany

Weste /ˈvɛstə/ die; ~, ~n waistcoat (Brit.); vest (Amer.); **eine weiße od. saubere ~ haben** (fig. ugs.) have a clean record; **jmdm. etw. unter die ~ jubeln** (fig. ugs.) shift or push sth. on to sb.

Westen der; ~s ▶ 266 **(a)** (Richtung) west; **nach ~:** westwards; to the west; **im/aus od. von od. vom ~:** in/from the west; **(b)** (Gegend) West; **im ~:** in the West; **der Wilde ~:** the Wild West; **(c)** (Geogr., Politik) der ~ the West; s. auch **Osten, Norden**

Westen·tasche die waistcoat (Brit.) or (Amer.) vest pocket; **etw. wie seine ~ kennen** (ugs.) know sth. like the back of one's hand

Western der; ~[s], ~: western

West·europa (das) Western Europe

west·europäisch Adj. West or Western European

West·indien (das) the West Indies pl

west·indisch Adj. West Indian

West·küste die west[ern] coast

westlich ▶ 266 **1** Adj. **(a)** (im Westen) western; **15 Grad ~er Länge** 15 degrees west [longitude]; **das ~e Frankreich** western France; **(b)** (nach, aus dem Westen) westerly;

(c) (des Westens, auch Politik) Western. **2** *Adv.* westwards; ～ **von** ...: [to the] west of ... **3** *Präp. mit Gen.* [to the] west of; *s. auch* **östlich**

wẹst-, Wẹst-: ～**seite** *die* western side; ～**wärts** *Adv.* ▶266❘ [to the] west; ～**wind** *der* west[erly] wind

wes·wegen *Adv.* ⇒ **warum**

Wẹtt-: ～**bewerb** *der;* ～**[e]s,** ～**e (a)** competition; **gut im** ～**bewerb liegen** have a good chance of winning the competition; **(b)** *o. Pl.* (Wirtsch.: Konkurrenz) competition *no indef. art.;* ～**bewerber** *der* competitor

Wette /'vɛtə/ *die;* ～**,** ～**n** bet; **was gilt die** ～**?** how much do you want to bet?; **what do you bet?; eine** ～ **[mit jmdm.] abschließen** make a bet [with sb.]; **[ich gehe] jede** ～ **[ein], dass** ...: I bet you anything [you like] that ...; **mit jmdm. um die** ～ **laufen** race sb.; **sie schwammen um die** ～: they raced each other at swimming

Wẹtt·eifer *der* competitiveness

wẹtt·eifern *itr. V.* compete (**mit** with, **um** for)

wetten 1 *itr. V.* bet; **mit jmdm.** ～: have a bet with sb.; **mit jmdm. um etw.** ～: bet sb. sth.; **auf etw.** *(Akk.)* ～: bet on sth.; put one's money on sth.; **[wollen wir]** ～**?** [do you] want to bet?; **ich wette hundert zu eins, dass** ... (ugs.) I'll bet [you] a hundred to one that ...; **so haben wir nicht gewettet** (ugs.) that was not the deal *or* not what we agreed; **auf Platz/Sieg** ～: make a place bet/bet on a win. **2** *tr. V.* **10 Mark** ～: bet 10 marks

Wetter *das;* ～**,** ～ **(a)** *o. Pl.* weather; **bei jedem** ～: in all weathers; **es ist schönes** ～: the weather is good *or* fine; **bei jmdm. gut** ～ **machen** (fig. ugs.) get on the right side of sb.; butter sb. up; **(b)** (Un～) storm; **(c)** *Pl.* (Bergbau) **schlagende** ～: firedamp

wetter-, Wetter-: ～**amt** *das* meteorological office; ～**aussichten** *Pl.* weather outlook *sing.;* ～**bericht** *der* weather report; (Voraussage) weather forecast; ～**besserung** *die* improvement in the weather; ～**beständig** *Adj.* weatherproof; ～**dienst** *der* weather *or* meteorological service; ～**fahne** *die* weathervane; ～**fest** *Adj.* weather-resistant; ～**fühlig** *Adj.* sensitive to [changes in] the weather *postpos.;* ～**fühligkeit** *die;* ～: sensitivity to [changes in] the weather; ～**hahn** *der* weathercock; ～**karte** *die* weather chart; weather map; ～**lage** *die* weather situation; (fig.) situation; climate; ～**leuchten** *itr. V.; unpers.* **es** ～**leuchtet** there is summer lightning; ～**leuchten** *das;* ～**s** sheet (*esp. summer*) lightning *no indef. art.*

wettern *itr. V.* (ugs.: schimpfen) curse; **gegen** *od.* **über etw./jmdn.** ～: loudly denounce sth./sb.

wetter-, Wetter-: ～**satellit** *der* weather satellite; ～**seite** *die* windward side; side exposed to the weather; ～**station** *die* weather station; ～**vorhersage** *die* weather forecast

wẹtt-, Wẹtt-: ～**fahrt** *die* race; ～**kampf** *der* competition; ～**kämpfer** *der* competitor; ～**lauf** *der* race; **einen** ～**lauf machen** run a race; **ein** ～**lauf mit der Zeit/dem Tod** (fig.) a race against time/with death; ～**|machen** *tr. V.* (ugs.) make up for; **etw. durch etw.** ～**machen** make up for sth. with sth.; (wieder gutmachen) make good ⟨*loss, mistake, etc.*⟩; ～**rennen** *das* (auch fig.) race; **ein** ～**rennen machen** have *or* run a race; ～**rüsten** *das;* ～**s** arms race; ～**streit** *der* contest

wetzen /'vɛtsn̩/ **1** *tr. V.* sharpen; whet. **2** *itr. V.; mit sein* (ugs.) dash

Wẹtz·stein *der* whetstone

WEZ *Abk.* **Westeuropäische Zeit** GMT

Whiskey /'vɪski/ *der;* ～**s** ～**s** whiskey; [American/Irish] whisky

Whisky /'vɪski/ *der;* ～**s,** ～**s** whisky

wich /vɪç/ *1. u. 3. Pers. Sg. Prät. v.* **weichen**

Wichse /'vɪksə/ *die;* ～**,** ～**n** (ugs.) [shoe-]polish

wichsen 1 *tr. V.* (ugs.) polish. **2** *itr. V.* (derb) wank (Brit. coarse); jerk off (coarse)

Wicht /vɪçt/ *der;* ～**[e]s,** ～**e (a)** (fam.: Kind) little rascal *or* imp (joc.); **(b)** (abwertend: Mensch) [insignificant] creature

Wichtel *der;* ～**s,** ～**, Wichtel·männchen** *das* gnome; (Kobold) goblin

wichtig /'vɪçtɪç/ *Adj.* important; **es ist mir** ～ **zu wissen, ob** ...: it is important to me to know if ...; **nichts Wichtigeres zu tun haben[, als** ...] (auch iron.) have nothing better to do [than ...]; **sich** ～ **machen** *od.* **tun** (ugs. abwertend) be full of one's own importance

Wichtigkeit *die;* ～ importance

Wichtigtuer /-tuːɐ/ *der;* ～**s,** ～ (ugs. abwertend) pompous ass

wichtigtuerisch 1 *Adj.* self-important; pompous. **2** *adv.* in a self-important manner; ⟨*behave, act*⟩ pompously

Wicke /'vɪkə/ *die;* ～**,** ～**n** vetch; (im Garten) sweet pea

Wickel *der;* ～**s,** ～: compress; **jmdn. am** *od.* **beim** ～ **haben/nehmen** (fig. ugs.) have/grab sb. by the scruff of his/her neck

Wickel-: ～**kind** *das* baby; infant; ～**kommode** *die* baby's changing-table

wickeln *tr. V.* **(a)** (auf～) wind; (ab～) unwind; **Wolle zu einem Knäuel** ～: wind wool into a ball; **etw. auf/um etw.** *(Akk.)* ～: wind sth. on to sth./round sth.; **(b)** (eindrehen) **sich/jmdm. die Haare** ～: put one's/sb.'s hair in curlers *or* rollers; **(c)** (ein～) wrap; (aus～) unwrap; **etw./jmdn./sich in etw.** *(Akk.)* ～: wrap sth./sb./oneself in sth.; **er hat sich [fest] in seinen Mantel gewickelt** he wrapped his coat tightly [a]round himself; **(d)** (windeln) **ein Kind** ～: change a baby's nappy; **er ist frisch gewickelt** he has had his nappy changed; **(e)** (bandagieren) bandage; **(f) schief gewickelt sein** (ugs.) be very much mistaken

Wickel-: ～**rock** *der* wrapover skirt; ～**tisch** *der* baby's changing-table

Widder /'vɪdɐ/ *der;* ～**s,** ～ **(a)** ram; **(b)** (Astron., Astrol.) Aries

wider /'viːdɐ/ *Präp. mit Akk.* **(a)** (veralt.) against; **(b)** (geh.: entgegen) contrary to; ～ **besseres Wissen/alle Vernunft** against one's better knowledge/all reason; ～ **Willen** against one's will

wider-, Wider-: ～**borstig 1** *Adj.* unruly, unmanageable ⟨*hair*⟩; (fig.) rebellious ⟨*person*⟩; unruly, rebellious ⟨*child*⟩; **2** *adv.* rebelliously; ～**fahren** /-'--/ *unr. itr. V.; mit sein* (geh.) **etw.** ～**fährt jmdm.** sth. happens to sb.; **ihm ist [ein] Unrecht** ～**fahren** he has been done an injustice; ～**haken** *der* barb; ～**hall** *der* echo; (fig.) **[bei jmdm.]** ～**hall finden** meet with a [positive] response [from sb.]; ～**|hallen** *itr. V.* echo; resound (**von** with); ～**legen** /-'--/ *tr. V.* **etw./jmdn.** ～**legen** refute *or* disprove sth./prove sb. wrong; ～**legung** /-'--/ *die;* ～**,** ～**en** refutation

widerlich (abwertend) **1** *Adj.* **(a)** revolting; repulsive; ～ **schmecken/riechen** taste/smell revolting; **(b)** repugnant, repulsive ⟨*person, behaviour, etc.*⟩; awful ⟨*headache etc.*⟩. **2** *adv.* revoltingly; ⟨*behave, act*⟩ in a repugnant *or* repulsive manner; awfully ⟨*cold, hot, sweet, etc.*⟩

wider-, Wider-: ～**natürlich** *Adj.* unnatural; ～**rechtlich 1** *Adj.* illegal; unlawful; ～**rechtliches Betreten eines Geländes/Gebäudes** trespass[ing] on a property/unlawful *or* illegal entry to a building; **2** *adv.* illegally; unlawfully; ～**rede** *die* argument; contradiction; **keine** ～**rede!** don't argue!; no arguing!; ～**ruf** *der* (einer Aussage) retraction; (eines Befehls, einer Anordnung, Erlaubnis usw.) revocation; withdrawal; **[bis] auf** ～**ruf** until revoked *or* cancelled; ～**rufen** /-'--/ *unr. tr., auch itr. V.* retract, withdraw ⟨*statement, claim, confession, etc.*⟩; revoke, cancel ⟨*order, permission, etc.*⟩; repeal ⟨*law*⟩; ～**sacher** *der;* ～**s,** ～**,** ～**sacherin** *die;* ～**,** ～**nen** (geh.) adversary; opponent; ～**schein** *der* (geh.) reflection; ～**setzen** /-'--/ *refl. V.* **sich jmdm./einer Sache** ～**setzen** oppose sb./sth.; ～**setzlich** /-'--/ **1** *Adj.* rebellious; **2** *adv.* rebelliously; ～**sinnig** *Adj.* absurd; ～**spenstig** ～/ʃpɛnstɪç/ **1** *Adj.* unruly; rebellious; wilful; unruly, unmanageable ⟨*hair*⟩; stubborn ⟨*horse, mule, etc.*⟩; **2** *adv.* wilfully; rebelliously; ～**spenstigkeit** *die;* ～: unruliness; rebelliousness; wilfulness; (von Haaren) unruliness; unmanageableness; (von Pferden usw.) stubbornness; ～**|spiegeln,** ～**spiegeln** /-'--/ **1** *tr. V.* reflect; (als Spiegelbild) mirror; (fig.) reflect; **2** *refl. V.* be reflected; (als Spiegelbild) be mirrored; (fig.) be reflected; ～**sprechen** /-'--/ *unr. itr. V.* **(a)** contradict; **jmdm./einer Sache/sich [selbst]** ～**sprechen** contradict sb./sth./oneself; **(b)** (im

Gegensatz stehen zu) contradict, be inconsistent with ⟨*facts, truth, etc.*⟩; **sich** (*Dat.*) **~sprechende Aussagen/Nachrichten** conflicting statements/news reports; **~spruch** *der* (**a**) *o. Pl.* opposition; protest; **es erhob sich allgemeiner ~spruch** there was a general protest; **auf ~spruch stoßen** meet with opposition *or* protests; (**b**) (etw. Unvereinbares) contradiction; **sich** (*Akk.*) **in ~sprüche verwickeln** get entangled *or* caught up in contradictions; **in ~spruch zu** *od.* **mit etw. stehen** contradict sth.; be contradictory to sth.; **~sprüchlich** *Adj.* contradictory ⟨*news, statements, etc.*⟩; inconsistent ⟨*behaviour, attitude, etc.*⟩; **~spruchs·los 1** *Adj.; nicht präd.* unprotesting; uncontradicting; **2** *adv.* without opposition *or* protest

Wider·stand *der* (**a**) resistance (**gegen** to); **jmdm./einer Sache ~ leisten** resist sb./sth.; put up resistance to sb./sth.; **bei jmdm. auf ~ stoßen** meet with *or* encounter resistance from sb.; **allen Widerständen zum Trotz** despite all opposition; **der ~** (Politik) the Resistance; *s. auch* **Weg c**; (**b**) (Elektrot.: Schaltungselement) resistor

widerstands·, Widerstands-: ~bewegung *die* resistance movement; **~fähig** *Adj.* robust; resistant ⟨*material etc.*⟩; hardy ⟨*animal, plant*⟩; **~fähig gegen etw. sein** be resistant to sth.; **~fähigkeit** *die; o. Pl.* robustness; (von Material usw.) resistance; (von Tier, Pflanze) hardiness; **~kämpfer** *der* resistance fighter; **~kraft** *die; o. Pl.* resistance; **~los 1** *Adj.* without resistance *postpos.*; **2** *adv.* without resistance

wider-, Wider-: ~stehen /-'--/ *unr. itr. V.* (**a**) (nicht nachgeben) [jmdm./einer Sache] **~stehen** resist [sb./sth.]; (**b**) (standhalten) **jmdm./einer Sache ~stehen** withstand sb./sth.; **~streben** /-'--/ *itr. V.* **etw. ~strebt jmdm.** sb. dislikes *or* detests sth.; **es ~strebt jmdm., etw. zu tun** sb. dislikes doing sth. *or* is reluctant to do sth.; **~d nachgeben/einwilligen** give in/agree reluctantly; **~streben** /--'--/ *das* reluctance; **~streit** *der; o. Pl.* conflict; **~streitend** /--'--/ *Adj.; nicht präd.* conflicting; **~wärtig** /~vɛrtɪç/ (abwertend) **1** *Adj.* (**a**) (unangenehm) disagreeable, unpleasant ⟨*conditions, situation, etc.*⟩; (**b**) (ekelhaft, abscheulich) revolting, repugnant ⟨*smell, taste, etc.*⟩; objectionable, offensive ⟨*person, behaviour, attitude, etc.*⟩; **2** *adv.* ⟨*behave, act, etc.*⟩ in an objectionable *or* offensive manner; **~wärtigkeit** *die; ~, -en* (**a**) *o. Pl.* offensiveness; objectionableness; repulsiveness; (**b**) (Umstand) disagreeable *or* unpleasant circumstance; **~wille** *der* aversion (**gegen** to); **~willig 1** *Adj.; nicht präd.* reluctant; unwilling; **2** *adv.* reluctantly; unwillingly; **etw. nur ~willig tun** do sth. only with reluctance; **~wort** *das:* **keine ~worte dulden** not tolerate any argument; **keine ~worte!** no arguments!

widmen /'vɪtmən/ **1** *tr. V.* (**a**) **jmdm. ein Buch/Gedicht** *usw.* **~:** dedicate a book/poem etc. to sb.; (**b**) (verwenden für/auf) **etw. jmdm./einer Sache ~** devote sth. to sb./sth. **2** *refl. V.* **sich jmdm./einer Sache ~:** attend to sb./sth.; (ausschließlich) devote oneself to sb./sth.

Widmung *die; ~, -en* dedication (**an** + *Akk.* to)

widrig /'vi:drɪç/ *Adj.* unfavourable; adverse

Widrigkeit *die; ~, -en* adversity

wie 1 *Interrogativadv.* (**a**) (auf welche Art u. Weise) how; **~ heißt er/das?** what is his/its name?; what is he/that called?; **~ [bitte]?** [I beg your] pardon?; (entrüstet) I beg your pardon!; **~ war das?** (ugs.) what was that?; what did you say?; **~ kommt es, dass ...?** how is it that ...?; **~ das?** (ugs.) how did that come about?; (b) (durch welche Merkmale gekennzeichnet) **~ war das Wetter?** what was the weather like?; how was the weather?; **~ ist dein neuer Chef?** what is your new boss like? (coll.); how is your new boss? (coll.); **~ geht es ihm?** how is he?; **~ war es in Spanien?** what was Spain like?; what was it like in Spain?; **~ findest du das Bild?** what do you think of the picture?; **~ gefällt er dir?** how do you like him?; **~ wär's mit ~:** how about ...; (**c**) (in welchem Grade) how; **~ lange/groß/hoch/oft/viel?** how long/big/high/often/much?; **~ spät ist es?** what time is it?; **wie alt bist du?** how old are you?; **und ~!** and how! (coll.); (**d**) (ugs.: nicht wahr) **das hat dir Spaß gemacht, ~?** you enjoyed that,

didn't you? **2** *Relativadv.* [**die Art,**] **~ er es tut** the way *or* manner in which he does it; **~ schon der Name sagt** as the name already implies. **3** *Konj.* (**a**) *Vergleichspartikel* as; [**so**] ... **~** ...: as ... as ...; **er macht es [genauso] ~ du** he does it [just] like you [do]; **ich fühlte mich ~ ...:** I felt as if I were ...; **„N" ~ „Nordpol"** N for November; **~ [zum Beispiel]** like; such as; **~ wenn** as if *or* though; (**b**) (und, sowie) as well as; both; **Männer ~ Frauen** men as well as women; both men and women; (**c**) (temporal: als) **~ ich an seinem Fenster vorbeigehe, höre ich ihn singen** as I pass by his window I hear him singing; (**d**) (ugs.: außer) **nichts ~ Ärger** nothing but trouble

wieder /'vi:dɐ/ *Adv.* (**a**) (erneut) again; **je/nie ~:** ever/ never again; **immer ~,** (geh.) **~ und ~:** again and again; time and [time] again; **nie ~ Krieg!** no more war!; **was ist denn jetzt schon ~ los?** what's happened 'now?; **etw. ~ aufnehmen** (fig.) resume sth.; **ein Thema/eine Idee ~ aufnehmen** take up a subject/an idea again; **Beziehungen ~ aufnehmen** re-establish relations; **ein Verfahren ~ aufnehmen** (Rechtspr.) reopen a case; **jmdn. ~ aufnehmen** readmit sb.; **~ auftauchen** (fig.) turn up again; **etw. ~ entdecken** rediscover sth.; **jmdn./etw. ~ erkennen** recognize sb./sth.; **er war kaum ~ zu erkennen** he was almost recognizable; **etw. ~ finden** find sth. again; (fig.) regain sth.; **sich ~ finden** be found; **jmdn./etw. ~ sehen** see sb./sth. again; **sich ~ sehen** see each other *or* meet again; **etw. ~ tun** do sth. again; **etw. ~ verwenden** reuse sth.; **jmdn. ~ wählen** re-elect sb.; (**b**) (unterscheidend: noch) **einige ..., andere ... und ~ andere ...:** some ..., others ..., and yet others ...; **das ist ~ etwas anderes** that is something else again; (**c**) (drückt Rückkehr in früheren Zustand aus) again; **alles ist ~ beim Alten** everything is back as it was before; **etw. ~ an seinen Platz zurückstellen** put sth. back in its place; **ich bin gleich ~ da** I'll be right back (coll.); I'll be back in a minute; **ein Land ~ vereinigen** reunify a country; **etw. ~ aufbauen** reconstruct sth.; rebuild sth.; **jmdn. ~ aufrichten** (fig.) give fresh heart to sb.; **jmdn. ~ beleben** revive *or* resuscitate sb.; **eine Freundschaft/einen Brauch ~ beleben** revive *or* resurrect a friendship/custom; **etw. ~ gutmachen** make sth. good; put sth. right; **den Schaden ~ gutmachen** pay for the damage; **ein nicht ~ gutzumachendes Unrecht** an irreparable injustice; (**d**) (andererseits, anders betrachtet) **das ist auch ~ wahr** that's true enough; **da hast du auch ~ recht** you're right there; (**e**) ⇒ **wiederum c**; (**f**) (zur Vergeltung/zum Dank) likewise; also; (**g**) (ugs.: noch) **wie heißt er ~?** what's his name again?; **wo/wann war das [gleich] ~?** where/when was that again?

wieder-, Wieder-: ~aufbau *der; o. Pl.* reconstruction; rebuilding; *****~auf|bauen** ⇒ **wieder c**; **~aufbereitungs·anlage** *die* recycling plant; (Kerntechnik) reprocessing plant; **~aufnahme** *die* (**a**) resumption; (von Beziehungen) re-establishment; **die ~aufnahme eines Verfahrens** (Rechtsspr.) the resumption *or* reopening of proceedings; (**b**) (als Mitglied) readmittance; (**c**) (eines Theaterstücks) revival; *****~auf|nehmen** ⇒ **wieder a**; *****~auf|richten** ⇒ **wieder c**; *****~auf|tauchen** ⇒ **wieder a**

wieder-, Wieder-: ~beginn *der* recommencement; resumption; **~|bekommen** *unr. tr. V.* get back; *****~|beleben** ⇒ **wieder c**; **~belebungs·versuch** *der* attempt at resuscitation; **bei jmdm. ~belebungsversuche machen** attempt to revive *or* resuscitate sb.; *****~|bringen** *unr. tr. V.* bring back; *****~|entdecken** ⇒ **wieder a**; *****~|erkennen** ⇒ **wieder a**; **~|finden** ⇒ **wieder a**; **~gabe** *die* (**a**) (Bericht) report; account; (**b**) (Übersetzung) rendering; (**c**) (Reproduktion) reproduction; **~|geben** *unr. tr. V.* (**a**) (zurückgeben) give back; return; (**b**) (berichten) report; give an account of; (wiederholen) repeat; (ausdrücken) express; (zitieren) quote; (**c**) (übersetzen) render; (**d**) (darstellen) portray; depict; (**e**) (hörbar, sichtbar machen) reproduce; **~|gewinnen** *unr. tr. V.* recover ⟨*lost item, money, etc.*⟩; regain ⟨*composure, equilibrium*⟩

*****wieder·gut|machen** ⇒ **wieder c**

wieder|haben *unr. tr. V.* (auch fig.) have back

wieder-, Wieder-: ~her|stellen; ich stelle wieder her *tr. V.* (**a**) re-establish ⟨*contact, peace*⟩; (**b**) (reparieren) restore ⟨*building*⟩; **(c) jmdn. ∼herstellen** restore sb. to health; get sb. on his/her feet again; **∼herstellung** *die* **(a)** re-establishment; **(b)** (Wiederinstandsetzung) restoration; **(c)** (Genesung) recovery; **∼holbar** *Adj.* repeatable; **∼holen** 1 *tr. V.* **(a)** repeat, replay ⟨*football match*⟩; retake ⟨*penalty kick*⟩; resit, retake ⟨*exam*⟩; hold ⟨*election*⟩ again; **(b)** (nochmals sagen) repeat, reiterate ⟨*question, demand, offer, etc.*⟩; **(c)** (repetieren) revise ⟨*lesson, vocabulary, etc.*⟩; **2** *refl. V.* **(a)** (wieder dasselbe sagen) repeat oneself; **(b)** (erneut geschehen) happen again; **(c)** (wiederkehren) be repeated; recur

wieder|holen *tr. V.* fetch *or* get back

wiederholt 1 *Adj.; nicht präd.* repeated; **zum ∼en Male** yet again. **2** *adv.* repeatedly

Wiederholung *die;* ∼, ∼**en (a)** repetition; (eines Fußballspiels usw.) replay; (eines Freistoßes, Elfmeters usw.) retaking; (einer Sendung) repeat; (einer Aufführung) repeat performance; **(b)** (des Schuljahrs, einer Prüfung usw.) repeating; **(c)** (von Lernstoff) revision

Wiederholungs-: ∼**zahlwort** *das* multiplicative; ∼**zeichen** *das* (Musik) repeat sign

Wieder·hören: [auf] ∼! goodbye! (*at end of telephone call*)

wieder-, Wieder-: ∼|**käuen** /-kɔyən/ **1** *itr. V.* ruminate; chew the cud; **2** *tr. V.* **(a)** chew again; **(b)** (fig. abwertend) rehash; ∼**käuer** *der;* ∼**s,** ∼: ruminant; ∼**kehr** *die;* ∼ (geh.) **(a)** (Rückkehr) return; **(b)** (Wiederholung) recurrence; ∼|**kehren** *itr. V.; mit sein* (geh.) **(a)** (zurückkehren) return; **(b)** (sich noch einmal ereignen) come again; **(c)** (sich wiederholen) be repeated; recur; ∼|**kommen** *unr. itr. V.; mit sein* **(a)** (zurückkommen) return, come back; **(b)** (noch einmal kommen) come back *or* again; **(c)** (sich noch einmal ereignen) ⟨*opportunity, past*⟩ come again; ∼|**kriegen** *tr. V.* (ugs.) get back; ∼**schauen:** [auf] ∼schauen! (südd., österr.) goodbye!; *∼|**sehen** ⇨ **wieder a;** ∼**sehen** *das;* ∼**s,** ∼: reunion; [auf] ∼**sehen!** goodbye!; **jmdm. Auf** *od.* **auf ∼sehen sagen** say goodbye to sb.

Wiedersehens·freude *die; o. Pl.* pleasure of seeing sb./each other again

wieder-, Wieder-: *∼|**tun** ⇨ **wieder a;** ∼**um** *Adv.* **(a)** (erneut) again; **(b)** (andererseits) on the other hand; **so weit würde ich ∼um nicht gehen** I wouldn't, however, go that far; **(c)** (meiner-, deinerseits usw.) in turn; *∼|**vereinigen** ⇨ **wieder c;** ∼**vereinigung** *die* reunification; *∼|**verwenden** ⇨ **wieder a;** ∼**verwendung** *die* reuse; ∼**wahl** *die* re-election; **sich zur ∼wahl stellen** stand *or* run for re-election; *∼|**wählen** ⇨ **wieder a**

Wiege /'vi:gə/ *die;* ∼, ∼**n** (auch fig.) cradle; **von der ∼ bis zur Bahre** (scherzh.) from the cradle to the grave

wiegen[1] *unr. tr., itr. V.* ▶228| weigh; **was** *od.* **wie viel wiegst du?** how much do you weigh?; what weight *or* how heavy are you?; **schwer ∼** (fig.) carry weight

wiegen[2] **1** *tr. V.* rock; shake ⟨*head*⟩ (*in doubt*); **die Hüften ∼:** sway one's hips; **einen ∼den Gang haben** have a rolling gait. **2** *refl. V.* ⟨*boat, cradle, etc.*⟩ rock; ⟨*person, branch, etc.*⟩ sway

Wiegen-: ∼**fest** *das* (geh.) birthday; ∼**lied** *das* lullaby; cradle-song

wiehern /'vi:ɐn/ *itr. V.* **(a)** whinny; (lauter) neigh; **(b)** [vor Lachen] ∼ (fig. ugs.) roar with laughter

Wien /'vi:n/ (*das*); ∼**s** ▶490| Vienna

Wiener[1] ▶490| **1** *der;* ∼**s,** ∼: Viennese. **2** *indekl. Adj.* Viennese; ∼ **Würstchen** wiener; frankfurter; ∼ **Schnitzel** Wiener schnitzel

Wiener[2] *die;* ∼, ∼: wiener [sausage]

Wienerin *die;* ∼, ∼**nen** Viennese

wienerisch *Adj.* ▶490| Viennese

wies /'vi:s/ *1. u. 3. Pers. Sg. Prät. v.* **weisen**

Wiese /'vi:zə/ *die;* ∼, ∼**n** meadow; (Rasen) lawn

Wiesel /'vi:zl/ *das;* ∼**s,** ∼: weasel; **wie ein ∼ laufen** run like a hare; *s. auch* **flink 1**

wie·so *Adv.* why

*****wie·viel** ⇨ **viel, wie, Uhr b**

wie·viel·mal /*od.* '-'--/ *Adv.* how many times

wievielt... /*od.* '--/ *Interrogativadj.;* ▶119| **als ∼er Läufer ist er durchs Ziel gekommen?** in what position did he finish?; **der ∼e Band?** which number volume?; **der Wievielte ist heute?** what is the date today?; **am Wievielten?** [on] what date?

wie·weit *Adv.* to what extent; how far

Wikinger /'vi:kɪŋɐ/ *der;* ∼**s,** ∼: Viking

wild /vɪlt/ **1** *Adj.* **(a)** wild; rugged, wild ⟨*countryside, area, etc.*⟩; wild, unruly ⟨*hair, beard, etc.*⟩; ∼**e Triebe** rank shoots; **(b)** (unerlaubt) unauthorized; illegal; ∼**es Parken** illegal parking; **in ∼er Ehe leben** (veralt.) live in sin; ∼**er Streik** wildcat strike; **(c)** (heftig, gewaltig) wild ⟨*panic, flight, passion, desire, etc.*⟩; fierce ⟨*battle, anger, determination, look*⟩; ∼ **auf etw.** (Akk.) **sein** (ugs.) be mad *or* crazy about sth. (coll.); ∼ **auf jmdn.** *od.* **nach jmdm. sein** (ugs.) be mad *or* crazy *or* wild about sb. (coll.); **(d)** (wütend) furious ⟨*curs ing, shouting, etc.*⟩; ∼ **werden** get furious; **den ∼en Mann spielen** (ugs.) get heavy (coll.); **(e)** (unbändig, ungestüm) wild, unruly ⟨*child*⟩; **(f)** (maßlos, wüst) wild ⟨*speculation, claim, rumour, accusation*⟩; vile ⟨*oaths, curses*⟩; **halb so ∼ sein** (ugs.) not be as bad as all that (coll.); **(g)** *nicht präd.* (primitiv) savage; wild. **2** *adv.* **(a)** wildly; ∼ **entschlossen sein** (ugs.) be absolutely determined; ∼ **um sich schlagen** hit out *or* lash out wildly; **wie ∼** (ugs.) like mad (coll.); **(b)** (unerlaubt) illegally; ∼ **zelten** camp in an unauthorized place; **(c)** ∼ **lebend** wild; living in the wild *postpos.*; ∼ **wachsend** wild

Wild *das;* ∼[e]**s** game; (einzelnes Tier) [wild] animal

Wild-: ∼**bahn** *die:* **in freier ∼bahn** in the wild; ∼**bret** /∼brɛt/ *das;* ∼**s** (geh.) game; ∼**dieb** *der* poacher

Wilde *der/die; adj. Dekl.* savage; **wie ein ∼r/die ∼n** (ugs.) like a mad thing/like mad things (coll.)

Wild·ente *die* wild duck

Wilderei *die;* ∼, ∼**en** poaching *no pl., no art.*

Wilderer *der;* ∼**s,** ∼: poacher

wildern **1** *itr. V.* **(a)** poach; go poaching; **(b)** ⟨*cat, dog*⟩ kill game. **2** *tr. V.* poach

wild·fremd *Adj.* completely strange; **ein ∼er Mensch** a complete stranger

Wild·gans *die* wild goose

Wildheit *die;* ∼: wildness; (eines Volkes usw.) savageness

wild-, Wild-: ∼**katze** *die* wild cat; *∼**lebend** ⇨ **wild 2 c;** ∼**leder** *das* suede

Wildnis *die;* ∼, ∼**se** wilderness

wild-, Wild-: ∼**pflanze** *die* wild plant; ∼**sau** *die* wild sow; ∼**schwein** *das* wild boar; *∼**wachsend** ⇨ **wild 2 c;** ∼**wechsel** *der* **(a)** game path; **(b)** *o. Pl.* (Vorgang) game crossing; ∼**westfilm** /-'--/ *der* western; Wild West film

Wilhelm /'vɪlhɛlm/ (*der*) William

will /vɪl/ *1. u. 3. Pers. Sg. Präsens v.* **wollen**

Wille *der;* ∼**ns** will; (Wunsch) wish; (Absicht) intention; **guter/böser ∼:** goodwill/ill will; **aus freiem ∼n** of one's own free will; **seinen ∼n durchsetzen** get one's own way; **lass ihm seinen ∼n** let him have his way; **beim besten ∼n** not with the best will in the world; **letzter ∼:** will; last will and testament (formal); **ich musste wider ∼n lachen** I couldn't help laughing

willen *Präp. mit Gen.* **um jmds./einer Sache ∼:** for sb.'s/sth.'s sake

Willen *der;* ∼**s** ⇨ **Wille**

willen·los **1** *Adj.* will-less; **völlig ∼ sein** have no will of one's own. **2** *adv.* will-lessly

willens *Adj.* ∼ **sein, etw. zu tun** (geh.) be willing to do sth.

willens-, Willens-: ∼**kraft** *die; o. Pl.* will-power; strength of will; ∼**schwach** *Adj.* weak-willed; ∼**stark** *Adj.* strong-willed

willentlich /'vɪləntlɪç/ **1** *Adj.; nicht präd.* deliberate. **2** *adv.* deliberately; on purpose

willig 1 *Adj.* willing. **2** *adv.* willingly

will·kommen *Adj.* welcome; **jmdm. ~ sein** be welcome to sb.; **jmdn. ~ heißen** welcome sb.

Will·kommen *das od.* (selten) *der;* **~s, ~:** welcome

Will·kür *die;* **~:** arbitrary use of power; **jmds. ~** (*Dat.*) **ausgeliefert sein** be at sb.'s mercy

Willkür-: ~akt *der* arbitrary act; **~herrschaft** *die* tyranny

willkürlich 1 *Adj.* arbitrary. **2** *adv.* arbitrarily

wimmeln /'vɪml̩n/ *itr. V.* **von Menschen ~:** be teeming *or* swarming with people; **von Fischen/Ungeziefer ~:** be teeming with fish/swarming with vermin; *unpers.* **in dem Artikel wimmelt es von Fehlern** the article is teeming with mistakes

wimmern /'vɪmɐn/ *itr. V.* whimper

Wimpel /'vɪmpl̩/ *der;* **~s, ~:** pennant

Wimper /'vɪmpɐ/ *die;* **~, ~n** [eye]lash; **ohne mit der ~ zu zucken** without batting an eyelid

Wimpern·tusche *die* mascara

Wind /vɪnt/ *der;* **~[e]s, ~e** (a) wind; **bei ~ und Wetter** in all weathers; **[schnell] wie der ~:** like the wind; (b) (fig.) **wissen/merken, woher der ~ weht** (ugs.) know/notice which way the wind's blowing; **~ machen** (ugs.) brag; **viel ~ um etw. machen** (ugs.) make a great fuss about sth.; **~ von etw. bekommen** (ugs.) get wind of sth.; **jmdm. den ~ aus den Segeln nehmen** (ugs.) take the wind out of sb.'s sails; **etw. in den ~ schlagen** turn a deaf ear *or* pay no heed to sth.; **in alle [vier] ~e** in all directions; **sein Mäntelchen nach dem ~e hängen** be a trimmer

Wind·bö[e] *die* gust of wind

Winde *die;* **~, ~n** (a) winch; (b) (Bot.) bindweed; convolvulus

Windel /'vɪndl̩/ *die;* **~, ~n** nappy (Brit.); diaper (Amer.)

Windel·höschen *das* nappy pants *pl.*

windel·weich *Adj.* (ugs.) **jmdn. ~ schlagen** *od.* **hauen** beat the living daylights out of sb. (coll.)

winden¹ 1 *unr. tr. V.* (geh.) make ⟨*wreath, garland*⟩; **etw. um etw. ~:** wind sth. around sth.; **jmdm. etw. aus der Hand ~:** wrest sth. from sb.'s hand. **2** *unr. refl. V.* (a) ⟨*plant, tendrils*⟩ wind (**um** around); ⟨*snake*⟩ coil [itself], wind itself (**um** around); (b) (sich krümmen) writhe; **sich ~ wie ein Aal** (fig.) try to wriggle out of it; (c) (sich schlängeln) ⟨*path, river*⟩ wind [its way]

winden² *itr. V.; unpers.* **es windet** it's windy

Windes·eile *die;* **in** *od.* **mit ~:** in next to no time

wind-, Wind-: ~fang *der* porch; **~geschützt** *Adj.* sheltered from the wind *postpos.;* sheltered; **~hose** *die* (Met.) whirlwind; **~hund** *der* (a) greyhound; **Afghanischer ~hund** Afghan hound; (b) (ugs. abwertend) careless and unreliable sort (coll.)

windig *Adj.* (a) windy; (b) (ugs. abwertend) shady; dubious ⟨*excuse*⟩

wind-, Wind-: ~jacke *die* wind-cheater (Brit.); windbreaker (Amer.); **~jammer** *der;* **~s, ~** (Seemannsspr.) windjammer; **~mühle** *die* windmill; **~pocken** *Pl.* ▶ 329 chickenpox *sing.;* **~rädchen** *das* windmill; **~richtung** *die* wind direction; **~rose** *die* compass card; **~schief** *Adj.* crooked; **~schutz·scheibe** *die* windscreen (Brit.); windshield (Amer.); **~spiel** *das* [small] greyhound; **~stärke** *die* wind force; **~still** *Adj.* windless; still; **es war völlig ~still** there was no wind at all; **~stille** *die* calm; **es herrschte völlige ~stille** there was no wind at all; **~stoß** *der* gust of wind; **~surfer** *der* windsurfer

Windung *die;* **~, ~en** (a) bend; (eines Flusses) meander; (des Darms, Gehirns) convolution; (b) (spiralförmiger Verlauf) spiral; (einer Spule o. ä.) winding

Wink /vɪŋk/ *der;* **~[e]s, ~e** (a) sign; (b) (Hinweis) hint; (Ratschlag) tip; hint; **ein ~ mit dem Zaunpfahl** (scherzh.) a strong hint

Winkel /'vɪŋkl̩/ *der;* **~s, ~** (a) angle; **toter ~:** blind spot; (b) (Ecke; auch fig.) corner; (c) (Ort) corner; spot; (d) (Werkzeug) [carpenter's] square; (T-förmig) T-square

Winkel-: ~messer *der* protractor; **~schleifer** *der* angle grinder; **~zug** *der; meist Pl.* shady trick *or* move

winken 1 *itr. V.* (a) wave; **mit etw. ~:** wave sth.; **jmdm. ~:** wave to sb.; (jmdn. heranwinken) beckon sb. over; (b) (fig.) **etw. winkt jmdm.** sth. is in prospect for sb.; **dem Sieger winkt eine Flasche Sekt** the winner will receive a bottle of champagne. **2** *tr. V.* (a) (heran~) beckon; **jmdn. zu sich ~:** beckon sb. over [to one]; **der Polizist winkte den Wagen zur Seite** the policeman waved the car over [to the side]; (b) (signalisieren) semaphore ⟨*message*⟩

winseln /'vɪnzl̩n/ *itr. V.* (a) ⟨*dog*⟩ whimper; (b) (abwertend) whine

Winter /'vɪntɐ/ *der;* **~s, ~:** ▶ 293 winter; *s. auch* **Frühling**

winter-, Winter-: ~anfang *der* beginning of winter; **~fest** *Adj.* (a) winter *attrib.* ⟨*clothing*⟩; (b) **~hart; ~garten** *der* conservatory; **~hart** *Adj.* (Bot.) hardy; **~kleidung** *die* winter clothes *pl.* or clothing

winterlich 1 *Adj.* ▶ 293 wintry; winter *attrib.* ⟨*clothing, break*⟩. **2** *adv.* ▶ 293 **~ kalt/öde** cold/bare and wintry

Winter-: ~mantel *der* winter coat; **~reifen** *der* winter tyre; **~sachen** *Pl.* winter things; **~saison** *die* winter season; **~schlaf** *der* (Zool.) hibernation; **~schlaf halten** hibernate; **~schluss·verkauf,** ***~schluß·verkauf** *der* winter sale[s *pl.*]; **~semester** *das* winter semester; **~sport** *der* winter sports *pl.;* **in den ~sport fahren** go on a winter sports holiday; **~sportler** *der* winter sportsman; **~tag** *der* winter['s] day; **~urlaub** *der* winter holiday; **~zeit** *die; o. Pl.* winter-time

Winzer /'vɪntsɐ/ *der;* **~s, ~, Winzerin** *die;* **~, ~nen** winegrower

winzig /'vɪntsɪç/ **1** *Adj.* tiny. **2** *adv.* **~ klein** tiny; minute

Winzigkeit *die;* **~** tininess; minuteness

Wipfel /'vɪpfl̩/ *der;* **~s, ~:** treetop

Wippe /'vɪpə/ *die;* **~, ~n** see-saw

wippen *itr. V.* bob up and down; (hin und her) bob about; (auf einer Wippe) see-saw; **er wippte in den Knien** he bobbed up and down, bending at the knees

wir /viːɐ/ *Personalpron.; 1. Pers. Pl. Nom.* we; **~ beide** *od.* **beiden** we two; the two of us; **Wer kommt mit? — Wir!** Who's coming? — We are!; **Wer ist es? — Wir sind's!** Who is it? — It's us!; *s. auch* **unser; uns**

wirb /vɪrp/ *Imperativ Sg. v.* **werben**

Wirbel /'vɪrbl̩/ *der;* **~s, ~** (a) (im Wasser) whirlpool; vortex; (in der Luft) whirlwind; (kleiner) eddy; (von Rauch, beim Tanz) whirl; (b) (Trubel) hurly-burly; (c) (Aufsehen) fuss; **um jmdn./etw. ~ machen** make a fuss about sb./sth.; (d) ▶ 326 (Anat.) vertebra; (e) (Haar~) crown; (f) (Trommel~) [drum] roll

Wirbellose *Pl.; adj. Dekl.* (Zool.) invertebrates

wirbeln 1 *itr. V.; mit Richtungsangabe mit sein* whirl; ⟨*water, snowflakes*⟩ swirl. **2** *tr. V.* swirl ⟨*leaves, dust*⟩; whirl ⟨*dancer*⟩

Wirbel-: ~säule *die* ▶ 326 (Anat.) vertebral column; spinal column; **~sturm** *der* cyclone; **~tier** *das* (Zool.) vertebrate; **~wind** *der* whirlwind

wirbt /vɪrpt/ *3. Pers. Sg. Präsens v.* **werben**

wird /vɪrt/ *3. Pers. Sg. Präsens v.* **werden**

wirf /vɪrf/ *Imperativ Sg. v.* **werfen**

wirft /vɪrft/ *3. Pers. Sg. Präsens v.* **werfen**

wirken /'vɪrkn̩/ **1** *itr. V.* (a) have an effect; **es wirkte erst nach einer Stunde** it only took effect after an hour; **schmerzstillend ~:** have a pain-killing effect; **gegen etw. ~:** be effective against sth.; **ihre Heiterkeit wirkte ansteckend** her cheerfulness was infectious; (b) (erscheinen) seem; appear; **sie wirkt sehr nett** she seems very nice; **er wirkt auf mich sehr sympathisch** I find him very congenial; (c) (beeindrucken) ⟨*person*⟩ make an impression (**auf** + *Akk.* on); ⟨*picture, design, etc.*⟩ be effective; (d) (tätig sein) work. **2** *tr. V.* (geh.) bring about; *s. auch* **Wunder a**

wirklich 1 *Adj.* real; actual, real ⟨*event, incident, state of affairs*⟩; real, true ⟨*friend*⟩. **2** *Adv.* really; (in der Tat) actually; really
Wirklichkeit *die;* ~, ~en reality; ~ **werden** become a reality; ⟨*dream*⟩ come true; **in** ~: in reality
wirksam /'vɪrkza:m/ **1** *Adj.* effective; **mit dem 1. Juli** ~ **werden** (Amtsspr.) take effect from 1 July. **2** *adv.* effectively
Wirksamkeit *die;* ~: effectiveness
Wirk·stoff *der* active agent
Wirkung *die;* ~, ~en effect (**auf** + *Akk.* on); **ohne** ~ **bleiben** have no effect; **seine** ~ **verfehlen** fail to have the desired effect; **mit** ~ **vom 1. Juli** (Amtsspr.) with effect from 1 July
wirkungs-, Wirkungs-: ~**los 1** *Adj.* .ineffective; **2** *adv.* ineffectively; ~**losigkeit** *die;* ~: ineffectiveness; ~**voll 1** *Adj.* effective; **2** *adv.* effectively
wirr /vɪr/ **1** *Adj.* (**a**) tousled ⟨*hair, beard*⟩; tangled ⟨*ropes, roots*⟩; **ein** ~**es Durcheinander** a chaotic muddle; (**b**) (verworren) confused. **2** *adv.* (**a**) **das Haar hing ihr** ~ **ins Gesicht** her tousled hair hung over her face; **alles lag** ~ **durcheinander** everything lay in a chaotic muddle; (**b**) (verworren) **sie träumte** ~: she had confused dreams
Wirren *Pl.* turmoil *sing.*
Wirrwarr /-var/ *der;* ~s chaos; (von Stimmen) clamour; (von Meinungen) welter; (von Haaren, Wurzeln, Vorschriften) tangle
Wirsing /'vɪrzɪŋ/ *der;* ~s, **Wirsing·kohl** *der* savoy [cabbage]
Wirt /vɪrt/ *der;* ~[e]s, ~e (**a**) landlord; (**b**) (Biol.) host
Wirtin *die;* ~, ~nen landlady
Wirtschaft *die;* ~, ~en (**a**) economy; (Geschäftsleben) commerce and industry; **in die** ~ **gehen** become a business man/woman; (**b**) (Gast~) public house (Brit.); pub (Brit.); bar (Amer.); (**c**) *o. Pl.* (ugs. abwertend: Unordnung) mess; shambles *sing.*
wirtschaften 1 *itr. V.* (**a**) **mit dem Geld gut** ~: manage one's money well; **mit Verlust/Gewinn** ~: run at a loss/profit; (**b**) (sich zu schaffen machen) busy oneself. **2** *tr. V.* **eine Firma in den Ruin** ~: ruin a company
wirtschaftlich 1 *Adj.* (**a**) *nicht präd.* economic; (**b**) *nicht präd.* (finanziell) financial; (**c**) (sparsam, rentabel) economical. **2** *adv.; s. Adj.*: economically; financially
Wirtschaftlichkeit *die;* ~: economic viability
wirtschafts-, Wirtschafts-: ~**beziehungen** *Pl.* economic relations; ~**gebäude** *Pl.* domestic offices; ~**geld** *das; o. Pl.* ⇒ **Haushaltsgeld;** ~**gemeinschaft** *die* economic community; ~**hilfe** *die* economic aid *no indef. art.;* ~**krise** *die* economic crisis; ~**lage** *die* economic situation; ~**minister** *der* minister for economic affairs; ~**ministerium** *das* ministry of economic affairs; ~**politik** *die* economic policy; ~**standort** *der* ⇒ **Standort c;** ~**system** *das* economic system; ~**union** *die* economic union; ~**wissenschaft** *die; meist Pl.* economics *sing., no art.;* economic science *no art.;* ~**wissenschaftler** *der* economist; ~**wunder** *das* (ugs.) economic miracle; ~**zeitung** *die* financial newspaper; ~**zweig** *der* economic sector
Wirts-: ~**haus** *das* pub (Brit.); (mit Unterkunft) inn; pub (Brit.); ~**leute** *Pl.* landlord and landlady; ~**stube** *die* bar
Wisch /vɪʃ/ *der;* ~[e]s, ~e (salopp abwertend) piece *or* bit of paper
wischen *itr., tr. V.* wipe; **etw. von etw.** ~: wipe sth. off *or* from sth.; **Staub** ~: do the dusting; dust
Wischer *der;* ~s, ~: wiper
Wischiwaschi /vɪʃi'vaʃi/ *das;* ~s (salopp abwertend) wish-wash
Wisch-: ~**lappen** *der,* ~**tuch** *das; Pl.* ~**tücher** cloth
Wisent /'vi:zɛnt/ *der;* ~s, ~e wisent; aurochs
Wismut /'vɪsmuːt/ *das;* ~[e]s bismuth
wispern /'vɪspɐn/ *itr., tr. V.* whisper
wiss-, *wiß-, Wiss-, *Wiß- : ~**begier,** ~**begierde** *die; o. Pl.* thirst for knowledge; ~**begierig** *Adj.* eager for knowledge; ⟨*child*⟩ eager to learn

wissen /'vɪsn̩/ **1** *unr. tr., auch itr. V.* know; **ich weiß [es]** I know; **ich weiß [es] nicht** I don't know; **etw. genau** ~: know sth. for certain; **soviel ich weiß** as far as I know; **ich weiß ein gutes Lokal** I know [of] a good pub (Brit.); **er weiß immer alles besser** he always knows better; **nicht, dass ich wüsste** not so far as I know; not that I know of; **woher soll ich das** ~? how should I know?; **weißt du was, wir fahren einfach hin** I'll tell you what, let's just go there; **jmdn. etw.** ~ **lassen** let sb. know sth.; **was weiß ich** (ugs.) I don't know; **man kann nie** ~ (ugs.) you never know; **gewusst, wie!** (ugs.) it's easy when you know how; **von jmdm./etw. nichts [mehr]** ~ **wollen** want to have nothing [more] to do with sb./sth.; **er tut, als sei es wer weiß wie wichtig** (ugs.) he behaves as if it were incredibly important (coll.); **ich weiß ihren Namen nicht mehr** I can't remember her name; **weißt du noch, wie arm wir damals waren?** do you remember how poor we were then?; *s. auch* **Gott a, b. 2** *unr. itr. V.* **von etw./um etw.** ~: know about sth.; **ich weiß von nichts** I don't know anything about it. **3** *unr. mod. V.* **etw. zu tun** ~: know how to do sth.; **er wusste zu berichten, dass ...:** he was able to report that ...
Wissen *das;* ~s knowledge; **meines** ~s: to my knowledge; **wider** *od.* **gegen besseres** ~: against one's better judgement; **nach bestem** ~ **und Gewissen** to the best of one's knowledge and belief
Wissenschaft *die;* ~, ~en science; **die** ~: science; **etw. ist eine** ~ **für sich** (ugs.) there's a real art to sth.
Wissenschaftler *der;* ~s ~, **Wissenschaftlerin** *die;* ~, ~nen ▶ 85⟩ academic; (Natur~) scientist
wissenschaftlich 1 *Adj.* scholarly; (natur~) scientific; ~**er Assistent** ≈ assistant lecturer. **2** *adv.* in a scholarly manner; (natur~) scientifically
wissens-, Wissens-: ~**durst** *der; o. Pl.* thirst for knowledge; ~**gebiet** *das* area *or* field of knowledge; ~**wert** *Adj.* ~**wert sein** be worth knowing; **viel Wissenswertes** a great deal of valuable and interesting information
wissentlich /'vɪsn̩tlɪç/ **1** *Adj.; nicht präd.* deliberate. **2** *adv.* knowingly; deliberately
witschen /'vɪtʃn̩/ *itr. V.; mit sein* (ugs.) slip
wittern /'vɪtɐn/ *tr. V.* get wind of; scent; (fig.: ahnen) sense
Witterung *die;* ~, ~en (**a**) weather *no indef. art;* (**b**) (Jägerspr.) (Geruchssinn) sense of smell; (Geruch) scent
Witwe /'vɪtvə/ *die;* ~, ~n widow; ~ **werden** be widowed
Witwer *der;* ~s, ~: widower; ~ **werden** be widowed
Witz /vɪts/ *der;* ~es, ~e (**a**) joke; **ich mache keine** ~e I'm not joking; **das soll wohl ein** ~ **sein** you/he *etc.* must be joking; (**b**) *o. Pl.* (Geist) wit; **mit** ~: wittily
Witz·bold /~bɔlt/ *der;* ~es, ~e joker; (der jmdm. elnen Streich spielt) practical joker; prankster
Witzelei *die;* ~, ~en (**a**) *o. Pl.* teasing; (**b**) (Bemerkung) joke
witzeln /'vɪtsl̩n/ *itr. V.* joke
Witz·figur *die* (ugs. abwertend) figure of fun
witzig 1 *Adj.* (**a**) (spaßig) funny; amusing; (**b**) (ugs.: seltsam) funny; odd; (**c**) (einfallsreich) imaginative. **2** *adv.; s. Adj.*: amusingly; oddly; imaginatively
witz·los 1 *Adj.* (**a**) dull; (**b**) (ugs.: sinnlos) pointless. **2** *adv.* (ohne Witz) unimaginatively
wo /vo:/ **1** *Adv.* (**a**) (interrogativ) where; **wo gibts denn so was!** (ugs.) who ever heard of such a thing!; (**b**) (relativisch) where; (temporal) when; **überall, wo** wherever; **wo immer er auch sein mag** wherever he may be. **2** *Konj.* (**a**) (da, weil) seeing that; (**b**) (obwohl) although; when; (**c**) (falls) **wo möglich** if possible
wo·anders *Adv.* somewhere else; elsewhere
wob /vo:p/ *1. u. 3. Pers. Sg. Prät. v.* **weben**
wo·bei *Adv.* (**a**) (interrogativ) ~ **hast du sie ertappt?** what did you catch her doing?; ~ **ist es kaputtgegangen?** how did it get broken?; (**b**) (relativisch) **er gab sechs Schüsse ab,** ~ **einer der Täter getötet wurde** he fired six shots — one of the criminals was killed
Woche /'vɔxə/ *die;* ~, ~n ▶ 595⟩ week; **in dieser/der nächsten/der letzten** ~: this/next/last week; **heute in/**

vor einer ~: a week today/a week ago today; **zweimal die** *od.* **in der** ~: twice a week; **unter der** ~ (landsch.) during the week

wochen-, Wochen-: ~**bett** *das:* im ~**bett liegen** be lying in; ~**blatt** *das* weekly; ~**ende** *das* weekend; **schönes** ~**ende!** have a nice weekend!; ~**end·haus** *das* weekend house; ~**karte** *die* weekly season ticket; ~**lang 1** *Adj.; nicht präd.* lasting weeks *postpos;* **2** *adv.* for weeks [on end]; ~**lohn** *der* weekly wages *pl.;* ~**markt** *der* weekly market; ~**tag** *der:* ▶595| **welcher** ~**tag ist heute?** what day of the week is it?; ~**tags** *Adv.* on weekdays [and Saturdays]

wöchentlich /'vœçn̩tlɪç/ **1** *Adj.* weekly. **2** *adv.* weekly; ~ **einmal** once a week

-wöchentlich 1 *Adj.* -weekly. **2** *adv.* every ... weeks; *s. auch* **achtwöchentlich**

Wochen·zeitung *die* weekly newspaper

-wöchig /-vœçɪç/ **(a)** (... Wochen alt) ... -week-old; **ein achtwöchiges Kind** an eight-week-old baby; **(b)** (... Wochen dauernd) ... -week; ... week's/weeks'; **eine vierwöchige Kur** a four-week course of treatment; **mit dreiwöchiger Verspätung** three weeks late

Wöchnerin /'vœçnərɪn/ *die;* ~, ~**nen** woman who has just given birth

Wodka /'vɔtka/ *der;* ~**s**, ~**s** vodka

wo·durch *Adv.* **(a)** (interrogativ) how; ~ **unterscheidet sie sich von den anderen?** in what way is she different from the others?; **(b)** (relativisch) as a result of which; **alles,** ~ **er sich verletzt fühlen könnte** anything that might offend him

wo·für *Adv.* **(a)** (interrogativ) for what; ~ **brauchst du es?** what do you need it for?; ~ **hältst du mich?** what do you take me for?; **(b)** (relativisch) for which

wog /voːk/ *1. u. 3. Pers. Sg. Prät. v.* **wiegen**

Woge /'voːɡə/ *die;* ~, ~**n** (auch fig.) wave

wo·gegen 1 *Adv.* **(a)** (interrogativ) against what; what ... against; ~ **ist sie allergisch?** what is she allergic to?; **(b)** (relativisch) against which; which ... against. **2** *Konj.* whereas

wogen /'voːɡn̩/ *itr. V.* (geh.) ⟨*sea*⟩ surge; (fig.) ⟨*corn*⟩ wave; ⟨*crowd*⟩ surge

wo·her *Adv.* **(a)** (interrogativ) where ... from; ~ **weißt du das?** how do you know that?; ~ **kennst du ihn?** where do you know him from?; **[ach]** ~ **denn!, ach** ~**!** (ugs.) good heavens, no!; not at all!; **(b)** (relativisch) where ... from

wohin *Adv.* **(a)** (interrogativ) where [... to]; ~ **damit?** (ugs.) where shall I put it/them?; **(b)** (relativisch) where; **(c)** (indefinit) **ich muss mal** ~ (ugs. verhüll.) I've got to pay a visit *or* a call (euphem.)

wo·hinein *Adv.* ⇒ **worein**

wo·hingegen *Konj.* whereas

wo·hinter *Adv.* **(a)** (interrogativ) behind what; what ... behind; **(b)** (relativisch) behind which

wohl /voːl/ **1** *Adv.* **(a)** well; **jmdm. ist nicht** ~, **jmd. fühlt sich nicht** ~: sb. does not feel well; ~ **bedacht** (geh.) well-considered; [carefully] considered ⟨*reply, judgement*⟩; ~ **begründet** (geh.) well-founded; (berechtigt) well-justified; ~ **bekannt** well-known; ~ **durchdacht** carefully thought-out; ~ **überlegt** well-considered; etw. **tut jmdm.** ~: sth. does sb. good; **jmdm.** ~ **wollen** wish sb. well; **(b)** (behaglich) at ease; happy; **mir ist nicht recht** ~ **bei der Sache** the whole thing makes me a bit uneasy; **leb** ~**!/leben Sie** ~**!** farewell!; ~ **oder übel** whether I/you *etc.* want to or not; **(c)** (durchaus) well; **ich bin mir dessen** ~ **bewusst** I'm quite or perfectly conscious of that; ~ **wissend, dass** ... (geh.) knowing full well that ...; **(d)** (ungefähr) about; **(e) sehr** ~**[, der** *od.* **mein Herr]** certainly[, sir]; very good [, sir]; **(f)** (jedoch) ..., ~ **aber** ...: but ...; however ...; **(g)** ~ **dem, der** ...! (geh. veralt.) happy the man who ...; **(h)** ⇒ **zwar a. 2** *Partikel* **(a)** (vermutlich) probably; ~ **kaum** hardly; **du bist** ~ **nicht recht bei Verstand?** have you taken leave of your senses?; **na** *od.* **ja, was/warum/wie** ~**?** need you ask what/why/how?;

das mag ~ *sein* that may well be; **das wird** ~ **so sein** that's probably the case; **ich habe** ~ **nicht recht gehört** I don't think I could have heard right; **(b)** (verstärkend) **wirst du** ~ **herkommen!** will you come here!; **siehst du** ~**!** there, you see!; **man wird doch** ~ **fragen dürfen** there's nothing wrong in asking, is there?

Wohl *das;* ~**[e]s** welfare; well-being; **das allgemeine/öffentliche** ~: the public good; **auf jmds.** ~ **trinken** drink sb.'s health; **[auf] dein** ~**!** your health!; **zum** ~**!** cheers!

wohl-, Wohl-: ~**auf** /-'-/ *Adj., nicht attr.* (geh.) ~**auf sein** be well *or* in good health; ***~**bedacht** ⇒ **wohl 1 a;** ~**befinden** *das* well-being; ***~**begründet** ⇒ **wohl 1 a;** ~**behagen** *das* sense of well-being; **etw. mit** ~**behagen essen** eat sth. with relish; ~**behalten** *Adj.* safe and well ⟨*person*⟩; undamaged ⟨*thing*⟩; ***~**bekannt** ⇒ **wohl 1 a;** ***~**durchdacht** ⇒ **wohl 1 a;** ~**ergehen** *das* ⇒ ~**befinden;** ~**erzogen** *Adj.* well brought-up; ~**fahrt** *die; o. Pl.* **(a)** (geh.) welfare; **(b)** (öffentliche Fürsorge) welfare services *pl.*

Wohlfahrts·staat *der* welfare state

wohl-, Wohl-: ~**gefallen** *das* pleasure; ~**gefällig 1** *Adj.* ⟨*smile, look*⟩ of pleasure; **2** *adv.* with pleasure; ~**geformt** *Adj.* well-formed; ~**gelitten** *Adj.* (geh.) well-liked; ~**gemerkt** *Adv.* please note; mark you; ~**genährt** *Adj.* (meist spött.) well-fed; ~**geraten** *Adj.* (geh.) fine *attrib.* ⟨*child*⟩; successful ⟨*piece of work, translation, etc.*⟩; ~**gesinnt** *Adj.* well-disposed; **jmdm./einer Sache** ~**gesinnt sein** be well-disposed towards sb./sth.; ~**habend** *Adj.* prosperous

wohlig 1 *Adj.; nicht präd.* pleasant; agreeable; (gemütlich) cosy. **2** *adv.* ⟨*sigh, purr, etc.*⟩ with pleasure; ⟨*stretch oneself*⟩ luxuriously

wohl, Wohl-: ~**meinend** *Adj.* (geh.) well-meaning; ~**proportioniert** *Adj.* (geh.) well-proportioned; ~**riechend** *Adj.* (geh.) fragrant; ~**schmeckend** *Adj.* (geh.) delicious; ~**sein** *das:* [zum] ~**sein!** your health!; ~**stand** *der; o. Pl.* prosperity

Wohlstands·gesellschaft *die; o. Pl.* (abwertend) affluent society

wohl, Wohl-: ~**tat** *die* **(a)** favour; **jmdm. eine** ~**tat erweisen** do sb. a good turn; **(b)** (etw., was Erleichterung bringt) blissful relief; ~**täter** *der* benefactor; ~**tätig** *Adj.* charitable; ~**tätigkeit** *die; o. Pl.* charity; charitableness

Wohltätigkeits- charity ⟨*event, concert, etc.*⟩

wohl-, Wohl-: ~**tuend 1** *Adj.* agreeable; **2** *adv.* agreeably; ***~|**tun,*****~**überlegt** ⇒ **wohl 1 a;** ~**verdient** *Adj.* well-earned; well-deserved ⟨*reward, honour, success, etc.*⟩; well-deserved ⟨*punishment, fate*⟩; ~**verhalten** *das* good behaviour *no indef. art.;* ~**weislich** /~**vaɪslɪç**/ *Adv.* deliberately; ***~**wollen** ⇒ **wohl 1 a;** ~**wollen** *das;* ~**s** goodwill; **mit** ~**wollen** benevolently; ~**wollend 1** *Adj.* benevolent; favourable ⟨*judgement, opinion*⟩; **2** *adv.* benevolently; ⟨*judge, consider*⟩ favourably

Wohn-: ~**anhänger** *der* caravan; trailer (Amer.); ~**block** *der; Pl.* ~**s,** (schweiz.) ~**blöcke** residential block

wohnen *itr. V.* live; (kurzfristig) stay; **sie** ~ **sehr hübsch** they have a lovely home; (der Lage nach) they live in a lovely spot; **wo** ~ **Sie?** where do you live/where are you staying?

wohn-, Wohn-: ~**gebiet** *das,* ~**gegend** *die* residential area; ~**gemeinschaft** *die* group sharing a flat (Brit.) *or* (Amer.) apartment/house; **in einer** ~**gemeinschaft leben** live in a shared flat (Brit.) *or* (Amer.) apartment/house; share a flat (Brit.) *or* (Amer.) apartment/house; ~**haft** *Adj.* resident; ~**haus** *das* [dwelling-]house; ~**heim** *das* home; (für Obdachlose, Lehrlinge) hostel; (für Studenten) hall of residence; ~**lage** *die:* **unsere** ~**lage ist optimal** our house/flat (Brit.) *or* (Amer.) apartment is ideally situated; **in ruhiger/guter** ~**lage** in a quiet/good area

wohnlich 1 *Adj.* homely. **2** *adv.* in a homely way

Wohnlichkeit *die;* ~: homeliness

Wohn-: ~**mobil** *das;* ~**s,** ~**e** motor home; motor caravan; ~**ort** *der; Pl.* ~**e** place of residence; ~**raum** *der* **(a)** living room; **(b)** *o. Pl.* (~**fläche**) living space;

Wochentage

Deutsch	Englisch	Abkürzung
Sonntag	Sunday	Sun
Montag	Monday	Mon
Dienstag	Tuesday	Tues
Mittwoch	Wednesday	Wed
Donnerstag	Thursday	Thurs
Freitag	Friday	Fri
Samstag	Saturday	Sat

Es ist zu beachten, dass im englischsprachigen Raum die Woche am Sonntag beginnt und am Samstag endet.

Wann?

Wie beim Datum wird am + Wochentag mit **on** übersetzt (ohne **the**). Dieses **on** kann nicht ausgelassen werden.

Ich fahre [am] Mittwoch nach Kairo	= I am going to Cairo on Wednesday

Selbstverständlich wird aber, wenn es sich um einen bestimmten, näher beschriebenen Tag handelt, ein Artikel eingesetzt.

am letzten Sonntag vor Pfingsten	= on the last Sunday before Whitsun
Es geschah an einem verregneten Montag	= It happened on a wet Monday

Aber:

Eines [schönen] Samstags trafen wir uns im Zoo	= One [fine] Saturday we met at the zoo

Wiederholtes

Hier fällt das **on** vor **every**, **most** und **some** weg. Vor der Pluralform (**Mondays**, **Fridays** usw.) fehlt das **on** im amerikanischen Englisch, wird aber im britischen Englisch meist nicht weggelassen.

Ich fahre freitags/jeden Freitag nach Hause	= I go home [on] Fridays/every Friday
jeden zweiten Donnerstag	= every other Thursday
jeden dritten Montag	= every third Monday
fast jeden Samstag	= almost every Saturday, most Saturdays
manchmal am Mittwoch	= sometimes on a Wednesday, some Wednesdays
ab und zu am Freitag	= occasionally on a Friday, on the occasional od. odd Friday

Vergangenes und Künftiges

letzten Donnerstag	= last Thursday
am vorangehenden Donnerstag	= [on] the preceding Thursday
vorletzten Donnerstag	= [on] the Thursday before last
Donnerstag vor einer Woche	= a week ago on Thursday

Ich werde sie [am] nächsten od. kommenden Montag sehen	= I will see her next Monday od. this [coming] Monday
Ich habe sie am [darauf] folgenden Montag gesehen	= I saw her the following od. the next Monday
übernächsten Montag	= the Monday after next
Montag in einer Woche	= a week on Monday
ab Samstag	= from Saturday [on]
Es muss bis Freitag fertig sein	= It must be ready by Friday

Tageszeiten

[am] Montagmorgen, Montag früh	= on Monday morning
[am] Dienstagmittag	= midday on Tuesday
[am] Mittwochnachmittag	= on Wednesday afternoon
[am] Donnerstagabend	= on Thursday evening; (am späten Abend) on Thursday night
Freitagnacht	= on Friday night

Und wenn es regelmäßig geschieht:

montagmorgens	= on Monday mornings
dienstagmittags	= midday on Tuesdays
mittwochnachmittags	= on Wednesday afternoons
donnerstagabends	= on Thursday evenings; (am späten Abend) on Thursday nights
freitagnachts	= on Friday nights

Heute

Welchen Tag haben wir heute?	= What day is it today?
Heute ist Dienstag	= It's Tuesday [today]

Adjektive und Zusammensetzungen

Im Englischen gibt es keine Adjektive, die dem deutschen sonntäglich, sonntägig usw. entsprächen. Man verwendet das Substantiv, mit oder ohne **'s**:

sein sonntäglicher Spaziergang	= his [regular] Sunday walk
ein sonntägiger Spaziergang	= a Sunday walk, a walk on a Sunday
ein Sonntagsfahrer	= a Sunday driver
die Sonntagszeitungen	= the Sunday papers

Vergleiche aber:

die Zeitung von Dienstag	= Tuesday's paper

Ferner:

die Züge am Montag	= Monday's trains
die Schulstunden am Mittwoch	= Wednesday's lessons

∿**siedlung** die residential estate; (mit gleichartigen Häusern) housing estate; ∿**sitz** der place of residence; domicile (formal); **ohne festen** ∿**sitz** of no fixed abode

Wohnung die; ∿, ∿**en** (a) flat (Brit.); apartment (Amer.); (b) o. Pl. (Unterkunft) lodging

Wohnungs-: ∿**schlüssel** der key to the flat (Brit.) or (Amer.) apartment; ∿**suche** die search for a flat (Brit.) or (Amer.) apartment; **auf** ∿**suche sein** be flat-hunting; ∿**tür** die door of the flat (Brit.) or (Amer.) apartment

Wohn-: ∿**verhältnisse** Pl. living conditions; ∿**viertel** das residential district; ∿**wagen** der caravan; trailer (Amer.); ∿**zimmer** das living room

wölben /'vœlbn̩/ **1** tr. V. curve; arch ‹brows, shoulders›; cup ‹hand›; bend ‹metal›; vault, arch ‹roof, ceiling›. **2** refl. V. curve; ‹sky, bridge, ceiling› arch; ‹chest› swell; ‹stomach, muscles› bulge; ‹metal› bend, buckle

Wölbung die; ∿, ∿**en** curve; (einer Decke, des Himmels) arch; vault; (von Augenbrauen) arch; (eines Bauches, Muskels) bulge

Wolf /vɔlf/ *der;* ~[e]s, **Wölfe** /'vœlfə/ (a) wolf; **ein** ~ **im Schafspelz sein** (fig.) be a wolf in sheep's clothing; **mit den Wölfen heulen** (fig. ugs.) run with the pack; (b) (ugs.: Fleisch~) mincer

Wölfin /'vœlfɪn/ *die;* ~, ~nen [wolf] bitch

Wolfram /'vɔlfram/ *das;* ~s (Chemie) tungsten

Wölkchen /'vœlkçən/ *das;* ~s, ~: small cloud

Wolke /'vɔlkə/ *die;* ~, ~n cloud; **aus allen** ~**n fallen** (fig. ugs.) be completely stunned

wolken-, Wolken-: ~**bruch** *der; Pl.* ~**brüche** cloudburst; ~**bruch·artig** *Adj.* torrential; ~**decke** *die* [unbroken] cloud *no indef. art.;* ~**kratzer** *der* skyscraper; ~**los** *Adj.* cloudless

wolkig *Adj.* cloudy

Woll·decke *die* [woollen] blanket

Wolle /'vɔlə/ *die;* ~, ~n wool; (fig.: Haar) hair; **sich in die** ~ **kriegen** (fig. ugs.) quarrel (**wegen** over); **sich in der** ~ **haben** (fig. ugs.) be at loggerheads

wollen[1] *Adj.; nicht präd.* woollen

wollen[2] **1** *unr. Modalverb; 2. Part.* ~ (a) etw. tun ~ (den Wunsch haben, etw. zu tun) want to do sth.; (die Absicht haben, etw. zu tun) be going to do sth.; **wir wollten gerade gehen** we were just about to go; **was will man da machen?** (ugs.) what can you do?; **ohne es zu** ~: without intending to; **dann will ich nichts gesagt haben** (ugs.) I take it all back; **das will ich meinen!** (ugs.) I absolutely agree; **wir** ~ **sehen** we'll see; (b) (in Aufforderungen) **wollt ihr wohl Ruhe geben/damit aufhören!** (ugs.) will you be quiet/stop that!; ~ **Sie bitte so freundlich sein und das heute noch erledigen** would you be so kind as to do it today; (c) **er will ein Dichter sein** he claims to be a poet; **sie will es [nicht] gesehen haben** she claims [not] to have seen it; (d) **die Wunde will [einfach] nicht heilen** the wound [just] won't heal; **der Motor wollte nicht anspringen** the engine wouldn't start; **es will [einfach] nicht gelingen** it just won't work; (e) **etw. will getan sein** sth. needs *or* (coll.) has got to be done; **das will gelernt sein** it has to be learned; (f) **das Buch will unterhalten** the book is intended *or* meant to entertain; (g) **das will nichts heißen/nicht viel sagen** that doesn't mean anything/much. **2** *unr. itr. V.* (a) **du musst nur** ~, **dann geht es auch** you only have to want to enough *or* have the will, then it's possible; **ob du willst oder nicht** whether you want to or not; **[ganz] wie du willst** just as you like; **wenn du willst, könnten wir** …: if you want [to], we could …; **das ist, wenn man so will,** …: that is, if you like, …; **[na] dann** ~ **wir mal!** (ugs.) [right] let's get started!; (b) (ugs.: irgendwohin zu gehen wünschen) **ich will nach Hause/ans Meer** I want to go home/to go to the seaside; **ich will hier raus** I want to get out of here; **zu wem** ~ **Sie?** whom do you want to see?; **er wollte zum Theater** he wanted to become an actor; (c) *verneint* (ugs.: funktionieren) **der Motor will nicht** the engine won't go; **seine Beine/Gelenke/Augen** ~ **nicht mehr** his legs/joints/eyes just aren't up to it any more. **3** *unr. tr. V.* (a) want; **das wollte ich nicht** I didn't mean to do that; **das habe ich nicht gewollt** I never meant that to happen; ~, **dass jmd. etw. tut** want sb. to do sth.; **da ist nichts [mehr] zu** ~ (ugs.) there's nothing we/you *etc.* can do about it; **ich wollte, er wäre hier/es wäre vorbei** I wish he were here/it were over; (b) **jmdm. nichts** ~ **können** (ugs.) be unable to harm sb.

Woll·gras *das* cotton grass

wollig *Adj.* woolly

Woll-: ~**jacke** *die* woollen cardigan; ~**kleid** *das* woollen dress; ~**knäuel** *das* ball of wool; ~**sachen** *Pl.* woollen things; woollies (coll.); ~**socke** *die* woollen sock; ~**stoff** *der* woollen cloth; ~**strumpf** *der* woollen stocking; (Kniestrumpf) woollen sock

Wollust /'vɔlʊst/ *die;* ~, **Wollüste** /'vɔlʏstə/ (geh.) lust; (Sinnlichkeit) sensuality; **etw. mit wahrer** ~ **tun** take great delight in doing sth.

wollüstig /'vɔlʏstɪç/ (geh.) **1** *Adj.* lustful; (sinnlich) sensual. **2** *Adj.* lustfully; (sinnlich) sensually

wo·mit *Adv.* (a) (interrogativ) ~ **schreibst du?** what do you write with?; (more formal) with what do you write?; (b) (relativisch) ~ **du schreibst** which *or* that you write with; (more formal) with which you write; ~ **ich nicht sagen will, dass** …: by which I don't mean to say that …

wo·möglich *Adv.* possibly

wo·nach *Adv.* (a) (interrogativ) after what; what … after; ~ **suchst du?** what are you looking for?; ~ **riecht es?** what does it smell of?; ~ **richtet ihr euch?** what do you go by?; (b) (relativisch) after which; which … after

Wonne /'vɔnə/ *die;* ~, ~n (geh.) bliss *no pl.;* ecstasy; (etw., was Freude macht) joy; delight; **es war eine** ~, **ihr zuzuhören** she was a joy *or* delight to listen to

wonnig *Adj.* sweet

woran /vo'ran/ *Adv.* (a) (interrogativ) ~ **hast du dich verletzt?** what did you hurt yourself on?; **man weiß nicht,** ~ **man ist** you don't know where you are; ~ **ist sie gestorben?** what did she die of?; ~ **denkst du?** what are you thinking of?; (b) (relativisch) **nichts,** ~ **man sich verletzen/anlehnen könnte** nothing one could hurt oneself on/one could lean against

worauf /vo'rauf/ (a) (interrogativ) ~ **sitzt er?** what is he sitting on?; ~ **wartest du?** what are you waiting for?; ~ **will er hinaus?** what is he getting at?; (b) (relativisch) **es gab nichts,** ~ **er sich hätte setzen können** there was nothing for him to sit on; **das Einzige,** ~ **es jetzt ankommt** the only thing that matters now; (c) (relativisch: woraufhin) whereupon

worauf·hin *Adv.* (a) (interrogativ) ~ **hat er das getan?** what made him do it?; what was the cause of his doing it?; (b) (relativisch) whereupon

woraus /vo'raus/ *Adv.* (a) (interrogativ) ~ **trinken wir den Wein?** what shall we drink the wine from?; ~ **ist das Gewebe?** what is the fabric made of?; ~ **schließt du das?** what do you infer that from?; (b) (relativisch) **es gab nichts,** ~ **wir den Wein hätten trinken können** there was nothing for us to drink the wine out of; **es gab nichts,** ~ **sie Werkzeuge machen konnten** there was nothing for them to make tools from

worden /'vɔrdn/ *2. Part. v.* **werden 2 c**

worein /vo'rain/ *Adv.* (a) (interrogativ) in what; what … in; (b) (relativisch) in which; which … in

worin /vo'rɪn/ *Adv.* (a) (interrogativ) in what; what … in; **ich weiß nicht,** ~ **der Unterschied liegt** I don't know what the difference is; (b) (relativisch) in which; which … in

Work·shop /'wɔːkʃɔp/ *der;* ~s, ~s workshop

Wort /vɔrt/ *das;* ~[e]s, **Wörter** /'vœrtɐ/ *od.* ~e (a) *Pl.* **Wörter,** (auch:) ~e word; ~ **für** ~: word for word; (b) *Pl.* ~e (Äußerung) word; **mir fehlen die** ~e I'm lost for words; **davon ist kein** ~ **wahr** not a word of it is true; **nicht viele** ~e **machen** not beat about the bush; **ich verstehe kein** ~e **[von]** I don't understand a word [of it]; **auf** jmds. ~e **hören** listen to what sb. says; **mit einem** ~: in a word; **mit anderen** ~en in other words; **ich glaube dir aufs** ~: I can well believe it; jmdn. **[nicht] zu** ~ **kommen lassen** [not] let sb. get a word in; **etw. mit keinem** ~ **erwähnen** not say a word about sth.; not mention sth. at all; **man verstand sein eigenes** ~ **nicht** you could not hear yourself speak; jmdm. **aufs** ~ **gehorchen** obey sb.'s every word; **ein** ~ **gab das andere** one thing led to another; **hast du [da noch] ein** ~e? what do you say to that?; **das ist das letzte/mein letztes** ~: that's the/my last word on the matter; **[immer] das letzte** ~ **haben wollen/müssen** want to have/have to have the last word; **Dr. Meyer hat das** ~: it's Dr Meyer's turn to speak; **das** ~ **ergreifen** *od.* **nehmen** start to speak; jmdm. **das** ~ **geben** *od.* **erteilen/entziehen** call upon sb. to speak/to finish speaking; **für** jmdn. **ein [gutes]** ~ **einlegen** put in a [good] word for sb.; jmdm. **das** ~ **aus dem Munde nehmen** take the words out of sb.'s mouth; jmdm. **das** ~ **im Munde herumdrehen** twist sb.'s words; **kein weiteres** ~ **über etw.** (*Akk.*) **verlieren** not say another word about sth.; jmdm. **ins** ~ **fallen** interrupt sb.; **ums** ~ **bitten** ask to speak; **sich zu** ~ **melden** indicate one's wish to speak; (c) *Pl.* ~e (Spruch) saying; (Zitat) quotation; **geflügelte** ~e well-known sayings and quotations; (d) *Pl.* ~e (geh.: Text) words *pl.;* **in**

~ **und Bild** in words and pictures; **(e)** *Pl.* ~**e** (Versprechen) word; [**sein**] ~ **halten** keep one's word; **sein** ~ **brechen** break one's word; **jmdm. sein** ~ [**auf etw.** (*Akk.*)] **geben** give sb. one's word [on sth.]; **auf mein** ~! I give you my word; **jmdn. beim** ~ **nehmen** take sb. at his/her word

Wort·art *die* (Sprachw.) part of speech
wort·brüchig *Adj.* ~ **werden** break one's word
Wörter·buch *das* dictionary
wort-, Wort-: ~**führer** *der*, ~**führerin** *die* spokesman/spokeswoman; spokesperson; ~**getreu** 1 *Adj.* word-for-word; 2 *adv.* word for word; ~**karg** 1 *Adj.* taciturn ‹*person*›; laconic ‹*reply, greeting, etc.*›; **ein** ~**karger Mann** a man of few words; 2 *adv.* taciturnly; ‹*reply, greet, etc.*› laconically; ~**klauberei** /~klaubə'rai/ *die;* ~, ~**en** quibbling; ~**laut** *der; o. Pl.* wording; **im** [**vollen**] ~**laut** verbatim

wörtlich /'vœrtlıç/ 1 *Adj.* **(a)** word-for-word; *s. auch* **Rede** e; **(b)** (der eigentlichen Bedeutung entsprechend) literal. 2 *adv.* **(a)** word for word; **das hat sie** ~ **gesagt** those were her very words; **(b)** (der eigentlichen Bedeutung entsprechend) literally

wort-, Wort-: ~**los** 1 *Adj.* silent; wordless; unspoken ‹*agreement, understanding*›; 2 *adv.* without saying a word; ~**meldung** *die:* **es liegen keine weiteren** ~**meldungen vor** no one else wishes to speak; ~**schatz** *der* vocabulary; ~**spiel** *das* play on words; (mit gleich od. ähnlich lautenden Wörtern) pun; play on words; ~**stellung** *die* (Sprachw.) word order; ~**wahl** *die; o. Pl.* choice of word; ~**wechsel** *der* exchange of words; ~**wörtlich** 1 *Adj.* word-for-word; 2 *adv.:* ⇒ **wörtlich** 2

worüber *Adv.* **(a)** (interrogativ) over what ...; what ... over; ~ **bist du gestolpert?** what did you trip over?; ~ **lachst du?** what are you laughing about?; **(b)** (relativisch) over which; which ... over

worum *Adv.* **(a)** (interrogativ) around what; what ... around; ~ **geht es denn?** what is it about then?; **(b)** (relativisch) around which; which ... around

worunter *Adv.* **(a)** (interrogativ) under what; what ... under; ~ **leidet er?** what is he suffering from?; **(b)** (relativisch) under which; which ... under

wo·von *Adv.* **(a)** (interrogativ) from where; where ... from; ~ **soll er leben?** what is he supposed to live on?; ~ **redest du?** what are you talking about?; ~ **ist er müde/krank?** what has made him tired/ill?; **(b)** (relativisch) from which; which ... from

wo·vor *Adv.* **(a)** (interrogativ) in front of what; what ... in front of; ~ **hast du Angst?** what are you afraid of?; **(b)** (relativisch) in front of which; which ... in front of; **das Einzige,** ~ **ich Angst habe** the only thing I am afraid of

wo·zu *Adv.* **(a)** (interrogativ) to what, what ... to; (wofür) what ... for; ~ **brauchst du das Geld?** what do you need the money for?; ~ **hast du dich entschlossen?** what have you decided [on]?; ~ **diese Umstände?** why all this fuss?; (als Ausdruck der Ablehnung) why should I/you *etc.*?; **(b)** (relativisch) **dann habe ich gebügelt,** ~ **ich keine Lust hatte** then I did some ironing, which I had no inclination to do; ~ **du dich auch entschließt** whatever you decide on

Wrack /vrak/ *das;* ~[**e**]**s**, ~**s** *od.* ~**e** (auch fig.) wreck
wrang /vraŋ/ *1. und 3. Pers. Sg. Prät. v.* **wringen**
wringen /'vrıŋən/ *unr. tr. V.* (bes. nordd.) wring
Wucher /'vu:xɐ/ *der;* ~**s** profiteering; (mit Zinsen) usury; [**mit etw.**] ~ **treiben** profiteer [on sth.]; (mit Zinsen) charge an extortionate rate/extortionate rates of interest [on sth.]
Wucherer *der;* ~**s**, ~: profiteer; (beim Verleihen von Geld) usurer
wuchern *itr. V.* **(a)** auch mit sein (stark wachsen) ‹*plants, weeds, etc.*› proliferate, run wild; (fig.) be rampant; **krebsartig** ~ (fig.) grow like a cancer; **(b)** (Wucher treiben) [**mit etw.**] ~: profiteer [on sth.]; (mit Zinsen) lend [sth.] at extortionate interest rates
Wucher·preis *der* extortionate price
Wucherung *die;* ~, ~**en** growth
wuchs /vu:ks/ *1. u. 3. Pers. Sg. Prät. v.* **wachsen**
Wuchs *der;* ~**es** (Gestalt) stature; **klein/groß von** ~ **sein** ‹*person*› be small/tall in stature

Wucht /vʊxt/ *die;* ~ **(a)** force; (von Schlägen) power; weight; **mit voller** ~: with full force; ‹*hit*› with all one's might; **(b) eine** ~ **sein** (salopp) be absolutely fantastic (coll.)
wuchten *tr. V.* heave
wuchtig *Adj.* massive
wühlen /'vy:lən/ 1 *itr. V.* **(a)** dig; (mit der Schnauze) root (**nach** for); ‹*mole*› tunnel, burrow; **(b)** (ugs.: suchen) rummage [around] (**nach** for). 2 *tr. V.* burrow; tunnel out ‹*burrow*›. 3 *refl. V.* **sich in etw.** (*Akk.*) /**durch etw.** ~: burrow into/through sth.
Wulst /vʊlst/ *der;* ~[**e**]**s**, **Wülste** /'vʏlstə/ *od.* ~**e** bulge; (Fett~) roll of fat; (an Flasche, Reifen) bead
wulstig *Adj.* bulging; thick ‹*lips*›
wund /vʊnt/ *Adj.* ▶ 329 | sore; **sich** ~ **laufen** walk until one's feet are sore; **sich** ~ **liegen** get bedsores (**an** + *Dat.* on); **sich** (*Dat.*) **den Rücken** ~ **liegen** get bedsores on one's back; *s. auch* **Fuß** b; **Punkt** d
Wunde *die;* ~, ~**n** wound; **der Krieg hat dem Land tiefe** ~**n geschlagen** (fig.) the war has left deep scars on the country
Wunder *das;* ~**s**, ~ **(a)** miracle; ~ **wirken** (fig. ugs.) work wonders; **ein/kein** ~ **sein** (ugs.) be a/no wonder; **was** ~, **wenn ...?** small *or* no wonder that ...; **er wird sein blaues** ~ **erleben** (ugs.) he's in for a nasty shock; **(b)** (etw. Erstaunliches) wonder; **ein** ~ **an ...** (*Dat.*) a miracle of ...; **ein technisches** ~: a technological marvel; **(c)** (ugs.) **er denkt, er sei** ~ **wer** he thinks he's really something; **er glaubt,** ~ **was geleistet zu haben** he thinks he's achieved something fantastic (coll.); **er bildet sich** ~ **was darauf ein** he's terribly pleased with himself about it (coll.)
wunderbar 1 *Adj.* **(a)** (übernatürlich erscheinend) miraculous; **auf** ~**e Weise** miraculously; **(b)** (herrlich) wonderful; marvellous. 2 *adv.* **(a)** (herrlich) wonderfully; marvellously; **(b)** (ugs.: sehr schön) wonderfully ‹*cosy, warm, etc.*›
wunder-, Wunder-: ~**glaube** *der* belief in miracles; ~**heiler** *der* faith healer; ~**hübsch** 1 *Adj.* wonderfully pretty; 2 *adv.* quite beautifully; ~**kerze** *die* sparkler; ~**kind** *das* child prodigy
wunderlich 1 *Adj.* strange; odd. 2 *adv.* strangely; oddly
Wunder·mittel *das* miracle cure
wundern 1 *tr. V.* surprise; **mich wundert, dass ...:** I'm surprised that ...; **es würde** *od.* **sollte mich [nicht]** ~, **wenn ...:** I should [not] be surprised *or* I wouldn't [not] surprise me if ... 2 *refl. V.* be surprised (**über** + *Akk.* at); **du wirst dich [noch mal]** ~ (ugs.) you're in for a shock; you've got a surprise in store
wunder-, Wunder-: ~**schön** 1 *Adj.* simply beautiful; (herrlich) simply wonderful; 2 *adv.* quite beautifully; (einwandfrei) perfectly; ~**tätig** *Adj.* miraculous; ~**tüte** *die* surprise packet; ~**voll** 1 *Adj.* wonderful; marvellous; 2 *adv.* wonderfully; marvellously; ~**werk** *das* marvel
wund-, Wund-: *~|**liegen** ⇒ **wund**; ~**sein** *das* ▶ 329 | soreness; ~**starrkrampf** *der* ▶ 329 | (Med.) tetanus
Wunsch /vʊnʃ/ *der;* ~[**e**]**s**, **Wünsche** /'vʏnʃə/ **(a)** wish (**nach** to have); (Sehnen) desire (**nach** for); **sich** (*Dat.*) **einen** ~ **erfüllen/versagen** grant/deny oneself something one wants; **haben Sie noch einen** ~? will there be anything else?; **auf jmds.** ~: at sb.'s wish; **alles geht nach** ~: everything's going as we want/he wants *etc.*; **(b)** *Pl.* ▶ 240 | **mit den besten/herzlichsten Wünschen** with best/warmest wishes
wünschbar *Adj.* (bes. schweiz.) desirable
Wunsch·denken *das* wishful thinking
Wünschel·rute /'vynʃl-/ *die* divining rod
wünschen /'vynʃn/ *tr. V.* **a)** **sich** (*Dat.*) **etw.** ~: want sth.; (im stillen) wish for sth.; **jmdm. Erfolg/nichts Gutes** ~: wish sb. success/no good; **jmdm. den Tod** ~: wish sb. dead; **was wünschst du dir?** what would you like?; **ich wünschte, du wärest hier** I wish you were here; **jmdn. weit weg** ~: wish sb. far away; **(b)** ▶ 240 | **jmdm. alles Gute/frohe Ostern** ~: wish sb. all the best/a happy Easter; **sie wünschte ihm gute Besserung** she said she hoped he would soon get better;

(c) *auch itr.* (begehren) want; **was ~ Sie?, Sie ~?** (von einem Bediensteten gesagt) yes, madam/sir?; (von einem Kellner gesagt) what would you like?; (von einem Verkäufer gesagt) can I help you?; **ganz, wie Sie ~:** just as you like; **die gewünschte Auskunft** the information asked for; **etw. lässt [viel]/lässt nichts zu ~ übrig** sth. leaves a great deal/nothing to be desired; **es verlief alles wie gewünscht** everything went as we/he *etc.* had wanted

wünschens·wert *Adj.* desirable

wunsch-, Wunsch-: **~gemäß** *Adv.* as desired; (einer Bitte gemäß) as requested; **~kind** *das* wanted child; **~konzert** *das* request concert; (im Rundfunk) request programme; **~los** **1** *Adj.* [perfectly] contented; perfect ‹*happiness*›; **2** *adv.* **~los glücklich sein** be perfectly contented; **~satz** *der* (Sprachw.) optative sentence; **~traum** *der* wishful dream; (unrealistisch) pipe dream; **~zettel** *der* list of presents one would like

wurde /'vʊrdə/ *1. u. 3. Pers. Sg. Prät. v.* **werden**

würde /'vʏrdə/ *1. u. 3. Pers. Sg. Konjunktiv II v.* **werden**

Würde *die; ~, ~n* **(a)** *o. Pl.* dignity; **sich in seiner ~ verletzt fühlen** feel that one's dignity has been affronted; **unter jmds. ~ sein** be beneath sb.'s dignity; **unter aller ~ sein** be beneath contempt; **(b)** (Rang) rank; (Amt) office; (Titel) title; (Auszeichnung) honour; **zu höchsten ~n gelangen** attain high office

würde·los **1** *Adj.* undignified. **2** *adv.* in an undignified way

Würdelosigkeit *die; ~:* lack of dignity

Würden·träger *der* dignitary

würde·voll **1** *Adj.* dignified. **2** *adv.* with dignity

würdig **1** *Adj.* **(a)** dignified; **(b)** (wert) worthy; suitable ‹*occasion*›; **jmds./einer Sache [nicht] ~ sein** [not] be worthy of sb./sth. **2** *adv.* **(a)** with dignity; ‹*dressed*› in a dignified manner; **(b)** (angemessen) worthily; ‹*celebrate*› in a/the appropriate manner

würdigen *tr. V.* **(a)** (anerkennen, beachten) recognize; (schätzen) appreciate; (lobend hervorheben) acknowledge; **etw. zu ~ wissen** appreciate sth.; **(b)** **jmdn. keines Blickes/keiner Antwort ~:** not deign to look at/answer sb.

Würdigung *die; ~, ~en* ⇒ **würdigen** a: recognition; appreciation; acknowledgement

Wurf /vʊrf/ *der; ~[e]s, Würfe* /'vʏrfə/ **(a)** throw; (beim Kegeln) bowl; (gezielt aufs Tor) shot; **(b)** *o. Pl.* (das Werfen) throwing/pitching/bowling; **beim ~:** when throwing/pitching/bowling; **(c)** (Zool.) litter

Würfel /'vʏrfl̩/ *der; ~s, ~* **(a)** cube; **Gemüse/Fleisch in ~ schneiden** dice vegetables/meat; **(b)** (Spiel~) dice; **die** (formal) **die ~ sind gefallen** (fig.) the die is cast

Würfel·becher *der* dice-cup

würfeln **1** *itr. V.* throw the dice; (mit Würfeln spielen) play dice; **hast du schon gewürfelt?** have you already thrown *or* had your throw?; **um etw. ~:** play dice for sth. **2** *tr. V.* **(a)** throw; **(b)** (in Würfel schneiden) dice ‹*vegetables, meat*›

Würfel-: **~spiel** *das* **(a)** (Glücksspiel) dice; (einzelne Partie) game of dice; **(b)** (Brettspiel) dice game; **~zucker** *der; o. Pl.* cube sugar; lump sugar

Wurf-: **~geschoss,** ***~geschoß** *das* missile; **~scheibe** *die* discus; **~sendung** *die* ⇒ **Postwurfsendung**

würgen /'vʏrgn̩/ **1** *tr. V.* strangle; throttle; (fig.) ‹*tie, collar*› strangle **2** *itr. V.* **(a)** (Brechreiz haben) retch; **(b)** (mühsam schlucken) **an etw.** (*Dat.*) **~:** have to force sth. down; *s. auch* **hängen² 1 d**

Wurm¹ /vʊrm/ *der; ~[e]s, Würmer* /'vʏrmɐ/ worm; (Made) maggot; **da ist der ~ drin** (fig. ugs.) there's something wrong there; **jmdm. die Würmer aus der Nase ziehen** (fig. ugs.) get sb. to spill the beans (fig. coll.)

Wurm² *das; ~[e]s, Würmer* (fam.) little mite

wurmen *tr., auch itr. V.* (ugs.) **jmdn. ~:** rankle with sb.

Wurm·fort·satz *der* ▶ 326] (Anat.) appendix

wurmig *Adj.,* **wurm·stichig** *Adj.* worm-eaten; (madig) maggoty

---

Wurscht /vʊrʃt/ (ugs.) **jmd./etw. ist jmdm. ~:** sb. doesn't care about sb./sth.; **das ist mir völlig ~:** I couldn't care less about that

wurscht·egal *Adj.* (ugs.) ⇒ **wurstegal**

Wurst /vʊrst/ *die; ~, Würste* /'vʏrstə/ **(a)** sausage; (Streich~) ≈ meat spread; **es geht um die ~** (fig. ugs.) the crunch has come; **(b)** (wurstähnliches Gebilde) roll; **eine ~ machen** (fam.) do a big one (child lang.); **(c)** (ugs.) ⇒ **Wurscht**

Wurst·brot *das* ⇒ **Wurst** a: open sausage/meat-spread sandwich; (zusammengeklappt) sausage/meat-spread sandwich

Würstchen /'vʏrstçən/ *das; ~s, ~* **(a)** [small] sausage; **Frankfurter/Wiener ~:** frankfurter/wienerwurst; **heiße ~:** hot sausages; **(b)** (ugs., oft abwertend) nobody; **(c)** **ein armes ~** (ugs.) a poor soul

wurst·egal *Adj.* (ugs.): **~ sein** not matter in the slightest

wursteln (ugs.) **1** *itr. V.* potter; **an etw.** (*Dat.*) **~:** potter about with sth. **2** *refl. V.* **sich durchs Leben ~:** muddle [along] through life

wurstig (ugs.) **1** *Adj.* couldn't-care-less *attrib.* ‹*attitude, behaviour, reply*›. **2** *adv.* in a couldn't-care-less way

Wurstigkeit *die; ~* (ugs.) couldn't-care-less attitude

Wurst-: **~salat** *der* piquant salad with pieces of sausage, onion rings, boiled eggs and/or cheese; **~waren** *Pl.* sausages; **~zipfel** *der* end of a/the sausage

Würze /'vʏrtsə/ *die; ~, ~n* **(a)** (Gewürz) spice; seasoning; **(b)** (Aroma) aroma; (fig.) spice; *s. auch* **Kürze c**

Wurzel /'vʊrtsl̩/ *die; ~, ~n* **(a)** (auch fig.) root; **~n schlagen** take root; (fig.) put down roots; **das Übel an der ~ fassen** *od.* **packen** (fig.) strike at the root of the problem; **(b)** ▶ 600] (Math.) root; **~n ziehen** calculate roots

wurzeln *itr. V.* (fig.) **das Misstrauen wurzelt tief in ihm** his mistrust is deep-rooted; **in etw.** (*Dat.*) **~** (seinen Ursprung haben in) be rooted in sth.; (verursacht sein durch) have its roots in sth.

Wurzel·werk *das; o. Pl.* roots *pl.*

würzen /'vʏrtsn̩/ *tr. V.* season; (fig.) spice

würzig *Adj.* tasty; full-flavoured ‹*beer, wine*›; aromatic ‹*fragrance, smell, tobacco*›; tangy ‹*air*›; (scharf) spicy

Würzigkeit *die; ~* ⇒ **würzig**: tastiness; full flavour; aromatic fragrance; tanginess; spiciness

wusch /vuːʃ/ *1. u. 3. Pers. Sg. Prät. v.* **waschen**

wuschelig *Adj.* (ugs.) frizzy; fuzzy

Wuschel·kopf *der* (ugs.) **(a)** shock *or* mopp of frizzy *or* fuzzy hair; **(b)** (Mensch) frizzy-haired *or* fuzzy-haired man/girl *etc*

wuselig *Adj.* (bes. südd., md.) busy; bustling

wuseln /'vuːzl̩n/ *itr. V.; mit sein* (bes. südd., md.) scurry

wusste, ***wußte** /'vʊstə/ *1. und 3. Pers. Sg. Prät. v.* **wissen**

wüsste, ***wüßte** /'vʏstə/ *1. und 3. Pers. Sg. Konjunktiv II v.* **wissen**

Wust /vuːst/ *der; ~[e]s* (abwertend) jumble; (fig.) welter

wüst /vyːst/ **1** *Adj.* **(a)** (öde) desolate; **(b)** (unordentlich) chaotic; tangled; tousled ‹*hair, beard, etc.*›; wild ‹*appearance*›; **(c)** (abwertend: wild, ungezügelt) wild; furious ‹*fight, shoot-out*›; **(d)** (abwertend: unanständig) rude; coarse ‹*oath, abuse*›; **(e)** (abwertend: furchtbar, abscheulich) terrible; foul (coll.), terrible (coll.) ‹*weather*›. **2** *adv.* **(a)** (unordentlich) chaotically; **das Haar hing ihr ~ ins Gesicht** her hair straggled down over her face; **(b)** (abwertend: wild, ungezügelt) wildly; **(c)** (abwertend: furchtbar, abscheulich) terribly

Wüste *die; ~, ~n* desert; (Eis~) waste; (fig.) wasteland; **jmdn. in die ~ schicken** (fig. ugs.) give sb. the push (Brit. coll.)

Wüstenei *die; ~, ~en* waste-land

Wüsten·sand *der* desert sand[s *pl.*]

Wüstling *der; ~s, ~e* (abwertend) lecher; debauchee

Wut /vuːt/ *die; ~:* rage; fury; **eine ~ auf jmdn. haben** be furious with sb.; **in ~ geraten** get furious; **jmdn. in ~ bringen** infuriate sb.

Wut-: **~anfall** *der* fit of rage; **~ausbruch** *der* outburst of rage *or* fury

---

***alte Schreibung (vgl. Hinweise auf S. xvi–xvii)

wüten /'vy:tn̩/ *itr. V.* (auch fig.) rage; (zerstören) wreak havoc
wütend 1 *Adj.* furious; angry ⟨*voice, mob*⟩; **auf jmdn.** **∼ sein** be furious with sb.; **über etw.** (*Akk.*) **∼ sein** be furious about sth. **2** *adv.* furiously; in a fury
wut·entbrannt *Adj.* infuriated; furious; in a fury *pred.*
Wüterich /'vy:tərɪç/ *der;* ∼**s**, ∼**e** (abwertend) hot-tempered person; (Gewaltmensch) brute
wut·schnaubend *Adj.* snorting with rage *pred.*
Wz *Abk.* **Warenzeichen** TM; ®

x¹, **X** /ɪks/ *das;* ∼, ∼**:** x, X; **jmdm. ein X für ein U** **vormachen** (fig.) dupe sb.; **er lässt sich** (*Dat.*) **kein X für ein U vormachen** you can't fool him; he's not easily fooled; *s. auch* **a, A**
x² *unbest. Zahlwort* (ugs.) umpteen (coll.)
X-Beine *Pl.* knock-knees; ∼ **haben** have knock-knees; be knock-kneed
x-beliebig *Adj.* (ugs.) **irgendein** ∼**er/irgendeine** ∼**e/** **irgendein** ∼**es** any old (coll. attrib.); **jeder** ∼**e Ort** any old place (coll.)
x-fach *Vervielfältigungsz.* **die** ∼**e Menge** x times the amount; (ugs.) umpteen times the amount (coll.)
X-fache *das;* ∼**n: das** ∼ **einer Zahl** X times a number; **das** ∼ **seines Einkommens** (ugs.) umpteen times his income (coll.)
x-mal *Adv.* (ugs.) umpteen times (coll.); any number of times
x-t... *Ordinalz.* ▶ 600 ◀ (ugs.) umpteenth (coll.); **das** ∼**e** *od.* **beim** ∼**en Mal** the umpteenth time (coll.); **das** ∼**e** *od.* **zum** ∼**en Mal** for the umpteenth time (coll.)
***x-te·mal,*x-ten·mal** ⇨ **x-t...**
Xylophon /ksylo'fo:n/ *das;* ∼**s**, ∼**e** xylophone

y, **Y** /'ʏpsilɔn/ *das;* ∼, ∼**:** y, Y; *s. auch* **a, A**
Yacht ⇨ **Jacht**
Yankee /'jɛnki/ *der;* ∼**s**, ∼**s** (oft abwertend) Yankee (Brit. coll.); Yank (Brit. coll.)
Yoga ⇨ **Joga**
Yogi[n] ⇨ **Jogi[n]**
Ypsilon /'ʏpsilɔn/ *das;* ∼**[s]**, ∼**s** y, Y; (im griechischen Alphabet) upsilon

Z z

z, Z /tsɛt/ *das;* ∼, ∼**:** z, Z; *s. auch* **a, A**
zack /tsak/ *Interj.* (salopp) ∼**!** ∼**!** get a move on! (coll.); make it snappy! (coll.); **bei ihm muss alles** ∼, ∼ **gehen** he likes things done at the double
Zacke *die;* ∼, ∼**n** point; peak; (einer Säge, eines Kamms) tooth; (einer Gabel, Harke) prong
zacken *tr. V.* serrate
Zacken *der;* ∼**s**, ∼ (a) ⇨ **Zacke**; (b) **sich** (*Dat.*) **keinen** ∼ **aus der Krone brechen** (fig. ugs.) not lose face
zackig 1 *Adj.* (a) jagged; (b) (schneidig) dashing; smart; rousing ⟨*music*⟩; brisk ⟨*orders*⟩. **2** *adv.* (a) (gezackt) jaggedly; (b) (schneidig) smartly; ⟨*play music*⟩ rousingly
zaghaft 1 *Adj.* timid; (zögernd) hesitant; tentative. **2** *adv.* timidly; (zögernd) hesitantly; tentatively
Zaghaftigkeit *die;* ∼**:** timidity; (Zögern) hesitancy
zäh /tsɛ:/ **1** *Adj.* (a) (fest) tough; heavy ⟨*dough, soil*⟩; (dickflüssig) glutinous; viscous ⟨*oil*⟩; (b) (schleppend) sluggish, dragging ⟨*conversation*⟩; (c) (widerstandsfähig) tough ⟨*person*⟩; (d) (beharrlich) tenacious; tough ⟨*negotiations*⟩; dogged ⟨*resistance*⟩. **2** *adv.* (a) (schleppend) sluggishly; (b) (beharrlich) tenaciously; ⟨*resist*⟩ doggedly
***Zäheit** ⇨ **Zähheit**
zäh·flüssig *Adj.* glutinous; viscous ⟨*oil*⟩; heavy ⟨*dough*⟩; (fig.: langsam) slow-moving ⟨*traffic*⟩
Zäh·flüssigkeit *die; o. Pl.* glutinousness; (von Öl) viscosity
Zähheit *die;* ∼ (a) (Festigkeit) toughness; (des Teigs, Bodens) heaviness; (Dickflüssigkeit) glutinousness; (von Öl) viscosity; (b) (schleppendes Tempo) sluggishness; (c) (Widerstandsfähigkeit) toughness; (d) (Beharrlichkeit) tenacity; (des Widerstands) doggedness
Zähigkeit *die;* ∼ (a) (Widerstandsfähigkeit) toughness; (b) (Beharrlichkeit) tenacity
Zahl /tsa:l/ *die;* ∼, ∼**en** ▶ 600 ◀ number; (Ziffer) numeral; (Zahlenangabe) figure; **in den roten/schwarzen** ∼**en** in the red/black; **acht** *usw.* **an der** ∼**:** eight *etc.* in number; **in großer** ∼**:** in great numbers
Zahl·adjektiv *das* numeral adjective
zahlbar *Adj.* (Kaufmannsspr.) payable
zählbar *Adj.* countable
zähleblg *Adj.* hardy ⟨*plant, animal*⟩; **ein** ∼**es Vorurteil** a prejudice which dies hard
zahlen 1 *tr. V.* (a) ▶ 216 ◀ pay ⟨*price, amount, rent, tax, fine, etc.*⟩ (**an** + *Akk.* to); **einen hohen Preis** ∼ (auch fig.) pay a high price; (b) ▶ 216 ◀ (ugs.: bezahlen) pay for ⟨*taxi, repair, etc.*⟩; **jmdm. etw.** ∼**:** give sb. the money for sth.; (spendieren) pay for sth. for sb. **2** ▶ 216 ◀ *itr. V.* pay; **er will nicht** ∼**:** he won't pay [up]; ∼ **bitte!** (im Lokal) [can I/we have] the bill, please!; **die Firma zahlt gut** the firm pays well
zählen /'tsɛ:lən/ **1** *itr. V.* (a) count; **ich zähle bis drei** I'll count up to three; (b) (gehören) belong (**zu** to); **diese Tage zählten zu den schönsten seines Lebens** these days were among *or* were some of the most wonderful in his life; (c) (gültig/wichtig sein) count; (d) **auf jmdn./etw.** ∼**:** count on sb./sth. **2** *tr. V.* (a) count; **Geld auf den Tisch** ∼**:** count money out on to the table; **seine Tage sind gezählt** (fig.) his days are numbered; (b) (geh.) **er zählt 90 Jahre** he is 90 years of age; **die Stadt zählt 500 000 Einwohner** the town has 500,000 inhabitants; (c) **jmdn. zu seinen Freunden** ∼**:** count sb. among one's friends; (d) (wert sein) be worth
zahlen-, Zahlen-: ∼**lotterie** *die,* ∼**lotto** *das* lottery in which entrants guess which set of figures will be drawn at random from a fixed sequence of numbers; ∼**mäßig 1** *Adj.:* nicht präd. numerical; **2** *adv.* numerically

Zahlen

Kardinalzahlen = Cardinal numbers

0 *(null)* = nought *(bes. brit.)*, zero[1]
1 *(eins, ein...)* = one
2 *(zwei)* = two
3 *(drei)* = three
4 *(vier)* = four
5 *(fünf)* = five
6 *(sechs)* = six
7 *(sieben)* = seven
8 *(acht)* = eight
9 *(neun)* = nine
10 *(zehn)* = ten
11 *(elf)* = eleven
12 *(zwölf)* = twelve
13 *(dreizehn)* = thirteen
14 *(vierzehn)* = fourteen
15 *(fünfzehn)* = fifteen
16 *(sechzehn)* = sixteen
17 *(siebzehn)* = seventeen
18 *(achtzehn)* = eighteen
19 *(neunzehn)* = nineteen
20 *(zwanzig)* = twenty
21 *(einundzwanzig)* = twenty-one
22 *(zweiundzwanzig)* = twenty-two
30 *(dreißig)* = thirty
40 *(vierzig)* = forty
50 *(fünfzig)* = fifty
60 *(sechzig)* = sixty
70 *(siebzig)* = seventy
80 *(achtzig)* = eighty
90 *(neunzig)* = ninety
100 *([ein]hundert)* = a *od.* one hundred[2]
101 *([ein]hundert[und]eins, [ein]hundert[und]ein...)* = a *od.* one hundred and one *(brit.)*, a *od.* one hundred one *(amerik.)*
555 *(fünfhundert[und]fünfundfünfzig)* = five hundred and fifty-five *(brit.)*, five hundred fifty-five *(amerik.)*
1,000 *([ein]tausend)* = a *od.* one thousand[2]
1,001 *([ein]tausend[und]eins, [ein]tausend[und]ein...)* = a *od.* one thousand and one *(brit.)*, a *od.* one thousand one *(amerik.)*
1,200 *([ein]tausendzweihundert od. zwölfhundert)* = one thousand two hundred, twelve hundred
100,000 *([ein]hunderttausend)* = a *od.* one hundred thousand
1,000,000 *(eine Million)* = a *od.* one million
3,536,000 *(drei Millionen fünfhundert-* = three million[3] five hundred and thirty-six *(brit.)* sechsunddreißigtausend) *od. (amerik.)* five hundred thirty-six thousand
1,000,000,000 *(eine Milliarde)* = a *od.* one billion, a *od.* one thousand million
1,000,000,000,000 *(eine Billion)* = a *od.* one trillion, a *od.* one million million

Anmerkungen

[1] 'Nought' wird hauptsächlich im britischen Englisch, 'zero' dagegen im amerikanischen Englisch für die Ziffer 0 verwendet. Wenn man eine Zahl ausspricht, die eine Null enthält, sagt man entweder 'oh' oder (besonders im amerikanischen Sprachraum) 'zero':

Die Vorwahl für London *(Mitte)* ist 0171 = The code for central London is 0171 (oh-one-seven-one *od. (bes. amerik.)* zero-one-seven-one)

der Peugeot 406 = the Peugeot 406 (four-oh-six)
Sie haben 4:0 gewonnen = They won 4-0 (four-nil *od. (amerik.)* four-zero)
Den ersten Satz gewann sie 6:0 = She won the first set 6-0 (six-love)
Tiefsttemperaturen um 4 Grad unter Null = Temperatures falling to *od. (bes. amerik.)* Lows around 4 degrees below zero

[2] **one** sagt man statt **a**, wenn man die Genauigkeit der Ziffer betonen will; **a hundred** (und **a thousand, a million** usw.) ist aber viel häufiger, vor allem bei zusammengesetzten Zahlen (z.B. **a hundred and twenty**).

[3] Wie bei **hundred** und **thousand**, verwendet man die Pluralform **millions** nicht in Zahlen, da **million** hier kein Substantiv ist; das gilt auch für unbestimmte Zahlwörter:

einige/ein paar Millionen [Pfund] = several/a couple of million [pounds]

millions kommt nur in ungenauen Ausdrücken vor, wie etwa:

Man kann Millionen von Pfund/Dollar verdienen = One can earn millions [of pounds/dollars]
Hunderte von Millionen = hundreds of millions

Brüche = Fractions

½	a half	1½	one and a half
⅓	a third	5⅔	five and two thirds
¼	a quarter	2¾	two and three quarters
⅕	a fifth	4⅘	four and four fifths
⅛	an eighth	8⅞	eight and seven eighths
¹⁄₃₂	one thirty-second	¹⁰⁄₇₁	ten seventy-firsts

Zur Bildung der Brüche dienen also die (substantivisch gebrauchten) Formen der Ordinalzahlen.

zwei Drittel des Weges = two thirds of the distance
drei Viertel aller Offiziere = three quarters of all officers

Nach dem Bruch folgt bei Maßeinheiten **of a**, und die Einheit steht dementsprechend im Singular.

ein Viertelliter = a quarter of a litre
fünf achtel Meilen = five eighths of a mile
sechs Hundertstel- sekunden = six hundredths of a second

Dezimalzahlen = Decimal numbers

0,1 = 0.1 (point one, oh *od. (brit.)* nought *od. (amerik.)* zero point one)
0,015 = 0.015 ([oh] point oh *od. (brit.)* [nought] point nought *od. (amerik.)* [zero] point zero one five)
1,43 = 1.43 (one point four three)
11,70 = 11.70 (eleven point seven oh)
12,3̄ = 12,3̄ (twelve point three recurring)

▶

▶ **Zahlen** (Fortsetzung)

Ordinalzahlen = Ordinal numbers
1. *(erst...)* = 1st (first)
2. *(zweit...)* = 2nd (second)
3. *(dritt...)* = 3rd (third)
4. *(viert...)* = 4th (fourth)
5. *(fünft...)* = 5th (fifth)
6. *(sechst...)* = 6th (sixth)
7. *(sieb[en]t...)* = 7th (seventh)
8. *(acht...)* = 8th (eighth)
9. *(neunt...)* = 9th (ninth)
10. *(zehnt...)* = 10th (tenth)
11. *(elft...)* = 11th (eleventh)
12. *(zwölft...)* = 12th (twelfth)
13. *(dreizehnt...)* = 13th (thirteenth)
14. *(vierzehnt...)* = 14th (fourteenth)
15. *(fünfzehnt...)* = 15th (fifteenth)
16. *(sechzehnt...)* = 16th (sixteenth)
17. *(siebzehnt...)* = 17th (seventeenth)
18. *(achtzehnt...)* = 18th (eighteenth)
19. *(neunzehnt...)* = 19th (nineteenth)
20. *(zwanzigst...)* = 20th (twentieth)
21. *(einundzwanzigst...)* = 21st (twenty-first)
22. *(zweiundzwanzigst...)* = 22nd (twenty-second)
30. *(dreißigst...)* = 30th (thirtieth)
40. *(vierzigst...)* = 40th (fortieth)
50. *(fünfzigst...)* = 50th (fiftieth)
60. *(sechzigst...)* = 60th (sixtieth)
70. *(siebzigst...)* = 70th (seventieth)
80. *(achtzigst...)* = 80th (eightieth)
90. *(neunzigst...)* = 90th (ninetieth)
100. *([ein]hundertst...)* = 100th ([one] hundredth)
101. *([ein]hundert[und]erst...)* = 101st ([one] hundred and first *(brit.)*, [one] hundred first *(amerik.)*)
555. *(fünfhundert[und]fünfundfünfzigst...)* = 555th (five hundred and fifty-fifth *(brit.)*, five hundred fifty-fifth *(amerik.)*)
1 000. *([ein]tausendst...)* = 1,000th ([one] thousandth)
1 001. *([ein]tausend[und]erst...)* = 1,001st (one thousand and first *(brit.)*, one thousand first *(amerik.)*)
1 200. *([ein]tausendzweihundertst... od. zwölfhundertst...)* = 1,200th (one thousand two hundredth, twelve hundredth)
100 000. *([ein]hunderttausendst...)* = 100,000th ([one] hundred thousandth)
1 000 000. *(millionst...)* = 1,000,000th ([one] millionth)
3 536 000. *(drei Millionen fünfhundertsechsund-dreißigtausendst...)* = 3,536,000th (three million five hundred and thirty-six *(brit.)* od. *(amerik.)* five hundred thirty-six thousandth)
1 000 000 000. *(milliardst...)* = 1,000,000,000th ([one] billionth, [one] thousand millionth)
1 000 000 000 000. *(billionst...)* = 1,000,000,000,000th ([one] trillionth, one million millionth)

Rechnen
7 + 3 = 10 (seven plus three is *od.* equals ten)
10 − 3 = 7 (ten minus three is *od.* equals seven)
10 x 3 = 30 (ten times three is *od.* equals thirty)
30 ÷ 3 = 10 (thirty divided by three is *od.* equals ten)

Potenzen = Powers
3^2 = *drei hoch zwei* = three squared
3^3 = *drei hoch drei* = three cubed
3^{10} = *drei hoch zehn* = three to the power of ten
$\sqrt{25}$ = *[Quadrat]wurzel aus fünfundzwanzig* = the square root of twenty-five

Siehe auch □ **Altersangaben, Datum, Entfernung, Fläche, Geld, Gewichte, Höhe und Tiefe, Länge und Breite, Rauminhalt, Temperaturen, Uhrzeit**

Zähler *der;* ~s, ~ (**a**) (Messgerät) meter; (**b**) (Math.) numerator
zahl-, Zahl-: ~**karte** *die* (Postw.) paying-in slip; ~**los** *Adj.* countless; innumerable; ~**meister** *der* (auch fig.) paymaster; (auf Schiffen) purser; ~**reich** 1 *Adj.* numerous. **2** *adv.* in large numbers
Zahlung *die;* ~, ~**en** ▶216 payment; **etw. in** ~ **nehmen/geben** (Kaufmannsspr.) take/give sth. in part exchange; take sth. as a trade-in/trade sth. in

Zählung *die;* ~, ~**en** count
zahlungs-, Zahlungs-: ~**bedingungen** *Pl.* (Wirtsch.) terms of payment; ~**empfänger** *der* payee; ~**fähig** *Adj.* solvent; ~**fähigkeit** *die; o. Pl.* solvency; ~**kräftig** *Adj.* (ugs.) affluent; ~**mittel** *das* means of payment; ~**unfähig** *Adj.* insolvent; ~**unfähigkeit** *die* insolvency; ~**weise** *die* method of payment ~**ziel** *das* (Kaufmannsspr.) ⇒ ~**frist**

Zahl-: ~**wort** *das; Pl.* ~**wörter** (Sprachw.) numeral; ~**zeichen** *das* numeral

zahm /tsa:m/ (auch fig.) **1** *Adj.* tame. **2** *adv.* tamely

zähmen /'tsɛ:mən/ *tr. V.* (a) (auch fig.) tame; subdue ‹*forces of nature*›; (b) (geh.) restrain ‹*curiosity, impatience, etc.*›

Zahn /tsa:n/ *der;* ~[e]s, **Zähne** /'tsɛ:nə/ (a) ▶ 326 J tooth; (an einer Briefmarke usw.) serration; **sich** (*Dat.*) **einen** ~ **ziehen lassen** have a tooth out; (b) (fig.) **der** ~ **der Zeit** (ugs.) the ravages *pl.* of time; **[jmdm.] die Zähne zeigen** (ugs.) show [sb.] one's teeth; **die Zähne zusammen-beißen** (ugs.) grit one's teeth; **sich** (*Dat.*) **an jmdm./etw. die Zähne ausbeißen** (ugs.) get nowhere with sb./sth.; **jmdm. auf den** ~ **fühlen** (ugs.) sound sb. out; **bis an die Zähne bewaffnet** armed to the teeth; (c) (ugs.: Tempo) **einen ganz schönen** ~ **draufhaben** be going like the clappers (sl.); **einen** ~ **zulegen** get a move on (coll.)

zahn-, Zahn-: ~**arzt** *der,* ~**ärztin** *die* ▶ 85 J dentist; ~**ärztlich 1** *Adj.; nicht präd.* dental ‹*treatment etc.*›; **2** *adv.* **jmdn.** ~**ärztlich behandeln** give sb. dental treatment; ~**bürste** *die* toothbrush; ~**creme** *die* ⇒ ~**pasta**

zähne-: ~**fletschend** *Adj.* baring its/their teeth *postpos.;* ~**klappernd** *Adj.* with chattering teeth *postpos.;* ~**knirschend** *Adv.* gnashing one's teeth; cursing silently

zahnen *itr. V.* ‹*baby*› be teething

zahn-, Zahn-: ~**fleisch** *das* ▶ 326 J gum; (als Ganzes) gums *pl.;* ~**kranz** *der* (a) sprocket [wheel]; (b) (~ paket) rear sprocket [cluster]; (c) ~**los** *Adj.* toothless; ~**lücke** *die* gap in one's teeth; ~**medizin** *die* dentistry *no art.;* ~**pasta** /~pasta/ *die;* ~, ~**pasten** toothpaste; ~**pro-these** *die* dentures *pl.;* [set *sing.* of] false teeth *pl.;* ~**pulver** *das* tooth powder; ~**putz·becher** *der* tooth mug; ~**rad** *das* gearwheel; (kleines) cog; (einer Uhr) [toothed] wheel; (für Ketten) sprocket; ~**rad·bahn** *die* rack-railway; ~**schmerzen** *Pl.* ▶ 329 J toothache *sing.;* ~**stein** *der; o. Pl.* tartar; ~**stocher** *der;* ~s, ~: toothpick; ~**weh** *das; o. Pl.* (ugs.) toothache

Zaire /za'i:r/ (*das*); ~s Zaire

Zairer /za'i:rɐ/ *der;* ~s, ~: ▶ 388 J Zairese

Zander /'tsandɐ/ *der;* ~s, ~: zander

Zange /'tsaŋə/ *die;* ~, ~**n** (a) (Werkzeug) pliers *pl.;* (Eiswür-fel~, Wäsche~, Zucker~) tongs *pl.;* (Geburts~) forceps *pl.;* (Kneif~) pincers *pl.;* (Loch~) punch; **eine** ~: a pair of pli-ers/tongs/forceps/pincers/a punch; **jmdn. in die** ~ **neh-men** (fig. ugs.) put the screws on sb.; (Fußballjargon) crowd sb. out; (b) (bei Tieren) pincer

Zank /tsaŋk/ *der;* ~[e]s squabble; row

Zank·apfel *der* bone of contention

zanken *refl., itr. V.* squabble, bicker (**um** *od.* **über** + *Akk.* over)

zänkisch *Adj.* quarrelsome

Zäpfchen /'tsɛpfçən/ *das;* ~s, ~ (Pharm.) suppository

zapfen /'tsapfn/ *tr. V.* tap, draw ‹*beer, wine*›

Zapfen *der;* ~s, ~ (a) (Bot.) cone; (b) (Stöpsel) bung; (c) (Eis~) icicle

Zapfen·streich *der* (Milit.) (a) (Signal) last post (Brit.); taps *pl.* (Amer.); **der Große** ~: the tattoo; (b) *o. Pl.* (Ende der Ausgehzeit) time for return to barracks

Zapf-: ~**hahn** *der* tap; ~**säule** *die* petrol pump (Brit.); gasoline pump (Amer.)

zappelig *Adj.* (ugs.) (a) wriggly; fidgety ‹*child*›; (b) (nervös) jittery (coll.)

zappeln /'tsapln/ *itr. V.* wriggle; ‹*child*› fidget; **mit den Beinen/Armen** ~: wave one's legs/arms about; **jmdn.** ~ **lassen** (fig. ugs.) keep sb. on tenterhooks

zappen /'tsɛpn/ (ugs.) **1** *itr. V.* zap (coll.). **2** *refl. V.* zap (coll.); **sich durch die Frühstückssendungen/zwanzig Ka-näle** ~: zap through the breakfast programmes/twenty channels

Zar /tsa:ɐ/ *der;* ~en, ~en (hist.) Tsar

Zaren·reich *das* (hist.) tsardom

Zarin *die;* ~, ~**nen** (hist.) Tsarina

zaristisch *Adj.* (hist.) tsarist

zart /tsa:ɐt/ **1** *Adj.* (a) delicate; soft ‹*skin*›; tender ‹*bud, shoot*›; fragile, delicate ‹*china*›; delicate, frail ‹*health, con-stitution, child*›; (b) (weich) tender ‹*meat, vegetables*›; soft ‹*filling*›; fine ‹*biscuits*›; (c) (leicht) gentle ‹*kiss, touch*›; deli-cate ‹*colour, complexion, fragrance, etc.*›; soft, gentle ‹*voice, sound, tune*›. **2** *adv.* delicately ‹*coloured, fragrant*›; ‹*kiss, touch*› gently; ~ **besaitet** ⇒ **zartbesaitet;** ~ **fühlend** ⇒ **zartfühlend**

zart-, Zart-: ~**besaitet** *Adj.* highly sensitive; ~**bitter** *Adj.* bittersweet ‹*chocolate*›; ~**blau** *Adj.* pale blue; ~**fühlend 1** *Adj.* tactful; **2** *adv.* tactfully; ~**ge-fühl** *das* tact; delicacy of feeling

Zartheit *die;* ~ (a) delicacy; (der Haut) softness; (von Porzel-lan) fragility; (von Spitzen, Seide) fineness; (der Gesundheit, ·Kon-stitution) delicateness; (Sensibilität) sensitivity; (b) (von Fleisch, Gemüse) tenderness; (c) (eines Kusses, einer Berührung) gentle-ness; (einer Farbe, eines Dufts) delicacy; (einer Stimme, eines Tons) softness; gentleness

zärtlich /'tsɛ:ɐtlɪç/ **1** *Adj.* tender; loving; ~ **werden** (ver-hüll.) start petting. **2** *adv.* tenderly; lovingly

Zärtlichkeit *die;* ~, ~**en** (a) *o. Pl.* tenderness; af-fection; (b) *meist Pl.* (Liebkosung) caress; **es kam zu** ~**en [zwischen ihnen]** (verhüll.) they became intimate

zart·rosa *Adj.* pale pink

Zäsur /tsɛ'zu:ɐ/ *die;* ~, ~**en** (a) (Verslehre, Musik) caesura; (b) (geh.: Einschnitt) break

Zauber /'tsaubɐ/ *der;* ~s, ~ (a) (auch fig.) magic; (magische Handlung) magic trick; (Bann) [magic] spell; **einen großen** ~ **auf jmdn. ausüben** (fig.) have a great fascination for sb.; (b) *o. Pl.* (ugs. abwertend: Aufheben) fuss; **ich halte nichts von dem ganzen** ~: the whole palaver means nothing to me (coll.)

Zauberei *die;* ~: magic

Zauberer *der;* ~s, ~: (a) magician; (b) (Zauberkünstler) conjurer

Zauber·formel *die* magic spell; (fig.) magic formula; panacea

zauber·haft 1 *Adj.* enchanting; delightful. **2** *adv.* en-chantingly; delightfully

Zauberin *die;* ~, ~**nen** (a) sorceress; (b) ⇒ **Zauberer b**

zauberisch (geh.) **1** *Adj.* magical. **2** *adv.* magically

Zauber-: ~**kunst** *die* (a) *o. Pl.* magic *no art.;* (eines Bühnenkünstlers) magic *no art.;* conjuring *no art.;* (b) *meist Pl.* (magische Fähigkeit) magic; ~**künstler** *der* conjurer; magician

zaubern 1 *itr. V.* (a) do magic; (b) (Zaubertricks ausführen) do conjuring tricks. **2** *tr. V.* (auch fig.) conjure; conjure up ‹*palace, horse*›; **eine Taube aus dem Hut** ~: produce a dove out of a hat

Zauber-: ~**stab** *der* magic wand; ~**trick** *der* conjur-ing trick

Zauderer *der;* ~s, ~: waverer; ditherer

zaudern /'tsaudɐn/ *itr. V.* (geh.) delay; ~, **etw. zu tun** delay in doing sth.

Zaum /tsaum/ *der;* ~[e]s, **Zäume** /'tsɔymə/ bridle; **sich/ seine Zunge/seine Leidenschaften im** ~ **halten** (fig. geh.) restrain *or* control oneself/control one's tongue/con-trol one's passions

zäumen /'tsɔymən/ *tr. V.* bridle

Zaum·zeug *das* bridle

Zaun /tsaun/ *der;* ~[e]s, **Zäune** /'tsɔynə/ fence; **einen Streit vom** ~ **brechen** (fig.) suddenly start a quarrel

Zaun-: ~**gast** *der* onlooker; ~**könig** *der* wren; ~**pfahl** *der* fence-post; *s. auch* **Wink b**

zausen /'tsauzn/ *tr. V.* (auch fig.) ruffle; ruffle, tousle ‹*hair*›

z. B. *Abk.* **zum Beispiel** e.g.

ZDF /tsɛt|de:'|ɛf/ *das;* ~ *Abk.* **Zweites Deutsches Fernsehen** Second German Television Channel

Zebra /'tse:bra/ *das;* ~s, ~s zebra
Zebra·streifen *der* zebra crossing (Brit.); pedestrian crossing
Zebu /'tse:bu/ *der od. das;* ~s, ~s zebu
Zeche *die* ~, ~n (a) bill (Brit.); check (Amer.); **die ~ prellen** (ugs.) leave without paying [the bill]; **die ~ bezahlen müssen** (fig.) have to foot the bill *or* pay the price; (b) (Bergwerk) pit; mine
zechen /'tsɛçn/ *itr. V.* (veralt., scherzh.) tipple
Zecher *der;* ~s, ~ (veralt., scherzh.) tippler
Zech-: ~**preller** *der;* ~s, ~ *person who leaves without paying the bill;* bill-dodger; ~**prellerei** *die;* ~, ~en *leaving without paying the bill;* bill-dodging
Zecke /'tsɛkə/ *die* ~, ~n tick
Zeder /'tse:dɐ/ *die* ~, ~n cedar
Zeh /tse:/ *der;* ~s, ~en, **Zehe** *die* ~, ~n (a) ▶ 326 | toe; **jmdm. auf die Zehen treten** (auch fig.) tread on sb.'s toes; (b) (Knoblauch~) clove
Zehen-: ~**nagel** *der* ▶ 326 | toenail; ~**spitze** *die:* **auf/auf die** ~**spitzen** (*Dat./Akk.*) on tiptoe
zehn /tse:n/ *Kardinalz.* ▶ 22 |, ▶ 530 |, ▶ 600 | ten; *s. auch* **acht¹**
Zehner *der;* ~s, ~ (a) (ugs.: Geldschein, Münze) ten; (b) (ugs.: Autobus) number ten; (c) (Math.) ten; (d) (Sprungturm) ten-metre platform
zehn·fach *Vervielfältigungsz.* tenfold; **die ~e Menge** ten times the quantity; *s. auch* **achtfach**
Zehnfache *das; adj. Dekl.* **das ~:** ten times as much; *s. auch* **Achtfache**
zehn-, Zehn-: ~**jährig** *Adj.* (10 Jahre alt) ten-year-old *attrib.;* ten years old *postpos.;* (10 Jahre dauernd) ten-year *attrib.; s. auch* **achtjährig;** ~**kampf** *der* (Sport) decathlon; ~**kämpfer** *der* decathlete; ~**mal** *Adv.* ten times; *s. auch* **achtmal;** ~**markschein** *der* ▶ 216 | ten-mark note; ~**pfennig·[brief]marke** *die* ten-pfennig stamp; ~**pfennigstück** *das* ▶ 216 | ten-pfennig piece; ~**stöckig** *Adj.* ten-storey ‹ *building* ›; *s. auch* **achtstöckig**
zehnt /tse:nt/ *in* **wir waren zu ~:** there were ten of us; *s. auch* **acht²**
zehnt... *Ordinalz.* ▶ 119 |, ▶ 600 | tenth; *s. auch* **acht...**
zehn-: ~**tägig** *Adj.* (10 Tage alt) ten-day-old *attrib.;* (10 Tage dauernd) ten-day *attrib.;* ~**tausend** *Kardinalz.* ▶ 600 | ten thousand; **die oberen** ~**tausend** (fig.: die vornehmen Leute) the élite of society
zehn·teilig *Adj.* ten-piece ‹ *tool-set etc.* ›; ten-part ‹ *serial* ›; *s. auch* **achtteilig**
zehntel /'tse:ntl/ *Bruchz.* ▶ 600 | tenth
Zehntel *das* (schweiz. meist der); ▶ 600 | ~s, ~: tenth
Zehntel-: ~**liter** *der* tenth of a litre; ~**sekunde** *die* tenth of a second
zehntens *Adv.* tenthly
zehren /'tse:rən/ *itr. V.* (a) **von etw.** ~: live on *or* off sth.; **von Erinnerungen** *usw.* ~ (fig.) sustain oneself on memories *etc.;* (b) **an jmdm./jmds. Kräften** ~: wear sb. down/sap sb.'s strength
Zeichen /'tsaiçn/ *das;* ~s, ~ (a) sign; (Laut, Wink) signal; **das ~ zum Angriff** the signal to attack; **jmdm. ein ~ geben** signal to sb.; **zum ~, dass ...:** to show that ...; as a sign that ...; (b) (Markierung) mark; (Waren~) [trade] mark; (am Briefkopf) reference; **[ein] ~ setzen** (fig.) set an example; point the way; (c) (Symbol) sign; (Chemie, Math., auf Landkarten usw.) symbol; (Satz~) punctuation mark; (Musik) accidental; (d) (An~) sign; indication; (einer Krankheit) sign; symptom; **ein ~ dafür, dass ...:** a [sure] sign that ...; **die ~ der Zeit erkennen** see which way the wind's blowing (fig.); (e) (Tierkreis~) sign [of the zodiac]; **ich bin im ~ des Krebses geboren** I was born under the sign of Cancer
Zeichen-: ~**block** *der; Pl.* ~s od. ~**blöcke** sketch pad; ~**brett** *das* drawing board; ~**erklärung** *die* legend; ~**feder** *die* drawing-pen; ~**setzung** *die* punctuation; ~**sprache** *die* sign language; ~**stift** *der* drawing-pencil; ~**trickfilm** *der* animated cartoon; ~**unterricht** *der* drawing lessons *pl.;* (Schulfach) art *no art.*

zeichnen **1** *tr. V.* (a) draw; (fig.) portray ‹ *character* ›; (b) **das Fell ist schön/auffallend gezeichnet** the fur has beautiful/striking markings; **er war von der Krankheit gezeichnet** (fig.) sickness had left its mark on him; (c) (bes. Kaufmannsspr.) sign ‹ *cheque* ›; subscribe for ‹ *share, loan* ›. **2** *itr. V.* (a) draw; (b) (bes. Kaufmannsspr.: unterschreiben) sign; **für etw. [verantwortlich]** ~ (fig.) be responsible for sth.
Zeichner *der;* ~s, ~, **Zeichnerin** *die;* ~, ~nen (a) graphic artist; (Technik) draughtsman/-woman; (b) (Kaufmannsspr.) subscriber
zeichnerisch **1** *Adj.* ‹ *talent* › as a draughtsman/-woman *or* for drawing. **2** *adv.* ~ **begabt sein** have a talent for drawing; **etw.** ~ **darstellen** make a drawing of sth.
Zeichnung *die;* ~, ~en (a) drawing; (fig.) portrayal; (b) (bei Tieren und Pflanzen) markings *pl.;* (c) (Kaufmannsspr.) subscriber
zeichnungs·berechtigt *Adj.* (Kaufmannsspr.) with signatory powers *postpos.;* ~ **sein** have signatory powers.
Zeige·finger *der* index finger; forefinger; **der erhobene** ~ (fig.) the wagging *or* monitory finger
zeigen /'tsaign/ **1** *tr. V.* point; **[mit dem Finger/einem Stock] auf jmdn./etw.** ~: point [one's finger/a stick] at sb./sth.. **2** *tr. V.* show; **jmdm. etw.** ~: show sb. sth.; show sth. to sb.; (jmdn. zu etw. hinführen) show sb. to sth.; **dem werd ichs** ~! (ugs.) I'll show him!; **zeig mal, was du kannst** show [us] what you can do. **3** *refl. V.* (a) (sich sehen lassen) appear; **mit ihr kann man sich überall** ~: you can take her anywhere; (b) (sich erweisen) **sich als etw.** ~: prove to be sth.; **es wird sich** ~, **wer schuld war** time will tell who was responsible; **es hat sich gezeigt, dass ...:** it turned out that ...
Zeiger *der;* ~s, ~: pointer; (Uhr~) hand
Zeige·stock *der; Pl.* ~**stöcke** pointer
zeihen /'tsaiən/ *unr. tr. V.* (geh.) **jmdn. einer Sache** (*Gen.*) ~: indict sb. of sth.
Zeile /'tsailə/ *die;* ~, ~n (a) line; **jmdm. ein paar** ~**n schreiben** drop sb. a line; **zwischen den** ~**n** (fig.) between the lines; (b) (Reihe) row
Zeisig /'tsaiziç/ *der;* ~s, ~e siskin
zeit /tsait/ *Präp. mit Gen.* ~ **meines** *usw.*/**unseres** *usw.* **Lebens** all my *etc.* life/our *etc.* lives
Zeit *die;* ~, ~en (a) *o. Pl.* time *no art.;* **im Laufe der** ~: in the course of time; **mit der** ~: with time; in time; (allmählich) gradually; **die** ~ **arbeitet für/gegen jmdn.** time is on sb.'s side/is against sb.; **keine** ~ **verlieren dürfen** have no time to lose; **die** ~ **drängt** time is pressing; there is [precious] little time; **die** ~ **[mit etw.] vertreiben** pass the time [with/doing sth.]; **jmdm.** ~/**drei Tage** *usw.* ~ **lassen** give sb. time/three days *etc.;* **sich** (*Dat.*) ~ **lassen** take one's time; **sich** (*Dat.*) **für jmdn./etw.** ~ **nehmen** make time for sb./sth.; **eine** ~ **lang** for a while *or* a time; (b) (~punkt) time; **seit der** *od.* **dieser** ~: since that time; **um diese** ~: at this time; **vor der** ~: prematurely; early; **von** ~ **zu** ~: from time to time; **zur** ~: at the moment; at present; (c) (~abschnitt, Lebensabschnitt) time; period; (Geschichtsabschnitt) age; period; **die erste** ~: at first; **auf** ~: temporarily; **ein Vertrag auf** ~: a fixed-term contract; **zu meiner** ~: in my day; (d) (Sport) time; **die** ~ **bei etw. stoppen** time sth.; **über die** ~ **kommen** (Boxen) go the distance; (e) (Sprachw.) tense
zeit-, Zeit-: ~**abschnitt** *der* period; ~**alter** *das* age; era; ~**ansage** *die* (im Radio) time check; (am Telefon) speaking clock; ~**aufwand** *der:* **viel** ~**aufwand erfordern** take up a great deal of time; ~**bombe** *die* (auch fig.) time bomb; ~**gefühl** *das; o. Pl.* sense of time; ~**geist** *der; o. Pl.* spirit of the age; ~**gemäß** *Adj.* contemporary ‹ *views* ›; (modern) up-to-date; ~**genosse** *der,* ~**genossin** *die* (a) contemporary; (b) (ugs.: Mensch) individual (coll.); ~**genössisch** /-gənœsɪʃ/ *Adj.* contemporary; ~**geschehen** *das:* **das [aktuelle]** ~**geschehen** current events *pl.;* ~**geschichte** *die; o. Pl.* contemporary history *no art.;* ~**geschichtlich** *Adj.; nicht präd.* contemporary ‹ *source etc.* ›; contemporary-history ‹ *teaching etc.* ›; ~**gleich** **1** *Adj.* (a) (Sport)

⟨*runners etc.*⟩ with the same time; **(b)** ⇒ **gleichzeitig 1;** 2 *adv.* ⇒ **gleichzeitig 2.**

zeitig *Adj., adv.* early

zeitigen *tr. V.* (geh.) produce, yield ⟨*result, success, etc.*⟩; provoke, precipitate ⟨*uproar*⟩

zeit-, Zeit-: ∼**karte** *die* season ticket; ∼**kritik** *die; o. Pl.* appraisal *or* analysis of contemporary issues; ∼**kritisch** *Adj.* ⟨*essay etc.*⟩ analysing contemporary issues; *∗∼**lang:** ⇒ **Zeit a;** ∼**läuf[t]e** /∼lɔyf(t)ə/ *Pl.* (geh.) times; **über alle** ∼**läuf[t]e hinweg** for all time; ∼**lebens** *Adv.* all my *etc.* life/our *etc.* lives

zeitlich **1** *Adj.* ⟨*length, interval*⟩ in time; chronological ⟨*order, sequence*⟩. **2** *adv.* with regard to time; **ich kann es** ∼ **nicht einrichten** I can't fit it in time-wise (coll.)

zeit-, Zeit-: ∼**los** **1** *Adj.* timeless; classic ⟨*fashion, shape*⟩; **2** *adv.* timelessly; ∼**los eingerichtet** furnished in a classic *or* timeless style; ∼**lupe** *die; o. Pl.* (Film) slow motion; ∼**lupen·tempo** *das:* **im** ∼**lupentempo** at a crawl; at a snail's pace; ∼**nah 1** *Adj.* topical ⟨*play etc.*⟩; ⟨*teaching, syllabus*⟩ relevant to the present day; **2** *adv.* topically; ∼**not** *die; o. Pl.* **in** ∼**not geraten** *od.* **kommen** become pressed for time; ∼**plan** *der* schedule; ∼**punkt** *der* moment; **zum jetzigen** ∼**punkt** at the present moment; at this point in time; ∼**raffer** *der* (Film) timelapse; ∼**raubend** *Adj.* timeconsuming; ∼**raum** *der* period; ∼**rechnung** *die* calendar; **vor unserer** ∼**rechnung** BC; before Christ; **unserer/christlicher** ∼**rechnung** AD; Anno Domini; ∼**schrift** *die* magazine; (bes. wissenschaftlich) journal; periodical; ∼**soldat** *der* soldier serving *for a fixed period;* ∼**spanne** *die* period

Zeitung *die;* ∼, ∼**en** [news]paper; **[die]** ∼ **lesen** read the paper

Zeitungs-: ∼**annonce** *die,* ∼**anzeige** *die* newspaper advertisement; ∼**artikel** *der* newspaper article; ∼**inserat** *das* newspaper advertisement; ∼**leser** *der* newspaper-reader; ∼**notiz** *die* newspaper item; ∼**papier** *das* **(a)** (alte Zeitung[en]) newspaper; **(b)** (unbedruckt) newsprint

zeit-, ∼Zeit-: ∼**verschwendung** *die* waste of time; ∼**verschwendung sein** be a waste of time; ∼**vertreib** *der;* ∼[e]s, ∼**e** pastime; **zum** ∼**vertreib** to pass the time; ∼**weilig 1** *Adj.; nicht präd.* temporary; **2** *adv.* temporarily; for a time; ∼**weise** *Adv.* **(a)** (gelegentlich) occasionally; at times; (von Zeit zu Zeit) from time to time; ∼**weise Regen** occasional rain; **(b)** (vorübergehend) for a time; for a while; ∼**wort** *das; Pl.* ∼**wörter** (Sprachw.) verb

zelebrieren /tsele'bri:rən/ *tr. V.* celebrate

Zelle /'tsɛlə/ *die;* ∼, ∼**n** cell; (Telefon∼) [tele]phone booth *or* (Brit.) box

Zell-: ∼**stoff** *der* cellulose; ∼**teilung** *die* (Biol.) cell division

Zellulitis /tsɛlu'li:tɪs/ *die;* ∼, **Zellulitiden** /tsɛluli'ti:dn̩/ (Med.) cellulitis

Zelluloid /tsɛlu'lɔyt/ *das;* ∼[e]s celluloid

Zellulose /tsɛlu'lo:zə/ *die;* ∼, ∼**n** cellulose

Zell·wolle *die* rayon

Zelt /tsɛlt/ *das;* ∼[e]s, ∼**e** tent; (Fest∼) marquee; (Zirkus∼) big top

zelten *itr. V.* camp; **wir waren** ∼: we went camping

Zelt-: ∼**lager** *das* camp; ∼**plane** *die* tarpaulin; ∼**platz** *der* camping site; campsite

Zement /tse'mɛnt/ *der;* ∼[e]s, ∼**e** cement

Zement·boden *der* concrete floor

zementieren *tr. V.* **(a)** cement; **(b)** (fig.) make ⟨*situation etc.*⟩ permanent

Zenit /tse'ni:t/ *der;* ∼[e]s zenith; **im** ∼ **stehen** be at its zenith

zensieren /tsɛn'zi:rən/ **1** *tr. V.* **(a)** (Schulw.) mark, (Amer.) grade ⟨*essay etc.*⟩; **(b)** (der Zensur unterziehen) censor ⟨*article, film, etc.*⟩. **2** *itr. V.* (Schulw.) **streng/milde** ∼: mark *or* (Amer.) grade severely/leniently

Zensur /tsɛn'zu:ɐ̯/ *die;* ∼, ∼**en (a)** (Schulw.) mark; grade (Amer.); **(b)** (Kontrolle) censorship; **(c)** (Behörde) censors *pl.*

Zenti·meter /'tsɛnti-, *auch:* --'--/ *der, auch: das* ▶277」, ▶340」 centimetre

Zentner /'tsɛntnɐ/ *der;* ∼**s**, ∼ ▶228」 **(a)** centner; metric hundredweight; **(b)** (österr., schweiz.) ⇒ **Doppelzentner**

Zentner·last *die* hundredweight load

zentner·schwer 1 *Adj.* (äußerst schwer) massively heavy. **2** *adv.* ∼ **auf jmdm. lasten** (fig.) weigh heavily on sb.

zentral /tsɛn'tra:l/ **1** *Adj.* central. **2** *adv.* centrally

Zentral·bank *die; Pl.* ∼**en** (Finanzw.) central bank

Zentrale *die;* ∼, ∼**n (a)** head *or* central office; (der Polizei, einer Partei) headquarters *sing. or pl.;* (Funk∼) control centre; **(b)** (Telefon∼) [telephone] exchange; (eines Hotels, einer Firma o. Ä.) switchboard

Zentral·heizung *die* central heating

zentralisieren *tr. V.* centralize

Zentral-: ∼**komitee** *das* Central Committee; ∼**speicher** *der* (DV) main memory; ∼**nerven·system** *das* central nervous system

Zentren ⇒ **Zentrum**

Zentrifugal·kraft /tsɛntrifu'ga:l-/ *die* (Physik) centrifugal force

Zentrifuge *die;* ∼, ∼**n** centrifuge

Zentripetal·kraft /tsɛntripe'ta:l-/ *die* (Physik) centripetal force

Zentrum /'tsɛntrʊm/ *das;* ∼**s, Zentren** centre; **im** ∼: at the centre; (im Stadt∼) in the town/city centre

Zeppelin /'tsɛpəli:n/ *der;* ∼**s**, ∼**e** Zeppelin

Zepter /'tsɛptɐ/ *das, auch: der;* ∼**s**, ∼: sceptre

zerbeißen *unr. tr. V.* bite in two; ⟨*flea, mosquito, etc.*⟩ bite ⟨*person etc.*⟩ all over

zerbersten *unr. itr. V.; mit sein* burst apart

zerbomben *tr. V.* bomb to pieces; destroy by bombing; **zerbombt** bombed ⟨*streets, houses*⟩

zerbrechen 1 *unr. itr. V.; mit sein* break [into pieces]; smash [to pieces]; ⟨*glass*⟩ shatter; (fig.) ⟨*marriage, relationship*⟩ break up. **2** *unr. tr. V.* break; smash, shatter ⟨*dishes, glass*⟩

zerbrechlich *Adj.* **(a)** fragile; „**Vorsicht,** ∼**!**" 'fragile; handle with care'; **(b)** (zart, schwach) frail

Zerbrechlichkeit *die;* ∼ ⇒ **zerbrechlich:** fragility; frailty

zerbröckeln 1 *itr. V.; mit sein* (auch fig.) crumble away. **2** *tr. V.* break into small pieces

zerdeppern /tsɛɐ̯'dɛpɐn/ *tr. V.* (ugs.) smash

zerdrücken *tr. V.* mash ⟨*potatoes, banana*⟩; squash ⟨*fly etc.*⟩; crease ⟨*clothes*⟩

Zeremonie /tseremo'ni:/ *die;* ∼, ∼**n** ceremony; (fig.) ritual

Zeremoniell /tseremo'niɛl/ *das;* ∼**s**, ∼**e** ceremonial

Zerfall *der;* ∼[e]s disintegration; (fig.: der Moral) breakdown; (einer Leiche) decomposition; (eines Gebäudes) decay

zerfallen *unr. itr. V.; mit sein* **(a)** (auch fig.) disintegrate (**in** + *Akk.,* **zu** into); ⟨*building*⟩ fall into ruin, decay; ⟨*corpse*⟩ decompose, decay; ∼**de Mauern** crumbling walls; **(b)** (unterteilt sein) be divided (**in** + *Akk.* into)

zerfetzen *tr. V.* rip *or* tear to pieces; rip *or* tear up ⟨*letter etc.*⟩ (**in** + *Akk.* into); tear apart ⟨*body, limb*⟩

zerfleddern *tr. V.* wear out

zerfleischen *tr. V.* tear ⟨*person, animal*⟩ limb from limb

zerfließen *unr. itr. V.; mit sein* **(a)** (schmelzen) melt [away]; **in** *od.* **vor Mitleid** ∼ (fig.) dissolve with pity; **(b)** (auseinander fließen) ⟨*paint, ink*⟩ run; ⟨*shapes*⟩ dissolve

zerfransen 1 *itr. V.; mit sein* fray. **2** *tr. V.* fray

zerfressen *unr. tr. V.* **(a)** eat away; ⟨*moth etc.*⟩ eat holes in; **von Motten** ∼: moth-eaten; **(b)** (zersetzen) corrode ⟨*metal*⟩

zerfurchen *tr. V.* **(a)** rut ⟨*track etc.*⟩; **(b)** furrow ⟨*brow, face*⟩

zergehen *unr. itr. V.; mit sein* melt; (sich auflösen) dissolve; **auf der Zunge** ∼: melt in the mouth

zerhacken *tr. V.* chop up

zerhauen *unr. tr. V.* chop up

zerkauen *tr. V.* chew [up]

zerkleinern /tsːɛɐ̯'klaɪnɐn/ *tr. V.* (zerhacken) chop up; (zerkauen) chew up ‹*food*›; (zermahlen) crush ‹*rock etc.*›

Zerkleinerung *die;* ~*, * ~**en** ⇒ **zerkleinern:** chopping up; chewing; crushing

zerklüftet *Adj.* fissured ‹*landscape*›; craggy ‹*mountains*›; deeply indented ‹*coastline*›

zerknallen *itr. V.; mit sein* (ugs.) burst [with a bang]

zerknautschen *tr. V.* (ugs.) crumple

zerknirscht **1** *Adj.* remorseful. **2** *adv.* remorsefully

zerknittern *tr. V.* crease; crumple

zerknüllen *tr. V.* crumple up [into a ball]

zerkochen **1** *itr. V.; mit sein* get overcooked. **2** *tr. V.* overcook

zerkratzen *tr. V.* scratch

zerkrümeln **1** *tr. V.* crumble up. **2** *itr. V.; mit sein* break into crumbs; crumble

zerlassen *unr. tr. V.* (Kochk.) melt

zerlegen *tr. V.* **(a)** dismantle; take to pieces; strip, dismantle ‹*engine*›; **etw. in seine Bestandteile** ~: reduce sth. to its component parts; **(b)** cut up ‹*animal, meat*›

zerlumpt *Adj.* ragged ‹*clothes, person*›; ~ **sein** ‹*clothes*› be in tatters, be torn; ~ **herumlaufen** go about in rags

zermahlen *unr. tr. V.* grind

zermalmen /tsɛɐ̯'malmən/ *tr. V.* crush

zermürben *tr. V.* wear ‹*person*› down; ~**d** wearing; trying

zernagen *tr. V.* gnaw away

zerpflücken *tr. V.* **(a)** pick ‹*flower, lettuce, etc.*› apart; **(b)** (fig.) pull ‹*book etc.*› to pieces; destroy ‹*alibi*›

zerplatzen *itr. V.; mit sein* burst

zerquetschen *tr. V.* crush; mash ‹*potatoes*›; **20 Mark und ein paar Zerquetschte** (ugs.) 20 marks and a bit

Zerr·bild *das* distorted image

zerreiben *unr. tr. V.* crush ‹*spices, paint colours, etc.*›

zerreißen **1** *unr. tr. V.* **(a)** tear up; (in kleine Stücke) tear to pieces; ‹*animal*› tear ‹*prey*› limb from limb; dismember ‹*prey*›; break ‹*thread*›; **ich kann mich nicht** ~: I can't be in two places at once; **(b)** (beschädigen) tear ‹*stocking, trousers, etc.*› **(an** + *Dat.* on). **2** *unr. itr. V.; mit sein* ‹*thread, string, rope*› break; ‹*paper, cloth, etc.*› tear; **ihre Nerven waren zum Zerreißen gespannt** her nerves were stretched to breaking point

zerren /'tsɛrən/ **1** *tr. V.* **(a)** drag; **(b) sich** (*Dat.*) **einen Muskel/eine Sehne** ~: pull a muscle/tendon. **2** *itr. V.* **an etw.** (*Dat.*) ~: tug *or* pull at sth.

zerrinnen *unr. itr. V.* melt; (fig.) ‹*time*› pass; **jmdm. unter den Händen** ~: slip through sb.'s fingers

zerrissen /tsɛɐ̯'rɪsn̩/ *Adj.* [innerlich] ~: at odds with oneself

Zerr·spiegel *der* distorting mirror

Zerrung *die;* ~*, * ~**en** (Muskel~) pulled muscle; (Sehnen~) pulled tendon

zerrupfen *tr. V.* tear to bits

zerrütten /tsɛɐ̯'rʏtn̩/ *tr. V.* ruin ‹*health*›; shatter ‹*nerves*›; ruin, wreck ‹*marriage*›

Zerrüttung *die;* ~*, * ~**en** (der Gesundheit) ruining; (der Nerven) shattering; (einer Ehe) [irretrievable] breakdown

zersägen *tr. V.* saw up

zerschellen *itr. V.; mit sein* be dashed *or* smashed to pieces

zerschlagen¹ **1** *unr. tr. V.* smash ‹*plate, windscreen, etc.*›; smash up ‹*furniture*›; (fig.) smash ‹*spy ring etc.*›; crush ‹*enemy, attack*›; break up ‹*cartel*›. **2** *unr. refl. V.* ‹*plan, deal*› fall through

zerschlagen² *Adj.* (erschöpft) worn out; whacked (Brit. coll.); tuckered [out] (Amer. coll.); shattered (Brit. coll.)

Zerschlagung *die;* ~*, * ~**en** smashing; destruction; (eines Gegners) crushing

zerschmelzen *unr. itr. V.; mit sein* (auch fig.) melt

zerschmettern *tr. V.* smash; shatter ‹*glass, leg, bone*›; (fig.) crush ‹*army, enemy*›

zerschneiden *unr. tr. V.* **(a)** cut; (in Stücke) cut up; (in zwei Teile) cut in two; carve ‹*joint*›; **(b)** (verletzen) cut [into] ‹*skin etc.*›

zerschnippeln *tr. V.* (ugs.) cut up *or* snip into small pieces

zerschunden /tsɛɐ̯'ʃʊndn̩/ *Adj.* covered in scratches *postpos.*

zersetzen **1** *tr. V.* **(a)** corrode ‹*metal*›; decompose ‹*organism*›; **(b)** (fig.) subvert ‹*ideals*›; undermine ‹*morale*›; ~**de Schriften** subversive writings. **2** *refl. V.* decompose; ‹*wood, compost*› rot

Zersetzung *die;* ~*, * ~**en** **(a)** ⇒ **zersetzen 2:** decomposition; rotting; **(b)** ⇒ **zersetzen 1 b:** subversion; undermining

zerspalten *unr. tr. V.* (auch fig.) split [up]

zersplittern *itr. V.; mit sein* ‹*wood, bone*› splinter; ‹*glass*› shatter; **das Land war in viele Kleinstaaten zersplittert** the country was fragmented into many small states

zersprengen *tr. V.* blow up; (in Stücke) blow to pieces

zerspringen *unr. itr. V.; mit sein* shatter; (Sprünge bekommen) crack

zerstampfen *tr. V.* pound, crush ‹*spices etc.*›; mash ‹*potatoes*›

zerstäuben *tr. V.* spray

Zerstäuber *der;* ~**s**, ~: atomizer

zerstechen *unr. tr. V.* **(a)** sting all over; ‹*mosquitoes*› bite all over; **(b)** (beschädigen) jab holes in ‹*cushion etc.*›; puncture, slit ‹*tyre*›

zerstieben *unr.* (auch regelm.) *itr. V.; mit sein* (geh.) scatter; ‹*crowd*› disperse

zerstören *tr. V.* destroy; ruin ‹*landscape, health, life*›; dash, destroy ‹*hopes, dreams*›; wreck, destroy ‹*marriage*›

Zerstörer *der;* ~**s**, ~ destroyer

zerstörerisch **1** *Adj.* destructive. **2** *adv.* ~ **wirken** have a destructive effect

Zerstörung *die* destruction; (der Gesundheit, Existenz) ruin[ation]; (einer Ehe) wrecking; destruction; (von Hoffnungen) dashing; destruction

zerstoßen *unr. tr. V.* crush ‹*berries etc.*›; (im Mörser) pound, crush ‹*peppercorns etc.*›

zerstreiten *unr. refl. V.* **sich mit jmdm.** ~: fall out with sb.

zerstreuen **1** *tr. V.* **(a)** scatter; disperse ‹*crowd*›; **(b)** (unterhalten) **jmdn./sich** ~: entertain sb./oneself; (ablenken) take sb.'s/one's mind off things; **(c)** (beseitigen) allay ‹*fear, doubt, suspicion*›; dispel ‹*worry, concern*›. **2** *refl. V.* disperse; (schneller) scatter

zerstreut **1** *Adj.* absent-minded. **2** *adv.* absent-mindedly

Zerstreutheit *die;* ~: absent-mindedness

Zerstreuung *die;* ~*, * ~**en** diversion; (Unterhaltung) entertainment; ~ **suchen** look for a distraction [to take one's mind off things]

zerstückeln *tr. V.* break ‹*sth.*› up into small pieces; (zerschneiden) cut *or* chop sth. up into small pieces; dismember ‹*corpse*›

Zerstückelung *die;* ~*, * ~**en** ⇒ **zerstückeln:** breaking up; cutting *or* chopping up; dismembering

zerteilen **1** *tr. V.* divide into pieces; (zerschneiden) cut into pieces; cut up. **2** *refl. V.* part

Zertifikat /tsɛrtifi'kaːt/ *das;* ~[**e**]**s**, ~**e** certificate

zertrampeln *tr. V.* trample all over ‹*flower bed etc.*›; trample ‹*child etc.*› underfoot

zertrennen *unr. tr. V.* take apart

zertreten *unr. tr. V.* stamp on; crush ‹*insect*› underfoot

zertrümmern *tr. V.* smash; smash, shatter ‹*glass*›; smash up ‹*furniture*›; wreck ‹*car, boat*›; reduce ‹*building, city*› to ruins

Zervelat·wurst /tsɛrvəˈlaːt-/ *die* cervelat [sausage]

zerwühlen *tr. V.* churn up ‹*bedclothes, soil*›; make a mess of, tousle ‹*hair*›

Zerwürfnis /tsɛɐ̯'vʏrfnɪs/ das; ~ses, ~se (geh.) quarrel; dispute; (Bruch) rift

zerzausen tr. V. ruffle; ruffle, tousle ‹hair›; **zerzaust aussehen** look dishevelled

zetern /'tse:tɐn/ itr. V. (abwertend) scold [shrilly]

Zettel /'tsɛtl/ der; ~s, ~: slip or piece of paper; (mit einigen Zeilen) note; (Bekanntmachung) notice; (Formular) form; (Kassen~) receipt; (Stimm~) [ballot-]paper

Zeug /tsɔʏk/ das; ~[e]s, ~e (a) o. Pl. (ugs., oft abwertend: Sachen) stuff; **sie hat das ~ zu etw.** (fig.) she has what it takes to be sth. or has the makings of sth.; **was das ~ hält** (fig. ugs.) for all one's worth; ‹drive› hell for leather; **sich [mächtig] ins ~ legen** (fig.) do one's utmost; (b) (ugs.) **dummes/albernes ~** (Gerede) nonsense; rubbish; **dummes ~ machen** mess about; (c) (Kleidung) things pl.

Zeuge /'tsɔʏɡə/ der; ~n, ~n witness; **~ einer Sache** (Gen.) **sein/werden** be a witness to sth.; witness sth.; **die ~n Jehovas** the Jehovah's Witnesses

zeugen[1] itr. V. **von etw. ~** (fig.) testify to sth.; (etw. zeigen) display sth.

zeugen[2] tr. V. father ‹child›

Zeugen·aussage die testimony; witness's statement

Zeugen-: ~stand der o. Pl. witness box (Brit.); witness stand (Amer.); ~vernehmung die examination of the witness/witnesses

Zeugin die; ~, ~nen witness

Zeugnis das; ~ses, ~se (a) (Schulw.) report; (b) (Arbeits~) reference; testimonial; (c) (Gutachten) certificate; (d) (geh.: Beweis) evidence; ~se einer früheren Kulturstufe evidence or testimony of an earlier stage of civilization

Zeugung die; ~, ~en fathering

z. Hd. Abk. **zu Händen** attn.

zickig (ugs. abwertend) **1** Adj. prim; (prüde) prudish. **2** adv. primly; (prüde) prudishly

Zicklein das; ~s, ~: kid

Zickzack der; ~[e]s, ~e zigzag; **im ~:** in a zigzag

Ziege /'tsi:ɡə/ die; ~, ~n (a) goat; (b) (Schimpfwort: Frau) cow (sl. derog.)

Ziegel /'tsi:ɡl/ der; ~s, ~ (a) brick; (b) (Dach~) tile

Ziegel·dach das tiled roof

Ziegelei die; ~, ~en brickworks sing.

Ziegel·stein der brick

Ziegen-: ~bart der goat's beard; (ugs.: Spitzbart) goatee beard; ~bock der he- or billy goat; ~käse der goat's cheese; ~milch die goat's milk; ~peter der; ~s, ~ (ugs.) mumps sing.

zieh /tsi:/ 1. u. 3. Pers. Sg. Prät. v. **zeihen**

ziehen /'tsi:ən/ **1** unr. tr. V. (a) pull; (sanfter) draw; (zerren) tug; (schleppen) drag; **jmdn. an sich ~:** draw sb. to one; **jmdn. am Ärmel ~:** pull sb. by the sleeve; **Perlen auf eine Schnur ~:** thread pearls/beads on to a string; **den Hut ins Gesicht ~:** pull one's hat down over one's face; **~ und ablegen** (DV) drag and drop; (b) (fig.) **es zog ihn zu ihr/zu dem Ort** he felt drawn to her/to the place; **alle Blicke auf sich ~:** attract or capture all the attention; **jmds. Zorn/Unwillen** usw. **auf sich ~:** incur sb.'s anger/displeasure etc.; **etw. nach sich ~:** result in sth.; entail sth.; (c) (heraus~) pull out ‹nail, cork, organ-stop, etc.›; extract ‹tooth›; take out, remove ‹stitches, splinter›; draw ‹cord, sword, pistol›; **den Hut ~:** raise or doff one's hat; **etw. aus der Tasche ~:** take sth. out of one's pocket; **Zigaretten/Süßigkeiten** usw. **~** (ugs.: aus Automaten) get cigarettes/sweets etc. from a slot machine; **die [Quadrat]wurzel ~** (Math.) extract the square root; (d) (dehnen) stretch ‹elastic etc.›; stretch out ‹sheets etc.›; (e) (Gesichtspartien bewegen) make ‹face, grimace›; **die Augenbrauen nach oben ~:** raise one's eyebrows; **die Stirn in Falten ~:** wrinkle or knit one's brow; (missmutig) frown; (f) (bei Brettspielen) move ‹chessman etc.›; (g) **er zog den Rauch in die Lungen** he inhaled the smoke [into his lungs]; (h) (zeichnen) draw ‹line, circle, arc, etc.›; (i) (anlegen) dig ‹trench›; build ‹wall›; erect ‹fence›; put up ‹washing-line›; run, lay ‹cable, wires›; draw ‹frontier›; trace ‹loop›;

---

*alte Schreibung (vgl. Hinweise auf S. xvi–xvii)

follow ‹course›; **sich** (Dat.) **einen Scheitel ~:** make a parting [in one's hair]; (j) (auf~) grow ‹plants, flowers›; breed ‹animals›; (k) (verblasst; auch als Funktionsverb) draw ‹lesson, conclusion, comparison›; s. auch **Konsequenz** a; **Rechenschaft; Verantwortung** a. **2** unr. itr. V. (a) (reißen) pull; **an etw.** (Dat.) **~:** pull on sth.; **der Hund zieht an der Leine** the dog is straining at the leash; **an einem** od. **am selben Strang ~** (fig.) be pulling in the same direction; (b) (funktionieren) ‹stove, pipe, chimney› draw; ‹car, engine› pull; (c) mit sein (um~) move (**nach, in** + Akk. to); **zu jmdm. ~:** move in with sb.; (d) mit sein (gehen) go; (marschieren) march; (umherstreifen) roam; rove; (fortgehen) go away; leave; ‹fog, clouds› drift; **durch etw. ~:** pass through sth.; **in den Krieg ~:** go or march off to war; **die Schwalben ~ nach Süden** the swallows are flying southwards; (e) (saugen) draw; **an einer Zigarette/Pfeife ~:** draw on a cigarette/pipe; **an einem Strohhalm ~:** suck at a straw; (f) ‹tea, coffee› draw; (g) (Kochk.) simmer; (h) unpers. **es zieht [vom Fenster her]** there's a draught [from the window]; (i) (ugs.: zum Erfolg führen) ‹trick› work; **das zieht bei mir nicht** that won't wash or won't cut any ice with me (fig. coll.); (j) (schmerzen) **es zieht [mir] im Rücken** I've got backache; **ein leichtes/starkes Ziehen im Bauch** a slight/intense stomach ache. **3** unr. refl. V. (a) ‹road› run, stretch; ‹frontier› run; (b) **der Weg zieht sich** (ugs.) the journey goes on and on

Zieh·harmonika die piano accordion

Ziehung die; ~, ~en draw; **die ~ des Hauptgewinns** the draw for the main prize

Ziel /tsi:l/ das; ~[e]s, ~e (a) destination; **am ~ der Reise anlangen** reach the end of one's journey; reach one's destination; (b) (Sport) finish; (c) (~scheibe; auch Milit.) target; **über das ~ hinausschießen** (fig.) go too far; (d) (Zweck) aim; goal; **sein ~ erreichen** achieve one's objective or aim; **[das] ~ unserer Bemühungen ist es, ... zu ...:** the object of our efforts is to ...; **sich** (Dat.) **ein ~ setzen** od. **stecken** set oneself a goal; **sich** (Dat.) **etw. zum ~ setzen** set oneself or take sth. as one's aim; **etw. zum ~ haben** have sth. as its goal

Ziel·band das Pl. ~bänder (Sport) finishing-tape

ziel·bewusst, *ziel·bewußt 1 Adj. purposeful; determined. **2** adv. purposefully; determinedly

zielen itr. V. (a) aim (**auf** + Akk. at); (b) **auf jmdn./etw. ~** (fig.) ‹reproach, plan, efforts, etc.› be aimed at sb./sth.

ziel-, Ziel-: ~gerade die (Sport) finishing straight; ~los **1** Adj. aimless; (ziel-)aimlessly; ~losigkeit die; ~: aimlessness; (auch fig.) target (Gen. for); ~setzung die; ~, ~en aims pl.; objectives pl.; ~sicher **1** Adj. decisive, purposeful ‹steps›; **2** adv. decisively; ~strebig **1** Adj. purposeful; (b) (energisch) single-minded ‹person›; **2** adv. (a) purposefully; (b) (energisch) single-mindedly; ~strebigkeit die; ~ ⇒ ~strebig: (a) purposefulness; (b) single-mindedness; ~wahl die (Fernspr.) one-touch dialling

ziemlich 1 Adj. (ugs.) fair, sizeable ‹quantity, number›; **mit ~er Lautstärke** quite loudly. **2** adv. (a) quite; fairly; (etwas intensiver) pretty; **du kommst ~ spät** you're rather late; **~ viele Leute** quite a few people; (b) (ugs.: fast) pretty well; more or less

Zier /tsi:ɐ̯/ die; ~ (veralt.) ⇒ **Zierde**

***Zierat** ⇒ **Zierrat**

Zierde die; ~, ~n (auch fig.) ornament; embellishment; **zur ~:** as decoration; **jmdm. zur ~ gereichen** (fig.) be a credit to sb.

zieren 1 tr. V. (geh.) adorn; decorate ‹room›. **2** refl. V. be coy; (sich bitten lassen) need some coaxing or pressing

zierlich 1 Adj. dainty; delicate; petite, dainty ‹woman, figure›. **2** adv. daintily; delicately

Zierlichkeit die; ~: daintiness; delicateness; (einer Frau, Gestalt) petiteness; daintiness

Zier·pflanze die ornamental plant

Zierrat /'tsi:ra:t/ der; ~[e]s, ~e (geh.) ornament[ation]; **bloßer ~ sein** be purely ornamental

Zier-: ∼**stich** *der* (Handarb.) ornamental stitch; ∼**strauch** *der* ornamental shrub

Ziffer /'tsɪfə/ *die;* ∼, ∼**n** numeral; (in einer mehrstelligen Zahl) digit; figure

Ziffer·blatt *das* dial; face

zig /tsɪç/ *unbest. Zahlwort* (ugs.) umpteen (coll.)

Zigarette /tsɪga'rɛtə/ *die;* ∼, ∼**n** cigarette

Zigaretten-: ∼**länge** *die:* auf *od.* für eine ∼**länge** (ugs.) just for a smoke; ∼**papier** *das* cigarette paper; ∼**pause** *die* (ugs.) break for a smoke; ∼**raucher** *der* cigarette-smoker

Zigarillo /tsɪga'rɪlo/ *der od. das;* ∼, ∼**s** cigarillo; small cigar

Zigarre /tsɪ'garə/ *die;* ∼, ∼**n** cigar

Zigarren·raucher *der* cigar-smoker

Zigeuner /tsɪ'ɡɔynɐ/ *der;* ∼**s**, ∼, **Zigeunerin** *die;* ∼, ∼**nen** gypsy

zig·mal *Adv.* (ugs.) umpteen times (coll.)

zigst ... *Ordinalz.* (ugs.) umpteenth (coll.)

zig·tausend *unbest. Zahlwort* (ugs.) umpteen thousand (coll.)

Zikade /tsi'ka:də/ *die;* ∼, ∼**n** cicada

Zimmer /'tsɪmɐ/ *das;* ∼**s**, ∼: ▶ **189**⌡ room

Zimmer-: ∼**flucht** *die; Pl.* ∼**en** suite [of rooms]; ∼**lautstärke** *die* domestic listening level; **das Radio auf** ∼**lautstärke stellen** turn the radio down to a reasonable volume [so as not to disturb the neighbours]; ∼**mädchen** *das* chambermaid; ∼**mann** *der; Pl.* ∼**leute** carpenter

zimmern 1 *tr. V.* make ⟨*shelves, coffin, etc.*⟩. 2 *itr. V.* do carpentry; **an einem Regal** ∼: be making a bookshelf

Zimmer-: ∼**suche** *die* room-hunt; **auf** ∼**suche sein** be looking for a room; ∼**temperatur** *die* room temperature; ∼**vermittlung** *die* accommodation office

zimperlich /'tsɪmpɐlɪç/ (abwertend) 1 *Adj.* timid; (leicht angeekelt) squeamish; (prüde) prissy; (übertrieben rücksichtsvoll) over-scrupulous. 2 *adv. s. Adj.* timidly; squeamishly; prissily; over-scrupulously

Zimperlichkeit *die;* ∼, ∼**en** (abwertend) ⇒ **zimperlich** 1: timidity; squeamishness; prissiness; over-scrupulousness

Zimt /tsɪmt/ *der;* ∼**[e]s**, ∼**e** cinnamon

Zink /tsɪŋk/ *das;* ∼**[e]s** zinc

Zinke *die;* ∼, ∼**n** prong; (eines Kamms) tooth

Zinn /tsɪn/ *das;* ∼**[e]s** (a) tin; (b) (Legierung) pewter; (c) (Gegenstände) pewter[ware]

Zinne *die;* ∼, ∼**n** merlon; ∼**n** battlements

Zinnie /'tsɪnjə/ *die;* ∼, ∼**n** (Bot.) zinnia

Zinn·soldat *der* tin soldier

Zins /tsɪns/ *der;* ∼**es**, ∼**en** interest; (∼satz) interest rate; ∼**en tragen** *od.* **bringen** earn interest; **jmdm. etw. mit** ∼**en od. mit** ∼ **und Zinseszins zurückzahlen** (fig.) make sb. pay dearly for sth.

Zinses·zins *der* compound interest; *s. auch* **Zins**

zins-, Zins-: ∼**los** 1 *Adj.* interest-free; 2 *adv.* free of interest; ∼**rechnung** *die* calculation of interest; ∼**satz** *der* interest rate

Zionismus /tsio'nɪsmʊs/ *der;* ∼, ∼: Zionism *no art.*

Zionist *der;* ∼**en**, ∼**en**, **Zionistin**, *die;* ∼, ∼**nen** Zionist

zionistisch *Adj.* Zionist

Zipfel /'tsɪpfl/ *der;* ∼**s**, ∼ (einer Decke usw.) corner; (Wurst∼) [tail-]end; (einer ∼**mütze**) point; (Spitze eines Sees usw.) tip

Zipfel·mütze *die* [long-]pointed cap

Zipp ⓦⓩ /tsɪp/ *der;* ∼**s**, ∼**s**, **Zipp·verschluss**, *****Zipp·verschluß** *der* (österr.) ⇒ **Reißverschluss**

zirka /'tsɪrka/ *Adv.* about; approximately

Zirkel /'tsɪrkl/ *der;* ∼**s**, ∼ (a) (Gerät) [pair *sing.* of] compasses *pl.;* (b) (Kreis, Gruppe) circle

zirkeln *tr. V.* measure out precisely

Zirkulation /tsɪrkula'tsɪo:n/ *die;* ∼, ∼**en** circulation

zirkulieren *itr. V.; auch mit sein* circulate

Zirkus /'tsɪrkʊs/ *der;* ∼, ∼**se** (a) circus; (b) **mach nicht so einen** ∼! (ugs.) don't make such a fuss!

Zirkus·zelt *das* big top

zirpen /'tsɪrpn/ *itr. V.* chirp

Zirrhose /tsɪ'ro:zə/ *die;* ∼, ∼**n** (Med.) cirrhosis

Zirrus /'tsɪrʊs/ *der;* ∼, ∼ *od.* **Zirren, Zirrus·wolke** *die* (Met.) cirrus [cloud]

zischen /'tsɪʃn/ 1 *itr. V.* (a) hiss; ⟨*hot fat*⟩ sizzle; (b) *mit sein* hiss; (ugs.: flitzen) whizz. 2 *tr. V.* (a) (zischend sprechen) hiss; (b) **ein Bier/einen** ∼ (ugs.) knock back a beer (coll.)/ knock one back (coll.)

Zisterne /tsɪs'tɛrnə/ *die;* ∼, ∼**n** [underground] tank *or* cistern

Zitadelle /tsita'dɛlə/ *die;* ∼, ∼**n** citadel

Zitat /tsi'ta:t/ *das;* ∼**[e]s**, ∼**e** quotation (aus from)

Zither /'tsɪtɐ/ *die;* ∼, ∼**n** zither

zitieren /tsi'ti:rən/ *tr. V.* (a) *auch itr.* quote (aus, nach from); (Rechtsspr.: anführen) cite; ..., **ich zitiere:** „...“ ... and I quote: '...'; **falsch** ∼: misquote; (b) (vorladen, rufen) summon (**vor** before, **zu** to)

Zitronat /tsitro'na:t/ *das;* ∼**[e]s** candied lemon-peel

Zitrone /tsi'tro:nə/ *die;* ∼, ∼**n** lemon; **jmdn. auspressen** *od.* **ausquetschen wie eine** ∼ (ugs.: ausfragen) pump sb.

zitronen-, Zitronen-: ∼**falter** *der* brimstone butterfly; ∼**gelb** *Adj.* lemon yellow; ∼**presse** *die* lemon-squeezer; ∼**saft** *der* lemon juice; ∼**säure** *die* citric acid; ∼**schale** *die* lemon-peel

Zitrus·frucht /'tsitrus-/ *die* citrus fruit

zittern /'tsɪtɐn/ *itr. V.* (a) tremble (**vor** + *Dat.* with); (vor Kälte) shiver; ⟨*needle, arrow, leaf, etc.*⟩ quiver; (beben) ⟨*walls, windows*⟩ shake; **mit** ∼**der Stimme** in a trembling *or* quavering voice; (b) (fig.) tremble; quake; **vor jmdm./ etw.** ∼: be terrified of sb./sth.

zittrig 1 *Adj.* shaky; doddery ⟨*old man*⟩. 2 *adv.* shakily

Zitze /'tsɪtsə/ *die;* ∼, ∼**n** teat

zivil /tsi'vi:l/ 1 *Adj.* (a) civilian ⟨*life, population*⟩; non-military ⟨*purposes*⟩; civil ⟨*aviation, marriage, law, defence*⟩; (b) (annehmbar) decent; reasonable. 2 *adv.* decently; reasonably

Zivil *das;* ∼**s** civilian clothes *pl.;* **Polizist in** ∼: plain-clothes policeman

Zivil-: ∼**bevölkerung** *die* civilian population; ∼**courage** *die* courage of one's convictions; ∼**dienst** *der; o. Pl.* ⇒ **Ersatzdienst**

Zivilisation /tsiviliza'tsɪo:n/ *die;* ∼, ∼**en** civilization

Zivilisations·krankheit *die* disease of modern civilization *or* society

zivilisieren *tr. V.* civilize

zivilisiert 1 *Adj.* civilized. 2 *adv.* in a civilized way

Zivilist *der;* ∼**en**, ∼**en** civilian

Zivil-: ∼**kleidung** *die* civilian clothes *pl;* ∼**luft·fahrt** *die* civil aviation; ∼**person** *die* civilian

ZK /tsɛt'ka:/ *das;* ∼**s**, ∼**s** *Abk.* **Zentralkomitee**

Zobel /'tso:bl/ *der;* ∼**s**, ∼ sable

Zofe /'tso:fə/ *die;* ∼, ∼**n** (hist.) lady's maid

Zoff /tsɔf/ *der;* ∼**s** (ugs.) rowing (coll.); squabbling; ∼ **machen** cause trouble

zog *1. u. 3. Pers. Sg. Prät. v.* **ziehen**

zögerlich /'tsø:ɡɐlɪç/ 1 *Adj.* hesitant; tentative. 2 *adv.* hesitantly; tentatively

zögern *itr. V.* hesitate; **ohne zu** ∼: without hesitation; **nach einigem Zögern** after a moment's hesitation; ∼**d vorangehen** proceed hesitantly

Zögling /'tsø:klɪŋ/ *der;* ∼**s**, ∼**e** (veralt.) boarding pupil; boarder

Zölibat /tsøli'ba:t/ *das od. der;* ∼**[e]s**,∼**e** celibacy *no art.*

Zoll¹ /tsɔl/ *der;* ∼**[e]s**, **Zölle** /'tsœlə/ (a) (Abgabe) [customs] duty; (b) *o. Pl.* (Behörde) customs *pl.*

Zoll² *der;* ∼**[e]s**, ∼: ▶ **340**⌡ inch

Zoll-: ∼**amt** *das* customs house *or* office; ∼**beamte** *der*, ∼**beamtin** *die* customs officer

zollen *tr. V.* (geh.) **jmdm. etw.** ∼: accord sb. sth.; **jmdm. Respekt/Bewunderung** ∼: show sb. respect/admiration; **jmdm./einer Sache Tribut** ∼: pay tribute to sb./ sth.

zoll-, Zoll-: ~erklärung die customs declaration; **~frei 1** Adj. duty-free; free of duty pred.; **2** adv. free of duty; **~kontrolle** die customs examination or check

Zöllner /'tsœlnɐ/ der; ~s, ~ (a) (ugs. veralt.) customs officer; (b) (hist.: Steuereintreiber) tax collector

Zoll·stock der folding rule

Zombie /'tsɔmbi/ der; ~s, ~s zombie

Zone /'tso:nə/ die; ~, ~n zone

Zoo /tso:/ der; ~s, ~s zoo; **im/in den ~:** at/to the zoo

Zoo·handlung die pet shop

Zoologe /tsoo'lo:gə/ der; ~n, ~n zoologist

Zoologie die; ~: zoology no art.

Zoologin die; ~, ~nen zoologist

zoologisch 1 Adj. zoological; **~er Garten** zoological gardens pl. **2** adv. zoologically

Zoom /zu:m/ das; ~s, ~s (Film, Fot.) zoom [lens]

Zoo-: ~tier das zoo animal; **~wärter** der zookeeper

Zopf /tsɔpf/ der; ~[e]s, **Zöpfe** /'tsœpfə/ plait; (am Hinterkopf) pigtail; **einen alten ~ abschneiden** (fig.) put an end to an antiquated custom or practice

Zopf·spange die hairslide (Brit.), barrette (Amer.) (for a pigtail)

Zorn /tsɔrn/ der; ~[e]s anger; (stärker) wrath; fury; **ihn packte der ~:** he flew into a rage; **einen ~ auf jmdn. haben** (ugs.) be furious with sb.; **im ~:** in a rage; in anger

Zorn·ausbruch der angry outburst; fit of rage

zornig Adj. furious (**über** + Akk. about, **auf** + Akk. with)

Zote /'tso:tə/ die; ~, ~n dirty joke

zotig 1 Adj. smutty; dirty (joke). **2** adv. smuttily

Zottel /'tsɔtl̩/ die; ~, ~n (ugs. abwertend: Haare) shaggy locks

zottelig Adj. shaggy

zotteln itr. V.; mit sein (ugs.) saunter; amble

zottig Adj. shaggy

Ztr. Abk. **Zentner** cwt.

zu /tsu:/ **1** Präp. mit Dat. (a) (Richtung) to; **zu … hin** towards …; **er kommt zu mir** (besucht mich) he is coming to my place; (b) (zusammen mit) with; **zu dem Käse gab es Wein** there was wine with the cheese; **das passt nicht zu Bier/zu dem Kleid** that doesn't go with beer/with that dress; (c) (Lage) at; **zu beiden Seiten** on both sides; **zu seiner Linken** (geh.) on his left; **er kam zu dieser Tür herein** he came in by this door; **der Dom zu Speyer** (veralt.) Speyer Cathedral; **das Gasthaus „Zu den drei Eichen"** the Three Oaks Inn; (d) (zeitlich) at; **zu Weihnachten** at Christmas; **was schenkst du ihnen zu Weihnachten** what will you give them for Christmas?; **er will zu Ostern verreisen** he wants to go away for Easter; **zu dieser Stunde** at this time; (e) (Art u. Weise) **zu meiner Zufriedenheit/Überraschung** to my satisfaction/surprise; **zu seinem Vorteil/Nachteil** to his advantage/disadvantage; (bei Mengenangaben o. Ä) **zu Dutzenden/zweien** by the dozen/in twos; **sie sind zu einem Drittel/zu 50 % arbeitslos** a third/50 % of them are jobless; **zu einem großen Teil** largely; to a large extent; (f) (ein Zahlenverhältnis ausdrückend) **ein Verhältnis von 3 zu 1** a ratio of 3 to 1; **das Ergebnis war 2 zu 1** the result was 2–1 or 2 to 1; (g) (einen Preis zuordnend) at; for; **fünf Briefmarken zu fünfzig [Pfennig]** five 50-pfennig stamps; (h) (eine Zahlenangabe zuordnend) **ein Fass zu zehn Litern** a ten-litre barrel; **Portionen zu je einem Pfund** portions weighing a pound each; (i) (Zweck) for; **sie sagte das zu seiner Beruhigung** she said it to allay his fears; (j) (Ziel, Ergebnis) into; **zu etw. werden** turn into sth.; **die Kartoffeln zu einem Brei zerstampfen** mash the potatoes into a puree; (k) (über) about; on; **sich zu etw. äußern** comment on sth.; **zu welchem Thema spricht er?** what is he going to speak about?; **was sagst du zu meinem Vorschlag?** what do you say to my proposal?; (l) (gegenüber) **freundlich/ hässlich zu jmdm. sein** be friendly/nasty to sb.; s. auch **zum; zur. 2** Adv. (a) (allzu) too; **zu sehr** too much; **er ist zu alt, um diese Reise zu unternehmen** he is too old to undertake this journey; **das ist ja zu schön/komisch!** that's really wonderful/

hilarious!; that's too wonderful/hilarious for words!; (b) nachgestellt (Richtung) towards; **der Grenze zu** towards the border; (c) (ugs.) **~ sein** be shut; **der Laden ist zu** the shop has shut; **Augen/Tür zu!** shut your eyes/the door!; (d) (ugs.: Aufforderung) **nur zu!** (fang/fangt an!) get going!; get down to it!; (mach/macht weiter!) get on with it! **3** Konj. (a) (mit Infinitiv) to; **du hast zu gehorchen** you must obey; **was gibts da zu lachen?** what is there to laugh about?; **das ist nicht zu glauben** it is unbelievable; **Haus zu verkaufen/vermieten** house for sale/to let; (b) (mit 1. Part.) **die zu gewinnenden Preise** the prizes to be won; **die zu erledigende Post** the letters pl. to be dealt with

zu·aller·erst Adv. first of all; (hauptsächlich) above all else

zu·aller·letzt Adv. last of all

zu|bauen tr. V. (ugs.) block (entrance, door); obstruct (view)

Zubehör /'tsu:bəhø:ɐ̯/ das; ~[e]s, ~e od. schweiz. ~den accessories pl.; (eines Staubsaugers, Mixers o. Ä.) attachments pl.; (Ausstattung) equipment

zu|beißen unr. itr. V. bite

zu|bekommen unr. tr. V. get (suitcase, door, etc.) shut; get (clothes, buttons) done up; manage to repair (leak); manage to mend (hole)

zu|bereiten tr. V. prepare (meal, food, cocktail, etc.); (kochen) cook (fish, meat, etc.)

Zu·bereitung die; ~, ~en preparation; (Kochen) cooking

Zu·bett·gehen das; ~s: **vorm/beim ~:** before/on going to bed

zu|bewegen 1 tr. V. etw. auf jmdn./etw. ~: move sth. towards sb./sth. **2** refl. V. **sich auf etw. ~:** move towards sth.

zu|billigen tr. V. jmdm. etw. ~: grant or allow sb. sth.; jmdm. ~, dass er in gutem Glauben gehandelt hat accept that sb. acted in good faith; **jmdm. mildernde Umstände ~:** allow sb.'s plea of extenuating circumstances

zu|binden unr. tr. V. tie [up]

zu|blinzeln itr. V. jmdm. ~: wink at sb.

zu|bringen unr. tr. V. (a) (verbringen) spend; (b) (landsch.) ⇒ zubekommen

Zu·bringer der; ~s, ~ (a) (Straße) access or feeder road; (b) (Verkehrsmittel) shuttle; (Flughafenbus o. ä.) courtesy bus

Zu·brot das; o. Pl. bit extra or on the side

zu|buttern tr., itr. V. (ugs.) chip in (coll.)

Zucht /tsʊxt/ die; ~, ~en (a) o. Pl. (von Tieren) breeding; (von Pflanzen) cultivation; (von Bakterien, Perlen) culture; **ein Pferd aus deutscher ~:** a German-bred horse; (b) (Einrichtung) breeding establishment; (für Pferde) stud; (für Pflanzen) plant-breeding establishment; (c) o. Pl. (geh.: Disziplin) discipline; **für ~ und Ordnung sorgen** keep order

züchten /'tsʏçtn̩/ tr. V. (auch fig.) breed; cultivate (plants); culture (bacteria, pearls)

Züchter der; ~s, ~, **Züchterin**, die; ~, ~nen breeder; (von Pflanzen) grower [of new varieties]; plant-breeder

Zucht·haus das (a) [long-stay] prison; penitentiary (Amer.); (b) o. Pl. (Strafe) [severest form of] imprisonment; imprisonment in a penitentiary (Amer.)

züchtigen /'tsʏçtɪgn̩/ tr. V. (geh.) beat; thrash

zucht·los (veralt.) **1** Adj. undisciplined. **2** adv. without discipline; in an undisciplined way

Zucht·perle die cultured pearl

Züchtung die; ~, ~en (a) breeding; (von Pflanzen) cultivation; (b) (Zuchtergebnis) strain

zuck /tsʊk/ ⇒ ruck, zuck

zuckeln /'tsʊkl̩n/ itr. V.; mit sein saunter; amble; (schleppend) trail; (cart etc.) trundle

zucken itr. V.; mit Richtungsangabe mit sein twitch; (body, arm, leg, etc.) jerk; (vor Schreck) start; (flames) flicker, flash up; (light, lightning) flicker, flash; **er zuckte zur Seite** he jumped to one side; **mit den Achseln** od. **Schultern ~:** shrug one's shoulders

zücken /'tsʏkn̩/ tr. V. draw (sword, dagger, knife); (scherzh.) take out, produce (wallet, notebook, camera, etc.)

zu, zum, zur

Wohin? = to

Sie gehen zur Schule/ *zur Arbeit*	= They are going to school/to work

Es ist zu beachten, dass bei diesen Ausdrücken im Englischen kein Artikel verwendet wird.

Beim Modalverb mit *zu* darf **go** im Englischen nicht fehlen:

Er will morgen zu ihr	= He wants to go and see her tomorrow
Ich muss zum Arzt	= I must go to the doctor's *od.* to see the doctor

Aber:

Er geht zum Militär/ *Theater*	= He is going into the army/the theatre

Adverbiale Zusätze wie *hin, hinaus, herüber* usw. verlangen andere Übersetzungen:

zur Küste hin	= towards the coast
zur Tür herein/hinaus	= in through/out of the door
Sie sah zu mir herüber/ *zum Himmel hinauf*	= She looked across at me/up at the sky

Beim übertragenen Gebrauch, der eine **Verwandlung** kennzeichnet, verwendet man oft auch **into**:

Das Wasser wurde zu *Eis*	= The water turned [in]to ice
Der Junge war zu *einem Mann geworden*	= The boy had grown into a man
Die Zutaten zu einem *Brei verrühren*	= Mix the ingredients [in]to a paste
Das machte ihn zum *Märtyrer*	= This made him into a martyr

Aber:

Ich machte/ernannte *ihn zu meinem* *Vertreter*	= I made/appointed him my representative

Wenn man ein **Verhältnis** beschreiben will, sagt man auch **to**:

in einem Verhältnis von *drei zu eins*	= in a ratio of three to one

Beim Spielstand aber wird das **to** meist ausgelassen, außer wenn die Worte 'goals', 'points', 'games', 'sets' usw. verwendet werden:

Das Ergebnis war zwei *zu null*	= The final score was two-nil *od.* two goals/points *etc.* to nil

Wo? Wann? Wie viel? = at

1. Ort

Ich bleibe zu Hause	= I am staying at home
Er lag zu ihren *Füßen*	= He lay at her feet
Zu ebener Erde haben *wir fünf Zimmer*	= We have five rooms at ground level *od.* on the ground floor

Aber:

zu beiden Seiten	= on both sides
zu meiner Linken	= on my left

2. Zeit

zu Anfang/Ende des *Jahres*	= at the beginning/end of the year
Zu Ostern/Zu *Weihnachten/Zum* *Wochenende wollen* *wir verreisen*	= We want to go away at *od.* for Easter/ Christmas/the weekend

Sie bekommen es zu *gegebener Zeit*	= You will get it at the appropriate time
Er kam zu später *Stunde* (geh.)	= He came at a late hour

Aber:

Es tritt zum 1. Januar *in Kraft*	= It comes into force on January 1st
Es muss [bis] zum 31. *August fertig werden*	= It must be finished by August 31st
zu diesem Anlass	= on this occasion
zum ersten/letzten Mal	= for the first/last time

3. Preis

Sie verkaufen alles zu *niedrigsten Preisen*	= They sell everything at rock-bottom prices
Kartoffeln zu 70 Pfennig *das Pfund*	= Potatoes at *od.* for 70 pfennigs a pound

Aber:

sechs Briefmarken zu *sieben Schilling*	= six seven schilling stamps

Was ist der Zweck? = for

Zu diesem Zweck gibt *es einen Notruf*	= There is an emergency line for this purpose
Sie fährt zu einer *Besprechung nach* *Berlin*	= She is going to Berlin for a meeting
Das haben wir nur zum *Spaß gemacht*	= We only did it for fun
das Öl zur Schmierung *od. zum Schmieren* *der Nockenwelle*	= the oil for the lubrication of *od.* for lubricating the camshaft

Hier verwendet man auch **to** + Infinitiv:

Zum Lesen braucht er *eine Brille*	= He needs spectacles for reading *od.* to read with
etwas zum Schreiben	= something to write with
ein paar Worte zur *Beruhigung*	= a few words to set your mind at rest

Aber:

ein paar Worte zur *Einführung/Erklärung/* *Entschuldigung*	= a few words by way of introduction/ explanation/apology

Wenn es sich um den Anlass für ein Geschenk oder dergleichen handelt, sagt man auch **for**:

Er hat es mir zu *Weihnachten/zum* *Geburtstag geschenkt*	= He gave it me for Christmas/my birthday
Zum 30. Jubiläum *überreichte ihm die* *Firma eine Uhr*	= For *od.* On the occasion of his 30th anniversary the firm presented him with a clock

Womit zusammen? = with

Diese Bluse kannst du *zu dem Rock tragen*	= You can wear this blouse with that skirt
Zum Essen gab es *Rotwein*	= There was red wine with the meal

Worüber? = on

Es gibt mehrere Bücher *zu diesem Thema*	= There are several books on this subject
Was meinen Sie zu *dieser Entwicklung?*	= What is your opinion on this development?
Er wurde zur Sache *vernommen*	= He was questioned on the matter

Zucker *der;* ~s, ~ (a) sugar; (b) *o. Pl.* (ugs.: ~krankheit) diabetes; ~ **haben** be a diabetic

Zucker·brot *das:* **mit** ~ **und Peitsche** with a carrot and a stick

zucker-, Zucker-: ~**dose** *die* sugar bowl; ~**hut** *der* sugar loaf; ~**krank** *Adj.* diabetic; ~**krankheit** *die* diabetes

Zuckerl *das;* ~s, ~[n] (südd., österr.) sweet (Brit.); candy (Amer.); (fig.) sweetener; enticement

zuckern *tr. V.* sugar

zucker-, Zucker-: ~**rohr** *das* sugar cane; ~**rübe** *die* sugar beet; ~**stange** *die* stick of rock; ~**streuer** *der* sugar-caster; ~**süß** 1 *Adj.* as sweet as sugar *postpos.;* beautifully sweet; (fig. abwertend) saccharine, sugary ⟨*picture, smile, etc.*⟩; 2 *adv.* ~**süß lächeln** (fig. abwertend) give a saccharine *or* sugary smile; ~**watte** *die* candy-floss

zuckrig *Adj.* sugary

Zuckung *die;* ~, ~**en** twitch

zu|decken *tr. V.* cover up; cover [over] ⟨*well, ditch*⟩; **sich** ~: tuck oneself up; **gut/warm zugedeckt** well/warmly tucked up

zu·dem *Adv.* (geh.) moreover; furthermore

zu|drehen 1 *tr. V.* (a) (abdrehen) turn off ⟨*tap, heating, water, gas*⟩; (schließen) screw ⟨*valve, container*⟩ shut; (b) ⇒ **zuwenden** 2 a. 2 *refl. V.* **sich jmdm./einer Sache** ~: turn to *or* towards sb./sth.

zu·dringlich *Adj.* pushy (coll.), pushing ⟨*person, manner*⟩; (sexuell) importunate ⟨*person, manner*⟩; prying ⟨*glance*⟩

Zu·dringlichkeit *die;* ~, ~**en** (a) *o. Pl.* pushiness (coll.); (sexuell) importunate manner; (b) *Pl.* insistent advances *or* attentions

zu|drücken *tr. V.* press shut; push ⟨*door*⟩ shut; **jmdm. die Kehle** ~: choke *or* throttle sb.; *s. auch* **Auge a**

zu|eignen *tr. V.* (geh.) **jmdm. etw.** ~: dedicate sth. to sb.

Zu·eignung *die;* ~, ~**en** dedication

zu|eilen *itr. V.; mit sein* **auf jmdn./etw.** ~: hurry *or* rush towards sb./sth.

zu·ein·ander *Adv.* to one another; ~ **finden** come together; ~ **halten** stick together; ~ **stehen** stand by one another; stick together; **Liebe** ~ **empfinden** have feelings of love towards one another; **gut/schlecht** ~ **passen** ⟨*things*⟩ go well together/not match; ⟨*people*⟩ be well-/ill-suited

***zueinander|finden** *usw.:* ⇒ **zueinander**

zu|erkennen *unr. tr. V.* **jmdm. eine Entschädigung/einen Preis** ~: award sb. compensation/a prize; **jmdm. einen Titel** ~: confer a title on sb.

Zuerkennung *die;* ~, ~**en** ⇒ **zuerkennen:** award; conferring

zu·erst *Adv.* (a) first; **er war** ~ **da** he was here first; he was the first to come; (b) (anfangs) at first; to start with; (c) (erstmals) first; for the first time

zu|fahren *unr. itr. V.; mit sein* (a) **auf jmdn./etw.** ~: head towards sb./sth.; **auf jmdn./etw. zugefahren kommen** come towards sb./sth.; (b) (ugs.: los-, weiterfahren) get a move on (coll.); **fahr zu!** step on it! (coll.)

Zu·fahrt *die* (a) *o. Pl.* access [for vehicles]; (b) (Straße, Weg) access road; (zum Haus) driveway

Zufahrts·straße *die* access road

Zu·fall *der* chance; (zufälliges Zusammentreffen von Ereignissen) coincidence; **es war [ein] reiner** ~: it was pure chance *or* coincidence; **es ist kein** ~, **dass ...:** it is no accident that ...; **durch** ~: by chance *or* accident; **dass wir uns dort begegneten, war** ~: our meeting there was a coincidence

zu|fallen *unr. itr. V.; mit sein* (a) ⟨*door etc.*⟩ slam shut; ⟨*eyes*⟩ close; **ihm fielen [vor Müdigkeit] die Augen zu** his eyelids were drooping [with tiredness]; (b) (zukommen) **jmdm.** ~ ⟨*task*⟩ fall to sb.; ⟨*prize, inheritance*⟩ go to sb.;

ihm fällt alles nur so zu everything just drops into his lap

zu·fällig 1 *Adj.* accidental; chance *attrib.* ⟨*meeting, acquaintance*⟩; random ⟨*selection*⟩. 2 *adv.* by chance; **ich bin** ~ **hier vorbeigekommen** I just happened to be passing; **wissen Sie** ~, **wie spät es ist?** (ugs.) do you by any chance know the time?

zufälliger·weise *Adv.* ⇒ **zufällig 2**

Zufalls-: ~ **auswahl** *die* random selection; ~**bekanntschaft** *die* chance acquaintance; ~**generator** *der* (Musik) random generator; ~**treffer** *der* fluke

zu|fassen *itr. V.* make a snatch *or* grab

zu|fliegen *unr. itr. V.; mit sein* (a) **auf jmdn./etw.** ~: fly towards sb./sth.; **es kam auf mich zugeflogen** it came flying towards me; (b) **jmdm.** ~ ⟨*bird*⟩ fly into sb.'s house; **ihm fliegen die Herzen zu** (fig.) all hearts surrender to his charms; (c) (ugs.: zufallen) ⟨*door etc.*⟩ slam shut

zu|fließen *unr. itr. V.; mit sein* **einer Sache** (*Dat.*) ~: flow towards sth.; **jmdm./einer Sache** ~ (fig.) ⟨*money etc.*⟩ go to sb./sth.

Zu·flucht *die* refuge ⟨**vor** + *Dat.* from⟩; (vor Unwetter o. Ä.) shelter ⟨**vor** + *Dat.* from⟩; **[seine]** ~ **zu etw. nehmen** (fig.) resort to sth.

Zufluchts·ort *der* place of refuge; sanctuary

Zu·fluss, ***Zu·fluß** *der* feeder stream/river

zu|flüstern *tr. V.* **jmdm. etw.** ~: whisper sth. to sb.

zu·folge *Präp. mit Dat.; nachgestellt* according to

zu·frieden 1 *Adj.* contented; (befriedigt) satisfied; **mit etw.** ~ **sein** be satisfied with sth.; **bist du jetzt** ~? are you satisfied [now]?; **ein** ~**es Gesicht machen** look contented *or* satisfied; **wir können** ~ **sein** we can't complain; **sich** ~ **geben** be satisfied; **jmdn.** ~ **stellen** satisfy sb. 2 *adv.* contentedly

***zufrieden|geben** ⇒ **zufrieden 1**

Zufriedenheit *die;* ~: contentment; (Befriedigung) satisfaction; **zu meiner vollen** ~: to my complete satisfaction

***zufrieden|stellen** ⇒ **zufrieden 1**

zufriedenstellend 1 *Adj.* satisfactory. 2 *adv.* satisfactorily

zu|frieren *unr. itr. V.; mit sein* freeze over

zu|fügen *tr. V.* **jmdm. etw.** ~: inflict sth. on sb.; **jmdm. Schaden/[ein] Unrecht** ~: do sb. harm/an injustice

Zufuhr /ˈtsuːfuːɐ̯/ *die;* ~: supply; (Material) supplies *pl.;* **die** ~ **milder Meeresluft** the stream of mild sea air

zu|führen 1 *itr. V.* **auf etw.** (*Akk.*) ~: lead towards sth. 2 *tr. V.* **einer Sache** (*Dat.*) **etw.** ~: supply sth. to sth.; supply sth. with sth.; **einer Firma Kunden/einer Partei Mitglieder** ~: bring new customers to a firm/new members to a party; **jmdn. der gerechten Strafe** ~: ensure that sb. gets condign punishment

Zug /tsuːk/ *der;* ~**[e]s, Züge** /ˈtsyːɡə/ (a) (Bahn) train; **ich nehme lieber den** ~ *od.* **fahre lieber mit dem** ~: I prefer to go by train *or* rail; **jmdn. vom** ~ **abholen/zum** ~ **bringen** meet sb. off/take sb. to the train; (b) (Kolonne) column; (Umzug) procession; (Demonstrations~) march; (c) (das Ziehen) pull; traction (Phys.); **das ist der** ~ **der Zeit** (fig.) this is the modern trend *or* the way things are going; (d) (Wanderung) migration; (Streif~, Beute~, Diebes~) expedition; (e) (beim Brettspiel) move; **du bist am** ~: it's your move; **zum** ~**e kommen** (fig.) get a chance; (f) (Schluck) swig (coll.); mouthful; (großer Schluck) gulp; **das Glas auf einen** *od.* **in einem** ~ **leeren** empty the glass at one go; **einen Roman in einem** ~ **durchlesen** (fig.) read a novel at one sitting; **er hat einen guten** ~ (ugs.) he can really knock it back (coll.); **etw. in vollen Zügen genießen** (fig.) enjoy sth. to the full; (g) (beim Rauchen) pull; puff; drag (coll.); (h) (Atem~) breath; **in tiefen** *od.* **vollen Zügen** in deep breaths; **in den letzten Zügen liegen** (ugs.) be at death's door; (fig. scherzh.) ⟨*car, engine, machine*⟩ be at its last gasp; ⟨*project etc.*⟩ be on the last lap; (i) *o. Pl.* (Zugluft; beim Ofen) draught; **im** ~ **sitzen** sit in a draught; (j) (Gesichts~) feature; trait; (Wesens~) characteristic; trait; **seine Züge** his features; **die Stadt trägt noch dörfliche Züge** the town still has something of the village about it; **das war kein schöner** ~ **von ihr** that did her

---

*alte Schreibung (vgl. Hinweise auf S. xvi–xvii)

no credit; **(k)** (landsch.: Schublade) drawer; **(l)** (Bewegung eines Schwimmers od. Ruderers) stroke; **(m)** (Milit.: Einheit) platoon; **(n)** (Schulw.: Zweig) side; **(o)** (Höhen∼) range; chain

Zu·gabe *die* **(a)** (Geschenk) [free] gift; **(b)** (im Konzert, Theater) encore; **(c)** *o. Pl.* (das Zugeben) addition

Zug·abteil *das* [train] compartment (Brit.)

Zu·gang *der* **(a)** (Weg) access; (Eingang) entrance; **(b)** (das Betreten, Hineingehen) access; **(c)** (fig.) access; ∼ **zu jmdm./ etw. finden** be able to relate to sb./sth.; **(d)** ⇒ **Neu- zugang**

zu·gange: ∼ **sein** (ugs.) be busy *or* occupied

zugänglich /ˈtsuːɡɛŋlɪç/ *Adj.* **(a)** accessible; (geöffnet) open; **schwer** ∼: difficult to reach *pred.;* **die Zimmer sind von der Terrasse her** ∼: the rooms can be reached from the terrace; **(b)** (zur Verfügung stehend) available (*Dat.,* **für** to); **(c)** (aufgeschlossen) approachable ⟨*person*⟩; **für neue Ideen** *usw.* ∼ **sein** be amenable *or* receptive to new ideas *etc.*

Zugänglichkeit *die;* ∼ **(a)** accessibility; **(b)** (Aufge- schlossenheit) receptiveness (**gegenüber** to)

Zug-: ∼**an·schluss,** *∼**an·schluß** der* [train] connection; ∼**brücke** *die* drawbridge

zu·geben *unr. tr. V.* **(a)** (hinzufügen) add (*Dat.* to); **(b)** (ge- stehen, zugestehen) admit; admit, confess ⟨*guilt, complicity*⟩; admit to, confess to ⟨*deed, crime*⟩; **sie gab zu, es ge- stohlen zu haben** she admitted stealing it *or* having stolen it; **es war, zugegeben, viel Glück dabei** true, there was a lot of luck involved

zu·gegebener·maßen *Adv.* admittedly

zu·gegen *Adj.:* ∼ **sein** (geh.) be present

zu|gehen *unr. itr. V.; mit sein* **(a) auf jmdn./etw.** ∼: approach sb./sth.; **aufeinander** ∼ (fig.) try to come to- gether; **dem Ende** ∼: be coming to an end; **(b)** (ugs.: voran- gehen) get a move on (coll.); step on it (coll.); **(c)** (Papierdt.) **jmdm.** ∼: be sent to sb.; **jmdm. etw.** ∼ **lassen** send sth. to sb.; **(d)** *unpers.* (verlaufen) **auf dem Fest ging es fröhlich zu** it was very jolly at the party; **es müsste seltsam** ∼, **wenn das nicht gelänge** something re- markable would have to happen for that not to succeed; **es geht nicht mit rechten Dingen zu** there is something fishy going on (coll.); **(e)** (ugs.: sich schließen) close; shut; **(f)** (ugs.: sich schließen lassen) **die Tür/der Knopf geht nicht zu** the door will not shut/the button will not fasten; **der Reißverschluss geht schwer zu** the zip is difficult to do up

zu|gehören *itr. V.* (geh.) **jmdm./einer Sache** ∼: be- long to sb./sth.

zu·gehörig *Adj.* belonging to it/them *postpos., not pred.;* **einer Sache** (*Dat.*) ∼: belonging to sth.; **sich jmdm./ einer Sache** (*Dat.*) ∼ **fühlen** have a feeling of belonging [to sb./sth.]

Zugehörigkeit *die;* ∼: belonging (**zu** to)

zu·geknöpft *Adj.* (fig. ugs.) tight-lipped; (nicht zugänglich) unapproachable

Zügel /ˈtsyːɡl̩/ *der;* ∼**s,** ∼ **(a)** rein; **ein Pferd am** ∼ **führen** lead a horse by the reins; **einem Pferd in die** ∼ **fallen** stop a horse by seizing the reins; **(b)** (fig.) **die** ∼ **[fest] in der Hand haben** be [firmly] in control; have things [firmly] under control; **die** ∼ **straffer anziehen** tighten up on things; **die** ∼ **schießen lassen** let things take their course; **die** ∼ **schleifen lassen** *od.* **lockern** slacken the reins

zügel·los (fig.) **1** *Adj.* unrestrained; unbridled ⟨*rage, passion*⟩; **ein** ∼**es Leben führen** live a life of licentious indulgence. **2** *adv.* without restraint; ∼ **leben** live a life of licentious indulgence

Zügellosigkeit *die;* ∼, ∼**en** lack of restraint

zügeln *tr. V.* **(a)** rein [in] ⟨*horse*⟩; **(b)** (fig.) curb, restrain ⟨*feeling, desire, curiosity, etc.*⟩; **sich** ∼: restrain oneself

Zügelung *die;* ∼, ∼**en** curbing; restraining

Zu·gereiste *der/die; adj. Dekl.* newcomer

zu|gesellen *refl. V.* **sich jmdm./einer Sache** ∼: join sb./sth.

Zu·geständnis *das* concession (**an** + *Akk.* to)

zu|gestehen *unr. tr. V.* **(a)** grant ⟨*right, claim, share, etc.*⟩; allow ⟨*discount, commission, time*⟩; **(b)** (zugeben) ad- mit; concede

zu·getan *Adj.:* **jmdm.** [herzlich] ∼ **sein** (geh.) be [very] attached to sb.; **den schönen Künsten** ∼ **sein** have a penchant for the fine arts

Zu·gewinn *der* gain (**an** + *Dat.* in)

Zu·gezogene *der/die; adj. Dekl.* newcomer

Zug·führer *der* **(a)** (Eisenb.) guard; **(b)** (Milit.) platoon ser- geant

zu|gießen *unr. tr. V.* add

zugig *Adj.* draughty, (im Freien) windy ⟨*corner etc.*⟩

zügig /ˈtsyːɡɪç/ **1** *Adj.* speedy; rapid. **2** *adv.* speedily; rapidly

Zügigkeit *die;* ∼: speediness; rapidity

Zug·kraft *die* (fig.) attraction

zug·kräftig *Adj.* effective ⟨*publicity*⟩; powerful ⟨*argument*⟩; influential ⟨*name*⟩; catchy ⟨*title, slogan*⟩

zu·gleich *Adv.* at the same time; **er ist Maler und Dichter** ∼: he is both a painter and a poet

Zug-: ∼**luft** *die; o. Pl.* draught; ∼**luft** [ab]**bekommen** be in a draught; ∼**pferd** *das* **(a)** draughthorse; **(b)** (fig.: Attraktion) big draw; crowd-puller

zu|greifen *unr. itr. V.* **(a)** take hold; **(b)** (sich bedienen) help oneself; **(c)** (fleißig arbeiten) [hart *od.* kräftig] ∼: [really] knuckle down to it

Zu·griff *der* **(a)** grasp; **sich dem** ∼ **der Polizei entziehen** escape the clutches of the police; **(b)** (fig.: Zugang) access (**auf** + *Akk.* to)

zu·grunde *Adv.* **(a)** ∼ **gehen** (sterben) die (**an** + *Dat.* of); (zerstört werden) be destroyed (**an** + *Dat.* by); ⟨*marriage*⟩ founder (**an** + *Dat.* owing to); ⟨*person*⟩ go under; (finanziell) be ruined; ⟨*company*⟩ go to the wall; ∼ **richten** destroy; (finanziell) ruin ⟨*company, person*⟩; **(b) etw.** ∼ **legen** use sth. as a basis; **etw. einer Sache** (*Dat.*) ∼ **legen** base sth. on sth.; **A liegt B** (*Dat.*) ∼**:** B is based on A

Zugs- (österr.) ⇒ **Zug-**

zu|gucken *itr. V.* (ugs.) ⇒ **zusehen**

Zug·unglück *das* train crash

zu·gunsten 1 *Präp. mit Gen.* in favour of. **2** *Adv.* ∼ **von** in favour of

zu·gut: **etw.** ∼ **haben** (schweiz., südd.) be owed sth.; **du hast [bei mir] 10 Mark** ∼**:** you've got ten marks to come [from me]

zu·gute *Adv.:* **jmdm. seine Jugend/Unerfahrenheit** *usw.* ∼ **halten** (geh.) take sb.'s youth/inexperience *etc.* into consideration; make allowances for sb.'s youth/inexperi- ence *etc.;* **jmdm./einer Sache** ∼ **kommen** stand sb./ sth. in good stead; **jmdm. etw.** ∼ **kommen lassen** let sb. have the benefit of *or* let sb. benefit from sth.

Zug-: ∼**verbindung** *die* rail *or* (Amer.) railroad ser- vice; ∼**verkehr** *der* rail *or* (Amer.) railroad traffic; ∼**vogel** *der* migratory bird

zu|haben *unr. itr. V.* (ugs.) **(a)** ⟨*shop, office*⟩ be shut *or* closed; **wir haben montags zu** we are closed on Mon- days; **(b) endlich hat sie den Koffer/Reißverschluss zu** at last she's managed to shut the suitcase/do up the zip

zu|haken *tr. V.* hook up; do up the hooks on

zu|halten 1 *unr. tr. V.* hold closed; (nicht öffnen) keep closed; **jmdm./sich die Augen/den Mund** *usw.* ∼**:** put one's hand[s] over sb.'s/one's eyes/mouth *etc.;* **sich** (*Dat.*) **die Nase** ∼**:** hold one's nose. **2** *itr. V.* **auf etw.** (*Akk.*) ∼**:** head for sth.

Zuhälter /ˈtsuːhɛltɐ/ *der;* ∼, ∼**:** pimp

zu|hängen *tr. V.* cover ⟨*window, cage*⟩

zu|hauen 1 *unr. itr. V.* **(a)** (ugs.) bang *or* slam ⟨*door, window*⟩ shut; **(b)** (behauen) hew into shape. **2** *unr. itr. V.* (ugs.) hit *or* strike out

Zu·hause *das;* ∼**s** home

zu|heilen *itr. V.; mit sein* heal [over]

zu·hinterst *Adv.* right at the back

zu|hören *itr. V.* listen (*Dat.* to); **nun hör mal zu** now listen; (drohend) now [you] listen here; **er kann gut** ∼**:** he's a good listener

Zu·hörer *der,* **Zu·hörerin** *die* listener

zu|jubeln *itr. V.* jmdm. **~:** cheer sb. [on]

zu|kehren *tr. V.* ⇒ **zuwenden 2 a**

zu|klappen 1 *tr. V.* close; fold ‹*penknife*› shut. 2 *itr. V.; mit sein* ‹*window, lid, etc.*› click to *or* shut

zu|kleben *tr. V.* (a) seal ‹*letter, envelope*›; (b) (vollkleben) cover

zu|knallen (ugs.) 1 *tr. V.* slam. 2 *itr. V.; mit sein* slam

zu|kneifen *unr. tr. V.* squeeze ‹*eye[s]*› shut; shut ‹*eye[s]*› tight; shut ‹*mouth*› tightly

zu|knöpfen *tr. V.* button up

zu|knoten *tr. V.* knot; tie up

zu|kommen *itr. V.; mit sein* (a) **auf** jmdn. **~:** approach sb.; (zu jmdm. kommen) come up to sb.; **er/es kam direkt auf mich zu** he/it came straight towards me; **er ahnte nicht, was noch auf ihn ~ sollte** (fig.) he had no idea what he was in for; **die Dinge auf sich ~ lassen** (fig.) take things as they come; (b) (geh.) jmdm. etw. **~ lassen** (schicken) send sb. sth.; (schenken) give sb. sth.; jmdm./ **einer Sache Pflege ~ lassen** devote care to sth.; (c) ⇒ **zustehen**; (d) (beizumessen sein) **dieser Entdeckung kommt große Bedeutung zu** great significance must be attached to this discovery

zu|korken *tr. V.* cork

zu|kriegen *tr. V.* (ugs.) ⇒ **zubekommen**

Zukunft /'tsu:kʊnft/ *die;* ~, **Zukünfte** /'tsu:kʏnftə/ (a) future; **für alle ~:** for all time; **~/keine ~ haben** have a/no future; **in naher/ferner ~:** in the near *or* immediate/distant future; **in ~:** in future; **ich wünsche Ihnen alles Gute für Ihre weitere ~:** I wish you all the best for the future; (b) (Sprachw.) future [tense]

zu·künftig 1 *Adj.* future. 2 *Adv.* in future

Zukünftige *der/die; adj. Dekl.* (ugs.) **mein ~r/meine ~:** my husband/wife-to-be; my intended (joc.)

Zukunfts-: ~forschung *die* futurology *no art.;* **~roman** *der* novel set in the future

zu|lächeln *itr. V.* jmdm. **~:** smile at sb.

Zulage *die* (vom Arbeitgeber) extra pay *no indef. art.;* additional allowance *no indef. art.;* (vom Staat) benefit

zu|langen *itr. V.* (ugs.) ⇒ **zugreifen b, c**

zu|länglich (geh.) 1 *Adj.* adequate. 2 *adv.* adequately

zu|lassen *unr. tr. V.* (a) (erlauben, dulden) allow; permit; **ich lasse keine Ausnahme zu** I do not allow *or* permit any exceptions; (b) (teilnehmen lassen) admit; (c) (mit einer Erlaubnis, Lizenz usw. versehen) jmdn. **als Arzt ~:** register sb. as a doctor; **der Anwalt ist beim Amtsgericht Mannheim zugelassen** the lawyer is registered to practise at Mannheim district court; jmdn. **zu einer Prüfung ~:** allow *or* permit sb. to take an examination; (d) (zur Benutzung, zum Verkauf usw. freigeben) allow; permit; **ein Medikament ~:** approve a medicine [for sale]; **für den öffentlichen Verkehr zugelassen sein** be authorized for use on public highways; (e) (Kfz-W.) register ‹*vehicle*›; (f) (geschlossen lassen) leave closed *or* shut; leave ‹*letter*› unopened; leave ‹*collar, coat*› fastened [up]

zu·lässig *Adj.* permissible

Zulässigkeit *die;* ~ permissibility

Zulassung *die;* ~, **~en** (a) (Erlaubnis, Lizenz) ~ **als Arzt** registration as a doctor; ~ **zur Teilnahme/zur Prüfung beantragen** apply for permission to attend/to take *or* (Brit.) sit an examination; **ihm ist die ~ zum Studium/zum Medizinstudium erteilt worden** he has been accepted at university/to study medicine; (b) (Freigabe) approval; authorization; (c) (Kfz-W.) registration

Zulassungs·stelle *die* vehicle registration office

zu·lasten 1 *Präp. mit Gen.* **die Verpackungskosten gehen ~ der Kunden** the cost of packaging will be charged to the customer. 2 *Adv.* **die Einsparungsmaßnahmen gehen vor allem ~ der Minderheiten** the burden of the economy measures falls heaviest on the minorities

Zu·lauf *der o. Pl.* ~ **haben** ‹*shop, restaurant, etc.*› enjoy a large clientele, be very popular; ‹*doctor, lawyer*› have a large practice, be very much in demand

zu|laufen *unr. itr. V.; mit sein* (a) **auf** jmdn./etw. **~** (auch fig.) run towards sb./sth.; **auf** jmdn./etw. **zugelaufen kommen** come running towards sb./sth.; (b) jmdm. **~** ‹*cat, dog, etc.*› adopt sb. as a new owner; (c) (hinzulaufen) ‹*water etc.*› run in; (d) (sich verjüngen) taper; **spitz ~:** taper to a point; (e) (ugs.: schnell laufen) get one's skates on (Brit. sl.); get a move on (coll.)

zu|legen 1 *refl. V.* **sich** (*Dat.*) etw. **~:** get oneself sth.; **er hat sich einen Bart zugelegt** (ugs.) he has grown a beard. 2 *itr. V.* (ugs.) (a) (sein Tempo steigern) step on it (coll.); (b) (wachsen) ‹*sales, output, turnover, etc.*› increase; **der Dollar hat [um vier Pfennige] zugelegt** the dollar has risen [four pfennigs]. 3 *tr. V.* (ugs.) add; **einen Schritt/** (ugs.) **Zahn ~:** get a move on (coll.)

zu·leid[e]: jmdm. etwas/nichts **~ tun** hurt *or* harm sb./not [do anything to] hurt *or* harm sb.; *s. auch* **Fliege a**

zu|leiten *tr. V.* (a) feed; supply; supply ‹*nourishment*›; (b) (schicken) send; forward

Zu·leitung *die* (a) *o. Pl.* ⇒ **zuleiten:** supply; sending; forwarding; (b) (Rohr, Kabel usw.) feed line

zu·letzt *Adv.* (a) last [of all]; **an sich selbst denkt sie immer ~:** she always thinks of herself last; **er kommt immer ~:** he always comes last; he is always [the] last; **das ~ geborene Kind** the child born last; (b) (fig.: am wenigsten) least of all; **nicht ~:** not least; (c) (das letzte Mal) last; **ich habe ihn ~ gestern Abend gesehen** I last saw him yesterday evening; (d) (schließlich) in the end; **bis ~:** [right up] to *or* until the end

zu·liebe *Adv.* jmdm./einer Sache **~:** for sb.'s sake/for the sake of sth.

Zu·liefer·betrieb *der* supplier (*Gen.* to)

zu|löten *tr. V.* solder; solder up ‹*hole*›

zum /tsʊm/ *Präp. + Art.* (a) = **zu dem;** (b) (räumlich: Richtung) to the; **ein Fenster ~ Hof** a window on to *or* facing the yard; **wo geht es ~ Stadion?** which is the way to the stadium?; (c) (räumlich: Lage) etw. **~ Fenster hinauswerfen** throw sth. out of the window; (d) (Zusammengehörigkeit, Hinzufügung) **Milch ~ Tee/Sahne ~ Kuchen nehmen** take milk with [one's] tea/have cream with one's cake; (e) (zeitlich) at the; **spätestens ~ 15. April** by 15 April at the latest; **~ Schluss/richtigen Zeitpunkt** at the end/the right moment; (f) (Zweck) **ein Gerät ~ Schneiden** an instrument for cutting [with]; **hol dir was ~ Schreiben** get something to write with; **~ Spaß/ Vergnügen** for fun/pleasure; **~ Lesen braucht er eine Brille** he needs glasses for reading; **~ Schutz** as *or* for protection; etw. **~ Essen/Lesen** (österr.) sth. to eat/read; (g) (Folge) **~ Ärger/Leidwesen seines Vaters** to the annoyance/sorrow of his father; (h) jmdn. **~ Direktor ernennen/~ Kanzler wählen** appoint sb. director/elect sb. chancellor; **~ Dieb werden** become a thief; (i) **~ ersten, ~ zweiten, ~ dritten!** (bei Versteigerung) going, going, gone!

zu|machen 1 *tr. V.* close; shut; fasten, do up ‹*dress*›; seal ‹*envelope, letter*›; turn off ‹*tap*›; put the top on ‹*bottle*›; (stilllegen) close *or* shut down ‹*factory, mine, etc.*›; **ich habe kein Auge zugemacht** I didn't sleep a wink. 2 *itr. V.* (a) close; shut; (b) (ugs., bes. nordd.: sich beeilen) get a move on (coll.)

zu·mal 1 *Adv.* especially; particularly; **~ da …:** especially *or* particularly since … 2 *Konj.* especially *or* particularly since

zu|marschieren *itr. V.; mit sein* **auf** jmdn./etw. **~:** march towards sb./sth.

zu|mauern *tr. V.* wall *or* brick up

zu·meist *Adj.* in the main; for the most part

zumindest *Adv.* at least

zumutbar *Adj.* reasonable; **das ist ihm kaum/ durchaus/nicht ~:** one can scarcely/quite well/not expect that of him

---

Zumutbarkeit *die;* ∼: reasonableness
zu·mute *Adj.* jmdm. **ist unbehaglich/elend** *usw.* ∼: sb. feels uncomfortable/wretched *etc.;* **mir war nicht danach** ∼: I didn't feel like it *or* in the mood; **mir war zum Weinen** ∼: I felt like crying
zu|muten *tr. V.* (a) (abverlangen) jmdm. etw. ∼: expect *or* ask sth. of sb.; **diese Arbeit möchte ich ihm nicht** ∼: I would not like to ask him to do this work *or* impose this work on him; **das ist ihm durchaus/nicht zuzumuten** it is perfectly reasonable to/one cannot expect *or* ask that of him; **sich zu viel** ∼: take on too much; overdo it; (b) (antun) jmdm. etw. ∼: expect sb. to put up with sth.; **diesen Anblick wollte ich ihm nicht** ∼: I wanted to spare him this sight
Zumutung *die;* ∼, ∼en (a) (Ansinnen) unreasonable demand; imposition; **eine** ∼ **sein** be unreasonable; **etw. als [eine]** ∼ **empfinden** consider sth. unreasonable; (b) (Belästigung) imposition; **eine** ∼ **für jmdn. sein** be an imposition on sb.; **das Essen war eine** ∼: the meal was an affront
zu·nächst *Adv.* (a) (als erstes) first; (anfangs) at first; ∼ **einmal** first; (b) (vorläufig) for the moment; for the time being
zu|nageln *tr. V.* nail up; etw. **mit Brettern** ∼: board sth. up
zu|nähen *tr. V.* sew up; *s. auch* **verdammt 1 a; verflixt 1 b**
Zunahme /ˈtsuːnaːmə/ *die;* ∼, ∼n increase (*Gen.,* **an** + *Dat.* in)
Zu·name *der* surname; last name
zündeln /ˈtsʏndl̩n/ *itr. V.* (auch fig.) play with fire
zünden /ˈtsʏndn̩/ **1** *tr. V.* ignite ⟨*gas, fuel, etc.*⟩; detonate ⟨*bomb, explosive device, etc.*⟩; let off ⟨*fireworks*⟩; fire ⟨*rocket*⟩. **2** *itr. V.* ⟨*rocket, engine*⟩ fire; ⟨*candle, lighter, match*⟩ light; ⟨*gas, fuel, explosive*⟩ ignite; (fig.) arouse enthusiasm
zündend *Adj.* (fig.) stirring, rousing ⟨*speech, song, tune, etc.*⟩
Zunder /ˈtsʊndɐ/ *der;* ∼s (a) tinder; **trocken wie** ∼: dry as tinder; tinder-dry; (b) (fig. ugs.) jmdm. ∼ **geben** lay into sb. (coll.); ∼ **kriegen** get it in the neck (coll.)
Zünder *der;* ∼s, ∼ igniter; (für Bombe, Mine) detonator
Zünd-: ∼**holz** *das* (bes. südd., österr.) match; ∼**kerze** *die* spark[ing]-plug; ∼**schloss, *∼schloß** *das* (Kfz-W.) ignition [lock]; ∼**schlüssel** *der* (Kfz-W.) ignition key; ∼**schnur** *die* fuse; ∼**stoff** *der* (fig.) fuel for conflict
Zündung *die;* ∼, ∼en (a) → **zünden 1**: ignition; detonation; letting off; firing; (b) (Kfz-W.: Anlage) ignition
zu|nehmen 1 *unr. itr. V.* (a) increase (**an** + *Dat.* in); ⟨*moon*⟩ wax; **in** ∼**dem Maße** to an increasing extent *or* degree; increasingly; **mit** ∼**dem Alter** with advancing age; (b) ▶ **228**| (schwerer werden) put on *or* gain weight; **er hat [um] ein Kilo zugenommen** he has put on *or* gained a kilo. **2** *unr. tr., auch itr. V.* (Handarb.) increase
zunehmend *Adv.* increasingly
Zu·neigung *die;* ∼, ∼en affection (**zu** for, towards); ∼ **zu jmdm. fassen** become fond of sb.
zünftig /ˈtsʏnftɪç/ (ugs.) **1** *Adj.* proper. **2** *adv.* properly
Zunge /ˈtsʊŋə/ *die;* ∼, ∼n ▶ **326**| (a) tongue; [jmdm.] **die** ∼ **herausstrecken** put one's tongue out [at sb.]; **auf der** ∼ **zergehen** melt in one's mouth; (b) (fig.) **eine spitze** *od.* **scharfe/lose** ∼ **haben** have a sharp/loose tongue; **böse** ∼**n behaupten, dass** …: malicious gossip has it that …; malicious tongues are saying that …; **seine** ∼ **hüten** *od.* **zügeln im Zaum halten** guard *or* mind one's tongue; **ich musste mir auf die** ∼ **beißen** I had to bite my tongue; **lieber beiße ich mir die** ∼ **ab** (ugs.) I would bite my tongue off first; **der Name liegt mir auf der** ∼: the name is on the tip of my tongue; **sich** *(Dat.)* **die** ∼ **abbrechen** tie one's tongue in knots; **mit [heraus]hängender** ∼: with [one's/its] tongue hanging out; (c) (eines Blasinstruments) reed; (einer Orgel) tongue; (eines Schuhs) tongue
züngeln /ˈtsʏŋl̩n/ *itr. V.* (a) ⟨*snake etc.*⟩ dart its tongue in and out; (b) *mit Richtungsangabe mit sein* ⟨*flame*⟩ flicker; dart

Zungen-: ∼**spitze** *die* tip of the tongue; ∼**wurst** *die* tongue sausage
Zünglein /ˈtsʏnlaɪn/ *das;* ∼s, ∼ (a) [little] tongue; (b) (einer Waage) [small] needle *or* pointer; **das** ∼ **an der Waage sein** (fig.) tip the scales
zu·nichte *Adj.* etw. ∼ **machen** ruin sth.; jmds. Hoffnungen ∼ **machen** shatter *or* dash sb.'s hopes
zu|nicken *itr. V.* jmdm./sich ∼: nod to sb./one another
zu·nutze *Adj.* sich *(Dat.)* etw. ∼ **machen** make use of sth.; (ausnutzen) take advantage of sth.
zu·oberst *Adv.* [right] on [the] top; *s. auch* **unter...** a
zu|ordnen *tr. V.* (a) relate (*Dat.* to); (b) (zurechnen) jmdn./etw. **einer Sache** *(Dat.)* ∼: classify sb./sth. as belonging to sth.; (c) (zuweisen) assign (*Dat.* to)
zu|packen *itr. V.* (a) grab it/them; **fest** ∼ **können** be able to grab things and grip them tightly; (b) (fig.) knuckle down to it; **er hat eine sehr** ∼**de Art** he has a very vigorous, purposeful manner
zupfen /ˈtsʊpfn̩/ **1** *itr. V.* **an etw.** *(Dat.)* ∼: pluck *or* pull at sth.; **sich** *(Dat.)* **am Ohrläppchen** ∼: pull [at] one's ear lobe. **2** *tr. V.* (a) etw. **aus/von** *usw.* etw. ∼: pull sth. out of/from *etc.* sth.; (b) (auszupfen) pull out; pluck ⟨*eyebrows*⟩; pull up ⟨*weeds*⟩; (c) pluck ⟨*string, guitar, tune*⟩; (d) jmdn. **am Ärmel/Bart** ∼: pull *or* tug [at] sb.'s sleeve/beard
zu|pflastern *tr. V.* pave over
zu|pressen *tr. V.* press shut
zu|prosten *itr. V.* jmdm. ∼: drink sb.'s health; raise one's glass to sb.
zur /tsuːɐ/ *Präp.* + *Art.* (a) = **zu der;** (b) (räumlich: Richtung) to the; **ein Fenster** ∼ **Straße** a window on to the street; **wo geht es** ∼ **Post?** which is the way to the post office?; (c) (räumlich: Lage) ∼ **Tür hereinkommen** come [in] through the door; (d) (Zusammengehörigkeit, Hinzufügung) ∼ **Hasenkeule empfehle ich einen Rotwein** I recommend a red wine with the haunch of hare; (e) (zeitlich) at the; ∼ **Stunde/Zeit** at the moment; at present; ∼ **Adventszeit** at Advent time; ∼ **Jahreswende** at New Year; **rechtzeitig** ∼ **Buchmesse** in [good] time for the book fair; (f) (Zweck) ∼ **Entschuldigung** by way of [an] excuse; ∼ **Inspektion in die Werkstatt müssen** have to go in for a check-up; (g) (Folge) ∼ **vollen Zufriedenheit ihres Chefs** to the complete satisfaction of her boss; ∼ **allgemeinen Erheiterung** to everybody's amusement; (h) **sie wurde** ∼ **Direktorin ernannt/**∼ **Präsidentin gewählt** she was appointed director/elected president; ∼ **Diebin werden** become a thief; **die Wahlen** ∼ **Knesseth** elections to the Knesset
zu rande *in* **mit etw. [nicht]** ∼ **kommen** (ugs.) [not] be able to cope with sth.
zu·rate *in* jmdn./etw. ∼ **ziehen** consult sb./sth.
zu|raten *unr. itr. V.* **ich würde dir** ∼: I would advise you to do so; **auf jmds. Zuraten [hin]** on sb.'s advice *or* recommendation; **ich möchte [dir] weder zu- noch abraten** I should not like to advise you one way or the other
Zürcher /ˈtsʏrçɐ/ ▶ **490**| **1** *indekl. Adj.; nicht präd.* Zurich *attrib.* **2** *der;* ∼s, ∼: inhabitant/native of Zurich; **er ist** ∼: he is from Zurich
zu|rechnen *tr. V.* jmdn./etw. **einer Sache** *(Dat.)* ∼: class sb./sth. as belonging to sth.
zurechnungs·fähig *Adj.* (a) sound of mind *pred.;* (b) (Rechtsw.: schuldfähig) responsible [for one's actions]
Zurechnungs·fähigkeit *die; o. Pl.* (a) soundness of mind; (b) (Rechtsw.: Schuldfähigkeit) responsibility [for one's actions]
zurecht-, Zurecht-: ∼**biegen** *unr. tr. V.* bend into shape; **er wird die Sache schon wieder** ∼**biegen** (fig.) he will get things straightened out *or* sorted out again; ∼**finden** *unr. refl. V.* find one's way [around]; **er findet sich im Leben/in der Welt nicht [mehr]** ∼: he is not able to cope with life/the world [any longer]; ∼**kommen** *unr. itr. V.; mit sein* get on (**mit** with); **mit etw.** ∼**kommen** cope with sth.; ∼**legen** *tr. V.* (a) lay out [ready] (*Dat.* for); (b) (fig.) get ready; prepare; **sich** *(Dat.)* **eine Erwiderung** ∼**gelegt haben** have a reply ready;

∼|**machen** *tr. V.* (ugs.) (a) (vorbereiten) get ready; (b) (herrichten) do up; (c) jmdn./sich ∼: get sb. ready/get [oneself] ready; (schminken) make sb. up/put on one's make-up; ∼|**rücken** *tr. V.* put or set ⟨*chair, crockery, etc.*⟩ in place; straighten ⟨*tie*⟩; adjust ⟨*spectacles, hat, etc.*⟩; (fig.: richtig stellen, korrigieren) put straight; *s. auch* **Kopf a;** ∼|**schneiden** *unr. tr. V.* cut to size/shape; trim ⟨*fringe, beard, hedge*⟩; ∼|**stutzen** *tr. V.* trim ⟨*hedge, beard, hair etc.*⟩; jmdn./etw. ∼stutzen (fig.) sort or straighten sb. out/get or knock sth. into shape; ∼|**weisen** *unr. tr. V.* rebuke; reprimand ⟨*pupil, subordinate, etc.*⟩; ∼**weisung** *die* ⇒ ∼weisen: rebuke; reprimand

zu|**reden** *itr. V.* jmdm. ∼: persuade sb.; (ermutigen) encourage sb.; jmdm. gut ∼: encourage sb.

zu·reichend (geh.) ⇒ zulänglich

Zürich /ˈzyːrɪç/ ⟨*das*⟩; ∼s ▶ 490 | Zurich

zu|**richten** *tr. V.* (a) (verletzen) injure; sie haben ihn übel zugerichtet they [really] knocked him about; (b) (beschädigen) make a mess of

zu|**riegeln** *tr. V.* bolt

Zur·schau·stellung *die* exhibition; display

zu·rück *Adv.* (a) back; ich bin gleich [wieder] ∼: I'll be right back (coll.); ein Schritt ∼: a step backwards; ∼! get or go back!; „∼ an Absender" 'return to sender'; … und 10 Pfennig ∼: … and 10 pfennigs change; *s. auch* **Dank a; hin d; Natur a;** (b) (weiter hinten; auch fig.) behind

Zurück *das in* es gibt kein ∼ [mehr] there is no going back

zurück-, Zurück-: ∼|**begleiten** *tr. V.* jmdn. ∼begleiten accompany sb. back; ∼|**behalten** *unr. tr. V.* (a) keep [back]; retain; (b) (nicht mehr loswerden) be left with ⟨*scar, heart defect, etc.*⟩; ∼|**bekommen** *unr. tr. V.* get back; Sie bekommen noch 10 Mark ∼: you get 10 marks change; ∼|**beordern** *tr. V.* order back; ∼|**beugen** 1 *tr. V.* bend back; 2 *refl. V.* lean or bend back; ∼|**bleiben** *unr. itr. V.; mit sein* (a) remain or stay behind; (b) (nicht mithalten) lag behind; (fig.) fall behind; hinter den Erwartungen ∼bleiben fall short of expectations; in seiner Entwicklung ∼bleiben ⟨*child*⟩ be retarded or backward in its development; (c) (bleiben) remain; von der Krankheit ist [bei ihm] nichts ∼geblieben the illness has left no lasting effects [on him]; (d) (wegbleiben) stay or keep back; *s. auch* zurückgeblieben; ∼|**blicken** *itr. V.* (auch fig.) look back ⟨*auf + Akk.* at, *fig.:* on⟩; (sich umblicken) look back or round; ∼|**bringen** *unr. tr. V.* bring/take back; return; ∼|**drängen** *tr. V.* force back; drive back ⟨*enemy*⟩; ∼|**drehen** *tr. V.* (a) turn back; turn down ⟨*heating, volume, etc.*⟩; (b) (rückwärts drehen) turn backwards; ∼|**eilen** *itr. V.; mit sein* hurry back; ∼|**erhalten** *unr. tr. V.* (geh.) be given back; get back; anliegend erhalten Sie ihre Bewerbungsunterlagen ∼: please find enclosed your application, which we are returning to you; ∼|**erinnern** *refl. V.* sich an etw. (*Akk.*) ∼erinnern remember or recall sth.; ∼|**erobern** *tr. V.* win back ⟨*votes, majority, etc.*⟩; regain ⟨*power, position, etc.*⟩; recapture ⟨*territory, town, etc.*⟩; ∼|**erstatten** *tr. V.* refund; jmdm. etw. ∼erstatten refund sth. to sb.; ∼|**erwarten** *tr. V.* jmdn. ∼erwarten expect sb. back; ∼|**fahren** 1 *unr. itr. V.; mit sein* (a) go/drive/ ride back; return; (b) (nach hinten fahren) go back[wards]; 2 *unr. tr. V.* jmdn./etw. ∼fahren drive sb./sth. back; ∼|**fallen** *unr. itr. V.; mit sein* (a) fall back; (b) (nach hinten fallen) fall back[wards]; (c) (fig.: in Rückstand geraten) fall behind; (d) (fig.: auf einen niedrigeren Rang) drop ⟨*auf + Akk.* to⟩; (e) (fig.: in einen früheren Zustand) in etw. (*Akk.*) ∼fallen fall back into sth.; (f) (fig.) an jmdn. ∼fallen ⟨*property*⟩ revert to sb.; (g) (fig.) auf jmdn. ∼fallen ⟨*actions, behaviour, etc.*⟩ reflect [up]on sb.; ∼|**finden** *unr. itr. V.* find one's way back; ∼|**fliegen** 1 *unr. itr. V.; mit sein* fly back; 2 *unr. tr. V.* jmdn./etw. ∼fliegen fly sb./sth. back; ∼|**fordern** *tr. V.* etw. ∼fordern ask for sth. back; (nachdrücklicher) demand sth. back; ∼|**fragen** *itr. V.* answer with a question; „…?" fragte er ∼: '…?', he asked in return; ∼|**führen** 1 *tr. V.* (a) jmdn. ∼führen take sb. back; (b) etw. ∼führen move sth. back; return sth.; (c) etw. auf etw.

(*Akk.*) ∼führen (auf Ursprung) trace sth. back to sth.; (auf Ursache) attribute sth. to sth.; put sth. down to sth.; (auf einfachere Form) reduce sth. to sth.; 2 *itr. V.* lead back; es führt kein anderer Weg ∼: there is no other way back; ∼|**geben** *unr. tr. V.* (a) give back; return; hand in ⟨*driver's licence, membership card*⟩; return ⟨*goods, unused ticket, etc.*⟩; relinquish ⟨*mandate, office, etc.*⟩; give back ⟨*freedom*⟩; jmdm. etw. ∼geben give sth. back to sb.; return sth. to sb.; (b) (erwidern) reply; (c) *auch itr.* (Ballspiele) return ⟨*ball, puck, service, pass, throw*⟩; (nach hinten geben) pass ⟨*ball*⟩ back; [den Ball] an jmdn. ∼geben return the ball to sb.; ∼**geblieben** *Adj.* retarded; ∼|**gehen** *unr. itr. V.; mit sein* (a) go back; return; (sich zurückbewegen) ⟨*pick-up arm, indicator, needle, etc.*⟩ return; (b) (nach hinten gehen) go back; ⟨*enemy*⟩ retreat; (c) (verschwinden) ⟨*bruise, ulcer*⟩ disappear; ⟨*swelling, inflammation*⟩ go down; ⟨*pain*⟩ subside; (bei sich verringern) decrease; go down; ⟨*fever*⟩ abate; ⟨*flood*⟩ subside; ⟨*business*⟩ fall off; (e) (zurückgeschickt werden) be returned or sent back; ein Essen ∼gehen lassen send a meal back; (f) auf jmdn. ∼gehen (jmds. Werk sein) go back to sb.; (von jmdm. abstammen) originate from or be descended from sb.; der Name geht auf ein lateinisches Wort ∼: the name comes from a Latin word; (g) (sich zurückbewegen lassen) ⟨*lever etc.*⟩ go back; ∼|**gewinnen** *unr. tr. V.* (a) win back; regain ⟨*confidence, title, strength, freedom, etc.*⟩; (b) (Wirtsch.) reclaim, recover ⟨*raw materials etc.*⟩; ∼|**gezogen** 1 *Adj.* secluded; 2 *adv.* ∼gezogen leben live a secluded life; ∼**gezogenheit** *die;* ∼: seclusion; ∼|**greifen** *unr. itr. V.* auf jmdn./etw. ∼greifen fall back on sb./sth.; ∼|**haben** *unr. tr. V.* have back; hast du es inzwischen ∼? have you got it back yet?; ∼|**halten** 1 *unr. tr. V.* (a) jmdn. ∼halten hold sb. back; er war durch nichts ∼zuhalten there was no stopping him; nothing would stop him; (b) (am Vordringen hindern) keep back ⟨*crowd, mob, etc.*⟩; (c) (behalten) withhold ⟨*news, letter, parcel, etc.*⟩; (d) (nicht austreten lassen) hold back ⟨*tears etc.*⟩; (e) (von etw. abhalten) jmdn. ∼halten stop sb.; jmdn. von etw. ∼halten keep sb. from sth.; 2 *unr. refl. V.* (a) (sich zügeln, sich beherrschen) restrain or control oneself; (b) (nicht aktiv werden) sich in einer Diskussion ∼halten keep in the background in a discussion; ∼**haltend** 1 *Adj.* (a) reserved; subdued, muted ⟨*colour*⟩; (b) (kühl, reserviert) cool, restrained ⟨*reception, response*⟩; (c) (sparsam) mit etw. ∼haltend ⟨*person*⟩ who is/was sparing with sth.; sparing with sth. *pred.;* 2 *adv.* ⟨*behave*⟩ with reserve or restraint; (b) (kühl, reserviert) coolly; ∼**haltung** *die; o. Pl.* reserve; (Kühle) coolness; ∼**haltung üben** (geh.) exercise restraint; ein Buch mit ∼haltung aufnehmen give a book a cool reception; ∼|**holen** *tr. V.* (a) fetch back; get back ⟨*money*⟩; bring back ⟨*satellite, missile*⟩; jmdn. ∼holen bring sb. back; (b) (∼rufen) call back; ∼|**kämmen** *tr. V.* comb back; backcomb; ∼**gekämmte Haare** backcombed hair; ∼|**kehren** *itr. V.; mit sein* return; come back; ∼|**kommen** *unr. itr. V.; mit sein* (a) come back; return; ⟨*letter*⟩ come back, be returned; (b) (zurückgelangen) get back; (c) ∼kommen auf (+ *Akk.*) come back to ⟨*subject, question, point, etc.*⟩; come back on ⟨*offer*⟩; ∼|**können** *unr. itr. V.* be able to go back or return; jetzt können wir nicht mehr ∼ (fig.) there's no going or turning back now; ∼|**kriegen** *tr. V.* ⇒ ∼bekommen; ∼|**lassen** *unr. tr. V.* (a) leave; (b) (zurückkehren lassen) jmdn. ∼lassen allow sb. to return; let sb. return; ∼**lassung** *die;* ∼: unter ∼lassung einer Sache/jmds. leaving sth./sb. behind; ∼|**laufen** *unr. itr. V.; mit sein* (a) run back; (b) (ugs.: zurückgehen) come/ go back; (c) (sich zurückbewegen) run back; das Tonband ∼laufen lassen run the tape back; ∼|**legen** 1 *tr. V.* (a) put back; (b) (nach hinten beugen) lean or lay ⟨*head*⟩ back; (c) (reservieren) put aside, keep (*Dat.,* für for); (d) (sparen) put away; put by; (e) (hinter sich bringen) cover ⟨*distance*⟩; 2 *refl. V.* lie back; (sich ∼lehnen, ∼neigen) lean back; ∼|**lehnen** *refl. V.* lean back; ∼|**liegen** *unr. itr. V.* (a) das Ereignis/das liegt einige Jahre ∼: the event took place/that was several years ago; (b) (bes. Sport) be behind; ∼|**melden** *refl. V.* report back (bei to); ∼|**müssen** *unr. itr. V.* (a) have to go back or return; (b) (zurückbefördert werden müssen) have to go back; ∼|**nehmen** *unr. tr. V.* (a) take back; (b) (widerrufen) take back; (c) (rückgängig machen) revoke, rescind ⟨*decision, ban, etc.*⟩; withdraw ⟨*complaint*⟩; ∼|**pfeifen** *unr. tr. V.* (a) whistle ⟨*dog*⟩ back; (b) (fig. salopp) jmdn. ∼pfeifen call sb. off; ∼|**prallen** *itr. V.; mit sein* (a) bounce back (**von** off); ⟨*bullet*⟩ ricochet (**von** from); (b) (fig.) start back; (entsetzt) recoil; ∼|**reichen 1** *tr. V.* hand back; **2** *itr. V.* go back; ∼|**rufen** *unr. tr. V.* (a) call back; recall ⟨*ambassador*⟩; (b) *auch itr.* (anrufen) call *or* (Brit.) ring back; (c) jmdm./ sich etw. ins Gedächtnis *od.* in die Erinnerung ∼rufen remind sb. of sth./call sth. to mind; (d) (als Antwort, nach hinten rufen) call *or* shout back; (e) (Wirtsch.) recall ⟨*defective goods, car, etc.*⟩; ∼|**schalten** *itr. V.* (in kleineren Gang schalten) change down; ∼|**schaudern** *itr. V.; mit sein* shrink back (**vor** + *Dat.* from); ∼|**schauen** *itr. V.* (bes. südd., österr., schweiz.) ⇒ ∼**blicken**; ∼|**scheuen** *itr. V.; mit sein* ⇒ ∼**schrecken²**; ∼|**schicken** *tr. V.* send back; ∼|**schieben** *unr. tr. V.* (a) push back; draw back ⟨*bolt, curtains*⟩; (b) (nach hinten schieben) push back[wards]; ∼|**schlagen 1** *unr. tr. V.* (a) (nach hinten schlagen) fold back ⟨*cover, hood, etc.*⟩; (zur Seite schlagen) pull *or* draw back ⟨*curtains*⟩; (b) (durch einen Schlag zurückbefördern) hit back; (mit dem Fuß) kick back; (c) (zum Rückzug zwingen, abwehren) beat off, repulse ⟨*enemy, attack*⟩; **2** *unr. itr. V.* (a) hit back; ⟨*enemy*⟩ strike back, retaliate; (b) *mit sein* ⟨*pendulum*⟩ swing back; ⟨*starting-handle*⟩ kick back; (c) auf etw. (*Akk.*) ∼schlagen (fig.) have repercussions on sth.; ∼|**schrecken¹** *tr. V.* jmdn. ∼schrecken deter sb.; ∼|**schrecken²** *regelm., veralt. unr. itr. V.; mit sein* (a) shrink back; recoil; (b) vor etw. (*Dat.*) ∼schrecken (fig.) shrink from sth.; er schreckt vor nichts ∼: he will stop at nothing; ∼|**sehnen** *refl. V.; sich zu jmdm./nach Italien ∼sehnen* long to be back with sb./in Italy; ∼|**senden** *unr. od. regelm. tr. V.* (geh.) ⇒ ∼**schicken**; ∼|**setzen 1** *tr. V.* (a) put back; (b) (nach hinten setzen) move back; (c) (zurückfahren) move back; reverse; back; (d) (fig.) jmdn. ∼setzen neglect sb.; sich ∼gesetzt fühlen feel neglected; **2** *refl. V.* (a) sit down again (**an** + *Akk.* at); (b) (sich nach hinten setzen) move back; **3** *itr. V.* (zurückfahren) move back[wards]; reverse; back; ∼**setzung** *die;* ∼, ∼**en** neglect; (Kränkung) insult, slight; ∼|**stecken 1** *tr. V.* (a) put back; (b) (nach hinten stecken) move back; **2** *itr. V.* (ugs.) lower one's sights; ∼|**stehen** *unr. itr. V.* (a) stand back; be set back; (fig.: übertroffen werden) be left behind; hinter jmdm. ∼stehen take second place to sb.; (c) (fig.: verzichten) miss out; ∼|**stellen** *tr. V.* (a) put back; (b) (nach hinten stellen) move back; (c) (niedriger einstellen) turn down ⟨*heating*⟩; put back ⟨*clock*⟩; (d) (reservieren) put aside, keep ⟨*Dat.*, **für** for⟩; (e) jmdn. vom Wehrdienst ∼stellen defer sb.'s military service; defer sb. (Amer.); (f) (aufschieben) postpone; defer; (g) (hintanstellen) put aside ⟨*reservations, doubts, etc.*⟩; ∼|**stoßen 1** *unr. tr. V.* (a) push back; (b) (von sich stoßen) push away; **2** *unr. itr. V.; mit sein* ⇒ ∼**setzen 3**; ∼|**treten** *unr. itr. V.* (a) *mit sein* step back; bitte von der Bahnsteigkante ∼treten please stand back from the edge of the platform; (b) *mit sein* (von einem Amt) resign; step down; ⟨*government*⟩ resign; als Vorsitzender/von einem Amt ∼treten step down as chairman/resign from an office; (c) *mit sein* (von einem Vertrag usw.) withdraw (**von** from); back out (**von** of); (d) *mit sein* (fig.: in den Hintergrund treten) become less important; fade in importance; hinter/ gegenüber etw. (*Dat.*) ∼treten take second place to sth.; ∼|**verlangen** *tr. V.* demand back; ∼|**versetzen 1** *tr. V.* (a) move or transfer back; (b) (fig.) take or transport back; **2** *refl. V.* think oneself back (**in** + *Akk.* to); ∼|**weichen** *unr. itr. V.; mit sein* draw back (**vor** + *Dat.* from); back away (**vor** + *Dat.* from); er wich keinen Schritt/Zentimeter ∼: he stood his ground; ∼|**weisen** *unr. tr. V.* (a) send back; (b) (abweisen, nicht akzeptieren) reject ⟨*proposal, question, demand, application, etc.*⟩; turn down, refuse ⟨*offer, request, invitation, help, etc.*⟩; turn away ⟨*petitioner, unwelcome guest*⟩; (c) (sich verwahren gegen) repudiate ⟨*accusation, claim, etc.*⟩; ∼**weisung** *die* ⇒ ∼**weisen**: sending back; rejection; turning down; refusal; turning away; repudiation; ∼|**werfen 1** *unr. tr. V.* (a) throw back; den Kopf/sein Haar ∼werfen throw *or* toss one's head back/toss one's hair back; (b) (reflektieren) reflect ⟨*light,*

sound⟩; (c) (Milit.) repulse ⟨*enemy*⟩; (d) (fig.: in einer Entwicklung) set back; **2** *unr. refl. V.* throw oneself back; ∼|**wollen 1** *unr. itr. V.* want to go back; **2** *unr. tr. V.* (ugs.) etw. ∼wollen want sth. back; ∼|**zahlen** *tr. V.* pay back; ∼|**ziehen 1** *unr. tr. V.* (a) pull back; draw back ⟨*bolt, curtains, one's hand, etc.*⟩; es zieht ihn in die Heimat/zu ihr ∼ (fig.) he is drawn back to his homeland/to her; (b) (abziehen, zurückbeordern) withdraw, pull back ⟨*troops*⟩; withdraw, recall ⟨*ambassador*⟩; (c) (rückgängig machen) withdraw; cancel ⟨*order, instruction*⟩; (d) (wieder aus dem Verkehr ziehen) withdraw ⟨*coin, stamp, etc.*⟩; **2** *unr. refl. V.* withdraw (**aus, von** from); ⟨*troops*⟩ withdraw, pull back; sich aufs Land/in sein Zimmer ∼: retreat to the country/retire to one's room; *s. auch* **zurückgezogen**; **3** *unr. itr. V.; mit sein* go back; return; ∼|**zucken** *itr. V.; mit sein* flinch; (erschrocken) start back; mit der Hand ∼zucken jerk one's hand away

Zu·ruf *der* shout

zu|rufen *unr. tr. V.* jmdm. etw. ∼: shout sth. to sb.

zur·zeit *Adv.* at the moment; at present

Zu·sage *die* (a) (auf eine Einladung hin) acceptance; (auf eine Stellenbewerbung hin) offer; (b) (Versprechen) promise; undertaking; jmdm. die *od.* seine ∼ geben, etw. zu tun promise sb. that one will do sth.

zu|sagen 1 *itr. V.* (a) (auf eine Einladung hin) [jmdm.] ∼/ fest ∼: accept/give sb. a firm acceptance; (b) (auf ein Angebot hin) accept; (c) (gefallen) jmdm. ∼: appeal to sb. **2** *tr. V.* (a) promise; jmdm. etw. ∼: promise sb. sth.; (b) *s. auch* **Kopf a**

zusammen /tsu'zaman/ *Adv.* together; ∼ sein (zusammenleben) be *or* live together; wir bestellten uns ∼ eine Flasche Wein we ordered a bottle of wine between us; ihr seid alle ∼ Feiglinge! (ugs.) you're cowards, the whole lot of you (coll.); er verdient mehr als alle anderen ∼: he earns more than the rest of them put together

zusammen-, Zusammen-: ∼**arbeit** *die; o. Pl.* cooperation *no indef. art.;* ∼|**arbeiten** *itr. V.* cooperate; work together; (kollaborieren) collaborate; ∼|**ballen** *tr. V.* [zu einem Klumpen] ∼ballen make into a ball; **2** *refl. V.* mass together; ∼|**beißen** *unr. tr. V.* die Zähne ∼beißen clench one's teeth together; *s. auch* **Zahn b**; ∼|**bekommen** *unr. tr. V.* (a) get together, raise ⟨*money, rent, etc.*⟩; manage to collect ⟨*signatures*⟩; (b) (zusammengesetzt/∼gebaut usw. bekommen) get together; (c) (fig. ugs.) remember; ∼|**binden** *unr. tr. V.* tie together; ∼|**bleiben** *unr. itr. V.; mit sein* stay together; ∼|**brauen 1** *tr. V.* (ugs.) concoct ⟨*drink*⟩; **2** *refl. V.* (fig.) ⟨*storm, bad weather, trouble, etc.*⟩ be brewing; ⟨*disaster*⟩ loom; da braut sich was ∼: there's something brewing there; ∼|**brechen** *unr. itr. V.; mit sein* (a) (einstürzen) collapse; (b) (zu Boden sinken) ⟨*person, animal*⟩ collapse; (fig.) ⟨*person*⟩ break down; (c) (fig.) collapse; ⟨*order, communications, system, telephone network*⟩ break down; ⟨*traffic*⟩ come to a standstill, be paralysed; ⟨*attack, front, resistance*⟩ crumble; ∼|**bringen** *unr. tr. V.* bring together; jmdn. mit jmdm. ∼bringen bring sb. together with sb.; ∼**bruch** *der* (a) (eines Menschen) collapse; (psychisch, nervlich) breakdown; dem ∼bruch nahe sein be near to collapse/breakdown; (b) (fig.) ⇒ ∼**brechen c:** collapse; breakdown; crumbling; ∼|**drängen 1** *tr. V.* push together; herd ⟨*crowd*⟩ together; **2** *refl. V.* crowd together; (fig.) be concentrated (**auf** + *Akk.* into); ∼|**drücken** *tr. V.* press together; (komprimieren) compress ⟨*gas*⟩; (b) (zerdrücken) crush; ∼|**fahren** *unr. itr. V.; mit sein* (a) collide (**mit** with); (b) (∼zucken) start; jump; ∼**fall** *der* coincidence; ∼|**fallen** *unr. itr. V.; mit sein* (a) collapse; das ganze Lügengebäude fiel in sich ∼ (fig.) the whole tissue of lies fell apart; (b) (∼sinken, schrumpfen) [in sich] ∼fallen ⟨*cake*⟩ sink [in the middle]; ⟨*froth, foam, balloon, etc.*⟩ collapse; (c) ⟨*person*⟩ become emaciated; (d) (zeitlich) [zeitlich] ∼fallen coincide; fall at the same time; (e) (räumlich) coincide; ∼|**falten** *tr. V.* fold up; ∼|**fassen** *tr. V.* (a) put together; (b) (in eine kurze Form bringen) summarize; etw. in einem Satz ∼fassen sum sth. up *or* summarize sth. in one sentence; ∼fassend kann man sagen ...: to sum up *or* in summary, one can say ...; ∼**fassung** *die* ⇒ ∼**fassen**: putting together; summary; ∼|**fegen** *tr. V.*

(bes. nordd.) sweep together; ~|**finden** unr. refl. V. (a) get together; (b) (zusammentreffen) meet up; ~|**flicken** tr. V. patch up; ~|**fließen** unr. itr. V.; mit sein ‹rivers, streams› flow into each other, join up; (fig.) ‹colours› run together; ‹sounds› blend together; ~**fluss** der ► 193 ┘ confluence; ~**fügen** 1 tr. V. fit together; 2 refl. V. fit together; ~**führen** tr. V. bring together; **getrennte Familien wieder ~führen** reunite divided families; ~|**gehen** unr. itr. V.; mit sein (a) (sich verbünden, sich zusammentun) join forces (mit with); (fusionieren) ‹firms› merge; (b) (zusammenpassen) go together; (c) (ugs.: zusammenlaufen, ~fließen usw.) join up; meet; (d) (ugs.: sich zusammenfügen, verbinden lassen) fit together; meet; ~|**gehören** itr. V. belong together; ~**gehörig** Adj. [closely] related or connected ‹subjects, problems, etc.›; matching attrib. ‹pieces of tea service, cutlery, etc.›; **die ~gehörigen Teile** the parts which belong together; ~**gehörigkeits·gefühl** das; o. Pl. sense or feeling of belonging together; ~**genommen** Adj.; nicht attr. **alle diese Dinge ~genommen** all these things together; ~**gewürfelt** Adj. oddly assorted; **ein bunt ~gewürfelter Haufen** a motley collection of people; ~**halt** der; o. Pl. cohesion; ~|**halten** 1 unr. tr. V. (a) hold together; (b) (beisammenhalten) keep together; **sein Geld ~halten** be careful with one's money; 2 unr. itr. V. (a) hold together; (b) (fig.) ‹friends, family, etc.› stick together; ~**hang** der connection; (einer Geschichte, Rede) coherence; (Kontext) context; **in [keinem] ~hang mit etw. stehen** be [in no way] connected with sth.; **etw. mit etw. in ~hang bringen** connect sth. with sth.; make a connection between sth. and sth.; **im ~hang mit ...:** in connection with ...; **etw. aus dem ~hang lösen/reißen** take sth. out of [its] context; ~|**hängen** unr. itr. V. (a) be joined [together]; **in ~hängenden Sätzen** in coherent sentences; (b) (fig.) **mit etw. ~hängen** (zu etw. eine Beziehung haben) be related to sth.; (durch etw. [mit] verursacht sein) be the result of sth.; **das hängt damit ~, dass ...:** that is connected with or has to do with the fact that ...; ~**hang·los** 1 Adj. incoherent, disjointed ‹speech, story, etc.›; 2 adv. ‹speak› incoherently; ~|**kehren** tr. V. (bes. südd.) ⇒ ~**fegen**; ~**klappbar** Adj. folding; ~**klappbar sein** fold up; ~|**klappen** 1 tr. V. fold up; 2 itr. V.; mit sein (ugs.) collapse; ~|**kleben** tr., itr. V. stick together; ~|**kneifen** unr. tr. V. press ‹lips› together; screw ‹eyes› up; ~|**knüllen** tr. V. crumple up; (fest) screw up; ~|**kommen** unr. itr. V.; mit sein (a) meet; **mit jmdm. ~kommen** meet sb.; (b) (zueinander kommen; auch fig.) get together; (c) (gleichzeitig auftreten) occur or happen together; (d) (sich summieren) accumulate; **da werden schon so an die 50 Leute ~kommen** there are sure to be getting on for 50 people there altogether; ~|**koppeln** tr. V. couple together; dock ‹spacecraft›; ~|**kriegen** tr. V. (ugs.) ⇒ ~**bekommen**; ~|**krümmen** refl. V. double up; writhe; ~**kunft** /-kʊnft/ die; ~, ~**künfte** /-kʏnftə/ meeting; ~|**laufen** unr. itr. V.; mit sein (a) ‹people, crowd› gather, congregate; (b) ‹rivers, streams› flow into each other, join up; (c) ‹water, oil, etc.› collect; (d) ‹colours› run together; ~|**leben** itr. V. live together; ~**leben** das; o. Pl. living together no art.; ~|**legen** 1 tr. V. (a) put or gather together; (b) (zusammenfalten) fold [up]; (c) amalgamate, merge ‹classes, departments, etc.›; combine ‹events›; (d) put ‹patients, guests, etc.› together [in the same room]; 2 itr. V. club together; pool our/your/their money; ~|**nähen** tr. V. sew together; **etw. mit etw. ~nähen** sew sth. to sth.; (b) (reparieren) sew up; ~|**nehmen** 1 unr. tr. V. summon or muster up ‹courage, strength, understanding›; collect ‹wits›; s. auch ~**genommen**; 2 unr. refl. V. get or take a grip on oneself; **nimm dich ~!** pull yourself together!; ~|**packen** 1 tr. V. pack up; (zusammen verpacken) pack up together; 2 itr. V. pack up; ~|**passen** itr. V. go together; ‹persons› be suited to each other; **mit etw. ~passen** go with sth.; ~**prall** der; ~**prall[e]s**, ~**pralle** collision; (fig.) clash; ~|**prallen** itr. V.; mit sein collide (mit with); (fig.) clash; ~|**pressen** tr. V. (a) squeeze; (b) (aneinander pressen) press ‹lips, hands› together; ~|**raffen** tr. V. gather up ‹possessions, papers, etc.›; bundle up ‹clothes›; ~|**rechnen** tr. V. add up; **etw.**

mit etw. ~rechnen add sth. to sth.; ~|**reißen** unr. refl. V. (ugs.) ⇒ ~|**nehmen** 2; ~|**rollen** 1 tr. V. roll up; 2 refl. V. ‹cat, dog, etc.› curl up; ‹hedgehog› roll [itself] up [into a ball]; ~|**rotten** refl. V. (abwertend) ‹crowds, groups, etc.› band together; ‹youths› gang together or up; (in Aufruhr) form a mob; ~|**rücken** 1 tr. V. move ‹chairs, tables, etc.› together; 2 itr. V.; mit sein (auch fig.) move closer together; ~|**rufen** unr. tr. V. call together; ~|**sacken** itr. V.; mit sein (ugs.) collapse; ~|**schlagen** 1 tr. V. (a) strike or bang together; clap ‹hands› [together]; **die Hacken ~schlagen** click one's heels; (b) (verprügeln) beat up; (c) (zertrümmern) smash up or to pieces; (d) (zusammenfalten) fold up; 2 unr. itr. V.; mit sein **über jmdm./etw. ~schlagen** (fig.) engulf sb./sth.; ~|**schluss**, *~**schluß** der joining together; union; (von Firmen) merger; amalgamation; ~|**schnüren** tr. V. (a) tie up (zu in); (b) (einschnüren) lace in ‹waist›; ~|**schreiben** unr. tr. V. (a) write together; (b) (abwertend: verfassen) dash off ‹report, letter, etc.›; ~|**schrumpfen** itr. V.; mit sein shrivel [up]; (fig.) dwindle; *~|**sein** ⇒ zusammen; ~**sein** das (a) being together no art.; (b) (Treffen) get-together; ~|**setzen** 1 tr. V. (a) put together; (b) (herstellen) make; **ein ~gesetztes Wort/Verb** a compound word/verb; (c) (zusammenbauen, -montieren) assemble; put together; (d) (beieinander sitzen lassen) seat or put together; **jmdn. mit jmdm. ~setzen** seat or put sb. next to sb.; 2 refl. V. (a) sit together; (zu einem Gespräch) get together; (b) **sich aus etw. ~setzen** be made up or composed of sth.; ~**setzung** die; ~, ~**en** (a) (Aufbau) composition; „~setzung: ...“ (als Aufschrift auf Medikamentenpackung) 'ingredients: ...'; (b) (Sprachw.) compound; ~|**sitzen** unr. itr. V. sit together; ~|**spielen** itr. V. play together; ‹actors› act together; **mit jmdm. ~spielen** play/act with sb.; ~|**stehen** unr. itr. V. (a) stand together; **mit jmdm. ~stehen** stand with sb.; (b) (fig.: zusammenhalten) stand by one another; ~|**stellen** 1 tr. V. (a) put together; (b) (aus Teilen gestalten) put together ‹programme, film, book, menu, exhibition, team, delegation›; draw up ‹list, timetable›; compile ‹report, broadcast›; work out ‹route, tour›; make up ‹flower arrangement›; (c) (in einer Übersicht, Liste usw.) draw together; compile ‹facts, data›; (d) (kombinieren) combine; 2 refl. V. stand together; ~**stellung** die (a) ⇒ ~**stellen** 1 b: putting together; drawing up; compilation; working out; making up; (b) (Übersicht) survey; (von Tatsachen, Daten) compilation; (c) (Kombination) combination; ~**stoß** der collision; (fig.) clash (mit with); **bei dem ~stoß [der beiden Züge]** in the collision [between the two trains]; ~|**stoßen** unr. itr. V.; mit sein collide (mit with); **wir stießen mit den Köpfen ~:** we banged or bumped our heads; ~|**strömen** itr. V.; mit sein (fig.) ‹people› congregate; ~|**stürzen** itr. V.; mit sein collapse; ~|**suchen** tr. V. collect bit by bit; hunt out ‹information› bit by bit; ~|**tragen** unr. tr. V. collect; ~|**treffen** unr. itr. V.; mit sein (a) meet; **mit jmdm. ~treffen** meet sb.; (b) (zeitlich) coincide; ~|**tun** (ugs.) 1 unr. tr. V. put together; 2 unr. refl. V. get together; ~|**zählen** tr. V. add up; ~|**ziehen** 1 unr. tr. V. (a) draw or pull together; draw or pull ‹noose, net› tight; (b) (konzentrieren) mass ‹troops, police›; 2 unr. refl. V. contract; 3 unr. itr. V.; mit sein move in with sb.; **mit jmdm. ~ziehen** move in with sb.; ~|**zucken** itr. V.; mit sein start; jump

Zu·satz der (a) addition; **ohne ~ von ...:** without the addition of ...; without adding ...; (b) (Additiv) additive

Zusatz·bremsleuchte die (Kfz-W.) high-level brake light

zusätzlich /ˈtsuːzɛtslɪç/ 1 Adj. additional; 2 adv. in addition

zu·schanden Adv. **etw. ~ machen** wreck or ruin sth.; **~ werden** be wrecked or ruined

zu|schanzen tr. V. (ugs.) **jmdm./sich etw. ~:** wangle sth. for sb./oneself (coll.)

zu|schauen tr. V. (südd., österr., schweiz.) ⇒ **zusehen**

Zu·schauer der, **Zu·schauerin** die; ~, ~**nen** spectator; (im Theater, Kino) member of the audience; (an einer Unfallstelle) onlooker; (Fernseh~) viewer; **die ~:** the spectators; the crowd sing./the audience sing./the onlookers/the audience sing.; the viewers

---

zu|schaufeln *tr. V.* fill in [with a shovel/shovels]

zu|schicken *tr. V.* jmdm. etw. ~: send sth. to sb.; send sb. sth.

zu|schieben *unr. tr. V.* (a) push ⟨*drawer, door*⟩ shut; **den Riegel** ~: put the bolt across; (b) jmdm. die Schuld/Verantwortung ~ (fig.) lay the blame/responsibility on sb.

zu|schießen 1 *unr. tr. V.* (als Zuschuss geben) contribute (**zu** towards). 2 *unr. itr. V.; mit sein* **auf jmdn./etw. zugeschossen kommen** come shooting towards sb.

Zu·schlag *der* (a) additional *or* extra charge; (auf Entgelt) additional *or* extra payment; (auf Fahrpreis) supplement; (b) (Eisenb.: Fahrschein) supplement ticket; (c) (bei einer Versteigerung) acceptance of a/the bid; (d) (bei Ausschreibung eines Auftrags) acceptance of a/the tender; **den ~ bekommen** get the contract

zu|schlagen 1 *unr. tr. V.* bang or slam ⟨*door, window, etc.*⟩ shut; close ⟨*book*⟩; (heftig) slam ⟨*book*⟩ shut. 2 *unr. itr. V.* (a) *mit sein* ⟨*door, trap*⟩ slam *or* bang shut; (b) (einen Schlag führen) throw a blow/blows; (losschlagen) hit *or* strike out; (fig.) ⟨*army, police, murderer*⟩ strike; **schlag doch zu!** [go on,] hit it/me/him *etc.!*

zuschlag·pflichtig /-ˈpflɪçtɪç/ *Adj.* (Eisenb.) ⟨*train*⟩ on which a supplement is payable

zu|schließen 1 *unr. tr. V.* lock. 2 *unr. itr. V.* lock up

zu|schnappen *itr. V.* (a) *mit sein* snap shut; (b) (zubeißen) snap

zu|schneiden *unr. tr. V.* cut out ⟨*material, dress, jacket, etc.*⟩; saw ⟨*plank, slat*⟩ to size; **auf jmdn./etw. zugeschnitten sein** (fig.) be tailor-made for sb./sth.

Zu·schnitt *der* (a) cut; (b) *o. Pl.* (das Zuschneiden) cutting [out]; (c) (fig.: Format) calibre

zu|schnüren *tr. V.* tie up; tie *or* do ⟨*shoes*⟩ up

zu|schrauben *tr. V.* screw the lid *or* top on ⟨*jar, flask*⟩; screw ⟨*lid, top*⟩ on

zu|schreiben *unr. tr. V.* (a) jmdm./einem Umstand etw. ~: attribute sth. to sb./a circumstance; **jmdm. das Verdienst/die Schuld an etw. (*Dat.*) ~:** credit sb. with/ blame sb. for sth.; **das hast du dir selbst zuzuschreiben** you only have yourself to blame [for this]

Zu·schrift *die* letter; (auf eine Anzeige) reply

zu·schulden *Adv.* sich (*Dat.*) etwas ~ kommen lassen do wrong

Zu·schuss, *Zu·schuß *der* contribution (**zu** towards); (regelmäßiger ~) allowance; [staatlicher] ~: state subsidy (**für, zu** towards)

zu|sehen *unr. itr. V.* (a) watch; **jmdm. beim Arbeiten** *usw.* ~: watch sb. working *etc.;* **vom [bloßen] Zusehen** [simply] by watching; (b) (dafür sorgen) make sure; see to it; **sieh zu, dass ...:** see that ...; make sure that ...; **er soll ~, wie er das hinkriegt** he'll just have to manage somehow; **sieh zu, wo du bleibst!** you're on your own!

zusehends /ˈtsuːzeːənts/ *Adv.* visibly

***zu·sein** ⇒ zu 2 c

zu|senden *unr. od. regelm. tr. V.* ⇒ **zuschicken**

Zu·sendung *die* sending

zu|setzen 1 *tr. V.* (a) einem Stoff etw. ~: add sth. to a substance; (b) (zuzahlen) pay out. 2 *itr. V.* (ugs.) **jmdm. ~:** (jmdn. angreifen) go for sb.; (jmdn. bedrängen) pester *or* badger sb.; ⟨*mosquitoes etc.*⟩ plague sb.; ⟨*illness, heat*⟩ take a lot out of sb.; **einer Sache (*Dat.*) ~** (etw. beschädigen) damage sth.

zu|sichern *tr. V.* jmdm. etw. ~: promise sb. sth.; assure sb. of sth.

Zu·sicherung *die* promise; assurance

Zu·spiel *das; o. Pl.* (Ballspiele) passing; (einzelner Spielzug) pass

zu|spielen *tr. V.* (a) jmdm. den Ball ~: pass the ball to sb.; (b) der Presse Informationen ~ (fig.) leak information to the press

zu|spitzen 1 *tr. V.* (a) sharpen to a point; (b) (fig.) aggravate ⟨*position, crisis*⟩; intensify ⟨*competition, conflict, etc.*⟩; (c) (fig.) make ⟨*question, answer*⟩ pointed. 2 *refl. V.* become aggravated

Zu·spitzung *die;* ~, ~en (fig.) ⇒ **zuspitzen b:** aggravation; intensification

zu|sprechen *unr. tr. V.* (a) **er sprach ihr Trost/Mut zu** his words gave her comfort/courage; (b) jmdm. ein Erbe *usw.* ~: award sb. an inheritance *etc.*

Zu·spruch *der; o. Pl.* [bei jmdm.] ~ finden (geh.) be popular [with sb.]

Zu·stand *der* (a) condition; (bes. abwertend) state; **in flüssigem ~:** in liquid form; **in betrunkenem ~:** while under the influence of alcohol; **geistiger/gesundheitlicher ~:** state of mind/health; **der ~ des Patienten** the patient's condition; **Zustände kriegen** (ugs.) have a fit (coll.); (b) (Stand der Dinge) state of affairs; situation; **das sind ja [schöne] Zustände!** that's a fine state of affairs!; these are fine goings-on!; **das ist doch kein ~!** that just won't do (coll.); *s. auch* **Rom**

zu·stande *Adv.* etw. ~ **bringen** [manage to] bring about sth.; ~ **kommen** come into being; (geschehen) take place

zu·ständig *Adj.* appropriate, proper, relevant ⟨*authority, office, etc.*⟩; **von ~er Seite** by the proper authority; [**für etw.**] **sein** (verantwortlich) be responsible [for sth.]; (kompetent) be competent [to deal with sth.]; ⟨*court*⟩ have jurisdiction [in sth.]

Zuständigkeit *die;* ~, ~en (Verantwortlichkeit) responsibility; (Kompetenz) competence; (eines Gerichts) jurisdiction

zu·statten *Adv.* jmdm./einer Sache ~ **kommen** be a help *or* be useful to sb./for sth.; (von Vorteil sein) be of advantage to sb./sth.

zu|stecken *tr. V.* jmdm. etw. ~: slip sb. sth.

zu|stehen *unr. itr. V.* etw. steht jmdm. zu sb. is entitled to sth.; **ein Urteil über ihn steht mir nicht zu** it is not for me to judge him

zu|steigen *unr. itr. V.; mit sein* get on; **ist noch jemand zugestiegen?** (im Bus) any more fares, please?; (im Zug) ≈ tickets, please!

zu|stellen *tr. V.* (a) block ⟨*entrance, passage, etc.*⟩; (b) (bringen) deliver ⟨*letter, parcel, etc.*⟩; **jmdm. etw. ~:** deliver sth. to sb.

Zu·stellung *die* delivery

zu|steuern 1 *itr. V.; mit sein* **auf jmdn./etw. ~:** head for sb./sth. 2 *tr. V.* etw. **auf jmdn./etw. ~:** steer *or* drive sth. towards sb./sth.

zu|stimmen *itr. V.* agree; jmdm. [in einem Punkt] ~: agree with sb. [on a point]; **dem kann ich nur ~:** I quite agree

Zu·stimmung *die* (Billigung) approval (**zu** of); (Einverständnis) agreement (**zu** to, with); ~ **finden** meet with approval; **jmdm. seine ~ zu etw. geben** give sb. one's consent to *or* for sth.

zu|stopfen *tr. V.* (a) plug, stop up; plug ⟨*ears*⟩; (b) (mit Nadel und Faden) darn, mend ⟨*hole*⟩

zu|stöpseln *tr. V.* (a) put a stopper in ⟨*bottle*⟩; (mit Korken) put a cork in, cork ⟨*bottle*⟩; (b) put a plug in ⟨*basin*⟩; plug ⟨*drain etc.*⟩

zu|stoßen 1 *unr. tr. V.* push ⟨*door etc.*⟩ shut. 2 *unr. itr. V.* (a) strike out; ⟨*snake etc.*⟩ strike; (mit einem Messer *usw.*) make a stab; stab; (b) *mit sein* jmdm. ~: happen to sb.

zu|streben *itr. V.; mit sein* einer Sache (*Dat.*) *od.* auf etw. (*Akk.*) ~: make for sth.; (fig.) strive for *or* aim at sth.

Zu·strom *der* (a) (auch fig.) flow; (b) (von Menschen) influx; stream

zu|tage *Adv.* ~ **kommen** *od.* **treten** become visible (lit. or fig.); ⟨*stream*⟩ come to the surface; (fig.) become evident; ⟨*story*⟩ come out, be made public; ⟨*differences etc.*⟩ come into the open; **etw. ~ bringen** *od.* **fördern** (aus der Tasche *usw.*) produce sth.; (fig.) bring sth. to light; reveal sth.; **offen ~ liegen** be perfectly clear *or* evident

Zu·tat *die* ingredient

zu·teil *Adv.* (geh.) **jmdm./einer Sache ~ werden** be granted *or* accorded to sb./sth.; **jmdm. etw. ~ werden lassen** accord sb. sth.; bestow sth. on sb.

zu|teilen *tr. V.* allot, assign (*Dat.* to); **jmdm. seine Portion ~:** mete out his/her share to sb.; **die zugeteilte Menge** the allocated amount

Zu·teilung *die* **(a)** allotting, assigning; (einer Ration) sharing out, allocation; (eines Mandats, Quartiers) allocation, assignment; **(b)** (Ration) allocation, ration

zu·tiefst *Adv.* profoundly; ~ **verletzt** deeply hurt *or* offended

zu|tragen *unr. refl. V.* (geh.) take place; occur

zuträglich /ˈtsuːtrɛːklɪç/ *Adj.* healthy ‹*climate*›; **jmdm./einer Sache** ~ **sein** be good for sb./sth.; be beneficial to sb./sth.

zu|trauen *tr. V.* **jmdm. etw.** ~: believe sb. [is] capable of [doing] sth.; **den Mut hätte ich ihm gar nicht zugetraut** I should never have thought he had the courage; **ich hätte ihm mehr Taktgefühl zugetraut** I should have thought he had more tact; **das ist ihm [durchaus] zuzutrauen** I could [well] believe it of him; **sich** (*Dat.*) **etw.** ~: think one can do *or* is capable of doing sth.; **er traut sich** (*Dat.*) **zu wenig zu** he has too little self-confidence

Zutrauen *das;* ~**s** confidence, trust (**zu** in)

zutraulich **1** *Adj.* trusting; trustful. **2** *adv.* trustingly; trustfully

Zutraulichkeit *die;* ~: trust[fulness]

zu|treffen *unr. itr. V.* **(a)** be correct; **(b) auf etw.** ~: apply to sth.

zutreffend **1** *Adj.* **(a)** correct; (treffend) accurate; **es ist** ~, **dass** …: it is correct *or* the case that …; **(b)** (geltend) applicable; relevant; **Zutreffendes bitte ankreuzen** please mark with a cross where applicable. **2** *adv.* correctly; (treffend) accurately

zu|trinken *unr. itr. V.* **jmdm.** ~: raise one's glass and drink to sb.

Zu·tritt *der* entry; admittance; „**kein** ~", „~ **verboten**" 'no entry'; 'no admittance'; ~ **[zu etw.] haben** have access [to sth.]

zu|tun *unr. tr. V.* **kein Auge** ~: not sleep a wink

Zu·tun *das;* ~**s: ohne jmds.** ~: without sb.'s being involved; **es geschah ohne mein** ~ I had nothing to do with it

zu·ungunsten *Präp. mit Gen.* to the disadvantage of

zu·unterst *Adv.* right at the bottom; *s. auch* **ober**… a

zuverlässig /ˈtsuːfɛɐlɛsɪç/ **1** *Adj.* reliable; (verlässlich) dependable ‹*person*›. **2** *adv.* **(a)** reliably; **er arbeitet sehr** ~: he is a very reliable worker; **(b)** (mit Gewissheit) ‹*confirm*› with certainty; ‹*know*› for sure, for certain

Zuverlässigkeit *die;* ~: reliability; (Verlässlichkeit) dependability

Zuversicht /ˈtsuːfɛɐzɪçt/ *die;* ~: confidence

zuversichtlich **1** *Adj.* confident; **sich** ~ **geben** express one's confidence. **2** *adv.* confidently

Zuversichtlichkeit *die;* ~: confidence

***zuviel** ⇨ **viel**; **kriegen 1 a**; **sagen 1 c**

zu·vor *Adv.* before; **tags/im Jahr** ~: the day/year before

zuvor|kommen *unr. itr. V.; mit sein* **(a) jmdm.** ~: beat sb. to it; get there first; **(b) einer Sache** (*Dat.*) ~: anticipate *or* forestall sth.

zuvorkommend **1** *Adj.* obliging; (höflich) courteous. **2** *adv.* obligingly; (höflich) courteously

Zuvorkommenheit *die;* ~: courteousness; courtesy

Zu·wachs *der;* ~**es, Zuwächse** /-vɛksə/ increase

zu|wachsen *unr. itr. V.; mit sein* become overgrown

Zu·wanderer *der* immigrant

zu|wandern *itr. V.; mit sein* immigrate

Zu·wanderung *die* immigration

zu|warten *itr. V.* wait

zu·wege *Adv.* **etw.** ~ **bringen** [manage to] achieve sth.

zu·weilen *Adv.* (geh.) now and again; at times

zu|weisen *unr. tr. V.* **jmdm. etw.** ~: allocate *or* allot sb. sth.

zu|wenden **1** *unr. od. regelm. refl. V.* **sich jmdm./einer Sache** ~ (auch fig.) turn to sb./sth.; (sich widmen) devote oneself to sb./sth.. **2** *unr. od. regelm. tr. V.* **(a) jmdm./einer Sache etw.** ~: turn sth. to[wards] sb./sth.; **jmdm. den**

Rücken ~: turn one's back on sb.; **(b) jmdm. Geld** ~ (geh.) give *or* donate money to sb.

Zu·wendung *die* **(a)** *o. Pl.* (Aufmerksamkeit) [loving] attention *or* care; **(b)** (Geldgeschenk) gift of money; (Unterstützung) [financial] contribution; (Geldspende) donation

***zu·wenig** ⇨ **wenig**; **viel**

zuwider *Adj.* **jmdm.** ~ **sein** be repugnant to sb.; **Spinat ist mir äußerst** ~: I absolutely detest spinach

zuwider-: ~**|handeln** *itr. V.* **dem Gesetz/einer Vorschrift** *usw.* ~**handeln** contravene *or* infringe the law/a regulation *etc.;* **einer Anordnung/einem Verbot** ~**handeln** defy an instruction/a ban; ~**|laufen** *unr. itr. V.; mit sein* **einer Sache** (*Dat.*) ~**laufen** go against *or* run counter to sth.

zu|winken *itr. V.* **jmdm.** ~: wave to sb.

zu|zahlen *tr. V.* pay ‹*five marks etc.*› extra; **einen Betrag** ~: pay an additional sum

zu|ziehen **1** *unr. tr. V.* **(a)** pull ‹*door*› shut; draw ‹*curtain*›; pull *or* draw ‹*knot, net*› tight; do up ‹*zip*›; **(b)** call in ‹*expert, specialist*›. **2** *unr. refl. V.* **(a) sich** (*Dat.*) **eine Krankheit/Infektion** ~: catch an illness/contract an infection; **sich** (*Dat.*) **einen Schädelbruch** ~: sustain a fracture of the skull; **sich** (*Dat.*) **jmds. Zorn** ~: incur sb.'s anger; **(b)** (sich schließen) ‹*knot, noose*› tighten, get tight. **3** *unr. itr. V.; mit sein* move here *or* into the area

Zu·zug *der* influx

zuzüglich /ˈtsuːtsyːklɪç/ *Präp. mit Gen.* plus

zu|zwinkern *itr. V.* **jmdm.** ~: wink at sb.

zwacken /ˈtsvakn̩/ *tr., auch itr. V.* (ugs.) ⇒ **zwicken**

zwang /tsvaŋ/ *1. u. 3. Pers. Sg. Prät. v.* **zwingen**

Zwang *der;* ~**[e]s, Zwänge** /ˈtsvɛŋə/ *o. Pl.* compulsion; **auf jmdn.** ~ **ausüben** exert pressure on sb.; **der** ~ **der Verhältnisse** the force of circumstance[s]; **soziale Zwänge** social constraints; the constraints of society; **(b)** (innerer Drang) irresistible urge; **aus einem** ~ **[heraus] handeln** act under a compulsion *or* on an irresistible impulse; **(c)** *o. Pl.* (Verpflichtung) obligation; **es besteht kein** ~ **zur Teilnahme/zum Kauf** there is no obligation to take part/to buy anything

zwängen /ˈtsvɛŋən/ **1** *tr. V.* squeeze. **2** *refl. V.* squeeze [oneself]

zwanglos **1** *Adj.* **(a)** informal; casual, free and easy ‹*behaviour*›; **(b)** (unregelmäßig) haphazard ‹*arrangement*›. **2** *adv.* **(a)** informally; freely; **es ging dort ziemlich** ~ **zu** things were pretty free and easy there; **(b)** (unregelmäßig) haphazardly ‹*arranged*›

Zwanglosigkeit *die;* ~ **(a)** informality; **(b)** (Unregelmäßigkeit) haphazard *or* casual manner

zwangs-, Zwangs-: ~**lage** *die* predicament; ~**läufig** /~ˌlɔyfɪç/ **1** *Adj.* inevitable; **2** *adv.* inevitably; ~**maßnahme** *die* coercive measure; sanction; ~**versteigern** *tr. V.* (Rechtsw.) put up for compulsory auction; ~**versteigerung** *die* (Rechtsw.) [compulsory] auction

zwanzig /ˈtsvantsɪç/ *Kardinalz.* ▶ **22** |, ▶ **530** |, ▶ **600** | twenty; *s. auch* **achtzig**

zwanziger *indekl. Adj.; nicht präd.* **die** ~ **Jahre** the twenties; *s. auch* **achtziger**

Zwanziger¹ *der;* ~**s,** ~ **(a)** twenty-year-old; **(b)** (Geldschein) twenty-mark/franc/schilling *etc.* note

Zwanziger² *die;* ~, ~ (ugs.) twenty-pfennig/schilling *etc.* stamp

Zwanziger·jahre ▶ **119** | *Pl.* twenties *pl.*

zwanzig·jährig *Adj.* (20 Jahre alt) twenty-year-old *attrib.;* (20 Jahre dauernd) twenty-year *attrib.*

Zwanzig·mark·schein *der* ▶ **216** | twenty-mark note

zwanzigst … *Ordinalz.* ▶ **119** |, ▶ **600** | twentieth; *s. auch* **acht**…; **achtzigst**…

zwar /tsvaːɐ/ *Adv.* **(a)** admittedly; **ich weiß es** ~ **nicht genau, aber** …: I'm not absolutely sure [I admit,] but …; **(b)** *usw.* to be precise; **er ist Zahnarzt, und** ~ **ein guter** he is a dentist, and a good one at that

Zweck /tsvɛk/ *der;* ~**[e]s,** ~**e (a)** purpose; **zu diesem** ~: for this purpose; **was ist der** ~ **Ihrer Reise?** what is the purpose of your journey?; **seinen** ~ **erfüllen** serve its purpose; **Geld für einen guten/wohltätigen** ~:

money for a good cause/for a charity; **der ~ der Übung** (ugs.) the object or point of the exercise; **(b)** (Sinn) point; **es hat keinen/wenig ~ [, das zu tun]** it's pointless or there is no point/there is little or not much point [in doing that]; **ohne [jeden] Sinn und ~:** completely pointless

zweck-, Zweck-: **~bau** der; Pl. **~bauten** functional building; **~dienlich** Adj. appropriate; helpful, relevant ‹information etc.›; **~entfremden** tr. V. use for another purpose; (für den falschen Zweck) misuse; **~los** Adj. pointless; **~mäßig 1** Adj. appropriate; expedient ‹behaviour, action›; functional ‹building, fittings, furniture›; **2** adv. appropriately ‹arranged, clothed›; ‹act› expediently; ‹equip, furnish› functionally; **~mäßigkeit** die appropriateness; (einer Handlung) expediency; (eines Gebäudes) functionalism

zwecks Präp. mit Gen. (Papierd.) for the purpose of

zwei /tsvai/ Kardinalz. ▶ 22 ⏐, ▶ 530 ⏐, ▶ 600 ⏐ two; **wir ~:** we two; the two of us; **sie waren/kamen zu ~en** there were two of them/two of them came; **für ~ essen/arbeiten** eat enough for two/do the work of two people; **dazu gehören immer noch ~!** (ugs.) it takes two [to do that]!; s. auch **acht¹**

Zwei die; **~, ~en (a)** (Zahl) two; **(b)** (Schulnote) B; **eine ~ schreiben/ bekommen** get a B; **er hat die Prüfung mit ~ bestanden** he got a B in the examination; s. auch **Acht¹ a, d, e, g**

zwei-, Zwei-: **~bändig** Adj. two-volume; **~bettzimmer** das twin-bedded room; **~deutig** /-dɔʏtɪç/ **1** Adj. **(a)** ambiguous; equivocal ‹smile›; **(b)** (fig.: schlüpfrig) suggestive ‹remark, joke›; **2** adv. **(a)** ambiguously; ‹smile› equivocally; **(b)** (fig.: schlüpfrig) suggestively; **~deutigkeit** die; **~, ~en** ⇒ **zweideutig 1: (a)** o. Pl. ambiguity; suggestiveness; **(b)** (Äußerung) ambiguity; double entendre; **~dimensional** /~dimɛnzjona:l/ **1** Adj. two-dimensional; **2** adv. twodimensionally; in two dimensions; **~ein·halb** Bruchz. ▶ 600 ⏐ two and a half

Zweier der; **~s, ~ (a)** (ugs.) ⇒ **Zwei b; (b)** (ugs.: Münze) two-pfennig piece; **(c)** (Ruderboot) pair

zweierlei Gattungsz.; indekl. **(a)** attr. two sorts or kinds of; two different ‹sizes, kinds, etc.›; **mit ~ Maß messen** use double standards; **(b)** allein stehend two [different] things; **es ist ~, ob man es sagt oder [ob man es] auch tut** it is one thing to say it and another [thing] to do it

zwei-, Zwei-: **~fach** Vervielfältigungsz. double; (~mal) twice; **die ~fache Menge/Länge** double or twice the amount/length; **etw. ~fach vergrößern/verkleinern** enlarge sth. to twice its size/reduce sth. to half-size; s. auch **achtfach; ~fache** das; adj. Dekl. **das ~fache** twice as much; s. auch **Achtfache; ~familien·haus** das two-family house; duplex (esp. Amer.); **~farbig 1** Adj. two-coloured; two-tone ‹scarf, paintwork, etc.›; **2** adv. in two colours

Zweifel /ˈtsvaifl̩/ der; **~s, ~:** doubt **(an + Dat.** about); **~ bekommen** become doubtful; **ich habe da so meine ~:** I have my doubts about that; **ich bin mir noch im ~, ob ...:** I am still uncertain whether ...; **etw. in ~ ziehen** question sth.; **[für jmdn.] außer ~ stehen** be beyond doubt [as far as sb. is concerned]; **über jeden od. allen ~ erhaben sein** be beyond any shadow of a doubt; **kein ~, ...:** there is/was no doubt about it, ...; **ohne ~:** without [any] doubt; **im ~:** in case of doubt; if in doubt

zweifelhaft Adj. **(a)** doubtful; **(b)** (fragwürdig) dubious

zweifel·los Adv. undoubtedly; without [any] doubt

zweifeln itr. V. doubt; **wenn man zweifelt** if one is in doubt or has any doubts; **an jmdm./etw. ~:** doubt sb./sth.; have doubts about sb./sth.; **~ daran, dass ..., ~, ob ...:** doubt whether ...; **daran ist nicht zu ~:** there can be no doubt about it

zweifels-, Zweifels-: **~fall** der case of doubt; doubtful or problematic case; **im ~fall[e]** in case of doubt; if in doubt; **~frei 1** Adj. definite; **~frei sein** beyond [any] doubt; **2** adv. beyond [any] doubt; **~ohne** Adv. undoubtedly; without doubt

Zweifler der; **~s, ~** doubter

Zweig /tsvaik/ der; **~[e]s, ~e (a)** [small] branch; (meist ohne Blätter) twig; **auf keinen grünen ~ kommen** (ugs.) not get anywhere; **(b)** (fig.) branch

zwei-: **~geschossig** Adj., adv. ⇒ **~stöckig; ~geteilt** Adj. divided; divided in two postpos.; **~gleisig** /-glaizɪç/ Adj. two-track; double-track; (fig.) two-way; **2** adv. **(a)** ‹run› on two tracks; **(b)** **~ fahren** (fig.) follow a dual-track policy

Zweig·stelle die branch [office]

zwei-, Zwei-: **~hundert** Kardinalz. ▶ 600 ⏐ two hundred; **~jährig** Adj. (zwei Jahre alt) two-year-old attrib.; (zwei Jahre dauernd) two-year attrib.; **~kampf** der **(a)** single combat; (Duell) duel; **(b)** (Sport) man-to-man tussle; duel; **~köpfig** Adj. **(a)** two-headed; **(b)** (aus zwei Personen bestehend) two-person attrib.; of two [people] postpos.; **~mal** Adv. twice; **das wird er sich** (Dat.) **~mal überlegen** he'll think twice about that; s. auch **achtmal; ~mark·stück** das ▶ 215 ⏐ two-mark piece; **~motorig** Adj. twin-engined; **~pfennig·stück** das ▶ 215 ⏐ two-pfennig piece; **~polig** Adj. double-pole; two-core ‹cable›; two-pin ‹plug, socket›; **~rad** das two-wheeler; **~reiher** der double-breasted suit/coat/ jacket; **~schneidig** Adj. double-edged; **ein ~schneidiges Schwert** (fig.) a double-edged sword; **~sprachig 1** Adj. bilingual; ‹sign› in two languages; **2** adv. bilingually; ‹labelled, written, printed, etc.› in two languages; **~spurig 1** Adj. **(a)** two-lane ‹road›; **(b)** two-track ‹vehicle›; **(c)** two- or twin-track ‹recording›; **2** adv. **(a)** in two lanes; **(b)** ‹record› on two tracks; **~stellig** Adj. two-figure attrib. ‹number, sum›; **~stöckig 1** Adj. two-storey attrib.; **~stöckig sein** have two storeys or floors; **2** adv. ‹build› two storeys high; **~strahlig** Adj. twin-engined ‹jet aircraft›; **~stündig** Adj. two-hour attrib.; (Schulw.) double-period attrib. ‹test, examination›; **nach ~stündiger Wartezeit** after waiting for two hours

zweit /tsvait/ **wir waren zu ~:** there were two of us; **sie sind zu ~ verreist** the two of them went away together; s. auch **acht²**

zweit... Ordinalz. ▶ 119 ⏐, ▶ 600 ⏐ second; **jeder ~e Einwohner** every other or second inhabitant; **jeder Zweite** every other one; **~er Klasse fahren/ liegen** travel second-class/be in a second-class hospital bed; **ich habe noch einen ~en** I have a second one; (als Ersatz) I have a spare; **wie kein Zweiter** as no one else can; like nobody else; s. auch **erst...**

zwei-, Zwei-: **~tägig** Adj. (2 Tage alt) two-day-old attrib.; (2 Tage dauernd) two-day attrib.; s. auch **achttägig; ~takter** der; **~s, ~** (Motor) two-stroke engine; (Fahrzeug) two-stroke; **~taktmotor** der two-stroke engine

zweit·ältest ... Adj. second oldest; **der/die Zweitälteste** the second oldest

zwei·tausend Kardinalz. ▶ 600 ⏐ two thousand

Zwei·tausender der mountain more than two thousand metres high

zweit·best... Adj. second best

zwei·teilig Adj. two-piece ‹suit, bathing suit, suite, etc.›; two-part ‹film, programme›

*zweite·mal, *zweiten·mal ⇒ **Mal¹**

zweitens Adv. secondly; in the second place

Zweite[r]-Klasse-Abteil das second-class compartment

zweit-, Zweit-: **~frisur** die wig; **~klässler, *~kläßler** der; **~s, ~** (südd., schweiz.) pupil in second class of primary school; second-year pupil; **~rangig** /~raŋɪç/ Adj. of secondary importance postpos.; secondary ‹importance›; **~stimme** die second vote

zwei·türig Adj. two-door ‹car›

Zweit-: **~wagen** der second car; **~wohnung** die second home

zwei-, Zwei-: **~wertig** Adj. (fachspr.) bivalent; **~zeiler** der; **~s, ~:** couplet; **~zimmerwohnung** /·'----⏐ die two-room flat (Brit.) or (Amer.) apartment

Zwerch·fell /ˈtsvɛrç-/ das ▶ 326 ⏐ (Anat.) diaphragm

Zwerg /tsvɛrk/ der; **~[e]s, ~e (a)** dwarf; (Garten~) gnome; **(b)** (abwertend: unbedeutender Mensch) [little] squirt (coll.); wretch

zwergenhaft *Adj.* dwarfish

Zwergin *die;* ~, ~nen dwarf

Zwerg·wuchs *der* dwarfism *no art.;* stunted growth *no art.*

Zwetsche /'tsvɛtʃə/ *die;* ~, ~n damson plum

Zwetschen-: ~kuchen *der* plum-flan; ~wasser *das; Pl.* ~wässer plum brandy

Zwetschken·knödel /'ts:vɛtʃkn̩-/ *der* (Kochk.) plum dumpling

zwicken /'tsvɪkn̩/ *tr., auch itr. V.* (a) pinch; **jmdm. od. jmdn. in den Arm** ~: pinch sb.'s arm; (b) (plagen) **es zwickte und zwackte ihn überall** he had twinges *or* little aches and pains all over

Zwick·mühle *die* (a) double mill; (b) (fig.: Dilemma) dilemma

Zwie·back /'tsvi:bak/ *der;* ~[e]s, ~e *od.* **Zwiebäcke** /'tsvi:bɛkə/ rusk; ~ **essen** eat rusks

Zwiebel /'tsvi:bl̩/ *die;* ~, ~n (a) onion; (b) (Blumen~) bulb

Zwiebel-: ~suppe *die* onion soup; ~turm *der* onion tower

zwie-, Zwie-: ~gespräch *das* (geh.) dialogue; ~licht *das; o. Pl.* (a) twilight; (b) (Mischung von Dämmer- und Kunstlicht) halflight (that is unpleasant for the eye); (c) **ins** ~licht **geraten** (fig.) become suspect; ⟨*person*⟩ come under suspicion; ~lichtig *Adj.* shady; dubious; ~spalt *der;* ~[e]s, ~e *od.* ~spälte /~ʃpɛltə/ [inner] conflict; **in einen** ~spalt **geraten** get into a state of conflict; ~spältig /~ʃpɛltɪç/ *Adj.* conflicting ⟨*mood, feelings*⟩; discordant ⟨*impression*⟩; ~tracht *die* (geh.) discord; ~tracht **säen** sow the seeds of discord

Zwilling /'tsvɪlɪŋ/ *der;* ~s, ~e (a) twin; (b) *Pl.* (Astron., Astrol.) Gemini; the Twins; (c) (Astrol.: Mensch) Gemini

Zwillings-: ~bruder *der* twin brother; ~paar *das* pair of twins; ~schwester *die* twin sister

zwingen /'tsvɪŋən/ **1** *unr. tr. V.* force; **jmdn.** [dazu] ~, etw. zu tun force *or* compel sb. to do sth.; make sb. do sth.; **jmdn. zu einem Geständnis** ~: force sb. into a confession *or* to make a confession; **sich gezwungen sehen, etw. zu tun** find oneself forced *or* compelled to do sth.; **man kann ihn nicht dazu** ~: he can't be forced *or* made to do it **2** *unr. refl. V.* force oneself

zwingend *Adj.* compelling ⟨*reason, logic*⟩; imperative; absolute ⟨*necessity*⟩

Zwinger *der;* ~s, ~ (a) (Hunde~) kennel; (ganze Anlage, auch Zucht) kennels *pl.;* (b) (Gehege) compound; enclosure; (für Bären) bear-pit

zwinkern /'tsvɪŋkɐn/ *itr. V.* **[mit den Augen]** ~: blink; (als Zeichen) wink

zwirbeln /'tsvɪrbl̩n/ *tr. V.* twirl; twist

Zwirn /tsvɪrn/ *der;* ~[e]s, ~e [strong] thread *or* yarn

Zwirns·faden *der* [strong] thread

zwischen /'tsvɪʃn̩/ *Präp. mit Dat./Akk.* (a) between; (b) (unter, inmitten) among[st]

zwischen-, Zwischen-: ~aufenthalt *der* stopover; ~bemerkung *die* interjection; ~durch /-'-/ *Adv.* (a) (zeitlich) between times; (von Zeit zu Zeit) from time to time; (b) (räumlich) here and there; ~fall *der* incident; ~frage *die* question; ~händler *der* (Wirtsch.) middleman; (fig.) go-between; ~hirn *das* (Anat.) diencephalon; ~hoch *das* (Met.) ridge of high pressure; ~lager *das* temporary *or* interim storage facility; ~lagern *tr. V.* store temporarily; ~landen *itr. V.; mit sein* **in X** ~landen land in X on the way; ~landung *die* stopover; ~lösung *die* interim solution; ~mahlzeit *die* snack [between meals]; ~menschlich **1** *Adj.* interpersonal ⟨*relations*⟩; ⟨*contacts*⟩ between people; **2** *adv.* on a personal level; ~prüfung *die* intermediate examination; ~raum *der* space; gap; (Lücke) gap; ~ruf *der* interruption; ~rufer *der* heckler; ~runde *die* (Sport) intermediate round; ~spurt *der* (Sport) spurt; burst [of speed]; ~stadium *das* intermediate stage; ~stufe *die* intermediate stage; ~ton *der* shade; nuance; (fig.) nuance; ~tür *die* connecting door; ~zeit *die* interim; (länger) intervening period; **in der** ~zeit in the meantime

Zwist /tsvɪst/ *der;* ~[e]s, ~e (geh.) strife *no indef. art.;* (Fehde) feud; dispute; **in od. im** ~ **leben** live in a state of strife

Zwistigkeit *die;* ~, ~en (geh.) dispute

zwitschern /'tsvɪtʃɐn/ **1** *itr., auch tr. V.* chirp. **2** *tr. V.* **einen** ~ (salopp) have a drink

Zwitter /'tsvɪtɐ/ *der;* ~s, ~ hermaphrodite; (fig.) cross (aus between)

zwittrig *Adj.* hermaphroditic

zwo /tsvo:/ *Kardinalz.* (ugs.; bes. zur Verdeutlichung) ⇒ **zwei**

zwölf /tsvœlf/ *Kardinalz.* ▶22|, ▶530|, ▶600| twelve; ~ **Uhr mittags/nachts** [twelve o'clock] midday/midnight; **es ist fünf [Minuten] vor** ~ (fig.) we are on the brink; *s. auch* **acht¹**

zwölf-, Zwölf- twelve-; *s. auch* **acht-, Acht-**

Zwölfer *der;* ~s, ~: twelve; *s. auch* **Achter c, d**

zwölf-, Zwölf-: ~fach *Vervielfältigungsz.* twelvefold; **die** ~fache **Menge** twelve times the quantity; *s. auch* **achtfach;** ~fache *das; adj. Dekl.;* **das** ~fache twelve times as much; *s. auch* **Achtfache;** ~fingerdarm *der* (Anat.) duodenum; ~jährig *Adj.* (12 Jahre alt) twelve-year-old *attrib.;* twelve years old *pred.;* (12 Jahre dauernd) twelve-year *attrib.; s. auch* **achtjährig;** ~mal *Adv.* twelve times; *s. auch* **achtmal**

zwölft /tsvœlft/ **wir waren zu** ~: there were twelve of us; *s. auch* **acht²**

zwölft... *Ordinalz.* ▶119|, ▶600| twelfth; *s. auch* **acht...**

zwölftel *Bruchz.* ▶600| twelfth; *s. auch* **achtel**

Zwölftel *das* (schweiz. meist *der*) ~s, ~: ▶600| twelfth

zwot... /tsvo:t.../ (ugs.; bes. bei Datumsangaben) ⇒ **zweit...**

Zyan·kali *das;* ~s (Chemie) potassium cyanide

Zyklen ⇒ **Zyklus**

zyklisch /'tsy:klɪʃ/ **1** *Adj.* cyclic[al]. **2** *adv.* cyclically; as a cycle

Zyklon /tsy'klo:n/ *der;* ~s, ~e (Met.) cyclone

Zyklus /'tsy:klʊs/ *der;* ~, **Zyklen** cycle

Zylinder /tsi'lɪndɐ/ *der;* ~s, ~ (a) cylinder; chimney; (b) (Hut) top hat

zylindrisch **1** *Adj.* cylindrical. **2** *adv.* cylindrically

Zyniker *der;* ~s, ~, **Zynikerin** *die;* ~, ~nen cynic

zynisch /'tsy:nɪʃ/ **1** *Adj.* cynical. **2** *adv.* cynically

Zynismus *der;* ~: cynicism

Zypern /'tsy:pɐn/ *(das);* ~s Cyprus

Zypresse /tsy'prɛsə/ *die;* ~, ~n cypress

Zypriot /tsypri'o:t/ *der;* ~en, ~en, **Zypriotin** *die;* ~, ~nen ▶388| Cypriot

zypriotisch, zyprisch *Adj.* ▶388| Cypriot

Zyste /'tsystə/ *die;* ~, ~n cyst

z. Z., z. Zt. *Abk.* zur Zeit

Vokabellisten zu ausgewählten Sachbereichen

Die folgenden thematischen Wortlisten sollen dem Benutzer dabei helfen, sich in der Fremdsprache auszudrücken. Sie können ihm beim Verfassen von Texten, wie Aufsätzen, Reden, geschäftlichen Berichten oder Artikeln, von großem Nutzen sein. Die Sachbereiche wurden nach ihrer Aktualität und nach ihrer Relevanz für die Bedürfnisse des Studenten von heute ausgewählt. Die Listen sollen nicht nur das benötigte Vokabular selbst liefern, sondern auch Hinweise zur grammatischen Konstruktion und zur Verwendungweise der Wörter geben, so dass der Benutzer in die Lage versetzt wird, seine Meinung zum Ausdruck zu bringen, seine Ansichten klar zu strukturieren und sich dabei einer idiomatischen Ausdruckweise zu bedienen.

Inhaltsverzeichnis

 ## Wie man seine Ansichten zum Ausdruck bringen kann/Expressing your opinion

Zustimmung und Ablehnung	Agreeing and Disagreeing
Zustimmung	Agreeing
Das ist eine gute Idee.	It's a good idea.
Wie X unterstrichen hat…	As X has emphasized…
Es ist richtig, dass …	It is true that…
Du musst zugeben, dass …	You have to admit that…
Es scheint mir absolut gerechtfertigt zu sein, … zu wollen.	It seems to me to be completely justified to want to…

Forsetzung…

Forsetzung...

Ich teile deine Sorge darum/deinen Widerwillen dagegen, das zu tun	I share your concern about this/reluctance to do this.
Ich teile deine Meinung.	I share your opinion.
Ich bin (ganz) deiner Meinung.	I agree (completely) with you.
In dieser Sache bin ich ganz der Meinung von X.	I agree completely with X about this.
Ganz meine Meinung.	I agree entirely.
Ich gebe zu, dass...	I grant you that...
Ich finde, es ist eine ausgezeichnete Idee, das zu tun	I think it is an excellent idea to do this.
Wir sind uns über die Notwendigkeit, das zu tun, einig.	We agree on the need to do this.
Du hast/Er hat völlig Recht.	You are/He is absolutely right.
X sagt völlig zu Recht, dass...	X states, quite rightly, that...

Ablehnung — Disagreeing

Es ist schade, dass...	It's a pity that...
Es is undenkbar, dass...	It is unthinkable that...
Man kann nicht sagen, dass...	You can't say that...
Es fällt freilich schwer, zu glauben, dass...	It is, however, difficult to believe that...
Es ist übertrieben, zu sagen, dass...	It is an exaggeration to say that...
Ich finde, wir dürfen nicht so hart urteilen.	I think that we must moderate our judgement.
Ich denke, es ist völlig unangemessen, das zu tun.	I think it is totally inappropriate to do this.
Mir scheint im Gegenteil, dass...	On the contrary, it seems to me that/the way I see it is that...
Ich muss leider ablehnen.	I'm afraid that I must refuse.
Ich kann leider nicht umhin, dir zu widersprechen.	Unfortunately, I feel that I must contradict you.
In dieser Sache bin ich anderer Meinung als X.	I disagree with X about this.
Ich teile nicht die Ansicht derer, die glauben, dass...	I disagree with those people who think that...
Ich bin völlig anderer Meinung.	I disagree completely.
Ich glaube einfach nicht, dass...	I refuse to believe that...
Ich bedaure (zutiefst), dass...	I (deeply) regret that...
Es tut mir Leid, dir widersprechen zu müssen, aber...	I am sorry to have to contradict you, but...
Es ist leicht, zu kritisieren, aber ich fände es hilfreicher, alternative Lösungen vorzuschlagen.	It is easy to be critical, but I think it would be more constructive to suggest some alternative solutions.
Wir sind darüber verschiedener Meinung.	We have different opinions on the matter.
Unsere Ansichten (über...) sind diametral entgegengesetzt.	We have diametrically opposed opinions (on/about ...)

Meinungsäusserungen — Giving your opinion

Meines Erachtens...; Nach meiner Meinung...; Meiner Ansicht nach...	In my opinion...; The way I see it,...
Es würde mich sehr überraschen, wenn...	I'd be very surprised if...
Es ist nicht zu leugnen, dass...	It is undeniable that...
Es fällt mir schwer, zu sagen, was ich über... denke.	It's difficult for me to give my opinion about...
Ich denke, es ist wichtig festzustellen/ zu betonen, dass...	I think it's important to say/to stress that...

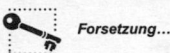 *Forsetzung...*

Mir scheint, dass…	It seems to me that…
Es dürfte klar sein, dass…	It seems obvious that…
Ich habe den Eindruck, dass…	I have/get the impression that…
Ich glaube, dass…	I believe that…
Ich finde es absolut normal/nicht normal, das zu tun.	I think it's completely normal/abnormal to do this.
Ich stelle es mir schwer vor, das zu tun	I imagine it must be difficult to do this.
Ich finde, dass…	I consider that…
Ich fürchte (sehr), dass…	I am (very much) afraid that…
Ich muss sagen, dass…	I must say that…
Ich habe wirklich Zweifel, ob…	I sincerely doubt whether…
Ich denke einfach, dass…	I just think that…
Ich möchte darüber kein Urteil abgeben, aber es scheint, dass…	I don't wish to pass judgement, but it appears that…
Ich sehe in…keinen Vorteil.	I see no advantage in…
Ich denke, dass…	I think that…
Ich bin sicher, dass…	I am certain that…
Ich bin (davon) überzeugt, dass…	I am convinced that…
Ich nehme an, dass…	I assume/suppose that…
Ich möchte betonen, dass…	I must stress that…
Ich persönlich bin nicht dafür.	Personally, I'm not in favour.
Warum tun wir es nicht?	Why don't we do this?
Da du mich nach meiner Meinung (dazu/darüber) fragst…	As you are asking me for my opinion (about/on this)…

Mittel zur Strukturierung von Meinungsäusserungen	Structuring your views
aber	but
zum Abschluss	in conclusion
abgesehen davon	having said that
vor allem	first of all
also	therefore; now
auch	also/as well
außerdem	in addition; then
und außerdem	moreover
andererseits	on the other hand; again
daher	hence
dann	then
darum	that is why; therefore
deshalb	therefore; that's the reason/that's why
ebenfalls	also/as well
auf jeden Fall	at any rate, in any case
folglich	consequently
im Gegenteil	on the contrary
gleich	in the first place
hauptsächlich; an erster Stelle	first (and foremost); most importantly
infolgedessen	consequently
jedoch	however
jetzt	now
kurz	in short
nichtsdestoweniger	none the less, nevertheless
nun	now
nur	only

Forsetzung...

obgleich; obwohl	although
schließlich	finally, at last
wie dem auch sei	be that as it may
auf der anderen Seite	on the other hand
sondern	but
in der Tat	indeed
tatsächlich	in fact; indeed
trotz	in spite of
trotzdem	nevertheless; still
von vornherein	from the start
wieder	again
mit anderen Worten	in other words
zudem	moreover
zuerst	in the first place; first (of all)
zuerst einmal, zunächst einmal	to begin with
zumindest	at least
zugegebenermaßen	admittedly
zusammenfassend	to sum up

Umwelt/Environment

Der Schutz der Umwelt/ Protection of the Environment

abbaubar:
- **biologisch abbaubar** • biodegradable

Abfallaufbereitung, *die*   waste processing

ansiedeln:
- **in einem Waldgebiet wieder Tiere ansiedeln** • to restock a forest

aufforsten:
- **einen Wald wieder aufforsten** • to replant a forest

ausrüsten:
- **ein Fahrzeug ausrüsten mit...** • to fit a vehicle with...

bedroht:
- **bedrohte Arten schützen** • to protect endangered species

Bioprodukt, *das*   organic product

bleifrei:
- **bleifreies Benzin** • unleaded petrol

CFK-freies Spray   CFC-free spray

Energie, *die:*   energy
- **Energie sparen** • to save energy

FCKW-freies Spray   CFC-free spray

Fußgängerzone, *die:*
- **ein Gebiet zur Fußgängerzone machen** • to pedestrianize an area

gesperrt:
- **(für den Fahrzeugverkehr) gesperrt** • closed to traffic

grün:
- **die Grünen** • the (German) Green Party

Hausmüllsammlung, *die*   household refuse collection

kämpfen für   to campaign for

Katalysator, *der*   catalytic converter

Luftqualität, *die*   air quality

Müll, *der:*
- **weniger Müll produzieren** • to limit waste production
- **Müllabfuhr,** *die* • refuse collection
- **Müll vermeiden** • to reduce waste

Naturschutz, *der*   nature conservation

ökologisch   ecological

ozonfreundlich   ozone-friendly

recycelbar   recyclable

Recycling, *das:*
- **Recycling von Glas/ Papier/Batterien** • glass/paper/battery recycling

Recyclingzentrum, *das*   recycling centre

Risiko, *das:*
- **die Risiken erkennen** • to realize the risks

Umweltschützer, *der/* **-in,** *die*   environmentalist

Umweltverschmutzung, *die:*
- **die Umweltverschmutzung bekämpfen** • to fight environmental pollution

umweltverträglich:
- **umweltverträgliches Produkt** • non-pollutant product

Verantwortungsbewusstsein, *das:*
- **bei der Öffentlichkeit Verantwortungsbewusstsein wecken** • to give the public a sense of responsibility

Wiederaufforstung, *die*   reforestation

wiederverwenden   to reclaim, reuse

Die Schädigung der Umwelt/ The Deterioration of the Environment

Atomkraftwerk, *das*   nuclear power station

ausgestorben   extinct

Aussterben, *das*   extinction

bedroht:
- **[vom Aussterben] bedrohte Arten** • endangered species

CFK, *der* **(Chlorfluorkohlenstoff,** *der*)   CFC (chlorofluorocarbon)

Desertifikation, *die*   desertification

Dürre, *die*   drought

Entwaldung, *die*   deforestation

Fauna, *die*   wildlife

FCKW, *der* **(Fluorchlorkohlenwasserstoff,** *der*)   CFC (chlorofluorocarbon)

Flora, *die*   flora

Giftmüll, *der*   toxic waste

Giftwolke, *die*   toxic cloud

Gleichgewicht, *das:*
- **das natürliche Gleichgewicht stören** • to upset the balance of nature

global:
- **globaler Temperaturanstieg** • global warming

Hungersnot, *die*   famine

Industrieabfall, *der;* **Industrieabfälle** *Pl.;* **Industriemüll,** *der*   industrial waste

Kernkraftwerk, *das*   nuclear power station

Klima, *das*   climate

Klimaschwankungen *Pl.*   climatic variation

Lärmbelastung, *die*   noise pollution

Luftverschmutzung, *die*   air pollution

nachhaltig   sustainable

Ölpest, *die*   black tide

Ressource, *die:*
- **natürliche Ressourcen erschöpfen** to exhaust natural resources

radioaktiv:
- **radioaktiver Abfall, radioaktive Abfälle** • radioactive waste

sauer:
- **saurer Regen** • acid rain

Sickerwasser, *das*   seepage (water)

Spray, *das*   spray

Spraydose, *die*   aerosol (can)

Treibgas, *das*   propellant

Treibhauseffekt, *der:*
- **den Treibhauseffekt verstärken/verringern** • to increase/reduce the greenhouse effect

Trockenheit, *die*   drought

Umweltkatastrophe, *die*   ecological disaster

verklappen   to dump

Verschmutzung, *die:*
- **Verschmutzung der Atmosphäre** • atmospheric pollution

• Verschmutzung, *die* der städtischen Umwelt	• urban pollution
Versickerung, *die*	seepage
Verwüstung, *die*	desertification
Wärmekraftwerk, *das*	thermal power station
Wasserverschmutzung, *die*	water pollution

Naturkatastrophen/Natural Disasters

Asche, *die*	ash
Epizentrum, *das*	epicentre
Erdbeben, *das*	earthquake
Erdrutsch, *der*	landslide
Erdstoß, *der*	earth tremor
evakuieren	to evacuate
flussabwärts	downstream
flussaufwärts	upstream
Flutwelle, *die*	tidal wave
Gewitter, *das*	storm
Hochwasser, *das*:	
• ein Hochwasser führender Fluss	• a river in spate
Hurrikan, *der*	hurricane
Katastrophe, *die*	disaster
Krater, *der*	crater
Lava, *die*	lava
Lawine, *die*	avalanche
Magma, *das*	magma
Natur, *die*:	nature
• die Natur zähmen	• to tame nature
• Launen der Natur	• vagaries of nature
Naturerscheinung, *die*; Naturphänomen, *das*	natural phenomenon
Notunterkunft, *die*	emergency shelter
Orkan, *der*	hurricane
Richterskala, *die*	Richter scale
Seismograf, *der*	seismograph
Seismologie, *die*	seismology
Steinschlag, *der*	rockfall
Strudel, *der*	whirlpool
Sturm, *der*	gale
Taifun, *der*	typhoon
Tornado, *der*	tornado
Überschwemmung, *die*	flood
Ufer, *das*:	
• über die Ufer treten	• to burst its banks
Unwetter, *das*	storm
Vulkan, *der*:	
• ein aktiver/tätiger Vulkan	• an active volcano
• ein erloschener Vulkan	• an extinct volcano
Vulkanausbruch, *der*	volcanic eruption
Waldbrand, *der*	forest fire
Wirbelsturm, *der*	cyclone
Wirbelwind, *der*	whirlwind
Zyklon, *der*	cyclone

 # Gesellschaft/Society

Politik/Politics

abgeben:	
• seine Stimme abgeben	• to cast one's vote
abstimmen	to vote
Außenminister, *der*/ -in, *die*	Foreign Minister (*Brit*); Secretary of State (*Amer*)
auszählen:	
• die Stimmen auszählen	• to count the votes
Beliebtheitsquote, *die*	popularity rating
bilden:	
• eine Regierung bilden	• to form a government
Bundesregierung, *die*	Federal Government
enthalten:	
• sich [der Stimme] enthalten	• to abstain
Enthaltung, *die*	abstention
Exekutive, *die*	executive
Extremist, *der*/-in, *die*	extremist
gemäßigt	moderate
Kandidat, *der*/-in, *die*	candidate
kandidieren	to stand for election
Kommunalwahl, *die*	local election
Kongress, *der*	Congress
Legislative, *die*	legislature
link...	left-wing
die Linke	the Left
links	left-wing
Mehrheit, *die*	majority
Meinung:	
• öffentliche Meinung	• public opinion
Meinungsumfrage, *die*	opinion poll
Minister, *der*/-in, *die*	minister
Ministerium, *das*	ministry
Opposition, *die*	opposition
Parlament, *das*	parliament
Parlamentswahl, *die*	general election
Partei, *die*:	
• einer Partei angehören; in einer Partei sein	• to belong to a party
Politiker, *der*/-in, *die*	politician
politischer Skandal; Politskandal, *der*	political scandal
Präsident, *der*/-in, *die*	president
Premierminister, *der*/ -in, *die*	prime minister
Präsidentschaftswahl, *die*	presidential election
recht...	right-wing
die Rechte	the Right
rechts	right-wing
Rede, *die*	speech
Referendum, *das*	referendum
Regierung, *die*	government
Republik, *die*	republic
Senat, *der*	Senate
Stellvertreter, *der*/ -in, *die*	deputy
Stimme, *die*	vote
Stimmenthaltung, *die*	abstention
Stimmzettel, *der*	ballot paper

Volksentscheid, *der*	referendum
wahlberechtigt sein	to have the right to vote
Wahlbeteiligung, *die*:	
• die Wahlbeteiligung war niedrig	• there was a low turnout (at the polls)
wählen:	to elect
• [zu etw.] gewählt werden	• to be elected [sth.]
• Wähler, *der/*-in, *die*	• voter
• Wählerschaft, *die*	• electorate
• Wählerverzeichnis, *das*	• electoral roll
• Wahlkabine, *die*	• polling booth
• Wahlkampf, *der*:	• election campaign
• Wahlkampf machen, einen Wahlkampf führen	• to campaign
• Wahlkreis, *der*	• constituency
• Wahllokal, *das*	• polling station
Wahlrecht, *das*:	
• allgemeines Wahlrecht	• universal suffrage
• jmdm. das Wahlrecht geben	• to give sb. the right to vote
• Wahlurne, *die*	• ballot box

Soziales/Social Issues

Abtreibung, *die*	abortion
Aids, *das*	Aids
Analphabetismus, *der*	illiteracy
antirassistische Bewegung	anti-racist movement
Antisemitismus, *der*	anti-Semitism
Arbeitslosigkeit, *die*	unemployment
Armut, *die*	poverty
Beihilfe, *die*	benefit
Droge, *die*:	
• Drogen nehmen	• to take drugs
Einelternfamilie, *die*	single-parent family
Empfängnisverhütung, *die*	contraception
Fremdenfeindlichkeit, *die*	xenophobia
Gleichheit, *die*	equality
Gruppe, *die*:	
• ethnische Gruppe	• ethnic group
Generationskonflikt, *der*; Generationsunterschied, *der*	generation gap
Kampf, *der*:	
• Kampf gegen Aids/ gegen den Rassismus	• fight against Aids/ against racism
Landstreicher, *der/* -in, *die*,	tramp
Minderheit, *die*; Minorität, *die*	minority
obdachlos	homeless
Obdachlose, *der/die*	homeless person
privilegiert	privileged
Qualifikation, *die*:	
• keinerlei Qualifikation haben	• to have no qualifications
Rand, *der*:	
• am Rande der Gesellschaft leben	• to live on the fringes of society
Rassentrennung, *die*	racial segregation
Rassismus, *der*	racism
rebellieren	to rebel
Selbstmordversuch, *der*	suicide attempt

Sexismus, *der*	sexism
Slumgürtel, *der*	slum belt
Sozialarbeiter, *der/* -in, *die*	social worker
Sozialwohnung, *die*	council flat
Stadtstreicher, *der/* -in, *die*	tramp
Umfeld, *das*:	
• familiäres Umfeld	• family environment
überdosis, *die*	overdose
Universität, *die*:	
• die Universität besuchen, [an der Universität] studieren	• to go to university
unterprivilegiert	underprivileged
Unterstützung, *die*	benefit
Vandalismus, *der*	vandalism
Vorstadt, *die*	suburb
Vorurteil, *das*	prejudice
Wohnsiedlung, *die*	housing estate
Wohnsitzlose, *der/die*	homeless person
Xenophobie, *die*	xenophobia

Auswanderung und Einwanderung/ Emigration and Immigration

abschieben	to deport
Arbeitserlaubnis, *die*	work permit
Asyl, *das*	(political) asylum
Asylbewerber, *der/* -in, *die*	asylum-seeker
Aufenthaltserlaubnis, *die*	resident's permit
Ausländer, *der/*-in, *die*	foreigner
Ausländerfeindlichkeit, *die*	xenophobia
ausländischer Mitbürger /ausländische Mitbürgerin	foreign resident
Auswanderer, *der/* Auswanderin, *die*	emigrant
auswandern	to emigrate
Braindrain, *der*	brain drain
einbürgern	to naturalize
Einbürgerung, *die*	naturalization
Einwanderer, *der/* Einwanderin, *die*	immigrant
einwandern	to immigrate
Einwanderungsgesetz, *das*	law on immigration
Einwanderungswelle, *die*	wave of immigration
Emigrant, *der/*-in, *die*	emigrant
entwurzelt	uprooted
Fluchtland, *das*	country of refuge
Flüchtling, *der*	refugee
Gastland, *das*	host country
Grenze, *die*:	
• an der Grenze zurückgewiesen werden	• to be turned back at the border
• die Grenzen schließen/ öffnen	• to close/open the borders
Herkunftsland, *das*	country of origin
illegaler Einwanderer/ illegale Einwanderin	illegal immigrant
Immigrant, *der/*-in, *die*	immigrant

Integration, *die*	integration
Intoleranz, *die*	intolerance
Kulturschock, *der*	culture shock
Massenflucht, *die*	mass exodus
naturalisieren	to naturalize
Staatsbürgerschaft, *die:*	
• **die amerikanische/ deutsche Staatsbürgerschaft erlangen**	• to acquire American/ German citizenship
• **Staatsbürgerschaftsgesetz,** *das*	• law on nationality
Studentenvisum, *das*	student visa
Touristenvisum, *das*	tourist visa
Visum, *das:*	visa
• **verlängerbares/ befristetes Visum**	• renewable/temporary visa
Wirtschaftsflüchtling, *der*	economic refugee
Zoll, *der:*	
• **durch den Zoll gehen**	• to go through customs

Geschäftswelt und Industrie/Business and Industry

Beschäftigung und Arbeitslosigkeit/ Employment and Unemployment

37,5-Stunden-Woche, *die*	37.5 hour week
Abfindung, *die*	redundancy payment
Achtstundentag, *der*	eight-hour day
Antragsformular, *das*	application form
Arbeit, *die:*	job; work
• **Arbeit haben/suchen**	• to have/look for a job
• **seine Arbeit verlieren**	• to lose one's job
arbeiten:	to work
• **ganztags arbeiten**	• to work full-time
• **Teilzeit arbeiten**	• to work part-time
• **Schicht arbeiten**	• to work shifts
Arbeitgeber, *der/ -in, die*	employer
Arbeitnehmer, *der/ -in, die*	employee
Arbeitsbedingungen *Pl.*	working conditions
arbeitslos:	unemployed
• **arbeitslos sein**	• to be unemployed; to be out of work
• **sich arbeitslos melden**	• to register as unemployed
Arbeitslose, *der/die*	unemployed person
Arbeitslosengeld, *das*	unemployment benefit
Arbeitslosigkeit, *die*	unemployment
Arbeitsmarkt, *der*	job market
Arbeitsplatz, *der*	job
Arbeitssuchende, *der/die*	job-seeker
Arbeitszeit, *die*	working hours
Beschäftigte, *der/die*	employee
Beschäftigung, *die*	employment
sich bewerben	to apply
Bewerbung, *die*	application

bezahlen:	
• **gut/schlecht bezahlt werden**	• to be well/badly paid
Blindbewerbung, *die*	unsolicited application
Bruttogehalt, *das*	gross salary
Bruttolohn, *der*	gross wage
Bürostunden *Pl.*	office hours
Dienstleistungssektor, *der*	service sector
einstellen	to hire
Einstellungsgespräch, *das*	job interview
entlassen	to dismiss; *(wegen Arbeitsmangels)* to make redundant
Entlassung, *die*	dismissal; *(wegen Arbeitsmangels)* redundancy
Erwachsenenbildung, *die*	adult education
Gehalt, *das*	salary
Gehaltsempfänger, *der /-in, die*	salaried employee
Job, *der*	job
Krankengeld, *das*	sick pay
kündigen	to hand in one's notice
Kündigung, *die*	notice
langzeitarbeitslos	long-term unemployed
Lebenslauf, *der*	CV, curriculum vitae
Lehrgang, *der*	training course
Lohn, *der*	wage
Mindestlohn, *der:*	
• **garantierter Mindestlohn**	• guaranteed minimum wage
Nettogehalt, *das*	net salary
Nettolohn, *der*	net wage
primärer Sektor	primary sector
Profil, *das:*	
• **das richtige Profil haben**	• to have the right profile
schaffen:	
• **neue Arbeitsplätze schaffen**	• to create new jobs
Schwarzarbeit, *die*	work done on the side *(without declaring one's earnings)*
Selbständige, *der/die*	self-employed person
soziale Sicherheit	social security
Sozialleistungen *Pl.*	benefits package
Sozialversicherung, *die*	social security
Stelle, *die*	job
Stellenvermittlung, *die*	employment agency
Sicherheit, *die:*	
• **Sicherheit des Arbeitsplatzes/der Arbeitsplätze**	• job security
Teilzeit, *die:*	
• **Teilzeit arbeiten**	• to work part-time
Teilzeitarbeit, *die*	part-time work
Überstunden *Pl.*	overtime
Vorstellungsgespräch, *das*	job interview
Wirtschaftskrise, *die*	economic crisis
Zeitarbeit, *die:*	
• **Zeitarbeit machen**	• to temp
Zeitarbeitskraft, *die*	temp

Handel und Gewerbe/Trade and Commerce

Absatz, *der*	sales
Alleinvertreiber, *der/-in, die*	sole distributor
Anbieter, *der/-in, die*	supplier
Angebot, *das:*	
• **Angebot und Nachfrage**	• supply and demand
Artikel, *der*	article, line
Auftrag, *der:*	order
• **einen Auftrag vergeben**	• to place an order
Ausfuhr, *die*	export
ausführen	to export
Außenhandel, *der*	foreign trade
Ausverkauf, *der*	(clearance) sale
ausverkaufen:	
• **ausverkauft sein**	• to be sold out
Automobilhersteller, *der*	car manufacturer
Automobilausstellung, *die;* **Autosalon**, *der*	motor show
Bankrott, *der:*	
• **Bankrott machen**	• to go bankrupt
bestellen	to order
Bestellung, *die*	order
Defizit, *das*	deficit
Einfuhr, *die*	import
einführen	to import; *(auf den Markt)* to launch
Einkaufszentrum, *das*	shopping centre
Einzelhandel, *der:*	retail trade
• **im Einzelhandel verkaufen**	• to sell retail
Erzeugnis, *das*	product
Export, *der*	export
exportieren	to export
Fertigprodukt, *das*	finished product
Filiale, *die*	branch
Freihandel, *der*	free trade
führen	to stock
Geschäft, *das:*	shop
• **ein Geschäft eröffnen/ aufmachen**	• to open a shop
• **ein Geschäft über- nehmen**	• to buy a shop
Geschäftsviertel, *das*	shopping area
Gewinn, *der*	profit
Großhandel, *der*	wholesale trade
Großhändler, *der/-in, die*	wholesaler
Grossist, *der/-in, die*	wholesaler
Handelsabkommen, *das*	trade agreement
Handelsbilanz, *die*	balance of trade
Handelskammer, *die*	chamber of commerce
Handelskette, *die*	chain of stores
Handelspartner, *der/ -in, die*	trading partner
Handelsvertreter, *der/ -in, die*	sales rep, sales representative
Hersteller, *der/-in, die*	manufacturer
Herstellungsfehler, *der*	manufacturing fault
Import, *der*	import
importieren	to import
inklusive	inclusive
Inventur, *die:*	
• **Inventur machen**	• to do the stocktaking

Kaufhaus, *das*	department store
Kaufkraft, *die*	purchasing power
Konkurrent, *der/-in, die*	competitor
Konkurrenz, *die*	competition
konkurrieren	to compete
Kundendienst, *der*	customer service; after- sales service
Laden, *der:*	shop
• **einen Laden eröffnen/ aufmachen**	• to open a shop
Ladeninhaber, *der/-in, die*	shopkeeper
Lagerhalle, *die*	warehouse
Lieferant, *der/-in, die*	supplier
liefern	to supply; to deliver
Lieferung, *die*	delivery
Marktsegment, *das*	market segment
Massenartikel, *der*	mass-produced article
Massenproduktion, *die*	mass production
in Massenproduktion herstellen	to mass-produce
Mehrwertsteuer, *die*	value-added tax
Messe, *die*	fair
Mitbewerber, *der/-in, die*	competitor
MWSt	VAT
Öffnungszeiten *Pl.*	opening hours
Produkt, *das:*	product
• **ein Produkt entwickeln**	• to develop a product
• **ein Produkt auf den Markt bringen**	• to launch a product
• **ein Produkt vertreiben**	• to distribute a product
Produktionsfehler, *der*	manufacturing fault
Produktlinie, *die*	product line
Profit, *der*	profit
Qualitätskontrolle, *die*	quality control
Rechnung, *die*	invoice
Reststück, *das*	oddment
Rohstoff, *der*	raw material
Selbstkostenpreis, *der*	cost price
sortieren:	to stock
• **gut sortiert sein**	• to be well-stocked
Supermarkt, *der*	supermarket
Sortiment, *das*	range of products
testen	to test
Verkauf, *der*	sale
verkaufen:	to sell
• **etw. im Einzelhandel/ Großhandel verkaufen**	• to retail/wholesale sth.
• **etw. mit Verlust verkaufen**	• to sell sth. at a loss
Verkäufer, *der/-in, die*	shop assistant
Verkaufszahlen *Pl.*	sales figures
Vertrieb, *der*	distribution
Warenhaus, *das*	department store
Wettbewerb, *der*	competition

Marketing und Publicity/ Marketing and Publicity

Absatzstrategie, *die*	sales strategy
Anzeige, *die*	advertisement
Antwortkarte, *die*	reply card
bewerben:	
• **ein Produkt bewerben**	• to promote a product

Einführungskampagne, *die*	launching a campaign	• **wer ist am Apparat?**	• Who is that speaking?
Fernsehspot, *der*	TV advert	**auflegen**	to hang up
Fernsehwerbung, *die:*		**Auskunft,** *die:*	
• 'aus der Fernsehwerbung'	• 'as seen on TV'	• **die Auskunft anrufen**	• to call directory enquiries
Gutschein, *der*	voucher	**ausrichten:**	
inserieren	to advertise (*in a newspaper*)	• **können Sie [ihm/ihr] etwas ausrichten?**	• could you take a message [for him/her]?
Marke, *die*	brand	**Autotelefon,** *das*	car phone
Markenimage, *das*	brand image	**besetzt**	engaged, busy
Markentreue, *die*	brand loyalty	**durchstellen:**	
Marketing, *das*	marketing	• **ich stelle Sie durch**	• I'm putting you through
Marketingabteilung, *die*	marketing department	**falsch:**	
Marketingetat, *der*	marketing budget	• **Sie sind falsch verbunden**	• you've got the wrong number
Markt, *der:*		**Fax,** *das*	fax
• **lebhafter Markt**	• buoyant market	**faxen**	to fax
• **in einem Markt Fuß fassen**	• to break into a market	**Fernabfrage,** *die:*	
Marktanteil, *der*	market share	• **Anrufbeantworter mit Fernabfrage**	• remote-access answering machine
Marktforschung, *die*	market research	**Freecallnummer,** *die*	freefone number
Marktlücke, *die:*		**Geheimnummer,** *die:*	
• **eine Marktlücke finden**	• to find a gap in the market	• **eine Geheimnummer haben**	• to be ex-directory
Markttrend, *der*	market trend	**die Gelben Seiten**	the Yellow Pages
PR	PR	**Gesprächsgebühr,** *die*	call charge
Publicrelations *Pl.*	public relations	**hallo**	hello
Rabatt, *der*	discount	**Handapparat,** *der*	handset
Radiospot, *der*	radio commercial	**Handy,** *das*	mobile phone
Slogan, *der*	slogan	**Hörer,** *der:*	receiver
Sonderangebot, *das*	special offer	• **den Hörer abnehmen**	• to pick up the receiver
sponsern	to sponsor	**Kartentelefon,** *das*	cardphone
Telefonmarketing, *das*	telephone sales	**Leitung,** *die*	line
Umfrage, *die*	survey	**melden:**	
Verbraucher, *der/-in, die*	consumer	• **es meldet sich niemand**	• there is no answer
Verbraucherbefragung, *die*	consumer survey	**Mobiltelefon,** *das*	mobile phone
		Nachricht, *die:*	
Verkaufsleiter, *der/ -in, die*	sales manager	• **nach dem Ton eine Nachricht hinterlassen**	• to leave a message after the tone
vermarkten	to market	**Nebenstellennummer,** *die*	extension number
Werbeabteilung, *die*	advertising department	**Notrufnummer,** *die*	emergency number
Werbeagentur, *die*	advertising agency	**Operator,** *der/-in, die*	operator
Werbefläche, *die*	advertising space	**R-Gespräch,** *das:*	
Werbekampagne, *die*	advertising campaign	• **jmdn. per R-Gespräch anrufen**	• to make a reverse-charge call to sb.
Werbeleiter, *der/-in, die*	advertising executive	**Sprachnachricht,** *die*	voice mail
Werbespot, *der*	commercial	**sprechen:**	
Werbespruch, *der*	slogan	• **Kann ich Herrn X sprechen?**	• could I speak to Mr X?
werben	to advertise	**Telefax,** *das*	fax
Werbung, *die*	advertising; (*im Fernsehen*) commercial	**Telefon,** *das:*	telephone
		• **schnurloses Telefon**	• cordless telephone
zielen auf	to target	• **öffentliches Telefon**	• public telephone
Zielgruppe, *die*	target group	• **ans Telefon gehen**	• to answer the phone
		• **das Telefon zehnmal klingeln lassen**	• to let the phone ring 10 times
		• **das Telefon klingeln hören**	• to hear the phone ring

Kommunikation/ Communication

		Telefonbuch, *das:*	directory; phonebook
		• **nicht im Telefonbuch stehen**	• to be ex-directory
		Telefonkarte, *die*	phonecard
		Telefonschnur, *die*	telephone cord
		Voicemail, *die*	voice mail

Telefon/Telephone

		wählen:	
Anrufbeantworter, *der*	answering machine	• **eine Nummer wählen**	• to dial a number
Apparat, *der:*		**verbinden:**	
• **bleiben Sie am Apparat**	• hold the line	• **ich verbinde**	• I'm putting you through

Vorwahl, *die*	dialling code
Wählscheibe, *die*	dial
Wählton, *der*:	
• den Wählton abwarten	• to wait for the dialling tone

Computertechnik/Computing

anklicken	to click on
anlegen:	
• ein Dokument/ eine Datei anlegen	• to create a document/ file
Anwendungsprogramm, *das*	application program
Ausdruck, *der*	hardcopy, printout
ausdrucken:	
• ein Dokument ausdrucken	• to print a document
benutzerfreundlich	user-friendly
Bildschirm, *der*	screen
Byte, *das*	byte
CD, *die*	CD
CD-I, *die*; **interaktive CD**	CD-I, interactive compact disk
CD-ROM, *die*	CD-ROM
CD-ROM-Laufwerk, *das*	CD-ROM drive
Chipkarte, *die*	smart card
Computereinsatz, *der*	computing
Computergrafik, *die*	computer graphics; computer-generated image
computerisieren	to computerize
Computerkurs, *der*	computer training course
Computerspiel, *das*	electronic game
Computertechnik, *die*	computing; computer technology
Computertechniker, *der/-in,* *die*	computer engineer
computerunterstützt	computer-aided
Computerwissenschaft- **ler,** *der/-in,* *die*	computer scientist
Cursor, *der*	cursor
Datei, *die*:	
• eine Datei auf eine Diskette kopieren	• to copy a file onto a floppy disk
• eine Datei sichern	• to save a file
Dateimanagement- **system,** *die*	file management system
Datenbank, *die*	database
Datenerfassung, *die*	data capture
Datenverarbeitung, *die*	data processing
Desktop(computer), *der*	desktop computer
Diskette, *die*	diskette, floppy disk
Diskettenlaufwerk, *das*	disk drive
Drucker, *der*	printer
E-Mail, *die*	email
Erfasser, *der/-in,* *die*	keyboarder
Fenster, *das*:	
• ein neues Fenster öffnen	• to open a new window
Festplatte, *die*	hard disk
Festspeicher, *der*	read only memory
formatieren	to format
Formatierung, *die*	formatting
Funktionstaste, *die*	function key
Hardware, *die*	hardware

Icon, *das*	icon
Informatik, *die*	information technology
KB, Kilobyte, *das*	KB, kilobyte
kopieren und einfügen	copy and paste
künstliche Intelligenz	artificial intelligence
Laptop[computer], *der*	laptop (computer)
Leertaste, *die*	space bar
Lernsoftware, *die*	educational software
löschen:	
• ein Dokument/eine Datei löschen	• to delete a document/file
Maus, *die*:	mouse
• mit der Maus klicken/ doppelklicken	• to click/double-click on the mouse
MB, Megabyte, *das*	MB, megabyte
Menü, *das*	menu
Mikroprozessor, *der*	microprocessor
Multimediacomputer, *der*	multimedia computer
Netz, *das*; **Netzwerk,** *das*	network
PC, *der*	PC
Programm, *das*	program
RAM, *das*	RAM, Random Access Memory
Rechnerkern, *der*	central processing unit, CPU
Rechtschreibprüf- **programm,** *das*	spellchecker
ROM, *das*	ROM, read-only memory
Schreib-Lese-Speicher, *der*	random access memory
scrollen	to scroll
Server, *der*	server
[Silizium]chip, *der*	(silicon) chip
Software, *die*	software
Speicher, *der*	memory
Spracherkennung, *die*	speech recognition
Systemanalytiker, *der/-in,die*	systems analyst
Tastatur, *die*	keyboard
Taste, *die*	key
Taster, *der/-in,* *die*	keyboarder
Textverarbeitung, *die*	word processing
Textverarbeitungs- **system,** *das*	word processor
Tischcomputer, *der*	desktop computer
tragbarer Computer	portable computer
Virus, *das*	virus
Zentraleinheit, *die*	central processing unit

Medien und Künste/ Media and Arts

Fernsehen/Television

Abendnachrichten *Pl.*	evening news
Abonnentenkanal, *der*	subscription (TV) channel
Ansager, *der/-in,* *die*	announcer
Antenne, *die*	aerial
Außenübertragung, *die*	outside broadcast
Bericht, *der*	report

Bildschirm, *der*	screen
Camcorder, *der*	camcorder
Decoder, *der*	decoder
Dokumentarbericht, *der*	documentary (report)
Dokumentarfilm, *der*	documentary (film)
Fernbedienung, *die*	remote control
Fernsehdebatte, *die*	televised debate
fernsehen	to watch television
Fernsehen, *das*:	
• hoch auflösendes Fernsehen	• high-definition television
• im Fernsehen auftreten	• to be on TV
• im Fernsehen gezeigt werden	• to be shown on TV
• etw. im Fernsehen übertragen	• to televise sth
Fernseher, *der*: tragbarer Fernseher	portable TV
Fernsehfilm, *der*	TV film
Fernsehsendung, *die*	TV programme
Fernsehserie, *die*	TV series
Fernsehspiel, *das*	television play
Folge, *die*	episode
Gameshow, *die*	game show
Kabelfernsehen, *das*	cable TV
Kanal, *der*	channel
Kathodenstrahlröhre, *die*	cathode-ray tube
Kinderprogramm, *das*	children's programme
Kommentarstimme, *die*	voice-over
Kommentator, *der/ -in, die*	commentator
live:	
• live senden	• to broadcast live
Moderator, *der/-in, die*	presenter
Nachrichten *Pl.*	news
Pay-TV-Kanal, *der*	subscription (TV) channel
Programm, *das*	programme
Rücklauf, *der*	rewind
Rundfunksatellit, *der*	broadcasting satellite
Satellitenschüssel, *die*	satellite dish
Seifenoper, *die*	soap opera, soap
Sender, *der*	channel; transmitter
privater Sender	commercial channel
staatlicher Sender	state-owned channel
Sendezeit, *die*:	
• beste Sendezeit	• peak viewing time
Sendung, *die*	broadcast programme
Serie, *die*	serial, series
Störung, *die*	interference
Unterhaltung, *die*	entertainment
verkabeln:	
• sich verkabeln lassen	• to get (hooked up to) cable TV
Video, *das*	video (tape)
Videokassette, *die*	video cassette
Videorekorder, *der*	video recorder, VCR
Voice-over, *die*	voice-over
Vorlauf, *der*:	
• schneller Vorlauf	• fast forward
Standbild, *das*	freeze-frame
Werbespot, *der*	commercial
Werbung, *die*	advertising
Wettervorhersage, *die*	weather forecast

Presse und Journalismus/Press and Journalism

Artikel, *der*	article
Auflage, *die*:	printrun
• eine Auflage von 10 000	• a circulation of 10,000
berichten:	to report
• über eine Veranstaltung berichten	• to report on/cover an event
Boulevardzeitung, *die*	tabloid
Druck, *der*:	
• eine Zeitung in Druck geben	• to put a paper to bed
Erhebung, *die*	survey
Fernsehnachrichten *Pl.*	TV news
Feuilleton, *das*	arts section
Filmkritiker, *der/-in, die*	film critic
Fotograf, *der/-in, die*	photographer
Fotojournalist, *der/-in, die*; Fotoreporter, *der/ -in, die*	photojournalist
Frauenzeitschrift, *die*	women's magazine
Herausgeber, *der/-in, die*	editor
Interview, *das*:	
• jmdm. ein Interview geben	• to give sb. an interview
Journalist, *der/-in, die*	journalist
Karikatur, *die*	cartoon
Kleinanzeige, *die*	classified advertisement
Korrespondent, *der/ -in, die*:	correspondent
Kurznachrichten *Pl.*	news in brief
Leitartikel, *der*	editorial, leader
Leserbrief, *der*:	reader's letter
• 'Leserbriefe'	• 'Letters to the Editor'
Literaturzeitschrift, *die*	literary journal
Massenblatt, *das*	mass circulation paper
Monatszeitschrift, *die*	monthly magazine
Nachrichten *Pl.*:	news
• die Nachrichten im Radio hören	• to listen to the news on the radio
Nachrichtenagentur, *die*	news agency
Nachrichtenmagazin, *das*	news magazine
Nachrichtensprecher, *der/-in, die*	news reader
Presseausweis, *der*	press pass
Pressefreiheit, *die*	freedom of the press
Presseinformation, *die*	press release
Pressekonferenz, *die*	press conference
Presseschau, *die*	review of the papers (*on TV*)
Redakteur, *der/-in, die*	copy-editor
Redaktion, *die*	editorial offices; editorial staff; editorial department
Redaktionsassistent, *der/-in, die*	sub-editor
Reporter, *der/-in, die*	reporter
Rezension, *die*	review
Schlagzeile, *die*:	
• Schlagzeilen machen; in den Schlagzeilen sein	• hit the headlines; be in the headlines
Sensationspresse, *die*	gutter press
Sonderausgabe, *die*	special edition

Sonderberichterstatter, der/-in, die	special correspondent
Spalte, die	column
Sportteil, der	sports section
Stellenanzeige, die	job advertisement
Tageszeitung, die	daily (paper)
Umfrage, die	survey
Untersuchung, die	survey
Wirtschaftsteil, der	business section
Wochenmagazin, das; **Wochenzeitschrift,** die	weekly magazine
Zeitschrift, die:	
• **[natur]wissenschaftliche Zeitschrift**	• scientific journal
Zeitung, die	newspaper, paper

Kino, Theater und Musik / Cinema, Theatre and Music

Abenteuerfilm, der	adventure film
anlaufen	to be released
aufführen	to perform
ausverkauft	sold out
Avantgardetheater, das	avant-garde theatre
Balkon, der	balcony
Band, die	band
Blaskapelle, die	brass band
Bühne, die:	
• **hinter der Bühne**	• backstage
• **ein Stück auf die Bühne bringen**	• to stage a play
Bühneneingang, der	stage door
Credits Pl.	credits
Dirigent, der/-in, die	conductor
dirigieren	to conduct
Drama, das	drama
Dreharbeiten Pl.	shooting
Drehbuchautor, der/-in, die	scriptwriter
Drehort, der	location
Farce, die	farce
Filmclub, der	film club
Filmfan, der	film fan, film buff
Filmkunsttheater, das	arthouse
Filmtheater, das	cinema, movie theatre
Freilichtbühne, die; **Freilichttheater,** das	open-air theatre
Hauptrolle, die:	lead-role, leading
• **die Hauptrolle in einem Film spielen**	• to play the lead/star in a film
inszenieren:	
• **ein Stück inszenieren**	• to stage/produce a play
Jazzband, die	jazz band
Kapelle, die	band
Kino, das:	cinema
der Film kommt in die Kinos	• the film is being released
Kinocenter, das	cinema complex
Klavierkonzert, das	piano concerto
Knüller, der	blockbuster
Komödie, die	comedy
Komparse, der/ **Komparsin,** die	extra
Komponist, der/-in, die	composer

Konzert, das:	
• **Konzert mit klassischer Musik**	• classical music concert
Konzerthalle, die	concert hall
Kostümprobe, die	dress rehearsal
Kriminalfilm, der	crime film; detective film
Kulisse, die:	
• **die Kulissen**	• the scenery; the wings
Lampenfieber, das	stage fright
Mitwirkende, der/die:	
• **Liste der Mitwirkenden**	• cast list
Montage, die	(final) editing
Multiplex, das	multiplex
Musical, das	musical
Musik, die	music
Musiker, der/-in, die	musician
Musikstück, das	piece of music
Muster[kopien] Pl.	rushes
Nahaufnahme, die	close-up
Nebenrolle, die	supporting part
Original, das:	
• **im Original**	• in the original language
Originalfassung, die	original version
Originalsprache, die	original language
Parkett, das	stalls
Pause, die	intermission, interval
Posse, die	farce
Preview, die	preview
Produzent, der/-in, die	producer
produzieren:	
• **einen Film produzieren**	• to produce a film
Programmkino, das	arthouse
Rang, der:	circle
• **erster Rang**	• dress circle
• **oberster Rang**	• balcony, gallery
Regie, die:	
• **bei einem Film Regie führen**	• to direct a film
Regisseur, der/-in, die	director
Rockkonzert, das	rock concert
Sänger, der/-in, die	singer
Schauspieler, der/-in die	actor/actress
Schnitt, der	editing
Sciencefictionfilm, der	sci-fi film
Soundtrack, der	soundtrack
Special Effects Pl.	special effects
spielen:	
• **in einem Stück spielen**	• to act in a play
Statist, der/-in, die	extra
synchronisieren	to dub
Szene, die	scene
Theater, das	theatre
Titel Pl.	titles
Tournee, die:	
• **auf Tournee gehen**	• to go on tour
Tragödie, die	tragedy
Trailer, der	trailer
Untertitel, der	subtitle
Varietee, das	variety show
verfilmen:	
• **einen Roman verfilmen**	• to make a film of a novel
zoomen auf; zuzoomen auf	to zoom in on

Kleiner Internet–Führer

Das Internet

Im explosionsartig wachsenden Internet spielt die englische Sprache eine überragende Rolle. 80% aller Informationen sind in Englisch. Obwohl die Software zunehmend auch auf Deutsch zu haben ist, sind Englischkenntnisse also unerlässlich, wenn man von dieser unerschöpflichen Informationsquelle in vollem Maße profitieren will.

Praktisch gesehen dürfte die elektronische Post (E-Mail) für die meisten der nützlichste Internet-Dienst sein. Per E-Mail kann man Nachrichten an andere Teilnehmer in der ganzen Welt schnell und billig verschicken; hierzu sind übrigens keine Englischkenntnisse erforderlich (Weiteres siehe unten). Und durch FTP (File Transfer Protocol) kann man auch ganze im Computer gespeicherte Dateien übersenden.

Zum Zweiten ist das beliebte Surfen im Web, wobei man mithilfe eines Browsers durchs Internet 'spaziert' und verschiedene Web-Seiten (Web sites) aufsucht, eine höchst interessante Beschäftigung. Hierbei stößt man größtenteils auf englischsprachige Informationen. Einige wenige Web-Seiten sind zweisprachig (in Englisch und Deutsch) gehalten (siehe unten).

Drittens kann man an den Newsgroups teilnehmen. Hiervon gibt es über 20 000 zu allen möglichen Themen, z.B. aus Bereichen wie Politik und Kunst bis hin zu den ausgefallensten Hobbys. Man kann entweder einfach die Informationen lesen oder auch eigene Beiträge bzw. Fragen hinterlassen.

Im wahrsten Sinne des Wortes interaktiv ist ein vierter, sehr beliebter Internet-Dienst, IRC (Internet Relay Chat), durch den man mit mehreren Internet-Teilnehmern gleichzeitig (aber natürlich auch mit nur einem) über die Computertastatur 'plaudern' kann.

Die nötige Software für E-Mail, das Surfen im Web und Newsgroups (auf Englisch sowie auf Deutsch) gibt es kostenlos zum Herunterladen auf den folgenden Web-Seiten:

Microsoft Internet Explorer
http://www.microsoft.com *oder* **http://www.microsoft.de**

Netscape Navigator
http://home.netscape.com/de

Die wohl populärste IRC-Software gibt es, ebenfalls kostenlos, zum Herunterladen von mIRC bei:
http://www.mirc.co.uk

Das Verschicken von E-Mails

Die Abbildung zeigt eine typische Oberfläche zum Verschicken von E-Mails.

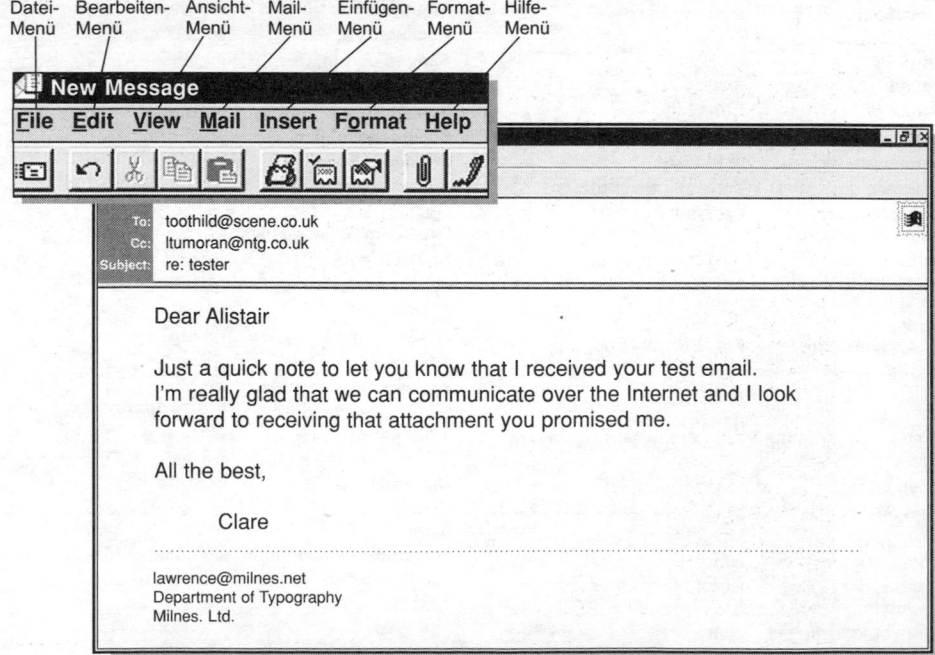

| Datei-Menü | Bearbeiten-Menü | Ansicht-Menü | Mail-Menü | Einfügen-Menü | Format-Menü | Hilfe-Menü |

New Message

File   Edit   View   Mail   Insert   Format   Help

To: toothild@scene.co.uk
Cc: ltumoran@ntg.co.uk
Subject: re: tester

Dear Alistair

Just a quick note to let you know that I received your test email.
I'm really glad that we can communicate over the Internet and I look forward to receiving that attachment you promised me.

All the best,

Clare

lawrence@milnes.net
Department of Typography
Milnes. Ltd.

● **File Menu**	Datei-Menü	**Columns**	Spalten
Open	Öffnen	**Sort by**	Sortieren
Print	Drucken	**Language**	Sprache
Save as	Speichern als	**Refresh**	Aktualisieren
Delete	Löschen		
Folder	Ordner	● **Mail Menu**	Mail-Menü
Address Book	Adressbuch	**New Message**	Neue Nachricht
Import	Importieren	**Reply to Sender**	Antwort an Absender
Export	Exportieren	**Reply to All**	Antwort an alle
Properties	Eigenschaften	**Forward**	Weiterleiten
Exit	Beenden	**Forward as attachment**	Weiterleiten als eingebundene Nachricht
● **Edit Menu**	Bearbeiten-Menü	**Move to**	In Ordner verschieben
Copy	Kopieren	**Copy to**	In Ordner kopieren
Select all	Alles markieren	**Send and Receive**	Nachrichten übermitteln
Mark as read	Als gelesen markieren		
Mark as unread	Als ungelesen markieren		
Find Message	Nachricht suchen	● **Insert Menu**	Einfügen-Menü
		Text File	Textdatei
● **View Menu**	Ansicht-Menü	**Attachment**	Anlage
Toolbar	Werkzeugleiste	**Signature**	Signatur*
Status bar	Statusleiste		
Preview Panel	Seitenansicht		

Weniger gebräuchlich; meist wird der englische Terminus verwendet.

Das Surfen im Web

Die Abbildung zeigt eine typische Oberfläche zum Surfen im Web.

Datei- Bearbeiten- Ansicht- Gehe- Lesezeichen- Hilfe-
Menü Menü Menü Menü Menü Menü

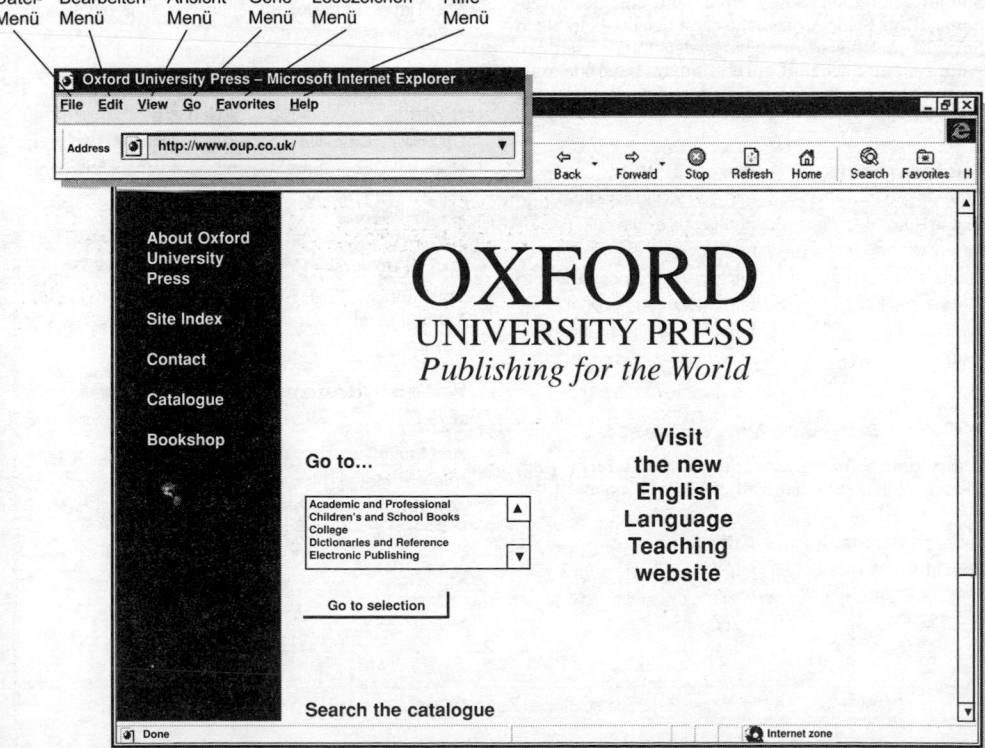

• File menu	Datei-Menü	Document source	Quelltext
Open	Öffnen	Options	Optionen
Save	Speichern		
Send to	Senden an	• Go to Menu	Gehe-Menü
Print preview	Seite einrichten	Back	Zurück
Print	Drucken	Forward	Vor
Exit	Beenden	Home	Anfang
		Search the Web	WWW-Suche
• Edit Menu	Bearbeiten-Menü	Best of Web	Empfehlungen
Cut	Ausschneiden	Read Mail	Mail lesen
Copy	Kopieren	Read News	Newsgroups lesen
Paste	Einfügen		
Select All	Alles markieren	• Favorites Menu	Lesezeichen-Menü
Find (on this page)	Suchen (aktuelles	Add Favorites	Lesezeichen hinzufügen
	Dokument)	Edit Favorites	Lesezeichen bearbeiten
• View Menu	Ansicht-Menü		
Toolbar	Werkzeugleiste		
Status bar	Statusleiste		
Fonts	Schriftarten		
Stop	Stopp		
Update	Aktualisieren		

Englischsprachige Webseiten*

Suchmaschinen (Search engines)

Die sogenannten Suchmaschinen sind wirklich unentbehrliche Internet-Werkzeuge, denn sie dienen als Web-Seiten-Verzeichnisse. Sie sind sehr leicht zu handhaben, und ermöglichen es dem Benutzer, themenspezifische Web-Seiten zu finden, eine Aufgabe, die sonst angesichts der gewaltigen Ausmaße des Webs so gut wie nicht zu bewältigen wäre. Man muss lediglich ein themenbezogenes Schlagwort eintippen, und die Suchmaschine zeigt eine Liste der einschlägigen Web-Seiten. Eine Schlagwortsuche kann in jeder beliebigen Sprache stattfinden, und bei vielen Suchmaschinen kann man die Suche auf ein bestimmtes Land oder eine bestimmte Sprache beschränken und so die Relevanz der gefundenen Seiten für das jeweilige Thema erhöhen.

Suchmaschine	Adresse
Alta Vista	http://www.altavista.com
Excite	http://www.excite.com
Infoseek	http://www.infoseek.com
Lycos	http://www.uk.lycos.de
Metacrawler	http://www.metacrawler.com
Webcrawler	http://www.webcrawler.com
Yahoo!	http://www.yahoo.com

▶ E-Mail-Adressen-Verzeichnisse

Diese funktionieren wie die Suchmaschinen und dienen zum Auffinden von E-Mail-Adressen in der ganzen Welt.

Adressenverzeichnis	Adresse
Four11 Email Directory	http://www.four11.com
The Ultimate Email Directory	http://www.theultimates.com

▶ Webseiten mit Nachrichten

Seite	Adresse
BBC	http://www.bbc.co./uk
CNN Interactive	http://www.cnn.com
The Economist	http://www.economist.co.uk
The New York Times	http://www.nytimes.com
Reuters	http://www.reuters.com
Time Magazine	http://www.time.com
The Times (London)	http://www.the-times.co.uk

▶ Webseiten mit Lernmaterial

Seite	Adresse
Discovery Channel	http://www.discovery.com
National Geographic	http://www.nationalgeographic.com
English Server	http://english-server.hss.cmu.edu
Oxford University Press	http://www.oup.co.uk
Travlang	http://www.travlang.com
Yahooligans!	http://www.yahooligans.com

▶ Webseiten zum Thema Kunst

Seite	Adresse
All Music Guide	http://www.allmusic.com
Internet Movie Database	http://www.imdb.com
Museum of Modern Art	http://www.moma.org

Thematic Wordfinder

This section of thematically organized vocabulary lists is designed as an aid to self-expression, and will be invaluable whether you are writing a paper, essay, speech, business report, or article. The subject areas covered have been chosen for their topicality and relevance to the needs of today's student. The lists are intended not only to provide the concrete vocabulary you require, but also to help with construction and usage, allowing you to express your opinion and structure your views clearly and idiomatically.

Contents

 Expressing your opinion / Wie man seine Ansichten zum Ausdruck bringen kann

Agreeing and Disagreeing	Zustimmung und Ablehnung
Agreeing	Zustimmung
It's a good idea.	Das ist eine gute Idee.
As X has emphasized...	Wie X unterstrichen hat...
It is true that...	Es ist richtig, dass...
You have to admit that...	Du musst zugeben, dass...
It seems to me to be completely justified to want to...	Es scheint mir absolut gerechtfertigt zu sein, ... zu wollen
I am delighted to accept (the invitation).	Ich nehme (die Einladung) sehr gerne an.
I share your concern about/reluctance to do this	Ich teile deine Sorge darum/deinen Widerwillen dagegen, das zu tun.
I share your opinion.	Ich teile deine Meinung.
I agree (completely) with you.	Ich bin (ganz) deiner Meinung.
I agree completely with X about this.	In dieser Sache bin ich ganz der Meinung von X.
I agree entirely.	Ganz meine Meinung.
I grant you that...	Ich gebe zu, dass...

continued...

 *continued...*

I think it is an excellent idea to do this.	Ich finde, es ist eine ausgezeichnete Idee, das zu tun.
We agree on the need to do this.	Wir sind uns über die Notwendigkeit, das zu tun, einig.
You are/He is absolutely right.	Du hast/Er hat völlig Recht.
X states, quite rightly, that...	X sagt völlig zu Recht, dass...

Disagreeing	Ablehnung
It's a pity that...	Es ist schade, dass...
It is unthinkable that...	Es is undenkbar, dass...
You can't say that...	Man kann nicht sagen, dass...
It is, however, difficult to believe that...	Es fällt freilich schwer, zu glauben, dass...
It is an exaggeration to say that...	Es ist übertrieben, zu sagen, dass...
I think that we must moderate our judgement.	Ich finde, wir dürfen nicht so hart urteilen.
I think it is totally inappropriate to do this.	Ich denke, es ist völlig unangemessen, das zu tun.
On the contrary, it seems to me that/the way I see it is that...	Mir scheint im Gegenteil, dass...
I'm afraid that I must refuse.	Ich muss leider ablehnen.
Unfortunately, I feel that I must contradict you.	Ich kann leider nicht umhin, dir zu widersprechen.
I disagree with X about this.	In dieser Sache bin ich anderer Meinung als X.
I disagree with those people who think that...	Ich teile nicht die Ansicht derer, die glauben, dass...
I disagree completely.	Ich bin völlig anderer Meinung.
I refuse to believe that...	Ich glaube einfach nicht, dass...
I (deeply) regret that...	Ich bedaure (zutiefst), dass...
I am sorry to have to contradict you, but...	Es tut mir leid, dir widersprechen zu müssen, aber...
It is easy to be critical, but I think it would be more constructive to suggest some alternative solutions.	Es ist leicht zu kritisieren, aber ich fände es hilfreicher, alternative Lösungen vorzuschlagen.
We have different opinions on the matter.	Wir sind darüber verschiedener Meinung.
We have diametrically opposed opinions (on/about...).	Unsere Ansichten (über...) sind diametral entgegengesetzt.

Giving your opinion | ## Meinungsäußerungen

In my opinion...	Meines Erachtens...; Nach meiner Meinung...; Meiner Ansicht nach...
I'd be very surprised if...	Es würde mich sehr überraschen, wenn...
It is undeniable that...	Es ist nicht zu leugnen, dass...
It's difficult for me to give my opinion about...	Es fällt mir schwer, zu sagen, was ich über... denke.
I think it's important to say/to stress that...	Ich denke, es ist wichtig festzustellen/zu betonen, dass
It seems to me that...	Mir scheint, dass...
It seems obvious that...	Es dürfte klar sein, dass...
I have/get the impression that...	Ich habe den Eindruck, dass...
I believe that...	Ich glaube, dass...
I think it's completely normal/abnormal to do this.	Ich finde es absolut normal/nicht normal, das zu tun.
I imagine it must be difficult to do this.	Ich stelle es mir schwer vor, das zu tun.
I consider that...	Ich finde, dass...
I am (very much) afraid that...	Ich fürchte (sehr), dass...
I must say that...	Ich muss sagen, dass...
I sincerely doubt whether...	Ich habe wirklich Zweifel, ob...
I just think that...	Ich denke einfach, dass...
I don't wish to pass judgement, but it appears that...	Ich möchte darüber kein Urteil abgeben, aber es scheint, dass...
I see no advantage in...	Ich sehe in...keinen Vorteil.
I think that...	Ich denke, dass...
I am certain that...	Ich bin sicher, dass...
I am convinced that...	Ich bin (davon) überzeugt, dass...
I assume/suppose that...	Ich nehme an, dass...
I must stress that...	Ich möchte betonen, dass...
Personally, I'm not in favour.	Ich persönlich bin nicht dafür.

 *continued...*

Why don't we do this?   Warum tun wir es nicht?
As you are asking me for my opinion   Da du mich nach meiner Meinung (dazu/darüber)
  (about/on this)…   fragst…

Structuring your views	Mittel zur Strukturierung von Meinungsäußerungen
admittedly	zugegebenermaßen
again	wieder; andererseits
also/as well	auch; ebenfalls
although	obwohl; obgleich
at any rate, in any case	auf jeden Fall
at last	schließlich
at least	zumindest
be that as it may	wie dem auch sei
to begin with	zunächst einmal; zuerst einmal
but	aber; sondern
consequently	folglich; infolgedessen
finally	schließlich
first of all	zuerst; vor allem
first (and foremost)	an erster Stelle; hauptsächlich
having said that	abgesehen davon
hence	daher
however	jedoch
in addition	außerdem
in conclusion	zum Abschluss
in fact	tatsächlich
In other words	mit anderen Worten
in short	kurz
in spite of	trotz
in the first place	zuerst; gleich
indeed	in der Tat; tatsächlich
moreover	und außerdem; zudem
most importantly	an erster Stelle; hauptsächlich
nevertheless	trotzdem; nichtsdestoweniger
none the less	nichtsdestoweniger
now	jetzt; nun; also
on the contrary	im Gegenteil
on the other hand	andererseits; auf der anderen Seite
only	nur
still	trotzdem
to sum up	zusammenfassend
that's the reason/that's why	deshalb; darum
then	dann; außerdem
therefore	deshalb; also

Environment/Umwelt

Protection of the Environment/ Der Schutz der Umwelt

air quality	Luftqualität, *die*
biodegradable	biologisch abbaubar
to campaign for	kämpfen für
catalytic converter	Katalysator, *der*
CFC-free spray	FCKW-freies Spray
closed to traffic	(für den Fahrzeug-verkehr) gesperrt
container	Behälter, *der*
ecological	ökologisch
economical car	sparsames Auto
energy: • to save energy	• Energie sparen
environmentalist	Umweltschützer, *der/* -in, *die*
to fit a vehicle with...	ein Fahrzeug mit... ausrüsten
Green Party	Grüne Partei (*in Germany*: die Grünen)
household refuse collection	Hausmüllsammlung, *die*; Müllabfuhr, *die*
nature conservation	Naturschutz, *der*
non-pollutant product	umweltverträgliches Produkt
nuclear fallout	nuklearer Fall-out
organic product	Bioprodukt, *das*
ozone-friendly	ozonfreundlich
to pedestrianize an area	ein Gebiet zur Fuß-gängerzone machen
pollution: • to fight pollution	• die Umweltverschmut-zung bekämpfen
to protect: • to protect endangered species • protected species	• bedrohte Arten schützen • geschützte Arten
to realize the risks	die Risiken erkennen
to reclaim	wiederverwenden
recyclable	recycelbar
recycling: • glass/paper/battery recycling • recycling centre	• Recycling, *das* von Glas/Papier/Batterien • Recyclingzentrum, *das*
to reduce waste	Müll vermeiden
reforestation	Wiederaufforstung, *die*
to replant a forest	einen Wald wieder auf-forsten
responsibility: • to give the public a sense of responsib-ility	• bei der Öffentlichkeit Verantwortungsbe-wusstsein wecken
to restock a forest	in einem Waldgebiet Tiere wieder ansiedeln
to salvage	für die Wiederverwen-dung sammeln
unleaded petrol	bleifreies Benzin
waste: • waste processing • to limit waste production	• Abfallaufbereitung, *die* • weniger Müll produzieren

The Deterioration of the Environment/ Die Schädigung der Umwelt

acid rain	saurer Regen
aerosol spray	Spray, *das* (mit Treibgas)
barrel	Barrel, *das*
black tide	Ölpest, *die*
CFC (chlorofluorocarbon)	CFK, *der* (Chlorfluorkohlenstoff), FCKW, *der* (Fluorchlor-kohlenwasserstoff)
climate	Klima, *das*
climatic variation	Klimaschwankungen, *Pl.*
deforestation	Entwaldung, *die*
desertification	Verwüstung, *die*; Desertifikation, *die*
destruction of wildlife/ flora	Vernichtung, *die* der Fauna/Flora
drought	Dürre, *die*
to dump toxic waste	Giftmüll verklappen
ecological disaster	Umweltkatastrophe, *die*
to exhaust natural resources	natürliche Ressourcen erschöpfen
extinct	ausgestorben
extinction	Aussterben, *das*
global warming	globaler Temperatur-anstieg
greenhouse effect: • to increase/reduce the greenhouse effect	• den Treibhauseffekt verstärken/verringern
groundwater	Grundwasser, *das*
heatwave	Hitzewelle, *die*
oil slick	Ölteppich, *der*
ozone layer	Ozonschicht, *die*
pollutant	Schadstoff, *der*
pollution: • air pollution • atmospheric pollution	• Luftverschmutzung, *die* • Verschmutzung, *die* der Atmosphäre
• noise pollution • urban pollution	• Lärmbelastung, *die* • Verschmutzung, *die* der städtischen Umwelt
• water pollution	• Wasserverschmutzung, *die*
power station: • nuclear power station • thermal power station	• Kernkraftwerk, *das*; Atomkraftwerk, *das* • Wärmekraftwerk, *das*
seepage	Versickerung, *die*
temperature	Temperatur, *die*
toxic: • toxic cloud • toxic waste	• Giftwolke, *die* • Giftmüll, *der*
to upset the balance of nature	das natürliche Gleichgewicht stören
waste: • industrial waste • radioactive waste	• Industrieabfall, *der*; Industrieabfälle *Pl.* • radioaktiver Abfall; radioaktive Abfälle

Natural Disasters/Naturkatastrophen

amplitude	Amplitude, *die*
ash	Asche, *die*
avalanche	Lawine, *die*

bed (of a river)	Bett, das; Flussbett, das
to burst its banks	über die Ufer treten
crater	Krater, der
cyclone	Zyklon, der; Wirbelsturm, der
disaster	Katastrophe, die
downstream	flussabwärts
earthquake	Erdbeben, das
earth tremor	Erdstoß, der; leichtes Erdbeben
emergency shelter	Notunterkunft, die
epicentre	Epizentrum, das
to evacuate an area	ein Gebiet evakuieren
flood	Überschwemmung, die
forest fire	Waldbrand, der
gale	Sturm, der
hurricane	Hurrikan, der; Orkan, der
landslide	Erdrutsch, der
lava	Lava, die
magma	Magma, das
natural phenomenon	Naturphänomen, das; Naturerscheinung, die
to overflow its bank	über die Ufer treten
Richter scale	Richterskala, die
rockfall	Steinschlag, der
seismograph	Seismograf, der
seismology	Seismologie, die
spate:	
• a river in spate	• ein Hochwasser führender Fluss
storm	Unwetter, das; Gewitter, das
to tame nature	die Natur zähmen
thaw	Tau, der
tidal wave	Flutwelle, die
tornado	Tornado, der
typhoon	Taifun, der
upstream	flussaufwärts
vagaries of nature	Launen Pl. der Natur
volcanic eruption	Vulkanausbruch, der
volcano:	
• an active volcano	• ein aktiver Vulkan; ein tätiger Vulkan
• an extinct volcano	• ein erloschener Vulkan
whirlpool	Strudel, der
whirlwind	Wirbelwind, der

¶¶ Society/Gesellschaft

Politics/Politik

to abstain	sich (der Stimme) enthalten
abstention	Stimmenthaltung, die; Enthaltung, die
to be appointed	ernannt werden
ballot box	Wahlurne, die
ballot paper	Stimmzettel, der
to campaign	Wahlkampf machen; einen Wahlkampf führen

candidate	Kandidat, der/-in, die
congress	Kongress, der
constituency	Wahlkreis, der
to count the votes	die Stimmen auszählen
deputy	Stellvertreter, der/-in, die
to elect	wählen
election:	
• general election	• Parlamentswahl, die
• local election	• Kommunalwahl, die
• presidential election	• Präsidentschaftswahl, die
• election campaign	• Wahlkampf, der
electoral roll:	
• to have oneself put on the electoral roll	• sich in das Wählerverzeichnis eintragen lassen
electorate	Wählerschaft, die
executive power	exekutive Gewalt; Exekutive, die
extremist	Extremist, der/-in, die
government:	
• to form a government	• eine Regierung bilden
the Left	die Linke
left-wing	link...; links
legislative power	legislative Gewalt; gesetzgebende Gewalt
legislature	Legislative, die
majority	Mehrheit, die
minister	Minister, der/-in, die
ministry	Ministerium, das
moderate	gemäßigt
MP (Member of Parliament)	Abgeordnete, der/die
opinion poll	Meinungsumfrage, die
opposition	Opposition, die
parliament	Parlament, das
party:	
• to belong to a party	• einer Partei angehören
policy:	
• economic policy	• Wirtschaftspolitik, die
• foreign policy	• Außenpolitik, die
• domestic policy	• Innenpolitik, die
political party	politische Partei
political scandal	politischer Skandal; Politskandal, der
politician	Politiker, der/-in, die
polling booth	Wahlkabine, die
polling card	Wahlausweis, der
polling station	Wahllokal, das
popularity rating	Beliebtheitsquote, die
president	Präsident, der/-in, die
prime minister	Premierminister, der/-in, die; Ministerpräsident, der/-in, die
public opinion	öffentliche Meinung
referendum	Volksentscheid, der; Referendum, das
republic	Republik, die
right:	
• to give sb. the right to vote	• jmdm. das Wahlrecht geben
• to have the right to vote	• wahlberechtigt sein
the Right	die Rechte
right-wing	recht...; rechts

Secretary of State	(*in den USA*) Außenminister, *der* /-in, *die*
Senate	Senat, *der*
speech	Rede, *die*
to stand for election	kandidieren
turnout:	
• there was a low turnout (at the polls)	• die Wahlbeteiligung war niedrig
universal suffrage	allgemeines Wahlrecht
vote	Stimme, *die*
to vote	wählen; abstimmen
voter	Wähler, *der*/-in, *die*

Social Issues/Soziales

abortion	Abtreibung, *die*
Aids	Aids, *das*
anti-racist movement	antirassistische Bewegung
anti-semitism	Antisemitismus, *der*
benefit	Beihilfe, *die*; Unterstützung, *die*
block of council flats	Block, *der* mit Sozialwohnungen
cardboard city	Obdachlosenschlafplatz, *der* im Freien
contraception	Empfängnisverhütung, *die*
discrimination against young people/women/disabled people/old people, *etc.*	Diskriminierung, *die* junger Menschen/von Frauen/Behinderter/ alter Menschen *usw.*
drug:	
• to take drugs	• Drogen nehmen
equality	Gleichheit, *die*; (*equal rights*) Gleichberechtigung, *die*; Gleichstellung, *die*
ethnic group	ethnische Gruppe
family environment	familiäres Umfeld
fight against Aids/racism	Kampf, *der* gegen Aids/ den Rassismus
fringe:	
• to live on the fringes of society	• am Rand der Gesellschaft leben
generation gap	Generationsunterschied, *der*; (*conflict*) Generationskonflikt, *der*
homeless:	
• homeless person	• Obdachlose, *der/die*
• homeless people	• Obdachlose *Pl.*; Wohnsitzlose *Pl.*
housing estate	Wohnsiedlung, *die*
illiteracy	Analphabetismus, *der*
to leave school at 16	mit 16 von der Schule abgehen
minority	Minderheit, *die*; Minorität, *die*
overdose	Überdosis, *die*
poverty	Armut, *die*
prejudice	Vorurteil, *das*
privileged/underprivileged background	privilegierter/unterprivilegierter Background
qualification:	
• to have no qualifications	• keinerlei Qualifikation haben
racism	Rassismus, *der*
to rebel	rebellieren

segregation	Rassentrennung, *die*
sexism	Sexismus, *der*
single-parent family	Einelternfamilie, *die*
slum belt	Slumgürtel, *der*
social worker	Sozialarbeiter, *der*/-in, *die*
suburb	Vorstadt, *die*
suicide attempt	Selbstmordversuch, *der*
tramp	Landstreicher, *der*/-in, *die*; (*in town*) Stadtstreicher, *der*/-in, *die*
unemployment	Arbeitslosigkeit, *die*
university:	
• to go to university	• die Universität besuchen; [an der Universität] studieren
vandalism	Vandalismus, *der*
xenophobia	Fremdenfeindlichkeit, *die*; Xenophobie, *die*

Emigration and Immigration/Auswanderung und Einwanderung

asylum-seeker	Asylbewerber, *der*/-in, *die*
border:	
• to be turned back at the border	• an der Grenze zurückgewiesen werden
• to close/open the borders	• die Grenzen schließen/ öffnen
brain drain	Braindrain, *der*
citizenship:	
• to acquire American/German citizenship	• die amerikanische/ deutsche Staatsbürgerschaft erlangen
country of origin	Herkunftsland, *das*
country of refuge	Fluchtland, *das*
culture shock	Kulturschock, *der*
customs:	
• to go through customs	• durch den Zoll gehen
deported	abgeschoben; ausgewiesen
economic refugee	Wirtschaftsflüchtling, *der*
emigrant	Emigrant, *der*/-in, *die*; Auswanderer, *der*/ Auswanderin, *die*
exodus	Exodus, *der*; Massenflucht, *die*
expatriate	Exilant, *der*/-in, *die*; Ausländer, *der*/-in, *die*
host country	Gastland, *das*
illegal immigrant	illegaler Einwanderer/ illegale Einwanderin
immigrant	Immigrant, *der*/-in, *die*; Einwanderer, *der*/Einwanderin, *die*
immigration	Einwanderung, *die*; Immigration, *die*
integration	Integration, *die*
intolerance	Intoleranz, *die*
law:	
• law on immigration	• Einwanderungsgesetz, *das*
• law on nationality	• Staatsbürgerschaftsgesetz, *das*
naturalization	Einbürgerung, *die*; Naturalisation, *die*
to naturalize	einbürgern; naturalisieren
permit:	
• resident's permit	• Aufenthaltserlaubnis, *die*

• work permit	• Arbeitserlaubnis, *die*	• to look for a job	• eine Stelle/einen Job suchen
political asylum	politisches Asyl	• to lose one's job	• seine Stelle/seinen Job verlieren
political refugee	politischer Flüchtling		
quota	Quote, *die*	labour	Arbeitskräfte *Pl.*
to turn back	zurückweisen; abweisen	lay-off	vorübergehende Entlassung
uprooted	entwurzelt		
visa:		long-term unemployed	langzeitarbeitslos
• renewable visa	• verlängerbares Visum	manufacturing industry sector	verarbeitende Industrie
• student visa	• Studentenvisum, *das*		
• temporary visa	• befristetes Visum	notice	Kündigung, *die*
• tourist visa	• Touristenvisum, *das*	office hours	Bürostunden *Pl.*
wave of immigration	Einwanderungswelle, *die*	overtime	Überstunden *Pl.*
		part-time work	Teilzeitarbeit, *die*

Business and Industry/Geschäftswelt und Industrie

		to pay:	
		• to be badly paid	• schlecht bezahlt werden
		primary sector	primärer Sektor
		profile:	
		• to have the right profile	• das richtige Profil haben
		to receive a salary/ receive benefit	ein Gehalt beziehen/ Sozialhilfe bekommen
		redundancy	Entlassung, *die*
		redundancy payment	Abfindung, *die*
		redundant:	

Employment and Unemployment/ Beschäftigung und Arbeitslosigkeit

39/35-*etc.* hour week	39-/35-Stunden-Woche, *die usw.*	• to make redundant	• entlassen
		to register as unemployed	sich arbeitslos melden
adult education	Erwachsenenbildung, *die*		
application:		to reintegrate	wieder eingliedern
• application form	• Antragsformular, *das*	to resign	kündigen
• unsolicited application	• Blindbewerbung, *die*	salaried employee	Gehaltsempfänger, *der* /-in, *die*
benefits package	Paket, *das* von Sozialleistungen		
		salary	Gehalt, *das*
to create:		self-employed person	Selbständige, *der/die*
• to help create new jobs	• zur Schaffung neuer Arbeitsplätze beitragen	service sector	Dienstleistungssektor, *der*
		shift:	
contract	Vertrag, *der*	• to work shifts	• Schicht arbeiten
CV, curriculum vitae	Lebenslauf, *der*	sick pay	Krankengeld, *das*
to dismiss	entlassen	to sign on at the unemployment office	sich arbeitslos melden, stempeln gehen (*ugs.*)
dismissal	Entlassung, *die*		
economic crisis	Wirtschaftskrise, *die*	social security	(*benefit*) Sozialhilfe, *die*
employee	Arbeitnehmer, *der*/-in, *die*; Beschäftigte, *der/die*	take-home pay	Nettolohn, *der*; (*salary*) Nettogehalt, *das*
employer	Arbeitgeber, *der*/-in, *die*	temp	Zeitarbeitskraft, *die*
employment agency	Stellenvermittlung, *die*	to temp	Zeitarbeit machen
full-time	ganztägig; ganztags	training course	Lehrgang, *der*
gross pay	Bruttolohn, *der*; Bruttogehalt, *das*	unemployed person	Arbeitslose, *der/die*
		unemployment:	Arbeitslosigkeit, *die*
guaranteed minimum wage	garantierter Mindestlohn	• unemployment benefit	• Arbeitslosengeld, *das*
		wage	Lohn, *der*
to hire	einstellen	wage earner	Lohnempfänger, *der*/-in, *die*
to interview sb (for a job)	mit jmdm. ein Vorstellungs- gespräch/Einstellungs- gespräch führen	to work:	
		• to work part-time/ full-time	• Teilzeit/ganztags arbeiten
job:		• to work without declar- ing one's earnings	• schwarz arbeiten
• job interview	• Vorstellungsgespräch, *das*; Einstellungs- gespräch, *das*	• working conditions	• Arbeitsbedingungen *Pl.*
		• working hours	• Arbeitszeit, *die*
• job market	• Arbeitsmarkt, *der*	• working population	• arbeitende Bevölkerung
• job security	• Sicherheit, *die* des Arbeitsplatzes/der Arbeitsplätze		
• job-seeker	• Arbeitssuchende, *der/die*		

Trade and Commerce/Handel und Gewerbe

• to change jobs	• den Arbeitsplatz/den Job/ die Stelle wechseln	after-sales service	Kundendienst, *der*
		balance of trade	Handelsbilanz, *die*
• to create job opportunities	• Arbeitsplätze schaffen	bankrupt:	
• to have a job	• eine Stelle/einen Job haben	• to go bankrupt	• Bankrott machen

to buy out a business	ein Unternehmen aufkaufen
to buy a shop	einen Laden/ ein Geschäft kaufen
car manufacturer	Automobilhersteller, der
chain of stores	Handelskette, die
chamber of commerce	Handelskammer, die
to clear goods	Waren ausverkaufen
to compete with	konkurrieren mit
competition	Konkurrenz, die; Wettbewerb, der
competitor	Konkurrent, der/-in, die
cost price	Selbstkostenpreis, der
customer service	Kundendienst, der
deficit	Defizit, das
delivery	Lieferung, die
department store	Kaufhaus, das; Warenhaus, das
to develop a product	ein Produkt entwickeln
to distribute a product	ein Produkt vertreiben
distribution	Vertrieb, der
to export	exportieren; ausführen
exportation	Export, der; Ausfuhr, die
exports	Exporte Pl.
fair	Messe, die
finished product	Fertigprodukt, das
foreign trade	Außenhandel, der
free trade	Freihandel, der
to import	importieren; einführen
importation	Import, der; Einfuhr, die
imports	Importe Pl.
inclusive of tax	inklusive Steuern
invoice	Rechnung, die
to launch a product	ein Produkt auf den Markt bringen; ein Produkt einführen
line	(product) Artikel, der; (of business) Branche, die
mail-order business	(trading) Versandhandel, der; (firm) Versandhaus, das
manufacturer	Hersteller, der/-in, die
manufacturing fault	Herstellungsfehler, der; Produktionsfehler, der
market:	
• lower end of the market	• unteres Marktsegment
• top end of the market	• oberes Marktsegment
to mass-produce	in Massenproduktion herstellen
motor show	Automobilausstellung, die
oddment	Reststück, das
to open a shop	einen Laden/ein Geschäft eröffnen/aufmachen
opening hours	Öffnungszeiten Pl.
order:	
• to place an order	• einen Auftrag vergeben
to order	bestellen
product	Produkt, das; Erzeugnis, das
profit:	
• to make a profit	• Gewinn machen
purchasing power	Kaufkraft, die
quality control	Qualitätskontrolle, die
range of products	Sortiment, das; Warenangebot, das

raw material	Rohstoff, der
to retail, to sell retail	im Einzelhandel verkaufen
retail trade	Einzelhandel, der
sale	Verkauf, der; (clearance sale) Ausverkauf, der
sales	Absatz, der; (figures) Verkaufszahlen Pl.
sales rep, sales representative	Handelsvertreter, der/ -in, die
to sell at a loss	mit Verlust verkaufen
shop	Laden, der; Geschäft, das
shop assistant	Verkäufer, der/-in, die
shopkeeper	Ladeninhaber, der/-in, die
shopping area	Geschäftsviertel, das
shopping centre	Einkaufszentrum, das
sole distributor	Alleinvertreiber, der/ -in, die
stock:	
• out of stock	• ausverkauft; nicht vorrätig
• to keep a line in stock	• eine Produktlinie führen
to stock:	
• to be well-stocked	• ein großes Lager haben; gut sortiert sein
stocktaking:	
• to do the stocktaking	• die Inventur machen
supplier	Lieferant, der/-in, die
supply and demand	Angebot und Nachfrage
to test a product	ein Produkt testen
trade agreements	Handelsabkommen, das
trade fair	Messe, die
trading partner	Handelspartner, der/-in, die
value:	
• to be (good) value for money	• seinen Preis wert sein
VAT, value-added tax	MWSt, Mehrwertsteuer, die
warehouse	Lagerhalle, die
to wholesale, to sell wholesale	im Großhandel verkaufen
wholesale trade	Großhandel, der
wholesaler	Großhändler, der/-in, die; Grossist, der/-in, die

Marketing and Publicity/ Marketing und Publicity

to advertise	werben; (in newspaper) inserieren
advertisement	Anzeige, die
advertising:	
• advertising agency	• Werbeagentur, die
• advertising campaign	• Werbekampagne, die
• advertising department	• Werbeabteilung, die
• advertising executive	• Werbeleiter, der/-in, die
• advertising space	• Platz, der für Anzeigen
'as seen on TV'	'aus der Fernsehwerbung'
brand	Marke, die
brand image	Markenimage, die
brand loyalty	Markentreue, die
buoyant market	lebhafter Markt
commercial	Werbespot, der; Werbung, die
consumer survey	Verbraucherbefragung, die
discount	Preisnachlass, der; Rabatt, der

launch campaign	Einführungskampagne, *die*
make	Marke, *die*
market:	
• market research	• Marktforschung, *die*
• market share	• Marktanteil, *der*
• market trends	• Markttrends *Pl.*
• to break into a market	• in einem Markt Fuß fassen
• to dominate a market	• einen Markt beherrschen
• to find a gap in the market	• eine Marktlücke finden
• to market a product	• ein Produkt vermarkten
marketing:	
• marketing budget	• Marketingetat, *der*
• Marketing Department	• Marketingabteilung, *die*
poster	Plakat, *das*; Poster, *das*
to promote a product	ein Produkt bewerben
PR	PR
promotional insert	Werbebeilage, *die*
promotional literature/ material	Werbematerial, *das*
public relations	Publicrelations *Pl.*
radio commercial	Radiospot, *der*
reply card	Antwortkarte, *die*
sales manager	Verkaufsleiter, *der*/-in, *die*
sales strategy	Absatzstrategie, *die*
slogan	Slogan, *der*, Werbespruch, *der*
special offer	Sonderangebot, *das*
to sponsor an event	eine Veranstaltung sponsern
survey	Umfrage, *die*
telephone sales	Telefonmarketing, *das*
to target	zielen auf
target group	Zielgruppe, *die*
TV advertising	Fernsehwerbung, *die*
voucher	Gutschein, *der*

Communication/ Kommunikation

Telephone/Telefon

answer:	
• there is no answer	• es meldet sich niemand
• to answer the phone	• ans Telefon gehen
• answering machine	• Anrufbeantworter, *der*
busy	besetzt
call charges	Gesprächsgebühren *Pl.*
car phone	Autotelefon, *das*
cardphone	Kartentelefon, *das*
cordless telephone	schnurloses Telefon
dial	Wählscheibe, *die*
to dial a number	eine Nummer wählen
dialling code	Vorwahl, *die*
dialling tone:	
• to wait for the dialling tone	• den Wählton abwarten
directory enquiries:	
• to call directory enquiries	• die Auskunft anrufen
electronic directory	elektronisches Verzeichnis
emergency number	Notrufnummer, *die*

engaged	besetzt
ex-directory:	
• to be ex-directory	• eine Geheimnummer haben; nicht im Telefonbuch stehen
extension number	Nebenstellennummer, *die*
fax	Fax, *das*; Telefax, *das*
to fax	faxen
freefone number	Freecallnummer, *die*
handset	Handapparat, *der*
to hang up	auflegen
hello	hallo
line:	
• hold the line	• bleiben Sie am Apparat
message:	
• could you take a message (for him/her)?	• können Sie [ihm/ihr] etwas ausrichten?
• to leave a message after the tone	• nach dem Ton eine Nachricht hinterlassen
mobile phone	Mobiltelefon, *das*; Handy, *das*
number	Nummer, *die*
operator	Operator, *der*/-in, *die*
phone	Telefon, *das*
phonebook	Telefonbuch, *das*
phonecard	Telefonkarte, *die*
public phone	öffentliches Telefon
to put through:	
• I'm putting you through	• ich stelle Sie durch; ich verbinde
receiver:	
• to pick up the receiver	• den Hörer abnehmen
remote-access answering machine	Anrufbeantworter, *der* mit Fernabfrage
reverse:	
• to make a reverse-charge call to sb	• jmdn. per R-Gespräch anrufen
to ring:	
• to hear the phone ring	• das Telefon klingeln hören
• to let the phone ring ten times	• das Telefon zehnmal klingeln lassen
to speak:	
• could I speak to Mr X?	• Kann ich Herrn X sprechen?
• who's that speaking?	• Wer ist am Apparat?
telephone:	
• telephone directory	• Telefonbuch, *das*
voice mail	Sprachnachricht, *die*; Voicemail, *die*
wrong:	
• you've got the wrong number	• Sie sind falsch verbunden
Yellow Pages	Gelbe Seiten

Computing/Computertechnik

application program	Anwendungsprogramm, *das*
artificial intelligence	künstliche Intelligenz
byte	Byte, *das*
CD, compact disk	CD, *die*
CD-I, interactive compact disk	CD-I, *die*; interaktive CD
CD-ROM	CD-ROM, *die*
CD-ROM disk drive	CD-ROM-Laufwerk, *das*

central processing unit, CPU	Zentraleinheit, *die*; Rechnerkern, *der*
(silicon) chip	(Silizium)chip, *der*
to click:	
• to click on sth	• etw. anklicken
• to click on the mouse	• mit der Maus klicken
• to double-click on the mouse	• mit der Maus doppel-klicken
computer:	
• computer engineer	• Computertechniker, *der*/-in, *die*
• computer game	• Computerspiel, *das*
• computer-generated image	• Computergrafik, *die*
• computer scientist	• Computerwissenschaft-ler, *der*/-in, *die*
• computer training course	• Computerkurs, *der*
• computer-aided	• computerunterstützt
to computerize	computerisieren
computing	Computertechnik, *die*; (*use*) Computereinsatz, *der*
to copy a file onto a floppy disk	eine Datei auf eine Diskette kopieren
to copy and paste	kopieren und einfügen
to create a document/ a file	ein Dokument/eine Datei anlegen
cursor	Cursor, *der*
data capture	Datenerfassung, *die*
data processing	Datenverarbeitung, *die*
database	Datenbank, *die*
to delete a document/ file	ein Dokument/eine Datei löschen
desktop computer	Tischcomputer, *der*; Desktop[computer], *der*
disk drive	Diskettenlaufwerk, *das*
diskette	Diskette, *die*
email	E-Mail, *die*
educational software	Lernsoftware, *die*
electronic data	elektronische Daten
electronical	elektronisch
file-management system	Dateimanagementsystem, *das*
floppy disk, diskette	Diskette, *die*
to format	formatieren
formatting	Formatierung, *die*
function key	Funktionstaste, *die*
hard disk	Festplatte, *die*
hardcopy	Ausdruck, *der*
hardware	Hardware, *die*
icon	Icon, *das*
information technology	Informatik, *die*
KB, kilobyte	KB; Kilobyte, *das*
key	Taste, *die*
keyboard	Tastatur, *die*
keyboarder	Taster, *der*/-in, *die*; Erfasser, *der*/-in, *die*
laptop (computer)	Laptop[computer], *der*
Mb, megabyte	MB, Megabyte, *das*
memory	Speicher, *der*
menu	Menü, *das*
microprocessor	Mikroprozessor, *der*
mouse	Maus, *die*
multimedia computer	Multimediacomputer, *der*
network	Netzwerk, *das*; Netz, *das*
to open a new window	ein neues Fenster öffnen

PC	PC, *der*
port	Anschluss, *der*; Port, *der*
portable computer	tragbarer Computer
to print a document	ein Dokument ausdrucken
printer	Drucker, *der*
printout	Ausdruck, *der*
program	Programm, *das*
RAM, random access memory	RAM, *das*; Schreib-Lese-Speicher, *der*
ROM, read-only memory	ROM, *das*; Festspeicher, *der*
to save a file	eine Datei sichern
screen	Bildschirm, *der*
to scroll	scrollen
server	Server, *der*
smart card	Chipkarte, *die*
software	Software, *die*
space bar	Leertaste, *die*
speech recognition	Spracherkennung, *die*
spellchecker	Rechtschreibprüf-programm, *das*
systems analyst	Systemanalytiker, *der*/-in, *die*
user-friendly	benutzerfreundlich
virus	Virus, *das*
window	Fenster, *das*
word processing	Textverarbeitung, *die*
word processor	Textverarbeitungssystem, *das*

(*see also* Guide to exploring the Internet)

 # Media and Arts/ Medien und Künste

Television/Fernsehen

aerial	Antenne, *die*
announcer	Ansager, *der*/-in, *die*
broadcasting satellite	Rundfunksatellit, *der*
cable TV	Kabelfernsehen, *das*
to get (hooked up to) cable TV	sich verkabeln lassen
camcorder	Camcorder, *der*
cathode-ray tube	Kathodenstrahlröhre, *die*
channel	Kanal, *der*; Programm, *das*
commercial/state-owned channel	privater/staatlicher Sender
children's programme	Kinderprogramm, *das*
commentator	Kommentator, *der*/-in, *die*
commercial	Werbespot, *der*
commercial TV	kommerzielles Fernsehen
decoder	Decoder, *der*
documentary	(*report*) Dokumentar-bericht, der; (*film*) Dokumentarfilm, *der*
entertainment programme	Unterhaltungssendung, *die*; Unterhaltungs-programm, *das*
episode	Folge, *die*

evening news	Abendnachrichten *Pl.*
fast forward	schneller Vorlauf
freeze-frame	Standbild, *das*
game show	Gameshow, *die*
high-definition television	hoch auflösendes Fernsehen
interference	Störung, *die*
live:	
• to broadcast live	• live senden
news	Nachrichten *Pl.*
outside broadcast	Außenübertragung, *die*
peak viewing time	beste Sendezeit; Hauptsendezeit, *die*
portable television	tragbarer Fernseher
presenter	Moderator, *der/-in, die*
programme	Programm, *das*; (*broadcast*) Sendung, *die*
remote control	Fernbedienung, *die*
report	Bericht, *der*
rewind	Rücklauf, *der*
satellite dish	Satellitenschüssel, *die*
screen	Bildschirm, *der*
serial	Serie, *die*
soap	Seifenoper, *die*; Soap, *die*
subscription (TV) channel	Abonnentenkanal, *der*; Pay-TV-Kanal, *der*
to televise:	
• televised debate	• Fernsehdebatte, *die*
television:	Fernsehen, *das*
• to watch television	• fernsehen
TV:	
• TV film	• Fernsehfilm, *der*
• TV licence	• (*durch Zahlung einer Gebühr zu erwerbende*) Fernsehempfangsberechtigung
• TV programme	• Fernsehsendung, *die*
• TV series	• Fernsehserie, *die*
• to be on TV	• im Fernsehen sein
video	(*tape*)Video, *das*; (*recorder*) Videorekorder, *der*
video cassette	Videokassette, *die*
video recorder, VCR	Videorekorder, *der*
voice-over	Voice-over, *die*; Kommentarstimme, *die*
weather forecast	Wettervorhersage, *die*

Press and Journalism/Presse und Journalismus

article	Artikel, *der*
bed:	
• to put a paper to bed	• eine Zeitung in Druck geben
book critic	Buchkritiker, *der*
book review	Buchbesprechung, *die*
burning issue	brennendes Thema
cartoon	Karikatur, *die*
circulation:	
• a circulation of 10,000	• eine Auflage von 10 000
classified advertisements	Kleinanzeigen *Pl.*
column	Spalte, *die*
copy-editor	Redakteur, *der/-in, die*

correspondent:	
• our New York correspondent	• unser New Yorker Korrespondent/ unsere New Yorker Korrespondentin
to cover an event	über eine Veranstaltung berichten
daily (paper)	Tageszeitung, *die*
editor	Herausgeber, *der/-in, die*
editorial	Leitartikel, *der*
editorial offices	Redaktion, *die*
editorial staff	Redaktion, *die*
to found a newspaper	eine Zeitung gründen
film critic	Filmkritiker, *der/-in, die*
freedom of the press	Pressefreiheit, *die*
front page	Titelseite, *die*; erste Seite
gutter press	Sensationspresse, *die*
headline:	
• to be in/ hit the headlines	• in den Schlagzeilen sein/ Schlagzeilen machen
interview:	
• to give sb an interview	• jmdm. ein Interview geben
investigation	Untersuchung, *die*
job advertisements	Stellenanzeigen *Pl.*
journal:	
• literary/scientific journal	• Literaturzeitschrift, *die*/ [natur]wissenschaftliche Zeitschrift
journalist	Journalist, *der/-in, die*
leader	Leitartikel, *der*
letters to the editor	Leserbriefe *Pl.*
to listen to the news on the radio	die Nachrichten im Radio hören
magazine:	
• women's/sport *etc.* magazine	• Frauenzeitschrift/ Sportzeitschrift, *die usw.*
mass circulation paper	Massenblatt, *das*
monthly magazine	Monatszeitschrift, *die*
news:	
• news agency	• Nachrichtenagentur, *die*
• news in brief	• Kurznachrichten *Pl.*
• news magazine	• Nachrichtenmagazin, *das*
newsreader	Nachrichtensprecher, *der/ -in, die*
newspaper	Zeitung, *die*
photographer	Fotograf, *der/-in, die*
photojournalist	Fotoreporter, *der/-in, die*; Fotojournalist, *der/-in, die*
press conference	Pressekonferenz, *die*
press pass	Presseausweis, *der*
press release	Presseinformation, *die*
reporter	Reporter, *der/-in, die*
review	Rezension, *die*
review of the papers	(*on TV*) Presseschau, *die*
section:	
• arts/sports section	• Feuilleton, *das*/ Sportteil, *der*
special correspondent	Sonderkorrespondent, *der/-in, die*; Sonderberichterstatter, *der/-in, die*
special edition	Sonderausgabe, *die*
sub-editor	Redaktionsassistent, *der/-in, die*
survey	Umfrage, *die*; Erhebung, *die*

tabloid	(kleinformatige) Boulevardzeitung
topical issue	aktuelles Thema
weekly magazine	Wochenzeitschrift, die; Wochenmagazin, das

Cinema, Theatre and Music/ Kino, Theater und Musik

to act in a play	in einem Stück spielen
actor/actress	Schauspieler, der/-in, die
to make a film of a novel	einen Roman verfilmen
arthouse	Programmkino, das; Filmkunsttheater, das
avant-garde theatre	Avantgardetheater, das
backstage	hinter der Bühne
balcony	Balkon, der; oberster Rang
band	Kapelle, die; Band, die
bit part	kleine Rolle
blockbuster	Knüller, der
brass band	Blaskapelle, die
choir	Chor, der
cinema	Kino, das; Filmtheater, das
cinema complex	Kinocenter, das
circle	Rang, der
close-up	Großaufnahme, die; Nahaufnahme, die
comedy	Komödie, die
composer	Komponist, der/-in, die
concert:	
• classical music concert	• Konzert, das mit klassischer Musik
• rock concert	• Rockkonzert, das
• concert hall	• Konzerthalle, die
concerto:	
• piano/violin concerto	• Klavier-/Violinkonzert, das
to conduct an orchestra	ein Orchester dirigieren
conductor	Dirigent, der/-in, die
credits	Credits Pl.; Titel Pl.
to direct a film	bei einem Film Regie führen
director	Regisseur, der/-in, die
drama	Drama, das
dress circle	erster Rang
dress rehearsal	Kostümprobe, die
to dub	synchronisieren
editing	Schnitt, der; Montage, die
extra	Statist, der/-in, die; Komparse, der/ Komparsin, die
farce	Farce, die; Posse, die
film:	Film, der
• adventure/detective/ sci-fi film	• Abenteuer-/Kriminal-/ Sciencefictionfilm, der
• film buff	• Filmliebhaber, der/-in, die
• film club	• Filmclub, der
intermission, interval	Pause, die
jazz band	Jazzband, die
lead, leading role	Hauptrolle, die
light comedy	leichte Komödie
light music	leichte Musik; Unterhaltungsmusik, die

to lip-sync	zu einem Playback synchrone Lippenbewe- gungen machen
to manage a theatre	ein Theater leiten
multiplex	Multiplex, das
musical	Musical, das
musician	Musiker, der/-in, die
open-air theatre	Freilichtbühne, die, Freilichttheater, das
orchestra	Orchester, das
original:	
• in the original language	• in der Originalsprache; im Original
• original version	• Originalfassung, die; Original, das
a piece of music	Musikstück, das
preview	Preview, die
to produce:	
• to produce a film	• einen Film produzieren
• to produce a play	• ein Stück inszenieren
producer	Produzent, der/-in, die
to release:	
• to be released	• in die Kinos kommen
rushes	Muster[kopien] Pl.
scene	Szene, die
scriptwriter	Drehbuchautor, der/-in, die
set:	
• on the set	• am Drehort
singer	Sänger, der/-in, die
sold out	ausverkauft
soundtrack	Soundtrack, der
special effects	Special Effects Pl.
spectacular	spektakulär
stage:	
• stage door	• Bühneneingang, der
• to have stage fright	• Lampenfieber haben
• to go on [the] stage	• auf die Bühne gehen
• to stage a play	• ein Stück aufführen; ein Stück auf die Bühne bringen
stalls	Parkett, das
to star in a film	eine Hauptrolle in einem Film spielen
subtitled	untertitelt; mit Untertiteln
supporting part	Nebenrolle, die
theatre	Theater, das
tour:	
• to go on tour	• auf Tournee gehen
tragedy	Tragödie, die
trailer	Trailer, der
variety show	Varietee, das
the wings	die Kulissen Pl.
to zoom in on	[zu]zoomen auf

Guide to Exploring the Internet

The Internet

Although English is the primary language of the Internet (*das Internet*) and by far the most widely used (80% of all information is in English), the Internet is becoming increasingly multilingual. German speakers use a mixture of German and English terms, which exist side by side in some cases (*die Datenautobahn* and *der Information-Highway*; *die Web-Seite* but *die Homepage*). The most immediately useful function of the Internet for most people is of course email (*die E-Mail*), and no knowledge of the foreign language is needed to use this, although for recognition purposes it is useful to note that German addresses usually end in *de* and Austrian ones in *at* (for further details see below). FTP (File Transfer Protocol) allows one to send whole files which have been saved on the computer. Browsing or surfing (*das Surfen*) means moving from site to site on the web and visiting those of interest, which can be highly enjoyable, interesting and informative. Many German-language sites can be accessed and even include some which are bilingual (see below). Then there are thou-

sands of newsgroups (*Newsgroups*) on specific subjects, from politics and the arts to the most obscure hobbies, where you can find information and also leave your own contribution or ask questions to be answered by other participants. The other popular and genuinely interactive function of the Internet is IRC (Internet Relay Chat), which allows you to communicate with one or several other users in any part of the world.

Software for email, Web browsing and newsgroups in German can be downloaded for free from the following Web sites:

Microsoft Internet Explorer
http://www.microsoft.com *or* **http://www.microsoft.de**

Netscape Navigator
http://home.netscape.com/de

The most popular IRC software is available to download (also free) from mIRC at:
http://www.mirc.co.uk

Sending an email

The illustration shows a typical interface for sending email.

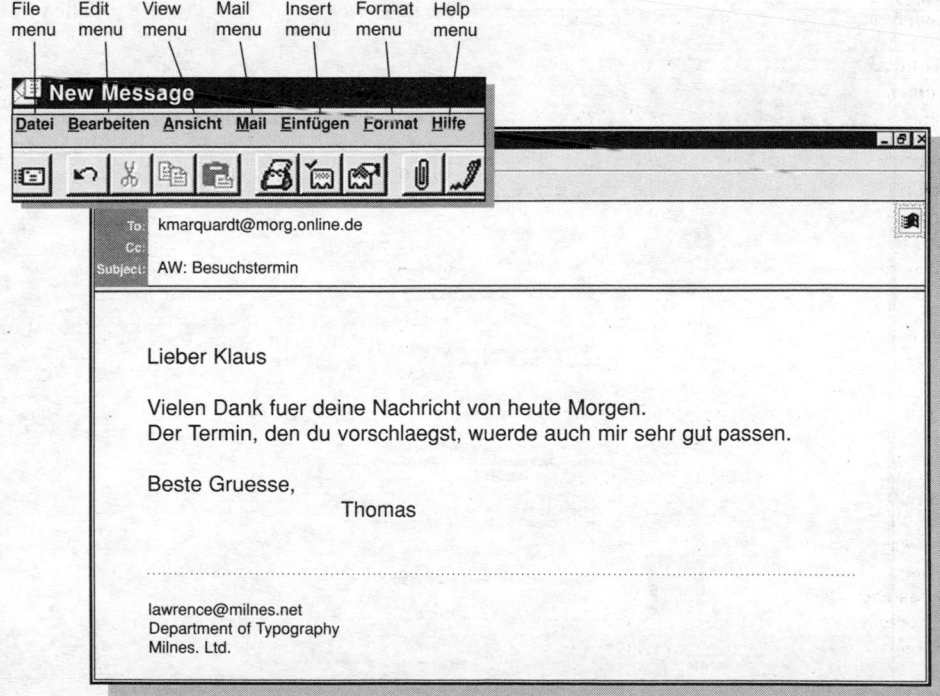

• **Datei-Menü**	File Menu	• **Bearbeiten-Menü**	Edit Menu
Öffnen	Open	**Kopieren**	Copy
Drucken	Print	**Alles markieren**	Select all
Speichern als	Save as	**Als gelesen markieren**	Mark as read
Löschen	Delete	**Als ungelesen**	Mark as unread
Ordner	Folder	**markieren**	
Adressbuch	Address book	**Nachricht suchen**	Find Message
Importieren	Import		
Exportieren	Export	• **Ansicht-Menü**	View Menu
Eigenschaften	Properties	**Werkzeugleiste**	Toolbar
Beenden	Exit	**Statusleiste**	Status bar
• **Mail-Menü**	Mail Menu	**Seitenansicht**	Preview Panel
Neue Nachricht	New Message	**Spalten**	Columns
Antwort an Absender	Reply to Sender	**Sortieren**	Sort by
Antwort an alle	Reply to All	**Language**	Sprache
Weiterleiten	Forward	**Aktualisieren**	Refresh
Weiterleiten als	Forward as attachment		
eingebundene		• **Einfügen-Menü**	Insert Menu
Nachricht		**Text datei**	Text File
In Ordner verschieben	Move to	**Anlage**	Attachment
In Ordner kopieren	Copy to	**Signatur***	Signature
Nachrichten	Send and Receive		
übermitteln			

* Less usual; the English term is more commonly used

Web browsing

The illustration shows a typical interface for browsing the Web.

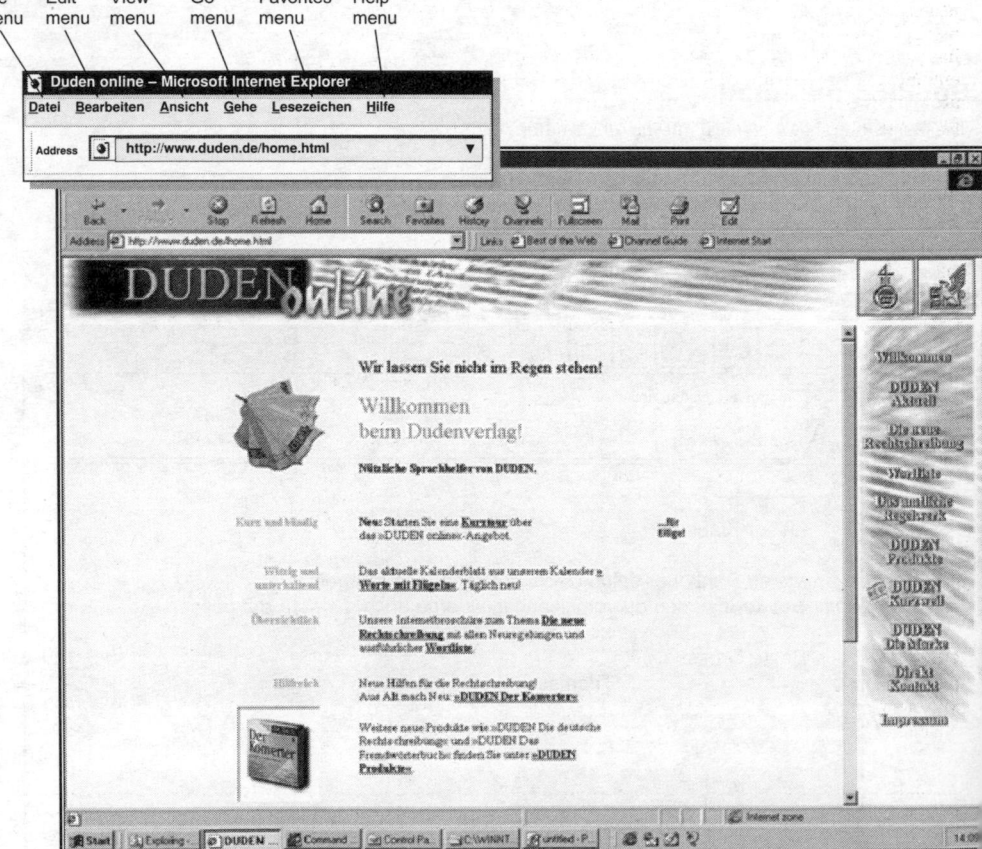

File   Edit   View   Go   Favorites   Help
menu menu menu menu menu menu

• **Datei-Menü**	File Menu	**Schriftarten**	Fonts
Öffnen	Open	**Stopp**	Stop
Speichern	Save	**Aktualisieren**	Update
Senden an	Send to	**Quelltext**	Document source
Seite einrichten	Print preview	**Optionen**	Options
Drucken	Print		
Beenden	Exit	• **Gehe-Menü**	Go to Menu
		Zurück	Back
• **Bearbeiten-Menü**	Edit Menu	**Vor**	Forward
Ausschneiden	Cut	**Anfang**	Home
Kopieren	Copy	**WWW-Suche**	Search the Web
Einfügen	Paste	**Empfehlungen**	Best of Web
Alles markieren	Select All	**Mail lesen**	Read Mail
Suchen	Find (on this page)	**Newsgroups lesen**	Read News
(aktuelles Dokument)			
		• **Lesezeichen-Menü**	Favorites Menu
• **Ansicht-Menü**	View Menu	**Lesezeichen hinzufügen**	Add Favorites
Werkzeugleiste	Toolbar	**Lesezeichen bearbeiten**	Edit Favorites
Statusleiste	Status bar		

German-language Web sites*

Search Engines

Search engines (Suchmaschinen) are really indispensable Internet tools, which serve as Web site directories. They are very easy to use and allow the user to find subject-specific Web sites, a task that would otherwise be next to impossible given the vastness of the Web. All one has to do is to type in a subject keyword, and the search engine shows the relevant 'hits' in a list of Web sites that are related to the subject. Keyword searches are possible in any language, and many search engines provide the facility to narrow down the search to a specific country or language, thus increasing the relevance of the 'hits' to one's chosen subject.

Search Engine	Address
Alta Vista	http://www.altavista.digital.com
DINO	http://www.dino-online.de
LEO	http://www.leo.org
Excite	http://www.excite.com
Infoseek	http://www.infoseek.com
Lycos	http://www.uk.lycos.de
Metacrawler	http://www.metacrawler.com
Webcrawler	http://www.webcrawler.com
Yahoo!	http://www.yahoo.com
Yahoo! Deutschland	http://www.yahoo.de

▶ Email Directories

These work like search engines, but find personal email addresses around the world.

Directory	Address
Four11 Email Directory	http://www.four11.com
The Ultimate Email Directory	http://www.theultimates. com.email

▶ News-related sites

All the main national and many regional newspapers in Germany and Austria are available on line, as well as weeklies and news from radio and TV organizations, for instance:

Site	Address
Bild-Zeitung	http://www.bild.de
Frankfurter Rundschau	http://www.fr-aktuell.de
Süddeutsche Zeitung	http://www.sueddeutsche.de
die tageszeitung	http://www.taz.de
Die Welt	http://www.welt.de
focus	http://www.focus.de
Der Spiegel	http://www.spiegel.de
Die Zeit	http://www.zeit.de
Stern	http://www.stern.de
ARD	http://www.ard.de
Deutsche Welle Radio International	http://www.dmc.net/dw.htm
ZDF	http://www.zdf.de

▶ Educational sites

Site	Address
Dudenredaktion	http://www.duden.de
Deutscher akademischer Austauschdienst	http://www.daad.de
Goethe-Institut	http://www.goethe.de
Institut für interkulturelle Kommunikation, Weimar	http://www.iik.com.

▶ Cultural and Tourist Information

All major towns and cities have Web sites, whose addresses take the usual form with the name of the town and de at the end, e.g.   http://www.berlin.de

Aa

A, a¹ /eɪ/ *n., pl.* **As** *or* **A's** **(a)** (letter) A, a, *das;* **from A to Z** von A bis Z; **A road** Straße 1. Ordnung; ≈ Bundesstraße, *die;* **(b)** (Mus.) A, a, *das;* **A sharp** ais, Ais, *das;* **A flat** as, As, *das;* **(c)** A 1 (coll.: first-rate) eins a (ugs.)

a² /ə, stressed eɪ/ *indef. art.* **(a)** ein/eine/ein; **he is a gardener/a Frenchman** er ist Gärtner/Franzose; **she did not say a word** sie sagte kein Wort; **(b)** (per) pro; **£40 a year** 40 Pfund pro Jahr; **it's 20p a pound** es kostet 20 Pence das Pfund; **two a penny** zwei Stück [für] einen Penny

AA *abbr.* (Brit.) **Automobile Association** britischer Automobilklub

aback /ə'bæk/ *adv.* **be taken** ∼: erstaunt sein (**by** über + *Akk.*)

abacus /'æbəkəs/ *n., pl.* ∼**es** *or* **abaci** /'æbəsaɪ/ Abakus, *der*

abandon /ə'bændən/ **1** *v.t.* **(a)** (forsake) verlassen ‹*Ort*›; verlassen, im Stich lassen ‹*Person*›; aussetzen ‹*Kind, Tier*›; aufgeben ‹*Prinzip*›; stehen lassen ‹*Auto*›; aufgeben, fallen lassen ‹*Gedanken, Plan*›; ∼ **hope** die Hoffnung aufgeben; ∼ **ship** das Schiff verlassen; ∼ **ship!** alle Mann von Bord!; **(b)** (surrender) ∼ **sth. to the enemy** etw. dem Feind übergeben *od.* überlassen; **(c)** (yield) ∼ **oneself to sth.** sich einer Sache (*Dat.*) hingeben. **2** *n., no pl.* **with** ∼: ungezwungen

abandonment /ə'bændənmənt/ *n., no pl.* (of right, claim) Preisgabe, *die;* (of plan, property) Aufgabe, *die*

abase /ə'beɪs/ *v.t.* demütigen, erniedrigen ‹*Person*›; ∼ **oneself** sich erniedrigen

abashed /ə'bæʃt/ *adj.* beschämt; verlegen

abate /ə'beɪt/ *v.i.* [an Stärke *od.* Intensität] abnehmen; nachlassen ‹*Zorn, Eifer, Sturm*›; abflauen, nachlassen

abattoir /'æbətwɑː(r)/ *n.* Schlachthof, *der;* ([part of] building) Schlachthaus, *das*

abbess /'æbɪs/ *n.* Äbtissin, *die*

abbey /'æbɪ/ *n.* Abtei, *die*

abbot /'æbət/ *n.* Abt, *der*

abbreviate /ə'briːvɪeɪt/ *v.t.* abkürzen ‹*Wort usw.*› (**to** mit)

ab'breviated dialling *n.* (Teleph.) Kurzwahl, *die*

abbreviation /əbriːvɪ'eɪʃn/ *n.* Abkürzung, *die*

ABC /eɪbiː'siː/ *n.* **(a)** (alphabet) ABC, *das;* **(b)** (fig.: rudiments) ABC, *das;* Einmaleins, *das*

abdicate /'æbdɪkeɪt/ *v.t.* abdanken; ∼ **[the throne]** auf den Thron verzichten

abdication /æbdɪ'keɪʃn/ *n.* Abdankung, *die;* Thronverzicht, *der*

abdomen /'æbdəmɪn/ *n.* (Anat.) Bauch, *der;* Unterleib, *der;* Abdomen, *das* (fachspr.)

abdominal /æb'dɒmɪnl/ *adj.* Bauch-; Abdominal- (fachspr.)

abduct /əb'dʌkt/ *v.t.* entführen

abduction /əb'dʌkʃn/ *n.* Entführung, *die*

aberration /æbə'reɪʃn/ *n.* Abweichung, *die;* **mental** ∼**[s]** geistige Verirrung

abet /ə'bet/ *v.t.*, **-tt-** helfen (+ *Dat.*); unterstützen; **aid and** ∼: Beihilfe leisten (+ *Dat.*)

abeyance /ə'beɪəns/ *n.* **be in/fall into** ∼: zeitweilig außer Kraft sein/treten

abhor /əb'hɔː(r)/ *v.t.*, **-rr-** hassen; (loathe) verabscheuen

abhorrence /əb'hɒrəns/ *n., no pl.* (loathing) Abneigung, *die* (**of** gegen)

abhorrent /əb'hɒrənt/ *adj.* abscheulich; **be** ∼ **to sb.** jmdm. zuwider sein

abide /ə'baɪd/ **1** *v.i.*, **abode** /ə'bəʊd/ *or* ∼**d** **(a)** *usu.* ∼**d**: ∼ **by** befolgen ‹*Gesetz, Regel, Vorschrift*›; [ein]halten ‹*Versprechen*›; **(b)** (arch: remain) bleiben; verweilen (geh.). **2** *v.t.* ertragen; **I can't** ∼ **dogs** ich kann Hunde nicht ausstehen

ability /ə'bɪlɪtɪ/ *n.* **(a)** (capacity) Können, *das;* Fähigkeit, *die;* **have the** ∼ **to do sth.** etw. können *od.* (geh.) vermögen; **make use of one's** ∼ *or* **abilities** seine Fähigkeiten einsetzen; **to the best of my** ∼: soweit es in meinen Kräften steht; **(b)** *no pl.* (cleverness) Intelligenz, *die;* **she is a girl of great** ∼: sie ist ein sehr intelligentes Mädchen; **(c)** (talent) Begabung, *die;* Talent, *das;* Anlagen *Pl.;* **he shows** *or* **has great musical** ∼: er ist musikalisch sehr begabt

abject /'æbdʒekt/ *adj.* elend; erbärmlich; bitter ‹*Armut*›; demütig ‹*Entschuldigung*›

abjure /əb'dʒʊə(r)/ *v.t.* abschwören (+ *Dat.*)

ablaze /ə'bleɪz/ *pred. adj.* **be** ∼: in Flammen stehen; **be** ∼ **with light** hell erleuchtet sein

able /'eɪbl/ *adj.* **(a)** **be** ∼ **to do sth.** etw. tun können; **I'd love to come but I don't know if I'll be** ∼ **[to]** ich würde sehr gern kommen, aber ich weiß nicht, ob es mir möglich sein wird; **(b)** (competent, talented) fähig

able: ∼**-bodied** /'eɪblbɒdɪd/ *adj.* kräftig; stark; tauglich ‹*Soldat, Matrose*›; ∼ **'seaman** *n.* Vollmatrose, *der*

ably /'eɪblɪ/ *adv.* geschickt; gekonnt

abnormal /æb'nɔːml/ *adj.* **(a)** abnorm ‹*Gestalt, Größe*›; a[b]normal ‹*Interesse, Verhalten*›; **mentally/physically** ∼: geistig/physisch anomal *od.* krank; **(b)** (unusual) ungewöhnlich; a[b]normal

abnormality /æbnɔː'mælɪtɪ/ *n.* Abnormität, *die;* Anomalie, *die*

abnormally /æb'nɔːməlɪ/ *adv.* ungewöhnlich

aboard /ə'bɔːd/ **1** *adv.* an Bord; **all** ∼**!** alle Mann an Bord!; (bus, train) alle[s] einsteigen! **2** *prep.* an Bord (+ *Gen.*); ∼ **the bus/train** im Bus/Zug; ∼ **ship** an Bord

abode¹ /ə'bəʊd/ *n.* (formal/joc.: dwelling place) Wohnstätte, *die;* Bleibe, *die;* **of no fixed** ∼: ohne festen Wohnsitz

abode² ⇒ **abide 1**

abolish /ə'bɒlɪʃ/ *v.t.* abschaffen

abolition /æbə'lɪʃn/ *n.* Abschaffung, *die*

abominable /ə'bɒmɪnəbl/ *adj.* abscheulich; scheußlich; **the A**∼ **Snowman** der Schneemensch; der Yeti

abominably /ə'bɒmɪnəblɪ/ *adv.* abscheulich; scheußlich

abomination /əbɒmɪ'neɪʃn/ *n.* **(a)** *no pl.* (abhorrence) Abscheu, *der* (**of** vor + *Dat.*); **(b)** (object of disgust) Abscheulichkeit, *die*

aborigine /æbə'rɪdʒɪnɪ/ *n.* Ureinwohner, *der;* Urbewohner, *der;* (in Australia) **A**∼: [australischer] Ureinwohner

abort /ə'bɔːt/ **1** *v.i.* eine Fehlgeburt haben; abortieren (Med.). **2** *v.t.* **(a)** (Med.) ∼ **a baby** eine Schwangerschaftsunterbrechung durchführen; [ein Baby] abtreiben; **(b)** (fig.: end) vorzeitig beenden; abbrechen ‹*Projekt, Unternehmen*›

abortion /ə'bɔːʃn/ *n.* **(a)** Schwangerschaftsunterbrechung, *die;* Abtreibung, *die;* **have/get an** ∼: die Schwangerschaft unterbrechen lassen; **back-street** ∼: illegale Abtreibung (*durch Engelmacherin*); **(b)** (involuntary) Frühod. Fehlgeburt, *die;* Abort, *der* (Med.)

a'bortion pill *n.* Abtreibungspille, *die*

abortive /ə'bɔːtɪv/ *adj.* misslungen ‹*Plan*›; fehlgeschlagen ‹*Versuch*›

abound /ə'baʊnd/ *v.i.* (a) (be plentiful) reichlich *od.* in Hülle und Fülle vorhanden sein *od.* da sein; (b) ~ **in sth.** an etw. *(Dat.)* reich sein; ~ **with** voll sein von

about /ə'baʊt/ **1** *adv.* (a) (all around) rings[her]um; (here and there) überall; **all** ~ ringsumher; **strewn/littered** ~ **all over the room** überall im Zimmer verstreut; (b) (near) **be** ~: da sein; hier sein; **is John** ~? ist John da?; **there was nobody** ~: es war niemand da; (c) **be** ~ **to do sth.** gerade etw. tun wollen; (d) (active) **be out and** ~: aktiv sein; **be up and** ~: auf sein (ugs.); (e) ▶**706**] (approximately) ungefähr; **[at]** ~ **5 p.m.** ungefähr um *od.* gegen 17 Uhr; (f) (round) herum; rum (ugs.); ~ **turn!**, (Amer.) ~ **face!** (Mil.) kehrt!; (g) **[turn and] turn** ~ (in rotation) abwechselnd. **2** *prep.* (a) (all around) um [... herum]; **there was litter lying** ~ **the park/streets** überall im Park/auf den Straßen lag der Abfall herum; (b) (with) **have sth.** ~ **one** etw. [bei sich] haben; (c) (concerning) über (+ *Akk.*); **an argument/a question** ~ **sth.** Streit wegen etw./eine Frage zu etw.; **talk/laugh** ~ **sth.** über etw. *(Akk.)* sprechen/ lachen; **cry** ~ **sth.** wegen etw. weinen; **know** ~ **sth.** von etw. wissen; **what was it** ~? worum ging es?; (d) (occupied with) **be quick/brief** ~ **it** beeil dich!; (in speaking) fasse dich kurz!; **while you're** ~ **it** da Sie gerade dabei sind

above /ə'bʌv/ **1** *adv.* (a) (position) oben; oberhalb; (higher up) darüber; **up** ~: oben; **from** ~: von oben [herab]; ~ **right** rechts oben; oben rechts; **the flat/floor** ~: die Wohnung/das Stockwerk darüber; (b) (direction) nach oben; hinauf; (upstream) stromauf[wärts]; (c) (earlier in text) weiter oben; **see** ~, p. 123 siehe oben, S. 123. **2** *prep.* (a) (position) über (+ *Dat.*); (upstream from) oberhalb (+ *Gen.*); ~ **oneself** (conceited) größenwahnsinnig (ugs.); (b) (direction) über (+ *Akk.*); (c) (more than) über (+ *Akk.*); **will anyone go** ~ **£2,000?** bietet jemand mehr als 2 000 Pfund?; **be** ~ **criticism/suspicion** über jede Kritik/jeden Verdacht erhaben sein; ~ **all [else]** vor allem; insbesondere; (d) (ranking higher than) über (+ *Dat.*); **she's in the class** ~ **me** sie ist eine Klasse über mir. **3** *adj.* obig ‹*Erklärung, Aufzählung, Ziffern*›; (~-mentioned) oben genannt. **4** *n.* **the** ~: das Obige; (person[s]) der/die Obengenannte/die Obengenannten

above: ~ **board** *pred. adj.* einwandfrei; korrekt; ~-**mentioned**, ~-**named** *adjs.* oben genannt; oben erwähnt

abrasion /ə'breɪʒn/ *n.* (graze) Hautabschürfung, *die*

abrasive /ə'breɪsɪv/ **1** *adj.* (a) scheuernd; Scheuer-; (b) (fig.: harsh) aggressiv; herausfordernd ‹*Ton*›. **2** *n.* Scheuermittel, *das*

abreast /ə'brest/ *adv.* (a) nebeneinander; Seite an Seite; (b) (fig.) **keep** ~ **of sth.** sich über etw. *(Akk.)* auf dem Laufenden halten

abridge /ə'brɪdʒ/ *v.t.* kürzen

abroad /ə'brɔːd/ *adv.* (a) im Ausland; (direction) ins Ausland; **from** ~: aus dem Ausland

abrupt /ə'brʌpt/ *adj.* (a) (sudden) abrupt, plötzlich ‹*Ende, Abreise, Wechsel*›; **come to an** ~ **halt** ‹*Fahrzeug:*› plötzlich *od.* abrupt anhalten; (b) (brusque) schroff, barsch ‹*Art, Ton*›; (c) (steep) jäh; steil

abruptly /ə'brʌptlɪ/ *adv.* (a) (suddenly) abrupt; plötzlich; (b) (brusquely) schroff; barsch; (c) (steeply) jäh; steil

ABS *abbr.* **anti-lock braking system** ABS

abscess /'æbsɪs/ *n.* (Med.) Abszess, *der*

abscond /əb'skɒnd/ *v.i.* sich entfernen

abseil /'æbseɪl, 'æbzaɪl/ (Mount.) **1** *v.i.* abseilen. **2** *n.* Abseilen, *das*

absence /'æbsəns/ *n.* (a) Abwesenheit, *die*; (from work) Fernbleiben, *das;* **his** ~**s from school** sein Fehlen in der Schule; ~ **makes the heart grow fonder** Trennung frischt die Liebe auf; (b) (lack) **the** ~ **of sth.** das Fehlen von etw.; (c) ~ **[of mind]** Geistesabwesenheit, *die*

absent 1 /'æbsənt/ *adj.* (a) abwesend; **be** ~: nicht da sein; **be** ~ **from school/work** in der Schule/am Arbeitsplatz fehlen; **be** ~ **without leave** sich unerlaubt entfernt haben; (b) (lacking) **be** ~: fehlen; (c) (abstracted) geistesabwesend. **2** /əb'sent/ *v. refl.* ~ **oneself [from sth.]** [einer Sache *(Dat.)*] fernbleiben

absentee /æbsən'tiː/ *n.* Abwesende, *der/die;* **there were a few** ~**s** ein paar fehlten

absent-minded /æbsənt'maɪndɪd/ *adj.* geistesabwesend; (habitually) zerstreut

absent-mindedly /æbsənt'maɪndɪdlɪ/ *adv.* geistesabwesend

absent-mindedness /æbsənt'maɪndɪdnɪs/ *n., no pl.* Geistesabwesenheit, *die*

absolute /'æbsəluːt, 'æbsəljuːt/ *adj.* absolut; unumstößlich ‹*Beweis, Tatsache*›; ausgemacht ‹*Lüge, Skandal*›; (unconditional) fest ‹*Versprechen*›; streng ‹*Verpflichtung*›; uneingeschränkt ‹*Macht*›; ~ **majority** absolute Mehrheit

absolutely /'æbsəluːtlɪ, 'æbsəljuːtlɪ/ *adv.* (a) absolut; strikt ‹*ablehnen*›; völlig ‹*verrückt*›; ausgesprochen ‹*kriminell, ekelhaft, schlimm*›; **you're** ~ **right!** du hast völlig Recht; (b) (positively) regelrecht; ~ **fabulous/gorgeous** echt toll (ugs.); ~ **not!** auf keinen Fall!; (c) /æbsə'luːtlɪ/ (coll.: yes indeed) hundertprozentig (ugs.)

absolution /æbsə'luːʃn, æbsə'ljuːʃn/ *n.* (Relig.) (forgiveness) Vergebung, *die;* (release) Erlass, *der* (from *Gen.*); **pronounce** ~: [die] Absolution erteilen

absolve /əb'zɒlv/ *v.t.* ~ **from** entbinden von ‹*Pflichten*›; vergeben ‹*Sünde, Verbrechen*›; lossprechen von ‹*Schuld*›; (Relig.) Absolution erteilen (+ *Dat.*)

absorb /əb'sɔːb, əb'zɔːb/ *v.t.* (a) aufsaugen ‹*Flüssigkeit*›; aufnehmen ‹*Flüssigkeit, Nährstoff, Wärme*›; (fig.) in sich *(Akk.)* aufnehmen ‹*Wissen*›; (b) (reduce in strength) absorbieren; abfangen ‹*Schlag, Stoß*›; (c) (incorporate) eingliedern, integrieren ‹*Abteilung, Gemeinde*›; (d) (consume) aufzehren ‹*Kraft, Zeit, Vermögen*›; (e) (engross) ausfüllen ‹*Person, Interesse, Gedanken*›

absorbed /əb'sɔːbd, əb'zɔːbd/ *adj.* versunken; **be/get** ~ **in sth.** in etw. *(Akk.)* vertieft sein/sich in etw. *(Akk.)* vertiefen

absorbency /əb'sɔːbənsɪ, əb'zɔːbənsɪ/ *n.* Saugfähigkeit, *die*

absorbent /əb'sɔːbənt, əb'zɔːbənt/ *adj.* saugfähig

absorbing /əb'sɔːbɪŋ, əb'zɔːbɪŋ/ *adj.* faszinierend

absorption /əb'sɔːpʃn, əb'zɔːpʃn/ *n.* (a) (incorporation, physical process) Absorption, *die* (fachspr.); (b) (of department, community) Integration, *die;* (c) (engrossment) Versunkenheit, *die*

abstain /əb'steɪn/ *v.i.* (a) enthaltsam sein; ~ **from sth.** sich einer Sache *(Gen.)* enthalten; (b) ~ **[from voting]** sich der Stimme enthalten

abstemious /əb'stiːmɪəs/ *adj.* enthaltsam

abstention /əb'stenʃn/ *n.* ~ **from the vote/from voting** Stimmenthaltung, *die;* **how many** ~**s were there?** wie viele Personen enthielten sich der Stimme?

abstinence /'æbstɪnəns/ *n.* Abstinenz, *die*

abstinent /'æbstɪnənt/ *adj.* abstinent

abstract 1 /'æbstrækt/ *adj.* abstrakt; ~ **noun** (Ling.) Abstraktum, *das;* **in the** ~: abstrakt. **2** /'æbstrækt/ *n.* (a) (summary) Zusammenfassung, *die;* Abstract, *das* (fachspr.); (of book) Inhaltsangabe, *die;* (b) (idea) Abstraktum, *das.* **3** /æb'strækt/ *v.t.* (remove) wegnehmen

abstruse /æb'struːs/ *adj.* abstrus

absurd /əb'sɜːd/ *adj.* absurd; (ridiculous) lächerlich

absurdity /əb'sɜːdɪtɪ/ *n.* Absurdität, *die*

absurdly /əb'sɜːdlɪ/ *adv.* lächerlich

ABTA *abbr.* (Brit.) **Association of British Travel Agents** Vereinigung der britischen Reiseveranstalter

abundance /ə'bʌndəns/ *n.* **[an]** ~ **of sth.** eine Fülle von etw.; **an** ~ **of love/energy** ein Übermaß an Liebe/ Energie *(Dat.)*; **in** ~: in Hülle und Fülle

abundant /ə'bʌndənt/ *adj.* reich (**in** an + *Dat.*); **an** ~ **supply of fish/fruit** Fisch/Obst im Überfluss

abundantly /ə'bʌndəntlɪ/ *adv.* überreichlich; **I made it** ~ **clear that ...**: ich habe es überdeutlich zum Ausdruck gebracht, dass ...

abuse 1 /ə'bjuːz/ *v.t.* (a) (misuse) missbrauchen ‹*Macht, Recht, Autorität, Vertrauen*›; (maltreat) peinigen, quälen ‹*Tier*›; **sexually** ~: sexuell missbrauchen; (b) (insult) beschimpfen. **2** /ə'bjuːs/ *n.* (a) (misuse) Missbrauch, *der;* (b) (unjust or corrupt practice) Missstand, *der;* (c) (insults) Beschimpfungen *Pl.;* **a term of** ~: ein Schimpfwort

abusive /ə'bjuːsɪv/ *adj.* beleidigend; ~ **language** Beleidigungen; Beschimpfungen; **become** *or* **get** ~: ausfallend werden

abut /ə'bʌt/ **1** *v.i.*, **-tt-:** **(a)** (border) ~ **on** grenzen an (+ *Akk.*); **(b)** (end) ~ **on/against** stoßen *od.* angrenzen an (+ *Akk.*). **2** *v.t.* **(a)** (border on) angrenzen an (+ *Akk.*); **(b)** (end on) anstoßen an (+ *Akk.*)

abysmal /ə'bɪzml/ *adj.* **(a)** grenzenlos ⟨ *Unwissenheit* ⟩; **(b)** (coll.: bad) katastrophal (ugs.)

abyss /ə'bɪs/ *n.* (lit. or fig.) Abgrund, *der*

AC *abbr.* (Electr.) **alternating current** Ws

a/c *abbr.* **account**

acacia /ə'keɪʃə/ *n.* (Bot.) Akazie, *die*

academic /ækə'demɪk/ **1** *adj.* akademisch; wissenschaftlich ⟨ *Fach*, *Studium* ⟩. **2** *n.* Wissenschaftler, *der*/Wissenschaftlerin, *die;* (scholar) Gelehrte, *der/die*

academically /ækə'demɪkəlɪ/ *adv.* wissenschaftlich; **be** ~ **very able** große intellektuelle Fähigkeiten haben

academy /ə'kædəmɪ/ *n.* Akademie, *die*

accede /æk'siːd/ *v.i.* **(a)** (assent) zustimmen (**to** *Dat.*); **(b)** beitreten (**to** *Dat.*) ⟨ *Abkommen*, *Bündnis* ⟩; antreten ⟨ *Amt* ⟩; ~ **[to the throne]** den Thron besteigen

accelerate /ək'seləreɪt/ **1** *v.t.* beschleunigen. **2** *v.i.* sich beschleunigen; ⟨ *Auto[fahrer]*, *Läufer:* ⟩ beschleunigen

acceleration /əkselə'reɪʃn/ *n.* Beschleunigung, *die*

accelerator /ək'seləreɪtə(r)/ *n.* ~ **[pedal]** Gas[pedal], *das*

accent 1 /'æksənt/ *n.* Akzent, *der;* (mark) Akzent, *der;* Akzentzeichen, *das;* **the** ~ **is on ...** (fig.) der Akzent liegt auf (+ *Dat.*) ... **2** /æk'sent/ *v.t.* betonen

accentuate /ək'sentjʊeɪt/ *v.t.* betonen; verstärken ⟨ *Schmerz*, *Kummer* ⟩

accept /ək'sept/ *v.t.* **(a)** (be willing to receive) annehmen; aufnehmen ⟨ *Mitglied* ⟩; (take formally) entgegennehmen ⟨ *Dank*, *Spende*, *Auszeichnung* ⟩; übernehmen ⟨ *Verantwortung*, *Aufgabe* ⟩; (agree to) annehmen ⟨ *Vorschlag*, *Plan*, *Heiratsantrag*, *Einladung* ⟩; ~ **sb. for a job/school** jmdm. eine Einstellungszusage geben/jmdn. in eine Schule aufnehmen; ~ **sb. for a course** jmdn. in einen Lehrgang aufnehmen; **(b)** (approve) akzeptieren; ~ **sb. as a member of the group** jmdn. als Mitglied der Gruppe anerkennen; **(c)** (acknowledge) akzeptieren; **it is** ~**ed that ...:** es ist unbestritten, dass ...; **an** ~**ed fact** eine anerkannte Tatsache; **(d)** (believe) ~ **sth. [from sb.]** [jmdm.] etw. glauben, **(e)** (tolerate) hinnehmen

acceptability /əkseptə'bɪlɪtɪ/ *n.*, *no pl.* Annehmbarkeit, *die;* (of salary, price) Angemessenheit, *die*

acceptable /ək'septəbl/ *adj.* akzeptabel; annehmbar ⟨ *Preis*, *Gehalt* ⟩

acceptance /ək'septəns/ *n.* **(a)** (willing receipt) Annahme, *die;* (of gift, offer) Annahme, *die;* Entgegennahme, *die;* (of duty, responsibility) Übernahme, *die;* (in answer) Zusage, *die;* (agreement) Annahme, *die;* Zustimmung, *die* (**of** zu); **(b)** *no pl.* (approval) Billigung, *die;* **(c)** *no pl.* (acknowledgement) Anerkennung, *die;* (toleration) Hinnahme, *die*

access /'ækses/ *n.* **1 (a)** *no pl.*, *no art.* (entering) Zutritt, *der* (**to** zu); (by vehicles) Einfahren, *das* (**into** in + *Akk.*); **this doorway is the only means of** ~: diese Tür ist der einzige Zugang; **(b)** (admission) **gain** *or* **obtain** *or* **get** ~: Einlass finden; **(c)** *no pl.* (opportunity to use or approach; also fig.) Zugang, *der* (**to** zu); **the father has** ~ **to the children** der Vater hat ein Recht zum Umgang mit den Kindern; **she was not allowed** ~ **to her personal file** man verweigerte ihr die Einsichtnahme in ihre Personalakte; **(d)** **easy/difficult of** ~: leicht/schwer zugänglich; **(e)** (way [in]) Zugang, *der;* (road) Zufahrt, *die;* (door) Eingang, *der.* **2** *v.t.* (Computing) ~ **the file/drive** *etc.* auf die Datei/das Laufwerk *usw.* zugreifen

accessible /ək'sesɪbl/ *adj.* **(a)** (reachable) **[more]** ~ **[to sb.]** [besser] erreichbar [für jmdn.]; **(b)** (available, open, understandable) zugänglich (**to** für)

accession /æk'seʃn/ *n.* Amtsantritt, *der;* ~ **to the throne** Thronbesteigung, *die*

accessory /ək'sesərɪ/ **1** *adj.* ~ **[to sth.]** zusätzlich [zu etw.]. **2** *n.* **(a)** (accompaniment) Extra, *das;* (attachments) Zubehör, *das;* **one of the accessories** eines der Zubehörteile; **(c)** (dress article) Accessoire, *das*

'access road *n.* Zufahrtsstraße, *die*

accident /'æksɪdənt/ *n.* **(a)** (unlucky event) Unfall, *der;* **road** ~: Verkehrsunfall, *der;* **have an** ~: einen Unfall haben; **(b)** (chance) Zufall, *der;* (unfortunate chance) Unglücksfall, *der;* **by** ~: zufällig; **(c)** (mistake) Versehen, *das;* **by** ~: versehentlich; **(d)** (mishap) Missgeschick, *das*

accidental /æksɪ'dentl/ *adj.* (happening by chance) zufällig; (unintended) unbeabsichtigt

accidentally /æksɪ'dentəlɪ/ *adv.* (by chance) zufällig; (by mistake) versehentlich

'accident-prone *adj.* **he was the most** ~ **of the children** er hatte von den Kindern immer die meisten Unfälle; **he's such an** ~ **boy** mit dem Jungen ist aber auch immer irgendwas (ugs.)

acclaim /ə'kleɪm/ *v.t.* (welcome) feiern; (hail as) ~ **sb. king** jmdn. zum König ausrufen

acclamation /æklə'meɪʃn/ *n.*, *no pl.* Beifall, *der*

acclimatization /əklaɪmətaɪ'zeɪʃn/ *n.* (lit. or fig.) Akklimatisation, *die*

acclimatize /ə'klaɪmətaɪz/ *v.t.* (lit. or fig.) akklimatisieren; ~ **sth./sb. to sth.** etw./jmdn. an etw. (*Akk.*) gewöhnen; **get** *or* **become** ~**d** sich akklimatisieren

accolade /'ækəleɪd, ækə'leɪd/ *n.* (praise) ~**[s]** Lob, *das;* (acknowledgement) Anerkennung, *die*

accommodate /ə'kɒmədeɪt/ *v.t.* **(a)** unterbringen; (hold, have room for) Platz bieten (+ *Dat.*); **(b)** (oblige) gefällig sein (+ *Dat.*)

accommodating /ə'kɒmədeɪtɪŋ/ *adj.* zuvorkommend

accommodation /əkɒmə'deɪʃn/ *n.*, *no pl.* Unterkunft, *die;* **can you provide us with** ~ **for the night?** können Sie uns ein Nachtquartier besorgen?; ~ **is very expensive** Wohnungen/Zimmer sind sehr teuer; **there is a lack of good hotel** ~ **in this town** in dieser Stadt fehlt es an guten Hotels; **student** ~ **is getting more expensive** Studentenunterkünfte *od.* -wohnungen werden [immer] teurer

accompaniment /ə'kʌmpənɪmənt/ *n.* (lit. or fig.; also Mus.) Begleitung, *die*

accompanist /ə'kʌmpənɪst/ *n.* (Mus.) Begleiter, *der*/Begleiterin, *die*

accompany /ə'kʌmpənɪ/ *v.t.* (also Mus.) begleiten

accomplice /ə'kʌmplɪs/ *n.* Komplize, *der*/Komplizin, *die*

accomplish /ə'kʌmplɪʃ/ *v.t.* (perform) vollbringen ⟨ *Tat* ⟩; erfüllen ⟨ *Aufgabe* ⟩

accomplished /ə'kʌmplɪʃt/ *adj.* fähig; **he is an** ~ **speaker/dancer** er ist ein erfahrener Redner/vollendeter Tänzer

accomplishment /ə'kʌmplɪʃmənt/ *n.* **(a)** *no pl.* (completion) Vollendung, *die;* (of task) Erfüllung, *die;* **(b)** (achievement) Leistung, *die;* (skill) Fähigkeit, *die*

accord /ə'kɔːd/ **1** *v.i.* ~ **[with sth.]** [mit etw.] übereinstimmen. **2** *v.t.* ~ **sb. sth.** jmdm. etw. gewähren. **3** *n.* **(a)** **of one's own** ~: aus eigenem Antrieb; **of its own** ~: von selbst; **(b)** (harmonious agreement) Übereinstimmung, *die;* **with one** ~: geschlossen

accordance /ə'kɔːdəns/ *n.* **in** ~ **with** in Übereinstimmung mit; gemäß (+ *Dat.*)

according /ə'kɔːdɪŋ/ *adv.* **(a)** ~ **as** (depending on how), je nachdem, wie; (depending on whether) je nachdem, ob; **(b)** ~ **to** nach; ~ **to him** (opinion) seiner Meinung nach; (account) nach seiner Aussage; ~ **to circumstances/the season** den Umständen/der Jahreszeit entsprechend

accordingly /ə'kɔːdɪŋlɪ/ *adv.* (as appropriate) entsprechend; (therefore) folglich

accordion /ə'kɔːdɪən/ *n.* Akkordeon, *das*

accost /ə'kɒst/ *v.t.* ansprechen

account /ə'kaʊnt/ *n.* **(a)** (Finance) Rechnung, *die;* **keep** ~**s/the** ~**s** Buch/die Bücher führen; **settle** *or* **square** ~**s with sb.** (lit. or fig.) mit jmdm. abrechnen; **on** ~: auf Rechnung; a conto; **on one's [own]** ~: auf eigene

Rechnung; (fig.) von sich aus; **(b)** (at bank, shop) Konto, *das;* **pay sth. into one's ~:** etw. auf sein Konto einzahlen; **draw sth. out of one's ~:** etw. von seinem Konto abheben; **on ~:** auf Rechnung; **(c)** (statement of facts) Rechenschaft, *die;* **give** *or* **render an ~ for sth.** über etw. (*Akk.*) Rechenschaft ablegen; **call sb. to ~:** jmdn. zur Rechenschaft ziehen; **give a good ~ of oneself** seinen Mann stehen; **(d)** (consideration) **take ~ of sth., take sth. into ~:** etw. berücksichtigen; **take no ~ of sth./sb., leave sth./sb. out of ~:** etw./jmdn. unberücksichtigt lassen *od.* nicht berücksichtigen; **don't change your plans on my ~:** ändert nicht meinetwegen eure Pläne; **on ~ of** wegen; **on no ~, not on any ~:** auf [gar] keinen Fall; **(e)** (importance) **of little/no ~:** von geringer/ ohne Bedeutung; **(f)** (report) **an ~ [of sth.]** ein Bericht [über etw. (*Akk.*)]; **give a full ~ of sth.** ausführlich über etw. (*Akk.*) berichten; **by** *or* **from all ~s** nach allem, was man hört

~ for *v.t.* **(a)** (give reckoning) Rechenschaft *od.* Rechnung ablegen über (+ *Akk.*); **(b)** (explain) erklären; **(c)** (represent in amount) ausmachen; ergeben

accountability /əkaʊntə'bɪlɪtɪ/ *n., no pl.* Verantwortlichkeit, *die* **(to** gegenüber**)**

accountable /ə'kaʊntəbl/ *adj.* verantwortlich **(for** für**); be ~ to sb.** jmdm. Rechenschaft schuldig sein

accountancy /ə'kaʊntənsɪ/ *n., no pl.* Buchhaltung, *die*

accountant /ə'kaʊntənt/ *n.* **▶ 887** [Bilanz]buchhalter, *der/*[Bilanz]buchhalterin, *die*

ac'count holder *n.* Kontoinhaber, *der/*-inhaberin, *die*

accounting /ə'kaʊntɪŋ/ *n.* **(a)** *no pl.* (Finance) Buchführung, *die;* **(b) there's no ~ for taste[s]** über Geschmack lässt sich [nicht] streiten

ac'count number *n.* Kontonummer, *die*

accredited /ə'kredɪtɪd/ *adj.* anerkannt 〈*Schule, Anstalt*〉; akkreditiert 〈*Botschafter, Diplomat*〉; zugelassen 〈*Journalist*〉

accrue /ə'kru:/ *v.i.* 〈*Zinsen:*〉 auflaufen; **~ to sb.** 〈*Macht:*〉 jmdm. zuwachsen; 〈*Reichtümer, Einnahmen:*〉 jmdm. zufließen

accumulate /ə'kju:mjʊleɪt/ **1** *v.t.* (gather) sammeln; machen, (fachspr.) akkumulieren 〈*Vermögen*〉; (along the way) einsammeln; (produce) einbringen 〈*Zinsen, Gewinne*〉 **(for sb.** jmdm.). **2** *v.i.* 〈*Menge, Staub:*〉 sich ansammeln; 〈*Schnee, Geld:*〉 sich anhäufen

accumulation /əkju:mjʊ'leɪʃn/ *n.* [An]sammeln, *das;* (being accumulated) Anhäufung, *die;* (growth) Zuwachs, *der* **(of** an + *Dat.*); (mass) Menge, *die*

accumulator /ə'kju:mjʊleɪtə(r)/ *n.* (Electr.) Akkumulator, *der;* Akku, *der* (ugs.); Sammler, *der*

accuracy /'ækjʊrəsɪ/ *n.* Genauigkeit, *die*

accurate /'ækjʊrət/ *adj.* (precise) genau; akkurat (geh.); (correct) richtig

accurately /'ækjʊrətlɪ/ *adv.* (precisely) genau; (correctly) richtig

accursed /ə'kɜ:st/ *adj.* (ill-fated) verflucht; verwünscht

accusation /ækju:'zeɪʃn/ *n.* Anschuldigung, *die* **(of** gegen**);** Anklage, *die* (Rechtsw.)

accusative /ə'kju:zətɪv/ (Ling.) **1** *adj.* Akkusativ-; akkusativisch; **~ case** Akkusativ, *der.* **2** *n.* Akkusativ, *der*

accuse /ə'kju:z/ *v.t.* beschuldigen; (Law) anklagen; **~ sb. of cowardice** jmdm. Feigheit vorwerfen; **~ sb. of doing sth.** *or* **of having done sth.** jmdn. beschuldigen, etw. getan zu haben; **~ sb. of theft/murder** jmdn. wegen Diebstahl[s]/Mord[es] anklagen; **the ~d** der/die Angeklagte; (*pl.*) die Angeklagten; **point an accusing finger at sb.** (lit. *or* fig.) anklagend mit dem Finger auf jmdn. zeigen

accustom /ə'kʌstəm/ *v.t.* **~ sb./sth. to sth.** jmdn./etw. an etw. (*Akk.*) gewöhnen; **grow/be ~ed to sth.** sich an etw. (*Akk.*) gewöhnen/an etw. (*Akk.*) gewöhnt sein

accustomed /ə'kʌstəmd/ *attrib. adj.* gewohnt; üblich

ace /eɪs/ *n.* (Cards, Tennis, person) Ass, *das;* **~ of trumps/ diamonds** Trumpf-/Karoass, *das;* **play one's ~** (fig.) seinen Trumpf ausspielen; **hold all the ~s** alle Trümpfe auf *od.* in der Hand haben; **he was within an ~ of doing it** (hair's breadth) er hätte es um ein Haar getan

acetylene /ə'setɪli:n/ *n.* Acetylen, *das*

ache /eɪk/ **1** *v.i.* **(a) ▶ 865** schmerzen; wehtun; **whereabouts does your leg ~?** wo tut [dir] das Bein weh?; **(b)** (fig.: long) **~ to do sth.** darauf brennen, etw. zu tun. **2** *n.* **▶ 865** Schmerz, *der;* **~s and pains** Wehwehchen *Pl.*

achieve /ə'tʃi:v/ *v.t.* zustande bringen; ausführen 〈*Aufgabe, Plan*〉; erreichen 〈*Ziel, Standard, Absicht*〉; herstellen, herbeiführen 〈*Frieden, Harmonie*〉; erzielen 〈*Rekord, Leistung, Erfolg*〉; erfüllen 〈*Zweck*〉

achievement /ə'tʃi:vmənt/ *n.* **(a)** *no pl.* ⇒ **achieve:** Zustandebringen, *das;* Ausführung, *die;* Erreichen, *das;* Herstellung, *die;* Herbeiführung, *die;* Erzielen, *das;* Erfüllung, *die;* **(b)** (thing accomplished) Leistung, *die;* Errungenschaft, *die*

acid /'æsɪd/ **1** *adj.* sauer. **2** *n.* Säure, *die*

acid: ~ drop *n.* (Brit.) saurer *od.* saures Drops; **~ house** *n.* Acidhouse, *das;* **~ house music/party** Acidhousemusik, *die/*Acidhouseparty, *die*

acidic /ə'sɪdɪk/ *adj.* säuerlich

acidity /ə'sɪdɪtɪ/ *n.* Säure, *die;* Acidität, *die* (fachspr.); Säuregrad, *der;* (excessive) Übersäuerung, *die*

acid: ~ 'rain *n.* saurer Regen; **~ test** *n.* (fig.) Feuerprobe, *die*

acknowledge /ək'nɒlɪdʒ/ *v.t.* **(a)** (admit) zugeben, eingestehen 〈*Tatsache, Notwendigkeit, Fehler, Schuld*〉; (accept) sich bekennen zu 〈*einer Verantwortung, Pflicht, Schuld*〉; (take notice of) grüßen 〈*Person*〉; (recognize) anerkennen 〈*Autorität, Recht, Forderung, Notwendigkeit*〉; **an ~d expert** ein anerkannter Fachmann; **~ sb./sth. [as** *or* **to be] sth.** jmdn./etw. als etw. anerkennen; **(b)** (express thanks for) sich erkenntlich zeigen für 〈*Dienste, Bemühungen, Gastfreundschaft*〉; erwidern 〈*Gruß*〉; **(c)** (confirm receipt of) bestätigen 〈*Empfang, Bewerbung*〉; **~ a letter** den Empfang eines Briefes bestätigen

acknowledg[e]ment /ək'nɒlɪdʒmənt/ *n.* **(a)** (admission of fact, necessity, error, guilt) Eingeständnis, *das;* (acceptance of a responsibility, duty, debt) Bekenntnis, *das* **(of** zu); (recognition of authority, right, claim) Anerkennung, *die;* **(b)** (thanks, appreciation) (of services, friendship) Dank, *der* **(of** für); (of greetings) Erwiderung, *die;* **(c)** (confirmation of receipt) Bestätigung, *die* [des Empfangs/einer Bewerbung]; **letter of ~:** Bestätigungsschreiben, *das;* **'~s** „Dank"

acne /'æknɪ/ *n.* (Med.) Akne, *die*

acorn /'eɪkɔ:n/ *n.* Eichel, *die*

acoustic /ə'ku:stɪk/ *adj.* akustisch; **~ guitar** Konzertgitarre, *die*

acoustics /ə'ku:stɪks/ *n. pl.* **(a)** (properties) Akustik, *die;* akustische Verhältnisse; **(b)** *constr. as sing.* (science) Akustik, *die*

acquaint /ə'kweɪnt/ *v.t.* **~ sb./oneself with sth.** jmdn./sich mit etw. vertraut machen; **be ~ed with sb.** mit jmdm. bekannt sein

acquaintance /ə'kweɪntəns/ *n.* **(a)** *no pl.* Vertrautheit, *die;* **~ with sb.** Bekanntschaft mit jmdm.; **a passing ~:** eine flüchtige Bekanntschaft; **make the ~ of sb.** jmds. Bekanntschaft machen; **(b)** (person) Bekannte, *der/die*

acquiesce /ækwɪ'es/ *v.i.* einwilligen **(in** in + *Akk.*); (under pressure) sich fügen

acquiescence /ækwɪ'esəns/ *n., no pl.* (acquiescing) Einwilligung, *die* **(in** in + *Akk.*); (state) Ergebenheit, *die;* (assent) Zustimmung, *die*

acquiescent /ækwɪ'esənt/ *adj.* fügsam; ergeben

acquire /ə'kwaɪə(r)/ *v.t.* **(a)** sich 〈*Dat.*〉 anschaffen 〈*Gegenstände*〉; erwerben 〈*Land, Besitz, Wohlstand, Kenntnisse*〉; **(b)** (take on) annehmen 〈*Tonfall, Farbe, Gewohnheit*〉; **~ a taste for sth.** Geschmack an etw. (*Dat.*) gewinnen; **this wine is an ~d taste** an diesen Wein muss man sich erst gewöhnen

acquisition /ækwɪ'zɪʃn/ *n.* **(a)** (of goods, wealth, land) Erwerb, *der;* (of knowledge) Aneignung, *die;* Erwerb, *der;* (of habit) Annahme, *die;* **(b)** (thing) Anschaffung, *die*

acquisitive /ə'kwɪzɪtɪv/ *adj.* raffsüchtig

acquit /ə'kwɪt/ *v.t.,* **-tt-:** **(a)** (Law) freisprechen; **~ sb. of sth.** jmdn. von etw. freisprechen; **(b) ~ oneself well** seine Sache gut machen

acquittal /ə'kwɪtl/ n. (Law) Freispruch, der

acre /'eɪkə(r)/ n. ▶ **643** | Acre, der; ≈ Morgen, der

acrid /'ækrɪd/ adj. beißend ‹Geruch, Dämpfe, Rauch›; bitter ‹Geschmack›

acrimonious /ækrɪ'məʊnɪəs/ adj. bitter; erbittert ‹Streit, Diskussion›

acrimony /'ækrɪmənɪ/ n., no pl. Bitterkeit, die; (of argument, discussion) Erbitterung, die

acrobat /'ækrəbæt/ n. (lit. or fig.) Akrobat, der/Akrobatin, die

acrobatic /ækrə'bætɪk/ adj. (lit. or fig.) akrobatisch

acrobatics /ækrə'bætɪks/ n., no pl. Akrobatik, die

acronym /'ækrənɪm/ n. Akronym, das; Initialwort, das

across /ə'krɒs/ 1 adv. (a) darüber; (in crossword puzzle) waagerecht; (from here to there) hinüber; **measure** or **be 9 miles** ∼: 9 Meilen breit sein; (b) (on the other side) drüben; ∼ **there/here** [da] drüben/hier drüben; ∼ **from** gegenüber von. 2 prep. (a) über (+ Akk.); **protests** ∼ **Canada** Proteste in ganz Kanada; (b) (on the other side of) auf der anderen Seite (+ Gen.); ∼ **the ocean/river** jenseits des Meeres/Flusses

a'cross-the-board adj. pauschal; **an** ∼ **pay rise** eine pauschale od. generelle Lohnerhöhung

acrylic /ə'krɪlɪk/ 1 adj. aus Acryl nachgestellt; Acryl-. 2 n. Acryl, das

act /ækt/ 1 n. (a) (deed) Tat, die; (official action) Akt, der; **an** ∼ **of God** höhere Gewalt; **Acts [of the Apostles]** (Bibl.) constr. as sing. Apostelgeschichte, die; (b) (process) **be in the** ∼ **of doing sth.** gerade dabei sein, etw. zu tun; **he was caught in the** ∼ **[of stealing]** er wurde [beim Stehlen] auf frischer Tat ertappt; (c) (in a play) Akt, der; Aufzug, der (geh.); **a one-**∼ **play** ein Einakter; (d) (theatre performance) Akt, der; Nummer, die; **get in on the** ∼ (fig. coll.) ins Geschäft einsteigen; mitmischen (ugs.); **he/she will be a hard** ∼ **to follow** (fig.) das macht ihm/ihr so leicht keiner nach; **get one's** ∼ **together** (coll.) sich am Riemen reißen (ugs.); (e) (pretence) Theater, das; Schau, die (ugs.); **it's all an** ∼ **with her** sie tut nur so; **put on an** ∼ (coll.) eine Schau abziehen (ugs.); Theater spielen; (f) (decree) Gesetz, das; **Act of Parliament** Parlamentsakte, die. 2 v.t. spielen ‹Stück, Rolle›. 3 v.i. (a) (perform actions) handeln; reagieren; ∼ **[up]on** folgen (+ Dat.) ‹Anweisung, Ratschlag›; (b) (behave) sich verhalten; (function) ∼ **as sb.** als jmd. fungieren od. tätig sein; ∼ **as sth.** als etw. dienen; (c) (perform special function) ‹Person:› handeln; ‹Gerät, Ding:› funktionieren; ‹Substanz, Mittel:› wirken (**on** auf + Akk.); (d) (perform play etc., lit. or fig.) spielen; schauspielern (ugs.). ∼ **'up** v.i. (coll.) Theater machen (ugs.); ‹Auto, Magen:› Zicken machen (ugs.)

acting /'æktɪŋ/ 1 adj. (temporary) stellvertretend. 2 n., no pl. (Theatre etc.) Schauspielerei, die; **an** ∼ **career** eine Karriere als Schauspieler

action /'ækʃn/ n. (a) (doing sth.) Handeln, das; **a man of** ∼: ein Mann der Tat; **take** ∼: Schritte od. etwas unternehmen; **put a plan into** ∼: einen Plan in die Tat umsetzen; **put sth. out of** ∼: etw. außer Betrieb setzen; **be/ be put out of** ∼: außer Betrieb sein/gesetzt werden; **a film full of** ∼: ein Film mit viel Handlung; (b) (effect) **the** ∼ **of salt on ice** die Wirkung von Salz auf Eis (Akk.); (c) (act) Tat, die; (d) (Theatre) Handlung, die; Geschehen, das; **where the** ∼ **is** (coll.) wo was los ist (ugs.); (e) (legal process) [Gerichts]verfahren, das; **bring an** ∼ **against sb.** eine Klage od. ein Verfahren gegen jmdn. anstrengen; (f) (fighting) Gefecht, das; Kampf, der; **he died in** ∼: er ist [im Kampf] gefallen; (g) (movement) Bewegung, die

actionable /'ækʃənəbl/ adj. [gerichtlich] verfolgbar od. strafbar

action: ∼**-packed** adj. spannend ‹Buch, Roman›; **an** ∼**-packed film** ein Film mit viel Aktion; **an** ∼**-packed holiday** ein Aktivurlaub; ∼ **'replay** n. Wiederholung [in Zeitlupe]; ∼ **stations** n. pl. (Mil.; also fig.) Stellung, die; ∼ **stations!** in die Stellungen!

activate /'æktɪveɪt/ v.t. (a) in Gang setzen ‹Vorrichtung, Mechanismus›; auslösen ‹Mechanismus›; (b) (Chem., Phys.) aktivieren; ∼**d carbon** or **charcoal** Aktivkohle, die

active /'æktɪv/ adj. aktiv; wirksam ‹Kraft, Mittel›; praktisch ‹Gebrauch, Versuch, Kenntnisse›; tätig ‹Vulkan›; **a very** ∼ **child** ein sehr lebhaftes Kind; **take an** ∼ **interest in sth.** regen Anteil an etw. (Dat.) nehmen; **take an** ∼ **part in sth.** sich aktiv an etw. (Dat.) beteiligen; **on** ∼ **service** or (Amer.) **duty** (Mil.) im aktiven Dienst

actively /'æktɪvlɪ/ adv. aktiv

activist /'æktɪvɪst/ n. Aktivist, der/Aktivistin, die

activity /æk'tɪvɪtɪ/ n. (a) no pl. Aktivität, die; **military** ∼: militärischer Einsatz; (b) (efforts) aktive Tätigkeit; rege [Mit]arbeit; (c) usu. in pl. (action) Aktivität, die; (occupation) Betätigung, die; **classroom activities** schulische Tätigkeiten; **outdoor activities** Betätigung an der frischen Luft

actor /'æktə(r)/ n. Schauspieler, der

actress /'æktrɪs/ n. Schauspielerin, die

actual /'æktʃʊəl/ adj. eigentlich, tatsächlich ‹Lage, Gegebenheiten›; wirklich ‹Name, Gegenstand›; konkret ‹Beispiel›; **in** ∼ **fact** tatsächlich; **no** ∼ **crime was committed** es wurde kein eigentliches Verbrechen begangen

actuality /æktʃʊ'ælɪtɪ/ n. Wirklichkeit, die; Realität, die; **in** ∼: in Wirklichkeit

actually /'æktʃʊəlɪ/ adv. (in fact) eigentlich; (by the way) übrigens; (believe it or not) sogar; ∼, **I must be going** ich muss jetzt wirklich gehen; **he** ∼ **had the cheek to suggest …:** er hatte tatsächlich die Unverfrorenheit, vorzuschlagen …

actuary /'æktʃʊərɪ/ n. ▶ **887** | Versicherungsmathematiker, der; Aktuar, der

actuate /'æktʃʊeɪt/ v.t. (activate) antreiben ‹Maschine›; auslösen ‹Mechanismus, Reaktion›

acumen /'ækjʊmen/ n. Scharfsinn, der; **business** ∼: Geschäftssinn, der

acupuncture /'ækjʊpʌnktʃə(r)/ n. (Med.) Akupunktur, die

acute /ə'kjuːt/ adj. ∼**r** /ə'kjuːtə(r)/, ∼**st** /ə'kjuːtɪst/ (a) (Geom.) ∼ **angle** spitzer Winkel; (b) (Med.) akut ‹Krankheit, Stadium›; (c) (critical) akut ‹Gefahr, Situation, Mangel›; (d) (keen) fein ‹Geruchssinn›; heftig ‹Schmerz›

AD abbr. ▶ **738** | Anno Domini n. Chr.

ad /æd/ n. (coll.) Annonce, die; Inserat, das; **small ad** Kleinanzeige, die

adage /'ædɪdʒ/ n. Sprichwort, das

adamant /'ædəmənt/ adj. unnachgiebig; **be** ∼ **that …:** darauf bestehen, dass …

Adam's apple /ædəmz 'æpl/ n. Adamsapfel, der

adapt /ə'dæpt/ 1 v.t. (a) (adjust) anpassen (**to** Dat.); variieren ‹Kleidung›; umstellen ‹Maschine› (**to** auf + Akk.); **be** ∼**ed for doing sth.** darauf eingestellt sein, etw. zu tun; (b) (modify) adaptieren, bearbeiten ‹Text, Theaterstück›. 2 v.i. (a) ‹Tier, Auge:› sich anpassen (**to** an + Akk.); (b) (to surroundings, circumstances) sich gewöhnen (**to** an + Akk.)

adaptable /ə'dæptəbl/ adj. anpassungsfähig; vielseitig ‹Maschine›; **be** ∼ **to** or **for sth.** an etw. (Akk.) angepasst werden können

adaptation /ædəp'teɪʃn/ n. (a) no pl. Anpassung, die (**to** an + Akk.); (of machine) Umstellung, die (**to** auf + Akk.); (b) (version) Adap[ta]tion, die; (of play, text) Bearbeitung, die

adaptor (**adapter**) /ə'dæptə(r)/ n. Adapter, der

add /æd/ 1 v.t. hinzufügen (**to** Dat.); hinzufügen, anfügen ‹weitere Worte›; beisteuern ‹Ideen, Vorschläge› (**to** zu); dazusetzen ‹Namen, Zahlen›; ∼ **two and two** zwei und zwei zusammenzählen; ∼ **two numbers together** zwei Zahlen addieren; ∼ **the flour to the liquid** geben Sie das Mehl in die Flüssigkeit. 2 v.i. ∼ **to** vergrößern ‹Schwierigkeiten, Einkommen›; verbessern ‹Ruf› ∼ **'up** 1 v.i. (a) these figures ∼ **up to** or **make 30** altogether diese Zahlen ergeben zusammen[gezählt] 30; **these things** ∼**/it** ∼**s up** (fig. coll.) all diese Dinge summieren sich/das summiert sich alles; ∼ **up to sth.** (fig.) auf etw. (Akk.) hinauslaufen; (b) (make sense) einen Sinn ergeben. 2 v.t. zusammenzählen

addenda /ə'dendə/ n. pl. (in book etc.) Addenda Pl.

adder /'ædə(r)/ n. (Zool.) Viper, die

addict 1 /ə'dɪkt/ v.t. **be** ∼**ed** süchtig sein; **become** ∼**ed [to sth.]** [nach etw.] süchtig werden; **be** ∼**ed to alcohol/**

drugs alkohol-/drogensüchtig sein. **2** /'ædɪkt/ *n.* Süchtige, *der*/*die;* (fig. coll.) [begeisterte] Anhänger, *der*/Anhängerin, *die;* **become an ~** (lit.) süchtig werden; **a TV ~** (fig. coll.) ein Fernsehnarr

addiction /ə'dɪkʃn/ *n.* Sucht, *die;* (fig. coll.) Fimmel, *der* (ugs.); **an ~ to sth.** die Sucht nach etw.

addictive /ə'dɪktɪv/ *adj.* **be ~:** süchtig machen; (fig. coll.) zu einer Sucht werden

'**adding machine** *n.* Rechenmaschine, *die*

addition /ə'dɪʃn/ *n.* **(a)** *no pl.* Hinzufügen, *das;* (of ingredient) Dazugeben, *das;* (adding up) Addieren, *das;* (process) Addition, *die;* **in ~:** außerdem; **in ~ to** zusätzlich zu; **(b)** (thing added) Ergänzung, *die* **(to** zu)

additional /ə'dɪʃənl/ *adj.* zusätzlich; **~ details** weitere Einzelheiten

additive /'ædɪtɪv/ *n.* Zusatz, *der*

'**add-on 1** *n.* (accessory) Zubehörteil, *das;* (for electrical appliance) Zusatzgerät, *das;* (addition) Zusatz, *der.* **2** *adj.* **accessory** Zubehörteil, *das;* (for electrical appliance) Zusatzgerät, *das;* **sth. can be bought as an ~ feature/accessory for sth.** etw. ist als Zubehör zu etw. erhältlich

address /ə'dres/ **1** *v.t.* **(a) ~ sth. to sb./sth.** etw. an jmdn./etw. richten; **(b)** (mark with ~) adressieren **(to** an + *Akk.*); mit Anschrift versehen; **(c)** (speak to) anreden 〈*Person*〉; sprechen zu 〈*Zuhörern*〉; **~ sb. as sth.** jmdn. mit etw. *od.* als etw. anreden; **(d)** (give attention to) angehen 〈*Problem*〉. **2** *n.* **(a)** (on letter or envelope) Adresse, *die;* Anschrift, *die;* (place of residence) Wohnsitz, *der;* **of no fixed ~:** ohne festen Wohnsitz; **(b)** (discourse) Ansprache, *die;* Rede, *die*

ad'dress book *n.* Adressbüchlein, *das*

addressee /ædre'si:/ *n.* Adressat, *der*/Adressatin, *die;* Empfänger, *der*/Empfängerin, *die*

ad'dress label *n.* Adressenaufkleber, *der*

adept /'ædept, ə'dept/ *adj.* geschickt **(in, at** in + *Dat.*)

adequacy /'ædɪkwəsɪ/ *n., no pl.* **(a)** Angemessenheit, *die;* Adäquatheit, *die;* **(b)** (sufficiency) **doubt/confirm the ~ of sth.** bezweifeln/bestätigen, dass etw. ausreichend ist *od.* ausreicht; **(c)** (acceptability) Annehmbarkeit, *die*

adequate /'ædɪkwət/ *adj.* **(a)** angemessen, adäquat **(to** *Dat.*); (suitable) passend; **(b)** (sufficient) ausreichend; **(c)** (acceptable) annehmbar

adequately /'ædɪkwətlɪ/ *adv.* **(a)** (sufficiently) ausreichend; **(b)** (suitably) angemessen 〈*gekleidet, qualifiziert usw.*〉

adhere /əd'hɪə(r)/ *v.i.* **(a)** (stick) haften, (by glue) kleben **(to** an + *Dat.*); **~ [to each other]** 〈*zwei Dinge:*〉 zusammenkleben; **(b)** (give support) **~ to sth./sb.** an jmdm./einer Sache festhalten; **(c) ~ to** sich halten an (+ *Akk.*) 〈*Abmachung, Versprechen, Regel*〉

adherence /əd'hɪərəns/ *n., no pl.* (to programme, agreement, promise, schedule) Einhalten, *das* **(to** *Gen.*); (to decision, tradition, principle) Festhalten, *das* **(to** an + *Dat.*); (to rule) Befolgen, *das* **(to** *Gen.*)

adherent /əd'hɪərənt/ *n.* Anhänger, *der*/Anhängerin, *die*

adhesion /əd'hi:ʒn/ *n., no pl.* (sticking) Haften, *das,* (by glue) Kleben, *das* **(to** an + *Dat.*)

adhesive /əd'hi:sɪv/ **1** *adj.* klebrig; gummiert 〈*Briefmarke, Umschlag*〉; Klebe〈*band, -schicht*〉; **be ~:** kleben/gummiert sein; **~ plaster** Heftpflaster, *das.* **2** *n.* Klebstoff, *der;* Klebemittel, *das*

adjacent /ə'dʒeɪsənt/ *adj.* angrenzend; Neben-; **~ to** (position) neben (+ *Dat.*); (direction) neben (+ *Akk.*)

adjective /'ædʒɪktɪv/ *n.* (Ling.) Adjektiv, *das;* Eigenschaftswort, *das*

adjoin /ə'dʒɔɪn/ **1** *v.t.* grenzen an (+ *Akk.*); **the room ~ing ours** das Zimmer neben unserem. **2** *v.i.* aneinander grenzen; nebeneinander liegen; **in the ~ing room** im Zimmer daneben *od.* nebenan

adjourn /ə'dʒɜ:n/ **1** *v.t.* (break off) unterbrechen; (put off) aufschieben. **2** *v.i.* (suspend proceedings) sich vertagen; **~ for lunch/for half an hour** eine Mittagspause/eine halbstündige Pause einlegen

adjournment /ə'dʒɜ:nmənt/ *n.* (suspending) (of court) Vertagung, *die;* (of meeting) Unterbrechung, *die*

adjudge /ə'dʒʌdʒ/ *v.t.* (pronounce) **~ sb./sth. [to be] sth.** jmdn./etw. für etw. erklären

adjudicate /ə'dʒu:dɪkeɪt/ *v.i.* (in court, tribunal) als Richter tätig sein; (in contest) Preisrichter sein **(at** bei, **in** + *Dat.*)

adjudication /ədʒu:dɪ'keɪʃn/ *n.* **(a)** (judging) Beurteilung, *die;* **(b)** (decision) Entscheidung, *die*

adjudicator /ə'dʒu:dɪkeɪtə(r)/ *n.* Schiedsrichter, *der*/Schiedsrichterin, *die*

adjunct /'ædʒʌŋkt/ *n.* Anhängsel, *das*

adjust /ə'dʒʌst/ **1** *v.t.* richtig [an]ordnen 〈*Gegenstände*〉; zurechtrücken 〈*Hut, Krawatte*〉; (regulate) regulieren, regeln 〈*Geschwindigkeit, Höhe usw.*〉; [richtig] einstellen 〈*Gerät, Motor, Maschine usw.*〉; (adapt) entsprechend ändern 〈*Plan, Bedingungen*〉; angleichen 〈*Gehalt, Lohn, Zinsen*〉; **~ sth. [to sth.]** etw. [an etw. (*Akk.*)] anpassen *od.* [auf etw. (*Akk.*)] einstellen; '**do not ~ your set**' „Störung". **2** *v.i.* **~ [to sth.]** sich [an etw. (*Akk.*)] gewöhnen *od.* anpassen; 〈*Gerät:*〉 sich [auf etw. (*Akk.*)] einstellen lassen

adjustable /ə'dʒʌstəbl/ *adj.* einstellbar **(to** auf + *Akk.*); verstellbar, justierbar 〈*Gerät*〉; regulierbar 〈*Temperatur*〉

adjustment /ə'dʒʌstmənt/ *n.* (of layout, plan) Ordnung, *die;* (of things) Anordnung, *die;* (of device, engine, machine) Einstellung, *die;* (to situation, lifestyle) Anpassung, *die* **(to** an + *Akk.*); (of eye) Adaption, *die;* Gewöhnung, *die*

ad lib /æd'lɪb/ **1** *adj.* Stegreif-, improvisiert 〈*Rede, Vortrag*〉. **2** *v.i.,* **-bb-** (coll.) improvisieren

Adm. *abbr.* **Admiral** Adm.

'**adman** *n.* Werbe-, Reklamefachmann, *der*

admin /'ædmɪn/ *n.* (coll.) Verwaltung, *die;* **an ~ problem** ein Verwaltungsproblem

administer /æd'mɪnɪstə(r)/ *v.t.* **(a)** (manage) verwalten; führen 〈*Geschäfte, Regierung*〉; **(b)** (give, apply) spenden 〈*Trost*〉; leisten, gewähren 〈*Hilfe, Unterstützung*〉; austeilen, verabreichen 〈*Schläge, Prügel*〉; verabreichen, geben 〈*Medikamente*〉; spenden, geben 〈*Sakramente*〉; **~ justice** Recht sprechen; **~ an oath to sb.** jmdn. vereidigen

administration /ədmɪnɪ'streɪʃn/ *n.* **(a)** Verwaltung, *die;* **(b)** (of sacraments) Spenden, *das;* Geben, *das;* (of medicine) Verabreichung, *die;* (of aid, relief) Gewährung, *die;* **~ of justice** Rechtspflege, *die;* **~ of an oath** Eidesabnahme, *die;* **(c)** (ministry, government) Regierung, *die;* (Amer.: President's period of office) Amtszeit, *die*

administrative /əd'mɪnɪstrətɪv/ *adj.* Verwaltungs-; administrativ 〈*Angelegenheit, Geschick*〉; **~ work** Verwaltungsarbeit, *die;* **an ~ job** ein Verwaltungsposten

administrator /əd'mɪnɪstreɪtə(r)/ *n.* ▶ **887** Administrator, *der;* Verwalter, *der*

admirable /'ædmərəbl/ *adj.* bewundernswert; erstaunlich; (excellent) vortrefflich

admirably /'ædmərəblɪ/ *adv.* bewundernswert; erstaunlich; (excellently) vortrefflich

admiral /'ædmərəl/ *n.* **(a)** ▶ **1152** Admiral, *der;* **(b)** (butterfly) **red ~:** Admiral, *der*

Admiralty /'ædmərəltɪ/ *n.* (Hist., except in titles) *britisches Marineministerium*

admiration /ædmə'reɪʃn/ *n., no pl.* Bewunderung, *die* **(of, for** für)

admire /əd'maɪə(r)/ *v.t.* bewundern **(for** wegen)

admirer /əd'maɪərə(r)/ *n.* Bewunderer, *der*/Bewunderin, *die;* (suitor) Verehrer, *der*/Verehrerin, *die*

admissible /əd'mɪsɪbl/ *adj.* **(a)** akzeptabel 〈*Plan, Vorschlag*〉; erlaubt, zulässig 〈*Abweichung, Schreibung*〉; **(b)** (Law) zulässig

admission /əd'mɪʃn/ *n.* **(a)** (entry) Zutritt, *der;* **~ to university** Zulassung [zum Studium] an einer Universität; **~ costs** *or* **is** 50p der Eintritt kostet 50 Pence; **(b)** (charge) Eintritt, *der;* **(c)** (confession) Eingeständnis, *das* **(of, to** *Gen.*); **by** *or* **on one's own ~:** nach eigenem Eingeständnis

admission: ~ charge, ~ fee, ~ price *ns.* Eintrittspreis, *der*

admit /əd'mɪt/ **1** *v.t.,* **-tt-:** **(a)** (let in) hinein-/hereinlassen; **persons under the age of 16 not ~ted** kein Zutritt für Jugendliche unter 16 Jahren; **~ sb. to a club** jmdn. in einen Klub aufnehmen; **be** ~**ted to hospital** ins Krankenhaus eingeliefert werden; **(b)** (accept as valid) **if we** ~ **that argument/evidence** wenn wir davon ausgehen, dass dieses Argument zutrifft/dass diese Beweise erlaubt sind; **(c)** (acknowledge) zugeben; eingestehen; ~ **to being drunk** zugeben, betrunken zu sein. **2** *v.i.*, **-tt-:** ~ **of sth.** etw. zulassen *od.* erlauben

admittance /əd'mɪtəns/ *n.* Zutritt, *der;* **no** ~ [**except on business**] Zutritt [für Unbefugte] verboten

admittedly /əd'mɪtɪdlɪ/ *adv.* zugegeben[ermaßen]

admonish /əd'mɒnɪʃ/ *v.t.* ermahnen

admonition /ædmə'nɪʃn/ *n.* Ermahnung, *die*

ad nauseam /æd 'nɔːsɪæm, æd 'nɔːzɪæm/ *adv.* bis zum Überdruss

ado /ə'duː/ *n.* **without more** *or* **with no further** ~: ohne weiteres Aufhebens

adolescence /ædə'lesns/ *n., no art.* die Zeit des Erwachsenwerdens

adolescent /ædə'lesnt/ **1** *n.* Heranwachsende, *der/die.* **2** *adj.* heranwachsend ‹*Person*›; pubertär ‹*Benehmen*›

adopt /ə'dɒpt/ *v.t.* **(a)** adoptieren; aufnehmen ‹*Tier*›; **(b)** (take over) annehmen, übernehmen ‹*Kultur, Sitte*›; annehmen ‹*Glaube, Religion*›; **(c)** (take·up) übernehmen, sich aneignen ‹*Methode*›; einnehmen ‹*Standpunkt, Haltung*›

adoption /ə'dɒpʃn/ *n.* **(a)** Adoption, *die;* **(b)** (of culture, custom) Annahme, *die;* Übernahme, *die;* (of belief) Annahme, *die;* **(c)** (taking up) (of method) Aneignung, *die;* Übernahme, *die;* (of point of view) Einnahme, *die*

adorable /ə'dɔːrəbl/ *adj.* bezaubernd; hinreißend

adoration /ædə'reɪʃn/ *n.* **(a)** Verehrung, *die;* **(b)** (worship of gods etc.) Anbetung, *die*

adore /ə'dɔː(r)/ *v.t.* **(a)** innig lieben; **his adoring girlfriend** seine schmachtende Freundin; **(b)** (coll.: like greatly) ~ **sth.** für etwas schwärmen; ~ **doing sth.** etw. für sein Leben gern tun (ugs.)

adorn /ə'dɔːn/ *v.t.* schmücken; ~ **oneself** sich schön machen

adornment /ə'dɔːnmənt/ *n.* **(a)** *no pl.* Verschönerung, *die;* **(b)** (ornament) Verzierung, *die;* ~**s** Schmuck, *der*

adrenalin, (*Amer.* **P**) /ə'drenəlɪn/ *n.* (Physiol., Med.) Adrenalin, *das*

Adriatic /eɪdrɪ'ætɪk/ *pr. n.* ~ [**Sea**] Adriatisches Meer; Adria, *die*

adrift /ə'drɪft/ *pred. adj.* **be** ~: treiben

adroit /ə'drɔɪt/ *adj.* geschickt, gewandt (**at** in + *Dat.*)

adulation /ædjʊ'leɪʃn/ *n., no pl.* (praise) Beweihräucherung, *die;* (admiration of person) Vergötterung, *die*

adult /'ædʌlt, ə'dʌlt/ **1** *adj.* erwachsen ‹*Person*›; reif ‹*Verhalten*›; ausgewachsen ‹*Tier, Pflanze*›; **an** ~ **film/book** *etc.* ein Film/Buch *usw.* [nur] für Erwachsene. **2** *n.* Erwachsene, *der/die;* '**A**~**s only**' „Nur für Erwachsene"; ~ **education** Erwachsenenbildung, *die*

adulterate /ə'dʌltəreɪt/ *v.t.* verunreinigen; panschen ‹*Wein, Milch*›

adulterous /ə'dʌltərəs/ *adj.* ehebrecherisch

adultery /ə'dʌltərɪ/ *n., no pl.* Ehebruch, *der*

adulthood /'ædʌlthʊd, ə'dʌlthʊd/ *n., no pl.* Erwachsenenalter, *das*

advance /əd'vɑːns/ **1** *v.t.* **(a)** (move forward) vorrücken lassen; **(b)** (put forward) vorbringen ‹*Plan, Meinung, These*›; **(c)** (bring forward) vorverlegen ‹*Termin*›; **(d)** (further) fördern; (pay before due date) vorschießen; ~ **sb. a week's pay** jmdm. einen Wochenlohn [als] Vorschuss geben; (loan) **the bank** ~**d me two thousand pounds** die Bank lieh mir zweitausend Pfund. **2** *v.i.* **(a)** (move forward; also Mil.) vorrücken; ‹*Prozession:*› sich vorwärts bewegen; ~ **towards sb./sth.** ‹*Person:*› auf jmdn./etw. zugehen; **(b)** (fig.: make progress) Fortschritte machen; vorankommen. **3** *n.* **(a)** (forward movement) Vorrücken, *das;* (fig.: progress) Fortschritt, *der;* **(b)** *usu. in pl.* (personal overture) Annäherungsversuch, *der;* **(c)** (payment beforehand) Vorauszahlung, *die;* (on salary) Vorschuss, *der* (**on** auf + *Akk.*); (loan) Darlehen, *das;* **(d) in** ~: im Voraus; **send sb./sth. in** ~: jmdn./etw. vorausschicken

ad'vance booking *n.* (for a film, play) [vorherige] Kartenreservierung; (of a table in a restaurant) [vorherige] Tischreservierung

advanced /əd'vɑːnst/ *adj.* fortgeschritten; **be** ~ **in years** in fortgeschrittenem Alter sein; ~ **level** ⇒ **A level**

advance 'guard *n.* (lit. or fig.) Vorhut, *die*

advancement /əd'vɑːnsmənt/ *n., no pl.* (furtherance) Förderung, *die*

advance: ~ '**notice** *n.* a week's ~ **notice** Benachrichtigung eine Woche [im] Voraus; **give sb.** ~ **notice of sth.** jmdn. im Voraus von etw. in Kenntnis setzen; ~ '**payment** *n.* Vorauszahlung, *die*

advantage /əd'vɑːntɪdʒ/ *n.* **(a)** (better position) Vorteil, *der;* **give sb. an** ~ **over sb.** für jmdn. einen Vorteil gegenüber jmdm. bedeuten; **gain an** ~ **over sb.** sich (*Dat.*) einen Vorteil gegenüber jmdm. verschaffen; **have an** ~ **over sb.** jmdm. gegenüber im Vorteil sein; **take** [**full/unfair**] ~ **of sth.** etw. [voll/unfairerweise] ausnutzen; **(b)** (benefit) Vorteil, *der;* **be to one's** ~: für jmdn. von Vorteil sein; **turn sth. to** [**one's**] ~: etw. ausnutzen

advantageous /ædvən'teɪdʒəs/ *adj.* vorteilhaft ‹*Verfahren, Übereinkunft*›; günstig ‹*Lage*›

advent /'ædvənt/ *n., no pl.* **(a)** (of thing) Beginn, *der;* Anfang, *der;* **(b)** *no art.* **A**~ (season) Advent, *der*

adventure /əd'ventʃə(r)/ *n.* Abenteuer, *die*

ad'venture: ~ **holiday** *n* Abenteuerurlaub, *der;* **they organize** ~ **holidays** sie bieten Abenteuerurlaub an; ~ **playground** *n.* Abenteuerspielplatz, *der*

adventurer /əd'ventʃərə(r)/ *n.* Abenteurer, *der*

adventurous /əd'ventʃərəs/ *adj.* **(a)** (eager for adventure) abenteuerlustig; **(b)** (filled with adventures) abenteuerlich

adverb /'ædvɜːb/ *n.* (Ling.) Adverb, *das;* Umstandswort, *das*

adverbial /əd'vɜːbɪəl/ *adj.* (Ling.) adverbial

adversary /'ædvəsərɪ/ *n.* (enemy) Widersacher, *der/*Widersacherin, *die;* (opponent) Kontrahent, *der/*Kontrahentin, *die*

adverse /'ædvɜːs/ *adj.* **(a)** (hostile) ablehnend (**to** gegenüber); **an** ~ **response** eine abschlägige Antwort; **(b)** (unfavourable) ungünstig ‹*Bedingung, Entwicklung*›; nachteilig ‹*Auswirkung*›; **(c)** (contrary) widrig ‹*Wind, Umstände*›

adversity /əd'vɜːsɪtɪ/ *n.* **(a)** *no pl.* Not, *die;* **in** ~: in der Not; in Notzeiten; **(b)** *usu. in pl.* (misfortune) Widrigkeit, *die*

advert /'ædvɜːt/ (Brit. coll.) ⇒ **advertisement**

advertise /'ædvətaɪz/ **1** *v.t.* werben für; (by small ad) inserieren; ausschreiben ‹*Stelle*›. **2** *v.i.* werben; (in newspaper) inserieren; annoncieren; ~ **for sb./sth.** jmdn./etw. [per Inserat] suchen

advertisement /əd'vɜːtɪsmənt/ *n.* Anzeige, *die;* **TV** ~: Fernsehspot, *der;* **classified** ~: Kleinanzeige, *die*

advertiser /'ædvətaɪzə(r)/ *n.* (in newspaper) Inserent, *der/*Inserentin, *die;* (on radio, TV) Auftraggeber/Auftraggeberin [der Werbesendung]

advertising /'ædvətaɪzɪŋ/ *n., no pl., no indef. art.* Werbung, *die;* ~ **agency/campaign/industry** Werbeagentur, *die/*-kampagne, *die/*-branche, *die*

Advertising 'Standards Authority *n.* (Brit.) Werbeaufsichtsbehörde

advice /əd'vaɪs/ *n., no pl., no indef. art.* (counsel) Rat, *der;* **on sb.'s** ~: auf jmds. Rat (*Akk.*) hin; **a piece of** ~: ein Rat[schlag]; **if you ask** *or* **want my** ~: wenn du meinen Rat hören willst; **ask sb.'s** ~ [**on sth.**] jmdn. [wegen etw.] um Rat bitten; **take sb.'s** ~: jmds. Rat (*Dat.*) folgen

advisable /əd'vaɪzəbl/ *adj.* ratsam

advise /əd'vaɪz/ *v.t.* **(a)** (offer advice to) beraten; **please** ~ **me** bitte geben Sie mir einen Rat; ~ **sb. to do sth.** jmdm. raten, etw. zu tun; ~ **sb. not to do** *or* **against doing sth.** jmdm. abraten, etw. zu tun; **(b)** (recommend) ~ **sth.** zu etw. raten; **(c)** (inform) unterrichten, informieren (**of** über + *Akk.*)

advised /əd'vaɪzd/ *adj.* [**well-**]~: wohl überlegt; **be well/better** ~: ‹*Person:*› wohl beraten/besser beraten sein

advisedly /əd'vaɪzɪdlɪ/ *adv.* bewusst

adviser, advisor /əd'vaɪzə(r)/ *n.* Berater, *der*/Beraterin, *die*

advisory /əd'vaɪzərɪ/ *adj.* beratend; ～ **committee** Beratungsausschuss, *der;* **in an** ～ **capacity** in beratender Funktion

advocate 1 /'ædvəkət/ *n.* ▸ 887▸ (of a cause) Befürworter, *der*/Befürworterin, *die;* Fürsprecher, *der*/Fürsprecherin, *die;* (for a person) Fürsprecher, *der*/Fürsprecherin, *die;* (Law) [Rechts]anwalt, *der*/[Rechts]anwältin, *die.* **2** /'ædvəkeɪt/ *v.t.* befürworten

advt. *abbr.* **advertisement**

Aegean /iːˈdʒiːən/ *pr. n.* ～ **[Sea]** Ägäisches Meer

aegis /'iːdʒɪs/ *n.* **under the** ～ **of sb./sth.** unter der Ägide (geh.) *od.* Schirmherrschaft von jmdm./etw.

aerial /'eərɪəl/ **1** *adj.* **(a)** (in the air) Luft-; **(b)** (atmospheric) atmosphärisch; **(c)** (Aeronaut.) Luft-. **2** *n.* Antenne, *die*

aero- /'eərə/ *in comb.* Aero-

aerobatics /eərə'bætɪks/ *n.* **(a)** *no pl.* Kunstflug, *der;* Aerobatik, *die;* **(b)** *pl.* (feats of flying skill) fliegerische Kunststücke

aerobic /eə'rəʊbɪk/ *adj.* aerob

aerobics /eə'rəʊbɪks/ *n., no pl.* Aerobic, *das*

aerodrome /'eərədrəʊm/ *n.* (Brit. dated) Aerodrom, *das* (veralt.); Flugplatz, *der*

aerody'namic /eərəʊdaɪ'næmɪk/ *adj.* aerodynamisch

'aerofoil *n.* Tragfläche, *die;* Tragflügel, *der* (fachspr.)

aero'nautical *adj.* aeronautisch

aeronautics /eərə'nɔːtɪks/ *n., no pl.* Aeronautik, *die*

'aeroplane *n.* (Brit.) Flugzeug, *das*

aerosol /'eərəsɒl/ *n.* (spray) Spray, *der od. das;* (container) ～ **[spray]** Spraydose, *die*

'aerospace *n., no pl., no art.* Erdatmosphäre und Weltraum; (technology) Luft- und Raumfahrt, *die*

aesthetic /iːsˈθetɪk/ *adj.* ästhetisch; schöngeistig ⟨Person⟩

aesthetics /iːsˈθetɪks/ *n., no pl.* Ästhetik, *die*

AF *abbr.* **audio frequency**

afar /ə'fɑː/ *adv.* weit fort; in weiter Ferne; **from** ～: aus der Ferne

affable /'æfəbl/ *adj.* freundlich

affair /ə'feə(r)/ *n.* **(a)** (concern, matter) Angelegenheit, *die;* **it's not my** ～: es geht mich nichts an; **that's 'his** ～: das ist seine Sache; **(b)** *in pl.* (everyday business) Geschäfte *Pl.;* (tägliche) Arbeit; (business dealings) Geschäfte *Pl.;* **state of** ～s Lage, *die;* **(c)** (love ～) Affäre, *die;* **(d)** (occurrence) Geschichte, *die* (ugs.); Angelegenheit, *die;* **(e)** (coll.: thing) Ding, *das*

affect¹ /ə'fekt/ *v.t.* (pretend to have) nachahmen; imitieren; (pretend to feel or do) vortäuschen; spielen; **the boy** ～**ed indifference** der Junge tat so, als sei es ihm gleichgültig

affect² *v.t.* **(a)** (produce effect on) sich auswirken auf (+ *Akk.*); **(b)** (emotionally) betroffen machen; **be** ～**ed by sth.** von etw. betroffen sein; **(c)** ⟨Vorschrift:⟩ betreffen; ⟨Krankheit:⟩ infizieren ⟨Person⟩, befallen ⟨Pflanze⟩

affectation /æfek'teɪʃn/ *n.* **(a)** (studied display) Verstellung, *die;* (artificiality) Affektiertheit, *die;* **(b)** *no pl.* (pretence) ～ **of sth.** Vortäuschung von etw.

affected /ə'fektɪd/ *adj.* affektiert; gekünstelt ⟨Sprache, Stil⟩

affection /ə'fekʃn/ *n.* Zuneigung, *die;* **have** *or* **feel** ～ **for sb./sth.** für jmdn. Zuneigung empfinden/an etw. (*Dat.*) hängen

affectionate /ə'fekʃənət/ *adj.* anhänglich ⟨Person, Kind, [Haus]tier⟩; liebevoll ⟨Umarmung⟩; zärtlich ⟨Lächeln, Erinnerung⟩

affectionately /ə'fekʃənətlɪ/ *adv.* liebevoll; **yours** ～: viele Grüße und Küsse

affidavit /æfɪ'deɪvɪt/ *n.* (Law) **[sworn]** ～: eidesstattliche Versicherung; **swear an** ～: eine eidesstattliche Versicherung abgeben

affiliate /ə'fɪlɪeɪt/ **1** *v.t.* (attach) **be** ～**d to** *or* **with sth.** an etw. (*Akk.*) angegliedert sein. **2** *n.* (person) assoziiertes Mitglied; (organization) Zweigorganisation, *die*

affiliation /əfɪlɪ'eɪʃn/ *n.* Angliederung, *die* **(to, with** an + *Akk.*)

affinity /ə'fɪnɪtɪ/ *n.* **(a)** (relationship, resemblance) Verwandtschaft, *die* **(to** mit); **(b)** (liking) Neigung, *die* **(for** zu); **feel an** ～ **to** *or* **for sb./sth.** sich zu jmdm./etw. hingezogen fühlen

affirm /ə'fɜːm/ *v.t.* (assert) bekräftigen ⟨Absicht⟩; beteuern ⟨Unschuld⟩; (state as a fact) bestätigen; ～ **sth. to sb.** jmdm. etw. versichern

affirmation /æfə'meɪʃn/ *n.* (of intention) Bekräftigung, *die;* (of fact) Bestätigung, *die*

affirmative /ə'fɜːmətɪv/ **1** *adj.* affirmativ; bestätigend ⟨Erklärung⟩; bejahend, zustimmend ⟨Antwort⟩. **2** *n.* **answer in the** ～: bejahend antworten

affix /ə'fɪks/ *v.t.* ～ **sth. to sth.** etw. an etw. (*Dat.*) befestigen; ～ **one's signature [to sth.]** seine Unterschrift [unter etw. (*Akk.*)] setzen

afflict /ə'flɪkt/ *v.t.* (physically) plagen; (mentally) quälen; peinigen; **be** ～**ed with sth.** von etw. befallen sein

affliction /ə'flɪkʃn/ *n.* **(a)** *no pl.* (distress) Bedrängnis, *die;* **endure sorrow and** ～: Kummer und Leid ertragen; **(b)** (cause of distress) Leiden, *das;* **bodily** ～s körperliche Gebrechen

affluence /'æfluəns/ *n., no pl.* **(a)** (wealth) Reichtum, *der;* **(b)** (plenty) Überfluss, *der*

affluent /'æfluənt/ *adj.* reich; **the** ～ **society** die Überflussgesellschaft

afford /ə'fɔːd/ *v.t.* **(a)** sich (*Dat.*) leisten; **be able to** ～ **sth.** sich (*Dat.*) etw. leisten können; **be able to** ～: aufbringen können ⟨Geld⟩; erübrigen können ⟨Zeit⟩; **(b)** (provide) bieten; gewähren ⟨Schutz⟩; bereiten ⟨Vergnügen⟩

affray /ə'freɪ/ *n.* Schlägerei, *die*

affront /ə'frʌnt/ **1** *v.t.* (insult) beleidigen; (offend) kränken. **2** *n.* (insult) Affront, *der* (geh.) **(to** gegen); Beleidigung, *die* **(to** *Gen.*); (offence) Kränkung, *die* **(to** *Gen.*)

Afghan /'æfgæn/ ▸ 897▸, ▸ 947▸ **1** *adj.* afghanisch. **2** *n.* **(a)** (person) Afghane, *der*/Afghanin, *die;* **(b)** (language) Afghanisch, *das; see also* **English 2 a**

Afghan 'hound *n.* Afghane, *der*

Afghanistan /æf'gænɪstɑːn/ *pr. n.* Afghanistan (*das*)

afield /ə'fiːld/ *adv.* **far** ～ (direction) weit hinaus; (place) weit draußen; **from as far** ～ **as** von so weit her wie

afloat /ə'fləʊt/ *pred. adj.* (floating) über Wasser; flott ⟨Schiff⟩; **get a boat** ～: ein Boot flott machen; **(b)** (at sea) auf See; **be** ～: auf dem Meer treiben

afoot /ə'fʊt/ *pred. adj.* (under way) im Gange; **set** ～: in Gang setzen; aufstellen ⟨Plan⟩; **plans were** ～ **to** …: es gab Pläne, zu …

aforementioned /ə'fɔːmenʃnd/, **aforesaid** /ə'fɔːsed/ *adjs.* oben erwähnt *od.* genannt

aforethought /ə'fɔːθɔːt/ *adj.* **with malice** ～: mit Vorbedacht

afraid /ə'freɪd/ *pred. adj.* **[not] be** ～ **[of sb./sth.]** [vor jmdm./etw.] [keine] Angst haben; **be** ～ **to do sth.** Angst davor haben, etw. zu tun; **be** ～ **of doing sth.** Angst haben, etw. zu tun; **I'm** ～ **[that] we must assume that** …: leider müssen wir annehmen, dass …; **I'm** ～ **so/not** ich fürchte ja/nein

afresh /ə'freʃ/ *adv.* von neuem

Africa /'æfrɪkə/ *pr. n.* Afrika (*das*)

African /'æfrɪkən/ **1** *adj.* ▸ 947▸ afrikanisch; **sb. is** ～: jmd. ist Afrikaner/Afrikanerin. **2** *n.* **(a)** ▸ 947▸ Afrikaner, *der*/Afrikanerin, *die;* **(b)** (Amer.: Negro) Neger, *der*/Negerin, *die*

Afrikaans /æfrɪ'kɑːns/ *n.* ▸ 897▸ Afrikaans, *das; see also* **English 2 a**

Afro /'æfrəʊ/ *adj.* Afro-; ～ **look** Afrolook, *der*

Afro-A'merican 1 *adj.* afroamerikanisch. **2** *n.* Afroamerikaner, *der*/-amerikanerin, *die*

Afro-Carib'bean 1 *adj.* afrokaribisch. **2** *n.* Mensch afrokaribischer Herkunft *od.* Abstammung

aft /ɑːft/ *adv.* (Naut., Aeronaut.) achtern; **go** ～: nach achtern gehen

after /'ɑːftə(r)/ **1** *adv.* **(a)** (later) danach; **two days** ～: zwei Tage danach *od.* später; **(b)** (behind) hinterher. **2** *prep.*

(a) (following in time, as result of) nach; ~ **six months** nach sechs Monaten; ~ **you** nach Ihnen; **time** ~ **time** wieder und wieder; **day** ~ **day** Tag für Tag; (b) (behind) hinter (+ *Dat.*); **what are you** ~? was suchst du denn?; (to questioner) was willst du wirklich wissen?; **she's only** ~ **his money** sie ist nur hinter seinem Geld her; (c) (about) **ask** ~ **sb.**/ **sth.** nach jmdm./etw. fragen; (d) (next in importance to) nach; (e) (in spite of) nach; ~ **all** schließlich; **so you've come** ~ **all!** du bist also doch gekommen!

after: ~**birth** *n.* Nachgeburt, *die;* ~**care** *n., no pl.* (after hospital stay) Nachsorge, *die;* (after prison sentence) Resozialisierung, *die;* ~**-'dinner speech** *n.* Tischrede, *die;* ~**-effect** *n., usu. in pl.* Nachwirkung, *die;* ~**life** *n.* Leben nach dem Tod

aftermath /'ɑːftəmæθ, 'ɑːftəmɑːθ/ *n., no pl.* Nachwirkungen *Pl.;* **the** ~ **of the war** die Folgen *od.* Auswirkungen des Krieges

afternoon /ɑːftə'nuːn/ *n.* ▶706|, ▶739| Nachmittag, *der; attrib.* Nachmittags-; **this/tomorrow** ~: heute/ morgen Nachmittag; **[early/late] in the** ~: am [frühen/ späten] Nachmittag; (regularly) [früh/spät] nachmittags; **at three in the** ~: um drei Uhr nachmittags; **on Monday** ~**s/**~: montagnachmittags/[am] Montagnachmittag; **one** ~: eines Nachmittags; ~**s, of an** ~: nachmittags

afters /'ɑːftəz/ *n. pl.* (Brit. coll.) Nachtisch, *der*

after: ~**-sales service** *n.* Kundendienst, *der;* ~**shave** *n.* Aftershave, *das;* ~**shock** *n.* Nachbeben, *das;* ~**taste** *n.* Nachgeschmack, *der;* ~**thought** *n.* nachträglicher Einfall; **be added as an** ~**thought** erst später hinzukommen

afterwards /'ɑːftəwədz/ (*Amer.:* **afterward** /'ɑːftəwəd/) *adv.* danach

again /ə'gen, ə'geɪn/ *adv.* (a) (another time) wieder; **see a film** ~: einen Film noch einmal sehen; **not** ~! nicht schon wieder!; ~ **and** ~, **time and [time]** ~: immer wieder; **back** ~: wieder zurück; **go back there** ~: wieder dorthin gehen; **half as much/many** ~: noch einmal halb so viel/so viele; (b) (besides) **[there]** ~: außerdem; (c) (on the other hand) **[then/there]** ~: andrerseits

against /ə'genst, ə'geɪnst/ *prep.* (a) gegen; **as** ~: gegenüber; **protect sth.** ~ **frost** etw. vor Frost schützen; **be warned** ~ **doing sth.** davor gewarnt werden, etw. zu tun; (b) (in return for) gegen; **rate of exchange** ~ **the dollar** Wechselkurs des Dollar

age /eɪdʒ/ **1** *n.* (a) ▶630| Alter, *das;* **the boys'** ~**s are 7, 6, and 3** die Jungen sind 7, 6 und 3 Jahre alt; **what** ~ **are you?, what is your** ~? wie alt bist du?; **at the** ~ **of** im Alter von; **at what** ~: in welchem Alter; **be six years of** ~: sechs Jahre alt sein; **when I was your** ~: als ich so alt war wie du; **come of** ~: mündig *od.* volljährig werden; (fig.) den Kinderschuhen entwachsen; **be/look under** ~: zu jung sein/aussehen; **be** *or* **act your** ~ (coll.) sei nicht so kindisch; (b) (advanced ~) Alter, *das;* (c) (generation) Generation, *die;* (d) (great period) Zeitalter, *das;* **wait [for]** ~**s** *or* **an** ~ **for sb./sth.** (coll.) eine Ewigkeit auf jmdn./etw. warten. **2** *v.i.* altern

'age bracket *n.* Altersstufe, *die;* **children in the 9–13** ~: Kinder im Alter von 9–13 Jahren

aged 1 *adj.* (a) /eɪdʒd/ **be** ~ **five** fünf Jahre alt sein; **a boy** ~ **five** ein fünfjähriger Junge; (b) /'eɪdʒɪd/ (elderly) bejahrt. **2** /'eɪdʒɪd/ *n. pl.* **the** ~: die alten Menschen

'age group *n.* Altersgruppe, *die*

ageism /'eɪdʒɪzm/ *n.* Diskriminierung auf Grund des Alters

ageist /'eɪdʒɪst/ *adj.* das Alter diskriminierend

'age limit *n.* Altersgrenze, *die*

agency /'eɪdʒənsɪ/ *n.* (a) (action) Handeln, *das;* **through/ by the** ~ **of sth.** durch [die Einwirkung von] etw.; **through/by the** ~ **of sb.** durch jmds. Vermittlung; (b) (business establishment) Geschäftsstelle, *die;* (news/advertising ~) Agentur, *die*

agenda /ə'dʒendə/ *n.* (lit. or fig.) Tagesordnung, *die;* Agenda, *die;* **[be] on the** ~: auf der Tagesordnung *od.* Agenda [stehen]; **six items on the** ~: sechs Tagesordnungspunkte; **be high on the** ~: obenan *od.* ganz oben

auf der Tagesordnung *od.* Agenda stehen; **have a hidden** ~: heimliche Absichten hegen *od.* verfolgen

agent /'eɪdʒənt/ *n.* (a) (substance) Mittel, *das;* **an oxidizing** ~: ein Oxidationsmittel; (b) (one who acts for another) Vertreter, *der/*Vertreterin, *die;* **be a free** ~: sein eigener Herr sein; (c) (spy) Agent, *der/*Agentin, *die*

age: ~**-old** *adj.* uralt; ~ **range** *n.* Altersstufe, *die;* **teach English across a very large** ~ **range** Schüler der verschiedensten Altersstufen in Englisch unterrichten; *see also* **age bracket**

aggravate /'ægrəveɪt/ *v.t.* (a) verschlimmern ‹*Krankheit, Zustand, Situation*›; verschärfen ‹*Streit*›; (b) (coll.: annoy) aufregen; ärgern; **be** ~**d by sth.** sich über etw. (*Akk.*) ärgern *od.* aufregen

aggravating /'ægrəveɪtɪŋ/ *adj.* (coll.) ärgerlich; lästig ‹*Kind, Lärm*›

aggravation /ægrə'veɪʃn/ *n., no pl.* (a) Verschlimmerung, *die;* (of dispute) Verschärfung, *die;* (b) (coll.: annoyance) Ärger, *der*

aggregate 1 /'ægrɪgət/ *n.* (sum total) Gesamtmenge, *die;* (assemblage) Ansammlung, *die.* **2** /'ægrɪgət/ *adj.* (collected into one) zusammengefügt; (collective) gesamt; **the** ~ **amount** der Gesamtbetrag. **3** /'ægrɪgeɪt/ *v.t.* (a) verbinden ‹*Material, Stoff*› (**into** zu); ansammeln ‹*Reichtum*›; (b) (unite) vereinigen

aggregation /ægrɪ'geɪʃn/ *n.* Ansammlung, *die;* Aggregation, *die* (bes. fachspr.)

aggression /ə'greʃn/ *n.* (a) *no pl.* Aggression, *die;* (b) (unprovoked attack) Angriff, *der*

aggressive /ə'gresɪv/ *adj.* aggressiv; angriffslustig ‹*Kämpfer*›; heftig ‹*Angriff*›

aggressively /ə'gresɪvlɪ/ *adv.* aggressiv

aggressiveness /ə'gresɪvnɪs/ *n., no pl.* Aggressivität, *die*

aggressor /ə'gresə(r)/ *n.* Aggressor, *der*

aggrieved /ə'griːvd/ (resentful) verärgert; (offended) gekränkt

aggro /'ægrəʊ/ *n., no pl.* (Brit. sl.) Zoff, *der* (ugs.); Krawall, *der;* **they are looking for** ~: sie suchen Streit

aghast /ə'gɑːst/ *pred. adj.* bestürzt; erschüttert

agile /'ædʒaɪl/ *adj.* beweglich; flink, behänd[e] ‹*Bewegung*›

agility /ə'dʒɪlɪtɪ/ *n., no pl.* ⇒ **agile**: Beweglichkeit, *die;* Flinkheit, *die;* Behändigkeit, *die*

agitate /'ædʒɪteɪt/ **1** *v.t.* (a) (shake) schütteln; (stir up) aufrühren; (b) (disturb) beunruhigen; erregen. **2** *v.i.* ~ **for/ against sth.** für/gegen etw. agitieren

agitation /ædʒɪ'teɪʃn/ *n.* (a) (shaking) Schütteln, *das;* (stirring up) Aufrühren, *das;* (b) (emotional disturbance) Erregung, *die;* (c) (campaign) Agitation, *die*

agitator /'ædʒɪteɪtə(r)/ *n.* (person) Agitator, *der*

AGM *abbr.* **Annual General Meeting** JHV

agnostic /æg'nɒstɪk/ **1** *adj.* agnostizistisch. **2** *n.* Agnostiker, *der/*Agnostikerin, *die*

agnosticism /æg'nɒstɪsɪzm/ *n., no pl.* Agnostizismus, *der*

ago /ə'gəʊ/ *adv.* **ten years** ~: vor zehn Jahren; **[not] long** ~: vor [nicht] langer Zeit; **how long** ~ **is it that …?** wie lange ist es her, dass …?; **no longer** ~ **than last Sunday** (only last Sunday) erst letzten Sonntag

agog /ə'gɒg/ *pred. adj.* gespannt (**for** auf + *Akk.*)

agonize /'ægənaɪz/ **1** *v.i.* (struggle) ringen; ~ **over sth.** sich (*Dat.*) den Kopf über etw. (*Akk.*) zermartern. **2** *v.t.* **an** ~**d scream** ein qualerfüllter Schrei; **an agonizing wait** (fig.) eine qualvolle Wartezeit

agony /'ægənɪ/ *n.* Todesqualen *Pl.;* **suffer** ~/**agonies** Todesqualen erleiden; **die in** ~: qualvoll sterben; **in an** ~ **of indecision** (fig.) in qualvoller Unentschlossenheit

agony: ~ **aunt** *n.* (coll.) Briefkastentante, *die* (ugs. scherzh.); ~ **column** *n.* (Brit. coll.: advice column) Spalte für die „Briefkastentante"

agoraphobia /ægərə'fəʊbɪə/ *n.* (Psych.) Agoraphobie, *die;* Platzangst, *die*

Age

How old?

How old is she?, What age is she?	= Wie alt ist sie?
She is forty [years old] or (more formal) *forty years of age*	= Sie ist vierzig [Jahre alt]
He has just turned sixty	= Er ist gerade sechzig geworden
at the age of twenty	= im Alter von zwanzig Jahren, mit zwanzig
Life begins at forty	= Mit vierzig fängt das Leben an
a man of fifty or *aged fifty*	= ein fünfzigjähriger Mann, ein Fünfzigjähriger
a girl of ten	= ein zehnjähriges Mädchen
a thirty-year-old (man)	= ein Dreißigjähriger
a thirty-year-old (woman)	= eine Dreißigjährige
an eighty-year-old pensioner	= ein achtzigjähriger Rentner
They have an eight-year-old and a five-year-old	= Sie haben ein achtjähriges und ein fünfjähriges Kind

Older and younger

I'm older than you (are)	= Ich bin älter als du
She's younger than him or *than he is*	= Sie ist jünger als er
He's four years older than me or (more formal) *four years my senior*	= Er ist vier Jahre älter als ich

You are twenty years younger than her or (more formal) *twenty years her junior*	= Du bist zwanzig Jahre jünger als sie
They are the same age	= Sie sind gleich alt or gleichaltrig
She is (exactly) the same age as John	= Sie ist [genau]so alt wie John

Approximate ages

He's about fifty	= Er ist ungefähr fünfzig or um die fünfzig
She's just over sixty	= Sie ist etwas über sechzig
He's nearly seventy or *just under seventy*	= Er ist fast or bald siebzig
He's getting on for seventy	= Er geht auf die siebzig zu or wird bald siebzig
She's in her sixties	= Sie ist in den Sechzigern
He's in his late/early sixties	= Er ist Ende/Anfang sechzig
Jane's in her mid-forties	= Jane ist Mitte vierzig
He's still a teenager or *in his teens*	= Er ist noch ein Teenager or in den Teenagerjahren
Her son's just ten	= Ihr Sohn ist gerade zehn geworden
She's barely twelve	= Sie ist noch keine zwölf Jahre alt
games for the under-twelves	= Spiele für Kinder unter 12 Jahren
only for the over-eighties	= nur für Leute über achtzig

---

agoraphobic /ægərə'fəʊbɪk/ *adj.* (Psych.) an Agoraphobie *od.* Platzangst leidend; **be ~:** an Agoraphobie *od.* Platzangst leiden

agree /ə'gri:/ **1** *v.i.* (a) (consent) einverstanden sein; **~ to** *or* **with sth./to do sth.** mit etw. einverstanden sein/damit einverstanden sein, etw. zu tun; (b) (hold similar opinion) einer Meinung sein; **they ~d [with me]** sie waren derselben Meinung [wie ich]; **~ with sb. about** *or* **on sth./that …:** jmdm. in etw. (*Dat.*) zustimmen/jmdm. darin zustimmen, dass …; **I ~:** stimmt; (c) (reach similar opinion) **~ on sth.** sich über etw. (*Akk.*) einigen; (d) (harmonize; also Ling.) übereinstimmen (**mit** with); (e) **~ with sb.** (suit) jmdm. bekommen. **2** *v.t.* (reach agreement about) vereinbaren

agreeable /ə'gri:əbl/ *adj.* (a) (pleasing) angenehm; erfreulich ⟨*Anblick*⟩; (b) (coll.: willing to agree) **be ~ [to sth.]** [mit etw.] einverstanden sein

agreeably /ə'gri:əblɪ/ *adv.* angenehm

agreed /ə'gri:d/ *adj.* einig; vereinbart ⟨*Summe, Zeit*⟩; **be ~ that …/about sth.** sich (*Dat.*) darüber einig sein, dass …/ sich (*Dat.*) über etw. (*Akk.*) einig sein; **~! **einverstanden!

agreement /ə'gri:mənt/ *n.* (a) Übereinstimmung, *die;* (mutual understanding) Übereinkunft, *die;* **be in ~ [about sth.]** sich (*Dat.*) [über etw. (*Akk.*)] einig sein; **enter into an ~:** eine Übereinkunft treffen; **come to** *or* **reach an ~ with sb. [about sth.]** mit jmdm. eine Einigung [über etw. (*Akk.*)] erzielen; (b) (treaty) Abkommen, *das;* (c) (Law) Abkommen, *das;* Vertrag, *der;* **legal ~:** rechtliche Vereinbarung; (d) (Ling.) Übereinstimmung, *die*

agricultural /ægrɪ'kʌltʃərl/ *adj.* landwirtschaftlich; **~ worker** Landarbeiter, *der*

agriculture /'ægrɪkʌltʃə(r)/ *n.* Landwirtschaft, *die*

aground /ə'graʊnd/ *pred. adj.* auf Grund gelaufen; **go** *or* **run ~:** auf Grund laufen

ah /ɑ:/ *int.* ach; (of pleasure) ah

aha /ɑ:'hɑ:/ *int.* aha

ahead /ə'hed/ *adv.* (a) (further forward in space) voraus; **~ of sb./sth.** vor jmdm./etw.; **keep going straight ~:** gehen Sie immer geradeaus; (b) (fig.) **be ~ of the others** den anderen voraus sein; **be ~ on points** nach Punkten führen; **get ~:** vorwärts kommen; (c) (further forward in time) **~ of us lay three days of intensive training** vor uns lagen drei Tage intensives Training; **finish ~ of schedule** *or* **time** früher als geplant fertig werden

ahoy /ə'hɔɪ/ *int.* (Naut.) ahoi

aid /eɪd/ **1** *v.t.* (a) **~ sb. [to do sth.]** jmdm. helfen[, etw. zu tun]; **~ed by** unterstützt von; *see also* **abet**; (b) (promote) fördern. **2** *n.* (a) *no pl.* (help) Hilfe, *die;* **come/go to the ~ of sb.** jmdm. zu Hilfe kommen; **with the ~ of sth./sb.** mithilfe einer Sache (*Gen.*) /mit jmds. Hilfe; mithilfe von etw./jmdm.; **in ~ of sb./sth.** zugunsten von jmdm./etw.; (b) (source of help) Hilfsmittel, *das* (**to** für)

aide /eɪd/ *n.* (a) ⇒ **aide-de-camp;** (b) (assistant) Berater, *der*/Beraterin, *die*

aide-de-camp /eɪddə'kã:/ *n., pl.* **aides-de-camp** /eɪddə'kã:/ (Mil.) Adjutant, *der*

Aids /eɪdz/ *n., no pl., no art.* ▶ 865 | Aids, *das;* **~ victim** Aidsopfer, *das;* **~ virus** Aidsvirus, *der,* (fachspr.) *das*

'Aids-related *adj.* **~ disease/illness** durch Aids hervorgerufene Krankheit

ail /eɪl/ *v.t.* (trouble) plagen

ailing /'eɪlɪŋ/ *adj.* (sickly) kränkelnd; kränklich

ailment /'eɪlmənt/ *n.* Gebrechen, *das;* **minor ~:** leichte Erkrankung

aim /eɪm/ **1** *v.t.* ausrichten ⟨*Schusswaffe, Rakete*⟩; **~ sth. at sb./sth.** etw. auf jmdn./ etw. richten; **that remark was not ~ed at you** (fig.) diese Bemerkung war nicht gegen Sie gerichtet; **~ a blow/shot at sb.** nach jmdm. schlagen/auf jmdn. schießen. **2** *v.i.* (a) zielen (**at** auf + *Akk.*); **~ high/wide** [zu] hoch/[zu] weit zielen; **~ high** (fig.) sich (*Dat.*) ein hohes Ziel stecken *od.* setzen; (b) (intend) **~ to do sth.** *or* **at doing sth.** beabsichtigen, etw. zu tun;

~ **at** or **for sth.** (fig.) etw. anstreben. **3** n. Ziel, das; his ~ **was true** er hatte genau gezielt; **take** ~ [at sth./sb.] [auf etw./jmdn.] zielen; **take** ~ **at the target** das Ziel anvisieren

aimless /'eɪmlɪs/ adj. ziellos ‹Leben, Aktivität›; sinnlos ‹Vorhaben, Beschäftigung›

aimlessly /'eɪmlɪslɪ/ adv. ziellos

ain't /eɪnt/ (coll.) **(a)** = **am not, is not, are not;** ⇒ **be; (b)** = **has not, have not;** ⇒ **have 2**

air /eə(r)/ **1** n. **(a)** Luft, die; **be/go on the** ~: senden; ‹Programm, Sendung:› gesendet werden; **be/go off the** ~: nicht/nicht mehr senden; ‹Programm:› beendet sein/ werden; **be in the** ~ (fig.) ‹Gerücht, Idee:› in der Luft liegen; **be up in the** ~ ‹Plan, Projekt:› in der Luft hängen; **be walking on** ~ (fig.) wie auf Wolken schweben (ugs.); **by** ~: mit dem Flugzeug; **travel by** ~: fliegen; **send a letter by** ~: einen Brief mit od. per Luftpost schicken; **from the** ~: aus der Vogelperspektive; **(b)** (appearance) **there was an** ~ **of absurdity about the whole exercise** die ganze Übung hatte etwas Absurdes; **(c)** (bearing) Auftreten, das; (facial expression) Miene, die; ~s **and graces** Allüren Pl. (abwertend); **give oneself** or **put on** ~s sich aufspielen; **(d)** (Mus.) Melodie, die. **2** v.t. **(a)** (ventilate) lüften ‹Zimmer, Matratze, Kleidung›; **(b)** (finish drying) nachtrocknen ‹Wäsche›; **(c)** (parade) zur Schau tragen; **(d)** (make public) [öffentlich] darlegen. **3** v.i. (be ventilated) lüften

air: ~ **bag** n. (Motor Veh.) Airbag, der; **side** ~ **bag** Seitenairbag, der; ~ **base** n. Luftwaffenstützpunkt, der; ~ **bed** n. Luftmatratze, die; ~**borne** adj. **be** ~**borne** sich in der Luft befinden; **become** ~**borne** sich in die Luft erheben; ~ **brake** n. Druckluftbremse, die; (flap) Luftbremse, die; ~ **bubble** n. Luftblase, die; **A**~**bus,** (P) n. Airbus, der; ~**-conditioned** adj. klimatisiert; ~**-conditioner** n. Klimaanlage, die; ~**conditioning** n., no pl. Klimatisierung, die; (system) Klimaanlage, die; ~**-cooled** adj. luftgekühlt; ~ **corridor** n. Luftkorridor, der; ~ **cover** n. Deckung aus der Luft

aircraft /'eəkrɑːft/ n., pl. same Luftfahrzeug, das; (aeroplane) Flugzeug, das

aircraft: ~**-carrier** n. Flugzeugträger, der; ~ **noise** n. Fluglärm, der

air: ~ **crew** n. Besatzung, die; Flugpersonal, das; ~ **cushion** n. **(a)** Luftkissen, das; **(b)** ~ **cushion vehicle** Luftkissenfahrzeug, das

airer /'eərə(r)/ n. Wäscheständer, der

air: ~ **fare** n. Flugpreis, der; ~**field** n. Flugplatz, der; ~ **filter** n. Luftfilter, der od. das; ~ **force** n. Luftstreitkräfte Pl.; Luftwaffe, die; ~ **freshener** n. Lufterfrischer, der; Luftverbesserer, der; ~**gun** n. Luftgewehr, das; ~ **hostess** n. ▶ 887 ⌋ Stewardess, die

airily /'eərɪlɪ/ adv. leichthin

airing /'eərɪŋ/ n. Auslüften, das; **these clothes need a good** ~ diese Kleider müssen gründlich gelüftet werden; ~ **cupboard** Trockenschrank, der

airless /'eəlɪs/ adj. stickig ‹Zimmer, Büro›; windstill ‹Nacht›

air: ~ **letter** n. Luftpostleichtbrief, der; Aerogramm, das; ~**lift 1** n. Luftbrücke, die (**of** für); **2** v.t. auf dem Luftweg od. über eine Luftbrücke transportieren; ~**line** n. Fluggesellschaft, die; Fluglinie, die; ~**line pilot** [für eine Fluggesellschaft fliegender] Pilot; ~**liner** n. Verkehrsflugzeug, das; ~**lock** n. **(a)** (of spacecraft etc.) Luftschleuse, die; **(b)** (stoppage) Luftblase, die; ~ **mail** n. Luftpost, die; **by** ~ **mail** mit od. per Luftpost; ~**-mail** v.t. mit od. per Luftpost befördern; ~**man** /'eəmən/ n., pl. ~**men** /'eəmən/ Flieger, der; ~**miss** n. Beinahezusammenstoß, der; ~**plane** (Amer.) ⇒ **aeroplane;** ~**play** n., no pl. (Radio) das Spielen einer Platte im Radio; **the record receives** or **gets no/a great deal of** ~**play** die Platte wird [überhaupt] nicht/wird sehr häufig im Radio gespielt; ~**pocket** n. Luftloch, das; ~ **pollution** n. Luftverschmutzung, die; ~**port** n. Flughafen, der; ~ **power** n. Schlagkraft der Luftwaffe; ~ **pressure** n. Luftdruck, der; ~ **pump** n. Luftpumpe, die; ~ **raid** n. Luftangriff, der; ~**-raid precautions**

Luftschutz, der; ~**-raid shelter** Luftschutzraum, der; ~**-raid siren** Luftschutzsirene, die; ~ **rifle** n. Luftgewehr, das; ~**-sea 'rescue** n. Seenotrettungseinsatz aus der Luft; ~**ship** n. Luftschiff, das; ~ **show** n. Flugschau, die; ~**sick** adj. luftkrank; ~**sickness** n. Luftkrankheit, die; ~**space** n. Luftraum, der; ~ **speed** n. (Aeronaut.) Eigengeschwindigkeit, die; ~**strip** n. Startund-Lande-Bahn, die; ~ **terminal** n. [Air-]Terminal, der od. das; ~**tight** adj. luftdicht; ~**-to**~ adj. Luft-Luft-; ~**-to**-~ **refuelling** Betanken in der Luft; ~ **traffic** n. (Aeronaut.) Flugverkehr, der; ~**-traffic control** Flugsicherung, die; ~**-traffic controller** Fluglotse, der; ~**waves** n. pl. Äther, der; ~**way** n. ~ (Aeronaut.) Luftstraße, die; **(b)** (Anat.) Luftweg, der; ~**worthy** adj. (Aeronaut.) lufttüchtig

airy /'eərɪ/ adj. **(a)** luftig ‹Büro, Zimmer›; **(b)** (superficial) vage; (flippant) leichtfertig

airy-fairy /eərɪ'feərɪ/ adj. (coll. derog.) aus der Luft gegriffen ‹Plan›; versponnen ‹Idee, Vorstellung›

aisle /aɪl/ n. Gang, der; (of church) Seitenschiff, das; **walk down the** ~ **with sb.** (fig.) mit jmdm. vor den Traualtar treten

aitch /eɪtʃ/ n. H, h, das; **drop one's** ~**es** das h [im Anlaut] nicht aussprechen

ajar /ə'dʒɑː(r)/ pred. adj. **be** or **stand** ~: einen Spaltbreit offen stehen; **leave** ~: offen lassen

akin /ə'kɪn/ pred. adj. **(a)** verwandt; **(b)** (fig.) ähnlich; **be** ~ **to sth.** einer Sache (Dat.) ähnlich sein

alabaster /'æləbɑːstə/ n. Alabaster, der

alacrity /ə'lækrɪtɪ/ n., no pl. Eilfertigkeit, die; **accept with** ~: mit [großer] Bereitwilligkeit annehmen

alarm /ə'lɑːm/ **1** n. **(a)** Alarm, der; **give** or **raise the** ~: Alarm schlagen; **(b)** (fear) Angst, die; (uneasiness) Besorgnis, die; **jump up in** ~: erschreckt aufspringen; **(c)** (mechanism) Alarmanlage, die; (of ~ clock) Weckmechanismus, der; (signal) Warnsignal, das; **sound the** ~: die Alarmanlage betätigen; **(d)** ⇒ **alarm clock. 2** v.t. **(a)** (make aware of danger) aufschrecken; **(b)** (cause anxiety to) beunruhigen

alarm: ~ **bell** n. Alarmglocke, die; Warnsignal, das; **the** ~ **bells started ringing [in my head]** (fig.) in meinem Kopf fing ein rotes Lämpchen an zu leuchten; ~ **call** n. Weck[an]ruf, der; ~ **clock** n. Wecker, der

alarming /ə'lɑːmɪŋ/ adj. alarmierend

alarmist /ə'lɑːmɪst/ **1** n. Panikmacher, der. **2** adj. ‹Reden, Behauptungen› von Panikmachern

alas /ə'læs, ə'lɑːs/ int. ach

Albania /æl'beɪnɪə/ pr. n. Albanien (das)

Albanian /æl'beɪnɪən/ ▶ 897⌋, ▶ 947⌋ **1** adj. albanisch; **sb. is** ~: jmd. ist Albaner/Albanerin. **2** n. **(a)** (person) Albaner, der/Albanerin, die; **(b)** (language) Albanisch, das

albatross /'ælbətrɒs/ n. Albatros, der

albeit /ɔːl'biːɪt/ conj. (literary) wenn auch; obgleich (geh.)

albino /æl'biːnəʊ/ n., pl. ~s Albino, der

album /'ælbəm/ n. Album, das

alchemist /'ælkəmɪst/ n. Alchimist, der; Alchemist, der

alchemy /'ælkəmɪ/ n., no pl. (lit. or fig.) Alchimie, die; Alchemie, die

alcohol /'ælkəhɒl/ n. Alkohol, der

'alcohol-free adj. alkoholfrei

alcoholic /ælkə'hɒlɪk/ **1** adj. alkoholisch; ~ **stupor** Vollrausch, der. **2** n. Alkoholiker, der/Alkoholikerin, die

alcoholism /'ælkəhɒlɪzm/ n., no pl. Alkoholismus, der; Trunksucht, die

alcopop /'ælkəʊpɒp/ n.: alkoholhaltiges Erfrischungsgetränk

alcove /'ælkəʊv/ n. Alkoven, der

alder /'ɔːldə(r)/ n. (Bot.) Erle, die

alderman /'ɔːldəmən/ n., pl. **aldermen** /'ɔːldəmən/ Stadtrat, der; Alderman, der

ale /eɪl/ n. **(a)** Ale, das; **(b)** (Hist.) Bier, das

'alehouse n. (Hist.) [Bier]schenke, die

alert /ə'lɜːt/ **1** adj. **(a)** (watchful) wachsam; **be** ~ **for trouble** auf der Hut sein; **be** ~ **to sth.** mit etw. rechnen; **(b)** (mentally lively) aufgeweckt. **2** n. (state of preparedness)

Alarmbereitschaft, *die;* **air-raid** ∼**:** Fliegeralarm, *der;* **be on the** ∼ **[for/against sth.]** [vor etw. (*Dat.*)] auf der Hut sein. **3** *v.t.* alarmieren; ∼ **sb.** **[to sth.]** jmdn. [vor etw. (*Dat.*)] warnen

A level /'eɪ levl/ *n.* (Brit. Sch.) ≈ Abitur, *das;* Abschluss der Sekundarstufe II; **take one's** ∼**s** ≈ das Abitur machen

alga /'ælgə/ *n., pl.* ∼**e** /'ældʒiː, 'ælgiː/ (Bot.) Alge, *die*

algebra /'ældʒɪbrə/ *n.* (Math.) Algebra, *die*

Algeria /æl'dʒɪərɪə/ *pr. n.* Algerien (*das*)

Algerian /æl'dʒɪərɪən/ **▶ 947 |** **1** *adj.* algerisch; **sb. is** ∼**:** jmd. ist Algerier/Algerierin. **2** *n.* Algerier, *der*/Algerierin, *die*

algorithm /'ælgərɪðm/ *n.* Algorithmus, *der*

alias /'eɪlɪəs/ **1** *adv.* alias. **2** *n.* angenommener Name; (of criminal) falscher Name

alibi /'ælɪbaɪ/ *n.* Alibi, *das*

alien /'eɪlɪən/ **1** *adj.* (a) (strange) fremd; **be** ∼ **to sb.** jmdm. fremd sein; (b) (foreign) ausländisch; (from another world) außerirdisch. **2** *n.* (a) (Admin.: foreigner) Ausländer, *der*/Ausländerin, *die;* (b) (a being from another world) Außerirdische, *der/die*

alienate /'eɪlɪəneɪt/ *v.t.* befremden ⟨*Person*⟩; **feel** ∼**d from society** sich der Gesellschaft entfremdet fühlen

alienation /eɪlɪə'neɪʃn/ *n., no pl.* Entfremdung, *die*

alight¹ /ə'laɪt/ *v.i.* (a) (dismount) ∼ **from a vehicle** aus einem Fahrzeug aussteigen; ∼ **from a horse** von einem Pferd absitzen; (b) ⟨*Vogel:*⟩ sich niedersetzen

alight² *pred. adj.* (on fire) **be/catch** ∼**:** brennen; **set sth.** ∼**:** etw. in Brand setzen

align /ə'laɪn/ *v.t.* (a) (place in a line) ausrichten; **the posts must be** ∼**ed** die Pfosten müssen in einer Linie ausgerichtet werden; (b) (bring into line) in eine Linie bringen; ∼ **the wheels** (Motor Veh.) die Spur einstellen

alignment /ə'laɪnmənt/ *n.* Ausrichtung, *die;* **in/out of** ∼**:** [genau] ausgerichtet/nicht richtig ausgerichtet

alike /ə'laɪk/ **1** *pred. adj.* ähnlich; (indistinguishable) [völlig] gleich. **2** *adv.* gleich; **in gleicher Weise; this concerns us all** ∼**:** es geht uns alle gleichermaßen an

alimentary /ælɪ'mentərɪ/ *adj.* Nahrungs-; ∼ **canal/organ** Verdauungskanal, *der*/-organ, *das*

alimony /'ælɪmənɪ/ *n.* Unterhaltszahlung, *die*

alive /ə'laɪv/ *pred. adj.* (a) lebendig; lebend; **stay** ∼**:** am Leben bleiben; **keep one's hopes** ∼**:** nicht die Hoffnung verlieren; **keep sb.'s hopes** ∼**:** jmdn. noch hoffen lassen; **come** ∼ (wieder aufl=eben); (b) (aware) **be** ∼ **to sth.** sich (*Dat.*) einer Sache (*Gen.*) bewusst sein; (c) (brisk) rege; munter; **be** ∼ **and kicking** gesund und munter sein; **look** ∼**!** ein bisschen munter!; (d) (swarming) **be** ∼ **with sth.** von etw. wimmeln

alkali /'ælkəlaɪ/ *n., pl.* ∼**s** *or* ∼**es** (Chem.) Alkali, *das*

alkaline /'ælkəlaɪn/ *adj.* (Chem.) alkalisch

all /ɔːl/ **1** *attrib. adj.* (a) (entire extent or quantity of) ganz; ∼ **day** den ganzen Tag; **for** ∼ **that** trotz allem; ∼ **his life** sein ganzes Leben; ∼ **my money** all mein Geld; **mein ganzes Geld; stop** ∼ **this noise/shouting!** hör mit dem Krach/Geschrei auf!; **thank you for** ∼ **your hard work** danke für all deine Anstrengungen; **get away from it** ∼**:** einmal von allem abschalten; **that says it** ∼**:** das sagt alles; (b) (entire number of) alle; ∼ **the books** alle Bücher; ∼ **my books** all[e] meine Bücher; **where are** ∼ **the glasses?** wo sind all die Gläser?; ∼ **ten men** alle zehn Männer; **we** ∼ **went to bed** wir gingen alle schlafen; ∼ **the others** alle anderen; ∼ **Goethe's works** sämtliche Werke Goethes; **why he** ∼ **of people?** warum ausgerechnet er?; **people of** ∼ **ages** Menschen jeden Alters; **All Fools' Day** der 1. April; (c) (any whatever) jeglicher/jegliche/jegliches; (d) (greatest possible) **in** ∼ **innocence** in aller Unschuld; **with** ∼ **speed** so schnell wie möglich. **2** *n.* (a) (∼ persons) alle; ∼ **present** alle Anwesenden; **one and** ∼**:** [alle] ohne Ausnahme; ∼ **and sundry** Krethi und Plethi; ∼ **of us** wir alle; **the happiest/most beautiful of** ∼**:** der/die Glücklichste/die Schönste unter allen; **most of** ∼**:** am meisten; **he ran fastest of** ∼**:** er lief am schnellsten; (b) (every bit) ∼ **of it/the money** alles/das ganze *od.* alles Geld; (c) ∼ **of** (coll.: as much as) **be** ∼ **of**

seven feet tall gut sieben Fuß groß sein; **(d)** (∼ things) alles; ∼ **I need is the money** ich brauche nur das Geld; ∼ **is not lost** es ist nicht alles verloren; **it's** ∼ **or nothing** es geht ums Ganze; **most of** ∼**:** am meisten; **give one's** ∼**:** sein Letztes geben; **it was** ∼ **but impossible** es war fast unmöglich; ∼ **in** ∼**:** alles in allem; **it's** ∼ **the same** *or* ∼ **one to me** es ist mir ganz egal *od.* völlig gleichgültig; **that's** ∼ **very well** das ist alles schön und gut; **can I help you at** ∼**?** kann ich Ihnen irgendwie behilflich sein?; **I do not care at** ∼**:** es ist mir völlig gleich; **you are not disturbing me at** ∼**:** du störst mich nicht im Geringsten; **were you surprised at** ∼**?** warst du denn überrascht?; **nothing at** ∼**:** gar nichts; **not at** ∼ **happy/well** überhaupt nicht glücklich/gesund; **not at** ∼**!** überhaupt nicht!; (acknowledging thanks) gern geschehen!; nichts zu danken!; **if at** ∼**:** wenn überhaupt; **in** ∼**:** insgesamt; **(e)** (Sport) **two [goals]** ∼**:** zwei zu zwei; (Tennis) **thirty** ∼**:** dreißig beide. **3** *adv.* ganz; ∼ **but fast; he** ∼ **but fell down** er wäre fast heruntergefallen; ∼ **the better/worse [for that]** um so besser/schlimmer; **I feel** ∼ **the better for it** das hat mir wirklich gut getan; ∼ **at once** (suddenly) plötzlich; (simultaneously) alle[s] zugleich; ∼ **too soon** allzu schnell; **be** ∼ **'for sth.** (coll.) sehr für etw. sein; **be** ∼ **'in** (exhausted) total *od.* völlig erledigt sein (ugs.); **go** ∼ **out [to do sth.]** alles daransetzen[, etw. zu tun]; **be** ∼ **ready [to go]** (coll.) fertig [zum Weggehen] sein (ugs.); **sth. is** ∼ **right** etw. ist in Ordnung; (tolerable) etw. ist ganz gut; **did you get home** ∼ **right?** sind Sie gut nach Hause gekommen?; **I'm** ∼ **right** mir geht es ganz gut; **work out** ∼ **right** gut gehen; klappen (ugs.); **that's her,** ∼ **right** das ist sie, ganz recht; **yes,** ∼ **right** ja, gut; **is it** ∼ **right if I go in?** kann ich reingehen?; **it's** ∼ **right by** *or* **with me** das ist mir recht; **lie** ∼ **round the room** überall im Zimmer herumliegen; **I don't think he's** ∼ **there** (coll.) ich glaube, er ist nicht ganz da (ugs.); ∼ **the same** trotzdem; **it's** ∼ **the same to me** es ist mir einerlei

Allah /'ælə/ *pr. n.* Allah (*der*)

allay /ə'leɪ/ *v.t.* (a) vermindern; zerstreuen ⟨*Besorgnis, Befürchtung*⟩; (b) (alleviate) stillen ⟨*Hunger, Durst*⟩; lindern ⟨*Schmerz*⟩

all: ∼**-'clear** *n.* Entwarnung, *die;* **sound the** ∼**-clear** entwarnen; ∼**-day** *adj.* ganztägig

allegation /ælɪ'geɪʃn/ *n.* Behauptung, *die;* **make** ∼**s against sb.** Beschuldigungen gegen jmdn. erheben; **reject all** ∼**s of corruption** jeglichen Vorwurf der Korruption zurückweisen

allege /ə'ledʒ/ *v.t.* ∼ **that …:** behaupten, dass …; ∼ **criminal negligence** den Vorwurf grober Fahrlässigkeit erheben

alleged /ə'ledʒd/ *adj.,* **allegedly** /ə'ledʒɪdlɪ/ *adv.* angeblich

allegiance /ə'liːdʒəns/ *n.* Loyalität, *die* (**to** gegenüber)

allegorical /ælɪ'gɒrɪkl/ *adj.* allegorisch

allegory /'ælɪgərɪ/ *n.* Allegorie, *die*

'all-embracing *adj.* alles umfassend

Allen key, (P) /'ælən kiː/ *n.* Inbusschlüssel, *der* (Ⓦ₂)

allergic /ə'lɜːdʒɪk/ *adj.* (Med.) allergisch (**to** gegen)

allergy /'ælədʒɪ/ *n.* (Med.) Allergie, *die* (**to** gegen)

alleviate /ə'liːvɪeɪt/ *v.t.* abschwächen

alley /'ælɪ/ *n.* [schmale] Gasse; **be up sb.'s** ∼ (coll.) jmds. Fall sein (ugs.)

alliance /ə'laɪəns/ *n.* Bündnis, *das;* (league) Allianz, *die;* **in** ∼ **with sb./sth.** im Verein mit jmdm./etw.

allied /'ælaɪd/ *adj.* **be** ∼ **to** *or* **with sb./sth.** mit jmdm./etw. verbündet sein; **the A**∼ **Powers** die Alliierten

alligator /'ælɪgeɪtə(r)/ *n.* Alligator, *der*

all: ∼**-important** *adj.* entscheidend; ∼**-in** *adj.* Pauschal-; **it costs £350** ∼**-in** es kostet 350 Pfund alles inklusive; ∼**-in wrestling** Freistilringen, *das*

alliteration /əlɪtə'reɪʃn/ *n.* Stabreim, *der;* Alliteration, *die*

'all-night *adj.* die ganze Nacht dauernd ⟨*Sitzung*⟩; nachts durchgehend geöffnet ⟨*Gaststätte*⟩

allocate /'æləkeɪt/ *v.t.* ∼ **sth. to sb./sth.** jmdm./einer Sache etw. zuweisen *od.* zuteilen

allocation /ælə'keɪʃn/ *n.* Verteilung, *die;* (ration) Zuteilung, *die*

allot /ə'lɒt/ *v.t.*, **-tt-:** ~ sth. to sb. jmdm. etw. zuteilen; **we ~ted two hours to the task** wir haben zwei Stunden für diese Arbeit vorgesehen

allotment /ə'lɒtmənt/ *n.* (a) Zuteilung, *die;* (b) (Brit.: plot of land) ≈ Schrebergarten, *der*

all: ~**-out** *attrib. adj.* mit allen [verfügbaren] Mitteln *nachgestellt;* ~**-over** *attrib. adj.* ~**-over tan** nahtlose Bräune

allow /ə'laʊ/ **1** *v.t.* (a) (permit) ~ sth. etw. erlauben *od.* zulassen *od.* gestatten; ~ sb. to do sth. jmdm. erlauben, etw. zu tun; **be ~ed to do sth.** etw. tun dürfen; **sb. is ~ed sth.** jmdm. ist etw. erlaubt; ~ **sb. in/out/past/ through** jmdn. hinein-/hinaus-/vorbei-/durchlassen; ~ **sth. to happen** zulassen, dass etw. geschieht; ~ **sb. a discount** jmdm. Rabatt geben; (b) (Law) bestätigen ‹Anspruch›; ~ **the appeal** der Berufung (*Dat.*) stattgeben; (c) (Sport) **the referee ~ed the goal** der Schiedsrichter gab das Tor. **2** *v.i.* ~ **of sth.** etw. zulassen *od.* erlauben; ~ **for sth.** etw. berücksichtigen

allowable /ə'laʊəbl/ *adj.* zulässig

allowance /ə'laʊəns/ *n.* (a) Zuteilung, *die;* (money for special expenses) Zuschuss, *der;* **your luggage ~ is 44 kg.** Sie haben 44 kg Freigepäck; **tax ~:** Steuerfreibetrag, *der;* (b) **make ~s for sth./sb.** etw./jmdn. berücksichtigen

alloy /'ælɔɪ/ *n.* Legierung, *die*

all: ~**-points bulletin** *n.* (Amer.) Fahndungsaufruf, *der;* ~**-'powerful** *adj.* allmächtig; ~**-purpose** *adj.* Universal-; Allzweck-; ~**-risks** *attrib. adj.* **an ~-risks insurance** eine alle gängigen Risiken abdeckende Versicherung; ~**-round** *adj.* Allround-; ~**-'rounder** *n.* Allroundtalent, *das;* (Sport) Allroundspieler, *der/*-spielerin, *die;* ~**-time** *adj.* ~**-time record** absoluter Rekord; ~**-time favourites** *or* **greats** unvergessene Publikumslieblinge; **hit** *or* **reach an ~-time high/low** eine Rekordhöhe/Rekordtiefe erreichen

allude /ə'lju:d, ə'lu:d/ *v.i.* ~ **to** sich beziehen auf (+ *Akk.*); (covertly) anspielen auf (+ *Akk.*)

allure /ə'ljʊə(r)/ **1** *v.t.* locken; (fascinate) faszinieren. **2** *n.*, *no pl.* Verlockung, *die;* (personal charm) Charme, *der*

alluring /ə'ljʊərɪŋ/ *adj.* verlockend; **an ~ appeal** eine Verlockung

allusion /ə'lju:ʒn, ə'lu:ʒn/ *n.* (a) Hinweis, *der;* **in an ~ to** unter Bezugnahme auf (+ *Akk.*); (b) (covert reference) Anspielung, *die* (**to** auf + *Akk.*)

alluvial /ə'lu:vɪəl/ *adj.* (Geol.) angeschwemmt

'all-weather *attrib. adj.* Allwetter-

ally 1 /ə'laɪ, 'ælaɪ/ *v.t.* ~ **oneself with sb./sth.** sich mit jmdm./etw. verbünden; *see also* **allied.** **2** /'ælaɪ/ *n.* Verbündete, *der/die;* **the Allies** die Alliierten

almanac /'ɔːlmənæk, 'ɒlmənæk/ *n.* Almanach, *der*

almighty /ɔːl'maɪtɪ/ **1** *adj.* (a) allmächtig; **the A~:** der Allmächtige; (b) (coll.: very great, hard, etc.) mächtig. **2** *adv.* (coll.) mächtig

almond /'ɑːmənd/ *n.* Mandel, *die*

almost /'ɔːlməʊst/ *adv.* fast; beinahe; **she ~ fell** sie wäre fast gefallen

alms /ɑːmz/ *n.*, *no pl.* Almosen, *das*

alone /ə'ləʊn/ **1** *pred. adj.* allein; alleine (ugs.); **he was not ~ in the belief that …:** er stand nicht allein mit der Überzeugung, dass … **2** *adv.* allein; **this fact ~:** schon allein dies; **go it ~:** es im Alleingang tun

along /ə'lɒŋ/ **1** *prep.* (a) (position) entlang (+ *Dat.*); ~ **one side of the street** auf der einen Straßenseite; **all ~ the wall** die ganze *od.* an der ganzen Mauer entlang; (b) (direction) entlang (+ *Akk.*); **walk ~ the river-bank/street** am Ufer *od.* das Ufer/die Straße entlanglaufen. **2** *adv.* (a) (onward) weiter; **he came running ~:** er kam herbei- *od.* angelaufen; (b) (with one) **bring/take sb./sth. ~:** jmdn./etw. mitbringen/mitnehmen; (c) (there) **I'll be ~ shortly** ich komme gleich; (d) **all ~:** die ganze Zeit [über]

alongside /əlɒŋ'saɪd/ **1** *adv.* daneben; ~ **of** ⇒ **2**. **2** *prep.* (position) neben (+ *Dat.*); (direction) neben (+ *Akk.*); (fig.)

neben (+ *Dat.*); **work ~ sb.** mit jmdm. zusammen arbeiten/(fig.) zusammenarbeiten

aloof /ə'lu:f/ **1** *adv.* abseits; **hold ~ from sb.** sich von jmdm. fernhalten; **keep ~:** Distanz wahren. **2** *adj.* distanziert; reserviert

aloud /ə'laʊd/ *adv.* laut; **read [sth.] ~:** [etw.] vorlesen

alpha /'ælfə/ *n.* (letter) Alpha, *das*

alphabet /'ælfəbet/ *n.* Alphabet, *das;* Abc, *das*

alphabetical /ælfə'betɪkl/ *adj.* alphabetisch; **in ~ order** in alphabetischer Reihenfolge

alpine /'ælpaɪn/ *adj.* (a) alpin; Hochgebirgs-; ~ **climate/ vegetation** Hochgebirgsklima, *das/*alpine Vegetation; ~ **flowers** Alpen-, Gebirgsblumen

Alps /ælps/ *pr. n. pl.* **the ~:** die Alpen

already /ɔːl'redɪ/ *adv.* schon; **it's ~ 8 o'clock** *or* **8 o'clock ~:** es ist schon 8 Uhr

Alsace /æl'sæs/ *pr. n.* Elsass, *das;* ~**-Lorraine** Elsass-Lothringen (*das*)

Alsatian /æl'seɪʃn/ *n.* [deutscher] Schäferhund

also /'ɔːlsəʊ/ *adv.* auch; (moreover) außerdem

altar /'ɔːltə(r), 'ɒltə(r)/ *n.* (a) (Communion table) Altar, *der;* **lead sb. to the ~** (fig.) jmdn. zum Traualtar führen; (b) (for sacrifice) Opferstätte, *die;* Opfertisch, *der*

alter /'ɔːltə(r), 'ɒltə(r)/ **1** *v.t.* ändern; verändern ‹Stadt, Wohnung›. **2** *v.i.* sich verändern; **he has ~ed a lot** (in appearance) er hat sich stark verändert; (in character) er hat sich sehr geändert

alteration /ɔːltə'reɪʃn, ɒltə'reɪʃn/ *n.* Änderung, *die;* (of text) Abänderung, *die;* (of house) Umbau, *der*

altercation /ɔːltə'keɪʃn, ɒltə'keɪʃn/ *n.* Auseinandersetzung, *die;* Streiterei, *die*

alternate 1 /ɔːl'tɜːnət, ɒl'tɜːnət/ *adj.* (a) (in turn) sich abwechselnd; **John and Mary come on ~ days** John und Mary kommen abwechselnd einen um den anderen Tag; (together) John und Mary kommen jeden zweiten Tag; (b) ⇒ **alternative 1.** **2** /'ɔːltəneɪt, 'ɒltəneɪt/ *v.t.* abwechseln lassen; **she has only two summer dresses, so she ~s them** sie hat nur zwei Sommerkleider, deshalb trägt sie sie abwechselnd; **he ~s his days off and** *or* **with his working days** er hat abwechselnd einen Tag frei und geht einen Tag zur Arbeit. **3** *v.i.* sich abwechseln; alternieren (fachspr.)

alternately /ɔːl'tɜːnətlɪ, ɒl'tɜːnətlɪ/ *adv.* abwechselnd

'alternating current *n.* (Electr.) Wechselstrom, *der*

alternative /ɔːl'tɜːnətɪv, ɒl'tɜːnətɪv/ **1** *adj.* alternativ; Alternativ-; ~ **possibility** Ausweich- *od.* Alternativmöglichkeit, *die;* ~ **suggestion** Alternativ- *od.* Gegenvorschlag, *der;* ~ **route** Alternativstrecke, *die;* (to avoid obstruction etc.) Ausweichstrecke, *die;* **the ~ society** die alternative Gesellschaft; ~ **fuel** Alternativkraftstoff, *der* (*für Verbrennungsmotore*); ~ **medicine** Alternativmedizin, *die.* **2** *n.* (a) (choice) Alternative, *die;* Wahl, *die;* **if I had the ~:** wenn ich vor die Wahl *od.* Alternative gestellt würde; **we have no ~ [but to …]** wir haben keine andere Wahl[, als zu …]; (b) (possibility) Möglichkeit, *die;* **there is no [other] ~:** es gibt keine Alternative *od.* andere Möglichkeit; **what are the ~s?** welche Alternativen gibt es?

alternatively /ɔːl'tɜːnətɪvlɪ, ɒl'tɜːnətɪvlɪ/ *adv.* oder aber; **or ~:** oder aber auch

alternator /'ɔːltəneɪtə(r), 'ɒltəneɪtə(r)/ *n.* (Electr.) Wechselstromgenerator, *der*

although /ɔːl'ðəʊ/ *conj.* obwohl

altitude /'æltɪtju:d/ *n.* ▶ 850 Höhe, *die;* **what is our ~?** wie hoch sind wir?; **from this ~:** aus dieser Höhe; **at an ~ of 2,000 ft.** ≈ in einer Höhe von 600 Metern; **at high ~:** in großer Höhe

alto /'æltəʊ/ *n.*, *pl.* ~**s** (Mus.) (voice, part) Alt, *der;* (male singer) Alt, *der;* Altist, *der;* Altsänger, *der;* (female singer) Alt, *der;* Altistin, *die;* Altsängerin, *die*

altogether /ɔːltə'geðə(r)/ **1** *adv.* völlig; (on the whole) im Großen und Ganzen; (in total) insgesamt; **not ~ [true/convincing]** nicht ganz [wahr/überzeugend]. **2** *n.* **in the ~** (coll.) im Evas-/Adamskostüm

altruism /'æltruːɪzm/ *n.*, *no pl.* Altruismus, *der;* Uneigennützigkeit, *die*

altruistic /ˈæltrʊˈɪstɪk/ *adj.* altruistisch; uneigennützig

aluminium /ˌæljʊˈmɪnɪəm/ (Brit.), **aluminum** /əˈluː mɪnəm/ (Amer.) *ns.* Aluminium, *das;* ~ **foil** Alufolie, *die*

always /ˈɔːlweɪz, ˈɔːlwɪz/ *adv.* (at all times) immer; (repeatedly) ständig; [an]dauernd (ugs.); (whatever the circumstances) jederzeit; **you can** ~ **come by train if you prefer** ihr könnt ja auch mit der Bahn kommen, wenn euch das lieber ist

Alzheimer's disease /ˈæltzhaɪməz dɪziːz/ *n.* Alzheimerkrankheit, *die*

a.m. /eɪˈem/ *adv.* ▶ 706 | vormittags; [at] one/four ~: [um] ein/vier Uhr nachts *od.* morgens *od.* früh; [at] **five/ eight** ~: [um] fünf/acht Uhr morgens *od.* früh; [at] **nine** ~: [um] neun Uhr morgens *od.* früh *od.* vormittags; [at] **ten/eleven** ~: [um] zehn/elf Uhr vormittags

AM *abbr.* **amplitude modulation** AM

am ⇒ **be**

amalgam /əˈmælgəm/ *n.* (a) (lit. or fig.: mixture) Mischung, *die;* (b) (alloy) Amalgam, *das*

amalgamate /əˈmælgəmeɪt/ **1** *v.t.* vereinigen; fusionieren ‹*Firmen*›. **2** *v.i.* sich vereinigen; ‹*Firmen:*› fusionieren

amalgamation /əmælgəˈmeɪʃn/ *n.* (a) (action) Vereinigung, *die;* (of firms) Fusion, *die;* (b) (result) Vereinigung, *die*

amass /əˈmæs/ *v.t.* [ein]sammeln; ~ **a [large] fortune** ein [großes] Vermögen anhäufen

amateur /ˈæmətə(r)/ *n.* (a) (non-professional) Amateur, *der;* (b) (derog.: trifler) Amateur, *der;* Dilettant, *der;* (c) *attrib.* Amateur-; Laien-

amateurish /ˈæmətərɪʃ/ *adj.* (derog.) laienhaft; amateurhaft

amaze /əˈmeɪz/ *v.t.* verblüffen; verwundern; **be** ~**d [by sth.]** [über etw. (*Akk.*)] verblüfft *od.* verwundert sein

amazement /əˈmeɪzmənt/ *n.,* no pl. Verblüffung, *die;* Verwunderung, *die*

amazing /əˈmeɪzɪŋ/ *adj.* (remarkable) erstaunlich; (astonishing) verblüffend

amazingly /əˈmeɪzɪŋlɪ/ *adv.* (a) as sentence-modifier (remarkably) erstaunlicherweise; (astonishingly) verblüffenderweise; (b) erstaunlich

Amazon¹ /ˈæməzən/ *pr. n.* ▶ 1048 | **the** ~: der Amazonas

Amazon² *n.* (a) (Mythol.: female warrior) Amazone, *die;* (b) (fig.) Mannweib, *das* (abwertend); Amazone, *die* (veralt.)

ambassador /æmˈbæsədə(r)/ *n.* ▶ 887 | Botschafter, *der/*Botschafterin, *die;* ~ **to a country/court** Botschafter in einem Land/an einem Hof

amber /ˈæmbə(r)/ **1** *n.* (a) Bernstein, *der;* (b) (traffic light) Gelb, *das.* **2** *adj.* Bernstein-; aus Bernstein *nachgestellt;* (colour) bernsteinfarben; gelb ‹*Verkehrslicht*›

ambidextrous /æmbɪˈdekstrəs/ *adj.* beidhändig; ambidexter (fachspr.)

ambience /ˈæmbɪəns/ *n.* Ambiente, *das* (geh.); Milieu, *das*

ambient /ˈæmbɪənt/ *adj.* Umgebungs-

ambiguity /æmbɪˈgjuːɪtɪ/ *n.* Zweideutigkeit, *die;* (having several meanings) Mehrdeutigkeit, *die*

ambiguous /æmˈbɪgjʊəs/ *adj.,* **ambiguously** /æm ˈbɪgjʊəslɪ/ *adv.* zweideutig; (with several meanings) mehrdeutig

ambiguousness /æmˈbɪgjʊəsnɪs/ *n.,* no pl. Zweideutigkeit, *die;* (having several meanings) Mehrdeutigkeit, *die*

ambition /æmˈbɪʃn/ *n.* Ehrgeiz, *der;* (aspiration) Ambition, *die*

ambitious /æmˈbɪʃəs/ *adj.* ehrgeizig; ambitioniert (geh.) ‹*Person*›

ambitiously /æmˈbɪʃəslɪ/ *adv.* voller Ehrgeiz; von Ehrgeiz erfüllt

ambivalent /æmˈbɪvələnt/ *adj.* ambivalent

amble /ˈæmbl/ **1** *v.i.* schlendern; gemütlich gehen. **2** *n.* Schlendern, *das*

ambulance /ˈæmbjʊləns/ *n.* Krankenwagen, *der*

ambulance: ~ **man** *n.* ▶ 887 | Sanitäter, *der;* ~ **service** *n.* Rettungsdienst, *der;* ~ **worker** *n.* Sanitäter, *der/*Sanitäterin, *die*

ambush /ˈæmbʊʃ/ **1** *n.* (concealment) Hinterhalt, *der;* (troops concealed) im Hinterhalt liegende Truppe; **lie in** ~ (lit. or fig.) im Hinterhalt liegen. **2** *v.t.* [aus dem Hinterhalt] überfallen

ameba /əˈmiːbə/ (Amer.) ⇒ **amoeba**

ameliorate /əˈmiːlɪəreɪt/ *v.t.* verbessern

amelioration /əmiːlɪəˈreɪʃn/ *n.* [Ver]besserung, *die*

amen /ɑːˈmen, eɪˈmen/ **1** *int.* amen. **2** *n.* Amen, *das*

amenable /əˈmiːnəbl/ *adj.* (a) (responsive) zugänglich, aufgeschlossen ‹*Person*› (to *Dat.*); (b) (subject) unterworfen ‹*Sache*› (to *Dat.*)

amend /əˈmend/ *v.t.* (correct) berichtigen; (improve) abändern, ergänzen ‹*Gesetzentwurf, Antrag*›; ändern ‹*Verfassung*›

amendment /əˈmendmənt/ *n.* (to motion) Abänderungsantrag, *der;* (to bill) Änderungsantrag, *der;* (to Constitution) Änderung, *die* (to *Gen.*); Amendement, *das* (Dipl.)

amends /əˈmendz/ *n. pl.* **make** ~ **[to sb.]** es [bei jmdm.] wieder gutmachen; **make** ~ **for sth.** etw. wieder gutmachen

amenity /əˈmiːnɪtɪ/ *n.* (pleasant feature) (of residence) Attraktivität, *die;* Wohnqualität, *die;* (of locality) Attraktivität, *die;* Reiz, *der;* **the amenities of a town** die kulturellen und Freizeiteinrichtungen einer Stadt; **a hotel with every** ~: ein Hotel mit allem Komfort

a'menity centre *n.* Freizeitzentrum, *das*

America /əˈmerɪkə/ *pr. n.* (a) Amerika (*das*); (b) **the** ~**s** Nord-, Süd- und Mittelamerika

American /əˈmerɪkən/ ▶ 947 | **1** *adj.* amerikanisch; **sb. is** ~: jmd. ist Amerikaner/Amerikanerin; ~ **studies** Amerikanistik, *die.* **2** *n.* (person) Amerikaner, *der/*Amerikanerin, *die*

American: ~ **'football** *n.* Football, *der;* ~ **'Indian 1** *n.* Indianer, *der/*Indianerin, *die;* **2** *adj.* indianisch

Americanise ⇒ **Americanize**

Americanism /əˈmerɪkənɪzm/ *n.* Amerikanismus, *der*

Americanize /əˈmerɪkənaɪz/ *v.t.* (a) amerikanisieren; (b) (naturalize) [in Amerika] einbürgern

Amerindian /æməˈrɪndɪən/ **1** *adj* indianisch. **2** *n.* Indianer, *der/*Indianerin, *die*

amethyst /ˈæmɪθɪst/ *n.* Amethyst, *der*

AMEX /ˈæmeks/ *abbr.* **American Stock Exchange** A.S.E.

amiable /ˈeɪmɪəbl/ *adj.* umgänglich; freundlich ‹*Person*›; entgegenkommend ‹*Haltung*›

amicable /ˈæmɪkəbl/ *adj.* freundschaftlich ‹*Gespräch, Beziehung*›; gütlich ‹*Einigung*›; friedlich ‹*Lösung*›

amicably /ˈæmɪkəblɪ/ *adv.* in [aller] Freundschaft

amid /əˈmɪd/ *prep.* inmitten; (fig.: during) bei

amidships /əˈmɪdʃɪps/ (Amer.: **amidship** /əˈmɪdʃɪp/) *adv.* (position) mittschiffs; Mitte Schiff (Seemannsspr.); (direction) [nach] mittschiffs

amidst /əˈmɪdst/ ⇒ **amid**

amino acid /əmiːnəʊ ˈæsɪd/ *n.* (Chem.) Aminosäure, *die*

amiss /əˈmɪs/ **1** *pred. adj.* (wrong) verkehrt; falsch; **is anything** ~? stimmt irgendetwas nicht? **2** *adv.* **take sth.** ~: etw. übel nehmen; **come or go** ~: ungelegen kommen

ammeter /ˈæmɪtə(r)/ *n.* (Electr.) Amperemeter, *das*

ammonia /əˈməʊnɪə/ *n.* Ammoniak, *das*

ammunition /æmjʊˈnɪʃn/ *n.,* no pl., no indef. art. (lit. or fig.) Munition, *die*

amnesia /æmˈniːzɪə/ *n.* (Med.) Amnesie, *die*

amnesty /ˈæmnɪstɪ/ *n.* Amnestie, *die;* **grant an** ~ **to sb.** jmdn. amnestieren

amoeba /əˈmiːbə/ *n.,* pl. ~**s** or ~**e** /əˈmiːbiː/ (Zool.) Amöbe, *die*

amok /əˈmɒk/ *adv.* **run** ~: Amok laufen

among[st] /əˈmʌŋ(st)/ *prep.* (a) unter (+ *Dat.;* seltener: + *Akk.*); ~ **us/you/friends** unter uns/euch/Freunden; ~ **other things** unter anderem; ~ **others** unter anderen; (b) (in/into the middle of, surrounded by) zwischen (+ *Dat./Akk.*); (c) (in the practice or opinion of, in the number of) unter (+ *Dat.*); ~ **men/scientists** unter Männern/Wissenschaftlern; **I count him** ~ **my friends** ich zähle ihn zu meinen

Freunden; **(d)** (between) unter (+ *Dat.; seltener:* + *Akk.*);
share the sweets ~ yourselves teilt euch die Bonbons;
(e) (reciprocally) **they often quarrel ~ themselves** sie
streiten oft miteinander; sie streiten sich oft; **(f)** (jointly) ~
you/them *etc.* gemeinsam; zusammen

amoral /eɪˈmɒrəl/ *adj.* amoralisch

amorous /ˈæmərəs/ *adj.* verliebt

amorphous /əˈmɔːfəs/ *adj.* formlos; ·amorph ‹*Masse*›;
(fig.) chaotisch ‹*Stil*›

amount /əˈmaʊnt/ **1** *v.i.* ~ **to sth.** sich auf etw. (*Akk.*)
belaufen; (fig.) etw. bedeuten; **all these arguments/pro-
posals don't** ~ **to much** diese Argumente/Vorschläge
bringen alle nicht viel; **my savings don't** ~ **to very
much** meine Ersparnisse sind nicht gerade groß; **what
this all** ~**s to is that** …: zusammenfassend kann man
sagen, dass … **2** *n.* **(a)** (total) Betrag, *der;* Summe, *die;* (full
significance) volle Bedeutung *od.* Tragweite; **(b) the** ~ **of a
bill** die Höhe einer Rechnung; **(c)** (quantity) Menge, *die;*
large ~**s of money** beträchtliche Geldsummen; **a tremendous** ~ **of** … (coll.) wahnsinnig viel … (ugs.); **no** ~
of money will make me change my mind und wenn
man mir noch soviel Geld gibt, meine Meinung werde ich
nicht ändern; *see also* **any 1 e**

amp /æmp/ *n.* **(a)** (Electr.) Ampere, *das;* **(b)** (coll.: amplifier)
Verstärker, *der*

ampere /ˈæmpeə(r)/ *n.* (Electr.) Ampere, *das*

ampersand /ˈæmpəsænd/ *n.* Et-Zeichen, *das*

amphetamine /æmˈfetəmiːn, æmˈfetəmɪn/ *n.* Ampheta-
min, *das*

amphibian /æmˈfɪbɪən/ (Zool.) **1** *adj.* amphibisch. **2** *n.*
Amphibie, *die;* Lurch, *der*

amphibious /æmˈfɪbɪəs/ *adj.* amphibisch; **toads are
~:** Kröten sind Amphibien; ~ **vehicle/tank/aircraft**
Amphibienfahrzeug, *das/*-panzer, *der/*-flugzeug, *das*

amphitheatre (Amer.: **amphitheater**) /ˈæmfɪθɪətə(r)/
n. Amphitheater, *das*

ample /ˈæmpl/ *adj.,* ~**r** /ˈæmplə(r)/, ~**st** /ˈæmplɪst/ **(a)**
(spacious) weitläufig ‹*Garten, Räume*›; groß ‹*Ausdehnung*›;
(extensive, abundant) reichhaltig ‹*Mahl, Bibliographie*›; weit
reichend, umfassend ‹*Vollmachten, Machtbefugnisse*›; **(b)**
(enough) ~ **room/food** reichlich Platz/zu essen; **(c)** (stout)
üppig ‹*Busen*›; stattlich ‹*Erscheinung*›

amplification /æmplɪfɪˈkeɪʃn/ *n.* **(a)** (Electr., Phys.) Verstärkung, *die;* **(b)** (further explanation) weitere *od.* zusätzliche
Erläuterungen

amplifier /ˈæmplɪfaɪə(r)/ *n.* Verstärker, *der*

amplify /ˈæmplɪfaɪ/ *v.t.* **(a)** (Electr., Phys.) verstärken; **(b)**
(enlarge on) weiter ausführen, näher *od.* ausführlicher erläutern ‹*Erklärung, Bericht*›

amplitude /ˈæmplɪtjuːd/ *n.* **(a)** (Electr.) Amplitude, *die;*
Schwingungsweite, *die;* **(b)** (Phys.) Amplitude, *die;* größte
Ausschlagweite; **(c)** *no pl.* (breadth) Breite, *die;* Weite, *die*

amply /ˈæmplɪ/ *adv.* reichlich ‹*breit, belohnen*›; zur
Genüge ‹*zeigen, demonstrieren*›

ampoule /ˈæmpuːl/ *n.* Ampulle, *die*

amputate /ˈæmpjʊteɪt/ *v.t.* amputieren

amputation /æmpjʊˈteɪʃn/ *n.* Amputation, *die*

amputee /æmpjʊˈtiː/ *n.* Amputierte, *der/die*

Amtrack, (**P**) /ˈæmtræk/ *n.: amerikanische Eisenbahngesellschaft*

amulet /ˈæmjʊlɪt/ *n.* (lit. or fig.) Amulett, *das*

amuse /əˈmjuːz/ *v.t.* **(a)** (interest) unterhalten; **keep a
child** ~**d** ein Kind richtig beschäftigen; ~ **oneself with
sth.** sich mit etw. beschäftigen; ~ **oneself by doing sth.**
sich (*Dat.*) die Zeit damit vertreiben, etw. zu tun; **(b)** (make
laugh or smile) belustigen; amüsieren; **be** ~**d by** *or* **at sth.**
sich über etw. (*Akk.*) amüsieren

amusement /əˈmjuːzmənt/ *n.* Belustigung, *die;* (pastime)
Freizeitbeschäftigung, *die*

a'musement arcade *n.* Spielhalle, *die*

amusing /əˈmjuːzɪŋ/ *adj.,* **amusingly** /əˈmjuːzɪŋlɪ/ *adv.*
amüsant

an /ən, *stressed* æn/ *indef. art. see also* **a²**: ein/eine/ein

anabolic steroid /ænəbɒlɪk ˈstɪərɔɪd, ænəbɒlɪk
ˈsterɔɪd/ *n.* (Physiol.) anaboles Steroid; Anabolikum, *das*

anachronism /əˈnækrənɪzm/ *n.* Anachronismus, *der*

anachronistic /ənækrəˈnɪstɪk/ *adj.* anachronistisch;
zeitwidrig

anaemia /əˈniːmɪə/ *n., no pl.* ▶ 865 (Med.) Blutarmut, *die;*
Anämie, *die*

anaemic /əˈniːmɪk/ *adj.* (Med.) blutarm; anämisch; (fig.)
blutleer; saft- und kraftlos

anaesthesia /ænɪsˈθiːzɪə/ *n.* (Med.) Narkose, *die;*
general ~: [Voll]narkose, *die;* Allgemeinanästhesie, *die*
(fachspr.); **local** ~: örtliche Betäubung; Lokalanästhesie,
die (fachspr.)

anaesthetic /ænɪsˈθetɪk/ *n.* Anästhetikum, *das;* **give
sb. an** ~: jmdm. eine Narkose geben; (local) jmdn. betäuben; **be under an** ~: in Narkose liegen; **general** ~:
Narkotikum, *das;* Narkosemittel, *das;* **local** ~: Lokalanästhetikum, *das*

anaesthetist /əˈniːsθətɪst/ *n.* ▶ 887 (Med.) Anästhesist,
*der/*Anästhesistin, *die;* Narkose[fach]arzt, *der/*-ärztin, *die*

anaesthetize /əˈniːsθətaɪz/ *v.t.* narkotisieren; betäuben; (fig.) abstumpfen (**to** gegenüber)

anagram /ˈænəgræm/ *n.* Anagramm, *das*

analgesia /ænælˈdʒiːzɪə/ *n.* (Med.) Analgesie, *die*

analgesic /ænælˈdʒiːsɪk/ *n.* (Med.) Analgetikum, *das*

analog (Amer.) ⇒ **analogue**

analogous /əˈnæləgəs/ *adj.* vergleichbar; analog; **be** ~
to sth. einer Sache (*Dat.*) entsprechen

analogue /ˈænəlɒg/ *n.* Entsprechung, *die;* ~ **computer**
Analogrechner, *der*

analogy /əˈnælədʒɪ/ *n.* (agreement; also Ling.) Analogie, *die;*
(similarity) Parallele, *die;* Analogie, *die;* **draw an** ~
between/with eine Parallele ziehen zwischen (+ *Dat.*)/zu

analyse /ˈænəlaɪz/ *v.t.* **(a)** analysieren; **(b)** (Chem.) untersuchen (**for** auf + *Akk.*)

analysis /əˈnælɪsɪs/ *n., pl.* **analyses** /əˈnælɪsiːz/ **(a)**
Analyse, *die;* (Chem., Med.: of sample) Untersuchung, *die;* **in
the final** *or* **last** ~: letzten Endes; **(b)** (Psych.) Analyse,
die

analyst /ˈænəlɪst/ *n.* ▶ 887 **(a)** Laboratoriumsingenieur,
der; **(b)** (Econ., Polit., etc.) Experte, *der;* Fachmann, *der;* **(c)**
(Psych.) Analytiker, *der/*Analytikerin, *die*

analytic /ænəˈlɪtɪk/, **analytical** /ænəˈlɪtɪkl/ *adj.* analytisch

analyze (Amer.) ⇒ **analyse**

anarchic /əˈnɑːkɪk/, **anarchical** /əˈnɑːkɪkl/ *adj.* anarchisch; (anarchistic) anarchistisch

anarchism /ˈænəkɪzm/ *n., no pl.* Anarchismus, *der*

anarchist /ˈænəkɪst/ *n.* Anarchist, *der/*Anarchistin, *die*

anarchistic /ænəˈkɪstɪk/ *adj.* anarchistisch

anarchy /ˈænəkɪ/ *n., no pl.* Anarchie, *die;* (fig.: disorder)
Chaos, *das*

anathema /əˈnæθəmə/ *n., no pl., no art.* **be** ~ **to sb.**
jmdm. verhasst *od.* ein Gräuel sein

anatomical /ænəˈtɒmɪkl/ *adj.* anatomisch

anatomist /əˈnætəmɪst/ *n.* Anatom, *der*

anatomy /əˈnætəmɪ/ *n., no pl.* Anatomie, *die*

ancestor /ˈænsestə(r)/ *n.* Vorfahr, *der;* Ahn[e], *der;* (fig.)
Ahn[e], *der*

ancestral /ænˈsestrl/ *adj.* angestammt ‹*Grundbesitz,
Land*›

ancestry /ˈænsestrɪ/ *n.* **(a)** (lineage) Abstammung, *die;*
Herkunft, *die;* **(b)** (ancestors) Vorfahren *Pl.*

anchor /ˈæŋkə(r)/ **1** *n.* Anker, *der;* **lie at** ~: vor Anker
liegen; **come to** *or* **cast** *or* **drop** ~: vor Anker gehen;
weigh ~: den Anker lichten. **2** *v.t.* **(a)** verankern; vor
Anker legen; (secure) befestigen (**to an** + *Dat.*); **(b)** (fig.) **be
~ed to sth.** an etw. (*Akk.*) gefesselt sein. **3** *v.i.* ankern

anchorage /ˈæŋkərɪdʒ/ *n.* Ankerplatz, *der*

'anchorman *n.* **(a)** (Sport) (in tug-of-war) hinterster *od.*
letzter Mann; (in relay race) Schlussläufer, *der;* (Mountaineering)
Seilletzte, *der;* **(b)** ▶ 887 (Telev., Radio) Moderator, *der;* Redakteur im Studio

anchovy /ˈæntʃəvɪ/ *n.* An[s]chovis, *die;* Sardelle, *die*

ancient /ˈeɪnʃənt/ *adj.* **(a)** (belonging to past) alt; (pertaining
to antiquity) antik; **that's** ~ **history** (fig.) das ist längst ein

alter Hut (ugs.); **the ~ Greeks** die alten Griechen; **(b)** (old) alt; historisch ‹ *Gebäude usw.* ›; **~ monument** (Brit. Admin.) [offiziell anerkanntes] historisches Denkmal

ancillary /'æn'sɪlərɪ/ **1** *adj.* **(a)** (auxiliary) **be ~ to sth.** für etw. Hilfsdienste leisten; **(b)** (subordinate) zweitrangig; **~ industries** Zulieferindustrien. **2** *n.* (Brit.) Hilfskraft, *die*

and /ənd, *stressed* ænd/ *conj.* **(a)** und; **two hundred ~ forty** zweihundert[und]vierzig; **a knife, fork, ~ spoon** Messer, Gabel und Löffel; **two ~ two are four** zwei und zwei ist *od.* sind vier; **(b)** *expr. condition* und; **take one more step ~ I'll shoot** noch einen Schritt, und ich schieße; **do that ~ you'll regret it** wenn du das tust, wirst du es noch bedauern; **(c)** *expr. continuation* und; **she cried ~ cried** sie weinte und weinte; **for weeks ~ weeks/years ~ years** wochen-/jahrelang; **for miles ~ miles** meilenweit; **better ~ better** immer besser

Andes /'ændiːz/ *pr. n. pl.* **the ~:** die Anden

anecdotal /ænɪk'dəʊtl/ *adj.* anekdotisch; anekdotenhaft

anecdote /'ænɪkdəʊt/ *n.* Anekdote, *die*

anemia, anemic (Amer.) ⇒ **anaem-**

anemone /ə'nemənɪ/ *n.* Anemone, *die*

anesthesia *etc.* (Amer.) ⇒ **anaesthesia** *etc.*

angel /'eɪndʒl/ *n.* (lit. or fig.) Engel, *der;* **be on the side of the ~s** (fig.) auf der Seite der Guten stehen; **be an ~ and ...** (coll.) sei so lieb und ...

'angel fish *n.* Engelfisch, *der*

angelic /æn'dʒelɪk/ *adj.* (like angel[s]) engelhaft; **she looked ~:** sie sah wie ein Engel aus

anger /'æŋgə(r)/ **1** *n., no pl.* Zorn, *der* (**at** über + *Akk.*); (fury) Wut, *die* (**at** über + *Akk.*); **be filled with ~:** erzürnt/ wütend sein; **in [a moment of] ~:** im Zorn/in der Wut. **2** *v.t.* verärgern; (infuriate) erzürnen (geh.)/wütend machen; **be ~ed by sth.** über etw. (*Akk.*) verärgert/erzürnt/wütend sein

angle¹ /'æŋgl/ **1** *n.* **(a)** (Geom.) Winkel, *der;* **acute/obtuse/right ~:** spitzer/stumpfer/rechter Winkel; **at an ~ of 60°** im Winkel von 60°; **at an ~:** schief; **at an ~ to the wall** schräg zur Wand; **(b)** (corner) Ecke, *die;* (recess) Winkel, *der;* **(c)** (direction) Perspektive, *die;* Blickwinkel, *der;* (fig.) Gesichtspunkt, *der;* Aspekt, *der;* **the committee examined the matter from various ~s** der Ausschuss prüfte die Angelegenheit von verschiedenen Seiten; **looking at it from a commercial ~:** aus kaufmännischer Sicht betrachtet. **2** *v.t.* **(a)** [aus]richten; **(b)** (coll.: bias) färben ‹ *Nachrichten, Formulierung* ›. **3** *v.i.* [im Winkel] abbiegen; **the road ~s sharply to the left** die Straße biegt scharf nach links ab

angle² *v.i.* (fish) angeln; (fig.) **~ for sth.** sich um etw. bemühen; **~ for compliments** nach Komplimenten fischen

angled /'æŋgəld/ *adj.* (angular) eckig ‹ *Form, Figur* ›; (placed obliquely) schief; (fig. coll.) tendenziös, gefärbt ‹ *Bericht, Kommentar* ›; **acute-/obtuse-/right-~:** spitz-/stumpf-/ rechtwinklig

angler /'æŋglə(r)/ *n.* Angler, *der*/Anglerin, *die*

Anglican /'æŋglɪkən/ **1** *adj.* anglikanisch. **2** *n.* Anglikaner, *der*/Anglikanerin, *die*

Anglicize /'æŋglɪsaɪz/ *v.t.* anglisieren

angling /'æŋglɪŋ/ *n.* Angeln, *das*

Anglo- /'æŋgləʊ/ *in comb.* anglo-/Anglo-

Anglo-A'merican ▶ 947 | **1** *adj.* angloamerikanisch; **an ~ agreement** ein englisch-/britisch-amerikanischer Vertrag. **2** *n.* Angloamerikaner, *der*/Angloamerikanerin, *die*

Anglo-'Indian ▶ 947 | **1** *adj.* angloindisch. **2** *n.* Anglo-Inder, *der*/Anglo-Inderin, *die*

Anglo-'Saxon 1 *n.* ▶ 947 | Angelsachse, *der*/Angelsächsin, *die;* (language) Angelsächsisch, *das.* **2** *adj.* angelsächsisch

angrily /'æŋgrɪlɪ/ *adv.* verärgert; (stronger) zornig

angry /'æŋgrɪ/ *adj.* **(a)** böse; verärgert ‹ *Person, Stimme, Geste* ›; (stronger) zornig; wütend; **be ~ at** *or* **about sth.** wegen etw. böse sein; **be ~ with** *or* **at sb.** mit jmdm. *od.* auf jmdn. böse sein; sich über jmdn. ärgern; **get ~:** böse werden; **get** *or* **make sb. ~:** jmdn. verärgern; (stronger)

jmdn. wütend machen; **(b)** (fig.) drohend, bedrohlich ‹ *Wolke, Himmel* ›

anguish /'æŋgwɪʃ/ *n., no pl.* Qualen *Pl.*

anguished /'æŋgwɪʃt/ *adj.* qualvoll; gequält ‹ *Herz, Gewissen* ›

angular /'æŋgjʊlə(r)/ *adj.* **(a)** (having angles) eckig ‹ *Gebäude, Struktur, Gestalt* ›; **(b)** (lacking plumpness, stiff) knochig ‹ *Körperbau* ›; kantig ‹ *Gesicht* ›; **(c)** (measured by angle) angular; winklig; **~ momentum** (Phys.) Drehimpuls, *der*

animal /'ænɪml/ **1** *n.* **(a)** Tier, *das;* (quadruped) Vierbeiner, *der;* (any living being) Lebewesen, *das;* **domestic ~:** Haustier, *das;* **~ rights** Tierrechte; **~ rights activists** aktive Tierschützer; Tierrechtler; **(b)** (fig. coll.) **there is no such ~ as a 'typical' criminal** so etwas wie den „typischen" Verbrecher gibt es gar nicht; **(c)** (carnal, sexual) körperlich ‹ *Triebe, Wünsche, Bedürfnisse* ›; tierisch, animalisch ‹ *Veranlagung, Natur* ›

animate 1 /'ænɪmeɪt/ *v.t.* **(a)** (enliven) beleben; **(b)** (inspire) anregen; **~ sb. with enthusiasm** jmdn. mit Begeisterung erfüllen; **(c)** (breathe life into) mit Leben erfüllen. **2** /'ænɪmət/ *adj.* beseelt ‹ *Leben, Körper* ›; belebt ‹ *Objekt, Welt* ›; lebendig ‹ *Seele* ›

animated /'ænɪmeɪtɪd/ *adj.* lebhaft ‹ *Diskussion, Unterhaltung, Ausdruck, Gebärde* ›; **~ cartoon** Zeichentrickfilm, *der*

animatedly /'ænɪmeɪtɪdlɪ/ *adv.* lebhaft

animation /ænɪ'meɪʃn/ *n.* **(a)** *no pl.* Lebhaftigkeit, *die;* **(b)** (Cinemat.) Animation, *die*

animosity /ænɪ'mɒsɪtɪ/ *n.* Animosität, *die* (geh.), Feindseligkeit, *die* (**against, towards** gegen)

aniseed /'ænɪsiːd/ *n.* Anis[samen], *der*

ankle /'æŋkl/ *n.* ▶ 672 | (joint) Fußgelenk, *das;* (part of leg) Knöchelgegend, *die;* Fessel, *die*

ankle: ~-deep *adj.* knöcheltief; **~ sock** *n.* Socke, *die;* (esp. for children) Söckchen, *das*

annals /'ænlz/ *n. pl.* (lit. or fig.) Annalen *Pl.*

annex 1 /ə'neks/ *v.t.* **(a)** (add) angliedern (**to** Dat.); (append) anfügen ‹ *Bemerkungen* › (**to** Dat.); **(b)** (incorporate) annektieren ‹ *Land, Territorium* ›; (coll.: take without right) sich (Dat.) unter den Nagel reißen (ugs.) ‹ *Gegenstände* ›. **2** /'æneks/ *n.* (supplementary building) Anbau, *der;* (built-on extension) Erweiterungsbau, *der;* (appendix) (to document) Zusatz, *der;* (to treaty) Anhang, *der*

annexation /ænɪk'seɪʃn/ *n.* (of land) Annexion, *die;* Annektierung, *die*

annexe ⇒ **annex 2**

annihilate /ə'naɪɪleɪt/ *v.t.* **(a)** vernichten ‹ *Armee, Bevölkerung, Menschheit* ›; zerstören ‹ *Stadt, Land* ›; **(b)** (fig.) zunichte machen; am Boden zerstören ‹ *Person* ›

annihilation /ənaɪɪ'leɪʃn/ *n.* **(a)** ⇒ **annihilate a:** Vernichtung, *die;* Zerstörung, *die;* **(b)** (fig.) Verderben, *das;* Untergang, *der*

anniversary /ænɪ'vɜːsərɪ/ *n.* Jahrestag, *der;* **wedding ~:** Hochzeitstag, *der;* **the university celebrated its 500th ~:** die Universität feierte ihr 500jähriges Jubiläum *od.* Bestehen; **the ~ of Shakespeare's birth** [die Wiederkehr von] Shakespeares Geburtstag; **the ~ of his death** sein Todestag

annotate /'ænəteɪt/ *v.t.* kommentieren; mit Anmerkungen versehen

announce /ə'naʊns/ *v.t.* **(a)** bekannt geben; ansagen ‹ *Programm* ›; (over Tannoy etc.) durchsagen; (in newspaper) anzeigen ‹ *Heirat usw.* ›; **(b)** (make known the approach of; fig.: signify) ankündigen

announcement /ə'naʊnsmənt/ *n.* Bekanntgabe, *die;* (over Tannoy etc.) Durchsage, *die;* **they made an ~ over the radio that ...:** sie gaben im Radio bekannt, dass ...; **did you read the ~ of his death in the paper?** haben Sie seine Todesanzeige in der Zeitung gelesen?

announcer /ə'naʊnsə(r)/ *n.* ▶ 897 | Ansager, *der*/Ansagerin, *die;* Sprecher, *der*/Sprecherin, *die*

annoy /ə'nɔɪ/ *v.t.* (a) ärgern; **his late arrival** ∼**ed me** ich habe mich über sein spätes Kommen geärgert; (b) (harass) schikanieren

annoyance /ə'nɔɪəns/ *n.* Verärgerung, *die;* (nuisance) Plage, *die*

annoyed /ə'nɔɪd/ *adj.* **be** ∼ **[at** *or* **with sb./sth.]** ärgerlich [auf *od.* über jmdn./über etw. (*Akk.*)] sein; **be** ∼ **to find that** ...: sich darüber ärgern, dass ...; **he got very** ∼: er hat sich darüber sehr geärgert

annoying /ə'nɔɪŋ/ *adj.* ärgerlich; lästig ⟨*Gewohnheit, Person*⟩; **the** ∼ **part of it is that** ...: das Ärgerliche daran ist, dass ...

annual /'ænjʊəl/ **1** *adj.* (a) (reckoned by the year) Jahres-; ∼ **rainfall** jährliche Regenmenge; (b) (recurring yearly) [all]jährlich ⟨*Ereignis, Feier*⟩; Jahres⟨*bericht, -hauptversammlung*⟩. **2** *n.* (a) (Bot.) einjährige Pflanze; (b) (book) Jahrbuch, *das;* (of comic etc.) Jahresalbum, *das*

annually /'ænjʊəlɪ/ *adv.* (per year) jährlich; (once a year) [all]jährlich

annuity /ə'njuːɪtɪ/ *n.* (grant, sum payable) Jahresrente, *die;* (investment) Rentenversicherung, *die*

annul /ə'nʌl/ *v.t.*, **-ll-** annullieren, für ungültig erklären ⟨*Gesetz, Vertrag, Ehe, Testament*⟩; auflösen ⟨*Vertrag*⟩

annulment /ə'nʌlmənt/ *n.* (of law, treaty, marriage, will) Annullierung, *die;* (of treaty also) Auflösung, *die*

Annunciation /ənʌnsɪ'eɪʃn/ *n.* (Eccl.) **the** ∼: Mariä Verkündigung

anoint /ə'nɔɪnt/ *v.t.* (esp. Relig.) salben

anomalous /ə'nɒmələs/ *adj.* anomal, anormal ⟨*Lage, Verhältnisse, Zustand*⟩; ungewöhnlich ⟨*Situation, Anblick*⟩

anomaly /ə'nɒməlɪ/ *n.* Anomalie, *die;* Absonderlichkeit, *die;* (exception) Ausnahme, *die*

anon. /ə'nɒn/ *abbr.* **anonymous [author]** anon.

anonymity /ænə'nɪmɪtɪ/ *n.* Anonymität, *die*

anonymous /ə'nɒnɪməs/ *adj.* anonym

anorak /'ænəræk/ *n.* Anorak, *der*

anorexia /ænə'reksɪə/ *n.* Anorexie, *die* (Med.); Magersucht, *die* (volkst.); ∼ **nervosa** /ænəreksɪə nɜː'vəʊsə/ nervöse Anorexie (Med.)

anorexic /ænə'reksɪk/ *adj.* anorektisch (fachspr.); magersüchtig; **be** ∼: an Anorexie (Med.) *od.* Magersucht leiden

another /ə'nʌðə(r)/ **1** *pron.* (a) (additional) noch einer/ eine/eins; ein weiterer/eine weitere/ein weiteres; **one thing leads to** ∼: eines ergibt sich aus dem anderen; **please have** ∼: nimm dir doch noch einen; (b) (counterpart) wieder einer/eine/eins; (c) (different) ein anderer/eine andere/ein anderes; **in one way or** ∼: so oder so; irgendwie; **for one reason or** ∼: aus irgendeinem Grund; *see also* **one 1** f, **3** b. **2** *adj.* (a) (additional) noch einer/eine/ eins; ein weiterer/eine weitere/ein weiteres; **give me** ∼ **chance** gib mir noch [einmal] eine Chance; **after** ∼ **six weeks** nach weiteren sechs Wochen; ∼ **100 pounds** weitere 100 Pfund; **he didn't say** ∼ **word** er sagte nichts mehr; (b) (a person like) ein neuer/eine neue/ein neues; ein zweiter/eine zweite/ein zweites; ∼ **Chaplin** ein neuer *od.* zweiter Chaplin; (c) (different) ein anderer/eine andere/ein anderes; **ask** ∼ **person** fragen Sie jemand anderen *od.* anders; ∼ **time, don't be so greedy** sei beim nächsten Mal nicht so geizig; **I'll do it** ∼ **time** ich tu's ein andermal; [and] [there's] ∼ **thing** [und] noch etwas

answer /'ɑːnsə(r)/ **1** *n.* (a) (reply) Antwort, *die* (to auf + *Akk.*); (reaction) Reaktion, *die;* **I tried to phone him, but there was no** ∼: ich habe versucht, ihn anzurufen, aber es hat sich niemand gemeldet; **there is no** ∼ **to that** dem ist nichts mehr hinzuzufügen; **by way of [an]** ∼: als Antwort; **in** ∼ **to sth.** als Antwort *od.* Reaktion auf etw. (*Akk.*); (b) (to problem) Lösung, *die* (to *Gen.*); (to calculation) Ergebnis, *das;* **have** *or* **know all the** ∼**s** (coll.) alles wissen. **2** *v.t.* (a) beantworten ⟨*Brief, Frage*⟩; antworten auf (+ *Akk.*) ⟨*Frage, Hilferuf, Einladung, Inserat*⟩; (react to) erwidern ⟨*Geste, Schlag*⟩; eingehen auf (+ *Akk.*), erfüllen ⟨*Bitte*⟩; sich stellen zu ⟨*Beschuldigung*⟩; ∼ **sb.** jmdm. antworten; ∼ **me!** antworte [mir]!; (b) ∼ **the door/bell** an die Tür gehen; *see also* **telephone 1**. **3** *v.i.* (a) (reply) antworten; ∼ **to sth.** sich zu etw. äußern; (b) (be responsible) ∼ **for sth.** für etw. die Verantwortung übernehmen;

∼ **to sb.** jmdm. [gegenüber] Rechenschaft ablegen; **he has a lot to** ∼ **for** er hat vieles zu verantworten; (c) (correspond) ∼ **to a description** einer Beschreibung (*Dat.*) entsprechen; (d) ∼ **to the name of** ...: auf den Namen ... hören; (e) ∼ **back** (coll.) widersprechen; Widerworte haben (ugs.)

answerable /'ɑːnsərəbl/ *adj.* (responsible) **be** ∼ **to sb.** jmdm. [gegenüber] verantwortlich sein; **be** ∼ **for sb./ sth.** für jmdn./etw. verantwortlich sein

'answering machine, (Brit.) **'answerphone** *ns.* Anrufbeantworter, *der*

ant /ænt/ *n.* Ameise, *die*

antacid /ænt'æsɪd/ **1** *n.* Antazidum, *das.* **2** *adj.* Magensäure bindend

antagonism /æn'tægənɪzm/ *n.* Feindseligkeit, *die* (towards, against gegenüber); (between two) Antagonismus, *der* (geh.)

antagonist /æn'tægənɪst/ *n.* Gegner, *der*/Gegnerin, *die;* (in debate etc.) Kontrahent, *der*/Kontrahentin, *die*

antagonistic /æntægə'nɪstɪk/ *adj.* feindlich ⟨*Mächte, Prinzipien*⟩; antagonistisch, gegensätzlich ⟨*Interessen*⟩; **be** ∼ **towards sb.** jmdn. anfeinden; **be** ∼ **towards sth.** gegen etw. eingestellt sein

antagonize /æn'tægənaɪz/ *v.t.* (a) sich (*Dat.*) ⟨*Person*⟩ zum Feind machen; (b) (counteract) entgegenwirken (+ *Dat.*)

antarctic /ænt'ɑːktɪk/ **1** *adj.* antarktisch; **A**∼ **Circle/ Ocean** südlicher Polarkreis/Südpolarmeer, *das.* **2** *pr. n.* **the A**∼: die Antarktis

Antarctica /ænt'ɑːktɪkə/ *pr. n.* Antarktis (*das*)

'anteater *n.* (Zool.) Ameisenfresser, *der*

antecedent /æntɪ'siːdənt/ *n.* (preceding event) früherer Umstand; vorangegangenes Ereignis; (preceding thing) Vorläufer, *der*

antedate /æntɪ'deɪt/ *v.t.* (precede) voraus-, vorangehen (+ *Dat.*)

antediluvian /æntɪdɪ'luːvɪən/ *adj.* (lit. or fig.) vorsintflutlich

antelope /'æntɪləʊp/ *n.* (Zool.) Antilope, *die*

antenatal /æntɪ'neɪtl/ *adj.* (a) (concerning pregnancy) Schwangerschafts-; Schwangeren-; ∼ **care** Schwangerenfürsorge, *die;* ∼ **clinic** Klinik für werdende Mütter; (b) (before birth) vorgeburtlich

antenna /æn'tenə/ *n.* (a) *pl.* ∼**e** /æn'teniː/ (Zool.) Fühler, *der;* Antenne, *die* (fachspr.); (b) *pl.* ∼**s** (Amer.: aerial) Antenne, *die*

ante-room /'æntɪruːm, 'æntɪrʊm/ *n.* Vorraum, *der;* (waiting room) Warteraum, *der*

anthem /'ænθəm/ *n.* (a) (Eccl. Mus.) Chorgesang, *der;* (b) (song of praise) Hymne, *die*

anther /'ænθə(r)/ *n.* (Bot.) Staubbeutel, *der*

anthill /'ænθɪl/ *n.* Ameisenhügel, *der*

anthology /æn'θɒlədʒɪ/ *n.* (by different writers) Anthologie, *die;* (by one writer) Auswahl, *die*

anthracite /'ænθrəsaɪt/ *n.* Anthrazit, *der*

anthrax /'ænθræks/ *n., no pl., no indef. art.* ▶ **865** | (Med., Vet. Med.) Milzbrand, *der;* Anthrax, *der* (fachspr.)

anthropoid /'ænθrəpɔɪd/ *n.* Anthropoid[e], *der;* Menschenaffe, *der*

anthropological /ænθrəpə'lɒdʒɪkl/ *adj.* anthropologisch

anthropologist /ænθrə'pɒlədʒɪst/ *n.* ▶ **887** | Anthropologe, *der*/Anthropologin, *die*

anthropology /ænθrə'pɒlədʒɪ/ *n., no pl.* Anthropologie, *die*

anti /'æntɪ/ *prep.* gegen

anti- /'æntɪ/ *pref.* anti-/Anti-

anti: ∼**-a'bortion** *attrib. adj.* ∼**-abortion protester** Abtreibungsgegner, *der*/-gegnerin, *die;* ∼**-abortion protest/law** Protest/Gesetz gegen Abtreibung; ∼**-abortion demonstration/movement** Abtreibungsdemonstration, *die*/-bewegung, *die;* ∼**-abortionist** /æntɪə'bɔːʃənɪst/ *n.* Abtreibungsgegner, *der*/-gegnerin, *die;* ∼**-'aircraft** *adj.* (Mil.) Flugabwehr-; ∼**-aircraft gun** Flak, *die;* ∼**-aircraft battery** Flakbatterie, *die*

antibiotic /ˌæntɪbaɪˈɒtɪk/ n. Antibiotikum, das

'**antibody** n. (Physiol.) Antikörper, der

antic /ˈæntɪk/ n. (trick) Mätzchen, das (ugs.); (of clown) Possen, der

anticipate /ænˈtɪsɪpeɪt/ v.t. (a) (expect) erwarten; (foresee) voraussehen; ~ **rain/trouble** mit Regen/Ärger rechnen; (b) (discuss or consider before due time) vorwegnehmen; antizipieren; (c) (forestall) ~ **sb./sth.** jmdm./einer Sache zuvorkommen

anticipation /ænˌtɪsɪˈpeɪʃn/ n., no pl. Erwartung, die; **in** ~ **of sth.** in Erwartung einer Sache (Gen.); **with** ~: erwartungsvoll; **thanking you in** ~: Ihnen im Voraus dankend

anti'climax n. (a) (ineffective end) Abstieg, der; Abfall, der; (b) (Lit.) Antiklimax, die

anti'clockwise 1 adv. gegen den Uhrzeigersinn. **2** adj. **in an** ~ **direction** gegen den od. entgegen dem Uhrzeigersinn

anti'cyclone n. (Meteorol.) Hochdruckgebiet, das; Antizyklone, die (Met.)

antidepressant /ˌæntɪdɪˈpresənt/ n. (Med.) Antidepressivum, das

antidote /ˈæntɪdəʊt/ n. Gegengift, -mittel, das (**for, against** gegen); (fig.) Gegenmittel, das (**to** gegen)

'**antifreeze** n. Gefrierschutzmittel, das; Frostschutzmittel, das

anti'histamine n. (Med.) Antihistamin[ikum], das

anti-lock 'braking system n. (Motor Veh.) Antiblockiersystem, das

anti'nuclear adj. Anti-Atom[kraft]-

antipathy /ænˈtɪpəθɪ/ n. Antipathie, die; Abneigung, die; ~ **to** or **for sb./sth.** Abneigung gegen jmdn./etw.

antiperspirant /ˌæntɪˈpɜːspɪrənt/ **1** adj. schweißhemmend; ~ **spray** Deodorantspray, der od. das. **2** n. Antitranspirant, das

antipodes /ænˈtɪpədiːz/ n. pl. entgegengesetzte od. antipodische Teile der Erde; (Australasia) Australien und Ozeanien

antiquarian /ˌæntɪˈkweərɪən/ adj. ~ **bookshop** Antiquariat, das; Antiquariatsbuchhandlung, die; ~ **bookseller** Antiquar, der; Antiquariatsbuchhändler, der

antiquated /ˈæntɪkweɪtɪd/ adj. (old-fashioned) antiquiert; veraltet; (out of date) überholt

antique /ænˈtiːk/ **1** adj. antik. **2** n. ▶ 887 Antiquität, die; ~ **dealer** Antiquitätenhändler, der/-händlerin, die; ~ **shop** Antiquitätenladen, der

antiquity /ænˈtɪkwɪtɪ/ n., no pl. (a) (ancientness) Alter, das; (b) no art. (old times) Antike, die

anti-'roll bar ⇒ **roll bar**

anti-Semitic /ˌæntɪsɪˈmɪtɪk/ adj. antisemitisch

anti-Semitism /ˌæntɪˈsemɪtɪzm/ n., no pl. Antisemitismus, der

anti: ~'**septic 1** adj. antiseptisch; **2** n. Antiseptikum, das; ~'**social** adj. (a) asozial; (b) (unsociable) ungesellig ⟨Person⟩ ~-'**terrorist** attrib. adj. antiterroristisch; ~-'**theft** attrib. adj. Antidiebstahl-

antithesis /ænˈtɪθəsɪs/ n., pl. **antitheses** /ænˈtɪθəsiːz/ (thing) Gegenstück, das (**of, to** zu)

anti'trust attrib. adj. (Amer.) Antitrust-

anti: ~'**virus** attrib. adj. (Computing) Antivirus-; ~-**virus software** Antivirensoftware, die; ~**vivisectionist** /ˌæntɪvɪvɪˈsekʃənɪst/ n. Vivisektionsgegner, der/-gegnerin, die

antler /ˈæntlə(r)/ n. Geweihstange, die; [**pair of**] ~s Geweih, das

antonym /ˈæntənɪm/ n. Antonym, das; Gegen[satz]wort, das

Antwerp /ˈæntwɜːp/ pr. n. ▶ 1159 Antwerpen (das)

anus /ˈeɪnəs/ n. (Anat.) After, der

anvil /ˈænvɪl/ n. Amboss, der

anxiety /æŋˈzaɪətɪ/ n. (a) (state) Angst, die; (concern about future) Sorge, die (**about** wegen); **anxieties** Sorgen Pl.; **cause sb.** ~: jmdm. Angst/Sorgen machen; (b) (desire) **his** ~ **to do sth.** sein Verlangen danach, etw. zu tun

anxious /ˈæŋkʃəs/ adj. (a) (troubled) besorgt; **be** ~ **about sth./sb.** um etw./jmdn. besorgt sein; **we were all so** ~ **about you** wir haben uns (Dat.) alle solche Sorgen um Sie gemacht; (b) (eager) sehnlich; **be** ~ **for sth.** ungeduldig auf etw. (Akk.) warten; **have an** ~ **desire to do sth.** ängstlich darauf bedacht sein, etw. zu tun; **he is** ~ **to please** er ist bemüht zu gefallen; (c) (worrying) **an** ~ **time** eine Zeit banger Sorge

anxiously /ˈæŋkʃəslɪ/ adv. (a) besorgt; (b) (eagerly) sehnsüchtig

any /ˈenɪ/ **1** adj. (a) (some) **have you** ~ **wool/**~ **statement to make?** haben Sie Wolle/[irgend]eine Erklärung abzugeben?; **if you have** ~ **difficulties** wenn du irgendwelche Schwierigkeiten hast; **not** ~: kein/keine; **without** ~: ohne jeden/jede/jedes; **have you** ~ **idea of the time?** hast du eine Ahnung, wie spät es ist?; (b) (one) ein/eine; **there isn't** ~ **hood on this coat** dieser Mantel hat keine Kapuze; **a book without** ~ **cover** ein Buch ohne Deckel; (c) (all) jeder/jede/jedes; **to avoid** ~ **delay** um jede Verzögerung zu vermeiden; (d) (every) jeder/jede/jedes; ~ **time I went there** jedes Mal od. immer, wenn ich dort hinging; [**at**] ~ **time** jederzeit; [**at**] ~ **time of day** zu jeder Tageszeit; (e) (whichever) jeder/jede/jedes [beliebige]; **choose** ~ [**one**] **book/**~ **books you like** suchen Sie sich irgendein Buch/irgendwelche Bücher aus; **choose** ~ **two numbers** nimm zwei beliebige Zahlen; **do it** ~ **way you like** machen Sie es, wie immer Sie wollen; [**at**] ~ **time** [**now**] jederzeit; ~ **day/minute** [**now**] jeden Tag/jede Minute; **you can count on him** ~ **time** (coll.) du kannst dich jederzeit auf ihn verlassen; **I'd prefer Mozart** ~ **day** (coll.) ich würde Mozart allemal (ugs.) od. jederzeit vorziehen; **not** [**just**] ~ **house** nicht irgendein beliebiges Haus; **take** ~ **amount you wish** nehmen Sie, so viel Sie wollen; ~ **amount of** jede Menge (ugs.); (f) (an appreciable) ein nennenswerter/eine nennenswerte/ein nennenswertes; **she didn't stay** ~ **length of time** sie ist nicht sehr lange geblieben. **2** pron. (a) (some) in condit., interrog., or neg. sentence (replacing sing. n.) einer/eine/ein[e]s; (replacing collect. n.) welcher/welche/welches; (replacing pl. n.) welche; **not** ~: keiner/keine/kein[e]s/Pl. keine; **without** ~: ohne; **I need to buy some sugar, we haven't got** ~ **at the moment** ich muss Zucker kaufen, wir haben im Augenblick keinen; **Here are some sweets. Would you like** ~**?** Hier sind ein paar Bonbons. Möchtest du welche?; **hardly** ~: kaum welche/etwas; **do you have** ~ **of them in stock?** haben Sie [irgend]welche davon vorrätig?; **he is not having** ~ **of it** (fig. coll.) er will nichts davon wissen; (b) (no matter which) irgendeiner/irgendeine/irgendein[e]s/irgendwelche Pl.; **Which numbers?** — **Any between 1 and 10** Welche Zahlen? — Irgendwelche zwischen 1 und 10. **3** adv. **do you feel** ~ **better today?** fühlen Sie sich heute [etwas] besser?; **if it gets** ~ **colder** wenn es noch kälter wird; **he didn't seem** ~ [**the**] **wiser after that** danach schien er auch nicht klüger zu sein; **I can't wait** ~ **longer** ich kann nicht [mehr] länger warten; **I don't feel** ~ **better** mir ist kein bisschen wohler

'**anybody** n. & pron. (a) (whoever) jeder; ~ **and everybody** jeder Beliebige; (b) (somebody) [irgend]jemand; **how could** ~ **be so cruel?** wie kann man nur so grausam sein?; **there wasn't** ~ **there** es war niemand da; **I've never seen** ~ **who ...:** ich habe noch keinen gesehen, der ...; **he is a match for** ~: er kann sich mit jedem od. jedermann messen; ~ **but** jeder[mann] außer; **it's** ~**'s match** das Spiel ist offen; **what will happen is** ~**'s guess** was geschehen wird, [das] weiß keiner; **he's not** [**just**] ~: er ist nicht [einfach] irgendwer; (c) (an important person) jemand; **everybody who was** ~ **was there** alles, was Rang und Namen hatte, war da

'**anyhow** adv. (a) ⇒ **anyway**; (b) (haphazardly) irgendwie; **the furniture was arranged** ~: die Möbel waren wahllos irgendwo hingestellt

'**anyone** ⇒ **anybody**

'**anyplace** (Amer. coll.) ⇒ **anywhere**

'**anything 1** n. & pron. (a) (whatever thing) was [immer]; alles, was; **you may do** ~ **you wish** Sie können [alles] tun, was Sie möchten; ~ **and everything** alles Mögliche;

Apologizing

Fairly formal

I owe you an apology or *I must apologize for accusing you wrongly*	= Ich muss mich bei Ihnen entschuldigen, dass ich Sie fälschlich beschuldigt habe
Please accept my humble apology	= Ich bitte vielmals um Entschuldigung
I take back all that I said and apologize unreservedly	= Ich nehme alles zurück und bitte tausendmal um Entschuldigung
I greatly or *very much regret that I have had to disappoint you*	= Ich bedaure sehr, dass ich Sie enttäuschen musste
I must ask you to forgive or *excuse my mistake*	= Ich muss Sie für meinen Fehler um Verzeihung bitten
Please excuse my oversight	= Bitte entschuldigen Sie mein Versehen
Please forgive me for being so late with these birthday wishes	= Bitte entschuldigen Sie, dass diese Geburtstagswünsche so verspätet eintreffen
I must apologize for the delay in replying to your letter	= Ich muss mich entschuldigen, dass ich Ihren Brief erst so spät beantworte
I am sorry or *I regret to have to inform you that ...*	= Ich muss Ihnen leider mitteilen, dass ..., Ich bedaure, Ihnen mitteilen zu müssen, dass ...

Less formal

I really am sorry that I've let you down	= Es tut mir aufrichtig Leid, dass ich dich im Stich gelassen habe
I'm sorry to be such a nuisance	= Tut mir Leid, dass ich dir so viel Mühe mache
Sorry! (e.g. when you bump into someone)	= Entschuldigung!
Sorry to bother you, but can you tell me ...	= Entschuldigung, wenn ich störe, aber können Sie mir sagen ...
I'm sorry, but or *Unfortunately I'll have to go now*	= Leider muss ich jetzt gehen
Sorry, but I can't help	= Tut mir Leid, da kann ich nicht helfen
Don't be cross that I haven't written before	= Sei mir nicht böse or Nimm es mir nicht übel, dass ich nicht früher geschrieben habe
Forgive me! It was all a stupid misunderstanding	= Verzeih! Es war alles nur ein dummes Missverständnis

(b) (something) irgendetwas; **is there ∼ wrong with you?** fehlt Ihnen [irgend] etwas?; **have you done ∼ silly?** hast du [irgend] etwas Dummes gemacht?; **can we do ∼ to help you?** können wir Ihnen irgendwie helfen?; **I don't want ∼ [further] to do with him** ich möchte nichts [mehr] mit ihm zu tun haben; **(c)** (a thing of any kind) alles; **∼ like that** so etwas; **as ... as ∼** (coll.) wahnsinnig ... (ugs.); **not for ∼ [in the world]** um nichts in der Welt; **∼ but ...** (∼ except) alles außer ...; (far from) alles andere als; **we don't want [just] ∼:** wir wollen nicht einfach irgendetwas [Beliebiges]. **2** *adv.* **not ∼ like as ... as** keineswegs so ... wie

ˈanyway *adv.* **(a)** (in any case, besides) sowieso; **we wouldn't accept your help ∼:** wir würden von Ihnen sowieso keine Hilfe annehmen; **(b)** (at any rate) jedenfalls; **∼, I must go now** wie dem auch sei, ich muss jetzt gehen

ˈanywhere 1 *adv.* **(a)** (in any place) (wherever) überall, wo; wo [immer]; (somewhere) irgendwo; **not ∼ near as ... as** (coll.) nicht annähernd so ... wie; **∼ but ...:** überall, außer ...; überall, nur nicht ...; **(b)** (to any place) (wherever) wohin [auch immer]; (somewhere) irgendwohin; **∼ but ...:** überallhin, außer ...; überallhin, nur nicht ...; **[just] ∼:** [einfach] irgendwohin. **2** *pron.* **if there's ∼ you'd like to see** wenn es irgendetwas gibt, was du sehen möchtest; **have you found ∼ to live yet?** haben Sie schon eine Wohnung gefunden?; **there's never ∼ open for milk after 6 p.m.** nach 18 Uhr kann man nirgends mehr Milch bekommen; **∼ but ...:** überall, außer ...; überall, nur nicht ...; **[just] ∼:** irgendein x-beliebiger Ort

apart /ə'pɑːt/ *adv.* **(a)** (separately) getrennt; **with one's legs ∼:** mit gespreizten Beinen; **∼ from ...** (except for) außer ...; bis auf ... (+ *Akk.*); (in addition to) außer ...; **(b)** (into pieces) auseinander; **he took the engine ∼:** er nahm den Motor auseinander; **take ∼** (fig.) (criticize) auseinander nehmen (ugs.) ‹*Theaterstück, Politiker*›; (analyse) zergliedern; **(c)** **∼ [from]** (to a distance) weg [von]; (at a distance) **ten kilometres ∼:** zehn Kilometer voneinander entfernt

apartheid /ə'pɑːtheɪt/ *n., no pl., no art.* Apartheid, *die*

apartment /ə'pɑːtmənt/ *n.* **(a)** (room) Apartment, *das;* Appartement, *das;* **∼s** (in a mansion etc.) Räume; Räumlichkeiten *Pl.;* **(b)** (Amer.) Wohnung, *die;* **∼ block** Wohnblock, *der*

apathetic /æpə'θetɪk/ *adj.* apathisch (**about** gegenüber)

apathy /'æpəθɪ/ *n., no pl.* Apathie, *die* (**about** gegenüber)

APB *abbr.* (Amer.) **all-points bulletin**

ape /eɪp/ **1** *n.* [Menschen]affe, *der;* (apelike person) Affe, *der.* **2** *v.t.* nachahmen; nachäffen (abwertend)

aperitif /əperɪ'tiːf/ *n.* Aperitif, *der*

aperture /'æpətʃə(r)/ *n.* Öffnung, *die*

apex /'eɪpeks/ *n., pl.* **∼es** *or* **apices** /'eɪpɪsiːz/ (tip) Spitze, *die;* (fig.) Gipfel, *der;* Höhepunkt, *der*

aphid /'eɪfɪd/ *n.* Blattlaus, *die*

aphorism /'æfərɪzm/ *n.* Aphorismus, *der*

aphrodisiac /æfrə'dɪzɪæk/ *n.* Aphrodisiakum, *das*

apices *pl. of* **apex**

apiece /ə'piːs/ *adv.* je; **we took two bags ∼:** wir nahmen je zwei Beutel; **they cost a penny ∼:** die kosten einen Penny das Stück

aplomb /ə'plɒm/ *n.* Sicherheit [im Auftreten]

apocalypse /ə'pɒkəlɪps/ *n.* Apokalypse, *die*

apocalyptic /əpɒkə'lɪptɪk/ *adj.* apokalyptisch

apocryphal /ə'pɒkrɪfl/ *adj.* apokryph

apolitical /eɪpə'lɪtɪkl/ *adj.* apolitisch; unpolitisch

apologetic /əpɒlə'dʒetɪk/ *adj.* **(a)** entschuldigend; **he was most ∼ about ...:** er entschuldigte sich vielmals für ...; **(b)** (diffident) zaghaft ‹*Lächeln, Ton*›; zurückhaltend, bescheiden ‹*Wesen, Art*›

apologetically /əpɒlə'dʒetɪkəlɪ/ *adv.* **(a)** entschuldigend; **(b)** (diffidently) zaghaft; bescheiden

apologize /ə'pɒlədʒaɪz/ *v.i.* sich entschuldigen; **∼ to sb. for sth./sb.** sich bei jmdm. für etw./jmdn. entschuldigen

apology /ə'pɒlədʒɪ/ *n.* **(a)** Entschuldigung, *die;* **make an ∼ [to sb.] for sth.** sich für etw. [bei jmdm.] entschuldigen; **you owe him an ∼:** Sie müssen sich bei ihm entschuldigen; **please accept our apologies** wir bitten vielmals um Entschuldigung; **(b)** (poor example of) **an ∼ for a ...:** ein erbärmliches Exemplar von ...

apoplectic /æpə'plektɪk/ *adj.* apoplektisch; **∼ stroke** *or* **fit** Schlaganfall, *der*

apoplexy /'æpəpleksɪ/ *n.* Apoplexie, *die* (fachspr.); Schlaganfall, *der*

apostle /ə'pɒsl/ n. (lit. or fig.) Apostel, der

apostrophe /ə'pɒstrəfɪ/ n. (sign) Apostroph, der; Auslassungszeichen, das

appal (*Amer.:* **appall**) /ə'pɔ:l/ v.t., **-ll-** (dismay) entsetzen; (terrify) erschrecken; **obscenity** ~**s her** sie empört sich über Obszönitäten

appalling /ə'pɔ:lɪŋ/ adj. (dismaying) entsetzlich; (terrifying) schrecklich; (coll.: unpleasant) fürchterlich

apparatus /æpə'reɪtəs/ n. (equipment) Gerät, das; (gymnastic ~) Geräte Pl.; (machinery, lit. or fig.) Apparat, der; **a piece of** ~: ein Apparat

apparel /ə'pærəl/ n. Kleidung, die; Gewänder Pl. (geh.)

apparent /ə'pærənt/ adj. (a) (clear) offensichtlich ⟨Ziel, Zweck, Wirkung, Begeisterung, Interesse⟩; offenbar ⟨Bedeutung, Wahrheit⟩; **it soon became** ~ **that** ...: es zeigte sich bald, dass ...; **heir** ~: recht- od. gesetzmäßiger Erbe; **(b)** (seeming) scheinbar

apparently /ə'pærəntlɪ/ adv. (a) (clearly) offensichtlich; offenbar; **(b)** (seemingly) scheinbar

apparition /æpə'rɪʃn/ n. (a) (appearance) [Geister]erscheinung, die; **(b)** (ghost) Gespenst, das

appeal /ə'pi:l/ **1** v.i. (Law etc.) Einspruch erheben od. einlegen (**to** bei); ~ **to a court** bei einem Gericht Berufung einlegen; ~ **against sth.** gegen etw. Einspruch/Berufung einlegen; **(b)** (refer) ~ **to** verweisen auf ⟨Erkenntnisse, Tatsachen⟩; **(c)** (make earnest request) ~ **to sb. for sth./to do sth.** jmdn. um etw. ersuchen/jmdn. ersuchen, etw. zu tun; **(d)** (address oneself) ~ **to sb./sth.** an jmdn./etw. appellieren; **(e)** (be attractive) ~ **to sb.** jmdm. zusagen. **2** n. **(a)** (Law etc.) Einspruch, der (**to** bei); (to higher court) Berufung, die (**to** bei); **lodge an** ~ **with sb.** bei jmdm. Einspruch/Berufung einlegen; **right of** ~: Einspruchs-/Berufungsrecht, das; **Court of A~:** Berufungsgericht, das; **(b)** (reference) Berufung, die; Verweisung, die; **make an** ~ **to sth.** sich auf etw. (Akk.) berufen; auf etw. (Akk.) verweisen; **(c)** (request) Appell, der; Aufruf, der; **an** ~ **to sb. for sth.** eine Bitte an jmdn. um etw.; **make an** ~ **to sb.** an jmdn. appellieren; **(d)** (addressing oneself) Appell, der; Aufruf, der; **make an** ~ **to sb.** einen Appell an jmdn. richten; **(e)** (attraction) Reiz, der

appealing /ə'pi:lɪŋ/ adj. (a) (imploring) flehend; **(b)** (attractive) ansprechend ⟨Farbe, Geschichte, Stil⟩; verlockend ⟨Essen, Idee⟩; reizvoll ⟨Haus, Beruf, Baustil⟩; angenehm ⟨Stimme, Charakter⟩

appear /ə'pɪə(r)/ v.i. (a) (become visible, be seen, arrive) erscheinen; ⟨Licht, Mond:⟩ auftauchen; ⟨Symptom, Darsteller:⟩ auftreten; (present oneself) auftreten; (Sport) spielen; **he was ordered to** ~ **before the court** er wurde vom Gericht vorgeladen; **he** ~**ed on a charge with murder** er stand wegen Mordes vor Gericht; **(b)** (occur) vorkommen; ⟨Irrtum:⟩ vorkommen, auftreten; ⟨Ereignis:⟩ vorkommen, eintreten; **(c)** (seem) ~ **[to be]** ...: scheinen ... [zu sein]; ~ **to do sth.** scheinen, etw. zu tun; **try to** ~ **relaxed** versuch, entspannt zu erscheinen; **he could at least** ~ **to be interested** er könnte zumindest so tun, als ob er interessiert wäre

appearance /ə'pɪərəns/ n. (a) (becoming visible) Auftauchen, das; (of symptoms) Auftreten, das; (arrival) Erscheinen, das; (of performer, speaker, etc.) Auftritt, der; **make an** or **one's** ~: erscheinen; **make a public** ~: in der Öffentlichkeit auftreten; **put in an** ~: sich sehen lassen; **(b)** (look) Äußere, das; **outward** ~: äußere Erscheinung; ~**s** Äußerlichkeiten Pl.; **to judge by** ~**s, to all** ~**s** allem Anschein nach; **for the sake of** ~**s, to keep up** ~**s** um den Schein zu wahren; **(c)** (semblance) Anschein, der; ~**s to the contrary,** ...: entgegen allem Anschein ...; ~**s can be deceptive** der Schein trügt; **(d)** (occurrence) Auftreten, das; Vorkommen, das

appease /ə'pi:z/ v.t. (a) (make calm) besänftigen; (Polit.) beschwichtigen; **(b)** (soothe) lindern ⟨Leid, Schmerz, Not⟩; mildern ⟨Beunruhigung, Erregung⟩; stillen ⟨Hunger, Durst⟩

appeasement /ə'pi:zmənt/ n. ⇒ **appease:** Besänftigung, die; Beschwichtigung, die; Linderung, die; Milderung, die; Stillen, das

append /ə'pend/ v.t. ~ **sth. to sth.** etw. an etw. (Akk.) anhängen; (add) etw. einer Sache (Dat.) anfügen

appendage /ə'pendɪdʒ/ n. (a) Anhängsel, das; (addition) Anhang, der; **(b)** (accompaniment) Zu-, Beigabe, die (**to** zu)

appendices pl. of **appendix**

appendicitis /əpendɪ'saɪtɪs/ n. ▶865| Blinddarmentzündung, die (volkst.); Appendizitis, die (fachspr.)

appendix /ə'pendɪks/ n., pl. **appendices** /ə'pendɪsi:z/ or ~**es** (a) Anhang, der (**to** zu); **(b)** ▶672| (Anat.) [**vermiform** /'vɜːmɪfɔːm/] ~: Blinddarm, der (volkst.); Wurmfortsatz [des Blinddarms]

appertain /æpə'teɪn/ v.i. ~ **to sth.** (relate) sich auf etw. (Akk.) beziehen; (belong) zu etw. gehören

appetite /'æpɪtaɪt/ n. (a) Appetit, der (**for** auf + Akk.); ~ **for sex** Lust auf Sex; **(b)** (fig.) Verlangen, das (**for** nach); ~ **for knowledge** Wissensdrang, der

appetizer /'æpɪtaɪzə(r)/ n. Appetitanreger, der

appetizing /'æpɪtaɪzɪŋ/ adj. appetitlich

applaud /ə'plɔːd/ **1** v.i. applaudieren; [Beifall] klatschen. **2** v.t. applaudieren (+ Dat.); Beifall spenden (+ Dat.); (approve of, welcome) billigen; (praise) loben; anerkennen

applause /ə'plɔːz/ n., no pl. Applaus, der; (praise) Lob, das; Anerkennung, die; **give** ~: Applaus od. Beifall spenden; **get** ~: Applaus od. Beifall ernten

apple /'æpl/ n. Apfel, der; **the** ~ **of sb.'s eye** (fig.) jmds. Liebling

apple: ~**-cart** n. upset the ~**-cart** (fig.) die Pferde od. Gäule scheu machen (ugs.); ~ **'pie** n. gedeckte Apfeltorte; ~ **'sauce** n. Apfelmus, das; ~ **tree** n. Apfelbaum, der

appliance /ə'plaɪəns/ n. (utensil) Gerät, das; (aid) Hilfsmittel, das

applicable /'æplɪkəbl, ə'plɪkəbl/ adj. (a) anwendbar (**to** auf + Akk.); **(b)** (appropriate) geeignet; angebracht; zutreffend ⟨Fragebogenteil usw.⟩

applicant /'æplɪkənt/ n. Bewerber, der/Bewerberin, die (**for** um); (claimant) Antragsteller, der/Antragstellerin, die

application /æplɪ'keɪʃn/ n. (a) (request) Bewerbung, die (**for** um); (for passport, licence, etc.) Antrag, der (**for** auf + Akk.); ~ **form** Antragsformular, das; **available on** ~: auf Anfrage erhältlich; **(b)** (diligence) Fleiß, der (**to** bei); (with enthusiasm) Eifer, der (**to** für); **(c)** (putting) Auftragen, das (**to** auf + Akk.); (administering) Anwendung, die; (of heat, liquids) Zufuhr, die; (employment; of rule etc.) Anwendung, die; **the** ~ **of new technology** der Einsatz neuer Technologien; **(d)** (Computing) Applikation, die

apply /ə'plaɪ/ **1** v.t. (a) anlegen ⟨Verband⟩; auftragen ⟨Creme, Paste, Farbe⟩ (**to** auf + Akk.); zuführen ⟨Wärme, Flüssigkeit⟩ (**to** Dat.); ~ **the brakes** bremsen; die Bremse betätigen; **(b)** (make use of) anwenden; **applied linguistics/mathematics** angewandte Sprachwissenschaft/Mathematik; **(c)** (devote) richten, lenken ⟨Gedanken, Überlegungen, Geist⟩ (**to** auf + Akk.); verwenden ⟨Zeit, Energie⟩ (**to** auf + Akk.); ~ **oneself [to sth.]** sich (Dat.) Mühe geben [mit etw.]; sich [um etw.] bemühen. **2** v.i. (a) (have relevance) zutreffen (**to** auf + Akk.); (be valid) gelten; **things which don't** ~ **to us** Dinge, die uns nicht betreffen; **(b)** (address oneself) ~ **[to sb.] for sth.** [jmdn.] um etw. bitten od. (geh.) ersuchen; (for passport, licence, etc.) [bei jmdm.] etw. beantragen; (for job) sich [bei jmdm.] um etw. bewerben

appoint /ə'pɔɪnt/ v.t. (a) (fix) bestimmen; festlegen ⟨Zeitpunkt, Ort⟩; **(b)** (choose for a job) einstellen; (assign to office) ernennen; ~ **sb. [to be** or **as] sth./to do sth.** jmdn. zu etw. ernennen/jmdn. dazu bereden, etw. zu tun; ~ **sb. to sth.** jmdn. in etw. (Akk.) einsetzen

appointed /ə'pɔɪntɪd/ adj. (a) (fixed) vereinbart; verabredet; **(b)** **well/badly** ~: gut/schlecht ausgestattet ⟨Zimmer usw.⟩

appointment /ə'pɔɪntmənt/ n. (a) (fixing) Festlegung, die; Festsetzung, die; **(b)** (assigning to office) Ernennung, die; Berufung, die; (being assigned to office) Ernennung, die (**as** zum/zur); (to job) Einstellung, die; ~ **to a position** Berufung auf einen Posten; **by** ~ **to Her Majesty the Queen, makers of fine confectionery** königlicher Hoflieferant für feines Konfekt; **(c)** (post) Stelle, die; Posten, *der;* **a teaching** ~**:** eine Stelle als Lehrer/Lehrerin; **(d)** (arrangement) Termin, *der;* **dental** ~**:** Termin beim Zahnarzt; **make an** ~ **with sb.** sich (*Dat.*) von jmdm. einen Termin geben lassen; **by** ~**:** mit Voranmeldung

apportion /əˈpɔːʃn/ *v.t.* **(a)** (allot) ~ **sth. to sb.** jmdm. etw. zuteilen; **(b)** (portion out) [gleichmäßig] verteilen (**among** an + *Akk.*)

apposite /ˈæpəzɪt/ *adj.* (appropriate) passend; geeignet; (well-chosen) treffend; ~ **to sth.** zutreffend auf etw. (*Akk.*)

appraisal /əˈpreɪzl/ *n.* Bewertung, *die*

appraise /əˈpreɪz/ *v.t.* bewerten

appreciable /əˈpriːʃəbl/ *adj.* (perceptible) nennenswert ‹ *Unterschied, Einfluss* ›; spürbar ‹ *Veränderung, Wirkung, Erfolg* ›; merklich ‹ *Verringerung, Anstieg* ›; (considerable) beträchtlich; erheblich

appreciably /əˈpriːʃəblɪ/ *adv.* (perceptibly) spürbar ‹ *verändern* ›; merklich ‹ *sich unterscheiden* ›; (considerably) beträchtlich; erheblich

appreciate /əˈpriːʃɪeɪt, əˈpriːsɪeɪt/ **1** *v.t.* **(a)** ([correctly] estimate value or worth of) [richtig] einschätzen; (understand) verstehen; (be aware of) sich (*Dat.*) bewusst sein (+ *Gen.*); (be receptive to) Gefallen finden an (+ *Dat.*); ~ **that/what** …**:** verstehen, dass/was …; **(b)** (be grateful for) anerkennen; schätzen; (enjoy) genießen; **I'd really** ~ **that** das wäre sehr nett von dir. **2** *v.i.* im Wert steigen

appreciation /əpriːʃɪˈeɪʃn, əpriːsɪˈeɪʃn/ *n.* **(a)** ([right] estimation) [richtige] Einschätzung; (understanding) Verständnis, *das* (**of** für); (awareness) Bewusstsein, *das;* (sensitivity) Sinn, *der* (**of** für); **(b)** (gratefulness) Dankbarkeit, *die;* (enjoyment) Gefallen, *das* (**of** an + *Dat.*); **(c)** (rise in value) Wertsteigerung, *die*

appreciative /əˈpriːʃətɪv/ *adj.* **(a)** **be** ~ **of sth./sb.** (aware of) fähig sein, etw./jmdn. [richtig] einzuschätzen; **she is very** ~ **of music** sie hat viel Sinn für Musik; **(b)** (grateful) dankbar (**of** für); (approving) anerkennend

apprehend /æprɪˈhend/ *v.t.* **(a)** (arrest) festnehmen; fassen; **(b)** (perceive) wahrnehmen; (understand) erfassen; begreifen

apprehension /æprɪˈhenʃn/ *n.* **(a)** (arrest) Festnahme, *die;* Verhaftung, *die;* **(b)** (uneasiness) Besorgnis, *die;* **(c)** (conception) Auffassung, *die;* Ansicht, *die* (**of** über + *Akk.*); (understanding) Verständnis, *das*

apprehensive /æprɪˈhensɪv/ *adj.* besorgt (**for** um + *Akk.*); ~ **of sth.** besorgt wegen etw.; **be** ~ **that** …**:** befürchten, dass …

apprehensively /æprɪˈhensɪvlɪ/ *adv.* besorgt

apprentice /əˈprentɪs/ **1** *n.* (learner) Lehrling, *der* (**to** bei); (beginner) Neuling, *der;* Anfänger, *der.* **2** *v.t.* **be** ~**d** [**to sb.**] [bei jmdm.] in der Lehre sein *od.* in die Lehre gehen

apprenticeship /əˈprentɪsʃɪp/ *n.* (training) Lehre, *die* (**to** bei); (learning period) Lehrzeit, *die;* Lehrjahre *Pl.;* **serve an/one's** ~**:** eine/seine Lehre machen; (fig.) ein/sein Volontariat machen

approach /əˈprəʊtʃ/ **1** *v.i.* (in space) sich nähern; näher kommen; ‹ *Sturm usw.* › aufziehen; (in time) nahen; **the train now** ~**ing platform 1** der auf Gleis 1 einfahrende Zug; **the time is fast** ~**ing when you will have to** …**:** es wird nicht mehr lange dauern und du musst … **2** *v.t.* **(a)** (come near to) sich nähern (+ *Dat.*); (set about) herangehen an (+ *Akk.*); angehen ‹ *Problem, Aufgabe, Thema* ›; **(b)** (be similar to) verwandt sein (+ *Dat.*); **(c)** (approximate to) nahe kommen (+ *Dat.*); **the temperature/weight** ~**es 100 °C/50 kg** die Temperatur/das Gewicht beträgt nahezu 100 °C/50 kg; **(d)** (appeal to) sich wenden an (+ *Akk.*). **3** *n.* **(a)** [Heran]nahen, *das;* (treatment) Ansatz, *der* (**to** zu); (attitude) Einstellung, *die* (**to** gegenüber); **(b)** (appeal) Herantreten, *das* (**to** an + *Akk.*); **make an** ~ **to sb. concerning sth.** sich wegen etw. an jmdn. wenden; **(c)** (advance) Annäherungsversuche *die;* **make** ~**es to sb.** Annäherungsversuche bei jmdm. machen; **(d)** (access) Zugang, *der;* (road) Zufahrtstraße, *die;* (fig.) Zugang, *der;* **(e)** (Aeronaut.) Landeanflug, *der;* Approach, *der*

approachable /əˈprəʊtʃəbl/ *adj.* **(a)** (friendly) umgänglich; (receptive) empfänglich; **(b)** (accessible) zugänglich; erreichbar

ap'proach road *n.* Zufahrtsstraße, *die*

approbation /æprəˈbeɪʃn/ *n.* (sanction) Genehmigung, *die;* (approval) Zustimmung, *die*

appropriate 1 /əˈprəʊprɪət/ *adj.* (suitable) geeignet (**to,** **for** für); **I feel it is** ~ **to say a few words** ich halte es für angebracht, ein paar Worte zu sagen; **the** ~ **authority** die zuständige Behörde. **2** /əˈprəʊprɪeɪt/ *v.t.* ~ **sth.** [**to oneself**] sich (*Dat.*) etw. aneignen

appropriately /əˈprəʊprɪətlɪ/ *adv.* gebührend; passend ‹ *dekoriert, gekleidet, genannt* ›

approval /əˈpruːvl/ *n.* **(a)** (sanctioning) (of plan, project, expenditure) Genehmigung, *die;* (of proposal, reform, marriage) Billigung, *die;* (agreement) Zustimmung, *die;* Einwilligung, *die* (**for** in + *Akk.*); **(b)** (esteem) Lob, *das;* Anerkennung, *die;* **does the plan meet with your** ~**?** findet der Plan Ihre Zustimmung?; **on** ~ (Commerc.) zur Probe; (to view) zur Ansicht

approve /əˈpruːv/ **1** *v.t.* **(a)** (sanction) genehmigen ‹ *Plan, Projekt, Ausgaben* ›; billigen ‹ *Vorschlag, Reform, Heirat* ›; ~**d hotel** empfohlenes Hotel; ~**d school** (Brit. Hist.) Erziehungsheim, *das;* **(b)** (find good) gutheißen; für gut halten. **2** *v.i.* ~ **of** billigen; zustimmen (+ *Dat.*) ‹ *Plan* ›; einverstanden sein mit ‹ *Tätigkeiten, Gewohnheiten, Verhalten* ›

approving /əˈpruːvɪŋ/ *adj.* zustimmend, beipflichtend ‹ *Worte* ›; anerkennend, bewundernd ‹ *Blicke* ›

approvingly /əˈpruːvɪŋlɪ/ *adv.* ⇒ **approving:** zustimmend; anerkennend

approximate 1 /əˈprɒksɪmət/ *adj.* (fairly correct) ungefähr *attr.;* **the figures given here are only** ~**:** dies hier sind nur ungefähre Zahlen. **2** /əˈprɒksɪmeɪt/ *v.t.* **(a)** (make similar) ~ **sth. to sth.** etw. einer Sache (*Dat.*) anpassen; **(b)** (come near to) nahe kommen (+ *Dat.*); annähernd erreichen (+ *Akk.*). **3** /əˈprɒksɪmeɪt/ *v.i.* **sth.** ~**s to sth.** etw. gleicht einer Sache (*Dat.*) annähernd

approximately /əˈprɒksɪmətlɪ/ *adv.* (roughly) ungefähr; (almost) fast; **the answer is** ~ **correct** die Antwort stimmt ungefähr; **very** ~**:** ganz grob

approximation /əprɒksɪˈmeɪʃn/ *n.* **(a)** Annäherung, *die* (**to** an + *Dat.*); **(b)** (estimate) Annäherungswert, *der*

Apr. *abbr.* **April** Apr.

APR *abbr.* **annualized percentage rate** Jahreszinssatz, *der*

apricot /ˈeɪprɪkɒt/ *n.* Aprikose, *die*

April /ˈeɪprəl/ *n.* ▶ **738**│ April, *der;* ~ **fool** April[s]narr, *der;* ~ **Fool's Day** der 1. April; *see also* **August**

apron /ˈeɪprən/ *n.* (garment) Schürze, *die;* **be tied to sb.'s** ~ **strings** jmdm. an der Schürze *od.* am Schürzenzipfel hängen

apropos /æprəˈpəʊ, ˈæprəpəʊ/ *adv.* ~ **of** in Bezug auf (+ *Akk.*); hinsichtlich (+ *Gen.*)

apse /æps/ *n.* Apsis, *die*

apt /æpt/ *adj.* **(a)** (suitable) passend ‹ *Ausdruck, Geschenk* ›; angemessen ‹ *Reaktion* ›; treffend ‹ *Zitat, Bemerkung* ›; **(b)** (tending) **be** ~ **to do sth.** dazu neigen, etw. zu tun

aptitude /ˈæptɪtjuːd/ *n.* **(a)** (propensity) Neigung, *die;* (ability) Begabung, *die;* **linguistic** ~**:** Sprachbegabung, *die;* **(b)** (tendency) Eignung, *die*

aptly /ˈæptlɪ/ *adv.* passend; ~ **chosen words** treffend gewählte Worte

aqualung /ˈækwəlʌŋ/ *n.* Tauchgerät, *das*

aquaplane /ˈækwəpleɪn/ **1** *v.i.* **(a)** ‹ *Reifen:* › aufschwimmen; ‹ *Fahrzeug:* › [durch Aquaplaning] ins Rutschen geraten; **(b)** (use ~) Wasserski laufen. **2** *n.* Monoski, *der;* Wasserski, *der*

aquarium /əˈkweərɪəm/ *n., pl.* ~**s** *or* **aquaria** /əˈkweərɪə/ Aquarium, *das*

Aquarius /əˈkweərɪəs/ *n.* (Astrol., Astron.) der Wassermann

aquatic /əˈkwætɪk/ *adj.* aquatisch; Wasser-; ~ **plant/bird** Wasserpflanze, *die/*-vogel, *der*

aqueduct /ˈækwɪdʌkt/ *n.* Aquädukt, *der od.* das

aquiline /ˈækwɪlaɪn/ *adj.* adlerartig; Adler-; ~ **eye/nose** Adlerauge, *das/*-nase, *die*

Arab /ˈærəb/ **1** *adj.* arabisch; ~ **horse** Araber, *der.* **2** ▶ **947**│ *n.* Araber, *der/*Araberin, *die*

Arabia /ə'reɪbɪə/ pr. n. Arabien (das)
Arabian /ə'reɪbɪən/ ▶ 947 | 1 adj. arabisch; the ~ Nights Tausendundeine Nacht. 2 n. Araber, der/Araberin, die
Arabic /'ærəbɪk/ 1 adj. arabisch. 2 n. ▶ 897 | Arabisch, das; see also **English** 2 a
Arab-Is'raeli attrib. adj. arabisch-israelisch
arable /'ærəbl/ adj. ~ land kultivierbares Land; (cultivated) Ackerland, das
arbiter /'ɑːbɪtə(r)/ n. (judge) Richter, der; (arbitrator) Vermittler, der
arbitrarily /'ɑːbɪtrərɪlɪ/ adv. (at random) willkürlich; (capriciously) aus einer Laune heraus
arbitrariness /'ɑːbɪtrərɪnɪs/ n., no pl. (randomness) Willkür, die
arbitrary /'ɑːbɪtrərɪ/ adj. (a) (random) willkürlich; arbiträr; (capricious) launenhaft; launisch ⟨Idee⟩; (b) (unrestrained) rücksichtslos ⟨Vorgehen, Bestrafung, Wesen, Haltung⟩
arbitrate /'ɑːbɪtreɪt/ 1 v.t. schlichten, beilegen ⟨Streit⟩. 2 v.i. ~ [upon sth.] [in einer Sache] vermitteln od. als Schiedsrichter fungieren
arbitration /ɑːbɪ'treɪʃn/ n. Vermittlung, die; (in industry) Schlichtung, die; go to ~: einen Schlichter anrufen od. einschalten
arbitrator /'ɑːbɪtreɪtə(r)/ n. (mediator) Vermittler, der; (in industry) Schlichter, der; (arbiter) Schiedsrichter, der; (judge) Richter, der
arc /ɑːk/ n. (a) [Kreis]bogen, der; (b) (Electr.) Lichtbogen, der; ~ lamp, ~ light Lichtbogenlampe, die
arcade /ɑː'keɪd/ n. Arkade, die; shopping ~: Einkaufspassage, die
arcane /ɑː'keɪn/ adj. geheimnisvoll
arch /ɑːtʃ/ 1 n. Bogen, der; (curvature; of foot) Wölbung, die; (of bridge) Bogen, der; Joch, das; (vault) Gewölbe, das. 2 v.i. sich wölben; ⟨Ast, Glied:⟩ sich biegen. 3 v.t. beugen ⟨Rücken, Arm⟩; the cat ~ed its back die Katze machte einen Buckel
arch- pref. Erz-; ~-villain Erzschurke, der; Erzgauner, der
archaeological /ɑːkɪə'lɒdʒɪkl/ adj. archäologisch
archaeologist /ɑːkɪ'ɒlədʒɪst/ n. ▶ 887 | Archäologe, der/Archäologin, die
archaeology /ɑːkɪ'ɒlədʒɪ/ n. Archäologie, die
archaic /ɑː'keɪɪk/ adj. (out of use) veraltet; (antiquated) altertümlich; überholt ⟨Methode, Gesetz⟩
archaism /'ɑːkeɪɪzm/ n. Archaismus, der
archangel /'ɑːkeɪndʒl/ n. Erzengel, der
arch'bishop n. Erzbischof, der
arch-'enemy n. Erzfeind, der
archeology etc. (Amer.) ⇒ **archaeology** etc.
archer /'ɑːtʃə(r)/ n. Bogenschütze, der
archery /'ɑːtʃərɪ/ n., no pl. Bogenschießen, das
archetypal /ɑːkɪtaɪpl/ adj. (original) archetypisch (geh.); (typical) typisch
archetype /'ɑːkɪtaɪp/ n. (original) Urfassung, die; Archetyp, der; (typical specimen) Prototyp, der
archipelago /ɑːkɪ'peləgəʊ/ n., pl. ~s or ~es Archipel, der; (islands) Inselgruppe, die; (sea) Inselmeer, das
architect /'ɑːkɪtekt/ n. ▶ 887 | Architekt, der/Architektin, die
architectural /ɑːkɪ'tektʃərl/ adj. architektonisch
architecture /'ɑːkɪtektʃə(r)/ n. (a) Architektur, die; Baukunst, die (geh.); (style) Bauweise, die; Architektur, die; naval/railway ~: Schiff[s]-/Eisenbahnbau, der; (b) (structure, lit. or fig.) Konstruktion, die; (Computing) [System]architektur, die
archive /'ɑːkaɪv/ 1 n., usu. in pl. Archiv, das. 2 v.t. archivieren
'archway n. (vaulted passage) Gewölbegang, der; Tunnel, der; (arched entrance) Durchgang, der; Torbogen, der
arctic /'ɑːktɪk/ 1 adj. (lit. or fig.) arktisch; A~ Circle/ Ocean nördlicher Polarkreis/Nordpolarmeer, das. 2 pr. n. the A~: die Arktis
ardent /'ɑːdənt/ adj. (eager) begeistert; (fervent) glühend ⟨Bewunderer, Leidenschaft⟩; hitzig ⟨Temperament, Wesen⟩;

brennend ⟨Wunsch⟩; leidenschaftlich ⟨Gedicht, Liebesbrief, Anbetung⟩; innigst, (geh.) inbrünstig ⟨Hoffnung, Liebe⟩
ardour (Brit.; Amer.: ardor) /'ɑːdə(r)/ n. (passionate emotion) Inbrunst, die (geh.); (fervour) Eifer, der; ~ for reform Reformeifer, der
arduous /'ɑːdjʊəs/ adj. schwer, anstrengend ⟨Aufgabe, Arbeit⟩; hart ⟨Arbeit, Tag⟩; beschwerlich ⟨Reise, Aufstieg, Fahrt⟩
arduously /'ɑːdjʊəslɪ/ adv. (laboriously) beschwerlich
are ⇒ **be**
area /'eərɪə/ n. (a) ▶ 643 | (surface measure) Flächenausdehnung, die; what is the ~ of your farm? wie groß ist Ihr Hof?; (b) (region) Gelände, das; (of wood, marsh, desert) Gebiet, das; (of city, country) Gegend, die; (of skin, wall, etc.) Stelle, die; in the Hamburg ~: im Hamburger Raum; (c) (defined space) Bereich, der; parking/picnic ~: Park-/Picknickplatz, der; no-smoking ~: Nichtraucherzone, die; (d) (subject field) Gebiet, das; (e) (scope) Raum, der; ~ of choice Wahlmöglichkeiten Pl.
'area code n. (Amer. Teleph.) Gebietsvorwahl[nummer], die
arena /ə'riːnə/ n. (at circus, bullfight) Arena, die; (fig.: scene of conflict) Bühne, die; (fig.: sphere of action) Bereich, der; the political ~: die politische Arena; enter the ~ (fig.) die Arena betreten
aren't /ɑːnt/ (coll.) = are not; ⇒ **be**
Argentina /ɑːdʒən'tiːnə/ pr. n. Argentinien (das)
Argentine /'ɑːdʒəntaɪn/ 1 pr. n. the ~: Argentinien (das). 2 n. ⇒ **Argentinian** 2. 3 adj. argentinisch
Argentinian /ɑːdʒən'tɪnɪən/ ▶ 947 | 1 adj. argentinisch; sb. is ~: jmd. ist Argentinier/Argentinierin. 2 n. Argentinier, der/Argentinierin, die
argon /'ɑːgɒn/ n. (Chem.) Argon, das
arguable /'ɑːgjʊəbl/ adj. (a) fragwürdig ⟨Angelegenheit, Punkt⟩; it's ~ whether ...: es ist noch die Frage, ob ...; (b) it is ~ that ... (can reasonably be argued that) man kann sich auf den Standpunkt stellen, dass ...
arguably /'ɑːgjʊəblɪ/ adv. möglicherweise
argue /'ɑːgjuː/ 1 v.t. (a) (maintain) ~ that ...: die Ansicht vertreten, dass ...; (b) (treat by reasoning) darlegen ⟨Grund, Standpunkt, Fakten⟩; (c) (persuade) ~ sb. into doing sth. jmdn. dazu überreden, etw. zu tun; ~ sb. out of doing sth. [es] jmdm. ausreden, etw. zu tun. 2 v.i. ~ with sb. sich mit jmdm. streiten; ~ against sb. jmdm. widersprechen; ~ for/against sth. sich für/gegen etw. aussprechen; ~ about sth. sich über etw. (Akk.) streiten
argument /'ɑːgjʊmənt/ n. (a) (reason) Begründung, die; ~s for/against sth. Argumente für/gegen etw.; (b) no pl. (reasoning process) Argumentieren, das; assume sth. for ~'s sake etw. rein theoretisch annehmen; (c) (debate) Auseinandersetzung, die; get into an ~/get into ~s with sb. mit jmdm. in Streit geraten
argumentation /ɑːgjʊmən'teɪʃn/ n. Argumentieren, das
argumentative /ɑːgjʊ'mentətɪv/ adj. widerspruchsfreudig
argy-bargy /ɑːdʒɪ'bɑːdʒɪ/ n. (joc.) Hickhack, der od. das (ugs.)
aria /'ɑːrɪə/ n. (Mus.) Arie, die
Arian /'eərɪən/ ⇒ **Aryan**
arid /'ærɪd/ adj. (a) (dry) trocken ⟨Klima, Land⟩; (Geog.) arid; ~ zone Trockengürtel, der; (b) (barren) karg
aridity /ə'rɪdɪtɪ/ n., no pl. ⇒ **arid**: Trockenheit, die; Aridität, die; Kargheit, die
Aries /'eəriːz/ n. (Astrol., Astron.) der Widder
aright /ə'raɪt/ adv. recht
arise /ə'raɪz/ v.i., arose /ə'rəʊz/, arisen /ə'rɪzn/ (a) (originate) entstehen; (b) (present itself) auftreten; ⟨Gelegenheit:⟩ sich bieten; a crisis has ~n in Turkey in der Türkei ist es zu einer Krise gekommen; (c) (result) ~ from or out of sth. auf etw. (Akk.) zurückzuführen sein; (d) ⟨Sonne, Nebel:⟩ aufsteigen; (e) ⟨See, Sturm:⟩ anschwellen; (f) (rise from the dead) auferstehen

Area (square measure)

1 square inch (sq. in.)	= 6,45 cm²	(sechs Komma vier fünf Quadratzentimeter)
144 square inches	= 1 square foot (sq. ft)	= 929 cm²
9 square feet	= 1 square yard (sq. yd)	= 0,836 m² (null Komma acht drei sechs Quadratmeter)
4,840 square yards	= 1 acre	= 0,4 ha (null Komma vier Hektar)
640 acres	= 1 square mile	= 2,59 km² (zwei Komma fünf neun Quadratkilometer)

What is the area of the room?   = Wie viel Quadratmeter hat das Zimmer?
The area of the room is 180 square feet   = Das Zimmer hat 16,72 Quadratmeter [Fläche]
2,000 square feet of office space   ≈ 186 Quadratmeter Bürofläche
He farms 1,000 acres [of land]   ≈ Er bewirtschaftet 400 Hektar [Land]
a farm of 1,000 acres   ≈ ein 400 Hektar großer Bauernhof, ein Bauernhof von 400 Hektar
an area of about 40 square miles   ≈ eine Fläche von etwa 100 Quadratkilometern

---

aristocracy /ærɪ'stɒkrəsɪ/ *n.* Aristokratie, *die*

aristocrat /'ærɪstəkræt/ *n.* Aristokrat, *der*/Aristokratin, *die*

aristocratic /ærɪstə'krætɪk/ *adj.* **(a)** aristokratisch; Aristokraten-; adelig; Adels-; **(b)** vornehm ‹*Aussehen, Auftreten*›; (refined) kultiviert; fein ‹*Manieren, Sitten*›; edel ‹*Geschmack, Wein*›

aristocratically /ærɪstə'krætɪkəlɪ/ *adv.* aristokratisch

Aristotle /'ærɪstɒtl/ *pr. n.* Aristoteles (*der*)

arithmetic[1] /ə'rɪθmətɪk/ *n.* **(a)** (science) Arithmetik, *die;* **(b)** (computation) Rechnen, *das;* **mental ~:** Kopfrechnen, *das*

arithmetic[2] /ærɪθ'metɪk/, **arithmetical** /ærɪθ'metɪkl/ *adj.* arithmetisch

ark /ɑːk/ *n.* **sth. looks as if it came** *or* **could have come straight out of the ~:** etw. sieht vorsintflutlich aus; *see also* **Noah's ark**

arm[1] /ɑːm/ *n.* **(a)** ▶ 672 | (also of sea etc.) Arm, *der;* **~ in ~:** Arm in Arm; **remain** *or* **keep at ~'s length from sb.** (fig.) eine gewisse Distanz zu jmdm. wahren; **as long as sb.'s ~** (fig.) ellenlang; **cost sb. an ~ and a leg** (fig.) jmdn. eine Stange Geld kosten (ugs.); **on sb.'s ~:** an jmds. Arm (*Dat.*); **under one's ~:** unter dem Arm; **take sb. in one's ~s** jmdn. in die Arme nehmen *od.* (geh.) schließen; **with open ~s** (lit. or fig.) mit offenen Armen; **(b)** (sleeve) Ärmel, *der;* **(c)** (support) Armlehne, *die*

arm[2] **1** *n.* **(a)** *usu. in pl.* (weapon) Waffe, *die;* **small ~s** Handfeuerwaffen; **lay down one's ~s** die Waffen niederlegen; **take up ~s** zu den Waffen greifen; **be up in ~s about sth.** (fig.) wegen etw. aufgebracht sein; **~s dealer** Waffenhändler, *der;* **~s race** Rüstungswettlauf, *der;* **(b)** *in pl.* (heraldic devices) Wappen, *das.* **2** *v.t.* **(a)** (furnish with weapons) bewaffnen; mit Waffen ausrüsten ‹*Schiff*›; **(b)** ~ **oneself with sth.** sich mit etw. wappnen; **(c)** scharf machen ‹*Bombe usw.*›

armada /ɑ'mɑːdə/ *n.* Armada, *die*

armadillo /ɑːmə'dɪləʊ/ *n.*, *pl.* **~s** (Zool.) Gürteltier, *das*

armament /'ɑːməmənt/ *n.* **~[s]** Kriegsgerät, *das*

arm: **~band** *n.* Armbinde, *die;* **~chair 1** *n.* Sessel, *der;* **2** *adj.* **~chair critic** Hobby- *od.* Amateurkritiker, *der;* **~chair travel** Reisen in der Fantasie

armed /ɑːmd/ *adj.* bewaffnet; ~ **forces** Streitkräfte *Pl.;* ~ **neutrality** bewaffnete Neutralität

-armed *adj. in comb.* mit ... Armen; **two-~:** zweiarmig

Armenia /ɑ'miːnɪə/ *pr. n.* Armenien (*das*)

Armenian /ɑː'miːnɪən/ ▶ 897 |, ▶ 947 | **1** *adj.* armenisch; **sb. is ~:** jmd. ist Armenier/Armenierin. **2** *n.* **(a)** (person) Armenier, *der*/Armenierin, *die;* **(b)** (language) Armenisch, *das; see also* **English 2 a**

armful /'ɑːmfʊl/ *n.* **an ~ of fruit** ein Arm voll Obst; **flowers by the ~:** ganze Arme voll Blumen

'armhole *n.* Armloch, *das*

armistice /'ɑːmɪstɪs/ *n.* Waffenstillstand, *der;* **A~ Day** *Gedenktag des Endes des 1. Weltkriegs*

armless /'ɑːmlɪs/ *adj.* armlos

armor, armored (Amer.) ⇒ **armour, armoured**

armorial /ɑː'mɔːrɪəl/ *adj.* Wappen-; ~ **bearings** Wappen, *das*

armour /'ɑːmə(r)/ *n.* (Brit.) **(a)** *no pl.* (Hist.) Rüstung, *die;* **suit of ~:** Harnisch, *der;* **(b)** *no pl.* (steel plates) **~[-plate]** Panzerung, *die;* **(c)** *no pl.* (~ed vehicles) Panzerfahrzeuge

armoured /'ɑːməd/ *adj.* (Brit.) ~ **car/train** Panzerwagen/-zug, *der;* ~ **cable** armiertes Kabel; ~ **division** Panzerdivision, *die;* ~ **glass** Panzerglas, *das*

arm: **~pit** *n.* Achselhöhle, *die;* **~rest** *n.* Armlehne, *die*

army /'ɑːmɪ/ *n.* **(a)** (fighting force) Heer, *das;* **(b)** *no pl.*, *no indef. art.* (military profession) Militär, *das;* **be in the ~:** beim Militär sein; **go into** *or* **join the ~:** zum Militär gehen; (as a career) die Militärlaufbahn einschlagen; **(c)** (large number) Heer, *das;* **an ~ of workmen/ants** ein Heer von Arbeitern/Ameisen

aroma /ə'rəʊmə/ *n.* Duft, *der*

aromatherapy /ərəʊmə'θerəpɪ/ *n.*, *no pl.* Aromatherapie, *die*

aromatic /ærə'mætɪk/ *adj.* aromatisch (auch Chem.); duftend ‹*Blütenblätter, Nelken usw.*›

arose ⇒ **arise**

around /ə'raʊnd/ **1** *adv.* **(a)** (on every side) **[all] ~:** überall; **he waved his arms ~:** er ruderte mit den Armen; **(b)** (round) herum; **come ~ to sb.'s house** bei jmdm. vorbeikommen; **show sb. ~:** jmdn. herumführen; **pass the hat ~:** den Hut herumgehen lassen; **get ~ to doing sth.** [endlich] einmal daran denken, etw. zu tun; **[have a] look ~:** sich [ein bisschen] umsehen; **(c)** (coll.: near) in der Nähe; **we'll always be ~ when you need us** wir werden immer da sein, wenn du uns brauchst; **(d)** (coll.: in existence) vorhanden; **there's not much leather ~ these days** zur Zeit gibt es nur wenig Leder; **(e)** (in various places) **ask/look ~:** herumfragen/-schauen; **he's been ~** (fig.) er ist viel herumgekommen. **2** *prep.* **(a)** um [... herum]; **they had their arms ~ each other** sie hielten sich umschlungen; **darkness closed in ~ us** die Dunkelheit umfing uns (geh.) *od.* schloss uns ein; ~ **the back of the house** (position) hinter dem Haus; (direction) hinter das Haus; **(b)** (here and there in) **we went ~ the town** wir gingen durch die Stadt; **(c)** (approximately at) ~ **3 o'clock** gegen 3 Uhr; **I saw him somewhere ~ the station** ich habe ihn irgendwo am Bahnhof gesehen; **(d)** (approximately equal to) ungefähr

arousal /ə'raʊzl/ *n.* ⇒ **arouse:** Aufwachen, *das;* Erregung, *die;* Erweckung, *die*

arouse /ə'raʊz/ *v.t.* **(a)** (awake) [auf]wecken; **(b)** (excite, also sexually) erregen; (call into existence) erwecken ‹*Interesse, Begeisterung*›; erregen ‹*Hass, Leidenschaften, Verdacht*›

arr. *abbr.* **(a)** (Mus.) **arranged by** Arr.; **(b)** **arrives** Ank.

arraign /ə'reɪn/ *v.t.* anklagen (**for** wegen)

arrange /ə'reɪndʒ/ **1** *v.t.* **(a)** (order) anordnen; (adjust) in Ordnung bringen; **(b)** (Mus., Radio, etc.: adapt) bearbeiten; **(c)** (settle beforehand) ausmachen ‹*Termin*›; **(d)** (plan) planen ‹*Urlaub*›; aufstellen ‹*Stundenplan*›; **don't ~ anything**

for tomorrow nimm dir für morgen nichts vor. **2** *v.i.* (a) (plan) sorgen (**about, for** für); **~ for sb./sth. to do sth.** veranlassen *od.* dafür sorgen, dass jmd./etw. etw. tut; **can you ~ to be at home?** kannst du es so einrichten, dass du zu Hause bist?; (b) (agree) **they ~d to meet the following day** sie verabredeten sich für den nächsten Tag; **~ with sb. about sth.** sich mit jmdm. über etw. (*Akk.*) einigen

arrangement /əˈreɪndʒmənt/ *n.* (a) (ordering, order) Anordnung, *die;* (thing ordered) Arrangement, *das;* **seating ~:** Anordnung der Sitze; (b) (Mus., Radio, etc.: adapting, adaptation) Bearbeitung, *die;* **a guitar ~:** eine Bearbeitung *od.* ein Arrangement für Gitarre; (c) (settling beforehand) Vereinbarung, *die;* (of plans) Aufstellung, *die;* **by ~:** nach Vereinbarung; (d) *in pl.* (plans) Vorkehrungen; **make ~s** Vorkehrungen treffen; **holiday ~s** Urlaubsvorbereitungen; (e) (agreement) Vereinbarung, *die;* **make an ~ to do sth.** vereinbaren, etw. zu tun; (f) (resolution) Einigung, *die;* **I'm sure we can come to some ~ about ...:** wir können uns sicher irgendwie einigen über (+ *Akk.*) ...

arrant /ˈærənt/ *adj.* Erz‹*lump, -schurke, -lügner, -feigling*›; **~ nonsense** barer Unsinn

array /əˈreɪ/ **1** *v.t.* (formal: dress) schmücken; **~ sb. in sth.** jmdn. in etw. (*Akk.*) kleiden *od.* (geh.) hüllen. **2** *n.* Reihe, *die*

arrears /əˈrɪəz/ *n. pl.* (debts) Schulden *Pl.;* **be in ~ with sth.** mit etw. im Rückstand sein; **be paid in ~:** rückwirkend bezahlt werden

arrest /əˈrest/ **1** *v.t.* (a) (stop) aufhalten; zum Stillstand bringen ‹*Fluss*›; (b) (seize) verhaften, (temporarily) festnehmen ‹*Person*›; (c) (catch) erregen ‹*Aufmerksamkeit, Interesse*›. **2** *n.* (a) (stoppage) Stillstand, *der;* **cardiac ~:** Herzstillstand, *der;* (b) (of person) Verhaftung, *die;* (temporary) Festnahme, *die;* **under ~:** festgenommen

arrival /əˈraɪvl/ *n.* (a) Ankunft, *die;* (fig.: at decision etc.) Gelangen, *das* (**at** zu); (of mail etc.: coming) Kommen, *das;* „**A~**" 'Ankunft'; **~s hall** Ankunftshalle, *die;* (b) (appearance) Auftauchen, *das;* (c) (person) Ankömmling, *der;* (thing) Lieferung, *die;* **new ~:** (coll.: newborn baby) Neugeborene, *das;* **new ~s** Neuankömmlinge

arrive /əˈraɪv/ *v.i.* (a) ankommen; **when do we arrive at Frankfurt?** wann kommen wir in Frankfurt an?; **~ at a conclusion/an agreement** zu einem Schluss/einer Einigung kommen; (b) (establish oneself) es schaffen; (c) (be brought) eintreffen; (coll.: be born) ankommen; (d) (come) ‹*Stunde, Tag, Augenblick*›› kommen

arrogance /ˈærəgəns/ *n., no pl.* Arroganz, *die;* (presumptuousness) Anmaßung, *die*

arrogant /ˈærəgənt/ *adj.* arrogant; (presumptuous) anmaßend

arrogantly /ˈærəgəntlɪ/ *adv.* arrogant; (presumptuously) anmaßend; anmaßenderweise ‹*behaupten, verlangen*›

arrow /ˈærəʊ/ **1** *n.* (missile) Pfeil, *der;* (pointer) [Hinweis-, Richtungs]pfeil, *der.* **2** *v.t.* mit einem Pfeil/mit Pfeilen markieren

arrow: **~head** *n.* Pfeilspitze, *die;* **~ key** *n.* (Computing) Cursortaste, *die;* Pfeiltaste, *die*

arse /ɑːs/ *n.* (coarse) Arsch, *der* (derb)
~ aˈbout, ~ around *v.i.* (Brit. coarse) rumalbern (ugs.); rumblödeln (ugs.)

'arsehole *n.* (coarse) Arschloch, *das* (derb)

arsenal /ˈɑːsənl/ *n.* [Waffen]arsenal, *das;* (fig.) Arsenal, *das*

arsenic /ˈɑːsənɪk/ *n.* (Chem.) (a) Arsenik, *das;* (b) (element) Arsen, *das*

arson /ˈɑːsn/ *n.* Brandstiftung, *die*

arsonist /ˈɑːsənɪst/ *n.* Brandstifter, *der*/Brandstifterin, *die*

art /ɑːt/ *n.* (a) Kunst, *die;* **the ~s ⇒ fine art c;** **works of ~:** Kunstwerke *Pl.;* **~s and crafts** Kunsthandwerk, *das;* Kunstgewerbe, *das;* (b) *in pl.* (branch of study) Geisteswissenschaften *Pl.;* **faculty of ~s** philosophische Fakultät; (c) (cunning) List, *die*

art: **~ collection** *n.* Kunstsammlung, *die;* **~ collector** *n.* Kunstsammler, *der*/sammlerin, *die* **~ college** ⇒ **~ school**

art deco /ɑːt ˈdekəʊ/ *n., no pl.* Art deco, *die*

artefact, artifact /ˈɑːtɪfækt/ *n.* Artefakt, *das*

arterial /ɑːˈtɪərɪəl/ *adj.* arteriell; **~ road** Hauptverkehrsstraße, *die*

artery /ˈɑːtərɪ/ *n.* (a) ▶672 (Anat.) Schlagader, *die;* Arterie, *die* (bes. fachspr.); (b) (fig.: road etc.) [Haupt]verkehrsader, *die*

artesian /ɑːˈtiːzɪən, ɑːˈtiːʒən/ *adj.* **~ well** artesischer Brunnen

'art form *n.* (form of composition) [Kunst]gattung, *die;* (medium of expression) Kunst[form], *die*

artful /ˈɑːtfl/ *adj.* schlau; **~ dodger** Schlawiner, *der*

artfully /ˈɑːtfəlɪ/ *adv.* schlau

artfulness /ˈɑːtflnɪs/ *n., no pl.* Schlauheit, *die*

'art gallery *n.* Kunstgalerie, *die*

arthritic /ɑːˈθrɪtɪk/ (Med.) **1** *adj.* arthritisch. **2** *n.* Arthritiker, *der*/Arthritikerin, *die*

arthritis /ɑːˈθraɪtɪs/ *n.* ▶865 (Med.) Arthritis, *die* (fachspr.); Gelenkentzündung, *die*

artichoke /ˈɑːtɪtʃəʊk/ *n.* **[globe] ~:** Artischocke, *die;* **Jerusalem ~:** /dʒəˈruːsələm/ Topinamburwurzel, *die*

article /ˈɑːtɪkl/ **1** *n.* (a) (of constitution, treaty) Artikel, *der;* (of agreement) [Vertrags]punkt, *der;* (of the law) Paragraph, *der;* **~s [of association]** Satzung, *die;* **~s of apprenticeship/employment** Lehr-/Arbeitsvertrag, *der;* **~ of faith** (fig.) Glaubensbekenntnis, *das* (fig.); (b) (in magazine, newspaper) Artikel, *der;* (in technical journal) Beitrag, *der;* (c) (Ling.) Artikel, *der;* **definite/indefinite ~:** bestimmter/unbestimmter Artikel; (d) (thing) Artikel, *der;* **an ~ of furniture/clothing** ein Möbel-/Kleidungsstück; **an ~ of value** ein Wertgegenstand. **2** *v.t.* in die Lehre geben (**to** bei); **be ~d to sb.** bei jmdm. in der Lehre sein

articled /ˈɑːtɪkld/ *adj.* **~ clerk** (Law) Rechtspraktikant, *der*/-praktikantin, *die;* ≈ Rechtsreferendar, *der*/-referendarin, *die*

articulate 1 /ɑːˈtɪkjʊlət/ *adj.* (a) (clear) verständlich; (b) (eloquent) redegewandt; **be ~/not very ~:** sich gut/nicht sehr gut ausdrücken [können]. **2** /ɑːˈtɪkjʊleɪt/ *v.t. a)* usu. *in pass.* durch Gelenke/ein Gelenk verbinden; **~d lorry** Sattelzug, *der;* (b) (pronounce) [deutlich] aussprechen; (utter, express) artikulieren. **3** *v.i.* (a) (speak distinctly) deutlich sprechen; (b) (form a joint) **~ with sth.** mit etw. Gelenke/ein Gelenk bilden

articulately /ɑːˈtɪkjʊlətlɪ/ *adv.* klar

articulation /ɑːtɪkjʊˈleɪʃn/ *n.* (a) (clear speech) deutliche Aussprache; (b) (act of speaking) Artikulation, *die*

artifice /ˈɑːtɪfɪs/ *n.* List, *die*

artificial /ɑːtɪˈfɪʃl/ *adj.* (a) (not natural) künstlich; Kunst-; (not real) unecht; imitiert; **~ sweetener** Süßstoff, *der;* **~ limb** Prothese, *die;* **~ eye** Glasauge, *das;* (b) (affected) affektiert; (insincere) gekünstelt; **she wore an ~ smile for the cameras** für die Fotografen setzte sie ein einstudiertes Lächeln auf

artificial: **~ hoˈrizon** *n.* Kreiselhorizont, *der;* **~ inseminaˈtion** /ɑːtɪfɪʃl ɪnsemɪˈneɪʃn/ *n.* künstliche Besamung; **~ inˈtelligence** *n.* künstliche Intelligenz

artificiality /ɑːtɪfɪʃɪˈælɪtɪ/ *n., no pl.* ⇒ **artificial:** Künstlichkeit, *die;* Unechtheit, *die;* Affektiertheit, *die;* Gekünsteltheit, *die*

artificial: **~ ˈkidney** ⇒ **kidney machine;** **~ ˈlanguage** *n.* Kunstsprache, *die*

artificially /ɑːtɪˈfɪʃəlɪ/ *adv.* (a) (unnaturally) künstlich; (b) (affectedly) affektiert; (insincerely) gekünstelt

artificial respiˈration *n.* künstliche Beatmung

artillery /ɑːˈtɪlərɪ/ *n.* Artillerie, *die*

artisan /ˈɑːtɪzn, ɑːtɪˈzæn/ *n.* [Kunst]handwerker, *der*

artist /ˈɑːtɪst/ *n.* ▶887 (a) (painter, musician, etc.; also fig.) Künstler, *der*/Künstlerin, *die;* (b) ⇒ **artiste**

artiste /ɑːˈtiːst/ *n.* Artist, *der*/Artistin, *die*

artistic /ɑːˈtɪstɪk/ *adj.* (a) (of art) Kunst-; künstlerisch; **~ movement** Kunstrichtung, *die;* (b) (of artists) Künstler-; künstlerisch; **~ circles** Künstlerkreise; (c) (made with art) kunstvoll; Kunst-; **a truly ~ piece of poetry/writing**

As

When used as a preposition or conjunction to mean *like,* the usual translation is **wie:**

as usual	= wie gewöhnlich
as explained below	= wie unten erklärt
as so often	= wie so oft
as you may have heard	= wie Sie vielleicht gehört haben
as was the custom there	= wie es dort Sitte war

Note also:

a coat the same colour as mine	= ein Mantel in derselben Farbe wie meiner
a writer such as Dickens	= ein Schriftsteller wie Dickens

However if the sense is *in the manner of* or *in the function of,* the translation is **als** (note that *a/an* is not translated):

dressed as a sailor	= als Matrose gekleidet
He works as an engineer	= Er arbeitet als Ingenieur
my duty as a father	= meine Pflicht als Vater

In comparisons *(as ... as ...)* the first *as* is translated by **so,** but this is often omitted in set similes:

She is as old as my mother	= Sie ist so alt wie meine Mutter
This car is not as fast as yours	= Dieses Auto ist nicht so schnell wie deins
He is not as good a cook as you	= Er ist kein so guter Koch wie du

He is as wily as a fox	= Er ist schlau wie ein Fuchs

Where a verb such as *can/could* or *want/like* comes after the *as,* **wie** is usually omitted:

Come as quickly as you can	= Komm, so schnell du kannst
Take as much as you like	= Nimm, so viel du willst

And where the sense of *as ... as* is the same as *however,* the translation is *wie ... auch:*

As fast as we rowed (= However fast we rowed), the others rowed faster	= Wie schnell wir auch ruderten, die anderen ruderten schneller

For the conjunction in time expressions, the translations are **als** (with the sense of *when*) or **während** (with the sense of *while*):

As I stepped into the house, I heard her voice	= Als ich in das Haus hineintrat, hörte ich ihre Stimme
As we were talking, the doorbell rang	= Während wir uns unterhielten, klingelte es

And expressing a reason with the sense of *since,* the translation is **da:**

As I am going to London I can take it with me	= Da ich nach London fahre, kann ich es mitnehmen

ein dichterisches/schriftstellerisches Kunstwerk; **(d)** (naturally skilled in art) künstlerisch begabt; **(e)** (appreciative of art) kunstverständig; ~ **sense** Kunstverständnis, *das*

artistically /ɑ:'tɪstɪkəlɪ/ *adv.* **(a)** (in art) künstlerisch; **(b)** (with art) kunstvoll ‹*geschmückt, gestaltet*›

artless /'ɑ:tlɪs/ *adj.* **(a)** (guileless) arglos; **(b)** (simple) schlicht; ~ **beauty/grace** natürliche Schönheit/Anmut

art nouveau /ɑ: nu:'vəʊ/ *n.* Jugendstil, *der*

'arts centre *n.* Kunstzentrum, *das*

art: ~ **school** *n.* Kunsthochschule, *die;* ~**work** *n.* Illustrationen *Pl.;* Bildmaterial, *das*

arty /'ɑ:tɪ/ *adj.* (coll.) auf Künstler machend; **he's an** ~ **type** er ist so ein Künstlertyp; ~**-[and-]crafty** (joc.) auf Kunstgewerbe gemacht

Aryan /'eərɪən/ **1** *adj.* indogermanisch. **2** *n.* **(a)** ▶ 897 | (language) Indogermanisch, *das;* **(b)** (person) Arier, *der*/Arierin, *die* (bes. ns.); Indogermane, *der*/Indogermanin, *die*

as /əz, stressed æz/ **1** *adv. in main sentence* (in same degree) **as ... [as ...]** so ... [wie ...]; **half as much** halb so viel; **they did as much as they could** sie taten, was sie konnten; **as good a player [as he]** nicht so guter Spieler [wie er]. **2** *rel. adv. or conj. in subord. clause* **(a)** *expr. degree* **[as** *or* **so]** ... **as** ...: [so ...] wie ...; **as quickly as possible** so schnell wie möglich; **as ... as you can** so ...[, wie] Sie können; **come as quickly as you can** kommen Sie, so schnell Sie können; **quick as a flash** blitzschnell; **(b)** (though) ... **as he** *etc.* **is/was** obwohl er *usw.* ... ist/war; **intelligent as she is,** ...: obwohl sie ziemlich intelligent ist, ...; **safe as it might be,** ...: obwohl es vielleicht ungefährlich ist, ...; **(c)** (however much) **try as he might/would, he could not concentrate** sosehr er sich auch bemühte, er konnte sich nicht konzentrieren; **(d)** *expr. manner* wie; **as it were** sozusagen; gewissermaßen; **as you were!** Kommando zurück!; **(e)** *expr. time* als; während; **as and when** wann immer; **as we climbed the stairs** als wir die Treppe hinaufgingen; **as we were talking** während wir uns unterhielten; **(f)** *expr. reason* da; **(g)** *expr. result* **so ... as to ...:** so ... zu; **would you be so kind as to help us?** würden Sie so freundlich sein und uns helfen?;

(h) *expr. purpose* **so as to ...:** um ... zu ...; **(i)** *expr. illustration* wie [zum Beispiel]; **industrial areas, as the northeast of England for example** Industriegebiete wie zum Beispiel der Nordosten Englands. **3** *prep.* **(a)** (in the function of) als; **as an artist** als Künstler; **speaking as a parent,** ...: als Mutter/Vater ...; **(b)** (like) wie; **they regard him as a fool** sie halten ihn für einen Dummkopf. **4** *rel. pron.* (which) **they danced, as was the custom there** sie tanzten, wie es dort Sitte war; **he was shocked, as were we all** er war wie wir alle schockiert; **the same as ...:** der-/die-/dasselbe wie ...; **such as** wie zum Beispiel; **they enjoy such foreign foods as ...:** sie essen gern ausländische Lebensmittel wie ... **5 as far** ⇒ **far 1 d; as for ...:** was ... angeht; **as from ...:** von ... an; **as [it] is** wie die Dinge liegen; wie es aussieht; **the place is untidy enough as it is** es ist schon liederlich genug[, wie es jetzt ist]; **as of ...** (Amer.) von ... an; **as to** hinsichtlich (+ *Gen.*); **nothing further was mentioned as to holiday plans** von Urlaubsplänen wurde nichts weiter gesagt; **as was** wie es einmal war; **Miss Tay as was** das frühere Fräulein Tay; **as yet** bis jetzt; **as yet the plan is only under discussion** der Plan wird noch diskutiert

a.s.a.p. *abbr.* **as soon as possible**

asbestos /æz'bestɒs, æs'bestɒs/ *n.* **(a)** Asbest, *der;* **(b)** (mineral) Amiant, *der*

ascend /ə'send/ **1** *v.i.* **(a)** (go up) hinaufgehen *od.* -steigen; (climb up) hinaufklettern; (by vehicle) hinauffahren; (come up) heraufkommen; **Christ** ~**ed into heaven** Christus fuhr auf gen Himmel (geh.); **(b)** (rise) aufsteigen; ‹*Hubschrauber:*› höhersteigen; **(c)** (slope upwards) ‹*Hügel, Straße:*› ansteigen; **the stairs** ~ **very steeply** die Treppe ist sehr steil. **2** *v.t.* **(a)** (go up) hinaufsteigen, hinaufgehen ‹*Treppe, Leiter, Berg*›; ~ **a rope** an einem Seil hochklettern; **(b)** (come up) heraufsteigen; **(c)** ~ **the throne** den Thron besteigen

ascendancy /ə'sendənsɪ/ *n., no pl.* Vorherrschaft, *die*

ascendant /ə'sendənt/ *n.* **(a)** (Astrol.) Aszendent, *der;* **(b)** **in the** ~**:** im Aufsteigen begriffen

Ascension /ə'senʃn/ *n.* (Relig.) **[the]** ~**:** [Christi] Himmelfahrt

A'scension Day n. Himmelfahrtstag, der

ascent /ə'sent/ n. (also fig.) Aufstieg, der

ascertain /æsə'teɪn/ v.t. feststellen; ermitteln ‹Daten, Fakten›

ascertainable /æsə'teɪnəbl/ adj. feststellbar; zu ermittelnd ‹Daten, Fakten›

ascetic /ə'setɪk/ **1** adj. asketisch. **2** n. **(a)** Asket, der/ Asketin, die; **(b)** (Relig. Hist.) Eremit, der

asceticism /ə'setɪsɪzm/ n., no pl. Askese, die

ascribe /ə'skraɪb/ v.t. **(a)** (regard as belonging) zuschreiben (**to** Dat.); **(b)** (attribute, impute) zurückführen (**to** auf + Akk.)

aseptic /er'septɪk/ adj. aseptisch

asexual /er'sekʃʊəl/ adj. asexuell

ash¹ /æʃ/ n. **(a)** (tree) Esche, die; **(b)** (wood) Eschenholz, das

ash² n. in sing. or pl. (powder) Asche, die

ashamed /ə'ʃeɪmd/ adj. be ∼: beschämt sein; sich schämen; **be ∼ of sb./sth.** sich jmds./einer Sache wegen schämen; **be/feel ∼ for sb./sth.** sich für jmdn./etw. schämen; **be ∼ of oneself for doing sth./be ∼ to do sth.** sich schämen, etw. zu tun; **I'm ∼ to admit that I told a lie** ich muss leider zugeben, dass ich gelogen habe

ash: ∼ blonde 1 adj. aschblond; **2** n. Aschblonde, die; **∼can** n. (Amer.) Mülleimer, der

ashen /'æʃn/ adj. (ash-coloured) aschfarben; aschfahl ‹Gesicht›; **∼ grey** aschgrau

ashore /ə'ʃɔː(r)/ adv. (position) an Land; am Ufer; (direction) an Land; ans Ufer

ash: ∼pan n. Aschkasten, der; **∼tray** n. Aschenbecher, der; **∼ tree** ⇒ **ash¹ a; Ash 'Wednesday** n. Aschermittwoch, der; **∼wood** ⇒ **ash¹ b**

Asia /'eɪʃə/ pr. n. Asien (das); **∼ 'Minor** Kleinasien (das)

Asian /'eɪʃən, 'eɪʒən/ **1** adj. asiatisch. **2** n. Asiat, der/ Asiatin, die

aside /ə'saɪd/ **1** adv. beiseite; zur Seite; **stand ∼!** treten Sie zur Seite!; **I pulled the curtain ∼:** ich zog den Vorhang zur Seite; **take sb. ∼:** jmdn. beiseite nehmen. **2** n. Apart, das; Beiseitesprechen, das

asinine /'æsɪnaɪn/ adj. dämlich

ask /ɑːsk/ **1** v.t. **(a)** fragen; **∼ [sb.] a question** [jmdm.] eine Frage stellen; **∼ sb.'s name** nach jmds. Namen fragen; **∼ sb. [sth.]** jmdn. [nach etw.] fragen; **∼ sb. about sth.** jmdn. nach etw. fragen; **I '∼ you!** (coll.) ich muss schon sagen!; **if you ∼ 'me** (coll.) [also] wenn du mich fragst; **(b)** (seek to obtain) **∼ sth.** um etw. bitten; **how much are you ∼ing for that car?** wieviel verlangen Sie für das Auto?; **∼ sb. to do sth.** jmdn. [darum] bitten, etw. zu tun; **∼ a lot of sb.** viel von jmdm. verlangen; **∼ing price** geforderter Preis; **it's yours for the ∼ing** du kannst es gern haben; **(c)** (invite) einladen; **∼ sb. to dinner** jmdn. zum Essen einladen; **∼ sb. out** jmdn. einladen. **2** v.i. **you may well ∼:** du hast allen Grund zu fragen; **∼ after sb./sth.** nach jmdm./etw. fragen; **∼ for sth./sb.** etw./jmdn. verlangen; **∼ for it** (coll.: invite trouble) es herausfordern

askance /ə'skæns, ə'skɑːns/ adv. **look ∼ at sb./sth.** jmdn. befremdet ansehen/etw. mit Befremden betrachten

askew /ə'skjuː/ adv., pred. adj. schief

asleep /ə'sliːp/ pred. adj. **(a)** (lit. or fig.) schlafend; **be/lie ∼:** schlafen; **fall ∼** (also euphem.) einschlafen; **(b)** (numb) eingeschlafen ‹Arm, Bein›

asparagus /ə'spærəgəs/ n. Spargel, der

aspect /'æspekt/ n. **(a)** Aspekt, der; **(b)** (position looking in a given direction) Lage, die; (front) Seite, die; **have a southern ∼:** nach Süden liegen

aspen /'æspən/ n. (Bot.) Espe, die

aspersion /ə'spɜːʃn/ n. Verunglimpfung, die; **cast ∼s on sb./sth.** jmdn./etw. in den Schmutz ziehen

asphalt /'æsfælt/ **1** n. Asphalt, der. **2** v.t. asphaltieren

asphyxia /æs'fɪksɪə/ n., no pl. (Med.) Asphyxie, die (fachspr.); Erstickung, die

asphyxiate /æs'fɪksɪeɪt/ (Med.) **1** v.t. ersticken; **be ∼d by sth.** an etw. (Dat.) ersticken. **2** v.i. ersticken

aspic /'æspɪk/ n. (jelly) Aspik, der

aspidistra /æspɪ'dɪstrə/ n. (Bot.) Schusterpalme, die

aspirant /ə'spaɪərənt, 'æspərənt/ adj. aufstrebend

aspiration /æspə'reɪʃn/ n. Streben, das; **have ∼s to sth.** nach etw. streben

aspire /ə'spaɪə(r)/ v.i. **∼ to** or **after sth.** nach etw. streben

aspirin /'æspərɪn/ n. (Med.) Aspirin (Wz), das; Kopfschmerztablette, die

aspiring /ə'spaɪərɪŋ/ adj. aufstrebend

ass¹ /æs/ n. (Zool.; also fig.) Esel, der; **make an ∼ of oneself** sich blamieren

ass² (Amer.) ⇒ **arse**

assail /ə'seɪl/ v.t. **(a)** angreifen; **(b)** (fig.) **∼ sb. with questions** jmdn. mit Fragen überschütten; **I was ∼ed with doubts** mich überkamen Zweifel

assailant /ə'seɪlənt/ n. Angreifer, der/Angreiferin, die

assassin /ə'sæsɪn/ n. Mörder, der/Mörderin, die

assassinate /ə'sæsɪneɪt/ v.t. ermorden; **be ∼d** einem Attentat zum Opfer fallen

assassination /əsæsɪ'neɪʃn/ n. Mord, der **(of** an + Dat.); **∼ attempt** Attentat, das **(on** auf + Akk.)

assault /ə'sɔːlt/ **1** n. **(a)** Angriff, der; (fig.) Anschlag, der; **verbal ∼** verbale Angriffe; **(b)** (Mil.) Sturmangriff, der; **∼ craft** Sturmboot, das; **∼ course** Hindernisbahn, die. **2** v.t. **(a)** (lit. or fig.) angreifen; **(b)** (Mil.) stürmen

assemblage /ə'semblɪdʒ/ n. **(a)** (of things, persons) Ansammlung, die; **(b)** (bringing together) Zusammentragen, das; (fitting together) Zusammensetzen, das

assemble /ə'sembl/ **1** v.t. **(a)** zusammentragen ‹Beweise, Material, Sammlung›; zusammenrufen ‹Personen›; **(b)** (fit together) zusammenbauen. **2** v.i. sich versammeln

assembly /ə'semblɪ/ n. **(a)** (coming together, meeting, deliberative body) Versammlung, die; (in school) (tägliche Versammlung aller Schüler und Lehrer zur Morgenandacht; **(b)** (fitting together) Zusammenbau, der; Montage, die; **(c)** (assembled unit) Einheit, die

as'sembly line n. Fließband, das

assent /ə'sent/ **1** v.i. zustimmen; **∼ to sth.** einer Sache (Dat.) zustimmen. **2** n. Zustimmung, die

assert /ə'sɜːt/ v.t. **(a)** geltend machen; **∼ oneself** sich durchsetzen; **(b)** (declare) behaupten; beteuern ‹Unschuld›

assertion /ə'sɜːʃn/ n. Geltendmachen, das; (declaration) Behauptung, die

assertive /ə'sɜːtɪv/ adj. energisch ‹Person›; bestimmt ‹Ton, Verhalten›; fest ‹Stimme›

assess /ə'ses/ v.t. **(a)** (evaluate) einschätzen; beurteilen; **(b)** (value) schätzen; taxieren; **(c)** (fix amount of) festsetzen ‹Steuer, Bußgeld usw.› **(at** auf + Akk.)

assessment /ə'sesmənt/ n. **(a)** (evaluation) Einschätzung, die; Beurteilung, die; **(b)** (valuation) Schätzung, die; Taxierung, die; **(c)** (fixing amount of damages or fine) Festsetzung, die; (of tax) Veranlagung, die; **(d)** (tax to be paid) Steuerbescheid, der

asset /'æset/ n. **(a)** Vermögenswert, der; **my [personal] ∼s** mein [persönlicher] Besitz; **(b)** (fig.) (useful quality) Vorzug, der **(to** für); (person) Stütze, die; (thing) Hilfe, die

'asset-stripping n. (Commerc.) Ankauf unrentabler Unternehmen, von denen einzelne Teile gewinnbringend weiterverkauft werden

assiduous /ə'sɪdjʊəs/ adj. **(a)** (diligent) eifrig; (conscientious) gewissenhaft; **(b)** (obsequiously attentive) beflissen

assign /ə'saɪn/ v.t. **(a)** (allot) **∼ sth. to sb.** jmdm. etw. zuweisen; (transfer) jmdm. etw. übereignen; **(b)** (appoint) zuteilen; **∼ sb. to a job/task** jmdn. mit einer Arbeit/Aufgabe betrauen; **∼ sb. to do sth.** jmdn. damit betrauen, etw. zu tun; **(c)** (specify) festsetzen ‹Zeit, Datum, Grenzwert›; **(d)** (ascribe) angeben; **∼ a cause to sth.** einen Grund für etw. angeben

assignment /ə'saɪnmənt/ n. **(a)** (allotting) Zuteilung, die; (of property) Übereignung, die; **(b)** (task) Aufgabe, die; (Amer. Sch. and Univ.) Arbeit, die; **(c)** (of reason, cause) Aufgabe, die

assimilate /ə'sɪmɪleɪt/ *v.t.* **(a)** (make like) angleichen; ∼ **sth. with** *or* **to sth.** etw. an etw. (*Akk.*) angleichen; **(b)** (fig.) aufnehmen ‹*Informationen, Einflüsse usw.*›

assimilation /əsɪmɪ'leɪʃn/ *n.* **(a)** (making or becoming like) Angleichung, *die* (**to, with** an + *Akk.*); **(b)** (fig.: of information, influences, etc.) Aufnahme, *die*

assist /ə'sɪst/ **1** *v.t.* (help) helfen (+ *Dat.*); voranbringen ‹*Vorgang, Prozess*›; ∼ **sb. to do** *or* **in doing sth.** jmdm. helfen, etw. zu tun; ∼ **sb. with sth.** jmdm. bei etw. helfen. **2** *v.i.* **(a)** (help) helfen; ∼ **with sth./in doing sth.** bei etw. helfen/helfen, etw. zu tun; **(b)** (take part) mitarbeiten (**in** an + *Dat.*)

assistance /ə'sɪstəns/ *n., no pl.* Hilfe, *die;* **give** ∼ **to sb.** jmdm. behilflich sein; **be of** ∼ [**to sb.**] [jmdm.] behilflich sein

assistant /ə'sɪstənt/ ▶ 887⟩ **1** *n.* (helper) Helfer, *der*/Helferin, *die;* (subordinate) Mitarbeiter, *der*/Mitarbeiterin, *die;* (of professor, artist) Assistent, *der*/Assistentin, *die;* (in shop) Verkäufer, *der*/Verkäuferin, *die.* **2** *attrib. adj.* ∼ **manager** stellvertretender Geschäftsführer; ∼ **editor** Redaktionsassistent, *der;* ∼ **professor** (Amer.) ≈ Assistenzprofessor, *der*

associate 1 /ə'səʊʃɪət, ə'səʊsɪət/ *n.* **(a)** (partner) Partner, *der*/Partnerin, *die;* Kompagnon, *der;* (colleague) Kollege, *der*/Kollegin, *die;* (of gangster) Komplize, *der*/Komplizin, *die;* **(b)** (subordinate member) außerordentliches Mitglied. **2** /ə'səʊʃɪət, ə'səʊsɪət/ *adj.* beigeordnet; außerordentlich ‹*Mitglied usw.*›. **3** /ə'səʊʃɪeɪt, ə'səʊsɪeɪt/ *v.t.* **(a)** (join) in Verbindung bringen; **be** ∼**d** in Verbindung stehen; **(b)** (connect in the mind) in Verbindung bringen, (Psych.) assoziieren (**mit** with); **(c)** ∼ **oneself with sth.** sich einer Sache (*Dat.*) anschließen. **4** *v.i.* ∼ **with sb.** mit jmdm. verkehren *od.* Umgang haben

association /əsəʊsɪ'eɪʃn/ *n.* **(a)** (organization) Verband, *der;* Vereinigung, *die;* **articles** *or* **deeds of** ∼: Satzung, *die;* **(b)** (mental connection) Assoziation, *die;* ∼ **of ideas** Gedankenassoziation, *die;* **have** ∼**s for sb.** bei jmdm. Assoziationen hervorrufen; **(c) A**∼ **football** (Brit.) Fußball, *der;* **(d)** (connection) Verbindung, *die;* **(e)** (cooperation) Zusammenarbeit, *die*

assorted /ə'sɔːtɪd/ *adj.* gemischt ‹*Bonbons, Sortiment*›; **cardigans of** ∼ **kinds** verschiedenerlei Strickjacken

assortment /ə'sɔːtmənt/ *n.* Sortiment, *das;* **a good** ∼ **of hats** eine gute Auswahl an Hüten

Asst. *abbr.* **Assistant** Ass.

assuage /ə'sweɪdʒ/ *v.t.* stillen; (soothe) besänftigen ‹*Person, Ärger*›; lindern ‹*Schmerz, Sorge*›

assume /ə'sjuːm/ *v.t.* **(a)** voraussetzen; ausgehen von; **assuming that** ...: vorausgesetzt, dass ...; **he's not so stupid as we** ∼**d** him to be er ist nicht so dumm, wie wir angenommen haben; **(b)** (undertake) übernehmen ‹*Amt, Pflichten*›; **(c)** (take on) annehmen ‹*Namen, Rolle*›; gewinnen ‹*Aspekt, Bedeutung*›; **under an** ∼**d name** unter einem Decknamen

assumption /ə'sʌmpʃn/ *n.* **(a)** Annahme, *die;* **going on the** ∼ **that** ...: vorausgesetzt, dass ...; **(b)** (undertaking) Übernahme, *die;* **(c) the A**∼ (Relig.) Mariä Himmelfahrt

assurance /ə'ʃʊərəns/ *n.* **(a)** Zusicherung, *die;* **I give you my** ∼ **that** ...: ich versichere Ihnen, dass ...; **I can give you no** ∼ **that** ...: ich kann Ihnen nicht versprechen, dass ...; **(b)** *no pl.* (self-confidence) Selbstsicherheit, *die;* **(c)** *no pl.* (Brit.: insurance) Versicherung, *die*

assure /ə'ʃʊə(r)/ *v.t.* **(a)** versichern (+ *Dat.*); ∼ **sb. of sth.** jmdm. einer Sache (*Gen.*) versichern (geh.); **(b)** (convince) ∼ **sb./oneself** jmdn./sich überzeugen; **(c)** (make certain or safe) gewährleisten; **(d)** (Brit.: insure) versichern

assured /ə'ʃʊəd/ *adj.* gesichert ‹*Tatsache*›; gewährleistet ‹*Erfolg*›; **be** ∼ **of sth.** sich (*Dat.*) einer Sache (*Gen.*) sicher sein

assuredly /ə'ʃʊərɪdlɪ/ *adv.* gewiss

aster /'æstə(r)/ *n.* Aster, *die*

asterisk /'æstərɪsk/ **1** *n.* Sternchen, *das.* **2** *v.t.* mit einem Sternchen versehen

astern /ə'stɜːn/ *adv.* (Naut., Aeronaut.) achtern; (towards the rear) achteraus; ∼ **of sth.** hinter etw. (*Dat.*); **full speed** ∼! volle Kraft zurück!

asteroid /'æstərɔɪd/ *n.* (Astron.) Asteroid, *der*

asthma /'æsmə/ *n.* ▶ 865⟩ (Med.) Asthma, *das*

asthmatic /æs'mætɪk/ (Med.) **1** *adj.* asthmatisch. **2** *n.* Asthmatiker, *der*/Asthmatikerin, *die*

astir /ə'stɜː(r)/ *pred. adj.* in Bewegung; (out of bed) auf den Beinen

astonish /ə'stɒnɪʃ/ *v.t.* erstaunen

astonishing /ə'stɒnɪʃɪŋ/ *adj.,* **astonishingly** /ə'stɒnɪʃɪŋlɪ/ *adv.* erstaunlich

astonishment /ə'stɒnɪʃmənt/ *n., no pl.* Erstaunen, *das;* **in utter** ∼: äußerst erstaunt

astound /ə'staʊnd/ *v.t.* verblüffen; [sehr] überraschen

astounding /ə'staʊndɪŋ/ *adj.* erstaunlich

astrakhan /æstrə'kæn/ *n.* Astrachan, *der*

astray /ə'streɪ/ **1** *adv.* in die Irre; **sb. goes** ∼: jmd. verirrt sich; **sth. goes** ∼ (is mislaid) etw. wird verlegt; (is lost) etw. geht verloren; **lead** ∼: irreführen; **go/lead** ∼ (fig.) in die Irre gehen/führen; (into sin) vom rechten Weg abkommen/abbringen. **2** *pred. adj.* **be** ∼: sich verirrt haben; (fig.: be in error) sich irren

astride /ə'straɪd/ **1** *adv.* rittlings ‹*sitzen*›; breitbeinig ‹*stehen*›; ∼ **of sth.** rittlings auf etw. (*Dat./Akk.*). **2** *prep.* **(a)** rittlings auf (+ *Dat.*); **(b)** (extending across) zu beiden Seiten (+ *Gen.*)

astringent /ə'strɪndʒənt/ **1** *adj.* **(a)** herb, streng ‹*Geschmack*›; stechend, beißend ‹*Geruch*›; **(b)** (styptic) adstringierend (Med.); blutstillend; **(c)** (severe) scharf. **2** *n.* Adstringens, *das*

astrologer /ə'strɒlədʒə(r)/ *n.* ▶ 887⟩ Astrologe, *der*/Astrologin, *die*

astrological /æstrə'lɒdʒɪkl/ *adj.* astrologisch

astrology /ə'strɒlədʒɪ/ *n., no pl.* Astrologie, *die*

astronaut /'æstrənɔːt/ *n.* ▶ 887⟩ Astronaut, *der*/Astronautin, *die*

astronautical /æstrə'nɔːtɪkl/ *adj.* astronautisch

astronautics /æstrə'nɔːtɪks/ *n., no pl.* Raumfahrt, *die*

astronomer /ə'strɒnəmə(r)/ *n.* ▶ 887⟩ Astronom, *der*/Astronomin, *die*

astronomical /æstrə'nɒmɪkl/ *adj.,* **astronomically** /æstrə'nɒmɪkəlɪ/ *adv.* (lit. or fig.) astronomisch

astronomy /ə'strɒnəmɪ/ *n., no pl.* Astronomie, *die*

astrophysics /æstrəʊ'fɪzɪks/ *n., no pl.* Astrophysik, *die*

astute /ə'stjuːt/ *adj.* scharfsinnig

asylum /ə'saɪləm/ *n.* Asyl, *das;* **grant sb.** ∼: jmdm. Asyl gewähren; **political** ∼: politisches Asyl; ∼ **seeker** Asylsuchende, *der/die*

asymmetric /æsɪ'metrɪk, eɪsɪ'metrɪk/, **asymmetrical** /æsɪ'metrɪkl, eɪsɪ'metrɪkl/ *adj.* asymmetrisch; unsymmetrisch

asymmetry /æ'sɪmɪtrɪ, eɪ'sɪmɪtrɪ/ *n.* Asymmetrie, *die*

at /ət, *stressed* æt/ *prep.* ▶ 648⟩ **(a)** *expr.* place an (+ *Dat.*); **at the station** am Bahnhof; **at the baker's/butcher's/grocer's** beim Bäcker/Fleischer/Kaufmann; **at the chemist's** in der Apotheke/Drogerie; **at the supermarket** im Supermarkt; **at my mother's** bei meiner Mutter; **at the party** auf der Party; **at the office/hotel** im Büro/Hotel; **at Dover** in Dover; **(b)** *expr. time* **at Christmas/Whitsun/Easter** [zu *od.* an] Weihnachten/Pfingsten/Ostern; **at six o'clock** um sechs Uhr; **at midnight** um Mitternacht; **at midday** am Mittag; mittags; **at [the age of]** 40 mit 40; im Alter von 40; **at this/the moment** in diesem/im Augenblick *od.* Moment; **at the first attempt** beim ersten Versuch; **(c)** *expr. price* **at £2.50 [each]** zu *od.* für [je] 2,50 Pfund; **(d) she's still 'at it** sie ist immer noch dabei; **while we're/you're etc. 'at it** wenn wir *usw.* schon dabei sind/bist *usw.;* **so while I was 'at it,...:** und wo *od.* da ich schon dabei war...; **at that** (at that point) dabei; (at that provocation) daraufhin; (moreover) noch dazu

ate ⇒ **eat**

atheism /'eɪθɪɪzm/ *n., no pl.* Atheismus, *der*

atheist /'eɪθɪɪst/ *n.* Atheist, *der*/Atheistin, *die*

Athenian /ə'θiːnɪən/ **1** *adj.* athenisch. **2** *n.* Athener, *der*/Athenerin, *die*

At

Where?

an + dative describes position:

at the corner of the street	= an der Straßenecke
at the royal court	= am königlichen Hof
at the side	= an der Seite

But note

at the top/bottom	= oben/unten
at the front/back	= vorne/hinten
at the top of the pile	= oben auf dem Stapel
at the bottom of page 4	= auf Seite 4 unten
at the back of the house	= (inside) hinten im Haus; (outside) hinterm Haus

When referring to someone's house or shop, **bei** + dative is used:

at my uncle's	= bei meinem Onkel
at the Robinsons	= bei Robinson
at the baker's	= beim Bäcker
at Woolworth's	= bei Woolworth

Note that there is usually no article with a name.

In the case of buildings, **an** indicates the general area (including outside), while **in** is used for the inside:

They are at the theatre (i.e. inside)	= Sie sind im Theater
We met at the theatre (i.e. inside/ just outside)	= Wir trafen uns im/am Theater

bei is also often used for a place of work:

He works at the bank	= Er arbeitet bei der Bank

but in the case of most offices and shops it is **in**:

at the bookshop	= in der Buchhandlung
at the supermarket	= im Supermarkt
at the office	= im Büro
at the travel agent's	= im Reisebüro

Cf. also

at school	= in der Schule
at university	= auf der Universität
at a party	= auf einer Party

With place names, use **in**:

You have to change at Cologne	= Sie müssen in Köln umsteigen

When?

With an actual time, *at* is translated by **um**:

at 9 a.m.	= um 9 Uhr (morgens)
at 9 p.m.	= um 9 Uhr abends or 21 Uhr
at midday/midnight	= um zwölf Uhr mittags/ um Mitternacht

But note

at a late hour	= zu später Stunde
at night	= bei Nacht
at sunrise/sunset	= bei Sonnenaufgang/ Sonnenuntergang

With the main church festivals, *at* is either not translated or **zu** (or in South Germany **an**) is used:

She's coming at Christmas/Easter	= Sie kommt [zu or an] Weihnachten/Ostern

Cf. also

at (5 minute) intervals	= in Abständen (von 5 Minuten)
at this moment	= in diesem Augenblick
at any moment or at any time	= jederzeit

How old?

at (the age of) sixty	= im Alter von sechzig
too old at forty	= mit vierzig schon zu alt
at her age	= in ihrem Alter

How much?

Expressing price, the translation is **zu**:

two pounds at fifty pence a pound	= zwei Pfund zu fünfzig Pence das Pfund
six oranges at 30p each	= sechs Orangen zu 30 Pence das Stück
at the same price	= zum gleichen Preis

With superlatives

She was at her most charming	= Sie zeigte sich von ihrer charmantesten Seite
I am not at my best in the morning	= Morgens bin ich nicht gerade in Höchstform
This is an example of Czech music at its most captivating	= Das ist eines der reizvollsten Beispiele tschechischer Musik

---

Athens /'æθɪnz/ *pr. n.* ▶ 1159 | Athen (*das*)
athlete /'æθliːt/ *n.* Athlet, *der*/Athletin, *die;* Sportler, *der*/ Sportlerin, *die;* (runner, jumper) Leichtathlet, *der*/Leichtathletin, *die;* ~'s **foot** (Med.) Fußpilz, *der*
athletic /æθ'letɪk/ *adj.* sportlich
athletics /æθ'letɪks/ *n., no pl.* (a) Leichtathletik, *die;* (b) (Amer.: physical sports) Sport, *der*
Atlantic /ət'læntɪk/ **1** *adj.* atlantisch; ~ **Ocean** Atlantischer Ozean. **2** *pr. n.* Atlantik, *der*
atlas /'ætləs/ Atlas, *der*
ATM *abbrev.* **automated teller machine**
atmosphere /'ætməsfɪə(r)/ *n.* (a) (lit. or fig.) Atmosphäre, *die;* (b) (air in a place) Luft, *die*
atmospheric /ætmə'sferɪk/ *adj.* (a) atmosphärisch; (b) (fig.: evocative) stimmungsvoll
atmospherics /ætmə'sferɪks/ *n. pl.* (Radio) atmosphärische Störungen
atoll /'ætɒl/ *n.* Atoll, *das*
atom /'ætəm/ *n.* Atom, *das;* **not an** ~ **of truth** (fig.) kein Körnchen Wahrheit
'atom bomb ⇒ **atomic bomb**
atomic /ə'tɒmɪk/ *adj.* (Phys.) Atom-
atomic: ~ **'bomb** *n.* Atombombe, *die;* ~ **'energy**

n., no pl. Atomenergie, *die;* ~ **'power** *n., no pl.* Atomkraft, *die;* ~ **'weight** *n.* (Phys., Chem.) Atomgewicht, *das*
atomize /'ætəmaɪz/ *v.t.* atomisieren; zerstäuben 〈Flüssigkeit〉
atomizer /'ætəmaɪzə(r)/ *n.* Zerstäuber, *der*
atone /ə'təʊn/ *v.i.* es wieder gutmachen; ~ **for sth.** etw. wieder gutmachen
atonement /ə'təʊnmənt/ *n.* (a) (atoning) Buße, *die;* (reparation) Wiedergutmachung, *die;* **make** ~ **for sth.** für etw. Buße tun; (b) (Relig.) Versöhnung, *die;* **Day of A**~: Versöhnungsfest, *das*
atrocious /ə'trəʊʃəs/ *adj.* grauenhaft; scheußlich 〈Wetter, Benehmen〉
atrociously /ə'trəʊʃəslɪ/ *adv.* grauenhaft; scheußlich 〈sich benehmen〉
atrocity /ə'trɒsɪtɪ/ *n.* (a) *no pl.* (extreme wickedness) Grauenhaftigkeit, *die;* (b) (atrocious deed) Gräueltat, *die* (geh.); Grausamkeit, *die*
atrophy /'ætrəfɪ/ **1** *n.* (Med.) Atrophie, *die;* **muscular** ~: Muskelatrophie, *die* (Med.); Muskelschwund, *der.* **2** *v.i.* atrophieren

attach /əˈtætʃ/ **1** v.t. **(a)** (fasten) befestigen (**to** an + Dat.); anhängen ‹Wagen› (**to** an + Dat.); **please find** ~**ed** ...: beigeheftet ist ...; **(b)** (assign) **be** ~**ed to sth.** einer Sache (Dat.) zugeteilt sein; **the research unit is** ~**ed to the university** die Forschungsabteilung ist der Universität (Dat.) angegliedert; **(c)** (fig.: ascribe) zuschreiben; ~ **no blame to sb.** jmdm. keine Schuld geben; **(d)** (attribute) beimessen; ~ **importance to sth.** einer Sache (Dat.) Gewicht beimessen. **2** v.i. **no blame** ~**es to sb.** jmdn. trifft keine Schuld

attaché /əˈtæʃeɪ/ n. Attaché, der

at'taché case n. Diplomatenkoffer, der

attached /əˈtætʃt/ adj. (emotionally) **be** ~ **to sb./sth.** an jmdm./etw. hängen; **become** ~ **to sb./sth.** jmdn./etw. lieb gewinnen

attachment /əˈtætʃmənt/ n. **(a)** (act or means of fastening) Befestigung, die; **(b)** (accessory) Zusatzgerät, das; **(c)** (ascribing) Zuordnung, die; **(d)** (attribution) Beimessung, die; **(e)** (affection) Anhänglichkeit, die (**to** an + Akk.); **have an** ~ **for sb.** an jmdm. hängen

attack /əˈtæk/ **1** v.t. **(a)** angreifen; (ambush, raid) überfallen; (fig.: criticize) attackieren; **(b)** ‹Krankheit:› befallen; **(c)** (start work on) in Angriff nehmen; **she** ~**ed the washing-up** sie machte sich an den Abwasch; **(d)** (act harmfully on) angreifen ‹Metall, Oberfläche›. **2** v.i. angreifen. **3** n. **(a)** (on enemy) Angriff, der; (on person) Überfall, der; (fig.: criticism) Attacke, die; Angriff, der; **be under** ~: angegriffen werden; **(b)** **make a spirited** ~ **on sth.** (start) etw. beherzt in Angriff nehmen

attacker /əˈtækə(r)/ n. (also Sport) Angreifer, der/Angreiferin, die

attacking /əˈtækɪŋ/ adj. offensiv ‹Spielweise, Spieler›

attain /əˈteɪn/ **1** v.t. erreichen ‹Ziel, Wirkung›; ~ **power** an die Macht gelangen; **she** ~**ed her hope** ihre Hoffnung erfüllte sich. **2** v.i. ~ **to sth.** zu etw. gelangen; ~ **to success** Erfolg haben

attainable /əˈteɪnəbl/ adj. erreichbar ‹Ziel›; realisierbar ‹Hoffnung, Ziel›

attainment /əˈteɪnmənt/ n. **(a)** no pl. Verwirklichung, die; **(b)** (thing attained) Leistung, die

attempt /əˈtempt/ **1** v.t. **(a)** versuchen; ~ **to do sth.** versuchen, etw. zu tun; **(b)** (try to accomplish) sich versuchen an (+ Dat.); **candidates should** ~ **5 out of 10 questions** die Kandidaten sollten 5 von 10 Fragen zu beantworten versuchen. **2** n. Versuch, der; **make an** ~ **to do sth.** den Versuch unternehmen, etw. zu tun; **make an** ~ **on sb.'s life** ein Attentat od. einen Mordanschlag auf jmdn. verüben

attend /əˈtend/ **1** v.i. **(a)** (give care and thought) aufpassen; ~ **to sth.** auf etw. (Akk.) achten; (deal with sth.) sich um etw. kümmern; **(b)** (be present) anwesend sein; **(c)** (wait) bedienen; aufwarten (veralt.); ~ **on sb.** jmdn. bedienen; jmdm. aufwarten (veralt.). **2** v.t. **(a)** (be present at) teilnehmen an (+ Dat.); (go regularly to) besuchen; **(b)** (follow as a result from) sich ergeben aus; **be** ~**ed by sth.** etw. zur Folge haben; **(c)** (wait on) bedienen; aufwarten (veralt.) (+ Dat.); **(d)** ‹Arzt:› behandeln

attendance /əˈtendəns/ n. **(a)** (being present) Anwesenheit, die; (going regularly) Besuch, der (**at** Gen.); **regular** ~ **at school** regelmäßiger Schulbesuch; **(b)** (number of people present) Teilnehmerzahl, die; **(c)** **be in** ~: anwesend sein

at'tendance centre n. (Brit.) Jugendarrestanstalt, die (in der Freizeitarrest verbüßt wird)

attendant /əˈtendənt/ **1** n. **(a)** ▶887 [**lavatory**] ~: Toilettenmann, der/Toilettenfrau, die; [**cloakroom**] ~: Garderobenmann, der/Garderobenfrau, die; **museum** ~: Museumswärter, der; **(b)** (member of entourage) Begleiter, der/Begleiterin, die. **2** adj. begleitend; **its** ~ **risks** die damit verbundenen Risiken

attention /əˈtenʃn/ **1** n. **(a)** no pl. Aufmerksamkeit, die; **pay** ~ **to sb./sth.** jmdn./etw. beachten; **pay** ~! gib acht!; **pass auf!**; **hold sb.'s** ~ jmds. Interesse wachhalten; **attract [sb.'s]** ~: [jmdn.] auf sich (Akk.) aufmerksam machen; **catch sb.'s** ~: jmds. Aufmerksamkeit erregen; **bring sth. to sb.'s** ~: jmdn. auf etw. (Akk.) aufmerksam

machen; **call** or **draw sb.'s** ~ **to sth./sth.** jmds. Aufmerksamkeit auf jmdn./etw. lenken; ~ **Miss Jones** (on letter) zu Händen [von] Miss Jones; **(b)** no pl. (consideration) **give sth. one's personal** ~: sich einer Sache (Gen.) persönlich annehmen; **(c)** (Mil.) **stand to** ~: stillstehen; strammstehen. **2** int. **(a)** Achtung; **(b)** (Mil.) stillgestanden

attentive /əˈtentɪv/ adj. aufmerksam; **be** ~ **to sth.** auf etw. (Akk.) achten; **be more** ~ **to one's studies** sich gewissenhafter seinen Studien widmen

attentively /əˈtentɪvlɪ/ adv. aufmerksam

attentiveness /əˈtentɪvnɪs/ n., no pl. Aufmerksamkeit, die

attest /əˈtest/ **1** v.t. (certify validity of) bestätigen; beglaubigen ‹Unterschrift, Urkunde›. **2** v.i. ~ **to sth.** etw. bezeugen; (fig.) von etw. zeugen

attic /ˈætɪk/ n. **(a)** (storey) Dachgeschoss, das; **(b)** (room) Dachboden, der; (habitable) Dachkammer, die

attire /əˈtaɪə(r)/ n., no pl. Kleidung, die

attitude /ˈætɪtjuːd/ n. **(a)** (posture, way of behaving) Haltung, die; **strike an** ~: eine Haltung einnehmen; **(b)** (mode of thinking) ~ **[of mind]** Einstellung, die (**to[wards]** zu); **(c)** (Aeron.) Fluglage, die

attorney /əˈtɜːnɪ/ n. ▶887 **(a)** (legal agent) Bevollmächtigte, der/die; **power of** ~: Vollmacht, die; **(b)** (Amer.: lawyer) [Rechts]anwalt, der/[Rechts]anwältin, die

Attorney-'General n., pl. **Attorneys-General** oberster Justizbeamter bestimmter Staaten; ≈ Generalbundesanwalt, der (Bundesrepublik Deutschland); (in USA) ≈ Justizminister, der

attract /əˈtrækt/ v.t. **(a)** (draw) anziehen; auf sich (Akk.) ziehen ‹Interesse, Blick, Kritik›; ‹Köder, Attraktion:› anlocken; **(b)** (arouse pleasure in) anziehend wirken auf (+ Akk.); **what** ~**s me about the girl** was ich an dem Mädchen anziehend finde; **(c)** (arouse interest in) reizen (**about** an + Dat.)

attraction /əˈtrækʃn/ n. **(a)** Anziehung, die; (force, lit. or fig.) Anziehung[skraft], die; **have little** ~ **for sb.** jmdn. nur wenig reizen; **(b)** (fig.: thing that attracts) Attraktion, die; (charm) Verlockung, die; Reiz, der

attractive /əˈtræktɪv/ adj. **(a)** anziehend; ~ **power/force** Anziehungskraft, die; **(b)** (fig.) attraktiv; reizvoll ‹Vorschlag, Möglichkeit, Idee›

attractiveness /əˈtræktɪvnɪs/ n., no pl. Attraktivität, die

attributable /əˈtrɪbjʊtəbl/ adj. **be** ~ **to sb./sth.** jmdm./einer Sache zuzuschreiben sein

attribute 1 /ˈætrɪbjuːt/ n. **(a)** (quality) Attribut, das; Eigenschaft, die; **(b)** (symbolic object) Attribut, das. **2** /əˈtrɪbjuːt/ v.t. (ascribe, assign) zuschreiben (**to** Dat.); (refer) zurückführen (**to** auf + Akk.)

attribution /ætrɪˈbjuːʃn/ n. (ascribing, assigning) Zuordnung, die (**to** Dat.); (referring) Zurückführung, die (**to** auf + Akk.)

attributive /əˈtrɪbjʊtɪv/ adj. (Ling.) attributiv

attrition /əˈtrɪʃn/ n., no pl. (wearing down) Zermürbung, die; **war of** ~ (lit. or fig.) Zermürbungskrieg, der

attune /əˈtjuːn/ v.t. (make accustomed) gewöhnen (**to** an + Akk.); **be** ~**d to sth.** auf etw. (Akk.) eingestellt sein

aubergine /ˈəʊbəʒiːn/ n. Aubergine, die

auburn /ˈɔːbən/ adj. rötlich braun

auction /ˈɔːkʃn/ **1** n. **(a)** Auktion, die; Versteigerung, die; **be put up for** ~: zur Versteigerung kommen; versteigert werden; **Dutch** ~: Abschlag, der; **(b)** (Cards) Bieten, das. **2** v.t. versteigern

auctioneer /ɔːkʃəˈnɪə(r)/ n. ▶887 Auktionator, der/Auktionatorin, die

audacious /ɔːˈdeɪʃəs/ adj. (daring) kühn; verwegen

audacity /ɔːˈdæsɪtɪ/ n., no pl. **(a)** (daringness) Kühnheit, die; Verwegenheit, die; **(b)** (impudence) Dreistigkeit, die

audibility /ɔːdɪˈbɪlɪtɪ/ n. Hörbarkeit, die

audible /ˈɔːdɪbl/ adj. hörbar; **every word was** ~: man konnte jedes Wort hören

audience /ˈɔːdɪəns/ n. **(a)** (listeners, spectators) Publikum, das; **(b)** (formal interview) Audienz, die (**with** bei); **private** ~: Privataudienz, die

audio /'ɔːdɪəʊ/ adj. Ton-; ~ **equipment** Audioanlage, die

audio: ~ **cassette** n. Audiokassette, die; Tonkassette, die; ~ **typist** n. ▶ 887 Phonotypist, der/-typistin, die; ~-**'visual** adj. audiovisuell (fachspr.)

audit /'ɔːdɪt/ 1 n. ~ [**of the accounts**] Rechnungsprüfung, die (Wirtsch.); **the** ~ **of the firm's books** die Revision der Firmengeschäftsbücher. 2 v.t. prüfen

audition /ɔː'dɪʃn/ 1 n. (singing) Probesingen, das; (dancing) Vortanzen, das; (acting) Vorsprechen, das. 2 v.i. (sing) vorsingen; probesingen; (dance) vortanzen; (act) vorsprechen; ~ **for a part** für eine Rolle vorsprechen. 3 v.t. vorsingen/vortanzen/vorsprechen lassen

auditor /'ɔːdɪtə(r)/ n. ▶ 887 Buchprüfer, der/-prüferin, die

auditorium /ɔːdɪ'tɔːrɪəm/ n., pl. ~s or **auditoria** /ɔːdɪ'tɔːrɪə/ Zuschauerraum, der

Aug. abbr. August Aug.

auger /'ɔːgə(r)/ n. Handbohrer, der; Stangenbohrer, der (Technik)

augment /ɔːg'ment/ v.t. verstärken ⟨Armee⟩; verbessern ⟨Einkommen⟩; aufstocken ⟨Fonds, finanzielle Mittel⟩

augur /'ɔːgə(r)/ 1 n. Augur, der. 2 v.t. (portend) bedeuten; versprechen ⟨Erfolg⟩. 3 v.i. ~ **well/ill for sth./sb.** ein gutes/schlechtes Zeichen für etw./jmdn. sein

augury /'ɔːgjʊrɪ/ n. Vorzeichen, das

August /'ɔːgəst/ n. ▶ 738 August, der; **in** ~: im August; **last/next** ~: letzten/nächsten August; **the first of/on the first of** ~ or **on** ~ [**the**] **first** der erste/am ersten August; **1st** ~ (as date on document) 1. August; **every** ~: jeden August; jedes Jahr im August; **an** ~ **day** ein Augusttag; **from** ~ **to October** von August bis Oktober

august /ɔː'gʌst/ adj. (venerable) ehrwürdig; (noble) erlaucht

auld /ɔːld/ adj. (Scot.) ⇒ **old; for** ~ **lang syne** um der guten, alten Zeiten willen

aunt /ɑːnt/ n. Tante, die

auntie, aunty /'ɑːntɪ/ n. (coll.) Tantchen, das; (with name) Tante, die

au pair /əʊ 'peə(r)/ 1 n. Aupairmädchen, das. 2 adj. ~ **girl** Aupairmädchen, das

aura /'ɔːrə/ n., pl. ~**e** /'ɔːriː/ or ~**s** Aura, die

aural /'ɔːrl/ adj. akustisch; aural (Med.)

auricle /'ɔːrɪkl/ n. Ohrmuschel, die

aurora /ɔː'rɔːrə/ n., pl. ~**s** or ~**e** /ɔː'rɔːriː/ Polarlicht, das; ~ **borealis** /bɔːrɪ'eɪlɪs/ Nordlicht, das

auspice /'ɔːspɪs/ n. (a) in pl. **under the** ~**s of sb./sth.** unter jmds./einer Sache Auspizien (geh.) od. Schirmherrschaft; (b) (sign) Auspizium, das (geh.); Vorzeichen, das

auspicious /ɔː'spɪʃəs/ adj. günstig; vielversprechend ⟨Anfang⟩

auspiciously /ɔː'spɪʃəslɪ/ adv. vielversprechend

Aussie /'ɒzɪ/ (coll.) 1 adj. australisch. 2 n. Australier, der/Australierin, die

austere /ɒ'stɪə(r), ɔː'stɪə(r)/ adj. (a) (morally strict, stern) streng; unbeugsam ⟨Haltung⟩; (b) (severely simple) karg; (c) (ascetic) asketisch ⟨Leben⟩

austerely /ɒ'stɪəlɪ, ɔː'stɪəlɪ/ adv. (a) (strictly, sternly) streng; (b) (severely simply) karg; ~ **simple** karg und schlicht

austereness /ɒ'stɪənɪs, ɔː'stɪənɪs/ ⇒ **austerity** a, b

austerity /ɒ'sterɪtɪ, ɔː'sterɪtɪ/ n. (a) no pl. (moral strictness) Strenge, die; (b) no pl. (severe simplicity) Kargheit, die; (c) no pl. (lack of luxuries) wirtschaftliche Einschränkung; (d) in pl. (deprivations) Entbehrungen

Australasia /ɒstrə'leɪʒə, ɔːstrə'leɪʒə/ pr. n. Australien und der südwestliche Pazifik

Australia /ɒ'streɪlɪə, ɔː'streɪlɪə/ pr. n. Australien (das)

Australian /ɒ'streɪlɪən, ɔː'streɪlɪən/ ▶ 947 1 adj. australisch; ~ **bear** Beutelbär, der; Koala, der; **sb. is** ~: jmd. ist Australier/Australierin. 2 n. Australier, der/Australierin, die

Austria /'ɒstrɪə, 'ɔːstrɪə/ pr. n. Österreich (das); ~-**Hungary** (Hist.) Österreich-Ungarn (das)

Austrian /'ɒstrɪən, 'ɔːstrɪən/ ▶ 947 1 adj. österreichisch; **sb. is** ~: jmd. ist Österreicher/Österreicherin. 2 n. Österreicher, der/Österreicherin, die

authentic /ɔː'θentɪk/ adj. authentisch; (genuine) authentisch; echt; unverfälscht ⟨Akzent⟩

authenticate /ɔː'θentɪkeɪt/ v.t. ~ **sth.** die Echtheit einer Sache (Gen.) bestätigen; ~ **a report** einen Bericht bestätigen

authentication /ɔːθentɪ'keɪʃn/ n., no pl. Bestätigung der Echtheit; (of report) Bestätigung, die

authenticity /ɔːθen'tɪsɪtɪ/ n., no pl. Echtheit, die; Authentizität, die; (of report) Zuverlässigkeit, die

author /'ɔːθə(r)/ 1 n. (a) ▶ 887 (writer) Autor, der/Autorin, die; (profession) Schriftsteller, der/Schriftstellerin, die; **the** ~ **of the book/article** der Autor od. Verfasser des Buches/Artikels; (b) (originator) Vater, der. 2 v.t. (write) verfassen

authoritarian /ɔːθɒrɪ'teərɪən/ adj. autoritär

authoritative /ɔː'θɒrɪtətɪv/ adj. (a) (recognized as reliable) maßgebend; zuverlässig ⟨Bericht, Information⟩; (official) amtlich; (b) (commanding) respekteinflößend

authoritatively /ɔː'θɒrɪtətɪvlɪ/ adv. (a) (reliably) zuverlässig ⟨berichten⟩; (officially) offiziell; **he talked** ~ **about his specialist field** er sprach als Fachmann über sein Spezialgebiet; (b) (commandingly) mit Bestimmtheit

authority /ɔː'θɒrɪtɪ/ n. (a) no pl. (power) Autorität, die; (delegated power) Befugnis, die; **have the/no** ~ **to do sth.** berechtigt od. befugt/nicht befugt sein, etw. zu tun; **have/exercise** ~ **over sb.** Weisungsbefugnis gegenüber jmdm. haben; **on one's own** ~: in eigener Verantwortung; [**be**] **in** ~: verantwortlich [sein]; (b) (body having power) **the authorities** die Behörde[n]; **the highest legal** ~: die höchste rechtliche Instanz; (c) (expert, book, quotation) Autorität, die; **have it on the** ~ **of sb./sth. that** ...: durch jmdn./etw. wissen, dass ...; **have it on good** ~ **that** ...: aus zuverlässiger Quelle wissen, dass ...; (d) no pl. **give** or **add** ~ **to sth.** einer Sache (Dat.) Gewicht verleihen; (e) no pl. (masterfulness) Souveränität, die

authorization /ɔːθəraɪ'zeɪʃn/ n. Genehmigung, die; **obtain/give** ~: die Genehmigung einholen/erteilen

authorize /'ɔːθəraɪz/ v.t. (a) (give authority to) ermächtigen; bevollmächtigen; autorisieren; ~ **sb. to do sth.** jmdn. ermächtigen, etw. zu tun; (b) (sanction) genehmigen

authorship /'ɔːθəʃɪp/ n., no pl. Autorschaft, die; **of unknown** ~: von einem unbekannten Autor od. Verfasser

autistic /ɔː'tɪstɪk/ adj. (Psych., Med.) autistisch

auto /'ɔːtəʊ/ n., pl. ~**s** (Amer. coll.) Auto, das

auto- /'ɔːtəʊ/ in comb. auto-/Auto-

autobio'graphic, autobio'graphical adj. autobiographisch

autobi'ography n. Autobiographie, die

autocracy /ɔː'tɒkrəsɪ/ n. Autokratie, die

autocrat /'ɔːtəkræt/ n. Autokrat, der

autocratic /ɔːtə'krætɪk/ adj. autokratisch

Autocue, (P) /'ɔːtəʊkjuː/ n. Teleprompter Ⓦ, der

'autofocus n., no pl. (Photog.) Autofokus, der

autograph /'ɔːtəgraːf/ 1 n. (a) (signature) Autogramm, das; (b) (manuscript) Autograph, das. 2 v.t. (sign) signieren

auto-im'mune adj. (Med.) autoimmun; ~ **response** Autoimmunantwort, die

automat /'ɔːtəmæt/ n. (Amer.) [Münz]automat, der

automate /'ɔːtəmeɪt/ v.t. automatisieren

automated 'teller machine n. Geldautomat, der

automatic /ɔːtə'mætɪk/ 1 adj. automatisch; **his reaction was completely** ~: er reagierte ganz automatisch; ~ **pilot** ⇒ **autopilot.** 2 n. (weapon) automatische Waffe; (vehicle) Fahrzeug mit Automatikgetriebe

automatically /ɔːtə'mætɪkəlɪ/ adv. automatisch

automation /ɔːtə'meɪʃn/ n., no pl. Automation, die; (automatic control) Automatisierung, die

automaton /ɔː'tɒmətən/ n., pl. ~**s** or **automata** /ɔː'tɒmətə/ Automat, der

automobile /'ɔ:təməbi:l/ *n.* (Amer.) Auto, *das*

automotive /ɔ:tə'məʊtɪv/ *adj.* Kraftfahrzeug-; ~ industry Auto[mobil]industrie, *die*

autonomous /ɔ:'tɒnəməs/ *adj.* (also Philos.) autonom

autonomy /ɔ:'tɒnəmɪ/ *n.*, *no pl.* (also Philos.) Autonomie, *die*

'**autopilot** *n.* Autopilot, *der;* [**fly**] **on** ~: mit Autopilot [fliegen]

autopsy /'ɔ:tɒpsɪ, ɔ:'tɒpsɪ/ *n.* Autopsie, *die;* Obduktion, *die*

'**auto-suggestion** *n.* Autosuggestion, *die*

'**autotimer** *n.* [automatische] Schaltuhr

autumn /'ɔ:təm/ *n.* ▶ 1065 (lit. or fig.) Herbst, *der;* **in** ~ 1969, **in the** ~ **of** 1969 im Herbst 1969; **in early/late** ~: im Frühherbst/Spätherbst; **last/next** ~: letzten/nächsten Herbst

autumnal /ɔ:'tʌmnl/ *adj.* (lit. or fig.) herbstlich

auxiliary /ɔ:g'zɪljərɪ/ **1** *adj.* (a) (helping) Hilfs-; **be** ~ **to sth.** etw. unterstützen *od.* fördern; (b) (subsidiary) zusätzlich; Zusatz-; (c) (Ling.) ~ **verb** Hilfsverb, *das.* **2** *n.* (a) Hilfskraft, *die;* **medical** ~: ärztliches Hilfspersonal; (b) (Ling.) Hilfsverb, *das*

avail /ə'veɪl/ **1** *n.*, *no pl.*, *no art.* **be of no** ~: nichts nützen; nutzlos *od.* vergeblich sein; **to no** ~: vergebens. **2** *v.i.* etwas nützen *od.* fruchten. **3** *v.t.* nützen; **it will** ~ **you nothing** es wird dir nichts nützen. **4** *v. refl.* ~ **oneself of sth.** von etw. Gebrauch machen; ~ **oneself of an opportunity** eine Gelegenheit nutzen

availability /əveɪlə'bɪlɪtɪ/ *n.*, *no pl.* Vorhandensein, *das;* **the** ~ **of sth.** die Möglichkeit, etw. zu bekommen; **the likely** ~ **of spare parts** die voraussichtliche Lieferbarkeit von Ersatzteilen

available /ə'veɪləbl/ *adj.* (a) (at one's disposal) verfügbar; **make sth.** ~ **to sb.** jmdm. etw. zur Verfügung stellen; **be** ~: zur Verfügung stehen; (b) (capable of use) gültig 〈*Fahrkarte, Angebot*〉; (c) (obtainable) erhältlich; lieferbar 〈*Waren*〉; verfügbar 〈*Unterkunft, Daten*〉; **have sth.** ~: etw. zur Verfügung haben

avalanche /'ævəlɑ:nʃ/ *n.* (lit. or fig.) Lawine, *die*

avant-garde /ævã'gɑ:d/ **1** *adj.* avantgardistisch. **2** *n.* Avantgarde, *die*

avarice /'ævərɪs/ *n.*, *no pl.* Geldgier, *die;* Habsucht, *die*

avaricious /ævə'rɪʃəs/ *adj.* geldgierig; habsüchtig

Ave. *abbr.* Avenue

Ave [Maria] /'aveɪ (mə'rɪə)/ *n.* Ave[-Maria], *das*

avenge /ə'vendʒ/ *v.t.* rächen; **be** ~**d/**~ **oneself on sb.** sich an jmdm. rächen; **be** ~**d for sth.** sich für etw. rächen

avenue /'ævənju:/ *n.* (broad street) Boulevard, *der;* (tree-lined road) Allee, *die;* (fig.) Weg, *der* (**to** zu); ~ **of approach** Zugang, *der*

aver /ə'vɜ:(r)/ *v.t.*, **-rr-** beteuern

average /'ævərɪdʒ/ **1** *n.* (a) Durchschnitt, *der;* **on** [**the** *or* **an**] ~: im Durchschnitt; durchschnittlich; im Schnitt (ugs.); **above/below** ~: über/unter dem Durchschnitt; **law of** ~**s** Wahrscheinlichkeitsgesetz, *das;* (b) (arithmetic mean) Mittelwert, *der.* **2** *adj.* (a) durchschnittlich; **he is of** ~ **height** er ist mittelgroß; (b) (mediocre) durchschnittlich; mittelmäßig. **3** *v.t.* (a) (find the ~ of) den Durchschnitt ermitteln von; (b) (amount on ~ to) durchschnittlich betragen; **the planks** ~**d three metres in length** die Bretter waren durchschnittlich drei Meter lang; (c) (do on ~) einen Durchschnitt von ... erreichen; **the train** ~**d 90 m.p.h.** der Zug fuhr im Durchschnitt mit 144 Kilometer pro Stunde. **4** *v.i.* ~ **out at** im Durchschnitt betragen

averse /ə'vɜ:s/ *pred. adj.* **be** ~ **to sth.** einer Sache (*Dat.*) abgeneigt sein; **be** ~ **to doing sth.** abgeneigt sein, etw. zu tun

aversion /ə'vɜ:ʃn/ *n.* (a) *no pl.* (dislike) Abneigung, *die;* Aversion, *die;* **have/take an** ~ **to sth.** eine Abneigung *od.* Aversion gegen etw. haben/bekommen; (b) (object) **my pet** ~ **is** ...: ein besonderer Gräuel ist mir ...

avert /ə'vɜ:t/ *v.t.* (a) (turn away) abwenden 〈*Blick, Gesicht, Aufmerksamkeit*〉; (b) (prevent) abwenden 〈*Katastrophe, Schaden, Niederlage*〉; verhüten 〈*Unfall*〉

aviary /'eɪvɪərɪ/ *n.* Vogelhaus, *das;* Aviarium, *das*

aviation /eɪvɪ'eɪʃn/ *n.*, *no pl.*, *no art.* Luftfahrt, *die;* ~ **fuel** Flugbenzin, *das;* ~ **industry** Flugzeugindustrie, *die*

aviator /'eɪvɪeɪtə(r)/ *n.* ▶ 887 Flieger, *der*/Fliegerin, *die*

avid /'ævɪd/ *adj.* (enthusiastic) begeistert; passioniert; **be** ~ **for sth.** (eager, greedy) begierig auf etw. (*Akk.*) sein

avionics /eɪvɪ'ɒnɪks/ *n.* Avionik, *die*

avocado /ævə'kɑ:dəʊ/ *n.*, *pl.* ~**s:** [**pear**] Avocado-[birne], *die*

avoid /ə'vɔɪd/ *v.t.* (a) (keep away from) meiden 〈*Ort*〉; ~ **an obstacle/a cyclist** einem Hindernis/Radfahrer ausweichen; (b) (refrain from) vermeiden; ~ **doing sth.** vermeiden, etw. zu tun; (c) (escape) vermeiden

avoidable /ə'vɔɪdəbl/ *adj.* vermeidbar

avoidance /ə'vɔɪdəns/ *n.*, *no pl.* Vermeidung, *die*

avow /ə'vaʊ/ *v.t.* bekennen; **be an** ~**ed opponent/supporter** ein erklärter Gegner/Befürworter

avowal /ə'vaʊəl/ *n.* Bekenntnis, *das*

avuncular /ə'vʌŋkjʊlə(r)/ *adj.* onkelhaft

await /ə'weɪt/ *v.t.* erwarten

awake /ə'weɪk/ **1** *v.i.*, **awoke** /ə'wəʊk/, **awoken** /ə'wəʊkn/ (lit. or fig.) erwachen; ~ **to sth.** (fig.) einer Sache (*Gen.*) gewahr werden. **2** *v.t.*, **awoke**, **awoken** (lit. or fig.) wecken; ~ **sb. to sth.** (fig.) jmdm. etw. bewusst machen. **3** *pred. adj.* (lit. or fig.) wach; **wide** ~: hellwach; **lie** ~: wach liegen; **be** ~ **to sth.** (fig.) sich (*Dat.*) einer Sache (*Gen.*) bewusst sein

awaken /ə'weɪkn/ **1** *v.t.* (esp. fig.) ⇒ **awake** 2. **2** *v.i.* (esp. fig.) ⇒ **awake** 1

awakening /ə'weɪknɪŋ/ *n.* **a rude** ~ (fig.) ein böses Erwachen

award /ə'wɔ:d/ **1** *v.t.* (grant) verleihen, zuerkennen 〈*Preis, Auszeichnung*〉; zusprechen 〈*Sorgerecht, Entschädigung*〉; gewähren 〈*Zahlung, Gehaltserhöhung*〉; ~ **sb. sth.** jmdm. etw. verleihen/zusprechen/gewähren; **he was** ~**ed the prize** der Preis wurde ihm zuerkannt. **2** *n.* (a) (judicial decision) Schiedsspruch, *der;* (b) (payment) Entschädigung[ssumme], *die;* (grant) Stipendium, *das;* (c) (prize) Auszeichnung, *die;* Preis, *der*

a'ward-winning *adj.* preisgekrönt

aware /ə'weə(r)/ *adj.* (a) *pred.* (conscious) **be** ~ **of sth.** sich (*Dat.*) einer Sache (*Gen.*) bewusst sein; **be** ~ **that** ...: sich (*Dat.*) [dessen] bewusst sein, dass ...; **as far as I am** ~: soweit ich weiß; **not that I am** ~ **of** nicht, dass ich wüsste; (b) (well-informed) informiert

awareness /ə'weənɪs/ *n.*, *no pl.* (consciousness) Bewusstsein, *das;* **raise public** ~ **of sth.** etw. der Öffentlichkeit zu Bewusstsein bringen; etw. ins allgemeine Bewusstsein bringen

awash /ə'wɒʃ/ *pred. adj.* auf gleicher Höhe mit dem Wasserspiegel; **be** ~ (flooded) unter Wasser stehen

away /ə'weɪ/ **1** *adv.* (a) (at a distance) entfernt; ~ **in the distance** weit in der Ferne; **play** ~ (Sport) auswärts spielen; **Christmas is still months** ~: bis Weihnachten dauert es noch Monate; (b) (to a distance) weg; fort; ~ **with you/him!** weg *od.* fort mit dir/ihm!; **throw sth.** ~: etw. wegwerfen *od.* fortwerfen; ~ **we go!** los geht's!; (c) (absent) nicht da; **be** ~ **on business** geschäftlich außer Haus sein; **be** ~ [**from school**] **with a cold** wegen einer Erkältung [in der Schule] fehlen; (d) **die/fade** ~: verhallen; **the water has all boiled** ~: das ganze Wasser ist verkocht; (e) (constantly) unablässig; **work** ~ **on sth.** ohne Unterbrechung an etw. (*Dat.*) arbeiten; **laugh** ~ **at sth.** unablässig über etw. (*Akk.*) lachen; (f) (without delay) gleich 〈*fragen usw.*〉; **fire** ~ (lit. or fig.) losschießen (ugs.). **2** *adj.* (Sport) auswärts *präd.;* Auswärts-; ~ **team** Gastmannschaft, *die*

awe /ɔ:/ **1** *n.* Ehrfurcht, *die* (**of** vor + *Dat.*); **be** *or* **stand in** ~ **of sb.** jmdn. fürchten; **hold sb. in** ~: jmdn. ehrfürchtig respektieren. **2** *v.t.* Ehrfurcht einflößen (+ *Dat.*); **be** ~**d by sth.** sich von etw. beeindrucken *od.* einschüchtern lassen

'**awe-inspiring** *adj.* Ehrfurcht gebietend; beeindruckend

awesome /'ɔ:səm/ *adj.* überwältigend; eindrucksvoll 〈*Schweigen*〉; übergroß 〈*Verantwortung*〉

awe: ~**stricken,** ~**struck** *adjs.* [von Ehrfurcht] ergriffen; ehrfurchtsvoll ⟨*Ausdruck, Staunen*⟩

awful /'ɔːfl/ *adj.* (coll.) furchtbar; fürchterlich; **too ~ for words** unbeschreiblich schlecht; **an ~ lot of money/people** ein Haufen Geld/Leute (ugs.); **an ~ long time/way** eine furchtbar lange Zeit/ein furchtbar weiter Weg

awfully /'ɔːfəlɪ, 'ɔːflɪ/ *adv.* (coll.) furchtbar; **not ~:** nicht besonders; **thanks ~:** tausend Dank

awkward /'ɔːkwəd/ *adj.* (a) (ill-adapted for use) ungünstig; **be ~ to use** unhandlich sein; **the parcel is ~ to carry** das Paket ist schlecht zu tragen; (b) (clumsy) unbeholfen; **be at an ~ age** in einem schwierigen Alter sein; (c) (embarrassing, embarrassed) peinlich; **feel ~:** sich unbehaglich fühlen; (d) (difficult) schwierig, unangenehm ⟨*Person*⟩; ungünstig ⟨*Zeitpunkt*⟩; schwierig, peinlich ⟨*Lage, Dilemma*⟩

awkwardly /'ɔːkwədlɪ/ *adv.* (a) (badly) ungünstig ⟨*geformt, angebracht*⟩; (b) (clumsily) ungeschickt, unbeholfen ⟨*gehen, sich ausdrücken*⟩; ungeschickt, unglücklich ⟨*fallen, sich ausdrücken*⟩; (c) (embarrassingly) peinlicherweise; (d) (unfavourably) ungünstig ⟨*gelegen*⟩

awkwardness /'ɔːkwədnɪs/ *n., no pl.* ⇒ **awkward:** (a) Unhandlichkeit, *die;* (b) Unbeholfenheit, *die;* (c) Peinlichkeit, *die;* (d) (of person) unangenehmes Wesen; (of situation, position) Schwierigkeit, *die*

awl /ɔːl/ *n.* Ahle, *die;* Pfriem, *der*

awning /'ɔːnɪŋ/ *n.* (on wagon) Plane, *die;* (on house) Markise, *die;* (of tent) Vordach, *das*

awoke, awoken ⇒ **awake** 1, 2

awry /ə'raɪ/ *adv.* schief; **go ~** (fig.) schiefgehen (ugs.); ⟨*Plan:*⟩ fehlschlagen

axe (*Amer.:* **ax**) /æks/ **1** *n.* Axt, *die;* Beil, *das;* **have an ~ to grind** (fig.) sein eigenes Süppchen kochen (ugs.). **2** *v.t.* (reduce) [radikal] kürzen; (eliminate) [radikal] einsparen ⟨*Stellen*⟩; (dismiss) entlassen; (abandon) aufgeben ⟨*Projekt*⟩

axes *pl. of* **axe, axis**

axiom /'æksɪəm/ *n.* Axiom, *das*

axiomatic /æksɪə'mætɪk/ *adj.* axiomatisch; **I have taken it as ~ that …:** ich gehe von dem Grundsatz aus, dass …

axis /'æksɪs/ *n., pl.* **axes** /'æksiːz/ Achse, *die;* ~ **of rotation** Rotationsachse, *die*

axle /'æksl/ *n.* Achse, *die*

ayatollah /aɪə'tɒlə/ *n.* Ajatollah, *der*

azalea /ə'zeɪlɪə/ *n.* (Bot.) Azalee, *die*

Azerbaijan /æzəbaɪ'dʒɑːn/ *pr. n.* Aserbaidschan (*das*); Aserbeidschan (*das*)

Aztec /'æztek/ **1** *adj.* aztekisch. **2** *n.* Azteke, *der*/Aztekin, *die*

azure /'æʒjə(r), 'eɪʒjə(r)/ **1** *n.* Azur[blau], *das.* **2** *adj.* azurblau

---

Bb

B, b /biː/ *n., pl.* **Bs** *or* **B's** (a) (letter) B, b, *das;* **B road** Straße 2. Ordnung; ≈ Landstraße, *die;* ~ **film** *or* (Amer.) **movie** Vorfilm, *der;* (b) **B** (Mus.) H, h, *das;* **B flat** B, b, *das*

BA *abbr.* (Univ.) **Bachelor of Arts;** *see also* **B.Sc.**

baa /bɑː/ **1** *n.* Blöken, *das.* **2** *v.i.*, **baaed** *or* **baa'd** /bɑːd/ mähen; blöken

babble /'bæbl/ **1** *v.i.* (a) (talk incoherently) stammeln; (b) (talk foolishly) [dumm] schwatzen; (c) (talk excessively) ~ **away** *or* **on** quasseln (ugs.); (d) ⟨*Bach:*⟩ plätschern. **2** *v.t.* (utter incoherently) stammeln. **3** *n.* (a) (incoherent speech) Gestammel, *das;* (childish or foolish speech) Gelalle, *das;* (b) (murmur of water) Geplätscher, *das*

baboon /bə'buːn/ *n.* Pavian, *der*

baby /'beɪbɪ/ *n.* (a) Baby, *das;* **have a ~/be going to have a ~:** ein Kind bekommen; **she has a young ~:** sie hat ein kleines Baby; **a ~ boy/girl** ein kleiner Junge/ein kleines Mädchen; **throw out** *or* **away the ~ with the bathwater** (fig.) das Kind mit dem Bade ausschütten; **be left holding** *or* **carrying the ~** (fig.) die Sache ausbaden müssen (ugs.); der Dumme sein (ugs.); **it's your/his** *etc.* ~ (fig.) das ist dein/sein *usw.* Bier (ugs.); (b) (youngest member) Jüngste, *der/die;* (male also) Benjamin, *der;* **the ~ of the family** das Küken der Familie; (c) (childish person) **be a ~:** sich wie ein kleines Kind benehmen; (d) (young lusanimal) Junge, *das;* ~ **bird/giraffe** Vogeljunge, *das*/Giraffenjunge, *das;* (e) (small thing) **be a ~:** winzig sein; (f) (coll.: sweetheart) Schatz, *der;* (in pop song also) Baby, *das;* (g) (sl.: young woman) Kleine, *die* (ugs.)

baby: ~ **clothes** *n. pl.* Babykleidung, *die;* ~ **food** *n.* Babynahrung, *die*

babyish /'beɪbɪɪʃ/ *adj.* kindlich ⟨*Aussehen*⟩; kindisch ⟨*Benehmen, Person*⟩

baby: ~-**minder** *n.* Tagesmutter, *die;* ~ **powder** *n.* Babypuder, *der;* ~**sit** *v.i., forms as* **sit** babysitten (ugs.); auf das Kind/die Kinder aufpassen; ~**sitter** *n.* Babysitter, *der;* ~**sitting** *n.* Babysitting, *das;* ~-**snatcher** /'beɪbɪsnætʃə(r)/ *n.* Kindesentführer, *der;* ~-**snatching** *n.* Kindesentführung, *die;* ~-**talk** *n.* Babysprache, *die;* ~-**walker** *n.* Laufstuhl, *der;* ~ **wipe** *n.* feuchtes Baby[pflege]tuch

bachelor /'bætʃələ(r)/ *n.* (a) (unmarried man) Junggeselle, *der;* (b) (Univ.) **B~ of Arts/Science** Bakkalaureus der philosophischen Fakultät/der Naturwissenschaften

bachelor: ~ **flat** *n.* Junggesellenwohnung, *die;* ~ **girl** *n.* Junggesellin, *die*

bacillus /bə'sɪləs/ *n., pl.* **bacilli** /bə'sɪlaɪ/ (Biol., Med.) Bazillus, *der*

back /bæk/ **1** *n.* (a) ▶672 (of person, animal) Rücken, *der;* **stand ~ to ~:** Rücken an Rücken stehen; **as soon as my ~ was turned** (fig.) sowie ich den Rücken gedreht hatte; **turn one's ~ on sb.** jmdm. den Rücken zuwenden; (fig.: abandon sb.) jmdn. im Stich lassen; **turn one's ~ on sth.** (fig.) sich um etw. nicht kümmern; **get** *or* **put sb.'s ~ up** (fig.) jmdn. wütend machen; **be glad to see the ~ of sb./sth.** (fig.) froh sein, jmdn./etw. nicht mehr sehen zu müssen; **have one's ~ to the wall** (fig.) mit dem Rücken zur Wand stehen; **get off my ~** (fig. coll.) lass mich zufrieden; **have sb./sth. on one's ~** (fig.) jmdn./etw. am Hals haben (ugs.); **put one's ~ into sth.** (fig.) sich für etw. mit allen Kräften einsetzen; (b) (outer or rear surface) Rücken, *der;* (of vehicle) Heck, *das;* (inside car) Rücksitz, *der;* **the car went into the ~ of me** (coll.) das Auto ist mir hinten reingefahren (ugs.); **with the ~ of one's hand** mit dem Handrücken; **know sth. like the ~ of one's hand** (fig.) etw. wie seine Westentasche kennen; **the ~ of one's/the head** der Hinterkopf; **the ~ of the leg** die Wade; (c) (of book) (spine) [Buch]rücken, *der;* (final pages) Ende, *das;* **at the ~ [of the book]** hinten [im Buch]; (d) (of dress) Rücken, *der;* (of knife) [Messer]rücken, *der;* (e) (more remote part) hinterer Teil; **at the ~ [of sth.]** hinten [in etw. (*Dat.*)]; im hinteren Teil [von etw.]; (f) (of chair) [Rücken]lehne, *die;* (of house, cheque) Rückseite, *die;* (~ wall) Rückseite, *die;* Rückwand, *die;* ~ **to front** verkehrt rum; **please get to the ~ of the queue** bitte, stellen Sie sich hinten an; **in ~ of sth.** (Amer.) hinter etw. (*Dat.*); (g) (Sport: player) Verteidiger, *der;* (h) (of ship) Kiel, *der.* **2** *adj., no compar.; superl.* ~**most** /'bækməʊst/ (a) (situated behind) hinter…; (b) (of the past) früher; ~ **issue** alte Ausgabe; (c) (overdue) rückständig ⟨*Lohn, Steuern*⟩. **3** *adv.* (a) (to the rear) zurück; **step ~:** zurücktreten; (b) (behind) zurück; weiter hinten; **we passed a pub two miles ~:** wir sind vor zwei Meilen an einem Pub vorbeigefahren; ~ **and forth** hin und her; ~ **of sth.** (Amer.) hinter etw. (*Dat.*); (c) (at a distance) **the house stands a long way ~ from the road** das Haus steht weit von der Straße zurück; (d) (to original position, home) [wieder] zurück; **I got my letter ~:** ich habe meinen Brief zurückbekommen; **the journey ~:** die Rückfahrt/der Rückflug; **there and ~:** hin und zurück; (e) (to original condition) wieder; (f) (in the past) zurück; **go a**

long way ~: weit zurückgehen; **a week/month** ~: vor einer Woche/vor einem Monat; **(g)** (in return) zurück; **I got a letter** ~: er/sie hat mir wiedergeschrieben. **4** *v.t.* **(a)** (assist) helfen (+ *Dat.*); unterstützen ‹*Person, Sache*›; **(b)** (bet on) wetten *od.* setzen auf (+ *Akk.*) ‹*Pferd, Gewinner, Favorit*›; ~ **the wrong/right horse** (lit. or fig.) aufs falsche/richtige Pferd setzen (ugs.); **(c)** (cause to move back) zurücksetzen [mit] ‹*Fahrzeug*›; rückwärts gehen lassen ‹*Pferd*›; **(d)** (put or act as a ~ to) [an der Rückseite] verstärken; **(e)** (endorse) indossieren ‹*Wechsel, Scheck*›; **(f)** (lie at the ~ of) ~ **sth.** hinten an etw. (*Akk.*) grenzen; **(g)** (Mus.) begleiten. **5** *v.i.* zurücksetzen; ~ **into/out of sth.** rückwärts in etw. (*Akk.*)/aus etw. fahren; ~ **on to sth.** hinten an etw. (*Akk.*) grenzen

~ **down** *v.i.* (fig.) nachgeben; einen Rückzieher machen (ugs.)

~ **up** **1** **(a)** *v.t.* unterstützen; untermauern ‹*Anspruch, Geschichte, These*›; **(b)** (Computing) sichern ‹*Daten, Dokumente*›; ~ **up a file on to a floppy disk** von einer Datei eine Sicherungskopie auf Diskette machen; **2** *v.i.* **(a)** ‹*Wasser:*› sich [auf]stauen; **(b)** (reverse) zurücksetzen; **(c)** (Amer.: form queue of vehicles) sich stauen. *see also* **back-up**

back: ~**ache** *n.*, *no pl.* Rückenschmerzen *Pl.;* ~**bencher** /bæk'bentʃə(r)/ *n.* (Brit. Parl.) [einfacher] Abgeordneter/[einfache] Abgeordnete; (derog.) Hinterbänkler, *der* (abwertend); ~**bone** *n.* Wirbelsäule, *die;* Rückgrat, *das;* ~**breaking** *adj.* äußerst mühsam; gewaltig ‹*Anstrengung*›; ~**breaking work** Knochenarbeit, *die;* ~ '**burner** *n.* **put sth. on the** ~ **burner** (fig. coll.) etw. zurückstellen; ~**chat** *n.*, *no pl.* (coll.) [freche] Widerrede; ~**comb** *v.t.* zurückkämmen; ~ **copy** ⇒ **back number;** ~**date** *v.t.* zurückdatieren (**to** auf + *Akk.*); ~ '**door** *n.* Hintertür, *die* (auch fig.)

backer /'bækə(r)/ *n.* Geldgeber, *der;* (of horse) Wetter, *der*

back'**fire** *v.i.* knallen; (fig.) fehlschlagen; **it** ~**fired on me/him** *etc.* der Schuss ging nach hinten los (ugs.)

backgammon /'bækgæmən/ *n.* Backgammon, *das*

back: ~**ground** *n.* **(a)** (lit. or fig.) Hintergrund, *der;* (social status) Herkunft, *die;* **be in the** ~**ground** im Hintergrund stehen; **against this** ~**ground** vor diesem Hintergrund; ~**ground music** Hintergrundmusik, *die;* ~**ground noise** (in a room etc.) Geräuschkulisse, *die;* (on a recording) Grundrauschen, *das;* **the level of** ~**ground noise** der Geräuschpegel; **I can't hear you because of all the** ~**ground noise** ich kann dich wegen des Lärms nicht verstehen; **(b)** ~**ground [information]** Hintergrundinformation, *die;* ~**hand** (Tennis etc.) **1** *adj.* Rückhand-; **2** *n.* Rückhand, *die;* ~**handed** /bæk'hændɪd/ *adj.* **(a)** ~**-handed stroke** (Tennis) Rückhandschlag, *der;* **(b)** (fig.) indirekt; zweifelhaft ‹*Kompliment*›; ~**hander** /'bæk'hændə(r)/ *n.* **(a)** (stroke) Rückhandschlag, *der* (Tennis usw.); (blow) Schlag [mit dem Handrücken]; **(b)** (coll.: bribe) Schmiergeld, *das*

backing /'bækɪŋ/ *n.* **(a)** (material) Rückenverstärkung, *die;* **(b)** (support) Unterstützung, *die*

back: ~ **issue** ⇒ **back number;** ~**lash** *n.* Rückstoß, *der;* (fig.) Gegenreaktion, *die;* **a right-wing** ~: eine Gegenbewegung nach rechts

backless /'bæklɪs/ *adj.* rückenfrei ‹*Kleid*›

back: ~**list** *n.* Verzeichnis der lieferbaren Titel; ~**log** *n.* Rückstand, *der;* ~**log of work** Arbeitsrückstand, *der;* ~ '**number** *n.* (of periodical, magazine) alte Nummer; ~**pack** **1** *n.* Rucksack, *der;* **2** *v.i.* mit dem Rucksack [ver]reisen; ~**packer** *n.* Rucksackreisende, *der/die;* Rucksacktourist, *der/*-touristin, *die;* (hiker) Wanderer, *der/* Wanderin, *die* mit Rucksack; ~**packing** *n.*, *no pl.* das [Ver]reisen mit dem Rucksack; (hiking) das Wandern mit dem Rucksack; *attrib.* ‹*Reise usw.*› mit dem Rucksack; ~**pay** *n.* ausstehender Lohn/ausstehendes Gehalt; **he was reinstated with** ~ **pay** er wurde wieder eingestellt und erhielt eine Lohn-/Gehaltsnachzahlung; **she was awarded £7,850 in** ~ **pay** sie erhielt eine Nachzahlung von £7,850; ~**pedal** *v.i.* **(a)** rückwärts treten; (brake) mit dem Rücktritt bremsen; **(b)** (fig.) einen Rückzieher machen (ugs.); ~**rest** *n.* Rückenlehne, *die;* ~ '**room** *n.* Hinterzimmer, *das;* ~**scratching** *n.* (fig. coll.) **[mutual]** ~**scratching** Klüngelei, *die* (abwertend); ~ '**seat**

n. Rücksitz, *der;* (in bus, coach) hinterer Sitzplatz; **take a** ~ **seat** (fig. coll.) in den Hintergrund treten; ~**-seat driver** /-'-/ *besserwisserischer Beifahrer, der immer dazwischenredet;* ~**side** *n.* Hinterteil, *das* (ugs.); Hintern, *der* (ugs.); **get [up] off one's** ~**side** seinen Hintern heben (ugs.); ~**sight** *n.* Visier, *das;* ~**slapping** *adj.* (fig.) plump-vertraulich; ~**slider** /'bækslaɪdə(r)/ *n.* Abtrünnige, *der/die;* ~**space** *v.i.* die Rücktaste betätigen; ~'**stage** *adj.* hinter der Bühne; **2** *adv.* **(a)** go ~**stage** hinter die Bühne gehen; **wait** ~**stage** hinter der Bühne warten; **(b)** (fig.) hinter den Kulissen; ~ '**stairs** *n. pl.* Hintertreppe, *die;* ~**stitch** **1** *v.t.* & *i.* steppen; **2** *n.* Steppstich, *der;* ~**street** *n.* kleine Seitenstraße; ~**stroke** *n.* (Swimming) Rückenschwimmen, *das;* ~ **talk** (Amer.) ⇒ ~**chat;** ~**track** *v.i.* wieder zurückgehen; (fig.) eine Kehrtwendung machen; ~**-up** *n.* **(a)** (support) Unterstützung, *die;* (of theory, claims) Untermauerung, *die;* **(b)** (reserve) Reserve, *die;* ~**-up supplies** Vorräte für den Bedarfs- *od.* Notfall; ~**-up copy** (Computing) Sicherungskopie, *die;* **make a** ~**-up [copy] [of a disk]** von einer Diskette eine Sicherungskopie machen; **(c)** (Amer.: queue of vehicles) Stau, *der;* **a** ~**-up of cars** eine Autoschlange; **(d)** ~**-up light** (Amer.) Rückfahrscheinwerfer, *der*

backward /'bækwəd/ **1** *adj.* **(a)** rückwärts gerichtet; Rückwärts-; ~ **movement** Rückwärtsbewegung, *die;* **(b)** (slow, retarded) zurückgeblieben ‹*Kind*›; (underdeveloped) rückständig, unterentwickelt ‹*Land, Region*›; ~ **in sth.** in etw. (*Dat.*) zurückgeblieben. **2** *adv.* ⇒ **backwards**

'**backward-looking** *adj.* „rückwärts gewandt"

backwardness /'bækwədnɪs/ *n.*, *no pl.* **(a)** (reluctance, shyness) Zurückhaltung, *die;* **(b)** (of child) Zurückgebliebenheit, *die;* (of country, region) Rückständigkeit, *die;* **the child's** ~ **in school** dass das Kind in der Schule zurückgeblieben ist/war

backwards /'bækwədz/ *adv.* **(a)** nach hinten; **the child fell [over]** ~ **into the water** das Kind fiel rückwärts ins Wasser; **bend** *or* **fall** *or* **lean over** ~ **to do sth.** (fig. coll.) sich zerreißen, um etw. zu tun (ugs.); **(b)** (oppositely to normal direction) rückwärts; ~ **and forwards** (to and fro, lit. or fig.) hin und her; **(c)** (into a worse state) **go** ~: sich verschlechtern; **(d)** (into past) **look** ~: an frühere Zeiten denken; **(e)** (reverse way) rückwärts; von hinten nach vorn; **you're doing everything** ~: du machst ja alles verkehrt herum; **know sth.** ~: etw. in- und auswendig kennen

back: ~**wash** *n.* Rückstrom, *der* (**from** *Gen.*); (fig.) Auswirkungen *Pl.;* ~**water** *n.* totes Wasser; (fig.) Kaff, *das* (ugs. abwertend); ~ '**yard** *n.* Hinterhof, *der;* **in one's own** ~ **yard** (fig.) vor der eigenen Haustür

bacon /'beɪkn/ *n.* [Frühstücks]speck, *der;* ~ **and eggs** Eier mit Speck; **bring home the** ~ (fig. coll.) es schaffen; **save one's** ~ (fig.) die eigene *od.* seine Haut retten

bacteria *pl. of* **bacterium**

bacterial /bæk'tɪərɪəl/ *adj.* bakteriell

bacteriological /bæktɪərɪə'lɒdʒɪkl/ *adj.* bakteriologisch

bacteriology /bæktɪərɪ'ɒlədʒɪ/ *n.* Bakteriologie, *die*

bacterium /bæk'tɪərɪəm/ *n.*, *pl.* **bacteria** /bæk'tɪərɪə/ Bakterie, *die*

bad /bæd/ **1** *adj.*, **worse** /wɜːs/, **worst** /wɜːst/ **(a)** schlecht; (worthless) wertlos, ungedeckt ‹*Scheck*›; (rotten) schlecht, verdorben ‹*Fleisch, Fisch, Essen*›; faul ‹*Ei, Apfel*›; (unpleasant) schlecht, unangenehm ‹*Geruch*›; **sth. gives sb. a** ~ **name** etw. trägt jmdm. einen schlechten Ruf ein; **sb. gets a** ~ **name** jmd. kommt in Verruf; **she is in** ~ **health** sie hat eine angegriffene Gesundheit; **[some]** ~ **news** schlechte *od.* schlimme Nachrichten; ~ **breath** Mundgeruch, *der;* **he is having a** ~ **day** er hat einen schwarzen Tag; ~ **hair day** (coll) schlechter Tag; **I'm having a** ~ **hair day** (coll) heute geht bei mir alles schief; ~ **business** ein schlechtes Geschäft; **it is a** ~ **business** (fig.) das ist eine schlimme Sache; **in the** ~ **old days** in den schlimmen Jahren; **not** ~ (coll.) nicht schlecht; nicht übel; **sth. is not a** ~ **idea** etw. ist keine schlechte Idee; **not half** ~ (coll.) [gar] nicht schlecht; **sth. is too** ~ (coll.) etw. ist ein Jammer; **too** ~! (coll.) so ein Pech! (auch iron.); **go** ~: schlecht werden; **(b)** (noxious) schlecht; schädlich; **(c)** (wicked) schlecht; (immoral) schlecht;

verdorben; (naughty) ungezogen, böse ‹*Kind, Hund*›; **(d)** (offensive) **[use]** ∼ **language** Kraftausdrücke [benutzen]; **(e)** (in ill health) **she's** ∼ **today** es geht ihr heute schlecht; **I have a** ∼ **pain/finger** ich habe schlimme Schmerzen/ (ugs.) einen schlimmen Finger; **be in a** ∼ **way** in schlechtem Zustand sein; **(f)** (serious) schlimm, böse ‹*Sturz, Krise*›; schwer ‹*Fehler, Krankheit, Unfall, Erschütterung*›; hoch ‹*Fieber*›; schrecklich ‹*Feuer*›; **(g)** (coll.: regretful) **a** ∼ **conscience** ein schlechtes Gewissen; **feel** ∼ **about sth./not having done sth.** etw. bedauern/bedauern, dass man etw. nicht getan hat; **I feel** ∼ **about him/her** ich habe seinetwegen/ihretwegen ein schlechtes Gewissen; **(h)** (Commerc.) **a** ∼ **debt** eine uneinbringliche Schuld (Wirtsch.). *See also* **worse 1; worst 1. 2** *n.* **be £100 to the** ∼: mit 100 Pfund in der Kreide stehen (ugs.); **go to the** ∼: auf die schiefe Bahn geraten

baddy /'bædɪ/ *n.* (coll.) Schurke, *der;* **the goodies and the baddies** die Guten und die Bösen (oft iron.)

bade ⇨ **bid 1 c**

badge /bædʒ/ *n.* **(a)** (as sign of office, membership, support) Abzeichen, *das;* (larger) Plakette, *die;* **(b)** (symbol) Symbol, *das*

badger /'bædʒə(r)/ **1** *n.* Dachs, *der.* **2** *v.t.* ∼ **sb. [into doing/to do sth.]** jmdm. keine Ruhe lassen[, bis er/sie etw. tut]; ∼ **sb. with questions** jmdn. mit Fragen löchern (ugs.)

'**badger baiting** *n.* Dachshetze, *die*

badly /'bædlɪ/ *adv.,* **worse** /wɜːs/, **worst** /wɜːst/ **(a)** schlecht; **(b)** (seriously) schwer ‹*verletzt, beschädigt*›; sehr ‹*schief sein, knarren*›; **he hurt himself** ∼: er hat sich (*Dat.*) schwer verletzt; **be** ∼ **beaten** schwer verprügelt werden (ugs.); (in game, battle) vernichtend geschlagen werden; **(c)** (urgently) dringend; **want sth.** ∼: sich (*Dat.*) etw. sehr wünschen; **(d)** (coll.: regretfully) **feel** ∼ **about sth.** etw. [sehr] bedauern. *See also* **worse 2; worst 2**

badminton /'bædmɪntən/ *n.* Federball, *der;* (als Sport) Badminton, *das*

bad-tempered /bæd'tempəd/ *adj.* griesgrämig

baffle /'bæfl/ **1** *v.t.* ∼ **sb.** jmdm. unverständlich sein; jmdn. vor ein Rätsel stellen. **2** *n.* ∼**[-plate]** Prallfläche, *die* (Technik)

baffled /'bæfld/ *adj.* verwirrt; **be** ∼: vor einem Rätsel stehen

bafflement /'bæflmənt/ *n.* Verwirrung, *die*

baffling /'bæflɪŋ/ *adj.* rätselhaft

bag /bæg/ **1** *n.* **(a)** Tasche, *die;* (sack) Sack, *der;* (hand∼) [Hand]tasche, *die;* (of plastic) Beutel, *der;* (small paper ∼) Tüte, *die;* **a** ∼ **of cement** ein Sack Zement; **be a** ∼ **of bones** (fig.) nur Haut und Knochen sein; **[whole]** ∼ **of tricks** (fig.) Trickkiste, *die* (ugs.); **his nomination is in the** ∼ (fig. coll.) er hat die Nominierung in der Tasche (ugs.); **(b)** (Hunting: amount of game) Jagdbeute, *die;* Strecke, *die* (Jägerspr.); **(c)** *in pl.* (coll.: large amount) ∼**s of** jede Menge (ugs.); **(d) have** ∼**s under** *or* **below one's eyes** Tränensäcke haben; **(e)** (sl. derog.: woman) **[old]** ∼: alte Schlampe (ugs. abwertend). **2** *v.t.,* **-gg-:** **(a)** (put in sacks) in Säcke füllen; (put in plastic ∼s) in Beutel füllen; (put in small paper ∼s) in Tüten füllen; **(b)** (Hunting) erlegen, erbeuten ‹*Tier*›; **(c)** (claim possession of) sich (*Dat.*) schnappen (ugs.)

bagful /'bægfʊl/ *n.* ⇨ **bag 1 a: a** ∼ **of** ein Sack [voll]/ eine Tasche/ein Beutel/eine Tüte [voll]

baggage /'bægɪdʒ/ *n.* Gepäck, *das;* **mental/cultural** ∼ (fig.) geistiges/kulturelles Rüstzeug

baggage: ∼ **allowance** *n.* Freigepäck, *das;* **be over/within one's** ∼ **allowance** Übergepäck/kein Übergepäck haben; ∼ **car** *n.* (Amer.) Gepäckwagen, *der;* ∼ **check** *n.* Gepäckkontrolle, *die;* ∼ **reclaim** *n.* Gepäckausgabe, *die*

bagginess /'bægɪnɪs/ *n., no pl.* Schlaffheit, *die*

baggy /'bægɪ/ *adj.* weit [geschnitten] ‹*Kleid*›; (through long use) ausgebeult ‹*Hose*›

bag: ∼**pipe[s]** *n.* Dudelsack, *der;* ∼**piper** *n.* Dudelsackpfeifer, *der*

bah /bɑː/ *int.* bah

Bahamas /bə'hɑːməz/ *pr. n. pl.* **the** ∼: die Bahamainseln

bail¹ /beɪl/ **1** *n.* **(a)** Kaution, *die;* (personal) Bürgschaft, *die;* **grant sb.** ∼: jmdm. die Freilassung gegen Kaution bewilligen; **be [out] on** ∼: gegen Kaution auf freiem Fuß sein; **put** *or* **release sb. on** ∼: jmdn. gegen Kaution freilassen; **(b)** (person[s] acting as surety) Bürge, *der;* **go** ∼ **for sb.** für jmdn. Bürge sein. **2** *v.t.* **(a)** (release) gegen Kaution freilassen; **(b)** (go ∼ for) bürgen für; ∼ **sb. out** jmdn. gegen Bürgschaft freibekommen; (fig.) jmdm. aus der Klemme helfen (ugs.)

bail² *n.* (Cricket) Querstab, *der*

bail³ *v.t.* (scoop) ∼ **[out]** ausschöpfen

∼ **out** *v.i.* (Aeronaut.) ‹*Pilot:*› abspringen, (Fliegerspr.) aussteigen

bailey /'beɪlɪ/ *n.* (wall) Burgmauer, *die;* (outer court) Zwinger, *der;* (inner court) Burghof, *der;* **the Old B**∼: das Old Bailey (*oberster Strafgerichtshof für London*)

bailiff /'beɪlɪf/ *n.* ▶ 887 | ≈ Justizbeamte, *der;* Büttel, *der* (veralt.); (issuing writs, making arrests) Gerichtsvollzieher, *der*

bairn /beən/ *n.* (Scot./N. Engl./literary) Kind, *das*

bait /beɪt/ **1** *v.t.* mit einem Köder versehen ‹*Falle*›; beködern ‹*Angelhaken*›. **2** *n.* (lit. or fig.) Köder, *der*

bake /beɪk/ **1** *v.t.* **(a)** (cook) backen; ∼**d beans** gebackene Bohnen [in Tomatensoße]; **(b)** (harden) brennen ‹*Ziegel, Keramik*›. **2** *v.i.* backen; gebacken werden; **I'm baking!** (fig.) mir ist wahnsinnig heiß! (ugs.)

'**bakehouse** *n.* Backstube, *die*

baker /'beɪkə(r)/ *n.* ▶ 887 | Bäcker, *der;* **at the** ∼'**s** beim Bäcker; in der Bäckerei; **go to the** ∼'**s** zum Bäcker *od.* zur Bäckerei gehen; **a** ∼'**s dozen** 13 Stück

bakery /'beɪkərɪ/ *n.* Bäckerei, *die*

baking /'beɪkɪŋ/ *adv.* **it's** ∼ **hot today** eine Hitze wie im Backofen ist das heute

baking: ∼ **dish** *n.* Auflaufform, *die;* ∼ **powder** *n.* Backpulver, *das;* ∼ **sheet** *n.* Backblech, *das;* ∼ **soda** *n.* Natron, *das;* ∼ **tin** *n.* Backform, *die;* ∼ **tray** *n.* Kuchenblech, *das*

Balaclava /bælə'klɑːvə/ *n.* ∼ **[helmet]** Balaklavamütze, *die* (*Wollmütze, die Kopf und Hals bedeckt und nur das Gesicht frei läßt*)

balalaika /bælə'laɪkə/ *n.* Balalaika, *die*

balance /'bæləns/ **1** *n.* **(a)** (instrument) Waage, *die;* ∼**[-wheel]** Unruh, *die;* **(b)** (fig.) **be** *or* **hang in the** ∼: in der Schwebe sein; **(c)** (even distribution) Gleichgewicht, *das;* (due proportion) ausgewogenes Verhältnis; **strike a** ∼ **between** den Mittelweg finden zwischen (+ *Dat.*); **(d)** (counterpoise, steady position) Gleichgewicht, *das;* **keep/lose one's** ∼ das Gleichgewicht halten/verlieren; (fig.) sein Gleichgewicht bewahren/verlieren; **off [one's]** ∼ (lit. or fig.) aus dem Gleichgewicht; **(e)** (preponderating weight or amount) Bilanz, *die;* **(f)** (Bookk.: difference) Bilanz, *die;* (state of bank account) Kontostand, *der;* (statement) Auszug, *der;* **on** ∼ (fig.) alles in allem; ∼ **sheet** Bilanz, *die;* **(g)** (Econ.) ∼ **of payments** Zahlungsbilanz, *die;* ∼ **of trade** Handelsbilanz, *die;* **(h)** (remainder) Rest, *der.* **2** *v.t.* **(a)** (weigh up) abwägen; ∼ **sth. with** *or* **by** *or* **against sth. else** etw. gegen etw. anderes abwägen; **(b)** (bring into or keep in ∼) balancieren; auswuchten ‹*Rad*›; ∼ **oneself** balancieren; **(c)** (equal, neutralize) ausgleichen; ∼ **each other, be** ∼**d** sich (*Dat.*) die Waage halten; **(d)** (make up for, exclude dominance of) ausgleichen; **(e)** (Bookk.) bilanzieren. **2** *v.i.* **(a)** (be in equilibrium) balancieren; **balancing act** (lit. or fig.) Balanceakt, *der;* **(b)** (Bookk.) ausgeglichen sein

balanced /'bælənst/ *adj.* ausgewogen; ausgeglichen ‹*Person, Team, Gemüt*›

balcony /'bælkənɪ/ *n.* Balkon, *der*

bald /bɔːld/ *adj.* **(a)** kahl ‹*Person, Kopf*›; kahlköpfig, glatzköpfig ‹*Person*›; **he is** ∼: er ist kahl[köpfig] *od.* hat eine Glatze; **go** ∼: eine Glatze bekommen; **(b)** (plain) einfach, schmucklos ‹*Rede, Prosa*›; knapp, nackt ‹*Behauptung*›; **(c)** (coll.: worn smooth) abgefahren ‹*Reifen*›

balderdash /'bɔːldədæʃ/ *n., no pl., no indef. art.* Unsinn, *der*

bald-headed /bɔːld'hedɪd/ *adj.* glatzköpfig, kahlköpfig

balding /'bɔːldɪŋ/ *adj.* mit beginnender Glatze nachgestellt; **be** ∼: kahl werden

baldness /'bɔːldnɪs/ *n., no pl.* ⇒ **bald** a, b: Kahlheit, *die;* Einfachheit, *die;* Knappheit, *die*

bale /beɪl/ **1** *n.* Ballen, *der.* **2** *v.t.* (pack) in Ballen verpacken; zu Ballen binden ‹*Heu*›

baleful /'beɪlfl/ *adj.* unheilvoll; (malignant) böse

balk /bɔːk, bɔːlk/ **1** *n.* (timber beam) Balken, *der.* **2** *v.t.* [be]hindern; **they were ~ed in their plan** ihr Plan wurde blockiert. **3** *v.i.* sich sträuben (**at** gegen); ‹*Pferd:*› scheuen (**at** vor + *Dat.*)

Balkan /'bɔːlkn/ **1** *adj.* Balkan-. **2** *n. pl.* **the ~s** der Balkan

ball¹ /bɔːl/ **1** *n.* (a) Kugel, *die;* **the animal rolled itself into a ~:** das Tier rollte sich [zu einer Kugel] zusammen; (b) (Sport, incl. Golf, Polo) Ball, *der;* (Billiards etc., Croquet) Kugel, *die;* **keep one's eye on the ~** (fig.) die Sache im Auge behalten; **start the ~ rolling** (fig.) den Anfang machen; **be on the ~** (fig. coll.) voll da sein (salopp); (be alert) auf Zack sein (ugs.); **play ~** (a) Ball spielen; (fig. coll.: cooperate) mitmachen; (c) (missile) Kugel, *die;* (d) (round mass) Kugel, *die;* (of wool, string, fluff, etc.) Knäuel, *das;* (e) (Anat.) Ballen, *der;* **~ of the hand/foot** Hand-/Fußballen, *der;* (f) *in pl.* (coarse: testicles) Eier *Pl.* (derb); **~s!** (fig.) Scheiße! (salopp abwertend). **2** *v.t.* zusammenballen; ballen ‹*Faust*›

ball² *n.* (dance) Ball, *der;* **have [oneself] a ~** (fig. coll.) sich riesig amüsieren (ugs.)

ballad /'bæləd/ *n.* Ballade, *die*

ballast /'bæləst/ *n.* (a) Ballast, *der;* (b) (coarse stone etc.) Schotter, *der*

ball: ~-'bearing *n.* (Mech.) Kugellager, *das;* **~boy** *n.* Balljunge, *der;* **~cock** *n.* Schwimmer[regel]ventil, *das* (Technik); **~ control** *n.* Ballführung, *die*

ballerina /bælə'riːnə/ *n.* ▶887▎ Ballerina, *die;* **prima ~:** Primaballerina, *die*

ballet /'bæleɪ/ *n.* Ballett, *das;* **~ dancer** Balletttänzer, *der/*-tänzerin, *die*

ball: ~ game *n.* (a) Ballspiel, *das;* (b) (Amer.) Baseballspiel, *das;* **a whole new ~ game** (fig. coll.) eine ganz neue Geschichte (ugs.); **~girl** *n.* Ballmädchen, *das*

ballistic /bə'lɪstɪk/ *adj.* ballistisch; **~ missile** ballistische Rakete

ballistics /bə'lɪstɪks/ *n., no pl.* Ballistik, *die*

balloon /bə'luːn/ **1** *n.* (a) Ballon, *der;* **hot-air ~:** Heißluftballon, *der;* **when the ~ goes up** (fig.) wenn es losgeht (ugs.); (b) (toy) Luftballon, *der;* (c) (coll.: in strip cartoon etc.) Sprechblase, *die.* **2** *v.i.* sich blähen

ballot /'bælət/ **1** *n.* (a) (voting) Abstimmung, *die;* **[secret] ~:** geheime Wahl; **hold** *or* **take a ~:** abstimmen; (b) (vote) Stimme, *die;* (c) (ticket, paper) Stimmzettel, *der.* **2** *v.i.* abstimmen; **~ for sb./sth.** für jmdn./etw. stimmen

ballot: ~ box *n.* Wahlurne, *die;* **~ paper** *n.* Stimmzettel, *der*

ball: ~ pen, ~point, ~point 'pen *ns.* Kugelschreiber, *der;* **~room** *n.* Tanzsaal, *der;* **~room dancing** *n.* Gesellschaftstanz, *der*

balls-up /'bɔːlzʌp/ *n.* (coarse) Scheiß, *der* (salopp abwertend); **make a ~ of sth.** bei etw. Scheiße bauen (derb)

'ball-tampering *n., no pl.:* die Manipulierung der Balloberfläche beim Kricketspiel

ballyhoo /bælɪ'huː/ *n.* (publicity) [Reklame]rummel, *der* (ugs.)

balm /bɑːm/ *n.* (lit. or fig.) Balsam, *der*

balmy /'bɑːmɪ/ *adj.* (a) (soft, mild) mild; (b) ⇒ **barmy**

balsa /'bɔːlsə, 'bɒlsə/ *n.* **~[-wood]** Balsaholz, *das*

balsam /'bɔːlsəm, 'bɒlsəm/ *n.* (lit. or fig.) Balsam, *der*

balsamic vinegar /bæl'sæmɪk/ *n.* Balsamessig, *der*

Balt /bɔːlt/ *n.* Balte, *der/*Baltin, *die*

Baltic /'bɔːltɪk, 'bɒltɪk/ **1** *pr. n.* Ostsee, *die.* **2** *adj.* baltisch; **~ coast** Ostseeküste, *die;* **the ~ Sea** die Ostsee; **the ~ States** das Baltikum

baluster /'bæləstə(r)/ *n.* Geländerpfosten, *der*

balustrade /bælə'streɪd/ *n.* Balustrade, *die*

bamboo /bæm'buː/ *n.* Bambus, *der*

bamboozle /bæm'buːzl/ *v.t.* (coll.) (a) (mystify) verblüffen; (b) (cheat) reinlegen (ugs.); **~ sb. into doing sth.** jmdn. so reinlegen, dass er etw. tut

ban /bæn/ **1** *v.t.,* **-nn-** verbieten; **~ sb. from doing sth.** jmdm. verbieten, etw. zu tun; **he was ~ned from driving/playing** er erhielt Fahr-/Spielverbot; **~ sb. from a place** jmdm. die Einreise/den Zutritt *usw.* verbieten; **~ sb. from a pub/the teaching profession** jmdm. Lokalverbot erteilen/jmdn. vom Lehrberuf ausschließen. **2** *n.* Verbot, *das;* **place a ~ on sth.** etw. mit einem Verbot belegen; **the ~ placed on these drugs** das Verbot dieser Drogen

banal /bə'nɑːl, bə'næl/ *adj.* banal

banality /bə'nælɪtɪ/ *n.* Banalität, *die*

banana /bə'nɑːnə/ *n.* Banane, *die;* **a hand of ~s** eine Hand Bananen (fachspr.); **go ~s** (Brit. coll.) verrückt werden (salopp)

banana: ~ republic *n.* (derog.) Bananenrepublik, *die* (abwertend); **~ skin** *n.* Bananenschale, *die;* **~ 'split** *n.* Bananensplit, *das*

band /bænd/ **1** *n.* (a) Band, *das;* **a ~ of light/colour** ein Streifen Licht/Farbe; (b) (range of values) Bandbreite, *die* (fig.); (c) (Radio) **long/medium ~:** Langwellen-/Mittelwellenband, *das;* (d) (organized group) Gruppe, *die;* (of robbers, outlaws, etc.) Bande, *die;* (e) (of musicians) [Musik]kapelle, *die;* (pop group, jazz ~) Band, *die;* Gruppe, *die;* (dance ~) [Tanz]kapelle, *die;* (military ~) Militärkapelle, *die.* **2** *v.t.* (a) **~ sth.** ein Band um etw. machen; (b) (mark with stripes) bändern. **3** *v.i.* **~ together [with sb.]** sich [mit jmdm.] zusammenschließen

bandage /'bændɪdʒ/ **1** *n.* (for wound, fracture) Verband, *der;* (for fracture, as support) Bandage, *die.* **2** *v.t.* verbinden ‹*[offene] Wunde usw.*›; bandagieren ‹*[verstauchtes] Gelenk usw.*›

b. & b. /biː ən 'biː/ *abbr.* **bed and breakfast**

'bandbox *n.* Bandschachtel, *die* (veralt.); ≈ Hutschachtel, *die*

bandit /'bændɪt/ *n.* Bandit, *der*

banditry /'bændɪtrɪ/ *n.* Banditen[un]wesen, *das*

band: ~master *n.* Kapellmeister, *der;* **~saw** *n.* Bandsäge, *die*

bandsman /'bændzmən/ *n., pl.* **bandsmen** /'bændzmən/ Mitglied der/einer Kapelle/Band

band: ~stand *n.* Musikertribüne, *die;* **~wagon** *n.* **climb** *or* **jump on [to] the ~wagon** (fig.) auf den fahrenden Zug aufspringen (fig.)

bandy¹ /'bændɪ/ *v.t.* (a) herumerzählen (ugs.) ‹*Geschichte*›; **insults were being bandied about** Beschimpfungen flogen hin und her; (b) (exchange) wechseln; **they were ~ing blows** sie tauschten Schläge aus; **don't ~ words with me** ich wünsche keine Diskussion

bandy² *adj.* krumm; **he has ~ legs** *or* **is ~-legged** er hat O-Beine (ugs.); **~-legged person** O-beinige Person (ugs.)

bane /beɪn/ *n.* Ruin, *der;* **he is the ~ of my life** er ist der Nagel zu meinem Sarg (ugs.)

bang /bæŋ/ **1** *v.t.* (a) knallen (ugs.); schlagen; zuknallen (ugs.), zuschlagen ‹*Tür, Fenster, Deckel*›; **~ one's head on** *or* **against the ceiling** mit dem Kopf an die Decke knallen (ugs.) *od.* schlagen; **he ~ed the nail in** er haute den Nagel rein (ugs.); (sl.: copulate with) bumsen (salopp). **2** *v.i.* (a) (strike) **~ [against sth.]** [gegen etw.] schlagen *od.* (ugs.) knallen; **~ at the door** gegen die Tür hämmern; (b) (make sound of blow or explosion) knallen; ‹*Trommeln:*› dröhnen; **~ away at sth.** (shoot) auf etw. (*Akk.*) ballern (ugs.); **~ shut** zuknallen (ugs.); zuschlagen. **3** *n.* (a) (blow) Schlag, *der;* (b) (noise) Knall, *der;* **the party went off with a ~** (fig.) die Party war eine Wucht (ugs.). **4** *adv.* (a) (with impact) mit voller Wucht; (b) (explosively) **go ~** ‹*Gewehr, Feuerwerkskörper:*› krachen; (c) **~ goes sth.** (fig.: sth. ends suddenly) aus ist es mit etw.; **~ went £50** 50 Pfund waren weg; (d) **~ off** (coll.: immediately) sofort; (e) (coll.: exactly) genau; **you are ~ on time** du bist pünktlich auf die Minute (ugs.)

banger /'bæŋə(r)/ *n.* (coll.) (a) (sausage) Würstchen, *das;* (b) (firework) Kracher, *der* (ugs.); (c) (car) Klapperkiste, *die* (ugs.)

Bangladesh /bæŋgləˈdeʃ/ *pr. n.* Bangladesch (*das*)
bangle /ˈbæŋgl/ *n.* Armreif, *der*
banish /ˈbænɪʃ/ *v.t.* verbannen (**from** aus); bannen ‹*Furcht*›
banishment /ˈbænɪʃmənt/ *n.* Verbannung, *die* (**from** aus)
banister /ˈbænɪstə(r)/ *n.* (**a**) (uprights and rail) [Treppen]geländer, *das;* (**b**) *usu. in pl.* (upright) Geländerpfosten, *der*
banjo /ˈbændʒəʊ/ *n., pl.* ∼s *or* ∼es Banjo, *das*
bank¹ /bæŋk/ 1 *n.* (**a**) (slope) Böschung, *die;* (**b**) ▶ 1048 (at side of river) Ufer, *das;* (**c**) (in bed of sea or river) Bank, *die;* (**d**) (mass) **a** ∼ **of clouds/fog** eine Wolken-/Nebelbank. 2 *v.t.* (**a**) überhöhen ‹*Straße, Kurve*›; (**b**) (heap) ∼ [**up**] aufschichten; ∼ [**up**] **the fire with coal** Kohlen auf das Feuer schichten; (**c**) in die Kurve legen ‹*Flugzeug*›. 3 *v.i.* ‹*Flugzeug:*› sich in die Kurve legen
bank² 1 *n.* (Commerc., Finance, Gaming) Bank, *die;* **central** ∼: Zentralbank, *die.* 2 *v.i.* (**a**) ∼ **at/with** …: ein Konto haben bei …; (**b**) ∼ **on sth.** (fig.) auf etw. (*Akk.*) zählen. 3 *v.t.* zur Bank bringen
bank³ *n.* (row) Reihe, *die*
bank: ∼ **account** *n.* Bankkonto, *das;* ∼ **balance** *n.* Kontostand, *der;* ∼ **card** *n.* Scheckkarte, *die;* ∼ **charges** *n. pl.* Kontoführungskosten *Pl.;* ∼ **clerk** *n.* ▶ 887 Bankangestellte, *der/die; das*
banker /ˈbæŋkə(r)/ *n.* ▶ 887 (Commerc., Finance) Bankier, *der;* Banker, *der* (ugs.)
banker's: ∼ **card** ⇨ **bank card;** ∼**'s draft** ⇨ **bank draft;** ∼ **order** *n.* Bankanweisung, *die*
bank 'holiday *n.* (**a**) Bankfeiertag, *der;* (**b**) (Brit.: public holiday) Feiertag, *der*
banking /ˈbæŋkɪŋ/ *n.* Bankwesen, *das;* **a career in** ∼: die Banklaufbahn; *attrib.* ∼ **hours** Schalterstunden *Pl.;* Öffnungszeiten *Pl.* (*der Bank*)
bank: ∼ **loan** *n.* Bankdarlehen, *das;* **take out a** ∼ **loan** bei einer Bank einen Kredit *od.* ein Darlehen aufnehmen; ∼ **manager** *n.* ▶ 887 Zweigstellenleiter, *der/* -leiterin, *die* [einer/der Bank]; ∼**note** *n.* Banknote, *die;* Geldschein, *der;* ∼ **raid** *n.* Banküberfall, *der;* ∼ **rate** *n.* Diskontsatz, *der;* ∼ **robber** *n.* Bankräuber, *der/* -räuberin, *die*
bankrupt /ˈbæŋkrʌpt/ 1 *n.* (**a**) (Law) Gemeinschuldner, *der;* (**b**) (insolvent debtor) Bankrotteur, *der.* 2 *adj.* (lit. or fig.) bankrott; **go** ∼: in Konkurs gehen; Bankrott machen. 3 *v.t.* Bankrott machen
bankruptcy /ˈbæŋkrʌptsɪ/ *n.* Konkurs, *der;* Bankrott, *der;* ∼ **proceedings** Konkursverfahren, *das*
bank: ∼ **statement** *n.* Kontoauszug, *der;* ∼ **transfer** *n.* Banküberweisung, *die*
banner /ˈbænə(r)/ 1 *n.* (**a**) (flag, ensign; also fig.) Banner, *das;* (**b**) (on two poles) Spruchband, *das;* Transparent, *das.* 2 *adj.* ∼ **headline** Balkenüberschrift, *die*
banns /bænz/ *n. pl.* Aufgebot, *das;* **publish/put up the** ∼: das Aufgebot verkünden/aushängen
banquet /ˈbæŋkwɪt/ 1 *n.* Bankett, *das* (geh.). 2 *v.i.* [festlich] tafeln (geh.); ∼**ing hall** Bankettsaal, *der*
banshee /ˈbænʃiː/ *n.* (Ir., Scot.) Banshee, *die* (Myth.); ≈ Weiße Frau
bantam /ˈbæntəm/ *n.* Zwerg-, Bantamhuhn, *das*
'bantamweight *n.* (Boxing etc.) Bantamgewicht, *das;* (person also) Bantamgewichtler, *der*
banter /ˈbæntə(r)/ *n.* (**a**) heiterer Spott; (**b**) (remarks) Spöttelei, *die*
bap /bæp/ *n.* ≈ Brötchen, *das*
baptise ⇨ **baptize**
baptism /ˈbæptɪzm/ *n.* Taufe, *die;* ∼ **of fire** (fig.) Feuertaufe, *die*
baptismal /bæpˈtɪzml/ *adj.* Tauf-; ‹*Wiedergeburt, Reinigung*› durch die Taufe
Baptist /ˈbæptɪst/ 1 *n.* (**a**) Baptist, *der*/Baptistin, *die;* (**b**) **John the** ∼: Johannes der Täufer. 2 *adj.* **the** ∼ **Church/a** ∼ **chapel** die Kirche/eine Kapelle der Baptisten

baptize /bæpˈtaɪz/ *v.t.* taufen; **be** ∼**d a Catholic/Protestant** katholisch/protestantisch getauft werden
bar /bɑː(r)/ 1 *n.* (**a**) (long piece of rigid material) Stange, *die;* (shorter, thinner also) Stab, *der;* (of gold, silver) Barren, *der;* **a** ∼ **of soap** ein Stück Seife; **a** ∼ **of chocolate** ein Riegel Schokolade; (slab) eine Tafel Schokolade; (**b**) (Sport) Stab, *der;* (cross∼) [Sprung]latte, *die;* **parallel** ∼**s** Barren, *der;* **high** *or* **horizontal** ∼: Reck, *das;* (**c**) (heating element) Heizelement, *das* (Elektrot.); (**d**) (band) Streifen, *der;* (on medal) silberner Querstreifen; (**e**) (rod, pole) Stange, *die;* (of cage, prison) Gitterstab, *der;* **behind** ∼**s** (in prison) hinter Gittern; (into prison) hinter Gitter; (**f**) (barrier, lit. or fig.) Barriere, *die* (**to** für); **a** ∼ **on recruitment/promotion** ein Einstellungs-/Beförderungsstopp; (**g**) (for refreshment) Bar, *der;* (counter) Theke, *die;* (**h**) (Law: place at which prisoner stands) ≈ Anklagebank, *die;* **the prisoner at the** ∼: der/die Angeklagte; (**i**) (Law: particular court) Gerichtshof, *der;* **be called to the** ∼: als Anwalt vor höheren Gerichten zugelassen werden; **the Bar** die höhere Anwaltschaft; (**j**) (Mus.) Takt, *der;* (**k**) (sandbank, shoal) Barre, *die;* Sandbank, *die.* 2 *v.t.,* -**rr**-: (**a**) (fasten) verriegeln; ∼**red window** vergittertes Fenster; (**b**) (obstruct) sperren ‹*Straße, Weg*› (**to** für); ∼ **sb.'s way** jmdm. den Weg versperren; (**c**) (prohibit, hinder) verbieten; ∼ **sb. from doing sth.** jmdn. daran hindern, etw. zu tun. 3 *prep.* abgesehen von; ∼ **none** ohne Einschränkung
barb /bɑːb/ *n.* Widerhaken, *der;* (fig.) Gehässigkeit, *die*
barbarian /bɑːˈbeərɪən/ 1 *n.* (lit. or fig.) Barbar, *der.* 2 *adj.* (lit. or fig.) barbarisch
barbaric /bɑːˈbærɪk/ *adj.,* **barbarically** /bɑːˈbærɪkəlɪ/ *adv.* barbarisch
barbarism /ˈbɑːbərɪzm/ *n., no pl.* Barbarei, *die*
barbarity /bɑːˈbærɪtɪ/ *n.* (**a**) *no pl.* Grausamkeit, *die;* **with** ∼: äußerst barbarisch; (**b**) (instance) Barbarei, *die*
barbarous /ˈbɑːbərəs/ *adj.* barbarisch
barbecue /ˈbɑːbɪkjuː/ 1 *n.* (**a**) (party) Grillparty, *die;* (**b**) (food) Grillgericht, *das;* ∼ **sauce** Grillsoße, *die;* Barbecuesoße, *die;* (**c**) (frame) Grill, *der.* 2 *v.t.* grillen
barbed wire /bɑːbd 'waɪər/ *n.* ∼ [**fence**] Stacheldraht[zaun], *der*
barber /ˈbɑːbə(r)/ *n.* ▶ 887 Friseur, *der;* Barbier, *der* (veralt.); **go to the** ∼**'s** zum Friseur gehen; ∼**'s pole** spiralig rot und weiß gestreifter Stab als Ladenschild des Friseurs
barbican /ˈbɑːbɪkən/ *n.* (Hist.) Barbakane, *die;* Torvorwerk, *das*
barbiturate /bɑːˈbɪtjʊrət/ *n.* (Chem.) Barbiturat, *das*
bar: ∼ **chart** *n.* Stabdiagramm, *das;* ∼ **code** *n.* Strichcode, *der*
bard /bɑːd/ *n.* Barde, *der*
bare /beə(r)/ 1 *adj.* (**a**) nackt; **with** *or* **in** ∼ **feet** barfuß; (**b**) (hatless) with one's head ∼: ohne Hut; (**c**) (leafless) kahl; (**d**) (unfurnished) kahl; nackt ‹*Boden*›; (**e**) (unconcealed) **lay** ∼ **sth.** etw. aufdecken; (**f**) (unadorned) nackt ‹*Wahrheit, Tatsache, Wand*›; (**g**) (empty) leer; (**h**) (scanty) knapp ‹*Mehrheit*›; [sehr] gering ‹*Menge, Teil*›; (**i**) (mere) äußerst ‹*Notwendige*›; karg ‹*Essen, Leben*›; **the** ∼ **necessities of life** das zum Leben Notwendigste; (**j**) (without tools) **with one's** ∼ **hands** mit den *od.* seinen bloßen Händen; (**k**) (unprovided with) ∼ **of** ohne. 2 *v.t.* entblößen ‹*Kopf, Arm, Bein*›; bloßlegen ‹*Draht eines Kabels*›; blecken ‹*Zähne*›
bare: ∼**back** 1 *adj.* ‹*Reiter, Reiten*› auf ungesatteltem Pferd; 2 *adv.* ohne Sattel; ∼**faced** /ˈbeəfeɪsd/ *adj.* (fig.) schamlos; ∼**foot** 1 *adj.* barfüßig; 2 *adv.* barfuß; ∼**handed** /beəˈhændɪd/ 1 *adj.* he was ∼**handed** (without gloves) er trug keine Handschuhe; (without weapon) er war unbewaffnet; 2 *adv.* mit bloßen Händen; ∼**headed** /beəˈhedɪd/ 1 *adj.* he was ∼**headed** er trug keine Kopfbedeckung; 2 *adv.* ohne Kopfbedeckung; ∼**legged** *adj.* mit bloßen Beinen
barely /ˈbeəlɪ/ *adv.* (**a**) (only just) kaum; knapp ‹*vermeiden, entkommen*›; (**b**) (scantily) karg
'barfly *n.* (coll.) Kneipenhocker, *der*/-hockerin, *die*
bargain /ˈbɑːgɪn/ 1 *n.* (**a**) (agreement) Abmachung, *die;* **into the** ∼, (Amer.) **in the** ∼: darüber hinaus; **make** *or* **strike a** ∼ **to do sth.** sich darauf einigen, etw. zu tun; (**b**) (thing bought) Kauf, *der;* **a good/bad** ∼: ein guter/ schlechter Kauf; (**c**) (thing offered cheap) günstiges Angebot;

(thing bought cheaply) guter Kauf. *See also* **best 3 e; hard 1 a. 2** *v.i.* **(a)** (discuss) handeln; ∼ **for sth.** um etw. handeln; **(b)** ∼ **for** *or* **on sth.** (expect sth.) mit etw. rechnen; **more than one had** ∼**ed for** mehr als man erwartet hatte

bargain: ∼ **'basement** *n.* Tiefgeschoss mit Sonderangeboten; ∼ **counter** *n.* Tisch mit Sonderangeboten ∼ **hunter** *n.* Schnäppchenjäger, *der/*-jägerin, *die*

bargaining /'bɑːɡɪnɪŋ/ *n.* Handel, *der;* (negotiating) Verhandlungen *Pl.;* ∼ **position** Verhandlungsposition, *die*

bargain: ∼ **'offer** *n.* Sonderangebot, *das;* ∼ **'price** *n.* Sonderpreis, *der*

barge /bɑːdʒ/ **1** *n.* Kahn, *der.* **2** *v.i.* **(a)** (lurch) ∼ **into sb.** jmdn. anrempeln; **(b)** ∼ **in** (intrude) hineinplatzen/hereinplatzen (ugs.) **(on** bei)

bargee /bɑː'dʒiː/ *n.* (Brit.) Flussschiffer, *der*

'bargepole *n.* **I wouldn't touch that with a** ∼**!** (fig.) ich würde das nicht mit der Beißzange anfassen! (ugs.)

baritone /'bærɪtəʊn/ (Mus.) **1** *n.* Bariton, *der;* (voice, part also) Baritonstimme, *die.* **2** *adj.* Bariton-

bark¹ /bɑːk/ **1** *n.* (of tree) Rinde, *die.* **2** *v.t.* (graze) aufschürfen

bark² **1** *n.* (of dog; also fig.) Bellen, *das;* **his** ∼ **is worse than his bite** (fig.) ≈ Hunde, die bellen, beißen nicht. **2** *v.i.* **(a)** (lit. or fig.) bellen; ∼ **at sb.** jmdn. anbellen; **be** ∼**ing up the wrong tree** auf dem Holzweg sein; **(b)** (bellow) brüllen. **3** *v.t.* **(a)** bellen; **(b)** (bellow) ∼ **[out] orders to sb.** jmdm. Befehle zubrüllen

barley /'bɑːlɪ/ *n.* Gerste, *die; see also* **pearl barley**

barley: ∼**corn** *n.* (grain) Gerstenkorn, *das;* ∼ **sugar** *n.* Gerstenzucker, *der;* ∼ **water** *n.* Gerstenwasser, *das* (veralt.)

bar: ∼**maid** *n.* ▶887 (Brit.) Bardame, *die;* ∼**man** /'bɑːmən/ *n., pl.* ∼**men** /'bɑːmən/ ▶887 Barmann, *der*

barmy /'bɑːmɪ/ *adj.* (coll.: crazy) bescheuert (salopp)

barn /bɑːn/ *n.* Scheune, *die*

barnacle /'bɑːnəkl/ *n.* (Zool.) Rankenfüßer, *der*

barn: ∼ **dance** *n.* ≈ Schottische, *der;* ∼ **owl** *n.* Schleiereule, *die;* ∼**storming** /'bɑːnstɔːmɪŋ/ *adj.* mitreißend; ∼**yard** *n.* Wirtschaftshof, *der*

barometer /bə'rɒmɪtə(r)/ *n.* (lit. or fig.) Barometer, *das*

barometric /bærə'metrɪk/ *adj.* barometrisch; ∼ **pressure** Luftdruck, *der*

baron /'bærn/ *n.* **(a)** ▶1152 (holder of title) Baron, *der;* Freiherr, *der;* **(b)** (powerful person) Papst, *der* (fig.); **press** ∼**:** Pressezar, *der;* **oil** ∼**:** Ölmagnat, *der*

baroness /'bærənɪs/ *n.* ▶1152 Baronin, *die;* Freifrau, *die*

baronet /'bærənɪt/ *n.* Baronet, *der*

baronial /bə'rəʊnɪəl/ *adj.* freiherrlich

baroque /bə'rɒk/ **1** *n.* Barock, *das.* **2** *adj.* **(a)** barock; Barock⟨*malerei, -musik usw.*⟩; **(b)** (grotesque) barock

barque /bɑːk/ *n.* Bark, *die*

barrack¹ /'bærək/ *n. usu. in pl., often constr. as sing.* Kaserne, *die*

barrack² **1** *v.i.* buhen (ugs.). **2** *v.t.* ausbuhen (ugs.)

barrack 'square *n.* Kasernenhof, *der*

barracuda /bærə'kuːdə/ *n., pl. same or* ∼**s** Barrakuda, *der*

barrage /'bærɑːʒ/ *n.* **(a)** (Mil.) Sperrfeuer, *das;* (fig.) **a** ∼ **of questions** ein Bombardement von Fragen; **a** ∼ **of cheers** stürmischer Jubel; **(b)** (dam) Talsperre, *die*

'barrage balloon *n.* Sperrballon, *der*

barrel /'bærl/ *n.* **(a)** (vessel) Fass, *das;* (measure) Barrel, *das;* **be over a** ∼ (fig.) in der Klemme sitzen (ugs.); **have sb. over a** ∼ (fig.) jmdn. in der Zange haben (ugs.); **scrape the** ∼ (fig.) das Letzte zusammenkratzen (ugs.); **(b)** (of gun) Lauf, *der;* (of cannon etc.) Rohr, *das*

barrel: ∼**-chested** /'bærlt∫estɪd/ *adj.* mit einem breiten, gewölbten Brustkorb *nachgestellt;* ∼ **organ** *n.* (Mus.) Leierkasten, *der;* Drehorgel, *die*

barren /'bærn/ *adj.* **(a)** (infertile) unfruchtbar; **(b)** (meagre, dull) nutzlos ⟨*Handlung, Arbeit*⟩; mager ⟨*Ergebnis*⟩; unfruchtbar ⟨*Periode, Beziehung*⟩; fruchtlos ⟨*Diskussion*⟩

barrenness /'bærnnɪs/ *n., no pl.* ⇒ **barren:** Unfruchtbarkeit, *die;* Nutzlosigkeit, *die;* Magerkeit, *die;* Fruchtlosigkeit, *die*

barricade /bærɪ'keɪd/ **1** *n.* Barrikade, *die.* **2** *v.t.* verbarrikadieren

barrier /'bærɪə(r)/ *n.* **(a)** (fence) Barriere, *die;* (at railway, frontier) Schranke, *die;* **(b)** (gate of railway station) Sperre, *die;* **(c)** (obstacle, lit. or fig.) Barriere, *die;* **a** ∼ **to progress** ein Hindernis für den Fortschritt

'barrier cream *n.* Schutzcreme, *die*

barring /'bɑːrɪŋ/ *prep.* außer im Falle (+ *Gen.*); ∼ **accidents** falls nichts passiert

barrister /'bærɪstə(r)/ *n.* ▶887 **(a)** (Brit.) ∼**[-at-law]** Barrister, *der;* ≈ [Rechts]anwalt/-anwältin vor höheren Gerichten, *der;* **(b)** (Amer.: lawyer) [Rechts]anwalt, *der/* -anwältin, *die*

barroom /'bɑːruːm/ *n.* (Amer.) Bar, *die*

barrow¹ /'bærəʊ/ *n.* **(a)** Karre, *die;* Karren, *der;* **(b)** ⇒ **wheelbarrow**

barrow² *n.* (Archaeol.) Hügelgrab, *das*

'barrow boy *n.* ▶887 (Brit.) Straßenhändler, *der*

'bartender *n.* ▶887 Barkeeper, *der*

barter /'bɑːtə(r)/ **1** *v.t.* [ein]tauschen (**for** für *od.* gegen); ∼ **away** etw. verspielen (fig.). **2** *v.i.* Tauschhandel treiben. **3** *n.* Tauschhandel, *der*

basalt /'bæsɔːlt/ *n.* Basalt, *der*

base¹ /beɪs/ **1** *n.* **(a)** (of lamp, pyramid, wall, mountain, microscope) Fuß, *der;* (of cupboard, statue) Sockel, *der;* (fig.) (support) Basis, *die;* (principle) Ausgangsbasis, *die;* (main ingredient) Hauptbestandteil, *der;* (of make-up) Grundlage, *die;* **(b)** (Mil.) Basis, *die;* Stützpunkt, *der;* (fig.: for sightseeing) Ausgangspunkt, *der;* **(c)** (Baseball) Mal, *das;* **get to first** ∼ (fig. coll.) [wenigstens] etwas erreichen; **(d)** (Archit., Geom., Surv., Math.) Basis, *die;* **(e)** (Chem.) Base, *die.* **2** *v.t.* **(a)** gründen (**on** auf + *Akk.*); **be** ∼**d on sth.** sich auf etw. (*Akk.*) gründen; ∼ **one's hopes on sth.** seine Hoffnung auf etw. (*Akk.*) gründen; **a book** ∼**d on newly discovered papers** ein Buch, das auf neu entdeckten Dokumenten basiert; **(b)** in *pass.* **be** ∼**d in Paris** (permanently) in Paris sitzen; (temporarily) in Paris sein; **computer-**∼**d accountancy** Buchführung über Computer; **land-**∼**d forces** landgestützte Streitkräfte; **(c)** ∼ **oneself on** sich stützen auf (+ *Akk.*)

base² *adj.* **(a)** (morally low) niederträchtig; niedrig ⟨*Beweggrund*⟩; **(b)** (cowardly) feige; (selfish) selbstsüchtig; (mean) niederträchtig

baseball /'beɪsbɔːl/ *n.* Baseball, *der*

'base camp *n.* Basislager, *das*

baseless /'beɪslɪs/ *adj.* unbegründet

'baseline *n.* Grundlinie, *die*

basement /'beɪsmənt/ *n.* Kellergeschoss, *das;* (esp. in department store) Untergeschoss, *das;* **a** ∼ **flat** eine Kellerwohnung

base 'metal *n.* unedles Metall

baseness /'beɪsnɪs/ *n., no pl.* ⇒ **base²:** Niederträchtigkeit, *die;* Niedrigkeit, *die*

'base rate *n.* (Finance) Eckzins, *der*

bases *pl. of* **base¹** *or* **basis**

bash /bæ∫/ **1** *v.t.* [heftig] schlagen; ∼ **one's head against sth.** sich (*Dat.*) den Kopf [heftig] an etw. (*Dat.*) anschlagen. **2** *n.* **(a)** heftiger Schlag; **(b)** (coll.: attempt) Versuch, *der;* **have a** ∼ **at sth.** etw. mal versuchen

bashful /'bæ∫fl/ *adj.* schüchtern

basic /'beɪsɪk/ *adj.* **(a)** (fundamental) grundlegend; Grund⟨*struktur, -prinzip, -bestandteil, -wortschatz, -lohn*⟩; Haupt⟨*problem, -grund, -sache*⟩; **be** ∼ **to sth.** wesentlich für etw. sein; **have a** ∼ **knowledge of sth.** Grundkenntnisse einer Sache (*Gen.*) haben; **a** ∼ **working day** ein normaler Arbeitstag; **(b)** (Chem.) basisch. *See also* **basics**

basically /'beɪsɪkəlɪ/ *adv.* im Grunde; grundsätzlich ⟨*übereinstimmen*⟩; (mainly) hauptsächlich

Basic 'English *n.* Basic English, *das; auf einem sehr einfachen Grundwortschatz beruhendes Englisch*

basics /'beɪsɪks/ *n. pl.* **stick to the** ∼**:** beim Wesentlichen bleiben; **the** ∼ **of maths/cooking** die

Grundlagen der Mathematik/das ABC der Kochkunst; **go** *or* **get back to** ~ (when learning) sich [zuerst] Grundkenntnisse aneignen; (return to moral values) wieder auf die [moralischen] Grundwerte zurückkommen

basil /'bæzɪl/ *n.* (Bot.) [**sweet**] ~: Basilikum, *das*

basilica /bə'zɪlɪkə/ *n.* (Archit., Eccl.) Basilika, *die*

basin /'beɪsn/ *n.* Becken, *das;* (wash-~) Waschbecken, *das;* (bowl) Schüssel, *die;* **the Amazon** ~: das Amazonasbecken

basis /'beɪsɪs/ *n., pl.* **bases** /'beɪsiːz/ (a) (ingredient) Grundbestandteil, *der;* (b) (foundation, principle, common ground) Basis, *die;* **on a purely friendly** ~: auf rein freundschaftlicher Basis; **on a first come first served** ~: nach dem Prinzip „Wer zuerst kommt, mahlt zuerst"; (c) (beginning) Ausgangspunkt, *der*

bask /bɑːsk/ *v.i.* (a) sich [wohlig] wärmen; sich aalen (ugs.); ~ **in the sun** sich sonnen; (b) (fig.) sich sonnen (**in** in + *Dat.*)

basket /'bɑːskɪt/ *n.* (a) Korb, *der;* (smaller, for bread etc.) Körbchen, *das;* (of chip pan) Drahteinsatz, *der;* (b) (quantity) **a** ~ [**full**] **of apples** ein Korb [voll] Äpfel

'basketball *n.* Basketball, *der*

basketful /'bɑːskɪtfʊl/ ⇒ **basket** b

basketry /'bɑːskɪtrɪ/ ⇒ **basketwork**

basket: ~ **weave** *n.* Panamabindung, *die* (Weberei); ~**work** *n.* (art) Korbflechterei, *die;* (activity) Korbflechten, *das;* (collectively) Korbwaren *Pl.;* **a piece of** ~**work** ein Korbgeflecht

basking 'shark *n.* Riesenhai, *der*

Basle /bɑːl/ *pr. n.* ▶ **1159** | Basel (*das*)

Basque /bæsk, bɑːsk/ ▶ **897** |, ▶ **947** | **1** *adj.* baskisch; **the** ~ **Country** das Baskenland. **2** *n.* (a) Baske, *der*/Baskin, *die;* (b) (language) Baskisch, *das*

bas-relief /'bæsrɪliːf/ *n.* (Art) Basrelief, *das*

bass¹ /bæs/ *n., pl. same or* ~**es** (Zool.) Barsch, *der*

bass² /beɪs/ (Mus.) **1** *n.* (a) Bass, *der;* (voice, part also) Bassstimme, *die;* (b) (coll.) (double ~) [Kontra]bass, *der;* (~ guitar) Bass, *der* **2** *adj.* Bass-

bass /beɪs/**:** ~ **clef** *n.* (Mus.) Bassschlüssel, *der;* ~ **drum** *n.* große Trommel

basset /'bæsɪt/ *n.* ~[**-hound**] Basset, *der*

bass guitar /beɪs gɪ'tɑː(r)/ *n.* Bassgitarre, *die*

bassoon /bə'suːn/ *n.* (Mus.) Fagott, *das*

bastard /'bɑːstəd/ **1** *adj.* (a) unehelich; (b) (hybrid) verfälscht ⟨*Sprache, Stil*⟩; (c) (Bot., Zool.) Bastard-. **2** *n.* (a) uneheliches Kind; (b) (sl.) (disliked person) Mistkerl, *der* (derb); (disliked thing) Scheißding, *das* (derb); **the poor** ~! (unfortunate person) das arme Schwein! (ugs.)

baste¹ /beɪst/ *v.t.* (stitch) heften

baste² *v.t.* [mit Fett/Bratensaft] begießen ⟨*Fleisch*⟩

bastion /'bæstɪən/ *n.* (lit. or fig.) Bastei, *die*

bat¹ /bæt/ *n.* (Zool.) Fledermaus, *die;* **blind as a** ~ (fig.) blind wie ein Maulwurf; **have** ~**s in the belfry** (coll.) einen Dachschaden haben (ugs.)

bat² **1** *n.* (a) (Sport) Schlagholz, *das;* (for table tennis) Schläger, *der;* **do sth. off one's own** ~ (fig.) etw. auf eigene Faust tun; **right off the** ~ (Amer. fig.) sofort; (b) (act of using) ~: Schlag, *der.* **2** *v.t. & i.* **-tt-** schlagen

bat³ *v.t.,* **-tt-:** **not** ~ **an eyelid** (fig.) nicht mit der Wimper zucken

batch /bætʃ/ *n.* (a) (of loaves) Schub, *der;* (b) (of people) Gruppe, *die;* (of books, papers, etc.) Stapel, *der;* (of rules, regulations) Bündel, *das*

batch: ~ **file** *n.* (Computing) Stapeldatei, *die;* ~ '**processing** *n.* (Computing) Stapelverarbeitung, *die;* ~ **production** *n.* Stapelfertigung, *die*

bate¹ /beɪt/ *v.t.* **with** ~**d breath** mit angehaltenem Atem

bate² *n.* (Brit. coll.) Rage, *die* (ugs.); **be in a** [**terrible**] ~: [schrecklich] in Rage sein; **get/fly into a** ~: in Rage geraten

bath /bɑːθ/ **1** *n., pl.* ~**s** /bɑːðz/ (a) Bad, *das;* **have** *or* **take a** ~: ein Bad nehmen; (b) (vessel) ~[**tub**] Badewanne, *die;* **room with** ~: Zimmer mit Bad; (c) *usu. in pl.* (building) Bad, *das;* [**swimming**] ~s Schwimmbad, *das.* **2** *v.t. & i.* baden

bath: **B**~ '**bun** *n.* ≈ Rosinenbrötchen mit Zuckerguss; ~ **cap** *n.* Duschhaube, *die;* ~ **chair** *n.* Rollstuhl, *der;* ~ **cube** *n.* Badesalzwürfel, *der*

bathe /beɪð/ **1** *v.t.* (a) baden; (b) (moisten) baden ⟨*Wunde, Körperteil*⟩; ~**d with** *or* **in sweat** schweißüberströmt; (c) ~**d in sunlight** von der Sonne beschienen. **2** *v.i.* baden; **go bathing** baden gehen. **3** *n.* Bad, *das* (im Meer usw.); **have a** ~: baden

bather /'beɪðə(r)/ *n.* Badende, *der/die*

bathing: ~ **beach** *n.* Badestrand, *der;* ~ **cap** *n.* Bademütze, *die;* ~ **costume** *n.* Badeanzug, *der;* ~ **suit** *n.* Badeanzug, *der;* ~ **trunks** *n. pl.* Badehose, *die*

bath: ~ **mat** *n.* Badematte, *die;* ~**robe** *n.* Bademantel, *der;* ~**room** *n.* Badezimmer, *das;* ~ **salts** *n. pl.* Badesalz, *das;* ~**time** *n.* Badezeit, *die;* ~ **towel** *n.* Badetuch, *das;* ~**tub** ⇒ **bath** 1 b; ~**water** *n.* Badewasser, *das; see also* **baby** a

batik /bə'tiːk/ *n.* Batik, *der od. die*

batman /'bætmən/ *n., pl.* **batmen** /'bætmən/ (Mil.) [Offiziers]bursche, *der*

baton /'bætn/ *n.* (a) (staff of office) Stab, *der;* (b) (truncheon) Schlagstock, *der;* (c) (Mus.) Taktstock, *der;* (d) (for relay race) [Staffel]stab, *der*

batsman /'bætsmən/ *n., pl.* **batsmen** /'bætsmən/ (Sport) Schlagmann, *der*

battalion /bə'tæljən/ *n.* (lit. or fig.) Bataillon, *das*

batten /'bætn/ **1** *n.* (Constr., Naut.) Latte, *die.* **2** *v.t.* (Naut.) ~ **down** [ver]schalken ⟨*Luke*⟩

batter¹ /'bætə(r)/ **1** *v.t.* (a) (strike) einschlagen auf (+ *Akk.*); ~ **down/in** einschlagen; ~ **sth. to pieces** etw. zerschmettern; (b) (attack with artillery) beschießen; (c) (bruise, damage) übel zurichten; misshandeln ⟨*Baby, Ehefrau*⟩; ~**ed by the gales** vom Sturm stark beschädigt; **a** ~**ed car** ein verbeultes Auto. **2** *v.i.* heftig klopfen; **they** ~**ed at** *or* **against the door** sie hämmerten gegen die Tür

batter² *n.* (Cookery) [Back]teig, *der;* (for pancake) [Eierkuchen]teig, *der*

'battering ram *n.* Rammbock, *der*

battery /'bætərɪ/ *n.* (a) (series; also Mil., Electr.) Batterie, *die;* **a** ~ **of specialists** (fig.) eine ganze Reihe von Spezialisten; (b) (Law) [**assault and**] ~: tätlicher Angriff

battery: ~ **charger** *n.* Batterieladegerät, *das;* ~ '**farming** *n.* Batteriehaltung, *die;* ~ '**hen** *n.* Batteriehuhn, *das;* ~**-operated** *adj.* batteriebetrieben

battle /'bætl/ **1** *n.* (a) (fight) Schlacht, *die;* **the** ~ **at Amman** die Schlacht bei Amman; **do** *or* **give** ~: kämpfen; **join** ~ **with sb.** jmdm. eine Schlacht liefern; **die in** ~: [in der Schlacht] fallen; (b) (fig.: contest) Kampf, *der;* ~ **of wits** geistiger Wettstreit; **sth. is half the** ~: mit etw. ist schon viel gewonnen. **2** *v.i.* kämpfen (**with** *or* **against** mit *od.* gegen, **for** für). **3** *v.t.* ~ **one's way through the crowd** sich durch die Menge kämpfen

battle: ~**axe** *n.* (a) Streitaxt, *die;* (b) (coll.: woman) Schreckschraube, *die* (ugs. abwertend); ~**dress** *n.* (Mil.) (for general service) Arbeitsanzug, *der;* (for field service) Kampfanzug, *der;* ~**field**, ~**ground** *ns.* Schlachtfeld, *das*

battlement /'bætlmənt/ *n., usu. in pl.* Zinne, *die*

'battleship *n.* Schlachtschiff, *das*

batty /'bætɪ/ *adj.* (coll.) bekloppt (salopp); **go** *or* **become** ~: überschnappen (ugs.)

bauble /'bɔːbl/ *n.* Flitter, *der*

Bavaria /bə'veərɪə/ *pr. n.* Bayern (*das*)

Bavarian /bə'veərɪən/ ▶ **897** |, ▶ **947** | **1** *adj.* bay[e]risch; **sb. is** ~: jmd. ist Bayer/Bayerin. **2** *n.* (a) (person) Bayer, *der*/Bayerin, *die;* (b) (dialect) Bay[e]risch[e], *das*

bawdy /'bɔːdɪ/ *adj.* zweideutig, (stronger) obszön ⟨*Sprache, Geschichte, Witz*⟩; obszön ⟨*Person*⟩

bawl /bɔːl/ **1** *v.t.* brüllen; ~ **sth. at sb.** jmdm. etw. zubrüllen; ~ **sb. out** (coll.) jmdn. zusammenstauchen (ugs.). **2** *v.i.* brüllen; ~ **out to sb.** nach jmdm. brüllen; ~ **at sb.** jmdn. anbrüllen

bay¹ /beɪ/ n. (of sea) Bucht, die; (larger also) Golf, der

bay² n. (a) (space in room) Erker, der; (b) **loading** ~: Ladeplatz, der; [**parking**] ~: Stellplatz, der; **sick**~ (Navy) Schiffshospital, das; (Mil.) Sanitätsbereich, der; (in school, college, office) Krankenzimmer, das

bay³ 1 n. (bark) Gebell, das; **hold** or **keep sb./sth. at** ~ (fig.) sich (Dat.) jmdn./etw. vom Leib halten. 2 v.i. bellen; ~ **at sb./sth.** jmdn./etw. anbellen

bay⁴ n. (Bot.) Lorbeer[baum], der

bay⁵ 1 adj. braun ‹Pferd›. 2 n. Braune, der

'bay leaf n. (Cookery) Lorbeerblatt, das

bayonet /'beɪənɪt/ 1 n. Bajonett, das; **with fixed** ~s mit aufgepflanzten Bajonetten 2 v.t. mit dem Bajonett aufspießen

bay 'window n. Erkerfenster, das

bazaar /bə'zɑ:(r)/ n. (oriental market) Basar, der; (sale) [Wohltätigkeits]basar, der

BBC abbr. **British Broadcasting Corporation** BBC, die

BC abbr. ▶ 738 **before Christ** v. Chr.

be /bi:/ v., pres. t. **I am** /əm, stressed æm/, neg. (coll.) **ain't** /emt/, **he is** /ɪz/, neg. (coll.) **isn't** /'ɪznt/; **we are** /ə(r), stressed ɑ:(r)/, neg. (coll.) **aren't** /ɑ:nt/; p.t. **I was** /wəz, stressed wɒz/, neg. (coll.) **wasn't** /'wɒznt/, **we were** /wə(r), stressed wɜ:(r), weə(r)/, neg. (coll.) **weren't** /wɜ:nt, weənt/; pres. p. **being** /'bi:ɪŋ/; p.p. **been** /bɪn, stressed bi:n/ 1 copula (a) indicating quality or attribute sein; **she'll be ten next week** sie ist nächste Woche zehn; **she is a mother/an Italian** sie ist Mutter/Italienerin; **being a Frenchman, he likes wine** als Franzose trinkt er gern Wein; **he is being nice to them/ sarcastic** er ist nett zu ihnen/jetzt ist er sarkastisch; (b) in exclamations **was she pleased!** war sie [vielleicht] froh!; **aren't you a big boy!** was bist du schon für ein großer Junge!; (c) **will be** indicating supposition [**I dare say**] **you'll be a big boy by now** du bist jetzt sicher schon ein großer Junge; **you'll be relieved to hear that** du wirst erleichtert sein, das zu hören; (d) indicating physical or mental welfare or state sein; sich fühlen; **I am hot** mir ist heiß; **I am freezing** mich friert es; **how are you/ is she?** wie geht's (ugs.) /geht es ihr?; (e) identifying the subject **it is the 5th today** heute haben wir den Fünften; **who's that?** wer ist das?; **it is she, it's her** sie ist's; **if I were you** an deiner Stelle; (f) indicating profession, pastime, etc. **be a teacher/a footballer** Lehrer/Fußballer sein; **she wants to be a surgeon** sie möchte Chirurgin werden; (g) with possessive **it is hers** es ist ihrs; es gehört ihr; (h) (cost) kosten; **how much are the eggs?** was kosten die Eier?; (i) (equal) sein; **two times three is six, two threes are six** zweimal drei ist od. sind od. gibt sechs; **sixteen ounces is a pound** sechzehn Unzen sind od. ergeben ein Pfund; (j) (constitute) bilden; **London is not England** London ist nicht [gleich] England; (k) (mean) bedeuten; **he was everything to her** er bedeutete ihr alles. 2 v.i. (a) (exist) [vorhanden] sein; existieren; **can such things be?** kann es so etwas geben?; kann so etwas vorkommen?; **I think, therefore I am** ich denke, also bin ich; **there is/are …:** es gibt …; **for the time being** vorläufig; **Miss Jones that was** das frühere Fräulein Jones; **be that as it may** wie dem auch sei; (b) (remain) bleiben; **I shan't be a moment** or **second** ich komme gleich; noch eine Minute; **she has been in her room for hours** sie ist schon seit Stunden in ihrem Zimmer; **let it be** lass es sein; **let him/her be** lass ihn/sie in Ruhe; **how long has he been here?** wie lange ist er schon hier?; (c) (happen) stattfinden; sein; **where will the party be?** wo ist die Party?; wo findet die Party statt?; (d) (go, come) **be off with you!** geh/geht!; **I'm off** or **for home** ich gehe jetzt nach Hause; **she's from Australia** sie stammt od. ist aus Australien; **are you for London?** wollen Sie nach London?; (e) (on visit etc.) sein; **have you [ever] been to London?** bist du schon einmal in London gewesen?; **has anyone been?** ist jemand da gewesen?; (f) **she's been and tidied the room** (coll.) sie hat doch wirklich das Zimmer aufgeräumt; **the children have been at the biscuits** die Kinder waren an den Keksen (ugs.); **I've been into this matter** ich habe mich mit der Sache befasst. 3

v. aux. (a) forming passive werden; **the child was found** das Kind wurde gefunden; **German is spoken here** hier wird Deutsch gesprochen; (b) forming continuous tenses, active **he is reading** er liest [gerade]; er ist beim Lesen; **I am leaving tomorrow** ich reise morgen [ab]; **the train was departing when I got there** der Zug fuhr gerade ab, als ich ankam; (c) forming continuous tenses, passive **the house is/was being built** das Haus wird/wurde [gerade] gebaut; (d) expr. obligation **be to** sollen; **I am to inform you** ich soll Sie unterrichten; **he is to be admired** er ist zu bewundern; (e) expr. arrangement **be to** sollen; **the Queen is to arrive at 3 p.m.** die Königin soll um 15 Uhr eintreffen; (f) expr. possibility **it was not to be seen** es war nicht zu sehen; **I was not to be sidetracked** ich ließ mich nicht ablenken; (g) expr. destiny **they were never to meet again** sie sollten sich nie wieder treffen; (h) expr. condition **if I were to tell you that …, were I to tell you that …:** wenn ich dir sagen würde, dass … 4 **bride-/husband-to-be** zukünftige Braut/ zukünftiger Ehemann; **mother-/father-to-be** werdende Mutter/werdender Vater; **the be-all and end-all** das A und O

beach /bi:tʃ/ 1 n. Strand, der; **on the** ~: am Strand. 2 v.t. auf [den] Strand setzen ‹Schiff usw.›; ans Ufer ziehen ‹Boot, Wal›

beach: ~**ball** n. Wasserball, der; ~**comber** /'bi:tʃ kəʊmə(r)/ n. Strandgutsammler, der; ~**head** n. (Mil.) Brückenkopf, der; ~**wear** n. Strandkleidung, die

beacon /'bi:kn/ n. (a) Leucht-, Signalfeuer, das; (Naut.) Leuchtbake, die; (b) (radio station) Funkfeuer, das; (c) (signal light) Signalleuchte, die; (for aircraft) Landelicht, das

bead /bi:d/ n. (a) Perle, die; (on rosary) Perle, die; **tell one's** ~s den Rosenkranz beten; ~s **of dew/ perspiration** or **sweat** Tau-/Schweißtropfen; (b) (gunsight) Korn, das

beady /'bi:dɪ/ adj. ~ **eyes** Knopfaugen; **those** ~ **eyes of hers don't miss anything** ihrem wachsamen Blick entgeht nichts; **I've got my** ~ **eye on you** ich lasse dich nicht aus den Augen

'beady-eyed adj. mit Knopfaugen nachgestellt; (watchful) mit wachen Augen nachgestellt

beagle /'bi:gl/ n. Beagle, der

beak¹ /bi:k/ n. Schnabel, der; (of turtle, octopus) Mundwerkzeug, das; (fig.: hooked nose) Hakennase, die; Zinken, der (salopp)

beak² n. (Brit. coll.: magistrate, judge) Kadi, der (ugs.)

beaked /bi:kt/ adj. geschnäbelt

beaker /'bi:kə(r)/ n. (a) Becher, der; (b) (Chem.) Becherglas, das

'be-all ⇒ **be** 4

beam /bi:m/ 1 n. (a) (timber etc.) Balken, der; (b) (Naut.) (ship's breadth) [größte] Schiffsbreite; (side of ship) [Schiffs]- seite, die; **on the port** ~: backbords; **broad in the** ~ (fig. coll.) breithüftig; (c) (ray etc.) [Licht]strahl, der; ~ **of light** Lichtstrahl, der; **the car's headlamps were on full** ~: die Scheinwerfer des Wagens waren aufgeblendet; (d) (Aeronaut., Mil., etc.: guide) Peil- od. Leitstrahl, der; **be off** ~ (fig. coll.) danebenliegen (ugs.); (e) (smile) Strahlen, das. 2 v.t. ausstrahlen. 3 v.i. (a) (shine) strahlen; **the sun** ~**ed down** die Sonne strahlte vom Himmel; (b) (smile) strahlen; ~ **at sb.** jmdn. anstrahlen

'beam-ends n. pl. **be on one's** ~ (fig.) pleite (ugs.) od. in großer Geldnot sein

beaming /'bi:mɪŋ/ adj. strahlend

bean /bi:n/ n. (a) Bohne, die; **full of** ~s (fig. coll.) putzmunter (ugs.); **he hasn't [got] a** ~ (fig. coll.) er hat keinen roten Heller (ugs.); (b) (Amer. coll.: head) Birne, die (fig. salopp)

bean: ~**bag** n. (a) mit Bohnen gefülltes Säckchen zum Spielen; (b) (cushion) Knautschsessel, der; ~ **curd** n. Soja- [bohnen]quark, der; ~**feast** n. (Brit. coll.) Gelage, das; ~**pole** n. (lit. or fig.) Bohnenstange, die; ~**sprout** n. Sojabohnenkeim, der; ~**stalk** n. Bohnenstängel, der

bear¹ /beə(r)/ n. (a) Bär, der; (b) (Astron.) **Great/Little B**~: Großer/Kleiner Bär

bear² 1 v.t., bore /bɔ:(r)/, borne /bɔ:n/ (a) (show) tragen ‹Wappen, Inschrift, Unterschrift›; aufweisen, zeigen

⟨*Merkmal, Spuren, Ähnlichkeit, Verwandtschaft*⟩; ~ **a resemblance** *or* **likeness to sb.** Ähnlichkeit mit jmdm. haben; **(b)** (be known by) tragen, führen ⟨*Namen, Titel*⟩; **(c)** ~ **some/little relation to sth.** einen gewissen/wenig Bezug zu etw. haben; **(d)** (poet./formal: carry) tragen ⟨*Waffe, Last*⟩; mit sich führen ⟨*Geschenk, Botschaft*⟩; **I was borne along by the fierce current** die starke Strömung trug mich mit [sich]; **(e)** (endure, tolerate) ertragen ⟨*Schmerz, Kummer*⟩; mit neg. aushalten ⟨*Schmerz*⟩; ausstehen ⟨*Geruch, Lärm, Speise*⟩; **(f)** (sustain) tragen, übernehmen ⟨*Verantwortlichkeit, Kosten*⟩; auf sich (*Akk.*) nehmen ⟨*Schuld*⟩; tragen, aushalten ⟨*Gewicht*⟩; **(g)** (be fit for) vertragen; **it does not ~ repeating** *or* **repetition** das lässt sich unmöglich wiederholen; **it does not ~ thinking about** daran darf man gar nicht denken; ~ **comparison with sth.** den *od.* einen Vergleich mit etw. aushalten; **(h)** (give birth to) gebären ⟨*Kind, Junges*⟩; *see also* **born**; **(i)** (yield) tragen ⟨*Blumen, Früchte usw.*⟩; ~ **fruit** (fig.) Früchte tragen (geh.). **2** *v.i.*, **bore**, **borne (a)** ~ **left** ⟨*Person:*⟩ sich links halten; **the path ~s to the left** der Weg führt nach links; **(b) bring to ~:** aufbieten ⟨*Kraft, Energie*⟩; ausüben ⟨*Druck*⟩; **bring one's influence to ~:** seinen Einfluss geltend machen

~ **a'way** *v.t.* wegtragen; davontragen ⟨*Preis usw.*⟩; **be borne away** fort- *od.* davongetragen werden

~ **'down** *v.i.* ~ **down on sb./sth.** auf jmdn./etw. zusteuern; ⟨*Wagen:*⟩ auf jmdn./etw. zufahren *od.* -steuern

~ **'off** ⇒ ~ **away**

~ **on** ⇒ ~ **upon**

~ **'out** *v.t.* (fig.) bestätigen ⟨*Bericht, Erklärung*⟩; ~ **sb. out** jmdm. recht geben

~ **'up** *v.i.* durchhalten; ~ **up well under sth.** etw. gut ertragen

~ **upon** *v.t.* (relate to) sich beziehen auf (+ *Akk.*)

~ **with** *v.t.* Nachsicht haben mit

bearable /'beərəbl/ *adj.* zum Aushalten *nachgestellt;* erträglich ⟨*Situation, Beruf*⟩

'bear cub *n.* Bärenjunge, *das*

beard /bɪəd/ **1** *n.* Bart, *der;* **full ~:** Vollbart, *der.* **2** *v.t.* ~ **the lion in his den** (fig.) sich in die Höhle des Löwen wagen

bearded /'bɪədɪd/ *adj.* bärtig; **be ~:** einen Bart haben

bearer /'beərə(r)/ *n.* (carrier) Träger, *der*/Trägerin, *die;* (of letter, message, cheque, banknote) Überbringer, *der*/Überbringerin, *die*

'bear-hug *n.* kräftige Umarmung

bearing /'beərɪŋ/ *n.* **(a)** (behaviour) Verhalten, *das;* (deportment) [Körper]haltung, *die;* **(b)** (relation) Zusammenhang, *der;* Bezug, *der;* **have some/no ~ on sth.** relevant/irrelevant *od.* von Belang/belanglos für etw. sein; **(c)** (Mech. Engin.) Lager, *das;* **(d)** (compass ~) Position, *die;* **take a compass ~:** den Kompasskurs feststellen; **get one's ~s** sich orientieren; (fig.) sich zurechtfinden; **I have lost my ~s** (lit. *or* fig.) ich habe die Orientierung verloren

bear: ~ **market** *n.* (St. Exch.) Markt mit fallenden Preisen; **~skin** *n.* **(a)** Bärenfell, *das;* **(b)** (Mil.) Bärenfellmütze, *die*

beast /biːst/ *n.* Tier, *das;* (ferocious, wild) Bestie, *die;* (fig.: brutal person) roher, brutaler Mensch; Bestie, *die* (abwertend); (disliked person) Scheusal, *das* (abwertend); **it was a ~ of a winter** das war ein scheußlicher Winter

beastly /'biːstlɪ/ *adj.*, *adv.* (coll.) scheußlich

beat /biːt/ **1** *v.t.*, **beat**, **beaten (a)** (strike repeatedly) schlagen ⟨*Trommel, Rhythmus, Eier, Teig*⟩; klopfen ⟨*Teppich*⟩; hämmern ⟨*Gold, Silber usw.*⟩; ~ **one's breast** (lit. *or* fig.) sich ⟨*Dat.*⟩ an die Brust schlagen; **(b)** (hit) schlagen; [ver]prügeln; **(c)** (defeat) schlagen ⟨*Mannschaft, Gegner*⟩; (surmount) in den Griff bekommen ⟨*Inflation, Arbeitslosigkeit, Krise*⟩; ~ **the deadline** den Termin noch einhalten; **(d)** (surpass) brechen ⟨*Rekord*⟩; übertreffen ⟨*Leistung*⟩; **hard to ~:** schwer zu schlagen; **you can't ~** *or* **nothing ~s French cuisine** es geht [doch] nichts über das französische Küche; ~ **that!** das soll mal einer nachmachen!; ~ **everything** (coll.) alles in den Schatten stellen; ~ **sb. to it** jmdm. zuvorkommen; **can you ~ it?** ist denn das zu fassen?; **(e)** (circumvent) umgehen; ~ **the system** sich gegen das bestehende System durchsetzen;

(f) (perplex) **it ~s me how/why …:** es ist mir ein Rätsel wie/warum …; **(g)** ~ **time** den Takt schlagen; **(h)** *p.p.* **beat: I'm ~** (coll.: exhausted) ich bin erledigt (ugs.). *See also* **beaten 2. 2** *v.i.*, **beat**, **beaten (a)** (throb) ⟨*Herz:*⟩ schlagen, klopfen; ⟨*Puls:*⟩ schlagen; **my heart seemed to stop ~ing** ich dachte, mir bleibt das Herz stehen; **(b)** ⟨*Sonne:*⟩ brennen (**on** auf + *Akk.*); ⟨*Wind, Wellen:*⟩ schlagen (**on** auf + *Akk.*, **against** gegen); ⟨*Regen, Hagel:*⟩ prasseln, trommeln (**against** gegen); **(c)** ~ **about the bush** um den [heißen] Brei herumreden (ugs.); **(d)** (knock) klopfen (**at** an + *Dat.*); **(e)** (Naut.) kreuzen. **3** *n.* **(a)** (stroke, throbbing) Schlag, *der;* (rhythm) Takt, *der;* **his heart missed a ~:** ihm stockte das Herz; **(b)** (Mus.) Schlag, *der;* (of metronome, baton) Taktschlag, *der;* **(c)** (of policeman, watchman) Runde, *die;* (area) Revier, *das;* **be off sb.'s [usual] ~** (fig.) nicht in jmds. Fach schlagen

~ **'back** *v.t.* zurückschlagen ⟨*Feind*⟩

~ **'down 1** *v.i.* ⟨*Sonne:*⟩ herniederbrennen; ⟨*Regen:*⟩ niederprasseln. **2** *v.t.* **(a)** einschlagen ⟨*Tür*⟩; **(b)** (in bargaining) herunterhandeln

~ **'in** *v.t.* einschlagen

~ **'off** *v.t.* abwehren ⟨*Angriff*⟩

~ **'out** *v.t.* heraushämmern ⟨*Rhythmus*⟩; aushämmern ⟨*Metall*⟩; ausschlagen ⟨*Feuer*⟩

~ **'up** *v.t.* zusammenschlagen ⟨*Person*⟩; schlagen ⟨*Sahne usw.*⟩

beaten /'biːtn/ **1** ⇒ **beat 1, 2. 2** *adj.* **(a)** off the ~ **track** (remote) weit abgelegen; **(b)** (hammered) gehämmert ⟨*Silber, Gold*⟩

beater /'biːtə(r)/ *n.* **(a)** (Cookery) Rührbesen, *der;* **(b)** (Hunting) Treiber, *der*

beatify /bɪˈætɪfaɪ/ *v.t.* (Relig.) selig sprechen

beating /'biːtɪŋ/ *n.* **(a)** (punishment) **a ~:** Schläge *Pl.;* Prügel *Pl.;* **give sb. a good ~:** jmdm. eine gehörige Tracht Prügel verpassen (ugs.); **(b)** (defeat) Niederlage, *die;* **(c)** (surpassing) **take some/a lot of ~:** nicht leicht zu übertreffen sein

'beat-up *adj.* (coll.) ramponiert (ugs.)

beau /bəʊ/ *n., pl.* **~x** /bəʊz/ *or* **~s (a)** (dandy) Dandy, *der* (geh.); **(b)** (Amer.: boyfriend) Verehrer, *der*

beaut /bjuːt/ *n.* (Austral., NZ, & Amer. sl.) Prachtexemplar, *das*

beautician /bjuːˈtɪʃn/ *n.* ▶ 887 Kosmetiker, *der*/Kosmetikerin, *die*

beautiful /'bjuːtɪfl/ *adj.* **(a)** [ausgesprochen] schön; wunderschön ⟨*Augen, Aussicht, Blume, Kleid, Morgen, Musik, Schmuck*⟩; **(b)** (enjoyable, impressive) großartig

beautifully /'bjuːtɪfəlɪ/ *adv.* wunderbar; (coll.: very well) prima (ugs.); (coll.: very) schön ⟨*weich, warm*⟩

beautify /'bjuːtɪfaɪ/ *v.t.* verschönern; (adorn) [aus]schmücken

beauty /'bjuːtɪ/ *n.* **(a)** *no pl.* Schönheit, *die;* (of action, response) Eleganz, *die;* (of idea, simplicity, sacrifice) Größe, *die;* ~ **is only skin deep** man kann nicht nach dem Äußeren urteilen; **(b)** (person or thing) Schönheit, *die;* (animal) wunderschönes Tier; **she is a real ~:** sie ist wirklich eine Schönheit; **(c)** (exceptionally good specimen) Prachtexemplar, *das;* **that last goal was a ~:** dieses letzte Tor war ein Bilderbuchtor; **(d)** (beautiful feature) Schöne, *das;* **her eyes are her great ~:** das Schöne an ihr sind ihre Augen; **the ~ of it/of living in California** das Schöne *od.* Gute daran/am Leben in Kalifornien

beauty: ~ **competition**, ~ **contest** *ns.* Schönheitswettbewerb, *der;* ~ **parlour** ⇒ ~ **salon;** ~ **queen** *n.* Schönheitskönigin, *die;* ~ **salon** *n.* Kosmetiksalon, *der;* ~ **spot** *n.* Schönheitsfleck, *der;* (place) schönes Fleckchen [Erde]

beaux *pl. of* **beau**

beaver /'biːvə(r)/ **1** *n.* **(a)** *pl. same or* **~s** Biber, *der;* **(b)** (fur) Biber[pelz], *der.* **2** *v.i.* (Brit.) ~ **away** eifrig arbeiten (**at** an + *Dat.*)

becalmed /bɪˈkɑːmd/ *adj.* **be ~** in einer Flaute *od.* Windstille treiben

became ⇒ **become**

because /bɪˈkɒz/ **1** *conj.* weil; **that is ~ you don't know German** das liegt daran, dass du kein Deutsch kannst. **2** *adv.* ~ **of** wegen (+ *Gen.*); **don't come just** ~ **of me** nur meinetwegen brauchen Sie nicht zu kommen; ~ **of which he** ...: weswegen er ...

beck /bek/ *n.* **be at sb.'s** ~ **and call** jmdm. zur Verfügung stehen

beckon /'bekn/ **1** *v.t.* (a) winken; ~ **sb. in/over** jmdn. herein-/herbei- *od.* herüberwinken; (b) (fig.: invite) locken. **2** *v.i.* (a) ~ **to sb.** jmdm. winken; (b) (fig.: be inviting) locken

become /bɪ'kʌm/ **1** *copula*, **became** /bɪ'keɪm/, **become** werden; ~ **a politician/dentist** Politiker/Zahnarzt werden; ~ **a nuisance/rule** zu einer Plage/zur Regel werden. **2** *v.i.*, **became**, **become** werden; **what has** ~ **of him?** was ist aus ihm geworden?; **what has** ~ **of that book?** wo ist das Buch geblieben? **3** *v.t.*, **became**, **become** (a) ⇒ **befit;** (b) (suit) ~ **sb.** jmdm. stehen; zu jmdm. passen

becoming /bɪ'kʌmɪŋ/ *adj.* (a) (fitting) schicklich (geh.); (b) (flattering) vorteilhaft ‹ *Hut, Kleid, Frisur* ›

bed /bed/ **1** *n.* (a) Bett, *das;* (without bedstead) Lager, *das;* **in** ~: im Bett; ~ **and board** Unterkunft und Verpflegung; ~ **and breakfast** Zimmer mit Frühstück; **get into/out of** ~: ins *od.* zu Bett gehen/aufstehen; **go to** ~: ins *od.* zu Bett gehen; **go to** ~ **with sb.** (fig.) mit jmdm. ins Bett gehen (ugs.); **make the** ~: das Bett machen; **put sb. to** ~: jmdn. ins *od.* zu Bett bringen; **life isn't a** *or* **is no** ~ **of roses** (fig.) das Leben ist kein reines Vergnügen; **have got out of** ~ **on the wrong side** (fig.) mit dem linken Fuß zuerst aufgestanden sein; **as you make your** ~ **so you must lie on it** (prov.) wie man sich bettet, so liegt man; **take to one's** ~: sich krank ins Bett legen; (b) (flat base) Unterlage, *die;* (of machine) Bett, *das;* (of road, railway, etc.) Unterbau, *der;* (c) (in garden) Beet, *das;* (d) (of sea, lake) Grund, *der;* Boden, *der;* (of river) Bett, *das;* (e) (layer) Schicht, *die.* **2** *v.t.*, **-dd-:** (a) ins Bett legen; (b) (fig. coll.) beschlafen ‹ *Frau* ›; (c) (plant) setzen ‹ *Pflanze, Sämling* ›.

~ **'down 1** *v.t.* **the troops were** ~**ded down in a barn** die Soldaten wurden über Nacht in einer Scheune einquartiert. **2** *v.i.* kampieren

~ **'in** *v.t.* einlassen

~ **'out** *v.t.* auspflanzen ‹ *Pflanze* ›

B. Ed. /biː'ed/ *abbr.* **Bachelor of Education** Bakkalaureus der Erziehungswissenschaften; *see also* **B.Sc.**

bed: ~**bug** *n.* [Bett]wanze, *die;* ~**clothes** *n. pl.* Bettzeug, *das*

bedding /'bedɪŋ/ *n.*, *no pl.*, *no indef. art.* Matratze und Bettzeug; (for animal) Streu, *das*

'bedding plant *n.* Freilandpflanze, *die*

beddy-byes /'bedɪbaɪz/ *n.* (child lang.) Heiabett, *das* (Kinderspr.); **off to** ~: ab in die Heia

bedeck /bɪ'dek/ *v.t.* schmücken; ~**ed with flags** mit Fahnen geschmückt

bedevil /bɪ'devl/ *v.t.*, (Brit.) **-ll-:** (a) (spoil) verderben; durcheinander bringen ‹ *System* ›; (b) (afflict) heimsuchen; ‹ *Pech:* › verfolgen

bed: ~**fellow** *n.* Bettgenosse, *der/*-genossin, *die;* **make** *or* **be strange** ~**fellows** (fig.) ‹ *Personen:* › ein merkwürdiges Gespann sein; ‹ *Staaten, Organisationen:* › eine eigenartige Kombination sein; ~**jacket** *n.* Bettjacke, *die*

bedlam /'bedləm/ *n.* Chaos, *die;* Durcheinander, *das*

'bedlinen *n.* Bettwäsche, *die*

bedouin /'beduːɪn/ *n.*, *pl. same* Beduine, *der/*Beduinin, *die*

bed: ~**pan** *n.* Bettpfanne, *die;* ~**post** *n.* Bettpfosten, *der*

bedraggled /bɪ'drægəld/ *adj.* [nass und] verschmutzt *od.* schmutzig

bed: ~**ridden** *adj.* bettlägerig; ~**rock** *n.* Felssohle, *die;* (fig.) Basis, *die;* **get** *or* **reach down to** ~**rock** (fig.) zum Kern der Sache kommen; ~**room** *n.* Schlafzimmer, *das;* ~**side** *n.* Seite des Bettes, *die;* **be at the** ~**side** am Bett sein; ~**side table/lamp** Nachttisch, *der/*Nachttischlampe, *die;* ~**side reading** Bettlektüre, *die;* **have a good** ~**side manner** ‹ *Arzt:* › gut mit Kranken umgehen können; ~**sit,** ~**'sitter** *ns.* (coll.), ~**'sitting room** *n.* (Brit.) Wohnschlafzimmer, *das;* ~**sore** *n.* wundgelegene

Stelle; ~**spread** *n.* Tagesdecke, *die;* ~**stead** /'bedsted/ *n.* Bettgestell, *das;* ~**time** *n.* Schlafenszeit, *die;* **it's past the children's** ~**time** die Kinder müssten schon im Bett sein; **will you have it finished by** ~**time?** bist du vor dem Schlafengehen damit fertig?; **a** ~**time story** eine Gutenachtgeschichte

beduin ⇒ **bedouin**

'bed-wetting *n.* Bettnässen, *das*

bee /biː/ *n.* Biene, *die;* **she's such a busy** ~ (fig.) sie ist so ein fleißiges Mädchen; **as busy as a** ~ (fig.) bienenfleißig; **she has a** ~ **in her bonnet about punctuality** sie hat einen Pünktlichkeitsfimmel (ugs.)

beech /biːtʃ/ *n.* (a) (tree) Buche, *die;* (b) (wood) Buche, *die;* Buchenholz, *das; attrib.* buchen

beech: ~**-nut** *n.* [Buch]ecker, *die;* ~**wood** ⇒ **beech b**

beef /biːf/ **1** *n.* (a) *no pl.* Rind[fleisch], *das;* (b) *no pl.* (coll.: muscles) Muskeln; **have plenty of** ~: sehr muskulös sein; (c) *usu. in pl.* **beeves** [biːvz] *or* (Amer.) ~**s** (ox) Mastrind, *das;* (d) *pl.* ~**s** (coll.: complaint) Meckerei, *die* (ugs.). **2** *v.t.* (coll.) ~ **up** stärken. **3** *v.i.* (coll.) meckern (ugs.) (**about** über + *Akk.*)

beef: ~**burger** *n.* Beefburger, *der;* ~**eater** *n.* (Brit.) Beefeater, *der;* ~**steak** *n.* Beefsteak, *das*

beefy /'biːfɪ/ *adj.* (a) (like beef) wie Rindfleisch *nachgestellt;* Rindfleisch-; (b) (coll.) (muscular) muskulös; (fleshy) massig

bee: ~**hive** *n.* Bienenstock, *der;* (rounded) Bienenkorb, *der;* (fig.: scene of activity) Taubenschlag, *der;* ~**-keeper** *n.* ▶ 887 | Imker, *der/*Imkerin, *die;* ~**-keeping** *n.* Imkerei, *die;* ~**line** *n.* **make a** ~**line for sth./sb.** schnurstracks auf etw./jmdn. zustürzen

been ⇒ **be**

beep /biːp/ **1** *n.* Piepton, *der;* (of car horn) Tuten, *das.* **2** *v.i.* piepen; ‹ *Signalhorn:* › hupen

beeper /'biːpə(r)/ *n.* Piepser, *der* (ugs.)

beer /bɪə(r)/ *n.* Bier, *das;* **order two** ~**s** zwei Bier bestellen; **brew various** ~**s** verschiedene Biere *od.* Biersorten brauen; **small** ~ (fig.: trifles) Kleinigkeiten *Pl.;* **that firm's turnover is only small** ~: der Umsatz dieser Firma ist kaum der Rede wert

beer: ~ **barrel** *n.* Bierfass, *das;* ~ **belly** *n.* (coll.) Bierbauch, *der* (ugs.); ~ **bottle** *n.* Bierflasche, *die;* ~ **can** *n.* Bierdose, *die;* ~ **cellar** *n.* Bierkeller, *der;* ~ **crate** *n.* Bierkasten, *der;* ~**-drinker** *n.* Biertrinker, *der;* ~ **garden** *n.* Biergarten, *der;* ~ **glass** *n.* Bierglas, *das;* ~ **mat** *n.* Bierdeckel, *der;* Bieruntersetzer, *der;* ~ **mug** *n.* Bierkrug, *der*

beeswax /'biːzwæks/ *n.* Bienenwachs, *das*

beet /biːt/ *n.* Rübe, *die*

beetle /'biːtl/ *n.* Käfer, *der*

'beetroot *n.* rote Beete *od.* Rübe

befall /bɪ'fɔːl/ **1** *v.i.*, *forms as* **fall 2** sich begeben (geh.); geschehen. **2** *v.t.*, *forms as* **fall 2** widerfahren (+ *Dat.*)

befit /bɪ'fɪt/ *v.t.*, **-tt-** sich ziemen *od.* gebühren für (geh.); **it ill** ~**s you to do that** es steht Ihnen schlecht an, das zu tun; **she behaved as** ~**ted a lady** sie benahm sich, wie es sich für eine Dame gebührte

befitting /bɪ'fɪtɪŋ/ *adj.* gebührend (geh.); schicklich (geh.) ‹ *Benehmen* ›

before /bɪ'fɔː(r)/ **1** *adv.* (a) (of time) vorher; zuvor; **the day** ~: am Tag zuvor; **long** ~: lange vorher *od.* früher; **not long** ~: kurz vorher; **the noise continued as** ~: der Lärm ging nach wie vor weiter; **you should have told me so** ~: das hättest du mir vorher *od.* früher *od.* eher sagen sollen; **I've seen that film** ~: ich habe den Film schon [einmal] gesehen; **I've heard that** ~: das habe ich schon einmal gehört; (b) (ahead in position) vor[aus]; (c) (in front) voran. **2** *prep.* (a) (of time) vor (+ *Dat.*); **the day** ~ **yesterday** vorgestern; **the year** ~ **last** vorletztes Jahr; **the year** ~ **that** das Jahr davor; **it was [well]** ~ **my time** es war vor meiner Zeit; **since** ~ **the war** schon vor dem Krieg; ~ **now** vorher; früher; ~ **Christ** vor Christus; vor Christi Geburt; **he got there** ~ **me** er war vor mir da; ~ **then** vorher; ~ **long** bald; ~ **leaving, he phoned/I will phone** bevor er wegging, rief er an/bevor ich weggehe, rufe ich an; ~ **tax** brutto; vor [Abzug (*Dat.*) der] Steuern; **(b)** (position) vor (+ *Dat.*); (direction) vor (+ *Akk.*); ~ **my very eyes** vor meinen Augen; **go ~ a court of law** vor ein Gericht kommen; **appear ~ the judge** vor dem Richter erscheinen; *see also* **carry 1 a; (c)** (awaiting) **have one's life ~ one** sein Leben noch vor sich (*Dat.*) haben; (confronting) **the matter ~ us** das uns (*Dat.*) vorliegende Thema; **the task ~ us** die Aufgabe, die vor uns (*Dat.*) liegt; **(d)** (more important than) vor (+ *Dat.*); **he puts work ~ everything** die Arbeit ist ihm wichtiger als alles andere. **3** *conj.* bevor; **it'll be ages ~ I finish this** es wird eine Ewigkeit dauern, bis ich damit fertig bin

beforehand /bɪˈfɔːhænd/ *adv.* vorher; (in anticipation) im Voraus; **I found out about it ~:** ich habe es schon vorher herausgefunden

befriend /brˈfrend/ *v.t.* **(a)** (act as a friend to) sich anfreunden mit; **(b)** (help) sich annehmen (+ *Gen.*)

beg /beg/ **1** *v.t.*, **-gg-: (a)** betteln um; erbetteln ⟨*Lebensunterhalt*⟩; **(b)** (ask earnestly) bitten; **she ~ged to come with us** sie bat darum, mit uns kommen zu dürfen; **I ~ to differ** da bin ich [aber] anderer Meinung; ~ **sb. for sth.** jmdn. um etw. bitten; ~ **sth. of sb.** etw. von jmdm. erbitten; ~ **a favour [of sb.]** [jmdn.] um einen Gefallen bitten; ~ **forgiveness** um Verzeihung bitten; *see also* **pardon 1 b; (d)** ~ **the question** (evade difficulty) der Frage (*Dat.*) ausweichen. **2** *v.i.*, **-gg-** ⟨*Bettler*⟩ betteln (**for** um); ⟨*Hund*⟩ Männchen machen; betteln; **a ~ging letter** ein Bettelbrief; **go [a-]/~ging** keinen Abnehmer finden

began ⇒ **begin**

beggar /ˈbegə(r)/ *n.* **(a)** Bettler, *der*/Bettlerin, *die;* **(b)** (coll.: person) Arme, *der/die;* **poor ~:** armer Teufel

begin /brˈgɪn/ **1** *v.t.*, **-nn-**, **began** /brˈgæn/, **begun** /brˈgʌn/ ~ **sth.** [mit] etw. beginnen; ~ **a new bottle** eine neue Flasche anbrechen; **she began life here** sie verbrachte ihre ersten Lebensjahre hier; ~ **school** in die Schule kommen; ~ **doing** *or* **to do sth.** anfangen *od.* beginnen, etw. zu tun; **I began to slip** ich kam ins Rutschen; **I am ~ning to get annoyed** so langsam werde ich ärgerlich; **the film does not ~ to compare with the book** der Film lässt sich nicht annähernd mit dem Buch vergleichen. **2** *v.i.* **-nn-**, **began**, **begun** anfangen; beginnen (oft geh.); ~**ning next month** vom nächsten Monat an; ~ **at the beginning** von vorne anfangen; ~ **with sth./sb.** bei *od.* mit etw./jmdm. anfangen *od.* beginnen; **to ~ with** zunächst *od.* zuerst einmal; **it is the wrong book, to ~ with** das ist schon einmal das falsche Buch

beginner /brˈgɪnə(r)/ *n.* Anfänger, *der*/Anfängerin, *die;* ~**'s luck** Anfängerglück, *das*

beginning /brˈgɪnɪŋ/ *n.* ▶ 738| Anfang, *der;* Beginn, *der;* **at** *or* **in the ~:** am Anfang; **at the ~ of February/the month** Anfang Februar/des Monats; **at the ~ of the day** zu Beginn des Tages; **from ~ to end** von Anfang bis Ende; von vorn bis hinten; **from the [very] ~:** [ganz] von Anfang an; **have its ~s in sth.** seine Anfänge *od.* seinen Ursprung in etw. (*Dat.*) haben; **[this is] the ~ of the end** [das ist] der Anfang vom Ende; **go back to the ~:** wieder von vorne anfangen

begonia /brˈgəʊnɪə/ *n.* (Bot.) Begonie, *die;* Schiefblatt, *das*

begrudge /brˈgrʌdʒ/ *v.t.* **(a)** (envy) ~ **sb. sth.** jmdm. etw. missgönnen; **(b)** (give reluctantly) **I ~ the time I have to spend** es ist mir leid um die Zeit; **(c)** (be dissatisfied with) ~ **doing sth.** etw. ungern tun

beguile /brˈgaɪl/ *v.t.* (delude) betören; verführen; ~ **sb. into doing sth.** jmdn. dazu verführen, etw. zu tun; **be ~d by sb./sth.** sich von jmdm./etw. täuschen lassen

begun ⇒ **begin**

behalf /brˈhɑːf/ *n., pl.* **behalves** /brˈhɑːvz/ **on** *or* (Amer.) **in ~ of sb./sth.** (as representing sb./sth.) für jmdn./etw.; (more formally) im Namen von jmdm./etw.

behave /brˈheɪv/ **1** *v.i.* **(a)** sich verhalten; sich benehmen; **he ~s more like a friend to them** er behandelt sie mehr wie Freunde; ~ **well/badly** sich gut/schlecht benehmen; ~ **well/badly towards sb.** jmdn. gut/schlecht behandeln; **well-/ill-** *or* **badly/nicely ~d** brav/ungezogen/lieb (ugs.); **(b)** (~ well) brav sein; sich benehmen; ~!

benimm dich! **2** *v. refl.* ~ **oneself** sich benehmen; ~ **yourself!** benimm dich!

behavior *etc.* (Amer.) ⇒ **behavior** *etc.*

behaviour /brˈheɪvjə(r)/ *n.* (conduct) Verhalten, *das* (**towards** gegenüber); Benehmen, *das* (**towards** gegenüber); (of child) Betragen, *das;* **be on one's best ~:** sein bestes Benehmen an den Tag legen; **put sb. on his/her best ~:** jmdm. raten, sich gut zu benehmen

behavioural 'science *n.* Verhaltensforschung, *die*

behaviourism /brˈheɪvjərɪzm/ *n., no pl.* (Psych.) Behaviorismus, *der*

behead /brˈhed/ *v.t.* enthaupten, köpfen ⟨*Person*⟩

beheld ⇒ **behold**

behest /brˈhest/ *n.* (literary) **at sb.'s ~:** auf jmds. Geheiß (*Akk.*)

behind /brˈhaɪnd/ **1** *adv.* **(a)** (at rear of sb./sth.) hinten; **from ~:** von hinten; **he glanced ~ before moving off** er schaute nach hinten, bevor er losfuhr; **we'll follow on ~:** wir kommen hinterher; **(b)** (further back) **be miles ~:** kilometerweit zurückliegen; **leave sb. ~:** jmdn. hinter sich (*Dat.*) lassen (*see also* **d**); **fall ~:** zurückbleiben; (fig.) in Rückstand geraten; **lag ~:** zurückbleiben; (fig.) im Rückstand sein; **be ~:** hinten sein; (be late) im Verzug sein; **(c)** (in arrears) **be/get ~ with one's rent** mit der Miete im Verzug sein/in Verzug geraten; **(d)** (remaining after sb.'s departure) **leave sb./sth. ~:** jmdn./etw. zurücklassen (*see also* **b**); **he left his gloves ~ by mistake** er ließ seine Handschuhe versehentlich liegen; **stay ~:** dableiben; (as punishment) nachsitzen. **2** *prep.* **(a)** (at rear of, on other side of; fig.: hidden by) hinter (+ *Dat.*); **he stepped out from ~ the wall** er trat hinter der Mauer hervor; **he came from ~ her** er kam von hinten; **one ~ the other** hintereinander; ~ **sb.'s back** (fig.) hinter jmds. Rücken (*Dat.*); **(b)** (towards rear of) hinter (+ *Akk.*); (fig.) **I don't want to go ~ his back** ich will nicht hinter seinem Rücken handeln; **put one** vergessen; **put the past ~ one** einen Strich unter die Vergangenheit ziehen; **(c)** (further back than) hinter (+ *Dat.*); **they were miles ~ us** sie lagen meilenweit hinter uns (*Dat.*) zurück; **be ~ the times** nicht auf dem Laufenden sein; **fall ~ sb./sth.** hinter jmdn./etw. zurückfallen; **(d)** (past) hinter (+ *Dat.*); **all that trouble is ~ me** ich habe den ganzen Ärger hinter mir; **(e)** (later than) ~ **schedule/time** im Rückstand; **(f)** (in support of) hinter (+ *Dat.*); **I'm right ~ you** ich stehe hinter dir; **the man ~ the project** der Mann, der hinter dem Projekt steht; **(g)** (remaining after departure of) **she left nothing ~ her** sie hinterließ nichts. **3** *n.* (buttocks) Hintern, *der* (ugs.)

behindhand /brˈhaɪndhænd/ *pred. adj.* **(a) be ~ with one's rent** mit der Miete im Verzug sein; **(b)** (backward) **be ~ in doing sth.** etw. zurückhaltend tun

behold /brˈhəʊld/ *v.t.*, **beheld** /brˈheld/ (arch./literary) **(a)** erblicken (geh.); **(b)** *in imper.* siehe/sehet

beholder /brˈhəʊldə(r)/ *n.* **beauty is in the eye of the ~:** schön ist, was gefällt

beige /beɪʒ/ **1** *n.* Beige, *das.* **2** *adj.* beige

being /ˈbiːɪŋ/ **1** *pres. p. of* **be. 2** *n.* **(a)** *no pl., no art.* (existence) Dasein, *das;* Leben, *das;* Existenz, *die;* **bring into ~:** einführen; **call into ~:** ins Leben rufen; **come into ~:** entstehen; **when the new system comes into ~:** wenn das neue System eingeführt wird; **(b)** (anything, esp. person, that exists) Wesen, *das;* Geschöpf, *das*

belabour (*Brit.; Amer.:* **belabor**) /brˈleɪbə(r)/ *v.t.* **(a)** (beat) einschlagen auf (+ *Akk.*); (fig.) überhäufen; **(b)** ⇒ **labour 3 b**

belated /brˈleɪtɪd/ *adj.* verspätet

belatedly /brˈleɪtɪdlɪ/ *adv.* verspätet; nachträglich

belch /beltʃ/ **1** *v.i.* heftig aufstoßen; rülpsen (ugs.). **2** *v.t.* ausstoßen ⟨*Rauch, Flüche usw.*⟩. **3** *n.* Rülpser, *der* (ugs.)

beleaguer /brˈliːgə(r)/ *v.t.* (lit. or fig.) belagern

belfry /ˈbelfrɪ/ *n.* Glockenturm, *der*

Belgian /ˈbeldʒən/ ▶ 947| **1** *n.* Belgier, *der*/Belgierin, *die.* **2** *adj.* belgisch; **sb. is ~:** jmd. ist Belgier/Belgierin

Belgium /'beldʒəm/ *pr. n.* Belgien (*das*)

Belgrade /bel'greɪd/ *pr. n.* ▶ 1159⌡ Belgrad (*das*)

belie /bɪ'laɪ/ *v.t.*, **belying** /bɪ'laɪɪŋ/ (fail to fulfil) enttäuschen ‹ *Versprechen, Vorstellung* ›; (give false notion of) hinwegtäuschen über (+ *Akk.*) ‹ *Tatsachen, wahren Zustand* ›

belief /bɪ'li:f/ *n.* Glaube[n], *der;* ~ **in sth.** Glaube an etw. (*Akk.*); **beyond** ~: unglaublich; **it is my** ~ **that** …: ich bin der Überzeugung, dass …; **in the** ~ **that** …: in der Überzeugung, dass …; **to the best of my** ~: meines Wissens

believable /bɪ'li:vəbl/ *adj.* glaubhaft; glaubwürdig

believe /bɪ'li:v/ **1** *v.i.* (a) ~ **in sth.** (put trust in truth of) an etw. (*Dat.*) glauben; **I** ~ **in free medical treatment for all** ich bin für die kostenlose ärztliche Behandlung aller; **I don't** ~ **in going to the dentist** ich halte nicht viel von Zahnärzten; (b) (have faith) glauben (**in** an + *Akk.*) ‹ *Gott, Himmel usw.* ›; (c) (suppose, think) glauben; denken; **I** ~ **so/not** ich glaube schon/nicht. **2** *v.t.* (a) ~ **sth.** etw. glauben; **I can well** ~ **it** das glaub' ich gerne; **if you** ~ **that, you'll** ~ **anything** wer's glaubt, wird selig (ugs. scherzh.); ~ **it or not** ob du es glaubst oder nicht; **would you** ~ **[it]** (coll.) stell dir mal vor (ugs.); ~ **sb.** jmdm. glauben; **I don't** ~ **you** das glaube ich dir nicht; ~ **[you] me** glaub/ glaubt mir!; **I couldn't** ~ **my eyes/ears** ich traute meinen Augen/Ohren nicht; (be of opinion that) glauben; der Überzeugung sein; **he is** ~**d to be in the London area** man vermutet ihn im Raum London; **people** ~**d her to be a witch** die Leute hielten sie für eine Hexe; **make** ~ [that …] so tun, als ob …

believer /bɪ'li:və(r)/ *n.* (a) Gläubige, *der/die;* (b) **be a great** *or* **firm** ~ **in sth.** viel von etw. halten

Belisha beacon /bəli:ʃə 'bi:kn/ *n.* (Brit.) gelbes Blinklicht an Zebrastreifen

belittle /bɪ'lɪtl/ *v.t.* herabsetzen

bell /bel/ *n.* (a) Glocke, *die;* (smaller) Glöckchen, *das;* **clear as a** ~: glockenklar; (understandable) [ganz] klar und deutlich; (b) (device to give ~-like sound) Klingel, *die;* (c) (ringing) Läuten, *das;* **the** ~ **has gone** es hat geläutet *od.* geklingelt; (d) (Boxing) Gong, *der*

bell-bottomed /'belbɒtəmd/ *adj.* ausgestellt

belle /bel/ *n.* Schönheit, *die;* Schöne, *die;* ~ **of the ball** Ballkönigin, *die*

belles-lettres /bel'letr/ *n. pl.* schöngeistige Literatur; Belletristik, *die*

bellicose /'belɪkəʊs/ *adj.* kriegerisch ‹ *Stimmung, Nation* ›; streitsüchtig ‹ *Person* ›

belligerent /bɪ'lɪdʒərənt/ **1** *adj.* (a) (eager to fight) kriegerisch ‹ *Nation* ›; streitlustig ‹ *Person, Benehmen* ›; aggressiv ‹ *Rede* ›; (b) (fighting a war) Krieg führend. **2** *n.* Krieg führende Partei

bellow /'beləʊ/ **1** *v.i.* ‹ *Tier, Person:* › brüllen; ~ **at sb.** jmdn. anbrüllen. **2** *v.t.* ~ **out** brüllen ‹ *Befehl* ›

bellows /'beləʊz/ *n. pl.* Blasebalg, *der;* **a pair of** ~: ein Blasebalg

bell: ~**-pull** *n.* Klingelzug, *der;* ~ **push** *n.* Klingel, *die;* ~**-ringer** *n.* Glöckner, *der;* ~**-ringing** *n.* Glockenläuten, *das;* ~**-shaped** *adj.* glockenförmig; ~ **tent** *n.* Rundzelt, *das;* ~ **tower** *n.* Glockenturm, *der*

belly /'belɪ/ *n.* Bauch, *der;* (stomach) Magen, *der*

belly: ~**ache** **1** *n.* Bauchschmerzen *Pl.;* Bauchweh, *das* (ugs.); **2** *v.i.* (sl.) jammern (**about** über + *Akk.*); ~ **button** *n.* (coll.) Bauchnabel, *der;* ~ **dance** *n.* Bauchtanz, *der;* ~ **dancer** *n.* Bauchtänzerin, *die*

bellyful /'belɪfʊl/ *n.* **have had a** ~ **of sth.** (fig.coll.) von etw. die Nase voll haben (ugs.)

belong /bɪ'lɒŋ/ *v.i.* (a) (be rightly assigned) ~ **to sb./sth.** jmdm./zu etw. gehören; (b) ~ **to** (be member of) ~ **to a club** einem Verein angehören; **she** ~**s to a trade union/ the club** sie ist Mitglied einer Gewerkschaft/des Vereins; (c) (be rightly placed) **feel that one doesn't** ~: das Gefühl haben, fehl am Platze zu sein *od.* dass man nicht dazugehört; **the cutlery** ~**s in this drawer** das Besteck gehört in diese Schublade

belongings /bɪ'lɒŋɪŋz/ *n. pl.* Habe, *die;* Sachen *Pl.;* **personal** ~: persönlicher Besitz; persönliches Eigentum; **all our** ~: unser ganzes Hab und Gut

beloved /bɪ'lʌvɪd/ **1** *adj.* geliebt; teuer; **be** ~ /bɪ'lʌvd/ **by** *or* **of sb.** von jmdm. geliebt werden; jmdm. lieb und teuer sein; **in** ~ **memory of sb.** in treuem Angedenken an jmdn. **2** *n.* Geliebte, *der/die*

below /bɪ'ləʊ/ **1** *adv.* (a) (position) unten; unterhalb; (lower down) darunter; (downstream) weiter unten; **down** ~: unten; **from** ~: von unten [herauf]; (b) (direction) nach unten; hinunter; hinab (geh.); ~ **left** links unten; unten links; (c) (later in text) unten; **see [p. 123]** ~: siehe unten[, S. 123]; **please sign** ~: bitte hier unterschreiben; (d) (downstairs) (position) unten; (direction) nach unten; (Naut.) unter Deck; **go** ~ (Naut.) unter Deck gehen; **the flat/floor** ~: die Wohnung/das Stockwerk darunter *od.* unter uns/ihnen *usw.* **2** *prep.* (a) (position) unter (+ *Dat.*); unterhalb (+ *Gen.*); (downstream from) unterhalb (+ *Gen.*); (b) (direction) unter (+ *Akk.*); (c) (ranking lower than) unter (+ *Dat.*); **she's in the class** ~ **me** sie ist eine Klasse unter mir

belt /belt/ **1** *n.* (a) Gürtel, *der;* (for carrying tools, weapons, etc.) Gurt, *der;* (on uniform) Koppel, *das;* **hit below the** ~ (lit. or fig.) unter die Gürtellinie schlagen; *see also* **tighten 1 a;** (b) (strip) Gurt, *der;* (region) Gürtel, *der;* **industrial** ~: Industrierevier, *das;* (c) (Mech. Engin.: drive ~) Riemen, *der;* (d) (coll.: heavy blow) Schlag, *der.* **2** *v.t.* (coll.: hit hard) schlagen; **I'll** ~ **you [one]** ich hau' dir eine runter (ugs.). **3** *v.i.* (coll.) ~ **up/down the motorway** über die Autobahn rasen; ~ **along** *v.i.* (coll.) rasen (ugs.); ~ **out** *v.t.* (coll.) schmettern; voll herausbringen ‹ *Rhythmus* ›; ~ **'up** *v.i.* (a) (Amer. coll., Brit. coll. joc.: put seat ~ on) sich anschnallen; (b) (Brit. sl.: be quiet) die Klappe halten (salopp)

belying ⇒ **belie**

bemoan /bɪ'məʊn/ *v.t.* beklagen

bemused /bɪ'mju:zd/ *adj.* verwirrt

bench /bentʃ/ *n.* (a) Bank, *die;* (b) (Law) **on the** ~: auf dem Richterstuhl; (c) (office of judge) Richteramt, *das;* (d) (Brit. Parl.) Bank, *die;* Reihe, *die;* (e) (work table) Werkbank, *die*

bench: ~**mark** *n.* (fig.) Maßstab, *der;* Fixpunkt, *der;* ~**marking** *n.*, *no pl.* Benchmarking, *das* (fachspr.); Leistungsvergleich, *der*

bend /bend/ **1** *n.* (a) Kurve, *die;* **there is a** ~ **in the road** die Straße macht eine Kurve; **a** ~ **in the river** eine Flussbiegung; **be round the** ~ (fig. coll.) spinnen (ugs.); verrückt sein (ugs.); **go round the** ~ (fig. coll.) überschnappen (ugs.); durchdrehen (ugs.); **drive sb. round the** ~ (fig. coll.) jmdn. wahnsinnig *od.* verrückt machen (ugs.); (b) **the** ~**s** (Med. coll.) Taucherkrankheit, *die.* **2** *v.t.*, **bent** /bent/ (a) biegen; verbiegen ‹ *Nadel, Messer, Eisenstange, Ast* ›; spannen ‹ *Bogen* ›; beugen ‹ *Arm, Knie* ›; anwinkeln ‹ *Arm, Bein* ›; krumm machen ‹ *Finger* ›; ~ **sth. back/forward/ up/down** etw. nach hinten/vorne/oben/unten biegen; *see also* **rule 1 a;** (b) **be bent on sth.** auf etw. (*Akk.*) erpicht sein; **he bent his mind to the problem** er dachte ernst über das Problem nach. **3** *v.i.*, **bent** sich biegen; sich krümmen; ‹ *Äste:* › sich neigen; **the road** ~**s** die Straße macht eine Kurve; **the river** ~**s/**~**s in and out** der Fluss macht eine Biegung/schlängelt sich; ~ **'down** *v.i.* sich bücken; sich hinunterbeugen; ~ **'over** *v.i.* sich bücken; sich nach vorn beugen; *see also* **backwards a**

bended /'bendɪd/ *adj.* **on** ~ **knee[s]** auf [den] Knien

beneath /bɪ'ni:θ/ **1** *prep.* (a) (unworthy of) ~ **sb.** jmds. unwürdig; unter jmds. Würde (*Dat.*); ~ **contempt** verachtenswert; (b) (arch./literary: under) unter (+ *Dat.*). **2** *adv.* (arch./literary) darunter

benediction /benɪ'dɪkʃn/ *n.* (Relig.) Segnung, *die*

benefactor /'benɪfæktə(r)/ *n.* Stifter, *der;* Gönner, *der*

beneficial /benɪ'fɪʃl/ *adj.* nutzbringend; vorteilhaft ‹ *Einfluss* ›; **be** ~ **to sth./sb.** zum Nutzen von etw./jmdm. sein

beneficiary /benɪ'fɪʃərɪ/ *n.* Nutznießer, *der/*Nutznießerin, *die*

benefit /'benɪfɪt/ **1** *n.* (a) Vorteil, *der;* **be of** ~ **to sb./ sth.** jmdm./einer Sache von Nutzen sein; **with the** ~ **of** mithilfe (+ *Gen.*); **for sb.'s** ~: in jmds. Interesse (*Dat.*); **give sb. the** ~ **of the doubt** im Zweifelsfall zu jmds.

Gunsten entscheiden; **(b)** (allowance) Beihilfe, *die;* **social security** ~: Sozialhilfe, *die;* **supplementary** ~ (Brit.) zusätzliche Hilfe zum Lebensunterhalt; **unemployment** ~: Arbeitslosenunterstützung, *die;* **sickness** ~: Krankengeld, *das;* **child** ~ (Brit.) Kindergeld, *das;* **(c)** ~ [**performance/match/concert**] Benefizveranstaltung, *das/* -spiel, *das/*-konzert, *das.* **2** *v.t.* ~ **sb./sth.** jmdm./einer Sache nützen *od.* gut tun. **3** *v.i.* ~ **by/from sth.** von etw. profitieren

'**benefit tourism** *n.* Sozialhilfetourismus, *der*

Benelux /ˈbenɪlʌks/ *pr. n.* **the** ~ **countries** die Beneluxländer

benevolence /bɪˈnevələns/ *n., no pl.* ⇒ **benevolent a**: Güte, *die;* Milde, *die;* Wohlwollen, *das*

benevolent /bɪˈnevələnt/ *adj.* **(a)** (desiring to do good) gütig; mild ⟨*Herrscher*⟩; wohlwollend ⟨*Behörde, Despot*⟩; **(b)** *attrib.* (charitable) wohltätig, mildtätig ⟨*Institution, Verein*⟩

benign /bɪˈnaɪn/ *adj.* **(a)** gütig ⟨*Person, Aussehen, Verständnis*⟩; wohlwollend ⟨*Person, Verhalten*⟩; mild, heilsam ⟨*Klima, Sonne*⟩; günstig ⟨*Stern, Einfluss*⟩; **(b)** (Med.) gutartig, (fachspr.) benigne ⟨*Tumor*⟩

benignly /bɪˈnaɪnlɪ/ *adv.* gütig; wohlwollend

bent /bent/ **1** ⇒ **bend 2, 3. 2** *n.* Neigung, *die;* Hang, *der;* **have a** ~ **for sth.** einen Hang zu etw. *od.* eine Vorliebe für etw. haben; **people with** *or* **of an artistic** ~: Menschen mit einer künstlerischen Ader *od.* Veranlagung. **3** *adj.* **(a)** krumm; gebogen; **(b)** (Brit. sl.: corrupt) link (salopp); nicht ganz sauber (salopp) ⟨*Händler usw.*⟩

benzene /ˈbenziːn/ *n.* (Chem.) Benzol, *das*

benzine /ˈbenziːn/ *n.* Leichtbenzin, *das*

bequeath /bɪˈkwiːð/ *v.t.* **(a)** ~ **sth. to sb.** jmdm. etw. vermachen; **(b)** (fig.) überliefern ⟨*Legende, Zeugnisse*⟩; vererben ⟨*Tradition*⟩

bequest /bɪˈkwest/ *n.* Vermächtnis, *das* (**to** an + *Akk.*); **make a** ~ **to sb. of sth.** jmdm. etw. vermachen

berate /bɪˈreɪt/ *v.t.* schelten

bereave /bɪˈriːv/ *v.t.* **be** ~**d** [**of sb.**] jmdn. verlieren; **the** ~**d** der/die Hinterbliebene/die Hinterbliebenen

bereavement /bɪˈriːvmənt/ *n.* Trauerfall, *der*

bereft /bɪˈreft/ *pred. adj.* **be** ~ **of sth.** etw. verloren haben

beret /ˈbereɪ, ˈberɪ/ *n.* Baskenmütze, *die;* (Mil.) Barett, *das*

berk /bɜːk/ *n.* (Brit. sl.) Dussel, *der* (ugs.); Blödmann, *der* (salopp)

Berlin /bɜːˈlɪn/ ▶ **1159**| **1** *pr. n.* Berlin (*das*). **2** *attrib. adj.* Berliner; (Ling.) berlinisch

Berliner /bɜːˈlɪnə(r)/ *n.* Berliner, *der*/Berlinerin, *die*

Bermuda shorts /bəmjuːdə ˈʃɔːts/ *n. pl.* Bermudashorts *Pl.*

Berne /bɜːn/ *pr. n.* ▶ **1159**| Bern (*das*)

berry /ˈberɪ/ *n.* Beere, *die*

berserk /bəˈsɜːk, bəˈzɜːk/ *adj.* rasend; **go** ~: durchdrehen (ugs.)

berth /bɜːθ/ **1** *n.* **(a) give sb./sth. a wide** ~ (fig.) einen großen Bogen um jmdn./etw. machen; **(b)** (ship's place at wharf) Liegeplatz, *der;* **(c)** (sleeping place) (in ship) Koje, *die;* Kajütenbett, *das;* (in train) Schlafwagenbett, *das;* (in aircraft) Sleeper, *der.* **2** *v.t.* festmachen ⟨*Schiff*⟩. **3** *v.i.* ⟨*Schiff:*⟩ festmachen, anlegen

beseech /bɪˈsiːtʃ/ *v.t.,* **besought** /bɪˈsɔːt/ *or* ~**ed** (literary) anflehen ⟨*Person*⟩; ~ **sb. to do sth.** jmdn. anflehen *od.* inständig bitten, etw. zu tun

beset /bɪˈset/ *v.t.,* **-tt-, beset** heimsuchen; plagen; ⟨*Probleme, Versuchungen:*⟩ bedrängen; ~ **by doubts** von Zweifeln geplagt

beside /bɪˈsaɪd/ *prep.* **(a)** (close to) neben ⟨*position:* + *Dat.; direction:* + *Akk.*⟩; an (+ *Dat.*); ~ **the sea/lake** am Meer/ See; **walk** ~ **the river** am Fluss entlanggehen; **(b)** (compared with) neben (+ *Dat.*); **(c)** ~ **oneself with joy/grief** außer sich vor Freude/Kummer

besides /bɪˈsaɪdz/ **1** *adv.* außerdem; **he was a historian** ~: er war außerdem noch Historiker; **do/say sth.** [**else**] ~: sonst noch etw. tun/sagen. **2** *prep.* außer; ~ **which, he was late** und obendrein *od.* außerdem kam er zu spät

besiege /bɪˈsiːdʒ/ *v.t.* belagern

besought ⇒ **beseech**

bespectacled /bɪˈspektəkld/ *adj.* bebrillt

best /best/ **1** *adj. superl. of* **good: (a)** best...; **be** ~ [**of all**] am [aller]besten sein; **the** ~ **thing about it** das Beste daran; **the** ~ **thing to do is to apologize** das Beste ist, sich zu entschuldigen; **may the** ~ **man win!** auf dass der Beste gewinnt!; **(b)** (most advantageous) best...; günstigst...; **which** *or* **what is the** ~ **way?** wie ist es am besten *od.* günstigsten?; **think it** ~ **to do sth.** es für das Beste halten, etw. zu tun; **(c)** (greatest) [**for**] **the** ~ **part of an hour** fast eine ganze Stunde. **2** *adv. superl. of* **well**[2] **2** am besten; **like sth.** ~ **of all** etw. am liebsten mögen; **as** ~ **we could** so gut wir konnten; **he is the person** ~ **able to do it** er ist der Fähigste, um das zu tun. **3** *n.* **(a) the** ~: der/die/das Beste; **their latest record is their** ~: ihre letzte Platte ist die beste; **(b)** (clothes) beste Sachen; Sonntagskleider *Pl.;* **wear one's** [**Sunday**] ~: seine Sonntagskleider tragen; **(c) play the** ~ **of three** [**games**] um zwei Gewinnsätze spielen; **get the** ~ **out of sth./sb.** das Beste aus etw./jmdm. herausholen; **he is not in the** ~ **of health** es geht ihm nicht sehr gut; **bring out the** ~ **in sb.** jmds. beste Seiten zum Vorschein bringen; **all the** ~**!** (coll.) alles Gute!; **(d) the** ~ *pl.* die Besten; **they are the** ~ **of friends** sie sind die besten Freunde; **with the** ~ **of intentions** in bester Absicht; **from the** ~ **of motives** aus den edelsten Motiven [heraus]; **(e) at** ~: bestenfalls; **be at one's** ~: in Hochform sein; [**even**] **at the** ~ **of times** schon normalerweise; **hope for the** ~: das Beste hoffen; **do one's** ~: sein Bestes *od.* Möglichstes tun; **do the** ~ **you can** machen Sie es, so gut Sie können; **look one's** ~: möglichst gut aussehen; **make the** ~ **of it/things** das Beste daraus machen; **make the** ~ **of a bad job** *or* **bargain** (coll.) das Beste daraus machen; **to the** ~ **of one's ability** nach besten Kräften; **to the** ~ **of my belief/knowledge** meines Wissens. **4** *v.t.* (Sport) schlagen; (outwit) übervorteilen

'**best-dressed** *attrib. adj.* bestgekleidet

bestial /ˈbestɪəl/ *adj.* (of or like a beast) tierisch; (brutish, barbarous) barbarisch; (savage) brutal; (depraved) bestialisch; tierisch

best: ~**-kept** *attrib. adj.* bestgepflegt; bestgehütet ⟨*Geheimnis*⟩; **the** ~**-kept village in England** das schönste Dorf Englands; ~**-known** *attrib. adj.* bekanntest...; ~**-loved** *attrib. adj.* meistgeliebt; ~ '**man** *n.* Trauzeuge, *der* (des Bräutigams)

bestow /bɪˈstəʊ/ *v.t.* verleihen ⟨*Titel*⟩, schenken ⟨*Wohlwollen, Gunst*⟩, zuteil werden lassen ⟨*Ehre, Segnungen*⟩ ([up]on *Dat.*)

best: ~ '**seller** *n.* Bestseller, *der;* (author) Bestsellerautor, *der;* ~**-selling** *attrib. adj.* meistverkauft ⟨*Schallplatte*⟩; ~**-selling book/novel** Bestseller, *der;* **a** ~**-selling author/novelist** ein Bestsellerautor

bet /bet/ **1** *v.t.,* **-tt-,** ~ *or* ~**ted** ⟨*Geld:*⟩ wetten; **I** ~ **him £10** ich habe mit ihm um 10 Pfund gewettet; **he** ~ **£10 on that horse** er hat 10 Pfund auf das Pferd gesetzt; **(b)** (coll.: be confident) wetten; **I** ~ **he's late** wetten, dass er zu spät kommt?; ~ [**you**] **I 'can** und ob ich kann; **you '**~ [**I am/ he will** *etc.*] und ob; allerdings. **2** *v.i.,* **-tt-,** ~ *or* ~**ted** wetten; ~ **on sth.** auf etw. (*Akk.*) setzen; [**do you**] **want to** ~? [wollen wir] wetten? **3** *n.* **(a)** Wette, *die;* (sum) Wetteinsatz, *der;* **make** *or* **have a** ~ **with sb. on sth.** mit jmdm. über etw. (*Akk.*) wetten; **(b)** (fig. coll.: choice) Tipp, *der;* **be a bad/good/safe** ~: ein schlechter/guter/sicherer Tipp sein; **be sb.'s best** ~: das Beste sein; **my** ~ **is that** ...: ich wette, dass ...

beta /ˈbiːtə/ *n.* (letter) Beta, *das*

betide /bɪˈtaɪd/ *v.t.* **woe** ~ **you if** ...: wehe dir, wenn ...

betoken /bɪˈtəʊkn/ *v.t.* ankündigen ⟨*Frühjahr, Krieg*⟩

betray /bɪˈtreɪ/ *v.t.* verraten (**to** an + *Akk.*); missbrauchen ⟨*jmds. Vertrauen*⟩; ~ **the fact that** ...: verraten, dass ...

betrayal /bɪˈtreɪəl/ *n.* Verrat, *der;* **an act of** ~: ein Verrat

betrothal /bɪˈtrəʊðl/ *n.* (arch.) Verlöbnis, *das*

betrothed /bɪˈtrəʊðd/ (arch.) **1** *adj.* versprochen (veralt.) (**to** *Dat.*). **2** *n.* Anverlobter, *der*/Anverlobte, *die* (veralt.)

better /'betə(r)/ **1** *adj. compar. of* **good 1** besser; something ∼: etwas Besseres; **do you know of anything** ∼? kennst du etwas Besseres?; **that's** ∼: so ist's schon besser; ∼ **and** ∼: immer besser; ∼ **still, let's phone** oder noch besser: rufen wir doch an; **be much** ∼ (recovered) sich viel besser fühlen; **he is much** ∼ **today** es geht ihm heute schon viel besser; **get** ∼ (recover) gesund werden; **be getting** ∼: auf dem Wege der Besserung sein; **I am/my ankle is getting** ∼: mir/meinem Knöchel geht es besser; **so much the** ∼: um so besser; **she is none/much the** ∼ **for it** das hat ihr nichts/sehr genützt; **my/his** ∼ **half** (joc.) meine/seine bessere Hälfte (scherzh.); **[for] the** ∼ **part of an hour** fast eine ganze Stunde; *see also* **all 3. 2** *adv. compar. of* **well² 2**: **(a)** (in a ∼ way) besser; **(b)** (to a greater degree) mehr; **I like Goethe** ∼ **than Schiller** ich mag Goethe lieber als Schiller; **he is** ∼ **liked than Carter** er ist beliebter als Carter; **(c) you ought to know** ∼ **than to** ...: du solltest es besser wissen und nicht ...; **you'd** ∼ **not tell her** Sie erzählen es ihr besser nicht; **I'd** ∼ **be off now** ich gehe jetzt besser; **hadn't you** ∼ **ask first?** sollten Sie nicht besser zuerst fragen?; **you'd** ∼! das will ich aber auch hoffen; *see also* **better off. 3** *n.* **(a)** Bessere, *das;* **get the** ∼ **of sb./sth.** jmdn./etw. unterkriegen (ugs.); **exhaustion got the** ∼ **of him** Erschöpfung übermannte ihn; **be a change for the** ∼: eine vorteilhafte Veränderung sein; **for** ∼ **or for worse** was immer daraus werden wird; **I thought** ∼ **of it** ich habe es mir anders überlegt; **(b)** *in pl.* one's ∼s Leute, die über einem stehen *od.* die einem überlegen sind. **4** *v.t.* **(a)** (surpass) übertreffen; **(b)** (improve) verbessern; ∼ **oneself** (rise socially) sich verbessern

better: ∼ **'off** *adj.* **(a)** (financially) [finanziell] besser gestellt; **(b) he is** ∼ **off than I am** ihm geht es besser als mir; **be** ∼ **off than sb.** besser als jmd. dran sein (ugs.); **be** ∼ **off without sth./sb.** ohne etw./jmdn. besser dran sein; ∼**-than-average** *attrib. adj.* überdurchschnittlich [gut/viel]

betting /'betɪŋ/ **1** *n.* Wetten, *das;* **there was heavy** ∼ **on that horse** auf das Pferd wurde sehr viel gesetzt; **what's the** ∼ **it rains?** (fig.) ob es wohl regnen wird? **2** *attrib. adj.* Wett-; **I'm not a** ∼ **man** ich wette nicht

betting: ∼ **office,** ∼ **shop** *ns.* Wettbüro, *das*

between /bɪ'twiːn/ **1** *prep.* **(a)** zwischen (*position:* + *Dat., direction:* + *Akk.*); ∼ **then and now** zwischen damals und jetzt; **[in]** ∼: zwischen; **(b)** (amongst) unter (+ *Dat.*); **the work was divided** ∼ **the volunteers** die Arbeit wurde zwischen den Freiwilligen aufgeteilt; ∼ **us had 40p** wir hatten zusammen 40 Pence; ∼ **ourselves,** ∼ **you and me** unter uns (*Dat.*) gesagt; **that's [just]** ∼ **ourselves** das bleibt aber unter uns (*Dat.*); **(c)** (by joint action of) ∼ **them/the four of them they dislodged the stone** gemeinsam/zu viert lösten sie den Stein. **2** *adv.* **[in]** ∼: dazwischen; (in time) zwischendurch; **the space** ∼: der Zwischenraum

bevel /'bevl/ **1** *n.* (slope) Schräge, *die;* ∼ **edge** Schrägkante, *die.* **2** *v.t.*, (Brit.) **-ll-** abschrägen

beverage /'bevərɪdʒ/ *n.* (formal) Getränk, *das*

bewail /bɪ'weɪl/ *v.t.* beklagen; (lament) bejammern

beware /bɪ'weə(r)/ *v.t. & i.; only in imper. and inf.* ∼ **[of]** **sb./sth.** sich vor jmdm./etw. hüten *od.* in Acht nehmen; ∼ **of doing sth.** sich davor hüten, etw. zu tun; '∼ **of pickpockets'** „vor Taschendieben wird gewarnt"; '∼ **of the dog'** „Vorsicht, bissiger Hund!"

bewilder /bɪ'wɪldə(r)/ *v.t.* verwirren; **be** ∼**ed by sth.** durch *od.* von etw. verwirrt werden/sein

bewildering /bɪ'wɪldərɪŋ/ *adj.* verwirrend

bewilderment /bɪ'wɪldəmənt/ *n., no pl.* Verwirrung, *die;* **in total** ∼: völlig verwirrt

bewitch /bɪ'wɪtʃ/ *v.t.* verzaubern; verhexen; (fig.) bezaubern

bewitching /bɪ'wɪtʃɪŋ/ *adj.* bezaubernd

beyond /bɪ'jɒnd/ **1** *adv.* **(a)** (in space) jenseits; (on other side of wall, mountain range, etc.) dahinter; **the world** ∼: das Jenseits; **(b)** (in time) darüber hinaus. **2** *prep.* **(a)** (at far side of) jenseits (+ *Gen.*); **when we get** ∼ **the river, we'll stop** wenn wir den Fluss überquert haben, machen wir Halt; **(b)** (in space: after) nach; **(c)** (later than) nach; **she never**

looks *or* **sees** ∼ **the present** sie sieht *od.* blickt nie über die Gegenwart hinaus; **(d)** (out of reach or comprehension or range) über ... (+ *Akk.*) hinaus; **it's [far** *or* (coll.) **way]** ∼ **me/him** *etc.* (too difficult) das ist mir/ihm *usw.* [bei weitem] zu schwer; (incomprehensible) das ist mir/ihm *usw.* [völlig] unverständlich; ∼ **reproach** tadellos; **(e)** (surpassing, exceeding) mehr als; **they're living** ∼ **their means** sie leben über ihre Verhältnisse; **(f)** (more than) weiter als; **(g)** (besides) außer; ∼ **this/that** weiter. **3** *n.* **the B**∼: das Jenseits; **at the back of** ∼: am Ende der Welt

bias /'baɪəs/ **1** *n.* **(a)** (tendency) Neigung, *die;* **have a** ∼ **towards** *or* **in favour of sth./sb.** etw./jmdn. bevorzugen; **have a** ∼ **against sth./sb.** gegen etw./jmdn. eingenommen sein; **(b)** (prejudice) Voreingenommenheit, *die;* **be without** ∼: unvoreingenommen sein. **2** *v.t.*, **-s-** *or* **-ss-** beeinflussen; **be** ∼**ed towards** *or* **in favour of sth./sb.** für etw./jmdn. eingestellt sein; **they are** ∼**ed in favour of women** sie bevorzugen Frauen; **be** ∼**ed against sth./sb.** gegen etw./jmdn. voreingenommen sein; **a** ∼**ed account** eine gefärbte *od.* tendenziöse Darstellung

bib /bɪb/ *n.* **(a)** (for baby) Lätzchen, *das;* **(b)** (of apron etc.) Latz, *der*

Bible /'baɪbl/ *n.* **(a)** (Christian) Bibel, *die;* **(b)** (of other religion) heiliges Buch; (fig.: authoritative book) Bibel, *die*

biblical /'bɪblɪkl/ *adj.* biblisch; Bibel-

bibliography /bɪblɪ'ɒgrəfɪ/ *n.* Bibliographie, *die*

bicarbonate /baɪ'kɑːbənɪt/ *n.* (Cookery) ∼ **[of soda]** Natron, *das*

bicentenary /baɪsen'tiːnərɪ, baɪsen'tenərɪ/, **bicentennial** /baɪsen'tenɪəl/ **1** *adjs.* Zweihundertjahr-. **2** *ns.* Zweihundertjahrfeier, *die*

biceps /'baɪseps/ *n.* (Anat.) Bizeps, *der*

bicker /'bɪkə(r)/ *v.i.* ∼ **[with sb. about** *or* **over sth.]** [sich mit jmdm. um etw.] zanken *od.* streiten

bicycle /'baɪsɪkl/ **1** *n.* **(a)** Fahrrad, *das;* **ride a** ∼: [mit dem] Fahrrad fahren; Rad fahren; **by** ∼: mit dem [Fahr]rad; **(b)** (attrib.) Fahrrad-; ∼ **clip/rack** Hosenklammer, *die*/Fahrradständer, *der.* **2** *v.i.* Rad fahren

bid /bɪd/ **1** *v.t.* **(a)** -dd-, **bid** (at auction) bieten; **(b)** -dd-, **bid** (Cards) reizen; **(c)** -dd-, **bade** /bæd/ *or* **bid**, **bidden** /'bɪdn/ *or* **bid**: ∼ **sb. welcome** jmdn. willkommen heißen; ∼ **sb. goodbye** sich von jmdm. verabschieden. **2** *v.i.*, **-dd-, bid (a)** werben **(for** um); **the President is** ∼**ding for re-election** der Präsident bewirbt sich um die Wiederwahl; ∼ **fair to be sth.** etw. zu werden versprechen; **(b)** (at auction) bieten; **(c)** (Cards) bieten; reizen. **3** *n.* **(a)** (at auction) Gebot, *das;* **(b)** (attempt) Bemühung, *die;* **make a** ∼ **for sth.** sich um etw. bemühen; **he made a strong** ∼ **for the Presidency** er griff nach dem Präsidentenamt; **the prisoner made a** ∼ **for freedom** der Gefangene versuchte, die Freiheit zu erlangen; **(c)** (Cards) Ansage, *die;* **make no** ∼: passen; **it's your** ∼: Sie bieten!

bidden ⇨ **bid 1 c**

bidder /'bɪdə(r)/ *n.* Bieter, *der*/Bieterin, *die;* **the highest** ∼: der/die Höchstbietende

bidding /'bɪdɪŋ/ *n.* **(a)** (at auction) Steigern, *das;* **open the** ∼: das erste Gebot machen; **(b)** (Cards) Bieten, *das;* Reizen, *das*

bide /baɪd/ *v.t.* ∼ **one's time** den rechten Augenblick abwarten

bidet /'biːdeɪ/ *n.* Bidet, *das*

biennial /baɪ'enɪəl/ **1** *adj.* **(a)** (lasting two years) zweijährig; **(b)** (once every two years) zweijährlich. **2** *n.* (Bot.) zweijährige Pflanze

bier /bɪə(r)/ *n.* Totenbahre, *die*

biff /bɪf/ (coll.) **1** *n.* Klaps, *der* (ugs.). **2** *v.t.* hauen; **he** ∼**ed me on the head with a book** er hat mir ein Buch auf den Kopf geknallt (ugs.)

bifocal /baɪ'fəʊkl/ **1** *adj.* Bifokal-. **2** *n. in pl.* Bifokalgläser *Pl.*

big /bɪg/ **1** *adj.* **(a)** (in size) groß; schwer, heftig ‹*Explosion, Zusammenstoß*›; schwer ‹*Unfall,* · *Niederlage*›; hart ‹*Konkurrenz*›; reichlich ‹*Mahlzeit*›; **earn** ∼ **money** das große Geld verdienen; **he is a** ∼ **man/she is a** ∼ **woman** (fat) er/sie ist wohlbeleibt; ∼ **words** geschraubte Ausdrücke (*see also* **g**); **in a** ∼ **way** (coll.) im großen Stil;

(b) (of largest size, larger than usual) groß ⟨*Appetit, Zehe, Buchstabe*⟩; **(c)** ~**ger** (worse) schwerer; ~**gest** (worst) größt...; **he is the** ~**gest liar/idiot** er ist der größte Lügner/Idiot; **(d)** (grown up, elder) groß; **(e)** (important) groß; wichtig ⟨*Nachricht, Entscheidung*⟩; **(f)** (coll.: outstanding) groß ⟨*Augenblick, Chance*⟩; **(g)** (boastful) **get** *or* **grow/be too** ~ **for one's boots** (coll.) größenwahnsinnig werden/sein (ugs.); ~ **talk** Großsprecherei, *die;* ~ **words** große Worte (*see also* **a**)*;* **(h)** (coll.: generous) großzügig; nobel (oft iron.); **(i)** (coll.: popular) **be** ~ ⟨*Schauspieler, Popstar:*⟩ gut ankommen. *See also* **idea d. 2** *adv.* **talk** ~: groß daherreden (ugs.); **think** ~: im großen Stil planen

bigamist /'bɪɡəmɪst/ *n.* Bigamist, *der*/Bigamistin, *die*

bigamy /'bɪɡəmɪ/ *n.* Bigamie, *die*

big: ~ '**bang** *n.* Urknall, *der;* **Big 'Brother** *n.* der Große Bruder; ~ '**business** *n.* das Großkapital; ~ '**deal** ⇒ **deal¹ 3 a;** ~ '**dipper** *n.* (Brit.) Achterbahn, *die;* ~ **game** *n.* Großwild, *das;* ~**head** *n.* (coll.) Fatzke, *der* (ugs. abwertend); ~'**headed** *adj.* (coll.) eingebildet; ~'**hearted** *adj.* großherzig; ~ **mouth** *n.* (fig. coll.) **(a)** /-'-/ **have a** ~ **mouth** ein Schwätzer/eine Schwätzerin sein (ugs.); **(b)** /'--/ **be a** ~ **mouth** ein Angeber/eine Angeberin sein (ugs.); ~ '**name** *n.* (person) Größe, *die;* ~ '**noise** *n.* (coll.) hohes Tier (ugs.)

bigot /'bɪɡət/ *n.* Eiferer, *der*/Eiferin, *die;* (Relig.) bigotter Mensch

bigoted /'bɪɡətɪd/ *adj.* eifernd; (Relig.) bigott

big: ~ **shot** ⇒ ~ **noise;** ~ **time** *n.* **be in the** ~ **time** (coll.) eine große Nummer sein (ugs.); **make it [in]to** *or* **hit the** ~ **time** (sl.) groß herauskommen (ugs.); ~ '**top** *n.* Zirkuszelt, *das;* ~ '**wheel** *n.* **(a)** (at fair) Riesenrad, *das;* **(b)** (coll.: person) hohes Tier (ugs.); ~**wig** *n.* (coll.) hohes Tier (ugs.)

bike /baɪk/ (coll.) **1** *n.* (bicycle) Rad, *das;* (motorcycle) Maschine, *die.* **2** *v.i.* (by bicycle) Rad fahren; radeln (ugs., bes. südd.); mit dem Fahrrad fahren; (by motorcycle) [mit dem] Motorrad fahren

biker /'baɪkə(r)/ *n.* (cyclist) Radfahrer, *der*/-fahrerin, *die;* (motorcyclist) Motorradfahrer, *der*/-fahrerin, *die*

bikini /bɪ'kiːnɪ/ *n.* Bikini, *der;* ~ **briefs** Slip, *der*

bilateral /baɪ'lætərl/ *adj.* bilateral

bilberry /'bɪlbərɪ/ *n.* Blau-, Heidelbeere, *die*

bile /baɪl/ *n.* (Physiol.) Gallenflüssigkeit, *die*

bilingual /baɪ'lɪŋɡwəl/ *adj.* zweisprachig

bilious /'bɪljəs/ *adj.* (Med.) Gallen-; (fig.: peevish) verdrießlich; ~ **attack** Gallenanfall, *der*

bill¹ /bɪl/ **1** *n.* (of bird) Schnabel, *der.* **2** *v.i.* ⟨*Vögel:*⟩ schnäbeln; ⟨*Personen:*⟩ sich liebkosen; ~ **and coo** ⟨*Vögel:*⟩ schnäbeln und gurren; ⟨*Personen:*⟩ [miteinander] turteln

bill² **1** *n.* **(a)** (Parl.) Gesetzentwurf, *der;* Gesetzesvorlage, *die;* **(b)** (note of charges) Rechnung, *die;* **could we have the** ~**, please?** wir möchten zahlen; **a** ~ **for £10** eine Rechnung über 10 Pfund (*Akk.*); (amount) **a large** ~: eine hohe Rechnung; **a** ~ **of £10** eine Rechnung von 10 Pfund; **(c)** (poster) Plakat, *das;* '[stick] no ~s' „Plakate ankleben verboten"; **(d)** ~ **of fare** Speisekarte, *die;* **(e)** ▶ 938⌋ (Amer.: banknote) Banknote, *die;* [Geld]schein, *der;* **(f)** (Commerc.) ~ [of exchange] Wechsel, *der;* Tratte, *die* (fachspr.); ~ **of lading** Konnossement, *das;* Seefrachtbrief, *der.* **2** *v.t.* **(a)** (announce) ankündigen; **(b)** (charge) eine Rechnung ausstellen (+ *Dat.*); ~ **sb. for sth.** jmdm. etw. in Rechnung stellen *od.* berechnen

'**billboard** *n.* Reklametafel, *die*

billet /'bɪlɪt/ **1** *n.* Quartier, *das;* Unterkunft, *die;* (for soldiers) Truppenunterkunft, *die.* **2** *v.t.* unterbringen, einquartieren (**with, on** bei; **in** in + *Dat.*)

'**billfold** *n.* (Amer.) Brieftasche, *die*

billiard /'bɪljəd/: ~ **ball** *n.* Billardkugel, *die;* ~ **cue** *n.* Queue, *das;* Billardstock, *der;* ~ **player** *n.* Billardspieler, *der;* ~ **room** *n.* Billardzimmer, *das*

billiards /'bɪljədz/ *n.* Billard[spiel], *das;* **a game of** ~: eine Partie Billard

'**billiard table** *n.* Billardtisch, *der*

billion /'bɪljən/ *n.* ▶ 956⌋ **(a)** (thousand million) Milliarde, *die;* **(b)** (esp. Brit. dated: million million) Billion, *die*

billionaire /bɪljə'neə(r)/ *n.* (Amer.) Milliardär, *der*/Milliardärin, *die*

billow /'bɪləʊ/ **1** *n.* ~ **of smoke** Rauchwolke, *die;* ~ **of fog** Nebelschwaden, *der.* **2** *v.i.* ⟨*Ballon, Segel:*⟩ sich [auf]blähen; ⟨*See, Meer:*⟩ wogen, sich [auf]türmen; ⟨*Rauch:*⟩ in Schwaden aufsteigen; ⟨*Kleid, Vorhang:*⟩ sich bauschen

bill: ~**poster,** ~**sticker** *n.* Plakatkleber, *der*

billy goat /'bɪlɪɡəʊt/ *n.* Ziegenbock, *der*

bimbo /'bɪmbəʊ/ *n.* Puppe, *die* (salopp)

bin /bɪn/ *n.* **(a)** (for storage) Behälter, *der;* (for bread) Brotkasten, *der;* (for rubbish) (inside house) Abfalleimer, *der;* Mülleimer, *der;* (outside house) Mülltonne, *die;* (in public place) Abfallkorb, *der*

binary /'baɪnərɪ/ *adj.* binär

'**bin bag** *n.* Müllbeutel, *der*

bind /baɪnd/ **1** *v.t.,* **bound** /baʊnd/ **(a)** (tie) fesseln ⟨*Person, Tier*⟩; (bandage) wickeln, binden ⟨*Glied*⟩; verbinden ⟨*Wunde*⟩ **(with** mit**); he was bound hand and foot** er war/wurde an Händen und Füßen gefesselt; **(b)** (fasten together) zusammenbinden; (fig.: unite) verbinden; **(c)** (Bookb.) binden; **(d) be bound up with sth.** (fig.) eng mit etw. verbunden sein; **(e)** (oblige) ~ **sb./oneself to sth.** jmdn./sich an etw. (*Akk.*) binden; **be bound to do sth.** (required) verpflichtet sein, etw. zu tun; **be bound by law** von Gesetzes wegen verpflichtet sein; **(f) be bound to do sth.** (certain) etw. ganz bestimmt tun; **it is bound to rain** es wird bestimmt *od.* sicherlich regnen; **(g) I'm bound to say that** ... (feel obliged) ich muss schon sagen, dass ...; **(h)** (Cookery) binden; **(i)** (Law) ~ **sb. over [to keep the peace]** jmdn. verwarnen *od.* rechtlich verpflichten[, die öffentliche Ordnung zu wahren]. **2** *v.i.,* **bound (a)** (cohere) binden; ⟨*Lehm, Ton:*⟩ fest *od.* hart werden; ⟨*Zement:*⟩ abbinden; **(b)** (be restricted) blockieren; ⟨*Kolben:*⟩ sich festfressen. **3** *n.* **(a)** (coll.: nuisance) **be a** ~: recht lästig sein; **what a** ~! wie unangenehm *od.* lästig!; **(b) be in a** ~ (Amer. coll.) in einer Klemme sitzen (ugs.)

binder /'baɪndə(r)/ *n.* **(a)** (substance) Bindemittel, *das;* Binder, *der;* **(b)** (book~) Buchbinder, *der*/-binderin, *die;* **(c)** (cover) (for papers) Hefter, *der;* (for magazines) Mappe, *die*

binding /'baɪndɪŋ/ **1** *adj.* bindend, verbindlich ⟨*Vertrag, Abkommen*⟩ **(on** für**). 2** *n.* **(a)** (cover of book) [Buch]einband, *der;* **(b)** (on ski) Bindung, *die*

bindweed /'baɪndwiːd/ *n.* (Bot.) Winde, *die*

binge /bɪndʒ/ *n.* (coll.: drinking bout) Sauferei, *die* (salopp); **go/be out on a** ~: auf Sauftour gehen/sein (salopp)

bingo /'bɪŋɡəʊ/ **1** *n.,* *no pl.* Bingo, *das; attrib.* ~ **hall** Bingohalle, *die.* **2** *int.* peng; zack

'**bin liner** *n.* Müllbeutel, *der*

binoculars /bɪ'nɒkjʊləz/ *n. pl.* **[pair of]** ~: Fernglas, *das;* Binokular, *das*

bint /bɪnt/ *n.* (sl. derog.) Weib[sstück], *das*

bio- /'baɪəʊ/ *in comb.* Bio-; Lebens-

bio'chemical *adj.* biochemisch

bio'chemistry *n.* Biochemie, *die*

biodegradable /baɪəʊdɪ'ɡreɪdəbl/ *adj.* biologisch abbaubar

biodi'versity *n.,* *no pl.* biologische Vielfalt

biographer /baɪ'ɒɡrəfə(r)/ *n.* ▶ 887⌋ Biograph, *der*/Biographin, *die*

biographic /baɪə'ɡræfɪk/, **biographical** /baɪə'ɡræfɪkl/ *adj.* biographisch

biography /baɪ'ɒɡrəfɪ/ *n.* Biographie, *die;* (branch of literature) biographische Literatur

biological /baɪə'lɒdʒɪkl/ *adj.* biologisch

biological: ~ '**clock** *n.* biologische Uhr; ~ '**control** *n.* biologische Schädlingsbekämpfung; ~ '**warfare** *n.* biologische Kriegführung; Bakterienkrieg, *der*

biologist /baɪ'ɒlədʒɪst/ *n.* ▶ 887⌋ Biologe, *der*/Biologin, *die*

biology /baɪ'ɒlədʒɪ/ *n.* Biologie, *die*

'**biorhythm** *n.* Biorhythmus, *der*

'**biosphere** *n.* Biosphäre, *die*

biotech'nology *n.* Biotechnik, *die*

bipartite /baɪ'pɑːtaɪt/ *adj.* (having two parts) zweiteilig; (involving two parties) zweiseitig ⟨*Dokument, Abkommen*⟩

biplane /'baɪpleɪn/ n. Doppeldecker, der

birch /bɜːtʃ/ n. (a) (tree) Birke, die; (b) (for punishment) [Birken]rute, die

bird /bɜːd/ n. (a) Vogel, der; ~s of a feather flock together (prov.) gleich und gleich gesellt sich gern (Spr.); it's [strictly] for the ~s (coll.) das kannste vergessen (salopp); kill two ~s with one stone (fig.) zwei Fliegen mit einer Klappe schlagen; a ~ in the hand is worth two in the bush (prov.) ein Spatz in der Hand ist besser als eine Taube auf dem Dach (Spr.); a little ~ told me mein kleiner Finger sagt mir das; (b) (sl.: girl) Mieze, die (salopp); (c) no art. (sl.: imprisonment) Knast, der (ugs.); do ~: Knast schieben (salopp). See also **early bird**

bird: ~ **bath** n. Vogelbad, das; ~**cage** n. Vogelkäfig, der; Vogelbauer, das od. der; ~ **call** n. Vogelruf, der

birdie /'bɜːdɪ/ n. Vögelchen, das

bird: ~ **sanctuary** n. Vogelschutzgebiet, das; ~'s-eye 'view n. Vogelperspektive, die; have/get a ~'s-eye view of sth. (lit. or fig.) etw. aus der Vogelperspektive sehen; ~'s nest n. Vogelnest, das; ~ table n. Futterstelle für Vögel; ~watcher n. Vogelbeobachter, der/ -beobachterin, die; ~watching n., no pl., no indef. art. das Beobachten von Vögeln

Biro, (P) /'baɪrəʊ/ n., pl. ~s Kugelschreiber, der; Kuli, der (ugs.)

birth /bɜːθ/ n. (a) Geburt, die; at the/at ~: bei der Geburt; [deaf] from or since ~: von Geburt an [taub]; date and place of ~: Geburtsdatum und -ort; give ~ ⟨Frau:⟩ entbinden; ⟨Tier:⟩ jungen; she gave ~ prematurely sie hatte eine Frühgeburt; give ~ to zur Welt bringen; (b) (of movement, fashion, etc.) Aufkommen, das; (of party, company) Gründung, die; (of nation, idea) Geburt, die; (of new era) Anbruch, der; Geburt, die; give ~ to sth. etw. entstehen lassen; (c) (parentage) Geburt, die; Abkunft, die (geh.); of humble ~: von niedriger Abstammung; of high ~: von hoher Geburt; [von] edler Abkunft (geh.); be a German by ~: [ein] gebürtiger Deutscher/[eine] gebürtige Deutsche sein

birth: ~ **certificate** n. Geburtsurkunde, die; ~ control n. Geburtenkontrolle od. -regelung, die; ~day n. ▶836| Geburtstag, der; attrib. Geburtstags⟨karte, -feier, -geschenk⟩; when is your ~day? wann haben Sie Geburtstag?; [be] in his/her ~day suit im Adams-/Evakostüm [sein]; ~ing pool /'bɜːθɪŋ/ n. Gebärwanne, die; ~mark n. Muttermal, das; ~place n. Geburtsort, der; (house) Geburtshaus, das; ~ rate n. Geburtenrate od. -ziffer, die; ~right n. Geburtsrecht, das

biscuit /'bɪskɪt/ 1 n. (a) (Brit.) Keks, der; coffee and ~s Kaffee und Gebäck; ~ tin Keksdose, die; (b) (Amer.: roll) [weiches] Brötchen; (c) (colour) Beige, das. See also **take** 1 c. 2 adj. beige

bisect /baɪ'sekt/ v.t. (into halves) in zwei Hälften teilen; halbieren; (into two) in zwei Teile teilen

bisexual /baɪ'seksjʊəl/ 1 adj. (a) (Biol.) zwittrig; doppelgeschlechtig; (b) (attracted by both sexes) bisexuell. 2 n. Bisexuelle, der/die

bishop /'bɪʃəp/ n. (a) (Eccl.) Bischof, der; (b) (Chess) Läufer, der

bison /'baɪsn/ n. (Zool.) (a) (Amer.: buffalo) Bison, der; (b) (European) Wisent, der

bit[1] /bɪt/ n. (a) (for horse) Gebiss, das; Gebissstange, die; take the ~ between one's teeth (fig.) aufmüpfig werden (ugs.); (b) (of drill) [Bohr]einsatz, der; Bohrer, der

bit[2] n. (a) (piece) Stück, das; (smaller) Stückchen, das; a little ~: ein kleines Stückchen; a ~ of cheese/sugar/wood/coal ein bisschen Käse/Zucker/ein Stück Holz/etwas Kohle; a ~ of trouble/luck ein wenig Ärger/Glück; the best ~s die besten Teile; it cost quite a ~: es kostete ziemlich viel; ~ by ~: Stück für Stück; (gradually) nach und nach; etwas Käse/Zucker/ein Stück Holz/etwas Kohle; a ~ of trouble/luck ein wenig Ärger/Glück; smashed to ~s in tausend Stücke zersprungen; ~s and pieces Verschiedenes; do one's ~: seinen Teil tun; (b) a ~ (somewhat): a ~ tired/too early ein bisschen müde/zu früh; a little ~, just a ~: ein klein bisschen; quite a ~: um einiges ⟨besser, stärker, hoffnungsvoller⟩; (c) a ~ of (rather): be a ~ of a coward/bully ein ziemlicher Feigling sein/den starken Mann

markieren (ugs.); a ~ of a disappointment eine ganz schöne Enttäuschung; (d) (short time) [for] a ~: eine Weile; wait a ~ longer noch ein Weilchen warten; (e) (short distance) a ~: ein Stückchen; a ~ closer ein bisschen näher; (f) (Amer.) two/four/six ~s 25/50/75 Cent

bit[3] n. (Computing) Bit, das

bit[4] ⇒ **bite** 1, 2

bitch /bɪtʃ/ 1 n. (a) (dog) Hündin, die; (b) (sl. derog.: woman) Miststück, das. 2 v.i. (coll.) meckern (ugs.) (about über + Akk.)

bite /baɪt/ 1 v.t., **bit** /bɪt/, **bitten** /'bɪtn/ beißen; (sting) ⟨Moskito usw.:⟩ stechen; ~ one's nails an den Nägeln kauen; (fig.) wie auf Kohlen sitzen; ~ one's lip (lit. or fig.) sich (Dat.) auf die Lippen beißen; he won't ~ you (fig. coll.) er wird dich schon nicht beißen; ~ the hand that feeds one (fig.) sich [seinem Gönner gegenüber] undankbar zeigen; ~ the dust (fig.) daran glauben müssen (ugs.); what's biting or bitten you? (fig. coll.) was ist mit dir los?; was hast du denn? 2 v.i., **bit, bitten** (a) beißen; (sting) stechen; ⟨Rad:⟩ fassen, greifen; ⟨Schraube:⟩ fassen; (take bait, lit. or fig.) anbeißen; (b) (have an effect) sich auswirken; greifen. 3 n. (a) (act) Biss, der; (piece) Bissen, der; (wound) Bisswunde, die; (by mosquito etc.) Stich, der; he took a ~ of the apple er biss in den Apfel; can I have a ~? darf ich mal [ab]beißen?; (b) (taking of bait) [An]beißen, das; I haven't had a ~ all day es hat den ganzen Tag noch keiner angebissen; (c) (food) Happen, der; Bissen, der; I haven't had a ~ [to eat] since breakfast ich habe seit dem Frühstück nichts mehr gegessen; have a ~ to eat eine Kleinigkeit essen; (d) (incisiveness) Bissigkeit, die; Schärfe, die ~ 'off v.t. abbeißen; the dog bit off the man's ear der Hund hat dem Mann ein Ohr abgebissen; ~ sb.'s head off (fig.) jmdm. den Kopf abreißen; ~ off more than one can chew (fig.) sich (Dat.) zu viel zumuten; sich übernehmen

'**bite-size** adj. (lit. or fig.) mundgerecht

biting /'baɪtɪŋ/ adj. (stinging) beißend; schneidend ⟨Kälte, Wind⟩; (sarcastic) scharf ⟨Angriff, Worte⟩; beißend ⟨Kritik⟩; bissig ⟨Bemerkung, Kommentar⟩

bitten ⇒ **bite** 1, 2

bitter /'bɪtə(r)/ 1 adj. (a) bitter; ~ lemon (drink) Bitter Lemon, das; (b) (fig.) scharf, heftig ⟨Antwort, Bemerkung, Angriff⟩; bitter ⟨Kampf, Kälte, Enttäuschung, Tränen⟩; verbittert ⟨Person⟩; erbittert ⟨Feind⟩; scharf, bitterkalt ⟨Wind, Wetter⟩; streng ⟨Winter⟩; to the ~ end bis zum bitteren Ende; be/feel ~ [about sth.] [über etw. (Akk.)] bitter od. verbittert sein. 2 n. (Brit.) bitteres Bier (halbdunkles, obergäriges Bier)

bitterly /'bɪtəlɪ/ adv. bitterlich ⟨weinen, sich beschweren⟩; bitter ⟨erwidern⟩; erbittert ⟨kämpfen, sich widersetzen⟩; scharf ⟨kritisieren⟩; ~ cold bitterkalt; be ~ opposed to sth. ein erbitterter Gegner einer Sache (Gen.) sein

bitterness /'bɪtənɪs/ n., no pl. ⇒ **bitter** 1: Bitterkeit, die; Schärfe, die; Heftigkeit, die; Verbitterung, die; bittere Kälte

bitter-'sweet adj. (lit. or fig.) bittersüß

bitty /'bɪtɪ/ adj. zusammengestoppelt (abwertend)

bitumen /'bɪtjʊmən/ n. Bitumen, das

bivouac /'bɪvʊæk/ 1 n. Biwak, das; Lager, das. 2 v.i., -ck- biwakieren; im Freien übernachten

bizarre /bɪ'zɑː(r)/ adj. bizarr; (eccentric) exzentrisch

blab /blæb/ v.i., -bb- (coll.) quatschen (abwertend)

black /blæk/ 1 adj. (a) schwarz; (very dark) dunkel; (b) B~ (dark-skinned) schwarz; B~ man/woman/child Schwarze, der/Schwarze, die/schwarzes Kind; B~ people Schwarze Pl.; B~ Africa Schwarzafrika (das); (c) (fig.) gloomy) düster; things look ~: es sieht böse od. düster aus; (d) (wicked) schwarz ⟨Gedanken⟩; he is not as ~ as he is painted er ist nicht so schlecht, wie er dargestellt wird; give sb. a ~ look jmdn. finster ansehen; (e) (dismal) a ~ day ein schwarzer Tag; (f) (macabre) schwarz ⟨Witz, Humor⟩. 2 n. (a) (colour) Schwarz, das; (b) B~ (person) Schwarze, der/die; (c) (credit) [be] in the ~: in den schwarzen Zahlen [sein]. 3 v.t. (a) (blacken) schwärzen; ~ sb.'s eye jmdm. ein blaues Auge machen; (b) (boycott) bestreiken ⟨Betrieb⟩; boykottieren ⟨Arbeit⟩

∼ 'out 1 *v.t.* verdunkeln. 2 *v.i.* das Bewusstsein verlieren

black: ∼ **and** '**blue** *pred. adj.* grün und blau; ∼ **and** '**white** 1 *pred. adj.* (in writing) schwarz auf weiß; (Cinemat., Photog., etc.) schwarzweiß; (fig.: comprising only opposite extremes) Schwarzweiß-; 2 *n.* [**sth. is there/down] in** ∼ **and** white (in writing) [etw. steht] schwarz auf weiß [geschrieben]; **this film is in** ∼ **and white** dieser Film ist in Schwarzweiß; **see/portray** *etc.* **things in** ∼ **and** white (fig.) schwarzweiß malen; ∼**-and-white** *attrib. adj.* Schwarzweiß-; ∼**berry** /'blækbərɪ/ *n.* Brombeere, *die;* **go** ∼**berrying** Brombeeren pflücken gehen; ∼**bird** *n.* Amsel, *die;* ∼**board** *n.* [Wand]tafel, *die;* ∼ '**books** *n. pl.* **be in sb.'s** ∼ **books** bei jmdm. schlecht angeschrieben sein; ∼ '**box** *n.* (flight recorder) Flugschreiber, *der;* ∼ '**bread** *n.* Schwarzbrot, *das;* **B**∼ **Country** *n.* (Brit.) *Industriegebiet von Staffordshire und Warwickshire;* ∼'**currant** *n.* schwarze Johannisbeere; **B**∼ '**Death** *n.* Schwarzer Tod; ∼ **e**'**conomy** *n.* Schattenwirtschaft, *die*

blacken /'blækn/ *v.t.* (a) (make dark[er]) verfinstern ⟨*Himmel*⟩; (make black[er]) schwärzen; (b) (fig.: defame) verunglimpfen; ∼ **sb.'s** [**good**] **name** jmds. [guten] Namen beschmutzen

black: ∼ '**eye** *n.* blaues Auge (fig.); Veilchen, *das* (ugs.); ∼**-eyed** *adj.* schwarzäugig; **be** ∼**-eyed** schwarze Augen haben; **B**∼ '**Forest** *pr. n.* Schwarzwald, *der;* **B**∼ **Forest** '**gateau** *n.* Schwarzwälder [Kirschtorte], *die;* ∼**head** *n.* Mitesser, *der;* ∼ '**hole** *n.* (Astron.) schwarzes Loch; ∼ '**ice** *n.* Glatteis, *das;* ∼**jack** *n.* (Cards) Vingt-[et-]un, *das;* ∼**leg** 1 *n.* (Brit.: strike-breaker) Streikbrecher, *der/* -brecherin, *die;* 2 *v.i.* Streikbrecher/-brecherin sein; ∼ '**list** *n.* schwarze Liste; ∼**list** *v.t.* auf die schwarze Liste setzen; ∼**mail** 1 *v.t.* erpressen; 2 *n.* Erpressung, *die;* **B**∼ **Maria** /blæk mə'raɪə/ *n.* grüne Minna (ugs.); ∼ '**mark** *n.* (fig.) Makel, *der;* ∼ '**market** *n.* schwarzer Markt

blackness /'blæknɪs/ *n., no pl.* (a) (black colour) Schwärze, *die;* (b) (darkness) Finsternis, *die;* (fig.: wickedness) Abscheulichkeit, *die*

black: ∼**out** *n.* (a) Verdunkelung, *die;* (Theatre, Radio) Blackout, *der;* **news** ∼**out** Nachrichtensperre, *die;* (b) (Med.) **I had a** ∼**out** ich verlor das Bewusstsein; ∼ '**pudding** *n.* Blutwurst, *die;* **B**∼ '**Sea** *pr. n.* Schwarze Meer, *das;* ∼**smith** *n.* ▶ 887 Schmied, *der;* ∼ '**spot** *n.* (fig.) schwarzer Fleck; (dangerous) Gefahrenstelle, *die;* ∼ '**tie** *n.* schwarze Fliege (*zur Smokingjacke getragen*); ∼ '**widow** *n.* (Zool.) Schwarze Witwe

bladder /'blædə(r)/ *n.* ▶ 672 Blase, *die*

blade /bleɪd/ *n.* (a) (of sword, knife, dagger, razor, plane) Klinge, *die;* (of chisel, scissors, shears) Schneide, *die;* (of saw, oar, paddle, spade, propeller) Blatt, *das;* (of paddle wheel, turbine) Schaufel, *die;* (b) (of grass etc.) Spreite, *die;* (c) (sword) Schwert, *das*

blame /bleɪm/ 1 *v.t.* (a) (hold responsible) ∼ **sb.** [**for sth.**] jmdm. die Schuld [an etw. (*Dat.*)] geben; **don't** ∼ **me** [**if** ...] geben Sie nicht mir die Schuld[, wenn ...]; ∼ **sth.** [**for sth.**] etw. [für etw.] verantwortlich machen; **be to** ∼ [**for sth.**] an etw. (*Dat.*) schuld sein; ∼ **sth. on sb./sth.** (coll.) jmdn./etw. für etw. verantwortlich machen; (b) (reproach) ∼ **sb./oneself** jmdm./sich Vorwürfe machen; **I don't** ∼ **you/him** (coll.) ich kann es Ihnen/ihm nicht verdenken; **don't** ∼ **yourself** machen Sie sich keine Vorwürfe; **have only oneself to** ∼: die Schuld bei sich selbst suchen müssen. 2 *n.* (responsibility) Schuld, *die;* **lay** *or* **put the** ∼ [**for sth.**] **on sb.** jmdm. [an etw. (*Dat.*)] die Schuld geben; **get the** ∼: die Schuld bekommen; **take the** ∼ [**for sth.**] die Schuld [für etw.] auf sich (*Akk.*) nehmen

blameless /'bleɪmlɪs/ *adj.* untadelig

blameworthy /'bleɪmwɜːðɪ/ *adj.* tadelnswert

blanch /blɑːnʃ/ 1 *v.t.* (whiten) bleichen; abziehen ⟨*Mandeln*⟩; (make pale) erbleichen lassen. 2 *v.i.* (grow pale) bleich werden

blancmange /blə'mɒnʒ/ *n.* Flammeri, *der*

bland /blænd/ *adj.* (gentle, suave) verbindlich; freundlich ⟨*Art, Stimmung*⟩; (not irritating, not stimulating) mild ⟨*Medizin, Nahrung*⟩; (unexciting) farblos

blandishment /'blændɪʃmənt/ *n.* (flattery) Schmeichelei, *die;* (cajolery) Beschwatzen, *das*

blandness /'blændnɪs/ *n., no pl.* ⇒ **bland:** Verbindlichkeit, *die;* Freundlichkeit, *die;* Milde, *die;* Farblosigkeit, *die*

blank /blæŋk/ 1 *adj.* (a) leer; kahl ⟨*Wand, Fläche*⟩; (b) (empty) frei; **leave a** ∼ **space** Platz frei lassen; (c) (fig.) leer, ausdruckslos ⟨*Gesicht, Blick*⟩; **look** ∼: ein verdutztes Gesicht machen; **my mind went** ∼: ich hatte ein Brett vor dem Kopf. 2 *n.* (a) (space) Lücke, *die;* **his memory was a** ∼: er hatte keinerlei Erinnerung; (b) (document with ∼s) Vordruck, *der;* (c) **draw a** ∼ (fig.) kein Glück haben; (d) (cartridge) Platzpatrone, *die*

blank: ∼ '**cartridge** *n.* Platzpatrone, *die;* ∼ '**cheque** *n.* Blankoscheck, *der;* (fig.) Blankovollmacht, *die*

blanket /'blæŋkɪt/ 1 *n.* (a) Decke, *die;* **wet** '∼ (fig.) Trauerkloß, *der;* (b) (thick layer) Decke, *die;* ∼ **of snow/fog** Schnee-/Nebeldecke, *die.* 2 *v.t.* zudecken. 3 *adj.* umfassend; ∼ **agreement** Pauschalabkommen, *das*

blankly /'blæŋklɪ/ *adv.* verdutzt

blank '**verse** *n.* (Pros.) Blankvers, *der*

blare /bleə(r)/ 1 *v.i.* ⟨*Lautsprecher:*⟩ plärren; ⟨*Trompete:*⟩ schmettern. 2 *v.t.* ∼ [**out**] [hinaus]plärren ⟨*Worte*⟩; [hinaus]schmettern ⟨*Melodie*⟩. 3 *n.* ⇒ 1: Plärren, *das;* Schmettern, *das*

blasé /'blɑːzeɪ/ *adj.* blasiert

blaspheme /blæs'fiːm/ *v.i.* lästern

blasphemy /'blæsfəmɪ/ *n.* Blasphemie, *die*

blast /blɑːst/ 1 *n.* (a) (gust) **a** ∼ [**of wind**] ein Windstoß; (b) (sound) Tuten, *das;* **give one** ∼ **of the horn** einmal ins Horn stoßen; (c) **at full** ∼ (fig.) auf Hochtouren *Pl.;* (d) (of explosion) Druckwelle, *die;* (coll.: explosion) Explosion, *die.* 2 *v.t.* (a) (blow up) sprengen ⟨*Felsen*⟩; (coll.: kick) donnern ⟨*Fußball*⟩; (b) (curse) ∼ **you/him!** zum Teufel mit dir/ ihm! 3 *v.i.* (coll.: shoot) **start** ∼**ing away** drauflosschießen (**at** auf + *Akk.*). 4 *int.* [**oh**] ∼**!** (coll.) verdammt!
∼ '**off** *v.i.* abheben

blasted /'blɑːstɪd/ *adj.* (damned) verdammt (salopp)

blast: ∼ **furnace** *n.* Hochofen, *der;* ∼**-off** *n.* Abheben, *das*

blatant /'bleɪtənt/ *adj.* (a) (flagrant) offensichtlich; (b) (unashamed) unverhohlen; unverfroren ⟨*Lüge*⟩

blatantly /'bleɪtəntlɪ/ *adv.* ⇒ **blatant:** offensichtlich; unverhohlen; unverfroren

blaze[1] /bleɪz/ 1 *n.* (a) (fire) Feuer, *das;* (in building) Feuer, *das;* Brand, *der;* (b) (display) **a** ∼ **of lights** ein Lichtermeer; **a** ∼ **of colour** eine Farbenpracht; ein Farbenmeer; **in a** ∼ **of glory** mit Glanz und Gloria; (coll.) **go to** ∼**s!** scher dich zum Teufel! (salopp); **like** ∼**s** wie verrückt (ugs.) ⟨*arbeiten, rennen usw.*⟩; **what the** ∼**s** [...]? was zum Teufel [...]? (salopp); **how/where/who/why the** ∼**s** ...? wie/wo/wer/warum zum Teufel ...? (salopp). 2 *v.i.* (burn) brennen; **the house was already blazing when the firemen arrived** das Haus stand schon in Flammen, als die Feuerwehr ankam; **a blazing fire** ein hell loderndes Feuer; **the blazing sun** die glühende Sonne; (b) (emit light) strahlen; (c) (fig.: with anger etc.) ⟨*Augen:*⟩ glühen; **a blazing row** ein heftiger Streit
∼ **a**'**way** *v.i.* [drauf]losschießen (**at** auf + *Akk.*)
∼ '**up** *v.i.* aufflammen

blaze[2] *v.t.* ∼ **a** *or* **the trail** (fig.) den Weg bahnen

blazer /'bleɪzə(r)/ *n.* Blazer, *der*

bleach /bliːtʃ/ 1 *v.t.* bleichen ⟨*Wäsche, Haar, Knochen*⟩. 2 *v.i.* bleichen. 3 *n.* Bleichmittel, *das*

bleak /bliːk/ *adj.* (a) (bare) öde ⟨*Landschaft usw.*⟩; karg ⟨*Zimmer*⟩; (b) (chilly) rau; kalt ⟨*Wetter, Tag*⟩; (c) (unpromising) düster; ∼ **prospect[s]** trübe Aussichten

bleary /'blɪərɪ/ *adj.* trübe ⟨*Augen*⟩; **look** ∼**-eyed** verschlafen aussehen

bleat /bliːt/ *v.i.* ⟨*Schaf, Kalb:*⟩ blöken; ⟨*Ziege:*⟩ meckern; (fig.) jammern; (plaintively) meckern

bled ⇒ **bleed**

bleed /bliːd/ 1 *v.i.,* **bled** /bled/ bluten. 2 *v.t.,* **bled** (draw blood from, lit. or fig.) zur Ader lassen

bleeding /'bliːdɪŋ/ 1 *n.* (loss of blood) Blutung, *die.* 2 *adj.* (Brit. coarse: damned) Scheiß- (derb). 3 *adv.* (Brit. coarse) ∼ **awful** total beschissen (derb); ∼ **stupid** saublöd (salopp)

bleep /bli:p/ **1** *n.* Piepen, *das;* **two faint** ∼s zwei schwache Piepser. **2** *v.i.* ‹*Geigerzähler, Funksignal:*› piepen. **3** *v.t.* ∼ **sb.** jmdn. über seinen Kleinempfänger *od.* (ugs.) Piepser rufen

bleeper /'bli:pə(r)/ *n.* Kleinempfänger, *der;* Piepser, *der* (ugs.)

blemish /'blemɪʃ/ **1** *n.* **(a)** (stain) Fleck, *der;* **(b)** (defect, lit. or fig.) Makel, *der;* (in character) Fehler, *der.* **2** *v.t.* **(a)** (spoil) verunstalten; **(b)** (fig.) ∼ **sth.** einer Sache (*Dat.*) schaden

blend /blend/ **1** *v.t.* **(a)** (mix) mischen ‹*Whisky-, Tee-, Tabaksorten*›; **(b)** (make indistinguishable) vermischen. **2** *v.i.* **(a)** sich mischen lassen; ∼ **in with/into sth.** [gut] zu etw. passen/mit etw. verschmelzen; **(b)** ‹*Whisky-, Tee-, Tabaksorten:*› sich [harmonisch] verbinden. **3** *n.* Mischung, *die*

blender /'blendə(r)/ *n.* **(a)** (person) [Ver]mischer, *der;* **(b)** (apparatus) Mixer, *der;* Mixgerät, *das*

bless /bles/ *v.t.,* **blessed** /blest/ *or* (poet.) **blest** /blest/ (consecrate, pronounce blessing on) segnen; **[God]** ∼ **you** Gottes Segen; (as thanks) das ist sehr lieb von dir/Ihnen; (to person sneezing) Gesundheit!; **goodbye and God** ∼: Wiedersehen, [und] mach's/macht's gut!; ∼ **me!**, **well I'm blest!**, ∼ **my soul!** du meine Güte! (ugs.); ∼ **me if it isn't Sid** ja das ist doch Sid!

blessed *adj.* /'blesɪd, pred.* blest/ **(a) be** ∼ **with sth.** (also iron.) mit etw. gesegnet sein; **(b)** (revered) heilig ‹*Gott, Mutter Maria*›; (in Paradise) selig; (RC Ch.: beatified) selig; (blissful) beglückend; **(c)** *attrib.* (euphem.: cursed) verdammt (salopp)

blessing /'blesɪŋ/ *n.* **(a)** (divine favour, grace at table) Segen, *der;* **do sth. with sb.'s** ∼ (fig.) etw. mit jmds. Segen tun (ugs.); **give sb./sth. one's** ∼ (fig.) jmdm./etw. seinen Segen geben (ugs.); **(b)** (divine gift) Segnung, *die;* **count one's** ∼s (fig.) dankbar sein; **(c)** (fig. coll.: welcome thing) Segen, *der;* **what a** ∼**!** welch ein Segen!; **be a** ∼ **in disguise** sich schließlich doch noch als Segen erweisen

blest ⇨ **bless;** (poet.) ⇨ **blessed** b

blew ⇨ **blow¹** 1, 2

blight /blaɪt/ **1** *n.* **(a)** (plant disease) Brand, *der;* (fig.) Geißel, *die;* **(b)** (fig.: unsightly urban area) Schandfleck, *der.* **2** *v.t.* **(a)** (affect with ∼) be ∼ed von Brand befallen werden/sein; **(b)** überschatten ‹*Freude, Leben*›; (frustrate) zunichte machen ‹*Hoffnung*›; **a** ∼**ed area** eine heruntergekommene Gegend

blighter /'blaɪtə(r)/ *n.* (Brit. coll.) **(a) the poor** ∼: der arme Kerl; **(b)** (derog.) Lümmel, *der* (abwertend)

blimey /'blaɪmɪ/ *int.* (Brit. sl.) Mensch (salopp)

blind /blaɪnd/ **1** *adj.* **(a)** blind ‹*Person, Tier*›; **a** ∼ **man/woman** ein Blinder/eine Blinde; **as** ∼ **as a bat** stockblind (ugs.); ∼ **in one eye** auf einem Auge blind; **go** *or* **become** ∼: blind werden; **turn a** ∼ **eye [to sth.]** (fig.) [bei etw.] ein Auge zudrücken; **(b)** (Aeronaut.) ∼ **landing/flying** Blindlandung, *die*/Blindflug, *der;* **(c)** (unreasoning) blind ‹*Vorurteil, Weigerung, Gehorsam, Vertrauen*›; **(d)** (oblivious) **be** ∼ **to sth.** blind gegenüber etw. sein; **(e)** (not ruled by purpose) blind ‹*Wut, Zorn*›; dunkel ‹*Instinkt*›; kopflos ‹*Panik*›. **2** *adv.* **(a)** blindlings; **the pilot had to fly/land** ∼: der Pilot musste blind fliegen/landen; **(b)** (completely) ∼ **drunk** stockbetrunken (ugs.); **swear** ∼: hoch und heilig versichern. **3** *n.* **(a)** (screen) Jalousie, *die;* (of cloth) Rouleau, *das;* (of shop) Markise, *die;* **(b)** (Amer. Hunting: hide) Jagdschirm, *der;* **(c)** (pretext) Vorwand, *der;* (cover) Tarnung, *die;* **be a** ∼ **for sth.** als Tarnung für etw. dienen; **(d)** *pl.* **the** ∼: die Blinden *Pl.;* **it's [a case of] the** ∼ **leading the** ∼ (fig.) das ist, wie wenn ein Blinder einen Lahmen [spazieren]führt. **4** *v.t.* (lit. or fig.) blenden; **be** ∼**ed** (accidentally) das Augenlicht verlieren; ∼ **sb. with science** jmdn. mit großen Worten beeindrucken

blind: ∼ **'alley** *n.* (lit. or fig.) Sackgasse, *die;* ∼ **'corner** *n.* unübersichtliche Ecke; ∼ **'date** *n.* Verabredung mit einem/einer Unbekannten; ∼**fold 1** *v.t.* die Augen verbinden (+ *Dat.*); **2** *adj.* mit verbundenen Augen *nachgestellt*

blinding /'blaɪndɪŋ/ *adj.* blendend ‹*Licht, Sonnenlicht, Blitz*›; grell ‹*Strahl*›; **a** ∼ **headache** rasende Kopfschmerzen *Pl.*

blindly /'blaɪndlɪ/ *adv.* [wie] blind; (fig.) blindlings

blind man's 'buff *n.* Blindekuh *o. Art.*

blindness /'blaɪndnɪs/ *n., no pl.* Blindheit, *die*

'blind spot *n.* (Anat.) blinder Fleck; (Motor Veh.) toter Winkel; (fig.: weak spot) schwacher Punkt

blink /blɪŋk/ **1** *v.i.* **(a)** blinzeln; **(b)** (shine intermittently) blinken; (shine momentarily) aufblinken. **2** *v.t.* ∼ **one's eyes** mit den Augen zwinkern. **3** *n.* **(a)** Blinzeln, *das;* **(b)** (coll.) **be on the** ∼: kaputt sein (ugs.)

blinker /'blɪŋkə(r)/ **1** *n. in pl.* Scheuklappen; **have/put** ∼s **on** (lit. or fig.) Scheuklappen tragen/anlegen. **2** *v.t.* Scheuklappen anlegen (+ *Dat.*); ∼**ed** (fig.) borniert

blinking /'blɪŋkɪŋ/ (Brit. coll. euphem.) **1** *adj.* verflixt (ugs.). **2** *adv.* verflixt (ugs.); **it's** ∼ **raining** verflixt [und zugenäht], es regnet

blip /blɪp/ *n.* **(a)** (sound) (of bursting bubble) leiser Knall; (on magnetic tape) leises Knacken; **(b)** (Radar: image) Echozeichen, *das*

bliss /blɪs/ *n.* (joy) [Glück]seligkeit, *die;* Glück, *das*

blissful /'blɪsfl/ *adj.* [glück]selig; ∼ **ignorance** (iron.) selige Unwissenheit

blister /'blɪstə(r)/ **1** *n.* (on skin, plant, metal, paintwork) Blase, *die.* **2** *v.t.* Blasen hervorrufen auf (+ *Dat.*) ‹*Haut, Metall, Anstrich*›. **3** *v.i.* ‹*Haut:*› Blasen bekommen; ‹*Metall, Anstrich:*› Blasen werfen

blistering /'blɪstərɪŋ/ *adj.* ätzend ‹*Kritik*›; **a** ∼ **attack** ein erbitterter Angriff

'blister pack *n.* Sichtpackung, *die*

blithely /'blaɪðlɪ/ *adv.* ∼ **ignore sth.** sich unbekümmert über etw. (*Akk.*) hinwegsetzen

blithering /'blɪðərɪŋ/ *adj.* (coll.) (utter) total; völlig; **a** ∼ **idiot** ein alter Idiot (salopp)

blitz /blɪts/ (coll.) **1** *n.* **(a)** (Hist.) Luftangriff, *der* (**on** auf + *Akk.*); **during the [London] B**∼: während der Luft- *od.* Bombenangriffe [auf London]; **(b)** (fig.: attack) Großaktion, *die* (fig.); **have a** ∼ **on one's room** in seinem Zimmer gründlich sauber machen. **2** *v.t.* [schwer] bombardieren

blizzard /'blɪzəd/ *n.* Schneesturm, *der*

bloated /'bləʊtɪd/ *adj.* **(a)** (having overeaten) aufgedunsen; **I feel** ∼: ich bin voll (ugs.); **(b) be** ∼ **with pride** aufgeblasen sein

blob /blɒb/ *n.* **(a)** (drop) Tropfen, *der;* (small mass) Klacks, *der* (ugs.); (of butter etc.) Klecks, *der;* **(b)** (spot of colour) Fleck, *der*

bloc /blɒk/ *n.* (Polit.) Block, *der;* **the Eastern** ∼**/Eastern** ∼ **countries** der Ostblock/die Ostblockstaaten; **the Western** ∼ **[countries]** die westlichen Staaten

block /blɒk/ **1** *n.* **(a)** (large piece) Klotz, *der;* ∼ **of wood** Holzklotz, *der;* **(b)** (for chopping on) Hackklotz, *der;* **(c)** (for beheading on) Richtblock, *der;* **(d)** (large mass of concrete or stone; building-stone) Block, *der;* **(e)** (coll.: head) **knock sb.'s** ∼ **off** jmdm. eins überziehen (salopp); **(f)** (of buildings) [Häuser]block, *der;* ∼ **of flats/offices** Wohnblock, *der*/Bürohaus, *das;* **(g)** (Amer.: area between streets) Block, *der;* **(h)** (large quantity) Masse, *die;* **a** ∼ **of shares** ein Aktienpaket; **a** ∼ **of seats** mehrere nebeneinander liegende Sitze; **(i)** (pad of paper) Block, *der;* **(j)** (obstruction) Verstopfung, *die;* **(k)** (mental barrier) **a mental** ∼: eine geistige Sperre; Mattscheibe *o. Art.* (salopp); **a psychological** ∼: ein psychologischer Block; **(l)** ∼ **and tackle** Flaschenzug, *der.* **2** *v.t.* **(a)** (obstruct) blockieren, versperren ‹*Tür, Straße, Durchgang, Sicht*›; blockieren ‹*Nase*›; blockieren ‹*Fortschritt*›; abblocken ‹*Ball, Torschuss*›; **(b)** (Commerc.) einfrieren ‹*Investitionen, Guthaben*›

∼ **'off** *v.t.* [ab]sperren ‹*Straße*›; blockieren ‹*Rohr, Verkehr*›

∼ **'out** *v.t.* ausschließen ‹*Licht, Lärm*›

∼ **'up** *v.t.* verstopfen; versperren ‹*Eingang*›

blockade /blɒ'keɪd/ **1** *n.* Blockade, *die.* **2** *v.t.* blockieren

blockage /'blɒkɪdʒ/ *n.* Block, *der;* (of pipe, gutter) Verstopfung, *die*

block: ∼**buster** *n.* Knüller, *der* (ugs.); ∼ **'capital** *n.* Blockbuchstabe, *der;* ∼**head** *n.* Dummkopf, *der* (abwertend); ∼ **'letters** *n. pl.* Blockschrift, *die*

bloke /bləuk/ *n.* (Brit. coll.) Typ, *der* (ugs.)

blond /blɒnd/ ⇒ **blonde 1**

blonde /blɒnd/ **1** *adj.* blond ⟨*Haar, Person*⟩; hell ⟨*Teint*⟩. **2** *n.* Blondine, *die*

blood /blʌd/ *n.* (a) ▶672 Blut, *das;* **sb.'s** ~ **boils** (fig.) jmd. ist in Rage; **it makes my** ~ **boil** es bringt mich in Rage; **sb.'s** ~ **turns** *or* **runs cold** (fig.) jmdm. erstarrt das Blut in den Adern; **be after** *or* **out for sb.'s** ~ (fig.) es auf jmdn. abgesehen haben; **it's like getting** ~ **out of** *or* **from a stone** das ist fast ein Ding der Unmöglichkeit; **do sth. in cold** ~ (fig.) etw. kaltblütig tun; (b) (relationship) Blutsverwandtschaft, *die;* ~ **is thicker than water** (prov.) Blut ist dicker als Wasser

blood: ~ **bank** *n.* Blutbank, *die;* ~**bath** *n.* Blutbad, *das;* ~ **cell** *n.* Blutkörperchen, *das;* ~ **clot** *n.* Blutgerinnsel, *das;* ~**-curdling** *adj.* grauenerregend; ~ **donor** ⇒ donor b; ~ **group** *n.* Blutgruppe, *die;* ~**hound** *n.* Bluthund, *der;* (fig.) Spürhund, *der*

bloodless /ˈblʌdlɪs/ *adj.* (a) (without bloodshed) unblutig; (b) (without blood, pale) blutleer

blood: ~**lust** *n.* Blutgier, *die;* ~ **money** *n.* Blutgeld, *das;* ~ **poisoning** *n.* Blutvergiftung, *die;* ~ **pressure** *n.* Blutdruck, *der;* ~**-red** *adj.* blutrot; ~ **relation** *n.* Blutsverwandte, *der/die;* ~ **sample** *n.* Blutprobe, *die;* ~**shed** *n.* Blutvergießen, *das;* ~**shot** *adj.* blutunterlaufen; ~ **sports** *n. pl.* Hetzjagd, *die;* ~**stain** *n.* Blutfleck, *der;* ~**stained** *adj.* (lit. or fig.) blutbefleckt; ~**stream** *n.* Blutstrom, *der;* ~**thirsty** *adj.* blutdürstig (geh.); blutrünstig; ~ **transfusion** *n.* Bluttransfusion, *die;* ~ **vessel** *n.* Blutgefäß, *das*

bloody /ˈblʌdɪ/ **1** *adj.* (a) blutig; (running with blood) blutend; (b) (sl.: damned) verdammt (salopp); **you** ~ **fool!** du Vollidiot! (salopp); ~ **hell!** verdammt noch mal! (salopp); (c) (Brit.) *as intensifier* einzig; **that/he is a** ~ **nuisance** das ist vielleicht ein Mist (salopp)/der geht einem vielleicht *od.* ganz schön auf den Wecker (ugs.). **2** *adv.* (a) (sl.: damned) verdammt (salopp); (b) (Brit.) *as intensifier* verdammt (salopp); **not** ~ **likely!** denkste! (salopp). **3** *v.t.* (make ~) blutig machen; (stain with blood) mit Blut beflecken

bloody-ˈminded *adj.* stur (ugs.)

bloom /bluːm/ **1** *n.* (a) Blüte, *die;* **be in** ~: in Blüte stehen; (b) (on fruit) Flaum, *der;* (flush) rosige Gesichtsfarbe; (c) (prime) **in the** ~ **of youth** in der Blüte der Jugend. **2** *v.i.* blühen; (fig.: flourish) in Blüte stehen

bloomers /ˈbluːməz/ *n. pl.* [Damen]pumphose, *die*

blossom /ˈblɒsəm/ **1** *n.* (a) (flower) Blüte, *die;* (b) *no pl., no indef. art.* (mass of flowers) Blüte, *die;* **be in** ~: in [voller] Blüte stehen *od.* sein; **have come into** ~: blühen. **2** *v.i.* (a) blühen; (b) (fig.) blühen ⟨*Person*⟩ aufblühen

blot /blɒt/ **1** *n.* (a) (spot of ink) Tintenklecks, *der;* (stain) Fleck, *der;* (blemish) Makel, *der;* Schandfleck, *der;* (b) (fig.) Makel, *der;* a ~ **on sb.'s character** ein Fleck auf jmds. weißer Weste (fig.). **2** *v.t.,* **-tt-:** (a) (dry) ablöschen ⟨*Tinte, Schrift, Papier*⟩; (b) (spot with ink) beklecksen; ~ **one's copybook** (fig. coll.) sich unmöglich machen

~ **'out** *v.t.* (a) (obliterate) einen Klecks machen auf (+ *Akk.*); unleserlich machen ⟨*Schrift*⟩; (b) (obscure) verdecken ⟨*Sicht*⟩; (c) auslöschen ⟨*Leben, Menschheit, Erinnerung*⟩

blotter /ˈblɒtə(r)/ *n.* Schreibunterlage, *die*

'blotting paper *n.* Löschpapier, *das*

blouse /blauz/ *n.* Bluse, *die*

blow¹ /bləu/ **1** *v.i.,* **blew** /bluː/, **blown** /bləun/ (a) ⟨*Wind:*⟩ wehen; ⟨*Sturm:*⟩ blasen; ⟨*Luft:*⟩ ziehen; **there is a gale** ~**ing out there** es stürmt draußen; (b) (exhale) blasen; ~ **on one's hands to warm them** in die Hände hauchen, um sie zu wärmen; ~ **hot and cold** (fig.) einmal hü und einmal hott sagen; (c) (puff, pant) ⟨*Person:*⟩ schwer atmen, schnaufen; ⟨*Tier:*⟩ schnaufen; (d) (be sounded by ~ing) geblasen werden; ⟨*Trompete, Flöte, Horn, Pfeife usw.:*⟩ ertönen; (e) (melt) ⟨*Sicherung, Glühfaden:*⟩ durchbrennen. **2** *v.t.,* **blew, blown** (see also **k**): (a) (breathe out) [aus]blasen, ausstoßen ⟨*Luft, Rauch*⟩; (b) (send by ~ing) ~ **sb. a kiss** jmdm. eine Kusshand zuwerfen; (c) blasen ⟨*Blätter, Schnee, Staub usw.*⟩; (d) (make by ~ing) blasen

⟨*Glas*⟩; machen ⟨*Seifenblasen*⟩; (e) (sound) blasen ⟨*Trompete, Flöte, Horn, Pfeife usw.*⟩; ~ **one's own trumpet** (fig.) sein Eigenlob singen; (f) (clear) ~ **one's nose** sich (*Dat.*) die Nase putzen; (g) (send flying) schleudern; ~ **sth. to pieces** etw. in die Luft sprengen; (h) (cause to melt) durchbrennen lassen ⟨*Sicherung, Glühlampe*⟩; durchhauen (ugs.) ⟨*Sicherung*⟩; (i) (break into) sprengen, aufbrechen ⟨*Tresor, Safe*⟩; (j) (coll.: reveal) verraten ⟨*Plan, Komplizen*⟩; (k) *p.t., p.p.* ~**ed** (coll.: curse) **[well,] I'm** *or* **I'll be** ~**ed** ich werde verrückt! (salopp); ~ **you, Jack!** du kannst mich mal gern haben! (salopp); ~**!** [so ein] Mist! (ugs.); ~ **the expense** es ist doch Wurscht, was es kostet (ugs.); (l) (sl.: squander) verpulvern, verplempern (ugs.) ⟨*Geld, Mittel, Erbschaft*⟩; ~ **it** (lose opportunity) es vermasseln (salopp)

~ **'off 1** *v.i.* weggeblasen werden. **2** *v.t.* wegblasen

~ **'out 1** *v.t.* (a) (extinguish) ausblasen ⟨*Kerze, Lampe*⟩; (b) (by explosion) **the explosion blew all the windows out** durch die Explosion flogen alle Fensterscheiben raus; ~ **sb.'s/one's brains out** jmdm./sich eine Kugel durch den Kopf jagen (ugs.). **2** *v.i.* ⟨*Reifen:*⟩ platzen; ⟨*Kerze, Lampe:*⟩ ausgeblasen werden. **3** *v. refl.* ⟨*Sturm:*⟩ sich legen

~ **'over 1** *v.i.* umgeblasen werden; ⟨*Streit, Sturm:*⟩ sich legen. **2** *v.t.* umblasen

~ **'up 1** *v.t.* (a) (shatter) [in die Luft] sprengen; (b) (inflate) aufblasen ⟨*Ballon*⟩; aufpumpen ⟨*Reifen*⟩; (c) (coll.: reprove) in der Luft zerreißen (ugs.); (d) (coll.: enlarge) vergrößern ⟨*Foto, Seite*⟩; (e) (coll.: exaggerate) hochspielen, aufbauschen ⟨*Ereignis, Bericht*⟩. **2** *v.i.* (a) (explode) explodieren; (b) (arise suddenly) ⟨*Krieg, Sturm, Konflikt:*⟩ ausbrechen; (c) (lose one's temper) [vor Wut] explodieren (ugs.)

blow² *n.* (a) (stroke) Schlag, *der;* (with axe) Hieb, *der;* (jolt, push) Stoß, *der;* **in** *or* **at one** ~ (lit. or fig.) mit einem Schlag; **come to** ~**s** handgreiflich werden; **a** ~**-by-**~ **account** ein Bericht in allen Einzelheiten; (b) (disaster) [schwerer] Schlag, *der* (fig.) (**to** für); **come as** *or* **be a** ~ **to sb.** ein schwerer Schlag für jmdn. sein

blow: ~**-dry** *v.t.* mit dem Fön frisieren; ~**lamp** *n.* Lötlampe, *die*

blown ⇒ **blow¹ 1, 2**

blow: ~**-out** *n.* (a) (burst tyre) Reifenpanne, *die;* (b) (coll.: meal) feudales Essen (ugs.); ~**pipe** *n.* (weapon) Blasrohr, *das;* ~**torch** (Amer.) ⇒ ~lamp; ~**-up** *n.* (coll.: enlargement) Vergrößerung, *die*

blowy /ˈbləuɪ/ *adj.* windig

blubber /ˈblʌbə(r)/ **1** *n.* (whale-fat) Walfischspeck, *der.* **2** *v.i.* (coll.: weep) heulen (ugs.)

blue /bluː/ **1** *adj.* (a) blau; **be** ~ **with cold/rage** blau gefroren/rot vor Zorn sein; (b) (depressed) **be/feel** ~: niedergeschlagen sein/sich bedrückt *od.* deprimiert fühlen; (c) (pornographic) pornografisch; Porno-; ~ **jokes** unanständige Witze. **2** *n.* (a) (colour) Blau, *das;* (b) (sky) Himmelsblau, *das;* **out of the** ~ (fig.) aus heiterem Himmel (ugs.); (c) **the** ~**s** (melancholy) Niedergeschlagenheit; **have the** ~**s** niedergeschlagen *od.* deprimiert sein; (d) **the** ~**s** (Mus.) der Blues; **play/sing the** ~**s** Blues spielen/singen

blue: ~ **'baby** *n.* (Med.) blausüchtiger Säugling; ~**bell** *n.* (campanula) [blaue Wiesen]glockenblume, *die;* (wild hyacinth) Sternhyazinthe, *die;* ~**berry** /ˈbluːbərɪ/ *n.* Heidelbeere, *die;* Blaubeere, *die;* ~ **'blood** *n.* blaues Blut; ~**bottle** *n.* Schmeißfliege, *die;* ~ **'cheese** *n.* Blauschimmelkäse, *der;* ~**-'collar** *adj.* ~**-collar worker** Arbeiter, *der/*Arbeiterin, *die;* ~**-collar union** Arbeitergewerkschaft, *die;* ~**-eyed** *adj.* blauäugig; **be** ~**-eyed** blaue Augen haben; ~**-eyed 'boy** *n.* (fig. coll.) Goldjunge, *der;* ~ **'jeans** *pl.* Blue jeans *Pl.;* ~ **'moon** *n.* **once in a** ~ **moon** alle Jubeljahre (ugs.); ~**print** *n.* (a) Blaupause, *die;* (b) (fig.) Plan, *der;* Entwurf, *der;* ~**stocking** *n.* Blaustrumpf, *der;* ~ **tit** *n.* (Ornith.) Blaumeise, *die*

bluff¹ /blʌf/ **1** *n.* (act) Täuschungsmanöver, *das;* Bluff, *der* (ugs.); *see also* **call 2 c. 2** *v.i. & t.* bluffen (ugs.)

bluff² *n.* (headland) Kliff, *das;* Steilküste, *die;* (inland) Steilhang, *der.* **2** *adj.* (abrupt, blunt, frank, hearty) raubeinig (ugs.)

bluish /ˈbluːɪʃ/ *adj.* bläulich

blunder /ˈblʌndə(r)/ **1** *n.* [schwerer] Fehler; **make a** ~: einen [schweren] Fehler machen. **2** *v.i.* (a) (make mistake) einen [schweren] Fehler machen; (b) (move blindly) tappen

blunt /blʌnt/ **1** *adj.* (a) stumpf; **a ∼ instrument** ein stumpfer Gegenstand; (b) (outspoken) direkt; unverblümt; (c) (uncompromising) glatt (ugs.) ⟨*Ablehnung*⟩. **2** *v.t.* ∼ [the edge of] stumpf machen ⟨*Messer, Schwert, Säge*⟩; dämpfen ⟨*Begeisterung, Mut*⟩; mildern ⟨*Trauer, Enttäuschung*⟩

bluntly /'blʌntlɪ/ *adv.* (a) (outspokenly) direkt, unverblümt ⟨*sprechen, antworten*⟩; (b) (uncompromisingly) glatt ⟨*ablehnen*⟩

bluntness /'blʌntnɪs/ *n., no pl.* ⇒ **blunt 1**: Stumpfheit, *die;* Direktheit, *die;* Unverblümtheit, *die*

blur /blɜː(r)/ **1** *v.t.*, **-rr-**: (a) (smear) verwischen, verschmieren ⟨*Schrift, Seite*⟩; (b) (make indistinct) verwischen ⟨*Schrift, Farben, Konturen*⟩; **become ∼red** ⟨*Farben, Schrift:*⟩ verwischt werden; (c) (dim) trüben ⟨*Sicht, Wahrnehmung*⟩; **my vision is ∼red** ich sehe alles verschwommen. **2** *n.* (a) (smear) [verschmierter] Fleck, *der;* (b) (dim image) verschwommener Fleck

blurb /blɜːb/ *n.* Klappentext, *der;* Waschzettel, *der*

blurt /blɜːt/ *v.t.* hervorstoßen ⟨*Worte, Beschimpfung*⟩; ∼ **sth. out** mit etw. herausplatzen (ugs.)

blush /blʌʃ/ **1** *v.i.* (a) rot werden; **make sb. ∼:** jmdn. rot werden lassen; (b) (be ashamed) sich schämen (**at** bei). **2** *n.* (a) (reddening) Erröten, *das* (geh.); **spare sb.'s ∼es** jmdn. nicht in Verlegenheit bringen; (b) (rosy glow) Röte, *die*

bluster /'blʌstə(r)/ *v.i.* (a) ⟨*Wind:*⟩ tosen, brausen; (b) ⟨*Person:*⟩ sich aufplustern (ugs.)

blustery /'blʌstərɪ/ *adj.* stürmisch ⟨*Wetter, Wind*⟩

BMX *abbr.* ∼ [**bike**] BMX-Rad, *das*

BO *abbr.* (coll.) **body odour** Körpergeruch, *der*

boa constrictor /'bəʊə kənstrɪktə(r)/ *n.* Boa constrictor, *die*

boar /bɔː(r)/ *n.* (a) (male pig) Eber, *der;* (b) (wild) Keiler, *der*

board /bɔːd/ **1** *n.* (a) Brett, *das;* **bare ∼s** bloße Dielen; (b) (black∼) Tafel, *die;* (c) (notice-∼) Schwarzes Brett; (d) (in game) Brett, *das;* (e) (spring∼) [Sprung]brett, *das;* (f) (meals) Verpflegung, *die;* ∼ **and lodging** Unterkunft und Verpflegung; **full ∼:** Vollpension, *die;* (g) (Admin. etc.) Amt, *das;* Behörde, *die;* **gas/water/electricity ∼:** Gas-/Wasser-/Elektrizitätsversorgungsgesellschaft, *die;* ∼ **of inquiry** Untersuchungsausschuss, *der;* (h) (Commerc., Industry) ∼ [**of directors**] Vorstand, *der;* (i) (Naut., Aeronaut., Transport) **on ∼:** an Bord; **on ∼ the ship/plane** an Bord des Schiffes/Flugzeugs; (j) **the ∼s** (Theatre) die Bühne; (k) **go by the ∼:** ins Wasser fallen; **above ∼:** korrekt; **across the ∼:** pauschal. **2** *v.t.* (go on ∼) ∼ **the ship/plane** an Bord des Schiffes/Flugzeugs gehen; ∼ **the train/bus** in den Zug/Bus einsteigen. **3** *v.i.* (a) (lodge) [in Pension] wohnen (**with** bei); (b) (∼ an aircraft) an Bord gehen; **'flight L 5701 now ∼ing [at] gate 15'** „Passagiere des Fluges L 5701 bitte zum Flugsteig 15" ∼ '**up** *v.t.* mit Brettern vernageln

boarder /'bɔːdə(r)/ *n.* (a) (lodger) Pensionsgast, *der;* (b) (Sch.) Internatsschüler, *der*/-schülerin, *die*

'**board game** *n.* Brettspiel, *das*

boarding: ∼ **house** *n.* Pension, *die;* ∼ **school** *n.* Internat, *das*

board: ∼ **meeting** *n.* Vorstands-/Aufsichtsrats-/Verwaltungsratssitzung, *die;* ∼**room** *n.* Sitzungssaal, *der*

boast /bəʊst/ **1** *v.i.* prahlen (**of, about** mit). **2** *v.t.* (possess) sich rühmen (+ *Gen.*). **3** *n.* (a) Prahlerei, *die;* (b) (cause of pride) Stolz, *der*

boastful /'bəʊstfl/ *adj.* prahlerisch; großspurig ⟨*Erklärung, Behauptung*⟩

boat /bəʊt/ **1** *n.* (a) Boot, *das;* **ship's ∼:** Beiboot, *das;* **go by ∼:** mit dem Schiff fahren; **be in the same ∼** (fig.) im gleichen Boot sitzen; (b) (ship) Schiff, *das;* (c) (for sauce etc.) Sauciere, *die.* **2** *v.i.* **go ∼ing** eine Bootsfahrt machen

boater /'bəʊtə(r)/ *n.* (a) (person) Bootsfahrer, *der*/-fahrerin, *die;* (b) (hat) steifer Strohhut

boat: ∼-**hook** *n.* Bootshaken, *der;* ∼**house** *n.* Bootshaus, *das;* ∼**load** *n.* Bootsladung, *die;* ∼ **race** *n.* Regatta, *die;* ∼**swain** /'bəʊsn/ *n.* Bootsmann, *der;* ∼-**train** *n.* Zug mit Schiffsanschluss

bob¹ /bɒb/ **1** *v.i.*, **-bb-:** (a) ∼ [**up and down**] sich auf und nieder bewegen; (jerkily) auf und nieder schnellen; ⟨[*Pferde*]*schwanz:*⟩ [auf und nieder] wippen; ∼ **up** hochschnellen; (b) (curtsy) knicksen. **2** *n.* (curtsy) Knicks, *der*

bob² **1** *n.* (hairstyle) Bubikopf, *der.* **2** *v.t.*, **-bb-** kurz schneiden ⟨*Haar*⟩; **wear one's hair ∼bed** einen Bubikopf tragen

bob³ *n., pl. same* (Brit. coll.) (a) (Hist.: shilling) Schilling, *der;* **she's not short of a ∼ or two** (fig.) sie hat schon ein paar Mark; (b) (5p) Fünfer, *der* (ugs.); **two/ten ∼:** 10/50 Pence

bob⁴ *n.* (∼sled) Bob, *der*

bobbin /'bɒbɪn/ *n.* Spule, *die*

bobble /'bɒbl/ *n.* Pompon, *der;* Bommel, *die* (bes. nordd.)

bobby /'bɒbɪ/ *n.* (Brit. coll.) Bobby, *der* (ugs.)

bob: ∼**sled,** ∼**sleigh** *ns.* Bob[schlitten], *der*

bode /bəʊd/ *v.i.* ∼ **ill/well** nichts Gutes/einiges erhoffen lassen

bodice /'bɒdɪs/ *n.* (part of dress) Oberteil, *das;* (undergarment, part of dirndl) Mieder, *das*

'**bodice-ripper** /'bɒdɪsrɪpə(r)/ *n.* (coll.) Verführungsschnulze, *die*

bodily /'bɒdɪlɪ/ **1** *adj.* körperlich; ∼ **harm** Körperverletzung, *die;* ∼ **needs** leibliche Bedürfnisse; ∼ **organs** Körperorgane. **2** *adv.* **he lifted her ∼:** er hob sie einfach hoch

body /'bɒdɪ/ *n.* (a) **▸ 672** (of person) Körper, *der;* Leib, *der* (geh.); (of animal) Körper, *der;* **enough to keep ∼ and soul together** genug, um am Leben zu bleiben; (b) (corpse) Leiche, *die;* Leichnam, *der* (geh.); **over my dead ∼!** nur über meine Leiche!; (c) (coll.: person) Mensch, *der;* (woman also) Person, *die;* (d) (group of persons) Gruppe, *die;* (having a particular function) Organ, *das;* **government ∼:** staatliche Einrichtung; (e) (mass) **a huge ∼ of water** große Wassermassen; (f) (main portion) Hauptteil, *der;* (g) (Motor Veh.) Karosserie, *die;* (Railw.) Aufbau, *der;* (h) (collection) Sammlung, *die;* **a ∼ of knowledge** ein Wissensschatz; **a ∼ of facts** Tatsachenmaterial, *das;* (i) (of wine) Körper, *der*

body: ∼ **bag** *n.* Leichensack, *der;* ∼-**building** *n.* Bodybuilding, *das;* ∼ **clock** ⇒ **biological clock;** ∼**guard** *n.* (single) Leibwächter, *der;* (group) Leibwache, *die;* ∼ **language** *n.* Körpersprache, *die;* ∼ **odour** *n.* Körpergeruch, *der;* ∼ **piercing** *n., no pl.* Piercing, *das;* ∼ **search** *n.* Leibesvisitation, *die;* ∼ **weight** *n.* Körpergewicht, *das;* ∼**work** *n., no pl.* (Motor Veh.) Karosserie, *die*

boffin /'bɒfɪn/ *n.* (Brit. coll.) Eierkopf, *der* (salopp)

bog /bɒg/ **1** *n.* (a) Moor, *das;* (marsh, swamp) Sumpf, *der;* (b) (Brit. sl.: lavatory) Lokus, *der* (salopp). **2** *v.t.*, **-gg-: be ∼ged down** festsitzen (fig.); nicht weiterkommen; **get ∼ged down in details** (fig.) sich in Details verzetteln

boggle /'bɒgl/ *v.i.* (be startled) sprachlos sein; **the mind ∼s [at the thought]** bei dem Gedanken wird einem schwindlig

boggy /'bɒgɪ/ *adj.* sumpfig; morastig

'**bog-standard** *adj.* stinknormal (salopp)

bogus /'bəʊgəs/ *adj.* falsch; gefälscht ⟨*Schmuck, Dokument*⟩; ∼ **firm** Schwindelfirma, *die*

Bohemia /bəʊ'hiːmɪə/ *pr. n.* Böhmen (*das*)

Bohemian /bəʊ'hiːmɪən/ **1** *adj.* (a) (socially unconventional) unkonventionell; unbürgerlich; **a ∼ person** ein Bohemien; (b) (Geog.) böhmisch. **2** *n.* (a) (socially unconventional person) Bohemien, *der;* (b) (native of Bohemia) Böhme, *der*/Böhmin, *die*

boil¹ /bɔɪl/ **1** *v.i.* (a) **▸ 1141** kochen; (Phys.) sieden; **the kettle's ∼ing** das Wasser [im Kessel] kocht; (b) (fig.) ⟨*Wasser, Wellen:*⟩ schäumen, brodeln; (c) (fig.: be angry) kochen; schäumen (**with** vor + *Dat.*); (d) (fig. coll.: be hot) **I'm ∼ing** mir ist heiß; **be ∼ing [hot]** sehr heiß sein. **2** *v.t.* kochen; ∼ **sth. dry** etw. verkochen; **it is necessary to ∼ the water** man muss das Wasser abkochen; ∼**ed potatoes** Salzkartoffeln; ∼ **the kettle** das Wasser heiß machen; ∼**ed sweet** (Brit.) hartes [Frucht]bonbon. **3** *n.* Kochen, *das;* **come to/go off the ∼:** zu kochen anfangen/

The body

German uses the definite article for parts of the body where English uses the possessive adjective, as long as it is clear whose body part it is (which usually means that it belongs to the person who is the subject of the sentence):

He raised his hand	= Er hob die Hand
She closed her eyes	= Sie schloss die Augen

But

She closed his eyes	= Sie schloss ihm die Augen
She passed her hand over my forehead	= Sie fuhr mir mit der Hand über die Stirn

From the last two examples it can be seen that where the owner of the part of the body is not the subject, i.e. not doing the action, German uses the dative of the personal pronoun plus the definite article. This also applies when the owner of the body part is responsible for the action (often an injury), but in this case the pronoun is reflexive (which only makes a difference in the third person):

I've broken my leg	= Ich habe mir das Bein gebrochen
He dislocated his arm	= Er hat sich (*Dat.*) den Arm ausgerenkt
You nearly dislocated his arm	= Du hast ihm fast den Arm ausgerenkt
She hit her head on the beam	= Sie hat sich den Kopf am Balken angestoßen *or* ist mit dem Kopf gegen den Balken gestoßen

Can you put some cream on my back (for me)?	= Kannst du mir den Rücken mit Creme einreiben?

Note the same construction with a noun:

She massaged her son's back	= Sie massierte ihrem Sohn den Rücken

Note also the following impersonal construction:

My head is spinning	= Mir dreht sich *or* schwirrt der Kopf
My feet were tingling	= Es kribbelte mir *or* mich in den Füßen

See also □ **Illnesses.**

Body features

There are many adjectives in German ending in **-ig** describing features corresponding to English adjectives ending in *-ed:*

blue-eyed	= blauäugig
dark-haired	= dunkelhaarig
long-legged	= langbeinig

These are usually used attributively, i.e. before the noun, not separately:

a long-legged blonde	= eine langbeinige Blondine

but

He is blue-eyed	= Er hat blaue Augen
She is dark-haired	= Sie hat dunkle Haare

See also □ **Colours, Height, Weight.**

---

aufhören; (fig.) sich zuspitzen/sich wieder beruhigen; **bring to the ~:** zum Kochen bringen

~ a'way *v.i.* **(a)** (continue ~ing) weiterkochen; **(b)** (evaporate completely) verkochen

~ 'down 1 *v.i.* einkochen; **~ down to sth.** (fig.) auf etw. (*Akk.*) hinauslaufen. **2** *v.t.* einkochen

~ 'over *v.i.* überkochen

~ 'up 1 *v.t.* kochen. **2** *v.i.* kochen; (fig.) sich zuspitzen

boil² *n.* (Med.) Furunkel, *der*

boiler /'bɔɪlə(r)/ *n.* **(a)** Kessel, *der;* **(b)** (hot-water tank) Boiler, *der*

boiler: ~ room *n.* Kesselraum, *der;* **~ suit** *n.* Overall, *der*

'boiling point *n.* ▶ 1141 Siedepunkt, *der;* **be at/reach ~** (fig.) auf dem Siedepunkt sein/den Siedepunkt erreichen

boisterous /'bɔɪstərəs/ *adj.* **(a)** (noisily cheerful) ausgelassen; **(b)** (rough) wild

boisterously /'bɔɪstərəslɪ/ *adv.* ⇒ **boisterous:** ausgelassen; wild

bold /bəʊld/ *adj.* **(a)** (courageous) mutig; (daring) kühn; **(b)** (forward) keck; kühn ‹*Worte*›; **make so ~ [as to …]** so kühn sein[, zu …]; **(c)** (striking) auffallend, kühn ‹*Farbe, Muster*›; kräftig ‹*Konturen*›; fett ‹*Schlagzeile*›; **bring out in ~ relief** deutlich hervortreten lassen; **(d)** (vigorous) kühn; ausdrucksvoll ‹*Stil, Beschreibung*›; **(e)** (Printing) fett; **in ~ [type]** im Fettdruck

boldly /'bəʊldlɪ/ *adv.* **(a)** (courageously) mutig; (daringly) kühn; **(b)** (forwardly) dreist; **(c)** mit kühnem Schwung ‹*malen*›; auffällig ‹*mustern*›

boldness /'bəʊldnɪs/ *n., no pl.* **(a)** (courage, daring) Kühnheit, *die;* **(b)** (forwardness) Dreistigkeit, *die;* **(c)** (strikingness) Kühnheit, *die;* (of description, style) Ausdruckskraft, *die*

Bolivia /bə'lɪvɪə/ *pr. n.* Bolivien (*das*)

Bolivian /bə'lɪvɪən/ ▶ 947 **1** *adj.* bolivianisch. **2** *n.* Bolivianer, *der*/Bolivianerin, *die*

bollard /'bɒlɑːd/ *n.* (Brit.) Poller, *der*

Bolshevik /'bɒlʃɪvɪk/ *n.* **(a)** (Hist.) Bolschewik, *der;* **(b)** (coll.: revolutionary) Bolschewist, *der*/Bolschewistin, *die* (ugs.)

bolshie, bolshy /'bɒlʃɪ/ *adj.* (coll.: uncooperative) aufsässig; rotzig (salopp)

bolster /'bəʊlstə(r)/ **1** *n.* (pillow) Nackenrolle, *die.* **2** *v.t.* (fig.) stärken; **~ sb. up** jmdm. Mut machen; **~ sth. up** etw. stärken

bolt /bəʊlt/ **1** *n.* **(a)** (on door or window) Riegel, *der;* (on gun) Kammerverschluss, *der;* **(b)** (metal pin) Schraube, *die;* (without thread) Bolzen, *der;* **(c)** (of crossbow) Bolzen, *der;* **(d)** **~ [of lightning]** Blitz[strahl], *der;* **[like] a ~ from the blue** (fig.) wie ein Blitz aus heiterem Himmel; **(e)** (sudden dash) **make a ~ for freedom** einen Fluchtversuch machen. **2** *v.i.* **(a)** davonlaufen; ‹*Pferd:*› durchgehen; **~ out of the shop** aus dem Laden rennen; **(b)** (Hort., Agric.) vorzeitig Samen bilden; ‹*Salat, Kohl:*› schießen. **3** *v.t.* **(a)** (fasten with ~) verriegeln; **~ sb. in/out** jmdn. einsperren/aussperren; **(b)** (fasten with ~s with/without thread) verschrauben/mit Bolzen verbinden; **~ sth. to sth.** etw. (*Akk.*) schrauben/mit Bolzen befestigen; **(c)** (gulp down) **~ [down]** hinunterschlingen ‹*Essen*›. **4** *adv.* **~ upright** kerzengerade

'bolt-hole *n.* (lit. or fig.) Schlupfloch, *das*

bomb /bɒm/ **1** *n.* **(a)** Bombe, *die;* **go like a ~** (fig. coll.) ein Bombenerfolg sein; **go down a ~ with** (fig. coll.) ein Bombenerfolg sein bei; **(b)** (coll.: large sum of money) **a ~:** 'ne Masse Geld (ugs.). **2** *v.t.* bombardieren

bombard /bɒm'bɑːd/ *v.t.* beschießen; (fig.) bombardieren

bombardment /bɒm'bɑːdmənt/ *n.* Beschuss, *der;* (fig.) Bombardierung, *die*

bombastic /bɒm'bæstɪk/ *adj.* bombastisch; schwülstig

bomb: ~ blast *n.* (blast wave) Druckwelle, *die;* (explosion) Bombenexplosion, *die;* **~ disposal** *n.* Räumung von Bomben

bomber /'bɒmə(r)/ *n.* **(a)** (Air Force) Bomber, *der* (ugs.); **(b)** (terrorist) Bombenattentäter, *der*/-attentäterin, *die;* Bombenleger, *der*/-legerin, *die* (ugs.)

'bomber jacket *n.* Bomberjacke, *die*

bombing /'bɒmɪŋ/ *n.* Bombardierung, *die*

bomb: ∼ **scare** n. Bombendrohung, die; ∼**shell** n. Bombe, die; (fig.) Sensation, die; **come as a** or **be something of a** ∼**shell** wie eine Bombe einschlagen; ∼**-site** n. Trümmergrundstück, das

bona fide /bəʊnə 'faɪdɪ/ adj. echt

bonanza /bə'nænzə/ n. **(a)** (unexpected success) Goldgrube, die (fig.); **(b)** (large output) reiche Ausbeute

bond /bɒnd/ **1** n. **(a)** Band, das; **(b)** in pl. (shackles, lit. or fig.) Fesseln; **(c)** (uniting force) Band, das; **(d)** (adhesion) Verbindung, die; **(e)** (Commerc.: debenture) Anleihe, die; Schuldverschreibung, die; **(f)** (agreement) Übereinkommen, das; **(g)** (Insurance) ≈ Vertrauensschadenversicherung, die. **2** v.t. **(a)** kleben (**to** an + Akk.); **(b)** (Commerc.) unter Zollverschluss nehmen

bondage /'bɒndɪdʒ/ n., no pl. (lit. or fig.) Sklaverei, die

bonded /'bɒndɪd/ adj. (Commerc.) unter Zollverschluss; ∼ **goods** Zollagergut, das; ∼ **warehouse** Zollager, das

bone /bəʊn/ **1** n. **(a)** ▶672⟩ Knochen, der; (of fish) Gräte, die; ∼s (fig.: remains) Gebeine Pl. (geh.); **be chilled to the** ∼ (fig.) völlig durchgefroren sein; **work one's fingers to the** ∼ (fig.) bis zum Umfallen arbeiten; **I feel it in my** ∼s (fig.) ich habe es im Gefühl; **the bare** ∼s (fig.) die wesentlichen Punkte; **close to the** or **near the** ∼ (fig.: indecent) gewagt; **(b)** (material) Knochen, der; **(c)** (stiffener) (in collar) Kragenstäbchen, das; (in corset) Korsettstange, die; **(d)** (subject of dispute) **find a** ∼ **to pick with sb.** mit jmdm. ein Hühnchen zu rupfen haben (ugs.); ∼ **of contention** Zankapfel, der; **make no** ∼s **about sth./doing sth.** keinen Hehl aus etw. machen/sich nicht scheuen, etw. zu tun. **2** v.t. den/die Knochen herauslösen aus, ausbeinen ⟨Fleisch, Geflügel⟩; entgräten ⟨Fisch⟩

bone: ∼ '**china** n. Knochenporzellan, das; ∼ '**dry** adj. knochentrocken (ugs.); ∼ '**idle,** ∼ '**lazy** adjs. stinkfaul (salopp); ∼ **marrow** n. (Anat.) Knochenmark, das; ∼**meal** n. Knochenmehl, das; ∼**shaker** n. Klapperkiste, die (salopp)

bonfire /'bɒnfaɪə(r)/ n. **(a)** (at celebration) Freudenfeuer, das; **B**∼ **Night** [Abend des] Guy Fawkes Day (mit Feuerwerk); **(b)** (for burning rubbish) Feuer, das

bonkers /'bɒŋkəz/ adj. (sl.) verrückt (salopp); wahnsinnig (ugs.)

bonnet /'bɒnɪt/ n. **(a)** (woman's) Haube, die; (child's) Häubchen, das; **(b)** (Brit. Motor Veh.) Motor- od. Kühlerhaube, die

bonny /'bɒnɪ/ adj. **(a)** (healthy-looking) prächtig ⟨Baby⟩; gesund ⟨Gesicht⟩; **(b)** (Scot. and N. Engl.: comely) hübsch

bonsai /'bɒnsaɪ/ n. **(a)** (tree) Bonsai[baum], der; **(b)** no pl., no art. (method) Bonsai, der

bonus /'bəʊnəs/ n. **(a)** zusätzliche Leistung; **(b)** (to shareholders, insurance-policy holder) Bonus, der; (to employee) **Christmas** ∼: Weihnachtsgratifikation, die

bony /'bəʊnɪ/ adj. **(a)** (of bone) beinern; knöchern; Knochen-; (like bone) knochenartig; **(b)** (big-boned) grobknochig; **(c)** (skinny) knochendürr (ugs.); spindeldürr; **(d)** (full of bones) grätig ⟨Fisch⟩; ⟨Fleisch⟩ mit viel Knochen

boo /buː/ **1** int. to surprise sb. huh; expr. disapproval, contempt buh; **he wouldn't say '**∼**' to a goose** er ist sehr schüchtern. **2** n. Buh, das (ugs.). **3** v.t. ausbuhen (ugs.); **he was** ∼**ed off the stage** er wurde so ausgebuht, dass er die Bühne verließ. **4** v.i. buhen (ugs.)

boob /buːb/ **1** n. **(a)** (Brit. coll.: mistake) Fehler, der; Schnitzer, der (ugs.); **(b)** (Brit. sl.: breast) Titte, die (derb). **2** (Brit. sl.) v.i. einen Schnitzer machen (ugs.)

booby /'buːbɪ/ n. ∼ **prize** n. Preis für den schlechtesten Teilnehmer an einem Wettbewerb; ∼ **trap** n. **(a)** Falle, mit der man jmdm. einen Streich spielen will; **(b)** (Mil.) versteckte Sprengladung; ∼**-trap** v.t. **(a)** [für einen Streich] präparieren; **(b)** (Mil.) **the door had been** ∼**-trapped** an der Tür war eine versteckte Sprengladung angebracht worden

book /bʊk/ **1** n. Buch, das; **be a closed** ∼ [**to sb.**] (fig.) [jmdm. od. für jmdn.] ein Buch mit sieben Siegeln sein; **throw the** ∼ **at sb.** (fig.) jmdn. kräftig zusammenstauchen (ugs.); **bring to** ∼ (fig.) zur Rechenschaft ziehen; **in my** ∼ (fig.) meiner Ansicht od. Meinung nach; **be in**

sb.'s good/bad ∼s (fig.) bei jmdm. gut/schlecht angeschrieben sein; **I can read you like a** ∼ (fig.) ich kann in dir lesen wie in einem Buch; **take a leaf out of sb.'s** ∼ (fig.) sich (Dat.) jmdn. zum Vorbild nehmen; **you could take a leaf out of his** ∼: du könntest dir von ihm eine Scheibe abschneiden (ugs.); **(b)** in pl. (records, accounts) Bücher; **do the** ∼s die Abrechnung machen; **balance the** ∼s die Bilanz machen od. ziehen; see also **keep 1** h; **(c)** in pl. (list of members) **be on the** ∼s auf der [Mitglieds]liste od. im Mitgliederverzeichnis stehen; **(d)** (record of bets) Wettbuch, das; **make** or **keep a** ∼ **on sth.** Wetten auf etw. (Akk.) annehmen; **(e)** ∼ **of tickets** Fahrscheinheft, das; ∼ **of stamps/matches** Briefmarkenheft/Streichholzbriefchen, das. **2** v.t. **(a)** buchen ⟨Reise, Flug, Platz [im Flugzeug]⟩; [vor]bestellen ⟨Eintrittskarte, Tisch, Zimmer, Platz [im Theater]⟩; anmelden ⟨Telefongespräch⟩; engagieren, verpflichten ⟨Künstler, Orchester⟩; **be fully** ∼**ed** ⟨Vorstellung⟩ ausverkauft sein; ⟨Flug[zeug]⟩ ausgebucht sein; ⟨Hotel:⟩ voll belegt od. ausgebucht sein; **(b)** (enter in ∼) eintragen; (for offence) aufschreiben (ugs.) **(for** wegen); **(c)** (issue ticket to) **we are** ∼**ed on a flight to Athens** man hat für uns einen Flug nach Athen gebucht. **3** v.i. buchen; (for travel, performance) vorbestellen

∼ '**in 1** v.i. sich eintragen; **we** ∼**ed in at the Ritz** wir sind im Ritz abgestiegen. **2** v.t. **(a)** (make reservation for) Zimmer/ein Zimmer vorbestellen od. reservieren für; **(b)** (register) eintragen

∼ '**up 1** v.i. buchen. **2** v.t. buchen; **the guest house is** ∼**ed up** die Pension ist ausgebucht od. voll belegt

book: ∼**case** n. Bücherschrank, der; ∼ **club** n. Buchklub, der; ∼**ends** n. pl. Buchstützen Pl.

bookie /'bʊkɪ/ n. (coll.) Buchmacher, der

booking /'bʊkɪŋ/ n. **(a)** Buchung, die; (of ticket) Bestellung, die; (of table, room, seat) Vorbestellung, die; **make/cancel a** ∼: buchen/eine Buchung rückgängig machen; (for tickets) bestellen/umbestellen; **change one's** ∼ umbuchen; (for tickets) umbestellen; **(b)** (of performer) Engagement, das

booking: ∼ **clerk** n. ▶887⟩ Schalterbeamte, der/ -beamtin, die; Fahrkartenverkäufer, der/-verkäuferin, die; ∼ **office** n. (in station) [Fahrkarten]schalter, der; (in theatre) [Theater]kasse, die; (selling tickets in advance) Vorverkaufsstelle, die

book: ∼ **jacket** n. Schutzumschlag, der; ∼**keeper** n. ▶887⟩ Buchhalter, der/-halterin, die; ∼**keeping** n. ▶887⟩ Buchführung, die; Buchhaltung, die

booklet /'bʊklɪt/ n. Broschüre, die

book: ∼**maker** n. ▶887⟩ (in betting) Buchmacher, der; ∼**mark,** ∼**marker** ns. Lese- od. Buchzeichen, das; ∼ **review** n. Buchbesprechung, die; ∼**seller** n. ▶887⟩ Buchhändler, der/-händlerin, die; ∼**shelf** n. Bücherbord, das; **on my** ∼**shelves** in meinen Bücherregalen; ∼**shop** n. Buchhandlung, die; ∼**stall** n. Bücherstand, der; ∼**store** (Amer.) ⇒ ∼**shop;** ∼ **token** n. Büchergutschein, der; ∼**worm** n. (lit. or fig.) Bücherwurm, der

boom[1] /buːm/ n. **(a)** (for camera or microphone) Ausleger, der; **(b)** (Naut.) Baum, der; **(c)** (floating barrier) [schwimmende] Absperrung

boom[2] **1** v.i. **(a)** dröhnen ⟨Kanone, Wellen, Brandung:⟩ dröhnen, donnern; **(b)** ⟨Geschäft, Verkauf, Stadt, Gebiet:⟩ sich sprunghaft entwickeln; ⟨Preise, Aktien:⟩ rapide steigen; **business is** ∼**ing** das Geschäft boomt od. erlebt einen Boom; die Geschäfte florieren. **2** n. **(a)** (of gun, waves) Dröhnen, das; Donnern, das; **(b)** (in business) [sprunghafter] Aufschwung, der; (in prices) [rapider] Anstieg; **a** ∼ **year** ein Boomjahr; **(c)** (period of economic expansion) Hochkonjunktur, die; Boom, der

∼ '**out 1** v.i. ⟨Stimme:⟩ donnern; ⟨Kanone:⟩ dröhnen, donnern. **2** v.t. brüllen ⟨Kommando, Befehl⟩

boomerang /'buːməræŋ/ **1** n. (lit. or fig.) Bumerang, der. **2** v.i. (fig.) sich als Bumerang erweisen

booming /'buːmɪŋ/ adj. **(a)** (deep, resonant) donnend ⟨Stimme⟩; schallend ⟨Lachen⟩; dröhnend ⟨Klang⟩ **(b)** (Econ.) boomend (ugs.) ⟨Wirtschaft, Konjunktur, Tourismus⟩

'**boom town** *n.* Stadt in sprunghaftem Aufschwung

boon /buːn/ *n.* (blessing) Segen, *der;* Wohltat, *die*

boor /bʊə(r)/ *n.* Rüpel, *der* (abwertend)

boorish /'bʊərɪʃ/ *adj.,* **boorishly** /'bʊərɪʃlɪ/ *adv.* flegelhaft (abwertend); rüpelhaft (abwertend)

boost /buːst/ **1** *v.t.* **(a)** steigern; ankurbeln ⟨*Wirtschaft*⟩; in die Höhe treiben ⟨*Preis, Wert, Aktienkurs*⟩; stärken, heben ⟨*Selbstvertrauen, Moral*⟩; **(b)** (Electr.) erhöhen ⟨*Spannung*⟩. **2** *n.* Auftrieb, *der;* (increase) Zunahme, *die;* **give sb./sth. a ~:** jmdn./einer Sache Auftrieb geben; **be given a ~:** Auftrieb erhalten

booster /'buːstə(r)/ *n.* (Med.) **~** [**shot** *or* **injection**] Auffrischimpfung, *die*

'**booster cushion**, '**booster seat** *ns.* Sitzerhöhung, *die*

boot /buːt/ **1** *n.* **(a)** Stiefel, *der;* **get the ~** (fig. coll.) rausgeschmissen werden (ugs.); **give sb. the ~** (fig. coll.) jmdn. rausschmeißen (ugs.); **the ~ is on the other foot** (fig.) es ist genau umgekehrt; **(b)** (Brit.: of car) Kofferraum, *der.* **2** *v.t.* **(a)** (coll.) treten; kicken (ugs.) ⟨*Ball*⟩; **~ sb. out** (fig. coll.) jmdn. rausschmeißen (ugs.); **(b)** (Computing) **~** [**up**] laden

bootable /'buːtəbl/ *adj.* (Computing) bootbar ⟨*System*⟩; **~ disk** Bootdiskette, *die*

booth /buːð/ *n.* **(a)** Bude, *die;* **(b)** (telephone ~) Telefonzelle, *die;* **(c)** (polling ~) Wahlkabine, *die*

'**bootleg** *adj.* geschmuggelt; (sold/made) schwarz (ugs.) *od.* illegal verkauft/gebrannt

booty /'buːtɪ/ *n., no pl.* Beute, *die*

booze /buːz/ (coll.) **1** *v.i.* saufen (derb). **2** *n., no pl.* (drink) Alkohol, *der*

'**booze-up** *n.* (coll.) Besäufnis, *das* (salopp); **have a ~:** sich voll laufen lassen (salopp)

bop /bɒp/ (coll.) **1** *v.i.* (zur Popmusik) tanzen. **2** *n.* Tanz, *der* (zur Popmusik); **have a ~:** tanzen

bordello /bɔː'deləʊ/ *n., pl.* **~s** (Amer.) Bordell, *das*

border /'bɔːdə(r)/ **1** *n.* **(a)** Rand, *der;* (of tablecloth, handkerchief, dress) Bordüre, *die;* **(b)** (of country) Grenze, *die;* **(c)** (flower bed) Rabatte, *die.* **2** *attrib. adj.* Grenz⟨*stadt, -gebiet, -streit*⟩. **3** *v.t.* **(a)** (adjoin) [an]grenzen an (+ *Akk.*); **be ~ed by** [an]grenzen an (+ *Akk.*); **(b)** (put a ~ to, act as ~ to) umranden; einfassen; **(c)** (resemble closely) grenzen an (+ *Akk.*). **4** *v.i.* **~ on** ⇒ **3 a, c**

'**borderline** *n.* Grenzlinie, *die;* (fig.) Grenze, *die.* **2** *adj.* **sb./sth. is ~** (fig.) jmd. ist/etw. liegt auf der Grenze; **a ~ case/candidate/type** (fig.) ein Grenzfall

bore¹ /bɔː(r)/ **1** *v.t.* (make hole in) bohren. **2** *v.i.* (drill) bohren (**for** nach). **3** *n.* **(a)** (of firearm, engine cylinder) Bohrung, *die;* (of tube, pipe) Innendurchmesser, *der;* **(b)** (calibre) Kaliber, *das*

bore² **1** *n.* **(a)** (nuisance) **it's a real ~:** es ist wirklich ärgerlich; **what a ~!** wie ärgerlich!; **(b)** (dull person) Langweiler, *der* (ugs. abwertend). **2** *v.t.* (weary) langweilen; **sb. is ~d with sth.** etw. langweilt jmdn.; **I'm ~d** ich langweile mich; ich habe Langeweile; **~ sb. to death** *or* **to tears** (coll.) jmdn. zu Tode langweilen

bore³ ⇒ **bear**²

boredom /'bɔːdəm/ *n., no pl.* Langeweile, *die*

'**borehole** *n.* Bohrloch, *das*

'**boring** /'bɔːrɪŋ/ *adj.* langweilig

born /bɔːn/ **1** *be ~:* geboren werden; **I was ~ in England** ich bin *od.* wurde in England geboren; **I wasn't ~ yesterday** (fig.) ich bin nicht von gestern (ugs.); **be ~ blind/lucky** blind (von Geburt sein/ein Glückskind sein; **be ~ a poet** zum Dichter geboren sein. **2** *adj.* **(a)** geboren; **~ again** (fig.) wieder geboren; **in all my ~ days** (fig. coll.) in meinem ganzen Leben; *see also* **breed 1 c; (b)** (destined to be) **be a ~ orator** der geborene Redner sein

borne ⇒ **bear**²

borough /'bʌrə/ *n.* **(a)** (Brit.: town sending members to Parliament) Stadt[bezirk] *mit Vertretung im Parlament;* **(b)** (Amer.) **the ~ of …** (town) die Stadt …; (village) die Gemeinde …; **(c)** (Amer.: district of New York or Alaska) Verwaltungsbezirk

borrow /'bɒrəʊ/ **1** *v.t.* **(a)** [sich (*Dat.*)] ausleihen; [sich (*Dat.*)] borgen; entleihen, ausleihen ⟨*Buch, Schallplatte usw. aus der Leihbücherei*⟩; [sich (*Dat.*)] leihen ⟨*Geld von*

der Bank⟩; [sich (*Dat.*)] leihen, [sich (*Dat.*)] borgen ⟨*Geld*⟩; **(b)** (fig.) übernehmen ⟨*Idee, Methode*⟩; entlehnen ⟨*Wort*⟩; **sb. is living on ~ed time** jmds. Uhr ist abgelaufen. **2** *v.i.* borgen; (from bank) Kredit aufnehmen (**from** bei)

borrower /'bɒrəʊə(r)/ *n.* (from bank) Kreditnehmer, *der;* (from library) Entleiher, *der*

borrowing /'bɒrəʊɪŋ/ *n.* (from bank) Kreditaufnahme, *die* (**from** bei); (from library) Entleihen, *das;* Ausleihen, *das;* (fig.) Übernahme, *die*

bos'n /'bəʊsn/ ⇒ **boatswain**

Bosnia /'bɒznɪə/ *n.* Bosnien (*das*)

Bosnia-Herzegovina /bɒznɪəhɜːtsəgə'viːnə/ *pr. n.* Bosnien-Herzegowina (*das*)

Bosnian /'bɒznɪən/ ▶ 947 | **1** *adj.* bosnisch; *sb.;* **sb. is ~:** jmd. ist Bosnier/Bosnierin. **2** *n.* Bosnier, *der*/Bosnierin, *die*

bosom /'bʊzm/ *n.* **(a)** (person's breast) Brust, *die;* Busen, *der* (bes. dichter.); **(b)** (fig.: enfolding relationship) Schoß, *der* (geh.); **in the ~ of one's family** im Schoße der Familie; *attrib.* **a ~ friend** ein guter Freund; ein Busenfreund

boss /bɒs/ (coll.) **1** *n.* Boss, *der* (ugs.); Chef, *der.* **2** *v.t.* **~ sb. [about** *or* **around]** jmdn. herumkommandieren (ugs.)

bossy /'bɒsɪ/ *adj.* (coll.) herrisch; **don't be so ~:** hör auf herumzukommandieren (ugs.)

bosun, bo'sun /'bəʊsn/ ⇒ **boatswain**

botanical /bə'tænɪkl/ *adj.* botanisch; **~ garden[s]** botanischer Garten

botanist /'bɒtənɪst/ *n.* ▶ 887 | Botaniker, *der*/Botanikerin, *die*

botany /'bɒtənɪ/ *n., no pl.* Botanik, *die;* Pflanzenkunde, *die*

botch /bɒtʃ/ *v.t.* **(a)** (bungle) pfuschen bei (ugs. abwertend) ⟨*Reparatur, Arbeit*⟩; **a ~ed job** eine gepfuschte Arbeit (ugs. abwertend); **(b)** (repair badly) [notdürftig] flicken

~ 'up *v.t.* **(a)** (bungle) verpfuschen (ugs. abwertend); **(b)** (repair badly) [notdürftig] flicken

both /bəʊθ/ **1** *adj.* beide; **we ~ like cooking** wir kochen beide gern; **~** [**the**] **brothers** beide Brüder; **~ our brothers** unsere beiden Brüder; **you can't have it ~ ways** beides [zugleich] geht nicht; *see also* **cut 2 a. 2** *pron.* beide; **~** [**of them**] **are dead** beide sind tot; **they are ~ dead** sie sind beide tot; **~ of you/them are …:** ihr seid/ sie sind beide …; **for them** ~: für sie beide; **go along to bed, ~ of you** ihr geht jetzt ins Bett, alle beide. **3** *adv.* **~ A and B** sowohl A als [auch] B; **~ you and I** wir beide

bother /'bɒðə(r)/ **1** *v.t.* **(a)** *in pass.* (take trouble) **I can't be ~ed** [**to do it**] ich habe keine Lust[, es zu machen]; **I can't be ~ed with details like that** ich kann mich nicht mit solchen Kleinigkeiten abgeben *od.* befassen; **(b)** (annoy) lästig sein *od.* fallen (+ *Dat.*); ⟨*Lärm, Licht:*⟩ stören; ⟨*Schmerz, Wunde, Zahn, Rücken:*⟩ zu schaffen machen (+ *Dat.*); **I'm sorry to ~ you, but …:** es tut mir Leid, dass ich Sie damit belästigen muss, aber …; **don't ~ me now** lass mich jetzt in Ruhe!; **(c)** (worry) Sorgen machen (+ *Dat.*); ⟨*Problem, Frage:*⟩ beschäftigen; **I'm not ~ed about him/the money** seinetwegen/wegen des Geldes mache ich mir keine Gedanken; **what's ~ing you/is something ~ing you?** was hast du denn/hast du etwas? **2** *v.i.* (trouble oneself) **don't ~ to do it** Sie brauchen es nicht zu tun; **you needn't have ~ed to come** Sie hätten wirklich nicht zu kommen brauchen; **you needn't/ shouldn't have ~ed** das wäre nicht nötig gewesen; **don't ~!** nicht nötig!; **~ with sth./sb.** sich mit etw./ jmdm. aufhalten; **~ about sth./sb.** sich (*Dat.*) über etw./ jmdn. Gedanken machen. **3** *n.* **(a)** (nuisance) **what a ~!** wie ärgerlich!; **it's a real/such a ~:** es ist wirklich lästig; **(b)** (trouble) Ärger, *der;* **it's no ~** [**for me**] es macht mir gar nichts aus; **the children were no ~ at all** ich hatte/ wir hatten mit den Kindern überhaupt keine Schwierigkeiten; **have a spot of ~ with sth.** Schwierigkeiten mit etw. haben; **go to the ~ of doing sth.** sich (*Dat.*) die Mühe machen, etw. zu tun. **4** *int.* (coll.) wie ärgerlich!

bottle /'bɒtl/ **1** *n.* **(a)** Flasche, *die;* **a beer ~:** eine Bierflasche; **a ~ of beer** eine Flasche Bier; **(b)** (fig. coll.: alcoholic drink) **be too fond of the ~:** dem Alkohol zu sehr zugetan sein; **be on the ~:** trinken; *see also* **hit 1 h. 2** *v.t.* **(a)** (put into ~s) in Flaschen [ab]füllen; **~d beer** Flaschenbier, *das;* **~d gas** Flaschengas, *das;* **(b)** (preserve in jars) einmachen ~ **'up** *v.t.* (conceal) in sich (*Dat.*) aufstauen

bottle: ~ **bank** *n.* Altglasbehälter, *der;* **~-fed** *adj.* mit der Flasche gefüttert; **~-green** *adj.* flaschengrün; **~neck** *n.* (fig.) Flaschenhals, *der* (ugs.); (in production process also) Engpass, *der;* ~ **opener** *n.* Flaschenöffner, *der;* ~ **party** *n.* Bottleparty, *die;* ~ **top** *n.* Flaschenverschluss, *der*

bottom /'bɒtəm/ **1** *n.* **(a)** (lowest part) unteres Ende; (of cup, glass, box, chest) Boden, *der;* (of valley, canyon, crevasse, well, shaft) Sohle, *die;* (of hill, slope, cliff, stairs) Fuß, *der;* **the ~ of the valley** die Talsohle; **[be] at the ~ of the page/list** unten auf der Seite/Liste [sein]; ~ **up** auf dem Kopf; verkehrt herum; **~s up!** (coll.) hoch die Tassen!; **the ~ fell** *or* **dropped out of her world/the market** (fig.) für sie brach eine Welt zusammen/der Markt brach zusammen; **(b)** ▸ **672┃** (buttocks) Hinterteil, *das* (ugs.); Po[dex], *der* (fam.); **(c)** (of chair) Sitz, *der;* Sitzfläche, *die;* **(d)** (of sea, lake) Grund, *der;* **go to the ~:** [ver]sinken; **touch ~:** Grund haben; (fig.) den Tiefpunkt erreichen; **(e)** (farthest point) **at the ~ of the garden/street** hinten im Garten/am Ende der Straße; **(f)** (underside) Unterseite, *die;* **(g)** (fig.) **start at the ~:** ganz unten anfangen; **be ~ of the class/league** der/die Letzte in der Klasse sein/Tabellenletzte[r] sein; **(h)** *usu. in pl.* **~[s]** (of track suit, pyjamas) Hose, *die;* **(i)** (fig.: basis, origin) **be at the ~ of sth.** hinter etw. (*Dat.*) stecken (ugs.); **get to the ~ of sth.** einer Sache (*Dat.*) auf den Grund kommen; **at ~:** im Grunde genommen; **(j)** (Naut.) Schiffsboden, *der;* **(k)** (Brit. Motor Veh.) **in ~:** im ersten Gang. **2** *adj.* **(a)** (lowest) unterst...; (lower) unter...; **(b)** (fig.: last) letzt...; **be ~:** der/ die/das Letzte sein

bottom 'drawer *n.* (fig.) Aussteuer, *die;* **put sth. [away] in one's ~ drawer** etw. für die Aussteuer beiseite legen

bottomless /'bɒtəmlɪs/ *adj.* bodenlos; unendlich tief ‹*Meer, Ozean*›; (fig.: inexhaustible) unerschöpflich

bottom 'line *n.* (fig. coll.) **the ~:** das Fazit

'botulism /'bɒtju:lɪzm/ *n.*, *no pl.*, *no art.* ▸ **865┃** (Med.) Botulismus, *der*

bough /baʊ/ *n.* Ast, *der*

bought ⇒ **buy 1**

boulder /'bəʊldə(r)/ *n.* Felsbrocken, *der*

bounce /baʊns/ **1** *v.i.* **(a)** (spring) springen; ~ **up and down on sth.** auf etw. (*Dat.*) herumspringen; **(b)** (coll.) ‹*Scheck:*› nicht gedeckt sein. **2** *v.t.* aufspringen lassen ‹*Ball*›; **he ~d the baby on his knee** er ließ das Kind auf den Knien reiten. **3** *n.* **(a)** (rebound) Aufprall, *der;* **on the ~:** beim Aufprall; **(b)** (rebounding power) ≈ Elastizität, *die;* (fig.: energy) Schwung, *der*

~ **'back** *v.i.* zurückprallen; (fig.) ‹*Person:*› [plötzlich] wieder da sein

~ **'off 1** *v.i.* abprallen. **2** *v.t.* ~ **sth. off sth.** etw. von etw. abprallen lassen; ~ **off sth.** von etw. abprallen

bouncer /'baʊnsə(r)/ *n.* (coll.) Rausschmeißer, *der* (ugs.)

bouncing /'baʊnsɪŋ/ *adj.* kräftig, stramm ‹*Baby*›

bouncy /'baʊnsɪ/ *adj.* **(a)** gut springend ‹*Ball*›; federnd ‹*Matratze, Bett*›; **(b)** (fig.: lively) munter

bound¹ /baʊnd/ **1** *n.* **(a)** *usu. in pl.* (limit) Grenze, *die;* **within the ~s of possibility** *or* **the possible** im Bereich des Möglichen; **go beyond the ~s of decency** die Grenzen des Anstands verletzen; **sth. is out of ~s [to sb.]** der Zutritt zu etw. ist [für jmdn.] verboten; **keep within the ~s of reason/propriety** vernünftig/im Rahmen bleiben; **(b)** (of territory) Grenze, *die.* **2** *v.t.*, *usu. in pass.* begrenzen

bound² **1** *v.i.* (spring) hüpfen; springen; ~ **into the room** ins Zimmer stürzen; **the dog came ~ing up** der Hund kam angesprungen. **2** *n.* (spring) Satz, *der;* **at** *or* **with one ~:** mit einem Satz

bound³ *pred. adj.* ▸ **715┃** **be ~ for home/Frankfurt** auf dem Heimweg/nach Frankfurt unterwegs sein; **homeward ~:** auf dem Weg nach Hause; **where are you ~ for?** wohin geht die Reise?; **all passengers ~ for Zurich** alle Passagiere nach Zürich

bound⁴ ⇒ **bind 1, 2**

boundary /'baʊndərɪ/ *n.* Grenze, *die*

boundless /'baʊndlɪs/ *adj.* grenzenlos

bountiful /'baʊntɪfl/ *adj.* (generous) großzügig; gütig ‹*Gott*›; (plentiful) reichlich ‹*Ernte, Gaben, Ertrag*›

bounty /'baʊntɪ/ *n.* (reward) Kopfgeld, *das;* (for capturing animal) Fangprämie, *die*

bouquet /bʊ'keɪ, bəʊ'keɪ, 'bu:keɪ/ *n.* **(a)** (bunch of flowers) Bukett, *das;* [Blumen]strauß, *der;* **(b)** (perfume of wine) Bukett, *das;* Blume, *die*

bourbon /'bɜ:bən, 'bʊəbən/ (Amer.) ~ **[whiskey]** Bourbon, *der*

bourgeois /'bʊəʒwɑ:/ **1** *n.*, *pl. same* **(a)** (middle-class person) Bürger, *der*/Bürgerin, *die;* **(b)** (person with conventional ideas, selfish materialist) Spießbürger, *der* (abwertend); Spießer, *der*/Spießerin, *die* (abwertend). **2** *adj.* **(a)** (middle-class) bürgerlich; **(b)** (conventional, selfishly materialist) spießbürgerlich (abwertend)

bourgeoisie /bʊəʒwɑ:'zi:/ *n.* **(a)** Bürgertum, *das;* **(b)** (capitalist class) Bourgeoisie, *die* (marx.)

bout /baʊt/ *n.* **(a)** (spell) Periode, *die;* **(b)** (contest) Wettkampf, *der;* **(c)** (fit) Anfall, *der;* **he's out on one of his drinking ~s again** er ist mal wieder auf einer seiner Zechtouren (ugs.)

boutique /bu:'ti:k/ *n.* Boutique, *die*

bow¹ /bəʊ/ **(a)** (curve, weapon, Mus.) Bogen, *der;* **have two strings to one's ~:** eine Alternative haben; **(b)** (tied knot or ribbon) Schleife, *die*

bow² /baʊ/ **1** *v.i.* **(a)** (submit) sich beugen (**to** *Dat.*); **(b)** ~ **[down to** *or* **before sb./sth.]** (bend) sich [vor jmdm./etw.] verbeugen *od.* verneigen; **(c)** (incline head) ~ **[to sb.]** sich [vor jmdm.] verbeugen. **2** *v.t.* (cause to bend) beugen; ~**ed down by** *or* **with care/responsibilities/age** (fig.) von Sorgen/Verpflichtungen niedergedrückt/vom Alter gebeugt. **3** *n.* Verbeugung, *die*

bow³ /baʊ/ *n.* (Naut.) *usu. in pl.* Bug, *der;* **in the ~s** im Bug; **on the ~:** am Bug

bowel /'baʊəl/ *n.* **(a)** ▸ **672┃** (Anat.) ~**s** *pl.*, (Med.) ~**:** Darm, *der;* **(b)** *in pl.* (interior) Innere, *das*

bowl¹ /bəʊl/ *n.* **(a)** (basin) Schüssel, *die;* (shallower) Schale, *die;* **mixing/washing-up ~:** Rühr-/Abwaschschüssel, *die;* **soup ~:** Suppentasse, *die;* **sugar ~:** Zuckerdose, *die;* **a ~ of water** eine Schüssel/Schale Wasser; **a ~ of soup** eine Tasse Suppe; **(b)** (of WC) Schüssel, *die;* (of spoon) Schöpfteil, *der;* (of pipe) [Pfeifen]kopf, *der*

bowl² **1** *n.* **(a)** (ball) Kugel, *die;* (in skittles) [Kegel]kugel, *die;* (in ten-pin bowling) [Bowling]kugel, *die;* **(b)** *in pl.* (game) Bowlsspiel, *das;* Bowls, *das.* **2** *v.i.* **(a)** (play ~s) Bowls spielen; (play skittles) kegeln; (play ten-pin bowling) bowlen; **(b)** (Cricket) werfen. **3** *v.t.* **(a)** (roll) rollen lassen; ~ **sb. over** (fig.) jmdn. überwältigen *od.* (ugs.) umhauen; **(b)** (Cricket etc.) werfen; ~ **the batsman [out]/side out** den Schlagmann/die Mannschaft ausschlagen

bow /bəʊ/**:** ~**-'legged** *adj.* krummbeinig; O-beinig (ugs.); **be ~-legged** krumme Beine *od.* (ugs.) O-Beine haben; ~**-'legs** *n. pl.* krumme Beine; O-Beine *Pl.* (ugs.)

bowler¹ /'bəʊlə(r)/ *n.* (Cricket) Werfer, *der*

bowler² *n.* ~ **[hat]** Bowler, *der*

bowling /'bəʊlɪŋ/ *n.* **[ten-pin] ~:** Bowling, *das;* **go ~:** bowlen gehen

bowling: ~ **alley** *n.* (for ten-pin ~) Bowlingbahn, *die;* (for skittles) Kegelbahn, *die;* ~ **green** *n.* Rasenfläche für Bowls

bow /bəʊ/**:** ~ **tie** *n.* Fliege, *die;* [Smoking-/Frack]schleife, *die;* ~ **window** *n.* Erkerfenster, *das*

box¹ /bɒks/ *n.* **(a)** (container) Kasten, *der;* (bigger) Kiste, *die;* (made of cardboard, thin wood, etc.) Schachtel, *die;* **a ~ of cigars** eine Schachtel Zigarren; **pencil ~:** Federkasten, *der;* **jewellery ~:** Schmuckkasten, *der;* **cardboard ~:** [Papp]karton, *der;* (smaller) [Papp]schachtel, *die;* **shoe~:** Schuhkarton, *der;* ~ **of matches** Streichholzschachtel, *die;* **(b)** ~ (coll.: television) der Kasten (ugs. abwertend); die Flimmerkiste (scherzh.); **(c)** (in theatre etc.) Loge, *die*

~ **'in** *v.t.* **(a)** (enclose in ~) in einem Gehäuse unterbringen; **(b)** (enclose tightly) einklemmen; **feel ~ed in** sich eingeengt fühlen

box² 1 *n.* (slap, punch) Schlag, *der;* **he gave him a ~ on the ear[s]** er gab ihm eine Ohrfeige. **2** *v.t.* **(a)** (slap, punch) schlagen; **he ~ed his ears** *or* **him round the ears** er ohrfeigte ihn; **get one's ears ~ed** eine Ohrfeige bekommen; **(b)** (fight with fists) **~ sb.** gegen jmdn. boxen. **3** *v.i.* boxen (**with, against** gegen)

box: ~ camera *n.* Box, *die;* **~car** *n.* (Amer. Railw.) gedeckter [Güter]wagen

boxer /'bɒksə(r)/ *n.* **(a)** ▶ 887 | Boxer, *der;* **(b)** (dog) Boxer, *der*

'boxer shorts *n. pl.* Boxershorts *Pl.*

boxing /'bɒksɪŋ/ *n.* Boxen, *das;* **professional/amateur ~:** Berufs-/Amateurboxen, *das*

boxing: B~ Day *n.* (Brit.) zweiter Weihnachtsfeiertag; **~ glove** *n.* Boxhandschuh, *der;* **~ match** *n.* Boxkampf, *der;* **~ ring** *n.* Boxring, *der*

box: ~ number *n.* (at newspaper office) Chiffre, *die;* (at post office) Postfach, *das;* **~ office** *n.* Kasse, *die;* **~room** *n.* (Brit.) Abstellraum, *der*

boy /bɔɪ/ **1** *n.* **(a)** Junge, *der;* **baby ~:** kleiner Junge; **~s' school** Jungenschule, *die;* **a ~'s name** ein Jungenname; **[my] ~** (as address) [mein] Junge; **~s will be ~s** so sind Jungs/Männer nun mal; **jobs for the ~s** Vetternwirtschaft, *die* (abwertend); **(b)** (servant) Boy, *der.* **2** *int.* **[oh] ~!** Junge, Junge! (ugs.)

boycott /'bɔɪkɒt/ **1** *v.t.* boykottieren. **2** *n.* Boykott, *der*

'boyfriend *n.* Freund, *der*

boyish /'bɔɪɪʃ/ *adj.* jungenhaft

bozo /'bəʊzəʊ/ *n.* (esp. Amer. sl.) Trottel, *der* (ugs. abwertend)

BR *abbr.* **British Rail[ways]** *britische Eisenbahngesellschaft*

bra /brɑː/ *n.* BH, *der* (ugs.)

brace /breɪs/ **1** *n.* **(a)** (buckle) Schnalle, *die;* (connecting piece) Klammer, *die;* (Dent.) [Zahn]spange, *die;* [Zahn]klammer, *die;* **(b)** *in pl.* (trouser straps) Hosenträger; **(c)** *pl. same* (pair) **a/two ~ of** zwei/vier; **(d)** (Printing, Mus.) geschweifte Klammer; Akkolade, *die;* **(e)** (strut) Strebe, *die.* **2** *v.t.* **(a)** (fasten) befestigen; (stretch) spannen; (string up) anspannen; (with struts) stützen; **(b)** (support) stützen. **3** *v. refl.* **~ oneself [up]** (fig.) sich zusammennehmen; **~ oneself [up] for sth.** (fig.) sich auf etw. (*Akk.*) [innerlich] vorbereiten

brace and 'bit *n.* Bohrwinde, *die*

bracelet /'breɪslɪt/ *n.* (band) Armband, *das;* (chain) Kettchen, *das;* (bangle) Armreif, *der*

bracing /'breɪsɪŋ/ *adj.* belebend

bracken /'brækn/ *n.* [Adler]farn, *der*

bracket /'brækɪt/ **1** *n.* **(a)** (support, projection) Konsole, *die;* (lamp support) Lampenhalter, *der;* **(b)** (mark) Klammer, *die;* **open/close ~s** Klammer auf/zu; **(c)** (group) Gruppe, *die.* **2** *v.t.* **(a)** (enclose in ~s) einklammern; **(b)** (couple with brace) mit einer Klammer verbinden; (fig.) in Verbindung bringen

brackish /'brækɪʃ/ *adj.* brackig

brag /bræg/ **1** *v.i.,* **-gg-** prahlen (**about** mit). **2** *v.t.,* **-gg-** prahlen; **he ~s that he has a Rolls Royce** er prahlt damit, dass er einen Rolls-Royce hat

braggart /'brægət/ *n.* Prahler, *der*/Prahlerin, *die*

braid /breɪd/ **1** *n.* **(a)** (plait) Flechte, *die* (geh.); Zopf, *der;* (band entwined with hair) Haarband, *das;* **(b)** (decorative woven band) Borte, *die;* **(c)** (on uniform) Litze, *die;* (with metal threads) Tresse, die. **2** *v.t.* **(a)** (plait; arrange in ~s) flechten; **(b)** zusammenbinden ‹*Haare*›; **(c)** (trim with ~) mit Borten/Litzen/Tressen besetzen

Braille /breɪl/ *n.* Blindenschrift, *die*

brain /breɪn/ **1** *n.* **(a)** Gehirn, *das;* **have [got] sex/ money on the ~:** nur Sex/Geld im Kopf haben; **use your ~[s]** gebrauch deinen Verstand; **he's got a good ~:** er ist ein kluger Kopf; **(b)** *in pl.* (Gastr.) Hirn, *das;* **(c)** (coll.: clever person) **she's the ~[s] of the class** sie ist die Intelligenteste in der Klasse. **2** *v.t.* **I'll ~ you!** (coll.) du kriegst gleich eins auf die Rübe! (ugs.)

brain: ~child *n.* (coll.) Geistesprodukt, *das;* **~-dead** *adj.* **(a)** (Med.) hirntot; **(b)** (coll. derog.) hirnlos (abwertend) ‹*Person*›; hirnverbrannt (abwertend), hirnrissig (abwertend)

⟨Ansicht, Idee⟩; ~ drain *n.* (coll.) Abwanderung [von Wissenschaftlern]; Braindrain, *der*

brainless /'breɪnlɪs/ *adj.* (stupid) hirnlos

brain: ~storm *n.* **(a)** Anfall geistiger Umnachtung; **(b)** (Amer. coll.) ⇒ **~wave; ~ surgeon** *n.* ▶ 887 | Gehirnchirurg, *der;* **~-teaser** *n.* Denk[sport]aufgabe, *die;* **~ tumour** *n.* Gehirntumor, *der;* **~wash** *v.t.* einer Gehirnwäsche unterziehen; **~wash sb. into doing sth.** jmdm. [ständig] einreden, etw. zu tun; **~washing** *n.* Gehirnwäsche, *die;* **~wave** *n.* (coll.: inspiration) genialer Einfall

brainy /'breɪnɪ/ *adj.* intelligent

braise /breɪz/ *v.t.* (Cookery) schmoren

brake /breɪk/ **1** *n.* (apparatus; coll.: pedal etc.) Bremse, *die;* **sth. acts as a ~ on sth.** etw. bremst etw.; **put on** *or* **apply the ~s** die Bremse betätigen; (fig.) zurückstecken; **put the ~[s] on sth.** (fig.) etw. bremsen. **2** *v.t. & i.* bremsen; **~ hard** scharf bremsen

brake: ~ block *n.* Bremsklotz, *der;* **~ drum** *n.* Bremstrommel, *die;* **~ fluid** *n.* Bremsflüssigkeit, *die;* **~ light** *n.* Bremslicht, *das;* **~ lining** *n.* Bremsbelag, *der;* **~ pad** *n.* Bremsbelag, *der;* **~ shoe** *n.* Bremsbacke, *die*

braking /'breɪkɪŋ/ *n.* Bremsen, *das;* **~ distance** Bremsweg, *der*

bramble /'bræmbl/ *n.* **(a)** (shrub) Dornenstrauch, *der;* (blackberry bush) Brombeerstrauch, *der;* **(b)** (fruit) Brombeere, *die*

bran /bræn/ *n.* Kleie, *die*

branch /brɑːnʃ/ **1** *n.* **(a)** (bough) Ast, *der;* (twig) Zweig, *der;* **(b)** (of nerve, artery, antlers) Ast, *der;* (of river) [Neben]arm, *der;* (local establishment) Zweigstelle, *die;* (shop) Filiale, *die.* **2** *v.i.* **(a)** sich verzweigen; **(b)** (diverge) **~ into sth.** (*Akk.*) aufspalten

~ 'off *v.i.* abzweigen; (fig.) sich abspalten
~ 'out *v.i.* **(a)** **~ ~ 2 a;** **(b)** (~ off) abzweigen; **(c)** (fig.) **~ out into sth.** sich auch mit etw. befassen

branch: ~ line *n.* (Railw.) Nebenstrecke, *die;* **~ manager** *n.* ▶ 887 | Filialleiter, *der*/-leiterin, *die;* **~ office** *n.* Zweigstelle, *die*

brand /brænd/ **1** *n.* **(a)** (trade mark) Markenzeichen, *das;* (goods of particular make) Marke, *die;* (fig.: type) Art, *die;* **~ of washing powder/soap** Waschpulvermarke, *die*/Seifenmarke, *die;* **(b)** (permanent mark, stigma) Brandmal, *das;* (on sheep, cattle) Brandzeichen, *das.* **2** *v.t.* **(a)** mit einem Brandzeichen markieren ‹*Tier*›; **(b)** (stigmatize [as]) **~ [as]** brandmarken als ‹*Verräter, Verbrecher usw.*›; **(c)** (Brit.: label with trade mark) mit einem Markenzeichen versehen; **~ed goods** Markenware, *die*

brand: ~ awareness *n.* Markenbewusstsein, *das;* **~ image** *n.* Markenimage, *das*

brandish /'brændɪʃ/ *v.t.* schwenken; schwingen ‹*Waffe*›

brand: ~ leader *n.* (product) marktführendes Produkt; (company) Marktführer, *der;* (brand) führende Marke; **~ name** *n.* Markenname, *der;* **~-'new** *adj.* nagelneu (ugs.)

brandy /'brændɪ/ *n.* Weinbrand, *der*

brash /bræʃ/ *adj.* (self-assertive) dreist; (garish) auffällig ‹*Kleidung*›

brass /brɑːs/ **1** *n.* **(a)** Messing, *das;* **do sth. as bold as ~:** die Unverfrorenheit haben, etw. zu tun; **(b)** (inscribed tablet) Grabplatte aus Messing; **(c)** [horse-]~es Messinggeschirr, *das;* **(d)** **the ~** (Mus.) das Blech (fachspr.); die Blechbläser; **(e)** ⇒ **brassware; (f)** *no pl., no indef. art.* (Brit. coll.: money) Kies, *der* (salopp); **(g)** [top] ~ (coll.: officers, leaders of industry etc.) hohe Tiere (ugs.). **2** *attrib. adj.* Messing-; **~ player** (Mus.) Blechbläser, *der*

brass 'band *n.* Blaskapelle, *die*

brassière /'bræzjə(r)/ *n.* (formal) Büstenhalter, *der*

brass: ~ 'plate *n.* Messingschild, *das;* **~ rubbing** *n.* **(a)** *no pl., no indef. art.* Frottage, *die* (von *Messingtafeln*); **(b)** (impression) Frottage, *die* (einer *Messingtafel*); **~ 'tacks** *n. pl.* **get** *or* **come down to ~ tacks** (coll.) zur Sache kommen; **~ware** *n., no pl.* Messingteile (utensils, candlesticks, etc.) Messinggerät, *das*

brat /bræt/ *n.* (derog.: child) Balg, *das od. der* (ugs., meist abwertend); (young rascal) Flegel, *der*

bravado /brəˈvɑːdəʊ/ *n., pl.* ~es *or* ~s Mut, *der;* **do sth. out of** ~: so waghalsig sein, etw. zu tun; (as pretence) den starken Mann markieren wollen und etw. tun (ugs.)

brave /breɪv/ **1** *adj.* mutig; (able to endure sth.) tapfer; **be** ~! nur Mut/sei tapfer! **2** *n.* [indianischer] Krieger. **3** *v.t.* trotzen (+ *Dat.*); mutig gegenübertreten (+ *Dat.*) ⟨*Kritiker, Interviewer*⟩; ~ **it out** sich durch nichts einschüchtern lassen

bravely /ˈbreɪvlɪ/ *adv.* mutig; (showing endurance) tapfer

bravery /ˈbreɪvərɪ/ *n., no pl.* Mut, *der;* (endurance) Tapferkeit, *die*

bravo /brɑːˈvəʊ/ *int.* bravo

brawl /brɔːl/ **1** *v.i.* sich schlagen. **2** *n.* Schlägerei, *die*

brawn /brɔːn/ *n.* (a) (muscle) Muskel, *der;* (muscularity) Muskeln; (b) (Gastr.) ≈ Presskopf, *der*

brawny /ˈbrɔːnɪ/ *adj.* muskulös

bray /breɪ/ **1** *n.* (of ass) Iah, *das.* **2** *v.i.* ⟨*Esel:*⟩ iahen, schreien

brazen /ˈbreɪzn/ **1** *adj.* dreist; (shameless) schamlos. **2** *v.t.* ~ **it out** (deny guilt) es abstreiten; (not admit guilt) es nicht zugeben

brazier /ˈbreɪzɪə(r), ˈbreɪʒə(r)/ *n.* Kohlenbecken, *das*

Brazil /brəˈzɪl/ *n.* (a) *pr. n.* Brasilien (*das*); (b) ⇒ **Brazil nut**

Brazilian /brəˈzɪlɪən/ ▶ 947 **1** *adj.* brasilianisch; **sb. is** ~: jmd. ist Brasilianer/Brasilianerin. **2** *n.* Brasilianer, *der*/Brasilianerin, *die*

Braˈzil nut *n.* Paranuss, *die*

breach /briːtʃ/ **1** *n.* (a) (violation) Verstoß, *der* (**of** gegen); ~ **of the peace** Störung von Ruhe und Ordnung; (by noise only) ruhestörender Lärm; ~ **of contract** Vertragsbruch, *der;* ~ **of promise** Wortbruch, *der;* (b) (of relations) Bruch, *der;* (c) (gap) Bresche, *die;* (fig.) Riß, *der;* **step into the** ~ (fig.) in die Bresche treten *od.* springen. **2** *v.t.* eine Bresche schlagen in (+ *Akk.*); **the wall/dike was** ~**ed** in die Mauer wurde eine Bresche geschlagen/der Deich wurde durchbrochen

bread /bred/ **1** *n.* (a) Brot, *das;* **a piece of** ~ **and butter** ein Butterbrot; **[some]** ~ **and butter** [ein paar] Butterbrote; ~ **and butter** (fig.) tägliches Brot; ~ **and water** (lit. or fig.) Wasser und Brot; **know which side one's** ~ **is buttered** wissen, wo etwas zu holen ist; (b) (sl.: money) Kies, *der* (salopp). **2** *v.t.* panieren

bread: ~ **bin** *n.* Brotkasten, *der;* ~**board** *n.* Brotbrett, *das;* ~**crumb** *n.* Brotkrume, *die;* ~**crumbs** (for coating e.g. fish) Paniermehl, *das;* ~ **knife** *n.* Brotmesser, *das;* ~**line** *n.* **live on/below the** ~**line** (fig.) gerade noch/nicht einmal mehr das Notwendigste zum Leben haben

breadth /bredθ/ *n.* (a) (broadness) Breite, *die;* (b) (extent) Weite, *die;* **with his** ~ **of experience/knowledge** bei seiner großen Erfahrung/bei seiner umfassenden Kenntnis

ˈbreadwinner *n.* Ernährer, *der*/Ernährerin, *die*

break /breɪk/ **1** *v.t.,* **broke** /brəʊk/, **broken** /ˈbrəʊkn/ (a) brechen; (so as to damage) zerbrechen; kaputtmachen (ugs.); aufschlagen ⟨*Ei zum Kochen*⟩; zerreißen ⟨*Seil*⟩; (fig.: interrupt) unterbrechen; brechen ⟨*Bann, Zauber, Schweigen*⟩; ~ **sth. in two/in pieces** etw. in zwei Teile/in Stücke brechen; **the TV/my watch is broken** der Fernseher/meine Uhr ist kaputt (ugs.); (b) ▶ 865 (fracture) sich (*Dat.*) brechen; (pierce) verletzen ⟨*Haut*⟩; **he broke his leg** er hat sich (*Dat.*) das Bein gebrochen; ~ **one's/sb.'s back** (fig.) sich/jmdn. kaputtmachen (ugs.); ~ **the back of sth.** (fig.) bei etw. das Schwerste hinter sich bringen; ~ **open** aufbrechen; (c) (violate) brechen ⟨*Vertrag, Versprechen*⟩; verletzen, verstoßen gegen ⟨*Regel, Tradition*⟩; nicht einhalten ⟨*Verabredung*⟩; überschreiten ⟨*Grenze*⟩; ~ **the law** gegen das Gesetz verstoßen; (d) (destroy) zerstören, ruinieren ⟨*Freundschaft, Ehe*⟩; (e) (surpass) brechen ⟨*Rekord*⟩; (f) (abscond from) ~ **jail** [aus dem Gefängnis] ausbrechen; (g) (weaken) brechen, beugen ⟨*Stolz*⟩; zusammenbrechen lassen ⟨*Streik*⟩; ~ **sb.'s heart** jmdm. das Herz brechen; ~ **sb.** (crush) jmdn. fertig machen (ugs.); ~ **the habit** es sich (*Dat.*) abgewöhnen; *see also* **make 1 o**; (h) (cushion) auffangen ⟨*Schlag, jmds. Fall*⟩; (i) (make bankrupt)

ruinieren; ~ **the bank** die Bank sprengen; **it won't** ~ **the bank** (fig. coll.) es kostet kein Vermögen; (j) (reveal) ~ **the news that** ...: melden, dass ...; (k) (solve) entschlüsseln, entziffern ⟨*Kode, Geheimschrift*⟩; (l) (Tennis) ~ **service/sb.'s service** den Aufschlag des Gegners/jmds. Aufschlag durchbrechen. *See also* **broken 2**. **2** *v.i.,* **broke, broken** (a) kaputtgehen (ugs.); entzweigehen; ⟨*Faden, Seil:*⟩ [zer]reißen; ⟨*Glas, Tasse, Teller:*⟩ zerbrechen; ⟨*Eis:*⟩ brechen; **sb.'s heart is** ~**ing** jmdm. bricht das Herz; ~ **in two/in pieces** entzweibrechen; (b) (crack) ⟨*Fenster-, Glasscheibe:*⟩ zerspringen; **my back was nearly** ~**ing** ich brach mir fast das Kreuz; (c) (sever links) ~ **with sb./sth.** mit jmdm./etw. brechen; (d) ~ **into** entbrechen in (+ *Akk.*) ⟨*Haus*⟩; aufbrechen ⟨*Safe*⟩; **he broke into a sweat** ihm brach der Schweiß aus; ~ **into a trot/run** *etc.* zu traben/laufen *usw.* anfangen; ~ **into a banknote** eine Banknote anbrechen; ~ **out of prison** *etc.* aus dem Gefängnis *usw.* ausbrechen; (e) ~ **free** *or* **loose [from sb./sb.'s grip]** sich [von jmdm./aus jmds. Griff] losreißen; ~ **free/loose [from prison]** [aus dem Gefängnis] ausbrechen; (f) ⟨*Welle:*⟩ sich brechen (**on/against** an + *Dat.*); (g) ⟨*Wetter:*⟩ umschlagen; (h) ⟨*Wolkendecke:*⟩ aufreißen; (i) ⟨*Tag:*⟩ anbrechen; (j) ⟨*Sturm:*⟩ losbrechen; (k) **sb.'s voice is** ~**ing** jmd. kommt in den Stimmbruch; (with emotion) jmdm. bricht die Stimme; (l) (have interval) ~ **for coffee/lunch** [eine] Kaffee-/Mittagspause machen; (m) (become public) bekannt werden. **3** *n.* (a) Bruch, *der;* (of rope) Reißen, *das;* ~ **[of service]** (Tennis) Break, *der od. das;* **a** ~ **with sb./sth.** ein Bruch mit jmdm./etw.; ~ **of day** Tagesanbruch, *der;* (b) (gap) Lücke, *die;* (Electr.: in circuit) Unterbrechung, *die;* (c) (sudden dash) **they made a sudden** ~ **[for it]** sie stürmten plötzlich davon; (d) (interruption) Unterbrechung, *die;* (e) (pause, holiday) Pause, *die;* **during the commercial** ~**s on TV** während der Werbespots im Fernsehen; **take** *or* **have a** ~: [eine] Pause machen; (f) (coll.: fair chance, piece of luck) Chance, *die;* **lucky** ~: große Chance; **that was a bad** ~ **for him** das war Pech für ihn

~ **aˈway 1** *v.t.* ~ **sth. away [from sth.]** etw. [von etw.] losbrechen *od.* abbrechen. **2** *v.i.* (a) ~ **away [from sth.]** [von etw.] losbrechen *od.* abbrechen; (separate itself/oneself) sich [von etw.] lösen; (escape) [aus etw.] entkommen; (b) (Footb.) sich freilaufen

~ **ˈdown 1** *v.i.* (a) (fail) zusammenbrechen ⟨*Verhandlungen*⟩ scheitern; (b) (cease to function) ⟨*Auto:*⟩ eine Panne haben; ⟨*Telefonnetz:*⟩ zusammenbrechen; **the machine has broken down** die Maschine funktioniert nicht mehr; (c) (be overcome by emotion) zusammenbrechen; (d) (Chem.) aufspalten. **2** *v.t.* (a) (demolish) aufbrechen ⟨*Tür*⟩; (b) (suppress) brechen ⟨*Widerstand*⟩; niederreißen ⟨*Barriere, Schranke*⟩; (c) (analyse) aufgliedern

~ **ˈin 1** *v.i.* einbrechen. **2** *v.t.* (a) (accustom to habit) eingewöhnen; (tame) zureiten ⟨*Pferd*⟩; (b) einlaufen ⟨*Schuhe*⟩

~ **into** ⇒ ~ **2 d**

~ **ˈoff 1** *v.t.* abbrechen; auflösen ⟨*Verlobung*⟩; ~ **it off [with sb.]** sich von jmdm. trennen. **2** *v.i.* (a) abbrechen; (b) (cease) aufhören

~ **ˈout** *v.i.* (escape, appear) ausbrechen; ~ **out in spots/a rash** *etc.* Pickel/einen Ausschlag *usw.* bekommen; **he broke out in a cold sweat** ihm brach der kalte Schweiß aus

~ **out of** ⇒ ~ **2 d**

~ **ˈthrough** *v.t. & i.* durchbrechen

~ **ˈup 1** *v.t.* (a) (~ into pieces) zerkleinern; ausschlachten ⟨*Auto*⟩; abwracken ⟨*Schiff*⟩; aufbrechen ⟨*Erde*⟩; (b) (disband) auflösen; auseinander reißen ⟨*Familie*⟩; zerstreuen ⟨*Menge*⟩; ~ **it up!** (coll.) auseinander!; (c) (end) zerstören ⟨*Freundschaft, Ehe*⟩. **2** *v.i.* (a) (~ into pieces, lit. or fig.) zerbrechen; ⟨*Erde, Straßenoberfläche:*⟩ aufbrechen; ⟨*Eis:*⟩ brechen; (b) (disband) sich auflösen ⟨*Schule:*⟩ schließen; ⟨*Schüler, Lehrer:*⟩ in die Ferien gehen; (c) (cease) abgebrochen werden; (end relationship) ~ **up [with sb.]** sich [von jmdm.] trennen

breakable /ˈbreɪkəbl/ **1** *adj.* zerbrechlich. **2** *n. in pl.* zerbrechliche Dinge

breakage /ˈbreɪkɪdʒ/ *n.* (a) (breaking) Zerbrechen, *das;* (b) (result of breaking) Bruchschaden, *der;* ~**s must be paid for** zerbrochene Ware muss bezahlt werden

break: ~**away 1** *n.* Ausbrechen, *das;* **2** *adj.* (Brit.) abtrünnig; ~**away group** Splittergruppe, *die;* ~**-dancing** *n.* Breakdancetanzen, *das;* ~**down** *n.* (a) (fig.: collapse) **a** ~**down in the system** (fig.) ein Zusammenbruch des Systems; (b) (mechanical failure) Panne, *die;* (in machine) Störung, *die; attrib.* ~**down service** Pannendienst, *der;* ~**down truck/van** Abschleppwagen, *der;* (c) (health or mental failure) Zusammenbruch, *der;* (d) (analysis) Aufschlüsselung, *die;* (e) (Chem.) Aufspaltung, *die*

breaker /'breɪkə(r)/ *n.* (wave) Brecher, *der*

break 'even *v.i.* die Kosten decken; **break-even point** Rentabilitätsschwelle, *die*

breakfast /'brekfəst/ **1** *n.* Frühstück, *das;* **for** ~: zum Frühstück; **eat** *or* **have [one's]** ~: frühstücken. **2** *v.i.* frühstücken

breakfast: ~ **cereal** *n.* ≈ Frühstücksflocken *Pl.;* ~ '**television** *n.* Frühstücksfernsehen, *das;* ~ **time** *n.* Frühstückszeit, *die*

'**break-in** *n.* Einbruch, *der;* **there has been a** ~ **at the bank** in der *od.* die Bank ist eingebrochen worden

'**breaking point** *n.* Belastungsgrenze, *die;* **be at** ~ (mentally) die Grenze der Belastbarkeit erreicht haben

break: ~**neck** *adj.* halsbrecherisch; ~**out** *n.* Ausbruch, *der;* ~**through** *n.* Durchbruch, *der;* ~**-up** *n.* (a) (disbanding, dispersal) Auflösung, *die;* (b) (of relationship) Bruch, *der;* ~**water** *n.* Wellenbrecher, *der*

breast /brest/ *n.* (lit. or fig.) Brust, *die;* **make a clean** ~ **[of sth.]** (fig.) [etw.] offen bekennen

breast: ~**bone** *n.* Brustbein, *das;* ~ **cancer** *n.* Brustkrebs, *der;* ~**feed** *v.t. & i.* stillen; ~**feeding** *n.* das Stillen; ~**stroke** *n.* (Swimming) Brustschwimmen, *das*

breath /breθ/ *n.* (a) Atem, *der;* **have bad** ~: Mundgeruch haben; **say sth. below** *or* **under one's** ~: etw. vor sich (*Akk.*) hin murmeln; **a** ~ **of fresh air** ein wenig frische Luft; **waste one's** ~: seine Worte verschwenden; **she caught her** ~: ihr stockte der Atem; **hold one's** ~: den Atem anhalten; **get one's** ~ **back** wieder zu Atem kommen; **be out of/short of** ~: außer Atem *od.* atemlos sein/kurzatmig sein; **take sb.'s** ~ **away** (fig.) jmdm. den Atem verschlagen; (b) (one respiration) Atemzug, *der;* **take** *or* **draw a [deep]** ~: [tief] einatmen; **in the same** ~: im selben Atemzug; (c) (air movement, whiff) Hauch, *der;* **there wasn't a** ~ **of air** es regte sich kein Lüftchen

breathalyser, (P) (*Amer.:* **breathalyzer**) /'breθəlaɪzə(r)/ *n.* Alcotest-Röhrchen ⓦⓩ, *das;* ~ **test** Alcotest ⓦⓩ, *der*

breathe /briːð/ **1** *v.i.* (lit. or fig.) atmen; ~ **in** einatmen; ~ **out** ausatmen; ~ **into sth.** [sanft] in etw. (*Akk.*) [hinein]blasen. **2** *v.t.* (a) ~ **one's last** seinen letzten Atemzug tun; ~ **[in/out]** ein-/ausatmen; (b) (utter) hauchen; **don't** ~ **a word about** *or* **of this to anyone** sag kein Sterbenswörtchen darüber zu irgendjemandem

breather /'briːðə(r)/ *n.* (brief pause) Verschnaufpause, *die*

breathing /'briːðɪŋ/ *n.* Atmen, *das*

breathing: ~ **apparatus** *n.* (a) (Med.) Beatmungsgerät, *das;* (b) (of fireman etc.) Atemschutzgerät, *das;* ~ **space** *n.* (time to breathe) Zeit zum Luftholen; (pause) Atempause, *die*

breathless /'breθlɪs/ *adj.* atemlos (**with** vor + *Dat.*); **leave sb.** ~ (lit. or fig.) jmdm. den Atem nehmen

breathlessness /'breθlɪsnɪs/ *n., no pl.* Atemlosigkeit, *die;* (caused by smoking or illness) Kurzatmigkeit, *die*

breath: ~**taking** *adj.* atemberaubend; ~ **test** *n.* Alcotest ⓦⓩ, *der*

bred ⇒ **breed 1, 2**

breech /briːtʃ/ *n.* [Geschütz]verschluss, *der*

breeches /'brɪtʃɪz/ *n. pl.* (short trousers) **[pair of]** ~: [Knie]bundhose, *die;* **[riding]** ~: Reithose, *die*

breed /briːd/ **1** *v.t.,* **bred** /bred/ (a) (be the cause of) erzeugen; hervorrufen; (b) (raise) züchten ‹*Tiere, Pflanzen*›; (c) (bring up) erziehen; **he was born and bred in London** er ist in London geboren und aufgewachsen. **2** *v.i.,* **bred** sich vermehren; ‹*Vogel:*› brüten; ‹*Tier:*› Junge haben; **they** ~ **like flies** *or* **rabbits** sie vermehren sich wie die Kaninchen. **3** *n.* Art, *die;* (of animals) Rasse, *die;* ~**s of cattle**

Rinderrassen; **the Jersey** ~ **[of cattle]** das Jerseyrind; **what** ~ **of dog is that?** zu welcher Rasse gehört dieser Hund?

breeder /'briːdə(r)/ *n.* ▶ 887 | Züchter, *der;* **be a** ~ **of sth.** etw. züchten; **dog-/horse-**~: Hunde-/Pferdezüchter, *der*

breeding /'briːdɪŋ/ *n.* Erziehung, *die;* **[good]** ~: gute Erziehung; **have** ~: eine gute Erziehung genossen haben

breeze /briːz/ **1** *n.* (gentle wind) Brise, *die;* **there is a** ~: es weht eine Brise. **2** *v.i.* (coll.) ~ **along** dahinrollen; (on foot) dahinschlendern; ~ **in** hereingeschneit kommen (ugs.)

breezy /'briːzɪ/ *adj.* (a) (windy) windig; (b) (coll.: brisk and carefree) [frisch und] unbekümmert

brevity /'brevɪtɪ/ *n.* Kürze, *die*

brew /bruː/ **1** *v.t.* (a) brauen ‹*Bier*›; keltern ‹*Apfelwein*›; ~ **[up]** kochen ‹*Kaffee, Tee, Kakao usw.*›; ~ **up** *abs.* Tee kochen; (b) (fig.: put together) ~ **[up]** [zusammen]brauen (ugs.); ausbrüten ‹*Plan usw.*›. **2** *v.i.* (a) ‹*Bier, Apfelwein:*› gären; ‹*Kaffee, Tee:*› ziehen; (b) (fig.: gather) ‹*Unwetter:*› sich zusammenbrauen; ‹*Rebellion, Krieg:*› drohen. **3** *n.* Gebräu, *das* (abwertend); ‹~**ed** beer/tea› Bier, *das*/Tee, *der*

brewer /'bruːə(r)/ *n.* (a) ▶ 887 | (person) Brauer, *der;* (b) (firm) Brauerei, *die*

brewery /'bruːərɪ/ *n.* Brauerei, *die*

briar ⇒ **brier**

bribe /braɪb/ **1** *n.* Bestechung, *die;* **a** ~ **[of £100]** ein Bestechungsgeld [in Höhe von 100 Pfund]; **take a** ~/~**s** sich bestechen lassen; **he won't accept** ~**s** er ist unbestechlich; **offer sb. a** ~: jmdn. bestechen wollen. **2** *v.t.* bestechen; ~ **sb. to do/into doing sth.** jmdn. bestechen, damit er etw. tut

bribery /'braɪbərɪ/ *n.* Bestechung, *die*

bric-à-brac /'brɪkəbræk/ *n.* Antiquarisches, (smaller things) Nippsachen *Pl.*

brick /brɪk/ **1** *n.* (a) (block) Ziegelstein, *der;* Backstein, *der;* (clay) Lehmziegel, *der;* **be** *or* **come down on sb. like a ton of** ~**s** (coll.) jmdn. unheimlich fertig machen *od.* zusammenstauchen (ugs.); (b) (toy) Bauklötzchen, *das.* **2** *adj.* Ziegelstein-; Backstein-. **3** *v.t.* ~ **up/in** zu-/einmauern

brick: ~**layer** *n.* ▶ 887 | Maurer, *der;* ~**laying** *n.* ▶ 887 | Mauern, *das;* ~**-red** *adj.* ziegelrot; ~**'wall** *n.* Backsteinmauer, *die;* **bang one's head against a** ~ **wall** (fig.) mit dem Kopf gegen die Wand rennen (fig.)

bridal /'braɪdl/ *adj.* (of bride) Braut-; (of wedding) Hochzeits-; ~ **couple/suite** Brautpaar, *das*/Hochzeitssuite, *die*

bride /braɪd/ *n.* Braut, *die*

'**bridegroom** *n.* Bräutigam, *der*

bridesmaid /'braɪdzmeɪd/ *n.* Brautjungfer, *die*

bridge[1] /brɪdʒ/ **1** *n.* (a) (lit. or fig.) Brücke, *die;* **cross that** ~ **when you come to it** (fig.) alles zu seiner Zeit; (b) (Naut.) [Kommando]brücke, *die;* (c) (of nose) Nasenbein, *das;* Sattel, *der;* (d) (of violin, spectacles) Steg, *der;* (e) (Dent.) [Zahn]brücke, *die.* **2** *v.t.* eine Brücke bauen *od.* errichten *od.* schlagen über (+ *Akk.*)

bridge[2] *n.* (Cards) Bridge, *das*

'**bridging loan** *n.* (Commerc.) Überbrückungskredit, *der*

bridle /'braɪdl/ **1** *n.* Zaumzeug, *das;* Zaum, *der.* **2** *v.t.* aufzäumen ‹*Pferd*›; (b) (fig.: restrain) zügeln ‹*Zunge*›; **im Zaum halten** ‹*Leidenschaft*›

bridle: ~ **path,** ~ **road** *ns.* Saumpfad, *der;* (for horses) Reitweg, *der*

brief[1] /briːf/ *adj.* (a) (of short duration) kurz; gering, geringfügig ‹*Verspätung*›; (b) (concise) knapp; **in** ~, **to be** ~: kurz gesagt; **make** *or* **keep it** ~: es kurz machen; **be** ~: sich kurz fassen

brief[2] **1** *n.* (a) (Law: summary of facts) Schriftsatz, *der;* (b) (Brit. Law: piece of work) Mandat, *das;* (c) (instructions) Instruktionen *Pl.;* Anweisungen *Pl.* **2** *v.t.* (a) (Brit. Law) mit der Vertretung eines Falles betrauen; (b) (Mil.: instruct) Anweisungen *od.* Instruktionen geben (+ *Dat.*); (c) (inform, instruct) unterrichten; informieren

'**briefcase** *n.* Aktentasche, *die*

briefing /'briːfɪŋ/ *n.* (a) Briefing, *das;* (of reporters or press) Unterrichtung, *die;* (before raid etc.) Einsatzbesprechung, *die;*

(b) (instructions) Instruktionen *Pl.;* Anweisungen *Pl.;* (information) Informationen *Pl.*

briefly /'briːflɪ/ *adv.* **(a)** (for a short time) kurz; **(b)** (concisely) knapp; kurz; **[to put it]** ~, ...: kurz gesagt ...

briefs /briːfs/ *n. pl.* **[pair of]** ~: Slip, *der*

brier /braɪə(r)/ *n.* (Bot.: rose) Wilde Rose

brig /brɪg/ *n.* (Naut.) Brigg, *die*

brigade /brɪ'geɪd/ *n.* (Mil.) Brigade, *die;* **the old** ~ (fig.) die alte Garde

brigadier [general] /brɪgə'dɪə(r) ('dʒenrl)/ *n.* **▶ 1152** (Mil.) Brigadegeneral, *der*

bright /braɪt/ **1** *adj.* **(a)** hell ‹Licht, Stern, Fleck›; grell ‹Scheinwerfer[licht], Sonnenlicht›; strahlend ‹Sonnenschein, Stern, Augen›; glänzend ‹Metall, Augen›; leuchtend, lebhaft ‹Farbe, Blume›; ~ **blue** *etc.* leuchtend blau *usw.;* **a** ~ **day** ein heiterer Tag; ~ **intervals/periods** Aufheiterungen; **the** ~ **lights of the city** (fig.) der Glanz der Großstadt; **look on the** ~ **side** (fig.) die Sache positiv sehen; **(b)** (cheerful) fröhlich, heiter ‹Person, Charakter, Stimmung›; strahlend ‹Lächeln›; freundlich ‹Zimmer, Farbe›; **(c)** (clever) intelligent; **he is a** ~ **boy** er ist ein heller *od.* aufgeweckter Junge; **(d)** (hopeful) viel versprechend ‹Zukunft›; glänzend ‹Aussichten›. **2** *adv.* **(a)** hell; **(b)** ~ **and early** in aller Frühe

brighten /'braɪtn/ **1** *v.t.* ~ **[up] (a)** aufhellen ‹Farbe›; **(b)** (make more cheerful) aufhellen, aufheitern ‹Zimmer›. **2** *v.i.* ~ **[up] (a)** ‹Himmel:› sich aufhellen; **the weather** *or* **it is** ~**ing [up]** es klärt sich auf; **(b)** (become more cheerful) ‹Person:› vergnügter werden; ‹Gesicht:› sich aufhellen; ‹Aussichten:› sich verbessern

brightly /'braɪtlɪ/ *adv.* **(a)** hell ‹scheinen, glänzen›; glänzend ‹poliert›; **(b)** (cheerfully) gut gelaunt

brightness /'braɪtnɪs/ *n., no pl.* ⇒ **bright 1: (a)** Helligkeit, *die;* Grelle, *die;* Grellheit, *die;* Strahlen, *das;* Glanz, *der;* Leuchtkraft, *die;* **(b)** Fröhlichkeit, *die;* Heiterkeit, *die;* **(c)** Intelligenz, *die*

brill /brɪl/ *adj.* (Brit. coll.) super (ugs.)

brilliance /'brɪljəns/ *n., no pl.* ⇒ **brilliant: (a)** Helligkeit, *die;* Funkeln, *das;* Leuchten, *das;* **(b)** Genialität, *die;* **(c)** Glanz, *der*

brilliant /'brɪljənt/ *adj.* **(a)** (bright) hell ‹Licht›; strahlend ‹Sonne›; funkelnd ‹Diamant, Stern›; leuchtend ‹Farbe›; **(b)** (highly talented) genial ‹Person, Erfindung, Gedanke, Schachzug, Leistung›; glänzend ‹Verstand, Aufführung, Vorstellung, Idee›; bestechend ‹Theorie, Argument›; **(c)** (illustrious) glänzend ‹Karriere, Erfolg, Sieg›; **a** ~ **achievement** eine Glanzleistung

brilliantly /'brɪljəntlɪ/ *adv.* **(a)** hell ‹scheinen, funkeln, schimmern›; **(b)** (with great talent) brillant; **(c)** (illustriously) glänzend ‹erfolgreich sein, triumphieren›

brim /brɪm/ **1** *n.* **(a)** (of cup, bowl, hollow) Rand, *der;* **full to the** ~: randvoll; **(b)** (of hat) [Hut]krempe, *die.* **2** *v.i.* **-mm-:** **be** ~**ming with sth.** randvoll mit etw. sein; (fig.) strotzen vor etw. (*Dat.*)

~ **'over** *v.i.* übervoll sein

brim-'full *pred. adj.* randvoll (**with** mit); **be** ~ **of energy/curiosity** (fig.) vor Energie (*Dat.*) sprühen/vor Neugierde (*Dat.*) platzen

brindled /'brɪndld/ *adj.* gestreift ‹Katze›; gestromt ‹Kuh, Hund›

brine /braɪn/ *n.* Salzwasser, *das;* (for preserving) [Salz]lake, *die*

bring /brɪŋ/ *v.t.,* **brought** /brɔːt/ **(a)** bringen; (as a present or favour) mitbringen; ~ **sth. with one** etw. mitbringen; **I haven't brought my towel** ich habe mein Handtuch nicht mitgebracht *od.* dabei; ~ **sth. [up]on oneself/sb.** sich selbst/jmdm. etw. einbrocken; **(b)** (result in) [mit sich] bringen; ~ **tears to sb.'s eyes** jmdm. Tränen in die Augen treiben; **(c)** (persuade) ~ **sb. to do sth.** jmdn. dazu bringen *od.* bewegen, etw. zu tun; **I could not** ~ **myself to do it** ich konnte es nicht über mich bringen, es zu tun; **(d)** (initiate, put forward) ~ **a charge/legal action against sb.** gegen jmdn. [An]klage erheben/einen Prozess anstrengen; ~ **a complaint** eine Beschwerde vorbringen; **(e)** (be sold for, earn) [ein]bringen ‹Geldsumme›

~ **a'bout** *v.t.* verursachen; herbeiführen; ~ **it about that** ...: es zustande bringen, dass ...

~ **a'long** *v.t.* **(a)** mitbringen; **(b)** ⇒ ~ **on b**

~ **'back** *v.t.* **(a)** (return) zurückbringen; (from a journey) mitbringen; **(b)** (recall) in Erinnerung bringen *od.* rufen; ~ **sth. back to sb.** ‹Musik, Foto usw.:› jmdn. an etw. (*Akk.*) erinnern; ~ **back memories** Erinnerungen wachrufen *od.* wecken; **(c)** (restore, reintroduce) wieder einführen ‹Sitten, Todesstrafe›; ~ **sb. back to life** jmdn. wieder beleben

~ **'down** *v.t.* **(a)** herunterbringen; **(b)** (shoot down out of the air) abschießen; herunterholen (ugs.); **(c)** (land) herunterbringen ‹Flugzeug, Drachen›; **(d)** (kill, wound) zur Strecke bringen ‹Gegner, Tier›; erlegen ‹Tier›; **(e)** (reduce) senken ‹Preise, Inflationsrate, Fieber›; **(f)** (cause to fall) zu Fall bringen ‹Gegner, Fußballer›; (fig.) stürzen, zu Fall bringen ‹Regierung›; *see also* **house 1 e**

~ **'forward** *v.t.* **(a)** nach vorne bringen; **(b)** (draw attention to) vorlegen ‹Beweise›; vorbringen ‹Argument›; zur Sprache bringen ‹Fall, Angelegenheit, Frage›; **(c)** (move to earlier time) vorverlegen ‹Termin› (**to** auf + *Akk.*); **(d)** (Bookk.) übertragen

~ **'in** *v.t.* **(a)** hereinbringen; auftragen ‹Essen›; einbringen ‹Ernte›; **(b)** (yield) einbringen ‹Verdienst, Summe›; **(c)** (Law) ~ **in a verdict of guilty/not guilty** einen Schuldspruch fällen/auf Freispruch erkennen; **(d)** (call in) hinzuziehen, einschalten ‹Experten›

~ **'off** *v.t.* **(a)** (rescue) retten; in Sicherheit bringen; **(b)** (conduct successfully) zustande bringen

~ **'on** *v.t.* **(a)** (cause) verursachen; **brought on by** ... ‹Krankheit› infolge von ...; **(b)** (advance progress of) wachsen *od.* sprießen lassen ‹Blumen, Getreide›; weiterbringen, fördern ‹Schüler, Sportler›; **(c)** (Sport) einsetzen

~ **'out** *v.t.* **(a)** herausbringen; **(b)** (show clearly) hervorheben, betonen ‹Unterschied›; verdeutlichen ‹Bedeutung›; herausbringen ‹Farbe›; **(c)** (cause to appear) herausbringen ‹Pflanzen, Blüte›; **the crisis brought out the best in him** die Krise brachte seine besten Seiten zum Vorschein *od.* ans Licht; **(d)** (begin to sell) einführen ‹Produkt›; herausbringen ‹Buch, Zeitschrift›

~ **'round** *v.t.* **(a)** mitbringen ‹Bekannte, Freunde usw.›; vorbeibringen ‹Gegenstände›; **(b)** (restore to consciousness) wieder zu sich bringen ‹Ohnmächtigen›; **(c)** (win over) überreden; herumkriegen (ugs.); ~ **sb. round to one's way of thinking** jmdn. von seiner Meinung überzeugen; **(d)** ~ **a conversation round to sth.** ein Gespräch auf etw. (*Akk.*) lenken

~ **'to** *v.t.* (restore to consciousness) wieder zu sich bringen

~ **'up** *v.t.* **(a)** heraufbringen; **(b)** (educate) erziehen; **(c)** (rear) aufziehen; großziehen; **(d)** (call attention to) zur Sprache bringen ‹Angelegenheit, Thema, Problem›; **(e)** (vomit) erbrechen

bring-and-'buy [sale] *n.* [Wohltätigkeits]basar, *der*

brink /brɪŋk/ *n.* (lit. or fig.) Rand, *der;* **be on the** ~ **of doing sth.** nahe daran sein, etw. zu tun; **be on the** ~ **of ruin/success** am Rand des Ruins sein *od.* stehen/dem Erfolg greifbar nahe sein

brinkmanship /'brɪŋkmənʃɪp/ *n., no pl.* gefährlicher Poker; **be playing a game of** ~: sich auf einen gefährlichen Poker eingelassen haben

brisk /brɪsk/ *adj.* flott ‹Gang, Bedienung›; forsch ‹Person, Art›; frisch ‹Wind›; (fig.) rege ‹Handel, Nachfrage›; lebhaft ‹Geschäft›

briskly /'brɪsklɪ/ *adv.* flott; **the wind blew** ~: es wehte ein frischer Wind; **sell** ~: sich gut verkaufen

bristle /'brɪsl/ **1** *n.* **(a)** Borste, *die;* **be made of** ~: aus Borsten bestehen; **(b)** ~**s** (of beard) [Bart]stoppeln. **2** *v.i.* **(a)** ~ **[up]** ‹Haare:› sich sträuben; **(b)** ~ **with** (fig.: have many) strotzen vor (+ *Dat.*); **(c)** ~ **[up]** (fig.: become angry) ‹Person:› ungehalten reagieren

bristly /'brɪslɪ/ *adj.* borstig; stopp[e]lig ‹Kinn›

Brit /brɪt/ *n.* (coll.) Brite, *der*/Britin, *die;* Engländer, *der*/ Engländerin, *die* (ugs.)

Britain /'brɪtn/ *pr. n.* Großbritannien (*das*)

British /'brɪtɪʃ/ **▶ 947** **1** *adj.* britisch; **he/she is** ~: er ist Brite/sie ist Britin; **sth. is** ~: etw. ist aus Großbritannien. **2** *n. pl.* **the** ~: die Briten

Britisher /ˈbrɪtɪʃə(r)/ *n.* Brite, *der*/Britin, *die*

British 'Isles *pr. n. pl.* Britische Inseln

Briton /ˈbrɪtn/ *n.* Brite, *der*/Britin, *die*

Britpop /ˈbrɪtpɒp/ *n.*, *no pl.*, *no art.* Britpop, *der*

Brittany /ˈbrɪtənɪ/ *pr. n.* Bretagne, *die*

brittle /ˈbrɪtl/ *adj.* spröde; zerbrechlich ⟨Glas⟩; schwach ⟨Knochen⟩; brüchig ⟨Gestein⟩

broach /brəʊtʃ/ *v.t.* **(a)** anzapfen; anstechen ⟨Fass⟩; **(b)** (fig.) anschneiden ⟨Thema⟩

broad /brɔːd/ *adj.* **(a)** ▶ 904 ⎮ breit; (extensive) weit ⟨Ebene, Meer, Land, Felder⟩; ausgedehnt ⟨Fläche⟩; **grow ~er** breiter werden; sich verbreitern; **make sth. ~er** etw. verbreitern; **it's as ~ as it is long** (fig.) es ist gehupft wie gesprungen (ugs.); **(b)** (explicit) deutlich, klar ⟨Hinweis⟩; **a ~ hint** ein Wink mit dem Zaunpfahl (scherzh.); **(c)** (clear, main) grob; wesentlich ⟨Fakten⟩; **in ~ outline** in groben *od.* großen Zügen; *see also* **daylight a**; **(d)** (generalized) allgemein; **in the ~est sense** im weitesten Sinne; **as a ~ indication** als Faustregel; **(e)** (strongly regional) stark ⟨Akzent⟩; breit ⟨Aussprache⟩

broad 'bean *n.* Saubohne, *die;* dicke Bohne

broadcast /ˈbrɔːdkɑːst/ **1** *n.* (Radio, Telev.) Sendung, *die;* (live) Übertragung, *die.* **2** *v.t.*, **broadcast (a)** (Radio, Telev.) senden; übertragen ⟨Livesendung, Sportveranstaltung⟩; **(b)** (spread) verbreiten ⟨Gerücht, Nachricht⟩. **3** *v.i.*, **broadcast** ⟨Rundfunk-, Fernsehstation:⟩ senden; ⟨Redakteur usw.:⟩ [im Rundfunk/Fernsehen] sprechen. **4** *adj.* (Radio, Telev.) im Rundfunk/Fernsehen gesendet; Rundfunk-/Fernseh-

broadcaster /ˈbrɔːdkɑːstə(r)/ *n.* ▶ 887 ⎮ (Radio, Telev.) *jmd., der durch häufige Auftritte im Rundfunk und Fernsehen, besonders als Interviewpartner, Diskussionsteilnehmer od. Kommentator, bekannt ist*

broadcasting /ˈbrɔːdkɑːstɪŋ/ *n.*, *no pl.* (Radio, Telev.) Senden, *das;* (live) Übertragen, *das;* **work in ~:** beim Funk arbeiten

broaden /ˈbrɔːdn/ **1** *v.t.* **(a)** verbreitern; **(b)** (fig.) ausweiten ⟨Diskussion⟩; **~ one's mind** seinen Horizont erweitern. **2** *v.i.* breiter werden; sich verbreitern; (fig.) sich erweitern

broadly /ˈbrɔːdlɪ/ *adv.* **(a)** deutlich ⟨hinweisen⟩; breit ⟨grinsen, lächeln⟩; **(b)** (in general) allgemein ⟨beschreiben⟩; **~ speaking** allgemein gesprochen

broad: ~-'minded *adj.* tolerant; **~sheet** *n.* Flugblatt, *das;* **~-'shouldered** *adj.* breitschultrig; **~side** *n.* **~side on [to sth.]** mit der Breitseite [nach etw.]; **fire [off] a ~side** (lit. or fig.) eine Breitseite abfeuern

brocade /brəˈkeɪd/ *n.* Brokat, *der*

broccoli /ˈbrɒkəlɪ/ *n.* Brokkoli, *der*

brochure /ˈbrəʊʃə(r)/ *n.* Broschüre, *die;* Prospekt, *der*

brogue¹ /brəʊg/ *n.* (shoe) Budapester, *der*

brogue² *n.* (accent) irischer Akzent

broil /brɔɪl/ *v.t.* braten; (on gridiron) grillen

broiler /ˈbrɔɪlə(r)/ *n.* **(a)** (chicken) Brathähnchen, *das;* [Gold]broiler, *der* (regional); **(b)** (utensil) Grill, *der;* Bratrost, *der*

broke /brəʊk/ **1** ⇒ **break 1, 2. 2** *pred. adj.* (coll.) pleite (ugs.); **go ~:** pleite gehen; **go for ~** (coll.) alles riskieren

broken /ˈbrəʊkn/ **1** ⇒ **break 1, 2. 2** *adj.* **(a)** zerbrochen; gebrochen ⟨Bein, Hals usw.⟩; verletzt ⟨Haut⟩; abgebrochen ⟨Zahn⟩; gerissen ⟨Seil⟩; kaputt (ugs.) ⟨Uhr, Fernsehen, Fenster⟩; **~ glass** Glasscherben; **get ~:** zerbrechen/brechen/reißen/kaputtgehen; **he got a ~ arm** er hat sich ⟨Dat.⟩ den Arm gebrochen; **(b)** (uneven) uneben ⟨Fläche⟩; **(c)** (imperfect) gebrochen; **in ~ English** in gebrochenem Englisch; **(d)** (fig.) ruiniert ⟨Ehe⟩; gebrochen ⟨Person, Herz, Stimme⟩; **come from a ~ home** aus zerrütteten Familienverhältnissen kommen

broken: ~-down *adj.* baufällig ⟨Gebäude⟩; kaputt (ugs.) ⟨Wagen, Maschine⟩; **~-hearted** /brəʊkn'hɑːtɪd/ *adj.* untröstlich

broker /ˈbrəʊkə(r)/ *n.* ▶ 887 ⎮ (Commerc., Insurance, St. Exch.) Makler, *der*

brolly /ˈbrɒlɪ/ *n.* (Brit. coll.) [Regen]schirm, *der*

bromide /ˈbrəʊmaɪd/ *n.* (Chem.) Bromsalz, *das*

bromine /ˈbrəʊmiːn/ *n.* (Chem.) Brom, *das*

bronchial /ˈbrɒŋkɪəl/ *adj.* (Anat., Med.) bronchial; Bronchial-; **~ tubes** Bronchien

bronchitis /brɒŋˈkaɪtɪs/ *n.*, *no pl.* ▶ 865 ⎮ (Med.) Bronchitis, *die*

bronze /brɒnz/ **1** *n.* **(a)** (metal, work of art, medal) Bronze, *die;* **the B~ Age** die Bronzezeit; **(b)** (colour) Bronze[farbe], *die.* **2** *attrib. adj.* Bronze-; (coloured like ~) bronzefarben; bronzen. **3** *v.t.* bräunen ⟨Gesicht, Haut⟩. **4** *v.i.* braun werden

bronzed /brɒnzd/ *adj.* [sonnen]gebräunt; braun[gebrannt]

brooch /brəʊtʃ/ *n.* Brosche, *die*

brood /bruːd/ **1** *n.* **(a)** Brut, *die;* (of hen) Küken *Pl.;* **(b)** (joc.: children) Kinderschar, *die.* **2** *v.i.* **(a)** (think) [vor sich ⟨Akk.⟩ hin] brüten; **~ over** *or* **upon sth.** über etw. ⟨Akk.⟩ [nach]grübeln; **(b)** (sit) ⟨Vogel:⟩ brüten

broody /ˈbruːdɪ/ *adj.* brütig; **~ hen** Glucke, *die*

brook¹ /brʊk/ *n.* Bach, *der*

brook² *v.t.* dulden; **~ no nonsense/delay** keinen Unfug/Aufschub dulden

broom /bruːm/ *n.* **(a)** Besen, *der;* **a new ~** (fig.) ein neuer Besen; **(b)** (Bot.) Ginster, *der*

broom: ~ cupboard *n.* Besenschrank, *der;* **~stick** *n.* Besenstiel, *der*

Bros. *abbr.* **Brothers** Gebr.

broth /brɒθ/ *n.* (thin soup) Bouillon, *die;* [Fleisch]brühe, *die*

brothel /ˈbrɒθl/ *n.* Bordell, *das*

brother /ˈbrʌðə(r)/ *n.* **(a)** Bruder, *der;* **my/your** *etc.* **~s and sisters** meine/deine *usw.* Geschwister; **have you any ~s or sisters?** haben Sie Geschwister?; **(b)** (fellow member of trade union) Kollege, *der*

brotherhood /ˈbrʌðəhʊd/ *n.* **(a)** *no pl.* Brüderschaft, *die;* brüderliches Verhältnis; **(b)** (association) Bruderschaft, *die*

'brother-in-law *n.*, *pl.* **brothers-in-law** Schwager, *der*

brotherly /ˈbrʌðəlɪ/ *adj.* brüderlich

brought ⇒ **bring**

brow /braʊ/ *n.* **(a)** (eye~) Braue, *die;* **(b)** (forehead) Stirn, *die;* **(c)** (of hill) [Berg]kuppe, *die*

'browbeat *v.t., forms as* **beat 1** unter Druck setzen; einschüchtern; **~ sb. into doing sth.** jmdn. so unter Druck setzen, dass er etw. tut

brown /braʊn/ **1** *adj.* braun. **2** *n.* Braun, *das.* **3** *v.t.* **(a)** bräunen ⟨Haut, Körper⟩; **(b)** (Cookery) [an]bräunen; anbraten ⟨Fleisch⟩; **(c)** (Brit. coll.) **be ~ed off with sth./sb.** etw./jmdn. satt haben (ugs.); **be ~ed off with doing sth.** es satt haben, etw. zu tun (ugs.). **4** *v.i.* **(a)** ⟨Haut:⟩ bräunen; **(b)** (Cookery) ⟨Fleisch:⟩ braun werden

brown: ~ 'ale *n.* dunkles Starkbier; **~ 'bear** *n.* Braunbär, *der;* **~ 'bread** *n.* ≈ Mischbrot, *das;* (wholemeal) Vollkornbrot, *das*

brownie /ˈbraʊnɪ/ *n.* **(a)** the B~s die Wichtel ⟨Pfadfinderinnen von 7–11 Jahren⟩; **get ~ points** (fig. coll.) Pluspunkte sammeln; **(b)** (elf) Heinzelmännchen, *das*

brownish /ˈbraʊnɪʃ/ *adj.* bräunlich

brown: ~ 'paper *n.* Packpapier, *das;* **~ 'rice** *n.* Naturreis, *der;* **~ 'sugar** *n.* brauner Zucker

browse /braʊz/ **1** *v.i.* **(a)** ⟨Vieh:⟩ weiden; ⟨Wild:⟩ äsen; **~ on sth.** etw. fressen; **(b)** (fig.) **~ through a magazine** in einer Zeitschrift blättern; **(c)** (Computing) suchen; **~ through sth.** etw. durchsuchen. **2** *v.t.* **(a)** abgrasen ⟨Weide⟩; abfressen ⟨Blätter⟩; **(b)** (Computing) **~ sth** in etw. ⟨Dat.⟩ suchen. **3** *n.* **have a ~:** sich umsehen; **it's worth a ~:** es ist das Reinschauen wert

browser /ˈbraʊzə(r)/ *n.* (Computing) Browser, *der*

Bruges /bruːʒ/ *pr. n.* ▶ 1159 ⎮ Brügge (*das*)

bruise /bruːz/ **1** *n.* **(a)** (Med.) blauer Fleck; **(b)** (on fruit) Druckstelle, *die.* **2** *v.t.* quetschen ⟨Obst, Pflanzen⟩; **~ oneself/one's leg** sich stoßen/sich am Bein stoßen; **he was badly ~d** er hat sich ⟨Dat.⟩ starke Prellungen zugezogen. **3** *v.i.* ⟨Person:⟩ blaue Flecken bekommen; ⟨Obst:⟩ Druckstellen bekommen

brunette /bruːˈnet/ **1** n. Brünette, die. **2** adj. brünett

Brunswick /ˈbrʌnzwɪk/ ▶ 1159 | **1** pr. n. Braunschweig (das). **2** attrib. adj. Braunschweiger

brunt /brʌnt/ n. bear the ~ of the attack/financial cuts von dem Angriff/von den Einsparungen am meisten betroffen sein

brush /brʌʃ/ **1** n. **(a)** Bürste, die; (for sweeping) Hand-, Kehrbesen, der; (with short handle) Handfeger, der; (for scrubbing) [Scheuer]bürste, die; (for painting or writing) Pinsel, der; **(b)** (quarrel, skirmish) Zusammenstoß, der; **have a ~ with the law** mit dem Gesetz in Konflikt kommen; **(c)** (light touch) flüchtige Berührung; **(d) give your hair/teeth a ~:** bürste dir die Haare/putz dir die Zähne; **give your shoes/clothes a ~:** bürste deine Schuhe/Kleider ab. **2** v.t. **(a)** (sweep) kehren, fegen; abbürsten ⟨Kleidung⟩; ~ one's teeth/hair sich (Dat.) die Zähne putzen/die Haare bürsten; **(b)** (Cookery) bepinseln, bestreichen ⟨Teigwaren, Gebäck⟩; **(c)** (touch in passing) flüchtig berühren; streifen. **3** v.i. ~ by or against or past sb./sth. jmdn./etw. streifen ~ a'side v.t. beiseite schieben ⟨Person, Hindernis⟩; abtun, vom Tisch wischen ⟨Einwand, Zweifel, Beschwerde⟩ ~ a'way v.t. abbürsten ⟨Schmutz, Staub usw.⟩; (with hand or cloth) abwischen; wegwischen ~ 'down v.t. abbürsten ⟨Kleidungsstück⟩ ~ 'off v.t. **(a)** abbürsten ⟨Schmutz, Staub usw.⟩; (with hand or cloth) abwischen; wegwischen, **(b)** (fig.: rebuff) abblitzen lassen (ugs.) ~ 'up **1** v.t. **(a)** zusammenfegen ⟨Krümel⟩; **(b)** auffrischen ⟨Sprache, Kenntnisse⟩. **2** v.i. ~ up on auffrischen

brush: ~-off n. Abfuhr, die; **give sb. the ~-off** jmdm. einen Korb geben (ugs.); ~ stroke n. Pinselstrich, der; ~-up n. **have a wash and ~-up** sich frisch machen

brusque /brʊsk, brʌsk/ adj. schroff

Brussels /ˈbrʌslz/ pr. n. ▶ 1159 | Brüssel (das)

Brussels 'sprouts n. pl. Rosenkohl, der; Kohlsprossen (österr.)

brutal /ˈbruːtl/ adj. brutal; (fig.) brutal, schonungslos ⟨Offenheit⟩

brutality /bruːˈtælɪtɪ/ n. Brutalität, die

brutally /ˈbruːtəlɪ/ adv. brutal

brute /bruːt/ **1** n. **(a)** (animal) Bestie, die; **(b)** (brutal person) Rohling, der; brutaler Kerl (ugs.); (thing) höllische Sache; **a ~ of a problem** (fig.) ein höllisches Problem; **a drunken ~:** ein brutaler Trunkenbold. **2** attrib. adj. (without capacity to reason) vernunftlos; irrational; **by ~ force** mit roher Gewalt

brutish /ˈbruːtɪʃ/ adj. brutal ⟨Flegel⟩; tierisch ⟨Leidenschaften, Gelüste⟩

BS abbr. **British Standard** Britische Norm

B. Sc. /biːesˈsiː/ abbr. **Bachelor of Science** Bakkalaureus der Naturwissenschaften; **he is a or has a ~:** ≈ er hat ein Diplom in Naturwissenschaften

BSE abbr. **bovine spongiform encephalopathy** BSE

BST abbr. **British Summer Time** Britische Sommerzeit

bubble /ˈbʌbl/ **1** n. **(a)** Blase, die; (small) Perle, die; (fig.) Seifenblase, die; **blow ~s** [Seifen]blasen machen; **(b)** (domed canopy) [Glas]kuppel, die. **2** v.i. **(a)** (form ~s) ⟨Wasser, Schlamm, Lava:⟩ Blasen bilden; ⟨Suppe, Flüssigkeiten:⟩ brodeln; (make sound of ~s) ⟨Bach, Quelle:⟩ plätschern; **(b)** (fig.) ~ with sth. vor etw. (Dat.) übersprudeln ~ 'over v.i. überschäumen; ~ over with excitement/joy (fig.) vor Aufregung übersprudeln/vor Freude überquellen ~ 'up v.i. ⟨Gas:⟩ in Blasen aufsteigen; ⟨Wasser:⟩ aufsprudeln

bubble: ~ bath n. Schaumbad, das; ~ gum n. Bubble-Gum, der; Ballonkaugummi, der

bubbly /ˈbʌblɪ/ **1** adj. **(a)** sprudelnd; schäumend ⟨Bade-, Spülwasser⟩; **(b)** (fig. coll.) quirlig (ugs.) ⟨Person⟩. **2** n. (Brit. coll.) Schampus, der

Bucharest /bjuːkəˈrest/ pr. n. ▶ 1159 | Bukarest (das)

buck¹ /bʌk/ **1** n. (deer, chamois) Bock, der; (rabbit, hare) Rammler, der. **2** v.i. ⟨Pferd:⟩ bocken. **3** v.t. ~ [off] ⟨Pferd:⟩ abwerfen

buck² n. (coll.) **pass the ~ to sb.** (fig.) jmdm. die Verantwortung aufhalsen; **the ~ stops here** (fig.) die Verantwortung liegt letzten Endes bei mir

buck³ (coll.) **1** v.i. ~ 'up **(a)** (make haste) sich ranhalten (ugs.); ~ up! los, schnell!; auf, los!; **(b)** (cheer up) ~ up! Kopf hoch! **2** v.t. ~ 'up **(a)** (cheer up) aufmuntern; **(b)** ~ one's ideas up (coll.) sich zusammenreißen

buck⁴ n. (Amer. and Austral. sl.: dollar) Dollar, der; **make a fast ~:** eine schnelle Mark machen (ugs.)

bucket /ˈbʌkɪt/ **1** n. Eimer, der; **a ~ of water** ein Eimer [voll] Wasser; **kick the ~** (fig. sl.) ins Gras beißen (salopp). **2** v.i. **the rain** or **it is ~ing down** es gießt wie aus Kübeln (ugs.)

bucketful /ˈbʌkɪtfʊl/ n. Eimer [voll]

'bucket shop n. [nicht ganz seriöses] Maklerbüro; (for air tickets) Reisebüro (das vor allem Billigflüge vermittelt)

buckle /ˈbʌkl/ **1** n. Schnalle, die. **2** v.t. **(a)** zuschnallen; ~ sth. on etw. anschnallen; ~ sth. up etw. zuschnallen; **(b)** (crumple) verbiegen ⟨Stoßstange, Rad⟩. **3** v.i. ⟨Rad, Metallplatte:⟩ sich verbiegen ~ 'down v.i. sich dahinter klemmen; ~ down to a task sich hinter eine Aufgabe klemmen

buck: ~-tooth n. vorstehender Zahn; Raffzahn, der (ugs.); ~wheat /ˈbʌkwiːt/ n. (Agric.) Buchweizen, der

bud /bʌd/ **1** n. Knospe, die; **come into ~/be in ~:** knospen; Knospen treiben; **nip sth. in the ~** (fig.) etw. im Keim ersticken. **2** v.i., **-dd-** knospen; Knospen treiben; ⟨Baum:⟩ ausschlagen; **a ~ding painter/actor** (fig.) ein angehender Maler/Schauspieler

Buddhism /ˈbʊdɪzm/ n. Buddhismus, der

Buddhist /ˈbʊdɪst/ **1** n. Buddhist, der/Buddhistin, die. **2** adj. buddhistisch

buddy /ˈbʌdɪ/ n. (coll.) Kumpel, der (ugs.)

budge /bʌdʒ/ **1** v.i. ⟨Person, Tier:⟩ sich [von der Stelle] rühren; ⟨Gegenstand:⟩ sich bewegen, nachgeben; (fig.: change opinion) nachgeben. **2** v.t. **(a)** bewegen; **I can't ~ this screw** ich kriege diese Schraube nicht los; **(b)** (fig.: change opinion) abbringen; **he refuses to be ~d** er lässt sich nicht umstimmen

budgerigar /ˈbʌdʒərɪgɑː(r)/ n. Wellensittich, der

budget /ˈbʌdʒɪt/ **1** n. Budget, das; Etat, der; Haushalt[splan], der; **keep within ~:** seinen Etat nicht überschreiten; ~ meal/holiday preisgünstige Mahlzeit/Ferien. **2** v.i. planen; ~ for sth. etw. [im Etat] einplanen

budgie /ˈbʌdʒɪ/ n. (coll.) Wellensittich, der

buff /bʌf/ **1** adj. gelbbraun. **2** n. **(a)** (coll.: enthusiast) Fan, der (ugs.); **(b)** (colour) Gelbbraun, das. **3** v.t. (polish) polieren, [blank] putzen ⟨Metall, Schuhe usw.⟩

buffalo /ˈbʌfələʊ/ n., pl. ~es or same Büffel, der

buffer /ˈbʌfə(r)/ n. Prellbock, der; (on vehicle; also fig.) Puffer, der

'buffer zone n. Pufferzone, die

buffet¹ /ˈbʌfɪt/ v.t. schlagen; ~ed by the wind/waves vom Wind geschüttelt/von den Wellen hin und her geworfen

buffet² /ˈbʊfeɪ/ n. (Brit.) **(a)** (place) Büfett, das; ~ car (Railw.) Büfettwagen, der; **(b)** (meal) Imbiss, der; ~ lunch/supper/meal Büfettessen, das; **a cold ~:** ein kaltes Büfett

bug /bʌg/ **1** n. **(a)** Wanze, die; **(b)** (Amer.: small insect) Insekt, das; Käfer, der; **(c)** (coll.: virus) Bazillus, der; **(d)** (coll.: disease) Infektion, die; Krankheit, die; **catch a ~:** sich (Dat.) was holen (ugs.); **(e)** (coll.: concealed microphone) Wanze, die (ugs.); **(f)** (coll.: defect) Macke, die (salopp). **2** v.t., **-gg-:** **(a)** (coll.: install microphone in) verwanzen ⟨Zimmer⟩ (ugs.); abhören ⟨Telefon, Konferenz⟩; **(b)** (coll.) (annoy) nerven (salopp); den Nerv töten (+ Dat.) (ugs.); (bother) beunruhigen; **what's ~ging you?** was ist mit dir?

bugbear /ˈbʌgbeə(r)/ n. Problem, das; Sorge, die

bugger /ˈbʌgə(r)/ **1** n. **(a)** (coarse) (fellow) Bursche, der (ugs.); Macker, der (salopp); (as insult) Scheißkerl, der (derb); **(b)** (coarse: thing) Scheißding, das (derb). **2** v.t. (coarse: damn) ~ you/him (dismissive) du kannst/der kann mich mal (derb); ~ this car/him! (angry) dieses Scheißauto/dieser Scheißkerl! (derb); ~ it! ach du Scheiße! (derb); (in surprise) well, ~ me *or* I'll be ~ed! ach du Scheiße! (derb) ~ a'bout, ~ a'round (coarse) 1 *v.i.* Scheiß machen (derb); rumblödeln (ugs.); ~ about with sth. mit etw. rumfummeln (ugs.). 2 *v.t.* verarschen (derb) ~ 'off *v.i.* (coarse) abhauen (ugs.) ~ 'up *v.t.* (coarse) verkorksen (ugs.)

buggy /ˈbʌgɪ/ *n.* (pushchair) Sportwagen, *der*

bugle /ˈbjuːgl/ *n.* Bügelhorn, *das*

build /bɪld/ 1 *v.t.*, **built** /bɪlt/ (a) bauen; errichten ‹Gebäude, Damm›; mauern ‹Schornstein, Kamin›; zusammenbauen *od.* -setzen ‹Fahrzeug›; **the house is still being built** das Haus ist noch im Bau; ~ sth. **from** *or* **out of sth.** etw. aus etw. machen *od.* bauen; (b) (fig.) aufbauen ‹System, Gesellschaft, Reich, Zukunft›; schaffen ‹bessere Zukunft, Beziehung›; begründen ‹Ruf›. 2 *v.i.*, **built** (a) bauen; (b) (fig.) ~ **on one's successes** auf seinen Erfolgen aufbauen. 3 *n.* Körperbau, *der*
~ 'in *v.t.* einbauen
~ **into** *v.t.* ~ sth. into sth. etw. in etw. (*Akk.*) einbauen
~ **on** *v.t.* (a) aufbauen auf (+ *Dat.*); bebauen ‹Gelände›; (b) (attach) ~ sth. on to sth. etw. an etw. (*Akk.*) anbauen
~ 'up 1 *v.t.* (a) bebauen ‹Land, Gebiet›; (b) (accumulate) aufhäufen ‹Reserven, Mittel, Kapital›; (c) (strengthen) stärken ‹Gesundheit, Widerstandskraft›; widerstandsfähig machen, kräftigen ‹Person, Körper›; (d) (increase) erhöhen, steigern ‹Produktion, Kapazität›; stärken ‹[Selbst]vertrauen›; ~ up sb.'s hopes [unduly] jmdm. [falsche] Hoffnung machen; (e) (develop) aufbauen ‹Firma, Geschäft›. 2 *v.i.* (a) ‹Spannung, Druck:› zunehmen, ansteigen; ‹Musik:› anschwellen; ‹Lärm:› sich steigern (**to** in + *Akk.*); ~ up to a crescendo sich zu einem Crescendo steigern; (b) ‹Schlange, Rückstau:› sich bilden; ‹Verkehr:› sich verdichten, sich stauen

builder /ˈbɪldə(r)/ *n.* ▶ 887 ◀ (a) Erbauer, *der;* (b) (contractor) Bauunternehmer, *der;* ~'s **labourer** Bauarbeiter, *der*

building /ˈbɪldɪŋ/ *n.* (a) *no pl.* Bau, *der;* (b) (structure) Gebäude, *das;* (for living in) Haus, *das*

building: ~ **contractor** *n.* ▶ 887 ◀ Bauunternehmer, *der;* ~ **site** *n.* Baustelle, *die;* ~ **society** *n.* (Brit.) Bausparkasse, *die*

'build-up *n.* (a) (publicity) Reklame[rummel], *der;* **give sb./sth. a good** ~: jmdn./etw. groß ankündigen; (b) (approach to climax) Vorbereitungen *Pl.* (**to** für); (c) (increase) Zunahme, *die;* (of forces) Verstärkung, *die;* **a** ~ **of traffic** ein [Verkehrs]stau

built ⇒ build 1, 2

built: ~-**in** *adj.* (a) eingebaut; **a** ~-**in cupboard/kitchen** ein Einbauschrank/eine Einbauküche; (b) (fig.: instinctive) angeboren; ~-**up** *adj.* bebaut; ~-**up area** Wohngebiet, *das;* (Motor Veh.) geschlossene Ortschaft

bulb /bʌlb/ *n.* (a) (Bot., Hort.) Zwiebel, *die;* (b) (of lamp) [Glüh]birne, *die;* (c) (of thermometer, chemical apparatus) [Glas]kolben, *der*

Bulgaria /bʌlˈgeərɪə/ *pr. n.* Bulgarien (*das*)

Bulgarian /bʌlˈgeərɪən/ ▶ 897 ◀, ▶ 947 ◀ 1 *adj.* bulgarisch; **he/she is** ~: er ist Bulgare/sie ist Bulgarin. 2 *n.* (a) (person) Bulgare, *der*/Bulgarin, *die;* (b) (language) Bulgarisch, *das; see also* **English 2 a**

bulge /bʌldʒ/ 1 *n.* (a) Ausbeulung, *die;* ausgebeulte Stelle; (in line) Bogen, *der;* (in tyre) Wulst, *der od. die;* (b) (coll.: increase) Anstieg, *der* (**in** Gen.). 2 *v.i.* (a) (swell outwards) sich wölben; (b) (be full) voll gestopft sein

bulging /ˈbʌldʒɪŋ/ *adj.* prall gefüllt ‹Einkaufstasche usw.›; voll gestopft ‹Hosentasche, Kiste›; rund ‹Bauch›

bulimia (nervosa) /bʊˈliːmɪə (nɜːˈvəʊsə)/ *n.* ▶ 865 ◀ Bulimie, *die;* Bulimia nervosa, *die* (fachspr.)

bulimic /bʊˈlɪmɪk/ 1 *n.* Bulimiker, *der*/Bulimikerin, *die.* 2 *adj.* bulimisch

bulk /bʌlk/ *n.* (a) (large quantity) **in** ~: in großen Mengen; (b) (large shape) massige Gestalt; (c) (size) Größe, *die;* (d) (volume) Menge, *die;* Umfang, *der;* (e) (greater part) **the** ~ **of the money** der Groß- *od.* Hauptteil des Geldes; **the** ~ **of the population** die Mehrheit der Bevölkerung; (f) (Commerc.) **in** ~: (loose) lose; unabgefüllt ‹Wein›; (wholesale) en gros

bulky /ˈbʌlkɪ/ *adj.* sperrig ‹Gegenstand›; massig, wuchtig ‹Gestalt, Körper›; unförmig ‹Kleidungsstück›; (unwieldy) unhandlich ‹Gegenstand, Paket›

bull /bʊl/ *n.* (a) Bulle, *der;* (for ~fight) Stier, *der;* **like a** ~ **in a china shop** (fig.) wie ein Elefant im Porzellanladen; **take the** ~ **by the horns** (fig.) den Stier bei den Hörnern fassen *od.* packen; (b) (whale, elephant) Bulle, *der;* (c) ⇒ **bull's eye**

bull: ~ **bar** *n.* Rammschutz, *der;* Rammbügel, *der;* ~**dog** *n.* Bulldogge, *die;* ~**dog clip** Flügelklammer, *die;* ~**doze** *v.t.* (a) planieren ‹Boden›; mit der Planierraupe wegräumen ‹Gebäude›; (b) (fig.: force) ~**doze sb. into doing sth.** jmdn. dazu zwingen, etw. zu tun; ~**dozer** /ˈbʊldəʊzə(r)/ *n.* Planierraupe, *die*

bullet /ˈbʊlɪt/ *n.* [Gewehr-, Pistolen]kugel, *die*

'bullet hole *n.* Einschuss, *der;* Einschussloch, *das*

bulletin /ˈbʊlɪtɪn/ *n.* Bulletin, *das*

'bulletin board *n.* (a) (Amer.) Anschlagtafel, *die;* (Sch., Univ.) Schwarzes Brett; (b) (Computing) Schwarzes Brett

'bulletproof *adj.* kugelsicher

bull: ~**fight** *n.* Stierkampf, *der;* ~**fighter** *n.* ▶ 887 ◀ Stierkämpfer, *der;* ~**fighting** *n.* Stierkämpfe; ~**finch** *n.* (Ornith.) Gimpel, *der;* ~**frog** *n.* Ochsenfrosch, *der*

bullion /ˈbʊljən/ *n., no pl., no indef. art.* **gold/silver** ~: ungemünztes Gold/Silber; (ingots) Gold-/Silberbarren *Pl.*

'bull market *n.* (St. Exch.) Haussemarkt, *der*

bullock /ˈbʊlək/ *n.* Ochse, *der*

bull: ~**ring** *n.* Stierkampfarena, *die;* ~'s-**eye** *n.* (of target) Schwarze, *das;* **score a** ~'s-**eye** (lit. *or* fig.) ins Schwarze treffen; ~**shit** *n.* (coarse) Scheiße, *die* (salopp abwertend)

bully /ˈbʊlɪ/ 1 *n.:* jmd., der gern Schwächere schikaniert *bzw.* tyrannisiert; (esp. schoolboy etc.) ≈ Rabauke, *der* (abwertend); (boss) Tyrann, *der.* 2 *v.t.* (persecute) schikanieren; (frighten) einschüchtern; ~ **sb. into/out of doing sth.** jmdn. so sehr einschüchtern, dass er etw. tut/lässt

bullying /ˈbʊlɪŋ/ 1 *n.* Schikanieren, *das.* 2 *adj.* tyrannisch

bulrush /ˈbʊlrʌʃ/ *n.* (a) (Bot.) Teichsimse, *die;* (b) (Bibl.) Rohr, *das*

bulwark /ˈbʊlwək/ *n.* (rampart) Wall, *der;* Bollwerk, *das* (auch fig.)

bum[1] /bʌm/ *n.* (Brit. sl.) Hintern, *der* (ugs.); Arsch, *der* (derb)

bum[2] (sl.) 1 *n.* (Amer.) (a) (tramp) Penner, *der* (salopp abwertend); Berber, *der* (salopp); (b) (lazy dissolute person) Penner, *der* (salopp abwertend); Gammler, *der* (ugs. abwertend). 2 *adj.* mies (ugs.). 3 *v.i.* -**mm**- ~ [**about** *or* **around**] rumgammeln (ugs.). 4 *v.t.* -**mm**- schnorren (ugs.) ‹Zigaretten usw.› (**off** bei)

bumble-bee /ˈbʌmblbiː/ *n.* Hummel, *die*

bumbling /ˈbʌmblɪŋ/ *adj.* stümperhaft

bumf /bʌmf/ *n.* (Brit. coll.) Papierkram, *der* (ugs.)

bump /bʌmp/ 1 *n.* (a) (sound) Bums, *der;* (impact) Stoß, *der;* **this car has had a few** ~s der Wagen hat schon einige Dellen abbekommen; (b) (swelling) Beule, *die;* (c) (hump) Buckel, *der* (ugs.). 2 *adv.* bums; rums, bums. 3 *v.t.* (a) anstoßen; **I** ~**ed the chair against the wall** ich stieß mit dem Stuhl an die Wand; (b) (hurt) ~ **one's head/knee** sich am Kopf/Knie stoßen. 4 *v.i.* (a) ~ **against sb./sth.** jmdn./an etw. (*Akk.*) *od.* gegen etw. stoßen; (b) (move with jolts) rumpeln
~ **into** *v.t.* (a) stoßen an (+ *Akk.*) *od.* gegen; (with vehicle) fahren gegen ‹Mauer, Baum›; ~ **into sb.** jmdn. anstoßen; (with vehicle) jmdn. anfahren; (b) (meet by chance) zufällig [wieder]treffen
~ 'off *v.t.* (sl.) kaltmachen (salopp)
~ up *v.t.* (coll.) aufschlagen ‹Preise›; aufbessern ‹Gehalt›

bumper /ˈbʌmpə(r)/ 1 *n.* (a) (Motor Veh.) Stoßstange, *die;* (b) (Amer. Railw.) Puffer, *der.* 2 *adj.* Rekord‹ernte, -jahr›

'bumper car *n.* [Auto]skooter, *der*

bumpkin /ˈbʌmpkɪn/ *n.* [**country**] ~: [Bauern]tölpel, *der* (abwertend)

bumpy /ˈbʌmpɪ/ *adj.* holp[e]rig ‹Straße, Fahrt, Fahrzeug›; uneben ‹Fläche›; unruhig ‹Flug›

bun /bʌn/ n. (a) süßes Brötchen; (currant ~) Korinthenbrötchen, das; (b) (hair) [Haar]knoten, der

bunch /bʌntʃ/ n. (a) (of flowers) Strauß, der; (of grapes, bananas) Traube, die; (of parsley, radishes) Bund, das; ~ of flowers/grapes Blumenstrauß, der/Traube, die; ~ of keys Schlüsselbund, der; (b) (lot) Anzahl, die; a whole ~ of ...: ein ganzer Haufen ... (ugs.); the best or pick of the ~: der/die/das Beste [von allen]; (c) (group) Haufen, der (ugs.)
~ **'up** 1 v.i. ⟨Personen:⟩ zusammenrücken; ⟨Kleid, Stoff:⟩ sich zusammenknüllen. 2 v.t. zusammenraffen ⟨Kleid⟩

bundle /'bʌndl/ 1 n. (a) Bündel, das; (of papers) Packen, der; (of hay) Bund, das; (of books) Stapel, der; (of fibres, nerves) Strang, der; she's a ~ of mischief/energy (fig.) sie hat nichts als Unfug im Kopf/ist ein Energiebündel; (b) (Computing) Paket, das. 2 v.t. (a) bündeln; (b) ~ sth. into the suitcase/back of the car etw. in den Koffer stopfen/hinten ins Auto werfen; ~ sb. into the car jmdn. ins Auto verfrachten; (c) (Computing) in einem od. als Paket verkaufen
~ **'up** v.t. (put in ~s) bündeln

bung /bʌŋ/ 1 n. Spund[zapfen], der. 2 v.t. (coll.) schmeißen (ugs.)
~ **'up** v.t. be/get ~ed up verstopft sein/verstopfen

bungalow /'bʌŋgələʊ/ n. Bungalow, der

bungee jumping /'bʌndʒɪ/ n., no pl. Bungeespringen, das

bungle /'bʌŋgl/ v.t. stümpern bei

bungler /'bʌŋglə(r)/ n. Stümper, der (abwertend)

bungling /'bʌŋglɪŋ/ adj. stümperhaft ⟨Versuch⟩; ~ person Stümper, der

bunk¹ /bʌŋk/ n. (in ship, aircraft, lorry) Koje, die; (in sleeping car, room) Bett, das

bunk² n. (coll.: nonsense) Quatsch, der (salopp); Mist, der (salopp)

bunk³ n. (Brit. sl.) do a ~: türmen (salopp)

'bunk bed n. Etagenbett, das

bunker /'bʌŋkə(r)/ n. (fuel-~, Mil., Golf) Bunker, der

bunny /'bʌnɪ/ n. Häschen, das

bunting n., no pl. (flags) [bunte] Fähnchen; Wimpel Pl.

buoy /bɔɪ/ 1 n. Boje, die. 2 v.t. ~ [up] über Wasser halten; (fig.: support, sustain) aufrechterhalten; I was ~ed [up] by the thought that ...: der Gedanke, dass ..., ließ mich durchhalten

buoyancy /'bɔɪənsɪ/ n. (a) Auftrieb, der; (b) (fig.) Schwung, der; Elan, der

buoyant /'bɔɪənt/ adj. (a) Auftrieb habend; schwimmend; be [more] ~: [einen größeren] Auftrieb haben; [besser] schwimmen; (b) (fig.) rege ⟨Markt⟩; heiter ⟨Person⟩; federnd ⟨Schritt⟩

burble /'bɜːbl/ v.i. (a) (speak lengthily) ~ [on] about sth. von etw. ständig quasseln (ugs.); (b) (make a murmuring sound) brummeln (ugs.)

burden /'bɜːdn/ 1 n. (lit. or fig.) Last, die; beast of ~: Lasttier, das; become a ~: zur Last werden; be a ~ to sb. für jmdn. eine Belastung sein; (less serious) jmdm. zur Last fallen. 2 v.t. belasten; (fig.) ~ sb./oneself with sth. jmdn./sich mit etw. belasten

burdensome /'bɜːdnsəm/ adj. (fig.) lästig ⟨Person, Pflicht, Verantwortung⟩; become/be ~ to sb. jmdm. zur Last werden/fallen

bureau /'bjʊərəʊ/ n., pl. ~x /'bjʊərəʊz/ or ~s (a) (Brit.: writing desk) Schreibschrank, der; (Amer.: chest of drawers) Kommode, die; (b) (office) Büro, das; (department) Abteilung, die; (Amer.: of government) Amt, das

bureaucracy /bjʊəˈrɒkrəsɪ/ n. Bürokratie, die

bureaucrat /'bjʊərəkræt/ n. Bürokrat, der/Bürokratin, die (abwertend)

bureaucratic /bjʊərəˈkrætɪk/ adj., **bureaucratically** /bjʊərəˈkrætɪklɪ/ adv. bürokratisch

burger /'bɜːgə(r)/ n. (coll.) Hamburger, der

'burger bar n. (coll.) Hamburgerlokal, das

burglar /'bɜːglə(r)/ n. Einbrecher, der

'burglar alarm n. Alarmanlage, die

burglarize /'bɜːgləraɪz/ (Amer.) ⇒ burgle

'burglar-proof adj. einbruch[s]sicher

burglary /'bɜːglərɪ/ n. Einbruch, der; (offence) [Einbruchs]diebstahl, der

burgle /'bɜːgl/ v.t. einbrechen in (+ Akk.); the shop/he was ~d in dem Laden/bei ihm wurde eingebrochen

Burgundy /'bɜːgəndɪ/ pr. n. Burgund (das)

burgundy n. Burgunder[wein], der

burial /'berɪəl/ n. Bestattung, die; Begräbnis, das; (funeral) Beerdigung, die; ~ at sea Seebestattung, die

'burial service n. Trauerfeier, die

burlesque /bɜːˈlesk/ n. (a) Varietee, das; (b) (book, play) Burleske, die; (parody) Parodie, die

burly /'bɜːlɪ/ adj. kräftig; stämmig; stramm ⟨Soldat⟩

Burma /'bɜːmə/ pr. n. Birma (das)

Burmese /bɜːˈmiːz/ ▶897 , ▶947 1 adj. birmanisch; sb. is ~: jmd. ist Birmane/Birmanin. 2 n., pl. same (a) (person) Birmane, der/Birmanin, die; (b) (language) Birmanisch, das; see also English 2 a

burn¹ /bɜːn/ 1 n. ▶865 (on the skin) Verbrennung, die; (on material) Brandfleck, der; (hole) Brandloch, das. 2 v.t., ~t or ~ed (a) verbrennen; ~ a hole in sth. ein Loch in etw. (Akk.) brennen; ~ one's boats or bridges (fig.) alle Brücken hinter sich ⟨Dat.⟩ abbrechen; (b) (use as fuel) als Brennstoff verwenden ⟨Gas, Öl usw.⟩; heizen mit ⟨Kohle, Holz, Torf⟩; verbrauchen ⟨Strom⟩; (use up) verbrauchen ⟨Treibstoff⟩; verfeuern ⟨Holz, Kohle⟩; ~ coal in the stove den Ofen mit Kohle feuern; (c) ▶865 (injure) verbrennen; ~ oneself/one's hand sich verbrennen/sich (Dat.) die Hand verbrennen; ~ one's fingers, get one's fingers ~t (fig.) sich (Dat.) die Finger verbrennen (fig.); (d) (spoil) anbrennen lassen ⟨Fleisch, Kuchen⟩; be ~t angebrannt sein; (e) (cause ~ing sensation to) verbrennen; (f) (put to death) ~ sb. [at the stake] jmdn. [auf dem Scheiterhaufen] verbrennen; (g) (corrode) ätzen; verätzen ⟨Haut⟩. 3 v.i., ~t or ~ed (a) brennen; ~ to death verbrennen; (b) (blaze) ⟨Feuer:⟩ brennen; ⟨Gebäude:⟩ in Flammen stehen; (c) (give light) ⟨Lampe, Kerze, Licht:⟩ brennen; (d) ▶865 (be injured) sich verbrennen; she/her skin ~s easily sie bekommt leicht einen Sonnenbrand; (e) (be spoiled) ⟨Kuchen, Milch, Essen:⟩ anbrennen; (f) (be corrosive) ätzen; ätzend sein
~ **'down** 1 v.t. niederbrennen. 2 v.i. ⟨Gebäude:⟩ niederbrennen, abbrennen; (less brightly) ⟨Feuer, Kerze:⟩ herunterbrennen
~ **'out** 1 v.t. (a) ausbrennen; (b) (fig.) feel ~ed out sich erschöpft fühlen; ~ oneself out sich völlig verausgaben. 2 v.i. (a) ⟨Kerze, Feuer:⟩ erlöschen, ausgehen; ⟨Rakete[nstufe]:⟩ ausbrennen; (b) (Electr.) durchbrennen
~ **'up** 1 v.t. verbrennen; verbrauchen ⟨Energie⟩. 2 v.i. (a) (begin to blaze) auflodern; (b) (be destroyed) ⟨Rakete, Meteor, Satellit:⟩ verglühen

burn² n. (Scot.) Bach, der

'burned-out adj. (lit. or fig.) ausgebrannt

burner /'bɜːnə(r)/ n. Brenner, der

burning /'bɜːnɪŋ/ 1 adj. (a) brennend; (b) (fig.) glühend ⟨Leidenschaft, Hass, Wunsch⟩; brennend ⟨Wunsch, Frage, Problem, Ehrgeiz⟩. 2 n. Brennen, das; a smell of ~: ein Brandgeruch

burnish /'bɜːnɪʃ/ v.t. polieren

'burn-out n. Burn-out, das (Med.); totale Erschöpfung od. Entkräftung; risk ~: Gefahr laufen, sich zu übernehmen

burnt ⇒ burn¹ 2, 3

burnt 'offering n. Brandopfer, das; (fig. joc.: burnt food) angebranntes Essen

'burnt-out ⇒ burned-out

burp /bɜːp/ (coll.) 1 n. Rülpser, der (ugs.); (of baby) Bäuerchen, das (fam.). 2 v.i. rülpsen (ugs.); aufstoßen. 3 v.t. ein Bäuerchen machen lassen (fam.) ⟨Baby⟩

burrow /'bʌrəʊ/ 1 n. Bau, der. 2 v.t. graben ⟨Loch, Höhle, Tunnel⟩; ~ one's way under/through sth. einen Weg *od.* Gang unter etw. (*Dat.*) durch/durch etw. graben. **3** *v.i.* [sich (*Dat.*)] einen Gang graben; ∼ **into sth.** (fig.) sich in etw. (*Akk.*) einarbeiten; ∼ **through sth.** (fig.) sich durch etw. hindurchwühlen

bursar /'bɜːsə(r)/ *n.* ▶ 887 | *Verwalter der geschäftlichen Angelegenheiten einer Schule/Universität*

bursary /'bɜːsərɪ/ *n.* Kasse, *die;* (scholarship) Stipendium, *das*

burst /bɜːst/ **1** *n.* (a) (split) Bruch, *der;* **a** ∼ **in a pipe** ein Rohrbruch; (b) (outbreak of firing) Feuerstoß, *der;* Salve, *die;* (c) (fig.) **a** ∼ **of applause** ein Beifallsausbruch; **there was a** ∼ **of laughter** man brach in Lachen aus. **2** *v.t.,* **burst** zum Platzen bringen; platzen lassen ⟨*Luftballon*⟩; platzen ⟨*Reifen*⟩; sprengen ⟨*Kessel*⟩; ∼ **pipe** Rohrbruch, *der;* **the river** ∼ **its banks** der Fluss trat über die Ufer; **he [almost]** ∼ **a blood vessel** (fig.) ihn traf [fast] der Schlag; ∼ **the door open** die Tür aufbrechen *od.* aufsprengen; ∼ **one's sides with laughing** (fig.) vor Lachen beinahe platzen. **3** *v.i.,* **burst** (a) platzen; ⟨*Granate, Bombe, Kessel:*⟩ explodieren; ⟨*Damm:*⟩ brechen; ⟨*Flussufer:*⟩ überschwemmt werden; ⟨*Furunkel, Geschwür:*⟩ aufgehen, aufplatzen; ⟨*Knospe:*⟩ aufbrechen; ∼ **open** ⟨*Tür, Deckel, Kiste, Koffer:*⟩ aufspringen; (b) (be full to overflowing) **be** ∼**ing with sth.** zum Bersten voll sein mit etw.; **be** ∼**ing with pride/impatience** (fig.) vor Stolz/Ungeduld platzen; **be** ∼**ing with excitement** (fig.) vor Aufregung außer sich sein; **I can't eat any more. I'm** ∼**ing** (fig.) Ich kann nichts mehr essen. Ich platze [gleich] (ugs.); **be** ∼**ing to say/do sth.** (fig.) es kaum abwarten können, etw. zu sagen/tun; (c) (appear, come suddenly) ∼ **through sth.** etw. durchbrechen

∼ **'in** *v.i.* hereinplatzen; hereinstürzen; ∼ **in [up]on sb./sth.** bei jmdm./etw. hereinplatzen

∼ **into** *v.t.* (a) eindringen in (+ *Akk.*); **we** ∼ **into the room** wir stürzten ins Zimmer; (b) ∼ **into tears/laughter** in Tränen/Gelächter ausbrechen; ∼ **into flames** in Brand geraten

∼ **'out** *v.i.* (a) herausstürzen; ∼ **out of a room** aus einem Raum [hinaus]stürmen *od.* stürzen; (b) (exclaim) losplatzen; (c) ∼ **out laughing/crying** in Lachen/Tränen ausbrechen

burton /'bɜːtn/ *n.* (Brit. coll.) **go for a** ∼ (be destroyed) kaputtgehen (ugs.); futsch gehen (salopp); (be lost) hopsgehen (salopp)

bury /'berɪ/ *v.t.* (a) begraben; beisetzen (geh.) ⟨*Toten*⟩; **where is Marx buried?** wo ist *od.* liegt Marx begraben?; (b) (hide) vergraben; (fig.) begraben; ∼ **the hatchet** or (Amer.) **tomahawk** (fig.) das Kriegsbeil begraben; ∼ **one's face in one's hands** das Gesicht in den Händen vergraben; (c) (bring underground) eingraben; abdecken ⟨*Wurzeln*⟩; **the houses were buried by a landslide** die Häuser wurden durch einen Erdrutsch verschüttet; (d) (plunge) ∼ **one's teeth in sth.** seine Zähne in etw. (*Akk.*) graben *od.* schlagen; (e) ∼ **oneself in one's studies/books** sich in seine Studien vertiefen/in seinen Büchern vergraben

bus /bʌs/ **1** *n.,* *pl.* ∼**es** (Amer.: ∼**ses**) [Auto-, Omni]bus, *der;* **go by** ∼: mit dem Bus fahren. **2** *v.i.,* (Amer.) **-ss-** mit dem Bus fahren. **3** *v.t.,* **-ss-** (Amer.) mit dem Bus befördern

busby /'bʌzbɪ/ *n.* (Brit.) Kalpak, *der;* (worn by guardsmen) Bärenfellmütze, *die*

bus: ∼ **company** *n.* ≈ Verkehrsbetrieb, *der;* ∼ **conductor** *n.* ▶ 887 | Busschaffner, *der;* ∼ **depot** ⇒ ∼ **garage;** ∼ **driver** *n.* ▶ 887 | Busfahrer, *der;* ∼ **fare** *n.* [Bus]fahrpreis, *der;* ∼ **garage** *n.* Busdepot, *das*

bush /bʊʃ/ *n.* (a) (shrub) Strauch, *der;* Busch, *der;* (b) (woodland) Busch, *der*

bushy /'bʊʃɪ/ *adj.* buschig

busily /'bɪzɪlɪ/ *adv.* eifrig

business /'bɪznɪs/ *n.* (a) (trading operation) Geschäft, *das;* (company, firm) Betrieb, *der;* (large) Unternehmen, *das;* (b) *no pl.* (buying and selling) Geschäfte *Pl.;* **on** ∼: geschäftlich; **he's in the wool** ∼: er ist in der Wollbranche; ∼ **is** ∼ (fig.) Geschäft ist Geschäft; **set up in** ∼: ein Geschäft *od.* eine Firma gründen; **go out of** ∼: pleite gehen (ugs.); **go into** ∼: Geschäftsmann/-frau werden; **do** ∼ **[with sb.]** [mit jmdm.] Geschäfte machen; **be in** ∼: Geschäftsmann/-frau

sein; (c) (task, duty, province) Aufgabe, *die;* Pflicht, *die;* **that is 'my** ∼**/none of 'your** ∼: das ist meine Angelegenheit/ nicht deine Sache; **what** ∼ **is it of yours?** was geht Sie das an?; **mind your own** ∼: kümmere dich um deine [eigenen] Angelegenheiten!; **he has no** ∼ **to do that** er hat kein Recht, das zu tun; (d) (matter to be considered) Angelegenheit, *die;* 'any other ∼' „Sonstiges"; (e) (serious work) **get down to [serious]** ∼: [ernsthaft] zur Sache kommen; (Commerc.) an die Arbeit gehen; **mean** ∼: es ernst meinen; ∼ **before pleasure** erst die Arbeit, dann das Vergnügen; (f) (derog.: affair) Sache, *die;* Geschichte, *die* (ugs.)

business: ∼ **address** *n.* Geschäftsadresse, *die;* ∼ **card** *n.* Geschäftskarte, *die;* ∼ **class** *n., no pl.* Businessklasse, *die; attrib.* Businessklasse-; **2** *adv.* **fly/travel** ∼ **class** in der Businessklasse fliegen/reisen; ∼ **hours** *n. pl.* Geschäftszeit, *die;* (in office) Dienstzeit, *die;* ∼ **letter** *n.* Geschäftsbrief, *der;* ∼**like** *adj.* geschäftsmäßig ⟨*Art*⟩; sachlich, nüchtern ⟨*Untersuchung*⟩; geschäftstüchtig ⟨*Person*⟩; ∼ **lunch** *n.* Arbeitsessen, *das;* ∼**man** *n.* ▶ 887 | Geschäftsmann, *der;* ∼ **park** *n.* Gewerbepark, *der;* ∼ **plan** *n.* Geschäftsplan, *der;* ∼ **school** *n.* kaufmännische Fachschule; ∼ **studies** *n. pl.* Wirtschaftslehre, *die;* ∼ **trip** *n.* Geschäftsreise, *die;* ∼**woman** *n.* ▶ 887 | Geschäftsfrau, *die*

busker /'bʌskə(r)/ *n.* Straßenmusikant, *der*

bus: ∼ **lane** *n.* (Brit.) Busspur, *die;* ∼ **ride** *n.* Busfahrt, *die;* ∼ **route** *n.* Buslinie, *die;* ∼ **service** *n.* Omnibusverkehr, *der;* (specific service) Busverbindung, *die;* ∼ **shelter** *n.* Wartehäuschen, *das;* ∼ **station** *n.* Omnibusbahnhof, *der;* ∼ **stop** *n.* Bushaltestelle, *die*

bust[1] /bʌst/ *n.* (a) (sculpture) Büste, *die;* (b) (woman's bosom) Busen, *der;* ∼ **[measurement]** Oberweite, *die*

bust[2] (coll.) **1** *adj.* (a) (broken) kaputt (ugs.); (b) (bankrupt) bankrott; pleite (ugs.); **go** ∼: pleite gehen. **2** *v.t.,* ∼**ed** or **bust** (break) kaputtmachen (ugs.); ∼ **sth. open** etw. aufbrechen. **3** *v.i.,* ∼**ed** or **bust** kaputtgehen (ugs.)

'bus ticket *n.* Busfahrkarte, *die;* Busfahrschein, *der*

bustle /'bʌsl/ **1** *v.i.* ∼ **about** geschäftig hin und her eilen; **the town centre was bustling with activity** im Stadtzentrum herrschte ein reges Treiben. **2** *v.t.* jagen (ugs.); treiben (ugs.). **3** *n.* Betrieb, *der;* (of fair, streets also) reges Treiben (**of** auf, in + *Dat.*)

bustling /'bʌslɪŋ/ *adj.* belebt ⟨*Stadt, Markt usw.*⟩; geschäftig ⟨*Person, Art*⟩; rege ⟨*Tätigkeit*⟩

'bust-up *n.* (coll.) Krach, *der* (ugs.); **have a** ∼: Krach haben (ugs.); sich verkrachen (ugs.)

busy /'bɪzɪ/ **1** *adj.* (a) (occupied) beschäftigt; **I'm** ∼ **now** ich habe jetzt zu tun; **be** ∼ **at** or **with sth.** mit etw. beschäftigt sein; **he was** ∼ **packing** er war mit Packen beschäftigt *od.* war gerade beim Packen; (b) (full of activity) arbeitsreich ⟨*Leben*⟩; ziemlich hektisch ⟨*Zeit*⟩; belebt ⟨*Stadt*⟩; ausgelastet ⟨*Person*⟩; rege ⟨*Verkehr*⟩; **a** ∼ **road** eine verkehrsreiche *od.* viel befahrene Straße; **the office was** ∼ **all day** im Büro war den ganzen Tag viel los; **I'm/he's a** ∼ **man** ich habe/er hat viel zu tun; (c) (Amer. Teleph.) besetzt. **2** *v. refl.* ∼ **oneself with sth.** sich mit etw. beschäftigen; ∼ **oneself [in] doing sth.** sich damit beschäftigen, etw. zu tun

'busybody *n.* G[e]schaftlhuber, *der* (südd., österr.); **don't be such a** ∼: misch dich nicht überall ein

but 1 /bət, *stressed* bʌt/ *conj.* (a) (contrasting) aber; **Sue wasn't there,** ∼ **her sister was** Sue war nicht da, dafür aber ihre Schwester; **we tried to do it** ∼ **couldn't** wir haben es versucht, aber nicht gekonnt; ∼ **I 'did!** hab' ich doch!; (b) (correcting after a negative sentence) **not that book** ∼ **this one** nicht das Buch, sondern dieses; **not only** ... ∼ **also** nicht nur ..., sondern auch; (c) (subordinating) ohne dass; **never a week passes** ∼ **he phones** keine Woche vergeht, ohne dass er anruft. **2** /bət/ *prep.* außer (+ *Dat.*); **all** ∼ **three** alle außer dreien; **the next** ∼ **one/two** der/die/das über-/überübernächste; **the last** ∼ **one/two** der/die/das vor-/vorvorletzte. **3** /bət/ *adv.* nur; bloß; **if I could** ∼ **talk to her** ...: wenn ich [doch] nur mit ihr sprechen könnte ...; **we can** ∼ **try** wir können es immerhin versuchen. **4** /bʌt/ *n.* Aber, *das;* **no** ∼**s [about it]!** kein Aber!

butane /'bjuːteɪn/ n. (Chem.) Butan, das

butch /bʊtʃ/ adj. betont männlich ‹Frau, Kleidung, Frisur›; betont maskulin, (salopp) macho ‹Mann›

butcher /'bʊtʃə(r)/ 1 n. (a) ▶887▏ Fleischer, der; Metzger, der (bes. westd., südd.); Schlachter, der (nordd.); ~'s [shop] Fleischerei, die; Metzgerei, die (bes. westd., südd.); see also **baker**; (b) (fig.: murderer) [Menschen]schlächter, der. 2 v.t. schlachten; (fig.: murder) niedermetzeln; abschlachten

butchery /'bʊtʃərɪ/ n. (a) ~ [trade or business] Fleischerhandwerk, das; (b) (fig.: needless slaughter) Metzelei, die

butler /'bʌtlə(r)/ n. ▶887▏ Butler, der

butt¹ /bʌt/ n. (vessel) Fass, das; (for rainwater) Tonne, die

butt² n. (a) (end) dickes Ende; (of rifle) Kolben, der; (b) (of cigarette, cigar) Stummel, der

butt³ n. (a) (object of teasing or ridicule) Zielscheibe, die; Gegenstand, der; (b) in pl. (shooting range) Schießstand, der; Waffenjustierstand, der

butt⁴ 1 n. (push) (by person) [Kopf]stoß, der; (by animal) Stoß [mit den Hörnern]. 2 v.i. ‹Person:› [mit dem Kopf] stoßen; ‹Stier, Ziege:› [mit den Hörnern] stoßen. 3 v.t. ‹Person:› mit dem Kopf stoßen; ‹Stier, Ziege:› mit den Hörnern stoßen; ~ **sb. in the stomach** jmdm. mit dem Kopf in den Bauch stoßen
~ **'in** v.i. (fig. coll.) dazwischenreden; **may I** ~ **in?** darf ich mal kurz stören?

butter /'bʌtə(r)/ 1 n. Butter, die; **he looks as if** ~ **wouldn't melt in his mouth** (fig.) er sieht aus, als ob er kein Wässerchen trüben könnte; **melted** ~: zerlassene Butter. 2 v.t. buttern; mit Butter bestreichen
~ **'up** v.t. ~ **sb. up** jmdm. Honig um den Mund od. Bart schmieren (fig.)

butter: ~**-bean** n. Mondbohne, die; Limabohne, die; ~**cup** n. (Bot.) Butterblume, die; ~ **dish** n. Butterdose, die; ~**-fingers** n. sing. Tollpatsch, der (beim Fangen usw.)

butterfly /'bʌtəflaɪ/ n. (a) Schmetterling, der; **have butterflies [in one's stomach]** (fig. coll.) ein flaues Gefühl im Magen haben; (b) ⇒ **butterfly stroke**

'butterfly stroke n. (Swimming) Delphinstil, der

butter: ~ **knife** n. Buttermesser, das; ~**milk** n. Buttermilch, die; ~**scotch** n. Buttertoffee, das

buttock /'bʌtək/ n. ▶672▏ (of person) Hinterbacke, die; ~s Gesäß, das

button /'bʌtn/ 1 n. (on clothing, of electric bell, etc.) Knopf, der. 2 v.t. (fasten) zuknöpfen; ~ **one's lip** (Amer. sl.) die Klappe halten (salopp). 3 v.i. [zu]geknöpft werden
~ **'up** v.t. zuknöpfen; (fig.) erledigen ‹Job›; **have the deal [all]** ~**ed up** das Geschäft unter Dach und Fach haben (ugs.). 2 v.i. [zu]geknöpft werden

button: ~**hole** 1 n. (a) Knopfloch, das; (b) (Brit.: flowers worn in coat-lapel) Knopflochsträußchen, das; (single flower) Knopflochblume, die; Blume im Knopfloch, das. 2 v.t. (detain) zu fassen kriegen (ugs.); **he was** ~**holed by X** X hat sich (Dat.) ihn geschnappt (ugs.); ~ **'mushroom** n. Champignon, der; ~**-through** adj. durchgeknöpft ‹Kleid›

buttress /'bʌtrɪs/ 1 n. (a) (Archit.) Mauerstrebe, die; (b) (fig.) Stütze, die. 2 v.t. ~ [up] (fig.) [unter]stützen; untermauern ‹Argument›

buxom /'bʌksəm/ adj. drall

buy /baɪ/ 1 v.t., **bought** /bɔːt/ (a) kaufen; lösen ‹Fahrkarte›; ~ **sb./oneself sth.** jmdm./sich etw. kaufen; ~ **and sell goods** Waren an- und verkaufen; ~ **sb. a pint** jmdm. einen Halben ausgeben; **he bought them a round** er spendierte ihnen eine Runde; (b) (fig.) erkaufen ‹Sieg, Ruhm, Frieden›; einsparen, gewinnen ‹Zeit›; (c) (bribe) bestechen; kaufen (ugs.); erkaufen ‹Zustimmung›; (d) (coll.) (believe) schlucken (ugs.); glauben; (accept) akzeptieren; **I'll** ~ **that** (believe) ich glaube es [mal]. 2 n. [Ein]kauf, der; **be a good** ~: preiswert sein
~ **'in** v.t. einkaufen ‹Vorräte, Fleisch usw.›
~ **'off** v.t. auszahlen ‹Forderung›; abfinden ‹Anspruchserhebenden›
~ **'out** v.t. auszahlen ‹Aktionär, Partner›; aufkaufen ‹Firma›
~ **'up** v.t. aufkaufen

buyer /'baɪə(r)/ n. (a) Käufer, der/Käuferin, die; **potential** ~: Kaufinteressent, der; (b) ▶887▏ (Commerc.) Einkäufer, der/Einkäuferin, die

'buying power /'baɪɪŋ/ n. Kaufkraft, die

'buyout n. Aufkauf, der; Management-Buy-Out, das (Wirtsch.)

buzz /bʌz/ 1 n. (a) (of insect) Summen, das; (of large insect) Brummen, das; (of smaller or agitated insect) Schwirren, das; (b) (sound of buzzer) Summen, das; **give one's secretary a** ~: über den Summer seine Sekretärin rufen; (c) (of conversation, movement) Gemurmel, das; (d) (coll.: telephone call) [Telefon]anruf, der; **give sb. a** ~: jmdn. anrufen; (e) (coll.: thrill) Nervenkitzel, der (ugs.). 2 v.i. (a) ⇒ **1a:** ‹Insekt:› summen/brummen/schwirren; (b) (signal with buzzer) [mit dem Summer] rufen; (c) ~ **with excitement** in heller Aufregung sein; **the rumour set the office** ~**ing** das Gerücht versetzte das Büro in helle Aufregung; **my ears are** ~**ing** mir sausen die Ohren. 3 v.t. (Aeronaut.) dicht vorbeifliegen an (+ Dat.)
~ **a'bout,** ~ **a'round** 1 v.i. herumschwirren; (fig.) ‹Person:› herumsausen. 2 v.t. ~ **around sth.** um etw. [herum]schwirren
~ **'off** v.i. (coll.) abhauen (salopp); abzischen (salopp)

buzzer /'bʌzə(r)/ n. Summer, der

'buzzword n. Schlagwort, das

by¹ /baɪ/ 1 prep. (a) (near, beside) an (+ Dat.); bei; (next to) neben; **by the window/river** am Fenster/Fluss; **she sat by me** sie saß neben mir; (b) (to position beside) zu; (c) (about, in the possession of) bei; **have sth. by one** etw. bei sich haben; (d) **north-east by east** Nordost auf Ost; (e) **by herself** etc. ⇒ **herself a;** (f) (along) entlang; **by the river** am od. den Fluss entlang; (g) (via) über (+ Akk.); **leave by the door/window** zur Tür hinausgehen/zum Fenster hinaussteigen; **we came by the quickest/shortest route** wir sind die schnellste/kürzeste Strecke gefahren; (h) (passing) vorbei an (+ Dat.); **run/drive by sb./sth.** an jmdm./etw. vorbeilaufen/vorbeifahren; (i) (during) bei; **by day/night** bei Tag/Nacht; tagsüber/nachts; (j) (through the agency of) von; **written by …:** geschrieben von …; (k) (through the means of) durch; **he was killed by lightning/a falling chimney** er ist vom Blitz/von einem umstürzenden Schornstein erschlagen worden; **heated by gas/oil** mit Gas/Öl geheizt; gas-/ölbeheizt; **by bus/ship** etc. mit dem Bus/Schiff usw.; **by air/sea** mit dem Flugzeug/Schiff; **have children by sb.** Kinder von jmdm. haben; (l) ▶706▏ (not later than) bis; **by now/this time** inzwischen; **by next week she will be in China** nächste Woche ist sie schon in China; **by the time this letter reaches you** bis dich dieser Brief erreicht; **by the 20th** bis zum 20.; (m) (indicating unit of time) pro; (indicating unit of length, weight, etc.) -weise; **by the second/minute/hour** pro Sekunde/Minute/Stunde; **rent a house by the year** ein Haus für jeweils ein Jahr mieten; **you can hire a car by the day or by the week** man kann sich (Dat.) ein Auto tageweise oder wochenweise mieten; **day by day/month by month,** **by the day/month** (as each day/month passes) Tag für Tag/Monat für Monat; **cloth by the metre** Stoff am Meter; **sell sth. by the packet/ton/dozen** etw. paket-/tonnenweise/im Dutzend verkaufen; **10 ft. by 20 ft.** 10 [Fuß] mal 20 Fuß; (n) (indicating amount) **by the thousands** zu Tausenden; **one by one** einzeln; **two by two/three by three/four by four** zu zweit/dritt/viert; **little by little** nach und nach; (o) (indicating factor) durch; **8 divided by 2 is 4** 8 geteilt durch 2 ist 4; (p) (indicating extent) um; **wider by a foot** um einen Fuß breiter; **win by ten metres** mit zehn Metern Vorsprung gewinnen; **passed by nine votes to two** mit neun zu zwei Stimmen angenommen; (q) (according to) nach; **by my watch** nach meiner Uhr; (r) (in oaths) bei; **by [Almighty] God** bei Gott[, dem Allmächtigen]. 2 adv. (a) (past) vorbei; **drive/run/flow by** vorbeifahren/-laufen/-fließen; (b) (near) **close/near by** in der Nähe; (c) **by and large** im großen und ganzen; **by and by** nach und nach; (in past) nach einer Weile

by² ⇒ **bye**²

bye¹ /baɪ/ int. (coll.) tschüs (ugs.); ~ **[for] now!** bis später!; tschüs! (ugs.)

bye² *n.* by the ∼ = by the way ⇒ **way 1 g**
bye-law ⇒ **by-law**
'by-election *n.* Nachwahl, *die*
'bygone 1 *n.* let ∼s be ∼s die Vergangenheit ruhen lassen. **2** *adj.* **[in]** ∼ **days** [in] vergangene[n] Tage[n]
'by-law *n.* (esp. Brit.) Verordnung, *die;* **the park** ∼s die Parkordnung
'bypass 1 *n.* (road) Umgehungsstraße, *die;* (channel; also Electr.) Nebenleitung, *die;* (Med.) Bypass, *der;* ∼ **surgery** (Med.) eine Bypassoperation/Bypassoperationen. **2** *v.t.* **(a)** **the road** ∼es **the town** die Straße führt um die Stadt herum; **(b)** (fig.: ignore) übergehen
'by-product *n.* Nebenprodukt, *das*
'by-road *n.* Nebenstraße, *die;* Seitenstraße, *die*
bystander /'baɪstændə(r)/ *n.* Zuschauer, *der*/Zuschauerin, *die*
byte /baɪt/ *n.* (Computing) Byte, *das*
'byway *n.* Seitenweg, *der*
'byword *n.* (notable example) Inbegriff, *der* (**for** *Gen.*)
Byzantine /bɪˈzæntaɪn, baɪˈzæntaɪn/ *adj.* byzantinisch

....

Cc

....

C, c /siː/ *n., pl.* **Cs** *or* **C's** **(a)** (letter) C, c, *das;* **(b)** **C** (Mus.) C, c, *das;* **C sharp** cis, Cis, *das*
C. *abbr.* **(a)** ▶1141 **Celsius** C; **(b)** ▶1141 **Centigrade** C; **(c)** (Geogr.) **Cape;** **(d)** (Polit.) **Conservative**
c. *abbr.* **(a)** circa ca.; **(b)** ▶938 **cent[s]** c
© *symb.* **copyright** ©
ca. *abbr.* circa ca.
cab /kæb/ *n.* **(a)** (taxi) Taxi, *das;* **(b)** (of lorry, truck) Fahrerhaus, *das;* (of train) Führerstand, *der*
CAB *abbr.* **Citizens' Advice Bureau** ≈ Bürgerbüro, *das*
cabaret /'kæbəreɪ/ *n.* Varietee, *das;* (satirical) Kabarett, *das*
cabbage /'kæbɪdʒ/ *n.* **(a)** Kohl, *der;* **red** ∼: Rotkohl, *der;* **a [head of]** ∼: ein Kopf Kohl; ein Kohlkopf; **(b)** (coll.: incapacitated person) **become a** ∼: dahinvegetieren
cabbage 'white *n.* (Zool.) Kohlweißling, *der*
cabby /'kæbɪ/ (coll.), **'cab driver** *ns.* Taxifahrer, *der*
cabin /'kæbɪn/ *n.* **(a)** (in ship) (for passengers) Kabine, *die;* (for crew) Kajüte, *die;* (in aircraft) Kabine, *die;* **(b)** (simple dwelling) Hütte, *die*
cabin: ∼ **boy** *n.* (Naut.) Kabinensteward, *der;* ∼ **cruiser** *n.* Kajütboot, *das*
cabinet /'kæbɪnɪt/ *n.* **(a)** Schrank, *der;* (in bathroom, for medicines) Schränkchen, *das;* (display ∼) Vitrine, *die;* **(b)** (Polit.) Kabinett, *das*
cabinet: ∼**maker** *n.* ▶887 Möbeltischler, *der;* **C**∼ **'Minister** *n.* Minister, *der*/Ministerin, *die*
cable /'keɪbl/ **1** *n.* **(a)** (rope) Kabel, *das;* (of ∼ car etc.) Seil, *das;* **(b)** (Electr., Teleph.) Kabel, *das;* **(c)** (telegram) Kabel, *das* (veralt.); [Übersee]telegramm, *das.* **2** *v.t.* (transmit) telegraphisch durchgeben, kabeln ⟨*Mitteilung, Nachricht*⟩; (inform) ∼ **sb.** jmdm. kabeln
cable: ∼ **car** *n.* Drahtseilbahn, *die;* (in street) gezogene Straßenbahn; ∼**-knit** *adj.* ∼**-knit sweater/cardigan** Pullover/Strickjacke mit Zopfmuster; ∼ **'railway** *n.* Standseilbahn, *die;* ∼ **'television** *n.* Kabelfernsehen, *das;* ∼ **TV** *n.* Kabelfernsehen, *das*
caboodle /kə'buːdl/ *n., no pl.* (coll.) **the whole** ∼: der ganze Kram (ugs.); das ganze Gelumpe (ugs.)
cache /kæʃ/ **1** *n.* geheimes [Waffen-/Proviant-]lager. **2** *v.t.* verstecken
cackle /'kækl/ **1** *n.* **(a)** (clucking of hen) Gackern, *das;* **(b)** (laughter) [meckerndes] Gelächter; (laugh) **he gave a loud**

∼: er prustete los (ugs.). **2** *v.i.* **(a)** ⟨*Henne:*⟩ gackern; **(b)** (laugh) meckernd lachen
cacophony /kə'kɒfənɪ/ *n.* Kakophonie, *die* (geh.); Missklang, *der*
cactus /'kæktəs/ *n., pl.* **cacti** /'kæktaɪ/ *or* ∼**es** Kaktus, *der*
CAD *abbr.* **computer-aided design** CAD
caddie /'kædɪ/ (Golf) **1** *n.* Caddie, *der.* **2** *v.i.* ∼ **for sb.** jmds. Caddie sein
caddy¹ /'kædɪ/ *n.* Behälter, *der;* (tin) Büchse, *die;* Dose, *die*
caddy² ⇒ **caddie**
cadet /kə'det/ *n.* Offiziersschüler, *der;* **naval/police** ∼: Marinekadett/Anwärter für den Polizeidienst
cadge /kædʒ/ **1** *v.t.* schnorren (ugs.); [sich (*Dat.*)] erbetteln; **could I** ∼ **a lift?** können Sie mich vielleicht [ein Stück] mitnehmen? **2** *v.i.* schnorren (ugs.)
cadger /'kædʒə(r)/ *n.* Schnorrer, *der* (ugs.)
CAE *abbr.* **computer-aided engineering** CAE
Caesar /'siːzə(r)/ *n.* Cäsar, Caesar (*der*)
Caesarean, Caesarian /sɪˈzeərɪən/ *adj. & n.* ∼ **[section]** Kaiserschnitt, *der*
café, cafe /'kæfeɪ/ *n.* Café, *das*
cafeteria /kæfɪˈtɪərɪə/ *n.* Selbstbedienungsrestaurant, *das*
cafetière /kæfə'tjeə/ *n.* Kaffeebereiter, *der*
caffeinated /'kæfɪneɪtɪd/ *adj.* koffeinhaltig
caffeine /'kæfiːn/ *n.* Koffein, *das;* (in tea) T[h]ein, *das*
caftan /'kæftæn/ *n.* Kaftan, *der*
cage /keɪdʒ/ **1** *n.* **(a)** Käfig, *der;* (for small birds) Bauer, *das;* **(b)** (of lift) Fahrkabine, *die.* **2** *v.t.* einsperren; käfigen (fachspr.) ⟨*Vögel*⟩
'cage bird *n.* Käfigvogel, *der*
cagey /'keɪdʒɪ/ *adj.* (coll.) (wary) vorsichtig (**about** bei); (secretive, uncommunicative) zugeknöpft (ugs.)
cagily /'keɪdʒɪlɪ/ *adv.* (coll.) vorsichtig
caginess /'keɪdʒɪnɪs/ *n.* (coll.) (caution) Vorsicht, *die;* (secretiveness) Zugeknöpftheit, *die* (ugs.)
cagoule /kə'guːl/ *n.* [leichter, knielanger] Anorak
cairn /keən/ *n.* Steinpyramide, *die*
Cairo /'kaɪrəʊ/ *pr. n.* ▶1159 Kairo (*das*)
cajole /kə'dʒəʊl/ *v.t.* ∼ **sb. into sth./into doing sth.** jmdm. etw. einreden/jmdm. einreden, etw. zu tun
cake /keɪk/ **1** *n.* **(a)** Kuchen, *der;* **a piece of** ∼: ein Stück Kuchen/Torte; (fig. coll.) ein Kinderspiel (ugs.); **a slice of** ∼: eine Scheibe Kuchen; **go** *or* **sell like hot** ∼s weggehen wie warme Semmeln (ugs.); **you cannot have your** ∼ **and eat it** (fig.) beides auf einmal geht nicht; *see also* **take 1 c;** **(b)** (block) **a** ∼ **of soap** ein Riegel *od.* Stück Seife. **2** *v.t.* (cover) verkrusten; ∼**d with dirt/blood** schmutz-/blutverkrustet. **3** *v.i.* (form a mass) verklumpen
cake: ∼ **shop** *n.* Konditorei, *die;* ∼ **slice** *n.* Tortenheber, *der;* ∼ **stand** *n.* Etagere, *die*
cal. *abbr.* **calorie[s]** cal.
CAL /kæl/ *abbr.* **computer-aided** *or* **computer-assisted learning** computergestütztes Lernen
calamity /kə'læmɪtɪ/ *n.* Unheil, *das;* Unglück, *das*
calcium /'kælsɪəm/ *n.* Kalzium, *das;* Calcium, *das* (fachspr.)
calculate /'kælkjʊleɪt/ **1** *v.t.* **(a)** (ascertain) berechnen; (by estimating) ausrechnen; **(b)** (plan) **be** ∼**d to do sth.** darauf abzielen, etw. zu tun; **(c)** (Amer. coll.: suppose) schätzen (ugs.). **2** *v.i.* **(a)** (Math.) rechnen; **(b)** ∼ **on doing sth.** damit rechnen, etw. zu tun
calculated /'kælkjʊleɪtɪd/ *adj.* vorsätzlich ⟨*Handlung, Straftat*⟩; bewusst ⟨*Zurückhaltung, Affront*⟩; kalkuliert ⟨*Risiko*⟩
calculating /'kælkjʊleɪtɪŋ/ *adj.* berechnend
calculation /kælkjʊ'leɪʃn/ *n.* **(a)** (result) Rechnung, *die;* **he is out in his** ∼s er hat sich verrechnet; **(b)** (calculating) Berechnung, *die;* **(c)** (forecast) Schätzung, *die;* **by my** ∼s nach meiner Schätzung

calculator /ˈkælkjʊleɪtə(r)/ n. Rechner, der

calculus /ˈkælkjʊləs/ n., pl. **calculi** /ˈkælkjʊlaɪ/ or **~es** (Math. etc.) Analysis, die; **[the] differential/integral** ~: [die] Differenzial-/Integralrechnung

Calcutta /kælˈkʌtə/ pr. n. ▶ 1159 | Kalkutta (das)

calendar /ˈkælɪndə(r)/ n. (a) Kalender, der; attrib. Kalender‹woche, -monat, -jahr›; **[church]** ~: Kirchenkalender, der; (b) (register, list) Verzeichnis, das

calf¹ /kɑːf/ n., pl. **calves** /kɑːvz/ (a) Kalb, das; (leather) Kalbsleder, das; (b) (of deer) Kalb, das; (of elephant, whale, rhinoceros) Junge, das

calf² n., pl. **calves** ▶ 672 | (Anat.) Wade, die

'calfskin n. (leather) Kalbsleder, das

caliber (Amer.) ⇒ **calibre**

calibrate /ˈkælɪbreɪt/ v.t. kalibrieren

calibration /kælɪˈbreɪʃn/ n. Kalibrierung, die

calibre /ˈkælɪbə(r)/ n. (Brit.) (a) (diameter) Kaliber, das; (b) (fig.) Format, das; **a man of your** ~: ein Mann von Ihrem Format

calico /ˈkælɪkəʊ/ **1** n., pl. **~es** Kattun, der. **2** adj. Kattun-

California /kælɪˈfɔːnɪə/ pr. n. Kalifornien (das)

caliper ⇒ **calliper**

call /kɔːl/ **1** v.i. (a) (shout) rufen; ~ **to sb.** jmdm. zurufen; ~ **[out] for help** um Hilfe rufen; ~ **[out] for sb.** nach jmdm. rufen; ~ **after sb.** jmdm. hinterherrufen; (b) (pay brief visit) [kurz] besuchen (at Akk.); vorbeikommen (ugs.) (at bei); ‹Zug:› halten (at in + Dat.); ~ **at a port/station** einen Hafen anlaufen/an einem Bahnhof halten; ~ **on sb.** jmdn. besuchen; bei jmdm. vorbeigehen (ugs.); **the postman ~ed to deliver a parcel** der Postbote war da und brachte ein Päckchen; ~ **round** vorbeikommen (ugs.); (c) (telephone) **who is ~ing, please?** wer spricht da, bitte?; **thank you for ~ing** vielen Dank für Ihren Anruf!; (broadcast) **this is London ~ing** hier spricht od. ist London. **2** v.t. (a) (cry out) rufen; aufrufen ‹Namen, Nummer›; (b) (cry to) rufen ‹Person›; (c) (summon) rufen; (to a duty, to do sth.) aufrufen; ~ **sb.'s bluff** es darauf ankommen lassen (ugs.); **that was ~ed in question** das wurde infrage gestellt od. in Zweifel gezogen; **please ~ me a taxi** or ~ **a taxi for me** bitte rufen Sie mir ein Taxi; (d) (radio/telephone) rufen/anrufen; (initially) Kontakt aufnehmen mit; **don't ~ us, we'll ~ you** wir sagen Ihnen Bescheid; (e) (rouse) wecken; (f) (announce) einberufen ‹Konferenz›; ausrufen ‹Streik›; ~ **a halt to sth.** mit etw. Schluss machen; ~ **time** (in pub) ≈ „Feierabend" rufen; (g) (name) nennen; **he is ~ed Bob** er heißt Bob; **you can ~ him by his first name** ihr könnt ihn mit Vornamen anreden; **what is it ~ed in English?** wie heißt das auf Englisch?; ~ **sb. names** jmdn. beschimpfen; (h) (consider) nennen; (i) (Cards etc.) ansagen. **3** n. (a) (shout, cry) Ruf, der; **a ~ for help** ein Hilferuf; **can you give me a ~ at 6 o'clock?** können Sie mich um 6 Uhr wecken?; **remain/be within ~:** in Rufweite bleiben/sein; **on ~:** dienstbereit; (b) (of bugle, whistle) Signal, das; (c) (visit) Besuch, der; **make** or **pay a ~ on sb., make** or **pay sb. a ~:** jmdn. besuchen; **have to pay a ~** (coll.: need lavatory) mal [verschwinden] müssen (ugs.); (d) (telephone) Anruf, der; Gespräch, das; **give sb. a ~:** jmdn. anrufen; **make a ~:** ein Telefongespräch führen; **receive a ~:** einen Anruf erhalten; (e) (invitation, summons) Aufruf, der; **the ~ of the sea/the wild** der Ruf des Meeres/der Wildnis; ~ **of nature** natürlicher Drang; **answer the ~ of duty** der Pflicht gehorchen; (f) (need, occasion) Anlass, der; Veranlassung, die; (g) (esp. Comm.: demand) Abruf, der; **have many ~s on one's purse/time** finanziell/zeitlich sehr in Anspruch genommen sein; (h) (Cards etc.) Ansage, die; **it's your ~:** du musst ansagen

~ **a'way** v.t. wegrufen; abrufen

~ **'back** **1** v.t. zurückrufen. **2** v.i. (come back) zurückkommen; noch einmal vorbeikommen (ugs.)

~ **'down** v.t. (invoke) herabflehen (geh.) ‹Segen›; herausfordern ‹Unwillen, Tadel›; ~ **down curses on sb.'s head** jmdn. verfluchen

~ **for** v.t. (a) (send for, order) [sich (Dat.)] kommen lassen, bestellen ‹Taxi, Essen, Person›; (b) (collect) abholen ‹Person, Güter›; **'to be ~ed for'** „wird abgeholt"; (c) (require, demand) erfordern; verlangen; **that remark was not**

~**ed for** die Bemerkung war unangebracht; **this ~s for a celebration** das muss gefeiert werden

~ **'in** **1** v.i. vorbeikommen (ugs.); **I'll ~ in on you** ich komme bei dir vorbei (ugs.); **I'll ~ in at your office** ich komme bei dir im Büro vorbei (ugs.). **2** v.t. (a) aus dem Verkehr ziehen ‹Waren, Münzen›; (b) ~ **in a specialist** einen Fachmann/Facharzt zurate ziehen

~ **'off** v.t. (cancel) absagen ‹Treffen, Verabredung›; rückgängig machen ‹Geschäft›; lösen ‹Verlobung›; (stop, end) abbrechen, (ugs.) abblasen ‹Streik›; ~ **off your dogs!** rufen Sie Ihre Hunde zurück!

~ **on** ⇒ ~ **[up]on**

~ **'out** **1** v.t. alarmieren ‹Truppen›; rufen ‹Wache›; zum Streik aufrufen ‹Arbeitnehmer›. **2** v.i. ⇒ ~ **1 a**

~ **'up** v.t. (a) (imagine, recollect) wachrufen ‹Erinnerungen, Bilder›; [herauf]beschwören, erwecken ‹böse Erinnerungen, Fantasien›; (b) (summon) anrufen, beschwören ‹Teufel, Geister›; (c) (telephone) anrufen; (d) (Mil.) einberufen

~ **[up]on** v.t. ~ **upon God** Gott anrufen; ~ **upon sb.'s generosity/sense of justice** an jmds. Großzügigkeit/Gerechtigkeitssinn (Akk.) appellieren; ~ **[up]on sb. to do sth.** jmdn. auffordern, etw. zu tun

call: ~ box n. Telefonzelle, die; ~ **centre** n Callcenter, das

caller /ˈkɔːlə(r)/ n. (visitor) Besucher, der/Besucherin, die; (on telephone) Anrufer, der/Anruferin, die

'call-girl n. Callgirl, das

calligraphy /kəˈlɪɡrəfɪ/ n. Kalligraphie, die; Schönschreiben, das

calling /ˈkɔːlɪŋ/ n. (a) (occupation, profession) Beruf, der; (b) (divine summons) Berufung, die

calliper /ˈkælɪpə(r)/ n. (a) in pl. **[pair of] ~s** Tasterzirkel, der; (b) ~ **[splint]** (Med.) Beinschiene, die

callous /ˈkæləs/ adj. gefühllos; herzlos ‹Handlung, Verhalten›

'call out n. Einsatz, der; **the ~ could come at any time** es kann jederzeit eine Einsatzanforderung kommen; ~ **fee/charge** Anfahrtskosten Pl.

callow /ˈkæləʊ/ adj. unreif ‹Junge, Student›; grün (ugs.) ‹Jüngling›

call: ~ sign, ~ signal ns. Rufzeichen, das; ~**-up** n. (Mil.) Einberufung, die

calm /kɑːm/ **1** n. (a) (stillness) Stille, die; (serenity) Ruhe, die; (b) (windless period) Windstille, die; **the ~ before the storm** (lit. or fig.) die Ruhe vor dem Sturm. **2** adj. (a) (tranquil, quiet, windless) ruhig; **keep ~:** ruhig bleiben; Ruhe bewahren; (b) (coll.: self-confident) gelassen. **3** v.t. besänftigen ‹Leidenschaften, Zorn›; ~ **sb. [down]** jmdn. beruhigen. **4** v.i. ~ **[down]** sich beruhigen; ‹Sturm:› abflauen

calmly /ˈkɑːmlɪ/ adv. ruhig; gelassen

calmness /ˈkɑːmnɪs/ n., no pl. Ruhe, die; (of water) Stille, die

Calor gas, (P) /ˈkælə ɡæs/ n. Butangas, das

calorie /ˈkælərɪ/ n. Kalorie, die

calve /kɑːv/ v.i. kalben

calves pl. of **calf¹, ²**

cam /kæm/ n. Nocken, der

CAM abbr. **computer-aided manufacturing** CAM

camber /ˈkæmbə(r)/ n. Wölbung, die

Cambodia /kæmˈbəʊdɪə/ pr. n. (Hist.) Kambodscha (das)

Cambodian /kæmˈbəʊdɪən/ (Hist.) ▶ 947 | **1** adj. kambodschanisch. **2** n. Kambodschaner, der/Kambodschanerin, die

camcorder /ˈkæmkɔːdə(r)/ n. Camcorder, der; Kamerarekorder, der

came ⇒ **come**

camel /ˈkæml/ n. (Zool.) Kamel, das

cameo /ˈkæmɪəʊ/ n., pl. ~**s** (a) (carving) Kamee, die; (b) (minor role) [winzige] Nebenrolle

camera /ˈkæmərə/ n. Kamera, die; (for still pictures) Fotoapparat, der; Kamera, die

camera: ~man n. ▶ 887 | Kameramann, der; ~**work** n., no pl., no indef. art. Kameraführung, die

Cameroon /'kæməru:n/ *pr. n.* Kamerun (*das*)

camomile /'kæməmaɪl/ *n.* (Bot.) Kamille, *die;* ∼ **tea** Kamillentee, *der*

camouflage /'kæməflɑ:ʒ/ **1** *n.* (lit. or fig.) Tarnung, *die.* **2** *v.t.* (lit. or fig.) tarnen

camp¹ /kæmp/ **1** *n.* Lager, *das;* (Mil.) Feldlager, *das;* **two opposing** ∼**s** (fig.) zwei entgegengesetzte Lager. **2** *v.i.* ∼ [**out**] campen; (in tent) zelten; **go** ∼**ing** Campen/Zelten fahren/gehen

camp² **1** *adj.* **(a)** (affected) affektiert ⟨*Person, Art, Benehmen*⟩; **(b)** (exaggerated) übertrieben ⟨*Gestik, Ausdrucksform*⟩. **2** *n.* Manieriertheit, *die.* **3** *v.t.* ∼ **it up** zu dick auftragen (ugs.)

campaign /kæm'peɪn/ **1** *n.* **(a)** (Mil.) Feldzug, *der;* **(b)** (organized course of action) Kampagne, *die;* **(c)** (for election) Wahlkampf, *der; see also* **presidential. 2** *v.i.* ∼ **for sth.** sich für etw. einsetzen; ∼ **against sth.** gegen etw. etwas unternehmen; **be** ∼**ing** (for election) ⟨*Politiker:*⟩ im Wahlkampf stehen; ∼ **hard** einen intensiven Wahlkampf führen

campaigner /kæm'peɪnə(r)/ *n.* **(a)** Vorkämpfer, *der*/Vorkämpferin, *die;* **(b)** (veteran) Veteran, *der;* alter Kämpfer; **an old** ∼: ein alter Kämpfer *od.* (veralt.) Kämpe; **(c)** ∼ **for** ...: Anhänger, *der*/Anhängerin, *die* (+ *Gen.*); ∼ **against** ...: Gegner, *der*/Gegnerin, *die* (+ *Gen.*)

cam'paign trail *n.* Wahlkampfreise, *die;* **on the** ∼: im Wahlkampf

'camp bed *n.* Campingliege, *die*

camper /'kæmpə(r)/ *n.* **(a)** Camper, *der*/Camperin, *die;* **(b)** ∼ [**van**] (vehicle) Wohnmobil, *das;* (adapted minibus) Campingbus, *der*

camp: ∼**fire** *n.* Lagerfeuer, *das;* ∼ **follower** *n.* Marketender, *der*/Marketenderin, *die;* (fig.: disciple, follower) Mitläufer, *der*/Mitläuferin, *die*

camping /'kæmpɪŋ/ *n.* Camping, *das;* (in tent) Zelten, *das*

camping: ∼ **ground** (Amer.) ⇒ ∼ **site;** ∼ **holiday** *n.* Campingurlaub, *der;* ∼ **site** *n.* Campingplatz, *der*

'campsite *n.* Campingplatz, *der*

campus /'kæmpəs/ *n.* Campus, *der;* Hochschulgelände, *das*

'camshaft *n.* Nockenwelle, *die*

can¹ /kæn/ **1** *n.* **(a)** (milk ∼, watering ∼) Kanne, *die;* (for oil, petrol) Kanister, *der;* (Amer.: for refuse) Eimer, *der;* Tonne, *die;* **a** ∼ **of paint** eine Büchse Farbe; (with handle) ein Eimer Farbe; **carry the** ∼ (fig. coll.) die Sache ausbaden (ugs.); **(b)** (container for preserving) [Konserven]dose, *die;* [Konserven]büchse, *die;* **a** ∼ **of tomatoes/sausages** eine Dose *od.* Büchse Tomaten/Würstchen; **a** ∼ **of beer** eine Dose Bier; **(c)** (Amer. sl.: lavatory) Lokus, *der* (ugs.). **2** *v.t.,* **-nn-** eindosen; einmachen ⟨*Obst*⟩

can² *v. aux., only in pres.* **can,** *neg.* **cannot** /'kænət/, (coll.) **can't** /kɑ:nt/, *past* **could** /kʊd/, *neg.* (coll.) **couldn't** /'kʊdnt/ können; (have right, be permitted) dürfen; können; **as much as one** ∼: so viel man kann; **as … as '**∼ **be** wirklich sehr ...; ∼ **do** (coll.) kein Problem; **he can't be more than 40** er kann nicht über 40 sein; **you can't smoke in this compartment** in diesem Abteil dürfen Sie nicht rauchen; **I can't hear what you're saying** ich kann Sie nicht verstehen; **how [ever] could you do this to me?** wie konnten Sie mir das bloß antun?; **I could have killed him** ich hätte ihn umbringen können; [**that**] **could be** [**so**] das könnte *od.* kann sein

Canada /'kænədə/ *pr. n.* Kanada (*das*)

Canadian /kə'neɪdɪən/ ▶**947**┙ **1** *adj.* kanadisch; **sb. is** ∼: jmd. ist Kanadier/Kanadierin. **2** *n.* Kanadier, *der*/Kanadierin, *die;* **the French/English** ∼**s** die Franko-/Anglokanadier

canal /kə'næl/ *n.* Kanal, *der;* **the Panama C**∼: der Panamakanal

ca'nal boat *n.: langes, enges Boot zum Befahren der Kanäle*

Canaries /kə'neərɪz/ *pr. n. pl.* Kanarische Inseln *Pl.*

canary /kə'neərɪ/ *n.* Kanarienvogel, *der*

canary: ∼ **'yellow** *n.* Kanariengelb, *das;* ∼**-yellow** *adj.* kanariengelb

cancan /'kænkæn/ *n.* Cancan, *der*

cancel /'kænsl/ **1** *v.t.,* (Brit.) **-ll-: (a)** (call off) absagen ⟨*Besuch, Urlaub, Reise, Sportveranstaltung*⟩; ausfallen lassen ⟨*Veranstaltung, Vorlesung, Zug, Bus*⟩; fallen lassen ⟨*Pläne*⟩; (annul, revoke) rückgängig machen ⟨*Einladung, Vertrag*⟩; zurücknehmen ⟨*Befehl*⟩; stornieren ⟨*Bestellung, Auftrag*⟩; streichen ⟨*Schuld[en]*⟩; kündigen ⟨*Abonnement*⟩; abbestellen ⟨*Zeitung*⟩; aufheben ⟨*Klausel, Gesetz, Recht*⟩; **the match had to be** ∼**led** das Spiel musste ausfallen; **the lecture has been** ∼**led** die Vorlesung fällt aus; **(b)** (balance, neutralize) aufheben; **the arguments** ∼ **each other out** die Argumente heben sich gegenseitig auf; **(c)** entwerten ⟨*Briefmarke, Fahrkarte*⟩; ungültig machen ⟨*Scheck*⟩. **2** *v.i.,* (Brit.) **-ll-:** ∼ [**out**] sich [gegenseitig] aufheben

cancellation /kænsə'leɪʃn/ *n.* ⇒ **cancel 1: (a)** Absage, *die;* Ausfall, *der;* Ausfallen, *das;* Fallenlassen, *das;* Rückgängigmachen, *das;* [Zu]rücknahme, *die;* Stornierung, *die;* Streichung, *die;* Kündigung, *die;* Abbestellung, *die;* Aufhebung, *die;* **(b)** Aufhebung, *die;* **(c)** Entwertung, *die;* Ungültigmachen, *das*

cancer /'kænsə(r)/ *n.* **(a)** ▶**865**┙ (Med.) Krebs, *der;* ∼ **of the liver** Leberkrebs, *der;* **(b) C**∼ (Astrol., Astron.) der Krebs; *see also* **tropic**

cancerous /'kænsərəs/ *adj.* Krebs⟨*geschwulst, -geschwür*⟩; krebsartig ⟨*Wucherung*⟩

candelabra /kændɪ'lɑ:brə/ *n.* Leuchter, *der;* (large) Kandelaber, *der*

candid /'kændɪd/ *adj.* offen; ehrlich ⟨*Ansicht, Bericht*⟩

candidate /'kændɪdət, 'kændɪdeɪt/ *n.* (Polit., examinee) Kandidat, *der*/Kandidatin, *die;* ∼ **for Mayor** Bürgermeisterkandidat/-kandidatin

candidly /'kændɪdlɪ/ *adv.* offen; ehrlich

candle /kændl/ *n.* Kerze, *die;* **burn the** ∼ **at both ends** (fig.) sich (*Dat.*) zu viel aufladen; **the game is not worth the** ∼ (fig.) die Sache ist nicht der Mühe (*Gen.*) wert

candle: ∼**light** *n.* Kerzenlicht, *das;* ∼**stick** *n.* Kerzenhalter, *der;* (elaborate) Leuchter, *der;* ∼**wick** *n.* (material) Frottierplüsch, *der*

candour (Brit.; Amer.: **candor**) /'kændə(r)/ *n.* Offenheit, *die;* Ehrlichkeit, *die*

candy /'kændɪ/ **1** *n.* (Amer.) (sweets) Süßigkeiten *Pl.;* (sweet) Bonbon, *das od. der.* **2** *v.t.* kandieren ⟨*Früchte*⟩; **candied lemon/orange peel** Zitronat/Orangeat, *das*

'candyfloss *n.* Zuckerwatte, *die*

cane /keɪn/ **1** *n.* **(a)** (stem of bamboo, rattan, etc.) Rohr, *das;* (of raspberry, blackberry) Spross, *der;* **(b)** (material) Rohr, *das;* **(c)** (stick) [Rohr]stock, *der;* **get the** ∼: eine Tracht Prügel bekommen. **2** *v.t.* (beat) [mit dem Stock] schlagen

cane: ∼ **chair** *n.* Rohrstuhl, *der;* ∼ **sugar** *n.* Rohrzucker, *der*

canine /'keɪnaɪn/ **1** *adj.* **(a)** (of dog[s]) Hunde-; **(b)** ∼ **tooth** Eckzahn, *der;* Augenzahn, *der.* **2** *n.* Eckzahn, *der;* Augenzahn, *der*

canister /'kænɪstə(r)/ *n.* Büchse, *die;* Dose, *die;* (for petrol, oil, DDT, etc.) Kanister, *der*

cannabis /'kænəbɪs/ *n.* (drug) Haschisch, *das;* Marihuana, *das*

canned /kænd/ *adj.* **(a)** Dosen-; in Dosen *nachgestellt;* ∼ **fish/meat/fruit** Fisch-/Fleisch-/Obstkonserven *Pl.;* ∼ **beer** Dosenbier; ∼ **food** [Lebensmittel]konserven *Pl.;* **(b)** (sl.: drunk) abgefüllt (ugs.); **(c)** (recorded) aufgezeichnet; ∼ **music** Musikkonserve, *die*

cannibal /'kænɪbl/ *n.* Kannibale, *der*/Kannibalin, *die;* Menschenfresser, *der*/-fresserin, *die* (ugs.)

cannibalism /'kænɪbəlɪzm/ *n.* Kannibalismus, *der;* Menschenfresserei, *die* (ugs.)

cannibalize /'kænɪbəlaɪz/ *v.t.* ausschlachten ⟨*Auto, Flugzeug, Maschine usw.*⟩

cannily /'kænɪlɪ/ *adv.* (shrewdly) schlau; (cautiously) vorsichtig

cannon /'kænən/ **1** *n.* Kanone, *die.* **2** *v.i.* (Brit.) ∼ **against sth.** gegen etw. prallen; ∼ **into sb./sth.** mit etw./jmdm. zusammenprallen

cannon: ∼ **ball** n. (Hist.) Kanonenkugel, die; ∼ **fodder** n. Kanonenfutter, das (salopp abwertend)

cannot ⇒ **can²**

canny /'kænɪ/ adj. (a) (shrewd) schlau; bauernschlau (ugs.); (thrifty) sparsam; (b) (cautious, wary) vorsichtig; umsichtig

canoe /kə'nu:/ **1** n. Paddelboot, das; (Indian ∼, Sport) Kanu, das. **2** v.i. paddeln; (in Indian ∼, Sport) Kanu fahren

canoeing /kə'nu:ɪŋ/ n. Paddeln, das; (Sport) Kanusport, der

canoeist /kə'nu:ɪst/ n. Paddelbootfahrer, der/-fahrerin, die; (Sport) Kanute, der/Kanutin, die

canon /'kænən/ n. (a) (rule) Grundregel, die; (b) ▶ 1152 | (priest) Kanoniker, der; (c) (list of sacred books) Kanon, der; (fig.) **the Shakespearean** ∼: das Gesamtwerk Shakespeares

canonisation, canonise ⇒ **canoniz-**

canonization /kænənaɪ'zeɪʃn/ n. Kanonisation, die

canonize /'kænənaɪz/ v.t. heilig sprechen

'can-opener n. Dosen-, Büchsenöffner, der

canopy /'kænəpɪ/ n. Baldachin, der (auch fig.); (over entrance) Vordach, das

cant¹ /kænt/ **1** v.t. kippen; ankippen, kanten ⟨Fass⟩; ∼ **over** umkippen. **2** v.i. sich neigen. **3** n. (tilted position) Schräglage, die

cant² n. (a) (derog.: language of class, sect, etc.) Kauderwelsch, das (abwertend); **thieves'** ∼: Rotwelsch, das; (b) (insincere talk) scheinheiliges Gerede

can't /kɑ:nt/ (coll.) = **cannot;** ⇒ **can²**

cantankerous /kæn'tæŋkərəs/ adj. streitsüchtig; knurrig (ugs.)

cantata /kæn'tɑ:tə/ n. (Mus.) Kantate, die

canteen /kæn'ti:n/ n. (a) Kantine, die; (b) (case of cutlery) Besteckkasten, der

canter /'kæntə(r)/ **1** n. Handgalopp, der; Kanter, Canter, der (fachspr.). **2** v.i. leicht galoppieren; kantern (fachspr.)

cantilever /'kæntɪli:və/ n. (a) (bracket) Konsole, die; Kragplatte, die; ∼ **brake** Cantileverbremse, die; (b) (beam) Träger, der

'cantilever bridge n. Auslegerbrücke, die

canton /'kæntɒn/ n. Kanton, der

Cantonese /kæntə'ni:z/ ▶ 897 |, ▶ 947 | **1** adj. kantonesisch. **2** n., pl. same (a) (person) Kantonese, der/Kantonesin, die; (b) (language) Kantonesisch (das)

canvas /'kænvəs/ n. (a) (cloth) Leinwand, die; (for tents, tarpaulins, etc.) Segeltuch, das; **under** ∼: im Zelt; (Naut.) unter Segel; (b) (Art) Leinwand, die; (painting) Gemälde, das; (for embroidery) Kanevas, der; Gitterleinwand, die

canvass /'kænvəs/ **1** v.t. (a) (solicit votes in or from) Wahlwerbung treiben in ⟨einem Wahlkreis, Gebiet⟩; Wahlwerbung treiben bei ⟨Wählern⟩; (b) (Brit.: propose) vorschlagen ⟨Plan, Idee⟩. **2** v.i. werben (**on behalf of** für); ∼ **for votes** um Stimmen werben

canvasser /'kænvəsə(r)/ n. (for votes) Wahlhelfer, der/ Wahlhelferin, die

canvassing /'kænvəsɪŋ/ n. (for votes) Wahlwerbung, die

canyon /'kænjən/ n. Cañon, der

cap /kæp/ **1** n. (a) Mütze, die; (nurse's, servant's) Haube, die; (bathing ∼) Badekappe, die; (with peak) Schirmmütze, die; (skull∼) Kappe, die; Käppchen, das; (Univ.) viereckige akademische Kopfbedeckung; ≈ Barett, das; **if the** ∼ **fits, [he etc. should]** **wear it** (fig.) wem die Jacke passt, der soll sie sich (Dat.) anziehen; **with** ∼ **in hand** (fig.) demütig; (b) (device to seal or close) [Verschluss]kappe, die; (petrol ∼, radiator ∼) Verschluss, der; (on milk bottle) Deckel, der; (of shoe) Kappe, die; (c) (Brit. Sport) Ziermütze als Zeichen der Aufstellung für die [National]mannschaft; (player) Nationalspieler, der/-spielerin, die; (d) (contraceptive) Pessar, das. **2** v.t., **-pp-:** (a) verschließen ⟨Flasche⟩; mit einer Schutzkappe versehen ⟨Zahn⟩; (b) (Brit. Sport: award ∼ to) aufstellen; (c) (crown with clouds or snow or mist) bedecken; (d) (follow with sth. even more noteworthy) überbieten ⟨Geschichte, Witz usw.⟩; **to** ∼ **it all** obendrein

capability /keɪpə'bɪlɪtɪ/ n. Fähigkeit, die; Vermögen, das (geh.)

capable /'keɪpəbl/ adj. (a) **be** ∼ **of sth.** ⟨Person:⟩ zu etw. imstande sein; **show him what you are** ∼ **of** zeig ihm, wozu du imstande bist od. wessen du fähig bist; (b) (gifted, able) fähig

capably /'keɪpəblɪ/ adv. gekonnt, kompetent ⟨leiten, führen⟩

capacitor /kə'pæsɪtə(r)/ n. (Electr.) Kondensator, der

capacity /kə'pæsɪtɪ/ n. (a) (power) Aufnahmefähigkeit, die; (to do things) Leistungsfähigkeit, die; (b) no pl. (maximum amount) Fassungsvermögen, das; **the machine is working to** ∼: die Maschine ist voll ausgelastet; **a seating** ∼ **of 300** 300 Sitzplätze; **filled to** ∼ ⟨Saal, Theater⟩ bis auf den letzten Platz besetzt; attrib. **the film drew** ∼ **audiences/houses for ten weeks** zehn Wochen lang waren alle Vorstellungen dieses Films ausverkauft; (c) ▶ 1193 | (measure) Rauminhalt, der; Volumen, das; (d) (position) Eigenschaft, die; Funktion, die; **in his** ∼ **as critic/lawyer** etc. in seiner Eigenschaft als Kritiker/Anwalt usw.

cape¹ /keɪp/ n. (garment) Umhang, der; Cape, das; (part of coat) Pelerine, die

cape² n. ▶ 1159 | (Geog.) Kap, das; **the C**∼ **[of Good Hope]** das Kap der guten Hoffnung; **C**∼ **Horn** Kap Hoorn (das); **C**∼ **Town** Kapstadt (das)

caper¹ /'keɪpə(r)/ **1** n. (a) (frisky movement) Luftsprung, der; (b) (wild behaviour) Kapriole, die; (coll.: activity, occupation) Masche, die (salopp). **2** v.i. ∼ **[about]** [herum]tollen [umher]tollen

caper² n. (Gastr.) ∼s Kapern Pl.

capful /'kæpfʊl/ n. **one** ∼: der Inhalt einer Verschlusskappe

capillary /kə'pɪlərɪ/ **1** adj. Kapillar⟨gefäß⟩; ∼ **tube** Kapillare, die (fachspr.). **2** n. Kapillare, die (fachspr.)

capital /'kæpɪtl/ **1** adj. (a) Todes⟨strafe, -urteil⟩; Kapital⟨verbrechen⟩; (b) attrib. Groß-, (fachspr.) Versal⟨buchstabe⟩; ∼ **letters** Großbuchstaben; Versalien (fachspr.); **with a** ∼ **A** etc. mit großem A usw. od. (fachspr.) mit Versal-A usw.; (c) attrib. (principal) Haupt⟨stadt⟩; (d) (Commerc.) ∼ **sum/expenditure** Kapitalbetrag, der/ -aufwendungen Pl. **2** n. (a) (letter) Großbuchstabe, der; **[large]** ∼s Großbuchstaben; Versalien (fachspr.); **small** ∼s Kapitälchen (fachspr.); **write one's name in [block]** ∼s seinen Namen in Blockbuchstaben schreiben; (b) (city, town) Hauptstadt, die; (c) (stock, accumulated wealth) Kapital, das; **make** ∼ **out of sth.** (fig.) aus etw. Kapital schlagen (ugs.)

capital 'gains tax n. (Brit.) Steuer auf Kapitalgewinn, die

capitalise ⇒ **capitalize**

capitalism /'kæpɪtəlɪzm/ n. Kapitalismus, der

capitalist /'kæpɪtəlɪst/ **1** n. Kapitalist, der/Kapitalistin, die. **2** adj. kapitalistisch

capitalize /'kæpɪtəlaɪz/ **1** v.t. groß schreiben ⟨Buchstaben, Wort⟩. **2** v.i. (fig.) ∼ **on sth.** von etw. profitieren; aus etw. Kapital schlagen (ugs.)

capitulate /kə'pɪtjʊleɪt/ v.i. kapitulieren

capitulation /kəpɪtjʊ'leɪʃn/ n. Kapitulation, die

caprice /kə'pri:s/ n. (change of mind or conduct) Laune, die; Kaprice, die (geh.); (inclination) Willkür, die

capricious /kə'prɪʃəs/ adj. launisch; kapriziös (geh.)

Capricorn /'kæprɪkɔ:n/ n. (Astrol., Astron.) der Steinbock; see also **tropic**

capsize /kæp'saɪz/ **1** v.t. zum Kentern bringen. **2** v.i. kentern

capstan /'kæpstən/ n. (Naut.) Winde, die; Spill, das (Seemannsspr.)

capsule /'kæpsjʊl/ n. Kapsel, die

captain /'kæptɪn/ **1** n. (a) ▶ 1152 | Kapitän, der; (in army) Hauptmann, der; (in navy) Kapitän [zur See]; ∼ **of a ship** Schiffskapitän, der; ∼ **of industry** (fig.) Industriekapitän, der (ugs.); (b) (Sport) Kapitän, der; Spielführer, der/ -führerin, die. **2** v.t. befehligen ⟨Soldaten, Armee⟩; ∼ **a team** Mannschaftskapitän sein

captaincy /'kæptɪnsɪ/ n. (Sport) Führung, die

caption /'kæpʃn/ n. (a) (heading) Überschrift, die; (b) (wording under photograph/drawing) Bildunterschrift, die; (Cinemat., Telev.) Untertitel, der

captivate /'kæptɪveɪt/ *v.t.* fesseln (fig.); gefangen nehmen (fig.)

captivating /'kæptɪveɪtɪŋ/ *adj.* bezaubernd; einnehmend ‹*Lächeln*›

captive /'kæptɪv/ **1** *adj.* gefangen; **be taken ~:** gefangen genommen werden; **hold sb. ~:** jmdn. gefangen halten. **2** *n.* Gefangener, *der*/Gefangene, *die*

captive 'audience *n.* unfreiwilliges Publikum

captivity /kæp'tɪvɪtɪ/ *n.* Gefangenschaft, *die;* **in ~:** in [der] Gefangenschaft; **be held in ~:** gefangen gehalten werden

captor /'kæptə(r)/ *n.* (of city, country) Eroberer, *der; his ~:* der, der/die, die ihn gefangen nahm

capture /'kæptʃə(r)/ **1** *n.* **(a)** (of thief etc.) Festnahme, *die;* (of town) Einnahme, *die;* **(b)** (thing or person ~d) Fang, *der.* **2** *v.t.* **(a)** festnehmen ‹*Person*›; [ein]fangen ‹*Tier*›; einnehmen ‹*Stadt*›; ergattern ‹*Preis*›; **~ sb.'s heart** jmds. Herz gewinnen; **they ~d the city from the Romans** sie nahmen den Römern die Stadt ab; **(b)** (Chess etc.) schlagen ‹*Figur*›; **(c)** (Computing) erfassen ‹*Daten*›

car /kɑː(r)/ *n.* **(a)** (motor ~) Auto, *das;* Wagen, *der;* **by ~:** mit dem Auto *od.* Wagen; **(b)** (railway carriage etc.) Wagen, *der;* **(c)** (Amer.: lift cage) Fahrkabine, *die*

carafe /kə'ræf/ *n.* Karaffe, *die*

caramel /'kærəml/ *n.* **(a)** (toffee) Karamelle, *die;* Karamellbonbon, *das;* **(b)** (burnt sugar or syrup) Karamell, *der*

carat /'kærət/ *n.* Karat, *das;* **a 22-~ gold ring** ein 22-karätiger Goldring

caravan /'kærəvæn/ *n.* **(a)** (Brit.) Wohnwagen, *der;* (used for camping) Wohnwagen, *der;* Caravan, *der;* **(b)** (company of merchants, pilgrims, etc.) Karawane, *die*

caravan: ~ park, ~ site *ns.* Campingplatz für Wohnwagen

caraway /'kærəweɪ/ *n.* Kümmel, *der*

'caraway seed *n.* Kümmelkorn, *das; in pl.* Kümmel, *der*

carbohydrate /kɑːbə'haɪdreɪt/ *n.* (Chem.) Kohle[n]hydrat, *das*

carbolic /kɑː'bɒlɪk/ *adj.* Karbol‹*säure*›; **~ soap** Karbolseife, *die*

'car bomb *n.* Autobombe, *die*

carbon /'kɑːbən/ *n.* **(a)** Kohlenstoff, *der;* **(b)** (copy) Durchschlag, *der;* (paper) Kohlepapier, *das*

carbonate /'kɑːbəneɪt/ *v.t.* mit Kohlensäure versetzen ‹*Getränke*›

carbon: ~ 'copy *n.* Durchschlag, *der;* (fig.) (imitation) Nachahmung, *die;* Abklatsch, *der* (abwertend); (identical counterpart) Ebenbild, *das;* **~ dating** *n.* Radiokarbonmethode, *die;* **~ di'oxide** *n.* (Chem.) Kohlendioxid, *das;* **~ mo'noxide** *n.* (Chem.) Kohlenmonoxid, *das;* **~ paper** *n.* Kohlepapier, *das*

car 'boot sale *n.:* Trödelmarkt, bei dem die Händler ihre Waren aus dem Kofferraum ihrer Autos heraus verkaufen

carbuncle /'kɑːbʌŋkl/ *n.* (abscess) Karbunkel, *der*

carburettor (*Amer.:* **carburetor**) /kɑːbə'retə(r)/ *n.* Vergaser, *der*

carcass (*Brit. also:* **carcase**) /'kɑːkəs/ *n.* **(a)** (dead body) Kadaver, *der;* (at butcher's) Rumpf, *der;* **(b)** (of ship, fortification, etc.) Skelett, *das*

carcinogen /kɑː'sɪnədʒən/ *n.* (Med.) Karzinogen, *das* (fachspr.); Krebserreger, *der*

carcinogenic /kɑːsɪnə'dʒenɪk/ *adj.* (Med.) karzinogen (fachspr.); Krebs erregend

car: ~ coat *n.* Autocoat, *der;* **~ crash** *n.* Autounfall, *der*

card /kɑːd/ *n.* **(a)** (playing ~) Karte, *die;* **read the ~s** Karten lesen; **be on the ~s** (fig.) zu erwarten sein; **put [all] one's ~s on the table** (fig.) [alle] seine Karten auf den Tisch legen; **have another ~ up one's sleeve** (fig.) noch einen Trumpf in der Hand haben; **(b)** *in pl.* (game) Karten *Pl.;* **play ~s** Karten spielen; **(c)** (~board, post~, visiting ~, greeting ~) Karte, *die;* **let me give you my ~:** ich gebe Ihnen meine Karte; **(d)** *in pl.* (coll.: employee's documents) Papiere *Pl.;* **ask for/get one's ~s** sich (*Dat.*) seine Papiere geben lassen/seine Papiere kriegen (ugs.).

card: ~board *n.* Pappe, *die;* Pappkarton, *der;* (fig) klischeehaft ‹*Figur*›; **~board box** ⇒ **box¹ a; ~ file** *n.* Kartei, *die;* (large) Kartothek, *die;* **~ game** *n.* Kartenspiel, *das;* **~holder** *n.* Karteninhaber, *der*/-inhaberin, *die*

cardiac /'kɑːdɪæk/ *adj.* Herz-

cardigan /'kɑːdɪgən/ *n.* Strickjacke, *die*

cardinal /'kɑːdml/ **1** *adj.* (fundamental) grundlegend ‹*Frage, Doktrin, Pflicht*›; Kardinal‹*fehler, -problem*›; (chief) hauptsächlich, Haupt‹*argument, -punkt, -merkmal*›. **2** *n.* **(a)** ▶1152⎥ (Eccl.) Kardinal, *der;* **(b)** ▶956⎥ ⇒ **cardinal number**

cardinal: ~ number *n.* ▶956⎥ Grund-, Kardinalzahl, *die;* **~ sin** *n.* Todsünde, *die*

'card index *n.* Kartei, *die*

cardiogram /'kɑːdɪəʊgræm/ *n.* Kardiogramm, *das* (Med.)

cardiology /kɑːdɪ'ɒlədʒɪ/ *n.* Kardiologie, *die*

'cardphone *n.* Kartentelefon, *das*

care /keə(r)/ **1** *n.* **(a)** (anxiety) Sorge, *die;* **she hasn't got a ~ in the world** sie hat keinerlei Sorgen; **(b)** (pains) Sorgfalt, *die;* **take ~:** sich bemühen; **he takes great ~ over his work** er gibt sich (*Dat.*) große Mühe mit seiner Arbeit; **(c)** (caution) Vorsicht, *die;* **take ~:** aufpassen; **take ~ to do sth.** darauf achten, etw. zu tun; **take more ~!** pass [doch] besser auf!; **(d)** (attention) **medical ~:** ärztliche Betreuung; **old people need special ~:** alte Menschen brauchen besondere Fürsorge; **~ in the community** ⇒ **community care; (e)** (concern) **~ for sb./sth.** die Sorge um jmdn./etw.; **(f)** (charge) Obhut, *die* (geh.); **be in ~:** in Pflege sein; **put sb. in ~:** jmdn. in Pflege geben; **take ~ of sb./sth.** (ensure safety of) auf jmdn./etw. aufpassen; (attend to, dispose of) sich um jmdn./etw. kümmern; **take ~ of oneself** für sich selbst sorgen; (as to health) sich schonen; **take ~ [of yourself]!** mach's gut! (ugs.). **2** *v.i.* **(a)** **~ for** or **about sb./sth.** (feel interest) sich für jmdn./etw. interessieren; **(b)** **~ for** or **about sb./sth.** (like) jmdn./etw. mögen; **would you ~ for a drink?** möchten Sie etwas trinken?; **(c)** (feel concern) **I don't ~ [whether/how/what** *etc.*] es ist mir gleich[, ob/wie/was *usw.*]; **for all I ~** (coll.) von mir aus (ugs.); **I couldn't ~ less** (coll.) es ist mir völlig einerlei *od.* (ugs.) egal; **what do I ~?** (coll.) mir ist es egal (ugs.); **who ~s?** (coll.) was soll's (ugs.); **(d)** (wish) **~ to do sth.** etw. tun mögen; **(e)** **~ for sb./sth.** (look after) sich um jmdn./etw. kümmern; **well ~d for** gepflegt; gut versorgt ‹*Person*›; gut erhalten ‹*Auto*›

career /kə'rɪə(r)/ **1** *n.* **(a)** (way of livelihood) Beruf, *der;* **a teaching ~:** der Beruf des Lehrers; **take up a ~ in journalism** or **as a journalist** den Beruf des Journalisten ergreifen; **(b)** (progress in life) [berufliche] Laufbahn; (very successful) Karriere, *die.* **2** *v.i.* rasen; ‹*Pferd, Reiter:*› galoppieren; **go ~ing down the hill** den Hügel hinunterrasen

career: ~ 'diplomat *n.* ▶887⎥ Berufsdiplomat, *der;* **~ girl** *n.* Karrierefrau, *die;* **~s adviser** *n.* ▶887⎥ Berufsberater, *der*/-beraterin, *die;* **~s office** *n.* Berufsberatung[sstelle], *die;* **~ woman** *n.* Karrierefrau, *die*

'carefree *adj.* sorgenfrei

careful /'keəfl/ *adj.* **(a)** (thorough) sorgfältig (watchful, cautious) vorsichtig; **[be] ~!** Vorsicht!; **be ~ to do sth.** darauf achten, etw. zu tun; **he was ~ not to mention the subject** er war darum bemüht, das Thema nicht zu erwähnen; **be ~ that ...:** darauf achten, dass ...; **be ~ of sb./sth.** (take care of) mit jmdm./etw. vorsichtig sein; (be cautious of) sich vor jmdm./etw. in Acht nehmen; **be ~ [about] how/what/where** *etc.* darauf achten, wie/was/ wo *usw.;* **be ~ about sth.** auf etw. (*Akk.*) achten; **be ~ about sb.** auf jmdn. aufpassen *od.* achten; **be ~ with sb./sth.** vorsichtig mit jmdm./etw. umgehen; **(b)** (showing care) sorgfältig; **a ~ piece of work** ein sorgfältig gearbeitetes Stück; **after ~ consideration** nach reiflicher Überlegung; **pay ~ attention to what he says** achte genau auf das, was er sagt

carefully /'keəfəlɪ/ *adv.* (thoroughly) sorgfältig; (attentively) aufmerksam; (cautiously) vorsichtig; **watch ~:** gut aufpassen

careless /'keəlɪs/ *adj.* **(a)** (inattentive) unaufmerksam; (thoughtless) gedankenlos; unvorsichtig, leichtsinnig

⟨*Fahrer*⟩; nachlässig ⟨*Arbeiter*⟩; **be ~ about** *or* **of sb./ sth.** wenig auf jmdn./etw. achten; **~ with sb./sth.** unvorsichtig mit jmdn./etw.; **be ~ [about** *or* **of] how/what** *etc.* wenig darauf achten, wie/was *usw.;* **(b)** (showing lack of care) unordentlich, nachlässig ⟨*Arbeit*⟩; unachtsam ⟨*Fahren*⟩; **a [very] ~ mistake** ein [grober] Flüchtigkeitsfehler

carelessly /'keəlɪslɪ/ *adv.* (without care) nachlässig; (thoughtlessly) gedankenlos; unvorsichtig, leichtsinnig ⟨*fahren*⟩

carelessness /'keəlɪsnɪs/ *n., no pl.* (lack of care) Nachlässigkeit, *die;* (thoughtlessness) Gedankenlosigkeit, *die*

carer /'keərə(r)/ *n.* Betreuer, *der*/Betreuerin, *die;* (for sick person also) Pfleger, *der*/Pflegerin, *die;* **be a ~ for** *or* **of sb.** jmdn. versorgen *od.* betreuen; sich um jmdn. bekümmern; (for sick person) jmdn. pflegen

caress /kə'res/ **1** *n.* Liebkosung, *die.* **2** *v.t.* liebkosen; **~ [each other]** sich *od.* einander liebkosen

care: **~taker** *n.* **(a)** ▶ 887⌋ Hausmeister, *der*/-meisterin, *die;* **(b)** **~taker government** Übergangsregierung, *die;* **~ worker** *n.* ▶ 887⌋ in einem Hilfsberuf Tätige, *der/ die;* **~worn** *adj.* von Sorgen gezeichnet

'car ferry, *die* Autofähre, *die*

cargo /'kɑːgəʊ/ *n., pl.* **~es** *or* (Amer.) **~s** Fracht, *die;* Ladung, *die*

cargo: **~ boat**, **~ ship** *ns.* Frachter, *der;* Frachtschiff, *das*

'car hire *n.* Autovermietung, *die*

Caribbean /kærɪ'biːən/ **1** *n.* **the ~:** die Karibik. **2** *adj.* karibisch

caribou /'kærɪbuː/ *n., pl. same* (Zool.) Karibu, *der od. das*

caricature /'kærɪkətjʊə(r)/ **1** *n.* Karikatur, *die;* (in mime) Parodie, *die;* **do a ~ of sb.** jmdn. karikieren/parodieren. **2** *v.t.* karikieren

carjacker /'kɑːdʒækə(r)/ *n.* Carjacker, *der*

carjacking /'kɑːdʒækɪŋ/ *n.* Carjacking, *das*

'carload *n.* Wagenladung, *die*

carnage /'kɑːnɪdʒ/ *n.* Gemetzel, *das*

carnal /'kɑːnl/ *adj.* körperlich; sinnlich; fleischlich (geh.)

carnation /kɑː'neɪʃn/ *n.* (Bot.) [Garten]nelke, *die*

carnet /'kɑːneɪ/ *n.* (of motorist) Triptyk, *das;* (of camper) Ausweis für Camper

carnival /'kɑːnɪvl/ *n.* **(a)** (festival) Volksfest, *das;* **(b)** (pre-Lent festivities) Karneval, *der;* Fastnacht, *die;* Fasching, *der* (bes. südd., österr.)

carnivore /'kɑːnɪvɔː(r)/ *n.* (animal) Fleischfresser, *der;* (plant) Fleisch fressende Pflanze

carnivorous /kɑː'nɪvərəs/ *adj.* Fleisch fressend

carol /'kærl/ *n.* **[Christmas] ~:** Weihnachtslied, *das;* **~ concert**, **~-singing** weihnachtliches Liedersingen; **~-singers** Leute, die von Haus zu Haus gehen und Weihnachtslieder vortragen; ≈ Weihnachtssänger

carouse /kə'raʊz/ *v.i.* zechen (veralt., noch scherzh.)

carousel /kærʊ'sel/ *n.* **(a)** (conveyor system) Ausgabeband, *das;* **(b)** ⇒ **carrousel**

carp[1] /kɑːp/ *n., pl. same* (Zool.) Karpfen, *der*

carp[2] *v.i.* nörgeln; **~ at sb./sth.** an jmdm./etw. herumnörgeln (ugs.)

'car park *n.* Parkplatz, *der;* (underground) Tiefgarage, *die;* (building) Parkhaus, *das*

carpenter /'kɑːpɪntə(r)/ *n.* ▶ 887⌋ Zimmermann, *der;* (for furniture) Tischler, *der*/Tischlerin, *die*

carpentry /'kɑːpɪntrɪ/ *n.* **(a)** (art) Zimmerhandwerk, *das;* (in furniture) Tischlerhandwerk, *das;* **(b)** (woodwork) **[piece of] ~:** Tischlerarbeit, *die*

carpet /'kɑːpɪt/ **1** *n.* **(a)** Teppich, *der;* **[fitted] ~:** Teppichboden, *der;* **stair-~:** [Treppen]läufer, *der;* **be on the ~** (coll.: be reprimanded) zusammengestaucht werden (ugs.); **sweep sth. under the ~** (fig.) etw. unter den Teppich kehren (ugs.); **~ of flowers** Blumenteppich, *der.* **2** *v.t.* **(a)** (cover) [mit Teppich(boden)] auslegen; (fig.) bedecken; **(b)** (coll.: reprimand) **be ~ed for sth.** wegen etw. zusammengestaucht werden (ugs.)

'carpet bombing *n.* Flächenbombardement, *das*

carpeting /'kɑːpɪtɪŋ/ *n.* Teppich[boden], *der;* **wall-to-wall ~:** Teppichboden, *der*

carpet: **~ slipper** *n.* Hausschuh, *der;* **~ sweeper** *n.* Teppichkehrer, *der*

car: **~ phone** *n.* Autotelefon, *das;* **~ pool** *n.* Fahrgemeinschaft, *die;* (of a firm etc.) Fahrzeugpark, *der;* **~port** *n.* Einstellplatz, *der;* **~ 'radio** *n.* Autoradio, *das;* **~ rental** ⇒ **car hire**

carriage /'kærɪdʒ/ *n.* **(a)** (horse-drawn vehicle) Kutsche, *die;* **~ and pair/four/six** *etc.* Zwei-/Vier-/Sechsspänner *usw., der;* **(b)** (Railw.) [Eisenbahn]wagen, *der;* **(c)** (Mech., of typewriter) Schlitten, *der;* **(d)** *no pl.* (conveying, being conveyed) Transport, *der;* **(e)** (cost of conveying) Frachtkosten *Pl.;* **~ paid** frachtfrei; **(f)** (bearing) Haltung, *die*

carriage: **~ clock** *n.* Reiseuhr, *die;* **~way** *n.* Fahrbahn, *die*

carrier /'kærɪə(r)/ *n.* **(a)** (bearer) Träger, *der;* **(b)** (Commerc.) (firm) Transportunternehmen, *das;* (person) Transportunternehmer, *der;* **(c)** (on bicycle etc.) Gepäckträger, *der;* **(d)** ⇒ **carrier bag**

carrier: **~ bag** *n.* Tragetasche, *die;* Tragetüte, *die;* **~ pigeon** *n.* Brieftaube, *die;* **by ~ pigeon** mit der Taubenpost

carrion /'kærɪən/ *n.* Aas, *das*

'carrion crow *n.* Rabenkrähe, *die*

carrot /'kærət/ *n.* **(a)** Möhre, *die;* Karotte, *die;* **grated ~[s]** geraspelte Möhren *od.* Karotten; **(b)** (fig.) Köder, *der;* **with ~ and stick** mit Zuckerbrot und Peitsche

carrousel /karʊ'sel/ *n.* (Amer.) Karussell, *das*

carry /'kærɪ/ **1** *v.t.* **(a)** (transport) tragen; (with emphasis on destination) bringen; ⟨*Strom:*⟩ spülen; ⟨*Verkehrsmittel:*⟩ befördern; **~ all before one** (fig.) nicht aufzuhalten sein; **(b)** (conduct) leiten; **~ sth. into effect** etw. in die Tat umsetzen; **(c)** (support) tragen; (contain) fassen; **~ responsibility** Verantwortung tragen; **(d)** (have with one) **~ [with one]** bei sich haben *od.* tragen; tragen ⟨*Waffe, Kennzeichen*⟩; **(e)** (possess) besitzen ⟨*Autorität, Gewicht*⟩; *see also* **conviction b;** **(f)** (hold) **she carries herself well** sie hat eine gute Haltung; **(g)** (prolong) **~ modesty/altruism** *etc.* **to excess** die Bescheidenheit/den Altruismus *usw.* bis zum Exzess treiben; **~ things to extremes** die Dinge auf die Spitze treiben; **(h)** (Math.: transfer) im Sinn behalten; **~ one** eins im Sinn; **(i)** (win) durchbringen ⟨*Antrag, Gesetzentwurf, Vorschlag*⟩; **the motion is carried** der Antrag ist angenommen; **~ one's audience with one** das Publikum überzeugen; **~ the day** den Sieg davontragen. **2** *v.i.* ⟨*Stimme, Laut:*⟩ zu hören sein

~ a'way *v.t.* forttragen; (by force) fortreißen; (fig.) **be** *or* **get carried away** (be inspired) hingerissen sein (**by** von); (lose self-control) sich hinreißen lassen

~ 'back *v.t.* **(a)** (return) zurückbringen; **(b)** ⇒ **take back b**

~ 'forward *v.t.* (Bookk.) vortragen

~ 'off *v.t.* **(a)** (from place) davontragen; (as owner or possessor) mit sich nehmen; (cause to die) dahinraffen (geh.); **(b)** (abduct) entführen ⟨*Person*⟩; **(c)** (win) gewinnen ⟨*Preis, Medaille*⟩; erringen ⟨*Sieg*⟩; **(d)** **~ it/sth. off [well]** es/etw. [gut] zustande bringen

~ 'on 1 *v.t.* (continue) fortführen ⟨*Tradition, Diskussion, Arbeit*⟩; **~ on the firm** die Firma übernehmen; **~ on [doing sth.]** weiterhin etw. tun. **2** *v.i.* **(a)** (continue) weitermachen; **~ on with a plan/project** einen Plan/ein Projekt weiterverfolgen; **(b)** (coll.: behave in unseemly manner) sich danebenbenehmen (ugs.); (make a fuss) Theater machen (ugs.); **(c)** **~ on with sb.** (have affair) mit jmdm. ein Verhältnis haben

~ 'out *v.t.* durchführen ⟨*Plan, Programm, Versuch*⟩; in die Tat umsetzen ⟨*Vorschlag, Absicht, Vorstellung*⟩; ausführen ⟨*Anweisung, Auftrag*⟩; halten ⟨*Versprechen*⟩; vornehmen ⟨*Verbesserungen*⟩; wahr machen ⟨*Drohung*⟩

~ 'over *v.t.* **(a)** (postpone) vertagen (**to** auf + *Akk.*); **(b)** (St. Exch.) prolongieren; **(c)** ⇒ **~ forward**

~ 'through *v.t.* (complete) durchführen

carry: **~cot** *n.* Babytragetasche, *die;* **~-on** *n.* (coll.) Theater, *das* (ugs.); **~-out** *n.* **~-out [meal]** Essen *od.*

Mahlzeit zum Mitnehmen; ~-out [restaurant] Restaurant mit Straßenverkauf; get a ~-out sich (*Dat.*) in einem Restaurant was zu essen holen; (to drink) sich (*Dat.*) was zu trinken holen

'carsick *adj.* children are often ~: Kindern wird beim Autofahren oft schlecht

cart /kɑːt/ 1 *n.* Karren, *der;* Wagen, *der;* horse and ~: Pferdewagen, *der;* put the ~ before the horse (fig.) das Pferd beim Schwanz aufzäumen. 2 *v.t.* (a) karren; (b) (fig. coll.: carry with effort) schleppen
~ 'off *v.t.* (coll.) abtransportieren

carte blanche /kɑːt 'blɑ̃ʃ/ *n.* unbeschränkte Vollmacht

cartel /kɑː'tel/ *n.* Kartell, *das*

'carthorse *n.* Arbeitspferd, *das*

cartilage /'kɑːtɪlɪdʒ/ *n.* Knorpel, *der*

cartography /kɑː'tɒgrəfɪ/ *n.* Kartographie, *die*

carton /'kɑːtn/ *n.* [Papp]karton, *der;* a ~ of milk eine Tüte Milch; a ~ of cigarettes eine Stange Zigaretten; a ~ of yoghurt ein Becher Joghurt

cartoon /kɑː'tuːn/ *n.* (a) (amusing drawing) humoristische Zeichnung; Cartoon, *der;* (satirical illustration) Karikatur, *die;* (sequence of drawings) [humoristische] Bilderserie; Cartoon, *der;* (b) (film) Zeichentrickfilm, *der*

cartoonist /kɑː'tuːnɪst/ *n.* ▶887 | Cartoonist, *der*/Cartoonistin, *die*

cartridge /'kɑːtrɪdʒ/ *n.* (a) (case for explosive) Patrone, *die;* (b) (spool of film, cassette) Kassette, *die;* (c) (of record player) Tonabnehmer, *der;* (d) (of pen) Patrone, *die*

'cartridge paper *n.* Zeichenpapier, *das*

cart: ~ track *n.* ≈ Feldweg, *der;* ~wheel *n.* (a) Wagenrad, *das;* (b) (Gymnastics) Rad, *das;* turn or do ~wheels radschlagen

carve /kɑːv/ 1 *v.t.* (a) (cut up) tranchieren ‹*Fleisch*›; (b) (from wood) schnitzen; (from stone) meißeln; ~ sth. out of wood/stone etw. aus Holz schnitzen/aus Stein meißeln. 2 *v.i.* (a) tranchieren; (b) ~ in wood/stone in Holz schnitzen/in Stein meißeln
~ out *v.t.* heraushauen
~ up *v.t.* aufschneiden ‹*Fleisch*›; aufteilen ‹*Erbe, Land*›

carver /'kɑːvə(r)/ *n.* (a) (in wood) [Holz]schnitzer, *der;* (in stone) Bildhauer, *der;* (b) *in pl.* (knife and fork) Tranchierbesteck, *das*

carving /'kɑːvɪŋ/ *n.* (a) (in or from wood) Schnitzerei, *die;* a ~ of a madonna in wood eine holzgeschnitzte Madonna; (b) (in or from stone) Skulptur, *die;* (on stone) eingeritztes Bild

'carving: ~ fork *n.* Tranchiergabel, *die;* ~ knife *n.* Tranchiermesser, *das*

cascade /kæs'keɪd/ 1 (lit. or fig.) Kaskade, *die.* 2 *v.i.* [in Kaskaden] herabstürzen

case¹ /keɪs/ *n.* (a) (instance, matter) Fall, *der;* if that's the ~: wenn das so ist; it is [not] the ~ that ...: es trifft [nicht] zu/stimmt [nicht], dass ...; it seems to be the ~ that they have ...: sie scheinen tatsächlich ... zu haben; as is generally the ~ with ...: wie das normalerweise bei ... der Fall ist; as the ~ may be je nachdem; in ~ ...: falls ...; für den Fall, dass ... (geh.); [just] in ~ (to allow for all possibilities) für alle Fälle; in ~ of fire/danger bei Feuer/Gefahr; in ~ of emergency im Notfall; in the ~ of bei; in any ~ (anything else) jedenfalls; I don't need it in any ~: ich brauche es sowieso nicht; in no ~ (certainly not) auf keinen Fall; in that ~: in diesem Fall; (b) (Med., Police, Soc. Serv., etc., or coll.: person afflicted) Fall, *der;* he is a mental/psychiatric ~: er ist ein Fall für den Psychiater; (c) (Law) Fall, *der;* (action) Verfahren, *das;* the ~ for the prosecution/defence die Anklage/Verteidigung; put one's ~: seinen Fall darlegen; (d) (fig.: set of arguments) Fall, *der;* (valid set of arguments) have a [good] ~ for doing sth./for sth. gute Gründe haben, etw. zu tun/für etw. haben; make out a ~ for sth. Argumente für etw. anführen; (e) (Ling.) Fall, *der;* Kasus, *der* (fachspr.); (f) (fig. coll.) (comical person) ulkiger Typ (ugs.); (comical woman) ulkige Nudel (ugs.)

case² 1 *n.* (a) Koffer, *der;* (small) Handkoffer, *der;* (brief~) [Akten]tasche, *die;* (for musical instrument) Kasten, *der;* (b) (sheath) Hülle, *die;* (for spectacles, cigarettes) Etui, *das;* (for jewellery) Schmuckkassette, *die;* (c) (crate) Kiste, *die;* ~ of oranges Kiste [mit] Apfelsinen; (d) (glass box) Vitrine, *die;* [display] ~: Schaukasten, *der;* (e) (cover) Gehäuse, *das.* 2 *v.t.* (a) (box) verpacken; (b) (sl.: examine) ~ the joint sich (*Dat.*) den Laden mal ansehen (ugs.)

case 'history *n.* (a) (record) [Vor]geschichte, *die;* (b) (Med.) Krankengeschichte, *die*

casement /'keɪsmənt/ *n.* [Fenster]flügel, *der*

'casement window *n.* Flügelfenster, *das*

case: ~ study *n.* Fallstudie, *die;* ~work *n.,* no pl., no indef. art. [auf den Einzelfall bezogene] Sozialarbeit;
~worker *n.* ▶887 | [Einzelfälle betreuender] Sozialarbeiter

cash /kæʃ/ 1 *n.,* no pl., no indef. art. ▶938 | (a) Bargeld, *das;* payment in ~ only nur Barzahlung; pay [in] ~, pay ~ down bar zahlen; we haven't got the ~: wir haben [dafür] kein Geld; be short of ~: knapp bei Kasse sein (ugs.); ~ on delivery per Nachnahme; (b) (Banking etc.) Geld, *das;* can I get ~ for these cheques? kann ich diese Schecks einlösen? 2 *v.t.* einlösen ‹*Scheck*›
~ in 1 /'--/ sich (*Dat.*) gutschreiben lassen ‹*Scheck*›. 2 /-'-/ *v.i.* ~ in on sth. (lit. or fig.) von etw. profitieren

cash: ~ and 'carry *n.: Verkaufssystem, bei dem der Kunde bar bezahlt und die Ware selbst nach Hause transportiert;* ~-and-carry [store] Cash-and-carry-Laden, *der;* ~-back *n.,* no pl., no art.: Barauszahlung eines Differenzbetrages bei Kauf mit Geldkarte; ~ box *n.* Geldkassette, *die;* ~ card *n.* Geldautomatenkarte, *die;* ~ desk *n.* (Brit.) Kasse, *die;* ~ dispenser *n.* Geldautomat, *der*

cashew /'kæʃuː/ *n.* (a) (nut) ⇒ cashew nut; (b) (tree) Nierenbaum, *der* (Bot.)

'cashew nut *n.* Cashewnuss, *die*

'cash flow *n.* (Econ.) Cashflow, *der*

cashier /kæ'ʃɪə(r)/ *n.* ▶887 | Kassierer, *der*/Kassiererin, *die;* ~'s office Kasse, *die*

cashmere /'kæʃmɪə(r)/ *n.* Kaschmir, *der*

cash: ~ payment *n.* Barzahlung, *die;* ~point *n.* Geldautomat, *der;* ~ register *n.* [Registrier]kasse, *die*

casing /'keɪsɪŋ/ *n.* Gehäuse, *das*

casino /kə'siːnəʊ/ *n.,* pl. ~s Kasino, *das;* (for gambling also) Spielkasino, *das;* Spielbank, *die*

cask /kɑːsk/ *n.* Fass, *das*

casket /'kɑːskɪt/ *n.* (a) Schatulle, *die* (veralt.); Kästchen, *das;* (b) (Amer.: coffin) Sarg, *der*

Caspian Sea /kæspɪən 'siː/ pr. *n.* Kaspische Meer, *das*

casserole /'kæsərəʊl/ *n.* (food, vessel) Schmortopf, *der*

cassette /kə'set, kæ'set/ *n.* Kassette, *die*

cassette: ~ deck *n.* Kassettendeck, *das;* ~ player *n.* Kassettengerät, *das;* ~ recorder *n.* Kassettenrekorder, *der*

cassock /'kæsək/ *n.* (Eccl.) Soutane, *die*

cast /kɑːst/ 1 *v.t.,* cast, cast (a) (throw) werfen; ~ sth. adrift etw. abtreiben lassen; ~ loose losmachen; ~ an or one's eye over sth. einen Blick auf etw. (*Akk.*) werfen; (fig.) Licht in etw. (*Akk.*) bringen; ~ the line/net die Angel[schnur]/das Netz auswerfen; ~ a shadow [on/over sth.] (lit. or fig.) einen Schatten [auf etw. (*Akk.*)] werfen; ~ one's vote seine Stimme abgeben; ~ one's mind back to sth. an etw. (*Akk.*) zurückdenken; (b) (shed) verlieren ‹*Haare, Winterfell*›; abwerfen ‹*Gehörn, Blätter, Hülle*›; the snake ~s its skin die Schlange häutet sich; ~ aside (fig.) beiseite schieben ‹*Vorschlag*›; ablegen ‹*Vorurteile, Gewohnheiten*›; vergessen ‹*Sorgen, Vorstellungen*›; fallen lassen ‹*Freunde, Hemmungen*›; (c) (shape, form) gießen; (d) (calculate) stellen ‹*Horoskop*›; (e) (assign role[s] of) besetzen; ~ Joe as sb./in the role of sb. jmdn./jmds. Rolle mit Joe besetzen; ~ a play/film die Rollen [in einem Stück/Film] besetzen. 2 *n.* (a) (Med.) Gipsverband, *der;* (b) (set of actors) Besetzung, *die;* (c) (model) Abdruck, *der;* (d) (Fishing) (throw of net) Auswerfen, *das;* (throw of line) Wurf, *der*
~ a'bout, ~ around *v.i.* ~ about or around [to find or for sth.] sich [nach etw.] umsehen
~ a'way *v.t.* (a) wegwerfen; (b) be ~ away on an

island auf einer Insel stranden
~ **'off** 1 *v.t.* **(a)** ablegen ‹*alte Kleider*›; **(b)** (Naut.) losmachen. 2 *v.i.* (Naut.) ablegen
~ **'up** *v.t.* (wash up) an Land spülen
castanet /kæstə'net/ *n., usu. in pl.* (Mus.) Kastagnette, *die*
castaway /'kɑːstəwer/ *n.* Schiffbrüchige, *der/die*
caste /kɑːst/ *n.* (lit. or fig.) **(a)** Kaste, *die;* **(b)** *no pl., no art.* (class system) Kastenwesen, *das*
caster /'kɑːstə(r)/ *n.* ⇨ **castor**
castigate /'kæstɪgeɪt/ *v.t.* (punish) züchtigen (geh.); (criticize) geißeln (geh.)
castigation /kæstɪ'geɪʃn/ *n.* (punishment) Züchtigung, *die* (geh.); (criticism) Geißelung, *die* (geh.)
casting /'kɑːstɪŋ/ *n.* **(a)** (Metallurgy: product) Gussstück, *das;* (Art) Abguss, *der;* **(b)** (Theatre, Cinemat.) Rollenbesetzung, *die*
casting 'vote *n.* ausschlaggebende Stimme (des Vorsitzenden bei Stimmengleichheit)
cast: ~ **'iron** *n.* Gusseisen, *das;* ~**-iron** *adj.* gusseisern; (fig.) eisern ‹*Konstitution, Magen*›; handfest, triftig ‹*Grund*›; hieb- und stichfest ‹*Alibi, Beweis*›; hundertprozentig ‹*Garantie*›
castle /'kɑːsl/ *n.* **(a)** (stronghold) Burg, *die;* (mansion) Schloss, *das;* ‹Windsor C~: Schloss Windsor; ~s in the air *or* in Spain Luftschlösser; **(b)** (Chess) Turm, *der*
castor /'kɑːstə(r)/ *n.* **(a)** (sprinkler) Streuer, *der;* **(b)** (wheel) Rolle, *die;* Laufrolle, *die* (Technik)
castor: ~ **'oil** *n.* Rizinusöl, *das;* Kastoröl, *das* (Kaufmannsspr.); ~ **sugar** *n.* (Brit.) Raffinade, *die*
castrate /kæ'streɪt/ *v.t.* kastrieren
castration /kæ'streɪʃn/ *n.* Kastration, *die*
casual /'kæʒʊəl, 'kæzjʊəl/ **1** *adj.* ungezwungen; zwanglos; leger ‹*Kleidung*›; beiläufig ‹*Bemerkung*›; flüchtig ‹*Bekannter, Bekanntschaft, Blick*›; unbekümmert, unbeschwert ‹*Haltung, Einstellung*›; salopp ‹*Ausdrucksweise*›; lässig ‹*Auftreten*›; **be ~ about sth.** etw. auf die leichte Schulter nehmen; ~ **sex** Sex ohne feste Bindung. **2** *n.* **(a)** *in pl.* (clothes) Freizeitkleidung, *die;* **(b)** ⇨ **casual labourer; (c)** ⇨ **casual shoe**
casual: ~ **'labour** *n., no pl.* Gelegenheitsarbeit, *die;* ~ **'labourer** *n.* Gelegenheitsarbeiter, *der*
casually /'kæʒʊəlɪ, 'kæzjʊəlɪ/ *adv.* ungezwungen; zwanglos; beiläufig ‹*bemerken*›; flüchtig ‹*anschauen*›; salopp ‹*sich ausdrücken*›; leger ‹*sich kleiden*›
casual 'shoe *n.* Freizeitschuh, *der*
casualty /'kæʒjʊəltɪ, 'kæzjʊəltɪ/ *n.* **(a)** (injured person) Verletzte, *der/die;* (in battle) Verwundete, *der/die;* (dead person) Tote, *der/die;* **(b)** (fig.) Opfer, *das;* **(c)** *no art.* (hospital department) Unfallstation, *die;* **work in ~:** auf der Unfallstation arbeiten
casualty: ~ **department** *n.* Unfallstation, *die;* ~ **ward** *n.* Unfallstation, *die*
cat /kæt/ *n.* **(a)** Katze, *die;* **she-~** Kätzin, *die;* [weibliche] Katze; **tom-~:** Kater, *der;* **the [great] Cats** die Großkatzen; **the ~ family** die Familie der Katzen; **play ~ and mouse with sb.** Katz und Maus mit jmdm. spielen (ugs.); **let the ~ out of the bag** (fig.) die Katze aus dem Sack lassen; **be like a ~ on hot bricks** wie auf glühenden Kohlen sitzen; **look like something the ~ brought in** (fig.) aussehen wie unter die Räuber gefallen; **curiosity killed the ~** (fig.) sei nicht so neugierig; **[fight] like ~ and dog** wie Hund und Katze [sein]; **not a ~ in hell's chance** nicht die geringste Chance; **a ~ may look at a king** (prov.) das ist doch auch nur ein Mensch; **put the ~ among the pigeons** (fig.) für Aufregung sorgen; **rain ~s and dogs** in Strömen regnen; **no room to swing a ~** (fig.) kaum Platz zum Umdrehen; **(b)** ⇨ **cat-o'-nine-tails**
cataclysm /'kætəklɪzm/ *n.* [Natur]katastrophe, *die*
cataclysmic /kætə'klɪzmɪk/ *adj.* katastrophal; verheerend
catacomb /'kætəkuːm, 'kætəkəʊm/ *n.* Katakombe, *die*
catalog (Amer.), **catalogue** /'kætəlɒg/ **1** *n.* Katalog, *der;* **subject ~:** Sachkatalog, *der* (Buchw.). **2** *v.t.* katalogisieren
catalyst /'kætəlɪst/ *n.* (Chem.; also fig.) Katalysator, *der*
catalytic converter /kætəlɪtɪk kən'vɜːtə(r)/ *n.* (Motor Veh.) Katalysator, *der*

catamaran /kætəmə'ræn/ *n.* (Naut.) Katamaran, *der*
catapult /'kætəpʌlt/ **1** *n.* Katapult, *das.* **2** *v.t.* katapultieren
cataract /'kætərækt/ *n.* **(a)** (lit. or fig.) Katarakt, *der;* **(b)** (Med.) grauer Star
catarrh /kə'tɑː(r)/ *n.* Schleimabsonderung, *die*
catastrophe /kə'tæstrəfɪ/ *n.* Katastrophe, *die;* **end in ~:** in einer Katastrophe enden
catastrophic /kætə'strɒfɪk/ *adj.* katastrophal
cat: ~ **burglar** *n.* Fassadenkletterer, *der*/Fassadenkletterin, *die;* ~**call** 1 *n.* ≈ Pfiff, *der;* 2 *v.i.* ≈ pfeifen
catch /kætʃ/ **1** *v.t.,* **caught** /kɔːt/ **(a)** (capture) fangen; (lay hold of) fassen; packen; ~ **sb. by the arm** jmdn. am Arm packen *od.* fassen; ~ **hold of sb./sth.** jmdn./etw. festhalten; (to stop oneself falling) sich an jmdm./etw. festhalten; **(b)** (intercept motion of) auffangen; fangen ‹*Ball*›; ~ **a thread** einen Faden vernähen; **get sth. caught** *or* ~ **sth. on/in sth.** mit etw. an/in etw. (*Dat.*) hängen bleiben; **I got my finger caught** *or* **caught my finger in the door** ich habe mir den Finger in der Tür eingeklemmt; **get caught on/in sth.** an/in etw. (*Dat.*) hängen bleiben; **(c)** (travel by) nehmen; (manage to see) sehen; (be in time for) [noch] erreichen; [noch] kriegen (ugs.) ‹*Bus, Zug*›; [noch] erwischen (ugs.) ‹*Person*›; **did you ~ her in?** hast du sie zu Hause erwischt? (ugs.); **(d)** (surprise) ~ **sb. at/doing sth.** jmdn. bei etw. erwischen (ugs.) /[dabei] erwischen, wie er etw. tut (ugs.); **caught in a thunderstorm** vom Sturm überrascht; **I caught myself thinking how ...:** ich ertappte mich bei dem Gedanken, wie ...; **(e)** (become infected with, receive) sich (*Dat.*) zuziehen *od.* (ugs.) holen; ~ **sth. from sb.** sich bei jmdm. mit etw. anstecken; ~ **[a] cold** sich erkälten/sich (*Dat.*) einen Schnupfen holen; (fig.) übel dran sein; ~ **it** (fig. coll.) etwas kriegen (ugs.); **you'll ~ it from me** du kannst von mir was erleben (ugs.); **(f)** (arrest) ~ **sb.'s attention** jmds. Aufmerksamkeit erregen; ~ **sb.'s fancy** jmdm. gefallen; jmdn. ansprechen; ~ **the Speaker's eye** (Parl.) das Wort erhalten; ~ **sb.'s eye** jmdm. auffallen; ‹*Gegenstand:*› jmdm. ins Auge fallen; (be impossible to overlook) jmdm. ins Auge springen; **(g)** (hit) ~ **sb. on/in sth.** jmdn. auf/in etw. (*Akk.*) treffen; ~ **sb. a blow [on/in sth.]** jmdm. einen Schlag [auf/in etw. (*Akk.*)] versetzen; **(h)** (grasp in thought) verstehen; mitbekommen; **did you ~ his meaning?** hast du verstanden *od.* mitbekommen, was er meint?; **(i)** ⇨ ~ **out a. 2** *v.i.,* **caught (a)** (begin to burn) [anfangen zu] brennen; **(b)** (become fixed) hängen bleiben; ‹*Haar, Faden:*› sich verfangen; **my coat caught on a nail** ich blieb mit meinem Mantel an einem Nagel hängen. **3** *n.* **(a)** (of ball) **make [several] good ~es** [mehrmals] gut fangen; **(b)** (amount caught, lit. or fig.) Fang, *der;* **(c)** (trick, difficulty) Haken, *der* (in an + *Dat.*); **the ~ is that ...:** der Haken an der Sache ist, dass ...; **it's ~-22** /kætʃtwentɪ'tuː/ (coll.) es ist ein Teufelskreis; **(d)** (fastener) Verschluss, *der;* (of door) Schnapper, *der;* **(e)** (Cricket etc.) ≈ Fang, *der;* **Abfangen des Balles, das den Schlagmann aus dem Spiel bringt;** **(f)** (catcher) **he is a good ~:** er kann gut fangen
~ **'on** *v.i.* (coll.) **(a)** (become popular) [gut] ankommen (ugs.); sich durchsetzen; **(b)** (understand) begreifen; kapieren (ugs.)
~ **'out** *v.t.* **(a)** (detect in mistake) [bei einem Fehler] ertappen; **(b)** (take unawares) erwischen (ugs.)
~ **'up** 1 *v.t.* **(a)** (reach) ~ **sb. up** jmdn. einholen; (in quality, skill) mit jmdm. mitkommen; **(b)** (absorb) **be caught up in sth.** in etw. (*Dat.*) [völlig] aufgehen; **(c)** (snatch) packen; **sth. gets caught up in sth.** etw. verfängt sich in etw. (*Dat.*). **2** *v.i.* (get level) ~ **up** einholen; ~ **up with sb.** (in quality, skill) mit jmdm. mitkommen; ~ **up on sth.** etw. nachholen; **I'm longing to ~ up on your news** ich bin gespannt, was für Neuigkeiten du hast
catching /'kætʃɪŋ/ *adj.* ansteckend
catchment area /'kætʃmənt eərɪə/ *n.* (lit. or fig.) Einzugsgebiet, *das*
catch: ~**phrase** *n.* Slogan, *der;* ~**word** *n.* (slogan) Schlagwort, *das*
catchy /'kætʃɪ/ *adj.* eingängig; **a ~ song** ein Ohrwurm (ugs.)

catechism /'kætɪkɪzm/ *n.* (Relig.) Katechismus, *der*

categorical /kætɪ'gɒrɪkl/ *adj.*, **categorically** /kætɪ'gɒrɪkəlɪ/ *adv.* kategorisch

category /'kætɪgərɪ/ *n.* Kategorie, *die*

cater /'keɪtə(r)/ *v.i.* (a) (provide or supply food) ~ [**for sb./ sth.**] [für jmdn./etw.] [die] Speisen und Getränke liefern; ~ **for weddings** Hochzeiten ausrichten; (b) (provide requisites etc.) ~ **for sb./sth.** auf jmdn./etw. eingestellt sein; ~ **for all ages** jeder Altersgruppe etwas bieten

caterer /'keɪtərə(r)/ *n.* ▶ 887 | Lieferant von Speisen und Getränken; Caterer, *der* (fachspr.)

catering /'keɪtərɪŋ/ *n.* (a) (trade) ~ [**business**] Gastronomie, *die;* (b) (service) Lieferung von Speisen und Getränken; Catering, *das* (fachspr.); **do the** ~**:** für Speisen und Getränke sorgen; ~ **firm/service** ⇨ **caterer**

caterpillar /'kætəpɪlə(r)/ *n.* (a) (Zool.) Raupe, *die;* (b) C~ [**tractor**] (P) (Mech.) Raupenfahrzeug, *das*

caterpillar: ~ **'track,** ~ **'tread** *ns.* Raupen-, Gleiskette, *die*

caterwaul /'kætəwɔːl/ *v.i.* ‹*Katze:*› schreien, [laut] miauen; ‹*Sänger:*› jaulen (abwertend)

cathedral /kə'θiːdrl/ *n.* ~ [**church**] Dom, *der;* Kathedrale, *die*

Catherine wheel /'kæθrɪn wiːl/ *n.* (firework) Feuerrad, *das*

catheter /'kæθɪtə(r)/ *n.* (Med.) Katheter, *der*

catholic /'kæθəlɪk, 'kæθlɪk/ **1** *adj.* (a) (all-embracing) umfassend; vielseitig ‹*Interessen*›; (b) C~ (Relig.) katholisch. **2** *n.* C~**:** Katholik, *der*/Katholikin, *die*

Catholicism /kə'θɒlɪsɪzm/ *n.* (Relig.) Katholizismus, *der*

catkin /'kætkɪn/ *n.* (Bot.) Kätzchen, *das*

cat: ~**nap** *n.* Nickerchen, *das* (ugs.); kurzes Schläfchen; ~**-o'-'nine-tails** *n.* neunschwänzige Katze; ~**'s-eye** *n.* (a) (stone) Katzenauge, *das;* (b) (Brit.: reflector) Bodenrückstrahler, *der* (Verkehrsw.)

cattle /'kætl/ *n. pl.* Vieh, *das;* Rinder *Pl.*

cattle: ~**-breeding** *n.* Rinderzucht, *die;* Viehzucht, *die;* ~ **market** *n.* Viehmarkt, *der;* ~ **truck** *n.* Viehtransporter, *der;* (Railw.) Viehwagen, *der*

catty /'kætɪ/ *adj.* gehässig

'catwalk *n.* Laufsteg, *der*

caucus /'kɔːkəs/ *n.* (Brit. derog., Amer.) (a) (committee) *den Wahlkampf und die Richtlinien der Politik bestimmendes regionales Gremium einer Partei;* (b) (party meeting) *den Wahlkampf und die Richtlinien der Politik bestimmende Sitzung der regionalen Parteiführung*

caught ⇨ **catch 1, 2**

cauldron /'kɔːldrən, 'kɒldrən/ *n.* Kessel, *der*

cauliflower /'kɒlɪflaʊə(r)/ *n.* Blumenkohl, *der*

causal /'kɔːzl/ *adj.* kausal

cause /kɔːz/ **1** *n.* (a) (what produces effect) Ursache, *die* (of für *od.* Gen.); (person) Verursacher, *der*/Verursacherin, *die;* **be the** ~ **of sth.** etw. verursachen; (b) (reason) Grund, *der;* Anlass, *der;* ~ **for/to do sth.** Grund *od.* Anlass zu etw./, etw. zu tun; **no** ~ **for concern** kein Grund zur Beunruhigung; **without good** ~**:** ohne triftigen Grund; (c) (aim, object of support) Sache, *die;* **freedom is our common** ~**:** Freiheit ist unser gemeinsames Anliegen *od.* Ziel; **be a lost** ~**:** aussichtslos sein; verlorene Liebesmühe sein (ugs.); [**in**] **a good** ~**:** [für] eine gute Sache. **2** *v.t.* (a) (produce) verursachen; erregen ‹*Aufsehen, Ärgernis*›; hervorrufen ‹*Verstimmung, Unruhe, Verwirrung*›; (b) (give) ~ **sb. worry/pain** etc. jmdm. Sorge/Schmerzen usw. bereiten; ~ **sb. trouble/bother** jmdm. Umstände machen; (c) (induce) ~ **sb. to do sth.** jmdn. veranlassen, etw. zu tun

causeway /'kɔːzweɪ/ *n.* Damm, *der*

caustic /'kɔːstɪk/ *adj.* beißend ‹*Spott*›; bissig ‹*Bemerkung, Worte*›; spitz, scharf ‹*Zunge*›; ~ **soda** Ätznatron, *das*

cauterize (cauterise) /'kɔːtəraɪz/ *v.t.* (Med.) kauterisieren

caution /'kɔːʃn/ **1** *n.* (a) (care) Vorsicht, *die;* **use** ~**:** vorsichtig sein; (b) (warning) Warnung, *die;* (warning and reprimand) Verwarnung, *die;* **just a word of** ~**:** noch ein guter Rat. **2** *v.t.* (warn) warnen; (warn and reprove) verwarnen (**for** wegen); ~ **sb. against sth./doing sth.** jmdn. vor etw. (Dat.) warnen/davor warnen, etw. zu tun; ~ **sb. to/not to do sth.** jmdn. ermahnen, etw. zu tun/nicht zu tun

cautious /'kɔːʃəs/ *adj.* vorsichtig; (circumspect) umsichtig

cautiously /'kɔːʃəslɪ/ *adv.* vorsichtig; (circumspectly) umsichtig

cavalier /kævə'lɪə(r)/ **1** *n.* Kavalier, *der.* **2** *adj.* (offhand) keck; (arrogant) anmaßend

cavalry /'kævlrɪ/ *n., constr. as sing. or pl.* Kavallerie, *die*

cave /keɪv/ **1** *n.* Höhle, *die.* **2** *v.i.* Höhlen erforschen ~ **'in** *v.i.* einbrechen; (fig.) (collapse) zusammenbrechen; (submit) nachgeben

caveat /'kævɪæt/ *n.* (warning) Warnung, *die*

cave: ~ **dweller,** ~**man** *ns.* Höhlenbewohner, *der;* (fig.) Wilde, *der*

cavern /'kævən/ *n.* (cave, lit. or fig.) Höhle, *die*

cavernous /'kævənəs/ *adj.* (like a cavern) höhlenartig

caviare (caviar) /'kævɪɑː(r), kævɪ'ɑː(r)/ *n.* Kaviar, *der*

cavil /'kævɪl/ *v.i.,* (Brit.) **-ll-** kritteln (abwertend); ~ **at/about sth.** etw. bekritteln (abwertend)

cavity /'kævɪtɪ/ *n.* Hohlraum, *der;* (in tooth) Loch, *das;* **nasal** ~**:** Nasenhöhle, *die*

'cavity wall *n.* Hohlmauer, *die*

cavort /kə'vɔːt/ *v.i.* (coll.) ~ [**about** *or* **around**] herumtollen (ugs.)

caw /kɔː/ **1** *n.* Krächzen, *das.* **2** *v.i.* krächzen

cayenne /keɪ'en/ *n.* ~ [**'pepper**] Cayennepfeffer, *der*

CB *abbr.* **citizens' band** CB

CBI *abbr.* **Confederation of British Industry** *britischer Unternehmerverband*

cc /siː'siː/ *abbr.* ▶ 1193 | **cubic centimetre(s)** cm³

CD *abbr.* (a) **civil defence;** (b) **Corps Diplomatique** CD; (c) **compact disc** CD; **CD player** CD-Spieler, *der*

CD-ROM /siːdiː'rɒm/ *n.* CD-ROM, *die;* ~ **drive** CD-ROM-Laufwerk, *das*

cease /siːs/ **1** *v.i.* aufhören; **without ceasing** ununterbrochen. **2** *v.t.* (a) (stop) aufhören; ~ **doing** *or* **to do sth.** aufhören, etw. zu tun; **sth. has** ~**d to exist** etw. existiert *od.* besteht nicht mehr; **it never** ~**s to amaze me** ich kann nur immer darüber staunen; (b) (end) aufhören mit; einstellen ‹*Bemühungen, Versuche*›; ~ **'fire** (Mil.) das Feuer einstellen

'ceasefire *n.* Waffenruhe, *die;* (signal) Befehl zur Feuereinstellung

ceaseless /'siːslɪs/ *adj.* endlos; unaufhörlich ‹*Anstrengung*›; ständig ‹*Wind, Regen, Lärm*›

cedar /'siːdə(r)/ *n.* (a) Zeder, *die;* (b) ⇨ **cedarwood**

'cedarwood *n.* Zedernholz, *das*

cede /siːd/ *v.t.* (surrender) abtreten ‹*Land, Rechte*› (**to** Dat., an + Akk.)

ceiling /'siːlɪŋ/ *n.* (a) Decke, *die;* (b) (upper limit) Maximum, *das;* (c) (Aeronaut.) Gipfelhöhe, *die*

celebrate /'selɪbreɪt/ **1** *v.t.* (observe) feiern; (Eccl.) zelebrieren, lesen ‹*Messe*›. **2** *v.i.* feiern

celebrated /'selɪbreɪtɪd/ *adj.* gefeiert, berühmt ‹*Person*›; berühmt ‹*Gebäude, Werk usw.*›

celebration /selɪ'breɪʃn/ *n.* (a) (observing) Feiern, *das;* (party etc.) Feier, *die;* **in** ~ **of** aus Anlass (+ Gen.); (with festivities) zur Feier (+ Gen.); **this calls for a** ~**!** das muss gefeiert werden!; (b) (performing) **the** ~ **of the wedding/ christening** die Trauung[szeremonie]/Taufe; **the** ~ **of Communion** die Feier der Kommunion

celebrity /sɪ'lebrɪtɪ/ *n.* (a) *no pl.* (fame) Berühmtheit, *die;* (b) (person) Berühmtheit, *die*

celery /'selərɪ/ *n.* [Bleich-, Stangen]sellerie, *der od. die*

celestial /sɪ'lestɪəl/ *adj.* (a) (heavenly) himmlisch; (b) (of the sky) Himmels-

celibate /'selɪbət/ *adj.* zölibatär (Rel.); ehelos; **remain** ~**:** im Zölibat leben (Rel.); ehelos bleiben

cell /sel/ n. (also Biol., Electr.) Zelle, die

cellar /'selə(r)/ n. Keller, der

cellist /'tʃelɪst/ n. ▶ 887 | (Mus.) Cellist, der/Cellistin, die

cello /'tʃeləʊ/ n., pl. ∼s (Mus.) Cello, das

Cellophane, cellophane, (P) /'seləfeɪn/ n. Cellophan Ⓦ, das

'cell phone n. Mobiltelefon, das

cellular /'seljʊlə(r)/ adj. (a) porös ‹Mineral, Gestein, Substanz›; (Biol.: of cells) zellular; Zell-; (b) (with open texture) luftdurchlässig; atmungsaktiv (Werbespr.)

cellular 'phone n. Mobiltelefon, das

cellulite /'seljʊlaɪt/ n. no pl., no indef. art.: überschüssige Fettdepots an Oberschenkeln und Hüften

celluloid /'seljʊlɔɪd/ n. (a) Zelluloid, das; (b) (cinema films) Kino, das; ∼ **hero** Leinwandheld, der

cellulose /'seljʊləʊs, 'seljʊləʊz/ n. (Chem.) Zellulose, die

Celsius /'selsɪəs/ adj. ▶ 1141 | Celsius

Celt /kelt, selt/ n. Kelte, der/Keltin, die

Celtic /'keltɪk, 'seltɪk/ **1** adj. keltisch. **2** n. Keltisch, das

cement /sɪ'ment/ **1** n. (a) (Building) Zement, der; (mortar) [Zement]mörtel, der; (b) (sticking substance) Klebstoff, der; (for mending broken vases etc. also) Kitt, der. **2** v.t. (a) mit Zement/ Mörtel zusammenfügen; (stick together) zusammenkleben; (fig.) zusammenkitten; zementieren ‹Freundschaft, Beziehung›; (b) (apply ∼ to) zementieren/mörteln

cemetery /'semɪtərɪ/ n. Friedhof, der

cenotaph /'senətɑːf, 'senətæf/ n. Kenotaph, das; Zenotaph, das

censor /'sensə(r)/ **1** n. (a) Zensor, der; (b) (judge) Kritiker, der. **2** v.t. zensieren

censorship /'sensəʃɪp/ n. Zensur, die

censure /'senʃə(r)/ **1** n. Tadel, der; **propose a vote of** ∼: einen Tadelsantrag stellen. **2** v.t. tadeln

census /'sensəs/ n. Zählung, die; **[national]** ∼: Volkszählung, die; Zensus, der

cent /sent/ n. ▶ 938 | Cent, der

centenarian /sentɪ'neərɪən/ n. Hundertjährige, der/die

centenary /sen'tiːnərɪ, sen'tenərɪ/ **1** adj. ∼ **celebrations/festival** Hundertjahrfeier, die. **2** n. Hundertjahrfeier, die

centennial /sen'tenɪəl/ **1** adj. hundertjährig; (occurring every 100 years) Jahrhundert-. **2** n. ⇨ **centenary 2**

center (Amer.) ⇨ **centre**

centi- /sentɪ/ in comb. Zenti-

'centigrade ⇨ **Celsius**

centime /'sɑ̃tiːm/ n. ▶ 938 | Centime, der

'centimetre (Brit.; Amer.: **centimeter**) n. ▶ 850 |, ▶ 904 |, ▶ 1193 | Zentimeter, der

centipede /'sentɪpiːd/ n. Hundertfüßer, der (Zool.); ≈ Tausendfüßler, der

central /'sentrl/ adj. zentral; **be** ∼ **to sth.** von zentraler Bedeutung für etw. sein; **in** ∼ **London** im Zentrum von London

Central: ∼ **A'merica** pr. n. Mittelamerika (das); ∼ **'Europe** pr. n. Mitteleuropa (das); ∼ **Euro'pean** adj. mitteleuropäisch; **c**∼ **'heating** n. Zentralheizung, die

centralize (centralise) /'sentrəlaɪz/ v.t. zentralisieren

central 'locking n. (Motor Veh.) Zentralverriegelung, die

centrally /'sentrəlɪ/ adv. (a) (in centre) zentral; (b) (in leading place) an zentraler Stelle

central: ∼ **'nervous system** n. (Anat., Zool.) Zentralnervensystem, das; ∼ **'processing unit** n. (Computing) Zentraleinheit, die; ∼ **reser'vation** n. (Brit.) Mittelstreifen, der; ∼ **'station** n. Hauptbahnhof, der

centre /'sentə(r)/ (Brit.) **1** n. (a) Mitte, die; (of circle, globe) Mitte, die; Zentrum, das; Mittelpunkt, der; (b) (town ∼) Innenstadt, die; Zentrum, das; (c) (filling of chocolate) Füllung, die; (d) (Polit.) Mitte, die; (e) (Sport: player) Mittelfeldspieler, der/-spielerin, die; (Basketball) Center, der; (f) **she likes to be the** ∼ **of attraction/attention** (fig.) sie steht gern im Mittelpunkt [des Interesses]. **2** adj. mittler...; ∼ **party** (Polit.) Partei der Mitte. **3** v.i. ∼ **on sth.** sich auf etw. (Akk.)

konzentrieren; **the novel** ∼**s on Prague** Prag steht im Mittelpunkt des Romans; ∼ **[a]round sth.** um etw. kreisen. **4** v.t. (a) (place in ∼) in der Mitte anbringen; in der Mitte aufhängen ‹Bild, Lampe›; zentrieren ‹Überschrift›; (b) (concentrate) ∼ **sth. on sth.** etw. auf etw. (Akk.) konzentrieren; **be** ∼**d [a]round sth.** etw. zum Mittelpunkt haben; (c) (Football, Hockey) [nach innen] flanken

centre: ∼ **'forward** n. (Sport) Mittelstürmer, der/-stürmerin, die; ∼ **'half** n. (Sport) Mittelläufer, der/-läuferin, die; (Football also) Vorstopper, der/-stopperin, die; ∼**piece** n. (ornament) ≈ Tafelschmuck, der (in der Mitte der Tafel); (principal item) Kernstück, das; ∼ **'spread** n. Doppelseite in der Mitte

centrifugal /sentrɪ'fjuːgl/ adj. zentrifugal; ∼ **force** Zentrifugalkraft, die; Fliehkraft, die

centrifuge /'sentrɪfjuːdʒ/ n. Zentrifuge, die

centurion /sen'tjʊərɪən/ n. (Roman Hist.) Zenturio, der

century /'sentʃərɪ/ n. (a) ▶ 738 | (period) Jahrhundert, das; (b) (Cricket) hundert Läufe

ceramic /sɪ'ræmɪk/ **1** adj. keramisch; Keramik‹vase, -kacheln›. **2** n. Keramik, die

ceramics /sɪ'ræmɪks/ n., no pl. Keramik, die

cereal /'sɪərɪəl/ n. (a) (kind of grain) Getreide, das; (b) (breakfast dish) Getreideflocken Pl.

cerebral /'serɪbrl/ adj. (a) (of the brain) Gehirn‹tumor, -blutung, -schädigung›; zerebral (Anat.); (b) (intellectual) intellektuell

ceremonial /serɪ'məʊnɪəl/ **1** adj. feierlich; (prescribed for ceremony) zeremoniell. **2** n. Zeremoniell, das

ceremonious /serɪ'məʊnɪəs/ adj. formell; förmlich ‹Höflichkeit›; (according to prescribed ceremony) zeremoniell

ceremony /'serɪmənɪ/ n. (a) Feier, die; (formal act) Zeremonie, die; (b) no pl., no art. (formalities) Zeremoniell, das; **stand on** ∼: Wert auf Förmlichkeiten legen; **without [great]** ∼: ohne große Förmlichkeit

cerise /sə'riːz, sə'riːs/ **1** adj. kirschrot. **2** n. Kirschrot, das

cert /sɜːt/ n. (Brit. coll.) (a) **that's a** ∼: das steht fest; (b) (as winner) todsicherer Tipp (ugs.)

certain /'sɜːtn/ adj. (a) (settled) bestimmt ‹Zeitpunkt›; (b) (unerring) sicher; (sure to happen) unvermeidlich; sicher ‹Tod›; **for** ∼: bestimmt; **I [don't] know for** ∼ **when** ...: ich weiß [nicht] genau, wann ...; **I can't say for** ∼ **that** ...: ich kann nicht mit Bestimmtheit sagen, dass ...; **make** ∼ **of sth.** (ensure) für etw. sorgen; (examine and establish) sich einer Sache (Gen.) vergewissern; **we made** ∼ **of a seat on the train** wir sicherten uns einen Sitzplatz im Zug; (c) (indisputable) unbestreitbar; (d) (confident) sicher; **of that I'm quite** ∼: dessen bin ich [mir] ganz sicher; (e) **be** ∼ **to do sth.** (inevitably) etw. bestimmt tun; (f) (particular but as yet unspecified) bestimmt; (g) (slight; existing but probably not already known) gewiss; **to a** ∼ **extent** in gewisser Weise; **a** ∼ **Mr Smith** ein gewisser Herr Smith

certainly /'sɜːtnlɪ/ (a) (admittedly) sicher[lich]; (definitely) bestimmt; (clearly) offensichtlich; (b) (in answer) [aber] gewiss; [aber] sicher; **[most]** ∼ **'not!** auf [gar] keinen Fall!

certainty /'sɜːtntɪ/ n. (a) **be a** ∼: sicher sein; feststehen; **regard sth. as a** ∼: etw. für sicher halten; (b) (absolute conviction, sure fact, assurance) Gewissheit, die; ∼ **of** or **about sth./sb.** Gewissheit über etw./jmdn.; ∼ **that** ...: Gewissheit [darüber], dass ...; **with some** ∼: mit einiger Sicherheit; **with** ∼, **for a** ∼: mit Sicherheit od. Bestimmtheit

certifiable /'sɜːtɪfaɪəbl/ adj. (a) nachweislich; überprüfbar ‹Ergebnis›; (b) (as insane) unzurechnungsfähig ‹Person›

certificate /sə'tɪfɪkət/ n. Urkunde, die; (of action performed) Schein, der; **doctor's** ∼: ärztliches Attest

certify /'sɜːtɪfaɪ/ v.t. (a) bescheinigen; bestätigen; (declare by certificate) berechtigen; **this is to** ∼ **that** ...: hiermit wird bescheinigt od. bestätigt, dass ...; (b) (declare insane) für unzurechnungsfähig erklären

certitude /'sɜːtɪtjuːd/ n. Gewissheit, die

cervical /sɜː'vaɪkl, 'sɜːvɪkl/ adj. (Anat.: of cervix) Gebärmutterhals-; zervikal (Anat.); ∼ **smear test** [Gebärmutterhals]abstrich, der

cervix /'sɜːvɪks/ n., pl. **cervices** /'sɜːvɪsiːz/ (Anat.: of uterus) Gebärmutterhals, der

Cesarean, Cesarian (Amer.) ⇒ **Caesarean**

cessation /se'seɪʃn/ n. Ende, das; (interval) Nachlassen, das

cesspit /'sespɪt/ n. (a) (refuse pit) Abfallgrube, die; (b) ⇒ **cesspool**

cesspool /'sespuːl/ n. Senk- od. Jauchegrube, die

cf. abbr. **compare** vgl.

CFC abbr. (Chem., Ecol.) **chlorofluorocarbon** FCKW

chafe /tʃeɪf/ 1 v.t. (make sore) aufscheuern; wund scheuern; (rub) reiben. 2 v.i. ⟨Person, Tier:⟩ sich scheuern; ⟨Gegenstand:⟩ scheuern ([up]on, against an + Dat.)

chaff /tʃɑːf/ (husks of corn, etc.) Spreu, die; (cattle food) Häcksel, das

chaffinch /'tʃæfɪnʃ/ n. (Ornith.) Buchfink, der

chagrin /'ʃægrɪn/ 1 n. Kummer, der; Verdruss, der; much to sb.'s ∼: zu jmds. großen Kummer od. Verdruss. 2 v.t. bekümmern; be or feel ∼ed at or by sth. wegen etw. niedergeschlagen sein

chain /tʃeɪn/ 1 n. (a) Kette, die; (fig.) Fessel, die; (jewellery) [Hals]kette, die; door ∼: Tür- od. Sicherungskette, die; (b) (series) Kette, die; Reihe, die; ∼ of events Reihe od. Kette von Ereignissen; ∼ of mountains Gebirgskette, die; ∼ of shops/hotels Laden-/Hotelkette, die; (c) (measurement) Chain, das (≈ 20 m). 2 v.t. (lit. or fig.) ∼ sb./sth. to sth. jmdn./etw. an etw. (Akk.) [an]ketten

chain: ∼ re'action n. (Chem., Phys.: also fig.) Kettenreaktion, die; ∼saw n. Kettensäge, die; ∼-smoke v.t. & i. Kette rauchen (ugs.); ∼-smoker n. Kettenraucher, der/-raucherin, die; ∼ store n. Kettenladen, der (Wirtsch.)

chair /tʃeə(r)/ 1 n. (a) Stuhl, der; (arm∼, easy ∼) Sessel, der; (b) (professorship) Lehrstuhl, der; (c) (at meeting) Vorsitz, der; (chairman) Vorsitzende, der/die; be or preside in/take the ∼: den Vorsitz haben od. führen/übernehmen. 2 v.t. (preside over) den Vorsitz haben od. führen bei

chair: ∼ back n. Rückenlehne, die; ∼lift n. Sessellift, der; ∼man /'tʃeəmən/ n., pl. **chairmen** /'tʃeəmən/ ▶887❘ Vorsitzende, der/die; Präsident, der/Präsidentin, die

chairmanship /'tʃeəmənʃɪp/ n. Vorsitz, der

chair: ∼person n. Vorsitzende, der/die; ∼woman n. Vorsitzende, die

chaise longue /ʃeɪz 'lɒŋɡ/ n. Chaiselongue, die

chalet /'ʃæleɪ/ n. Chalet, das

chalice /'tʃælɪs/ n. (poet./Eccl.) Kelch, der

chalk /tʃɔːk/ 1 n. Kreide, die; as white as ∼: kreidebleich; not by a long ∼ (Brit. coll.) bei weitem nicht; as different as ∼ and cheese so verschieden wie Tag und Nacht. 2 v.t. mit Kreide schreiben/malen/zeichnen usw. ∼ 'up v.t. (a) [mit Kreide] an- od. aufschreiben; (b) (fig.: register) für sich verbuchen können ⟨Erfolg⟩; (c) ∼ it up (fig.) es auf die Rechnung setzen

challenge /'tʃælɪndʒ/ 1 n. (a) (to contest or duel; also Sport) Herausforderung, die (to Gen.); issue a ∼ to sb. jmdn. herausfordern; (b) (of sentry) Aufforderung, die; (call for password) Anruf, der; (c) (person, task) Herausforderung, die. 2 v.t. (a) (to contest etc.) herausfordern (to zu); ∼ sb. to a duel jmdn. zum Duell [heraus]fordern; (b) (fig.) auffordern; ∼ sb.'s authority jmds. Autorität od. Befugnis infrage stellen; (c) (demand password etc. from) ⟨Wachposten:⟩ anrufen; (d) (question) infrage stellen; anzweifeln; ∼ a verdict ein Urteil kritisieren

challenged /'tʃælɪndʒd/ adj. (euphem. or joc.) behindert; physically/vertically ∼: körperbehindert/kleinwüchsig; mentally ∼: geistig behindert

challenger /'tʃælɪndʒə(r)/ n. Herausforderer, der/Herausforderin, die

challenging /'tʃælɪndʒɪŋ/ adj. herausfordernd; fesselnd, faszinierend ⟨Problem⟩; anspruchsvoll ⟨Arbeit⟩

chamber /'tʃeɪmbə(r)/ n. (a) (poet./arch.: room) Gemach, das (geh.); (bedroom) [Schlaf]gemach, das (geh.); (b) Upper-/

Lower C∼ (Parl.) Ober-/Unterhaus, das; (c) (Anat.; in machinery, etc.) Kammer, die

chamber: ∼maid n. ▶887❘ Zimmermädchen, das; ∼ music n. Kammermusik, die; C∼ of 'Commerce n. Industrie- und Handelskammer, die; ∼ pot n. Nachttopf, der

chameleon /kə'miːlɪən/ n. (Zool.; also fig.) Chamäleon, das

chamois /'ʃæmwɑː/ n., pl. same /'ʃæmwɑːz/ (a) (Zool.) Gämse, die; (b) (leather) Chamois[leder], das; ∼ leather /'ʃæmɪ-, 'ʃæmi-/ Chamoisleder, das

champagne /ʃæm'peɪn/ n. Sekt, der; (from Champagne) Champagner, der

champion /'tʃæmpɪən/ 1 n. (a) (defender) Verfechter, der/Verfechterin, die; (b) (Sport) Meister, der/Meisterin, die; Champion, der; world ∼: Weltmeister, der/-meisterin, die; (c) (animal or plant best in contest) Sieger, der; be a ∼: prämiert od. preisgekrönt sein; (d) attrib. ∼ dog preisgekrönter Hund; ∼ boxer Champion im Boxen. 2 v.t. verfechten ⟨Sache⟩; ∼ a person sich für eine Person einsetzen

championship /'tʃæmpɪənʃɪp/ n. (a) (Sport) Meisterschaft, die; defend the ∼: den Titel od. die Meisterschaft verteidigen; attrib. ∼ title/match Titel-, der/Titelkampf, der; (b) (advocacy) ∼ of a cause Engagement für eine Sache

chance /tʃɑːns/ 1 n. (a) no art. (fortune) Zufall, der; attrib. Zufalls-; zufällig; leave sth. to ∼: es dem Zufall od. Schicksal überlassen; pure ∼: reiner Zufall; by ∼: zufällig; durch Zufall; (b) (trick of fate) Zufall, der; could you by any ∼ give me a lift? könntest du mich vielleicht mitnehmen?; (c) (opportunity) Chance, die; Gelegenheit, die; (possibility) Chance, die; Möglichkeit, die; give sb. a ∼: jmdm. eine Chance geben; give sb. half a ∼: jmdm. nur die [geringste] Chance geben; given the ∼: wenn ich usw. die Gelegenheit dazu hätte; give sth. a ∼ to do sth. einer Sache (Dat.) Gelegenheit geben, etw. zu tun; get a/the ∼ to do sth. eine/die Gelegenheit haben, etw. zu tun; this is my big ∼: das ist die Chance für mich; now's your ∼! das ist deine Chance!; on the [off] ∼ of doing sth./that …: in der vagen Hoffnung, etw. zu tun/dass …; stand a ∼ of doing sth. die Chance haben, etw. zu tun; (d) in sing. or pl. (probability) have a good/fair ∼ of doing sth. gute Aussichten haben, etw. zu tun; [is there] any ∼ of your attending? besteht eine Chance, dass Sie kommen können?; there is every/not the slightest ∼ that…: es ist sehr gut möglich/es besteht keine Möglichkeit, dass …; the ∼s are that …: es ist wahrscheinlich, dass …; (e) (risk) take one's ∼: es darauf ankommen lassen; take a ∼/∼s ein Risiko/Risiken eingehen; es riskieren; take a ∼ on sth. es bei etw. auf einen Versuch ankommen lassen. 2 v.t. riskieren; ∼ it es riskieren od. darauf ankommen lassen; we'll have to ∼ that happening wir müssen es riskieren; ∼ one's arm (Brit. coll.) es riskieren

chancel /'tʃɑːnsl/ n. (Eccl.) Altarraum, der; (choir) Chor, der

chancellor /'tʃɑːnsələ(r)/ n. (Polit., Law, Univ.) Kanzler, der; C∼ of the Exchequer (Brit.) Schatzkanzler, der

chancery /'tʃɑːnsərɪ/ n. (a) C∼ (Brit. Law) Gerichtshof des Lordkanzlers; (b) (Brit. Diplom.) ≈ Botschaft, die/Gesandtschaft, die

chancy /'tʃɑːnsɪ/ adj. riskant; gewagt

chandelier /ʃændə'lɪə(r)/ n. Kronleuchter, der

change /tʃeɪndʒ/ 1 n. (a) (of name, address, lifestyle, outlook, condition, etc.) Änderung, die; (of job, surroundings, government, etc.) Wechsel, der; there has been a ∼ of plan der Plan ist geändert worden; a ∼ in the weather ein Witterungsod. Wetterumschlag; a ∼ for the better/worse eine Verbesserung/Verschlechterung; a ∼ of air would do her good eine Luftveränderung täte ihr gut; the ∼ [of life] die Wechseljahre; a ∼ of heart ein Sinneswandel; (b) no pl., no art. (process of changing) Veränderung, die; be for/against ∼: für/gegen eine Veränderung sein; (c) (for the sake of variety) Abwechslung, die; [just] for a ∼: [nur so] zur Abwechslung; make a ∼ (be different) mal etwas anderes sein (from als); a ∼ is as good as a rest (prov.) Abwechslung wirkt Wunder; (d) no pl., no indef. art. ▶938❘ (money) Wechselgeld, das; [loose or small] ∼: Kleingeld, das; give ∼, (Amer.) make ∼: herausgeben;

give sb. 40 p in ∿: jmdm. 40 p [Wechselgeld] herausgeben; **can you give me** ∿ **for 50 p?** können Sie mir 50 p wechseln?; **I haven't got** ∿ **for a pound** ich kann auf ein Pfund nicht herausgeben; **[you can] keep the** ∿: behalten Sie den Rest; [es] stimmt so; **(e) a** ∿ **[of clothes]** (fresh clothes) Kleidung zum Wechseln. **2** *v.t.* **(a)** (switch) wechseln; auswechseln ‹*Glühbirne, Batterie, Zündkerzen*›; ∿ **one's clothes** sich umziehen; ∿ **one's address/ name** seine Anschrift/seinen Namen ändern; ∿ **trains/ buses** umsteigen; ∿ **schools/one's doctor** die Schule/ den Arzt wechseln; **he's always changing jobs** er wechselt ständig den Job; ∿ **the bed** das Bett frisch beziehen; ∿ **the baby** das Baby [frisch] wickeln *od.* trockenlegen; **(b)** (transform) verwandeln; (alter) ändern; ∿ **sth./sb. into sth./sb.** etw./jmdn. in etw./jmdn. verwandeln; ∿ **direction** die Richtung ändern; **(c)** (exchange) eintauschen; ∿ **seats** die Plätze tauschen; ∿ **seats with sb.** mit jmdm. den Platz tauschen; **take sth. back to the shop and** ∿ **it for sth.** etw. [zum Laden zurückbringen und] gegen etw. umtauschen; **(d)** ▶ **938**] (in currency or denomination) wechseln ‹*Geld*›; ∿ **one's money into Deutschmarks** sein Geld in DM umtauschen. **3** *v.i.* **(a)** (alter) sich ändern; ‹*Person, Land:*› sich verändern; ‹*Wetter:*› umschlagen, sich ändern; **she'll never** ∿! sie wird sich nie ändern!; **wait for the lights to** ∿: warten, dass es grün/rot wird; ∿ **for the better** sich verbessern; **conditions** ∿d **for the worse** die Lage verschlechterte sich; **(b)** (into something else) sich verwandeln; **the wind** ∿s **from east to west** der Wind dreht von Ost nach West; **(c)** (exchange) tauschen; ∿ **with sb.** mit jmdm. tauschen; **(d)** (put on other clothes) sich umziehen; ∿ **out of/into sth.** etw. ausziehen/anziehen; **(e)** (take different train or bus) umsteigen

∿ **'over** *v.i.* **(a)** ∿ **over from sth. to sth.** von etw. zu etw. übergehen; **they** ∿d **over from one system to another** sie stellten das System auf ein anderes um; **(b)** (exchange places) die Plätze wechseln; (Sport) [die Seiten] wechseln

∿ **'round** *v.t.* umstellen ‹*Möbel, Tagesordnung[spunkte]*›; umräumen ‹*Zimmer*›

changeable /'tʃeɪndʒəbl/ *adj.* veränderlich; unbeständig ‹*Charakter, Wetter*›; wankelmütig ‹*Person*›; wechselhaft, veränderlich ‹*Wetter*›; wechselnd ‹*Wind, Stimmung*›

changeless /'tʃeɪndʒlɪs/ *adj.* unveränderlich

changing /'tʃeɪndʒɪŋ/ *adj.* wechselnd; sich ändernd

'changing room *n.* (Brit.) **(a)** (Sport) Umkleideraum, *der;* **(b)** (in shop) Umkleidekabine, *die*

channel /'tʃænl/ **1** *n.* **(a)** Kanal, *der;* (gutter) Rinnstein, *der;* (navigable part of waterway) Fahrrinne, *die;* **the C**∿ (Brit.) der [Ärmel]kanal; **(b)** (fig.) Kanal, *der;* **your application will go through the usual** ∿s Ihre Bewerbung wird auf dem üblichen Weg weitergeleitet; **(c)** (Telev., Radio) Kanal, *der;* **(d)** (on recording tape etc.) Spur, *die;* **(e)** (groove) Rille, *die.* **2** *v.t.*, (Brit.) **-ll-** (fig.: guide, direct) lenken, richten (**into** auf + *Akk.*)

Channel: ∿ **Islands** *pr. n. pl.* Kanalinseln *Pl.;* ∿ **'Tunnel** *n.* [Ärmel]kanaltunnel, *der*

chant /tʃɑ:nt/ **1** *v.t.* **(a)** (Eccl.) singen; **(b)** (utter rhythmically) skandieren. **2** *v.i.* **(a)** (Eccl.) singen; **(b)** (utter slogans etc.) Sprechchöre anstimmen. **3** *n.* **(a)** (Eccl., Mus.) Gesang, *der;* **(b)** (sing-song) Singsang, *der*

chaos /'keɪɒs/ *n., no indef. art.* Chaos, *das*

chaotic /keɪ'ɒtɪk/ *adj.* chaotisch

chap¹ /tʃæp/ *n.* (Brit. coll.) Bursche, *der;* Kerl, *der;* **old** ∿: alter Knabe (ugs.)

chap² **1** *v.t.*, **-pp-** aufplatzen lassen. **2** *n. usu. in pl.* Riss, *der*

chapel /'tʃæpl/ *n.* Kapelle, *die*

chaperon /'ʃæpərəʊn/ **1** *n.* Anstandsdame, *die;* (joc.) Anstandswauwau, *der* (ugs. scherzh.). **2** *v.t.* beaufsichtigen; (escort) begleiten

chaplain /'tʃæplɪn/ *n.* Kaplan, *der*

chapter /'tʃæptə(r)/ *n.* **(a)** (of book) Kapitel, *das;* **give** ∿ **and verse for sth.** etw. hieb- und stichfest belegen; **(b)** (fig.) ∿ **in** *or* **of sb.'s life** Abschnitt in jmds. Leben; **(c)** (Eccl.) Kapitel, *das*

char¹ /tʃɑ:(r)/ *v.t. & i.*, **-rr-** (burn) verkohlen

char² *n.* ▶ **887**] (Brit.: cleaner) Putzfrau, *die*

character /'kærɪktə(r)/ *n.* **(a)** (mental or moral qualities, integrity) Charakter, *der;* **be of good** ∿: ein guter Mensch sein; einen guten Charakter haben; **a woman of** ∿: eine Frau mit Charakter; **strength of** ∿: Charakterstärke, *die;* **(b)** *no pl.* (individuality, style) Charakter, *der;* **the town has a** ∿ **all of its own** die Stadt hat einen ganz eigenen Charakter; **have no** ∿: charakterlos *od.* ohne Charakter sein; **(c)** (in novel etc.) Charakter, *der;* (part played by sb.) Rolle, *die;* **be in/out of** ∿ (fig.) typisch/untypisch sein; **his behaviour was quite out of** ∿ (fig.) sein Betragen war ganz und gar untypisch für ihn; **(d)** (coll.: extraordinary person) Original, *das;* **be [quite] a** ∿/**a real** ∿: ein [echtes/richtiges] Original sein; **(e)** (coll.: individual) Mensch, *der;* (derog.) Individuum, *das*

character: ∿ **actor** *n.* Chargenspieler, *der;* ∿ **actress** *n.* Chargenspielerin, *die*

characterisation, characterise ⇒ **characteriz-**

characteristic /kærɪktə'rɪstɪk/ **1** *adj.* charakteristisch (**of** für). **2** *n.* charakteristisches Merkmal; **one of the main** ∿s eines der charakteristischsten Merkmale

characteristically /kærɪktə'rɪstɪkəlɪ/ *adv.* in charakteristischer Weise

characterization /kærɪktərəɪ'zeɪʃn/ *n.* Charakterisierung, *die*

characterize /'kærɪktəraɪz/ *v.t.* charakterisieren

characterless /'kærɪktəlɪs/ *adj.* nichtssagend

charade /ʃə'rɑ:d/ *n.* Scharade, *die;* (fig.) Farce, *die*

charcoal /'tʃɑ:kəʊl/ *n.* **(a)** Holzkohle, *die;* (for drawing) Kohle, *die;* **(b)** ⇒ **charcoal grey**

charcoal: ∿ **'grey** *n.* [Kohlen]grau, *das;* ∿ **pencil** *n.* Kohlestift, *der*

charge /tʃɑ:dʒ/ **1** *n.* **(a)** (price) Preis, *der;* (payable to telephone company, bank, authorities, etc., for services) Gebühr, *die;* **is there a** ∿ **for it?** kostet das etwas?; **(b)** (care) Verantwortung, *die;* (task) Auftrag, *der;* (person entrusted) Schützling, *der;* **be in** ∿ **of a child** ein Kind betreuen; **the patients in** *or* **under her** ∿: die ihr anvertrauten Patienten; **be under sb.'s** ∿: unter jmds. Obhut stehen; **the officer/ teacher in** ∿: der Dienst habende Offizier/der verantwortliche Lehrer; **be in** ∿: die Verantwortung haben; **be in** ∿ **of sth.** für etw. die Verantwortung haben; (be leader) etw. leiten; **put sb. in** ∿ **of sth.** jmdn. mit der Verantwortung für etw. betrauen; **take** ∿: die Verantwortung übernehmen; **take** ∿ **of sth.** (become responsible for) etw. übernehmen; **(c)** (Law: accusation) Anklage, *die;* **make a** ∿ **against sb.** jmdn. beschuldigen; **bring a** ∿ **of sth. against sb.** jmdn. wegen etw. beschuldigen/verklagen; **press** ∿s Anzeige erstatten; **on a** ∿ **of** wegen; **(d)** (allegation) Beschuldigung, *die;* **(e)** (attack) Angriff, *der;* Attacke, *die;* **(f)** (of explosives etc.) Ladung, *die;* **(g)** (of electricity) Ladung, *die;* **put the battery on** ∿: die Batterie an das Ladegerät anschließen. **2** *v.t.* **(a)** (demand payment of or from) ∿ **sb. sth.,** ∿ **sth. to sb.** jmdm. etw. berechnen; ∿ **sb. £1 for sth.** jmdm. ein Pfund für etw. berechnen ; ∿ **sth. [up] to sb.'s account** jmdm. Konto mit etw. belasten; **(b)** (Law: accuse) anklagen; ∿ **sb. with sth.** jmdn. wegen etw. anklagen; **(c)** (formal: entrust) ∿ **sb. with sth.** jmdn. mit etw. betrauen; **(d)** (load) laden ‹*Gewehr*›; **(e)** (Electr.) laden; [auf]laden ‹*Batterie*›; ∿d **with emotion** (fig.) voller Gefühl; **(f)** (rush at) angreifen; **(g)** (formal: command) befehlen; ∿ **sb. to do sth.** jmdm. befehlen, etw. zu tun. **3** *v.i.* **(a)** (attack) angreifen; ∿! Angriff!; Attacke!; ∿ **at sb./sth.** jmdn./etw. angreifen; **he** ∿d **into a wall** (fig.) er krachte gegen eine Mauer; **(b)** (coll.: hurry) sausen

chargeable /'tʃɑ:dʒəbl/ *adj.* **be** ∿ **to sb.** auf jmds. Kosten gehen

'charge card *n.* Kreditkarte, *die*

chargé d'affaires /ʃɑ:ʒeɪ dæ'feə(r)/ *n., pl.* **chargés d'affaires** /ʃɑ:ʒeɪ dæ'feə(r)/ Chargé d'affaires, *der;* [diplomatischer] Geschäftsträger

charger /'tʃɑ:dʒə(r)/ *n.* (Electr.) [Batterie]ladegerät, *das*

chariot /'tʃærɪət/ *n.* (Hist.) [zweirädriger] Streitwagen

charisma /kə'rɪzmə/ *n., pl.* ∿**ta** /kə'rɪzmətə/ Charisma, *das*

charismatic /kærɪz'mætɪk/ *adj.* charismatisch

charitable /'tʃærɪtəbl/ *adj.* **(a)** (generous, lenient) großzügig; **(b)** (of or for charity) karitativ

charity /'tʃærɪtɪ/ *n.* **(a)** (Christian love) Nächstenliebe, *die;* **(b)** (kindness) Güte, *die;* **(c)** (generosity in giving) Wohltätigkeit, *die;* **live on** ∼**/accept** ∼: von Almosen leben/Almosen annehmen; ∼ **begins at home** (prov.) man muss zuerst an die eigenen Leute denken; **give money to** ∼: Geld für wohltätige Zwecke spenden; **(d)** (institution) wohltätige Organisation

'charity shop *n.: Secondhandladen, dessen Erlöse einem wohltätigen Zweck dienen*

charlady /'tʃɑːleɪdɪ/ (Brit.) ⇒ **char²**

charlatan /'ʃɑːlətən/ *n.* Scharlatan, *der*

charm /tʃɑːm/ **1** *n.* **(a)** (act) Zauber, *der;* (thing) Zaubermittel, *das;* (words) Zauberspruch, *der;* Zauberformel, *die;* **lucky** ∼: Glücksbringer, *der;* **work like a** ∼: Wunder wirken, **(b)** (talisman) Talisman, *der;* **(c)** (trinket) Anhänger, *der;* **(d)** (attractiveness) Reiz, *der;* (of person) Charme, *der;* **turn on the** ∼ (coll.) auf charmant machen (ugs.). **2** *v.t.* **(a)** (captivate) bezaubern; **(b)** (by magic) verzaubern; **lead a** ∼**ed life** unter einem Glücksstern geboren sein

charming /'tʃɑːmɪŋ/ *adj.* bezaubernd; ∼**!** (iron.) [wie] charmant! (iron.)

chart /tʃɑːt/ **1** *n.* **(a)** (map) Karte, *die;* **weather** ∼: Wetterkarte, *die;* **(b)** (graph etc.) Schaubild, *das;* (diagram) Diagramm, *das;* **(c)** (tabulated information) Tabelle, *die;* **the** ∼**s** (of pop records) die Hitliste. **2** *v.t.* grafisch darstellen; (map) kartographisch erfassen; (fig.: describe) schildern

charter /'tʃɑːtə(r)/ **1** *n.* Charta, *die;* (of foundation also) Gründungs- *od.* Stiftungsurkunde, *die;* (fig.) Freibrief, *der.* **2** *v.t.* (Transport) chartern ⟨ *Schiff, Flugzeug* ⟩; mieten ⟨ *Bus* ⟩

chartered ac'countant *n.* ▶ 887 | (Brit.) Wirtschaftsprüfer, *der*/-prüferin, *die*

charter: ∼ **flight** *n.* Charterflug, *der;* ∼ **plane** *n.* Charterflugzeug, *das*

charwoman /'tʃɑːwʊmən/ ⇒ **char²**

chary /'tʃeərɪ/ *adj.* **(a)** (sparing, ungenerous) zurückhaltend **(of** mit); **(b)** (cautious) vorsichtig; **be** ∼ **of doing sth.** darauf bedacht sein, etw. nicht zu tun

chase /tʃeɪs/ **1** *n.* Verfolgungsjagd, *die;* **car** ∼: Verfolgungsjagd im Auto; **give** ∼ **[to the thief]** [dem Dieb] hinterherjagen. **2** *v.t.* (pursue) jagen; ∼ **sth.** (fig.) einer Sache (*Dat.*) nachjagen. **3** *v.i.* ∼ **after sb./sth.** hinter jmdm./ etw. herjagen

∼ **a'bout,** ∼ **a'round** *v.i.* herumrasen (ugs.)

∼ **a'way** *v.t.* wegjagen

∼ **round** ⇒ ∼ **around**

∼ **'up** *v.t.* (coll.) ausfindig machen

chaser /'tʃeɪsə(r)/ *n.* **drink sth. as a** ∼ (coll.) etw. zum Nachspülen trinken (ugs.); **drink beer with vodka** ∼**s** Bier trinken und mit Wodka nachspülen

chasm /'kæzm/ *n.* (lit. or fig.) Kluft, *die*

chassis /'ʃæsɪ/ *n., pl. same* /'ʃæsɪz/ (Motor Veh.) Chassis, *das;* Fahrgestell, *das*

chaste /tʃeɪst/ *adj.* keusch

chasten /'tʃeɪsn/ *v.t.* **(a)** züchtigen (geh.); strafen; **(b)** (fig.) dämpfen ⟨ *Stimmung* ⟩; demütigen ⟨ *Person* ⟩

chastening /'tʃeɪsənɪŋ/ *adj.* ernüchternd

chastise /tʃæ'staɪz/ *v.t.* **(a)** (punish) züchtigen (geh.); bestrafen; **(b)** (thrash) züchtigen (geh.)

chastisement /tʃæ'staɪzmənt/ *n.* Züchtigung, *die* (geh.); Strafe, *die*

chastity /'tʃæstɪtɪ/ *n., no pl.* Keuschheit, *die*

chat /tʃæt/ **1** *n.* **(a)** Schwätzchen, *die;* **have a** ∼ **about sth.** sich über etw. (*Akk.*) unterhalten; **(b)** *no pl., no indef. art.* (∼ting) Geplauder, *das.* **2** *v.i.*, **-tt-** plaudern; ∼ **with** *or* **to sb. about sth.** sich mit jmdm. über etw. (*Akk.*) unterhalten

∼ **'up** *v.t.* (Brit. coll.) sich heranmachen an (+ *Akk.*) (ugs.); (amorously) anmachen (ugs.)

'chat show *n.* Talk-Show, *die*

chattel /'tʃætl/ *n., usu. in pl.* ∼**[s]** bewegliche Habe (geh.)

chatter /'tʃætə(r)/ **1** *v.i.* **(a)** schwatzen; **(b)** (rattle) ⟨ *Zähne* ⟩ klappern; **his teeth** ∼**ed** er klapperte mit den Zähnen. **2** *n.* **(a)** Schwatzen, *das;* **(b)** (of teeth) Klappern, *das*

chatterbox /'tʃætəbɒks/ *n.* Quasselstrippe, *die* (ugs.); (child) Plappermäulchen, *das*

chatty /'tʃætɪ/ *adj.* gesprächig

chauffeur /'ʃəʊfə(r), ʃəʊ'fɜː(r)/ **1** *n.* ▶ 887 | Fahrer, *der;* Chauffeur, *der;* ∼**-driven car** Wagen mit Chauffeur. **2** *v.t.* fahren

chauvinism /'ʃəʊvɪnɪzm/ *n., no pl.* Chauvinismus, *der;* **male** ∼: männlicher Chauvinismus

chauvinist /'ʃəʊvɪnɪst/ *n.* Chauvinist, *der*/Chauvinistin, *die;* **male** ∼/**[male]** ∼ **pig** Chauvinist, *der*/Chauvinistenschwein, *das*

chauvinistic /ʃəʊvɪ'nɪstɪk/ *adj.* chauvinistisch

cheap /tʃiːp/ **1** *adj.* **(a)** billig; (at reduced rate) verbilligt; **be** ∼ **and nasty** billiger Ramsch sein; **be** ∼ **at the price** sehr preiswert sein; (fig.) es wert sein; **on the** ∼ (coll.) billig, **(b)** (worthless) billig ⟨ *Aussehen* ⟩; gemein ⟨ *Lügner* ⟩; schäbig ⟨ *Verhalten, Betragen* ⟩. **2** *adv.* billig; **be going** ∼: besonders günstig sein (ugs.)

cheapen /'tʃiːpn/ *v.t.* (fig.) herabsetzen; ∼ **oneself** sich [selbst] herabsetzen

cheaply /'tʃiːplɪ/ *adv.* ⇒ **cheap 1**: billig; gemein; schäbig

cheat /tʃiːt/ **1** *n.* **(a)** (person) Schwindler, *der*/Schwindlerin, *die;* **(b)** (act) Schwindel, *der;* **that's a** ∼**!** das ist Betrug! **2** *v.t.* betrügen; ∼ **sb./sth. [out] of sth.** jmdn./etw. um etw. betrügen. **3** *v.i.* betrügen; (Sch.) täuschen; ∼ **at cards** beim Kartenspielen mogeln

Chechenia, Chechnya /tʃetʃ'nɪɑː/ *pr. ns.* Tschetschenien (*das*)

check¹ /tʃek/ **1** *n.* **(a)** (stoppage, thing that restrains) Hindernis, *die;* (restraint) Kontrolle, *die;* **[hold** *or* **keep sth.] in** ∼: [etw.] unter Kontrolle [halten]; **act as a** ∼ **upon sth.** etw. unter Kontrolle halten; **(b)** (for accuracy) Kontrolle, *die;* **make a** ∼ **on sth./sb.** etw./jmdn. überprüfen *od.* kontrollieren; **keep a** ∼ **on** überprüfen; kontrollieren; überwachen ⟨ *Verdächtigen* ⟩; **(c)** (Amer.: bill) Rechnung, *die;* **(d)** (Amer.) ⇒ **cheque; (e)** (Chess) Schach, *das;* **be in** ∼: im Schach stehen. **2** *v.t.* **(a)** (restrain) unter Kontrolle halten; unterdrücken ⟨ *Ärger, Lachen* ⟩; ∼ **oneself** sich beherrschen; **(b)** (examine accuracy of) nachprüfen; nachsehen ⟨ *Hausaufgaben* ⟩; kontrollieren ⟨ *Fahrkarte* ⟩; (Amer.: mark with tick) abhaken. **3** *v.i.* ∼ **on sth.** etw. überprüfen; ∼ **with sb.** bei jmdm. nachfragen. **4** *int.* (Chess) Schach

∼ **'in** *v.t.* (at airport) ∼ **in one's luggage** sein Gepäck abfertigen lassen *od.* einchecken. **2** *v.i.* (arrive at hotel) ankommen; (report one's arrival) sich melden; (at airport) einchecken

∼ **'off** *v.t.* abhaken

∼ **'out 1** *v.t.* überprüfen. **2** *v.i.* ∼ **out [of one's hotel]** abreisen

∼ **'over** *v.t.* durchsehen

∼ **'up** *v.i.* überprüfen; ∼ **up on sb./sth.** jmdn./etw. überprüfen *od.* kontrollieren

check² *n.* (pattern) Karo, *das*

checked /tʃekt/ *adj.* (patterned) kariert

checkerboard /'tʃekəbɔːd/ *n.* (Amer.) Schachbrett, *das*

checkers /'tʃekəz/ *n., no pl.* (Amer.) ⇒ **draughts**

'check-in *n.* Abfertigung, *die; attrib.* Abfertigungs-

'checking account *n.* (Amer.) Girokonto, *das*

check: ∼**list** *n.* Checkliste, *die;* ∼**mate 1** *n.* [Schach]matt, *das;* **2** *int.* [schach]matt; ∼**out** *n.* Abreise, *die;* ∼**out [desk** *or* **point** *or* **counter] Kasse, *die;* ∼**point** *n.* Kontrollpunkt, *der;* ∼**-up** *n.* (Med.) Untersuchung, *die*

Cheddar /'tʃedə(r)/ *n.* Cheddar[käse], *der*

cheek /tʃiːk/ *n.* **(a)** ▶ 672 | Backe, *die;* Wange, *die* (geh.); **turn the other** ∼ (fig.) die andere Wange darbieten; **(b)** (impertinence) Frechheit, *die;* **have the** ∼ **to do sth.** die Frechheit besitzen, etw. zu tun

cheekily /'tʃiːkɪlɪ/ *adv.,* **cheeky** /'tʃiːkɪ/ *adj.* frech

cheep /tʃiːp/ **1** *v.i.* piep[s]en. **2** *n.* Piep[s]en, *das*

cheer /tʃɪə(r)/ **1** *n.* **(a)** (applause) Beifallsruf, *der;* **give three** ∼**s for sb.** jmdn. [dreimal] hochleben lassen; **(b)** *in pl.* (Brit. coll.: as a toast) prost; **(c)** *in pl.* (Brit. coll.: thank you) danke; **(d)** *in pl.* (Brit. coll.: goodbye) tschüs (ugs.). **2** *v.t.* **(a)** (applaud) ∼ **sth./sb.** etw. bejubeln/jmdm. zujubeln; **(b)** (gladden) aufmuntern; aufheitern. **3** *v.i.* jubeln

~ **'on** v.t. anfeuern ‹*Sportler, Wettkämpfer*›
~ **'up 1** v.t. aufheitern. **2** v.i. bessere Laune bekommen;
~ up! Kopf hoch!

cheerful /'tʃɪəfl/ adj. (in good spirits) fröhlich; gut gelaunt; (bright, pleasant) heiter; erfreulich ‹*Aussichten*›; lustig ‹*Feuer*›

cheerfully /'tʃɪəfəlɪ/ adv. vergnügt; **the fire blazed ~:** das Feuer brannte lustig

cheerily /'tʃɪərɪlɪ/ adv. fröhlich

cheering /'tʃɪərɪŋ/ **1** adj. (a) (gladdening) fröhlich stimmend; (b) (applauding) jubelnd. **2** n. Jubeln, das

cheerio /tʃɪərɪ'əʊ/ int. (Brit. coll.) tschüs (ugs.)

cheerless /'tʃɪəlɪs/ adj. freudlos; düster ‹*Aussichten*›

cheery /'tʃɪərɪ/ adj. fröhlich

cheese /tʃi:z/ n. **(a)** (food) Käse, der; ~s Käsesorten; **(b)** (whole) Käselaib, der

cheese: ~**board** n. Käseplatte, die; ~**cake** n. Käsetorte, die; ~**cloth** n. [indischer] Baumwollstoff

cheesed off /tʃi:zd 'ɒf/ adj. (Brit. coll.) angeödet (ugs.)

cheetah /'tʃi:tə/ n. (Zool.) Gepard, der

chef /ʃef/ n. ▶ 887 | Küchenchef, der; (as profession) Koch, der

chemical /'kemɪkl/ **1** adj. chemisch. **2** n. Chemikalie, die

chemical 'warfare n. chemische Krieg[s]führung

chemist /'kemɪst/ n. ▶ 887 | **(a)** (scientist) Chemiker, der/ Chemikerin, die; **(b)** (Brit.: pharmacist) Drogist, der/Drogistin, die; ~**'s [shop]** Drogerie, die

chemistry /'kemɪstrɪ/ n., no pl. **(a)** no indef. art. Chemie, die; **(b)** (fig.) unerklärliche Wirkungskraft

chemistry: ~ **laboratory** n. Chemiesaal, der; ~ **set** n. Chemiebaukasten, der

chemotherapy /ki:mə'θerəpɪ/ n. Chemotherapie, die

cheque /tʃek/ n. ▶ 938 | Scheck, der; **write a ~:** einen Scheck ausfüllen; **pay by ~:** mit [einem] Scheck bezahlen

cheque: ~**book** n. Scheckbuch, das; ~**book journalism** n. Scheckbuchjournalismus, der; ~ **card** n. Scheckkarte, die

chequered /'tʃekəd/ adj. **(a)** kariert; **(b)** (fig.) bewegt ‹*Geschichte, Leben, Laufbahn*›

cherish /'tʃerɪʃ/ v.t. **(a)** (value and keep) hegen ‹*Hoffnung, Gefühl*›; in Ehren halten ‹*[Erinnerungs]gegenstand*›; **(b)** (foster) ~ sb. [liebevoll] für jmdn. sorgen

cherry /'tʃerɪ/ **1** n. Kirsche, die. **2** adj. kirschrot

cherry: ~ **blossom** n. Kirschblüte, die; ~ '**brandy** n. Cherrybrandy, der; ≈ Kirschlikör, der; ~**pick 1** v.t. sich (*Dat.*) [her]aussuchen (*from* aus); **2** v.i. sich (*Dat.*) die Rosinen herauspicken; ~ **stone** n. Kirschkern, der

cherub /'tʃerəb/ n., pl. ~s (Art) Putte, die; (child) Engelchen, das

chess /tʃes/ n., no pl., no indef. art. das Schach[spiel]; **play ~:** Schach spielen

chess: ~**board** n. Schachbrett, das; ~**man** n. Schachfigur, die; ~ **player** n. Schachspieler, der/-spielerin, die

chest /tʃest/ n. **(a)** Kiste, die; (for clothes or money) Truhe, die; **(b)** ▶ 672 | (part of body) Brust, die; **get sth. off one's ~** (fig. coll.) sich (*Dat.*) etw. von der Seele reden

chest: ~ **expander** n. Expander, der; ~ **measurement** n. Brustumfang, der

chestnut /'tʃesnʌt/ **1** n. **(a)** Kastanie, die; **(b)** (colour) Kastanienbraun, das; **(c)** (stale story or topic) **[old]** ~**:** alte od. olle Kamelle (ugs.); **(d)** (horse) Fuchs, der. **2** adj. (colour) ~**[-brown]** kastanienbraun

'chestnut tree n. Kastanienbaum, der

chest of 'drawers n. Kommode, die

chew /tʃu:/ **1** v.t. kauen; ~ **one's fingernails** an den [Finger]nägeln kauen; *see also* **bite off; cud. 2** v.i. kauen **(on** auf + *Dat.*); ~ **on** or **over sth.** (fig.) sich (*Dat.*) etw. durch den Kopf gehen lassen. **3** n. Kauen, das

---

'chewing gum n. Kaugummi, der od. das

chewy /'tʃu:ɪ/ adj. zäh ‹*Fleisch, Bonbon*›

chic /ʃi:k/ **1** adj. schick; elegant. **2** n. Schick, der

chicane /ʃɪ'keɪn/ n. (Sport) Schikane, die

chick /tʃɪk/ n. **(a)** Küken, das; **(b)** (sl.: young woman) Biene, die (ugs.)

chicken /'tʃɪkɪn/ **1** n. **(a)** Huhn, das; (grilled, roasted) Hähnchen, das; **don't count your ~s [before they are hatched]** (prov.) man soll den Pelz nicht verkaufen, ehe man den Bären erlegt hat; **(b) she's no ~** (coll.: is no longer young) sie ist nicht mehr die Jüngste; **(c)** (coll.: coward) Angsthase, der. **2** adj. (coll.) feig[e]. **3** v.i. ~ **out** (coll.) kneifen

chicken: ~**-and-'egg** adj. Huhn-Ei-‹*Frage*›; ~ **feed** n. **(a)** Hühnerfutter, das; **(b)** (fig. coll.) eine lächerliche Summe; ~**pox** n. ▶ 865 | (Med.) Windpocken *Pl.;* ~ '**soup** n. Hühnersuppe, die

'chickpea n. Kichererbse, die

chicory /'tʃɪkərɪ/ n. (plant) Chicorée, der od. die; (for coffee) Zichorie, die

chief /tʃi:f/ **1** n. **(a)** (of state, town, clan) Oberhaupt, das; (of tribe) Häuptling, der; **(b)** (of department) Leiter, der; (coll.: one's superior, boss) Chef, der; Boss, der; ~ **of police** Polizeipräsident, der; ~ **of staff** (of a service) Generalstabschef, der; (commander) Stabschef, der. **2** adj., usu. attrib. **(a)** Ober-; ~ **engineer** erster Maschinist (Seew.); **[Lord] C~ Justice** (Brit.) [Lord] Oberrichter, der; **(b)** (first in importance, influence, etc.) Haupt-; ~ **reason/aim** Hauptgrund, der/-ziel, das

chiefly /'tʃi:flɪ/ adv. hauptsächlich; vor allem

chieftain /'tʃi:ftən/ n. (of Highland clan) Oberhaupt, das; (of tribe) Stammesführer, der

chiffon /'ʃɪfɒn/ **1** n. (Textiles) Chiffon, der. **2** adj. Chiffon-

chihuahua /tʃɪ'wɑ:wə/ n. Chihuahua, der

chilblain /'tʃɪlbleɪn/ n. Frostbeule, die

child /tʃaɪld/ n., pl. ~**ren** /'tʃɪldrən/ Kind, das; **when I was a ~:** als ich klein war; **[be] with ~** (dated) schwanger [sein]

child: ~ **abuse** n. Kindesmisshandlung, die; (sexual) sexueller Missbrauch von Kindern; ~ '**benefit** n. (Brit.) Kindergeld, das; ~**birth** n. Geburt, die; ~ **care** n. **(a)** Betreuung von Kindern; **(b)** (social services department) Kinderfürsorge, die

childhood /'tʃaɪldhʊd/ n. Kindheit, die; **in ~:** als Kind; **from** or **since ~:** schon als Kind; **be in one's second ~:** an Altersschwachsinn leiden

childish /'tʃaɪldɪʃ/ adj., **childishly** /'tʃaɪldɪʃlɪ/ adv. kindlich; (derog.) kindisch

childishness /'tʃaɪldɪʃnɪs/ n., no pl. (derog.: behaviour) kindisches Benehmen

childless /'tʃaɪldlɪs/ adj. kinderlos

childlike /'tʃaɪldlaɪk/ adj. kindlich

child: ~**minder** n. ▶ 887 | (Brit.) Tagesmutter, die; ~ '**prodigy** n. Wunderkind, das; ~**proof** adj. kindersicher

children pl. of **child**

child: ~**'s play** n., no pl. (fig.) **it's ~'s play!** es ist ein Kinderspiel; **C~ Sup'port Agency** n. (Brit.) staatliche Einrichtung zur Durchsetzung von Unterhaltsansprüchen für Kinder; ~ '**welfare** n. Kinderfürsorge, die

Chile /'tʃɪlɪ/ pr. n. Chile (das)

Chilean /'tʃɪlɪən/ ▶ 947 | **1** adj. chilenisch; **sb. is ~:** jmd. ist Chilene/Chilenin. **2** n. Chilene, der/Chilenin, die

chili ⇨ **chilli**

chill /tʃɪl/ **1** n. **(a)** (cold sensation) Frösteln, das; (feverish shivering) Schüttelfrost, der; (illness) Erkältung, die; **catch a ~:** sich verkühlen od. erkälten; **(b)** (unpleasant coldness) Kühle, die; (fig.) Abkühlung, die; **take the ~ off [sth.]** etw. leicht erwärmen; **there's a ~ in the air** es ist ziemlich kühl [draußen]. **2** v.t. kühlen. **3** v.i. **(a)** abkühlen; **(b)** (Amer.) ⇨ ~ **out. 4** adj. (literary; lit. or fig.) kühl

~ **out** v.i. (Amer. coll.) (relax) sich entspannen; (calm down) sich abregen (ugs.)

'chill factor ⇨ **wind-chill factor**

chilli /'tʃɪlɪ/ n., pl. ~**es** Chili, der; ~ **con carne** /tʃɪlɪ kɒn 'kɑ:nɪ/ (Gastr.) Chili con carne

chilling /'tʃɪlɪŋ/ *adj.* (fig.) ernüchternd; frostig ‹*Art, Worte, Blick*›

chilly /'tʃɪlɪ/ *adj.* (lit. or fig.) kühl; **I am rather ～:** mir ist ziemlich kühl

chime /tʃaɪm/ **1** *n.* (a) Geläute, *das;* (b) (set of bells) Glockenspiel, *das.* **2** *v.i.* läuten; ‹*Turmuhr:*› schlagen; **chiming clock** Schlaguhr, *die.* **3** *v.t.* erklingen lassen ‹*Melodie*›; schlagen ‹*Stunde, Mitternacht*›

～ 'in *v.i.* (a) (Mus.) einstimmen; (fig.) übereinstimmen (**with** mit); (b) (interject remark) sich [in die Unterhaltung] einmischen

chimney /'tʃɪmnɪ/ *n.* (of house, factory, etc.) Schornstein, *der;* (of house also) Kamin, *der* (bes. südd.); **the smoke goes up the ～:** der Rauch zieht durch den Kaminschacht ab; **come down the ～:** durch den Kaminstein kommen; **smoke like a ～** (fig.) wie ein Schlot rauchen

chimney: ～ breast *n.* Kaminmantel, *der;* **～ pot** *n.* ≈ Schornsteinkopf, *der;* **～ sweep** *n.* ▶ 887 Schornsteinfeger, *der*

chimp /tʃɪmp/ (coll.), **chimpanzee** /tʃɪmpən'zi:/ *ns.* Schimpanse, *der*

chin /tʃɪn/ *n.* ▶ 672 Kinn, *das;* **keep one's ～ up** (fig.) den Kopf nicht hängen lassen; **～ up!** Kopf hoch!; **take it on the ～** (endure sth. courageously) es mit Fassung tragen

China /'tʃaɪnə/ *pr. n.* China (*das*)

china *n.* Porzellan, *das;* (crockery) Geschirr, *das*

china 'clay *n.* Porzellanerde, *die*

China: ～man /'tʃaɪnəmən/ *n., pl.* **～men** /'tʃaɪnəmən/ (derog.) Chinese, *der;* **～ 'tea** *n.* Chinatee, *der*

chinchilla /tʃɪn'tʃɪlə/ *n.* (Zool.) Chinchilla, *die*

Chinese /tʃaɪ'ni:z/ ▶ 897, ▶ 947 **1** *adj.* chinesisch; **sb. is ～:** jmd. ist Chinese/Chinesin. **2** *n.* (a) *pl. same* (person) Chinese, *der*/Chinesin, *die;* (b) (language) Chinesisch, *das; see also* **English 2 a**

Chinese 'lantern *n.* Lampion, *der*

chink¹ /tʃɪŋk/ *n.* (a) Spalt, *der;* **a ～ in sb.'s armour** (fig.) jmds. schwache Stelle; (b) **a ～ of light** ein Lichtspalt

chink² **1** *n.* (sound) ⇒ **clink¹** 1. **2** *v.i. & t.* ⇒ **clink¹** 2, 3

'chinstrap *n.* Kinnriemen, *der*

chintz /tʃɪnts/ *n.* Chintz, *der*

'chinwag (coll.) **1** *n.* Schwatz, *der.* **2** *v.i.* schwatzen

chip /tʃɪp/ **1** *n.* (a) Splitter, *der;* **have a ～ on one's shoulder** (fig.) einen Komplex haben; (b) *in pl.* (Brit.: fried potatoes) Pommes frites *Pl.;* (Amer.: crisps) Kartoffelchips *Pl.;* (c) **there is a ～ in this cup/paintwork** diese Tasse ist angeschlagen/etwas Farbe ist abgeplatzt; (d) (Gambling) Chip, *der;* Jeton, *der;* **when the ～s are down** (fig. coll.) wenn's ernst wird; (e) (Electronics) Chip, *der.* **2** *v.t.,* **-pp-:** (a) anschlagen ‹*Geschirr*›; **～ [off]** abschlagen; **the paint is ～ped** die Farbe ist abgesprungen; (b) **～ped potatoes** Pommes frites

～ 'in (coll.) **1** *v.i.* (a) (interrupt) sich einmischen; (b) (contribute money) etwas beisteuern; **～ in with £5** sich mit 5 Pfund an etw. (*Dat.*) beteiligen. **2** *v.t.* (contribute) beisteuern

'chipboard *n.* Spanplatte, *die*

chipmunk /'tʃɪpmʌŋk/ *n.* (Zool.) Chipmunk, *das*

chipolata /tʃɪpə'lɑːtə/ *n. kleine Wurst;* Chipolata, *die*

'chip pan *n.* Fritteuse, *die*

chippings /'tʃɪpɪŋz/ *n. pl.* (Road Constr.) Splitt, *der;* 'loose ～' „Rollsplitt"

'chip shop *n.* (Brit. coll.) Frittenbude, *die* (ugs.)

chiropodist /kɪ'rɒpədɪst/ *n.* ▶ 887 Fußpfleger, *der*/-pflegerin, *die*

chiropody /kɪ'rɒpədɪ/ *n.* Fußpflege, *die*

chirp /tʃɜːp/ *v.i.* zwitschern; ‹*Sperling:*› tschilpen; ‹*Grille:*› zirpen. **2** *n.* ⇒ **1:** Zwitschern, *das;* Tschilpen, *das;* Zirpen, *das*

chirrup /'tʃɪrəp/ **1** *v.i.* zwitschern; ‹*Sperling:*› tschilpen. **2** *n.* Zwitschern, *das;* (of sparrow) Tschilpen, *das*

chisel /'tʃɪzl/ **1** *n.* Meißel, *der;* (for wood) Stemmeisen, *das;* Beitel, *der.* **2** *v.t.,* (Brit.) **-ll-** meißeln; (in wood) hauen; stemmen

chit /tʃɪt/ *n.* (note) Notiz, *die;* (certificate) Zeugnis, *das*

chit-chat /'tʃɪttʃæt/ *n.* Plauderei, *die*

chivalrous /'ʃɪvlrəs/ *adj.,* **chivalrously** /'ʃɪvlrəslɪ/ *adv.* ritterlich

chivalry /'ʃɪvlrɪ/ *n., no pl.* (a) Ritterlichkeit, *die;* (b) **Age of C～:** Ritterzeit, *die*

chives /tʃaɪvz/ *n. pl.* Schnittlauch, *der*

chiv[v]y /'tʃɪvɪ/ *v.t.* hetzen; **～ sb. into doing sth.** jmdn. drängen, etw. zu tun; **～ sb. about sth.** jmdn. wegen etw. drängen

～ a'long *v.t.* antreiben

chloride /'klɔːraɪd/ *n.* (Chem.) Chlorid, *das*

chlorinate /'klɔːrɪneɪt/ *v.t.* chloren

chlorine /'klɔːriːn/ *n.* Chlor, *das*

chlorofluorocarbon /klɔːrəʊflʊərəʊ'kɑːbən/ *n.* Chlorfluorkohlenstoff, *der*

chloroform /'klɒrəfɔːm/ **1** *n.* Chloroform, *das.* **2** *v.t.* chloroformieren

chlorophyll /'klɒrəfɪl/ *n.* (Bot.) Chlorophyll, *das*

choc ice /'tʃɒkaɪs/ *n.* Eis mit Schokoladenüberzug

chock /tʃɒk/ **1** *n.* Bremsklotz, *der.* **2** *v.t.* blockieren

'chock-a-block *pred. adj.* voll gepfropft

'chock-full *pred. adj.* gestopft voll (ugs.); **～ with sth.** mit etw. voll gepfropft

chocolate /'tʃɒkələt, 'tʃɒklət/ **1** *n.* Schokolade, *die;* (sweet with ～ coating) Praline, *die;* **drinking ～:** Trinkschokolade, *die.* **2** *adj.* (a) (with flavour of ～) Schokoladen-; (b) (with colour of ～) **～[-brown]** schokoladenbraun

chocolate: ～ 'biscuit *n.* Schokoladenkeks, *der;* **～ box 1** *n.* Pralinenschachtel, *die;* **2** *adj.* (fig.) kitschig

choice /tʃɔɪs/ **1** *n.* (a) Wahl, *die;* **take your ～:** suchen Sie sich (*Dat.*) einen/eine/eins aus; **make a [good] ～:** eine [gute] Wahl treffen; **give sb. the ～:** jmdm. die Wahl lassen; **the ～ is yours** Sie haben die Wahl; **do sth. from ～:** etw. freiwillig tun; **have no ～ but to do sth.** keine andere Wahl haben, als etw. zu tun; **leave sb. no ～:** jmdm. keine [andere] Wahl lassen; **you have several ～s** Sie haben mehrere Möglichkeiten; (b) (thing chosen) **his ～ of wallpaper was …:** die Tapete, die er sich ausgesucht hatte, war …; (c) (variety) Auswahl, *die;* **there is a ～ of three** es gibt drei zur Auswahl; **be spoilt for ～:** die Qual der Wahl haben; **have a ～:** die Auswahl haben. **2** *adj.* ausgewählt; **～ fruit** Obst erster Wahl

choir /'kwaɪə(r)/ *n.* Chor, *der*

'choirboy *n.* Chorknabe, *der*

choke /tʃəʊk/ **1** *v.t.* (a) (lit. or fig.) ersticken; (b) (strangle) **～ [to death]** erdrosseln; (c) (fill chock-full) voll stopfen; (block up) verstopfen. **2** *v.i.* (temporarily) keine Luft [mehr] bekommen; (permanently) ersticken (**on** an + *Dat.*). **3** *n.* (Motor Veh.) Choke, *der*

～ 'back *v.t.* unterdrücken ‹*Wut*›; zurückhalten ‹*Tränen*›; hinunterschlucken (ugs.) ‹*Wut, Worte*›

choker /'tʃəʊkə(r)/ *n.* (high collar) Stehkragen, *der;* (necklace) Halsband, *das*

cholera /'kɒlərə/ *n.* ▶ 865 (Med.) Cholera, *die*

cholesterol /kə'lestərɒl/ *n.* (Med.) Cholesterin, *das*

choose /tʃuːz/ **1** *v.t.,* **chose** /tʃəʊz/, **chosen** /'tʃəʊzn/ (a) (select) wählen; (from a group) auswählen; **～ sb. as or to be or for leader** jmdn. zum Anführer wählen; (b) (decide) **～/～ not to do sth.** sich dafür/dagegen entscheiden, etw. zu tun; **there's nothing/not much/little to ～ between them** sie unterscheiden sich in nichts/nicht sehr/nur wenig voneinander. **2** *v.i.,* **chose, chosen** wählen; **when I ～:** wenn es mir passt; **～ from sth.** aus etw./(from several) unter etw. (*Dat.*) [aus]wählen

choos[e]y /'tʃuːzɪ/ *adj.* (coll.) wählerisch

chop¹ /tʃɒp/ **1** *n.* (a) Hieb, *der;* (b) (of meat) Kotelett, *das;* (c) (coll.) **get the ～** (be dismissed) rausgeworfen werden (ugs.); **sth. gets the ～:** etw. wird abgeschafft; **give sb. the ～:** jmdn. rauswerfen (ugs.); **be due for the ～:** die längste Zeit existiert haben (ugs.). **2** *v.t.,* **-pp-:** (a) hacken ‹*Holz*›; klein schneiden ‹*Fleisch, Gemüse*›; **～ped herbs** gehackte Kräuter; (b) (Sport) schneiden ‹*Ball*›. **3** *v.i.,* **-pp-:** **～ [away] at sth.** auf etw. (*Akk.*) einhacken; **～ through the bone** den Knochen durchhacken

~ **'down** *v.t.* fällen ‹*Baum*›; umhauen ‹*Busch, Pfosten*›
~ **'off** *v.t.* abhacken
~ **'up** *v.t.* klein schneiden ‹*Fleisch, Gemüse*›; zerhacken ‹*Möbel*›

chop² *v.i.*, **-pp-: she's always** ~**ping and changing** sie überlegt es sich (*Dat.*) dauernd anders

chopper /'tʃɒpə(r)/ *n.* **(a)** (axe) Beil, *das;* (cleaver) Hackbeil, *das;* **(b)** (coll.: helicopter) Hubschrauber, *der*

chopping board /'tʃɒpɪŋbɔːd/ *n.* Hackbrett, *das*

choppy /'tʃɒpɪ/ *adj.* bewegt; kabbelig (Seemannsspr.)

'chopstick *n.* [Eß]stäbchen, *das*

choral /'kɔːrl/ *adj.* Chor-

'choral society *n.* Gesangverein, *der*

chord¹ /kɔːd/ *n.* **strike a [familiar/responsive]** ~ **with sb.** (fig.) bei jmdm. eine Saite zum Erklingen bringen/ bei jmdm. Echo finden; **touch the right** ~ (fig.) den richtigen Ton anschlagen *od.* treffen

chord² *n.* (Mus.) Akkord, *der*

chore /tʃɔː(r)/ *n.* [lästige] Routinearbeit; **do the household** ~**s** die üblichen Hausarbeiten erledigen; **writing letters is a** ~: Briefe zu schreiben ist eine lästige Pflicht

choreographer /kɒrɪ'ɒgrəfə(r)/ *n.* ▶ 887 ◀ Choreograph, *der*/Choreographin, *die*

choreography /kɒrɪ'ɒgrəfɪ/ *n.* Choreographie, *die*

chorister /'kɒrɪstə(r)/ *n.* (choirboy) Chorknabe, *der*

chortle /'tʃɔːtl/ **1** *v.i.* vor Lachen glucksen. **2** *n.* Glucksen, *das*

chorus /'kɔːrəs/ **1** *n.* **(a)** (utterance) Chor, *der;* **say sth. in** ~: etw. im Chor sagen; **(b)** (of singers) Chor, *der;* (of dancers) Ballett, *das;* **(c)** (of song) Chorus, *der;* **(d)** (composition) Chor, *der.* **2** *v.t.* im Chor singen/sprechen

'chorus girl *n.* [Revue]girl, *das*

chose, chosen ⇒ **choose**

choux /ʃuː/ *n.* ~ **[pastry]** Brandteig, *der*

chow /tʃaʊ/ *n.* **(a)** (dog) Chow-Chow, *der;* **(b)** (Amer. sl.: food) Futterage, *die* (ugs.); Futter, *das* (salopp)

chowder /'tʃaʊdə(r)/ *n.* (Amer.) *Suppe od. Eintopf mit Fisch od. Muscheln, Pökelfleisch od. Schinken, Milch, Kartoffeln u. Gemüse*

Christ /kraɪst/ **1** *n.* Christus (*der*); *see also* **before 2 a.** **2** *int.* (sl.) [**oh**] ~**!**, ~ **almighty!** Herrgott noch mal! (ugs.)

christen /'krɪsn/ *v.t.* **(a)** taufen; **she was** ~**ed Martha** sie wurde [auf den Namen] Martha getauft; **(b)** (coll.: use for first time) einweihen (ugs. scherzh.)

christening /'krɪsnɪŋ/ *n.* Taufe, *die;* **her** ~ **will be next Sunday** sie wird nächsten Sonntag getauft

Christian /'krɪstjən/ **1** *adj.* christlich. **2** *n.* Christ, *der*/Christin, *die*

Christianity /krɪstɪ'ænɪtɪ/ *n.*, *no pl.*, *no art.* das Christentum

'Christian name *n.* Vorname, *der*

Christmas /'krɪsməs/ *n.* ▶ 836 ◀ Weihnachten, *das od. Pl.;* **merry** *or* **happy** ~**:** frohe *od.* fröhliche Weihnachten; **what did you get for** ~? was hast du zu Weihnachten bekommen?; **at** ~: [zu *od.* an] Weihnachten

Christmas: ~ **cake** *n.* Weihnachtskuchen, *der; mit Marzipan und Zuckerguss verzierter, reichhaltiger Gewürzkuchen;* ~ **card** *n.* Weihnachtskarte, *die;* ~ **'carol** *n.* Weihnachtslied, *das;* ~ **'Day** *n.* erster Weihnachtsfeiertag; ~ **'Eve** *n.* Heiligabend, *der;* ~ **present** *n.* Weihnachtsgeschenk, *das;* ~ **'pudding** *n.* Plumpudding, *der;* ~ **time** *n.* Weihnachtszeit, *die;* **at** ~ **time** in der *od.* zur Weihnachtszeit; ~ **tree** *n.* Weihnachtsbaum, *der*

chromatic /krə'mætɪk/ *adj.* chromatisch

chrome /krəʊm/ *n.* **(a)** (chromium-plate) Chrom, *das;* **(b)** (colour) Chromgelb, *das*

chromium /'krəʊmɪəm/ *n.* Chrom, *das*

chromium: ~**-plate 1** *n.* Chrom, *das;* **2** *v.t.* verchromen; ~**-plated** *adj.* verchromt

chromosome /'krəʊməsəʊm/ *n.* (Biol.) Chromosom, *das*

chronic /'krɒnɪk/ *adj.* **(a)** chronisch; ~ **sufferers from arthritis** Personen, die an chronischer Arthritis leiden; ~ **fatigue syndrome** chronisches Müdigkeitssyndrom;

(b) (Brit. coll.: bad, intense) katastrophal (ugs.); **be** ~**:** eine [einzige] Katastrophe sein (ugs.)

chronicle /'krɒnɪkl/ **1** *n.* **(a)** Chronik, *die;* **(b)** (account) Schilderung, *die.* **2** *v.t.* [chronologisch] aufzeichnen

chronological /krɒnə'lɒdʒɪkl/ *adj.* chronologisch

chronology /krə'nɒlədʒɪ/ *n.* Chronologie, *die;* (table) Zeittafel, *die*

chrysalis /'krɪsəlɪs/ *n.*, *pl.* ~**es** (Zool.) **(a)** (pupa) Chrysalide, *die* (Zool.); Puppe, *die;* **(b)** (case enclosing pupa) Puppenhülle, *die*

chrysanth /krɪ'sænθ/ (coll.), **chrysanthemum** /krɪ'sænθɪməm/ *ns.* (Bot.) **(a)** (flower) Chrysantheme, *die;* **(b)** (plant) Chrysanthemum, *das;* Wucherblume, *die*

chubby /'tʃʌbɪ/ *adj.* pummelig; rundlich ‹*Gesicht*›; ~ **cheeks** Pausbacken (fam.)

chuck¹ /tʃʌk/ *v.t.* (coll.) **(a)** (throw) schmeißen (ugs.); **(b)** (throw out) wegschmeißen (ugs.); ~ **the whole thing** alles hinschmeißen

~ **a'way** *v.t.* (coll.) wegschmeißen (ugs.); (fig.: waste) zum Fenster rauswerfen (ugs.) ‹*Geld*› (**on** für); vertun ‹*Chance, Gelegenheit*›

~ **'out** *v.t.* (coll.) wegschmeißen (ugs.); (fig.: eject) rausschmeißen (ugs.)

chuck² *n.* (of drill, lathe) Futter, *das*

chuckle /'tʃʌkl/ **1** *v.i.* leise [vor sich hin] lachen (**at** über + *Akk.*). **2** *n.* leises, glucksendes Lachen; **have a** ~ [**to oneself**] **about sth.** leise über etw. (*Akk.*) vor sich hin lachen

chuffed /tʃʌft/ *pred. adj.* (Brit. coll.) zufrieden (**about, at, with** über + *Akk.*); **be** ~**:** sich freuen

chug /tʃʌg/ **1** *v.i.*, **-gg-** ‹*Motor:*› tuckern. **2** *n.* Tuckern, *das*

chum /tʃʌm/ *n.* (coll.) Kumpel, *der* (salopp)

chunk /tʃʌŋk/ *n.* dickes Stück; (broken off) Brocken, *der*

chunky /'tʃʌŋkɪ/ *adj.* **(a)** (containing chunks) ‹*Orangenmarmelade, Hundefutter*› mit ganzen Stücken; **(b)** (small and sturdy, short and thick) stämmig; **(c)** (made of thick material) dick ‹*Pullover, Strickjacke*›

Chunnel /'tʃʌnl/ *n.* (coll.) [Ärmel]kanaltunnel, *der*

church /tʃɜːtʃ/ *n.* **(a)** Kirche, *die;* **in** *or* **at** ~**:** in der Kirche; **go to** ~**:** in die *od.* zur Kirche gehen; **(b)** **C**~ (body) die Kirche; **the C**~ **of England** die Kirche von England

church: ~**goer** *n.* Kirchgänger, *der*/-gängerin, *die;* ~**warden** *n.* Kirchenvorsteher, *der*/-vorsteherin, *die;* ~**yard** *n.* Friedhof, *der* (bei einer Kirche)

churlish /'tʃɜːlɪʃ/ *adj.* (ill-bred) ungehobelt; (surly) griesgrämig

churn /tʃɜːn/ **1** *n.* (Brit.) **(a)** (for making butter) Butterfass, *das;* **(b)** (milk-can) Milchkanne, *die.* **2** *v.t.* **(a)** ~ **butter** buttern; **(b)** aufwühlen ‹*Wasser, Schlamm*›. **3** *v.i.* ‹*Meer:*› wallen (geh.); ‹*Schiffsschraube:*› wirbeln; **my stomach was** ~**ing** mir drehte sich der Magen um

~ **'out** *v.t.* massenweise produzieren (ugs.)

~ **'up** *v.t.* aufwühlen

chute /ʃuːt/ *n.* Schütte, *die;* (for persons) Rutsche, *die*

chutney /'tʃʌtnɪ/ *n.* Chutney, *das*

CI *abbr.* (Brit.) **Channel Islands**

CIA *abbr.* (Amer.) **Central Intelligence Agency** CIA, *der od. die*

cicada /sɪ'kɑːdə/ *n.* (Zool.) Zikade, *die*

CID *abbr.* (Brit.) **Criminal Investigation Department** C. I. D.; **the** ~**:** die Kripo

cider /'saɪdə(r)/ *n.* ≈ Apfelwein, *der*

cider: ~ **apple** *n.* Mostapfel, *der;* ~ **press** *n.* Mostpresse, *die*

cig /sɪg/ *n.* (coll.) Glimmstängel, *der* (ugs.)

cigar /sɪ'gɑː(r)/ *n.* Zigarre, *die*

cigarette /sɪgə'ret/ *n.* Zigarette, *die*

cigarette: ~ **card** *n.* Zigarettenbild, *das;* ~ **case** *n.* Zigarettenetui, *das;* ~ **end** *n.* Zigarettenstummel, *der;* ~ **lighter** *n.* Feuerzeug, *das;* (in car) Zigarettenanzünder, *der;* ~ **packet** *n.* Zigarettenschachtel, *die;* ~ **paper** *n.* Zigarettenpapier, *das*

cigar: ~ **lighter** ⇨ **cigarette lighter;** ~-**shaped** *adj.* zigarrenförmig

C.-in-C. *abbr.* (Mil.) **Commander-in-Chief**

cinch /sɪntʃ/ *n.* (coll.) (easy thing) Klacks, *der* (ugs.); Kinderspiel, *das;* (Amer.: sure thing) todsichere Sache (ugs.)

cinder /'sɪndə(r)/ *n.* ausgeglühtes Stück Holz/Kohle; ~s Asche, *die;* **burnt to a** ~: völlig verkohlt

Cinderella /sɪndə'relə/ *n.* Aschenbrödel, *das;* Aschenputtel, *das*

cine /'sɪnɪ/: ~ **camera** *n.* Filmkamera, *die;* ~ **film** *n.* Schmalfilm, *der*

cinema /'sɪnɪmə/ *n.* (a) (Brit.: building) Kino, *das;* go to the ~: ins Kino gehen; **what's on at the** ~? was gibt's im Kino?; (b) *no pl., no art.* (cinematography) Kinematographie, *die;* (c) (films, film production) Film, *der*

cinema: ~ **complex** *n.* Kinocenter, *das;* ~-**goer** *n.* (Brit.) Kinogänger, *der/*-gängerin, *die*

cinematography /sɪnɪmə'tɒɡrəfɪ/ *n., no pl.* Kinematographie, *die*

cinnamon /'sɪnəmən/ *n.* Zimt, *der*

cipher /'saɪfə(r)/ *n.* (a) (code, secret writing) Chiffre, *die;* Geheimschrift, *die;* **in** ~: chiffriert; (b) (symbol for zero) [Ziffer] Null, *die;* (c) (fig.: nonentity) Nummer, *die*

circa /'sɜːkə/ *prep.* zirka

circle /'sɜːkl/ **1** *n.* (a) (also Geom.) Kreis, *der;* **fly/stand in a** ~: im Kreis fliegen/stehen; **run round in** ~s (fig. coll.) hektisch herumlaufen (ugs.); **go round in** ~s im Kreis laufen; (fig.) sich im Kreis drehen; ~ **of friends** Freundeskreis, *der;* **come full** ~ (fig.) zum Ausgangspunkt zurückkehren; (b) (seats in theatre or cinema) Rang, *der.* **2** *v.i.* kreisen; (walk in a ~) im Kreis gehen. **3** *v.t.* (a) (move in a ~ round) umkreisen; **the aircraft** ~**d the airport** das Flugzeug kreiste über dem Flughafen; (b) (draw ~ round) einkreisen

~ **'back** *v.i.* auf einem Umweg zurückkehren

~ **'round** *v.i.* kreisen

circuit /'sɜːkɪt/ *n.* (a) (Electr.) Schaltung, *die;* (path of current) Stromkreis, *der;* (b) (Motor racing) Rundkurs, *der;* (c) (journey round) Runde, *die;* (by car etc.) Rundfahrt, *die*

circuitous /sə'kjuːɪtəs/ *adj.* umständlich; **the path followed a** ~ **route** der Pfad machte einen weiten Bogen

circuitry /'sɜːkɪtrɪ/ *n.* (Electr.) Schaltungen *Pl.*

circular /'sɜːkjʊlə(r)/ **1** *adj.* (a) (round) kreisförmig; (b) (moving in circle) Kreis⟨bahn, -bewegung⟩; (c) (Logic) **that argument is** ~: das ist ein Zirkelschluss *od.* -beweis. **2** *n.* (letter, notice) Rundschreiben, *das;* (advertisement) Werbeprospekt, *der*

circular: ~ **'letter** ⇨ **circular 2;** ~ **'saw** *n.* Kreissäge, *die;* ~ **'tour** *n.* (Brit.) Rundfahrt, *die* (**of** durch)

circulate /'sɜːkjʊleɪt/ **1** *v.i.* ⟨Blut, Flüssigkeit:⟩ zirkulieren; ⟨Geld, Gerüchte:⟩ kursieren; ⟨Nachrichten:⟩ sich herumsprechen; ⟨Verkehr:⟩ fließen; ⟨Personen, Wein usw.:⟩ die Runde machen (ugs.). **2** *v.t.* in Umlauf setzen ⟨Gerücht⟩; verbreiten ⟨Nachricht, Information⟩; zirkulieren lassen ⟨Aktennotiz, Rundschreiben⟩; herumgehen lassen ⟨Buch, Bericht⟩ (**around** in + *Dat.*)

circulation /sɜːkjʊ'leɪʃn/ *n.* (a) (Physiol.) Kreislauf, *der;* Zirkulation, *die;* (of sap, water) Zirkulation, *die;* **poor** ~ (Physiol.) schlechte Durchblutung; Kreislaufstörungen *Pl.;* (b) (of news, rumour, publication) Verbreitung, *die;* **have a wide** ~: große Verbreitung finden; (c) (of notes, coins) Umlauf, *der;* **withdraw from** ~: aus dem Umlauf ziehen; **put/come into** ~: in Umlauf bringen/kommen; (d) (fig.) **be back in** ~: wieder auf dem Posten sein; **be out of** ~: aus dem Verkehr gezogen sein (ugs. scherzh.); (e) (number of copies sold) verkaufte Auflage

circumcise /'sɜːkəmsaɪz/ *v.t.* beschneiden

circumcision /sɜːkəm'sɪʒn/ *n.* Beschneidung, *die*

circumference /sə'kʌmfərəns/ *n.* Umfang, *der;* (periphery) Kreislinie, *die*

circumflex /'sɜːkəmfleks/ *n.* Zirkumflex, *der*

circumnavigate /sɜːkəm'nævɪɡeɪt/ *v.t.* umfahren; (by sail) umsegeln

circumscribe /'sɜːkəmskraɪb/ *v.t.* (lay down limits of) eingrenzen; einschränken ⟨Macht, Handlungsfreiheit usw.⟩

circumspect /'sɜːkəmspekt/ *adj.* umsichtig

circumstance /'sɜːkəmstəns/ *n.* (a) *usu. in pl.* Umstand, *der;* **in** *or* **under the** ~s unter den gegebenen *od.* diesen Umständen; **in certain** ~s unter [gewissen] Umständen; **under no** ~s unter [gar] keinen Umständen; (b) *in pl.* (financial state) Verhältnisse

circumstantial /sɜːkəm'stænʃl/ *adj.* ~ **evidence** Indizienbeweise; **be purely** ~ ⟨Beweis:⟩ nur auf Indizien gegründet sein

circumvent /sɜːkəm'vent/ *v.t.* umgehen; hinters Licht führen

circus /'sɜːkəs/ *n.* Zirkus, *der*

cirrhosis /sɪ'rəʊsɪs/ *n., pl.* **cirrhoses** /sɪ'rəʊsiːz/ ▶ 865 | (Med.) Zirrhose, *die;* ~ **of the liver** Leberzirrhose, *die*

cissy /'sɪsɪ/ ⇨ **sissy**

cistern /'sɪstən/ *n.* Wasserkasten, *der;* (in roof) Wasserbehälter, *der*

citadel /'sɪtədəl/ *n.* Zitadelle, *die*

citation /saɪ'teɪʃn/ *n.* (a) *no pl.* (citing) Zitieren, *das;* (b) (quotation) Zitat, *das*

cite /saɪt/ *v.t.* (quote) zitieren; anführen ⟨Beispiel⟩

citizen /'sɪtɪzən/ *n.* (a) (of town, city) Bürger, *der/*Bürgerin, *die;* (b) (of state) [Staats]bürger, *der/*-bürgerin, *die;* **he is a British** ~: er ist britischer Staatsbürger *od.* Brite; **C**~**'s Advice Bureau** (Brit.) Bürgerberatungsstelle, *die;* ~**'s arrest** Festnahme durch eine Zivilperson; ~**s' band radio** CB-Funk, *der;* (radio set) CB-Funkgerät, *das*

citizenship /'sɪtɪzənʃɪp/ *n.* Staatsbürgerschaft, *die*

citric acid /sɪtrɪk 'æsɪd/ *n.* (Chem.) Zitronensäure, *die*

citrus /'sɪtrəs/ *n.* ~ [**fruit**] Zitrusfrucht, *die*

city /'sɪtɪ/ *n.* ▶ 1159 | (a) [Groß]stadt, *die;* **the C**~: die [Londoner] City; das Londoner Banken- und Börsenviertel; (b) (Brit.) Stadt, *die* (Ehrentitel für bestimmte Städte, meist Bischofssitze); (c) (Amer.) ≈ Stadtgemeinde, *die;* (d) *attrib.* [Groß]stadt⟨leben, -verkehr⟩; ~ **lights** Lichter der Großstadt

city 'centre *n.* Stadtzentrum, *das;* Innenstadt, *die*

civic /'sɪvɪk/ *adj.* (a) (of citizens, citizenship) [Staats]bürger-; [staats]bürgerlich; **my** ~ **responsibility** meine Verantwortung als Staatsbürger; (b) (of city) Stadt-; städtisch; ~ **centre** Verwaltungszentrum der Stadt

civies ⇨ **civvies**

civil /'sɪvɪl, 'sɪvl/ *adj.* (a) (not military) zivil; **in** ~ **life** im Zivilleben; (b) (polite, obliging) höflich; (c) (Law) Zivil⟨gerichtsbarkeit, -prozess, -verfahren⟩; zivilrechtlich; (d) (of citizens) bürgerlich; Bürger⟨krieg, -recht, -pflicht⟩

civil: ~ **avi'ation** *n.* Zivilluftfahrt, *die;* ~ **de'fence** *n.* Zivilschutz, *der;* ~ **diso'bedience** *n.* ziviler Ungehorsam; ~ **engi'neer** *n.* ▶ 887 | Bauingenieur, *der/*-ingenieurin, *die;* ~ **engi'neering** *n.* Hoch- und Tiefbau, *der*

civilian /sɪ'vɪljən/ **1** *n.* Zivilist, *der.* **2** *adj.* Zivil-; **wear** ~ **clothes** Zivil[kleidung] tragen

civilise *etc.* ⇨ **civiliz-**

civility /sɪ'vɪlɪtɪ/ *n., no pl.* Höflichkeit, *die*

civilization /sɪvɪlaɪ'zeɪʃn/ *n.* Zivilisation, *die*

civilize /'sɪvɪlaɪz/ *v.t.* zivilisieren

civilized /'sɪvɪlaɪzd/ *adj.* zivilisiert; (refined) kultiviert

civil 'law *n.* Zivilrecht, *das*

civilly /'sɪvɪlɪ, 'sɪvəlɪ/ *adv.* höflich

civil: ~ **'marriage** *n.* Ziviltrauung, *die;* standesamtliche Trauung; ~ **'rights** *n. pl.* Bürgerrechte; ~ **'servant** *n.* ▶ 887 | ≈ [Staats]beamte, *der/*-beamtin, *die;* **C**~ **'Service** *n.* öffentlicher Dienst; ~ **'war** *n.* Bürgerkrieg, *der*

civvies /'sɪvɪz/ *n. pl.* (Brit. coll.) Zivil, *das;* Zivilklamotten *Pl.* (ugs.)

Civvy Street /'sɪvɪ striːt/ *n., no pl., no art.* (Brit. coll.) das Zivilleben

CJD *abbr.* **Creuzfeldt-Jakob disease**

clad /klæd/ *adj.* (arch./literary) gekleidet (**in** in + *Akk.*)

cladding /'klædɪŋ/ *n.* Verkleidung, *die*

claim /kleɪm/ **1** *v.t.* (a) (demand as one's due property) Anspruch erheben auf (+ *Akk.*), beanspruchen ⟨Thron,

Gebiete); fordern ‹*Lohnerhöhung, Schadenersatz*›; beantragen ‹*Arbeitslosenunterstützung, Sozialhilfe usw.*›; abholen ‹*Fundsache*›; ∼ **one's luggage** sein Gepäck [ab]holen; **(b)** (represent oneself as having) für sich beanspruchen, in Anspruch nehmen ‹*Sieg*›; **(c)** (profess, contend) behaupten; **the new system is** ∼**ed to have many advantages** das neue System soll viele Vorteile bieten; **(d)** (result in loss of) fordern ‹*Opfer, Menschenleben*›. **2** *v.i.* **(a)** (Insurance) Ansprüche geltend machen; **(b)** (for costs) ∼ **for damages/expenses** Schadenersatz fordern/sich (*Dat.*) Auslagen rückerstatten lassen. **3** *n.* **(a)** Anspruch, *der* (**to** auf + *Akk.*); **lay** ∼ **to sth.** auf etw. (*Akk.*) Anspruch erheben; **make too many** ∼**s on sth.** etw. zu sehr in Anspruch nehmen; **(b)** (assertion) **make** ∼**s about sth.** Behauptungen über etw. (*Akk.*) aufstellen; **(c)** (pay ∼) Forderung, *die* (for nach); **(d)** ∼ **[for expenses]** Spesenabrechnung, *die* (**for** über + *Akk.*); ∼ **for damages** Schadenersatzforderung, *die;* **(e) stake a** ∼ **to sth.** (fig.) ein Anrecht auf etw. (*Akk.*) anmelden

∼ **'back** *v.t.* zurückfordern

claimant /'kleɪmənt/ *n.* (for rent rebate, state benefit) Antragsteller, *der/*-stellerin, *die;* (for inheritance) Erbberechtigte, *der/die*

clairvoyant /kleə'vɔɪənt/ **1** *n.* Hellseher, *der/*Hellseherin, *die.* **2** *adj.* hellseherisch

clam /klæm/ **1** *n.* Klaffmuschel, *die;* **shut up like a** ∼ (fig.) ausgesprochen wortkarg werden. **2** *v.i.,* -**mm-:** ∼ **up** (coll.) den Mund nicht [mehr] aufmachen

clamber /'klæmbə(r)/ *v.i.* klettern; ‹*Baby:*› krabbeln; ∼ **up a wall** auf eine Mauer klettern; eine Mauer hochklettern

clammy /'klæmɪ/ *adj.* feucht; kalt und schweißig ‹*Hände, Gesicht, Haut*›; klamm ‹*Kleidung usw.*›; nasskalt ‹*Luft usw.*›

clamour (*Brit.; Amer.:* **clamor**) /'klæmə(r)/ **1** *n.* **(a)** (noise, shouting) Lärm, *der;* lautes Geschrei; **(b)** (protest) [lautstarker] Protest; (demand) [lautstarke] Forderung (**for** nach). **2** *v.i.* **(a)** (shout) schreien; **(b)** (protest, demand) ∼ **against sth.** gegen etw. [lautstark] protestieren; ∼ **for sth.** nach etw. schreien; ∼ **to be let out** lautstark fordern, herausgelassen zu werden

clamp /klæmp/ **1** *n.* Klammer, *die;* (Woodw.) Schraubzwinge, *die; see also* **wheel clamp. 2** *v.t.* **(a)** klemmen; einspannen ‹*Werkstück*›; (Med.) klammern; ∼ **two pieces of wood together** zwei Holzstücke miteinander verklammern; **(b)** ∼ **a vehicle** an einem Fahrzeug eine Parkralle anbringen. **3** *v.i.* ∼ **down on sb./sth.** gegen jmdn./ etw. rigoros vorgehen

'clampdown *n.* rigoroses Vorgehen (**on** gegen)

clan /klæn/ *n.* Sippe, *die;* (of Scottish Highlanders) Clan, *der*

clandestine /klæn'destɪn/ *adj.* heimlich

clang /klæŋ/ **1** *n.* (of bell) Läuten, *das;* (of hammer) Klingen, *das;* (of sword) Klirren, *das.* **2** *v.i.* ‹*Glocke:*› läuten; ‹*Hammer:*› klingen; ‹*Schwert:*› klirren

clanger /'klæŋə(r)/ *n.* (Brit. coll.) Schnitzer, *der* (ugs.); **drop a** ∼: sich (*Dat.*) einen Schnitzer leisten (ugs.)

clank /klæŋk/ **1** *n.* Klappern, *das;* (of sword, chain) Klirren, *das.* **2** *v.i.* klappern; ‹*Schwert, Kette:*› klirren; ‹*Kette:*› rasseln. **3** *v.t.* klirren mit ‹*Schwert, Kette*›

clap /klæp/ **1** *n.* **(a)** Klatschen, *das;* **give sb. a** ∼: jmdm. applaudieren *od.* Beifall klatschen; **(b)** (slap) Klaps, *der* (ugs.); **(c)** ∼ **of thunder** Donnerschlag, *der.* **2** *v.i.,* -**pp-:** klatschen. **3** *v.t.,* -**pp-:** **(a)** ∼ **one's hands** in die Hände klatschen; ∼ **sth.** etw. beklatschen; ∼ **sb.** jmdm. Beifall klatschen; **(b)** ∼ **sb. in prison** jmdn. ins Gefängnis werfen *od.* (ugs.) stecken; ∼ **eyes on sb./sth.** jmdn./etw. zu Gesicht bekommen; **(c)** ∼**ped out** (coll.) schrottreif (ugs.) ‹*Auto, Flugzeug*›; kaputt (ugs.) ‹*Person, Idee*›

clapper /'klæpə(r)/ *n.* (of bell) Klöppel, *der;* Schwengel, *der*

clapping /'klæpɪŋ/ *n., no pl.* Beifall, *der;* Applaus, *der*

claptrap /'klæptræp/ *n., no pl.* **(a)** (pretentious assertions) [leere] Phrasen; **(b)** (coll.: nonsense) Geschwafel, *das* (ugs. abwertend)

claret /'klærət/ **1** *n.* roter Bordeauxwein. **2** *adj.* weinrot

clarification /klærɪfɪ'keɪʃn/ *n.* Klärung, *die;* (explanation) Klarstellung, *die*

clarify /'klærɪfaɪ/ *v.t.* klären ‹*Situation, Problem usw.*›; (by explanation) klarstellen; erläutern ‹*Aussage, Bemerkung usw.*›

clarinet /klærɪ'net/ *n.* (Mus.) Klarinette, *die*

clarinettist (*Amer.:* **clarinetist**) /klærɪ'netɪst/ *n.* ▶ **887 |** (Mus.) Klarinettist, *der/*Klarinettistin, *die*

clarity /'klærɪtɪ/ *n., no pl.* Klarheit, *die*

clash /klæʃ/ **1** *v.i.* **(a)** scheppern (ugs.); ‹*Becken:*› dröhnen; ‹*Schwerter:*› aneinander schlagen; **(b)** (meet in conflict) zusammenstoßen (**with** mit); **(c)** (disagree) sich streiten; ∼ **with sb.** mit jmdm. eine Auseinandersetzung haben; **(d)** (be incompatible) aufeinander prallen; ‹*Interesse, Ereignis:*› kollidieren (**with** mit); ‹*Persönlichkeit, Stil:*› nicht zusammenpassen (**with** mit); ‹*Farbe:*› sich beißen (ugs.) (**with** mit). **2** *v.t.* gegeneinander schlagen. **3** *n.* **(a)** (of cymbals) Dröhnen, *das;* (of swords) Aneinanderschlagen, *das;* **(b)** (meeting in conflict) Zusammenstoß, *der;* **(c)** (disagreement) Auseinandersetzung, *die;* **(d)** (incompatibility) Unvereinbarkeit, *die;* (of personalities, styles, colours) Unverträglichkeit, *die;* (of events) Überschneidung, *die*

clasp /klɑːsp/ **1** *n.* **(a)** Verschluss, *der;* (of belt) Schnalle, *die;* **(b)** (embrace) Umarmung, *die;* **(c)** (grasp) Griff, *der.* **2** *v.t.* **(a)** (embrace) drücken (**to** an + *Akk.*); **(b)** (grasp) umklammern

class /klɑːs/ **1** *n.* **(a)** (group in society) Gesellschaftsschicht, *die;* Klasse, *die* (Soziol.); (system) Klassensystem, *das;* **(b)** (Educ.) Klasse, *die;* (Sch.: lesson) Stunde, *die;* (Univ.: seminar etc.) Übung, *die;* **a French** ∼: eine Französischstunde; **(c)** (group [according to quality]) Klasse, *die;* **be in a** ∼ **by itself** *or* **on its own/of one's own** *or* **by oneself** eine Klasse für sich sein; **(d)** (coll.: quality) Klasse, *die* (ugs.). **2** *v.t.* einordnen; ∼ **sth. as sth.** etw. als etw. einstufen

class: ∼**-conscious** *adj.* klassenbewusst; ∼**-consciousness** *n.* Klassenbewusstsein, *das;* ∼ **distinction** *n.* Klassenunterschied, *der*

classic /'klæsɪk/ **1** *adj.* klassisch. **2** *n.* **(a)** *in pl.* (classical studies) Altphilologie, *die;* **(b)** (book, play, film) Klassiker, *der*

classical /'klæsɪkl/ *adj.* klassisch; ∼ **studies** Altphilologie, *die;* **the** ∼ **world** die Antike; ∼ **education** humanistische [Schul]bildung

classicist /'klæsɪsɪst/ *n.* Altphilologe, *der/*-philologin, *die*

classifiable /'klæsɪfaɪəbl/ *adj.* klassifizierbar

classification /klæsɪfɪ'keɪʃn/ *n.* Klassifikation, *die*

classified /'klæsɪfaɪd/ *adj.* **(a)** (arranged in classes) gegliedert; unterteilt; ∼ **advertisement** Kleinanzeige, *die;* **(b)** (officially secret) geheim

classify /'klæsɪfaɪ/ *v.t.* klassifizieren; ∼ **books by subjects** Bücher nach Fachgebieten [ein]ordnen

classless /'klɑːslɪs/ *adj.* klassenlos ‹*Gesellschaft*›

class: ∼**mate** *n.* Klassenkamerad, *der/*-kameradin, *die;* ∼**room** *n.* (Sch.) Klassenzimmer, *das;* Klasse, *die;* ∼ **struggle,** ∼ **war** *ns.* Klassenkampf, *der*

classy /'klɑːsɪ/ *adj.* (coll.) klasse (ugs.); nobel ‹*Vorort, Hotel*›

clatter /'klætə(r)/ **1** *n.* Klappern, *das;* **the kettle fell with a** ∼ **to the ground** der Kessel fiel scheppernd zu Boden. **2** *v.i.* **(a)** klappern; **(b)** (move or fall with a ∼) poltern. **3** *v.t.* klappern mit

clause /klɔːz/ *n.* **(a)** Klausel, *die;* **(b)** (Ling.) Teilsatz, *der;* **[subordinate]** ∼**:** Nebensatz, *der*

claustrophobia /klɒstrə'fəʊbɪə/ *n., no pl.* (Psych.) Klaustrophobie, *die*

claustrophobic /klɒstrə'fəʊbɪk/ *adj.* beengend ‹*Ort, Atmosphäre*›; an Klaustrophobie leidend ‹*Person*›

claw /klɔː/ **1** *n.* (of bird, animal) Kralle, *die;* (of crab, lobster, etc.) Schere, *die;* (foot with ∼) Klaue, *die.* **2** *v.t.* kratzen. **3** *v.i.* ∼ **at sth.** sich an etw. (*Akk.*) krallen

∼ **'back** *v.t.* wieder eintreiben ‹*Geld, Unterstützung*›; wettmachen ‹*Defizit*›

clay /kleɪ/ *n.* Lehm, *der;* (for pottery) Ton, *der*

clay 'pigeon shooting *n.* Tontaubenschießen, *das*

clean /kliːn/ **1** *adj.* **(a)** sauber; frisch ‹*Wäsche, Hemd*›; **(b)** (unused, fresh) sauber; (free of defects) einwandfrei; sauber; **make a** ∼ **start** noch einmal neu anfangen; **come** ∼

(coll.) (confess) auspacken (ugs.); (tell the truth) mit der Wahrheit [he]rausrücken (ugs.); **(c)** (regular, complete) glatt ⟨*Bruch*⟩; glatt, sauber ⟨*Schnitt*⟩; **make a ∼ break [with sth.]** (fig.) einen Schlussstrich [unter etw. (*Akk.*)] ziehen; **(d)** (coll.: not obscene or indecent) sauber; stubenrein (scherzh.) ⟨*Witz*⟩; **be good ∼ fun** völlig harmlos sein; **(e)** (sportsmanlike, fair) sauber. **2** *adv.* glatt; einfach ⟨*vergessen*⟩; **we're ∼ out of whisky** wir haben überhaupt keinen Whisky mehr; **the fox got ∼ away** der Fuchs ist uns/ihnen *usw.* glatt entwischt. **3** *v.t.* sauber machen; putzen ⟨*Zimmer, Haus, Fenster, Schuh*⟩; reinigen ⟨*Teppich, Möbel, Käfig, Kleidung, Wunde*⟩; fegen, kehren ⟨*Kamin*⟩; (with cloth) aufwischen ⟨*Fußboden*⟩; **∼ one's hands/teeth** sich (*Dat.*) die Hände waschen/Zähne putzen. **4** *v.i.* sich reinigen lassen. **5** *n.* **this carpet needs a good ∼:** dieser Teppich muss gründlich gereinigt werden; **give your shoes a ∼:** putz deine Schuhe

∼ 'out *v.t.* **(a)** (remove dirt from) sauber machen; ausmisten ⟨*Stall*⟩; **(b)** (coll.) **∼ sb. out** (take all sb.'s money) jmdn. [total] schröpfen (ugs.); **the tobacconist was ∼ed out of cigarettes** beim Tabakhändler war alles an Zigaretten aufgekauft worden

∼ 'up 1 *v.t.* **(a)** aufräumen ⟨*Zimmer, Schreibtisch*⟩; beseitigen ⟨*Trümmer, Unordnung*⟩; **(b)** **∼ oneself up** sich sauber machen; (get washed) sich waschen; **(c)** (fig.) säubern ⟨*Stadt*⟩; aufräumen mit ⟨*Korruption usw.*⟩. **2** *v.i.* **(a)** aufräumen; **(b)** (coll.: make money) absahnen (ugs.)

'clean-cut *adj.* klar [umrissen]; **his ∼ features** seine klar geschnittenen Gesichtszüge

cleaner /'kli:nə(r)/ *n.* **(a)** ▸ 887 | (person) Raumpfleger, *der*/-pflegerin, *die;* (woman also) Putzfrau, *die;* **(b)** (vacuum ∼) Staubsauger, *der;* (substance) Reinigungsmittel, *das;* **(c)** *usu. in pl.* (dry-∼) Reinigung, *die;* **take sth. to the ∼s** etw. in die Reinigung bringen; **take sb. to the ∼s** (coll.) jmdn. bis aufs Hemd ausziehen (ugs.)

cleanliness /'klenlɪnɪs/ *n., no pl.* Reinlichkeit, *die;* Sauberkeit, *die*

cleanly /'klenlɪ/ *adj.* sauber

cleanness /'kli:nnɪs/ *n., no pl.* **(a)** Sauberkeit, *die;* **(b)** **the ∼ of the ship's lines** die klare Linienführung des Schiffes; **(c)** (regularity of cut or break) Glätte, *die*

'clean-out *n.* **give sth. a ∼:** etw. sauber machen

cleanse /klenz/ *v.t.* **(a)** (spiritually purify) läutern; **∼d of** *or* **from sin** von der Sünde befreit; **(b)** (clean) [gründlich] reinigen

cleanser /'klenzə(r)/ *n.* **(a)** Reinigungsmittel, *das;* Reiniger, *der;* **(b)** (for skin) Reinigungscreme, *die*

'clean-shaven *adj.* glatt rasiert

cleansing /'klenzɪŋ/**: ∼ cream** *n.* Reinigungscreme, *die;* **∼ department** *n.* Stadtreinigung, *die*

clear /klɪə(r)/ **1** *adj.* **(a)** klar; rein ⟨*Haut, Teint*⟩; **(b)** (distinct) scharf ⟨*Bild, Foto, Umriss*⟩; deutlich ⟨*Abbild*⟩; klar ⟨*Ton*⟩; klar verständlich ⟨*Wort*⟩; **(c)** (obvious, unambiguous) klar ⟨*Aussage, Vorteil, Vorsprung, Mehrheit, Sieg, Fall*⟩; **make oneself ∼:** sich deutlich *od.* klar [genug] ausdrücken; **make sth. ∼:** etw. deutlich zum Ausdruck bringen; **make it ∼ [to sb.] that …:** [jmdm.] klar und deutlich sagen, dass …; **(d)** (free) frei; (Horse-riding) fehlerfrei ⟨*Runde*⟩; **be ∼ of suspicion** nicht unter Verdacht stehen; **we're in the ∼** (free of suspicion) auf uns fällt kein Verdacht; (free of trouble) wir haben es geschafft; **be three points ∼:** drei Punkte Vorsprung haben; **(e)** (complete) **three ∼ days/lines** drei volle *od.* volle drei Tage/Zeilen; **(f)** (open, unobstructed) frei; **keep sth. ∼** (not block) etw. frei halten; **have a ∼ run** freie Fahrt haben; **all ∼** (one will not be detected) die Luft ist rein (ugs.); *see also* **all-clear; the way is [now] ∼ [for sb.] to do sth.** (fig.) es steht [jmdm.] nichts [mehr] im Wege, etw. zu tun; **(g)** (discerning) klar; **keep a ∼ head** einen klaren *od.* kühlen Kopf bewahren; **(h)** (certain, confident) **be ∼ [on** *or* **about sth.]** sich (*Dat.*) [über etw. (*Akk.*)] im klaren sein. **2** *adv.* **keep ∼ of sth./sb.** etw./jmdn. meiden; **'keep ∼'** (don't approach) „Vorsicht [Zug *usw.*]"; **please stand** *or* **keep ∼ of the door** bitte von der Tür zurücktreten; **move sth. ∼ of sth.** etw. von etw. wegräumen; **the driver was pulled ∼ of the wreckage** man zog den Fahrer aus dem Wrack seines Wagens. **3** *v.t.* **(a)** (make ∼) klären ⟨*Flüssigkeit*⟩; **∼ the air**

lüften; (fig.) die Atmosphäre reinigen; **(b)** (free from obstruction) räumen ⟨*Straße*⟩; abräumen ⟨*Regal, Schreibtisch*⟩; freimachen ⟨*Abfluss, Kanal*⟩; **∼ the streets of snow** den Schnee von den Straßen räumen; **∼ a space for sb./sth.** für jmdn./etw. Platz machen; **∼ one's throat** sich räuspern; *see also* **deck 1 a; way 1 f; (c)** (make empty) räumen; leeren ⟨*Briefkasten*⟩; **∼ the room** das Zimmer räumen; **∼ the table** den Tisch abräumen; **∼ one's desk** seinen Schreibtisch ausräumen; **∼ one's plate** seinen Teller leer essen; **(d)** (remove) wegräumen; beheben ⟨*Verstopfung*⟩; **∼ sth. out of the way** etw. aus dem Weg räumen; **(e)** (pass over without touching) nehmen ⟨*Hindernis*⟩; überspringen ⟨*Latte*⟩. **(f)** (show to be innocent) freisprechen; **∼ oneself** seine Unschuld beweisen; **∼ sb. of sth.** jmdn. von etw. freisprechen; **∼ one's name** seine Unschuld beweisen; **(g)** (declare fit to have secret information) für unbedenklich erklären; **(h)** (get permission for) **∼ sth. with sb.** etw. von jmdm. genehmigen lassen; (give permission for) **∼ a plane for take-off/landing** einem Flugzeug Start-/Landeerlaubnis erteilen; **(i)** (at customs) **∼ customs** vom Zoll abgefertigt werden; **(j)** (pay off) begleichen ⟨*Schuld*⟩. **4** *v.i.* **(a)** (become ∼) klar werden; sich klären ⟨*Wetter, Himmel:*⟩ sich aufheitern; (fig.) ⟨*Gesicht:*⟩ sich aufhellen; **(b)** (disperse) ⟨*Nebel:*⟩ sich verziehen

∼ a'way 1 *v.t.* wegschaffen; (from the table) abräumen ⟨*Geschirr, Besteck*⟩. **2** *v.i.* **(a)** abräumen; **(b)** (disperse) ⟨*Nebel:*⟩ sich verziehen

∼ 'off 1 *v.t.* begleichen ⟨*Schulden*⟩; abzahlen ⟨*Hypothek*⟩; aufarbeiten ⟨*Rückstand*⟩. **2** *v.i.* (coll.) abhauen (salopp)

∼ 'out 1 *v.t.* ausräumen. **2** *v.i.* (coll.) verschwinden

∼ 'up 1 *v.t.* **(a)** beseitigen ⟨*Unordnung*⟩; wegräumen ⟨*Abfall*⟩; aufräumen ⟨*Platz, Sachen*⟩; **(b)** (explain, solve) klären. **2** *v.i.* **(a)** aufräumen; Ordnung machen; **(b)** (become ∼) ⟨*Wetter:*⟩ sich aufhellen; **(c)** (disappear) ⟨*Symptome, Ausschlag:*⟩ zurückgehen

clearance /'klɪərəns/ *n.* **(a)** (of obstruction) Beseitigung, *die;* (of forest) Abholzung, *die;* **(b)** (to land/take off) Lande-/ Starterlaubnis, *die;* **(c)** (security ∼) Einstufung als unbedenklich [im Sinne der Sicherheitsbestimmungen]; (document) ≈ Sonderausweis, *der;* **(d)** (clear space) Spielraum, *der;* (headroom) lichte Höhe; **(e)** (Sport) Abwehr, *die;* **make a poor ∼:** schlecht abwehren

clearance: ∼ order *n.* Räumungsbefehl, *der;* **∼ sale** *n.* Räumungsverkauf, *der*

'clear-cut *adj.* klar umrissen; klar ⟨*Abgrenzung, Ergebnis, Entscheidung*⟩; [gestochen] scharf ⟨*Umriss, Raster*⟩

clearing /'klɪərɪŋ/ *n.* (land) Lichtung, *die*

'clearing bank *n.* (Commerc.) Clearingbank, *die*

clearly /'klɪəlɪ/ *adv.* **(a)** (distinctly) klar; deutlich ⟨*sprechen*⟩; **(b)** (obviously, unambiguously) eindeutig; klar ⟨*denken*⟩

clearness /'klɪənɪs/ *n., no pl.* ⇒ **clear 1 a–c:** Klarheit, *die;* Reinheit, *die;* Schärfe, *die;* Deutlichkeit, *die*

clear: ∼-out *n.* Entrümpelung, *die;* **have a ∼-out** eine Aufräum- *od.* Entrümpelungsaktion starten; **∼-up** *n.* Aufräumen, *das;* **have a [good] ∼-up** [gründlich] aufräumen; **∼way** *n.* (Brit.) Straße mit Halteverbot

cleat /kli:t/ *n.* (to prevent rope from slipping) Klampe, *die* (Seemannsspr.)

cleavage /'kli:vɪdʒ/ *n.* **(a)** (act of splitting) Spaltung, *die;* **(b)** (between breasts) Dekolleté, *das*

cleave /kli:v/ *v.t.,* **∼d** *or* **clove** /kləʊv/ *or* **cleft** /kleft/, **∼d** *or* **cloven** /'kləʊvn/ *or* **cleft** (literary) **(a)** (split) spalten; **(b)** (make way through) durchpflügen ⟨*Wellen, Wasser*⟩. See *also* **cleft² 2; cloven 2**

cleaver /'kli:və(r)/ *n.* Hackbeil, *das*

clef /klef/ *n.* (Mus.) Notenschlüssel, *der*

cleft¹ /kleft/ *n.* Spalte, *die*

cleft² /kleft/ **1** ⇒ **cleave. 2** *adj.* gespalten; **∼ palate** Gaumenspalte, *die;* **be [caught] in a ∼ stick** (fig.) in der Klemme sitzen (ugs.)

clematis /'klemətɪs, klə'meɪtɪs/ *n.* (Bot.) Klematis, *die*

clemency /'klemənsɪ/ *n., no pl.* Nachsicht, *die;* **show ∼ to sb.** jmdm. gegenüber Nachsicht walten lassen

clench /klentʃ/ *v.t.* **(a)** (close tightly) zusammenpressen; **∼ one's fist** *or* **fingers** die Faust ballen; **with [one's] ∼ed**

fist mit geballter Faust; ~ **one's teeth** die Zähne zusammenbeißen; **(b)** (grasp firmly) umklammern

clergy /'klɜːdʒɪ/ n. pl. Geistlichkeit, die; Klerus, der

clergyman /'klɜːdʒɪmən/ n., pl. ~**men** /'klɜːdʒɪmən/ ▶ 887 | Geistliche, der

cleric /'klerɪk/ n. Kleriker, der

clerical /'klerɪkl/ adj. **(a)** (of clergy) klerikal; geistlich; **(b)** (of or by clerk) Büro‹arbeit, -personal›; ~ **error** Schreibfehler, der; ~ **worker** ▶ 887 | Büroangestellte, der/die; Bürokraft, die

clerk /klɑːk/ n. ▶ 887 | **(a)** Angestellte, der/die; (in bank) Bankangestellte, der/die; (in office) Büroangestellte, der/die; **(b)** (in charge of records) Schriftführer, der/Schriftführerin, die

clever /'klevə(r)/ adj., ~**er** /'klevərə(r)/, ~**est** /'klevərɪst/ **(a)** gescheit; klug; **be** ~ **at mathematics/thinking up excuses** gut in Mathematik/findig im Ausdenken von Entschuldigungen sein; **(b)** (skilful) geschickt; **be** ~ **with one's hands** geschickte Hände haben; **(c)** (ingenious) brillant, geistreich ‹Idee, Argument, Rede, Roman, Gedicht›; geschickt ‹Täuschung, Vorgehen›; glänzend (ugs.) ‹Idee, Erfindung, Mittel›; **(d)** (smart, cunning) clever; raffiniert ‹Schritt, Taktik, Täuschung›; schlau, raffiniert ‹Person›

'**clever Dick** n. (coll. derog.) Schlaumeier, der (ugs.)

cleverly /'klevəlɪ/ adv. **(a)** klug; **(b)** (skilfully) geschickt; **(c)** (cunningly) trickreich

cleverness /'klevənɪs/ n., no pl. **(a)** Klugheit, die; (talent) Begabung, die (**at für**); **(b)** (skill) Geschicklichkeit, die; **(c)** (ingenuity) Brillanz, die; **(d)** (smartness) Cleverness, die; Raffiniertheit, die; (of person also) Schläue, die

cliché /'kliːʃeɪ/ n. Klischee, das

click /klɪk/ **1** n. Klicken, das. **2** v.t. zuschnappen lassen ‹Schloss, Tür›; ~ **the shutter of a camera** den Verschluss einer Kamera auslösen; ~ **one's tongue** mit der Zunge schnalzen. **3** v.i. **(a)** klicken; ‹Absätze, Stricknadeln:› klappern; **(b)** (coll.: fall into context) **it's just** ~**ed** ich hab's (ugs.); ~ **with sb.** (coll.) mit jmdm. gleich prima auskommen (ugs.)

client /'klaɪənt/ n. **(a)** (of lawyer, social worker) Klient, der/Klientin, die; (of architect) Auftraggeber, der/-geberin, die; **(b)** (customer) Kunde, der/Kundin, die

clientele /kliːɒn'tel/ n. (of shop) Kundschaft, die

cliff /klɪf/ n. (on coast) Kliff, das; (inland) Felswand, die

'**cliffhanger** n. Thriller, der

climate /'klaɪmət/ n. Klima, das; **the** ~ **of opinion** (fig.) die allgemeine Meinung

climax /'klaɪmæks/ **1** n. Höhepunkt, der. **2** v.i. seinen Höhepunkt erreichen

climb /klaɪm/ **1** v.t. hinaufsteigen ‹Treppe, Leiter, Hügel, Berg›; hinaufklettern ‹Mauer, Seil, Mast›; klettern auf ‹Baum›; ‹Auto:› hinaufkommen ‹Hügel›; **this mountain had never been** ~**ed before** dieser Berg war noch nie zuvor bestiegen worden; **the prisoners escaped by** ~**ing the wall** die Gefangenen entkamen, indem sie über die Mauer kletterten. **2** v.i. **(a)** klettern (**up** auf + Akk.); ~ **into/out of** steigen in (+ Akk.)/aus ‹Auto, Bett›; ~ **aboard** einsteigen; **(b)** ‹Flugzeug, Sonne:› aufsteigen; **(c)** (slope upwards) ansteigen. **3** n. (ascent) Aufstieg, der; (of aeroplane) Steigflug, der

~ '**down** v.i. **(a)** hinunterklettern; (from horse) absteigen; **(b)** (fig.: retreat, give in) nachgeben; einlenken; ~ **down over an issue** in einer Frage nachgeben

'**climbdown** n. Rückzieher, der (ugs.)

climber /'klaɪmə(r)/ n. **(a)** (mountaineer) Bergsteiger, der; (of cliff, rock face) Kletterer, der; **(b)** (plant) Kletterpflanze, die

climbing: ~ **boot** n. Kletterschuh, der; ~ **frame** n. Klettergerüst, das

clinch /klɪntʃ/ **1** v.t. zum Abschluss bringen ‹Angelegenheit›; perfekt machen (ugs.) ‹Geschäft, Handel›; **that** ~**es it** damit ist der Fall klar. **2** n. (Boxing) Clinch, der

cling /klɪŋ/ v.i., **clung** /klʌŋ/ **(a)** ~ **to sth./sb.** sich an etw./jmdn. klammern; ‹Schmutz:› einer Sache/jmdm. anhaften; ‹Staub:› sich auf etw./jmdn. setzen; **his sweat-soaked shirt clung to his back** das durchgeschwitzte

Hemd klebte ihm am Rücken; ~ **together** aneinander haften; **(b)** (remain stubbornly faithful) ~ **to sb./sth.** sich an jmdn./etw. klammern

'**cling film** n. Klarsichtfolie, die

clinic /'klɪnɪk/ n. [Abteilung einer] Klinik; (occasion) Sprechstunde, die; (private hospital) Privatklinik, die; **dental** ~: Zahnklinik, die

clinical /'klɪnɪkl/ adj. **(a)** (Med.) klinisch ‹Medizin, Tod›; **(b)** (dispassionate) nüchtern; (coldly detached) kühl

clinical: ~ **psy'chologist** n. klinischer Psychologe/klinische Psychologin; ~ **psy'chology** n. klinische Psychologie

clink¹ /klɪŋk/ **1** n. (of glasses, bottles) Klirren, das; (of coins, keys) Klimpern, das. **2** v.i. ‹Flaschen, Gläser:› klirren; ‹Münzen, Schlüssel:› klimpern. **3** v.t. klirren mit ‹Glas›

clink² n. (sl.: prison) Knast, der (salopp)

clip¹ /klɪp/ **1** n. **(a)** Klammer, die; (for paper) Büroklammer, die; (of pen) Klipp, der; (of piece of jewellery) Klipp, der; Clip, der. **2** v.t., **-pp-:** ~ **sth. [on] to sth.** etw. an etw. (Akk.) klammern; ~ **papers together** Schriftstücke zusammenklammern

~ '**on** v.t. anlegen ‹Ohrring›; anstecken ‹Brosche, Mikrofon›

clip² **1** v.t., **-pp-:** **(a)** (cut) schneiden ‹Fingernägel, Haar, Hecke›; scheren ‹Wolle›; stutzen ‹Flügel›; **(b)** scheren ‹Schaf›; trimmen ‹Hund›; **(c)** lochen, entwerten ‹Fahrkarte›. **2** n. **(a)** (of fingernails, hedge) Schneiden, das; (of sheep) Schur, die; (of dog) Trimmen, das; **give the hedge a** ~: die Hecke schneiden; **(b)** (extract from film) [Film]ausschnitt, der; **(c)** (blow with hand) Schlag, der; ~ **round or on or over the ear** Ohrfeige, die

clip: art n. (Computing) Clipart, die; ~**board** **(a)** n. Klemmbrett, das; **(b)** (Computing) Zwischenablage, die; ~ **frame** n. [rahmenloser] Bilderhalter; ~ **joint** n. (sl. derog.) Nepplokal, das (ugs. abwertend); ~**-on** adj. ~**-on sunglasses** eine Sonnenbrille zum Aufstecken

clipped /klɪpt/ adj. abgehackt ‹Wörter›

clipper /'klɪpə(r)/ n. (Naut.) Klipper, der

clipping /'klɪpɪŋ/ n. **(a)** (piece clipped off) Schnipsel, der od. das; **(b)** (newspaper cutting) Ausschnitt, der

clique /kliːk/ n. Clique, die

clitoris /'klɪtərɪs/ n. (Anat.) Kitzler, der; Klitoris, die (fachspr.)

cloak /kləʊk/ **1** n. Umhang, der; Mantel, der (hist.); **under the** ~ **of darkness** im Schutz der Dunkelheit; **use sth. as a** ~ **for sth.** etw. als Deckmantel für etw. benutzen; **a** ~ **of secrecy** ein Mantel des Schweigens. **2** v.t. **(a)** [ein]hüllen; **(b)** (fig.) ~**ed in mist/darkness** in Nebel/Dunkel gehüllt; **sth. is** ~**ed in secrecy** über etw. (Akk.) wird der Mantel des Schweigens gebreitet

cloak: ~**-and-'dagger** adj. mysteriös; Spionage‹stück, -tätigkeit›; ~**room** n. Garderobe, die; (Brit. euphem.: lavatory) Toilette, die; ~**room attendant** ▶ 887 | Garderobier, der/Garderobiere, die/Toilettenmann, der/-frau, die

clock /klɒk/ **1** n. **(a)** ▶ 706 | Uhr, die; [work] **against the** ~: gegen die Zeit [arbeiten]; **beat the** ~ **[by ten minutes]** [10 Minuten] früher fertig werden; **put or turn the** ~ **back** (fig.) die Zeit zurückdrehen; **round the** ~: rund um die Uhr; **watch the** ~ (fig.) [dauernd] auf die Uhr sehen (weil man ungeduldig auf den Arbeitsschluss wartet); **(b)** (coll.) (speedometer) Tacho, der (ugs.); (milometer) ≈ Kilometerzähler, der; (taximeter) Taxameter, das. **2** v.t. ~ **[up]** zu verzeichnen haben ‹Sieg, Zeit, Erfolg›; erreichen ‹Geschwindigkeit›; zurücklegen ‹Entfernung›

~ '**in**, ~ '**on** v.i. [bei Arbeitsantritt] stechen od. stempeln

~ '**off**, ~ '**out** v.i. [bei Arbeitsschluss] stechen od. stempeln

clock: ~**-face** n. Zifferblatt, das; ~ **radio** n. Radiowecker, der; ~ **tower** n. Uhr[en]turm, der

'**clockwise** **1** adv. im Uhrzeigersinn. **2** adj. im Uhrzeigersinn nachgestellt; **in a** ~ **direction** im Uhrzeigersinn

The clock

What time is it?	= Wie viel Uhr ist es?, Wie spät ist es?
Could you tell me the time?	= Könnten Sie mir sagen, wie spät es ist?
What time do you make it?	= Wie viel Uhr hast du?
By my watch it's five to/ten past nine	= Nach meiner Uhr ist es fünf vor/zehn nach neun
My watch is fast/slow	= Meine Uhr geht vor/nach
It's just after or just gone ten	= Es ist etwas nach zehn
It's gone eleven	= Es ist elf Uhr vorbei
It's coming up to seven	= Es ist gleich sieben

Unlike English, German uses the twenty-four hour clock most of the time, even sometimes in conversation, and it is certainly the only possibility when quoting times in print or on radio and television. Note that when such times are spoken, the word **Uhr** is never omitted, and it is immediately followed by the number of minutes – these cannot come before with **vor** or **nach**, nor can **Viertel** be used for "quarter" or **halb** for "half". However the twelve hour clock is also used in conversation and letters, followed by **nachmittags, abends** ("in the afternoon", "in the evening"), etc. if it is necessary to make this clear.

WRITTEN	SPOKEN
1.00 a.m./0100	*one [a.m. or in the morning]/one hundred hours*
= 1 Uhr	eins, ein Uhr [nachts *or* morgens]/ein Uhr
1.00 p.m./1300	*one [p.m. or in the afternoon]/thirteen hundred hours*
= 13 Uhr	eins, ein Uhr [mittags]/dreizehn Uhr
2.05 a.m./0205	*five past two (in the morning)/[o] two o five*
= 2.05 Uhr	fünf [Minuten] nach zwei [Uhr nachts *or* morgens]/zwei Uhr fünf
2.05 p.m./1405	*five past two [in the afternoon]/fourteen o five*
= 14.05 Uhr	fünf [Minuten] nach zwei [Uhr nachmittags]/vierzehn Uhr fünf
4.15 a.m./0415	*four fifteen [a.m.], a quarter past four [in the morning]/[o] four fifteen*
= 4.15 Uhr	Viertel nach vier [morgens]/ vier Uhr fünfzehn
4.15 p.m./1615	*four fifteen [p.m.], a quarter past four [in the afternoon]*
= 16.15 Uhr	Viertel nach vier [nachmittags]/sechzehn Uhr fünfzehn
5.30 a.m./0530	*five thirty [a.m.], half past five [in the morning]/[o] five thirty*
= 5.30 Uhr	halb sechs [morgens]/ fünf Uhr dreißig
5.30 p.m./1730	*five thirty [p.m.], half past five [in the afternoon]/seventeen thirty*
= 17.30 Uhr	halb sechs [abends]/siebzehn Uhr dreißig
7.45 a.m./0745	*seven forty-five [a.m.], a quarter to eight [in the morning]/[o] seven forty-five*
= 7.45 Uhr	Viertel vor acht [morgens]/sieben Uhr fünfundvierzig
7.45 p.m./1945	*seven forty-five p.m., a quarter to eight [in the evening]/nineteen forty-five*
= 19.45 Uhr	Viertel vor acht [abends]/neunzehn Uhr fünfundvierzig
12.00 [midnight]/, 0000, 2400	*twelve [o'clock], [twelve midnight/oo double o, twenty-four hundred hours*
= 0 Uhr, 24 Uhr	zwölf, zwölf Uhr [nachts]/null Uhr, vierundzwanzig Uhr
12 [noon]/1200	*twelve [o'clock], [twelve] noon/twelve hundred hours*
= 12 Uhr	zwölf, zwölf Uhr [mittags]/zwölf Uhr

N.B. When using the twenty-four hour clock, 0000 = null Uhr indicates the beginning of the day, 2400 = vierundzwanzig Uhr the end of the day.

When?

at with a time is **um:**

He came at eight o'clock	= Er kam um acht Uhr
[At] what time do you want breakfast?	= Um wie viel Uhr wollen Sie frühstücken?
at half past	= um halb
at half past eight, at half eight	= um halb neun
at six exactly, on the dot of six	= genau um sechs, [um] Punkt sechs
at about ten	= gegen zehn
at twelve at the latest	= spätestens um zwölf
It must be ready by eleven	= Es muss bis elf fertig sein
I won't be there until six	= Ich bin erst um sechs dort
closed from 1 to 2 p.m.	= von 13 bis 14 Uhr geschlossen
every hour on the hour	= stündlich zur vollen Stunde

'**clockwork** *n.* Uhrwerk, *das;* **as regular as** ~ (fig.) absolut regelmäßig; **go like** ~ (fig.) klappen wie am Schnürchen (ugs.)

clod /klɒd/ *n.* Klumpen, *der;* (of earth) Scholle, *die*

clog /klɒg/ **1** *n.* Holzschuh, *der;* ([fashionable] wooden-soled shoe) Clog, *der.* **2** *v.t.,* **-gg-:** ~ **[up]** verstopfen ‹*Rohr, Poren*›; blockieren ‹*Rad, Maschinerie*›; **be** ~**ged [up] with sth.** mit etw. verstopft/durch etw. blockiert sein

cloister /'klɔɪstə(r)/ *n.* **(a)** (covered walk) Kreuzgang, *der;* **(b)** (convent, monastery; monastic life) Kloster, *das*

cloistered /'klɔɪstəd/ *adj.* (fig.) klösterlich ‹*Abgeschiedenheit, Dasein*›

clone /kləʊn/ (Biol.) **1** *n.* Klon, *der;* (fig.: copy) [schlechte] Kopie. **2** *v.t.* klonen

close **1** /kləʊs/ *adj.* **(a)** (near in space) dicht; nahe; **be** ~ **to sth.** nahe bei *od.* an etw. (*Dat.*) sein; **how** ~ **is London**

to the South coast? wie weit ist London von der Südküste entfernt?; **you're too** ~ **to the fire** du bist zu dicht *od.* nah am Feuer; **I wish we lived** ~**r to your parents** ich wünschte, wir würden näher bei deinen Eltern wohnen; **be** ~ **to tears/breaking point** den Tränen/einem Zusammenbruch nahe sein; **at** ~ **quarters, the building looked less impressive** aus der Nähe betrachtet, wirkte das Gebäude weniger imposant; **at** ~ **range** aus kurzer Entfernung; **(b)** (near in time) nahe **(to** an + *Dat.*); **(c)** eng ⟨*Freund, Freundschaft, Beziehung, Zusammenarbeit, Verbindung*⟩; nahe ⟨*Verwandte, Bekanntschaft*⟩; **be/become** ~ **to sb.** jmdm. nahe stehen/nahekommen; **(d)** (rigorous, painstaking) eingehend, genau ⟨*Untersuchung, Prüfung, Befragung usw.*⟩; **pay** ~ **attention** genau aufpassen; **(e)** (stifling) stickig ⟨*Luft, Raum*⟩; drückend, schwül ⟨*Wetter*⟩; **(f)** (nearly equal) hart ⟨[*Wett*]*kampf, Spiel*⟩; knapp ⟨*Ergebnis*⟩; **a** ~ **race** ein Kopf-an-Kopf-Rennen; **that was a** ~ **call** *or* **shave** *or* **thing** (coll.) das war knapp!; **(g)** (nearly matching) wortgetreu ⟨*Übersetzung*⟩; getreu, genau ⟨*Imitation, Kopie*⟩; groß ⟨*Ähnlichkeit*⟩; **be the** ~**st equivalent to sth.** einer Sache (*Dat.*) am ehesten entsprechen; **bear a** ~ **resemblance to sb.** jmdm. sehr ähnlich sehen; **(h)** eng ⟨*Schrift*⟩. **2** /kləʊs/ *adv.* **(a)** (near) nah[e]; **come** ~ **to the truth** der Wahrheit nahe kommen; **be** ~ **at hand** in Reichweite sein; ~ **by** in der Nähe; ~ **by the river** nahe am Fluss; ~ **on 60 years** fast 60 Jahre; ~ **on 2 o'clock** kurz vor 2 [Uhr]; ~ **to sb./sth.** nahe bei jmdm./etw.; **don't stand so** ~ **to the edge of the cliff** stell dich nicht so nah *od.* dicht an den Rand des Kliffs; ~ **together** dicht beieinander; **it brought them** ~**r together** (fig.) es brachte sie einander näher; ~ **behind** dicht dahinter; **be/come** ~ **to tears** den Tränen nahe sein; **(b)** fest ⟨*schließen*⟩; genau ⟨*hinsehen*⟩; **on looking** ~**r** bei genauerem Hinsehen. **3** /kləʊz/ *v.t.* **(a)** (shut) schließen, (ugs.) zumachen ⟨*Augen, Tür, Fenster, Geschäft*⟩; zuziehen ⟨*Vorhang*⟩; (declare shut) schließen ⟨*Laden, Geschäft, Fabrik, Betrieb, Werk, Zeche*⟩; stilllegen ⟨*Betrieb, Werk, Zeche, Bahnlinie*⟩; sperren ⟨*Straße, Brücke*⟩; **(b)** (conclude) schließen, beenden ⟨*Besprechung, Rede, Diskussion*⟩; schließen ⟨*Versammlung, Sitzung*⟩; ~ **an account** ein Konto auflösen; **(c)** (make smaller) schließen (auch fig.) ⟨*Lücke*⟩. **4** /kləʊz/ *v.i.* **(a)** (shut) sich schließen ⟨*Tür:*⟩ zugehen (ugs.), sich schließen; **the door/lid doesn't** ~ **properly** die Tür/der Deckel schließt nicht richtig; **(b)** ⟨*Laden, Geschäft, Fabrik:*⟩ schließen, (ugs.) zumachen; (permanently) ⟨*Betrieb, Werk, Zeche:*⟩ geschlossen *od.* stillgelegt werden; ⟨*Geschäft:*⟩ geschlossen werden, (ugs.) zumachen; **(c)** (come to an end) zu Ende gehen; enden; (finish speaking) schließen. **5** *n.* **(a)** /kləʊz/ *no pl.* Ende, das; Schluss, *der;* **come** *or* **draw to a** ~: zu Ende gehen; **bring** *or* **draw sth. to a** ~: einer Sache (*Dat.*) ein Ende bereiten; etw. zu Ende bringen; **(b)** /kləʊs/ (cul-de-sac) Sackgasse, *die*

~ **'down** /kləʊz/ **1** *v.t.* schließen; (ugs.) zumachen; stilllegen ⟨*Werk, Zeche*⟩; einstellen ⟨*Betrieb, Arbeit*⟩. **2** *v.i.* geschlossen werden; zugemacht werden (ugs.); ⟨*Werk, Zeche:*⟩ stillgelegt werden; (Brit.) ⟨*Rundfunkstation:*⟩ Sendeschluss haben

~ **'in** *v.i.* ⟨*Nacht, Dunkelheit:*⟩ hereinbrechen; ⟨*Tage:*⟩ kürzer werden; ~ **in [up]on sb./sth.** (draw nearer) sich jmdm./etw. nähern; ⟨*draw around*⟩ jmdn./etw. umzingeln

~ **'off** *v.t.* [ab]sperren; abriegeln

~ **'up 1** *v.i.* **(a)** aufrücken; **(b)** ⟨*Blume:*⟩ sich schließen; **(c)** (lock up) abschließen. **2** *v.t.* abschließen

closed /kləʊzd/ *adj.* **(a)** (no longer open) geschlossen ⟨*Laden, Geschäft, Fabrik*⟩; **we're** ~: wir haben geschlossen; "~" „Geschlossen"; **the subject is** ~: das Thema ist [für mich] erledigt; **(b)** (restricted) [der Öffentlichkeit] nicht frei zugänglich

'closed-circuit *adj.* ~ **television** interne Fernsehanlage; (for supervision) Fernsehüberwachungsanlage, *die*

close-down /'kləʊzdaʊn/ *n.* **(a)** (closing) Schließung, *die;* (of works, railway, mine) Stilllegung, *die;* (of project, operation) Einstellung, *die;* **(b)** (Radio, Telev.) Sendeschluss, *der*

closed 'shop *n.* Closed Shop, *der;* **we have** *or* **operate a** ~ **in this factory** in unserer Fabrik besteht Gewerkschaftszwang

close-fitting /'kləʊsfɪtɪŋ/ *adj.* eng anliegend; knapp sitzend ⟨*Anzug*⟩

closely /'kləʊslɪ/ *adv.* **(a)** dicht; **follow me** ~: bleib *od.* geh dicht hinter mir!; **look** ~ **at** genau betrachten; **look** ~ **into** (fig.) näher untersuchen; **(b)** (intimately) eng; **we're not** ~ **related** wir sind nicht nah miteinander verwandt; **(c)** (rigorously, painstakingly) genau; genau, eingehend ⟨*befragen, prüfen*⟩; streng, scharf ⟨*bewachen*⟩; **a** ~ **guarded secret** ein streng *od.* sorgsam gehütetes Geheimnis; **(d)** (nearly equally) ~ **fought/contested** hart umkämpft; **(e)** (exactly) genau; ~ **resemble sb.** jmdm. sehr ähneln; **(f)** ~ **printed/written** eng bedruckt/beschrieben; ~ **reasoned** (fig.) schlüssig

closeness /'kləʊsnɪs/ *n., no pl.* **(a)** (nearness in space or time) Nähe, *die;* **(b)** (intimacy) Enge, *die;* **(c)** (rigorousness) Genauigkeit, *die;* (of questioning) Nachdrücklichkeit, *die;* **(d)** (of atmosphere, air) Schwüle, *die;* **(e)** (exactness) **the** ~ **of the fit** der genaue Sitz; **the** ~ **of a translation** die Worttreue einer Übersetzung

close season /'kləʊs siːzn/ *n.* Schonzeit, *die*

closet /'klɒzɪt/ *n.* **(a)** (Amer.: cupboard) Schrank, *der;* **come out of the** ~ (fig.) sich nicht länger verstecken; **(b)** (water ~) Klosett, *das*

closeted /'klɒzɪtɪd/ *adj.* **be** ~ **together/with sb.** eine Besprechung/mit jmdm. eine Besprechung hinter verschlossenen Türen haben

close-up /'kləʊsʌp/ *n.* (Cinemat., Telev.) ~ **[picture/shot]** Nahaufnahme *die;* (of face etc.) Großaufnahme, *die;* **in** ~**:** in Nah-/Großaufnahme

closing /'kləʊzɪŋ/**:** ~ **date** *n.* (for competition) Einsendeschluss, *der;* (to take part) Meldefrist, *die;* **the** ~ **date for applications for the job is …:** Bewerbungen bitte bis zum … einreichen; ~ **time** *n.* (of public house) Polizeistunde, *die;* (of shop) Ladenschlusszeit, *die*

closure /'kləʊʒə(r)/ *n.* **(a)** (closing) Schließung, *die;* (of factory, pit also) Stilllegung, *die;* (of road, bridge) Sperrung, *die;* **(b)** (cap, stopper) [Flaschen]verschluss, *der*

clot /klɒt/ **1** *n.* **(a)** Klumpen, *der;* **(b)** (Brit. coll.: stupid person) Trottel, *der* (ugs. abwertend). **2** *v.i.* **-tt-** ⟨*Blut:*⟩ gerinnen; ⟨*Sahne:*⟩ klumpen

cloth /klɒθ/ *n., pl.* ~**s** /klɒθs/ **(a)** Stoff, *der;* Tuch, *das;* **cut one's coat according to one's** ~ (fig.) sich nach der Decke strecken (ugs.); **(b)** (piece of ~) Tuch, *das;* (dish~) Spültuch, *das;* (table~) Tischtuch, *das;* [Tisch]decke, *die;* (duster) Staubtuch, *das*

clothe /kləʊð/ *v.t.* (lit. or fig.) kleiden

clothes /kləʊðz/ *n. pl.* Kleider *Pl.;* (collectively) Kleidung, *die;* **with one's** ~ **on** angezogen; **put one's** ~ **on** sich anziehen; **take one's** ~ **off** sich ausziehen

clothes: ~ **brush** *n.* Kleiderbürste, *die,* ~ **hanger** *n.* Kleiderbügel, *der;* ~ **horse** *n.* Wäscheständer, *der;* ~ **line** *n.* Wäscheleine, *die;* ~**-peg** (Brit.), ~**-pin** (Amer.) *ns.* Wäscheklammer, *die*

clothing /'kləʊðɪŋ/ *n., no pl.* Kleidung, *die;* **article of** ~**:** Kleidungsstück, *das*

clotted cream /klɒtɪd 'kriːm/ *n.: sehr fetter Rahm*

cloud /klaʊd/ **1** *n.* **(a)** Wolke, *die;* (collective) Bewölkung, *die;* **go round with** *or* **have one's head in the** ~**s** (fig.) (be unrealistic) in den Wolken schweben; (be absent-minded) mit seinen Gedanken ganz woanders sein; **every** ~ **has a silver lining** (prov.) es hat alles seine Gutes; **(b)** ~ **of dust/smoke** Staub-/Rauchwolke, *die;* **(c)** (fig.: cause of gloom or suspicion) dunkle Wolke; **he left under a** ~: unter zweifelhaften Umständen schied er aus dem Dienst. **2** *v.t.* **(a)** verdunkeln ⟨*Himmel*⟩; blind machen ⟨*Fenster[scheibe]*, Spiegel*⟩; **(b)** (fig.: cast gloom or trouble on) trüben ⟨*Glück, Freude, Aussicht*⟩; überschatten ⟨*Zukunft*⟩; (make unclear) trüben ⟨*Urteilsvermögen, Verstand, Bewusstsein*⟩

~ **'over** *v.i.* sich bewölken; ⟨*Spiegel:*⟩ beschlagen

cloud: ~**burst** *n.* Wolkenbruch, *der;* ~**-'cuckooland** *n.* Wolkenkuckucksheim, *das* (geh.)

cloudless /'klaʊdlɪs/ *adj.* wolkenlos

cloudy /'klaʊdɪ/ *adj.* bewölkt, bedeckt, wolkig ⟨*Himmel*⟩; trübe ⟨*Wetter, Flüssigkeit, Glas*⟩

clout /klaʊt/ **1** *n.* **(a)** (coll.: hit) Schlag, *der;* **(b)** (coll.: power, influence) Schlagkraft, *die.* **2** *v.t.* (coll.) hauen (ugs.); ~ **sb. round the ear** jmdm. eins hinter die Ohren geben (ugs.); ~ **sb. [one]** jmdm. eine runterhauen (salopp)

clove[1] /kləʊv/ n. Brutzwiebel, die; (of garlic) [Knoblauch]zehe, die

clove[2] n. (spice) [Gewürz]nelke, die

clove[3] ⇨ **cleave**

cloven /'kləʊvn/ 1 ⇨ **cleave**. 2 adj. ∼ foot/hoof Spaltfuß, der (veralt.)/Spalthuf, der (veralt.); (of devil) Pferdefuß, der

clover /'kləʊvə(r)/ n. Klee, der

'cloverleaf n. (also Road Constr.) Kleeblatt, das

clown /klaʊn/ 1 n. (a) Clown, der; **act** or **play the** ∼: den Clown spielen; (b) (ignorant person) Dummkopf, der (ugs.); (ill-bred person) ungehobelter Klotz. 2 v.i. ∼ [about or around] den Clown spielen (abwertend)

cloy /klɔɪ/ v.t. übersättigen; überfüttern

cloying /'klɔɪɪŋ/ adj. (lit. or fig.) süßlich

club /klʌb/ 1 n. (a) Keule, die; (golf ∼) Golfschläger, der; (b) (association) Klub, der; Club, der; Verein, der; **join the** ∼ (fig.) mitmachen; **join the** or **welcome to the** ∼! (fig.) du also auch!; (c) (premises) Klub, der; (buildings/grounds) Klubhaus/-gelände, das; (d) (Cards) Kreuz, das; **the ace/ seven of** ∼s das Kreuzas/die Kreuzsieben. 2 v.t., **-bb-** (beat) prügeln; (with ∼) knüppeln. 3 v.i., **-bb-:** ∼ **together** sich zusammentun; (in order to buy something) zusammenlegen

'clubhouse n. Klubhaus, das

cluck /klʌk/ v.i. gackern; (to call chicks) glucken

clue /kluː/ n. (a) (fact, principle) Anhaltspunkt, der; (in criminal investigation) Spur, die; (b) (fig. coll.) **give sb. a** ∼: jmdm. einen Tipp geben; **not have a** ∼: keine Ahnung haben (ugs.); (c) (in crossword) Frage, die

clueless /'kluːlɪs/ adj. (coll. derog.) unbedarft (ugs.) ⟨Person⟩

clump /klʌmp/ 1 n. (of trees, bushes, flowers) Gruppe, die; (of grass) Büschel, das. 2 v.i. (tread) stapfen. 3 v.t. zusammengruppieren; in Gruppen anordnen

clumsiness /'klʌmzɪnɪs/ n., no pl. ⇨ **clumsy:** Schwerfälligkeit, die; Plumpheit, die

clumsy /'klʌmzɪ/ adj. (a) (awkward) schwerfällig, unbeholfen ⟨Person, Bewegungen⟩; plump ⟨Form, Figur⟩; tollpatschig ⟨Heranwachsender⟩; (b) (ill-contrived) plump ⟨Verse, Nachahmung⟩; unbeholfen ⟨Worte⟩; primitiv ⟨Vorrichtung, Maschine⟩; (c) (tactless) plump

clung ⇨ **cling**

cluster /'klʌstə(r)/ 1 n. (a) (of grapes, berries) Traube, die; (of fruit, flowers, curls) Büschel, das; (of trees, shrubs) Gruppe, die; (b) (of stars, cells) Haufen, der. 2 v.i. ∼ [a]round sb./ sth. sich um jmdn./etw. scharen od. drängen

clutch /klʌtʃ/ 1 v.t. umklammern. 2 v.i. ∼ at sth. nach etw. greifen; (fig.) sich an etw. ⟨Akk.⟩ klammern. 3 n. (a) in pl. (fig.: control) **fall into sb.'s** ∼es jmdm. in die Klauen fallen; (b) (Motor Veh., Mech.) Kupplung, die; **let in the** ∼, **put the** ∼ **in** einkuppeln; **disengage the** ∼, **let the** ∼ **out** auskuppeln

clutter /'klʌtə(r)/ 1 n. Durcheinander, das. 2 v.t. ∼ [up] **the table/room** überall auf dem Tisch/im Zimmer herumliegen; **be** ∼ed [up] **with sth.** ⟨Zimmer:⟩ mit etw. voll gestopft sein; ⟨Tisch:⟩ mit etw. übersät sein

cm. abbr. ▶ 850|, ▶ 904|, ▶ 1193| centimetre[s] cm

CND abbr. (Brit.) **Campaign for Nuclear Disarmament** Kampagne für atomare Abrüstung

Co. abbr. (a) **company** Co.; **and Co.** /ənd kəʊ/ (coll.) und Co. (ugs.); (b) **county**

c/o abbr. **care of** bei; c/o

coach /kəʊtʃ/ 1 n. (a) (road vehicle) Kutsche, die; (state ∼) [Staats]karosse, die; (b) (railway carriage) Wagen, der; (c) (bus) [Reise]bus, der; **by** ∼: mit dem Bus, der; (tutor) Privat- od. Nachhilfelehrer, der/-lehrerin, die; (sport instructor) Trainer, der/Trainerin, die. 2 v.t. trainieren; ∼ **a pupil for an examination** einen Schüler auf eine Prüfung vorbereiten

coaching /'kəʊtʃɪŋ/ n., no pl. (a) (teaching) Privatunterricht, der; (b) (sports) Training

coach: ∼ **party** n. Reisegesellschaft, die; ∼ **station** n. Busbahnhof, der; ∼ **tour** n. Rundreise [im Omnibus]; Omnibusreise, die

coagulate /kəʊ'ægjʊleɪt/ 1 v.t. gerinnen lassen; koagulieren (fachspr.). 2 v.i. gerinnen; koagulieren (fachspr.)

coal /kəʊl/ n. (a) Kohle, die; (hard ∼) Steinkohle, die; (b) (piece of ∼) Stück Kohle; **live** ∼s Glut, die; **haul sb. over the** ∼s (fig.) jmdm. die Leviten lesen (ugs.); **carry** ∼s **to Newcastle** (fig.) Eulen nach Athen tragen (fig.)

coal: ∼ **cellar** n. Kohlenkeller, der; ∼ **dust** n. Kohlenstaub, der; ∼**face** n. Streb, der; **at the** ∼**face** im Streb od. vor Ort; ∼**field** n. Kohlenrevier, das; ∼ **fire** n. Kohlenfeuer, das

coalition /kəʊə'lɪʃn/ n. (Polit.) Koalition, die

coal: ∼ **merchant** n. ▶ 887| Kohlenhändler, der; ∼ **mine** n. ▶ 887| Kohlen[berg]werk, das; ∼ **miner** n. ▶ 887| [im Kohlenbergbau tätiger] Grubenarbeiter; ∼ **mining** n. Kohlenbergbau, der; ∼ **oil** n. (Amer.) Paraffin, das

coarse /kɔːs/ adj. (a) (in texture) grob; rau, grob ⟨Haut, Teint⟩; (b) (unrefined, rude, obscene) derb; roh ⟨Geschmack, Kraft⟩; primitiv ⟨Person, Geist⟩; ungehobelt ⟨Manieren, Person⟩; gemein ⟨Lachen, Witz, Geräusch⟩

coast /kəʊst/ 1 n. Küste, die. 2 v.i. (a) (ride) im Freilauf fahren; (b) (fig.: progress) **they are just** ∼**ing along in their work** sie tun bei der Arbeit nur das Nötigste; **he** ∼s **through every examination** er schafft jede Prüfung spielend

coastal /'kəʊstl/ adj. Küsten-

coaster /'kəʊstə(r)/ n. (a) (mat) Untersetzer, der; (b) (ship) Küstenmotorschiff, das; Kümo, das

coast: ∼**guard** n. ▶ 887| (person) Angehörige[r] der Küstenwacht; (b) (organization) Küstenwache, -wacht, die; ∼**line** n. Küste, die

coat /kəʊt/ 1 n. (a) Mantel, der; (b) (layer) Schicht, die; (c) (animal's hair, fur, etc.) Fell, das; (d) ⇨ **coating**. 2 v.t. überziehen; (with paint) streichen

coated /'kəʊtɪd/ adj. belegt ⟨Zunge⟩; ∼ **with dust/ sugar** staubbedeckt/mit Zucker überzogen

coat: ∼**hanger** n. Kleiderbügel, der; ∼ **hook** n. Kleiderhaken, der

coating /'kəʊtɪŋ/ n. (of paint) Anstrich, der; (of dust, snow, wax, polish, varnish) Schicht, die

coat of 'arms n. Wappen, das

co-author /kəʊ'ɔːθə(r)/ n. Mitautor, der/-autorin, die

coax /kəʊks/ v.t. überreden; ∼ **sb. into doing sth.** jmdn. herumkriegen (ugs.), etw. zu tun; ∼ **a smile/some money out of sb.** jmdm. ein Lächeln/etw. Geld entlocken

cob /kɒb/ n. (a) (nut) Haselnuss, die; (b) (swan) männlicher Schwan; (c) ⇨ **corn cob**

cobalt /'kəʊbɔːlt, 'kəʊbɒlt/ n. (element) Kobalt, das

cobber /'kɒbə(r)/ n. (Austral. and NZ coll.) Kumpel, der (ugs.)

cobble[1] /'kɒbl/ 1 n. Pflaster-, Kopfstein, der; Katzenkopf, der. 2 v.t. pflastern ⟨Straße⟩; ∼d **streets** Straßen mit Kopfsteinpflaster

cobble[2] v.t. (put together, mend) flicken

cobbler /'kɒblə(r)/ n. ▶ 887| Schuster, der

'cobblestone ⇨ **cobble**[1] 1

'cobnut ⇨ **cob a**

cobra /'kɒbrə/ n. Kobra, die

cobweb /'kɒbweb/ n. Spinnengewebe, das; Spinnennetz, das

cocaine /kə'keɪn/ n. Kokain, das

cock /kɒk/ 1 n. (a) (bird, lobster, crab, salmon) Männchen, das; (domestic fowl) Hahn, der; (b) (spout, tap, etc.) Hahn, der; (c) (coarse: penis) Schwanz, der (salopp). 2 v.t. (a) aufstellen, (fig.) spitzen ⟨Ohren⟩; (b) **a** ∼**ed hat** ein Hut mit hoher Krempe; (triangular hat) ein Dreispitz; **knock sb./sth. into a** ∼**ed hat** (fig.: surpass) jmdn./etw. weit übertreffen; jmdn./ etw. in den Sack stecken (fig. ugs.); (c) ∼ **a/the gun** den Hahn spannen

∼ **'up** v.t. (Brit. sl.) versauen (salopp)

cock-a-doodle-doo /kɒkədu:dl'du:/ n. Kikeriki, das

cock-a-hoop /kɒkə'hu:p/ adj. überschwänglich; (boastful) triumphierend

cock and 'bull story n. Lügengeschichte, die

cockatoo /kɒkə'tu:/ n. Kakadu, der

cockchafer /'kɒktʃeɪfə(r)/ n. Maikäfer, der

cockerel /'kɒkərəl/ n. junger Hahn

cock-eyed /'kɒkaɪd/ adj. (a) (crooked) schief; (b) (absurd) verrückt

cockle /ˈkɒkl/ n. Herzmuschel, die

cockney /ˈkɒknɪ/ **1** adj. Cockney-. **2** n. (a) (person) waschechter Londoner/waschechte Londonerin; Cockney, der; (b) (dialect) Cockney, das

'cockpit n. Cockpit, das

cockroach /ˈkɒkrəʊtʃ/ n. [Küchen-, Haus-]schabe, die

cocksure /kɒkˈʃʊə(r)/ adj. (a) (convinced) todsicher; (b) (self-confident) selbstsicher

cocktail /ˈkɒkteɪl/ n. Cocktail, der

cocktail: ∼ **cabinet** n. Hausbar, die; ∼ **dress** n. Cocktailkleid, das; ∼ **party** n. Cocktailparty, die; ∼ **shaker** n. Mixbecher, der

'cock-up n. (Brit. sl.) Schlamassel, der (ugs.); **make a** ∼ **of sth.** bei etw. Scheiße bauen (derb)

cocky /ˈkɒkɪ/ adj. anmaßend

cocoa /ˈkəʊkəʊ/ n. Kakao, der

coconut /ˈkəʊkənʌt/ n. Kokosnuss, die

coconut: ∼ **'matting** n. Kokosmatten Pl.; ∼ **milk** n. Kokosmilch, die; ∼ **palm** n. Kokospalme, die; ∼ **shy** n. Wurfbude, die

cocoon /kəˈkuːn/ **1** n. (a) (Zool.) Kokon, der; (b) (covering) Hülle, die. **2** v.t. einmummen

cod /kɒd/ n., pl. same Kabeljau, der; (in Baltic) Dorsch, der

COD abbr. **cash on delivery; collect on delivery** (Amer.) p. Nachn.

coddle /ˈkɒdl/ v.t. [ver]hätscheln ‹Kind›; verwöhnen ‹Kranken›

code /kəʊd/ **1** n. (a) (collection of statutes etc.) Kodex, der; Gesetzbuch, das; ∼ **of honour** Ehrenkodex, der; ∼s of behaviour Verhaltensnormen; (b) (system of signals) Kode, Code, der; (coded word, etc.) Chiffre, die; **be in** ∼: verschlüsselt sein; **put sth. into** ∼: etw. verschlüsseln. **2** v.t. chiffrieren; verschlüsseln

code: ∼ **name** n. Deckname, der; ∼ **number** n. Kenn-, Tarnzahl, die; ∼ **word** n. Kennwort, das

codger /ˈkɒdʒə(r)/ n. (coll.) Knacker, der (salopp)

cod-liver 'oil n. Lebertran, der

co-driver /ˈkəʊdraɪvə(r)/ n. Beifahrer, der/-fahrerin, die

coed /ˈkəʊed/ (esp. Amer. coll.) **1** n. Studentin, die. **2** adj. koedukativ; Koedukations-; ∼ **school** gemischte Schule

coeducation /kəʊedjʊˈkeɪʃn/ n. Koedukation, die

coeducational /kəʊedjʊˈkeɪʃənl/ adj. koedukativ; Koedukations-

coefficient /kəʊɪˈfɪʃənt/ n. (Math., Phys.) Koeffizient, der

coerce /kəʊˈɜːs/ v.t. zwingen; ∼ **sb. into sth.** jmdn. zu etw. zwingen; ∼ **sb. into doing sth.** jmdn. dazu zwingen, etw. zu tun

coercion /kəʊˈɜːʃn/ n. Zwang, der

coexist /kəʊɪgˈzɪst/ v.i. ‹Ideen, Überzeugungen:› nebeneinander bestehen, koexistieren; ∼ **[together] with sb./ sth.** neben jmdm./etw. bestehen; mit jmdm./etw. koexistieren

coexistence /kəʊɪgˈzɪstəns/ n. Koexistenz, die

C. of E. /siːəvˈiː/ abbr. **Church of England**

coffee /ˈkɒfɪ/ n. Kaffee, der; **drink** or **have a cup of** ∼: eine Tasse Kaffee trinken; **three black/white** ∼s drei [Tassen] Kaffee ohne/mit Milch

coffee: ∼ **bar** n. Café, das; ∼ **bean** n. Kaffeebohne, die; ∼ **break** n. Kaffeepause, die; ∼ **cup** n. Kaffeetasse, die; ∼ **filter** n. Kaffeefilter, der; ∼ **grinder** n. Kaffeemühle, die; ∼ **grounds** n. pl. Kaffeesatz, der; ∼ **morning** n. Morgenkaffee, der; ∼ **pot** n. Kaffeekanne, die; ∼ **shop** n. Kaffeestube, die; Café, das; (selling ∼ beans etc.) Kaffeegeschäft, das; ∼ **table** n. Couchtisch, der

coffin /ˈkɒfɪn/ n. Sarg, der

cog /kɒg/ n. (Mech.) Zahn, der; **be just a** ∼ **[in the wheel/ machine]** (fig.) bloß ein Rädchen im Getriebe sein

cogent /ˈkəʊdʒənt/ adj. (convincing) überzeugend ‹Argument›; zwingend ‹Grund›; (valid) stichhaltig ‹Kritik, Analyse›

cogitate /ˈkɒdʒɪteɪt/ v.i. (formal/joc.) nachsinnen, nachdenken (**on** über + Akk.)

cognac /ˈkɒnjæk/ n. Cognac, der ⓌⓏ

cognate /ˈkɒgneɪt/ adj. (Ling.) verwandt

cog: ∼ **railway** n. (esp. Amer.) Zahnradbahn, die; ∼**wheel** n. Zahnrad, das

cohabit /kəʊˈhæbɪt/ v.i. zusammenleben

cohere /kəʊˈhɪə(r)/ v.i. ‹Teile, Ganzes, Gruppe:› zusammenhalten

coherence /kəʊˈhɪərəns/ n. Zusammenhang, der; Kohärenz, die (geh.); (in work, system, form) Geschlossenheit, die

coherent /kəʊˈhɪərənt/ adj. (a) (cohering) zusammenhängend; (b) (fig.) zusammenhängend; kohärent (geh.); in sich (Dat.) geschlossen ‹System, Ganzes, Werk, Aufsatz, Form›

coherently /kəʊˈhɪərəntlɪ/ adv. zusammenhängend; im Zusammenhang

cohesive /kəʊˈhiːsɪv/ adj. geschlossen, in sich (Dat.) ruhend ‹Ganzes, Einheit, Form›; stimmig ‹Stil, Argument›; kohäsiv ‹Masse, Mischung›

coil /kɔɪl/ **1** v.t. (a) (arrange) aufwickeln; **the snake** ∼ed itself round a branch die Schlange wand sich um einen Ast; (b) (twist) aufdrehen; **the snake** ∼ed itself up die Schlange rollte sich auf. **2** v.i. (a) (twist) ∼ **round sth.** etw. umschlingen; (b) (move sinuously) sich winden; ‹Rauch:› sich ringeln. **3** n. (a) ∼s of rope/wire/piping aufgerollte Seile Pl./aufgerollter Draht/aufgerollte Leitungen Pl.; (b) (single turn of ∼ed thing) Windung, die; (c) (length of ∼ed rope etc.) Stück, das; (d) (contraceptive device) Spirale, die; (e) (Electr.) Spule, die

coin /kɔɪn/ **1** n. ▶ **938**] Münze, die; (metal money) Münzen Pl.; **the other side of the** ∼ (fig.) die Kehrseite der Medaille. **2** v.t. (a) (invent) prägen ‹Wort, Redewendung›; ..., **to** ∼ **a phrase** (iron.) ..., um mich ganz originell auszudrücken; (b) (make) prägen ‹Geld›

'coin-box telephone n. Münzfernsprecher, der

coincide /kəʊɪnˈsaɪd/ v.i. (in space) sich decken; ∼ **with one another** sich decken; (b) (in time) ‹Ereignisse, Veranstaltungen:› zusammenfallen; (c) (agree together) übereinstimmen (**with** mit)

coincidence /kəʊˈɪnsɪdəns/ n. Zufall, der; **by pure** or **sheer** ∼: rein zufällig; **by a curious** ∼: durch einen merkwürdigen Zufall

coincidental /kəʊɪnsɪˈdentl/ adj. zufällig

coincidentally /kəʊɪnsɪˈdentəlɪ/ adv. gleichzeitig; (by coincidence) zufälligerweise

Coke, (P) /kəʊk/ n. (drink) Coke, das ⓌⓏ

coke /kəʊk/ n. Koks, der

colander /ˈkʌləndə(r)/ n. Sieb, das; Durchschlag, der

cold /kəʊld/ **1** adj. (a) kalt; **I feel** ∼: ich friere; mir ist kalt; **her hands/feet were** ∼: sie hatte kalte Hände/ Füße; (b) kalt ‹Intellekt, Herz›; [betont] kühl ‹Person, Ansprache, Aufnahme, Begrüßung›; eiskalt ‹Handlung›; **leave sb.** ∼: jmdn. kaltlassen (ugs.); (c) (coll.: unconscious) bewusstlos; k.o. (ugs.); **he laid him out** ∼: er schlug ihn k.o.; (d) (sexually frigid) [gefühls]kalt; (e) (chilling, depressing) kalt ‹Farbe›; nackt ‹Tatsache, Statistik›. **2** adv. kalt. **3** n. (a) Kälte, die; **be left out in the** ∼ (fig.) links liegengelassen werden; (b) ▶ **865**] (illness) Erkältung, die; ∼ **[in the head]** Schnupfen, der

cold: ∼-**blooded** /ˈkəʊldblʌdɪd/ adj. (a) wechselwarm ‹Tier›; kaltblütig (selten); ∼-**blooded animals** Kaltblüter Pl.; (b) (callous) kaltblütig ‹Person, Mord›; ∼ **cream** n. Coldcream, die od. das

coldly /ˈkəʊldlɪ/ adv. [betont] kühl; [eis]kalt ‹handeln›

cold: ∼ **'storage** n. Kühllagerung, die; ∼ **store** n. Kühlhaus, das; ∼ **'sweat** n. kalter Schweiß; **break out in a** ∼ **sweat** in kalten Schweiß ausbrechen; ∼ **'turkey** n. (Amer. sl.) Totalentzug, der; Coldturkey, der (Drogenjargon); ∼ **'war** n. kalter Krieg

coleslaw /ˈkəʊlslɔː/ n. Kohl-, Krautsalat, der

colic /ˈkɒlɪk/ n. Kolik, die

collaborate /kəˈlæbəreɪt/ v.i. (a) (work jointly) zusammenarbeiten; ∼ **[with sb.] on sth.** zusammen [mit jmdm.] an etw. (Dat.) arbeiten; ∼ **[with sb.] on** or **in doing sth.** mit jmdm. bei etw. zusammenarbeiten; (b) (cooperate with enemy) kollaborieren

collaboration /kəlæbəˈreɪʃn/ n. Zusammenarbeit, die; (with enemy) Kollaboration, die

collaborator /kə'læbəreɪtə(r)/ n. Mitarbeiter, der/-arbeiterin, die; (with enemy) Kollaborateur, der/Kollaborateurin, die

collage /'kɒlɑːʒ/ n. Collage, die

collapse /kə'læps/ 1 n. (a) (of person) (physical or mental breakdown) Zusammenbruch, der; (heart attack; of lung, blood vessel, circulation) Kollaps, der; (b) (of tower, bridge, structure, wall, roof) Einsturz, der; (c) (fig.: failure) Zusammenbruch, der; (of negotiations, plans, hopes) Scheitern, das. 2 v.i. (a) ⟨Person:⟩ zusammenbrechen; ⟨Lunge, Gefäß, Kreislauf:⟩ kollabieren; ~ with laughter (fig.) sich vor Lachen kugeln; (b) ⟨Zelt:⟩ in sich zusammenfallen; ⟨Tisch, Stuhl:⟩ zusammenbrechen; ⟨Turm, Brücke, Gebäude, Mauer, Dach:⟩ einstürzen; (c) (fig.: fail) ⟨Verhandlungen, Pläne, Hoffnungen:⟩ scheitern; ⟨Geschäft, Unternehmen usw.:⟩ zusammenbrechen; (d) (fold down) ⟨Regenschirm, Fahrrad, Tisch:⟩ sich zusammenklappen lassen

collapsible /kə'læpsɪbl/ adj. Klapp-, zusammenklappbar ⟨Stuhl, Tisch, Fahrrad⟩; Falt-, faltbar ⟨Boot⟩

collar /'kɒlə(r)/ 1 n. (a) Kragen, der; with ~ and tie mit Krawatte; hot under the ~ (fig.) (embarrassed) verlegen; (angry) wütend; (b) (for dog) [Hunde]halsband, das. 2 v.t. (seize) am Kragen kriegen (ugs.); schnappen (ugs.)

'collarbone n. (Anat.) Schlüsselbein, das

collate /kə'leɪt/ v.t. (a) (Bibliog.: compare) kollationieren (Buchw.) ⟨Manuskripte, Druckbögen⟩; ~ a copy with the original eine Abschrift mit dem Original vergleichen; (b) (put together) zusammenstellen ⟨Daten, Beweismaterial⟩

collateral /kə'lætərl/ n. (Finance) ~ [security] Sicherheiten Pl.

colleague /'kɒliːg/ n. Kollege, der/Kollegin, die

collect /kə'lekt/ 1 v.i. (a) (assemble) sich versammeln; (b) (accumulate) ⟨Staub, Müll usw.:⟩ sich ansammeln. 2 v.t. (a) (assemble) sammeln; aufsammeln ⟨Müll, leere Flaschen usw.⟩; ~ [up] one's belongings seine Siebensachen (ugs.) zusammensuchen; ~ dust Staub anziehen; (b) (fetch, pick up) abholen ⟨Person, Dinge⟩; ~ a parcel from the post office ein Paket bei od. auf der Post abholen; ~ sb. from the station jmdn. am Bahnhof od. von der Bahn abholen; (c) eintreiben ⟨Steuern, Zinsen, Schulden⟩; kassieren ⟨Miete, Fahrgeld⟩; beziehen ⟨Zahlungen, Sozialhilfe⟩; (d) (as hobby) sammeln ⟨Münzen, Bücher, Briefmarken, Gemälde usw.⟩; (e) ~ one's wits/thoughts seine Gedanken sammeln

collected /kə'lektɪd/ adj. (a) (gathered) gesammelt; (b) (calm) gesammelt; gelassen

collection /kə'lekʃn/ n. (a) (collecting) Sammeln, das; (of rent, fares) Kassieren, das; (of taxes, interest, debts) Eintreiben, das; (of goods, persons) Abholen, das; (amount of money collected) Sammlung, die; (in church) Kollekte, die; (c) (of mail) Abholung, die; (from postbox) Leerung, die; (d) (group collected) (of coins, books, stamps, paintings, etc.) Sammlung, die; (of fashionable clothes) Kollektion, die; (of people) Ansammlung, die; (e) (accumulated quantity) Ansammlung, die

collective /kə'lektɪv/ 1 adj. kollektiv nicht präd.; gesamt nicht präd. 2 n. Genossenschaftsbetrieb, der

collective: ~ 'bargaining n. Tarifverhandlungen Pl.; ~ 'noun n. (Ling.) Kollektivum, das

collector /kə'lektə(r)/ n. (of stamps, coins, etc.) Sammler, der/Sammlerin, die; (of taxes) Einnehmer, der/Einnehmerin, die; (of rent, cash) Kassierer, der/Kassiererin, die

college /'kɒlɪdʒ/ n. (a) (esp. Brit.: independent corporation in university) College, das; (b) (place of further education) Fach[hoch]schule, die; go to ~ (esp. Amer.) studieren; start ~ (esp. Amer.) sein Studium aufnehmen; (c) (esp. Brit.: school) Internatsschule, die; Kolleg, das

College of Edu'cation Pädagogische Hochschule

collide /kə'laɪd/ v.i. (a) (come into collision) zusammenstoßen (with mit); ⟨Schiff:⟩ kollidieren; (b) (be in conflict) zusammenprallen; kollidieren

collie /'kɒlɪ/ n. Collie, der

colliery /'kɒljərɪ/ n. Kohlengrube, die

collision /kə'lɪʒn/ n. (a) (colliding) Zusammenstoß, der; (between ships) Kollision, die; come into ~: zusammenstoßen; ⟨Schiffe:⟩ in Kollision geraten, kollidieren; a head-on ~ between a car and a bus ein Frontalzusammenstoß eines PKW mit einem Bus; (b) (fig.) Konflikt, der; Kollision, die

col'lision course n. (lit. or fig.) Kollisionskurs, der; on a ~: auf Kollisionskurs

collocator /'kɒləkeɪtə(r)/ n. (Ling.) Kollokator, der

colloquial /kə'ləʊkwɪəl/ adj. umgangssprachlich; ~ language Umgangssprache, die

collusion /kə'ljuːʒn, kə'luːʒn/ n. geheime Absprache

Cologne /kə'ləʊn/ ▶1159| 1 pr. n. Köln (das). 2 attrib. adj. Kölner

cologne ⇒ eau-de-Cologne

Colombia /kə'lɒmbɪə/ pr. n. Kolumbien (das)

colon¹ /'kəʊlən/ n. Doppelpunkt, der

colon² /'kəʊlən, 'kəʊlɒn/ n. ▶672| (Anat.) Grimmdarm, der

colonel /kɜːnl/ n. ▶1152| Oberst, der

colonial /kə'ləʊnɪəl/ adj. Kolonial-; kolonial

colonialism /kə'ləʊnɪəlɪzm/ n. Kolonialismus, der

colonisation, colonise ⇒ coloniz-

colonist /'kɒlənɪst/ n. Siedler, der/Siedlerin, die; Kolonist, der/Kolonistin, die

colonization /kɒlənaɪ'zeɪʃn/ n. Kolonisation, die; Kolonisierung, die

colonize /'kɒlənaɪz/ v.t. kolonisieren; besiedeln ⟨unbewohntes Gebiet⟩

colonnade /kɒlə'neɪd/ n. (Archit.) Säulengang, der; Kolonnade, die

colony /'kɒlənɪ/ n. Kolonie, die

color etc. (Amer.) ⇒ **colour** etc.

coloration /kʌlə'reɪʃn/ n. (a) (act of colouring) Kolorierung, die; (b) (colour) Färbung, die

colossal /kə'lɒsl/ adj. ungeheuer; gewaltig ⟨Bauwerk⟩; riesenhaft, kolossal ⟨Mann, Statue⟩

colour /'kʌlə(r)/ (Brit.) 1 n. (a) Farbe, die; primary ~s Grundfarben Pl.; secondary ~s Mischfarben Pl.; what ~ is it? welche Farbe hat es?; (b) (complexion) [Gesichts]farbe, die; change ~: die Farbe ändern; (go red/pale) rot/blass werden; he is/looks a bit off ~ today ihm ist heute nicht besonders gut/er sieht heute nicht besonders gut aus; (c) (racial) Hautfarbe, die; (d) (character, tone, quality, etc.) Charakter, der; add ~ to a story einer Erzählung Farbe od. Kolorit geben; local ~: Lokalkolorit, das; (e) in pl. (ribbon, dress, etc., worn as symbol of party, club, etc.) Farben Pl.; show one's [true] ~s sein wahres Gesicht zeigen; (f) in pl. (national flag) Farben Pl.; (g) (flag) Fahne, die; (of ship) Flagge, die; pass with flying ~s (fig.) glänzend abschneiden; nail one's ~s to the mast (fig.) Farbe bekennen. 2 v.t. (a) (give ~ to) Farbe geben (+ Dat.); (b) (paint) malen; ~ in ausmalen ⟨Bild, Figur⟩; ~ a wall red eine Wand rot anmalen; (c) (stain, dye) färben ⟨Material, Stoff⟩; (d) (misrepresent) [schön]färben ⟨Nachrichten, Bericht⟩; (e) (fig.: influence) beeinflussen. 3 v.i. (blush) ~ [up] erröten; rot werden

colouration (Brit.) ⇒ **coloration**

colour: ~ bar n. Rassenschranke, die; ~-blind adj. farbenblind; a ~-blind person ein Farbenblinder/eine Farbenblinde

coloured /'kʌləd/ (Brit.) 1 adj. (a) farbig; ~ pencil Farbstift, der; (b) (of non-white descent) farbig; ~ people Farbige Pl. 2 n. Farbige, der/die

colour: ~-fast adj. farbecht; ~ film n. Farbfilm, der

colourful /'kʌləfl/ adj. (Brit.) bunt; farbenfroh, bunt ⟨Bild, Schauspiel⟩; farbig, anschaulich ⟨Sprache, Stil, Bericht⟩; buntbewegt ⟨Zeitepoche, Leben⟩

colouring /'kʌlərɪŋ/ n. (Brit.) (a) (colours) Farben Pl.; (b) (facial complexion) Teint, der; (c) ~ [matter] (in food etc.) Farbstoff, der

colourless /'kʌləlɪs/ adj. (Brit.) (a) (without colour) farblos ⟨Flüssigkeit, Gas⟩; (pale) blass ⟨Teint⟩; (dull-hued) grau, düster ⟨Bild, Stoff, Himmel⟩; (b) (fig.) farblos, langweilig ⟨Geschichte, Schilderung⟩; unauffällig ⟨Person⟩

colour: ~ photograph n. Farbfotografie, -aufnahme, die; ~ photography n. Farbfotografie, die; ~ scheme n. Farb[en]zusammenstellung, die; ~ supplement n. Farbbeilage, die; ~ television n. (a) Farbfernsehen, das; (b) (set) Farbfernsehgerät, das; ~ transparency n. Farbdia, das

colt /kəʊlt/ n. [Hengst]fohlen, das

column /'kɒləm/ n. **(a)** (Archit., of smoke) Säule, die; **(b)** (division of page, table, etc.) Spalte, die; Kolumne, die; **(c)** (in newspaper) Spalte, die; Kolumne, die; **the sports** ~: der Sportteil; **the gossip** ~: die Klatschspalte (ugs. abwertend); **(d)** (of troops, vehicles, ships) Kolonne, die

columnist /'kɒləmɪst/ n. Kolumnist, der/Kolumnistin, die

coma /'kəʊmə/ n. (Med.) Koma, das; **be in a** ~: im Koma liegen; **go into a** ~: ins Koma fallen

comb /kəʊm/ **1** n. Kamm, der; **give one's hair a** ~: sich (Dat.) die Haare kämmen. **2** v.t. **(a)** kämmen ⟨Haare, Flachs, Wolle⟩; ~ **sb.'s/one's hair** jmdm./sich die Haare kämmen; jmdn./sich kämmen; **(b)** (search) durchkämmen ⟨Gelände, Wald⟩

combat /'kɒmbæt/ **1** n. Kampf, der. **2** v.t. (fig.: strive against) bekämpfen

combatant /'kɒmbətənt/ n. (in war) Kombattant, der; (in duel) Kämpfer, der

combative /'kɒmbətɪv/ adj. streitlustig

combed /kəʊmd/ adj. gekämmt

combination /kɒmbɪ'neɪʃn/ n. Kombination, die; **in** ~: zusammen

combi'nation lock n. Kombinationsschloss, das

combine 1 /kəm'baɪn/ v.t. **(a)** (join together) kombinieren; zusammenfügen (**into** zu); **(b)** (possess together) vereinigen; in sich (Dat.) vereinigen ⟨Eigenschaften⟩. **2** /kəm'baɪn/ v.i. **(a)** (join together) ⟨Stoffe:⟩ sich verbinden; **(b)** (cooperate) zusammenwirken; ⟨Parteien:⟩ sich zusammentun. **3** /'kɒmbaɪn/ n. **(a)** (Commerc.) Konzern, der; **(b)** (machine) ~ **[harvester]** Mähdrescher, der; Kombine, die

combined /kəm'baɪnd/ adj. vereint; **a** ~ **operation** eine gemeinsame Operation

combustible /kəm'bʌstɪbl/ adj. brennbar

combustion /kəm'bʌstʃn/ n. Verbrennung, die; ~ **chamber** (of jet engine) Brennkammer, die; (of internal-~ engine) Verbrennungsraum, der

come /kʌm/ v.i., **came** /keɪm/, **come** /kʌm/ **(a)** kommen; ~ **here!** komm [mal] her!; **[I'm] coming!** [ich] komme schon!; ~ **running** angelaufen kommen; ~ **running into the room** ins Zimmer gerannt kommen; **not know whether** or **if one is coming or going** nicht wissen, wo einem der Kopf steht; **they came to a house/ town** sie kamen zu einem Haus/in eine Stadt; **Christmas/Easter is coming** bald ist Weihnachten/Ostern; **he has** ~ **a long way** er kommt von weit her; ~ **to sb.'s notice** or **attention/knowledge** jmdm. auffallen/zu Ohren kommen; **the train came into the station** der Zug fuhr in den Bahnhof ein; **(b)** (occur) kommen; (in list etc.) stehen; **(c)** (become, be) **the shoelaces have** ~ **undone** die Schnürsenkel sind aufgegangen; **the handle has** ~ **loose** der Griff ist lose; **it all came right in the end** es ging alles gut aus; **have** ~ **to believe/ realize that** …: zu der Überzeugung/Einsicht gelangt sein, dass …; **(d)** (become present) kommen; **in the coming week/month** kommende Woche/kommenden Monat; **to** ~ (future) künftig; **in years to** ~: in künftigen Jahren; **for some time to** ~: [noch] für einige Zeit; **(e)** (be result) kommen; **nothing came of it** es ist nichts daraus geworden; **the suggestion came from him** der Vorschlag war od. stammte von ihm; **(f)** (happen) **how** ~**s it that you** …? wie kommt es, dass du …?; **how** ~? (coll.) wieso?; weshalb?; ~ **what may** komme, was wolle (geh.); ganz gleich, was kommt; **(g)** (be available) ⟨Waren:⟩ erhältlich sein; **this dress** ~**s in three sizes** dies Kleid gibt es in drei Größen od. ist in drei Größen erhältlich; **(h)** (coll.: play a part) ~ **the bully with sb.** bei jmdm. den starken Mann markieren (salopp); **don't** ~ **the innocent with me** spiel mir nicht den Unschuldsengel vor! (ugs.); **don't** ~ **that game with me!** komm mir bloß nicht mit dieser Tour od. Masche! (salopp)

~ **a'bout** v.i. passieren; **how did it** ~ **about that** …? wie kam es, dass …?

~ **across 1** /-'-/ v.i. **(a)** (be understood) ⟨Bedeutung:⟩ verstanden werden; ⟨Mitteilung, Rede:⟩ ankommen (ugs.); **(b)**

(coll.: make an impression) wirken (**as** wie). **2** /'---/ v.t. ~ **across sb./sth.** jmdm./einer Sache begegnen; **have you** ~ **across my watch?** ist dir meine Uhr begegnet? (ugs.)

~ **a'long** v.i. **(a)** (hurry up) ~ **along!** komm/kommt!; nun mach/macht schon! (ugs.); **(b)** (make progress) ~ **along nicely** gute Fortschritte machen; **(c)** (arrive, present oneself/ itself) ⟨Person:⟩ ankommen; ⟨Gelegenheit, Stelle:⟩ sich bieten; **he'll take any job that** ~**s along** er nimmt jeden Job, der sich ihm bietet; **(d)** (to place) mitkommen (**with** mit)

~ **a'way** v.i. **(a)** (leave) weggehen; **(b)** (become detached) sich lösen (**from** von); **(c)** (be left) ~ **away with the impression/feeling that** …: mit dem Eindruck/Gefühl gehen, dass …

~ '**back** v.i. **(a)** (return) zurückkommen; ⟨Gedächtnis, Vergangenes:⟩ wiederkehren; **(b)** (return to memory) **it will** ~ **back [to me]** es wird mir wieder einfallen; **(c)** ~ **back [into fashion]** wiederkommen; wieder in Mode kommen; **(d)** (retort) ~ **back at sb. with sth.** jmdm. etw. entgegnen

~ **between** v.t. treten zwischen (+ Akk.)

~ **by 1** /'--/ v.t. (obtain, receive) kriegen (ugs.); bekommen. **2** /'-'-/ v.i. vorbeikommen

~ '**down** v.i. **(a)** (collapse) herunterfallen; runterfallen (ugs.); (fall) ⟨Schnee, Regen, Preis:⟩ fallen; **(b)** (~ to place regarded as lower) herunterkommen; runterkommen (ugs.); (~ southwards) runterkommen (ugs.); **(c)** (land) [not]landen; (crash) abstürzen; ~ **down in a field** auf einem Acker [not]landen/auf einem Acker stürzen; **(d)** (be passed on) ⟨Sage, Brauch:⟩ überliefert werden; **(e)** ~ **down to** (reach) reichen bis; **(f)** ~ **down to** (be reduced to) hinauslaufen auf (+ Akk.); **(g)** ~ **down to** (be a question of) ankommen (**to** auf + Akk.); **(h)** (suffer change for the worse) **she has** ~ **down in the world** sie hat einen Abstieg erlebt; ~ **down to sth.** (be forced to resort to sth.) auf etw. (Akk.) angewiesen sein; **(i)** ~ **down with** bekommen ⟨Krankheit⟩

~ '**in** v.i. **(a)** (enter) hereinkommen; reinkommen (ugs.); ~ **in!** herein!; **(b)** ⟨Flut:⟩ kommen; **(c)** (be received) ⟨Nachrichten, Bericht:⟩ hereinkommen; **(d)** (in radio communication) melden; **C**~ **in, Tom,** ~ **in, Tom.** Over Tom melden, Tom melden. Ende; **(e)** (contribute to discussion etc.) sich einschalten; **(f)** (become fashionable) in Mode kommen; aufkommen; **(g)** (in race) einlaufen als od. durchs Ziel gehen als ⟨Erster usw.⟩; **(h)** (play a part) **where do I** ~ **in?** welche Rolle soll ich spielen?; ~ **in on sth.** sich an etw. (Dat.) beteiligen; **(i)** ~ **in for** erregen ⟨Bewunderung, Aufmerksamkeit⟩; auf sich (Akk.) ziehen, hervorrufen ⟨Kritik⟩

~ **into** v.t. **(a)** (enter) hereinkommen in (+ Akk.); ⟨Zug:⟩ einfahren in ⟨Bahnhof⟩; ⟨Schiff:⟩ einlaufen in ⟨Hafen⟩; **(b)** (inherit) erben ⟨Vermögen⟩; **(c)** (play a part) **wealth does not** ~ **into it** Reichtum spielt dabei keine Rolle; **where do I** ~ **into it?** welche Rolle soll ich [dabei] spielen?

~ **near** v.t. ~ **near [to] doing sth.** drauf und dran sein, etw. zu tun (ugs.)

~ **off 1** /-'-/ v.i. **(a)** (become detached) ⟨Griff, Knopf:⟩ abgehen; (be removable) sich abnehmen lassen; ⟨Fleck:⟩ weg-, rausgehen (ugs.); **(b)** (fall from sth.) runterfallen; **(c)** (emerge from contest etc.) abschneiden; **(d)** (succeed) ⟨Pläne, Versuche:⟩ Erfolg haben, (ugs.) klappen; **(e)** (take place) stattfinden; **their wedding/holiday did not** ~ **off** aus ihrer Hochzeit/ihrem Urlaub wurde nichts. **2** /-'-/ v.t. ~ **off a horse/ bike** vom Pferd/Fahrrad fallen; ~ '**off it!** (coll.) nun mach mal halblang! (ugs.)

~ **on 1** /-'-/ v.i. **(a)** (continue coming, follow) kommen; ~ **on!** komm, komm/kommt, kommt!; (encouraging) na, komm; (impatient) na, komm schon; (incredulous) ach komm!; **I'll** ~ **on later** ich komme später nach; **(b)** (make progress) **my work is coming on very well** meine Arbeit macht gute Fortschritte; **(c)** (begin to arrive) ⟨Nacht, Dunkelheit, Winter:⟩ anbrechen; **(d)** (appear on stage or scene) auftreten. **2** /-'-/ v.t. ⇒ ~ **upon**

~ '**out** v.i. **(a)** herauskommen; ~ **out [on strike]** in den Streik treten; **(b)** (appear, become visible) ⟨Sonne, Knospen, Blumen:⟩ herauskommen, (ugs.) rauskommen ⟨Sterne:⟩ zu sehen sein; **(c)** (be revealed) ⟨Wahrheit, Nachrichten:⟩ herauskommen, (ugs.) rauskommen; **(d)** (be published, declared, etc.) herauskommen; rauskommen (ugs.); ⟨Ergebnisse, Zensuren:⟩ bekannt gegeben werden; **(e)** (declare oneself) ~ **out for** or **in favour of sth.** sich für etw. aussprechen;

~ **out against sth.** sich gegen etw. aussprechen; **(f)** (be covered) **she came out in a rash** sie bekam einen Ausschlag; **(g)** (be removed) ⟨*Fleck, Schmutz:*⟩ rausgehen (ugs.); **(h)** ~ **out with** herausrücken mit (ugs.) ⟨*Wahrheit, Fakten*⟩; loslassen (ugs.) ⟨*Flüche, Bemerkungen*⟩
~ **'over 1** *v.i.* **(a)** (~ from some distance) herüberkommen; **(b)** (change sides or opinions) ~ **over to sb./sth.** sich jmdm./ einer Sache anschließen; **(c)** ⇨ ~ **across 1 b; (d) she came over funny/dizzy** ihr wurde auf einmal ganz komisch/schwindlig (ugs.). **2** *v.t.* (coll.) kommen über (+ *Akk.*); **what has** ~ **over him?** was ist über ihn gekommen?
~ **'round** *v.i.* **(a)** (make informal visit) vorbeischauen; **(b)** (recover) wieder zu sich kommen; **(c)** (be converted) es sich [anders] (*Dat.*) überlegen; **he came round to my way of thinking** er hat sich meiner Auffassung (*Dat.*) angeschlossen; **(d)** (recur) **Christmas** ~s **round again** wir haben wieder Weihnachten
~ **'through 1** *v.i.* durchkommen. **2** *v.t.* (survive) überleben
~ **to 1** /'--/ *v.t.* **(a)** (amount to) ⟨*Rechnung, Gehalt, Kosten:*⟩ sich belaufen auf (+ *Akk.*); **his plans came to nothing** aus seinen Plänen wurde nichts; **he/it will never** ~ **to much** aus ihm wird nichts Besonderes werden/daraus wird nicht viel; **(b)** (inherit) erben ⟨*Vermögen*⟩; **(c)** (arrive at) **what is the world coming to?** wohin ist es mit der Welt gekommen?; **this is what he has** ~ **to** so weit ist es also mit ihm gekommen. **2** /-'-/ *v.i.* wieder zu sich kommen
~ **to'gether** *v.i.* ⟨*Personen:*⟩ zusammenkommen; ⟨*Ereignisse:*⟩ zusammenfallen
~ **under** *v.t.* **(a)** (be classed as or among) kommen unter (+ *Akk.*); **(b)** (be subject to) geraten *od.* kommen unter (+ *Akk.*)
~ **'up** *v.i.* **(a)** (~ to place regarded as higher) hochkommen; heraufkommen; (~ northwards) raufkommen (ugs.); **he** ~s **up to London every other weekend** er kommt jedes zweite Wochenende nach London; **(b)** ~ **up to sb.** auf jmdn. zukommen; **(c)** (arise out of ground) herauskommen; rauskommen (ugs.); **(d)** (be discussed) ⟨*Frage, Thema:*⟩ angeschnitten werden, aufkommen; ⟨*Name:*⟩ genannt werden; ⟨*Fall:*⟩ verhandelt werden; **(e)** (present itself) sich ergeben; ~ **up for sale/renewal** zum Kauf angeboten werden/erneuert werden müssen; **(f)** ~ **up to** (reach) reichen bis an (+ *Akk.*); (be equal to) entsprechen (+ *Dat.*) ⟨*Erwartungen, Anforderungen*⟩; **(g)** ~ **up against sth.** (fig.) auf etw. (*Akk.*) stoßen; **(h)** ~ **up with** vorbringen ⟨*Vorschlag*⟩; wissen ⟨*Lösung, Antwort*⟩; haben ⟨*Erklärung, Idee*⟩
~ **upon** *v.t.* (meet by chance) begegnen (+ *Dat.*)
~ **with** *v.t.* (be supplied together with) **this model** ~s **with** ...: zu diesem Modell gehört ...
'comeback *n.* **(a)** (return to profession etc.) Come-back, *das;* **(b)** (coll.: retort) Reaktion, *die*
comedian /kə'miːdɪən/ *n.* ▶ **887** Komiker, *der*
comedienne /kəmiːdr'en, kəmedɪ'en/ *n.* ▶ **887** Komikerin, *die*
'comedown *n.* (loss of prestige etc.) Abstieg, *der*
comedy /'kɒmɪdɪ/ *n.* **(a)** (play) Lustspiel, *das;* Komödie, *die;* **(b)** (humour) Witz, *der;* Witzigkeit, *die*
comely /'kʌmlɪ/ *adj.* gut aussehend; ansehnlich
comer /'kʌmə(r)/ *n.* **the competition is open to all** ~s an dem Wettbewerb kann sich jeder beteiligen; **the first** ~: derjenige, der zuerst kommt
comet /'kɒmɪt/ *n.* (Astron.) Komet, *der*
comeuppance /kʌm'ʌpəns/ *n.* **get one's** ~: die Quittung kriegen (fig.)
comfort /'kʌmfət/ **1** *n.* **(a)** (consolation) Trost, *der;* **it is a** ~/**no** ~ **to know that** ...: es ist tröstlich/alles andere als tröstlich zu wissen, dass ...; **he takes** ~ **from the fact that** ...: er tröstet sich mit der Tatsache, dass ...; **(b)** (physical well-being) Behaglichkeit, *die;* **live in great** ~: sehr behaglich *od.* bequem leben; **(c)** (person) Trost, *der;* **(d)** *in pl.* (things that make life easy) Komfort, *der o. Pl.* **2** *v.t.* trösten; (give help to) sich annehmen (+ *Gen.*).
comfortable /'kʌmfətəbl/ *adj.* **(a)** bequem ⟨*Bett, Sessel, Schuhe, Leben*⟩; komfortabel ⟨*Haus, Hotel, Zimmer*⟩; (fig.) ausreichend ⟨*Einkommen, Rente*⟩; **a** ~ **victory** ein leichter Sieg; **a** ~ **majority** eine gute Mehrheit; **(b)** (at

ease) **be/feel** ~: sich wohl fühlen; **make yourself** ~: machen Sie es sich (*Dat.*) bequem
comfortably /'kʌmfətəblɪ/ *adv.* bequem; komfortabel ⟨*eingerichtet*⟩; gut, leicht ⟨*gewinnen*⟩; **they are** ~ **off** es geht ihnen gut
comforting /'kʌmfətɪŋ/ *adj.* beruhigend ⟨*Gedanke*⟩; tröstend ⟨*Worte*⟩; wohlig ⟨*Wärme*⟩
'comfort station *n.* (Amer.) öffentliche Toilette
comfy /'kʌmfɪ/ *adj.* (coll.) bequem; gemütlich ⟨*Haus, Zimmer*⟩
comic /'kɒmɪk/ **1** *adj.* komisch; humoristisch ⟨*Dichtung, Dichter*⟩. **2** *n.* **(a)** ▶ **887** (comedian) Komiker, *der*/Komikerin, *die;* **(b)** (periodical) Comic-Heft, *das;* **(c)** (amusing person) Witzbold, *der;* ulkiger Vogel (ugs.)
comical /'kɒmɪkl/ *adj.* ulkig; komisch
coming /'kʌmɪŋ/ **1** ⇨ **come. 2** *n.* (of person) Ankunft, *die;* (of time) Beginn, *der;* (of institution) Einführung, *die;* ~s **and goings** das Kommen und Gehen
comma /'kɒmə/ *n.* Komma, *das*
command /kə'mɑːnd/ **1** *v.t.* **(a)** (order, bid) befehlen (**sb.** jmdm.); **(b)** (be in ~ of) befehligen ⟨*Schiff, Armee, Streitkräfte*⟩; (have authority over or control of) gebieten über (+ *Akk.*) (geh.); beherrschen; **(c)** (have at one's disposal) verfügen über (+ *Akk.*) ⟨*Gelder, Ressourcen, Wortschatz*⟩; **(d)** (deserve and get) verdient haben ⟨*Achtung, Respekt*⟩; **(e) the hill** ~s **a fine view of** ...: der Berg bietet eine schöne Aussicht auf ... (+ *Akk.*). **2** *n.* **(a)** Kommando, *das;* (in writing) Befehl, *der;* **at** *or* **by sb.'s** ~: auf jmds. Befehl (*Akk.*) [hin]; **(b)** (exercise or tenure) Kommando, *das;* Befehlsgewalt, *die;* **be in** ~ **of an army/ship** eine Armee/ein Schiff befehligen; **have/take** ~ **of** ...: das Kommando über (+ *Akk.*) ... haben/übernehmen; **officer in** ~: befehlshabender Offizier; **(c)** (control, mastery, possession) Beherrschung, *die;* **have a good** ~ **of French** das Französische gut beherrschen; **(d)** (Computing) Befehl, *der*
commandant /kɒmən'dænt/ *n.* Kommandant, *der*
commandeer /kɒmən'dɪə(r)/ *v.t.* **(a)** (take arbitrary possession of) sich (*Dat.*) aneignen; requirieren (scherzh.); **(b)** (seize for military service) einziehen ⟨*Männer*⟩; beschlagnahmen, requirieren ⟨*Pferde, Vorräte, Gebäude*⟩
commander /kə'mɑːndə(r)/ *n.* ▶ **1152** **(a)** Führer, *der;* Leiter, *der;* **(b)** (naval officer below captain) Fregattenkapitän, *der;* **(c) C**~-**in-Chief** Oberbefehlshaber, *der*
commanding /kə'mɑːndɪŋ/ *adj.* **(a)** gebieterisch ⟨*Persönlichkeit, Erscheinung, Stimme*⟩; imposant, eindrucksvoll ⟨*Statur, Gestalt*⟩; **(b)** beherrschend ⟨*Ausblick, Lage*⟩
commanding 'officer *n.* Befehlshaber, *der*/Befehlshaberin, *die*
commandment /kə'mɑːndmənt/ *n.* Gebot, *das;* **the Ten C**~s die Zehn Gebote
commando /kə'mɑːndəʊ/ *n., pl.* ~s **(a)** (unit) Kommando, *das;* Kommandotrupp, *der;* **(b)** (member of ~) Angehöriger eines Kommando[trupp]s
com'mand performance *n.* königliche Galavorstellung
commemorate /kə'meməreɪt/ *v.t.* gedenken (+ *Gen.*)
commemoration /kəmemə'reɪʃn/ *n.* (act) Gedenken, *das;* **in** ~ **of** zum Gedenken an (+ *Akk.*); **the** ~ **of sb.'s death** das Gedenken an jmds. Tod (*Akk.*)
commemorative /kə'memərətɪv/ *adj.* Gedenk-
commence /kə'mens/ *v.t. & i.* beginnen; **building** ~d mit dem Bau wurde begonnen; ~ **to do** *or* ~ **doing sth.** beginnen, etw. zu tun
commencement /kə'mensmənt/ *n.* Beginn, *der*
commend /kə'mend/ *v.t.* **(a)** (praise) loben; ~ **sb. [up]on sth.** jmdn. wegen etw. loben; ~ **sb./sth. to sb.** jmdn./etw. empfehlen; **(b)** (entrust or commit to person's care) anvertrauen
commendable /kə'mendəbl/ *adj.* lobenswert; löblich
commendation /kɒmen'deɪʃn/ *n.* (praise) Lob, *das;* (official) Belobigung, *die;* (award) Auszeichnung, *die*
commensurate /kə'menʃərət, kə'mensjərət/ *adj.* ~ **to** *or* **with** entsprechend (+ *Dat.*); **be** ~ **to** *or* **with sth.** einer Sache (*Dat.*) entsprechen

comment /'kɒment/ **1** n. Bemerkung, die (**on** über + Akk.); (marginal note) Anmerkung, die (**on** über + Akk.); **no** ∼**!** (coll.) kein Kommentar! **2** v.i. ∼ **on sth.** über etw. (Akk.) Bemerkungen machen; **he** ∼**ed that** ...: er bemerkte, dass ...; ∼ **on a text/manuscript** einen Text/ein Manuskript kommentieren

commentary /'kɒmøntørı/ n. (**a**) (series of comments, treatise) Kommentar, der (**on** zu); (comment) Erläuterung, die (**on** zu); (**b**) (Radio, Telev.) [**live** or **running**] ∼: Live-Reportage, die

commentate /'kɒmønteıt/ v.i. ∼ **on sth.** etw. kommentieren

commentator /'kɒmønteıtø(r)/ n. ▶887▶ Kommentator, der/Kommentatorin, die; (Sport) Reporter, der/Reporterin, die

commerce /'kɒmɜ:s/ n. Handel, der; (between countries) Handel[sverkehr], der

commercial /kø'mɜ:ʃl/ **1** adj. (**a**) Handels-; kaufmännisch ⟨Ausbildung⟩; (**b**) (interested in financial return) kommerziell. **2** n. Werbespot, der

commercial: ∼ **'art** n. Gebrauchs-, Werbegrafik, die; ∼ **'bank** n. private Geschäftsbank; ∼ **'break** n. Werbepause, die

commercialise ⇒ commercialize

commercialism /kø'mɜ:ʃølızm/ n. Kommerzialismus, der

commercialize /kø'mɜ:ʃølaız/ v.t. kommerzialisieren

commercial: ∼ **'television** n. kommerzielles Fernsehen; Werbefernsehen, das; ∼ **'traveller** n. ▶887▶ Handelsvertreter, der/-vertreterin, die; ∼ **'vehicle** n. Nutzfahrzeug, das

commiserate /kø'mızøreıt/ v.i. ∼ **with sb.** mit jmdm. mitfühlen; (express one's commiseration) jmdm. sein Mitgefühl aussprechen (**on** zu)

commiseration /kømızø'reıʃn/ n. (**a**) Mitgefühl, das; (**b**) in sing. or pl. (condolence) Teilnahme, die; Beileid, das

commission /kø'mıʃn/ **1** n. (**a**) (official body) Kommission, die; (**b**) (instruction, piece of work) Auftrag, der; (**c**) (in armed services) Ernennungsurkunde, die; **get one's** ∼: zum Offizier ernannt werden; **resign one's** ∼: aus dem Offiziersdienst ausscheiden; (**d**) (pay of agent) Provision, die; **sell goods on** ∼: Waren auf Provisionsbasis verkaufen; (**e**) **in/out of** ∼ ⟨Kriegsschiff⟩ in/außer Dienst; ⟨Auto, Maschine, Lift usw.⟩ in/außer Betrieb. **2** v.t. (**a**) beauftragen ⟨Künstler⟩; in Auftrag geben ⟨Gemälde usw.⟩; (**b**) (empower) bevollmächtigen; ∼**ed officer** Offizier, der; (**c**) (give command of ship to) zum Kapitän ernennen; (**d**) (prepare for service) in Dienst stellen ⟨Schiff⟩; (**e**) (bring into operation) in Betrieb setzen ⟨Kraftwerk, Fabrik⟩

commissionaire /kømıʃø'neø(r)/ n. ▶887▶ (esp. Brit.) Portier, der

commissioner /kø'mıʃønø(r)/ n. (**a**) (person appointed by commission) Beauftragte, der/die; (of police) Präsident, der; (**b**) (member of commission) Kommissions-, Ausschussmitglied, das; (**c**) (representative of supreme authority) Kommissar, der; (**d**) **C**∼ **for Oaths** Notar, der/Notarin, die

commit /kø'mıt/ v.t., **-tt-:** (**a**) (perpetrate) begehen, verüben ⟨Mord, Selbstmord, Verbrechen, Raub⟩; begehen ⟨Dummheit, Bigamie, Fehler, Ehebruch⟩; (**b**) (pledge, bind) ∼ **oneself/sb. to doing sth.** sich/jmdn. verpflichten, etw. zu tun; ∼ **oneself to a course of action** sich auf eine Vorgehensweise festlegen; (**c**) (entrust) anvertrauen (**to** Dat.); ∼ **sth. to a person/a person's care** jmdm. etw. anvertrauen/etw. jmds. Obhut (Dat.) anvertrauen; (**d**) ∼ **sb. for trial** jmdn. dem Gericht überstellen

commitment /kø'mıtmønt/ n. (to course of action or opinion) Verpflichtung (**to** gegenüber); (by dedication) Engagement, das (**to** für)

committed /kø'mıtıd/ adj. (**a**) verpflichtet (**to** zu); festgelegt (**to** auf + Akk.); (**b**) (morally dedicated) engagiert

committee /kø'mıtı/ n. Ausschuss, der (auch Parl.); Komitee, das

commodity /kø'mɒdıtı/ n. (**a**) (utility item) **household** ∼: Haushaltsartikel, der; **a rare/precious** ∼ (fig.) etwas Seltenes/Kostbares; (**b**) (St. Exch.) [vertretbare] Ware; (raw material) Rohstoff, der

common /'kɒmøn/ **1** adj., ∼**er** /'kɒmønø(r)/, ∼**est** /'kɒmønıst/ (**a**) (belonging equally to all) gemeinsam ⟨Ziel, Interesse, Sache, Unternehmung, Vorteil, Merkmal, Sprache⟩; ∼ **to all birds** allen Vögeln gemeinsam; (**b**) (belonging to the public) öffentlich; **the** ∼ **good** das Gemeinwohl; **a** ∼ **belief** [ein] allgemeiner Glaube; **have the** ∼ **touch** volkstümlich sein; (**c**) (usual) gewöhnlich; normal; (frequent) häufig ⟨Vorgang, Erscheinung, Ereignis, Erlebnis⟩; allgemein verbreitet ⟨Sitte, Wort, Redensart⟩; ∼ **honesty/courtesy** [ganz] normale Ehrlichkeit/Höflichkeit; (**d**) (without rank or position) einfach; (**e**) (vulgar) gemein; gewöhnlich (abwertend), ordinär (ugs. abwertend) ⟨Ausdrucksweise, Mundart, Aussehen, Benehmen⟩. **2** n. (**a**) (land) Gemeindeland, das; Allmende, die; (**b**) **have sth./nothing/a lot in** ∼ [**with sb.**] etw./nichts/viel [mit jmdm.] gemein[sam] haben

common: ∼ **'cold** n. ▶865▶ Erkältung, die; ∼ **de-'nominator** n. (Math.) gemeinsamer Nenner, der

commoner /'kɒmønø(r)/ n. Bürgerliche, der/die

common: ∼ **'knowledge** n. it's [a matter of] ∼ **knowledge that** ...: es ist allgemein bekannt, dass ...; ∼**-law** adj. she's his ∼**-law wife** sie lebt mit ihm in eheähnlicher Gemeinschaft

commonly /'kɒmønlı/ adv. (**a**) (generally) im Allgemeinen; (**b**) (vulgarly) gewöhnlich (abwertend)

Common 'Market n. Gemeinsamer Markt

commonplace /'kɒmønpleıs/ **1** n. (platitude) Gemeinplatz, der; (anything usual or trite) Alltäglichkeit, die. **2** adj. nichtssagend, banal ⟨Bemerkung, Buch⟩; alltäglich ⟨Angelegenheit, Ereignis⟩

common: C∼ **'Prayer** n. Liturgie, die (der Kirche von England); ∼ **room** n. (Brit.) Gemeinschaftsraum, der; (for lecturers) Dozentenzimmer, das

Commons /'kɒmønz/ n. pl. **the** [**House of**] ∼: das Unterhaus

common: ∼ **'sense** n. gesunder Menschenverstand; ∼**-sense** adj. vernünftig; gesund ⟨Ansicht, Standpunkt⟩

Commonwealth /'kɒmønwelθ/ n. **the** [**British**] ∼ [**of Nations**] das Commonwealth

commotion /kø'møʊʃn/ n. Tumult, der

communal /'kɒmjʊnl/ adj. (**a**) (of or for the community) gemeindlich; ∼ **living/life** Gemeinschaftsleben, das; (**b**) (for the common use) gemeinsam; Gemeinschafts⟨küche, -schüssel, -grab⟩

commune¹ /'kɒmju:n/ n. Kommune, die

commune² /kø'mju:n/ v.i. ∼ **with sb./sth.** mit jmdm./ etw. Zwiesprache halten (geh.)

communicate /kø'mju:nıkeıt/ **1** v.t. übertragen ⟨Wärme, Bewegung, Krankheit⟩; übermitteln ⟨Nachrichten, Informationen⟩; vermitteln ⟨Gefühle, Ideen⟩. **2** v.i. (**a**) ∼ **with sb.** mit jmdm. kommunizieren; (**b**) (have common door) verbunden sein

communication /kømju:nı'keıʃn/ n. (**a**) (of disease, motion, heat, etc.) Übertragung, die; (of news, information) Übermittlung, die; (of ideas) Vermittlung, die; (**b**) (information given) Mitteilung, die (**to** an + Akk.); (**c**) (interaction with sb.) Verbindung, die; **be in** ∼ **with sb.** mit jmdm. in Verbindung stehen; (**d**) in pl. (conveying information) Kommunikation, die; (science, practice) Kommunikationswesen, das

communication: ∼ **cord** n. Notbremse, die; ∼**s satellite** n. Nachrichten- od. Kommunikationssatellit, der

communicative /kø'mju:nıkøtıv/ adj. gesprächig

communion /kø'mju:nıøn/ n. (**a**) [**Holy**] **C**∼ (Protestant Ch.) das [heilige] Abendmahl; (RC Ch.) die [heilige] Kommunion; **receive** or **take** [**Holy**] **C**∼: das [heilige] Abendmahl/die [heilige] Kommunion empfangen; (**b**) (fellowship) Gemeinschaft, die

communiqué /kø'mju:nıkeı/ n. Kommuniqué, das

communism /'kɒmjʊnızm/ n. Kommunismus, der; **C**∼: der Kommunismus

Communist, communist /'kɒmjʊnıst/ **1** n. Kommunist, der/Kommunistin, die. **2** adj. kommunistisch

community /kø'mju:nıtı/ n. (**a**) (organized body) Gemeinwesen, das; **the Jewish** ∼: die jüdische Gemeinde;

a ~ of monks eine Mönchsgemeinde; (b) *no pl.* (public) Öffentlichkeit, *die*

community: ~ 'care *n., no pl.* ≈ ambulante Betreuung; ~ centre *n.* Gemeindezentrum, *das;* ~ 'charge *n.* (Brit.) Gemeindesteuer, *die;* ~ re'lations *n. pl.* Verhältnis zwischen den Bevölkerungsgruppen; ~ 'service *n.* [*freiwilliger od. als Strafe auferlegter*] sozialer *Dienst*

commute /kə'mju:t/ 1 *v.t.* (a) umwandeln ‹*Strafe*› (to in + *Akk.*); (b) (change to sth. different) umwandeln. 2 *v.i.* pendeln

commuter /kə'mju:tə(r)/ *n.* Pendler, *der*/Pendlerin, *die*

com'muter train *n.* Pendlerzug, *der*

compact¹ /kəm'pækt/ 1 *adj.* kompakt; komprimiert ‹*Stil*›. 2 *v.t.* zusammenpressen

compact² /'kɒmpækt/ *n.* Puderdose [mit Puder(stein)]

compact³ /'kɒmpækt/ *n.* (agreement) Vertrag, *der*

compact disc /'kɒmpækt 'dɪsk/ *n.* Compactdisc, *die;* Kompaktschallplatte, *die;* ~ player CD-Spieler, *der*

companion /kəm'pænjən/ *n.* (a) (one accompanying) Begleiter, *der*/Begleiterin, *die;* (b) (associate) Kamerad, *der*/Kameradin, *die;* (c) (matching thing) Gegenstück, *das;* Pendant, *das*

companionable /kəm'pænjənəbl/ *adj.* freundlich

companionship /kəm'pænjənʃɪp/ *n.* Gesellschaft, *die;* (fellowship) Kameradschaft, *die*

company /'kʌmpənɪ/ *n.* (a) (persons assembled, companionship) Gesellschaft, *die;* expect/receive ~: Besuch *od.* Gäste *Pl.* erwarten/empfangen; for ~: zur Gesellschaft; two is ~, three is a crowd zu zweit ist es gemütlich, ein Dritter stört; keep sb. ~: jmdm. Gesellschaft leisten; part ~ with sb./sth. sich von jmdm./etw. trennen; (b) (firm) Gesellschaft, *die;* Firma, *die;* ~ car Firmenwagen, *der;* ~ policy Unternehmenspolitik, *die;* Firmenpolitik, *die;* (c) (of actors) Truppe, *die;* Ensemble, *das;* (d) (Mil.) Kompanie, *die;* (e) (Navy) ship's ~: Besatzung, *die*

comparable /'kɒmpərəbl/ *adj.* vergleichbar (to, with mit)

comparative /kəm'pærətɪv/ 1 *adj.* (a) vergleichend ‹*Anatomie, Sprachwissenschaft usw.*›; (b) (estimated by comparison) the ~ merits/advantages of the proposals die Vorzüge/Vorteile der Vorschläge im Vergleich; (c) (relative) relativ; in ~ comfort relativ *od.* verhältnismäßig komfortabel; (d) (Ling.) komparativ (fachspr.); a ~ adjective/ adverb ein Adjektiv/Adverb im Komparativ. 2 *n.* (Ling.) Komparativ, *der*

comparatively /kəm'pærətɪvlɪ/ *adv.* (a) (by means of comparison) vergleichend; (b) (relatively) relativ; verhältnismäßig

compare /kəm'peə(r)/ 1 *v.t.* vergleichen (to, with mit); ~ two/three *etc.* things zwei/drei *usw.* Dinge [miteinander] vergleichen; ~d with *or* to sb./sth. verglichen mit *od.* im Vergleich zu jmdm./etw. 2 *v.i.* sich vergleichen lassen. 3 *n.* (literary) beyond *or* without ~: unvergleichlich

comparison /kəm'pærɪsn/ *n.* (act of comparing, simile) Vergleich, *der;* in *or* by ~ [with sb./sth.] im Vergleich [zu jmdm./etw.]; there's no ~ between them man kann sie einfach nicht vergleichen

compartment /kəm'pɑ:tmənt/ *n.* (in drawer, desk, etc.) Fach, *das;* (of railway carriage) Abteil, *das*

compass /'kʌmpəs/ *n.* (a) *in pl.* [a pair of] ~es ein Zirkel; (b) ▶ 715 | (for navigating) Kompass, *der;* (c) (extent) Gebiet, *das;* (fig.: scope) Rahmen, *der*

compassion /kəm'pæʃn/ *n., no pl.* Mitgefühl, *das* (for, on mit)

compassionate /kəm'pæʃənət/ *adj.* mitfühlend; on ~ grounds aus persönlichen Gründen; (for family reasons) aus familiären Gründen

compatibility /kəmpætr'bɪlɪtɪ/ *n., no pl.* (consistency, mutual tolerance) Vereinbarkeit, *die;* (of people) Zueinanderpassen, *das*

compatible /kəm'pætɪbl/ *adj.* (consistent, mutually tolerant) vereinbar; zueinander passend ‹*Personen*›; aufeinander abgestimmt, zueinander passend, (Computing) kompatibel ‹*Geräte, Maschinen*›

compatriot /kəm'pætrɪət, kəm'peɪtrɪət/ *n.* Landsmann, *der*/-männin, *die*

compel /kəm'pel/ *v.t.,* -ll- zwingen; ~ sb. to do sth. jmdn. [dazu] zwingen, etw. zu tun

compelling /kəm'pelɪŋ/ *adj.* bezwingend

compendium /kəm'pendɪəm/ *n., pl.* ~s *or* compendia /kəm'pendɪə/ Abriss, *der;* (summary) Kompendium, *das;* ~ of games Spielemagazin, *das*

compensate /'kɒmpenseɪt/ 1 *v.i.* ~ for sth. etw. ersetzen; ~ for injury *etc.* für Verletzung *usw.* Schaden[s]ersatz leisten. 2 *v.t.* ~ sb. for sth. jmdn. für etw. entschädigen

compensation /kɒmpen'seɪʃn/ *n.* Ersatz, *der;* (for damages, injuries, etc.) Schaden[s]ersatz, *der;* (for requisitioned property) Entschädigung, *die*

compère /'kɒmpeə(r)/ (Brit.) 1 *n.* Conférencier, *der.* 2 *v.t.* konferieren ‹*Show*›

compete /kəm'pi:t/ *v.i.* konkurrieren (for um); (Sport) kämpfen; ~ with sb./sth. mit jmdm./etw. konkurrieren; ~ with one another miteinander wetteifern

competence /'kɒmpɪtəns/, competency /'kɒmpɪtənsɪ/ *n.* (a) (ability) Fähigkeiten *Pl.;* (b) (Law) Zuständigkeit, *die*

competent /'kɒmpɪtənt/ *adj.* fähig; befähigt; not ~ to do sth. nicht kompetent, etw. zu tun

competently /'kɒmpɪtəntlɪ/ *adv.* sachkundig; kompetent

competition /kɒmpɪ'tɪʃn/ *n.* (a) (contest) Wettbewerb, *der;* (in magazine) Preisausschreiben, *das;* (b) (those competing) Konkurrenz, *die;* (Sport) Gegner *Pl.*

competitive /kəm'petɪtɪv/ *adj.* (a) Leistungs-; ~ sports Wettkampf- *od.* Leistungssport, *der;* ~ spirit Konkurrenz- *od.* Wettbewerbsdenken, *das;* (b) (comparable with rivals) leistungs-, wettbewerbsfähig ‹*Preis, Unternehmen*›

competitor /kəm'petɪtə(r)/ *n.* Konkurrent, *der*/Konkurrentin, *die;* (in contest, race) Teilnehmer, *der*/-nehmerin, *die;* (for job) Mitbewerber, *der*/-bewerberin, *die;* our ~s unsere Konkurrenz

compilation /kɒmpɪ'leɪʃn/ *n.* Zusammenstellung, *die*

compile /kəm'paɪl/ *v.t.* zusammenstellen; verfassen ‹*Wörterbuch, Reiseführer*›

compiler /kəm'paɪlə(r)/ *n.* Verfasser, *der*/Verfasserin, *die*

complacency /kəm'pleɪsənsɪ/ *n., no pl.* Selbstzufriedenheit, *die*

complacent /kəm'pleɪsənt/ *adj.* selbstzufrieden; selbstgefällig

complain /kəm'pleɪn/ *v.i.* sich beklagen *od.* beschweren (about, at über + *Akk.*); ~ of sth. über etw. (*Akk.*) klagen

complaint /kəm'pleɪnt/ *n.* (a) Beanstandung, *die;* Beschwerde, *die;* Klage, *die;* (formal accusation, expression of grief) Klage, *die;* (b) ▶ 865 | (ailment) Leiden, *das*

complement 1 /'kɒmplɪmənt/ *n.* (a) (what completes) Vervollständigung, *die;* (b) (full number) a [full] ~: die volle Zahl; (of people) die volle Stärke; the ship's ~: die volle Schiffsbesatzung; (c) (Ling.) Ergänzung, *die.* 2 /'kɒmplɪment/ *v.t.* ergänzen

complementary /kɒmplɪ'mentərɪ/ *adj.* (a) (completing) ergänzend; (b) (completing each other) einander ergänzend

complementary 'medicine *n.* Komplementärmedizin, *die*

complete /kəm'pli:t/ 1 *adj.* (a) vollständig; (in number) vollzählig; komplett; a ~ edition eine Gesamtausgabe; (b) (finished) fertig; abgeschlossen ‹*Arbeit*›; (c) (absolute) völlig; total, komplett ‹*Idiot, Reinfall, Ignoranz*›; absolut ‹*Chaos, Katastrophe*›; vollkommen ‹*Ruhe*›; total, (ugs.) blutig ‹*Anfänger, Amateur*›; a ~ stranger ein völlig Fremder. 2 *v.t.* (a) (finish) beenden; fertig stellen ‹*Gebäude, Arbeit*›; abschließen ‹*Vertrag*›; (b) (make whole) vervollkommnen, vollkommen machen ‹*Glück*›; vervollständigen ‹*Sammlung*›; (c) (make whole amount of) vollzählig machen; (d) ausfüllen ‹*Fragebogen, Formular*›

Points of the compass

COMPASS POINT	DIRECTION, AREA	ABBR	ADJECTIVE, ADVERB, PREPOSITION
north	Nord	Norden	N	nördlich
south	Süd	Süden	S	südlich
east	Ost	Osten	O	östlich
west	West	Westen	W	westlich
north-east	Nordost	Nordosten	NO	nordöstlich
north-west	Nordwest	Nordwesten	NW	nordwestlich
south-east	Südost	Südosten	SO	südöstlich
south-west	Südwest	Südwesten	SW	südwestlich
north-north-east	Nordnordost	Nordnordosten	NNO	nordnordöstlich
north-north-west	Nordnordwest	Nordnordwesten	NNW	nordnordwestlich
south-south-east	Südsüdost	Südsüdosten	SSO	südsüdöstlich
south-south-west	Südsüdwest	Südsüdwesten	SSW	südsüdwestlich
east-north-east	Ostnordost	Ostnordosten	ONO	ostnordöstlich
west-north-west	Westnordwest	Westnordwesten	WNW	westnordwestlich
east-south-east	Ostsüdost	Ostsüdosten	OSO	ostsüdöstlich
west-south-west	Westsüdwest	Westsüdwesten	WSW	westsüdwestlich

The forms **Nord, Süd, Ost** and **West** and their derivatives have no gender (except in the nautical sense of a wind) and exist mainly as labels for the points of the compass. They are also used in nautical and meteorological contexts, without an article. The more commonly used forms are **Norden, Süden, Osten** and **Westen** and their combinations, which are masculine and can be used with the article, indicating either a direction or an area.

Directions

The wind is from the north/the north-east	= Der Wind kommt von Norden/Nordosten *or (Meteorol., Naut.)* von Nord/Nordost
We are going north tomorrow	= Wir fahren morgen nach Norden
They were travelling westwards or *in a westerly direction*	= Sie fuhren in Richtung Westen *or* in westliche Richtung
The road runs due north	= Die Straße führt genau nach Norden
the northbound train	= der Zug in Richtung Norden
The aircraft/ship is southward bound	= Das Flugzeug fliegt/ Das Schiff fährt nach Süden
The sitting room faces north	= Das Wohnzimmer geht nach Norden

Locations

the South of England	= der Süden Englands *or* von England, Südengland
the Deep South	= der tiefe Süden
the far North	= der hohe Norden
the Middle/Far East	= der Nahe/Ferne Osten
They live in the South-West	= Sie wohnen im Südwesten
She comes from the North-East	= Sie stammt aus dem Nordosten
It's a few miles to the west	= Es liegt ein paar Meilen westlich *or* nach Westen
further [to the] east	= weiter östlich *or* nach Osten
25 miles [to the] north of London	= 40 Kilometer nördlich von London
just to the south of the island/of Crete	= etwas südlich der Insel/von Kreta

The terms **nördlich, südlich** etc. operate in combination with **von** + dative or as prepositions with the genitive in the sense *[to the] north of, south of* etc. The use with the genitive is more common where there is an article, that is, with nouns rather than place names.

Adjectives

The English adjectives *north/northern, south/southern* etc. are frequently translated by the combining forms **Nord-, Süd-** etc. rather than the adjectives **nördlich, südlich** etc. This is especially the case with countries and other geographical names:

Northern/Southern Italy	= Norditalien/Süditalien
North/South America	= Nordamerika/ Südamerika
West/East Africa	= Westafrika/Ostafrika
the Southern States	= die Südstaaten
the West Coast	= die Westküste
the north face of the Eiger	= die Eigernordwand
the south side	= die Südseite

nördlich, südlich etc. are generally used for less specific terms, as is illustrated by the difference between

South Africa	= Südafrika
southern Africa	= das südliche Afrika
the north wind	= der Nordwind
northerly winds	= nördliche Winde, Winde aus nördlichen Richtungen

However it would be a mistake to think that the German adjectives are straightforward equivalents for the English *northern, southern* etc. Consider for instance:

East or *Eastern Germany*	= Ostdeutschland
West or *Western Germany*	= Westdeutschland

Cf. also:

a southern climate	= ein südliches Klima
the easternmost or *most easterly point*	= der östlichste Punkt
Western journalists	= westliche Journalisten
the Western countries	= die westlichen Länder

But:

the Western Powers	= die Westmächte
the Eastern Bloc	= der Ostblock

completely /kəm'pliːtlɪ/ *adv.* völlig; absolut ⟨*erfolgreich*⟩

completion /kəm'pliːʃn/ *n.* Beendigung, *die;* (of building, work) Fertigstellung, *die;* (of contract) Abschluss, *der;* (of questionnaire, form) Ausfüllen, *das;* **on ~ of the course** nach Abschluss des Kurses

complex /'kɒmpleks/ **1** *adj.* **(a)** (complicated) kompliziert; **(b)** (composite) komplex. **2** *n.* (also Psych.) Komplex, *der;* **a [building] ~:** ein Gebäudekomplex

complexion /kəm'plekʃn/ *n.* Gesichtsfarbe, *die;* Teint, *der;* (fig.) Gesicht, *das;* **that puts a different ~ on the matter** dadurch sieht die Sache schon anders aus

complexity /kəm'pleksɪtɪ/ *n.* ⇒ **complex** 1: Kompliziertheit, *die;* Komplexität, *die*

compliance /kəm'plaɪəns/ *n.* **(a)** (action) Zustimmung, *die* **(with** zu); **(b)** (submission) Unterwürfigkeit, *die*

compliant /kəm'plaɪənt/ *adj.* unterwürfig

complicate /'kɒmplɪkeɪt/ *v.t.* komplizieren

complicated /'kɒmplɪkeɪtɪd/ *adj.* kompliziert

complication /kɒmplɪ'keɪʃn/ *n.* **(a)** Kompliziertheit, *die;* **(b)** (circumstance; also Med.) Komplikation, *die*

complicity /kəm'plɪsɪtɪ/ *n.* Mittäterschaft, *die* **(in** bei)

compliment **1** /'kɒmplɪmənt/ *n.* **(a)** (polite words) Kompliment, *das;* **pay sb. a ~** [on sth.] jmdm. [wegen etw.] ein Kompliment machen; **return the ~:** das Kompliment erwidern; (fig.) zurückschlagen; **(b)** *in pl.* (formal greetings) Grüße *Pl.;* Empfehlung, *die.* **2** /'kɒmplɪment/ *v.t.* **~ sb. on sth.** jmdm. Komplimente wegen etw. machen

complimentary /kɒmplɪ'mentərɪ/ *adj.* **(a)** (expressing compliment) schmeichelhaft; **(b)** (given free) Frei-

comply /kəm'plaɪ/ *v.i.* **~ with sth.** sich nach etw. richten; **he refused to ~:** er wollte sich nicht danach richten

component /kəm'pəʊnənt/ **1** *n.* Bestandteil, *der;* (of machine) [Einzel]teil, *das.* **2** *adj.* **a ~ part** ein Bestandteil

compose /kəm'pəʊz/ *v.t.* **(a)** (make up) bilden; **be ~d of** sich zusammensetzen aus; **(b)** (construct) verfassen ⟨*Rede, Gedicht, Liedertext, Libretto*⟩; abfassen, aufsetzen ⟨*Brief*⟩; **(c)** (Mus.) komponieren; **(d)** (calm) **~ oneself** sich zusammennehmen

composed /kəm'pəʊzd/ *adj.* (calm) gefasst

composer /kəm'pəʊzə(r)/ *n.* **(a)** ▶ 887 | (of music) Komponist, *der*/Komponistin, *die;* **(b)** (of poem etc.) Verfasser, *der*/Verfasserin, *die*

composition /kɒmpə'zɪʃn/ *n.* **(a)** (act) Zusammenstellung, *die;* (construction) Herstellung, *die;* **(b)** (constitution) (of soil, etc.) Zusammensetzung, *die;* (of picture) Aufbau, *der;* **(c)** (piece of writing) Darstellung, *die;* (essay) Aufsatz, *der;* (piece of music) Komposition, *die;* **(d)** (construction in writing) (of sentences) Konstruktion, *die;* (of prose, verse) Verfassen, *das;* (Mus.) Komposition, *die*

compost /'kɒmpɒst/ **1** *n.* Kompost, *der.* **2** *v.t.* kompostieren

compost: ~ heap, ~ pile *ns.* Komposthaufen, *der*

composure /kəm'pəʊʒə(r)/ *n.* Gleichmut, *der;* **lose/regain one's ~:** die Fassung verlieren/wieder finden; **upset sb.'s ~:** jmdn. aus der Fassung bringen

compote /'kɒmpəʊt/ *n.* Kompott, *das*

compound¹ **1** /'kɒmpaʊnd/ *adj.* **(a)** (of several ingredients) zusammengesetzt; **(b)** (of several parts) kombiniert; **a ~ word** ein zusammengesetztes Wort; eine Zusammensetzung; **(c)** (Zool.) **~ eye** Facettenauge, *das;* **(d)** (Med.) **~ fracture** komplizierter Bruch. **2** /'kɒmpaʊnd/ *n.* **(a)** (Ling.) Kompositum, *das;* Zusammensetzung, *die;* **(b)** (Chem.) Verbindung, *die.* **3** /kəm'paʊnd/ *v.t.* (increase, complicate) verschlimmern ⟨*Schwierigkeiten, Verletzung usw.*⟩

compound² /'kɒmpaʊnd/ *n.* (enclosed space) umzäuntes Gebiet *od.* Gelände; **prison ~:** Gefängnishof, *der*

compound 'interest *n.* (Finance) Zinseszinsen *Pl.*

comprehend /kɒmprɪ'hend/ *v.t.* begreifen; verstehen

comprehensible /kɒmprɪ'hensɪbl/ *adj.* verständlich **(to** *Dat.*)

comprehension /kɒmprɪ'henʃn/ *n.* **(a)** (understanding) Verständnis, *das;* **(b)** **~ [exercise/test]** Übung zum Textverständnis

comprehensive /kɒmprɪ'hensɪv/ **1** *adj.* **(a)** (inclusive) umfassend; universal ⟨*Verstand*⟩; **(b)** **~ school** Gesamtschule, *die;* **go ~** ⟨*Schule:*⟩ zur Gesamtschule [gemacht] werden; **(c)** (Insurance) Vollkasko-; **~ policy** Vollkaskoversicherung, *die.* **2** *n.* (Sch.) Gesamtschule, *die*

comprehensively /kɒmprɪ'hensɪvlɪ/ *adv.* umfassend; **~ beaten** deutlich geschlagen

compress **1** /kəm'pres/ *v.t.* **(a)** (squeeze) zusammenpressen **(into** zu); **(b)** komprimieren ⟨*Luft, Gas, Bericht*⟩; **(c)** (Computing) komprimieren. **2** /'kɒmpres/ *n.* (Med.) Kompresse, *die*

compressed 'air *adj.* Druck-, Pressluft, *die*

compression /kəm'preʃn/ *n.* Kompression, *die*

compressor /kəm'presə(r)/ *n.* Kompressor, *der*

comprise /kəm'praɪz/ *v.t.* (include) umfassen; (not exclude) einschließen; (consist of) bestehen aus; (make up) bilden

compromise /'kɒmprəmaɪz/ **1** *n.* Kompromiss, *der.* **2** *v.i.* Kompromisse/einen Kompromiss schließen; **~ with sb. over sth.** mit jmdm. einen Kompromiss in etw. (*Dat.*) schließen. **3** *v.t.* (bring under suspicion) kompromittieren; (bring into danger) schaden (+ *Dat.*); **~ oneself** sich kompromittieren

compulsion /kəm'pʌlʃn/ *n.* (also Psych.) Zwang, *der;* **be under no ~ to do sth.** keinesfalls etw. tun müssen

compulsive /kəm'pʌlsɪv/ *adj.* **(a)** zwanghaft; **he is a ~ eater/gambler** er leidet unter Esszwang/er ist dem Spiel verfallen; **(b)** (irresistible) **this book is ~ reading** von diesem Buch kann man sich nicht losreißen

compulsorily /kəm'pʌlsərɪlɪ/ *adv.* zwangsweise

compulsory /kəm'pʌlsərɪ/ *adj.* obligatorisch; **be ~:** obligatorisch *od.* Pflicht sein

compunction /kəm'pʌŋkʃn/ *n.* Schuldgefühle *Pl.*

computation /kɒmpjʊ'teɪʃn/ *n.* Berechnung, *die*

compute /kəm'pjuːt/ *v.t.* berechnen **(at** auf + *Akk.*)

computer /kəm'pjuːtə(r)/ *n.* Computer, *der*

computer: ~-aided, ~-assisted *adjs.* computergestützt; **~-aided design** computergestütztes Entwerfen; **~-aided engineering** computergestütztes Konstruieren; **~ crime** *n.* **(a)** *no pl.* Computerkriminalität, *die;* **(b)** (individual crime) Fall von Computerkriminalität; **~ game** *n.* Computerspiel, *das;* **~ 'graphics** *n. pl.* Computergrafik, *die*

computerize (**computerise**) /kəm'pjuːtəraɪz/ *v.t.* computerisieren

computer: ~-'literate *adj.* mit Computern vertraut; **~-'operated** *adj.* computergesteuert; **~ processing** *n.* elektronische Datenverarbeitung; **~ program** *n.* Programm, *das;* **~ programmer** *n.* ▶ 887 | Programmierer, *der*/Programmiererin, *die;* **~ programming** *n.* Programmieren, *das;* **~ 'science** *n.* Computerwissenschaft, *die;* **~ terminal** *n.* Terminal, *das;* **~ virus** *n.* [Computer]virus, *das od. der*

computing /kəm'pjuːtɪŋ/ *n.* EDV, *die;* elektronische Datenverarbeitung; **personal ~:** PC-Nutzung, *die; attrib.* Computer-; **~ skills** Computerkenntnisse *Pl.;* **~ time** Rechenzeit, *die*

comrade /'kɒmreɪd, 'kɒmrɪd/ *n.* Kamerad, *der*/Kameradin, *die;* **~-in-arms** Kampfgefährte, *der*

comradeship /'kɒmreɪdʃɪp/ *n.*, *no pl.* Kameradschaft, *die*

con¹ /kɒn/ (coll.) **1** *n.* (trick) Schwindel, *der.* **2** *v.t.*, **-nn-** **(a)** (swindle) reinlegen (ugs.); **~ sb. out of sth.** jmdm. etw. abschwindeln *od.* (ugs.) abgaunern; **(b)** (persuade) beschwatzen (ugs.); **~ sb. into sth.** jmdm. etw. aufschwatzen (ugs.)

con² ⇒ **pro¹**

concave /'kɒnkeɪv/ *adj.* konkav; **~ mirror/lens** Konkav- *od.* Hohlspiegel, *der*/Konkavlinse, *die*

conceal /kən'siːl/ *v.t.* verbergen **(from** vor + *Dat.*); **~ the true state of affairs from sb.** jmdm. den wirklichen Sachverhalt verheimlichen

concealed /kən'siːld/ *adj.* verdeckt; **~ lighting** indirekte Beleuchtung

concealment /kən'siːlmənt/ *n.* ⇒ **conceal:** Verbergen, *das;* Verheimlichung, *die*

concede /kən'si:d/ *v.t.* (admit, allow) zugeben; (grant) zugestehen, einräumen ‹*Recht, Privileg*›

conceit /kən'si:t/ *n.*, *no pl.* (vanity) Einbildung, *die*

conceited /kən'si:tɪd/ *adj.* eingebildet

conceivable /kən'si:vəbl/ *adj.* vorstellbar; **it's scarcely ~ that ...:** man kann sich (*Dat.*) kaum vorstellen, dass ...

conceivably /kən'si:vəblɪ/ *adv.* möglicherweise; **he cannot ~ have done it** er kann es unmöglich getan haben

conceive /kən'si:v/ 1 *v.t.* (a) empfangen ‹*Kind*›; (b) (form in mind) sich (*Dat.*) vorstellen *od.* denken; haben, kommen auf (+ *Akk.*) ‹*Idee, Plan*›; **~ a dislike for sb./sth.** eine Abneigung gegen jmdn./etw. entwickeln; (c) (think) meinen; glauben. 2 *v.i.* (a) (become pregnant) empfangen; (b) **~ of sth.** sich (*Dat.*) etw. vorstellen

concentrate /'kɒnsəntreɪt/ 1 *v.t.* **~ one's efforts [up]on sth.** seine Bemühungen auf etw. (*Akk.*) konzentrieren; **~ one's mind on sth.** sich auf etw. (*Akk.*) konzentrieren. 2 *v.i.* sich konzentrieren (**on** auf + *Akk.*); **~ on doing sth.** sich darauf konzentrieren, etw. zu tun. 3 *n.* Konzentrat, *das*

concentrated /'kɒnsəntreɪtɪd/ *adj.* konzentriert

concentration /kɒnsən'treɪʃn/ *n.* (also Chem.) Konzentration, *die;* **power[s] of ~:** Konzentrationsfähigkeit, *die;* **lose one's ~:** sich nicht mehr konzentrieren können

concen'tration camp *n.* Konzentrationslager, *das;* KZ, *das*

concept /'kɒnsept/ *n.* Begriff, *der;* (idea) Vorstellung, *die*

conception /kən'sepʃn/ (a) (idea) Vorstellung, *die* (of von); (b) (conceiving) **great powers of ~:** ein großes Vorstellungsvermögen; (c) (of child) Empfängnis, *die*

conceptual /kən'septjʊəl/ *adj.* begrifflich

concern /kən'sɜ:n/ 1 *v.t.* (a) (affect) betreffen; **so far as ... is ~ed** was ... betrifft; '**to whom it may ~**' ≈ „Bestätigung"; (on certificate, testimonial) ≈ „Zeugnis"; (b) (interest) **~ oneself with** *or* **about sth.** sich mit etw. befassen; (c) (trouble) **the news/her health greatly ~s me** ich bin über diese Nachricht tief beunruhigt/ihre Gesundheit bereitet mir große Sorgen. 2 *n.* (a) (relation) **have no ~ with sth.** mit etw. nichts zu tun haben; (b) (anxiety) Besorgnis, *die;* (interest) Interesse, *das;* **express ~:** Sorge ausdrücken; (c) (matter) Angelegenheit, *die;* **that's no ~ of mine** das geht mich nichts an; (d) (firm) Unternehmen, *das*

concerned /kən'sɜ:nd/ *adj.* (a) (involved) betroffen; (interested) interessiert; **the people ~:** die Betroffenen; **where work/health is ~:** wenn es um die Arbeit/die Gesundheit geht; **as** *or* **so far as I'm ~:** was mich betrifft *od.* anbelangt; (b) (implicated) verwickelt (**in** in + *Akk.*); (c) (troubled) besorgt; **I am ~ to hear that ...:** ich höre mit Sorge, dass ...; **I was ~ at the news** die Nachricht beunruhigte mich

concerning /kən'sɜ:nɪŋ/ *prep.* bezüglich

concert /'kɒnsət/ *n.* (a) (of music) Konzert, *das;* (b) **work in ~ with sb.** mit jmdm. zusammenarbeiten

concerted /kən'sɜ:tɪd/ *adj.* vereint; gemeinsam

concert: ~-goer *n.* Konzertbesucher, *der/*-besucherin, *die;* **~ hall** *n.* Konzertsaal, *der;* (building) Konzerthalle, *die*

concertina /kɒnsə'ti:nə/ *n.* (Mus.) Konzertina, *die*

concerto /kən'tʃeətəʊ/ *n.*, *pl.* **~s** *or* **concerti** /kən'tʃeəti/ (Mus.) Konzert, *das*

concert: ~ pianist *n.* Konzertpianist, *der/*-pianistin, *die;* **~ pitch** *n.* Kammerton, *der*

concession /kən'seʃn/ *n.* Konzession, *die*

concessionary /kən'seʃənərɪ/ *adj.* Konzessions-; **~ rate/fare** ermäßigter Tarif

conciliate /kən'sɪlɪeɪt/ *v.t.* (a) (reconcile) in Einklang bringen ‹*Gegensätze, Theorien*›; (b) (pacify) besänftigen

conciliation /kənsɪlɪ'eɪʃn/ *n.* (a) (reconcilement) Versöhnung, *die;* (b) (pacification) Besänftigung, *die;* (c) (in industrial relations) Schlichtung, *die*

conciliatory /kən'sɪljətərɪ/ *adj.* versöhnlich; (pacifying) beschwichtigend

concise /kən'saɪs/ *adj.* kurz und prägnant; knapp, konzis ‹*Stil*›; **be ~** ‹*Person:*› sich knapp fassen; **a ~ dictionary** ein Handwörterbuch

concisely /kən'saɪslɪ/ *adv.* kurz und prägnant; knapp, konzis ‹*schreiben*›

conclude /kən'klu:d/ 1 *v.t.* (a) (end) beschließen; beenden; (b) (infer) schließen; folgern; (c) (reach decision) beschließen; (d) (agree on) schließen ‹*Bündnis, Vertrag*›. 2 *v.i.* (end) schließen

concluding /kən'klu:dɪŋ/ *attrib. adj.* abschließend

conclusion /kən'klu:ʒn/ *n.* (a) (end) Abschluss, *der;* **in ~:** zum Abschluss; (b) (result) Ausgang, *der;* (c) (decision reached) Beschluss, *der;* (d) (inference) Schluss, *der;* (Logic) [Schluss]folgerung, *die*

conclusive /kən'klu:sɪv/ *adj.* schlüssig

conclusively /kən'klu:sɪvlɪ/ *adv.* schlüssig ‹*beweisen, belegen*›

concoct /kən'kɒkt/ *v.t.* zubereiten; zusammenbrauen ‹*Trank*›; (fig.) sich (*Dat.*) ausdenken ‹*Geschichte*›; sich (*Dat.*) zurechtlegen ‹*Ausrede, Alibi*›

concoction /kən'kɒkʃn/ *n.* (drink) Gebräu, *das*

concord /'kɒŋkɔ:d, 'kɒŋkɔ:d/ *n.* (agreement) Eintracht, *die*

concourse /'kɒŋkɔ:s, 'kɒŋkɔ:s/ *n.* (of public building) Halle, *die;* **station ~:** Bahnhofshalle, *die*

concrete /'kɒŋkri:t/ 1 *adj.* (specific) konkret; **~ noun** (Ling.) Konkretum, *das.* 2 *n.* Beton, *der; attrib.* Beton-; aus Beton *präd.* 3 *v.t.* betonieren; (embed in **~**) **~ [in]** einbetonieren

'**concrete mixer** *n.* Betonmischer, *der*

concur /kən'kɜ:(r)/ *v.i.*, **-rr-** (agree) **~ [with sb.] [in sth.]** [jmdm.] [in etw. (*Dat.*)] zustimmen *od.* beipflichten

concurrent /kən'kʌrənt/ *adj.* gleichzeitig; **be ~ with sth.** gleichzeitig mit etw. stattfinden; **~ sentences** zu einer Gesamtstrafe zusammengefasste Einzelstrafen

concurrently /kən'kʌrəntlɪ/ *adv.* gleichzeitig; **run ~** ‹*Gefängnisstrafen:*› zu einer Gesamtstrafe zusammengefasst sein/werden

concuss /kən'kʌs/ *v.t.* **be ~ed** eine Gehirnerschütterung haben

concussion /kən'kʌʃn/ *n.* (Med.) Gehirnerschütterung, *die*

condemn /kən'dem/ *v.t.* (a) (censure) verdammen; (b) (Law: sentence) verurteilen; (fig.) verdammen; **~ sb. to death** jmdn. zum Tode verurteilen; **a ~ed man** ein zum Tode Verurteilter; **~ed cell** Todeszelle, *die;* (c) (declare unfit) für unbewohnbar erklären ‹*Gebäude*›; für ungenießbar erklären ‹*Fleisch*›

condemnation /kɒndem'neɪʃn/ *n.* (a) (censure) Verdammung, *die;* (b) (Law: conviction) Verurteilung, *die*

condensation /kɒnden'seɪʃn/ *n.* (a) *no pl.* (condensing) Kondensation, *die;* (b) (what is condensed) Kondensat, *das;* (water) Kondenswasser, *das;* (c) (abridgement) [Ver]kürzung, *die;* (abridged form) Kurzfassung, *die*

condense /kən'dens/ 1 *v.t.* (a) komprimieren; **~d milk** Kondensmilch, *die;* (b) (Phys., Chem.) kondensieren; (c) (make concise) zusammenfassen; **in a ~d form** in verkürzter Form. 2 *v.i.* kondensieren

condenser /kən'densə(r)/ *n.* (of steam engine; Electr.) Kondensator, *der*

condescend /kɒndɪ'send/ *v.i.* **~ to do sth.** sich dazu herablassen, etw. zu tun; **~ to sb.** jmdn. von oben herab behandeln

condescending /kɒndɪ'sendɪŋ/ *adj.* herablassend

condescension /kɒndɪ'senʃn/ *n.* Herablassung, *die*

condiment /'kɒndɪmənt/ *n.* Gewürz, *das*

condition /kən'dɪʃn/ 1 *n.* (a) (stipulation) [Vor]bedingung, *die;* Voraussetzung, *die;* **make it a ~ that ...:** es zur Bedingung machen, dass ...; **on [the] ~ that ...:** unter der Voraussetzung *od.* Bedingung, dass ...; (b) (in pl.: circumstances) Umstände *Pl.;* **weather/light ~s** Witterungsverhältnisse/Lichtverhältnisse; **under** *or* **in present ~s** unter den gegenwärtigen Umständen *od.* Bedingungen; **living/working ~s** Unterkunfts-/Arbeitsbedingungen; (c) (of athlete, etc.) Kondition, *die;* Form, *die;* (of thing) Zustand, *der;* (of invalid, patient, etc.) Verfassung, *die;* **keep sth. in good** ∼: etw. in gutem Zustand erhalten; **be out of** ∼/ **in [good]** ∼ ‹*Person:*› schlecht/gut in Form sein; **(d)** ▶ 865⌋ (Med.) Leiden, *das;* **have a heart/lung** *etc.* ∼: ein Herz-/Lungenleiden *usw.* haben. **2** *v.t.* bestimmen

conditional /kən'dɪʃənl/ *adj.* **(a)** bedingt; **be** ∼ **[up]on sth.** von etw. abhängen; **(b)** (Ling.) konditional; ∼ **clause** Konditionalsatz, *der*

conditionally /kən'dɪʃənəlɪ/ *adv.* mit *od.* unter Vorbehalt

condolence /kən'dəʊləns/ *n.* Anteilnahme, *die;* Mitgefühl, *das;* (on death) Beileid, *das;* **letter of** ∼: Beileidsbrief, *der;* Kondolenzbrief, *der*

condom /'kɒndɒm/ *n.* Kondom, *das od. der;* Präservativ, *das*

condominium /kɒndə'mɪnɪəm/ *n.* (Amer.) Appartementhaus [mit Eigentumswohnungen]; (single dwelling) Eigentumswohnung, *die*

condone /kən'dəʊn/ *v.t.* **(a)** hinwegsehen über (+ *Akk.*); (approve) billigen; **(b)** (Law) in Kauf nehmen; stillschweigend billigen

conducive /kən'dju:sɪv/ *adj.* **be** ∼ **to sth.** einer Sache (*Dat.*) förderlich sein; zu etw. beitragen

conduct 1 /'kɒndʌkt/ *n.* **(a)** (behaviour) Verhalten, *das;* **good** ∼: gute Führung; **(b)** (way of ∼ing) Führung, *die;* (of inquiry, operation) Durchführung, *die.* **2** /kən'dʌkt/ *v.t.* **(a)** (Mus.) dirigieren; **(b)** führen ‹*Geschäfte, Krieg, Gespräch*›; durchführen ‹*Operation, Untersuchung*›; **(c)** (Phys.) leiten ‹*Wärme, Elektrizität*›; **(d)** ∼ **oneself** sich verhalten; **(e)** (guide) führen; **a** ∼**ed tour [of a museum/factory]** eine [Museums-/Werks]führung

conduction /kən'dʌkʃn/ *n.* (Phys.) Leitung, *die*

conductor /kən'dʌktə(r)/ *n.* **(a)** ▶ 887⌋ (Mus.) Dirigent, *der*/Dirigentin, *die;* **(b)** ▶ 887⌋ (of bus, tram) Schaffner, *der;* (Amer.: of train) Zugführer, *der;* Schaffner, *der* (ugs.); **(c)** (Phys.) Leiter, *der*

conductress /kən'dʌktrɪs/ *n.* ▶ 887⌋ Schaffnerin, *die*

conduit /'kɒndɪt, 'kɒndjʊɪt/ *n.* Leitung, *die;* Kanal, *der* (auch fig.)

cone /kəʊn/ *n.* **(a)** Kegel, *der;* Konus, *der* (fachspr.); (traffic ∼) Leitkegel, *der;* **(b)** (Bot.) Zapfen, *der;* **(c)** ice cream ∼: Eistüte, *die*

confection /kən'fekʃn/ *n.* Konfekt, *das*

confectioner /kən'fekʃənə(r)/ *n.* (maker) Hersteller von Süßigkeiten; (retailer) Süßwarenhändler, *der;* ∼**'s [shop]** Süßwarengeschäft, *das;* ∼**s' sugar** (Amer.) Puderzucker, *der*

confectionery /kən'fekʃənərɪ/ *n.* Süßwaren *Pl.*

confederate /kən'fedərət/ **1** *adj.* verbündet. **2** *n.* Verbündete, *der/die;* (accomplice) Komplize, *der*/Komplizin, *die*

confederation /kənfedə'reɪʃn/ *n.* **(a)** (Polit.) [Staaten]bund, *der;* **(b)** (alliance) Bund, *der;* **C**∼ **of British Industry** britischer Unternehmerverband

confer /kən'fɜ:(r)/ **1** *v.t.,* **-rr-:** ∼ **a title/degree/knighthood [up]on sb.** jmdm. einen Titel/Grad verleihen/jmdn. zum Ritter schlagen. **2** *v.i.,* **-rr-:** ∼ **with sb.** sich mit jmdm. beraten

conference /'kɒnfərəns/ *n.* **(a)** (meeting) Konferenz, *die;* Tagung, *die;* **(b)** (consultation) Beratung, *die;* (business discussion) Besprechung, *die;* **be in** ∼: in einer Besprechung sein

conference: ∼ **room** *n.* Konferenzraum, *der;* (smaller) Besprechungszimmer, *das;* ∼ **table** *n.* Konferenztisch, *der*

conferment /kən'fɜ:mənt/ *n.* Verleihung, *die*

confess /kən'fes/ **1** *v.t.* **(a)** zugeben; gestehen; **(b)** (Eccl.) beichten. **2** *v.i.* **(a)** ∼ **to sth.** etw. gestehen; **(b)** (Eccl.) beichten **(to sb.** jmdm.)

confession /kən'feʃn/ *n.* **(a)** (of offence etc.; thing confessed) Geständnis, *das;* **on** *or* **by one's own** ∼: nach eigenem Geständnis; **(b)** (Eccl.: of sins etc.) Beichte, *die;* **(c)** (Relig.: denomination) Konfession, *die;* **(d)** (Eccl.: confessing) Bekenntnis, *das*

confessional /kən'feʃənl/ *n.* (Eccl.) (stall) Beichtstuhl, *der*

confessor /kən'fesə(r)/ *n.* (Eccl.) Beichtvater, *der*

confetti /kən'fetɪ/ *n.* Konfetti, *das*

confidant /'kɒnfɪdænt, kɒnfɪ'dænt/ *n.* Vertraute, *der*

confidante /'kɒnfɪdænt, kɒnfɪ'dænt/ *n.* Vertraute, *die*

confide /kən'faɪd/ **1** *v.i.* ∼ **in sb.** sich jmdm. anvertrauen; ∼ **to sb. about sth.** jmdm. etw. anvertrauen. **2** *v.t.* ∼ **sth. to sb.** jmdm. etw. anvertrauen; **he** ∼**d that he** …: er gestand, dass er …

confidence /'kɒnfɪdəns/ *n.* **(a)** (firm trust) Vertrauen, *das;* **have [complete** *or* **every/no]** ∼ **in sb./sth.** [volles/ kein] Vertrauen zu jmdm./etw. haben; **have [absolute]** ∼ **that** …: [absolut] sicher sein, dass …; **(b)** (assured expectation) Gewissheit, *die;* Sicherheit, *die;* **(c)** (self-reliance) Selbstvertrauen, *das;* **(d) in** ∼: im Vertrauen; **this is in [strict]** ∼: das ist [streng] vertraulich; **take sb. into one's** ∼: jmdn. ins Vertrauen ziehen; **(e)** (thing told in ∼) Vertraulichkeit, *die*

confidence: ∼ **game** (Amer.) ⇒ ∼ **trick;** ∼ **man** *n.* Trickbetrüger, *der;* Bauernfänger, *der* (ugs.); ∼ **trick** *n.* (Brit.) Trickbetrug, *der;* Bauernfängerei, *die* (ugs.); ∼ **trickster** (Brit.) ⇒ ∼ **man**

confident /'kɒnfɪdənt/ *adj.* **(a)** (trusting, fully assured) zuversichtlich **(about** in Bezug auf + *Akk.*); **be** ∼ **that** …: sicher sein, dass …; **be** ∼ **of sth.** auf etw. (*Akk.*) vertrauen; **(b)** (self-assured) selbstbewusst

confidential /kɒnfɪ'denʃl/ *adj.* vertraulich

confidentiality /kɒnfɪdenʃɪ'ælɪtɪ/ *n., no pl.* Vertraulichkeit, *die*

confidentially /kɒnfɪ'denʃəlɪ/ *adv.* vertraulich

confidently /'kɒnfɪdəntlɪ/ *adv.* zuversichtlich

configuration /kənfɪgjʊ'reɪʃn/ *n.* **(a)** (arrangement, outline) Gestaltung, *die;* **(b)** (Computing) Konfiguration, *die*

configure /kən'fɪgə(r)/ *v.t.* (Computing) konfigurieren

confine /kən'faɪn/ *v.t.* **(a)** einsperren; **be** ∼**d to bed/the house** ans Bett/Haus gefesselt sein; **be** ∼**d to barracks** keinen Ausgang bekommen; **(b)** (fig.) ∼ **sb./sth. to sth.** jmdn./etw. auf etw. (*Akk.*) beschränken; ∼ **oneself to sth./doing sth.** sich auf etw. (*Akk.*) beschränken/sich darauf beschränken, etw. zu tun

confined /kən'faɪnd/ *adj.* begrenzt

confinement /kən'faɪnmənt/ *n.* (imprisonment) Einsperrung, *die;* **put/keep sb. in** ∼: jmdn. in Haft nehmen/halten

confines /'kɒnfaɪnz/ *n. pl.* Grenzen

confirm /kən'fɜ:m/ *v.t.* **(a)** bestätigen; **(b)** (Protestant Ch.) konfirmieren; (RC Ch.) firmen

confirmation /kɒnfə'meɪʃn/ *n.* **(a)** Bestätigung, *die;* **(b)** (Protestant Ch.) Konfirmation, *die;* Einsegnung, *die;* (RC Ch.) Firmung, *die*

confirmed /kən'fɜ:md/ *adj.* (unlikely to change) eingefleischt ‹*Junggeselle*›; überzeugt ‹*Atheist, Vegetarier*›

confiscate /'kɒnfɪskeɪt/ *v.t.* beschlagnahmen; konfiszieren; ∼ **sth. from sb.** jmdm. etw. wegnehmen

confiscation /kɒnfɪs'keɪʃn/ *n.* Beschlagnahme, *die*

conflict 1 /'kɒnflɪkt/ *n.* **(a)** (fight) Kampf, *der;* (prolonged) Krieg, *der;* **come into** ∼ **with sb./sth.** mit jmdm./etw. in Konflikt geraten; **be in** ∼ **with sb./sth.** (fig.) mit jmdm./etw. im Kampf liegen; **(b)** (clashing) Konflikt, *der.* **2** /kən'flɪkt/ *v.i.* (be incompatible) sich (*Dat.*) widersprechen; ∼ **with sth.** einer Sache (*Dat.*) widersprechen

conflicting /kən'flɪktɪŋ/ *adj.* widersprüchlich

conform /kən'fɔ:m/ *v.i.* **(a)** entsprechen **(to** *Dat.*); **(b)** (comply) ∼ **to** *or* **with sth./with sb.** sich nach etw./jmdm. richten

conformism /kən'fɔ:mɪzm/ *n.* Konformismus, *der*

conformist /kən'fɔ:mɪst/ *n.* Konformist, *der*/Konformistin, *die*

conformity /kən'fɔ:mɪtɪ/ *n.* Übereinstimmung, *die* **(with, to** mit)

confound /kən'faʊnd/ *v.t.* **(a)** ∼ **it!** verflixt noch mal! (ugs.); **(b)** (confuse) verwirren; **(c)** (discomfit) ins Unrecht setzen

confounded /kən'faʊndɪd/ *adj.* (coll. derog.) verdammt

confront /kən'frʌnt/ *v.t.* (a) gegenüberstellen; konfrontieren; ~ **sb. with sth./sb.** jmdn. mit etw./[mit] jmdm. konfrontieren; (b) (stand facing) gegenüberstehen (+ *Dat.*); (c) (face in defiance) ins Auge sehen (+ *Dat.*)

confrontation /kɒnfrən'teɪʃn/ *n.* Konfrontation, *die*

confuse /kən'fju:z/ *v.t.* (a) (disorder) durcheinander bringen; verwirren; (blur) verwischen; ~ **the issue** den Sachverhalt unklar machen; **it simply ~s matters** das verwirrt die Sache nur; (b) (mix up mentally) verwechseln; (c) (perplex) konfus machen; verwirren

confused /kən'fju:zd/ *adj.* konfus; wirr ‹*Gedanken, Gerüchte*›; verworren ‹*Lage, Situation*›; (embarrassed) verlegen

confusing /kən'fju:zɪŋ/ *adj.* verwirrend

confusion /kən'fju:ʒn/ *n.* (a) (disordering) Verwirrung, *die*; (mixing up) Verwechslung, *die*; (b) (state) Verwirrung, *die*; (embarrassment) Verlegenheit, *die*; **throw sb./sth. into ~:** jmdn./etw. [völlig] durcheinander bringen

conga /'kɒŋgə/ *n.* Conga, *die*

congeal /kən'dʒi:l/ **1** *v.i.* gerinnen. **2** *v.t.* gerinnen lassen

congenial /kən'dʒi:nɪəl/ *adj.* (agreeable) angenehm

congenital /kən'dʒenɪtl/ *adj.* angeboren; **a ~ idiot** ein von Geburt an Schwachsinniger

conger /'kɒŋgə(r)/ *n.* (Zool.) ~ **[eel]** Meer- *od.* Seeaal, *der*

congest /kən'dʒest/ *v.t.* verstopfen

congested /kən'dʒestɪd/ *adj.* überfüllt, verstopft ‹*Straße*›; **my nose is ~:** ich habe eine verstopfte Nase

congestion /kən'dʒestʃn/ *n.* (of traffic etc.) Stauung, *die*; **nasal ~:** verstopfte Nase

conglomerate 1 /kən'glɒməreɪt/ *v.i.* sich zusammenballen; (fig.) sich versammeln. **2** /kən'glɒmərət/ *n.* (Commerc.) Großkonzern, *der*

conglomeration /kənglɒmə'reɪʃn/ *n.* Konglomerat, *das*; (collection) Ansammlung, *die*

congratulate /kən'grætjʊleɪt/ *v.t.* gratulieren (+ *Dat.*); ~ **sb./oneself [up]on sth.** jmdm./sich zu etw. gratulieren

congratulation /kəngrætjʊ'leɪʃn/ **1** *int.* ~**s!** herzlichen Glückwunsch! (**on** zu). **2** *n.* (a) *in pl.* Glückwünsche *Pl.;* (b) (action) Gratulation, *die*

congregate /'kɒŋgrɪgeɪt/ *v.i.* sich versammeln

congregation /kɒŋgrɪ'geɪʃn/ *n.* (Eccl.) Gemeinde, *die*

congress /'kɒŋgres/ *n.* (a) (meeting of heads of state etc.) Kongress, *der*; **a party ~:** ein Parteitag; (b) **C~** (Amer.: legislature) der Kongress

congressional /kən'greʃənl/ *adj.* Kongress-

Congressman /'kɒŋgresmən/ *n., pl.* **Congressmen** /'kɒŋgresmən/ (Amer.) Kongressabgeordnete, *der*

congruent /'kɒŋgrʊənt/ *adj.* (Geom.) kongruent

conic /'kɒnɪk/ *adj.* Kegel-

conical /'kɒnɪkl/ *adj.* konisch; kegelförmig

conifer /'kɒnɪfə(r)/ *n.* Nadelbaum, *der*

conjecture /kən'dʒektʃə(r)/ **1** *n.* Mutmaßung, *die* (geh.); Vermutung, *die.* **2** *v.t.* mutmaßen (geh.); vermuten. **3** *v.i.* (guess) Mutmaßungen (geh.) *od.* Vermutungen anstellen

conjugal /'kɒndʒʊgl/ *adj.* ehelich; ~ **bliss/worries** Eheglück, *das/*Ehesorgen *Pl.*

conjugate /'kɒndʒʊgeɪt/ *v.t.* (Ling.) konjugieren

conjugation /kɒndʒʊ'geɪʃn/ *n.* (Ling.) Konjugation, *die*

conjunction /kən'dʒʌŋkʃn/ *n.* (a) Verbindung, *die*; **in ~ with sb./sth.** in Verbindung mit jmdm./etw.; (b) (Ling.) Konjunktion, *die*; Bindewort, *das*

conjure /'kʌndʒə(r)/ *v.i.* zaubern; **conjuring trick** Zaubertrick, *der*

~ **'up** *v.t.* beschwören ‹*Geister, Teufel*›; (fig.) heraufbeschwören

conjurer, conjuror /'kʌndʒərə(r)/ *n.* Zauberkünstler, *der/*-künstlerin, *die;* Zauberer, *der/*Zauberin, *die*

conk /kɒŋk/ *v.i.* ~ **'out** (coll.) ‹*Maschine, Auto usw.*› den Geist aufgeben (scherzh.), kaputtgehen (ugs.)

conker /'kɒŋkə(r)/ *n.* (horse chestnut) [Roß]kastanie, *die*; **play ~s** *ein Wettspiel mit Kastanien machen*

'conman (coll.) ⇒ **confidence man**

connect /kə'nekt/ **1** *v.t.* (a) verbinden (**to, with** mit); (Electr.) anschließen (**to, with** an + *Akk.*); (b) (associate) verbinden; ~ **sth. with sth.** etw. mit etw. verbinden *od.* in Verbindung bringen; **be ~ed with sb./sth.** mit jmdm./ etw. in Verbindung stehen. **2** *v.i.* ~ **with sth.** mit etw. zusammenhängen *od.* verbunden sein; ‹*Zug, Schiff usw.*:› Anschluss haben an etw. (*Akk.*)

~ **'up** *v.t.* anschließen

connected /kə'nektɪd/ *adj.* (logically joined) zusammenhängend; (related) verwandt

connecting: ~ **door** *n.* Verbindungstür, *die;* ~ **rod** *n.* (Mech. Engin.) Pleuelstange, *die*

connection /kə'nekʃn/ *n.* (a) (act, state) Verbindung, *die*; (Electr.: of telephone) Anschluss, *der*; **cut the ~:** die Verbindung abbrechen; (b) (fig.: of ideas) Zusammenhang, *der*; **in ~ with sth.** im Zusammenhang mit etw.; (c) (part) Verbindung, *die*; Verbindungsstück, *das;* (d) (train, boat, etc.) Anschluss, *der*; **miss/catch** *or* **make a ~:** einen Anschluss verpassen/erreichen *od.* (ugs.) kriegen

connexion (Brit.) ⇒ **connection**

conning tower /'kɒnɪŋtaʊə(r)/ *n.* (Naut.) Kommandoturm, *der*

connivance /kə'naɪvəns/ *n.* stillschweigende Duldung

connive /kə'naɪv/ *v.i.* ~ **at sth.** über etw. (*Akk.*) hinwegsehen; etw. stillschweigend dulden; ~ **with sb.** mit jmdm. gemeinsame Sache machen (**in** bei)

connoisseur /kɒnə'sɜ:(r)/ *n.* Kenner, *der*

connotation /kɒnə'teɪʃn/ *n.* Assoziation, *die*; Konnotation, *die* (Sprachw.)

conquer /'kɒŋkə(r)/ *v.t.* besiegen ‹*Gegner, Leidenschaft, Gewohnheit*›; erobern ‹*Land*›; bezwingen ‹*Berg, Gegner*›

conqueror /'kɒŋkərə(r)/ *n.* Sieger, *der/*Siegerin, *die* (**of** über + *Akk.*); (of a country) Eroberer, *der*

conquest /'kɒŋkwest/ *n.* Eroberung, *die*

conscience /'kɒnʃəns/ *n.* Gewissen, *das;* **have a good** *or* **clear/bad** *or* **guilty ~:** ein gutes/schlechtes Gewissen haben; **with a clear** *or* **easy ~:** mit gutem Gewissen; **have sth. on one's ~:** wegen etw. ein schlechtes Gewissen haben

conscientious /kɒnʃɪ'enʃəs/ *adj.* pflichtbewusst; (meticulous) gewissenhaft; ~ **objector** Wehrdienstverweigerer, *der* [aus Gewissensgründen]

conscientiously /kɒnʃɪ'enʃəslɪ/ *adv.* pflichtbewusst; (meticulously) gewissenhaft

conscious /'kɒnʃəs/ *adj.* (a) **I was ~ that …:** mir war bewusst, dass …; **but he is not ~ of it** aber es ist ihm nicht bewusst; (b) *pred.* (awake) bei Bewusstsein *präd.;* (c) (realized by doer) bewusst ‹*Handeln, Versuch, Bemühung*›

consciously /'kɒnʃəslɪ/ *adv.* bewusst

consciousness /'kɒnʃəsnɪs/ *n., no pl.* (a) Bewusstsein, *das;* **lose/recover** *or* **regain ~:** das Bewusstsein verlieren/wiedererlangen; (b) (totality of thought; perception) Bewusstsein, *das*

conscript 1 /kən'skrɪpt/ *v.t.* einberufen ‹*Soldaten*›; ausheben ‹*Armee*›. **2** /'kɒnskrɪpt/ *n.* Einberufene, *der/die*

conscription /kən'skrɪpʃn/ *n.* Einberufung, *die;* (compulsory military service) Wehrpflicht, *die*

consecrate /'kɒnsɪkreɪt/ *v.t.* (Eccl.; also fig.) weihen

consecration /kɒnsɪ'kreɪʃn/ *n.* (Eccl.; also fig.) Weihe, *die*

consecutive /kən'sekjʊtɪv/ *adj.* aufeinander folgend ‹*Monate, Jahre*›; fortlaufend ‹*Zahlen*›; **this is the fifth ~ day that …:** heute ist schon der fünfte Tag, an dem …

consecutively /kən'sekjʊtɪvlɪ/ *adv.* hintereinander

consensus /kən'sensəs/ *n.* Einigkeit, *die;* **the general ~ is that …:** es besteht allgemeine Einigkeit darüber, dass …

consent /kən'sent/ **1** *v.i.* zustimmen; ~ **to do sth.** einwilligen, etw. zu tun. **2** *n.* (a) (agreement) Zustimmung, *die* (**to** zu); Einwilligung, *die* (**to in** + *Akk.*); **by common** *or* **general ~:** nach allgemeiner Auffassung; (as wished by all) auf allgemeinen Wunsch; **age of ~:** *Alter, in dem man hinsichtlich Heirat und Geschlechtsleben nicht mehr als minderjährig gilt;* ≈ Ehemündigkeitsalter, *das;* (b) (permission) Zustimmung, *die*

consequence /'kɒnsɪkwəns/ *n.* **(a)** (result) Folge, *die;* **in** ~**:** folglich; **in** ~ **of** als Folge (+ *Gen.*); **as a** ~**:** infolgedessen; **(b)** (importance) Bedeutung, *die;* **be of no** ~**:** unerheblich *od.* ohne Bedeutung sein

consequent /'kɒnsɪkwənt/ *adj.* (resultant) daraus folgend; (following in time) darauf folgend

consequently /'kɒnsɪkwəntlɪ/ *adv.* infolgedessen; folglich

conservation /kɒnsə'veɪʃn/ *n.* **(a)** (preservation) Schutz, *der;* Erhaltung, *die;* (wise utilization) sparsamer Umgang (**of** mit); **wildlife** ~**:** Schutz wild lebender Tierarten; **(b)** (Phys.) ~ **of energy/momentum** Erhaltung der Energie/ des Impulses

conser'vation area *n.* (Brit.) (rural) Landschaftsschutzgebiet, *das;* (urban) unter Denkmalschutz stehendes Gebiet

conservationist /kɒnsə'veɪʃənɪst/ *n.* Naturschützer, *der/-*schützerin, *die*

conservatism /kən'sɜ:vətɪzm/ *n.* Konservati[vi]smus, *der*

conservative /kən'sɜ:vətɪv/ **1** *adj.* **(a)** (averse to change) konservativ; **(b)** (not too high) vorsichtig, eher zu niedrig ⟨*Zahlen, Schätzung*⟩; **(c)** (avoiding extremes) konservativ ⟨*Geschmack, Ansichten, Baustil*⟩; **(d) C**~ (Brit. Polit.) konservativ; **the C**~ **Party** die Konservative Partei. **2** *n.* **C**~ (Brit. Polit.) Konservative, *der/die*

conservatively /kən'sɜ:vətɪvlɪ/ *adv.* vorsichtig, eher zu niedrig ⟨*geschätzt*⟩

conservatory /kən'sɜ:vətərɪ/ *n.* Wintergarten, *der*

conserve /kən'sɜ:v/ **1** *v.t.* erhalten ⟨*Gebäude, Kunstwerk, Wälder*⟩; schonen ⟨*Gesundheit, Kräfte*⟩. **2** *n. often in pl.* Eingemachte, *das*

consider /kən'sɪdə(r)/ *v.t.* **(a)** (look at) betrachten; (think about) ~ **sth.** an etw. (*Akk.*) denken; **(b)** (weigh merits of) denken an (+ *Akk.*); **he's** ~**ing emigrating** er denkt daran, auszuwandern; **(c)** (reflect) sich (*Dat.*) überlegen; **(d)** (regard as) halten für; **I** ~ **him [to be** *or* **as] a swindler** ich halte ihn für einen Betrüger; **(e)** (allow for) berücksichtigen; ~ **other people's feelings** auf die Gefühle anderer Rücksicht nehmen; **all things** ~**ed** alles in allem

considerable /kən'sɪdərəbl/ *adj.* beträchtlich; erheblich ⟨*Schwierigkeiten, Ärger*⟩; groß ⟨*Freude, Charakterstärke*⟩; eingehend ⟨*Überlegung*⟩; (Amer.: large) ansehnlich ⟨*Gebäude, Edelstein*⟩

considerably /kən'sɪdərəblɪ/ *adv.* erheblich; (in amount) beträchtlich

considerate /kən'sɪdərət/ *adj.* rücksichtsvoll (**towards** gegenüber); (thoughtfully kind) entgegenkommend

consideration /kənsɪdə'reɪʃn/ *n.* **(a)** Überlegung, *die;* (meditation) Betrachtung, *die;* **take sth. into** ~**:** etw. berücksichtigen *od.* in Erwägung ziehen; **give sth. one's** ~**:** etw. in Erwägung ziehen; **the matter is under** ~**:** die Angelegenheit wird geprüft; **leave sth. out of** ~**:** etw. unberücksichtigt lassen; **(b)** (thoughtfulness) Rücksichtnahme, *die* **(for** auf + *Akk.*)**; show** ~ **for sb.** Rücksicht auf jmdn. nehmen; **(c)** (sth. as reason) Umstand, *der;* **(d)** (payment) **for a** ~**:** gegen Entgelt

considered /kən'sɪdəd/ *adj.* **(a)** ~ **opinion** ernsthafte Überzeugung; **(b) be highly** ~ **[by others]** [bei anderen] in hohem Ansehen stehen

considering /kən'sɪdərɪŋ/ *prep.* ~ **sth.** wenn man etw. bedenkt

consign /kən'saɪn/ *v.t.* **(a)** anvertrauen (**to** *Dat.*); ~ **sth. to the scrap heap** (lit. or fig.) etw. auf den Schrotthaufen werfen; **(b)** (Commerc.) übersenden, (fachspr.) konsignieren ⟨*Güter*⟩ (**to** an + *Akk.*)

consignment /kən'saɪnmənt/ *n.* (Commerc.) **(a)** (consigning) Übersendung, *die* (**to** an + *Akk.*); **(b)** (goods) Sendung, *die;* (large) Ladung, *die*

consist /kən'sɪst/ *v.i.* **(a)** ~ **of** bestehen aus; **(b)** ~ **in** bestehen in (+ *Dat.*)

consistency /kən'sɪstənsɪ/ *n.* **(a)** (density) Konsistenz, *die;* **(b)** (being consistent) Konsequenz, *die*

consistent /kən'sɪstənt/ *adj.* **(a)** (compatible) [miteinander] vereinbar; **be** ~ **with sth.** mit etw. übereinstimmen; mit etw. vereinbar sein; **(b)** (uniform) beständig; gleich bleibend ⟨*Qualität*⟩; einheitlich ⟨*Vorgehen, Darstellung*⟩

consistently /kən'sɪstəntlɪ/ *adv.* in Übereinstimmung ⟨*handeln*⟩; einheitlich ⟨*gestalten*⟩; konsistent ⟨*denken*⟩; konsequent ⟨*behaupten, verfolgen, handeln*⟩

consolation /kɒnsə'leɪʃn/ *n.* **(a)** (act) Tröstung, *die;* Trost, *der;* **words of** ~**:** Worte des Trostes; **(b)** (consoling circumstance) Trost, *der*

conso'lation prize *n.* Trostpreis, *der*

console¹ /kən'səʊl/ *v.t.* trösten

console² /'kɒnsəʊl/ *n.* **(a)** (Mus.) Spieltisch, *der;* **(b)** (panel) [Schalt]pult, *das*

consolidate /kən'sɒlɪdeɪt/ *v.t.* **(a)** konsolidieren ⟨*Stellung, Einfluss, Macht*⟩; **(b)** (combine) zusammenlegen ⟨*Territorien, Grundstücke, Firmen*⟩; konsolidieren ⟨*Anleihen, Schulden*⟩

consolidation /kənsɒlɪ'deɪʃn/ *n., no pl.* **(a)** Konsolidierung, *die;* **(b)** (combining) Zusammenlegung, *die*

consoling /kən'səʊlɪŋ/ *adj.* tröstlich

consommé /kən'sɒmeɪ/ *n.* (Gastr.) Kraftbrühe, *die*

consonant /'kɒnsənənt/ *n.* Konsonant, *der;* Mitlaut, *der*

consort¹ /'kɒnsɔ:t/ *n.* Gemahl, *der/*Gemahlin, *die*

consort² /kən'sɔ:t/ *v.i.* (keep company) verkehren (**with** mit)

consortium /kən'sɔ:tɪəm/ *n., pl.* **consortia** /kən'sɔ:tɪə/ Konsortium, *das*

conspicuous /kən'spɪkjʊəs/ *adj.* **(a)** (clearly visible) unübersehbar; **(b)** (obvious, noticeable) auffallend

conspicuously /kən'spɪkjʊəslɪ/ *adv.* **(a)** (very visibly) unübersehbar; **(b)** (obviously) auffallend

conspiracy /kən'spɪrəsɪ/ *n.* (conspiring) Verschwörung, *die;* (plot) Komplott, *das;* ~ **of silence** verabredetes Stillschweigen

conspirator /kən'spɪrətə(r)/ *n.* Verschwörer, *der/* Verschwörerin, *die*

conspiratorial /kənspɪrə'tɔ:rɪəl/ *adj.* verschwörerisch

conspire /kən'spaɪə(r)/ *v.i.* (lit. or fig.) sich verschwören

constable /'kʌnstəbl, 'kɒnstəbl/ *n.* ▶887| **(a)** (Brit.) ⇒ **police constable; (b)** (Brit.) **Chief C**~**:** ≈ Polizeipräsident, *der/*-präsidentin, *die*

constabulary /kən'stæbjʊlərɪ/ **1** *n.* Polizei, *die;* (unit) Polizeieinheit, *die.* **2** *adj.* Polizei-

constancy /'kɒnstənsɪ/ *n.* **(a)** (steadfastness) Standhaftigkeit, *die;* **(b)** (faithfulness) Treue, *die;* **(c)** (unchangingness) Beständigkeit, *die*

constant /'kɒnstənt/ **1** *adj.* **(a)** (unceasing) ständig; anhaltend ⟨*Regen*⟩; **there was a** ~ **stream of traffic** der Verkehr floss ununterbrochen; **(b)** (unchanging) gleich bleibend; konstant; **(c)** (steadfast) standhaft; **(d)** (faithful) treu. **2** *n.* (Phys., Math.) Konstante, *die*

constantly /'kɒnstəntlɪ/ *adv.* **(a)** (unceasingly) ständig; **(b)** (unchangingly) konstant; **(c)** (steadfastly) standhaft

constellation /kɒnstə'leɪʃn/ *n.* Sternbild, *das*

consternation /kɒnstə'neɪʃn/ *n.* Bestürzung, *die;* (confusion) Aufregung, *die;* **in** ~**:** bestürzt/aufgeregt; **be filled with** ~**:** sehr bestürzt/aufgeregt sein

constipation /kɒnstɪ'peɪʃn/ *n.* ▶865| Verstopfung, *die*

constituency /kən'stɪtjʊənsɪ/ *n.* (voters) Wählerschaft, *die* (eines Wahlkreises); (area) Wahlkreis, *der*

constituent /kən'stɪtjʊənt/ **1** *adj.* ~ **part** Bestandteil, *der.* **2** *n.* **(a)** (component part) Bestandteil, *der;* **(b)** (member of constituency) Wähler, *der/*Wählerin, *die* (eines Wahlkreises)

constitute /'kɒnstɪtju:t/ *v.t.* **(a)** (form, be) sein; ~ **a threat to** eine Gefahr sein für; **(b)** (make up) bilden; begründen ⟨*Anspruch*⟩; **(c)** (establish) gründen ⟨*Partei, Organisation*⟩

constitution /kɒnstɪ'tju:ʃn/ *n.* **(a)** (of person) Konstitution, *die;* **(b)** (mode of State organization) Staatsform, *die;* **(c)** (body of laws and principles) Verfassung, *die*

constitutional /kɒnstɪ'tju:ʃənl/ **1** *adj.* **(a)** (of bodily constitution) konstitutionell; **(b)** (Polit.) (of constitution) der Verfassung *nachgestellt;* (authorized by or in harmony with constitution) verfassungsmäßig; konstitutionell ⟨*Monarchie*⟩; ~ **law** Verfassungsrecht, *das.* **2** *n.* Spaziergang, *der*

constrain /kən'streɪn/ v.t. zwingen

constraint /kən'streɪnt/ n. (a) Zwang, der; (b) (limitation) Einschränkung, die

constrict /kən'strɪkt/ v.t. verengen

constriction /kən'strɪkʃn/ n. Verengung, die

construct 1 /kən'strʌkt/ v.t. (a) (build) bauen; (fig.) aufbauen; erstellen ‹Plan›; (b) (Ling.; Geom.: draw) konstruieren. 2 /'kɒnstrʌkt/ n. Konstrukt, das

construction /kən'strʌkʃn/ n. (a) (constructing) Bau, der; (of sentence) Konstruktion, die; (fig.: of plan, syllabus) Erstellung, die; ~ **work** Bauarbeiten Pl.; **be under** ~: im Bau sein; (b) (thing constructed) Bauwerk, das; (fig.) Gebilde, das; (c) (Ling.; Geom.: drawing) Konstruktion, die; (d) (interpretation) Deutung, die

constructive /kən'strʌktɪv/ adj. konstruktiv

construe /kən'stru:/ v.t. auslegen; auffassen; **I** ~**d his words as meaning that** …: ich habe ihn so verstanden, dass …

consul /'kɒnsl/ n. Konsul, der

consular /'kɒnsjʊlə(r)/ adj. konsularisch; ~ **rank** Rang eines Konsuls

consulate /'kɒnsjʊlət/ n. Konsulat, das

consult /kən'sʌlt/ 1 v.i. sich beraten (with mit); ~ **together** sich miteinander beraten. 2 v.t. (seek information from) konsultieren; befragen ‹Orakel›; fragen, konsultieren, zu rate ziehen ‹Arzt, Fachmann›; ~ **a list/book** in einer Liste/einem Buch nachsehen; ~ **one's watch** auf die Uhr sehen; ~ **a dictionary** in einem Wörterbuch nachschlagen

consultant /kən'sʌltənt/ 1 n. ▶ 887 ▌ (a) (adviser) Berater, der/Beraterin, die; (b) (physician) ≈ Chefarzt, der/-ärztin, die. 2 attrib. adj. ⇨ **consulting**

consultation /kɒnsəl'teɪʃn/ n. Beratung, die (on über + Akk.); **have a** ~ **with sb.** sich mit jmdm. beraten; **by** ~ **of a dictionary/of an expert** durch Konsultation eines Wörterbuchs/Experten; **act in** ~ **with sb.** in Absprache mit jmdm. handeln

consulting /kən'sʌltɪŋ/ attrib. adj. beratend ‹Architekt, Ingenieur›

consumable /kən'sju:məbl/ adj. (a) kurzlebig ‹Konsumgüter›; (b) (edible, drinkable) genießbar

consume /kən'sju:m/ v.t. (a) (use up) verbrauchen; ‹Person.› aufwenden, ‹Sache.› kosten ‹Zeit, Energie›; (b) (destroy) vernichten; (eat, drink) konsumieren; verkonsumieren (ugs.); (c) (fig.) **be** ~**d with love/passion** sich in Liebe/Leidenschaft verzehren; **be** ~**d with jealousy/envy** sich vor Eifersucht/Neid verzehren (geh.)

consumer /kən'sju:mə(r)/ n. (Econ.) Verbraucher, der/Verbraucherin, die; Konsument, der/Konsumentin, die

consumer: ~ **goods** n. pl. Konsumgüter; ~ **pro'tection** n. Verbraucherschutz, der

consummate 1 /kən'sʌmət/ adj. (a) (perfect) vollkommen; **with** ~ **ease** mühelos; (b) (accomplished) perfekt; **a** ~ **artist** ein vollendeter Künstler. 2 /'kɒnsəmeɪt/ v.t. vollenden, zum Abschluss bringen ‹Diskussion, Geschäftsverhandlungen›; vollziehen ‹Ehe›

consummation /kɒnsə'meɪʃn/ n. (of marriage) Vollzug, der

consumption /kən'sʌmpʃn/ n. (a) (using up, eating, drinking) Verbrauch, der (of an + Dat.); (act of eating or drinking) Verzehr, der (of von); ~ **of fuel/sugar** Kraftstoff-/Zuckerverbrauch, der; ~ **of alcohol** Alkoholkonsum, der; (b) (Econ.) Verbrauch, der; Konsum, der; (c) (Med. dated) ▶ 865 ▌ Schwindsucht, die (veralt.)

cont. abbr. **continued** Forts.

contact 1 /'kɒntækt/ n. (a) (state of touching) Berührung, die; Kontakt, der; (fig.) Verbindung, die; Kontakt, der; **point of** ~: Berührungspunkt, der; **be in** ~ **with sth.** etw. berühren; **be in** ~ **with sb.** (fig.) mit jmdm. in Verbindung stehen od. Kontakt haben; **come in** or **into** ~ **[with sth.]** [mit etw.] in Berührung kommen; **come into** ~ **with sb./sth.** (fig.) mit jmdm./etw. in Berührung kommen; **come into** ~ **with sb./sth.** (fig.) mit jmdm./etw. etwas zu tun haben; **make** ~ **with sb.** (fig.) mit jmdm. Kontakt aufnehmen; **lose** ~ **with sb.** (fig.) den Kontakt mit jmdm. verlieren; (b) (Electr.: connection) Kontakt, der; **make/break a** ~: einen Kontakt

herstellen/unterbrechen. 2 /'kɒntækt, kən'tækt/ v.t. (a) (get into touch with) sich in Verbindung setzen mit; **can I** ~ **you by telephone?** sind Sie telefonisch zu erreichen?; (b) (begin dealings with) Kontakt aufnehmen mit

contact: ~ **lens** n. Kontaktlinse, die; ~ **man** n. Kontaktmann, der; Mittelsmann, der

contagious /kən'teɪdʒəs/ adj. (lit. or fig.) ansteckend

contain /kən'teɪn/ v.t. (a) (hold as contents, include) enthalten; (comprise) umfassen; (b) (prevent from spreading; also Mil.) aufhalten; (restrain) unterdrücken; **he could hardly** ~ **himself for joy** er konnte vor Freude kaum an sich (Akk.) halten

container /kən'teɪnə(r)/ n. Behälter, der; (cargo ~) Container, der; **cardboard/wooden** ~: Pappkarton, der/ Holzkiste, die

containerize /kən'teɪnəraɪz/ v.t. in Container verpacken

con'tainer ship n. Containerschiff, das

contaminate /kən'tæmɪneɪt/ v.t. verunreinigen; (with radioactivity) verseuchen

contamination /kəntæmɪ'neɪʃn/ n. Verunreinigung, die; (with radioactivity) Verseuchung, die

contemplate /'kɒntəmpleɪt/ v.t. (a) betrachten; (mentally) nachdenken über (+ Akk.); (b) (expect) rechnen mit; (consider) in Betracht ziehen; ~ **sth./doing sth.** an etw. (Akk.) denken/daran denken, etw. zu tun

contemplation /kɒntəm'pleɪʃn/ n. (a) Betrachtung, die; (mental) Nachdenken, das (of über + Akk.); (b) (expectation) Erwartung, die; (consideration) Erwägung, die

contemplative /kən'templətɪv, 'kɒntəmpleɪtɪv/ adj. besinnlich; kontemplativ (geh.)

contemporary /kən'tempərərɪ/ 1 adj. zeitgenössisch; (present-day) heutig; zeitgenössisch; **A is** ~ **with B** A und B finden zur gleichen Zeit statt. 2 n. (a) (person belonging to same time) Zeitgenosse, der/-genossin, die (to von); **we were contemporaries** or **he was a** ~ **of mine at university/school** wir waren im Studium Studienkollege od. Kommilitone/Schulkamerad von mir; (b) (person of same age) Altersgenosse, der/-genossin, die; **they are contemporaries** sie sind gleichaltrig od. Altersgenossen

contempt /kən'tempt/ n. (a) Verachtung, die (of, for für); (b) (disregard) Missachtung, die; (c) **have** or **hold sb. in** ~: jmdn. verachten; see also **beneath 1 a**; (d) (Law) ~ **of court** ≈ Ungebühr vor Gericht

contemptible /kən'temptɪbl/ adj. verachtenswert

contemptuous /kən'temptjʊəs/ adj. verächtlich; überheblich ‹Person›; **be** ~ **of sth./sb.** etw./jmdn. verachten

contend /kən'tend/ 1 v.i. (a) (strive) ~ **[with sb. for sth.]** [mit jmdm. um etw.] kämpfen; (b) (struggle) **be able/ have to** ~ **with** fertig werden können/müssen mit; **I've got enough to** ~ **with at the moment** ich habe schon so genug um die Ohren (ugs.). 2 v.t. ~ **that** …: behaupten, dass …

contender /kən'tendə(r)/ n. Bewerber, der/Bewerberin, die

content¹ /'kɒntent/ n. (a) in pl. Inhalt, der; (of medicine) Zusammensetzung, die; **the** ~**s of the room had all been damaged** alles im Zimmer war beschädigt worden; **[table of]** ~**s** Inhaltsverzeichnis, das; (b) (amount contained) Gehalt, der (of an + Dat.); (c) (constituent elements, substance) Gehalt, der

content² /kən'tent/ 1 pred. adj. zufrieden (with mit); **be** ~ **to do sth.** bereit sein, etw. zu tun. 2 n. **to one's heart's** ~: nach Herzenslust. 3 v.t. zufriedenstellen; befriedigen; ~ **oneself with sth./sb.** sich mit etw./jmdm. zufrieden geben

contented /kən'tentɪd/ adj. zufrieden (with mit); glücklich ‹Kindheit, Ehe, Leben›

contentedly /kən'tentɪdlɪ/ adv. zufrieden

contention /kən'tenʃn/ n. (a) (dispute) Streit, der; **sth. is the subject of much** ~: etw. wird heftig diskutiert; (b) (point asserted) Behauptung, die

contentious /kən'tenʃəs/ adj. strittig ‹Punkt, Frage, Thema›; umstritten ‹Verhalten, Argument›

contentment /kən'tentmənt/ *n.* Zufriedenheit, *die*

contest 1 /'kɒntest/ *n.* (competition) Wettbewerb, *der;* (Sport) Wettkampf, *der.* **2** /kən'test/ *v.t.* **(a)** (dispute) bestreiten; anfechten ‹*Anspruch, Recht*›; infrage stellen ‹*Behauptung, These*›; **(b)** (fight for) kämpfen um; **(c)** (Brit.) (compete in) kandidieren bei; (compete for) kandidieren für

contestant /kən'testənt/ *n.* (competitor) Teilnehmer, *der/* Teilnehmerin, *die* (**in** an + *Dat.*, bei); (in fight) Gegner, *der/* Gegnerin, *die*

context /'kɒntekst/ *n.* Kontext, *der;* **in/out of** ∼: im/ ohne Kontext; **in this** ∼: in diesem Zusammenhang

continent /'kɒntɪnənt/ *n.* Kontinent, *der;* Erdteil, *der;* **the** ∼**s of Europe, Asia, Africa** die Erdteile Europa, Asien, Afrika; **the C**∼: das europäische Festland; der Kontinent

continental /kɒntɪ'nentl/ **1** *adj.* **(a)** kontinental; ∼ **Europe** Kontinentaleuropa (*das*); **(b) C**∼ (mainland European) kontinental[europäisch]. **2** *n.* **C**∼: Kontinentaleuropäer, *der/*-europäerin, *die*

continental: ∼ **'breakfast** *n.* kontinentales Frühstück (im Unterschied zum englischen Frühstück); ∼ **quilt** *n.* (Brit.) [Stepp]federbett, *das*

contingency /kən'tɪndʒənsɪ/ *n.* (chance event) Eventualität, *die;* (possible event) Eventualfall, *der;* ∼ **plan** Alternativplan, *der*

contingent /kən'tɪndʒənt/ **1** *adj.* **(a)** (fortuitous) zufällig; **(b)** (conditional) abhängig ([up]on von). **2** *n.* (Mil.; also fig.) Kontingent, *das*

continual /kən'tɪnjʊəl/ *adj.* (frequently happening) ständig; (without cessation) unaufhörlich; **there have been** ∼ **quarrels** es gab ständig *od.* dauernd Streit

continually /kən'tɪnjʊəlɪ/ *adv.* (frequently) ständig; immer wieder; (without cessation) unaufhörlich; ∼ **tired** immer müde

continuance /kən'tɪnjʊəns/ *n.* Fortbestand, *der;* (of happiness, noise, rain) Fortdauer, *die*

continuation /kəntɪnjʊ'eɪʃn/ *n.* Fortsetzung, *die;* **a** ∼ **of these good relations** eine Fortdauer dieser guten Beziehungen

continue /kən'tɪnjuː/ **1** *v.t.* fortsetzen; '**to be** ∼**d**' „Fortsetzung folgt"; '∼**d on page 2**' „Fortsetzung auf S. 2"; ∼ **doing** *or* **to do sth.** etw. weiter tun; **it** ∼**d to rain** es regnete weiter; **it** ∼**s to be a problem** es ist weiterhin ein Problem; '...', **he** ∼**d** „...", fuhr er fort. **2** *v.i.* **(a)** (persist) ‹*Wetter, Zustand, Krise usw.*› andauern; (persist in doing etc. sth.) weitermachen (ugs.); nicht aufhören; (last) dauern; **if the rain** ∼**s** wenn der Regen anhält; **if you** ∼ **like this** wenn Sie so weitermachen (ugs.); ∼ **with sth.** mit etw. fortfahren; ∼ **with a plan** einen Plan weiterverfolgen; ∼ **on one's way** seinen Weg fortsetzen; **(b)** (stay) bleiben; ∼ **in power** an der Macht bleiben

continued /kən'tɪnjuːd/ *adj.* fortgesetzt ‹*Bemühungen*›; ∼ **existence** Weiterbestehen, *das*

continuity /kɒntɪ'njuːɪtɪ/ *n., no pl.* Kontinuität, *die*

conti'nuity girl *n.* ▸ 887 | Skriptgirl, *das*

continuous /kən'tɪnjʊəs/ *adj.* **(a)** ununterbrochen; anhaltend ‹*Regen, Sonnenschein, Anstieg*›; ständig ‹*Kritik, Streit, Änderung*›; fortlaufend ‹*Mauer*›; durchgezogen ‹*Linie*›; **(b)** (Ling.) ∼ [**form**] Verlaufsform, *die;* **present** ∼ *or* ∼ **present/past** ∼ *or* ∼ **past** Verlaufsform des Präsens/Präteritums

continuously /kən'tɪnjʊəslɪ/ *adv.* (in space) durchgehend; (in time or sequence) ununterbrochen; ständig ‹*sich ändern*›

continuum /kən'tɪnjʊəm/ *n., pl.* **continua** /kən'tɪnjʊə/ Kontinuum, *das*

contort /kən'tɔːt/ *v.t.* verdrehen (auch fig.); verzerren ‹*Gesicht, Gesichtszüge*›; verrenken, verdrehen ‹*Körper*›

contortion /kən'tɔːʃn/ *n.* Verzerrung, *die;* (of body) Verdrehung, *die;* Verrenkung, *die*

contour /'kɒntʊə(r)/ *n.* Kontur, *die;* ∼ **map/line** Höhenlinienkarte, *die/*Höhenschichtlinie, *die*

contraband /'kɒntrəbænd/ **1** *n.* Schmuggelware, *die.* **2** *adj.* geschmuggelt; ∼ **goods** Schmuggelware, *die*

contraception /kɒntrə'sepʃn/ *n.* Empfängnisverhütung, *die*

contraceptive /kɒntrə'septɪv/ **1** *adj.* empfängnisverhütend; ∼ **device/method** Verhütungsmittel, *das/*-methode, *die.* **2** *n.* Verhütungsmittel, *das*

contract 1 /'kɒntrækt/ *n.* Vertrag, *der;* ∼ **of employment** Arbeitsvertrag, *der;* **be under** ∼ **to do sth.** vertraglich verpflichtet sein, etw. zu tun; **exchange** ∼**s** (Law) die Vertragsurkunden austauschen. **2** /kən'trækt/ *v.t.* **(a)** (cause to shrink, make smaller) schrumpfen lassen; (draw together) zusammenziehen; **(b)** (become infected with) sich (*Dat.*) zuziehen; ∼ **sth. from sb.** sich mit etw. bei jmdm. anstecken; ∼ **sth. from** ...: an etw. (*Dat.*) durch ... erkranken; **(c)** (incur) machen ‹*Schulden*›. **3** /kən'trækt/ *v.i.* **(a)** (enter into agreement) Verträge/einen Vertrag schließen; ∼ **for sth.** etw. vertraglich zusichern; ∼ **to do sth.** sich vertraglich verpflichten, etw. zu tun; **(b)** (shrink, become smaller, be drawn together) sich zusammenziehen

∼ **'out 1** *v.i.* ∼ **out [of sth.]** sich [an etw. (*Dat.*)] nicht beteiligen; (withdraw) [aus etw.] aussteigen (ugs.). **2** *v.t.* ∼ **work out [to another firm]** Arbeit [an eine andere Firma] vergeben

contract bridge /'kɒntrækt 'brɪdʒ/ *n.* Kontraktbridge, *das*

contraction /kən'trækʃn/ *n.* **(a)** (shrinking) Kontraktion, *die* (Physik); **(b)** (Physiol.: of muscle) Zusammenziehung, *die;* Kontraktion, *die* (Med.); **(c)** (Ling.) Kontraktion, *die;* **(d)** (catching) Ansteckung, *die* (**of** mit)

contractor /kən'træktə(r)/ *n.* ▸ 887 | Auftragnehmer, *der/*-nehmerin, *die*

contractual /kən'træktjʊəl/ *adj.* vertraglich

contradict /kɒntrə'dɪkt/ *v.t.* widersprechen (+ *Dat.*)

contradiction /kɒntrə'dɪkʃn/ *n.* Widerspruch, *der* (**of** gegen); **in** ∼ **to sth./sb.** im Widerspruch *od.* Gegensatz zu etw./jmdm.; **be a** ∼ **to** *or* **of sth.** im Widerspruch zu etw. stehen; **a** ∼ **in terms** ein Widerspruch in sich selbst

contradictory /kɒntrə'dɪktərɪ/ *adj.* widersprechend; (mutually opposed) widersprüchlich

contraflow /'kɒntrəfləʊ/ *n.* Gegenverkehr auf einem Fahrstreifen

contralto /kən'træltəʊ/ *n., pl.* ∼**s** (Mus.) **(a)** (voice) Alt, *der;* (very low) Kontraalt, *der;* **(b)** (singer) Altistin, *die;* Alt, *der* (selten); (with very low voice) Kontraalt, *der*

contraption /kən'træpʃn/ *n.* (coll.) (machine) Apparat, *der* (ugs.); (device) [komisches] Gerät

contrary /'kɒntrərɪ/ **1** *adj.* **(a)** entgegengesetzt; **be** ∼ **to sth.** im Gegensatz zu etw. stehen; **the result was** ∼ **to expectation** das Ergebnis entsprach nicht den Erwartungen; **(b)** (opposite) entgegengesetzt; **(c)** /kən'treərɪ/ (coll.: perverse) widerspenstig; widerborstig. **2** *n.* **the** ∼: das Gegenteil; **be/do completely the** ∼: das genaue Gegenteil sein/tun; **on the** ∼: im Gegenteil. **3** *adv.* ∼ **to sth.** entgegen einer Sache; ∼ **to expectation** wider Erwarten

contrast 1 /kən'trɑːst/ *v.t.* gegenüberstellen; ∼ **sth. with sth.** etw. von etw. [deutlich] abheben. **2** /kən'trɑːst/ *v.i.* ∼ **with sth.** mit etw. kontrastieren; sich von etw. abheben. **3** /'kɒntrɑːst/ *n.* **(a)** Kontrast, *der* (**with** zu); **what a** ∼! welch ein Gegensatz!; **in** ∼, ...: im Gegensatz dazu, ...; [**be**] **in** ∼ **with sth.** im Gegensatz *od.* Kontrast zu etw. [stehen]; **(b)** (thing) **a** ∼ **to sth.** ein Gegensatz zu etw.; (person) **be a** ∼ **to sb.** [ganz] anders sein als jmd.

contrasting /kən'trɑːstɪŋ/ *adj.* gegensätzlich; kontrastierend ‹*Farbe*›; (very different) sehr unterschiedlich

contravene /kɒntrə'viːn/ *v.t.* verstoßen gegen ‹*Recht, Gesetz*›

contravention /kɒntrə'venʃn/ *n.* Verstoß, *der* (**of** gegen); **be in** ∼ **of sth.** im Widerspruch zu etw. stehen

contretemps /'kɔ̃trətɑ̃/ *n., pl.* **same** /'kɔ̃trətɑ̃z/ Missgeschick, *das;* Malheur, *das* (ugs.)

contribute /kən'trɪbjuːt/ *v.t.* ∼ **sth. [to** *or* **towards sth.]** etw. [zu etw.] beitragen/(cooperatively) beisteuern; ∼ **money towards sth.** für etw. Geld beisteuern/(for charity) spenden; **he regularly** ∼**s articles to the 'Guardian'** er schreibt regelmäßig für den „Guardian". **2** *v.i.* **everyone** ∼**d towards the production** jeder trug etwas zur Aufführung bei; ∼ **to charity** für karitative Zwecke spenden; ~ **to sb.'s misery/disappointment** jmds. Kummer/Enttäuschung vergrößern; ~ **to a newspaper** für eine Zeitung schreiben; ~ **to the success of sth.** zum Erfolg einer Sache (*Gen.*) beitragen

contribution /kɒntrɪˈbjuːʃn/ *n.* (a) make a ~ **to a fund** etw. für einen Fonds spenden; **the ~ of clothing and money to sth.** das Spenden von Kleidern und Geld für etw.; (b) (thing contributed) Beitrag, *der;* (for charity) Spende, *die* (**to** für); ~**s of clothing and money** Kleider- und Geldspenden; **make a ~ to sth.** einen Beitrag zu etw. leisten

contributor /kənˈtrɪbjʊtə(r)/ *n.* (a) (giver) Spender, *der/* Spenderin, *die;* (b) (to encyclopaedia, dictionary, etc.) Mitarbeiter, *der/*Mitarbeiterin, *die* (**to** *Gen.*); **be a regular ~ to the 'Guardian'** regelmäßig für den „Guardian" schreiben

'**con trick** (coll.) ⇒ **confidence trick**

contrite /ˈkɒntraɪt/ *adj.* zerknirscht

contrition /kənˈtrɪʃn/ *n.* Reue, *die*

contrivance /kənˈtraɪvəns/ *n.* (a) (contriving) Plan, *der;* (b) (inventing) Ersinnen, *das;* (c) (device) Gerät, *das*

contrive /kənˈtraɪv/ *v.t.* (a) (manage) ~ **to do sth.** es fertig bringen *od.* zuwege bringen, etw. zu tun; **they ~d to meet** es gelang ihnen, sich zu treffen; (b) (devise) sich (*Dat.*) ausdenken; ersinnen (geh.)

contrived /kənˈtraɪvd/ *adj.* künstlich

control /kənˈtrəʊl/ **1** *n.* (a) (power of directing, restraint) Kontrolle, *die* (**of** über + *Akk.*); (management) Leitung, *die;* **governmental ~:** Regierungsgewalt, *die;* **have ~ of sth.** die Kontrolle über etw. (*Akk.*) haben; (take decisions) für etw. zuständig sein; **take ~ of** die Kontrolle übernehmen über (+ *Akk.*); **keep ~ of sth.** etw. unter Kontrolle halten; **be in ~ [of sth.]** die Kontrolle [über etw. (*Akk.*)] haben; **be in ~ of the situation** die Situation unter Kontrolle haben; [**go** *or* **get**] **out of ~:** außer Kontrolle [geraten]; [**get sth.**] **under ~:** [etw.] unter Kontrolle [bringen]; **gain ~ of sth.** etw. unter Kontrolle bekommen; **lose/regain ~ of oneself** die Beherrschung verlieren/wiedergewinnen; **have some/complete/no ~ over sth.** eine gewisse/die absolute/keine Kontrolle über etw. (*Akk.*) haben; (b) (device) Regler, *der;* ~**s** (as a group) Schalttafel, *die;* (of TV, stereo system) Bedienungstafel, *die;* **be at the ~s** ⟨*Fahrer, Pilot:*⟩ am Steuer sitzen. **2** *v.t.,* **-ll-:** (a) (have ~ of) kontrollieren; steuern, lenken ⟨*Auto*⟩; **he ~s the financial side of things** er ist für die Finanzen zuständig; ~**ling interest** (Commerc.) Mehrheitsbeteiligung, *die;* (b) (hold in check) beherrschen; zügeln ⟨*Zorn, Ungeduld, Temperament*⟩; (regulate) kontrollieren; regulieren ⟨*Geschwindigkeit, Temperatur*⟩; einschränken ⟨*Export, Ausgaben*⟩; regeln ⟨*Verkehr*⟩

control: ~ **centre** *n.* Kontrollzentrum, *das;* ~ **desk** *n.* Schaltpult, *das;* ~ **panel** *n.* Schalttafel, *die;* ~ **room** *n.* Kontrollraum, *der;* (Radio, Telev.) Regieraum, *der;* (in power station) Schaltwarte, *die;* ~ **tower** *n.* Kontrollturm, *der*

controversial /kɒntrəˈvɜːʃl/ *adj.* umstritten ⟨*Mode, Kunstwerk, Gesetz, Idee*⟩; strittig ⟨*Frage, Punkt, Angelegenheit*⟩; (given to controversy) streitsüchtig

controversy /ˈkɒntrəvɜːsɪ, kənˈtrɒvəsɪ/ *n.* Kontroverse, *die;* Auseinandersetzung, *die;* **much ~:** eine längere Kontroverse *od.* Auseinandersetzung

contusion /kənˈtjuːʒn/ *n.* Prellung, *die*

conundrum /kəˈnʌndrəm/ *n.* (*auf einem Wortspiel beruhendes*) Rätsel

conurbation /kɒnɜːˈbeɪʃn/ *n.* Konurbation, *die* (Soziol.); ≈ Stadtregion, *die*

convalesce /kɒnvəˈles/ *v.i.* ▶865⟩ genesen; rekonvaleszieren (Med.)

convalescence /kɒnvəˈlesəns/ *n.* ▶865⟩ Genesung, *die;* Rekonvaleszens, *die* (Med.)

convalescent /kɒnvəˈlesənt/ ▶865⟩ **1** *adj.* rekonvaleszent (Med.). **2** *n.* Rekonvaleszent, *der/*Rekonvaleszentin, *die* (Med.); Genesende, *der/die*

convection /kənˈvekʃn/ *n.* (Phys., Meteorol.) Konvektion, *die;* ~ **current** Konvektionsstrom, *der*

convector /kənˈvektə(r)/ *n.* Konvektor, *der*

convene /kənˈviːn/ **1** *v.t.* einberufen. **2** *v.i.* zusammenkommen; ⟨*Gericht, gewählte Vertreter:*⟩ zusammentreten; ⟨*Konferenz, Versammlung:*⟩ beginnen

convener /kənˈviːnə(r)/ *n.* (Brit.) *jmd., der eine Versammlung einberuft/leitet*

convenience /kənˈviːnɪəns/ *n.* (a) *no pl.* (suitableness) Annehmlichkeit, *die;* **its ~ to** *or* **for the city centre** seine günstige Lage zum Stadtzentrum; (b) (personal satisfaction) Bequemlichkeit, *die;* **for sb.'s ~, for ~'s sake** zu jmds. Bequemlichkeit; **at your ~:** wann es Ihnen passt; (c) (advantage) **be a ~ to sb.** angenehm *od.* praktisch für jmdn. sein; (d) (advantageous thing) Annehmlichkeit, *die;* (e) (esp. Admin.: toilet) Toilette, *die;* **public ~:** öffentliche Toilette *od.* (Amtsspr.) Bedürfnisanstalt

con'venience food *n.* Fertignahrung, *die*

convenient /kənˈviːnɪənt/ *adj.* (a) (suitable, not troublesome) günstig; (useful) praktisch; angenehm; **be ~ to** *or* **for sb.** günstig für jmdn. sein; **would it be ~ to you?** würde es Ihnen passen?; **it's not very ~ at the moment** es passt im Augenblick nicht gut; (b) (of easy access) **be ~ to** *or* **for sth.** günstig zu etw. liegen; **a ~ taxi** ein Taxi, das gerade dasteht/angefahren kommt

conveniently /kənˈviːnɪəntlɪ/ *adv.* (a) günstig ⟨*gelegen, angebracht*⟩; leicht ⟨*gesehen werden*⟩; **we're ~ situated for the shops** wir haben es nicht weit zu den Geschäften; (b) (opportunely) angenehmerweise

convenor ⇒ **convener**

convent /ˈkɒnvənt/ *n.* Kloster, *das*

convention /kənˈvenʃn/ *n.* (a) (a practice) Brauch, *der;* **it is the ~ to do sth.** es ist Brauch, etw. zu tun; (b) *no art.* (established customs) Konvention, *die;* **break with ~:** sich über die Konventionen hinwegsetzen; (c) (formal assembly) Konferenz, *die;* (d) (agreement between States) Konvention, *die* (bes. Völkerrecht)

conventional /kənˈvenʃənl/ *adj.* konventionell; (not spontaneous) formell

conventionally /kənˈvenʃənəlɪ/ *adv.* konventionell

converge /kənˈvɜːdʒ/ *v.i.* ~ **[on each other]** aufeinander zulaufen; ⟨*Gedanken, Meinungen, Ansichten:*⟩ sich [einander] annähern; ~ **on sb.** auf jmdn. zulaufen

convergence /kənˈvɜːdʒəns/ *n.* Annäherung, *die;* Konvergenz, *die* (geh.); (of roads, rivers) Zusammentreffen, *das*

convergent /kənˈvɜːdʒənt/ *adj.* aufeinander zulaufend

conversant /kənˈvɜːsənt/ *pred. adj.* vertraut (**with** mit)

conversation /kɒnvəˈseɪʃn/ *n.* Unterhaltung, *die;* Gespräch, *das;* (in language teaching) Konversation, *die;* **be in ~ [with sb.]** sich [mit jmdm.] unterhalten; **be deep in ~:** in ein Gespräch vertieft sein; **make [polite] ~ with sb.** mit jmdm. Konversation machen; **come up in ~:** gesprächsweise erwähnt werden; **have a ~ with sb.** mit jmdm. ein Gespräch führen

conversational /kɒnvəˈseɪʃənl/ *adj.* gesprächig ⟨*Person*⟩; ungezwungen ⟨*Art*⟩; ~ **English** gesprochenes Englisch

converse[1] /kənˈvɜːs/ *v.i.* (formal) ~ **[with sb.] [about** *or* **on sth.]** sich [mit jmdm.] [über etw. (*Akk.*)] unterhalten

converse[2] /ˈkɒnvɜːs/ **1** *adj.* entgegengesetzt; umgekehrt ⟨*Fall, Situation*⟩. **2** *n.* Gegenteil, *das*

conversely /kənˈvɜːslɪ/ *adv.* umgekehrt

conversion /kənˈvɜːʃn/ *n.* (a) (transforming) Umwandlung, *die* (**into** in + *Akk.*); (b) (adaptation, adapted building) Umbau, *der;* **do a ~ on sth.** etw. umbauen; (c) (of person) Bekehrung, *die* (**to** zu); Konversion, *die* (Rel.); (d) (to different units or expression) Übertragung, *die* (**into** in + *Akk.*); (e) (Theol., Psych., Phys.) Konversion, *die;* (calculation) Umrechnung, *die;* (f) (Rugby, Amer. Footb.) Erhöhung, *die*

convert /kənˈvɜːt/ *v.t.* (a) (transform, change in function) umwandeln (**into** in + *Akk.*); (b) (adapt) ~ **sth. [into sth.]** etw. [zu etw.] umbauen; (c) (bring over) ~ **sb. [to sth.]** (lit. *or* fig.) jmdn. [zu etw.] bekehren; (d) (to different units or expressions) übertragen (**into** in + *Akk.*); (e) (calculate) umrechnen (**into** in + *Akk.*); (f) (Rugby, Amer. Footb.) erhöhen. **2** /kənˈvɜːt/ *v.i.* (a) ~ **into sth.** sich in etw. (*Akk.*) umwandeln lassen; (b) (be adaptable) sich umbauen lassen; (c) (to new method etc.) umstellen (**to** auf + *Akk.*). **3** /'kɒnvɜ:t/ *n.* (Relig.) Konvertit, *der*/Konvertitin, *die*

convertible /kən'vɜ:tɪbl/ **1** *adj.* **(a) be ~ into sth.** (transformable) sich in etw. (*Akk.*) umwandeln lassen; **(b)** (able to be altered) **be ~ [into sth.]** sich zu etw. umbauen lassen. **2** *n.* Kabrio[lett], *das;* (with four or more seats) Kabriolimousine, *die*

convex /'kɒnveks/ *adj.* konvex; *attrib.* Konvex‹*linse*, *-spiegel*›

convey /kən'veɪ/ *v.t.* **(a)** (transport) befördern; (transmit) übermitteln ‹*Nachricht, Grüße*›; **(b)** (impart) vermitteln; **words cannot ~ it** Worte können es nicht wiedergeben; **the message ~ed nothing whatever to me** die Nachricht sagte mir überhaupt nichts

conveyance /kən'veɪəns/ *n.* **(a)** (transportation) Beförderung, *die;* **(b)** (formal: vehicle) Beförderungsmittel, *das;* **(c)** (Law) Übertragung, *die;* Überschreibung, *die*

conveyancing /kən'veɪənsɪŋ/ *n.* (Law) **~ [of property]** [Eigentums]übertragung, *die*

conveyer, conveyor /kən'veɪə(r)/ *n.* Förderer, *der* (Technik); **~ [belt]** (Industry) Förderband, *das;* (in manufacture also) Fließband, *das*

convict 1 /'kɒnvɪkt/ *n.* Strafgefangene, *der*/*die*. **2** /kən'vɪkt/ *v.t.* **(a)** (declare guilty) für schuldig befinden; verurteilen; **be ~ed** verurteilt werden; **(b)** (prove guilty) **~ sb. of sth.** jmdn. einer Sache (*Gen.*) überführen

conviction /kən'vɪkʃn/ *n.* **(a)** (Law) Verurteilung, *die* (**for** wegen); **have you [had] any previous ~s?** sind Sie vorbestraft?; **(b)** (settled belief) Überzeugung, *die;* **it is their ~ that ...:** sie sind der Überzeugung, dass ...; **carry ~:** überzeugend sein

convince /kən'vɪns/ *v.t.* überzeugen; **~ sb. that ...:** jmdn. davon überzeugen, dass ...; **be ~d that ...:** davon überzeugt sein, dass ...

convincing /kən'vɪnsɪŋ/ *adj.*, **convincingly** /kən'vɪnsɪŋlɪ/ *adv.* überzeugend

convivial /kən'vɪvɪəl/ *n.* fröhlich

convoluted /'kɒnvəlu:tɪd/ *adj.* **(a)** (twisted) verschlungen; **(b)** (complex) kompliziert

convoy /'kɒnvɔɪ/ *n.* Konvoi, *der;* **in ~:** im Konvoi

convulse /kən'vʌls/ *v.t.* **(a) be ~d** von Krämpfen geschüttelt werden; **(b)** (shake, lit. or fig.) erschüttern

convulsion /kən'vʌlʃn/ *n.* **(a)** in pl. Schüttelkrampf, *der* (Med.); Krämpfe; **(b)** (shaking, lit. or fig.) Erschütterung, *die*

coo /ku:/ **1** *int.* (of person) oh; (of dove) ruckedigu. **2** *n.* (of dove) **the ~[s]** das Gurren. **3** *v.i.* gurren; ‹*Baby:*› gurren (fig.)

cook /kʊk/ **1** *n.* ▶ 887 ◀ Koch, *der*/Köchin, *die*. **2** *v.t.* **(a)** garen; zubereiten, kochen ‹*Mahlzeit*›; (fry, roast) braten; (boil) kochen; **how would you ~ this piece of meat?** wie würden Sie dieses Stück Fleisch zubereiten?; **~ed in the oven** im Backofen zubereitet *od.* (Kochk.) gegart; **~ed meal** warme Mahlzeit; *abs.* **do you ~ with gas or electricity?** kochen Sie mit Gas oder mit Strom?; **she knows how to ~:** sie kann gut kochen *od.* kocht gut; **~ sb.'s goose [for him]** (fig.) jmdm. alles verderben; **(b)** (fig. coll.: falsify) frisieren (ugs.). **3** *v.i.* kochen; garen (Kochk.); **the meat was ~ing slowly** das Fleisch garte langsam; **what's ~ing?** (fig. coll.) was liegt an? (ugs.)

~ 'up *v.t.* sich (*Dat.*) ausbrüten, (ugs.) aushecken ‹*Plan*›; erfinden ‹*Geschichte*›

cooker /'kʊkə(r)/ *n.* **(a)** (Brit.: stove) Herd, *der;* **electric/gas ~:** Elektroherd/Gasherd, *der;* **(b)** (fruit) **are those apples eaters or ~s?** sind diese Äpfel zum Essen oder zum Kochen?

cookery /'kʊkərɪ/ *n.* Kochen, *das*

'cookery book *n.* (Brit.) Kochbuch, *das*

cookhouse /'kʊkhaʊs/ *n.* (Mil.) Feldküche, *die*

cookie /'kʊkɪ/ *n.* **(a)** (Scot.: plain bun) Plätzchen, *das;* **(b)** (Amer.: biscuit) Keks, *der*

cooking /'kʊkɪŋ/ *n.* Kochen, *das;* **German ~:** die deutsche Küche; **do one's own ~:** für sich selbst kochen; **do the ~:** kochen

cooking: **~ apple** *n.* Kochapfel, *der;* **~ fat** *n.* Bratfett, *das;* **~ salt** *n.* Speisesalz, *das;* **~ utensil** *n.* Küchengerät, *das*

'cookout *n.* (Amer.) ≈ Grillparty, *die*

cool /ku:l/ **1** *adj.* **(a)** kühl; luftig ‹*Kleidung*›; **'store in a ~ place'** „kühl aufbewahren"; **(b)** (calm) **he kept or stayed ~:** er blieb ruhig *od.* bewahrte die Ruhe; **play it ~** (coll.) ruhig bleiben; cool vorgehen (salopp); **he was ~, calm, and collected** er war ruhig und gelassen; **keep a ~ head** einen kühlen Kopf bewahren; **(c)** (unemotional, unfriendly) kühl; (calmly audacious) kaltblütig. **2** *n.* Kühle, *die*. **3** *v.i.* abkühlen; **the weather has ~ed** es ist kühler geworden; (fig.) **our relationship has ~ed** unsere Beziehung ist kühler geworden; **~ towards sb./sth.** an jmdm./etw. das Interesse verlieren. **4** *v.t.* kühlen; (from high temperature) abkühlen; (fig.) abkühlen ‹*Leidenschaft, Raserei*›; **~ one's heels** (fig.) lange warten

~ 'down 1 *v.i.* **(a)** ‹*Tee:*› abkühlen; ‹*Luft:*› sich abkühlen; **(b)** (fig.) sich beruhigen. **2** *v.t.* abkühlen

~ 'off 1 *v.i.* **(a)** abkühlen; **the weather has ~ed off** es ist kühler geworden; **we need a few minutes to ~ off** wir brauchen ein paar Minuten, um uns abzukühlen; **(b)** (fig.) sich beruhigen; ‹*Zorn, Begeisterung, Interesse:*› sich legen, nachlassen. **2** *v.t.* abkühlen; (fig.) beruhigen

'cool box *n.* Kühlbox, *die*

cooler /'ku:lə(r)/ *n.* Kühler, *der*

coolie /'ku:lɪ/ *n.* Kuli, *der*

coolly /'ku:llɪ/ *adv.* **(a)** kühl; **(b)** (fig.) (calmly) ruhig; (unemotionally, in unfriendly manner) kühl; (audaciously) kaltblütig; unverfroren ‹*verlangen, fordern*›

coolness /'ku:lnɪs/ *n.*, no pl. Kühle, *die;* (fig.) (calmness) Ruhe, *die;* (unemotional nature, unfriendliness) Kühle, *die;* (audacity) Kaltblütigkeit, *die*

coop /ku:p/ *n.* (cage) Geflügelkäfig, *der;* (for poultry) Hühnerstall, *der;* (fowl-run) Auslauf, *der*

cooperate /kəʊ'ɒpəreɪt/ *v.i.* mitarbeiten (**in** bei); (with each other) zusammenarbeiten (**in** bei); (not obstruct) mitmachen (ugs.); **~ with sb.** mit jmdm. zusammenarbeiten

cooperation /kəʊɒpə'reɪʃn/ *n.* Mitarbeit, *die;* Zusammenarbeit, *die;* Kooperation, *die;* **with the ~ of** unter Mitarbeit von; **in ~ with** in Zusammenarbeit mit

cooperative /kəʊ'ɒpərətɪv/ **1** *adj.* kooperativ; (helpful) hilfsbereit. **2** *n.* Genossenschaft, *die;* Kooperative, *die* (bes. in der ehemaligen DDR); (shop) Genossenschaftsladen, *der;* **workers' ~:** Produktivgenossenschaft, *die*

co-opt /kəʊ'ɒpt/ *v.t.* kooptieren; hinzuwählen; **be ~ed [on] to a committee** von einem Komitee kooptiert werden

coordinate 1 /kəʊ'ɔ:dɪnət/ *n.* **(a)** (Math.) Koordinate, *die;* **(b)** in pl. (clothes) Kombination, *die.* **2** /kəʊ'ɔ:dɪneɪt/ *v.t.* koordinieren; **coordinating conjunction** koordinierende Konjunktion

coordination /kəʊɔ:dɪ'neɪʃn/ *n.* Koordination, *die*

cop¹ /kɒp/ *n.* (coll.: police officer) Bulle, *der* (salopp)

cop² (sl.) **1** *v.t.*, **-pp-:** **(a)** when ..., **you'll ~ it** (be punished) wenn ..., dann kannst du was erleben; **(b)** they **~ped it** (were killed) sie mussten dran glauben (salopp). **2** *n.* **it's a fair ~!** guter Fang!; **no ~, not much ~:** nichts Besonderes

~ 'out *v.i.* (sl.) **(a)** (escape) abhauen (salopp); **~ out of society** [aus der Gesellschaft] aussteigen (ugs.); **(b)** (give up) alles hinwerfen (ugs.)

cope /kəʊp/ *v.i.* **~ with sb./sth.** mit jmdm./etw. fertig werden; **~ with a handicapped child** mit einem behinderten Kind zurechtkommen

Copenhagen /kəʊpn'heɪgn/ *pr. n.* ▶ 1159 ◀ Kopenhagen (*das*)

copier /'kɒpɪə(r)/ *n.* (machine) Kopiergerät, *das;* Kopierer, *der* (ugs.)

co-pilot /'kəʊpaɪlət/ *n.* Kopilot, *der*/Kopilotin, *die*

copious /'kəʊpɪəs/ *adj.* (plentiful) reichhaltig; (informative) umfassend

'cop-out *n.* (sl.) Drückebergerei, *die* (ugs. abwertend); **that's a ~:** das ist Drückebergerei

copper¹ /'kɒpə(r)/ **1** *n.* **(a)** Kupfer, *das;* **(b)** (coin) Kupfermünze, *das;* **a few ~s** etwas Kupfergeld; **(c)** (for laundry) Waschkessel, *der.* **2** *attrib. adj.* **(a)** (made of ~) kupfern; Kupfer‹*münze, -kessel, -rohr*›; **(b)** (coloured like ~) kupferfarben; kupfern

copper² (Brit. coll.) ⇒ **cop¹**

copper: ~ **'beech** n. Blutbuche, die; ~**-coloured** adj. kupferfarben; ~**plate** 1 n. (a) (metal plate) Kupferplatte, die; (b) (print) Kupferstich, der; 2 adj. ~**plate writing** ≈ Schönschrift, die

coppice /ˈkɒpɪs/, **copse** /kɒps/ ns. Wäldchen, das; Niederwald, der (Forstw.)

copula /ˈkɒpjʊlə/ n. (Ling.) Kopula, die

copulate /ˈkɒpjʊleɪt/ v.i. kopulieren

copulation /kɒpjʊˈleɪʃn/ n. Kopulation, die

copy /ˈkɒpɪ/ 1 n. (a) (reproduction) Kopie, die; (imitation) Nachahmung, die; (with carbon paper etc.) (typed) Durchschlag, der; (written) Durchschrift, die; (b) (specimen) Exemplar, das; **have you a** ~ **of today's 'Times'?** haben Sie die „Times" von heute?; **send three copies of the application** die Bewerbung in dreifacher Ausfertigung schicken; **top** ~: Original, das. 2 v.t. (a) (make ~ of) kopieren; (by photocopier) [foto]kopieren; (transcribe) abschreiben; (b) (imitate) nachahmen. 3 v.i. (a) kopieren; ~ **from sb./sth.** jmdn./etw. kopieren; (b) (in exam etc.) abschreiben; ~ **from sb./sth.** bei jmdm./aus etw. abschreiben
~ **'out** v.t. abschreiben

'copybook attrib. adj. wie im Bilderbuch nachgestellt; see also **blot 2 b**

copyright /ˈkɒpɪraɪt/ 1 n. Copyright, das; Urheberrecht, das; **be out of** ~: gemeinfrei [geworden] sein; **protected by** ~: urheberrechtlich geschützt. 2 adj. urheberrechtlich geschützt

'copy typist n. ▶887┃ Schreibkraft (die nur nach schriftlichen Vorlagen arbeitet)

coral /ˈkɒrl/ 1 n. Koralle, die. 2 attrib. adj. korallen; Korallen‹insel, -riff, -rot›

cord /kɔːd/ n. (a) Kordel, die; (b) (cloth) Cord, der

cordial /ˈkɔːdɪəl/ 1 adj. herzlich; **a** ~ **dislike for sb.** eine tief empfundene Abneigung gegenüber jmdm. 2 n. (drink) Sirup, der

cordially /ˈkɔːdɪəlɪ/ adv. herzlich; ~ **dislike sb.** eine tief empfundene Abneigung gegenüber jmdm. haben

cordon /ˈkɔːdn/ 1 n. Kordon, der; see also **throw around** b. 2 v.t. ~ **[off]** absperren; abriegeln

corduroy /ˈkɔːdərɔɪ, ˈkɔːdjʊrɔɪ/ n. Cordsamt, der

core /kɔː(r)/ 1 n. (a) (of fruit) Kerngehäuse, das; (b) (Geol.) (rock sample) [Bohr]kern, der; (of earth) [Erd]kern, der; (c) (fig.: innermost part) **rotten to the** ~: verdorben bis ins Mark; **English to the** ~: durch und durch englisch; **shake sb. to the** ~: jmdn. zutiefst erschüttern. 2 v.t. entkernen ‹Apfel, Birne›

co-respondent /kəʊrɪˈspɒndənt/ n. Mitbeklagte, der/die (im Scheidungsprozeß)

corgi /ˈkɔːgɪ/ n. [Welsh] ~: Welsh Corgi, der

coriander /kɒrɪˈændə(r)/ n. Koriander, der; ~ **seed** Koriander, der

cork /kɔːk/ 1 n. (a) (bark) Kork, der; (b) (bottle-stopper) Korken, der. 2 v.t. zukorken; verkorken
~ **'up** v.t. zukorken; verkorken

'corkscrew n. Korkenzieher, der

cormorant /ˈkɔːmərənt/ n. (Ornith.) Kormoran, der

corn¹ /kɔːn/ n. (a) (cereal) Getreide, das; (esp. rye, wheat also) Korn, das; [**sweet**]~ (maize) Mais, der; ~ **on the cob** [gekochter/gerösteter] Maiskolben; (b) (seed) Korn, das

corn² n. (on foot) Hühnerauge, das

corn: ~ **cob** n. Maiskolben, der; ~ **dolly** n. Strohpuppe, die

cornea /ˈkɔːnɪə/ n. (Anat.) Hornhaut, die; Cornea, die (fachspr.)

corned beef /kɔːnd ˈbiːf/ n. Cornedbeef, das

corner /ˈkɔːnə(r)/ 1 n. (a) Ecke, die; (curve) Kurve, die; **on the** ~: an der Ecke/in der Kurve; **at the** ~: an der Ecke; ~ **of the street** Straßenecke, die; **cut** [**off**] **a/the** ~: eine/die Kurve schneiden; **cut** ~s (fig.) auf die Schnelle arbeiten (ugs.); [**sth. is**] **just** [**a**]**round the** ~: [etw. ist] gleich um die Ecke; **Christmas is just round the** ~ (fig. coll.) Weihnachten steht vor der Tür; **turn the** ~: um die Ecke biegen; **he has turned the** ~ now (fig.) er ist jetzt

über den Berg (ugs.); (b) (hollow angle between walls) Ecke, die; (of mouth, eye) Winkel, der; (c) (Boxing, Wrestling) Ecke, die; (d) (secluded place) Eckchen, das; Plätzchen, das; (remote region) Winkel, der; **from the four** ~s of the earth aus aller Welt; (e) (Hockey, Footb.) Ecke, die; (f) (Commerc.) Corner, der; Schwänze, die. 2 v.t. (a) (drive into ~) in eine Ecke treiben; (fig.) in die Enge treiben; **have** [**got**] **sb.** ~**ed** jmdn. in der Falle haben; (b) (Commerc.) ~ **the market in coffee** die Kaffeevorräte aufkaufen; den Kaffeemarkt aufschwänzen (fachspr.). 3 v.i. die Kurve nehmen; ~ **well/badly** ‹Fahrzeug:› eine gute/schlechte Kurvenlage haben

corner: ~ **flag** n. (Sport) Eckfahne, die; ~ **kick** n. (Footb.) Eckball, der; Eckstoß, der; ~ **seat** n. Ecksitz, der; ~ **shop** n. Tante-Emma-Laden, der (ugs.); ~**stone** n. Eckstein, der; (fig.) Eckpfeiler, der

cornet /ˈkɔːnɪt/ n. (a) (Brit.: wafer) [Eis]tüte, die; Eishörnchen, das; (b) (Mus.) Kornett, das

corn: ~**field** n. Kornfeld, das; (Amer.) Maisfeld, das; ~**flakes** n. pl. Corn-flakes Pl.; ~**flour** n. (a) (Brit.: ground maize) Maismehl, das; (b) (flour of rice etc.) Stärkemehl, das; ~**flower** n. Kornblume, die

cornice /ˈkɔːnɪs/ n. (Archit.) Kranzgesims, das

Cornish /ˈkɔːnɪʃ/ 1 adj. kornisch. 2 n. Kornisch, das

'cornstarch (Amer.) ⇒ **cornflour a**

corny /ˈkɔːnɪ/ adj. (coll.) (old-fashioned) altmodisch ‹Witz usw.›; (trite) abgedroschen (ugs.)

corollary /kəˈrɒlərɪ/ n. (proposition) Korollar[ium], das (Logik); (consequence) [logische od. natürliche] Folge

coronary /ˈkɒrənərɪ/ 1 adj. (Anat.) koronar. 2 n. (Med.) ⇒ **coronary thrombosis**

coronary throm'bosis n. (Med.) Koronarthrombose, die

coronation /kɒrəˈneɪʃn/ n. Krönung, die

coroner /ˈkɒrənə(r)/ n. Coroner, der; Beamter, der gewaltsame od. unnatürliche Todesfälle untersucht

coronet /ˈkɒrənet/ n. Krone, die

corpora pl. of **corpus**

corporal¹ /ˈkɔːpərl/ adj. körperlich

corporal² n. ▶1152┃ Korporal, der (hist.; österr.); ≈ Hauptgefreite, der

corporate /ˈkɔːpərət/ adj. körperschaftlich; ~ **body**, **body** ~: Körperschaft, die

corporation /kɔːpəˈreɪʃn/ n. (a) (civic authority) [**municipal**] ~: Gemeindeverwaltung, die; (of borough, city) Stadtverwaltung, die; (b) (united body) Körperschaft, die; Korporation, die

corporeal /kɔːˈpɔːrɪəl/ adj. (a) (bodily) körperlich; (b) (material) materiell; stofflich

corps /kɔː(r)/ n., pl. same /kɔːz/ Korps, das

corpse /kɔːps/ n. Leiche, die; Leichnam, der (geh.)

corpulent /ˈkɔːpjʊlənt/ adj. korpulent

corpus /ˈkɔːpəs/ n., pl. **corpora** /ˈkɔːpərə/ Sammlung, die; Korpus, das

Corpus Christi /kɔːpəs ˈkrɪstɪ/ n. (Eccl.) Fronleichnam (der); Fronleichnamsfest, das

corpuscle /ˈkɔːpʌsl/ n. (Anat.) [**blood**] ~: Blutkörperchen, das

corral /kəˈrɑːl/ n. (Amer.) Pferch, der

correct /kəˈrekt/ 1 v.t. (a) (amend) korrigieren; verbessern, korrigieren ‹Fehler, Formulierung, jmds. Englisch/Deutsch›; ~ **me if I'm wrong** ich könnte mich natürlich irren; (b) (counteract) ausgleichen ‹etw. Schädliches›; (c) (admonish) zurechtweisen (**for** wegen). 2 adj. richtig; korrekt; (precise) korrekt; akkurat; **that is** ~: das stimmt; **have you the** ~ **time?** haben Sie die genaue Uhrzeit?; **am I** ~ **in assuming that …?** gehe ich recht in der Annahme, dass …?

correction /kəˈrekʃn/ n. Korrektur, die; **the pupils had to write out** or **do their** ~s die Schüler mussten die Verbesserung od. Berichtigung schreiben

corrective /kəˈrektɪv/ adj. korrigierend; **take** ~ **action** korrigierend eingreifen

correctly /kəˈrektlɪ/ adv. richtig; korrekt; (precisely) korrekt; akkurat; **behave very** ~: sich sehr korrekt benehmen

correlate /'kɒrɪleɪt/ **1** v.i. einander entsprechen; ~ **with** or **to sth.** einer Sache (Dat.) entsprechen. **2** v.t. ~ **sth. with sth.** etw. zu etw. in Beziehung setzen

correlation /kɒrɪ'leɪʃn/ n. [Wechsel]beziehung, die; Korrelation, die (bes. Math., Naturw.); (connection) Zusammenhang, der

correspond /kɒrɪ'spɒnd/ v.i. **(a)** (be analogous, agree in amount) ~ **[to each other]** einander entsprechen; ~ **to sth.** einer Sache (Dat.) entsprechen; **(b)** (agree in position) ~ **[to sth.]** [mit etw.] übereinstimmen; (be in harmony) ~ **[with** or **to sth.]** [mit etw.] zusammenpassen; **(c)** (communicate) ~ **with sb.** mit jmdm. korrespondieren

correspondence /kɒrɪ'spɒndəns/ n. **(a)** Übereinstimmung (**with**, **to** mit); **(b)** (communication, letters) Briefwechsel, der; Korrespondenz, die

correspondence: ~ **college** n. Fernschule, die; ~ **column** n. Rubrik „Leserbriefe"; ~ **course** n. Fernkurs, der

correspondent /kɒrɪ'spɒndənt/ n. **(a)** Briefschreiber, der/-schreiberin, die; (penfriend) Brieffreund, der/-freundin, die; (to newspaper) Leserbriefschreiber, der/-schreiberin, die; **(b)** ▶ 887 ◀ (Radio, Telev., Journ., etc.) Berichterstatter, der/-erstatterin, die; Korrespondent, der/Korrespondentin, die

corresponding /kɒrɪ'spɒndɪŋ/ adj. entsprechend (**to** Dat.)

correspondingly /kɒrɪ'spɒndɪŋlɪ/ adv. entsprechend

corridor /'kɒrɪdɔː(r)/ n. **(a)** (inside passage) Flur, der; Gang, der; Korridor, der; (outside passage) Galerie, die; **in the ~s of power** (fig.) in den politischen Schaltstellen; **(b)** (Railw.) [Seiten]gang, der

corroborate /kə'rɒbəreɪt/ v.t. bestätigen

corroboration /kərɒbə'reɪʃn/ n. Bestätigung, die; **in ~ of sth.** als od. zur Bestätigung einer Sache (Gen.)

corrode /kə'rəʊd/ **1** v.t. zerfressen; korrodieren, zerfressen ⟨Metall, Gestein⟩. **2** v.i. zerfressen werden; ⟨Gestein, Metall:⟩ korrodieren, zerfressen werden

corrosion /kə'rəʊʒn/ n. Zerfall, der; (of metal, stone) Korrosion, die

corrosive /kə'rəʊsɪv/ **1** adj. zerstörend; korrosiv (bes. Chemie, Geol.); ätzend ⟨Chemikalien⟩; (fig.) zerstörerisch. **2** n. Korrosion verursachender Stoff

corrugate /'kɒrʊgeɪt/ v.t. zerfurchen; ~d **cardboard/paper** Wellpappe, die; ~d **iron** Wellblech, das

corrugation /kɒrʊ'geɪʃn/ n. **(a)** Zerfurchung, die; **(b)** (wrinkle, ridge mark) Furche, die; (ridge made by bending) Rille, die

corrupt /kə'rʌpt/ **1** adj. (depraved) verkommen; verdorben (geh.); (influenced by bribery) korrupt. **2** v.t. (deprave) korrumpieren; (bribe) bestechen

corruption /kə'rʌpʃn/ n. **(a)** (moral deterioration) Verdorbenheit, die (geh.); **(b)** (use of corrupt practices) Korruption, die; **(c)** (perversion) Korrumpierung, die

corset /'kɔːsɪt/ n., in sing. or pl. Korsett, das

Corsica /'kɔːsɪkə/ pr. n. Korsika (das)

Corsican /'kɔːsɪkən/ ▶ 947 ◀ **1** adj. korsisch; **sb. is ~:** jmd. ist Korse/Korsin. **2** n. (person) Korse, der/Korsin, die

cortège /kɔː'teɪʒ/ n. Trauerzug, der

cortisone /'kɔːtɪzəʊn/ n. Kortison, das (Med.); Cortison, das (fachspr.)

corvette /kɔː'vet/ n. (Naut.) Korvette, die

cos¹ /kɒs/ n. Römischer Salat; Sommerendivie, die

cos², **'cos** /kɒz/ (coll.) ⇒ **because**

cosh /kɒʃ/ (Brit. coll.) **1** n. Totschläger, der; Knüppel, der. **2** v.t. niederknüppeln

cosily /'kəʊzɪlɪ/ adv. bequem; gemütlich, behaglich ⟨plaudern, wohnen⟩

cosine /'kəʊsaɪn/ n. (Math.) Kosinus, der

cosmetic /kɒz'metɪk/ **1** adj. (lit. or fig.) kosmetisch; ~ **surgery** Schönheitschirurgie, die. **2** n. Kosmetikum, das

cosmic /'kɒzmɪk/ adj. (lit. or fig.) kosmisch; ~ **radiation** or **rays** kosmische Strahlung

cosmonaut /'kɒzmənɔːt/ n. ▶ 887 ◀ Kosmonaut, der/Kosmonautin, die

cosmopolitan /kɒzmə'pɒlɪtən/ adj. kosmopolitisch

cosmos /'kɒzmɒs/ n. Kosmos, der

Cossack /'kɒsæk/ n. Kosak, der

cosset /'kɒsɪt/ v.t. [ver]hätscheln

cost /kɒst/ **1** n. **(a)** Kosten Pl.; **the ~ of bread/gas/oil** der Brot-/Gas-/Ölpreis; **the ~ of heating a house** die Heizkosten für ein Haus; **regardless of ~, whatever the ~:** ganz gleich, was es kostet; **(b)** (fig.) Preis, der; **at all ~s, at any ~:** um jeden Preis; **at the ~ of sth.** auf Kosten einer Sache (Gen.); **whatever the ~:** koste es, was es wolle; **to my/his** etc. **~:** zu meinem/seinem usw. Nachteil; **as I know to my ~:** wie ich aus bitterer Erfahrung weiß; see also **count¹** 2 a; **(c)** in pl. (Law) [Gerichts]kosten Pl. **2** v.t. **(a)** p.t., p.p. **cost** (lit. or fig.) kosten; **how much does it ~?** was kostet es?; **whatever it may ~:** koste es, was es wolle; ~ **sb. dear[ly]** jmdm. od. jmdn. teuer zu stehen kommen; **(b)** p.t., p.p. ~**ed** (Commerc.: fix price of) ~ **sth.** den Preis für etw. kalkulieren

co-star /'kəʊstɑː(r)/ (Cinemat., Theatre) **1** n. **be a/the ~:** eine der Hauptrollen/die zweite Hauptrolle spielen. **2** v.i., **-rr-** eine der Hauptrollen spielen

'cost-effective adj. rentabel

coster[monger] /'kɒstə(mʌŋgə(r))/ n. (Brit.) Straßenhändler, der/-händlerin, die

costing /'kɒstɪŋ/ n. **(a)** (estimation of costs) Kostenberechnung, die; **(b)** (costs) Kosten Pl.

costly /'kɒstlɪ/ adj. **(a)** teuer; kostspielig; **(b)** (fig.) **a ~ victory** ein teuer erkaufter Sieg; **a ~ error** ein folgenschwerer Irrtum

cost: ~ **of 'living** n. Lebenshaltungskosten Pl.; ~ **price** n. Selbstkostenpreis, der

costume /'kɒstjuːm/ n. Kleidermode, die; (theatrical ~) Kostüm, das; **historical ~s** historische Kostüme

cosy /'kəʊzɪ/ **1** adj. gemütlich; behaglich ⟨Atmosphäre⟩; bequem ⟨Sessel⟩; **feel ~:** sich wohl od. behaglich fühlen; **be ~:** es gemütlich haben. **2** n. ⇒ **tea cosy**

cot /kɒt/ n. (Brit.: child's bed) Kinderbett, das

'cot death (Brit.) plötzlicher Kindstod; Cotdeath, der (Med.)

cottage /'kɒtɪdʒ/ n. Cottage, das; Häuschen, das

cottage: ~ **'cheese** n. Hüttenkäse, der; ~ **industry** n. Heimarbeit, die; ~ **'pie** n. mit Kartoffelbrei überbackenes Hackfleisch

cotter /'kɒtə(r)/ n. ~**[pin]** Splint, der

cotton /'kɒtn/ **1** n. Baumwolle, die; (thread) Baumwollgarn, das; (cloth) Baumwollstoff, der. **2** attrib. adj. Baumwoll-. **3** v.i. ~ **'on** (coll.) kapieren (ugs.)

cotton-: ~ **mill** n. Baumwollspinnerei, die; ~ **plant** n. Baumwollpflanze, die; ~ **reel** n. [Näh]garnrolle, die; ~ **'waste** n. Putzwolle, die; ~ **'wool** n. Watte, die; ~**wool ball** Wattebausch, der; **wrap sb. up** or **keep sb. in ~ wool** (fig.) jmdn. in Watte packen

couch /kaʊtʃ/ **1** n. (sofa) Couch, die. **2** v.t. formulieren

couchette /kuː'ʃet/ n. (Railw.) Liegewagen, der; (berth) Liegesitz, der

cough /kɒf/ **1** n. (act of ~ing, condition) Husten, der; **give a ~:** husten; **have a [bad] ~:** [einen schlimmen] Husten haben. **2** v.i. **(a)** husten; **(b)** ⟨Motor:⟩ stottern. **3** v.t. ~ **out** [her]aushusten; ~ **up** [her]aushusten; (coll.: pay) ausspucken (ugs.)

coughing /'kɒfɪŋ/ n. Husten, das; Gehuste, das

cough: ~ **medicine** n. Hustenmittel, das; ~ **mixture** n. Hustensaft, der

could ⇒ **can²**

couldn't /'kʊdnt/ (coll.) = **could not**; ⇒ **can²**

council /'kaʊnsl/ n. **(a)** Ratsversammlung, die; **(b)** (administrative/advisory body) Rat, der; **local ~:** Gemeinderat, der; **city/town ~:** Stadtrat, der

council: ~ **estate** n. Wohnviertel mit Sozialwohnungen; ~ **flat** n. Sozialwohnung, die; ~ **house** n. Haus des sozialen Wohnungsbaus; ~ **housing** n. sozialer Wohnungsbau

councillor /'kaʊnsələ(r)/ n. ▶ 887 ◀ Ratsmitglied, das; **town ~:** Stadtrat, der/-rätin, die

council: ∼ **of 'war** *n.* (lit. or fig.) Kriegsrat, *der;* ∼ **tax** *n.* (Brit.) Gemeindesteuer, *die*

counsel /'kaʊnsl/ **1** *n.* **(a)** (consultation) Beratung, *die;* **take/hold** ∼ **with sb.** [about sth.] sich mit jmdm. [über etw. (*Akk.*)] beraten; **(b)** Rat[schlag], *der;* **keep one's own** ∼: seine Meinung für sich behalten; **(c)** *pl. same* (Law) Rechtsanwalt, *der*/-anwältin, *die;* ∼ **for the defence** Verteidiger, *der*/Verteidigerin, *die;* ∼ **for the prosecution** Anklagevertreter, *der*/-vertreterin, *die;* Staatsanwalt, *der*/ -anwältin, *die;* **Queen's/King's C**∼: Anwalt/Anwältin der Krone; Kronanwalt, *der*/-anwältin, *die.* **2** *v.t.,* (Brit.) **-ll-** (advise) beraten; ∼ **sb. to do sth.** jmdm. raten *od.* den Rat geben, etw. zu tun

counselling (*Amer.:* **counseling**) /'kaʊnsəlɪŋ/ *n.* Beratung, *die*

counsellor, (Amer.) **counselor** /'kaʊnsələ(r)/ *n.* ▶ 887 ⎥ Berater, *der*/Beraterin, *die;* **marriage-guidance** ∼: Eheberater, *der*/-beraterin, *die*

count¹ /kaʊnt/ **1** *n.* **(a)** Zählen, *das;* Zählung, *die;* **keep** ∼ **[of sth.]** [etw.] zählen; **lose** ∼ beim Zählen durcheinander geraten; **lose** ∼ **of sth.** etw. gar nicht mehr zählen können; **have/take/make a** ∼: zählen; **on the** ∼ **of three** bei „drei"; **(b)** (Law) Anklagepunkt, *der;* **on that** ∼ (fig.) in diesem Punkt; **(c)** (Boxing) Auszählen, *das;* **be out for the** ∼: ausgezählt werden; (fig.) hinüber sein (ugs.). **2** *v.t.* **(a)** zählen; ∼ **ten** bis zehn zählen; ∼ **the votes** die Stimmen [aus]zählen; ∼ **again** nachzählen; ∼ **the pennies** (fig.) jeden Pfennig umdrehen; ∼ **the cost** (fig.) unter den Folgen zu leiden haben; **(b)** (include) mitzählen; **be** ∼**ed against sb.** gegen jmdn. sprechen; **not** ∼**ing** abgesehen von; *see also* **nothing 1 a; (c)** (consider) halten für; ∼ **one-self lucky** sich glücklich schätzen können. **3** *v.i.* **(a)** zählen; ∼ **[up] to ten** bis zehn zählen; ∼**ing from now** von jetzt an [gerechnet]; ab jetzt; **(b)** (be included) zählen; **every moment** ∼**s** jede Sekunde zählt; ∼ **against sb.** gegen jmdn. sprechen; ∼ **for much/little** viel/wenig zählen

∼ **'in** *v.t.* mitrechnen; **you can** ∼ **me in** ich bin dabei

∼ **on** *v.t.* ∼ **on sb./sth.** sich auf jmdn./etw. verlassen

∼ **'out** *v.t.* **(a)** (one by one) abzählen; **(b)** (exclude) **[you can]** ∼ **me out** ich komme/mache nicht mit; **(c)** (Boxing) auszählen

∼ **'up** *v.t.* zusammenzählen; zusammenrechnen

∼ **upon** ⇒ ∼ **on**

count² *n.* ▶ 1152 ⎥ (nobleman) Graf, *der*

'countdown *n.* Count-down, *der od. das*

countenance /'kaʊntɪnəns/ **1** *n.* **(a)** (literary: face) Antlitz, *das* (dichter.); **(b)** (formal: expression) Gesichtsausdruck, *der.* **2** *v.t.* (formal: approve) gutheißen

counter¹ /'kaʊntə(r)/ *n.* **(a)** ▶ 887 ⎥ (in shop) Ladentisch, *der;* (in cafeteria, restaurant, train) Büfett, *das;* (in post office, bank) Schalter, *der;* ∼ **clerk** Schalterbeamte, *der*/-beamtin, *die;* **[buy/sell sth.] under the** ∼ (fig.) [etwas] unter dem Ladentisch [kaufen/verkaufen]; **(b)** (disc for games) Spielmarke, *die;* **(c)** (apparatus for counting) Zähler, *der*

counter² **1** *adj.* entgegengesetzt; Gegen-/gegen-. **2** *v.t.* **(a)** (oppose, contradict) begegnen (+ *Dat.*); **(b)** (take action against) kontern. **3** *v.i.* (take opposing action) antworten. **4** *adv.* **act** ∼ **to** zuwiderhandeln (+ *Dat.*); **go** ∼ **to** zuwiderlaufen (+ *Dat.*)

counter: ∼**'act** *v.t.* entgegenwirken (+ *Dat.*); ∼**-attack** (lit. or fig.) **1** *n.* Gegenangriff, *der;* **2** *v.t.* ∼**-attack sb.** gegen jmdn. einen Gegenangriff richten; **3** *v.i.* zurückschlagen; ∼**-attraction** *n.* **(a)** (rival) Konkurrenz, *die;* **(b)** (of contrary tendency) entgegengesetzte Anziehungskraft; ∼**balance** *v.t.* ein Gegengewicht bilden zu; (fig.: neutralize) ausgleichen; ∼**-'clockwise** ⇒ **anti-clockwise;** ∼**-'espionage** *n.* Spionageabwehr, *die*

counterfeit /'kaʊntəfɪt, 'kaʊntəfiːt/ **1** *adj.* falsch, unecht ⟨*Schmuck*⟩; falsch, gefälscht ⟨*Unterschrift, Münze, Banknote*⟩; ∼ **money** Falschgeld, *das.* **2** *v.t.* fälschen

counterfeiter /'kaʊntəfɪtə(r)/ *n.* Fälscher, *der*/Fälscherin, *die*

counter: ∼**foil** *n.* Kontrollabschnitt, *der;* ∼**-intelligence** ⇒ ∼**-espionage**

countermand /kaʊntə'mɑːnd/ *v.t.* (revoke) widerrufen

counter: ∼**measure** *n.* Gegenmaßnahme, *die;* ∼**-offensive** *n.* (Mil.) Gegenoffensive, *die;* ∼**part** *n.* Gegenstück, *das* (of zu); ∼**-pro'ductive** *adj.* das Gegenteil des Gewünschten bewirkend; **sth. is** ∼**-productive** etw. bewirkt das Gegenteil des Gewünschten; ∼**sign** *v.t.* gegenzeichnen; ∼**sink** *v.t.,* ∼**sunk** /'kaʊntəsʌŋk/ (Woodw., Metalw.) senken ⟨*Loch*⟩; versenken ⟨*Schraube*⟩; ∼**weight** *n.* Gegengewicht, *das*

countess /'kaʊntɪs/ *n.* ▶ 1152 ⎥ Gräfin, *die*

countless /'kaʊntlɪs/ *adj.* zahllos; ∼ **numbers of** eine zahllose Menge von

country /'kʌntrɪ/ *n.* **(a)** Land, *das;* **sb.'s [home]** ∼: jmds. Heimat; **fight/die for one's** ∼: für sein [Vater]land kämpfen/sterben; **farming** ∼: Ackerland, *das;* **(b)** (rural district) Land, *das;* (countryside) Landschaft, *die;* **[be/live** etc.**] in the** ∼: auf dem Land [sein/leben *usw.*]; **to the** ∼: aufs Land; **(c)** (Brit.: population) Volk, *das;* **appeal** *or* **go to the** ∼: den Wähler entscheiden lassen

country: ∼ **'dancing** *n.* Kontertanz, *der;* ∼ **'house** *n.* Landhaus, *das;* ∼**man** /'kʌntrɪmən/ *n., pl.* ∼**men** /'kʌntrɪmən/ **(a)** (national) Landsmann, *der;* [my/her etc.] **fellow** ∼**man** [mein/ihr *usw.*] Landsmann; **(b)** (rural) Landbewohner, *der;* ∼**side** *n.* **(a)** (rural areas) Land, *das;* **(b)** (rural scenery) Landschaft, *die;* ∼**-wide** *adj.* landesweit; ∼**woman** *n.* **(a)** (national) Landsmännin, *die;* **(b)** (rural) Landbewohnerin, *die*

county /'kaʊntɪ/ *n.* (Brit.) Grafschaft, *die*

county: ∼ **'council** *n.* Grafschaftsrat, *der;* ∼ **'town** *n.* (Brit.) Verwaltungssitz einer Grafschaft

coup /kuː/ *n.* **(a)** Coup, *der;* **(b)** ⇒ **coup d'état**

coup d'état /kuː deɪˈtɑː/ *n.* Staatsstreich, *der*

coupé /'kuːpeɪ/ (*Amer.:* **coupe** /kuːp/) *n.* Coupé, *das*

couple /kʌpl/ **1** *n.* **(a)** (pair) Paar, *das;* (married) [Ehe]paar, *das;* **(b) a** ∼ **[of]** (a few) ein paar; (two) zwei; **a** ∼ **of people/things/days/weeks** etc. ein paar/zwei Leute/Dinge/Tage/Wochen *usw.* **2** *v.t.* **(a)** (associate) verbinden; **(b)** (fasten together) koppeln

couplet /'kʌplɪt/ *n.* (Pros.) Verspaar, *das;* (rhyming) Reimpaar, *das*

coupling /'kʌplɪŋ/ *n.* (Railw., Mech. Engin.) Kupplung, *die*

coupon /'kuːpɒn/ *n.* (for rationed goods) Marke, *die;* (in advertisement) Gutschein, *der;* Coupon, *der;* (entry form for football pool etc.) Tippschein, *der*

courage /'kʌrɪdʒ/ *n.* Mut, *der;* **have/lack the** ∼ **to do sth.** den Mut haben/nicht den Mut haben, etw. zu tun; **take one's** ∼ **in both hands** sein Herz in beide Hände nehmen

courageous /kəˈreɪdʒəs/ *adj.,* **courageously** /kəˈreɪdʒəslɪ/ *adv.* mutig

courgette /kʊəˈʒet/ *n.* (Brit.) Zucchino, *der*

courier /'kʊrɪə(r)/ *n.* ▶ 887 ⎥ **(a)** (Tourism) Reiseleiter, *der*/ -leiterin, *die;* **(b)** (messenger) Kurier, *der*

course /kɔːs/ *n.* **(a)** (of ship, plane) Kurs, *der;* **change [one's]** ∼ (lit. or fig.) den Kurs wechseln; ∼ **[of action]** Vorgehensweise, *die;* **what are our possible** ∼**s of action?** welche Möglichkeiten haben wir?; **the most sensible** ∼ **would be to** …: das Vernünftigste wäre, zu …; **the** ∼ **of nature/history** der Lauf der Dinge/Geschichte; **run** *or* **take its** ∼: seinen/ihren Lauf nehmen; **let things take their** ∼: den Dingen ihren Lauf lassen; **off/on** ∼: vom Kurs abgekommen/auf Kurs; **(b) of** ∼: natürlich; **[do sth.] as a matter of** ∼: selbstverständlich [tun]; **(c)** (progression) Lauf, *der;* **in due** ∼: zu gegebener Zeit; **in the** ∼ **of the lesson/the day/his life** im Lauf[e] der Stunde/des Tages/seines Lebens; **(d)** (of river etc.) Lauf, *der;* **(e)** (of meal) Gang, *der;* **(f)** (Sport) Kurs, *der;* (for race) Rennstrecke, *die;* **[golf]** ∼: [Golf]platz, *der;* **(g)** (Educ.) Kurs[us], *der;* (for employee also) Lehrgang, *der;* (book) Lehrbuch, *das;* **go to** *or* **attend/do a** ∼ **in sth.** einen Kurs in etw. (*Dat.*) besuchen/machen; **(h)** (Med.) **a** ∼ **of treatment** eine Kur

court /kɔːt/ *n.* **(a)** (yard) Hof, *der;* **(b)** (Sport) Spielfeld, *das;* (Tennis, Squash also) Platz, *der;* **(c)** (of sovereign) Hof, *der;* **hold** ∼ (fig.) hofhalten (scherzh.); **(d)** (Law) Gericht, *das;* ∼ **of law** *or* **justice** Gerichtshof, *der;* **take sb. to** ∼: jmdn.

vor Gericht bringen *od.* verklagen; **appear in** ∼: vor Gericht erscheinen. **2** *v.t.* **(a)** (woo) ∼ **sb.** jmdn. umwerben; ∼**ing couple** Liebespärchen, *das;* **(b)** (fig.) suchen ‹*Gunst, Ruhm, Gefahr*›; **he is** ∼**ing disaster/danger** er wandelt am Rande des Abgrunds (fig. geh.)

courteous /'kɜ:tɪəs/ *adj.* höflich

courtesy /'kɜ:təsɪ/ *n.* Höflichkeit, *die;* **by** ∼ **of the museum** mit freundlicher Genehmigung des Museums

'**courtesy light** *n.* (Motor Veh.) Innenbeleuchtung, *die*

'**courthouse** *n.* (Law) Gerichtsgebäude, *das*

courtier /'kɔ:tɪə(r)/ *n.* Höfling, *der*

court: ∼ '**martial** *n., pl.* ∼**s martial** (Mil.) Kriegsgericht, *das;* **be tried by** ∼ **martial** vor das/ein Kriegsgericht kommen; ∼'**martial** *v.t.*, (Brit.) -**ll**- vor das/ein Kriegsgericht stellen; ∼**room** *n.* (Law) Gerichtssaal, *der*

courtship /'kɔ:tʃɪp/ *n.* Werben, *das*

court: ∼ **shoe** *n.* Pumps, *der;* ∼**yard** *n.* Hof, *der*

cousin /'kʌzn/ *n.* [**first**] ∼: Cousin, *der*/Cousine, *die;* Vetter, *der*/(veralt.) Base, *die;* [**second**] ∼: Cousin/Cousine zweiten Grades

cove /kəʊv/ *n.* (Geog.) [kleine] Bucht

covenant /'kʌvənənt/ **1** *n.* formelle Übereinkunft. **2** *v.t.* (also Law) [vertraglich] vereinbaren

Coventry /'kɒvəntrɪ/ *n.* **send sb. to** ∼ (fig.) jmdn. [demonstrativ] schneiden

cover /'kʌvə(r)/ **1** *n.* **(a)** (piece of cloth) Decke, *die;* (of cushion, bed) Bezug, *der;* (lid) Deckel, *der;* (of hole, engine, typewriter, etc.) Abdeckung, *die;* **put a** ∼ **on** *or* **over** zudecken; abdecken ‹*Loch, Fußboden, Grab, Fahrzeug, Maschine*›; beziehen ‹*Kissen, Bett*›; **(b)** (of book) Einband, *der;* (of magazine) Umschlag, *der;* (of record) [Platten]hülle, *die;* **read sth. from** ∼ **to** ∼: etw. von vorn bis hinten lesen; **on the [front/back]** ∼: auf dem [vorderen/hinteren] Buchdeckel; (of magazine) auf der Titelseite/hinteren Umschlagseite; **(c)** (Post: envelope) [Brief]umschlag, *der;* **under plain** ∼: in neutralem Umschlag; [**send sth.**] **under separate** ∼: [etw.] mit getrennter Post [schicken]; **(d)** *in pl.* (bedclothes) Bettzeug, *das;* **(e)** (hiding place, shelter) Schutz, *der;* **take** ∼ [**from sth.**] Schutz [vor etw. (*Dat.*)] suchen; [**be] go] under** ∼ (from bullets etc.) in Deckung [sein/gehen]; **under** ∼ (from rain) überdacht ‹*Sitzplatz*›; regengeschützt; **keep sth. under** ∼: etw. abgedeckt halten; **under** ∼ **of darkness** im Schutz der Dunkelheit; **(f)** (Mil.: supporting force) Deckung, *die;* **(g)** (protection) Deckung, *die;* **give sb./ sth.** ∼: jmdm. Deckung geben; **(h)** (pretence) Vorwand, *der;* (false identity, screen) Tarnung, *die;* **(i)** (Insurance) [**insurance**] ∼: Versicherung, *die;* **get** ∼ **against sth.** sich gegen etw. versichern; **have adequate** ∼: ausreichend versichert sein; **(j)** (of song etc.) ∼ [**version**] Coverversion, *die.* **2** *v.t.* **(a)** bedecken; ∼ **a book with leather** ein Buch in Leder binden; ∼ **a chair with chintz** einen Stuhl mit Chintz beziehen; ∼ **a pan with a lid** eine Pfanne mit einem Deckel zudecken; **she** ∼**ed her face with her hands** sie verbarg das Gesicht in den Händen; **the roses are** ∼**ed with greenfly** die Rosen sind voller Blattläuse; **sb. is** ∼**ed in** *or* **with confusion/shame** (fig.) jmd. ist ganz verlegen/sehr beschämt; **(b)** (conceal, lit. or fig.) verbergen; (for protection) abdecken; **(c)** (travel) zurücklegen; **(d)** *in p.p.* (having roof) überdacht; **(e)** (deal with) behandeln; (include) abdecken; **(f)** (Journ.) berichten über (+ *Akk.*); **(g)** ∼ **expenses** die Kosten decken; **£10 will** ∼ **my needs for the journey** 10 Pfund werden für die Reisekosten reichen; **(h)** (shield) decken; **I'll keep you** ∼**ed** ich gebe dir Deckung; **(i)** ∼ **oneself** (fig.) sich absichern; (Insurance) ∼ **oneself against sth.** sich gegen etw. versichern; **(j)** (aim gun at) in Schach halten (ugs.); **I've got you** ∼**ed** ich habe meine Waffe auf dich gerichtet

∼ **for** *v.t.* einspringen für

∼ '**in** *v.t.* überdachen; (fill in) zuschütten

∼ '**up 1** *v.t.* (conceal) zudecken; (fig.) vertuschen. **2** *v.i.* (fig.: conceal) es vertuschen; ∼ **up for sb.** jmdn. decken

coverage /'kʌvərɪdʒ/ *n., no pl.* **(a)** (Journ., Radio, Telev.: treatment) Berichterstattung, *die* (**of** über + *Akk.*); **newspaper/broadcast** ∼: Berichterstattung in der Presse/in Funk und Fernsehen; **give sth.** [**full/limited**] ∼: [ausführlich/kurz] über etw. (*Akk.*) berichten; **(b)** (Advertising) Abdeckung des Marktes

coverall /'kʌvərɔ:l/ *n., usu. in pl.* (esp. Amer.) Overall, *der;* (for baby) Strampelanzug, *der*

cover: ∼ **charge** *n.* [Preis für das] Gedeck; ∼ **girl** *n.* Covergirl, *das*

covering /'kʌvərɪŋ/ *n.* (material) Decke, *die;* (of chair, bed) Bezug, *der*

covering: ∼ **letter** *n.* Begleitbrief, *der;* ∼ **note** *n.* [kurzes] Begleitschreiben

'**cover note** *n.* (Insurance) Deckungskarte, *die*

covert /'kʌvət/ *adj.* versteckt

'**cover-up** *n.* Verschleierung, *die*

covet /'kʌvɪt/ *v.t.* begehren (geh.)

covetous /'kʌvɪtəs/ *adj.* begehrlich (geh.)

cow[1] /kaʊ/ *n.* **(a)** Kuh, *die;* **till the** ∼**s come home** (fig. coll.) bis in alle Ewigkeit (ugs.); **(b)** (sl. derog.: woman) Kuh, *die* (salopp abwertend)

cow[2] *v.t.* einschüchtern; ∼ **sb. into submission** jmdn. so einschüchtern, dass er sich unterordnet

coward /'kaʊəd/ *n.* Feigling, *der*

cowardice /'kaʊədɪs/ *n.* Feigheit, *die*

cowardly /'kaʊədlɪ/ *adj.* feig[e]

'**cowboy** *n.* Cowboy, *der;* (Brit. coll.: unscrupulous businessman, tradesman, etc.) Betrüger, *der*

cower /'kaʊə(r)/ *v.i.* sich ducken; (squat) kauern

'**cowherd** *n.* ▶ **887**] Kuhhirte, *der*

cowl /kaʊl/ *n.* **(a)** (of monk) Kutte, *die;* (hood) Kapuze, *die;* **(b)** (of chimney) Schornsteinaufsatz, *der*

co-worker /'kəʊwɜ:kə(r)/ *n.* Kollege, *der*/Kollegin, *die*

cow: ∼**shed** *n.* Kuhstall, *der;* ∼**slip** *n.* Schlüsselblume, *die*

cox /kɒks/ **1** *n.* Steuermann, *der.* **2** *v.t. & i.* (esp. Rowing) steuern

coxswain /'kɒkswein, 'kɒksn/ ⇒ **cox 1**

coy /kɔɪ/ *adj.* gespielt schüchtern; geziert ‹*Benehmen, Ausdruck*›

coyote /kə'jəʊtɪ, 'kɔɪəʊt/ *n.* (Zool.) Kojote, *der*

cozily, cozy (Amer.) ⇒ **cos-**

crab /kræb/ *n.* Krabbe, *die*

'**crab apple** *n.* Holzapfel, *der*

crack /kræk/ **1** *n.* **(a)** (noise) Krachen, *das;* **give sb./have a fair** ∼ **of the whip** (fig.) jmdm. eine Chance geben/eine Chance haben; **(b)** (in china, glass, eggshell, ice, etc.) Sprung, *der;* (in rock) Spalte, *die;* (chink) Spalt, *der;* **there's a** ∼ **in the ceiling** die Decke hat einen Riß; **(c)** (blow) Schlag, *der;* **(d)** (coll.: try) Versuch, *der;* **have a** ∼ **at sth./at doing sth.** etw. in Angriff nehmen/versuchen, etw. zu tun; **(e)** **the/at the** ∼ **of dawn** (coll.) der/bei Tagesanbruch; **(f)** (coll.: wisecrack) [geistreicher] Witz; **(g)** (sl.: drug) ∼ [**cocaine**] Crack, *das.* **2** *adj.* (coll.) erstklassig. **3** *v.t.* **(a)** (break, lit. or fig.) knacken ‹*Nuss, Problem*›; knacken (salopp) ‹*Safe, Kode*›; **(b)** (make a ∼ in) anschlagen ‹*Porzellan, Glas*›; **(c)** ∼ **a whip** mit einer Peitsche knallen; ∼ **the whip** (fig.) Druck machen (ugs.); **(d)** ∼ **a joke** einen Witz machen. **4** *v.i.* **(a)** ‹*Porzellan, Glas*›: einen Sprung/Sprünge bekommen; ‹*Haut*›: aufspringen, rissig werden; ‹*Eis*›: Risse bekommen; **(b)** (make sound) ‹*Peitsche*›: knallen; ‹*Gelenk*›: knacken; ‹*Gewehr*›: krachen; **(c)** (coll.) **get** ∼**ing!** mach los! (ugs.); **let's get** ∼**ing** fangen wir endlich an; **get** ∼**ing** [**with sth.**] [mit etw.] loslegen (ugs.)

∼ '**down** *v.i.* (coll.) ∼ **down** [**on sb./sth.**] [gegen jmdn./ etw.] [hart] vorgehen

∼ '**up** (coll.) **1** *v.i.* ‹*Flugzeug usw.*›: auseinander brechen; ‹*Gesellschaft, Person*›: zusammenbrechen. **2** *v.t.* **she/it is not all she/it is** ∼**ed up to be** so toll ist sie/es nun auch wieder nicht[, wie sie/es dargestellt wird]

cracked /krækt/ *adj.* **(a)** gesprungen ‹*Porzellan, Ziegel, Glas*›; rissig, aufgesprungen ‹*Haut, Erdboden*›; rissig ‹*Verputz*›; **(b)** (coll.: crazy) übergeschnappt (ugs.)

cracker /'krækə(r)/ *n.* **(a)** [**Christmas**] ∼ ≈ Knallbonbon, *der od. das;* **(b)** (firework) Knallkörper, *der;* **(c)** (biscuit) Cracker, *der*

crackers /'krækəz/ *pred. adj.* (Brit. coll.) übergeschnappt (ugs.)

crackle /'krækl/ **1** *v.i.* knistern; ‹*Feuer*›: prasseln. **2** *n.* Knistern, *das;* (of fire) Prasseln, *das*

crackling /'kræklɪŋ/ *n.*, *no pl.*, *no indef. art.* (Cookery) Kruste, *die*

'crackpot *n.* (coll.) Spinner, *der*/Spinnerin, *die* (ugs.); *attrib.* ~ **ideas/schemes** hirnrissige Ideen/Pläne (abwertend)

cradle /kreɪdl/ **1** *n.* (cot, lit. or fig.) Wiege, *die;* **from the** ~ **to the grave** von der Wiege bis zur Bahre. **2** *v.t.* wiegen; ~ **sb./sth. in one's arms** jmdn. in den Armen/etw. im Arm halten

craft /krɑːft/ *n.* **(a)** (trade) Handwerk, *das;* (art) Kunsthandwerk, *das;* **(b)** *no pl.* (skill) Kunstfertigkeit, *die;* **(c)** *no pl.* (cunning) List, *die;* **(d)** *pl. same* (boat) Boot, *das*

craftsman /'krɑːftsmən/ *n.*, *pl.* **craftsmen** /'krɑːftsmən/ Handwerker, *der*

craftsmanship /'krɑːftsmənʃɪp/ *n.*, *no pl.* (skilled workmanship) handwerkliches Können

crafty /'krɑːftɪ/ *adj.* listig

crag /kræg/ *n.* Felsspitze, *die*

craggy /'krægɪ/ *adj.* (rugged) zerklüftet; zerfurcht ⟨*Gesicht*⟩; (rocky) felsig

cram /kræm/ **1** *v.t.*, **-mm-:** **(a)** (overfill) voll stopfen (ugs.); (force) stopfen; **the bus was** ~**med** der Bus war gerammelt voll (ugs.) *od.* war überfüllt; **(b)** (for examination) ~ **pupils** mit Schülern pauken (ugs.); **(c)** (feed to excess) mästen. **2** *v.i.*, **-mm-** (for examination) büffeln (ugs.); pauken (ugs.)

cramp /kræmp/ **1** *n.* (Med.) Krampf, *der;* **suffer an attack of** ~: einen Krampf bekommen; **have** ~ **[in one's leg/arm]** einen Krampf [im Bein/Arm] haben. **2** *v.t.* (confine) einengen; ~ **[up]** zusammenpferchen; ~ **sb.'s style** jmdn. einengen

cramped /kræmpt/ *adj.* eng ⟨*Raum*⟩; gedrängt ⟨*Handschrift*⟩

cranberry /'krænbərɪ/ *n.* Preiselbeere, *die*

crane /kreɪn/ **1** *n.* **(a)** (machine) Kran, *der;* **(b)** (Ornith.) Kranich, *der.* **2** *v.t.* ~ **one's neck** den Hals recken. **3** *v.i.* den Hals recken; ~ **forward** den Hals [nach vorn] recken

crane-fly *n.* Schnake, *die*

crank¹ /kræŋk/ **1** *n.* (Mech. Engin.) [Hand]kurbel, *die.* **2** *v.t.* ~ **[up]** ankurbeln

crank² *n.* Irre, *der/die* (salopp); **health** ~: Gesundheitsfanatiker, *der*/-fanatikerin, *die* (ugs.)

'crankshaft *n.* (Mech. Engin.) Kurbelwelle, *die*

cranky /'kræŋkɪ/ *adj.* **(a)** (eccentric) schrullig; verschroben; **(b)** (Amer.: ill-tempered) griesgrämig

cranny /'krænɪ/ *n.* Ritze, *die; see also* **nook**

crap /kræp/ (coarse) **1** *n.* **(a)** (faeces) Scheiße, *die* (derb); **have a** ~: scheißen (derb); **(b)** (nonsense) Scheiß, *der* (salopp abwertend). **2** *v.i.*, **-pp-** scheißen (derb)

craps /kræps/ *n. pl.* (Amer.: dice game) Craps, *das*

crash /kræʃ/ **1** *n.* **(a)** (noise) Krachen, *das;* **fall with a** ~: mit einem lauten Krach fallen; **a sudden** ~ **of thunder** ein plötzlicher Donnerschlag; **(b)** (collision) Zusammenstoß, *der;* **plane/train** ~: Flugzeug-/Eisenbahnunglück, *das;* **have a** ~: einen Unfall haben; **in a [car]** ~: bei einem [Auto]unfall; **(c)** (Finance etc.) Zusammenbruch, *der.* **2** *v.i.* **(a)** (make a noise, go noisily) krachen; **(b)** (have a collision) einen Unfall haben; ⟨*Flugzeug, Flieger:*⟩ abstürzen; ~ **into sth.** gegen etw. krachen; **(c)** (Finance etc., Computing) zusammenbrechen. **3** *v.t.* **(a)** (smash) schmettern; **(b)** (cause to have collision) einen Unfall haben mit

crash: ~ **barrier** *n.* Leitplanke, *die;* ~ **course** *n.* Intensivkurs, *der;* ~ **helmet** *n.* Sturzhelm, *der;* ~**land** **1** *v.t.* ~**-land a plane** mit einem Flugzeug bruchlanden; **2** *v.i.* bruchlanden

crass /kræs/ *adj.* krass; grob ⟨*Benehmen*⟩; haarsträubend ⟨*Dummheit, Unwissenheit*⟩; (very stupid) strohdumm

crate /kreɪt/ *n.* Kiste, *die;* **a** ~ **of beer/lemonade** ein Kasten Bier/Limonade

crater /'kreɪtə(r)/ *n.* Krater, *der*

cravat /krə'væt/ *n.* (scarf) Halstuch, *das;* (necktie) Krawatte, *die*

crave /kreɪv/ **1** *v.t.* **(a)** (beg) erbitten; erflehen ⟨*Gnade*⟩; **(b)** (long for) sich sehnen nach. **2** *v.i.* ~ **for** *or* **after** ⇒ **1**

craving /'kreɪvɪŋ/ *n.* Verlangen, *das;* **have a** ~ **for sth.** ein [dringendes] Verlangen nach etw. haben

crawl /krɔːl/ **1** *v.i.* **(a)** kriechen; **the baby/insect** ~**s along the ground** das Baby/Insekt krabbelt über den Boden; **(b)** (coll.: behave abjectly) kriechen (abwertend); ~ **to sb.** vor jmdm. buckeln *od.* kriechen; **(c)** **be** ~**ing** (be covered or filled) wimmeln (**with** von); **(d)** ⇒ **creep 1** b. **2** *n.* **(a)** ▶ **1102** Kriechen, *das;* (of insect, baby also) Krabbeln, *das;* (slow speed) Schneckentempo, *das;* **move/go at a** ~: sich im Schneckentempo bewegen/im Schneckentempo fahren; **(b)** (swimming stroke) Kraulen, *das*

crawler lane /'krɔːlə leɪn/ *n.* Kriechspur, *die*

crayfish /'kreɪfɪʃ/ *n.*, *pl. same* Flusskrebs, *der*

crayon /'kreɪən/ *n.* (pencil) **[coloured]** ~: Buntstift, *der;* (of wax) Wachsmalstift, *der;* (of chalk) Kreidestift, *der*

craze /kreɪz/ **1** *n.* Begeisterung, *die;* Fimmel, *der* (ugs. abwertend); **there's a** ~ **for doing sth.** es ist gerade große Mode, etw. zu tun. **2** *v.t.* **be [half]** ~**d with pain/grief** *etc.* [halb] wahnsinnig vor Schmerz/Kummer *usw.* sein; **a** ~**d look/expression [on sb.'s face]** ein vom Wahnsinn verzerrtes Gesicht

crazy /'kreɪzɪ/ *adj.* **(a)** (mad) verrückt; wahnsinnig; **go** ~: verrückt *od.* wahnsinnig werden; **drive** *or* **send sb.** ~: jmdn. verrückt *od.* wahnsinnig machen (ugs.); **(b)** (coll.: enthusiastic) **be** ~ **about sb./sth.** nach jmdm./etw. verrückt sein (ugs.); **(c)** ~ **paving** gestückeltes Pflaster

creak /kriːk/ **1** *n.* (of gate, door) Quietschen, *das;* (of floorboard, door, chair) Knarren, *das.* **2** *v.i.* ⟨*Tor, Tür:*⟩ quietschen; ⟨*Diele, Tür, Stuhl:*⟩ knarren

cream /kriːm/ **1** *n.* **(a)** Sahne, *die;* **(b)** (Cookery) (sauce) Sahnesoße, *die;* (dessert) Creme, *die;* ~ **of mushroom soup** Champignoncremesuppe, *die;* **(c)** (cosmetic preparation) Creme, *die;* **(d)** (fig.: best) Beste, *das;* **the** ~ **of society** die Creme der Gesellschaft; **(e)** (colour) Creme, *das.* **2** *adj.* ~**[coloured]** creme[farben]. **3** *v.t.* cremig rühren *od.* schlagen; schaumig rühren ⟨*Butter*⟩; ~**ed potatoes** Kartoffelpüree, *das*

~ **'off** *v.t.* ~ **off the best players** die besten Spieler wegschnappen (ugs.)

cream: ~ **cake** *n.* Cremetorte, *die;* (with whipped ~) Sahnetorte, *die;* ~ **'cheese** *n.* ≈ Frischkäse, *der;* ~ **'tea** *n.* Tee mit Marmeladetörtchen und Sahne

creamy /'kriːmɪ/ *adj.* (with cream) sahnig; (like cream) cremig

crease /kriːs/ **1** *n.* (pressed) Bügelfalte, *die;* (accidental; in skin) Falte, *die;* (in fabric) Falte, *die;* Knitter, *der;* **put a** ~ **in trousers** Bügelfalten in Hosen bügeln. **2** *v.t.* (press) eine Falte/Falten bügeln in (+ *Akk.*); (accidentally) knittern; (extensively) zerknittern. **3** *v.i.* Falten bekommen; knittern

'crease-resistant *adj.* knitterfrei

create /kriˈeɪt/ **1** *v.t.* **(a)** schaffen; erschaffen (geh.); verursachen ⟨*Verwirrung*⟩; machen ⟨*Eindruck*⟩; ⟨*Sache:*⟩ mit sich bringen, ⟨*Person:*⟩ machen ⟨*Schwierigkeiten*⟩; ~ **a scene** eine Szene machen; ~ **a sensation** für eine Sensation sorgen; **(b)** (design) schaffen; kreieren ⟨*Mode, Stil*⟩; **(c)** (invest with rank) ernennen; ~ **sb. a peer** jmdn. zum Peer erheben *od.* ernennen. **2** *v.i.* (Brit. coll.: make a fuss) Theater machen (ugs.)

creation /kriˈeɪʃn/ *n.* **(a)** *no pl.* (act of creating) Schaffung, *die;* (of the world) Erschaffung, *die;* Schöpfung, *die* (geh.); **(b)** *no pl.* (all created things) Schöpfung, *die;* **(c)** (Fashion) Kreation, *die*

creative /kriˈeɪtɪv/ *adj.* schöpferisch; kreativ

creator /kriˈeɪtə(r)/ *n.* Schöpfer, *der*/Schöpferin, *die;* **the C**~: der Schöpfer

creature /'kriːtʃə(r)/ *n.* **(a)** (created being) Geschöpf, *das;* **all living** ~**s** alle Lebewesen; **(b)** (human being) Geschöpf, *das;* (derog.) Kerl, *der* (abwertend); (woman) **the** ~ **with the red hair** die mit den roten Haaren (ugs.); ~ **of habit** Gewohnheitsmensch, *der*

crèche /kreʃ/ *n.* [Kinder]krippe, *die*

credential /krɪˈdenʃl/ *n.*, *usu. in pl.* (testimonial) Zeugnis, *das*

credibility /kredɪˈbɪlɪtɪ/ *n.* Glaubwürdigkeit, *die*

credible /'kredɪbl/ *adj.* glaubwürdig ⟨*Person, Aussage*⟩

credibly /'kredɪblɪ/ *adv.* glaubwürdig; glaubhaft

credit /'kredɪt/ **1** *n.* **(a)** *no pl.* (commendation) Anerkennung, *die;* (honour) Ehre, *die;* **give sb. [the]** ~ **for sth.**

jmdm. für etw. Anerkennung zollen (geh.); **take the ∼ for sth.** die Anerkennung für etw. einstecken; [**we must give**] **∼ where ∼ is due** Ehre, wem Ehre gebührt; **it is** [**much** or **greatly/little**] **to sb.'s/sth.'s ∼ that ...:** es macht jmdm./einer Sache [große/wenig] Ehre, dass ...; **it is to his ∼ that ...:** es ehrt ihn, dass ...; **be a ∼ to sb./ sth.** jmdm./einer Sache Ehre machen; (**b**) **∼s, ∼ titles** (at beginning of film) Vorspann, *der;* (at end) Nachspann, *der;* (**c**) *no pl., no art.* (belief) Glaube, *der;* **gain ∼:** an Glaubwürdigkeit gewinnen; (**d**) *no pl.* (Commerc.) Kredit, *der;* **give** [**sb.**] **∼:** [jmdm.] Kredit geben; **their ∼ is excellent** sie sind unbedingt kreditwürdig; (**e**) *no pl.* (Finance, Bookk.) Guthaben, *das;* **be in ∼** ⟨*Konto:*⟩ im Haben sein; ⟨*Person:*⟩ mit seinem Konto im Haben sein; (**f**) (fig.) **have sth. to one's ∼:** etw. vorzuweisen haben; **he's cleverer than I gave him ∼ for** er ist klüger, als ich dachte. **2** *v.t.* (**a**) (believe) glauben; (**b**) (accredit) **∼ sb. with sth.** jmdm. etw. zutrauen; **∼ sth. with sth.** einer Sache (*Dat.*) etw. zuschreiben; (**c**) (Finance, Bookk.) gutschreiben; **∼ £10 to sb./sb.'s account** jmdm./jmds. Konto 10 Pfund gutschreiben

creditable /'krɛdɪtəbl/ *adj.* anerkennenswert

credit: ∼ card *n.* ▸938⏌ Kreditkarte, *die;* **∼ facilities** *n. pl.* [Kredit]fazilität, *die* (fachspr.); **∼ limit** *n.* Kreditlinie, *die;* **∼ note** *n.* Gutschein, *der*

creditor /'krɛdɪtə(r)/ *n.* Gläubiger, *der/*Gläubigerin, *die*

credit: ∼ rating *n.* Einschätzung der Kreditwürdigkeit; **have a good/bad ∼ rating** als kreditwürdig/kreditunwürdig eingeschätzt werden; **∼ sale** *n.* Kreditkauf, *der;* **∼ side** *n.* (Finance) Habenseite, *die;* (fig.) **on the ∼ side she has experience** für sie spricht ihre Erfahrung; **∼ squeeze** *n.* Kreditrestriktion, *die;* **∼worthy** *adj.* kreditwürdig

credulity /krɪ'dju:lɪtɪ/ *n., no pl.* Leichtgläubigkeit, *die*

credulous /'krɛdjʊləs/ *adj.* leichtgläubig

creed /kri:d/ *n.* (lit. or fig.) Glaubensbekenntnis, *das*

creek /kri:k/ *n.* (**a**) (Brit.: inlet on sea-coast) [kleine] Bucht; (**b**) (short arm of river) [kurzer] Flussarm; (**c**) **be up the ∼** (coll.: be in difficulties or trouble) in der Klemme *od.* Tinte sitzen (ugs.)

creep /kri:p/ **1** *v.i.*, **crept** /krɛpt/ (**a**) kriechen; (move timidly, slowly, stealthily) schleichen; **∼ and crawl** (fig.) kriechen; (**b**) **make sb.'s flesh ∼:** jmdm. eine Gänsehaut über den Rücken jagen. **2** *n., in pl.* (coll.) **give sb. the ∼s** jmdm. nicht [ganz] geheuer sein

∼ 'in *v.i.* [sich] hinein-/hereinschleichen; (fig.) ⟨*Irrtum, Enttäuschung usw.:*⟩ sich einschleichen

∼ 'on *v.i.* **time is ∼ing on** die Zeit verrinnt [unaufhaltsam]

∼ 'up *v.i.* (approach) sich anschleichen; **∼ up on sb.** sich an jmdn. anschleichen

creeper /'kri:pə(r)/ *n.* (Bot.) (growing along ground) Kriechpflanze, *die;* (growing up wall etc.) Kletterpflanze, *die*

creepy /'kri:pɪ/ *adj.* unheimlich; gruselig, schaurig ⟨*Geschichte, Film*⟩

cremate /krɪ'meɪt/ *v.t.* einäschern

cremation /krɪ'meɪʃn/ *n.* Einäscherung, *die*

crematorium /krɛmə'tɔ:rɪəm/ *n., pl.* **crematoria** /krɛmə'tɔ:rɪə/ or **∼s** Krematorium, *das*

creosote /'kri:əsəʊt/ **1** *n.* Kreosot, *das.* **2** *v.t.* mit Kreosot behandeln

crêpe /kreɪp/ *n.* Krepp, *der*

crept ⇒ **creep 1**

crescendo /krɪ'ʃɛndəʊ/ *n., pl.* **∼s** (Mus.) Crescendo, *das;* (fig.) Zunahme, *die;* **reach a ∼** (fig. coll.) einen Höhepunkt erreichen

crescent /'krɛsənt/ **1** *n.* (**a**) Mondsichel, *die;* (as emblem) Halbmond, *der;* **∼-shaped** halbmondförmig; (**b**) (Brit.: street) [kleinere] halbkreisförmige Straße. **2** *adj.* **the ∼ moon** die Mondsichel

cress /krɛs/ *n.* Kresse, *die*

crest /krɛst/ *n.* (**a**) (on bird's or animal's head) Kamm, *der;* (**b**) (top of mountain or wave) Kamm, *der;* [**be/ride**] **on the ∼ of a** or **the wave** (fig.) ganz oben [sein/schwimmen]; (**c**) (Her.) Helmzier, *die;* (emblem) Emblem, *das*

'crestfallen *adj.* (fig.) niedergeschlagen

Crete /kri:t/ *pr. n.* Kreta (*das*)

cretin /'krɛtɪn/ *n.* (**a**) (Med.) Kretin, *der;* (**b**) (coll.: fool) Trottel, *der* (ugs. abwertend)

Creutzfeldt-Jakob disease /'krɔɪtsfɛlt'jækɒb/ *n.* ▸865⏌ (Med.) Creutzfeldt-Jakob-Krankheit, *die*

crevasse /krɪ'væs/ *n.* Gletscherspalte, *die*

crevice /'krɛvɪs/ *n.* Spalt, *der*

crew /kru:/ **1** *n.* (**a**) (of ship, aircraft, etc.) Besatzung, *die;* Crew, *die;* (excluding officers) Mannschaft, *die;* Crew, *die;* (Sport) Mannschaft, *die;* Crew, *die;* (**b**) (associated body) Gruppe, *die;* (set, often derog.) Haufen, *der;* **a motley ∼:** ein bunt zusammengewürfelter Haufen. **2** *v.i.* die Mannschaft/ Mitglied der Mannschaft sein. **3** *v.t.* **∼ a boat** Mitglied der Mannschaft/die Mannschaft eines Bootes sein

'crew cut *n.* Bürstenschnitt, *der*

crib /krɪb/ **1** *n.* (**a**) (cot) Gitterbett, *das;* (**b**) (model of manger-scene; manger) Krippe, *die;* (**c**) (coll.: translation) Klatsche, *die* (Schülerspr.). **2** *v.t.*, **-bb-** (coll.: plagiarize) abkupfern (salopp)

crick /krɪk/ **1** *n.* **a ∼ [in one's neck/back]** ein steifer Hals/Rücken. **2** *v.t.* **∼ one's neck/back** einen steifen Hals/Rücken bekommen

cricket[1] /'krɪkɪt/ *n.* (Sport) Kricket, *das;* **it's/that's not ∼** (Brit. dated coll.) das ist nicht die feine Art (ugs.)

cricket[2] *n.* (Zool.) Grille, *die*

cricket: ∼ ball *n.* Kricketball, *der;* **∼ bat** *n.* Schlagholz, *das*

cricketer /'krɪkɪtə(r)/ *n.* ▸887⏌ Kricketspieler, *der/*-spielerin, *die*

cricket: ∼ match *n.* Kricketspiel, *das;* **∼ pitch** *n.* Kricketfeld, *das* (*zwischen den Toren*)

crime /kraɪm/ *n.* (**a**) Verbrechen, *das;* (**b**) collect., *no pl.* **a wave of ∼:** eine Welle von Straftaten; **∼ doesn't pay** Verbrechen lohnen sich nicht; (**c**) (fig. coll.: shameful action) Sünde, *die*

'crime rate *n.* Kriminalitätsrate, *die*

criminal /'krɪmɪnl/ **1** *adj.* (**a**) (illegal) kriminell; strafbar; (concerned with criminals and crime) Straf-; **∼ act** or **deed/ offence** Straftat, *die;* **take ∼ proceedings against sb.** strafrechtlich gegen jmdn. vorgehen; (**b**) (fig. coll.) kriminell (ugs.); **it's a ∼ waste** es ist eine sträfliche Verschwendung. **2** *n.* Kriminelle, *der/die*

criminal: ∼ charge *n.* Anklage, *die;* **face ∼ charges** [**for sth.**] sich [wegen etw.] vor Gericht zu verantworten haben; **there are ∼ charges against him** er steht unter Anklage; **C∼ Investigation Department** *n.* (Brit.) Kriminalpolizei, *die;* **∼ 'law** *n.* Strafrecht, *das*

criminally /'krɪmɪnəlɪ/ *adv.* kriminell; (according to criminal law) strafrechtlich

criminal 'record *n.* Strafregister, *das;* **have a ∼:** vorbestraft sein

criminology /krɪmɪ'nɒlədʒɪ/ *n.* Kriminologie, *die*

crimson /'krɪmzn/ **1** *adj.* purpurrot; **turn ∼** ⟨*Himmel:*⟩ sich blutrot färben; (with anger) ⟨*Person:*⟩ rot anlaufen; (blush) puterrot werden. **2** *n.* Purpurrot, *das*

cringe /krɪndʒ/ *v.i.* zusammenzucken; ⟨*Hund:*⟩ sich ducken, zusammenzucken; **∼ at sth.** bei etw. zusammenzucken; **∼ away** or **back** [**from sb./sth.**] [vor jmdm./etw.] zurückschrecken; **it makes me ∼** (in disgust) da wird mir schlecht

cringing /'krɪndʒɪŋ/ *adj.* kriecherisch (abwertend)

crinkle /'krɪŋkl/ **1** *n.* Knick, *der;* (in fabric) Knitterfalte, *die;* (in hair) Kräusel, *die.* **2** *v.t.* knicken; zerknittern ⟨*Stoff, Papier*⟩; kräuseln ⟨*Haar*⟩. **3** *v.i.* ⟨*Stoff, Papier:*⟩ knittern; ⟨*Haar:*⟩ sich kräuseln

crinoline /'krɪnəlɪn, 'krɪnəli:n/ *n.* (Hist.) Krinoline, *die*

cripple /'krɪpl/ **1** *n.* (lit. or fig.) Krüppel, *der.* **2** *v.t.* zum Krüppel machen; (fig.) lähmen

crippled /'krɪpld/ *adj.* verkrüppelt ⟨*Arm, Baum, Bettler*⟩; **be ∼ with rheumatism** durch Rheuma gelähmt sein; **industry was ∼ by the strikes** die Streiks haben die ganze Industrie lahmgelegt

crisis /'kraɪsɪs/ n., pl. **crises** /'kraɪsiːz/ Krise, die

crisp /krɪsp/ **1** adj. knusprig ⟨Brot, Keks, Speck⟩; knackig ⟨Apfel, Gemüse⟩; trocken ⟨Herbstblätter, Zweige⟩; frisch [gebügelt/gestärkt] ⟨Wäsche⟩; [druck]frisch ⟨Banknote⟩; verharscht ⟨Schnee⟩; scharf ⟨Umrisse, Kanten⟩; knapp [und klar] ⟨Stil⟩. **2** n. (a) usu. in pl. (Brit.: potato ～) [Kartoffel]chip, der; **be burned to a ～:** verbrannt sein

'crispbread n. Knäckebrot, das

crispy /'krɪspɪ/ adj. knusprig ⟨Brot, Keks, Speck⟩; knackig ⟨Apfel, Gemüse⟩

criss-cross /'krɪskrɒs/ **1** adj. ～ **pattern** Muster aus gekreuzten Linien. **2** adv. kreuz und quer. **3** v.t. (intersect repeatedly) wiederholt schneiden

criterion /kraɪ'tɪərɪən/ n., pl. **criteria** /kraɪ'tɪərɪə/ Kriterium, das

critic /'krɪtɪk/ n. ▶ 887 | Kritiker, der/Kritikerin, die; **literary ～:** Literaturkritiker, der/-kritikerin, die

critical /'krɪtɪkl/ adj. (a) kritisch; **be ～ of sb./sth.** jmdn./etw. kritisieren; **cast a ～ eye over sth.** etw. mit kritischen Augen betrachten; **the play received ～ acclaim** das Stück fand die Anerkennung der Kritik; **(b)** (involving risk, crucial) kritisch ⟨Zustand, Punkt, Phase⟩; entscheidend ⟨Faktor, Test⟩

critically /'krɪtɪkəlɪ/ adv. kritisch; **be ～ ill** ernstlich krank sein

criticise ⇨ criticize

criticism /'krɪtɪsɪzm/ n. Kritik, die **(of** an + Dat.); **come in for a lot of ～:** heftig kritisiert werden; **be open to ～:** der Kritik ausgesetzt sein; **literary ～:** Literaturkritik, die

criticize /'krɪtɪsaɪz/ v.t. kritisieren **(for** wegen); **～ sb. for sth.** jmdn. wegen etw. kritisieren

critique /krɪ'tiːk/ n. Kritik, die

croak /krəʊk/ **1** n. (of frog) Quaken, das; (of raven, person) Krächzen, das. **2** v.i. ⟨Frosch:⟩ quaken; ⟨Rabe, Person:⟩ krächzen. **3** v.t. krächzen

Croat /'krəʊæt/ ▶ 897 |, ▶ 947 | n. (a) (person) Kroate, der/ Kroatin, die; (b) (language) Kroatisch, das

Croatia /krəʊ'eɪʃə/ pr. n. Kroatien (das)

crochet /'krəʊʃeɪ, 'krəʊʃɪ/ **1** n. Häkelarbeit, die; ～ **hook** Häkelhaken, der. **2** v.t., p.t. and p.p. ～**ed** /'krəʊ ʃeɪd, 'krəʊʃɪd/ häkeln

crock¹ /krɒk/ n. (pot) Topf, der (aus Ton)

crock² n. (coll.) (a) (person) Wrack, das (fig.); (b) (vehicle) [Klapper]kiste, die (ugs.)

crockery /'krɒkərɪ/ n. Geschirr, das

crocodile /'krɒkədaɪl/ n. Krokodil, das; (skin) Krokodilleder, das

'crocodile tears n. pl. Krokodilstränen Pl. (ugs.)

crocus /'krəʊkəs/ n. Krokus, der

croft /krɒft/ n. (Brit.) (a) [kleines] Stück Acker-/Weideland; (b) (smallholding) [kleines] Pachtgut

crony /'krəʊnɪ/ n. Kumpel, der; (female) Freundin, die; **they were old cronies** sie waren gute, alte Freunde

crook /krʊk/ **1** n. (a) (coll.: rogue) Gauner, der; (b) (staff) Hirtenstab, der; (of bishop) [Krumm]stab, der; (c) (hook) Haken, der; (of arm) [Arm]beuge, die. **2** v.t. biegen; ～ **one's finger** seinen Finger krümmen

crooked /'krʊkɪd/ adj. krumm; schief ⟨Lächeln⟩; (fig.: dishonest) betrügerisch; **the picture is ～:** das Bild hängt schief; **you've got your hat on ～:** dein Hut sitzt schief; **a ～ person** ein Gauner; **～ dealings** krumme Geschäfte

croon /kruːn/ v.t. & i. [leise] singen; ⟨Popsänger:⟩ schmachtend singen, schnulzen (ugs. abwertend)

crop /krɒp/ **1** n. (a) (Agric.) [Feld]frucht, die; (season's total yield) Ernte, die; (fig.) [An]zahl, die; ～ **of apples** Apfelernte, die; (b) (of bird) Kropf, der; (c) (of whip) [Peitschen]stiel, der; (d) (of hair) kurzer Haarschnitt; (style) Kurzhaarfrisur, die. **2** v.t., **-pp-** (cut off) abschneiden; (cut short) stutzen ⟨Bart, Haare, Hecken, Flügel⟩; ⟨Tier:⟩ abweiden ⟨Gras⟩

～ **up** v.i. (a) (occur) auftauchen; (be mentioned) erwähnt werden

cropper /'krɒpə(r)/ n. (coll.) **come a ～:** einen Sturz bauen (ugs.); (fig.) auf die Nase fallen (ugs.)

croquet /'krəʊkeɪ, 'krəʊkɪ/ n. Krocket[spiel], das

croquette /krɒ'ket/ n. (Cookery) Krokette, die

cross /krɒs/ **1** n. (a) Kreuz, das; (monument) [Gedenk]kreuz, das; (sign) Kreuzzeichen, das; **the C～:** das Kreuz [Christi]; (b) (～-shaped thing or mark) Kreuz[zeichen], das; (c) (mixture, compromise) Mittelding, das **(between** zwischen + Dat.); Mischung, die **(between** aus); (d) (affliction, cause of trouble) Kreuz, das; (e) (intermixture of breeds) Kreuzung, die; (f) (Footb.) Querpass, der; (Boxing) Cross, der. **2** v.t. (a) [über]kreuzen; ～ **one's arms/legs** die Arme verschränken/die Beine übereinander schlagen; ～ **one's fingers** or **keep one's fingers ～ed** [for sb.] (fig.) [jmdm.] die od. den Daumen drücken/halten; **I got a ～ed line** (Teleph.) es war jemand in der Leitung; (b) (go across) kreuzen; überqueren ⟨Straße, Gewässer, Gebirge⟩; durchqueren ⟨Land, Wüste, Zimmer⟩; ～ **the road** über die Straße gehen; **we can ～** abs. die Straße ist frei; **the bridge ～es the river** die Brücke führt über den Fluss; ～ **sb.'s mind** (fig.) jmdm. einfallen; ～ **sb.'s path** (fig.) jmdm. über den Weg laufen (ugs.); (c) (Brit.) ～ **a cheque** einen Scheck zur Verrechnung ausstellen; **a ～ed cheque** ein Verrechnungsscheck; (d) (make sign of ～ on) ～ **oneself** sich bekreuzigen; (e) (cause to interbreed) kreuzen; (～-fertilize) kreuzbefruchten. **3** v.i. (meet and pass) aneinander vorbeigehen; ～ **[in the post]** ⟨Briefe:⟩ sich kreuzen. **4** adj. (a) (transverse) Quer-; ～ **traffic** kreuzender Verkehr; (b) (coll.: peevish) verärgert; ärgerlich ⟨Worte⟩; **sb. will be ～:** jmd. wird ärgerlich od. böse werden; **be ～ with sb.** böse auf jmdn. od. mit jmdm. sein

～ **'off** v.t. streichen; ～ **a name off a list** einen Namen von einer Liste streichen

～ **'out** v.t. ausstreichen

～ **'over** v.t. überqueren; abs. hinübergehen

cross: ～**bar** n. (a) [Fahrrad]stange, die; (b) (Sport) Querlatte, die; ～**-bencher** /'krɒsbentʃə(r)/ n. Abgeordnete, der/die weder der Regierungspartei noch der Opposition angehört; ～**bow** /'krɒsbəʊ/ n. Armbrust, die; ～**breed 1** n. Hybride, die; (animal) Bastard, der; **2** v.t. kreuzen; ～**Channel** adj. ～**-Channel traffic/ferry** Verkehr/Fähre über den Kanal; ～**-check 1** n. Gegenprobe, die; **2** v.t. [nochmals] nachprüfen; nachkontrollieren; ～**-country 1** adj. Querfeldein-; ～**-country running** Crosslauf, der; **2** adv. querfeldein; ～**-examination** n. Kreuzverhör, das; ～**-examine** v.t. ins Kreuzverhör nehmen; ～**-eyed** /'krɒsaɪd/ adj. [nach innen] schielend; **be ～-eyed** schielen; ～**-'fertilize** v.t. fremdbestäuben; ～**fire** n. (lit. or fig.) Kreuzfeuer, das

crossing /'krɒsɪŋ/ n. (a) (act of going across) Überquerung, die; (b) (road or rail intersection) Kreuzung, die; (c) (pedestrian ～) Überweg, der

cross-legged /'krɒslegd/ adv. mit gekreuzten Beinen; (with feet across thighs) im Schneidersitz

crossly /'krɒslɪ/ adv. verärgert

cross: ～**patch** n. Griesgram, der; Miesepeter, der; ～**'purposes** n. pl. **talk at ～ purposes** aneinander vorbeireden; ～**-'reference 1** n. Querverweis, der; **2** v.t. verweisen ⟨Person, Stichwort⟩ **(to** auf + Akk.); mit Querverweisen versehen ⟨Eintrag, Werk⟩; ～**roads** n. sing. Kreuzung, die; (fig.) Wendepunkt, der; **be at/the ～roads** (fig.) am Scheideweg stehen; ～**-section** n. Querschnitt, der; (fig.) repräsentative Auswahl; **a ～-section of the population** ein Querschnitt durch die Bevölkerung; ～**wind** n. Seitenwind, der; ～**word** n. ～**word [puzzle]** Kreuzworträtsel, das

crotchet /'krɒtʃɪt/ n. (Brit. Mus.) Viertelnote, die

crouch /kraʊtʃ/ v.i. [sich zusammen]kauern; ～ **down** sich niederkauern; ⟨Person:⟩ sich hinhocken

croupier /'kruːpɪə(r), 'kruːpɪeɪ/ n. ▶ 887 | Croupier, der

crow /krəʊ/ **1** n. (a) (bird) Krähe, die; **as the ～ flies** Luftlinie; (b) (cry of cock) Krähen, das. **2** v.i. (a) ⟨Hahn:⟩ krähen; (b) (exult) ～ **over** [hämisch] frohlocken über (+ Akk.)

'crowbar n. Brechstange, die

crowd /kraʊd/ **1** n. (a) (large number of persons) Menschenmenge, die; ～**[s] of people** Menschenmassen Pl.; **stand out from the ～:** aus der Menge herausragen; (b) (mass of spectators, audience) Zuschauermenge, die; (c) (multitude) breite Masse; **follow the** ~ (fig.) mit der Herde laufen; **(d)** (coll.: company, set) Clique, *die;* **(e)** (large number of things) Menge, *die.* **2** *v.t.* **(a)** (fill, occupy, cram) füllen; ~ **sth. with sth.** etw. mit etw. voll stopfen; **the streets were ~ed with people** die Straßen waren voll mit Leuten; **(b)** (fig.: fill) ausfüllen. **3** *v.i.* (collect) sich sammeln; ~ **around sb./ sth.** sich um jmdn./etw. drängen *od.* scharen ~ **'out** *v.t.* herausdrängen

crowded /'kraʊdɪd/ *adj.* überfüllt; voll ⟨*Programm*⟩; ereignisreich ⟨*Tag, Leben, Karriere*⟩

crown /kraʊn/ **1** *n.* **(a)** Krone, *die;* **the C~:** die Krone; **(b)** (of head) Scheitel, *der;* (of tree, tooth) Krone, *die;* (of hat) Kopfteil, *das;* (thing that forms the summit) Gipfel, *der.* **2** *v.t.* **(a)** krönen; ~ **sb. king/queen** jmdn. zum König/zur Königin krönen; **(b)** (put finishing touch to) krönen; **to** ~ **[it] all** zur Krönung des Ganzen; (to make things even worse) um das Maß voll zu machen; **(c)** (Dent.) überkronen

Crown 'Court *n.* (Brit. Law) Krongericht, *das*

crowning /'kraʊnɪŋ/ **1** *n.* Krönung, *die.* **2** *adj.* krönend

crown: ~ **'jewels** *n. pl.* Kronjuwelen; **C~ 'prince** *n.* (lit. or fig.) Kronprinz, *der*

'crow's-nest *n.* (Naut.) Krähennest, *das;* Mastkorb, *der*

crucial /'kruːʃl/ *adj.* entscheidend (**to** für)

crucifix /'kruːsɪfɪks/ *n.* Kruzifix, *das*

crucifixion /kruːsɪ'fɪkʃn/ *n.* Kreuzigung, *die*

crucify /'kruːsɪfaɪ/ *v.t.* kreuzigen

crude /kruːd/ *adj.* **(a)** (in natural or raw state) roh; Roh-; ~ **oil/ore** Rohöl, *das*/Roherz, *das;* **(b)** (fig.: rough, unpolished) primitiv; simpel; grob ⟨*Entwurf, Skizze*⟩; **(c)** (rude, blunt) ungehobelt, ungeschliffen ⟨*Person, Benehmen*⟩; grob, derb ⟨*Worte*⟩; ordinär ⟨*Witz*⟩

crudeness /'kruːdnɪs/ *n., no pl.* **(a)** (roughness) Primitivität, *die;* (of theory, design, plan) Skizzenhaftigkeit, *die;* **(b)** (rudeness, bluntness) (of person, behaviour, manners) Ungeschliffenheit, *die;* (of words) Derbheit, *die;* (of joke) Geschmacklosigkeit, *die*

crudity /'kruːdɪtɪ/ *n.* **(a)** *no pl.* ⇒ **crudeness; (b)** (crude remark) Grobheit, *die*

cruel /'kruːəl/ *adj.*, (Brit.) **-ll-** grausam; **be** ~ **to animals** ein Tierquäler sein; **be** ~ **to be kind** in jmds. Interesse unbarmherzig sein müssen

cruelty /'kruːəltɪ/ *n.* Grausamkeit, *die;* ~ **to animals** Tierquälerei, *die;* ~ **to children** Kindesmisshandlung, *die*

cruise /kruːz/ **1** *v.i.* **(a)** (sail for pleasure) eine Kreuzfahrt machen; **(b)** (at random) ⟨*Fahrzeug, Fahrer:*⟩ herumfahren; **(c)** (at economical speed) ⟨*Fahrzeug:*⟩ mit Dauergeschwindigkeit fahren; ⟨*Flugzeug:*⟩ mit Reisegeschwindigkeit fliegen; **cruising speed** Reisegeschwindigkeit, *die.* **2** *n.* Kreuzfahrt, *die;* **go on** *or* **for a** ~: eine Kreuzfahrt machen

'cruise missile *n.* Marschflugkörper, *der*

cruiser /'kruːzə(r)/ *n.* Kreuzer, *der*

crumb /krʌm/ *n.* Krümel, *der;* Brösel, *der;* (fig.) Brocken, *der;* ~**[s] of comfort** kleiner Trost

crumble /'krʌmbl/ **1** *v.t.* zerbröckeln ⟨*Brot*⟩; zerkrümeln ⟨*Keks, Kuchen*⟩. **2** *v.i.* ⟨*Brot, Kuchen:*⟩ krümeln; ⟨*Gestein:*⟩ [zer]bröckeln; ⟨*Mauer:*⟩ zusammenfallen. **3** *n.* (Cookery) *mit Streuseln bestreutes und überbackenes* [*Apfel-, Rhabarber- usw.*]*dessert*

crumbly /'krʌmblɪ/ *adj.* krümelig ⟨*Keks, Kuchen, Brot*⟩; bröckelig ⟨*Gestein, Erde*⟩

crumpet /'krʌmpɪt/ *n.: weiches Hefeküchlein zum Toasten*

crumple /'krʌmpl/ **1** *v.t.* **(a)** (crush) zerdrücken; zerquetschen; **(b)** (ruffle, wrinkle) zerknittern ⟨*Kleider, Papier, Stoff*⟩; ~ **[up] a piece of paper** ein Stück Papier zerknüllen. **2** *v.i.* ⟨*Kleider, Stoff, Papier:*⟩ knittern

'crumple zone *n.* (Motor Veh.) Knautschzone, *die*

crunch /krʌntʃ/ **1** *v.t.* [geräuschvoll] knabbern ⟨*Keks, Zwieback*⟩. **2** *v.i.* ⟨*Schnee, Kies:*⟩ knirschen; ⟨*Eis:*⟩ [zer]splittern; **the wheels ~ed on the gravel** der Kies knirschte unter den Rädern. **3** *n.* (~ing noise) Knirschen, *das;* **when it comes to the** ~: wenn es hart auf hart geht

crunchy /'krʌntʃɪ/ *adj.* knusprig ⟨*Gebäck, Nüsse*⟩; knackig ⟨*Apfel*⟩

crusade /kruː'seɪd/ *n.* (Hist.; also fig.) Kreuzzug, *der*

crusader /kruː'seɪdə(r)/ *n.* (Hist.) Kreuzfahrer, *der*

crush /krʌʃ/ **1** *v.t.* **(a)** (compress with violence) quetschen; auspressen ⟨*Trauben, Obst*⟩; (kill, destroy) zerquetschen; zermalmen; **(b)** (reduce to powder) zerstampfen; zermahlen; zerstoßen ⟨*Gewürze, Tabletten*⟩; **(c)** (fig.: subdue, overwhelm) niederwerfen, niederschlagen ⟨*Aufstand*⟩; vernichten ⟨*Feind*⟩; zunichte machen ⟨*Hoffnungen*⟩; **(d)** (crumple, crease) zerknittern ⟨*Kleid, Stoff*⟩; zerdrücken, verbeulen ⟨*Hut*⟩. **2** *n.* **(a)** (crowded mass) Gedränge, *das;* **(b)** (coll.: infatuation) Schwärmerei, *die;* **have a** ~ **on sb.** in jmdn. verknallt sein (ugs.)

crust /krʌst/ *n.* **(a)** (of bread) Kruste, *die;* **(b)** (hard surface) Kruste, *die;* **the earth's** ~: die Erdkruste; **(c)** (of pie) Teigdeckel, *der*

crustacean /krʌ'steɪʃn/ *n.* Krusten- *od.* Krebstier, *das*

crusty /'krʌstɪ/ *adj.* **(a)** (crisp) knusprig; **(b)** (irritable) barsch

crutch /krʌtʃ/ *n.* (lit. or fig.) Krücke, *die*

crux /krʌks/ *n., pl.* ~**es** *or* **cruces** /'kruːsiːz/ (decisive point) Kern[punkt], *der;* **the** ~ **of the matter** der springende Punkt bei der Sache

cry /kraɪ/ **1** *n.* **(a)** (of grief) Schrei, *der;* (of words) Schreien, *das;* Geschrei, *das;* (of hounds or wolves) Heulen, *das;* **a** ~ **of pain/rage** ein Schmerzens-/Wutschrei; **a far** ~ **from ...** (fig.) etwas ganz anderes als ...; **(b)** (appeal, entreaty) Appell, *der;* **a** ~ **for help** ein Hilferuf; **(c)** (fit or spell of weeping) **have a good** ~: sich ausweinen. **2** *v.t.* **(a)** rufen; (loudly) schreien; **(b)** (weep) weinen; ~ **one's eyes out** sich (*Dat.*) die Augen ausweinen; ~ **oneself to sleep** sich in den Schlaf weinen. **3** *v.i.* **(a)** rufen; (loudly) schreien; ~ **[out] for sth./sb.** nach etw./jmdm. rufen *od.* schreien; ~ **with pain** vor Schmerz[en] schreien; **(b)** (weep) weinen (**over** wegen); ~ **for sth.** nach etw. weinen; (fig.) einer Sache (*Dat.*) nachweinen; **(c)** ⟨*Möwe:*⟩ schreien ~ **'off** *v.i.* absagen; einen Rückzieher machen (ugs.) ~ **'out** *v.i.* aufschreien; *see also* ~ **3 a**

crying /'kraɪɪŋ/ *attrib. adj.* weinend ⟨*Kind*⟩; schreiend ⟨*Unrecht*⟩; dringend ⟨*Bedürfnis, Notwendigkeit*⟩; **it is a** ~ **shame** es ist eine wahre Schande

crypt /krɪpt/ *n.* Krypta, *die*

cryptic /'krɪptɪk/ *adj.* **(a)** (secret, mystical) geheimnisvoll; **(b)** (obscure in meaning) undurchschaubar; kryptisch

crystal /'krɪstl/ **1** *n.* **(a)** (Chem., Min., etc.) Kristall, *der;* **(b)** ⇒ **crystal glass.** **2** *adj.* (made of ~ glass) kristallen

crystal: ~ **'ball** *n.* Kristallkugel, *die;* ~ **clear** *adj.* kristallklar; kristallen (geh.); (fig.) glasklar; ~**-gazing** *n.* Hellseherei, *die;* ~ **'glass** *n.* Bleikristall, *das;* Kristallglas, *das*

crystallisation, crystallise ⇒ **crystalliz-**

crystallization /krɪstəlar'zeɪʃn/ *n.* Kristallbildung, *die;* Kristallisation, *die*

crystallize /'krɪstəlaɪz/ **1** *v.t.* auskristallisieren ⟨*Salze*⟩; kandieren ⟨*Früchte*⟩. **2** *v.i.* kristallisieren; (fig.) feste Form annehmen

CSA *abbr.* (Brit.) **Child Support Agency**

cub /kʌb/ *n.* **(a)** Junge, *das;* (of wolf, fox, dog) Welpe, *der;* Junge, *das;* **(b)** Cub ⇒ **Cub Scout**

Cuba /'kjuːbə/ *n.* Kuba (*das*)

Cuban /'kjuːbn/ ▶ 947 **1** *adj.* kubanisch; **sb. is** ~: jmd. ist Kubaner/Kubanerin. **2** *n.* Kubaner, *der*/Kubanerin, *die*

cubby[hole] /'kʌbɪ(həʊl)/ *n.* Kämmerchen, *das;* (snug place) Kuschelecke, *die*

cube /kjuːb/ *n.* **(a)** Würfel, *der;* Kubus, *der* (fachspr.); **(b)** (Math.) dritte Potenz

cube 'root *n.* Kubikwurzel, *die*

cubic /'kjuːbɪk/ *adj.* **(a)** würfelförmig; **(b)** ▶ 1193 (of three dimensions) Kubik-; ~ **metre/centimetre/foot/yard** Kubikmeter/-zentimeter/-fuß/-yard, *der*

cubicle /'kjuːbɪkl/ *n.* **(a)** (sleeping compartment) Bettnische, *die;* **(b)** (for dressing, private discussion, etc.) Kabine, *die*

'Cub Scout *n.* Wölfling, *der*

cuckoo /'kʊkuː/ **1** *n.* Kuckuck, *der.* **2** *adj.* (coll.) meschugge *nicht attr.* (salopp)

'cuckoo clock n. Kuckucksuhr, *die*

cucumber /'kju:kʌmbə(r)/ n. [Salat]gurke, *die;* **be as cool as a** ~ (fig.) einen kühlen Kopf behalten

cud /kʌd/ n. wiedergekäutes Futter; **chew the** ~: wiederkäuen

cuddle /'kʌdl/ **1** n. Liebkosung, *die;* **give sb. a** ~: jmdn. drücken *od.* in den Arm nehmen; **have a** ~: schmusen. **2** *v.t.* schmusen mit; hätscheln ‹*kleines Kind*›. **3** *v.i.* schmusen

cuddly /'kʌdlɪ/ adj. (given to cuddling) verschmust

cuddly 'toy n. Kuscheltier, *das*

cudgel /'kʌdʒl/ **1** n. Knüppel, *der;* **take up the** ~**s for sb./sth.** (fig.) [energisch] für jmdn./etw. eintreten. **2** *v.t.*, (Brit.) **-ll-** knüppeln

cue¹ /kju:/ n. (Billiards etc.) Queue, *das;* Billardstock, *der*

cue² n. **(a)** (Theatre) Stichwort, *das;* (Music) Stichnoten *Pl.;* (Cinemat., Broadcasting) Zeichen zum Aufnahmebeginn; be/speak/play **on** ~: rechtzeitig einsetzen; **(b)** (sign when or how to act) Wink, *der;* **take one's** ~ **from sb.** (lit. or fig.) sich nach jmdm. richten

cuff¹ /kʌf/ n. **(a)** Manschette, *die;* **off the** ~ (fig.) aus dem Stegreif; **(b)** (Amer.: trouser turn-up) [Hosen]aufschlag, *der*

cuff² *v.t.* ~ **sb.'s ears,** ~ **sb. over the ears** jmdm. eins hinter die Ohren geben (ugs.); ~ **sb.** jmdm. einen Klaps geben

'cuff link n. Manschettenknopf, *der*

cuisine /kwɪ'zi:n/ n. Küche, *die*

cul-de-sac /'kʌldəsæk/ n., pl. **culs-de-sac** /'kʌldəsæk/ Sackgasse, *die*

culinary /'kʌlɪnərɪ/ adj. kulinarisch

cull /kʌl/ *v.t.* erlegen; (shoot) abschießen

culminate /'kʌlmɪneɪt/ *v.i.* gipfeln; kulminieren; ~ **in sth.** in etw. (*Dat.*) seinen Höchststand erreichen

culmination /kʌlmɪ'neɪʃn/ n. Höhepunkt, *der*

culottes /kju:'lɒt/ n. pl. Hosenrock, *der*

culpable /'kʌlpəbl/ adj. schuldig ‹*Person*›; strafbar ‹*Handlung*›; ~ **negligence** grobe Fahrlässigkeit

culprit /'kʌlprɪt/ n. (guilty of crime) Schuldige, *der/die;* Täter, *der/*Täterin, *die;* (guilty of wrong) Übeltäter, *der/*-täterin, *die*

cult /kʌlt/ n. Kult, *der; attrib.* Kult‹*film, -figur usw.*›

cultivate /'kʌltɪveɪt/ *v.t.* **(a)** (for crops) kultivieren; bestellen, bebauen ‹*Feld, Land*›; **(b)** anbauen, züchten ‹*Pflanzen*›; **(c)** (fig.) kultivieren, entwickeln ‹*Geschmack*›; kultivieren ‹*Freundschaft, Gefühl, Gewohnheit*›; entwickeln ‹*Kunst, Fertigkeit*›

cultivation /kʌltɪ'veɪʃn/ n. (lit. or fig.) Kultivierung, *die;* (of a skill) Entwicklung, *die;* ~ **of land** Landbau, *der;* Pflanzenbau, *der*

cultural /'kʌltʃərl/ adj. kulturell ‹*Entwicklung, Ereignis, Interessen, Beziehungen*›; ~ **revolution/anthropology** Kulturrevolution/-anthropologie, *die*

culture /'kʌltʃə(r)/ n. **(a)** Kultur, *die;* **(b)** (Agric., of bacteria) Kultur, *die;* (tillage of the soil) Landbau, *der;* (rearing, production) Zucht, *die*

cultured /'kʌltʃəd/ adj. **(a)** (cultivated, refined) kultiviert; gebildet; **(b)** ~ **pearl** Zuchtperle, *die*

cumbersome /'kʌmbəsəm/ adj. lästig, hinderlich ‹*Kleider*›; sperrig ‹*Gepäck, Pakete*›; schwerfällig ‹*Bewegung, Stil, Arbeitsweise*›

cumulate /'kju:mjʊleɪt/ n., **cumulation** /kju:mjʊ'leɪʃn/ ⇒ **accumul-**

cumulative /'kju:mjʊlətɪv/ adj. **(a)** (increased by successive additions) kumulativ (geh.); ~ **strength/effect** Gesamtstärke/-wirkung, *die;* ~ **evidence** Häufung von Beweismaterial; **(b)** (formed by successive additions) zusätzlich; Zusatz-

cunning /'kʌnɪŋ/ **1** n. Schläue, *die;* Gerissenheit, *die.* **2** adj. schlau; gerissen

cup /kʌp/ **1** n. **(a)** Tasse, *die;* **(b)** (prize, competition) Pokal, *der;* **(c)** (~ful) Tasse, *die;* **a** ~ **of coffee/tea** eine Tasse Kaffee/Tee; **it's [not] my** ~ **of tea** (fig. coll.) das ist [nicht] mein Fall (ugs.); **(d)** (of brassière) Körbchen, *das.* **2** *v.t.,* **-pp-:** **(a)** ~ **one's chin in one's hand** das Kinn in die Hand stützen; **(b)** (make ~-shaped) hohl machen; ~ **one's hand to one's ear** die Hand ans Ohr halten

cupboard /'kʌbəd/ n. Schrank, *der*

'cupboard love n. geheuchelte Zuneigung

Cup 'Final n. (Footb.) Pokalendspiel, *das*

cupful /'kʌpfʊl/ n. Tasse, *die;* **a** ~ **of water** eine Tasse Wasser

cupola /'kju:pələ/ n. Kuppel, *die*

curable /'kjʊərəbl/ adj. heilbar

curate /'kjʊərət/ n. (Eccl.) Kurat, *der;* Hilfsgeistliche, *der*

curator /kjʊə'reɪtə(r)/ n. ▶**887** | (of museum) Direktor, *der/* Direktorin, *die*

curb /kɜ:b/ **1** *v.t.* (lit. or fig.) zügeln. **2** n. **(a)** (chain or strap for horse) Kandare, *die;* **(b)** ⇒ **kerb**

curdle /'kɜ:dl/ **1** *v.t.* (lit. or fig.) gerinnen lassen. **2** *v.i.* (lit. or fig.) gerinnen

curds /kɜ:dz/ n. pl. ≈ Quark, *der*

cure /kjʊə(r)/ ▶**865** | **1** n. **(a)** (thing that ~s) [Heil]mittel, *das* (**for** gegen); (fig.) Mittel, *das;* **(b)** (restoration to health) Heilung, *die;* **(c)** (treatment) Behandlung, *die;* **take a** ~ **at a spa** in *od.* zur Kur gehen. **2** *v.t.* **(a)** heilen; kurieren; ~ **sb. of a disease** jmdn. von einer Krankheit heilen; **(b)** (fig.) kurieren; **(c)** (preserve) [ein]pökeln ‹*Fleisch*›; räuchern ‹*Fisch*›; trocknen ‹*Häute, Tabak*›

'cure-all n. Allheilmittel, *das*

curfew /'kɜ:fju:/ n. Ausgangssperre, *die*

curio /'kjʊərɪəʊ/ n., pl. ~**s** Kuriosität, *die*

curiosity /kjʊərɪ'ɒsɪtɪ/ n. **(a)** (desire to know) Neugier[de], *die* (**about** in Bezug auf + *Akk.*); ~ **killed the cat** (fig.) die Neugier ist schon manchem zum Verhängnis geworden; **(b)** (strange or rare object) Wunderding, *das;* Rarität, *die;* (strange matter) Kuriosität, *die*

curious /'kjʊərɪəs/ adj. **(a)** (inquisitive) neugierig; (eager to learn) wissbegierig; **be** ~ **about sth.** (eagerly awaiting) auf etw. (*Akk.*) neugierig sein; **be** ~ **about sb.** in Bezug auf jmdn. neugierig sein; **be** ~ **to know sth.** etw. gern wissen wollen; **(b)** (strange, odd) merkwürdig; seltsam; **how [very]** ~**!** [sehr] seltsam!

curiously /'kjʊərɪəslɪ/ adv. neugierig ‹*fragen, gucken*›; seltsam, merkwürdig ‹*sprechen, sich verhalten*›; ~ **[enough]** as sentence-modifier merkwürdigerweise; seltsamerweise

curl /kɜ:l/ **1** n. **(a)** (of hair) Locke, *die;* **(b)** (sth. spiral or curved inwards) **the** ~ **of a leaf/wave** ein gekräuseltes Blatt/eine gekräuselte Welle; **a** ~ **of smoke** ein Rauchkringel. **2** *v.t.* **(a)** (cause to form coils) locken; (tightly) kräuseln; **she** ~**ed her hair** sie legte ihr Haar in Locken (*Akk.*); **(b)** (bend, twist) kräuseln ‹*Blätter, Lippen*›. **3** *v.i.* **(a)** (grow in coils) sich locken; (tightly) sich kräuseln; **(b)** ‹*Straße, Fluss:*› sich winden, sich schlängeln
 ~ **'up 1** *v.t.* hochbiegen; ~ **oneself up** sich zusammenrollen. **2** *v.i.* sich zusammenrollen; ~ **up with a book** es sich (*Dat.*) mit einem Buch gemütlich machen

curler /'kɜ:lə(r)/ n. Lockenwickler, *der;* **in** ~**s** mit Lockenwicklern

curlew /'kɜ:lju:/ n. (Ornith.) Brachvogel, *der*

curling /'kɜ:lɪŋ/ n. Curling, *das;* ≈ Eisschießen, *das*

curly /'kɜ:lɪ/ adj. lockig, (tightly) kraus ‹*Haar*›

'curly-haired /'kɜ:lɪheəd/ adj. lockenköpfig

currant /'kʌrənt/ n. **(a)** (dried fruit) Korinthe, *die;* **(b)** (fruit) Johannisbeere, *die*

currency /'kʌrənsɪ/ n. ▶**938** | (money) Währung, *die;* **foreign currencies** Devisen *Pl.;* **(b)** (other commodity) Zahlungsmittel, *das;* **(c)** (prevalence) (of word, idea, story, rumour) Verbreitung, *die;* (of expression) Gebräuchlichkeit, *die*

current /'kʌrənt/ **1** adj. **(a)** (in general circulation or use) kursierend, umlaufend ‹*Geld, Geschichte, Gerücht*›; verbreitet ‹*Meinung*›; gebräuchlich ‹*Wort*›; gängig ‹*Redensart*›; **(b)** laufend ‹*Jahr, Monat*›; **in the** ~ **year** in diesem Jahr; **(c)** (belonging to the present time) aktuell ‹*Ereignis, Mode*›; Tages‹*politik, -preis*›; gegenwärtig ‹*Krise, Aufregung*›; ~ **issue/edition** letzte Ausgabe/neueste Auflage; ~ **affairs** Tagespolitik, *die;* aktuelle Fragen. **2** n. **(a)** (of water, air) Strömung, *die;* **air/ocean** ~: Luft-/Meeresströmung, *die;* **swim against/with the** ~: gegen den/mit dem Strom schwimmen; **(b)** (Electr.) Strom, *der;* (intensity) Stromstärke, *die;* (**c**) (running stream) Strömung, *die;* (**d**) (tendency of events, opinions, etc.) Tendenz, *die;* Trend, *der*

'**current account** *n.* Girokonto, *das*

currently /'kʌrəntlɪ/ *adv.* gegenwärtig; momentan; **he is ~ writing a book** er schreibt gerade *od.* zur Zeit an einem Buch

curriculum /kə'rɪkjʊləm/ *n., pl.* **curricula** /kə'rɪkjʊlə/ Lehrplan, *der*

curriculum vitae /kərɪkjʊləm 'viːtaɪ/ *n.* Lebenslauf, *der*

curry¹ /'kʌrɪ/ *n.* (Cookery) Curry[gericht], *das*

curry² *v.t.* **~ favour [with sb.]** sich [bei jmdm.] einschmeicheln

'**curry powder** *n.* Currypulver, *das*

curse /kɜːs/ **1** *n.* (**a**) Fluch, *der;* **be under a ~:** unter einem Fluch stehen; (**b**) (great evil) Geißel, *die;* Plage, *die.* **2** *v.t.* (**a**) (utter ~ against) verfluchen; (**b**) (as oath) **~ it/you!** verflucht!; verdammt!; (**c**) (afflict) strafen. **3** *v.i.* fluchen (**at** über + *Akk.*)

cursed /'kɜːsɪd/ *adj.* verflucht

cursor /'kɜːsə(r)/ *n.* Läufer, *der;* (on screen) Cursor, *der*

cursory /'kɜːsərɪ/ *adj.* flüchtig ⟨*Blick*⟩; oberflächlich ⟨*Untersuchung, Bericht, Studium*⟩

curt /kɜːt/ *adj.* kurz und schroff ⟨*Brief, Mitteilung*⟩; kurz angebunden ⟨*Person, Art*⟩

curtail /kɜː'teɪl/ *v.t.* kürzen; abkürzen ⟨*Urlaub*⟩; beschneiden ⟨*Macht*⟩

curtain /'kɜːtən/ *n.* (**a**) Vorhang, *der;* (with net ~s) Übergardine, *die;* **draw** *or* **pull the ~s** (open) die Vorhänge aufziehen; (close) die Vorhänge zuziehen; **draw** *or* **pull back the ~s** die Vorhänge aufziehen; (**b**) (fig.) **a ~ of fog/mist** ein Nebelschleier; **a ~ of smoke/flames/rain** eine Rauch-/Flammen-/Regenwand; (**c**) (Theatre) Vorhang, *der;* (end of play) Schlussszene, *die;* (rise of ~ at start of play) Aufgehen des Vorhanges; Aktbeginn, *der;* (fall of ~ at end of scene) Fallen des Vorhanges; Aktschluss, *der;* **the ~ rises/ falls** der Vorhang hebt sich/fällt

~ 'off *v.t.* mit einem Vorhang abteilen

curtain: ~ call *n.* Vorhang, *der;* **~ rail** *n.* Gardinenstange, *die;* **~-raiser** /'kɜː'tənreɪzə(r)/ *n.* [kurzes] Vorspiel; (fig.) Auftakt, *der;* **~ rod** *n.* Gardinenstange, *die;* **~ track** *n.* Gardinenleiste, *die*

curtsy (**curtsey**) /'kɜːtsɪ/ **1** *n.* Knicks, *der;* **make** *or* **drop a ~ to sb.** vor jmdm. einen Knicks machen. **2** *v.i.* **~ to sb.** vor jmdm. knicksen

curvaceous /kɜː'veɪʃəs/ *adj.* (coll.) kurvenreich (ugs.); **a ~ figure** eine üppige Figur

curvature /'kɜːvətʃə(r)/ *n.* Krümmung, *die*

curve /kɜːv/ **1** *v.t.* krümmen. **2** *v.i.* ⟨*Straße, Fluss*⟩ (once) eine Biegung machen, (repeatedly) sich winden; ⟨*Horizont*⟩ sich krümmen; ⟨*Linie*⟩ einen Bogen machen; **the road ~s round the town** die Straße macht einen Bogen um die Stadt. **3** *n.* (**a**) Kurve, *die;* (**b**) (surface; curved form or thing) Rundung, *die*

curved /kɜːvd/ *adj.* krumm; gebogen; gekrümmt ⟨*Raum, Linie*⟩

cushion /'kʊʃn/ **1** *n.* (**a**) Kissen, *das;* (**b**) (for protection) Kissen, *das;* Polster, *das.* **2** *v.t.* (**a**) [aus]polstern ⟨*Stuhl*⟩; (**b**) (absorb) dämpfen ⟨*Aufprall, Stoß*⟩

cushy /'kʊʃɪ/ *adj.* (coll.) bequem

cuss /kʌs/ (coll.) **1** *n.* Fluch, *der;* Beschimpfung, *die;* **sb. does not give** *or* **care a ~:** jmdm. ist es vollkommen schnuppe (ugs.); **he/it is not worth a tinker's ~:** er/es ist keinen Pfifferling *od.* roten Heller wert (ugs.). **2** *v.i.* fluchen; schimpfen. **3** *v.t.* verfluchen; beschimpfen

cussed /'kʌsɪd/ *adj.* (coll.: perverse, obstinate) stur (ugs.)

cussedness /'kʌsɪdnɪs/ *n., no pl.* Sturheit, *die;* **from sheer ~:** aus reiner Sturheit

custard /'kʌstəd/ *n.* (**a**) ~ [**pudding**] ≈ Vanillepudding, *der;* (**b**) (sauce) ≈ Vanillesoße, *die*

custard: ~ 'pie *n.* (pie) Kuchen mit einer Füllung aus *Vanillepudding;* (in comedy) Sahnetorte, *die;* **~ powder** *n.* Vanillesoßenpulver, *das*

custodian /kʌs'təʊdɪən/ *n.* ▶887 (of public building) Wärter, *der*/Wärterin, *die;* (of park, museum) Wächter, *der*/Wächterin, *die;* (of valuables, traditions, culture) Hüter, *der*/Hüterin, *die*

custody /'kʌstədɪ/ *n.* (**a**) (guardianship, care) Obhut, *die;* **be in the ~ of sb.** unter jmds. Obhut (*Dat.*) stehen; **the mother was given [the] ~ of the children** die Kinder wurden der Mutter zugesprochen; (**b**) (imprisonment) [**be**] **in ~:** in Haft [sein]; **take sb. into ~:** jmdn. verhaften *od.* festnehmen

custom /'kʌstəm/ *n.* (**a**) Brauch, *der;* Sitte, *die;* **it was his ~ to smoke a cigar after dinner** er pflegte nach dem Essen eine Zigarre zu rauchen; (**b**) *in pl.* (duty on imports) Zoll, *der;* [**the**] **C~s** (government department) der Zoll; **go through C~s** durch den Zoll gehen (ugs.); (**c**) (Law) Gewohnheitsrecht, *das;* (**d**) (business patronage) Kundschaft, *die* (veralt.); **we should like to have your ~:** wir hätten Sie gern zum/zur *od.* als Kunden/Kundin

customary /'kʌstəmərɪ/ *adj.* üblich

'**custom-built** *adj.* spezial[an]gefertigt; **~ clothes** (Amer.) maßgeschneiderte Kleidung

customer /'kʌstəmə(r)/ *n.* (**a**) Kunde, *der*/Kundin, *die;* (of restaurant) Gast, *der;* (of theatre) Besucher, *der*/Besucherin, *die;* (**b**) (coll.: person) Kerl, *der* (ugs.); **a queer/an awkward ~:** ein schwieriger Kunde (ugs.)

'**custom-made** *adj.* spezial[an]gefertigt; maßgeschneidert ⟨*Kleidung*⟩

customs: ~ clearance *n.* Zollabfertigung, *die;* **~ declaration** *n.* Zollerklärung, *die;* **~ duty** *n.* Zoll, *der;* **~ inspection** *n.* Zollkontrolle, *die;* **~ officer** *n.* ▶887 Zollbeamter, *der*/-beamtin, *die*

cut /kʌt/ **1** *v.t.*, **-tt-**, **cut** (**a**) (penetrate, wound) schneiden; **~ one's finger/leg** sich (*Dat. od. Akk.*) in den Finger/ins Bein schneiden; **he ~ himself on broken glass** er hat sich an einer Glasscherbe geschnitten; **the remark ~ him to the quick** (fig.) die Bemerkung traf ihn ins Mark; (**b**) (divide) (with knife) schneiden; durchschneiden ⟨*Seil*⟩; (with axe) durchhacken; **~ sth. in half/two/three** etw. halbieren/zweiteilen/dreiteilen; **~ one's ties** *or* **links** alle Verbindungen abbrechen; **~ no ice with sb.** (fig. coll.) keinen Eindruck auf jmdn. machen; (**c**) (detach, reduce) abschneiden; schneiden, stutzen ⟨*Hecke*⟩; mähen ⟨*Getreide, Gras*⟩; **~** (*p.p.*) **flowers** Schnittblumen; **~ one's nails** sich (*Dat.*) die Nägel schneiden; (**d**) (shape, fashion) schleifen ⟨*Glas, Edelstein, Kristall*⟩; hauen, schlagen ⟨*Stufen*⟩; **~ a key** einen Schlüssel feilen *od.* anfertigen; **~ figures in wood/stone** Figuren aus Holz schnitzen/aus Stein hauen; (**e**) (meet and cross) ⟨*Straße, Linie, Kreis*⟩ schneiden; (**f**) (fig.) (renounce, refuse to recognize) schneiden; (**g**) (carve) [auf]schneiden ⟨*Fleisch, Geflügel*⟩; abschneiden ⟨*Scheibe*⟩; (**h**) (reduce) senken ⟨*Preise*⟩; verringern, einschränken ⟨*Menge, Produktion*⟩; mindern ⟨*Qualität*⟩; kürzen ⟨*Ausgaben, Lohn*⟩; verkürzen ⟨*Arbeitszeit, Urlaub*⟩; (cease, stop) einstellen ⟨*Dienstleistungen, Lieferungen*⟩; abstellen ⟨*Strom*⟩; (**i**) (absent oneself from) schwänzen ⟨*Schule, Unterricht*⟩; **~ one's losses** höherem Verlust vorbeugen; (**k**) **~ sth. short** (lit. or fig.: interrupt, terminate) etw. abbrechen; **~ sb. short** jmdn. unterbrechen; (impatiently) jmdm. ins Wort fallen; **to ~ a long story short** um kurzer Rede kurzer Sinn; (**l**) (Cards) abheben; (**m**) **~ a tooth** einen Zahn bekommen; (**n**) **be ~ and dried** genau festgelegt *od.* abgesprochen sein; (**o**) (Computing) **~ and paste** ausschneiden und einfügen. **2** *v.i.*, **-tt-**, **cut** (**a**) ⟨*Messer, Schwert usw.*⟩ schneiden; ⟨*Papier, Tuch, Käse*⟩ sich schneiden lassen; **~ both ways** (fig.) ein zweischneidiges Schwert sein (fig.); (**b**) (cross, intersect) sich schneiden; (**c**) (pass) **~ through** *or* **across the field/park** [quer] über das Feld/durch den Park gehen; (**d**) (Cinemat.) (stop the cameras) abbrechen; (go quickly to another shot) überblenden (**to** zu). **3** *n.* (**a**) (act of cutting) Schnitt, *der;* (**b**) (stroke, blow) (with knife) Schnitt, *der;* (with sword, whip) Hieb, *der;* (injury) Schnittwunde, *die;* (**c**) (reduction) (in wages, expenditure, budget) Kürzung, *die;* (in prices) Senkung, *die;* (in working hours, holiday, etc.) Verkürzung, *die;* (in services) Verringerung, *die;* (in production, output, etc.) Einschränkung, *die;* (**d**) (of meat) Stück, *das;* (**e**) (coll.: commission, share) Anteil, *der;* (**f**) (of hair: style) [Haar]schnitt, *der;* (of clothes) Schnitt, *der;* (in play, book, etc.) Streichung, *die;* (in film) Schnitt, *der;* **make ~s** Streichungen/Schnitte vornehmen

~ a'way ⇨ ~ off a

~ 'back 1 *v.t.* (a) (reduce) einschränken ‹*Produktion*›; verringern ‹*Investitionen*›; (b) (prune) stutzen. 2 *v.i.* (reduce) ~ back on sth. etw. einschränken

~ 'down 1 *v.t.* (a) (fell) fällen; (b) (kill) töten; (c) (reduce) einschränken; ~ sb. down to size (fig.) jmdn. auf seinen Platz verweisen. 2 *v.i.* (reduce) ~ down on sth. etw. einschränken

~ 'in *v.i.* (a) (come in abruptly, interpose) sich einschalten; ~ in on sb./sth. jmdn./etw. unterbrechen; (b) (after overtaking) schneiden; (c) ‹*Motor usw.*› sich einschalten

~ 'off *v.t.* (a) (remove by ~ting) abschneiden; abtrennen; (with axe etc.) abschlagen; (b) (interrupt, make unavailable) abschneiden; (c) ‹*Strom, Gas, Wasser*›: abstellen ‹*Strom, Gas, Wasser*›; unterbrechen ‹*Telefongespräch, Sprecher am Telefon*›; (c) (isolate) abschneiden; be ~ off by the snow/tide durch den Schnee/die Flut abgeschnitten sein; (d) (prevent, block) abschneiden; their retreat was ~ off ihnen wurde der Rückzug abgeschnitten; (e) (exclude from contact) ~ sb. off from the outside world jmdn. von der Außenwelt abschneiden; ~ oneself off sich absondern

~ 'out 1 *v.t.* (a) (remove by ~ting) ausschneiden (out of aus); (b) (stop doing or using) aufhören mit; ~ out cigarettes/alcohol aufhören, Zigaretten zu rauchen/Alkohol zu trinken; ~ it *or* that out! (coll.) hör/hört auf damit!; (c) be ~ out for sth. für etw. geeignet sein; he was not ~ out to be a teacher er war nicht zum Lehrer gemacht. 2 *v.i.* ‹*Motor:*› aussetzen; ‹*Gerät:*› sich abschalten

~ 'up *v.t.* zerschneiden; in Stücke schneiden ‹*Fleisch, Gemüse*›; be ~ up about sth. (fig.) zutiefst betroffen über etw. (*Akk.*) sein

'cutback *n.* (reduction) Kürzung, *die*

cute /kju:t/ *adj.* (coll., esp. Amer.) süß, niedlich ‹*Kind, Mädchen*›; entzückend ‹*Stadt, Haus*›

cut 'glass *n.* Kristall[glas], *das*

cuticle /'kju:tɪkl/ *n.* Epidermis, *die* (fachspr.); Oberhaut, *die;* (of nail) Nagelhaut, *die*

cutlery /'kʌtlərɪ/ *n.* Besteck, *das*

cutlet /'kʌtlɪt/ *n.* (a) (of mutton or lamb) Kotelett, *das;* (b) veal ~: Frikandeau, *das;* (c) (minced meat etc. in shape of ~) Hacksteak, *das*

cut: ~-off *n.* Trennung, *die; attrib.* ~-off point Trennungslinie, *die;* ~-price *adj.* herabgesetzt; ~-price goods Waren zu herabgesetzten Preisen; ~-rate *adj.* verbilligt; herabgesetzt

cutter /'kʌtə(r)/ *n.* (a) (person) (of cloth) Zuschneider, *der/* Zuschneiderin, *die;* (of films) Cutter, *der/*Cutterin, *die;* (b) (machine) Schneidegerät, *das;* (c) (Naut.) Kutter, *der*

'cutthroat 1 *n.* Strolch, *der;* (murderer) Killer, *der* (ugs.). 2 *adj.* (a) mörderisch, gnadenlos ‹*Wettbewerb*›; (b) ~ razor Rasiermesser, *das*

cutting /'kʌtɪŋ/ 1 *adj.* beißend ‹*Bemerkung, Antwort*›; ~ edge Schneide, *die.* 2 *n.* (a) (esp. Brit.: from newspaper) Ausschnitt, *der;* (b) (esp. Brit.: excavation for railway, road etc.) Einschnitt, *der;* (c) (of plant) Ableger, *der*

'cutting ~ edge *n.* be at the ~ of technology auf dem Gebiet der Technologie führend sein; die Speerspitze der Technologie sein; be at the ~ edge of fashion auf dem Gebiet der Mode führend sein

cuttle[fish] /'kʌtl(fɪʃ)/ *n.* Tintenfisch, *der;* Sepia, *die* (fachspr.)

c.v. *abbr.* curriculum vitae

cwt. *abbr.* hundredweight ≈ Ztr.

cyanide /'saɪənaɪd/ *n.* Cyanid, *das*

cyber: ~sex /'saɪbəseks/ *n., no pl., no art.* Cybersex, *der;* ~space /'saɪbəspeɪs/ *n., no pl., no art.* Cyberspace, *der*

cyclamen /'sɪkləmən/ *n.* (Bot.) Alpenveilchen, *das*

cycle /'saɪkl/ 1 *n.* (a) Zyklus, *der;* (period of completion) Turnus, *der;* ~ per second (Phys., Electr.) Schwingung pro Sekunde; (b) (bicycle) Rad, *das.* 2 *v.i.* Rad fahren; mit dem [Fahr]rad fahren; go cycling Rad fahren

cycle: ~ lane *n.* Fahrradspur, *die;* ~ track *n.* Rad-[fahr]weg, *der;* (for racing) Radrennbahn, *die*

cyclic /'saɪklɪk/, cyclical /'saɪklɪkl/ *adj.* zyklisch

cycling /'saɪklɪŋ/ *n.* (activity) Radfahren, *das;* (sport) Radsport, *der;* amateur ~: Amateur-Radrennsport, *der; attrib.* ~ enthusiast Radsportfan, *der;* ~ shorts Radlerhose, *die*

cyclist /'saɪklɪst/ *n.* Radfahrer, *der/*-fahrerin, *die*

cyclone /'saɪkləʊn/ *n.* (system of winds) Tiefdruckgebiet, *das;* Zyklon, *die* (fachspr.); (violent hurricane) Zyklon, *der*

cygnet /'sɪgnɪt/ *n.* junger Schwan

cylinder /'sɪlɪndə(r)/ *n.* (also Geom., Motor Veh.) Zylinder, *der;* (for compressed or liquefied gas) Gasflasche, *die;* (of diving apparatus) [Sauerstoff]flasche, *die;* (of typewriter, mower) Walze, *die*

cylinder: ~ block *n.* Motorblock, *der;* ~ head *n.* Zylinderkopf, *der*

cylindrical /sɪ'lɪndrɪkl/ *adj.* zylindrisch

cymbal /'sɪmbl/ *n.* (Mus.) Beckenteller, *der;* ~s Becken *Pl.*

cynic /'sɪnɪk/ *n.* Zyniker, *der*

cynical /'sɪnɪkl/ *adj.* zynisch; bissig ‹*Artikel, Bemerkung, Worte*›

cynicism /'sɪnɪsɪzm/ *n.* Zynismus, *der*

cypher ⇨ cipher

cypress /'saɪprɪs/ *n.* Zypresse, *die*

Cypriot /'sɪprɪət/ ▶ 947 | 1 *adj.* zyprisch; zypriotisch. 2 *n.* Zypriot, *der/*Zypriotin, *die*

Cyprus /'saɪprəs/ *pr. n.* Zypern (*das*)

Czech /tʃek/ ▶ 897 |, ▶ 947 | 1 *adj.* tschechisch. 2 *n.* (a) (language) Tschechisch, *das;* (b) (person) Tscheche, *der/* Tschechin, *die*

Czechoslovakia /tʃekəʊslə'vækɪə/ *n.* (*Hist.*) die Tschechoslowakei

Czechoslovakian /tʃekəʊslə'vækɪən/ ▶ 947 | (*Hist.*) 1 *adj.* tschechoslowakisch. 2 *pr. n.* Tschechoslowake, *der/* Tschechoslowakin, *die*

Czech Republic *n.* Tschechische Republik; Tschechien, (*das*)

....

Dd

....

D, d /di:/ *n., pl.* Ds *or* D's (a) (letter) D, d, *das;* (b) D (Mus.) D, d, *das;* D sharp dis, Dis, *das;* D flat des, Des, *das*

d. *abbr.* (a) died gest.; (b) (Brit. Hist.) penny/pence d.

DA *abbr.* (Amer.) District Attorney

dab¹ /dæb/ 1 *n.* Tupfer, *der.* 2 *v.t.*, -bb- (press with sponge etc.) abtupfen; ~ sth. on *or* against sth. etw. auf etw. (*Akk.*) tupfen. 3 *v.i.*, -bb-: ~ at sth. etw. ab- *od.* betupfen

dab² (Brit. coll.: expert) 1 *n.* Könner, *der.* 2 *adj.* geschickt; be a ~ hand at cricket/making omelettes ein As im Kricket/Eierkuchenbacken sein (ugs.)

dabble /'dæbl/ 1 *v.t.* (wet slightly) befeuchten; ~ one's feet in the water mit den Füßen im Wasser planschen. 2 *v.i.* ~ in/at sth. sich in etw. (*Dat.*) versuchen

dachshund /'dækshʊnd/ *n.* Dackel, *der*

dad /dæd/ *n.* (coll.) Vater, *der*

daddy /'dædɪ/ *n.* (coll.) Vati, *der* (fam.); Papa, *der* (fam.)

daddy-'long-legs *n. sing.* (Zool.) (a) (crane-fly) Schnake, *die;* (b) (Amer.: harvestman) Weberknecht, *der;* Kanker, *der*

daffodil /'dæfədɪl/ *n.* Gelbe Narzisse; Osterglocke, *die*

daft /dɑ:ft/ *adj.* doof (ugs.); blöd[e] (ugs.)

dagger /'dægə(r)/ *n.* Dolch, *der;* be at ~s drawn with sb. (fig.) mit jmdm. auf Kriegsfuß stehen; look ~s at sb. jmdm. finstere Blicke zuwerfen

dago /'deɪgəʊ/ *n., pl.* ~s *or* ~es (sl. derog.: Spaniard, Portuguese, Italian) Welsche, *der* (veralt. abwertend); Kanake, *der* (derb abwertend)

dahlia /'deɪlɪə/ n. Dahlie, die
daily /'deɪlɪ/ **1** adj. täglich; ~ **[news]paper** Tageszeitung, die. **2** adv. täglich; jeden Tag; (constantly) Tag für Tag. **3** n. (a) (newspaper) Tageszeitung, die; (b) (Brit. coll.: charwoman) Reinemachefrau, die
dainty /'deɪntɪ/ **1** adj. zierlich; anmutig ⟨Bewegung, Person⟩; zart, fein ⟨Gesichtszüge⟩. **2** n. (lit. or fig.) Delikatesse, die; Leckerbissen, der
dairy /'deərɪ/ n. (a) Molkerei, die; (b) (shop) Milchladen, der
dairy: ~ **cattle** n. Milchvieh, das; ~**man** /'deə rɪmən/ n., pl. ~**men** /'deərɪmən/ Milchmann, der; ~ **produce** n., ~ **products** n. pl. Molkereiprodukte Pl.
dais /'deɪɪs/ n. Podium, das
daisy /'deɪzɪ/ n. Gänseblümchen, das; (ox-eye) Margerite, die
dale /deɪl/ n. (literary/N. Engl.) Tal, das; see also **up** 2 a
dally /'dælɪ/ v.i. (a) ~ **with sb.** mit jmdm. spielen od. leichtfertig umgehen; (flirt) mit jmdm. schäkern (ugs.) od. flirten; (b) (idle, loiter) [herum]trödeln (ugs.); ~ **[over sth.]** mit etw. trödeln (ugs.)
Dalmatian /dæl'meɪʃn/ n. Dalmatiner, der
dam¹ /dæm/ **1** n. [Stau]damm, der; (made by beavers) Damm, der. **2** v.t., -**mm-:** (a) (lit. or fig.) ~ **[up/back]** sth. etw. abblocken; (b) (furnish or confine with ~) aufstauen
dam² n. (Zool.) Muttertier, das
damage /'dæmɪdʒ/ **1** n. (a) no pl. Schaden, der; **do a lot of** ~ **to sb./sth.** jmdm./einer Sache großen Schaden zufügen; (b) in pl. (Law) Schadenersatz, der. **2** v.t. (a) beschädigen; **smoking can** ~ **your health** Rauchen gefährdet die Gesundheit; (b) (detract from) schädigen
damaging /'dæmɪdʒɪŋ/ adj. schädlich (**to** für)
dame /deɪm/ n. (a) **D**~ (Brit.) Dame (Titel der weiblichen Träger verschiedener Orden im Ritterstand); (b) **D**~ (literary/poet.: title of woman of rank) Dame, die; (c) (arch./poet./joc./Amer. sl.) Weib, das
damfool /'dæmfuːl/ (coll.) **1** adj. idiotisch (ugs.); blöd (ugs.). **2** n. Idiot, der (ugs.)
dammit /'dæmɪt/ int. (coll.) verdammt noch mal (ugs.); **as near as** ~: jedenfalls so gut wie (ugs.)
damn /dæm/ **1** v.t. (a) (condemn, censure) verreißen ⟨Buch, Film, Theaterstück⟩; (b) (doom to hell, curse) verdammen; (c) (coll.) ~ **[it]!** verflucht [noch mal]! (ugs.); ~ **you/him!** hol dich/ihn der Teufel! (salopp); **[well,] I'll be** or **I'm** ~**ed** ich werd verrückt (ugs.); [**I'll be** or **I'm**] ~**ed if I know** ich habe nicht die leiseste Ahnung. **2** n. (a) (curse) Fluch, der; (b) **he didn't give** or **care a** ~ **[about it]** ihm war es völlig Wurscht (ugs.). **3** adj. verdammt (ugs.). **4** adv. verdammt
damnation /dæm'neɪʃn/ **1** n. Verdammnis, die. **2** int. verdammt [noch mal] (ugs.)
damned /dæmd/ (coll.) **1** adj. (a) (infernal, unwelcome) verdammt (ugs.); **what a** ~ **nuisance!** verdammter Mist! (ugs.); (b) **do/try one's** ~**est** sein Möglichstes tun. **2** adv. verdammt (ugs.); **I should** ~ **well hope so** das will ich aber [auch] schwer hoffen (ugs.)
damning /'dæmɪŋ/ adj. vernichtend ⟨Urteil, Kritik, Worte⟩; belastend ⟨Beweise⟩
damp /dæmp/ **1** adj. feucht; **a** ~ **squib** (fig.) ein Reinfall. **2** v.t. (a) befeuchten; (b) ~ **[down]** a fire ein Feuer ersticken; (c) (Mus., Phys.) dämpfen; (d) dämpfen ⟨Eifer, Begeisterung⟩; ~ **sb.'s spirits** jmdm. den Mut nehmen. **3** n. Feuchtigkeit, die
'damp course ⇒ **damp-proof**
dampen /'dæmpn/ ⇒ **damp** 2 a, d
damper /'dæmpə(r)/ n. (a) **put a** ~ **on sth.** einer Sache (Dat.) einen Dämpfer aufsetzen; (b) (Mus.) Dämpfer, der; (c) (in flue) Luftklappe, die
'damp-proof adj. feuchtigkeitsbeständig; ~ **course** Sperrschicht, die (gegen aufsteigende Bodenfeuchtigkeit)
damsel /'dæmzl/ n. (arch./literary) Maid, die (veralt.); **a** ~ **in distress** (joc.) eine hilflose junge Dame
damson /'dæmzn/ n. Haferpflaume, die
dance /dɑːns/ **1** v.i. tanzen; (jump about, skip) herumtanzen. **2** v.t. (a) tanzen; (b) (move up and down) schaukeln. **3** n. (a)

Tanz, der; **lead sb. a [merry]** ~ (fig.) jmdn. [schön] an der Nase herumführen; (b) (party) Tanzveranstaltung, die; (private) Tanzparty, die
dance: ~ **band** n. Tanzkapelle, die; ~ **hall** n. Tanzsaal, der
dancer /'dɑːnsə(r)/ n. Tänzer, der/Tänzerin, die
dancing /'dɑːnsɪŋ/**:** ~ **girl** n. Tänzerin, die; ~ **partner** n. Tanzpartner, der/-partnerin, die
dandelion /'dændɪlaɪən/ n. Löwenzahn, der
dandruff /'dændrʌf/ n. [Kopf]schuppen Pl.
dandy /'dændɪ/ n. Dandy, der (geh.); Geck, der (abwertend)
Dane /deɪn/ n. Däne, der/Dänin, die
danger /'deɪndʒə(r)/ n. Gefahr, die; **a** ~ **to sb./sth.** eine Gefahr für jmdn./etw.; **'**~**!** „Vorsicht!"; **there is [a]** ~ **of war** es besteht Kriegsgefahr; **in** ~: in Gefahr; **be in** ~ **of doing sth.** ⟨Person:⟩ Gefahr laufen, etw. zu tun; ⟨Sache:⟩ drohen, etw. zu tun; **out of** ~: außer Gefahr
danger: ~ **list** n. **be on/off the** ~ **list** in/außer Lebensgefahr sein; ~ **money** n. Gefahrenzulage, die
dangerous /'deɪndʒərəs/ adj., **dangerously** /'deɪndʒə rəslɪ/ adv. gefährlich
'danger signal n. Warnzeichen, das
dangle /'dæŋgl/ **1** v.i. baumeln (**from** an + Dat.). **2** v.t. baumeln lassen; ~ **sth. in front of sb.** (fig.) jmdm. etw. in Aussicht stellen
Danish /'deɪnɪʃ/ ▶ **897** ▶ **947** **1** adj. dänisch; **sb. is** ~: jmd. ist Däne/Dänin. **2** n. Dänisch, das; see also **English 2 a**
Danish: ~ **'blue** n. dänischer Blauschimmelkäse; ~ **'pastry** n. Plunderstück, das
dank /dæŋk/ adj. feucht
Danube /'dænjuːb/ ▶ **1048** pr. n. Donau, die
dapper /'dæpə(r)/ adj. adrett; schmuck (veralt.)
dappled /'dæpld/ adj. gesprenkelt; gefleckt ⟨Pferd, Kuh⟩
dare /deə(r)/ **1** v.t., pres. **he** ~ or ~**s**, neg. ~ **not**, (coll.) ~**n't** /deənt/ (a) (venture) [es] wagen; sich (Akk.) trauen; **if you** ~ **[to] give away the secret** wenn du es wagst, das Geheimnis zu verraten; **we** ~ **not/**~**d not** or (coll.) **didn't** ~ **tell him the truth** wir wagen/wagten [es] nicht od. trauen/trauten uns nicht, ihm die Wahrheit zu sagen; **you wouldn't** ~: das wagst du nicht; du traust dich nicht; **just you/don't you** ~**!** untersteh dich!; **how** ~ **you!** was fällt dir ein!; (formal) was erlauben Sie sich!; **I** ~ **say** (supposing) ich nehme an; (confirming) das glaube ich gern; (b) (challenge) ~ **sb. to do sth.** jmdn. dazu aufstacheln, etw. zu tun; **I** ~ **you!** trau dich! **2** n. **do sth. for/as a** ~: etw. als Mutprobe tun
'daredevil n. Draufgänger, der/-gängerin, die
daring /'deərɪŋ/ **1** adj. kühn; waghalsig ⟨Kunststück, Tat⟩. **2** n., no pl. Kühnheit, die
dark /dɑːk/ **1** adj. (a) dunkel; dunkel, finster ⟨Nacht, Haus, Straße⟩; (gloomy) düster; (b) dunkel ⟨Farbe⟩; (browncomplexioned) dunkelhäutig; (dark-haired) dunkelhaarig; ~**blue/-brown** etc. dunkelblau/-braun usw.; (c) (evil) finster; (d) (cheerless) finster; düster ⟨Bild⟩. **2** n. (a) Dunkel, das; **in the** ~: im Dunkeln; (b) **keep sb. in the** ~ **about/as to sth.** jmdn. über etw. (Akk.) im Dunkeln lassen; **it was a shot in the** ~: es war aufs Geratewohl geraten/versucht; **a leap in the** ~: ein Sprung ins Ungewisse
'Dark Ages n. pl. [frühes] Mittelalter
darken /'dɑːkn/ **1** v.t. (a) verdunkeln; (b) (fig.) verdüstern; **never** ~ **my door again!** du betrittst mir meine Schwelle nicht mehr! **2** v.i. ⟨Zimmer:⟩ dunkel werden; ⟨Wolken, Himmel:⟩ sich verfinstern
dark: ~ **'glasses** n. pl. dunkle Brille; ~**-haired** /'dɑːkheəd/ adj. dunkelhaarig; ~ **'horse** n. (fig.: secretive person) **be a** ~ **horse** ein stilles Wasser sein
darkness /'dɑːknɪs/ n., no pl. Dunkelheit, die
'darkroom n. Dunkelkammer, die
darling /'dɑːlɪŋ/ **1** n. Liebling, der; **she was his** ~: sie war seine Liebste od. sein Schatz. **2** adj. geliebt
darn¹ /dɑːn/ **1** v.t. stopfen. **2** n. gestopfte Stelle
darn² (coll.: damn) **1** v.t. ~ **you** etc.**!** zum Kuckuck mit dir usw.! (salopp); ~ **[it]!** verflixt [und zugenäht]! (ugs.). **2** adj. verflixt (ugs.)

darned /dɑːnd/ (coll.) **1** adj. verflixt (ugs.). **2** adv. verflixt (ugs.)

darning /'dɑːnɪŋ/ n. Stopfen, das

'darning needle n. Stopfnadel, die

dart /dɑːt/ **1** n. (a) (missile) Pfeil, der; (b) (Sport) Wurfpfeil, der; ~s sing. (game) Darts, das. **2** v.i. sausen

'dartboard n. Dartscheibe, die

dash /dæʃ/ **1** v.i. (move quickly) sausen; (coll.: hurry) sich eilen; ~ **down/up [the stairs]** [die Treppe] hinunter-/hinaufstürzen. **2** v.t. (a) (shatter) ~ **sth. [to pieces]** etw. [in tausend Stücke] zerschlagen od. zerschmettern; (b) (fling) schleudern; schmettern; (c) (frustrate) **sb.'s hopes are** ~ed jmds. Hoffnungen haben sich zerschlagen. **3** n. (a) **make a** ~ **for sth.** zu etw. rasen (ugs.); **make a** ~ **for shelter** rasch Schutz suchen; **make a** ~ **for freedom** plötzlich versuchen, wegzulaufen; (b) (horizontal stroke) Gedankenstrich, der; (c) (Morse signal) Strich, der; (d) (small amount) Schuss, der; **a** ~ **of salt** eine Prise Salz

~ **a'way** v.i. (rush) davonjagen; (coll: hurry) **they had to** ~ **away** sie mussten schnell weg

~ **'off 1** v.i. ⇒ ~ **away**. **2** v.t. rasch schreiben

'dashboard n. (Motor Veh.) Armaturenbrett, das

dashing /'dæʃɪŋ/ adj. schneidig

data /'deɪtə, 'dɑːtə/ n. pl., constr. as pl. or sing. Daten Pl.

data: ~ **bank** n. Datenbank, die; ~**base** n. Datenbank, die; ~**base management system** Datenbankmanagementsystem, das; ~ **capture** n. Datenerfassung, die; ~ **communications** n. pl. (Computing) Datenaustausch, der; ~ **entry** n., no. pl., no art. (Computing) Dateneingabe, die; ~ **file** n. (Computing) Datei, die; ~**glove** n. (Computing) Datenhandschuh, der; ~ **handling** n. (Computing) Datenverarbeitung, die; ~ **link** n. (Computing) Datenleitung, die; ~ **processing** ⇒ ~ **handling;** ~ **processor** n. (Computing) Datenverarbeitungsanlage, die; ~ **pro'tection** n. (Computing) Datenschutz, der; ~ **security** n. (Computing) Datensicherung, die; ~ **storage** n. (Computing) Datenspeicherung, die; (capacity) Speicherkapazität, die; Speicherplatz, der; ~ **transmission** n. (Computing) Datenübertragung, die

date¹ /deɪt/ n. (Bot.) Dattel, die

date² **1** n. (a) Datum, das; (on coin etc.) Jahreszahl, die; ~ **of birth** Geburtsdatum, das; (b) (coll.: appointment) Verabredung, die; **have/make a** ~ **with sb.** mit jmdm. verabredet sein/sich mit jmdm. verabreden; **go [out] on a** ~ **with sb.** mit jmdm. ausgehen; (c) (Amer. coll.: person) Freund, der/Freundin, die; (d) **be out of** ~: altmodisch sein; (expired) nicht mehr gültig sein; **to** ~: bis heute. See also **up to date. 2** v.t. (a) datieren; (b) (coll: make seem old) alt machen. **3** v.i. (a) ~ **back to/** ~ **from a certain time** aus einer bestimmten Zeit stammen; (b) (coll.: become out of ~) aus der Mode kommen

dated /'deɪtɪd/ adj. (coll.) altmodisch

date: ~ **line** n. (Geog.) Datumsgrenze, die; ~ **palm** n. Dattelpalme, die; ~ **rape** n.: Vergewaltigung der eigenen Freundin oder Vergewaltigung einer Frau während einer Verabredung mit ihr; ~ **stamp** n. Datumsstempel, der; ~**-stamp** v.t. abstempeln

'dating agency /'deɪtɪŋ/ n. Partnervermittlung, die

dative /'deɪtɪv/ (Ling.) **1** adj. Dativ; dativisch; ~ **case** Dativ, der. **2** n. Dativ, der

daub /dɔːb/ v.t. (a) (coat) bewerfen; (smear, soil) beschmieren; (b) (spread crudely) schmieren

daughter /'dɔːtə(r)/ n. (lit. or fig.) Tochter, die

'daughter-in-law n., pl. **daughters-in-law** Schwiegertochter, die

daunt /dɔːnt/ v.t. entmutigen; schrecken (geh.); **nothing** ~ed unverzagt

dawdle /'dɔːdl/ v.i. bummeln (ugs.)

dawn /dɔːn/ **1** v.i. (a) dämmern; **day[light]** ~ed der Morgen dämmerte; (b) (fig.) ⟨Zeitalter:⟩ anbrechen; ⟨Idee:⟩ aufkommen; **sth.** ~s **on** or **upon sb.** etw. dämmert jmdm.; **hasn't it** ~ed **on you that** ...? ist dir nicht langsam klar geworden, dass ...? **2** n. [Morgen]dämmerung, die; **from** ~ **to dusk** von früh bis spät; **at** ~: im Morgengrauen

dawn 'chorus n. morgendlicher Gesang der Vögel

day /deɪ/ n. (a) ▶ 739 ↓ Tag, der; **all** ~ **[long]** den ganzen Tag [lang]; **take all** ~ (fig.) eine Ewigkeit brauchen; **all** ~ **and every** ~: tagaus, tagein; **to this** ~, **from that** ~ **to this** bis zum heutigen Tag; **for two** ~s zwei Tage [lang]; **what's the** ~ or **what** ~ **is it today?** welcher Tag ist heute?; **twice a** ~: zweimal täglich od. am Tag; **in a** ~/**two** ~s (within) in od. an einem Tag/in zwei Tagen; **[on] the** ~ **after/before** am Tag danach/davor; **[the] next/[on] the following/[on] the previous** ~: am nächsten/folgenden/vorhergehenden Tag; **the** ~ **before yesterday/after tomorrow** vorgestern/übermorgen; **the other** ~: neulich; **from this/that** ~ **[on]** von heute an/von diesem Tag an; **one of these [fine]** ~s eines [schönen] Tages; **some** ~: eines Tages; irgendwann einmal; **for the** ~: für einen Tag; ~ **after** ~: Tag für Tag; ~ **by** ~, **from** ~ **to** ~: von Tag zu Tag; ~ **in** ~ **out** tagaus, tagein; **call it a** ~ (end work) Feierabend machen; (more generally) Schluss machen; **at the end of the** ~ (fig.) letzten Endes; **it's not my** ~: ich habe [heute] einen schlechten Tag; (b) in sing. or pl. (period) **in the** ~s **when** ...: zu der Zeit, als ...; **these** ~s heutzutage; **in those** ~s damals; zu jener Zeit; **in this** ~ **and age** heutzutage; **have seen/known better** ~s bessere Tage gesehen/gekannt haben; **those were the** ~s das waren noch Zeiten; **in one's** ~: zu seiner Zeit; (during lifetime) in seinem Leben; **every dog has its** ~: jeder hat einmal seine Chance; **it has had its** ~: es hat ausgedient (ugs.); (c) (victory) **win** or **carry the** ~: den Sieg davontragen

-day adj. in comb. -tägig; **three-**~**[s]-old** drei Tage alt; **five-**~ **week** Fünftagewoche, die

day: ~**-boy** n. (Brit.) externer Schüler; ~**break** n. Tagesanbruch, der; **at** ~**break** bei Tagesanbruch; ~ **care** n. Ganztagsbetreuung, die; ~**-care centre** Tagesstätte, die; (for children) Kindertagesstätte, die; [Kinder]krippe, die; (for the elderly) Altenzentrum, das; Altentagesstätte, die; (for invalids or the disabled) Tagesbetreuungsstätte, die; ~**dream 1** n. Tagtraum, der; **2** v.i. träumen; ~**dreamer** n. Tagträumer, der/-träumerin, die; ~**girl** n. (Brit.) externe Schülerin; ~**light** n. (a) (light of ~) Tageslicht, das; **go on working while it's still** ~**light** weiterarbeiten, solange es noch hell ist; **in broad** ~**light** am helllichten Tag[e]; ~**light saving [time]** Sommerzeit, die; (b) (dawn) **at** or **by/before** ~**light** bei/vor Tagesanbruch; (c) (fig.) **I see** ~**light** ich denke, die Situation lichtet sich; **it's** ~**light robbery** es ist der reine Wucher; ~ **re'lease** n. tageweise Freistellung [zur Fortbildung]; **on** ~ **release** unter Inanspruchnahme von tageweiser Freistellung; ~**-release course** Fortbildungskurs, der; Fortbildung, die ~ **re'turn** n. Tagesrückfahrkarte, die ~ **shift** n. Tagschicht, die; **be on [the]** ~ **shift** Tagschicht haben; ~**time** n. Tag, der; **in** or **during the** ~**time** während des Tages; ~**-to-**~ adj. [tag]täglich; ~**-to-**~ **life** Alltagsleben, das; ~ **trip** n. Tagesausflug, der; ~ **tripper** n. Tagesausflügler, der/-ausflüglerin, die

daze /deɪz/ v.t. benommen machen; **be** ~d benommen sein (at von)

dazzle /'dæzl/ v.t. (lit. or fig.: delude) blenden; (fig.: confuse, impress) überwältigen

DBMS abbr. (Computing) **database management system** DBMS

DC abbr. (Electr.) **direct current** GS

D-Day /'diːdeɪ/ n.: Tag der Landung der Alliierten in der Normandie 1944; (fig.) der Tag

DDT abbr. DDT

deacon /'diːkn/ n. Diakon, der

dead /ded/ **1** adj. (a) tot; [as] ~ **as a doornail/as mutton** mausetot (ugs.); **I wouldn't be seen** ~ **in a place like that** (coll.) keine zehn Pferde würden mich an solch einen Ort bringen (ugs.); (b) tot ⟨Materie⟩; erloschen ⟨Vulkan, Gefühl, Interesse⟩; verbraucht, leer ⟨Batterie⟩; tot ⟨Telefon, Leitung, Saison, Kapital, Ball, Sprache⟩; **the phone has gone** ~: die Leitung ist tot; **the motor is** ~: der Motor läuft nicht; (c) expr. completeness plötzlich

Dates

Unlike English which has several variations (May 10, 10 May, May 10th, 10th May etc.), dates in German are always written in the same way:

der 10. Mai

The accusative form is used at the head of letters, preceded by the name of the place:

Amstetten, den 25. August 1997

Dates written all in numbers are found in German as in English, particularly in business letters:

Frankfurt a.M., den 15.1.1997

With reference to your letter of the 4.1.1997 or (Amer.) 1.4.1997 = Bezug nehmend auf Ihr Schreiben vom 4.1.1997 (*spoken*: vom vierten Ersten neunzehnhundertsiebenundneunzig)

Saying dates

What's the date?	= Welches Datum haben wir heute?, Der Wievielte ist heute?
It's May the tenth	= Es ist der zehnte Mai
What date is the wedding?	= Wann ist die Hochzeit?; (*if the month is known*) Am Wievielten ist die Hochzeit?
The wedding is on the 22nd (twenty-second)	= Die Hochzeit ist am 22. (Zweiundzwanzigsten)

	WRITTEN	SPOKEN
May 1st, May 1	der 1. Mai	der erste Mai
May 21st, May 21	der 21. Mai	der einundzwanzigste Mai
May 30th, May 30	der 30. Mai	der dreißigste Mai
Monday May 3rd 1994	Montag, der 3. Mai 1994	Montag, der dritte Mai neunzehnhundertvierundneunzig
21.5.66 or (Amer.) 5.21.66	21.5.66	der einundzwanzigste Fünfte sechsundsechzig
1900	1900	neunzehnhundert
the year 2000	das Jahr 2000	das Jahr zweitausend
2001	2001	zweitausend-[und]eins
230 AD	230 n.Chr.	zweihundertdreißig nach Christus
55 BC	55 v.Chr.	fünfundfünfzig vor Christus
the 16th century	das 16. Jahrhundert or Jh.	das sechzehnte Jahrhundert

Saying when

on with days and dates is translated by **an** with the definite article, conflated to **am,** whether there is a definite article in English or not:

on Friday	= am Freitag*
on March 6th	= am 6. März (*spoken* am sechsten März)
on Friday March 6th	= am Freitag, den *or* dem 6. März
on the first of next month	= am nächsten Ersten

An exception is not unnaturally:

It happened on a Tuesday	= Es geschah an einem Dienstag

If an adjective follows *a* or *one*, the genitive construction can be used:

on a fine Sunday, one fine Sunday	= eines schönen Sonntags

*With days of the week the **am** can be omitted colloquially:

She's coming on Friday	= Sie kommt Freitag

in with months is **in** plus the definite article, conflated to **im:**

in June	= im Juni
last June	= voriges Jahr im Juni
next June	= im Juni nächsten Jahres

But note:

at the end/beginning of June	= Ende/Anfang Juni
in the middle of July	= Mitte Juli

When giving the year when something happened in German, the year is usually given on its own without any preposition, although "im Jahre" can be added in more formal language or when "v.Chr." or "n.Chr" follow:

He died in 1945	= Er starb 1945
in 55 BC	= im Jahre 55 v.Chr.
in 27 AD	= im Jahre 27 n.Chr.

Other phrases:

from November/ November 5th (onwards)	= ab November/ab dem 5. November, vom November an/vom 5. November an
from next Tuesday	= ab kommendem Dienstag
from the 21st to the 30th	= vom 21. bis zum 30.
It will be ready by Friday/by the 14th	= Es wird bis Freitag/bis zum 14. fertig
It won't be ready until Friday	= Es wird erst [am] Freitag fertig
around May 16th	= um den 16. Mai [herum]
in the sixties or 60s	= in den Sechzigerjahren *or* 60er-Jahren
in the 1880s	= in den Achtzigerjahren des 19. Jahrhunderts, in den 1880er-Jahren
the 1912 uprising	= der Aufstand von 1912
the 19th century novel	= der Roman des 19. Jahrhunderts
a 17th century composer	= ein Komponist des 17. Jahrhunderts
a 14th century building	= ein Gebäude aus dem 14. Jahrhundert

---

⟨*Halt*⟩; völlig ⟨*Stillstand*⟩; genau ⟨*Mitte*⟩; ∼ **silence** *or* **quiet** Totenstille, *die;* ∼ **calm** Flaute, *die;* ∼ **faint** [totenähnliche] Ohnmacht; (**d**) (benumbed) taub; (**e**) (exhausted) erschöpft; kaputt (ugs.). **2** *adv.* (**a**) (completely) völlig; ∼ **straight** schnurgerade; ∼ **tired** todmüde; ∼ **easy** *or* **simple/slow** kinderleicht/ganz langsam; '∼ **slow**'

„Schritt fahren"; ∼ **drunk** stockbetrunken (ugs.); be ∼ **against sth.** absolut gegen etw. sein; (**b**) (exactly) ∼ **on target** genau im Ziel; ∼ **on time** auf die Minute; ∼ **on two [o'clock]** Punkt zwei [Uhr]. **3** *n.* (**a**) **in the** ∼ **of winter/night** mitten im Winter/in der Nacht; (**b**) *pl.* **the** ∼**:** die Toten *Pl.*

Days of the week

ENGLISH	GERMAN	ABBREVIATION
Monday	**Montag**	**Mo**
Tuesday	**Dienstag**	**Di**
Wednesday	**Mittwoch**	**Mi**
Thursday	**Donnerstag**	**Do**
Friday	**Freitag**	**Fr**
Saturday	**Samstag***	**Sa**
Sunday	**Sonntag**	**So**

Note that the week is considered as beginning on Monday. The abbreviations given are used mainly in printed matter, such as calendars, diaries, timetables and notices giving opening times, rather than in private or business correspondence. All the days of the week are masculine.

*An alternative for **Samstag** used mainly in North Germany is **Sonnabend**.

Saying when

As with dates, the English *on* is translated by **am:**

| *I am leaving on Wednesday* | = Ich fahre am Mittwoch |

Sometimes this is omitted in speech or a letter, especially where there are further details in the sentence:

| *I am leaving on Wednesday for Cairo* | = Ich fahre Mittwoch nach Kairo |

One exception to the use of **am** is naturally enough when the indefinite article *a* or *one* is used for a particular occasion:

Her birthday is on a Tuesday	= Ihr Geburtstag ist an einem Dienstag
It happened one wet Sunday	= Es geschah an einem verregneten Sonntag
One Saturday I met him at the zoo	= Eines Samstags traf ich ihn im Zoo

Repeated events are another exception to the use of **am:**

| *I go home on Fridays/ every Friday* | = Ich fahre freitags/jeden Freitag nach Hause |
| *Her evening class is on Mondays or on a Monday* | = Ihr Abendkurs ist montags |

Notice that the adverbial forms **montags, dienstags** etc. are written with a small letter.

Some more expressions for less frequent or regular events:

every other Thursday	= jeden zweiten Donnerstag
every third Monday	= jeden dritten Montag
most Saturdays	= fast jeden Samstag
some Wednesdays	= manchmal am Mittwoch
on the occasional or odd Friday	= ab und zu am Freitag

Looking backwards and forwards

last Thursday	= letzten Donnerstag
[on] the preceding Thursday	= am vorangehenden Donnerstag
[on] the Thursday before last	= vorletzten Donnerstag

a week ago on Thursday	= Donnerstag vor einer Woche
I shall see her next Monday or this [coming] Monday	= Ich werde sie [am] nächsten or kommenden Montag sehen
I saw her the next or the following Monday	= Ich habe sie am [darauf] folgenden Montag gesehen
the Monday after next	= übernächsten Montag
a week on Monday	= Montag in einer Woche
from Saturday [on]	= ab Samstag, von Samstag an
It has to be ready by Friday	= Es muss bis Freitag fertig sein

Times of day

on Monday morning	= [am] Montagmorgen
on Wednesday afternoon	[am] Mittwoch- nachmittag
on Thursday evening	= [am] Donnerstagabend
on Friday night	= *(early)* [am] Freitagabend; *(late)* Freitagnacht

And if it's habitual:

on Monday mornings	= montagmorgens
on Wednesday afternoons	= mittwochnachmittags
on Thursday evenings	= donnerstagabends
on Friday nights	= *(early)* freitagabends; *(late)* freitagnachts

Today

| *What day is it [today]?* | = Welchen Tag haben wir heute? |
| *It's Tuesday [today]* | = Heute ist Dienstag |

Belonging to a certain day

German has more than one way of expressing this, where in English we have simply the name of the day with or without an apostrophe s; there are adjectives for all the days of the week except Wednesday (**Mittwoch**) which relate to a habitual occurrence, or a compound can be formed, especially for a particular institution:

his [regular] Sunday walk	= sein sonntäglicher Spaziergang
the Sunday papers	= die Sonntagszeitungen
a Sunday driver	= ein Sonntagsfahrer
Monday's trains	= die Züge am Montag
Wednesday's classes	= die Schulstunden am Mittwoch
Tuesday's paper	= die Zeitung von Dienstag
There will be a Saturday [train] service	= Die Züge werden wie an einem Samstag verkehren
Wednesday's sailing is cancelled	= Das Schiff am Mittwoch fällt aus

See also □ **Dates**

---

dead 'beat *pred. adj.* (exhausted) völlig zerschlagen

deaden /'dedn/ *v.t.* dämpfen; abstumpfen ‹*Gefühl*›; betäuben ‹*Nerv, Körperteil, Schmerz*›

dead: ∼ **'end** *n.* (closed end) Absperrung, *die;* (street; also fig.) Sackgasse, *die;* ∼**-end** *attrib. adj.* **(a)** ∼-end street/

road Sackgasse, *die;* **(b)** (fig.) aussichtslos; **she's in a** ∼**-end job** in ihrem Job hat sie keine Aufstiegschancen; ∼ **'heat** *n.* totes Rennen; ∼ **'letter** *n.* **(a)** (law) Gesetz, das nicht angewendet wird; **be a** ∼ **letter** nur noch auf dem Papier bestehen; **(b)** (letter) unzustellbarer Brief; ∼**line** *n.* [letzter] Termin; **meet the** ∼**line** den Termin einhalten;

set a ~line for sth. eine Frist für etw. setzen; ~**lock** *n.* völliger Stillstand; **come to a** *or* **reach** [a] ~**lock/be at** ~**lock** an einem toten Punkt anlangen/angelangt sein; **the negotiations had reached** ~**lock** die Verhandlungen waren festgefahren; ~ '**loss** *n.* (coll.) (worthless thing) totaler Reinfall (ugs.); (person) hoffnungsloser Fall (ugs.)

deadly /'dedlɪ/ **1** *adj.* tödlich; (fig. coll.: awful) fürchterlich; (very boring) todlangweilig; (very dangerous) lebensgefährlich; ~ **enemy** Todfeind, *der;* **I'm in** ~ **earnest about this** es ist mir todernst damit. **2** *adv.* tod-; (extremely) äußerst; ~ **pale** totenblass; ~ **dull** todlangweilig

deadly 'nightshade *n.* (Bot.) Tollkirsche, *die*

dead: ~ '**on** *adj., adv.* [ganz] genau; ~**pan** *adj.* unbewegt; **he had a** ~**pan expression** er verzog keine Miene; ~ **ringer** /ded 'rɪŋə(r)/ *n.* (coll.) Doppelgänger, *der/*-gängerin, *die;* **a** ~ **ringer for Trotski** ein Doppelgänger *od.* Double Trotzkis; **a** ~ **ringer for his father** ein Ebenbild seines Vaters; **be a** ~ **ringer for sb.** jmdm. zum Verwechseln ähnlich sehen; **D**~ '**Sea** *pr. n.* Tote Meer, *das;* ~ **weight** *n.* (inert mass) Eigengewicht, *das;* (fig.) schwere Bürde

deaf /def/ *adj.* (a) taub; ~ **and dumb** taubstumm; ~ **in one ear** auf einem Ohr taub; (b) (insensitive) **be** ~ **to sth.** kein Ohr für etw. haben; (fig.) taub gegenüber etw. sein; **turn a** ~ **ear [to sth./sb.]** sich [gegenüber etw./jmdm.] taub stellen; **fall on** ~ **ears** kein Gehör finden

'**deaf aid** *n.* Hörgerät, *das*

deafen /'defn/ *v.t.* ~ **sb.** bei jmdm. zur Taubheit führen; **I was** ~**ed by the noise** (fig.) ich war von dem Lärm wie betäubt

deafening /'defnɪŋ/ ohrenbetäubend ‹*Lärm, Musik, Geschrei*›

deaf 'mute *n.* Taubstumme, *der/die*

deafness /'defnɪs/ *n., no pl.* Taubheit, *die*

deal¹ /diːl/ **1** *v.t.,* **dealt** /delt/ (a) (Cards) austeilen; **who** ~**t the cards?** wer hat gegeben?; (b) ~ **sb. a blow** (lit. or fig.) jmdm. einen Schlag versetzen. **2** *v.i.,* **dealt** (a) (do business) ~ **with sb.** mit jmdm. Geschäfte machen; ~ **in sth.** mit etw. handeln; (b) (occupy oneself) ~ **with sth.** sich mit etw. befassen; (manage) mit etw. fertig werden; (c) (take measures) ~ **with sb.** mit jmdm. fertig werden. **3** *n.* (a) (coll.: arrangement, bargain) Geschäft, *das;* **make a** ~ **with sb.** mit jmdm. ein Geschäft abschließen; **it's a** ~! abgemacht!; **big** ~! (iron.) na und?; **fair** ~ (treatment) faire *od.* gerechte Behandlung; **raw** *or* **rough** ~ ungerechte Behandlung; (b) (coll.: agreement) **make** *or* **do a** ~ **with sb.** mit jmdm. eine Vereinbarung treffen; (c) (Cards) **it's your** ~: du gibst

~ '**out** *v.t.* verteilen

deal² *n.* **a great** *or* **good** ~, (coll.) **a** ~: viel; (often) ziemlich viel; **a great** *or* **good** ~ **of,** (coll.) **a** ~ **of** eine [ganze] Menge

dealer /'diːlə(r)/ *n.* (a) ▶ 887 | (trader) Händler, *der;* **he's a** ~ **in antiques** er ist Antiquitätenhändler *od.* handelt mit Antiquitäten; (b) (Cards) Geber, *der;* **he's the** ~: er gibt

dealership /'diːləʃɪp/ *n.* (Commerc.) Vertretung, *die;* **a network of Ford** ~**s** ein Netz von Fordvertragshändlern

dealing /'diːlɪŋ/ *n.* **have** ~**s with sb.** mit jmdm. zu tun haben

dealt ⇨ **deal**¹ 1, 2

dean /diːn/ *n.* (a) (Eccl.) Dechant, *der;* Dekan, *der;* (b) (in college, university, etc.) Dekan, *der*

dear /dɪə(r)/ **1** *adj.* (a) (beloved; also iron.) lieb; geliebt; (sweet; also iron.) entzückend; **my** ~ **sir/madam** [mein] lieber Herr/[meine] liebe Dame; **my** ~ **man/woman** guter Mann/gute Frau; **my** ~ **child/girl** [mein] liebes Kind/liebes Mädchen; **sb./sth. is [very]** ~ **to sb.['s heart]** jmd. liebt jmdn./etw. [über alles]; **sb. holds sb./sth.** ~: jmd./etw. liegt jmdm. [sehr] am Herzen; **run for** ~ **life** um sein Leben rennen; (b) (beginning letter) **D**~ **Sir/ Madam** Sehr geehrter Herr/Sehr verehrte gnädige Frau; **D**~ **Mr Jones/Mrs Jones** Sehr geehrter Herr Jones/ Sehr verehrte Frau Jones; **D**~ **Malcolm/Emily** Lieber Malcolm/Liebe Emily; (c) (expensive) teuer. **2** *int.* ~, ~!, ~ **me!, oh** ~! [ach] du liebe *od.* meine Güte! **3** *n.* (a)

she is a ~: sie ist ein Schatz; (b) [**my**] ~ (to wife, husband, younger relative) [mein] Liebling; [mein] Schatz; (to little girl/ boy) [meine] Kleine/[mein] Kleiner; ~**est** Liebling (*der*). **4** *adv.* teuer

dearly /'dɪəlɪ/ *adv.* (a) von ganzem Herzen; **I'd** ~ **love to do that** ich würde das liebend gern tun; (b) (at high price) teuer

dearth /dɜːθ/ *n.* Mangel, *der* (**of** an + *Dat.*); **there is no** ~ **of sth.** es fehlt nicht an etw. (*Dat.*)

death /deθ/ *n.* (a) Tod, *der;* **after** ~: nach dem Tod; **meet one's death** den Tod finden (geh.); **catch one's** ~ [**of cold**] (coll.) sich (*Dat.*) den Tod holen (ugs.); … **to** ~: zu Tode …; **bleed to** ~: verbluten; **freeze to** ~: erfrieren; **beat sb. to** ~: jmdn. totschlagen; **I'm scared to** ~ (fig.) mir ist angst und bange (**about** *vor* + *Dat.*); **be sick to** ~ **of sth.** (fig.) etw. gründlich satt haben; [**fight**] **to the** ~: auf Leben und Tod [kämpfen]; **be at** ~'**s door** an der Schwelle des Todes stehen; (b) (instance) Todesfall, *der*

death: ~**bed** *n.* **on one's** ~**bed** auf dem Sterbebett; ~ **certificate** *n.* Totenschein, *der;* ~-**defying** *adj.* todesmutig

deathly /'deθlɪ/ **1** *adj.* tödlich; ~ **stillness/hush** Totenstille, *die.* **2** *adv.* tödlich; ~ **pale** totenblass; ~ **still/quiet** totenstill

death: ~ **penalty** *n.* Todesstrafe, *die;* ~ **rate** *n.* Sterblichkeitsziffer, *die;* ~'**s head** *n.* Totenkopf, *der;* ~ **squad** *n.* Todesschwadron, *die;* Killerkommando, *das;* ~ **threat** *n.* Morddrohung, *die;* ~ **throes** *n. pl.* Todeskampf, *der;* Agonie, *die* (geh.); **be in one's [last]** ~ **throes** mit dem Tode[e] ringen; in Agonie liegen (geh.); ‹*Tier.:*› **be in its [last]** ~ **throes** am Verenden sein; (fig.) ‹*politisches System:*› in Agonie liegen (geh.); ~ **toll** *n.* Zahl der Todesopfer; ~ **trap** *n.* lebensgefährliche Sache; ~ **warrant** *n.* Exekutionsbefehl, *der;* (fig.) Todesurteil, *das;* ~-**watch** [**beetle**] *n.* (Zool.) Totenuhr, *die*

debar /dɪ'bɑː(r)/ *v.t.,* -**rr**- ausschließen; ~ **sb. from doing sth.** jmdn. davon ausschließen, etw. zu tun

debase /dɪ'beɪs/ *v.t.* (a) verschlechtern; herabsetzen, entwürdigen ‹*Person*›; ~ **oneself** sich erniedrigen; (b) ~ **the coinage** den Wert der Währung mindern

debatable /dɪ'beɪtəbl/ *adj.* (questionable) fraglich

debate /dɪ'beɪt/ **1** *v.t.* debattieren über (+ *Akk.*); **be** ~**d** diskutiert *od.* debattiert werden. **2** *n.* Debatte, *die;* **there was much** ~ **about whether** … es wurde viel darüber debattiert, ob …

debauchery /dɪ'bɔːtʃərɪ/ *n.* (literary) Ausschweifung, *die*

debenture /dɪ'bentʃə(r)/ *n.* (Finance) Schuldverschreibung, *die*

debility /dɪ'bɪlɪtɪ/ *n.* Schwäche, *die*

debit /'debɪt/ **1** *n.* (Bookk.) Soll, *das;* ~ **balance** Lastschrift, *die* (Finance) Sollseite, *die.* **2** *v.t.* belasten; ~ **sb./sb.'s account with a sum** jmdn./jmds. Konto mit einer Summe belasten

debonair /debə'neə(r)/ *adj.* frohgemut

debrief /diː'briːf/ *v.t.* (coll.) befragen (bei Rückkehr von einem Einsatz usw.)

debriefing /diː'briːfɪŋ/ *n.* (coll.) Befragung, *die;* **hold a** ~ **session** sich Bericht erstatten lassen

debris /'debriː, 'deɪbriː/ *n., no pl.* Trümmer *Pl.*

debt /det/ *n.* Schuld, *die;* **National D**~: Staatsverschuldung, *die;* **be in** ~: verschuldet sein; **get** *or* **run into** ~: in Schulden geraten; sich verschulden; **get out of** ~: aus den Schulden herauskommen; **be in sb.'s** ~: in jmds. Schuld stehen

'**debt collector** *n.* ▶ 887 | Inkassobevollmächtigte, *der/die*

debtor /'detə(r)/ *n.* Schuldner, *der/*Schuldnerin, *die*

debug /diː'bʌg/ *v.t.,* -**gg**- (remove microphones from) von Wanzen befreien; (remove defects from) von Fehlern befreien

debunk /diː'bʌŋk/ *v.t.* (coll.) (remove false reputation from) entlarven; (expose falseness of) bloßstellen

debut (*also:* **début**) /'deɪbuː, 'deɪbjuː/ *n.* Debüt, *das;* **make one's** ~: debütieren

debutante (*also:* **débutante**) /'debju:tɑ:nt, 'deɪbju:tɑ:nt/ *n.* Debütantin, *die*

Dec. *abbr.* **December** Dez.

decade /'dekeɪd/ *n.* Jahrzehnt, *das;* Dekade, *die*

decadence /'dekədəns/ *n.* Dekadenz, *die*

decadent /'dekədənt/ *adj.* dekadent

decaf, decaff /'di:kæf/ *n.* (coll.) *or* (**P**) koffeinfreier Kaffee

decaffeinated /di:'kæfɪneɪtɪd/ *adj.* entkoffeiniert; koffeinfrei (veralt.)

decamp /dɪ'kæmp/ *v.i.* verschwinden (ugs.)

decant /dɪ'kænt/ *v.t.* abgießen; dekantieren ‹ *Wein* ›

decanter /dɪ'kæntə(r)/ *n.* Karaffe, *die*

decapitate /dɪ'kæpɪteɪt/ *v.t.* köpfen

decathlon /dɪ'kæθlən/ *n.* (Sport) Zehnkampf, *der*

decay /dɪ'keɪ/ **1** *v.i.* (a) (become rotten) verrotten; [ver]faulen; ‹ *Zahn:* › faul *od.* (fachspr.) kariös werden; ‹ *Gebäude:* › zerfallen; (**b**) (decline) verfallen. **2** *n.* (**a**) (rotting) Verrotten, *das;* (of tooth) Fäule, *die;* (of building) Zerfall, *der;* (**b**) (decline) Verfall, *der*

decease /dɪ'si:s/ *n.* (Law/formal) Ableben, *das* (geh.)

deceased /dɪ'si:st/ (Law/formal) **1** *adj.* verstorben. **2** *n.* Verstorbene, *der/die*

deceit /dɪ'si:t/ *n.* Täuschung, *die;* Betrug, *der;* (being deceitful) Falschheit, *die*

deceitful /dɪ'si:tfl/ *adj.* falsch ‹ *Person, Art, Charakter* ›; hinterlistig ‹ *Trick* ›

deceitfulness /dɪ'si:tflnɪs/ *n., no pl.* ⇒ **deceitful:** Falschheit, *die;* Hinterlistigkeit, *die*

deceive /dɪ'si:v/ *v.t.* täuschen; (be unfaithful to) betrügen; ∼ **sb. into doing sth.** jmdn. [durch Täuschung] dazu bringen, etw. zu tun; ∼ **oneself** sich täuschen; (delude oneself) sich (*Dat.*) etwas vormachen (ugs.)

decelerate /di:'seləreɪt/ **1** *v.t.* verlangsamen. **2** *v.i.* ‹ *Fahrzeug, Fahrer:* › langsamer fahren

December /dɪ'sembə(r)/ *n.* ▶ **738** Dezember, *der; see also* **August**

decency /'di:sənsɪ/ *n.* (propriety) Anstand, *der;* (of manners, literature, language) Schicklichkeit, *die* (geh.); (fairness, respectability) Anständigkeit, *die; **it is [a matter of] common** ∼:* es ist eine Frage des Anstands

decent /'di:sənt/ *adj.* (**a**) (seemly) schicklich (geh.); anständig ‹ *Person* ›; (**b**) (passable, respectable) annehmbar; anständig ‹ *Person, ugs. auch Preis, Gehalt* ›

decentralisation, decentralise ⇒ **decentraliz-**

decentralization /di:sentrəlaɪ'zeɪʃn/ *n.* Dezentralisierung, *die*

decentralize /di:'sentrəlaɪz/ *v.t.* dezentralisieren

deception /dɪ'sepʃn/ *n.* (**a**) (deceiving, trickery) Betrug, *der;* (being deceived) Täuschung, *die; use* ∼: betrügen; (**b**) (trick) Betrügerei, *die*

deceptive /dɪ'septɪv/ *adj.* trügerisch

decibel /'desɪbel/ *n.* Dezibel, *das*

decide /dɪ'saɪd/ **1** *v.t.* (**a**) (settle, judge) entscheiden über (+ *Akk.*); ∼ **that** …: entscheiden, dass …; (**b**) (resolve) ∼ **that** …: beschließen, dass …; ∼ **to do sth.** sich entschließen, etw. zu tun. **2** *v.i.* sich entscheiden (**in favour of** zugunsten von, **on** für); ∼ **against doing sth.** sich dagegen entscheiden, etw. zu tun

decided /dɪ'saɪdɪd/ *adj.* (**a**) (unquestionable) entschieden; eindeutig; (**b**) (not hesitant) bestimmt

decidedly /dɪ'saɪdɪdlɪ/ *adv.* (**a**) (unquestionably) entschieden; deutlich; (**b**) (firmly) bestimmt

decider /dɪ'saɪdə(r)/ *n.* (game) Entscheidungsspiel, *das*

deciduous /dɪ'sɪdjʊəs/ *adj.* (Bot.) ∼ **leaves** Blätter, die abgeworfen werden; ∼ **tree** laubwerfender Baum; ≈ Laubbaum, *der*

decimal /'desɪml/ *adj.* ▶ **956** **1** *adj.* Dezimal-; **go** ∼: sich auf das Dezimalsystem umstellen. **2** *n.* Dezimalbruch, *der*

decimal: ∼ **'coinage,** ∼ **'currency** *ns.* Dezimalwährung, *die;* ∼ **'fraction** *n.* Dezimalbruch, *der*

decimalize (decimalise) /'desɪməlaɪz/ *v.t.* (express as decimal) als Dezimalzahl schreiben; (convert to decimal system) dezimalisieren

decimal: ∼ **'place** *n.* Dezimale, *die;* **calculate sth. to five** ∼ **places** etw. auf fünf Stellen nach dem Komma ausrechnen; ∼ **'point** *n.* Komma, *das;* ∼ **system** *n.* Dezimalsystem, *das*

decimate /'desɪmeɪt/ *v.t.* dezimieren

decipher /dɪ'saɪfə(r)/ *v.t.* entziffern

decision /dɪ'sɪʒn/ *n.* Entscheidung, *die* (**on** über + *Akk.*); **it's 'your** ∼: die Entscheidung liegt ganz bei dir; **come to** *or* **reach a** ∼: zu einer Entscheidung kommen; **make** *or* **take a** ∼: eine Entscheidung treffen

decisive /dɪ'saɪsɪv/ *adj.* (**a**) (conclusive) entscheidend; (**b**) (decided) entschlussfreudig ‹ *Person* ›; bestimmt ‹ *Charakter, Art* ›

deck /dek/ **1** *n.* (**a**) (of ship) Deck, *das;* **above** ∼: auf Deck; **below** ∼**[s]** unter Deck; **clear the** ∼**s** [**for action** *etc.*] das Schiff klarmachen [zum Gefecht *usw.*]; **on** ∼: an Deck; **all hands on** ∼! alle Mann an Deck!; (**b**) (of bus etc.) Deck, *das;* **the upper** ∼: das Oberdeck; (**c**) (tape ∼) Tape-deck, *das;* (record ∼) Plattenspieler, *der.* **2** *v.t.* ∼ **sth.** [**with sth.**] etw. [mit etw.] schmücken

∼ **'out** *v.t.* herausputzen ‹ *Person* ›; [aus]schmücken ‹ *Raum* ›

'deckchair *n.* Liegestuhl, *der;* (on ship) Liege- *od.* Deckstuhl, *der*

declaim /dɪ'kleɪm/ *v.i.* eifern; deklamieren (veralt.)

declaration /deklə'reɪʃn/ *n.* Erklärung, *die;* (at customs) Deklaration, *die;* ∼ **of war** Kriegserklärung, *die;* **make a** ∼: eine Erklärung abgeben

declare /dɪ'kleə(r)/ *v.t.* (**a**) (announce) erklären; (state explicitly) kundtun (geh.) ‹ *Wunsch, Absicht* ›; Ausdruck verleihen (+ *Dat.*) (geh.) ‹ *Hoffnung* ›; (**b**) (pronounce) ∼ **sth./sb.** [**to be**] **sth.** etw./jmdn. für etw. erklären

declassify /di:'klæsɪfaɪ/ *v.t.* freigeben

declension /dɪ'klenʃn/ *n.* (Ling.) Deklination, *die*

decline /dɪ'klaɪn/ **1** *v.i.* (**a**) (fall off) nachlassen; ‹ *Moral:* › sinken, nachlassen; ‹ *Preis, Anzahl:* › sinken, zurückgehen; ‹ *Gesundheitszustand:* › sich verschlechtern; (**b**) (refuse) ∼ **with thanks** (also iron.) dankend ablehnen. **2** *v.t.* (**a**) (refuse) ablehnen; ∼ **to do sth.** [es] ablehnen, etw. zu tun; (**b**) (Ling.) deklinieren. **3** *n.* Nachlassen, *das* (**in** *Gen.*); **a** ∼ **in prices/numbers** ein Sinken der Preise/Anzahl; **be on the** ∼: nachlassen

declutch /di:'klʌtʃ/ *v.i.* (Motor Veh.) auskuppeln; **double-**∼: Zwischengas geben

decode /di:'kəʊd/ *v.t.* dekodieren, dechiffrieren ‹ *Mitteilung, Signal* ›; entschlüsseln ‹ *Schrift, Hieroglyphen* ›

decommission /di:kə'mɪʃən/ *v.t.* stilllegen; außer Dienst stellen ‹ *Schiff* ›

decompose /di:kəm'pəʊz/ *v.i.* sich zersetzen

decomposition /di:kɒmpə'zɪʃn/ *n.* Zersetzung, *die*

decompress /di:kəm'pres/ *v.t.* (Computing) dekomprimieren

decompression /di:kəm'preʃn/ *n.* Dekompression, *die*

decontaminate /di:kən'tæmɪneɪt/ *v.t.* dekontaminieren (fachspr.); entseuchen

decontamination /di:kəntæmɪ'neɪʃn/ *n.* Dekontamination, *die* (fachspr.); Entseuchung, *die*

decor (*also:* **décor**)/'deɪkɔ:(r)/ *n.* Ausstattung, *die*

decorate /'dekəreɪt/ *v.t.* (**a**) schmücken ‹ *Raum, Straße, Baum* ›; verzieren ‹ *Kuchen, Kleid* ›; dekorieren ‹ *Schaufenster* ›; (with wallpaper) tapezieren; (with paint) streichen; (**b**) (invest with order etc.) auszeichnen

decoration /dekə'reɪʃn/ *n.* (**a**) ⇒ **decorate** a: Schmücken, *das;* Verzieren, *das;* Dekoration, *die;* Tapezieren, *das;* Streichen, *das;* (**b**) (adornment) (thing) Schmuck, *der;* (in shop window) Dekoration, *die;* (**c**) (medal etc.) Auszeichnung, *die;* (**d**) *in pl.* **Christmas** ∼**s** Weihnachtsschmuck, *der*

decorative /'dekərətɪv/ *adj.* dekorativ

decorator /'dekəreɪtə(r)/ *n.* ▶ **887** Maler, *der*/Malerin, *die;* (paper-hanger) Tapezierer, *der*/Tapeziererin, *die*

decorum /dɪ'kɔ:rəm/ *n.* Schicklichkeit, *die* (geh.); **behave with** ∼: sich schicklich benehmen

decoy /dɪ'kɔɪ, 'di:kɔɪ/ *n.* (Hunting; also person) Lockvogel, *der*

decrease 1 /dɪˈkriːs/ *v.i.* abnehmen; ⟨*Anzahl, Einfuhr, Produktivität:*⟩ abnehmen, zurückgehen; ⟨*Stärke, Gesundheit:*⟩ nachlassen; ∼ **in value/size/weight** an Wert/Größe/Gewicht verlieren; ∼ **in price** im Preis fallen. **2** /dɪˈkriːs/ *v.t.* reduzieren; [ver]mindern ⟨*Wert, Lärm, Körperkraft*⟩; schmälern ⟨*Popularität, Macht*⟩. **3** /ˈdiːkriːs/ *n.* Rückgang, *der;* (in weight, stocks) Abnahme, *die;* (in strength, power, energy) Nachlassen, *das;* (in value, noise) Minderung, *die;* **a** ∼ **in speed** eine Minderung der Geschwindigkeit; **be on the** ∼ ⇒ **1**

decree /dɪˈkriː/ **1** *n.* **(a)** (ordinance) Dekret, *das;* Erlass, *der;* **(b)** (Law) Urteil, *das;* ∼ **nisi/absolute** vorläufiges/endgültiges Scheidungsurteil. **2** *v.t.* (ordain) verfügen

decrepit /dɪˈkrepɪt/ *adj.* altersschwach; (dilapidated) heruntergekommen ⟨*Haus, Stadt*⟩

decriminalize /diːˈkrɪmɪnəlaɪz/ *v.t.* entkriminalisieren

decry /dɪˈkraɪ/ *v.t.* verwerfen

dedicate /ˈdedɪkeɪt/ *v.t.* **(a)** ∼ **sth. to sb.** jmdm. etw. widmen; **(b)** (give up) ∼ **one's life to sth.** sein Leben einer Sache (*Dat.*) weihen; **(c)** (devote solemnly) weihen

dedicated /ˈdedɪkeɪtɪd/ *adj.* **(a)** (devoted) **be** ∼ **to sth./sb.** nur für etw./jmdn. leben; **(b)** (devoted to vocation) hingebungsvoll; **a** ∼ **teacher** ein Lehrer mit Leib und Seele

dedication /dedɪˈkeɪʃn/ *n.* **(a)** Widmung, *die* (**to** *Dat.*); **(b)** (devotion) Hingabe, *die*

deduce /dɪˈdjuːs/ *v.t.* ableiten, schließen auf (**from** aus); ∼ **from sth. that** …: aus etw. schließen, dass …

deduct /dɪˈdʌkt/ *v.t.* abziehen (**from** von)

deductible /dɪˈdʌktɪbl/ *adj.* **be** ∼: einbehalten werden [können]

deduction /dɪˈdʌkʃn/ *n.* **(a)** (deducting) Abzug, *der;* **(b)** (deducing, thing deduced) Ableitung, *die;* **(c)** (amount) Abzüge *Pl.*

deductive /dɪˈdʌktɪv/ *adj.* deduktiv

deed /diːd/ *n.* **(a)** Tat, *die;* **(b)** (Law) [gesiegelte] Urkunde

deejay /ˈdiːˈdʒeɪ/ *n.* (coll.) Diskjockey, *der*

deem /diːm/ *v.t.* erachten für; [as] **I** ∼**ed** wie mir schien

deep /diːp/ **1** *adj.* **(a)** ▶ 850] (lit. or fig.) tief; **water ten feet** ∼: drei Meter tiefes Wasser; **take a** ∼ **breath** tief Atem holen; **ten feet** ∼ **in water** drei Meter tief unter Wasser; **be** ∼ **in thought/prayer** in Gedanken/im Gebet versunken sein; **be** ∼ **in debt** hoch verschuldet sein; **be standing three** ∼: drei hintereinander stehen; **(b)** (profound) tief ⟨*Grund*⟩; gründlich ⟨*Studium, Forschung*⟩; tiefgründig ⟨*Bemerkung*⟩; **give sth.** ∼ **thought** über etw. (*Akk.*) gründlich nachdenken; **he's a** ∼ **one** (coll.) er ist ein stilles Wasser (ugs.); **(c)** (heartfelt) tief; aufrichtig ⟨*Interesse, Dank*⟩. **2** *adv.* tief; **still waters run** ∼ (prov.) stille Wasser sind tief (Spr.); ∼ **down** (fig.) im Innersten

deepen /ˈdiːpn/ **1** *v.t.* **(a)** tiefer machen; vertiefen; **(b)** (increase, intensify) vertiefen; intensivieren ⟨*Farbe*⟩. **2** *v.i.* **(a)** tiefer werden; **(b)** (intensify) sich vertiefen

deep: ∼**'freeze 1** *n.* (also Amer. **P**) **D**∼**freeze** Tiefkühltruhe, *die;* **2** *v.t.* tiefgefrieren; ∼**-fried** *adj.* frittiert

deeply /ˈdiːplɪ/ *adv.* (lit. or fig.) tief; äußerst ⟨*interessiert, dankbar, selbstbewusst*⟩; **be** ∼ **in love** sehr verliebt sein; **be** ∼ **indebted to sb.** jmdm. sehr zu Dank verpflichtet sein

deep: ∼**-rooted** *adj.* tief ⟨*Abneigung*⟩; tief verwurzelt ⟨*Tradition*⟩; ∼**-sea** *adj.* Tiefsee; ∼**-'seated** *adj.* tief sitzend; ∼ **space** *n.* [erdferner] Weltraum; All, *das*

deer /dɪə(r)/ *n., pl. same* Hirsch, *der;* (roe ∼) Reh, *das*

deer: ∼ **park** *n.* Wildpark, *der;* ∼**skin** *n.* Rehleder, *das;* ∼**stalker** /ˈdɪəstɔːkə(r)/ *n.* (hat) ≈ Sherlock-Holmes-Mütze, *die*

de-escalation /diːeskəˈleɪʃn/ *n., no pl.* Deeskalation, *die* (geh.); (of a conflict) Entschärfung, *die*

deface /dɪˈfeɪs/ *v.t.* verunstalten; verschandeln ⟨*Gebäude*⟩

defamation /defəˈmeɪʃn, diːfəˈmeɪʃn/ *n.* Diffamierung, *die*

defamatory /dɪˈfæmətərɪ/ *adj.* diffamierend

defame /dɪˈfeɪm/ *v.t.* diffamieren; beschmutzen ⟨*Name, Ansehen*⟩

default /dɪˈfɔːlt, dɪˈfɒlt/ **1** *n.* **in** ∼ **of** mangels (+ *Gen.*); in Ermangelung (geh.) (+ *Gen.*); **lose/go by** ∼: durch Abwesenheit verlieren/nicht zur Geltung kommen; **win by** ∼: durch Nichterscheinen des Gegners gewinnen. **2** *v.i.* versagen; ∼ **on one's payments/debts** seinen Zahlungsverpflichtungen nicht nachkommen

defeat /dɪˈfiːt/ **1** *v.t.* **(a)** (overcome) besiegen; zu Fall bringen ⟨*Antrag, Vorschlag*⟩; **(b)** (baffle) **sth.** ∼**s me** ich kann etw. nicht begreifen; (frustrate) **the task has** ∼**ed us** diese Aufgabe hat uns überfordert; ∼ **the object/purpose of sth.** etw. völlig sinnlos machen. **2** *n.* (being ∼ed) Niederlage, *die;* (∼ing) Sieg, *der* (**of** über + *Akk.*)

defeatism /dɪˈfiːtɪzm/ *n.* Defätismus, *der*

defeatist /dɪˈfiːtɪst/ **1** *n.* Defätist, *der.* **2** *adj.* defätistisch

defecate /ˈdefəkeɪt/ *v.i.* Kot ausscheiden; defäkieren (Med.)

defect 1 /ˈdiːfekt/ *n.* **(a)** (lack) Mangel, *der;* **(b)** (shortcoming) Fehler, *der;* (in construction, body, mind, etc. also) Defekt, *der.* **2** /dɪˈfekt/ *v.i.* überlaufen (**to** zu)

defection /dɪˈfekʃn/ *n.* Abfall, *der;* (desertion) Flucht, *die*

defective /dɪˈfektɪv/ *adj.* **(a)** (faulty) defekt ⟨*Maschine*⟩; fehlerhaft ⟨*Material, Arbeiten, Methode, Plan*⟩; **sb./sth. is** ∼ **in sth.** es mangelt jmdm./einer Sache an etw. (*Dat.*); **(b)** (mentally deficient) geistig gestört

defector /dɪˈfektə(r)/ *n.* Überläufer, *der*/-läuferin, *die;* (from a cause or party) Abtrünnige, *der/die*

defence /dɪˈfens/ *n.* (Brit.) **(a)** (defending) Verteidigung, *die;* (of body against disease) Schutz, *der;* **in** ∼ **of** zur Verteidigung (+ *Gen.*); **(b)** (thing that protects, means of resisting attack) Schutz, *der;* **(c)** (justification) Rechtfertigung, *die;* **in sb.'s** ∼: zu jmds. Verteidigung; **(d)** (military resources) Verteidigung, *die;* **(e)** *in pl.* (fortification) Befestigungsanlagen *Pl.;* **(f)** (Sport, Law) Verteidigung, *die;* **the case for the** ∼: die Verteidigung; ∼ **witness** Zeuge/Zeugin der Verteidigung

defenceless /dɪˈfenslɪs/ *adj.* (Brit.) wehrlos

defend /dɪˈfend/ **1** *v.t.* **(a)** (protect) schützen (**from** vor + *Dat.*); (by fighting) verteidigen; **(b)** (uphold by argument, speak or write in favour of) verteidigen; verteidigen, rechtfertigen ⟨*Politik, Handeln*⟩; **(c)** (Sport, Law) verteidigen. **2** *v.i.* (Sport) verteidigen

defendant /dɪˈfendənt/ *n.* (Law) (accused) Angeklagte, *der/die;* (sued) Beklagte, *der/die*

defender /dɪˈfendə(r)/ *n.* (also Sport) Verteidiger, *der*/Verteidigerin, *die*

defense, defenseless (Amer.) ⇒ **defence, defenceless**

defensive /dɪˈfensɪv/ **1** *adj.* **(a)** (protective) defensiv ⟨*Strategie, Handlung*⟩; ∼ **player** Defensivspieler, *der;* ∼ **wall** Schutzwall, *der;* **(b)** (excessively self-justifying) **he's always so** ∼ **when he's criticized** er will sich immer um jeden Preis rechtfertigen, wenn er kritisiert wird. **2** *n.* Defensive, *die;* **be on the** ∼: in der Defensive sein

defer¹ /dɪˈfɜː(r)/ *v.t.*, **-rr-** aufschieben

defer² *v.i.*, **-rr-:** ∼ **[to sb.]** sich [jmdm.] beugen; ∼ **to sb.'s wishes** sich jmds. Wünschen fügen

deference /ˈdefərəns/ *n.* Respekt, *der;* Ehrerbietung, *die* (geh.); **in** ∼ **to sb./sth.** aus Achtung vor jmdm./etw.

deferential /defəˈrenʃl/ *adj.* respektvoll; groß ⟨*Respekt*⟩; **be** ∼ **to sb./sth.** jmdm./einer Sache mit Respekt begegnen

deferment /dɪˈfɜːmənt/ *n.* Aufschub, *der*

defiance /dɪˈfaɪəns/ *n.* Aufsässigkeit, *die;* (open disobedience) Missachtung, *die;* **in** ∼ **of sb./sth.** jmdm./einer Sache zum Trotz

defiant /dɪˈfaɪənt/ *adj.*, **defiantly** /dɪˈfaɪəntlɪ/ *adv.* aufsässig

deficiency /dɪˈfɪʃənsɪ/ *n.* **(a)** (lack) Mangel, *der* (**of, in** an + *Dat.*); **nutritional** ∼: Ernährungsmangel, *der;* **(b)** (inadequacy) Unzulänglichkeit, *die*

deficient /dɪˈfɪʃənt/ *adj.* **(a)** (not having enough) **sb./sth. is** ∼ **in sth.** jmdm./einer Sache mangelt es an etw. (*Dat.*); **be [mentally]** ∼: geistig behindert sein; **(b)** (not being enough) nicht ausreichend; (in quality also) unzulänglich

deficit /'defɪsɪt/ n. Defizit, das (of an + Dat.)

defile¹ /'diːfaɪl/ n. (gorge) Hohlweg, der

defile² /dɪ'faɪl/ v.t. (a) verschandeln; verpesten ‹Luft›; (b) (desecrate) beflecken ‹Unschuld, Reinheit›

define /dɪ'faɪn/ v.t. definieren; **be ~d [against sth.]** sich [gegen etw.] abzeichnen; **~ one's position** (fig.) Stellung beziehen (**on** zu)

definite /'defɪnɪt/ adj. (having exact limits) bestimmt; (precise) eindeutig, definitiv ‹Antwort, Entscheidung›; eindeutig ‹Beschluss, Verbesserung, Standpunkt›; eindeutig, klar ‹Vorteil›; klar umrissen ‹Ziel, Plan, Thema›; klar ‹Konzept, Linie, Vorstellung›; deutlich ‹Konturen, Umrisse›; genau ‹Zeitpunkt›; **you don't seem to be very ~:** Sie scheinen sich nicht ganz sicher zu sein; **but that is not yet ~:** aber das ist noch nicht endgültig

definitely /'defɪnɪtlɪ/ **1** adv. eindeutig ‹festlegen, größer sein, verbessert, erklären›; endgültig ‹entscheiden, annehmen›; fest ‹vereinbaren›; **she's ~ going to America** sie fährt auf jeden Fall nach Amerika. **2** int. (coll.) na, klar (ugs.)

definition /defɪ'nɪʃn/ n. (a) Definition, die; **by ~:** per definitionem (geh.); (b) (making or being distinct, degree of distinctness) Schärfe, die; **improve the ~ on the TV** den Fernseher schärfer einstellen

definitive /dɪ'fɪnɪtɪv/ adj. (a) (decisive) endgültig, definitiv ‹Beschluss, Antwort, Urteil›; (b) (most authoritative) maßgeblich

deflate /dɪ'fleɪt/ **1** v.t. (a) **~ a tyre/balloon** die Luft aus einem Reifen/Ballon ablassen; (b) (cause to lose conceitedness) ernüchtern; (c) (Econ.) deflationieren. **2** v.i. (Econ.) deflationieren

deflation /dɪ'fleɪʃn/ n. (Econ.) Deflation, die

deflationary /dɪ'fleɪʃənərɪ/ adj. (Econ.) deflationär

deflect /dɪ'flekt/ v.t. beugen ‹Licht›; **~ sb./sth. [from sb./sth.]** jmdn./etw. [von jmdn./einer Sache] ablenken

deflection, (Brit. also) **deflexion** /dɪ'flekʃn/ n. (deviation) Ablenkung, die

deforestation /diːfɒrɪ'steɪʃn/ n. Entwaldung, die; Abholzung, die

deform /dɪ'fɔːm/ v.t. (a) (deface) deformieren; verunstalten; (b) (misshape) verformen

deformed /dɪ'fɔːmd/ adj. entstellt ‹Gesicht›; verunstaltet ‹Person, Körperteil›

deformity /dɪ'fɔːmɪtɪ/ n. (being deformed) Missgestalt, die; (malformation) Verunstaltung, die

defraud /dɪ'frɔːd/ v.t. **~ sb. [of sth.]** jmdn. [um etw.] betrügen

defray /dɪ'freɪ/ v.t. bestreiten ‹Kosten›

defrost /diː'frɒst/ v.t. abtauen ‹Speisen›; abtauen ‹Kühlschrank›; enteisen ‹Windschutzscheibe, Fenster›

deft /deft/ adj., **deftly** /'deftlɪ/ adv. sicher und geschickt

defunct /dɪ'fʌŋkt/ adj. defekt ‹Maschine›; veraltet ‹Gesetz›; eingegangen ‹Zeitung›; überholt, vergessen ‹Brauch, Idee, Mode›

defuse /diː'fjuːz/ v.t. (lit. or fig.) entschärfen

defy /dɪ'faɪ/ v.t. (a) (resist openly) **~ sb.** jmdm. trotzen od. Trotz bieten; (refuse to obey) **~ sb./sth.** sich jmdm./einer Sache widersetzen; (b) (present insuperable obstacles to) widerstehen; **it defies explanation** das spottet jeder Erklärung

degenerate 1 /dɪ'dʒenəreɪt/ v.i. **~ [into sth.]** [zu etw.] verkommen od. degenerieren. **2** /dɪ'dʒenərət/ adj. degeneriert

degeneration /dɪdʒenə'reɪʃn/ n. Degeneration, die

degradation /degrə'deɪʃn/ n. (abasement) Erniedrigung, die

degrade /dɪ'greɪd/ v.t. (abase) erniedrigen; herabsetzen ‹Ansehen, Maßstab›

degrading /dɪ'greɪdɪŋ/ adj. entwürdigend; erniedrigend

degree /dɪ'griː/ n. (a) ▶ 1141 (Math., Phys.) Grad, der; **an angle/a temperature of 45 ~s** ein Winkel/eine Temperatur von 45 Grad; (b) (stage in scale or extent) Grad, der; **by ~s** allmählich; **a certain ~ of imagination** ein gewisses Maß an Fantasie; **to some** or **a certain ~:** [bis] zu einem gewissen Grad; (c) (academic rank) [akademischer]

Grad; **take/receive a ~ in sth.** einen akademischen Grad in etw. (Dat.) erwerben/verliehen bekommen; **have a ~ in physics/maths** einen Hochschulabschluss in Physik/Mathematik haben

dehydrate /diː'haɪdreɪt/ v.t. das Wasser entziehen (+ Dat.), austrocknen ‹Körper›; **~d** dehydratisiert (fachspr.); getrocknet

de-ice /diː'aɪs/ v.t. enteisen

de-icer /diː'aɪsə(r)/ n. (spray) Defroster, der

deign /deɪn/ v.t. **~ to do sth.** sich [dazu] herablassen, etw. zu tun

deity /'diːɪtɪ/ n. Gottheit, die

dejected /dɪ'dʒektɪd/ adj. niedergeschlagen

dejection /dɪ'dʒekʃn/ n. Niedergeschlagenheit, die

delay /dɪ'leɪ/ **1** v.t. (postpone) verschieben; (make late) aufhalten; verzögern ‹Ankunft, Abfahrt›; (hinder) aufhalten; **be ~ed** ‹Veranstaltung:› verspätet od. später erfolgen. **2** v.i. (wait) warten; (loiter) trödeln (ugs.); **don't ~:** warte nicht damit; **~ in doing sth.** zögern, etw. zu tun. **3** n. (a) Verzögerung, die (**to** bei); **what's the ~ now?** weshalb geht es jetzt nicht weiter?; **without ~:** unverzüglich; (b) (Transport) Verspätung, die; **trains are subject to ~:** es ist mit Zugverspätungen zu rechnen

delayed-action /dɪleɪd'ækʃn/ adj. **~ bomb** Bombe mit Zeitzünder; **~ mechanism** (Photog.) Selbstauslöser, der

delectable /dɪ'lektəbl/ adj. köstlich

delegate 1 /'delɪgət/ n. Delegierte, der/die. **2** /'delɪgeɪt/ v.t. (a) (depute) delegieren; (b) (commit) **~ sth. [to sb.]** etw. [an jmdn.] delegieren; abs. **he does not know how to ~:** er will alles selbst erledigen

delegation /delɪ'geɪʃn/ n. Delegation, die (**to** an + Akk.)

delete /dɪ'liːt/ v.t. streichen (**from** in + Dat.); (Computing) löschen; **~ where inapplicable** Nichtzutreffendes streichen

de'lete key n. (Computing) Löschtaste, die

deletion /dɪ'liːʃn/ n. Streichung, die; (Computing) Löschung, die

deli /'delɪ/ (coll.) ⇒ **delicatessen**

deliberate 1 /dɪ'lɪbərət/ adj. (a) (intentional) absichtlich; bewusst ‹Lüge, Irreführung›; vorsätzlich ‹Verbrechen›; (b) (unhurried and considered) bedächtig. **2** /dɪ'lɪbəreɪt/ v.i. (a) (think carefully) **~ on sth.** über etw. (Akk.) [sorgfältig] nachdenken; (b) (debate) **~ over** or **on** or **about sth.** über etw. (Akk.) beraten

deliberately /dɪ'lɪbərətlɪ/ adv. (a) (intentionally) absichtlich; mit Absicht; vorsätzlich ‹ein Verbrechen begehen›; (b) (with full consideration) [**very**] **~:** [ganz] bewusst; (c) (in unhurried manner) bedächtig

deliberation /dɪlɪbə'reɪʃn/ n. (a) no pl. (unhurried nature) Bedächtigkeit, die; (b) no pl. (careful consideration) Überlegung, die; (c) (discussion) Beratung, die

delicacy /'delɪkəsɪ/ n. (a) (tactfulness and care) Feingefühl, das; Delikatesse, die (geh.); (b) (fineness) Zartheit, die; (c) (weakliness) Zartheit, die; (d) (need of discretion etc.) Delikatheit, die; (e) (food) Delikatesse, die

delicate /'delɪkət/ adj. (a) (easily injured) empfindlich ‹Organ›; zart ‹Gesundheit, Konstitution›; (sensitive) sensibel, empfindlich ‹Person, Natur›; empfindlich ‹Waage, Instrument›; (b) (requiring careful handling) empfindlich; (fig.) delikat, heikel ‹Frage, Angelegenheit, Problem›; (c) (fine, of exquisite quality) zart; delikat; (dainty) delikat; (d) (subtle) fein; (e) (deft, light) geschickt; zart; (f) (tactful) taktvoll; behutsam

delicatessen /delɪkə'tesən/ n. Feinkostgeschäft, das; Delikatessengeschäft, das

delicious /dɪ'lɪʃəs/ adj. köstlich, lecker ‹Speise, Geschmack›

delight /dɪ'laɪt/ **1** v.t. erfreuen. **2** v.i. **sb. ~s in doing sth.** es macht jmdm. Freude, etw. zu tun. **3** n. (a) (great pleasure) Freude, die (at über + Akk.); **~ in sth./in doing sth.** Freude an etw. (Dat.) /daran, etw. zu tun; **to my ~:** zu meiner Freude; **sb. takes ~ in doing sth.** es macht jmdm. Freude, etw. zu tun; (b) (cause of pleasure) Vergnügen, das

delighted /dɪ'laɪtɪd/ *adj.* freudig ‹*Schrei*›; **be ~** ‹*Person:*› hocherfreut sein; **be ~ by** *or* **with sth.** sich über etw. (*Akk.*) freuen; **be ~ to do sth.** sich freuen, etw. zu tun

delightful /dɪ'laɪtfl/ *adj.* wunderbar; köstlich ‹*Geschmack, Klang*›; reizend ‹*Person, Landschaft*›

delightfully /dɪ'laɪtfəlɪ/ *adv.* wunderbar; bezaubernd ‹*singen, tanzen, hübsch*›

delimit /dɪ'lɪmɪt/ *v.t.* begrenzen ‹*Gebiet, Region*›; (fig.) eingrenzen

delineate /dɪ'lɪnɪeɪt/ *v.t.* (draw) zeichnen; (describe) darstellen

delinquency /dɪ'lɪŋkwənsɪ/ *n.*, *no pl.* Kriminalität, *die*

delinquent /dɪ'lɪŋkwənt/ **1** *n.* (*bes. jugendlicher*) Randalierer, *der.* **2** *adj.* kriminell

delirious /dɪ'lɪrɪəs/ *adj.* (a) delirant (Med.); **be ~:** im Delirium sein; (b) (wildly excited) **be ~ [with sth.]** außer sich (*Dat.*) [vor etw. (*Dat.*)] sein

delirium /dɪ'lɪrɪəm/ *n.* Delirium, *das*

deliver /dɪ'lɪvə(r)/ *v.t.* (a) (utter) halten ‹*Rede, Vorlesung, Predigt*›; vorbringen ‹*Worte*›; vortragen ‹*Verse*›; (pronounce) verkünden ‹*Urteil, Meinung, Botschaft*›; (b) werfen ‹*Ball*›; versetzen ‹*Stoß, Schlag, Tritt*›; vortragen ‹*Angriff*›; (c) (hand over) bringen; liefern ‹*Ware*›; zustellen ‹*Post, Telegramm*›; überbringen ‹*Botschaft*›; **~ sth. to the door** etw. ins Haus liefern; **~ [the goods]** (fig.) es schaffen (ugs.); (fulfil promise) halten, was man versprochen hat; (d) (give up) aushändigen; (e) (render) geben, liefern ‹*Bericht*›; stellen ‹*Ultimatum*›; (f) (assist in giving birth, aid in being born) entbinden; (g) (save) **~ sb./sth. from sb./sth.** jmdn./ etw. von jmdm./etw. erlösen

deliverance /dɪ'lɪvərəns/ *n.* Erlösung, *die* (**from** von)

delivery /dɪ'lɪvərɪ/ *n.* (a) (handing over) Lieferung, *die;* (of letters, parcels) Zustellung, *die;* **take ~ of sth.** etw. annehmen; **pay on ~:** bei Lieferung bezahlen; (Post) per Nachnahme bezahlen; (b) (manner of uttering) Vortragsweise, *die;* Vortrag, *der;* (c) (childbirth) Entbindung, *die*

delivery: ~ date *n.* Liefertermin, *der;* **~ van** *n.* Lieferwagen, *der*

dell /del/ *n.* [bewaldetes] Tal

delphinium /del'fɪnɪəm/ *n.* (Bot.) Rittersporn, *der*

delta /'deltə/ *n.* Delta, *das*

delude /dɪ'lju:d, dɪ'lu:d/ *v.t.* täuschen; **~ sb. into believing that ...:** jmdm. weismachen, dass ...

deluge /'delju:dʒ/ **1** *n.* (a) (rain) sintflutartiger Regen; (b) (Bibl.) **the D~:** die Sintflut. **2** *v.t.* (lit. or fig.) überschwemmen

delusion /dɪ'lu:ʒn, dɪ'lu:ʒn/ *n.* Illusion, *die;* (as symptom of madness) Wahnvorstellung, *die;* **be under a ~:** einer Täuschung unterliegen; **be under the ~ that ...:** sich (*Dat.*) der Täuschung hingeben, dass ...

de luxe /də'lʌks, də'lu:ks/ *adj.* Luxus-

delve /delv/ *v.i.* **~ into sth. [for sth.]** tief in etw. (*Akk.*) greifen[, um etw. herauszuholen]

demagogue (*Amer.:* **demagog**) /'deməgɒg/ *n.* Demagoge, *der*/Demagogin, *die*

demand /dɪ'mɑ:nd/ **1** *n.* (a) (request) Forderung, *die* (**for** nach); **final ~:** letzte Mahnung; (b) (desire for commodity) Nachfrage, *die* (**for** nach); **by popular ~:** auf vielfachen Wunsch; **sth./sb. is in [great] ~:** etw. ist [sehr] gefragt/ jmd. ist [sehr] begehrt; (c) (claim) **make ~s on sb.** jmdn. beanspruchen. **2** *v.t.* (a) (ask for, require, need) verlangen (**of, from** von); fordern ‹*Recht, Genugtuung*›; **~ to know/see sth.** etw. zu wissen/zu sehen verlangen; (b) (insist on being told) unbedingt wissen wollen; **he ~ed my business** or fragte mich nachdrücklich, was ich wünschte

demanding /dɪ'mɑ:ndɪŋ/ *adj.* anspruchsvoll

demarcate /'di:mɑ:keɪt/ *v.t.* festlegen ‹*Grenze*›; demarkieren (geh.)

demarcation /di:mɑ:'keɪʃn/ *n.* (of frontier) Demarkation, *die* (geh.)

demar'cation dispute *n.* Streit um die Abgrenzung der Zuständigkeitsbereiche

demeaning /dɪ'mi:nɪŋ/ *adj.* erniedrigend

demeanour (*Brit.; Amer.:* **demeanor**) /dɪ'mi:nə(r)/ *n.* Benehmen, *das*

demented /dɪ'mentɪd/ *adj.* wahnsinnig

demerara /demə'reərə/ *n.* **~ [sugar]** brauner Zucker

demi- /'demɪ/ *pref.* Halb-

'demigod *n.* Halbgott, *der*

demilitarize (**demilitarise**) /di:'mɪlɪtəraɪz/ *v.t.* entmilitarisieren

demise /dɪ'maɪz/ *n.* (death) Ableben, *das* (geh.); (fig.) Verschwinden, *das;* (of firm, party, creed, etc.) Untergang, *der*

demist /di:'mɪst/ *v.t.* (Brit.) trockenblasen; (with cloth etc.) trockenreiben

demister /di:'mɪstə(r)/ *n.* (Brit.) Defroster, *der;* Gebläse, *das*

demo /'deməʊ/ *n.*, *pl.* **~s** (coll.) Demo, *die* (ugs.)

demob /di:'mɒb/ *v.t.* (Brit. coll.), **-bb-** aus dem Kriegsdienst entlassen

demobilize (**demobilise**) /di:'məʊbɪlaɪz/ *v.t.* demobilisieren ‹*Armee, Kriegsschiff*›; aus dem Kriegsdienst entlassen ‹*Soldat*›

democracy /dɪ'mɒkrəsɪ/ *n.* Demokratie, *die*

democrat /'deməkræt/ *n.* Demokrat, *der*/Demokratin, *die;* **D~** (Amer. Polit.) Demokrat, *der*/Demokratin, *die*

democratic /demə'krætɪk/ *adj.* demokratisch; **D~ Party** (Amer. Polit.) Demokratische Partei

democratically /demə'krætɪkəlɪ/ *adv.* demokratisch

demolish /dɪ'mɒlɪʃ/ *v.t.* (a) (pull down) abreißen; (break to pieces) zerstören; demolieren; (b) abschaffen ‹*System, Privilegien*›; widerlegen, umstoßen ‹*Theorie*›; entkräften ‹*Einwand*›; zerstören ‹*Legende, Mythos*›

demolition /demə'lɪʃn, di:mə'lɪʃn/ *n.* ⇒ **demolish a:** Abriss, *der;* Zerstörung, *die;* Demolierung, *die; attrib.* **~ contractors** Abbruchunternehmen, *das;* **~ work** Abbrucharbeit, *die*

demon /'di:mən/ *n.* (a) Dämon, *der;* (b) (person) Teufel, *der*

demonstrable /'demənstrəbl, dɪ'mɒnstrəbl/ *adj.* beweisbar

demonstrably /'demənstrəblɪ, dɪ'mɒnstrəblɪ/ *adv.* nachweislich

demonstrate /'demənstreɪt/ **1** *v.t.* (a) (by examples, experiments, etc.) zeigen; demonstrieren; (show, explain) vorführen ‹*Vorrichtung, Gerät*›; (b) (be, provide, proof of) beweisen; (c) zeigen ‹*Gefühl, Bedürfnis, Gutwilligkeit*›. **2** *v.i.* (a) (protest etc.) demonstrieren; (b) **~ on sth./sb.** etw./ jmdn. als Demonstrationsobjekt benutzen

demonstration /demən'streɪʃn/ *n.* (a) (also meeting, procession) Demonstration, *die;* (b) (showing of appliances etc.) Vorführung, *die;* **give sb. a ~ of sth.** jmdm. etw. vorführen; (c) (proof) Beweis, *der*

demonstrative /dɪ'mɒnstrətɪv/ *adj.* (a) offen ‹*Person*›; (b) (Ling.) Demonstrativ-; hinweisend

demonstrator /'demənstreɪtə(r)/ *n.* (protestor etc.) Demonstrant, *der*/Demonstrantin, *die*

demoralisation, demoralise ⇒ **demoraliz-**

demoralization /dɪmɒrəlaɪ'zeɪʃn/ *n.* Demoralisierung, *die*

demoralize /dɪ'mɒrəlaɪz/ *v.t.* demoralisieren

demote /di:'məʊt/ *v.t.* degradieren (**to** zu)

demotion /di:'məʊʃn/ *n.* Degradierung, *die* (**to** zu)

demur /dɪ'mɜ:(r)/ *v.i.*, **-rr-** Einwände erheben (**to** gegen)

demure /dɪ'mjʊə(r)/ *adj.* (a) (affectedly quiet and serious) betont zurückhaltend; (b) (grave, composed) ernst; gesetzt ‹*Benehmen*›

den /den/ *n.* (a) (of wild beast) Höhle, *die;* **fox's ~:** Fuchsbau, *der;* (b) **~ of thieves, thieves' ~:** Diebeshöhle, *die;* Diebesnest, *das;* (c) (coll.: small room) Bude, *die* (ugs.)

denationalize (**denationalise**) /di:'næʃənəlaɪz/ *v.t.* privatisieren

denial /dɪ'naɪəl/ *n.* (refusal) Verweigerung, *die;* (of request, wish) Ablehnung, *die*

denigrate /'denɪgreɪt/ *v.t.* verunglimpfen

denim /'denɪm/ *n.* (a) (fabric) Denim Ⓦ, *der;* Jeansstoff, *der;* **~ jacket** Jeansjacke, *die;* (b) *in pl.* (garment) Bluejeans *Pl.*

Denmark /'denmɑːk/ *pr. n.* Dänemark (*das*)

denomination /dɪnɒmɪ'neɪʃn/ *n.* (a) (class of units) Einheit, *die;* **coins/paper money of the smallest ~:** Münzen/Papiergeld mit dem geringsten Nennwert; (b) (Relig.) Glaubensgemeinschaft, *die;* Konfession, *die*

denominator /dɪ'nɒmɪneɪtə(r)/ *n.* (Math.) Nenner, *der; see also* **common denominator**

denote /dɪ'nəʊt/ *v.t.* (a) (indicate) hindeuten auf (+ *Akk.*); **~ that** ...: darauf hindeuten, dass ...; (b) (designate) bedeuten

denouement (*also:* **dénouement**) /deɪ'nuːmɑ̃/ *n.* Ausgang, *der;* Auflösung, *die*

denounce /dɪ'naʊns/ *v.t.* (inform against) denunzieren (**to** bei); (accuse publicly) beschuldigen; **~ sb. as a spy** jmdn. beschuldigen, ein Spion zu sein

dense /dens/ *adj.* (a) dicht; massiv ‹*Körper*›; (b) (crowded together) dicht gedrängt; eng ‹*Schrift*›; (c) (stupid) dumm; **he's pretty ~:** er ist ziemlich schwer von Begriff

densely /'denslɪ/ *adv.* dicht; **~ packed** dicht gedrängt

denseness /'densnɪs/ *n., no pl.* (a) Dichte, *die;* (b) (stupidity) Begriffsstutzigkeit, *die*

density /'densɪtɪ/ *n.* (also Phys.) Dichte, *die;* **population ~:** Bevölkerungsdichte, *die*

dent /dent/ **1** *n.* Beule, *die;* (fig. coll.) Loch, *das.* **2** *v.t.* einbeulen; eindellen (ugs.) ‹*Holz, Tisch*›; (fig.) anknacksen (ugs.)

dental /'dentl/ *adj.* Zahn-; **~ care** Zahnpflege, *die*

dental: ~ floss *n.* Zahnseide, *die;* **~ surgeon** *n.* ▶ 887 | Zahnarzt, *der/*-ärztin, *die*

dentist /'dentɪst/ *n.* ▶ 887 | Zahnarzt, *der/*-ärztin, *die;* **at the ~['s]** beim Zahnarzt; **~'s chair** Zahnarztstuhl, *der*

dentistry /'dentɪstrɪ/ *n., no pl.* Zahnheilkunde, *die*

denture /'dentʃə(r)/ *n.* **~[s]** Zahnprothese, *die;* [künstliches] Gebiss; **partial ~:** Teilprothese, *die*

denunciation /dɪnʌnsɪ'eɪʃn/ *n.* Denunziation, *die;* (public accusation) Beschuldigung, *die*

deny /dɪ'naɪ/ *v.t.* (a) (declare untrue) bestreiten; zurückweisen ‹*Beschuldigung*›; **there is no ~ing the fact that** ...: es lässt sich nicht bestreiten *od.* leugnen, dass ...; **~ all knowledge of sth.** bestreiten, irgendetwas von etw. zu wissen; (b) (refuse) verweigern; **~ sb. sth.** jmdm. etw. verweigern; (c) (disavow, repudiate; refuse access to) verleugnen; ablehnen ‹*Verantwortung*›

deodorant /diː'əʊdərənt/ **1** *adj.* **~ spray** Deo[dorant]spray, *der od. das.* **2** *n.* Deodorant, *das*

dep. *abbr.* **departs** (Railw.) Abf.; (Aeronaut.) Abfl.

depart /dɪ'pɑːt/ **1** *v.i.* (a) (go away, take one's leave) weggehen; fortgehen; (b) (set out, start, leave) abfahren ‹*Flugzeug:*› abfliegen; (on one's journey) abreisen; (c) (fig.: deviate) **~ from sth.** von etw. abweichen. **2** *v.t.* (literary) **~ this life/world** aus dem Leben/aus dieser Welt scheiden (geh.)

departed /dɪ'pɑːtɪd/ **1** *adj.* (deceased) dahingeschieden (geh. verhüll.). **2** *n.* **the ~:** der/die Dahingeschiedene/die Dahingeschiedenen (geh. verhüll.)

department /dɪ'pɑːtmənt/ *n.* (a) (of municipal administration) Amt, *das;* (of state administration) Ministerium, *das;* (of university) Seminar, *das;* (of shop) Abteilung, *die;* **the personnel ~:** die Personalabteilung; **D~ for Education and Employment** (Brit.) Ministerium für Erziehung und Arbeit; **D~ of Trade and Industry** (Brit.) Ministerium für Handel und Industrie; ≈ Wirtschaftsministerium, *das;* **D~ of Social Security** (Brit.) Sozialversicherungsministerium, *das;* (b) (fig.: area of activity) Ressort, *das;* **it's not my ~** (not my responsibility) dafür bin ich nicht zuständig

departmental /diːpɑːt'mentl/ *adj.* ⇒ **department** a: Amts-; Ministerial-; Seminar-; Abteilungs-

de'partment store *n.* Kaufhaus, *das*

departure /dɪ'pɑːtʃə(r)/ *n.* (a) (going away) Abreise, *die;* (b) (deviation) **~ from sth.** Abweichen von etw.; (c) (of train, bus, ship) Abfahrt, *die;* (of aircraft) Abflug, *der;* (d) **point of ~:** Ansatzpunkt, *der;* **this product is a new ~ for us** mit diesem Produkt schlagen wir einen neuen Weg ein

departure: ~ lounge *n.* Abflughalle, *die;* **~ time** *n.* (of train, bus) Abfahrtzeit, *die;* (of aircraft) Abflugzeit, *die*

depend /dɪ'pend/ *v.i.* (a) **~ [up]on** abhängen von; **it [all] ~s on whether/what/how** ...: das hängt [ganz] davon ab *od.* kommt ganz darauf an, ob/was/wie ...; **that ~s es kommt darauf an; ~ing on how** ...: je nachdem, wie ...; (b) (rely, trust) **~ [up]on** sich verlassen auf (+ *Akk.*); (have to rely on) angewiesen sein auf (+ *Akk.*)

dependable /dɪ'pendəbl/ *adj.* verlässlich; zuverlässig

dependant /dɪ'pendənt/ *n.* Abhängige, *der/die*

dependence /dɪ'pendəns/ *n.* (a) Abhängigkeit, *die* ([up]on von); (b) (reliance) **put** *or* **place ~ [up]on sb.** sich auf jmdn. verlassen

dependency /dɪ'pendənsɪ/ *n.* (a) (country) Territorium, *das;* (b) Abhängigkeit, *die* (on von); **~ culture** (Sociol.) Kultur der Abhängigkeit [vom Staat]

dependent /dɪ'pendənt/ **1** *n.* ⇒ **dependant.** **2** *adj.* (a) (also Ling.) abhängig; **be ~ on sth.** von etw. abhängen *od.* abhängig sein; (b) **be ~ on** (be unable to do without) angewiesen sein auf (+ *Akk.*); abhängig sein von ‹*Droge*›

depict /dɪ'pɪkt/ *v.t.* darstellen

depilatory /dɪ'pɪlətərɪ/ *n.* Enthaarungsmittel, *das*

deplete /dɪ'pliːt/ *v.t.* erheblich verringern; **our stores are ~d** unser Vorrat ist zusammengeschrumpft

depletion /dɪ'pliːʃn/ *n.* Verringerung, *die*

deplorable /dɪ'plɔːrəbl/ *adj.* beklagenswert

deplore /dɪ'plɔː(r)/ *v.t.* (a) (disapprove of) verurteilen; (b) (bewail, regret) beklagen; **sth. is to be ~d** etw. ist beklagenswert

deploy /dɪ'plɔɪ/ **1** *v.t.* (also Mil.) einsetzen. **2** *v.i.* (Mil.) eingesetzt werden

deployment /dɪ'plɔɪmənt/ *n.* Einsatz, *der*

depopulate /diː'pɒpjʊleɪt/ *v.t.* entvölkern

deport /dɪ'pɔːt/ *v.t.* deportieren; (from country) ausweisen

deportation /diːpɔː'teɪʃn/ *n.* Deportation, *die;* (from country) Ausweisung, *die*

depose /dɪ'pəʊz/ *v.t.* absetzen

deposit /dɪ'pɒzɪt/ **1** *n.* (a) (in bank) Depot, *das;* (credit) Guthaben, *das;* (Brit.: at interest) Sparguthaben, *das;* **make a ~:** etwas einzahlen; (b) (payment as pledge) Kaution, *die;* (first instalment) Anzahlung, *die;* **pay a ~:** eine Kaution zahlen; eine Anzahlung leisten; **there is a five pence ~ on the bottle** auf der Flasche sind fünf Pence Pfand; (c) (of sand, mud, lime, etc.) Ablagerung, *die;* (in glass, bottle) Bodensatz, *der.* **2** *v.t.* (a) (put down in a place) ablegen; abstellen ‹*etw. Senkrechtes, auch Tablett, Teller usw.*›; absetzen ‹*Mitfahrer*›; (b) (leave lying) ‹*Wasser usw.:*› ablagern; (c) (in bank) deponieren, [auf ein Konto] einzahlen ‹*Geld*›; (Brit.: at interest) [auf ein Sparkonto] einzahlen

de'posit account *n.* (Brit.) Sparkonto, *das*

depositor /dɪ'pɒzɪtə(r)/ *n.* (Banking) Einleger, *der/*Einlegerin, *die*

depository /dɪ'pɒzɪtərɪ/ *n.* (storehouse) Lagerhaus, *das;* (place for safe keeping) Aufbewahrungsort, *der;* (fig.) Fundgrube, *die*

depot /'depəʊ/ *n.* (a) Depot, *das;* (b) (storehouse) Lager, *das;* (c) **[bus] ~** (Brit.) Depot, *das;* Omnibusgarage, *die;* (Amer.: bus station) Omnibusbahnhof, *der;* (Amer.: railway station) Bahnhof, *der*

depraved /dɪ'preɪvd/ *adj.* verdorben; lasterhaft ‹*Gewohnheit*›

depravity /dɪ'prævɪtɪ/ *n.* Lasterhaftigkeit, *die;* Verderbtheit, *die* (geh.)

deprecate /'deprɪkeɪt/ *v.t.* (disapprove of) missbilligen

depreciate /dɪ'priːʃɪeɪt, dɪ'priːsɪeɪt/ **1** *v.t.* abwerten. **2** *v.i.* an Wert verlieren

depreciation /dɪpriːʃɪ'eɪʃn, dɪpriːsɪ'eɪʃn/ *n.* (of money, currency, property) Wertverlust, *der*

depress /dɪ'pres/ *v.t.* (a) (deject) deprimieren; (b) (push or pull down) herunterdrücken; (c) (reduce activity of) unterdrücken; sich nicht entfalten lassen ‹*Handel, Wirtschaftswachstum*›

depressant /dɪ'presənt/ (Med.) **1** *adj.* beruhigend; sedativ (fachspr.). **2** *n.* Beruhigungsmittel, *das;* Sedativ[um], *das* (fachspr.)

depressed /dɪ'prest/ *adj.* deprimiert ⟨*Person, Stimmung*⟩; geschwächt ⟨*Industrie*⟩; ~ **area** unter [wirtschaftlicher] Depression leidendes Gebiet

depressing /dɪ'presɪŋ/ *adj.*, **depressingly** /dɪ'presɪŋlɪ/ *adv.* deprimierend

depression /dɪ'preʃn/ *n.* (a) Depression, *die;* (b) (sunk place) Vertiefung, *die;* (c) (Meteorol.) Tief[druckgebiet], *das;* (d) (Econ.) **the D~:** die Weltwirtschaftskrise; **economic ~:** Wirtschaftskrise, *die;* Depression, *die*

depressive /dɪ'presɪv/ *adj.* bedrückend; deprimierend

deprival /dɪ'praɪvl/, **deprivation** /deprɪ'veɪʃn/ *ns.* Entzug, *der;* (of one's rights, liberties, or title) Aberkennung, *die*

deprive /dɪ'praɪv/ *v.t.* (a) ~ sb. of sth. jmdm. etw. nehmen; (debar from having) jmdm. etw. vorenthalten; ~ **sb. of citizenship** jmdm. die Staatsbürgerschaft aberkennen; **be ~d of light** nicht genug Licht haben; (b) (prevent from having normal life) benachteiligen

deprived /dɪ'praɪvd/ *adj.* benachteiligt ⟨*Kind, Familie usw.*⟩

Dept. *abbr.* **Department** Amt/Min./Seminar/Abt.

depth /depθ/ *n.* (a) ▶ 850 | (lit. or fig.) Tiefe, *die;* **at a ~ of 3 metres** in einer Tiefe von 3 Metern; **3 feet in ~:** 3 Fuß tief; **what is the ~ of the pond?** wie tief ist der Teich?; **from/in the ~s of the forest/ocean** aus/in der Tiefe des Waldes/des Ozeans; **in the ~s of winter** im tiefen Winter; (b) **in ~:** gründlich, intensiv ⟨*studieren*⟩; **an in~ study/analysis** *etc.* eine gründliche Untersuchung/ Analyse *usw.;* (c) **be out of one's ~:** nicht mehr stehen können; keinen Grund mehr unter den Füßen haben; (fig.) ins Schwimmen kommen (ugs.); **get out of one's ~** (lit. or fig.) den Grund unter den Füßen verlieren

'depth charge *n.* Wasserbombe, *die*

deputation /depjʊ'teɪʃn/ *n.* Abordnung, *die;* Delegation, *die*

depute /dɪ'pjuːt/ *v.t.* (a) (commit task or authority to) ~ sb. to do sth. jmdn. beauftragen, etw. zu tun; (b) (appoint as deputy) ~ sb. to do sth. jmdn. [als Stellvertreter] damit betrauen, etw. zu tun

deputize (deputise) /'depjʊtaɪz/ *v.i.* als Stellvertreter einspringen; ~ **for sb.** jmdn. vertreten

deputy /'depjʊtɪ/ *n.* (a) [Stell]vertreter, *der*/-vertreterin, *die; attrib.* stellvertretend; **act as ~ for sb.** jmdn. vertreten; (b) (parliamentary representative) Abgeordnete, *der*/*die*

derail /dɪ'reɪl, diː'reɪl/ *v.t.* **be ~ed** entgleisen

derailleur /dɪ'reɪlə(r), diː'reɪljə(r)/ *n.* ~ **[gear]** Kettenschaltung, *die*

derailment /dɪ'reɪlmənt, diː'reɪlmənt/ *n.* Entgleisung, *die*

deranged /dɪ'reɪndʒd/ *adj.* **[mentally] ~:** geistesgestört

deregulate /diː'regjʊleɪt/ *v.t.* deregulieren (fachspr.); dem freien Wettbewerb überlassen

deregulation /diːregjʊ'leɪʃn/ *n.* Deregulation, *die* (fachspr.); Deregulierung, *die* (fachspr.)

derelict /'derɪlɪkt/ **1** *adj.* verlassen und verfallen. **2** *n.* (person) Ausgestoßene, *der*/*die*

dereliction /derɪ'lɪkʃn/ *n.* (a) Vernachlässigung, *die;* (state) verkommener Zustand; (b) ~ **of duty** Pflichtverletzung, *die*

deride /dɪ'raɪd/ *v.t.* (treat with scorn) sich lustig machen über (+ *Akk.*); (laugh scornfully at) verlachen

derision /dɪ'rɪʒn/ *n.* Spott, *der;* **be an object of ~:** Zielscheibe des Spottes sein

derisive /dɪ'raɪsɪv/ *adj.* (ironical) spöttisch; (scoffing) verächtlich

derisory /dɪ'raɪsərɪ, dɪ'raɪzərɪ/ *adj.* (a) (ridiculously inadequate) lächerlich; (b) (scoffing) verächtlich; (ironical) spöttisch

derivation /derɪ'veɪʃn/ *n.* (a) (obtaining from a source) Herleitung, *die;* (b) (extraction, origin) Herkunft, *die;* (c) (Ling.) Ableitung, *die;* Derivation, *die* (fachspr.)

derivative /dɪ'rɪvətɪv/ **1** *adj.* abgeleitet; (lacking originality) nachahmend; epigonal. **2** *n.* (a) (word) Ableitung, *die;* (b) (Fin.) ~s Derivate *Pl.,* ~s **market** Derivatenmarkt, *der;* ~s **trader** Derivatenhändler, *der*

derive /dɪ'raɪv/ **1** *v.t.* ~ sth. from sth. etw. aus etw. gewinnen; **the river ~s its name from a Greek god** der Name des Flusses geht auf eine griechische Gottheit zurück; ~ **pleasure from sth.** Freude an etw. (*Dat.*) haben. **2** *v.i.* ~ **from** beruhen auf (+ *Dat.*); **the word ~s from Latin** das Wort stammt *od.* kommt aus dem Lateinischen

dermatitis /dɜːmə'taɪtɪs/ *n.* ▶ 865 | (Med.) Hautentzündung, *die*

derogatory /dɪ'rɒgətərɪ/ *adj.* abfällig; abschätzig; ~ **sense [of a word]** abwertende Bedeutung [eines Wortes]

derrick /'derɪk/ *n.* [Derrick]kran, *der;* (over oil-well) Bohrturm, *der*

derv /dɜːv/ *n.* (Brit. Motor Veh.) Diesel[kraftstoff], *der*

dervish /'dɜːvɪʃ/ *n.* Derwisch, *der*

descant /'deskænt/ *n.* (Mus.) Diskant, *der*

'descant recorder *n.* (Mus.) Sopranflöte, *die*

descend /dɪ'send/ **1** *v.i.* (a) (go down) hinuntergehen/ -steigen/-klettern/-fahren; (come down) herunterkommen; (sink) niedergehen (**on** auf + *Dat.*); **the lift ~ed** der Aufzug fuhr nach unten; ~ **in the lift** mit dem Aufzug nach unten fahren; (b) (slope downwards) abfallen; **the hill ~s into/ towards the sea** der Hügel fällt zum Meer hin ab; (c) (in quality, thought, etc.) herabsinken; (d) (in pitch) fallen; sinken; (e) (make sudden attack) ~ **on sth.** über etw. (*Akk.*) herfallen; ~ **on sb.** (lit., or fig.: arrive unexpectedly) jmdn. überfallen; (f) (fig.: lower oneself) ~ **to sth.** sich zu etw. erniedrigen; (g) (derive) **descend** (**from** von); (have origin) zurückgehen (**from** auf + *Akk.*). **2** *v.t.* (go/come down) hinunter-/heruntergehen/-steigen/-klettern/-fahren; hinab-/herabsteigen (geh.)

descendant /dɪ'sendənt/ *n.* Nachkomme, *der;* **be ~s/ ~ of** abstammen von

descended /dɪ'sendɪd/ *adj.* **be ~ from sb.** von jmdm. abstammen

descent /dɪ'sent/ *n.* (a) (of person) Abstieg, *der;* (of parachute, plane, bird, avalanche) Niedergehen, *das;* (b) (way) Abstieg, *der;* (c) (slope) Abfall, *der;* **the ~ was very steep** das Gefälle war sehr stark; (d) (lineage) Abstammung, *die;* Herkunft, *die;* **be of Russian ~:** russischer Abstammung sein

describe /dɪ'skraɪb/ *v.t.* (a) beschreiben; schildern; ~ **[oneself] as …:** [sich] als … bezeichnen; (b) (move in, draw) beschreiben ⟨*Kreis, Bogen, Kurve*⟩

description /dɪ'skrɪpʃn/ *n.* (a) Beschreibung, *die;* Schilderung, *die;* **he answers [to] *or* fits the ~:** er entspricht der Beschreibung (*Dat.*); (b) (sort, class) **cars of every ~:** Autos aller Art; (c) (designation) Bezeichnung, *die*

descriptive /dɪ'skrɪptɪv/ *adj.* (a) anschaulich; beschreibend ⟨*Lyrik*⟩; deskriptiv ⟨*Analyse*⟩; (b) (not expressing feelings or judgements) deskriptiv

desecrate /'desɪkreɪt/ *v.t.* entweihen; schänden

desegregate /diː'segrɪgeɪt/ *v.t.* die Rassentrennung aufheben an (+ *Dat.*)

desert¹ /'dezət/ *n. in pl.* (what is deserved) Verdienste *Pl.;* **get one's [just] ~s** das bekommen, was man verdient hat

desert² /'dezət/ **1** *n.* Wüste, *die;* (fig.) Einöde, *die;* **the Sahara ~:** die Wüste Sahara. **2** *adj.* öde; Wüsten⟨*klima, -stamm*⟩

desert³ /dɪ'zɜːt/ **1** *v.t.* verlassen; im Stich lassen ⟨*Frau, Familie usw.*⟩. **2** *v.i.* ⟨*Soldat:*⟩ desertieren

deserted /dɪ'zɜːtɪd/ *adj.* verlassen; **the streets were ~:** die Straßen waren wie ausgestorben

deserter /dɪ'zɜːtə(r)/ *n.* Deserteur, *der;* Fahnenflüchtige, *der*/*die*

desertion /dɪ'zɜːʃn/ *n.* Verlassen, *das;* (Mil.) Desertion, *die;* Fahnenflucht, *die;* ~ **to the enemy** Überlaufen zum Feind

desert island /dezət 'aɪlənd/ *n.* einsame Insel

deserve /dɪ'zɜːv/ *v.t.* verdienen; **he ~s to be punished** er verdient [es], bestraft zu werden; **what have I done to ~ this?** womit habe ich das verdient?; **he got what he ~d** er hat es nicht besser verdient

deservedly /dɪˈzɜːvɪdlɪ/ *adv.* verdientermaßen

deserving /dɪˈzɜːvɪŋ/ *adj.* (a) (worthy) verdienstvoll; **donate money to a ~ cause** Geld für einen guten Zweck geben; (b) **be ~ of sth.** etw. verdienen

desiccated /ˈdesɪkeɪtɪd/ *adj.* getrocknet; (fig.) vertrocknet ‹*Person*›

design /dɪˈzaɪn/ 1 *n.* (a) (preliminary sketch) Entwurf, *der;* (b) (pattern) Muster, *das;* (c) *no art.* (art) Design, *das;* Gestaltung, *die* (geh.); (d) (established form of a product) Entwurf, *der;* (of machine, engine, etc.) Bauweise, *die;* (e) (general idea, construction from parts) Konstruktion, *die;* (f) *in pl.* **have ~s on sb./sth.** es auf jmdn./etw. abgesehen haben; (g) (purpose) Absicht, *die;* **by ~:** mit Absicht; absichtlich; (h) (end in view) Ziel, *das.* 2 *v.t.* (a) (draw plan of, sketch) entwerfen; konstruieren, entwerfen ‹*Maschine, Fahrzeug, Flugzeug*›; (b) **be ~ed to do sth.** ‹*Maschine, Werkzeug, Gerät:*› etw. tun sollen; (c) (set apart) vorsehen; **be ~ed for sb./sth.** für jmdn./etw. gedacht *od.* vorgesehen sein

designate 1 /ˈdezɪgnət/ *postpos. adj.* designiert. 2 /ˈdezɪgneɪt/ *v.t.* (a) (serve as name of, describe) bezeichnen; (serve as distinctive mark of) kennzeichnen; (b) (appoint to office) designieren (geh.)

designation /dezɪgˈneɪʃn/ *n.* (a) Bezeichnung, *die;* (b) (appointing to office) Designation, *die*

designer /dɪˈzaɪnə(r)/ *n.* ▶887┃ Designer, *der*/Designerin, *die;* (of machines, buildings) Konstrukteur, *der*/Konstrukteurin, *die; attrib.* Modell‹*kleidung, -jeans*›; **~ drug** Designerdroge, *die*

desirable /dɪˈzaɪərəbl/ *adj.* (a) (worth having or wishing for) wünschenswert; '**knowledge of French ~**' „Französischkenntnisse erwünscht"; (b) (causing desire) attraktiv; begehrenswert ‹*Frau*›

desire /dɪˈzaɪə(r)/ 1 *n.* (a) (wish, request) Wunsch, *der* (**for** nach); (longing) Sehnsucht, *die* (**for** nach); **~ to do sth.** Wunsch, etw. zu tun; **I have no ~ to see him** ich habe nicht den Wunsch, ihn zu sehen; (b) (thing ~d) **she is my heart's ~:** sie ist die Frau meines Herzens; (c) (lust) Verlangen, *das;* **fleshly ~s** fleischliche Begierden. 2 *v.t.* (a) (wish) sich (*Dat.*) wünschen; (long for) sich sehnen nach; **he only ~d her happiness** er wollte nur ihr Glück; **leave much to be ~d** viel zu wünschen übrig lassen; (b) (request) wünschen; (c) (sexually) begehren ‹*Mann, Frau*›

desirous /dɪˈzaɪərəs/ *pred. adj.* (formal) **be ~ of sth.** etw. wünschen

desist /dɪˈzɪst, dɪˈsɪst/ *v.i.* (literary) einhalten (geh.); **~ from sth.** von etw. ablassen (geh.); **~ in one's efforts to do sth.** von seinen Bemühungen ablassen, etw. zu tun

desk /desk/ *n.* (a) Schreibtisch, *der;* (in school) Tisch, *der;* (teacher's raised ~) Pult, *das;* **~ copy** Arbeitsexemplar, *das;* (b) (for cashier) Kasse, *die;* (for receptionist) Rezeption, *die;* **information ~:** Auskunft, *die;* **sales ~:** Verkauf, *der;* (c) (section of newspaper office) Ressort, *das*

desk: ~ calendar, ~ diary *ns.* Tischkalender, *der;* **~ lamp** *n.* Schreibtischlampe, *die;* **~top** *adj.* **~top publishing** Desktoppublishing, *das;* **~top computer** Tischcomputer, *der*

desolate 1 /ˈdesələt/ *adj.* (a) (ruinous, neglected, barren) trostlos ‹*Haus, Ort*›; desolat ‹*Zustand*›; (b) (uninhabited) öde; verlassen; (c) (forlorn, wretched) trostlos ‹*Leben*›; verzweifelt ‹*Schrei*›. 2 /ˈdesəleɪt/ *v.t.* (a) (devastate) verwüsten ‹*Land*›; (b) (make wretched) in Verzweiflung stürzen

desolation /desəˈleɪʃn/ *n.* (a) (desolating) Verwüstung, *die;* (b) (neglected or barren state) Öde, *die;* (state of ruin) Verwüstung, *die;* (c) (loneliness, being forsaken) Verlassenheit, *die;* (d) (wretchedness) Verzweiflung, *die*

despair /dɪˈspeə(r)/ 1 *n.* (a) Verzweiflung, *die;* (b) (cause) **be the ~ of sb.** jmdn. zur Verzweiflung bringen. 2 *v.i.* verzweifeln; **~ of doing sth.** die Hoffnung aufgeben, etw. zu tun; **~ of sth.** die Hoffnung auf etw. (*Akk.*) aufgeben

despatch (Brit.) ⇒ **dispatch**

desperate /ˈdespərət/ *adj.* (a) verzweifelt; (coll.: urgent) dringend; **get *or* become ~:** verzweifeln; **feel ~:** verzweifelt sein; **be ~ for sth.** etw. dringend brauchen; (b) extrem ‹*Maßnahmen, Lösung*›; (c) verzweifelt ‹*Lage, Situation*›

desperately /ˈdespərətlɪ/ *adv.* (a) verzweifelt; **be ~ ill *or* sick** todkrank sein; (b) (appallingly, shockingly, extremely) schrecklich (ugs.)

desperation /despəˈreɪʃn/ *n.* Verzweiflung, *die;* **out of *or* in [sheer] ~:** aus [lauter] Verzweiflung

despicable /ˈdespɪkəbl/ *adj.* verabscheuungswürdig

despise /dɪˈspaɪz/ *v.t.* verachten

despite /dɪˈspaɪt/ *prep.* trotz; **~ what she said** ungeachtet dessen, was sie sagte

despondency /dɪˈspɒndənsɪ/ *n., no pl.* Niedergeschlagenheit, *die*

despondent /dɪˈspɒndənt/ *adj.* niedergeschlagen; bedrückt; **be ~ about sth.** wegen etw. *od.* über etw. (*Akk.*) bedrückt sein; **feel ~:** niedergeschlagen sein; **grow *or* get ~:** mutlos werden

despot /ˈdespət/ *n.* Despot, *der*

despotic /dɪˈspɒtɪk/ *adj.* despotisch

despotism /ˈdespətɪzm/ *n.* Despotie, *die;* (political system) Despotismus, *der*

dessert /dɪˈzɜːt/ *n.* (a) süße Nachspeise; (b) (Brit.: after dinner) Dessert, *das;* Nachtisch, *der*

dessert: ~spoon *n.* Dessertlöffel, *der;* **~spoonful** *n.* Esslöffel, *der*

destination /destɪˈneɪʃn/ *n.* (of person) Reiseziel, *das;* (of goods) Bestimmungsort, *der;* (of train, bus) Zielort, *der;* **arrive at one's ~:** am Ziel ankommen

destine /ˈdestɪn/ *v.t.* bestimmen; **~ sb. for sth.** jmdn. für etw. bestimmen; ‹*Schicksal:*› jmdn. für etw. vorbestimmen; **be ~d to do sth.** dazu ausersehen *od.* bestimmt sein, etw. zu tun; **we were ~d [never] to meet again** wir sollten uns [nie] wieder sehen

destiny /ˈdestɪnɪ/ *n.* (a) Schicksal, *das;* Los, *das;* (b) *no art.* (power) das Schicksal

destitute /ˈdestɪtjuːt/ *adj.* mittellos; **the ~:** die Mittellosen

destitution /destɪˈtjuːʃn/ *n., no pl.* Armut, *die;* Not, *die*

destroy /dɪˈstrɔɪ/ *v.t.* (a) zerstören; kaputtmachen (ugs.) ‹*Tisch, Stuhl, Uhr, Schachtel*›; vernichten ‹*Ernte, Papiere, Dokumente*›; (b) (kill, annihilate) vernichten ‹*Feind, Insekten*›; **the dog will have to be ~ed** der Hund muss eingeschläfert werden; (c) (fig.) zunichte machen ‹*Hoffnungen, Chancen*›; ruinieren ‹*Zukunft*›; zerstören ‹*Glück, Freundschaft*›

destroyer /dɪˈstrɔɪə(r)/ *n.* (also Naut.) Zerstörer, *der*

destruction /dɪˈstrʌkʃn/ *n.* (a) Zerstörung, *die;* (b) (cause of ruin) Untergang, *der*

destructive /dɪˈstrʌktɪv/ *adj.* zerstörerisch; verheerend ‹*Sturm, Feuer, Krieg*›; zersetzend ‹*Einfluss, Haltung, Tendenz*›; destruktiv ‹*Person, Kritik, Vorstellung, Einfluss, Ziel*›

desultory /ˈdesəltərɪ/ *adj.* (a) sprunghaft; zwanglos, ungezwungen ‹*Gespräch*›; (b) (unmethodical) planlos

detach /dɪˈtætʃ/ *v.t.* (a) entfernen; ablösen ‹*Aufgeklebtes*›; abbrechen ‹*Angewachsenes*›; abtrennen ‹*zu Entfernendes*›; abnehmen ‹*wieder zu Befestigendes*›; abhängen ‹*Angekuppeltes*›; herausnehmen ‹*innen Befindliches*›; (b) (Mil., Navy) abkommandieren (**from** aus)

detachable /dɪˈtætʃəbl/ *adj.* abnehmbar; herausnehmbar ‹*Futter*›

detached /dɪˈtætʃt/ *adj.* (a) (impartial) unvoreingenommen; (unemotional) unbeteiligt; (b) **~ house** Einzelhaus, *das*

detachment /dɪˈtætʃmənt/ *n.* (a) (detaching) ⇒ **detach a:** Entfernen, *das;* Ablösen, *das;* Abbrechen, *das;* Abtrennen, *das;* Abnehmen, *das;* Abhängen, *das;* Herausnehmen, *das;* (b) (Mil., Navy) Abteilung, *die;* (c) (independence of judgement) Unvoreingenommenheit, *die*

detail /ˈdiːteɪl/ 1 *n.* (a) (item) Einzelheit, *die;* Detail, *das;* **enter *or* go into ~s** ins Detail gehen; auf Einzelheiten eingehen; (b) (dealing with things item by item) **in ~:** Punkt für Punkt; **in great *or* much ~:** in allen Einzelheiten; **go into ~:** ins Detail gehen; auf Einzelheiten eingehen; (c) (in building, picture, etc.) Detail, *das.* 2 *v.t.* (a) (list) einzeln aufführen; (b) (Mil.) abkommandieren

detailed /'di:teɪld/ adj. detailliert; eingehend ⟨Studie⟩

detain /dɪ'teɪn/ v.t. (a) (keep in confinement) festhalten; (take into confinement) verhaften; (b) (delay) aufhalten

detainee /diːteɪ'niː/ n. Verhaftete, der/die

detect /dɪ'tekt/ v.t. entdecken; bemerken ⟨Trauer, Verärgerung⟩; wahrnehmen ⟨Bewegung⟩; aufdecken ⟨Irrtum, Verbrechen⟩; durchschauen ⟨Beweggrund⟩; feststellen ⟨Strahlung⟩

detectable /dɪ'tektəbl/ adj. feststellbar; wahrnehmbar ⟨Bewegung⟩

detection /dɪ'tekʃn/ n. (a) ⇒ detect: Entdeckung, die; Bemerken, das; Wahrnehmung, die; Aufdeckung, die; Durchschauen, das; Feststellung, die; try to escape ∼: versuchen, unentdeckt zu bleiben; (b) (work of detective) Ermittlungsarbeit, die

detective /dɪ'tektɪv/ 1 n. ▶ 887 | Detektiv, der; (policeman) Kriminalbeamte, der/Kriminalbeamtin, die; private ∼: Privatdetektiv, der. 2 attrib. adj. Kriminal-; ∼ work Ermittlungsarbeit, die; ∼ story Detektivgeschichte, die

detector /dɪ'tektə(r)/ n. Detektor, der

détente /deɪ'tɑ̃t/ n. (Polit.) Entspannung, die

detention /dɪ'tenʃn/ n. (a) Festnahme, die; (confinement) Haft, die; (b) (Sch.) Nachsitzen, das

de'tention camp n. (prison camp) [Gefangenen]lager, das; (internment camp) [Internierungs]lager, das

deter /dɪ'tɜː(r)/ v.t., -rr- abschrecken; ∼ sb. from sth. jmdn. von etw. abhalten; ∼ sb. from doing sth. jmdn. davon abhalten, etw. zu tun; be ∼red by sth. sich durch etw. abschrecken lassen

detergent /dɪ'tɜːdʒənt/ n. Reinigungsmittel, das; (for washing) Waschmittel, das

deteriorate /dɪ'tɪərɪəreɪt/ v.i. sich verschlechtern; ⟨Haus:⟩ verfallen, verkommen; ⟨Holz, Leder:⟩ verrotten; his work has ∼d seine Arbeit hat nachgelassen

deterioration /dɪtɪərɪə'reɪʃn/ n. ⇒ deteriorate: Verschlechterung, die; Verfall, der; Verrottung, die

determinate /dɪ'tɜːmɪnət/ adj. (a) (limited, finite) begrenzt; (b) (distinct) bestimmt

determination /dɪtɜːmɪ'neɪʃn/ n. (a) (ascertaining, defining) Bestimmung, die; (b) (resoluteness) Entschlossenheit, die; with [sudden] ∼: [kurz] entschlossen; (c) (intention) [feste] Absicht

determine /dɪ'tɜːmɪn/ 1 v.t. (a) (decide) beschließen; (b) (make decide) veranlassen; ∼ sb. to do sth. jmdn. dazu veranlassen, etw. zu tun; (c) (be a decisive factor for) bestimmen; (d) (ascertain, define) feststellen; bestimmen. 2 v.i. (decide) ∼ on doing sth. beschließen, etw. zu tun

determined /dɪ'tɜːmɪnd/ adj. (a) (resolved) be ∼ to do or on doing sth. fest entschlossen sein, etw. zu tun; sb. is ∼ that …: es ist für jmdn. beschlossene Sache, dass …; (b) (resolute) entschlossen; resolut ⟨Person⟩

deterrence /dɪ'terəns/ n. Abschreckung, die

deterrent /dɪ'terənt/ 1 adj. abschreckend. 2 n. Abschreckungsmittel, das (to für)

detest /dɪ'test/ v.t. verabscheuen; ∼ doing sth. es verabscheuen, etw. zu tun

detestable /dɪ'testəbl/ adj. verabscheuenswert

detestation /diːte'steɪʃn/ n., no pl. Abscheu, der (of vor + Dat.)

detonate /'detəneɪt/ 1 v.i. detonieren. 2 v.t. zur Explosion bringen; zünden

detonation /detə'neɪʃn/ n. Detonation, die

detonator /'detəneɪtə(r)/ n. Sprengkapsel, die; Detonator, der

detour /'diːtʊə(r)/ n. Umweg, der; (in a road) Bogen, der; Schleife, die; (diversion) Umleitung, die; make a ∼: einen Umweg machen

detox (coll.) 1 /'diːtɒks/ n. Entzug, der; be in ∼: auf Entzug sein. 2 /diː'tɒks/ v.t. entziehen (ugs.) ⟨Drogensüchtigen, Alkoholiker⟩. 3 /diː'tɒks/ v.i. einen Entzug machen.

detoxification /diːtɒksɪfɪ'keɪʃn/ n., no pl. Entgiftung, die; Detoxikation, die (fachspr.)

detoxify /diː'tɒksɪfaɪ/ 1 v.t. entgiften; unschädlich machen ⟨Gift usw.⟩. 2 v.i sich entgiften

detract /dɪ'trækt/ v.i. ∼ from sth. etw. beeinträchtigen

detraction /dɪ'trækʃn/ n. Beeinträchtigung, die (from Gen.)

detriment /'detrɪmənt/ n. to the ∼ of sth. zum Nachteil od. Schaden einer Sache (Gen.); without ∼ to ohne Schaden für

detrimental /detrɪ'mentl/ adj. schädlich; be ∼ to sth. einer Sache (Dat.) schaden od. (geh.) abträglich sein

detritus /dɪ'traɪtəs/ n., no pl. Überbleibsel, das

deuce¹ /djuːs/ n. (Tennis) Einstand, der

deuce² n. (coll.) who/where/what etc. the ∼: wer/wo/was usw. zum Teufel? (salopp); there will be the ∼ to pay da ist der Teufel los (ugs.)

Deutschmark /'dɔɪtʃmɑːk/ n. ▶ 938 | Deutsche Mark

devaluation /diːvæljuː'eɪʃn/ n. (also Econ.) Abwertung, die

devalue /diː'væljuː/ v.t. (also Econ.) abwerten

devastate /'devəsteɪt/ v.t. verwüsten; verheeren; (fig.) niederschmettern

devastating /'devəsteɪtɪŋ/ adj. verheerend; (fig.) niederschmetternd ⟨Nachricht, Analyse⟩; vernichtend ⟨Spielweise, Kritik⟩

devastation /devə'steɪʃn/ n., no pl. Verwüstung, die; Verheerung, die

develop /dɪ'veləp/ 1 v.t. (a) (also Photog.) entwickeln; aufbauen ⟨Handel, Handelszentrum⟩; entfalten ⟨Persönlichkeit, Individualität⟩; erschließen ⟨natürliche Ressourcen⟩; ∼ a business from scratch ein Geschäft neu aufziehen; (b) (expand; make more sophisticated) weiterentwickeln; ausbauen ⟨Verkehrsnetz, System, Handel, Verkehr, Position⟩; ∼ sth. further etw. weiterentwickeln; (c) (begin to exhibit, begin to suffer from) annehmen ⟨Gewohnheit⟩; bei sich entdecken ⟨Vorliebe⟩; bekommen ⟨Krankheit, Fieber, Lust⟩; entwickeln ⟨Talent, Stärke⟩; erkranken an (+ Dat.) ⟨Krebs, Tumor⟩; ∼ a taste for sth. Geschmack an etw. (Akk.) finden; the car ∼ed a fault an dem Wagen ist ein Defekt aufgetreten; (d) (construct buildings etc. on, convert to new use) erschließen; sanieren ⟨Altstadt⟩. 2 v.i. (a) sich entwickeln (from aus; into zu); ⟨Defekt, Symptome, Erkrankungen:⟩ auftreten; (b) (become fuller) sich [weiter]entwickeln (into zu)

developer /dɪ'veləpə(r)/ n. (a) (Photog.) Entwickler, der; (b) (person who develops real estate) ≈ Bauunternehmer, der; (c) late or slow ∼ (person) Spätentwickler, der

de'veloping country n. Entwicklungsland, das

development /dɪ'veləpmənt/ n. (a) (also Photog.) Entwicklung, die (from aus, into zu); (of individuality, talent) Entfaltung, die; (of natural resources etc.) Erschließung, die; (b) (expansion) Ausbau, der; Weiterentwicklung, die; (c) (of land etc.) Erschließung, die; (d) (full-grown state) Vollendung, die; (e) (developed product or form) a ∼ of sth. eine Fortentwicklung od. Weiterentwicklung einer Sache

de'velopment area n. (Brit.) Entwicklungsgebiet, das

deviant /'diːvɪənt/ adj. abweichend

deviate /'diːvɪeɪt/ v.i. (lit. or fig.) abweichen

deviation /diːvɪ'eɪʃn/ n. Abweichung, die

device /dɪ'vaɪs/ n. (a) (apparatus, aid) Gerät, das; (as part of sth.) Vorrichtung, die; nuclear ∼: atomarer Sprengkörper; (b) (plan, scheme) List, die; (c) leave sb. to his own ∼s jmdn. sich (Dat.) selbst überlassen

devil /'devl/ n. (a) (Satan) the D∼: der Teufel; (b) or D∼ (coll.) who/where/what etc. the ∼? wer/wo/was usw. zum Teufel? (salopp); the ∼ take him! hol' ihn der Teufel! (salopp); the ∼! Teufel auch! (salopp); there will be the ∼ to pay da ist der Teufel los (ugs.); [you can] go to the ∼! scher dich zum Teufel! (salopp); work like the ∼: wie ein Besessener arbeiten; run like the ∼: wie der Teufel rennen (ugs.); between the ∼ and the deep [blue] sea in einer Zwickmühle (ugs.); better the ∼ one knows lieber das bekannte Übel; speak or talk of the ∼ [and he will appear] wenn man vom Teufel spricht[, kommt er]; (c) a ∼ or the ∼ of a mess ein verteufelter Schlamassel (ugs.); have the ∼ of a time es verteufelt schwer haben; (d) (able, clever person) As, das (ugs.); he's a clever ∼: er ist ein schlauer Hund (ugs.); you ∼! (ugs.) du Schlingel!; a

poor ∼**:** ein armer Teufel; **lucky** ∼**:** Glückspilz, *der* (ugs.); **cheeky** ∼**:** Frechdachs, *der* (fam., meist scherzh.)

devilish /'devəlɪʃ/ *adj.* (llt. or fig.) teuflisch ‹*Künste, Zauberei*›

'devil-may-care *adj.* sorglos-unbekümmert

devilment /'devlmənt/ *n.* (mischief) Unfug, *der;* (wild spirits) Übermut, *der*

devil's 'advocate *n.* Advocatus Diaboli, *der*

devious /'diːvɪəs/ *adj.* (a) (winding) verschlungen; **take a** ∼ **route** einen Umweg fahren; (b) (unscrupulous, insincere) verschlagen ‹*Person*›; hinterhältig ‹*Person, Methode, Tat*›

devise /dɪ'vaɪz/ *v.t.* entwerfen; schmieden ‹*Pläne*›; kreieren ‹*Mode, Stil*›; ausarbeiten ‹*Programm*›

devoid /dɪ'vɔɪd/ *adj.* ∼ **of sth.** (lacking) ohne etw.; bar einer Sache (*Gen.*) (geh.); (free from) frei von etw.

devolution /diːvə'luːʃn/ *n.* (deputing, delegation) Übertragung, *die;* (Polit.) Dezentralisierung, *die*

devote /dɪ'vəʊt/ *v.t.* widmen; bestimmen ‹*Geld*› (**to** für); ∼ **one's thoughts/energy to sth.** sein Denken/seine Energie auf etw. (*Akk.*) verwenden

devoted /dɪ'vəʊtɪd/ *adj.* treu; ergeben ‹*Diener*›; aufrichtig ‹*Freundschaft, Liebe, Verehrung*›; **he is very** ∼ **to his work/his wife** er geht in seiner Arbeit völlig auf/liebt seine Frau innig

devotee /devə'tiː/ *n.* Anhänger, *der*/Anhängerin, *die;* (of music, art) Liebhaber, *der*/Liebhaberin, *die*

devotion /dɪ'vəʊʃn/ *n.* (a) (addiction, loyalty, devoutness) ∼ **to sb./sth.** Hingabe an jmdn./etw.; ∼ **to music/the arts** Liebe zur Musik/Kunst; ∼ **to duty** Pflichteifer, *der;* (b) (devoting) Weihung, *die*

devour /dɪ'vaʊə(r)/ *v.t.* verschlingen

devout /dɪ'vaʊt/ *adj.* fromm; sehnlich ‹*Wunsch*›; inständig ‹*Hoffnung*›

dew /djuː/ *n.* Tau, *der*

dewy /'djuːɪ/ *adj.* taufeucht

'dewy-eyed *adj.* naiv; **go all** ∼ ganz feuchte Augen bekommen

dexterity /dek'sterɪtɪ/ *n., no pl.* (skill) Geschicklichkeit, *die*

dextrous /'dekstrəs/ *adj.* geschickt

DFE *abbr.* (Brit.) **Department for Education and Employment**

diabetes /daɪə'biːtiːz/ *n., pl. same* ▶ **865|** (Med.) Zuckerkrankheit, *die;* Diabetes, *der* (fachspr.)

diabetic /daɪə'betɪk, daɪə'hiːtɪk/ (Med.) **1** *adj.* (a) (of diabetes) diabetisch; (b) (having diabetes) diabetisch (Med.); zuckerkrank; (c) (for diabetics) Diabetiker‹*nahrung, -schokolade usw.*›. **2** *n.* Diabetiker, *der*/Diabetikerin, *die*

diabolic /daɪə'bʊlɪk/, **diabolical** /daɪə'bʊlɪkl/ *adjs.* teuflisch; diabolisch; (coll.: extremely bad) mörderisch (ugs.) ‹*Hitze*›; teuflisch (ugs.) ‹*Kälte, Wetter*›

diagnose /daɪəg'nəʊz/ *v.t.* diagnostizieren ‹*Krankheit*›; feststellen ‹*Fehler*›

diagnosis /daɪəg'nəʊsɪs/ *n., pl.* **diagnoses** /daɪəg'nəʊsiːz/ (a) (of disease) Diagnose, *die;* **make a** ∼**:** eine Diagnose stellen; (b) (of difficulty, fault) Feststellung, *die*

diagnostic /daɪəg'nɒstɪk/ *adj.* diagnostisch

diagonal /daɪ'æɡənl/ **1** *adj.* diagonal. **2** *n.* Diagonale, *die*

diagonally /daɪ'æɡənəlɪ/ *adv.* diagonal

diagram /'daɪəɡræm/ *n.* (a) (sketch) schematische Darstellung; **I'll make a** ∼ **to show you how to get there** ich zeichne Ihnen auf, wie Sie dorthin kommen; (b) (graphic or symbolic representation; Geom.) Diagramm, *das*

dial /'daɪəl/ **1** *n.* (a) (of clock or watch) Zifferblatt, *das;* (b) (of gauge, meter, etc.; on radio or television) Skala, *die;* (c) (Teleph.) Wählscheibe, *die.* **2** *v.t.,* (Brit.) **-ll-** (Teleph.) wählen; ∼ **[London] direct** [nach London] durchwählen. **3** *v.i.,* (Brit.) **-ll-** (Teleph.) wählen

dialect /'daɪəlekt/ *n.* Dialekt, *der;* Mundart, *die*

dialling (Amer.: **dialing**) /'daɪəlɪŋ/**:** ∼ **code** *n.* Vorwahl, *die;* Ortsnetzkennzahl, *die* (Amtsspr.); ∼ **tone** *n.* Freizeichen, *das;* Wählton, *der* (fachspr.)

dialogue /'daɪəlɒg/ *n.* Dialog, *der*

'dialogue box *n.* (Computing) Dialogbox, *die;* Dialogfenster, *das*

'dial tone (Amer.) ⇨ **dialling tone**

dialysis /daɪ'ælɪsɪs/ *n., pl.* **dialyses** /daɪ'ælɪsiːz/ (a) (Chem.) Dialyse, *die;* (b) (Med.) [Hämo]dialyse, *die* (fachspr.); Blutwäsche, *die;* ∼ **machine** Dialyseapparat, *der*

diameter /daɪ'æmɪtə(r)/ *n.* Durchmesser, *der*

diametrical /daɪə'metrɪkl/ *adj.,* **diametrically** /daɪə'metrɪkəlɪ/ *adv.* diametral

diamond /'daɪəmənd/ **1** *n.* (a) Diamant, *der;* (b) (figure) Raute, *die;* Rhombus, *der;* (Cards) Karo, *das; see also* **club 1 d. 2** *adj.* (made of ∼[s]) diamanten; (set with ∼[s]) diamantenbesetzt; Diamant‹*ring, -staub, -schmuck*›

diamond: ∼ **'jubilee** *n.* 60-jähriges/75-jähriges Jubiläum; ∼ **'wedding** *n.* diamantene Hochzeit

diaper /'daɪəpə(r)/ *n.* (Amer.) Windel, *die*

diaphragm /'daɪəfræm/ *n.* Diaphragma, *das* (fachspr.); (Anat. also) Zwerchfell, *das;* (contraceptive also) Pessar, *das*

diarrhoea (Amer.: **diarrhea**) /daɪə'riːə/ *n.* Durchfall, *der;* Diarrhö[e], *die* (Med.)

diary /'daɪərɪ/ *n.* (a) Tagebuch, *das;* **keep a** ∼**:** [ein] Tagebuch führen; (b) (for appointments) Terminkalender, *der;* **pocket/desk** ∼**:** Taschen-/Tischkalender, *der*

dice /daɪs/ **1** *n., pl. same* (a) (cube) Würfel, *der;* **throw** ∼**:** würfeln; **throw** ∼ **for sth.** etw. auswürfeln; **no** ∼**!** (fig. coll.) kommt nicht in Frage!; (b) *in sing.* (game) Würfelspiel, *das;* **play** ∼**:** würfeln. **2** *v.i.* ∼ **with death** mit seinem Leben spielen. **3** *v.t.* (Cookery) würfeln

dicey /'daɪsɪ/ *adj.* (coll.) riskant

dichotomy /daɪ'kɒtəmɪ, dɪ'kɒtəmɪ/ *n.* Dichotomie, *die*

dick /dɪk/ *n.* (sl.: detective) Schnüffler, *der* (ugs. abwertend)

dicky /'dɪkɪ/ *adj.* (Brit. coll.) mies (ugs. abwertend); klapprig (ugs.) ‹*Herz*›

'dicky bird *n.* (child lang./coll.) Piepvogel, *der* (Kinderspr.)

Dictaphone, (P) /'dɪktəfəʊn/ *n.* Diktaphon, *das* (fachspr.); Diktiergerät, *das*

dictate 1 /dɪk'teɪt/ *v.t. & i.* diktieren; (prescribe) vorschreiben; ∼ **to** Vorschriften machen (+ *Dat.*); **I will not be** ∼**d to** ich lasse mir keine Vorschriften machen. **2** /'dɪkteɪt/ *n., usu. in pl.* Diktat, *das*

dic'tating machine *n.* Diktiergerät, *das*

dictation /dɪk'teɪʃn/ *n.* Diktat, *das;* **take a** ∼**:** ein Diktat aufnehmen

dictator /dɪk'teɪtə(r)/ *n.* (lit. or fig.) Diktator, *der;* **be a** ∼ (fig.) diktatorisch sein

dictatorial /dɪktə'tɔːrɪəl/ *adj.* diktatorisch

dictatorship /dɪk'teɪtəʃɪp/ *n.* (lit. or fig.) Diktatur, *die*

diction /'dɪkʃn/ *n.* Diktion, *die* (geh.)

dictionary /'dɪkʃənərɪ/ *n.* Wörterbuch, *das*

did ⇨ **do¹**

didactic /dɪ'dæktɪk, daɪ'dæktɪk/ *adj.* (a) didaktisch; (b) (authoritarian) schulmeisterlich

diddle /'dɪdl/ *v.t.* (coll.) übers Ohr hauen (ugs.); ∼ **sb. out of sth.** jmdm. etw. abluchsen (salopp)

didn't /'dɪdnt/ (coll.) = **did not;** ⇨ **do¹**

die¹ /daɪ/ **1** *v.i.,* **dying** /'daɪŋ/ (a) sterben ‹*Tier, Pflanze:*› eingehen, (geh.) sterben; ‹*Körperteil:*› absterben; **be dying** sterben; ∼ **from** *or* **of sth.** an etw. (*Dat.*) sterben; ∼ **of a heart attack/a brain tumour** einen Herzanfall/Hirntumor erliegen; ∼ **from one's injuries** seinen Verletzungen erliegen; **sb. would** ∼ **rather than do sth.** um nichts in der Welt würde jmd. etw. tun; **never say** ∼ (fig.) nur nicht den Mut verlieren; (fig.) **be dying for sth.** etw. unbedingt brauchen; **be dying for a cup of tea** nach einer Tasse Tee lechzen; **be dying to do sth.** darauf brennen, etw. zu tun; **be dying of boredom** vor Langeweile sterben; ∼ **with** *or* **of shame** sich zu Tode schämen; (c) (disappear) in Vergessenheit geraten; ‹*Gefühl, Liebe, Ruhm:*› vergehen; ‹*Ton:*› verklingen; ‹*Flamme:*› verlöschen. **2** *v.t.,* **dying:** ∼ **a natural/violent death** eines natürlichen/gewaltsamen Todes sterben

∼ **'down** *v.i.* ‹*Sturm, Wind, Protest, Aufruhr:*› sich legen; ‹*Flammen:*› kleiner werden; ‹*Feuer:*› herunterbrennen;

⟨*Lärm*.⟩ leiser werden; ⟨*Kämpfe*:⟩ nachlassen

~ **'off** *v.i.* ⟨*Pflanzen, Tiere*:⟩ [nacheinander] eingehen; ⟨*Blätter*:⟩ [nacheinander] absterben; ⟨*Personen*:⟩ [nacheinander] sterben

~ **'out** *v.i.* aussterben

die² *n., pl.* **dice** /daɪs/ (formal) Würfel, *der;* **the ~ is cast** die Würfel sind gefallen; **as straight** *or* **true as a ~:** schnurgerade ⟨*Weg, Linie*⟩

'diehard 1 *n.* hartnäckiger Typ; (reactionary) Ewiggestrige, *der/die.* **2** *adj.* hartnäckig; (dyed-in-the-wool) eingefleischt; (reactionary) ewiggestrig

diesel /'diːzl/ *n.* ~ **[engine]** Diesel[motor], *der;* (Railw.) Diesellok, *die;* ~ **[lorry/car]** Diesel, *der;* ~ **[train]** (Railw.) [Zug mit] Dieseltriebwagen, ~ **[fuel]** Diesel[kraftstoff], *der*

'diesel oil *n.* Dieseltreibstoff, *der*

diet /'daɪət/ **1** *n.* **(a)** (for slimming) Diät, *die;* Schlankheitskur, *die;* **be/go on a ~:** eine Schlankheitskur *od.* Diät machen; **(b)** (Med.) Diät, *die;* Schonkost, *die;* **(c)** (habitual food) Kost, *die.* **2** *v.i.* eine Schlankheitskur *od.* Diät machen

dietitian (dietician) /daɪə'tɪʃn/ *n.* ▶887┃ Diätassistent, *der/*-assistentin, *die*

differ /'dɪfə(r)/ *v.i.* **(a)** (vary, be different) sich unterscheiden; **opinions/ideas ~:** die Meinungen/ Vorstellungen gehen auseinander; **tastes/temperaments ~:** die Geschmäcker *die;* **be/go on a ~** / Temperamente sind verschieden; ~ **from sb./sth. in that …:** sich von jmdm./etw. dadurch *od.* darin unterscheiden, dass …; **(b)** (disagree) anderer Meinung sein

difference /'dɪfərəns/ *n.* **(a)** Unterschied, *der;* ~ **in age** Altersunterschied, *der;* **have a ~ of opinion [with sb.]** eine Meinungsverschiedenheit [mit jmdm.] haben; **it makes a ~:** es ist ein *od.* (ugs.) macht einen Unterschied; **what ~ would it make if …?** was würde es schon ausmachen, wenn …?; **make all the ~ [in the world]** ungeheuer viel ausmachen; **make no ~ [to sb.]** [jmdm.] nichts ausmachen; **(b)** (between amounts) Differenz, *die;* **pay the ~:** den Rest[betrag] bezahlen; **split the ~:** sich (*Dat.*) den Rest[betrag] teilen; **(c)** (dispute) **have a ~ with sb.** mit jmdm. eine Auseinandersetzung haben; **settle one's ~s** seine Differenzen beilegen

different /'dɪfərənt/ *adj.* verschieden; (pred. also) anders; (attrib. also) ander…; **be ~ from** *or* (esp. Brit.) **to** *or* (Amer.) **than …:** anders sein als …; ~ **viewpoints/cultures** unterschiedliche Standpunkte/Kulturen; **how are they ~?** worin *od.* wodurch unterscheiden sie sich?

differential /dɪfə'renʃl/ *n.* **(a)** (Commerc.) **[wage] ~:** [Einkommens]unterschied, *der;* **price ~s** Preisunterschiede; **(b)** (Motor Veh.) Differenzial[getriebe], *das*

differentiate /dɪfə'renʃɪeɪt/ **1** *v.t.* unterscheiden. **2** *v.i.* **(a)** (recognize the difference) unterscheiden; differenzieren; **(b)** (treat sth. differently) einen Unterschied machen; differenzieren

differently /'dɪfərəntlɪ/ *adv.* anders (**from**, esp. Brit.: **to** als); ~ **[to** *or* **from each other]** verschieden; (with different result, at various times) unterschiedlich

differing /'dɪfərɪŋ/ *adj.* unterschiedlich

difficult /'dɪfɪkəlt/ *adj.* **(a)** schwer; schwierig; **he finds it ~ to do sth.** ihm fällt es schwer, etw. zu tun; **make things ~ for sb.** es jmdm. nicht leicht machen; **(b)** (unaccommodating) schwierig; **he is being ~:** er macht Schwierigkeiten

difficulty /'dɪfɪkəltɪ/ *n.* **(a)** Schwierigkeit, *die;* **with [great] ~:** [sehr] mühsam; **with the greatest ~:** unter größten Schwierigkeiten; **without [great] ~:** ohne große Probleme; mühelos; **have ~ [in] doing sth.** Schwierigkeiten haben, etw. zu tun; **(b)** *usu. in pl.* (trouble) **be in ~** *or* **difficulties** in Schwierigkeiten sein; **fall** *or* **get into difficulties** in Schwierigkeiten kommen *od.* geraten

diffident /'dɪfɪdənt/ *adj.* zaghaft; (modest) zurückhaltend

diffuse 1 /dɪ'fjuːz/ *v.t.* verbreiten; diffundieren (fachspr.). **2** /dɪ'fjuːz/ *v.i.* sich ausbreiten (**through** in + *Dat.*); diffundieren (fachspr.). **3** /dɪ'fjuːs/ *adj.* diffus

diffusion /dɪ'fjuːʒn/ *n.* Verbreitung, *die*

dig /dɪg/ **1** *v.i.,* **-gg-, dug** /dʌg/ **(a)** graben (**for** nach); **(b)** (Archaeol.: excavate) Ausgrabungen machen; graben. **2** *v.t.,* **-gg-, dug** **(a)** graben; ~ **a hole [in sth.]** ein Loch [in etw.

(*Akk.*)] graben; **(b)** (turn up with spade etc.) umgraben; **(c)** (Archaeol.) ausgraben; **(d)** (sl.: appreciate) stark finden (Jugendspr.); (understand) schnallen (salopp). **3** *n.* **(a)** Grabung, *die;* **(b)** (Archaeol. coll.) Ausgrabung, *die;* (site) Ausgrabungsort, *der;* **(c)** (fig.) Anspielung, *die* (**at** auf + *Akk.*); **have** *or* **make a ~ at sb./sth.** eine [spitze] Bemerkung über jmdn./etw. machen

~ **'in** *v.i.* (Mil.) sich eingraben; (fig.)˙sich festsetzen. **2** *v.t.* **(a)** (Mil.) eingraben; ~ **oneself in** sich eingraben; (fig.) sich etablieren; **(b)** (thrust) **the cat dug its claws in** die Katze krallte sich fest; ~ **one's heels** *or* **toes in** (fig. coll.) sich auf die Hinterbeine stellen (ugs.); **(c)** (mix with soil) eingraben

~ **'out** *v.t.* (lit. or fig.) ausgraben

~ **'up** *v.t.* umgraben ⟨*Garten, Rasen, Erde*⟩; ausgraben ⟨*Pflanzen, Knochen, Leiche, Schatz*⟩

digest 1 /dɪ'dʒest, daɪ'dʒest/ *v.t.* **(a)** (assimilate, lit or fig.) verdauen; **(b)** (consider) durchdenken. **2** /'daɪdʒest/ *n.* (periodical) Digest, *der od. das*

digestible /dɪ'dʒestɪbl, daɪ'dʒestɪbl/ *adj.* verdaulich

digestion /dɪ'dʒestʃn, daɪ'dʒestʃn/ *n.* Verdauung, *die*

digestive /dɪ'dʒestɪv, daɪ'dʒestɪv/ **1** *adj.* Verdauungs-; ~ **biscuit** (Brit.) ⇒ **2. 2** *n.* (Brit.: biscuit) Keks, *der (aus Vollkornmehl)*

digger /'dɪgə(r)/ *n.* (Mech.) Bagger, *der*

digit /'dɪdʒɪt/ *n.* **(a)** (numeral) Ziffer, *die;* **a six-~ number** eine sechsstellige Zahl; **(b)** (Zool., Anat.) (finger) Finger, *der;* (toe) Zehe, *die*

digital /'dɪdʒɪtl/ *adj.* digital; ~ **clock/watch** Digitaluhr, *die;* ~ **computer** Digitalrechner, *der;* ~ **recording** Digitalaufnahme, *die;* ~ **audio tape** Digitaltonband, *das*

dignified /'dɪgnɪfaɪd/ *adj.* würdig; (self-respecting) würdevoll

dignify /'dɪgnɪfaɪ/ *v.t.* **(a)** (make stately) Würde verleihen (+ *Dat.*); **(b)** (give distinction to) Glanz verleihen (+ *Dat.*); auszeichnen ⟨*Person*⟩; **(c)** (give grand title to) aufwerten (fig.)

dignitary /'dɪgnɪtərɪ/ *n.* Würdenträger, *der;* **dignitaries** (prominent people) Honoratioren *Pl.*

dignity /'dɪgnɪtɪ/ *n.* Würde, *die;* **be beneath one's ~:** unter seiner Würde sein

digress /daɪ'gres/ *v.i.* abschweifen (**from** von, **on** zu)

digression /daɪ'greʃn/ *n.* Abschweifung, *die;* (passage) Exkurs, *der*

digs /dɪgz/ *n. pl.* (Brit. coll.) Bude, *die* (ugs.)

dike /daɪk/ *n.* **(a)** (flood-wall) Deich, *der;* **(b)** (ditch) Graben, *der;* **(c)** (causeway) Damm, *der*

dilapidated /dɪ'læpɪdeɪtɪd/ *adj.* verfallen ⟨*Gebäude*⟩; verwahrlost ⟨*Äußeres, Erscheinung*⟩

dilapidation /dɪlæpɪ'deɪʃn/ *n., no pl.* Verfall, *der*

dilate /daɪ'leɪt/ **1** *v.i.* sich weiten. **2** *v.t.* ausdehnen

dilation /daɪ'leɪʃn/ *n.* Dilatation, *die;* (Phys. also) Ausdehnung, *die;* (Med. also) Erweiterung, *die*

dilatory /'dɪlətərɪ/ *adj.* langsam; zögernd ⟨*Antwort, Reaktion*⟩; (causing delay) **be ~ in** sich (*Dat.*) [viel] Zeit lassen bei

dilemma /dɪ'lemə, daɪ'lemə/ *n.* Dilemma, *das;* **be on the horns of** *or* **faced with a ~:** vor einem Dilemma stehen

dilettante /dɪlɪ'tæntɪ/ *n., pl.* **dilettanti** /dɪlɪ'tæntiː/ *or* ~**s** Dilettant, *der/*Dilettantin, *die;* Laie, *der*

diligence /'dɪlɪdʒəns/ *n.* Fleiß, *der;* (purposefulness) Eifer, *der*

diligent /'dɪlɪdʒənt/ *adj.* fleißig; (purposeful) eifrig; sorgfältig, gewissenhaft ⟨*Arbeit, Suche*⟩

diligently /'dɪlɪdʒəntlɪ/ *adv.* fleißig; (purposefully) eifrig

dill /dɪl/ *n.* (Bot.) Dill, *der*

dilly-dally /'dɪlɪdælɪ/ *v.i.* (coll.) trödeln

dilute 1 /daɪ'ljuːt, 'daɪljuːt/ *adj.* verdünnt. **2** /daɪ'ljuːt/ *v.t.* **(a)** verdünnen; **(b)** (fig.) abschwächen; entschärfen

dim /dɪm/ **1** *adj.* **(a)** schwach, trüb ⟨*Licht, Flackern*⟩; matt, gedeckt ⟨*Farbe*⟩; dämmrig, dunkel ⟨*Zimmer*⟩; undeutlich, verschwommen ⟨*Gestalt*⟩; **grow ~:** schwächer werden; **(b)** (fig.) blass; verschwommen; **in the ~ and distant past** in ferner Vergangenheit; **(c)** (indistinct) schwach, getrübt ⟨*Seh-, Hörvermögen*⟩; **(d)** (coll.: stupid) beschränkt; **(e) take a** ∼ **view of sth.** (coll.) von etw. nicht erbaut sein. **2** *v.i.*, **-mm-** (lit. or fig.) schwächer werden. **3** *v.t.*, **-mm-** verdunkeln; (fig.) trüben; dämpfen; ∼ **the lights** (Theatre, Cinemat.) die Lichter langsam verlöschen lassen

dime /daɪm/ *n.* (Amer.) Zehncentstück, *das;* ≈ Groschen, *der* (ugs.)

dimension /dɪ'menʃn, daɪ'menʃn/ *n.* (lit. or fig.) Dimension, *die;* (measurement) Abmessung, *die*

diminish /dɪ'mɪnɪʃ/ **1** *v.i.* nachlassen; ⟨*Zahl:*⟩ sich verringern; ⟨*Vorräte, Autorität, Einfluss:*⟩ abnehmen; ⟨*Wert, Bedeutung, Ansehen:*⟩ geringer werden; ∼ **in value/ number** an Wert verlieren/an Zahl od. zahlenmäßig abnehmen. **2** *v.t.* vermindern; verringern; (fig.) herabwürdigen ⟨*Person*⟩; schmälern ⟨*Ansehen, Ruf*⟩

diminished /dɪ'mɪnɪʃt/ *adj.* geringer ⟨*Wert, Anzahl, Einfluss, Popularität*⟩; vermindert ⟨*Stärke, Fähigkeit*⟩; ∼ **responsibility** (Law) verminderte Zurechnungsfähigkeit

diminishing /dɪ'mɪnɪʃɪŋ/ *adj.* sinkend; abnehmend ⟨*Vorräte*⟩; schwindend ⟨*Kraft, Einfluss, Macht*⟩

diminutive /dɪ'mɪnjʊtɪv/ **1** *adj.* **(a)** winzig; **(b)** (Ling.) diminutiv. **2** *n.* (Ling.) Diminutiv[um], *das*

dimly /'dɪmlɪ/ *adv.* schwach; undeutlich ⟨*sehen*⟩; ungefähr ⟨*begreifen*⟩; **I** ∼ **remember it** ich erinnere mich noch dunkel daran

dimmer /'dɪmə(r)/ *n.* **(a)** Dimmer, *der;* **(b)** (Amer. Motor Veh.: switch) Abblendschalter, *der*

dimple /'dɪmpl/ *n.* Grübchen, *das;* (on golf-ball etc.) kleine Vertiefung

dim: ∼**wit** *n.* (coll.) Dummkopf, *der* (ugs.); ∼**-witted** /'dɪmwɪtɪd/ *adj.* (coll.) dusselig (salopp)

din /dɪn/ **1** *n.* Lärm, *der.* **2** *v.t.*, **-nn-:** ∼ **sth. into sb.** jmdm. etw. einhämmern *od.* einbläuen

dine /daɪn/ *v.i.* (at midday/in the evening) [zu Mittag/zu Abend] essen *od.* (geh.) speisen; ∼ **off/on sth.** (eat) etw. [zum Mittag-/Abendessen] verzehren; ∼ **off sth.** (eat from) von etw. speisen

∼ **'out** *v.i.* **(a)** auswärts [zu Mittag/Abend] essen; **(b)** ∼ **out on sth.** wegen etw. zum Essen eingeladen werden

diner /'daɪnə(r)/ *n.* Gast, *der* (*zum Abendessen*)

ding-dong /'dɪŋdɒŋ/ *n.* Bimbam, *das*

dinghy /'dɪŋgɪ, 'dɪŋɪ/ *n.* Ding[h]i, *das;* (inflatable) Schlauchboot, *das*

dingo /'dɪŋgəʊ/ *n., pl.* ∼**es** Dingo, *der*

dingy /'dɪndʒɪ/ *adj.* schmuddelig

dining /'daɪnɪŋ/**:** ∼ **area** *n.* ≈ Essecke, *die;* ∼ **car** *n.* (Railw.) Speisewagen, *der;* ∼ **chair** *n.* Esszimmerstuhl, *der;* ∼ **hall** *n.* Speisesaal, *der;* ∼ **room** *n.* (in private house) Esszimmer, *das;* (in hotel etc.) Speisesaal, *der;* ∼ **table** *n.* Esstisch, *der*

dinkum /'dɪŋkəm/ *adj.* (Austral. and NZ coll.) astrein (ugs.)

dinner /'dɪnə(r)/ *n.* Essen, *das;* (at midday also) Mittagessen, *das;* (in the evening also) Abendessen, *das;* (formal event) Diner, *das;* **have** *or* **eat** [one's] ∼**:** zu Mittag/Abend essen; **go out to** ∼**:** [abends] essen gehen; **be having** *or* **eating** [one's] ∼**:** gerade beim Essen sein; **have people to** *or* **for** ∼**:** Gäste zum Essen haben

dinner: ∼ **dance** *n.* Abendessen mit anschließendem Tanz; ∼ **jacket** *n.* (Brit.) Dinnerjacket, *das;* ∼ **lady** *n.* (Brit.) Servlererin beim Mittagessen in der Schule; ∼ **party** *n.* Abendeinladung (mit Essen), *die;* (more formal) Abendgesellschaft, *die;* ∼ **service** *n.* Essgeschirr, *das;* ∼ **table** *n.* Esstisch, *der;* ∼ **time** *n.* Essenszeit, *die;* **at** ∼ **time** zur Essenszeit; (12–2 p.m.) mittags

dinosaur /'daɪnəsɔː(r)/ *n.* Dinosaurier, *der*

dint /dɪnt/ *n.* **by** ∼ **of** durch; **by** ∼ **of doing sth.** indem jmd. etw. tut

diocesan /daɪ'ɒsɪsən/ *adj.* (Eccl.) diözesan

diocese /'daɪəsɪs/ *n.* (Eccl.) Diözese, *die*

dioxin /daɪ'ɒksɪn/ *n.* (Chem.) Dioxin, *das*

dip /dɪp/ **1** *v.t.*, **-pp-:** **(a)** [ein]tauchen (**in** in + *Akk.*); **she** ∼**ped her hand into the sack** sie griff in den Sack; **(b)** (Agric.) dippen ⟨*Schaf*⟩; **(c)** (Brit. Motor Veh.) ∼ **one's [head]lights** abblenden; **[drive with** *or* **on]** ∼**ped headlights** [mit] Abblendlicht [fahren]. **2** *v.i.*, **-pp-:** **(a)** (go down)

sinken; **(b)** (incline downwards, lit. or fig.) abfallen. **3** *n.* **(a)** (∼ping) [kurzes] Eintauchen; **(b)** (bathe) [kurzes] Bad; **(c)** (in road) Senke, *die;* **(d)** (Gastr.) Dip, *der*

∼ **into** *v.t.* **(a)** greifen in (+ *Akk.*); (fig.) ∼ **into one's pocket** *or* **purse** [tief] in die Tasche greifen; ∼ **into one's savings** seine Ersparnisse angreifen; **(b)** (look cursorily at) einen flüchtigen Blick werfen in (+ *Akk.*)

diphtheria /dɪf'θɪərɪə/ *n.* (Med.) Diphtherie, *die*

diphthong /'dɪfθɒŋ/ *n.* Diphthong, *der* (fachspr.); Doppellaut, *der*

diploma /dɪ'pləʊmə/ *n.* (Educ.) Diplom, *das*

diplomacy /dɪ'pləʊməsɪ/ *n.* (Polit.; also fig.) Diplomatie, *die*

diplomat /'dɪpləmæt/ *n.* ▶ **887** (Polit.; also fig.) Diplomat, *der*/Diplomatin, *die*

diplomatic /dɪplə'mætɪk/ *adj.*, **diplomatically** /dɪplə'mætɪkəlɪ/ *adv.* (Polit.; also fig.) diplomatisch

diplomatic: ∼ **'bags** *n. pl.* Kuriergepäck, *das;* ∼ **corps** *n.* diplomatisches Korps

dip: ∼**stick** *n.* [Öl-/Benzin]messstab, *der;* ∼ **switch** *n.* (Brit. Motor Veh.) Abblendschalter, *der*

dire /'daɪə(r)/ *adj.* **(a)** (dreadful) entsetzlich; furchtbar; **(b)** (extreme) ∼ **necessity** dringende Notwendigkeit; **be in** ∼ **need of sth.** etw. dringend benötigen; **be in** ∼ **[financial] straits** in einer ernsten [finanziellen] Notlage sein

direct /dɪ'rekt, daɪ'rekt/ **1** *v.t.* **(a)** ▶ **1199** (turn) richten (**to[wards]** auf + *Akk.*); ∼ **sb.'s attention to sth.** jmds. Aufmerksamkeit auf etw. (*Akk.*) lenken; **the remark was** ∼**ed at you** die Bemerkung galt dir; **the bomb/missile was** ∼**ed at ...** die Bombe/das Geschoss galt ... *Dat.*; ∼ **sb. to a place** jmdm. den Weg zu einem Ort beschreiben *od.* sagen; **(b)** (control) leiten; beaufsichtigen ⟨*Arbeitskräfte, Arbeitsablauf*⟩; regeln, dirigieren ⟨*Verkehr*⟩; **(c)** (order) anweisen; ∼ **sb. to do sth.** jmdn. anweisen, etw. zu tun; **as** ∼**ed [by the doctor]** wie [vom Arzt] verordnet; **(d)** (Theatre, Cinemat., Telev., Radio) Regie führen bei. **2** *adj.* **(a)** direkt; durchgehend ⟨*Zug*⟩; unmittelbar ⟨*Ursache, Gefahr, Auswirkung*⟩; (immediate) unmittelbar, persönlich ⟨*Erfahrung, Verantwortung, Beteiligung*⟩; **(b)** (diametrical) genau ⟨*Gegenteil*⟩; direkt ⟨*Widerspruch*⟩; diametral ⟨*Gegensatz*⟩; **(c)** (frank) direkt; offen; glatt ⟨*Absage*⟩. **3** *adv.* direkt

direct: ∼ **'debit** *n.* (Brit.) Lastschriftverfahren, *das;* ∼ **'current** *n.* (Electr.) Gleichstrom, *der;* ∼ **dialling** *n.* Durchwahl, *die;* **we will soon have** ∼ **dialling** wir werden bald ein Durchwahlsystem haben; ∼ **'hit** *n.* Volltreffer, *der*

direction /dɪ'rekʃn, daɪ'rekʃn/ *n.* **(a)** (guidance) Führung, *die;* (of firm, orchestra) Leitung, *die;* (of play, film, TV or radio programme) Regie, *die;* **(b)** ▶ **1199** *usu. in pl.* (order) Anordnung, *die;* Gebrauchsanweisung, *die;* on *or* by sb.'s ∼**:** auf jmds. Anordnung (*Akk.*) [hin]; **give sb.** ∼**s to the museum/to York** jmdm. den Weg zum Museum/nach York beschreiben; **(c)** (point moved towards *or* from, lit. *or* fig.) Richtung, *die;* **from which** ∼**?** aus welcher Richtung?; **travel in a southerly** ∼**/in the** ∼ **of London** in südliche[r] Richtung/in Richtung London reisen; **sense of** ∼**:** Orientierungssinn, *der;* (fig.) Orientierung, *die;* **lose all sense of** ∼ (lit. *or* fig.) jede Orientierung verlieren

di'rection indicator *n.* (Motor Veh.) [Fahrt]richtungsanzeiger, *der*

directive /dɪ'rektɪv, daɪ'rektɪv/ *n.* Weisung, *die;* Direktive, *die*

directly /dɪ'rektlɪ, daɪ'rektlɪ/ **1** *adv.* **(a)** direkt; unmittelbar ⟨*folgen, verantwortlich sein*⟩; **(b)** (exactly) direkt; wörtlich ⟨*zitieren, abschreiben*⟩; **(c)** (at once) direkt; umgehend; (shortly) gleich; sofort. **2** *conj.* (Brit. coll.) sowie

directness /dɪ'rektnɪs, daɪ'rektnɪs/ *n., no pl.* **(a)** (of route, course) Geradheit, *die;* **(b)** (fig.) Direktheit, *die*

director /dɪ'rektə(r), daɪ'rektə(r)/ *n.* ▶ **887** **(a)** (Commerc.) Direktor, *der*/Direktorin, *die;* (of project) Leiter, *der*/Leiterin, *die;* **board of** ∼**s** Aufsichtsrat, *der;* **(b)** (Theatre, Cinemat., Telev., Radio) Regisseur, *der*/Regisseurin, *die*

directorship /dɪ'rektəʃɪp, daɪ'rektəʃɪp/ *n.* (Commerc.) Leitung, *die;* **hold two** ∼**s** in zwei Aufsichtsräten sein

directory /dɪˈrektərɪ, daɪˈrektərɪ/ *n.* **(a)** (telephone ∼) Telefonbuch, *das;* (of tradesmen etc.) Branchenverzeichnis, *das;* *attrib.* ∼ **enquiries** (Brit.), ∼ **information** (Amer.) [Fernsprech]auskunft, *die;* **(b)** (Computing) Verzeichnis, *das*

direct 'speech *n.* (Ling.) direkte Rede

dirge /dɜːdʒ/ *n.* **(a)** (for the dead) Grabgesang, *der;* **(b)** (mournful song) Klagegesang, *der*

dirt /dɜːt/ *n., no pl.* **(a)** Schmutz, *der;* Dreck, *der* (ugs.)**; be covered in** ∼: ganz schmutzig sein; (stronger) vor Schmutz starren; ∼ **cheap** spottbillig; **treat sb. like** ∼: jmdn. wie [den letzten] Dreck behandeln (salopp); **(b)** (soil) Erde, *die*

dirty /ˈdɜːtɪ/ **1** *adj.* **(a)** schmutzig; dreckig (ugs.)**; get one's shoes/hands** ∼: sich (*Dat.*) die Schuhe/Hände schmutzig machen; **get sth.** ∼: etw. schmutzig machen; **(b)** ∼ **weather** stürmisches Wetter; Dreckwetter, *das* (ugs. abwertend); **(c)** ∼ **look** (coll.) giftiger Blick; **(d)** (fig.: obscene) schmutzig; schlüpfrig; (sexually illicit) **spend a** ∼ **weekend together** ein Liebeswochenende zusammen verbringen; ∼ **old man** alter Lustmolch (ugs. abwertend); geiler alter Bock (salopp abwertend); **(e)** (despicable, sordid) schmutzig ⟨*Lüge, Gerücht, Geschäft*⟩; dreckig (salopp abwertend), gemein ⟨*Lügner, Betrüger*⟩; (unsportsmanlike) unfair; **do the** ∼ **on sb.** (coll.) jmdn. [he]reinlegen (ugs.); ∼ **trick** gemeiner Trick; ∼ **work** (coll.) schmutziges Geschäft; **do the/sb.'s** ∼ **work** sich (*Dat.*)/sich (*Dat.*) für jmdn. die Finger schmutzig machen. **2** *v.t.* schmutzig machen; beschmutzen

dirty 'word *n.* unanständiges Wort

disability /dɪsəˈbɪlɪtɪ/ *n.* Behinderung, *die;* **suffer from** *or* **have a** ∼: behindert sein

disable /dɪsˈeɪbl/ *v.t.* **(a)** ∼ **sb.** [physically] jmdn. zum Invaliden machen; **be** ∼**d by sth.** durch etw. behindert sein; **(b)** (make unable to fight) kampfunfähig machen ⟨*Feind, Schiff, Panzer, Flugzeug*⟩

disabled /dɪsˈeɪbld/ **1** *adj.* **(a)** behindert; **physically/ mentally** ∼: körperbehindert/geistig behindert; **(b)** (unable to fight) kampfunfähig ⟨*Schiff, Panzer, Flugzeug*⟩. **2** *n. pl.* **the** [**physically/mentally**] ∼: die [Körper]behinderten/[geistig] Behinderten *Pl.*

disablement /dɪsˈeɪblmənt/ *n., no pl.* Behinderung, *die*

disadvantage /dɪsədˈvɑːntɪdʒ/ **1** *n.* Nachteil, *der;* **be at a** ∼: im Nachteil sein; benachteiligt sein; **be to sb.'s/ sth.'s** ∼: sich zu jmds. Nachteil/zum Nachteil einer Sache auswirken. **2** *v.t.* benachteiligen

disadvantaged /dɪsədˈvɑːntɪdʒd/ *adj.* benachteiligt

disadvantageous /dɪsædvənˈteɪdʒəs/ *adj.* nachteilig

disagree /dɪsəˈɡriː/ *v.i.* **(a)** anderer Meinung sein; ∼ **with sb./sth.** mit jmdm./etw. nicht übereinstimmen; ∼ [**with sb.**] **about** *or* **over sth.** sich [mit jmdm.] über etw. (*Akk.*) nicht einig sein; **(b)** (quarrel) eine Auseinandersetzung haben; **(c)** (be mutually inconsistent) nicht übereinstimmen; **(d)** ∼ **with sb.** (have bad effects on) jmdm. nicht bekommen

disagreeable /dɪsəˈɡriːəbl/ *adj.* unangenehm

disagreement /dɪsəˈɡriːmənt/ *n.* **(a)** (difference of opinion) Uneinigkeit, *die;* **be in** ∼: geteilter Meinung sein; **be in** ∼ **with sb./sth.** mit jmdm./etw. nicht übereinstimmen; **(b)** (strife, quarrel) Meinungsverschiedenheit, *die;* **(c)** (discrepancy) Diskrepanz, *die*

disallow /dɪsəˈlaʊ/ *v.t.* nicht gestatten; abweisen ⟨*Antrag, Anspruch, Klage*⟩; (refuse to admit) nicht anerkennen; nicht gelten lassen; (Sport) nicht geben ⟨*Tor*⟩

disappear /dɪsəˈpɪə(r)/ *v.i.* verschwinden; ⟨*Brauch, Kunst, Tierart:*⟩ aussterben

disappearance /dɪsəˈpɪərəns/ *n.* Verschwinden, *das;* (of customs; extinction) Aussterben, *das*

disappoint /dɪsəˈpɔɪnt/ *v.t.* enttäuschen; **be** ∼**ed in** *or* **by** *or* **with sb./sth.** von jmdm./etw. enttäuscht sein

disappointing /dɪsəˈpɔɪntɪŋ/ *adj.* enttäuschend

disappointment /dɪsəˈpɔɪntmənt/ *n.* Enttäuschung, *die*

disapproval /dɪsəˈpruːvl/ *n.* Missbilligung, *die*

disapprove /dɪsəˈpruːv/ **1** *v.i.* dagegen sein; ∼ **of sb./ sth.** jmdn. ablehnen/etw. missbilligen; ∼ **of sb. doing sth.** es missbilligen, wenn jmd. etw. tut. **2** *v.t.* missbilligen

disapproving /dɪsəˈpruːvɪŋ/ *adj.* missbilligend

disarm /dɪsˈɑːm/ *v.t.* (lit. or fig.) entwaffnen

disarmament /dɪsˈɑːməmənt/ *n.* Abrüstung, *die; attrib.* ∼ **talks** Abrüstungsgespräche

disarming /dɪsˈɑːmɪŋ/ *adj.* entwaffnend

disarray /dɪsəˈreɪ/ *n.* Unordnung, *die;* (confusion) Wirrwarr, *der;* **be in** ∼: in Unordnung sein; *see also* **throw 1 b**

disaster /dɪˈzɑːstə(r)/ *n.* **(a)** Katastrophe, *die;* **air** ∼: Flugzeugunglück, *das;* **a railway/mining** ∼: ein Eisenbahn-/Grubenunglück; **end in** ∼: in einer Katastrophe enden; **(b)** (complete failure) Fiasko, *das;* Katastrophe, *die*

di'saster area *n.* Katastrophengebiet, *das*

disastrous /dɪˈzɑːstrəs/ *adj.* katastrophal; verhängnisvoll ⟨*Irrtum, Entscheidung, Politik*⟩; verheerend, katastrophal ⟨*Überschwemmung, Wirbelsturm*⟩

disband /dɪsˈbænd/ **1** *v.t.* auflösen. **2** *v.i.* sich auflösen

disbelief /dɪsbɪˈliːf/ *n.* Unglaube, *der;* **in** ∼: ungläubig

disbelieve /dɪsbɪˈliːv/ *v.t.* ∼ **sb./sth.** jmdm. etw. nicht glauben

disc /dɪsk/ *n.* **(a)** Scheibe, *die;* **(b)** (CD) CD, *die;* (gramophone record) [Schall]platte, *die;* **(c)** (Computing) ⇒ **disk**

discard 1 /dɪˈskɑːd/ *v.t.* **(a)** wegwerfen; ablegen ⟨*Kleidung*⟩; fallen lassen ⟨*Vorschlag, Idee, Person*⟩; **(b)** (Cards) abwerfen. **2** /ˈdɪskɑːd/ *n.* Ausschuss, *der*

disc brake *n.* Scheibenbremse, *die*

discern /dɪˈsɜːn/ *v.t.* wahrnehmen; **sth. can be** ∼**ed** etw. ist zu erkennen; ∼ **from sth. whether** …: an etw. (*Dat.*) erkennen, ob …

discernible /dɪˈsɜːnɪbl/ *adj.* erkennbar

discerning /dɪˈsɜːnɪŋ/ *adj.* fein ⟨*Gaumen, Ohr, Geschmack*⟩; scharf ⟨*Auge*⟩; urteilsfähig ⟨*Richter, Kritiker*⟩; kritisch ⟨*Leser, Kunde, Zuschauer, Kommentar*⟩

discharge 1 /dɪsˈtʃɑːdʒ/ *v.t.* **(a)** (dismiss, allow to leave) entlassen (**from** aus); freisprechen ⟨*Angeklagte*⟩; (exempt from liabilities) befreien (**from** von); **(b)** abschießen ⟨*Pfeil, Torpedo*⟩; ablassen ⟨*Flüssigkeit, Gas*⟩; absondern ⟨*Eiter*⟩; **(c)** (fire) abfeuern ⟨*Gewehr, Kanone*⟩; **(d)** erfüllen ⟨*Pflicht, Verbindlichkeiten, Versprechen*⟩; bezahlen ⟨*Schulden*⟩. **2** /dɪsˈtʃɑːdʒ/ *v.i.* entladen werden; ⟨*Schiff auch:*⟩ gelöscht werden; ⟨*Batterie:*⟩ sich entladen. **3** /dɪsˈtʃɑːdʒ, ˈdɪstʃɑːdʒ/ *n.* **(a)** (dismissal) Entlassung, *die* (**from** aus); (of defendant) Freispruch, *der;* (exemption from liabilities) Befreiung, *die;* **(b)** (emission) Ausfluss, *der;* (of gas) Austritt, *der;* (of pus) Absonderung, *die;* (Electr.) Entladung, *die;* (of gun) Abfeuern, *das;* **(c)** (of debt) Begleichung, *die;* (of duty) Erfüllung, *die*

disciple /dɪˈsaɪpl/ *n.* **(a)** (Relig.) Jünger, *der;* **(b)** (follower) Anhänger, *der/*Anhängerin, *die*

disciplinarian /dɪsɪplɪˈneərɪən/ *n.* [strenger] Erzieher

disciplinary /ˈdɪsɪplɪnərɪ, dɪsɪˈplɪnərɪ/ *adj.* Disziplinar-; disziplinarisch

discipline /ˈdɪsɪplɪn/ **1** *n.* Disziplin, *die;* **maintain** ∼: die Disziplin aufrechterhalten. **2** *v.t.* **(a)** disziplinieren; **(b)** (punish) bestrafen; (physically also) züchtigen (geh.)

disciplined /ˈdɪsɪplɪnd/ *adj.* diszipliniert

'disc jockey *n.* ▶ **887** | Diskjockey, *der*

disclaim /dɪsˈkleɪm/ *v.t.* abstreiten

disclaimer /dɪsˈkleɪmə(r)/ *n.* Gegenerklärung, *die;* (Law) Verzichterklärung, *die*

disclose /dɪsˈkləʊz/ *v.t.* enthüllen; bekannt geben ⟨*Information, Nachricht*⟩; **he didn't** ∼ **why he'd come** er verriet nicht, warum er gekommen war

disclosure /dɪsˈkləʊʒə(r)/ *n.* Enthüllung, *die;* (of information, news) Bekanntgabe, *die*

disco /ˈdɪskəʊ/ *n., pl.* ∼**s** (coll.: discothèque, party) Disko, *die*

discolor (Amer.) ⇒ **discolour**

discoloration /dɪskʌləˈreɪʃn/ *n.* Verfärbung, *die*

discolour /dɪsˈkʌlə(r)/ (Brit.) **1** *v.t.* verfärben; (fade) ausbleichen. **2** *v.i.* sich verfärben

discolouration (Brit.) ⇒ **discoloration**

discomfit /dɪsˈkʌmfɪt/ *v.t.* verunsichern

discomfiture /dɪsˈkʌmfɪtʃə(r)/ *n.* Verunsicherung, *die*

discomfort /dɪsˈkʌmfət/ *n.* **(a)** *no pl.* (uneasiness of body) Beschwerden *Pl.;* **(b)** *no pl.* (uneasiness of mind) Unbehagen, *das;* **(c)** (hardship) Unannehmlichkeit, *die*

disconcert /dɪskən'sɜːt/ v.t. irritieren

disconnect /dɪskə'nekt/ v.t. (a) abtrennen; (b) (Electr., Teleph.) ~ **the electricity from a house** ein Haus von der Stromversorgung abtrennen; ~ **the TV** den Stecker des Fernsehers herausziehen; **if you don't pay your telephone bill you will be** ~**ed** wenn Sie Ihre Telefonrechnung nicht bezahlen, wird Ihr Telefon abgestellt

disconnected /dɪskə'nektɪd/ adj. (a) abgetrennt; abgestellt ‹Telefon›; **is the cooker/TV** ~? ist der Stecker beim Herd/Fernseher herausgezogen?; (b) (incoherent) unzusammenhängend

disconsolate /dɪs'kɒnsələt/ adj. untröstlich

discontent /dɪskən'tent/ n. Unzufriedenheit, die

discontented /dɪskən'tentɪd/ adj. unzufrieden (**with, about** mit)

discontentment /dɪskən'tentmənt/ n., no pl. Unzufriedenheit, die

discontinue /dɪskən'tɪnjuː/ v.t. einstellen; abbestellen ‹Abonnement›; abbrechen ‹Behandlung›

discord /'dɪskɔːd/ n. (a) Zwietracht, die; (quarrelling) Streit, der; (b) (Mus.) Dissonanz, die

discordant /dɪs'kɔːdənt/ adj. (a) (conflicting) gegensätzlich; (b) (dissonant) misstönend

discotheque /'dɪskətek/ n. Diskothek, die

discount 1 /'dɪskaʊnt/ n. (Commerc.) Rabatt, der; **give or offer [sb.] a** ~ **on sth.** [jmdm.] Rabatt auf etw. (Akk.) geben od. gewähren; ~ **for cash** Skonto, der od. das; **at a** ~: mit Rabatt; (fig.) nicht gefragt. 2 /dɪs'kaʊnt/ v.t. (disbelieve) unberücksichtigt lassen; (discredit) widerlegen ‹Beweis, Theorie›; (underrate) zu gering einschätzen

discourage /dɪs'kʌrɪdʒ/ v.t. (a) (dispirit) entmutigen; (b) (advise against) abraten; ~ **sb. from sth.** jmdm. von etw. abraten; (c) (stop) abhalten ‹Person›; verhindern ‹Handlung›; ~ **sb. from doing sth.** jmdn. davon abhalten, etw. zu tun

discouragement /dɪs'kʌrɪdʒmənt/ n. (a) Entmutigung, die; (b) (deterrent) Abschreckung, die; (c) (depression) Mutlosigkeit, die

discouraging /dɪs'kʌrɪdʒɪŋ/ adj. entmutigend

discourteous /dɪs'kɜːtɪəs/ adj. unhöflich

discourtesy /dɪs'kɜːtəsɪ/ n. Unhöflichkeit, die

discover /dɪs'kʌvə(r)/ v.t. entdecken; (by search) herausfinden

discoverer /dɪs'kʌvərə(r)/ n. Entdecker, der/Entdeckerin, die

discovery /dɪs'kʌvərɪ/ n. Entdeckung, die; **voyage of** ~: Entdeckungsreise, die

discredit /dɪs'kredɪt/ 1 n. (a) no pl. Misskredit, der; **bring** ~ **on sb./sth., bring sb./sth. into** ~: jmdn./ etw. in Misskredit (Akk.) bringen; (b) (sb. or sth. that ~s) **be a** ~ **to sb./sth.** jmdm./einer Sache keine Ehre machen. 2 v.t. (a) (disbelieve) keinen Glauben schenken (+ Dat.); (cause to be disbelieved) unglaubwürdig machen; (b) (disgrace) diskreditieren (geh.); in Verruf bringen

discreet /dɪs'kriːt/ adj., ~**er** /dɪs'kriːtə(r)/, ~**est** /dɪs'kriːtɪst/ diskret; taktvoll; (unobtrusive) diskret; dezent ‹Parfüm, Kleidung›

discreetly /dɪs'kriːtlɪ/ adv. diskret; dezent ‹gekleidet›

discrepancy /dɪs'krepənsɪ/ n. Diskrepanz, die

discrete /dɪs'kriːt/ adj. eigenständig; (Math., Phys.) diskret

discretion /dɪs'kreʃn/ n. (a) (prudence) Umsicht, die; (reservedness) Diskretion, die; **use** ~: diskret sein; ~ **is the better part of valour** (prov.) Vorsicht ist besser als Nachsicht (ugs. scherzh.); (b) (liberty to decide) Ermessen, das; **leave sth. to sb.'s** ~: etw. in jmds. Ermessen (Akk.) stellen; **at sb.'s** ~: nach jmds. Ermessen; **use one's** ~: nach eigenem Ermessen od. Gutdünken handeln

discriminate /dɪs'krɪmɪneɪt/ v.i. (a) (distinguish) unterscheiden; ~ **between [two things]** unterscheiden zwischen [zwei Dingen]; (b) ~ **against/in favour of sb.** jmdn. diskriminieren/bevorzugen

discriminating /dɪs'krɪmɪneɪtɪŋ/ adj. kritisch ‹Urteil, Auge, Kunde, Kunstsammler›; fein ‹Geschmack, Gaumen, Ohr›

discrimination /dɪskrɪmɪ'neɪʃn/ n. (a) (discernment) [kritisches] Urteilsvermögen; (b) (differential treatment) Diskriminierung, die (**against** Gen.); ~ **against Blacks/ women** Diskriminierung von Schwarzen/Frauen; ~ **in favour of** Bevorzugung (+ Gen.); **racial** ~: Rassendiskriminierung, die

discus /'dɪskəs/ n. (Sport) Diskus, der

discuss /dɪs'kʌs/ v.t. (a) (talk about) besprechen; **I'm not willing to** ~ **this matter at present** ich möchte jetzt nicht darüber sprechen; (b) (debate) diskutieren über (+ Akk.); (examine) erörtern; diskutieren

discussion /dɪs'kʌʃn/ n. (a) (conversation) Gespräch, das; (more formal) Unterredung, die; (b) (debate) Diskussion, die; (examination) Erörterung, die; **be under** ~: zur Diskussion stehen

disdain /dɪs'deɪn/ 1 n. Verachtung, die; **with** ~: verächtlich; **a look of** ~: ein verächtlicher od. geringschätziger Blick. 2 v.t. verachten; verächtlich ablehnen ‹Rat, Hilfe›; ~ **to do sth.** zu stolz sein, etw. zu tun

disdainful /dɪs'deɪnfl/ adj. verächtlich, geringschätzig ‹Lachen, Ton, Blick, Kommentar›; **look** ~: verächtlich dreinblicken

disease /dɪ'ziːz/ n. (lit. or fig.) Krankheit, die

diseased /dɪ'ziːzd/ adj. (lit. or fig.) krank

disembark /dɪsɪm'bɑːk/ 1 v.t. ausschiffen. 2 v.i. von Bord gehen

disembodied /dɪsɪm'bɒdɪd/ adj. körperlos ‹Seele, Geist›; geisterhaft ‹Stimme›

disenchant /dɪsɪn'tʃɑːnt/ v.t. (a) entzaubern (geh.); (b) (disillusion) ernüchtern; **he became** ~**ed with her/it** sie/ es hat ihn desillusioniert

disengage /dɪsɪn'geɪdʒ/ v.t. lösen (**from** aus, von); ~ **the clutch** auskuppeln

disentangle /dɪsɪn'tæŋgl/ v.t. (a) (extricate) befreien (**from** aus); (fig.) herauslösen (**from** aus); (b) (unravel) entwirren

disfavour (Brit.; Amer.: **disfavor**) /dɪs'feɪvə(r)/ n. (displeasure, disapproval) Missfallen, das; (being out of favour) Ungnade, die; **incur sb.'s** ~: jmds. Unwillen erregen

disfigure /dɪs'fɪgə(r)/ v.t. entstellen

disfigurement /dɪs'fɪgəmənt/ n. Entstellung, die

disgorge /dɪs'gɔːdʒ/ v.t. ausspucken; ausspeien (geh.); (fig.) ausspeien (geh.)

disgrace /dɪs'greɪs/ 1 n., no pl. (a) (ignominy) Schande, die; Schmach, die (geh.); (deep disfavour) Ungnade, die; **bring** ~ **on sb./sth.** Schande über jmdn./etw. bringen; (b) **be a** ~ **[to sb./sth.]** [für jmdn./etw.] eine Schande sein. 2 v.t. ‹Person:› Schande machen (+ Dat.); ‹Person, Handlung:› Schande bringen über (+ Akk.); ~ **oneself** sich blamieren

disgraceful /dɪs'greɪsfl/ adj. erbärmlich; miserabel ‹Handschrift›; skandalös ‹Benehmen, Enthüllung, Bedingungen, Verstoß, Behandlung, Tat›; **it's [absolutely or really or quite]** ~: es ist [wirklich] ein Skandal

disgracefully /dɪs'greɪsfəlɪ/ adv. erbärmlich; schändlich ‹verraten, betrügen, behandeln›; **behave** ~: sich schändlich od. (geh.) schimpflich benehmen

disgruntled /dɪs'grʌntld/ adj. verstimmt

disguise /dɪs'gaɪz/ 1 v.t. (a) verkleiden ‹Person›; verstellen ‹Stimme›; tarnen ‹Gegenstand›; ~ **oneself** sich verkleiden; (b) (misrepresent) verschleiern; **there is no disguising the fact that** ...: es lässt sich nicht verheimlichen, dass ...; (c) (conceal) verbergen. 2 n. Verkleidung, die; (fig.) Maske, die; **wear a** ~: verkleidet sein; **in the** ~ **of** verkleidet als; **in** ~: verkleidet

disgust /dɪs'gʌst/ 1 n. (nausea) Ekel, der (**at** vor + Dat.); (revulsion) Abscheu, der (**at** vor + Dat.); (indignation) Empörung, die (**at** über + Akk.); **in/with** ~: angewidert; (with indignation) empört. 2 v.t. anwidern; (fill with nausea) anwidern; ekeln; (fill with indignation) empören

disgusted /dɪs'gʌstɪd/ adj. angewidert; (nauseated) angewidert; angeekelt; (indignant) empört

disgusting /dɪs'gʌstɪŋ/ adj. widerlich; widerwärtig; (nauseating also) ekelhaft

dish /dɪʃ/ n. (a) (for food) Schale, die; (flatter) Platte, die; (deeper) Schüssel, die; (b) in pl. (crockery) Geschirr, das;

wash *or* (coll.) **do the** ~**es** Geschirr spülen; abwaschen; **(c)** (type of food) Gericht, *das;* **(d)** (coll.: woman, girl) klasse Frau (ugs.); **(e)** (receptacle) Schale, *die*
~ **'out** *v.t.* **(a)** austeilen ‹*Essen*›; **(b)** (coll.: distribute) verteilen
~ **'up** *v.t.* auftragen, servieren ‹*Essen*›
'dishcloth *n.* **(a)** (for washing) Abwaschlappen, *der;* Spültuch, *das;* **(b)** (Brit.: for drying) Geschirrtuch, *das*
dishearten /dɪs'hɑːtn/ *v.t.* entmutigen; **be** ~**ed** den Mut verlieren/verloren haben
disheartening /dɪs'hɑːtənɪŋ/ *adj.* entmutigend
dishevelled (*Amer.:* **disheveled**) /dɪ'ʃevld/ *adj.* unordentlich ‹*Kleidung*›; zerzaust ‹*Haar, Bart*›; ungepflegt ‹*Erscheinung*›
dishonest /dɪs'ɒnɪst/ *adj.* unehrlich ‹*Person*›; unaufrichtig ‹*Person, Antwort*›; unlauter (geh.) ‹*Geschäftsgebaren, Vorhaben*›; unredlich ‹*Geschäftsmann*›; unreell ‹*Geschäft, Gewinn*›; **be** ~ **with sb.** unehrlich od. unaufrichtig gegen jmdn. sein
dishonestly /dɪs'ɒnɪstlɪ/ *adv.* unehrlich; unaufrichtig; unlauter (geh.) ‹*handeln*›; unredlich ‹*sich verhalten*›
dishonesty /dɪs'ɒnɪstɪ/ *n.* Unehrlichkeit, *die;* Unaufrichtigkeit, *die;* (of methods) Unlauterkeit, *die* (geh.)
dishonor *etc.* (*Amer.*) ⇒ **dishonour** *etc.*
dishonour /dɪs'ɒnə(r)/ **1** *n.* Schande, *die.* **2** *v.t.* beleidigen
dishonourable /dɪs'ɒnərəbl/ *adj.* unehrenhaft
dish: ~ **rack** *n.* Abtropfgestell, *das;* (in dishwasher) Geschirrwagen, *der;* ~ **towel** *n.* Geschirrtuch, *das;* ~**washer** *n.* Geschirrspülmaschine, *die;* Geschirrspüler, *der* (ugs.); ~**water** *n.* Abwaschwasser, *das;* Spülwasser, *das*
disillusion /dɪsɪ'ljuːʒn, dɪsɪ'luːʒn/ **1** *n., no pl.* Desillusion, *die* (with über + *Akk.*). **2** *v.t.* ernüchtern
disillusioned /dɪsɪ'ljuːʒnd, dɪsɪ'luːʒnd/ *adj.* desillusioniert; **become** ~ **with sth.** seine Illusionen über etw. (*Akk.*) verlieren
disillusionment /dɪsɪ'ljuːʒnmənt, dɪsɪ'luːʒnmənt/ *n.* Desillusionierung, *die*
disincentive /dɪsɪn'sentɪv/ *n.* Hemmnis, *das;* **act as** *or* **be a** ~ **to sb. to do sth.** jmdn. davon abhalten, etw. zu tun
disinclination /dɪsɪnklɪ'neɪʃn/ *n.* Abneigung, *die* (for, to gegen)
disincline /dɪsɪn'klaɪn/ *v.t.* abgeneigt machen (for, to gegen)
disinclined /dɪsɪn'klaɪnd/ *adj.* abgeneigt
disinfect /dɪsɪn'fekt/ *v.t.* desinfizieren
disinfectant /dɪsɪn'fektənt/ **1** *adj.* desinfizierend. **2** *n.* Desinfektionsmittel, *das*
disingenuous /dɪsɪn'dʒenjʊəs/ *adj.* unaufrichtig
disintegrate /dɪs'ɪntɪgreɪt/ **1** *v.i.* zerfallen; (shatter suddenly) zerbersten; (fig.) sich auflösen. **2** *v.t.* zerstören
disintegration /dɪsɪntɪ'greɪʃn/ *n.* Zerfall, *der;* (fig.) Auflösung, *die*
disinter /dɪsɪn'tɜː(r)/ *v.t.*, **-rr-** ausgraben
disinterested /dɪs'ɪntrəstɪd, dɪs'ɪntrɪstɪd/ *adj.* **(a)** (impartial) unvoreingenommen; unparteiisch; (free from selfish motive) selbstlos; uneigennützig; **(b)** (coll.: uninterested) desinteressiert
disjointed /dɪs'dʒɔɪntɪd/ *adj.* unzusammenhängend; zusammenhanglos
disk /dɪsk/ *n.* (Computing) [**magnetic**] ~: Magnetplatte, *die;* **floppy** ~: Floppy disk, *die;* Diskette, *die;* **hard** ~ (fixed) Festplatte, *die*
'disk drive *n.* (Computing) Diskettenlaufwerk, *das*
diskette /dɪ'sket/ *n.* (Computing) Diskette, *die*
dislike /dɪs'laɪk/ **1** *v.t.* nicht mögen; ~ **sb./sth. greatly** *or* **intensely** jmdn./etw. ganz und gar nicht leiden können; **I don't** ~ **it** ich finde es nicht schlecht; ~ **doing sth.** es nicht mögen, etw. zu tun; etw. ungern tun. **2** *n.* (a) *no pl.* Abneigung, *die* (of, for gegen); **she took an instant** ~ **to him/the house** sie empfand sofort eine Abneigung gegen ihn/das Haus; **(b)** (object) **one of my greatest** ~**s**

is …: zu den Dingen, die ich am wenigsten leiden kann, gehört …
dislocate /'dɪsləkeɪt/ *v.t.* (Med.) ausrenken; auskugeln ‹*Schulter, Hüfte*›
dislodge /dɪs'lɒdʒ/ *v.t.* entfernen (**from** aus); (detach) lösen (**from** von)
disloyal /dɪs'lɔɪəl/ *adj.* illoyal (**to** gegenüber); treulos ‹*Freund, Ehepartner*›; **be** ~: nicht loyal sein
disloyalty /dɪs'lɔɪəltɪ/ *n.* Illoyalität, *die* (**to** gegenüber); (to spouse, friend) Treulosigkeit, *die*
dismal /'dɪzməl/ *adj.* trist; düster; trostlos ‹*Landschaft, Ort*›; (coll.: feeble) kläglich ‹*Zustand, Leistung, Versuch*›; **a** ~ **failure** ein völliger Reinfall (ugs.)
dismantle /dɪs'mæntl/ *v.t.* zerlegen; demontieren; (fig.) demontieren; abbauen ‹*Schuppen, Gerüst*›
dismay /dɪs'meɪ/ **1** *v.t.* bestürzen; **he was** ~**ed to hear that** …: mit Bestürzung hörte er, dass … **2** *n.* Bestürzung, *die* (at über + *Akk.*); **watch in** *or* **with** ~: bestürzt zusehen
dismiss /dɪs'mɪs/ *v.t.* **(a)** entlassen; auflösen; aufheben ‹*Versammlung*›; **(b)** (from the mind) verwerfen; (reject) ablehnen; (treat very briefly) abtun
dismissal /dɪs'mɪsl/ *n.* **(a)** Entlassung, *die;* (of gathering etc.) Auflösung, *die;* Aufhebung, *die;* **(b)** (from the mind) Aufgabe, *die;* (rejection) Ablehnung, *die;* (very brief treatment) Abtun, *das*
dismissive /dɪs'mɪsɪv/ *adj.* abweisend; (disdainful) abschätzig; **be** ~ **about sth.** etw. abtun
dismount /dɪs'maʊnt/ **1** *v.i.* absteigen. **2** *v.t.* abwerfen ‹*Reiter*›
disobedience /dɪsə'biːdɪəns/ *n.* Ungehorsam, *der;* **act of** ~: ungehorsames Verhalten
disobedient /dɪsə'biːdɪənt/ *adj.* ungehorsam; **be** ~ **to sb.** jmdm. nicht gehorchen
disobey /dɪsə'beɪ/ *v.t.* nicht gehorchen (+ *Dat.*); nicht befolgen; missachten ‹*Befehl, Vorschrift usw.*›; übertreten ‹*Gesetz*›
disobliging /dɪsə'blaɪdʒɪŋ/ *adj.* ungefällig
disorder /dɪs'ɔːdə(r)/ *n.* **(a)** Unordnung, *die;* Durcheinander, *das;* **everything was in [complete]** ~: alles war ein einziges[, heilloses] Durcheinander; **the meeting broke up in** ~: die Versammlung endete in einem heillosen Durcheinander; **(b)** (rioting, disturbance) Unruhen *Pl.;* **(c)** (Med.) [Funktions]störung, *die;* **suffer from a mental** ~: geisteskrank sein; **a stomach/liver** ~: ein Magen-/Leberleiden
disordered /dɪs'ɔːdəd/ *adj.* unordentlich; ungeordnet ‹*Wortschwall, Gedanken[gang]*›
disorderly /dɪs'ɔːdəlɪ/ *adj.* **(a)** (untidy) unordentlich; ungeordnet ‹*Ansammlung*›; **(b)** (unruly) undiszipliniert; aufrührerisch ‹*Mob*›; ~ **conduct** ungebührliches Benehmen
disorganization /dɪsɔːgənaɪ'zeɪʃn/ *n., no pl.* Desorganisation, *die;* (muddle) Durcheinander, *das*
disorganize /dɪs'ɔːgənaɪz/ *v.t.* durcheinander bringen
disorganized /dɪs'ɔːgənaɪzd/ *adj.* chaotisch
disorient /dɪs'ɔːrɪənt/, **disorientate** /dɪs'ɔːrɪənteɪt/ *v.t.* die Orientierung nehmen (+ *Dat.*); (fig.) verwirren
disorientated /dɪs'ɔːrɪənteɪtɪd/, **disoriented** /dɪs'ɔːrɪəntɪd/ *adj.* verwirrt, desorientiert
disown /dɪs'əʊn/ *v.t.* verleugnen
disparage /dɪ'spærɪdʒ/ *v.t.* herabsetzen
disparagement /dɪ'spærɪdʒmənt/ *n.* Herabsetzung, *die*
disparaging /dɪ'spærɪdʒɪŋ/ *adj.* abschätzig
disparate /'dɪspərət/ *adj.* [völlig] verschieden; disparat (geh.)
disparity /dɪ'spærɪtɪ/ *n.* Unterschied, *der;* (lack of parity) Ungleichheit, *die*
dispassionate /dɪ'spæʃənət/ *adj.* (impartial) unvoreingenommen
dispatch /dɪ'spætʃ/ **1** *v.t.* **(a)** (send off) schicken; ~ **sb. [to do sth.]** jmdn. entsenden [, um etw. zu tun]; **(b)** (deal with) erledigen; **(c)** (kill) töten. **2** *n.* **(a)** (official report, Journ.) Bericht, *der;* **(b)** (sending off) Absenden, *das;* (of troops, messenger, delegation) Entsendung, *die* (geh.)

dispel /dɪ'spel/ v.t., **-ll-** vertreiben; zerstreuen ‹Besorgnis, Befürchtung›; verdrängen, unterdrücken ‹Gefühl, Erinnerung›

dispensable /dɪ'spensəbl/ adj. entbehrlich

dispensary /dɪ'spensərɪ/ n. (Pharm.) Apotheke, die

dispensation /dɪspen'seɪʃn/ n. **(a)** (distribution) Verteilung, die **(to** an + Akk.); (of favours) Gewährung, die; **(b)** (exemption) Sonderregelung, die

dispense /dɪ'spens/ **1** v.i. ~ **with** verzichten auf (+ Akk.); (do away with) überflüssig machen. **2** v.t. **(a)** (distribute, administer) verteilen **(to** an + Akk.); gewähren ‹Gastfreundschaft›; zuteil werden lassen ‹Gnade›; **the machine** ~**s hot drinks** der Automat gibt heiße Getränke aus; **(b)** (Pharm.) dispensieren (fachspr.)

dispenser /dɪ'spensə(r)/ n. (vending machine) Automat, der; (container) Spender, der

dispensing 'chemist n. ▶887│ Apotheker, der/Apothekerin, die

dispersal /dɪ'spɜːsl/ n. Zerstreuung, die; (diffusion) Ausbreitung, die; (of mist, oil slick) Auflösung, die

disperse /dɪ'spɜːs/ **1** v.t. zerstreuen; (dispel) auflösen ‹Dunst, Öl›; vertreiben ‹Wolken, Gase›. **2** v.i. sich zerstreuen

dispersion /dɪ'spɜːʃn/ n. (scattering) Zerstreuung, die; (diffusion) Ausbreitung, die

dispirited /dɪ'spɪrɪtɪd/ adj. entmutigt

dispiriting /dɪ'spɪrɪtɪŋ/ adj. entmutigend

displace /dɪs'pleɪs/ v.t. **(a)** (move from place) verschieben; **(b)** (supplant) ersetzen; (crowd out) verdrängen

displaced 'person n. Vertriebene, der/die

displacement /dɪs'pleɪsmənt/ n. **(a)** (moving) Verschiebung, die; **(b)** (supplanting) Ersetzung, die; **(c)** (Naut.: weight displaced) [Wasser]verdrängung, die

display /dɪ'spleɪ/ **1** v.t. **(a)** zeigen, tragen ‹Abzeichen›; aufstellen ‹Trophäe›; (to public view) ausstellen; (on noticeboard) aushängen; (standing) aufstellen ‹Schild›; (attached) aufhängen ‹Schild, Fahne›; **(b)** (flaunt) zur Schau stellen; **(c)** (Commerc.) ausstellen. **2** n. **(a)** Aufstellung, die; (to public view) Ausstellung, die; **a** ~ **of ill will/courage** eine Demonstration von jmds. Übelwollen/Mut; **(b)** (exhibition) Ausstellung, die; (Commerc.) Auslage, die; **a fashion** ~: eine Modenschau; **an air** ~: eine Flugschau; **be on** ~: ausgestellt werden; **(c)** (ostentatious show) Zurschaustellung, die; **make a** ~ **of one's affection** seine Gefühle zur Schau stellen; **(d)** (Computing etc.) Display, das; Anzeige, die

display: ~ **cabinet,** ~ **case** ⇒ case² **1 d**

displease /dɪs'pliːz/ v.t. **(a)** (earn disapproval of) ~ **sb.** jmds. Missfallen erregen; **(b)** (annoy) verärgern; **be** ~**d [with sb./at sth.]** [über jmdn./etw.] verärgert sein

displeasure /dɪs'pleʒə(r)/ n., no pl. Missfallen, das **(at** über + Akk.)

disposable /dɪ'spəʊzəbl/ adj. **(a)** (to be thrown away after use) Wegwerf-; ~ **bottle/container/syringe** Einwegflasche/-behälter/-spritze; **be** ~: nach Gebrauch weggeworfen werden; **(b)** (available) verfügbar; ~ **income** verfügbares Einkommen

disposal /dɪ'spəʊzl/ n. **(a)** (getting rid of, killing) Beseitigung, die; (of waste) Entsorgung, die; **(b)** (putting away) Forträumen, das; **(c)** (settling) Erledigung, die; **(d)** (treating) Abhandlung, die; **(e)** (control) Verfügung, die; **place** or **put sth./sb. at sb.'s [complete]** ~: jmdm. etw./jmdn. [ganz] zur Verfügung stellen; **have sth./sb. at one's** ~: etw./jmdn. zur Verfügung haben; **be at sb.'s** ~: jmdm. zur Verfügung stehen

dispose /dɪ'spəʊz/ v.t. **(a)** (make inclined) ~ **sb. to do sth.** jmdn. dazu veranlassen, etw. zu tun; **(b)** (arrange) anordnen; (Mil.) aufstellen ‹Truppen›
~ **of** v.t. **(a)** (do as one wishes with) ~ **of sth./sb.** über etw./jmdn. frei verfügen; **(b)** (kill, get rid of) beseitigen ‹Rivalen, Leiche, Abfall›; erlegen, töten ‹Gegner›; **(c)** (put away) wegräumen; **(d)** (eat up) aufessen; verputzen (ugs.); **(e)** (settle, finish) erledigen; **(f)** (disprove) widerlegen

disposed /dɪ'spəʊzd/ adj. **be** ~ **to sth.** zu etw. neigen; **be** ~ **to do sth.** dazu neigen, etw. zu tun; **be well/ill** ~ **towards sb.** jmdm. wohl/übel gesinnt sein; **be well/ill** ~ **towards sth.** einer Sache (Dat.) positiv/ablehnend gegenüberstehen

disposition /dɪspə'zɪʃn/ n. **(a)** (arrangement) Aufstellung, die; (of seating, figures) Anordnung, die; **(b)** (temperament) Veranlagung, die; Disposition, die; **she has a/is of a rather irritable** ~: sie ist ziemlich reizbar; **(c)** (inclination) Hang, der; Neigung, die **(towards** zu); **have a** ~ **to do sth./to[wards] sth.** dazu neigen, etw. zu tun/zu etw. neigen

dispossess /dɪspə'zes/ v.t. ~ **sb. of sth.** jmdm. etw. entziehen; (fig.) jmdm. etw. rauben

disproportion /dɪsprə'pɔːʃn/ n. Missverhältnis, das

disproportionate /dɪsprə'pɔːʃənət/ adj. vom Normalen abweichend; unangemessen; **be [totally]** ~ **to sth.** in einem [völligen] Missverhältnis od. in [gar] keinem Verhältnis zu etw. stehen

disprove /dɪs'pruːv/ v.t. widerlegen

disputable /dɪ'spjuːtəbl/ adj. strittig

dispute /dɪ'spjuːt/ **1** n. **(a)** no pl. (controversy) Streit, der; **a matter of much** ~: eine sehr umstrittene Frage; **that is [not] in** ~: darüber wird [nicht] gestritten; **be beyond** ~: außer Frage stehen; **(b)** (argument) Streit, der **(over** um); see also **industrial dispute**. **2** v.t. **(a)** sich streiten über (+ Akk.); ~ **whether …/how …:** sich darüber streiten, ob …/wie …; **(b)** (oppose) bestreiten; anfechten ‹Rechtsanspruch›; angreifen ‹Entscheidung›; **(c)** (contend for) streiten um

disqualification /dɪskwɒlɪfɪ'keɪʃn/ n. Ausschluss, der **(from** von); (Sport) Disqualifikation, die

disqualify /dɪs'kwɒlɪfaɪ/ v.t. **(a)** (debar) ausschließen **(from** von); (Sport) disqualifizieren; **(b)** (make unfit) ungeeignet machen; ~ **sb./sth. for sth.** jmdn./etw. für etw. ungeeignet machen

disquiet /dɪs'kwaɪət/ n. Unruhe, die

disquieting /dɪs'kwaɪətɪŋ/ adj. beunruhigend

disregard /dɪsrɪ'gɑːd/ **1** v.t. ignorieren; nicht berücksichtigen ‹Tatsache›; ~ **a request** einer Bitte (Dat.) nicht nachkommen. **2** n. Missachtung, die **(of,** for Gen.); (of wishes, feelings) Gleichgültigkeit, die **(for,** of gegenüber)

disrepair /dɪsrɪ'peə(r)/ n. (of building) schlechter [baulicher] Zustand; (of furniture etc.) schlechter Zustand

disreputable /dɪs'repjʊtəbl/ adj. zwielichtig; übelbeleumdet ‹Person›; verrufen ‹Etablissement, Gegend›; schäbig ‹Aussehen›

disrepute /dɪsrɪ'pjuːt/ n. Verruf, der; (of area) Verrufenheit, die; **bring sb./sth. into** ~: jmdn./etw. in Verruf bringen

disrespect /dɪsrɪ'spekt/ n. Missachtung, die; **show** ~ **for sb./sth.** keine Achtung vor jmdm./etw. haben

disrespectful /dɪsrɪ'spektfl/ adj. respektlos

disrupt /dɪs'rʌpt/ v.t. unterbrechen; stören ‹Klasse, Sitzung›

disruption /dɪs'rʌpʃn/ n. Unterbrechung, die; (of class, meeting) Störung, die

disruptive /dɪs'rʌptɪv/ adj. störend

dissatisfaction /dɪsætɪs'fækʃn/ n., no pl. Unzufriedenheit, die **(with** mit)

dissatisfied /dɪs'sætɪsfaɪd/ adj. unzufrieden **(with** mit)

dissect /dɪ'sekt/ v.t. **(a)** (cut into pieces) zerschneiden, zerlegen **(into** in + Akk.); **(b)** (Med., Biol.) präparieren

dissection /dɪ'sekʃn/ n. **(a)** (cutting into pieces) Zerlegung, die; **(b)** (Med., Biol.) Präparation, die

disseminate /dɪ'semɪneɪt/ v.t. (lit. or fig.) verbreiten

dissension /dɪ'senʃn/ n. Dissens, der; Streit, der **(on** über + Akk.); ~**s** Streitigkeiten

dissent /dɪ'sent/ **1** v.i. **(a)** (refuse to assent) nicht zustimmen; ~ **from sth.** mit etw. nicht übereinstimmen; **(b)** (disagree) ~ **from sth.** von etw. abweichen. **2** n. Ablehnung, die; (from majority) Abweichung, die

dissenter /dɪ'sentə(r)/ n. Andersdenkende, der/die

dissertation /dɪsə'teɪʃn/ n. (spoken) Vortrag, der; (written) Abhandlung, die; (for Ph.D.) Dissertation, die

disservice /dɪs'sɜːvɪs/ n. **do sb. a** ~: jmdm. einen schlechten Dienst erweisen

Distance

1 yard = 0,914 m (null Komma neun eins vier Meter)
1 mile = 1,61 km (eins Komma sechs eins Kilometer)

How far is it or *What's the distance from London to Edinburgh?*	= Wie weit ist es von London nach Edinburgh?	*A and B are the same distance away*	= A und B sind gleich weit entfernt
It's/The distance is 365 miles	= Es sind/Die Entfernung beträgt 588 Kilometer	*He hit the target from a distance of 50 metres*	= Er traf das Ziel aus einer Entfernung von 50 Metern
It's quite a long way [away]	= Es ist ziemlich weit [entfernt]	*a fifty mile drive*	= eine Autofahrt von achtzig Kilometern
The house is just a few hundred yards from here	= Das Haus liegt nur ein paar hundert Meter von hier [entfernt]	*an hour's drive*	= eine Stunde Fahrt [mit dem Auto], eine Autostunde
Manchester is further from the sea than Chester	= Manchester liegt *or* ist weiter vom Meer entfernt als Chester	*It's only a ten minute walk*	= Es sind nur zehn Minuten zu Fuß
Reading is nearer to London than Oxford	= Reading liegt näher an London als Oxford		

dissident /'dɪsɪdənt/ **1** *adj.* anders denkend; **hold a ~ view** *or* **opinion** eine abweichende Meinung vertreten. **2** *n.* Dissident, *der*/Dissidentin, *die*

dissimilar /dɪ'sɪmɪlə(r)/ *adj.* unähnlich; unterschiedlich, verschieden ‹*Ideen, Ansichten, Geschmack*›; **be ~ to sth./ sb.** anders als etw./jmd. sein

dissimilarity /dɪsɪmɪ'lærɪtɪ/ *n.* Unähnlichkeit, *die*

dissipate /'dɪsɪpeɪt/ *v.t.* **(a)** (dispel) auflösen ‹*Nebel, Dunst*›; zerstreuen ‹*Befürchtungen, Zweifel*›; **(b)** (fritter away) vergeuden; durchbringen ‹*Vermögen, Erbschaft*›

dissipated /'dɪsɪpeɪtɪd/ *adj.* ausschweifend; zügellos

dissipation /dɪsɪ'peɪʃn/ *n.* (intemperate living) Ausschweifung, *die*

dissociate /dɪ'səʊʃɪeɪt, dɪ'səʊsɪeɪt/ *v.t.* trennen; **~ oneself from sth./sb.** sich von etw./jmdm. distanzieren

dissolute /'dɪsəluːt, 'dɪsəljuːt/ *adj.* (licentious) ausschweifend; zügellos ‹*Benehmen*›

dissolution /dɪsə'luːʃn, dɪsə'ljuːʃn/ *n.* **(a)** (disintegration) Zersetzung, *die;* **(b)** (undoing, dispersal) Auflösung, *die*

dissolve /dɪ'zɒlv/ **1** *v.t.* auflösen. **2** *v.i.* sich auflösen; **~ into tears/laughter** in Tränen/Gelächter ausbrechen

dissonance /'dɪsənəns/ *n.* Dissonanz, *die*

dissonant /'dɪsənənt/ *adj.* (Mus.) dissonant

dissuade /dɪ'sweɪd/ *v.t.* **~ sb. from sth.** jmdn. von etw. abbringen; **~ sb. from doing sth.** jmdn. davon abbringen, etw. zu tun

distance /'dɪstəns/ **1** *n.* **(a)** Entfernung, *die* (**from** zu); **their ~ from each other** die räumliche Entfernung zwischen ihnen; **keep [at] a [safe] ~ [from sb./sth.]** jmdm./einer Sache nicht zu nahe kommen; **(b)** (fig.: aloofness) Abstand, *der;* **keep one's ~ [from sb./sth.]** Abstand [zu jmdm./etw.] wahren; **(c)** (way to cover) Strecke, *die;* Weg, *der;* (gap) Abstand, *der;* **from this ~:** aus dieser Entfernung; **at a ~ of …** [from sb./sth.] in einer Entfernung von … [von jmdm./etw.]; **a short ~ away** ganz in der Nähe; **(d)** (remoter field of vision) Ferne, *die;* **in/into the ~:** in der Ferne; **(e)** (distant point) Entfernung, *die;* **at a ~/[viewed] from a ~:** von weitem; **(f)** (space of time) Abstand, *der;* **at a ~ of 20 years** aus einem Abstand von 20 Jahren. **2** *v.t.* **~ oneself from sb./sth.** sich von jmdm./ etwas distanzieren

distant /'dɪstənt/ *adj.* **(a)** (far) fern; **be ~ [from sb.]** weit [von jmdm.] weg sein; **(b)** (fig.: remote) entfernt ‹*Ähnlichkeit, Verwandtschaft, Verwandte, Beziehung*›; **it's a ~ prospect/possibility** das ist Zukunftsmusik; **(c)** (in time) fern; **in the ~ past/future** in ferner Vergangenheit/Zukunft; **(d)** (cool) reserviert, distanziert ‹*Person, Haltung*›

distaste /dɪs'teɪst/ *n.* Abneigung, *die;* **[have] a ~ for sb./sth.** eine Abneigung gegen jmdn./etw. [haben]; **in ~:** aus Abneigung

distasteful /dɪs'teɪstfl/ *adj.* unangenehm; **be ~ to sb.** jmdm. zuwider sein

distemper¹ /dɪ'stempə(r)/ **1** *n.* (paint) Temperafarbe, *die.* **2** *v.t.* mit Temperafarbe bemalen

distemper² *n.* (animal disease) Staupe, *die*

distend /dɪ'stend/ *v.t.* aufblähen, auftreiben ‹*Leib, Bauch*›; blähen ‹*Nüstern*›; erweitern ‹*Gefäße, Darm, Ader*›

distil, (Amer.) **distill** /dɪ'stɪl/ *v.t.*, **-ll-** (lit. *or* fig.) destillieren; brennen ‹*Branntwein*›; **~ sth. from sth.** (fig.) etw. aus etw. [heraus]destillieren

distillation /dɪstɪ'leɪʃn/ *n.* Destillation, *die;* (fig.) Herausdestillieren, *das;* (result) Destillat, *das*

distiller /dɪ'stɪlə(r)/ *n.* Destillateur, *der;* Branntweinbrenner, *der*

distillery /dɪ'stɪlərɪ/ *n.* [Branntwein]brennerei, *die*

distinct /dɪ'stɪŋkt/ *adj.* **(a)** (different) verschieden; **keep two things ~:** zwei Dinge auseinander halten; **as ~ from** im Unterschied zu; **(b)** (clearly perceptible, decided) deutlich; klar ‹*Stimme, Sicht*›; **(c)** (separate) unterschiedlich

distinction /dɪ'stɪŋkʃn/ *n.* **(a)** (making a difference) Unterscheidung, *die;* **by way of ~, for ~:** zur Unterscheidung; **(b)** (difference) Unterschied, *der;* **make** *or* **draw a ~ between A and B** einen Unterschied zwischen A und B machen; **(c)** **have the ~ of being …** ‹*Person:*› sich dadurch auszeichnen, dass man … ist; **(d)** **gain** *or* **get a ~ in one's examination** das Examen mit Auszeichnung bestehen; **a scientist of ~:** ein Wissenschaftler von Rang [und Namen]

distinctive /dɪ'stɪŋktɪv/ *adj.* unverwechselbar; **be ~ of sth.** für etw. charakteristisch sein

distinctly /dɪ'stɪŋktlɪ/ *adv.* **(a)** (clearly) deutlich; **(b)** (decidedly) merklich

distinguish /dɪ'stɪŋgwɪʃ/ **1** *v.t.* **(a)** (make out) erkennen; **(b)** (differentiate) unterscheiden; (characterize) kennzeichnen; **(c)** (make prominent) **~ oneself [by sth.]** sich [durch etw.] hervortun; **~ oneself by doing sth.** sich dadurch hervortun, dass man etw. tut. **2** *v.i.* unterscheiden; **~ between persons/things** Personen/Dinge auseinander halten

distinguishable /dɪ'stɪŋgwɪʃəbl/ *adj.* erkennbar

distinguished /dɪ'stɪŋgwɪʃt/ *adj.* **(a)** (eminent) namhaft, angesehen ‹*Persönlichkeit, Schule, Firma*›; glänzend ‹*Laufbahn*›; **a ~ politician** ein Politiker von Rang [und Namen]; **(b)** (looking eminent) vornehm, (geh.) distinguiert ‹*Aussehen, Mensch*›

distort /dɪ'stɔːt/ *v.t.* **(a)** verzerren; ‹*Schmerz, Krankheit:*› entstellen; **(b)** (misrepresent) entstellt *od.* verzerrt wiedergeben; verdrehen ‹*Worte, Wahrheit*›

distortion /dɪ'stɔːʃn/ *n.* Verzerrung, *die*

distract /dɪ'strækt/ *v.t.* ablenken; **~ sb.['s attention from sth.]** jmdn. [von etw.] ablenken

distracted /dɪ'stræktɪd/ *adj.* **(a)** (mad) von Sinnen *nachgestellt;* außer sich *nachgestellt;* (worried) besorgt; beunruhigt; **(b)** (mentally far away) abwesend

distraction /dɪ'strækʃn/ *n.* **(a)** (frenzy) Wahnsinn, *der;* **drive sb. to ~:** jmdn. wahnsinnig machen *od.* zum Wahnsinn treiben; **(b)** (diversion) Ablenkung, *die;* **(c)** (interruption) Störung, *die;* **be a ~:** ein Störfaktor sein; **(d)** (amusement) Zerstreuung, *die*

distraught /dɪ'strɔ:t/ *adj.* aufgelöst **(with** vor + *Dat.*); verstört ‹*Blick, Gesichtsausdruck*›

distress /dɪ'stres/ **1** *n.* **(a)** (anguish) Kummer, *der* **(at** über + *Akk.*); **(b)** (suffering caused by want) Not, *die;* Elend, *das;* **(c)** (danger) **an aircraft/a ship in ~:** ein Flugzeug in Not/ ein Schiff in Seenot; **(d)** (exhaustion) Erschöpfung, *die;* (severe pain) Qualen *Pl.* **2** *v.t.* **(a)** (worry) bedrücken; bekümmern; (cause anguish to) ängstigen; (upset) nahe gehen (+ *Dat.*); mitnehmen; **we were most ~ed** wir waren zutiefst betroffen; **(b)** (exhaust) erschöpfen

distressed /dɪ'strest/ *adj.* **(a)** (anguished) leidvoll; betrübt; **(b)** (impoverished) notleidend ‹*Volkswirtschaft, Dritte Welt*›; verarmt ‹*Adel*›; armselig ‹*Verhältnisse*›

distressing /dɪ'stresɪŋ/ *adj.* **(a)** (upsetting) erschütternd; **be ~ to sb.** jmdn. sehr belasten; **(b)** (regrettable) beklagenswert

di'stress signal *n.* Notsignal, *das*

distribute /dɪ'strɪbju:t/ *v.t.* verteilen **(to** an + *Akk.,* **among** unter + *Akk.*)

distribution /dɪstrɪ'bju:ʃn/ *n.* Verteilung, *die* **(to** an + *Akk.,* **among** unter + *Akk.*); (Econ.: of goods) Distribution, *die* (fachspr.); Vertrieb, *der;* (of films) Verleih, *der;* **the ~ of wealth** die Vermögensverteilung

distributor /dɪ'strɪbjʊtə(r)/ *n.* **(a)** Verteiler, *der/*Verteilerin, *die;* (Econ.) Vertreiber, *der;* (firm) Vertrieb, *der;* (of films) Verleih[er], *der;* **(b)** (Motor Veh.) [Zünd]verteiler, *der*

district /'dɪstrɪkt/ *n.* **(a)** (administrative area) Bezirk, *der;* **(b)** (Brit.: part of county) Distrikt, *der;* **(c)** (Amer.: political division) Wahlkreis, *der;* **(d)** (tract of country, area) Gegend, *die;* **country ~s** ländliche Gegenden

district: ~ at'torney *n.* (Amer. Law) [Bezirks]staatsanwalt, *der/*-anwältin, *die;* **~ 'council** *n.* (Brit.) Rat des Distrikts; **Newbury D~ Council** der Rat des Distrikts Newbury; **~ 'nurse** *n.* (Brit.) Gemeindeschwester, *die*

distrust /dɪs'trʌst/ **1** *n.* Misstrauen, *das* **(of** gegen). **2** *v.t.* misstrauen (+ *Dat.*); (because of bad experiences) mit Argwohn *od.* Misstrauen begegnen (+ *Dat.*)

distrustful /dɪs'trʌstfl/ *adj.* misstrauisch; **be ~ of sb./ sth.** jmdm./einer Sache nicht trauen

disturb /dɪ'stɜ:b/ *v.t.* **(a)** (break calm of) stören; aufscheuchen ‹*Vögel*›; aufhalten, behindern ‹*Fortschritt*›; '**do not ~!**' „bitte nicht stören!"; **~ing the peace** Ruhestörung, *die;* **(b)** (move from settled position) durcheinander bringen; **(c)** (worry) beunruhigen; (agitate) nervös machen; **don't be ~ed** beunruhigen Sie sich nicht

disturbance /dɪ'stɜ:bəns/ *n.* **(a)** (interruption) Störung, *die;* (nuisance) Belästigung, *die;* **(b)** (agitation, tumult) Unruhe, *die;* **political ~s** politische Unruhen

disturbed /dɪ'stɜ:bd/ *adj.* besorgt ‹*Eindruck, Ausdruck*›; unruhig ‹*Nacht*›; **be [mentally] ~:** geistig gestört sein

disturbing /dɪs'tɜ:bɪŋ/ *adj.* bestürzend

disuse /dɪs'ju:s/ *n.* (discontinuance) Außer-Gebrauch-Kommen, *das;* (disappearance) Verschwinden, *das;* (abolition) Abschaffung, *die;* **fall into ~:** außer Gebrauch kommen

disused /dɪs'ju:zd/ *adj.* stillgelegt ‹*Bergwerk, Eisenbahnlinie*›; leerstehend ‹*Gebäude*›; ausrangiert (ugs.) ‹*Fahrzeug, Möbel*›

ditch /dɪtʃ/ **1** *n.* Graben, *der;* (at side of road) Straßengraben, *der.* **2** *v.t.* (coll.: abandon) sitzen lassen ‹*Familie, Freunde*›; sausen lassen (ugs.) ‹*Plan*›

'ditchwater *n.* stehendes, fauliges Wasser; **[as] dull as ~:** sterbenslangweilig

dither /'dɪðə(r)/ **1** *v.i.* schwanken. **2** *n.* (coll.) **be all of a ~ or in a ~:** am Rotieren sein (ugs.)

ditto /'dɪtəʊ/ *n., pl.* **~s: p. 5 is missing, p. 19 ~:** S. 5 fehlt, ebenso S. 19; **~ marks** Unterführungszeichen, *das;* **I'm hungry. — D~:** Ich habe Hunger. — Ich auch

ditty /'dɪtɪ/ *n.* Weise, *die*

divan /dɪ'væn/ *n.* **(a)** (couch, bed) [Polster]liege, *die;* **(b)** (long seat) Chaiselongue, *die*

di'van bed ⇒ **divan a**

dive /daɪv/ **1** *v.i.,* **~d** *or* (Amer.) **dove** /dəʊv/ **(a)** einen Kopfsprung machen; springen; (when already in water) [unter]-tauchen; **(b)** (plunge downwards) ‹*Vogel, Flugzeug usw.*› einen Sturzflug machen; ‹*Unterseeboot usw.*› abtauchen (Seemannsspr.), tauchen; **(c)** (dart down) sich hinwerfen; **(d)** (dart) **~ [out of sight]** sich schnell verstecken. **2** *n.* **(a)** (plunge) Kopfsprung, *der;* (of bird, aircraft, etc.) Sturzflug, *der* **(towards** auf + *Akk.*); (of submarine etc.) [Unter]tauchen; **(b)** (sudden darting movement) Sprung, *der;* **(c)** (coll.: disreputable place) Spelunke, *die* (abwertend)

~ 'in *v.i.* [mit dem Kopf voraus] hineinspringen

dive: ~-bomb *v.t.* (Mil.) im Sturzflug bombardieren; **~-bomber** *n.* (Mil.) Sturzkampfflugzeug, *das*

diver /'daɪvə(r)/ *n.* **(a)** (Sport) Kunstspringer, *der/*-springerin, *die;* **(b)** ▶ **887** (as profession) Taucher, *der/*Taucherin, *die*

diverge /daɪ'vɜ:dʒ/ *v.i.* **(a)** auseinander gehen; **here the road ~s from the river** hier entfernt die Straße sich vom Fluss; **(b)** (fig.) ‹*Berufswege, Pfade*›› sich trennen; (from norm etc.) abweichen; **(c)** ‹*Meinungen, Aussichten*›› voneinander abweichen

divergence /daɪ'vɜ:dʒəns/ *n.* **(a)** Divergenz, *die* (fachspr.); Auseinandergehen, *das;* **(b)** (fig.) **~ of opinions/views** Meinungsverschiedenheit, *die*

divergent /daɪ'vɜ:dʒənt/ *adj.* **(a)** divergent (fachspr.); auseinander gehend *od.* laufend ‹*Routen, Wege*›; **(b)** (differing) unterschiedlich, voneinander abweichend ‹*Ansichten, Methoden*›

diverse /daɪ'vɜ:s/ *adj.* **(a)** (unlike) verschieden[artig]; unterschiedlich; **(b)** (varied) vielseitig, breit gefächert ‹[*Aus*]*bildung, Interessen, Kenntnisse*›; bunt [gewürfelt] ‹*Mischung*›

diversify /daɪ'vɜ:sɪfaɪ/ **1** *v.t.* abwechslungsreich[er] gestalten. **2** *v.i.* (Commerc.) diversifizieren

diversion /daɪ'vɜ:ʃn/ *n.* **(a)** (diverting of attention) Ablenkung, *die;* **(b)** (feint) Ablenkungsmanöver, *das;* **create a ~:** ein Ablenkungsmanöver durchführen; **(c)** *no pl.* (recreation) Unterhaltung, *die;* (distraction) Zerstreuung, *die;* Abwechslung, *die;* **(d)** (amusement) [Möglichkeit der] Freizeitbeschäftigung; (e) (of river, traffic) Ableitung, *die;* **(f)** (Brit.: alternative route) Umleitung, *die*

diversionary /daɪ'vɜ:ʃənərɪ/ *adj.* Ablenkungs‹*angriff, -bombardement, -manöver*›

diversity /daɪ'vɜ:sɪtɪ/ *n.* Vielfalt, *die;* **~ of opinion** Meinungsvielfalt, *die*

divert /daɪ'vɜ:t/ *v.t.* **(a)** umleiten ‹*Verkehr, Fluss, Fahrzeug*›; ablenken ‹*Aufmerksamkeit*›; lenken ‹*Energien, Aggressionen*›; **(b)** (distract) ablenken; **(c)** (entertain) unterhalten

diverting /daɪ'vɜ:tɪŋ/ *adj.* (entertaining) unterhaltsam

divest /daɪ'vest, dɪ'vest/ *v.t.* **~ sb./sth. of sth.** (deprive) jmdn./etw. einer Sache (*Gen.*) berauben

divide /dɪ'vaɪd/ **1** *v.t.* **(a)** teilen; (subdivide) aufteilen; (with precision) einteilen; (into separated pieces) zerteilen; **~ sth. in[to] parts** (separate) etw. in Stücke (*Akk.*)] aufteilen; **~ sth. into sth.** halbieren/vierteln; **~ sth. in two** etw. [in zwei Teile] zerteilen; **(b)** (by marking out) **~ sth. into sth.** etw. in etw. (*Akk.*) unterteilen; **(c)** (part by marking) trennen; **~ sth./sb. from or and sth./sb.** etw./jmdn. von etw./jmdm. trennen; **(d)** (mark off) **~ sth. from sth. else** etw. von etw. anderem abgrenzen; **dividing line** Trennungslinie, *die;* **(e)** (distinguish) unterscheiden; **(f)** (cause to disagree) entzweien; **be ~d over an issue in** einer Angelegenheit nicht einig sein; **be ~d against itself** zerstritten sein; **(g)** (distribute) aufteilen **(among** unter + *Akk. od. Dat.*); **(h)** (Math.) dividieren (fachspr.), teilen **(by** durch); **~ three into nine** neun durch drei dividieren *od.* teilen. **2** *v.i.* **(a)** (separate) **~ [in** *or* **into parts]** sich [in Teile] teilen; ‹*Buch, Urkunde usw.*›› sich [in Teile] gliedern, [in Teile] gegliedert sein; **~ into two** sich in zwei Teile teilen; **(b)** **~ [from sth.]** von etw. abzweigen; **(c)** (Math.) **~ [by a number]** sich [durch eine Zahl] dividieren (fachspr.) *od.* teilen lassen

~ 'off 1 *v.t.* trennen; **~ off an area** einen Bereich abtrennen *od.* abteilen. **2** *v.i.* **~ off from sth.** sich von etw. trennen

~ **'out** *v.t.* ~ sth. out [among/between persons] etw. unter Personen (*Akk. od. Dat.*) aufteilen

~ **'up 1** *v.t.* aufteilen. **2** *v.i.* ~ **up into sth.** sich in etw. (*Akk.*) aufteilen lassen

divided 'skirt *n.* Hosenrock, *der*

dividend /'dɪvɪdend/ *n.* (**a**) (Commerc., Finance) Dividende, *die;* (**b**) *in pl.* (fig.: benefit) Vorteil, *der;* **pay** ~s sich auszahlen *od.* rentieren; **reap the** ~s die Früchte ernten

divider /dɪ'vaɪdə(r)/ *n.* (**a**) (screen) Trennwand, *die;* (**b**) ~s *pl.* Stechzirkel, *der*

divine /dɪ'vaɪn/ **1** *adj.*, ~r /dɪ'vaɪnə/, ~st /dɪ'vaɪnɪst/ (**a**) göttlich; (devoted to God) gottgeweiht; (**b**) (coll.: delightful) traumhaft. **2** *v.t.* deuten

diving /'daɪvɪŋ/ *n.* (Sport) Kunstspringen, *das*

diving: ~ **board** *n.* Sprungbrett, *das;* ~ **suit** *n.* Taucheranzug, *der*

divinity /dɪ'vɪnɪtɪ/ *n.* (**a**) (god) Gottheit, *die;* (**b**) *no pl.* (being a god) Göttlichkeit, *die;* (**c**) *no pl.* (theology) Theologie, *die*

divisible /dɪ'vɪzɪbl/ *adj.* (**a**) (separable) aufteilbar; **be** ~ **into …:** sich in … aufteilen lassen; (**b**) (Math.) **be** ~ **[by a number]** [durch eine Zahl] teilbar sein

division /dɪ'vɪʒn/ *n.* (**a**) ⇒ **divide 1 a:** Teilung/Auf-/Ein-/Zerteilung, *die;* (**b**) (parting) (of things) Abtrennung, *die;* (of persons) Trennung, *die;* (marking off) Abgrenzung, *die;* (**c**) (distinguishing) Unterscheidung, *die;* Abgrenzung, *die* (from gegenüber); (**d**) (distributing) Verteilung, *die* (**between/among** an + *Akk.*); (sharing) Teilen, *das;* (**e**) (disagreement) Unstimmigkeit, *die;* (**f**) (Math.) Teilen, *das;* Dividieren, *das;* Division, *die* (fachspr.); **do** ~: dividieren; **long** ~: ausführliche Division (*mit Aufschreiben der Zwischenprodukte*); **short** ~: verkürzte Division (*ohne Aufschreiben der Zwischenprodukte*); (**g**) (separation in voting) Abstimmung [durch Hammelsprung]; (**h**) (part) Unterteilung, *die;* Abschnitt, *der;* (**i**) (section) Abteilung, *die;* (group) Gruppe, *die;* (Mil. etc.) Division, *die;* (of police) Einheit, *die;* (**j**) (Footb. etc.) Liga, *die;* Spielklasse, *die;* (in British football) Division, *die*

di'vision sign *n.* Divisionszeichen, *das*

divisive /dɪ'vaɪsɪv/ *adj.* spalterisch

divisor /dɪ'vaɪzə(r)/ *n.* (Math.) Divisor, *der;* Teiler, *der*

divorce /dɪ'vɔːs/ **1** *n.* (**a**) [Ehe]scheidung, *die;* **want a** ~: sich scheiden lassen wollen; **get** *od.* **obtain a** ~: sich scheiden lassen; *attrib.* ~ **court** Scheidungsgericht, *das;* ~ **proceedings** [Ehe]scheidungsverfahren, *das;* (**b**) (fig.) Trennung, *die.* **2** *v.t.* (dissolve marriage of) scheiden ⟨*Ehepartner*⟩; (**b**) ~ **one's husband/wife** sich von seinem Mann/seiner Frau scheiden lassen

divorcee /dɪvɔː'siː/ *n.* Geschiedene, *der/die;* **be a** ~: geschieden sein

divot /'dɪvət/ *n.* (Golf) ausgehacktes Rasenstück

divulge /daɪ'vʌldʒ/ *v.t.* preisgeben; enthüllen ⟨*Identität*⟩; bekannt geben ⟨*Nachrichten*⟩

Dixie /'dɪksɪ/ *n.* (**a**) die Südstaaten [der USA]; (**b**) (Mus.) Dixie, *der*

'Dixieland *n.* (**a**) (Mus.) Dixie[land], *der;* (**b**) ⇒ **Dixie a**

DIY *abbr.* **do-it-yourself**

dizzy /'dɪzɪ/ *adj.* (**a**) (giddy) schwind[e]lig; **I feel** ~: mir ist schwindlig; **he felt** ~: ihm wurde schwindlig; (**b**) (making giddy) schwindelerregend

DJ /diː'dʒeɪ/ *abbr.* **a disc jockey** Diskjockey, *der;* (**b**) (Brit.: dinner jacket) Smokingjacke, *die*

DNA *abbr.* **deoxyribonucleic acid** DNS

do[1] /də, *stressed* duː/ **1** *v.t., neg. coll.* **don't** /dəʊnt/, *pres. t.* **he does** /dʌz/, *neg.* (coll.) **doesn't** /'dʌznt/, *p.t.* **did** /dɪd/, *neg.* (coll.) **didn't** /'dɪdnt/, *pres. p.* **doing** /'duːɪŋ/, *p.p.* **done** /dʌn/ (**a**) (perform) machen ⟨*Hausaufgaben, Hausarbeit, Examen, Handstand*⟩; vollbringen ⟨*Tat*⟩; tun, erfüllen ⟨*Pflicht*⟩; tun, verrichten ⟨*Arbeit*⟩; ausführen ⟨*Malerarbeiten*⟩; vorführen ⟨*Trick, Striptease, Nummer, Tanz*⟩; durchführen ⟨*Test*⟩; aufführen ⟨*Stück*⟩; singen ⟨*Lied*⟩; mitmachen ⟨*Rennen, Wettbewerb*⟩; spielen ⟨*Musikstück, Rolle*⟩; tun ⟨*Buße*⟩; **do the shopping/washing up/cleaning** einkaufen [gehen]/abwaschen/sauber machen; **do a lot of reading/walking** etc. viel lesen/

spazieren gehen *usw.;* **do a dance/the foxtrot** tanzen/Foxtrott tanzen; **have nothing to do** nichts zu tun haben; **do sth. to sth./sb.** etw. mit etw./jmdm. machen; **what can I do for you?** was kann ich für Sie tun?; (in shop) was darf's sein?; **not know what to do with oneself** nicht wissen, was man machen soll; **that does it** jetzt reicht's (ugs.); **that's done it** (caused a change for the worse) das hat das Fass zum Überlaufen gebracht; (caused a change for the better) das hätten wir; **that will/should do it** so müsste es gehen; (is enough) das müsste genügen; **do a Garbo** (coll.) es der Garbo (*Dat.*) gleichtun; **how many miles has this car done?** wie viele Kilometer hat der Wagen gefahren?; **the car does/was doing about 100 m.p.h./does 45 miles to the gallon** das Auto schafft/fuhr mit ungefähr 160 Stundenkilometern/frisst (ugs.) *od.* braucht sechs Liter pro 100 Kilometer; (**b**) (spend) **do a spell in the armed forces** eine Zeit lang bei der Armee sein; **how much longer have you to do at college?** wie lange musst du noch aufs College gehen?; (**c**) (produce) machen ⟨*Übersetzung, Kopie*⟩; anfertigen ⟨*Bild, Skulptur*⟩; herstellen ⟨*Artikel, Produkte*⟩; schaffen ⟨*Pensum*⟩; (**d**) (provide) haben ⟨*Vollpension, Mittagstisch*⟩; (coll.: offer for sale) führen; (**e**) (prepare) machen ⟨*Bett, Frühstück*⟩; (work on) machen (ugs.), fertig machen ⟨*Garten, Hecke*⟩; (clean) sauber machen ⟨*Schuhe, Fenster*⟩; machen (ugs.) ⟨*Treppe*⟩; (arrange) [zurecht]machen ⟨*Haare*⟩; fertig machen ⟨*Korrespondenz, Zimmer*⟩; (make up) schminken ⟨*Lippen, Augen, Gesicht*⟩; machen (ugs.) ⟨*Nägel*⟩; (cut) schneiden ⟨*Nägel*⟩; schneiden ⟨*Gras, Hecke*⟩; (paint) machen (ugs.) ⟨*Zimmer*⟩; streichen ⟨*Haus, Möbel*⟩; (attend to) sich kümmern um ⟨*Bücher, Rechnungen, Korrespondenz*⟩; (repair) in Ordnung bringen; (**f**) (cook) braten; **well done** durch[gebraten]; (**g**) (solve) lösen ⟨*Problem, Rätsel*⟩; machen ⟨*Puzzle, Kreuzworträtsel*⟩; (**h**) (study, work at) machen; haben ⟨*Abiturfach*⟩; (**i**) (sl.: swindle) reinlegen (ugs.); **do sb. out of sth.** jmdn. um etw. bringen; (**j**) (sl.: defeat, kill) fertig machen (ugs.); (**k**) (traverse) schaffen ⟨*Entfernung*⟩; (**l**) (sl.: undergo) absitzen, (salopp) abreißen ⟨*Strafe*⟩; (**m**) (coll.: visit) besuchen; **do Europe in three weeks** Europa in drei Wochen absolvieren *od.* abhaken (ugs.); (**n**) (satisfy) zusagen (+ *Dat.*); (suffice for, last) reichen (+ *Dat.*). **2** *v.i., forms as* **1:** (**a**) (act) tun; (perform) spielen; **you can do just as you like** du kannst machen, was du willst; **do as they do** mach es wie sie; **do or die** kämpfen oder untergehen; (**b**) (fare) **how are you doing?** wie geht's dir?; (**c**) (get on) vorankommen; (in exams) abschneiden; **how are you doing at school?** wie geht es in der Schule?; **do well/badly at school** gut/schlecht in der Schule sein; (**d**) ▶ **836|** **how do you do?** (formal) guten Tag/Morgen/Abend!; (**e**) (coll.: manage) **how are we doing for time?** wie steht es mit der Zeit *od.* (ugs.) sieht es mit der Zeit aus?; (**f**) (serve purpose) es tun; (suffice) [aus]reichen; (be suitable) gehen; **that won't do** das geht nicht; **that will do!** jetzt aber genug!; (**g**) (be usable) **do for** *or* **as sth.** etw. benutzt werden können; (**h**) (happen) **what's doing?** was ist los?; **there's nothing doing on the job market** es tut sich nichts auf dem Arbeitsmarkt (ugs.); **Nothing doing. He's not interested** Nichts zu machen (ugs.). Er ist nicht interessiert. *See also* **doing; done. 3** *v. substitute, forms as* **1:** (**a**) *replacing v.: usually not translated;* **you mustn't act as he does** du darfst nicht so wie er handeln; (**b**) *replacing v. and obj. etc.* **he read the Bible every day as his father did before him** er las täglich in der Bibel, wie es schon sein Vater vor ihm getan hatte *od.* wie sie vor ihm sein Vater; **as they did in the Middle Ages** wie sie es im Mittelalter taten; (**c**) *as ellipt. aux.* **You went to Paris, didn't you?** — Yes, I did Du warst doch in Paris, oder *od.* nicht wahr? — Ja[, stimmt *od.* war ich]; (**d**) *with* 'so', 'it', *etc.* **I knew John Lennon. — So did I** Ich kannte John Lennon. — Ich auch; **go ahead and do it** nur zu; (**e**) *in tag questions* **I know you from somewhere, don't I?** wir kennen uns doch irgendwoher, nicht? **4** *v. aux.* + *inf. as pres. or past, forms as* **1:** (**a**) *for special emphasis* **I do love Greece** Griechenland gefällt mir wirklich gut; **I do apologize** es tut mit wirklich leid; **you do look glum** du siehst ja so bedrückt aus; **but I tell you, I did see him** aber ich sage dir doch, dass ich ihn gesehen habe; (**b**) *for inversion* **little did he know that …:** er hatte keine Ahnung, dass …; (**c**) *in questions* **do you know him?** kennst du ihn?; **what does he want?** was will er?; **didn't they look wonderful?** haben sie nicht wundcrhübsch ausgesehen?; **(d)** *in negation* **I don't** *or* **do not wish to take part** ich möchte nicht teilnehmen; **(e)** *in neg. commands* **don't** *or* **do not expect to find him in a good mood** erwarten Sie nicht, dass Sie ihn in guter Stimmung antreffen; **children, do not forget** …: Kinder, vergesst [ja] nicht …; **don't be so noisy!** seid [doch] nicht so laut!; **don't!** tu's/tut's/tun Sie's nicht!; **(f)** + *inf. as imper. for emphasis etc.* **do sit down, won't you?** bitte setzen Sie sich doch!; **do be quiet, Paul!** Paul, sei doch mal ruhig!; **do hurry up!** beeil dich doch!

do a'way with *v.t.* (coll.) abschaffen

'do by *v.t.* **do well by sb.** jmdn. gut behandeln; **he felt hard done by** er fühlte sich zurückgesetzt *od.* schlecht behandelt

do 'down *v.t.* (coll.) schlechtmachen; heruntermachen (ugs.)

'do for *v.t.* **(a)** ⇒ **do¹ 2 g; (b)** (coll.: destroy) **do for sb.** jmdn. fertig machen *od.* schaffen (ugs.); **do for sth.** etw. kaputtmachen (ugs.); **if we don't do better next time we're done for** wenn wir das nächste Mal nicht besser sind, sind wir erledigt; **(c)** (Brit. coll.: keep house for) **do for sb.** für jmdn. sorgen; ‹*Putzfrau:*› für *od.* bei jmdm. putzen

do 'in *v.t.* (sl.) kaltmachen (salopp)

do 'out *v.t.* (coll.: clean) sauber machen; (redecorate) streichen; (in wallpaper) tapezieren; (decorate, furnish) herrichten

do 'up 1 *v.t.* **(a)** (fasten) zumachen; binden ‹*Schnürsenkel, Fliege*›; **(b)** (wrap) einpacken; verpacken; (arrange) zurechtmachen; **(c)** (coll.: adorn) zurechtmachen ‹*Menschen*›; dekorieren ‹*Haus*›. **2** *v.i.* ‹*Kleid, Reißverschluss, Knopf usw.:*› zugehen

'do with *v.t.* **(a)** (get by with) auskommen mit; (get benefit from) **I could do with a glass of orange juice** ich könnte ein Glas Orangensaft vertragen (ugs.); **he could do with a good hiding** eine Tracht Prügel würde ihm nicht schaden; **(b)** **have to do with** zu tun haben mit; **have something/nothing to do with sth./sb.** etwas/nichts mit etw./jmdm. zu tun haben

'do without *v.t.* **do without sth.** ohne etw. auskommen; auf etw. (*Akk.*) verzichten

do² /du:/ *n., pl.* **dos** *or* **do's** /du:z/ **(a)** (sl.: swindle) Schwindel, *der;* krumme Sache (ugs.); **(b)** (Brit. coll.: festivity) Feier, *die;* Fete, *die* (ugs.); **(c)** *in pl.* **the dos and don'ts** die Ge- und Verbote (**of** *Gen.*)

doc /dɒk/ *n.* (coll.) Doktor, *der* (ugs.)

docile /'dəʊsaɪl/ *adj.* sanft; (submissive) unterwürfig

dock¹ /dɒk/ **1** *n.* **(a)** Dock, *das;* **the ship came into ~:** das Schiff ging in[s] Dock; **be in ~:** im Dock liegen; **(b)** *usu. in pl.* (area) Hafen, *der;* **down by the ~[s]** unten im Hafen. **2** *v.t.* (Naut.) [ein]docken; (Astronaut.) docken. **3** *v.i.* (Naut.) anlegen; (Astronaut.) docken

dock² *n.* (in lawcourt) ≈ Anklagebank, *die;* **stand/be in the ~** (lit. *or* fig.) ≈ auf der Anklagebank sitzen

dock³ *v.t.* **(a)** (cut short) kupieren ‹*Hund, Pferd, Schwanz*›; **(b)** kürzen ‹*Lohn, Stipendium usw.*›; **he had his pay ~ed by £14,** he had £14 **~ed from his pay** sein Lohn wurde um 14 Pfund gekürzt

docker /'dɒkə(r)/ *n.* ▶ 887 | Hafenarbeiter, *der*

'dockyard *n.* Schiffswerft, *die*

doctor /'dɒktə(r)/ **1** *n.* ▶ 887 |, ▶ 1152 | **(a)** Arzt, *der*/Ärztin, *die;* Doktor, *der* (ugs.); *as title* Doktor, *der; as address* Herr/Frau Doktor; **~'s orders** ärztliche Anweisung; **just what the ~ ordered** [ganz] genau das Richtige!; **(b)** (Amer.: dentist) Zahnarzt, *der*/-ärztin, *die;* **(c)** (Amer.: veterinary surgeon) Tierarzt, *der*/-ärztin, *die;* **(d)** (holder of degree) Doktor, *der;* **D~ of Medicine** Doktor der Medizin. **2** *v.t.* (coll.) (falsify) verfälschen ‹*Dokumente, Tonbänder*›; frisieren (ugs.) ‹*Bilanzen, Bücher*›; (adulterate) panschen (ugs.) ‹*Wein*›; verwürzen ‹*Gericht*›

doctorate /'dɒktərət/ *n.* Doktorwürde, *die;* **do a ~:** seinen Doktor machen (ugs.); promovieren

doctrinaire /dɒktrɪ'neə(r)/ *adj.* doktrinär

doctrine /'dɒktrɪn/ *n.* **(a)** (principle) Lehre, *die;* **the ~ of free speech** der Grundsatz der Redefreiheit; **(b)** (body of instruction) Doktrin, *die;* Lehrmeinung, *die*

document 1 /'dɒkjʊmənt/ *n.* Dokument, *das;* Urkunde, *die.* **2** /'dɒkjʊment/ *v.t.* **(a)** (prove by ~[s]) dokumentieren; **(b)** **be well ~ed** ‹*Leben, Zeit usw.:*› gut belegt sein

documentary /dɒkjʊ'mentərɪ/ **1** *adj.* dokumentarisch; urkundlich ‹*Beweis*›; (factual) dokumentarisch; **~ film** Dokumentarfilm, *der.* **2** *n.* (film) Dokumentarfilm, *der*

documentation /dɒkjʊmen'teɪʃn/ *n.* **(a)** (documenting) Dokumentation, *die;* **(b)** (material) beweiskräftige Dokumente

document: ~ case *n.* Kollegmappe, *die;* **~ holder** *n.* Konzepthalter, *der*

doddery /'dɒdərɪ/ *adj.* tatterig (ugs.) ‹*alter Mann*›; zittrig ‹*Beine, Bewegungen*›

doddle /'dɒdl/ *n.* (Brit. coll.) Kinderspiel, *das* (fig.)

dodge /dɒdʒ/ **1** *v.i.* **(a)** (move quickly) ausweichen; **~ behind the hedge** hinter die Hecke springen; **~ out of the way** zur Seite springen; **(b)** (move to and fro) ständig in Bewegung sein; **~ through the traffic** sich durch den Verkehr schlängeln. **2** *v.t.* ausweichen (+ *Dat.*) ‹*Schlag, Hindernis usw.*›; entkommen (+ *Dat.*) ‹*Polizei, Verfolger*›; (avoid) sich drücken vor (+ *Dat.*) ‹*Wehrdienst*›; umgehen ‹*Steuer*›; aus dem Weg gehen (+ *Dat.*) ‹*Frage, Problem*›; **~ doing sth.** es umgehen, etw. zu tun. **3** *n.* **(a)** (move) Sprung zur Seite; **(b)** (trick) Trick, *der;* **he's up to all the ~s** er ist mit allen Wassern gewaschen

dodgem /'dɒdʒəm/ *n.* [Auto]skooter, *der; in pl.* [Auto]-skooterbahn, *die;* **have a ride/go on the ~s** Autoskooter fahren

dodgy /'dɒdʒɪ/ *adj.* (Brit. coll.) (unreliable) unsicher; schwach ‹*Knie, Herz usw.*›; (awkward) verzwickt; vertrackt; (tricky) knifflig; (risky) gewagt; heikel

dodo /'dəʊdəʊ/ *n., pl.* **~s** *or* **~es** Dodo, *der;* Dronte, *die;* **[as] dead as the** *or* **a ~:** völlig ausgestorben

doe /dəʊ/ *n.* **(a)** (deer) Damtier, *das;* Damgeiß, *die;* **(b)** (hare) Häsin, *die;* **(c)** (rabbit) [Kaninchen]weibchen, *das*

DOE *abbr.* (Brit.) **Department of the Environment** Umweltministerium, *das*

does /dʌz/ ⇒ **do¹**

doesn't /'dʌznt/ (coll.) = **does not;** ⇒ **do¹**

doff /dɒf/ *v.t.* lüften, ziehen ‹*Hut*›

dog /dɒg/ **1** *n.* **(a)** Hund, *der;* **not [stand** *or* **have] a ~'s chance** nicht die geringste Chance [haben]; **dressed up/done up like a ~'s dinner** (coll.) aufgeputzt wie ein Pfau (ugs.); ‹*Frau:*› aufgetakelt wie eine Fregatte (ugs.); **give a ~ a bad name** einmal in Verruf gekommen, bleibt man immer verdächtig; **go to the ~s** vor die Hunde gehen (ugs.); **a ~ in the manger** ein Biest, das keinem was gönnt; **~-in-the-manger** missgünstig ‹*Benehmen*›; **be like a ~ with two tails** sich freuen wie ein Schneekönig (ugs.); **the ~s** (Brit. coll.: greyhound-racing) das Windhundrennen; **(b)** (male ~) Rüde, *der;* **(c)** (despicable person; coll.: fellow) Hund, *der* (derb); **wise old ~/cunning [old] ~:** schlauer Fuchs (ugs.). **2** *v.t.,* **-gg-** verfolgen; (fig.) heimsuchen; verfolgen

dog: ~ biscuit *n.* Hundekuchen, *der;* **~-breeder** ⇒ **breeder;** **~ collar** *n.* **(a)** [Hunde]halsband, *das;* **(b)** (joc.: clerical collar) Kollar, *das;* **~-eared** /'dɒgɪəd/ *adj.* a **~-eared book** ein Buch mit Eselsohren; **~fight** *n.* **(a)** Hundekampf, *der;* (fig.) Handgemenge, *das;* **(b)** (between aircraft) Luftkampf, *der*

dogged /'dɒgɪd/ *adj.* hartnäckig ‹*Weigerung, Verurteilung*›; zäh ‹*Durchhaltevermögen, Ausdauer*›; beharrlich ‹*Haltung, Kritik*›

doggerel /'dɒgərəl/ *n.* Knittelvers, *der*

doggie ⇒ **doggy**

doggo /'dɒgəʊ/ *adv.* (coll.) **lie ~:** sich nicht mucksen (ugs.)

doggy /'dɒgɪ/ *n.* (coll.) Hündchen, *das*

'doggy bag *n.* (coll.) Tüte, in der man Essensreste [*bes. von einer Mahlzeit im Restaurant*] mit nach Hause nimmt

dog: ~house *n.* **(a)** (Amer.) Hundehütte, *die;* **(b)** **be in the ~house** (coll.: in disgrace) in Ungnade sein; **~-leg** *n.* Knick, *der;* **~ licence** *n.* Hundesteuerbescheinigung, *die*

dogma /'dɒgmə/ *n.* Dogma, *das*

dogmatic /dɒg'mætɪk/ *adj.* dogmatisch; **be ~ about sth.** in etw. (*Dat.*) dogmatisch sein

dogmatism /'dɒgmətɪzm/ *n.* Dogmatismus, *der*

do-gooder /duːˈgʊdə(r)/ *n.* Wohltäter, *der* (iron.); (reformer) Weltverbesserer, *der* (iron.)

dog: ∼**rose** *n.* (Bot.) Hundsrose, *die;* ∼**sbody** *n.* (Brit. coll.) Mädchen für alles; ∼**'s life** *n.* a ∼'s life ein Hundeleben; ∼ **'tag** *n.* (lit. or fig.) Hundemarke, *die;* ∼**'tired** *adj.* hundemüde; ∼**trot** *n.* gemächlicher Trott; ∼**watch** *n.* (Naut.) (from 4 p.m. to 6 p.m./from 6 p.m. to 8 p.m.) 1./2. Plattfuß, *der* (Seemannsspr.); ∼**wood** *n.* (Bot.) Hartriegel, *der;* Hornstrauch, *der*

doily /'dɔɪlɪ/ *n.* [Spitzen-, Zier]deckchen, *das*

doing /'duːɪŋ/ **1** *pres. p. of* **do**¹. **2** *n.* **(a)** *vbl. n. of* **do**¹; **(b)** *no pl.* Tun, *das;* be [of] sb.'s ∼: jmds. Werk sein; **it was not [of]** *or* **none of his** ∼: er hatte nichts damit zu tun; **that takes a lot of/some** ∼: da gehört sehr viel/ schon etwas dazu; **(c)** *in pl.* **sb.'s** ∼**s** (actions) jmds. Tun und Treiben; **the** ∼**s** (coll.) die Dinger (ugs.); (thing with unknown name) das Dings (ugs.)

do-it-yourself /duːɪtjəˈself/ **1** *adj.* Do-it-yourself-. **2** *n.* Heimwerken, *das*

doldrums /'dɒldrəmz/ *n. pl.* **(a) in the** ∼ (in low spirits) niedergeschlagen; **(b)** (Naut.) **in the** ∼**:** ohne Wind; (fig.) in einer Flaute

dole /dəʊl/ **1** *n.* (Brit. coll.) **the** ∼**:** Stempelgeld, *das* (ugs.); Stütze, *die* (ugs.); **be/go on the** ∼**:** stempeln gehen (ugs.). **2** *v.t.* ∼ **out** verteilen; austeilen

doleful /'dəʊlfl/ *adj.* traurig ⟨*Augen*, *Blick*, *Gesichtsausdruck*⟩

doll /dɒl/ **1** *n.* **(a)** Puppe, *die;* **(b)** (sl.: young woman) Mieze, *die* (ugs.). **2** *v.t.* ∼ **up** herausputzen

dollar /'dɒlə(r)/ *n.* ▶ **938**▮ Dollar, *der;* **feel/look like a million** ∼**s** (coll.) sich pudelwohl fühlen (ugs.) /tipptopp aussehen (ugs.); **sixty-four [thousand]** ∼ **question** (lit. or fig.) Preisfrage, *die*

dollar: ∼ **'bill** *n.* ▶ **938**▮ Dollarnote, *die;* Dollarschein, *der;* ∼ **sign** *n.* Dollarzeichen, *das*

'dollhouse (Amer.) ⇒ **doll's house**

dollop /'dɒləp/ *n.* (coll.) Klacks, *der* (ugs.)

'doll's house *n.* Puppenhaus, *das*

dolly /'dɒlɪ/ *n.* Puppe, *die;* Püppchen, *das;* (child language) Püppi, *die* (Kinderspr.)

'dolly-bird *n.* (Brit. coll.) Mieze, *die* (ugs.)

Dolomites /'dɒləmaɪts/ *pr. n. pl.* **the** ∼**:** die Dolomiten

dolphin /'dɒlfɪn/ *n.* Delphin, *der*

dolt /dəʊlt/ *n.* Tölpel, *der*

domain /də'meɪn/ *n.* **(a)** (estate) Gut, *das;* Ländereien *Pl.;* **(b)** (field) Domäne, *die* (geh.); Gebiet, *das*

dome /dəʊm/ *n.* Kuppel, *die*

domestic /də'mestɪk/ *adj.* **(a)** (household) häuslich ⟨*Verhältnisse*, *Umstände*⟩; (family) familiär ⟨*Atmosphäre*, *Angelegenheit*, *Reibereien*⟩; ⟨*Wasserversorgung*, *Ölverbrauch*⟩ der privaten Haushalte; ∼ **servant** Hausgehilfe, *der*/ -gehilfin, *die;* ∼ **help** Haushaltshilfe, *die;* ∼ **appliance** Haushaltgerät, *das* **(b)** (of one's own country) inländisch; einheimisch ⟨*Produkt*⟩; innenpolitisch ⟨*Problem*, *Auseinandersetzungen*⟩; **(c)** (kept by man) ∼ **animal** Haustier, *das;* ∼ **rabbit/cat** Hauskaninchen, *das*/Hauskatze, *die*

domesticated /də'mestɪkeɪtɪd/ *adj.* **(a)** domestiziert (fachspr.), gezähmt ⟨*Tier*⟩; **(b)** häuslich ⟨*Person*⟩

domestic 'science *n.*, *no pl.* Hauswirtschaftslehre, *die*

domicile /'dɒmɪsaɪl/ **1** *n.* Heimat, *die.* **2** *v.t.* ansiedeln

dominance /'dɒmɪnəns/ *n.*, *no pl.* Dominanz, *die;* Vorherrschaft, *die* (**over** über + *Akk.*); (of colours etc.) Vorherrschen, *das*

dominant /'dɒmɪnənt/ *adj.* dominierend (geh.); beherrschend; hervorstechend, herausragend ⟨[*Wesens*]*merkmal*, *Eigenschaft*⟩; vorherrschend ⟨*Kultur*, *Farbe*, *Geschmack*⟩; **have a** ∼ **position** eine beherrschende Stellung einnehmen; **be** ∼ **over** dominieren über (+ *Akk.*)

dominate /'dɒmɪneɪt/ **1** *v.t.* beherrschen. **2** *v.i.* **(a)** ∼ **over sb./sth.** jmdn./etw. beherrschen; **(b)** (be the most influential) dominieren

domination /dɒmɪ'neɪʃn/ *n.*, *no pl.* [Vor]herrschaft, *die* (**over** über + *Akk.*); **under Roman** ∼**:** unter römischer Herrschaft

domineering /dɒmɪ'nɪərɪŋ/ *adj.* herrisch, herrschsüchtig ⟨*Person*⟩

dominion /də'mɪnjən/ *n.* **(a)** (control) Herrschaft, *die* (**over** über + *Akk.*); **[be] under Roman** ∼**:** unter römischer Herrschaft [stehen]; **(b)** *usu. in pl.* (territory of sovereign or government) Reich, *das;* **(c)** (Commonwealth Hist.) Dominion, *das*

domino /'dɒmɪnəʊ/ *n.*, *pl.* ∼**es** Domino[stein], *der;* ∼**es** *sing.* (game) Domino[spiel], *das;* **play** ∼**es** Domino spielen

don¹ /dɒn/ *n.* ▶ **887**▮ (Univ.) [Universitäts]dozent, *der* (bes. in Oxford und Cambridge)

don² *v.t.*, **-nn-** anlegen (geh.); anziehen ⟨*Mantel usw.*⟩; aufsetzen ⟨*Hut*⟩

donate /də'neɪt/ *v.t.* spenden ⟨*Organe*⟩; stiften, spenden ⟨*Geld*, *Kleidung*⟩

donation /də'neɪʃn/ *n.* Spende, *die* (**to[wards]** für); (largescale) Stiftung, *die;* **a** ∼ **of money/clothes** eine Geld-/ Kleiderspende; **make a** ∼ **of £1,000 [to charity]** 1 000 Pfund [für wohltätige Zwecke] spenden *od.* stiften

done /dʌn/ *adj.* **(a)** (coll.: acceptable) **it's not** ∼ **[in this country]** das macht man [hierzulande] nicht; **it's [not] the** ∼ **thing** es ist [nicht] üblich; **(b)** *as int.* (accepted) abgemacht!; **(c)** (finished) **be** ∼**:** vorbei sein; **be** ∼ **with sth.** mit etw. fertig sein; **is your plate** ∼ **with?** brauchen Sie Ihren Teller noch?; **(d) have** ∼ **[doing sth.]** (have stopped) aufgehört haben, etw. zu tun; **have** ∼ **with sth./ doing sth.** (stop) mit etw. aufhören/aufhören, etw. zu tun

donkey /'dɒŋkɪ/ *n.* (lit. or fig.) Esel, *der;* **she could talk the hind leg[s] off a** ∼**!** (fig.) die kann einem die Ohren abreden! (ugs.)

'donkey work *n.* Schwerarbeit, *die*

donor /'dəʊnə(r)/ *n.* **(a)** (of gift) Schenker, *der*/Schenkerin, *die;* (to institution etc.) Stifter, *der*/Stifterin, *die;* **(b)** (of blood, organ, etc.) Spender, *der*/Spenderin, *die;* **blood** ∼**:** Blutspender, *der*/-spenderin, *die*

don't /dəʊnt/ **1** *v.i.* (coll.) = **do not;** ⇒ **do**¹. **2** *n.* Nein, *das;* Verbot, *das;* **dos and** ∼**s** ⇒ **do²** c

doodle /'duːdl/ **1** *v.i.* ≈ Männchen malen; [herum]kritzeln. **2** *n.* Kritzelei, *die*

doom /duːm/ **1** *n.* (fate) Schicksal, *das;* (ruin) Verhängnis, *das;* **meet one's** ∼**:** vom Schicksal heimgesucht *od.* (geh.) ereilt werden. **2** *v.t.* verurteilen; verdammen; ∼ **sb./sth. to sth.** jmdn./eine Sache zu etw. verdammen *od.* verurteilen; **be** ∼**ed to fail** *or* **failure** zum Scheitern verurteilt sein; **be** ∼**ed** verloren sein

doomsday /'duːmzdeɪ/ *n.* der Jüngste Tag; **till** ∼ (fig.) bis zum Jüngsten Tag

door /dɔː(r)/ *n.* **(a)** Tür, *die;* (of castle, barn) Tor, *das;* '∼s open at 7' „Einlass ab 7 Uhr"; **he put his head round the** ∼**:** er streckte den Kopf durch die Tür; **lay sth. at sb.'s** ∼ (fig.) jmdm. etw. anlasten *od.* zur Last legen; **next** ∼**:** nebenan; **live next** ∼ **to sb.** neben jmdm. wohnen; **from** ∼ **to** ∼**:** von Haus zu Haus; von Tür zu Tür; **(b)** (fig.: entrance) Zugang, *der* (**to** zu); **all** ∼**s are open/closed to him** ihm stehen alle Türen offen/sind alle Türen verschlossen; **close the** ∼ **to sth.** etw. unmöglich machen; **have/get one's foot in the** ∼**:** mit einem Fuß *od.* Bein drin sein; **leave the** ∼ **open for sth.** die Tür für *od.* zu etw. offenhalten; **open the** ∼ **to** *or* **for sth.** etw. möglich machen; **show sb. the** ∼**:** jmdm. die Tür weisen; **(c)** (∼way) [Tür]eingang, *der;* **walk through the** ∼**:** zur Tür hineingehen/hereinkommen; **shop** ∼**:** Geschäftseingang, *der;* **(d) out of** ∼**s** im Freien; draußen; **go out of** ∼**s** nach draußen gehen

door: ∼**bell** *n.* Türklingel, *die;* ∼**frame** *n.* Türrahmen, *der;* ∼ **handle** *n.* Türklinke, *die;* ∼**keeper** *n.* ▶ **887**▮ Pförtner, *der;* Portier, *der;* ∼**knob** *n.* Türknopf, -knauf, *der;* ∼ **knocker** ⇒ **knocker a;** ∼**man** *n.* ▶ **887**▮ Portier, *der;* ∼**mat** *n.* Fußmatte, *die;* (fig.) Fußabtreter, *der;* ∼**post** *n.* Türpfosten, *der;* ∼**step** *n.* Eingangsstufe, *die;* Türstufe, *die;* **on one's/the** ∼**step** (fig.) vor jmds./der Tür; ∼**stop** *n.* Türanschlag, *der;* (stone, wedge, etc.) Türstopper, *der;* **∼-to-∼** *adj.* **∼-to-∼ col-lection** Haussammlung, *die;* **∼way** *n.* Eingang, *der*

dope /dəʊp/ **1** *n.* **(a)** (stimulant) Aufputschmittel, *das;* (sl.: narcotic) Stoff, *der* (salopp); **∼ test** Dopingkontrolle, *die;* **(b)** (sl.: information) Informationen *Pl.;* **(c)** (coll.: fool) Dussel, *der* (ugs.). **2** *v.t.* dopen ⟨*Pferd, Athleten*⟩; (administer narcotic to) Rauschgift verabreichen (+ *Dat.*); (stupefy) betäuben

dopey /ˈdəʊpɪ/ *adj.* (coll.) benebelt (ugs.)

dormant /ˈdɔːmənt/ *adj.* untätig ⟨*Vulkan*⟩; ruhend ⟨*Tier, Pflanze*⟩; verborgen, schlummernd ⟨*Talent, Fähigkeiten*⟩; **lie ∼** ⟨*Tier:*⟩ schlafen; ⟨*Pflanze, Ei:*⟩ ruhen; ⟨*Talent, Fähigkeiten:*⟩ schlummern

dormer /ˈdɔːmə(r)/ *n.* **∼ [window]** Mansardenfenster, *das*

dormitory /ˈdɔːmɪtərɪ/ *n.* **(a)** Schlafsaal, *der;* **(b)** *attrib.* **∼ suburb** *or* **town** Schlafstadt, *die*

dormouse /ˈdɔːmaʊs/ *n., pl.* **dormice** /ˈdɔːmaɪs/ Haselmaus, *die*

dos *pl. of* **do²**

DOS /dɒs/ *abbr.* (Computing) **disk operating system** DOS

dosage /ˈdəʊsɪdʒ/ *n.* **(a)** (giving of medicine) Dosierung, *die;* **(b)** (size of dose) Dosis, *die*

dose /dəʊs/ **1** *n.* **(a)** (lit. or fig.) Dosis, *die;* **take a ∼ of medicine** Medizin [ein]nehmen; **in small ∼s** (fig.) in kleinen Mengen; **(b)** (amount of radiation) Strahlen-, Bestrahlungsdosis, *die.* **2** *v.t.* **∼ sb. with sth.** jmdm. etw. geben *od.* verabreichen

doss-house /ˈdɒshaʊs/ *n.* (Brit. sl.) Nachtasyl, *das*

dossier /ˈdɒsɪə(r), ˈdɒsjeɪ/ *n.* Akte, *die;* (bundle of papers) Dossier, *das*

dot /dɒt/ **1** *n.* **(a)** Punkt, *der;* (smaller) Pünktchen, *das;* **(b)** **on the ∼:** auf den Punkt genau. **2** *v.t.,* **-tt-: (a)** (mark with ∼) Punkten/einem Punkt markieren; **(b) ∼ one's i's/j's** i-/j-Punkte machen; **(c)** (mark as with ∼s) [be]sprenkeln; **the sky was ∼ted with stars** der Himmel war von Sternen übersät; **(d)** (scatter) verteilen

dotage /ˈdəʊtɪdʒ/ *n.* **be in one's ∼:** senil sein

dote /dəʊt/ *v.i.* **[absolutely] ∼ on sb./sth.** jmdn./etw. abgöttisch lieben

doting /ˈdəʊtɪŋ/ *adj.* vernarrt

dotted /ˈdɒtɪd/ *adj.* gepunktet ⟨*Kleid, Linie*⟩; **sign on the ∼ line** (fig.) unterschreiben

dotty /ˈdɒtɪ/ *adj.* (coll.) **(a)** (silly) dümmlich; **be ∼ over** *or* **about sb./sth.** in jmdn./etw. vernarrt sein; **(b)** (feeble-minded) schrullig (ugs. abwertend); vertrottelt (ugs. abwertend); **go ∼:** vertrotteln; **(c)** (absurd) blödsinnig (ugs.); verrückt ⟨*Idee*⟩

double /ˈdʌbl/ **1** *adj.* **(a)** (consisting of two parts etc.) doppelt ⟨*Anstrich, Stofflage, Sohle*⟩; **(b)** (twofold) doppelt ⟨*Sandwich, Futter, Fenster, Boden*⟩; **(c)** (with pl.: two) zwei ⟨*Punkte, Klingen*⟩; **(d)** (for two persons) Doppel-; **∼ seat** Doppelsitz, *der;* **∼ bed/room** Doppelbett, *das/*-zimmer, *das;* **(e)** folded **∼:** einmal *od.* einfach gefaltet; **be bent ∼ with pain** sich vor Schmerzen (*Dat.*) krümmen; **(f)** (having some part **∼**) Doppel⟨*adler, -heft, -stecker*⟩; **(g)** (dual) doppelt ⟨*Sinn,* [*Verwendungs*]*zweck*⟩; **(h)** (twice as much) doppelt ⟨*Anzahl*⟩; **a room ∼ the size of this** ein doppelt so großes Zimmer wie dieses; **be ∼ the height/width/time** doppelt so hoch/breit/lang sein; **be ∼ the cost** doppelt so teuer sein; **at ∼ the cost** zum doppelten Preis; **(i)** (twice as many) doppelt so viele wie (etc.) doppelt ⟨*Portion, Lautstärke, Kognak, Whisky*⟩; **(k)** (of extra size etc.) doppelt so groß ⟨*Anstrengung, Mühe, Schwierigkeit, Problem, Anreiz*⟩; **(l)** (deceitful) falsch ⟨*Spiel*⟩. **2** *adv.* doppelt. **3** *n.* **(a)** (∼ quantity) Doppelte, *der;* **(b)** (∼ measure of whisky etc.) Doppelte, *der;* (∼ room) Doppelzimmer, *das;* **(c)** (twice as much) das Doppelte; doppelt soviel; (twice as many) doppelt so viele; **∼ or quits** doppelt oder nichts; **(d)** (identical person) Doppelgänger, *der/*-gängerin, *die;* **(e) at the ∼:** unverzüglich; (Mil.) aufs schnellste; **(f)** (pair of victories) Doppelerfolg, *der;* (pair of championships) Double, *das;* Doppel, *das;* **(g)** in *pl.* (Tennis etc.) Doppel, *das;* **women's** *or* **ladies'/men's/mixed ∼s** Damen-/Herrendoppel, *das/*gemischtes Doppel. **4** *v.t.* verdoppeln; (make **∼**) doppelt nehmen ⟨*Decke*⟩. **5** *v.i.*

(a) sich verdoppeln; **(b)** (have two functions) doppelt verwendbar sein; **the sofa ∼s as a bed** man kann das Sofa auch als Bett benutzen

∼ 'back *v.i.* kehrtmachen (ugs.)

∼ 'up 1 *v.i.* **(a)** sich krümmen; **∼ up with pain** sich vor Schmerzen (*Dat.*) krümmen; **(b)** (fig.) **∼ up with laughter** sich vor Lachen krümmen; **(c)** (share quarters) sich (*Dat.*) eine Unterkunft teilen; (in hotel etc.) sich (*Dat.*) ein Zimmer teilen. **2** *v.t.* (fold) einmal falten

double: ∼ 'agent *n.* Doppelagent, *der/*-agentin, *die;* **∼-barrelled** (*Amer.:* **∼-barreled**) /ˈdʌblbærəld/ *adj.* doppelläufig; **∼-barrelled surname** (Brit.) Doppelname, *der;* **∼ bass** /dʌblˈbeɪs/ *n.* (Mus.) Kontrabass, *der;* **∼-'book** *v.t.* doppelt reservieren; doppelt buchen ⟨*Flug*⟩; **∼-'check** *v.t.* **(a)** (verify twice) zweimal kontrollieren; **(b)** (verify in two ways) zweifach überprüfen; **∼ 'chin** *n.* Doppelkinn, *das;* **∼-click** (Computing) **1** *v.i.* doppelklicken; **2** *v.t.* **∼-click sth.** auf etw. (*Dat.*) doppelklicken; **∼ 'cream** *n.* Sahne mit hohem Fettgehalt; **∼-'cross 1** *n.* Doppelspiel, *das;* **2** *v.t.* ein Doppelspiel treiben mit; reinlegen (ugs.); **∼-dealing 1** /-'-/ *n.* Betrügerei, *die;* **2** /----/ *adj.* betrügerisch; **∼-decker** /dʌblˈdekə(r)/ **1** /'----/ *adj.* Doppeldecker-; Doppelstock- (Amtsspr.); **∼-decker bus** Doppeldeckerbus, *der;* **a ∼-decker sandwich** ein doppelter Sandwich; ein Doppeldecker (ugs.); **2** /-'--/ *n.* Doppeldecker, *der;* **∼-de'clutch** ⇒ **declutch; ∼ 'door** *n.* (door with two parts) Flügeltür, *die;* (twofold door) Doppeltür, *die;* **∼ 'Dutch** ⇒ **Dutch 2 c; ∼-edged** *adj.* (lit. or fig.) zweischneidig

double entendre /duːbl ɑ̃ˈtɑːdr/ *n.* Zweideutigkeit, *die*

double: ∼ 'feature *n.* Doppelprogramm, *das;* **∼-'glazed** *adj.* Doppel⟨*fenster*⟩; **∼ 'glazing** *n.* Doppelverglasung, *die;* **∼-'jointed** *adj.* sehr gelenkig; **∼ 'parking** *n.* Parken in der zweiten Reihe; **∼-quick 1** /'--/ *adj.* **(a)** in **∼-quick time/at a ∼-quick pace** im Laufschritt; **(b)** (fig.) ganz schnell; **2** /-'-/ *adv.* (Mil.) im Laufschritt; (fig.) ganz schnell; **∼ 'room** *n.* Doppelzimmer, *das;* **∼-'spaced** *adj.* mit doppeltem Zeilenabstand *nachgestellt;* **∼ 'standard** *n.* Doppelmoral, *die;* **apply** *or* **operate a ∼ standard** *or* **∼ standards** mit zweierlei Maß messen; **∼ 'take** *n.* he did a **∼ take a moment after he saw her walk by** nachdem sie vorbeigegangen war, stutzte er und sah ihr nach; **∼ 'time** *n.* doppelter Stundenlohn; **be on ∼ time** 100% Zuschlag bekommen; **∼ 'vision** *n.* (Med.) Doppeltsehen, *das;* **∼ whammy** /dʌbl ˈwæmɪ/ *n.* (coll.) doppelter Schlag; **be hit by a ∼ whammy** doppelt *od.* in zweifacher Weise getroffen werden; **∼ yellow 'lines** *n. pl.:* am Fuhrbahnrand verlaufende gelbe Doppellinie, die ein Halteverbot signalisiert

doubly /ˈdʌblɪ/ *adv.* doppelt; **make ∼ sure that …:** [ganz] besonders darauf achten, dass …

doubt /daʊt/ **1** *n.* **(a)** Zweifel, *der;* **∼[s] [about** *or* **as to sth./as to whether …]** (as to future) Ungewissheit, (as to fact) Unsicherheit [über etw. (*Akk.*) /darüber, ob …]; **∼[s] about** *or* **as to sth., ∼ of sth.** (inclination to disbelieve) Zweifel an etw. (*Dat.*); **there's no ∼ that …:** es besteht kein Zweifel daran, dass …; **∼[s]** (hesitations) Bedenken *Pl.;* **have [one's] ∼s about doing sth.** [seine] Bedenken haben, ob man etw. tun soll [oder nicht]; **when** *or* **if in ∼:** im Zweifelsfall; **no ∼** (certainly) gewiss; (probably) sicherlich; (admittedly) wohl; **cast ∼ on sth.** etw. in Zweifel ziehen; **(b)** *no pl.* (uncertain state of things) Ungewissheit, *die;* **be in ∼:** ungewiss sein; **beyond [all] ∼, without [a] ∼:** ohne [jeden] Zweifel. **2** *v.t.* anzweifeln; zweifeln an (+ *Dat.*); **she ∼ed him** sie zweifelte an ihm; **I don't ∼ that** *or* **it** ich zweifle nicht daran; **I ∼ whether** *or* **if** *or* **that …:** ich bezweifle, dass …

doubter /ˈdaʊtə(r)/ *n.* Zweifler, *der/*Zweiflerin, *die*

doubtful /ˈdaʊtfl/ *adj.* **(a)** (sceptical) skeptisch ⟨*Mensch, Wesen*⟩; **(b)** (showing doubt) ungläubig ⟨*Gesicht, Blick, Stirnrunzeln*⟩; **(c)** (uncertain) zweifelnd; **be ∼ as to** *or* **about sth.** an etw. (*Dat.*) (causing doubt) fraglich; **(e)** (uncertain in meaning etc.) ungewiss ⟨*Ergebnis, Ausgang, Herkunft, Aussicht*⟩; (questionable) zweifelhaft ⟨*Ruf, Charakter, Wert, Autorität*⟩; (ambiguous) unklar

‹*Bedeutung*›; (unsettled) unsicher ‹*Lage*›; (**f**) (unreliable) zweifelhaft ‹*Maßstab, Stütze*›; (**g**) (giving reason to suspect evil) bedenklich ‹*Gewohnheit, Spiel, Botschaft*›

doubtfully /'daʊtfəlɪ/ *adv.* skeptisch

doubtless /'daʊtlɪs/ *adv.* (**a**) (certainly) gewiss; (**b**) (probably) sicherlich; (**c**) (admittedly) wohl

dough /dəʊ/ *n.* (**a**) Teig, *der;* (**b**) (sl.: money) Knete, *die* (salopp)

'**doughnut** *n.* [Berliner] Pfannkuchen, *der*

dour /dʊə(r)/ *adj.* hartnäckig; düster ‹*Blick, Gesicht*›

douse /daʊs/ *v.t.* (**a**) (extinguish) ausmachen ‹*Licht, Kerze, Feuer*›; (**b**) (throw water on) übergießen ‹*Feuer, Flamme, Menschen*›

dove¹ /dʌv/ *n.* (also Polit.) Taube, *die*

dove² ⇨ dive 1

dove: ~**cot**, ~**cote** /'dʌvkɒt/ *n.* Taubenschlag, *der;* ~**tail** 1 *n.* (Carpentry) Schwalbenschwanzverbindung, *die;* 2 *v.i.* (fig.: fit together) ‹*Vorbereitungen, Zeitpläne:*› aufeinander abgestimmt sein

dowager /'daʊədʒə(r)/ *n.* Witwe von Stand

dowdy /'daʊdɪ/ *adj.* unansehnlich; (shabby) schäbig

dowel /'daʊəl/ *n.* (Carpentry) [Holz]dübel, *der*

down¹ /daʊn/ *n.* (Geog.) [baumloser] Höhenzug; *in pl.* Downs *Pl. (an der Südküste Englands)*

down² *n.* (**a**) (of bird) Daunen *Pl.;* Flaum, *der;* (**b**) (hair) Flaum, *der*

down³ 1 *adv.* (**a**) (to lower place, to ~stairs, southwards) runter (bes. ugs.); herunter/hinunter (bes. schriftsprachlich); (in lift) abwärts; (in crossword puzzle) senkrecht; [**right**] ~ **to sth.** [ganz] bis zu etw. her-/hinunter; **go** ~ **to the shops/the end of the road** zu den Läden/zum Ende der Straße hinuntergehen; (**b**) (Brit.: from capital) raus (bes. ugs.); heraus/hinaus (bes. schriftsprachlich); **get** ~ **to Reading from London** von London nach Reading raus-/hinausfahren; **come** ~ **from Edinburgh to London** von Edinburgh nach London [he]runterkommen; (**c**) (of money: at once) sofort; **pay for sth. cash** ~: etw. [in] bar bezahlen; (**d**) (into prostration) ‹*fallen, -geschlagen werden*›; **shout the place/house** ~ (fig.) schreien, dass die Wände zittern; (**e**) (on to paper) **copy sth.** ~ **from the board** etw. von der Tafel abschreiben; (**f**) (on programme) **put a meeting** ~ **for 2 p.m.** ein Treffen für *od.* auf 14 Uhr ansetzen; (**g**) *as int.* runter! (bes. ugs.); (to dog) leg dich!; nieder!; (Mil.) hinlegen!; ~ **with imperialism/the president!** nieder mit dem Imperialismus/dem Präsidenten!; (**h**) (in lower place, ~stairs, in fallen position, in south) unten; ~ **on the floor** auf dem Fußboden; **low/lower** ~: tief/tiefer unten; ~ **under the table** unter dem Tisch; **wear one's hair** ~: sein Haar offen tragen; ~ **there/here** da/hier unten; **X metres** ~: X Meter tief; **his flat is on the next floor** ~: seine Wohnung ist ein Stockwerk tiefer; ~ **in Wales/in the country** weit weg in Wales/draußen auf dem Lande; ~ **south** unten im Süden (ugs.); ~ **south/east** (Amer.) in den Südstaaten/im Osten; ~ [**on the floor**] (Boxing) am Boden; auf den Brettern; ~ **and out** (Boxing) k. o.; (fig.) fertig (ugs.); (**i**) (prostrate) auf dem Fußboden/der Erde; **be** ~ **with an illness** eine Krankheit haben; (**j**) (on paper) **be** ~ **in writing/on paper/in print** niedergeschrieben/zu Papier gebracht/gedruckt sein; (**k**) (on programme) angesetzt ‹*Termin, Treffen*›; (**l**) (facing ~wards, bowed) zu Boden; **keep one's eyes** ~: zu Boden sehen; **be** ~ (brought to the ground) am Boden liegen; (**m**) (in depression) ~ [**in the mouth**] niedergeschlagen; (**n**) (now cheaper) [jetzt] billiger; (**o**) **be** ~ **to** ... (have only ... left) nichts mehr haben außer ...; **we're** ~ **to our last £100** wir haben nur noch 100 Pfund; **now it's** ~ **to him to do something** nun liegt es bei ihm, an ihm, etwas zu tun; (**p**) (to reduced consistency or size) **thin gravy** ~: Soße verdünnen; **the water had boiled right** ~: das Wasser war fast verdampft; **wear the soles** ~: die Sohlen ablaufen; (**q**) (including lower limit) **from** ... ~ **to** ...: von ... bis zu ... hinunter; (**r**) (in position of lagging or loss) weniger; **be three points/games** ~: mit drei Punkten/Spielen zurückliegen; **be** ~ **on one's earnings of the previous year** weniger verdienen als im Vorjahr; **be** ~ **on one's luck** eine Pechsträhne haben. *See also* up 1. 2 *prep.* (**a**) (~wards along, from top to bottom of) runter (bes. ugs.); herunter/

hinunter (bes. schriftsprachlich); **lower** ~ **the river** weiter unten am Fluss; **fall** ~ **the stairs/steps** die Treppe/Stufen herunterstürzen; **his eye travelled** ~ **the list** sein Auge wanderte über die Liste; **walk** ~ **the hill/road** den Hügel/die Straße heruntergehen; (**b**) (~wards through) durch; (**c**) (~wards into) rein in (+ *Akk.*) (bes. ugs.); hinein in (+ *Akk.*) (bes. schriftsprachlich); **fall** ~ **a hole/ditch** in ein Loch/einen Graben fallen; (**d**) (~wards over) über (+ *Akk.*); **spill water all** ~ **one's skirt** sich (*Dat.*) Wasser über den Rock gießen; (**e**) (~wards in time) **the tradition has continued** ~ **the ages** die Tradition ist von Generation zu Generation weitergegeben worden; (**f**) (along) **come** ~ **the street** die Straße herunter- *od.* entlangkommen; **go** ~ **the pub/disco** (Brit. coll.) in die Kneipe/Disko gehen; (**g**) (at or in a lower position in or on) [weiter] unten; **further** ~ **the ladder/coast** weiter unten auf der Leiter/an der Küste; **live just** ~ **the road** ein Stück weiter unten in der Straße wohnen; (**h**) (from top to bottom along) an (+ *Dat.*); ~ **the side of a house** an der Seite eines Hauses; (**i**) (all over) überall auf (+ *Dat.*); **I've got coffee [all]** ~ **my skirt** mein ganzer Rock ist voll Kaffee; (**j**) (Brit. coll.: in, at) ~ **the pub/café/town** in der Kneipe/im Café/in der Stadt. 3 *adj.* (directed ~wards) nach unten führend ‹*Rohr, Kabel*›; ‹*Rolltreppe*› nach unten; nach unten gerichtet ‹*Kolbenhub, Sog*›; aus der Hauptstadt herausführend ‹*Bahnlinie*›. 4 *v.t.* (coll.) (**a**) (knock ~) auf die Bretter schicken ‹*Boxer*›; (**b**) (drink ~) leer machen (ugs.) ‹*Flasche, Glas*›; schlucken (ugs.) ‹*Getränk*›; (**c**) ~ **tools** (cease work) zu arbeiten aufhören; (take a break) die Arbeit unterbrechen; (go on strike) die Arbeit niederlegen; (**d**) (shoot ~) abschießen, (ugs.) runterholen ‹*Flugzeug*›. 5 *n.* (coll.) **have a** ~ **on sb./sth.** jmdn./etw. auf dem Kieker haben (ugs.); *see also* up 4

down: ~**and-out** *n.* Stadtstreicher, *der/*Stadtstreicherin, *die;* Penner, *der/*Pennerin, *die* (ugs.); ~**beat** *n.* (Mus.) erster/betonter Taktteil; ~**cast** *adj.* niedergeschlagen ‹*Blick, Gesicht*›; ~**fall** *n.* Untergang, *der;* ~**grade** *v.t.* niedriger einstufen; ~**hearted** *adj.* niedergeschlagen; ~**hill** 1 /'--/ *adj.* bergab führend ‹*Fahrt*›; ‹*Strecke, Weg*› bergab; **he's on the** ~**hill path** (fig.) es geht bergab mit ihm; **be** ~**hill all the way** (fig.) ganz einfach sein; 2 /'--/ *adv.* bergab; **come** ~**hill** den Berg herunterkommen; 3 /'--/ *n.* (**a**) Gefällstrecke, *die;* (**b**) (Skiing) Abfahrtslauf, *der;* ~**land** *n.* [baumloses] Hügelland; ~'**load** *v.t.* (Computing) herunterladen; ~**market** *adj.* weniger anspruchsvoll; **go** ~**market** weniger anspruchsvoll werden; ~ **payment** *n.* Anzahlung, *die;* ~**pipe** *n.* [Regenab]fallrohr, *das;* ~**pour** *n.* Regenguss, *der;* ~**right** 1 *adj.* ausgemacht ‹*Frechheit, Dummheit, Idiot, Lügner*›; glatt ‹*Lüge*›; 2 *adv.* geradezu; ausgesprochen; **it would be** ~**right stupid to do that** es wäre eine ausgemachte Dummheit, das zu versuchen; ~**size** 1 *v.t.* verschlanken; 2 *v.i.* abspecken; ~**stage** *adv.* (Theatre) im Vordergrund der Bühne; **move** ~**stage** sich zum Vordergrund der Bühne bewegen; ~**stairs** 1 /'--/ *adv.* die Treppe hinunter‹*gehen, -fallen, -kommen*›; unten ‹*wohnen, sein*›; 2 /'--/ *adj.* im Parterre *od.* Erdgeschoss *nachgestellt;* Parterre‹*wohnung*›; 3 /'--/ *n.* Untergeschoss, *das;* ~**stream** ▶ 1048| 1 /'--/ *adv.* flussabwärts; 2 /'--/ *adj.* flussabwärts gelegen ‹*Ort*›; ~ **time** *n.* (Computing) Ausfallzeit, *die;* ~**to-earth** *adj.* praktisch, nüchtern ‹*Person*›; realistisch ‹*Plan, Vorschlag*›; ~**town** (Amer.) 1 *adj.* im Stadtzentrum *nachgestellt;* ~**town** Manhattan das Stadtzentrum Manhattan; 2 *adv.* ins Stadtzentrum ‹*gehen, fahren*›; im Stadtzentrum ‹*leben, liegen, sein*›; ~**trodden** *adj.* geknechtet; unterdrückt; ~**turn** *n.* (Econ., Commerc.) Abschwung, *der;* ~'**under** (coll.) 1 *adv.* in/(to) nach Australien/Neuseeland; 2 *n.* (Australia) Australien (*das*); (New Zealand) Neuseeland (*das*)

downward /'daʊnwəd/ 1 *adj.* nach unten *nachgestellt;* nach unten gerichtet; ~ **movement/trend** (lit. or fig.) Abwärtsbewegung, *die/*-trend, *der;* ~ **gradient** *or* **slope** Gefälle, *das.* 2 *adv.* abwärts ‹*sich bewegen*›; nach unten ‹*sehen, gehen*›; *see also* face down[ward]

downwards /'daʊnwədz/ ⇨ downward 2

'**downwind** *adv.* mit dem Wind; vor dem Wind ‹*segeln*›; **be** ~ **of sth.** im Windschatten einer Sache (*Gen.*) sein

dowry /'daʊrɪ/ *n.* Mitgift, *die* (veralt.); Aussteuer, *die*

doyley ⇒ **doily**

doz. *abbr.* **dozen** Dtzd.

doze /dəʊz/ **1** *v.i.* dösen (ugs.); [nicht tief] schlafen; **lie dozing** im Halbschlaf liegen. **2** *n.* Nickerchen, *das* (ugs.) ∼ **'off** *v.i.* eindösen (ugs.)

dozen /'dʌzn/ *n.* **(a)** *pl. same* (twelve) Dutzend, *das;* **six** ∼ **bottles of wine** sechsmal zwölf Flaschen Wein; **a** ∼ **times/reasons** (fig. coll.: many) dutzendmal/Dutzende von Gründen; **half a** ∼: sechs; **(b)** *pl.* ∼**s** (set of twelve) Dutzend, *das;* **by the** ∼ (in twelves) im Dutzend; (fig. coll.: in great numbers) in großen Mengen; **(c)** *in pl.* (coll.: many) Dutzende *Pl.;* ∼**s of times** dutzendmal

DP *abbr.* **data processing** DV

Dr *abbr.* **(a)** ▶ 1152 | **Doctor** (as prefix to name) Dr.; **(b)** **debtor** Sch.

drab /dræb/ *adj.* **(a)** (dull brown) gelblich braun; (dull-coloured) matt; **(b)** (dull, monotonous) langweilig ‹ *Ort, Gebäude* ›

draft /drɑːft/ **1** *n.* **(a)** (rough copy) (of speech) Konzept, *das;* (of treaty, parliamentary bill) Entwurf, *der; attrib.* ∼ **copy/version** Konzept, *das;* **(b)** (plan of work) Skizze, *die;* [Bau-, Riß]zeichnung, *die;* **(c)** (Mil.: detaching for special duty) Sonderkommando, *das;* (Brit.: those detached) Abkommandierte *Pl.;* **(d)** (Amer. Mil.: conscription) Einberufung, *die;* (those conscripted) Wehrpflichtige *Pl.;* Einberufene *Pl.;* **(e)** (Commerc.: cheque drawn) Wechsel, *der;* Tratte, *die;* **(f)** (Amer.) ⇒ **draught. 2** *v.t.* **(a)** (make rough copy of) entwerfen; **(b)** (Mil.) abkommandieren; **(c)** (Amer. Mil.: conscript) einberufen

drafty (Amer.) ⇒ **draughty**

drag /dræg/ **1** *n.* **(a)** (difficult progress) **it was a long** ∼ **up the hill** der Aufstieg auf den Hügel war ein ganz schöner Schlauch (ugs.); **(b)** (obstruction) Hindernis, *das* (**on** für); Hemmnis, *das* (**on** für); **(c)** *no pl.* (coll.: women's dress worn by men) Frauenkleider *Pl.* **2** *v.t.,* **-gg-:** **(a)** [herum]schleppen; **(b)** (move with effort) ∼ **oneself** sich schleppen; ∼ **one's feet** [mit den Füßen] schlurfen; ∼ **one's feet** *or* **heels** (fig.) sich (*Dat.*) Zeit lassen (**over, in** mit); **(c)** (fig. coll.: take despite resistance) **he** ∼**ged me to a dance** er schleifte mich (ugs.) zu einer Tanzveranstaltung; ∼ **sb. into sth.** jmdn. in etw. (*Akk.*) hineinziehen; **(d)** (search) [mit einem Schleppnetz] absuchen ‹ *Fluss-, Seegrund* ›. **(e)** (Computing) ziehen; ∼ **and drop** ziehen und ablegen. **3** *v.i.,* **-gg-:** **(a)** schleifen; ∼ **on** *or* **at a cigarette** (coll.) an einer Zigarette ziehen; **(b)** (fig.: pass slowly) sich [hin]schleppen ∼ **'in** *v.t.* hineinziehen ∼ **'on** *v.i.* (continue) sich [da]hinschleppen; **time** ∼**ged on die Zeit verstrich;** ∼ **on for months** sich über Monate hinziehen ∼ **'out** *v.t.* (protract unduly) hinausziehen

'dragnet *n.* (lit. or fig.) Schleppnetz, *das;* (fig.) Netz, *das*

dragon /'drægn/ *n.* Drache, *der;* (fig.: person) Drachen, *der*

'dragonfly *n.* (Zool.) Libelle, *die*

drain /dreɪn/ **1** *n.* **(a)** Abflussrohr, *das;* (underground) Kanalisationsrohr, *das;* (grating at roadside) Gully, *der;* **down the** ∼ (fig. coll.) für die Katz (ugs.); **go down the** ∼ (fig. coll.) für die Katz sein (ugs.); **that was money [thrown] down the** ∼ (fig. coll.) das Geld war zum Fenster hinausgeworfen (ugs.); **(b)** (fig.: constant demand) Belastung, *die* (**on** *Gen.*). **2** *v.t.* **(a)** trockenlegen ‹ *Teich* ›; entwässern ‹ *Land* ›; ableiten ‹ *Wasser* ›; **(b)** (Cookery) abgießen ‹ *Wasser, Kartoffeln, Gemüse* ›; **(c)** (drink all contents of) austrinken; **(d)** (fig.: deprive) ∼ **a country of its wealth** *or* **resources/**∼ **sb. of his energy** ein Land/jmdn. auslaugen. **3** *v.i.* **(a)** ‹ *Geschirr, Gemüse:* › abtropfen; ‹ *Flüssigkeit:* › ablaufen; **(b)** **the colour** ∼**ed from her face** (fig.) die Farbe wich aus ihrem Gesicht

drainage /'dreɪnɪdʒ/ *n.* Entwässerung, *die;* (system) Entwässerungssystem, *das;* (of city, house, etc.) Kanalisation, *die*

'draining board /'dreɪnɪŋ bɔːd/ (Brit.; Amer.: **'drainboard**) *n.* Abtropfbrett, *das*

'drainpipe *n.* **(a)** (to carry off rainwater) Regen[abfall]rohr, *das;* **(b)** (to carry off sewage) Abwasserleitung, *die;* (underground) Kanalisationsleitung, *die*

drake /dreɪk/ *n.* Enterich, *der*

dram /dræm/ *n.* **(a)** (Pharm.) (weight) Drachme, *die;* **(b)** (small drink) Schlückchen, *das* (ugs.)

drama /'drɑːmə/ *n.* (lit. or fig.) Drama, *das;* (dramatic art) Schauspielkunst, *die; attrib.* ∼ **critic** Theaterkritiker, *der*

dramatic /drə'mætɪk/ *adj.* (lit. or fig.) dramatisch; ∼ **art** Dramatik, *die*

dramatise ⇒ **dramatize**

dramatist /'dræmətɪst/ *n.* Dramatiker, *der/*Dramatikerin, *die*

dramatize /'dræmətaɪz/ *v.t.* (lit. or fig.) dramatisieren

drank ⇒ **drink** 2, 3

drape /dreɪp/ **1** *v.t.* **(a)** (cover, adorn) ∼ **oneself/sb. in sth.** sich/jmdn. in etw. (*Akk.*) hüllen; **(b)** (put loosely) legen; drapieren. **2** *n.* **(a)** (cloth) Tuch, *das;* **(b)** *usu. in pl.* (Amer.: curtain) Vorhang, *der*

draper /'dreɪpə(r)/ *n.* ▶ 887 | (Brit.) Textilkaufmann, *der;* **the** ∼**'s [shop]** das Textilgeschäft

drapery /'dreɪpərɪ/ *n.* **(a)** (Brit.: cloth) Stoffe; **(b)** (Brit.: trade) Textilgewerbe, *das;* ∼ **shop** Textilgeschäft, *das;* **(c)** (arrangement of cloth) Draperie, *die*

drastic /'dræstɪk/ *adj.* drastisch; erheblich ‹ *Wandel, Verbesserung* ›; durchgreifend, rigoros ‹ *Mittel* ›; dringend ‹ *Bedarf* ›; einschneidend ‹ *Veränderung* ›; erschreckend ‹ *Mangel* ›; **something** ∼ **will have to be done** drastische Maßnahmen müssen ergriffen werden

drat /dræt/ *v.t.* (coll.) ∼ **[it]/him!** verflucht!/verfluchter Kerl! (salopp)

draught /drɑːft/ *n.* **(a)** (of air) [Luft]zug, *der;* **be [sitting] in a** ∼**:** im Zug sitzen; **there's a** ∼ **[in here]** es zieht [hier]; **feel the** ∼ (fig. coll.) [finanziell] in der Klemme sitzen (ugs.); **(b)** **[beer] on** ∼**:** [Bier] vom Fass; **(c)** (swallow) Zug, *der;* (amount) Schluck, *der;* **(d)** (Naut.) Tiefgang, *der*

draught: ∼ **'beer** *n.* Fassbier, *das;* ∼**board** *n.* (Brit.) Damebrett, *das;* ∼**-proof 1** *adj.* winddicht; **2** *v.t.* winddicht machen

draughts /drɑːfts/ *n., no pl.* (Brit.) Damespiel, *das*

draughtsman /'drɑːftsmən/ *n., pl.* **draughtsmen** /'drɑːftsmən/ ▶ 887 | (Brit.) Zeichner, *der/*Zeichnerin, *die*

draughty /'drɑːftɪ/ *adj.* zugig

draw /drɔː/ **1** *v.i.,* **drew** /druː/, **drawn** /drɔːn/ **(a)** (pull) ziehen; ∼ **the curtains/blinds** (open) die Vorhänge aufziehen/die Jalousien hochziehen; (close) die Vorhänge zuziehen/die Jalousien herunterlassen; ∼ **the bolt** (unfasten) den Riegel zurückschieben; **(b)** (attract, take in) anlocken ‹ *Publikum, Menge, Kunden* ›; **be** ∼**n to sb.** von jmdm. angezogen werden; **he refused to be** ∼**n** er ließ sich nichts entlocken; **(c)** (take out) herausziehen; ziehen (from aus); ∼ **money from the bank/one's account** Geld bei der Bank holen/von seinem Konto abheben; ∼ **water from a well** Wasser an einem Brunnen holen *od.* schöpfen; **(d)** (derive, elicit) finden; ∼ **comfort from sth.** Trost in etw. (*Dat.*) finden; ∼ **reassurance/encouragement from sth.** Zuversicht/Mut aus etw. schöpfen; **(e)** (as one's due) erhalten; bekommen; beziehen ‹ *Gehalt, Rente, Arbeitslosenunterstützung* ›; **(f)** (select at random) ∼ **straws** Lose ziehen; ∼ **cards from a pack** Karten von einem Haufen abheben; ∼ **a winner** ein Gewinnlos ziehen; **(g)** (trace) ziehen ‹ *Strich* ›; zeichnen ‹ *geometrische Figur, Bild* ›; ∼ **the line at sth.** (fig.) bei etw. nicht mehr mitmachen; **(h)** (formulate) ziehen ‹ *Parallele, Vergleich* ›; herstellen ‹ *Analogie* ›; herausstellen ‹ *Unterschied* ›; **(i)** (end with neither side winner) unentschieden beenden ‹ *Spiel* ›; **the match was** ∼**n** das Spiel ging unentschieden aus. **2** *v.i.,* **drew, drawn (a)** (make one's way, move) ‹ *Person:* › gehen; ‹ *Fahrzeug:* › fahren; ∼ **into sth.** ‹ *Zug:* › in etw. (*Akk.*) einfahren; ‹ *Schiff:* › in etw. (*Akk.*) einlaufen; ∼ **towards sth.** sich einer Sache (*Dat.*) nähern; ∼ **to an end** zu Ende gehen; **(b)** (∼ lots) ziehen; losen; ∼ **[for partners]** [die Partner] auslosen. **3** *n.* **(a)** (raffle) Tombola, *die;* (for matches, contests) Auslosung, *die;* **(b)** ([result of] drawn game) Unentschieden, *das;* **end in a** ∼**:** mit einem Unentschieden enden; **(c)** (film, play) Publikumserfolg, *der;* **(d) be quick/slow on the** ∼**:** den Finger schnell/zu langsam am Abzug haben

∼ **a'side** *v.t.* zur Seite ziehen; ∼ **sb. aside** jmdn. beiseite nehmen

∼ **a'way** *v.i.* (a) (move ahead) ∼ **away from sth./sb.** sich von etw. entfernen/jmdm. davonziehen; (b) (set off) losfahren

∼ **'back** 1 *v.t.* zurückziehen; aufziehen ‹ *Vorhang* ›. 2 *v.i.* zurückweichen; (fig.) sich zurückziehen

∼ **'in** 1 *v.i.* (a) (move in and stop) einfahren; **the car drew in to the side of the road** das Auto fuhr an den Straßenrand heran; (b) ‹ *Tage:* › kürzer werden; ‹ *Abende:* › länger werden. 2 *v.t.* (fig.) hineinziehen ‹ *Person* ›; zum Mitmachen überreden

∼ **on** 1 /'-'-/ *v.i.* ‹ *Zeit:* › vergehen; (approach) ‹ *Winter, Nacht:* › nahen. 2 /'--/ *v.t.* (a) anziehen ‹ *Kleidung* ›; (b) zurückgreifen auf ‹ *Ersparnisse, Vorräte* ›; schöpfen aus ‹ *Wissen, Erfahrungen* ›

∼ **'out** 1 *v.t.* (extend) ausdehnen; in die Länge ziehen; **long ∼n out** ausgedehnt. 2 *v.i.* (a) abfahren; **the train drew out of the station** der Zug fuhr aus dem Bahnhof aus; (b) ‹ *Tage:* › länger werden; ‹ *Abende:* › kürzer werden

∼ **'up** 1 *v.t.* (a) (formulate) abfassen; aufsetzen ‹ *Vertrag* ›; aufstellen ‹ *Liste* ›; entwerfen ‹ *Plan, Budget* ›; (b) (pull closer) heranziehen; (c) ∼ **oneself up [to one's full height]** sich [zu seiner vollen Größe] aufrichten. 2 *v.i.* [an]halten

∼ **upon** ⇨ ∼ **on 2 b**

draw: ∼**back** *n.* Nachteil, *der;* ∼**bridge** *n.* Zugbrücke, *die*

drawer *n.* (a) /drɔː(r), 'drɔːə(r)/ (in furniture) Schublade, *die;* (b) *in pl.* /drɔːz/ (dated/joc.: woman's garment) Schlüpfer *Pl.*

drawing /'drɔːɪŋ/ *n.* (sketch) Zeichnung, *die*

drawing: ∼ **board** *n.* Zeichenbrett, *das;* **so it's back to the ∼ board** dann müssen wir wohl wieder von vorne beginnen; ∼ **office** *n.* Konstruktionsbüro, *das;* ∼ **pin** *n.* (Brit.) Reißzwecke, *die;* ∼ **room** *n.* Salon, *der*

drawl /drɔːl/ 1 *v.i.* gedehnt sprechen. 2 *v.t.* dehnen; gedehnt aussprechen. 3 *n.* gedehntes Sprechen; **speak with a ∼:** gedehnt sprechen

drawn /drɔːn/ 1 ⇨ **draw** 1, 2. 2 *adj.* verzogen ‹ *Gesicht* ›; **look ∼** (from tiredness) abgespannt aussehen; (from worries) abgehärmt aussehen

'drawstring *n.* Durchziehband, *das*

dread /dred/ 1 *v.t.* sich sehr fürchten vor (+ *Dat.*); **the ∼ed day/moment** der gefürchtete Tag/Augenblick; **I ∼ to think [what may have happened]** ich mag gar nicht daran denken[, was passiert sein könnte]. 2 *n., no pl.* (terror) Angst, *die;* **be** or **live in ∼ of sth./sb.** in [ständiger] Furcht vor etw./jmdm. leben

dreadful /'dredfl/ *adj.* schrecklich; furchtbar; (coll.: very bad) fürchterlich; **I feel ∼** (unwell) ich fühle mich scheußlich (ugs.); (embarrassed) es ist mir fürchtbar peinlich

dreadfully /'dredfəlɪ/ *adv.* (a) schrecklich; entsetzlich; furchtbar ‹ *leiden* ›; (coll.: very badly) grauenhaft; fürchterlich; (b) (coll.: extremely) schrecklich; furchtbar

dream /driːm/ 1 *n.* (a) Traum, *die.* (a) von jmdm./etw. träumen; **it was all a bad ∼:** das ganze war wie ein böser Traum; **in a ∼:** im Traum; **go/work like a ∼** (coll.) wie eine Eins fahren/funktionieren (ugs.); (b) (ambition, vision) Traum, *der;* **never in one's wildest ∼s** nicht in seinen kühnsten Träumen; (c) *attrib.* traumhaft; Traum‹ *haus, -auto, -urlaub* ›. 2 *v.i.,* ∼**t** /dremt/ or ∼**ed** träumen (about, of von); (while awake) vor sich (*Akk.*) hin träumen; **he wouldn't ∼ of doing it** (fig.) er würde nicht im Traum daran denken, das zu tun. 3 *v.t.,* ∼**t** or ∼**ed** träumen; **she never ∼t that she'd win** sie hätte sich (*Dat.*) nie träumen lassen, dass sie gewinnen würde

∼ **'up** *v.t.* sich (*Dat.*) ausdenken

dreamer /'driːmə(r)/ *n.* (day-∼) Träumer, *der*/Träumerin, *die*

dreamless /'driːmlɪs/ *adj.* traumlos

dreamt ⇨ **dream** 2, 3

dreary /'drɪərɪ/ *adj.* trostlos; monoton ‹ *Musik* ›; langweilig ‹ *Unterricht, Lehrbuch* ›

dredge /dredʒ/ *v.t.* ausbaggern; ∼ **[up]** (fig.) ausgraben

dredger /'dredʒə(r)/ *n.* Bagger, *der;* (boat) Schwimmbagger, *der*

dregs /dregz/ *n. pl.* (a) [Boden]satz, *der;* **drain one's glass to the ∼:** sein Glas bis zur Neige leeren; (b) (fig.) Abschaum, *der*

drench /drentʃ/ *v.t.* durchnässen; **get completely ∼ed, get ∼ed to the skin** nass bis auf die Haut werden

dress /dres/ 1 *n.* (a) (woman's or girl's frock) Kleid, *das;* (b) *no pl.* (clothing) Kleidung, *die;* **articles of ∼:** Kleidungsstücke; (c) *no pl.* (manner of dressing) Kleidung, *die.* 2 *v.t.* (a) (clothe) anziehen; **be ∼ed** angezogen sein; **be well ∼ed** gut gekleidet sein; **get ∼ed** sich anziehen; (b) (provide clothes for) einkleiden ‹ *Familie* ›; (c) (deck, adorn) schmücken; beflaggen ‹ *Schiff* ›; dekorieren ‹ *Schaufenster* ›; (d) (Med.) verbinden, versorgen ‹ *Wunde* ›; (e) (Cookery) zubereiten; (f) (treat, prepare) gerben ‹ *tierische Häute, Felle* ›; (put finish on) appretieren ‹ *Gewebe, Holz, Leder* ›. 3 *v.i.* (wear clothes) sich anziehen; sich kleiden; (get ∼ed) sich anziehen; ∼ **for dinner** sich zum Abendessen umziehen

∼ **'down** *v.t.* (fig.) zurechtweisen

∼ **'up** 1 *v.t.* (a) (in formal clothes) feinmachen; (b) (disguise) verkleiden; (c) (smarten) verschönern. 2 *v.i.* (a) (wear formal clothes) sich feinmachen; (b) (disguise oneself) sich verkleiden

dressage /'dresɑːʒ/ *n.* Dressurreiten, *das*

'dress circle *n.* (Theatre) erster Rang

dresser¹ /'dresə(r)/ *n.* Anrichte, *die;* Büfett, *das*

dresser² *n.* (a) **he's a careless/elegant ∼:** er kleidet sich nachlässig/elegant; (b) ▶ 887 ⫘ (Theatre) Garderobier, *der*/Garderobiere, *die*

dressing /'dresɪŋ/ *n.* (a) *no pl.* Anziehen, *das;* (b) (Cookery) Dressing, *das;* (c) (Med.) Verband, *der;* (d) (Agric.) Dünger, *der*

dressing: ∼ **'down** *n.* **give sb. a ∼ down** jmdm. eine Standpauke halten (ugs.); ∼ **gown** *n.* Bademantel, *der;* ∼ **room** *n.* (a) (of actor or actress) [Schauspieler]garderobe, *die;* [Künstler]garderobe, *die;* (b) (Sport) Umkleideraum, *der;* ∼ **table** *n.* Frisierkommode, *die*

dress: ∼**maker** *n.* ▶ 887 ⫘ Damenschneider, *der*/-schneiderin, *die;* ∼**making** *n.* Damenschneiderei, *die;* ∼ **rehearsal** *n.* (lit. or fig.) Generalprobe, *die;* ∼ **shirt** *n.* Smokinghemd, *das;* ∼ **suit** *n.* Abendanzug, *der;* ∼ **uniform** *n.* (Mil.) Paradeuniform, *die*

drew ⇨ **draw** 1, 2

dribble /'drɪbl/ 1 *v.i.* (a) (trickle) tropfen; (b) (slobber) ‹ *Baby:* › sabbern; (c) (Sport) dribbeln. 2 *v.t.* (a) ‹ *Baby:* › kleckern; (b) (Sport) dribbeln mit ‹ *Ball* ›

dribs *n. pl.* ∼ **and drabs** /drɪbz n 'dræbz/ kleine Mengen; **in ∼ and drabs** kleckerweise (ugs.)

dried /draɪd/ *adj.* getrocknet; ∼ **fruit[s]** Dörr- od. Backobst, *das;* ∼ **milk/meat** Trockenmilch, *die*/-fleisch, *das*

drier¹ ⇨ **dry** 1

drier² /'draɪə(r)/ *n.* (for hair) Trockenhaube, *die;* (hand-held) Fön ⓦ, *der;* Haartrockner, *der;* (for laundry) [Wäsche]trockner, *der*

driest ⇨ **dry** 1

drift /drɪft/ 1 *n.* (a) (flow, steady movement) Wanderung, *die;* (b) (fig.: trend, shift, tendency) Tendenz, *die;* (c) (flow of air or water) Strömung, *die;* (d) (Naut., Aeronaut.: deviation from course) Abdrift, *die* (fachspr.); (e) (of snow or sand) Verwehung, *die;* (f) (fig.: gist, import) das Wesentliche; **get** or **catch the ∼ of sth.** etw. im Wesentlichen verstehen. 2 *v.i.* (a) (be borne by current; fig.: move passively or aimlessly) treiben; ‹ *Wolke:* › ziehen; ∼ **out to sea** aufs Meer hinaustreiben; ∼ **off course** abtreiben; ∼ **into crime** in die Kriminalität [ab]driften; ∼ **into unconsciousness** in Bewusstlosigkeit versinken; **months ∼ed by** die Monate vergingen; (b) (coll.: come or go casually) ∼ **in** hereinschneien (ugs.); ∼ **out** abziehen (ugs.); (c) (form ∼s) zusammengeweht werden; ∼**ing sand** Treibsand, *der*

drifter /'drɪftə(r)/ *n.* (a) (Naut.) Drifter, *der;* (b) (person) **be a ∼:** sich treiben lassen

drift: ∼**-net** *n.* Treibnetz, *das;* ∼**wood** *n.* Treibholz, *das*

drill /drɪl/ 1 *n.* (a) (tool) Bohrer, *der;* (Dent.) Bohrinstrument, *das;* (Carpentry, Building) Bohrmaschine, *die;* (b) (Mil.: training) Drill, *der;* (c) (Educ.: also fig.) Übung, *die;* (d) (Brit. coll.: agreed procedure) Prozedur, *die;* **know the ∼:** wissen, wie es gemacht wird. **2** *v.t.* **(a)** (bore) bohren ‹*Loch, Brunnen*›; an-, ausbohren ‹*Zahn*›; ~ **sth.** (right through) etw. durchbohren; **(b)** (Mil.: instruct) drillen; **(c)** (Educ.; also fig.) ~ **sb. in sth.**, ~ **sth. into sb.** mit jmdm. etw. systematisch einüben; jmdm. etw. eindrillen (ugs.). **3** *v.i.* bohren (**for** nach)

drill: ~ **bit** *n.* Bohrer, *der;* ~ **chuck** *n.* Bohrfutter, *das*

drink /drɪŋk/ **1** *n.* **(a)** Getränk; *das;* **have a** ~: [etwas] trinken; **would you like a** ~ **of milk?** möchten Sie etwas Milch [trinken]?; **give sb. a** ~ **[of fruit juice]** jmdm. etwas [Fruchtsaft] zu trinken geben; **(b)** (glass of alcoholic liquor) Glas, *das;* (not with food) Drink, *der;* Glas, *das;* **have a** ~: ein Glas trinken; **let's have a** ~! trinken wir einen!; **he has had a few** ~**s** er hat einige getrunken (ugs.); **(c)** *no pl., no art.* (intoxicating liquor) Alkohol, *der;* [**strong**] ~: scharfe *od.* hochprozentige Getränke; **the worse for** ~: betrunken; **drive sb. to** ~: jmdn. zum Trinker werden lassen. **2** *v.t.,* **drank** /dræŋk/, **drunk** /drʌŋk/ trinken ‹*Kaffee, Glas Milch, Flasche Whisky*›; ~ **down** *or* **off [in one gulp]** [in einem *od.* auf einen Zug] austrinken; ~ **oneself to death** sich zu Tode trinken. **3** *v.i.,* **drank, drunk** trinken; ~ **from a bottle** aus einer Flasche trinken; ~**ing and driving,** ~**-driving** Alkohol am Steuer; ~ **to sb./sth.** auf jmdn./etw. trinken ~ **'in** *v.t.* einsaugen ‹*Luft; fig.: Schönheit*›; begierig aufnehmen ‹*Worte, Geschichten*› ~ **'up** *v.t. & i.* austrinken

drinkable /'drɪŋkəbl/ *adj.* trinkbar

drinker /'drɪŋkə(r)/ *n.* Trinker, *der*/Trinkerin, *die*

drinking /'drɪŋkɪŋ/: ~ **fountain** *n.* Trinkbrunnen, *der;* ~**'up time** *n.* (Brit.) Zeit zwischen dem Ende des Ausschanks und der Schließung der Gaststätte (meist 10 Minuten); ~ **water** *n.* Trinkwasser, *das*

'drinks cabinet, drinks cupboard *n.* Barschrank, *der*

drip /drɪp/ **1** *v.i.,* **-pp-: (a)** tropfen; (overflow in drops) triefen; **be** ~**ping with moisture** triefend nass sein; **(b)** (fig.) **be** ~**ping with** überladen sein mit ‹*Schmuck*›; triefen von *od.* vor ‹*Ironie, Sentimentalität usw.*›. **2** *v.t.,* **-pp-** tropfen lassen. **3** *n.* **(a)** Tropfen, *das;* **(b)** (Med.) Tropfinfusion, *die;* **the patient was on a** ~: der Patient hing am Tropf; **(c)** (coll.: feeble person) Schlappschwanz, *der* (salopp abwertend)

drip-dry (Textiles) **1** /·'·/ *v.i.* knitterfrei trocknen. **2** /'··/ *adj.* bügelfrei; schnelltrocknend

dripping /'drɪpɪŋ/ **1** *adv.* ~ **wet** tropf- *od.* (ugs.) patsch-*od.* (ugs.) klitschnass. **2** *n.* (Cookery) Schmalz, *das;* **bread and** ~: Schmalzbrot, *das*

drive /draɪv/ **1** *n.* **(a)** Fahrt, *die;* **a nine-hour** ~, **a** ~ **of nine hours** eine neunstündige Autofahrt; **have a long** ~ **to work** eine lange Anfahrt zur Arbeit haben; **(b)** (street) Straße, *die;* **(c)** (private road) Zufahrt, *die;* (entrance to large building) Auffahrt, *die;* **(d)** (energy to achieve) Tatkraft, *die;* **(e)** (Commerc., Polit., etc.: vigorous campaign) Aktion, *die;* Kampagne, *die;* **export/sales/recruiting** ~: Export-/ Verkaufs-/Anwerbekampagne, *die;* **(f)** (Psych.) Trieb, *der;* **(g)** (Motor Veh.: position of steering wheel) **left-hand/right-hand** ~: Links-/Rechtssteuerung *od.* -lenkung, *die;* **be left-hand** ~: Linkssteuerung haben; **(h)** (Motor Veh., Mech. Engin.: transmission of power) Antrieb, *der;* **front-wheel/rear-wheel** ~: Front-/Heckantrieb, *der.* **2** *v.t.,* **drove** /drəʊv/, **driven** /'drɪvn/ **(a)** fahren ‹*Auto, Lkw, Route, Strecke, Fahrgast*›; lenken ‹*Kutsche, Streitwagen*›; treiben ‹*Tier*›; **(b)** (as job) ~ **a lorry/train** Lkw-Fahrer/Lokomotivführer sein; **(c)** (compel to move) vertreiben; ~ **sb. out of** *or* **from a place/country** jmdn. von einem Ort/aus einem Land vertreiben; **(d)** (chase, urge on) treiben ‹*Vieh, Wild*›; **(e)** (fig.) ~ **sb. to sth.** jmdn. zu etw. treiben; ~ **sb. out of his mind** *or* **wits** jmdn. in den Wahnsinn treiben; **(f)** ‹*Wind, Wasser:*› treiben; **be** ~**n off course** abgetrieben werden; **(g)** (cause to penetrate) ~ **sth. into sth.** etw. in etw. (*Akk.*) treiben; **(h)** (power) antreiben ‹*Mühle, Maschine*›; **be steam-**~**n** *or* ~**n by steam** dampfgetrieben sein; **(i)** (incite to action) antreiben; ~ **oneself [too] hard** sich [zu sehr] schinden. **3** *v.i.,* **drove, driven (a)** fahren; **in Great Britain we** ~ **on the left** bei uns in Großbritannien ist Linksverkehr; ~ **at 30 m.p.h.** mit 50 km/h

fahren; **learn to** ~: [Auto]fahren lernen; den Führerschein machen (ugs.); **can you** ~? kannst du Auto fahren?; **(b)** (go by car) mit dem [eigenen] Auto fahren; **(c)** ‹*Hagelkörner, Wellen:*› schlagen; **clouds were driving across the sky** Wolken jagten über den Himmel ~ **at** *v.t.* hinauswollen auf (+ *Akk.*); **what are you driving at?** worauf wollen Sie hinaus? ~ **a'way 1** *v.i.* wegfahren. **2** *v.t.* **(a)** wegfahren, wegbringen ‹*Ladung, Fahrzeug*›; (chase away) wegjagen; **(b)** (fig.) zerstreuen ‹*Bedenken, Befürchtungen*› ~ **'back** *v.t.* (force to retreat) zurückschlagen ‹*Eindringlinge*› ~ **'off 1** *v.i.* **(a)** wegfahren; **(b)** (Golf) abschlagen. **2** *v.t.* (repel) zurückschlagen ‹*Angreifer*› ~ **'on 1** *v.i.* weiterfahren. **2** *v.t.* (impel) treiben (**to** zu) ~ **'out** *v.t.* hinauswerfen ‹*Person*›; hinausjagen ‹*Hund*› ~ **'up 1** *v.i.* vorfahren (**to** vor + *Dat.*). **2** *v.t.* hochtreiben ‹*Kosten*›

'drive-in *adj.* Drive-in-; ~ **bank** Bank mit Autoschalter; ~ **cinema** *or* (Amer.) **movie [theater]** Autokino, *das*

drivel /'drɪvl/ *n.* Gefasel, *das* (ugs. abwertend); **talk** ~: faseln (ugs. abwertend)

driven ⇒ **drive** 2, 3

'drive-on *adj.* ~ **car ferry** Autofährschiff, *das*

driver /'draɪvə(r)/ *n.* Fahrer, *der*/Fahrerin, *die;* (of locomotive) Führer, *der*/Führerin, *die;* **be in the** ~**'s seat** (fig.) das Steuer in der Hand haben (fig.)

drive: ~**shaft** *n.* Antriebswelle, *die;* ~**-time** *n.* attrib. ‹*Sender, Sendung*› für Autofahrer im Berufsverkehr; ~**way** ⇒ ~ 1 d

driving /'draɪvɪŋ/ **1** *n.* Fahren, *das; his* ~ **is awful** er fährt furchtbar. **2** *adj.* **(a)** ~ **rain** peitschender Regen; **(b)** (fig.) treibend

driving: ~ **force** *n.* treibende Kraft; Triebfeder, *die;* **the** ~ **force behind sth.** die treibende Kraft hinter etw.; ~ **instructor** *n.* ▶ 887 Fahrlehrer, *der*/-lehrerin, *die;* ~ **lesson** *n.* Fahrstunde, *die;* ~ **licence** *n.* Führerschein, *der;* ~ **mirror** *n.* Rückspiegel, *der;* ~ **school** *n.* Fahrschule, *die;* ~ **seat** *n.* Fahrersitz, *der;* **be in the** ~ **seat** das Steuer in der Hand haben (fig.); ~ **test** *n.* Fahrprüfung, *die;* **take/pass/fail one's** ~ **test** die Fahrprüfung ablegen/bestehen/nicht bestehen

drizzle /'drɪzl/ **1** *n.* Sprühregen, *der;* Nieseln, *das.* **2** *v.i.* **it's drizzling** es nieselt; **drizzling rain** Nieselregen, *der*

dromedary /'drɒmɪdərɪ/ *n.* (Zool.) Dromedar, *das*

drone /drəʊn/ **1** *n.* **(a)** (of bees, flies) Summen, *das;* (of machine) Brummen, *das;* **(b)** (derog.: monotonous tone of speech) Geleier, *das;* **(c)** (Zool.: bee; Aeronaut.) Drohne, *die.* **2** *v.i.* **(a)** (buzz, hum) ‹*Biene:*› summen; ‹*Maschine:*› brummen; **(b)** (derog.) ‹*Rezitator:*› leiern. **3** *v.t.* leiern

drool /druːl/ *v.i.* ~ **over sb./sth.** über jmdn./etw. in Verzückung geraten

droop /druːp/ *v.i.* **(a)** herunterhängen; ‹*Blume:*› den Kopf hängen lassen; **her head** ~**ed forwards** ihr Kopf sank nach vorn; **his eyelids were** ~**ing** ihm fielen die Augen zu; **(b)** ‹*Person:*› ermatten

drop /drɒp/ **1** *n.* **(a)** Tropfen, *der;* ~**s of rain/dew/ blood/sweat** Regen- / Tau- / Bluts- / Schweißtropfen; ~ **by** ~, **in** ~**s** tropfenweise; **be a** ~ **in the ocean** *or* **in the** *or* **a bucket** (fig.) ein Tropfen auf einen heißen Stein sein; (fig.: small amount) **[just] a** ~: [nur] ein kleiner Tropfen; **(b)** (fig. coll.: of alcohol) Gläschen, *das;* **have had a** ~ **too much** ein Glas über den Durst getrunken haben (ugs.); **(c)** *in pl.* (Med.) Tropfen *Pl.;* **(d)** (vertical distance) **there was a** ~ **of 50 metres from the roof to the ground below** vom Dach bis zum Boden waren es 50 Meter; **(e)** (abrupt descent of land) plötzlicher Abfall; Absturz, *der;* **(f)** (fig.: decrease) Rückgang, *der;* ~ **in temperature/prices** Temperatur-/Preisrückgang, *der;* **a** ~ **in the cost of living** ein Sinken der Lebenshaltungskosten; **a** ~ **in salary/ wages/income** eine Gehalts-/Lohn-/Einkommensminderung. **2** *v.i.,* **-pp-: (a)** (fall) (accidentally) [herunter]fallen; (deliberately) sich [hinunter]fallen lassen; ~ **out of** *or* **from sb.'s hand** jmdm. aus der Hand fallen; **(b)** (sink to ground) ‹*Person:*› fallen; ~ **to the ground** umfallen; zu Boden fallen; ~ **[down] dead** tot umfallen; ~ **dead!** (coll.) scher dich zum Teufel!; ~ **into bed/an armchair** ins Bett/in einen

Sessel sinken; **be fit** *or* **ready to** ~ (coll.) zum Umfallen müde sein; **(c)** (in amount etc.) sinken; ‹*Wind:*› abflauen, sich legen; ‹*Stimme:*› sich senken; ‹*Kinnlade:*› herunterfallen; **(d)** (move, go) ~ **back** (Sport) zurückfallen; **(e)** (fall in ~s) ‹*Flüssigkeit:*› tropfen (**from** aus); **(f)** ~ **[back] into one's old routine** in den alten Trott verfallen; ~ **into the habit** *or* **way of doing sth.** die Gewohnheit annehmen, etw. zu tun; **(g)** (cease) **the affair was allowed to** ~: man ließ die Angelegenheit auf sich (*Dat.*) beruhen; **(h) let** ~: beiläufig erwähnen ‹*Tatsache, Absicht*›; fallen lassen ‹*Bemerkung*›; **let** [**it**] ~ **that/when** ...: beiläufig erwähnen, dass/wann ... **3** *v.t.*, **-pp-:** **(a)** (let fall) fallen lassen; abwerfen ‹*Bomben, Flugblätter, Nachschub*›; absetzen ‹*Fallschirmjäger, Truppen*›; ~ **a letter in the letter box** einen Brief einwerfen; ~ **the latch on the door** den Türriegel vorlegen; **(b)** (by mistake) fallen lassen; **she** ~**ped crumbs on the floor/ juice on the table** ihr fielen Krümel auf den Boden/tropfte Saft auf den Tisch; **he** ~**ped the glass** ihm fiel das Glas herunter; **(c)** (let fall in ~s) tropfen; **(d)** (utter casually) fallen lassen ‹*Namen*›; ~ **a hint** eine Anspielung machen; **(e)** (send casually) ~ **sb. a note** *or* **line** jmdm. [ein paar Zeilen] schreiben; **(f)** (set down, unload from car) absetzen ‹*Mitfahrer, Fahrgast*›; **(g)** (omit) (in writing) auslassen; (in speech) nicht aussprechen; ~ **a name from a list** einen Namen von einer Liste streichen; **(h)** (discontinue, abandon) fallen lassen ‹*Plan, Thema, Anklage*›; einstellen ‹*Untersuchung, Ermittlungen*›; beiseite lassen ‹*Formalitäten*›; aufgeben, Schluss machen mit ‹*Verstellung, Heuchelei*›; ~ **it!** lass das!; **shall we** ~ **the subject?** wollen wir nicht lieber von was anderem sprechen?; **(i)** ~ **sb. from a team** jmdn. aus einer Mannschaft nehmen; **(j)** ~ **one's voice** die Stimme senken; **(k)** ~**ped handlebars** Rennlenker, *der*
~ **'by** *v.i.* vorbeikommen
~ **'in 1** *v.t.* (deliver) vorbeibringen. **2** *v.i.* **(a)** hineinfallen; **(b)** (visit) hereinschauen; vorbeikommen; ~ **in on sb.** *or* **at sb.'s house** bei jmdm. hereinschauen
~ **'off 1** *v.i.* **(a)** (fall off) abfallen; (become detached) abgehen; **(b)** (fall asleep) einnicken; **(c)** (decrease) ‹*Teilnahme, Geschäft:*› zurückgehen; ‹*Unterstützung, Interesse:*› nachlassen. **2** *v.t.* **(a)** (fall off) abfallen von; **(b)** (set down) absetzen ‹*Fahrgast*›
~ **'out** *v.i.* **(a)** (fall out) herausfallen (**of** aus); **(b)** (withdraw beforehand) seine Teilnahme absagen; (withdraw while in progress) aussteigen (ugs.) (**of** aus); **(c)** (cease to take part) aussteigen (ugs.) (**of** aus); ‹*Student:*› das Studium abbrechen; ~ **out** [**of society**] aussteigen (ugs.)
~ **'round** *v.i.* vorbeikommen
drop: ~**-dead** *adv.* (coll.) umwerfend (ugs.) ‹*schön*›; unverschämt (ugs.) ‹*gut aussehen*›; ~**-down menu** *n.* (Computing) Dropdownmenü, *das* ~**-handlebars** *n. pl.* Rennlenker, *der;* ~**-in centre** *n.* (*jedermann zugängliche, auch Rat und Hilfe anbietende*) Begegnungsstätte
droplet /'drɒplɪt/ *n.* Tröpfchen, *das*
'drop-out *n.* (coll.) (from college etc.) Abbrecher, *der*/Abbrecherin, *die;* (from society) Aussteiger, *der*/Aussteigerin, *die* (ugs.)
droppings /'drɒpɪŋz/ *n. pl.* Mist, *der;* (of horse) Pferdeäpfel *Pl.*
'drop shot *n.* (Tennis etc.) Stoppball, *der*
drought /draʊt/, (Amer., Scot., Ir./poet.) **drouth** /draʊθ/ *n.* Dürre, *die;* **a period of** ~: eine Dürreperiode
drove ⇨ **drive** 2, 3
drown /draʊn/ **1** *v.i.* ertrinken. **2** *v.t.* **(a)** ertränken; **be** ~**ed** ertrinken; **(b)** (fig.) ~ **one's sorrows** seine Sorgen ertränken; **(c)** übertönen ‹*Geräusch, Musik*›
drowse /draʊz/ *v.i.* [vor sich hin]dösen
drowsy /'draʊzɪ/ *adj.* **(a)** (half asleep) schläfrig; (on just waking) verschlafen; **(b)** (soporific) einschläfernd
drudge /drʌdʒ/ *n.* Schwerarbeiter, *der* (fig.); Kuli, *der* (ugs.)
drudgery /'drʌdʒərɪ/ *n.* Schufterei, *die;* Plackerei, *die*
drug /drʌg/ **1** *n.* **(a)** (Med., Pharm.) Medikament, *das;* [Arznei]mittel, *das;* **(b)** (narcotic, opiate, etc.) Droge, *die;* Rauschgift, *das;* **he can't kick the** ~ **habit** er kommt von der Droge nicht los; ~**s ring** Drogenring, *der.* **2** *v.t.*, **-gg-:** **he was** ~**ged and kidnapped** er wurde betäubt und

entführt; ~ **sb.'s food/drink** jmds. Essen/Getränk (*Dat.*) ein Betäubungsmittel beimischen
drug: ~ **abuse** *n.* Drogenmissbrauch, *der;* ~ **abuser** *n.* Drogenmissbrauch Treibende, *der/die;* ~ **addict** *n.* Drogen- *od.* Rauschgiftsüchtige, *der/die;* ~ **addiction** *n.* Drogen- *od.* Rauschgiftsucht, *die;* ~ **dealer** *n.* Drogenhändler, *der/*-händlerin, *die;* Dealer, *der/*Dealerin, *die* (ugs.)
druggist /'drʌgɪst/ *n.* ▶ 887 Drogist, *der*/Drogistin, *die*
drug: ~ **pusher** *n.* Pusher, *der* (Drogenszene); ~**-related** *adj.* Drogen‹*-tote, -kriminalität, -delikt, -probleme*›; ~**-store** *n.* (Amer.) Drugstore, *der;* ~**-taking** *n., no pl.* Drogenkonsum, *der;* ~ **test** *n.* Dopingtest, *der;* ~ **trafficker** *n.* Drogenhändler, *der/*-händlerin, *die;* ~ **trafficking** *n.* Drogenhandel, *der;* ~ **user** *n.* Drogenkonsument, *der/*-konsumentin, *die;* **be a regular** ~ **user** regelmäßig Drogen nehmen
Druid /'druːɪd/ *n.* Druide, *der*
drum /drʌm/ **1** *n.* **(a)** Trommel, *die;* **(b)** *in pl.* (in jazz or pop) Schlagzeug, *das;* (section of band etc.) Trommeln *Pl.;* **(c)** (container for oil etc.) Fass, *das.* **2** *v.i.*, **-mm-** trommeln. **3** *v.t.*, **-mm-:** ~ **one's fingers on the desk** mit den Fingern auf den Tisch trommeln
~ **into** *v.t.* ~ **sth. into sb.** jmdm. etw. einhämmern (ugs.)
~ **'up** *v.t.* auftreiben ‹*Kunden, Unterstützung*›; zusammentrommeln (ugs.) ‹*Helfer, Anhänger*›; anbahnen ‹*Geschäfte*›
drum: ~ **'major** *n.* (Mil.) Tambourmajor, *der;* ~ **majorette** /drʌm meɪdʒə'ret/ *n.* Tambourmajorette, *die*
drummer /'drʌmə(r)/ *n.* ▶ 887 Schlagzeuger, *der*
'drumstick *n.* **(a)** (Mus.) Trommelschlägel, *der;* **(b)** (of fowl) Keule, *die*
drunk /drʌŋk/ **1** *adj.* **be** ~: betrunken sein; **get** ~ [**on gin**] [von Gin] betrunken werden; (intentionally) sich [mit Gin] betrinken; **be** ~ **as a lord** (coll.) voll wie eine Haubitze sein (ugs.); ~ **in charge** [**of a vehicle**] betrunken am Steuer. **2** *n.* Betrunkene, *der/die*
drunkard /'drʌŋkəd/ *n.* Trinker, *der*/Trinkerin, *die*
drunken /'drʌŋkn/ *attrib. adj.* **(a)** betrunken; (habitually drunk) versoffen (derb); **(b)** **a** ~ **brawl** *or* **fight** eine Schlägerei zwischen Betrunkenen; ~ **driving** Trunkenheit am Steuer
drunkenness /'drʌŋknnɪs/ *n., no pl.* **(a)** (temporary) Betrunkenheit, *die;* **(b)** (habitual) Trunksucht, *die*
dry /draɪ/ **1** *adj.*, **drier** /'draɪə(r)/, **driest** /'draɪɪst/ **(a)** trocken, (not fresh) trocken; (~) herb ‹*Wein*›; ausgetrocknet ‹*Fluss, Flussbett*›; **go** ~: austrocknen; **as** ~ **as a bone** völlig trocken; ~ **shave/shampoo** Trockenrasur, *die/* -shampoo, *das;* **(b)** (not rainy) trocken ‹*Wetter, Klima*›; **(c)** (coll.: thirsty) durstig; **I'm a bit** ~: ich habe eine trockene Kehle; **(d)** ausgetrocknet, versiegt ‹*Brunnen*›; **(e)** (fig.) trocken ‹*Humor*›; (impassive, cold) kühl ‹*Art, Bemerkung usw.*›; **(f)** (dull) trocken ‹*Stoff, Bericht, Vorlesung*›. **2** *v.t.* **(a)** trocknen ‹*Haare, Wäsche*›; abtrocknen ‹*Geschirr, Baby*›; ~ **oneself** sich abtrocknen; ~ **one's eyes** *or* **tears/ hands** sich (*Dat.*) die Tränen abwischen/die Hände abtrocknen; **(b)** (preserve) trocknen ‹*Kräuter, Holz, Blumen*›; dörren ‹*Obst, Fleisch*›. **3** *v.i.* trocknen; trocken werden
~ **'out 1** *v.t.* **(a)** trocknen; **(b)** einer Entziehungskur unterziehen ‹*Alkoholiker, Drogenabhängigen*›. **2** *v.i.* trocknen
~ **'up 1** *v.t.* abtrocknen. **2** *v.i.* **(a)** (~ the dishes) abtrocknen; **(b)** ‹*Brunnen, Quelle:*› versiegen; ‹*Fluss, Teich:*› austrocknen; **(c)** (fig.) ‹*Ideen, Erfindergeist:*› versiegen
dry: ~**'clean** *v.t.* chemisch reinigen; **have sth.** ~**-cleaned** etw. in die Reinigung geben; ~**'cleaners** *n. pl.* chemische Reinigung; ~**'cleaning** *n.* chemische Reinigung; ~ **'dock** *n.* Trockendock, *das*
dryer ⇨ **drier²**
drying-'up *n.* Abtrocknen, *das;* **do the** ~: abtrocknen; *attrib.* ~**-up cloth** Geschirrtuch, *das*
dry 'land *n.* Festland, *das;* **be back on** ~: wieder festen Boden unter den Füßen haben

dryness /'draɪnɪs/ *n., no pl.* (lit. or fig.) Trockenheit, *die*

dry: ~ **'rot** *n.* Trockenfäule, *die;* ~ **'run** *n.* (coll.) Probelauf, *der*

DSS *abbr.* (Brit.) **Department of Social Security** Amt für Sozialwesen

DTI *abbr.* (Brit.) **Department of Trade and Industry**

dual /dju:əl/ *adj.* doppelt; Doppel-; ~ **role/function** Doppelrolle, *die/*-funktion, *die*

dual: ~ **'carriageway** *n.* (Brit.) zweispurige Straße; ~-**'purpose** *adj.* zweifach verwendbar

dub¹ /dʌb/ *v.t.* **-bb-** (Cinemat.) synchronisieren

dub² *v.t.* **-bb-:** (a) ~ **sb.** [a] **knight** jmdn. zum Ritter schlagen; (b) (call, nickname) titulieren

dubious /'dju:bɪəs/ *adj.* (a) (doubting) unschlüssig; **I'm** ~ **about accepting the invitation** ich weiß nicht recht, ob ich die Einladung annehmen soll; (b) (suspicious, questionable) zweifelhaft

dubiously /'dju:bɪəslɪ/ *adv.* (a) (doubtingly) unschlüssig; (b) (suspiciously) dubios

duchess /'dʌtʃɪs/ *n.* ▶ 1152 | Herzogin, *die*

duchy /'dʌtʃɪ/ *n.* Herzogtum, *das*

duck /dʌk/ **1** *n.* (a) *pl.* ~**s** *or* (collect.) *same* Ente, *die;* **wild** ~: Wildente, *die;* **it was [like] water off a** ~**'s back** (fig.) das lief alles an ihm/ihr *usw.* ab; **take to sth. like a** ~ **to water** bei etw. gleich in seinem Element sein; (b) (Brit. coll.: *my*) ~: Schätzchen; (c) (Cricket) **be out for a** ~: ohne einen Punkt zu machen aus sein. **2** *v.i.* (a) (bend down) sich [schnell] ducken; (b) (coll.: move hastily) türmen (ugs.). **3** *v.t.* (a) ~ **sb.** [**in water**] jmdn. untertauchen; (b) ~ **one's head** den Kopf einziehen

duck: ~**boards** *n. pl.* Lattenrost, *der;* ~-**egg** *n.* Entenei, *das*

duckie /'dʌkɪ/ ⇒ **duck 1 b**

ducking /'dʌkɪŋ/ *n.* [Ein-, Unter]tauchen, *das;* **give sb. a** ~: jmdn. untertauchen

duckling /'dʌklɪŋ/ *n.* Entenküken, *das;* (as food) junge Ente

'duck pond *n.* Ententeich, *der*

duct /dʌkt/ *n.* (for fluid, gas, cable) [Rohr]leitung, *die;* Rohr, *das;* (for air) Ventil, *das*

dud /dʌd/ (coll.) **1** *n.* (a) (useless thing) Niete, *die* (ugs.); (counterfeit) Fälschung, *die;* (banknote) Blüte, *die* (ugs.); **this battery/ballpoint is a** ~: diese Batterie/dieser Kugelschreiber taugt nichts; (b) (bomb etc.) Blindgänger, *der.* **2** *adj.* (a) mies (ugs.); schlecht; (fake) gefälscht; **a** ~ **banknote** eine Blüte (ugs.); (b) **a** ~ **bullet/shell/bomb** ein Blindgänger

dude /du:d/ *n.* (Amer. sl.) feiner Pinkel aus der Stadt (ugs.)

dudgeon /'dʌdʒn/ *n.* **in high** ~: äußerst empört

due /dju:/ **1** *adj.* (a) (owed) geschuldet; zustehend ⟨*Eigentum, Recht usw.*⟩; **the share/reward** ~ **to him** der Anteil, der/die Belohnung, die ihm zusteht; **the amount** ~: der zu zahlende Betrag; **there's sth.** ~ **to me, I've got sth.** ~, **I'm** ~ **for sth.** mir steht etw. zu; (b) (immediately payable, lit. or fig.) fällig; **be more than** ~ (fig.) überfällig sein; (c) (that it is proper to give, use) gebührend; geziemend (geh.); angemessen ⟨*Belohnung*⟩; reiflich ⟨*Überlegung*⟩; **be** ~ **to sb.** jmdm. gebühren; **recognition** ~ **to sb.** Anerkennung, die jmdm. gebührt; **with all** ~ **respect, madam** bei allem gebotenen Respekt, meine Dame; **with** ~ **allowance** *or* **regard** unter gebührender Berücksichtigung (**for** *Gen.*); **with** ~ **caution/care** mit der nötigen Vorsicht/Sorgfalt; **they were given** ~ **warning** sie wurden hinreichend gewarnt; **in** ~ **time** rechtzeitig; (d) (attributable) ~ **to negligence** aufgrund von Nachlässigkeit; **the mistake was** ~ **to negligence** der Fehler war durch Nachlässigkeit verursacht; **it's** ~ **to her that we missed the train** ihretwegen verpassten wir den Zug; **be** ~ **to the fact that** ...: darauf zurückzuführen sein, dass ...; (e) (scheduled, expected, under instructions) **be** ~ **to do sth.** etw. tun sollen; **I'm** ~ (my plan is) **to leave tomorrow** ich werde morgen abfahren; **be** ~ [**to arrive**] ankommen sollen; **the train is now** ~: planmäßig müßte der Zug jetzt ankommen; **when are we** ~ **to land?** wann landen wir?; **the baby is** ~ **in two weeks' time** das Baby kommt in zwei Wochen; (**f**) (likely to get, deserving) **be** ~ **for sth.** etw. verdienen; **he is** ~ **for promotion** seine Beförderung ist fällig. **2** *adv.* (a) ▶ 715 | ~ **north** genau nach Norden; (b) ~ **to** auf Grund (+ *Gen.*); aufgrund (+ *Gen.*). **3** *n.* (a) *in pl.* (debt) Schulden *Pl.;* **pay one's** ~**s** seine Schulden bezahlen; (b) *no pl.* (fig.: just deserts, reward) **sb.'s** ~: das, was jmdm. zusteht; **that was no more than his** ~: das hatte er auch verdient; **give sb. his** ~: jmdm. Gerechtigkeit widerfahren lassen; (c) *usu. in pl.* (fee) Gebühr, *die;* **membership** ~**s** Mitgliedsbeiträge *Pl.*

duel /'dju:əl/ **1** *n.* (a) Duell, *das;* (Univ.) Mensur, *die;* **fight a** ~: ein Duell/eine Mensur austragen; (b) (fig.: contest) Kampf, *der;* ~ **of wits** geistiger Wettstreit. **2** *v.i.* (Brit.) **-ll-** sich duellieren; (Univ.) eine Mensur austragen *od.* schlagen

duet /dju:'et/ *n.* (Mus.) (for voices) Duett, *das;* (instrumental) Duo, *das*

duffle /'dʌfl/: ~ **bag** *n.* Matchbeutel, *der;* (waterproof, also) Seesack, *der;* ~ **coat** *n.* Dufflecoat, *der*

dug ⇒ **dig 1, 2**

'dugout *n.* (a) (canoe) Einbaum, *der;* (b) (Mil.) Unterstand, *der*

duke /dju:k/ *n.* ▶ 1152 | Herzog, *der*

dukedom /'dju:kdəm/ *n.* (a) (territory) Herzogtum, *das;* (b) (rank) Herzogwürde, *die*

dulcimer /'dʌlsɪmə(r)/ *n.* (Mus.) Hackbrett, *das*

dull /dʌl/ **1** *adj.* (a) (stupid) beschränkt; (slow to understand) begriffsstutzig (abwertend); (b) (boring) langweilig; stumpfsinnig ⟨*Arbeit, Routine*⟩; (c) (gloomy) trübe ⟨*Wetter, Tag*⟩; (d) (not bright) matt, stumpf ⟨*Farbe, Glanz, Licht, Metall*⟩; trübe ⟨*Augen*⟩; blind ⟨*Spiegel*⟩; (not sharp) dumpf ⟨*Geräusch, Aufprall, Schmerz, Gefühl*⟩; (e) (listless) lustlos; (f) (blunt) stumpf. **2** *v.t.* (a) (make less acute) schwächen; trüben; betäuben ⟨*Schmerz*⟩; (b) (make less bright or sharp) stumpf werden lassen; verblassen lassen ⟨*Farbe*⟩; (c) (blunt) stumpf machen; (d) (fig.) dämpfen ⟨*Freude, Enthusiasmus*⟩; abstumpfen ⟨*Geist, Sinne, Verstand, Vorstellungskraft*⟩

dullness /'dʌlnɪs/ *n., no pl.* (a) (stupidity) Beschränktheit, *die;* (slow-wittedness) Begriffsstutzigkeit, *die* (abwertend); [geistige] Trägheit; (b) (boringness) Langweiligkeit, *die;* (of work, life, routine) Stumpfsinn, *der;* (c) (of colour, light, metal) Stumpfheit, *die;* Mattheit, *die*

dull-witted /dʌl'wɪtɪd/ ⇒ **dull 1 a**

duly /'dju:lɪ/ *adv.* (a) (rightly, properly) ordnungsgemäß; (b) (sufficiently) ausreichend; hinreichend

dumb /dʌm/ **1** *adj.,* ~**er** /'dʌmə(r)/, ~**est** /'dʌmɪst/ (a) stumm; **a** ~ **person** ein Stummer/eine Stumme; ~ **animals** *or* **creatures** die Tiere; **die stumme Kreatur** (dichter.); **he was [struck]** ~ **with amazement** vor Staunen verschlug es ihm die Sprache; (b) (coll.: stupid) doof (ugs.); **act** ~: sich dumm stellen; **a** ~ **blonde** eine dümmliche Blondine (ugs.). **2** *n. pl.* **the** ~: die Stummen; **the deaf and** ~: die Taubstummen

'dumb-bell *n.* Hantel, *die*

dumbfound /dʌm'faʊnd/ *v.t.* sprachlos machen; verblüffen

dumbfounded /dʌm'faʊndɪd/ *adj.* sprachlos; verblüfft

dumb: ~ **show** *n.* **in** ~ **show** durch Mimik; ~ **'waiter** *n.* (a) (trolley) stummer Diener; (b) (lift) Speisenaufzug, *der*

dummy /'dʌmɪ/ **1** *n.* (a) (of tailor) Schneiderpuppe, *die;* (in shop) Modepuppe, *die;* Schaufensterpuppe, *die;* (of ventriloquist) Puppe, *die;* (coll.: stupid person) Dummkopf, *der* (ugs.); Doofi, *der* (ugs.); **like a stuffed** ~: wie ein Ölgötze (ugs.); (b) (imitation) Attrappe, *die;* Dummy, *der;* (Commerc.) Schaupackung, *die;* (esp. Brit.: for baby) Schnuller, *der.* **2** *attrib. adj.* unecht; blind ⟨*Tür, Fenster*⟩; Übungs- (Mil.); ~ **gun** Gewehrattrappe, *die;* ~ **run** Probelauf, *der*

dump /dʌmp/ **1** *n.* (a) (place) Müllkippe, *die;* (heap) Müllhaufen, *der;* (permanent) Müllhalde, *die;* (b) (Mil.) Depot, *das;* Lager, *das;* (c) (coll. derog.: unpleasant place) Dreckloch, *das* (salopp abwertend); (boring town) Kaff, *das* (ugs. abwertend). **2** *v.t.* (a) (dispose of) werfen; (deposit) abladen, kippen ⟨*Sand, Müll usw.*⟩; (leave) lassen; (place) abstellen; (b) (Commerc.: send abroad) zu Dumpingpreisen verkaufen; (c) (fig. coll.: abandon) abladen (ugs.)

dumpling /'dʌmplɪŋ/ n. (a) (Gastr.) Kloß, der; **apple** ∼: Apfel im Schlafrock; (b) (coll.: short, plump person) Tönnchen, das (ugs.)

dumps /dʌmps/ n. pl. (coll.) **be** or **feel [down] in the** ∼: ganz down sein (ugs.)

'dump truck n. Kipper, der

dumpy /'dʌmpɪ/ adj. pummelig (ugs.)

dun /dʌn/ 1 adj. graubraun. 2 n. Graubraun, das

dunce /dʌns/ n. Niete, die (ugs. abwertend); **the** ∼ **of the class** das Schlusslicht der Klasse (ugs.); ∼'s **cap** (Hist.) Spotthut, der (für schlechte Schüler)

dune /dju:n/ n. Düne, die

dung /dʌŋ/ n. Dung, der; Mist, der

dungarees /dʌŋgə'ri:z/ n. pl. Latzhose, die; **a pair of** ∼: eine Latzhose

dungeon /'dʌndʒn/ n. Kerker, der; Verlies, das

'dunghill n. Misthaufen, der

dunk /dʌŋk/ v.t. tunken; stippen (bes. nordd.)

duo /'dju:əʊ/ n., pl. ∼**s** Paar, das; **comedy** ∼: Komikerpaar, das

duodenal /dju:ə'di:nl/ adj. (Anat.) duodenal (fachspr.); Zwölffingerdarm-

duodenum /dju:ə'di:nəm/ n. (Anat.) Duodenum, das (fachspr.); Zwölffingerdarm, der

dupe /dju:p/ 1 v.t. düpieren (geh.); übertölpeln; **be** ∼**d [into doing sth.]** sich übertölpeln lassen [und etw. tun]. 2 n. Dumme, der/die; Gelackmeierte, der/die (salopp scherzh.)

duplex /'dju:pleks/ adj. (esp. Amer.) (two-storey) zweistöckig ⟨Wohnung⟩; (two-family) Zweifamilien⟨haus⟩

duplicate 1 /'dju:plɪkət/ adj. (a) (identical) Zweit; ∼ **key** Nach- od. Zweitschlüssel, der; ∼ **copy** Zweit- od. Abschrift, die; Doppel, das; (b) (twofold) doppelt. 2 /'dju:plɪkət/ n. (a) Kopie, die; (second copy of letter/document/key) Duplikat, das; (b) **prepare/complete sth. in** ∼: etw. in doppelter Ausfertigung machen/ausfüllen. 3 /'dju:plɪkeɪt/ v.t. (a) (make a copy of, make in ∼) ∼ **sth.** eine zweite Anfertigung von etw. machen; etw. nachmachen (ugs.); (b) (be exact copy of) genau gleichen (+ Dat.); (c) (on machine) vervielfältigen; (d) (unnecessarily) [unnötigerweise] noch einmal tun

duplication /dju:plɪ'keɪʃn/ n. Wiederholung, die

duplicator /'dju:plɪkeɪtə(r)/ n. Vervielfältigungsgerät, das

duplicity /dju:'plɪsɪtɪ/ n. Falschheit, die

durability /djʊərə'bɪlɪtɪ/ n., no pl. (a) (of friendship, peace, etc.) Dauerhaftigkeit, die; (of person) Unverwüstlichkeit, die; (b) (of garment, material) Haltbarkeit, die; Strapazierfähigkeit, die

durable /'djʊərəbl/ 1 adj. (a) dauerhaft ⟨Friede, Freundschaft usw.⟩; (b) (resisting wear) solide; strapazierfähig, haltbar ⟨Kleidung, Stoff⟩; widerstandsfähig ⟨Metall, Bauelement⟩; ∼ **goods** ⇒ 2. 2 n. in pl. **consumer** ∼**s** langlebige Konsumgüter

duration /djʊə'reɪʃn/ n. Dauer, die; **be of short/long** ∼: von kurzer/langer Dauer sein

duress /djʊə'res, 'djʊəres/ n., no pl. Zwang, der

during /'djʊərɪŋ/ prep. während; (at a point in) in (+ Dat.); ∼ **the night** während od. in der Nacht

dusk /dʌsk/ n. [Abend]dämmerung, die; Einbruch der Dunkelheit; **at** ∼: bei Einbruch der Dunkelheit

dusky /'dʌskɪ/ adj. dunkelhäutig ⟨Person, Schönheit⟩

dust /dʌst/ 1 n., no pl. Staub, der. See also **bite** 1; **raise** 1 b. 2 v.t. (a) abstauben ⟨Möbel⟩; ∼ **a room/ house** in einem Zimmer/Haus Staub wischen; (sprinkle; also Cookery) ∼ **sth. with sth.** etw. mit etw. bestäuben; (with talc etc.) etw. mit etw. pudern. 3 v.i. Staub wischen

dust: ∼**bin** n. (Brit.) Mülltonne, die; Abfalltonne, die; ∼**cart** n. (Brit.) Müllwagen, der; ∼ **cover** n. (on record player) Abdeckhaube, die; (on book) ⇒ **dust jacket**

duster /'dʌstə(r)/ n. Staubtuch, das

dusting /'dʌstɪŋ/ n. ⇒ **dust** 2 a: Abstauben, das; Staubwischen, das; **give a room a** ∼: in einem Zimmer Staub wischen

dust: ∼ **jacket** n. Schutzumschlag, der; ∼**man** /'dʌstmən/ n., pl. ∼**men** /'dʌstmən/ ▶887⏐ (Brit.)

Müllwerker, der; Müllmann, der; ∼**pan** n. Kehrschaufel, die; ∼ **sheet** n. Staubdecke, die; ∼**trap** n. Staubfänger, der (abwertend); ∼**-up** n. (coll.) Krach, der (ugs.)

dusty /'dʌstɪ/ adj. staubig ⟨Straße, Stadt, Zimmer⟩; verstaubt ⟨Bücher, Möbel⟩

Dutch /dʌtʃ/ ▶897⏐, ▶947⏐ 1 adj. (a) holländisch; niederländisch; **sb. is** ∼: jmd. ist Holländer/Holländerin; (b) **go** ∼ **[with sb.] [on sth.]** (coll.) getrennte Kasse [mit jmdm.] [bei etw.] machen. 2 n. (a) constr. as pl. **the** ∼: die Holländer od. Niederländer; (b) (language) Holländisch, das; Niederländisch, das; (c) **it was all double** ∼ **to him** das waren alles böhmische Dörfer für ihn. See also **English** 2 a

Dutch: ∼ **'auction** ⇒ **auction** 1 a; ∼ **'barn** n. offene Scheune; ∼ **'courage** n. angetrunkener Mut; **give oneself** or **get** ∼ **courage** sich (Dat.) Mut antrinken; ∼ **'elm disease** n. (Bot.) Ulmensterben, das; ∼**man** /'dʌtʃmən/ n., pl. ∼**men** /'dʌtʃmən/ (a) Holländer, der; Niederländer, der; (b) (fig. coll.) **or I'm a** ∼**man** wenn ich will Emil heißen (ugs.); ∼**woman** n. Holländerin, die; Niederländerin, die

dutiable /'dju:tɪəbl/ adj. (Customs) zollpflichtig; abgabenpflichtig

dutiful /'dju:tɪfl/ adj. pflichtbewusst ⟨Ehefrau, Arbeiter, Bürger⟩

duty /'dju:tɪ/ n. (a) no pl. (obligation) Pflicht, die; Verpflichtung, die; ∼ **calls** die Pflicht ruft; **have a** ∼ **to do sth.** die Pflicht haben, etw. zu tun; **do one's** ∼ **[by sb.]** [jmdm. gegenüber] seine Pflicht [und Schuldigkeit] tun; (b) (specific task, esp. professional) Aufgabe, die; Pflicht, die; **take up one's duties** seinen Dienst antreten; **your duties will consist of ...:** zu Ihren Aufgaben gehören ...; **the** ∼**nurse** die Dienst habende Schwester; **on** ∼: im Dienst; **be on** ∼: Dienst haben; **go/come on** ∼ **at 7 p.m.** um 19 Uhr seinen Dienst antreten; **off** ∼: nicht im Dienst; **be off** ∼: keinen Dienst haben; ⟨ab ... Uhr⟩ dienstfrei sein; **go/come off** ∼ **at 8 a.m.** seinen Dienst um 8 Uhr beenden; attrib. ∼ **chemist** Apotheke, die Nachtdienst hat; **which is the** ∼ **chemist tonight?** welche Apotheke hat heute Nachtdienst?; (c) (Econ.: tax) Zoll, der; **pay** ∼ **on sth.** Zoll für etw. bezahlen; etw. verzollen

duty: ∼**-bound** adj. **be/feel [oneself]** ∼**-bound to do sth.** verpflichtet sein/sich verpflichtet fühlen, etw. zu tun; ∼**-free** adj. zollfrei ⟨Ware, Preis⟩; ∼**-frees** n. pl. (coll.) zollfreie Waren Pl.; ∼**-free 'shop** n. Duty-free-Shop, der; ∼ **officer** n. (Mil.) Offizier vom Dienst

duvet /'du:veɪ/ n. Federbett, das; ∼ **cover** Bettbezug, der

dwarf /dwɔ:f/ 1 n., pl. ∼**s** or **dwarves** /dwɔ:vz/ (a) (person) Liliputaner, der/Liliputanerin, die; Zwerg, der/Zwergin, die (auch abwertend); (b) (Mythol.) Zwerg, der/Zwergin, die. 2 adj. Zwerg⟨baum, -stern⟩. 3 v.t. (a) (cause to look small) klein erscheinen lassen; (b) (fig.) in den Schatten stellen

dweeb /dwi:b/ n. (esp. Amer. sl.) trübe Tasse (ugs. abwertend)

dwell /dwel/ v.i., **dwelt** /dwelt/ (literary) wohnen; weilen (geh.)
∼ **[up]on** v.t. (in discussion) sich länger od. ausführlich befassen mit; (in thought) in Gedanken verweilen bei

dwelling /'dwelɪŋ/ n. (Admin. lang./literary) Wohnung, die

'dwelling place n. Wohnsitz, der

dwelt ⇒ **dwell**

dwindle /'dwɪndl/ v.i. ∼ **[away]** abnehmen; ⟨Unterstützung, Interesse:⟩ nachlassen; ⟨Vorräte, Handel, Hoheitsgebiet:⟩ schrumpfen; ⟨Macht, Einfluss, Tageslicht:⟩ schwinden (geh.); ∼ **away to nothing** dahinschwinden

dye /daɪ/ 1 n. (a) (substance) Färbemittel, das; (b) (colour) Farbe, die. 2 v.t., ∼**ing** /'daɪɪŋ/ färben; ∼**d-in-the-wool** eingefleischt, (ugs.) in der Wolle gefärbt ⟨Konservative, Reaktionär usw.⟩

'dyestuff n. Färbemittel, das

dying /'daɪɪŋ/ 1 adj. (a) sterbend ⟨Person, Tier⟩; eingehend ⟨Pflanze⟩; absterbend ⟨Baum⟩; aussterbend ⟨Kunst, Kultur, Tradition, [Tier]art, Menschenschlag⟩; zu Ende gehend ⟨Jahr⟩; (b) (related to time of death) letzt...; **to my** ∼ **day** bis an mein Lebensende. 2 n. pl. **the** ∼: die Sterbenden. See also **die**¹

dyke ⇨ **dike**

dynamic /daɪ'næmɪk/ *adj.*, **dynamically** /daɪ'næmɪkəlɪ/ *adv.* (lit. or fig.; also Mus.) dynamisch

dynamism /'daɪnəmɪzm/ *n.* Dynamik, *die*

dynamite /'daɪnəmaɪt/ **1** *n.* **(a)** Dynamit, *das;* **(b)** (fig.: politically dangerous thing) Sprengstoff, *der;* **(c)** (fig.: sensational person or thing) **be** ~ ⟨*Person:*⟩ eine Wucht sein (salopp); ⟨*Sache:*⟩ eine Sensation sein. **2** *v.t.* mit Dynamit sprengen

dynamo /'daɪnəməʊ/ *n., pl.* ~**s** Dynamomaschine, *die;* (of car) Lichtmaschine, *die;* (of bicycle) Dynamo, *der*

dynasty /'dɪnəstɪ/ *n.* (lit. or fig.) Dynastie, *die*

dysentery /'dɪsəntərɪ/ *n.* ▶865│ (Med.) Ruhr, *die;* Dysenterie, *die* (fachspr.)

dysfunctional /dɪs'fʌŋkʃənl/ *adj.* [funktions]gestört ⟨*Modem, Telefonleitung*⟩; **a** ~ **family** eine nicht [mehr] intakte Familie

dyslexia /dɪs'leksɪə/ *n.* (Med., Psych.) Dyslexie, *die* (fachspr.); Lesestörung, *die*

dyslexic /dɪs'leksɪk/ (Med., Psych.) **1** *adj.* dyslektisch (fachspr.); **a** ~ **child** ein Kind mit einer Lesestörung. **2** *n.* Dyslektiker, *der*/Dyslektikerin, *die* (fachspr.); Mensch mit einer Lesestörung

dyspepsia /dɪs'pepsɪə/ *n.* ▶865│ (Med.) Dyspepsie, *die* (fachspr.); Verdauungsstörung, *die*

∙∙∙

∙∙∙

E, e /iː/ *n., pl.* **Es** *or* **E's** **(a)** (letter) E, e, *das;* **(b)** E (Mus.) E, e, *das;* **E flat** es, Es, *das*

E. *abbr.* **(a)** ▶715│ **east** O; **(b)** ▶715│ **eastern** ö; **(c)** (sl.) **Ecstasy** E; XTC

each /iːtʃ/ **1** *adj.* jeder/jede/jedes; **they cost** *or* **are a pound** ~: sie kosten ein Pfund pro Stück *od.* je[weils] ein Pfund; **they** ~ **have …**: sie haben jeder …; jeder von ihnen hat …; **books at £1** ~: Bücher zu je einem Pfund *od.* für je ein Pfund; **two teams with 10 players** ~: zwei Mannschaften mit je 10 Spielern; **I gave them a book** ~ *or* ~ **a book** ich habe jedem von ihnen ein Buch *od.* ihnen je ein Buch gegeben; ~ **one of them** jeder/jede/jedes einzelne von ihnen. **2** *pron.* **(a)** jeder/jede/jedes; **have some of** ~: von jedem etwas nehmen/haben; **(b)** ~ **other** sich [gegenseitig]; **they are cross with** ~ **other** sie sind böse aufeinander; **they wore** ~ **other's hats** jeder trug den Hut des anderen; **be in love with** ~ **other** ineinander verliebt sein; **live next door to** ~ **other** Tür an Tür wohnen

eager /'iːgə(r)/ *adj.* eifrig; **be** ~ **to do sth.** etw. unbedingt tun wollen; **be** ~ **for sth.** etw. unbedingt haben wollen

eagerly /'iːgəlɪ/ *adv.* eifrig ⟨*ja sagen, zustimmen*⟩; gespannt, ungeduldig ⟨*warten, aufblicken*⟩; **look forward** ~ **to sth.** sich sehr auf etw. (*Akk.*) freuen

eagerness /'iːgənɪs/ *n., no pl.* Eifer, *der;* ~ **to learn** Lerneifer, *der;* Lernbegier[de], *die;* ~ **to succeed** Erfolgshunger, *der*

eagle /'iːgl/ *n.* Adler, *der*

'eagle-eyed *adj.* adleräugig

ear¹ /ɪə(r)/ *n.* **(a)** ▶672│ Ohr, *das;* ~**, nose, and throat hospital/specialist** Hals-Nasen-Ohren-Klinik, *die*/-Arzt, *der*/-Ärztin, *die;* **smile from** ~ **to** ~: von einem Ohr zum anderen strahlen (ugs.); **be out on one's** ~ (fig. coll.) auf der Straße stehen (ugs.); **up to one's** ~**s in work/debt** bis zum Hals in Arbeit/Schulden; **have a word in sb.'s** ~: jmdm. ein Wort im Vertrauen sagen; **keep one's** ~**s open** (fig.) die Ohren offenhalten; **have/keep an** ~ **to the ground** sein Ohr ständig am Puls der Masse haben (ugs. scherzh.); **be[come] all** ~**s** [plötzlich] ganz Ohr sein; **go in [at] one** ~ **and out [at] the other** (coll.) zum einen Ohr herein, zum anderen wieder hinausgehen; **(b)** *no pl.*

(sense) Gehör, *das;* **have an** ~ *or* **a good** ~/**no** ~ **for music** ein [gutes]/kein Gehör für Musik haben; **play by** ~ (Mus.) nach dem Gehör spielen; *see also* **play 3 a**

ear² *n.* (Bot.) Ähre, *die;* ~ **of corn** Kornähre, *die*

ear: ~**ache** *n.* ▶865│ (Med.) Ohrenschmerzen *Pl.;* ~**drum** *n.* ▶672│(Anat.) Trommelfell, *das*

earl /ɜːl/ *n.* ▶1152│ Graf, *der*

'earlobe *n.* ▶672│ Ohrläppchen, *das*

early /'ɜːlɪ/ **1** *adj.* früh; **I am a bit** ~: ich bin etwas zu früh gekommen (ugs.) dran; **the train was 10 minutes** ~: der Zug kam 10 Minuten zu früh; **have an** ~ **night** früh ins Bett gehen; ~ **riser** Frühaufsteher, *der*/-aufsteherin, *die;* **at the earliest** frühestens; **in the** ~ **afternoon/evening** am frühen Nachmittag/Abend; **into the** ~ **hours** bis in die frühen Morgenstunden; **at/from an** ~ **age** in jungen Jahren/von klein auf; **at an** ~ **stage, in its** ~ **stages** im Frühstadium; **an** ~ **work of an author** ein Frühwerk eines Autors. **2** *adv.* früh; ~ **next week** Anfang der nächsten Woche; ~ **next Wednesday** nächsten Mittwoch früh; ~ **in June** Anfang Juni; **as** ~ **as tomorrow** schon *od.* bereits morgen; **the earliest I can come is Friday** ich kann frühestens Freitag kommen; ~ **on** schon früh; **earlier on this week/year** früher in der Woche/im Jahr

early: ~ **bird** *n.* (joc.) jmd., der etw. frühzeitig tut; (getting up) Frühaufsteher, *der*/-aufsteherin, *die;* **the** ~ **bird catches the worm** (prov.) Morgenstunde hat Gold im Munde (Spr.); ~ **'closing** *n.* **it is** ~ **closing** die Geschäfte haben nachmittags geschlossen; ~**-'closing day** *n.* Tag, an dem die Geschäfte nachmittags geschlossen haben; ~**-'warning** *attrib. adj.* Frühwarn-

ear: ~**mark** *v.t.* (fig.) vorsehen; ~**muffs** *n. pl.* Ohrenschützer *Pl.*

earn /ɜːn/ *v.t.* **(a)** ⟨*Person, Tat, Benehmen:*⟩ verdienen; ~**ed income** Einkommen aus Arbeit; **it** ~**ed him much respect** es trug ihm viel Respekt ein; **(b)** (bring in as income or interest) einbringen; **(c)** (incur) eintragen; einbringen

earner /'ɜːnə(r)/ *n.* **be a nice little** ~ (coll.) ganz schön was einbringen (ugs.)

earnest /'ɜːnɪst/ **1** *adj.* **(a)** (serious) ernsthaft; **(b)** (ardent) innig ⟨*Wunsch, Gebet, Hoffnung*⟩; leidenschaftlich ⟨*Appell*⟩. **2** *n.* **in** ~: mit vollem Ernst; **this time I'm in** ~ **[about it]** diesmal ist es mir Ernst *od.* meine ich es ernst [damit]

earnestly /'ɜːnɪstlɪ/ *adv.* ernsthaft

earnings /'ɜːnɪŋz/ *n. pl.* Verdienst, *der;* (of business etc.) Ertrag, *der*

ear: ~**phones** *n. pl.* Kopfhörer, *der;* ~**plug** *n.* Ohropax, *das* ⓌⓏ; ~**ring** *n.* Ohrring, *der;* ~**shot** *n.* **out of/within** ~**shot** außer/in Hörweite; ~**-splitting** *adj.* ohrenbetäubend

earth /ɜːθ/ **1** *n.* **(a)** (land, soil) Erde, *die;* (ground) Boden, *der;* **be brought/come down** *or* **back to** ~ **[with a bump]** (fig.) (schnell) wieder auf den Boden der Tatsachen zurückgeholt werden/zurückkommen; **(b)** *or* **E**~ (planet) Erde, *die;* **(c)** (world) Erde, *die;* **on** ~ (existing anywhere) auf der Welt; **nothing on** ~ **will stop me** keine Macht der Welt kann mich aufhalten; **how/what** *etc.* **on** ~ **…?** wie/was *usw.* in aller Welt …?; **who on** ~ **is that?** wer ist das bloß?; **what on** ~ **do you mean?** was meinst du denn nur?; **where on** ~ **has she got to?** wo ist sie denn bloß hingegangen?; **look like nothing on** ~ (be unrecognizable) nicht zu erkennen sein; (look repellent) furchtbar aussehen; **(d)** (of animal) Bau, *der;* **have gone to** ~ (fig.) untergetaucht sein; **run to** ~ (fig.) aufspüren; **(e)** (coll.) **charge/cost/pay the** ~: ein Vermögen *od.* (ugs.) eine ganze Stange Geld verlangen/kosten/bezahlen; **(f)** (Brit. Electr.) Erde, *die;* Erdung, *die.* **2** *v.t.* (Brit. Electr.) erden

~ **'up** *v.t.* mit Erde bedecken

earthenware /'ɜːθnweə(r)/ **1** *n., no pl.* (pots etc.) Tonwaren *Pl.* **2** *adj.* Ton-; tönern

earthly /'ɜːθlɪ/ *adj.* irdisch; **no** ~ **use** *etc.* (coll.) nicht der geringste Nutzen *usw.*

earth: ~**-moving** *adj.* ~**-moving vehicle** Fahrzeug für Erdarbeiten; ~**quake** *n.* Erdbeben, *das;* ~**shaking,** ~**-shattering** *adjs.* (fig.) weltbewegend; ~**worm** *n.* Regenwurm, *der*

earthy /'ɜːθɪ/ *adj.* (a) erdig; (b) derb ‹*Person*›

'earwax *n.* Ohrenschmalz, *das*

earwig /'ɪəwɪg/ *n.* Ohrwurm, *der*

ease /iːz/ **1** *n.* (a) (freedom from pain or trouble) Ruhe, *die;* (b) (leisure) Muße, *die;* (idleness) Müßiggang, *der;* (c) (freedom from constraint) Entspanntheit, *die;* **at** [**one's**] ~**:** entspannt; behaglich; **be** *or* **feel at** [**one's**] ~**:** sich wohl fühlen; **put** *or* **set sb. at his** ~**:** jmdn. die Befangenheit nehmen; (d) **with** ~ (without difficulty) mit Leichtigkeit. **2** *v.t.* (a) (relieve) lindern ‹*Schmerz, Kummer*›; (make lighter, easier) erleichtern ‹*Last*›; entspannen ‹*Lage*›; (b) (give mental ~ to) erleichtern; ~ **sb.'s mind** jmdn. beruhigen; (c) (relax, adjust) lockern ‹*Griff, Knoten*›; verringern ‹*Druck, Spannung, Geschwindigkeit*›; (d) (cause to move) behutsam bewegen; ~ **the clutch in** die Kupplung langsam kommen lassen; ~ **the cap off a bottle** eine Flasche vorsichtig öffnen. **3** *v.i.* (a) ‹*Belastung, Druck, Wind, Sturm:*› nachlassen; (b) ~ **off** *or* **up** (begin to take it easy) sich entspannen; (drive more slowly) ein bisschen langsamer fahren

easel /'iːzl/ *n.* Staffelei, *die*

easily /'iːzɪlɪ/ *adv.* (a) leicht; (b) (without doubt) zweifelsohne; **it is** ~ **a hundred metres deep** es ist gut und gerne hundert Meter tief

easiness /'iːzɪnɪs/ *n.* Leichtigkeit, *die*

east /iːst/ ▶**715** **1** *n.* (a) (direction) Osten, *der;* **the** ~**:** Ost (Met., Seew.); **in/to**[**wards**]**/from the** ~**:** im/nach/von Osten; **to the** ~ **of** östlich von; östlich (+ *Gen.*); (b) *usu.* **E**~ (also Polit.) Osten, *der;* **from the E**~**:** aus dem Osten. **2** *adj.* östlich; Ost‹*küste, -wind, -grenze, -tor*›. **3** *adv.* ostwärts; nach Osten; ~ **of** östlich von; östlich (+ *Gen.*)

East: ~ **'Africa** *pr. n.* Ostafrika (*das*); ~ **Ber'lin** *pr. n.* (Hist.) Ost-Berlin (*das*); **e**~**bound** *adj.* ▶**715** ‹*Zug, Verkehr usw.*› in Richtung Osten; ~ **'End** *n.* (Brit.) Londoner Osten

Easter /'iːstə(r)/ *n.* ▶**836** Ostern, *das od. Pl.;* **at** ~**:** [zu *od.* an] Ostern; **next/last** ~**:** nächste/letzte Ostern

Easter: ~ **'Day** *n.* Ostersonntag, *der;* ~ **egg** *n.* Osterei, *das*

easterly /'iːstəlɪ/ ▶**715** (a) (in position or direction) östlich; **in an** ~ **direction** nach Osten; (b) (from the east) ‹*Wind*› aus östlichen Richtungen

eastern /'iːstən/ *adj.* ▶**715** östlich; Ost‹*grenze, -hälfte, -seite*›; ~ **Germany** Ostdeutschland

Eastern 'Europe *pr. n.* Osteuropa (*das*)

easternmost /'iːstənməʊst/ *adj.* ▶**715** östlichst...

Easter: ~ **'Sunday** ⇒ **Easter Day;** ~ **week** *n.*, *no art.* Osterwoche, *die*

East: ~ **'German** (Hist.) **1** *adj.* ostdeutsch; **2** *n.* Ostdeutsche, *der/die;* ~ **'Germany** *pr. n.* (Hist.) Ostdeutschland (*das*)

eastward /'iːstwəd/ ▶**715** **1** *adj.* nach Osten gerichtet; (situated towards the east) östlich; **in an** ~ **direction** nach Osten; [in] Richtung Osten. **2** *adv.* ostwärts; **they are** ~**bound** sie fahren nach *od.* [in] Richtung Osten. **3** *n.* Osten, *der*

eastwards /'iːstwədz/ *adv.* ▶**715** ostwärts

easy /'iːzɪ/ **1** *adj.* (a) (not difficult) leicht; ~ **to clean/see** *etc.* leicht zu reinigen/sehen *usw.;* **it is** ~ **to see that ...:** es ist offensichtlich, dass ...; man sieht sofort, dass ...; **it's as** ~ **as anything** (coll.) es ist kinderleicht; **it is** ~ **for him to talk** er hat leicht *od.* gut reden; **on** ~ **terms** auf Raten ‹*kaufen*›; (b) (free from pain, anxiety, etc.) sorglos, angenehm ‹*Leben, Zeit*›; **make it** *or* **things** ~ **for sb.** es jmdm. leicht machen; (c) (free from constraint, strictness, etc.) ungezwungen; unbefangen ‹*Art*›; **he is** ~ **to get on with/work with** mit ihm kann man gut auskommen / zusammenarbeiten; **I'm** ~ (coll.) es ist mir egal. **2** *adv.* leicht; **easier said than done** leichter gesagt als getan; ~ **does it** immer langsam *od.* sachte; **go** ~**:** vorsichtig sein; **go** ~ **on** *or* **with** sparsam umgehen mit; **go** ~ **on** *or* **with sb.**

mit jmdm. nachsichtig sein; **take it** ~**!** (calm down!) beruhige dich!; **take it** *or* **things** *or* **life** ~**:** sich nicht übernehmen

easy: ~ **'chair** *n.* Sessel, *der;* ~**going** *adj.* (calm, placid) gelassen; (lax) nachlässig

eat /iːt/ **1** *v.t.*, **ate** /et, eɪt/, **eaten** /'iːtn/ (a) ‹*Person:*› essen; ‹*Tier:*› fressen; **he won't** ~ **you!** (fig.) er wird dich schon nicht fressen (ugs.); ~ **sb. out of house and home** jmdn. arm essen; **what's** ~**ing you?** (coll.) was hast du denn?; ~ **one's words** seine Worte zurücknehmen; (b) (destroy, consume, make hole in) fressen; ~ **its way into/through sth.** sich in etw. (*Akk.*) hineinfressen/durch etw. hindurchfressen. **2** *v.i.*, **ate, eaten** (a) ‹*Person:*› essen; ‹*Tier:*› fressen; (b) (make a way by gnawing or corrosion) ~ **into** sich hineinfressen in (+ *Akk.*); ~ **through** sich durchfressen durch

~ **'out** *v.i.* essen gehen

~ **'up 1** *v.t.* (a) (consume) ‹*Person:*› aufessen; ‹*Tier:*› auffressen; (b) (traverse rapidly) **our car** ~**s up the miles** unser Auto frisst die Meilen nur so (ugs.). **2** *v.i.* aufessen

eatable /'iːtəbl/ *adj.* genießbar; essbar

eaten ⇒ **eat**

eater /'iːtə(r)/ *n.* Esser, *der*/Esserin, *die;* **a big** ~**:** ein guter Esser

eating /'iːtɪŋ/ *n.* Essen, *das;* **make good** ~**:** ein gutes Essen sein; **not for** ~**:** nicht zum Essen [geeignet]

eating: ~ **apple** *n.* Essapfel, *der;* ~ **disorder** *n.* Essstörung, *die* (*meist Pl.*)*;* ~ **habits** *n. pl.* Essgewohnheiten *Pl.*

eau-de-Cologne /əʊdəkə'ləʊn/ *n.* Eau de Cologne, *das;* Kölnisch Wasser, *das*

eaves /iːvz/ *n. pl.* Dachgesims, *das*

eaves: ~**drop** *v.i.* lauschen; ~**drop on sth./sb.** etw./jmdn. belauschen; ~**dropper** /'iːvsdrɒpə(r)/ *n.* Lauscher, *der*/Lauscherin, *die*

ebb /eb/ **1** *n.* (a) (of tide) Ebbe, *die;* **the tide is on the** ~**:** es ist Ebbe; (b) (decline, decay) Niedergang, *der;* **their morale was at its lowest** ~**:** ihre Moral war auf dem Tiefpunkt angelangt; **the** ~ **and flow** das Auf und Ab. **2** *v.i.* (a) (flow back) zurückgehen; (b) (recede, decline) schwinden; ~ **away** dahinschwinden

'ebb tide *n.* Ebbe, *die*

ebony /'ebənɪ/ **1** *n.* Ebenholz, *das.* **2** *adj.* Ebenholz‹*baum*›; ebenholzfarben ‹*Haar, Haut*›; ~ **box** *etc.* Kiste *usw.* aus Ebenholz

ebullient /ɪ'bʌlɪənt, ɪ'bʊlənt/ *adj.* überschwänglich; überschäumend ‹*Temperament, Laune*›

EC *abbr.* **European Community** EG

eccentric /ɪk'sentrɪk/ **1** *adj.* exzentrisch. **2** *n.* Exzentriker, *der*/Exzentrikerin, *die*

eccentricity /eksən'trɪsɪtɪ/ *n.* Exzentrizität, *die*

ecclesiastical /ɪkliːzɪ'æstɪkl/ *adj.* kirchlich; Kirchen‹*gebäude, -amt, -jahr*›; ~ **music** geistliche Musik; Kirchenmusik, *die*

echelon /'eʃəlɒn/ ⇒ **upper 1 b**

echo /'ekəʊ/ **1** *n., pl.* ~**es** (a) Echo, *das;* (b) (fig.) Anklang, *der* (**of** an + *Akk.*). **2** *v.i.* (a) ‹*Ort:*› hallen (**with** von); **it** ~**s in here** hier gibt es ein Echo; (b) ‹*Geräusch:*› widerhallen. **3** *v.t.* (a) (repeat) zurückwerfen; (b) (repeat words of) echoen; wiederholen; (imitate words or opinions of) widerspiegeln

éclair /eɪ'kleə(r)/ *n.* Eclair, *das*

eclipse /ɪ'klɪps/ **1** *n.* (Astron.) Eklipse, *die* (fachspr.); Finsternis, *die;* ~ **of the sun, solar** ~**:** Sonnenfinsternis, *die;* ~ **of the moon, lunar** ~**:** Mondfinsternis, *die.* **2** *v.t.* (a) verfinstern ‹*Sonne, Mond*›; (b) (fig.: outshine, surpass) in den Schatten stellen

eco-friendly /'iːkəʊfrendlɪ/ *adj.* umweltfreundlich

ecological /iːkə'lɒdʒɪkl/ *adj.* ökologisch

ecology /iː'kɒlədʒɪ/ *n.* Ökologie, *die*

economic /iːkə'nɒmɪk, ekə'nɒmɪk/ *adj.* (a) (of economics) Wirtschafts‹*politik, -system, -modell*›; ökonomisch, wirtschaftlich ‹*Entwicklung, Zusammenbruch*›; (b) (giving adequate return) wirtschaftlich ‹*Miete*›

economical /iːkə'nɒmɪkl, ekə'nɒmɪkl/ *adj.* wirtschaftlich; ökonomisch; sparsam ‹*Person*›; **be ~ with sth.** mit etw. haushalten; **the car is ~ to run** das Auto ist wirtschaftlich

economically /iːkə'nɒmɪkəli, ekə'nɒmɪkəli/ *adv.* (a) (with reference to economics) wirtschaftlich; (b) (not wastefully) sparsam; **be ~ minded** wirtschaftlich denken

economics /iːkə'nɒmɪks, ekə'nɒmɪks/ *n., no pl.* (a) Wirtschaftswissenschaft, *die* (*meist Pl.*); [politische] Ökonomie; (b) (economic considerations) wirtschaftlicher Aspekt

economise ⇒ **economize**

economist /ɪ'kɒnəmɪst/ *n.* ▶ 887 Wirtschaftswissenschaftler, *der*/-wissenschaftlerin, *die*

economize /ɪ'kɒnəmaɪz/ *v.i.* sparen; **~ on sth.** etw. sparen

economy /ɪ'kɒnəmi/ *n.* (a) (frugality) Sparsamkeit, *die;* (of effort, motion) Wirtschaftlichkeit, *die;* (b) (instance) Einsparung, *die;* **make economies** zu Sparmaßnahmen greifen; (c) (of country etc.) Wirtschaft, *die*

economy: ~ class *n.* Touristenklasse, *die;* **~ size** *n.* Haushaltspackung, *die;* Sparpackung, *die;* **an ~-size packet of salt** eine Haushaltspackung Salz

ecosystem /'iːkəʊsɪstəm/ *n.* Ökosystem, *das*

ecstasy /'ekstəsi/ *n.* (a) Ekstase, *die;* Verzückung, *die;* **be in/go into ecstasies [over sth.]** in Ekstase [über etw. (*Akk.*)] sein/geraten; (b) **E~** (drug) Ecstasy, *das*

ecstatic /ɪk'stætɪk/ *adj.*, **ecstatically** /ɪk'stætɪkəli/ *adv.* ekstatisch; verzückt

ectopic /ek'tɒpɪk/ *adj.* (Med.) **~ pregnancy** ektopische Schwangerschaft; (tubal pregnancy) Eileiterschwangerschaft, *die*

ECU, ecu /'eɪkjuː/ *abbr.* ▶ 938 **European currency unit** Ecu, *der od. die*

Ecuador /ekwa'dɔː(r)/ *pr. n.* Ekuador (*das*)

ecumenical /iːkjʊ'menɪkl, ekjʊ'menɪkl/ *adj.* (Relig.) ökumenisch

eczema /'eksɪmə/ *n.* ▶ 865 (Med.) Ekzem, *das* (fachspr.); Hautausschlag, *der*

eddy /'edɪ/ *n.* (a) (whirlpool) Strudel, *der;* (b) (of smoke etc.) Wirbel, *der*

edge /edʒ/ 1 *n.* (a) (of knife, razor, weapon) Schneide, *die;* **the knife has lost its ~:** das Messer ist stumpf geworden *od.* ist nicht mehr scharf; **take the ~ off sth.** etw. stumpf machen; (fig.) etw. abschwächen; **that took the ~ off our hunger** das nahm uns erst einmal den Hunger; **be on ~ [about sth.]** [wegen etw.] nervös *od.* gereizt sein; **set sb.'s teeth on ~:** jmdm. durch Mark und Bein gehen; **have the ~ [on sb./sth.]** (coll.) jmdm./einer Sache überlegen *od.* (ugs.) über sein; (b) (of solid, bed, brick, record, piece of cloth) Kante, *die;* (of dress) Saum, *der;* **~ of a table** Tischkante, *die;* **roll off the ~ of the table** vom Tisch hinunterrollen; (c) (boundary) (of sheet of paper, road, forest, desert, cliff) Rand, *der;* (of sea, lake, river) Ufer, *das;* (of estate) Grenze, *die;* **~ of the paper/road** Papier-/Straßenrand, *der;* **on the ~ of sth.** (fig.) am Rande einer Sache (*Gen.*). 2 *v.i.* (move cautiously) sich schieben; **~ along sth.** sich an etw. (*Dat.*) entlangschieben; **~ away from sb./sth.** sich allmählich von jmdm./etw. entfernen; **~ out of the room** sich aus dem Zimmer stehlen. 3 *v.t.* (a) (furnish with border) säumen ‹*Straße, Platz*›; besetzen ‹*Kleid, Hut*›; einfassen ‹*Garten, Straße*›; (b) (push gradually) [langsam] schieben; **~ one's way through a crowd** sich [langsam] durch eine Menschenmenge schieben *od.* drängen

edgeways /'edʒweɪz/, **edgewise** /'edʒwaɪz/ *adv.* (a) mit der Schmalseite voran; **stand sth. ~:** etw. hochkant stellen; (b) (fig.) **I can't get a word in ~!** ich komme überhaupt nicht zu Wort!

edging /'edʒɪŋ/ *n.* (of dress) Borte, *die;* (of garden) Einfassung, *die*

edgy /'edʒɪ/ *adj.* nervös

edible /'edɪbl/ *adj.* essbar; genießbar

edict /'iːdɪkt/ *n.* Erlass, *der;* Edikt, *das* (hist.)

edifice /'edɪfɪs/ *n.* Gebäude, *das*

Edinburgh /'edɪnbərə/ ▶ 1159 1 *pr. n.* Edinburgh (*das*); Edinburg (*das*). 2 *attrib. adj.* Edinburger

edit /'edɪt/ *v.t.* (a) (act as editor of) herausgeben ‹*Zeitung*›; (b) (prepare for publication) redigieren ‹*Buch, Artikel, Manuskript*›; (c) (prepare an edition of) bearbeiten; **~ the works of Homer** die Werke Homers neu herausgeben; (d) schneiden, cutten, montieren ‹*Film, Bandaufnahme*›

edition /ɪ'dɪʃn/ *n.* (a) (form of work, one copy; also fig.) Ausgabe, *die;* **paperback ~:** Taschenbuchausgabe, *die;* **first ~:** Erstausgabe, *die;* (b) (printing) Auflage, *die;* **morning/evening ~ of a newspaper** Morgen-/Abendausgabe einer Zeitung

editor /'edɪtə(r)/ *n.* ▶ 887 (a) (who prepares the work of others) Redakteur, *der*/Redakteurin, *die;* (of particular work) Bearbeiter, *der*/Bearbeiterin, *die;* (scholarly) Herausgeber, *der*/-geberin, *die;* (b) (of newspaper or periodical) Herausgeber, *der*/-geberin, *die;* **sports/business ~:** Sport-/Wirtschaftsredakteur, *der*

editorial /edɪ'tɔːrɪəl/ 1 *n.* Leitartikel, *der.* 2 *adj.* (of an editor) redaktionell; Redaktions‹*assistent, -angestellte*›; **~ department** Redaktion, *die*

EDP *abbr.* **electronic data processing** EDV

educate /'edjʊkeɪt/ *v.t.* (a) (bring up) erziehen; (b) (provide schooling for) **he was ~d at Eton and Cambridge** er hat seine Ausbildung in Eton und Cambridge erhalten; (c) (give intellectual and moral training to) bilden; **~ oneself** sich [weiter]bilden; (d) (train) schulen ‹*Geist, Körper*›; [aus]-bilden ‹*Geschmack*›; **~ oneself to do sth.** sich dazu erziehen, etw. zu tun

educated /'edjʊkeɪtɪd/ *adj.* gebildet; **make an ~ guess** eine wohlbegründete *od.* fundierte Vermutung anstellen

education /edjʊ'keɪʃn/ *n.* (instruction) Erziehung, *die;* (course of instruction) Ausbildung, *die;* (system) Erziehungs[-und Ausbildungs]wesen, *das;* (science) Erziehungswissenschaften *Pl.;* Pädagogik, *die;* **~ is free** die Schulausbildung ist kostenlos; **receive a good ~:** eine gute Ausbildung genießen

educational /edjʊ'keɪʃənl/ *adj.* pädagogisch; erzieherisch; Lehr‹*film, -spiele, -anstalt*›; Erziehungs‹*methoden, -arbeit*›

educationalist /edjʊ'keɪʃənəlɪst/ *n.* Pädagoge, *der*/Pädagogin, *die;* Erziehungswissenschaftler, *der*/-wissenschaftlerin, *die*

educator /'edjʊkeɪtə(r)/ *n.* Pädagoge, *der*/Pädagogin, *die;* Erzieher, *der*/Erzieherin, *die*

Edwardian /ed'wɔːdɪən/ 1 *adj.* Edwardianisch. 2 *n.* Edwardianer, *der*

EEC *abbr.* **European Economic Community** EWG

eel /iːl/ *n.* Aal, *der*

eerie /'ɪərɪ/ *adj.* unheimlich ‹*Ort, Gebäude, Form*›; schaurig ‹*Klang*›; schauerlich ‹*Schrei*›

efface /ɪ'feɪs/ *v.t.* (a) (rub out) beseitigen ‹*Inschrift*›; (b) (fig.: obliterate) auslöschen; tilgen (geh.)

effect /ɪ'fekt/ 1 *n.* (a) (result) Wirkung, *die* (**on** auf + *Akk.*); **her words had little ~ on him** ihre Worte erzielten bei ihm nur eine geringe Wirkung; **the ~s of sth. on sth.** die Auswirkungen einer Sache (*Gen.*) auf etw. (*Akk.*); die Folgen einer Sache (*Gen.*) für etw.; **with the ~ that …:** mit der Folge *od.* dem Resultat, dass …; **take ~:** wirken; die erwünschte Wirkung erzielen; **in ~:** in Wirklichkeit; praktisch; (b) (*no art.* (impression) Wirkung, *die;* Effekt, *der;* **solely** *or* **only for ~:** nur des Effekts wegen; aus reiner Effekthascherei (abwertend); (c) (meaning) Inhalt, *der;* Sinn, *der;* **or words to that ~:** oder etwas in diesem Sinne; **we received a letter to the ~ that …:** wir erhielten ein Schreiben des Inhalts, dass …; (d) (validity) Kraft, *die;* Gültigkeit, *die;* **be in ~:** gültig *od.* in Kraft sein; **come into ~:** gültig *od.* wirksam werden; (*bes. Gesetz:*) in Kraft treten; **put into ~:** in Kraft setzen ‹*Gesetz*›; verwirklichen ‹*Plan*›; **take ~:** in Kraft treten; **with ~ from Monday** mit Wirkung von Montag; (e) **in** *pl.* (property) Vermögenswerte *Pl.;* Eigentum, *das;* **personal ~s** persönliches Eigentum; Privateigentum, *das;* **household ~s** Hausrat, *der.* 2 *v.t.* durchführen; herbeiführen ‹*Einigung*›; erzielen ‹*Übereinstimmung, Übereinkommen*›; tätigen ‹*Umsatz, Kauf*›; abschließen ‹*Versicherung*›; leisten ‹*Zahlung*›

effective /ɪ'fektɪv/ *adj.* **(a)** (having an effect) wirksam ‹*Mittel*›; effektiv ‹*Maßnahmen*›; **be ~** ‹*Arzneimittel:*› wirken; **(b)** (in operation) gültig; **~ from/as of** mit Wirkung von; **the law is ~ as from 1 September** das Gesetz tritt ab 1. September in Kraft *od.* wird ab 1. September wirksam; **(c)** (powerful in effect) überzeugend ‹*Rede, Redner, Worte*›; **(d)** (striking) wirkungsvoll; effektvoll; **(e)** (existing) wirklich, tatsächlich ‹*Hilfe*›; effektiv ‹*Gewinn, Umsatz*›

effectively /ɪ'fektɪvlɪ/ *adv.* (in fact) effektiv; (with effect) wirkungsvoll; effektvoll

effectiveness /ɪ'fektɪvnɪs/ *n., no pl.* Wirksamkeit, *die;* Effektivität, *die*

effeminate /ɪ'femmət/ *adj.* unmännlich; (geh.) effeminiert

effervesce /efə'ves/ *v.i.* sprudeln

effervescence /efə'vesəns/ *n., no pl.* Sprudeln, *das;* (fig.) Übersprudeln, *das;* Überschäumen, *das*

effervescent /efə'vesənt/ *adj.* sprudelnd; (fig.) übersprudelnd, überschäumend ‹*Freude, Verhalten*›; **~ tablets** Brausetabletten

effete /e'fi:t/ *adj.* (exhausted, worn out) verbraucht; saft- und kraftlos ‹*Person*›; überlebt ‹*System*›

efficacious /efɪ'keɪʃəs/ *adj.* wirksam ‹*Methode, Mittel, Medizin*›

efficiency /ɪ'fɪʃənsɪ/ *n.* **(a)** (of person) Fähigkeit, *die;* Tüchtigkeit, *die;* (of machine, factory, engine) Leistungsfähigkeit, *die;* (of organization, method) Rationalität, *die;* Effizienz, *die* (geh.); **(b)** (Mech., Phys.) Wirkungsgrad, *der*

efficient /ɪ'fɪʃənt/ *adj.* effizient (geh.); fähig ‹*Person*›; tüchtig ‹*Arbeiter, Sekretärin*›; leistungsfähig ‹*Maschine, Abteilung, Fabrik*›; rationell ‹*Methode, Organisation*›

efficiently /ɪ'fɪʃəntlɪ/ *adv.* einwandfrei; gut; effizient (geh.)

effigy /'efɪdʒɪ/ *n.* Bildnis, *das;* **hang/burn sb. in ~:** jmdn. in Effigie hängen/verbrennen (geh.)

effluent /'eflʊənt/ *n.* Abwässer *Pl.*

effort /'efət/ *n.* **(a)** (exertion) Anstrengung, *die;* Mühe, *die;* **make an/every ~** (physically) sich anstrengen; (mentally) sich bemühen; **without [any] ~:** ohne Anstrengung; mühelos; **[a] waste of time and ~:** vergebliche Liebesmüh; **make every possible ~ to do sth.** jede nur mögliche Anstrengung machen, etw. zu tun; **he makes no ~ at all** er gibt sich überhaupt keine Mühe; **(b)** (attempt) Versuch, *der;* **in an ~ to do sth.** beim Versuch, etw. zu tun; **make no ~ to be polite** sich (*Dat.*) nicht die Mühe machen, höflich zu sein; **(c)** (coll.: result) Leistung, *die;* **that was a pretty poor ~:** das war ein ziemlich schwaches Bild (ugs.); **whose is this rather poor ~?** welcher Stümper hat das denn verbrochen? (ugs.); **the book was one of his first ~s** das Buch war einer seiner ersten Versuche

effortless /'efətlɪs/ *adj.* mühelos; leicht; flüssig, leicht ‹*Stil*›

effrontery /ɪ'frʌntərɪ/ *n.* Dreistigkeit, *die;* **have the ~ to do sth.** die Stirn besitzen, etw. zu tun (geh.)

effusive /ɪ'fju:sɪv/ *adj.* überschwänglich; exaltiert (geh.) ‹*Person, Stil, Charakter*›

EFL *abbr.* **English as a foreign language**

e.g. /i:'dʒi:/ *abbr.* **for example** z. B.

egg[1] /eg/ *n.* Ei, *das;* **a bad ~** (fig. coll.: person) eine üble Person; **have *or* put all one's ~s in one basket** (fig. coll.) alles auf eine Karte setzen; **as sure as ~s is *or* are ~s** (coll.) so sicher wie das Amen in der Kirche (ugs.); **have ~ on *or* all over one's face** (fig.) dumm *od.* blöd dastehen (ugs.); dumm aus der Wäsche gucken (salopp)

egg[2] *v.t.* **~ sb. on [to do sth.]** jmdn. anstacheln[, etw. zu tun]

egg: **~cup** *n.* Eierbecher, *der;* **~ 'custard** *n.* Eierkrem, *die;* **~head** *n.* (coll.) Eierkopf, *der* (abwertend); **~plant** *n.* Aubergine, *die;* **~-shaped** *adj.* eiförmig; **~shell** *n.* Eierschale, *die;* **~-spoon** *n.* Eierlöffel, *der;* **~-timer** *n.* Eieruhr, *die;* **~ whisk** *n.* Schneebesen, *der;* **~ white** *n.* Eiweiß, *das;* **~ yolk** *n.* Eigelb, *das;* Eidotter, *der od. das*

EGM *abbr.* **extraordinary general meeting** aoHV, ao.HV (*außerordentliche Hauptversammlung*); (of club) aoMV, ao.MV (*außerordentliche Mitgliederversammlung*)

ego /'i:gəʊ/ *n., pl.* **~s** **(a)** (Psych.) Ego, *das;* (Metaphys.) Ich, *das;* **(b)** (self-esteem) Selbstbewusstsein, *das;* **inflated ~:** übersteigertes Selbstbewusstsein; **boost sb.'s ~:** jmds. Selbstbewusstsein stärken; jmdm. Auftrieb geben

egocentric /i:gəʊ'sentrɪk/ *adj.* egozentrisch; ichbezogen

egoism /'i:gəʊɪzm/ *n., no pl.* **(a)** (systematic selfishness) Egoismus, *der;* Selbstsucht, *die* (abwertend); **(b)** (arrogance) Selbstherrlichkeit, *die*

egoist /'i:gəʊɪst/ *n.* Egoist, *der*/Egoistin, *die*

egomania /i:gəʊ'meɪnɪə/ *n.* Egomanie, *die*

egomaniac /i:gəʊ'meɪnɪæk/ *n.* Egomane, *der*/Egomanin, *die*

egotism /'i:gətɪzm/ *n., no pl.* **(a)** Egotismus, *der* (fachspr.); Ichbezogenheit, *die;* **(b)** (self-conceit) Egotismus, *der;* Selbstgefälligkeit, *die*

egotist /'i:gətɪst/ *n.* Egotist, *der*/Egotistin, *die* (fachspr.); (self-centred person) Egozentriker, *der*/Egozentrikerin, *die*

egotistic /i:gə'tɪstɪk/, **egotistical** /i:gə'tɪstɪkl/ *adj.* **(a)** ichbezogen ‹*Rede*›; **(b)** selbstsüchtig, selbstgefällig (abwertend) ‹*Person*›

Egypt /'i:dʒɪpt/ *pr. n.* Ägypten (*das*)

Egyptian /ɪ'dʒɪpʃn/ ▶ 947 ͏ 1 *adj.* ägyptisch; **sb. is ~:** jmd. ist Ägypter/Ägypterin. 2 *n.* (person) Ägypter, *der*/Ägypterin, *die*

eh /eɪ/ *int.* (coll.) *expr. inquiry or surprise* wie?; wie bitte?; *inviting assent* nicht [wahr]?; *asking for sth. to be repeated or explained* was?; hä? (salopp); **wasn't that good, eh?** war das nicht gut?; **let's not have any more fuss, eh?** Schluss mit dem Theater, ja? (ugs.)

eider /'aɪdə(r)/: **~down** *n.* Daunenbett, *das;* Federbett, *das;* **~ duck** *n.* Eiderente, *die*

eight /eɪt/ ▶ 630 ͏, ▶ 706 ͏, ▶ 956 ͏ 1 *adj.* acht; **at ~:** um acht; **it's ~ [o'clock]** es ist acht [Uhr]; **half past ~:** halb neun; **~ thirty** acht Uhr dreißig; **~ ten/fifty** zehn nach acht/vor neun; (esp. in timetable) acht Uhr zehn/fünfzig; **around ~**, **at about ~:** gegen acht [Uhr]; **half ~** (coll.) halb neun; **girl of ~:** Mädchen von acht Jahren; **~-year-old boy** achtjähriger Junge; **~-year-old** Achtjähriger, *der*/Achtjährige, *die;* **be ~ [years old]** acht [Jahre alt] sein; **at [the age of] ~**, **aged ~:** mit acht Jahren; im Alter von acht Jahren; **he won ~-six** er hat acht zu sechs gewonnen; **Book/Volume/Part/Chapter E~:** Buch/Band/Teil/Kapitel acht; achtes Buch/achter Band/achter Teil/achtes Kapitel; **~-figure number** achtstellige Zahl; **~-page** achtseitig; **~-storey[ed] building** achtstöckiges *od.* achtgeschossiges Gebäude; **~-sided** achtseitig; **bet at ~ to one** acht zu eins wetten; **~ times** achtmal. 2 *n.* **(a)** (number, symbol) Acht, *die;* **the first/last ~:** die ersten/letzten acht; **there were ~ of us** wir waren [zu] acht; **come ~ at a time/in ~s** acht auf einmal/zu je acht kommen; **stack the boxes in ~s** die Kisten zu achten stapeln; **the [number] ~ [bus]** die Buslinie Nr. 8; der Achter (ugs.); **(b)** (8-shaped figure) **[figure of] ~:** Achter, *der* (ugs.); Acht, *die;* **(c)** (Cards) **~ [of hearts/ trumps]** [Herz-/Trumpf]acht, *die;* **(d)** (size) **a size ~ dress** ein Kleid [in] Größe 8; **wear size ~ shoes** [Schuh]größe 8 haben *od.* tragen; **wear an ~**, **be size ~:** Größe 8 tragen *od.* haben; **(e)** (Rowing: crew) Achtermannschaft, *die*

eighteen /eɪ'ti:n/ ▶ 630 ͏, ▶ 706 ͏, ▶ 956 ͏ 1 *adj.* achtzehn; *see also* **eight** 1. 2 *n.* Achtzehn, *die;* **~ seventy** achtzehnhundertsiebzig; **in the ~ seventies** in den siebziger Jahren des neunzehnten Jahrhunderts; *see also* **eight** 2 a, d

eighteenth /eɪ'ti:nθ/ ▶ 738 ͏, ▶ 956 ͏ 1 *adj.* achtzehnt...; *see also* **eighth** 1. 2 *n.* (fraction) Achtzehntel, *das; see also* **eighth** 2

eighth /eɪtθ/ ▶ 738 ͏, ▶ 956 ͏ 1 *adj.* acht...; **be/come ~:** achter sein/als achter ankommen; **~ largest** achtgrößt... 2 *n.* (in sequence, rank) Achte, *der/die/das;* (fraction) Achtel, *das;* **be the ~ to do sth.** der/die achte sein, der/die/ das etw. tut; **the ~ of May** der achte Mai; **the ~ [of the month]** der Achte [des Monats]

'eighth note n. (Amer. Mus.) Achtelnote, die

eightieth /ˈeɪtɪɪθ/ ▶956| adj. achtzigst...; see also eighth 1

eighty /ˈeɪtɪ/ ▶630|, ▶956| 1 adj. achtzig; see also eight 1. 2 n. Achtzig, die; be in one's eighties in den Achtzigern sein; be in one's early/late eighties Anfang/Ende Achtzig sein; the eighties (years) die Achtzigerjahre; the temperature will be rising [well] into the eighties die Temperatur steigt auf [gut] über 30 Grad; see also eight 2 a

eighty: ∼-'first etc. adj. ▶956| einundachtzigst... usw.; see also eighth 1; ∼-'one etc. ▶956| 1 adj. einundachtzig usw.; see also eight 1; 2 n. Einundachtzig usw., die; see also eight 2 a

Eire /ˈeərə/ pr. n. Irland, das; Eire, das

either /ˈaɪðə(r), ˈiːðə(r)/ 1 adj. (a) (each) at ∼ end of the table an beiden Enden des Tisches; on ∼ side of the road auf beiden Seiten der Straße; ∼ way so oder so; (b) (one or other) [irgend]ein ... [von beiden]; take ∼ one nimm einen/eine/eins von [den] beiden. 2 pron. (a) (each) beide Pl.; ∼ is possible beides ist möglich; I can't cope with ∼: ich kann mit keinem von beiden fertig werden; I don't like ∼ [of them] ich mag beide nicht; (b) (one or other) einer/eine/ein[e]s [von beiden]; ∼ of the buses jeder der beiden Busse; beide Busse. 3 adv. (a) (any more than the other) auch [nicht]; 'I don't like that ∼: ich mag es auch nicht; I don't like 'that ∼: auch das mag ich nicht; (b) (moreover, furthermore) noch nicht einmal; there was a time, and not so long ago ∼: früher, noch gar nicht einmal so lange her. 4 conj. ∼ ... or ...: entweder ... oder ...; (after negation) weder ... noch ...

ejaculate /ɪˈdʒækjʊleɪt/ 1 v.t. ausstoßen ⟨Fluch, Gebet⟩. 2 v.i. (Physiol.) ejakulieren

ejaculation /ɪdʒækjʊˈleɪʃn/ n. (a) (cry) Ausruf, der; (b) (Physiol.) Ejakulation, die; Samenerguss, der

eject /ɪˈdʒekt/ 1 v.t. (from hall, meeting) hinauswerfen (from aus); (from machine gun) auswerfen. 2 v.i. sich hinauskatapultieren

ejection /ɪˈdʒekʃn/ n. (of intruder etc.) Vertreibung, die; (of heckler, drunk) Hinauswurf, der; (of empty cartridge) Auswerfen, das

ejector seat /ɪˈdʒektə siːt/ n. Schleudersitz, der

eke /iːk/ v.t. ∼ out strecken ⟨Vorräte, Essen, Einkommen⟩; ∼ out a living or an existence sich (Dat.) seinen Lebensunterhalt [notdürftig od. mühsam] verdienen

elaborate 1 /ɪˈlæbərət/ adj. kompliziert; ausgefeilt ⟨Stil⟩; durchorganisiert ⟨Studium, Forschung⟩; kunstvoll [gearbeitet] ⟨Arrangement, Verzierung, Kleidungsstück⟩; üppig ⟨Menü⟩. 2 /ɪˈlæbəreɪt/ v.t. weiter ausarbeiten; weiter ausführen ⟨Arbeit, Plan, Thema⟩. 3 v.i. mehr ins Detail gehen; could you ∼ [on that]? könnten Sie das näher ausführen?

elapse /ɪˈlæps/ v.i. ⟨Zeit:⟩ vergehen

elastic /ɪˈlæstɪk/ 1 adj. (a) elastisch; (b) (fig.: flexible) flexibel. 2 n. (∼-band) Gummiband, das; (fabric) elastisches Material

elasticated /ɪˈlæstɪkeɪtɪd/ adj. elastisch

elastic 'band n. Gummiband, das

elasticity /ɪlæsˈtɪsɪtɪ/ n., no pl. (a) Elastizität, die; (b) (fig.: flexibility) Flexibilität, die

elated /ɪˈleɪtɪd/ adj. freudig erregt; ∼ mood, ∼ state of mind Hochstimmung, die; be or feel ∼: in Hochstimmung sein

elation /ɪˈleɪʃn/ n., no pl. freudige Erregung

elbow /ˈelbəʊ/ 1 n. ▶672| (also of garment) Ell[en]bogen, der; at one's ∼: bei sich; in Reichweite. 2 v.t. ∼ one's way sich mit den Ellenbogen einen Weg bahnen; sich drängeln (ugs.); ∼ sb. aside jmdn. mit den Ellenbogen zur Seite stoßen; ∼ sb. out (fig.) jmdn. hinausdrängeln

elbow: ∼ grease n., no pl. (joc.) Muskelkraft, die; ∼ room n. (lit. or fig.) Ell[en]bogenfreiheit, die; (fig.) Spielraum, der

elder¹ /ˈeldə(r)/ 1 attrib. adj. älter... 2 n. (a) our ∼s and betters die Älteren mit mehr Lebenserfahrung; the village ∼s die Dorfältesten; (b) (official in Church) [Kirchen]älteste, der/die

elder² n. (Bot.) Holunder, der

'elderberry n. Holunderbeere, die

elderly /ˈeldəlɪ/ 1 adj. älter; my parents are both quite ∼ now meine Eltern sind beide inzwischen ziemlich alt geworden. 2 n. pl. the ∼: ältere Menschen

elder 'statesman n. Elder Statesman, der (Politik)

eldest /ˈeldɪst/ adj. ältest...

elect /ɪˈlekt/ 1 postpos. adj. gewählt; the President ∼: der gewählte od. designierte Präsident. 2 v.t. (a) wählen; ∼ sb. chairman/MP etc. jmdn. zum Vorsitzenden/ Abgeordneten usw. wählen; ∼ sb. to the Senate jmdn. in den Senat wählen; (b) (choose) ∼ to do sth. sich dafür entscheiden, etw. zu tun

election /ɪˈlekʃn/ n. Wahl, die; presidential ∼s (Amer.) Präsidentschaftswahlen Pl.; general/local ∼: allgemeine/kommunale Wahlen; ∼ as chairman Wahl zum Vorsitzenden; ∼ results Wahlergebnisse Pl.

e'lection campaign n. Wahlkampf, der

electioneering /ɪlekʃəˈnɪərɪŋ/ n., no pl. Agitation, die (for für)

elector /ɪˈlektə(r)/ n. Wähler, der/Wählerin, die; Wahlberechtigte, der/die

electoral /ɪˈlektərl/ adj. Wahl⟨liste, -system, -bezirk, -berechtigung⟩; Wähler⟨liste, -wille⟩

electorate /ɪˈlektərət/ n. Wähler Pl.; Wählerschaft, die

electric /ɪˈlektrɪk/ adj. elektrisch ⟨Strom, Feld, Licht, Orgel usw.⟩; Elektro⟨kabel, -motor, -herd, -kessel⟩; (fig.) spannungsgeladen ⟨Atmosphäre⟩; elektrisierend ⟨Wirkung⟩

electrical /ɪˈlektrɪkl/ adj. elektrisch ⟨Defekt, Kontakt⟩; Elektro⟨abteilung, -handel, -geräte⟩

electrical: ∼ engi'neer n. ▶887| Elektroingenieur, der/-ingenieurin, die; ∼ engi'neering n. Elektrotechnik, die

electrically /ɪˈlektrɪkəlɪ/ adv. elektrisch; (fig.) [wie] elektrisiert

electric: ∼ 'blanket n. Heizdecke, die; ∼ 'chair n. elektrischer Stuhl; ∼ 'fire n. [elektrischer] Heizofen; Heizstrahler, der

electrician /ɪlekˈtrɪʃn/ n. ▶887| Elektriker, der/Elektrikerin, die

electricity /ɪlekˈtrɪsɪtɪ/ n., no pl. (a) Elektrizität, die; (b) (supply) Strom, der; (c) (fig.) Spannung, die

electricity: ∼ bill n. Stromrechnung, die; ∼ meter n. Stromzähler, der

electric 'shock n. Stromschlag, der; [elektrischer] Schlag

electrify /ɪˈlektrɪfaɪ/ v.t. (a) (convert) elektrifizieren ⟨Eisenbahnstrecke⟩; (b) (fig.) elektrisieren

electrocute /ɪˈlektrəkjuːt/ v.t. durch Stromschlag töten

electrocution /ɪlektrəˈkjuːʃn/ n. Tod durch Stromschlag

electrode /ɪˈlektrəʊd/ n. Elektrode, die

electromag'netic adj. elektromagnetisch

electron /ɪˈlektrɒn/ n. Elektron, das

electronic /ɪlekˈtrɒnɪk, elekˈtrɒnɪk/ adj. elektronisch; Elektronen⟨uhr, -orgel, -blitz⟩; ∼ news-gathering elektronische Berichterstattung

electronic mail n. elektronische Post

electronics /ɪlekˈtrɒnɪks, elekˈtrɒnɪks/ n., no pl. Elektronik, die

electron 'microscope n. Elektronenmikroskop, das

e'lectroplate v.t. galvanisieren

elegance /ˈelɪgəns/ n., no pl. Eleganz, die

elegant /ˈelɪgənt/ adj., **elegantly** /ˈelɪgəntlɪ/ adv. elegant

element /ˈelɪmənt/ n. (a) (component part) Element, das; an ∼ of truth ein Körnchen Wahrheit; an ∼ of chance/ danger in sth. eine gewisse Zufälligkeit/Gefahr bei etw.; (b) (Chem.) Element, das; Grundstoff, der; (c) in pl. (weather) Elemente Pl.; (d) be in one's ∼ (fig.) in seinem Element sein; (e) (Electr.) Heizelement, das; (f) in pl. (rudiments of learning) Grundlagen Pl.; Elemente Pl.

elementary /elɪˈmentərɪ/ adj. elementar; grundlegend ⟨Fakten, Wissen⟩; schlicht ⟨Fabel, Stil⟩;

Grundschul⟨*lehrer, -bildung*⟩; Grund⟨*stufe, -kurs, -ausbildung, -rechnen, -kenntnisse*⟩; Ausgangs⟨*text, -thema*⟩; Anfangs⟨*stadium*⟩; **course in** ∼ **German** Grundkurs in Deutsch

ele'mentary school *n.* Grundschule, *die*

elephant /'elɪfənt/ *n.* Elefant, *der*

elevate /'elɪveɪt/ *v.t.* [empor]heben ⟨*Gerät, Gegenstand*⟩; aufrichten ⟨*Blick, Geschützrohr*⟩

elevated /'elɪveɪtɪd/ *adj.* **(a)** (raised) gehoben ⟨*Stellung*⟩; erhöht ⟨*Lage, Platzierung*⟩; aufgeschüttet ⟨*Damm, Straße*⟩; **(b)** (above ground level) Hoch⟨*bahn, -straße*⟩; **(c)** (formal, dignified) gehoben ⟨*Stil, Rede, Wortwahl*⟩

elevation /elɪ'veɪʃn/ *n.* **(a)** (of mind, thought) Erhebung, *die*; (state) Erhabenheit, *die*; **(b)** (height) Höhe, *die*; ∼ **of the ground** Bodenerhebung, *die*; Anhöhe *die*; **(c)** (drawing, diagram) Aufriss, *der*

elevator /'elɪveɪtə(r)/ *n.* **(a)** (machine) Förderwerk, *das*; Elevator, *der*; **(b)** (Amer.) ⇒ **lift 3 b**

eleven /ɪ'levn/ ▶630|, ▶706|, ▶956| **1** *adj.* elf; *see also* **eight 1. 2** *n.* Elf, *die*; *see also* **eight 2 a, d**

elevenses /ɪ'levnzɪz/ *n. sing. or pl.* (Brit. coll.) ≈ zweites Frühstück [gegen elf Uhr]

eleventh /ɪ'levnθ/ ▶738|, ▶956| **1** *adj.* elft...; **at the** ∼ **hour** im letzten Augenblick; in letzter Minute; *see also* **eighth 1. 2** *n.* (fraction) Elftel, *das*; *see also* **eighth 2**

elf /elf/ *n., pl.* **elves** /elvz/ **(a)** (Mythol.) Elf, *der*/Elfe, *die*; **(b)** (mischievous creature) [boshafter] Schelm; Kobold, *der*

elicit /ɪ'lɪsɪt/ *v.t.* entlocken ⟨*Antwort, Auskunft, Wahrheit, Geheimnis*⟩ **(from** *Dat.*); gewinnen ⟨*Unterstützung*⟩ **(amongst** bei)

eligibility /elɪdʒɪ'bɪlɪtɪ/ *n., no pl.* (fitness) Qualifikation, *die*; (for a job) Eignung, *die*; (entitlement) Berechtigung, *die* **(for** zu)

eligible /'elɪdʒɪbl/ *adj.* be ∼ **for sth.** (fit) für etw. qualifiziert *od.* geeignet sein; (entitled) zu etw. berechtigt sein; **be** ∼ **to do sth.** etw. tun dürfen; **an** ∼ **bachelor** ein begehrter Junggeselle

eliminate /ɪ'lɪmɪneɪt/ *v.t.* **(a)** (remove) beseitigen ⟨*Zweifel, Fehler, Gegner*⟩; ausschließen ⟨*Möglichkeit*⟩; **(b)** (exclude) ausschließen; **the team was** ∼**d in the third round** die Mannschaft schied in der dritten Runde aus

elimination /ɪlɪmɪ'neɪʃn/ *n.* **(a)** (removal) Beseitigung, *die*; **process of** ∼: Ausleseverfahren, *das*; **by a process of** ∼: durch Eliminierung; **(b)** (exclusion) Ausschluss, *der*; (Sport) Ausscheiden, *das*

élite /eɪ'li:t/ *n.* Elite, *die*

élitism /eɪ'li:tɪzm/ *n.* Elitedenken, *das*

élitist /eɪ'li:tɪst/ **1** *adj.* Elite⟨*denken*⟩. **2** *n.* elitär Denkender/Denkende

elixir /ɪ'lɪksə(r)/ *n.* Heilmittel, *das*; ∼ **[of life]** [Lebens]elixier, *das*

Elizabethan /ɪlɪzə'bi:θn/ *adj.* elisabethanisch

elk /elk/ *n., pl.* ∼**s** *or same* (moose) Riesenelch, *der*

ellipse /ɪ'lɪps/ *n.* Ellipse, *die*

elliptical /ɪ'lɪptɪkl/ *adj.* elliptisch; Ellipsen⟨*bogen, -bahn*⟩

elm /elm/ *n.* Ulme, *die*

elocution /elə'kju:ʃn/ *n., no pl.* Sprechkunst, *die*; **give lessons in** ∼: Sprechunterricht geben

elongate /'i:lɒŋgeɪt/ *v.t.* länger werden lassen ⟨*Schatten*⟩; strecken ⟨*Körper*⟩; recken ⟨*Hals*⟩

elongated /'i:lɒŋgeɪtɪd/ *adj.* lang gestreckt ⟨*Gestalt, Gliedmaße*⟩; langgereckt ⟨*Hals*⟩

elongation /i:lɒŋ'geɪʃn/ *n.* Verlängerung, *die*; (of limbs, neck) [Aus]recken, *das*; (of forms, shapes) Strecken, *das*

elope /ɪ'ləʊp/ *v.i.* durchbrennen (ugs.)

elopement /ɪ'ləʊpmənt/ *n.* Durchbrennen, *das* (ugs.)

eloquence /'eləkwəns/ *n.* Beredtheit, *die*; **a man of great** ∼: ein sehr beredter Mann

eloquent /'eləkwənt/ *adj.* **(a)** gewandt ⟨*Stil, Redner*⟩; beredt ⟨*Person*⟩; **(b)** (fig.) beredt ⟨*Blick, Schweigen*⟩

else /els/ *adv.* **(a)** (besides, in addition) sonst [noch]; **anybody/anything** ∼? sonst noch jemand/etwas?; **don't mention it to anybody** ∼: erwähnen Sie es gegenüber

niemandem sonst; **somebody/something** ∼: [noch] jemand anders/noch etwas; **everybody/everything** ∼: alle anderen/alles andere; **nobody** ∼: niemand sonst; sonst niemand; **nothing** ∼: sonst *od.* weiter nichts; **that is something** ∼ **again** das ist wieder etwas anderes; **anywhere** ∼? anderswo? (ugs.); woanders?; **not anywhere** ∼: sonst nirgendwo; **somewhere** ∼: anderswo (ugs.); woanders; **go somewhere** ∼: anderswohin (ugs.) *od.* woandershin gehen; **everywhere** ∼: auch sonst überall; **nowhere** ∼: sonst nirgendwo; **little** ∼: kaum noch etwas; nur noch wenig; **much** ∼: [noch] vieles andere *od.* mehr; **not much** ∼: nicht mehr viel; nur noch wenig; **who/what/when/how** ∼? wer/was/wann/wie sonst noch?; **where** ∼? wo/wohin sonst noch?; **(b)** (instead) ander...; **sb.** ∼'**s hat** der Hut von jmd. anders *od.* jmd. anderem (ugs.); **anybody/anything** ∼? [irgend] jemand anders/etwas anderes?; **anyone** ∼ **but Joe would have realized that** jeder [andere] außer Joe hätte das bemerkt; **somebody/something** ∼: jemand anders/etwas anderes; **everybody/everything** ∼: alle anderen/alles andere; **nobody/nothing** ∼: niemand anders/nichts anderes; **there's nothing** ∼ **for it** es hilft nichts; **anywhere** ∼? anderswo? (ugs.); woanders?; **somewhere** ∼: anderswo (ugs.); woanders; **go somewhere** ∼: woandershin gehen; **his mind was/his thoughts were somewhere** ∼: im Geist/mit seinen Gedanken war er woanders; **everywhere** ∼: überall anders; überall sonst; **nowhere** ∼: nirgendwo sonst; **there's not much** ∼ **we can do but** ...: wir können kaum etwas anderes tun, als ...; **who** ∼ **[but]?** wer anders [als]?; **what** ∼ **can I do?** was kann ich anderes machen?; **why** ∼ **would I have done it?** warum hätte ich es sonst getan?; **where** ∼ **could we go?** wohin könnten wir statt dessen gehen?; **how** ∼ **would you do it?** wie würden Sie es anders *od.* sonst machen?; **(c)** (otherwise) sonst; anderenfalls; **or** ∼: oder aber; **do it or** ∼ ...! tun Sie es, sonst ...!; **do it or** ∼! (coll.) tu es gefälligst!

'elsewhere *adv.* woanders; **go** ∼: woandershin gehen; **his mind was/his thoughts were** ∼: im Geist/mit seinen Gedanken war er woanders

elucidate /ɪ'lu:sɪdeɪt/ *v.t.* erläutern; aufklären ⟨*Geheimnis*⟩

elude /ɪ'lu:d/ *v.t.* (avoid) ausweichen (+ *Dat.*) ⟨*Person, Angriff, Blick, Frage*⟩; (escape from) entkommen (+ *Dat.*); ∼ **the police** sich dem Zugriff der Polizei entziehen; **the name** ∼**s me at the moment** der Name fällt mir im Moment nicht ein

elusive /ɪ'lu:sɪv/ *adj.* **(a)** (avoiding grasp or pursuit) schwer zu erreichen ⟨*Person*⟩; schwer zu fassen ⟨*Straftäter*⟩; scheu ⟨*Fuchs, Waldbewohner*⟩; **(b)** (short-lived) flüchtig ⟨*Freude, Glück*⟩; **(c)** (hard to define) schwer definierbar

elves *pl. of* **elf**

emaciated /ɪ'meɪsɪeɪtɪd, ɪ'meɪʃɪeɪtɪd/ *adj.* ausgemergelt; abgezehrt

e-mail /'i:meɪl/ **1** *n.* E-Mail, *die*; *attrib.* ∼ **address** E-Mail-Adresse, *die*; ∼ **message** E-Mail, *die.* **2** *v.t.* per E-Mail übermitteln ⟨*Ergebnisse, Datei usw.*⟩; ∼ **sb.** jmdm. eine E-Mail schicken; ∼ **sb with sth.** jmdm. etw. per E-Mail mitteilen

emanate /'eməneɪt/ *v.i.* **(a)** (originate) ausgehen **(from** von); **(b)** (proceed, issue) ausgestrahlt werden **(from** von); **(c)** (formal: be sent out) ⟨*Befehle:*⟩ erteilt *od.* erlassen werden; ⟨*Briefe, Urkunden:*⟩ ausgestellt *od.* ausgefertigt werden

emancipate /ɪ'mænsɪpeɪt/ *v.t.* emanzipieren

emancipated /ɪ'mænsɪpeɪtɪd/ *adj.* emanzipiert ⟨*Frau, Vorstellung, Einstellung*⟩; **become** ∼: sich emanzipieren; ∼ **slave** freigelassener Sklave

emancipation /ɪmænsɪ'peɪʃn/ *n.* Emanzipation, *die*; (of slave) Freilassung, *die*

embalm /ɪm'bɑ:m/ *v.t.* einbalsamieren

embankment /ɪm'bæŋkmənt/ *n.* Damm, *der*; [railway] ∼: Bahndamm, *der*; **the Thames E**∼: die Themse-Uferstraße (in London)

embargo /ɪm'bɑ:gəʊ/ **1** *n., pl.* ∼**es** Embargo, *das.* **2** *v.t.* mit einem Embargo belegen

embark /ɪmˈbɑːk/ **1** v.t. einschiffen ‹Passagiere, Waren›. **2** v.i. (a) sich einschiffen (**for** nach); (b) (start) ~ [**up**]**on sth.** etw. in Angriff nehmen

embarkation /embɑːˈkeɪʃn/ n. Einschiffung, die

embarrass /ɪmˈbærəs/ v.t. in Verlegenheit bringen; **be ~ed by lack of money** in Geldverlegenheit sein

embarrassed /ɪmˈbærəst/ adj. verlegen ‹Person, Blick, Lächeln, Benehmen, Schweigen›; **feel ~:** verlegen sein; **now don't be ~!** geniere dich nicht!; **make sb. feel ~:** jmdn. verlegen machen

embarrassing /ɪmˈbærəsɪŋ/ adj. peinlich ‹Benehmen, Schweigen, Situation, Augenblick, Frage, Thema›; beschämend ‹Großzügigkeit›; verwirrend ‹Auswahl›

embarrassment /ɪmˈbærəsmənt/ n. Verlegenheit, die; (instance) Peinlichkeit, die; **much to his ~:** zu seiner großen Verlegenheit

embassy /ˈembəsi/ n. Botschaft, die

embed /ɪmˈbed/ v.t., **-dd-:** (a) (fix) einlassen; ~ **sth. in concrete** etw. einbetonieren; (b) (fig.) **be firmly ~ded in sth.** fest in etw. (Dat.) verankert sein

embellish /ɪmˈbelɪʃ/ v.t. (a) (beautify) schmücken; beschönigen ‹Wahrheit›; (b) ausschmücken ‹Geschichte, Bericht›

embellishment /ɪmˈbelɪʃmənt/ n. (a) (arrangement) Verzierung, die; (b) no pl. (ornamentation of story) Ausschmückung, die

ember /ˈembə(r)/ n., usu. in pl. (lit. or fig.) Glut, die

embezzle /ɪmˈbezl/ v.t. unterschlagen

embezzlement /ɪmˈbezlmənt/ n. Unterschlagung, die

embitter /ɪmˈbɪtə(r)/ v.t. vergiften ‹Beziehungen›; verschärfen ‹Auseinandersetzung›; verbittern ‹Person›

emblem /ˈembləm/ n. (symbol) Emblem, das; Wahrzeichen, das

embodiment /ɪmˈbɒdɪmənt/ n. Verkörperung, die

embody /ɪmˈbɒdi/ v.t. verkörpern

emboss /ɪmˈbɒs/ v.t. prägen ‹Metall, Papier, Leder usw.›; **an ~ed design** ein erhabenes Muster

embrace /ɪmˈbreɪs/ **1** v.t. (a) umarmen; (b) (fig.: surround) umgeben; (c) (accept) wahrnehmen ‹Gelegenheit›; annehmen ‹Angebot›; (d) (adopt) annehmen; ~ **a cause** eine Sache zu seiner eigenen machen; ~ **Catholicism** sich zum Katholizismus bekennen; (e) (include) umfassen. **2** v.i. sich umarmen. **3** n. Umarmung, die

embroider /ɪmˈbrɔɪdə(r)/ v.t. sticken ‹Muster›; besticken ‹Tuch, Kleid›; (fig.) ausschmücken ‹Erzählung, Wahrheit›

embroidery /ɪmˈbrɔɪdəri/ n. (a) Stickerei, die; (b) no pl. (fig.: ornament) Ausschmückungen Pl.

embroil /ɪmˈbrɔɪl/ v.t. **become/be ~ed in a war/dispute** in einen Krieg/Streit verwickelt werden/sein

embryo /ˈembrɪəʊ/ n., pl. ~**s** Embryo, der; **in ~** (fig.) im Keim

embryonic /embrɪˈɒnɪk/ adj. (Biol., fig.) Embryonal-; unausgereift ‹Vorstellung›

emend /ɪˈmend/ v.t. (Lit.) emendieren (fachspr.); berichtigen

emerald /ˈemərəld/ **1** n. (a) Smaragd, der; (b) ~ [**green**] Smaragdgrün, das. **2** adj. (a) smaragdgrün; (b) **the E~ Isle** (Ireland) die Grüne Insel

emerge /ɪˈmɜːdʒ/ v.i. (a) (come out) auftauchen (**from** aus, **from behind** hinter + Dat., **from beneath** or **under** unter + Dat. hervor); **the sun ~d from behind the clouds** die Sonne trat hinter den Wolken hervor; **the caterpillar ~d from the egg** die Raupe schlüpfte aus dem Ei; (b) (arise) hervorgehen (**from** aus); ‹Leben:› entstammen (**from** + Dat.); **difficulties may ~:** es können Schwierigkeiten auftreten; (c) (become known) ‹Wahrheit:› an den Tag kommen; **it ~s that …:** es zeigt sich od. stellt sich heraus, dass …

emergence /ɪˈmɜːdʒəns/ n. (a) (rising out of liquid) Auftauchen, das; (b) (coming forth) Hervortreten, das; (of school of thought, new ideas) Aufkommen, das

emergency /ɪˈmɜːdʒənsi/ **1** n. (a) Notfall, der; **in an** or **in case of ~:** im Notfall; ~ [**case**] (Med.) Notfall, der; (b) (Polit.) Ausnahmezustand, der; **declare a state of ~:** den Ausnahmezustand erklären. **2** adj. Not‹bremse, -ruf, -ausgang, -landung›; ~ **ward** Unfallstation, die

e'mergency services n. pl. Rettungsdienste Pl.

emergent /ɪˈmɜːdʒənt/ adj. jung, aufstrebend ‹Volk›

emery /ˈeməri/: ~ **board** n. Schleifbrett, das; (strip for fingernails) Sandblattfeile, die; ~ **paper** n. Schmirgelpapier, das

emetic /ɪˈmetɪk/ n. (Med.) Emetikum, das (fachspr.); Brechmittel, das

emigrant /ˈemɪɡrənt/ n. Auswanderer, der/Auswanderin, die; Emigrant, der/Emigrantin, die

emigrate /ˈemɪɡreɪt/ v.i. auswandern, emigrieren (**to** nach, **from** aus)

emigration /emɪˈɡreɪʃn/ n. Auswanderung, die, Emigration, die (**to** nach, **from** aus)

émigré /ˈemɪɡreɪ/ n. Emigrant, der/Emigrantin, die

eminence /ˈemɪnəns/ n. no pl. (distinguished superiority) hohes Ansehen; **person of great ~:** bedeutender od. hochangesehener Mensch

eminent /ˈemɪnənt/ adj. (a) (distinguished) bedeutend, hochangesehen ‹Redner, Gelehrter, Künstler›; ~ **guest** hoher Gast; (b) (remarkable) ausnehmen ‹Eigenschaft›

eminently /ˈemɪnəntli/ adv. ausnehmend; vorzüglich ‹geeignet›; überaus ‹erfolgreich›; ~ **respectable** hochangesehen

emissary /ˈemɪsəri/ n. Abgesandte, der/die

emission /ɪˈmɪʃn/ n. (a) (giving off or out) Aussendung, die; (of vapour) Ablassen, das; (of liquid) Ausscheidung, die; ~ **of light/heat** Licht-/Wärmeausstrahlung, die; (b) (thing given off) Abstrahlung, die

emit /ɪˈmɪt/ v.t., **-tt-** aussenden ‹Strahlen›; ausstrahlen ‹Wärme, Licht›; ausstoßen ‹Rauch, Schrei›; ausscheiden ‹Flüssigkeit›; abgeben ‹Geräusch›

emoticon /ɪˈmɒtɪkɒn/ n. (Computing) Emoticon, das

emotion /ɪˈməʊʃn/ n. (a) (state) Ergriffenheit, die; Bewegtheit, die; **be overcome with ~:** von Gefühl übermannt sein; **show no ~:** keine Gefühlsregung zeigen; (b) (feeling) Gefühl, das; Emotion, die

emotional /ɪˈməʊʃənl/ adj. (a) (of emotions) emotional; Gefühls‹ausdruck, -leben, -erlebnis, -reaktion›; Gemüts‹zustand, -störung›; gefühlsgeladen ‹Worte, Musik, Geschichte, Film›; gefühlvoll ‹Stimme, Ton›; (b) (liable to excessive emotion) leicht erregbar ‹Person›

emotionally /ɪˈməʊʃənəli/ adv. emotional; ~ **exhausted/disturbed** seelisch erschöpft/gestört; **get ~ involved with sb.** eine gefühlsmäßige Bindung mit jmdm. eingehen

emotive /ɪˈməʊtɪv/ adj. emotional; gefühlsbetont; emotiv (Psych., Sprachw.)

empathize /ˈempəθaɪz/ v.i. ~ **with sb.** sich in jmdn. hineinversetzen; ~ **with sth.** etw. nachempfinden

empathy /ˈempəθi/ n. Empathie, die (Psych.); Einfühlung, die

emperor /ˈempərə(r)/ n. ▶**1152**| Kaiser, der

emphasis /ˈemfəsɪs/ n., pl. **emphases** /ˈemfəsiːz/ (a) (in speech etc.) Betonung, die; **the ~ is on sth.** die Betonung liegt auf etw. (Dat.); **lay ~ on sth.** etw. betonen; (b) (intensity) Nachdruck, der; **with ~:** nachdrücklich; (c) (importance attached) Gewicht, das; **lay** or **put [considerable] ~ on sth.** [großes] Gewicht auf etw. (Akk.) legen; **the ~ has shifted** der Akzent hat sich verlagert

emphasize (**emphasise**) /ˈemfəsaɪz/ v.t. (lit. or fig.) betonen; (attach importance to) Gewicht auf etw. (Akk.) legen

emphatic /ɪmˈfætɪk/ adj. nachdrücklich; (forcible) demonstrativ ‹Rückzug, Ablehnung›; eindringlich ‹Demonstration›; **be quite ~ that …:** durchaus darauf bestehen, dass …

emphatically /ɪmˈfætɪkəli/ adv. nachdrücklich; eindringlich ‹sprechen›; (decisively) entschieden ‹bestreiten usw.›

empire /ˈempaɪə(r)/ n. (a) Reich, das; (b) (commercial organization) Imperium, das (fig.)

empirical /ɪmˈpɪrɪkl/ adj. empirisch; empirisch begründet ‹Argument, Wissen, Schlussfolgerung›

employ /ɪmˈplɔɪ/ **1** v.t. (a) (take on) einstellen; (have working for one) beschäftigen; **be ~ed by a company** bei einer

Firma beschäftigt sein; **(b)** (use services of) ~ **sb. on sth.** jmdn. für etw. einsetzen; ~ **sb. to do sth.** jmdn. dafür einsetzen, etw. zu tun; **(c)** (use) einsetzen (**for, in, on** für); anwenden ‹*Methode, List*› (**for, in, on** bei). **2** *n., no pl., no indef. art.* **be in the** ~ **of sb.** bei jmdm. beschäftigt sein

employee (*Amer.:* **employe**) /emplɔɪˈiː, emˈplɔɪiː/ *n.* Angestellte, *der/die;* (in contrast to employer) Arbeitnehmer, *der/*-nehmerin, *die;* **the firm's** ~**s** die Belegschaft der Firma

employer /ɪmˈplɔɪə(r)/ *n.* Arbeitgeber, *der/*-geberin, *die*

employment /ɪmˈplɔɪmənt/ *n., no pl.* **(a)** (work) Arbeit, *die;* **be in/without regular** ~: eine/keine feste Anstellung haben; **(b)** (regular trade or profession) Beschäftigung, *die*

em'ployment agency *n.* Stellenvermittlung, *die*

empower /ɪmˈpaʊə(r)/ *v.t.* (authorize) ermächtigen; (enable) befähigen

empress /ˈemprɪs/ *n.* Kaiserin, *die*

emptiness /ˈemptɪnɪs/ *n., no pl.* (lit. or fig.) Leere, *die*

empty /ˈemptɪ/ **1** *adj.* **(a)** leer; frei ‹*Sitz, Parkplatz*›; ~ **of sth.** ohne etw.; **(b)** (coll.: hungry) **I feel a bit** ~: ich bin ein bisschen hungrig; **(c)** (fig.) (foolish) dumm; hohl ‹*Kopf*›; (meaningless) leer. **2** *n.* (bottle) leere Flasche; (container) leerer Behälter. **3** *v.t.* **(a)** (remove contents of) leeren; (finish using contents of) aufbrauchen; (eat/drink whole contents of) leer essen ‹*Teller*›/leeren ‹*Glas*›; **(b)** (transfer) umfüllen (**into** in + *Akk.*); (pour) schütten (**over** über + *Akk.*). **4** *v.i.* **(a)** (become ~) sich leeren; **(b)** (discharge) ~ **into** ‹*Fluss, Abwasserkanal:*› münden in (+ *Akk.*)

empty: ~**-handed** /emptɪˈhændɪd/ *pred. adj.* mit leeren Händen; ~**-headed** /ˈemptɪhedɪd/ *adj.* hohlköpfig (abwertend)

EMS *abbr.* **European Monetary System** EWS

emu /ˈiːmjuː/ *n.* (Ornith.) Emu, *der*

EMU *abbr.* **Economic and Monetary Union** WWU

emulate /ˈemjʊleɪt/ *v.t.* nacheifern (+ *Dat.*)

emulsion /ɪˈmʌlʃn/ *n.* **(a)** Emulsion, *die;* **(b)** ⇒ **emulsion paint**

e'mulsion paint *n.* Dispersionsfarbe, *die*

enable /ɪˈneɪbl/ *v.t.* ~ **sb. to do sth.** es jmdm. ermöglichen, etw. zu tun; ~ **sth.** [**to be done**] etw. ermöglichen

enact /ɪˈnækt/ *v.t.* **(a)** (make law) erlassen; **(b)** (act out) aufführen ‹*Theaterstück*›; spielen ‹*Rolle*›

enamel /ɪˈnæml/ **1** *n.* **(a)** Emaille, *die;* Email, *das;* (paint) Lack, *der;* **(b)** (Anat.) [Zahn]schmelz, *der.* **2** *attrib. adj.* emailliert. **3** *v.t.,* (Brit.) **-ll-** emaillieren

encase /ɪnˈkeɪs/ *v.t.* einschließen

enchant /ɪnˈtʃɑːnt/ *v.t.* **(a)** (bewitch) verzaubern; **(b)** (delight) entzücken

enchanting /ɪnˈtʃɑːntɪŋ/ *adj.* (delightful) entzückend; bezaubernd

enchantment /ɪnˈtʃɑːntmənt/ *n.* (delight) Entzücken, *das* (**with** über + *Akk.*)

encircle /ɪnˈsɜːkl/ *v.t.* **(a)** einkreisen; ‹*Bäume, Zaun usw.:*› umgeben; **(b)** (mark with circle) einkreisen ‹*Buchstabe, Antwort*›

encl. *abbr.* **enclosed, enclosure[s]** Anl.

enclave /ˈenkleɪv/ *n.* (lit. or fig.) Enklave, *die*

enclose /ɪnˈkləʊz/ *v.t.* **(a)** (surround) umgeben; (shut up or in) einschließen; ~ **land with barbed wire** Land mit Stacheldraht einzäunen; **(b)** (put in envelope with letter) beilegen (**with, in** *Dat.*); **please find** ~**d,** ~**d please find** als Anlage übersenden wir Ihnen; anbei erhalten Sie; **the** ~**d brochure** der beiliegende Prospekt; **a cheque is** ~**d** beiliegend finden Sie einen Scheck

enclosure /ɪnˈkləʊʒə(r)/ *n.* **(a)** (act) Einzäunung, *die;* **(b)** (place) (in zoo) Gehege, *das;* (paddock) Koppel, *die;* **(c)** (fence) Umzäunung, *die;* **(d)** (with letter) Anlage, *die*

encode /ɪnˈkəʊd/ *v.t.* verschlüsseln; chiffrieren

encore /ˈɒŋkɔː(r)/ **1** *int.* Zugabe. **2** *n.* Zugabe, *die;* **give an** ~: eine Zugabe spielen/singen. **3** *v.t.* als Zugabe verlangen ‹*Lied, Tanz usw.*›

encounter /ɪnˈkaʊntə(r)/ **1** *v.t.* **(a)** (as adversary) treffen auf (+ *Akk.*); **(b)** (by chance) begegnen (+ *Dat.*); **(c)** (meet

with) stoßen auf (+ *Akk.*) ‹*Problem, Schwierigkeit, Kritik, Widerstand usw.*›. **2** *n.* **(a)** (in combat) Zusammenstoß, *der;* **(b)** (chance meeting, introduction) Begegnung, *die*

encourage /ɪnˈkʌrɪdʒ/ *v.t.* **(a)** (stimulate, incite) ermutigen; **bread** ~**s rats** Brot lockt Ratten an; **(b)** (promote) fördern; ~ **a smile/a response from sb.** jmdm. ein Lächeln/eine Reaktion entlocken; ~ **bad habits** schlechte Angewohnheiten unterstützen; **we do not** ~ **smoking** wir unterstützen es nicht, dass geraucht wird; **(c)** (urge) ~ **sb. to do sth.** jmdn. dazu ermuntern, etw. zu tun; **(d)** (cheer) **be** [**much**] ~**d by sth.** durch etw. neuen Mut schöpfen; **we were** ~**d to hear …:** wir schöpften neuen Mut, als wir hörten …

encouragement /ɪnˈkʌrɪdʒmənt/ *n.* **(a)** (support, incitement) Ermutigung, *die* (**from** durch); **give sb.** ~: jmdn. ermutigen; **get** *or* **receive** ~ **from sth.** durch etw. ermutigt werden; **(b)** (urging) Ermunterung, *die;* **(c)** (stimulus) Ansporn, *der*

encouraging /ɪnˈkʌrɪdʒɪŋ/ *adj.* ermutigend

encroach /ɪnˈkrəʊtʃ/ *v.i.* (lit. or fig.) ~ [**on sth.**] [in etw. (*Akk.*)] eindringen; **the sea is** ~**ing** [**on the land**] das Meer dringt vor; ~ **on sb.'s time** jmds. Zeit über Gebühr in Anspruch nehmen

encrust /ɪnˈkrʌst/ *v.t.* ~**ed with diamonds** über und über mit Diamanten besetzt

encumber /ɪnˈkʌmbə(r)/ *v.t.* **(a)** (hamper) behindern; ~ **oneself/sb. with sth.** sich/jmdn. mit etw. belasten; **(b)** (burden) ~ **sb. with debt** jmdn. mit Schulden belasten

encumbrance /ɪnˈkʌmbrəns/ *n.* **(a)** (impediment) Hindernis, *das* (**to** für); **(b)** (burden) Last, *die*

encyclopaedia /ɪnsaɪkləˈpiːdɪə/ *n.* Lexikon, *das;* Enzyklopädie, *die*

encyclopaedic /ensaɪkləˈpiːdɪk, ɪnsaɪkləˈpiːdɪk/ *adj.* enzyklopädisch

end /end/ **1** *n.* **(a)** (farthest point) Ende, *das;* (of nose, hair, tail, branch, finger) Spitze, *die;* **that was the** ~ (coll.) (no longer tolerable) da war Schluss (ugs.); (very bad) das war das Letzte (ugs.); **at an** ~: zu Ende; **come to an** ~: enden (*see also* **1g**); **my patience has come to** *or* **is now at an** ~: meine Geduld ist jetzt am Ende; **look at a building/a pencil** ~ **on** ein Gebäude von der Schmalseite/einen Bleistift von der Spitze her betrachten; **from** ~ **to** ~: von einem Ende zum anderen; ~ **to** ~: längs hintereinander; **lay** ~ **to** ~: aneinander reihen; **keep one's** ~ **up** (fig.) seinen Mann stehen; **make** [**both**] ~**s meet** (fig.) [mit seinem Geld] zurechtkommen; **no** ~ (coll.) unendlich viel; **there is no** ~ **to sth.** (coll.) etw. nimmt kein Ende; **put an** ~ **to sth.** einer Sache (*Dat.*) ein Ende machen; **(b)** (of box, packet, tube, etc.) Schmalseite, *die;* (top/bottom surface) Ober-/Unterseite, *die;* **sb.'s hair stands on** ~ (fig.) jmdm. stehen die Haare zu Berge (ugs.); **(c)** (remnant) Rest, *der;* (of cigarette, candle) Stummel, *der;* **(d)** (side) Seite, *die;* **be on the receiving** ~ **of sth.** etw. abbekommen *od.* einstecken müssen; **how are things at your** ~? wie sieht es bei dir aus?; **(e)** (half of sports pitch or court) Spielfeldhälfte, *die;* **(f)** (of swimming pool) **deep/shallow** ~ [**of the pool**] tiefer/flacher Teil [des Schwimmbeckens]; **(g)** ▶ **738** | (conclusion, lit. or fig.) Ende, *das;* (of lesson, speech, story, discussion, meeting, argument, play, film, book, sentence) Schluss, *der;* Ende, *das;* **by the** ~ **of the week/meeting** als die Woche herum war/als die Versammlung zu Ende war; **at the** ~ **of 1987/March** Ende 1987/März; **that's the** ~ **of 'that** (fig.) damit ist die Sache erledigt; **be at an** ~: zu Ende sein; **bring a meeting** *etc.* **to an** ~: eine Versammlung *usw.* beenden; **come to an** ~: ein Ende nehmen (*see also* **1a**); **have come to the** ~ **of sth.** mit etw. fertig sein; **in the** ~: schließlich; **on** ~ ununterbrochen (*see also* **b**); **(h)** (downfall, destruction) Ende, *das;* (death) Ende, *das* (geh. verhüll.); **meet one's** ~: den Tod finden (geh.); **sb. comes to a bad** ~: es nimmt ein böses *od.* schlimmes Ende mit jmdm.; **(i)** (purpose, object) Ziel, *das;* Zweck, *der;* **be an** ~ **in itself** (the only purpose) das eigentliche Ziel sein; **the** ~ **justifies the means** der Zweck heiligt die Mittel; **with this** ~ **in view** mit diesem Ziel vor Augen; **to this/what** ~: zu diesem/welchem Zweck. **2** *v.t.* **(a)** (bring to an ~) beenden; kündigen ‹*Abonnement*›; ~ **one's life/days** (spend last part of life) sein Leben/seine

Tage beschließen; **(b)** (put an ∼ to, destroy) ein Ende setzen (+ *Dat.*); ∼ **it** [**all**] (coll.: kill oneself) [mit dem Leben] Schluss machen (ugs.); **(c)** (stand as supreme example of) **a feast/race** *etc.* **to** ∼ **all feasts/races** *etc.* ein Fest/Rennen *usw.*, das alles [bisher Dagewesene] in den Schatten stellt. **3** *v.i.* enden; **where will it all** ∼? wo soll das noch hinführen?; **the match** ∼**ed in a draw** das Spiel ging unentschieden aus

∼ '**up** *v.i.* enden; ∼ **up** [**as**] **a teacher/an alcoholic** (coll.) schließlich Lehrer/zum Alkoholiker werden; **I always** ∼ **up doing all the work** (coll.) am Ende bleibt die ganze Arbeit immer an mir hängen

'**end-all** ⇒ **be 4**

endanger /ɪn'deɪndʒə(r)/ *v.t.* gefährden; **an** ∼**ed species** eine vom Aussterben bedrohte Art

endear /ɪn'dɪə(r)/ *v.t.* ∼ **sb./sth./oneself to sb.** jmdn./ etw./sich bei jmdm. beliebt machen

endearing /ɪn'dɪərɪŋ/ *adj.* reizend; gewinnend 〈*Lächeln*, *Art*〉

endearment /ɪn'dɪəmənt/ *n.* Zärtlichkeit, *die;* **term of** ∼: Kosename, *der*

endeavour (*Brit.; Amer.:* **endeavor**) /ɪn'devə(r)/ **1** *v.i.* ∼ **to do sth.** sich bemühen, etw. zu tun. **2** *n.* Bemühung, *die;* (attempt) Versuch, *der;* **make every** ∼ **to do sth.** alle Anstrengungen unternehmen, um etw. zu tun; **despite his best** ∼**s** obwohl er sich nach Kräften bemühte

endemic /en'demɪk/ *adj.* verbreitet

ending /'endɪŋ/ *n.* Schluss, *der;* (of word) Endung, *die*

endive /'endaɪv/ *n.* Endivie, *die*

endless /'endlɪs/ *adj.* endlos; (coll.: innumerable) unzählig; (eternal, infinite) unendlich; unendlich lang 〈*Liste*〉; **have an** ∼ **wait, wait an** ∼ **time** endlos lange warten

endlessly /'endlɪslɪ/ *adv.* unaufhörlich 〈*streiten*, *schwatzen*〉

endorse /ɪn'dɔ:s/ *v.t.* **(a)** (sign one's name on back of) indossieren 〈*Scheck, Wechsel*〉; **(b)** (support) beipflichten (+ *Dat.*) 〈*Meinung, Aussage*〉; billigen, gutheißen 〈*Entscheidung, Handlung, Einstellung*〉; unterstützen 〈*Vorschlag, Kandidaten*〉; **(c)** (Brit.: make entry regarding offence on) einen Strafvermerk machen auf (+ *Akk. od. Dat.*)

endorsement /ɪn'dɔ:smənt/ *n.* **(a)** (of cheque) Indossament, *das;* **(b)** (support) Billigung, *die;* (of proposal, move, candidate) Unterstützung, *die;* **(c)** (Brit.: entry regarding offence) Strafvermerk, *der*

endow /ɪn'daʊ/ *v.t.* **(a)** (give permanent income to) [über Stiftungen/eine Stiftung] finanzieren 〈*Einrichtung, Krankenhaus usw.*〉; stiften 〈*Preis, Lehrstuhl*〉; **(b)** (fig.) **be** ∼**ed with charm/a talent for music** *etc.* Charme/musikalisches Talent *usw.* besitzen

endowment /ɪn'daʊmənt/ *n.* **(a)** (endowing, fund, etc.) Stiftung, *die;* **(b)** (talent) Begabung, *die*

en'dowment policy *n.* abgekürzte *od.* gemischte Lebensversicherung

end: ∼ **product** *n.* (lit. or fig.) Endprodukt, *das;* (fig.) Resultat, *das;* ∼ **re'sult** *n.* Ergebnis, *das;* (consequence) Folge, *die*

endurable /ɪn'djʊərəbl/ *adj.* erträglich

endurance /ɪn'djʊərəns/ *n.* **(a)** Widerstandskraft, *die;* (ability to withstand strain) Ausdauer, *die;* (patience) Geduld, *die;* **past** *or* **beyond** ∼: unerträglich; **(b)** (lasting quality) Dauerhaftigkeit, *die*

en'durance test *n.* Belastungsprobe, *die*

endure /ɪn'djʊə(r)/ **1** *v.t.* (undergo, tolerate) ertragen; (submit to) über sich ergehen lassen. **2** *v.i.* fortdauern

enduring /ɪn'djʊərɪŋ/ *adj.* dauerhaft; beständig 〈*Glaube, Tradition*〉

'**end user** *n.* **(a)** (Econ.) Endverbraucher, *der;* **(b)** (Computing) Endbenutzer, *der/*-benutzerin, *die*

enema /'enɪmə/ *n.* (Med.) Einlauf, *der;* Klistier, *das* (Med.)

enemy /'enəmɪ/ **1** *n.* (lit. or fig.) Feind, *der* (**of, to** *Gen.*); **make an** ∼ **of sb.** sich (*Dat.*) jmdn. zum Feind machen; **be one's own worst** ∼: sich (*Dat.*) selbst im Wege stehen. **2** *adj.* feindlich; **destroyed by** ∼ **action** durch Feindeinwirkung zerstört

energetic /enə'dʒetɪk/ *adj.* **(a)** (very active) energiegeladen; tatkräftig 〈*Mitarbeiter*〉; lebhaft 〈*Kind*〉; **I don't feel** ∼ **enough** ich habe nicht genug Energie; **(b)** (vigorous) schwungvoll; entschieden, energisch 〈*Zustimmung, Ablehnung*〉; kräftig 〈*Rühren*〉

energetically /enə'dʒetɪkəlɪ/ *adv.* schwungvoll; entschieden 〈*sich äußern*〉

energy /'enədʒɪ/ *n.* **(a)** (vigour) Energie, *die;* (active operation) Kraft, *die;* **save your** ∼! schone deine Kräfte!; **I've no** ∼ **left** ich habe keine Energie mehr; **(b)** *in pl.* (individual's powers) Kraft, *die;* **(c)** (Phys.) Energie, *die;* **sources of** ∼: Energiequellen

energy: ∼ **crisis** *n.* Energiekrise, *die;* ∼**-giving** *adj.* Energie spendend; ∼ **resources** *n. pl.* Energieressourcen *Pl.;* ∼**-saving** *adj.* Energie sparend

enervate /'enəveɪt/ *v.t.* schwächen

enervating /'enəveɪtɪŋ/ *adj.* enervierend (geh.), ermüdend 〈*Auseinandersetzung, Streben*〉; schlapp machend 〈*Klima, Feuchtigkeit*〉; kräftezehrend 〈*Krankheit*〉; lähmend 〈*Hitze*〉

enfeeble /ɪn'fi:bl/ *v.t.* schwächen

enforce /ɪn'fɔ:s/ *v.t.* **(a)** durchsetzen; sorgen für 〈*Disziplin*〉; ∼ **the law** dem Gesetz Geltung verschaffen; ∼**d** erzwungen 〈*Schweigen*〉; unfreiwillig 〈*Untätigkeit*〉; **(b)** (give more force to) Nachdruck verleihen (+ *Dat.*)

enforceable /ɪn'fɔ:səbl/ *adj.* durchsetzbar

enforcement /ɪn'fɔ:smənt/ *n.* Durchsetzung, *die*

ENG *abbr.* **electronic news-gathering** EB

engage /ɪn'geɪdʒ/ **1** *v.t.* **(a)** (hire) einstellen 〈*Arbeiter*〉; engagieren 〈*Sänger*〉; **(b)** (employ busily) beschäftigen (**in** mit); (involve) verwickeln (**in** in + *Akk.*); **(c)** (attract and hold fast) wecken [und wachhalten] 〈*Interesse*〉; auf sich (*Akk.*) ziehen 〈*Aufmerksamkeit*〉; fesseln 〈*Person*〉; in Anspruch nehmen 〈*Konzentration*〉; gewinnen 〈*Sympathie, Unterstützung*〉; **(d)** (enter into conflict with) angreifen; (e) (Mech.) ∼ **the clutch/gears** einkuppeln/einen Gang einlegen. **2** *v.i.* **(a)** ∼ **in sth.** sich an etw. (*Dat.*) beteiligen; ∼ **in politics** sich politisch engagieren; ∼ **in a sport** eine Sportart betreiben; **(b)** (Mech.) ineinander greifen

engaged /ɪn'geɪdʒd/ *adj.* **(a)** (to be married) verlobt; **be** ∼ [**to be married**] [**to sb.**] [mit jmdm.] verlobt sein; **become** *or* **get** ∼ [**to be married**] [**to sb.**] sich [mit jmdm.] verloben; **(b)** (bound by promise) verabredet; **be otherwise** ∼: etwas anderes vorhaben; **(c)** (occupied with business) beschäftigt; **(d)** (occupied or used by person) besetzt 〈*Toilette, Taxi*〉; (Teleph.) besetzt; **you're always** ∼: bei dir ist immer besetzt; ∼ **signal** *or* **tone** (Brit.) Besetztzeichen, *das*

engagement /ɪn'geɪdʒmənt/ *n.* **(a)** (to be married) Verlobung, *die* (**to** mit); **(b)** (appointment made with another) Verabredung, *die;* **have a previous** *or* **prior** ∼: schon anderweitig festgelegt sein; **(c)** (booked appearance) Engagement, *das;* **(d)** (Mil.) Kampfhandlung, *die*

en'gagement ring *n.* Verlobungsring, *der*

engaging /ɪn'geɪdʒɪŋ/ *adj.* bezaubernd; gewinnend 〈*Lächeln*〉; einnehmend 〈*Persönlichkeit, Art*〉

engender /ɪn'dʒendə(r)/ *v.t.* zur Folge haben; erzeugen

engine /'endʒɪn/ *n.* **(a)** Motor, *der;* (rocket/jet ∼) Triebwerk, *das;* **(b)** (locomotive) Lok[omotive], *die*

'**engine driver** *n.* ▶ 887 | (Brit.) Lok[omotiv]führer, *der*

engineer /endʒɪ'nɪə(r)/ **1** *n.* **(a)** Ingenieur, *der/*Ingenieurin, *die;* (service ∼, installation ∼) Techniker, *der/*Technikerin, *die;* **(b)** (maker or designer of engines) Maschinenbauingenieur, *der;* **(c)** [ship's] ∼: Maschinist, *der.* **2** *v.t.* **(a)** (coll.: contrive) arrangieren; entwickeln 〈*Plan*〉; **(b)** (manage construction of) konstruieren

engineering /endʒɪ'nɪərɪŋ/ *n., no pl.* **(a)** Technik, *die;* **(b)** *attrib.* technisch 〈*Arbeiten, Fähigkeiten*〉; ∼ **science** Ingenieurwesen, *das;* ∼ **company** *or* **firm** Maschinenbaufirma, *die*

'**engine room** *n.* Maschinenhaus, *das;* Maschinenraum, *der*

England /'ɪŋglənd/ *pr. n.* England (*das*)

English /'ɪŋglɪʃ/ ▶ 897 |, ▶ 947 | **1** *adj.* englisch; **he/she is** ∼: er ist Engländer/sie ist Engländerin. **2** *n.* **(a)** (language) Englisch, *das;* **say sth. in** ∼: etw. auf Englisch sagen; **speak** ~: Englisch sprechen; **be speaking** ~: englisch sprechen; **I [can] speak/read** ~: ich spreche Englisch/kann Englisch lesen; **I cannot** *or* **do not speak/read** ~: ich spreche kein Englisch/kann Englisch nicht lesen; **translate into/from [the]** ~: ins Englische/ aus dem Englischen übersetzen; **write sth. in** ~: etw. [auf *od.* in] Englisch schreiben; **her** ~ **is very good** sie schreibt/spricht ein sehr gutes Englisch; **the King's/ Queen's** ~: die englische Hochsprache; **Old** ~: Altenglisch, *das;* **in plain** ~: in einfachen Worten; **(b)** *pl.* **the** ~: die Engländer. *See also* **pidgin English**

English: ~ **'Channel** *pr. n.* the ~ Channel der [Ärmel]kanal; **~man** /'ɪŋglɪʃmən/ *n., pl.* **~men** /'ɪŋ glɪʃmən/ Engländer, *der;* **~woman** *n.* Engländerin, *die*

engrave /ɪn'ɡreɪv/ *v.t.* gravieren; ~ **sth. with a name** *etc.* einen Namen *usw.* in etw. (*Akk.*) [ein]gravieren

engraving /ɪn'ɡreɪvɪŋ/ *n.* **(a)** (design, marks) Gravur, *die;* **(b)** (Art: print) Stich, *der;* (from wood) Holzschnitt, *der*

engross /ɪn'ɡrəʊs/ *v.t.* be ~**ed in sth.** in etw. (*Akk.*) vertieft sein; **become** *or* **get** ~**ed in sth.** sich in etw. (*Akk.*) vertiefen

engrossing /ɪn'ɡrəʊsɪŋ/ *adj.* fesselnd

engulf /ɪn'ɡʌlf/ *v.t.* (lit. *or* fig.) verschlingen; **the house was** ~**ed in flames** das Haus stand in hellen Flammen

enhance /ɪn'hɑːns/ *v.t.* verbessern ‹*Aussichten, Stellung*›; erhöhen ‹*Wert, [An]reiz, Macht, Schönheit*›; steigern ‹*Qualität, Wirkung*›; heben ‹*Aussehen*›

enhancement /ɪn'hɑːnsmənt/ *n.* ⇒ **enhance**: Verbesserung, *die;* Erhöhung, *die;* Steigerung, *die;* Hebung, *die*

enigma /ɪ'nɪɡmə/ *n.* Rätsel, *das*

enigmatic /enɪɡ'mætɪk/ *adj.* rätselhaft

enjoin /ɪn'dʒɔɪn/ *v.t.* ~ **sb. [not] to do sth.** jmdn. eindringlich ermahnen, etw. [nicht] zu tun

enjoy /ɪn'dʒɔɪ/ **1** *v.t.* **(a) I** ~**ed the film** der Film hat mir gefallen; **are you** ~**ing your meal?** schmeckt dir das Essen?; **he** ~**s reading** er liest gern; **he** ~**s music** er mag Musik; **we really** ~**ed seeing you again** wir haben uns wirklich gefreut, euch wiederzusehen; **(b)** (have use of) genießen ‹*Recht, Privileg, Vorteil*›; sich erfreuen (+ *Gen.*) ‹*hohen Einkommens*›. **2** *v. refl.* sich amüsieren; **we thoroughly** ~**ed ourselves in Spain** wir hatten viel Spaß in Spanien; ~ **yourself at the theatre!** viel Spaß im Theater!

enjoyable /ɪn'dʒɔɪəbl/ *adj.* schön; angenehm ‹*Empfindung, Unterhaltung, Arbeit*›; unterhaltsam ‹*Buch, Film, Stück*›

enjoyment /ɪn'dʒɔɪmənt/ *n.* (delight) Vergnügen, *das* (**of** an + *Dat.*)

enlarge /ɪn'lɑːdʒ/ **1** *v.t.* vergrößern; (widen) erweitern ‹*Wissen*›. **2** *v.i.* **(a)** sich vergrößern; größer werden; (widen) sich verbreitern; **(b)** ~ **[up]on sth.** etw. weiter ausführen

enlargement /ɪn'lɑːdʒmənt/ *n.* **(a)** Vergrößerung, *die;* **(b)** (further explanation) weitere Ausführung

enlighten /ɪn'laɪtn/ *v.t.* aufklären (**on, as to** über + *Akk.*); **let me** ~ **you** ich will es dir erklären

enlightened /ɪn'laɪtnd/ *adj.* aufgeklärt

enlightenment /ɪn'laɪtnmənt/ *n., no pl.* Aufklärung, *die*

enlist /ɪn'lɪst/ **1** *v.t.* **(a)** (Mil.) anwerben; **(b)** (obtain) gewinnen. **2** *v.i.* in die Armee/Marine eintreten

enlistment /ɪn'lɪstmənt/ *n.* (Mil.) Anwerbung, *die*

enliven /ɪn'laɪvn/ *v.t.* beleben; in Schwung bringen (ugs.) ‹*Person, Schulklasse usw.*›; lebhafter gestalten ‹*Tanz, Unterricht*›

enmity /'enmɪtɪ/ *n.* Feindschaft, *die*

enormity /ɪ'nɔːmɪtɪ/ *n.* **(a)** (atrocity) Ungeheuerlichkeit, *die* (abwertend); **(b)** ⇒ **enormousness**

enormous /ɪ'nɔːməs/ *adj.* **(a)** enorm; riesig, gewaltig ‹*Figur, Tier, Fluss, Wüste, Menge*›; gewaltig, enorm ‹*Veränderung, Unterschied, Liebe, Hass, Widerspruch, Größe, Ausgabe, Kraft*›; ungeheuer ‹*Mut, Charme, Problem*›; **(b)** (fat) ungeheuer dick

enormously /ɪ'nɔːməslɪ/ *adv.* ungeheuer; enorm

enormousness /ɪ'nɔːməsnɪs/ *n., no pl.* ungeheure Größe; Riesenhaftigkeit, *die;* (of size, length, height) ungeheures Ausmaß

enough /ɪ'nʌf/ **1** *adj.* genug; genügend; **there's** ~ **room** *or* **room** ~: es ist Platz genug *od.* genügend Platz; **more than** ~: mehr als genug. **2** *n., no pl., no art.* genug; **be** ~ **to do sth.** genügen, etw. zu tun; **are there** ~ **of us?** sind wir genug [Leute]?; **four people are quite** ~: vier Leute genügen völlig; **that [amount] will be** ~ **to go round** das reicht für alle; ~ **of ...:** genug von ...; **are there** ~ **of these books to go round?** reichen diese Bücher für alle?; **[that's]** ~ **[of that]!** [jetzt ist es] genug!; ~ **of your nonsense!** Schluss mit dem Unsinn!; **have had** ~ **[of sb./sth.]** genug [von jmdm./etw.] haben; **I've had** ~**!** jetzt reicht's mir aber!; jetzt habe ich aber genug!; **more than** ~: mehr als genug; **[that's]** ~ **about ...:** genug über ... (*Akk.*) geredet; ~ **said** mehr braucht man dazu nicht zu sagen; ~ **is** ~: mal muss es auch genug sein (ugs.); **it's** ~ **to make you weep** es ist zum Weinen; **as if that were not** ~: als ob das noch nicht genügte. **3** *adv.* genug; **the meat is not cooked** ~: das Fleisch ist nicht genügend durch; **he is not trying hard** ~: er gibt sich nicht genug *od.* genügend Mühe; **they were friendly** ~ **towards us** sie waren soweit recht nett zu uns; **oddly/ funnily** ~: merkwürdiger-/(ugs.) komischerweise; **sure** ~: natürlich; **be good/kind** ~ **to do sth.** so gut sein, etw. zu tun

enquire *etc.* ⇒ **inquire** *etc.*

enrage /ɪn'reɪdʒ/ *v.t.* wütend machen; reizen ‹*wildes Tier*›; **be** ~**d by sth.** über etw. (*Akk.*) wütend werden; **be** ~**d at sb./sth.** auf jmdn./etw. wütend sein

enrich /ɪn'rɪtʃ/ *v.t.* **(a)** (make wealthy) reich machen; **(b)** (fig.) bereichern; anreichern ‹*Nahrungsmittel, Boden, Uran*›; verbessern ‹*Haut*›

enrichment /ɪn'rɪtʃmənt/ *n.* (lit. *or* fig.) Bereicherung, *die;* (of soil, food, uranium) Anreicherung, *die*

enrol (*Amer.:* **enroll**) /ɪn'rəʊl/ **1** *v.i.,* **-ll-** sich anmelden; sich einschreiben [lassen]; (Univ.) sich einschreiben; sich immatrikulieren; ~ **for a course** sich zu einem Kurs anmelden. **2** *v.t.,* **-ll-** einschreiben ‹*Studenten, Kursteilnehmer*›; anwerben ‹*Rekruten*›; aufnehmen ‹*Schüler, Mitglied, Rekrut*›; ~ **sb. for a course/the army** jmdn. für einen Kurs annehmen/in die Armee aufnehmen

enrolment (*Amer.:* **enrollment**) /ɪn'rəʊlmənt/ *n.* Anmeldung, *die;* (Univ.) Immatrikulation, *die;* Einschreibung, *die;* (in army) Eintritt, *der*

en route /ɑ̃ 'ruːt/ *adv.* unterwegs; auf dem Weg; ~ **to Scotland/for Perth** unterwegs *od.* auf dem Weg nach Schottland/Perth

ensemble /ɑ̃'sɑ̃bl/ *n.* Ensemble, *das*

ensign /'ensaɪn, 'ensn/ *n.* **(a)** (banner) Hoheitszeichen, *das;* **(b)** (Brit.) **blue/red/white** ~: Flagge der britischen Marinereserve/Handelsflotte/Marine

enslave /ɪn'sleɪv/ *v.t.* versklaven

ensnare /ɪn'sneə(r)/ *v.t.* (lit. *or* fig.) fangen

ensue /ɪn'sjuː/ *v.i.* **(a)** (follow) sich daran anschließen; **(b)** (result) sich daraus ergeben; ~ **from sth.** sich aus etw. ergeben

ensuing /ɪn'sjuːɪŋ/ *adj.* darauf folgend

ensure /ɪn'ʃʊə(r)/ *v.t.* **(a)** ~ **that ...** (satisfy oneself that) sich vergewissern, dass ...; (see to it that) gewährleisten, dass ...; **(b)** (secure) ~ **sth.** etw. gewährleisten; **this will** ~ **victory for the Party** dies wird der Partei den Sieg sichern

entail /ɪn'teɪl/ *v.t.* mit sich bringen; **what exactly does your job** ~**?** worin besteht Ihre Arbeit ganz genau?; **sth.** ~**s doing sth.** etw. bedeutet, dass man etw. tun muss

entangle /ɪn'tæŋɡl/ *v.t.* **(a)** (catch) sich verfangen lassen; **get [oneself]** *or* **become** ~**d in** *or* **with sth.** sich in etw. (*Dat.*) verfangen; **be** ~**d in sth.** sich in etw. (*Dat.*) verfangen haben; **(b)** (fig.: involve) verwickeln; **be/become** ~**d in sth.** in etw. (*Akk.*) verwickelt sein/werden; **(c)** (make tangled) völlig durcheinander bringen; **get sth.** ~**d [with sth.]** etw. [mit etw.] durcheinander bringen

entanglement /ɪn'tæŋglmənt/ n. (a) Verwicklung, die; (b) (fig.: involvement) **his ~ in a divorce case** seine Verwicklung in eine Scheidungsaffäre; (c) (entangled things) Durcheinander, das; (Mil.) [Draht]verhau, der

enter /'entə(r)/ 1 v.i. (a) (go in) hineingehen; ‹Fahrzeug:› hineinfahren; (come in) hereinkommen; (walk into room) eintreten; (come on stage) auftreten; **~ Macbeth** (Theatre) Auftritt Macbeth; **~ into a building/another world** ein Gebäude/eine andere Welt betreten; 'E~!' „Herein!"; (b) (announce oneself as competitor in race etc.) sich zur Teilnahme anmelden (**for** an + Dat.). 2 v.t. (a) (go into) [hinein]gehen in (+ Akk.); ‹Fahrzeug:› [hinein]fahren in (+ Akk.); ‹Flugzeug:› [hinein]fliegen in (+ Akk.); betreten ‹Gebäude, Zimmer›; eintreten in (+ Akk.) ‹Zimmer›; einlaufen in (+ Akk.) ‹Hafen›; einreisen in (+ Akk.) ‹Land›; (drive into) hineinfahren in (+ Akk.); (come into) [herein]kommen in (+ Akk.); **has it ever ~ed your mind that ...?** ist dir nie der Gedanke gekommen, dass ...?; (b) (become a member of) beitreten (+ Dat.) ‹Verein, Organisation, Partei›; eintreten in (+ Akk.) ‹Kirche, Kloster›; ergreifen ‹Beruf›; **~ the army/[the] university** zum Militär/auf die od. zur Universität gehen; **~ teaching/medicine** den Lehr-/Arztberuf ergreifen; **~ the law** die juristische Laufbahn einschlagen; (c) (participate in) sich beteiligen an (+ Dat.) ‹Diskussion, Unterhaltung›; teilnehmen an (+ Dat.) ‹Rennen, Wettbewerb›; (d) (write) eintragen (**in** in + Akk.); **~ sth. in a dictionary/an index** etw. in ein Wörterbuch/ein Register aufnehmen; (e) **~ sb./sth./one's name for** jmdn./etw./sich anmelden für ‹Rennen, Wettbewerb, Prüfung›; (f) (Computing) eingeben ‹Daten usw.›; **press ~:** 'Enter' drücken

~ into v.t. (a) (engage in) anknüpfen ‹Gespräch›; sich beteiligen an (+ Dat.) ‹Diskussion, Debatte, Wettbewerb›; aufnehmen ‹Beziehung, Verhandlungen›; (bind oneself by) eingehen ‹Verpflichtung, Ehe, Beziehung›; schließen ‹Vertrag›; (b) (form part of) Bestandteil sein von; **that doesn't ~ into it at all** das hat damit gar nichts zu tun **~ on** v.t. beginnen ‹Karriere, Laufbahn, Amtsperiode›; in Angriff nehmen ‹Aufgabe, Projekt›

~ 'up v.t. eintragen

~ upon ⇨ **~ on**

'enter key n. (Computing) Entertaste, die; Eingabetaste, die

enterprise /'entəpraɪz/ n. (a) (undertaking) Unternehmen, das; **commercial ~:** Handelsunternehmen, das; **free/private ~:** freies/privates Unternehmertum; (b) no indef. art. (readiness to undertake new ventures) Unternehmungsgeist, der

enterprising /'entəpraɪzɪŋ/ adj. unternehmungslustig, rührig ‹Geschäftsmann›; kühn ‹Reise, Gedanke, Idee›

entertain /entə'teɪn/ v.t. (a) (amuse) unterhalten; **we were greatly ~ed by ...:** wir haben uns köstlich über ... (Akk.) amüsiert; (b) (receive as guest) bewirten; **~ sb. to lunch/dinner** (Brit.) jmdn. zum Mittag-/Abendessen einladen; (c) (have in the mind) haben ‹Meinung, Vorstellung›; hegen (geh.) ‹Gefühl, Vorurteil, Verdacht, Zweifel, Groll›; (consider) in Erwägung ziehen; **he would never ~ the idea of doing that** er würde es nie ernstlich erwägen, das zu tun

entertainer /entə'teɪnə(r)/ n. ▸ **887** Entertainer, der/ Entertainerin, die

entertaining /entə'teɪnɪŋ/ 1 adj. unterhaltsam. 2 n., no pl., no indef. art. **they enjoy ~:** sie haben gern Gäste; **do some** or **a bit of/a lot of ~:** manchmal/sehr oft Gäste einladen; **she's not very good at ~:** sie ist keine sehr gute Gastgeberin

entertainment /entə'teɪnmənt/ n. (a) (amusement) Unterhaltung, die; **the world of ~:** die Welt des Showbusiness; (b) (public performance, show) Veranstaltung, die

enthral (Amer.: **enthrall**) /ɪn'θrɔːl/ v.t., **-ll-:** (a) (captivate) gefangen nehmen (fig.); (b) (delight) begeistern; entzücken

enthrone /ɪn'θrəʊn/ v.t. inthronisieren

enthuse /ɪn'θjuːz, ɪn'θuːz/ (coll.) 1 v.i. in Begeisterung ausbrechen (**about, over** über + Akk.). 2 v.t. begeistern

enthusiasm /ɪn'θjuːzɪæzəm, ɪn'θuːzɪæzəm/ n. (a) no pl. Enthusiasmus, der; Begeisterung, die (**for, about** für); (b) (thing about which sb. is enthusiastic) Leidenschaft, die

enthusiast /ɪn'θjuːzɪæst, ɪn'θuːzɪæst/ n. Enthusiast, der; (for sport, pop music) Fan, der; **a DIY ~:** ein begeisterter Heimwerker

enthusiastic /ɪnθjuːzɪ'æstɪk, ɪnθuːzɪ'æstɪk/ adj. begeistert (**about** von); **not be very ~ about doing sth.** keine große Lust haben, etw. zu tun

enthusiastically /ɪnθjuːzɪ'æstɪkəlɪ, ɪnθuːzɪ'æstɪkəlɪ/ adv. begeistert

entice /ɪn'taɪs/ v.t. locken (**into** in + Akk.); **~ sb./sth. [away] from sb./sth.** jmdn./etw. von jmdm./etw. fortlocken; **~ sb. into doing** or **to do sth.** jmdn. dazu verleiten, etw. zu tun

enticement /ɪn'taɪsmənt/ n. (thing) Lockmittel, das

enticing /ɪn'taɪsɪŋ/ adj. verlockend

entire /ɪn'taɪə(r)/ adj. (a) (whole) ganz; (b) (intact) vollständig ‹Ausgabe, Buch, Manuskript, Service›; **remain ~:** unversehrt bleiben

entirely /ɪn'taɪəlɪ/ adv. (a) (wholly) völlig; **not ~ suitable for the occasion** dem Anlass nicht ganz angemessen; (b) (solely) ganz ‹für sich behalten›; allein, voll ‹verantwortlich sein›; **it's up to you ~:** es liegt ganz bei dir

entirety /ɪn'taɪərətɪ/ n., no pl. **in its ~:** in seiner/ihrer Gesamtheit

entitle /ɪn'taɪtl/ v.t. (a) (give title of) **~ a book/film ...:** einem Buch/Film den Titel ... geben; (b) (give rightful claim) berechtigen (**to** zu); **~ sb. to do sth.** jmdn. berechtigen od. jmdm. das Recht geben, etw. zu tun; **be ~d to [claim] sth.** Anspruch auf etw. (Akk.) haben; **be ~d to do sth.** das Recht haben, etw. zu tun

entitlement /ɪn'taɪtlmənt/ n. (rightful claim) Anspruch, der (**to** auf + Akk.)

entity /'entɪtɪ/ n. (thing that exists) [**separate**] **~:** eigenständiges Gebilde

entomologist /entə'mɒlədʒɪst/ n. ▸ **887** Entomologe, der/Entomologin, die

entomology /entə'mɒlədʒɪ/ n. Entomologie, die; Insektenkunde, die

entourage /ɒntʊ'rɑːʒ/ n. Gefolge, das

entrails /'entreɪlz/ n. pl. Eingeweide Pl.; Gedärm, das

entrance¹ /'entrəns/ n. (a) (entering) Eintritt, der (**into** in + Akk.); (of troops) Einzug, der; (of vehicle) Einfahrt, die; (b) (on to stage, lit. or fig.) Auftritt, der; **make an** or **one's ~:** seinen Auftritt haben; (c) (way in) Eingang, der (**to** Gen. od.); (for vehicle) Einfahrt, die; (d) no pl., no art. (right of admission) Aufnahme, die (**to** in + Akk.); **~ to the concert is by ticket only** man kommt nur mit einer Eintrittskarte in das Konzert; (e) (fee) Eintritt, der

entrance² /ɪn'trɑːns/ v.t. hinreißen; bezaubern; **be ~d by** or **with sth.** von etw. hingerissen od. bezaubert sein

entrance /'entrəns/: **~ examination** n. Aufnahmeprüfung, die; **~ fee** n. Eintrittsgeld, das; (for competition) Teilnahmegebühr, die; (on joining club) Aufnahmegebühr, die; **~ hall** n. Eingangshalle, die

entrancing /ɪn'trɑːnsɪŋ/ adj. bezaubernd; hinreißend

entrant /'entrənt/ n. (a) (into a profession etc.) Anfänger, der/Anfängerin, die; (b) (for competition, race, etc.) Teilnehmer, der/Teilnehmerin, die (**for** Gen., an + Dat.)

entrap /ɪn'træp/ v.t., **-pp-** (trick) **~ sb. into doing sth.** jmdn. verleiten, etw. zu tun

entreat /ɪn'triːt/ v.t. anflehen

entreaty /ɪn'triːtɪ/ n. flehentliche Bitte

entrecôte /'ɒntrəkəʊt/ n. (Gastr.) **~ [steak]** Entrecote, das

entrench /ɪn'trentʃ/ v.t. **become ~ed** (fig.) ‹Vorurteil, Gedanke:› sich festsetzen; ‹Tradition:› sich verwurzeln

entrepreneur /ɒntrəprə'nɜː(r)/ n. Unternehmer, der/Unternehmerin, die

entrust /ɪn'trʌst/ v.t. **~ sb. with sth.** jmdm. etw. anvertrauen; **~ sb./sth. to sb./sth.** jmdm./etw. jmdm./einer Sache anvertrauen; **~ a task to sb., ~ sb. with a task** jmdn. mit einer Aufgabe betrauen

entry /'entrɪ/ n. (a) Eintritt, der (**into** in + Akk.); (of troops) Einzug, der; (into organization) Beitritt, der (**into** zu); (into country) Einreise, die; (ceremonial entrance) [feierlicher]

Einzug; **gain ~ to the house** ins Haus gelangen; '**no ~**' (for people) „Zutritt verboten"; (for vehicle) „Einfahrt verboten"; **a 'no ~' sign** ein Schild mit der Aufschrift „Zutritt/Einfahrt verboten"; **(b)** (on to stage) Auftritt, *der;* **(c)** (way in) Eingang, *der;* (for vehicle) Einfahrt, *die;* **(d)** (registration, item registered) Eintragung, *die* (**in, into** in + *Akk. od. Dat.*); (in dictionary, encyclopaedia, yearbook, index) Eintrag, *der;* **make an ~:** eine Eintragung vornehmen; **(e)** (person or thing in competition) Nennung, *die;* (set of answers etc.) Lösung, *die*

entry: ~ fee ⇒ **entrance fee; ~ form** *n.* Anmeldeformular, *das;* (for competition) Teilnahmeschein, *der;* **~ permit** *n.* Einreiseerlaubnis, *die;* **~ visa** *n.* Einreisevisum, *das*

entwine /ɪn'twaɪn/ *v.t.* **~ sth. round sb./sth.** etw. um jmdn./etw. schlingen *od.* (geh.) winden; **~ sth. with sth.** etw. mit etw. umschlingen *od.* (geh.) umwinden

enumerate /ɪ'njuːməreɪt/ *v.t.* (einzeln) aufzählen

enumeration /ɪnjuːmə'reɪʃn/ *n.* Aufzählung, *die*

enunciate /ɪ'nʌnsɪeɪt/ *v.t.* artikulieren

enunciation /ɪnʌnsɪ'eɪʃn/ *n.* Artikulation, *die;* [deutliche] Aussprache

envelop /ɪn'veləp/ *v.t.* [ein]hüllen (**in** in + *Akk.*); **be ~ed in flames** ganz von Flammen umgeben sein

envelope /'envələʊp, 'ɒnvələʊp/ *n.* [Brief]umschlag, *der*

enviable /'envɪəbl/ *adj.* beneidenswert

envious /'envɪəs/ *adj.* neidisch (**of** auf + *Akk.*)

environment /ɪn'vaɪərənmənt/ *n.* **(a)** (natural surroundings) **the ~:** die Umwelt; **the Department of the E~** (Brit.) das Umweltministerium; **(b)** (surrounding objects, region) Umgebung, *die;* (social surroundings) Milieu, *das;* **physical/ working ~:** Umwelt, *die*/Arbeitswelt, *die;* **home/family ~:** häusliches Milieu/Familienverhältnisse *Pl.*

environmental /ɪnvaɪərən'mentl/ *adj.* Umwelt-

environmental 'health *n.* Umwelthygiene, *die;* **~ officer** Umwelthygienebeauftragte, *der;* **~ department** Umwelthygieneamt, *das*

environmentalism /ɪnvaɪərən'mentəlɪzm/ *n., no pl., no art.* Engagement für die Umwelt; (as political movement) Ökologismus, *der*

environmentalist /ɪnvaɪərən'mentəlɪst/ *n.* Umweltschützer, *der*/-schützerin, *die*

environmentally /ɪnvaɪərən'mentəlɪ/ *adv.* ökologisch; **~ friendly** umweltfreundlich; **~ sensitive** ökologisch sensibel; (~ friendly) umweltverträglich; umweltschonend; **~ sound** umweltverträglich; umweltgerecht

envisage /ɪn'vɪzɪdʒ/ *v.t.* sich (*Dat.*) vorstellen; **what do you ~ doing [about it]?** was gedenkst du [in der Sache] zu tun?

envoy /'envɔɪ/ *n.* (messenger) Bote, *der*/Botin, *die;* (Diplom. etc.) Gesandte, *der*/Gesandtin, *die*

envy /'envɪ/ **1** *n.* **(a)** Neid, *der;* **feelings of ~:** Neidgefühle; **(b)** (object) **his new sports car was the ~ of all his friends** alle seine Freunde beneideten ihn um seinen neuen Sportwagen. **2** *v.t.* beneiden; **~ sb. sth.** jmdn. um etw. beneiden; **I don't ~ you** dich kann ich nicht beneiden

enzyme /'enzaɪm/ *n.* (Chem.) Enzym, *das*

EOC *abbr.* (Brit.) **Equal Opportunities Commission**

ephemeral /ɪ'femərl/ *adj.* ephemer[isch] (geh.); kurzlebig

epic /'epɪk/ **1** *adj.* **(a)** episch; **(b)** (of heroic type or scale, lit. or fig.) monumental; **~ film** Filmepos, *das.* **2** *n.* Epos, *das*

epicentre (Brit.; Amer.: **epicenter**) /'epɪsentə(r)/ *n.* Epizentrum, *das*

epidemic /epɪ'demɪk/ (Med.; also fig.) **1** *adj.* epidemisch. **2** *n.* Epidemie, *die*

epigram /'epɪgræm/ *n.* Epigramm, *das;* Sinngedicht, *das*

epilepsy /'epɪlepsɪ/ *n.* ▶865| (Med.) Epilepsie, *die*

epileptic /epɪ'leptɪk/ (Med.) **1** *adj.* epileptisch; *see also* fit¹ a. **2** *n.* Epileptiker, *der*/Epileptikerin, *die*

epilogue (Amer.: **epilog**) /'epɪlɒg/ *n.* (Lit.) Epilog, *der*

Epiphany /ɪ'pɪfənɪ/ *n.* **[Feast of the] ~:** Epiphanias, *das;* Dreikönigsfest, *das*

episcopal /ɪ'pɪskəpl/ *adj.* episkopal; bischöflich

episode /'epɪsəʊd/ *n.* **(a)** Episode, *die;* **(b)** (instalment of serial) Folge, *die*

epistle /ɪ'pɪsl/ *n.* (Bibl., Lit., or usu. joc.: letter) Epistel, *die*

epitaph /'epɪtɑːf/ *n.* Epitaph, *das;* Grab[in]schrift, *die*

epithet /'epɪθet/ *n.* **(a)** Beiname, *der;* **(b)** (Ling.) Epitheton, *das* (fachspr.); Beiwort, *das*

epitome /ɪ'pɪtəmɪ/ *n.* Inbegriff, *der*

epitomize /ɪ'pɪtəmaɪz/ *v.t.* **~ sth.** der Inbegriff einer Sache (*Gen.*) sein

epoch /'iːpɒk/ *n.* Epoche, *die*

'epoch-making *adj.* epochal ⟨*Bedeutung*⟩; epochemachend ⟨*Entdeckung*⟩

equable /'ekwəbl/ *adj.* ausgeglichen ⟨*Wesen, Person, Klima*⟩; (equally proportioned) ausgewogen ⟨*Maße, System, Proportionen*⟩

equal /'iːkwl/ **1** *adj.* **(a)** gleich; **~ in** *or* **of ~ height/ weight/size/importance** *etc.* gleich hoch/schwer/groß/ wichtig *usw.;* **not ~ in length** verschieden lang; **divide a cake into ~ parts/portions** einen Kuchen in gleich große Stücke/Portionen aufteilen; **~ amounts of milk and water** gleich viel Milch und Wasser; **be ~ in size to sth.** ebenso groß wie etw. sein; **Michael came ~ third** *or* **third ~ with Richard in the class exams** bei den Klassenprüfungen kam Michael zusammen mit Richard auf den dritten Platz; **be on ~ terms [with sb.]** [mit jmdm.] gleichgestellt sein; **all/other things being ~:** wenn nichts dazwischen kommt; **~ rights** gleiche Rechte; Gleichberechtigung, *die;;* **(b) be ~ to sth./sb.** (strong, clever, etc. enough) einer Sache/jmdm. gewachsen sein; **be ~ to doing sth.** imstande sein, etw. zu tun; **(c) they were all given ~ treatment** sie wurden alle gleich behandelt; **(d)** (evenly balanced) ausgeglichen. **2** *n.* Gleichgestellte, *der*/*die;* **be sb.'s/sth.'s ~:** jmdm. ebenbürtig sein/ einer Sache (*Dat.*) gleichkommen; **he/she/it has no** *or* **is without ~:** er/sie/es hat nicht seines-/ihresgleichen. **3** *v.t.,* (Brit.) **-ll-: (a)** (be equal to) **~ sb./sth. [in sth.]** jmdm./ einer Sache [in etw. (*Dat.*)] entsprechen; **three times four ~s twelve** drei mal vier ist [gleich] zwölf; **(b)** (do sth. equal to) **~ sb.** es jmdm. gleichtun

equalise, equaliser ⇒ **equaliz-**

equality /ɪ'kwɒlɪtɪ/ *n.* Gleichheit, *die;* (equal rights) Gleichberechtigung, *die;* **racial ~:** Gleichberechtigung der Rassen; **~ between the sexes** Gleichheit von Mann und Frau

equalize /'iːkwəlaɪz/ **1** *v.t.* ausgleichen ⟨*Druck, Temperatur*⟩. **2** *v.i.* (Sport) den Ausgleich[streffer] erzielen

equalizer /'iːkwəlaɪzə(r)/ *n.* (Sport) Ausgleich[streffer], *der*

equally /'iːkwəlɪ/ *adv.* **(a)** ebenso; **be ~ close to a and b** von a und b gleich weit entfernt sein; **the two are ~ gifted** die beiden sind gleich begabt; **(b)** (in equal shares) in gleiche Teile ⟨*aufteilen*⟩; gleichmäßig ⟨*verteilen*⟩; **(c)** (according to the same rule and measurement) in gleicher Weise; gleich ⟨*behandeln*⟩

Equal Opportunities Commission *n.* (Brit.) Ausschuss für Chancengleichheit; ≈ Gleichstellungsausschuss, *der*

equal oppor'tunity *n.* Chancengleichheit, *die;* **an ~** *or* **equal opportunities employer** ein Arbeitgeber, der Chancengleicheit praktiziert

'equals sign *n.* (Math.) Gleichheitszeichen, *das*

equanimity /ekwə'nɪmɪtɪ/ *n., no pl.* Gleichmut, *der*

equate /ɪ'kweɪt/ *v.t.* **~ sth. [to** *or* **with sth.]** etw. [einer Sache (*Dat.*) *od.* mit etw.] gleichsetzen

equation /ɪ'kweɪʒn/ *n.* (Math., Chem.) Gleichung, *die*

equator /ɪ'kweɪtə(r)/ *n.* (Geog., Astron.) Äquator, *der*

equestrian /ɪ'kwestrɪən/ *adj.* reiterlich; Reit⟨*turnier, -talent*⟩

equidistant /iːkwɪ'dɪstənt/ *adj.* gleich weit entfernt (**from** von)

equilateral /iːkwɪ'lætərl/ *adj.* (Math.) gleichseitig

equilibrium /iːkwɪ'lɪbrɪəm/ *n., pl.* **equilibria** /iːkwɪ'lɪbrɪə/ *or* **~s** Gleichgewicht, *das;* **mental/emotional ~:**

geistige/emotionale Ausgeglichenheit; **in** ∼: im Gleichgewicht

equinox /'iːkwɪnɒks, 'ekwɪnɒks/ *n.* Tagundnachtgleiche, *die*

equip /ɪ'kwɪp/ *v.t.* **-pp-** ausrüsten ⟨*Fahrzeug, Armee, Person*⟩; ausstatten ⟨*Zimmer, Küche*⟩; **fully ∼ped** komplett ausgerüstet/ausgestattet

equipment /ɪ'kwɪpmənt/ *n.* Ausrüstung, *die;* (of kitchen, laboratory, etc.) Ausstattung, *die;* (sth. needed for activity) Geräte *Pl.;* **breathing/recording** ∼: Sauerstoffgerät, *das*/Aufnahmegeräte *Pl.;* **climbing/diving** ∼: Bergsteiger-/Taucherausrüstung, *die*

equitable /'ekwɪtəbl/ *adj.* gerecht; **in an** ∼ **manner** gerecht

equity /'ekwɪtɪ/ *n.* **(a)** (fairness) Gerechtigkeit, *die;* **(b)** *in pl.* (stocks and shares without fixed interest) [Stamm]aktien *Pl.*

equity: ∼ **'capital** *n.* (Commerc.) Eigenkapital, *das;* ∼ **market** *n.* (Commerc.) Aktienmarkt, *der*

equivalence /ɪ'kwɪvələns/ *n.* **(a)** (being equivalent) Gleichwertigkeit, *die;* (of two amounts) Wertgleichheit, *die;* **(b)** (having equivalent meaning) ∼ **[in meaning]** Bedeutungsgleichheit, *die*

equivalent /ɪ'kwɪvələnt/ **1** *adj.* **(a)** (equal, having same result) gleichwertig; (corresponding) entsprechend; **be** ∼ **to sth.** einer Sache (*Dat.*) entsprechen; **be** ∼ **to doing sth.** dasselbe sein, wie wenn man etw. tut; **(b)** (meaning the same) äquivalent (Sprachw.); entsprechend; **these two words are [not]** ∼ **in meaning** diese beiden Wörter sind [nicht] bedeutungsgleich. **2** *n.* **(a)** (∼ or corresponding thing or person) Pendant, *das,* Gegenstück, *das* (**of** zu); **(b)** (word etc. having same meaning) Entsprechung, *die* (**of** zu); Äquivalent, *das* (**of** für); **(c)** (thing having same result) **be the** ∼ **of sth.** einer Sache (*Dat.*) entsprechen

equivocal /ɪ'kwɪvəkl/ *adj.* **(a)** (ambiguous) zweideutig; **(b)** (questionable) zweifelhaft

equivocate /ɪ'kwɪvəkeɪt/ *v.i.* ausweichen

er /ɜː(r)/ *int.* äh

era /'ɪərə/ *n.* Ära, *die*

eradicate /ɪ'rædɪkeɪt/ *v.t.* ausrotten

erase /ɪ'reɪz/ *v.t.* **(a)** (rub out) auslöschen; (with rubber, knife) ausradieren; **(b)** (obliterate) tilgen (geh.) (**from** aus); **(c)** (from recording tape; also Computing) löschen

eraser /ɪ'reɪzə(r)/ *n.* **[pencil]** ∼: Radiergummi, *der;* **[blackboard]** ∼: Block mit Filzbelag o. ä. zum Löschen von Kreideschrift

erect /ɪ'rekt/ **1** *adj.* **(a)** (upright, vertical; also fig.) aufrecht; gerade ⟨*Rücken, Wuchs*⟩; **(b)** (Physiol.) erigiert. **2** *v.t.* errichten; aufbauen ⟨*Gerüst*⟩; aufstellen ⟨*Standbild, Verkehrsschild*⟩; aufschlagen, aufstellen ⟨*Zelt*⟩

erection /ɪ'rekʃn/ *n.* **(a)** ⇒ **erect 2:** Errichtung, *die;* Aufbau, *der;* Aufstellen, *das;* Aufschlagen, *das;* **(b)** (structure) Bauwerk, *das;* (other than a building) Konstruktion, *die;* **(c)** (Physiol.) Erektion, *die*

ergonomic /ɜːgə'nɒmɪk/ *adj.* ergonomisch

ergonomics /ɜːgə'nɒmɪks/ *n., no pl.* Ergonomie, *die*

ERM *abbr.* **exchange rate mechanism** ⇒ **exchange 3 c**

ermine /'ɜːmɪn/ *n.* **(a)** (fur; also Her.) Hermelin, *der;* **(b)** (Zool.) Hermelin, *das*

erode /ɪ'rəʊd/ *v.t.* **(a)** ⟨*Säure, Rost:*⟩ angreifen; ⟨*Wasser, Regen, Meer:*⟩ auswaschen; ⟨*Wasser, Regen, Meer, Wind:*⟩ erodieren (Geol.); **(b)** (fig.) unterminieren

erosion /ɪ'rəʊʒn/ *n.* **(a)** ⇒ **erode a:** Angreifen, *das;* Auswaschung, *die;* Erosion, *die* (Geol.); **(b)** (fig.) Unterminierung, *die*

erotic /ɪ'rɒtɪk/ *adj.,* **erotically** /ɪ'rɒtɪkəlɪ/ *adv.* erotisch

err /ɜː(r)/ *v.i.* sich irren; **to** ∼ **is human** (prov.) Irren ist menschlich; **let's** ∼ **on the safe side and …:** um sicher zu gehen, wollen wir …

errand /'erənd/ *n.* Botengang, *der;* (shopping) Besorgung, *die;* **go on** *or* **run an** ∼: einen Botengang/eine Besorgung machen

errand: ∼**-boy** *n.* Laufbursche, *der;* Bote[njunge], *der;* ∼**-girl** *n.* Laufmädchen, *das;* Botin, *die*

erratic /ɪ'rætɪk/ *adj.* unregelmäßig; sprunghaft ⟨*Wesen, Person, Art*⟩; unbeständig ⟨*Charakter, Leistung*⟩; launenhaft ⟨*Verhalten*⟩; ungleichmäßig ⟨*Bewegung, Verlauf*⟩

erroneous /ɪ'rəʊnɪəs/ *adj.* falsch; irrig ⟨*Schlussfolgerung, Eindruck, Ansicht, Auffassung, Annahme*⟩

erroneously /ɪ'rəʊnɪəslɪ/ *adv.* fälschlich; irrigerweise

error /'erə(r)/ *n.* **(a)** (mistake) Fehler, *der;* **gross** ∼ **of judgement** grobe Fehleinschätzung; **(b)** (wrong opinion) Irrtum, *der;* **realize the** ∼ **of one's ways** seine Fehler einsehen; **in** ∼: irrtümlich[erweise]

'error message *n.* (Computing) Fehlermeldung, *die*

erudite /'erʊdaɪt/ *adj.* gelehrt ⟨*Abhandlung, Vortrag*⟩; gebildet, gelehrt ⟨*Person*⟩

erudition /erʊ'dɪʃn/ *n., no pl.* Gelehrsamkeit, *die* (geh.)

erupt /ɪ'rʌpt/ *v.i.* **(a)** ⟨*Vulkan, Geysir:*⟩ ausbrechen; ∼ **with anger/into a fit of rage** (fig.) einen Wutanfall bekommen; **(b)** ⟨*Hautausschlag:*⟩ ausbrechen

eruption /ɪ'rʌpʃn/ *n.* (of volcano, geyser) Ausbruch, *der;* Eruption, *die* (Geol.)

escalate /'eskəleɪt/ **1** *v.i.* sich ausweiten (**into** zu); eskalieren (geh.) (**into** zu); ⟨*Preise, Kosten:*⟩ [ständig] steigen. **2** *v.t.* ausweiten (**into** zu); eskalieren (geh.) (**into** zu)

escalator /'eskəleɪtə(r)/ *n.* Rolltreppe, *die*

escalope /'eskələʊp/ *n.* (Gastr.) Schnitzel, *das*

escapade /'eskəpeɪd/ *n.* Eskapade, *die* (geh.)

escape /ɪ'skeɪp/ **1** *n.* **(a)** (lit. or fig.) Flucht, *die* (**from** aus); (from prison) Ausbruch, *der* (**from** aus); **there is no** ∼ (lit. or fig.) es gibt kein Entkommen; ∼ **vehicle** Fluchtfahrzeug, *das;* **make one's** ∼ **[from sth.]** [aus etw.] entkommen; **have a narrow** ∼: gerade noch einmal davonkommen; **have a lucky** ∼: glücklich davonkommen; **(b)** (leakage of gas etc.) Austritt, *der;* Entweichen, *das.* **2** *v.i.* **(a)** (lit. or fig.) fliehen (**from** aus); entfliehen (geh.) (**from** *Dat.*); (successfully) entkommen (**from** *Dat.*); (from prison) ausbrechen (**from** aus); ⟨*Großtier:*⟩ ausbrechen; ⟨*Kleintier:*⟩ entlaufen (**from** *Dat.*); ⟨*Vogel:*⟩ entfliegen (**from** *Dat.*); **while trying to** ∼: auf der Flucht; ∼**d prisoner/convict** entflohener Gefangener/Sträfling; **(b)** (leak) ⟨*Gas:*⟩ ausströmen; ⟨*Flüssigkeit:*⟩ auslaufen; **(c)** (avoid harm) davonkommen; ∼ **alive** mit dem Leben davonkommen; **(d)** (Computing) **press** ∼: 'Escape' drücken. **3** *v.t.* **(a)** entkommen (+ *Dat.*) ⟨*Verfolger, Angreifer, Feind*⟩; entgehen (+ *Dat.*) ⟨*Bestrafung, Gefangennahme, Tod, Entdeckung*⟩; verschont bleiben von ⟨*Katastrophe, Krankheit, Zerstörung, Auswirkungen*⟩; **she narrowly** ∼**d being killed** sie wäre fast getötet worden; **(b)** (not be remembered by) entfallen sein (+ *Dat.*); **(c)** ∼ **sb.['s notice]** (not be seen) jmdm. entgehen; ∼ **notice** nicht bemerkt werden; ∼ **sb.'s attention** jmds. Aufmerksamkeit (*Dat.*) entgehen

escape: ∼ **attempt** *n.* Fluchtversuch, *der;* (from prison) Ausbruchsversuch, *der;* ∼ **key** *n.* (Computing) Escapetaste, *die;* ∼ **route** *n.* Fluchtweg, *der;* ∼ **valve** *n.* Sicherheitsventil, *das*

escapism /ɪ'skeɪpɪzm/ *n.* Realitätsflucht, *die*

escort 1 /'eskɔːt/ *n.* **(a)** (armed guard) Eskorte, *die;* Geleitschutz, *der* (Milit.); **police** ∼: Polizeieskorte, *die;* **with an** ∼, **under** ∼: mit einer Eskorte; **(b)** (person[s] protecting or guiding) Begleitung, *die;* **be sb.'s** ∼: jmdn. begleiten; **(c)** (hired companion) Begleiter, *der*/Begleiterin, *die;* (woman also) ≈ Hostess, *die.* **2** /ɪ'skɔːt/ *v.t.* **(a)** begleiten; (Mil.) eskortieren; **(b)** (take forcibly) bringen

escort: /'eskɔːt/: ∼ **agency** *n.* Agentur für Begleiter/Begleiterinnen, *die;* ∼ **vessel** *n.* (Navy) Geleitschiff, *das*

Eskimo /'eskɪməʊ/ **1** *adj.* Eskimo-. **2** *n.* **(a)** *no pl.* ▶ **897** (language) Eskimoisch, *das; see also* **English 2 a;** **(b)** *pl.* ∼**s** *or same* Eskimo, *der*/Eskimofrau, *die;* **the** ∼**[s]** die Eskimos

esoteric /esə'terɪk, iːsə'terɪk/ *adj.* esoterisch (geh.)

ESP *abbr.* (Psych.) **extra-sensory perception** ASW

especial /ɪ'speʃl/ *attrib. adj.* [ganz] besonder…

especially /ɪ'speʃəlɪ/ *adv.* besonders; **what** ∼ **do you want to see?** was möchten Sie insbesondere sehen?; ∼ **as** zumal; **more** ∼: ganz besonders

Esperanto /espə'ræntəʊ/ *n.*, *no pl.* ▶897 | Esperanto, *das; see also* **English 2 a**

espionage /'espɪənɑːʒ/ *n.* Spionage, *die*

esplanade /esplə'neɪd, esplə'nɑːd/ *n.* Esplanade, *die* (geh.)

espouse /ɪ'spaʊz/ *v.t.* eintreten für

espresso /e'spresəʊ/ *n.*, *pl.* ~s (coffee) Espresso, *der*

e'spresso bar *n.* Espressobar, *die;* Espresso, *das*

Esq. *abbr.* **Esquire** ▶1152 | ≈ Hr.; (on letter) ≈ Hrn.; **James Smith**, ~: Hr./Hrn. James Smith

essay /'eseɪ/ *n.* Essay, *der;* Aufsatz, *der* (bes. Schulw.)

essence /'esəns/ *n.* **(a)** Wesen, *das;* (gist) Wesentliche, *das;* (of problem, teaching) Kern, *der;* **in** ~: im Wesentlichen; **be of the** ~: von entscheidender Bedeutung sein; **(b)** (Cookery) Essenz, *die*

essential /ɪ'senʃl/ **1** *adj.* **(a)** (fundamental) wesentlich ‹ *Unterschied, Merkmal, Aspekt* ›; entscheidend ‹ *Frage* ›; **(b)** (indispensable) unentbehrlich; lebenswichtig ‹ *Nahrungsmittel, Güter* ›; unabdingbar ‹ *Erfordernis, Qualifikation, Voraussetzung* ›; unbedingt notwendig ‹ *Bestandteile, Maßnahmen, Ausrüstung* ›; wesentlich, entscheidend ‹ *Rolle* ›; ~ **to life** lebensnotwendig; **it is [absolutely** *or* **most]** ~ **that** …: es ist unbedingt notwendig, dass … **2** *n.*, *esp. in pl.* **(a)** (indispensable element) Notwendigste, *das;* **the bare** ~s das Allernotwendigste; **(b)** (fundamental element) Wesentliche, *das;* **the** ~s **of French grammar** die Grundzüge der französischen Grammatik

essentially /ɪ'senʃəlɪ/ *adv.* im Grunde

establish /ɪ'stæblɪʃ/ **1** *v.t.* **(a)** (set up, create, found) schaffen ‹ *Einrichtung, Präzedenzfall, Ministerposten* ›; gründen ‹ *Organisation, Institut* ›; errichten ‹ *Geschäft, Lehrstuhl, System* ›; einsetzen, bilden ‹ *Regierung, Ausschuss* ›; herstellen ‹ *Kontakt, Beziehungen* › (with zu); aufstellen ‹ *Rekord* ›; ins Leben rufen, begründen ‹ *Bewegung* ›; ~ **one's authority** sich (*Dat.*) Autorität verschaffen; ~ **law and order** Recht und Ordnung herstellen; **(b)** (secure acceptance for) etablieren; **become** ~**ed** sich einbürgern; ~ **one's reputation** sich (*Dat.*) einen Namen machen; **(c)** (prove) beweisen ‹ *Schuld, Unschuld, Tatsache* ›; unter Beweis stellen ‹ *Können* ›; nachweisen ‹ *Anspruch* ›; **(d)** (discover) feststellen; ermitteln ‹ *Umstände, Aufenthaltsort* ›. **2** *v. refl.* ~ **oneself [at** *or* **in a place]** sich [an einem Ort] niederlassen

established /ɪ'stæblɪʃt/ *adj.* **(a)** eingeführt ‹ *Geschäft usw.* ›; bestehend ‹ *Ordnung* ›; etabliert ‹ *Schriftsteller* ›; **(b)** (accepted) üblich; etabliert ‹ *Gesellschaftsordnung* ›; geltend ‹ *Norm* ›; fest ‹ *Brauch* ›; feststehend ‹ *Tatsache* ›; **become** ~: sich durchsetzen; **(c)** (Eccl.) ~ **church/religion** Staatskirche/-religion, *die*

establishment /ɪ'stæblɪʃmənt/ *n.* **(a)** (setting up, creation, foundation) Gründung, *die;* (of government, committee) Einsetzung, *die;* (of movement) Begründung, *die;* (of relations) Schaffung, *die;* **(b)** (institution) **[business]** ~: Unternehmen, *das;* **commercial/industrial** ~ Handels-/Industrieunternehmen, *das;* **(c)** (Brit.) **the E**~: das Establishment

estate /ɪ'steɪt/ *n.* **(a)** (landed property) Gut, *das;* **(b)** (Brit.) (housing ~) **[Wohn]**siedlung, *die;* (industrial ~) Industriegebiet, *das;* (trading ~) Gewerbegebiet, *das;* **(c)** (total assets) (of deceased person) Erbmasse, *die* (Rechtsspr.); Nachlass, *der;* (of bankrupt) Konkursmasse, *die* (Wirtsch., Rechtsspr.)

estate: ~ **agent** *n.* ▶887 | (Brit.) Grundstücksmakler, *der;* Immobilienmakler, *der;* ~ **car** *n.* (Brit.) Kombiwagen, *der*

esteem /ɪ'stiːm/ **1** *n.*, *no pl.* Wertschätzung, *die* (geh.) **(for Gen., für)**; **hold sb./sth. in [high** *or* **great]** ~: [hohe *od.* große] Achtung vor jmdm./etw. haben. **2** *v.t.* **(a)** (think favourably of) schätzen; **highly** *or* **much** *or* **greatly** ~**ed** hochgeschätzt (geh.); sehr geschätzt; **(b)** (consider) ~ **[as]** erachten für (geh.); ansehen als

estimate 1 /'estɪmət/ *n.* **(a)** (of number, amount, etc.) Schätzung, *die;* **at a rough** ~: grob geschätzt; **(b)** (of character, qualities, etc.) Einschätzung, *die;* **(c)** (Commerc.) Kostenvoranschlag, *der.* **2** /'estɪmeɪt/ *v.t.* schätzen ‹ *Größe, Entfernung, Zahl, Umsatz* › (at auf + *Akk.*); einschätzen ‹ *Fähigkeiten, Durchführbarkeit, Aussichten* ›

estimation /estɪ'meɪʃn/ *n.* Schätzung, *die;* (of situation etc.) Einschätzung, *die;* Beurteilung, *die;* **in sb.'s** ~: nach jmds. Schätzung; **go up/down in sb.'s** ~: in jmds. Achtung steigen/sinken

Estonia /e'stəʊnɪə/ *pr. n.* Estland (*das*)

estrange /ɪ'streɪndʒ/ *v.t.* entfremden **(from** *Dat.*); **be/become** ~**d from sb.** jmdm. entfremdet sein/sich jmdm. entfremden

estuary /'estjʊərɪ/ *n.* (Geog.) Mündung, *die*

etc. *abbr.* **et cetera** usw.

etcetera /et'setərə, ɪt'setərə/ und so weiter; et cetera

etch /etʃ/ *v.t.* **(a)** ätzen **(on** auf *od.* in + *Akk.*); (on metal also) ‹ *bes. Künstler:* › radieren; **(b)** (fig.) einprägen **(in, on** *Dat.*)

etching /'etʃɪŋ/ *n.* Ätzung, *die;* (piece of art) Radierung, *die*

eternal /ɪ'tɜːnl, iː'tɜːnl/ *adj.* **(a)** ewig; **life** ~: das ewige Leben; ~ **triangle** Dreiecksverhältnis, *das;* **(b)** (coll.: unceasing) ewig (ugs.)

eternity /ɪ'tɜːnɪtɪ, iː'tɜːnɪtɪ/ *n.* **(a)** Ewigkeit, *die;* **for all** ~: [bis] in alle Ewigkeit; **(b)** (coll.: long time) Ewigkeit, *die* (ugs.)

ether /'iːθə(r)/ *n.* Äther, *der*

ethic /'eθɪk/ *n.* Ethik, *die* (geh.)

ethical /'eθɪkl/ *adj.* **(a)** (relating to morals) ethisch; ~ **philosophy** Ethik, *die;* **(b)** (morally correct) moralisch einwandfrei

ethics /'eθɪks/ *n.*, *no pl.* **(a)** Moral, *die;* (moral philosophy) Ethik, *die;* **(b)** *usu. constr. as pl.* (moral code) Ethik, *die* (geh.); **professional** ~: Berufsethos, *das*

Ethiopia /iːθɪ'əʊpɪə/ *pr. n.* Äthiopien (*das*)

Ethiopian /iːθɪ'əʊpɪən/ ▶947 | **1** *adj.* äthiopisch; **sb. is** ~ jmd. is Äthiopier/Äthiopierin. **2** *n.* Äthiopier, *der*/Äthiopierin, *die*

ethnic /'eθnɪk/ *adj.* **(a)** ethnisch; Volks‹ *gruppe, -musik, -tanz* ›; ~ **minority** ethnische Minderheit; **(b)** (from specified group) Volks‹ *chinesen, -deutsche usw.* ›

ethos /'iːθɒs/ *n.* (guiding beliefs) Gesinnung, *die;* (fundamental values) Ethos, *das* (geh.)

etiquette /'etɪket/ *n.* Etikette, *die;* **breach of** ~: Verstoß gegen die Etikette

etymological /etɪmə'lɒdʒɪkl/ *adj.* (Ling.) etymologisch

etymology /etɪ'mɒlədʒɪ/ *n.* (Ling.) Etymologie, *die*

EU *abbr.* **European Union**

eucalyptus /juːkə'lɪptəs/ *n.* **(a)** ~ **[oil]** (Pharm.) Eukalyptusöl, *das;* **(b)** (Bot.) Eukalyptus[baum], *der*

Eucharist /'juːkərɪst/ *n.* (Eccl.) Eucharistie, *die*

eulogy /'juːlədʒɪ/ *n.* Lobrede, *die;* (Amer.: funeral oration) Grabrede, *die*

eunuch /'juːnək/ *n.* Eunuch, *der*

euphemism /'juːfəmɪzm/ *n.* Euphemismus, *der* (bes. Sprachw.); verhüllende Umschreibung

euphemistic /juːfə'mɪstɪk/ *adj.* euphemistisch (bes. Sprachw.); verhüllend

euphoria /juː'fɔːrɪə/ *n.*, *no pl.* Euphorie, *die* (geh.)

euphoric /juː'fɒrɪk/ *adj.* euphorisch (geh.)

eureka /jʊə'riːkə/ *int.* heureka (geh.); ich hab's (ugs.)

Euro /'jʊərəʊ/ *n.* Euro, *der*

Euro- /'jʊərəʊ/ *in comb.* euro-/Euro-

Euro: ~**bond** *n.* (Commerc.) Eurobond, *der;* Euroanleihe, *die;* ~**cheque** *n.* (Commerc.) Euroscheck, *der;* ~**currency** *n.* ▶938 | Eurowährung, *die;* ~**dollar** *n.* ▶938 | (Econ.) Eurodollar, *der;* ~**market** *n.* **(a)** (Commerc.) Euro[geld]markt, *der;* **(b)** (European Community) europäischer Markt; [EU-]Binnenmarkt, *der;* ~-**MP** *n.* Europaabgeordnete, *der/die*

Europe /'jʊərəp/ *pr. n.* **(a)** Europa (*das*); **(b)** (Brit. coll.: EC) EG, *die;* **go into** ~: der EG beitreten

European /jʊərə'piːən/ ▶947 | **1** *adj.* europäisch; **sb. is** ~: jmd. ist Europäer/Europäerin. **2** *n.* Europäer, *der*/Europäerin, *die*

European: ~ **Com'mission** *n.* Europäische Kommission; ~ **Eco'nomic Community** *n.* Europäische Wirtschaftsgemeinschaft; ~ **currency unit** *n.* Europäische Währungseinheit; ~ '**Monetary System** *n.* Europäisches Währungssystem; ~ **Monetary**

'Union *n.* Europäische Währungsunion; ~ **'Union** *n.* Europäische Union

Euro-: ~**-rebel** *n.* (esp. Brit.) [innerparteilicher] Europagegner/[innerparteiliche] Europagegnerin; ~**sceptic** *n.* Euroskeptiker, *der*/-skeptikerin, *die;* ~**star** (P) *n.* Eurostar, *der;* **go by** ~**star** mit dem Eurostar fahren

euthanasia /juːθəˈneɪzɪə/ *n.* Euthanasie, *die*

evacuate /ɪˈvækjʊeɪt/ *v.t.* (a) (remove from danger, clear of occupants) evakuieren **(from** aus); (b) (esp. Mil.: cease to occupy) räumen

evacuation /ɪvækjʊˈeɪʃn/ *n.* (a) (removal of people or things, clearance of place) Evakuierung, *die* **(from** aus); (b) (esp. Mil.) **the ~ of a territory** die Räumung eines Gebietes

evacuee /ɪvækjuːˈiː/ *n.* Evakuierte, *der*/*die;* (attrib.) ~ **children** evakuierte Kinder

evade /ɪˈveɪd/ *v.t.* ausweichen (+ *Dat.*) ‹*Angriff, Angreifer, Blick, Problem, Schwierigkeit, Tatsache, Frage, Thema*›; sich entziehen (+ *Dat.*) ‹*Verhaftung, Ergreifung, Wehrdienst, Gerechtigkeit, Pflicht, Verantwortung*›; entkommen (+ *Dat.*) ‹*Polizei, Verfolger, Verfolgung*›; hinterziehen ‹*Steuern, Zölle*›; umgehen ‹*Gesetz, Vorschrift*›; ~ **doing sth.** vermeiden, etw. zu tun

evaluate /ɪˈvæljʊeɪt/ *v.t.* (a) (value) schätzen ‹*Wert, Preis, Schaden, Kosten*›; (b) (appraise) einschätzen; auswerten ‹*Daten*›

evaluation /ɪvæljʊˈeɪʃn/ *n.* (a) Schätzung, *die;* (b) (appraisal) Einschätzung, *die;* (of data) Auswertung, *die*

evangelical /iːvænˈdʒelɪkl/ *adj.* (a) (Protestant) evangelikal; (b) (evangelizing) missionarisch (fig.)

evangelise ⇒ **evangelize**

evangelism /ɪˈvændʒəlɪzm/ *n., no pl.* Evangelisation, *die*

evangelist /ɪˈvændʒəlɪst/ *n.* Evangelist, *der*

evangelize /ɪˈvændʒəlaɪz/ *v.t.* evangelisieren

evaporate /ɪˈvæpəreɪt/ *v.i.* (a) verdunsten; (b) (fig.) sich in Luft auflösen; ‹*Furcht, Begeisterung:*› verfliegen

evaporated 'milk *n.* Kondensmilch, *die*

evaporation /ɪvæpəˈreɪʃn/ *n.* Verdunstung, *die*

evasion /ɪˈveɪʒn/ *n.* (a) (avoidance) Umgehung, *die;* (of duty) Vernachlässigung, *die;* (of responsibility, question) Ausweichen, *das* **(of** vor + *Dat.*); (b) (evasive statement) Ausrede, *die;* ~**s** Ausflüchte *Pl.*

evasive /ɪˈveɪsɪv/ *adj.* ausweichend ‹*Antwort*›; **be/become [very]** ~: [ständig] ausweichen; **be** ~ **about sth.** um etw. herumreden; **take** ~ **action** ein Ausweichmanöver machen

Eve /iːv/ *pr. n.* (Bibl.) Eva (*die*)

eve *n.* Vorabend, *der;* (day) Vortag, *der;* **the** ~ **of** der Abend/Tag vor (+ *Dat.*); der Vorabend/Vortag (+ *Gen.*)

even /ˈiːvn/ **1** *adj.,* ~**er** /ˈiːvənə(r)/, ~**est** /ˈiːvənɪst/ (a) (smooth, flat) eben ‹*Boden, Fläche*›; **make sth.** ~: etw. ebnen; (b) (level) gleich hoch ‹*Stapel, Stuhl-, Tischbein*›; gleich lang ‹*Vorhang, Stuhl-, Tischbein usw.*›; **be of** ~ **height/length** gleich hoch/lang sein; ~ **with** genauso hoch/lang wie; **on an** ~ **keel** (fig.) ausgeglichen; (c) (straight) gerade ‹*Saum, Kante*›; (d) (parallel) parallel **(with** zu); (e) (regular) regelmäßig ‹*Zähne*›; (steady) gleichmäßig ‹*Schrift, Rhythmus, Atmen, Schlagen*›; stetig ‹*Fortschritt*›; (f) (equal) gleich [groß] ‹*Menge, Abstand*›; gleichmäßig ‹*Verteilung, Aufteilung*›; **the odds are** ~, **it's an** ~ **bet** die Chancen stehen fünfzig zu fünfzig *od.* (ugs.) fifty-fifty; **break** ~: die Kosten decken; (g) (balanced) im Gleichgewicht; (h) (quits, fully revenged) **be** *or* **get** ~ **with sb.** es jmdm. heimzahlen; (i) (divisible by two, so numbered) gerade ‹*Zahl, Seite, Hausnummer*›. **2** *adv.* (a) sogar; selbst; **hard, unbearable** ~: hart, ja unerträglich; **do sth.** ~ **without being told** etw. auch ohne Aufforderung tun; (b) *with negative* **not** *or* **never** ~ ...: [noch] nicht einmal ...; **without** ~ **saying goodbye** ohne wenigstens auf Wiedersehen zu sagen; (c) *with compar. adj. or adv.* sogar noch ‹*komplizierter, weniger, schlimmer usw.*›; (d) ~ **if Arsenal win** selbst wenn Arsenal gewinnt; ~ **if Arsenal won** selbst wenn Arsenal gewinnen würde; (fact) obgleich Arsenal gewann; ~ **so** [aber] trotzdem *od.* dennoch; ~ **now/ then** selbst *od.* sogar jetzt/dann

~ **'out** *v.t.* (a) (make smooth) glätten; (b) ausgleichen ‹*Unterschiede*›

~ **'up** *v.t.* ausgleichen; **so as to** ~ **things up** zum Ausgleich

evening /ˈiːvnɪŋ/ *n.* (a) ▶**706**], ▶**739**] Abend, *der;* attrib. Abend‹*vorstellung, -ausgabe, -messe*›; **this/tomorrow** ~: heute/morgen Abend; **during the** ~: am Abend; **[early/late] in the** ~: am [frühen/späten] Abend; (regularly) [früh/spät] abends; **at eight in the** ~: um acht Uhr abends; **on Wednesday** ~**s**/~: mittwochabends/am Mittwoch abend; **one** ~: eines Abends; ~**s, of an** ~: abends; (b) ▶**836** (coll.: greeting) 'n Abend! (ugs.)

evening: ~ **class** *n.* Abendkurs, *der;* **take** *or* **do** ~ **classes in pottery** *etc.* Abendkurse im Töpfern *usw.* besuchen; ~ **dress** *n.* (a) *no pl.* Abendkleidung, *die;* **in [full]** ~ **dress** in Abendkleidung; (b) Abendkleid, *das;* ~ **gown** *n.* Abendkleid, *das;* ~ **'paper** *n.* Abendzeitung, *die*

evenly /ˈiːvnlɪ/ *adv.* gleichmäßig; **be** ~ **spaced** den gleichen Abstand voneinander haben; **the runners are** ~ **matched** die Läufer sind einander ebenbürtig

'even-numbered *adj.* gerade

'evensong *n.* (Eccl.) Abendandacht, *die*

event /ɪˈvent/ *n.* (a) **in the** ~ **of his dying** *or* **death** im Falle seines Todes; **in the** ~ **of sickness/war** im Falle einer Krankheit/im Kriegsfalle; **in that** ~: in dem Falle; (b) (outcome) **in any/either** ~ = **in any case** ⇒ **case**[1] a; **at all** ~**s** auf jeden Fall; **in the** ~: letzten Endes; (c) (occurrence) Ereignis, *das;* (d) (Sport) Wettkampf, *der*

even-'tempered *adj.* ausgeglichen

eventful /ɪˈventfl/ *adj.* ereignisreich ‹*Tag, Zeiten*›; bewegt ‹*Leben, Jugend, Zeiten*›

eventual /ɪˈventjʊəl/ *adj.* **predict sb.'s** ~ **downfall** vorhersagen, dass jmd. schließlich zu Fall kommen wird; **the rise of Napoleon and his** ~ **defeat** der Aufstieg Napoleons und schließlich seine Niederlage

eventuality /ɪventjʊˈælɪtɪ/ *n.* Eventualität, *die;* **in certain eventualities** in bestimmten [möglichen] Fällen; **be ready for all eventualities** auf alle Eventualitäten gefasst sein

eventually /ɪˈventjʊəlɪ/ *adv.* schließlich

ever /ˈevə(r)/ *adv.* (a) (always, at all times) immer; stets; **for** ~: für immer ‹*weggehen, gelten*›; ewig ‹*lieben, da sein, leben*›; **for** ~ **and** ~: immer und ewig; **for** ~ **and a day** eine Ewigkeit; ~ **since [then]** seit [dieser Zeit]; ~ **since I've known her** solange ich sie kenne; ~ **since I can remember** soweit ich zurückdenken kann; (b) *in comb. with compar. adj. or adv.* noch; immer; **get** ~ **deeper into debt** sich noch *od.* immer mehr verschulden; ~ **further** noch immer weiter; (c) *in comb. with participles etc.* ~**-increasing** ständig zunehmend; ~**-present** allgegenwärtig; (d) (at any time) je[mals]; **not** ~: noch nie; ~ **before** je zuvor; **never** ~: nie im Leben; **nothing** ~ **happens** es passiert nie etwas; **his best performance** ~: seine beste Vorstellung überhaupt; **it hardly** ~ **rains** es regnet so gut wie nie; **don't you** ~ **do that again!** mach das bloß nicht noch mal!; **better than** ~: besser denn je; **as** ~: wie gewöhnlich; (iron.) wie gehabt; **if I** ~ **catch you doing that again** wenn ich dich dabei noch einmal erwische; **the greatest tennis player** ~: der größte Tennisspieler, den es je gegeben hat; (e) (coll.) *emphasizing question* **what** ~ **does he want?** was will er nur?; **how** ~ **did I drop it?/could I have dropped it?** wie konnte ich es nur fallen lassen?; **why** ~ **not?** warum denn nicht?; (f) *intensifier* **before** ~ **he opened his mouth** bevor er seinen Mund aufmachte; **as soon as** ~ **I can** so bald wie irgend möglich; **I'm** ~ **so sorry** (coll.) mir tut es ja so leid; **thanks** ~ **so [much]** (coll.) vielen herzlichen Dank; **it was** ~ **such a shame** (coll.) es war so schade

'evergreen 1 *adj.* (a) immergrün ‹*Baum, Strauch*›; (b) (fig.) immer wieder aktuell ‹*Problem, Thema*›; immer wieder gern gehört ‹*Lied, Schlager, Sänger*›; ~ **song** Evergreen, *der.* **2** *n.* immergrüne Pflanze/immergrüner Baum

ever'lasting *adj.* (a) (eternal) immer während; ewig ‹*Leben, Höllenqualen, Gott, Gedenken*›; unvergänglich ‹*Ruhm, Ehre*›; (b) (incessant) ewig (ugs.); endlos

everlastingly /evəˈlɑːstɪŋlɪ/ *adv.* (a) (eternally) ewig ‹*leben, leiden*›; (b) (incessantly) ewig (ugs.); ständig

ever'more *adv.* auf ewig; **for ~:** in [alle] Ewigkeit

every /'evrɪ/ *adj.* **(a)** (each single) jeder/jede/jedes; **have ~ reason** allen Grund haben; **~ [single] time/on ~ [single] occasion** [aber auch] jedes Mal; **he ate ~ last** *or* **single biscuit** (coll.) er hat die ganzen Kekse aufgegessen (ugs.); **~ one** jeder/jede/jedes [einzelne]; **(b)** *after possessive adj.* **your ~ wish** all[e] deine Wünsche; **his ~ thought** all[e] seine Gedanken; **(c)** (indicating recurrence) **she comes [once] ~ day** sie kommt jeden Tag [einmal]; **~ three/few days** alle drei/paar Tage; **~ other** (~ second, or fig.: almost ~) jeder/jede/jedes zweite; **~ now and then** *or* **again, ~ so often, ~ once in a while** hin und wieder; **(d)** (the greatest possible) unbedingt, uneingeschränkt ⟨*Vertrauen*⟩; voll ⟨*Beachtung*⟩; all ⟨*Respekt, Aussicht*⟩; **I wish you ~ happiness/success** ich wünsche dir alles Gute/viel Erfolg

'everybody *n. & pron.* jeder; **~ else** alle anderen; **~ knows ~ else round here** hier kennt jeder jeden; **he asked ~ to be quiet** er bat alle um Ruhe; **opera isn't [to] ~'s taste** Oper ist nicht jedermanns Sache

'everyday *attrib. adj.* alltäglich; Alltags⟨*kleidung, -sprache*⟩; **in ~ life** im Alltag; im täglichen Leben

everyone /'evrɪwʌn, 'evrɪwən/ ⇒ **everybody**

'everyplace (Amer.) ⇒ **everywhere**

'everything *n. & pron.* **(a)** alles; **~ else** alles andere; **~ interesting/valuable** alles Interessante/Wertvolle; **there's a [right] time for ~:** alles zu seiner Zeit; **(b)** (coll.: all that matters) alles; **looks aren't ~:** das Aussehen [allein] ist nicht alles

'everywhere *adv.* **(a)** (in every place) überall; **(b)** (to every place) **go ~:** überall hingehen/-fahren; **~ you go/look** wohin man auch geht/sieht

evict /ɪ'vɪkt/ *v.t.* **~ sb. [from his/her home]** jmdn. zur Räumung [seiner Wohnung] zwingen

eviction /ɪ'vɪkʃn/ *n.* Zwangsräumung, *die;* **the ~ of the tenant** die zwangsweise Vertreibung des Mieters [aus seiner Wohnung]

evidence /'evɪdəns/ *n.* **(a)** Beweis, *der;* **be ~ of sth.** etw. beweisen; **provide ~ of sth.** den Beweis *od.* Beweise für etw. liefern; **there was no ~ of a fight** nichts deutete auf einen Kampf hin; **(b)** (Law) Beweismaterial, *das;* (testimony) [Zeugen]aussage, *die;* **give ~:** [als Zeuge] aussagen; **piece of ~:** Beweisstück, *das;* (statement) Beweis, *der;* **(c) be [much] in ~:** [stark] in Erscheinung treten; **he was nowhere in ~:** er war nirgends zu sehen; **sth. is very much in ~:** überall sieht man etw.

evident /'evɪdənt/ *adj.* offensichtlich; deutlich ⟨*Verbesserung*⟩; **be ~ to sb.** jmdm. klar sein; **it soon became ~ that ...:** es stellte sich bald heraus, dass ...

evidently /'evɪdəntlɪ/ *adv.* offensichtlich

evil /'i:vl, 'i:vɪl/ **1** *adj.* **(a)** böse; schlecht ⟨*Charakter, Beispiel, Einfluss, System*⟩; übel, verwerflich ⟨*Praktiken*⟩; **(b)** (unlucky) verhängnisvoll, unglückselig ⟨*Tag, Stunde*⟩; **~ days** *or* **times** schlechte *od.* schlimme Zeiten; **put off** *or* **postpone the evil hour** das Unvermeidliche hinauszögern; **(c)** (disagreeable) übel ⟨*Geruch, Geschmack*⟩. **2** *n.* **(a)** *no pl.* (literary) Böse, *das;* **the root of all ~:** die Wurzel allen Übels; **(b)** (bad thing) Übel, *das;* **necessary ~:** notwendiges Übel; **the lesser ~:** das kleinere Übel

evil: ~doer /'i:vlduːə(r)/ *n.* Übeltäter, *der*/Übeltäterin, *die;* **~-'minded** *adj.* bösartig; **~-'smelling** *adj.* übel riechend

evince /ɪ'vɪns/ *v.t.* ⟨*Person:*⟩ an den Tag legen; ⟨*Äußerung, Handlung:*⟩ zeugen von

evocation /evə'keɪʃn/ *n.* Heraufbeschwören, *das*

evocative /ɪ'vɒkətɪv/ *adj.* (thought-provoking) aufrüttelnd (fig.); **be ~ of sth.** an etw. (*Akk.*) erinnern; etw. heraufbeschwören; **an ~ scent** ein Duft, der Erinnerungen weckt

evoke /ɪ'vəʊk/ *v.t.* heraufbeschwören; hervorrufen ⟨*Bewunderung, Überraschung, Wirkung*⟩; erregen ⟨*Interesse*⟩

evolution /i:və'lu:ʃn, evə'lu:ʃn/ *n.* **(a)** (development) Entwicklung, *die;* **(b)** (Biol.: of species etc.) Evolution, *die;* **theory of ~:** Evolutionstheorie, *die*

evolutionary /i:və'lu:ʃənərɪ, evə'lu:ʃənərɪ/ *adj.* evolutionär

evolve /ɪ'vɒlv/ **1** *v.i.* sich entwickeln (**out of, from** aus; **into** zu). **2** *v.t.* entwickeln (**from** aus)

ewe /ju:/ *n.* Mutterschaf, *das*

ex- *pref.* Ex-⟨*Freundin, Präsident, Champion*⟩; Alt⟨*bundes*]*kanzler, -bundespräsident*⟩; ehemalig

exacerbate /ek'sæsəbeɪt/ *v.t.* verschlimmern ⟨*Schmerz, Krankheit, Wut*⟩; verschlechtern ⟨*Zustand*⟩; verschärfen ⟨*Lage*⟩

exact /ɪg'zækt/ **1** *adj.* genau; exakt, genau ⟨*Daten, Berechnung*⟩; **those were his ~ words** das waren genau seine Worte; **on the ~ spot where ...:** genau an der Stelle, wo ...; **could you give me the ~ money?** könnten Sie mir das Geld passend geben? **2** *v.t.* fordern, verlangen; erheben ⟨*Gebühr*⟩

exacting /ɪg'zæktɪŋ/ *adj.* anspruchsvoll; streng ⟨*Lehrer, Maßstab*⟩; hoch ⟨*Anforderung, Maßstab*⟩

exactitude /ɪg'zæktɪtju:d/ *n., no pl.* Genauigkeit, *die*

exactly /ɪg'zæktlɪ/ *adv.* **(a)** genau; **when ~** *or* **~ when did he leave?** wann genau ging er?; **at ~ the right moment** genau im richtigen Moment; **~!** genau!; **at four o'clock ~:** Punkt vier Uhr; **not ~** (coll. iron.) nicht gerade; **(b)** (with perfect accuracy) [ganz] genau

exactness /ɪg'zæktnɪs/ *n., no pl.* Genauigkeit, *die*

exaggerate /ɪg'zædʒəreɪt/ *v.t.* übertreiben; **you are exaggerating his importance** du machst ihn wichtiger, als er ist

exaggerated /ɪg'zædʒəreɪtɪd/ *adj.* übertrieben

exaggeration /ɪgzædʒə'reɪʃn/ *n.* Übertreibung, *die;* **it is a wild/is no ~ to say that ...:** es ist stark/nicht übertrieben, wenn man sagt, dass ...

exalt /ɪg'zɔ:lt/ *v.t.* [lob]preisen

exalted /ɪg'zɔ:ltɪd/ *adj.* **(a)** (high-ranking) hoch; **(b)** (lofty, sublime) hoch ⟨*Ideal*⟩; erhaben ⟨*Thema, Stil, Stimmung, Gedanke*⟩

exam /ɪg'zæm/ (coll.) ⇒ **examination c**

examination /ɪgzæmɪ'neɪʃn/ *n.* **(a)** (inspection) Untersuchung, *die;* (of accounts) [Über]prüfung, *die;* **be under ~:** untersucht *od.* überprüft werden; **(b)** (Med.) Untersuchung, *die;* **undergo an ~:** sich untersuchen lassen; **(c)** (test of knowledge or ability) Prüfung, *die;* (final ~ at university) Examen, *das;* **(d)** (of witness, accused) Verhör, *das;* Vernehmung, *die;* (of case) Untersuchung, *die*

exami'nation paper *n.* **(a)** **~[s]** schriftliche Prüfungsaufgaben; **(b)** (with candidate's answers) ≈ Klausurarbeit, *die*

examine /ɪg'zæmɪn/ *v.t.* **(a)** (inspect) untersuchen (**for** auf + *Akk.*); prüfen ⟨*Dokument, Gewissen, Geschäftsbücher*⟩; **(b)** (Med.) untersuchen; **(c)** (test knowledge or ability of) prüfen (**in** in + *Dat.*); **~ sb. on his knowledge of French** jmds. Französischkenntnisse prüfen; **(d)** (Law) verhören; vernehmen

examinee /ɪgzæmɪ'ni:/ *n.* Prüfungskandidat, *der*/-kandidatin, *die;* Prüfling, *der;* (Univ. also) Examenskandidat, *der*/-kandidatin, *die*

examiner /ɪg'zæmɪnə(r)/ *n.* Prüfer, *der*/Prüferin, *die;* **board of ~s** Prüfungsausschuss, *der*

example /ɪg'zɑ:mpl/ *n.* Beispiel, *das;* **by way of [an] ~:** als Beispiel; **take sth. as an ~:** etw. zum Beispiel nehmen; **for ~:** zum Beispiel; **set an ~** *or* **a good ~ to sb.** jmdm. ein Beispiel geben; **make an ~ of sb.** ein Exempel an jmdm. statuieren

exasperate /ɪg'zæspəreɪt, ɪg'zɑ:spəreɪt/ *v.t.* (irritate) verärgern; (infuriate) zur Verzweiflung bringen; **be ~d at** *or* **by sb./sth.** über jmdn./etw. verärgert/verzweifelt sein; **become** *or* **get ~d [with sb.]** sich [über jmdn.] ärgern

exasperating /ɪg'zæspəreɪtɪŋ, ɪg'zɑ:spəreɪtɪŋ/ *adj.* ärgerlich; ⟨*Aufgabe*⟩ die einen zur Verzweiflung bringt; **be ~:** einen zur Verzweiflung bringen

exasperation /ɪgzæspə'reɪʃn, ɪgzɑ:spə'reɪʃn/ *n.* ⇒ **exasperate:** Ärger, *der*/Verzweiflung, *die* (**with** über + *Akk.*); **in ~:** verärgert/verzweifelt

excavate /'ekskəveɪt/ v.t. (a) ausschachten; (with machine) ausbaggern; fördern, abbauen ‹Erz, Metall›; (b) (Archaeol.) ausgraben

excavation /ekskə'veɪʃn/ n. (a) Ausschachtung, die; (with machine) Ausbaggerung, die; (of ore, metals) Förderung, die; Abbau, der; (b) (Archaeol.) Ausgrabung, die; (place) Ausgrabungsstätte, die

excavator /'ekskəveɪtə(r)/ n. (machine) Bagger, der

exceed /ɪk'si:d/ v.t. (a) (be greater than) übertreffen (**in** an + Dat.); ‹Kosten, Summe, Anzahl:› übersteigen (**by** um); not **∼ing** bis zu; (b) (go beyond) überschreiten; hinausgehen über (+ Akk.) ‹Auftrag, Befehl›

exceedingly /ɪk'si:dɪŋlɪ/ adv. äußerst; ausgesprochen ‹hässlich, dumm›

excel /ɪk'sel/ 1 v.t., -ll- übertreffen; ∼ **oneself** (lit. or iron.) sich selbst übertreffen. 2 v.i., -ll- sich hervortun (**at, in** in + Dat.)

excellence /'eksələns/ n. hervorragende Qualität

excellency /'eksələnsɪ/ n. Exzellenz, die

excellent /'eksələnt/ adj. ausgezeichnet; hervorragend; exzellent (geh.); vorzüglich ‹Wein, Koch, Speise›

except /ɪk'sept/ 1 prep. ∼ [(coll.) for] außer (+ Dat.); ∼ **for** (in all respects other than) bis auf (+ Akk.); abgesehen von; ∼ **[for the fact] that** …, (coll.) ∼ …: abgesehen davon, dass …; **there was nothing to be done** ∼ **[to] stay there** man konnte nichts anderes tun als dableiben. 2 v.t. ausnehmen (**from** bei); ∼**ed** ausgenommen

excepting /ɪk'septɪŋ/ prep. außer (+ Dat.); not ∼ **Peter** Peter nicht ausgenommen; ∼ **that** …, (coll.) ∼ …: abgesehen davon, dass …

exception /ɪk'sepʃn/ n. (a) Ausnahme, die; **with the** ∼ **of** mit Ausnahme (+ Gen.); **with the** ∼ **of her/myself** mit Ausnahme von ihr/mir; **the** ∼ **proves the rule** (prov.) Ausnahmen bestätigen die Regel; **make an** ∼ **[of/for sb.]** [bei jmdm.] eine Ausnahme machen; (b) **take** ∼ **to sth.** an etw. (Dat.) Anstoß nehmen

exceptional /ɪk'sepʃənl/ adj. außergewöhnlich; **in** ∼ **cases** in Ausnahmefällen

exceptionally /ɪk'sepʃənəlɪ/ adv. (a) (as an exception) ausnahmsweise; (b) (remarkably) ungewöhnlich; außergewöhnlich

excerpt /'eksɜ:pt/ n. Auszug, der (**from, of** aus)

excess /ɪk'ses/ n. (a) (inordinate degree or amount) Übermaß, das (**of** an + Dat.); **eat/drink to** ∼: übermäßig essen/trinken; **in** ∼: im Übermaß; (b) esp. in pl. (immoderate act) Exzess, der; (savage also) Ausschreitung, die; (**c**) **be in** ∼ **of sth.** etw. übersteigen; **in** ∼ **of a million** über eine Million; (d) (surplus) Überschuss, der (**of** an + Dat.); ∼ **weight** Übergewicht, das; (e) (esp. Brit. Insurance) Selbstbeteiligung, die

excess /'ekses/: ∼ '**baggage** n. Mehrgepäck, das; ∼ '**fare** n. Mehrpreis, der; **pay the** ∼ **fare** nachlösen

excessive /ɪk'sesɪv/ adj. übermäßig; übertrieben ‹Forderung›; zu stark ‹Schmerz, Belastung›; unmäßig ‹Esser, Trinker›

excessively /ɪk'sesɪvlɪ/ adv. übertrieben; unmäßig ‹essen, trinken›

exchange /ɪks'tʃeɪndʒ/ 1 v.t. (a) tauschen ‹Plätze, Zimmer, Ringe, Küsse›; umtauschen, wechseln ‹Geld›; austauschen ‹Adressen, [Kriegs]gefangene, Erinnerungen, Gedanken, Erfahrungen›; wechseln ‹Blicke, Worte, Ringe›; ∼ **letters** einen Briefwechsel führen; ∼ **blows/insults** sich schlagen/sich gegenseitig beleidigen; (b) (give in place of another) eintauschen (**for** für, gegen); umtauschen ‹[gekaufte] Ware› (**for** gegen); austauschen ‹Spion› (**for** gegen). 2 v.i. tauschen. 3 n. (a) Tausch, der; (of prisoners, spies, compliments, greetings, insults) Austausch, der; **an** ∼ **of ideas/blows** ein Meinungsaustausch/Handgreiflichkeiten Pl.; **in** ∼: dafür; **in** ∼ **for sth.** für etw.; (b) (Educ.) Austausch, der; attrib. Austausch-; **an** ∼ **student** ein Austauschstudent/eine Austauschstudentin; (c) (of money) Umtausch, der; ∼ **[rate]** Wechselkurs, der; ∼ **rate mechanism** Wechselkursmechanismus, der; (d) ⇒ **telephone exchange**

exchequer /ɪks'tʃekə(r)/ n. (Brit.) Schatzamt, das; Finanzministerium, das

excise¹ /'eksaɪz/ n. Verbrauchsteuer, die; **Customs and E**∼ **[Department]** (Brit.) Amt für Zölle und Verbrauchsteuer

excise² /ɪk'saɪz/ v.t. (a) (from book, article) entfernen (**from** aus); (from film also) herausschneiden (**from** aus); (b) (Med.) entfernen; exzidieren (fachspr.)

excitable /ɪk'saɪtəbl/ adj. leicht erregbar

excite /ɪk'saɪt/ v.t. (a) (thrill) begeistern; **she was/became** ∼**d by the idea** die Idee begeisterte sie; (b) (agitate) aufregen; **be/become** ∼**d by sth.** sich über etw. (Akk.) aufregen od. erregen; (c) (stimulate sexually) erregen

excited /ɪk'saɪtɪd/ adj. (a) (thrilled) aufgeregt (**at** über + Akk.); **you don't seem very** ∼ **[about it]** du scheinst [davon] nicht sehr begeistert zu sein; **it's nothing to get** ∼ **about** es ist nichts Besonderes; **don't get** ∼, **it's only Tom** keine Aufregung, es ist nur Tom; (b) (agitated) erregt; aufgeregt; **it's nothing to get** ∼ **about** es besteht kein Grund zur Aufregung; **don't get** ∼, **it's only Tom** keine Panik, es ist nur Tom; **don't get so** ∼: reg dich nicht so auf; (c) (sexually) erregt

excitement /ɪk'saɪtmənt/ n., no pl. Aufregung, die; (enthusiasm) Begeisterung, die

exciting /ɪk'saɪtɪŋ/ adj. aufregend; (full of suspense) spannend

exclaim /ɪk'skleɪm/ 1 v.t. ausrufen; ∼ **that** …: rufen, dass … 2 v.i. aufschreien

exclamation /ekskləˈmeɪʃn/ n. Ausruf, der

excla'mation mark n. Ausrufezeichen, das

exclude /ɪk'sklu:d/ v.t. (a) (keep out) ausschließen (**from** von); **sb. is** ∼**d from a profession/the Church** jmdm. ist die Ausübung eines Berufes/die Zugehörigkeit zur Kirche verwehrt; (b) (leave out of account) nicht berücksichtigen (**from** bei)

excluding /ɪk'sklu:dɪŋ/ prep. ∼ **drinks/VAT** Getränke ausgenommen/ohne Mehrwertsteuer

exclusion /ɪk'sklu:ʒn/ n. Ausschluss, der; **[talk about sth.] to the** ∼ **of everything else** ausschließlich [über etw. (Akk.) sprechen]

exclusive /ɪk'sklu:sɪv/ adj. (a) (not shared) alleinig ‹Besitzer, Kontrolle›; Allein‹eigentum›; (Journ.) Exklusiv‹bericht, -interview›; ∼ **right** Alleinrecht, das; **have** ∼ **rights** die Alleinrechte/Exklusivrechte haben; (b) (select) exklusiv; (c) (excluding) ausschließlich; ∼ **of** ohne; ∼ **of drinks** Getränke ausgenommen; **the price is** ∼ **of postage** Versandkosten sind im Preis nicht inbegriffen; **be mutually** ∼: sich gegenseitig ausschließen

exclusively /ɪk'sklu:sɪvlɪ/ adv. ausschließlich; (Journ.) exklusiv

excommunicate /ekskə'mju:nɪkeɪt/ v.t. (Eccl.) exkommunizieren

excommunication /ekskəmju:nɪ'keɪʃn/ n. (Eccl.) Exkommunikation, die

excrement /'ekskrɪmənt/ n. in sing. or pl. Exkremente Pl. (bes. Med.); Kot, der (geh.)

excruciating /ɪk'skru:ʃɪeɪtɪŋ/ adj. unerträglich; qualvoll ‹Tod›; **an** ∼ **pun** ≈ ein schlimmer Kalauer

excursion /ɪk'skɜ:ʃn/ n. Ausflug, der; **day** ∼: Tagesausflug, der

excusable /ɪk'skju:zəbl/ adj. entschuldbar; verzeihlich

excuse 1 /ɪk'skju:z/ v.t. (a) ▶ 639 ⎪ (forgive, exonerate) entschuldigen; ∼ **oneself** (apologize) sich entschuldigen; ∼ **me** Entschuldigung; Verzeihung; **please** ∼ **me** bitte entschuldigen Sie; ∼ **me[, what did you say]?** (Amer.) Verzeihung[, was haben Sie gesagt]?; ∼ **me if I don't get up** entschuldigen Sie, wenn ich nicht aufstehe; ∼ **sb. sth.** etw. bei jmdm. entschuldigen; **I can be** ∼**d for confusing them** es ist verzeihlich, dass ich sie verwechselt habe; (b) (release) befreien; ∼ **sb. [from] sth.** jmdn. von etw. befreien; (c) (allow to leave) entschuldigen; ∼ **oneself** sich entschuldigen; **if you will** ∼ **me** wenn Sie mich bitte entschuldigen wollen; **you are** ∼**d** ihr könnt gehen; **may I be** ∼**d?** (euphem.: to go to the toilet) darf ich mal austreten? 2 /ɪk'skju:s/ n. Entschuldigung, die; **give or offer an** ∼ **for sth.** sich für etw. entschuldigen; **there is no** ∼ **for what I did** was ich getan habe, ist nicht zu entschuldigen;

I'm not trying to make ~s, but …: das soll keine Entschuldigung sein, aber …; **any ~ for a drink!** zum Trinken gibt es immer einen Grund!

ex-di'rectory *adj.* (Brit. Teleph.) Geheim‹*nummer, -anschluss*›

exec /ɪgˈzek/ *n.* (coll.) ⇒ **executive 1 a**

execute /ˈeksɪkjuːt/ *v.t.* (a) (kill) hinrichten; exekutieren (Milit.); (b) (put into effect) ausführen; durchführen ‹*Vorschrift, Gesetz*›; (c) (Law) vollstrecken ‹*Testament*›; unterzeichnen ‹*Urkunde*›

execution /eksɪˈkjuːʃn/ *n.* (a) (killing) Hinrichtung, *die;* Exekution, *die* (Milit.); (b) (putting into effect) Ausführung, *die;* (of instruction, law) Durchführung, *die;* **in the ~ of one's duty** in Erfüllung seiner Pflicht

executioner /eksɪˈkjuːʃənə(r)/ *n.* Scharfrichter, *der*

executive /ɪgˈzekjʊtɪv/ **1** *n.* (a) (person) leitender Angestellter/leitende Angestellte; (b) (administrative body) **the ~** (of government) die Exekutive; (of political organization, trade union) der Vorstand. **2** *adj.* (a) (Commerc.) leitend ‹*Stellung, Funktion*›; (b) (relating to government) exekutiv

executive: **~ com'mittee** *n.* [geschäftsführender] Vorstand; **~ 'stress** *n.* Managerstress, *der;* **~ 'toy** *n.* Managerspielzeug, *das*

executor /ɪgˈzekjʊtə(r)/ *n.* (Law) Testamentsvollstrecker, *der/*-vollstreckerin, *die*

exemplary /ɪgˈzemplərɪ/ *adj.* (a) (model) vorbildlich; (b) (deterrent) exemplarisch

exemplify /ɪgˈzemplɪfaɪ/ *v.t.* veranschaulichen

exempt /ɪgˈzempt/ **1** *adj.* befreit (**from** von). **2** *v.t.* befreien (**from** von)

exemption /ɪgˈzempʃn/ *n.* Befreiung, *die*

exercise /ˈeksəsaɪz/ **1** *n.* (a) *no pl., no indef. art.* (physical exertion) Bewegung, *die;* **take ~:** sich (*Dat.*) Bewegung verschaffen; (b) (task set, activity; also Mus., Sch.) Übung, *die;* **the object of the ~:** der Sinn der Übung; (c) (to improve fitness) [Gymnastik]übung, *die;* (d) *no pl.* (employment, application) Ausübung, *die;* (e) *usu. in pl.* (Mil.) Übung, *die.* **2** *v.t.* (a) ausüben ‹*Recht, Macht, Einfluss*›; walten lassen ‹*Vorsicht*›; sich üben in (+ *Dat.*) ‹*Zurückhaltung, Diskretion*›; (b) **~ the mind** die geistigen Fähigkeiten herausfordern; (c) (physically) trainieren ‹*Körper, Muskeln*›; bewegen ‹*Pferd*›. **3** *v.i.* sich (*Dat.*) Bewegung verschaffen

exercise: **~ bicycle,** (coll.) **~ bike** *ns.* Heimtrainer, *der;* **~ book** *n.* [Schul]heft, *das*

exert /ɪgˈzɜːt/ *v.t.* aufbieten ‹*Kraft, Beredsamkeit*›; ausüben ‹*Einfluss, Druck, Macht*›. **2** *v. refl.* sich anstrengen

exertion /ɪgˈzɜːʃn/ *n.* (a) *no pl.* (of strength, force) Aufwendung, *die;* (of influence, pressure, force) Ausübung, *die;* (b) (effort) Anstrengung, *die*

exhale /eksˈheɪl/ **1** *v.t.* ausatmen. **2** *v.i.* ausatmen; exhalieren (Med.)

exhaust /ɪgˈzɔːst/ **1** *v.t.* (a) (use up) erschöpfen; erschöpfend behandeln ‹*Thema*›; (b) (tire) erschöpfen; **have ~ed oneself** sich völlig verausgabt haben. **2** *n.* (Motor Veh.) (a) **~ [system]** Auspuff, *der;* (b) (what is expelled) Auspuffgase *Pl.*

exhausted /ɪgˈzɔːstɪd/ *adj.* erschöpft

exhausting /ɪgˈzɔːstɪŋ/ *adj.* anstrengend

exhaustion /ɪgˈzɔːstʃn/ *n., no pl.* Erschöpfung, *die*

exhaustive /ɪgˈzɔːstɪv/ *adj.* umfassend

ex'haust pipe *n.* (Motor Veh.) Auspuffrohr, *das*

exhibit /ɪgˈzɪbɪt/ **1** *v.t.* (a) (display) vorzeigen; (show publicly) ausstellen; (b) (manifest) zeigen ‹*Mut, Verachtung, Symptome, Neigung, Angst*›. **2** *n.* (a) Ausstellungsstück, *das;* (b) (Law) Beweisstück, *das*

exhibition /eksɪˈbɪʃn/ *n.* (a) (public display) Ausstellung, *die;* (b) (derog.) **make an ~ of oneself** sich unmöglich aufführen

exhibitionist /eksɪˈbɪʃənɪst/ *n.* Exhibitionist, *der/*Exhibitionistin, *die*

exhibitor /ɪgˈzɪbɪtə(r)/ *n.* Aussteller, *der/*Ausstellerin, *die*

exhilarated /ɪgˈzɪləreɪtɪd/ *adj.* belebt; (gladdened) fröhlich gestimmt; (stimulated) angeregt

exhilarating /ɪgˈzɪləreɪtɪŋ/ *adj.* belebend; fröhlich stimmend ‹*Nachricht, Musik, Anblick*›

exhilaration /ɪgzɪləˈreɪʃn/ *n.* [feeling of] **~:** Hochgefühl, *das*

exhort /ɪgˈzɔːt/ *v.t.* (ernsthaft) ermahnen

exhortation /eksɔːˈteɪʃn/ *n.* Ermahnung, *die*

exile /ˈeksaɪl, ˈegzaɪl/ **1** *n.* (a) Exil, *das;* (forcible also) Verbannung, *die* (**from** aus); **in ~:** im Exil; **into ~:** ins Exil; (b) (person, lit. or fig.) Verbannte, *der/die.* **2** *v.t.* verbannen

exist /ɪgˈzɪst/ *v.i.* (a) (be in existence) existieren ‹*Zweifel, Gefahr, Problem, Brauch, Einrichtung:*› bestehen; **fairies do ~:** es gibt Feen; **the biggest book that has ever ~ed** das größte Buch aller Zeiten; (b) (survive) existieren; überleben; **~ on sth.** von etw. leben; (c) (be found) sth. **~s only in Europe** es gibt etw. nur in Europa

existence /ɪgˈzɪstəns/ *n.* (a) (existing) Existenz, *die;* **doubt sb.'s ~/the ~ of sth.** bezweifeln, dass es jmdn./ etw. gibt; **be in ~:** existieren; **the only such plant in ~:** die einzige Pflanze dieser Art, die es gibt; **come into ~:** entstehen; **go out of ~:** verschwinden; (b) (mode of living) Dasein, *das;* (survival) Existenz, *die*

existential /egzɪˈstenʃl/ *adj.* (Philos.) existenziell

existentialism /egzɪˈstenʃəlɪzm/ *n., no pl.* (Philos.) Existenzialismus, *der*

existing /ɪgˈzɪstɪŋ/ *adj.* bestehend ‹*Ordnung, Schwierigkeiten*›; gegenwärtig ‹*Lage, Führung, Stand der Dinge*›

exit /ˈeksɪt/ **1** *n.* (a) (way out) Ausgang, *der* (**from** aus); (for vehicle) Ausfahrt, *die;* (b) (from stage) Abgang, *der;* **make one's ~:** abgehen; (c) (from room) Hinausgehen, *das.* **2** *v.i.* (a) hinausgehen (**from** aus); (from stage) abgehen (**from** von); (b) (Theatre: as stage direction) ab

exit: **~ permit** *n.* Ausreiseerlaubnis, *die;* **~ visa** *n.* Ausreisevisum, *das*

exodus /ˈeksədəs/ *n.* Auszug, *der;* Exodus, *der* (geh.); **general ~:** allgemeiner Aufbruch

exonerate /ɪgˈzɒnəreɪt/ *v.t.* entlasten

exorbitant /ɪgˈzɔːbɪtənt/ *adj.* [maßlos] überhöht ‹*Preis, Miete, Gewinn, Anforderung, Rechnung*›; maßlos ‹*Ehrgeiz, Forderung*›; **£10 — that's ~!** 10 Pfund — das ist unverschämt viel! (ugs.)

exorcise ⇒ **exorcize**

exorcism /ˈeksɔːsɪzm/ *n.* Exorzismus, *der;* Teufelsaustreibung, *die*

exorcist /ˈeksɔːsɪst/ *n.* Exorzist, *der*

exorcize /ˈeksɔːsaɪz/ *v.t.* austreiben; exorzieren

exotic /ɪgˈzɒtɪk/ *adj.* exotisch

expand /ɪkˈspænd/ **1** *v.i.* (a) (get bigger) sich ausdehnen; ‹*Unternehmen, Stadt, Staat:*› expandieren; ‹*Institution:*› erweitert werden; **~ into sth.** zu etw. anwachsen; (b) **~ on a subject** ein Thema weiter ausführen. **2** *v.t.* (a) (enlarge) ausdehnen; erweitern ‹*Horizont, Wissen*›; dehnen ‹*Körper*›; **~ sth. into sth.** etw. zu etw. erweitern; (b) (Commerc.: develop) erweitern; **~ the economy** das Wirtschaftswachstum fördern; (c) (amplify) weiter ausführen ‹*Gedanken, Notiz, Idee*›

expanse /ɪkˈspæns/ *n.* [weite] Fläche; **~ of water** Wasserfläche, *die*

expansion /ɪkˈspænʃn/ *n.* (a) Ausdehnung, *die;* (of territorial rule also) Expansion, *die;* (of knowledge, building) Erweiterung, *die;* (b) (Commerc.) Expansion, *die*

expansive /ɪkˈspænsɪv/ *adj.* offen; (responsive) zugänglich

expatriate /eksˈpætrɪət/ **1** *attrib. adj.* im Ausland lebend. **2** *n.* (exile) Exilant, *der/*Exilantin, *die;* (foreigner) Ausländer, *der/*Ausländerin, *die*

expect /ɪkˈspekt/ *v.t.* (a) erwarten; **~ to do sth.** damit rechnen, etw. zu tun; **~ sb. to do sth.** damit rechnen, dass jmd. etw. tut; **I ~ you'd like something to eat** ich nehme an, dass du gern etwas essen möchtest; **don't ~ me to help you out** von mir hast du keine Hilfe zu erwarten; **it is ~ed that …:** man erwartet, dass …; **that was [not] to be ~ed** das war [auch nicht] zu erwarten; **be ~ing a baby/child** ein Baby/Kind erwarten; **~ sb. to do sth.** von jmdm. erwarten, dass er etw. tut; **~ sth. from** *or* **of sb.** etw. von jmdm. erwarten; (b) (coll.: think, suppose) glauben; **I ~ so** ich glaube schon; **I don't ~ so**

ich glaube nicht; **I ～ it was/he did** *etc.* das glaube ich gern

expectancy /ɪk'spektənsɪ/ *n., no pl.* Erwartung, *die*

expectant /ɪk'spektənt/ *adj.* (**a**) erwartungsvoll; (**b**) ～ **mother** werdende Mutter

expectantly /ɪk'spektəntlɪ/ *adv.* erwartungsvoll; gespannt ⟨*warten*⟩

expectation /ekspek'teɪʃn/ *n.* (**a**) *no pl.* (expecting) Erwartung, *die;* **in the ～ of** sth. in Erwartung einer Sache (*Gen.*); (**b**) *usu. in pl.* (thing expected) Erwartung, *die;* **come up to ～[s]/sb.'s ～s** den/jmds. Erwartungen entsprechen; **contrary to ～** *or* **to all ～s** wider Erwarten

expediency /ɪk'spiːdɪənsɪ/ *n.* Zweckmäßigkeit, *die*

expedient /ɪk'spiːdɪənt/ **1** *adj.* (**a**) (appropriate, advantageous) angebracht; (**b**) (politic) zweckmäßig. **2** *n.* Mittel, *das*

expedite /'ekspɪdaɪt/ *v.t.* (hasten) beschleunigen; vorantreiben

expedition /ekspɪ'dɪʃn/ *n.* (**a**) Expedition, *die;* (**b**) (Mil.) Feldzug, *der;* (**c**) (excursion) Ausflug, *der*

expel /ɪk'spel/ *v.t.,* **-ll-:** (**a**) ausweisen; ～ **from school** von der Schule verweisen; ～ **sb. from a country** jmdn. aus einem Land ausweisen; ～ **from a club** aus einem Verein ausschließen; (**b**) (with force) vertreiben (**from** aus)

expend /ɪk'spend/ *v.t.* (**a**) aufwenden ([**up**]**on** für); (**b**) (use up) aufbrauchen ([**up**]**on** für)

expendable /ɪk'spendəbl/ *adj.* entbehrlich

expenditure /ɪk'spendɪtʃə(r)/ *n.* (**a**) (amount spent) Ausgaben *Pl.* (**on** für); (**b**) (using up of fuel or effort) Aufwand, *der* (**of** an + *Dat.*)

expense /ɪk'spens/ *n.* (**a**) Kosten *Pl.;* **at one's own ～:** auf eigene Kosten; **go to the ～ of travelling first-class** sogar noch das Geld für die erste Klasse ausgeben; **go to some/great ～:** sich in Unkosten/große Unkosten stürzen; (**b**) (expensive item) teure Angelegenheit; **be** *or* **prove a great** *or* **big ～:** mit großen Ausgaben verbunden sein; (**c**) *usu. in pl.* (Commerc. etc.) Spesen *Pl.;* **with** [**all**] **～s paid** auf Spesen; (**d**) (fig.) Preis, *der;* [**be**] **at the ～ of** sth. auf Kosten von etw. [gehen]; **at sb.'s ～:** auf jmds. Kosten (*Akk.*)

ex'pense account *n.* Spesenabrechnung, *die*

expensive /ɪk'spensɪv/ *adj.* teuer

experience /ɪk'spɪərɪəns/ **1** *n.* (**a**) *no pl., no indef. art.* Erfahrung, *die;* **have ～ of** sth./sb. Erfahrung in etw. (*Dat.*) /mit jmdm. haben; **have ～ of doing** sth. Erfahrung darin haben, etw. zu tun; **learn from ～:** durch eigene *od.* aus eigener Erfahrung lernen; **in/from my** [**own**] [**previous**] **～:** nach meiner/aus eigener Erfahrung; (**b**) (event) Erfahrung, *die;* Erlebnis, *das.* **2** *v.t.* erleben; stoßen auf (+ *Akk.*) ⟨*Schwierigkeiten*⟩; kennen lernen ⟨*Lebensweise*⟩; empfinden ⟨*Hunger, Kälte, Schmerz*⟩

experienced /ɪk'spɪərɪənst/ *adj.* erfahren (**in** in + *Dat.*); **an ～ eye** ein geschulter Blick

experiment 1 /ɪk'sperɪmənt/ *n.* (**a**) Experiment, *das,* Versuch, *der* (**on** an + *Dat.*); **do an ～:** ein Experiment machen; (**b**) (fig.) Experiment, *das;* **as an ～:** versuchsweise. **2** /ɪk'sperɪment/ *v.i.* experimentieren (**on** an + *Dat.,* **with** mit)

experimental /ɪksperɪ'mentl/ *adj.* (**a**) experimentell; Experimental⟨*physik, -psychologie*⟩; Experimentier⟨*theater*⟩; Versuchs⟨*labor, -bedingungen*⟩; Versuchs⟨*tier*⟩; **at the/an ～ stage** im Versuchsstadium; (**b**) (fig.: tentative) vorläufig

experimentation /ɪksperɪmen'teɪʃn/ *n.* Experimentieren, *das*

expert /'ekspɜːt/ **1** *adj.* (**a**) ausgezeichnet; **be ～ in** *or* **at** sth. Fachmann *od.* Experte in etw. (*Dat.*) sein; **be ～ in** *or* **at doing** sth. etw. ausgezeichnet können; (**b**) (of an ～) fachmännisch; ～ **witness** sachverständiger Zeuge; **an ～ opinion** die Meinung eines Fachmanns; ～ **knowledge** Fachkenntnis, *die.* **2** *n.* Fachmann, *der;* Experte, *der*/Expertin, *die;* (Law) Sachverständige, *der/die;* **be an ～ in** *or* **at/on** sth. Fachmann *od.* Experte in etw. (*Dat.*)/für etw. sein

expertise /ekspɜː'tiːz/ *n.* Fachkenntnisse; (skill) Können, *das*

expertly /'ekspɜːtlɪ/ *adv.* meisterhaft; fachmännisch ⟨*reparieren, beraten, beurteilen*⟩

expert 'witness *n.* sachverständiger Zeuge

expire /ɪk'spaɪə(r)/ *v.i.* (**a**) (become invalid) ablaufen; ⟨*Vertrag, Amtszeit:*⟩ auslaufen; (**b**) (literary: die) versterben (geh.)

expiry /ɪk'spaɪərɪ/ *n.* Ablauf, *der;* ～ **date, date of ～** (of contract, credit card, etc.) Ablaufdatum, *das;* (of voucher, medicine, etc.) Verfallsdatum, *das*

explain /ɪk'spleɪn/ **1** *v.t., also abs.* erklären; erläutern ⟨*Grund, Motiv, Gedanken*⟩; darlegen ⟨*Absicht, Beweggrund*⟩; **how do you ～ that?** wie erklären Sie sich (*Dat.*) das? **2** *v. refl.* (**a**) *often abs.* (justify one's conduct) **please ～ [yourself]** bitte erklären Sie mir das; **he refused to ～:** er wollte mir keine Erklärung dafür geben; (**b**) (make one's meaning clear) **please ～ yourself** bitte erklären Sie das [näher]

～ a'way *v.t.* eine [plausible] Erklärung finden für

explanation /eksplə'neɪʃn/ *n.* Erklärung, *die;* **need ～:** einer Erklärung (*Gen.*) bedürfen

explanatory /ɪk'splænətərɪ/ *adj.* erklärend; erläuternd ⟨*Bemerkung*⟩

expletive /ɪk'spliːtɪv, ek'spliːtɪv/ *n.* Kraftausdruck, *der*

explicable /ɪk'splɪkəbl/ *adj.* erklärbar

explicit /ɪk'splɪsɪt/ *adj.* (stated in detail) ausführlich; (openly expressed) offen; unverhüllt; (definite) klar; ausdrücklich ⟨*Zustimmung, Erwähnung*⟩

explicitly /ɪk'splɪsɪtlɪ/ *adv.* ausdrücklich

explode /ɪk'spləʊd/ **1** *v.i.* (lit. or fig.) explodieren; ⟨*Bevölkerung:*⟩ rapide zunehmen. **2** *v.t.* (**a**) zur Explosion bringen; (**b**) (fig.) widerlegen ⟨*Vorstellung, Doktrin, Theorie*⟩

exploit 1 /'eksplɔɪt/ *n.* (feat; also: exc.: deed) Heldentat, *die.* **2** /ɪk'splɔɪt/ *v.t.* (**a**) (derog.) ausbeuten ⟨*Arbeiter, Kolonie usw.*⟩; ausnutzen ⟨*Gutmütigkeit, Freund, Unwissenheit*⟩; (**b**) (utilize) nutzen; nützen; ausnutzen ⟨*Gelegenheit, Situation*⟩; ausbeuten ⟨*Grube*⟩

exploitation /eksplɔɪ'teɪʃn/ *n.* ⇒ **exploit 2:** Ausbeutung, *die;* Ausnutzung, *die;* Nutzung, *die*

exploration /eksplə'reɪʃn/ *n.* (**a**) Erforschung, *die;* (of town, house) Erkundung, *die;* **voyage of ～:** Entdeckungsreise, *die;* (**b**) (fig.) Untersuchung, *die*

exploratory /ɪk'splɒrətərɪ/ *adj.* Forschungs-; ～ **talks** Sondierungsgespräche; ～ **operation** (Med.) explorative Operation

explore /ɪk'splɔː(r)/ *v.t.* (**a**) erforschen; erkunden ⟨*Stadt, Haus*⟩; (**b**) (fig.) untersuchen

explorer /ɪk'splɔːrə(r)/ *n.* Entdeckungsreisende, *der/die;* **Arctic ～:** Arktisforscher, *der/*-forscherin, *die*

explosion /ɪk'spləʊʒn/ *n.* (**a**) (lit.: fig.: rapid increase) Explosion, *die;* (noise) [Explosions]knall, *der;* (**b**) (fig.: of anger etc.) Ausbruch, *der*

explosive /ɪk'spləʊsɪv/ **1** *adj.* (**a**) explosiv; ～ **device** Sprengkörper, *der;* (**b**) (fig.) explosiv; brisant ⟨*Thema*⟩. **2** *n.* Sprengstoff, *der;* **high ～:** hochexplosiver Stoff

exponent /ɪk'spəʊnənt/ *n.* Vertreter, *der*/Vertreterin, *die*

exponential /ekspə'nenʃl/ *adj.* exponentiell; Exponential-

exponentially /ekspə'nenʃəlɪ/ *adv.* exponentiell

export 1 /ɪk'spɔːt/ *v.t.* exportieren; ausführen; ～**ing country** Ausfuhrland, *das;* **oil-～ing countries** [erdöl]exportierende Länder. **2** /'ekspɔːt/ *n.* (**a**) (process, amount ～ed) Export, *der;* Ausfuhr, *die;* (～ed articles) Exportgut, *das;* ～**s of sugar** Zuckerexporte *od.* -ausfuhren; (**b**) *attrib.* Export⟨*leiter, -handel, -markt, -kaufmann*⟩

exporter /ɪk'spɔːtə(r)/ *n.* Exporteur, *der*

expose /ɪk'spəʊz/ **1** *v.t.* (**a**) (uncover) freilegen; entblößen ⟨*Haut, Körper, Knie*⟩; (**b**) (make known) offenbaren ⟨*Schwäche, Tatsache, Geheimnis, Plan*⟩; aufdecken ⟨*Irrtum, Missstände, Verbrechen, Verrat*⟩; entlarven ⟨*Täter, Verräter, Spion*⟩; (**c**) (subject) ～ **to** sth. einer Sache (*Dat.*) aussetzen; (**d**) (Photog.) belichten. **2** *v. refl.* sich [unsittlich] entblößen

exposed /ɪk'spəʊzd/ *adj.* (unprotected) ungeschützt

exposition /ekspə'zɪʃn/ *n.* (**a**) (statement) Darstellung, *die;* (**b**) (exhibition) Ausstellung, *die*

expostulate /ık'spɒstjʊleıt/ *v.i.* protestieren

expostulation /ıkspɒstjʊ'leıʃn/ *n.* Protest, *der*

exposure /ık'spəʊʒə(r)/ *n.* **(a)** (to air, cold, etc.) (being exposed) Ausgesetztsein, *das;* (exposing) Aussetzen, *das;* **die of/suffer from** ~ **[to cold]** an Unterkühlung (*Dat.*) sterben/leiden; **indecent** ~: Entblößung in schamverletzender Weise; **media** ~: Publicity, *die;* **(b)** (of fraud etc.) Enthüllung, *die;* (of criminal) Entlarvung, *die;* **(c)** (Photog.) (exposing time) Belichtung, *die;* (picture) Aufnahme, *die*

ex'posure meter *n.* (Photog.) Belichtungsmesser, *der*

expound /ık'spaʊnd/ *v.t.* darlegen ‹Theorie, Doktrin› (**to** *Dat.*)

express /ık'spres/ **1** *v.t.* **(a)** (indicate) ausdrücken; **(b)** (put into words) äußern ‹Meinung, Wunsch›; zum Ausdruck bringen ‹Dank, Bedauern, Liebe›; ~ **sth. in another language** etw. in einer anderen Sprache ausdrücken; ~ **one-self** sich ausdrücken; **(c)** (represent by symbols) ausdrücken ‹Zahl, Wert›. **2** *attrib. adj.* **(a)** (fast) ‹brief, -bote usw.›: Schnell‹paket, -sendung›; *see also* **express train; (b)** (particular) besonder...; bestimmt; ausdrücklich ‹Absicht›; **(c)** (stated) ausdrücklich ‹Wunsch, Befehl usw.›. **3** *adv.* als Eilsache ‹senden›. **4** *n.* (train) Schnellzug, *der;* D-Zug, *der*

expression /ık'spreʃn/ *n.* Ausdruck, *der;* **the** ~ **on his face, his facial** ~: sein Gesichtsausdruck; **full of/without** ~: ausdrucksvoll/-los

expressionism /ık'spreʃənızm/ *n., no pl.* Expressionismus, *der*

expressive /ık'spresıv/ *adj.* ausdrucksvoll; vielsagend ‹Schweigen›

expressively /ık'spresıvlı/ *adv.* ausdrucksvoll

expressly /ık'preslı/ *adv.* ausdrücklich

express: ~ **'train** *n.* Schnellzug, *der;* D-Zug, *der;* ~**way** *n.* (Amer.) Schnell[verkehrs]straße, *die*

expulsion /ık'spʌlʃn/ *n.* (from school, college) Verweisung, *die* (**from** von); (from country) Ausweisung, *die* (**from** aus); (from club) Ausschluss, *der* (**from** aus)

expurgate /'ekspəgeıt/ *v.t.* ~**d version/edition** zensierte Fassung/Ausgabe

exquisite /'ekskwızıt, ık'skwızıt/ *adj.* **(a)** erlesen; exquisit, bezaubernd ‹Aussicht, Muster, Melodie, Anmut›; **(b)** heftig ‹Schmerz, Freude›; unerträglich ‹Leiden, Schmerzen›

exquisitely /'ekskwızıtlı, ık'skwızıtlı/ *adv.* **(a)** vorzüglich; kunstvoll ‹verziert, geschnitzt›; **(b)** (acutely) äußerst; außerordentlich

extend /ık'stend/ **1** *v.t.* **(a)** (stretch out) ausstrecken ‹Arm, Bein, Hand›; ausziehen ‹Leiter, Teleskop›; ausbreiten ‹Flügel›; ~ **one's hand to sb.** jmdm. die Hand reichen; **the table can be** ~**ed** der Tisch ist ausziehbar; **(b)** (make longer) (in space) verlängern; ausdehnen ‹Grenze›; ausbauen ‹Bahnlinie, Straße›; (in time) verlängern; verlängern lassen ‹Leihbuch, Visum›; ~ **the time limit** den Termin hinausschieben; **(c)** (enlarge) ausdehnen ‹Einfluss, Macht›; erweitern ‹Wissen, Wortschatz, Bedeutung, Freundeskreis, Besitz, Geschäft›; ausbauen, vergrößern ‹Haus, Geschäft›; **(d)** (offer) gewähren, zuteil werden lassen ‹Gast[freund]schaft, Schutz, Hilfe, Kredit› (**to** *Dat.*); (accord) aussprechen ‹Dank, Einladung, Glückwunsch› (**to** *Dat.*); ausrichten ‹Gruß› (**to** *Dat.*); ~ **a welcome to sb.** jmdm. willkommen heißen. **2** *v.i.* sich erstrecken; **the wall** ~**s for miles** die Mauer zieht sich meilenweit hin; **the season** ~**s from November to March** die Saison geht von November bis März

extension /ık'stenʃn/ *n.* **(a)** (stretching out) (of arm, leg, hand) [Aus]strecken, *das;* (of wings) Ausbreiten, *das;* **(b)** (prolonging) Verlängerung, *die;* (of road, railway) Ausbau, *der;* **ask for an** ~: um Verlängerung bitten; **be granted** *or* **get an** ~: Verlängerung bekommen; **(c)** (enlargement) (of power, influence, research, frontier) Ausdehnung, *die;* (of enterprise, trade, knowledge) Erweiterung, *die;* **(d)** (additional part) (of house) Anbau, *der;* (of office, university, hospital, etc.) Erweiterungsbau, *der;* **(e)** (telephone) Nebenanschluss, *der;* (number) Apparat, *der*

ex'tension lead *n.* (Brit.) Verlängerungsschnur, *die*

extensive /ık'stensıv/ *adj.* ausgedehnt ‹Ländereien, Reisen, Stadt, Wald, Besitz[tümer], Handel, Forschungen›; umfangreich ‹Reparatur, Investitionen, Wissen, Nachforschungen, Studien, Auswahl, Sammlung›; beträchtlich ‹Schäden, Geldmittel, Anstrengungen›; weit reichend ‹Änderungen, Reformen, Einfluss›; ausführlich ‹Bericht, Einleitung›

extensively /ık'stensıvlı/ *adv.* beträchtlich ‹ändern, beschädigen›; ausführlich ‹berichten, schreiben›

extent /ık'stent/ *n.* **(a)** (space) Ausdehnung, *die;* (of wings) Spannweite, *die;* **(b)** (scope) (of knowledge, power, authority) Umfang, *der;* (of damage, disaster) Ausmaß, *das;* (of debt, loss) Höhe, *die;* **to what** ~? inwieweit?; **to a great** *or* **large** ~: in hohem Maße; **to some** *or* **a certain** ~: in gewissem Maße; **to a greater or lesser** ~: mehr oder weniger; **to such an** ~ **that** ...: in solchem Maße, dass ...

extenuating /ık'stenjʊeıtıŋ/ *adj.* ~ **circumstances** mildernde Umstände

exterior /ık'stıərıə(r)/ **1** *adj.* **(a)** äußer...; Außen‹fläche, -wand, -anstrich›; **(b)** ([coming] from) outside) äußer...; außerhalb gelegen. **2** *n.* **(a)** Äußere, *das;* (of house) Außenwände *Pl.;* **(b)** (appearance) Äußere, *das*

exterminate /ık'stɜːmıneıt/ *v.t.* ausrotten; vertilgen ‹Ungeziefer›

extermination /ıkstɜːmı'neıʃn/ *n.* Ausrottung, *die;* (of pests) Vertilgung, *die*

external /ık'stɜːnl/ *adj.* **(a)** äußer...; Außen‹fläche, -druck, -winkel, -abmessungen›; **purely** ~: nur äd. rein äußerlich; **(b)** (applied to outside) äußerlich ‹Heilmittel›; **for** ~ **use only** nur äußerlich anzuwenden; **(c)** (of foreign affairs) Außen‹minister, -handel, -politik›

externally /ık'stɜːnəlı/ *adv.* äußerlich

extinct /ık'stıŋkt/ *adj.* erloschen ‹Vulkan, Leidenschaft, Liebe, Hoffnung›; ausgestorben ‹Art, Rasse, Volk, Gattung›; **become** ~: aussterben

extinction /ık'stıŋkʃn/ *n., no pl.* Aussterben, *das;* **threatened with** ~: vom Aussterben bedroht

extinguish /ık'stıŋgwıʃ/ *v.t.* löschen; erlöschen lassen ‹Liebe, Hoffnung›; auslöschen ‹Leben›

extinguisher /ık'stıŋgwıʃə(r)/ *n.* (for fire) Feuerlöscher, *der*

extol /ık'stəʊl, ık'stɒl/ *v.t.,* **-ll-** rühmen; preisen

extort /ık'stɔːt/ *v.t.* erpressen (**out of, from** von); ~ **a confession from sb.** ein Geständnis aus jmdm. herauspressen

extortion /ık'stɔːʃn/ *n.* (of money, taxes) Erpressung, *die;* **£50? That's sheer** ~! 50 Pfund? Das ist ja Wucher!

extortionate /ık'stɔːʃənət/ *adj.* Wucher‹preis, -zinsen usw.›; horrend ‹Gebühr, Steuer›; maßlos überzogen ‹Forderung›

extra /'ekstrə/ **1** *adj.* **(a)** (additional) zusätzlich; Mehr‹arbeit, -kosten, -ausgaben, -aufwendungen›; Sonder‹bus, -zug›; ~ **charge** Aufpreis, *der;* **all we need is an** ~ **hour/three pounds** wir brauchen nur noch eine Stunde/drei Pfund [zusätzlich]; **(b)** (more than is necessary) überzählig ‹Exemplar, Portion›; **an** ~ **pair of gloves** noch ein *od.* ein zweites Paar Handschuhe. **2** *adv.* **(a)** (more than usually) besonders; extra ‹lang, stark, fein›; überaus ‹froh›; **an** ~ **large blouse** eine Bluse in Übergröße; **an** ~ **special occasion** eine ganz besondere Gelegenheit; **(b)** (additionally) extra; **packing and postage** ~: zuzüglich Verpackung und Porto. **3** *n.* **(a)** (added to services, salary, etc.) zusätzliche Leistung; (on car etc. offered for sale) Extra, *das;* **(b)** (sth. with ~ charge) **be an** ~: zusätzlich berechnet werden; **(c)** (in play, film, etc.) Statist, *der*/Statistin, *die*

extract **1** /'ekstrækt/ *n.* **(a)** (substance) Extrakt, *der* (fachspr. auch: das); **(b)** (from book, music, etc.) Auszug, *der;* Extrakt, *der* (geh.). **2** /ık'strækt/ *v.t.* **(a)** ziehen, (fachspr.) extrahieren ‹Zahn›; ~ **sth. from sb.** (fig.) etw. aus jmdm. herausholen; ~ **a promise/confession from sb.** jmdm. ein Versprechen/Geständnis abpressen; ~ **papers from a folder** einem Aktenordner Unterlagen entnehmen; **(b)** (obtain) extrahieren; ~ **the juice from apples** Äpfel entsaften; ~ **metal from ore** Metall aus Erz gewinnen; **(c)** (derive) erfassen ‹Bedeutung, Hauptpunkte›

extraction /ık'strækʃn/ *n.* **(a)** (of tooth) Extraktion, *die;* (of juice, honey, metal) Gewinnung, *die;* **(b)** **be of German** ~: deutscher Abstammung *od.* Herkunft sein

extractor fan /ɪk'stræktə fæn/ *n.* Entlüfter, *der*
extradite /'ekstrədaɪt/ *v.t.* **(a)** ausliefern ‹ *Verbrecher* ›; **(b)** (obtain extradition of) ~ **sb.** jmds. Auslieferung erwirken
extradition /ekstrə'dɪʃn/ *n.* Auslieferung, *die;* ~ **treaty** Auslieferungsvertrag, *der*
extra-'marital *adj.* außerehelich
extra'mural *adj.* (Univ.) außerhalb der Universität *nach*gestellt
extraneous /ɪk'streɪnɪəs/ *adj.* **(a)** (from outside) von außen; **(b)** (irrelevant) belanglos; **be** ~ **to sth.** für etw. ohne Belang sein
extraordinarily /ɪk'strɔːdɪnərɪlɪ, ekstrə'ɔːdɪnərɪlɪ/ *adv.* außergewöhnlich; überaus ‹ *merkwürdig* ›
extraordinary /ɪk'strɔːdɪnərɪ, ekstrə'ɔːdɪnərɪ/ *adj.* (exceptional) außergewöhnlich; (unusual, peculiar) ungewöhnlich ‹ *Gabe* ›; merkwürdig ‹ *Zeichen, Benehmen, Angewohnheit* ›; außerordentlich ‹ *Verdienste, Einfluss* ›; (additional) außerordentlich ‹ *Versammlung* ›; **how** ~**!** wie seltsam!
extra'ordinary general meeting *n.* (of shareholders) außerordentliche Hauptversammlung; (of club) außerordentliche Mitgliederversammlung
extra-'sensory *adj.* ~ **perception** außersinnliche Wahrnehmung
extra 'time *n.* (Sport) **after** ~: nach einer Verlängerung; **play** ~: in die Verlängerung gehen
extravagance /ɪk'strævəgəns/ *n.* **(a)** *no pl.* (being extravagant) Extravaganz, *die;* (of claim, wish, order, demand) Übertriebenheit, *die;* (of words, thoughts, ideas) Verstiegenheit, *die;* (with money) Verschwendungssucht, *die;* **(b)** (extravagant thing) Luxus, *der*
extravagant /ɪk'strævəgənt/ *adj.* **(a)** (wasteful) verschwenderisch; aufwendig ‹ *Lebensstil* ›; teuer ‹ *Geschmack* ›; **(b)** (immoderate) übertrieben ‹ *Benehmen, Lob, Eifer, Begeisterung usw.* ›; **(c)** (beyond bounds of reason) abwegig ‹ *Theorie, Frage, Einfall* ›
extravagantly /ɪk'strævəgəntlɪ/ *adv.* extravagant ‹ *ausstatten, sich kleiden* ›; verschwenderisch ‹ *benutzen, verbrauchen* ›; luxuriös, aufwendig ‹ *leben* ›; überschwänglich ‹ *loben* ›
'extra-virgin *adj.* [extra]nativ ‹ *Olivenöl* ›
extreme /ɪk'striːm/ **1** *adj.* **(a)** (outermost, utmost) äußerst... ‹ *Spitze, Rand, Ende* ›; extrem, krass ‹ *Gegensätze* ›; **at the** ~ **edge/left** ganz am Rand/ganz links; **in the** ~ **North** im äußersten Norden; **(b)** (reaching high degree) extrem; gewaltig ‹ *Entfernung, Unterschied* ›; höchst... ‹ *Gefahr* ›; äußerst... ‹ *Notfall, Höflichkeit, Bescheidenheit* ›; stärkst... ‹ *Schmerzen* ›; heftigst... ‹ *Zorn* ›; tiefst... ‹ *Hass, Dankbarkeit* ›; größt... ‹ *Wichtigkeit* ›; **(c)** (not moderate) extrem ‹ *Person, Ideen, Kritik* ›; ~ **right-wing views** rechtsextreme Ansichten; **(d)** (severe) drastisch ‹ *Maßnahme* ›. **2** *n.* Extrem, *das;* [krasser] Gegensatz; **the** ~**s of wealth and poverty** größter Reichtum und äußerste Armut; ~**s of temperature** extreme Temperaturunterschiede; **go to** ~**s** vor nichts zurückschrecken; **go to the other** ~: ins andere Extrem verfallen; **go from one** ~ **to another** von od. aus einem Extrem ins andere fallen; ... **in the** ~: äußerst ...; *see also* **carry 1 g**
extremely /ɪk'striːmlɪ/ *adv.* äußerst; **Did you enjoy the party? — Yes,** ~**:** Hat dir die Party gefallen? — Ja, sehr sogar!
extremist /ɪk'striːmɪst/ *n.* **(a)** Extremist, *der*/Extremistin, *die;* **right-wing** ~**:** Rechtsextremist, *der*/-extremistin, *die;* **(b)** *attrib.* extremistisch
extremity /ɪk'stremɪtɪ/ *n.* **(a)** (of branch, road) äußerstes Ende; (of region) Rand, *der;* **(b)** *in pl.* (hands and feet) Extremitäten *Pl.*
extricate /'ekstrɪkeɪt/ *v.t.* ~ **sth. from sth.** etw. aus etw. herausziehen; ~ **oneself/sb. from sth.** sich/jmdn. aus etw. befreien
extrovert /'ekstrəvɜːt/ **1** *n.* extrovertierter Mensch; **be an** ~**:** extrovertiert sein. **2** *adj.* extrovertiert
extroverted /'ekstrəvɜːtɪd/ *adj.* extrovertiert
exuberance /ɪg'zjuːbərəns/ *n.* **(a)** (vigour) Überschwang, *der;* ~ **of youth** jugendlicher Überschwang; **(b)** (of language, style) Lebendigkeit, *die*

exuberant /ɪg'zjuːbərənt/ *adj.* **(a)** (overflowing) überschäumend ‹ *Kraft, Freude, Eifer* ›; **(b)** (effusive) überschwänglich
exude /ɪg'zjuːd/ *v.t.* absondern ‹ *Flüssigkeit, Harz* ›; ausströmen ‹ *Geruch* ›; (fig.) ausstrahlen ‹ *Charme, Zuversicht* ›
exult /ɪg'zʌlt/ *v.i.* (literary) frohlocken (geh.) **(in, at, over** über + *Akk.*)
exultant /ɪg'zʌltənt/ *adj.* (literary) jubelnd; **be** ~**:** jubeln
exultation /egzʌl'teɪʃn/ *n.* Jubel, *der*
eye /aɪ/ **1** *n.* **(a)** ▶672 Auge, *das;* ~**s** (look, glance, gaze) Blick, *der;* **the sun/light is [shining] in my** ~**s** die Sonne/das Licht blendet mich; **out of the corner of one's** ~**:** aus den Augenwinkeln; **with one's own** *or* **very** ~**s** mit eigenen Augen; **before sb.'s very** ~**s** vor jmds. Augen (*Dat.*); **measure a distance by** ~**:** einen Abstand nach Augenmaß schätzen; **paint/draw sth. by** ~**:** etw. nach der Natur malen/zeichnen; **look sb. in the** ~**:** jmdm. gerade in die Augen sehen; **be unable to take one's** ~**s off sb./sth.** die Augen od. den Blick nicht von jmdm./etw. abwenden können; **keep an** ~ **on sb./sth.** auf jmdn./etw. aufpassen; **have [got] an** ~ *or* **one's** ~**[s] on sb./sth.** ein Auge auf jmdn./etw. geworfen haben; **I've got my** ~ **on you!** ich lasse dich nicht aus den Augen!; **keep an** ~ **open** *or* **out [for sb./sth.]** [nach jmdm./etw.] Ausschau halten; **keep one's** ~**s open** *or* (coll.) **peeled** *or* (coll.) **skinned for sth.** nach etw. Ausschau halten; **with one's** ~**s open** (fig.) mit offenen Augen; **with one's** ~**s shut** (fig.) (without full awareness) blind; (with great ease) im Schlaf; **be all** ~**s** gespannt zusehen; **[an]** ~ **for [an]** ~**:** Auge um Auge; **have an** ~ **to sth./doing sth.** auf etw. (*Akk.*) bedacht sein/darauf bedacht sein, etw. zu tun; **that was one in the** ~ **for him** (coll.) das war ein Schlag ins Kontor für ihn (ugs.); **see** ~ **to** ~ **[on sth. with sb.]** [mit jmdm.] einer Meinung [über etw. (*Akk.*)] sein; **be up to one's** ~**s** (fig.) bis über beide Ohren drinstecken (ugs.); **be up to one's** ~**s in work/debt** bis über beide Ohren in der Arbeit/in Schulden stecken (ugs.); **have a keen/good** ~ **for sth.** einen geschärften/einen sicheren od. den richtigen Blick für etw. haben; **make** ~**s at sb.** jmdm. [schöne] Augen machen; **(b)** (of needle, fish-hook) Öhr, *das;* (metal loop) Öse, *die.* **2** *v.t.,* ~**ing** *or* **eying** /'aɪɪŋ/ beäugen; ~ **sb. up and down** jmdn. von oben bis unten mustern
eye: ~**ball** *n.* Augapfel, *der;* ~**brow** *n.* ▶672 Augenbraue, *die;* **raise an** ~**brow** *or* **one's** ~**brows [at sth.]** (fig.: in surprise) die Stirn runzeln (at über + *Akk.*); **it will raise a few** ~**brows** das wird einiges Stirnrunzeln hervorrufen; ~**-catching** *adj.* ins Auge springend od. fallend ‹ *Inserat, Plakat, Buchhülle usw.* ›; ~ **drops** *n. pl.* (Med.) Augentropfen *Pl.*
eyeful /'aɪfʊl/ *n.* (coll.) **get an** ~ **[of sth.]** einiges [von etw.] zu sehen bekommen
'eyelash *n.* ▶672 Augenwimper, *die*
eyelet /'aɪlɪt/ *n.* Öse, *die*
eye: ~ **level** *n.* Augenhöhe, *die; attrib.* ~**-level** in Augenhöhe *nachgestellt;* ~**lid** *n.* ▶672 Augenlid, *das;* ~ **make-up** *n.* Augen-Make-up, *das;* ~**-opener** *n.* (surprise, revelation) Überraschung, *die;* **the book was an** ~**-opener to the public** das Buch hat der Öffentlichkeit (*Dat.*) die Augen geöffnet; ~**piece** *n.* (Optics) Okular, *das;* ~**-shade** *n.* Augenschirm, *der;* ~**shadow** *n.* Lidschatten, *der;* ~**sight** *n.* Sehkraft, *die;* **have good** ~**sight** gute Augen haben; **his** ~**sight is poor** er hat schlechte Augen; ~**sore** *n.* Schandfleck, *der;* **the building is an** ~**sore** das Gebäude beleidigt das Auge; ~**strain** *n.* Überanstrengung der Augen; ~ **test** *n.* Sehtest, *der;* ~**-tooth** *n.* Eckzahn, *der;* ~**wash** *n.* **(a)** (Med.: lotion) Augenwasser, *das;* **(b)** *no pl.* (coll.) (nonsense) Gewäsch, *das* (ugs. abwertend); (concealment) Augen[aus]wischerei, *die* (ugs.); ~**witness** *n.* Augenzeuge, *der*/-zeugin, *die; attrib.* ~**witness account** *or* **report** Augenzeugenbericht, *der*
eyrie /'ɪərɪ/ *n.* (nest) Horst, *der*

Ff

F, f /ef/ *n., pl.* **Fs** *or* **F's** **(a)** (letter) F, f, *das;* **(b)** F (Mus.) F, f, *das;* **F sharp** fis, Fis, *das*

F. *abbr.* **(a)** ▶**1141** **Fahrenheit** F; **(b)** ▶**938** **franc** F

f. *abbr.* **(a)** **female** weibl.; **(b)** **feminine** f.; **(c)** **focal length** f; f/8 (Photog.) Blende 8; **(d)** **following [page]** f.; **(e)** **forte** f

fable /'feɪbl/ *n.* **(a)** (myth, lie) Märchen, *das;* **(b)** (thing that does not really exist, brief story) Fabel, *die*

fabled /'feɪbld/ *adj.* **(a)** **it is ~ that …:** es heißt, dass …; **(b)** (mythical) Fabel⟨*land, -wesen, -tier*⟩; **(c)** (celebrated) berühmt **(for** für**)**

fabric /'fæbrɪk/ *n.* **(a)** (material, construction, texture) Gewebe, *das;* **woven/knitted ~:** Web-/Strickware, *die;* **(b)** (of building) bauliche Substanz; **(c)** (fig.) **the ~ of society** die Struktur der Gesellschaft

fabricate /'fæbrɪkeɪt/ *v.t.* **(a)** (invent) erfinden; (forge) fälschen; **(b)** (manufacture) herstellen

fabrication /fæbrɪ'keɪʃn/ *n.* **(a)** (of story etc.) Erfindung, *die;* **the story is [a] pure ~:** die Geschichte ist frei erfunden; **(b)** (manufacture) Herstellung, *die*

'fabric softener *n.* Weichspülmittel, *das;* Weichspüler, *der*

fabulous /'fæbjʊləs/ *adj.* **(a)** sagenhaft; Fabel⟨*tier, -wesen*⟩; **(b)** (coll.: marvellous) fabelhaft (ugs.)

façade /fə'sɑ:d/ *n.* (lit. or fig.) Fassade, *die*

face /feɪs/ **1** *n.* **(a)** ▶**672** Gesicht, *das;* **wash one's ~:** sich (*Dat.*) das Gesicht waschen; **go blue in the ~** (with cold) blau im Gesicht werden; **go red** *or* **purple in the ~** (with exertion or passion or shame) rot im Gesicht werden; **the stone struck me in the ~:** der Stein traf mich ins Gesicht; **bring A and B ~ to ~:** A und B einander (*Dat.*) gegenüberstellen; **meet sb. ~ to ~:** jmdn. persönlich kennen lernen; **come** *or* **be brought ~ to ~ with sb.** mit jmdm. konfrontiert werden; **come ~ to ~ with the fact that …:** vor der Tatsache stehen, dass …; **in [the] ~ of sth.** (despite) trotz; **slam the door in sb.'s ~:** jmdm. die Tür vor der Nase zuknallen (ugs.); **fall [flat] on one's ~** (lit. or fig.) auf die Nase fallen (ugs.); **look sb./sth. in the ~:** jmdm./einer Sache ins Gesicht sehen; **show one's ~:** sich sehen *od.* blicken lassen; **tell sb. to his ~ what …:** jmdm. [offen] ins Gesicht sagen, was …; **till one is blue in the ~:** bis man verrückt wird (ugs.); **save one's ~:** das Gesicht wahren *od.* retten; **lose ~ [with sb.] [over sth.]** das Gesicht [vor jmdm.] [wegen etw.] verlieren; **make** *or* **pull a ~/~s [at sb.]** (to show dislike) ein Gesicht/Gesichter machen *od.* ziehen; (to amuse or frighten) eine Grimasse/Grimassen schneiden; **don't make a ~!** mach nicht so ein Gesicht!; **on the ~ of it** dem Anschein nach; **put a brave ~ on it** gute Miene zum bösen Spiel machen; **(b)** (front) (of mountain, cliff) Wand, *die;* (of building) Stirnseite, *die;* (of clock, watch) Zifferblatt, *das;* (of coin, medal, banknote, playing card) Vorderseite, *die;* (of golf club, cricket bat, hockey stick, tennis racket) Schlagfläche, *die;* **(c)** (surface) **the ~ of the earth** die Erde; **disappear off** *or* **from the ~ of the earth** spurlos verschwinden; **(d)** (Geom.: also of crystal, gem) Fläche, *die;* **(e)** ⇒ **typeface.** *See also* **face down[ward]; face up[ward].** **2** *v.t.* **(a)** ▶**715** (look towards) sich wenden zu; **sb. ~s the front** jmd. sieht nach vorne; **[stand] facing one another** sich (*Dat.*) *od.* (meist geh.) einander gegenüber [stehen]; **the window ~s the garden/front** das Fenster geht zum Garten/zur Straße hinaus; **sit facing the engine** (in a train) in Fahrtrichtung sitzen; **(b)** (fig.: have to deal with) ins Auge sehen (+ *Dat.*) ⟨*Tod, Vorstellung*⟩; gegenübertreten (+ *Dat.*) ⟨*Kläger*⟩; sich stellen (+ *Dat.*) ⟨*Anschuldigung, Kritik*⟩; stehen vor (+ *Dat.*) ⟨*Ruin, Entscheidung*⟩; **~ trial for murder, ~ a charge of murder** sich wegen Mordes vor Gericht verantworten müssen; **(c)** (not shrink from) ins Auge sehen (+ *Dat.*) ⟨*Tatsache, Wahrheit*⟩; mit Fassung gegenübertreten

(+ *Dat.*) ⟨*Kläger*⟩; **~ the music** (fig.) die Suppe auslöffeln (ugs.); **let's ~ it** (coll.) machen wir uns (*Dat.*) doch nichts vor (ugs.); **let's ~ it** (coll.) machen wir uns (*Dat.*) doch nichts vor (ugs.); **~d with sth.** sich einer Sache (*Dat.*) gegenübersehen; **~d with these facts** mit diesen Sachen konfrontiert; **(e)** (coll.: bear) verkraften. **3** *v.i.* **~ forwards/backwards** ⟨*Person, Bank, Sitz:*⟩ in/entgegen Fahrtrichtung sitzen/aufgestellt sein; **in which direction was he facing?** in welche Richtung blickte er?; **stand facing away from sb.** mit dem Rücken zu jmdm. stehen; **~ away from the road/on to the road/east[wards** *or* **to[wards] the east** ⟨*Fenster, Zimmer:*⟩ nach hinten/vorn/Osten liegen; **the side of the house ~s to[wards] the sea** die Seite des Hauses liegt zum Meer

~ 'up to *v.t.* ins Auge sehen (+ *Dat.*); sich abfinden mit ⟨*Möglichkeit*⟩; auf sich nehmen ⟨*Verantwortung*⟩

face: **~cloth** *n.* Waschlappen [für das Gesicht]; **~ cream** *n.* Gesichtscreme, *die;* **~ 'down[ward]** *adv.* mit der Vorderseite nach unten; **lie ~ down[ward]** ⟨*Person/Buch:*⟩ auf dem Bauch/Gesicht liegen; **~-flannel** (Brit.) ⇒ **~-cloth**

faceless /'feɪslɪs/ *adj.* (anonymous) anonym (fig.)

face: **~lift** *n.* **(a)** Facelifting, *das;* **have** *or* **get a ~lift** sich liften lassen; **(b)** (fig.) Verschönerung, *die;* **~ pack** *n.* [Gesichts]maske, *die;* **~-saving** *adj.* zur Wahrung des Gesichts *nachgestellt;* **as a ~-saving gesture** um das Gesicht zu wahren

facet /'fæsɪt/ *n.* **(a)** (of cut stone etc.) Facette, *die;* **(b)** (aspect) Seite, *die;* **every ~:** alle Seiten

facetious /fə'si:ʃəs/ *adj.* (gewollt) witzig; **[not] be ~ [about sth.]** [keine] Witze [über etw. (*Akk.*)] machen (ugs.)

face: **~-to-~** *adj.* unmittelbar ⟨*Gegenüberstellung*⟩; persönlich ⟨*Gespräch, Treffen*⟩; **~ 'up[ward]** *adv.* mit der Vorderseite nach oben; **lie ~ up[ward]** ⟨*Person:*⟩ auf dem Rücken liegen; (open) ⟨*Buch:*⟩ aufgeschlagen liegen; **~ value** *n.* (Finance) Nennwert, *der;* **accept sth. at [its] ~ value** (fig.) etw. für bare Münze nehmen; **take sb. at [his/her] ~ value** (fig.) jmdn. nach seinem Äußeren beurteilen

facial /'feɪʃl/ **1** *adj.* Gesichts-. **2** *n.* Gesichtsmassage, *die;* **have a ~:** sich (*Dat.*) das Gesicht massieren lassen

facile /'fæsaɪl/ *adj.* (often derog.) leicht ⟨*Sieg, Aufgabe*⟩; nichtssagend, banal ⟨*Bemerkung*⟩

facilitate /fə'sɪlɪteɪt/ *v.t.* erleichtern

facility /fə'sɪlɪtɪ/ *n.* **(a)** *esp. in pl.* Einrichtung, *die;* **cooking/washing facilities** Koch-/Waschgelegenheit, *die;* **sports facilities** Sportanlagen; **(b)** (opportunity) Möglichkeit, *die;* **(c)** (ease) Leichtigkeit, *die;* (dexterity) Gewandtheit, *die*

facing /'feɪsɪŋ/ *n.* **(a)** (on garment) Aufschlag, *der;* Besatz, *der;* **(b)** (covering) Verkleidung, *die*

facsimile /fæk'sɪmɪlɪ/ *n.* **(a)** Faksimile, *das;* **(b)** (Telecommunications) ⇒ **fax 1**

fact /fækt/ *n.* **(a)** (true thing) Tatsache, *die;* **~s and figures** Fakten und Zahlen; **the ~ remains that …:** Tatsache bleibt: …; **the true ~s of the case** *or* **matter** der wahre Sachverhalt; **know for a ~ that …:** genau *od.* sicher wissen, dass …; **is that a ~?** (coll.) Tatsache? (ugs.); **and that's a ~:** und daran gibt's nichts zu zweifeln (ugs.); **the reason lies in the ~ that …:** der Grund besteht darin, dass …; **face [the] ~s** den Tatsachen ins Gesicht sehen; **it is a proven ~ that …:** es ist erwiesen, dass …; **the ~ [of the matter] is that …:** die Sache ist die, dass …; **[it is a] ~ of life** [das ist die] harte *od.* rauhe Wirklichkeit; **tell** *or* **teach sb. the ~s of life** (coll. euphem.) jmdn. [sexuell] aufklären; **(b)** (reality) Wahrheit, *die;* Tatsachen *Pl.;* **distinguish ~ from fiction** Fakten und Fiktion (*od.* Dichtung und Wahrheit) unterscheiden; **in ~:** tatsächlich; **I don't think he'll come back; in ~ I know he won't** ich glaube nicht, dass er zurückkommt, ich weiß es sogar; *see also* **matter 1 d; (c)** (thing assumed to be ~) Faktum, *das;* **deny the ~ that …:** [die Tatsache] abstreiten, dass …

'fact-finding *attrib. adj.* Erkundungs⟨*fahrt, -trupp*⟩; **~ committee/trip** Untersuchungsausschuss, *der*/Informationsreise, *die*

faction /ˈfækʃn/ n. Splittergruppe, die

factor /ˈfæktə(r)/ n. (also Math.) Faktor, der

factory /ˈfæktərɪ/ n. Fabrik, die; Werk, das

factory: ∼ **farm** n. [voll]automatisierter landwirtschaftlicher Betrieb; Agrarfabrik, die (abwertend); ∼ **farming** n. [fabrikmäßige] Massentierhaltung; **the** ∼ **farming of salmon** die massenweise Lachsproduktion; ∼ **ship** n. Fabrikschiff, das; ∼ **worker** n. ▶ 887 | Fabrikarbeiter, der/-arbeiterin, die

'fact sheet n. Infoblatt, das

factual /ˈfæktʃʊəl/ adj. sachlich ⟨Bericht, Darlegung⟩; auf Tatsachen beruhend ⟨Punkt, Beweis⟩; ∼ **error** Sachfehler, der

faculty /ˈfækltɪ/ n. (a) (physical capability) Fähigkeit, die; Vermögen, das; ∼ **of sight/speech/hearing/thought** Seh-/Sprach-/Hör-/Denkvermögen, das; (b) (mental power) **in [full] possession of [all] one's [mental] faculties** im [Voll]besitz [all] seiner [geistigen] Kräfte; (c) (Univ.: department) Fakultät, die; Fachbereich, der; (d) (Amer. Sch., Univ.: staff) Lehrkörper, der

fad /fæd/ n. Marotte, die; Spleen, der (ugs.)

fade /feɪd/ **1** v.i. (a) (droop, wither) ⟨Blätter, Blumen:⟩ [ver]welken, welk werden; (b) (lose freshness, vigour) verblassen; [v]erlöschen; ⟨Läufer:⟩ langsamer werden; ⟨Schönheit:⟩ verblühen; (c) (lose colour) bleichen; ∼ **[in colour]** [ver]bleichen; (d) (grow pale, dim) **the light** ∼**d [into darkness]** es dunkelte; (e) (fig.: lose strength) ⟨Erinnerung:⟩ verblassen; ⟨Eingebung, Kreativität, Optimismus:⟩ nachlassen; ⟨Freude, Lust, Liebe:⟩ erlöschen; ⟨Ruhm:⟩ verblassen; ⟨Traum, Hoffnung:⟩ zerrinnen; (f) (grow faint) ⟨Laut:⟩ verklingen; ∼ **into the distance** in der Ferne entschwinden; ⟨Laut, Stimme:⟩ in der Ferne verklingen; (g) (blend) übergehen (into in + Akk.). **2** v.t. ausbleichen ⟨Vorhang, Teppich, Farbe⟩

∼ **a'way** v.i. schwinden; ⟨Laut:⟩ verklingen (into in + Dat.); ⟨Erinnerung, Augenlicht, Kraft:⟩ nachlassen; ⟨Interesse, Hoffnung:⟩ erlöschen; (joc.) ⟨dünne Person:⟩ immer weniger werden (scherzh.)

∼ **'in** v.t. (Radio, Telev., Cinemat.) einblenden

∼ **'out** (Radio, Telev., Cinemat.) **1** v.i. ausgeblendet werden. **2** v.t. (Radio, Telev., Cinemat.) ausblenden

faded /ˈfeɪdɪd/ adj. welk ⟨Blume, Blatt, Laub⟩; verblichen ⟨Stoff, Jeans, Farbe, Gemälde, Ruhm, Teppich⟩; verblüht ⟨Schönheit⟩

'fade-in n. (Radio, Telev., Cinemat.) Einblendung, die

'fade-out n. (Radio, Telev., Cinemat.) Ausblendung, die

faeces /ˈfiːsiːz/ n. pl. Fäkalien Pl.

fag /fæg/ **1** v.i., **-gg-** (toil) sich [ab]schinden (ugs.) ([**away**] at mit). **2** v.t., **-gg-:** ∼ **sb.** [**out**] jmdn. schlauchen (ugs.); ∼ **oneself out** sich [ab]schinden (ugs.); **be** ∼**ged out** geschlaucht sein (ugs.). **3** n. (a) (Brit. coll.) Schinderei, die (ugs. abwertend); (b) (coll.: cigarette) Glimmstängel, der (ugs. scherzh.)

'fag end n. (a) (remnant) Schluss, der; Ende, das; (b) (coll.: cigarette end) Kippe, die (ugs.)

faggot (Amer.: **fagot**) /ˈfægət/ n. (a) Reisigbündel, das; (b) usu. in pl. (Gastr.) Leberknödel, der

Fahrenheit /ˈfærənhaɪt/ adj. ▶ 1141 | Fahrenheit

fail /feɪl/ **1** v.i. (a) (not succeed) scheitern (in mit); ∼ **in one's duty** seine Pflicht versäumen; ∼ **as a human being/a doctor** als Mensch/Arzt versagen; (b) (miscarry, come to nothing) scheitern; fehlschlagen; **if all else** ∼**s** wenn alle Stricke od. Stränge reißen (ugs.); (c) (become bankrupt) Bankrott machen; (d) (in examination) nicht bestehen (in Akk.); (e) (become weaker) ⟨Augenlicht, Gehör, Gedächtnis, Stärke:⟩ nachlassen; ⟨Mut:⟩ sinken; **his health is** ∼**ing** sein Gesundheitszustand verschlechtert sich; (f) (break down, stop) ⟨Versorgung:⟩ zusammenbrechen; ⟨Motor, Radio:⟩ aussetzen; ⟨Generator, Batterie, Pumpe:⟩ ausfallen; ⟨Bremse, Herz:⟩ versagen; (g) ⟨Ernte:⟩ schlecht ausfallen. **2** v.t. (a) ∼ **to do sth.** (not succeed in doing) etw. nicht tun [können]; ∼ **to reach a decision** zu keinem Entschluss kommen; ∼ **to achieve one's purpose/aim** seine Absicht/sein Ziel verfehlen; (b) (be unsuccessful in) nicht bestehen ⟨Prüfung⟩; (c) (reject) durchfallen lassen (ugs.) ⟨Prüfling⟩; (d) ∼ **to do sth.** (not do) etw. nicht tun; (neglect

to do) [es] versäumen, etw. zu tun; **not** ∼ **to do sth.** etw. tun; **I** ∼ **to see why ...:** ich sehe nicht ein, warum ...; (e) (not suffice for) im Stich lassen; **words** ∼ **sb.** jmdm. fehlen die Worte. **3** n. **without** ∼: auf jeden Fall; garantiert

failed /feɪld/ attrib. adj. nicht bestanden ⟨Prüfung⟩; durchgefallen (ugs.) ⟨Prüfling⟩; gescheitert ⟨Geschäft, Ehe, Versuch⟩

failing /ˈfeɪlɪŋ/ **1** n. Schwäche, die. **2** prep. ∼ **that** or **this** andernfalls; wenn nicht. **3** adj. sich verschlechternd ⟨Gesundheitszustand⟩; nachlassend ⟨Kraft⟩; sinkend ⟨Mut⟩; dämmrig ⟨Licht⟩

'fail-safe adj. ausfallsicher; abgesichert ⟨Methode⟩; Fail-safe-⟨Vorkehrung, Prinzip⟩ (fachspr.)

failure /ˈfeɪljə(r)/ n. (a) (omission, neglect) Versäumnis, das; ∼ **to do sth.** das Versäumnis, etw. zu tun; ∼ **to observe the rule** Nichtbeachtung der Regel; ∼ **to pass an exam** Nichtbestehen einer Prüfung; (b) (lack of success) Scheitern, das; **end in** ∼: scheitern; (c) (unsuccessful person or thing) Versager, der; **the party/play was a** ∼: das Fest/Stück war ein Misserfolg; **our plan/attempt was a** ∼: unser Plan/Versuch war fehlgeschlagen; (d) (of supply) Zusammenbruch, der; (of engine, generator) Ausfall, der; **signal/engine** ∼: Ausfall des Signals/des Motors; **power** ∼: Stromausfall, der; **crop** ∼: Missernte, die; (e) (bankruptcy) Zusammenbruch, der

faint /feɪnt/ **1** adj. (a) matt ⟨Licht, Farbe, Stimme, Lächeln⟩; schwach ⟨Geruch, Duft⟩; leise ⟨Geräusch, Stimme, Ton⟩; entfernt ⟨Ähnlichkeit⟩; undeutlich ⟨Umriss, Linie, Gestalt, Spur, Fotokopie⟩; leise ⟨Hoffnung, Verdacht, Ahnung⟩; gering ⟨Chance⟩; **not have the** ∼**est idea** nicht die geringste od. blasseste Ahnung haben; (b) (giddy, weak) matt; schwach; **she felt** ∼: ihr war schwindelig; (c) (feeble) schwach ⟨Lob, Widerstand⟩; zaghaft ⟨Versuch, Bemühung⟩. **2** v.i. ohnmächtig werden, in Ohnmacht fallen (**from** vor + Dat.). **3** n. Ohnmacht, die

faint-hearted /feɪntˈhɑːtɪd/ adj. hasenherzig (abwertend); zaghaft ⟨Versuch⟩

faintly /ˈfeɪntlɪ/ adv. undeutlich ⟨markieren, hören⟩; kaum ⟨sichtbar⟩; schwach ⟨riechen, scheinen⟩; entfernt ⟨sich ähneln⟩; wenig ⟨interessieren⟩; leicht ⟨enttäuschen⟩; zaghaft ⟨lächeln⟩

faintness /ˈfeɪntnɪs/ n., no pl. (a) (of marking, outline) Undeutlichkeit, die; (of resemblance) Entferntheit, die; (of colour) Mattheit, die; **the** ∼ **of the light** das schwache Licht; (b) (dizziness) Schwäche, die

fair¹ /feə(r)/ n. (a) (gathering) Markt, der; (with shows, merry-go-rounds) Jahrmarkt, der; (b) ⇒ **funfair**; (c) (exhibition) Messe, der; **antiques/book/trade** ∼: Antiquitäten-/Buch-/Handelsmesse, die

fair² **1** adj. (a) (just) gerecht; begründet ⟨Beschwerde, Annahme⟩; berechtigt ⟨Frage⟩; fair ⟨Spiel, Kampf, Prozess, Preis, Handel⟩; (representative) typisch, markant ⟨Beispiel, Kostprobe⟩; **be** ∼ **with** or **to sb.** gerecht gegen jmdn. od. zu jmdm. sein; **it's only** ∼ **to do sth./for sb. to do sth.** es ist nur recht und billig, etw. zu tun/dass jmd. etw. tut; **that's not** ∼: das ist ungerecht od. unfair; ∼ **enough!** (coll.) dagegen ist nichts einzuwenden; (OK) na gut; **all's in love and war** in der Liebe und im Krieg ist alles erlaubt; ∼ **play** Fairness, die; (b) (not bad, pretty good) ganz gut ⟨Bilanz, Vorstellung, Anzahl, Kenntnisse, Chance⟩; ziemlich ⟨Maß, Geschwindigkeit⟩; **a** ∼ **amount of work** ein schönes Stück Arbeit; (c) (favourable) schön ⟨Wetter, Tag, Abend⟩; günstig ⟨Wetterlage, Wind⟩; heiter ⟨Wetter, Tag⟩; (d) ▶ 672 | (blond) blond ⟨Haar, Person⟩; (not dark) hell ⟨Teint, Haut⟩; hellhäutig ⟨Person⟩; (e) (poet. or literary: beautiful) hold (dichter. veralt.) ⟨Maid, Prinz, Gesicht⟩; **the** ∼ **sex** das schöne Geschlecht. **2** adv. (a) fair ⟨kämpfen, spielen⟩; gerecht ⟨behandeln⟩; (b) (coll.: completely) völlig; **the sight** ∼ **took my breath away** der Anblick hat mir glatt (ugs.) den Atem verschlagen; (c) ∼ **and square** (honestly) offen und ehrlich; (accurately) voll, genau ⟨schlagen, treffen⟩. **3** n. ∼**'s** ∼ (coll.) Gerechtigkeit muss sein

fair: ∼ **'copy** n. Reinschrift, die; **make a** ∼ **copy of sth.** etw. ins Reine schreiben; ∼**ground** n. Festplatz, der; ∼**-haired** /ˈfeəheəd/ adj. ▶ 672 | blond

fairly /'feəlɪ/ adv. (a) fair ⟨kämpfen, spielen⟩; gerecht ⟨bestrafen, beurteilen, behandeln⟩; (b) (tolerably, rather) ziemlich; (c) (completely) völlig; **it ~ took my breath away** es hat mir glatt (ugs.) den Atem verschlagen; (d) (actually) richtig; **I ~ jumped for joy** ich habe einen regelrechten Freudensprung gemacht; (e) ~ **and squarely** (honestly) offen und ehrlich; **beat sb. ~ and squarely** jmdn. nach allen Regeln der Kunst (ugs.) besiegen

fair-'minded adj. unvoreingenommen

fairness /'feənɪs/ n., no pl. Gerechtigkeit, die; **in all ~ [to sb.]** um fair [gegen jmdn.] zu sein

fair: ~**-sized** /'feəsaɪzd/ adj. recht ansehnlich; ~**way** n. (a) (channel) Fahrrinne, die; (b) (Golf) Fairway, das

fairy /'feərɪ/ n. (Mythol.) Fee, die; (in a household) Kobold, der

fairy: ~ **'godmother** n. (lit. or fig.) gute Fee; **F~land** n. (land of fairies) Feenland, das; (enchanted region) Märchenland, das; ~ **lights** n. pl. kleine farbige Lichter; ~ **'ring** n. (Bot.) Hexenring, der; ~ **story** ⇒ ~ **tale** 1; ~ **tale** 1 n. (lit. or fig.) Märchen, das; 2 adj. Märchen⟨landschaft⟩; märchenhaft schön ⟨Szene, Wirkung, Kleid⟩

fait accompli /feɪt æ'kɔpli:, feɪt ə'kɒmplɪ/ n. vollendete Tatsache

faith /feɪθ/ n. (a) (reliance, trust) Vertrauen, das; **have ~ in sb./sth.** Vertrauen zu jmdm./etw. haben; auf jmdn./etw. vertrauen; **lose ~ in sb./sth.** das Vertrauen zu jmdm./ etw. verlieren; (b) ([religious] belief) Glaube, der; **different Christian ~s** verschiedene christliche Glaubensrichtungen; (c) **keep ~ with sb.** jmdm. treu bleiben od. die Treue halten; (d) **in good ~:** ohne Hintergedanken; (unsuspectingly) in gutem Glauben; **in bad ~:** in böser Absicht

faithful /'feɪθfl/ 1 adj. (a) (loyal) treu (to Dat.); (b) (conscientious) pflichttreu; [ge]treu ⟨Diener⟩; (c) (accurate) [wahrheits]getreu; originalgetreu ⟨Wiedergabe, Kopie⟩. 2 n. pl. the ~: die Gläubigen; **the party ~:** die treuen Anhänger der Partei

faithfully /'feɪθfəlɪ/ adv. (a) (loyally) treu ⟨dienen⟩; hoch und heilig, fest ⟨versprechen⟩; (b) originalgetreu ⟨wiedergeben⟩; genau ⟨befolgen⟩; (c) **yours ~** (in letter) mit freundlichen Grüßen; (more formally) hochachtungsvoll

faith: ~ **healer** n. Gesundbeter, der/-beterin, die; ~ **healing** n. Gesundbeten, das

fake /feɪk/ 1 adj. unecht; gefälscht ⟨Dokument, Banknote, Münze⟩. 2 n. (a) (imitation) Imitation, die; (painting) Fälschung, die; (b) (person) Schwindler, der/Schwindlerin, die. 3 v.t. (a) fälschen ⟨Unterschrift, Gemälde⟩; vortäuschen ⟨Krankheit, Unfall⟩; erfinden ⟨Geschichte⟩; (b) (alter so as to deceive) verfälschen

fakir /'feɪkɪə(r)/ n. Fakir, der

falcon /'fɔːlkn, 'fɔːkn/ n. (Ornith.) Falke, der

fall /fɔːl/ 1 n. (a) (act or manner of ~ing) Fallen, das; (of person) Sturz, der; ~ **of snow/rain** Schnee-/Regenfall, der; **in a ~:** bei einem Sturz; **have a ~:** stürzen; (b) (collapse, defeat) Fall, der; (of dynasty, empire) Untergang, der; (of government) Sturz, der; (c) (slope) Abfall, der (to zu, nach); (d) **▶ 1065** (Amer.: autumn) Herbst, der. 2 v.i. **fell** /fel/, ~**en** /'fɔːln/ (a) fallen; ⟨Person:⟩ [hin]fallen, stürzen; ⟨Pferd:⟩ stürzen; ~ **off sth.**, ~ **down from sth.** von etw. [herunter]fallen; ~ **down [into] sth.** in etw. (Akk.) [hinein]fallen; ~ **to the ground** zu Boden fallen; ~ **down dead** tot umfallen; ~ **down the stairs** die Treppe herunter-/hinunterfallen; ~ **[flat] on one's face** (lit. or fig.) auf die Nase fallen (ugs.); ~ **into the trap** in die Falle gehen; ~ **from a great height** aus großer Höhe abstürzen; **rain/ snow is ~ing** es regnet/schneit; ~ **from power** entmachtet werden; (b) ⟨Nacht, Dunkelheit:⟩ hereinbrechen; ⟨Abend:⟩ anbrechen; ⟨Stille:⟩ eintreten; (c) (fig.: be uttered) fallen; ~ **from sb.'s lips** über jmds. Lippen (Akk.) kommen; **let ~ a remark** eine Bemerkung fallen lassen; (d) (become detached) ⟨Blätter:⟩ [ab]fallen; ~ **out** ⟨Haare, Federn:⟩ ausfallen; (e) (sink to lower level) sinken; ⟨Barometer:⟩ fallen; ⟨Absatz, Verkauf:⟩ zurückgehen; ~ **into sin/ temptation** eine Sünde begehen/der Versuchung er- od. unterliegen; (f) (subside) ⟨Wasserspiegel, Gezeitenhöhe:⟩ fallen; ⟨Wind:⟩ sich legen; (g) (show dismay) **his/her face fell** er/sie machte ein langes Gesicht (ugs.); (h) (be defeated) ⟨Festung, Stadt:⟩ fallen; ⟨Monarchie, Regierung:⟩ gestürzt

werden; ⟨Reich:⟩ untergehen; **the fortress fell to the enemy** die Festung fiel dem Feind in die Hände; (i) (perish) ⟨Soldat:⟩ fallen; **the ~en** die Gefallenen; (j) (collapse, break) einstürzen; ~ **to pieces**, ~ **apart** ⟨Buch, Wagen:⟩ auseinander fallen; ~ **apart at the seams** an den Nähten aufplatzen; (k) (come by chance, duty, etc.) fallen (**to** an + Akk.); **it fell to me** or **to my lot to do it** das Los, es tun zu müssen, hat mich getroffen; ~ **into decay** ⟨Gebäude:⟩ verfallen; ~ **ill** krank werden; ~ **into a swoon** or **faint** in Ohnmacht fallen; **they fell to fighting among themselves** es kam zu einer Schlägerei zwischen ihnen; (l) ⟨Auge, Strahl, Licht, Schatten:⟩ fallen (**upon** auf + Akk.); (m) (have specified place) liegen (**on, to** auf + Dat., **within** in + Dat.); ~ **into** or **under a category** in od. unter eine Kategorie fallen; (n) (occur) fallen (**on** auf + Akk.)

~ **a'bout** v.i. ~ **about [laughing** or **with laughter]** sich [vor Lachen] kringeln (ugs.)

~ **a'way** v.i. (have slope) abfallen (**to** zu)

~ **'back** v.i. zurückweichen; ⟨Armee:⟩ sich zurückziehen; (lag) zurückbleiben

~ **'back on** v.t. zurückgreifen auf (+ Akk.)

~ **behind** 1 v.t. zurückfallen hinter (+ Akk.). 2 v.i. zurückbleiben; ~ **behind with sth.** mit etw. in Rückstand geraten

~ **'down** v.i. (a) ⇒ ~ 2 a; (b) (collapse) ⟨Brücke, Gebäude:⟩ einstürzen; ⟨Person:⟩ hinfallen; ~ **down [on sth.]** (fig. coll.) [bei etw.] versagen

~ **for** v.t. (coll.) (a) (~ in love with) sich verknallen in (ugs.); (b) (be persuaded by) hereinfallen auf (+ Akk.) (ugs.)

~ **'in** v.i. (a) hineinfallen; (b) (Mil.) antreten (**for** zu); ~ **in!** angetreten!; (c) (collapse) ⟨Gebäude, Wand usw.:⟩ einstürzen

~ **'in with** v.t. (a) (meet and join) stoßen zu; (b) (agree) beipflichten (+ Dat.) ⟨Person, Meinung, Vorschlag usw.⟩; eingehen auf (+ Akk.) ⟨Plan, Person, Bitte⟩

~ **'off** v.i. (a) ⇒ ~ 2 a; (b) ⟨Nachfrage, Produktion, Anzahl:⟩ zurückgehen; ⟨Dienstleistungen, Gesundheit, Geschäft:⟩ sich verschlechtern; ⟨Interesse:⟩ nachlassen

~ **on** v.t. (be borne by) ~ **on sb.** jmdm. zufallen; ⟨Verdacht, Schuld, Los:⟩ auf jmdn. fallen

~ **'out** v.i. (a) herausfallen; (b) ⇒ ~ 2 d; (c) (quarrel) ~ **out [with sb. over sth.]** sich [mit jmdm. über etw. (Akk.)] [zer]streiten; (d) (come to happen) vonstatten gehen; **see how things ~ out** abwarten, wie sich die Dinge entwickeln

~ **over** 1 v.t. (a) /'---/ (stumble over) fallen über (+ Akk.); ~ **over one's own feet** über seine eigenen Füße stolpern; (b) /---/ ~ **over oneself to do sth.** (fig. coll.) sich vor Eifer überschlagen, um etw. zu tun (ugs.). 2 /---/ v.i. umfallen; ⟨Person:⟩ [hin]fallen

~ **'through** v.i. (fig.) ins Wasser fallen (ugs.)

fallacious /fə'leɪʃəs/ adj. (a) (containing a fallacy) irrig; ~ **conclusion** Fehlschluss, der; (b) (deceptive, delusive) irreführend

fallacy /'fæləsɪ/ n. (a) (delusion, error) Irrtum, der; (b) (unsoundness, delusiveness) Irrigkeit, die

fallen ⇒ **fall** 2

'fall guy n. (coll.: scapegoat) Prügelknabe, der (ugs.)

fallible /'fælɪbl/ adj. (a) (liable to err) fehlbar ⟨Person⟩; (b) (liable to be erroneous) nicht unfehlbar

'fall-off n. (in quality) [Ver]minderung, die (**in** Gen.); (in quantity) Rückgang, der (**in** Gen.); **there has been a ~ in support for the government** die Regierung hat an Rückhalt verloren

Fallopian tube /fə'ləʊpɪən tjuːb/ n. (Anat.) Eileiter, der

'fallout n. radioaktiver Niederschlag; (fig.: side effects) Abfallprodukte; attrib. ~ **shelter** Atombunker, der

fallow /'fæləʊ/ adj. (lit. or fig.) brachliegend; ~ **ground/ land** Brache, die/Brachland, das; **lie ~** (lit. or fig.) brachliegen

'fallow deer n. Damhirsch, der

false /fɔːls, fɒls/ adj. falsch; Fehl⟨deutung, -urteil⟩; Falsch⟨meldung, -eid, -aussage⟩; treulos ⟨Geliebte[r]⟩; gefälscht ⟨Urkunde, Dokument⟩; künstlich ⟨Wimpern, Auge⟩; geheuchelt ⟨Bescheidenheit⟩; **under a ~ name** unter falschem Namen

false: ～ a**'larm** *n.* blinder Alarm; ～ **'bottom** *n.* doppelter Boden

falsehood /'fɔ:lshʊd, 'fɒlshʊd/ *n.* **(a)** *no pl.* (falseness) Unrichtigkeit, *die;* **(b)** (untrue thing) Unwahrheit, *die*

falsely /'fɔ:lslɪ, 'fɒlslɪ/ *adv.* **(a)** (dishonestly) unaufrichtig ⟨*sprechen*⟩; falsch ⟨*schwören*⟩; **(b)** (incorrectly, unjustly) falsch ⟨*auslegen, verstehen*⟩; fälschlich[erweise] ⟨*annehmen, glauben, behaupten, beschuldigen*⟩

false 'move ⇒ **false step**

falseness /'fɔ:lsnɪs, 'fɒlsnɪs/ *n., no pl.* **(a)** (incorrectness) Unrichtigkeit, *die;* Falschheit, *die;* **(b)** (faithlessness) Treulosigkeit, *die* (**to** gegenüber)

false: ～ **pre'tences** *n. pl.* Vorspiegelung falscher Tatsachen; ～ **'start** *n.* (Sport; also fig.) Fehlstart, *der;* ～ **'step** *n.* (lit. or fig.) falscher Schritt; ～ **'teeth** *n. pl.* [künstliches] Gebiss; Prothese, *die*

falsetto /fɔ:l'setəʊ, fɒl'setəʊ/ *n., pl.* ～**s** (voice) Kopfstimme, *die;* (Mus.: of man) Falsett, *das*

falsify /'fɔ:lsɪfaɪ, 'fɒlsɪfaɪ/ *v.t.* (alter) fälschen; (misrepresent) verfälschen ⟨*Tatsache, Geschichte, Ereignis, Wahrheit*⟩

falsity /'fɔ:lsɪtɪ, 'fɒlsɪtɪ/ *n., no pl.* **(a)** (incorrectness) Falschheit, *die;* **(b)** (falsehood) Unwahrheit, *die*

falter /'fɔ:ltə(r), 'fɒltə(r)/ **1** *v.i.* **(a)** (waver) stocken; ⟨*Mut:*⟩ sinken; ～ **in one's determination** in seiner Entschlossenheit schwankend werden; **(b)** (stumble) wanken; **with** ～**ing steps** mit [sch]wankenden Schritten. **2** *v.t.* ～ **sth.** etw. stammeln

fame /feɪm/ *n., no pl.* Ruhm, *der;* **rise to** ～: zu Ruhm kommen *od.* gelangen; **ill** ～: schlechter Ruf

famed /feɪmd/ *adj.* berühmt (**for** für, wegen)

familiar /fə'mɪljə(r)/ *adj.* **(a)** (well acquainted) bekannt; **be** ～ **with sb.** jmdn. näher kennen; **(b)** (having knowledge) vertraut (**with** mit); **(c)** (well known) vertraut; bekannt ⟨*Gesicht, Name, Lied*⟩; (common, usual) geläufig ⟨*Ausdruck*⟩; gängig ⟨*Vorstellung*⟩; **he looks** ～: er kommt mir bekannt vor; **(d)** (informal) familiär ⟨*Ton, Begrüßung*⟩; ungezwungen ⟨*Art, Sprache, Stil*⟩; **(e)** (presumptuous) plump-vertraulich (abwertend)

familiarise ⇒ **familiarize**

familiarity /fəmɪlɪ'ærɪtɪ/ *n.* **(a)** *no pl.* (acquaintance) Vertrautheit, *die;* **(b)** *no pl.* (relationship) familiäres Verhältnis; **(c)** (of action, behaviour) Vertraulichkeit, *die;* ～ **breeds contempt** (prov.) zu große Vertraulichkeit erzeugt Verachtung

familiarize /fə'mɪljəraɪz/ *v.t.* vertraut machen (**with** mit)

family /'fæməlɪ/ *n.* **(a)** Familie, *die; attrib.* Familien-; familiär ⟨*Hintergrund*⟩; **be one of the** ～: zur Familie gehören; **start a** ～: eine Familie gründen; **run in the** ～: in der Familie liegen; **(b)** (group, race) Geschlecht, *das*

family: ～ **al'lowance** *n.* Kindergeld, *das;* ～ **'doctor** *n.* Hausarzt, *der;* ～ **'income supplement** *n.* (Brit.) ≈ Familienzulage, *die;* ～ **man** *n.* Familienvater, *der;* (home-loving man) häuslich veranlagter Mann; ～ **name** *n.* Familienname, *der;* Nachname, *der;* ～ **'planning** *n.* Familienplanung, *die;* ～ **'planning clinic** *n.* ≈ Familienberatung[sstelle], *die;* ～ **'room** *n.* **(a)** (in a house) Familienzimmer, *das;* **(b)** (Brit.: in a pub) Familienraum, *der;* ～ **'tree** *n.* Stammbaum, *der* ～ **viewing** *n.* **be** ～ **viewing/suitable for** ～**viewing** ⟨*Film usw.:*⟩ für die ganze Familie geeignet sein; **this programme is** ～ **viewing** dies ist ein Familienprogramm *od.* eine Familiensendung

famine /'fæmɪn/ *n.* Hungersnot, *die*

famished /'fæmɪʃt/ *adj.* ausgehungert; **I'm absolutely** ～ (coll.) ich sterbe vor Hunger (ugs.)

famous /'feɪməs/ *adj.* berühmt; **a** ～ **victory** ein rühmlicher Sieg

fan[1] /fæn/ **1** *n.* **(a)** (held in hand) Fächer, *der;* **(b)** (apparatus) Ventilator, *der.* **2** *v.t.,* **-nn-** fächeln ⟨*Gesicht*⟩; anfachen ⟨*Feuer*⟩; ～ **oneself/sb.** sich/jmdm. Luft zufächeln; ～ **the flame[s]** (fig.) das Feuer schüren

～ **'out** *v.t.* fächern; auffächern ⟨*Spielkarten*⟩. **2** *v.i.* fächern; ⟨*Soldaten:*⟩ ausfächern

fan[2] *n.* (devotee) Fan, *der*

fanatic /fə'nætɪk/ **1** *adj.* fanatisch. **2** *n.* Fanatiker, *der*/Fanatikerin, *die*

fanatical /fə'nætɪkl/ ⇒ **fanatic 1**

fanaticism /fə'nætɪsɪzm/ *n.* Fanatismus, *der*

'fan belt *n.* (Motor Veh.) Keilriemen, *der*

fancier /'fænsɪə(r)/ *n.* Liebhaber, *der*/Liebhaberin, *die*

fanciful /'fænsɪfl/ *adj.* versponnen ⟨*Person*⟩; abstrus, überspannt ⟨*Vorstellung, Gedanke*⟩; fantastisch ⟨*Gemälde, Design*⟩

'fan club *n.* Fanklub, *der*

fancy /'fænsɪ/ **1** *n.* **(a)** (taste, inclination) **he has taken a** ～ **to a new car/her** ein neues Auto/sie hat es ihm angetan; **take** *or* **catch sb.'s** ～: jmdm. gefallen; jmdn. ansprechen; **(b)** (whim) Laune, *die;* **just as the** ～ **takes me** ganz nach Lust und Laune; **tickle sb.'s** ～: jmdn. reizen; **(c)** (notion) merkwürdiges Gefühl; (delusion, belief) Vorstellung, *die;* **(d)** (faculty of imagining) Fantasie, *die;* **(e)** (mental image) Fantasievorstellung, *die; just a* ～: nur Einbildung. **2** *attrib. adj.* **(a)** (ornamental) kunstvoll ⟨*Arbeit, Muster*⟩; ～ **jewellery** Modeschmuck, *der;* **nothing** ～: etwas ganz Schlichtes; **(b)** (extravagant) stolz (ugs.); ～ **prices** gepfefferte Preise (ugs.). **3** *v.t.* **(a)** (imagine) sich ⟨*Dat.*⟩ einbilden; **(b)** (coll.) *in imper. as excl. of surprise* ～ **meeting you here!** na, so etwas, Sie hier zu treffen!; ～ **that!** sieh mal einer an!; also so etwas!; **(c)** (suppose) glauben; denken; ..., **I** ～: ..., möchte ich meinen; **(d)** (wish to have) mögen; **what do you** ～ **for dinner?** was hättest du gern zum Abendessen?; **he fancies [the idea of] doing sth.** er würde etw. gern tun; **do you think she fancies him?** glaubst du, sie mag ihn?; **(e)** (coll.: have high opinion of) ～ **oneself** von sich eingenommen sein; ～ **oneself as a singer** sich für einen [großen] Sänger halten; ～ **one's/sb.'s chances** seine/jmds. Chancen hoch einschätzen

fancy: ～ **'dress** *n.* [Masken]kostüm, *das;* **in** ～ **dress** kostümiert; *attrib.* ～**-dress party** Kostümfest, *das;* ～ **'free** *adj.* frei und ungebunden; ～ **goods** *n. pl.* Geschenkartikel

fanfare /'fænfeə(r)/ *n.* Fanfare, *die*

fang /fæŋ/ *n.* **(a)** (canine tooth) Reißzahn, *der;* Fang[zahn], *der;* (of boar, joc.: of person) Hauer, *der;* **(b)** (of snake) Giftzahn, *der*

fan: ～ **heater** *n.* Heizlüfter, *der;* ～**light** *n.* Oberlicht, *das;* (～-shaped) Fächerfenster, *das* (Archit.); ～ **mail** *n.* Fanpost, *der;* ～**-shaped** *adj.* fächerförmig

fantasia /fæn'teɪzɪə/ *n.* (Mus.) Fantasie, *die*

fantastic /fæn'tæstɪk/ *adj.* **(a)** (grotesque, quaint) bizarr; (fanciful) fantastisch; **(b)** (coll.: excellent, extraordinary) fantastisch (ugs.)

fantastically /fæn'tæstɪkəlɪ/ *adv.* **(a)** fantastisch; **(b)** (coll.: excellently, extraordinarily) fantastisch (ugs.)

fantasy /'fæntəzɪ/ *n.* Fantasie, *die;* (mental image) Fantasiegebilde, *das*

FAQ /fæk/ *abbr.* (Computing) FAQ, *das od. die*

far /fɑ:(r)/ **1** *adv.,* **farther, further; farthest, furthest** ▶ 756 **(a)** (in space) weit; ～ **away** weit entfernt; ～ **[away] from** weit entfernt von; **see sth. from** ～ **away** etw. aus der Ferne sehen; **I won't be** ～ **away** ich werde ganz in der Nähe sein; ～ **above/below** hoch über/tief unter (+ *Dat.*); *adv.* hoch oben/tief unten; **fly as** ～ **as Munich** bis [nach] München fliegen; ～ **and wide** weit und breit; **from** ～ **and near** *or* **wide** von fern und nah; **(b)** (in time) weit; ～ **into the night** bis spät *od.* tief in die Nacht; **as** ～ **back as I can remember** soweit ich zurückdenken kann; **(c)** (by much) weit; ～ **too** viel zu; ～ **longer/ better** weit[aus] länger/besser; **(d)** (fig.) **as** ～ **as** (to whatever extent, to the extent of) so weit [wie]; **I haven't got as** ～ **as phoning her** ich bin noch nicht dazu gekommen, sie anzurufen; **not as** ～ **as I know** nicht, dass ich wüsste; **as** ～ **as I remember/know** soweit ich mich erinnere/weiß; **go so** ～ **as to do sth.** so weit gehen und etw. tun; **in so** ～ **as** insofern *od.* insoweit als; **so** ～ (until now) bisher; **so** ～ **so good** so weit, so gut; **by** ～: bei weitem; **better by** ～: weitaus besser; ～ **from easy/good** alles andere als leicht/gut; ～ **from it!** ganz im Gegenteil!; **go too** ～: zu weit gehen; **carry** *or* **take sth. too** ～: etw. zu weit treiben. **2** *adj.,* **farther, further; farthest, furthest (a)** (remote) weit entfernt; (remote in time) fern; **in the** ～ **distance** in weiter Ferne; **(b)** (more remote) weiter entfernt;

the ~ **bank of the river/side of the road** das andere Flussufer/die andere Straßenseite

'faraway *attrib. adj.* **(a)** (remote in space) entlegen; abgelegen; (remote in time) fern; **(b)** (dreamy) verträumt ‹ *Stimme, Blick, Augen* ›

farce /fɑːs/ *n.* **(a)** Farce, *die;* **(b)** (Theatre) Posse, *die;* Farce, *die*

farcical /'fɑːsɪkl/ *adj.* **(a)** (absurd) farcenhaft; absurd; **(b)** (Theatre) possenhaft ‹ *Stück, Element* ›

fare /feə(r)/ **1** *n.* **(a)** (price) Fahrpreis, *der;* (money) Fahrgeld, *das;* **what** *or* **how much is the ~?** was kostet die Fahrt/(by air) der Flug/(by boat) die Überfahrt?; **any more ~s?** noch jemand ohne [Fahrschein]?; **(b)** (passenger) Fahrgast, *der;* **(c)** (food) Kost, *die.* **2** *v.i.* **I don't know how he is faring/how he ~d on his travels** ich weiß nicht, wie es ihm geht/wie es ihm auf seinen Reisen ergangen ist

Far: ~ **'East** *n.* **the** ~ **East** der Ferne Osten; Fernost *o. Art.;* ~ **'Eastern** *adj.* fernöstlich; des Fernen Ostens *nachgestellt*

'fare stage *n.* Teilstrecke, *die;* (end of section) Zahlgrenze, *die*

farewell /feə'wel/ **1** *int.* leb[e] wohl (veralt.). **2** *n.* **(a)** **make one's ~s** sich verabschieden; **(b)** *attrib.* ~ **speech/gift** Abschiedsrede, *die*/-geschenk, *das*

far: ~**-fetched** /'fɑːfetʃt/ *adj.* weit hergeholt; an *od.* bei den Haaren herbeigezogen (ugs.); ~**-flung** *adj.* (widely spread) weit ausgedehnt; (distant) weit entfernt

farm /fɑːm/ **1** *n.* [Bauern]hof, *der;* (larger) Gut, *das;* Gutshof, *der;* (in English-speaking countries outside Europe) Farm, *die;* **poultry/chicken** ~: Geflügel-/Hühnerfarm, *die;* ~ **bread/eggs** Landbrot, *das*/Landeier *Pl.;* ~ **animals** Vieh, *das.* **2** *v.t.* bebauen, bewirtschaften ‹ *Land* ›; züchten ‹ *Lachs, Forellen* ›. **3** *v.i.* Landwirtschaft betreiben ~ **'out** *v.t.* **(a)** verpachten ‹ *Land* ›; **(b)** vergeben ‹ *Arbeit* › (**to** an + *Akk.*)

farmer /'fɑːmə(r)/ *n.* ▶ 887 ⦚ Landwirt, *der*/-wirtin, *die;* Bauer, *der*/Bäuerin, *die;* **poultry** ~: Geflügelzüchter, *der*/ -züchterin, *die*

farm: ~**hand** *n.* ▶ 887 ⦚ Landarbeiter, *der*/-arbeiterin, *die;* ~**house** *n.* Bauernhaus, *das;* (larger) Gutshaus, *das*

farming /'fɑːmɪŋ/ *n., no pl., no indef. art.* Landwirtschaft, *die;* ~ **of crops** Ackerbau, *der;* ~ **of animals** Viehzucht, *die*

farm: ~**stead** /'fɑːmsted/ *n.* Bauernhof, *der;* Gehöft, *das;* ~**worker** ▶ 887 ⦚ *n.* Landarbeiter, *der*/-arbeiterin, *die;* ~**yard** *n.* Hof, *der*

Faroes /'feərəʊz/ *pr. n. pl.* Färöer *Pl.*

far: ~**-off** *adj.* (in space) [weit] entfernt; (in time) fern; ~ **out** *adj.* **(a)** (distant) [weit] entfernt; **(b)** (fig. coll.: excellent) toll (ugs.); super (ugs.); ~**-reaching** *adj.* weit reichend ‹ *Konsequenzen, Bedeutung, Wirkung* ›; ~**-seeing** *adj.* weitblickend; ~**-sighted** *adj.* **(a)** (able to see a great distance) scharfsichtig; **(b)** (having foresight) weitblickend

fart /fɑːt/ (coarse) **1** *v.i.* furzen (derb). **2** *n.* Furz, *der* (derb)

farther /'fɑːðə(r)/ ⇒ **further** 1 a, 2 a

farthest /'fɑːðɪst/ ⇒ **furthest**

farthing /'fɑːðɪŋ/ *n.* (Brit. Hist.) Farthing, *der*

Far 'West *n.* (Amer.) **the** ~: der Westen der USA

fascinate /'fæsɪneɪt/ *v.t.* fesseln; faszinieren (geh.); **it ~s me how …:** ich finde es faszinierend, wie …

fascinated /'fæsɪneɪtɪd/ *adj.* fasziniert

fascinating /'fæsɪneɪtɪŋ/ *adj.* faszinierend (geh.); bezaubernd; hochinteressant ‹ *Thema, Faktum* ›; spannend, fesselnd ‹ *Buch* ›

fascination /fæsɪ'neɪʃn/ *n., no pl.* Faszination, *die* (geh.); (quality of fascinating) Zauber, *der;* Reiz, *der;* **have a ~ for sb.** einen besonderen Reiz auf jmdn. ausüben

Fascism /'fæʃɪzm/ *n.* Faschismus, *der*

Fascist /'fæʃɪst/ **1** *n.* Faschist, *der*/Faschistin, *die.* **2** *adj.* faschistisch

fashion /'fæʃn/ **1** *n.* **(a)** Art [und Weise]; **talk/behave in a peculiar ~:** merkwürdig sprechen/sich merkwürdig verhalten; **walk crab-~/in a zigzag ~:** im Krebsgang/ Zickzack gehen; **after** *or* **in the ~ of** im Stil *od.* nach Art

von; **after** *or* **in a ~:** schlecht und recht; einigermaßen; **(b)** (custom, esp. in dress) Mode, *die;* **the latest summer/ autumn ~s** die neusten Sommer-/Wintermodelle; **it is the ~:** es ist Mode *od.* modern; **be all the ~:** große Mode *od.* groß in Mode sein; **in ~:** in Mode; modern; **be out of ~:** aus der Mode *od.* nicht mehr modern sein; **come into/ go out of ~:** in Mode/aus der Mode kommen; **it was the ~ in those days** das war damals Sitte *od.* Brauch. **2** *v.t.* formen, gestalten (out of, from aus; [in]to zu)

fashionable /'fæʃənəbl/ *adj.* modisch ‹ *Kleider, Person, Design* ›; vornehm ‹ *Gegend, Hotel, Restaurant* ›; Mode‹ *farbe, -krankheit, -wort, -autor* ›; **it isn't ~ any more** es ist nicht mehr modern *od.* in Mode

fashionably /'fæʃənəblɪ/ *adv.* modisch ‹ *sich kleiden* ›

fashion: ~**-conscious** *adj.* modebewusst; ~ **magazine** *n.* Modezeitschrift, *die;* ~ **show** *n.* Mode[n]schau, *die*

fast¹ /fɑːst/ **1** *v.i.* fasten; **a day of ~ing** ein Fast[en]tag. **2** *n.* (going without food) Fasten, *das;* (hunger strike) Hungerstreik, *der;* **a 40-day ~:** eine Fastenzeit von 40 Tagen

fast² **1** *adj.* **(a)** (fixed, attached) fest; **the rope is ~:** das Tau ist fest[gemacht]; **make [the boat] ~:** das Boot festmachen; **hard and ~:** fest; bindend, verbindlich ‹ *Regeln* ›; **(b)** (not fading) farbecht ‹ *Stoff* ›; echt, beständig ‹ *Farbe* ›; **(c)** (rapid) schnell; ~ **train** Schnellzug, *der;* D-Zug, *der;* ~ **speed** hohe Geschwindigkeit; **he is a ~ worker** (lit. or fig.) er arbeitet schnell; (in amorous activities) er geht mächtig ran (ugs.); **pull a ~ one [on sb.]** (coll.) jmdn. übers Ohr hauen *od.* reinlegen (ugs.); **(d) be ~ [by ten minutes], be [ten minutes]** ~ ‹ *Uhr:* › [zehn Minuten] vorgehen. **2** *adv.* **(a)** (lit. or fig.) fest; **hold ~ to sth.** sich an etw. (*Dat.*) festhalten; (fig.) an etw. (*Dat.*) festhalten; **(b)** (soundly) **be ~ asleep** fest schlafen; (when one should be awake) fest eingeschlafen sein; **(c)** (quickly) schnell; **not so ~!** nicht so hastig!; **(d) play ~ and loose with sb.** mit jmdm. ein falsches *od.* doppeltes Spiel treiben

fasten /'fɑːsn/ **1** *v.t.* **(a)** festmachen, befestigen (**on, to** an + *Dat.*); festziehen, anziehen ‹ *Schraube* ›; zumachen ‹ *Kleid, Spange, Knöpfe, Jacke* ›; schließen ‹ *Tür, Fenster* ›; anstecken ‹ *Brosche* › (**to** an + *Akk.*); ~ **sth. together with a clip** etw. zusammenheften; ~ **one's safety belt** sich anschnallen; ~ **up one's shoes** seine Schuhe binden *od.* schnüren; **(b)** heften ‹ *Blick* › ([up]on auf + *Akk.*); ~ **one's attention on sb.** jmdm. seine Aufmerksamkeit zuwenden. **2** *v.i.* **(a)** sich schließen lassen; **the skirt ~s at the back** der Rock wird hinten zugemacht; **(b)** ~ [up]on **sth.** (single out) etw. herausgreifen; (seize upon) etw. aufs Korn nehmen (ugs.)

fastener /'fɑːsnə(r)/, **fastening** /'fɑːsnɪŋ/ *ns.* Verschluss, *der*

fast: ~ **'food** *n.:* im Schnellrestaurant angebotenes Essen; Fast food, *das;* ~ **food restaurant** Schnellrestaurant, *das;* ~ **'forward** *n.* schneller Vorlauf; (playback) Zeitrafferwiedergabe, *die;* **watch sth. on** ~ **forward** etw. im Zeitraffer ansehen; ~**-forward** **1** *attrib. adj.* Vorspul‹ *taste, -funktion* ›; **2** *v.t. & i.* vorspulen; ~**-growing** *adj.* schnell wachsend

fastidious /fæ'stɪdɪəs/ *adj.* (hard to please) heikel, (ugs.) pingelig (**about** in Bezug auf + *Akk.*); (carefully selective) wählerisch (**about** in Bezug auf + *Akk.*)

'fast lane *n.* Überholspur, *die;* **life in the** ~ (fig.) Leben auf vollen Touren (ugs.)

fat /fæt/ **1** *adj.* **(a)** dick; fett (abwertend); rund ‹ *Wangen, Gesicht* ›; fett ‹ *Schwein* ›; **grow** *or* **get** ~: dick werden; **(b)** fett ‹ *Essen, Fleisch, Brühe* ›; **(c)** (fig.) dick ‹ *Bündel, Buch, Zigarre* ›; üppig, fett ‹ *Gewinn, Gehalt, Scheck* ›; **(d)** (coll. iron.) ~ **lot of good 'you are** du bist mir 'ne schöne Hilfe (iron.); **a** ~ **lot [of good it would do me]** [das würde mir] herzlich wenig [helfen]. **2** *n.* Fett, *das;* **low in** ~: fettarm ‹ *Nahrungsmittel* ›; **put on** ~: Fett ansetzen; **run to** ~: [zu] dick werden; **the** ~ **is in the fire** (fig.) der Teufel ist los (ugs.); **live off** *or* **on the** ~ **of the land** (fig.) wie die Made im Speck leben (ugs.)

fatal /'feɪtl/ *adj.* **(a)** (ruinous, disastrous) verheerend (**to** für); fatal; schicksalsschwer ‹ *Tag, Moment* ›; **it would be** ~: das wäre das Ende; **(b)** (deadly) tödlich ‹ *Unfall, Verletzung* ›;

deal sb. a ∼ **blow** jmdm. einen vernichtenden Schlag versetzen

fatalism /'feɪtəlɪzm/ *n., no pl.* Fatalismus, *der* (geh.); Schicksalsergebenheit, *die*

fatalist /'feɪtəlɪst/ *n.* Fatalist, *der*/ Fatalistin, *die*

fatalistic /feɪtə'lɪstɪk/ *adj.* fatalistisch; schicksalsergeben ‹*Person*›

fatality /fə'tælɪtɪ/ *n.* Todesfall, *der;* (in car crash, war, etc.) [Todes]opfer, *das*

fatally /'feɪtəlɪ/ *adv.* tödlich ‹*verwunden*›; (disastrously) verhängnisvoll; unwiderstehlich ‹*attraktiv*›; **be** ∼ **wrong** *or* **mistaken** einem verhängnisvollen Irrtum unterliegen; **be** ∼ **ill** todkrank sein

fate /feɪt/ *n.* Schicksal, *das;* **an accident** *or* **stroke of** ∼: eine Fügung des Schicksals

fated /'feɪtɪd/ *adj.* (doomed) zum Scheitern verurteilt ‹*Plan, Projekt*›; **be** ∼ **to fail** *or* **to be unsuccessful** zum Scheitern verurteilt sein; **be** ∼: unter einem ungünstigen Stern stehen

fateful /'feɪtfl/ *adj.* **(a)** (important, decisive) schicksalsschwer ‹*Tag, Stunde, Entscheidung*›; entscheidend ‹*Worte*›; **(b)** (controlled by fate) schicksalhaft ‹*Begegnung, Treffen, Ereignis*›; **(c)** (prophetic) schicksalverkündend; (of misfortune) unheilverkündend

fat: ∼**-free** *adj.* fettfrei; ∼**-head** *n.* Dummkopf, *der* (ugs.); ∼**-headed** *adj.* dumm; blöd (ugs.)

father /'fɑːðə(r)/ **1** *n.* **(a)** (lit. or fig.) Vater, *der;* **become a** ∼: Vater werden; **he is a** *or* **the** ∼ **of six** er hat sechs Kinder; **like** ∼ **like son** der Apfel fällt nicht weit vom Stamm (ugs. scherzh., Spr.); **our heavenly F**∼: unser himmlischer Vater; **(b)** ▶ 1152│ (priest) Pfarrer, *der;* (monk) Pater, *der;* **F**∼ (as title: priest) Herr Pfarrer; (as title: monk) Pater. **2** *v.t.* zeugen

father: F∼ **'Christmas** *n.* der Weihnachtsmann; ∼ **figure** *n.* Vaterfigur, *die*

fatherhood /'fɑːðəhʊd/ *n., no pl.* Vaterschaft, *die*

father: ∼**-in-law** *n., pl.* ∼**s-in-law** Schwiegervater, *der;* ∼**land** *n.* Vaterland, *das*

fatherly /'fɑːðəlɪ/ *adj.* väterlich

fathom /'fæðəm/ **1** *n.* (Naut.) Fathom, *das* (geh.); Faden, *der.* **2** *v.t.* **(a)** (measure) mit dem Lot messen; **(b)** (fig.: comprehend) verstehen; ∼ **sb./sth. out** jmdn./etw. ergründen

fatigue /fə'tiːg/ **1** *n.* **(a)** Ermüdung, *die;* Erschöpfung, *die;* **extreme** ∼: Übermüdung, *die;* **(b)** (of metal etc.) Ermüdung, *die.* **2** *v.t.* ermüden; **be/look** ∼**d** erschöpft sein/ aussehen

fatten /'fætn/ *v.t.* herausfüttern ‹*Person*›; mästen ‹*Tier*›

fattening /'fætnɪŋ/ *adj.* dick machend ‹*Nahrungsmittel*›; ∼ **foods** Dickmacher *Pl.* (ugs.); **be** ∼: dick machen

fatty /'fætɪ/ **1** *adj.* **(a)** fett ‹*Fleisch*›; fetthaltig ‹*Nahrung, Speise*›; fettig ‹*Substanz*›; **(b)** (consisting of fat) Fett-. **2** *n.* (coll.) Dickerchen, *das* (scherzh.)

fatuous /'fætjʊəs/ *adj.* albern; töricht; einfältig ‹*Grinsen*›

faucet /'fɔːsɪt/ *n.* (Amer.) Wasserhahn, *der*

fault /fɔːlt, fɒlt/ **1** *n.* **(a)** Fehler, *der;* **to a** ∼: allzu übertrieben; übermäßig; **find** ∼ **[with sb./sth.]** etwas [an jmdm./etw.] auszusetzen haben; **(b)** (responsibility) Schuld, *die;* Verschulden, *das; whose* ∼ **was it?** wer war schuld [daran]?; **it's all your own** ∼! das ist deine eigene Schuld!; **it isn't my** ∼: es ist nicht meine Schuld; **be at** ∼: im Unrecht sein; **(c)** (Tennis etc.) Fehler, *der;* **double** ∼: Doppelfehler, *der;* **(d)** (in gas or water supply; Electr.) Defekt, *der;* **(e)** (Geol.) Verwerfung, *die.* **2** *v.t.* Fehler finden an (+ *Dat.*); etwas auszusetzen haben an (+ *Dat.*)

fault: ∼**finder** *n.* Krittler, *der*/ Krittlerin, *die;* ∼**finding 1** *n.* Krittelei, *die;* **2** *adj.* krittelig

faultless /'fɔːltlɪs, 'fɒltlɪs/ *adj.* einwandfrei; fehlerlos, fehlerfrei ‹*Übersetzung, Englisch*›

faulty /'fɔːltɪ, 'fɒltɪ/ *adj.* fehlerhaft; unzutreffend ‹*Argument*›; defekt ‹*Gerät usw.*›; ∼ **design** Fehlkonstruktion, *die*

fauna /'fɔːnə/ *n., pl.* ∼**e** /'fɔːniː/ *or* ∼**s** (Zool.) Fauna, *die*

faux pas /fəʊ 'pɑː/ *n., pl.* same /fəʊ 'pɑːz/ Fauxpas, *der*

favor *etc.* (Amer.) ⇒ **favour** *etc.*

favour /'feɪvə(r)/ (Brit.) **1** *n.* **(a)** Gunst, *die;* Wohlwollen, *das;* **find/lose** ∼ **with sb.** ‹*Sache:*› bei jmdm. Anklang

finden/jmdm. nicht mehr gefallen; ‹*Person:*› jmds. Wohlwollen gewinnen/verlieren; **be in** ∼ **[with sb.]** [bei jmdm.] beliebt sein; ‹*Idee, Kleidung usw.:*› [bei jmdm.] in Mode sein; **be out of** ∼ **[with sb.]** [bei jmdm.] unbeliebt sein; ‹*Idee, Kleidung usw.:*› [bei jmdm.] nicht mehr in Mode sein; **(b)** (kindness) Gefallen, *der;* Gefälligkeit, *die;* **ask a** ∼ **of sb.**, **ask sb. a** ∼: jmdn. um einen Gefallen bitten; **do sb. a** ∼, **do a** ∼ **for sb.** jmdm. einen Gefallen tun; **as a** ∼: aus Gefälligkeit; **as a** ∼ **to sb.** jmdm. zuliebe; **(c)** (support) **be in** ∼ **of sth.** für etw. sein; **in** ∼ **of** zugunsten (+ *Gen.*); **all those in** ∼: alle, die dafür sind; **in sb.'s** ∼: zu jmds. Gunsten; **(d)** (partiality) Begünstigung, *die;* **show** ∼ **to[wards] sb.** jmdn. begünstigen. **2** *v.t.* **(a)** (approve) für gut halten, gutheißen ‹*Plan, Idee, Vorschlag*›; (think preferable) bevorzugen; **I** ∼ **the first proposal** ich bin für den ersten Vorschlag; **(b)** (oblige) beehren (**with** mit) (geh.); **(c)** (treat with partiality) bevorzugen; **(d)** (prove advantageous to) begünstigen

favourable /'feɪvərəbl/ *adj.* (Brit.) **(a)** günstig ‹*Eindruck, Licht*›; gewogen ‹*Haltung, Einstellung*›; wohlmeinend ‹*Urteil*›; **be** ∼ **to[wards] sth.** ‹*Person:*› einer Sache (*Dat.*) positiv gegenüberstehen; **(b)** (praising) freundlich ‹*Erwähnung*›; positiv, günstig ‹*Bericht[erstattung]*, Bemerkung*›; **(c)** (promising) vielversprechend; gut ‹*Omen, Zeichen*›; **(d)** (helpful) günstig (**to** für) ‹*Wetter, Wind, Umstand*›; **(e) give sb. a** ∼ **answer** jmdm. eine Zusage geben

favourably /'feɪvərəblɪ/ *adv.* (Brit.) **(a)** wohlwollend ‹*ansehen, anhören, denken, urteilen*›; **be** ∼ **impressed with sb./sth.** von jmdm./etw. sehr angetan sein; **be** ∼ **disposed towards sb./sth.** jmdm./einer Sache positiv gegenüberstehen; **(b)** lobend ‹*erwähnen*›; positiv ‹*vermerken*›

favoured /'feɪvəd/ *adj.* (Brit.) (privileged) bevorzugt; (well-liked) Lieblings‹*platz, -buch, -gericht*›

favourite /'feɪvərɪt/ (Brit.) **1** *adj.* Lieblings-. **2** *n.* **(a)** (film/food/pupil etc.) Lieblingsfilm, *der*/-essen, *das*/-schüler, *der usw.;* (person) Liebling, *der;* **this/he is my** ∼: das/ihn mag ich am liebsten; **(b)** (Sport) Favorit, *der*/Favoritin, *die*

favouritism /'feɪvərɪtɪzm/ *n., no pl.* (Brit.) Begünstigung, *die;* (when selecting sb. for a post etc.) Günstlingswirtschaft, *die*

fawn¹ /fɔːn/ **1** *n.* **(a)** (fallow deer) [Dam]kitz, *das;* (buck) Bockkitz, *das;* (doe) Geißkitz, *das;* **(b)** (colour) Rehbraun, *das.* **2** *adj.* rehfarben; ∼ **colour** Rehbraun, *das*

fawn² *v.i.* **(a)** ‹*Hund:*› [bellen und] mit dem Schwanz wedeln; **(b)** (behave servilely) ∼ **[on** *or* **upon sb.]** [vor jmdm.] katzbuckeln (abwertend)

fax /fæks/ **1** *n.* [Tele]fax, *das;* Fernkopie, *die.* **2** *v.t.* faxen; fernkopieren; **I'll** ∼ **it [through] to you** ich faxe es dir zu

fax: ∼ **machine** *n.* Faxgerät, *das;* Fernkopierer, *der;* ∼ **modem** *n.* (Computing) Faxmodem, *das;* ∼ **number** *n.* Faxnummer, *die*

FBI *abbr.* (Amer.) **Federal Bureau of Investigation** FBI, *das*

fear /fɪər/ **1** *n.* **(a)** Furcht, *die*, Angst, *die* (of vor + *Dat.*); ∼ **of death** *or* **dying/heights** Todes-/Höhenangst, *die;* ∼ **of doing sth.** Angst od. Furcht davor, etw. zu tun; **in** ∼ **of being caught** in der Angst, gefasst zu werden; **strike** ∼ **into sb.** jmdn. in Angst versetzen; **(b)** (object of ∼) Furcht, *die; in pl.* Befürchtungen *Pl.;* **(c)** (anxiety for sb.'s/ sth.'s safety) Sorge, *die* (**for** um); **go** *or* **be in** ∼ **of one's life** Angst um sein Leben haben; **(d)** (coll.: risk) Gefahr, *die;* **no** ∼! (coll.) keine Bange! (ugs.). **2** *v.t.* **(a)** (be afraid of) ∼ **sb./sth.** vor jmdm./etw. Angst haben; jmdn./etw. fürchten; ∼ **to do** *or* **doing sth.** Angst haben od. sich fürchten, etw. zu tun; **you have nothing to** ∼: Sie haben nichts zu befürchten; ∼ **the worst** das Schlimmste befürchten; **(b)** (be worried about) befürchten; ∼ **[that …]** fürchten[, dass …]. **3** *v.i.* sich fürchten; ∼ **for sb./sth.** um jmdn./etw. bangen (geh.) *od.* fürchten; **never** ∼ (also joc. iron.) keine Bange (ugs.)

fearful /'fɪəfl/ *adj.* **(a)** (terrible) furchtbar; **(b)** (frightened) ängstlich; **be** ∼ **of sth./sb.** vor etw./jmdm. Angst haben; **be** ∼ **of doing sth.** Angst [davor] haben, etw. zu tun

fearfully /'frəfəlɪ/ *adv.* ängstlich

fearless /'frəlɪs/ *adj.* furchtlos; **be ~ [of sth./sb.]** keine Angst [vor etw./jmdm.] haben *od.* kennen

fearlessly /'frəlɪslɪ/ *adv.* furchtlos; ohne Angst

fearsome /'frəsəm/ *adj.* furchteinflößend; furchterregend

feasibility /fi:zɪ'bɪlɪtɪ/ *n., no pl.* Durchführbarkeit, *die;* (of method) Anwendbarkeit, *die;* (possibility) Möglichkeit, *die*

feasible /'fi:zɪbl/ *adj.* durchführbar ‹*Plan, Vorschlag*›; anwendbar ‹*Methode*›; (possible) möglich

feast /fi:st/ **1** *n.* (a) (Relig.) Fest, *das;* **movable/immovable ~:** beweglicher/unbeweglicher Feiertag; **(b)** (banquet) Festessen, *das;* **a ~ for the eyes/ears** eine Augenweide/ein Ohrenschmaus. **2** *v.i.* schlemmen; schwelgen; **~ on sth.** sich an etw. (*Dat.*) gütlich tun. **3** *v.t.* festlich bewirten; (fig.) **he ~ed his eyes on her beauty** er labte sich an ihrer Schönheit (geh.)

feat /fi:t/ *n.* (action) Meisterleistung, *die;* (thing) Meisterwerk, *das;* **a ~ of intellect/strength** eine intellektuelle Meisterleistung/ein Kraftakt

feather /'feðə(r)/ **1** *n.* (a) Feder, *die;* (on arrow) [Pfeil]feder, *die;* **as light as a ~:** federleicht; **a ~ in sb.'s cap** (fig. coll.) ein Grund für jmdn., stolz zu sein; **you could have knocked me down with a ~:** ich war völlig von den Socken (ugs.); **(b)** *collect.* (plumage) Gefieder, *das. See also* **bird a. 2** *v.t.* **~ one's nest** (fig.) auf seinen finanziellen Vorteil bedacht sein

feather: ~ 'bed *n.* mit Federn gefüllte Matratze; **~bed** *v.t.* [ver]hätscheln; **~-brained** /'feðəbreɪnd/ *adj.* schwachköpfig (ugs.); **~ 'duster** *n.* Federwisch, *der;* **~weight** *n.* (a) (very light thing/person) Fliegengewicht, *das;* **(b)** (Boxing etc.) Federgewicht, *das;* (person also) Federgewichtler, *der*

feathery /'feðərɪ/ *adj.* (a) (covered with feathers) befiedert; gefiedert; **(b)** (feather-like) (in quality) federnartig; (in weight) federleicht; locker ‹*Kuchenteig*›

feature /'fi:tʃə(r)/ **1** *n.* (a) *usu. in pl.* (part of face) Gesichtszug, *der;* **(b)** (distinctive characteristic) [charakteristisches] Merkmal; **be a ~ of sth.** charakteristisch für etw. sein; **make a ~ of sth.** etw. [sehr] betonen *od.* herausstellen; **(c)** (Journ. etc.) Reportage, *die;* Feature, *das;* **(d)** (Cinemat.) **~ [film]** Hauptfilm, *der;* Spielfilm *der;* **(e)** (Radio, Telev.) **~ [programme]** Feature, *das.* **2** *v.t.* (make attraction of) vorrangig vorstellen; (give special prominence to) (in film) in der Hauptrolle zeigen; (in show) als Stargast präsentieren. **3** *v.i.* **(a)** (be ~) vorkommen; **(b)** (be [important] participant) **~ in sth.** eine [bedeutende] Rolle bei etw. spielen

featureless /'fi:tʃələs/ *adj.* eintönig

Feb. *abbr.* **February** Febr.

February /'februərɪ/ *n.* ▶738 | Februar, *der; see also* **August**

feces (Amer.) ⇒ **faeces**

feckless /'feklɪs/ *adj.* (feeble) schwächlich ‹*Person*›; nutzlos, vertan ‹*Leben*›; (inefficient) untauglich; (aimless) ziellos

fed /fed/ **1** ⇒ **feed 1, 2. 2** *pred. adj.* (coll.) **be/get ~ up with sb./sth.** jmdn./etw. satt haben (ugs.); **be/get ~ up with doing sth.** es satt haben, etw. zu tun (ugs.)

federal /'fedərl/ *adj.* Bundes-; föderativ ‹*System*›; föderalistisch ‹*Partei usw.*›

federalism /'fedərəlɪzəm/ *n., no pl.* Föderalismus, *der*

federalist /'fedərəlɪst/ **1** *adj.* föderalistisch. **2** *n.* Föderalist, *der*/Föderalistin, *die*

federation /fedə'reɪʃn/ *n.* (group of states) Bündnis, *das;* Föderation, *die;* (society) Bund, *der*

fee /fi:/ *n.* (a) Gebühr, *die;* (of doctor, lawyer, etc.) Honorar, *das;* (of performer) Gage, *die;* **registration ~:** Aufnahmegebühr, *die;* **school ~s** Schulgeld, *das;* **(b)** (administrative charge) Bearbeitungsgebühr, *die*

feeble /'fi:bl/ *adj.* (a) (weak) schwach; **(b)** (deficient) schwächlich; (in resolve, argument) halbherzig; **(c)** (lacking energy) schwach ‹*Leistung, Kampf, Applaus*›; wenig überzeugend ‹*Argument, Entschuldigung, Erklärung*›; zaghaft, kläglich ‹*Versuch, Bemühung*›; lahm (ugs.) ‹*Witz*›; **(d)** (indistinct) schwach ‹*[Licht]schein, Herzschlag*›

feeble-'minded *adj.* (a) töricht; **(b)** (Psych.) geistesschwach

feed /fi:d/ **1** *v.t.,* **fed** /fed/ (a) (give food to) füttern; **~ sb./an animal with sth.** jmdm. etw. zu essen/einem Tier [etw.] zu fressen geben; **~ a baby/an animal on** *or* **with sth.** ein Baby/Tier mit etw. füttern; **~ [at the breast]** stillen; **~ oneself** allein *od.* ohne Hilfe essen; **(b)** (provide food for) ernähren; **~ sb./an animal on** *or* **with sth.** jmdn./ein Tier mit etw. ernähren; **(c)** (give out) verfüttern ‹*Viehfutter*› (**to an + Akk.**); **(d)** (keep supplied) speisen ‹*Wasserreservoir*›; (supply with material) versorgen; **~ a film into the projector** einen Film in das Vorführgerät einlegen; **~ data into the computer** Daten in den Computer eingeben. **2** *v.i.,* **fed** ‹*Tier:*› fressen (**from** aus); ‹*Person:*› essen (**off** von); **~ on sth.** ‹*Tier:*› etw. fressen; ‹*Person:*› sich von etw. [er]nähren. **3** *n.* (a) (instance of eating) (of animals) Fressen, *das;* (of baby) Mahlzeit, *die;* **have [quite] a ~:** [ordentlich] futtern (ugs.); [kräftig] zulangen; **(b)** (fodder) **[cattle/pig] ~:** [Vieh-/Schweine]futter, *das* **~ 'back** *v.t.* zurückleiten; weiterleiten, -geben ‹*Informationen*›; **be fed back** zurückfließen

'feedback *n.* (a) (information about result, response) Reaktion, *die;* Feedback, *das* (fachspr.); **(b)** (Electr.) Rückkopplung, *die*

feeder /'fi:də(r)/ *n.* (a) (animal) Fresser, *der;* **plankton ~** Planktonfresser, *der;* **the larvae are voracious ~s** die Larven sind gefräßig; **(b)** (dispenser) Futterspender, *der*

'feeder road *n.* Zubringer, *der;* Zubringerstraße, *die*

feeding /'fi:dɪŋ/**: ~ bottle** *n.* [Saug]flasche, *die;* **~ time** *n.* Fütterungszeit, *die*

feel /fi:l/ **1** *v.t.,* **felt** /felt/ (a) (explore by touch) befühlen; **~ sb.'s pulse** jmdm. den Puls fühlen; **~ one's way** sich (*Dat.*) seinen Weg ertasten; (fig.: try sth. out) sich vorsichtig vor[an]tasten; **(b)** (perceive by touch) fühlen; (become aware of) bemerken; (be aware of) merken; (have sensation of) spüren; **(c)** empfinden ‹*Mitleid, Dank, Eifersucht*›; verspüren ‹*Drang, Wunsch*›; **~ the cold/ heat** unter der Kälte/Hitze leiden; **~ one's age** sein Alter spüren; **make itself felt** zu spüren sein; (have effect) sich bemerkbar machen; **(d)** (experience) empfinden; (be affected by) zu spüren bekommen; **(e)** (have vague or emotional conviction) **~ [that]** …: das Gefühl haben, dass …; **(f)** (think) **~ [that]** …: glauben, dass …; **if that's what you ~ about the matter** wenn du so darüber denkst. **2** *v.i.,* **felt (a) ~ [about] in sth. [for sth.]** [nach etw.] [herum]suchen; **~ [about] [after** *or* **for sth.] with sth.** mit etw. [nach etw.] [umher]tasten; **(b)** (have sense of touch) fühlen; **(c)** (be conscious that one is) sich … fühlen; **~ angry/delighted/disappointed** böse/froh/enttäuscht sein; **I felt such a fool** ich kam mir wie ein Idiot vor; **~ inclined to do sth.** dazu neigen, etw. zu tun; **the child did not ~ loved/wanted** das Kind hatte das Gefühl, ungeliebt/unerwünscht zu sein; **~ quite hopeful** guter Hoffnung sein; **I felt sorry for him** er tat mir leid; **how do you ~ today?** wie fühlst du dich *od.* wie geht es dir heute?; **~ like sth./doing sth.** (coll.: wish to have/do) auf etw. (*Akk.*) Lust haben/Lust haben, etw. zu tun; **do you ~ like a cup of tea?** möchtest du eine Tasse Tee?; **we ~ as if** *or* **as though** …: es kommt uns vor, als ob …; (have the impression that) wir haben das Gefühl, dass …; **how do you ~ about the idea?** was hältst du von der Idee?; **if that's how** *or* **the way you ~ about it** wenn du so darüber denkst; **(d)** (be emotionally affected) **passionately/bitterly about sth.** sich für etw. begeistern/über etw. (*Akk.*) verbittert sein; **(e)** (be consciously perceived as) sich … anfühlen; **~ like sth.** sich wie etw. anfühlen; **it ~s nice/uncomfortable** es ist ein angenehmes/unangenehmes Gefühl. **3** *n.* **have a silky ~:** sich seidig anfühlen; **let me have a ~:** lass mich mal fühlen; **get/have a ~ for sth.** (fig.) ein Gespür für etw. bekommen/haben

~ for *v.t.* **~ for sb.** mit jmdm. Mitleid haben

~ 'out *v.t.* (sound out) **~ sb. out** jmds. Ansichten feststellen

~ with *v.t.* Mitgefühl haben mit

feeler /'fi:lə(r)/ *n.* Fühler, *der;* **put out ~s** (fig.) seine Fühler ausstrecken

feeling /'fi:lɪŋ/ *n.* (a) (sense of touch) [sense of] **~:** Tastsinn, *der;* **have no ~ in one's legs** kein Gefühl in den

Beinen haben; **(b)** (physical sensation, emotion) Gefühl, *das;* **what are your ~s for each other?** was empfindet ihr füreinander?; **say sth. with ~:** etw. mit Nachdruck sagen; **~s were running high** Emotionen wurden geweckt; **bad ~** (jealousy) Neid, *der;* (annoyance) Verstimmung, *die;* **(c)** *in pl.* (sensibilities) Gefühle; **hurt sb.'s ~s** jmdn. verletzen; **(d)** (belief) Gefühl, *das;* **have a/the ~ [that]** …: das Gefühl haben, dass …; **(e)** (sentiment) Ansicht, *die;* **the general ~ was that** …: man war allgemein der Ansicht, dass …

'fee-paying *adj.* **~ school** schulgeldpflichtige Schule; **~ pupil/student** Schulgeld/Studiengebühren zahlender Schüler/Student

feet *pl. of* **foot**

feign /feɪn/ *v.t.* vorspiegeln; vortäuschen; **~ ignorance** sich dumm stellen; **~ to do sth.** vorgeben, etw. zu tun

feint /feɪnt/ *n.* (Boxing, Fencing) Finte, *die;* **make a ~:** eine Finte ausführen; fintieren

feline /'fiːlaɪn/ **1** *adj.* (of cat[s]) Katzen-; (catlike) katzenhaft. **2** *n.* Katze, *die;* **the ~s** die Katzen *od.* (fachspr.) Feliden

fell¹ ⇨ **fall 2**

fell² /fel/ *v.t.* **(a)** (cut down) fällen 〈*Baum*〉; **(b)** (strike down) niederstrecken 〈*Gegner*〉

fell³ *n.* (Brit.) **(a)** (in names: hill) Berg, *der;* **(b)** (stretch of high moorland) Hochmoor, *das*

fell⁴ *adj.* **at** *or* **in one ~ swoop** auf einen Schlag

fellow /'feləʊ/ **1** *n.* **(a)** *usu. in pl.* (comrade) Kamerad, *der;* **a good ~:** ein guter Kumpel (ugs.); **(b)** *usu. in pl.* (equal) Gleichgestellte, *der/die;* **(c)** (Brit. Univ.) Fellow, *der;* (member of academy or society) Fellow, *der;* Mitglied, *das;* **(d)** (coll.: man, boy) Bursche, *der* (ugs.); Kerl, *der* (ugs.); **well, young ~:** nun, junger Mann; **old** *or* **dear ~:** alter Junge *od.* Knabe (ugs.). **2** *attrib. adj.* Mit-; **~ worker** Kollege, *der/*Kollegin, *die;* **~ man** *or* **human being** Mitmensch, *der;* **~ sufferer** Leidensgenosse, *der/*-genossin, *die;* **my ~ teachers/workers** *etc.* meine Lehrer-/Arbeitskollegen *usw.;* **~ student** Kommilitone, *der/*Kommilitonin, *die*

fellow: ~ 'countryman ⇨ **countryman a; ~ 'feeling** *n.* **(a)** (sympathy) Mitgefühl, *das;* **have a ~ feeling for sb.** mit jmdm. fühlen; **(b)** (mutual understanding) Zusammengehörigkeitsgefühl, *das*

fellowship /'feləʊʃɪp/ *n.* **(a)** *no pl.* (companionship) Gesellschaft, *die;* **(b)** *no pl.* (community of interest) Zusammengehörigkeit, *die;* **(c)** (Univ. etc.) Status eines Fellows; Fellowship, *die*

fellow-'traveller *n.* Mitreisende, *der/die*

felony /'feləni/ *n.* Kapitalverbrechen, *das*

felt¹ /felt/ *n.* (cloth) Filz, *der;* **~ hat** Filzhut, *der*

felt² ⇨ **feel 1, 2**

felt[-tipped] pen /felt(tɪpt) 'pen/ *n.* Filzstift, *der*

female /'fiːmeɪl/ **1** *adj.* weiblich; Frauen〈*stimme, -station, -chor, -verein*〉; **~ animal/bird/fish/insect** Weibchen, *das;* **~ child/doctor** Mädchen, *das/*Ärztin, *die.* **2** *n.* **(a)** (person) Frau, *die;* (foetus, child) Mädchen, *das;* (animal) Weibchen, *das;* **(b)** (derog.: woman) Weib[sbild], *das* (ugs. abwertend)

feminine /'femɪnɪn/ *adj.* **(a)** (of women) weiblich; Frauen〈*angelegenheit, -problem, -leiden*〉; **(b)** (womanly) fraulich; feminin; **(c)** (Ling.) weiblich; feminin (fachspr.)

feminism /'femɪnɪzm/ *n., no pl.* Feminismus, *der*

feminist /'femɪnɪst/ **1** *n.* Feministin, *die/*Feminist, *der.* **2** *adj.* feministisch; Feministen〈*bewegung, -blatt, -gruppe*〉

femur /'fiːmə(r)/ **▶ 672** *n., pl.* **~s** *or* **femora** /'femərə/ (Anat.) Oberschenkelknochen, *der;* Femur, *der* (fachspr.)

fen /fen/ *n.* Sumpfland, *das;* Fenn, *das;* **the Fens** die Fens

fence /fens/ **1** *n.* **(a)** (Zaun, *der;* **sit on the ~** (fig.) sich nicht einmischen; sich neutral verhalten; **(b)** (for horses to jump) Hindernis, *das;* **(c)** (coll.: receiver) Hehler, *der/*Hehlerin, *die.* **2** *v.i.* (Sport) fechten. **3** *v.t.* (surround with fence) einzäunen, (fig.) absichern (**with** durch)

~ 'in *v.t.* einzäunen; (fig.) einengen (**with** durch)

~ 'off *v.t.* abzäunen

fencer /'fensə(r)/ *n.* Fechter, *der/*Fechterin, *die*

fencing /'fensɪŋ/ *n., no pl.* **(a)** Einzäunen, *das;* **(b)** (Sport/ Hist.) Fechten, *das; attrib.* Fecht-; **(c)** (fences) Zäune *Pl.*

fend /fend/ *v.i.* **~ for oneself** für sich selbst sorgen; (in hostile surroundings) sich allein durchschlagen

~ 'off *v.t.* abwehren; von sich fernhalten

fender /'fendə(r)/ *n.* **(a)** (for fire) Kaminschutz, *der;* **(b)** (Amer.) (car mudguard or wing) Kotflügel, *der;* (bicycle mudguard) Schutzblech, *das*

fennel /'fenl/ *n.* (Bot.) Fenchel, *der*

ferment 1 /fə'ment/ *v.i.* (lit. or fig.) gären. **2** *v.t.* zur Gärung bringen; (fig.) heraufbeschwören 〈*Unzufriedenheit, Unruhe*〉. **3** /'fɜːment/ *n.* **(a)** (fermentation) Gärung, *die;* Fermentation, *die* (fachspr.); **(b)** (agitation) Unruhe, *die;* Aufruhr, *der;* **in ~:** in Unruhe *od.* Aufruhr

fermentation /fɜːmen'teɪʃn/ *n.* Gärung, *die;* Fermentation, *die* (fachspr.)

fern /fɜːn/ *n.* Farnkraut, *das*

ferocious /fə'rəʊʃəs/ *adj.* wild 〈*Tier, Person, Aussehen, Blick, Lachen*〉; grimmig 〈*Stimme*〉; heftig 〈*Schlag, Kampf, Stoß*〉; (fig.) scharf 〈*Kritik, Angriff*〉; heftig 〈*Streit, Auseinandersetzung*〉

ferocity /fə'rɒsɪti/ *n., no pl.* ⇨ **ferocious:** Wildheit, *die;* Grimmigkeit, *die;* Heftigkeit, *die;* Schärfe, *die*

ferret /'ferɪt/ **1** *n.* Frettchen, *das.* **2** *v.i.* **~ [about** *or* **around]** herumstöbern (ugs.); herumschnüffeln (abwertend)

~ 'out *v.t.* aufspüren; aufstöbern (ugs.)

Ferris wheel /'ferɪs wiːl/ *n.* Riesenrad, *das*

ferrule /'feruːl, 'ferl/ *n.* Zwinge, *die*

ferry /'feri/ **1** *n.* **(a)** Fähre, *die;* **(b)** (service) Fährverbindung, *die;* Fähre, *die* (ugs.). **2** *v.t.* **(a)** (convey in boat) **~ [across** *or* **over]** übersetzen; **(b)** (transport) befördern, bringen 〈*Güter, Personen*〉

ferry: ~ boat *n.* Fährboot, *das;* **~man** /'ferɪmən/ *n., pl.* **~men** /'ferɪmən/ Fährmann, *der*

fertile /'fɜːtaɪl/ *adj.* **(a)** (fruitful) fruchtbar (**in** an + *Dat.*); **have a ~ imagination** viel Fantasie haben; **(b)** (capable of developing) befruchtet; **(c)** (able to become parent) fortpflanzungsfähig

fertilisation, fertilise, fertiliser ⇨ **fertiliz-**

fertility /fɜː'tɪlɪti/ *n., no pl.* **(a)** (lit. or fig.) Fruchtbarkeit, *die;* **(b)** (ability to become parent) Fortpflanzungsfähigkeit, *die*

fer'tility drug *n.* (Med.) Hormonpräparat, *das* (*zur Steigerung der Fruchtbarkeit*)

fertilization /fɜːtɪlaɪ'zeɪʃn/ *n.* (Biol.) Befruchtung, *die*

fertilize /'fɜːtɪlaɪz/ *v.t.* **(a)** (Biol.) befruchten; **(b)** (Agric.) düngen

fertilizer /'fɜːtɪlaɪzə(r)/ *n.* Dünger, *der*

fervent /'fɜːvənt/ *adj.* leidenschaftlich; inbrünstig 〈*Gebet, Wunsch, Hoffnung*〉; glühend 〈*Verehrer, Liebe, Hass*〉

fervour (Brit.; Amer.: **fervor**) /'fɜːvə(r)/ *n.* Leidenschaftlichkeit, *die;* (of love, belief) Inbrunst, *die*

fester /'festə(r)/ *v.i.* (lit or fig) eitern

festival /'festɪvl/ *n.* **(a)** (feast day) Fest, *das;* **(b)** (performances, plays, etc.) Festival, *das;* Festspiele *Pl.;* (rock ~, jazz ~, single event) Festival, *das*

festive /'festɪv/ *adj.* festlich; **the ~ season** die Weihnachtszeit

festivity /fe'stɪvɪti/ *n.* **(a)** *no pl.* (gaiety) Feststimmung, *die;* **(b)** (festive celebration) Feier, *die;* **festivities** Feierlichkeiten *Pl.*

festoon /fe'stuːn/ **1** *n.* Girlande, *die.* **2** *v.t.* schmücken (**with** mit)

fetal (Amer.) ⇨ **foetal**

fetch /fetʃ/ **1** *v.t.* **(a)** holen; (collect) abholen (**from** von); **~ sb. sth., ~ sth. for sb.** jmdm. etw. holen; **(b)** (be sold for) erzielen 〈*Preis*〉; **my car ~ed £500** ich habe für den Wagen 500 Pfund bekommen; **(c)** (deal) **~ sb. a blow/ punch** jmdm. einen Schlag versetzen. **2** *v.i.* **~ and carry [for sb.]** [bei jmdm.] Mädchen für alles sein (ugs.)

~ 'up *v.i.* (coll.) landen (ugs.)

fetching /'fetʃɪŋ/ *adj.* einnehmend, gewinnend 〈*Lächeln, Stimme, Wesen, Benehmen*〉

fête /feɪt/ **1** *n.* **(a)** [Wohltätigkeits]basar, *der;* **(b)** (festival) Fest, *das;* Feier, *die.* **2** *v.t.* feiern

fetid /'fetɪd/ *adj.* stinkend; übel riechend; ~ **smell/ odour/stench** Gestank, *der*

fetish /'fetɪʃ/ *n.* Fetisch, *der;* **she has a** ~ **about tidiness** Sauberkeit ist bei ihr zur Manie geworden

fetishism /'fetɪʃɪzm/ *n.* Fetischismus, *der*

fetishist /'fetɪʃɪst/ *n.* Fetischist, *der*/Fetischistin, *die*

fetlock /'fetlɒk/ *n.* Köte, *die*

fetter /'fetə(r)/ **1** *n.* **(a)** (shackle) Fußfessel, *die;* **(b)** *in pl.* (bonds; fig.: captivity) Fesseln *Pl.* **2** *v.t.* fesseln; (fig.) hemmen ‹Fortschritt, Entwicklung›

fettle /'fetl/ *n.* **be in good** *or* **fine/poor** ~**:** sich in guter/schlechter Verfassung befinden

fetus (Amer.) ⇒ **foetus**

feud /fju:d/ **1** *n.* Zwist, *der;* Zwistigkeiten *Pl.;* (Hist./fig.) Fehde, *die.* **2** *v.i.* ~ **[with sb./each other]** [mit jmdm./ miteinander] im Streit liegen

feudal /'fju:dl/ *adj.* Feudal-; feudalistisch; **in** ~ **Britain** im feudalistischen England

'feudal system *n.* (Hist.) Feudalsystem, *das*

fever /'fi:və(r)/ *n.* ▶ 865 | **(a)** *no pl.* (Med.: high temperature) Fieber, *das;* **have a [high]** ~**:** [hohes] Fieber haben; **a** ~ **of 105 °F** 40,5 °C Fieber; **(b)** (Med.: disease) Fieberkrankheit, *die;* **(c)** (nervous excitement) Erregung, *die;* Aufregung, *die;* **in a** ~ **of anticipation** im Fieber der Erwartung

feverish /'fi:vərɪʃ/ *adj.* ▶ 865 | **(a)** (Med.) fiebrig; Fieber‹zustand, -traum›; **be** ~**:** fiebern; Fieber haben; **(b)** fiebrig ‹Erwartung›; fieberhaft ‹Aufregung, Eifer, Kampf, Eile›

'fever pitch *n.* Siedepunkt, *der* (fig.); **reach** ~**:** auf dem Siedepunkt angelangt sein; **at** ~**:** auf dem Siedepunkt

few /fju:/ **1** *adj.* **(a)** (not many) wenige; ~ **people** [nur] wenige [Leute]; **very** ~ **housewives know that** das wissen die wenigsten Hausfrauen; **his** ~ **belongings** seine paar Habseligkeiten; **[all] too** ~ **people** [viel] zu wenig Leute; ~ **and far between** rar; **they were** ~ **in number** sie waren nur sehr wenige; **a** ~ ...: wenige ...; **not a** ~ ...: eine ganze Reihe ...; **[just** *or* **only] a** ~ **troublemakers** einige [wenige] Störenfriede; **just a** ~ **words from you** nur ein paar Worte von dir; **(b)** (some) wenige; **a** ~ ...: einige od. ein paar ...; **every** ~ **minutes** alle paar Minuten; **a good** ~ [...]/**quite a** ~ [...] (coll.) eine ganze Menge [...]/ziemlich viele [...]. **2** *n.* **(a)** (not many) wenige; **a** ~**:** wenige; **a very** ~**:** nur wenige; **the** ~**:** die wenigen; ~ **of us/them** nur wenige von uns/nur wenige [von ihnen]; ~ **of the people** nur wenige [Leute]; **just a** ~ **of you/her friends** nur ein paar von euch/ ihrer Freunde; **not a** ~ **of them** eine ganze Reihe von ihnen; **not a** ~**:** nicht wenige; **(b)** (some) **the/these/those** ~ **who** diejenigen, die; **there were a** ~ **of us who** ...: es gab einige unter uns, die ...; **with a** ~ **of our friends** mit einigen od. ein paar unserer Freunde; **a** ~ **[more] of these biscuits** [noch] ein paar von diesen Keksen; **a good** ~/**quite a** ~ (coll.) eine ganze Menge/ziemlich viele [Leute]

fewer /'fju:ə(r)/ *adj.* weniger; **become** ~ **and** ~**:** immer weniger werden

fewest /'fju:ɪst/ **1** *adj.* **[the]** ~ [...] die wenigsten [...]. **2** *n.* **the** ~ **[of us/them]** die wenigsten [von uns/ihnen]; **at the** ~**:** mindestens

fiancé /fɪ'ɒseɪ/ *n.* Verlobte, *der*

fiancée /fɪ'ɒseɪ/ *n.* Verlobte, *die*

fiasco /fɪ'æskəʊ/ *n., pl.* ~**s** Fiasko, *das*

fib /fɪb/ **1** *n.* Flunkerei, *die* (ugs.); **tell** ~**s** flunkern (ugs.); **that was a** ~**:** das war geschwindelt. **2** *v.i.,* **-bb-** schwindeln; flunkern (ugs.)

fibber /'fɪbə(r)/ *n.* Flunkerer, *der* (ugs.); Schwindler, *der*/ Schwindlerin, *die*

fibre (Brit.; Amer.: **fiber**) /'faɪbə(r)/ *n.* **(a)** Faser, *die;* **(b)** (substance consisting of ~s) [Faser]gewebe, *das;* **(c)** (roughage) Ballaststoffe *Pl.;* **(d)** **moral** ~**:** Charakterstärke, *die*

fibre: ~**glass** (Amer.: **fiber glass**) *n.* (fibrous glass) Glasfaser, *die;* (plastic) glasfaserverstärkter Kunststoff; ~

optic cable *n.* Glasfaserkabel, *das;* ~ **'optics** *n.* Faseroptik, *die*

fibrous /'faɪbrəs/ *adj.* faserig; Faser‹gewebe, -holz, -stoff›

fiche /fi:ʃ/ *n., pl. same or* ~**s** ⇒ **microfiche**

fickle /'fɪkl/ *adj.* unberechenbar; launisch

fiction /'fɪkʃn/ *n.* **(a)** (literature) erzählende Literatur; **(b)** (thing feigned or imagined) ~/~**s** eine Erfindung

fictional /'fɪkʃənl/ *adj.* belletristisch; erfunden ‹Geschichte›; ~ **literature** erzählende Literatur; ~ **characters** fiktive Figuren

'fiction writer *n.* Belletrist, *der*/Belletristin, *die*

fictitious /fɪk'tɪʃəs/ *adj.* **(a)** (counterfeit) fingiert; unwahr ‹Behauptung, Darstellung›; **(b)** (assumed) falsch ‹Name, Identität›; **(c)** (imaginary) [frei] erfunden ‹Person, Figur, Geschichte›

fiddle /'fɪdl/ **1** *n.* **(a)** (Mus.) (coll./derog.) Fidel, *die;* (violin for traditional or folk music) Geige, *die;* Fidel, *die;* **[as] fit as a** ~**:** kerngesund; **play first/second** ~ (fig.) die erste/zweite Geige spielen (ugs.); **play second** ~ **to sb.** in jmds. Schatten (Dat.) stehen; **(b)** (coll.: swindle) Gaunerei, *die;* **it's all a** ~**:** das ist alles Schiebung (ugs.); **be on the** ~**:** krumme Dinger machen (ugs.). **2** *v.i.* **(a)** ~ **about** (coll.: waste time) herumtrödeln (ugs.); ~ **about with sth.** (work on to adjust etc.) an etw. (Dat.) herumfummeln (ugs.); (tinker with) an etw. (Dat.) herumbasteln (ugs.); ~ **with sth.** (play with) mit etw. herumspielen; **(b)** (coll.: deceive) krumme Dinger drehen (ugs.). **3** *v.t.* (coll.) (falsify) frisieren (ugs.) ‹Bücher, Rechnungen›; (get by cheating) [sich (Dat.)] ergaunern (ugs.)

fiddler /'fɪdlə(r)/ *n.* **(a)** (player) Geiger, *der*/Geigerin, *die;* **(b)** (coll.: swindler etc.) Gauner, *der*/Gaunerin, *die* (abwertend)

'fiddlesticks *int.* (coll.) dummes Zeug (ugs.); Schnickschnack (ugs.)

fiddling /'fɪdlɪŋ/ *adj.* **(a)** (petty) belanglos; **(b)** ⇒ **fiddly**

fiddly /'fɪdlɪ/ *adj.* (coll.) **(a)** (awkward to do) knifflig; **(b)** (awkward to use) umständlich

fidelity /fɪ'delɪtɪ/ *n.* **(a)** (faithfulness) Treue, *die* (**to** zu); **(b)** (Radio, Telev., etc.) Wiedergabetreue, *die;* (of sound) Klangtreue, *die;* (of picture) Bildtreue, *die*

fidget /'fɪdʒɪt/ **1** *n.* **(a)** **have/get the** ~**s** zappelig sein/ werden (ugs.); **(b)** (person) Zappelphilipp, *der* (ugs.). **2** *v.i.* ~ **[about]** [herum]zappeln (ugs.); herumrutschen

fidgety /'fɪdʒɪtɪ/ *adj.* unruhig ‹Person, Pferd, Stimmung›; zappelig ‹Kind›; nervös ‹Bewegungen, Zuckungen›

field /fi:ld/ **1** *n.* **(a)** (cultivated) Feld, *das;* Acker, *der;* (for grazing) Weide, *die;* (meadow) Wiese, *die;* **work in the** ~**s** auf dem Feld arbeiten; **(b)** (area rich in minerals etc.) Lagerstätte, *die;* **gas-**~**:** Gasfeld, *das;* **(c)** (battlefield) Schlachtfeld, *das;* (fig.) Feld, *das;* **leave sb. a clear** *or* **the** ~ (fig.) jmdm. das Feld überlassen; **(d)** (playing ~) Sportplatz, *der;* (ground marked out for game) Platz, *der;* [Spiel]feld, *das;* **send sb. off the** ~**:** jmdn. vom Platz schicken; **take the** ~**:** das Spielfeld betreten; **(e)** (competitors in sports event) Feld, *das;* (fig.) Teilnehmerkreis, *der;* **(f)** (area of operation, subject area, etc.) Fach, *das;* [Fach]gebiet, *das;* **in the** ~ **of medicine** auf dem Gebiet der Medizin; ~ **of vision** *or* **view** Blickfeld, *das;* **(g)** (Phys.) **magnetic/gravitational** ~**:** Magnet-/ Gravitationsfeld, *das.* **2** *v.i.* (Cricket, Baseball, etc.) als Fänger spielen. **3** *v.t.* **(a)** (Cricket, Baseball, etc.) (stop) fangen ‹Ball›; (stop and return) auffangen und zurückwerfen; **(b)** (put into ~) aufstellen, aufs Feld schicken ‹Mannschaft, Spieler›; **(c)** (fig.: deal with) fertig werden mit; parieren ‹Fragen›

'field day *n.* **have a** ~**:** seinen großen Tag haben

fielder /'fi:ldə(r)/ *n.* (Cricket, Baseball, etc.) Feldspieler, *der*

field: ~ **events** *n. pl.* (Sport) technische Disziplinen; ~ **glasses** *n. pl.* Feldstecher, *der;* **F**~ **'Marshal** *n.* ▶ 1152 | (Brit. Mil.) Feldmarschall, *der;* ~ **mouse** *n.* Brandmaus, *die;* ~ **sports** *n. pl.* Sport im Freien (bes. Jagen und Fischen); ~ **test** *n.* ⇒ **trial;** ~**-test** *v.t.* in der Praxis erproben; ~ **trial** *n.* Feldversuch, *der;* ~ **trip** *n.* Exkursion, *die;* ~**work** *n.* (of surveyor etc.) Arbeit im Gelände; (of sociologist, collector of scientific data, etc.) Feldforschung, *die;* ~**worker** *n.* ▶ 887 | Feldforscher, *der*/ -forscherin, *die*

fiend /fi:nd/ *n.* **(a)** (very wicked person) Scheusal, *das;* Unmensch, *der;* **(b)** (evil spirit) böser Geist; **(c)** (coll.: mischievous or tiresome person) Plagegeist, *der;* **(d)** (devotee) Fan, *der;* **fresh-air** ~: Frischluftfanatiker, *der*/-fanatikerin, *die*

fiendish /'fiːndɪʃ/ *adj.* **(a)** (fiendlike) teuflisch; **(b)** (extremely awkward) höllisch

fiendishly /'fiːndɪʃlɪ/ *adv.* **(a)** teuflisch; **(b)** ~ **clever** (coll.) gerissen und schlau; **(c)** (extremely awkwardly) höllisch

fierce /'fɪəs/ *adj.* **(a)** (violently hostile) wild; erbittert ⟨*Widerstand, Kampf*⟩; wuchtig ⟨*Schlag*⟩; heftig ⟨*Angriff*⟩; **(b)** (raging) wütend; grimmig ⟨*Hass, Wut*⟩; scharf ⟨*Kritik*⟩; wild ⟨*Tier*⟩; **(c)** heftig ⟨*Andrang, Streit*⟩; heiß ⟨*Wettbewerb*⟩; leidenschaftlich ⟨*Stolz, Wille*⟩; **(d)** (unpleasantly strong or intense) unerträglich; **(e)** (violent in action) hart ⟨*Bremsen, Ruck*⟩

fiercely /'fɪəslɪ/ *adv.* **(a)** heftig ⟨*angreifen, Widerstand leisten*⟩; wütend, grimmig ⟨*brüllen*⟩; **(b)** wütend ⟨*toben*⟩; aufs heftigste ⟨*kritisieren, bekämpfen*⟩; **(c)** äußerst ⟨*stolz, unabhängig sein*⟩; wild ⟨*entschlossen, kämpfen*⟩

fiery /'faɪərɪ/ *adj.* **(a)** (consisting of or flaming with fire) glühend; feurig ⟨*Atem*⟩; (looking like fire) feurig; **(b)** (producing burning sensation) feurig ⟨*Geschmack, Gewürz*⟩; scharf ⟨*Getränk*⟩; **(c)** (irascible, impassioned) hitzig ⟨*Temperament*⟩; feurig ⟨*Rede, Redner*⟩; **have a** ~ **temper** ein Hitzkopf sein

fiesta /fiːˈestə/ *n.* Fest, *das*

fife /faɪf/ *n.* Pfeife, *die*

fifteen /fɪfˈtiːn/ ▶630⌋, ▶706⌋, ▶956⌋ **1** *adj.* fünfzehn; *see also* **eight** 1. **2** *n.* Fünfzehn, *die; see also* **eight** 2 a, d; **eighteen** 2

fifteenth /fɪfˈtiːnθ/ ▶738⌋, ▶956⌋ **1** *adj.* fünfzehnt...; *see also* **eighth** 1. **2** *n.* (fraction) Fünfzehntel, *das; see also* **eighth** 2

fifth /fɪfθ/ ▶738⌋, ▶956⌋ **1** *adj.* fünft...; *see also* **eighth** 1. **2** *n.* (in sequence, rank) Fünfte, *der/die/das;* (fraction) Fünftel, *das; see also* **eighth** 2

fiftieth /'fɪftɪθ/ ▶956⌋ **1** *adj.* fünfzigst...; *see also* **eighth** 1. **2** *n.* (fraction) Fünfzigstel, *das; see also* **eighth** 2

fifty /'fɪftɪ/ ▶630⌋, ▶956⌋ **1** *adj.* fünfzig; *see also* **eight** 1. **2** *n.* Fünfzig, *die; see also* **eight** 2 a; **eighty** 2

fifty: ~-'~ *adv., adj.* fifty-fifty (ugs.); halbe-halbe (ugs.); **go** ~-'~: fifty-fifty od. halbpart machen; ~-'**first** *etc. adj.* ▶956⌋ einundfünfzigst... *usw.; see also* **eighth** 1; ~-'**one** *etc.* ▶956⌋ **1** *adj.* einundfünfzig *usw.; see also* **eight** 1; **2** *n.* Einundfünfzig *usw., die; see also* **eight** 2 a

fig /fɪɡ/ *n.* Feige, *die;* **not care** *or* **give a** ~ **about sth.** sich keinen Deut für etw. interessieren

fig. *abbr.* **figure** Abb.

fight /faɪt/ **1** *v.i.,* **fought** /fɔːt/ **(a)** (lit. or fig.) kämpfen; (with fists) sich schlagen; ~ **shy of sb./sth.** jmdm./einer Sache aus dem Weg gehen; **(b)** (squabble) [sich] streiten, [sich] zanken (**about** wegen). **2** *v.t.,* **fought (a)** (in battle) ~ **sb./sth.** gegen jmdn./etw. kämpfen; (using fists) ~ **sb.** sich mit jmdm. schlagen; ⟨*Boxer:*⟩ gegen jmdn. boxen; **(b)** (seek to overcome) bekämpfen; (resist) ~ **sb./sth.** gegen jmdn./etw. ankämpfen; **(c)** ~ **a battle** einen Kampf austragen; **be** ~**ing a losing battle** (fig.) auf verlorenem Posten stehen *od.* kämpfen; **(d)** führen ⟨*Kampagne*⟩; kandidieren bei ⟨*Wahl*⟩; **(e)** ~ **one's way** sich (*Dat.*) den Weg freikämpfen; (fig.) sich (*Dat.*) seinen Weg bahnen; ~ **one's way to the top** (fig.) sich an die Spitze kämpfen. **3** *n.* **(a)** Kampf, *der* (**for** um); (brawl) Schlägerei, *die;* **make a** ~ **of it, put up a** ~: sich wehren; (fig.) sich zur Wehr setzen; **give in without a** ~ (fig.) klein beigeben; **(b)** (squabble) Streit, *der;* **they are always having** ~**s** zwischen ihnen gibt es dauernd Streit; **(c)** (ability to ~) Kampffähigkeit, *die;* (appetite for ~ing) Kampfgeist, *der;* **all the** ~ **had gone out of him** (fig.) sein Kampfgeist war erloschen

~ **against** *v.t.* (lit. or fig.) kämpfen gegen; ankämpfen gegen ⟨*Wellen, Wind, Gefühle*⟩

~ '**back** **1** *v.i.* zurückschlagen; sich zur Wehr setzen. **2** *v.t.* (suppress) zurückhalten

~ '**down** *v.t.* zurückhalten

~ **for** *v.t.* (lit. or fig.) kämpfen für; ~ **for one's life** um sein Leben kämpfen

~ '**off** *v.t.* (lit. or fig.) abwehren; abwimmeln (ugs.) ⟨*Reporter, Fans, Bewunderer*⟩; bekämpfen ⟨*Erkältung*⟩; ~ **off the desire** dem Wunsch widerstehen

~ '**out** *v.t.* (lit. or fig.) ausfechten

~ **over** *v.t.* **(a)** (~ with regard to) [sich] streiten über (+ *Akk.*); **(b)** (~ to gain possession of) kämpfen um; (squabble to gain possession of) [sich] streiten um

~ **with** *v.t.* **(a)** kämpfen mit; **(b)** (squabble with) [sich] streiten mit

fighter /'faɪtə(r)/ *n.* ▶887⌋ **(a)** Kämpfer, *der*/Kämpferin, *die;* (warrior) Krieger, *der;* (boxer) Fighter, *der;* **(b)** (aircraft) Kampfflugzeug, *das;* ~ **pilot** Jagdflieger, *der*

fighting /'faɪtɪŋ/ **1** *adj.* Kampf⟨*truppen, -schiff*⟩. **2** *n.* Kämpfe *Pl.*

fighting: ~ '**chance** *n.* **have a** ~ **chance of succeeding/of doing sth.** Aussicht auf Erfolg haben/gute Chancen haben, etw. zu tun; ~ '**fit** *adj.* topfit (ugs.); ~ '**words** *n. pl.* (coll.) Kampfparolen *Pl.*

'**fig leaf** *n.* (lit. or fig.) Feigenblatt, *das*

figment /'fɪɡmənt/ *n.* Hirngespinst, *das;* **a** ~ **of one's** *or* **the imagination** pure Einbildung

'**fig tree** *n.* Feigenbaum, *der*

figurative /'fɪɡjʊrətɪv, 'fɪɡərətɪv/ *adj.* übertragen; figurativ (Sprachw.)

figure /'fɪɡə(r)/ **1** *n.* **(a)** (shape) Form, *die;* **(b)** (Geom.) Figur, *die;* **(c)** (one's bodily shape) Figur, *die;* **keep one's** ~: sich (*Dat.*) seine Figur bewahren; **lose one's** ~: dick werden; **(d)** (person as seen) Gestalt, *die;* (literary ~) Figur, *die;* (historical etc. ~) Persönlichkeit, *die;* **a fine** ~ **of a man/woman** eine stattliche Erscheinung; **(e)** (simile etc.) ~ **[of speech]** Redewendung, *die;* (Rhet.) Redefigur, *die;* **(f)** (illustration) Abbildung, *die;* **(g)** (Dancing, Skating) Figur, *die;* **(h)** (numerical symbol) Ziffer, *die;* (number so expressed) Zahl, *die;* (amount of money) Betrag, *der;* **double** ~**s** zweistellige Zahlen; **go** *or* **run into three** ~**s** sich auf dreistellige Zahlen belaufen; **three-/four-**~: drei-/vierstellig; **(i)** *in pl.* (accounts, result of calculations) Zahlen *Pl.;* **can you check my** ~**s?** kannst du mal nachrechnen? **2** *v.t.* **(a)** (picture mentally) sich (*Dat.*) vorstellen; **(b)** (calculate) schätzen. **3** *v.i.* **(a)** vorkommen; erscheinen; (in play) auftreten; **children don't** ~ **in her plans for the future** Kinder spielen in ihren Zukunftsplänen keine Rolle; **(b)** (coll.: be likely, understandable) **that** ~**s** das kann gut sein

~ '**out** *v.t.* **(a)** (work out by arithmetic) ausrechnen; **(b)** (Amer.: estimate) ~ **out that ...:** damit rechnen, dass ...; **(c)** (understand) verstehen; **I can't** ~ **him out** ich werde nicht schlau aus ihm; **(d)** (ascertain) herausfinden

figure: ~**head** *n.* (lit. or fig.) Galionsfigur, *die;* ~ **skating** *n.* Eiskunstlauf, *der*

Fiji /'fiːdʒiː/ *pr. n.* Fidschi (*das*)

filament /'fɪləmənt/ *n.* **(a)** Faden, *der;* **(b)** (conducting wire or thread) Glühfaden, *der*

filch /fɪltʃ/ *v.t.* stibitzen (ugs.)

file¹ /faɪl/ **1** *n.* Feile, *die;* (nail-~) [Nagel]feile, *die.* **2** *v.t.* feilen ⟨*Fingernägel*⟩; mit der Feile bearbeiten ⟨*Holz, Eisen*⟩

~ **a'way** *v.t.* abfeilen

~ '**down** *v.t.* abfeilen

file² **1** *n.* **(a)** (holder) Ordner, *der;* (box) Kassette, *die;* [Dokumenten]schachtel, *die;* **on** ~: in der Kartei/in *od.* bei den Akten; **put sth. on** ~: etw. in die Akten/Kartei aufnehmen; **(b)** (set of papers) Ablage, *die;* (as cards) Kartei, *die;* **open/keep a** ~ **on sb./sth.** eine Akte über jmdn./etw. anlegen/führen. **2** *v.t.* **(a)** (place in a ~) (in die Kartei) einordnen/[in die Akten] aufnehmen; ablegen (Bürow.); **(b)** (submit) einreichen ⟨*Antrag*⟩; **(c)** ⟨*Journalist:*⟩ einsenden ⟨*Bericht*⟩

~ **a'way** *v.t.* ablegen (Bürow.)

file³ **1** *n.* Reihe, *die;* [**in**] **single** *or* **Indian** ~: [im] Gänsemarsch. **2** *v.i.* in einer Reihe hintereinander hergehen

~ **a'way** *v.i.* [einer nach dem anderen] weggehen

~ '**off** ⇒ ~ **away**

'**file card** *n.* Karteikarte, *die*

filibuster /'fɪlɪbʌstə(r)/ **1** *n.* (obstruction) Verschleppungstaktik, *die;* Filibuster, *das;* **2** *v.i.* obstruieren; Dauerreden halten

filigree /'fɪlɪɡriː/ *n.* (lit. or fig.) Filigran, *das*

filing /'faɪlɪŋ/ *n.* ~**s** (particles) Späne

filing: ~ **cabinet** *n.* Aktenschrank, *der;* ~ **clerk** *n.* ▶887⌋ Archivkraft, *die*

Filipino /ˌfɪlɪ'piːnəʊ/ ▶ 947 | **1** *adj.* philippinisch. **2** *n.*, *pl.* ~**s** Filipino, *der*/Filipina, *die*

fill /fɪl/ **1** *v.t.* **(a)** (make full) ~ sth. [with sth.] etw. [mit etw.] füllen; ~**ed with** voller ‹*Reue, Bewunderung, Neid, Verzweiflung*› (at über + *Akk.*); **be** ~**ed with people/ flowers/fish** *etc.* voller Menschen/Blumen/Fische *usw.* sein; **(b)** (occupy whole capacity of, spread over) füllen; besetzen ‹*Sitzplätze*›; (fig.) ausfüllen ‹*Gedanken, Zeit*›; **the room was** ~**ed to capacity** der Raum war voll besetzt; ~ **the bill** (fig.) den Erwartungen entsprechen; (be appropriate) angemessen sein; **(c)** (pervade) erfüllen; **light** ~**ed the room** Licht strömte in das Zimmer; **(d)** (block up) füllen ‹*Lücke*›; füllen, (veralt.) plombieren ‹*Zahn*›; **(e)** (Cookery) (stuff) füllen; (put layer of sth. solid in) belegen; (put layer of sth. spreadable in) bestreichen; **(f)** (hold) innehaben ‹*Posten*›; versehen ‹*Amt*›; (take up) ausfüllen ‹*Position*›; (appoint sb. to) besetzen ‹*Posten, Lehrstuhl*›. **2** *v.i.* ~ **[with sth.]** sich [mit etw.] füllen; (fig.) sich [mit etw.] erfüllen. **3** *n.* **eat/drink one's** ~: sich satt essen/trinken; **have had one's** ~ seinen Hunger und Durst gestillt haben; **have had one's** ~ **of sth./doing sth.** genug von etw. haben/etw. zur Genüge getan haben

~ **'in** **1** *v.t.* **(a)** füllen; zuschütten, auffüllen ‹*Erdloch*›; **(b)** (complete) ausfüllen ‹*Formular usw.*›; ergänzen ‹*Auslassungen*›; **(c)** (insert) einsetzen; **(d)** überbrücken ‹*Zeit*›; **(e)** (coll.: inform) ~ **sb. in [on sth.]** jmdn. [über etw. (*Akk.*)] ins Bild setzen. **2** *v.i.* ~ **in for sb.** für jmdn. einspringen

~ **'out** **1** *v.t.* **(a)** (enlarge to proper size or extent) ausfüllen; **(b)** (complete) ausfüllen ‹*Formular usw.*›. **2** *v.i.* **(a)** (become enlarged) sich ausdehnen; **(b)** (become plumper) voller werden

~ **'up** **1** *v.t.* **(a)** (make full) ~ **sth. up [with sth.]** etw. [mit etw.] füllen; ~ **up sb.'s glass** jmdm. noch einmal einschenken; **(b)** (put petrol into) ~ **up [the tank]** tanken; ~ **her up!** (coll.) voll[tanken]!; **(c)** auffüllen ‹*Loch*›; **(d)** (complete) ausfüllen ‹*Formular usw.*›. **2** *v.i.* ‹*Theater, Zimmer, Zug usw.*› sich füllen; ‹*Becken, Spülkasten*› voll laufen

filler /'fɪlə(r)/ *n.* (to fill cavity) Füllmasse, *die*

'filler cap *n.* Tankverschluss, *der*

fillet /'fɪlɪt/ **1** *n.* (Gastr.) Filet, *das*; ~ **[steak]** (slice) Filetsteak, *das*; (cut) Filet, *das*; ~ **of pork/cod** Schweine-/Kabeljaufilet, *das*. **2** *v.t.* filetieren; (remove bones from) entgräten ‹*Fisch*›

filling /'fɪlɪŋ/ **1** *n.* **(a)** (for teeth) Füllung, *die*; Plombe, *die* (veralt.); **have a** ~: sich (*Dat.*) einen Zahn füllen lassen; **(b)** (for pancakes etc.) Füllung, *die*; (for sandwiches etc.) Belag, *der*; (for spreading) Aufstrich, *der*. **2** *adj.* sättigend

'filling station *n.* Tankstelle, *die*

fillip /'fɪlɪp/ *n.* (stimulus) Anreiz, *der*; Ansporn, *der*; **give sb. a** ~: jmdn. anspornen

filly /'fɪlɪ/ *n.* junge Stute; Stutfohlen, *das*

film /fɪlm/ **1** *n.* **(a)** (thin layer) Schicht, *die*; ~ **[of oil/ slime]** [Öl-/Schmier]film, *der*; **(b)** (Photog.; Cinemat.: story etc.) Film, *der*; **(c)** *in pl.* (cinema industry) Kino, *das*; Film, *der*; **go into** ~s zum Kino *od.* Film gehen; **(d)** *no pl.* (as artform) der Film. **2** *v.t.* filmen; drehen ‹*Kinofilm, Szene*›; verfilmen ‹*Buch usw.*›

film: ~ **clip** ⇒ **clip²** 2 b; ~ **crew** *n.* Kamerateam, *das*; ~ **director** *n.* ▶ 887 | Filmregisseur, *der*/-regisseurin, *die*; ~ **industry** *n.* Filmindustrie, *die*; ~ **projector** *n.* Filmprojektor, *der*; ~ **script** *n.* Drehbuch, *das*; ~ **set** *n.* Dekoration, *die*; ~ **show** *n.* Filmvorführung, *die*; ~ **star** *n.* Filmstar, *der*; ~**strip** *n.* Filmstreifen, *der*

Filofax, (P) /'faɪləʊfæks/ *n.* ≈ Terminplaner, *der*

filter /'fɪltə(r)/ **1** *n.* **(a)** Filter, *der*; **(b)** (Brit.) (route) Abbiegespur, *die*; (light) grünes Licht für Abbieger. **2** *v.t.* filtern. **3** *v.i.* **(a)** ‹*Flüssigkeiten*› sickern; **(b)** (make way gradually) ~ **through/into sth.** durch etw. hindurch-/in etw. (*Akk.*) hineinsickern; **(c)** (at road junction) sich einfädeln

~ **'out** **1** *v.t.* (lit. or fig.) herausfiltern. **2** *v.i.* durchsickern

filter: ~ **ciga'rette** *n.* Filterzigarette, *die*; ~ **coffee** *n.* Filterkaffee, *der*; ~ **lane** *n.* (Brit.) Abbiegespur, *die*; ~ **tip** *n.* **(a)** Filter, *der*; **(b)** ~ **tip [cigarette]** Filterzigarette, *die*

filth /fɪlθ/ *n., no pl.* **(a)** (disgusting dirt) Dreck, *der*; **(b)** (obscenity) Schmutz [und Schund]

filthy /'fɪlθɪ/ **1** *adj.* **(a)** (disgustingly dirty) dreckig (ugs.); schmutzig; (fig.) widerlich ‹*Angewohnheit*›; **(b)** (vile) gemein ‹*Lügner, Trick*›; ~ **lucre** schnöder Mammon (abwertend, auch scherzh.); **(c)** (obscene) schweinisch (ugs.); obszön, unflätig ‹*Sprache*›; **a** ~ **devil** ein Schweinigel (ugs.). **2** *adv.* ~ **dirty** völlig verdreckt (ugs.); ~ **rich** (coll.) stinkreich (ugs.)

fin /fɪn/ *n.* (Zool.; on boat) Flosse, *die;* (flipper) [Schwimm]flosse, *die*

final /'faɪnl/ **1** *adj.* **(a)** (ultimate) letzt...; End‹*spiel, -stadium, -stufe, -ergebnis*›; Schluss‹*bericht, -szene, -etappe, -phase*›; ~ **examination** Abschlussprüfung, *die;* **give a** ~ **wave** ein letztes Mal winken; **(b)** (conclusive) endgültig ‹*Urteil, Entscheidung*›; **is this your** ~ **decision/word?** ist das Ihr letztes Wort?; **I'm not coming with you, and that's** ~! ich komme nicht mit, und damit basta! (ugs.). **2** *n.* **(a)** (Sport etc.) Finale, *das;* (of quiz game) Endrunde, *die;* **(b)** *in pl.* (examination) Abschlussprüfung, *die;* (at university) Examen, *das*

finale /fɪ'nɑːlɪ/ *n.* Finale, *das*

finalise ⇒ **finalize**

finalist /'faɪnəlɪst/ *n.* Teilnehmer/Teilnehmerin in der Endausscheidung; (Sport) Finalist, *der*/Finalistin, *die*

finality /faɪ'nælɪtɪ/ *n., no pl.* Endgültigkeit, *die;* (of tone of voice) Entschiedenheit, *die*

finalize /'faɪnəlaɪz/ *v.t.* [endgültig] beschließen; unter Dach und Fach bringen ‹*Geschäft, Vertrag*›; (complete) zum Abschluss bringen

finally /'faɪnəlɪ/ *adv.* **(a)** (in the end) schließlich; (expressing impatience etc.) endlich; **(b)** (in conclusion) zum Schluss; (once for all) ein für allemal

finance /fɪ'næns, 'faɪnæns/ **1** *n.* **(a)** *in pl.* (resources) Finanzen *Pl.;* **(b)** (management of money) Geldwesen, *das;* **(c)** (support) Gelder *Pl.* (ugs.); Geldmittel *Pl.* **2** *v.t.* finanzieren; finanziell unterstützen ‹*Person*›

financial /faɪ'nænʃl, fɪ'nænʃl/ *adj.* finanziell; Finanz‹*mittel, -quelle, -experte, -lage*›; Geld‹*mittel, -geber, -sorgen*›; Wirtschafts‹*nachrichten, -bericht*›

financially /faɪ'nænʃəlɪ, fɪ'nænʃəlɪ/ *adv.* finanziell

financial 'year *n.* Geschäftsjahr, *das;* (im öffentlichen Haushalt) Rechnungsjahr, *das*

financier /faɪ'nænsɪə(r), fɪ'nænsɪə(r)/ *n.* Finanzier, *der*

finch /fɪnʃ/ *n.* (Ornith.) Fink[envogel], *der*

find /faɪnd/ **1** *v.t.*, **found** /faʊnd/ **(a)** (get possession of by chance) finden; (come across unexpectedly) entdecken; ~ **that** ...: herausfinden *od.* entdecken, dass ...; **he was found dead/injured** er wurde tot/verletzt aufgefunden; **(b)** (obtain) finden ‹*Zustimmung, Erleichterung, Trost, Gegenliebe*›; **have found one's feet** (be able to walk) laufen können; (be able to act by oneself) auf eigenen Füßen stehen; **(c)** (recognize as present) sehen ‹*Veranlassung, Schwierigkeit*›; (acknowledge or discover to be) finden; ~ **no difficulty in doing sth.** etw. nicht schwierig finden; ~ **sb. in/out** jmdn. antreffen/ nicht antreffen; ~ **sb./sth. to be** ...: feststellen, dass jmd./etw. ... ist/war; **(d)** (discover by trial or experience to be or do) für ... halten; **do you** ~ **him easy to get on with?** finden Sie, dass sich gut mit ihm auskommen lässt?; **she** ~**s it hard to come to terms with his death** es fällt ihr schwer, sich mit seinem Tod abzufinden; ~ **sth. necessary** etw. für nötig befinden *od.* erachten; ~ **sth./ sb. to be** ...: herausfinden, dass etw./jmd. ... ist/war; **you will** ~ **[that]** ...: Sie werden sehen *od.* feststellen, dass ...; **(e)** (discover by search) finden; **want to** ~ **sth.** etw. suchen; ~ **[again]** wieder finden; **(f)** (succeed in obtaining) finden ‹*Zeit, Mittel und Wege, Worte*›; auftreiben ‹*Geld, Gegenstand*›; aufbringen ‹*Kraft, Energie*›; ~ **it in oneself** *or* **one's heart to do sth.** es über sich *od.* übers Herz bringen, etw. zu tun; **(g)** (ascertain by study or calculation or inquiry) finden; ~ **what time the train leaves** herausfinden, wann der Zug [ab]fährt; ~ **one's way home** nach Hause zurückfinden; **(h)** (supply) besorgen; ~ **sb. sth.** *or* **sth. for sb.** jmdn. mit etw. versorgen; **all found** bei freier Kost und Logis. **2** *n.* **(a)** Fund, *der;* **make a** ~/**two** ~**s** einmal/zweimal fündig werden; **(b)** (person) Entdeckung, *die*

~ **for** *v.t.* (Law) ~ **for the defendant/plaintiff** zugunsten der Verteidigung/des Klägers entscheiden; ~

for the accused auf Freispruch erkennen
~ 'out *v.t.* (a) (discover, devise) herausfinden; bekommen 〈*Informationen*〉; **manage to ~ out how …**: herauskommen, wie …; ~ **out about** (get information on) sich informieren über (+ *Akk.*); (learn of) erfahren von; (b) (detect in offence, act of deceit, etc.) erwischen, ertappen 〈*Dieb usw.*〉

findable /'faɪndəbl/ *pred. adj.* **be [easily] ~**: [leicht] zu finden sein

finder /'faɪndə(r)/ *n.* (of sth. lost) Finder, *der*/Finderin, *die*; (of sth. unknown) Entdecker, *der*/Entdeckerin, *die*; **~s keepers** (coll.) wer's findet, dem gehört's (ugs.)

finding /'faɪndɪŋ/ *n. usu. in pl.* (conclusion) Ergebnis, *das*; (verdict) Urteil, *das*

fine¹ /faɪn/ **1** *n.* Geldstrafe, *die*; (for minor offence) Bußgeld, *das*. **2** *v.t.* mit einer Geldstrafe belegen; **we were ~d £10** wir mussten ein Bußgeld von 10 Pfund bezahlen; **be ~d for speeding** ein Bußgeld wegen überhöhter Geschwindigkeit zahlen müssen

fine² **1** *adj.* (a) (of high quality) gut; hochwertig 〈*Qualität, Lebensmittel*〉; fein 〈*Besteck, Gewebe, Spitze*〉; edel 〈*Holz, Wein*〉; (b) (delicately beautiful) zart 〈*Porzellan, Spitze*〉; fein 〈*Muster, Kristall, Stickerei, Gesichtszüge*〉; (c) (refined) edel 〈*Empfindungen*〉; fein 〈*Taktgefühl, Geschmack*〉; **sb.'s ~r feelings** das Gute in jmdm.; (d) (delicate in structure or texture) fein; (e) (thin) fein; hauchdünn; **cut it ~** knapp kalkulieren; **we'd be cutting it ~ if …** es wird etwas knapp werden, wenn …; (f) (in small particles) [hauch]fein 〈*Sand, Staub*〉; ~ **rain** Nieselregen, *der*; (g) (sharp, narrow-pointed) scharf 〈*Spitze, Klinge*〉; spitz 〈*Nadel, Schreibfeder*〉; (h) ~ **print** ⇒ **small print**; (i) (capable of delicate discrimination) fein 〈*Gehör*〉; scharf 〈*Auge*〉; genau 〈*Werkzeug*〉; empfindlich 〈*Messgerät*〉; (j) (perceptible only with difficulty) fein 〈*Unterschied, Nuancen*〉; (precise) klein 〈*Detail*〉; **the ~r points** die Feinheiten; (k) (excellent) schön; ausgezeichnet 〈*Sänger, Schauspieler*〉; **a ~ time to do sth.** (iron.) ein passender Zeitpunkt, etw. zu tun (iron.); **you 'are a ~ one!** (iron.) du bist mir vielleicht einer! (ugs.); **(l)** (satisfactory) schön; gut; **that's ~ with** *or* **by me** ja, ist mir recht; **everything is ~**: es ist alles in Ordnung; **(m)** (well conceived or expressed) schön 〈*Worte, Ausdruck usw.*〉; gelungen 〈*Rede, Übersetzung usw.*〉; **(n)** (of handsome appearance or size) schön; stattlich 〈*Mann, Baum, Tier*〉; **(o)** (in good health or state) gut; **feel ~**: sich wohl fühlen; **How are you? — F~, thanks** Wie geht es Ihnen? — Gut, danke; **(p)** (bright and clear) schön 〈*Wetter, Sommerabend*〉; ~ **and sunny** heiter und sonnig; **(q)** (ornate) prächtig 〈*Kleidung*〉; **(r)** (affectedly ornate) geziert; schönklingend 〈*Worte*〉. **2** *adv.* (a) (into small particles) fein 〈*mahlen, raspeln, hacken*〉; **(b)** (coll.: well) gut

fine 'art *n.* (a) (subject) bildende Kunst; (b) **get sth. [down] to a ~**: etw. zu einer richtigen Kunst entwickeln; (c) **the ~s** die Schönen Künste

finely /'faɪnlɪ/ *adv.* (a) (exquisitely, delicately) fein; genau 〈*ausbalanciert*〉; (b) **a ~-sharpened blade** eine sorgfältig geschärfte Klinge; **a ~-drawn line** eine fein od. dünn [aus]gezogene Linie; (c) (into small particles) fein 〈*mahlen*〉

finery /'faɪnərɪ/ *n., no pl.* Pracht, *die*; (garments etc.) Staat, *der*

finesse /fɪ'nes/ *n.* (refinement) Feinheit, *die*; (of diplomat) Gewandtheit, *die*; (delicate manipulation) Finesse, *die*

fine-tooth 'comb *n.* **go through a manuscript** *etc.*/ **house** *etc.* **with a ~** (fig.) ein Manuskript *usw.* Punkt für Punkt durchgehen/ein Haus *usw.* durchkämmen

fine-'tune *v.t.* abstimmen 〈*Computersystem, Pläne, Ausrüstung*〉; präzise einstellen 〈*Gerät, Maschine*〉; optimieren 〈*Wirtschaft*〉

finger /'fɪŋgə(r)/ **1** *n.* ▶672 Finger, *der*; **lay a ~ on sb.** (fig.) jmdm. ein Härchen krümmen (ugs.); **they never lift** *or* **raise a ~ to help her** (fig.) sie rühren keinen Finger, um ihr zu helfen; **pull** *or* **take one's ~ out** (fig. sl.) Dampf dahinter machen (ugs.); **point a** *or* **one's ~ at sb./sth.** mit dem Finger/(fig. ugs.) mit Fingern auf jmdn./etw. zeigen; **put the ~ on sb.** (fig. sl.) jmdn. verpfeifen (ugs. abwertend); **put** *or* **lay one's ~ on sth.** (fig.) etw. genau ausmachen; **sth. slips through sb.'s ~s** etw. gleitet jmdm. durch die Finger; **his ~s are [all] 'thumbs**, **he is all ~s and thumbs** er hat zwei linke Hände (ugs.); **a ~ of toast** ein

Streifen Toast. **2** *v.t.* berühren 〈*Ware*〉; (toy or meddle with) befingern; herumfingern an (+ *Dat.*)

finger: ~**board** *n.* Griffbrett, *das*; ~ **bowl** *n.* Fingerschale, *die*; ~**end** *n.* Fingerspitze, *die*; ~**mark** *n.* Fingerabdruck, *der*; ~**nail** *n.* Fingernagel, *der*; ~**print 1** *n.* Fingerabdruck, *der*; **2** *v.t.* ~**print sb.** jmdm. die Fingerabdrücke abnehmen; ~**tip** *n.* Fingerspitze, *die*; **have sth. at one's ~tips** (fig.) etw. aus dem Effeff können *od.* im kleinen Finger haben (ugs.)

finicky /'fɪnɪkɪ/ *adj.* heikel 〈*Person*〉; kniff[e]lig 〈*Arbeit, Stickerei*〉

finish /'fɪnɪʃ/ **1** *v.t.* (a) (bring to an end) beenden 〈*Unterhaltung*〉; erledigen 〈*Arbeit*〉; abschließen 〈*Kurs, Ausbildung*〉; **have ~ed sth.** etw. fertig haben; mit etw. fertig sein; **have you ~ed the letter/book?** hast du den Brief/das Buch fertig?; ~ **writing/reading sth.** etw. zu Ende schreiben/lesen; **have you quite ~ed?** sind Sie fertig?; (b) (get through) aufessen 〈*Mahlzeit*〉; auslesen 〈*Buch, Zeitung*〉; austrinken 〈*Flasche, Glas*〉; (c) (kill) umbringen; (coll.: overcome) schaffen (ugs.); (overcome completely) bezwingen 〈*Feind*〉; (ruin) zugrunde richten; **any more stress would ~ him** noch mehr Stress würde ihn kaputtmachen (ugs.); **it almost ~ed me!** das hat mich fast geschafft! (ugs.); **(d)** (perfect) vervollkommnen; den letzten Schliff geben (+ *Dat.*); ~ **a seam** einen Saum vernähen; **(e)** (complete manufacture of by surface treatment) eine schöne Oberfläche geben (+ *Dat.*); glätten 〈*Papier, Holz*〉; appretieren 〈*Gewebe, Leder*〉; **the ~ed article** *or* **product** das fertige Produkt. **2** *v.i.* (a) (reach the end) aufhören 〈*Geschichte, Episode*〉 enden; **when does the concert ~?** wann ist das Konzert aus?; (b) (come to end of race) das Ziel erreichen; ~ **first** als erster durchs Ziel gehen; erster werden; ~ **badly/well** nicht durchhalten/einen guten Endspurt haben; (c) ~ **by doing sth.** zum Schluss etw. tun. **3** *n.* (a) (termination, cause of ruin) Ende, *das*; **it would be the ~ of him as a politician** das würde das Ende seiner Karriere als Politiker bedeuten; (b) (point at which race etc. ends) Ziel, *das*; **arrive at the ~**: das Ziel erreichen; durchs Ziel gehen; (c) (what serves to give completeness) letzter Schliff; **a ~ to sth.** die Vervollkommnung *od.* Vollendung einer Sache; (d) (mode of finishing) [technische] Ausführung; Finish, *das*; **paintwork with a matt/gloss ~**: Matt-/Hochglanzlack, *der*

~ 'off *v.t.* (a) ⇒ **1 c, d**; (b) (provide with ending) abschließen; beenden; (c) (finish or trim neatly) sauber verarbeiten

~ 'up *v.i.* (a) ⇒ **2 c**; (b) = **end up**

~ **with** *v.t.* (a) (complete one's use of) **have you ~ed with the sugar?** brauchen Sie den Zucker noch?; **have ~ed with a book** ein Buch aus- *od.* fertig gelesen *od.* zu Ende gelesen haben; (b) (end association with) brechen mit; **she ~ed with her boyfriend** sie hat mit ihrem Freund Schluss gemacht

finishing: ~ **post** *n.* Zielpfosten, *der*; ~ **'touch** *n.* **as a ~ touch to sth.** zur Vollendung *od.* Vervollkommnung einer Sache; um eine Sache abzurunden; **put the ~ touches to sth.** einer Sache (*Dat.*) den letzten Schliff geben

finite /'faɪnaɪt/ (a) (bounded) begrenzt; ~ **number** (Math.) endliche Zahl; (b) (Ling.) finit

Finland /'fɪnlənd/ *pr. n.* Finnland (*das*)

Finn /fɪn/ *n.* ▶947 Finne, *der*/Finnin, *die*

Finnish /'fɪnɪʃ/ ▶897, ▶947 **1** *adj.* finnisch; **sb. is ~**: jmd. ist Finne/Finnin; **the ~ language** das Finnische. **2** *n.* Finnisch, *das; see also* **English 2 a**

fiord /fjɔːd/ *n.* Fjord, *der*

fir /fɜː(r)/ *n.* (a) (tree) Tanne, *die*; (b) (wood) Tanne, *die*; Tannenholz, *das*

'fir cone *n.* Tannenzapfen, *der*

fire /'faɪə(r)/ **1** *n.* (a) Feuer, *das*; **set ~ to sth.** 〈*Person*〉 etw. anzünden; **be on ~**: brennen (auch fig.); in Flammen stehen; **catch ~**: Feuer fangen 〈*Wald, Gebäude*〉 in Brand geraten; **set sth. on ~**: etw. anzünden; (in order to destroy) etw. in Brand stecken; (deliberately) Feuer an etw. (*Akk.*) legen; (b) (in grate) [offenes] Feuer; (electric or gas ~) Heizofen, *der*; (in the open air) Lagerfeuer, *das*; **open ~**: Kaminfeuer, *das*; **turn up the ~** (electric) die Heizung/(gas) das Gas höher drehen *od.* aufdrehen; **play with ~** (lit. or fig.)

mit dem Feuer spielen; **light the** ∼: den Ofen anstecken; (in grate) das [Kamin]feuer anmachen; **(c)** (destructive burning) Brand, *der;* **in case of** ∼: bei Feuer; **where's the** ∼? (coll. iron.) wo brennt's denn? **(d)** (fervour) Feuer, *das;* **the** ∼ **with which he speaks** die Leidenschaft, mit der er spricht; **(e)** (firing of guns) Schießen, *das;* Schießerei, *die;* **pistol** ∼: [Pistolen]schüsse; **cannon** ∼: Kanonenfeuer, *das;* **line of** ∼ (lit. or fig.) Schusslinie, *die;* **be/come under** ∼: beschossen werden/unter Beschuss geraten. **2** *v.t.* **(a)** (fill with enthusiasm) begeistern, in Begeisterung versetzen ⟨*Person*⟩; **(b)** (supply with fuel) befeuern ⟨*Ofen*⟩; [be]heizen ⟨*Lokomotive*⟩; **(c)** (discharge) abschießen ⟨*Gewehr*⟩; abfeuern ⟨*Kanone*⟩; ∼ **one's gun/pistol/rifle at sb.** auf jmdn. schießen; **(d)** (propel from gun etc.) abgeben, abfeuern ⟨*Schuss*⟩; ∼ **questions at sb.** jmdn. mit Fragen bombardieren; Fragen auf jmdn. abfeuern; **(e)** (coll.: dismiss) feuern (ugs.) ⟨*Angestellten*⟩; **(f)** brennen ⟨*Tonwaren, Ziegel*⟩. **3** *v.i.* **(a)** (shoot) schießen; feuern; ∼! [gebt] Feuer!; **be the first to** ∼: das Feuer eröffnen; ∼ **at/on sth./sb.** auf etw./ jmdn. schießen; **(b)** ⟨*Motor:*⟩ zünden

∼ **a'way** *v.i.* **(a)** (fig. coll.) losschießen (fig. ugs.); ∼ **away!** schieß los!; fang an!

fire: ∼ **alarm** *n.* Feuermelder, *der;* ∼**arm** *n.* Schusswaffe, *die;* ∼**ball** *n.* (ball of flame) Feuerball, *der;* ∼**bomb 1** *n.* Brandsatz, *der;* (aerial bomb) Brandbombe, *die;* ∼ **bomb attack** Brandanschlag, *der;* **2** *v.t.* ∼**bomb sth.** einen Brandanschlag auf etw. (*Akk.*) verüben; ∼**break** *n.* Brandschneise, *die;* ∼**brigade** (Brit.) *n.* Feuerwehr, *die;* ∼ **chief** *n.* (Amer.) Branddirektor, *der;* ∼ **department** *n.* (Amer.) Feuerwehr, *die;* ∼ **drill** *n.* Probe[feuer]alarm, *der;* (for ∼men) Feuerwehrübung, *die;* ∼**-eater** *n.* Feuerschlucker, *der;* ∼ **engine** *n.* Löschfahrzeug, *das;* ∼ **escape** *n.* (staircase) Feuertreppe, *die;* (ladder) Feuerleiter, *die;* ∼ **exit** *n.* Notausgang, *der;* ∼ **extinguisher** *n.* Feuerlöscher, *der;* ∼**fighter** *n.* ▶ 887 Feuerwehrmann, *der*/-frau, *die;* ∼**fly** *n.* Leuchtkäfer, *der;* ∼**guard** *n.* Kamingitter, *das;* ∼ **hazard** *n.* Brandrisiko, *das;* ∼ **hose** *n.* Feuerwehrschlauch, *der;* ∼ **insurance** *n.* Feuer- *od.* Brandversicherung, *die;* ∼**lighter** *n.* (Brit.) Feueranzünder, *der;* ∼**man** /'faɪəmən/ *n., pl.* ∼**men** /'faɪəmən/ ▶ 887 **(a)** (member of ∼ brigade) Feuerwehrmann, *der;* **(b)** (Railw.) Heizer, *der;* ∼**place** *n.* Kamin, *der;* ∼**power** *n.* Feuerkraft, *die* (Milit.); ∼**-practice** ⇒ ∼ **drill;** ∼**proof 1** *adj.* feuerfest; **2** *v.t.* feuerfest machen; ∼**-resistant** *adj.* feuerbeständig; schwer entflammbar; **F**∼ **Service** *n.* Feuerwehr, *die;* ∼**side** *n.* Kaminecke, *die;* **at** *or* **by the** ∼**side am** Kamin; ∼ **station** *n.* Feuerwache, *die;* ∼**wall** *n.* **(a)** Feuer[schutz]wand, *die;* **(b)** (Computing) Firewall, *die od. der;* ∼**wood** *n.* Brennholz, *das;* ∼**work** *n.* **(a)** Feuerwerkskörper, *der;* ∼**work display** Feuerwerk, *das;* **(b)** *in pl.* (display) Feuerwerk, *das;* **there were** *or* **it caused** ∼**works** (fig.) da war was los *od.* flogen die Funken (ugs.)

firing /'faɪərɪŋ/ *n.* **(a)** (of pottery) Brennen, *das;* **(b)** *no pl.* (of guns) Abfeuern, *das;* **we could hear** ∼ **in the distance** in der Ferne konnten wir Schüsse hören

firing: ∼ **line** *n.* (lit. or fig.) Feuerlinie, *die;* ∼ **squad** *n.* (at military execution) Exekutionskommando, *das*

firm[1] /fɜːm/ *n.* Firma, *die;* ∼ **of architects/decorators** Architektenbüro, *das*/Malerbetrieb, *der*

firm[2] **1** *adj.* **(a)** fest; stabil ⟨*Verhältnis, Konstruktion, Stuhl*⟩; straff ⟨*Busen*⟩; verbindlich ⟨*Angebot*⟩; **be on** ∼ **ground again** (lit. or fig.) wieder festen Boden unter den Füßen haben; **they are** ∼ **friends** sie sind gut befreundet; **the chair is not** ∼: der Stuhl ist wacklig *od.* wackelt; **(b)** (resolute) entschlossen ⟨*Blick*⟩; bestimmt, entschieden ⟨*Ton*⟩; **be a** ∼ **believer in sth.** fest an etw. (*Akk.*) glauben; **(c)** (insisting on obedience etc.) bestimmt; **be** ∼ **with sb.** jmdm. gegenüber bestimmt auftreten. **2** *adv.* **stand** ∼! (fig.) sei standhaft!; **hold** ∼ **to sth.** (fig.) an einer Sache festhalten. **3** *v.t.* fest werden lassen; festigen, straffen ⟨*Muskulatur, Körper*⟩

firmly /'fɜːmlɪ/ *adv.* **(a)** fest; **a** ∼**-built structure** eine stabile Konstruktion; **(b)** (resolutely) beharrlich ⟨*unterstützen, sich widersetzen*⟩; bestimmt, energisch ⟨*reden*⟩

firmness /'fɜːmnɪs/ *n., no pl.* **(a)** (solidity) Festigkeit, *die;* (of foundations, building) Stabilität, *die;* **(b)** (resoluteness) Entschlossenheit, *die;* (of voice) Bestimmtheit, *die;* **(c)** (insistence on obedience etc.) Bestimmtheit, *die*

'**firmware** *n., no pl., no indef. art.* (Computing) Firmware, *die*

first /fɜːst/ ▶ 956 **1** *adj.* erst...; (for the ∼ time ever) Erst⟨*aufführung, -besteigung*⟩; (of an artist's ∼ achievement) Erstlings⟨*film, -roman, -stück, -werk*⟩; **he was** ∼ **to arrive** er kam als erster an; **for the [very]** ∼ **time** zum [aller]ersten Mal; **the** ∼ **two** die ersten beiden *od.* zwei; **come in** ∼ (win race) [das Rennen] gewinnen; **head/feet** ∼: mit dem Kopf/den Füßen zuerst *od.* voran; ∼ **thing in the morning** gleich frühmorgens; (coll.: tomorrow) gleich morgen früh; ∼ **things** ∼ (coll.) eins nach dem anderen; **he's always [the]** ∼ **to help** er ist immer als erster zur Stelle, wenn Hilfe benötigt wird; **not know the** ∼ **thing about sth.** von einer Sache nicht das geringste verstehen. **2** *adv.* **(a)** (before anyone else) zuerst; als erster/erste ⟨*sprechen, ankommen*⟩; (before anything else) an erster Stelle ⟨*stehen, kommen*⟩; (when listing: firstly) zuerst; als erstes; **ladies** ∼! Ladys first!; den Damen der Vortritt!; **you [go]** ∼ (as invitation) Sie haben den Vortritt; bitte nach Ihnen; ∼ **come** ∼ **served** wer zuerst kommt, mahlt zuerst (Spr.); **say** ∼ **one thing and then another** erst so und dann wieder so sagen (ugs.); **(b)** (beforehand) vorher; ...**but** ∼ **we must** ...: ... aber zuerst *od.* erst müssen wir ...; **(c)** (for the ∼ time) zum ersten Mal; (at first) erstmals ⟨*bekannt geben, sich durchsetzen*⟩; **(d)** (in preference) eher; lieber; **(e)** ∼ **of all** zuerst; (in importance) vor allem; ∼ **and foremost** (basically) zunächst einmal. **3** *n.* **(a) the** ∼ (in sequence, rank) der/die/das Erste; **be the** ∼ **to arrive** als Erster/Erste ankommen; **she is the** ∼ **in the class** sie ist Klassenbeste; **this is the** ∼ **I've heard of it** das höre ich zum ersten Mal; **(b) at** ∼: zuerst; anfangs; **from the** ∼: von Anfang an; **from** ∼ **to last** von Anfang bis Ende; **(c)** ▶ 738 (day) **the** ∼ **of May** der erste Mai; **the** ∼ **[of the month]** der Erste [des Monats]

first: ∼ **'aid** *n.* Erste Hilfe; **give [sb.]** ∼ **aid** [jmdm.] Erste Hilfe leisten; ∼**-born 1** *adj.* erstgeboren; **2** *n.* Erstgeborene, *der/die;* ∼ '**class** *n.* **(a)** erste Kategorie; **(b)** (Transport, Post) erste Klasse; **(c)** (Brit. Univ.) ≈ Eins, *die;* ∼**-class 1** /'--/ *adj.* **(a)** (of the ∼ class) erster Klasse nachgestellt; Erster-Klasse-⟨*Fahrkarte, Abteil, Passagier, Post, Brief usw.*⟩; ∼**-class stamp** Briefmarke für einen Erster-Klasse-Brief; **(b)** (excellent) erstklassig; **2** /-'-/ *adv.* erster Klasse ⟨*fahren*⟩; ∼**-class letter** ∼**-class** *einen Brief mit Erster-Klasse-Post schicken;* ∼ '**cousin** ⇒ **cousin;** ∼ **e'dition** *n.* Erstausgabe, *die;* ∼ '**floor** ⇒ **floor 1 b** ∼ '**gear** *n., no pl.* (Motor Veh.) erster Gang; *see also* **gear 1 a;** ∼**hand** *adj.* aus erster Hand nachgestellt; **from** ∼**hand experience** aus eigener Erfahrung; ∼ '**light** *n.* **at** ∼ **light** im *od.* beim Morgengrauen

firstly /'fɜːstlɪ/ *adv.* zunächst [einmal]; (followed by 'secondly') erstens

first: ∼ **name** *n.* Vorname, *der;* ∼ '**night** *n.* (Theatre) Premiere, *die;* ∼ '**officer** *n.* (Naut.) Erster Offizier; ∼**-rate** *adj.* erstklassig; ∼ **school** *n.* (Brit.) ≈ Grundschule, *die*

'**fir tree** ⇒ **fir a**

fiscal /'fɪskl/ *adj.* fiskalisch; finanzpolitisch

fish /fɪʃ/ **1** *n., pl. same* **(a)** Fisch, *der;* ∼ **and chips** Fisch mit Pommes frites; **[be] like a** ∼ **out of water** [sich] wie ein Fisch auf dem Trockenen [fühlen]; **there are plenty more** ∼ **in the sea** (fig. coll.) es gibt noch andere auf der Welt; **(b)** (coll.: person) **queer** ∼: komischer Kauz; **big** ∼: großes Tier (ugs., scherzh.). **2** *v.i.* **(a)** fischen; (with rod) angeln; **go** ∼**ing** fischen/angeln gehen; **(b)** (fig. coll.) (try to get information) auf Informationen aus sein; (delve) ∼ **around in one's bag** in der Tasche herumsuchen. **3** *v.t.* fischen; (with rod) angeln

∼ **for** *v.t.* **(a)** fischen/angeln; fischen/angeln auf (+ *Akk.*) (Anglerjargon); **(b)** (fig. coll.) suchen nach

∼ '**out** *v.t.* (fig. coll.) herausfischen (ugs.)

fish: ∼ **bone** *n.* [Fisch]gräte, *die;* ∼ **cake** *n.* (Cookery) Fischfrikadelle, *die*

fisherman /'fɪʃəmən/ n., pl. **fishermen** /'fɪʃəmən/ ▶ 887 | Fischer, der; (angler) Angler, der

fishery /'fɪʃərɪ/ n. (part of sea) Fischfanggebiet, das; Fischereigewässer, das

fish: ∼ **'finger** n. Fischstäbchen, das; ∼-**hook** n. Angelhaken, der

fishing: ∼ **boat** n. Fischerboot, das; ∼ **net** n. Fischernetz, das; ∼ **rod** n. Angelrute, die; ∼ **tackle** n. Angelgeräte

fish: ∼ **knife** n. Fischmesser, das; ∼**monger** /'fɪʃmʌŋgə(r)/ n. ▶ 887 | (Brit.) Fischhändler, der/-händlerin, die; ∼**net** n. Fischnetz, das; ∼**net stockings** Netzstrümpfe; ∼ **shop** n. Fischgeschäft, das; ∼ **slice** n. Wender, der; ∼ **tank** n. Fischkasten, der; Fischbehälter, der

fishy /'fɪʃɪ/ adj. (a) fischartig; ∼ **taste/smell** Fischgeschmack/-geruch, der; (b) (coll.: suspect) verdächtig

fission /'fɪʃn/ n. (Nucl. Phys.) [Kern]spaltung, die; Fission, die (fachspr.)

fissure /'fɪʃə(r)/ n. Riß, der

fist /fɪst/ n. Faust, die

fistful /'fɪstfʊl/ n. Handvoll, die

fit¹ /fɪt/ n. (a) Anfall, der; ∼ **of coughing** Hustenanfall, der; **epileptic** ∼: epileptischer Anfall; (b) (fig.) [plötzliche] Anwandlung; **have** or **throw a** ∼: einen Anfall bekommen; **[almost] have** or **throw a** ∼ (fig.) [fast] Zustände kriegen (ugs.); **be in** ∼**s of laughter** sich vor Lachen biegen; **sb./sth. has sb. in** ∼**s [of laughter]** jmd. ruft dröhnendes Gelächter bei jmdm. hervor

fit² 1 adj. (a) (suitable) geeignet; ∼ **to eat** or **to be eaten/ for human consumption** essbar/zum Verzehr geeignet; (b) (worthy) würdig; wert; (c) (right and proper) richtig; **see** or **think** ∼ **[to do sth.]** es für richtig od. angebracht halten[, etw. zu tun]; (d) (ready) **be** ∼ **to drop** zum Umfallen müde sein; (e) (healthy) gesund; fit (ugs.); in Form (ugs.); ∼ **for duty** or **service** dienstfähig od. -tauglich; see also **fiddle** 1 a. 2 n. Passform, die; **it is a good/bad** ∼: es sitzt od. passt gut/nicht gut; **I can just get it in the suitcase, but it's a tight** ∼ (fig.) ich kriege es noch in den Koffer, aber nur gerade so (ugs.). 3 v.t., -**tt-:** (a) ⟨Kleider:⟩ passen (+ Dat.); ⟨Schlüssel:⟩ passen in (+ Akk.); ⟨Deckel, Bezug:⟩ passen auf (+ Akk.); (b) (make suitable) anpassen ⟨Kleidungsstück, Brille⟩; (c) (correspond to, suit) entsprechen (+ Dat.); (make correspond) abstimmen (**to** auf + Akk.); anpassen (**to** an + Akk.); (d) (put into place) anbringen (**to** an + Dat. od. Akk.); einbauen ⟨Motor, Ersatzteil⟩; einsetzen ⟨Scheibe, Tür, Schloss⟩; (equip) ausstatten. 4 v.i., -**tt**- passen; (agree) zusammenpassen; übereinstimmen; ∼ **well** ⟨Kleidungsstück:⟩ gut sitzen

∼ **'in** 1 v.t. (a) unterbringen; (b) (to a schedule) einen Termin geben (+ Dat.); unterbringen, einschieben ⟨Treffen, Besuch, Sitzung⟩. 2 v.i. (a) hineinpassen; (b) (be in accordance) ∼ **in with sth.** mit etw. übereinstimmen; ∼ **in with sb.'s plan/ideas** in jmds. Plan/Konzept (Akk.) passen; (c) (settle harmoniously) ⟨Person:⟩ sich anpassen (**with** an + Akk.); ∼ **in easily with a group** sich leicht in eine Gruppe einfügen

∼ **'out** v.t. ausstatten; (for expedition etc.) ausrüsten

fitful /'fɪtfl/ adj. unbeständig; unruhig ⟨Schlaf⟩; launisch ⟨Brise⟩

fitment /'fɪtmənt/ n. (piece of furniture) Einrichtungsgegenstand, der; (piece of equipment) Zubehörteil, das

fitness /'fɪtnɪs/ n., no pl. (a) (physical) Fitness, die; (b) (suitability) Eignung, die; (appropriateness) Angemessenheit, die

fitted /'fɪtɪd/ adj. (a) (suited) geeignet (**for** für, zu); (b) tailliert, auf Taille gearbeitet ⟨Kleider⟩; ∼ **carpet** Teppichboden, der; ∼ **kitchen/cupboards** Einbauküche, die/ Einbauschränke

fitter /'fɪtə(r)/ n. ▶ 887 | Monteur, der; (of pipes) Installateur, der; (of machines) Maschinenschlosser, der; **electrical** ∼: Elektriker, der

fitting /'fɪtɪŋ/ 1 adj. (appropriate) passend; angemessen; geeignet ⟨Moment, Zeitpunkt⟩; günstig, passend ⟨Gelegenheit⟩; (becoming) schicklich (geh.) ⟨Benehmen⟩. 2 n. (a) usu. in pl. (fixture) Anschluss, der; ∼**s** (furniture) Ausstattung, die; (b) (of clothes) Anprobe, die

five /faɪv/ ▶ 630 |, ▶ 706 |, ▶ 956 | 1 adj. (a) fünf; see also **eight** 1; (b) ∼ **o'clock shadow** [nachmittäglicher] Stoppelbart (ugs.). 2 n. Fünf, die; see also **eight** 2 a, c, d

five-and-'dime, **five-and-'ten** n. (Amer.) Billigkaufhaus, das

fiver /'faɪvə(r)/ n. (coll.) (Brit.) Fünfpfundschein, der; (Amer.) Fünfdollarschein, der

fix /fɪks/ 1 v.t. (a) (place firmly, attach, prevent from moving) befestigen; festmachen; ∼ **sth. to/on sth.** etw. an/auf etw. (Dat.) befestigen od. festmachen; ∼ **shelves to the wall/ a handle on the door** Regale an der Wand/eine Klinke an der Tür anbringen; ∼ **sth. in one's mind** sich (Dat.) etw. fest einprägen; (b) (direct steadily) richten ⟨Blick, Gedanken, Augen⟩ ([up]on auf + Akk.); (c) (decide, specify) festsetzen, festlegen ⟨Termin, Preis, Strafe, Grenze⟩; (settle, agree on) ausmachen; **it was** ∼**ed that** …: es wurde beschlossen od. vereinbart, dass …; (d) (repair) in Ordnung bringen; reparieren; (e) (arrange) arrangieren; ∼ **a rehearsal for Friday** eine Probe für od. auf Freitag (Akk.) ansetzen; **nothing definite has been** ∼**ed yet** es ist noch nichts Endgültiges vereinbart od. ausgemacht; (f) (manipulate fraudulently) manipulieren ⟨Rennen, Kampf⟩; **the whole thing was** ∼**ed** das war eine abgekartete Sache (ugs.); (g) (Amer. coll.: prepare) machen ⟨Essen, Kaffee, Drink⟩; (h) (sl.: deal with) in Ordnung bringen; regeln; ∼ **sb.** (get even with) es jmdm. heimzahlen; (kill) jmdn. kaltmachen (salopp). 2 n. (a) (coll.: predicament) Klemme, die (ugs.); **be in a** ∼: in der Klemme sein (ugs.); (b) (sl.: of drugs) Fix, der (Drogenjargon)

∼ **on** v.t. (a) /'-'-/ anbringen; (b) /'--/ (decide on) sich entscheiden für

∼ **'up** v.t. (a) (arrange) arrangieren; festsetzen, ausmachen ⟨Termin, Treffpunkt⟩; **we've nothing** ∼**ed up for tonight** wir haben noch nichts vor [für] heute Abend; (b) (provide) versorgen; (provide with accommodation) unterbringen; ∼ **sb. up with sth.** jmdm. etw. verschaffen od. besorgen

fixation /fɪk'seɪʃn/ n. Fixierung, die

fixed /fɪkst/ adj. (a) pred. (coll.: placed) **how are you/is he** etc. ∼ **for cash/fuel?** wie sieht's bei dir/ihm usw. mit dem Geld/Treibstoff aus? (ugs.); (b) (not variable) fest; starr ⟨Lächeln, Gesichtsausdruck⟩; ∼ **assets** Anlagevermögen, das

fixed: ∼ **price** n. Festpreis, der; ∼-**rate** attrib. adj. Festzins od. festem Zins nachgestellt

fixture /'fɪkstʃə(r)/ n. (a) (furnishing) eingebautes Teil; (accessory) festes Zubehörteil; ∼**s and fittings** Ausstattung und Installationen; (b) (Sport) Veranstaltung, die

fizz /fɪz/ 1 v.i. [zischend] sprudeln. 2 n. (effervescence) Sprudeln, das

fizzle /'fɪzl/ v.i. zischen

∼ **'out** v.i. ⟨Feuerwerk:⟩ zischend verlöschen; ⟨Begeisterung:⟩ sich legen; ⟨Kampagne:⟩ im Sande verlaufen

fizzy /'fɪzɪ/ adj. sprudelnd; ∼ **lemonade** Brause[limonade], die; ∼ **drinks** kohlensäurehaltige Getränke

flab /flæb/ n. (coll.) Fett, das; Speck, der (ugs.)

flabbergast /'flæbəga:st/ v.t. verblüffen; umhauen (ugs.)

flabby /'flæbɪ/ adj. schlaff ⟨Muskeln, Bauch, Fleisch, Hände, Wangen, Brüste⟩; wabbelig (ugs.), schwammig ⟨Bauch, Fleisch⟩

flag¹ /flæg/ n. Fahne, die; (small paper etc. device) Fähnchen, das; (national ∼, on ship) Flagge, die; **keep the** ∼ **flying** (fig.) die Fahne hochhalten

∼ **'down** v.t. [durch Winken] anhalten

flag² v.i., -**gg**- ⟨Person:⟩ abbauen; ⟨Kraft, Interesse, Begeisterung:⟩ nachlassen; **business is** ∼**ging** die Geschäfte lassen nach

'flag day n. (Brit.) Tag der Straßensammlung für wohltätige Zwecke

flagon /'flægən/ n. Kanne, die

'flagpole n. Flaggenmast, der

flagrant /'fleɪgrənt/ adj. eklatant; flagrant ⟨Verstoß⟩; (scandalous) ungeheuerlich; himmelschreiend ⟨Unrecht⟩

flag: ∼**ship** n. (Navy) Flaggschiff, das; (fig. attrib.) führend…; ∼**stone** n. Steinplatte, die; (for floor) Fliese, die; in pl. (pavement) Straßenpflaster, das

flail /fleɪl/ *v.i.* [wild] um sich schlagen; **with arms ~ing he tried to keep his balance** mit den Armen fuchtelnd, versuchte er, das Gleichgewicht zu halten

flair /fleə(r)/ *n.* Gespür, *das;* (special ability) Talent, *das;* [natürliche] Begabung; **have a ~ for sth.** (talent) ein Talent *od.* eine Begabung für etw. haben

flak /flæk/ *n.* Flakfeuer, *das* (Milit.); **get a lot of ~ for sth.** (fig.) wegen etw. [schwer] unter Beschuss geraten

flake /fleɪk/ **1** *n.* (of snow, soap, cereals) Flocke, *die;* (of dry skin) Schuppe, *die;* (of enamel, paint) ≈ Splitter, *der.* **2** *v.i.* ⟨*Stuck, Verputz, Stein:*⟩ abbröckeln; ⟨*Farbe, Rost, Emaille:*⟩ abblättern; ⟨*Haut:*⟩ sich schuppen

flaky /ˈfleɪkɪ/ *adj.* bröcklig ⟨*Farbe, Gips, Rost*⟩; blättrig ⟨*Kruste*⟩; schuppig ⟨*Haut*⟩; **~ pastry** Blätterteig, *der*

flamboyance /flæmˈbɔɪəns/ *n.* Extravaganz, *die;* (of clothes, lifestyle) Pracht, *die*

flamboyant /flæmˈbɔɪənt/ *adj.* extravagant; prächtig ⟨*Farben, Federkleid*⟩

flame /fleɪm/ *n.* **1** (a) Flamme, *die;* **be in ~s** in Flammen stehen; **burst into ~:** in Brand geraten; (b) (joc.: boyfriend/girlfriend) Flamme, *die* (ugs.); **old ~:** alte Flamme (ugs. veralt.); (c) (Computing) Flame, *die.* **2** *v.t.* (Computing) ~ **sb.** jmdm. eine Flame/Flames schicken; **the PC was ~d** die PC wurde mit Flames überzogen

flamenco /fləˈmeŋkəʊ/ *n., pl.* **~s** Flamenco, *der*

'flame-proof *adj.* nicht entflammbar; flammfest

flaming /ˈfleɪmɪŋ/ **1** *adj.* (a) (bright-coloured) feuerrot; flammend ⟨*Rot, Abendhimmel*⟩; (b) (very hot) glühend heiß; (coll.: passionate) heftig, leidenschaftlich ⟨*Auseinandersetzung*⟩; (c) (coll.: damned) verdammt. **2** *adv.* (coll.: damned) **he is too ~ idle** *or* **lazy** er ist, verdammt noch mal, einfach zu faul (ugs.)

flamingo /fləˈmɪŋgəʊ/ *n., pl.* **~s** *or* **~es** (Ornith.) Flamingo, *der*

flammable /ˈflæməbl/ ⇒ **inflammable a**

flan /flæn/ *n.* [fruit] **~:** [Obst]torte, *die*

Flanders /ˈflɑːndəz/ *pr. n.* Flandern (*das*)

flange /flændʒ/ *n.* Flansch, *der*

flank /flæŋk/ *n.* (of person) Seite, *die;* (of animal; also Mil.) Flanke, *die*

flannel /ˈflænl/ *n.* (a) (fabric) Flanell, *der;* (b) (Brit.: for washing oneself) Waschlappen, *der;* (c) (Brit. coll.: verbose nonsense) Geschwafel, *das* (ugs. abwertend)

flap /flæp/ **1** *v.t.* **-pp-** schlagen; **~ its wings** mit den Flügeln schlagen; (at short intervals) [mit den Flügeln] flattern. **2** *v.i.* **-pp-:** (a) ⟨*Flügel:*⟩ schlagen; ⟨*Segel, Fahne, Vorhang:*⟩ flattern; (b) **sb.'s ears were ~ping** (was very interested) jmd. spitzte die Ohren; (c) (fig. coll.: panic) die Nerven verlieren. **3** *n.* (a) Klappe, *die;* (seal on envelope, tongue of shoe) Lasche, *die;* (b) (fig. coll.: panic) **be in a ~:** furchtbar aufgeregt sein

flare /fleə(r)/ **1** *v.i.* (a) (blaze) flackern; (fig.) ausbrechen; **tempers ~d** die Gemüter erhitzten sich; (b) (widen) sich erweitern. **2** *n.* (a) (as signal; also Naut.) Leuchtsignal, *das;* (from pistol) Leuchtkugel, *die;* (b) (blaze of light) Lichtschein, *der;* (c) (widening) **skirt/trousers with ~s** ausgestellter Rock/ausgestellte Hose

~ 'up *v.i.* (a) (burn more fiercely) aufflackern; auflodern; (b) (break out) [wieder] ausbrechen; (c) (become angry) aufbrausen; aus der Haut fahren (ugs.)

flash /flæʃ/ **1** *n.* (a) (of light) Aufleuchten, *das;* Aufblinken, *das;* (as signal) Lichtsignal, *das;* **~ of lightning** Blitz, *der;* **~ in the pan** (fig. coll.) Zufallstreffer, *der;* (b) (Photog.) Blitzlicht, *das;* (c) (fig.) **~ of genius** *or* **inspiration** *or* **brilliance** Geistesblitz, *der;* **~ of insight** *or* **intuition** Eingebung, *die;* (d) (instant) **be over in a ~:** gleich *od.* (ugs.) im Nu vorbei sein. **2** *v.t.* (a) aufleuchten lassen; **~ the/one's headlights** aufblenden; die Lichthupe betätigen; (b) (fig.) **her eyes ~ed fire** ihre Augen sprühten Feuer *od.* funkelten böse; **~ sb. a smile/glance** jmdm. ein Lächeln/einen Blick zuwerfen; (c) (display briefly) kurz zeigen; **~ one's money about** *or* **around** mit [dem] Geld um sich werfen (ugs.); (d) (Communications) durchgeben. **3** *v.i.* (a) aufleuchten; **the lightning ~ed** es blitzte; **~ at sb. with one's headlamps** jmdn. anblinken *od.* mit der Lichthupe anblinken; (b) (fig.) **her eyes ~ed in anger**

ihre Augen blitzten vor Zorn; (c) (move swiftly) **~ by** *or* **past** vorbeiflitzen (ugs.); (fig.) ⟨*Zeit, Ferien:*⟩ wie im Fluge vergehen; (d) (burst suddenly into perception) **sth. ~ed through my mind** etw. schoß mir durch den Kopf; (e) (Brit. sl.: expose oneself) sich [unsittlich] entblößen

flash: **~back** *n.* (Cinemat. etc.) Rückblende, *die* (to auf + Akk.); **~bulb** *n.* (Photog.) Blitzbirnchen, *das;* **~cube** *n.* (Photog.) Blitzwürfel, *der;* **~ flood** *n.* Überschwemmung, *die* (durch heftige Regenfälle;) **~gun** *n.* (Photog.) Blitzlichtgerät, *das;* **~light** *n.* (a) (for signals) Blinklicht, *das;* (b) (Photog.) Blitzlicht, *das;* (c) (Amer.: torch) Taschenlampe, *die;* **~point** *n.* Flammpunkt, *der;* (fig.) Siedepunkt, *der*

flashy /ˈflæʃɪ/ *adj.* auffällig; protzig (ugs. abwertend)

flask /flɑːsk/ *n.* (a) ⇒ **Thermos; vacuum flask;** (b) (for wine, oil) [bauchige] Flasche; (Chem.) Kolben, *der*

flat¹ /flæt/ *n.* (Brit.: dwelling) Wohnung, *die*

flat² **1** *adj.* (a) flach; eben ⟨*Fläche*⟩; platt ⟨*Nase, Reifen*⟩; **spread the blanket ~ on the ground** die Decke glatt auf dem Boden ausbreiten; (b) (fig.) (monotonous) eintönig; (dull) lahm (ugs.); fade; (stale) schal, abgestanden ⟨*Bier, Sekt*⟩; (Electr.) leer ⟨*Batterie*⟩; **fall ~:** nicht ankommen (ugs.); seine Wirkung verfehlen; (c) (downright) glatt (ugs.); [and] that's **~:** und damit basta (ugs.); (d) (Mus.) [um einen Halbton] erniedrigt ⟨*Note*⟩. **2** *adv.* (a) (coll.: completely) **~ broke** total pleite; (b) (coll.: exactly) **in two hours ~:** in genau zwei Stunden. **3** *n.* (a) flache Seite; **~ of the hand** Handfläche, *die;* (b) (level ground) Ebene, *die;* (c) (Mus.) erniedrigter Ton

flat: **~-chested** /flæt'tʃestɪd/ *adj.* flachbrüstig; flachbusig; **~ 'feet** *n. pl.* Plattfüße; **~fish** *n.* Plattfisch, *der;* **~-footed** /flæt'fʊtɪd/ *adj.* plattfüßig

flatly /ˈflætlɪ/ *adv.* rundweg; glatt (ugs.)

'flatmate *n.* (Brit.) Mitbewohner, *der*/Mitbewohnerin, *die;* **they were ~s** sie haben eine Wohnung geteilt

flatness /ˈflætnɪs/ *n., no pl.* Flachheit, *die;* (of nose) Plattheit, *die*

flat: **~ 'out** *adv.* ▶ 1102 **he ran/worked ~ out** er rannte/arbeitete, so schnell er konnte; **~-pack** *adj.* ⟨*Möbel*⟩ zum Selbstbauen; **~ race** *n.* Flachrennen, *das*

flatten /ˈflætn/ **1** *v.t.* flach *od.* platt drücken ⟨*Schachtel*⟩; dem Erdboden gleichmachen ⟨*Stadt, Gebäude*⟩. **2** *v. refl.* **~ oneself against sth.** sich flach *od.* platt gegen etw. drücken

flatter /ˈflætə(r)/ **1** *v.t.* schmeicheln (+ *Dat.*). **2** *v. refl.* **~ oneself [on being/having sth.]** sich (*Dat.*) einbilden[, etw. zu sein/haben]

flatterer /ˈflætərə(r)/ *n.* Schmeichler, *der*/Schmeichlerin, *die*

flattering /ˈflætərɪŋ/ *adj.* schmeichelhaft; schmeichlerisch ⟨*Person*⟩; vorteilhaft ⟨*Kleid, Licht, Frisur*⟩

flattery /ˈflætərɪ/ *n.* Schmeichelei, *die*

flat 'tyre *n.* Reifenpanne, *die;* (the tyre itself) platter Reifen

flatulence /ˈflætjʊləns/ *n.* Blähungen; Flatulenz, *die* (Med.)

flaunt /flɔːnt/ *v.t.* zur Schau stellen

flautist /ˈflɔːtɪst/ *n.* ▶ 887 Flötist, *der*/Flötistin, *die*

flavor etc. (Amer.) ⇒ **flavour** etc.

flavour /ˈfleɪvə(r)/ (Brit.) **1** *n.* (a) Aroma, *das;* (taste) Geschmack, *der;* **the dish lacks ~:** das Gericht schmeckt fade; **be ~ of the month** (fig.) hoch im Kurs stehen; **I'm not ~ of the month with him at the moment** er ist zur Zeit nicht gut auf mich zu sprechen; (b) (fig.) Touch, *der* (ugs.); Anflug, *der.* **2** *v.t.* (a) abschmecken; würzen; (b) (fig.) Würze verleihen (+ *Dat.*)

flavouring /ˈfleɪvərɪŋ/ *n.* (Brit.) Aroma, *das*

flaw /flɔː/ *n.* (imperfection) Makel, *der;* (in plan, argument) Fehler, *der;* (in goods) Mangel, *der*

flawless /ˈflɔːlɪs/ *adj.* (a) makellos ⟨*Schönheit*⟩; einwandfrei, fehlerlos ⟨*Aussprache, Verarbeitung*⟩; (b) (masterly) vollendet ⟨*Aufführung, Wiedergabe*⟩; (c) lupenrein ⟨*Edelstein*⟩

flax /flæks/ *n.* (a) (Bot.) Flachs, *der;* (b) (Textiles: fibre) Flachsfaser, *die;* Flachs, *der*

'flaxen-haired adj. flachsblond

flay /fleɪ/ v.t. **(a)** häuten; **(b)** (fig.: criticize) heruntermachen (ugs.)

flea /fliː/ n. Floh, der; **send sb. away** or **off with a ∼ in his/her ear** (fig. coll.) jmdn. abblitzen lassen (ugs.)

'flea bite n. Flohbiss, der; **it's just a ∼** (fig.) es ist nur eine Kleinigkeit od. (ugs.) ein Klacks

fleck /flek/ **1** n. **(a)** Tupfen, der; (small) Punkt, der; (blemish on skin) Fleck, der; **(b)** (speck) Flocke, die. **2** v.t. sprenkeln

fled ⇨ **flee**

fledg[e]ling /'fledʒlɪŋ/ n. Jungvogel, der

flee /fliː/ **1** v.i., **fled** /fled/ fliehen; **∼ from sth./sb.** aus etw./vor jmdm. flüchten od. fliehen. **2** v.t., **fled** fliehen aus; **∼ the country** aus dem Land fliehen od. flüchten

fleece /fliːs/ **1** n. Vlies, das; [Schaf]fell, das. **2** v.t. (fig.) ausplündern; (charge excessively) neppen (ugs. abwertend)

fleecy /'fliːsɪ/ adj. flauschig; **∼ cloud** Schäfchenwolke, die

fleet /fliːt/ n. **(a)** (Navy) Flotte, die; **(b)** (in operation together) (vessels) Flotte, die; (aircraft) Geschwader, das; **(c)** (under same ownership) Flotte, die (fig.); **he owns a ∼ of cars** ihm gehört ein ganzer Wagenpark

fleeting /'fliːtɪŋ/ adj. flüchtig; vergänglich ‹Natur, Schönheit›; **∼ visit** Stippvisite, die (ugs.)

Flemish /'flemɪʃ/ ▶947| **1** adj. flämisch. **2** n. Flämisch, das; see also **English 2 a**

flesh /fleʃ/ n., no pl., no indef. art. **(a)** Fleisch, das; **∼ and blood** Fleisch und Blut; **(b)** (of fruit, plant) [Frucht]fleisch, das; **(c)** (fig.: body) Fleisch, das (geh.); **go the way of all ∼:** den Weg allen Fleisches gehen (geh.)

flesh wound /'fleʃwuːnd/ n. Fleischwunde, die

fleshy /'fleʃɪ/ adj. (fat, boneless) fett; fleischig ‹Hände›

flew ⇨ **fly²** 1, 2

flex¹ /fleks/ n. (Brit. Electr.) Kabel, das

flex² v.t. **(a)** (Anat.) beugen ‹Arm, Knie›; **(b)** **∼ one's muscles** (lit. or fig.) seine Muskeln spielen lassen

flexibility /fleksɪ'bɪlɪtɪ/ n., no pl. **(a)** Biegsamkeit, die; Elastizität, die; **(b)** (fig.) Flexibilität, die

flexible /'fleksɪbl/ adj. **(a)** biegsam; elastisch; **(b)** (fig.) flexibel; dehnbar ‹Vorschriften›; schwach ‹Wille›; **∼ working hours** or **time** gleitende Arbeitszeit

flexitime /'fleksɪtaɪm/ (Brit.), **flextime** /'flekstaɪm/ (Amer.) ns. Gleitzeit, die

flick /flɪk/ **1** n. **∼ of the wrist** kurze, schnelle Drehung des Handgelenks; **a ∼ of the switch** ein einfaches Klicken des Schalters. **2** v.t. schnippen; anknipsen ‹Schalter›; verspritzen ‹Tinte›; **∼ one's fingers** mit den Fingern schnipsen

∼ through v.t. durchblättern

flicker /'flɪkə(r)/ **1** v.i. flackern; ‹Fernsehapparat:› flimmern; **a smile ∼ed round her lips** ein Lächeln spielte um ihre Lippen. **2** n. Flackern, das; (of TV) Flimmern, das; (fig.) Aufflackern, das; (of smile) Anflug, der

'flick knife n. (Brit.) Schnappmesser, das

flight¹ /flaɪt/ n. **(a)** (flying) Flug, der; **in ∼:** im Flug; **(b)** (journey) Flug, der; (migration of birds) Zug, der; **(c)** **∼ [of stairs** or **steps]** Treppe, die; **(d)** (flock of birds) Schwarm, der; **(e)** (Air Force) ≈ Staffel, die; **in the first** or **top ∼** (fig.) in der Spitzengruppe

flight² n. (fleeing) Flucht, die; **take [to] ∼:** die Flucht ergreifen

flight: ∼ attendant n. ▶887| Flugbegleiter, der/-begleiterin, die; **∼ deck** n. **(a)** (of aircraft-carrier) Flugdeck, das; **(b)** (of aircraft) Cockpit, das; **∼ path** n. (Aeronaut.) Flugweg, der; **∼ recorder** n. Flugschreiber, der

flimsy /'flɪmzɪ/ adj. **(a)** dünn; fadenscheinig ‹Kleidung, Vorhang›; nicht [sehr] haltbar ‹Verpackung›; **(b)** (fig.) fadenscheinig (abwertend) ‹Entschuldigung, Argument›

flinch /flɪntʃ/ v.i. **(a)** zurückschrecken; **∼ from sth.** vor einer Sache zurückschrecken; **∼ from one's responsibilities** sich seinen Pflichten entziehen; **(b)** (wince) zusammenzucken

fling /flɪŋ/ **1** n. **(a)** (fig.: attempt) **have a ∼ at sth., give sth. a ∼:** es mit etw. versuchen; **(b)** (fig.: indulgence) **have**

one's **∼:** sich ausleben. **2** v.t., **flung** /flʌŋ/ **(a)** werfen; **∼ back one's head** den Kopf zurückwerfen; **∼ sth. away** (lit. or fig.) etw. fortwerfen; **∼ down the money** das Geld hinschmeißen (ugs.); **∼ on one's jacket** [sich (Dat.)] die Jacke überwerfen; **(b)** (fig.) **∼ sb. into jail** jmdn. ins Gefängnis werfen; **∼ caution to the winds/∼ aside one's scruples** alle Vorsicht/seine Skrupel über Bord werfen. **3** v. refl., **flung (a) ∼ oneself at sb.** sich auf jmdn. stürzen; **∼ oneself in front of/upon** or **on to sth.** sich vor/auf etw. (Akk.) werfen; **(b)** (fig.) **∼ oneself into sth.** sich in etw. (Akk.) stürzen

flint /flɪnt/ n. Feuerstein, der; Flint, der (veralt.)

flip /flɪp/ **1** n. Schnipsen, das; **give sth. a ∼:** etw. hochschnipsen. **2** v.t., **-pp-** schnipsen; **∼ [over]** (turn over) umdrehen. **3** v.i. (sl.) ausflippen (ugs.)

∼ through v.t. durchblättern

'flip chart n. Flipchart, das

flippant /'flɪpənt/ adj. unernst; leichtfertig

flipper /'flɪpə(r)/ n. Flosse, die

flipping /'flɪpɪŋ/ (Brit. sl.) adj., adv. verdammt (salopp)

'flip side n. B-Seite, die

flirt /flɜːt/ **1** n. **he/she is just a ∼:** er/sie will nur flirten. **2** v.i. **(a) ∼ [with sb.]** [mit jmdm.] flirten; **(b)** (fig.) **∼ with sth.** mit etw. liebäugeln; **∼ with danger/death** die Gefahr [leichtfertig] herausfordern/mit dem Leben spielen

flirtation /flɜː'teɪʃn/ n. Flirt, der

flirtatious /flɜː'teɪʃəs/ adj. kokett ‹Blick, Art›

flit /flɪt/ v.i., **-tt-** huschen; **recollections/thoughts ∼ted through his mind** Erinnerungen/Gedanken schossen ihm durch den Kopf

float /fləʊt/ **1** v.i. **(a)** (on water) treiben; **∼ away** wegtreiben; **(b)** (through air) schweben; **∼ across sth.** ‹Wolke, Nebel:› über etw. (Akk.) ziehen; **(c)** (fig.) **∼ about** or **[a]round** umgehen; im Umlauf sein; **(d)** (coll.: move casually) **∼ [around** or **about]** herumziehen (ugs.); **(e)** (Finance) floaten. **2** v.t. **(a)** (convey by water, on rafts) flößen; (set afloat) flott machen ‹Schiff›; **(b)** (fig.: circulate) in Umlauf bringen; **(c)** (Finance) floaten lassen; freigeben; **(d)** (Commerc.) ausgeben, auf den Markt bringen ‹Aktien›; gründen ‹Unternehmen›; lancieren ‹Plan, Idee›. **3** n. **(a)** (for carnival) Festwagen, der; (Brit.: delivery cart) Wagen, der; **(b)** (petty cash) Bargeld, das; **(c)** (Angling) Floß, das (fachspr.); Schwimmer, der

floating /'fləʊtɪŋ/ adj. treibend; schwimmend ‹Hotel›; **∼ exchange rate** flexibler od. frei schwankender Wechselkurs

floating 'voter n. Wechselwähler, der/-wählerin, die

flock /flɒk/ **1** n. **(a)** (of sheep, goats; also Eccl.) Herde, die; (of birds) Schwarm, der; **(b)** (of people) Schar, die. **2** v.i. strömen; **∼ round sb.** sich um jmdn. scharen; **∼ in/out/together** [in Scharen] hinein-/heraus-/zusammenströmen

floe /fləʊ/ n. Eisscholle, die

flog /flɒg/ v.t., **-gg-: (a)** auspeitschen; **∼ a dead horse** (fig.) seine Kraft und Zeit verschwenden; **∼ sth. to death** (fig.) etw. zu Tode reiten; **(b)** (Brit. sl.: sell) verscheuern (salopp)

flood /flʌd/ **1** n. **(a)** Überschwemmung, die; **the F∼** (Bibl.) die Sintflut; **attrib. ∼ area** Überschwemmungsgebiet, das; **(b)** ▶1048| (of tide) Flut, die. **2** v.i. **(a)** ‹Fluss:› über die Ufer treten; **there's danger of ∼ing** es besteht Überschwemmungsgefahr; **(b)** (fig.) strömen. **3** v.t. **(a)** überschwemmen; (deluge) unter Wasser setzen; **the cellar was ∼ed** der Keller stand unter Wasser; **(b)** (fig.) überschwemmen; **∼ed with light** lichtdurchflutet

flood: ∼ damage n. Hochwasserschaden, der; **the area suffered extensive ∼ damage** in dem Gebiet gab es beträchtliche Hochwasserschäden; **∼gate** n. (Hydraulic Engin.) Schütze, die; **open the ∼gates to sth.** (fig.) einer Sache (Dat.) Tür und Tor öffnen; **∼light 1** n. Scheinwerfer, der; (illumination in a broad beam) Flutlicht, das; **2** v.t., **∼lit** /'flʌdlɪt/ anstrahlen ‹Bauwerk›; beleuchten ‹Weg, Straße›; **∼ water** n. Hochwasser, das; (in motion) anflutendes Wasser

floor /flɔː(r)/ **1** n. **(a)** Boden, der; (of room) [Fuß]boden, der; **take the ∼** (dance) sich aufs Parkett begeben (see also **c**); **(b)** (storey) Stockwerk, das; **first ∼** (Amer.) Erdgeschoss, das; **first ∼** (Brit.), **second ∼** (Amer.) erster Stock; **ground**

~: Erdgeschoss, *das;* Parterre, *das;* **(c)** (in debate, meeting) Sitzungssaal, *der;* (Parl.) Plenarsaal, *der;* **be given** *or* **have the ~:** das Wort haben; **take the ~** (Amer.: speak) das Wort ergreifen (*see also* **a**). **2** *v.t.* **(a)** (confound) überfordern; (overcome, defeat) besiegen; **(b)** (knock down) zu Boden schlagen *od.* strecken

floor: **~board** *n.* Dielenbrett, *das;* **~cloth** *n.* (Brit.) Scheuertuch, *das*

flooring /ˈflɔːrɪŋ/ *n.* Fußboden[belag], *der*

floor: **~-polish** *n.* Bohnerwachs, *das;* **~ show** *n.* ≈ Unterhaltungsprogramm, *das*

floozie (floosie) /ˈfluːzɪ/ *n.* (coll.) Flittchen, *das* (ugs. abwertend)

flop /flɒp/ **1** *v.i.,* **-pp-:** **(a)** plumpsen; **she ~ped into a chair** sie ließ sich in einen Sessel plumpsen; **(b)** (coll.: fail) fehlschlagen; ein Reinfall sein (ugs.); ‹*Theaterstück, Show:*› durchfallen. **2** *n.* (coll.: failure) Reinfall, *der* (ugs.); Flop, *der* (ugs.)

floppy /ˈflɒpɪ/ *adj.* weich und biegsam; **~ disc** ⇒ **disc c;** **~ ears/hat** Schlappohren/Schlapphut, *der*

flora /ˈflɔːrə/ *n., pl.* **~e** /ˈflɔːriː/ *or* **~s** Flora, *die*

floral /ˈflɔːrl, ˈflɒrl/ *adj.* geblümt ‹*Kleid, Stoff, Tapete*›; Blumen‹*gesteck, -arrangement, -muster*›

Florence /ˈflɒrəns/ *pr. n.* ▶ 1159 Florenz (*das*)

florid /ˈflɒrɪd/ *adj.* **(a)** (over-ornate) schwülstig (abwertend); blumig ‹*Stil, Redeweise*›; **(b)** (high-coloured) gerötet ‹*Teint*›

florist /ˈflɒrɪst/ *n.* ▶ 887 Florist, *der*/Floristin, *die;* **~'s [shop]** Blumenladen, *der*

flotation /fləʊˈteɪʃn/ *n.* (Commerc.) (of company) Gründung, *die;* (of shares) Ausgabe, *die*

flotilla /fləˈtɪlə/ *n.* Flottille, *die*

flotsam /ˈflɒtsəm/ *n.* **~ [and jetsam]** Treibgut, *das*

flounce /flaʊns/ *v.i.* stolzieren

flounder¹ /ˈflaʊndə(r)/ *v.i.* taumeln; (stumble, lit. or fig.) stolpern

flounder² *n.* (Zool.) Flunder, *die*

flour /ˈflaʊə(r)/ *n.* Mehl, *das*

flourish /ˈflʌrɪʃ/ **1** *v.i.* **(a)** gedeihen; ‹*Handel, Geschäft:*› florieren, gut gehen; **(b)** (be active) seine Blütezeit erleben *od.* haben. **2** *v.t.* schwingen. **3** *n.* **(a) do sth. with a ~:** etw. schwungvoll *od.* mit einer schwungvollen Bewegung tun; **(b)** (in writing) Schnörkel, *der;* **(c)** (Mus.: fanfare) Fanfare, *die*

flout /flaʊt/ *v.t.* missachten; sich hinwegsetzen über (+ Akk.) ‹*Ratschlag, Wunsch, öffentliche Meinung*›

flow /fləʊ/ **1** *v.i.* **(a)** ▶ 1048 fließen; ‹*Körner, Sand:*› rinnen, rieseln; ‹*Gas:*› strömen; **the river ~ed over its banks** der Fluss trat über die Ufer; **(b)** (fig.) fließen; ‹*Personen:*› strömen; **keep the traffic ~ing smoothly** den Verkehr fließend halten; **(c)** (abound) **~ freely** *or* **like water** reichlich *od.* in Strömen fließen; **(d)** **~ from** (be derived from) sich ergeben aus. **2** *n.* **(a)** Fließen, *das;* (progress) Fluss, *der;* (volume) Durchflussmenge, *die;* **~ of water/people** Wasser-/Menschenstrom, *der;* **~ of electricity/information/conversation** Strom-/Informations-/Gesprächsfluss, *der;* **(b)** (of tide, river) Flut, *die* **~ a'way** *v.i.* abfließen

'flow chart *n.* Flussdiagramm, *das*

flower /ˈflaʊə(r)/ **1** *n.* **(a)** (blossom) Blüte, *die;* (plant) Blume, *die;* **come into ~:** zu blühen beginnen; **(b)** *no pl.* (fig.: best part) Zierde, *die;* **in the ~ of youth** in der Blüte der Jugend. **2** *v.i.* blühen; (fig.) erblühen (**into** zu)

flower: **~ arrangement** *n.* Blumenarrangement, *das;* (smaller also) Gesteck, *das;* **~ bed** *n.* Blumenbeet, *das*

flowered /ˈflaʊəd/ *adj.* geblümt ‹*Stoff, Teppich, Tapete*›; **purple-~:** purpurblühend ‹*Pflanze*›

flower: **~ garden** *n.* Blumengarten, *der;* **~pot** *n.* Blumentopf, *der;* **~ shop** *n.* Blumenladen, *der;* **~ show** *n.* Blumenschau, *die*

flowery /ˈflaʊərɪ/ *adj.* geblümt ‹*Stoff, Muster*›; blumig ‹*Duft, Wein*›; (fig.) blumig ‹*Sprache, Ausdruck*›

flowing /ˈfləʊɪŋ/ *adj.* fließend; wallend ‹*Haar, Bart, Gewand*›

flown ⇒ **fly²** 1, 2

fl oz *abbr.* **fluid ounce**

flu /fluː/ *n.* ▶ 865 (coll.) Grippe, *die;* **get** *or* **catch [the] ~:** Grippe bekommen

fluctuate /ˈflʌktjʊeɪt/ *v.i.* schwanken

fluctuation /flʌktjʊˈeɪʃn/ *n.* Schwankung, *die;* Fluktuation, *die* (bes. Wirtsch., Soziol.)

flue /fluː/ *n.* **(a)** (in chimney) Rauchabzug, *der;* **(b)** (for passage of hot air) Luftkanal, *der*

fluency /ˈfluːənsɪ/ *n.* Gewandtheit, *die;* (in speaking) Redegewandtheit, *die*

fluent /ˈfluːənt/ *adj.* gewandt ‹*Stil, Redeweise, Redner, Schreiber, Erzähler*›; **be ~ in Russian, speak ~ Russian, be a ~ speaker of Russian** fließend Russisch sprechen

fluff /flʌf/ **1** *n.* Fusseln *Pl.;* (on birds, rabbits, etc.) Flaum, *der.* **2** *v.t.* **(a) the bird ~ed itself/its feathers [up]** der Vogel plusterte sich/seine Federn auf; **(b)** (coll.: bungle) verpatzen (ugs.)

fluffy /ˈflʌfɪ/ *adj.* [flaum]weich ‹*Kissen, Küken, Haar*›; flauschig ‹*Spielzeug, Stoff, Decke*›; locker ‹*Omelett*›; schaumig ‹*Eiweiß*›

fluid /ˈfluːɪd/ **1** *n.* **(a)** (liquid) Flüssigkeit, *die;* **(b)** (liquid or gas) Fluid, *das* (Technik, Chemie). **2** *adj.* **(a)** (liquid) flüssig; **(b)** (liquid or gaseous) fluid (Technik, Chemie); **(c)** (fig.) ungewiss, unklar ‹*Lage*›

fluid 'ounce *n.* ▶ 1193 Fluid Ounce, *die* (*Brit.: 28,41 cm³; Amer.: 29,57 cm³*)

fluke /fluːk/ *n.* (piece of luck) Glücksfall, *der;* **by a** *or* **some [pure] ~:** [nur] durch einen glücklichen Zufall

fluky /ˈfluːkɪ/ *adj.* glücklich ‹*Zufall, Zusammentreffen, Sieg*›; zufällig ‹*Ergebnis, Relikt*›; Zufalls‹*treffer, -ergebnis*›

flung ⇒ **fling** 2, 3

flunkey, flunky /ˈflʌŋkɪ/ *n.* (usu. derog.) Lakai, *der* (abwertend)

fluorescent /fluːəˈresənt/ *adj.* fluoreszierend; **~ material** Leuchtstoff, *der;* (fabric) fluoreszierendes Material

fluorescent: **~ 'lamp,** **~ 'light** *ns.* Leuchtstofflampe, *die* (Elektrot.); ≈ Neonlampe, *die*

fluoride /ˈfluːəraɪd/ *n.* Fluorid, *das;* **~ toothpaste** fluorhaltige Zahnpasta

flurry /ˈflʌrɪ/ **1** *n.* **(a)** Aufregung, *die;* **there was a sudden ~ of activity** es herrschte plötzlich rege Betriebsamkeit; **(b)** (of rain/snow) [Regen-/Schnee]schauer, *der.* **2** *v.t.* durcheinander bringen; **don't let yourself be flurried** lass dich nicht nervös *od.* (ugs.) verrückt machen

flush¹ /flʌʃ/ **1** *v.i.* rot werden; erröten (**with** vor + *Dat.*). **2** *v.t.* ausspülen ‹*Becken*›; durch-, ausspülen ‹*Rohr*›; **the toilet** *or* **lavatory** spülen. **3** *n.* **(a)** (blush) Erröten, *das;* **hot ~es** Hitzewallungen; **(b)** (elation) **in the [first] ~ of victory** *or* **conquest** im [ersten] Siegestaumel

flush² *adj.* **(a)** (level) bündig; **be ~ with sth.** mit etw. bündig abschließen; **(b)** *usu. pred.* (plentiful) reichlich vorhanden *od.* im Umlauf ‹*Geld*›; **be ~ [with money]** gut bei Kasse sein (ugs.)

flushed /flʌʃt/ *adj.* gerötet ‹*Wangen, Gesicht*›; **~ with pride** vor Stolz glühend

flush 'out *v.t.* aufscheuchen (fig.) ‹*Spion, Verbrecher*›

fluster /ˈflʌstə(r)/ *v.t.* aus der Fassung bringen

flustered /ˈflʌstəd/ *adj.* **be/become ~:** nervös sein/werden

flute /fluːt/ *n.* (Mus.) Flöte, *die*

flutter /ˈflʌtə(r)/ **1** *v.i.* **(a)** ‹*Vogel, Motte, Papier, Vorhang, Fahne, Segel, Drachen, Flügel:*› flattern; ‹*Blumen, Gräser usw.:*› schaukeln; **(b)** (beat abnormally) ‹*Herz:*› schneller *od.* höher schlagen. **2** *v.t.* flattern mit ‹*Flügel*›; **~ one's eyelashes** mit den Wimpern klimpern; **~ one's eyelashes at sb.** jmdm. mit den Wimpern zuklimpern. **3** *n.* **(a)** Flattern, *das;* **(b)** (fig.) (stir) [leichte] Unruhe; (nervous state) Aufregung, *die;* **(c)** (Brit. coll.: bet) Wette, *die;* **have a ~:** ein paar Scheinchen riskieren (ugs.)

flux /flʌks/ *n.* (change) **be in a state of ~:** im Fluss sein; sich verändern

fly¹ /flaɪ/ n. (Zool.) Fliege, die; **the only ~ in the ointment** (fig.) der einzige Haken [bei der Sache] (ugs.); **he wouldn't hurt a ~** (fig.) er kann keiner Fliege etwas zuleide tun; **[there are] no flies on him** (fig. coll.) ihm kann man nichts vormachen (ugs.)

fly² 1 v.i., **flew** /fluː/, **flown** /fləʊn/ (a) fliegen; **~ about/away** or **off** umher-/weg- od. davonfliegen; (b) (float, flutter) fliegen; **rumours are ~ing about** (fig.) es gehen Gerüchte um; (c) (move quickly) fliegen; **come ~ing towards sb.** jmdm. entgegengeflogen kommen; **~ open** auffliegen; **knock** or **send sb./sth. ~ing** jmdn./etw. umstoßen; **~ into a temper** or **rage** einen Wutanfall bekommen; (d) (fig.) **~ [by** or **past]** wie im Fluge vergehen; **how time flies!, doesn't time ~!** wie die Zeit vergeht!; (e) ⟨Fahne:⟩ gehisst sein; (f) (attack angrily) **~ at sb.** (lit. or fig.) über jmdn. herfallen; **let ~:** zuschlagen; (fig.: use strong language) losschimpfen; **let ~ with** abschießen ⟨Pfeil, Rakete, Gewehr⟩; werfen ⟨Stein⟩; (g) (flee) fliehen; (coll.: depart hastily) eilig aufbrechen; **I really must ~** (coll.) jetzt muss ich aber schnell los. 2 v.t., **flew**, **flown** (a) fliegen ⟨Flugzeug, Fracht, Einsatz⟩; fliegen über (+ Akk.) ⟨Strecke⟩; (travel over) überfliegen; überqueren; **~ Concorde/Lufthansa** mit der Concorde/mit Lufthansa fliegen; (b) führen ⟨Flagge⟩; **~ a kite** einen Drachen steigen lassen. 3 n. in sing. or pl. (on trousers) Hosenschlitz, der

~ 'in 1 v.i. (arrive in aircraft) [mit dem Flugzeug] eintreffen (from aus); (come in to land) landen. 2 v.t. landen ⟨Flugzeug⟩; (bring by aircraft) einfliegen

~ 'off v.i. (a) abfliegen; (b) (become detached) abgehen; ⟨Hut:⟩ wegfliegen

~ 'out 1 v.i. abfliegen (**of** von). 2 v.t. ausfliegen

fly: ~-drive 1 attrib. adj. Fly-drive-⟨Paket, Vereinbarung, Urlaub⟩; 2 n. Fly-drive-Paket, das; Fly-drive-Urlaub, der; **~-by-night** 1 adj. zwielichtig; 2 n. jmd., der sich nachts heimlich aus dem Staub macht

flyer /'flaɪə(r)/ n. (a) (pilot) Flieger, der/Fliegerin, die; (b) (handbill) Handzettel, der

flying /'flaɪɪŋ/ 1 adj. Kurz-; **~ visit** Stippvisite, die (ugs.). 2 n. Fliegen, das; attrib. Flug⟨wetter, -zeit, -geschwindigkeit, -erfahrung⟩

flying: ~ bomb n. V-Waffe, die; **~ fish** n. fliegender Fisch; **~ 'jump, ~ 'leap** ns. Sprung mit Anlauf; großer Satz (ugs.); **~ machine** n. Luftfahrzeug, das; Flugmaschine, die (veralt.); **~ 'saucer** n. fliegende Untertasse; **~ squad** n. (Police) Überfallkommando, das; **~ 'start** n. (Sport) fliegender Start; **get off to** or **have a ~ start** (fig.) einen glänzenden Start haben

fly: ~leaf n. Vorsatzblatt, das; **~-on-the-wall** attrib. adj. von einer bewusst im Hintergrund gehaltenen Kamera aufgenommen ⟨Dokumentarfilm⟩; die Kamera bewusst möglichst im Hintergrund haltend ⟨Aufnahmetechnik, -stil⟩; **~over** n. (Brit.) [Straßen]überführung, die; Fly-over, der; **~-past** n. Luftparade, die; **~sheet** n. (a) (of tent) Überzelt, das; (b) (circular) Prospekt, der; **~ spray** n. Insektenspray, der od. das; **~ swatter** n. Fliegenklatsche, die; **~weight** n. (Boxing etc.) Fliegengewicht, das; (person also) Fliegengewichtler, der; **~wheel** n. Schwungrad, das

FM abbr. **frequency modulation** FM

foal /fəʊl/ n. Fohlen, das

foam /fəʊm/ 1 n. (a) Schaum, der; (b) ⇒ **foam rubber.** 2 v.i. (lit. or fig.) schäumen (**with** vor + Dat.); **~ at the mouth** Schaum vorm Mund haben; (fig. coll.) [vor Wut] schäumen

foam: ~ bath n. Schaumbad, das; **~ 'rubber** n. Schaumgummi, der

fob /fɒb/ v.t., **-bb-: ~ sb. off with sth.** jmdn. mit etw. abspeisen (ugs.)

focal /'fəʊkl/: **~ 'distance, ~ 'length** ns. Brennweite, die

foc's'le /'fəʊksl/ ⇒ **forecastle**

focus /'fəʊkəs/ 1 n., pl. **~es** or **foci** /'fəʊsaɪ/ (a) (Optics, Photog.) Brennpunkt, der; (focal length) Brennweite, die; (adjustment of eye or lens) Scharfeinstellung, die; **out of/in ~:** unscharf/scharf eingestellt ⟨Kamera, Teleskop⟩; unscharf/scharf ⟨Foto, Film, Vordergrund usw.⟩; **get sth. in ~** (fig.) etw. klarer erkennen; (b) (fig.: centre, central object) Mittelpunkt, der; **be the ~ of attention** im Brennpunkt des Interesses stehen. 2 v.t., **-s-** or **-ss-:** (a) (Optics, Photog.) einstellen (**on** auf + Akk.); **~ one's eyes on sth./sb.** die Augen auf etw./jmdn. richten; (b) (concentrate) bündeln ⟨Licht, Strahlen⟩; (fig.) konzentrieren (**on** auf + Akk.). 3 v.i., **-s-** or **-ss-:** (a) **the camera ~es automatically** die Kamera hat automatische Scharfeinstellung; (b) ⟨Licht, Strahlen:⟩ sich bündeln; (fig.) sich konzentrieren (**on** auf + Akk.)

fodder /'fɒdə(r)/ n. [Vieh]futter, das

foe /fəʊ/ n. (poet./rhet.) Feind, der

FoE abbr. **Friends of the Earth**

foetal /'fiːtl/ adj. fötal; fetal

foetid /'fiːtɪd/ ⇒ **fetid**

foetus /'fiːtəs/ n. Fötus, der; Fetus, der

fog /fɒg/ n. Nebel, der; **be in a [complete] ~** (fig.) [völlig] verunsichert sein

'fogbound adj. (a) (surrounded) in Nebel gehüllt; (b) (immobilized) durch Nebel festgehalten

foggy /'fɒgɪ/ adj. (a) neblig; (b) (fig.) nebelhaft ⟨Vorstellung, Sprache, Bewusstsein⟩; **[I] haven't the foggiest [idea** or **notion]** (coll.) [ich] hab' keinen blassen Schimmer

fog: ~horn n. (Naut.) Nebelhorn, das; **~ lamp, ~light** ns. (Motor Veh.) Nebelscheinwerfer, der

fogy /'fəʊgɪ/ n. **[old] ~:** [alter od. rückständiger] Opa (salopp) /[alte od. rückständige] Oma (salopp)

foible /'fɔɪbl/ n. Eigenheit, die

foil¹ /fɔɪl/ n. (a) (metal as thin sheet) Folie, die; (b) (to wrap or cover food etc.) Folie, die; (c) (sb./sth. contrasting) ≈ Kontrast, der

foil² v.t. vereiteln ⟨Versuch, Plan, Flucht⟩; durchkreuzen ⟨Vorhaben, Plan⟩

foil³ n. (sword) Florett, das

foist /fɔɪst/ v.t. **~ [off] on to** or **[up]on sb.** jmdm. andrehen (ugs.) ⟨schlechte Waren⟩; jmdm. zuschieben ⟨Schuld, Verantwortung⟩; auf jmdn. abwälzen ⟨Probleme, Verantwortung⟩; **~ oneself on sb.** sich jmdm. aufdrängen

fold /fəʊld/ 1 v.t. (a) (double over on itself) [zusammen]falten; zusammenlegen ⟨Laken, Wäsche⟩; (b) (embrace) **~ sb. in one's arms** jmdn. in die Arme schließen; (c) **~ one's arms** die Arme verschränken; (d) (envelop) **~ sth./sb. in** sth. etw./jmdn. in etw. (Akk.) einhüllen. 2 v.i. (a) (become ~ed) sich zusammenlegen; sich zusammenfalten; (b) (collapse) zusammenklappen; (go bankrupt) Konkurs od. Bankrott machen; (c) (be able to be ~ed) sich falten lassen; **it ~s easily** es ist leicht zu falten. 3 n. (a) (doubling) Falte, die; (b) (act of ~ing) Faltung, die; (c) (line made by ~ing) Knick, der

~ a'way 1 v.t. zusammenklappen. 2 v.i. zusammenklappbar sein; sich zusammenklappen lassen

~ 'back 1 v.t. zurückschlagen, aufschlagen ⟨Laken⟩; zurückklappen ⟨Rücksitz⟩; umknicken ⟨Papier⟩. 2 v.i. sich zurückschlagen lassen

~ 'down 1 v.t. zusammenklappen; (~ back) zurückschlagen. 2 v.i. sich zusammenklappen lassen; (~ back) sich zurückschlagen lassen

~ 'out v.i. ⟨Landkarte:⟩ sich auseinander falten lassen; ⟨Tisch:⟩ sich hochklappen lassen

~ 'up 1 v.t. (a) zusammenfalten; zusammenlegen ⟨Laken, Wäsche⟩; (b) zusammenklappen ⟨Stuhl, Tisch usw.⟩. 2 v.i. (a) sich zusammenfalten lassen; (b) ⟨Stuhl, Tisch usw.:⟩ sich zusammenklappen lassen

folder /'fəʊldə(r)/ n. (a) Mappe, die; (b) (Computing) Ordner, der

folding: ~ 'door n. Falttür, die; **~ 'doors** n. pl. Falttür, die; (of hangar, barn, etc.) Falttor, das

foliage /'fəʊlɪdʒ/ n., no pl. (leaves) Blätter Pl.; (of tree also) Laub, das

folk /fəʊk/ n., pl. same or **~s** (a) (a people) Volk, das; (b) in pl. **~[s]** (people) Leute Pl.; (people in general) die Leute; **[the] rich/poor ~:** die Reichen/Armen; **old ~[s]** alte Leute; (c) in pl. **~s** (coll., as address: people, friends) Leute Pl.

(ugs.); **(d)** *in pl.* ~**s** (coll.: one's relatives) Verwandte *Pl.;* Leute *Pl.* (ugs.); **(e)** *attrib.* (of the people, traditional) Volks-

folk: ~ **dance** *n.* Volkstanz, *der;* ~**lore** *n.* **(a)** (traditional beliefs) [volkstümliche] Überlieferung; Folklore, *die;* **(b)** (study) Volkskunde, *die;* Folklore, *die;* ~ **music** *n.* Volksmusik, *die;* ~ **song** *n.* Volkslied, *das;* (modern) Folksong, *der;* ~ **tale** *n.* Volksmärchen, *das*

follow /ˈfɒləʊ/ **1** *v.t.* **(a)** folgen (+ *Dat.*); **you're being** ~**ed** Sie werden verfolgt; **(b)** (go along) folgen (+ *Dat.*); entlanggehen/-fahren ⟨ *Straße usw.* ⟩; **(c)** (come after in order or time) folgen (+ *Dat.*); folgen auf (+ *Akk.*); **A is** ~**ed by B** auf A folgt B; **(d)** (accompany) [nach]folgen (+ *Dat.*); **(e)** (provide with sequel) ~ **sth. with sth.** einer Sache *(Dat.)* etw. folgen lassen; **(f)** (result from) die Folge sein von; hervorgehen aus; **(g)** (treat or take as guide or leader) folgen (+ *Dat.*); sich orientieren an (+ *Dat.*); (adhere to) anhängen (+ *Dat.*); **(h)** (act according to) folgen (+ *Dat.*) ⟨ *Prinzip, Instinkt, Trend* ⟩; verfolgen ⟨ *Politik* ⟩; befolgen ⟨ *Vorschrift, Regel, Anweisung, Rat, Warnung* ⟩; handeln nach ⟨ *Gefühl, Wunsch* ⟩; sich halten an (+ *Akk.*) ⟨ *Konventionen, Diät, Maßstab* ⟩; **(i)** (keep up with mentally, grasp meaning of) folgen (+ *Dat.*); **do you** ~ **me?, are you** ~**ing me?** verstehst du, was ich meine?; **(j)** (be aware of the present state or progress of) verfolgen ⟨ *Ereignisse, Nachrichten, Prozess* ⟩. **2** *v.i.* **(a)** (go, come) ~ **after sb./sth.** jmdm./einer Sache folgen; **(b)** (go or come after person or thing) folgen; ~ **in the wake of sth.** etw. ablösen; auf etw. *(Akk.)* folgen; **(c)** (come next in order or time) folgen; **as** ~**s** wie folgt; **(d)** ~ **from sth.** (result) die Folge von etw. sein; (be deducible) aus etw. folgen
~ **'on** *v.i.* (continue) ~ **on from sth.** die Fortsetzung von etw. sein
~ **'through 1** *v.t.* zu Ende verfolgen; durchziehen (ugs.). **2** *v.i.* (Sport) durchschwingen
~ **'up** *v.t.* **(a)** (add further action etc. to) ausbauen ⟨ *Erfolg, Sieg* ⟩; **(b)** (investigate further) nachgehen (+ *Dat.*) ⟨ *Hinweis* ⟩; **(c)** (consider further) berücksichtigen ⟨ *Bitte, Angebot* ⟩

follower /ˈfɒləʊə(r)/ *n.* Anhänger, *der*/Anhängerin, *die*

following /ˈfɒləʊɪŋ/ **1** *adj.* **(a)** (now to be mentioned) folgend; **in the** ~ **way** folgendermaßen; **the** ~**:** folgendes; (persons) folgende; **(b)** ~ **wind** Rückenwind, *der.* **2** *prep.* nach. **3** *n.* Anhängerschaft, *die*

'follow-up *n.* Fortsetzung, *die;* **as a** ~**:** im Anschluss (**to** an + *Akk.*); *attrib.* ~ **letter/visit** Nachfassbrief, *der*/-besuch, *der* (Werbespr.)

folly /ˈfɒlɪ/ *n.* **(a)** Torheit, *die* (geh.); **it would be [sheer]** ~**:** es wäre [äußerst] töricht (geh.); **(b)** (costly structure considered useless) nutzloser Prunkbau

foment /fəˈment, fəʊˈment/ *v.t.* schüren

fond /fɒnd/ *adj.* **(a)** (tender) zärtlich; (affectionate) liebevoll ⟨ *Blick* ⟩; lieb ⟨ *Erinnerung* ⟩; **be** ~ **of sb.** jmdn. mögen *od.* gern haben; **be** ~ **of doing sth.** etw. gern tun; **I'm not very** ~ **of sweets** ich mache mir nicht viel aus Süßigkeiten; **(b)** (foolishly credulous or hopeful) kühn ⟨ *Hoffnung, Traum* ⟩; gutgläubig ⟨ *Person* ⟩; allzu zuversichtlich ⟨ *Glaube* ⟩

fondant /ˈfɒndənt/ *n.* Fondant, *der od. das*

fondle /ˈfɒndl/ *v.t.* streicheln

fondness /ˈfɒndnɪs/ *n.* **(a)** (tenderness) Zärtlichkeit, *die;* (affection) Liebe, *die;* ~ **for sth./doing sth.** (special liking) Vorliebe für etw./dafür, etw. zu tun

fondue /ˈfɒndjuː/ *n.* (Gastr.) Fondue, *das od. die*

font /fɒnt/ *n.* Taufstein, *der*

food /fuːd/ *n.* **(a)** *no pl., no art.* Nahrung, *die;* (for animals) Futter, *das;* **(b)** *no pl., no art.* (as commodity) Lebensmittel *Pl.;* **(c)** *no pl.* (in solid form) Essen, *das;* **some** ~**:** etwas zu essen; **he's very keen on Italian** ~**:** er mag die italienische Küche; er isst gern italienisch; **(d)** (for animals) Futter, *das;* (for humans) Nahrungsmittel, *das;* Kost, *die;* (for animals) Futter, *das;* **canned** ~**s** Konserven *Pl.;* **(e)** (fig.) ~ **for thought** Stoff zum Nachdenken

food: ~ **chain** *n.* (Ecol.) Nahrungskette, *die;* ~ **poisoning** *n.* Lebensmittelvergiftung, *die;* ~ **processor** *n.* Küchenmaschine, *die;* ~ **shop,** ~ **store** *ns.* Lebensmittelgeschäft, *das;* ~**stuff** *n.* Nahrungsmittel, *das*

fool /fuːl/ **1** *n.* **(a)** Dummkopf, *der* (ugs.); **what a** ~ **I am!** wie dumm von mir!; **be no** *or* **nobody's** ~**:** nicht dumm *od.* (ugs.) nicht auf den Kopf gefallen sein; **make a** ~ **of oneself** sich lächerlich machen; **(b)** (Hist.: jester, clown) Narr, *der;* **(c)** (dupe) **make a** ~ **of sb.** jmdn. zum Narren halten. **2** *v.i.* herumalbern (ugs.). **3** *v.t.* **(a)** (cheat) ~ **sb. into doing sth.** jmdn. [durch Tricks] dazu bringen, etw. zu tun; **(b)** (dupe) täuschen; hereinlegen (ugs.); **you could have** ~**ed me** (iron.) ach, was du nicht sagst!
~ **a'bout,** ~ **a'round** *v.i.* (play the ~) herumalbern (ugs.); (idle) herumtrödeln (ugs.); ~ **about** *or* **around with sth./sb.** mit etw./jmdm. herumspielen
~ **with** *v.t.* [herum]spielen mit

foolhardy /ˈfuːlhɑːdɪ/ *adj.* tollkühn ⟨ *Handlung, Behauptung, Person* ⟩; draufgängerisch ⟨ *Person* ⟩

foolish /ˈfuːlɪʃ/ *adj.* **(a)** töricht; verrückt (ugs.) ⟨ *Idee, Vorschlag* ⟩; **don't do anything** ~**:** mach keinen Unsinn; **what a** ~ **thing to do/say** wie kann man nur so etwas Dummes tun/sagen; **(b)** (ridiculous) albern (ugs.) ⟨ *Verhalten* ⟩; blöd, dumm (ugs.) ⟨ *Grinsen, Bemerkung* ⟩; lächerlich ⟨ *Aussehen* ⟩

foolishly /ˈfuːlɪʃlɪ/ *adv., as sentence-modifier* törichterweise

fool: ~**proof** *adj.* (not open to misuse) wasserdicht (fig.); (infallible) absolut sicher; (that cannot break down) narrensicher (ugs.); ~**scap** /ˈfuːlskæp, ˈfuːlzkæp/ *n.* **(a)** (size of paper) Kanzleiformat, *das;* **(b)** (paper of this size) Kanzleipapier, *das;* ~**'s 'paradise** *n.* Traumwelt, *die*

foot /fʊt/ **1** *n., pl.* **feet** /fiːt/ (**▶ 672**) Fuß, *der;* **at sb.'s feet** zu jmds. Füßen; **put one's best** ~ **forward** (fig.) (hurry) sich beeilen; (do one's best) sein Bestes tun; **feet first** mit den Füßen zuerst *od.* voran; **go into sth. feet first** (fig.) sich Hals über Kopf (ugs.) in etw. hineinstürzen; **have one** ~ **in the grave** (fig.) mit einem Fuß im Grabe stehen; **have both [one's] feet on the ground** (fig.) mit beiden Beinen [fest] auf der Erde stehen; **on** ~**:** zu Fuß; **on one's/its feet** (lit. or fig.) auf den Beinen; **put one's** ~ **down** (fig.) (be firmly insistent or repressive) energisch werden; (accelerate motor vehicle) [Voll]gas geben; **put one's** ~ **in it** (fig. coll.) ins Fettnäpfchen treten (ugs.); **put one's feet up** die Beine hochlegen; **start [off]** *or* **get off on the right/wrong** ~ (fig.) einen guten/schlechten Start haben; **set** ~ **in/on sth.** etw. betreten; **be rushed off one's feet** (fig.) in Trab gehalten werden (ugs.); **stand on one's own [two] feet** auf eigenen Füßen stehen; **rise** *or* **get to one's feet** sich erheben; aufstehen; **never put a** ~ **wrong** (fig.) nie etwas falsch machen; **get/have cold feet** kalte Füße kriegen/gekriegt haben (ugs.); **catch sb. on the wrong** ~ (fig.) jmdn. auf dem falschen Fuß erwischen; **have two left feet** (fig.) zwei linke Füße haben (ugs.); **(b)** (far end) unteres Ende; (of bed) Fußende, *das;* (lowest part) Fuß, *der;* **at the** ~ **of the list/page** unten auf der Liste/Seite; **(c)** (of stocking etc.) Fuß, *der;* Füßling, *der;* **(d)** (Pros.: metrical unit) [Vers]fuß, *der;* **(e)** *pl.* **feet** *or same* **▶ 850**, **▶ 904** (linear measure) Fuß, *der* (30,48 cm); **7** ~ *or* **feet** 7 Fuß; **(f)** (base) Fuß, *der;* (of statue, pillar) Sockel, *der.* **2** *v.t.* (pay) ~ **the bill** die Rechnung bezahlen

footage /ˈfʊtɪdʒ/ *n., no pl., no indef. art.* [Film]material, *das;* **documentary** ~**:** Dokumentaraufnahmen *Pl.*

foot-and-'mouth [disease] *n.* Maul- und Klauenseuche, *die*

football /ˈfʊtbɔːl/ *n.* (game, ball) Fußball, *der*

'football boot *n.* Fußballschuh, *der*

footballer /ˈfʊtbɔːlə(r)/ *n.* (**▶ 887**) Fußballspieler, *der*/-spielerin, *die*

football: ~ **pitch** *n.* Fußballplatz, *der;* ~ **pools** *n. pl.* **the** ~ **pools** das Fußballtoto

foot: ~ **brake** *n.* Fußbremse, *die;* ~ **bridge** *n.* Steg, *der;* (across road, railway, etc.) Fußgängerbrücke, *die;* ~**hill** *n., usu. pl.* [Gebirgs]ausläufer, *der;* ~**hold** *n.* Halt, *der;* (fig.) Stützpunkt, *der;* **get a** ~**hold** (fig.) Fuß fassen

footing /ˈfʊtɪŋ/ *n.* **(a)** (fig.: status) Stellung, *die;* **be on an equal** ~ **[with sb.]** [jmdm.] gleichgestellt sein; **place sth. on a firm** ~**:** etw. auf eine feste Basis stellen; **be on a war** ~**:** sich im Kriegszustand befinden; **(b)** (foothold) Halt, *der*

foot: **~lights** *n. pl.* (Theatre) Rampenlicht, *das;* **~loose** *adj.* ungebunden; **~loose and fancy-free** frei und ungebunden; **~man** /'futmən/ *n., pl.* **~men** /'futmən/ Lakai, *der;* Diener, *der;* **~note** *n.* Fußnote, *die;* **~ passenger** *n.* Fußpassagier, *der;* **~path** *n.* (path) Fußweg, *der;* **~print** *n.* Fußabdruck, *der;* **~prints in the snow** Fußspuren im Schnee; **~rest** *n.* Fußstütze, *die;* **~step** *n.* Schritt, *der;* **follow** *or* **tread in sb.'s ~steps** (fig.) in jmds. Fußstapfen treten; **~stool** *n.* Fußbank, *die;* Fußschemel, *der;* **~wear** *n., no pl., no indef. art.* Schuhe *Pl.;* Schuhwerk, *das;* Fußbekleidung, *die* (Kaufmannsspr.); **~work** *n., no pl.* (Sport, Dancing) Beinarbeit, *die*

for /fə(r), *stressed* fɔ:(r)/ ▶ 810 ⌋ **1** *prep.* **(a)** (representing, on behalf of, in exchange against) für; (in place of) für; anstelle von; **what is the German ~ 'buzz'?** wie heißt „buzz" auf Deutsch?; **(b)** (in defence, support, or favour of) für; **be ~ doing sth.** dafür sein, etw. zu tun; **it's each [man]** *or* **every man ~ himself** jeder ist auf sich selbst gestellt; **(c)** (to the benefit of) für; **do sth. ~ sb.** für jmdn. etw. tun; **(d)** (with a view to) für; **they invited me ~ Christmas/Monday/ supper** sie haben mich zu Weihnachten/für Montag/zum Abendessen eingeladen; **what is it ~?** wofür/wozu ist das? **be saving up ~ sth.** auf etw. (*Akk.*) sparen; **(e)** (being the motive of) für; (having as purpose) zu; **reason ~ living** Grund zu leben; **a dish ~ holding nuts** eine Schale für Nüsse; **(f)** (to obtain, win, save) **a request ~ help** eine Bitte um Hilfe; **study ~ a university degree** auf einen Hochschulabschluss hin studieren; **phone ~ a doctor** nach einem Arzt telefonieren; **take sb. ~ a ride in the car/a walk** jmdn. im Auto spazieren fahren/mit jmdm. einen Spaziergang machen; **work ~ a living** für den Lebensunterhalt arbeiten; **run/jump** *etc.* **~ it** loslaufen/-springen *usw.;* **(g)** (to reach) nach; **set out ~ England/ the north/an island** nach England/nach Norden/zu einer Insel aufbrechen; **(h)** (to be received by) für; **that's Jim ~ you** das sieht Jim mal wieder ähnlich; **(i)** (as regards) **checked ~ accuracy** auf Richtigkeit geprüft; **be dressed/ready ~ dinner** zum Dinner angezogen/fertig sein; **open ~ business** eröffnet; **have sth. ~ breakfast/pudding** etw. zum Frühstück/Nachtisch haben; **enough ... ~:** genug ... für; **that's quite enough ~ me** das reicht mir völlig; **too ... ~:** zu ... für; **there is nothing ~ it but to do sth.** es gibt keine andere Möglichkeit, als etw. zu tun; **(j)** (to the amount of) **cheque/ bill ~ £5** Scheck/Rechnung über *od.* in Höhe von 5 Pfund; **(k)** (to affect, as if affecting) für; **things don't look very promising ~ the business** was die Geschäfte angeht, sieht das alles nicht sehr viel versprechend aus; **it is wise/advisable ~ sb. to do sth.** es ist vernünftig/ratsam, dass jmd. etw. tut; **it's hopeless ~ me to try and explain the system** es ist sinnlos, dir das System erklären zu wollen; **(l)** (as being) für; **what do you take me ~** wofür hältst du mich?; **I/you** *etc.* **~ one** ich/ du *usw.* für mein[en]/ dein[en] *usw.* Teil; **(m)** (on account of, as penalty of) wegen; **famous/well-known ~ sth.** berühmt/ bekannt wegen *od.* für etw.; **jump/ shout ~ joy** vor Freude in die Luft springen/schreien; **were it not ~ you/ your help, I should not be able to do it** ohne dich/deine Hilfe wäre ich dazu nicht in der Lage; **(n)** (on the occasion of) **~ the first time** zum ersten Mal; **why can't you help ~ once?** warum kannst du nicht einmal helfen?; **what shall I give him ~ his birthday?** was soll ich ihm zum Geburtstag schenken?; **(o)** (in spite of) **~ all ...:** trotz ...; **~ all that, ...:** trotzdem ...; **(p)** (on account of the hindrance of) vor (+ *Dat.*); **~ fear of ...:** aus Angst vor (+ *Dat.*); **but ~ ..., except ~ ...:** wenn nicht ... gewesen wäre, [dann] ...; **(q)** (so far as concerns) **~ all I know/care ...:** möglicherweise/was mich betrifft, ...; **~ one thing, ...:** zunächst einmal ...; **(r)** (considering the usual nature of) für; **not bad ~ a first attempt** nicht schlecht für den ersten Versuch; **(s)** (during) seit; **we've/we haven't been here ~ three years** wir sind seit drei Jahren hier/nicht mehr hier gewesen; **we waited ~ hours/three hours** wir warteten stundenlang/drei Stunden lang; **how long are you here ~?** wie lange bleiben Sie hier?; **sit here ~ now** *or* **~ the moment** bleiben Sie im Augenblick hier sitzen; **(t)** (to the extent of) **walk ~ 20 miles/~ another**

20 miles 20 Meilen [weit] gehen/weiter gehen; **(u) be 'for it** (coll.) dran sein (ugs.); sich auf was gefasst machen können (ugs.). **2** *conj.* (since, as proof) denn

forage /'fɒrɪdʒ/ **1** *n.* (food for horses or cattle) Futter, *das.* **2** *v.i.* auf Nahrungssuche sein; **~ for sth.** auf der Suche nach etw. sein

foray /'fɒreɪ/ *n.* Streifzug, *der;* (Mil.) Ausfall, *der*

forbad, forbade ⇒ **forbid**

forbear¹ /'fɔ:beə(r)/ *n., usu. in pl.* Vorfahr, *der*

forbear² /fɔ:'beə(r)/ *v.i.,* **forbore** /fɔ:'bɔ:(r)/, **forborne** /fɔ:'bɔ:n/ **(a)** (refrain) **~ from doing sth.** davon Abstand nehmen, etw. zu tun; **(b)** (be patient) sich gedulden

forbearance /fɔ:'beərəns/ *n., no pl.* Nachsicht, *die*

forbid /fə'bɪd/ *v.t.,* **-dd-**, **forbade** /fə'bæd, fə'beɪd/ *or* **forbad** /fə'bæd/, **forbidden** /fə'bɪdn/ **(a) ~ sb. to do sth.** jmdm. verbieten, etw. zu tun; **~ [sb.] sth.** [jmdm.] etw. verbieten; **it is ~den [to do sth.]** es ist verboten *od.* nicht gestattet[, etw. zu tun]; **(b)** (make impossible) nicht zulassen; nicht erlauben; **God/Heaven ~ [that ...]!** Gott/der Himmel bewahre[, dass ...]!

forbidding /fə'bɪdɪŋ/ *adj.* furchteinflößend ‹Aussehen, Stimme›; unwirtlich ‹Landschaft›; (fig.) düster ‹Aussicht›

forbore, forborne ⇒ **forbear²**

force /fɔ:s/ **1** *n.* **(a)** *no pl.* (strength, power) Stärke, *die;* (of bomb, explosion, attack, storm) Wucht, *die;* (physical strength) Kraft, *die;* **achieve sth. by brute ~:** etw. mit roher Gewalt erreichen; **(b)** *no pl.* (fig.: power, validity) Kraft, *die;* **by ~ of** auf Grund (+ *Gen.*); **argue with much ~:** sehr überzeugend argumentieren; **in ~** (in effect) in Kraft; **come into ~** ‹Gesetz usw.› in Kraft treten; **put in[to] ~:** in Kraft setzen; **(c)** (coercion, violence) Gewalt, *die;* **use** *or* **employ ~ [against sb.]** Gewalt [gegen jmdn.] anwenden; **by ~:** gewaltsam; mit Gewalt; **(d)** (organized group) (of workers) Kolonne, *die;* Trupp, *der;* (of police) Einheit, *die;* (Mil.) Armee, *die;* **the ~s** die Armee; **be in the ~s** beim Militär sein; **(e)** (forceful agency or person) Kraft, *die;* Macht, *die;* **there are ~s in action/at work here ...:** hier walten Kräfte/sind Kräfte am Werk ...; **he is a ~ in the land** (fig.) /**a ~ to be reckoned with** er ist ein einflussreicher Mann im Land/eine Macht, die nicht zu unterschätzen ist; **(f)** (meaning) Bedeutung, *die;* **(g)** (Phys.) Kraft, *die.* **2** *v.t.* **(a)** zwingen; **~ sb./oneself [to do sth.]** jmdn./sich zwingen[, etw. zu tun]; **be ~d to do sth.** gezwungen sein *od.* sich gezwungen sehen, etw. zu tun; **I was ~d to accept/into accepting the offer** (felt obliged) ich fühlte mich verpflichtet, das Angebot anzunehmen; **~ sb.'s hand** (fig.) jmdn. zwingen zu handeln, **(b)** (take by ~) **~ sth. from sb.** jmdm. etw. entreißen; **he ~d it out of her hands** er riss es ihr aus der Hand; **~ a confession from sb.** (fig.) jmdn. zu einem Geständnis zwingen; **(c)** (push) **~ sth. into sth.** etw. in etw. (*Akk.*) [hinein]zwängen; **(d)** (impose, inflict) **~ sth. [up]on sb.** jmdm. etw. aufzwingen *od.* aufnötigen; **he ~d his attention on her** er drängte sich ihr mit seinen Aufmerksamkeiten auf; **(e)** (break open) **~ [open]** aufbrechen; **(f)** (effect by violent means) sich (*Dat.*) erzwingen ‹Zutritt›; **~ one's way in[to a building]** sich (*Dat.*) mit Gewalt Zutritt [zu einem Gebäude] verschaffen; **(g)** (produce with effort) sich zwingen zu; **~ a smile** sich zu einem Lächeln zwingen

~ 'down *v.t.* **(a)** drücken ‹Preis›; **(b)** zur Landung zwingen ‹Flugzeug›; **(c)** (make oneself eat) herunterwürgen (ugs.) ‹Nahrung›

~ 'up *v.t.* hochtreiben ‹Preis›

forced /fɔ:st/ *adj.* **(a)** (contrived, unnatural) gezwungen; gewollt ‹Geste, Vergleich, Metapher›; gekünstelt ‹Benehmen›; **(b)** (compelled by force) erzwungen; Zwangs‹arbeit, -anleihe›

forced: ~ 'landing *n.* Notlandung, *die;* **~ 'march** *n.* (Mil.) Gewaltmarsch, *der*

'force-feed *v.t.* zwangsernähren

forceful /'fɔ:sfl/ *adj.* stark ‹Persönlichkeit, Charakter›; energisch ‹Person, Art, Maßnahme›; schwungvoll ‹Rede-, Schreibweise›; eindrucksvoll ‹Sprache›; eindringlich ‹Worte›

For

The most frequent translation of the preposition *for*, with the related senses *on behalf of*, *in place of*, *in favour of*, *for the benefit* or *use of* etc., is **für:**

a bed for two	= ein Bett für zwei
I did it for him	= Ich habe es für ihn gemacht*

*This translation works whether the stress is on *him*, meaning "for his benefit", or on *for*, meaning "in his place", which could also be "an seiner Stelle".

Expressing purpose

Where purpose is involved and where a verbal noun or other noun describing action follows, the translation is **zu:**

a device for removing stones from cherries	= ein Gerät zum Entkernen von Kirschen
We met for a discussion	= Wir trafen uns zu einer Besprechung
She did it for pleasure	= Sie machte es zum Vergnügen *or* zum Zeitvertreib
What's that for?	= Wozu dient denn das?

This also applies to meals:

We had meat for lunch/ a mousse for dessert	= Bei uns gab es zum Mittagessen Fleisch/ zum Nachtisch eine Mousse

But on the other hand:

a dish for nuts	= eine Schale für Nüsse

The construction *for sb.* + infinitive expressing purpose can be rendered by a clause with **damit:**

For him to be able to come we will have to change the date	= Wir werden den Termin ändern müssen, damit er mitkommen kann
I took a piece for her to try	= Ich nahm ein Stück mit, damit sie es probieren konnte, Ich nahm ihr ein Stück zum Probieren mit

Expressing reasons

With the sense *because of*, **wegen** can be used, although **für** is also found with some adjectives:

The area is well known/famous for its wines	= Die Gegend ist bekannt/berühmt für ihre Weine *or* wegen ihrer Weine
He was sentenced to death for murder	= Er wurde wegen Mordes zum Tode verurteilt

aus also occurs with a governing emotion:

for fear of waking her	= aus Angst, sie zu wecken
for love of his country	= aus Liebe zum Vaterland

Expressing direction

Where the sense is simply *going to*, the translation is **nach:**

the train for Bath	= der Zug nach Bath

We left for Scotland	= Wir sind nach Schottland abgefahren

But with a more general indication of direction rather than destination (meaning *towards*), **auf ... zu** or **in Richtung** can be used in German:

The ship was heading for the rocks	= Das Schiff steuerte auf die Felsen zu
They were making for London	= Sie fuhren in Richtung London

Expressing time

The translation will depend on the tense, which is not always the same in German:

PERFECT CONTINUOUS
I have been living here for two years (and am still living here)	= Ich wohne seit zwei Jahren hier

PAST CONTINUOUS
I had been living here for two years (and was still living here at the time)	= Ich wohnte seit zwei Jahren hier

PAST
I lived here for two years (and no longer live here)	= Ich habe zwei Jahre [lang] hier gewohnt

FUTURE
You will have to wait for an hour	= Sie werden eine Stunde warten müssen
I am going to the USA for two weeks	= Ich fahre für zwei Wochen in die USA

Note that **lang** is placed after the noun, and is often omitted in speech, especially referring to short periods:

I was in Paris for a few days	= Ich war ein paar Tage in Paris

However the translation of the phrase *for hours* is **stundenlang:**

I had to wait for hours	= Ich musste stundenlang warten

Similarly

for weeks	= wochenlang
for months	= monatelang
for years	= jahrelang

With personal pronouns

In most cases *für* can be used, but the dative of the personal pronoun is often found with adjectives and nouns expressing difficulty, impossibility, unpleasantness etc. and also more positive feelings:

It's good for you	= Es ist gut für dich, Es tut dir gut
This makes it impossible for me	= Das macht es mir unmöglich
Your visit is inconvenient for her	= Dein Besuch ist *or* kommt ihr ungelegen
The whole business is very embarrassing for them	= Die ganze Sache ist ihnen sehr peinlich
It's a great pleasure/ honour for me	= Es ist mir eine große Freude/Ehre

---

forceps /'fɔːseps/ *n.*, *pl. same* [**pair of**] ～: Zange, *die*

forcible /'fɔːsɪbl/ *adj.* gewaltsam

forcibly /'fɔːsɪblɪ/ *adv.* gewaltsam; mit Gewalt

ford /fɔːd/ **1** *n.* Furt, *die.* **2** *v.t.* durchqueren; (wade through) durchwaten

fore /fɔː(r)/ **1** *adj.*, *esp. in comb.* vorder...; Vorder‹teil, -front usw.›. **2** *n.* [**be/come**] **to the** ～: im Vordergrund [stehen]/in den Vordergrund [rücken]. **3** *adv.* (Naut.) vorn; ～ **and aft** längs[schiffs]

'forearm *n.* ▶ **672** Unterarm, *der*

forebear ⇨ **forbear¹**

foreboding /fɔːˈbəʊdɪŋ/ *n.* Vorahnung, *die;* (unease caused by premonition) ungutes Gefühl

ˈ**forecast** **1** *v.t.,* ∼ *or* ∼ed vorhersagen. **2** *n.* Voraussage, *die;* (Meteorol.) [Wetter]vorhersage, *die*

forecastle /ˈfəʊksl/ *n.* (Naut.) Back, *die*

ˈ**forecourt** *n.* Vorhof, *der;* ∼ **attendant** ≈ Tankwart, *der*

ˈ**forefather** *n., usu. in pl.* Vorfahr, *der;* **our** ∼**s** unsere Vorväter

ˈ**forefinger** *n.* ▶ **672** Zeigefinger, *der*

ˈ**forefront** *n.* [**be**] **in the** ∼ **of** in vorderster Linie (+ *Gen.*) [stehen]

forego ⇨ **forgo**

foregoing /ˈfɔːˈgəʊɪŋ/ *adj.* vorhergehend

ˈ**foregone** *adj.* **be a** ∼ **conclusion** (be predetermined) von vornherein feststehen; (be certain) so gut wie sicher sein

ˈ**foreground** *n.* Vordergrund, *der*

ˈ**forehand** (Tennis etc.) **1** *adj.* Vorhand-. **2** *n.* Vorhand, *die*

forehead /ˈfɒrɪd, ˈfɔːhed/ *n.* ▶ **672** Stirn, *die*

foreign /ˈfɒrɪn/ *adj.* (**a**) (from abroad) ausländisch; Fremd⟨*herrschaft, -kapital, -sprache*⟩; fremdartig ⟨*Gebräuche*⟩; ∼ **worker** Gastarbeiter, *der*/-arbeiterin, *die;* **he is** ∼: er ist Ausländer; (**b**) (abroad) fremd; Auslands⟨*reise, -niederlassung, -markt*⟩; ∼ **countries** das Ausland; ∼ **travel** Reisen ins Ausland; (**c**) (related to countries abroad) außenpolitisch; Außen⟨*politik, -handel*⟩; **affairs** auswärtige Angelegenheiten; (**d**) (from outside) fremd; ∼ **body** *or* **substance** Fremdkörper, *der;* (**e**) (alien) fremd; **be** ∼ **to sb./sb.'s nature** jmdm. fremd sein/nicht jmds. Art sein

foreign: ∼ **ˈaid** *n.* Entwicklungshilfe, *die;* **F**∼ **and ˈCommonwealth Office** *n.* (Brit.) Außenministerium, *das;* ∼ **correˈspondent** *n.* ▶ **887** (Journ.) Auslandskorrespondent, *der*/ -korrespondentin, *die*

foreigner /ˈfɒrɪnə(r)/ *n.* Ausländer, *der*/Ausländerin, *die*

foreign: ∼ **exˈchange** *n.* (dealings) Devisenhandel, *der;* (currency) Devisen *Pl.;* ∼ **ˈlanguage** *n.* Fremdsprache, *die;* ∼ **ˈlegion** *n.* Fremdenlegion, *die;* **F**∼ **ˈMinister** *n.* Außenminister, *der;* **F**∼ **Office** *n.* (Brit. Hist./coll.) Außenministerium, *das;* **F**∼ **ˈSecretary** *n.* ▶ **887** (Brit.) Außenminister, *der;* ∼ **service** *n.* diplomatischer Dienst

ˈ**foreleg** *n.* Vorderbein, *das*

foreman /ˈfɔːmən/ *n., pl.* **foremen** /ˈfɔːmən/ ▶ **887** (**a**) Vorarbeiter, *der;* (**b**) (Law) Sprecher [der Geschworenen/(in Germany) der Schöffen]

foremost /ˈfɔːməʊst/ *adj.* (**a**) vorderst...; (**b**) (fig.) führend

ˈ**forename** *n.* Vorname, *der*

forensic /fəˈrensɪk/ *adj.* gerichtlich; forensisch (fachspr.); ∼ **medicine** Gerichtsmedizin, *die*

ˈ**foreplay** *n.* Vorspiel, *das*

ˈ**forerunner** *n.* Vorläufer, *der*/Vorläuferin, *die*

foresaw ⇨ **foresee**

foresee /fɔːˈsiː/ *v.t., forms as* **see** voraussehen

foreseeable /fɔːˈsiːəbl/ *adj.* vorhersehbar; **in the** ∼ **future** in nächster Zukunft

foreseen ⇨ **foresee**

foreˈshadow *v.t.* vorausahnen lassen; vorausdeuten auf (+ *Akk.*)

foreˈshorten *v.t.* (**a**) (Art, Photog.) [perspektivisch] verkürzen; (**b**) (shorten, condense) verkürzen

ˈ**foresight** *n., no pl.* Weitblick, *der;* Voraussicht, *die*

ˈ**foreskin** *n.* (Anat.) Vorhaut, *die*

forest /ˈfɒrɪst/ *n.* Wald, *der;* (commercially exploited) Forst, *der*

foreˈstall *v.t.* zuvorkommen (+ *Dat.*); (prevent by prior action) vermeiden

forester /ˈfɒrɪstə(r)/ *n.* Förster, *der*

forestry /ˈfɒrɪstrɪ/ *n.* Forstwirtschaft, *die;* (science) Forstwissenschaft, *die*

ˈ**foretaste** *n.* Vorgeschmack, *der*

foreˈtell *v.t.,* **foretold** vorhersagen; voraussagen

ˈ**forethought** *n.* (prior deliberation) [vorherige] Überlegung; (care for the future) Vorausdenken, *das*

foretold ⇨ **foretell**

forever /fəˈrevə(r)/ *adv.* (**a**) (constantly, persistently) ständig; (**b**) (Amer.) = **for ever;** ⇨ **ever a**

foreˈwarn *v.t.* vorwarnen; ∼ed **is** foreˈarmed (prov.) wer gewarnt ist, ist gewappnet

foreˈwarning *n.* Vorwarnung, *die*

ˈ**foreword** *n.* Vorwort, *das*

forfeit /ˈfɔːfɪt/ **1** *v.t.* verlieren (auch fig.); einbüßen (geh., auch fig.); verwirken (geh.) ⟨*Recht, jmds. Gunst*⟩. **2** *n.* Strafe, *die*

forgave ⇨ **forgive**

forge¹ /fɔːdʒ/ **1** *n.* (**a**) (workshop) Schmiede, *die;* (**b**) (blacksmith's hearth) Esse, *die;* (furnace for melting or refining metal) Schmiedeofen, *der.* **2** *v.t.* (**a**) schmieden (**into** zu); (**b**) (fig.) schmieden ⟨*Plan, Verbindung*⟩; schließen ⟨*Vereinbarung, Freundschaft*⟩; (**c**) (counterfeit) fälschen

forge² *v.i.* ∼ **ahead** [das Tempo] beschleunigen; ⟨*Wettläufer:*⟩ vorstoßen; (fig.) vorankommen; Fortschritte machen

forger /ˈfɔːdʒə(r)/ *n.* Fälscher, *der*/Fälscherin, *die*

forgery /ˈfɔːdʒərɪ/ *n.* Fälschung, *die*

forget /fəˈget/ **1** *v.t.,* **-tt-,** **forgot** /fəˈgɒt/, **forgotten** / fəˈgɒtn/ vergessen; (∼ learned ability) verlernen; vergessen; **gone but not forgotten** in bleibender Erinnerung; **I** ∼ **his name** (have forgotten) ich habe seinen Namen vergessen; ∼ **doing sth./having done sth.** vergessen, dass man etw. getan hat; **don't** ∼ **that** …: vergiss nicht *od.* denk[e] daran, dass …; ∼ **how to dance** das Tanzen verlernen; **and don't you** ∼ **it** (coll.) vergiss das ja nicht; ∼ **it!** (coll.) schon gut!; vergiss es! **2** *v.i.,* **-tt-,** **forgot, forgotten** es vergessen; ∼ **about sth.** etw. vergessen; ∼ **about it!** (coll.) schon gut!; **I forgot about Joe** ich habe gar nicht an Joe gedacht. **3** *v. refl.,* **-tt-,** **forgot, forgotten** (**a**) (act unbecomingly) sich vergessen; (**b**) (neglect one's own interests) sich selbst vergessen

forgetful /fəˈgetfl/ *adj.* (**a**) (absent-minded) vergesslich; (**b**) ∼ **of sth.** ohne an etw. (*Akk.*) zu denken; **be** ∼ **of one's duty** seine Pflicht vernachlässigen

forgetfulness /fəˈgetflnɪs/ *n., no pl.* Vergesslichkeit, *die*

forˈget-me-not *n.* (Bot.) Vergissmeinnicht, *das*

forgettable /fəˈgetəbl/ *adj.* easily ∼: leicht zu vergessen

forgive /fəˈgɪv/ *v.t.,* **forgave** /fəˈgeɪv/, **forgiven** /fəˈgɪvn/ ▶ **639** vergeben ⟨*Sünden*⟩; verzeihen ⟨*Unrecht*⟩; entschuldigen, verzeihen ⟨*Unterbrechung, Neugier, Ausdrucksweise*⟩; ∼ **sb.** [**sth.** *or* **for sth.**] jmdm. [etw.] verzeihen *od.* (geh.) vergeben; **God** ∼ **me** möge Gott mir vergeben; **am I** ∼**n?** verzeihst du mir?; **you are** ∼**n** ich verzeihe dir; ∼ **me for saying so, but** …: entschuldigen *od.* verzeihen Sie[, dass ich es sage], [aber] …

forgiveness /fəˈgɪvnɪs/ *n., no pl.* Verzeihung, *die;* (esp. of sins) Vergebung, *die;* **ask/beg** [**sb.'s**] ∼: [jmdn.] um Verzeihung/(geh.) Vergebung bitten

forgiving /fəˈgɪvɪŋ/ *adj.* versöhnlich

forgo /fɔːˈgəʊ/ *v.t., forms as* **go** verzichten auf (+ *Akk.*)

forgone ⇨ **forgo**

forgot, forgotten ⇨ **forget**

fork /fɔːk/ **1** *n.* (**a**) Gabel, *die;* **the knives and** ∼**s** das Besteck; (**b**) ([point of] division into branches) Gabelung, *die;* (one branch) Abzweigung, *die;* (of tree) Astgabel, *die.* **2** *v.i.* (**a**) (divide) sich gabeln; (**b**) (turn) abbiegen; ∼ [**to the**] **left** [**for**] [nach] links abbiegen [nach]

∼ **ˈout,** ∼ **ˈup** (coll.) **1** *v.t.* lockermachen (ugs.). **2** *v.i.* ∼ **out** *or* **up** [**for sth.**] [für etw.] blechen (ugs.)

forked /fɔːkt/ *adj.* gegabelt

forked ˈlightning *n., no pl., no indef. art.* Linienblitz, *der* '**fork-lift truck** *n.* Gabelstapler, *der*

forlorn /fəˈlɔːn/ *adj.* (a) (desperate) verzweifelt; ~ **hope** (faint hope) verzweifelte Hoffnung; (desperate enterprise) aussichtsloses Unterfangen; (b) (forsaken) [einsam und] verlassen

form /fɔːm/ 1 *n.* (a) (type, style) Form, *die;* ~ **of address** [Form der] Anrede; **in human** ~: in menschlicher Gestalt; in Menschengestalt; **in the** ~ **of** in Form von *od.* + *Gen.;* **in book** ~: in Buchform; als Buch; (b) *no pl.* (shape, visible aspect) Form, *die;* Gestalt, *die;* **take** ~: Gestalt annehmen *od.* gewinnen; (c) (printed sheet) Formular, *das;* (d) (Brit. Sch.) Klasse, *die;* (e) (bench) Bank, *die;* (f) *no pl., no indef. art.* (Sport: physical condition) Form, *die;* **peak** ~: Bestform, *die;* **out of** ~: außer Form; nicht in Form; **in [good]** ~ (lit. or fig.) [gut] in Form; **she was in great** ~ **at the party** (fig.) bei der Party war sie groß in Form; **on/off** ~ (lit. or fig.) in/nicht in Form; (g) (Sport: previous record) bisherige Leistungen; **on/judging by [past/present]** ~ (fig.) nach der Papierform; **true to** ~ (fig.) wie üblich *od.* zu erwarten; (h) (etiquette) **for the sake of** ~: der Form halber; **good/bad** ~: gutes/schlechtes Benehmen; (i) (figure) Gestalt, *die;* (j) (Ling.) Form, *die.* 2 *v.t.* (a) (make; also Ling.) bilden; **be** ~**ed from sth.** aus etw. entstehen; (b) (shape, mould) formen, gestalten (**into** zu); (fig.) formen ‹*Charakter usw.*›; (c) sich (*Dat.*) bilden ‹*Meinung, Urteil*›; gewinnen ‹*Eindruck*›; fassen ‹*Entschluss, Plan*›; kommen zu ‹*Schluss*›; (acquire, develop) entwickeln ‹*Vorliebe, Gewohnheit, Wunsch*›; schließen ‹*Freundschaft*›; (d) (constitute, compose, be, come) bilden; **Schleswig once** ~**ed [a] part of Denmark** Schleswig war einmal ein Teil von Dänemark; (e) (establish, set up) bilden ‹*Regierung*›; gründen ‹*Bund, Verein, Firma, Partei, Gruppe*›. 3 *v.i.* (come into being) sich bilden; ‹*Idee*:› sich formen, Gestalt annehmen

formal /ˈfɔːml/ *adj.* (a) formell; förmlich ‹*Person, Art, Einladung, Begrüßung*›; steif ‹*Person, Begrüßung*›; (official) offiziell; **wear** ~ **dress** *or* **clothes** Gesellschaftskleidung tragen; (b) (explicit) formell; ~ **education/knowledge** ordentliche Schulbildung/reales Wissen

formality /fɔːˈmælɪtɪ/ *n.* (a) (requirement) Formalität, *die;* (b) *no pl.* (being formal, ceremony) Förmlichkeit, *die*

formalize /ˈfɔːməlaɪz/ *v.t.* (a) (specify) formalisieren; (b) (make official) formell bekräftigen

format /ˈfɔːmæt/ *n.* 1 (a) (of book) (layout) Aufmachung, *die;* (shape and size) Format, *das;* (b) (Telev., Radio) Aufbau, *der.* 2 *v.t.* **-tt-** (Computing) formatieren

formation /fɔːˈmeɪʃn/ *n.* (a) *no pl.* (forming) (of substance, object) Bildung, *die;* (of character) Formung, *die;* (of plan) Entstehung, *die;* (establishing) Gründung, *die;* (b) (Mil., Aeronaut., Dancing) Formation, *die*

formative /ˈfɔːmətɪv/ *adj.* formend, prägend ‹*Einfluss*›; **the** ~ **years of life** die entscheidenden Lebensjahre

former /ˈfɔːmə(r)/ *attrib. adj.* (a) (earlier) früher; (ex-) ehemalig; Ex-; **in** ~ **times** früher; (b) (first-mentioned) **in the** ~ **case** im ersteren Fall; **the** ~: der/die/das erstere; *pl.* die ersteren

formerly /ˈfɔːməlɪ/ *adv.* früher

Formica, (P) /fɔːˈmaɪkə/ *n.* ≈ Resopal, *das* ⓌＺ

formidable /ˈfɔːmɪdəbl/ *adj.* gewaltig; ungeheuer; bedrohlich, gefährlich ‹*Gegner, Herausforderung*›; (awe-inspiring) formidabel; beeindruckend

formula /ˈfɔːmjʊlə/ *n., pl.* ~**s** *or* (esp. as tech. term) ~**e** /ˈfɔːmjʊliː/ (a) (also Math., Chem., Phys.) Formel, *die;* (b) (set form) Schema, *das;* (prescription, recipe) Rezeptur, *die;* (fig.) Rezept, *das*

formulate /ˈfɔːmjʊleɪt/ *v.t.* formulieren; (devise) entwickeln

fornicate /ˈfɔːnɪkeɪt/ *v.i.* Unzucht treiben; huren (abwertend)

for-'profit *attrib. adj.* gewinnorientiert ‹*Organisation*›

forsake /fəˈseɪk/ *v.t.,* **forsook** /fəˈsʊk/, ~**n** /fəˈseɪkn/ (a) (give up) entsagen (geh.) (+ *Dat.*); verzichten auf (+ *Akk.*); (b) (desert) verlassen

forsaken /fəˈseɪkn/ *adj.* verlassen

forsook ⇒ **forsake**

fort /fɔːt/ *n.* (Mil.) Fort, *das;* **hold the** ~ (fig.) die Stellung halten

forte /ˈfɔːteɪ/ *n.* Stärke, *die;* starke Seite (ugs.)

forth /fɔːθ/ *adv.* (a) **and so** ~: und so weiter; (b) **from this/that day** *etc.* ~: von diesem/jenem Tag *usw.* an; von Stund an (geh.)

forthcoming /ˈfɔːθkʌmɪŋ, fɔːθˈkʌmɪŋ/ *adj.* (a) (approaching) bevorstehend; (about to appear) in Kürze zu erwartend ...; in Kürze anlaufend ‹*Film*›; in Kürze erscheinend ‹*Ausgabe, Buch usw.*›; **be** ~: bevorstehen; (about to appear) in Kürze zu erwarten sein/anlaufen/erscheinen; (b) *pred.* (made available) **be** ~ ‹*Geld, Antwort:*› kommen; ‹*Hilfe:*› geleistet werden; **not be** ~: ausbleiben; (c) (responsive) mitteilsam ‹*Person*›

forthright /ˈfɔːθraɪt/ *adj.* direkt; offen ‹*Blick*›

forthwith /fɔːθˈwɪθ, fɔːθˈwɪð/ *adv.* unverzüglich

fortieth /ˈfɔːtɪɪθ/ ▶956] 1 *adj.* vierzigst...; *see also* **eighth** 1. 2 *n.* (fraction) Vierzigstel, *das; see also* **eighth** 2

fortification /fɔːtɪfɪˈkeɪʃn/ *n.* (Mil.) (a) *no pl.* (fortifying) Befestigung, *die;* (b) *usu. in pl.* (defensive works) Befestigung, *die;* Festungsanlage, *die*

fortify /ˈfɔːtɪfaɪ/ *v.t.* (a) (Mil.) befestigen; (b) (strengthen, lit. or fig.) stärken; (c) aufspriten ‹*Wein*›

fortitude /ˈfɔːtɪtjuːd/ *n., no pl.* innere Stärke

fortnight /ˈfɔːtnaɪt/ *n.* vierzehn Tage; zwei Wochen; **a** ~ **[from] today** heute in vierzehn Tagen

fortnightly /ˈfɔːtnaɪtlɪ/ 1 *adj.* vierzehntäglich; zweiwöchentlich. 2 *adv.* alle vierzehn Tage; alle zwei Wochen

fortress /ˈfɔːtrɪs/ *n.* Festung, *die*

fortuitous /fɔːˈtjuːɪtəs/ *adj.*, **fortuitously** /fɔːˈtjuːɪtəslɪ/ *adv.* zufällig

fortunate /ˈfɔːtʃənət, ˈfɔːtʃənət/ *adj.* glücklich; **it is** ~ **for sb. [that ...]** es ist jmds. Glück[, dass ...]; **sb. is** ~ **to be alive** jmd. kann von Glück sagen *od.* reden, dass er noch lebt; **it was very** ~ **that ...:** es war ein Glück, dass ...

fortunately /ˈfɔːtʃənətlɪ, ˈfɔːtʃənətlɪ/ *adv.* (luckily) glücklicherweise; zum Glück

fortune /ˈfɔːtʃən, ˈfɔːtʃuːn/ *n.* (a) (private wealth) Vermögen, *das;* **make a** ~: ein Vermögen machen; (b) (prosperous condition) Glück, *das;* (of country) Wohl, *das;* (c) (luck, destiny) Schicksal, *das;* **bad/good** ~: Pech, *das*/Glück, *das;* **by sheer good** ~ **there was ...:** es war reines Glück, dass ... war; **thank one's good** ~ **that ...:** dem Glück dafür danken, dass ...; **tell sb.'s** ~: jmdm. wahrsagen *od.* sein Schicksal vorhersagen; **tell** ~**s** wahrsagen

fortune: ~**-teller** *n.* Wahrsager, *der*/Wahrsagerin, *die;* ~**-telling** *n., no pl.* Wahrsagerei, *die*

forty /ˈfɔːtɪ/ ▶630], ▶956] 1 *adj.* vierzig; **have** ~'**winks** ein Nickerchen (fam.) machen *od.* halten; *see also* **eight** 1. 2 *n.* Vierzig, *die; see also* **eight** 2 a; **eighty** 2

forty: ~-'**first** *etc. adj.* ▶956] einundvierzigst... *usw.; see also* **eighth** 1; ~-'**one** *etc.* ▶956] 1 *adj.* einundvierzig *usw.; see also* **eight** 1; 2 *n.* Einundvierzig *usw., die; see also* **eight** 2 a

forum /ˈfɔːrəm/ *n.* (also Roman Hist.) Forum, *das*

forward /ˈfɔːwəd/ 1 *adv.* (a) (in direction faced) vorwärts; **take three steps** ~: drei Schritte vortreten; (b) (towards end of room etc. faced) nach vorn; vor‹*laufen, -rücken, -schieben*›; (c) (closer) heran; **he came** ~ **to greet me** er kam auf mich zu, um mich zu begrüßen; (d) (ahead, in advance) voraus‹*schicken, -gehen*›; (e) (into future) voraus‹*schauen, -denken*›; (f) **come** ~ (present oneself) ‹*Zeuge, Helfer:*› sich melden. 2 *adj.* (a) (directed ahead) vorwärts gerichtet; vorn nach‹*gestellt*›; (b) (at or to the front) Vorder-; vorder...; (c) (advanced) frühreif ‹*Kind, Pflanze, Getreide*›; fortschrittlich ‹*Vorstellung, Ansicht, Maßnahme*›; (d) (bold) dreist; (e) (Commerc.) Termin‹*geschäft, -verkauf*›; Zukunfts‹*planung*›. 3 *n.* (Sport) Stürmer, *der*/Stürmerin, *die.* 4 *v.t.* (a) (send on) nachschicken ‹*Brief, Paket, Post*› (**to** an + *Akk.*); (dispatch) abschicken ‹*Waren*› (**to** an + *Akk.*); '**please** ~' „bitte nachsenden"; ~**ing address** Nachsendeanschrift, *die;* (b) (pass on) weiterreichen, weiterleiten ‹*Vorschlag, Plan*› (**to** an + *Akk.*); (c) (promote) voranbringen ‹*Karriere, Vorbereitung*›

forward 'planning n. Vorausplanung, die

forwards /'fɔ:wədz/ ⇒ **forward 1 a, b**

forwent ⇒ **forgo**

fossil /'fɒsɪl/ n. Fossil, das; ~ **fuel** fossiler Brennstoff

fossilize (fossilise) /'fɒsɪlaɪz/ v.t. fossilisieren lassen (Paläont.); versteinern lassen (auch fig.); ~**d** fossil (Paläont.)

foster /'fɒstə(r)/ **1** v.t. **(a)** (encourage) fördern; pflegen ⟨Freundschaft⟩; (harbour) hegen (geh.); **(b)** in Pflege haben ⟨Kind⟩. **2** adj. ~-: Pflege⟨kind, -mutter, -eltern, -sohn usw.⟩

fought ⇒ **fight 1, 2**

foul /faʊl/ **1** adj. **(a)** (offensive to the senses) abscheulich; übel ⟨Geruch, Geschmack⟩; **(b)** (polluted) verschmutzt ⟨Wasser, Luft⟩; **(c)** (coll.: awful) scheußlich (ugs.); mies (ugs. abwertend); **(d)** (morally vile) anstößig, unanständig ⟨Sprache, Gerede⟩; niederträchtig ⟨Verleumdung, Tat⟩; **(e)** (unfair) unerlaubt, unredlich ⟨Mittel⟩; ~ **play** (Sport) Foulspiel, das; **the police do not suspect** ~ **play** die Polizei vermutet kein Verbrechen; **(f)** fall or run ~ of (fig.) kollidieren od. in Konflikt geraten mit ⟨Vorschrift, Gesetz, Polizei⟩. **2** n. (Sport) Foul, das; **commit a** ~: foulen; ein Foul begehen. **3** v.t. **(a)** (make ~) beschmutzen (auch fig.); verunreinigen (abwertend); verpesten ⟨Luft⟩; **(b)** (be entangled with) sich verfangen in (+ Dat.); **(c)** (Sport) foulen ~ '**up** v.t. (coll.: spoil) vermasseln (salopp)

foul: ~-**mouthed** /'faʊlmaʊðd/ adj. unanständig; unflätig; ~-**smelling** adj. übel riechend

found¹ /faʊnd/ v.t. **(a)** (establish) gründen; stiften ⟨Krankenhaus, Kloster⟩; begründen ⟨Wissenschaft, Religion, Glauben, Kirche⟩; **(b)** (fig.: base) begründen; ~ sth. **[up]on** etw. auf etw. (Akk.) gründen; **be** ~**ed [up]on sth.** [sich] auf etw. (Akk.) gründen

found² ⇒ **find 1**

foundation /faʊn'deɪʃn/ n. **(a)** (establishing) Gründung, die; (of hospital, monastery) Stiftung, die; (of school of painting, of religion) Begründung, die; **(b)** (institution) Stiftung, die; **(c)** usu. in pl. ~[s] (underlying part of building; also fig.) Fundament, das; **be without** or **have no** ~ (fig.) unbegründet sein; **lay the** ~ **of/for sth.** (fig.) das Fundament od. die Grundlage zu etw. legen; **(d)** (cosmetic) Grundierung, die

foundation: ~ **course** n. (Univ. etc.) Grundkurs, der; ~ **cream** n. Grundierungscreme, die; ~ **stone** n. (lit. or fig.) Grundstein, der

founder¹ /'faʊndə(r)/ n. Gründer, der/Gründerin, die; (of hospital, or with an endowment) Stifter, der/Stifterin, die

founder² v.i. **(a)** ⟨Schiff:⟩ sinken, untergehen; **(b)** (fig.: fail) sich zerschlagen

foundry /'faʊndrɪ/ n. (Metallurgy) Gießerei, die

fount /faʊnt, fɒnt/ n. (Printing) Schrift, die

fountain /'faʊntɪn/ n. **(a)** (jet[s] of water) Fontäne, die; (structure) Springbrunnen, der; **(b)** (fig.: source) Quelle, die

'fountain pen n. Füllfederhalter, der; Füller, der (ugs.)

four /fɔ:(r)/ ▶ 630], ▶ 706], ▶ 956] **1** adj. vier; see also **eight 1. 2** n. Vier, die; **on all** ~s auf allen vieren (ugs.); see also **eight 2 a, c, d**

four: ~-**door** attrib. adj. viertürig ⟨Auto⟩; ~-**footed** /'fɔ:fʊtɪd/ adj. vierfüßig; ~-**leaf clover**, ~-**leaved clover** n. vierblättriges Kleeblatt; ~-**letter 'word** n. vulgärer Ausdruck; ~-**poster** n. Himmelbett, das

foursome /'fɔ:səm/ n. **(a)** Quartett, das; **go in** or **as a** ~: zu viert gehen; **(b)** (Golf) Vierer, der

'four-stroke adj. (Mech. Engin.) Viertakt⟨motor, -verfahren⟩

fourteen /fɔ:'ti:n/ ▶ 630], ▶ 706], ▶ 956] **1** adj. vierzehn; see also **eight 1. 2** n. Vierzehn, die; see also **eight 2 a, d; eighteen 2**

fourteenth /fɔ:'ti:nθ/ ▶ 738], ▶ 956] **1** adj. vierzehnt...; see also **eighth 1. 2** n. (fraction) Vierzehntel, das; see also **eighth 2**

fourth /fɔ:θ/ ▶ 738], ▶ 956] **1** adj. **(a)** viert...; **the** ~ **finger** der kleine Finger; see also **eighth 1; (b)** ~ **dimension** vierte Dimension. **2** n. (in sequence, rank) Vierte, der/die/das; (fraction) Viertel, das; see also **eighth 2**

fourth 'gear n., no pl. (Motor Veh.) vierter Gang; see also **gear 1 a**

fourthly /'fɔ:θlɪ/ adv. viertens

four-wheel 'drive n. (Motor Veh.) Vier- od. Allradantrieb, der

fowl /faʊl/ n., pl. ~s or same Haushuhn, das; (collectively) Geflügel, das

fox /fɒks/ **1** n. Fuchs, der. **2** v.t. verwirren

fox: ~ **cub** n. Fuchswelpe, der; ~**glove** n. (Bot.) Fingerhut, der; ~-**hunt** n. Fuchsjagd, die; ~ **'terrier** n. Foxterrier, der; ~**trot** n. Foxtrott, der

foyer /'fɔɪeɪ, 'fwɑjeɪ/ n. Foyer, das

fraction /'frækʃn/ n. **(a)** ▶ 956] (Math.) Bruch, der; **(b)** (small part) Bruchteil, der; **the car missed me by a** ~ **of an inch** das Auto hätte mich um Haaresbreite überfahren

fractional /'frækʃənl/ adj., **fractionally** /'frækʃənəlɪ/ adv. (fig.) geringfügig

fractious /'frækʃəs/ adj. (unruly) aufsässig; (peevish) quengelig ⟨Kind⟩

fracture /'fræktʃə(r)/ ▶ 865] **1** n. (also Med.) Bruch, der. **2** v.t. (also Med.) brechen; ~ **one's jaw** etc. sich (Dat.) den Kiefer usw. brechen; ~ **one's skull** sich (Dat.) einen Schädelbruch zuziehen. **3** v.i. (Med.) brechen

fragile /'frædʒaɪl/ adj. **(a)** zerbrechlich; zart ⟨Teint, Hand⟩; '~ — **handle with care**„ „Vorsicht, zerbrechlich!"; **(b)** (fig.) unsicher ⟨Frieden⟩; zart ⟨Gesundheit, Konstitution⟩; zerbrechlich ⟨alte Frau⟩

fragment 1 /'frægmənt/ n. Bruchstück, das; (of document, conversation) Fetzen, der; (of china) Scherbe, die; (Lit., Mus.) Fragment, das. **2** /fræg'ment/ v.t. & i. zersplittern

fragmentary /'frægməntərɪ/ adj. bruchstückhaft; fragmentarisch

fragmented /fræg'mentɪd/ adj. bruchstückhaft

fragrance /'freɪɡrəns/ n. Duft, der

fragrant /'freɪɡrənt/ adj. duftend

frail /freɪl/ adj. zerbrechlich; zart ⟨Gesundheit⟩; gebrechlich ⟨Greis, Greisin⟩; schwach ⟨Stimme⟩

frailty /'freɪltɪ/ n. **(a)** no pl. Zerbrechlichkeit, die; (of health) Zartheit, die; **(b)** esp. in pl. (fault) Schwäche, die

frame /freɪm/ **1** n. **(a)** (of vehicle, bicycle) Rahmen, der; (of easel, rucksack, bed, umbrella) Gestell, das; (of ship, aircraft) Gerüst, das; **(b)** (border) Rahmen, der; [spectacle] ~s [Brillen]gestell, das; **(c)** (of person, animal) Körper, der; **(d)** (Photog., Cinemat.) [Einzel]bild, das. **2** v.t. **(a)** rahmen ⟨Bild, Spiegel⟩; **(b)** (compose) formulieren ⟨Frage, Antwort, Satz⟩; aufbauen ⟨Rede, Aufsatz⟩; (devise) entwerfen ⟨Gesetz, Politik, Plan⟩; ausarbeiten ⟨Plan, Methode, Denksystem⟩; **(c)** (coll.: incriminate unjustly) ~ **sb.** jmdm. etwas anhängen (ugs.)

frame: ~-**up** n. (coll.) abgekartetes Spiel (ugs.); ~**work** n. (of ship etc., fig.: of project) Gerüst, das; [with]in the ~**work of** (as part of) im Rahmen (+ Gen.); (in relation to) im Zusammenhang mit

franc /fræŋk/ n. ▶ 938] Franc, der; (Swiss) Franken, der

France /frɑːns/ pr. n. Frankreich (das)

franchise /'fræntʃaɪz/ n. **(a)** Stimmrecht, das; (esp. for Parliament) Wahlrecht, das; **(b)** (Commerc.) Lizenz, die

frank¹ adj. (candid) offen ⟨Bekenntnis, Aussprache, Blick, Gesicht, Person⟩; freimütig ⟨Geständnis, Äußerung⟩; **be** ~ **with sb.** zu jmdm. offen sein; **to be [quite]** ~ (as sentence-modifier) offen gesagt

frank² v.t. (Post) **(a)** (in lieu of postage stamp) freistempeln; **(b)** (put postage stamp on) frankieren

frankfurter /'fræŋkfɜ:tə(r)/ (Amer.: **frankfurt** /'fræŋkfɜ:t/) n. Frankfurter [Würstchen]

frankincense /'fræŋkɪnsens/ n. Weihrauch, der

franking machine /'fræŋkɪŋməʃiːn/ n. (Brit. Post) Frankiermaschine, die; Freistempler, der

frankly /'fræŋklɪ/ adv. (candidly) offen; frank und frei; (honestly) offen od. ehrlich gesagt; (openly, undisguisedly) unverhohlen ⟨kritisch, materialistisch usw.⟩

frankness /'fræŋknɪs/ n., no pl. Offenheit, die; Freimütigkeit, die

frantic /'fræntɪk/ adj. **(a)** verzweifelt ⟨Hilferufe, Gestikulieren⟩; **be** ~ **with fear/rage** etc. außer sich (Dat.)

sein vor Angst/Wut *usw.;* **drive sb. ~:** jmdn. in den Wahnsinn treiben; **(b)** (very anxious, noisy, uncontrolled) hektisch ‹*Aktivität, Suche, Getriebe*›

fraternal /frə'tɜːnl/ *adj.* brüderlich

fraternise ⇒ **fraternize**

fraternity /frə'tɜːnɪtɪ/ *n.* **(a) the teaching/medical/ legal ~:** die Lehrer-/Ärzte-/Juristenzunft; die Zunft der Lehrer/Ärzte/Juristen; **(b)** (Amer. Univ.) [studentische] Verbindung; **(c)** *no pl.* (brotherliness) Brüderlichkeit, *die*

fraternize /'frætənaɪz/ *v.i.* ~ **[with sb.]** sich verbrüdern [mit jmdm.]

fraud /frɔːd/ *n.* **(a)** *no pl.* (cheating, deceit) Betrug, *der;* Täuschung, *die;* (Law) [arglistige] Täuschung; **(b)** (trick, false thing) Schwindel, *der;* **(c)** (person) Betrüger, *der*/Betrügerin, *die;* Schwindler, *der*/Schwindlerin, *die*

fraudulent /'frɔːdjʊlənt/ *adj.* betrügerisch

fraught /frɔːt/ *adj.* **(a) be ~ with danger** voller Gefahren sein; **~ with obstacles/difficulties** voller Hindernisse/Schwierigkeiten; **(b)** (coll.: distressingly tense) stressig (ugs.) ‹*Atmosphäre, Situation, Diskussion*›; gestresst (ugs.) ‹*Person*›

fray¹ /freɪ/ *n.* (fight) [Kampf]getümmel, *das;* (noisy quarrel) Streit, *der;* **be eager/ready for the ~** (lit. or fig.) kampflustig/kampfbereit sein; **enter** *or* **join the ~** (lit. or fig.) sich in den Kampf *od.* ins Getümmel stürzen

fray² **1** *v.i.* [sich] durchscheuern; ‹*Hosenbein, Teppich, Seilende:*› ausfransen; **our nerves/tempers began to ~** (fig.) wir verloren langsam die Nerven/unsere Gemüter erhitzten sich. **2** *v.t.* durchscheuern; ausfransen ‹*Hosenbein, Teppich, Seilende*›

freak /friːk/ *n.* **(a)** (monstrosity) Missgeburt, *die;* (plant) missgebildete Pflanze; **~ of nature** Laune der Natur; *attrib.* ungewöhnlich ‹*Wetter, Ereignis*›; völlig überraschend ‹*Sieg, Ergebnis*›; **(b)** (coll.: fanatic) Freak, *der;* **health ~:** Gesundheitsfanatiker, *der*

freckle /'frekl/ *n.* Sommersprosse, *die*

freckled /'frekld/ *adj.* sommersprossig

free /friː/ **1** *adj.,* **freer** /'friːə(r)/, **freest** /'friːɪst/ **(a)** frei; **get ~:** freikommen; sich befreien; **go ~** (escape unpunished) straffrei ausgehen; **let sb. go ~** (leave captivity) jmdn. freilassen; (unpunished) jmdn. freisprechen; **set ~:** freilassen; (fig.) erlösen; **~ of sth.** (without) frei von etw.; **~ of charge/ cost** gebührenfrei/kostenlos; **~ and easy** ungezwungen; locker (ugs.); **give ~ rein to sth.** einer Sache (*Dat.*) freien Lauf lassen; **(b)** (having liberty) **sb. is ~ to do sth.** es steht jmdm. frei, etw. zu tun; **you're ~ to choose** du kannst frei [aus]wählen; **leave sb. ~ to do sth.** es jmdm. ermöglichen, etw. zu tun; **feel ~!** nur zu! (ugs.); **feel ~ to correct me** du darfst mich gerne korrigieren; **it's a ~ country** (coll.) wir leben in einem freien Land; **~ from sth.** frei von etw.; **~ from pain/troubles** schmerz-/sorgenfrei; **(c)** (provided without payment) kostenlos; frei ‹*Überfahrt, Unterkunft, Versand, Verpflegung*›; Frei‹*karte, -exemplar, -fahrt*›; Gratis‹*probe, -vorstellung*›; **'admission ~'** „Eintritt frei"; **have a ~ ride on the train** umsonst mit der Bahn fahren; **for ~** (coll.) umsonst; **(d)** (not occupied, not reserved, not being used) frei; **~ time** Freizeit, *die;* **when would you be ~ to start work?** wann könnten Sie mit der Arbeit anfangen?; **he's ~ in the mornings** er hat morgens Zeit; **(e)** (generous) **be ~ with sth.** mit etw. großzügig umgehen; **(f)** (frank, open) offen; freimütig; **(g)** (not strict) frei ‹*Übersetzung, Interpretation, Bearbeitung usw.*›. **2** *adv.* (without cost or payment) gratis; umsonst. **3** *v.t.* (set at liberty) freilassen; (disentangle) befreien (**of, from** von); **~ sb./oneself from** jmdn./sich befreien von ‹*Tyrannei, Unterdrückung, Tradition*›; jmdn./ sich befreien aus ‹*Gefängnis, Sklaverei, Umklammerung*›; **~ sb./oneself of** jmdn./sich od. freimachen von

free 'agent *n.* **be a ~ agent** sein eigener Herr sein

freebie /'friːbɪ/ (Amer. coll.) **1** *n.* Gratisprobe, *die;* Werbegeschenk, *das.* **2** *adj.* Gratis ‹*essen-, -getränk*›; **~ ticket** Freikarte, *die*

freedom /'friːdəm/ *n.* **(a)** Freiheit, *die;* **give sb. his ~:** jmdn. freigeben; (from prison, slavery) jmdn. freilassen; **~ of the press** Pressefreiheit, *die;* **~ of action/speech/ movement** Handlungs-/Rede-/Bewegungsfreiheit, *die;* **(b)**

(privilege) **[give sb.** *or* **present sb. with] the ~ of the city** [jmdn.] die Ehrenbürgerrechte [verleihen]

'freedom fighter *n.* Freiheitskämpfer, *der*/-kämpferin, *die*

free: ~ **'enterprise** *n.* freies Unternehmertum; ~ **'fall** *n.* freier Fall

Freefone, (P) /'friːfəʊn/ *n., no pl.* Freecall; ≈ Service 130; ~ **line** *or* **number/hotline** gebührenfreie Servicenummer/Hotline; **phone us on ~ 0800 343 027** rufen Sie uns unter 0800 343 027 zum Nulltarif an

free: ~**-for-all** *n.* [allgemeine] Schlägerei; (less violent) [allgemeines] Gerangel; ~ **'gift** *n.* Gratisgabe, *die;* ~**hold 1** *n.* Besitzrecht, *das;* **2** *adj.* Eigentums-; ~**hold land** freier Grundbesitz; ~ **house** *n.* (Brit.) brauereiunabhängiges Wirtshaus; ~ **'kick** *n.* (Footb.) Freistoß, *der;* ~**lance 1** *n.* freier Mitarbeiter/freie Mitarbeiterin; **2** *adj.* freiberuflich; **3** *v.i.* freiberuflich arbeiten; ~**lancer** /'friːlɑːnsə(r)/ ⇒ **freelance 1**; ~**'loader** *n.* (coll.) Nassauer, *der* (ugs.)

freely /'friːlɪ/ *adv.* **(a)** (willingly) großzügig; freimütig ‹*eingestehen*›; **(b)** (without restriction, loosely) frei; **(c)** (frankly) offen

free: ~ **'market** *n.* (Econ.) freier Markt; **F~mason** *n.* Freimaurer, *der*

Freephone ⇒ **Freefone**

freer ⇒ **free 1**

'free-range *adj.* freilaufend ‹*Huhn*›; ~ **eggs** Eier von frei laufenden Hühnern

freesia /'friːzɪə/ *n.* (Bot.) Freesie, *die*

free 'speech *n.* Redefreiheit, *die*

freest ⇒ **free 1**

free: ~ **'trade** *n.* Freihandel, *der;* ~**ware** /'friːweə(r)/ *n., no pl., no indef. art.* (Computing) Freeware, *die;* kostenlose Software; ~**way** *n.* (Amer.) Autobahn, *die;* ~**-wheel** *v.i.* im Freilauf fahren

freeze /friːz/ **1** *v.i.,* **froze** /frəʊz/, **frozen** /'frəʊzn/ **(a)** frieren; **it will ~** (Meteorol.) es wird Frost geben; **(b)** (become covered with ice) ‹*See, Fluss, Teich:*› zufrieren; ‹*Straße:*› vereisen; **(c)** (solidify) ‹*Flüssigkeit:*› gefrieren; ‹*Rohr, Schloss:*› einfrieren; **(d)** (become rigid) steif frieren; (fig.) ‹*Lächeln:*› gefrieren (geh.); **(e)** (be or feel cold) sehr frieren; (fig.) erstarren (**with** vor + *Dat.*); ‹*Blut:*› gefrieren (geh.); **my hands are freezing** meine Hände sind eiskalt; **~ to death** meine Hände (fig.) bitterlich frieren; **(f)** (make oneself motionless) erstarren. **2** *v.t.,* **froze, frozen (a)** zufrieren lassen ‹*Teich, Fluss*›; gefrieren lassen ‹*Rohr*›; (fig.) erstarren lassen; **we were frozen stiff** (fig.) wir waren steif gefroren; **(b)** (preserve) tiefkühlen, tiefgefrieren ‹*Lebensmittel*›; **(c)** einfrieren ‹*Kredit, Guthaben, Gelder, Löhne, Preise usw.*›; **(d)** (fig.) erstarren lassen. **3** *n.* (fixing) Einfrieren, *das* (**on** *Gen.*); **price/wage ~:** Preis-/Lohnstopp, *der*

~ **'up 1** *v.i.* ‹*Fluss, Teich:*› zufrieren; ‹*Schloss, Rohr:*› einfrieren. **2** *v.t.* ⇒ **1:** zufrieren/einfrieren lassen

'freeze-dry *v.t.* gefriertrocknen

freezer /'friːzə(r)/ *n.* (deep freeze) Tiefkühltruhe, *die;* Gefriertruhe, *die;* **[upright] ~:** Tiefkühlschrank, *der;* Gefrierschrank, *der; attrib.* ~ **compartment** Tiefkühlfach, *das;* Gefrierfach, *das*

freezing /'friːzɪŋ/ **1** *adj.* (lit. or fig.) frostig; ~ **temperatures** Temperaturen unter null Grad; **it is ~ in here** es ist eiskalt hier drinnen. **2** *n., no pl.* ▶ 1141 | (~ point) **above/below ~:** über/unter dem/den Gefrierpunkt. **3** *adv.* ~ **cold** eiskalt

freezing: ~ **'fog** *n.* gefrierender Nebel; ~ **point** *n.* ▶ 1141 | Gefrierpunkt, *der*

freight /freɪt/ **1** *n.* Fracht, *die.* **2** *v.t.* befrachten

'freight car *n.* (Amer. Railw.) Güterwagen, *der*

freighter /'freɪtə(r)/ *n.* (ship) Frachter, *der;* Frachtschiff, *das;* (aircraft) Frachtflugzeug, *das*

French /frentʃ/ ▶ 897 |, ▶ 947 | **1** *adj.* französisch; **he/ she is ~:** er ist Franzose/sie ist Französin. **2** *n.* **(a)** Französisch, *das; see also* **English 2 a; (b)** *constr. as pl.* **the ~:** die Franzosen

French: ~ **'bean** n. (Brit.) Gartenbohne, die; [grüne] Bohne; ~ **Ca'nadian** n. ▶947| Frankokanadier, der/ -kanadierin, die; ~**Ca'nadian** adj. ▶947| frankokanadisch; ~ **'door** ⇒ ~ **window;** ~ **'dressing** n. Vinaigrette, die; ~ **'fries** n. pl. Pommes frites Pl.; ~ **'horn** n. (Mus.) [Wald]horn, das; ~ **'letter** n. (Brit. coll.) Pariser, der (salopp); ~**man** /'frentʃmən/ n., pl. ~**men** /'frentʃmən/ Franzose, der; ~ **'polish** n. Schellackpolitur, die; ~ **'window** n., in sing. or pl. französisches Fenster; ~**woman** n. Französin, die

frenetic /frɪ'netɪk/ adj. verzweifelt ‹Hilferuf, Versuch›

frenzied /'frenzɪd/ adj. rasend; wahnsinnig ‹Tat›

frenzy /'frenzɪ/ n. (a) (derangement) Wahnsinn, der; (b) (fury, agitation) Raserei, die; **in a ~ of despair/passion** in einem Anfall von Verzweiflung/von wilder Leidenschaft übermannt

frequency /'fri:kwənsɪ/ n. (a) Häufigkeit, die; (b) (Phys., Statistics) Frequenz, die

'frequency band n. (Radio, Telev., Phys.) Frequenzband, das

frequent **1** /'fri:kwənt/ adj. (a) häufig; **it's a ~ occurrence** es kommt häufig vor; (b) (habitual, constant) eifrig ‹[Kino-, Theater]besucher, Briefschreiber›. **2** /frɪ'kwent/ v.t. frequentieren (geh.); häufig besuchen ‹Café, Klub usw.›; **much ~ed** stark frequentiert (geh.)

frequently /'fri:kwəntlɪ/ adv. häufig

fresco /'freskəʊ/ n., pl. ~**es** or ~**s** (a) no pl., no art. (method) Freskomalerei, die; (b) (a painting) Fresko, das

fresh /freʃ/ **1** adj. (a) frisch; neu ‹Beweise, Anstrich, Ideen›; frisch, neu ‹Energie, Mut, Papierbogen›; **a ~ approach** ein neuer Ansatz; ~ **supplies** Nachschub, der (of an + Dat.); **make a ~ start** noch einmal von vorn anfangen; (fig.) neu beginnen; ~ **from** or **off the press** druckfrisch; frisch aus der Presse; **get some ~ air** frische Luft schnappen (ugs.); **as ~ as a daisy/as paint** ganz frisch; (in appearance) frisch wie der junge Morgen (meist scherzh.); (b) (cheeky) keck; **get ~ with sb.** jmdm. frech kommen (ugs.). **2** adv. frisch; **we're ~ out of eggs** (coll.) uns sind gerade die Eier ausgegangen

freshen /'freʃn/ v.i. (increase) ‹Wind:› auffrischen ~ **'up** v.i. sich frisch machen

freshly /'freʃlɪ/ adv. frisch

freshman /'freʃmən/ n., pl. **freshmen** /'freʃmən/ Erstsemester, das

freshness /'freʃnɪs/ n., no pl. Frische, die; (of idea, approach) Neuartigkeit, die

fresh: ~ **'water** n. Süßwasser, das; ~**water** adj. Süßwasser-

fret[1] /fret/ v.i., -**tt**- beunruhigt sein; besorgt sein; **don't ~!** sei unbesorgt!; ~ **at** or **about** or **over sth.** sich über etw. (Akk.) od. wegen etw. aufregen

fret[2] n. (Mus.) Bund, der

fretful /'fretfl/ adj. (peevish) verdrießlich; quengelig (ugs.) ‹Kleinkind›; (restless) unruhig

Freudian /'frɔɪdɪən/ adj. freudianisch; ~ **slip** Freudsche Fehlleistung

Fri. abbr. ▶739| **Friday** Fr.

friar /'fraɪə(r)/ n. Ordensbruder, der

fricassee /'frɪkəsɪ:/ n. (Cookery) Frikassee, das

friction /'frɪkʃn/ n. Reibung, die

Friday /'fraɪdeɪ, 'fraɪdɪ/ ▶739| **1** n. Freitag, der; **on ~:** [am] Freitag; **on a ~, on ~s** freitags; **we got married on a ~:** wir haben an einem Freitag geheiratet; ~ **13 August** Freitag, der 13. August; (at top of letter etc.) Freitag, den 13. August; **on ~ 13 August** am Freitag, den od. dem 13. August; **next/last ~:** [am] nächsten/letzten od. vergangenen Freitag; **we were married a year [ago] last/next ~:** vergangenen/kommenden Freitag vor einem Jahr haben wir geheiratet; **[last] ~'s newspaper** die Zeitung vom [letzten] Freitag; **Good ~:** Karfreitag, der; **man/girl ~:** Mädchen für alles (ugs.). **2** adv. (coll.) (a) ~ **[week]** Freitag [in einer Woche]; (b) ~**s** freitags; Freitag (ugs.); **she comes ~s** sie kommt freitags

fridge /frɪdʒ/ n. (Brit. coll.) Kühlschrank, der; ~**-freezer** Kühl- und Gefrier-Kombination, die

fried ⇒ **fry**[1]

friend /frend/ n. (a) Freund, der/Freundin, die; **be ~s with sb.** mit jmdm. befreundet sein; **make ~s [with sb.]** [mit jmdm.] Freundschaft schließen; **a ~ in need is a ~ indeed** (prov.) Freunde in der Not gehn hundert od. tausend auf ein Lot (Spr.); **between ~s** unter Freunden; ~**s in high places** einflussreiche Freunde; (b) **the Society of F~s** die Quäker

friendless /'frendlɪs/ adj. ohne Freund[e] nachgestellt

friendliness /'frendlɪnɪs/ n., no pl. Freundlichkeit, die

friendly /'frendlɪ/ **1** adj. (a) freundlich (**to** zu); freundschaftlich ‹Rat, Beziehungen, Wettkampf, Gespräch›; **be on ~ terms** or **be ~ with sb.** mit jmdm. auf freundschaftlichem Fuße stehen; (b) (not hostile) freundlich [gesinnt] ‹Bewohner›; befreundet ‹Staat›; zutraulich ‹Tier›; (c) (well-wishing) wohlwollend ‹Erwähnung›. **2** n. (Sport) Freundschaftsspiel, das

friendly 'fire n. (Milit.) eigenes Feuer

friendship /'frendʃɪp/ n. Freundschaft, die; **strike up a ~ with sb.** sich mit jmdm. anfreunden

Friends of the Earth pr. n. sing. or pl. Friends of the Earth (Umweltschutzvereinigung)

fries /fraɪz/ n. pl. (Amer.) Pommes frites Pl.

Friesian /'fri:zɪən, 'fri:ʒən/ (Agric.) **1** adj. schwarzbunt. **2** n. Schwarzbunte, die

frigate /'frɪgət/ n. (Naut.) Fregatte, die

fright /fraɪt/ n. Schreck, der; Schrecken, der; **take ~:** erschrecken; **give sb. a ~:** jmdm. einen Schreck[en] einjagen; **get** or **have a ~:** einen Schreck[en] bekommen; **be** or **look a ~:** zum Fürchten aussehen (ugs.)

frighten /'fraɪtn/ v.t. ‹Explosion, Schuss:› erschrecken; ‹Gedanke, Drohung:› angst machen (+ Dat.); **be ~ed at** or **by sth.** vor etw. (Dat.) erschrecken; ~ **sb. out of his wits** jmdn. furchtbar erschrecken; **be ~ed to death** (fig.) zu Tode erschrocken sein
~ **a'way,** ~ **'off** v.t. vertreiben; (put off) abschrecken

frightened /'fraɪtnd/ adj. verängstigt; angsterfüllt ‹Stimme›; **be ~ [of sth.]** [vor etw. (Dat.)] Angst haben

frightening /'fraɪtnɪŋ/ adj. furchterregend

frightful /'fraɪtfl/ adj. furchterlich; furchtbar; (coll.: terrible) furchtbar (ugs.)

frightfully /'fraɪtfəlɪ/ adv. furchtbar; schrecklich; (coll.: extremely) furchtbar (ugs.)

frigid /'frɪdʒɪd/ adj. (formal, unfriendly) frostig; (sexually unresponsive) frigid[e] ‹Frau›

frill /frɪl/ n. (a) (ruffled edge) Rüsche, die; (b) in pl. (embellishments) Beiwerk, das; Ausschmückungen (fig.); **with no ~s** ‹Ferienhaus, Auto› ohne besondere Ausstattung

frilly /'frɪlɪ/ adj. mit Rüschen besetzt; Rüschen‹kleid, -bluse›

fringe /frɪndʒ/ n. (a) (bordering) Fransen; Fransenkante, die (on an + Dat.); (b) (hair) [Pony]fransen (ugs.); (c) (edge) Rand, der; attrib. Rand‹geschehen, -gruppe, -gebiet›; **live on the ~[s] of the city** in den Randgebieten der Stadt wohnen; **lunatic ~:** Extremisten; attrib. ~ **benefits** zusätzliche Leistungen

frisk /frɪsk/ **1** v.i. ~ **[about]** [herum]springen. **2** v.t. (coll.) filzen (ugs.)

frisky /'frɪskɪ/ adj. munter

fritter[1] /'frɪtə(r)/ n. (Cookery) **apple/sausage ~s** Apfelstücke/Würstchen in Pfannkuchenteig

fritter[2] v.t. ~ **away** vergeuden; verplempern (ugs.)

frivolity /frɪ'vɒlɪtɪ/ n., no pl. Oberflächlichkeit, die; Leichtfertigkeit, die

frivolous /'frɪvələs/ adj. (a) (not serious) frivol; extravagant ‹Kleidung›; (b) (trifling, futile) belanglos

fro /frəʊ/ ⇒ **to 2 b**

frock /frɒk/ n. Kleid, das

frog /frɒg/ n. Frosch, der; **have a ~ in the** or **one's throat** (coll.) einen Frosch im Hals haben (ugs.)

frog: ~**man** /'frɒgmən/ n., pl. ~**men** /'frɒgmən/ Froschmann, der; ~**march** v.t. (carry) zu viert an Händen und Füßen tragen; (hustle) ≈ im Polizeigriff abführen; ~**spawn** n. Froschlaich, der

frolic /'frɒlɪk/ v.i., **-ck-:** ~ **[about** or **around]** [herum]springen

from /frəm, stressed frɒm/ prep. **(a)** expr. starting point von; (~ within) aus; [**come**] ~ **Paris/Munich** aus Paris/ München [kommen]; ~ **Paris to Munich** von Paris nach München; **where have you come** ~? woher kommen Sie?; **(b)** ▶ **1205 |** expr. beginning von; ~ **the year 1972 we never saw him again** seit 1972 haben wir ihn nie mehr [wieder]gesehen; ~ **tomorrow [until ...]** von morgen an [bis ...]; **start work** ~ **2 August** am 2. August anfangen zu arbeiten; ~ **now on** von jetzt an; ~ **then on** seitdem; **(c)** expr. lower limit von; **blouses [ranging]** ~ **£2 to £5** Blusen [im Preis] zwischen 2 und 5 Pfund; **dresses** ~ **£20 [upwards]** Kleider von 20 Pfund aufwärts od. ab 20 Pfund; ~ **4 to 6 eggs** 4 bis 6 Eier; ~ **the age of 18 [upwards]** ab 18 Jahre od. Jahren; ~ **a child** (since childhood) schon als Kind; **(d)** expr. distance von; **be a mile** ~ **sth.** eine Meile von etw. entfernt sein; **away** ~ **home** von zu Hause weg; **(e)** expr. removal, avoidance von; expr. escape von (+ Dat.); **(f)** expr. change von; ~ ... **to** ...: von ... zu ...; (relating to price) von ... auf ...; ~ **crisis to crisis,** ~ **one crisis to another** von einer Krise zur anderen; **(g)** expr. source, origin aus; **pick apples** ~ **a tree** Äpfel vom Baum pflücken; **buy everything** ~ **the same shop** alles im selben Laden kaufen; **where do you come** ~?, **where are you** ~? woher kommen Sie?; ~ **the country** vom Land; **(h)** expr. viewpoint von [... aus]; **(i)** expr. giver, sender von; **take it** ~ **me that** ...: lass dir gesagt sein, dass ...; **(j)** (after the model of) **painted** ~ **life/nature** nach dem Leben/nach der Natur gemalt; **(k)** expr. reason, cause **she was weak** ~ **hunger/tired** ~ **so much work** sie war schwach vor Hunger/müde von der vielen Arbeit; ~ **what I can see/have heard ...:** wie ich das sehe/wie ich gehört habe, ...; **(l)** with adv. von (unten, oben, innen, außen); **(m)** with prep. ~ **behind/under[neath] sth.** hinter/unter etw. (Dat.) hervor

front /frʌnt/ **1** n. **(a)** Vorderseite, die; (of door) Außenseite, die; (of house) Vorderfront, die; (of queue) vorderes Ende; (of procession) Spitze, die; (of book) vorderer Deckel; **in** or **at the** ~ **[of sth.]** vorn [in etw. position: Dat.; movement: Akk.]; **sit in the** ~ **of the car** vorne sitzen; **the index is at the** ~: das Register ist vorn; **to the** ~: nach vorn; **in** ~: vorn[e]; **be in** ~ **of sth./sb.** vor etw./jmdm. sein; **walk in** ~ **of sb.** (preceding) vor jmdm. gehen; (to position) vor jmdn. gehen; **he was murdered in** ~ **of his wife** er wurde vor den Augen seiner Frau ermordet; **(b)** (Mil.; also fig.) Front, die; **on the Western** ~: an der Westfront; **be attacked on all** ~s an allen Fronten/(fig.) von allen Seiten angegriffen werden; **(c)** (at seaside) Strandpromenade, die; **(d)** (Meteorol.) Front, die; **cold/warm** ~: Kalt-/Warmluftfront, die; **(e)** (outward appearance) Aussehen, das; (bluff) Fassade, die (oft abwertend); (pretext, façade) Tarnung, die; **put on a brave** ~: nach außen hin gefasst bleiben; **it's all a** ~: das ist alles nur Fassade (abwertend). **2** adj. vorder...; Vorder(rad, -zimmer, -zahn); ~ **garden** Vorgarten, der; ~ **row** erste Reihe

frontage /'frʌntɪdʒ/ n. **(a)** (extent) Frontbreite, die; **(b)** (façade) Fassade, die

frontal /'frʌntl/ adj. **(a)** Frontal-; **(b)** (Art) frontal (Darstellung); **[full]** ~: frontal dargestellt (Akt)

front: ~ **'bench** n. (Brit. Parl.) vorderste Bank; ~ **'door** n. (of flat) Wohnungstür, die; (of house; also fig.) Haustür, die

frontier /'frʌntɪə(r)/ n. (lit. or fig.) Grenze, die

frontispiece /'frʌntɪspiːs/ n. Frontispiz, das; Titelbild, das

front: ~ **'line** n. Front[linie], die; ~**man** n. **(a)** (of criminal organization) [An]führer, der; **(b)** (of television programme) Moderator, der; **(c)** (of rock group etc.) Frontmann, der; ~ **'page** n. Titelseite, die; **make the** ~ **page** auf die Titelseite kommen; ~**rank** adj. (fig.) herausragend; ~ **runner** n. (fig.) Spitzenkandidat, der; ~ **'seat** n. (in theatre) Platz in den ersten Reihen; (in car) Vordersitz, der; (in bus, coach) vorderer Sitzplatz; ~**-wheel drive** **1** n. Vorderradantrieb, der; Frontantrieb, der; **2** adj. a ~**wheel drive vehicle** ein Fahrzeug mit Vorderrad- od.

Frontantrieb; **the car is** ~**-wheel drive** das Auto hat Vorderrad- od. Frontantrieb.

frost /frɒst/ **1** n. Frost, der; (frozen dew or vapour) Reif, der; **ten degrees of** ~ (Brit.) zehn Grad minus. **2** v.t. **(a)** (esp. Amer. Cookery) mit Zucker bestreuen; (ice) glasieren; **(b)** ~**ed glass** Mattglas, das ~ **'over 1** v.t. be ~ed over vereist sein. **2** v.i. vereisen

frost: ~**bite** n. Erfrierung, die; ~**bitten** adj. durch Frost geschädigt; **sb. is** ~**bitten** jmd. hat Erfrierungen; **his toes are** ~**bitten** er hat Frost od. Erfrierungen in den Zehen

frosting /'frɒstɪŋ/ n. (esp. Amer. Cookery) Zucker, der; (icing) Glasur, die

frosty /'frɒstɪ/ adj. (lit. or fig.) frostig; (with hoar frost) bereift

froth /frɒθ/ **1** n. (foam) Schaum, der. **2** v.i. schäumen; ~ **at the mouth** Schaum vor dem Mund haben

frothy /'frɒθɪ/ adj. schaumig; schäumend (Bier, Brandung, Maul)

frown /fraʊn/ **1** v.i. die Stirn runzeln (at, [up]on über + Akk.); ~ **at sth./sb.** etw./jmdn. stirnrunzelnd ansehen. **2** n. Stirnrunzeln, das; **with a [deep/worried/puzzled]** ~: mit [stark/sorgenvoll/verwirrt] gerunzelter Stirn; **a** ~ **of disapproval** ein missbilligender Blick

froze ⇒ **freeze 1, 2**

frozen /'frəʊzn/ **1** ⇒ **freeze 1, 2. 2** adj. **(a)** gefroren; zugefroren (Fluss, See); erfroren (Tier, Person, Pflanze); eingefroren (Wasserleitung); **I am** ~ **stiff** (fig.) ich bin ganz steif gefroren; **my hands are** ~ (fig.) meine Hände sind eiskalt; **(b)** (to preserve) tiefgekühlt; ~ **food** Tiefkühlkost, die

frugal /'fruːgl/ adj. sparsam (Hausfrau); genügsam (Lebensweise, Person); frugal (Mahl)

fruit /fruːt/ n. Frucht, die; (collectively) Obst, das; Früchte; **bear** ~ (lit. or fig.) Früchte tragen

fruiterer /'fruːtərə(r)/ n. ▶ **887 |** Obsthändler, der/-händlerin, die

fruitful /'fruːtfl/ adj. (lit. or fig.) fruchtbar

fruition /fruːˈɪʃn/ n. **bring to** ~: verwirklichen (Plan, Ziel); **come to** ~ (Plan:) Wirklichkeit werden

'fruit juice n. Fruchtsaft, der

fruitless /'fruːtlɪs/ adj. nutzlos (Versuch); fruchtlos (Verhandlung, Bemühung, Suche)

fruit: ~ **machine** n. (Brit.) Spielautomat, der; ~ **'salad** n. Obstsalat, der; ~ **tree** n. Obstbaum, der

fruity /'fruːtɪ/ adj. **(a)** fruchtig (Geschmack, Wein); **(b)** (coll.: rich in tone) volltönend (Stimme); herzhaft (Lachen)

frump /frʌmp/ n. (derog.) Vogelscheuche, die (ugs.)

frumpy /'frʌmpɪ/ adj. (derog.) ohne jeden Schick nachgestellt

frustrate /frʌˈstreɪt/ v.t. vereiteln, durchkreuzen (Plan, Vorhaben, Versuch); zunichte machen (Hoffnung, Bemühungen); enttäuschen (Erwartung)

frustrated /frʌˈstreɪtɪd/ adj. frustriert

frustrating /frʌˈstreɪtɪŋ/ adj. frustrierend; ärgerlich (Angewohnheit)

frustration /frʌˈstreɪʃn/ n. Frustration, die; (of plans, efforts) Scheitern, das

fry¹ /fraɪ/ v.t. braten; **fried eggs/potatoes** Spiegeleier/ Bratkartoffeln ~ **'up** v.t. aufbraten (Reste)

fry² n. (young fishes etc.) Brut, die; **'small** ~ (fig.) unbedeutende Leute

frying pan /'fraɪŋpæn/ n. Bratpfanne, die; **[fall/jump] out of the** ~ **into the fire** vom Regen in die Traufe [kommen] (ugs.)

fry: ~**pan** (Amer.) ⇒ **frying pan;** ~**-up** n. Pfannengericht, das

ft. abbr. ▶ **850 |, ▶ 904 | feet, foot** ft.

fuchsia /'fjuːʃə/ n. (Bot.) Fuchsie, die

fuck /fʌk/ (coarse) **1** v.t. & i. ficken (vulg.); **[oh,]** ~!, **[oh,]** ~ **it!** [au,] Scheiße! (derb); ~ **you!** leck mich am Arsch! (derb). **2** n. (act) Fick, der (vulg.)

fuddle /'fʌdl/ v.t. **(a)** (intoxicate) **slightly** ~**d** [leicht] beschwipst (ugs.); **(b)** (confuse) verwirren

fuddy-duddy /ˈfʌdɪdʌdɪ/ (coll.) **1** *adj.* verkalkt (ugs.). **2** *n.* Fossil, *das* (fig.)

fudge¹ /fʌdʒ/ *n.* (sweet) Karamellbonbon, *der od. das*

fudge² **1** *v.t.* frisieren (ugs.) ⟨*Geschäftsbücher*⟩; sich (*Dat.*) aus den Fingern saugen ⟨*Ausrede, Geschichte, Entschuldigung*⟩. **2** *n.* Schwindel, *der*

fuel /ˈfjuːəl/ **1** *n.* Brennstoff, *der;* (for vehicle) Kraftstoff, *der;* (for ship, aircraft, spacecraft) Treibstoff, *der;* **add ∼ to the flames** *or* **fire** (fig.) Öl ins Feuer gießen. **2** *v.t.,* (Brit.) **-ll-** auftanken ⟨*Schiff, Flugzeug*⟩; (fig.: stimulate) Nahrung geben (+ *Dat.*) ⟨*Verdacht, Spekulationen*⟩; anheizen ⟨*Inflation*⟩

fuel: **∼ consumption** *n.* (of vehicle) Kraftstoffverbrauch, *der;* **∼-efficient** *adj.* sparsam ⟨*Motor, Auto usw.*⟩; **∼ pump** *n.* Kraftstoffpumpe, *die;* **∼ tank** *n.* (of vehicle) Kraftstofftank, *der;* (for storage) Kraftstoffbehälter, *der*

fug /fʌg/ *n.* (coll.) Mief, *der* (salopp)

fugitive /ˈfjuːdʒɪtɪv/ **1** *adj.* (lit. or fig.) flüchtig. **2** *n.* **(a)** Flüchtige, *der/die;* **be a ∼ from justice/from the law** auf der Flucht vor der Justiz/dem Gesetz sein; **(b)** (exile) Flüchtling, *der*

fugue /fjuːg/ *n.* (Mus.) Fuge, *die*

fulfil (*Amer.*: **fulfill**) /fʊlˈfɪl/ *v.t.,* **-ll-** erfüllen; stillen ⟨*Verlangen, Bedürfnisse*⟩; entsprechen (+ *Dat.*) ⟨*Erwartungen*⟩; ausführen ⟨*Befehl*⟩; halten ⟨*Versprechen*⟩; **be fulfilled** ⟨*Wunsch, Hoffnung, Prophezeiung:*⟩ sich erfüllen; **be** *or* **feel fulfilled [in one's job]** [in seinem Beruf] Erfüllung finden

fulfilment (*Amer.*: **fulfillment**) /fʊlˈfɪlmənt/ *n.* Erfüllung, *die;* (of an order) Ausführung, *die;* **bring sth. to ∼:** etw. erfüllen

full /fʊl/ **1** *adj.* **(a)** voll; **the jug is ∼ of water** der Krug ist voll Wasser; **the bus was completely ∼:** der Bus war voll besetzt; **∼ of hatred/holes** voller Hass/Löcher; **∼ up** (coll.) voll [besetzt] sein; ⟨*Behälter:*⟩ randvoll sein; ⟨*Liste:*⟩ voll sein; ⟨*Flug:*⟩ völlig ausgebucht sein (*see also* **c**); **(b) ∼ of** (engrossed with): **be ∼ of oneself/one's own importance** sehr von sich eingenommen sein/sich sehr wichtig nehmen; **she's been ∼ of it ever since** seitdem spricht sie von nichts anderem [mehr]; **the newspapers are ∼ of the crisis** die Zeitungen sind voll von Berichten über die Krise; **(c)** (replete with food) voll ⟨*Magen*⟩; satt ⟨*Person*⟩; **I'm ∼ [up]** (coll.) ich bin voll [bis obenhin] (ugs.) (*see also* **a**); **(d)** (comprehensive) ausführlich, umfassend ⟨*Bericht, Beschreibung*⟩; (satisfying) vollwertig ⟨*Mahlzeit*⟩; erfüllt ⟨*Leben*⟩; (complete) ganz ⟨*Stunde, Tag, Jahr, Monat, Semester, Seite*⟩; voll ⟨*Name, Fahrpreis, Gehalt, Bezahlung, Unterstützung, Mitgefühl, Verständnis*⟩; **[the] ∼ details** alle Einzelheiten; **in ∼ daylight** am helllichten Tag; **the moon is ∼:** es ist Vollmond; **in ∼ bloom** in voller Blüte; **∼ member** Vollmitglied, *das;* **in ∼ view of sb.** [direkt] vor jmds. Augen; **at ∼ speed** mit Höchstgeschwindigkeit; **be at ∼ strength** ⟨*Mannschaft, Ausschuss, Kabinett:*⟩ vollzählig sein; **(e)** (intense in quality) hell, voll ⟨*Licht*⟩; voll ⟨*Klang, Stimme, Aroma*⟩; **(f)** (rounded, plump) voll ⟨*Gesicht, Busen, Lippen, Mund, Segel*⟩; füllig ⟨*Figur*⟩; weit geschnitten ⟨*Rock*⟩. **2** *n.* **(a) in ∼:** vollständig; **write your name [out] in ∼:** schreiben Sie Ihren Namen aus; **(b) enjoy sth. to the ∼:** etw. in vollen Zügen genießen. **3** *adv.* **(a)** (very) **know ∼ well that …:** ganz genau *od.* sehr wohl wissen, dass …; **(b)** (exactly, directly) genau; **∼ in the face** direkt ins Gesicht ⟨*schlagen, scheinen*⟩; **look sb. ∼ in the face** jmdn. voll ansehen

full: **∼-blooded** /fʊlbˈlʌdɪd/ *adj.* (vigorous) vollblütig; **∼-blown** *adj.* ausgewachsen ⟨*Skandal*⟩; ausgereift ⟨*Theorie, Plan, Gedanke*⟩; umfassend ⟨*Bericht*⟩; **∼-blown Aids** Vollbild-Aids, *das;* **∼ 'board** *n.* Vollpension, *die;* **∼-bodied** /fʊlbˈɒdɪd/ *adj.* vollmundig, (fachspr.) körperreich ⟨*Wein*⟩; voll ⟨*Ton, Klang*⟩; **∼-cream milk** *n.* Vollmilch, *die;* **∼ em'ployment** *n.* Vollbeschäftigung, *die;* **∼-grown** *adj.* ausgewachsen ⟨*Person, Tier*⟩; **∼ 'house** *n.* (Theatre) ausverkauftes *od.* volles Haus; **∼ 'length** *adv.* der Länge nach ⟨*hinfallen, liegen*⟩; **∼ length** *adj.* abendfüllend ⟨*Film, Theaterstück*⟩; **∼ length portrait** Ganzporträt, *das;* **∼-length dress**

langes Kleid; **∼ 'marks** *n. pl., no art.* die höchste Bewertung; (Sch., Univ.) die beste Note; **∼ marks!** (fig. coll.) ausgezeichnet!; **give sb. ∼ marks** (fig.) jmdm. höchstes Lob zollen; **∼ 'moon** *n.* Vollmond, *der*

fullness /ˈfʊlnɪs/ *n., no pl.* (of skirt) weiter Schnitt; (of figure) Fülligkeit, *die;* (of face) Rundheit, *die;* **in the ∼ of time** (literary) wenn die Zeit dafür gekommen ist/als die Zeit dafür gekommen war

full: **∼-page** *adj.* ganzseitig; **∼ 'point** *n.* Punkt, *der;* **∼-scale** *adj.* **(a)** in Originalgröße *nachgestellt;* **(b)** groß angelegt ⟨*Werbekampagne, Untersuchung, Suchaktion*⟩; umfassend ⟨*Umarbeitung, Revision*⟩; **∼-size, ∼-sized** *adjs.* **(a)** (standard-size) normal groß; **∼-size trees** ausgewachsene *od.* große Bäume; **(b)** (not scaled down) in Originalgröße *postpos.* **∼ 'stop** *n.* **(a)** Punkt, *der;* **(b)** (fig. coll.) **come to a ∼ stop** zum Stillstand kommen; **I'm not going, ∼ stop!** ich gehe nicht, [und damit] basta! (ugs.); **∼ 'time** *adv.* ganztags ⟨*arbeiten*⟩; **∼-time** *adj.* ganztägig; Ganztags⟨*arbeit, -beschäftigung*⟩

fully /ˈfʊlɪ/ *adv.* **(a)** voll [und ganz]; fest ⟨*entschlossen*⟩; ausführlich ⟨*erklären usw.*⟩; restlos ⟨*überzeugt*⟩; **(b)** (at least) **∼ two hours** volle zwei Stunden; **∼ three weeks ago** vor gut drei Wochen

fully: **∼-fledged** /ˈfʊlɪfledʒd/ *attrib. adj.* flügge ⟨*Vogel*⟩; (fig.) fertig ⟨*Lehrer, Pilot, usw.*⟩; richtig ⟨*Demokratie*⟩; **∼-qualified** *attrib adj.* vollqualifiziert

fulsome /ˈfʊlsəm/ *adj.* übertrieben ⟨*Lob, Kompliment*⟩

fumble /ˈfʌmbl/ *v.i.* **∼ at** *or* **with** [herum]fingern an (+ *Dat.*); **∼ with one's papers** in seinen Papieren kramen (ugs.); **∼ in one's pockets for sth.** in seinen Taschen nach etw. fingern *od.* (ugs.) kramen; **∼ for the light switch** nach dem Lichtschalter tasten; **∼ [about** *or* **around] in the dark** im Dunkeln herumtasten

fume /fjuːm/ **1** *n. in pl.* **petrol/ammonia ∼s** Benzin-/Ammoniakdämpfe; **∼s of wine/whisky** Alkohol-/Whiskydunst, *der.* **2** *v.i.* vor Wut schäumen; **∼ at sb.** auf *od.* über jmdn. wütend sein; **∼ at** *or* **about sth.** wegen etw. wütend sein

fumigate /ˈfjuːmɪgeɪt/ *v.t.* ausräuchern

fun /fʌn/ **1** *n.* Spaß, *der;* **have ∼ doing sth.** Spaß daran haben, etw. zu tun; **have ∼!** viel Spaß!; **make ∼ of** *or* **poke ∼ at sb./sth.** sich über jmdn./etw. lustig machen; **in ∼:** im Spaß; **for ∼, for the ∼ of it** zum Spaß; **spoil the** *or* **sb.'s ∼:** jmdm. den Spaß verderben; **sth. is [good** *or* **great/no] ∼:** etw. macht [großen/keinen] Spaß; **it's no ∼ being unemployed** es ist kein Vergnügen, arbeitslos zu sein; **we had the usual ∼ and games with him** (iron.: trouble) wir hatten wieder das übliche Theater mit ihm (ugs.). **2** *adj.* (coll.) lustig; amüsant

function /ˈfʌŋkʃn/ **1** *n.* **(a)** (role) Aufgabe, *die;* **in his ∼ as surgeon** in seiner Funktion *od.* Eigenschaft als Chirurg; **(b)** (mode of action) Funktion, *die;* **(c)** (reception) Empfang, *der;* (official ceremony) Feierlichkeit, *die;* **(d)** (Math.) Funktion, *die.* **2** *v.i.* ⟨*Maschine, System, Organisation:*⟩ funktionieren; ⟨*Organ:*⟩ arbeiten; **∼ as** (have the ∼ of) fungieren als; (serve as) dienen als

functional /ˈfʌŋkʃənl/ *adj.* **(a)** (useful, practical) funktionell; **(b)** (working) funktionsfähig; **be ∼ again** wieder funktionieren

function: **∼ key** *n.* (Computing) Funktionstaste, *die;* **∼ word** *n.* Funktionswort, *das*

fund /fʌnd/ **1** *n.* **(a)** (of money) Fonds, *der;* **(b)** (fig.: stock, store) Fundus, *der* (**of** von, an + *Dat.*); **(c)** *in pl.* (resources) Mittel *Pl.;* Gelder *Pl.;* **be short of ∼s** knapp *od.* schlecht bei Kasse sein (ugs.). **2** *v.t.* finanzieren

fundamental /fʌndəˈmentl/ *adj.* grundlegend (**to** für); elementar ⟨*Bedürfnisse*⟩; (primary, original) Grund⟨*struktur, -form, -typus*⟩

fundamentally /fʌndəˈmentəlɪ/ *adv.* grundlegend; von Grund auf ⟨*verschieden, ehrlich*⟩; **∼ opposed to sth.** grundsätzlich gegen etw.; **man is ∼ good** der Mensch ist von Natur aus gut

fundholder *n.* (Brit.) *praktischer Arzt mit eigenständig verwaltetem Budget*

fundholding /ˈfʌndhəʊldɪŋ/ (Brit.) **1** *adj.* **∼ practitioner** praktischer Arzt mit eigenständig verwaltetem

Budget; ~ **practice** [Arzt]praxis mit eigenständig verwaltetem Budget. **2** *n.* Eigenbudgetierung, *die*

funding /'fʌndɪŋ/ *n.*, *no pl.*, *no indef. art.* **(a)** (providing funds) Finanzierung, *die;* **(b)** (resources) Finanzierungsmittel *Pl.*

fund: ~ **manager** *n.* Fondsverwalter, *der*/-verwalterin, *die;* Fondsmanager, *der*/-managerin, *die* (fachspr.); ~-**raiser** /'fʌndreɪzə(r)/ *n.* **(a)** (person) Geldbeschaffer, *der*/ -beschafferin, *die;* **(b)** (event) Benefizveranstaltung, *die;* ~-**raising** /'fʌndreɪzɪŋ/ *n.*, *no pl.* Geldbeschaffung, *die;* *attrib.* zur Geldbeschaffung *nachgestellt*

funeral /'fju:nərl/ *n.* **(a)** Beerdigung, *die;* **(b)** *attrib.* ▶ 887 ǀ ~ **director** Bestattungsunternehmer, *der;* ~ **procession** Leichenzug, *der* (geh.); ~ **service** Trauerfeier, *die;* **(c)** (coll.: concern) that's my ~: das ist mein Problem

funereal /fju:'nɪəriəl/ *adj.* düster; ~ **expression** Trauermiene, *die* (ugs.); trauervolle Miene

'**funfair** *n.* (Brit.) Jahrmarkt, *der*

fungus /'fʌŋgəs/ *n.*, *pl.* **fungi** /'fʌŋgaɪ/ *or* ~**es** Pilz, *der*

funicular /fju:'nɪkjʊlə(r)/ *adj.* ~ **[railway]** [Stand]seilbahn, *die*

funk /fʌŋk/ (coll.) **1** *n.* Bammel, *der* (salopp); Schiss, *der* (salopp); **be in a [blue]** ~: [mächtig] Bammel *od.* Schiss haben (salopp). **2** *v.t.* kneifen vor (+ *Dat.*) (ugs.); **he** ~**ed it** er hat gekniffen (ugs.)

funnel /'fʌnl/ **1** *n.* **(a)** (cone) Trichter, *der;* **(b)** (of ship etc.) Schornstein, *der.* **2** *v.i.*, (Brit.) **-ll-** strömen

funnily /'fʌnɪlɪ/ *adv.* komisch; ~ **enough** komischerweise (ugs.)

funny /'fʌnɪ/ *adj.* **(a)** (comical) komisch; lustig; witzig ⟨*Person, Einfall, Bemerkung*⟩; **are you being** *or* **trying to be** ~? das soll wohl ein Witz sein?; **(b)** (strange) komisch; seltsam; **the** ~ **thing 'is that …:** das Komische [daran] ist, dass …; **have a** ~ **feeling that …:** das komische Gefühl haben, dass …; **there's something** ~ **going on here** hier ist doch was faul (ugs.)

'**funny bone** *n.* (Anat.) Musikantenknochen, *der*

fur /fɜ:(r)/ *n.* **(a)** (coat of animal) Fell, *das;* (for or as garment) Pelz, *der; attrib.* ~ **coat/hat** Pelzmantel, *der*/-mütze, *die;* **trimmed/lined with** ~: mit Pelz besetzt *od.* verbrämt/ gefüttert; **(b)** (coating formed by hard water) Wasserstein, *der;* (in kettle) Kesselstein, *der.* **2** *v.i.*, **-rr-: the kettle has/pipes have** ~**red** [**up**] im Kessel hat sich Kesselstein/in den Rohren hat sich Wasserstein gebildet

furious /'fjʊərɪəs/ *adj.* wütend; heftig ⟨*Streit, Kampf, Sturm, Lärm*⟩; wild ⟨*Tanz, Sturm, Tempo, Kampf*⟩; **be** ~ **with sb./at sth.** wütend auf jmdn./über etw. (*Akk.*) sein

furiously /'fjʊərɪəslɪ/ *adv.* wütend; wild ⟨*kämpfen, tanzen*⟩; wie wild (ugs.) ⟨*arbeiten, in die Pedale treten*⟩

furlong /'fɜ:lɒŋ/ *n.* Achtelmeile, *die*

furnace /'fɜ:nɪs/ *n.* Ofen, *der;* (blast-~) Hochofen, *der;* (smelting ~) Schmelzofen, *der*

furnish /'fɜ:nɪʃ/ *v.t.* **(a)** möblieren; **live in** ~**ed accommodation** möbliert wohnen; ~**ing fabrics** Möbel- und Vorhangstoffe; **(b)** (provide, supply) liefern ⟨*Vorräte*⟩; ~ **sb. with sth.** jmdm. etw. liefern

furnishings /'fɜ:nɪʃɪŋz/ *n. pl.* Einrichtungsgegenstände *Pl.*

furniture /'fɜ:nɪtʃə(r)/ *n.*, *no pl.* Möbel *Pl.;* **piece of** ~: Möbel[stück], *das*

furniture: ~ **polish** *n.* Möbelpolitur, *die;* ~ **van** *n.* Möbelwagen, *der*

furore /fjʊə'rɔ:rɪ/ (*Amer.:* **furor** /'fjʊərɔ:(r)/) *n.* **create** *or* **cause a** ~: Furore machen; (cause a scandal) einen Skandal verursachen

furrier /'fʌrɪə(r)/ *n.* (one who prepares fur) Kürschner, *der*/ Kürschnerin, *die;* (dealer) Pelzhändler, *der*/-händlerin, *die*

furrow /'fʌrəʊ/ **1** *n.* (lit. or fig.) Furche, *die.* **2** *v.t.* (mark with wrinkles) ~**ed face** zerfurchtes Gesicht

furry /'fɜ:rɪ/ *adj.* haarig; flauschig ⟨*Stoff*⟩; belegt ⟨*Zunge*⟩

further /'fɜ:ðə(r)/ **1** *adj. compar. of* **far:** **(a)** (of two) ander…; (in space) weiter entfernt; **on the** ~ **bank of the river/side of town** am anderen Ufer/Ende der Stadt; **(b)** (additional) weiter…; **till** ~ **notice/orders** bis auf weiteres; **will there be anything** ~? darf es noch etwas sein?;

haben Sie sonst noch einen Wunsch?; ~ **details** *or* **particulars** weitere *od.* nähere Einzelheiten. **2** *adv. compar. of* **far:** **(a)** weiter; **not let it go any** ~ (keep it secret) es nicht weitersagen; **until you hear** ~ **from us** bis Sie wieder von uns hören; **nothing was** ~ **from his thoughts** nichts lag ihm ferner; **(b)** (moreover) außerdem. **3** *v.t.* fördern; ~ **one's career** beruflich vorankommen

furtherance /'fɜ:ðərəns/ *n.*, *no pl.* Förderung, *die;* Unterstützung, *die;* **in** ~ **of sth.** zur Förderung *od.* Unterstützung einer Sache (*Gen.*)

further edu'cation *n.* Weiterbildung, *die;* (for adults also) Erwachsenenbildung, *die*

furthermore /fɜ:ðə'mɔ:(r)/ *adv.* außerdem

furthermost /'fɜ:ðəməʊst/ *adj.* äußerst…; entlegenst…; **to the** ~ **ends of the earth** bis ans Ende der Welt

furthest /'fɜ:ðɪst/ **1** *adj. superl. of* **far** am weitesten entfernt; **ten miles at the** ~: höchstens zehn Meilen. **2** *adv. superl. of* **far** am weitesten ⟨*springen, laufen*⟩; am weitesten entfernt ⟨*sein, wohnen*⟩

furtive /'fɜ:tɪv/ *adj.* verstohlen; **his** ~ **behaviour** seine offenkundige Bemühtheit, nicht aufzufallen

furtively /'fɜ:tɪvlɪ/ *adv.* verstohlen

fury /'fjʊərɪ/ *n.* **(a)** Wut, *die;* (of storm, sea, battle, war) Wüten, *das;* **in a** ~: wütend; **fly into a/be in a** ~: einen Wutanfall bekommen/haben; **(b)** **like** ~ (coll.) wie wild (ugs.)

fuse[1] /fju:z/ **1** *v.t.* (blend) verschmelzen (**into** zu). **2** *v.i.* (blend) ~ **together** miteinander verschmelzen; ~ **with sth.** (fig.) sich mit etw. verbinden

fuse[2] *n.* **[time-]**~: [Zeit]zünder, *der;* (cord) Zündschnur, *die*

fuse[3] (Electr.) **1** *n.* Sicherung, *die.* **2** *v.t.* ~ **the lights** die Sicherung [für die Lampen] durchbrennen lassen. **3** *v.i.* **the lights have** ~**d** die Sicherung [für die Lampen] ist durchgebrannt

'**fuse box** *n.* (Electr.) Sicherungskasten, *der*

fuselage /'fju:zəlɑ:ʒ/ *n.* (Aeronaut.) [Flugzeug]rumpf, *der*

fusion /'fju:ʒn/ *n.* **(a)** Verschmelzung, *die;* (fig.) Verbindung, *die;* **(b)** (Phys.) Fusion, *die*

fuss /fʌs/ **1** *n.* Theater, *das* (ugs.); **without any** ~: ohne großes Theater (ugs.); **kick up a** ~: ein großes Theater machen; **make a** ~ **[about sth.]** Aufhebens [von etw.] *od.* einen Wirbel [um etw.] machen; **make a** ~ **of** [einen] Wirbel machen um ⟨*Person, Tier*⟩. **2** *v.i.* Wirbel machen; (get agitated) sich [unnötig] aufregen; **she is always** ~**ing over sb./sth.** sie macht immer ein Theater mit jmdm./ etw. (ugs.)

fussy /'fʌsɪ/ *adj.* **(a)** (fastidious) eigen; penibel; **be** ~ **about one's food** *or* **what one eats** mäklig im Essen sein (ugs.); **I'm not** ~ (I don't mind) ich bin nicht wählerisch; **(b)** (full of unnecessary decoration) verspielt

futile /'fju:taɪl/ *adj.* vergeblich ⟨*Versuch, Bemühungen, Vorschlag usw.*⟩; zum Scheitern verurteilt ⟨*Plan, Vorgehen usw.*⟩

futility /fju:'tɪlɪtɪ/ *n.*, *no pl.* (of effort, attempt, etc.) Vergeblichkeit, *die;* (of plan) Zwecklosigkeit, *die;* (of war) Sinnlosigkeit, *die*

future /'fju:tʃə(r)/ **1** *adj.* **(a)** [zu]künftig; **at some** ~ **date** zu einem späteren Zeitpunkt; **(b)** (Ling.) futurisch; ~ **tense** Futur, *das;* Zukunft, *die;* ~ **perfect** Futur II, *das.* **2** *n.* **(a)** Zukunft, *die;* **a man with a** ~: ein Mann mit Zukunft; **in** ~: in Zukunft; künftig; **see sb. in the** ~: jmdn. demnächst sehen; **there's no** ~ **in it** das hat keine Zukunft; **(b)** (Ling.) Futur, *das;* Zukunft, *die*

futuristic /fju:tʃə'rɪstɪk/ *adj.* futuristisch

fuze (Amer.) ⇒ **fuse**[2]

fuzz /fʌz/ *n.* **(a)** (fluff) Flaum, *der;* **(b)** (frizzy hair) Kraushaar, *das;* **(c)** *no pl.* (sl.: police) Polente, *die* (salopp)

fuzzy /'fʌzɪ/ *adj.* **(a)** (like fluff) flaumig; **(b)** (frizzy) kraus; **(c)** (blurred) verschwommen; unscharf

G, g /dʒiː/ *n., pl.* **Gs** *or* **G's** (a) (letter) G, g, *das;* (b) G (Mus.) G, g, *das;* **G sharp** gis, Gis, *das;* **G flat** ges, Ges, *das* **g.** *abbr.* (a) ▶ 1202 | **gram[s]** g; (b) **gravity** g

gab /gæb/ *n.* (coll.) **have the gift of the** ∼: reden können

gabble /'gæbl/ **1** *v.i.* (inarticulately) brabbeln (ugs.); (volubly) schnattern (fig.). **2** *v.t.* herunterschnurren (salopp) ‹*Gebet, Gedicht*›. **3** *n.* Gebrabbel, *das* (ugs.)

gable /'geɪbl/ *n.* (a) Giebel, *der;* (b) ⇒ **gable-end**

gabled /'geɪbld/ *adj.* gegiebelt; Giebel‹*dach, -haus*›

'gable-end *n.* Giebelseite, *die*

gad /gæd/ *v.i.*, **-dd-** (coll.) ∼ **about** *or* **around** herumziehen; sich herumtreiben (ugs. abwertend)

gadget /'gædʒɪt/ *n.* Gerät, *das;* (larger) Apparat, *der;* ∼s (derog.) [technischer] Krimskrams (ugs.)

gadgetry /'gædʒɪtrɪ/ *n., no pl.* [hoch technisierte] Ausstattung

Gaelic /'geɪlɪk, 'gælɪk/ **1** *adj.* gälisch. **2** *n.* ▶ 897 | Gälisch, *das; see also* **English 2 a**

gaff /gæf/ *n.* (coll.) **blow the** ∼: plaudern (**on** über + *Akk.*)

gaffe /gæf/ *n.* Fauxpas, *der;* Fehler, *der;* **make** *or* **commit a** ∼: einen Fauxpas begehen

gaffer /'gæfə(r)/ *n.* (coll.) (a) (old fellow) Alte, *der;* (b) (Brit.: boss) Boss, *der* (ugs.)

gag /gæg/ **1** *n.* (a) Knebel, *der;* (b) (joke) Gag, *der.* **2** *v.t.*, **-gg-:** ∼ sb. jmdn. knebeln; (fig.) jmdn. zum Schweigen bringen

gaga /'gɑːgɑː/ *adj.* (coll.: senile) verkalkt (ugs.); **go** ∼: verkalken (ugs.)

gage (Amer.) ⇒ **gauge**

gaggle /'gægl/ *n.* ∼ **[of geese]** Schar [Gänse], *die*

gaiety /'geɪətɪ/ *n., no pl.* Fröhlichkeit, *die*

gaily /'geɪlɪ/ *adv.* (a) (cheerfully) fröhlich; (b) (brightly, showily) in leuchtenden Farben ‹*bemalt, geschmückt*›; ∼ **coloured** farbenfroh

gain /geɪn/ **1** *n.* (a) Gewinn, *der;* **be to sb.'s** ∼: für jmdn. von Vorteil sein; **ill-gotten** ∼ unrechtmäßig erworbener Besitz; (b) (increase) Zunahme, *die* (**in** an + *Dat.*). **2** *v.t.* (a) (obtain) gewinnen; finden ‹*Zugang, Zutritt*›; erwerben ‹*Wissen, Ruf*›; erlangen ‹*Freiheit, Ruhm*›; erzielen ‹*Vorteil, Punkte*›; verdienen ‹*Lebensunterhalt, Geldsumme*›; ∼ **possession of sth.** in den Besitz einer Sache (*Gen.*) kommen; (b) (win) gewinnen ‹*Preis, Schlacht*›; erringen ‹*Sieg*›; (c) (obtain as increase) ∼ **weight/five pounds [in weight]** zunehmen/fünf Pfund zunehmen; ∼ **speed** schneller werden; (d) (reach) gewinnen (geh.), erreichen ‹*Gipfel, Ufer*›; (e) (become fast by) **my watch** ∼s **two minutes a day** meine Uhr geht pro Tag zwei Minuten vor. **3** *v.i.* (a) (make a profit) ∼ **by sth.** von etw. profitieren; (b) (obtain increase) ∼ **in influence/prestige** an Einfluss/Prestige gewinnen; ∼ **in wisdom** weiser werden; ∼ **in knowledge** sein Wissen vergrößern; ∼ **in weight** zunehmen; (c) (become fast) ‹*Uhr:*› vorgehen; (d) ∼ **on sb.** (come closer) jmdm. [immer] näher kommen; (increase lead) den Vorsprung zu jmdm. vergrößern

gainful /'geɪnfl/ *adj.* bezahlt; ∼ **employment** Erwerbstätigkeit, *die*

gait /geɪt/ *n.* Gang, *der;* **with a slow** ∼: mit langsamen Schritten

gal. *abbr.* ▶ 1193 | **gallon[s]** gal.; gall.

gala /'gɑːlə, 'geɪlə/ *n.* (a) (fête) Festveranstaltung, *die; attrib.* Gala‹*abend, -diner, -vorstellung*›; (b) (Brit. Sport) Sportfest, *das;* **swimming** ∼ Schwimmfest, *das*

galaxy /'gæləksɪ/ *n.* (a) (star system) Galaxie, *die;* (b) (Milky Way) **the G**∼: die Milchstraße

gale /geɪl/ *n.* Sturm, *der;* ∼ **force** Sturmstärke, *die;* ∼ **warning** Sturmwarnung, *die*

gall¹ /gɔːl/ *n.* (a) (Physiol.) Galle, *die;* (b) (coll.: impudence) Unverschämtheit, *die;* Frechheit, *die*

gall² *v.t.* (fig.) (annoy) ärgern; (vex) schmerzen; **be** ∼**ed by sth.** unter etw. (*Dat.*) leiden

gallant *adj.* (a) /'gælənt/ (brave) tapfer; (chivalrous) ritterlich; (b) /'gælənt, gə'lænt/ (attentive to women) galant

gallantly *adv.* (a) /'gæləntlɪ/ (bravely) tapfer; (b) /'gæləntlɪ, gə'læntlɪ/ (with courtesy) galant

gallantry /'gæləntrɪ/ *n.* (a) (bravery) Tapferkeit, *die;* (b) (courtesy) Galanterie, *die* (geh.)

'gall-bladder *n.* ▶ 672 | (Anat.) Gallenblase, *die*

galleon /'gælɪən/ *n.* (Hist.) Galeone, *die*

gallery /'gælərɪ/ *n.* (a) (Archit.) Galerie, *die;* (b) (Theatre) dritter Rang; **play to the** ∼ (fig. coll.) für die Galerie spielen; (c) (art ∼) (building) Galerie, *die;* (room) Ausstellungsraum, *der*

galley /'gælɪ/ *n.* (a) (Hist.) Galeere, *die;* (b) (kitchen) (of ship) Kombüse, *die;* (of aircraft) Bordküche, *die;* (c) (Printing) Satzschiff, *das;* ∼ **[proof]** [Druck]fahne, *die*

'galley-slave *n.* Galeerensklave, *der*

Gallic /'gælɪk/ *adj.* gallisch

Gallicism /'gælɪsɪzm/ *n.* (a) Gallizismus, *der;* (b) (characteristic) französische Eigenart

galling /'gɔːlɪŋ/ *adj.* (a) (irritating) ärgerlich; (b) (humiliating) erniedrigend

gallivant /gælɪ'vænt/ *v.i.* (coll.) herumziehen (ugs.) (**about, around** in + *Dat.*)

gallon /'gælən/ *n.* ▶ 1193 | Gallone, *die;* **drink** ∼s **of water** *etc.* (fig. coll.) literweise Wasser *usw.* trinken

gallop /'gæləp/ **1** *n.* Galopp, *der;* **at a** ∼: im Galopp. **2** *v.i.* (a) ‹*Pferd, Reiter:*› galoppieren; (b) (fig.) ∼ **through** im Galopp (fig.) durchlesen ‹*Buch*›; rasch herunterspielen ‹*Musikstück*›; im Galopp (fig.) erledigen ‹*Arbeit*›; ∼**ing inflation** (fig.) galoppierende Inflation

gallows /'gæləʊz/ *n. sing.* Galgen, *der*

'gallstone *n.* (Med.) Gallenstein, *der*

galore /gə'lɔː(r)/ *adv.* im Überfluss; in Hülle und Fülle

galvanize (galvanise) /'gælvənaɪz/ *v.t.* (a) (fig.: rouse) wachrütteln ‹*Volk, Partei usw.*›; ∼ **sb. into action** jmdn. veranlassen, sofort aktiv zu werden; (b) (coat with zinc) verzinken

gambit /'gæmbɪt/ *n.* (Chess) Gambit, *das;* (fig.: trick, device) Schachzug, *der;* **[opening]** ∼ (fig.) einleitender Schachzug; (in conversation) einleitende Bemerkung

gamble /'gæmbl/ **1** *v.i.* (a) [um Geld] spielen; ∼ **at cards/on horses** mit Karten um Geld spielen/auf Pferde wetten; (b) (fig.) spekulieren; ∼ **on the Stock Exchange/in oil shares** an der Börse/in Öl[aktien] spekulieren; ∼ **on sth.** sich auf etw. (*Akk.*) verlassen. **2** *v.t.* (a) verspielen; (b) (fig.) riskieren, aufs Spiel setzen ‹*Vermögen*›. **3** *n.* (lit. *or* fig.) Glücksspiel, *das;* **take a** ∼: ein Wagnis auf sich (*Akk.*) nehmen

∼ **a'way** *v.t.* verspielen; (on the Stock Exchange) verspekulieren

gambler /'gæmblə(r)/ *n.* Glücksspieler, *der*

gambling /'gæmblɪŋ/ *n.* Spiel[en], *das;* Glücksspiel, *das;* (on horses, dogs) Wetten, *das*

'gambling debts *n. pl.* Spielschulden

gambol /'gæmbl/ *v.i.*, (Brit.) **-ll-** ‹*Kind, Lamm:*› herumspringen

game¹ /geɪm/ *n.* (a) (form of contest) Spiel, *das;* (a contest) (with ball) Spiel, *das;* (at [table-]tennis, chess, cards, billiards, cricket) Partie, *die;* **have** *or* **play a** ∼ **of tennis/chess** *etc.* **[with sb.]** eine Partie Tennis/Schach *usw.* [mit jmdn.] spielen; **have** *or* **play a** ∼ **of football [with sb.]** Fußball [mit jmdn.] spielen; **be on/off one's** ∼: gut in Form/nicht in Form sein; **beat sb. at his own** ∼ (fig.) jmdn. mit seinen eigenen Waffen schlagen (geh.); **play the** ∼ (fig.) sich an die Spielregeln halten (fig.); **[I'll show her that] two can play at that** ∼ (fig.) was sie kann, kann ich auch; (b) (fig.: scheme, undertaking) Vorhaben, *das;* **play sb.'s** ∼: jmdm. in die Hände arbeiten; (for one's own benefit) jmds. Spiel mitspielen; **the** ∼ **is up** (coll.) das Spiel ist aus; **give the** ∼ **away** alles verraten; **what's his** ∼? (coll.) was hat er vor?; **what's the** ∼? (coll.) was soll das?; (c) (business, activity)

Gewerbe, *das;* Branche, *die;* **be new to the** ~ (fig.) neu im Geschäft sein (auch fig. ugs.); **be/go on the** ~ ‹*Prostituierte:*› anschaffen gehen (salopp); **(d)** (diversion) Spiel, *das;* (piece of fun) Scherz, *der;* Spaß, *der;* **don't play** ~**s with me** versuch nicht, mich auf den Arm zu nehmen (ugs.); **(e)** *in pl.* (athletic contests) Spiele; (in school) (sports) Schulsport, *der;* (athletics) Leichtathletik, *die;* **good at** ~**s** gut im Sport; **(f)** (portion of contest) Spiel, *das;* **two** ~**s all** zwei beide; zwei zu zwei; ~ **to Graf** (Tennis) Spiel Graf; ~, **set, and match** (Tennis) Spiel, Satz und Sieg; **(g)** *no pl.* (Hunting, Cookery) Wild, *das;* **fair** ~ (fig.) Freiwild, *das;* **easy** ~ (fig. coll.) leichte Beute; **big** ~: Großwild, *das*

game² *adj.* mutig; **be** ~ **to do sth.** (be willing) bereit sein, etw. zu tun; **be** ~ **for sth./anything** zu etw./allem bereit sein

'**gamekeeper** *n.* ▶ 887 | Wildheger, *der*

gamely /'geɪmlɪ/ *adv.* mutig

game: ~ **park** *ns.* Wildreservat, *das;* ~ **plan** *n.* (Sport) Taktik, *die;* (fig.) Strategie, *die;* ~ **reserve** ⇒ ~ **park**

gamesmanship /'geɪmzmənʃɪp/ *n., no pl.* Gerissenheit, *die od.* Gewieftheit, *die* (ugs.) beim Spiel

'**game warden** *n.* ▶ 887 | Wildhüter, *der*

gaming /'geɪmɪŋ/**:** ~ **machine** *n.* Münzspielgerät, *das;* ~ **table** *n.* Spieltisch, *der*

gamma /'gæmə/ *n.* (letter) Gamma, *das*

'**gamma rays** *n. pl.* (Phys.) Gammastrahlen *Pl.*

gammon /'gæmən/ *n.* (ham cured like bacon) Räucherschinken, *der*

gamut /'gæmət/ *n.* (fig.: range) Skala, *die;* **run the whole** ~ **of …:** die ganze Skala von … durchgehen

gander /'gændə(r)/ *n.* **(a)** (Ornith.) Gänserich, *der;* **(b)** (coll.: look, glance) **have a** ~ **at/round sth.** sich (*Dat.*) etw. ansehen

gang /gæŋ/ **1** *n.* **(a)** (of workmen, slaves, prisoners) Trupp, *der;* **(b)** (of criminals) Bande, *die;* Gang, *die;* ~ **of thieves/criminals/terrorists** Diebes-/Verbrecher-/Terroristenbande, *die;* **(c)** (coll.: group of friends etc.) Haufen, *der;* Bande, *die* (scherzh.). **2** *v.i.* **(a)** ~ **up [with sb.]** (join) sich [mit jmdm.] zusammentun (ugs.); **(b)** ~ **up against** *or* **on** (coll.: combine against) sich zusammenschließen gegen

gangling /'gæŋglɪŋ/ *adj.* schlaksig (ugs.) ‹*Person, Gang, Gestalt*›

'**gangplank** *n.* (Naut.) Laufplanke, *die*

gangrene /'gæŋgriːn/ *n.* ▶ 865 | (Med.) Gangrän, *die od. das;* Brand, *der*

gangrenous /'gæŋgrɪnəs/ *adj.* (Med.) brandig

gangster /'gæŋstə(r)/ *n.* Gangster, *der*

'**gangway** *n.* **(a)** (for boarding ship or plane) Gangway, *die;* **(b)** (Brit.: between rows of seats) Gang, *der;* **leave a** ~ (fig.) einen Durchgang freilassen

gantry /'gæntrɪ/ *n.* (crane) Portal, *das;* (on road) Schilderbrücke, *die;* (Railw.) Signalbrücke, *die;* (Astronaut.) Startrampe, *die*

gaol /dʒeɪl/ (Brit. in official use) ⇒ **jail**

gaoler /'dʒeɪlə(r)/ (Brit. in official use) ⇒ **jailer**

gap /gæp/ *n.* **(a)** Lücke, *die;* **a** ~ **in the curtains** ein Spalt im Vorhang; **(b)** (in time) Pause, *die;* **(c)** (fig.: contrast, divergence in views etc.) Kluft, *die;* **fill a** ~: eine Lücke füllen *od.* schließen; **stop** *or* **close** *or* **bridge a** ~: eine Kluft überbrücken *od.* überwinden

gape /geɪp/ *v.i.* **(a)** (open mouth) den Mund aufsperren; (be open wide) ‹*Schnabel, Mund:*› aufgesperrt sein; ‹*Loch, Abgrund, Wunde:*› klaffen; **(b)** (stare) Mund und Nase aufsperren (ugs.); ~ **at sb./sth.** jmdn./etw. mit offenem Mund anstarren

gaping /'geɪpɪŋ/ *adj.* **(a)** (open wide) gähnend ‹*Loch*›; klaffend ‹*Wunde*›; **(b)** (staring) erstaunt starrend

garage /'gærɑːʒ, 'gærɪdʒ/ *n.* **(a)** (for parking) Garage, *die;* **bus** ~: Busdepot, *das;* **(b)** (for selling petrol) Tankstelle, *die;* (for repairing cars) [Kfz-]Werkstatt, *die;* (for selling cars) Autohandlung, *die*

garb /gɑːb/ *n.* Tracht, *die;* **strange** ~: seltsame Kleidung

garbage /'gɑːbɪdʒ/ *n.* **(a)** Abfall, *der;* Müll, *der;* **(b)** (fig.: rubbishy literature) Schund, *der;* **(c)** (coll.: nonsense) Quatsch, *der* (salopp)

garbage: ~ **can** (Amer.) ⇒ **dustbin;** ~ **collection** *n.* (Amer.) Müllabfuhr, *die;* ~ **collector** (Amer.) ⇒ **dustman;** ~ **dis'posal unit**, ~ **disposer** /'gɑːbɪdʒ dɪspəʊzə(r)/ *ns.* Abfallvernichter, *der;* Müllwolf, *der;* ~ **truck** *n.* (Amer.) Müllwagen, *der*

garble /'gɑːbl/ *v.t.* **(a)** verstümmeln, entstellen ‹*Bericht, Korrespondenz, Tatsache*›; **(b)** (confuse) durcheinander bringen

garden /gɑːdn/ *n.* Garten, *der;* **lead sb. up the** ~ **path** (fig. coll.) jmdn. an der Nase herumführen (ugs.)

garden: ~ **centre** *n.* Gartencenter, *das;* ~ '**city** *n.* Gartenstadt, *die*

gardener /'gɑːdnə(r)/ *n.* ▶ 887 | Gärtner, *der*/Gärtnerin, *die*

gardening /'gɑːdnɪŋ/ *n.* Gartenarbeit, *die; attrib.* Garten‹*gerät, -buch, -handschuh*›; **he likes** ~: er gärtnert gern

garden: ~ **party** *n.* Gartenfest, *das;* ~ '**shed** *n.* Geräteschuppen, *der*

gargle /'gɑːgl/ **1** *v.i.* gurgeln. **2** *n.* **(a)** (liquid) Gurgelmittel, *das;* **(b)** (act) **have a** ~: gurgeln

gargoyle /'gɑːgɔɪl/ *n.* (Archit.) Wasserspeier, *der*

garish /'geərɪʃ/ *adj.* grell ‹*Farbe, Licht, Beleuchtung*›; knallbunt ‹*Kleidung, Verzierung, Muster*›

garishly /'geərɪʃlɪ/ *adv.* grell ‹*beleuchten*›; knallbunt ‹*kleiden, tapezieren*›

garland /'gɑːlənd/ *n.* Girlande, *die;* ~ **of flowers/laurel** Blumen-/Lorbeerkranz, *der*

garlic /'gɑːlɪk/ *n.* Knoblauch, *der*

garment /'gɑːmənt/ *n.* Kleidungsstück, *das; in pl.* (clothes) Kleidung, *die;* Kleider

garnish /'gɑːnɪʃ/ **1** *v.t.* (lit. or fig.) garnieren. **2** *n.* (Cookery) Garnierung, *die*

garret /'gærɪt/ *n.* (room on top floor) Dachkammer, *die*

garrison /'gærɪsn/ **1** *n.* Garnison, *die.* **2** *v.t.* **(a)** (furnish with ~) mit einer Garnison belegen ‹*Stadt*›; **(b)** (place as ~) in Garnison legen ‹*Truppen*›

'**garrison town** *n.* Garnison[s]stadt, *die*

garrulous /'gærʊləs/ *adj.* (talkative) gesprächig; geschwätzig

garter /'gɑːtə(r)/ *n.* Strumpfband, *das*

gas /gæs/ **1** *n., pl.* ~**es** /'gæsɪz/ **(a)** Gas, *das;* **natural** ~: Erdgas, *das;* **cook by** *or* **with** ~: mit Gas kochen; **(b)** (Amer. coll.: petrol) Benzin, *das;* **(c)** (anaesthetic) Narkotikum, *das;* Lachgas, *das;* **(d)** (for lighting) Leuchtgas, *das.* **2** *v.t.,* -**ss**- mit Gas vergiften. **3** *v.i.,* -**ss**- (coll.: talk idly) schwafeln (ugs. abwertend) (**about** von)

gas: ~**bag** *n.* (coll. derog.: talker) Schwafler, *der*/Schwaflerin, *die* (ugs. abwertend); ~ **cylinder** *n.* Gasflasche, *die;* ~ '**fire** *n.* Gasofen, *der;* ~**-fired** /'gæsfaɪəd/ *adj.* mit Gas betrieben; Gas‹*boiler, -ofen usw.*›

gash /gæʃ/ **1** *n.* (wound) Schnittwunde, *die;* (cleft) [klaffende] Spalte; (in sack etc.) Schlitz, *der.* **2** *v.t.* aufritzen ‹*Haut*›; aufschlitzen ‹*Sack*›; ~ **one's finger/knee** sich (*Dat. od. Akk.*) in den Finger schneiden/sich (*Dat.*) das Knie aufschlagen

'**gasholder** *n.* Gasbehälter, *der*

gasket /'gæskɪt/ *n.* Dichtung, *die*

gas: ~ **lamp** *n.* Gaslampe, *die;* (in street etc.) Gaslaterne, *die;* ~**light** *n.* **(a)** ⇒ ~ **lamp; (b)** *no pl.* (illumination) Gaslicht, *das;* ~ **lighter** *n.* **(a)** [Gas]anzünder, *der;* **(b)** (cigarette lighter) Gasfeuerzeug, *das;* ~ **main** *n.* Hauptgasleitung, *die;* ~**man** *n.* ▶ 887 | (fitter) Gasinstallateur, *der;* (meter-reader, collector) Gasableser, *der;* Gasmann, *der* (ugs.); ~ **mask** *n.* Gasmaske, *die;* ~ **meter** *n.* Gaszähler, *der*

gasoline (gasolene) /'gæsəliːn/ *n.* (Amer.) Benzin, *das*

gasometer /gæ'sɒmɪtə(r)/ *n.* Gasometer, *der*

'**gas oven** *n.* Gasherd, *der*

gasp /gɑːsp/ **1** *v.i.* nach Luft schnappen (**with** vor); **make sb.** ~ (fig.) jmdm. den Atem nehmen; **leave sb.** ~**ing [with sth.]** jmdm. [vor etw.] den Atem verschlagen *od.* rauben; **he was** ~**ing for air** *or* **breath** er rang nach

Luft. **2** *v.t.* ~ **out** hervorstoßen ⟨*Bitte, Worte*⟩. **3** *n.* Keuchen, *das;* **give a** ~ **of fear/surprise** vor Furcht/ Überraschung die Luft einziehen; **be at one's last** ~: in den letzten Zügen liegen (ugs.)

gas: ~ **pipe** *n.* Gasleitung, *die;* ~ **ring** *n.* Gasbrenner, *der;* ~ **station** *n.* (Amer.) Tankstelle, *die;* ~ **stove** *n.* Gasherd, *der*

gassy /'gæsɪ/ *adj.* (fizzy) sprudelnd; schäumend ⟨*Bier*⟩

gas: ~ **tank** *n.* (a) Gastank, *der;* (b) (Amer.: petrol tank) Benzintank, *der;* ~ **tap** *n.* Gashahn, *der*

gastric /'gæstrɪk/**:** ~ **'flu** (coll.), ~ **influ'enza** *ns.* ▶ 865 Darmgrippe, *die;* ~ **'ulcer** *n.* ▶ 865 Magengeschwür, *das*

gastronomic /gæstrə'nɒmɪk/ *adj.* gastronomisch; kulinarisch ⟨*Genüsse*⟩

gastronomy /gæ'strɒnəmɪ/ *n.* Gastronomie, *die;* French ~: französische Küche

'gasworks *n. sing., pl. same* Gaswerk, *das*

gate /geɪt/ *n.* (a) (lit. or fig.) Tor, *das;* (barrier) Sperre, *die;* (to field etc.) Gatter, *das;* (in garden fence) [Garten]pforte, *die;* (Railw.: of level crossing) [Bahn]schranke, *die;* (in airport) Flugsteig, *der;* (b) (Sport: number to see match) Besucherzahl, *die*

gateau /'gætəʊ/ *n., pl.* ~**s** *or* ~**x** /'gætəʊz/ Torte, *die*

gate: ~**crash** *v.t.* ohne Einladung einfach hingehen zu; ~**crasher** /'geɪtkræʃə(r)/ *n.* ungeladener Gast; ~ **money** *n.* Eintrittsgelder *Pl.;* Einnahmen *Pl.;* ~**post** *n.* Torpfosten, *der;* **between you and me and the** ~**post** (coll.) unter uns (*Dat.*) gesagt; ~**way** *n.* (a) (~, lit. or fig.) Tor, *das* (**to** zu); (b) (Archit.) (structure) Torbau, *der;* (frame) Torbogen, *der*

gather /'gæðə(r)/ **1** *v.t.* (a) sammeln; zusammentragen ⟨*Informationen*⟩; pflücken ⟨*Obst, Blumen*⟩; ~ **sth.** [**together**] etw. zusammensuchen *od.* -sammeln; ~ **[in] the harvest** die Ernte einbringen; (b) (infer, deduce) schließen (**from** aus); ~ **from sb. that** ...: von jmdm. erfahren, dass ...; **as far as I can** ~: soweit ich weiß; **as you will have** ~**ed** wie Sie sicherlich vermutet haben; (c) ~ **speed/force** schneller/stärker werden; (d) (summon up) ~ [**together**] zusammennehmen ⟨*Kräfte, Mut*⟩; ~ **oneself** [**together**] sich zusammennehmen; ~ **one's thoughts** seine Gedanken ordnen; ~ **one's breath/strength** [wieder] zu Atem kommen/Kräfte sammeln; (e) **she** ~**ed her shawl round her neck** sie schlang den Schal um den Hals; (f) (Sewing) ankrausen. **2** *v.i.* (a) sich versammeln; ⟨*Wolken:*⟩ sich zusammenziehen; ⟨*Staub:*⟩ sich ansammeln; ⟨*Schweißperlen:*⟩ sich sammeln; **be** ~**ed** [**together**] versammelt sein; ~ **round** zusammenkommen; ~ **round sb./sth.** sich um jmdn./etw. versammeln; (b) (increase) zunehmen; **darkness was** ~**ing** es wurde dunkler. **3** *n. in pl.* (Sewing) Kräusel[falten]

~ **'up** *v.t.* (a) (bring together and pick up) aufsammeln; zusammenpacken ⟨*Habseligkeiten, Werkzeug*⟩; (b) (draw) hochraffen ⟨*Rock*⟩; (summon) sammeln ⟨*Kräfte, Gedanken usw.*⟩

gathering /'gæðərɪŋ/ *n.* (assembly, meeting) Versammlung, *die*

gauche /gəʊʃ/ *adj.* linkisch

gaudy /'gɔːdɪ/ *adj.* protzig (abwertend); grell ⟨*Farben*⟩

gauge /geɪdʒ/ **1** *n.* (a) (standard measure) [Normal]maß, *das;* (of rail) Spurweite, *die;* **narrow** ~: Schmalspur, *die;* (b) (instrument) Messgerät, *das;* (for dimensions of tools or wire) Lehre, *die;* (c) (fig.: criterion, test) Kriterium, *das;* Maßstab, *der.* **2** *v.t.* (a) (measure) messen; (b) (fig.) beurteilen (**by** nach)

gaunt /gɔːnt/ *adj.* hager; (from suffering) verhärmt; karg ⟨*Landschaft*⟩

gauntlet¹ /'gɔːntlɪt/ *n.* Stulpenhandschuh, *der;* **fling** *or* **throw down the** ~ (fig.) jmdm. den Fehdehandschuh hinwerfen

gauntlet² *n.* **run the** ~: Spießruten laufen

gauze /gɔːz/ *n.* (fabric, wire) Gaze, *die*

gave ⇒ **give 1, 2**

gawky /'gɔːkɪ/ *adj.* linkisch; unbeholfen; (lanky) schlaksig (ugs.)

gay /geɪ/ **1** *adj.* (a) fröhlich; fidel (ugs.) ⟨*Person, Gesellschaft*⟩; (b) (showy, bright-coloured) farbenfroh ⟨*Stoff,*

Ausstattung⟩; fröhlich, lebhaft ⟨*Farbe*⟩; (c) (coll.: homosexual) schwul (ugs.); Schwulen⟨*lokal, -blatt*⟩. **2** *n.* (coll.) Schwule, *der* (ugs.)

gay: ~ **libe'ration** *n.* Schwulenemanzipation, *die;* ~ **liberation movement** Schwulenbewegung, *die;* ~ **'rights** *n. pl.* Schwulenrechte *Pl.;* ~ **rights group/demonstration** Schwulengruppe, *die/~demonstration, die*

gaze /geɪz/ *v.i.* blicken; (more fixedly) starren; ~ **at sb./sth.** jmdn./etw. anstarren *od.* ansehen

gazelle /gə'zel/ *n.* Gazelle, *die*

gazette /gə'zet/ *n.* (a) (Brit.: official journal) Amtsblatt, *das;* (b) (newspaper) Zeitung, *die*

gazetteer /gæzɪ'tɪə(r)/ *n.* alphabetisches [Orts]verzeichnis

gazump /gə'zʌmp/ *v.t.* (coll.) *durch nachträgliches Überbieten um die Chance bringen, ein Haus zu kaufen*

GB *abbr.* **Great Britain** GB

GBH *abbr.* (Brit.) **grievous bodily harm**

GCE *abbr.* (Brit. Hist.) **General Certificate of Education**

GCSE *abbr.* (Brit.) **General Certificate of Secondary Education**

GDR *abbr.* (Hist.) **German Democratic Republic** DDR, *die*

gear /gɪə(r)/ **1** *n.* (a) (Motor Veh.) Gang, *der;* **first** *or* **bottom/top** ~ (Brit.) der erste/höchste Gang; **high/low** ~: hoher/niedriger Gang; **change** ~: schalten; **change into second/a higher/lower** ~: in den zweiten Gang/in einen höheren/niedrigeren Gang schalten; **a bicycle with ten-speed** ~**s** ein Fahrrad mit Zehngangschaltung; **put the car into** ~: einen Gang einlegen; **leave the car in** ~: den Gang drin lassen; (b) (combination of wheels, levers, etc.) Getriebe, *das;* (c) (clothes) Aufmachung, *die;* **travelling** ~: Reisekleidung, *die;* (d) (equipment, tools) Gerät, *das;* Ausrüstung, *die.* **2** *v.t.* (adjust, adapt) ausrichten (**to** auf + *Akk.*)

gear: ~**box** *n.* Getriebekasten, *der;* **five-speed** ~**box** Fünfganggetriebe, *das;* ~ **lever**, (Amer.) ~ **shift**, ~**stick** *ns.* Schalthebel, *der;* ~**wheel** *n.* Zahnrad, *das*

gee /dʒiː/ *int.* (coll.) Mann (salopp); Mensch [Meier] (salopp)

geese *pl. of* **goose**

gee 'whiz ⇒ **gee**

geezer /'giːzə(r)/ *n.* (sl.: old man) Opa, *der* (ugs. scherzh. *od.* abwertend)

Geiger counter /'gaɪgə kaʊntə(r)/ *n.* (Phys.) Geigerzähler, *der*

gel /dʒel/ **1** *n.* Gel, *das.* **2** *v.i.,* **-ll-:** (a) gelatinieren; gelieren; (b) (fig.) Gestalt annehmen

gelatin /'dʒelətɪn/, (esp. Brit.) **gelatine** /'dʒeləti:n/ *n.* Gelatine, *die*

gelding /'geldɪŋ/ *n.* kastriertes Tier; (male horse) Wallach, *der*

gelignite /'dʒelɪgnaɪt/ *n.* Gelatinedynamit, *das*

gem /dʒem/ *n.* (a) Edelstein, *der;* (cut also) Juwel, *das od. der;* (b) (fig.) Juwel, *das;* Perle, *die;* (choicest part) Glanzstück, *das*

Gemini /'dʒemɪnaɪ, 'dʒemɪnɪ/ *n.* (Astrol., Astron.) Zwillinge *Pl.*

gen /dʒen/ *n.* (Brit. coll.) notwendige Angaben

Gen. *abbr.* ▶ 1152 **General** Gen.

gender /'dʒendə(r)/ *n.* (a) (Ling.) [grammatisches] Geschlecht; Genus, *das;* (b) (coll.: one's sex) Geschlecht, *das;* ~ **gap** Unterschied zwischen den Geschlechtern

gene /dʒiːn/ *n.* (Biol.) Gen, *das;* ~ **pool** Genpool, *der*

genealogy /dʒiːnɪ'ælədʒɪ/ *n.* Genealogie, *die* (fachspr.); (pedigree) Ahnentafel, *die* (geh.)

genera *pl. of* **genus**

general /'dʒenrl/ **1** *adj.* (a) allgemein; **the** ~ **public** weite Kreise der Öffentlichkeit *od.* Bevölkerung; **in** ~ **use** allgemein verbreitet; **his** ~ **health/manner** sein Allgemeinbefinden/sein Benehmen im Allgemeinen; **he has had a good** ~ **education** er hat eine gute Allgemeinbildung; (b) (prevalent, widespread, usual) allgemein; weitverbreitet ⟨*Übel, Vorurteil, Aberglaube, Ansicht*⟩; **it is the** ~ **custom** *or* **rule** es ist allgemein üblich *od.* ist Sitte *od.*

Brauch; (**c**) (not limited in application) allgemein; (true of [nearly] all cases) allgemein gültig; generell; **as a ~ rule, in ~:** im Allgemeinen; (**d**) (not detailed, vague) allgemein; ungefähr, vage ⟨ *Vorstellung, Beschreibung, Ähnlichkeit usw.* ⟩; **the ~ idea** *or* **plan is that we …:** wir haben uns das so vorgestellt, dass wir … 2 *n.* ▶ 1152 | (Mil.) General, *der*

general: ~ anaes'thetic ⇒ **anaesthetic; G~ Certificate of Edu'cation** *n.* (Brit. Hist.) (ordinary level) ≈ mittlere Reife; (advanced level) ≈ Abitur, *das;* **G~ Certificate of Secondary Edu'cation** *n.* (Brit.) *Abschluss der Sekundarstufe;* **~ e'lection** ⇒ **election**

generalisation, generalise ⇒ **generaliz-**

generality /dʒenəˈrælɪtɪ/ *n.* (**a**) **talk in generalities** verallgemeinern; (**b**) (majority) (of mankind, electorate, etc.) Großteil, *der;* (of voters, individuals, etc.) Mehrheit, *die*

generalization /dʒenrəlaɪˈzeɪʃn/ *n.* Verallgemeinerung, *die*

generalize /ˈdʒenrəlaɪz/ 1 *v.t.* verallgemeinern. 2 *v.i.* **~ [about sth.]** [etw.] verallgemeinern; **~ about the French** die Franzosen alle über einen Kamm scheren

general 'knowledge *n.* Allgemeinwissen, *das*

generally /ˈdʒenrəlɪ/ *adv.* (**a**) (extensively) allgemein; **~ available** überall erhältlich; (**b**) **~ speaking** im Allgemeinen; (**c**) (usually) im Allgemeinen; normalerweise; (**d**) (summarizing the situation) ganz Allgemein

general: ~ 'manager *n.* ▶ 887 | [leitender] Direktor/ [leitende] Direktorin; **~ 'practice** *n.* (Med.) Allgemeinmedizin, *die;* **~ prac'titioner** *n.* ▶ 887 | (Med.) Arzt/ Ärztin für Allgemeinmedizin; **~ 'staff** *n.* Generalstab, *der;* **~ 'strike** *n.* Generalstreik, *der*

generate /ˈdʒenəreɪt/ *v.t.* (produce) erzeugen (**from** aus); (result in) führen zu

generating station /ˈdʒenəreɪtɪŋ steɪʃn/ *n.* Elektrizitätswerk, *das*

generation /dʒenəˈreɪʃn/ *n.* (**a**) Generation, *die;* **the present/rising ~:** die heutige/heranwachsende *od.* junge Generation; **first-/second-~ computers** *etc.* Computer *usw.* der ersten/zweiten Generation; *attrib.* **~ gap** Generationsunterschied, *der;* (**b**) (production) Erzeugung, *die;* **~ of electricity** Stromerzeugung, *die*

generator /ˈdʒenəreɪtə(r)/ *n.* Generator, *der;* (in motor car also) Lichtmaschine, *die*

generic /dʒɪˈnerɪk/ *adj.* (**a**) **~ term** *or* **name** Ober- *od.* Gattungsbegriff, *der;* (**b**) (Biol.) Gattungs⟨ *name, -bezeichnung* ⟩

generosity /dʒenəˈrɒsɪtɪ/ *n.* Großzügigkeit, *die;* (magnanimity) Großmut, *die*

generous /ˈdʒenərəs/ *adj.* (**a**) großzügig; (noble-minded) großmütig; (**b**) (ample, abundant) großzügig; reichhaltig ⟨ *Mahl* ⟩; reichlich ⟨ *Nachschub, Vorrat, Portion* ⟩; üppig ⟨ *Figur, Formen, Mahl* ⟩

generously /ˈdʒenərəslɪ/ *adv.* großzügig; (magnanimously) großmütig

genesis /ˈdʒenɪsɪs/ *n., pl.* **geneses** /ˈdʒenɪsiːz/ (**a**) **G~** *no pl.* Schöpfungsgeschichte, *die;* (**b**) (origin) Herkunft, *die;* (development into being) Entstehung, *die*

genetic /dʒɪˈnetɪk/ *adj.,* **genetically** /dʒɪˈnetɪkəlɪ/ *adv.* genetisch

genetic: ~ engi'neering *n.* Gentechnologie, *die;* **~ 'fingerprinting, ~ profiling** /ˈprəʊfaɪlɪŋ/ *ns., no pl.* DNA-Fingerprintmethode, *die*

genetics /dʒɪˈnetɪks/ *n., no pl.* Genetik, *die*

genetic 'testing *n., no pl.* Gentests *Pl.*

Geneva /dʒɪˈniːvə/ ▶ 1159 | 1 *pr. n.* Genf (*das*); **Lake ~:** der Genfer See. 2 *attrib. adj.* Genfer

genial /ˈdʒiːnɪəl/ *adj.* (jovial, kindly) freundlich; (sociable) jovial, leutselig ⟨ *Person, Art* ⟩

geniality /dʒiːnɪˈælɪtɪ/ *n., no pl.* Freundlichkeit, *die*

genital /ˈdʒenɪtl/ 1 *n. in pl.* ▶ 672 | Geschlechtsorgane; Genitalien. 2 *adj.* Geschlechts⟨ *teile, -organe* ⟩

genitalia /dʒenɪˈteɪlɪə/ *n. pl.* Genitalia (Med.)

genitive /ˈdʒenɪtɪv/ (Ling.) 1 *adj.* Genitiv-; genitivisch; **~ case** Genitiv, *der.* 2 *n.* Genitiv, *der*

genius /ˈdʒiːnɪəs/ *n., pl.* **~es** *or* **genii** /ˈdʒiːnɪaɪ/ (**a**) *pl.* **~es** (person) Genie, *das;* (**b**) (natural ability; also iron.) Talent,

das; Begabung, *die;* (extremely great) Genie, *das;* **a man of ~:** ein genialer Mensch; ein Genie

Genoa /ˈdʒenəʊə/ *pr. n.* ▶ 1159 | Genua (*das*)

genocide /ˈdʒenəsaɪd/ *n.* Völkermord, *der*

genome /ˈdʒiːnəʊm/ *n.* (Biol.) Genom, *das*

genre /ˈʒɑːrə/ *n.* Genre, *das;* Gattung, *die*

gent /dʒent/ *n.* (**a**) (coll./joc.) Gent, der (iron.); (**b**) **~s'** Herren⟨ *friseur, -ausstatter* ⟩; (**c**) **the G~s** (Brit. coll.) die Herrentoilette

genteel /dʒenˈtiːl/ *adj.* vornehm; fein

Gentile /ˈdʒentaɪl/ 1 *n.* Nichtjude, *der*/-jüdin, *die.* 2 *adj.* nichtjüdisch

gentility /dʒenˈtɪlɪtɪ/ *n., no pl.* Vornehmheit, *die*

gentle /ˈdʒentl/ *adj.,* **~r** /ˈdʒentlə(r)/, **~st** /ˈdʒentlɪst/ sanft; sanftmütig ⟨ *Wesen* ⟩; liebenswürdig, freundlich ⟨ *Person, Verhalten, Ausdrucksweise* ⟩; leicht, schwach ⟨ *Brise* ⟩; ruhig ⟨ *Fluss, Wesen* ⟩; leise ⟨ *Geräusch* ⟩; gemäßigt ⟨ *Tempo* ⟩; mäßig ⟨ *Hitze* ⟩; gemächlich ⟨ *Tempo, Schritte, Spaziergang* ⟩; sanft ⟨ *Abhang usw.* ⟩; mild ⟨ *Reinigungsmittel, Shampoo usw.* ⟩; wohlig ⟨ *Wärme* ⟩; zahm, lammfromm ⟨ *Tier* ⟩; **be ~ with sb./sth.** sanft mit jmdm./ etw. umgehen; **a ~ reminder/hint** ein zarter Wink/eine zarte Andeutung; **the ~ sex** das zarte Geschlecht (ugs. scherzh.)

gentleman /ˈdʒentlmən/ *n., pl.* **gentlemen** /ˈdʒentlmən/ (**a**) (man of good manners and breeding) Gentleman, *der;* (**b**) (man) Herr, *der;* **[Ladies and] Gentlemen!** meine [Damen und] Herren!; **Gentlemen, …** (in formal, business letter) Sehr geehrte Herren!; **~'s agreement** Gentleman's Agreement, *das;* **gentlemen's** Herren⟨ *friseur, -schneider* ⟩

gentlemanly /ˈdʒentlmənlɪ/ *adj.* gentlemanlike *nicht attrib.;* eines Gentlemans *nachgestellt*

gentleness /ˈdʒentlnɪs/ *n., no pl.* Sanftheit, *die;* (of nature) Sanftmütigkeit, *die;* (of shampoo, cleanser, etc.) Milde, *die*

gently /ˈdʒentlɪ/ *adv.* (tenderly) zart; zärtlich; (mildly) sanft; (carefully) vorsichtig; behutsam; (quietly, softly) leise; (moderately) sanft; (slowly) langsam; **she broke the news to him ~:** sie brachte ihm die Nachricht schonend bei; **~ does it!** immer sachte! (ugs.); **~!** [sachte] sachte!

gentry /ˈdʒentrɪ/ *n. pl.* niederer Adel; Gentry, *die*

genuine /ˈdʒenjʊɪn/ *adj.* (**a**) (real) echt; authentisch ⟨ *Text* ⟩; **the ~ article** die echte Ausgabe (fig.); (**b**) (true) aufrichtig; wahr ⟨ *Grund, Not* ⟩; echt ⟨ *Tränen* ⟩; ernsthaft, ernst gemeint ⟨ *Angebot* ⟩

genuinely /ˈdʒenjʊɪnlɪ/ *adv.* wirklich

genus /ˈdʒiːnəs, ˈdʒenəs/ *n., pl.* **genera** /ˈdʒenərə/ (Biol.) Gattung, *die*

geographer /dʒɪˈɒɡrəfə(r)/ *n.* ▶ 887 | Geograph, *der*/Geographin, *die*

geographical /dʒiːəˈɡræfɪkl/ *adj.,* **geographically** /dʒiːəˈɡræfɪkəlɪ/ *adv.* geographisch

geography /dʒɪˈɒɡrəfɪ/ *n.* Geographie, *die;* Erdkunde, *die* (Schulw.)

geological /dʒiːəˈlɒdʒɪkl/ *adj.,* **geologically** /dʒiːəˈlɒdʒɪkəlɪ/ *adv.* geologisch

geologist /dʒɪˈɒlədʒɪst/ *n.* ▶ 887 | Geologe, *der*/Geologin, *die*

geology /dʒɪˈɒlədʒɪ/ *n.* Geologie, *die*

geometric /dʒiːəˈmetrɪk/, **geometrical** /dʒiːəˈmetrɪkl/ *adjs.,* **geometrically** /dʒiːəˈmetrɪkəlɪ/ *adv.* geometrisch

geometry /dʒɪˈɒmɪtrɪ/ *n.* Geometrie, *die*

Georgian /ˈdʒɔːdʒɪən/ *adj.* (Brit. Hist.) georgianisch

geranium /dʒəˈreɪnɪəm/ *n.* Geranie, *die;* Pelargonie, *die*

gerbil /ˈdʒɜːbɪl/ *n.* (Zool.) Wüstenmaus, *die;* Rennmaus, *die*

geriatric /dʒerɪˈætrɪk/ *adj.* geriatrisch

germ /dʒɜːm/ *n.* (lit. *or* fig.) Keim, *der;* **I don't want to catch your ~s** ich möchte mich nicht bei dir anstecken; **wheat ~:** Weizenkeim, *der*

German /ˈdʒɜːmən/ ▶ 897 |, ▶ 947 | 1 *adj.* deutsch; **a ~ person** ein Deutscher/eine Deutsche; **the ~ people** die Deutschen; **he/she is ~:** er ist Deutscher/sie ist Deutsche; **he is a native ~ speaker** seine Muttersprache ist Deutsch. *See also* **East German 1; West German 1.** 2 *n.* (**a**) (person) Deutsche, *der/die;* **he/she is a ~:** er ist

Deutscher/sie ist Deutsche; **(b)** (language) Deutsch, *das;* **High** ~: Hochdeutsch, *das;* **Low** ~: Niederdeutsch, *das. See also* **East German 2; English 2 a; West German 2**

German Democratic Re'public *pr. n.* (Hist.) Deutsche Demokratische Republik

Germanic /dʒɜː'mænɪk/ *adj.* germanisch

German: ~ **'measles** *n. sing.* ▶ 865 Röteln *Pl.;* ~ **'shepherd [dog]** *n.* [Deutscher] Schäferhund

Germany /'dʒɜːmənɪ/ *pr. n.* Deutschland *(das);* **Federal Republic of** ~: Bundesrepublik Deutschland, *die; see also* **East Germany; West Germany**

germinate /'dʒɜːmɪneɪt/ **1** *v.i.* keimen; (fig.) entstehen. **2** *v.t.* zum Keimen bringen

germination /dʒɜːmɪ'neɪʃn/ *n.* Keimung, *die;* Keimen, *das*

germ 'warfare *n.* Bakterienkrieg, *der;* biologische Krieg[s]führung

gerund /'dʒerənd/ *n.* (Ling.) Gerundium, *das*

gestation /dʒe'steɪʃn/ *n.* (of animal) Trächtigkeit, *die;* (of woman) Schwangerschaft, *die*

gesticulate /dʒe'stɪkjʊleɪt/ *v.i.* gestikulieren

gesticulation /dʒestɪkjʊ'leɪʃn/ *n.* ~[s *pl.*] Gesten

gesture /'dʒestʃə(r)/ **1** *n.* Geste, *die* (auch fig.); Gebärde, *die* (geh.); **a** ~ **of resignation** eine resignierte Geste. **2** *v.i.* gestikulieren; ~ **to sb. to do sth.** jmdm. zu verstehen geben *od.* (geh.) jmdm. bedeuten, etw. zu tun. **3** *v.t.* ~ **sb. to do sth.** jmdm. bedeuten, etw. zu tun (geh.)

get /get/ **1** *v.t.,* **-tt-,** *p.t.* **got** /gɒt/, *p.p.* **got** *or* (*in comb./ arch./ Amer. except in sense* **m**) **gotten** /'gɒtn/ (**got** *also coll. abbr. of* **has got** *or* **have got**) **(a)** (obtain) bekommen; kriegen (ugs.); (by buying) kaufen; sich (*Dat.*) anschaffen ⟨*Auto usw.*⟩; (by one's own effort for special purpose) sich (*Dat.*) besorgen ⟨*Visum, Genehmigung, Arbeitskräfte*⟩; sich (*Dat.*) beschaffen ⟨*Geld*⟩; einholen ⟨*Gutachten*⟩; (by contrivance) kommen zu; (find) finden ⟨*Zeit*⟩; **where did you** ~ **that?** wo hast du das her?; **he got him by the leg/arm** er kriegte ihn am Bein/Arm zu fassen; ~ **sb. a job/taxi,** ~ **a job/taxi for sb.** jmdm. einen Job verschaffen/ein Taxi besorgen *od.* rufen; ~ **oneself sth./a job** sich (*Dat.*) etw. zulegen/einen Job finden; **you can't** ~ **this kind of fruit in the winter months** dieses Obst gibt es im Winter nicht zu kaufen; ~ **something to eat** etwas zu essen holen; **(b)** (fetch) holen; **what can I** ~ **you?** was kann ich Ihnen anbieten?; **is there anything I can** ~ **you in town?** soll ich dir etwas aus der Stadt mitbringen?; **(c)** ~ **the bus** *etc.* (be in time for, catch) den Bus *usw.* erreichen *od.* (ugs.) kriegen; (travel by) den Bus nehmen; **(d)** (prepare) machen (ugs.), zubereiten ⟨*Essen*⟩; **(e)** (coll.: eat) essen; (be given) etwas zu essen bekommen; **(f)** (gain) erreichen; **what do I** ~ **out of it?** was habe ich davon?; **(g)** (by calculation) herausbekommen; **(h)** (receive) bekommen; erhalten, (ugs.) kriegen ⟨*Geldsumme*⟩; **the country** ~**s very little sun/ rain** die Sonne scheint/es regnet nur sehr wenig in dem Land; **he got his jaw broken in a fight** bei einer Schlägerei wurde ihm der Kiefer gebrochen; **(i)** (receive as penalty) bekommen, (ugs.) kriegen ⟨*6 Monate Gefängnis, Geldstrafe, Tracht Prügel*⟩; **you'll** ~ **it** (coll.) du kriegst Prügel (ugs.); es setzt was (ugs.); (be scolded) du kriegst was zu hören (ugs.); **(j)** (kill) töten; erlegen ⟨*Wild*⟩; (hit, injure) treffen; **(k)** (win) bekommen; finden ⟨*Anerkennung*⟩; sich (*Dat.*) verschaffen ⟨*Ansehen*⟩; erzielen ⟨*Tor, Punkt, Treffer*⟩; gewinnen ⟨*Preis, Belohnung*⟩; belegen ⟨*ersten usw. Platz*⟩; ~ **permission** die Erlaubnis erhalten; **(l)** (come to have) finden ⟨*Schlaf, Ruhe*⟩; bekommen ⟨*Einfall, Vorstellung, Gefühl*⟩; gewinnen ⟨*Eindruck*⟩; (contract) bekommen ⟨*Kopfschmerzen, Grippe, Malaria*⟩; ~ **some rest** sich ausruhen; ~ **an idea/a habit from sb.** von jmdm. eine Idee/Angewohnheit übernehmen; **(m)** **have got** (coll.: have) haben; **give it all you've got** gib dein Bestes; **have got a toothache/a cold** Zahnschmerzen/eine Erkältung haben *od.* erkältet sein; **have got to do sth.** etw. tun müssen; **something has got to be done [about it]** dagegen muss etwas unternommen werden; **(n)** (succeed in bringing, placing, etc.) bringen; kriegen (ugs.); **I must** ~ **a message to her** ich muss ihr eine Nachricht zukommen lassen; **(o)** (bring into some state) ~ **a machine going** eine Maschine in Gang

setzen *od.* bringen; ~ **things going** *or* **started** die Dinge in Gang bringen; ~ **everything packed/prepared** alles [ein]packen/vorbereiten; ~ **sth. ready/done** etw. fertig machen; ~ **one's feet wet** nasse Füße kriegen; ~ **one's hands dirty** sich (*Dat.*) die Hände schmutzig machen; **I didn't** ~ **much done today** ich habe heute nicht viel geschafft; **you'll** ~ **yourself thrown out/arrested** du schaffst es noch, dass du rausgeworfen/verhaftet wirst; ~ **sb. talking/drunk/interested** jmdn. zum Reden bringen/betrunken machen/jmds. Interesse wecken; ~ **one's hair cut** sich (*Dat.*) die Haare schneiden lassen; **(p)** (induce) ~ **sb. to do sth.** jmdn. dazu bringen, etw. zu tun; ~ **sth. to do sth.** es schaffen, dass etw. etw. tut; **I can't** ~ **the car to start/the door to shut** ich kriege das Auto nicht in Gang/die Tür nicht zu; **(q)** (Radio, Telev.: pick up) empfangen ⟨*Sender*⟩; **(r)** (contact by telephone) ~ **sb.** **[on the phone]** jmdn. [telefonisch] erreichen; **(s)** (answer) **I'll** ~ **it!** ich geh schon!; (answer doorbell) ich mach auf!; (answer the phone) ich gehe ran (ugs.) *od.* nehme ab!; **(t)** (coll.: perplex) **in** Verwirrung bringen; **you've got me there; I don't know** da bin ich überfragt — ich weiß es nicht; **(u)** (coll.) (understand) kapieren (ugs.); verstehen ⟨*Personen*⟩; (hear) mitkriegen (ugs.); ~ **it?** alles klar? (ugs.); **(v)** (coll.: annoy) aufregen (ugs.). **2** *v.i.,* **-tt-, got, gotten (a)** (succeed in coming or going) kommen; ~ **to London before dark** London vor Einbruch der Dunkelheit erreichen; **when did you get here to school?** wann bist du gekommen?/wann warst du in der Schule?; **we got as far as Oxford** wir kamen bis Oxford; **how did that** ~ **here?** wie ist das hierher gekommen?; **(b)** (come to be) ~ **talking [to sb.]** [mit jmdm.] ins Gespräch kommen; ~ **going** *or* **started** (leave) losgehen; aufbrechen; (start talking) loslegen (ugs.); (become lively or operative) in Schwung kommen; ~ **going on** *or* **with sth.** mit etw. anfangen; **(c)** ~ **to know sb.** jmdn. kennen lernen; **he got to like/hate her** mit der Zeit mochte er sie/begann er, sie zu hassen; ~ **to hear of sth.** von etw. erfahren; ~ **to do sth.** (succeed in doing) etw. tun können; **(d)** (become) werden; ~ **ready/washed** sich fertig machen/waschen; ~ **frightened/hungry** Angst/Hunger kriegen; ~ **excited about sth.** sich auf etw. (*Akk.*) freuen; ~ **interested in sth.** sich für etw. interessieren; ~ **caught in the rain** vom Regen überrascht werden; ~ **well soon!** gute Besserung!

~ **a'bout** *v.i.* **(a)** (move) sich bewegen; (travel) herumkommen; **(b)** ⟨*Gerücht:*⟩ sich verbreiten

~ **across 1** /-'-'-/ *v.i.* **(a)** (to/from other side) rüberkommen (ugs.); **(b)** (coll.: be communicated) rüberkommen (ugs.); ~ **across [to sb.]** ⟨*Person:*⟩ sich [jmdm.] verständlich machen; ⟨*Witz, Idee:*⟩ [bei jmdm.] ankommen. **2** [*stress varies*] *v.t.* **(a)** (cross) überqueren; ~ **sb./sth. across [sth.]** (transport to/from other side) jmdn./etw. [über etw. (*Akk.*)] hin-/herüberbringen; **(b)** (coll.: communicate) vermitteln, klarmachen (**to** *Dat.*)

~ **a'long** *v.i.* **(a)** (advance, progress) ~ **along well** [gute] Fortschritte machen; **how is he** ~**ting along with his work?** wie kommt er mit seiner Arbeit voran?; **(b)** (manage) zurechtkommen; **(c)** (agree or live sociably) auskommen; ~ **along with each other** *or* **together** miteinander auskommen; (get along) sich auf den Weg machen

~ **at** *v.t.* **(a)** herankommen an (+ *Akk.*); **(b)** (find out) [he]rausfinden ⟨*Wahrheit, Ursache usw.*⟩; **(c)** (coll.) **what are you/is he getting at?** worauf wollen Sie/will er hinaus?; (referring to) worauf spielen Sie/spielt er jetzt an?; **(d)** (coll.: attack, taunt) anmachen (salopp)

~ **a'way 1** *v.i.* **(a)** wegkommen; **I can't** ~ **away from work** ich kann nicht von der Arbeit weg; **there is no** ~**ting away from the fact that ...:** man kommt nicht um die Tatsache *od.* darum herum, dass ...; ~ **away from it all** ⇒ **all 1 a; (b)** (escape) entkommen; entwischen (ugs.); **(c)** *in imper.* (coll.) ~ **away [with you]!** ach, geh *od.* komm! (ugs.); ach, erzähl mir doch nichts! (ugs.). **2** *v.t.* wegnehmen; ~ **sth. away from sb.** jmdm. etw. wegnehmen

~ **a'way with** *v.t.* **(a)** (steal and escape with) entkommen mit; **(b)** (coll.: go unpunished for) ungestraft davonkommen mit; **the things he** ~**s away with!** was der sich (*Dat.*) alles erlauben kann!; ~ **away with it** es sich (*Dat.*) erlauben können; (succeed) damit durchkommen

~ **'back 1** *v.i.* **(a)** (return) zurückkommen; ~ **back**

home nach Hause kommen; **(b)** (stand away) zurücktreten. **2** *v.t.* **(a)** (recover) wieder- *od.* zurückbekommen; ∼ **one's strength back** wieder zu Kräften kommen; **(b)** (return) zurücktun; **I can't** ∼ **the lid back on** [**it**] ich kriege den Deckel nicht wieder drauf (ugs.); **(c)** ∼ **one's 'own back** [**on sb.**] (coll.) sich [an jmdm.] rächen

∼ **'back to** *v.t.* ∼ **back to sb.** auf jmdn. zurückkommen; **I'll** ∼ **back to you on that** ich komme darauf noch zurück; ∼ **back to work** wieder an die Arbeit gehen

∼ **be'hind** *v.i.* zurückbleiben; ins Hintertreffen geraten (ugs.); (with payments) in Rückstand geraten

∼ **'by 1** *v.i.* **(a)** (move past) passieren; vorbeikommen; **let sb.** ∼ **by** jmdn. vorbeilassen; **(b)** (coll.: be acceptable, adequate) **she should** [**just about**] ∼ **by in the exam** sie müsste die Prüfung [gerade so] schaffen; **(c)** (coll.: manage) über die Runden kommen (on mit). **2** *v.t.* **(a)** (move past) ∼ **by sb./sth.** an jmdm./etw. vorbeikommen; **(b)** (pass unnoticed) entgehen (+ *Dat.*)

∼ **down 1** /ˈ-ˈ-/ *v.i.* **(a)** (come down) heruntersteigen; (go down) hinuntersteigen; **(b)** (leave table) aufstehen; **(c)** (bend down) sich bücken; ∼ **down on one's knees** niederknien. **2** [stress varies] *v.t.* **(a)** (come down) heruntersteigen; herunterkommen; (go down) hinuntersteigen; hinuntergeben; **(b)** ∼ **sb./sth. down** (manage to bring down) jmdn./etw. hin-/herunterbringen; (with difficulty) jmdn./etw. hin-/herunterbekommen; (take down from above) jmdn./etw. hin-/herunterholen; **(c)** (swallow) hinunterschlucken; **(d)** (record, write) ∼ **sth. down** [**on paper**] etw. schriftlich festhalten *od.* zu Papier bringen; **(e)** (coll.: depress) fertig machen (ugs.); **(f)** senken ⟨Fieber, Preis⟩; (by bargaining) herunterdrücken ⟨Preis⟩

∼ **'down to** *v.t.* ∼ **down to sth.** sich an etw. (*Akk.*) machen; ∼ **down to writing a letter** sich hinsetzen und einen Brief schreiben

∼ **'in 1** *v.i.* **(a)** (into bus etc.) einsteigen; (into bath) hineinsteigen; (into bed) sich hinlegen; (into room, house, etc.) eintreten; (intrude) eindringen; **(b)** (arrive) ankommen; (get home) heimkommen; **(c)** (be elected) gewählt werden; **(d)** (obtain place) (at institution etc.) angenommen werden; (at university) einen Studienplatz bekommen. **2** *v.t.* **(a)** (bring in) einbringen ⟨Ernte⟩; hineinbringen, ins Haus bringen ⟨Einkäufe, Kind⟩; einlagern ⟨Kohlen, Kartoffeln⟩; reinholen ⟨Wäsche⟩; (Brit.: fetch and pay for) holen ⟨Getränke⟩; **(b)** (coll.: enter) einsteigen in (+ *Akk.*) ⟨Auto, Zug⟩; **(c)** (submit) abgeben ⟨Artikel, Hausarbeit⟩; einreichen ⟨Bewerbung, Bericht⟩; **(d)** (receive) erhalten; reinkriegen (ugs.); **(e)** (send for) holen; rufen ⟨Arzt, Polizei⟩; hinzuziehen ⟨Spezialist⟩; **(f)** (fit in) reinkriegen (ugs.); einschieben ⟨Unterrichtsstunde⟩; **try to** ∼ **in a word about sth.** sich zu etw. äußern wollen

∼ **'in on** *v.t.* (coll.) sich beteiligen an (+ *Dat.*); ∼ **in on the act** mitmischen (ugs.)

∼ **into** *v.t.* **(a)** (bring into) fahren ⟨Auto usw.⟩ in (+ *Akk.*) ⟨Garage⟩; bringen in (+ *Akk.*) ⟨Haus, Bett, Hafen⟩; **(b)** (enter) gehen/(as intruder) eindringen in (+ *Akk.*) ⟨Haus⟩; [ein]steigen in (+ *Akk.*) ⟨Auto usw.⟩; [ein]treten in (+ *Akk.*) ⟨Zimmer⟩; steigen in (+ *Akk.*) ⟨Wasser⟩; **the coach** ∼**s into the station at 9 p.m.** der Bus kommt um 21.00 Uhr am Busbahnhof an; **(c)** (gain admission to) eingelassen werden in (+ *Akk.*); einen Studienplatz erhalten an (+ *Dat.*) ⟨Universität⟩; genommen werden von ⟨Firma⟩; ∼ **into Parliament** ins Parlament einziehen; **(d)** (coll.) ∼ **into one's clothes** sich anziehen; **I can't** ∼ **into these trousers** ich komme in diese Hose nicht rein (ugs.); **(e)** (penetrate) [ein]dringen in (+*Akk.*); **(f)** (begin to undergo) geraten in (+ *Akk.*); kommen in (+ *Akk.*) ⟨Schwierigkeiten⟩; (cause to undergo) stürzen in (+ *Akk.*) ⟨Schulden, Unglück⟩; bringen in (+ *Akk.*) ⟨Schwierigkeiten⟩; **(g)** (accustom to, become accustomed to) annehmen ⟨Gewohnheit⟩; ∼ **into the job/work** sich einarbeiten; *see also* **habit a**; **(h)** geraten in (+ *Akk.*) ⟨Wut, Panik⟩; **(i) what's got into him?** was ist nur in ihn gefahren?

∼ **'in with** *v.t.* (coll.) ∼ **in** [**well**] **with sb.** sich mit jmdm. gut stellen; **he got in with a bad crowd** er geriet in schlechte Gesellschaft

∼ **off 1** /ˈ-ˈ-/ *v.i.* **(a)** (alight) aussteigen; (dismount) absteigen; **tell sb. where he** ∼**s off** *or* **where to** ∼ **off** (fig. coll.) jmdn. in seine Grenzen verweisen; **(b)** (not remain on sb./sth.)

runtergehen; (from chair) aufstehen; (from ladder, table, carpet) herunterkommen; (let go) loslassen; **(c)** (start) aufbrechen; ∼ **off to school/to work** zur Schule/Arbeit losgehen/ -fahren; ∼ **off to a good** *etc.* **start** einen guten *usw.* Start haben; **(d)** (escape punishment or injury) davonkommen; ∼ **off lightly** glimpflich davonkommen; **(e)** (fall asleep) einschlafen; **(f)** (leave) [weg]gehen; ∼ **off early** [schon] früh [weg]gehen. **2** [stress varies] *v.t.* **(a)** (dismount from) [ab]-steigen von ⟨Fahrrad⟩; steigen von ⟨Pferd⟩; (alight from) aussteigen aus ⟨Bus, Zug usw.⟩; steigen aus ⟨Boot⟩; **(b)** (not remain on) herunterkommen von ⟨Teppich, Mauer, Leiter, Tisch⟩; aufstehen von ⟨Stuhl⟩; verschwinden von, verlassen ⟨Gelände⟩; ∼ **off the subject** vom Thema abkommen; **(c)** (cause to start) [los]schicken; **it takes ages to** ∼ **the children off to school** es dauert eine Ewigkeit, die Kinder für die Schule fertig zu machen; **(d)** (remove) ausziehen ⟨Kleidung usw.⟩; entfernen ⟨Fleck, Farbe usw.⟩; abbekommen ⟨Deckel, Ring⟩; ∼ **sth. off sth.** etw. von etw. entfernen/abbekommen; ∼ **sb. off a subject** jmdn. von einem Thema abbringen; **(e)** (send, dispatch) abschicken; aufgeben ⟨Telegramm, Paket⟩; **(f)** (cause to escape punishment) davonkommen lassen; **(g)** (not have to do, go to, etc.) frei haben; ∼ **time/a day of** [**work**] freibekommen/einen Tag freibekommen; ∼ **off work** [**early**] [früher] Feierabend machen; **I have got the afternoon off** ich habe den Nachmittag frei

∼ **on 1** /ˈ-ˈ-/ *v.i.* **(a)** (on bicycle) aufsteigen; (on horse) aufsitzen; (enter vehicle) einsteigen; **(b)** (make progress) vorankommen; ∼ **on in life/the world** es zu etwas [im Leben] bringen; (fare) **how did you** ∼ **on there?** wie ist es dir dort ergangen?; **he's** ∼**ting on well** es geht ihm gut; **I didn't** ∼ **on too well in my exams** meine Prüfungen sind nicht besonders gut gelaufen (ugs.); **(d)** (become late) vorrücken; **it's** ∼**ting on for five** es geht auf fünf zu; **it's** ∼**ting on for six months since** …: es sind bald sechs Monate, seit …; **time is** ∼**ting on** es wird langsam spät; **(e)** ▶630 (advance in age) älter werden; **be** ∼**ting on in years/for seventy** langsam älter werden/auf die siebzig zugehen; **(f) there were** ∼**ting on for fifty people** es waren an die fünfzig Leute da; **(g)** (manage) zurechtkommen; **(h)** ⇒ ∼ **along c. 2** [stress varies] *v.t.* **(a)** (climb on) steigen auf (+ *Akk.*) ⟨Fahrrad, Pferd⟩; (enter, board) einsteigen in (+ *Akk.*) ⟨Zug, Bus, Flugzeug⟩; gehen auf (+ *Akk.*) ⟨Schiff⟩; **(b)** (put on) anziehen ⟨Kleider, Schuhe⟩; aufsetzen ⟨Hut, Kessel⟩; (load) [auf]laden auf (+ *Akk.*); ∼ **the cover** [**back**] **on** den Deckel [wieder] draufbekommen; **(c)** (coll.) ∼ **something on sb.** (discover sth. incriminating) etwas gegen jmdn. in der Hand haben

∼ **'on to** *v.t.* **(a)** ⇒ ∼ **on 2 a;** **(b)** (contact) sich in Verbindung setzen mit; (by telephone) anrufen; **(c)** (realize) ∼ **on to sth.** hinter etw. (*Akk.*) kommen; ∼ **on to the fact that** …: dahinter kommen, dass …; **(d)** (move on to discuss, study, etc.) übergehen zu

∼ **'on with** *v.t.* **(a)** weitermachen mit; **let sb.** ∼ **on with it** (coll.) jmdn. [allein weiter]machen lassen; **enough to be** ∼**ting on with** genug für den Anfang *od.* fürs Erste; **(b)** = ∼ **along with** ⇒ ∼ **along a, c**

∼ **'out 1** *v.i.* **(a)** (walk out) rausgehen (**of** aus); (drive out) rausfahren (**of** aus); (alight) aussteigen (**of** aus); (climb out) rausklettern (**of** aus); ∼ **out** [**of my room**]**!** raus [aus meinem Zimmer]!; **(b)** (leak) austreten (**of** aus); (escape from cage, jail) ausbrechen, entkommen (**of** aus); (fig.) ⟨Geheimnis:⟩ herauskommen; ⟨Nachrichten:⟩ durchsickern. **2** *v.t.* **(a)** (cause to leave) rausbringen (**of** aus); (send out) rausschicken (**of** aus); (throw out) rauswerfen (**of** aus); ∼ **a stain out/out of sth.** einen Fleck wegbekommen/aus etw. herausbekommen; **(b)** (bring or take out) herausholen (**of** aus); herausziehen ⟨Korken⟩; (drive out) herausfahren (**of** aus); **(c)** (withdraw) abheben ⟨Geld⟩ (**of** von)

∼ **'out of** *v.t.* **(a)** (leave) verlassen ⟨Zimmer, Haus, Stadt, Land⟩; (cause to leave) entfernen aus; (extract from) herausziehen aus; (bring or take out of) herausholen aus; (leak from) austreten aus; (withdraw from) abheben ⟨Geld⟩ von; ∼ **a book out of the library** ein Buch aus der Bibliothek ausleihen; ∼ **him out of my sight!** schaff ihn mir aus den Augen!; ∼ **sth. out of one's head** *or* **mind** sich (*Dat.*) etw. aus dem Kopf schlagen; **(b)** (escape) herauskommen aus; (avoid) herumkommen um (ugs.); sich drücken vor (+ *Dat.*) (ugs.)

⟨*Arbeit*⟩; **(c)** (gain from) herausholen ⟨*Geld*⟩ aus; machen (ugs.) *od.* erzielen ⟨*Gewinn*⟩ bei; **~ a word/the truth/a confession out of sb.** aus jmdm. ein Wort/die Wahrheit/ein Geständnis herausbringen; **~ the best/most out of sb./sth.** das Beste/Meiste aus jmdm./etw. herausholen
~ 'over 1 *v.i.* **(a)** (cross) **~ over to the other side** auf die andere Seite gehen; **(b)** ⇒ **~ across 1 b.** **2** *v.t.* **(a)** (cross) gehen über (+ *Akk.*); setzen über (+ *Akk.*) ⟨*Fluss*⟩; (climb) klettern über (+ *Akk.*); (cause to cross) [hinüber]-bringen über (+ *Akk.*); **(b)** ⇒ **~ across 2 b.**; **(c)** (overcome, recover from) überwinden; hinwegkommen über (+ *Akk.*); verwinden (geh.) ⟨*Verlust*⟩; sich erholen von ⟨*Krankheit*⟩; **(d)** (fully believe) **I can't ~ over his cheek/the fact that …:** solche Frechheit kann ich nicht begreifen/ich kann gar nicht fassen, dass …
~ 'over with *v.t.* (coll.) **~ sth. over with** etw. hinter sich (*Akk.*) bringen
~ 'past 1 *v.i.* ⇒ **~ by 1 a.** **2** *v.t.* ⇒ **~ by 2**
~ 'round 1 *v.i.* **(a)** ⇒ **~ about;** **(b)** **~ round to doing sth.** dazu kommen, etw. zu tun. **2** *v.t.* **(a)** (avoid) umgehen ⟨*Gesetz, Bestimmungen*⟩; **(b)** **~ round sb.** (get one's way with) jmdn. herumkriegen (ugs.); (persuade) jmdn. überzeugen (**to** von); **(c)** (overcome) lösen ⟨*Problem usw.*⟩; überwinden ⟨*Hindernis usw.*⟩; umgehen ⟨*Schwierigkeit usw.*⟩
~ through 1 /-'-/ *v.i.* **(a)** (pass obstacle) durchkommen; (make contact) durchkommen (ugs.); Verbindung bekommen (**to** mit); **(b)** (be transmitted) durchkommen (ugs.); durchdringen (**to** bis zu *od.* nach); **(c)** (win heat or round) gewinnen; **~ through to the finals** in die Endrunde kommen; **(d)** **~ through [to sb.]** (make sb. understand) sich [jmdm.] verständlich machen; **(e)** (pass) bestehen; durchkommen (ugs.); **(f)** (be approved) angenommen werden; durchkommen (ugs.). **2** [stress varies] *v.t.* **(a)** (pass through) [durch]kommen durch; **(b)** (help to make contact) **~ sb. through** to jmdn. verbinden mit; **(c)** (bring) [durch]bringen; übermitteln ⟨*Nachricht*⟩ (**to** *Dat.*); **~ a message through to sb.** jmdm. eine Nachricht zukommen lassen; **(d)** (communicate) **~ sth. through to sb.** jmdm. etw. klarmachen; **(e)** (pass) durchkommen bei (ugs.), bestehen ⟨*Prüfung*⟩; **(f)** (consume, use up) verbrauchen; verqualmen (ugs. abwertend) ⟨*Zigaretten*⟩; aufessen ⟨*Essen*⟩; (spend) durchbringen ⟨*Geld, Vermögen*⟩; **(g)** (survive) durchstehen; überstehen; kommen durch; **(h)** fertig werden mit, erledigen ⟨*Arbeit*⟩; durchkriegen ⟨*Buch*⟩
~ to *v.t.* **(a)** (reach) kommen zu ⟨*Gebäude*⟩; erreichen ⟨*Person, Ort*⟩; **he is ~ting to the age when …:** er wird bald das Alter erreicht haben, wo …; **I haven't got to the end [of the novel] yet** ich habe [den Roman] noch nicht zu Ende gelesen; **where has the child/the book got to?** wo ist das Kind hin/das Buch hingekommen?; **(b)** (begin) **~ to doing sth.** anfangen, etw. zu tun; **(c)** **~ to sb.** (coll.: annoy) jmdm. auf die Nerven gehen (ugs.)
~ to'gether 1 *v.i.* zusammenkommen; **why not ~ together after work?** wollen wir uns nach Feierabend treffen? **2** *v.t.* **(a)** (collect) zusammenbringen; **~ one's things together** seine Sachen zusammenpacken; **(b)** (coll.: organize) **~ it** *or* **things together** die Dinge auf die Reihe kriegen (ugs.)
~ up 1 /-'-/ *v.i.* **(a)** (rise from bed, chair, floor; leave table) aufstehen; **please don't ~ up!** bitte bleiben Sie sitzen!; **(b)** (climb) [auf]steigen, aufsitzen (**on** auf + *Dat. od. Akk.*); **(c)** (rise, increase in force) zunehmen; **the sea is ~ting up** die See wird immer wilder. **2** [stress varies] *v.t.* **(a)** (call, awaken) wecken; (cause to leave bed) aus dem Bett holen; **(b)** (cause to stand up) aufhelfen (+ *Dat.*); **(c)** (climb) hinaufsteigen; **your car will not ~ up that hill** dein Auto kommt den Berg nicht hinauf; **(d)** (carry up) **~ sb./sth. up [sth.]** jmdn./etw. [etw.] her-/hinaufbringen; (with difficulty) jmdn. etw. [etw.] her-/hinaufbekommen; **(e)** (organize) organisieren; auf die Beine stellen; auf die Beine bringen ⟨*Personen*⟩; **(f)** (arrange appearance of, dress up) zurechtmachen; herrichten ⟨*Zimmer*⟩; **~ sb./oneself up as sb.** jmdn./sich als jmdn. ausstaffieren
~ 'up to *v.t.* **(a)** (reach) erreichen ⟨*Leistungsniveau*⟩; (cause to reach) bringen auf (+ *Akk.*); **(b)** (indulge in) aus sein auf (+ *Akk.*); **~ up to mischief** etwas anstellen; **what have you been ~ting up to?** was hast du getrieben *od.* angestellt?

get: ~away *n.* Flucht, *die; attrib.* Flucht⟨*plan, -wagen*⟩; **make one's ~away** entkommen; **~-together** *n.* (coll.) Zusammenkunft, *die;* (informal social gathering) gemütliches Beisammensein; **have a ~-together** sich treffen; zusammenkommen; **~-up** *n.* (coll.) Aufmachung, *die;* **~-up-and-'go** *n.* (coll.) Elan, *der;* Schwung, *der*
geyser *n.* **(a)** /'giːzə(r), 'geɪzə(r)/ (hot spring) Geysir, *der;* **(b)** /'giːzə(r)/ (Brit.: water heater) Durchlauferhitzer, *der*
Ghana /'gɑːnə/ *pr. n.* Ghana (*das*)
Ghanaian /gɑː'neɪən/ **1** *adj.* ghanaisch. **2** *n.* Ghanaer, *der/*Ghanaerin, *die*
ghastly /'gɑːstlɪ/ *adj.* **(a)** grauenvoll; grässlich; entsetzlich ⟨*Verletzungen*⟩; schrecklich ⟨*Geschichte, Fehler, Irrtum*⟩; **(b)** (coll.: objectionable, unpleasant) scheußlich (ugs.); grässlich (ugs.); **I feel ~:** ich fühle mich scheußlich
gherkin /'gɜːkɪn/ *n.* Essiggurke, *die*
ghetto /'getəʊ/ *n., pl.* **~s** Getto, *das*
ghetto blaster /'getəʊ blɑːstə(r)/ *n.* (coll.) [großer tragbarer] Radiorekorder
ghost /gəʊst/ **1** *n.* Geist, *der;* Gespenst, *das;* **give up the ~:** den *od.* seinen Geist aufgeben (veralt., scherzh.); (fig.: give up hope) die Hoffnung aufgeben; **not have the** *or* **a ~ of a chance** nicht die geringste Chance haben. **2** *v.t.* **~ sb.'s speech** *etc.* für jmdn. eine Rede *usw.* [als Ghostwriter] schreiben
ghostly /'gəʊstlɪ/ *adj.* gespenstisch; geisterhaft
ghost: ~ story *n.* Gespenstergeschichte, *die;* **~ town** *n.* Geisterstadt, *die;* **~ writer** *n.* Ghostwriter, *der*
ghoulish /'guːlɪʃ/ *adj.* teuflisch ⟨*Freude*⟩; schaurig ⟨*Gelächter*⟩; makaber ⟨*Geschichte*⟩
GI /'dʒiːaɪ, dʒiː'aɪ/ **1** *adj.* GI-⟨*Uniform, Haarschnitt*⟩. **2** *n.* GI, *der*
giant /'dʒaɪənt/ **1** *n.* Riese, *der.* **2** *attrib. adj.* riesig; Riesen- (ugs.)
giant 'panda *n.* Bambusbär, *der;* Riesenpanda, *der*
gibber /'dʒɪbə(r)/ *v.i.* plappern; ⟨*Affe:*⟩ schnattern
gibberish /'dʒɪbərɪʃ/ *n.* Kauderwelsch, *das*
gibbon /'gɪbən/ *n.* (Zool.) Gibbon, *der*
gibe /dʒaɪb/ **1** *n.* Spöttelei, *die* (ugs.); Stichelei, *die* (ugs.). **2** *v.i.* **~ at sb./sth.** über jmdn./etw. spötteln
giblets /'dʒɪblɪts/ *n. pl.* [Geflügel]klein, *das*
Gibraltar /dʒɪ'brɔːltə(r)/ *pr. n.* Gibraltar (*das*)
giddiness /'gɪdɪnɪs/ *n., no pl.* Schwindel, *der*
giddy /'gɪdɪ/ *adj.* schwind[e]lig; Schwindel erregend ⟨*Höhe, Abgrund*⟩; **I feel ~:** mir ist schwindlig
gift /gɪft/ *n.* **(a)** (present) Geschenk, *das;* Gabe, *die* (geh.); **it was given to me as a ~:** ich habe es geschenkt bekommen; **a ~ box/pack** eine Geschenkpackung; **(b)** (talent etc.) Begabung, *die;* **have a ~ for languages/mathematics** sprachbegabt/mathematisch begabt sein; **(c)** (easy task etc.) **be a ~:** geschenkt sein (ugs.)
gifted /'gɪftɪd/ *adj.* begabt (**in, at** für); **be ~ in** *or* **at languages** sprachbegabt sein
gift: ~-horse *n.* never *or* don't look a **~-horse in the mouth** (prov.) einem geschenkten Gaul schaut man nicht ins Maul (Spr.); **~ shop** *n.* Geschenkboutique, *die;* **~ token,** **~ voucher** *ns.* Geschenkgutschein, *der;* **~-wrap** *v.t.* als Geschenk einpacken
giga /'gɪgə/ *pref.* giga-/Giga-; **~byte** Gigabyte, *das*
gigantic /dʒaɪ'gæntɪk/ *adj.* gigantisch; riesig; enorm, gewaltig ⟨*Verbesserung, Appetit, Portion*⟩
giggle /'gɪgl/ **1** *n.* **(a)** Kichern, *das;* Gekicher, *das;* **with a ~:** kichernd; **[a fit of] the ~s** ein Kicheranfall; **(b)** (coll.) (amusing person) Witzbold, *der;* (amusing thing, joke) Spaß, *der;* **we did it for a ~:** wir wollten unseren Spaß haben. **2** *v.i.* kichern
gild /gɪld/ *v.t.* vergolden; **~ the lily** des Guten zu viel tun
gill /gɪl/ *n., usu. in pl.* ▶ **1193**] Kieme, *die*
gilt /gɪlt/ **1** *n.* (gilding) Goldauflage, *die;* (paint) Goldfarbe, *die.* **2** *adj.* vergoldet
gilt-edged /'gɪltedʒd/ *adj.* (Commerc.) **~ securities/stocks** mündelsichere Wertpapiere

gimmick /'gɪmɪk/ n. (coll.) Gag, der; **a publicity** ∼: ein Werbegag

gimmickry /'gɪmɪkrɪ/ n. (coll.) Firlefanz, der (ugs.); Pipifax, der (ugs.); **advertising** ∼: Werbetricks od. -gags

gimmicky /'gɪmɪkɪ/ adj. (coll.) vergagt

gin /dʒɪn/ n. (drink) Gin, der; ∼ **and tonic** Gin [und] Tonic, der

ginger /'dʒɪndʒə(r)/ **1** n. (a) Ingwer, der; (b) (colour) Rötlichgelb, das. **2** adj. (a) (flavour) Ingwer‹gebäck, -geschmack›; (b) (colour) rötlich gelb; rotblond ‹Bart, Haare›

ginger: ∼ **'ale** n. Gingerale, das; ∼ **'beer** n. Ingwerbier, das; Ginger beer, das; ∼**bread** n. Pfefferkuchen, der

gingerly /'dʒɪndʒəlɪ/ adv. behutsam; [übertrieben] vorsichtig

gipsy ⇒ **gypsy**

giraffe /dʒɪ'rɑːf, dʒɪ'ræf/ n. Giraffe, die

girder /'gɜːdə(r)/ n. [Eisen-/Stahl]träger, der

girdle /'gɜːdl/ n. (corset) Hüfthalter, der; Hüftgürtel, der

girl /gɜːl/ n. (a) Mädchen, das; (teenager) junges Mädchen; ([young] woman) Frau, die; (daughter) Mädchen, das (ugs.); Tochter, die; **baby** ∼: kleines Mädchen; ∼**s' school** Mädchenschule, die; **a** ∼**'s name** ein Mädchenname; **[my]** ∼ (as address) [mein] Mädchen; **the** ∼**s** (female friends) meine/ihre usw. Freundinnen; **the** ∼ **at the cash-desk/switchboard** die Kassiererin/Telefonistin; (b) (sweetheart) Mädchen, das; Freundin, die

girl: ∼ **'Friday** ⇒ **Friday** 1; ∼**friend** n. Freundin, die; ∼ **'guide** ⇒ **guide** 1 c

girlie /'gɜːlɪ/ n. **1** adj. mit nackten Mädchen nachgestellt. **2** n. [kleines] Mädchen

girlish /'gɜːlɪʃ/ adj. mädchenhaft

giro /'dʒaɪrəʊ/ n., pl. ∼**s** Giro, das; attrib. Giro-; **post office/bank** ∼: Postgiro- od. (veralt.) Postscheck-/Giroverkehr, der

girth /gɜːθ/ n. (a) (circumference) Umfang, der; (at waist) Taillenumfang, der; (b) (for horse) Bauchgurt, der

gismo /'gɪzməʊ/ n. (coll.) Ding, das (ugs.)

gist /dʒɪst/ n. Wesentliche, das; (of tale, argument, question, etc.) Kern, der; **this is the** ∼ **of what he said** das hat er im Wesentlichen gesagt; **get the** ∼ **of sth.** das Wesentliche einer Sache mitbekommen; **could you give me the** ∼ **of it?** könntest du mir sagen, worum es hier geht?

give /gɪv/ **1** v.t., **gave** /geɪv/, **given** /'gɪvn/ (a) (hand over, pass) geben; (transfer from one's authority, custody, or responsibility) überbringen; übergeben (**to** an + Akk.); **she gave him her bag to carry** sie gab ihm ihre Tasche zum Tragen; **G**∼ **it to me! I'll do it** Gib her! Ich mache das; ∼ **me** … (on telephone) geben Sie mir …; verbinden Sie mich mit …; (b) (as gift) schenken; (donate) spenden; geben; (bequeath) vermachen; ∼ **sb. sth.,** ∼ **sth. to sb.** jmdm. etw. schenken; **the book was** ∼**n [to] me by my son** das Buch hat mir mein Sohn geschenkt; **I wouldn't have it if it was** ∼**n [to] me** ich würde es nicht mal geschenkt nehmen; abs. ∼ **towards sth.** zu etw. beisteuern; ∼ **blood** Blut spenden; ∼ **[a donation] to charity** für wohltätige Zwecke spenden; ∼ **and take** (fig.) Kompromisse eingehen; (in marriage etc.) geben und nehmen; (c) (sell) verkaufen; geben; (pay) zahlen; geben (ugs.); (sacrifice) geben; opfern; ∼ **sb. sth. [in exchange] for sth.** jmdm. etw. für etw. [im Tausch] geben; **I would** ∼ **anything** or **my right arm/a lot to be there** ich würde alles/viel darum geben, wenn ich dort sein könnte; (d) (assign) aufgeben ‹Hausaufgaben, Strafarbeit usw.›; (sentence to) geben ‹10 Jahre Gefängnis usw.›; (e) (grant, award) geben ‹Erlaubnis, Arbeitsplatz, Interview, Rabatt, Fähigkeit, Kraft›; verleihen ‹Preis, Titel, Orden usw.›; **be** ∼**n sth.** etw. bekommen; **he was** ∼**n the privilege/honour of doing it** ihm wurde das Vorrecht/die Ehre zuteil, es zu tun; ∼ **sb. to understand** or **believe that** …: jmdn. glauben lassen, dass …; (f) (entrust sb. with) übertragen (**to** Dat.); ∼ **sb. the power to do sth.** jmdn. ermächtigen, etw. zu tun; (g) (allow sb. to have) geben ‹Recht, Zeit, Urteil›; lassen ‹Wahl, Zeit›; **they gave me [the use of] their car for the weekend** sie überließen mir ihr Auto übers Wochenende; **I will** ∼ **you a day to think it over** ich lasse dir einen Tag Bedenkzeit; ∼ **yourself**

time to think about it lass dir Zeit, und denk darüber nach; ∼ **me London any day** or **time** or **every time** (fig. coll.) London ist mir zehnmal lieber; **I['ll]** ∼ **you/him** etc. **that** (fig. coll.: grant) das gebe ich zu; zugegeben; **you've got to** ∼ **it to him** (fig. coll.) das muss man ihm lassen; **it cost £5,** ∼ **or take a few pence** es hat so um die fünf Pfund gekostet (ugs.); ∼**n that** (because) da; (if) wenn; ∼**n the right tools** mit dem richtigen Werkzeug; ∼**n time,** **I'll do it** wenn ich Zeit habe, mache ich es; (h) (offer to sb.) geben, reichen ‹Arm, Hand usw.›; **please** ∼ **me your attention** ich bitte um Ihre Aufmerksamkeit; ∼ **sb. in marriage** jmdn. verheiraten; (i) (cause sb./sth. to have) geben; verleihen ‹Charme, Reiz, Gewicht, Nachdruck›; bereiten, machen ‹Freude, Mühe, Kummer›; bereiten, verursachen ‹Schmerz›; bieten ‹Abwechslung, Schutz›; leisten ‹Hilfe›; gewähren ‹Unterstützung›; **I was** ∼ **the guest room** man gab mir das Gästezimmer; ∼ **a clear picture** (Telev.) ein gutes Bild haben; ∼ **hope to sb.** jmdm. Hoffnung machen; ∼ **sb. what for** (sl.) es jmdm. geben (ugs.); (j) (convey in words, tell, communicate) angeben ‹Namen, Anschrift, Alter, Grund, Zahl›; nennen ‹Grund, Einzelheiten, Losungswort›; geben ‹Rat, Beispiel, Befehl, Anweisung, Antwort›; fällen ‹Urteil, Entscheidung›; sagen ‹Meinung›; bekannt geben ‹Nachricht, Ergebnis›; machen ‹Andeutung›; erteilen ‹Verweis, Rüge›; (present, set forth) ‹Wörterbuch, Brief:› enthalten; ‹Zeitung:› bringen ‹Bericht›; ∼ **details of sth.** Einzelheiten einer Sache (Gen.) darlegen; ∼ **sth. a mention** etw. erwähnen; ∼ **sb. the facts** jmdn. mit den Fakten vertraut od. bekannt machen; **she gave us the news** sie teilte es uns mit; ∼ **sb. a decision** jmdm. eine Entscheidung mitteilen; ∼ **him my best wishes** richte ihm meine besten Wünsche aus; **don't** ∼ **me 'that!** (coll.) erzähl mir [doch] nichts! (ugs.); (k) ∼**n** (specified) gegeben; (l) (perform, read, sing, etc.) geben ‹Vorstellung, Konzert›; halten ‹Vortrag, Seminar›; vorlesen ‹Gedicht, Erzählung›; singen ‹Lied›; spielen ‹Schauspiel, Oper, Musikstück›; ∼ **us a song** sing mal was; (m) ausbringen ‹Toast, Trinkspruch›; (as toast) **ladies and gentlemen, I** ∼ **you the Queen** meine Damen, meine Herren, I auf die Königin od. das Wohl der Königin; (n) (produce) geben ‹Licht, Milch›; tragen ‹Früchte›; ergeben ‹Zahlen, Resultat›; erbringen ‹Ernte›; (o) (cause to develop) machen; **sth.** ∼**s me a headache** von etw. bekomme ich Kopfschmerzen; **running** ∼**s me an appetite** Laufen macht mich hungrig; (p) (make sb. undergo) geben; versetzen ‹Schlag, Stoß›; verabreichen (geh.), geben ‹Arznei›; ∼ **sb. a [friendly] look** jmdm. einen [freundlichen] Blick zuwerfen; **he gave her hand a squeeze** er drückte ihr die Hand; ∼ **as good as one gets** (coll.) es jmdm. mit gleicher Münze heimzahlen; (q) (execute, make, show) geben ‹Zeichen, Stoß, Tritt›; machen ‹Satz, Ruck›; ausstoßen ‹Schrei, Seufzer, Pfiff›; ∼ **a [little] smile** [schwach] lächeln; ∼ **sth./sb. a look** sich (Dat.) etw./jmdn. ansehen; (r) (devote, dedicate) widmen; **be** ∼**n to sth./doing sth.** zu etw. neigen/etw. gern tun; ∼ **[it] all one's got** (coll.) sein Möglichstes tun; (s) (be host at) geben ‹Party, Empfang, Essen usw.›; (t) ∼ **sb./sth. two months/a year** jmdm./einer Sache zwei Monate/ein Jahr geben. **2** v.i., **gave, given** (a) (yield, bend) nachgeben (auch fig.); ‹Knie:› weich werden; ‹Bett:› federn; (break down) zusammenbrechen; ‹Brücke:› einstürzen; (fig.) nachlassen; (b) (lead) ∼ **on to the street/garden** ‹Tür usw.:› auf die Straße hinausführen/in den Garten führen. **3** n. (a) Nachgiebigkeit, die; (elasticity) Elastizität, die; **have [no]** ∼: [nicht] nachgeben; (b) ∼ **and take** (compromise) Kompromiss, der; (exchange of concessions) Geben und Nehmen, das
∼ **a'way** v.t. (a) (without charge, as gift) verschenken; (b) (in marriage) dem Bräutigam zuführen; (c) (distribute) verteilen, vergeben ‹Preise›; (d) (fig.: betray) verraten
∼ **'back** v.t. (lit. or fig.) zurückgeben; wiedergeben
∼ **in 1** /'--/ v.t. abgeben. **2** /-'-/ v.i. nachgeben (**to** Dat.)
∼ **'off** v.t. ausströmen ‹Rauch, Geruch›; aussenden ‹Strahlen›
∼ **out 1** /'--/ v.t. (a) (distribute) verteilen ‹Prospekte, Karten, Preise›; austeilen ‹Stifte, Hefte usw.›; vergeben ‹Arbeit›; (b) (declare) bekannt geben ‹Nachricht›. **2** /-'-/ v.i. ‹Vorräte:› ausgehen; ‹Maschine:› versagen; ‹Kraft:› nachlassen

~ **'over** v.t. (a) be ~n over to sth. für etw. beansprucht werden; (b) (abandon) ~ sth./sb. over to sb. etw. jmdm. überlassen/jmdm. jmdm. ausliefern; (c) (coll.: stop) ~ over [doing sth.] aufhören[, etw. zu tun]

~ **'up** 1 v.i. aufgeben. 2 v.t. (a) (renounce) aufgeben; ablegen ‹Gewohnheit›; widmen ‹Zeit›; (relinquish) verzichten auf (+ Akk.) ‹Territorium, Süßigkeiten›; ~ sth. up (abandon habit) sich (Dat.) etw. abgewöhnen; ~ sb./sth. up as a bad job (coll.) jmdn./etw. abschreiben (ugs.); (b) ~ sb. up (as not coming) jmdn. nicht mehr erwarten; (as beyond help) jmdn. aufgeben; (c) (hand over to police etc.) übergeben (to Dat.); ~ oneself up [to sb.] sich [jmdm.] stellen

~ **'way** v.i. (a) (yield, lit. or fig.) nachgeben; (collapse) ‹Brücke, Balkon:› einstürzen; his legs gave way under him er knickte [in den Knien] ein; ~ way to anger seinem Ärger Luft machen; ~ way to fear der Angst erliegen; (b) (in traffic) ~ way [to traffic from the right] [dem Rechtsverkehr] die Vorfahrt lassen; 'G~ Way' „Vorfahrt beachten"; (c) (be succeeded by) ~ way to sth. einer Sache (Dat.) weichen

'give-away n. (coll.) (a) (what betrays) the tremble in her voice was the ~: mit ihrer zitternden Stimme hat sie sich verraten; it was a dead ~: es verriet alles; (b) attrib. (Commerc.) ~ prices Schleuderpreise

given ⇒ give 1, 2

giver /'gɪvə(r)/ n. Geber, der/Geberin, die; (donor) Spender, der/Spenderin, die

give-'way sign n. (Brit.) Vorfahrtsschild, das

gizmo ⇒ gismo

glacé /'glæseɪ/ adj. glasiert

glacial /'gleɪsɪəl, 'gleɪʃl/ adj. (a) (icy) eisig; (fig.) eiskalt; (b) (Geol.) Gletscher-

glacier /'glæsɪə(r)/ n. Gletscher, der

glad /glæd/ adj. pred. froh; be ~ about sth. sich über etw. (Akk.) freuen; be ~ that ...: sich freuen, dass ...; (be relieved) froh sein [darüber], dass ...; [I'm] ~ to meet you es freut mich od. ich freue mich, Sie kennen zu lernen; be ~ to hear sth. sich zu hören; (relieved) froh sein, etw. zu hören; he's ~ to be alive er ist froh, dass er lebt; ..., you'll be ~ to know/hear: ..., das freut Sie sicherlich; I'd be ~ to [help you] Ihnen gern [helfe ich Ihnen]; Take your gloves. You'll be ~ of them Nimm deine Handschuhe mit. Du wirst sie gebrauchen können

gladden /'glædn/ v.t. erfreuen

glade /gleɪd/ n. Lichtung, die

gladiator /'glædɪeɪtə(r)/ n. Gladiator, der

gladiolus /glædɪ'əʊləs/ n., pl. gladioli /glædɪ'əʊlaɪ/ or ~es (Bot.) Gladiole, die

gladly /'glædlɪ/ adv. (a) (willingly) gern; (b) (with joy) freudig

glamor (Amer.) ⇒ glamour

glamorize (**glamorise**) /'glæməraɪz/ v.t. (add glamour to) [mehr] Glanz verleihen (+ Dat.); (idealize) verherrlichen (into zu); glorifizieren

glamorous /'glæmərəs/ adj. glanzvoll; glamourös ‹Filmstar, Lebenswandel›; mondän ‹Kleidung›; a ~ job ein Traumberuf

glamour /'glæmə(r)/ n. Glanz, der; (of person) Ausstrahlung, die

glance /glɑːns/ 1 n. Blick, der; cast or take or have a [quick] ~ at sth./sb. einen [kurzen] Blick auf etw./jmdn. werfen; at a ~: auf einen Blick. 2 v.i. (a) blicken; schauen; ~ at sb./sth. jmdn./etw. anblicken; ~ at one's watch auf seine Uhr blicken; she ~d at herself in the mirror sie warf einen Blick in den Spiegel; ~ down/up [at sth.] [auf etw. (Akk.)] hinunter-/[zu etw.] aufblicken; ~ through the newspaper etc. die Zeitung usw. durchblättern; ~ at the newspaper etc. einen Blick in die Zeitung usw. werfen; ~ round [the room] sich [im Zimmer] umsehen; (b) ~ [off sth.] abprallen [an etw. (Dat.)]; ‹Messer, Schwert:› abgleiten [an etw. (Dat.)]; strike sb. a glancing blow jmdn. nur streifen

gland /glænd/ n. Drüse, die

glandular /'glændjʊlə(r)/ adj. Drüsen-

glare /gleə(r)/ 1 n. (a) (dazzle) grelles Licht; the ~ of the sun die grelle Sonne; amidst the ~/in the full ~

of publicity (fig.) im Rampenlicht der Öffentlichkeit; (b) (hostile look) feindseliger Blick; with a ~: feindselig. 2 v.i. (a) (glower) [finster] starren; ~ at sb./sth. jmdn./etw. anstarren; (b) ‹Licht:› grell scheinen

glaring /'gleərɪŋ/ adj. (dazzling) grell [strahlend/scheinend usw.]; gleißend hell ‹Licht›; (fig.: conspicuous) schreiend; eklatant; grob ‹Fehler›; krass ‹Gegensatz›

glasnost /'glæsnɒst/ n. Glasnost, die

glass /glɑːs/ 1 n. (a) no pl. (substance) Glas, das; pieces of/broken ~: Glasscherben Pl.; (smaller) Glassplitter Pl.; (b) (drinking ~) Glas, das; a ~ of milk ein Glas Milch; wine by the ~: offener Wein; (c) (of spectacles, watch) Glas, das; (pane, covering picture) [Glas]scheibe, die; (d) in pl. (spectacles) [a pair of] ~es eine Brille. 2 attrib. adj. Glas-; people who live in ~ houses should not throw stones (prov.) wer im Glashaus sitzt, soll nicht mit Steinen werfen (Spr.)

glass: ~-**blower** n. Glasbläser, der/Glasbläserin, die; ~-**blowing** n. Glasblasen, das; ~ **'ceiling** n. (fig.) unsichtbare Barriere; ~ **'door** n. Glastür, die; ~ **'fibre** n. Glasfaser, die

glassful /'glɑːsfʊl/ n. Glas, das (of von); a ~ of milk ein Glas Milch

glass: ~**house** n. (a) (Brit.: greenhouse) Gewächshaus, das; Glashaus, das; (b) (Brit. sl.: military prison) Bunker, der (Soldatenspr. salopp); ~**ware** n. Glas, das

glassy /'glɑːsɪ/ adj. gläsern; (fig.) glasig ‹Blick›

glaucoma /glɔː'kəʊmə/ n. ▶865| (Med.) Glaukom, das (fachspr.); grüner Star

glaze /gleɪz/ 1 n. (on food or pottery) Glasur, die; (of paint) Lasur, die; (on paper, fabric) Appretur, die. 2 v.t. (a) (cover with ~) glasieren ‹Esswaren, Töpferwaren›; satinieren ‹Papier, Kunststoff›; lasieren ‹Farbe, bemalte Fläche›; ~d tile Kachel, die; (b) (fit with glass) ~ [in] verglasen ‹Fenster, Haus usw.›. 3 v.i. ~ [over] ‹Augen:› glasig werden

glazier /'gleɪzɪə(r), 'gleɪʒə(r)/ n. ▶887| Glaser, der

gleam /gliːm/ 1 n. (a) (brighter) Schein, der; (fainter) Schimmer, der; ~ of light Lichtschein, der; (b) (fig.: faint trace) Anflug, der (of von); ~ of hope/truth Hoffnungsschimmer, der/ Funke Wahrheit. 2 v.i. ‹Sonne, Licht:› scheinen; ‹Fußboden, Fahrzeug, Stiefel:› glänzen; ‹Zähne:› blitzen; ‹Augen:› leuchten

gleaming /'gliːmɪŋ/ adj. glänzend ‹Wasser, Metall, Fahrzeug›

glean /gliːn/ v.t. (a) zusammentragen ‹Informationen, Nachrichten usw.›; herausfinden ‹Inhalt eines Briefes usw.›; ~ sth. from sth. einer Sache (Dat.) etw. entnehmen, (b) (Agric.) nachlesen ‹Getreide›

glee /gliː/ n. Freude, die; (gloating joy) Schadenfreude, die

gleeful /'gliːfl/ adj. freudig; vergnügt; (gloatingly joyful) schadenfroh; hämisch

glen /glen/ n. [schmales] Tal

glib /glɪb/ adj. (derog.) aalglatt ‹Person›; (impromptu, offhand) leicht dahingesagt ‹Antwort›; (facile in the use of words) zungenfertig ‹Person›; flink ‹Zunge›; flinkzüngig ‹Antwort›

glide /glaɪd/ v.i. (a) gleiten; (through the air) schweben; (b) ‹Segelflugzeug:› gleiten, schweben; ‹Flugzeug:› im Gleitflug fliegen

glider /'glaɪdə(r)/ n. Segelflugzeug, das

gliding /'glaɪdɪŋ/ n. (Sport) Segelfliegen, das; attrib. Segelflug-

glimmer /'glɪmə(r)/ 1 n. (of light) [schwacher] Schein, Schimmer, der (of von) (auch fig.); (of fire) Glimmen, das. 2 v.i. glimmen

glimpse /glɪmps/ 1 n. [kurzer] Blick; catch or have or get a ~ of sb./sth. jmdn./etw. [kurz] zu sehen od. zu Gesicht bekommen. 2 v.t. flüchtig sehen

glint /glɪnt/ 1 n. Schimmer, der; (reflected flash) Glitzern, das; (of eyes) Funkeln, das; (of knife, dagger) Blitzen, das. 2 v.i. blinken; glitzern

glisten /'glɪsn/ v.i. glitzern; see also glitter 1

glitter /'glɪtə(r)/ 1 v.i. glitzern; ‹Augen, Juwelen, Sterne:› funkeln; all that ~s or glistens is not gold (prov.) es ist nicht alles Gold, was glänzt (Spr.). 2 n. Glitzern, das; (of diamonds) Funkeln, das

glitterati /glɪtə'rɑːtɪ/ *n. pl.* Schickeria, *die* (Jargon)

gloat /gləʊt/ *v.i.* ~ **over sth.** (look at with selfish delight) sich an etw. (*Dat.*) weiden *od.* ergötzen; (derive sadistic pleasure from) sich hämisch über etw. (*Akk.*) freuen

global /'gləʊbl/ *adj.* global; weltweit; weltumspannend ⟨*Kommunikationssystem*⟩; ~ **warming** globaler Temperaturanstieg; **the ~ village** das Weltdorf

globalize /'gləʊbəlaɪz/ *v.t.* globalisieren

globe /gləʊb/ *n.* (a) (sphere) Kugel, *die;* (b) (sphere with map) Globus, *der;* (c) (world) **the ~:** der Erdball

'**globe-trotter** *n.* Globetrotter, *der;* Weltenbummler, *der*

globular /'glɒbjʊlə(r)/ *adj.* kugelförmig

globule /'glɒbjuːl/ *n.* Kügelchen, *das;* (of liquid) Tröpfchen, *das*

gloom /gluːm/ *n.* (a) (darkness) Dunkel, *das* (geh.); (b) (despondency) düstere Stimmung

gloomy /'gluːmɪ/ *adj.* (a) (dark) düster; finster; dämmrig ⟨*Tag, Nachmittag usw.*⟩; (b) (depressing) düster, finster [stimmend]; bedrückend; (depressed) trübsinnig ⟨*Person*⟩; bedrückt ⟨*Gesicht*⟩; **he always tends to see the ~ side of things** er sieht immer gleich schwarz; **feel ~ about the future** der Zukunft pessimistisch entgegensehen

glorification /glɔːrɪfɪ'keɪʃn/ *n.* Verherrlichung, *die*

glorify /'glɔːrɪfaɪ/ *v.t.* (extol) verherrlichen; **he's just a glorified messenger boy** er ist nichts weiter als ein besserer Botenjunge

glorious /'glɔːrɪəs/ *adj.* (a) (illustrious) ruhmreich ⟨*Held, Sieg, Geschichte*⟩; (b) (delightful) wunderschön; herrlich

glory /'glɔːrɪ/ **1** *n.* (a) (splendour) Schönheit, *die;* (majesty) Herrlichkeit, *die;* (b) (fame) Ruhm, *der;* (c) ~ **[be] to God in the highest** Ehre sei Gott in der Höhe. **2** *v.i.* ~ **in sth./doing sth.** (be pleased by) etw. genießen/es genießen, etw. zu tun; (be proud of) sich einer Sache (*Gen.*) rühmen/ sich rühmen, etw. zu tun; ~ **in the name of ...:** den stolzen Namen ... besitzen *od.* führen

gloss¹ /glɒs/ *n.* (a) (sheen) Glanz, *der;* ~ **paint** Lackfarbe, *die;* (b) (fig.) Anstrich, *der*

~ **over** *v.t.* bemänteln; beschönigen ⟨*Fehler*⟩; (conceal) unter den Teppich kehren (ugs.)

gloss² **1** *n.* [Wort]erklärung, *die.* **2** *v.t.* glossieren

glossary /'glɒsərɪ/ *n.* Glossar, *das*

glossy /'glɒsɪ/ *adj.* glänzend; ~ **print** Glanzabzug, *der;* ~ **magazine** Hochglanzzeitschrift, *die*

glottal stop /glɒtl 'stɒp/ *n.* (Phonet.) Glottisschlag, *der;* Knacklaut, *der*

glove /glʌv/ *n.* Handschuh, *der;* **sth. fits sb. like a ~:** etw. passt jmdm. wie angegossen (ugs.)

'**glove compartment** *n.* Handschuhfach, *das*

glow /gləʊ/ **1** *v.i.* (a) glühen ⟨*Lampe, Leuchtfarbe:*⟩ schimmern, leuchten; (b) (fig.) (with warmth or pride) ⟨*Gesicht, Wangen:*⟩ glühen (**with** vor + *Dat.*); (with health or vigour) strotzen (**with** vor + *Dat.*); (c) (be suffused with warm colour) [warm] leuchten. **2** *n.* (a) Glühen, *das;* (of candle, lamp) Schein, *der;* (of embers, sunset) Glut, *die;* (b) (fig.) Glühen, *das;* **his cheeks had a healthy ~:** seine Wangen hatten eine blühende Farbe

glower /'glaʊə(r)/ *v.i.* finster dreinblicken; ~ **at sb.** jmdn. finster anstarren

glowing /'gləʊɪŋ/ *adj.* glühend (auch fig.); (fig.: enthusiastic) begeistert ⟨*Bericht, Beschreibung*⟩; **describe sth. in ~ colours** etw. in glühenden Farben beschreiben

'**glow-worm** *n.* Glühwürmchen, *das*

glucose /'gluːkəʊs, 'gluːkəʊz/ *n.* Glucose, *die*

glue /gluː/ **1** *n.* Klebstoff, *der.* **2** *v.t.* (a) kleben; ~ **sth. together/on** etw. zusammen-/ankleben; ~ **sth. to sth.** etw. an etw. (*Dat.*) an- *od.* festkleben; (b) (fig.) **be ~d to sth./sb.** an etw./jmdn. kleben (ugs.); **their eyes** *or* **they were ~d to the TV screen** sie starrten auf den Bildschirm

glum /glʌm/ *adj.* trübsinnig ⟨*Person*⟩; bedrückt ⟨*Gesicht*⟩

glut /glʌt/ (Commerc.) **1** *n.* Überangebot, *das* (**of** an, von + *Dat.*); **a ~ of apples** eine Apfelschwemme. **2** *v.t.*, **-tt-** überschwemmen

glutinous /'gluːtɪnəs/ *adj.* klebrig

glutton /'glʌtn/ *n.* Vielfraß, *der* (ugs.); **a ~ for punishment** (iron.)/**work** (fig.) ein Masochist (fig.)/ein Arbeitstier (fig.)

gluttonous /'glʌtənəs/ *adj.* gefräßig

gluttony /'glʌtənɪ/ *n.* Gefräßigkeit, *die*

glycerine /'glɪsəriːn/ (*Amer.:* **glycerin** /'glɪsərɪn/) *n.* Glyzerin, *das*

gm. *abbr.* ▶ **1202 | gram[s]** g

GMT *abbr.* **Greenwich mean time** GMT; WEZ

gnarled /nɑːld/ *adj.* knorrig; knotig ⟨*Finger, Hand*⟩

gnash /næʃ/ *v.t.* ~ **one's teeth [in anger]** [vor Zorn] mit den Zähnen knirschen; ~**ing of teeth** Zähneknirschen, *das*

gnat /næt/ *n.* [Stech]mücke, *die*

gnaw /nɔː/ **1** *v.i.* ~ **[away] at sth.** (lit. or fig.) an etw. (*Dat.*) nagen; ~ **through a rope/sack** ein Seil/einen Sack durchnagen. **2** *v.t.* nagen an (+ *Dat.*); abnagen ⟨*Knochen*⟩; kauen an *od.* auf (+ *Dat.*) ⟨*Fingernägeln*⟩; ~ **a hole in sth.** ein Loch in etw. (*Akk.*) nagen

gnawing /'nɔːɪŋ/ *adj.* nagend ⟨*Hunger, Schmerz, Zweifel, Kummer usw.*⟩; quälend ⟨*Zahnschmerzen, Angst*⟩

gnome /nəʊm/ *n.* Gnom, *der;* (in garden) Gartenzwerg, *der*

GNP *abbr.* **gross national product** BSP

gnu /nuː, njuː/ *n.* (Zool.) Gnu, *das*

go /gəʊ/ **1** *v.i., pres.* **he goes** /gəʊz/, *p.t.* **went** /went/, *pres. p.* **going** /'gəʊɪŋ/, *p.p.* **gone** /gɒn/ (a) gehen; ⟨*Fahrzeug:*⟩ fahren; ⟨*Flugzeug:*⟩ fliegen; ⟨*Vierfüßer:*⟩ laufen; ⟨*Reptil:*⟩ kriechen; (on horseback etc.) reiten; (on skis, roller skates) laufen; (in wheelchair, pram, lift) fahren; **go by bicycle/ car/bus/train** *or* **rail/boat** *or* **sea** *or* **ship** mit dem [Fahr]rad/Auto/Bus/Zug/Schiff fahren; **go by plane** *or* **air** fliegen; **go on foot** zu Fuß gehen; laufen (ugs.); **as one goes [along]** (fig.) nach und nach; **do sth. as one goes [along]** (lit.) etw. beim Gehen *od.* unterwegs tun; **go on a journey** eine Reise machen; verreisen; **go first-class/at 50 m.p.h.** erster Klasse reisen *od.* fahren/80 Stundenkilometer fahren; **have far to go** weit zu gehen *od.* zu fahren haben; es weit haben; **the doll/dog goes everywhere with her** sie hat immer ihre Puppe/ihren Hund dabei; **who goes there?** (sentry's challenge) wer da?; **there you go** (coll., giving sth.) bitte!; da! (ugs.); (b) (proceed as regards purpose, activity, destination, or route) ⟨*Bus, Zug, Lift, Schiff:*⟩ fahren; (use means of transportation) fahren; (fly) fliegen; (proceed on outward journey) weg-, abfahren; (travel regularly) ⟨*Verkehrsmittel:*⟩ verkehren (**from ... to** zwischen + *Dat.* ... und); **his hand went to his pocket** er griff nach seiner Tasche; **go to the toilet/cinema/moon/a museum/a funeral** auf die Toilette/ins Kino gehen/zum Mond fliegen/ins Museum/zu einer Beerdigung gehen; **go to a dance** tanzen gehen; **go to the doctor['s]** *etc.* zum Arzt *usw.* gehen; **go [out] to China** nach China gehen; **go [over] to America** nach Amerika [hinüber]fliegen/-fahren; **go [off] to London** nach London [ab]fahren/[ab]fliegen; **last year we went to Italy** letztes Jahr waren wir in Italien; **go this/that way** hier/da entlanggehen/-fahren; **go out of one's way** einen Umweg machen; (fig.) keine Mühe scheuen; **go towards sth.** auf etw./jmdn. zugehen; **don't go on the grass** geh nicht auf den Rasen; **go by sth./sb.** ⟨*Festzug usw.:*⟩ an etw./jmdm. vorbeiziehen; ⟨*Bus usw.:*⟩ an etw./ jmdn. vorbeifahren; **go in and out [of sth.]** [in etw. (*Dat.*)] ein- und ausgehen; **go into sth.** in etw. (*Akk.*) [hinein]gehen; **go looking for sb.** jmdn. suchen gehen; **go chasing after sth./sb.** hinter etw./jmdm. herrennen (ugs.); **go to live in Berlin** nach Berlin ziehen; **go to see sb.** jmdn. aufsuchen; **I went to water the garden** ich ging den Garten sprengen; **go and do sth.** [gehen und] etw. tun; **I'll go and get my coat** ich hole jetzt meinen Mantel; **go and see whether ...:** nachsehen [gehen], ob ...; **go on a pilgrimage** *etc.* eine Pilgerfahrt *usw.* machen; **go on TV/the radio** im Fernsehen/Radio auftreten; **I'll go!** (at door etc.) (answer phone) ich gehe ran *od.* nehme ab; (answer door) ich mache auf; '**you go!** (to the phone) geh du mal ran!; (c) (start) losgehen; (in vehicle) losfahren; **let's go!** (coll.) fangen wir an!; **here goes!** (coll.) dann mal los!; **whose turn is it to go?** (in game) wer ist an der Reihe?;

go first (in game) anfangen; **from the word go** (fig. coll.) [schon] von Anfang an; **(d)** (pass, circulate, be transmitted) gehen; **a shiver went up** *or* **down my spine** ein Schauer lief mir über den Rücken *od.* den Rücken hinunter; **go to** (be given to) ⟨*Preis, Sieg, Gelder, Job:*⟩ gehen an (+ *Akk.*); ⟨*Titel, Krone, Besitz:*⟩ übergehen auf (+ *Akk.*); ⟨*Ehre, Verdienst:*⟩ zuteil werden (*Dat.*); **go towards** (be of benefit to) zugute kommen (+ *Dat.*); **go according to** (be determined by) sich richten nach; **(e)** (make specific motion, do something specific) **go round** ⟨*Rad:*⟩ sich drehen; **there he** *etc.* **goes again** (coll.) da, schon wieder!; **here we go again** (coll.) jetzt geht das wieder los!; **(f)** (act, work, function effectively) gehen; ⟨*Mechanismus, Maschine:*⟩ laufen; **get the car to go** das Auto ankriegen (ugs.) *od.* starten; **at midnight we were still going** um Mitternacht waren wir immer noch dabei *od.* im Gange; **go by electricity** mit Strom betrieben werden; **keep going** (in movement) weitergehen/ -fahren; (in activity) weitermachen; (not fail) sich aufrecht halten; **keep sb. going** (enable to continue) jmdn. aufrecht halten; **that'll keep me going** damit komme ich aus; **keep sth. going** etw. in Gang halten; **make sth. go, get/ set sth. going** etw. in Gang bringen; **(g) go to** (attend): **go to work** zur Arbeit gehen; **go to church/school** in die Kirche/die Schule gehen; **go to a comprehensive school** eine Gesamtschule besuchen; auf eine Gesamtschule gehen; **(h)** (have recourse) **go to the originals** auf die Quellen zurückgreifen; **go to the relevant authority/ UN** sich an die zuständige Behörde/UN wenden; **where do we go from here?** (fig.) und was nun? (ugs.); **(i)** (depart) gehen; ⟨*Bus, Zug:*⟩ [ab]fahren; ⟨*Post:*⟩ rausgehen (ugs.); **I must be going now** ich muss allmählich gehen; **time to go!** wir müssen/ihr müsst *usw.* gehen!; **to go** (Amer.) ⟨*Speisen, Getränke:*⟩ zum Mitnehmen; **(j)** (euphem.: die) sterben; **be dead and gone** tot sein; **after I go** wenn ich einmal nicht mehr bin; **(k)** (fail) ⟨*Gedächtnis, Kräfte:*⟩ nachlassen; (cease to function) kaputtgehen; ⟨*Maschine, Computer usw.:*⟩ ausfallen; ⟨*Sicherung:*⟩ durchbrennen; (break) brechen; ⟨*Seil usw.:*⟩ reißen; (collapse) einstürzen; (fray badly) ausfransen; **the jacket has gone at the elbows** die Jacke ist an den Ellbogen durchgescheuert; **(l)** (disappear) verschwinden; ⟨*Geruch, Rauch:*⟩ sich verziehen; ⟨*Geld, Zeit:*⟩ draufgehen (ugs.) (in, on für); (be relinquished) aufgegeben werden; ⟨*Tradition:*⟩ abgeschafft werden; (be dismissed) ⟨*Arbeitskräfte:*⟩ entlassen werden; **be gone from sight** außer Sicht geraten sein; **my coat/the stain has gone** mein Mantel/der Fleck ist weg; **where has my hat gone?** wo ist mein Hut [geblieben]?; **all his money goes on women** er gibt sein ganzes Geld für Frauen aus; **(m)** (elapse) ⟨*Zeit:*⟩ vergehen; ⟨*Interview usw.:*⟩ vorüher-, vorbeigehen; **that has all gone by** das ist jetzt alles vorbei; **in days gone by** in längst vergangenen Zeiten; **(n) to go** (still remaining): **have sth. [still] to go** [noch] etw. übrig haben; **there's hours to go** es dauert noch Stunden; **one week** *etc.* **to go to** …: noch eine Woche *usw.* bis …; **there's only another mile to go** [es ist] nur noch eine Meile; **still have a mile to go** noch eine Meile vor sich (*Dat.*) haben; **one down, two to go** einer ist bereits erledigt, bleiben noch zwei übrig (salopp); **(o)** (be sold) weggehen (ugs.); verkauft werden; **it went for £1** es ging für 1 Pfund weg; **going! going! gone!** zum Ersten! zum Zweiten! zum Dritten!; **(p)** (run) ⟨*Grenze, Straße usw.:*⟩ verlaufen, gehen; (afford access, lead) gehen; führen; (extend) reichen; ⟨*Zug:*⟩ gehen; **as** *or* **so far as he/it goes** so weit; **(q)** (turn out, progress) ⟨*Ereignis, Projekt, Interview, Abend:*⟩ verlaufen, gehen; **go against sb./sth.** ⟨*Wahl, Kampf:*⟩ zu jmds./ einer Sache Ungunsten ausgehen; ⟨*Entscheidung, Urteil:*⟩ zu jmds./einer Sache Ungunsten ausfallen; **how did your holiday/party go?** wie war Ihr Urlaub/Ihre Party?; **how is the book going?** was macht [denn] das Buch?; **things have been going well/badly/smoothly** *etc.* in der letzten Zeit läuft alles gut/schief/glatt *usw.;* **how are things going?, how is it going?** wie steht's *od.* (ugs.) läuft's?; **(r)** (be, have form or nature, be in temporary state) sein; ⟨*Sprichwort, Gedicht, Titel:*⟩ lauten; **this is how things go, that's the way it goes** so ist es nun mal; **go against sth.** mit etw. nicht übereinstimmen; **go against one's principles** gegen seine Prinzipien gehen; **go hungry** hungern; hungrig bleiben; **go without food/water** es

ohne Essen/Wasser aushalten; **go in fear of one's life** in beständiger Angst um sein Leben leben; *see also* **go against**; **(s)** (become) werden; **the tyre has gone flat** der Reifen ist platt; **the phone has gone dead** die Leitung ist tot; **the constituency/York went Tory** der Wahlkreis/York ging an die Tories; **(t)** (have usual place) kommen; (belong) gehören; **where does the box go?** wo kommt *od.* gehört die Kiste hin?; **where do you want this chair to go?** wo soll *od.* kommt der Stuhl hin?; **(u)** (fit) passen; **go in[to] sth.** in etw. (*Akk.*) gehen *od.* [hinein]- passen; **go through sth.** durch etw. [hindurch]gehen *od.* [hindurch]passen; **six into twelve goes twice** sechs geht zweimal in zwölf; **five goes into forty exactly** vierzig durch fünf geht auf; **(v)** (harmonize, match) passen (**with** zu); **the two colours don't go** die beiden Farben passen nicht zusammen *od.* beißen sich; **(w)** (serve, contribute) dienen; **the qualities that go to make a leader** die Eigenschaften, die einen Führer ausmachen; **it just goes to show that** …: daran zeigt sich, dass …; **(x)** (make sound of specified kind) machen; (emit sound) ⟨*Turmuhr, Gong:*⟩ schlagen; ⟨*Glocke:*⟩ läuten; **There goes the bell. School is over** Es klingelt. Die Schule ist aus; **the fire alarm went at 3 a.m.** der Feueralarm ging um 3 Uhr morgens los; **a police car with its siren going** ein Polizeiwagen mit eingeschalteter Sirene; **(y)** *as intensifier* (coll.) **don't go making** *or* **go and make him angry** verärgere ihn bloß nicht; **don't go looking for trouble** such keinen Streit; **I gave him a £10 note and, of course, he had to go and lose it** (iron.) ich gab ihm einen 10-Pfund-Schein, und er musste ihn natürlich prompt verlieren; **now you've been and gone and done it!** (coll.) du hast ja was Schönes angerichtet! (ugs. iron.); **go tell him I'm ready** (coll./Amer.) geh und sag ihm, dass ich fertig bin; **(z)** (coll.: be acceptable or permitted) erlaubt sein; gehen (ugs.); **everything/anything goes** es ist alles erlaubt; **it/that goes without saying** es/das ist doch selbstverständlich; **what he** *etc.* **says, goes** was er *usw.* sagt, gilt. *See also* **going; gone.** **2** *v.t., forms as* **1:** **(a)** (Cards) spielen; **(b)** (coll.) **go it** es toll treiben; (work hard) rangehen; **he has been going it a bit too hard** er hat es etwas zu weit getrieben; **go it!** los!; weiter! **3** *n., pl.* **goes** /gəʊz/ (coll.) **(a)** (attempt, try) Versuch, *der;* (chance) Gelegenheit, *die;* **have a go** es versuchen *od.* probieren; **have a go at doing sth.** versuchen, etw. zu tun; **have a go at sth.** sich an etw. (*Dat.*) versuchen; **let me have/ can I have a go?** lass mich [auch ein]mal/kann ich [auch ein]mal? (ugs.); **it's my go** ich bin an der Reihe *od.* dran; **in two/three goes** bei zwei/drei Versuchen; **at the first go** auf Anhieb; **(b)** **have a go at sb.** (scold) sich (*Dat.*) jmdn. vornehmen *od.* vorknöpfen (ugs.); (attack) über jmdn. herfallen; **(c)** (period of activity) **in one go** auf einmal; **he downed his beer in one go** er trank sein Bier in einem Zug aus; **(d)** (energy) Schwung, *der;* **be full of go** voller Schwung *od.* Elan sein; **have plenty of go** einen enormen Schwung *od.* Elan haben; **(e)** (vigorous activity) **it's all go** es ist alles eine einzige Hetzerei (ugs.); **it's all go at work** es ist ganz schön was los bei der Arbeit; **be on the go** auf Trab sein (ugs.); **keep sb. on the go** jmdn. auf Trab halten (ugs.); **make a go of sth.** mit etw. Erfolg haben; **it's no go** da ist nichts zu machen. **4** *adj.* (coll.) **all systems go** alles klar

go about **1** /-´-/ *v.i.* **(a)** (move from place to place) herumgehen/-fahren; **go about in groups** in Gruppen herumziehen; **go about in leather gear/dressed like a tramp** in Lederkleidung/wie ein Landstreicher herumlaufen; **go about doing sth.** (be in the habit of) etw. immer tun; **(b)** (circulate) ⟨*Gerücht, Geschichte, Grippe:*⟩ umgehen. **2** /-´--/ *v.t.* **(a)** (set about) erledigen ⟨*Arbeit*⟩; angehen ⟨*Problem*⟩; **how does one go about it?** wie geht man da vor?; **(b)** (busy oneself with) nachgehen (+ *Dat.*) ⟨*Arbeit usw.*⟩

'go after *v.t.* (hunt) jagen; zu stellen versuchen; (fig.) anstreben; sich bemühen um ⟨*Job*⟩

'go against *v.t.* zuwiderhandeln (+ *Dat.*); handeln gegen ⟨*Prinzip, Gesetz*⟩; **go against sb.** sich jmdm. in den Weg stellen *od.* widersetzen; *see also* **go 1 q, r**

go a'head *v.i.* **(a)** (in advance) vorausgehen (**of** *Dat.*); **You go ahead. I'll meet you there** Geh mal schon vor. Wir treffen uns dann dort; **(b)** (proceed) weitermachen; (make progress) ⟨*Arbeit:*⟩ fortschreiten, vorangehen; **go ahead with a plan** einen Plan durchführen; **go ahead and do it** es einfach machen; **go ahead!** nur zu!

go a'long 1 *v.i.* dahingehen/-fahren; (attend) hingehen. **2** *v.t.* entlanggehen/-fahren

go a'long with *v.t.* **go along with sth.** (share sb.'s opinion) einer Sache (*Dat.*) zustimmen; (agree to) sich einer Sache (*Dat.*) anschließen; **go along with sb.** mit jmdm. übereinstimmen

go a'round ⇨ **go about 1** a, b; **go round**

'**go at** *v.t.* **go at sb.** (attack) auf jmdn. losgehen; **go at sth./it** (work at) sich an etw. (*Akk.*) machen/sich dranmachen

go a'way *v.i.* weggehen; (on holiday or business) wegfahren; verreisen; **the problem won't go away** das Problem kann man nicht einfach ignorieren

go 'back *v.i.* **(a)** (return) zurückgehen/-fahren; (fig.) zurückgehen; **go back to a subject** auf ein Thema zurückkommen; **go back to the beginning** noch mal von vorne anfangen; **(b)** (be returned) zurückgegeben werden; ⟨*Waren:*⟩ zurückgehen **(to** an + *Akk.*); **(c)** (be put back) ⟨*Uhren:*⟩ zurückgestellt werden

'**go by** *v.t.* **go by sth.** sich nach etw. richten; (adhere to) sich an etw. (*Akk.*) halten; **if the report is anything to go by** wenn man nach dem Bericht gehen kann; **go by appearances** nach dem Äußeren gehen; *see also* **go 1 a, b, m**

go 'down *v.i.* **(a)** hinuntergehen/-fahren; ⟨*Taucher:*⟩ [hinunter]tauchen; (set) ⟨*Sonne:*⟩ untergehen; (sink) ⟨*Schiff:*⟩ sinken, untergehen; (fall to ground) ⟨*Flugzeug usw.:*⟩ abstürzen; **go down to the bottom of the garden/to the beach** zum hinteren Ende des Gartens gehen/an den Strand gehen; **(b)** (be swallowed) hinuntergeschluckt werden; **go down the wrong way** in die falsche Kehle geraten; **(c)** (become less) sinken; ⟨*Umsatz, Schwellung:*⟩ zurückgehen; ⟨*Vorräte usw.:*⟩ abnehmen; ⟨*Währung:*⟩ fallen; (become lower) fallen; (subside) ⟨*Wind usw.:*⟩ nachlassen; **go down in sb.'s estimation/in the world** in jmds. Achtung (*Dat.*) sinken/sich verschlechtern; **(d) go down well/all right** *etc.* **[with sb.]** [mit jmdm.] gut *usw.* klarkommen (ugs.); ⟨*Film, Schauspieler, Vorschlag:*⟩ [bei jmdm.] gut *usw.* ankommen (ugs.); **that didn't go down [at all] well with his wife** das hat ihm seine Frau nicht abgenommen; **(e)** (be defeated) unterliegen; **go down to sb.** gegen jmdn. verlieren

go 'down with *v.t.* bekommen ⟨*Krankheit*⟩; *see also* **go down** d

'**go for** *v.t.* **(a)** (go to fetch) **go for sb./sth.** jmdn./etw. holen; **(b)** (apply to) **go for sb./sth.** für jmdn./etw. gelten; **that goes for me too** das gilt auch für mich; ich auch; **(c)** (like) **go for sb./sth.** jmdn./etw. gut finden. *See also* **go 1 o; going 2 e**

go 'forward *v.i.* **(a)** weitergehen/-fahren; (fig.) voranschreiten; **(b)** (be put forward) ⟨*Uhren:*⟩ vorgestellt werden

go 'in *v.i.* **(a)** (go indoors) hineingehen; reingehen (ugs.); **(b)** (be covered by cloud) verschwinden; weggehen (ugs.); **(c)** (be learnt) [in den Kopf] reingehen (ugs.) *See also* **go 1 b, u**

go 'in for *v.t.* **go in for sth.** (choose as career) etw. [er]lernen wollen; (enter) an etw. (*Dat.*) teilnehmen; (indulge in, like) für etw. zu haben sein; (have as one's hobby, pastime, etc.) sich auf etw. (*Akk.*) verlegen; **go in for teaching** Lehrer/Lehrerin werden; **go in for wearing loud colours** gern knallige Farben tragen

'**go into** *v.t.* **(a)** (join) eintreten in (+ *Akk.*) ⟨*Orden, Geschäft usw.*⟩; gehen in (+ *Akk.*) ⟨*Industrie, Politik*⟩; gehen zu ⟨*Film, Fernsehen, Armee*⟩; beitreten (+ *Dat.*) ⟨*Bündnis*⟩; **go into law/the church** Jurist/Geistlicher werden; **go into nursing** Krankenschwester/-pfleger werden; **go into publishing** ins Verlagswesen gehen; **go into general practice** (Med.) sich als allgemeiner Mediziner niederlassen; **(b)** (go and live in) gehen in (+ *Akk.*) ⟨*Krankenhaus, Heim usw.*⟩; ziehen in (+ *Akk.*) ⟨*Wohnung, Heim*⟩; **(c)** /-'--/ (consider) eingehen auf (*Akk.*); (investigate, examine) sich befassen mit; (explain) darlegen; **(d)** (crash into) [hinein]fahren in (+ *Akk.*); fahren gegen ⟨*Baum usw.*⟩. *See also* **go 1 b, u**

go 'in with *v.t.* **go in with sb.** [mit jmdm.] mitmachen

go off 1 /-'-/ *v.i.* **(a)** (Theatre) abgehen; **(b) go off with sb./sth.** sich mit jmdm./etw. auf- und davonmachen (ugs.); **his wife has gone off with the milkman** seine Frau ist mit dem Milchmann durchgebrannt (ugs.); **(c)** ⟨*Alarm, Klingel, Schusswaffe:*⟩ losgehen; ⟨*Wecker:*⟩ klingeln; ⟨*Bombe:*⟩ hochgehen; **(d)** (turn bad) schlecht werden; (turn sour) sauer werden; (fig.) sich verschlechtern; **(e)** ⟨*Strom, Gas, Wasser:*⟩ ausfallen; **(f) go off [to sleep]** einschlafen; **(g)** (be sent) abgehen **(to** an + *Akk.*); **(h) go off well** *etc.* gut *usw.* verlaufen. *See also* **go 1 b. 2** /'--, -'-/ *v.t.* (begin to dislike) **go off sth.** von etw. abkommen; **go/have gone off sb.** jmdn. nicht mehr mögen; **I have gone off the cinema** ich mache mir nichts mehr aus Kino

go on 1 /-'-/ *v.i.* **(a)** weitergehen/-fahren; (by vehicle) die Reise/Fahrt *usw.* fortsetzen; (go ahead) vorausgehen/-fahren; **(b)** (continue) weitergehen; ⟨*Kämpfe:*⟩ anhalten; ⟨*Verhandlungen, Arbeiten:*⟩ [an]dauern; (continue to act) weitermachen; (continue to live) weiterleben; **I can't go on** ich kann nicht mehr; **go on for weeks** *etc.* Wochen *usw.* dauern; **this has been going on for months** das geht schon seit Monaten so; **go on to say** *etc.* fortfahren und sagen *usw.;* **go on and on** kein Ende nehmen wollen; **go on [and on]** (coll.: chatter) reden und reden; **go on about sb./sth.** (coll.) (talk) stundenlang von jmdm./etw. erzählen; (complain) sich ständig über jmdn./etw. beklagen; **go on at sb.** (coll.) auf jmdm. herumhacken (ugs.); **(c)** (elapse) ⟨*Zeit:*⟩ vergehen; **as time/the years went on** im Laufe der Zeit/Jahre; **(d)** (happen) passieren; nur sich gehen; **there's more going on in the big cities** in den großen Städten ist mehr los; **what's going on?** was geht vor?; was ist los?; **(e) be going on [for]** … (be nearly) fast … sein; **he is going on [for] ninety** er geht auf die neunzig zu; **it is going on [for] ten o'clock** es geht auf 10 Uhr zu; **(f)** (behave) sich benehmen; sich aufführen; **(g)** ⟨*Kleidung:*⟩ passen; **my dress wouldn't go on** ich kam nicht in mein Kleid rein (ugs.); **(h)** (Theatre) auftreten; **(i)** ⟨*Licht:*⟩ angehen; ⟨*Strom, Wasser:*⟩ kommen; **go on again** ⟨*Strom, Gas, Wasser:*⟩ wiederkommen; **(j) go on!** (proceed) los, mach schon! (ugs.); (resume) fahren Sie fort!; (coll.: stop talking nonsense) ach, geh *od.* komm! (ugs.). **2** /'--/ *v.t.* **(a)** (ride on) fahren mit; **go on the Big Dipper** Achterbahn fahren; **(b)** (continue) **go on working/talking** *etc.* weiterarbeiten/-reden *usw.;* **go on trying** es weiter[hin] versuchen; **(c)** (coll.: be guided by) sich stützen auf (+ *Akk.*); **(d)** (begin to receive) bekommen, erhalten ⟨*Arbeitslosengeld, Sozialfürsorge*⟩; *see also* **dole 1; (e)** (start to take) nehmen ⟨*Medikament, Drogen*⟩; **go on a diet** eine Abmagerungs- *od.* Schlankheitskur machen; **(f)** (coll.: like) ⇨ **much 3** d. *See also* **go 1 a, b, l**

go 'on for ⇨ **go on 1** e

go 'on to *v.t.* übergehen zu; **he went on to become …:** er wurde schließlich …

go 'on with *v.t.* **go on with sth.** mit etw. weitermachen; **something/enough to go on with** *or* **be going on with** etwas/genug für den Anfang *od.* für fürs Erste; **here's £10 to be going on with** hier sind erst [ein]mal 10 Pfund [für den Anfang] (ugs.)

go 'out *v.i.* **(a)** (from home) ausgehen; **go out to work/for a meal** arbeiten/essen gehen; **out you go!** hinaus *od.* (ugs.) raus mit dir!; **go out with sb.** (regularly) mit jmdm. gehen (ugs.); **(b)** (be extinguished) ⟨*Feuer, Licht, Zigarre usw.:*⟩ ausgehen; **go out like a light** (fig. coll.: fall asleep) sofort weg sein (ugs.) *od.* einschlafen; **(c)** (ebb) ⟨*Ebbe, Wasser:*⟩ ablaufen, zurückgehen; **the tide has gone out** es ist Ebbe; **(d)** (be issued) verteilt werden; (Radio, Telev.: be transmitted) ausgestrahlt werden

go over 1 /-'--/ *v.i.* **(a) he went over to the fireplace** er ging zum Kamin hinüber; **we're going over to our friends'** wir fahren zu unseren Freunden; **(b)** (be received) ⟨*Rede, Ankündigung, Plan:*⟩ ankommen **(with** bei); **(c)** (Radio, Telev.) **go over to sb./Belfast** zu jmdm./nach Belfast umschalten. *See also* **go 1 b; go over to. 2** /'--, -'--/ *v.t.* **(a)** (re-examine, think over, rehearse) durchgehen; **go over sth./the facts in one's head** *or* **mind** etw. im Geiste durchgehen/die Fakten überdenken; **(b)** (clean) sauber machen; (inspect and repair) durchsehen ⟨*Maschine, Auto usw.*⟩

go 'over to *v.t.* hinübergehen zu; übertreten zu

‹*Glauben, Partei*›; überwechseln zu ‹*Revolutionären*›; ‹*Verräter:*› überlaufen zu ‹*Feind*›; *see also* **go 1 b; go over 1 a, c**

go round 1 /-'-/ *v.i.* **(a)** (call) **go round and** *or* **to see sb.** jmdn. besuchen; bei jmdm. vorbeigehen (ugs.); **go round to sb.'s house** (call at) jmdn. aufsuchen; **(b)** (look round) sich umschauen; **(c)** (suffice) reichen; langen (ugs.); **enough coffee to go round** genug Kaffee für alle; **(d)** (spin) sich drehen; **my head is going round** mir dreht sich alles; **(e)** (circulate) **the word went round that** …: es ging die Parole um, dass … 2 /'-/ *v.t.* **(a)** (inspect) besichtigen; **(b)** ‹*Gürtel:*› herumreichen um ‹*Taille*›

go through 1 /-'-/ *v.i.* ‹*Ernennung, Gesetzesvorlage:*› durchkommen; ‹*Geschäft:*› [erfolgreich] abgeschlossen werden; ‹*Antrag, Bewerbung:*› durchgehen; **go through to the final** in die Endrunde kommen. 2 /'--/ *v.t.* **(a)** (execute, undergo) erledigen ‹*Formalität, Anforderung*›; **(b)** (rehearse) durchgehen; **(c)** (examine) durchsehen ‹*Post, Unterlagen*›; (search) durchsuchen ‹*Taschen*›; **(d)** (endure) durchmachen ‹*schwere Zeiten*›; (suffer) erleiden ‹*Schmerzen*›; **(e)** (use up) verbrauchen; durchbringen ‹*Erbschaft*›; aufbrauchen ‹*Vorräte*›. *See also* **go 1 u**

go 'through with *v.t.* zu Ende führen; ausführen ‹*Hinrichtung*›

go to'gether *v.i.* **(a)** (coincide) zusammengehen; **(b)** (match) zusammenpassen

go 'under *v.i.* (sink below surface) untergehen; (fig.: fail) ‹*Unternehmen:*› eingehen

go 'up *v.i.* **(a)** hinaufgehen/-fahren; ‹*Ballon:*› aufsteigen; (Theatre) ‹*Vorhang:*› aufgehen, hochgehen; ‹*Lichter:*› angehen; **(b)** (increase) ‹*Bevölkerung, Zahl:*› wachsen; ‹*Preis, Wert, Zahl, Niveau:*› steigen; (in price) ‹*Ware:*› teurer werden; **(c)** (be constructed) ‹*Gebäude, Barrikade:*› errichtet werden; **(d)** (be destroyed) in die Luft fliegen (ugs.); hochgehen (ugs.)

'go with *v.t.* **(a)** (be commonly found together with) einhergehen mit; **(b)** (be included with) gehören zu. *See also* **go 1 a, v**

go without 1 /'---/ *v.t.* verzichten auf (+ *Akk.*); **have to go without sth.** ohne etw. auskommen müssen. 2 /--'-/ *v.i.* (willingly) verzichten; **[have to] go without** (not from choice) leer ausgehen

goad /gəʊd/ *v.t.* ~ **sb. into sth./doing sth.** jmdn. zu etw. anstacheln/dazu anstacheln, etw. zu tun
~ **'on** *v.t.* ~ **sb. on** jmdn. anstiften

'go-ahead 1 *adj.* (enterprising) unternehmungslustig; (progressive) fortschrittlich. 2 *n.* **give sb./sth. the** ~: jmdm./ einer Sache grünes Licht geben

goal /gəʊl/ *n.* **(a)** (aim) Ziel, *das;* **attain one's** ~: sein Ziel erreichen; **(b)** (Footb., Hockey) Tor, *das;* (Rugby) Mal, *das;* **[play] in** ~: im Tor [stehen]; **score/kick a** ~: einen Treffer erzielen

goalie /'gəʊlɪ/ *n.* (coll.) Tormann, *der;* Schlussmann, *der* (ugs.)

goal: ~**keeper** *n.* ▶ **887** | Torwart, *der;* ~ **'kick** *n.* (Assoc. Footb.) Abstoß, *der;* (Rugby) Tritt nach dem Mal; ~**post** *n.* Torpfosten, *der;* **move the** ~**posts** (fig. coll.) sich nicht an die Spielregeln halten

goat /gəʊt/ *n.* Ziege, *die;* **get sb.'s** ~ (fig. coll.) jmdn. aufregen (ugs.)

gob /gɒb/ *n.* (sl.) Schnauze, *die* (derb abwertend)

gobble /'gɒbl/ 1 *v.t.* ~ **[down** *or* **up]** hinunterschlingen. 2 *v.i.* schlingen
~ **up** *v.t.* (fig. coll.) verschlingen

gobbledegook, gobbledygook /'gɒbldɪgu:k/ *n.* Kauderwelsch, *das*

'go-between *n.* Vermittler, *der*/Vermittlerin, *die*

goblet /'gɒblɪt/ *n.* Kelchglas, *das*

goblin /'gɒblɪn/ *n.* Kobold, *der*

gobsmacked /'gɒbsmækt/ *adj.* (Brit. coll.) geplättet (salopp); baff (salopp)

'gobstopper *n.* (Brit.) Riesenlutscher, *der*

god /gɒd/ *n.* **(a)** Gott, *der;* **be** *or* **lie in the lap of the** ~**s** im Schoß der Götter liegen; **(b)** God *no pl.* (Theol.) Gott; **God knows** (as God is witness) weiß Gott (ugs.); **God [only] knows** (nobody knows) weiß der Himmel (ugs.); **an act of God** höhere Gewalt; **[oh/my/dear] God!** [ach *od.* o/

mein/lieber] Gott!; **good God!** großer *od.* allmächtiger *od.* guter Gott!; **for God's sake!** um Himmels *od.* Gottes willen!; **thank God!** Gott sei Dank!; **God damn it!** zum Teufel noch mal! (ugs.); **God help you/him** *etc.* Gott steh dir/ihm *usw.* bei; **(c)** (fig.) Gott, *der;* Götze, *der* (geh., abwertend); **(d)** (Theatre) **the** ~**s** der Olymp (ugs. scherzh.)

'God-awful *adj.* (sl.) fürchterlich

god: ~**child** *n.* Patenkind, *das;* ~**dam**, ~**damn**, ~**damned** (sl.) 1 *adjs.* gottverdammt (derb); **[it is] none of your** ~**dam business** das geht dich einen Dreck an (salopp); 2 *advs.* gottverdammt (derb); **you're** ~**dam right!** du hast, verdammt noch mal, recht! (derb); ~**daughter** *n.* Patentochter, *die*

goddess /'gɒdɪs/ *n.* Göttin, *die*

'godfather *n.* Pate, *der*

'godforsaken *adj.* gottverlassen

godly /'gɒdlɪ/ *adj.* gottgefällig; gottergeben

god: ~**mother** *n.* Patin, *die;* ~**parent** *n.* (male) Pate, *der;* (female) Patin, *die;* ~**parents** Paten; ~**send** *n.* Gottesgabe, *die;* **be a** ~**send to sb.** für jmdn. ein Geschenk des Himmels sein; ~**son** *n.* Patensohn, *der*

goes ⇒ **go**

go-getter /'gəʊgetə(r)/ *n.* (coll.) Draufgänger, *der*

goggle /'gɒgl/ 1 *n. in pl.* **[a pair of]** ~**s** eine Schutzbrille. 2 *v.i.* glotzen (ugs.); ~ **at sb./sth.** jmdn./etw. anglotzen (ugs.)

'goggle-eyed *adj.* glotzäugig (ugs.)

going /'gəʊɪŋ/ 1 *n.* **(a) 150 miles in two hours, that is good** ~: 150 Meilen in zwei Stunden, das ist wirklich gut; **the journey was slow** ~: die Reise zog sich [in die Länge]; **this book is heavy** ~: dieses Buch liest sich schwer; **while the** ~ **is good** solange noch Zeit dazu ist *od.* es noch geht; **(b)** (Horseracing, Hunting, etc.) Geläuf, *das.* 2 *adj.* **(a)** (available) erhältlich; **there is sth.** ~: es gibt etw.; **take any job** ~: jede Arbeit annehmen, die es nur gibt; **(b) be** ~ **to do sth.** etw. tun [werden/wollen]; **he's** ~ **to be a ballet dancer when he grows up** wenn er groß ist, wird er Balletttänzer; **I was** ~ **to say** ich wollte sagen; **I was not** ~ (did not intend) **to do sth.** ich hatte nicht die Absicht, etw. zu tun; **(c)** (current) [derzeit/damals/ dann] geltend; **(d) a** ~ **concern** eine gesunde Firma; **(e) have a** ~ **lot/nothing** *etc.* ~ **for one** (coll.) viel/nichts *usw.* haben, was für einen spricht; **(f) to be** ~ **on with** ⇒ **go on with**

going-'over *n.* **(a)** (coll.: overhaul of engine etc.) Überholung, *die;* **give sth. a [good etc.]** ~: eine Sache [gründlich *usw.*] durchgehen *od.* durchsehen; **(b)** (sl.: thrashing) **give sb. a [good]** ~: jmdn. ordentlich verprügeln (ugs.)

goings-on /gəʊɪŋz'ɒn/ *n. pl.* Ereignisse; Vorgänge; **there have been some strange** ~: es sind seltsame Dinge passiert

go-kart /'gəʊkɑ:t/ *n.* Gokart, *der*

gold /gəʊld/ 1 *n.* **(a)** *no pl., no indef. art.* Gold, *das;* **be worth one's weight in** ~: nicht mit Gold aufzuwiegen sein; **a heart of** ~: ein goldenes Herz; **(b)** (colour, medal) Gold, *das.* 2 *attrib. adj.* golden; Gold‹*münze, -stück, -kette, -krone usw.*›

'gold-coloured *adj.* goldfarben

golden /'gəʊldn/ *adj.* **(a)** golden; ~ **brown** goldbraun; **(b)** (fig.) golden; einmalig ‹*Gelegenheit*›

golden: ~ **age** *n.* goldenes Zeitalter; ~ **'eagle** *n.* Steinadler, *der;* ~ **he'llo** *n.* ≈ Handgeld, *das;* ~ **'hamster** *n.* Goldhamster, *der;* ~ **'handshake** *n.* Abfindung[ssumme], *die;* ~ **re'triever** *n.* Golden Retriever, *der;* ~ **'rule** *n.* goldene Regel; ~ **'syrup** *n.* (Brit.) Sirup, *der;* ~ **'wedding** *n.* goldene Hochzeit

gold: ~**finch** *n.* Stieglitz, *der;* Distelfink, *der;* ~**fish** *n.* Goldfisch, *der;* ~**fish bowl** *n.* Goldfischglas, *das;* ~ **'leaf** *n.* Blattgold, *das;* ~ **'medal** *n.* Goldmedaille, *die;* ~ **'medallist** *n.* Goldmedaillengewinner, *der*/-gewinnerin, *die;* ~ **mine** *n.* Goldmine, *die;* (fig.) Goldgrube, *die;* ~ **'plate** *n., no pl., no indef. art.* vergoldete Ware; (coating) Goldauflage, *die;* ~**smith** *n.* ▶ **887** | Goldschmied, *der*/ -schmiedin, *die*

golf /gɒlf/ *n., no pl.* Golf, *das; attrib.* Golf‹*platz, -schlag usw.*›

golf: ∼ **ball** *n.* (a) Golfball, *der;* (b) (coll.: in typewriter) Kugelkopf, *der;* ∼ **club** *n.* (a) (implement) Golfschläger, *der;* (b) (association) Golfclub, *der;* ∼**course** *n.* Golfplatz, *der*

golfer /'gɒlfə(r)/ *n.* Golfer, *der*/Golferin, *die;* Golfspieler, *der*/Golfspielerin, *die*

gondola /'gɒndələ/ *n.* Gondel, *die*

gondolier /gɒndə'lɪə(r)/ *n.* Gondoliere, *der*

gone /gɒn/ *pred. adj.* (a) (away) weg; **it's time you were** ∼: es ist *od.* wird Zeit, dass du gehst; **he has been** ∼ **ten minutes** (coll.) er ist seit zehn Minuten fort *od.* weg; **he will be** ∼ **a year** er wird ein Jahr lang weg sein; (b) (of time: after) nach; **it's** ∼ **ten o'clock** es ist zehn Uhr vorbei; (c) (used up) **be all** ∼: alle sein (ugs.); (d) **be** ∼ **on sb./ sth.** (coll.) ganz weg von jmdm./etw. sein (ugs.). *See also* **far 1 d; forget 1; go 1 k**

goner /'gɒnə(r)/ *n.* (sl.) **he is a** ∼: er hat die längste Zeit gelebt (ugs.)

gong /gɒŋ/ *n.* Gong, *der*

gonna /'gɒnə/ (sl./Amer. coll.) = **going to**; ⇒ **going 2 c**

gonorrhoea (*Amer.:* **gonorrhea**) /gɒnə'rɪə/ *n.* ▶ 865 (Med.) Tripper, *der;* Gonorrhö, *die* (fachspr.)

goo /guː/ *n.* (coll.) Schmiere, *die* (ugs.)

good /gʊd/ **1** *adj.,* **better** /'betə(r)/, **best** /best/ (a) (satisfactory) gut; (reliable) gut; zuverlässig; (sufficient) gut; ausreichend ⟨ *Vorrat* ⟩; ausgiebig ⟨ *Mahl* ⟩; (competent) gut; geeignet; **his** ∼ **eye/leg** sein gesundes Auge/Bein; **Late again! It's just not** ∼ **enough!** (coll.) Schon wieder zu spät. So geht es einfach nicht!; **in** ∼ **time** frühzeitig; **all in** ∼ **time** alles zu seiner Zeit; **take** ∼ **care of sb.** gut für jmdn. sorgen; **be** ∼ **at sth.** in etw. (*Dat.*) gut sein; **be** ∼ **at doing sth.** etw. gut können; **speak** ∼ **English** gut[es] Englisch sprechen; **be** ∼ **with people** *etc.* mit Menschen *usw.* gut *od.* leicht zurechtkommen; (b) (favourable, advantageous) gut; günstig ⟨ *Gelegenheit, Augenblick, Angebot* ⟩; **a** ∼ **chance of succeeding** gute Erfolgschancen; **too** ∼ **to be true** zu schön, um wahr zu sein; **the** ∼ **thing about it is that** ...: das Gute daran ist, dass ...; **be too much of a** ∼ **thing** zu viel des Guten sein; **you can have too much of a** ∼ **thing** man kann es auch übertreiben; **be** ∼ **for sb./sth.** gut für jmdn./etw. sein; **apples are** ∼ **for you** Äpfel sind gesund; **eat more than is** ∼ **for one** mehr essen, als einem gut tut; **it's a** ∼ **thing you told him** nur gut, dass du es ihm gesagt hast; (c) (prosperous) gut; ∼ **times** eine schöne Zeit; (d) (enjoyable) schön ⟨ *Leben, Urlaub, Wochenende* ⟩; **the** ∼ **things in life** Annehmlichkeiten; **the** ∼ **old days** die gute alte Zeit; **the** ∼ **life** das angenehme[, sorglose] Leben; **have a** ∼ **time!** viel Spaß *od.* Vergnügen!; **have a** ∼ **journey!** gute Reise!; **it's** ∼ **to be home again** es ist schön, wieder zu Hause zu sein; **Did you have a** ∼ **day at the office?** Wie war es heute im Büro?; (e) (cheerful) gut; angenehm ⟨ *Patient* ⟩; ∼ **humour** *or* **spirits** *or* **mood** gute Laune; **feel** ∼: sich wohl fühlen; **I'm not feeling too** ∼ (coll.) mir geht es nicht sehr gut; (f) (well-behaved) gut; brav; **be** ∼!, **be a** ∼ **girl/ boy!** sei brav *od.* lieb!; **[as]** ∼ **as gold** ganz artig *od.* brav; (g) (virtuous) rechtschaffen; (kind) nett; gut ⟨ *Absicht, Wünsche, Benehmen, Tat* ⟩; **the** ∼ **guy** der Gute; **be** ∼ **to sb.** gut zu jmdm. sein; **would you be so** ∼ **as to** *or* ∼ **enough to do that?** wären Sie so freundlich *od.* nett, das zu tun?; **how** ∼ **of you!** wie nett von Ihnen!; **that/it is** ∼ **of you** das/es ist nett *od.* lieb von dir; (h) (commendable) gut; ∼ **for 'you** *etc.* (coll.) bravo!; ∼ **old Jim** *etc.* (coll.) der gute alte Jim *usw.* (ugs.); **my** ∼ **man/friend** (coll.) mein lieber Herr/Freund (ugs.: auch iron.); **that's a** ∼ **one** (coll.) der ist gut! (ugs.); (iron.) das ist'n Ding! (ugs.); (i) (attractive) schön; gut ⟨ *Figur, Haltung* ⟩; gepflegt ⟨ *Erscheinung, Äußeres* ⟩; wohlgeformt ⟨ *Beine* ⟩; **look** ∼: gut aussehen; (j) (thorough) gut; **take a** ∼ **look round** sich gründlich umsehen; **give sth. a** ∼ **polish** etw. ordentlich polieren; **have a** ∼ **weep/rest/sleep** sich richtig ausweinen/ausruhen/[sich] richtig ausschlafen (ugs.); (k) (considerable) [recht] ansehnlich ⟨ *Menschenmenge* ⟩; ganz schön, ziemlich (ugs.) ⟨ *Stück Wegs, Entfernung, Zeitraum, Strecke* ⟩; gut, anständig ⟨ *Preis, Erlös* ⟩; hoch ⟨ *Alter* ⟩; (l) (sound, valid) gut ⟨ *Grund, Rat, Gedanke* ⟩; berechtigt ⟨ *Anspruch* ⟩; (Commerc.)

solide ⟨ *Kunde* ⟩; sicher ⟨ *Anleihe, Kredit* ⟩; ∼ **sense** Vernünftigkeit, *die;* **have the** ∼ **sense to do sth.** so vernünftig sein, etw. zu tun; **(m)** (in greetings) ∼ **afternoon/ day** guten Tag!; ∼ **evening/morning** guten Abend/ Morgen!; ∼ **night** gute Nacht!; **(n)** *in exclamation* gut; **very** ∼, **sir** sehr wohl!; ∼ **God/Lord** *etc. see nouns;* **(o)** (best) gut ⟨ *Geschirr, Anzug* ⟩; **(p)** (correct, fitting) gut; (appropriate) angebracht; ratsam; **(q) as** ∼ **as** so gut wie; **(r) make** ∼ (succeed) erfolgreich sein; (effect) in die Tat umsetzen; ausführen ⟨ *Plan* ⟩; erfüllen ⟨ *Versprechen* ⟩; (compensate for) wieder gutmachen ⟨ *Fehler* ⟩; (indemnify) ersetzen ⟨ *Schaden, Ausgaben* ⟩. *See also* **best 1; better 1. 2** *adv. as intensifier* (coll.) ∼ **and** ...: richtig ...; **hit sb.** ∼ **and proper** jmdn. ordentlich verprügeln. *See also* **best 2; better 2. 3** *n.* (a) (use) Nutzen, *der;* **be some** ∼ **to sb./ sth.** jmdm./einer Sache nützen; **he'll never be any** ∼? aus dem wird nichts Gutes werden; **is this book any** ∼? taugt dieses Buch etwas?; **be no** ∼ **to sb./sth.** für jmdn./ etw. nicht zu gebrauchen sein; **it is no/not much** ∼ **doing sth.** es hat keinen/kaum einen Sinn, etw. zu tun; **what's the** ∼ **of ...?, what** ∼ **is ...?** was nützt ...?; **(b)** (benefit) **for your/his** *etc.* **own** ∼: zu deinem/seinem *usw.* Besten *od.* eigenen Vorteil; **for the** ∼ **of mankind/the country** zum Wohl[e] der Menschheit/des Landes; **do no/ little** ∼: nichts/wenig helfen *od.* nützen; **do sb./sth.** ∼: jmdm./einer Sache nützen; ⟨ *Ruhe, Erholung:* ⟩ jmdm./einer Sache gut tun; ⟨ *Arznei:* ⟩ jmdm./einer Sache helfen; **I'll tell him, but what** ∼ **will that do?** ich sag es ihm, aber was nützt *od.* hilft das schon?; **this development was all to the** ∼: diese Entwicklung war nur von Vorteil; **come home £10 to the** ∼ mit 10 Pfund plus nach Hause kommen; **come to no** ∼: kein gutes Ende nehmen; **(c)** (goodness) Gute, *das;* **there's** ∼ **and bad in everyone** in jedem steckt Gutes und Böses; **the difference between** ∼ **and bad** *or* **evil** der Unterschied zwischen Gut und Böse; **(d)** (kind acts) Gute, *das;* **be up to no** ∼: nichts Gutes im Sinn haben *od.* im Schilde führen; **do** ∼: Gutes tun; **(e) for** ∼ **[and all]** (finally) ein für alle Mal; (permanently) für immer [und ewig]; endgültig; *constr. as pl.* (virtuous people) **the** ∼: die Guten; **(g)** *in pl.* (wares etc.) Waren; (Brit. Railw.) Fracht, *die; attrib.* Güter⟨ *bahnhof, -wagen, -zug* ⟩; ∼**s and chattels** Sachen; **in pl. the** ∼**s** (coll.: what is wanted) das Gewünschte; das Verlangte; **deliver the** ∼**s** (fig.) halten, was man verspricht

good: ∼**'bye** (*Amer.:* ∼**'by**) **1** *int.* ▶ 836 auf Wiedersehen!; (on telephone) auf Wiederhören!; **2** *n., pl.* ∼**byes** (*Amer.:* ∼**bys**) (saying '∼-bye') Lebewohl, *das* (geh.); (parting) Abschied, *der;* **say** ∼**bye to sb.** jmdm. auf Wiedersehen sagen; **say** ∼**bye** sich verabschieden; **wave** ∼**bye** zum Abschied winken; **say** ∼**bye to sth., kiss sth.** ∼**bye** (fig.: accept its loss) etw. abschreiben (ugs.); ∼**-for-nothing** (derog.) **1** *adj.* nichtsnutzig; **2** *n.* Taugenichts, *der;* **G**∼**'Friday** ⇒ **Friday 1;** ∼**-humoured** /gʊd'hjuːməd/ *adj.* gutmütig

goodies /'gʊdɪz/ *n. pl.* (coll.) (food) Naschereien; (sweets) Süßigkeiten; (attractive things) Attraktionen; tolle Sachen

good: ∼**-'looking** *adj.* gut aussehend; ∼**-natured** /gʊd'neɪtʃəd/ *adj.* gutwillig; gutmütig

goodness /'gʊdnɪs/ **1** *n., no pl.* (a) (virtue) Güte, *die;* (b) (of food) Nährgehalt, *der;* Güte, *die.* **2** *int.* **[my]** ∼ *expr.* surprise meine Güte! (ugs.); **[oh] my** ∼ *expr. shock* lieber Himmel!; ∼ **gracious** *or* **me!** [ach] du lieber Himmel *od.* liebe Güte! (ugs.); **for** ∼' **sake** um Himmels willen; ∼ **[only] knows** weiß der Himmel (ugs.)

goods ⇒ **good 3 g, h**

good: ∼**-'tempered** /gʊd'tempəd/ *adj.* gutmütig; verträglich ⟨ *Person* ⟩; ∼**'will** *n.* (a) (friendly feeling) guter Wille; *attrib.* Goodwill⟨ *botschaft, -reise usw.* ⟩; (b) (willingness) Bereitwilligkeit, *die;* (c) (Commerc.) Goodwill, *der*

goody¹ /'gʊdɪ/ *n.* (coll.: hero) Gute, *der/die; see also* **goodies, baddy**

goody² *int.* (coll.) toll; prima

gooey /'guːɪ/ *adj.,* **gooier** /'guːɪə(r)/, **gooiest** /'guːɪəst/ (coll.) klebrig

goof /guːf/ (sl.) **1** *n.* (gaffe) Schnitzer, *der* (ugs.). **2** *v.i.* Mist machen *od.* bauen (salopp)

goose /gu:s/ *n., pl.* **geese** /gi:s/ Gans, *die; see also* **boo 1; cook 2 a**

gooseberry /'gʊzbərɪ/ *n.* **(a)** Stachelbeere, *die;* **(b)** play ⁓: das fünfte Rad am Wagen sein (ugs.)

goose: ⁓-**flesh** *n., no pl.* Gänsehaut, *die;* ⁓ **pimples** *n. pl.* have ⁓ **pimples** eine Gänsehaut haben; ⁓-**step** **1** *n.* Stechschritt, *der;* **2** *v.i.* im Stechschritt marschieren

gopher /'gəʊfə(r)/ *n.* **(a)** (Zool.) Taschenratte, *die;* (squirrel) Ziesel, *der;* **(b)** (Computing) Gopher, *der*

gore[1] /gɔ:(r)/ *v.t.* be ⁓**d** **[to death] by a bull** von den Hörnern eines Stieres durchbohrt [und tödlich verletzt] werden

gore[2] *n.* (blood) Blut, *das*

gorge /gɔ:dʒ/ **1** *n.* Schlucht, *die.* **2** *v.i. & refl.* ⁓ **[one-self]** sich voll stopfen (**on** mit) (ugs.)

gorgeous /'gɔ:dʒəs/ *adj.* **(a)** (magnificent) prächtig; hinrei-ßend ⟨*Frau, Mann, Lächeln*⟩; (richly coloured) farbenprächtig; **(b)** (coll.: splendid) sagenhaft (ugs.)

gorilla /gə'rɪlə/ *n.* Gorilla, *der*

gormless /'gɔ:mlɪs/ *adj.* (Brit. coll.) dämlich (ugs.)

gorse /gɔ:s/ *n.* Stechginster, *der*

gory /'gɔ:rɪ/ *adj.* **(a)** blutbefleckt ⟨*Hände*⟩; blutig ⟨*Schlacht*⟩; **(b)** (fig.: sensational) blutrünstig

gosh /gɒʃ/ *int.* (coll.) Gott!

gosling /'gɒzlɪŋ/ *n.* Gänseküken, *das;* Gössel, *das* (nordd.)

'go-slow *n.* (Brit.) Bummelstreik, *der*

gospel /'gɒspl/ *n.* Evangelium, *das;* **take sth. as** ⁓ (fig.) etw. für bare Münze nehmen

gospel 'truth *n.* absolute *od.* reine Wahrheit

gossamer /'gɒsəmə(r)/ *n.* Altweibersommer, *der; attrib.* hauchdünn

gossip /'gɒsɪp/ **1** *n.* **(a)** (person) Klatschbase, *die* (ugs. abwertend); **(b)** (talk) Schwatz, *der;* (malicious) Klatsch, *der* (ugs. abwertend). **2** *v.i.* schwatzen; (maliciously) klatschen (ugs. abwertend)

gossip: ⁓ **column** *n.* Klatschspalte, *die* (ugs. abwer-tend); ⁓ **columnist** *n.* Klatschkolumnist, *der*/-kolum-nistin, *die* (abwertend)

got ⇨ **get**

Gothic /'gɒθɪk/ *adj.* **(a)** gotisch; **(b)** (Lit.) ⁓ **novel** Schauerroman, *der*

gotten ⇨ **get**

gouge /gaʊdʒ/ **1** *v.t.* aushöhlen; ⁓ **a channel** ⟨*Fluss:*⟩ eine Rinne auswaschen. **2** *n.* Hohleisen, *das* ⁓ **out** *v.t.* ausschneiden; ⁓ **sb.'s eye out** jmdm. ein Auge ausstechen

goulash /'gu:læʃ/ *n.* (Gastr.) Gulasch, *das od. der*

gourd /gʊəd/ *n.* (fruit, plant) [Flaschen]kürbis, *der*

gourmand /'gʊəmənd/ *n.* (glutton) Gourmand, *der*

gourmet /'gʊəmeɪ/ *n.* Gourmet, *der; attrib.* ⁓ **meal/res-taurant** Feinschmeckergericht, *das*/-lokal, *das*

gout /gaʊt/ *n.* ▶ 865 | (Med.) Gicht, *die*

govern /'gʌvn/ **1** *v.t.* **(a)** (rule) regieren ⟨*Land, Volk*⟩; (administer) verwalten ⟨*Provinz, Kolonie*⟩; **(b)** (dictate) bestim-men; **be** ⁓**ed by sth.** sich von etw. leiten lassen; **(c)** (regu-late) ⟨*Vorschriften:*⟩ regeln; **(d)** (Ling.) verlangen; regieren ⟨*Kasus*⟩. **2** *v.i.* regieren

governess /'gʌvənɪs/ *n.* ▶ 887 | Gouvernante, *die* (veralt.); Hauslehrerin, *die*

governing /'gʌvənɪŋ/ *adj.* **(a)** (ruling) regierend; **(b)** (guid-ing) dominierend ⟨*Einfluss*⟩; ⁓ **body** leitendes Gremium

government /'gʌvnmənt/ *n.* Regierung, *die; attrib.* Re-gierungs-; ⁓ **money** Staatsgelder *Pl.;* ⁓ **securities** *or* **stocks** Staatspapiere *od.* -anleihen

government: ⁓ **de'partment** *n.* Regierungsstelle, *die;* ⁓-**funded** *adj.* staatlich finanziert; ⁓ **official** *n.* Regierungsbeamte, *der*/Regierungsbeamtin, *die*

governor /'gʌvənə(r)/ *n.* ▶ 887 | **(a)** (ruler) Herrscher, *der;* **(b)** (of province, town, etc.) Gouverneur, *der;* **(c)** (of State of US) Gouverneur, *der;* **(d)** (of institution, prison) Direktor, *der*/ Direktorin, *die;* **[board of]** ⁓**s** Vorstand, *der;* (of school) Schulleitung, *die;* (of bank, company) Direktorium, *das;*

Direktion, *die;* **(e)** (sl.: employer) Boss, *der* (ugs.); **(f)** (Mech.) Regler, *der*

Govt. *abbr.* **Government** Reg.

gown /gaʊn/ *n.* **(a)** [elegantes] Kleid; **bridal** ⁓: Braut-kleid, *das;* **(b)** (official or uniform robe) Talar, *der;* Robe, *die;* **(c)** (surgeon's overall) [Operations]kittel, *der*

GP *abbr.* **general practitioner**

GPO *abbr.* (Hist.) **General Post Office** Post, *die*

grab /græb/ **1** *v.t.,* **-bb-** greifen nach; (seize) packen; (cap-ture, arrest) schnappen (ugs.); ⁓ **sb. by the arm** *etc.* jmdn. am Arm *usw.* packen; ⁓ **some food** *or* **a bite to eat** (coll.) schnell etwas essen; ⁓ **hold of sb./sth.** sich ⟨*Dat.*⟩ jmdn./ etw. schnappen (ugs.). **2** *v.i.,* **-bb-:** ⁓ **at sth.** nach etw. greifen. **3** *n.* **(a)** **make a** ⁓ **at** *or* **for sb./sth.** nach jmdm./etw. greifen *od.* (ugs.) grapschen; **be up for** ⁓**s** (coll.) zu erwerben sein; ⟨*Posten:*⟩ frei sein; **(b)** (Mech.) Greifer, *der*

grace /greɪs/ **1** *n.* **(a)** (charm) Anmut, *die* (geh.); Grazie, *die;* **(b)** (attractive feature) Charme, *der;* **airs and** ⁓**s** vor-nehmes Getue (ugs. abwertend); affektiertes Benehmen; **(c)** (accomplishment) **social** ⁓**s** Umgangsformen *Pl.;* **(d)** (de-cency) Anstand, *der;* **have the** ⁓ **to do sth.** so anständig sein und etw. tun; (civility) **with [a] good/bad** ⁓: bereitwil-lig/widerwillig; **he accepted my criticism with good/ bad** ⁓: er trug meine Kritik mit Fassung/nahm meine Kritik mit Verärgerung hin; **(e)** (favour) Wohlwollen, *das;* Gunst, *die;* **he fell from** ⁓: er fiel in Ungnade; **(f)** (delay) Frist, *die;* (Commerc.) Zahlungsfrist, *die;* **give sb. a day's** ⁓: jmdm. einen Tag Aufschub gewähren; **(g)** (prayers) Tischgebet, *das;* **say** ⁓: das Tischgebet sprechen; **(h)** ▶ 1152 | *in address* **Your G**⁓: Euer Gnaden. **2** *v.t.* **(a)** (adorn) zieren (geh.); schmücken; **(b)** (honour) auszeichnen; ehren

graceful /'greɪsfl/ *adj.* elegant; graziös ⟨*Bewegung, Eleganz*⟩; geschmeidig ⟨*Katze, Pferd*⟩

gracefully /'greɪsfəlɪ/ *adv.* elegant, grazios ⟨*tanzen, sich bewegen*⟩; **grow old** ⁓: mit Würde alt werden

gracious /'greɪʃəs/ **1** *adj.* **(a)** liebenswürdig; freund-lich; ⁓ **living** kultivierter Lebensstil; **(b)** (merciful) gnädig. **2** *int.* ⁓!, **good[ness]** ⁓!, **[goodness]** ⁓ **me!** [ach] du meine *od.* liebe Güte!

graciously /'greɪʃəslɪ/ *adv.* liebenswürdig; freundlich; (with condescension) gnädig

grade /greɪd/ **1** *n.* **(a)** Rang, *der;* (Mil.) Dienstgrad, *der;* (salary ⁓) Gehaltsstufe, *die;* (of goods) [Handels-, Güte]klasse, *die;* (of textiles) Qualität, *die;* (position, level) Stufe, *die;* **(b)** (Amer. Sch.: class) Klasse, *die;* **(c)** (Sch., Univ.: mark) Note, *die;* Zensur, *die;* **(d)** (Amer.: gradient) (ascent) Steigung, *die;* (des-cent) Neigung, *die;* **(e) make the** ⁓: es schaffen. **2** *v.t.* **(a)** einstufen ⟨*Arbeit nach Gehalt, Schüler nach Fähigkeiten, Leistungen*⟩; [nach Größe/Qualität] sortieren ⟨*Eier, Kartoffeln*⟩; **(b)** (mark) benoten; zensieren

'grade school *n.* (Amer.) Grundschule, *die*

gradient /'greɪdɪənt/ *n.* (ascent) Steigung, *die;* (descent) Ge-fälle, *das;* (inclined part of road) Neigung, *die;* **a** ⁓ **of 1 in 10** eine Steigung/ein Gefälle von 10 %

gradual /'grædʒʊəl/ *adj.* allmählich; sanft ⟨*Steigung, Ge-fälle usw.*⟩

gradually /'grædʒʊəlɪ/ *adv.* allmählich; sanft ⟨*ansteigen, abfallen*⟩

graduate **1** /'grædʒʊət/ *n.* Graduierte, *der*/*die;* (who has left university) Akademiker, *der*/Akademikerin, *die;* **uni-versity** ⁓: Hochschulabsolvent, *der*/-absolventin, *die.* **2** /'grædʒʊeɪt/ *v.i.* **(a)** einen akademischen Grad/Titel erwerben; **when did you** ⁓? wann haben Sie Ihr Stu-dium abgeschlossen?; **(b)** (Amer.: from [the School]ab-schlussprüfung bestehen (**from** an + *Dat.*). **3** /'grædʒʊeɪt/ *v.t.* (mark) mit Gradeinteilung versehen; gradu-ieren (bes. Technik) ⟨*Thermometer*⟩

graduation /grædʒʊ'eɪʃn/ *n.* **(a)** (Univ.) Graduierung, *die;* **(b)** (Amer. Sch.) Entlassung, *die;* **(c)** *attrib.* Abschluss-; **(d)** (mark) Graduation, *die* (bes. Technik)

graffiti /grə'fi:ti:/ *n. sing. or pl.* Graffiti *Pl.;* ⁓ **artist** Graf-fitikünstler, *der*/-künstlerin, *die*

graft¹ /grɑːft/ **1** n. **(a)** (Bot.) Pfropfreis, das; **(b)** (Med.) (operation) Transplantation, die (fachspr.); (thing ~ed) Transplantat, das; **(c)** (Brit. coll.: work) Plackerei, die (ugs.). **2** v.t. **(a)** (Bot.) pfropfen; **(b)** (Med.) transplantieren (fachspr.); verpflanzen. **3** v.i. **(a)** pfropfen; **(b)** (Brit. coll.: work) schuften (ugs.).

graft² n. (coll.) (dishonesty) Gaunerei, die; (profit) Fischzug, der

grain /greɪn/ n. **(a)** Korn, das; (collect.: [species of] corn) Getreide, das; Korn, das; **(b)** (particle) Korn, das; **(c)** (unit of weight) Gran, das (veralt.); **a ~ of truth** (fig.) ein Gran od. Körnchen Wahrheit; **(d)** (texture) Korn, das (fachspr.); Griff, der; (in wood) Maserung, die; (in paper) Faser, die; Faserverlauf, der; (in leather) Narbung, die; **go against the ~** [for sb.] (fig.) jmdm. gegen den Strich gehen (ugs.)

grainy /ˈgreɪnɪ/ adj. körnig; gemasert ‹Holz›; genarbt ‹Leder›

gram /græm/ n. ▶ 1202 | Gramm, das

grammar /ˈgræmə(r)/ n. (also book) Grammatik, die; **sth. is bad ~:** etw. ist grammat[ikal]isch nicht richtig od. korrekt

grammar: **~ book** n. Grammatik, die; **~ school** n. **(a)** (Brit.) ≈ Gymnasium, das; **(b)** (Amer.) ≈ Realschule, die

grammatical /grəˈmætɪkl/ adj. **(a)** grammat[ikal]isch richtig od. korrekt; **(b)** (of grammar) grammatisch

grammatically /grəˈmætɪkəlɪ/ adv. grammat[ikal]isch ‹richtig, falsch›; **speak English ~:** grammatisch richtiges od. korrektes Englisch sprechen

gramme ⇒ **gram**

gramophone /ˈgræməfəʊn/ n. Plattenspieler, der

granary /ˈgrænərɪ/ n. Getreidesilo, der od. das; Kornspeicher, der

grand /grænd/ **1** adj. **(a)** (most or very important) groß; **~ finale** großes Finale; see also **slam²**; **(b)** (final) **~ total** Gesamtsumme, die; **(c)** (splendid) grandios; (conducted with solemnity, splendour, etc.) glanzvoll; **(d)** (distinguished) vornehm; **(e)** (dignified, lofty) erhaben; groß ‹Versprechungen, Pläne, Worte›; (noble, admirable) ehrwürdig; **(f)** (coll.: excellent) großartig. **2** n. (piano) Flügel, der

grandad /ˈgrændæd/ n. (coll./child lang.) Großpapa, der (fam.); Opa, der (Kinderspr./ugs.)

grand: **~child** n. Enkel, der/Enkelin, die; Enkelkind, das; **~dad[dy]** /ˈgrændæd(ɪ)/ ⇒ **grandad; ~daughter** n. Enkelin, die

grandeur /ˈgrændʒə(r), ˈgrændjə(r)/ n. **(a)** Erhabenheit, die; **(b)** (splendour of living, surroundings, etc.) Großartigkeit, die; Glanz, der; **(c)** (nobility of character) Größe, die; Erhabenheit, die

grandfather n. Großvater, der; **~ clock** Standuhr, die

grandiose /ˈgrændɪəʊs/ adj. **(a)** (impressive) grandios; **(b)** (pompous) bombastisch (abwertend)

grandly /ˈgrændlɪ/ adv. großartig; aufwendig ‹sich kleiden›; in großem Stil ‹leben›

grand: **~ma** n. (coll./child lang.) Großmama, die (fam.); Oma, die (Kinderspr./ugs.); **~mother** n. Großmutter, die; **~ 'opera** n. große Oper; **~pa** n. (coll./child lang.) Großpapa, der (fam.); Opa, der (Kinderspr./ugs.); **~parent** n. (male) Großvater, der; (female) Großmutter, die; **~parents** Großeltern Pl.; **~ pi'ano** n. [Konzert]flügel, der; **G~ Prix** /grɑ̃ ˈpriː/ n. Grand Prix, der; **~son** n. Enkel, der; **~stand** n. [Haupt]tribüne, die

granite /ˈgrænɪt/ n. Granit, der

granny (grannie) /ˈgrænɪ/ n. (coll./child lang.) Großmama, die (fam.); Oma, die (Kinderspr./ugs.)

granny flat n. Einliegerwohnung, die;

grant /grɑːnt/ **1** v.t. **(a)** (consent to fulfil) erfüllen ‹Wunsch›; stattgeben (+ Dat.) ‹Gesuch›; **(b)** (concede, give) gewähren; bewilligen ‹Geldmittel›; zugestehen ‹Recht›; erteilen ‹Erlaubnis›; **(c)** (in argument) zugeben; einräumen (geh.); **~ed that ...:** zugegeben, dass ...; **take sb./sth. [too much] for ~ed** sich (Dat.) jmds. [allzu] sicher sein/etw. für [allzu] selbstverständlich halten. **2** n. Zuschuss, der; (financial aid [to student]) [Studien]beihilfe, die; (scholarship) Stipendium, das

granular /ˈgrænjʊlə(r)/ adj. körnig; granulös (Med.)

granulated sugar /ˈgrænjʊleɪtɪd ˈʃʊgə(r)/ n. [Zucker]raffinade, die; Kristallzucker, der

granule /ˈgrænjuːl/ n. Körnchen, das

grape /greɪp/ n. Weintraube, die; Weinbeere, die; **a bunch of ~s** eine Traube; **[it's] sour ~s** (fig.) die Trauben hängen zu hoch

grape: **~fruit** n., pl. same Grapefruit, die; **~juice** n. Traubensaft, der; **~vine** n. **(a)** Wein, der; **(b)** (fig.) **I heard [it] on the ~vine that ...:** es wird geflüstert, dass ...

graph /græf, grɑːf/ n. grafische Darstellung

graphic /ˈgræfɪk/ **1** adj. **(a)** grafisch; **~ art[s]** Grafik, die; **(b)** (clear, vivid) plastisch; anschaulich; **in ~ detail** in allen Einzelheiten. **2** n. **(a)** (product) Grafik, die; **(b)** in pl. ⇒ **graphics**

graphically /ˈgræfɪkəlɪ/ adv. **(a)** (clearly, vividly) plastisch; anschaulich; **(b)** (by use of graphic methods) grafisch

graphics /ˈgræfɪks/ n. (design and decoration) grafische Gestaltung; (use of diagrams) grafische Darstellung; **computer ~:** Computergrafik, die

graphite /ˈgræfaɪt/ n. Graphit, der

graph paper n. Diagrammpapier, das

grapple /ˈgræpl/ v.i. handgemein werden; **~ with** (fig.) sich auseinander setzen od. (ugs.) herumschlagen mit

grasp /grɑːsp/ **1** v.i. **~ at** (lit. or fig.) ergreifen; (fig.) stürzen auf (+ Akk.) ‹Angebot›. **2** v.t. **(a)** (clutch at, seize) ergreifen (auch fig.); **manage to ~:** zu fassen bekommen; **(b)** (hold firmly) festhalten; **~ sb. in one's arms** jmdn. [fest] in den Armen halten; **~ the nettle** (fig.) das Problem beherzt anpacken; **(c)** (understand) verstehen; erfassen ‹Bedeutung›. **3** n. **(a)** (firm hold) Griff, der; **he had my hand in a firm ~:** er hielt meine Hand mit festem Griff; **sth. is within/beyond sb.'s ~:** etwas ist in/außer jmds. Reichweite (Dat.); **(b)** (mental hold) **have a good ~ of sth.** etw. gut beherrschen; **sth. is beyond/within sb.'s ~:** etw. überfordert jmds. [intellektuelle] Fähigkeiten/kann von jmdm. verstanden werden

grasping /ˈgrɑːspɪŋ/ adj. (greedy) habgierig

grass /grɑːs/ **1** n. **(a)** Gras, das; **(b)** no pl. (lawn) Rasen, der; **(c)** no pl. (grazing, pasture) Weide, die; (pastureland) Weideland, das; **put** or **turn out to ~:** auf die Weide treiben od. führen; (fig.) in den Ruhestand versetzen; **(d)** (sl.: marijuana) Gras, das (ugs.); **(e)** (Brit. coll.: police informer) Spitzel, der. **2** v.t. (cover with turf) mit Rasen bedecken. **3** v.i. (Brit. coll.: inform police) singen (salopp); **~ on sb.** jmdn. verpfeifen (ugs.)

grass: **~hopper** n. Grashüpfer, der; **~land** n. Grasland, das; (for grazing) Weideland, das; **~root[s]** attrib. adj. (Polit.) Basis-; **~ roots** n. pl. (fig.) (source) Wurzeln; (Polit.) Basis, die; **~ 'skirt** n. Baströckchen, das; **~ snake** n. **(a)** (Brit.: ringed snake) Ringelnatter, die; **(b)** (Amer.: greensnake) Grasnatter, die; **~ widow** n. Strohwitwe, die (ugs. scherzh.); **~ widower** n. Strohwitwer, der (ugs. scherzh.)

grassy /ˈgrɑːsɪ/ adj. mit Gras bewachsen

grate¹ /greɪt/ n. Rost, der; (fireplace) Kamin, der

grate² **1** v.t. **(a)** (reduce to particles) reiben; (less finely) raspeln; **(b)** (grind) **~ one's teeth in anger** vor Wut mit den Zähnen knirschen; **(c)** (utter in harsh tone) [durch die Zähne] knirschen. **2** v.i. **(a)** (rub, sound harshly) knirschen; **(b)** **~ [up]on sb./sb.'s nerves** jmdm. auf die Nerven gehen

grateful /ˈgreɪtfl/ adj. dankbar (**to** Dat.)

gratefully /ˈgreɪtfəlɪ/ adv. dankbar

grater /ˈgreɪtə(r)/ n. Reibe, die; (less fine) Raspel, die

gratify /ˈgrætɪfaɪ/ v.t. **(a)** (please) freuen; **be gratified by** or **with** or **at sth.** über etw. (Akk.) erfreut sein; **(b)** (satisfy) befriedigen ‹Neugier, Bedürfnis, Eitelkeit›; stillen ‹Sehnsucht, Verlangen›

gratifying /ˈgrætɪfaɪɪŋ/ adj. erfreulich

grating /ˈgreɪtɪŋ/ n. (framework) Gitter, das

gratis /ˈgrɑːtɪs/ **1** adv. gratis ‹bekommen, abgeben›; umsonst ‹tun›. **2** adj. gratis nicht attr.; Gratis‹mahlzeit, -vorstellung usw.›

gratitude /'grætɪtjuːd/ *n., no pl.* Dankbarkeit, *die* (**to ge-**genüber); **show one's ~ to sb.** sich jmdm. gegenüber dankbar zeigen

gratuitous /grə'tjuːɪtəs/ *adj.* (uncalled-far, motiveless) grundlos; unnötig; (without logical reason) unbegründet

gratuity /grə'tjuːɪtɪ/ *n.* (formal: tip) Trinkgeld, *das*

grave[1] /greɪv/ *n.* Grab, *das;* **it was as quiet *or* silent as the ~:** es herrschte Grabesstille; **dig one's own ~** (fig.) sich (*Dat.*) selbst sein Grab graben (fig.); **he would turn in his ~** (fig.) er würde sich im Grabe herumdrehen

grave[2] *adj.* (**a**) (important, dignified, solemn) ernst; (**b**) (formidable, serious) schwer, gravierend ⟨*Fehler, Verfehlung*⟩; ernst ⟨*Lage, Schwierigkeit*⟩; groß ⟨*Gefahr, Risiko, Verantwortung*⟩; schlimm ⟨*Nachricht, Zeichen*⟩

'gravedigger *n.* ▶ 887 | Totengräber, *der*

gravel /'grævl/ *n.* Kies, *der; attrib.* **~ path/pit** Kiesweg, *der/*-grube, *die*

gravelly /'grævəlɪ/ *adj.* rau, heiser ⟨*Stimme*⟩

gravely /'greɪvlɪ/ *adv.* (**a**) (solemnly) ernst; (**b**) (seriously) ernstlich

grave: ~**stone** *n.* Grabstein, *der;* ~**yard** *n.* Friedhof, *der*

gravitate /'grævɪteɪt/ *v.i.* **sb. ~s towards sb./sth.** es zieht jmdn. zu jmdm./etw.

gravity /'grævɪtɪ/ *n.* (**a**) (importance) (of mistake, offence) Schwere, *die;* (of situation) Ernst, *der;* (**b**) (Phys., Astron.) Gravitation, *die;* Schwerkraft, *die;* **the law/force of ~:** das Gravitationsgesetz/die Schwerkraft; **centre of ~** (lit. or fig.) Schwerpunkt, *der*

gravy /'greɪvɪ/ *n.* (**a**) (juices) Bratensaft, *der;* (**b**) (dressing) [Braten]soße, *die;* ~ **boat** Sauciere, *die*

gray *etc.* (Amer.) ⇒ **grey** *etc.*

graze[1] /greɪz/ *v.i.* (**a**) grasen; weiden; (**b**) (snack) zwischendurch dies und jenes naschen; **I had been grazing all day** ich hatte den ganzen Tag herumgenascht (ugs.); ~ **on sth.** etw. essen *od.* naschen

graze[2] **1** *n.* Schürfwunde, *die.* **2** *v.t.* (**a**) (touch lightly) streifen; (**b**) (scrape) abschürfen ⟨*Haut*⟩; zerkratzen ⟨*Oberfläche*⟩; ~ **one's knee/elbow** sich (*Dat.*) das Knie/den Ellbogen aufschürfen

grease /griːs/ **1** *n.* Fett, *das;* (lubricant) Schmierfett, *das.* **2** *v.t.* einfetten; (lubricate) schmieren; **like ~d lightning** (coll.) wie ein geölter Blitz (ugs.)

grease: ~ **gun** *n.* Fettpresse, *die* (Technik); ~**-paint** *n.* [Fett]schminke, *die;* ~**proof 'paper** *n.* Pergamentpapier, *das*

greasy /'griːsɪ/ *adj.* (**a**) fettig; fett ⟨*Essen*⟩; speckig ⟨*Kleidung*⟩; (lubricated) geschmiert; (slippery, dirty with lubricant) schmierig; (**b**) (fig.) schmierig (abwertend)

great /greɪt/ **1** *adj.* (**a**) (large) groß; ~ **big** (coll.) riesengroß (ugs.); **a ~ many** sehr viele; (**b**) (beyond the ordinary) groß; sehr gut ⟨*Freund*⟩; **a ~ age** ein hohes Alter; **take ~ care of/a ~ interest in** sich sehr kümmern um/interessieren für; (**c**) (important) groß ⟨*Tag, Ereignis, Attraktion, Hilfe*⟩; (powerful, able) groß ⟨*Person, Komponist, Schriftsteller*⟩; (impressive) großartig; **the ~ thing is …:** die Hauptsache ist …; **Peter the G~:** Peter der Große; **be ~ at sth.** (skilful) in etw. (*Dat.*) ganz groß sein (ugs.); **be a ~ one for sth.** etw. sehr gern tun; (**d**) (coll.: splendid) großartig; (**e**) (in relationship) Groß⟨*onkel, -tante, -neffe, -nichte*⟩; Ur⟨*großmutter, -großvater, -enkel, -enkelin*⟩. **2** *n.* (person) Größe, *die; as pl.* **the ~s:** die Großen [der Geschichte/Literatur *usw.*]; **the ~est** (coll.) der/die Größte/die Größten (ugs.)

Great: ~ **'Britain** *pr. n.* Großbritannien (*das*); ~ **'Dane** *n.* Deutsche Dogge

Greater 'London *pr. n.* Groß-London

greatly /'greɪtlɪ/ *adv.* sehr; höchst ⟨*verärgert*⟩; stark ⟨*beeinflusst, beunruhigt*⟩; bedeutend ⟨*verbessert*⟩; **it doesn't ~ matter** es ist nicht so wichtig

greatness /'greɪtnɪs/ *n., no pl.* Größe, *die*

Great 'War *n.* erster Weltkrieg

Grecian /'griːʃn/ *adj.* griechisch

Greece /griːs/ *pr. n.* Griechenland (*das*)

greed /griːd/ *n.* Gier, *die* (**for** nach); (gluttony) Gefräßigkeit, *die* (abwertend); (of animal) Fressgier, *die;* ~ **for money/power** Geld-/Machtgier, *die*

greedily /'griːdɪlɪ/ *adv.* gierig

greedy /'griːdɪ/ *adj.* gierig; (gluttonous) gefräßig (abwertend); **be ~ for sth.** nach etw. gieren; ~ **for money/power** geldgierig/machthungrig

Greek /griːk/ ▶ 897 |, ▶ 947 | **1** *adj.* griechisch; **sb. is ~:** jmd. ist Grieche/Griechin. **2** *n.* (**a**) (person) Grieche, *der/* Griechin, *die;* (**b**) (language) Griechisch, *das;* **it's all ~ to me** (fig.) das sind mir *od.* für mich böhmische Dörfer; *see also* **English 2 a**

green /griːn/ **1** *adj.* (**a**) grün; **have ~ fingers** (fig.) eine grüne Hand haben (ugs.); ~ **vegetables** Grüngemüse, *das;* (**b**) (Polit.) **G~:** grün; **he/she is G~:** er ist ein Grüner/sie ist eine Grüne; **the G~s** die Grünen; (**c**) (environmentally safe) ökologisch; (**d**) (unripe, young) grün ⟨*Obst, Zweig*⟩; (**e**) **be/turn ~ with envy** vor Neid grün sein/werden; (**f**) (gullible) naiv; einfältig; (inexperienced) grün. **2** *n.* (**a**) (colour, traffic light) Grün, *das;* (**b**) (piece of land) Grünfläche, *die;* **village ~:** Dorfanger, *der;* (**c**) *in pl.* (~ vegetables) Grüngemüse, *das*

green: ~ **'belt** *n.* Grüngürtel, *der;* ~ **'card** *n.* (Insurance) grüne Karte (Verkehrsw.)

greenery /'griːnərɪ/ *n., no pl.* Grün, *das*

green: ~**-eyed** *adj.* grünaugig; **be ~-eyed** grüne Augen haben; ~**field site** *n.* Bauplatz in Grünen; ~**fly** *n.* (Brit.) grüne Blattlaus; ~**gage** /'griːngeɪdʒ/ *n.* Reineclaude, *die;* ~**grocer** *n.* (Brit.) Obst- und Gemüsehändler, *der/*-händlerin, *die; see also* **baker;** ~**house** *n.* Gewächshaus, *das;* ~**house effect/gas** (Ecol.) Treibhauseffekt, *der/den Treibhauseffekt bewirkendes Gas*

greenish /'griːnɪʃ/ *adj.* grünlich

Greenland /'griːnlənd/ *pr. n.* Grönland (*das*)

green: ~ **'light** *n.* (**a**) grünes Licht; (as signal) Grün, *das;* (**b**) (fig. coll.) **give sb./get the ~ light** jmdm. grünes Licht geben/grünes Licht erhalten; **G~ 'Paper** *n.* (Brit.) *öffentliches Diskussionspapier über die Regierungspolitik;* **G~ Party** *n.* (Polit.) die Grünen; ~ **'pepper** ⇒ **pepper 1 b**

Greenwich /'grenɪdʒ, 'grenɪtʃ/ *n.* ~ **[mean] time** Greenwicher Zeit

greet /griːt/ *v.t.* (**a**) begrüßen; (in passing) grüßen; (receive) empfangen; ~ **sb. with sth.** jmdn. mit etw. begrüßen/grüßen/empfangen; (**b**) (meet) empfangen; ~ **sb.'s eyes/ears** sich jmds. Augen (*Dat.*) darbieten/an jmds. Ohr (*Akk.*) dringen

greeting /'griːtɪŋ/ *n.* ▶ 836 | Begrüßung, *die;* (in passing) Gruß, *der;* (words) Grußformel, *die;* (reception) Empfang, *der;* **please give my ~s to your parents** grüßen Sie bitte Ihre Eltern von mir; **my husband also sends his ~s** mein Mann lässt auch grüßen

'greeting[s] card *n.* Grußkarte, *die;* (for anniversary, birthday) Glückwunschkarte, *die*

gregarious /grɪ'geərɪəs/ *adj.* (**a**) (Zool.) gesellig; *attrib.* Herden-; (**b**) (fond of company) gesellig

gremlin /'gremlɪn/ *n.* (coll. joc.) ≈ Kobold, *der*

grenade /grɪ'neɪd/ *n.* Granate, *die*

grew ⇒ **grow**

grey /greɪ/ **1** *adj.* (lit. or fig.) grau; **he *or* his hair went *or* turned ~:** er wurde grau *od.* ergraute; ~ **area** (fig.) Grauzone, *die.* **2** *n.* Grau, *das*

grey: ~ **e'conomy** *n.* graue Wirtschaft; ~**-haired**, ~**-headed** *adjs.* grauhaarig; ~**hound** *n.* Windhund, *der;* ~**hound racing** *n.* Windhundrennen, *das*

greyish /'greɪɪʃ/ *adj.* gräulich

grey: ~ **matter** *n.* (fig.: intelligence) graue Zellen; ~ **'squirrel** *n.* Grauhörnchen, *das*

grid /grɪd/ *n.* (**a**) (grating) Rost, *der;* (**b**) (of lines) Gitter[netz], *das;* (**c**) (for supply) [Versorgungs]netz, *das;* (**d**) (Motor racing) Startmarkierung, *die*

grid: ~ **iron** *n.* (**a**) (Cookery) Bratrost, *der;* (**b**) (Amer.: football field) Footballfeld, *das;* ~**lock** *n.* Verkehrsinfarkt, *der;* (fig.) völliger Stillstand; **save the city centre from the threat of ~lock** das Stadtzentrum vor dem Verkehrsinfarkt bewahren; ~**locked** /'grɪdlɒkt/ *adj.* total verstopft ⟨*Straße, Stadt*⟩; (fig.) festgefahren; **the traffic is ~locked** der Verkehr ist völlig zusammengebrochen; ~ **reference** *n.* Positionsangabe, *die*

Greetings (See also □ Letter-writing)

On a postcard

Greetings or Best wishes from Freiburg	=	Schöne or Herzliche Grüße aus Freiburg
Having a wonderful time	=	Es gefällt uns hier ausgezeichnet
Wish you were here!	≈	Das hättest Du alles sehen sollen!
See you soon	=	Bis bald
All best wishes, Steve and Cathy	=	Herzlichst or Herzliche Grüße or Es grüßen recht herzlich Steve und Cathy

For a birthday

Many happy returns [of the day], Happy birthday	=	Herzlichen Glückwunsch zum Geburtstag
All good or best wishes for your birthday	=	Alles Gute zum Geburtstag

For Christmas and the New Year

Happy Christmas!	=	Frohe Weihnachten!
[Best wishes for] a Merry or Happy Christmas and a Prosperous New Year	=	Frohe Weihnachten or Fröhliche Weihnachten or Ein gesegnetes Weihnachtsfest und viel Glück im neuen Jahr
Happy New Year!	=	Glückliches neues Jahr!; (when drinking) Prost or Prosit Neujahr!

For Easter

[Best wishes for a] Happy Easter	=	Frohe Ostern or Ein fröhliches Osterfest

For a wedding

Every good wish to the happy couple or to the bride and groom on their wedding day and in the years to come	=	Dem glücklichen Paar alles Schöne am Hochzeitstag und viel Glück in der Zukunft

For an exam

Every success in your [forthcoming] exams	=	Viel Erfolg bei deiner or der bevorstehenden Prüfung
All good wishes for your A levels/GCSEs	≈	Alles Gute zum Abitur

For a house move

Every happiness in your new home	=	Viel Glück im neuen Heim

For an illness

Get well soon!	=	Gute Besserung!
Best wishes for a speedy recovery	=	Die besten Wünsche zur baldigen Genesung

Spoken greetings

Equivalents can only be approximate in some cases, and in others do not really exist.

Meeting someone

Hello or Hallo or Hullo [there]!, Hi!	=	Hallo! (more colloquial); Guten Tag! (more formal); Grüß Gott! (South German)
Good morning!	=	Guten Morgen!
Good afternoon!	=	no equivalent; say Guten Tag!
Good evening!	=	Guten Abend!
How are you?	=	Wie geht es Ihnen? (formal); Wie gehts? (more colloquial)
How do you do?	≈	(when being introduced) Freut mich!; Angenehm! (dated)

Saying goodbye

Goodbye!	=	Auf Wiedersehen!
'Bye now!	=	Wiedersehen!; Tschüs! (more colloquial)
Look after yourself!, Take care!	=	Machs gut!

---

grief /gri:f/ n. (a) Kummer, der (over, at über + Akk., um); (at loss of sb.) Trauer, die (for um); **come to ~** (fail) scheitern; (b) **good ~!** großer Gott!

grievance /'gri:vəns/ n. (complaint) Beschwerde, die; (grudge) Groll, der; **air one's ~s** seine Beschwerden vorbringen

grieve /gri:v/ 1 v.t. betrüben; bekümmern. 2 v.i. trauern (for um); **~ over sb./sth.** jmdm./einer Sache nachtrauern

grievous /'gri:vəs/ adj. schwer ‹Verwundung, Krankheit›; groß ‹Schmerz›; **~ bodily harm** (Brit. Law) schwere Körperverletzung

grill¹ /grɪl/ 1 v.t. (a) (cook) grillen; (b) (fig.: question) in die Mangel nehmen (ugs.). 2 n. (a) (Gastr.) Grillgericht, das; **mixed ~:** Mixedgrill, der; gemischte Grillplatte; (b) (on cooker) Grill, der

grille (**grill²**) n. (a) (grating) Gitter, das; (b) (Motor Veh.) [Kühler]grill, der

grim /grɪm/ adj. (stern) streng; grimmig ‹Lächeln, Gesicht, Blick, Schweigen, Humor, Entschlossenheit›; (unrelenting, merciless, severe) erbittert ‹Widerstand, Kampf, Schlacht›; (sinister, ghastly) grauenvoll ‹Aufgabe, Anblick, Nachricht›; trostlos ‹Winter, Tag, Landschaft, Aussichten›; **hold** or **hang** or **cling on [to sth.] like ~ death** sich mit aller Kraft [an etw. (Dat.)] festklammern

grimace /grɪ'meɪs/ 1 n. Grimasse, die; **make a ~:** eine Grimasse machen od. schneiden. 2 v.i. Grimassen machen

od. schneiden; **~ with pain** vor Schmerz das Gesicht verziehen

grime /graɪm/ n. Schmutz, der; (soot) Ruß, der

grimly /'grɪmlɪ/ adv. grimmig; eisern ‹entschlossen sein, sich festhalten›; erbittert ‹kämpfen›

grimy /'graɪmɪ/ adj. schmutzig; rußgeschwärzt ‹Gebäude›

grin /grɪn/ 1 n. Grinsen, das. 2 v.i., **-nn-** grinsen; **~ at sb.** jmdn. angrinsen; **~ and bear it** gute Miene zum bösen Spiel machen

grind /graɪnd/ 1 v.t., **ground** /graʊnd/ (a) (reduce to small particles) **~ [up]** zermahlen; pulverisieren ‹Metall›; mahlen ‹Kaffee, Pfeffer, Getreide›; (b) (sharpen) schleifen ‹Schere, Messer›; schärfen ‹Klinge›; (smooth, shape) schleifen ‹Linse, Edelstein›; (c) (rub harshly) zerquetschen; **~ one's teeth** mit den Zähnen knirschen; (d) (produce by ~ing) mahlen ‹Mehl›; (e) (fig.: oppress, harass) auspressen (fig.); **~ing poverty** erdrückende Armut. 2 v.i., **ground: ~ to a halt, come to a ~ing halt** ‹Fahrzeug:› quietschend zum Stehen kommen; (fig.) ‹Verkehr:› zum Erliegen kommen; ‹Maschine:› stehen bleiben; ‹Projekt:› sich festfahren. 3 n. Plackerei, die (ugs.); **the daily ~** (coll.) der alltägliche Trott

~ a'way v.t. abschleifen

~ 'down v.t. (fig.) ‹Tyrann, Regierung:› unterdrücken; ‹Armut, Verantwortung:› erdrücken

grinder /'graɪndə(r)/ n. Schleifmaschine, die; (coffee-~ etc.) Mühle, die

'grindstone n. Schleifstein, der; **keep one's/sb.'s nose to the ~** (fig.) sich dahinter klemmen (ugs.) /dafür sorgen, dass jmd. sich dahinter klemmt (ugs.); **gct back to the ~:** sich wieder an die Arbeit machen

grip /grɪp/ 1 n. (a) (firm hold) Halt, der; (fig.: power) Umklammerung, die; **have a ~ on sth.** etw. festhalten; **loosen one's ~:** loslassen; **get** or **take a ~ on oneself** (fig.) sich zusammenreißen (ugs.); **have/get a ~ on sth.** (fig.) etw. im Griff haben/in den Griff bekommen; **come** or **get to ~s with sth./sb.** (fig.) mit etw. fertigwerden/sich (Dat.) jmdn. vorknöpfen od. vornehmen (ugs.); **be in the ~ of** (fig.) beherrscht werden von ‹Angst, Leidenschaft, Furcht›; heimgesucht werden von ‹Naturkatastrophe, Armut, Krieg›; **lose one's ~** (fig.) nachlassen; **(b)** (strength or way of ~ping, part which is held) Griff, der; **(c)** (bag) Reisetasche, die. 2 v.t., **-pp-** greifen nach; ‹Reifen:› greifen; (fig.) ergreifen; fesseln ‹Publikum, Aufmerksamkeit›. 3 v.i., **-pp-** ‹Räder, Bremsen usw.:› greifen

gripe /graɪp/ 1 n. (a) (coll.: complaint) Meckern, das (ugs. abwertend); **have a good ~ about sth./at sb.** sich über etw. (Akk.) ausschimpfen/jmdn. tüchtig ausschimpfen; **(b)** in pl. (colic) **the ~s** Bauchschmerzen; Bauchweh (ugs.). 2 v.i. (coll.) meckern (ugs. abwertend) **(about** über + Akk.)

gripping /'grɪpɪŋ/ adj. (fig.) packend

grisly /'grɪzlɪ/ adj. grausig

grist /grɪst/ n. **it's all ~ to the/sb.'s mill** man kann aus allem etwas machen/jmd. versteht es, aus allem etwas zu machen

gristle /'grɪsl/ n. Knorpel, der

grit /grɪt/ 1 n. (a) Sand, der; (b) (coll.: courage) Schneid, der (ugs.). 2 v.t., **-tt-:** (a) streuen ‹vereiste Straßen›; (b) **~ one's teeth** die Zähne zusammenbeißen (ugs.)

gritty /'grɪtɪ/ adj. sandig

grizzly /'grɪzlɪ/ n. ~ **[bear]** Grisliybär, der

groan /grəʊn/ 1 n. (of person) Stöhnen, das; (of thing) Ächzen, das (fig.). 2 v.i. ‹Person:› [auf]stöhnen **(at** bei); ‹Tisch, Planken:› ächzen (fig.)

grocer /'grəʊsə(r)/ n. Lebensmittelhändler, der/-händlerin, die; see also **baker**

grocery /'grəʊsərɪ/ n. (a) in pl. (goods) Lebensmittel Pl.; **(b)** ~ **[store]** Lebensmittelgeschäft, das

grog /grɒg/ n. Grog, der

groggy /'grɒgɪ/ adj. groggy (ugs.) präd.

groin /grɔɪn/ n. ▶ 672 | Leistengegend, die

groom /gruːm/ 1 n. (a) (stable-boy) Stallbursche, der; (b) (bride~) Bräutigam, der. 2 v.t. (a) striegeln ‹Pferd›; **~ oneself** sich zurechtmachen; **(b)** (fig.: prepare) **~ sb. for a career** jmdn. auf od. für eine Laufbahn vorbereiten

groove /gruːv/ n. (a) (channel) Nut, die (bes. Technik); (of gramophone record) Rille, die; (b) (fig.: routine) **be stuck in a ~:** aus dem Trott nicht mehr herauskommen

grope /grəʊp/ 1 v.i. tasten **(for** nach); **~ for the right word/truth** nach dem richtigen Wort/der Wahrheit suchen. 2 v.t. **~ one's way [along]** sich [entlang]tasten; (fig.) [sich durch]lavieren (ugs. abwertend)

gross¹ /grəʊs/ 1 adj. (a) (flagrant) grob ‹Fahrlässigkeit, Fehler, Irrtum›; übel ‹Laster, Beleidigung›; schreiend ‹Ungerechtigkeit›; **(b)** (obese) fett (abwertend); **(c)** (coarse, rude) ordinär (abwertend); **(d)** (total) Brutto-; **earn £15,000 ~:** 15 000 Pfund brutto verdienen; **~ national product** Bruttosozialprodukt, das; **(e)** (dull, not delicate) grob ‹Person, Geschmack›. 2 v.t. [insgesamt] einbringen ‹Geld›

gross² n., pl. same Gros, das; **by the ~:** en gros

grossly /'grəʊslɪ/ adv. (a) (flagrantly) äußerst; grob ‹übertreiben›; schwer ‹beleidigen›; (b) (coarsely, rudely) ordinär ‹sich benehmen, sprechen›

grotesque /grəʊ'tesk/ adj., **grotesquely** /grəʊ'tesklɪ/ adv. grotesk

grotto /'grɒtəʊ/ n., pl. **~es** or **~s** Grotte, die

grotty /'grɒtɪ/ adj. (Brit. coll.) mies (ugs.)

grouch /graʊtʃ/ (coll.) 1 v.i. schimpfen; mosern (ugs.). 2 n. (a) (person) Miesepeter, der (ugs. abwertend); (b) (cause) Ärger, der; **have a ~ against sb.** auf jmdn. sauer sein (salopp)

grouchy /'graʊtʃɪ/ adj. (coll.) griesgrämig

ground¹ /graʊnd/ 1 n. (a) Boden, der; **work above/ below ~:** über/unter der Erde arbeiten; **deep under the ~:** tief unter der Erde; **uneven, hilly ~:** unebenes, hügeliges Gelände; **on high ~:** in höheren Lagen; **(b)** (fig.) **cut the ~ from under sb.'s feet** jmdn. den Wind aus den Segeln nehmen (ugs.); **suit sb. down to the ~** (coll.) genau das Richtige für jmdn. sein; **get off the ~** (coll.) konkrete Gestalt annehmen; **get sth. off the ~** (coll.) etw. in die Tat umsetzen; **go to ~** ‹Fuchs usw.:› im Bau verschwinden; ‹Person:› untertauchen; **run sb./oneself into the ~** (coll.) jmdn./sich kaputtmachen (ugs.); **run a car into the ~** (coll.) ein Auto so lange fahren, bis es schrottreif ist; **on the ~** (in practice) an Ort und Stelle; **thin/thick on the ~:** dünn/dicht gesät; **cover much** or **a lot of ~:** weit vorankommen; **give** or **lose ~:** an Boden verlieren; **hold** or **keep** or **stand one's ~:** nicht nachgeben; **(c)** (special area) Gelände, das; **[sports]** ~: Sportplatz, der; **[cricket]** ~: Cricketfeld, das; **(d)** in pl. (attached to house) Anlage, die; **(e)** (motive, reason) Grund, der; **on the ~[s] of, on ~s of** auf Grund (+ Gen.); (giving as one's reason) unter Berufung auf (+ Akk.); **on the ~s that ...:** unter Berufung auf die Tatsache, dass ...; **on health/religious** etc. ~**s** aus gesundheitlichen/religiösen usw. Gründen; **the ~s for divorce are ...:** als Scheidungsgrund gilt ...; **have no ~s for sth./to do sth.** keinen Grund für etw. haben/keinen Grund haben, etw. zu tun; **have no ~s for complaint** keinen Grund zur Klage haben; **(f)** in pl. (sediment) Satz, der; (of coffee) Kaffeesatz, der; **(g)** (Electr.) Erde, die. 2 v.t. (a) (cause to run ashore) auf Grund setzen; **be ~ed** auf Grund gelaufen sein; (b) (base, establish) gründen (on auf + Akk.); **be ~ed on** gründen auf (+ Dat.); **(c)** (Aeronaut.) am Boden festhalten; (prevent from flying) nicht fliegen lassen ‹Piloten›. 3 v.i. (run ashore) ‹Schiff:› auf Grund laufen

ground² 1 ⇒ **grind** 1, 2. 2 adj. gemahlen ‹Kaffee, Getreide›; **~ meat** (Amer.) Hackfleisch, das; **~ coffee** Kaffeepulver, das

ground: ~ control n. (Aeronaut.) Flugsicherungskontrolldienst, der; **~ 'floor** ⇒ **floor** 1 b; **~ frost** n. Bodenfrost, der

grounding /'graʊndɪŋ/ n. (basic knowledge) Grundkenntnisse Pl.; Grundwissen, das; **give sb./receive a ~ in sth.** jmdn. die Grundlagen einer Sache (Gen.) vermitteln/die Grundlagen einer Sache (Gen.) vermittelt bekommen

groundless /'graʊndlɪs/ adj. unbegründet; **these reports** etc. **are ~:** diese Berichte usw. entbehren jeder Grundlage

ground: ~ level n. above/below ~ **level** oberhalb/ unterhalb der ebenen Erde; **on** or **at ~ level** ebenerdig; **~ plan** n. Grundriss, der; **~ 'rice** n. Reismehl, das; **~ rule** n. (a) (Sport) Platzregel, die; (b) (basic principle) Grundregel, die; **~sheet** n. Bodenplane, die; **~sman** /'graʊndzmən/ n., pl. **~smen** /'graʊndzmən/ (Sport) Platzwart, der; **~ staff** n. (Aeronaut.) Bodenpersonal, das; **~work** n. Vorarbeiten Pl.

group /gruːp/ 1 n. (a) Gruppe, die; attrib. Gruppen‹verhalten, -dynamik, -therapie, -diskussion›; **~ of houses/islands/trees** Häuser-/Insel-/Baumgruppe, die; **(b)** (Commerc.) [Unternehmens]gruppe, die; **(c)** ⇒ **pop group.** 2 v.t. gruppieren; **~ books according to their subjects** Bücher nach ihrer Thematik ordnen

group: ~ captain n. (Air Force) Oberst der Luftwaffe; **~ practice** n. Gemeinschaftspraxis, die

grouse¹ /graʊs/ n. (a) pl. same Raufußhuhn, das; **[red] ~** (Brit.) Schottisches Moorschneehuhn; (b) no pl. (as food) Waldhuhn, das; schottisches Moorhuhn

grouse² (coll.) 1 v.i. meckern (ugs.) **(about** über + Akk.). 2 n. Meckerei, die (ugs.)

grout /graʊt/ n. Mörtelschlamm, der

grove /grəʊv/ n. Wäldchen, das; Hain, der (dichter. veralt.)

grovel /'grɒvl/ v.i., **-ll-:** (a) sich auf die Knie werfen; **be ~ling on the floor** auf dem Fußboden kriechen; (b) (fig.: be subservient) katzbuckeln (abwertend)

grow /grəʊ/ 1 v.i., **grew** /gruː/, **grown** /grəʊn/ (a) wachsen; ‹Bevölkerung:› zunehmen, wachsen; **~ out of** or

from sth. (develop) sich aus etw. entwickeln; (from sth. abstract) von etw. herrühren; ⟨*Situation, Krieg usw.*⟩ die Folge von etw. sein; ⟨*Plan.*⟩ aus etw. erwachsen; **∼ in** gewinnen an (+ *Dat.*) ⟨*Größe, Bedeutung, Autorität, Popularität, Weisheit*⟩; **(b)** (become) werden; **∼ used to sth./sb.** sich an etw./jmdn. gewöhnen; **∼ apart** (fig.) sich auseinander leben; **∼ to be sth.** allmählich etw. werden; **he grew to be a man** er wuchs zum Manne heran (geh.); **∼ to love/ hate** *etc.* **sb./sth.** jmdn./etw. lieben lernen/hassen lernen *usw.;* **∼ to like sb./sth.** nach und nach Gefallen an jmdm./etw. finden. See also **growing; grown** 2. **2** *v.t.,* **grew, grown** **(a)** (cultivate) (on a small scale) ziehen; (on a large scale) anpflanzen; züchten ⟨*Blumen*⟩; **(b)** **∼ one's hair [long]** sich (*Dat.*) die Haare [lang] wachsen lassen **∼ a beard** sich (*Dat.*) einen Bart wachsen lassen

∼ into *v.t.* **(a)** (become) werden zu; **(b)** (become big enough for) hineinwachsen in (+ *Akk.*) ⟨*Kleidung*⟩

∼ on *v.t.* **it ∼s on you** man findet mit der Zeit Gefallen daran

∼ 'out of *v.t.* **(a)** (become too big for) herauswachsen aus ⟨*Kleidung*⟩; **(b)** (lose eventually) ablegen ⟨*Angewohnheit*⟩; entwachsen (+ *Dat.*) ⟨*Kindereien*⟩; überwinden ⟨*Zustand*⟩; *see also* **∼ 1 a**

∼ 'up *v.i.* **(a)** (spend early years) aufwachsen; (become adult) erwachsen werden; **what do you want to be** *or* **do when you ∼ up?** was willst du denn mal werden, wenn du groß bist?; **(b)** (fig.: behave [more] maturely) erwachsen werden; **∼ up!** werde endlich erwachsen!; **(c)** (develop) ⟨*Freundschaft, Feindschaft.*⟩ sich entwickeln; ⟨*Legende.*⟩ entstehen; ⟨*Tradition, Brauch.*⟩ sich herausbilden

∼ 'up into *v.t.* werden *od.* sich entwickeln zu

grower /ˈgrəʊə(r)/ *n. usu. in comb.* (person) Produzent, *der*/ Produzentin, *die;* **fruit-/vegetable-∼:** Obst-/Gemüsebauer, *der*

growing /ˈgrəʊɪŋ/ *adj.* wachsend; immer umfangreicher werdend ⟨*Sachgebiet*⟩; sich immer mehr verbreitend ⟨*Praktik*⟩

'growing pains *n. pl.* Wachstumsschmerzen *Pl.;* (fig.) Anfangsschwierigkeiten *Pl.*

growl /graʊl/ **1** *n.* Knurren, *das;* (of bear) Brummen, *das.* **2** *v.i.* knurren; ⟨*Bär.*⟩ [böse] brummen; **∼ at sb.** jmdn. anknurren/anbrummen

grown /grəʊn/ **1** ⇒ **grow. 2** *adj.* erwachsen; **fully ∼:** ausgewachsen

'grown-up 1 *n.* Erwachsene, *der*/*die.* **2** *adj.* erwachsen; **∼ books/clothes** Bücher/Kleider für Erwachsene

growth /grəʊθ/ *n.* **(a)** (of industry, economy, population) Wachstum, *das* **(of, in** *Gen.*); (of interest, illiteracy) Zunahme, *die* **(of, in** *Gen.*); *attrib.* Wachstums⟨*hormon, -rate*⟩; **(b)** (of organisms, amount grown) Wachstum, *das;* **(c)** (thing grown) Vegetation, *die;* Pflanzenwuchs, *der;* **(d)** (Med.) Geschwulst, *die;* Gewächs, *das*

growth: ∼ area *n.* Wachstumsbereich, *der;* **∼ industry** *n.* Wachstumsindustrie, *die;* **∼ rate** *n.* Wachstumsrate, *die;* **∼ ring** *n.* Wachstumsring, *der*

grub /grʌb/ **1** *n.* **(a)** Larve, *die;* (maggot) Made, *die;* **(b)** (sl.: food) Fressen, *das* (salopp); (provisions) Fressalien *Pl.* (ugs.); **∼['s] up!** ran an die Futterkrippe!; **lovely ∼!** ein Spitzenfraß! (salopp). **2** *v.i.,* **-bb-** wühlen (**for** nach); **∼ about [herum]**wühlen

grubby /ˈgrʌbɪ/ *adj.* schmudd[e]lig (ugs. abwertend)

grudge /grʌdʒ/ **1** *v.t.* **∼ sb. sth.** jmdm. etw. missgönnen; **I don't ∼ him his success** ich gönne ihm seinen Erfolg; **∼ doing sth.** (be unwilling to do sth.) nicht bereit sein, etw. zu tun; (do sth. reluctantly) etw. ungern tun; **I ∼ paying £20 for this** es geht mir gegen den Strich, dafür 20 Pfund zu zahlen (ugs.). **2** *n.* Groll, *der;* **have** *or* **hold a ∼ against sb.** einen Groll *od.* (ugs.) Hass auf jmdn. haben; jmdm. grollen; **bear sb. a ∼** *or* **a ∼ against sb.** jmdm. gegenüber nachtragend sein

grudging /ˈgrʌdʒɪŋ/ *adj.* widerwillig ⟨*Lob, Bewunderung, Unterstützung*⟩; widerwillig gewährt ⟨*Zuschuss*⟩

grudgingly /ˈgrʌdʒɪŋlɪ/ *adv.* widerwillig

gruel /ˈgruːəl/ *n.* Schleimsuppe, *die*

gruelling (*Amer.:* **grueling**) /ˈgruːəlɪŋ/ *adj.* aufreibend; zermürbend; [äußerst] strapaziös ⟨*Reise, Marsch*⟩; mörderisch (ugs.) ⟨*Tempo, Rennen*⟩

gruesome /ˈgruːsəm/ *adj.* grausig; schaurig

gruff /grʌf/ *adj.* barsch; schroff; ruppig ⟨*Benehmen, Wesen*⟩; rau ⟨*Stimme*⟩

grumble /ˈgrʌmbl/ **1** *v.i.* murren; **∼ about** *or* **over sth.** sich über etw. (*Akk.*) beklagen. **2** *n.* (act) Murren, *das;* (complaint) Klage, *die;* **without a ∼:** ohne Murren

grumbler /ˈgrʌmblə(r)/ *n.* Querulant, *der*/Querulantin, *die*

grumpily /ˈgrʌmpɪlɪ/ *adv.,* **grumpy** /ˈgrʌmpɪ/ *adj.* unleidlich; grantig (ugs.)

grunge /grʌndʒ/ *n., no. pl.* **(a)** (Amer. sl.: grime) Dreck, *der* (ugs.); Siff, *der* (salopp); **(b)** (music) Grunge, *der;* **(c)** (fashion) Grunge[look], *der*/-[stil], *der*

grunt /grʌnt/ **1** *n.* Grunzen, *das;* **give a ∼:** grunzen. **2** *v.i.* grunzen

'G-string *n.* (garment) ≈ Cache-sex, *das;* G-String, *die od. der*

guarantee /gærənˈtiː/ **1** *v.t.* **(a)** garantieren für; [eine] Garantie geben auf (+ *Akk.*); **the clock is ∼d for a year** die Uhr hat ein Jahr Garantie; **∼d wage** Garantielohn, *der;* **∼d genuine** *etc.* garantiert echt *usw.;* **(b)** (promise) garantieren (ugs.); (ensure) bürgen für ⟨*Qualität*⟩; garantieren ⟨*Erfolg*⟩; **be ∼d to do sth.** etw. garantiert tun. **2** *n.* **(a)** (Commerc. etc.) Garantie, *die;* (document) Garantieschein, *der;* **there's a year's ∼ on this radio, this radio has a year's ∼:** auf dieses Radio gibt es *od.* dieses Radio hat ein Jahr Garantie; **is it still under ∼?** ist noch Garantie darauf?; **(b)** (coll.: promise) Garantie, *die* (ugs.); **give sb. a ∼ that …:** jmdm. garantieren, dass …; **be a ∼ of sth.** (ensure) eine Garantie für etw. sein

guard /gɑːd/ ▶ 887 | **1** *n.* **(a)** (Mil.: guardsman) Wach[t]posten, *der;* **(b)** *no pl.* (Mil.: group of soldiers) Wache, *die;* Wachmannschaft, *die;* **∼ of honour** Ehrenwache, *die;* Ehrengarde, *die;* **(c)** **G∼s** (Brit. Mil.: household troops) Garderegiment, *das;* Garde, *die;* **(d)** (watch; also Mil.) Wache, *die;* **be on ∼:** Wache haben; **keep** *or* **stand ∼:** Wache halten *od.* stehen; **keep** *or* **stand ∼ over** bewachen; **be on [one's] ∼ [against sb./sth.]** (lit. or fig.) sich [vor jmdm./ etw.] hüten; **be off [one's] ∼** (fig.) nicht auf der Hut sein; **be caught** *or* **taken off ∼** *or* **off one's ∼ [by sth.]** (fig.) [von etw.] überrascht werden; **put sb. on [his/her] ∼:** jmdn. misstrauisch machen; **under ∼:** unter Bewachung; **be [kept/held] under ∼:** unter Bewachung stehen; **keep** *or* **hold/put under ∼:** bewachen/unter Bewachung stellen; **(e)** (Brit. Railw.) [Zug]schaffner, *der*/-schaffnerin, *die;* **(f)** (Amer.: prison warder) [Gefängnis]wärter, *der*/-wärterin, *die;* **(g)** (safety device) Schutz, *der;* Schutzvorrichtung, *die;* (worn on body) Schutz, *der;* **(h)** (posture) (Boxing, Fencing) Deckung, *die;* **drop** *or* **lower one's ∼:** die Deckung fallen lassen; (fig.) seine Reserve aufgeben. **2** *v.t.* (watch over) bewachen; (keep safe) hüten ⟨*Geheimnis, Schatz*⟩; schützen ⟨*Leben*⟩; beschützen ⟨*Prominenten*⟩; **∼ sb. against sth.** jmdn. vor etw. (*Dat.*) beschützen

∼ against *v.t.* sich hüten vor (+ *Dat.*); verhüten ⟨*Unfall*⟩; vorbeugen (+ *Dat.*) ⟨*Krankheit, Gefahr, Irrtum*⟩; **∼ against doing sth.** sich [davor] hüten, etw. zu tun

guard: ∼ dog *n.* Wachhund, *der;* **∼ duty** *n.* Wachdienst, *der;* **be on** *or* **do ∼ duty** Wachdienst haben

guarded /ˈgɑːdɪd/ *adj.* zurückhaltend; vorsichtig

guardian /ˈgɑːdɪən/ *n.* **(a)** Hüter, *der;* Wächter, *der;* **(b)** (Law) Vormund, *der*

guard: ∼ rail *n.* Geländer, *das;* **∼room** *n.* (Mil.) Wachstube, *die;* Wachlokal, *das*

guardsman /ˈgɑːdzmən/ *n., pl.* **guardsmen** /ˈgɑːdzmən/ ▶ 887 | Wach[t]posten, *der;* (in Guards) Gardist, *der*

guerrilla /gəˈrɪlə/ *n.* Guerillakämpfer, *der*/-kämpferin, *die; attrib.* Guerilla-

guess /ges/ **1** *v.t.* **(a)** (estimate) schätzen; (surmise) raten; (surmise correctly) erraten; raten ⟨*Rätsel*⟩; **can you ∼ his weight?** schätz mal, wieviel er wiegt; **∼ what!** (coll.) stell dir vor!; **you'd never ∼ that …:** man würde nie vermuten, dass …; **I ∼ed as much** das habe ich mir schon gedacht; **(b)** (esp. Amer.: suppose) **I ∼:** ich glaube; ich schätze (ugs.); **I ∼ we'll have to** wir müssen wohl; **I ∼ so/not** ich glaube schon *od.* ja/nicht *od.* kaum. **2** *v.i.* (estimate) schätzen; (make assumption) vermuten; (surmise correctly) es erraten; ~ **at sth.** etw. schätzen; (surmise) über etw. (*Akk.*) Vermutungen anstellen; **I'm just** ~**ing** das ist nur eine Schätzung/eine Vermutung; **you've** ~**ed right/wrong** deine Vermutung ist richtig/falsch; **keep sb.** ~**ing** (coll.) jmdn. im Unklaren *od.* Ungewissen lassen; **you'll never** ~! darauf kommst du nie! **3** *n.* Schätzung, *die*; **at a** ~: schätzungsweise; **make** *or* **have a** ~: schätzen; **have a** ~! rate *od.* schätz mal!; **my** ~ **is [that]** ...: ich schätze, dass ...; **I'll give you three** ~**es** (coll.) dreimal darfst du raten (ugs.)

guesstimate /'gestɪmət/ *n.* (coll.) grobe Schätzung

'guesswork *n., no pl., no indef. art.* **be** ~: eine Vermutung sein

guest /gest/ *n.* Gast, *der;* **be my** ~ (fig. coll.) tun Sie sich/ tu dir keinen Zwang an; ~ **of honour** Ehrengast, *der*

guest: ~ **house** *n.* Pension, *die;* ~ **room** *n.* Gästezimmer, *das;* ~ **worker** *n.* Gastarbeiter, *der/*-arbeiterin, *die*

guffaw /gʌ'fɔ:/ **1** *n.* brüllendes Gelächter; **give a [great]** ~: in brüllendes Gelächter ausbrechen. **2** *v.i.* brüllend lachen

guidance /'gaɪdəns/ *n., no pl., no indef. art.* **(a)** (leadership, direction) Führung, *die;* (by teacher, tutor, etc.) [An]leitung, *die;* **(b)** (advice) Rat, *der;* **give sb.** ~ **on sth.** jmdn. in etw. (*Dat.*) beraten

guide /gaɪd/ **1** *n.* **(a)** Führer, *der/*Führerin, *die;* (Tourism) [Fremden]führer, *der/*-führerin, *die;* (professional mountainclimber) [Berg]führer, *der/*-führerin, *die;* **(b)** (indicator) **be a [good]** ~ **to sth.** ein [guter] Anhaltspunkt für etw. sein; **be no** ~ **to sth.** keine Rückschlüsse auf etw. (*Akk.*) zulassen; **(c)** (Brit.) **[Girl] G**~: Pfadfinderin, *die;* **the G**~**s** die Pfadfinderinnen; **(d)** (handbook) Handbuch, *das;* **a** ~ **to healthier living** ein Ratgeber für ein gesünderes Leben; **(e)** (book for tourists) [Reise]führer, *der;* **a** ~ **to York** ein Führer für *od.* durch York. **2** *v.t.* **(a)** führen ‹*Personen, Pflug, Maschinenteil usw.*›; **(b)** (fig.) bestimmen ‹*Handeln, Urteil*›; anleiten ‹*Schüler, Lehrling*›; **be** ~**d by sth./sb.** sich von etw./jmdm. leiten lassen

'guidebook ⇒ **guide 1 e**

guided missile /gaɪdɪd 'mɪsaɪl/ *n.* Lenkflugkörper, *der*

'guide dog *n.* ~ **[for the blind]** Blindenhund, *der*

guided tour /gaɪdɪd 'tʊə(r)/ *n.* Führung, *die* **(of** durch)

'guideline *n.* (fig.) Richtlinie, *die*

guild /gɪld/ *n.* **(a)** Verein, *der;* **(b)** (Hist.) (of merchants) Gilde, *die;* (of artisans) Zunft, *die*

guile /gaɪl/ *n., no pl.* Hinterlist, *die*

guillotine /'gɪlətiːn/ **1** *n.* **(a)** Guillotine, *die;* Fallbeil, *das;* **(b)** (for paper) Papierschneidemaschine, *die.* **2** *v.t.* **(a)** (behead) mit der Guillotine *od.* dem Fallbeil hinrichten; **(b)** (cut) schneiden

guilt /gɪlt/ *n., no pl.* **(a)** Schuld, *die* **(of** an + *Dat.*); **(b)** (guilty feeling) Schuldgefühle *Pl.*

guiltily /'gɪltɪlɪ/ *adv.* schuldbewusst

guiltless /'gɪltlɪs/ *adj.* unschuldig **(of** an + *Dat.*)

guilty /'gɪltɪ/ *adj.* **(a)** schuldig; **the** ~ **person** der/die Schuldige; **be** ~ **of murder** des Mordes schuldig sein; **find sb.** ~**/not** ~ **[of sth.]** jmdn. [an etw. (*Dat.*)] schuldig sprechen/freisprechen; **[return** *or* **find a verdict of]** ~**/not** ~: [auf] „schuldig"/„nicht schuldig" [erkennen]; **feel** ~ **about sth./having done sth.** (coll.) ein schlechtes Gewissen haben wegen etw./, weil man etw. getan hat; **everyone is/we're all** ~ **of that** (coll.) das tut jeder/das tun wir alle; **(b)** (prompted by guilt) schuldbewusst ‹*Miene, Blick, Verhalten*›; schlecht ‹*Gewissen*›

guinea /'gɪnɪ/ *n.* (Hist.) Guinee, *die*

'guinea pig *n.* **(a)** (animal) Meerschweinchen, *das;* **(b)** (fig.: subject of experiment) Versuchskaninchen, *das* (ugs. abwertend); **act as** ~: Versuchskaninchen spielen

guise /gaɪz/ *n.* Gestalt, *die;* **in the** ~ **of** in Gestalt (+ *Gen.*)

guitar /gɪ'tɑ:(r)/ *n.* Gitarre, *die; attrib.* Gitarren‹*musik, -spieler*›

guitarist /gɪ'tɑ:rɪst/ *n.* ▶ 887 | Gitarrist, *der/*Gitarristin, *die*

gulch /gʌltʃ/ *n.* (Amer.) Schlucht, *die;* Klamm, *die*

gulf /gʌlf/ *n.* **(a)** (portion of sea) Golf, *der;* Meerbusen, *der;* **the [Arabian** *or* **Persian] G**~: der [Persische] Golf; **the G**~ **of Mexico** der Golf von Mexiko; **(b)** (wide difference) Kluft, *die;* **(c)** (chasm) Abgrund, *der*

Gulf: ~ **States** *pr. n. pl.* Golfstaaten *Pl.;* ~ **Stream** *pr. n.* Golfstrom, *der;* ~ **War** *n.* Golfkrieg, *der*

gull /gʌl/ *n.* Möwe, *die*

gullet /'gʌlɪt/ *n.* **(a)** (food-passage) Speiseröhre, *die;* **(b)** (throat) Kehle, *die;* Gurgel, *die*

gullible /'gʌlɪbl/ *adj.* leichtgläubig; (trusting) gutgläubig

gully /'gʌlɪ/ *n.* **(a)** (artificial channel) Abzugskanal, *der;* **(b)** (drain) Gully, *der;* **(c)** (water-worn ravine) [Erosions]rinne, *die*

gulp /gʌlp/ **1** *v.t.* hinunterschlingen; hinuntergießen ‹*Getränk*›. **2** *n.* **(a)** (act of ~ing, effort to swallow) Schlucken, *das;* **swallow in** *or* **at one** ~: mit einem Schluck herunterstürzen ‹*Getränk*›; in einem Bissen herunterschlingen ‹*Speise*›; **(b)** (large mouthful of drink) kräftiger Schluck

~ **'down** ⇒ ~ **1**

gum¹ /gʌm/ *n., usu. in pl.* (Anat.) ~**[s]** Zahnfleisch, *das*

gum² **1** *n.* **(a)** (natural substance) Gummi, *das;* **(b)** (glue) Klebstoff, *der;* **(b)** (sweet) Gummibonbon, *der od. das;* **(c)** (Amer.) ⇒ **chewing gum. 2** *v.t., -mm-:* **(a)** (smear with ~) gummieren ‹*Briefmarken, Etiketten usw.*›; **(b)** (fasten with ~) kleben

~ **'up** *v.t.* ~ up the works (sl) alles vermasseln (salopp)

gum: ~**boil** *n.* Zahnfleischabszess, *der;* ~**boot** *n.* Gummistiefel, *der*

gumption /'gʌmpʃn/ *n., no pl., no indef. art.* (coll.) (resourcefulness) Grips, *der* (ugs.); (enterprising spirit) Unternehmungsgeist, *der*

'gum tree *n.* **be up a** ~ (fig.) in der Klemme sitzen (ugs.)

gun /gʌn/ *n.* **(a)** Schusswaffe, *die;* (piece of artillery) Geschütz, *das;* (rifle) Gewehr, *das;* (pistol) Pistole, *die;* (revolver) Revolver, *der;* **big** ~ (coll.: important person) hohes *od.* großes Tier (ugs.); **be going great** ~**s** laufen wie geschmiert (ugs.); ‹*Person:*› toll in Schwung sein (ugs.); **stick to one's** ~**s** (fig.) auf seinem Standpunkt beharren; **(b)** (starting pistol) Startpistole, *die;* **jump the** ~: einen Fehlstart verursachen; (fig.) vorpreschen; (by saying sth.) vorzeitig etwas bekannt werden lassen

~ **'down** *v.t.* niederschießen

~ **for** *v.t.* (fig.) auf dem Kieker haben (ugs.)

gun: ~ **battle** *n.* Schießerei, *die;* ~**boat** *n.* Kanonenboot, *das;* ~ **carriage** *n.* [fahrbare] Geschützlafette; ~**fight** *n.* (Amer. coll.) Schießerei, *die;* ~**fighter** *n.* Revolverheld, *der;* ~**fire** *n.* Geschützfeuer, *das;* (of small arms) Schießerei, *die*

gunge /gʌndʒ/ *n.* (Brit. coll.) Schmiere, *die*

gun: ~ **laws** *pl.* Waffengesetze, *Pl.;* ~**man** /'gʌnmən/ *n., pl.* ~**men** /'gʌnmən/ [mit einer Schusswaffe] bewaffneter Mann

gunner /'gʌnə(r)/ *n.* Artillerist, *der;* (private soldier) Kanonier, *der*

gun: ~**point** ⇒ **point 1 b;** ~**powder** *n.* Schießpulver, *das;* **Gunpowder Plot** (Hist.) Pulververschwörung, *die;* ~**shot** *n.* **(a)** (shot) Schuss, *der;* **(b)** within/out of ~**shot** in/außer Schussweite; ~**smith** *n.* ▶ 887 | Büchsenmacher, *der*

gunwale /'gʌnl/ *n.* (Naut.) Schandeck, *das;* Schandeckel, *der;* (of rowing boat) Dollbord, *der*

gurgle /'gɜ:gl/ **1** *n.* Gluckern, *das;* (of brook) Plätschern, *das.* **2** *v.i.* gluckern; ‹*Bach:*› plätschern; ‹*Baby:*› lallen; (with delight) glucksen

guru /'guru:/ *n.* **(a)** Guru, *der;* **(b)** (mentor) Mentor, *der*

gush /gʌʃ/ **1** *n.* **(a)** (sudden stream) Schwall, *der;* **(b)** (effusiveness) Überschwänglichkeit, *die;* **(c)** (excessive enthusiasm) Schwärmerei, *die.* **2** *v.i.* **(a)** strömen; schießen; ~ **out** herausströmen; herausschießen; **(b)** (fig.: speak or act effusively) überschwänglich sein; **(c)** (fig.: speak with excessive enthusiasm) schwärmen. **3** *v.t.* **sth.** ~**es water/oil/blood** Wasser/Öl/Blut schießt aus etw. hervor

gushing /'gʌʃɪŋ/ *adj.* **(a)** reißend ‹*Strom*›; **(b)** (effusive) exaltiert

gusset /'gʌsɪt/ n. Zwickel, der; Keil, der

gust /gʌst/ **1** n. ∼ [of wind] Windstoß, der; Bö[e], die. **2** v.i. böig wehen

gusto /'gʌstəʊ/ n., no pl. (enjoyment) Genuss, der; (vitality) Schwung, der

gusty /'gʌstɪ/ adj. böig

gut /gʌt/ **1** n. **(a)** (material) Darm, der; **(b)** in pl. (bowels) Eingeweide Pl.; Gedärme Pl.; **hate sb.'s ∼s** (coll.) jmdn. auf den Tod nicht ausstehen können; **sweat** or **work one's ∼s out** (coll.) sich dumm und dämlich schuften (ugs.); **(c)** in pl. (fig.: contents) Innereien Pl. (scherzh.); **(d)** in pl. (coll.: courage) Schneid, der (ugs.); Mumm, der (ugs.); **(e)** (intestine) Darm, der. **2** v.t., **-tt-: (a)** (take out ∼s of) ausnehmen; **(b)** (remove or destroy fittings in) ausräumen; **the house was ∼ted [by the fire]** das Haus brannte aus. **3** attrib. adj. (instinctive) gefühlsmäßig ‹Reaktion›

gutless /'gʌtlɪs/ adj. feige; **be ∼:** keinen Mumm haben (ugs.)

gutter /'gʌtə(r)/ **1** n. (below edge of roof) Dach- od. Regenrinne, die; (at side of street) Rinnstein, der; Gosse, die; **the ∼** (fig.) die Gosse. **2** v.i. ‹Kerze:› tropfen; ‹Flamme:› [immer schwächer] flackern

gutter: **∼ press** n. Sensationspresse, die (abwertend); **∼snipe** n. Gassenjunge, der (abwertend)

guttural /'gʌtərl/ adj. (from the throat) guttural; kehlig

guy¹ /gaɪ/ n. (rope) Halteseil, das

guy² n. **(a)** (coll.: man) Typ, der (ugs.); **(b)** in pl. (Amer.: everyone) [**listen,**] **you ∼s!** [hört mal,] Kinder! (ugs.); **(c)** (Brit.: effigy) Guy-Fawkes-Puppe, die; **Guy Fawkes Day** Festtag (5. November) zum Gedenken an die Pulververschwörung

'guy-rope n. Zelt[spann]leine, die

guzzle /'gʌzl/ **1** v.t. (eat) hinunterschlingen; (drink) hinuntergießen. **2** v.i. schlingen

gym /dʒɪm/ n. (coll.) **(a)** (gymnasium) Turnhalle, die; **(b)** no pl., no indef. art. (gymnastics) Turnen, das

gymkhana /dʒɪm'kɑːnə/ n. Gymkhana, das

gymnasium /dʒɪm'neɪzɪəm/ n., pl. **∼s** or **gymnasia** /dʒɪm'neɪzɪə/ Turnhalle, die

gymnast /'dʒɪmnæst/ n. Turner, der/Turnerin, die

gymnastic /dʒɪm'næstɪk/ adj. turnerisch ‹Können›; **∼ equipment** Turngeräte Pl.

gymnastics /dʒɪm'næstɪks/ n., no pl. Gymnastik, die; (esp. with apparatus) Turnen, das; attrib. Gymnastik-/Turn‹stunde, -lehrer›

gym: **∼ shoe** n. Turnschuh, der; **∼slip,** **∼ tunic** ns. Trägerrock, der (für die Schule)

gynaecological /gaɪnɪkə'lɒdʒɪkl/ adj. (Med.) gynäkologisch

gynaecologist /gaɪnɪ'kɒlədʒɪst/ n. ▶ 887 ⎪ (Med.) Gynäkologe, der/Gynäkologin, die; Frauenarzt, der/Frauenärztin, die

gynaecology /gaɪnɪ'kɒlədʒɪ/ n. (Med.) Gynäkologie, die; Frauenheilkunde, die

gynecological etc. (Amer.) ⇒ **gynaec-**

gypsy (Gypsy) /'dʒɪpsɪ/ n. Zigeuner, der/Zigeunerin, die

gyrate /dʒaɪə'reɪt/ v.i. sich drehen

gyration /dʒaɪə'reɪʃn/ n. Drehung, die; kreiselnde Bewegung

gyroscope /'dʒaɪərəskəʊp/ n. (Phys., Naut., Aeronaut.) Kreisel, der; (for scientific purposes) Gyroskop, das

H h

H¹, h /eɪtʃ/ n., pl. **Hs** or **H's** /'eɪtʃɪz/ (letter) H, h, das

h abbr. ▶ 706 ⎪ **hour[s]** Std[n]; **at 1700h** um 17.00h

H² abbr. (on pencil) **hard** H

habeas corpus /heɪbɪəs 'kɔːpəs/ n., no pl. (Law) Anordnung eines Haftprüfungstermins

haberdashery /'hæbədæʃərɪ/ n. **(a)** (goods) (Brit.) Kurzwaren Pl.; (Amer: menswear) Herrenmoden Pl.; **(b)** (shop) (Brit.) Kurzwarengeschäft, das; (Amer.) Herrenmodengeschäft, das

habit /'hæbɪt/ n. **(a)** (set practice) Gewohnheit, die; **good/ bad ∼:** gute/schlechte [An]gewohnheit; **the ∼ of smoking** das [gewohnheitsmäßige] Rauchen; **have a** or **the ∼ of doing sth.** die Angewohnheit haben, etw. zu tun; **out of ∼, from [force of] ∼:** aus Gewohnheit; **old ∼s die hard** der Mensch ist ein Gewohnheitstier (ugs.); **be in the ∼ of doing sth.** die Gewohnheit haben, etw. zu tun; **not be in the ∼ of doing sth.** es nicht gewohnt sein, etw. zu tun; **get** or **fall into a** or **the ∼ of doing sth.** [es] sich (Dat.) angewöhnen, etw. zu tun; **get** or **fall into** or (coll.) **pick up bad ∼s** schlechte [An]gewohnheiten annehmen; **get out of the ∼ of doing sth.** [es] sich (Dat.) abgewöhnen, etw. zu tun; **(b)** (coll.) (addiction) Süchtigkeit, die; [Drogen]abhängigkeit, die; **(c)** (dress) Habit, der od. das

habitable /'hæbɪtəbl/ adj. bewohnbar

habitat /'hæbɪtæt/ n. (of animals, plants) Habitat, das (Zool., Bot.); Lebensraum, der; Standort, der (Bot.)

habitation /hæbɪ'teɪʃn/ n. **fit/unfit** or **not fit for human ∼:** bewohnbar/unbewohnbar

habitual /hə'bɪtjʊəl/ adj. **(a)** (usual) gewohnt; **(b)** (continual) ständig; **(c)** (given to habit) gewohnheitsmäßig ‹Lügner›; **Gewohnheits‹trinker›**

habitually /hə'bɪtjʊəlɪ/ adv. **(a)** (regularly, recurrently) regelmäßig; **(b)** (incessantly) ständig

habitué /hə'bɪtjʊeɪ/ n. regelmäßiger Besucher; (of hotel, casino, etc.) Stammgast, der

hack¹ /hæk/ **1** v.t. **(a)** hacken ‹Holz›; **∼ sb./sth. to bits** or **pieces** jmdn. zerstückeln/etw. in Stücke hacken; **∼ one's way [through/along/out of sth.]** sich (Dat.) einen Weg [durch etw./entlang/aus etw. heraus] [frei]schlagen; **(b)** (Computing) eindringen in (+ Akk.) ‹Computersystem›. **2** v.i. **(a)** **∼ at** herumhacken auf (+ Dat.); **∼ through the undergrowth** sich (Dat.) einen Weg durchs Unterholz schlagen; **(b)** **∼ing cough** trockener Husten; Reizhusten, der; **(c)** (Computing) **∼ into sth.** in etw. (Akk.) eindringen

∼ 'off v.t. abhacken; abschlagen

hack² **1** n. **(a)** (writer) Schreiberling, der (abwertend); **newspaper ∼:** Zeitungsschreiber, der; **publisher's ∼:** Lohnschreiber, der; **(b)** (hired horse) Mietpferd, das. **2** adj. **(a)** **∼ writer** Lohnschreiber, der; **(b)** (mediocre) Nullachtfünfzehn- (ugs. abwertend)

hacker /'hækə(r)/ n. (Computing) Hacker, der

hacking jacket /'hækɪŋ dʒækɪt/ n. Reitjackett, das; (sports jacket) Sportjacke, die

hackle /'hækl/ n. **sb.'s ∼s rise** (fig.) jmd. gerät in Harnisch; **get sb.'s ∼s up, make sb.'s ∼s rise** (fig.) jmdn. wütend machen

hackney /'hæknɪ/: **∼ 'cab,** **∼ 'carriage** ns. Droschke, die (veralt.); Taxe, die

hackneyed /'hæknɪd/ adj. abgegriffen; abgedroschen (ugs.)

'hacksaw n. [Metall]bügelsäge, die

had ⇒ **have 1, 2**

haddock /'hædək/ n., pl. same Schellfisch, der; **smoked ∼:** Haddock, der

hadn't /'hædnt/ (coll.) = **had not;** ⇒ **have 1, 2**

haemoglobin /hiːmə'gləʊbɪn/ n. (Anat., Zool.) Hämoglobin, das

haemophilia /hiːməˈfɪlɪə/ n. ▶ 865| (Med.) Hämophilie, die (fachspr.); Bluterkrankheit, die

haemophiliac /hiːməˈfɪlɪæk/ n. (Med.) Bluter, der/Bluterin, die

haemorrhage /ˈhemərɪdʒ/ (Med.) **1** n. Hämorrhagie, die (fachspr.); Blutung, die. **2** v.i. starke Blutungen haben

haemorrhoid /ˈheməroɪd/ n. Hämorrhoide, die

hag /hæg/ n. (a) (old woman) [alte] Hexe; (b) (witch) Hexe, die

haggard /ˈhægəd/ adj. (worn) ausgezehrt; (with worry) abgehärmt; (tired) abgespannt

haggis /ˈhægɪs/ n. (Gastr.) Haggis, der; gefüllter Schafsmagen

haggle /ˈhægl/ v.i. sich zanken (**over, about** wegen); (over price) feilschen (abwertend) (**over, about** um)

Hague /heɪg/ pr. n. **The ~:** Den Haag (das)

hail[1] /heɪl/ **1** n. (a) no pl., no indef. art. (Meteorol.) Hagel, der; (b) (fig.: shower) Hagel, der; (of insults, questions, etc.) Schwall, der; Flut, die; **a ~ of bullets/arrows** ein Kugel-/Pfeilhagel od. -regen. **2** v.i. (a) impers. (Meteorol.) **it ~s** or **is ~ing** es hagelt; (b) (fig.) **~ down** niederprasseln (**on** auf + Akk.); **~ down on sb.** (Beschimpfungen, Vorwürfe usw.:) auf jmdn. einprasseln. **3** v.t. niederhageln od. niederprasseln lassen

hail[2] **1** v.t. (a) (call out to) anrufen, (fachspr.) anpreien ⟨Schiff⟩; (signal to) heranwinken, anhalten ⟨Taxi⟩; (b) (acclaim) zujubeln (+ Dat.); bejubeln (**as** als); **~ sb. king** jmdm. als König zujubeln. **2** int. (arch.) sei gegrüßt (geh.); **~ Macbeth/to thee, O Caesar** Heil Macbeth/dir, o Cäsar; **H~ Mary** ⇒ **Ave Maria; ~-fellow-well-met** kumpelhaft

hail: ~stone n. (Meteorol.) Hagelkorn, das; **~storm** n. (Meteorol.) Hagelschauer, der

hair /heə(r)/ n. ▶ 672| (a) (one strand) Haar, das; **without turning a ~** (fig.) ohne eine Miene zu verziehen; **not harm a ~ of sb.'s head** (fig.) jmdm. kein Haar krümmen; (b) collect., no pl. (many strands, mass) Haar, das; Haare Pl.; attrib. Haar-; **do one's/sb.'s ~** sich/jmdm. das Haar machen (ugs.); **have** or **get one's ~ done** sich (Dat.) das Haar od. die Haare machen (ugs.) lassen; **pull sb.'s ~:** jmdn. an den Haaren ziehen; **he's losing his ~** ihm gehen die Haare aus; **keep your ~ on!** (coll.) geh [mal] nicht gleich an die Decke! (ugs.); **let one's ~ down** (give free expression to one's feelings etc.) aus sich herausgehen; (have a good time) auf den Putz hauen (ugs.); **sb.'s ~ stands on end** (fig.) jmdm. stehen die Haare zu Berge (ugs.); **get in sb.'s ~** (fig. coll.) jmdn. auf die Nerven od. den Wecker gehen od. fallen (ugs.). See also **bad 1 a**

hair: ~brush n. Haarbürste, die; **~ conditioner** n. Pflegespülung, die; **~cut** n. (a) (act) Haareschneiden, das; **go for/need a ~cut** zum Friseur gehen/müssen; **give sb. a ~cut** jmdm. die Haare schneiden; **get/have a ~cut** sich (Dat.) die Haare schneiden lassen; (b) (style) Haarschnitt, der; **~do** n. (coll.) (a) give sb. a **~do** jmdm. das Haar machen (ugs.); (b) (style) Frisur, die; **~dresser** n. ▶ 887| Friseur, der/Friseurin, die; **men's ~dresser** Herrenfriseur, der/-friseurin, die; **ladies' ~dresser** Damenfriseur, der/-friseurin, die; **go to the ~dresser['s]** zum Friseur gehen; **~dressing** n. der Friseurberuf; (attrib.) **~dressing salon** Friseursalon, der; **~drier** n. Haartrockner, der; Föhn, der; (with a hood) Trockenhaube, die

-haired /heəd/ adj. in comb. **black-/frizzy-~:** schwarz-/kraushaarig

hair: ~grip n. (Brit.) Haarklammer, die; **~ lacquer** ⇒ **~spray; ~line** n. (a) (edge of hair) Haaransatz, der; **his ~line is receding, he has a receding ~line** er bekommt eine Stirnglatze; (b) (narrow line) haarfeine Linie; haarfeiner Strich; (c) **~line [crack]** haarfeiner Riss; **~net** n. Haarnetz, das; **~piece** n. Haarteil, das; **~pin** n. Haarnadel, die; **~pin 'bend** n. Haarnadelkurve, die; **~-raising** /ˈheəreɪzɪŋ/ adj. furchterregend; (very bad) haarsträubend; mörderisch ⟨Rennstrecke, Abstieg vom Berg usw.⟩; **~'s breadth** n. **by [no more than] a ~'s breadth** [nur] um Haaresbreite ⟨verfehlen⟩; nur knapp ⟨gewinnen⟩; **~slide** n. (Brit.) Haarspange, die; **~splitting** (derog.) **1** adj. haarspalterisch (abwertend); **2** n.

Haarspalterei, die (abwertend); **~spray** n. Haarspray, das; **~style** n. Frisur, die

hairy /ˈheərɪ/ adj. (a) (having hair) behaart; flauschig ⟨Schal, Pullover, Teppich⟩; (b) (sl.: difficult, dangerous) haarig; (c) (sl.: unpleasant, frightening) eklig (ugs.)

hake /heɪk/ n., pl. same (Zool.) Seehecht, der

'halcyon days /ˈhælsɪən deɪz/ n. pl. glückliche Zeiten Pl.

hale /heɪl/ adj. kräftig ⟨Körper, Konstitution⟩; rege ⟨Geist⟩; **~ and hearty** gesund und munter

half /hɑːf/ **1** n., pl. **halves** /hɑːvz/ (a) ▶ 956| (part) Hälfte, die; **~ [of sth.]** die Hälfte [von etw.]; **~ of Europe** halb Europa; **I've only ~ left** ich habe nur noch die Hälfte; **~ [of] that** die Hälfte [davon]; **cut sth. in ~** or **into [two] halves** etw. in zwei Hälften schneiden; **divide sth. in ~** or **into halves** etw. halbieren; **one/two and a ~ hours, one hour/two hours and a ~:** anderthalb od. eineinhalb/zweieinhalb Stunden; **she is three and a ~:** sie ist dreieinhalb; **not/never do anything/things by halves** keine halben Sachen machen; **be too cheeky/big by ~:** entschieden zu frech/groß sein; **go halves** or **go ~ and ~ [with sb.]** halbe-halbe [mit jmdm.] machen (ugs.); **how the other ~ lives** wie andere Leute leben; **that's only** or **just** or **not the ~ of it** das ist noch nicht alles; (b) (coll.: ~-pint) kleines Glas; (of beer) kleines Bier; Kleine, das (ugs.); **a ~ of bitter** etc. ein kleines Bitter usw.; (c) (Footb. etc.: period) Halbzeit, die. **2** adj. halb; **~ the house/books/staff/time** die Hälfte des Hauses/der Bücher/des Personals/der Zeit; **he is drunk ~ the time** (very often) er ist fast immer betrunken; **~ an hour** eine halbe Stunde. **3** adv. (a) (to the extent of ~) zur Hälfte; halb ⟨öffnen, schließen, aufessen, fertig, voll, geöffnet⟩; (almost) fast ⟨fallen, ersticken, tot sein⟩; **~ as much/many/big/heavy** halb so viel/viele/groß/schwer; **~ run [and] ~ walk** teils laufen, teils gehen; **I ~ wished/hoped that ...:** ich wünschte mir/hoffte fast, dass ...; **only ~ hear what ...:** nur zum Teil hören, was ...; **~ listen for/to** mit halbem Ohr horchen auf (+ Akk.)/zuhören (+ Dat.); **~ cook sth.** etw. halb gar werden lassen; (b) ▶ 706| (by the amount of a ~-hour) halb; **~ past** or (coll.) **~ one/two/three** etc. halb zwei/drei/vier usw.; **~ past twelve** halb eins

half- in comb. halb ⟨gar, verbrannt, betrunken, voll, leer⟩; **~-starved** halb verhungert; **a ~-dozen** ein halbes Dutzend; **~-pound bag/~-litre glass** Halbpfundtüte, die/ -literglas, das; **~-year** Halbjahr, das; halbes Jahr

half: ~-and-'~ 1 n. Does it contain a or b? — **H~-and-~:** Enthält es a oder b? — Halb und halb; **2** adj. **~-and-~ mixture of a and b** Mischung, die je zur Hälfte aus a und b besteht; **3** adv. zu gleichen Teilen; **they divide their earnings ~-and-~:** sie teilen ihre Einkünfte gleichmäßig untereinander auf; **~-baked** /hɑːf'beɪkt/ adj. unausgegoren (abwertend), unausgereift ⟨Plan, Aufsatz⟩; **~-breed** n. (a) Mischling, der; Halbblut, das; (b) ⇒ **cross-breed 1; ~-brother** n. Halbbruder, der; **~-caste 1** n. Mischling, der; Halbblut, das; **2** adj. Mischlings-; **~-conscious** adj. [nur] halb bewusst ⟨Wunsch, Wahrnehmung usw.⟩; **be only ~-conscious** ⟨Person:⟩ nicht bei vollem Bewusstsein sein; **~-'crown** n. (Brit. Hist.) Halfcrown, die; **~-day** n. halber Tag; attrib. halbtägig ⟨Kurs, Test⟩; **take a ~-day's holiday** einen halben Tag Urlaub nehmen; **it's ~-day closing today** heute ist nur halbtägig geöffnet; **~-hearted** /hɑːf'hɑːtɪd/ adj., **~-heartedly** /hɑːf'hɑːtɪdlɪ/ adv. halbherzig; **~-'hour** n. halbe Stunde; **~-'hourly 1** adj. halbstündlich; halbstündlich verkehrend ⟨Bus usw.⟩; **the bus service is ~-hourly** der Bus verkehrt halbstündlich; **2** adv. jede halbe Stunde; halbstündlich; **~-life** n. (Phys.) Halbwertszeit, die; **~-light** n. Halblicht, das; **~-'mast** n. **be [flown] at ~-mast** ⟨Flagge:⟩ auf halbmast gehisst sein od. stehen; **~ measure** n. (a) **~ measure of whisky** ein halber Whisky; (b) in pl. halbe Maßnahme; Halbheit, die (abwertend); **~ 'moon** n. Halbmond, der; **~ 'note** n. (Amer. Mus.) ⇒ **minim; ~ 'pay** n. Ruhegehalt, das; Pension, die; **be on ~ pay** Ruhegehalt od. Pension beziehen; **~penny** /ˈheɪpnɪ/, n. pl. usu. **~pennies** /ˈheɪpnɪz/ for separate coins, **~pence** /ˈheɪpəns/ for sum of money (Brit. Hist.) (coin) Halfpenny, der;

(sum) halber Penny; ~-'**pint** *n.* halbes Pint; ~-'**price 1** *n.* halber Preis; **reduce sth. to** ~-price etw. um die Hälfte heruntersetzen; **2** *adj.* zum halben Preis *nachgestellt;* **3** *adv.* zum halben Preis; ~-**sister** *n.* Halbschwester, *die;* ~-'**term** *n.* (Brit.) **(a) it is nearly** ~-term das Trimester ist fast zur Hälfte vorüber; **by/at** ~-**term** bis zur/in der Mitte des Trimesters; **(b)** (holiday) ~-**term [holiday/ break]** Ferien in der Mitte des Trimesters; **before** ~-term in der ersten Trimesterhälfte; ~-**timbered** / hɑːf'tɪmbəd/ *adj.* Fachwerk‹*haus, -bauweise*›; **be** ~-**timbered** ein Fachwerkbau sein; ~-'**time** *n.* (Sport) Halbzeit, *die; attrib.* |'--| Halbzeit‹*pfiff, -stand*›; **at** ~-**time** bei *od.* bis zur Halbzeit; (during interval) in der Halbzeitpause; ~-**tone** *n.* (Amer. Mus.) ⇒ **semitone;** ~-**truth** *n.* Halbwahrheit, *die;* ~-'**volley** *n.* Halfvolley, *der;* ~'**way 1** *adj.* ~**way point** Mitte, *die;* ~**way house** (compromise) Kompromiss, *der;* Mittelweg, *der;* ~**way line** (Footb.) Mittellinie, *die;* **2** *adv.* die Hälfte des Weges ‹*begleiten, fahren*›; ~**wit** *n.* Schwachkopf, *der;* ~-**witted** /'hɑːfwɪtɪd/ *adj.* dumm; (mentally deficient) debil; schwachsinnig; ~-'**yearly 1** *adj.* halbjährlich; **2** *adv.* halbjährlich; jedes halbe Jahr

halibut /'hælɪbət/ *n., pl.* same (Zool.) Heilbutt, *der*

halitosis /hælɪˈtəʊsɪs/ *n., pl.* **halitoses** /hælɪˈtəʊsiːz/ (Med.) Halitose, *die* (fachspr.); [übler] Mundgeruch

hall /hɔːl/ *n.* **(a)** (large [public] room) Saal, *der;* (public building) Halle, *die;* (for receptions, banquets) Festsaal, *der;* (in medieval house: principal living room) Wohnsaal, *der;* **school/church** ~**:** Aula, *die*/Gemeindehaus, *das;* **(b)** (Univ.) (residential building) ~ **[of residence]** Studentenwohnheim, *das;* **live in** ~**:** im [Studenten]wohnheim wohnen; **(c)** (entrance passage) Diele, *die;* Flur, *der*

'**hallmark 1** *n.* [Feingehalts]stempel, *der;* Repunze, *die;* (fig.: distinctive mark) Kennzeichen, *das;* **be the** ~ **of quality/perfection** (fig.) für Qualität/Vollkommenheit bürgen *od.* stehen. **2** *v.t.* stempeln; repunzieren

hallo /həˈləʊ/ **1** *int.* **(a)** (to call attention) hallo; **(b)** (Brit.) ⇒ **hello 1. 2** *n., pl.* ~**s** Hallo, *das*

hallow /'hæləʊ/ *v.t.* heiligen; ~**ed** geheiligt (auch fig.); heilig ‹*Boden*›

Hallowe'en /hæləʊˈiːn/ *n.* Halloween, *das; Abend vor Allerheiligen;* **on** *or* **at** ~**:** [an] Halloween

hall: ~ '**porter** *n.* (Brit.) [Hotel]portier, *der;* ~ **stand** *n.* [Flur]garderobe, *die*

hallucinate /həˈluːsɪneɪt/ *v.i.* halluzinieren (Med., Psych.); Halluzinationen haben

hallucination /həluːsɪˈneɪʃn/ *n.* (act) Halluzinieren, *das;* (instance, imagined object) Halluzination, *die;* Sinnestäuschung, *die*

hallucinogenic /həluːsɪnəˈdʒenɪk/ *adj.* (Med.) halluzinogen

'**hallway** *n.* **(a)** ⇒ **hall c; (b)** (corridor) Flur, *der;* Korridor, *der*

halo /'heɪləʊ/ *n., pl.* ~**es (a)** (Meteorol.) Halo, *der* (fachspr.); Hof, *der;* **(b)** (around head) Heiligen-, Glorienschein, *der*

halogen /'hælədʒən/ *n.* (Chem.) Halogen, *das;* ~ **lamp** Halogenlampe, *die*

halt /hɒlt, hɔːlt/ **1** *n.* **(a)** (temporary stoppage) Pause, *die;* (on march or journey) Rast, *die;* Pause, *die;* (esp. Mil. also) Halt, *der;* **make a** ~**:** Rast/eine Pause machen/haltmachen; **call a** ~**:** eine Pause machen lassen/haltmachen lassen; **let's call a** ~**:** machen wir eine Pause!; **(b)** (interruption) Unterbrechung, *die;* **(c)** (Brit. Railw.) Haltepunkt, *der.* **2** *v.i.* **(a)** (stop) ‹*Fußgänger, Tier:*› stehen bleiben; ‹*Fahrer:*› anhalten; (for a rest) eine Pause machen; (esp. Mil.) Halt machen; ~**, who goes there?** (Mil.) halt, wer da?; **(b)** (end) eingestellt werden. **3** *v.t.* **(a)** (cause to stop) anhalten; haltmachen lassen ‹*Marschkolonne usw.*›; **(b)** (cause to end) stoppen ‹*Diskussion*›; einstellen ‹*Projekt*›

halter /'hɒltə(r), 'hɔːltə(r)/ *n.* **(a)** (for horse) Halfter, *das;* **(b)** (Dressmaking) (strap) Nackenträger, *der;* ~ **dress/top** Kleid/Oberteil *od.* Top mit Nackenträger

halting /'hɒltɪŋ, 'hɔːltɪŋ/ *adj.* schleppend ‹*Stimme, Redeweise, Fortschritt*›; holprig ‹*Verse*›; zögernd ‹*Antwort*›

halve /hɑːv/ *v.t.* **(a)** (divide) halbieren; **(b)** (reduce) halbieren; auf *od.* um die Hälfte verringern

halves *pl. of* **half**

ham /hæm/ **1** *n.* **(a)** ([meat from] thigh of pig) Schinken, *der;* **(b)** (coll.) (amateur) Amateur, *der;* (poor actor) Schmierenkomödiant, *der* (abwertend). **2** *v.i.,* -**mm**- (coll.) überziehen. **3** *v.t.,* -**mm**- (coll.) überzogen spielen

~ '**up** *v.t.* (coll.) überzogen spielen ‹*Stück*›; ~ **it up** überziehen

hamburger /'hæmbɜːgə(r)/ *n.* (beef cake) Hacksteak, *das;* (filled roll) Hamburger, *der*

ham: ~-**fisted** /hæm'fɪstɪd/, ~-**handed** /hæm 'hændɪd/ *adjs.* (coll.) tollpatschig (ugs.) ‹*Person, Art*›

hamlet /'hæmlɪt/ *n.* Weiler, *der*

hammer /'hæmə(r)/ **1** *n.* **(a)** Hammer, *der;* **go** *or* **be at sth.** ~ **and tongs** sich bei etw. schwer ins Zeug legen (ugs.); **go** *or* **be at it** ~ **and tongs** (quarrel) sich streiten, dass die Fetzen fliegen; **(b)** (of gun) Hahn, *der;* **(c)** (Athletics) [Wurf]hammer, *der;* **[throwing] the** ~ (event) das Hammerwerfen. **2** *v.t.* **(a)** hämmern; (fig.) hämmern auf (*Akk.*) ‹*Tasten, Tisch*›; ~ **a nail into sth.** einen Nagel in etw. (*Akk.*) hämmern *od.* schlagen; ~ **sth. into sb.['s head]** (fig.) jmdm. etw. einhämmern; **(b)** (coll.: inflict heavy defeat on) abservieren (ugs.) ‹*Gegner*›; vernichtend schlagen ‹*Feind*›. **3** *v.i.* hämmern; klopfen; ~ **at sth.** an etw. (*Dat.*) [herum]hämmern

~ **a'way** *v.i.* hämmern; ~ **away at** herumhämmern auf (+ *Dat.*)

~ '**out** *v.t.* **(a)** (make smooth) ausklopfen ‹*Delle, Beule*›; ausbeulen ‹*Kotflügel usw.*›; glatt klopfen ‹*Blech usw.*›; **(b)** (fig.: devise) ausarbeiten ‹*Plan, Methode, Vereinbarung*›

hammock /'hæmək/ *n.* Hängematte, *die*

hamper¹ /'hæmpə(r)/ *n.* **(a)** (basket) [Deckel]korb, *der;* **(b)** (consignment of food) Präsentkorb, *der*

hamper² *v.t.* behindern; hemmen ‹*Entwicklung, Wachstum usw.*›

hamster /'hæmstə(r)/ *n.* Hamster, *der; see also* **golden hamster**

'**hamstring 1** *n.* (Anat.) Kniesehne, *die.* **2** *v.t.,* hamstrung *or* ~**ed** (fig.) lähmen

hand /hænd/ **1** *n.* **(a)** ▶ 672 (Anat., Zool.) Hand, *die;* **eat from** *or* **out of sb.'s** ~ (lit. or fig.) jmdm. aus der Hand fressen; **get one's** ~**s dirty** (lit. or fig.) sich (*Dat.*) die Hände schmutzig machen; **give sb. one's** ~ (reach, shake) jmdm. die Hand geben *od.* reichen; **give** *or* **lend [sb.] a** ~ **[with** *or* **in sth.]** [jmdm.] [bei etw.] helfen; **pass** *or* **go through sb.'s** ~**s** (fig.) durch jmds. Hand *od.* Hände gehen; ~ **in** ~**:** Hand in Hand; **go** ~ **in** ~ **[with sth.]** (fig.) [mit etw.] Hand in Hand gehen; **the problem/matter in** ~**:** das vorliegende Problem/die vorliegende Angelegenheit; **hold** ~**s** Händchen halten (ugs. scherzh.); sich bei den Händen halten; **hold sb.'s** ~**:** jmds. Hand halten; jmdm. die Hand halten; (fig.: give sb. close guidance) jmdn. bei der Hand nehmen; (fig.: give sb. moral support or backing) jmdm. das Händchen halten (iron.); ~**s off!** Hände *od.* Finger weg!; **take/keep one's** ~**s off sb./sth.** jmdn./etw. loslassen/nicht anfassen; **keep one's** ~**s off sth.** (fig.) die Finger von etw. lassen (ugs.); ~**s up [all those in favour]** wer dafür ist, hebt die Hand!; ~**s up!** (as sign of surrender) Hände hoch!; ~**s down** (fig.) (easily) mit links (ugs.); (without a doubt, by a large margin) ganz klar (ugs.); **turn one's** ~ **to sth.** sich einer Sache (*Dat.*) zuwenden; **have sth. at** ~**:** etw. zur Hand haben; **have sb. at** ~**:** jmdn. bei sich haben; **be at** ~ (be nearby) in der Nähe sein; (be about to happen) unmittelbar bevorstehen; **out of** ~ (summarily) kurzerhand; **be** ~ (be readily available, within reach) zur Hand sein; (be received) ‹*Brief, Notiz, Anweisung:*› vorliegen; **fight** ~ **to** ~**:** Mann gegen Mann kämpfen; **go/pass from** ~ **to** ~**:** von Hand zu Hand gehen; **live from** ~ **to mouth** von der Hand in den Mund leben; **be** ~ **in glove [with]** unter einer Decke stecken [mit]; **wait on sb.** ~ **and foot** (fig.) jmdm. vorne und hinten bedienen (ugs.); **have one's** ~**s full** die Hände voll haben; (fig.: be fully occupied) alle Hände voll zu tun haben (ugs.); ~ **on heart** (fig.) Hand aufs Herz; **get one's** ~**s on sb./sth.** jmdn. erwischen *od.* (ugs.) in die Finger kriegen/ etw. auftreiben; **lay** *or* **put one's** ~ **on sth.** etw. finden; **by** ~ (manually) mit der *od.* von Hand; (in handwriting) handschriftlich; (by messenger) durch Boten; **be made by** ~**:** Handarbeit sein; **I could do that with one** ~ **tied**

behind my back das mache ich doch mit links (ugs.); **(b)** (fig.: authority) **with a firm/iron** ~: mit starker Hand/eiserner Faust ‹*regieren*›; **he needs a father's** ~: er braucht die väterliche Hand; **get out of** ~: außer Kontrolle geraten; *see also* **take 1 f**; **upper 1 a**; **give sb. a free** ~: jmdm. freie Hand lassen; **have a free** ~ **to do sth.** freie Hand haben, etw. zu tun; **(c)** *in pl.* (custody) **in sb.'s** ~s, **in the** ~s **of sb.** (in sb.'s possession) in jmds. Besitz; (in sb.'s care) in jmds. Obhut; **may I leave the matter in your** ~s? darf ich die Angelegenheit Ihnen überlassen?; **fall into sb.'s** ~s ‹*Person, Geld:*› jmdm. in die Hände fallen; **have [got] sth./sb. on one's** ~s sich um etw./jmdn. kümmern müssen; **he's got such a lot/enough on his** ~s **at the moment** er hat augenblicklich so viel/genug um die Ohren (ugs.); **have time on one's** ~s [viel] Zeit haben; (too much) mit seiner Zeit nichts anzufangen wissen; **take sb./sth. off sb.'s** ~s jmdm. jmdn./etw. abnehmen; **change** ~s den Besitzer wechseln; **(d)** (disposal) **have sth. in** ~: etw. zur Verfügung haben; (not used up) etw. [übrig] haben; **keep in** ~: in Reserve halten ‹*Geld*›; **have on** ~: dahaben; **be on** ~: da sein; **(e)** (share) **have a** ~ **in sth.** bei etw. seine Hände im Spiel haben; **take a** ~ **[in sth.]** sich [an etw. *(Dat.)*] beteiligen; **(f)** (agency) Wirken, *das* (geh.); **the** ~ **of a craftsman has been at work here** hier war ein Fachmann am Werk; **the** ~ **of God** die Hand Gottes; **suffer/seek injustice at the** ~s **of sb.** unter jmdm./jmds. Ungerechtigkeit zu leiden haben; **(g)** (pledge of marriage) **ask for** *or* **seek sb.'s** ~ **[in marriage]** um jmds. Hand bitten *od.* (geh.) anhalten; **(h)** (worker) Arbeitskraft, *die;* Arbeiter, *der;* (Naut.: seaman) Hand, *die* (fachspr.); Matrose, *der;* **the ship sank with all** ~s das Schiff sank mit der gesamten Mannschaft; **(i)** (person having ability) **be a good/poor** ~ **at tennis** ein guter/ schwacher Tennisspieler sein; **I'm no** ~ **at painting** ich kann nicht malen; **(j)** (source) Quelle, *die;* **at first/second/third** ~: aus erster/zweiter/dritter Hand; *see also* **first-hand**; **second-hand**; **(k)** (skill) Geschick, *das;* **get one's** ~ **in** wieder in Übung kommen *od.* (ugs.) reinkommen; **keep one's** ~ **in** in der Übung bleiben; **(l)** (style of ~writing) Handschrift, *die;* (signature) Unterschrift, *die;* **(m)** (of clock or watch) Zeiger, *der;* **(n)** (side) Seite, *die;* **on the right/left** ~: rechts/links; rechter/linker Hand; **on sb.'s right/left** ~: rechts/links von jmdm.; zu jmds. Rechten/Linken; **on every** ~ von allen Seiten ‹*umringt sein*›; ringsum ‹*etw. sehen*›; **on the one** ~ ..., **[but] on the other [**~**]** ...: einerseits ..., andererseits ...; auf der einen Seite ..., auf der anderen Seite ...; **(o)** (measurement) Handbreit, *die;* **(p)** (coll.: applause) Beifall, *der;* Applaus, *der;* **give him a big** ~, **let's have a big** ~ **for him** viel Applaus *od.* Beifall für ihn!; **(q)** (cards) Karte, *die;* (period of play) Runde, *die; see also* **throw in d. 2** *v.t.* geben; ‹*Überbringer:*› übergeben ‹*Sendung, Lieferung*›; ~ **sth. from one to another** etw. von einem zum anderen weitergeben; ~ **sth. [a]round** (pass round, circulate) etw. herumgeben; (among group) etw. herumgehen lassen; **you've got to** ~ **it to them/her** *etc.* (fig. coll.) das muss man ihnen/ihr *usw.* lassen

~ **'back** *v.t.* (return) zurückgeben

~ **'down** *v.t.* **(a)** (pass on) überliefern ‹*Geschichte, Tradition*›; weitergeben ‹*Gegenstand*› **(to** an + *Akk.*); [weiter]vererben ‹*Erbstück*› **(to** an + *Akk.*); **(b)** (Law) verhängen ‹*Strafe*› **(to** über + *Akk.*); fällen ‹*Entscheidung*›; verkünden ‹*Urteil*›

~ **'in** *v.t.* abgeben ‹*Klausur, Arbeit, Aufsatz*› **(to, at** bei); einreichen ‹*Petition, Bewerbung*› **(to, at** bei)

~ **'on** *v.t.* weitergeben **(to** an + *Akk.*)

~ **'out** *v.t.* aus-, verteilen **(to** an + *Akk.*, **among** unter + *Dat.*); geben ‹*Ratschläge, Tips, Winke*› **(to** an + *Akk.*)

~ **'over** *v.t.* **(a)** (deliver) übergeben **(to** *Dat.*); freilassen ‹*Geisel*›; ~ **over your guns/money!** Waffen/Geld her!; **(b)** (transfer) übergeben *od.* -reichen **(to** *Dat.*); (pass) herüber- *od.* rübergeben *od.* -reichen **(to** *Dat.*); (allow to have) abgeben. **2** *v.i.* (to next speaker/one's successor) das Wort/die Arbeit übergeben **(to** an + *Akk.*)

hand- *in comb.* **(a)** (operated by hand, held in the hand) Hand-; **(b)** (done by hand) hand‹*gestickt*›; mit der Hand *od.* von Hand ‹*glasiert, verziert, gebacken*›

hand: ~**bag** *n.* Handtasche, *die;* ~ **baggage** *n.* Handgepäck, *das;* ~**bill** *n.* Handzettel, *der;* ~**book** *n.* Handbuch, *das;* (guidebook) Führer, *der;* ~**brake** *n.* Handbremse, *die;* ~**cart** *n.* Handwagen, *der;* ~**clap** *n.* **(a)** (single clap) In-die-Hände-Klatschen, *das;* **give three** ~**claps** dreimal in die Hände klatschen; **(b)** (applause) [Hände]klatschen, *das;* ~ **cream** *n.* Handcreme, *die;* ~**cuff 1** *n., usu. in pl.* Handschelle, *die;* **2** *v.t.* in Handschellen *(Akk.)* legen ‹*Hände*›; ~**cuff sb.** jmdm. Handschellen anlegen

handful /'hændfʊl/ *n.* **(a)** **a few** ~s **of nuts** ein paar Hand voll Nüsse; **(b)** (fig. coll.: troublesome person[s] or thing[s]) **these children are/this dog is a real** ~: die Kinder halten/der Hund hält einen ständig auf Trab (ugs.)

hand: ~ **grenade** *n.* Handgranate, *die;* ~**gun** *n.* Faustfeuerwaffe, *die;* ~**hold** *n.* Halt, *der;* **provide** ~**holds/a** ~**hold for sb.** jmdm. Halt bieten

handicap /'hændɪkæp/ **1** *n.* **(a)** (Sport: advantage) Handikap, *das* (fachspr.); Vorgabe, *die;* **(b)** (race, competition) Handikaprennen, *das;* Ausgleichsrennen, *das;* **(c)** (fig.: hindrance) Handikap, *das;* **have a mental/physical** ~: geistig behindert/körperbehindert sein. **2** *v.t.*, **-pp-: (a)** (Sport: impose a ~ on) mit einem Handikap festlegen für; **(b)** (fig.: put at a disadvantage) benachteiligen; handikapen (ugs.)

handicapped /'hændɪkæpt/ **1** *adj.* behindert; **mentally/physically** ~: geistig behindert/körperbehindert. **2** *n. pl.* **the [mentally/physically]** ~: die [geistig/körperlich] Behinderten

handicraft /'hændɪkrɑːft/ *n.* [Kunst]handwerk, *das;* (knitting, weaving, needlework) Handarbeit, *die*

handily /'hændɪlɪ/ *adv.* praktisch; günstig ‹*gelegen*›

handiwork /'hændɪwɜːk/ *n., no pl., no indef. art.* **(a)** (working) handwerkliche Arbeit; **(b)** **this ring is all my own** ~: diesen Ring habe ich selbst gemacht; **whose** ~ **is this?** (derog.) wer hat das [denn] verbrochen? (ugs.)

handkerchief /'hæŋkətʃɪf, 'hæŋkətʃiːf/ *n., pl.* ~**s** *or* **handkerchieves** /'hæŋkətʃiːvz/ Taschentuch, *das*

handle /'hændl/ **1** *n.* **(a)** (part held) [Hand]griff, *der;* (of bag etc.) [Trag]griff, *der;* (of knife, chisel) Heft, *das;* Griff, *der;* (of axe, brush, comb, broom, saucepan) Stiel, *der;* (of handbag) Bügel, *der;* (of door) Klinke, *die;* (of bucket, watering can, cup, jug) Henkel, *der;* (of pump) Schwengel, *der;* **fly off the** ~ (fig. coll.) an die Decke gehen (ugs.); **(b)** (coll.: title) Titel, *der.* **2** *v.t.* **(a)** (touch, feel) anfassen; **'Fragile! H**~ **with care!'** „Vorsicht! Zerbrechlich!"; **(b)** (deal with) umgehen mit ‹*Person, Tier, Situation*›; führen ‹*Verhandlung*›; erledigen ‹*Korrespondenz, Telefonat usw.*›; (cope with) fertigwerden *od.* zurechtkommen mit ‹*Person, Tier, Situation*›; **(c)** (control) handhaben ‹*Fahrzeug, Flugzeug*›; **(d)** (process, transport) umschlagen ‹*Fracht*›; **Heathrow** ~**s x passengers per year** in Heathrow werden pro Jahr x Passagiere abgefertigt

handlebar /'hændlbɑː(r)/ *n.* Lenkstange, *die;* Lenker, *der;* ~ **moustache** Schnauzbart, *der*

handler /'hændlə(r)/ *n.* **(a)** ▶ 887 (of police dog) Hundeführer, *der/*-führerin, *die;* **(b)** **a** ~ **of stolen goods** ein Hehler

handling /'hændlɪŋ/ *n., no pl.* **(a)** (management) Handhabung, *die;* (of troops, workforce, bargaining, discussion) Führung, *die;* (of situation, class, crowd) Umgang, *der* (of mit); **(b)** (use) Handhabung, *die;* (Motor Veh.) Fahrverhalten, *das;* Handling, *das;* **(c)** (treatment) Behandlung, *die;* **the child needs firm** ~: das Kind braucht eine feste Hand; **(d)** (processing) Beförderung, *die;* (of passengers) Abfertigung, *die*

'handling charge *n.* Bearbeitungsgebühr, *die*

hand: ~ **lotion** *n.* Handlotion, *die;* ~ **luggage** *n.* Handgepäck, *das;* ~**made** *adj.* handgearbeitet; handgeschöpft ‹*Papier*›; ~**me-down** *adj.* abgelegt *od.* gebrauchtes Kleidungsstück **(from** *Gen.*); ~**out** *n.* **(a)** (alms) Almosen, *das;* Gabe, *die;* **(b)** (information) Handout, *das;* (press release) Presseerklärung, *die;* ~**over** *n.* Übergabe, *die;* ~**painted** *adj.* handbemalt ‹*Gegenstand*›; handgemalt ‹*Muster, Bild*›; ~**'picked** *adj.* sorgfältig ausgewählt; handverlesen (ugs. scherzh.); ~**rail** *n.* Geländer, *das;* Handlauf, *der* (Bauw.); (on ship) Handläufer, *der;* ~**set** *n.*

(Teleph.) Handapparat, *der;* ~**shake** *n.* Händedruck, *der;* Handschlag, *der*

hands: ~'**off** *adj.* have a ~-**off** approach sich heraushalten (**to** aus); **be a** ~-**off manager** seinen Mitarbeitern freie Hand lassen; ~-'**on** *adj.* (**a**) praxisbezogen, praxisnahe ⟨*Ausbildung, Lernen*⟩; praktisch ⟨*Erfahrung, Kurs*⟩; **learn sth. through a** ~-**on approach** etw. durch Praxis lernen; (**b**) **have a** ~-**on approach to sth.** etw. tatkräftig angehen; **be a** ~-**on manager** ein tatkräftiger Manager sein

handsome /'hænsəm/ *adj.*, ~**r** /'hænsəmə(r)/, ~**st** /'hænsəmɪst/ (**a**) (good-looking) gut aussehend ⟨*Mann, Frau*⟩; schön, edel ⟨*Tier, Möbel*⟩; (**b**) (generous) großzügig ⟨*Geschenk, Belohnung, Mitgift*⟩; nobel ⟨*Behandlung, Verhalten, Empfang*⟩; (considerable) stattlich, ansehnlich ⟨*Vermögen, Summe, Preis*⟩

handsomely /'hænsəmlɪ/ *adv.* großzügig; mit großem Vorsprung ⟨*gewinnen*⟩

hand: ~**spring** *n.* Handstandüberschlag, *der;* ~**stand** *n.* Handstand, *der;* ~-**to**-~ *adj.* ~-**to**-~ **combat** ein Kampf Mann gegen Mann; ~-**to-mouth** *adj.* kärglich, kümmerlich ⟨*Leben, Dasein*⟩; **eke out/lead a** ~-**to-mouth life/existence** von der Hand in den Mund leben; ~ **towel** *n.* [Hände]handtuch, *das;* ~**writing** *n.* [Hand]schrift, *die;* ~'**written** *adj.* handgeschrieben

handy /'hændɪ/ *adj.* (**a**) (ready to hand) griffbereit; **keep/have sth.** ~: etw. griffbereit haben; **the house is very** ~ **for the town centre** von dem Haus aus ist man sehr schnell in der Stadt; (**b**) (useful) praktisch; nützlich; **come in** ~: sich als nützlich erweisen; **that'll come in** ~! das kann ich gebrauchen!; (**c**) (adroit) geschickt; **be [quite/very]** ~ **with sth.** [ganz gut/sehr gut] mit etw. umgehen können

'**handyman** *n.* Handwerker, *der;* [**home**] ~: Heimwerker, *der*

hang /hæŋ/ **1** *v.t.,* **hung** /hʌŋ/ (*see also* **e**): (**a**) (support from above) hängen; aufhängen ⟨*Gardinen*⟩; ~ **sth. from sth.** etw. an etw. (*Dat.*) aufhängen; (**b**) (place on wall) aufhängen ⟨*Bild, Gemälde, Zeichnung*⟩; (**c**) (paste up) ankleben ⟨*Tapete*⟩; (**d**) (Cookery) abhängen lassen ⟨*Fleisch, Wild*⟩; (**e**) *p.t., p.p.* **hanged** (execute) hängen, *usw.*) aufhängen (**for** wegen); ~ **oneself** sich erhängen *od.* (ugs.) aufhängen; **I'll be** *or* **I am** ~**ed if** … (fig.) der Henker soll mich holen, wenn …; ~ **the expense!** die Kosten interessieren mich nicht; (**f**) (let droop) ~ **one's head in shame** beschämt den Kopf senken. **2** *v.i.,* **hung** (**a**) (be supported from above) hängen; ⟨*Kleid usw.*⟩ fallen; ~ **from the ceiling** an der Decke hängen; ~ **by a rope** an einem Strick hängen; ~ **in there!** (coll.) halte durch!; **time** ~**s heavily** *or* **heavy on sb.** die Zeit wird jmdm. lang; (**b**) (be executed) hängen; (**c**) (droop) **the dog's ears and tail hung** [**down**] der Hund ließ die Ohren und den Schwanz hängen; **his head hung** er hielt den Kopf gesenkt. **3** *n., no pl.* **get the** ~ **of** (fig. coll.: get the knack of, understand) klarkommen mit (ugs.) ⟨*Gerät, Arbeit*⟩; **you'll soon get the** ~ **of it/doing it** du wirst den Bogen bald raushaben (ugs.)/wirst bald raushaben, wie man es macht

~ **about** (Brit.), ~ **around 1** /-'-/ *v.i.* (loiter about) herumlungern (salopp); **we** ~ **about** *or* **around there all evening** wir hängen da den ganzen Abend rum (ugs.). **2** /'---/ *v.t.* herumlungern an/in/*usw.* (+ *Dat.*) (salopp)

~ '**back** *v.i.* (**a**) (be reluctant) sich zieren; (**b**) (keep to the rear) zurückbleiben

~ **on 1** /-'-/ *v.i.* (**a**) (hold fast) sich festhalten; ~ **on to** (lit.: grasp) sich festhalten an (+ *Dat.*) ⟨*Gegenstand*⟩; (fig. coll.: retain) behalten ⟨*Eigentum, Stellung*⟩; (**b**) (stand firm, survive) durchhalten; (**c**) (coll.: wait) warten; ~ **on** [**a minute**]! Moment *od.* (ugs.) Sekunde mal!; (**d**) (coll.: not ring off) dranbleiben (ugs.). **2** /'--/ *v.t.* ~ **on sth.** (fig.) von etw. abhängen; ~ **on sb.'s words** jmdm. gespannt zuhören

~ '**out 1** *v.t.* (**a**) aufhängen ⟨*Wäsche*⟩; (**b**) heraushängen lassen ⟨*Zunge, Tentakel*⟩. **2** *v.i.* (**a**) (protrude) heraushängen; **let it all** ~ **out** (fig. sl.) die Sau rauslassen (ugs.); (**b**) (sl.) (reside) wohnen; seine Bude haben (ugs.); (be often present) sich herumtreiben (ugs.)

~ **to'gether** *v.i.* (**a**) (be coherent) ⟨*Teile eines Ganzen*⟩ sich zusammenfügen; ⟨*Aussagen*⟩ zusammenstimmen; (**b**) (be or remain associated) zusammenhalten

~ '**up 1** *v.t.* (**a**) aufhängen; ~ **up sth. on a hook** etw. an einen Haken hängen; (**b**) (coll.) **be hung up about sth.** ein gestörtes Verhältnis zu etw. haben. **2** *v.i.* (Teleph.) einhängen; auflegen; ~ **up on sb.** einfach einhängen *od.* auflegen

hangar /'hæŋə(r), 'hæŋgə(r)/ *n.* Hangar, *der;* Flugzeughalle, *die*

'**hangdog** *adj.* zerknirscht

hanger /'hæŋə(r)/ *n.* (**a**) (for clothes) Bügel, *der;* (**b**) (loop on clothes etc.) Aufhänger, *der*

hanger-'on *n.* **there are many hangers-on in every political party** in jeder politischen Partei gibt es viele, denen es nur um den persönlichen Vorteil geht; **the rock group with its usual** [**crowd of**] **hangers-on** die Rockgruppe mit ihrem üblichen Anhang

hang: ~-**glider** *n.* Hängegleiter, *der;* Drachen, *der;* ~-**glider pilot** Drachenflieger, *der*/-fliegerin, *die;* ~-**gliding** *n.* Drachenfliegen, *das*

hanging /'hæŋɪŋ/ **1** *n.* (**a**) ⇒ **hang 1:** [Auf]hängen, *das;* Ankleben, *das;* Abhängen, *das;* (**b**) (execution) Hinrichtung [durch den Strang]; (**c**) *in pl.* (drapery) Behang, *der.* **2** *adj.* ~ **basket** Hängekorb, *der*

hang: ~**man** /'hæŋmən/ *n., pl.* ~**men** /'hæŋmən/ Henker, *der;* ~**over** *n.* (**a**) (after-effects) Kater, *der* (ugs.); (**b**) (remainder) Relikt, *das;* ~-**up** *n.* (coll.) (**a**) (inhibition) Macke, *die* (ugs.); **have a** ~-**up about sth.** ein gestörtes Verhältnis zu etw. haben; (**b**) (fixation) Komplex, *der* (**about** wegen)

hank /hæŋk/ *n.* Strang, *der*

hanker /'hæŋkə(r)/ *v.i.* ~ **after** *or* **for** ein [heftiges] Verlangen haben nach ⟨*Person, etwas Neuem, Zigarette*⟩; sich (*Dat.*) sehnlichst wünschen ⟨*Gelegenheit*⟩

hankering /'hæŋkərɪŋ/ *n.* (craving) Verlangen, *das* (**after, for** nach); (longing) Sehnsucht, *die* (**after, for** nach)

hanky /'hæŋkɪ/ *n.* (coll.) Taschentuch, *das*

hanky-panky /hæŋkɪ'pæŋkɪ/ *n., no pl., no indef. art.* (coll.) Mauschelei, *die* (abwertend); **there's been some** ~: es ist gemauschelt worden (ugs. abwertend)

Hanover /'hænəʊvə(r)/ *pr. n.* **▶ 1159** Hannover (*das*)

Hansard /'hænsɑːd/ *n.* Hansard, *der; die britischen Parlamentsberichte*

Hanseatic /hænsɪ'ætɪk/ *adj.* (Hist.) hansisch; ~ **town** Hansestadt, *die;* **the** ~ **League** der Hansebund

haphazard /hæp'hæzəd/ **1** *adj.* willkürlich ⟨*Auswahl*⟩; unbedacht ⟨*Bemerkung*⟩; **the whole thing was rather** ~: das Ganze geschah ziemlich planlos. **2** *adv.* (at random) willkürlich; wahllos

haphazardly /hæp'hæzədlɪ/ *adv.* willkürlich; wahllos

happen /'hæpn/ *v.i.* (**a**) (occur) geschehen; ⟨*Vorhergesagtes:*⟩ eintreffen; **these things** [**do**] ~: das kommt vor; **what's** ~**ing?** was ist los?; **what's** ~**ing this evening?** was ist für heute Abend geplant?; **I can't** *or* **don't see** '**that** ~**ing** das kann ich mir nicht vorstellen; **nothing ever** ~**s here** hier ist nichts los; **don't let it** ~ **again!** dass mir das nicht wieder vorkommt!; **that's what** ~**s!** das kommt davon!; ~ **to sb.** jmdm. passieren; **what has** ~**ed to him/her arm?** was ist mit ihm/ihrem Arm?; **what can have** ~**ed to him?** was mag mit ihm los sein?; **it all** ~**ed so quickly that** …: es ging alles so schnell, dass …; **it's all** ~**ing** (coll.) es ist was los (ugs.); (**b**) (chance) ~ **to do sth.** zufällig etw. tun; **it so** ~**s** *or* **as it** ~**s I have** …: zufällig habe ich *od.* ich habe zufällig …; **how does it** ~ **that** …? wie kommt es, dass …?; **do you** ~ **to know him?** kennen Sie ihn zufällig?

~ [**up**]**on** *v.t.* zufällig treffen ⟨*Person*⟩; zufällig finden ⟨*Arbeit, Gegenstand*⟩

happening /'hæpnɪŋ/ *n.* (**a**) *usu. in pl.* (event) Ereignis, *das;* **a regrettable** ~: ein bedauerlicher Vorfall; (**b**) (improvised performance) Happening, *das*

happily /'hæpɪlɪ/ *adv.* (**a**) glücklich ⟨*lächeln*⟩; fröhlich, vergnügt ⟨*spielen, lachen*⟩; (**b**) (gladly) mit Vergnügen; (**c**) (aptly) gut; treffend, passend ⟨*ausdrücken, formulieren*⟩; (**d**) (fortunately) glücklicherweise; zum Glück; **it ended** ~: es ging gut aus

happiness /'hæpɪnɪs/ *n., no pl.* ⇨ **happy a:** Glück, *das;* Heiterkeit, *die;* Zufriedenheit, *die*

happy /'hæpɪ/ *adj.* ▸ 836⌋ (a) (joyful) glücklich; heiter ⟨*Bild, Veranlagung, Ton*⟩; (contented) zufrieden; (causing joy) erfreulich ⟨*Gedanke, Erinnerung, Szene*⟩; froh ⟨*Ereignis*⟩; glücklich ⟨*Zeiten*⟩; **I'm not** ∼ **with her work** ich bin mit ihrer Arbeit nicht zufrieden; **not be** ∼ **about sth./ doing sth.** nicht froh über etw. (*Akk.*) sein/etw. nicht gern tun; ∼ **event** (euphem.: birth) freudiges Ereignis (verhüll.); a ∼ **medium** der goldene Mittelweg; **strike a** ∼ **medium** den goldenen Mittelweg wählen; **(b)** (glad) **be** ∼ **to do sth.** etw. gern *od.* mit Vergnügen tun; **yes, I'd be** ∼ **to** (as reply to request) ja, gern *od.* mit Vergnügen; **(c)** (lucky) glücklich; **by a** ∼ **chance/coincidence** durch einen glücklichen Zufall

happy: ∼ **'ending** *n.* Happyend, *das;* ∼**-go-'lucky** *adj.* sorglos; unbekümmert

harangue /hə'ræŋ/ **1** *n.* Tirade, *die* (abwertend). **2** *v.t.* eine Ansprache halten an (+ *Akk.*)

harass /'hærəs/ *v.t.* schikanieren; **constantly** ∼ **the enemy** den Feind nicht zur Ruhe kommen lassen; ∼ **sb. into doing sth.** jmdm. so sehr zusetzen, dass er etw. tut

harassed /'hærəst/ *adj.* geplagt **(with** von); gequält ⟨*Blick, Ausdruck*⟩

harassment /'hærəsmənt/ *n.* Schikanierung, *die;* **sexual** ∼**:** [sexuelle] Belästigung

harbour (*Brit.; Amer.:* **harbor**) /'hɑːbə(r)/ **1** *n.* Hafen, *der;* **in** ∼**:** im Hafen. **2** *v.t.* Unterschlupf gewähren (+ *Dat.*) ⟨*Verbrecher, Flüchtling*⟩; (fig.) hegen (geh.) ⟨*Groll, Verdacht*⟩

hard /hɑːd/ **1** *adj.* **(a)** hart; stark, heftig ⟨*Regen*⟩; gesichert ⟨*Beweis, Zahlen, Daten, Information*⟩; **drive a** ∼ **bargain** hart verhandeln; **(b)** (difficult) schwer; schwierig; **this is** ∼ **to believe** das ist kaum zu glauben; **it is** ∼ **to do sth.** es ist schwer, etw. zu tun; **make it** ∼ **for sb.** [**to do sth.**] es jmdm. schwer machen[, etw. zu tun]; **[choose to] go about/do sth. the** ∼ **way** es sich (*Dat.*) bei etw. unnötig schwer machen; **learn sth. the** ∼ **way** etw. durch schlechte Erfahrungen lernen; **be** ∼ **of hearing** schwerhörig sein; **be** ∼ **going** ⟨*Buch:*⟩ sich schwer lesen; ⟨*Arbeit:*⟩ anstrengend sein; **play** ∼ **to get** (coll.) so tun, als sei man nicht interessiert; **have a** ∼ **time doing sth.** Schwierigkeiten haben, etw. zu tun; **it's a** ∼ **life** (joc.) das Leben ist schwer; **it is [a bit]** ∼ **on him** es ist [schon] schlimm für ihn; ∼ **luck** (coll.) Pech; **(c)** (strenuous) hart; beschwerlich ⟨*Reise*⟩; leidenschaftlich ⟨*Spieler*⟩; **be a** ∼ **drinker** viel trinken; **try one's** ∼**est to do sth.** sich nach Kräften bemühen, etw. zu tun; **(d)** (vigorous) heftig ⟨*Angriff, Schlag*⟩; kräftig ⟨*Schlag, Stoß, Tritt*⟩; (severe) streng ⟨*Winter*⟩; **(e)** (unfeeling) hart; **be** ∼ **[up]on sb.** streng mit jmdm. sein; **take a** ∼ **line [with sb. on sth.]** [in Bezug auf etw. (*Akk.*)] eine harte Linie [gegenüber jmdm.] vertreten. **2** *adv.* **(a)** (strenuously) hart ⟨*arbeiten, trainieren*⟩; fleißig ⟨*lernen, studieren, üben*⟩; genau ⟨*überlegen, beobachten*⟩; scharf ⟨*nachdenken*⟩; gut ⟨*aufpassen, zuhören, sich festhalten*⟩; konzentriere ∼/**er** sich sehr/ mehr konzentrieren; **try** ∼**:** sich sehr bemühen; **be** ∼ **at work on sth.** an etw. (*Dat.*) intensiv *od.* konzentriert arbeiten; **be** ∼ '**at it** schwer arbeiten; **(b)** (vigorously) heftig; fest ⟨*schlagen, drücken, klopfen*⟩; **(c)** (severely, drastically) hart; streng ⟨*zensieren*⟩; **cut back** ∼ **on sth.** etw. drastisch einschränken; **be** ∼ **up** knapp bei Kasse sein (ugs.); **(d) be** ∼ **put to it [to do sth.]** große Schwierigkeiten haben[, etw. zu tun]; **(e)** hart ⟨*kochen*⟩; fest ⟨*gefrieren [lassen]*⟩; **set** ∼**:** fest werden

hard: ∼ **and 'fast** ⇨ **fast²** 1 a; ∼**back** (Printing) **1** *n.* gebundene Ausgabe; **in** ∼**back** gebunden; mit festem Einband; **2** *adj.* gebunden; ∼**bitten** *adj.* hartgesotten; abgebrüht (ugs.) ⟨*Veteran, Journalist, Karrieremacher*⟩; ∼**board** *n.* Hartfaserplatte, *die;* ∼**-boiled** *adj.* **(a)** (boiled solid) hart gekocht; **(b)** (fig.) (shrewd) ausgekocht (ugs.); (tough) hartgesotten; ∼ **'cash** *n.* **(a)** (coins) Hartgeld, *das;* **(b)** (actual money) Bargeld, *das;* **in** ∼ **cash** in bar ⟨*bezahlen*⟩; ∼ **'copy** *n.* (Computing) Hardcopy, *die;* Ausdruck, *der;* ∼ **core** *n.* **(a)** /-'-/ (nucleus) harter Kern; (of a problem) Kern, *der;* **(b)** /'--/ (Brit.: material) Packlage, *die* (Bauw.); ∼**-core** *attrib. adj.* hart ⟨*Pornographie*⟩; zum harten

Kern gehörend ⟨*Terrorist*⟩; ∼ **'court** *n.* (Tennis) Hartplatz, *der;* ∼ **'currency** *n.* (Econ.) harte Währung; ∼**-drinking** *attrib. adj.* ⟨*Mann/Frau,*⟩ der/die viel [Alkohol] trinkt; ∼ **drug** *n.* harte Droge; ∼**-earned** *adj.* schwer verdient

harden /'hɑːdn/ **1** *v.t.* **(a)** (make hard) härten; **(b)** (fig.: reinforce) ∼ **sb.'s attitude/conviction** jmdn. in seiner Haltung/Überzeugung bestärken; **(c)** (make robust) abhärten **(to** gegen); **(d)** (make tough) unempfindlich machen **(to** gegen); ∼ **sb./oneself to sth.** jmdn./sich gegenüber etw. hart machen; **he** ∼**ed his heart against her** er verhärtete sich gegen sie. **2** *v.i.* **(a)** (become hard) hart werden; **(b)** (become confirmed) sich verhärten; **(c)** (become severe) ⟨*Gesicht:*⟩ einen harten Ausdruck annehmen; ⟨*Gesichtsausdruck:*⟩ hart werden

hardened /'hɑːdnd/ *adj.* **(a)** verhärtet ⟨*Arterie*⟩; **(b)** (grown tough) abgehärtet, unempfindlich **(to, against** gegen); hartgesotten ⟨*Verbrecher, Krieger*⟩; **be/become** ∼ **to sth.** gegen etw. unempfindlich sein/werden

hardening /'hɑːdnɪŋ/ *n.* **(a)** (of steel) Härten, *das;* **(b)** (of arteries) Verhärtung, *die*

hard: ∼**-featured** *adj.* ⟨*Person*⟩ mit harten Gesichtszügen; ∼ **'feelings** *n. pl.* (coll.) **no** ∼ **feelings** schon gut; ∼**-fought** *adj.* heftig ⟨*Kampf*⟩; hart ⟨*Spiel*⟩; ∼**-headed** *adj.* sachlich; nüchtern; ∼**-hearted** /hɑːd'hɑːtɪd/ *adj.* hartherzig **(towards** gegenüber); ∼**- 'hitting** *adj.* schlagkräftig; (fig.) aggressiv ⟨*Rede, Politik, Kritik*⟩; ∼ **'labour** *n.* Zwangsarbeit, *die;* ∼**line** *adj.* kompromisslos; ∼**liner** *n.* Befürworter einer harten Linie **(on** gegenüber); ∼**-'luck story** *n.* Leidensgeschichte, *die*

hardly /'hɑːdlɪ/ *adv.* kaum; **he can** ∼ **have arrived yet** er kann kaum jetzt schon angekommen sein; ∼ **anyone** *or* **anybody/anything** kaum jemand/etwas; ∼ **any wine/ beds** kaum Wein/Betten; ∼ **ever** so gut wie nie; ∼ **at all** fast überhaupt nicht

hardness /'hɑːdnɪs/ *n., no pl.* Härte, *die;* (of blow) Heftigkeit, *die;* (of person) Strenge, *die*

hard: ∼**-nosed** /'hɑːdnəʊzd/ *adj.* (coll.) abgebrüht; ∼**- 'pressed** *adj.* hart bedrängt; **be** ∼**-pressed** große Schwierigkeiten haben; ∼ **sell** *n.* aggressive Verkaufsmethoden; *attrib.* aggressiv ⟨*Werbung,* [*Verkaufs*]*methode*⟩

hardship /'hɑːdʃɪp/ *n.* **(a)** *no pl., no indef. art.* Not, *die;* Elend, *das;* **(b)** (instance) Notlage, *die;* ∼**s** Not, *die;* **(c)** (sth. causing suffering) Unannehmlichkeit, *die*

hard: ∼ **'shoulder** *n.* Standspur, *die;* ∼ **'standing** *n., no pl., no indef. art.* befestigte Abstellfläche; ∼**ware** *n., no pl., no indef. art.* **(a)** (goods) Eisenwaren *Pl.;* (for domestic use also) Haushaltswaren *Pl.; attrib.* Eisen-/ Haushaltswaren⟨*geschäft*⟩; **(b)** (Computing) Hardware, *die;* ∼**-wearing** *adj.* strapazierfähig; ∼**wood** *n.* Hartholz, *das; attrib.* Hartholz-; ∼ **'words** *n. pl.* (angry) harte Worte; ∼**-working** *adj.* fleißig ⟨*Person*⟩

hardy /'hɑːdɪ/ *adj.* **(a)** (robust) abgehärtet; zäh, robust ⟨*Rasse*⟩; **(b)** (Hort.) winterhart

hardy: ∼ **'annual** *n.* (Hort.) winterharte einjährige Pflanze; ∼ **per'ennial** *n.* **(a)** (Hort.) winterharte mehrjährige Pflanze; **(b)** (fig. joc.) Dauerbrenner, *der* (ugs.)

hare /heə(r)/ **1** *n.* Hase, *der;* **[as] mad as a March** ∼ (fig.) völlig verrückt (ugs.). **2** *v.i.* sausen (ugs.); **go haring about** herumsausen (ugs.)

hare: ∼**-brained** /'heəbreɪnd/ *adj.* unüberlegt; ∼**'lip** *n.* Hasenscharte, *die*

harem /'hɑːriːm/ *n.* Harem, *der*

hark /hɑːk/ *v.i.* **(a)** (arch.: listen) ∼**!** horch!/horcht!; **(b)** (coll.) **just** ∼ **at him!** hör ihn dir/hört ihn euch nur an!

∼ **'back** *v.i.* ∼ **back to** (come back to) zurückkommen auf (+ *Akk.*); zurückgreifen auf (+ *Akk.*) ⟨*Tradition*⟩; wieder anfangen von ⟨*alten Zeiten*⟩; (go back to) ⟨*Idee, Brauch:*⟩ zurückgehen auf (+ *Akk.*)

harm /hɑːm/ **1** *n.* Schaden, *der;* **do** ∼**:** Schaden anrichten; **do** ∼ **to sb., do sb.** ∼**:** jmdm. schaden; (injure) jmdn. verletzen; **it won't do you any** ∼ (iron.) es würde dir nichts schaden; **do** ∼ **to sth.** einer Sache (*Dat.*) schaden; **sb./sth. comes to no** ∼**:** jmdm./einer Sache passiert nichts; **there is no ~ done** nichts ist passiert; **there's no ~ in doing sth.**, it will do no ~ to do sth. (could be of benefit) es kann nicht schaden, etw. zu tun; **there's no ~ in asking** Fragen kostet nichts; **it will do more ~ than good** es wird mehr schaden als nützen; **where's *or* what's the ~ in it?** was ist denn schon dabei?; **keep out of ~'s way** der Gefahr fernbleiben; von der Gefahr fernhalten ⟨*Person*⟩. **2** *v.t.* etwas [zuleide] tun (+ *Dat.*); schaden (+ *Dat.*) ⟨*Beziehungen, Land, Karriere, Ruf*⟩

harmful /'hɑːmfl/ *adj.* schädlich (**to** für); schlecht ⟨*Angewohnheit*⟩

harmless /'hɑːmlɪs/ *adj.* harmlos; **make *or* render ~:** unschädlich machen; entschärfen ⟨*Bombe*⟩

harmonica /hɑːˈmɒnɪkə/ *n.* (Mus.) Mundharmonika, *die*

harmonious /hɑːˈməʊnɪəs/ *adj., adv.* harmonisch

harmonise ⇒ **harmonize**

harmonium /hɑːˈməʊnɪəm/ *n.* (Mus.) Harmonium, *das*

harmonize /'hɑːmənaɪz/ **1** *v.t.* **(a)** (bring into harmony) aufeinander abstimmen; **(b)** (Mus.) harmonisieren. **2** *v.i.* (be in harmony) harmonieren (**with** mit); ⟨*Interessen, Ansichten, Wort und Tat:*⟩ miteinander im *od.* in Einklang stehen

harmony /'hɑːmənɪ/ *n.* **(a)** Harmonie, *die;* **live in perfect ~:** völlig harmonisch *od.* in vollkommener Harmonie zusammenleben; **be in ~** ⇒ **harmonize 2**; **be in ~ with sth.** mit etw. im *od.* in Einklang stehen; **(b)** (Mus.) Harmonie, *die;* **sing in ~:** mehrstimmig singen

harness /'hɑːnɪs/ **1** *n.* **(a)** Geschirr, *das;* **(b)** (on parachute) Gurtzeug, *das;* (for toddler, dog) Laufgeschirr, *das;* (for window cleaner, steeplejack, etc.) Sicherheitsgürtel, *der;* **die in ~** (fig.) in den Sielen sterben. **2** *v.t.* **(a)** (put ~ on) anschirren; **~ a horse to a cart** ein Pferd vor einen Wagen spannen; **(b)** (fig.) nutzen

harp /hɑːp/ **1** *n.* Harfe, *die.* **2** *v.i.* **~ on** [**about**] **sth.** [immer wieder] von etw. reden; (critically) auf etw. ⟨*Dat.*⟩ herumreiten (salopp); **don't ~ on about it!** hör auf damit!

harpoon /hɑːˈpuːn/ **1** *n.* Harpune, *die.* **2** *v.t.* harpunieren

harpsichord /'hɑːpsɪkɔːd/ *n.* (Mus.) Cembalo, *das*

harrow /'hærəʊ/ *n.* Egge, *die*

harrowing /'hærəʊɪŋ/ *adj.* entsetzlich; (horrific) grauenhaft ⟨*Anblick, Geschichte*⟩

harry /'hærɪ/ *v.t.* **(a)** **~** [**continuously**] wiederholt angreifen; **(b)** (harass) bedrängen

harsh /hɑːʃ/ *adj.* **(a)** rau ⟨*Gewebe, Oberfläche, Gegend, Land, Klima*⟩; schrill ⟨*Ton, Stimme*⟩; grell ⟨*Licht, Farbe*⟩; hart ⟨*Bedingungen*⟩; **(b)** (excessively severe) [sehr] hart; [äußerst] streng ⟨*Richter, Disziplin*⟩; rücksichtslos ⟨*Tyrann, Herrscher, Politik*⟩; **don't be ~ on him** sei nicht zu streng mit ihm

harvest /'hɑːvɪst/ **1** *n.* Ernte, *die;* **find/reap a** [**rich**] **~** (fig.) einen [tollen] Fang machen. **2** *v.t.* ernten; lesen ⟨*Weintrauben*⟩

harvester /'hɑːvɪstə(r)/ *n.* **(a)** (machine) Erntemaschine, *die; see also* **combine 3 b**; **(b)** (person) Erntearbeiter, *der/* -arbeiterin, *die*

harvest: ~ 'festival *n.* Erntedankfest, *das;* **~ 'home** *n.* Erntefest, *das*

has ⇒ **have 1, 2**

has-been /'hæzbiːn/ *n.* (coll.) **be** [**a bit of**] **a ~:** seine besten Jahre hinter sich (*Dat.*) haben

hash¹ /hæʃ/ *n.* (Cookery) Haschee, *das;* **make a ~ of sth.** (coll.) etw. verpfuschen (ugs.) **~ 'up** *v.t.* (coll.) verpfuschen (ugs.)

hash² *n.* (coll.: drug) Hasch, *das* (ugs.)

'hash browns *n. pl.* Bratkartoffeln *mit Zwiebeln;* ≈ Rösti mit Zwiebeln

hashish /'hæʃɪʃ/ *n.* Haschisch, *das*

hasn't /'hæznt/ = **has not;** ⇒ **have 1, 2**

hasp /hɑːsp/ *n.* Haspe, *die;* (fastener snapping into a lock) [Schnapp]schloss, *das*

hassle /'hæsl/ (coll.) **1** *n.* **~**[**s**] Krach, *der* (ugs.); (trouble, problem) Ärger, *der;* **it's a real ~:** das ist ein echtes Problem; **it's too much** [**of a**]**/such a ~:** das macht zu viel/ so viel Umstände. **2** *v.t.* schikanieren

hassock /'hæsək/ *n.* (cushion) Kniekissen, *das*

haste /heɪst/ *n., no pl.* Eile, *die;* (rush) Hast, *die;* **in his ~:** in seiner Hast; **more ~, less speed** (prov.) eile mit Weile (Spr.); **make ~:** sich beeilen

hasten /'heɪsn/ **1** *v.t.* (cause to hurry) drängen; (accelerate) beschleunigen. **2** *v.i.* eilen; **~ to do sth.** sich beeilen, etw. zu tun; **I ~ to add/say** ich muss *od.* möchte gleich hinzufügen/sagen

hastily /'heɪstɪlɪ/ *adv.* (hurriedly) eilig; (precipitately) hastig; (rashly) übereilt; (quick-temperedly) hitzig; **judge sb. too ~:** jmdn. vorschnell beurteilen

hasty /'heɪstɪ/ *adj.* (hurried) eilig; flüchtig ⟨*Skizze, Blick*⟩; (precipitate) hastig; (rash) übereilt; (quick-tempered) hitzig; **beat a ~ retreat** sich schnellstens zurückziehen *od.* (ugs.) aus dem Staub machen

hat /hæt/ *n.* **(a)** Hut, *der;* [**sailor's/woollen/knitted**] **~:** [Matrosen- / Woll- / Strick]mütze, *die;* **raise one's ~ to sb.** vor jmdm. den Hut ziehen; **take one's ~ off to sb./ sth.** (lit. or fig.) vor jmdm./etw. den Hut ziehen; **(b)** (fig.) **at the drop of a ~:** auf der Stelle; **sb. will eat his ~ if ...:** jmd. frisst einen Besen, wenn ... (salopp); **be old ~** (coll.) ein alter Hut sein (ugs.); **produce sth. out of a ~:** etw. aus dem Ärmel schütteln; **pass the ~ round** (coll.) den Hut herumgehen lassen; **keep sth. under one's ~:** etw. für sich behalten; [**when he is**] **wearing his ... ~:** in seiner Rolle als ...

hatch¹ /hætʃ/ *n.* **(a)** (opening) Luke, *die;* **down the ~!** (fig. coll.) runter damit! (ugs.); **(b)** (serving-~) Durchreiche, *die*

hatch² **1** *v.t.* (lit. or fig.) ausbrüten. **2** *v.i.* [aus]schlüpfen **~ 'out** *v.i.* ausschlüpfen; **the eggs have ~ed out** die Eier sind ausgebrütet. **2** *v.t.* ausbrüten

'hatchback *n.* **(a)** (door) Heckklappe, *die;* **(b)** (vehicle) Schräghecklimousine, *die*

hatchet /'hætʃɪt/ *n.* Beil, *das;* **bury the ~** (fig.) das Kriegsbeil begraben

hatchet: ~ job *n.* **do a ~ job on sb./sth.** jmdn./ etw. in der Luft zerreißen (salopp); **~ man** *n.* **(a)** (professional killer) Killer, *der;* **(b)** (henchman) Erfüllungsgehilfe, *der* (fig. abwertend)

hate /heɪt/ **1** *n.* **(a)** Hass, *der;* **~ for sb.** Hass auf *od.* gegen jmdn.; **(b)** (coll.: object of dislike) **be sb.'s ~:** jmdm. verhasst sein; **my pet ~ is ...:** ... hasse ich am meisten. **2** *v.t.* hassen; **I ~ having to get up at seven** ich hasse es, um sieben Uhr aufstehen zu müssen; **I ~ to say this** (coll.) ich sage das nicht gern; **I ~ to think what would have happened if ...** (coll.) ich darf gar nicht daran denken, was geschehen wäre, wenn ...

hateful /'heɪtfl/ *adj.* abscheulich

'hate mail *n.* hasserfüllte Briefe *Pl.*

hatred /'heɪtrɪd/ *n.* Hass, *der;* **feel ~ for *or* of sb./sth.** Hass auf *od.* gegen jmdn./etw. empfinden

'hatstand *n.* Hutständer, *der*

hatter /'hætə(r)/ *n.* Hutmacher, *der;* [**as**] **mad as a ~** (fig.) völlig verrückt (ugs.)

'hat-trick *n.* Hattrick, *der*

haughty /'hɔːtɪ/ *adj.* hochmütig

haul /hɔːl/ **1** *v.t.* **(a)** (pull) ziehen; schleppen; **~ down** einholen ⟨*Flagge, Segel*⟩; **(b)** (transport) transportieren; befördern. **2** *v.i.* ziehen. **3** *n.* **(a)** Ziehen, *das;* Schleppen, *das;* **(b)** (catch) Fang, *der;* (fig.) Beute, *die*

haulage /'hɔːlɪdʒ/ *n., no pl.* **(a)** (hauling) Transport, *der;* **(b)** (charges) Transportkosten *Pl.*

haunch /hɔːntʃ/ *n.* **(a)** **sit on one's/its ~es** auf seinem Hinterteil sitzen; **(b)** (Gastr.) Keule, *die*

haunt /hɔːnt/ **1** *v.t.* **(a)** **~ a house/castle** in einem Haus/Schloss spuken *od.* umgehen; **(b)** (fig.: trouble) ⟨*Erinnerung, Gedanke:*⟩ plagen, verfolgen. **2** *n.* **a favourite ~ of artists** ein beliebter Treffpunkt für Künstler

haunted /'hɔːntɪd/ *adj.* **(a)** **a ~ house** ein Haus, in dem es spukt; **(b)** (fig.: troubled) gehetzt ⟨*Blick, Eindruck*⟩

haunting /'hɔːntɪŋ/ *adj.* sehnsüchtig ⟨*Klänge, Musik*⟩; lastend ⟨*Erinnerung*⟩

have 1 /hæv/ *v.t., pres.* **he has** /hæz/, *p.t. & p.p.* **had** /hæd/ **(a)** (possess) haben; **I ~ it!** ich hab's[!]; **and what ~ you** (coll.) und so weiter; **(b)** (obtain) bekommen; **let's**

not ∼ any ...: lass uns ... vermeiden; **come on, let's ∼ it!** (coll.) rück schon raus damit! (ugs.); **(c)** (take) nehmen; **(d)** (keep) behalten; haben; **(e)** (eat, drink, etc.) ∼ **breakfast/ dinner/lunch** frühstücken/zu Abend/zu Mittag essen; **(f)** (experience) haben ⟨*Spaß, Vergnügen*⟩; **(g)** (suffer) haben ⟨*Krankheit, Schmerz, Enttäuschung, Abenteuer*⟩; (show) haben ⟨*Güte, Freundlichkeit, Frechheit*⟩; **(h)** (engage in) ∼ **a game of football** Fußball spielen; **(i)** (accept) **I won't ∼ it** das lasse ich mir nicht bieten; **(j)** (give birth to) bekommen; **(k)** (coll.: swindle) **I was had** ich bin [he]reingelegt worden (ugs.); **ever been had!** da bist du ganz schön reingefallen (ugs.); **(l)** (know) **I ∼ it on good authority that** ...: ich weiß es aus zuverlässiger Quelle, dass ...; **(m)** (as guest) ∼ **sb. to stay** jmdn. zu Besuch haben; **(n)** (summon) **he had me into his office** er hat mich in sein Büro beordert; **(o)** (in coll. phrases) **you've had it now** (coll.) jetzt ist es aus (ugs.); **this car/dress has had it** (coll.) dieser Wagen/dieses Kleid hat ausgedient. **2** /həv, əv, *stressed* hæv/ *v. aux.*, **he has** /həz, əz, *stressed* hæz/, **had** /həd, əd, *stressed* hæd/ **(a)** *forming past tenses* **I ∼/I had read** ich habe/hatte gelesen; **I ∼/I had gone** ich bin/war gegangen; **having seen him** (because) weil ich ihn gesehen habe/hatte; (after) wenn ich ihn gesehen habe/nachdem ich ihn gesehen hatte; **if I had known** ...: wenn ich gewusst hätte ...; **(b)** (cause to be) ∼ **sth. made/repaired** etw. machen/reparieren lassen; ∼ **the painters in** die Maler haben; ∼ **sb. do sth.** jmdn. etw. tun lassen; ∼ **a tooth extracted** sich (*Dat.*) einen Zahn ziehen lassen; **(c) she had her purse stolen** man hat ihr das Portemonnaie gestohlen; **(d)** *expr. obligation* ∼ **to** müssen; **I only ∼ to do the washing-up** ich muss nur noch den Abwasch machen; **I ∼ only to see him to feel annoyed** ich brauche ihn nur zu sehen, und ich ärgere mich; **he 'has to be guilty** er ist fraglos schuldig. **3** *n.* **the ∼s and the ∼-nots** die Besitzenden und die Besitzlosen

∼ **off** *v.t.* **(a)** abmachen; **(b)** ∼ **it off [with sb.]** (sl.) es [mit jmdm.] treiben (salopp)

∼ **'on** *v.t.* **(a)** (wear) tragen; **(b)** (Brit. coll.: deceive) ∼ **sb. on** jmdn. auf den Arm nehmen (ugs.)

∼ **'out** *v.t.* **(a)** ∼ **a tooth/one's tonsils out** sich (*Dat.*) einen Zahn ziehen lassen/sich (*Dat.*) die Mandeln herausnehmen lassen; **(b)** (discuss and settle) ∼ **sth. out** sich über etw. (*Akk.*) offen [mit jmdm.] aussprechen; ∼ **it out with sb.** mit jmdm. offen sprechen

haven /'heɪvn/ *n.* geschützte Anlegestelle; (fig.) Zufluchtsort, *der*

have-not ⇒ have 3

haven't /'hævnt/ = have not; ⇒ have 1, 2

haversack /'hævəsæk/ *n.* Brotbeutel, *der*

havoc /'hævək/ *n., no pl.* **(a)** (devastation) Verwüstungen *Pl.;* **cause** *or* **wreak ∼:** Verwüstungen anrichten; **(b)** (confusion) Chaos, *das;* **play ∼ with sth.** etw. völlig durcheinander bringen

Hawaii /hə'waɪɪ/ *pr. n.* Hawaii (*das*)

Hawaiian /hə'waɪən/ ▶947⎮ **1** *adj.* hawaiisch. **2** *n.* (person) Hawaiianer, *der*/Hawaiianerin, *die*

hawk¹ /hɔːk/ *n.* (also Polit.) Falke, *der;* **watch sb. like a ∼:** jmdn. mit Argusaugen beobachten; **have eyes like a ∼:** Augen wie ein Luchs *od.* Adleraugen haben

hawk² *v.t.* (peddle) ∼ **sth.** (at door) mit etw. hausieren [gehen]; (in street) etw. [auf der Straße] verkaufen

hawker /'hɔːkə(r)/ *n.* Hausierer, *der*/Hausiererin, *die*

hawthorn /'hɔːθɔːn/ *n.* (Bot.) (white) Weißdorn, *der;* (red) Rotdorn, *der*

hay /heɪ/ *n., no pl.* Heu, *das;* **make ∼ while the sun shines** (prov.) die Zeit nutzen

hay: ∼ **fever** *n., no pl.* ▶865⎮ Heuschnupfen, *der;* ∼**making** *n., no pl.* Heuernte, *die;* ∼**rick**, ∼**stack** *ns.* Heuschober, *der* (südd.); Heudieme, *die* (nordd.); *see also* **needle** ⎮

haywire /'heɪwaɪə(r)/ *adj.* (coll.) **go ∼** ⟨*Instrument:*⟩ verrückt spielen (ugs.); ⟨*Plan:*⟩ über den Haufen geworfen werden (ugs.)

hazard /'hæzəd/ **1** *n.* Gefahr, *die;* (on road) Gefahrenstelle, *die.* **2** *v.t.* ∼ **a guess** mit Raten probieren

'hazard lights, **hazard 'warning lights** *ns. pl.* (Motor Veh.) Warnblinkanlage, *die*

hazardous /'hæzədəs/ *adj.* (dangerous) gefährlich; (risky) riskant

haze /heɪz/ *n.* Dunst[schleier], *der*

hazel /'heɪzl/ **1** *n.* (Bot.) Haselnussstrauch, *der.* **2** *adj.* haselnussbraun

'hazelnut *n.* Haselnuss, *die*

hazy /'heɪzɪ/ *adj.* dunstig, diesig ⟨*Wetter, Tag*[*eszeit*]⟩; verschwommen, unscharf ⟨*Konturen*⟩; (fig.) vage

H-bomb /'eɪtʃbɒm/ *n.* H-Bombe, *die*

HDTV *abbr.* **high-definition television** HDTV

he¹ /hɪ/, *stressed* hiː/ *pron. referring to personified things or animals which correspond to German feminines/neuters* sie/es; **it was he** (formal) er war es; **he who** wer; *see also* **him; himself; his**

he² /hiː/ *int.* haha

head /hed/ **1** *n.* **(a)** ▶672⎮ Kopf, *der;* Haupt, *das* (geh.); **mind your ∼!** Vorsicht, dein Kopf!; (on sign) Vorsicht — geringe Durchgangshöhe!; ∼ **first** mit dem Kopf zuerst/ voran; ∼ **over heels** kopfüber; ∼ **over heels in love** bis über beide Ohren verliebt (ugs.); **keep one's ∼:** einen klaren Kopf behalten; **lose one's ∼** (fig.) den Kopf verlieren; **be unable to make ∼ or tail of sth./sb.** aus etw./jmdm. nicht klug werden; **(b)** (mind) Kopf, *der;* **in one's ∼:** im Kopf; **enter sb.'s ∼:** jmdm. in den Sinn kommen; **two ∼s are better than one** (prov.) zwei Köpfe sind besser als einer; **I've got a good/bad ∼ for figures** ich kann gut rechnen/rechnen kann ich überhaupt nicht; **use your ∼:** gebrauch deinen Verstand; **not quite right in the ∼** (coll.) nicht ganz richtig [im Kopf] (ugs.); **get sth. into one's ∼:** etw. begreifen; **have got it into one's ∼ that** ...: fest [davon] überzeugt sein, dass ...; **the first thing that comes into sb.'s ∼:** das Erste, was jmdm. einfällt; **(c)** (person) *a* or *per* ∼: pro Kopf; **(d)** *pl. same* (in counting) Stück [Vieh], *das;* **(e)** *in pl.* (on coin) ∼**s or tails?** Kopf oder Zahl?; **(f)** (working end etc.; also Mus.) Kopf, *der;* **playback/erasing ∼:** Wiedergabe-/Löschkopf, *der;* **(g)** (on beer) Blume, *die;* **(h)** (highest part) Kopf, *der;* (of stairs) oberes Ende; (of list, column) oberste Reihe; **(i)** (upper or more important end) Kopf, *der;* (of bed) Kopfende, *das;* **(j)** (leader) Leiter, *der*/Leiterin, *die;* ∼ **of government** Regierungschef, *der*/-chefin, *die;* ∼ **of state** Staatsoberhaupt, *das;* **(k)** ⇒ **headmaster; headmistress. 2** *attrib. adj.* ∼ **waiter** Oberkellner, *der;* ∼ **office** Hauptverwaltung, *die;* (Commerc.) Hauptbüro, *das.* **3** *v.t.* **(a)** (provide with heading) überschreiben; betiteln; ∼**ed notepaper** Briefpapier mit Kopf; **(b)** (stand at top of) anführen ⟨*Liste*⟩; (lead) leiten; führen ⟨*Bewegung*⟩; **(c)** (direct) **we were ∼ed towards Plymouth** wir fuhren mit Kurs auf Plymouth; **(d)** (Footb.) köpfen; **(e)** (overtake and stop) ∼ **sb./sth. [off]** jmdn./etw. abdrängen. **4** *v.i.* steuern; ∼ **for London** ⟨*Flugzeug, Schiff:*⟩ Kurs auf London nehmen; ⟨*Auto:*⟩ in Richtung London fahren; ∼ **towards** or **for sb./the buffet** auf jmdn./ das Büfett zusteuern; **you're ∼ing for trouble** du wirst Ärger bekommen

head: ∼**ache** *n.* ▶865⎮ Kopfschmerzen *Pl.;* (fig. coll.) Problem, *das;* ∼**board** *n.* Kopfende, *das;* ∼ **case** *n.* (coll.) Hirni, *der* (ugs.); **be some sort of ∼ case** sie nicht alle haben (ugs.); ∼**dress** *n.* Kopfschmuck, *der*

-headed /'hedɪd/ *adj. in comb.* -köpfig

header /'hedə(r)/ *n.* (Footb.) Kopfball, *der*

head: ∼**gear** *n., no pl.* Kopfbedeckung, *die;* **protective ∼gear** Kopfschutz, *der;* ∼**hunter** *n.* (lit. or fig.) Kopfjäger, *der*

heading /'hedɪŋ/ *n.* Überschrift, *die;* (in encyclopaedia) Stichwort, *das;* (fig.: category) Rubrik, *die*

head: ∼**lamp** *n.* Scheinwerfer, *der;* ∼**lamp flasher** Lichthupe, *die;* ∼**land** /'hedlənd, 'hedlænd/ *n.* (Geog.) Landspitze, *die;* ∼**light** *n.* Scheinwerfer, *der;* ∼**line** *n.* Schlagzeile, *die;* **hit the ∼lines, be ∼line news** Schlagzeilen machen; **the [news] ∼lines** (Radio, Telev.) die Kurznachrichten; (within news programme) der [Nachrichten]überblick

headless /'hedlɪs/ *adj.* ohne Kopf; **run around like a ∼ chicken** herumrennen wie ein aufgescheuchtes Huhn '**headlong 1** *adv.* **(a)** (head first) **fall/plunge** ~ **into sth.** kopfüber in etw. fallen/springen; **(b)** (uncontrollably) blindlings. **2** *attrib. adj.* ~ **dive** Kopfsprung, *der*

head: ~**man** *n.* Häuptling, *der;* ~'**master** *n.* ▶887|, ▶1152| Schulleiter, *der;* ~'**mistress** *n.* ▶887|, ▶1152| Schulleiterin, *die;* ~**-on 1** /'--/ *adj.* frontal; offen ⟨*Konfrontation, Konflikt*⟩; **a** ~**-on collision** *or* **crash** ein Frontalzusammenstoß; **2** /-'-/ *adv.* frontal; **meet sth./sb.** ~**-on** (fig.: resolutely) einer Sache/jmdm. entschieden entgegentreten; ~**phones** *n. pl.* Kopfhörer, *der;* ~'**quarters** *n. sing. or pl.* Hauptquartier, *das;* (of firm) Zentrale, *die;* ~**rest** *n.* Kopfstütze, *die;* ~**room** *n.,* no pl. [lichte] Höhe, *die;* (in car) Kopffreiheit, *die;* ~**scarf** *n.* Kopftuch, *das;* ~ '**start** *n.* **a** ~ **start** [over sb.] eine Vorgabe [gegenüber jmdm.]; ~**strong** *adj.* eigensinnig; ~ '**teacher** ⇨ **headmaster; headmistress;** ~**way** *n.,* no pl. **make** ~**way** Fortschritte machen; ~ **wind** *n.* Gegenwind, *der;* ~**word** *n.* Stichwort, *das*

heady /'hedɪ/ *adj.* (intoxicating) berauschend

heal /hi:l/ **1** *v.t.* (lit. or fig.) heilen; **time** ~**s all** (fig.) die Zeit heilt [alle] Wunden. **2** *v.i.* ~ [**up**] [ver]heilen

healing /'hi:lɪŋ/ *n.* Heilung, *die*

health /helθ/ *n.* **(a)** no pl. (state) Gesundheitszustand, *der;* (healthiness) Gesundheit, *die;* **in good** ~: bei guter Gesundheit; **be in poor** ~: in schlechtem gesundheitlichen Zustand sein; **(b)** (toast) **drink sb.'s** ~ auf jmds. Gesundheit trinken; **good** *or* **your** ~! auf deine Gesundheit!

health: ~ **care** *n.* Gesundheitsfürsorge, *die;* ~ **care worker** im Gesundheitswesen Beschäftigte, *der/die;* **inadequate** ~ **care** unzureichende medizinische Versorgung; ~ **centre** *n.* medizinisches Versorgungszentrum; Poliklinik, *die;* ~ **certificate** *n.* Gesundheitszeugnis, *das;* ~ **check** *n.* Gesundheitsuntersuchung, *die;* ~ **education** *n.* Gesundheitslehre, *die;* ~ **farm** *n.* Gesundheitsfarm, *die;* ~ **food** *n.* Reformhauskost, *die;* ~**food shop** Reformhaus, *das;* ~ **hazard** *n.* Gesundheitsrisiko, *das;* ~ **insurance** *n.* Krankenversicherung, *die;* ~ **resort** *n.* Kurort, *der;* **H**~ **Secretary** *n.* (Brit.) Gesundheitsminister, *der/*~ministerin, *die;* ~ **service** *n.* Gesundheitsdienst, *der;* ~ **visitor** *n.* ▶887| Krankenschwester/-pfleger im Sozialdienst; ~ **warning** *n.* Warnhinweis, *der; Hinweis auf die Gesundheitsgefährdung*

healthy /'helθɪ/ *adj.* gesund

heap /hi:p/ **1** *n.* **(a)** Haufen, *der;* **lying in a** ~/**in** ~**s** auf einem/in Haufen liegen; **he was lying in a** ~ **on the ground** er lag zusammengesackt am Boden; **(b)** (fig. coll.: quantity) ~**s of** jede Menge (ugs.). **2** *v.t.* aufhäufen

hear /hɪə(r)/ **1** *v.t.,* **heard** /hɜ:d/ **(a)** hören; **they** ~**d the car drive away** sie hörten den Wagen abfahren; **I can hardly** ~ **myself think/speak** ich kann keinen klaren Gedanken fassen/kann mein eigenes Wort nicht verstehen; **(b)** (understand) verstehen; **(c)** (Law) [an]hören; verhandeln ⟨*Fall*⟩. **2** *v.i.,* **heard:** ~ **about sb./sth.** von jmdm./etw. [etwas] hören; ~ **from sb.** von jmdm. hören; **he wouldn't** ~ **of it** er wollte nichts davon hören. **3** *int.* **H**~! **H**~! bravo!; richtig! ~'**out** *v.t.* ausreden lassen

heard ⇨ **hear 1, 2**

hearing /'hɪərɪŋ/ *n.* Gehör, *das;* **have good** ~: gut hören können; **be hard of** ~: schwerhörig sein; **within/out of** ~: in/außer Hörweite

'**hearing aid** *n.* Hörgerät, *das*

hearsay /'hɪəseɪ/ *n.,* no pl., no indef. art. Gerücht, *das;* **it is only** ~: es ist nur ein Gerücht

hearse /hɜ:s/ *n.* Leichenwagen, *der*

heart /hɑ:t/ *n.* **(a)** ▶672| (lit. or fig.) Herz, *das;* **know/learn sth. by** ~: etw. auswendig wissen/lernen; **at** ~: im Grunde seines/ihres Herzens; **from the bottom of one's** ~: aus tiefstem Herzen; **my** ~ **goes out to them** ich verspüre großes Mitleid mit ihnen; **set one's** ~ **on sth./on doing sth.** sein Herz an etw. (*Akk.*) hängen/daran hängen, etw. zu tun; **take sth. to** ~: sich (*Dat.*) etw. zu Herzen nehmen; (accept) beherzigen ⟨*Rat*⟩; **it does my** ~ **good** es erfreut mein Herz; **somebody after my own** ~: jemand ganz nach meinem Herzen; **not have the** ~ **to do sth.** nicht das Herz haben, etw. zu tun; **take** ~: Mut schöpfen (**from** bei); **lose** ~: Mut verlieren; **my** ~ **sank** mein Mut sank; **the** ~ **of the matter** der wahre Kern der Sache; **(b)** (Cards) Herz, *das. See also* **break**[1] **g, 2 a; change 1 a; club 1 d; desire 1 b; gold 1 a**

heart: ~**ache** *n.* [seelische] Qual; ~ **attack** *n.* ▶865| Herzanfall, *der;* (fatal) Herzschlag, *der;* ~**beat** *n.* Herzschlag, *der;* ~**breaking** *adj.* herzzerreißend; ~**broken** *adj.* **she was** ~**broken** ihr Herz war gebrochen; ~**burn** *n.,* no pl. (Med.) Sodbrennen, *das;* ~ **disease** *n.,* no pl. ▶865| Herzkrankheiten *Pl.;* **die of/from** ~ **disease** einem Herzleiden erliegen

hearten /'hɑ:tn/ *v.t.* ermutigen

heartening /'hɑ:tənɪŋ/ *adj.* ermutigend

heart: ~ **failure** *n.* Herzversagen, *das;* ~**felt** *adj.* tief empfunden ⟨*Beileid*⟩; aufrichtig ⟨*Dankbarkeit*⟩

hearth /hɑ:θ/ *n.* Platz vor dem Kamin

'**hearthrug** *n.* Kaminvorleger, *der*

heartily /'hɑ:tɪlɪ/ *adv.* von Herzen; **eat** ~: tüchtig essen; **be** ~ **sick of sth.** etw. herzlich leid sein

heartless /'hɑ:tlɪs/ *adj.,* **heartlessly** /'hɑ:tlɪslɪ/ *adv.* herzlos; unbarmherzig

heart: ~ **rate** *n.* Herzfrequenz, *die;* **an abnormally rapid** ~ **rate** ein abnorm schneller Herzschlag; ~**rending** /'hɑ:trendɪŋ/ *adj.* herzzerreißend; ~**searching** *n.* Gewissenserforschung, *die;* ~**-shaped** *adj.* herzförmig; ~**throb** *n.* (person) Idol, *das;* ~**-to-**~ *attrib. adj.* **have a** ~**-to-**~ **talk** offen und ehrlich miteinander sprechen; ~ **transplant** *n.* (operation) Herztransplantation, *die* (fachspr.); Herzverpflanzung, *die;* (transplanted heart) Herztransplantat, *das* (fachspr.); **receive a** ~ **transplant from sb.** jmds. Herz eingepflanzt od. implantiert bekommen; ~ **trouble** *n.* Probleme *Pl.* mit dem Herzen; ~**-warming** *adj.* herzerfreuend

hearty /'hɑ:tɪ/ *adj.* **(a)** (whole-hearted) ungeteilt ⟨*Unterstützung, Zustimmung*⟩; (enthusiastic, unrestrained) herzlich; begeistert ⟨*Gesang*⟩; **(b)** (large) herzhaft ⟨*Mahlzeit*⟩; gesund ⟨*Appetit*⟩; *see also* **hale**

heat /hi:t/ **1** *n.* **(a)** (hotness) Hitze, *die;* **(b)** (Phys.) Wärme, *die;* **(c)** (Zool.) Brunst, *die;* **be in** *or* **on** ~: brünstig sein; **(d)** (Sport) Vorlauf, *der.* **2** *v.t.* heizen ⟨*Raum*⟩; erhitzen ⟨*Substanz, Lösung*⟩ ~ '**up** *v.t.* heiß machen ⟨*Essen, Wasser*⟩

heated /'hi:tɪd/ *adj.* hitzig; **a** ~ **exchange** ein heftiger Schlagabtausch (fig.)

heatedly /'hi:tɪdlɪ/ *adv.* hitzig

heater /'hi:tə(r)/ *n.* Ofen, *der;* (for water) Boiler, *der*

heath /hi:θ/ *n.* Heide, *die*

'**heat haze** *n.* Hitzeschleier, *der;* **sth. shimmers in the** ~ **haze** etw. flimmert in der Hitze; **through the shimmering** ~ **haze** durch die flimmernde Hitze

heathen /'hi:ðn/ **1** *adj.* heidnisch. **2** *n.* Heide, *der/*Heidin, *die*

heather /'heðə(r)/ *n.* Heidekraut, *das*

heating /'hi:tɪŋ/ *n.,* no pl. Heizung, *die*

heat: ~**-resistant** *adj.* hitzebeständig; ~**stroke** *n.* Hitzschlag, *der;* ~**wave** *n.* Hitzewelle, *die*

heave /hi:v/ **1** *v.t.* **(a)** (lift) heben; wuchten (ugs.); **(b)** *p.t.* & *p.p.* **hove** /həʊv/ (coll.: throw) werfen; schmeißen (ugs.); **(c)** ~ **a sigh [of relief]** [erleichtert] aufseufzen. **2** *v.i.* **(a)** (pull) ziehen; ~ **ho!** hau ruck!; **(b)** (retch) sich übergeben; **(c)** *p.t.* & *p.p.* **hove** (move) ~ **in sight** in Sicht kommen. **3** *n.* (pull) Zug, *der*

heaven /'hevn/ *n.* **(a)** Himmel, *der;* **in** ~: im Himmel; **go to** ~: in den Himmel kommen; **it was** ~ [**to her**] (fig.) es war der Himmel auf Erden [für sie]; **(b)** *in pl.,* (poet.) *in sing.* (sky) Firmament, *das;* **(c)** (God, Providence) **for H**~'**s sake** um Gottes od. Himmels willen; **thank H**~[**s**] Gott sei Dank; *see also* **forbid b**

heavenly /'hevnlɪ/ *adj.* **(a)** himmlisch; **(b)** ~ **body** Himmelskörper, *der*

heavily /'hevɪlɪ/ *adj.* **(a)** schwer; **(b)** (to a great extent) stark; schwer ⟨*bewaffnet*⟩; tief ⟨*schlafen*⟩; dicht ⟨*bevölkert*⟩; **smoke/drink** ~: ein starker Raucher/Trinker sein; **rely** ~ **on sb./sth.** von jmdm./etw. [vollkommen] abhängig sein; **(c)** (with great force) **it rained**/

snowed ~: es regnete/schneite stark; **fall** ~: hart fallen

heaviness /'hevɪnɪs/ n., no pl. **(a)** (weight) Gewicht, das; **(b)** (clinging quality) Schwere, die

heavy /'hevɪ/ adj. **(a)** ▶ 1202 | (in weight) schwer; dick ⟨Mantel⟩; fest ⟨Schuh⟩; ~ **traffic** (dense) hohes Verkehrsaufkommen; **(b)** (severe) schwer ⟨Schaden, Verlust, Strafe, Kampf⟩; hoch ⟨Steuern, Schulden, Anforderungen⟩; massiv ⟨Druck, Unterstützung⟩; **(c)** (excessive) unmäßig ⟨Trinken, Essen, Rauchen⟩; **a** ~ **smoker/drinker** ein starker Raucher/Trinker; **(d)** (violent) schwer ⟨Schlag, Sturm, Regen, Sturz, Seegang⟩; **make** ~ **weather of sth.** (fig.) die Dinge unnötig komplizieren; **(e)** (clinging) schwer ⟨Boden⟩; see also **going 1 a**; **(f)** (tedious) schwerfällig; (serious) seriös ⟨Zeitung⟩; ernst ⟨Musik, Theaterrolle⟩

heavy: ~**-duty** adj. strapazierfähig ⟨Kleidung, Material⟩; schwer ⟨Werkzeug, Maschine⟩; ~ '**goods vehicle** n. Schwerlastwagen, der; ~**-handed** /hevɪ'hændɪd/ adj. (clumsy) ungeschickt ⟨Person⟩; (oppressive) unbarmherzig; ~ '**industry** n. Schwerindustrie, die; ~**weight** n. (Boxing etc.) Schwergewicht, das; (person also) Schwergewichtler, der; (fig.) Größe, die

Hebrew /'hi:bru:/ **1** adj. hebräisch. **2** n. **(a)** (Israelite) Hebräer, der/Hebräerin, die; **(b)** no pl. ▶ 897 | (language) Hebräisch, das; see also **English 2 a**

heckle /'hekl/ v.t. ~ **sb./a speech** jmdn./eine Rede durch Zwischenrufe unterbrechen

heckler /'heklə(r)/ n. Zwischenrufer, der

hectare /'hektɑ:(r), 'hekteə(r)/ n. ▶ 643 | Hektar, das od. der

hectic /'hektɪk/ adj. hektisch

he'd /hɪd, stressed hi:d/ **(a)** = **he had**; **(b)** = **he would**

hedge /hedʒ/ **1** n. Hecke, die; (fig.: barrier) Mauer, die. **2** v.t. **(a)** mit einer Hecke umgeben; **(b)** (protect) ~ **one's bets** mit verteiltem Risiko wetten; (fig.) nicht alles auf eine Karte setzen. **3** v.i. (avoid commitment) sich nicht festlegen

'**hedge-clippers** n. pl. Heckenschere, die

hedge: ~**hog** /'hedʒhɒg/ n. Igel, der; ~**-hop** v.i. im Tiefflug fliegen; ~**row** /'hedʒrəʊ/ n. Hecke, die [als Feldbegrenzung]

heebie-jeebies /hi:bɪ'dʒi:bɪz/ n. pl. (coll.) **give sb. the** ~: jmdn. kribb[e]lig machen (ugs.)

heed /hi:d/ **1** v.t. beachten; berücksichtigen ⟨Rat, Lektion⟩; ~ **the danger/risk** sich (Dat.) der Gefahr/des Risikos bewusst sein. **2** n., no art., no pl. **give** or **pay** ~ **to**, **take** ~ **of** Beachtung schenken (+ Dat.); **give** or **pay no** ~ **to**, **take no** ~ **of** nicht beachten

heedless /'hi:dlɪs/ adj. unachtsam; **be** ~ **of sth.** auf etw. (Akk.) nicht achten

heel /hi:l/ **1** n. **(a)** ▶ 672 | Ferse, die; ~ **of the hand** Handballen, der; **Achilles'** ~ (fig.) Achillesferse, die; **bring a dog to** ~: einen Hund bei Fuß rufen; **bring sb. to** ~ (fig.) jmdn. auf Vordermann bringen (ugs.); **take to one's** ~**s** (fig.) Fersengeld geben (ugs.); see also **dig in 2 b**; **(b)** (of shoe) Absatz, der; (of stocking) Ferse, die; **down at** ~: abgetreten; (fig.) heruntergekommen (ugs.). **2** v.t. ~ **a shoe** einen Schuh mit einem [neuen] Absatz versehen

hefty /'heftɪ/ adj. kräftig; (heavy) schwer; (fig.: large) hoch ⟨Rechnung, Summe, Strafe, Anteil⟩; deutlich ⟨Mehrheit⟩; stark ⟨Erhöhung⟩

heifer /'hefə(r)/ n. Färse, die

height /haɪt/ n. **(a)** Höhe, die; (of person, animal, building) Größe, die; **be three metres in** ~: drei Meter hoch sein; **be six feet in** ~ ⟨Person:⟩ 1,80 m groß sein; **at a** ~ **of three metres** in einer Höhe von drei Metern; **(b)** (fig.: highest point) Höhepunkt, der; **the** ~ **of folly** der Gipfel der Dummheit

heighten /'haɪtn/ v.t. aufstocken; (fig.: intensify) verstärken

heinous /'heɪnəs/ adj. schändlich

heir /eə(r)/ n. (lit. or fig.) Erbe, der/Erbin, die

heiress /'eərɪs/ n. Erbin, die

heirloom /'eəlu:m/ n. Erbstück, das; (fig.) Erbe, das

heist /haɪst/ (Amer. coll.) **1** n. Raubüberfall, der. **2** v.t. (steal) rauben; (rob) ausrauben

---

held ⇒ **hold²** 1, 2

helical /'helɪkl/ adj. spiralförmig; spiralig

helices pl. of **helix**

helicopter /'helɪkɒptə(r)/ n. Hubschrauber, der

Heligoland /'helɪgəlænd/ pr. n. Helgoland (das)

heliport /'helɪpɔ:t/ n. Heliport, der

helium /'hi:lɪəm/ n. Helium, das

helix /'hi:lɪks/ n., pl. **helices** /'hi:lɪsi:z/ Spirale, die

hell /hel/ n. **(a)** Hölle, die; **all** ~ **was let loose** (fig.) es war die Hölle los; see also **raise 1 g**; **(b)** (coll.) [**oh**] ~! verdammter Mist! (ugs.); **what the** ~! ach, zum Teufel! (ugs.); **to** or **the** ~ **with it!** ich hab's satt (ugs.); **a** or **one** ~ **of a [good] party** eine unheimlich gute Party (ugs.); **work/run like** ~: wie der Teufel arbeiten/rennen (ugs.); **it hurt like** ~: es tat höllisch weh (ugs.)

he'll /hɪl, stressed hi:l/ = **he will**

hell: ~**-'bent** adj. **be** ~**-bent on doing sth.** (coll.) wild entschlossen sein, etw. zu tun (ugs.); ~**fire** n. Höllenfeuer, das

hellish /'helɪʃ/ adj. höllisch ⟨Qual, Schmerz⟩; scheußlich ⟨Arbeit, Zeit⟩

hello /hə'ləʊ, he'ləʊ/ **1** int. ▶ 836 | (greeting) hallo; (surprise) holla. **2** n. Hallo, das

hell's 'angel n. Rocker, der

helm /helm/ n. (Naut.) Ruder, das

helmet /'helmɪt/ n. Helm, der

helmsman /'helmzmən/ n., pl. **helmsmen** /'helmzmən/ (Naut.) Rudergänger, der

help /help/ **1** v.t. **(a)** ~ **sb. [to do sth.]** jmdm. helfen [, etw. zu tun]; ~ **oneself** sich (Dat.) selbst helfen; **can I** ~ **you?** was kann ich für Sie tun?; (in shop also) was möchten Sie bitte?; **(b)** (serve) ~ **oneself** sich (Dat.) nehmen; sich bedienen; ~ **oneself to sth.** sich (Dat.) etw. nehmen; (coll.: steal) etw. mitgehen lassen (ugs.); **(c)** (avoid) **if I/you can** ~ **it** wenn es irgend zu vermeiden ist; **not if I can** ~ **it** nicht, wenn ich es verhindern kann; **it can't be** ~**ed** es lässt sich nicht ändern; **I can't** ~ **it** (remedy) ich kann nichts dafür (ugs.); **(d)** (refrain from) **I can't** ~ **thinking** or **can't** ~ **but think that** …: ich kann mir nicht helfen, ich glaube, …; **I can't** ~ **laughing** ich muss einfach lachen. **2** n. Hilfe, die; **be of [some]/no/much** ~ **to sb.** jmdm. eine gewisse/keine/eine große Hilfe sein; **there's no** ~ **for it** daran lässt sich nichts ändern ~ **'out 1** v.i. aushelfen. **2** v.t. ~ **sb. out** jmdm. helfen

'**help desk** n. Help Desk, das (fachspr.); Auskunftsstelle für Computerbenutzer

helper /'helpə(r)/ n. Helfer, der/Helferin, die; (paid assistant) Aushilfskraft, die

helpful /'helpfl/ adj. (willing) hilfsbereit; (useful) hilfreich; nützlich

helping /'helpɪŋ/ **1** attrib. adj. **lend [sb.] a** ~ **hand [with sth.]** (fig.) [jmdm.] [bei etw.] helfen. **2** n. Portion, die

helpless /'helplɪs/ adj. hilflos; (powerless) machtlos

'**helpline** n. Hotline, die; **a** ~ **for parents** ein telefonischer Beratungsdienst für Eltern; **the AIDS** ~: das AIDS-Telefon

helter-skelter /heltəskeltə(r)/ **1** adv. in wildem Durcheinander. **2** n. (in funfair) [spiralförmige] Rutschbahn

hem /hem/ **1** n. Saum, der. **2** v.t. **-mm-:** **(a)** säumen; **(b)** (surround) ~ **sb./sth. in** or **about** jmdn./etw. einschließen; **feel** ~**med in** (fig.) sich eingeengt fühlen

he-man /'hi:mæn/ n. **a real** ~: ein richtiger Mann

'**hemisphere** n. Halbkugel, die; Hemisphäre, die

'**hemline** n. Saum, der; ~**s are up/down** die Röcke sind kurz/lang

hemo- (Amer.) ⇒ **haemo-**

hemp /hemp/ n. **(a)** (Bot., Textiles) Hanf, der; **(b)** (drug) Haschisch, das od. der

hen /hen/ n. Huhn, das; Henne, die (bes. im Gegensatz zu „Hahn")

hence /hens/ adv. **(a)** (therefore) daher; **(b)** (from this time) **a week/ten years** ~: in einer Woche/zehn Jahren

Height and depth

1 inch = 25,4 mm
1 foot = 30,48 cm

Height

People

How tall is she?, What height is she?	= Wie groß ist sie?
She's five foot six	= Sie ist ein Meter achtundsechzig (1,68 m) groß
He's smaller or less tall than his brother	= Er ist kleiner als sein Bruder
A is the same height or as tall as B	= A ist [genau]so groß wie B
They are the same height	= Sie sind gleich groß
an athlete six feet tall	= ein 1,80 Meter großer Athlet

Things

How high is it?, What height is it?	= Wie hoch ist es?
It's about thirty feet high or in height	= Es ist ungefähr neun Meter hoch
A is lower/higher than B	= A ist niedriger/höher als B
A is the same height or as high as B	= A ist [genau]so hoch wie B
The towers are the same height	= Die Türme sind gleich hoch
The aircraft was flying at a height or an altitude of 10,000 feet	= Die Maschine flog in einer Höhe von 3 000 Metern

The treeline is at a height of about 6,500 feet	= Die Baumgrenze liegt bei etwa 2 000 Meter Höhe or bei etwa 2 000 Metern
waves ten feet high	= drei Meter hohe Wellen
a mountain of over 20,000 feet or over 20,000 feet in height	= ein Berg von über 6 000 Metern or von über 6 000 Meter Höhe

Depth

How deep or What depth is the river?	= Wie tief ist or Welche Tiefe hat der Fluss?
It's ten feet deep	≈ Er ist drei Meter tief or hat eine Tiefe von drei Metern
The treasure is at a depth of fifty feet or is fifty feet down	≈ Der Schatz liegt in einer Tiefe von fünfzehn Metern or fünfzehn Meter tief
A is the same depth as B	= A hat die gleiche Tiefe wie B
A and B are the same depth	= A und B sind gleich tief
A is shallower than B	= A ist flacher or seichter als B
a hole ten feet deep	≈ ein drei Meter tiefes Loch

hence'forth, hence'forward *advs.* von nun an
henchman /'hentʃmən/ *n., pl.* **henchmen** /'hentʃmən/ (derog.) Handlanger, *der*
henna /'henə/ *n.* (dye) Henna, *das*
hen: ~**-party** *n.* (coll.) [Damen]kränzchen, *das;* ~**pecked** /'henpekt/ *adj.* a ~**pecked husband** ein Pantoffelheld (ugs.); be ~**pecked** unter dem Pantoffel stehen (ugs.).
hepatitis /hepə'taɪtɪs/ *n.* ▶865 (Med.) Leberentzündung, *die;* Hepatitis, *die* (fachspr.)
her[1] /hə(r), *stressed* hɜː(r)/ *pron.* sie; *as indirect object* ihr; *reflexively* sich; *referring to personified things or animals which correspond to German masculines/neuters* ihn/es; *as indirect object* ihm; **it was** ~: sie war's; ~ **and me** (coll.) sie und ich; **if I were** ~ (coll.) wenn ich sie wäre
her[2] *poss. pron. attrib.* ihr; *referring to personified things or animals which correspond to German masculines/neuters* sein; **she opened** ~ **eyes/mouth** sie öffnete die Augen/den Mund; ~ **father and mother** ihr Vater und ihre Mutter; **she has a room of** ~ **own** sie hat ein eigenes Zimmer; **he complained about** ~ **being late** er beklagte sich darüber, dass sie zu spät kam
herald /'herəld/ **1** *n.* **(a)** Herold, *der;* **(b)** (messenger) Bote, *der;* (fig.: forerunner) Vorbote, *der.* **2** *v.t.* (lit. or fig.) ankündigen
heraldic /he'rældɪk/ *adj.* heraldisch
heraldry /'herəldrɪ/ *n., no pl.* Wappenkunde, *die;* Heraldik, *die*
herb /hɜːb/ *n.* Kraut, *das;* (Cookery) Gewürzkraut, *das*
herbaceous /hɜː'beɪʃəs/ *adj.* (Bot.) krautartig ‹*Pflanze*›; ~ **border** Staudenrabatte, *die*
herbal /'hɜːbl/ **1** *attrib. adj.* Kräuter‹tee, -arznei›; ‹*Behandlung*› mit Heilkräutern. **2** *n.* Pflanzenbuch, *das*
herbivorous /hɜː'bɪvərəs/ *adj.* pflanzenfressend
herd /hɜːd/ **1** *n.* **(a)** Herde, *die;* (of wild animals) Rudel, *das;* **(b)** (fig.) Masse, *die;* **follow the** ~ (fig.) der Herde folgen; mit der Herde laufen. **2** *v.t.* **(a)** (lit. or fig.) treiben; ~

[people] together (fig.) [Menschen] zusammenpferchen; **(b)** (tend) hüten
'herdsman /'hɜːdzmən/ *n., pl.* ~**smen** /'hɜːdzmən/ Hirt[e], *der*
here /hɪə(r)/ **1** *adv.* **(a)** (in or at this place) hier; **Schmidt** ~ (on telephone) Schmidt; **spring is** ~: der Frühling ist da; **down/in/up** ~: hier unten/drin/oben; ~ **goes!** (coll.) dann mal los! (ugs.); ~, **there, and everywhere** überall; ~ **you are** (coll.: giving sth.) hier; ~ **we are** (on arrival) da sind *od.* wären wir; **(b)** (to this place) hierher; **in[to]** ~: hierherein; ~ **comes/bring** ~: hierher kommen/bringen; herkommen/-bringen; ~ **comes the bus** hier *od.* da kommt der Bus. **2 up to** ~, **as far as** ~: bis hierhin; **from** ~ on von nun an; **where do we go from** ~? (fig.) was machen wir jetzt? **3** *int.* (attracting attention) he
here: ~**a'bout[s]** *adv.* hier [in dieser Gegend]; ~**'after** *adv.* (formal) im folgenden; ~**'by** *adv.* (formal) hiermit
hereditary /hɪ'redɪtərɪ/ *adj.* **(a)** erblich ‹Titel, Amt›; ererbt ‹Reichtum›; ~ **monarchy/right** Erbmonarchie, *die*/ Erbrecht, *das;* **(b)** (Biol.) angeboren ‹Instinkt, Verhaltensweise›
heredity /hɪ'redɪtɪ/ *n.* (Biol.) **(a)** (transmission of qualities) Vererbung, *die;* **(b)** (genetic constitution) Erbgut, *das*
heresy /'herɪsɪ/ *n.* Ketzerei, *die;* Häresie, *die* (geh.)
heretic /'herɪtɪk/ *n.* Ketzer, *der*/Ketzerin, *die;* Häretiker, *der*/Häretikerin, *die* (geh.)
heretical /hɪ'retɪkl/ *adj.* ketzerisch; häretisch (geh.)
here: ~**u'pon** *adv.* hierauf; ~**'with** *adv.* (with this) in der Anlage; **we enclose** ~**with your cheque** wir legen Ihren Scheck diesem Schreiben bei
heritage /'herɪtɪdʒ/ *n.* (lit. or fig.) Erbe, *das*
hermetic /hɜː'metɪk/ *adj.* luftdicht; (fig.) hermetisch (geh.)
hermetically /hɜː'metɪkəlɪ/ *adv.* hermetisch
hermit /'hɜːmɪt/ *n.* Einsiedler, *der*/Einsiedlerin, *die*
hernia /'hɜːnɪə/ *n., pl.* ~**s** *or* ~**e** /'hɜːnɪiː/ (Med.) Bruch, *der;* Hernie, *die* (Med.)

hero /'hɪərəʊ/ *n., pl.* **~es** Held, *der;* (demigod) Heros, *der;* ~ **of the hour** Held des Tages

heroic /hɪ'rəʊɪk/ *adj.* (a) heldenhaft; heroisch (geh.); (b) (Lit.) ~ **epic/legend** Heldenepos, *das/-*legende, *die*

heroics /hɪ'rəʊɪks/ *n. pl.* (language) Theatralische, *das;* (foolhardiness) Draufgängertum, *das*

heroin /'herəʊɪn/ *n., no pl.* Heroin, *das*

heroine /'herəʊɪn/ *n.* Heldin, *die;* Heroin, *die* (geh.); Heroine, *die* (Theater)

heroism /'herəʊɪzm/ *n., no pl.* Heldentum, *das*

heron /'hern/ *n.* Reiher, *der*

'**hero-worship** 1 *n.* Heldenverehrung, *die.* 2 *v.t.* vergöttern

herpes /'hɜːpiːz/ *n.* ▶865] (Med.) Herpes, *der*

herring /'herɪŋ/ *n.* Hering, *der*

hers /hɜːz/ *poss. pron. pred.* ihrer/ihre/ihres; der/die/das ihre *od.* ihrige (geh.); **the book is ~**: das Buch gehört ihr; **some friends of ~**: ein paar Freunde von ihr; **those children of ~**: ihre Gören (ugs.); **~ is a difficult job** sie hat einen schwierigen Job (ugs.)

herself /hɜː'self/ *pron.* (a) *emphat.* selbst; **she ~ said so** sie selbst hat das gesagt; **she saw it ~**: sie hat es selbst gesehen; **she was just being ~**: sie gab sich einfach so, wie sie ist; **she is [quite] ~ again** sie ist wieder ganz die alte; (after an illness) sie ist wieder auf der Höhe (ugs.); **all right in ~**: im Wesentlichen gesund; **[all] by ~** (on her own, by her own efforts) [ganz] allein[e]; (b) *refl.* sich; allein[e] ⟨*tun, wählen*⟩; **she wants to see for ~**: sie will [es] selbst sehen; **younger than/as heavy as ~**: jünger als/so schwer wie sie selbst; ... **she thought to ~**: ... dachte sie sich [im Stillen]; ... dachte sie bei sich

he's /hɪz, *stressed* hiːz/ (a) = **he is;** (b) = **he has**

hesitant /'hezɪtənt/ *adj.* zögernd ⟨*Reaktion*⟩; stockend ⟨*Rede*⟩; unsicher ⟨*Person, Stimme*⟩; **be ~ to do sth.** *or* **about doing sth.** Bedenken haben, etw. zu tun

hesitate /'hezɪteɪt/ *v.i.* (a) (show uncertainty) zögern; **he who ~s is lost** (prov.) man muss die Gelegenheit beim Schopfe fassen; (b) (falter) ins Stocken geraten; (c) ~ **to do sth.** Bedenken haben, etw. zu tun

hesitation /hezɪ'teɪʃn/ *n.* (a) *no pl.* (indecision) Unentschlossenheit, *die;* **without the slightest ~**: ohne im Geringsten zu zögern; (b) (instance of faltering) Unsicherheit, *die;* (c) *no pl.* (reluctance) Bedenken *Pl.*

hessian /'hesɪən/ *n.* Sackleinen, *das;* Hessian, *das* (fachspr.)

het /het/ *adj.* (coll.) ~ **up** aufgeregt; **get ~ up over sth.** sich über etw. (*Akk*) aufregen

heterogeneous /hetərə'dʒiːnɪəs, hetərə'dʒenɪəs/ *adj.* ungleichartig; heterogen

heterosexual /hetərəʊ'seksjʊəl/ 1 *adj.* heterosexuell. 2 *n.* Heterosexuelle, *der/die*

heterosexuality /hetərəʊseksjʊ'ælɪtɪ/ *n., no pl.* Heterosexualität, *die*

hew /hju:/ 1 *v.t., p.p.* **~n** /hju:n/ *or* **~ed** /hju:d/ (cut) hacken ⟨*Holz*⟩; fällen ⟨*Baum*⟩; schlagen ⟨*Kohle, Gestein*⟩. 2 *v.i., p.p.* **~n** *or* **~ed** zuschlagen

hex /heks/ *n.* (Amer.) **put a ~ on sb./sth.** jmdm./etw. verhexen

hexagon /'heksəgən/ *n.* (Geom.) Sechseck, *das;* Hexagon, *das* (fachspr.)

hey /heɪ/ *int.* he; ~ **presto!** simsalabim!

heyday /'heɪdeɪ/ *n., no pl.* Blütezeit, *die*

HGV *abbr.* (Brit.) **heavy goods vehicle**

hi /haɪ/ *int.* hallo (ugs.)

hiatus /har'eɪtəs/ *n.* (gap) Bruch, *der;* (interruption) Unterbrechung, *die*

hibernate /'haɪbəneɪt/ *v.i.* Winterschlaf halten

hibernation /haɪbə'neɪʃn/ *n.* Winterschlaf, *der*

hiccup /'hɪkʌp/ 1 *n.* (a) Schluckauf, *der;* **have/get [the] ~s** [den] Schluckauf haben/bekommen; (b) (fig.: stoppage) Störung, *die;* **without any ~s** reibungslos. 2 *v.i.* schlucksen (ugs.); hick machen (ugs.); (many times) den Schluckauf haben

hid ⇨ **hide¹** 1, 2

hidden ⇨ **hide¹** 1, 2

hide¹ /haɪd/ 1 *v.t.,* **hid** /hɪd/, **hidden** /'hɪdn/ (a) verstecken ⟨*Gegenstand, Person usw.*⟩ (**from** vor + *Dat.*); ~ **one's face in one's hands** sein Gesicht in den Händen bergen; (b) (keep secret) verbergen ⟨*Gefühle, Sinn, Freude usw.*⟩ (**from** vor + *Dat.*); verheimlichen ⟨*Tatsache, Absicht, Grund usw.*⟩ (**from** *Dat.*); **have nothing to ~**: nichts zu verbergen haben; (c) (obscure) verdecken; ~ **sth. [from view]** etw. verstecken; (by covering) etw. verdecken; ⟨*Nebel, Rauch usw.*⟩ etw. einhüllen. 2 *v.i.,* **hid, hidden** sich verstecken *od.* verbergen (**from** vor + *Dat.*). 3 *n.* (Brit.) Versteck, *das;* (hunter's ~) Ansitz, *der* (Jägerspr.)

~ **a'way** *v.i.* sich verstecken *od.* verbergen

~ '**out,** ~ '**up** *v.i.* sich versteckt *od.* verborgen halten

hide² *n.* (animal's skin) Haut, *die;* (of furry animal) Fell, *das;* (dressed) Leder, *das;* (joc.: human skin) Haut, *die;* Fell, *das;* **tan sb.'s ~**: jmdm. das Fell gerben *od.* versohlen (salopp)

hide: ~-**and-'seek** *n.* Versteckspiel, *das;* **play ~-and-seek** Verstecken spielen; ~**bound** *adj.* engstirnig; borniert

hideous /'hɪdɪəs/ *adj.* (a) scheußlich; (horrific) entsetzlich; grauenhaft; (b) (coll.: unpleasant) furchtbar (ugs.)

'**hideout** *n.* Versteck, *das;* (of bandits, partisans, etc.) Versteck, *das;* Unterschlupf, *der*

hiding¹ /'haɪdɪŋ/ *n.* **go into ~** (to avoid police, public attention) untertauchen; **be in ~** sich versteckt halten; **come out of ~**: wieder auftauchen

hiding² *n.* (coll.: beating) Tracht Prügel; (fig.) Schlappe, *die;* **give sb. a [good] ~**: jmdm. eine [ordentliche] Tracht Prügel verpassen; (fig.) jmdm. eine [klare] Abfuhr erteilen; **be on a ~ to nothing** eine undankbare Rolle haben

'**hiding place** *n.* Versteck, *das*

hierarchic /haɪə'rɑːkɪk/, **hierarchical** /haɪə'rɑːkɪkl/ *adjs.* hierarchisch

hierarchy /'haɪərɑːkɪ/ *n.* Hierarchie, *die*

hieroglyphics /haɪərə'glɪfɪks/ *n. pl.* (also joc.) Hieroglyphen

hi-fi /'haɪfaɪ/ (coll.) 1 *adj.* Hi-Fi-. 2 *n.* (equipment) Hi-Fi-Anlage, *die*

higgledy-piggledy /hɪgldɪ'pɪgldɪ/ 1 *adv.* wie Kraut und Rüben (ugs.). 2 *adj.* wirr, kunterbunt ⟨*Ansammlung usw.*⟩

high /haɪ/ 1 *adj.* (a) ▶850] hoch ⟨*Berg, Gebäude, Mauer*⟩; (b) (above normal level) hoch ⟨*Stiefel*⟩; **the river/water is ~**: der Fluss/das Wasser steht hoch; **be left ~ and dry** (fig.) auf dem Trock[e]nen sitzen (ugs.); (c) (far above ground or sea level) hoch ⟨*Gipfel, Punkt*⟩; groß ⟨*Höhe*⟩; (d) (to or from far above the ground) hoch ⟨*Aufstieg, Sprung*⟩; ~ **diving** Turmspringen, *das; see also* **bar** 1 b; (e) (of exalted rank) hoch ⟨*Beamter, Amt, Gericht*⟩; **a ~er court** eine höhere Instanz; ~ **and mighty** (coll.: ~handed) selbstherrlich; (coll.: superior) hochnäsig (ugs.); **be born** *od.* **destined for ~er things** zu Höherem geboren *od.* bestimmt sein; **those in ~ places** die Oberen; (f) (great in degree) hoch; groß ⟨*Gefallen, Bedeutung*⟩; stark ⟨*Wind*⟩; **be held in ~ regard/esteem** hohes Ansehen/hohe Wertschätzung genießen; ~ **blood pressure** Bluthochdruck, *der;* **have a ~ opinion of sb./sth.** eine hohe Meinung von jmdm./ etw. haben (geh.); viel von jmdm./etw. halten; (g) (noble, virtuous) hoch ⟨*Ideal, Ziel, Prinzip, Berufung*⟩; edel ⟨*Charakter*⟩; (h) (of ~ birth) von hoher Geburt (geh.); (i) (of time, season) **it is ~ time you left** es ist *od.* wird höchste Zeit, dass du gehst; ~ **noon** Mittag; ~ **summer** Hochsommer, *der;* (i) (luxurious, extravagant) üppig ⟨*Leben*⟩; (j) (enjoyable) **have a ~ [old] time** sich bestens amüsieren; (k) (coll.: on a drug) high *nicht attr.* (ugs.) (**on** von); **get ~ on** sich anturnen mit (ugs.) ⟨*Haschisch, LSD usw.*⟩; (l) (in pitch) hoch ⟨*Ton, Stimme, Lage, Klang usw.*⟩; (m) (slightly decomposed) angegangen (landsch.) ⟨*Fleisch*⟩; (n) (Cards) hoch; **ace is ~**: Ass ist hoch. 2 *adv.* (a) (in or to a ~ position) hoch; ~ **on our list of priorities** weit oben auf unserer Prioritätenliste; **search** *or* **hunt** *or* **look ~ and low** überall suchen; (b) (to a ~ level) hoch; **prices have gone too ~**: die Preise sind zu stark gestiegen; **I'll go as ~ as two thousand pounds** ich gehe bis zweitausend Pfund. 3 *n.*

(a) (~est level/figure) Höchststand, *der; see also* **all-time;**
(b) (~ position) **on** ~**:** hoch oben *od.* (geh., südd., österr.) droben; (in heaven) im Himmel; **(c)** (Meteorol.) Hoch, *das*

high: ~ **'altar** *n.* (Eccl.) Hochaltar, *der;* ~ **'beam** *n.* Fernlicht, *das;* **I was on** ~ **beam most of the time** ich fuhr die meiste Zeit mit Fernlicht; ~**-brow** (coll.) *adj.* intellektuell ‹ *Person, Gerede usw.* ›; hochgestochen (abwertend) ‹ *Person, Gerede, Musik, Literatur usw.* ›; ~ **chair** *n.* (for baby) Hochstuhl, *der;* **H~** **'Church** *n.* High Church, *die;* Hochkirche, *die;* ~**-class** *adj.* hochwertig ‹ *Erzeugnis* ›; erstklassig ‹ *Unterkunft, Konditor usw.* ›; **H~** **'Court [of Justice]** *n.* (Brit. Law) *oberster Gerichtshof für Zivil- und Strafsachen;* ~**-definition** **'television** *n.* hoch auflösendes Fernsehen; ~ **'diving** *n.* Turmspringen, *das*

higher /'haɪə(r)/**:** ~ **edu'cation** *n., no pl., no art.* Hochschul[aus]bildung, *die;* ~ **mathe'matics** *n.* höhere Mathematik

high: ~ **ex'plosive** ⇒ explosive 2; ~**-flown** *adj.* geschwollen (abwertend) ‹ *Stil, Ausdrucksweise* ›; hochfliegend ‹ *Ideen, Pläne* ›; ~**-'flyer** *n.* (able person) Hochbegabte, *der/die;* ~**'frequency** *n.* hohe Frequenz; (radio frequency) Hochfrequenz, *die;* ~**-grade** *adj.* hochwertig; ~**-grade** **steel** Edelstahl, *der;* ~**-handed** /haɪ'hændɪd/ *adj.* selbstherrlich; ~ **'heel** *n.* (a) hoher Absatz; **(b)** *in pl.* (shoes) hochhackige Schuhe; ~**-heeled** /haɪ'hiːld/ *adj.* ‹ *Schuhe* › mit hohen Absätzen; ~**-income** *adj.* einkommensstark; ~**-income** **earners** Bezieher hoher Einkommen; ~**-income** **area/country** Gebiet/Land mit hohem Pro-Kopf-Einkommen; ~**-income** **investment** Investition mit hoher Rendite; ~ **jinks** /'haɪ dʒɪŋks/ *n. pl.* [übermütige] Ausgelassenheit; ~ **jump** *n., no pl.* **(a)** (Sport) Hochsprung, *der;* **(b)** (fig.: reprimand, punishment) **he is for the** ~ **jump** er kann sich auf was gefasst machen (ugs.); ~**land** /'haɪlənd/ **1** *n., usu. in pl.* Hochland, *das;* **the H~lands** (in Scotland) die Highlands; **2** *adj.* hochländisch; ~**-level** *adj.* ‹ *Verhandlungen usw.* › auf hoher Ebene; ~ **life** *n., no pl.* **(a)** (life of upper class) das Leben der Oberschicht; **(b)** (luxurious living) **the** ~ **life** das Leben auf großem Fuße; ~**light** **1** *n.* **(a)** (outstanding moment) Höhepunkt, *der;* **(b)** (bright area) Licht, *das;* **(c)** *usu. pl.* (in hair) Strähnchen, *das;* **2** *v.t.,* ~**lighted** ein Schlaglicht werfen auf (+ *Akk.*) ‹ *Probleme usw.* ›; markieren ‹ *Text, Wort etc.* ›

highly /'haɪlɪ/ *adv.* **(a)** (to a high degree) sehr; äußerst; hoch ‹ *begabt, -interessant, -angesehen, -bezahlt, -gebildet, -modern, -aktuell* ›; leicht ‹ *entzündlich* ›; stark ‹ *gewürzt* ›; **feel** ~ **honoured** sich hoch geehrt fühlen; **I can** ~ **recommend the restaurant** ich kann dieses Restaurant sehr empfehlen; **(b)** (favourably) **think** ~ **of sb./sth.,** **regard sb./sth.** ~**:** eine hohe Meinung von jmdm./etw. haben

'highly strung *adj.* übererregbar

high-minded /haɪ'maɪndɪd/ *adj.* hochgesinnt ‹ *Person* ›; hoch, (geh.) hehr ‹ *Prinzipien, Dienstauffassung usw.* ›

Highness /'haɪnɪs/ *n.* ▶**1152** Hoheit, *die;* **His/Her/Your [Royal]** ~**:** Seine/Ihre/Eure [Königliche] Hoheit

high: ~**-pitched** *adj.* **(a)** hoch ‹ *Ton, Stimme* ›; **(b)** (Archit.) steil ‹ *Dach* ›; ~ **point** *n.* Höhepunkt, *der;* Gipfelpunkt, *der;* ~**-powered** /'haɪpaʊəd/ *adj.* **(a)** (powerful) stark ‹ *Fahrzeug, Motor, Glühbirne usw.* ›; **(b)** (forceful) dynamisch ‹ *Geschäftsmann, Manager usw.* ›; ~**'pressure** *n.* **(a)** (Meteorol.) Hochdruck, *der;* **an area of** ~ **pressure** ein Hochdruckgebiet; **(b)** (Mech. Engin.) Überdruck, *der;* **(c)** (fig.: high degree of activity) Hochdruck, *der;* ~**-pressure** *adj.* Hochdruck-; (fig.: persuasive) aggressiv ‹ *Verkaufsmethoden* ›; ~ **'priest** *n.* Hohepriester, *der;* ~**-ranking** *adj.* hochrangig; von hohem Rang *nachgestellt;* ~**-rise** *adj.* ~**-rise building** Hochhaus, *das;* ~**-rise [block of] flats/office block** Wohn-/Bürohochhaus, *das;* ~**-risk** *attrib. adj.* risikoreich; Risiko‹ *gruppe, -sportart* ›; hochgradig gefährdet ‹ *Person* ›; **take a** ~**-risk gamble** viel aufs Spiel setzen, viel riskieren; **a** ~**-risk investment** eine Geldanlage mit hohem Risiko; ~ **road** *n.* Hauptstraße, *die;* ~ **school** *n.* ≈ Oberschule, *die;* ~ **'seas** *n. pl.* **the** ~ **seas** die hohe See; ~ **season** *n.* Hochsaison, *die;* ~**speed** *adj.* schnell [fahrend]; ~**-speed train** Hochgeschwindigkeitszug, *der;* ~**-spirited** ⇒ spirited b;

~ **'spirits** ⇒ spirit 1 g; ~ **street** *n.* Hauptstraße, *die;* ~ **'tea** ⇒ tea b; ~**-tech** /'haɪtek/ *adj.* (coll.) Hightech-; ~ **tech** /haɪ'tek/ (coll.), ~ **tech'nology** *ns.* Spitzentechnologie, *die;* Hochtechnologie, *die;* ~**-technology** *adj.* hoch technisiert; Hightech-; ~ **'tide** ⇒ tide 1 a; ~ **'treason** ⇒ treason; ~**-'voltage** *adj.* (Electr.) Hochspannungs-; ~ **'water** *n.* Hochwasser, *das;* ~ **'water mark** *n.* Hochwassermarke, *die;* ~**way** *n.* **(a)** (public road) öffentliche Straße; **(b)** (main route) Verkehrsweg, *der;* **H~way 'Code** *n.* (Brit.) Straßenverkehrsordnung, *die;* ~**wayman** /'haɪweɪmən/ *n., pl.* ~**waymen** /'haɪweɪmən/ (Hist.) Straßenräuber, *der;* Wegelagerer, *der*

hijack /'haɪdʒæk/ **1** *v.t.* in seine Gewalt bringen; **they** ~**ed an aircraft to Cuba** sie haben ein Flugzeug nach Kuba entführt. **2** *n.* (of aircraft) Entführung, *die* (of *Gen.*); (of vehicle) Überfall, *der* (of auf + *Akk.*)

hijacker /'haɪdʒækə(r)/ *n.* Entführer, *der;* (of aircraft) Hijacker, *der;* Flugzeugentführer, *der*

hike /haɪk/ **1** *n.* Wanderung, *die;* **go on a** ~**:** eine Wanderung machen; wandern gehen. **2** *v.i.* wandern; eine Wanderung machen

hiker /'haɪkə(r)/ *n.* Wanderer, *der/*Wanderin, *die*

hilarious /hɪ'leərɪəs/ *adj.* urkomisch; rasend komisch (ugs.)

hilariously /hɪ'leərɪəslɪ/ *adv.* **be** ~ **funny** rasend komisch sein (ugs.)

hilarity /hɪ'lærɪtɪ/ *n., no pl.* **(a)** (gaiety) Fröhlichkeit, *die;* **(b)** (merriment) übermütige Ausgelassenheit; (loud laughter) Heiterkeit, *die*

hill /hɪl/ *n.* **(a)** (mound) Hügel, *der;* (higher) Berg, *der;* **built on a** ~**:** am Hang gebaut; **be over the** ~ (fig. coll.) auf dem absteigenden Ast sein (ugs.); (past the crisis) über den Berg sein (ugs.); **[as] old as the** ~**s** (fig.) uralt; ‹ *Person* › [so] alt wie Methusalem; *see also* **up 2 a; (b)** (heap) Hügel, *der;* (ant~, dung~, mole~) Haufen, *der;* **(c)** (sloping road) Steigung, *die*

hill-billy /'hɪlbɪlɪ/ *n.* (Amer.) Hinterwäldler, *der/*Hinterwäldlerin, *die* (spött.)

hillock /'hɪlək/ *n.* [kleiner] Hügel

hill: ~**side** *n.* Hang, *der;* ~**top** *n.* [Berg]gipfel, *der*

hilly /'hɪlɪ/ *adj.* hüg[e]lig; (higher) bergig

hilt /hɪlt/ *n.* Griff, *der;* Heft, *das* (geh., fachspr.); **[up] to the** ~ (fig.) voll und ganz ‹ *unterstützen usw.* ›

him /ɪm, *stressed* hɪm/ *pron.* ihn; *as indirect object* ihm; *reflexively* sich; *referring to personified things or animals which correspond to German feminines/neuters* sie/es; *as indirect object* ihr/ihm; **it was** ~**:** er war's; ~ **and me** (coll.) er und ich; **if I were** ~**:** wenn ich er wäre

Himalayas /hɪmə'leɪəz/ *pr. n. pl.* Himalaya, *der*

himself /hɪm'self/ *pron.* **(a)** *emphat.* selbst; **(b)** *refl.* sich. *See also* **herself**

hind /haɪnd/ *n.* Hirschkuh, *die*

hind² *adj.* hinter...; ~ **legs** Hinterbeine

hinder /'hɪndə(r)/ *v.t.* (impede) behindern; (delay) verzögern ‹ *Vollendung einer Arbeit, Vorgang* ›; aufhalten ‹ *Person* ›; ~ **sb. from doing sth.** jmdn. daran hindern, etw. zu tun

Hindi /'hɪndiː/ **1** *adj.* Hindi-. **2** *n.* ▶**947** Hindi, *das; see also* **English 2 a**

hind: ~**most** *adj.* hinterst...; **it was devil take the** ~**most** es galt nur noch: Rette sich, wer kann!; ~**quarters** *n. pl.* Hinterteil, *das;* (of large quadruped) Hinterteil, *das;* Hinterhand, *die* (fachspr.)

hindrance /'hɪndrəns/ *n.* **(a)** (action) Behinderung, *die; see also* **let²; (b)** (obstacle) Hindernis, *das* (to für); **he is more of a** ~ **than a help** er stört mehr, als dass er hilft

'hindsight *n.* **in** ~**, with [the benefit of]** ~**:** im Nachhinein

Hindu /'hɪnduː:, hɪn'duː/ **1** *n.* Hindu, *der.* **2** *adj.* hinduistisch; Hindu‹ *gott, -tempel* ›

hinge /hɪndʒ/ **1** *n.* Scharnier, *das;* (continuous) Klavierband, *das;* **off its** ~**s** ‹ *Tür* › aus den Angeln gehoben. **2** *v.t.* mit Scharnieren/einem Scharnier versehen. **3** *v.i.* (fig.) abhängen (**[up]on** von)

hint /hɪnt/ **1** *n.* **(a)** (suggestion) Wink, *der;* Hinweis, *der;* **give a ~ that …**: andeuten, dass …; *see also* **broad b; drop 3 d; take 1 v; (b)** (slight trace) Spur, *die* **(of** von**); the ~/no ~ of a smile** der Anflug/nicht die Spur eines Lächelns; **a ~ of aniseed** ein Hauch von Anis; **(c)** (practical information) Tipp, *der* **(on** für**). 2** *v.t.* andeuten; **nothing has yet been ~ed about it** darüber hat man noch nichts herausgelassen (ugs.). **3** *v.i.* **~ at** andeuten

hip[1] /hɪp/ *n.* **(a)** ▶ 672 | Hüfte, *die;* **with one's hands on one's ~s** die Arme in die Hüften gestemmt; **(b)** *in sing. or pl.* **(~-measurement)** Hüftumfang, *der;* Hüftweite, *die;* (of man, boy) Gesäßumfang, *der;* Gesäßweite, *die*

hip[2] *n.* (Bot.) Hagebutte, *die*

hip: ~ bone *n.* ▶ 672 | (Anat.) Hüftbein, *das;* Hüftknochen, *der;* **~ flask** *n.* Taschenflasche, *die;* **~ joint** *n.* ▶ 672 | (Anat.) Hüftgelenk, *das*

hippie /'hɪpɪ/ *n.* (coll.) Hippie, *der*

hippo /'hɪpəʊ/ *n.*, *pl.* **~s** (coll.) ⇒ **hippopotamus**

hip 'pocket *n.* Gesäßtasche, *die*

hippopotamus /hɪpə'pɒtəməs/ *n.*, *pl.* **~es** *or* **hippopotami** /hɪpə'pɒtəmaɪ/ (Zool.) Nilpferd, *das;* Flusspferd, *das*

hippy /'hɪpɪ/ ⇒ **hippie**

hire /haɪə(r)/ **1** *n.* **(a)** (action) Mieten, *das;* (of servant) Einstellen, *das;* **(b)** (condition) **be on ~ [to sb.]** [an jmdn.] vermietet sein; **for** *or* **on ~**: zu vermieten. **2** *v.t.* **(a)** (employ) anwerben; engagieren ‹Anwalt, Berater usw.›; **(b)** (obtain use of) mieten; **~ sth. from sb.** etw. bei jmdm. mieten; **(c)** (grant use of) vermieten; **~ sth. to sb.** etw. jmdm. od. an jmdn. vermieten **~ 'out** *v.t.* vermieten

hire: ~ car *n.* Mietwagen, *der;* Leihwagen, *der;* **~ 'purchase** *n.*, *no pl.*, *no art.* (Brit.) Ratenkauf, *der;* Teilzahlungskauf, *der; attrib.* Raten-; Teilzahlungs-; **pay for/ buy sth. on ~ purchase** etw. in Raten bezahlen/auf Raten *od.* Teilzahlung kaufen

his /ɪz, stressed hɪz/ *poss. pron.* **(a)** *attrib.* sein; *referring to personified things or animals which correspond to German feminines/neuters* ihr/sein; *see also* **her**[2]; **(b)** *pred.* (the one[s] belonging to him) seiner/seine/sein[e]s; der/die/das seine *od.* seinige (geh.); *see also* **hers**

hiss /hɪs/ **1** *n.* (of goose, snake, escaping steam, crowd, audience) Zischen, *das;* (of cat, locomotive) Fauchen, *das.* **2** *v.i.* ‹Gans, Schlange, Dampf, Publikum, Menge:› zischen; ‹Katze, Lokomotive:› fauchen. **3** *v.t.* auszischen ‹Redner, Schauspieler›

historian /hɪ'stɔːrɪən/ *n.* ▶ 887 | **(a)** (writer of history) Geschichtsschreiber, *der*/-schreiberin, *die;* **(b)** (scholar of history) Historiker, *der*/Historikerin, *die*

historic /hɪ'stɒrɪk/ *adj.* historisch

historical /hɪ'stɒrɪkl/ *adj.* **(a)** historisch; geschichtlich ‹Belege, Hintergrund›; **(b)** (belonging to the past) in früheren Zeiten üblich ‹Methode›

history /'hɪstərɪ/ *n.* **(a)** (continuous record) Geschichte, *die;* **histories** historische Darstellungen; **(b)** *no pl.*, *no art.* Geschichte, *die;* (study of past events) Geschichte, *die;* Geschichtswissenschaft, *die;* **make ~**: Geschichte machen; **and the rest is ~**: und das Weitere ist [ja] bekannt; **(c)** (train of events) Geschichte, *die;* (of person) Werdegang, *der;* **have a ~ of asthma/shoplifting** schon lange an Asthma leiden/eine Vorgeschichte als Ladendieb haben; **(d)** (eventful past career) Geschichte, *die*

'history book *n.* Geschichtsbuch, *das*

hit /hɪt/ **1** *v.t.*, **-tt-, hit (a)** (strike with blow) schlagen; (strike with missile) treffen; ‹Geschoss, Ball usw.:› treffen; **I've been ~!** (struck by bullet) ich bin getroffen!; **I could ~ him** (fig. coll.) ich könnte ihm eine runterhauen (ugs.); **~ sb. over the head** jmdm. eins überziehen (ugs.); **~ by lightning** vom Blitz getroffen; **(b)** (come forcibly into contact with) ‹Fahrzeug:› prallen gegen ‹Mauer usw.›; ‹Schiff:› laufen gegen ‹Felsen usw.›; **the aircraft ~ the ground** das Flugzeug schlug auf den Boden auf; **~ the roof** *or* **ceiling** (fig. coll.: become angry) an die Decke *od.* in die Luft gehen (ugs.); **(c)** (cause to come into contact) [an]stoßen; [an]schlagen; **~ one's head on sth.** mit dem Kopf gegen etw. stoßen; sich (Dat.) den Kopf an etw. (Dat.) stoßen; **(d)** (fig.: cause to suffer) **~ badly** *or* **hard** schwer treffen; **(e)** (fig.: affect)

treffen; **have been ~ by frost/rain** *etc.* durch Frost/Regen *usw.* gelitten haben; **(f)** (fig.: light upon) finden; stoßen *od.* treffen auf (+ *Akk.*); finden ‹Bodenschätze›; **(g)** (fig. coll.: arrive at) erreichen ‹Höchstform, bestimmten Ort, bestimmte Höhe, bestimmtes Alter usw.›; **I think we've ~ a snag** ich glaube, jetzt gibt's Probleme; **~ town** ankommen; *see also* **all-time; (h)** (fig. coll.: indulge in) zuschlagen bei (+ Dat.) (salopp); **[begin to] ~ the bottle** das Trinken anfangen; **(i)** (Cricket) erzielen ‹Lauf›; **~ the ball for six** (Brit.) sechs Läufe auf einmal erzielen; **~ sb. for six** (fig.) jmdn. übertrumpfen. **2** *v.i.*, **-tt-, hit (a)** (direct a blow) schlagen; **~ hard** fest *od.* hart zuschlagen; **~ at sb./sth.** auf jmdn./etw. einschlagen; **~ and run** ‹Autofahrer:› Fahrer- *od.* Unfallflucht begehen; ‹Angreifer:› einen Blitzüberfall machen; **(b)** (come into forcible contact) **~ against** *or* **upon sth.** gegen *od.* auf etw. (*Akk.*) stoßen. **3** *n.* **(a)** (blow) Schlag, *der;* **(b)** (shot or bomb striking target) Treffer, *der;* **(c)** (success) Erfolg, *der;* Knüller, *der* (ugs.); (success in entertainment) Schlager, *der;* Hit, *der* (ugs.); **make a ~:** gut ankommen

~ 'back 1 *v.t.* zurückschlagen. **2** *v.i.* zurückschlagen; (verbally) kontern; sich wehren; **~ back at sb.** (fig.) jmdm. Kontra geben

~ 'off *v.t.* **(a)** (characterize) genau treffen; treffend charakterisieren; **~ it off [with each other]** gut miteinander auskommen; **~ it off with sb.** gut mit jmdm. auskommen

~ 'out *v.i.* drauflosschlagen; **~ out at** *or* **against sb./ sth.** (fig.) jmdn./etw. scharf angreifen

~ upon *v.t.* stoßen auf (+ *Akk.*); finden ‹richtige Antwort, Methode›; kommen auf (+ *Akk.*) ‹Idee›

hit: ~-and-'miss ⇒ **~-or-miss; ~-and-'run** *adj.* unfallflüchtig ‹Fahrer›; **~-and-run accident** Unfall mit Fahrerflucht

hitch /hɪtʃ/ **1** *v.t.* **(a)** (move by a jerk) rücken; **(b)** (fasten) [fest]binden ‹Tier› **(to an** + *Akk.*); binden ‹Seil› **(round um** + *Akk.*); [an]koppeln ‹Anhänger usw.› **(to an** + *Akk.*); spannen ‹Zugtier, -maschine usw.› **(to vor** + *Akk.*). **2** *v.i.* ⇒ **hitch-hike 1. 3** *n.* **(a)** (stoppage) Unterbrechung, *die;* **(b)** (impediment) Problem, *das;* Schwierigkeit, *die;* **have one ~:** einen Haken haben (ugs.)

~ 'up *v.t.* hochheben ‹Rock›

hitch: ~-hike 1 *v.i.* per Anhalter fahren; trampen; **2** *n.* Tramptour, *die;* **~-hiker** *n.* Anhalter, *der*/Anhalterin, *die;* Tramper, *der*/Tramperin, *die;* **~-hiking** *n.* Trampen, *das*

hither /'hɪðə(r)/ *adv.* (literary) hierher; **~ and thither** *or* **yon** hierhin und dorthin

hitherto /'hɪðətʊ, hɪðə'tuː/ *adv.* (literary) bisher; bislang

hit: ~ list *n.* **(a)** (charts) ⇒ **~ parade; (b)** (coll.: victims) Abschussliste, *die* (fig.); **~ man** *n.* (coll.) Killer, *der* (salopp); **~-or-'miss** *adj.* (coll.) (random) unsicher, unzuverlässig ‹Methode›; (careless) schlampig, schluderig (ugs. abwertend) ‹Arbeit›; **it was a very ~-or-miss affair** es ging alles aufs Geratewohl (ugs.); **~ parade** *n.* Hitparade, *die;* **~ 'record** *n.* Hit, *der* (ugs.)

HIV *abbr.* (Med.) **human immunodeficiency virus** HIV; **HIV-positive/-negative** HIV-positiv/-negativ

hive /haɪv/ *n.* [Bienen]stock, *der;* (of straw) Bienenkorb, *der;* **what a ~ of industry!** der reinste Bienenstock! (ugs.)

~ 'off (Brit.) *v.t.* (separate and make independent) verselbstständigen; **the firm was ~d off from the parent company** die Firma wurde aus der Muttergesellschaft ausgegliedert

HM *abbr.* (Brit.) **(a) Her/His Majesty** I. M./S. M.; **(b) Her/His Majesty's**

HMS *abbr.* (Brit.) **Her/His Majesty's Ship** H.M.S.

ho /həʊ/ *int. expr.* *surprise* oh; nanu; *expr. admiration* oh; *expr. triumph* ha; *drawing attention* he; heda; *expr. derision* haha

hoard /hɔːd/ **1** *n.* **(a)** (store laid by) Vorrat, *der;* **make/collect a ~ of sth.** etw. horten; **(b)** (fig.: amassed stock) Sammlung, *die.* **2** *v.t.* **~ [up]** horten ‹Geld, Brennmaterial, Lebensmittel usw.›; hamstern ‹Lebensmittel›

hoarder /'hɔːdə(r)/ *n.* Hamsterer, *der*/Hamsterin, *die*

hoarding /'hɔːdɪŋ/ *n.* **(a)** (fence) Bretterzaun, *der;* Bretterwand, *die;* (round building site) Bauzaun, *der;* **(b)** (Brit.: for advertisements) Reklamewand, *die;* Plakatwand, *die*

hoar frost /'hɔːfrɒst/ *n.* [Rau]reif, *der*

hoarse /hɔːs/ *adj.* **(a)** (rough, husky) heiser, rau ‹*Stimme*›; (croaking) krächzend ‹*Laut*›; (with emotion) belegt ‹*Stimme*›; **(b)** (having a dry, husky voice) heiser

hoary /'hɔːrɪ/ *adj.* **(a)** (grey) grau; ergraut (geh.); (white) [schloh]weiß; **(b)** (very old) altehrwürdig ‹*Gebäude*›; ~ **old joke** uralter Witz

hoax /həʊks/ **1** *v.t.* anführen (ugs.); foppen; zum Besten haben *od.* halten; ~ **sb. into believing sth.** jmdm. etw. weismachen. **2** *n.* (deception) Schwindel, *der;* (false report) Falschmeldung, *die;* Ente, *die* (ugs.); (practical joke) Streich, *der;* (false alarm) blinder Alarm

hob /hɒb/ *n.* (of cooker) Kochmulde, *die* (Fachspr.); [Koch]platte, *die;* Kochstelle, *die*

hobble /'hɒbl/ **1** *v.i.* ~ **[about]** [herum]humpeln *od.* -hinken. **2** *n.* Humpeln, *das;* Hinken, *das*

hobby /'hɒbɪ/ *n.* Hobby, *das;* Steckenpferd, *das*

'hobby horse *n.* (child's toy) Steckenpferd, *das*

hob: ~**nail** *n.* [starker] Schuh- *od.* Stiefelnagel; ~**nailed** /'hɒbneɪld/ *adj.* Nagel‹*schuh, -stiefel*›

hobo /'həʊbəʊ/ *n., pl.* ~**es** (Amer.) Landstreicher, *der*/-streicherin, *die*

hock¹ /hɒk/ *n.* (Brit.: wine) Rheinwein, *der*

hock² (esp. Amer.) **1** *v.t.* versetzen. **2** *n.* **be in** ~**:** versetzt sein

hockey /'hɒkɪ/ *n.* Hockey, *das*

'hockey stick *n.* Hockeystock, *der;* Hockeyschläger, *der*

hocus-pocus /həʊkəs'pəʊkəs/ *n.* Zauberei, *die*

hod /hɒd/ *n.* Tragmulde, *die*

hoe /həʊ/ **1** *n.* Hacke, *die.* **2** *v.t.* hacken ‹*Beet, Acker*›

hog /hɒg/ **1** *n.* **(a)** (domesticated pig) [Mast]schwein, *das;* **go the whole** ~ (coll.) Nägel mit Köpfen machen (ugs.); **(b)** (fig.: person) Schwein, *das* (derb); Sau, *die* (derb); Ferkel, *das* (derb). **2** *v.t.*, **-gg-** (coll.) mit Beschlag belegen

Hogmanay /'hɒgməneɪ/ *n.* (Scot., N. Engl.) Silvester, *der od. das*

hoist /hɔɪst/ **1** *v.t.* **(a)** (raise aloft) hoch-, aufziehen, hissen ‹*Flagge usw.*›; heißen (Seemannsspr.) ‹*Flagge usw.*›; **(b)** (raise by tackle etc.) hieven ‹*Last*›; setzen ‹*Segel*›. **2** *n.* (goods lift) [Lasten]aufzug, *der.* **3** *adj.* **be** ~ **with one's own petard** sich in seiner eigenen Schlinge fangen

hoity-toity /hɔɪtɪ'tɔɪtɪ/ *adj.* (coll.) hochnäsig (abwertend); eingebildet; (petulant) pikiert

hold¹ /həʊld/ *n.* (of ship) Laderaum, *der;* (of aircraft) Frachtraum, *der*

hold² **1** *v.t.,* **held** /held/ **(a)** (grasp) halten; (carry) tragen; (keep fast) festhalten; ~ **sb. by the arm** jmdn. am Arm festhalten; **(b)** (support) ‹*tragendes Teil:*› halten, stützen, tragen ‹*Decke, Dach usw.*›; aufnehmen ‹*Gewicht, Kraft*›; **(c)** (keep in position) halten; ~ **the door open for sb.** jmdm. die Tür aufhalten; **(d)** (grasp to control) halten ‹*Kind, Hund, Zügel*›; **(e)** (keep in particular attitude) ~ **oneself still** stillhalten; ~ **oneself ready** *or* **in readiness** sich bereit *od.* in Bereitschaft halten; ~ **one's head high** (fig.) (be confident) selbstbewusst sein *od.* auftreten; (be proud) den Kopf hoch tragen; **(f)** (contain) enthalten; bergen ‹*Gefahr, Geheimnis*›; (be able to contain) fassen ‹*Liter, Personen usw.*›; **the room** ~**s ten people** in dem Raum haben 10 Leute Platz; der Raum bietet 10 Leuten Platz; ~ **water** ‹*Behälter:*› wasserdicht sein; Wasser halten; (fig.) ‹*Argument, Theorie:*› stichhaltig sein, hieb- und stichfest sein; **(g)** (not be intoxicated by) **he can/can't** ~ **his drink** *or* **liquor** er kann etwas/nichts vertragen; **(h)** (possess) besitzen; haben; **(i)** (have gained) halten ‹*Rekord*›; haben ‹*Diplom, Doktorgrad*›; **(j)** (keep possession of) halten ‹*Stützpunkt, Stadt, Stellung*›; (Mus.: sustain) [aus]halten ‹*Ton*›; ~ **one's own** (fig.) sich behaupten; ~ **one's position** (fig.) auf seinem Standpunkt beharren; **(k)** (occupy) innehaben, (geh.) bekleiden ‹*Posten, Amt, Stellung*›; ~ **office** im Amt sein; ~ **the line** (Teleph.) am Apparat bleiben; **(l)** (engross) fesseln, (geh.) gefangen halten ‹*Aufmerksamkeit, Publikum*›; **(m)**

(keep in specified condition) halten; ~ **the ladder steady** die Leiter festhalten; *see also* **bay³ 1; ransom 1;** **(n)** (detain) (in custody) in Haft halten, festhalten; (imprison) festsetzen; inhaftieren; (arrest) festnehmen; **be held in a prison** in einem Gefängnis einsitzen; **(o)** (oblige to adhere) ~ **sb. to the terms of the contract/to a promise** darauf bestehen, dass jmd. sich an die Vertragsbestimmungen hält/dass jmd. ein Versprechen hält *od.* einlöst; **(p)** (Sport: restrict) ~ **one's opponent [to a draw]** ein Unentschieden [gegen den Gegner] halten *od.* verteidigen; **(q)** (cause to take place) stattfinden lassen; abhalten ‹*Veranstaltung, Konferenz, Gottesdienst, Sitzung, Prüfung*›; veranstalten ‹*Festival, Auktion*›; austragen ‹*Meisterschaften*›; führen ‹*Unterhaltung, Gespräch, Korrespondenz*›; durchführen ‹*Untersuchung*›; geben ‹*Empfang*›; halten ‹*Vortrag, Rede*›; **be held** stattfinden; **(r)** (restrain) [fest]halten; ~ **one's fire** [noch] nicht schießen; (fig.: refrain from criticism) mit seiner Kritik zurückhalten; **(s)** (coll.: withhold) zurückhalten; ~ **it!** [einen] Moment mal!; *see also* **horse a;** **(t)** (think, believe) ~ **a view** *or* **an opinion** eine Ansicht haben (on über + *Akk.*); ~ **that ...:** dafürhalten, dass ...; der Ansicht sein, dass ...; ~ **sb./oneself guilty/blameless** jmdn./sich für schuldig/unschuldig halten (for an + *Dat.*); ~ **oneself responsible for sth.** sich für etw. verantwortlich fühlen; ~ **sth. against sb.** jmdm. etw. vorwerfen; *see also* **dear 1 a; responsible a. 2** *v.i.,* **held (a)** (not give way) ‹*Seil, Nagel, Anker, Schloss, Angeklebtes:*› halten; ‹*Damm:*› [stand]halten; **(b)** (remain unchanged) anhalten; [an]dauern; ‹*Wetter:*› sich halten, so bleiben; ‹*Angebot, Versprechen:*› gelten; **his luck held** er hatte auch weiterhin Glück; **(c)** (remain steadfast) ~ **to sth.** bei etw. bleiben; an etw. (*Dat.*) festhalten; **(d)** (be valid) ~ **[good** *or* **true]** gelten; Gültigkeit haben. **3** *n.* **(a)** (grasp) Griff, *der;* **grab** *or* **seize** ~ **of sth.** etw. ergreifen; **get** *or* **lay** *or* **take** ~ **of sth.** etw. fassen *od.* packen; **keep** ~ **of sth.** etw. festhalten; **lose one's** ~**:** den Halt verlieren; **take** ~ (fig.) sich durchsetzen; ‹*Krankheit:*› fortschreiten; **get** ~ **of sth.** (fig.) etw. bekommen *od.* auftreiben; **get** ~ **of sb.** (fig.) jmdn. erreichen; **get a** ~ **on oneself** sich fassen; **have a** ~ **over sb.** jmdn. in der Hand halten; *see also* **catch 1 a;** **(b)** (influence) Einfluss, *der* (on, over auf + *Akk.*); **(c)** (Sport) Griff, *der;* **there are no** ~**s barred** (fig.) alles ist erlaubt; **(d)** (thing to hold by) Griff, *der;* **(e)** put on ~**:** auf Eis legen ‹*Plan, Programm*›

~ **'back 1** *v.t.* **(a)** (restrain) zurückhalten; ~ **sb. back from doing sth.** jmdn. [daran] hindern, etw. zu tun; **(b)** (impede progress of) hindern; **(c)** (withhold) zurückhalten; ~ **sth. back from sb.** jmdm. etw. vorenthalten. **2** *v.i.* zögern; ~ **back from doing sth.** zögern, etw. zu tun

~ **'down** *v.t.* **(a)** festhalten; (repress) unterdrücken; niederhalten ‹*Volk*›; (fig.: keep at low level) niedrig halten ‹*Preise, Löhne usw.*›; **(b)** (keep) sich halten in (+ *Dat.*) ‹*Stellung, Position*›

~ **'forth 1** *v.t.* (offer) anpreisen. **2** *v.i.* sich in langen Reden ergehen; ~ **forth about** *or* **on sth.** sich über etw. (*Akk.*) auslassen

~ **'off 1** *v.t.* (keep at bay) von sich fernhalten, (ugs.) sich (*Dat.*) vom Leib halten ‹*Fans, Presse*›; abwehren ‹*Angriff*›. **2** *v.i.* ‹*Käufer usw.:*› sich zurückhalten; ‹*Feind:*› sich ruhig verhalten; ‹*Regen, Monsun, Winter:*› ausbleiben, auf sich (*Akk.*) warten lassen

~ **'on 1** *v.t.* (keep in position) [fest]halten. **2** *v.i.* **(a)** sich festhalten; ~ **on to sb./sth.** sich an jmdm./etw. festhalten; (fig.: retain) jmdn./etw. behalten; **(b)** (stand firm) durchhalten; aushalten; **(c)** (Teleph.) am Apparat bleiben; dranbleiben (ugs.); **(d)** (coll.: wait) warten; ~ **on!** einen Moment!

~ **'out 1** *v.t.* **(a)** ausstrecken ‹*Hand, Arm usw.*›; ausbreiten ‹*Arme*›; hinhalten ‹*Tasse, Teller*›; **(b)** (fig.: offer) in Aussicht stellen (to *Dat.*); **he did not** ~ **out much hope** er hat mir/dir *usw.* nicht viel Hoffnung gemacht. **2** *v.i.* **(a)** (maintain resistance) sich halten; **(b)** (last) ‹*Vorräte:*› vorhalten; ‹*Motor:*› halten; **(c)** ~ **out for sth.** etw. herauszuschinden versuchen (ugs.)

~ **'over** *v.t.* vertagen (till auf + *Akk.*)

~ **'up 1** *v.t.* **(a)** (raise) hochhalten; hochheben ‹*Person*›; [hoch]heben ‹*Hand, Kopf*›; **(b)** (fig.: offer as an example) ~ **sb. up as ...:** jmdn. als ... hinstellen; ~ **sb./sth. up to**

ridicule/scorn jmdn./etw. dem Spott/Hohn preisgeben; **(c)** (support) stützen; tragen ⟨*Dach usw.*⟩; ∼ **sth. up with sth.** etw. mit etw. abstützen; **(d)** (delay) aufhalten; behindern ⟨*Verkehr, Versorgung*⟩; verzögern ⟨*Friedensvertrag*⟩; (halt) ins Stocken bringen ⟨*Produktion*⟩; **(e)** (rob) überfallen [und ausrauben]. **2** *v.i.* (under scrutiny) sich als stichhaltig erweisen

∼ **with** *v.t.* ∼/**not** ∼ **with sth.** mit etw. einverstanden sein/etw. ablehnen

'holdall /'həʊldɔːl/ *n.* Reisetasche, *die*

holder /'həʊldə(r)/ *n.* **(a)** (of post) Inhaber, *der*/Inhaberin, *die;* **(b)** (of title) Träger, *der*/Trägerin, *die;* (Sport) Titelhalter, -inhaber, *der;* **(c)** ⟨*Zigaretten*⟩spitze, *die;* ⟨*Papier-, Feder-, Zahnputzglas*⟩halter, *der*

'hold-up *n.* **(a)** (robbery) [Raub]überfall, *der;* **(b)** (stoppage) Unterbrechung, *die;* (delay) Verzögerung, *die*

hole /həʊl/ **1** *n.* **(a)** Loch, *das;* **make a** ∼ **in sth.** (fig.) eine ganze Menge von etw. verschlingen; **pick** ∼**s in** (fig.: find fault with) zerpflücken (ugs.); auseinander nehmen (ugs.); madig machen (ugs.) ⟨*Person*⟩; ∼ **in the heart** Loch in der Herzscheidewand; **(b)** (burrow) (of fox, badger, rabbit) Bau, *der;* (of mouse) Loch, *das;* **(c)** (coll.) (dingy abode) Loch, *das* (salopp abwertend); (wretched place) Kaff, *das* (ugs. abwertend); Nest, *das* (ugs. abwertend); **(d)** (Golf) Loch, *das;* (space between tee and ∼) [Spiel]bahn, *die;* ∼ **in one** Hole-in-One, *das;* Ass, *das.* **2** *v.t.* **(a)** Löcher/ein Loch machen in (+ *Akk.*); **(b)** (Naut.) be ∼d leckschlagen (Seemannsspr.)

∼ **'up** *v.i.* (Amer. coll.) sich verkriechen (ugs.)

'hole-in-the-wall *adj.* ∼ [**cash**] **machine** Geldautomat, *der*

holiday /'hɒlɪdeɪ, 'hɒlɪdɪ/ **1** *n.* **(a)** (day of recreation) [arbeits]freier Tag; (day of festivity) Feiertag, *der;* **tomorrow is a** ∼: morgen ist frei/Feiertag; **(b)** *in sing. or pl.* (Brit.: vacation) Urlaub, *der;* (Sch.) [Schul]ferien *Pl.;* **need a** ∼: urlaubsreif sein; **have a good** ∼! schönen Urlaub!; **take** *or* **have a/one's** ∼: Urlaub nehmen *od.* machen/seinen Urlaub nehmen; **on** ∼, **on one's** ∼**s** im *od.* in seinem Urlaub. **2** *attrib. adj.* Urlaubs-/Ferien⟨*stimmung, -pläne*⟩. **3** *v.i.* Urlaub/Ferien machen; urlauben (ugs.)

holiday: ∼ **camp** *n.* Feriendorf, *das;* Ferienpark, *der;* ∼ **home** *n.* Feriendomizil, *das;* ∼ **job** *n.* Ferienjob, *der;* ∼**-maker** *n.* Urlauber, *der*/Urlauberin, *die;* ∼ **resort** *n.* Ferienort, *der*

holiness /'həʊlɪnɪs/ *n., no pl.* ▶ 1152 | Heiligkeit, *die;* **His H**∼**:** Seine Heiligkeit

Holland /'hɒlənd/ *pr. n.* Holland (*das*)

hollow /'hɒləʊ/ **1** *adj.* **(a)** (not solid) hohl; Hohl⟨*ziegel, -mauer, -zylinder, -kugel*⟩; **(b)** (sunken) eingefallen ⟨*Wangen, Schläfen*⟩; hohl, tief liegend ⟨*Augen*⟩; **(c)** (echoing) hohl ⟨*Ton, Klang*⟩; **(d)** (fig.: empty) wertlos; **(e)** (fig.: cynical) verlogen; leer ⟨*Versprechen*⟩; gequält ⟨*Lachen*⟩. **2** *n.* [Boden]senke, *die;* [Boden]vertiefung, *die;* **hold sth. in the** ∼ **of one's hand** etw. in der hohlen Hand halten. **3** *adv.* **beat sb.** ∼ (coll.) jmdn. um Längen schlagen (ugs.). **4** *v.t.* ∼ **out** aushöhlen; graben ⟨*Höhle*⟩

holly /'hɒlɪ/ *n.* (tree) Stechpalme, *die;* Ilex, *der* (fachspr.)

'hollyhock *n.* (Bot.) Stockrose, *die*

holocaust /'hɒləkɔːst/ *n.* Massenvernichtung, *die;* the **H**∼**:** der Holocaust; die Judenvernichtung

hologram /'hɒləgræm/ *n.* Hologramm, *das*

holster /'həʊlstə(r)/ *n.* [Pistolen]halfter, *die od. das*

holy /'həʊlɪ/ *adj.* heilig; fromm ⟨*Zweck*⟩; ∼ **saints** Heilige

Holy: ∼ **'Bible** *n.* Heilige Schrift; ∼ **Com'munion** ⇒ **communion a;** ∼ **'Ghost** ⇒ ∼ **Spirit;** ∼ **Grail** *n.* Heiliger Gral; ∼ **Land** *n.* the ∼ **Land** das Heilige Land; ∼ **Roman 'Empire** *n.* (Hist.) Heiliges Römisches Reich [Deutscher Nation]; ∼ **'Spirit** *n.* (Relig.) Heiliger Geist; ∼ **Week** *n.* Karwoche, *die*

homage /'hɒmɪdʒ/ *n.* (tribute) Huldigung, *die* (**to an** + *Akk.*); **pay** *or* **do** ∼ **to sb./sth.** jmdm./einer Sache huldigen

home /həʊm/ **1** *n.* **(a)** Heim, *das;* (flat) Wohnung, *die;* (house) Haus, *das;* (household) [Eltern]haus, *das;* **my** ∼ **is in Leeds** ich bin in Leeds zu Hause *od.* wohne in Leeds; **a** ∼ **of one's own** ein eigenes Zuhause; **leave/have left** ∼**:** aus dem Haus gehen/sein; **live at** ∼**:** im Elternhaus

wohnen; **they had no** ∼/∼**s** [of their own] sie hatten kein Zuhause; **at** ∼**:** zu Hause; (not abroad) im Inland; **be/feel at** ∼ (fig.) sich wohl fühlen; **make sb. feel at** ∼**:** es jmdm. behaglich machen; **make yourself at** ∼**:** fühl dich wie zu Hause; **he is quite at** ∼ **in French** er ist im Französischen ganz gut zu Hause; ∼ **from** ∼**:** zweites Zuhause; **(b)** (fig.) **to take an example nearer** ∼, ...**:** um ein Beispiel zu nehmen, das uns näher liegt, ...; **(c)** (native country) die Heimat; **at** ∼**:** zu Hause; in der Heimat; **(d)** (institution) Heim, *das;* (coll.: mental ∼) Anstalt, *die* (salopp). **2** *adj.* **(a)** (connected with ∼) Haus-; Haushalts⟨*gerät usw.*⟩; **(b)** (done at ∼) häuslich; Selbst⟨*backen, ∼brauen usw.*⟩; **(c)** (in the neighbourhood of ∼) nahe gelegen; **(d)** (Sport) Heim⟨*spiel, -sieg, -mannschaft*⟩; ⟨*Anhänger, Spieler*⟩ der Heimmannschaft; ∼ **ground** eigener Platz; **(e)** (not foreign) [ein]heimisch; inländisch. **3** *adv.* **(a)** (to ∼) nach Hause; **on one's way** ∼**:** auf dem Weg nach Hause; Nachhauseweg; **he takes** ∼ **£200 a week after tax** er verdient 200 Pfund netto in der Woche; **nothing to write** ∼ **about** (coll.) nichts Besonderes *od.* Aufregendes; **(b)** (arrived at ∼) zu Hause; **be** ∼ **and dry** (fig.) aus dem Schneider sein (ugs.); **(c)** (as far as possible) **push** ∼**:** [ganz] hineinschieben ⟨*Schublade*⟩; ausnutzen ⟨*Vorteil*⟩; **press** ∼**:** [ganz] hinunterdrücken ⟨*Hebel*⟩; forcieren ⟨*Angriff*⟩; [voll] ausnutzen ⟨*Vorteil*⟩; **drive** ∼**:** [ganz] einschlagen ⟨*Nagel*⟩; **(d) come** *or* **get** ∼ **to sb.** (become fully realized) jmdm. in vollem Ausmaß bewusst werden; *see also* **roost 1. 4** *v.i.* **(a)** ⟨*Vogel usw.*⟩ zurückkehren; **(b)** (be guided) **these missiles** ∼ [**in**] **on their targets** diese Flugkörper suchen sich (*Dat.*) ihr Ziel; **(c)** ∼ **in/on sth.** (fig.) etw. herausgreifen

home: ∼ **address** *n.* Privatanschrift, *die;* ∼**-'brew** *n.* selbst gebrautes Bier; ∼**coming** *n.* Heimkehr, *die;* ∼ **com'puter** *n.* Heimcomputer, *der;* **H**∼ **Counties** *n. pl.* (Brit.) **the H**∼ **Counties** die Home Countys; die Grafschaften um London; ∼ **eco'nomics** *n. sing.* ⇒ **domestic science;** ∼ **'ground** *n.* on [one's] ∼ **ground** auf heimischem Boden; (fig.) zu Hause (ugs.); ∼**-grown** *adj.* selbst gezogen ⟨*Gemüse, Obst*⟩; ∼ **'help** *n.* (Brit.) Haushaltshilfe, *die;* ∼**land** *n.* **(a)** Heimat, *die;* Heimatland, *das;* **(b)** (in South Africa) Homeland, *das*

homeless /'həʊmlɪs/ **1** *adj.* obdachlos. **2** *n.* the ∼**:** die Obdachlosen

'home-loving *adj.* häuslich

homely /'həʊmlɪ/ *adj.* einfach, schlicht ⟨*Worte, Stil, Sprache usw.*⟩; warmherzig ⟨*Person*⟩

home: ∼**-made** *adj.* selbst gemacht; selbst gebacken ⟨*Brot*⟩; hausgemacht ⟨*Lebensmittel*⟩; ∼ **'movie** *n.* Amateurfilm, *der;* **H**∼ **Office** *n.* (Brit.) Innenministerium, *das*

homeopathic *etc.* (Amer.) ⇒ **homoeo-**

home: ∼**owner** *n.* Eigenheimbesitzer, *der*/-besitzerin, *die;* ∼ **page** *n.* (Computing) Homepage, *die;* **H**∼ **'Secretary** *n.* (Brit.) Innenminister, *der;* ∼ **'shopping** *n.* Teleshopping, *das;* ∼**sick** *adj.* heimwehkrank; **become/be** ∼**sick** Heimweh bekommen/haben; ∼**spun** *adj.* **(a)** (spun [and woven] at ∼) selbst gesponnen [und gewoben]; (of ∼ manufacture) in Heimarbeit gesponnen; **(b)** (unsophisticated) schlicht; einfach; ∼ **'town** *n.* Heimatstadt, *die;* Vaterstadt, *die* (geh.); (town of residence) Wohnort, *der;* ∼ **'truth** *n.* unangenehme Wahrheit; **tell sb. a few** ∼ **truths** jmdm. [gehörig] die Meinung sagen

homeward /'həʊmwəd/ **1** *adj.* nach Hause *nachgestellt;* Nachhause⟨*weg*⟩; (return) Rück⟨*fahrt, -reise, -weg*⟩; *see also* **bound³. 2** *adv.* nach Hause; heimwärts

'homework *n.* (Sch.) Hausaufgaben *Pl.;* **piece of** ∼**:** Hausaufgabe, *die;* **do one's** ∼ (fig.) sich mit der Materie vertraut machen; seine Hausaufgaben machen (scherzh.)

homicidal /ˌhɒmɪ'saɪdl/ *adj.* gemeingefährlich

homicide /'hɒmɪsaɪd/ *n.* Tötung, *die;* (manslaughter) Totschlag, *der*

homily /'hɒmɪlɪ/ *n.* **(a)** (sermon) Homilie, *die* (Theol.); **(b)** (tedious talk) Moralpredigt, *die*

homing /'həʊmɪŋ/ *attrib. adj.* zielsuchend ⟨*Flugkörper, Torpedo*⟩; ∼ **instinct** Heimfindevermögen, *das*

'homing pigeon *n.* Brieftaube, *die*

homo- /'həʊməʊ, 'hɒməʊ/ *in comb.* homo-/Homo-

homoeopathic /ˌhəʊmɪə'pæθɪk, ˌhɒmɪə'pæθɪk/ *adj.* homöopathisch

homoeopathy /həʊmɪˈɒpəθɪ, hɒmɪˈɒpəθɪ/ n. Homöopathie, *die*

homogeneous /hɒməˈdʒiːnɪəs, həʊməˈdʒiːnɪəs/ *adj.* homogen

homogenize (homogenise) /həˈmɒdʒɪnaɪz/ *v.t.* (lit. or fig.) homogenisieren

homonym /ˈhɒmənɪm/ n. (Ling.) Homonym, *das*

homo'sexual 1 *adj.* homosexuell. 2 *n.* Homosexuelle, *der/die*

homosexu'ality n., *no pl.* Homosexualität, *die*

Honduras /hɒnˈdjʊərəs/ *pr. n.* Honduras (*das*)

hone /həʊn/ *v.t.* wetzen ‹ *Messer, Klinge usw.* ›

honest /ˈɒnɪst/ *adj.* (a) ehrlich; (showing righteousness) redlich; ehrenhaft ‹ *Absicht, Tat, Plan* ›; ehrlich ‹ *Arbeit* ›; **the ~ truth** die reine Wahrheit; **make an ~ living** sein Leben auf ehrliche Weise verdienen; (b) (unsophisticated) [gut und] einfach; (unadulterated) rein

honestly /ˈɒnɪstlɪ/ *adv.* ehrlich; redlich ‹ *handeln* ›; **~!** ehrlich!; (annoyed) also wirklich!

honesty /ˈɒnɪstɪ/ n. Ehrlichkeit, *die;* (upright conduct) Redlichkeit, *die;* **in all ~:** ganz ehrlich; **~ is the best policy** (prov.) ehrlich währt am längsten (Spr.)

honey /ˈhʌnɪ/ n. (a) Honig, *der;* (b) (Amer., Ir.: darling) Schatz, *der* (ugs.)

honey: ~ bee n. Honigbiene, *die;* **~comb** n. Bienenwabe, *die;* (filled with ~) Honigwabe, *die;* **~moon** 1 n. (a) Flitterwochen *Pl.;* Honigmond, *der* (scherzh.); (journey) Hochzeitsreise, *die;* **go on one's ~moon** in die Flitterwochen fahren; (b) (fig.: initial period) anfängliche Begeisterung; 2 *v.i.* seine Flitterwochen verbringen; **~suckle** n. (Bot.) Geißblatt, *das*

honk /hɒŋk/ 1 n. (a) (of horn) Hupen, *das;* (b) (of goose or seal) Schrei, *der.* 2 *v.i.* (a) ‹ *Fahrzeug, Fahrer:* › hupen; (b) ‹ *Gans, Seehund:* › schreien

honor, honorable (Amer.) ⇒ **honour, honourable**

honorary /ˈɒnərərɪ/ *adj.* ▶ 1152 | (a) ehrenamtlich; Ehren ‹ *mitglied, -präsident, -doktor, -bürger* ›; (b) (conferred as an honour) Ehren-; **~ degree** ehrenhalber verliehener akademischer Grad

honour /ˈɒnə(r)/ (Brit.) 1 n. (a) *no indef. art.* (reputation) Ehre, *die;* **do ~ to sb./sth.** jmdm./einer Sache zur Ehre gereichen (geh.); jmdm./einer Sache Ehre machen; (b) (respect) Hochachtung, *die;* **do sb. ~, do sth. to sb.** jmdm. Ehre erweisen; (show appreciation of) jmdn. würdigen; **in ~ of sb.** jmdm. zu Ehren; **in ~ of sth.** um etw. gebührend zu feiern; (c) (privilege) Ehre, *die;* **may I have the ~ [of the next dance]?** darf ich [um den nächsten Tanz] bitten?; (d) *no art.* (ethical quality) Ehre, *die;* **he is a man of ~:** er ist ein Ehrenmann *od.* Mann von Ehre; **feel [in] ~ bound to do sth.** sich moralisch verpflichtet fühlen, etw. zu tun; **promise [up]on one's ~:** sein Ehrenwort geben; (e) (distinction) Auszeichnung, *die;* (title) Ehrentitel, *der; in pl.* (Univ.) **she gained ~s in her exam, she passed [the exam] with ~s** sie hat das Examen mit Auszeichnung bestanden; (f) *in pl.* **do the ~s** (coll.) (introduce guests) die Honneurs machen; (serve guests) den Gastgeber spielen; (g) *in title* **your H~** (Brit. Law) hohes Gericht; Euer Ehren; (h) (person or thing that brings credit) **be an ~ to sb./sth.** jmdm./einer Sache Ehre machen. 2 *v.t.* (a) ehren; würdigen ‹ *Verdienste, besondere Eigenschaften* ›; **be ~ed as an artist** als Künstler Anerkennung finden; **~ sb. with one's presence** (iron.) jmdn. mit seiner Gegenwart beehren; (b) (acknowledge) beachten ‹ *Vorschriften* ›; respektieren ‹ *Gebräuche, Rechte* ›; (c) (fulfil) sich halten an (+ *Akk.*); (Commerc.) honorieren; begleichen ‹ *Rechnung, Schuld* ›

honourable /ˈɒnərəbl/ *adj.* (Brit.) (a) (worthy of respect) ehrenwert (geh.); (b) (bringing credit) achtbar; (consistent with honour) ehrenvoll ‹ *Frieden, Rückzug, Entlassung* ›; (c) (ethical) rechtschaffen; redlich ‹ *Geschäftsgebaren* ›; (d) ▶ 1152 | *in title* **the H~ ...:** ≈ der/die ehrenwerte ...; **the ~ gentleman/lady, the ~ member [for X]** (Brit. Parl.) der Herr/die Frau Abgeordnete [für den Wahlkreis X]; ≈ der [verehrte] Herr Kollege/die [verehrte] Frau Kollegin

hood /hʊd/ n. (a) Kapuze, *die;* (b) (of vehicle) (Brit.: waterproof top) Verdeck, *das;* (Amer.: bonnet) [Motor]haube, *die*

hoodlum /ˈhuːdləm/ n. (young thug) Rowdy, *der* (abwertend)

hoodoo /ˈhuːduː/ n. (a) (bad spell) Fluch, *der;* **there is a ~ on ...:** es liegt ein Fluch auf ... (+ *Dat.*); (b) (bringer of bad luck) **be a ~:** Unglück bringen

hoodwink /ˈhʊdwɪŋk/ *v.t.* hinters Licht führen; täuschen

hoof /huːf/ 1 n., *pl.* **~s** *or* **hooves** /huːvz/ Huf, *der;* **buy cattle on the ~** (for meat) Lebendvieh kaufen; **on the ~** (fig.) auf der Stelle. *See also* **cloven** 2. 2 *v.t.* (coll.) (walk) **~ it** tippeln (ugs.)

hook /hʊk/ 1 n. (a) Haken, *der;* (Fishing) [Angel]haken, *der;* **~ and eye** Haken und Öse; **swallow sth. ~, line, and sinker** (fig.) etw. blind glauben; **get sb. off the ~** (fig. coll.) jmdn. herauspauken (ugs.); **that lets me/him off the ~** (fig. coll.) da bin ich/ist er noch einmal davongekommen; **by ~ or by crook** mit allen Mitteln; (b) (telephone cradle) Gabel, *die;* (c) (Boxing) Haken, *der.* 2 *v.t.* (a) (grasp) mit Haken/mit einem Haken greifen; (b) (fasten) mit Haken/mit einem Haken befestigen (**to** an + *Dat.*); festhaken ‹ *Tor* › (**to** an + *Akk.*); haken ‹ *Bein, Finger* › (**over** über + *Akk.*, **in** in + *Akk.*); (c) **be ~ed [on sth./sb.]** (coll.) (addicted harmfully) [von etw./jmdn.] abhängig sein; (addicted harmlessly) [auf etw./jmdn.] stehen (ugs., bes. Jugendspr.); (captivated) [von etw./jmdn.] fasziniert sein; (d) (catch) an die Angel bekommen ‹ *Fisch* ›; (fig.) sich (*Dat.*) angeln

~ 'on 1 *v.t.* anhaken (**to** an + *Akk.*); anhängen ‹ *Wagen, Anhänger* › (**to** an + *Akk.*). 2 *v.i.* angehakt werden (**to** an + *Akk.*)

~ 'up 1 *v.t.* (a) festhaken (**to** an + *Akk.*); zuhaken ‹ *Kleid* ›; (b) (Radio and Telev. coll.) zusammenschalten ‹ *Sender* ›. 2 *v.i.* ‹ *Kleid:* › mit Haken geschlossen werden

hooked /hʊkt/ *adj.* (a) (hook-shaped) hakenförmig; (b) (having hook[s]) mit Haken/mit einem Haken versehen. *See also* **hook** 2 c

hooker /ˈhʊkə(r)/ n. (a) (Rugby) Hakler, *der;* (b) (Amer. sl.: prostitute) Nutte, *die* (salopp)

hook: ~-'nose n. Hakennase, *die;* **~-up** n. (Radio and Telev. coll.) Zusammenschaltung, *die* (*zu einer Gemeinschaftssendung*)

hooligan /ˈhuːlɪɡən/ n. Rowdy, *der*

hooliganism /ˈhuːlɪɡənɪzm/ n., *no pl.* Rowdytum, *das*

hoop /huːp/ n. Reifen, *der;* (in circus, show, etc.) Springreifen, *der;* **put sb. through the ~[s]** (fig.) jmdn. durch die Mangel drehen (salopp)

hooray ⇒ **hurray**

hoot /huːt/ 1 *v.i.* (a) (call out) johlen; (b) ‹ *Eule:* › schreien; (c) ‹ *Fahrzeug, Fahrer:* › hupen, tuten; ‹ *Sirene, Nebelhorn usw.:* › heulen, tuten; **~ at sb./sth.** jmdn./etw. anhupen. 2 *v.t.* heulen *od.* tuten lassen ‹ *Sirene, Nebelhorn* ›. 3 n. (a) (shout) **~s of derision/scorn** verächtliches Gejohle; (b) (owl's cry) Schrei, *der;* (c) (signal) (of vehicle) Hupen, *das;* (of siren, fog-horn) Heulen, *das;* Tuten, *das;* (d) (coll.) **I don't care** *or* **give a ~ or two ~s what you do** es ist mir völlig piepegal *od.* schnuppe (ugs.), was du tust

hooter /ˈhuːtə(r)/ n. (Brit.) (a) (siren) Sirene, *die;* (b) (motor horn) Hupe, *die*

hoover /ˈhuːvə(r)/ (Brit.) 1 n. (a) **H~** (P) [Hoover]staubsauger, *der;* (b) (made by any company) Staubsauger, *der.* 2 *v.t.* (coll.) staubsaugen; saugen ‹ *Boden, Teppich* ›; absaugen ‹ *Möbel* ›. 3 *v.i.* (coll.) [staub]saugen

hop¹ /hɒp/ n. (Bot.) (plant) Hopfen, *der; in pl.* (cones) Hopfendolden *Pl.*

hop² /hɒp/ 1 *v.i.*, **-pp-:** (a) hüpfen; ‹ *Hase:* › hoppeln; **be ~ping mad [about** *or* **over sth.]** (coll.) [wegen etw.] fuchsteufelswild sein (ugs.); (b) (fig. coll.) **~ out of bed** aus dem Bett springen; **~ into the car/on [to] the bus/train/bicycle** sich ins Auto/in den Bus/Zug/aufs Fahrrad schwingen (ugs.); **~ off/out** aussteigen. 2 *v.t.*, **-pp-:** (a) (jump over) springen über (+ *Akk.*); (b) (coll.: jump aboard) aufspringen auf (+ *Akk.*); (c) **~ it** (Brit. coll.: go away) sich verziehen (ugs.). 3 n. (a) (action) Hüpfer, *der;* Hopser, *der* (ugs.); (b) **keep sb. on the ~** (Brit. coll.: bustling about) jmdn. in Trab halten (ugs.); (c) **catch sb. on the ~** (Brit. coll.: unprepared) jmdn. überraschen *od.* überrumpeln; (d) (distance flown) Flugstrecke, *die;* (stage of journey) Teilstrecke, *die;* Etappe, *die*

hope /həʊp/ **1** *n.* Hoffnung, *die;* **give up** ∼: die Hoffnung aufgeben; **hold out** ∼ **[for sb.]** [jmdm.] Hoffnung machen; **beyond** *or* **past** ∼: hoffnungslos; **in the** ∼/**in** ∼[s] **of sth.**/**doing sth.** in der Hoffnung auf etw. (*Akk.*) / , etw. zu tun; **I have some** ∼[s] **of success** *or* **of succeeding** es besteht die Hoffnung, dass ich Erfolg habe; **set** *or* **put** *or* **place one's** ∼s **on** *or* **in sth.**/**sb.** seine Hoffnung auf etw./jmdn. setzen; **raise sb.'s** ∼s jmdm. Hoffnung machen; **high** ∼s große Hoffnungen; **have high** ∼s **of sth.** sich (*Dat.*) große Hoffnungen auf etw. (*Akk.*) machen; **not have a** ∼ **[in hell] [of sth.]** (coll.) sich (*Dat.*) keine[rlei] Hoffnung [auf etw. (*Akk.*)] machen können; **what a** ∼! (coll.), **some** ∼[s]! (coll. iron.) schön wär's!; **be hoping against** ∼ **that** …: trotz allem die Hoffnung nicht aufgeben, dass … **2** *v.i.* hoffen **(for** auf + *Akk.*); **I** ∼ **so/not** hoffentlich/hoffentlich nicht; ich hoffe es/ich hoffe nicht; ∼ **for the best** das Beste hoffen. **3** *v.t.* ∼ **to do sth.**/**that sth. may be so** hoffen, etw. zu tun/dass etw. so eintrifft; **I** ∼ **to go to Paris** (am planning) ich habe vor, nach Paris zu fahren

hopeful /'həʊpfl/ **1** *adj.* **(a)** zuversichtlich; **I'm** ∼/**not** ∼ **that** …: ich hoffe zuversichtlich/bezweifle, dass …; **be** ∼ **of sth.**/**of doing sth.** auf etw. (*Akk.*) hoffen/voller Hoffnung sein, etw. zu tun; **(b)** (promising) vielversprechend; aussichtsreich ⟨*Kapitalanlage, Kandidat*⟩. **2** *n.* [young] ∼: hoffnungsvoller junger Mensch

hopefully /'həʊpfli/ *adv.* **(a)** (expectantly) voller Hoffnung; **(b)** (promisingly) vielversprechend; **(c)** (coll.: it is hoped that) hoffentlich; ∼, **all our problems should now be over** wir wollen hoffen, dass unsere ganzen (ugs.) Probleme jetzt beseitigt sind

hopeless /'həʊplɪs/ *adj.* **(a)** hoffnungslos; **(b)** (inadequate, incompetent) miserabel; **be** ∼, **be a** ∼ **case** ein hoffnungsloser Fall sein (ugs.) **(at** in + *Dat.*); **be** ∼ **at doing sth.** etw. überhaupt nicht können

hopelessly /'həʊplɪslɪ/ *adv.* **(a)** hoffnungslos; **(b)** (inadequately) miserabel

hopper /'hɒpə(r)/ *n.* (Mech.) Trichter, *der*

'hopscotch *n.* Himmel-und-Hölle-Spiel, *das;* **play** ∼: „Himmel und Hölle" spielen

horde /hɔːd/ *n.* große Menge; (derog.) Horde, *die;* **in [their]** ∼s in Scharen

horizon /hə'raɪzn/ *n.* (lit. or fig.) Horizont, *der;* **on/over the** ∼: am Horizont; **there is trouble on the** ∼ (fig.) am Horizont tauchen Probleme auf; **there's nothing on the** ∼ (fig.) da ist nichts in Sicht (ugs.)

horizontal /hɒrɪ'zɒntl/ **1** *adj.* horizontal; waagerecht; *see also* **bar** 1 b. **2** *n.* Horizontale, *die;* Waagerechte, *die*

horizontally /hɒrɪ'zɒntəlɪ/ *adv.* horizontal, (flat) waagerecht; flach ⟨*liegen*⟩

hormone /'hɔːməʊn/ *n.* (Biol., Pharm.) Hormon, *das*

hormone re'placement therapy *n.* (Med.) Hormonsubstitutionstherapie, *die*

horn /hɔːn/ *n.* **(a)** (of animal or devil) Horn, *das;* (of deer) Geweihstange, *die* (Jägerspr.); ∼s Geweih, *das;* **lock** ∼s **[with sb.]** (fig.) [mit jmdm.] die Klinge[n] kreuzen (geh.); **draw in one's** ∼s (fig.) sich zurückhalten; (restrain one's ambition) zurückstecken; **(b)** (substance) Horn, *das;* **(c)** (Mus.) Horn, *das;* **[French]** ∼: [Wald]horn, *das;* **(d)** (of vehicle) Hupe, *die;* (of ship) [Signal]horn, *das;* (of factory) [Fabrik]sirene, *die;* **sound** *or* **blow** *or* **hoot one's** ∼ **[at sb.]** ⟨*Fahrer:*⟩ [jmdn. an]hupen; **(e)** (Geog.) **the H**∼: das Kap Hoorn. *See also* **dilemma**

horned /hɔːnd/ *adj.* gehörnt

hornet /'hɔːnɪt/ *n.* Hornisse, *die;* **stir up** *or* **walk into a** ∼s' **nest** (fig.) in ein Wespennest stechen *od.* greifen (ugs.)

'hornpipe *n.* (Mus.) Hornpipe, *die*

'horn-rimmed *adj.* ∼ **spectacles** *or* **glasses** Hornbrille, *die*

horny /'hɔːnɪ/ *adj.* **(a)** (hard) hornig ⟨*Fußsohlen, Haut, Hände*⟩; **(b)** (made of horn) aus Horn *nachgestellt;* (like horn) hornartig; **(c)** (sl.: sexually aroused) spitz (salopp)

horoscope /'hɒrəskəʊp/ *n.* (Astrol.) Horoskop, *das;* **draw up** *or* **cast sb.'s** ∼: jmdm. das Horoskop stellen

horrendous /hə'rendəs/ *adj.* (coll.) schrecklich (ugs.); entsetzlich (ugs.) ⟨*Dummheit*⟩; horrend ⟨*Preis*⟩

horrible /'hɒrɪbl/ *adj.* **(a)** grauenhaft; grausig ⟨*Monster, Geschichte*⟩; grauenvoll ⟨*Verbrechen, Albtraum*⟩; schauerlich ⟨*Maske*⟩; **I find all insects** ∼: mir graust vor jeder Art von Insekten; **(b)** (coll.: unpleasant, excessive) grauenhaft (ugs.); horrend ⟨*Ausgaben, Kosten*⟩; **I have a** ∼ **feeling that** …: ich habe das ungute Gefühl, dass …

horribly /'hɒrɪblɪ/ *adv.* **(a)** entsetzlich ⟨*entstellt*⟩; scheußlich ⟨*grinsen*⟩; **(b)** (coll.: unpleasantly, excessively) entsetzlich (ugs.); fürchterlich (ugs.) ⟨*aufregen*⟩; horrend ⟨*teuer*⟩

horrid /'hɒrɪd/ *adj.* scheußlich; **don't be so** ∼ **to me** (coll.) sei nicht so garstig zu mir

horrific /hə'rɪfɪk/ *adj.* schrecklich; (coll.) horrend ⟨*Preis*⟩

horrify /'hɒrɪfaɪ/ *v.t.* **(a)** (excite horror in) mit Schrecken erfüllen; **(b)** (shock, scandalize) **be horrified** entsetzt sein **(at, by** über + *Akk.*)

horrifying /'hɒrɪfaɪɪŋ/ *adj.* grauenhaft; grausig ⟨*Film*⟩; **it is** ∼ **to think that** …: der Gedanke, dass …, ist schrecklich

horror /'hɒrə(r)/ **1** *n.* **(a)** Entsetzen, *das* (**at** über + *Akk.*); (repugnance) Grausen, *das;* **have a** ∼ **of sb.**/**sth.**/**doing sth.** einen Horror vor jmdn./etw. haben/einen Horror davor haben, etw. zu tun (ugs.); **(b)** (horrifying quality) Grauenhaftigkeit, *die;* (horrifying thing) Gräuel, *der;* (horrifying person) Scheusal, *das.* **2** *attrib. adj.* Horror⟨*comic, -film, -geschichte*⟩

horror: ∼-**stricken**, ∼-**struck** *adjs.* von Entsetzen gepackt

hors d'œuvre /ɔː'dɜːvr, ɔː'dɜːv/ *n.* (Gastr.) Horsd'œuvre, *das;* ≈ Vorspeise, *die*

horse /hɔːs/ *n.* **(a)** Pferd, *das;* (adult male) Hengst, *der;* **be/get on one's high** ∼ (fig.) auf dem hohen Roß sitzen/sich aufs hohe Roß setzen (ugs.); **hold your** ∼s! (fig.) immer sachte mit den jungen Pferden! (ugs.); **as strong as a** ∼: bärenstark (ugs.); **eat/work like a** ∼: wie ein Scheunendrescher essen (salopp) /wie ein Pferd arbeiten; **I could eat a** ∼ (coll.) ich habe einen Bärenhunger (ugs.); **[right** *or* **straight] from the** ∼'s **mouth** (fig.) aus erster Hand *od.* Quelle; **it's [a question** *or* **matter of]** ∼s **for courses** (fig.) jeder sollte die Aufgaben übernehmen, für die er am besten geeignet ist; **(b)** (Gymnastics) **[vaulting]** ∼: [Sprung]pferd, *das;* **(c)** (framework) Gestell, *das;* **[clothes]-** ∼: Wäscheständer, *der*

horse: ∼**back** *n.* **on** ∼**back** zu Pferd; ∼**box** *n.* (trailer) Pferdeanhänger, *der;* (Motor Veh.) Pferdetransporter, *der;* ∼ '**chestnut** *n.* (Bot.) Roßkastanie, *die;* ∼-**drawn** *attrib. adj.* pferdebespannt; von Pferden gezogen; ∼-**drawn vehicle** Pferdewagen, *der;* ∼**hair** *n.* **(a)** (single hair) Pferdehaar, *das,* **(b)** *no pl., no indef. art.* (mass of hairs) Roßhaar, *das;* ∼**man** /'hɔːsmən/ *n., pl.* ∼**men** /'hɔːsmən/ ([skilled] rider) [guter] Reiter

horsemanship /'hɔːsmənʃɪp/ *n., no pl.* **[skills of]** ∼: reiterliches Können

horse: ∼**play** *n.* Balgerei, *die;* ∼**power** *n., pl. same* (Mech.) Pferdestärke, *die;* **a 40** ∼**power car** ein Auto mit 40 PS; ∼**racing** *n.* Pferderennsport, *der;* ∼**radish** *n.* Meerrettich, *der;* ∼**shoe** *n.* Hufeisen, *das;* ∼**whip 1** *n.* Reitpeitsche, *die;* **2** *v.t.* auspeitschen; ∼**woman** *n.* Reiterin, *die*

horsy (horsey) /'hɔːsɪ/ *adj.* **(a)** (horselike) pferdeähnlich; **(b)** (much concerned with horses) pferdenärrisch

horticultural /hɔːtɪ'kʌltʃərl/ *adj.* gartenbaulich; Gartenbau⟨*zeitschrift, -ausstellung*⟩

horticulture /'hɔːtɪkʌltʃə(r)/ *n.* Gartenbau, *der*

hose /həʊz/ **1** *n.* Schlauch, *der.* **2** *v.t.* sprengen; ∼ '**down** *v.t.* abspritzen

'hosepipe *n.* Schlauch, *der*

hosiery /'həʊzɪərɪ/ *n., no pl.* Strumpfwaren *Pl.*

hospice /'hɒspɪs/ *n.* **(a)** (Brit.) (for the destitute) Heim für Mittellose; (for the terminally ill) Sterbehospiz, *das;* **(b)** (for travellers or students) Hospiz, *das*

hospitable /'hɒspɪtəbl/ *adj.* (welcoming) gastfreundlich ⟨*Person, Wesensart*⟩; gastlich ⟨*Haus, Hotel, Klima*⟩

hospital /'hɒspɪtl/ *n.* Krankenhaus, *das;* **in** ∼ (Brit.), **in the** ∼ (Amer.) im Krankenhaus; **into** *or* **to** ∼ (Brit.), **to the** ∼ (Amer.) ins Krankenhaus ⟨*gehen, bringen*⟩

hospital: ~ **bed** *n.* Krankenhausbett, *das;* ~ **case** *n.* Fall fürs Krankenhaus

hospitalise ⇒ hospitalize

hospitality /hɒspɪˈtælɪti/ *n., no pl.* (of person) Gastfreundschaft, *die*

hospitalize /ˈhɒspɪtəlaɪz/ *v.t.* ins Krankenhaus einweisen

hospital: ~ **nurse** *n.* ▶ 887 | Krankenschwester, *die/* Krankenpfleger, *der;* ~ **porter** *n.* ▶ 887 | ≈ Krankenpflegehelfer, *der/*-helferin, *die*

host¹ /həʊst/ *n.* (large number) Menge, *die;* **in [their]** ~s in Scharen

host² 1 *n.* (a) Gastgeber, *der/*Gastgeberin, *die;* **be** *or* **play** ~ **to sb.** jmdn. zu Gast haben; (b) (compère) Moderator, *der.* 2 *v.t.* (a) (act as host at) Gastgeber sein bei; (b) (compère) moderieren

hostage /ˈhɒstɪdʒ/ *n.* Geisel, *die;* **hold/take sb.** ~: jmdn. als Geisel festhalten/nehmen; **a** ~ **to fortune** etwas, was einem das Schicksal nehmen kann

hostel /ˈhɒstl/ *n.* (Brit.) (a) Wohnheim, *das;* (b) ⇒ **youth hostel**

hostess /ˈhəʊstɪs/ *n.* (a) Gastgeberin, *die;* (b) (in nightclub) Animierdame, *die;* (c) (in passenger transport) Hostess, *die;* (d) (compère) Moderatorin, *die*

hostile /ˈhɒstaɪl/ *adj.* (a) feindlich; (b) (unfriendly) feindselig (**to, towards** gegenüber); **be** ~ **to sth.** etw. ablehnen; (c) (inhospitable) unwirtlich; feindselig ‹ *Atmosphäre* ›

hostility /hɒˈstɪlɪti/ *n.* (a) *no pl.* (enmity) Feindschaft, *die;* (b) *no pl.* (antagonism) Feindseligkeit, *die* (**to[wards]** gegenüber); **feel no** ~ **towards anybody** niemandem feindlich gesinnt sein; (c) (state of war, act of warfare) Feindseligkeit, *die*

hot /hɒt/ *adj.* (a) heiß; (cooked) warm ‹ *Mahlzeit, Essen* ›; (fig.: potentially dangerous, difficult) heiß (ugs.) ‹ *Thema, Geschichte* ›; ungemütlich, gefährlich ‹ *Lage* ›; ~ **and cold running water** fließend warm und kalt Wasser; **be too** ~ **to handle** (fig.) eine zu heiße Angelegenheit sein (ugs.); **make it** *or* **things [too]** ~ **for sb.** (fig.) jmdm. die Hölle heiß machen (ugs.); (b) (feeling heat) **I am/feel** ~: mir ist heiß; (c) (pungent) scharf ‹ *Gewürz, Senf usw.* ›; (d) (passionate, lustful) heiß ‹ *Küsse, Tränen, Umarmung* ›; **be** ~ **for sth.** heiß auf etw. (*Akk.*) sein (ugs.); **he's really** ~ **on her** (sexually) er ist richtig scharf auf sie (ugs.); (e) (agitated, angry) hitzig; **get [all]** ~ **and bothered** sich [fürchterlich (ugs.)] aufregen; (f) (coll.: good) toll (ugs.); **be** ~ **at sth.** in etw. (*Dat.*) [ganz] groß sein (ugs.); **I'm not too** ~ **at that** darin bin ich nicht besonders umwerfend (ugs.); **be** ~ **on sth.** (knowledgeable) sich in *od.* mit etw. (*Dat.*) gut auskennen (ugs.); (g) (recent) noch warm ‹ *Nachrichten* ›; **this is really** ~ **[news]** das ist wirklich das Neueste vom Neuen; (h) (close) **you are getting** ~/**are** ~ (in children's games) es wird schon wärmer/[jetzt ist es] heiß; **follow** ~ **on sb.'s heels** jmdm. dicht auf den Fersen folgen (ugs.); (i) (coll.: in demand) zugkräftig; **a** ~ **property** (singer, actress, etc.) eine ertragreiche Zugnummer; (company, invention, etc.) eine ertragreiche Geldanlage; (j) (Sport; also fig.) heiß (ugs.) ‹ *Tipp, Favorit* ›; (k) (sl.: illegally obtained) heiß ‹ *Ware, Geld* ›. *See also* **blow¹** 1 b; **cake** 1 a; **collar** 1 a; **potato**

~ **'up** (Brit. coll.) 1 *v.t.* (a) (heat) warm machen; (b) (excite) auf Touren bringen (ugs.); (c) (make more exciting) in Schwung bringen; (make more dangerous) verschärfen; (d) (intensify) anheizen (ugs.). 2 *v.i.* (a) (rise in temperature) heiß werden; **the weather** ~s **up** es wird wärmer; (b) (become exciting) in Schwung kommen; (become dangerous) sich verschärfen; (c) (become more intense) sich verstärken; ‹ *Wortgefecht:* › ~ werden ‹ zunehmend hitziger werden

hot: ~ **'air** *n.* (coll.: idle talk) leeres Gerede (ugs.); ~**bed** *n.* (Hort.) Mistbeet, *das;* Frühbeet, *das;* (fig.) Nährboden, *der* (**of** für); (of vice, corruption, etc.) Brutstätte, *die* (**of** für)

hotchpotch /ˈhɒtʃpɒtʃ/ *n.* (mixture) Mischmasch, *der* (ugs.) (**of** aus)

hot: ~ **cross 'bun** *n.:* mit einem Kreuz aus Teig verziertes Rosinenbrötchen, das am Karfreitag gegessen wird; ~**-'desking** *n.:* Mehrfachnutzung von Arbeitsplätzen; ~ **dog** *n.* (coll.) Hotdog, *das od. der*

hotel /həˈtel, həʊˈtel/ *n.* Hotel, *das*

hotelier /həˈteliə(r)/ *n.* ▶ 887 | Hotelier, *der*

hot: ~**foot** 1 *adv.* stehenden Fußes; 2 *v.t.* ~**foot it** sich hastig davonmachen; ~**head** *n.* Hitzkopf, *der;* ~**house** *n.* Treibhaus, *das;* ~**line** *n.* Hotline, *die;* (Polit.) heißer Draht

hotly /ˈhɒtli/ *adv.* heftig

hot: ~**plate** *n.* Kochplatte, *die;* (for keeping food ~) Warmhalteplatte, *die;* ~ **rod** *n.* (Motor Veh.) hochfrisiertes Auto (ugs.); ~ **seat** *n.* (coll.) (uneasy situation) Folterbank, *die* (fig.); (involving heavy responsibility) **be in the** ~ **seat** den Kopf hinhalten müssen (ugs.); ~**shot** *n.* (coll.) As, *das* (ugs.); ~ **spot** *n.* (a) heiße Gegend; (b) (difficult situation) **get into a** ~ **spot** in die Bredouille kommen *od.* geraten (ugs.); ~ **'stuff** *n., no pl., no art.* (coll.) **sb./sth. is** ~ **stuff** jmd./etw. ist große Klasse (ugs.); ~**-tempered** *adj.* heißblütig; ~ **'water** *n.* (fig. coll.) **be in** ~ **water** in der Bredouille sein (ugs.); ~**-'water bottle** *n.* Wärmflasche, *die*

hound /haʊnd/ 1 *n.* Jagdhund, *der;* **the [pack of]** ~s (Brit. Hunting) die Meute (Jägerspr.). 2 *v.t.* jagen; (fig.) verfolgen

~ **'out** *v.t.* (a) (hunt out) aufspüren; (b) (force to leave) vertreiben (**of** aus); verjagen (**of** aus)

hour /ˈaʊə(r)/ *n.* (a) ▶ 706 | Stunde, *die;* **half an** ~: eine halbe Stunde; **an** ~ **and a half** anderthalb Stunden; **be paid by the** ~: stundenweise bezahlt werden; **a two-**~ **session** eine zweistündige Sitzung; **the 24-**~ *or* **twenty-four-**~ **clock** die Vierundzwanzigstundenuhr; (b) (time o'clock) Zeit, *die;* **on the** ~: zur vollen Stunde; **at this late** ~: zu so später Stunde (geh.); **at all** ~s zu jeder [Tages- oder Nacht]zeit; (late at night) spät in der Nacht; **the small** ~s **[of the morning]** die frühen Morgenstunden; 0100/0200/1700/1800 ~s (on 24-~ clock) 1.00/2.00/17.00/18.00 Uhr; (c) *in pl.* **doctor's** ~s Sprechstunde, *die;* **post-office** ~s Schalterstunden *der* Post; **what** ~s **do you work?** wie ist deine Arbeitszeit?; **work long** ~s einen langen Arbeitstag haben; **during school** ~s während der Schulstunden *od.* des Unterrichts; **out of/after** ~s (in office, bank, etc.) außerhalb der Dienstzeit; (in shop) außerhalb der Geschäftszeit; (in pub) außerhalb der Ausschankzeit; (d) (particular time) Stunde, *die;* **sb.'s finest** ~: jmds. größte Stunde; **the question** *etc.* **of the** ~: das Problem *usw.* der Stunde; (e) (distance) Stunde, *die;* **they are two** ~s **from us by train** sie wohnen zwei Bahnstunden von uns entfernt

hour: ~**glass** *n.* Sanduhr, *die;* Stundenglas, *das* (veralt.); ~ **hand** *n.* Stundenzeiger, *der;* kleiner Zeiger; ~**-long** *attrib. adj.* einstündig

hourly /ˈaʊəli/ 1 *adj.* (happening every hour) stündlich; **at** ~ **intervals** jede Stunde; stündlich; **there are** ~ **trains to London** jede *od.* alle Stunde fährt ein Zug nach London; **he is paid an** ~ **rate of** £6 er hat einen Stundenlohn von 6 Pfund; **two-**~: zweistündlich. 2 *adv.* stündlich; **be paid** ~: stundenweise bezahlt werden

house 1 /haʊs/ *n., pl.* ~s /ˈhaʊzɪz/ (a) Haus, *das;* **to/at my** ~: zu mir [nach Hause]/bei mir [zu Hause]; **keep** ~ **[for sb.]** [jmdm.] den Haushalt führen; **put** *or* **set one's** ~ **in order** (fig.) seine Angelegenheiten in Ordnung bringen; **[as] safe as** ~s absolut sicher; **[get on] like a** ~ **on fire** (fig.) prächtig [miteinander auskommen]; (b) (Parl.) (building) Parlamentsgebäude, *das;* (assembly) Haus, *das;* **the H**~ (Brit.) das Parlament; *see also* **Commons; lord 1 c; parliament; representative 1 b;** (c) (institution) Haus, *das;* **fashion** ~: Modehaus, *das;* (d) (inn etc.) Wirtshaus, *das;* **on the** ~: auf Kosten des Hauses; (e) (Theatre) (audience) Publikum, *das;* (performance) Vorstellung, *die;* **an empty** ~: ein leeres Haus; **bring the** ~ **down** stürmischen Beifall auslösen; (cause laughter) Lachstürme entfesseln. 2 /haʊz/ *v.t.* (a) (provide with home) ein Heim geben (+ *Dat.*); **be** ~d **in sth.** in etw. (*Dat.*) untergebracht sein; (b) (keep, store) unterbringen; einlagern ‹ *Waren* ›

house: ~ **arrest** *n.* Hausarrest, *der;* ~**boat** *n.* Hausboot, *das;* ~**breaking** *n., no pl.* (burglary) Einbruch, *der;* ~**coat** *n.* Hausmantel, *der;* Morgenmantel, *der;* ~ **guest** *n.* Logiergast, *der*

household /ˈhaʊshəʊld/ *n.* Haushalt, *der; attrib.* Haushalts-; ~ **chores** Hausarbeit, *die*

householder /ˈhaʊshəʊldə(r)/ n. (home-owner) Wohnungsinhaber, der/-inhaberin, die

household: ～ **ˈmanagement** n. Hauswirtschaft, die; ～ **ˈname** n. geläufiger Name; **be a** ～ **name** ein Begriff sein

house /haʊs/: ～**-hunting** n., no pl. Suche nach einem Haus; **go** ～**-hunting** sich nach einem Haus umsehen; ～ **keeper** n. ▸ 887 | (woman managing household affairs) Haushälterin, die; Wirtschafterin, die; (person running own home) Hausfrau, die/Hausmann, der; ～**keeping** n. (a) (management) Hauswirtschaft, die; Haushaltsführung, die; (b) (fig.: maintenance, record-keeping, etc.) Wirtschaften, das; ～**maid** n. ▸ 887 | Hausgehilfin, die; ～**-painter** n. ▸ 887 | Maler, die/Malerin, die; Anstreicher, der/Anstreicherin, die; ～ **plant** n. Zimmerpflanze, die; ～**-proud** adj. he/she is ～**-proud** Ordnung und Sauberkeit [im Haushalt] gehen ihm/ihr über alles; ～**room** n., no pl., no indef. art. **find** ～**room for sth.** einen Platz für etw. [in der Wohnung] finden; **I wouldn't give it** ～**room** so etwas wollte ich nicht im Haus haben; ～**-sit** v.i. das Haus hüten; ～**-sitter** n. Housesitter, der (ugs.); Person, die für jemanden das Haus hütet; ～**-to-**～: adj. make ～**-to-**～ **enquiries** von Haus zu Haus gehen und fragen; ～**-train** v.t. (Brit.) ～**-train a cat/child** eine Katze/ein Kleinkind dazu bringen, dass sie stubenrein/dass es sauber wird; ～**-trained** adj. (Brit.) stubenrein ⟨Hund, Katze⟩; sauber ⟨Kleinkind⟩; ～**-warming** /ˈhaʊswɔ:mɪŋ/ n. ～**-warming [party]** Einzugsfeier, die; ～**wife** n. Hausfrau, die; ～**work** n., no pl. Hausarbeit, die

housing /ˈhaʊzɪŋ/ n. (a) no pl. (dwellings collectively) Wohnungen; (provision of dwellings) Wohnungsbeschaffung, die; attrib. Wohnungs-; ～ **programme** Wohnungsbauprogramm, das; (b) no pl. (shelter) Unterkunft, die

housing: ～ **association** n. (Brit.) Gesellschaft für sozialen Wohnungsbau; ～ **benefit** n. (Brit.) Wohngeld, das; ～ **estate** n. (Brit.) Wohnsiedlung, die

hove ⇒ **heave 1 b, 2 c**

hovel /ˈhɒvl/ n. [armselige] Hütte; (joc.) Bruchbude, die (ugs. abwertend)

hover /ˈhɒvə(r)/ v.i. (a) schweben; (b) (linger) sich herumdrücken (ugs.); (c) (waver) schwanken; ～ **between life and death** (fig.) zwischen Leben und Tod schweben

hover: ～**craft** n., pl. same Hovercraft, das; Luftkissenfahrzeug, das; ～ **mower** n. Luftkissenmäher, der

how /haʊ/ adv. wie; **learn** ～ **to ride a bike/swim** etc. Rad fahren/schwimmen usw. lernen; **this is** ～ **to do it** so macht man das; ～ **do you know that?** woher weißt du das?; ～**'s that?** (～ did that happen?) wie kommt das [denn]?; (is that as it should be?) ist es so gut?; (will you agree to that?) was hältst du davon?; ～ **so?** wieso [das]?; ～ **would it be if ...?** wie wäre es, wenn ...?; ～ **is she/the car?** (after accident) wie geht es ihr?/was ist mit dem Auto?; ～**'are you?** wie geht es dir?; (greeting) guten Morgen/Tag/Abend!; ～ **do you 'do?** (formal) guten Morgen/Tag/Abend!; ～ **much?** wie viel?; ～ **many?** wie viel?; wie viele?; ～ **many times?** wie oft?; ～ **far** (to what extent) inwieweit; ～ **right/wrong you are!** da hast du völlig recht/da irrst du dich gewaltig!; ～ **naughty of him!** das war aber frech von ihm; **and** ～! (coll.) und wie! (ugs.); ～ **about ...?** wie ist es mit ...?; (in invitation, proposal, suggestion) wie wäre es mit ...?; ～ **about tomorrow?** wie sieht's morgen aus? (ugs.); ～ **about it?** na, wie ist das?; (is that acceptable?) was hältst du davon?

however /haʊˈevə(r)/ adv. (a) wie ... auch; egal, wie (ugs.); **I shall never win this race,** ～ **hard I try** ich werde dieses Rennen nie gewinnen, und wenn ich mich noch so anstrenge od. wie sehr ich mich auch anstrenge; (b) (nevertheless) jedoch; aber; **I don't like him very much. H**～, **he has never done me any harm** Ich mag ihn nicht sehr. Er hat mir allerdings noch nie etwas getan; ～, **the rain soon stopped, and ...**: es hörte jedoch od. aber bald auf zu regnen, und ...

howitzer /ˈhaʊɪtsə(r)/ n. (Mil.) Haubitze, die

howl /haʊl/ 1 n. (of animal) Heulen, das; (of distress) Schrei, der; **a** ～ **of pain** or **agony** ein Schmerzensschrei; ～**s of laughter** brüllendes Gelächter; ～**s of derision/scorn** verächtliches Gejohle. 2 v.i. ⟨Tier, Wind:⟩ heulen; (with distress) schreien; ～ **in** or **with pain/hunger** etc. vor Schmerz/Hunger usw. schreien. 3 v.t. [hinaus]schreien ～ **'down** v.t. niederbrüllen

howler /ˈhaʊlə(r)/ n. (coll.: blunder) Schnitzer, der (ugs.); **make a** ～: sich (Dat.) einen Schnitzer leisten

HP abbr. (a) /eɪtʃˈpi:/ (Brit.) **hire purchase; on** ～: auf Teilzahlungsbasis; (b) **horsepower** PS

HQ abbr. **headquarters** HQ

hr[s]. abbr. **hour[s]** Std[n].; **at 0800 hrs.** um 8.00 Uhr

HRT abbr. **hormone replacement therapy**

hub /hʌb/ n. (a) (of wheel) [Rad]nabe, die; (b) (fig.: central point) Mittelpunkt, der; Zentrum, das; **the** ～ **of the universe** (fig.) der Nabel der Welt (geh.)

hubbub /ˈhʌbʌb/ n. Lärm, der; **a** ～ **of conversation/voices** ein Stimmengewirr

'hubcap n. Radkappe, die

huddle /ˈhʌdl/ 1 v.i. sich drängen; (curl up, nestle) sich kuscheln; ～ **against each other/together** sich aneinander drängen/sich zusammendrängen. 2 v.t. (a) (put on) ～ **one's coat around one** sich in den Mantel hüllen; (b) (crowd together) [eng] zusammendrängen. 3 n. (a) (tight group) dicht gedrängte Menge od. Gruppe; (b) (coll.: conference) Besprechung, die; **be in a** ～**/go [off] in[to] a** ～: die Köpfe zusammenstecken (ugs.) ～ **'up** v.i. (nestle up) sich zusammenkauern; (crowd together) sich [zusammen]drängen

hue[1] /hju:/ n. (a) Farbton, der; **the sky took on a reddish** ～: der Himmel färbte sich rötlich; (b) (fig.: aspect) Schattierung, die

hue[2] n. ～ **and cry** (outcry) lautes Geschrei; (protest) Gezeter, das (abwertend); **raise a** ～ **and cry against sb./sth.** ein lautes Geschrei/Gezeter über jmdn./etw. anstimmen

huff /hʌf/ 1 v.i. ～ **and puff** schnaufen und keuchen. 2 n. **be in a** ～: beleidigt od. (ugs.) eingeschnappt sein; **go off in a** ～: beleidigt od. eingeschnappt abziehen (ugs.)

hug /hʌg/ 1 n. Umarmung, die; (of animal) Umklammerung, die; **give sb. a** ～: jmdn. umarmen. 2 v.t., **-gg-:** (a) umarmen; ⟨Tier:⟩ umklammern; ～ **sb./sth. to oneself** jmdn./etw. an sich (Akk.) drücken od. pressen; **the bear** ～**ged him to death** der Bär drückte ihn zu Tode; (b) (keep close to) sich dicht halten an (+ Dat.); ⟨Schiff, Auto usw.:⟩ dicht entlangfahren an (+ Dat.); (c) (fit tightly around) eng anliegen an (+ Dat.); **a pullover that** ～**s the figure** ein Pullover, der die Figur betont

huge /hju:dʒ/ adj. riesig; gewaltig ⟨Unterschied, Verbesserung, Interesse⟩; **the problem is** ～: das Problem ist außerordentlich schwierig

hulk /hʌlk/ n. (a) (body of ship) [Schiffs]rumpf, der; (as store etc.) Hulk, die od. der (Seew.); (b) (wreck of car, machine, etc.) Wrack, das; (c) (fig.) (big thing) Klotz, der; (big person) Koloß, der (ugs. scherzh.); **a** ～ **of a man** ein Klotz von [einem] Mann (fig. ugs.)

hulking /ˈhʌlkɪŋ/ adj. (coll.) (bulky) wuchtig; (clumsy) klotzig (abwertend); **a** ～ **great person/thing** ein klobiger Mensch/ein klobiges Etwas

hull /hʌl/ n. (Naut.) Schiffskörper, der; (Aeronaut.) Rumpf, der

hullabaloo /ˌhʌləbəˈlu:/ n. (a) (noise) Radau, der (ugs.); Lärm, der; (of show-business life, city) Trubel, der; (b) (controversy) Aufruhr, der; **make a** ～ **about sth.** viel Lärm um etw. machen

hullo /həˈləʊ/ ⇒ **hallo; hello**

hum /hʌm/ 1 v.i., **-mm-:** (a) summen; ⟨Motor, Maschine, Kreisel:⟩ brummen; ～ **and ha** or **haw** (coll.) herumdrucksen (ugs.); (b) (coll.: be in state of activity) voller Leben od. Aktivität sein. 2 v.t., **-mm-** summen ⟨Melodie, Lied⟩. 3 n. (a) Summen, das; (of spinning top, machinery, engine) Brummen, das; (b) (inarticulate sound) Hm, das; (c) (of voices, conversation) Gemurmel, das; (of insects and small creatures) Gesumme, das; (of traffic) Brausen, das. 4 int. hm

human /ˈhju:mən/ 1 adj. menschlich; **the** ～ **race** die menschliche Rasse; **I'm only** ～: ich bin auch nur ein Mensch; ～ **error** menschliches Versagen; **lack the** ～ **touch** menschliche Wärme vermissen lassen; **be** ～! sei kein Unmensch!; see also **nature d.** 2 n. Mensch, der

human 'being n. Mensch, der

humane /hju:'meɪn/ adj. (a) human; (b) (tending to civilize) humanistisch

humanise ⇨ **humanize**

humanism /'hju:mənɪzm/ n., no pl. (a) Humanität, die; (b) (literary culture; also Philos.) Humanismus, der

humanist /'hju:mənɪst/ n. Humanist, der/Humanistin, die

humanitarian /hju:mænɪˈteərɪən/ 1 adj. humanitär. 2 n. (philanthropist) Menschenfreund, der; (promoter of human welfare) Humanitarist, der/Humanitaristin, die

humanity /hju:'mænɪtɪ/ n. (a) no pl., no art. (mankind) Menschheit, die; (people collectively) Menschen; (b) no pl. (being humane) Humanität, die; Menschlichkeit, die; (c) in pl. (cultural learning) [the] humanities [die] Geisteswissenschaften

humanize /'hju:mənaɪz/ v.t. (a) (make human) vermenschlichen; (b) (adapt to human use) den menschlichen Bedürfnissen anpassen; humanisieren ⟨Industrie⟩; (c) (make humane) humanisieren ⟨Strafvollzug⟩

humanly /'hju:mənlɪ/ adv. menschlich; (by human means) mit menschlichen Mitteln; do everything ~ possible alles Menschenmögliche tun

human: ~ re'sources n. (a) pl. [Arbeits]kräfte Pl.; Personal, das; (b) sing. (department) Personalabteilung, die; ~ 'right, ~ 'rights n. pl. Menschenrechte Pl.; attrib. ~ rights group Menschenrechtsorganisation, die; ~ rights activist Menschenrechtler, der/-rechtlerin, die

humble /'hʌmbl/ 1 adj. (a) (modest) bescheiden; ergeben ⟨Untertan, Diener, Gefolgsmann⟩; unterwürfig (oft abwertend) ⟨Haltung, Knechtschaft⟩; please accept my ~ apologies ich bitte ergebenst um Verzeihung; eat ~ pie klein beigeben; (b) (low-ranking) einfach; niedrig ⟨Status, Rang usw.⟩; (c) (unpretentious) einfach; bescheiden ⟨Zuhause, Wohnung, Anfang⟩. 2 v.t. (a) (abase) demütigen; ~ oneself sich demütigen od. erniedrigen; (b) (defeat decisively) [vernichtend] schlagen

humbly /'hʌmblɪ/ adv. (with humility) demütig; ergebenst ⟨um Verzeihung bitten⟩; (in formal address) höflichst ⟨bitten, ersuchen⟩

humbug /'hʌmbʌɡ/ n. (a) no pl., no art. (deception, nonsense) Humbug, der (ugs. abwertend); (b) (Brit.: sweet) [Pfefferminz]bonbon, der od. das

humdrum /'hʌmdrʌm/ adj. (a) alltäglich; eintönig ⟨Leben⟩; (b) (monotonous) stumpfsinnig; the ~ routine of life/things das tägliche Einerlei

humid /'hju:mɪd/ adj. feucht; humid (Geogr.)

humidity /hju:'mɪdɪtɪ/ n. (a) no pl. Feuchtigkeit, die; (b) (degree of moisture) ~ [of the atmosphere] Luftfeuchtigkeit, die (Met.)

humiliate /hju:'mɪlɪeɪt/ v.t. demütigen; I was or felt totally ~d ich war zutiefst beschämt

humiliation /hju:mɪlɪˈeɪʃn/ n. Demütigung, die

humility /hju:'mɪlɪtɪ/ n. Demut, die; (of servant) Ergebenheit, die; (absence of pride or arrogance) Bescheidenheit, die

'hummingbird n. Kolibri, der

hummock /'hʌmək/ n. (hillock) [kleiner] Hügel

humor (Amer.) ⇨ **humour**

humorist /'hju:mərɪst/ n. (a) (facetious person) Spaßvogel, der; Komiker, der (fig.); (b) (talker, writer) Humorist, der/Humoristin, die

humorless (Amer.) ⇨ **humourless**

humorous /'hju:mərəs/ adj. lustig, komisch ⟨Geschichte, Name, Situation⟩; witzig ⟨Bemerkung⟩; humorvoll ⟨Person⟩

humour /'hju:mə(r)/ (Brit.) 1 n. (a) no pl., no indef. art. (faculty, comic quality) Humor, der; (of situation) Komische, das; sense of ~: Sinn für Humor; (b) no pl., no indef. art. (facetiousness) Witzigkeit, die; (c) (mood) Laune, die; in good ~: gut gelaunt; be out of ~: schlechte Laune haben. 2 v.t. ~ sb. jmdm. seinen Willen lassen; ~ sb.'s taste jmds. Geschmack od. Vorliebe (Dat.) entsprechen; do it just to ~ her/him tu's doch, damit sie ihren/er seinen Willen hat

humourless /'hju:məlɪs/ adj. (Brit.) humorlos

hump /hʌmp/ 1 n. (a) (human) Buckel, der; Höcker, der (ugs.); (of animal) Höcker, der; he has a ~ on his back er hat einen Buckel; (b) (mound) Hügel, der. 2 v.t. (Brit. coll.: carry) schleppen

hump: ~back 'bridge n. gewölbte Brücke; ~backed /'hʌmpbækt/ ⇨ hunchbacked

humus /'hju:məs/ n. Humus, der

hunch¹ /hʌntʃ/ v.t. hochziehen ⟨Schultern⟩; sit ~ed in a corner zusammengekauert in einer Ecke sitzen ~ 'up v.t. hochziehen; ~ oneself up einen Buckel machen

hunch² n. (intuitive feeling) Gefühl, das

hunch: ~back n. (a) (back) Buckel, der; (b) (person) Bucklige, der/die; be a ~back einen Buckel haben; ~backed /'hʌntʃbækt/ adj. buck[e]lig

hundred /'hʌndrəd/ ▶630◀, ▶706◀, ▶956◀ 1 adj. (a) hundert; a or one ~: [ein]hundert; two/several ~: zweihundert/mehrere hundert; a or one ~ and one [ein]hundert[und]eins; a or one ~ and one people hundert[und]ein Menschen od. Mensch; the ~ metres race der Hundertmeterlauf; (b) a ~ [and one] (fig.: innumerable) hundert (ugs.); (c) a or one ~ per cent hundertprozentig; I'm not a ~ per cent at the moment (fig.) momentan geht es mir nicht sehr gut. See also eight 1. 2 n. (a) (number) Hundert, die; a or one/two ~: [ein]hundert/ zweihundert; not if I live to be a ~: nie im Leben; in or by ~s hundertweise; the seventeen-~s etc. das achtzehnte usw. Jahrhundert; a ~ and one etc. [ein]hundert[und]eins usw.; it's a ~ to one that ...: die Chancen stehen hundert zu eins, dass ...; (b) (symbol, written figure) Hundert, die; (~-pound etc. note) Hunderter, der; (c) (indefinite amount) ~s Hunderte Pl.; ~s of times hundert Mal. See also eight 2 a

hundredth /'hʌndrədθ/ ▶956◀ 1 adj. hundertst...; a ~ part ein Hundertstel. 2 n. (fraction) Hundertstel, das; (in sequence, rank) Hundertste, der/die/das

hundredweight /'hʌndrədweɪt/ n., pl. same or ~s ▶1202◀ (Brit.) 50,8 kg; ≈ Zentner, der

hung ⇨ **hang 1, 2**

Hungarian /hʌŋˈɡeərɪən/ ▶897◀, ▶947◀ 1 adj. ungarisch; sb. is ~: jmd. ist Ungar/Ungarin. 2 n. (a) (person) Ungar, der/Ungarin, die; (b) (language) Ungarisch, das; see also English 2 a

Hungary /'hʌŋɡərɪ/ pr. n. Ungarn (das)

hunger /'hʌŋɡə(r)/ 1 n. (lit. or fig.) Hunger, der; pang[s] of ~: quälender Hunger; die of ~: verhungern; (fig.: be very hungry) vor Hunger sterben (ugs.). 2 v.i. ~ after or for sb./sth. [heftiges] Verlangen nach jmdm./etw. haben

hunger: ~ march n. Hungermarsch, der; ~ marcher n. Hungermarschierer, der; ~ strike n. Hungerstreik, der; go on ~ strike in den Hungerstreik treten; ~ striker n. Hungerstreikende, der/die

hung: ~'over adj. (coll.) verkatert (ugs.); ~ 'parliament n. Parlament, in dem keine Partei die absolute Mehrheit hat

hungrily /'hʌŋɡrɪlɪ/ adv. (a) hungrig; (b) (fig.: longingly) sehnsüchtig ⟨an etw. denken⟩; [be]gierig ⟨etw. verfolgen⟩

hungry /'hʌŋɡrɪ/ adj. (a) (feeling hunger) hungrig; (regularly feeling hunger) hungernd; (showing hunger) hungrig, gierig ⟨Augen, Blick⟩; be ~: Hunger haben; hungrig sein; go ~: hungern; hungrig bleiben; (b) (fig.: eager, avaricious) be ~ for sth. nach etw. hungern (geh.); ~ for success/power/ knowledge/love erfolgs-/macht-/bildungs-/liebeshungrig

hunk /hʌŋk/ n. (a) (large piece) [großes] Stück, der; (of bread) Brocken, der; (b) (coll.: large person) stattliche Erscheinung; he is a gorgeous great ~: er ist ein blendend aussehender, stattlicher Mann

hunt /hʌnt/ 1 n. (a) (pursuit of game) Jagd, die; (b) (search) Suche, die; (strenuous search) Jagd, die; be on the ~ for sb./sth. auf der Suche/Jagd nach jmdm./etw. sein; (c) (body of fox-hunters) Jagd[gesellschaft], die; (association) Jagdverband, der. 2 v.t. (a) jagen; Jagd machen auf (+ Akk.); (b) (search for) Jagd machen auf (+ Akk.) ⟨Mörder usw.⟩; fahnden nach ⟨vermisster Person⟩; (c) (drive, lit. or fig.) jagen; he was ~ed out of society er wurde aus der

Gesellschaft ausgestoßen. **3** *v.i.* **(a)** jagen; **go ~ing** jagen; auf die Jagd gehen; **(b)** (seek) **~ after** *or* **for sb./sth.** nach jmdm./etw. suchen; **the police are ~ing for him** die Polizei ist auf der Suche nach ihm

~ a'bout, **~ a'round** *v.i.* **~ about** *or* **around for sb./sth.** [überall] nach jmdm./etw. suchen

~ 'down *v.t.* **(a)** (bring to bay) hetzen und stellen; **(b)** (pursue and overcome) zur Strecke bringen ⟨*Person*⟩; abschießen ⟨*feindliches Flugzeug*⟩; **(c)** (fig.: track down) aufstöbern

~ 'out *v.t.* **(a)** (drive from cover) aufstöbern; **(b)** (seek out) suchen; **(c)** (fig.: track down) ausfindig machen ⟨*Tatsachen, Antworten*⟩

~ 'up *v.t.* aufspüren

hunted /ˈhʌntɪd/ *adj.* **(a)** (pursued) gejagt; **(b)** (expressing fear) gejagt, gehetzt ⟨*Blick, Gesichtsausdruck*⟩

hunter /ˈhʌntə(r)/ *n.* **(a)** Jäger, *der;* **(b)** (fig.: seeker) **auto-graph-~:** Autogrammjäger, *der;* **bargain-~s** *Leute, die ständig auf der Suche nach Sonderangeboten, nach einem Gelegenheitskauf sind;* **(c)** (horse) Jagdpferd, *das*

hunting /ˈhʌntɪŋ/ *n., no pl.* die Jagd **(of** auf + *Akk.*); das Jagen **(of** *Gen.*)

'hunt saboteur *n.* Jagdsaboteur, *der*

huntsman /ˈhʌntsmən/ *n., pl.* **huntsmen** /ˈhʌntsmən/ (hunter) Jäger, *der;* (riding to hounds) Jagdreiter, *der*

hurdle /ˈhɜːdl/ **1** *n.* (Athletics) Hürde, *die;* **~ race**, **~s** Hürdenlauf, *der;* **fall at the last ~** (fig.) an der letzten Hürde scheitern. **2** *v.t.* überspringen ⟨*Zaun, Hecke usw.*⟩

hurdler /ˈhɜːdlə(r)/ *n.* (Athletics) Hürdenläufer, *der/*-läuferin, *die*

hurl /hɜːl/ *v.t.* werfen; (violently) schleudern; (throw down) stürzen; **she ~ed herself to her death from a 15th-floor window** sie stürzte sich aus einem Fenster im 15. Stock zu Tode; **~ insults at sb.** jmdm. Beleidigungen ins Gesicht schleudern

hurly-burly /ˈhɜːlɪbɜːlɪ/ *n.* Tumult, *der*

hurrah /həˈrɑː, hʊˈrɑː/, **hurray** /həˈreɪ, hʊˈreɪ/ *int.* hurra; **~ for sb./sth.!** jmd./etw. lebe hoch!; **hip, hip, ~!** hipp, hipp, hurra!

hurricane /ˈhʌrɪkən/ *n.* (tropical cyclone) Hurrikan, *der;* (storm, lit. or fig.) Orkan, *der*

'hurricane lamp *n.* Sturmlaterne, *die*

hurried /ˈhʌrɪd/ *adj.* eilig; überstürzt ⟨*Abreise*⟩; eilig *od.* hastig geschrieben ⟨*Brief, Aufsatz*⟩; in Eile ausgeführt ⟨*Arbeit*⟩

hurry /ˈhʌrɪ/ **1** *n.* **(a)** (great haste) Eile, *die;* **what is** *or* **why the [big] ~?** warum die Eile?; **in a ~:** eilig; **be in a [great** *or* **terrible] ~** ⟨ɑ⟩ [furchtbar] eilig haben; **do sth. in a ~:** etw. in Eile tun; **leave in a ~:** davoneilen; **I need it in a ~:** ich brauche es dringend; **I shan't ask again in a ~** (coll.) ich frage so schnell nicht wieder; **be in a/not be in a** *or* **be in no ~ to do sth.** es eilig/nicht eilig haben, etw. zu tun; **(b)** (urgent requirement) **there is a ~ for sth.** etw. ist sehr gefragt; **what's the [big] ~?** wozu die Eile?; **there's no ~:** es eilt nicht; es hat keine Eile. **2** *v.t.* (transport fast) schnell bringen; (urge to go or act faster) antreiben; (consume fast) hinunterschlingen ⟨*Essen*⟩; **~ one's work** seine Arbeit in zu großer Eile erledigen. **3** *v.i.* sich beeilen; (to or from place) eilen; **~ downstairs/out/in** nach unten/nach draußen/nach drinnen eilen

~ a'long 1 *v.i.* (coll.) sich beeilen. **2** *v.t.* zur Eile antreiben; beschleunigen ⟨*Vorgang*⟩

~ 'on 1 *v.i.* weitereilen; **I must ~ on** ich muss [rasch] weiter. **2** *v.t.* antreiben

~ through *v.t.* **(a)** /-ʹ-/ beschleunigen; **(b)** /ʹ---/ schnell durcheilen; (fig.) möglichst schnell durchziehen (ugs.)

~ 'up 1 *v.i.* (coll.) sich beeilen. **2** *v.t.* antreiben; vorantreiben ⟨*Vorgang*⟩

hurt /hɜːt/ **1** *v.t.*, **hurt (a)** weh tun (+ *Dat.*); (injure physically) verletzen; **~ one's arm/back** sich (*Dat.*) den Arm/am Rücken weh tun; (injure) sich (*Dat.*) den Arm/am Rücken verletzen; **you are ~ing me/my arm** du tust mir weh/am Arm weh; **my arm is ~ing me** mein Arm tut [mir] weh; mir tut der Arm weh; **he wouldn't ~ a fly** (fig.) er tut keiner Fliege etwas zuleide; **sth. won't** *or* **wouldn't ~ sb.** etw. tut nicht weh; (fig.) etw. würde jmdm. nichts schaden (ugs.); **~ oneself** sich (*Dat.*) weh tun; (injure oneself) sich verletzen;

(b) (damage, be detrimental to) schaden (+ *Dat.*); **sth. won't** *or* **wouldn't ~ sth.** etw. würde einer Sache (*Dat.*) nichts schaden; **(c)** (emotionally) verletzen, kranken ⟨*Person*⟩; verletzen ⟨*Ehrgefühl, Stolz*⟩; **~ sb.'s feelings** jmdn. verletzen. **2** *v.i.*, **hurt (a)** ▸ 865 weh tun; schmerzen; **my leg ~s** mein Bein tut [mir] weh; **does your hand ~?** tut dir die Hand weh?; **(b)** (cause damage, be detrimental) schaden; **(c)** (cause emotional distress) weh tun; ⟨*Worte, Beleidigungen:*⟩ verletzen; ⟨*Person:*⟩ verletzend sein. **3** *adj.* gekränkt ⟨*Tonfall, Miene*⟩. **4** *n.* (emotional pain) Schmerz, *der*

hurtful /ˈhɜːtfl/ *adj.* (emotionally wounding) verletzend; **what a ~ thing to say/do!** wie kann man nur so etwas Verletzendes sagen/tun!

hurtle /ˈhɜːtl/ *v.i.* rasen (ugs.); **he went hurtling down the street/round the corner** er raste die Straße hinunter/um die Ecke

husband /ˈhʌzbənd/ *n.* Ehemann, *der;* **my/your/her ~:** mein/dein/ihr Mann; **~ and wife** Mann und Frau

husbandry /ˈhʌzbəndrɪ/ *n., no pl.* **animal/dairy ~:** Viehzucht, *die/*Milchviehhaltung, *die*

hush /hʌʃ/ **1** *n.* **(a)** (silence) Schweigen, *das;* **a sudden ~ fell over them** sie verstummten plötzlich; **(b)** (stillness) Stille, *die.* **2** *v.t.* (silence) zum Schweigen bringen; (still) beruhigen; besänftigen. **3** *v.i.* still sein; (become silent) verstummen; **~!** still!

~ 'up *v.t.* **(a)** (make silent) zum Schweigen bringen; **(b)** (keep secret) **~ sth. up** etw. vertuschen

hushed /hʌʃt/ *adj.* gedämpft ⟨*Flüstern, Stimme*⟩

hush: ~-hush *adj.* (coll.) geheim; **keep sth. ~-hush** etw. geheim halten; **~ money** *n.* Schweigegeld, *das*

husk /hʌsk/ *n.* Schale, *die;* (of wheat, grain, rice) Spelze, *die;* (fig.: useless remainder) Hülse, *die*

husky¹ /ˈhʌskɪ/ *adj.* (hoarse) heiser

husky² *n.* (dog) Eskimohund, *der;* (sledge dog) Schlittenhund, *der*

hussar /hʊˈzɑː(r)/ *n.* (Mil.) Husar, *der*

hustings /ˈhʌstɪŋz/ *n. pl., constr. as sing. or pl.* (proceedings) Wahlveranstaltungen *Pl.*

hustle /ˈhʌsl/ **1** *v.t.* **(a)** drängen **(into** zu); **(b)** (jostle) anrempeln (salopp); (thrust) [hastig] drängen; **the guide ~d the tourists along** der Führer scheuchte die Touristen voran. **2** *v.i.* **(a)** (push roughly) **~ through the crowds** sich durch die Menge drängeln; **(b)** (hurry) hasten; **~ and bustle about** geschäftig hin und her eilen *od.* sausen. **3** *n.* **(a)** (jostling) Gedränge, *das;* **(b)** (hurry) Hetze, *die;* **~ and bustle** Geschäftigkeit, *die;* (in street) geschäftiges Treiben

hut /hʌt/ *n.* Hütte, *die;* (Mil.) Baracke, *die*

hutch /hʌtʃ/ *n.* Stall, *der*

hyacinth /ˈhaɪəsɪnθ/ *n.* (Bot.) Hyazinthe, *die*

hybrid /ˈhaɪbrɪd/ **1** *n.* **(a)** (Biol.) Hybride, *die od. der* **(between** aus); Kreuzung, *die;* **(b)** (fig.: mixture) Mischung, *die.* **2** *adj.* **(a)** (Biol.) hybrid ⟨*Züchtung*⟩; **(b)** (fig.: mixed) gemischt; Misch⟨*kultur, -sprache*⟩

hydrangea /haɪˈdreɪndʒə/ *n.* (Bot.) Hortensie, *die*

hydrant /ˈhaɪdrənt/ *n.* Hydrant, *der*

hydraulic /haɪˈdrɔːlɪk/ *adj.* (Mech. Engin.) hydraulisch; **~ engineering** Wasserbau, *der*

hydrocarbon /haɪdrəˈkɑːbən/ *n.* (Chem.) Kohlenwasserstoff, *der*

hydrochloric acid /haɪdrəklɔːrɪk ˈæsɪd/ *n.* (Chem.) Salzsäure, *die*

hydroelectric /haɪdrəʊˈlektrɪk/ *adj.* (Electr.) hydroelektrisch; **~ power plant** *or* **station** Wasserkraftwerk, *das*

hydrofoil /ˈhaɪdrəfɔɪl/ *n.* (Naut.: vessel) Tragflächenboot, *das*

hydrogen /ˈhaɪdrədʒən/ *n.* Wasserstoff, *der*

'hydrogen bomb *n.* Wasserstoffbombe, *die*

hydrometer /haɪˈdrɒmɪtə(r)/ *n.* Hydrometer, *das*

hydroponics /haɪdrəˈpɒnɪks/ *n., no pl.* (Hort.) Hydroponik, *die* (fachspr.); Hydrokultur, *die*

hydroxide /haɪˈdrɒksaɪd/ *n.* (Chem.) Hydroxid, *das*

hyena /haɪˈiːnə/ *n.* (Zool.) Hyäne, *die;* **laugh like a ~:** wie eine Hyäne kreischen

hygiene /ˈhaɪdʒiːn/ *n., no pl.* Hygiene, *die;* **dental ~:** Zahnhygiene, *die; see also* **personal**

hygienic /haɪˈdʒiːnɪk/ *adj.* hygienisch; **not** ~: unhygienisch

hygienist /haɪˈdʒiːnɪst/ *n.* ▶ 887┘ Hygieniker, *der*/Hygienikerin, *die;* **dental** ~: Zahnhygieniker, *der*/-hygienikerin, *die*

hymn /hɪm/ *n.* Hymne, *die*

'hymn book *n.* Gesangbuch, *das*

hype /haɪp/ *n.* (coll.: misleading publicity) Reklameschwindel, *der* (ugs.)
~ **up** *v.t* (coll.) hochputschen (ugs.); **be/feel** ~**d up** überdreht sein (ugs.)

hyper /ˈhaɪpə(r)/ *adj.* (sl.) aufgedreht (ugs.); überdreht (ugs.); **there's no need to get so** ~! kein Grund zur Panik! (ugs.)

hyperactive /haɪpəˈræktɪv/ *adj.* überaktiv

hyperbola /haɪˈpɜːbələ/ *n., pl.* ~**s** or ~**e** /haɪˈpɜːbəli:/ (Geom.) Hyperbel, *die*

hyper: ~**'critical** *adj.* hyperkritisch; ~**link** *n.* (Computing) Hyperlink, *der;* ~**market** *n.* Verbrauchermarkt, *der;* ~**'sensitive** *adj.* hypersensibel; überempfindlich; **be** ~**sensitive to sth.** überempfindlich auf etw. (*Akk.*) reagieren; ~**text** *n., no pl.* (Computing) Hypertext, *der;* ~ **link** Hyperlink, *der;* ~**'ventilate** *v.i.* hyperventilieren (Med.)

hyphen /ˈhaɪfn/ **1** *n.* (a) Bindestrich, *der;* (b) (connecting separate syllables) Trennungsstrich, *der;* Divis, *das* (fachspr.). **2** *v.t.* mit Bindestrich schreiben

hyphenate /ˈhaɪfəneɪt/ ⇒ **hyphen** 2

hyphenation /haɪfəˈneɪʃn/ *n., no pl.* Kopp[e]lung, *die*

hypnosis /hɪpˈnəʊsɪs/ *n., pl.* **hypnoses** /hɪpˈnəʊsi:z/ Hypnose, *die;* (act, process) Hypnotisierung, *die;* **under** ~: in Hypnose (*Dat.*)

hypnotic /hɪpˈnɒtɪk/ *adj.* hypnotisch; (producing hypnotism) hypnotisch; hypnotisierend ⟨*Wirkung, Blick*⟩

hypnotism /ˈhɪpnətɪzm/ *n.* Hypnotik, *die;* (act) Hypnotisieren, *das*

hypnotist /ˈhɪpnətɪst/ *n.* Hypnotiseur, *der*/Hypnotiseuse, *die*

hypnotize /ˈhɪpnətaɪz/ *v.t.* (lit. or fig.) hypnotisieren; (fig.: fascinate) faszinieren

hypochondria /haɪpəˈkɒndrɪə/ *n.* Hypochondrie, *die*

hypochondriac /haɪpəˈkɒndrɪæk/ *n.* Hypochonder, *der*

hypocrisy /hɪˈpɒkrɪsɪ/ *n.* (a) Heuchelei, *die;* (b) (simulation of virtue) Scheinheiligkeit, *die*

hypocrite /ˈhɪpəkrɪt/ *n.* (a) Heuchler, *der*/Heuchlerin, *die;* (b) (person feigning virtue) Scheinheilige, *der*/*die*

hypocritical /hɪpəˈkrɪtɪkl/ *adj.* heuchlerisch; (feigning virtue) scheinheilig

hypodermic /haɪpəˈdɜːmɪk/ (Med.) **1** *adj.* subkutan ⟨*Injektion*⟩; ~ **syringe** Injektionsspritze, *die.* **2** *n.* (syringe) Injektionsspritze, *die*

hypotenuse /haɪˈpɒtənjuːz/ *n.* (Geom.) Hypotenuse, *die*

hypothermia /haɪpəˈθɜːmɪə/ *n.* (Med.) Hypothermie, *die* (fachspr.); Unterkühlung, *die*

hypothesis /haɪˈpɒθɪsɪs/ *n., pl.* **hypotheses** /haɪˈpɒθɪsi:z/ Hypothese, *die*

hypothetical /haɪpəˈθetɪkl/ *adj.* hypothetisch

hysterectomy /hɪstəˈrektəmɪ/ *n.* (Med.) Hysterektomie, *die*

hysteria /hɪˈstɪərɪə/ *n.* Hysterie, *die*

hysterical /hɪˈsterɪkl/ *adj.* hysterisch

hysterically /hɪˈsterɪkəlɪ/ *adv.* hysterisch; ~ **funny** urkomisch

hysterics /hɪˈsterɪks/ *n. pl.* (laughter) hysterischer Lachanfall; (crying) hysterischer Weinkrampf; **have** ~: hysterisch lachen/weinen

Hz *abbr.* **hertz** Hz

I¹, i /aɪ/ *n., pl.* **Is** or **I's** I, i, *das; see also* **dot** 2 b

I² *pron.* ich; **it is I** (formal) ich bin es; *see also* **me¹; mine²; my; myself**

I. *abbr.* (a) **Island[s]** I.; (b) **Isle[s]** I.

IBA *abbr.* (Brit.) **Independent Broadcasting Authority** Kontrollgremium für den privaten Rundfunk und das Privatfernsehen

Iberia /aɪˈbɪərɪə/ *pr. n.* (Hist., Geog.) Iberische Halbinsel

Iberian Peninsula /aɪˈbɪərɪən pɪˈnɪnsjʊlə(r)/ *pr. n.* (Geog.) Iberische Halbinsel

ice /aɪs/ **1** *n.* (a) *no pl.* Eis, *das;* **feel/be like** ~ (be very cold) eiskalt sein; **there was** ~ **over the pond** eine Eisschicht bedeckte den Teich; **fall through the** ~: auf dem Eis einbrechen; **be on** ~ (coll.) ⟨*Plan:*⟩ auf Eis (*Dat.*) liegen (ugs.); **put on** ~ (coll.) auf Eis (*Akk.*) legen (ugs.); **be on thin** ~ (fig.) sich auf dünnes Eis begeben haben; **break the** ~ (fig.: break through reserve) das Eis brechen; (b) (Brit.: ~ cream) [Speise]eis, *das;* Eiscreme, *die;* **an** ~/**two** ~**s** ein/zwei Eis. **2** *v.t.* (a) (cool with ~) [mit Eis] kühlen; ~**d coffee/tea** Eiskaffee, *der*/Tee mit Eis; **be** ~**d** eisgekühlt sein; (b) glasieren ⟨*Kuchen*⟩
~ **'over** *v.i.* ⟨*Gewässer:*⟩ zufrieren; ⟨*Straße:*⟩ vereisen
~ **'up** *v.i.* (a) (freeze) ⟨*Wasserleitung:*⟩ einfrieren; (b) ⇒ ~ over

'ice age *n.* Eiszeit, *die*

iceberg /ˈaɪsbɜːɡ/ *n.* Eisberg, *der;* **the tip of the** ~ (fig.) die Spitze des Eisbergs

ice: ~**-blue 1** /'-ˈ-/ *n.* Eisblau, *das;* **2** /'-ˈ-/ *adj.* eisblau; ~**-bound** *adj.* eingefroren ⟨*Schiff*⟩; durch Vereisung abgeschnitten ⟨*Hafen, Küste*⟩; ~ (Amer.) Kühlschrank, *der;* ~**-breaker** *n.* (Naut.) Eisbrecher, *der;* ~ **bucket** *n.* Eiskübel, *der;* ~**-cold** *adj.* eiskalt; ~ **'cream** *n.* Eis, *das;* Eiscreme, *die;* **one** ~ **cream/two** ~ **creams** ein/zwei Eis; ~ **'cream parlour** *n.* Eisdiele, *die;* Eiscafé, *das;* ~ **cube** *n.* Eiswürfel, *der;* ~ **floe** *n.* Eisscholle, *die;* ~ **hockey** *n.* Eishockey, *das*

Iceland /ˈaɪslənd/ *pr. n.* Island (*das*)

Icelander /ˈaɪsləndə(r)/ *n.* Isländer, *der*/Isländerin, *die*

Icelandic /aɪsˈlændɪk/ ▶ 897┘, ▶ 947┘ **1** *adj.* isländisch; **sb. is** ~: jmd. ist Isländer/Isländerin. **2** *n.* Isländisch, *das; see also* **English** 2 a

ice: ~ **'lolly** ⇒ **lolly** ~ **pack** *n.* (a) (to relieve pain) Eispackung, *die;* (b) (to keep food cold) Kühlakku, *der* (ugs.); ~ **rink** *n.* Schlittschuh-, Eisbahn, *die;* ~**-skate 1** *n.* Schlittschuh, *der;* **2** *v.i.* Schlittschuh laufen; Eis laufen; ~**-skating** *n.* Schlittschuhlaufen, *das*

icicle /ˈaɪsɪkl/ *n.* Eiszapfen, *der*

icily /ˈaɪsɪlɪ/ *adv.* eisig; (fig.) kalt ⟨*ablehnend, lächelnd*⟩; eisig, frostig ⟨*begrüßen, anblicken*⟩

icing /ˈaɪsɪŋ/ *n.* (Cookery) Zuckerguss, *der;* Zuckerglasur, *die;* **[the]** ~ **on the cake** (fig.) das Tüpfelchen auf dem i

'icing sugar *n.* (Brit.) Puderzucker, *der*

icon /ˈaɪkən, ˈaɪkɒn/ *n.* (a) (Orthodox Ch.) Ikone, *die;* (b) (Computing) Icon, *das*

iconoclastic /aɪkɒnəˈklæstɪk/ *adj.* (lit. or fig.) bilderstürmerisch

icy /ˈaɪsɪ/ *adj.* (a) vereist ⟨*Berge, Landschaft, Straße, See*⟩; eisreich ⟨*Region, Land*⟩; **in** ~ **conditions** bei Eis; (b) (very cold) eiskalt; eisig; (fig.) frostig ⟨*Ton*⟩

ID /aɪˈdiː/ *n.* **ID card, ID plate** ⇒ **identification; have you [got] some** or **any ID?** können Sie sich ausweisen?

I'd /aɪd/ (a) = **I had;** (b) = **I would**

idea /aɪˈdɪə/ *n.* (a) (conception) Idee, *die;* Gedanke, *der;* **arrive at an** ~: auf eine Idee *od.* einen Gedanken kommen; **the** ~ **of going abroad** der Gedanke *od.* die Vorstellung, ins Ausland zu fahren; **give/get some** ~ **of sth.** einen Überblick über etw. (*Akk.*) geben/einen Eindruck von etw.

bekommen; **get the** ~ **[of sth.]** verstehen, worum es [bei etw.] geht; **sb.'s** ~ **of sth.** (coll.) jmds. Vorstellung von etw.; **not my** ~ **of** ... (coll.) nicht, was ich mir unter ... (*Dat.*) vorstelle; **he has no** ~ (coll.) er hat keine Ahnung (ugs.); **(b)** (mental picture) Vorstellung, *die;* **what gave you 'that** ~**?** wie bist du darauf gekommen?; **get the** ~ **that** ...: den Eindruck bekommen, dass ...; **get** *or* **have** ~**s** (coll.) (be rebellious) auf dumme Gedanken kommen (ugs.); (be ambitious) sich (*Dat.*) Hoffnungen machen; **put** ~**s into sb.'s head** jmdn. auf dumme Gedanken bringen; **(c)** (vague notion) Ahnung, *die;* Vorstellung, *die;* **have you any** ~ **[of] how** ...? weißt du ungefähr, wie ...?; **you can have no** ~ **[of] how** ...: du kannst dir gar nicht vorstellen, wie ...; **not have the remotest** *or* **slightest** *or* **faintest** *or* (coll.) **foggiest** ~**:** nicht die entfernteste *od.* mindeste *od.* leiseste Ahnung haben; **I suddenly had the** ~ **that** ...: mir kam plötzlich der Gedanke, dass ...; **I've an** ~ **that** ...: ich habe so eine Ahnung, dass ...; **the [very]** ~**!, what an** ~**!** (coll.) unvorstellbar!; allein die Vorstellung!; **(d)** (plan) Idee, *die;* **good** ~**!** [das ist eine] gute Idee!; **'that's an** ~ (coll.) das ist eine gute Idee; **that gives me an** ~: das hat mich auf eine Idee gebracht; **the** ~ **was that** ...: der Plan war, dass ...; **have big** ~**s** große Rosinen im Kopf haben; **what's the big** ~**?** (iron.) was soll das?; was soll der Blödsinn? (ugs.)

ideal /aɪˈdɪəl/ **1** *adj.* **(a)** ideal; vollendet ‹*Ehemann, Gastgeber*›; vollkommen ‹*Glück, Welt*›; **(b)** (embodying an idea, existing only in idea) ideell; gedacht. **2** *n.* Ideal, *das*

idealise ⇒ **idealize**

idealism /aɪˈdɪəlɪzm/ *n.*, *no pl.* Idealismus, *der*

idealist /aɪˈdɪəlɪst/ *n.* Idealist, *der*/Idealistin, *die*

idealistic /aɪdɪəˈlɪstɪk/ *adj.* idealistisch

idealize /aɪˈdɪəlaɪz/ *v.t.* idealisieren

ideally /aɪˈdɪəlɪ/ *adv.* ideal; ~, **the work should be finished in two weeks** im Idealfalle *od.* idealerweise sollte die Arbeit in zwei Wochen abgeschlossen sein

identical /aɪˈdentɪkl/ *adj.* **(a)** (same) identisch; **the** ~ **species** dieselbe Art; **(b)** (agreeing in every detail) identisch; sich (*Dat.*) gleichend; **be** ~**:** sich (*Dat.*) völlig gleichen; ~ **twins** eineiige Zwillinge

identifiable /aɪˈdentɪfaɪəbl/ *adj.* erkennbar (by an + *Dat.*); nachweisbar ‹*Stoff, Substanz*›; bestimmbar ‹*Pflanzen-, Tierart*›

identification /aɪdentɪfɪˈkeɪʃn/ *n.* Identifizierung, *die;* (of plants or animals) Bestimmung, *die;* **means of** ~: Ausweispapiere *Pl.;* **have you any means of** ~? können Sie sich ausweisen?; ~ **card** [Personal]ausweis, *der;* ~ **plate** Kennzeichenschild, *das*

identifi'cation parade *n.* (Brit.) Gegenüberstellung, *die* [zur Identifizierung]

identify /aɪˈdentɪfaɪ/ **1** *v.t.* **(a)** (treat as identical) gleichsetzen (**with** mit); **(b)** (associate) identifizieren (**with** mit); **(c)** (recognize) identifizieren; bestimmen ‹*Pflanze, Tier*›; **(d)** (establish) ermitteln. **2** *v.i.* ~ **with sb.** sich mit jmdm. identifizieren

Identikit, (P) /aɪˈdentɪkɪt/ *n.* Phantombild, *das*

identity /aɪˈdentɪtɪ/ *n.* **(a)** (sameness) Übereinstimmung, *die;* **(b)** (individuality, being specified person) Identität, *die;* **proof of** ~**:** Identitätsnachweis, *der;* **[case of] mistaken** ~**:** [Personen]verwechslung, *die;* **(c)** ~ **card/plate** ⇒ **identification**

i'dentity parade ⇒ **identification parade**

ideological /aɪdɪəˈlɒdʒɪkl, ɪdɪəˈlɒdʒɪkl/ *adj.* ideologisch

ideology /aɪdɪˈɒlədʒɪ, ɪdɪˈɒlədʒɪ/ *n.* Ideologie, *die;* Weltanschauung, *die*

idiocy /ˈɪdɪəsɪ/ *n.* Dummheit, *die;* Idiotie, *die*

idiom /ˈɪdɪəm/ *n.* [Rede]wendung, *die;* idiomatischer Ausdruck

idiomatic /ɪdɪəˈmætɪk/ *adj.* idiomatisch

idiosyncrasy /ɪdɪəˈsɪŋkrəsɪ/ *n.* Eigentümlichkeit, *die;* Eigenheit, *die*

idiosyncratic /ɪdɪəsɪŋˈkrætɪk/ *adj.* eigenwillig

idiot /ˈɪdɪət/ *n.* Idiot, *der* (ugs.); Trottel, *der* (ugs.)

idiotic /ɪdɪˈɒtɪk/ *adj.* idiotisch (ugs.); **what an** ~ **thing to do/say** was für ein Schwachsinn

idle /ˈaɪdl/ **1** *adj.* **(a)** (lazy) faul; träge; **(b)** (not in use) außer Betrieb *nachgestellt;* **be** *or* **stand** ~ ‹*Maschinen, Fabrik:*› stillstehen; *see also* **lle²** **2 b; (c)** (having no special purpose) bloß ‹*Neugier*›; nutzlos, leer ‹*Geschwätz*›; **(d)** (groundless) unbegründet ‹*Annahme, Mutmaßung*›; bloß, rein ‹*Spekulation, Gerücht*›; **no** ~ **boast** *or* **jest** (iron.) kein leeres Versprechen; **(e)** (ineffective) sinnlos, (geh.) müßig ‹*Diskussion, Streit*›; leer ‹*Versprechen*›; **(f)** (unoccupied) frei ‹*Zeit, Stunden, Tag*›; **(g)** (unemployed) **be made** ~ ‹*Arbeiter:*› arbeitslos werden. **2** *v.i.* ‹*Motor:*› leer laufen, im Leerlauf laufen

~ **a'way** *v.t.* vertun ‹*Zeit, Leben*›

idleness /ˈaɪdlnɪs/ *n.*, *no pl.* (being unoccupied) Untätigkeit, *die;* (avoidance of work) Müßiggang, *der* (geh.)

idler /ˈaɪdlə(r)/ *n.* Faulenzer, *der*/Faulenzerin, *die;* Faulpelz, *der* (fam.)

idly /ˈaɪdlɪ/ *adv.* **(a)** (carelessly) leichtsinnig; gedankenlos; **(b)** (inactively) untätig; **stand** ~ **by while** ... (fig.) untätig zusehen, wie ...; **(c)** (indolently) faul

idol /ˈaɪdl/ *n.* **(a)** (false god) Götze, *der;* (image of deity) Götzenbild, *das;* **(b)** (person venerated) Idol, *das;* (thing venerated) Götze, *der*

idolatry /aɪˈdɒlətrɪ/ *n.* Götzenverehrung, *die*

idolize (idolise) /ˈaɪdəlaɪz/ *v.t.* **(a)** (make an idol of) anbeten; verehren; **(b)** (fig.: venerate) vergöttern; zum Idol erheben

idyll /ˈɪdɪl/ Idyll, *das*

idyllic /aɪˈdɪlɪk, ɪˈdɪlɪk/ *adj.* idyllisch

i.e. /aɪˈiː/ *abbr.* **that is** d. h.; i. e.

if /ɪf/ **1** *conj.* **(a)** wenn; **if anyone should ask** ...: falls jemand fragt, ...; wenn jemand fragen sollte, ...; **if you would lend me some money** ...: wenn du mir Geld leihen würdest, ...; **if I knew what to do** ...: wenn ich wüsste, was ich tun soll ...; **if I were you** an deiner Stelle; **better, if anything** vielleicht etwas besser; **tell me what I can do to help, if anything** falls ich irgendwie helfen kann, sag es mir; **if so/not** wenn ja/nein *od.* nicht; **if then/that/at all** wenn überhaupt; **if only for today** wenn auch nur für heute; **if only because/to** ...: schon allein, weil/um ... zu ...; **as if** als ob; **as if you didn't know!** als ob du es nicht gewusst hättest!; **it isn't** *or* **it's not as if we were** *or* (coll.) **we're rich** es ist nicht etwa so, dass wir reich wären; **(b)** (whenever) [immer] wenn; **(c)** (whether) ob; **(d)** *in excl. of wish* **if I only knew, if only I knew!** wenn ich das nur wüsste!; das wüsste ich gern!; **if only you could have seen it!** wenn du es nur hättest sehen können!; **(e)** *expr. surprise etc.* **if it isn't Ronnie!** das ist doch Ronnie!; **(f)** *in polite request* **if you will wait a moment** wenn Sie einen Augenblick warten wollen; **if you wouldn't mind holding the door open** wenn Sie so freundlich wären und die Tür aufhielten; **(g)** (though) und wenn; auch *od.* selbst wenn; **even if he did say that**, ...: selbst wenn er das gesagt hat, ...; **(h)** (despite being) wenn auch; **likeable, if somewhat rough** liebenswürdig, wenn auch etwas derb. **2** *n.* Wenn, *das;* **ifs and buts** Wenn und Aber, *das*

igloo /ˈɪgluː/ *n.* Iglu, *der od.* das

ignite /ɪgˈnaɪt/ **1** *v.t.* anzünden; entzünden (geh.). **2** *v.i.* sich entzünden

ignition /ɪgˈnɪʃn/ *n.* **(a)** (igniting) Zünden, *das;* Entzünden, *das* (geh.); **(b)** (Motor Veh.) Zündung, *die*

ig'nition key *n.* (Motor Veh.) Zündschlüssel, *der*

ignoble /ɪgˈnəʊbl/ *adj.* niedrig ‹*Geburt, Herkunft*›; niederträchtig ‹*Person*›; schändlich ‹*Tat*›

ignominious /ɪgnəˈmɪnɪəs/ *adj.* verwerflich (geh.) ‹*Tat, Idee, Praktik*›; (humiliating) schändlich

ignominy /ˈɪgnəmɪnɪ/ *n.* Schande, *die*

ignoramus /ɪgnəˈreɪməs/ *n.* Ignorant, *der;* Nichtswisser, *der*

ignorance /ˈɪgnərəns/ *n.*, *no pl.* Ignoranz, *die* (abwertend); Unwissenheit, *die;* **keep sb. in** ~ **of sth.** jmdn. in Unkenntnis über etw. (*Akk.*) lassen; ~ **is bliss** was ich nicht weiß, macht mich nicht heiß (Spr.); **his** ~ **of physics** seine mangelnden Kenntnisse in Physik

ignorant /ˈɪgnərənt/ *adj.* **(a)** (lacking knowledge) unwissend; ungebildet; **(b)** (behaving in uncouth manner) unkultiviert (abwertend); **(c)** (uninformed) **be ~ of sth.** über etw. (*Akk.*) nicht informiert sein; **remain ~ of sth.** über etw. (*Akk.*) nie etwas erfahren; **be ~ in** *or* **of mathematics** mangelnde Kenntnisse in Mathematik haben

ignore /ɪgˈnɔː(r)/ *v.t.* ignorieren; nicht beachten; nicht befolgen ‹ *Befehl, Rat* ›; übergehen, überhören ‹ *Frage, Bemerkung* ›; **I shall ~ that remark!** ich habe das nicht gehört!

ilk /ɪlk/ *n.* (coll.) **Bill and [others of] his ~:** Bill und seinesgleichen; **he's another of the same ~:** er gehört auch zu derselben Sorte; **people of that ~:** solche Leute

ill /ɪl/ **1** *adj.*, **worse** /wɜːs/, **worst** /wɜːst/ **(a)** ▶ 865 (sick) krank; **be ~ with flu** an Grippe (*Dat.*) erkrankt sein; **be ~ with worry** vor Sorgen [ganz] krank sein; *see also* **fall 2 k**; **take 1 i**; **(b)** (harmful) ~ **effects** schädliche Wirkungen; **(c)** (unfavourable) widrig ‹ *Schicksal, Umstand* ›; ~ **fate** *or* **fortune** *or* **luck** Pech, *das;* **it's an ~ wind that blows nobody [any] good** (prov.) des einen Leid, des andern Freud (Spr.); **as ~ luck would have it** wie es das Unglück wollte. **2** *n.* **(a)** (evil) Übel, *das;* **for good or ~:** komme, was will; **(b)** (harm) Schlechte, *das;* Unglück, *das;* **wish sb. ~:** jmdm. nichts Gutes *od.* nur das Schlechteste wünschen; **speak ~ of sb./sth.** Schlechtes über jmdn. *od.* von jmdm./von etw. sagen; **(c)** *in pl.* (misfortunes) Missstände *Pl.* **3** *adv.*, **worse**, **worst (a)** (badly) schlecht, unschicklich ‹ *sich benehmen* ›; **(b)** (imperfectly) schlecht, unzureichend ‹ *versorgt, ausgestattet* ›; **he can ~ afford it** er kann es sich (*Dat.*) kaum leisten; ~ **at ease** verlegen

I'll /aɪl/ = **I shall**; **(b)** = **I will**

ill: ~-**advised** *adj.* unklug; schlecht beraten ‹ *Kunde* ›; **be ~-advised** ‹ *Person:* › schlecht beraten sein; ~-**behaved** ⇒ **behave 1 a**; ~-**bred** *adj.* schlecht erzogen ‹ *Kind, Jugendlicher* ›; unkultiviert (abwertend) ‹ *Leute, Kerl usw.* ›; ~-**conceived** *adj.* schlecht durchdacht; ~-**defined** *adj.* ungenau definiert, unklar ‹ *Verfahren, Vorgehen* ›

illegal /ɪˈliːgl/ *adj.* ungesetzlich; illegal; (Sport) regelwidrig; unerlaubt; **it is ~ to drive a car without a licence** es ist verboten, ohne Führerschein Auto zu fahren

illegality /ɪliˈgælɪti/ *n. no pl.* Ungesetzlichkeit, *die*

illegally /ɪˈliːgəli/ *adv.* illegal; **bring sth. into the country ~:** etw. illegal einführen

illegible /ɪˈledʒɪbl/ *adj.* unleserlich

illegitimate /ɪlɪˈdʒɪtɪmət/ *adj.* **(a)** unehelich ‹ *Kind* ›; **(b)** (not authorized by law) unrechtmäßig ‹ *Machtergreifung, Geschäft* ›; mit dem Gesetz unvereinbar ‹ *Maßnahme, Vorgehen, Beweggrund* ›; **(c)** (wrongly inferred) unzulässig

ill: ~-**'fated** *adj.* unglückselig; verhängnisvoll ‹ *Entscheidung, Stunde, Tag* ›; ~ **'feeling** *n.* Verstimmung, *die;* **cause ~ feeling** böses Blut machen *od.* schaffen; **no ~ feeling[s]?** sind Sie jetzt verstimmt *od.* (fam.) böse?; ~-**founded** /ˈɪlfaʊndɪd/ *adj.* haltlos ‹ *Theorie, Gerücht* ›; **be ~-founded** völlig haltlos sein; ~-**gotten** *adj.* unrechtmäßig erworben; ~ **'health** *n.* schwache Gesundheit; ~-**humoured** /ɪlˈhjuːməd/ *adj.* schlecht gelaunt

illicit /ɪˈlɪsɪt/ *adj.* verboten ‹ *Glücksspiel* ›; unerlaubt ‹ [*Geschlechts*]*verkehr, Beziehung* ›; Schwarz‹ *handel, -verkauf, -arbeit* ›

'ill-informed *adj.* schlecht informiert; auf Unkenntnis beruhend ‹ *Bemerkung, Schätzung, Urteil* ›

illiteracy /ɪˈlɪtərəsi/ *n., no pl.* Analphabetentum, *das*

illiterate /ɪˈlɪtərət/ **1** *adj.* **(a)** des Lesens und Schreibens unkundig; analphabetisch ‹ *Bevölkerung* ›; **he is ~:** er ist Analphabet; **(b)** (showing lack of learning) primitiv (abwertend); **musically ~:** musikalisch völlig unbedarft. **2** *n.* Analphabet, *der*/Analphabetin, *die*

ill: ~-**judged** *adj.* unklug; (rash) unüberlegt; leichtfertig; ~-**mannered** /ɪlˈmænəd/ *adj.* rüpelhaft (abwertend); ungezogen ‹ *Kind* ›

illness /ˈɪlnɪs/ *n.* Krankheit, *die;* **children's ~:** Kinderkrankheit, *die;* **because of ~:** wegen [einer] Krankheit

illogical /ɪˈlɒdʒɪkl/ *adj.* unlogisch

ill: ~-**tempered** /ɪlˈtempəd/ *adj.* schlecht gelaunt; ~-**timed** *adj.* [zeitlich] ungelegen; unpassend ‹ *Bemerkung* ›;

~-**'treat** *v.t.* misshandeln ‹ *Lebewesen* ›; nicht schonend behandeln ‹ *Gegenstand* ›; ~-**'treatment** *n., no pl.* (of living thing) Misshandlung, *die;* (of object) wenig pflegliche Behandlung

illuminate /ɪˈljuːmɪneɪt, ɪˈluːmɪneɪt/ *v.t.* **(a)** ‹ *Lampe usw.:* › beleuchten; ‹ *Mond, Sonne:* › erleuchten; **(b)** (give enlightenment to) erleuchten; **(c)** (help to explain) erhellen; [näher] beleuchten; **(d)** (decorate with lights) festlich beleuchten; illuminieren; ~**d advertisements** Leuchtreklamen *Pl.*; **(e)** ausmalen, (fachspr.) illuminieren ‹ *Handschriften usw.* ›

illuminating /ɪˈljuːmɪneɪtɪŋ, ɪˈluːmɪneɪtɪŋ/ *adj.* aufschlussreich

illumination /ɪljuːmɪˈneɪʃn, ɪluːmɪˈneɪʃn/ *n.* **(a)** (lighting) Beleuchtung, *die;* **(b)** (enlightenment) Erleuchtung, *die;* **(c)** (decorative lights) *often in pl.* ~[s] Festbeleuchtung, *die;* Illumination, *die*

illusion /ɪˈljuːʒn, ɪˈluːʒn/ *n.* Illusion, *die;* (misapprehension) falsche Vorstellung; Illusion, *die;* **be under an ~:** sich Illusionen (*Dat.*) hingeben; **be under the ~ that ...:** sich (*Dat.*) einbilden, dass ...; **have no ~s about sb./sth.** sich (*Dat.*) über jmdn./etw. keine Illusionen machen

illusory /ɪˈljuːsəri, ɪˈluːsəri/ *adj.* (deceptive) illusorisch

illustrate /ˈɪləstreɪt/ *v.t.* **(a)** (serve as example of) veranschaulichen; illustrieren; **(b)** (elucidate by pictures) [bildlich] darstellen ‹ *Vorgang, Ablauf* ›; illustrieren ‹ *Buch, Erklärung* ›; **(c)** (explain) verdeutlichen; erläutern; (make clear by examples) anschaulicher machen; illustrieren

illustration /ɪləˈstreɪʃn/ *n.* **(a)** (example) Beispiel, *das* (of für); (drawing) Abbildung, *die;* **(b)** (picture) Abbildung, *die;* Illustration, *die;* **(c)** *no pl.* (with example) Illustration, *die;* **by way of ~:** zur Illustration *od.* Verdeutlichung

illustrative /ˈɪləstrətɪv/ *adj.* erläuternd; illustrativ; **be ~ of sth.** beispielhaft für etw. sein

illustrator /ˈɪləstreɪtə(r)/ *n.* ▶ 887 Illustrator, *der*/Illustratorin, *die*

illustrious /ɪˈlʌstrɪəs/ *adj.* berühmt ‹ *Person* › (for wegen); ruhmreich ‹ *Tat, Herrschaft* ›

ill 'will *n.* Böswilligkeit, *die*

I'm /aɪm/ = **I am**

image /ˈɪmɪdʒ/ *n.* **(a)** Bildnis, *das* (geh.); (statue) Standbild, *das;* (Optics, Math.) Bild, *das;* **(c)** (semblance) Bild, *das;* (counterpart) Ebenbild, *das* (geh.); **she is the [very] ~ of her mother** sie ist das [getreue] Ebenbild ihrer Mutter; **(d)** (Lit.: simile, metaphor) Bild, *das;* **(e)** (mental representation) Bild, *das;* (conception) Vorstellung, *die;* **(f)** (perceived character) Image, *das;* **improve one's ~:** sein Image aufbessern; **public ~:** Image [in der Öffentlichkeit]

'image-conscious *adj.* imagebewusst

imagery /ˈɪmɪdʒəri, ˈɪmɪdʒri/ *n., no pl.* (Lit.) Metaphorik, *die*

imaginable /ɪˈmædʒɪnəbl/ *adj.* erdenklich; **the biggest lie ~:** die unverschämteste Lüge, die man sich (*Dat.*) vorstellen kann

imaginary /ɪˈmædʒɪnəri/ *adj.* imaginär (geh.); konstruiert ‹ *Bildnis* ›; eingebildet ‹ *Krankheit* ›

imagination /ɪmædʒɪˈneɪʃn/ *n.* **(a)** *no pl., no art.* Fantasie, *die;* **use your ~!** hab doch ein bisschen Fantasie! (ugs.); **(b)** *no pl., no art.* (fancy) Einbildung, *die;* **catch sb.'s ~:** jmdn. begeistern; **it's just your ~:** das bildest du dir nur ein

imaginative /ɪˈmædʒɪnətɪv/ *adj.* fantasievoll; (showing imagination) einfallsreich

imagine /ɪˈmædʒɪn/ *v.t.* **(a)** (picture to oneself, guess, think) sich (*Dat.*) vorstellen; **can you ~?** stell dir vor!; ~ **things** sich (*Dat.*) Dinge einbilden[, die gar nicht stimmen]; ~ **sth. to be easy/difficult** *etc.* sich (*Dat.*) etw. leicht/ schwer *usw.* vorstellen; **do not ~ that ...:** bilden Sie sich (*Dat.*) bloß nicht ein, dass ...; **as you can ~** wie du dir denken *od.* vorstellen kannst; **(b)** (coll.: suppose) glauben; **(c)** (get the impression) ~ **[that] ...:** sich (*Dat.*) einbilden[, dass] ...

imbalance /ɪmˈbæləns/ *n.* Unausgeglichenheit, *die*

imbecile /ˈɪmbɪsiːl, ˈɪmbɪsaɪl/ **1** *adj.* schwachsinnig (ugs. abwertend). **2** *n.* Idiot, *der* (ugs.)

Illnesses, aches and pains

Injuries

Where does it hurt?	= Wo haben Sie Schmerzen?; *(to child)* Wo tut es weh?
My right arm is hurting	= Der rechte Arm tut mir weh, Mir tut der rechte Arm weh
She has hurt her foot	= *(e.g. twisted it)* Sie hat sich am Fuß weh getan; *(wounded it, e.g. cut it or stuck something into it)* Sie hat sich am Fuß verletzt
I have sprained my ankle	= Ich habe mir den Fuß verstaucht
He has broken his leg	= Er hat sich das Bein gebrochen
She has a fractured skull/pelvis	= Sie hat einen Schädelbruch/ Beckenbruch
You've burnt your hand	= Du hast dir die Hand verbrannt

Note the number of expressions where the English possessive with a part of the body is translated by a definite article and a personal pronoun in the dative (*see also* □ **The body**).

Aches and pains

I've got toothache/ a headache/a stomach ache	= Ich habe Zahnschmerzen/ Kopfschmerzen/ Magenschmerzen *or (coll.)* Zahnweh/ Kopfweh/Magenweh
She has a pain in her knee	= Sie hat Schmerzen im Knie
something to relieve the pain	= etwas gegen die Schmerzen
a stab of pain	= ein stechender Schmerz
A gnawing pain went right through him	= Ein bohrender Schmerz durchfuhr ihn

Note that **Schmerz** referring to physical pain is mostly used in the plural for continuing or repeated pain, and in the singular only when a single occurrence is meant.

Being ill

I feel ill	= Ich fühle mich krank; *(esp. sick)* Mir ist übel *or* schlecht
He is ill with flu, He has [got] flu	= Er ist an Grippe erkrankt, Er hat [die] Grippe
He is seriously/ terminally ill	= Er ist schwer krank/ unheilbar krank
She has caught or gone down with a cold	= Sie hat sich erkältet *or* sich *(Dat.)* eine Erkältung zugezogen
You'll catch pneumonia	= Du holst dir eine Lungenentzündung
They suffer from asthma/bronchitis	= Sie leiden an Asthma/Bronchitis
a bout of malaria	= ein Malariaanfall
an asthma attack	= ein Asthmaanfall

Illnesses and conditions

More permanent illnesses are usually translated as **-leiden**:

He has a heart condition/ a stomach complaint	= Er hat ein Herzleiden/ ein Magenleiden

But:

a skin complaint	= eine Hautkrankheit

Indicating often general and less well defined pain or discomfort, the German **-beschwerden** (plural) corresponds approximately to the English "trouble" (also translated by **-probleme**):

heart/stomach trouble	= Herzbeschwerden *or* Herzprobleme/ Magenbeschwerden *or* Magenprobleme
She suffers from back trouble	= Sie hat Rücken- probleme, Sie hats mit dem Rücken *(coll.)*

In some cases, the noun describing the person is used rather than the word for the illness:

He has epilepsy	= Er ist Epileptiker

German forms many words for people with certain illnesses by adding **-kranke(r)**:

people with Aids or Aids sufferers	= Aidskranke
a cancer patient or victim	= ein Krebskranker/eine Krebskranke

Treatment

She is having or receiving treatment [from a specialist]	= Sie ist [bei einem Facharzt] in Behandlung
He is being treated for cancer/a stomach ulcer	= Er wird wegen Krebs/eines Magengeschwürs behandelt

In this last example **auf** + accusative can also be used, but this gives the phrase the sense "given the treatment for", i.e. the condition has not necessarily been diagnosed (or not correctly):

They treated him for a stomach ulcer, but it turned out that he had cancer	= Sie haben ihn auf ein Magengeschwür behandelt, aber es stellte sich heraus, dass er Krebs hatte
What can I take for hay fever?	= Was kann ich gegen Heuschnupfen nehmen?
To be taken three times a day	= Dreimal täglich einzunehmen
Shake the bottle	= Vor Gebrauch schütteln
There is no cure for Aids	= Es gibt kein Mittel gegen Aids, Aids ist nicht heilbar
I had four operations	= Ich bin viermal operiert worden
Have you been vaccinated against cholera?	= Sind Sie gegen Cholera geimpft [worden]?
She gave me an injection	= Sie gab mir eine Spritze

Recovery

He is getting better or is on the mend or on the road to recovery	= Er ist auf dem Wege der Besserung
She is much better	= Es geht ihr *or* Sie fühlt sich viel besser
I am completely cured/fully recovered	= Ich bin völlig geheilt/ habe mich vollständig erholt

imbibe /ɪmˈbaɪb/ *v.t.* **(a)** (drink) trinken; **(b)** (fig.: assimilate) in sich (*Akk.*) aufsaugen

imbue /ɪmˈbjuː/ *v.t.* durchdringen

IMF *abbr.* **International Monetary Fund** IWF, *der*

imitate /ˈɪmɪteɪt/ *v.t.* **(a)** (mimic) nachahmen; nachmachen (ugs.); ~ **sb.** (follow example of) es jmdm. gleichtun; **(b)** (produce sth. like) kopieren; **(c)** (be like) imitieren

imitation /ɪmɪˈteɪʃn/ **1** *n.* **(a)** (imitating) Nachahmung, *die;* **a style developed in** ~ **of classical models** ein nach klassischen Vorbildern entwickelter Stil; **do** ~**s of sb.** jmdn. imitieren od. nachahmen; **he sings, tells jokes, and does** ~**s** er singt, erzählt Witze und ahmt andere Leute nach; **(b)** (copy) Kopie, *die;* (counterfeit) Imitation, *die.* **2** *adj.* imitiert; Kunst‹*leder, -horn*›; ~ **marble/fur** *etc.* Marmor-/Pelzimitation *usw., die*

imitative /ˈɪmɪtətɪv, ˈɪmɪteɪtɪv/ *adj.* **(a)** uneigenständig; **be** ~ **of sb./sth.** jmdn./etw. nachahmen; **(b)** (prone to copy) imitativ (geh.)

imitator /ˈɪmɪteɪtə(r)/ *n.* Nachahmer, *der*/Nachahmerin, *die;* Imitator, *der*/Imitatorin, *die*

immaculate /ɪˈmækjʊlət/ *adj.* **(a)** (spotless) makellos ‹*Kleidung, Weiß*›; **(b)** (faultless) tadellos

immaculately /ɪˈmækjʊlətlɪ/ *adv.* **(a)** (spotlessly) makellos; **(b)** (faultlessly) tadellos

immaterial /ɪməˈtɪərɪəl/ *adj.* unerheblich; **it's quite** ~ **to me** das ist für mich vollkommen uninteressant

immature /ɪməˈtjʊə(r)/ *adj.* unreif; noch nicht voll entwickelt ‹*Lebewesen*›; noch nicht voll ausgereift ‹*Begabung, Talent*›

immaturity /ɪməˈtjʊərɪtɪ/ *n. no pl.* Unreife, *die*

immeasurable /ɪˈmeʒərəbl/ *adj.* unermesslich

immediate /ɪˈmiːdjət/ *adj.* **(a)** unmittelbar; (nearest) nächst... ‹*Nachbar[schaft], Umgebung, Zukunft*›; engst... ‹*Familie*›; unmittelbar ‹*Kontakt*›; **your** ~ **action must be to ...:** als Erstes müssen Sie ...; **his** ~ **plan is to ...:** zunächst einmal will er ...; **(b)** (occurring at once) prompt; unverzüglich ‹*Handeln, Maßnahmen*›; umgehend ‹*Antwort*›

immediately /ɪˈmiːdjətlɪ/ **1** *adv.* **(a)** unmittelbar; direkt; **(b)** (without delay) sofort. **2** *conj.* (coll.) sobald

immemorial /ɪmɪˈmɔːrɪəl/ *adj.* undenklich; **from time** ~**:** seit undenklichen Zeiten

immense /ɪˈmens/ *adj.* **(a)** ungeheuer; immens; **(b)** (coll.: great) enorm

immensely /ɪˈmenslɪ/ *adv.* **(a)** ungeheuer; **(b)** (coll.: very much) unheimlich (ugs.)

immensity /ɪˈmensɪtɪ/ *n., no pl.* Ungeheuerlichkeit, *die*

immerse /ɪˈmɜːs/ *v.t.* **(a)** (dip) [ein]tauchen; **(b)** (cause to be under water) versenken; ~**d in water** unter Wasser; **(c)** **be** ~**d in thought/one's work** (fig.: involved deeply) in Gedanken versunken/in seine Arbeit vertieft sein

immersion /ɪˈmɜːʃn/ *n.* Eintauchen, *das*

im'mersion heater *n.* Heißwasserbereiter, *der;* (small, portable) Tauchsieder, *der*

immigrant /ˈɪmɪɡrənt/ **1** *n.* Einwanderer, *der*/Einwanderin, *die;* Immigrant, *der*/Immigrantin, *die.* **2** *adj.* Einwanderer-; ~ **population** Einwanderer *Pl.;* ~ **workers** ausländische Arbeitnehmer *Pl.*

immigrate /ˈɪmɪɡreɪt/ *v.i.* einwandern, immigrieren (**into** nach, **from** aus)

immigration /ɪmɪˈɡreɪʃn/ *n.* Einwanderung *die,* Immigration, *die* (**into** nach, **from** aus); *attrib.* Einwanderungs‹*kontrolle, -gesetz*›; ~ **officer** Beamte/Beamtin der Einwanderungsbehörde; **go through** ~**:** durch die Passkontrolle gehen; ~ **authorities** Einwanderungsbehörden *Pl.;* **I**~ **Service** Einwanderungsbehörde, *die*

imminent /ˈɪmɪnənt/ *adj.* unmittelbar bevorstehend; drohend ‹*Gefahr*›; **be** ~**:** unmittelbar bevorstehen/drohen

immobile /ɪˈməʊbaɪl/ *adj.* **(a)** (immovable) unbeweglich; **(b)** (motionless) bewegungslos

immobilise ⇨ **immobilize**

immobility /ɪməˈbɪlɪtɪ/ *n., no pl.* **(a)** (immovableness) Unbeweglichkeit, *die;* **(b)** (motionlessness) Bewegungslosigkeit, *die*

immobilize /ɪˈməʊbɪlaɪz/ *v.t.* **(a)** (fix immovably) verankern; (fig.) lähmen; **(b)** gegen Wegfahren sichern ‹*Fahrzeug*›

immobilizer /ɪˈməʊbɪlaɪzə(r)/ *n.* (Motor Veh.) Wegfahrsperre, *die*

immoderate /ɪˈmɒdərət/ *adj.* **(a)** (excessive) unmäßig ‹*Rauchen, Trinken*›; **(b)** (extreme) extrem ‹*Ansichten, Politiker*›; maßlos ‹*Lebensstil*›

immodest /ɪˈmɒdɪst/ *adj.* **(a)** (impudent) unbescheiden; **(b)** (improper) unanständig

immoral /ɪˈmɒrəl/ *adj.* **(a)** (not conforming od. morality) unmoralisch; unsittlich; sittenwidrig (Rechtsspr.); **(b)** (morally evil) pervers; **(c)** (in sexual matters) sittenlos

immorality /ɪməˈrælɪtɪ/ *n.* **(a)** *no pl.* Unsittlichkeit, *die;* Unmoral, *die;* Sittenwidrigkeit, *die* (Rechtsspr.); **(b)** *no pl.* (wickedness) Verdorbenheit, *die;* **(c)** (in sexual matters) Sittenlosigkeit, *die;* **(d)** (morally wrong act) Unsittlichkeit, *die*

immortal /ɪˈmɔːtl/ *adj.* unsterblich

immortalise ⇨ **immortalize**

immortality /ɪmɔːˈtælɪtɪ/ *n., no pl.* Unsterblichkeit, *die*

immortalize /ɪˈmɔːtəlaɪz/ *v.t.* unsterblich machen

immovable /ɪˈmuːvəbl/ *adj.* **(a)** unbeweglich; **(b)** (motionless) bewegungslos; **(c)** (steadfast) unerschütterlich

immovably /ɪˈmuːvəblɪ/ *adv.* fest; **be** ~ **stuck** feststecken

immune /ɪˈmjuːn/ *adj.* **(a)** (exempt) sicher (**from** vor + *Dat.*); geschützt (**from, against** vor + *Dat.*); **(b)** (insusceptible) unempfindlich (**to** gegen); (to hints, suggestions, etc.) unempfänglich (**to** für); immun (**to** gegen); **(c)** (Med.) immun (**to** gegen); ~ **system** Immunsystem, *das*

immunisation, immunise ⇨ **immunize-**

immunity /ɪˈmjuːnɪtɪ/ *n.* **(a)** ~ **from prosecution** Schutz vor Strafverfolgung; **give sb.** ~ **from prosecution** ‹*Person:*› jmdn. von der Bestrafung ausnehmen; ‹*Umstand:*› jmdn. vor Strafe schützen; **diplomatic** ~**:** diplomatische Immunität; ⇨ **immune b:** Unempfindlichkeit, *die* (**to** gegen)/Unempfänglichkeit, *die* (**to** für); Immunität, *die* (**to** gegen); **(c)** (Med.) Immunität, *die*

immunization /ɪmjʊnaɪˈzeɪʃn/ *n.* (Med.) Immunisierung, *die*

immunize /ˈɪmjʊnaɪz/ *v.t.* (Med.) immunisieren

immunodeficiency /ɪmjuːnəʊdɪfɪˈʃənsɪ/ *n.* (Med.) Immunschwäche, *die*

immunology /ɪmjʊˈnɒlədʒɪ/ *n.* (Med.) Immunologie, *die*

immutable /ɪˈmjuːtəbl/ *adj.* unveränderlich

imp /ɪmp/ *n.* **(a)** Kobold, *der;* **(b)** (fig.: mischievous child) Racker, *der* (fam.)

impact 1 /ˈɪmpækt/ *n.* **(a)** Aufprall, *der* (**on, against** auf + *Akk.*); (of shell or bomb) Einschlag, *der;* (collision) Zusammenprall, *der;* **(b)** (fig.: effect) Wirkung, *die;* **have an** ~ **on sb./sth.** Auswirkungen auf jmdn./etw. haben; **make an** ~ **on sb./sth.** Eindruck auf jmdn./etw. machen. **2** /ɪmˈpækt/ *v.t.* pressen

impacted /ɪmˈpæktɪd/ *adj.* (Dent.) impaktiert ‹*Zahn*›

impair /ɪmˈpeə(r)/ *v.t.* **(a)** (damage) beeinträchtigen; schaden (+ *Dat.*) ‹*Gesundheit*›; **(b)** (weaken) beeinträchtigen; ~**ed vision** Sehschwäche, *die;* ~**ed hearing** Schwerhörigkeit, *die*

impale /ɪmˈpeɪl/ *v.t.* aufspießen; (Hist.) pfählen

impart /ɪmˈpɑːt/ *v.t.* **(a)** (give) [ab]geben (**to** an + *Akk.*); vermachen (**to** *Dat.*); **(b)** (communicate) kundtun (geh.) (**to** *Dat.*); vermitteln ‹*Kenntnisse*› (**to** *Dat.*)

impartial /ɪmˈpɑːʃl/ *adj.* unparteiisch; gerecht ‹*Entscheidung, Behandlung, Urteil*›

impartiality /ɪmpɑːʃɪˈælɪtɪ/ *n., no pl.* Unparteilichkeit, *die*

impassable /ɪmˈpɑːsəbl/ *adj.* unpassierbar (**to** für); (to vehicles) unbefahrbar (**to** für)

impasse /ˈæmpɑːs, ˈɪmpɑːs/ *n.* (lit. or fig.) Sackgasse, *die;* **the negotiations have reached an** ~**:** die Verhandlungen sind in eine Sackgasse geraten

impassioned /ɪmˈpæʃnd/ *adj.* leidenschaftlich

impassive /ɪmˈpæsɪv/ *adj.* **(a)** ausdruckslos; **(b)** (incapable of feeling emotion) leidenschaftslos

impatience /ɪmˈpeɪʃəns/ *n., no pl.* (a) Ungeduld, *die* (at über + *Akk.*); (b) (intolerance) Unduldsamkeit, *die* (of gegen); (c) (eager desire) [ungeduldige] Erwartung (for *Gen.*)

impatient /ɪmˈpeɪʃənt/ *adj.* (a) ungeduldig; ~ at sth./with sb. ungeduldig über etw. (*Akk.*) /mit jmdm.; (b) (intolerant) unduldsam (of gegen); (c) (eagerly desirous) be ~ for sth. etw. kaum erwarten können; be ~ to do sth. unbedingt etw. tun wollen

impatiently /ɪmˈpeɪʃəntlɪ/ *adv.* ungeduldig

impeach /ɪmˈpiːtʃ/ *v.t.* (a) (call in question) infrage stellen; (b) (Law) anklagen (of *Gen.*, wegen)

impeachment /ɪmˈpiːtʃmənt/ *n.* (Law) Impeachment, *das*

impeccable /ɪmˈpekəbl/ *adj.* makellos; tadellos ⟨*Manieren*⟩

impede /ɪmˈpiːd/ *v.t.* behindern

impediment /ɪmˈpedɪmənt/ *n.* (a) Hindernis, *das* (to für); (b) (speech defect) Sprachfehler, *der*

impel /ɪmˈpel/ *v.t.*, **-ll-** treiben, antreiben ⟨*Turbine usw.*⟩; feel ~led to do sth. sich genötigt *od.* gezwungen fühlen, etw. zu tun

impend /ɪmˈpend/ *v.i.* (be about to happen) bevorstehen; ⟨*Gefahr:*⟩ drohen

impenetrable /ɪmˈpenɪtrəbl/ *adj.* (a) undurchdringlich (by, to für); unbezwingbar, uneinnehmbar ⟨*Festung*⟩; (b) (inscrutable) unergründlich

imperative /ɪmˈperətɪv/ **1** *adj.* (a) (commanding) gebieterisch (geh.) ⟨*Stimme, Geste*⟩; (b) (urgent) dringend erforderlich. **2** *n.* (a) Befehl, *der;* (b) (Ling.) Imperativ, *der*

imperceptible /ɪmpəˈseptɪbl/ *adj.* (a) nicht wahrnehmbar (to für); unsichtbar ⟨*Schranke (fig.)*⟩; be ~ to sb./the senses von jmdm./den Sinnen nicht wahrgenommen werden können; (b) (very slight or gradual) unmerklich; (subtle) kaum zu erkennen *nicht attr.;* kaum zu erkennend *nicht präd.;* minimal ⟨*Unterschied*⟩

imperfect /ɪmˈpɜːfɪkt/ **1** *adj.* (a) (not fully formed) unfertig; (incomplete) unvollständig; slightly ~ stockings/pottery *etc.* Strümpfe/Keramik *usw.* mit kleinen Fehlern; (b) (faulty) mangelhaft. **2** *n.* (Ling.) Imperfekt, *das*

imperfection /ɪmpəˈfekʃn/ *n.* (a) *no pl.* (incompleteness) Unvollständigkeit, *die;* (b) *no pl.* (faultiness) Mangelhaftigkeit, *die;* (c) (fault) Mangel, *der*

imperfectly /ɪmˈpɜːfɪktlɪ/ *adv.* (a) (incompletely) unvollständig; (b) (faultily) fehlerhaft; mangelhaft

imperial /ɪmˈpɪərɪəl/ *adj.* (a) kaiserlich; Reichs⟨*adler, -insignien*⟩; (b) (of an emperor) Kaiser-; (c) (fixed by statute) britisch ⟨*Maße, Gewichte*⟩

imperialism /ɪmˈpɪərɪəlɪzm/ *n., no pl.* (derog.) Imperialismus, *der;* US/Soviet ~: der US-/Sowjetimperialismus

imperialist /ɪmˈpɪərɪəlɪst/ *n.* (derog.) Imperialist, *der*/Imperialistin, *die*

imperil /ɪmˈperɪl/ *v.t.*, (Brit.) **-ll-** gefährden

imperious /ɪmˈpɪərɪəs/ *adj.* (overbearing) herrisch; gebieterisch

imperishable /ɪmˈperɪʃəbl/ *adj.* alterungsbeständig ⟨*Material*⟩; unverderblich ⟨*Lebensmittel*⟩

impermeable /ɪmˈpɜːmɪəbl/ *adj.* undurchlässig

impermissible /ɪmpəˈmɪsɪbl/ *adj.* unzulässig

impersonal /ɪmˈpɜːsənl/ *adj.* unpersönlich

impersonate /ɪmˈpɜːsəneɪt/ *v.t.* (for entertainment) imitieren; nachahmen; (for purpose of fraud) sich ausgeben als

impersonation /ɪmpɜːsəˈneɪʃn/ *n.* (a) (personification) Verkörperung, *die;* (b) (imitation) Imitation, *die;* Nachahmung, *die;* he does ~s er ist Imitator; do an ~ of sb. jmdn. imitieren *od.* nachahmen

impersonator /ɪmˈpɜːsəneɪtə(r)/ *n.* (entertainer) Imitator, *der*/Imitatorin, *die*

impertinence /ɪmˈpɜːtɪnəns/ *n.* Unverschämtheit, *die*

impertinent /ɪmˈpɜːtɪnənt/ *adj.* unverschämt

imperturbable /ɪmpəˈtɜːbəbl/ *adj.* gelassen; be completely ~: durch nichts zu erschüttern sein; die Ruhe weghaben (ugs.)

impervious /ɪmˈpɜːvɪəs/ *adj.* (a) undurchlässig; ~ to water/bullets/rain wasserdicht/kugelsicher/regendicht;

(b) be ~ to sth. (fig.) unempfänglich für etw. sein; be ~ to argument Argumenten unzugänglich sein

impetuosity /ɪmpetjʊˈɒsɪtɪ/ *n.* (a) *no pl.* (quality) Impulsivität, *die;* (b) (act, impulse) Ausbruch, *der*

impetuous /ɪmˈpetjʊəs/ *adj.* impulsiv ⟨*Person*⟩; unüberlegt ⟨*Handlung, Entscheidung*⟩; (vehement) stürmisch; ungestüm ⟨*Person, Angriff*⟩

impetus /ˈɪmpɪtəs/ *n.* (a) Kraft, *die;* (of impact) Wucht, *die;* (b) (fig.: impulse) Motivation, *die*

impinge /ɪmˈpɪndʒ/ *v.i.* (a) (make impact) ~ [up]on sth. auf etw. (*Akk.*) auftreffen; (b) (encroach) ~ [up]on sth. auf etw. (*Akk.*) Einfluss nehmen

impish /ˈɪmpɪʃ/ *adj.* lausbübisch; diebisch ⟨*Freude*⟩

implacable /ɪmˈplækəbl/ *adj.* unversöhnlich; erbittert ⟨*Gegner*⟩; erbarmungslos ⟨*Verfolgung*⟩; unerbittlich ⟨*Schicksal*⟩

implant 1 /ɪmˈplɑːnt/ *v.t.* (a) (Med.) implantieren (fachspr.), einpflanzen (in *Dat.*); (b) (fig.: instil) einpflanzen (in *Dat.*). **2** /ˈɪmplɑːnt/ *n.* (Med.) Implantat, *das*

implausible /ɪmˈplɔːzɪbl/ *adj.* unglaubwürdig

implement 1 /ˈɪmplɪmənt/ *n.* Gerät, *das.* **2** /ˈɪmplɪment/ *v.t.* erfüllen ⟨*Versprechen, Vertrag*⟩; einhalten ⟨*Termin usw.*⟩; vollziehen ⟨*Erlass usw.*⟩; [in die Tat] umsetzen ⟨*Politik, Plan usw.*⟩

implementation /ɪmplɪmenˈteɪʃn/ *n.* ⇒ **implement** 2: Erfüllung, *die;* Einhaltung, *die;* Vollzug, *der;* Umsetzung [in die Tat], *die*

implicate /ˈɪmplɪkeɪt/ *v.t.* (show to be involved) belasten ⟨*Verdächtigen usw.*⟩; be ~d in a scandal in einen Skandal verwickelt sein

implication /ɪmplɪˈkeɪʃn/ *n.* (a) *no pl.* (implying) Implikation, *die* (geh.); by ~: implizit; implizite (geh.); (b) *no pl.* (being involved) Verwicklung, *die* (in in + *Akk.*); (c) *no pl.* (being affected) Betroffenheit, *die* (in von); (d) (thing implied) Implikation, *die*

implicit /ɪmˈplɪsɪt/ *adj.* (a) (implied) implizit; unausgesprochen ⟨*Drohung, Zweifel*⟩; (b) (virtually contained) be ~ in sth. in etw. (*Dat.*) enthalten sein; (c) (resting on authority) unbedingt; blind ⟨*Vertrauen*⟩

implode /ɪmˈpləʊd/ **1** *v.i.* implodieren. **2** *v.t.* implodieren lassen

implore /ɪmˈplɔː(r)/ *v.t.* (a) (beg for) erflehen (geh.); flehen um; 'please', she ~d "bitte", flehte sie; (b) (entreat) anflehen (for um)

imploring /ɪmˈplɔːrɪŋ/ *adj.* flehend

imploringly /ɪmˈplɔːrɪŋlɪ/ *adv.* flehentlich (geh.)

imply /ɪmˈplaɪ/ *v.t.* (a) (Involve the existence of) implizieren (geh.); (by inference) schließen lassen auf (+ *Akk.*); be implied in sth. in etw. (*Dat.*) enthalten sein; (b) (express indirectly) hindeuten auf (+ *Akk.*); (insinuate) unterstellen; are you ~ing that …? willst du damit etwa sagen, dass …?

impolite /ɪmpəˈlaɪt/ *adj.*, ~r /ɪmpəˈlaɪtə(r)/, ~st /ɪmpəˈlaɪtɪst/ unhöflich; ungezogen ⟨*Kind*⟩

impoliteness /ɪmpəˈlaɪtnɪs/ *n., no pl.* Unhöflichkeit, *die;* (of child) Ungezogenheit, *die*

imponderable /ɪmˈpɒndərəbl/ *adj.* unwägbar

import 1 /ɪmˈpɔːt/ *v.t.* (a) importieren, einführen ⟨*Waren*⟩ (from aus, into nach); (b) (signify) bedeuten. **2** /ˈɪmpɔːt/ *n.* (a) (process, amount ~ed) Import, *der;* Einfuhr, *die;* (b) (article ~ed) Importgut, *das;* (c) (meaning, importance) Bedeutung, *die;* an event of great ~: ein sehr bedeutungsvolles Ereignis

importance /ɪmˈpɔːtəns/ *n., no pl.* (a) Bedeutung, *die;* Wichtigkeit, *die;* be of great ~ to sb./sth. für jmdn./etw. äußerst wichtig sein; (b) (significance) Bedeutung, *die;* (of decision) Tragweite, *die;* be of/without ~: wichtig/unwichtig sein; full of one's own ~: von seiner eigenen Wichtigkeit überzeugt

important /ɪmˈpɔːtənt/ *adj.* (a) bedeutend; (in a particular matter) wichtig (to für); the most ~ thing is …: die Hauptsache ist …; (b) (momentous) wichtig ⟨*Entscheidung*⟩; bedeutsam ⟨*Tag*⟩; (c) (having high rank) wichtig ⟨*Persönlichkeit*⟩; (d) (considerable) beträchtlich; erheblich

importantly /ɪmˈpɔːtəntlɪ/ *adv.* (a) bear ~ [up]on sth. auf etw. (*Akk.*) bedeutsame Auswirkungen haben;

more/most ~ *as sentence-modifier* was noch wichtiger/ am wichtigsten ist; **(b)** (pompously) wichtigtuerisch

'import duty *n.* Einfuhrzoll, *der*

importer /ɪm'pɔːtə(r)/ *n.* Importeur, *der;* **be an** ~ **of cotton** Baumwollimporteur sein; ⟨*Land:*⟩ Baumwolle importieren

'import permit *n.* Einfuhrerlaubnis, *die*

impose /ɪm'pəʊz/ **1** *v.t.* **(a)** auferlegen (geh.) ⟨*Bürde, Verpflichtung*⟩ **([up]on** *Dat.*); erheben ⟨*Steuer, Zoll*⟩ **(on** auf + *Akk.*); verhängen ⟨*Kriegsrecht*⟩; anordnen ⟨*Rationierung*⟩; verhängen ⟨*Sanktionen*⟩ **(on** gegen); ~ **a ban on sth.** etw. mit einem Verbot belegen; ~ **a tax on sth.** etw. mit einer Steuer belegen; **(b)** (compel compliance with) ~ **sth. [up]on sb.** jmdm. etw. aufdrängen. **2** *v.i.* **(a)** (exert influence) imponieren; Eindruck machen; **(b)** (take advantage) **I do not want** *or* **wish to** ~: ich will nicht aufdringlich sein. **3** *v. refl.* ~ **oneself on sb.** sich jmdm. aufdrängen

~ **on,** ~ **upon** *v.t.* ausnutzen ⟨*Gutmütigkeit, Toleranz usw.*⟩; ~ **on sb.** sich jmdm. aufdrängen

imposing /ɪm'pəʊzɪŋ/ *adj.* imposant

imposition /ɪmpə'zɪʃn/ *n.* **(a)** *no pl.* (action) Auferlegung, *die;* (of tax) Erhebung, *die;* **(b)** *no pl.* (enforcement) Durchsetzung, *die;* **(c)** (piece of advantage-taking) Ausnützung, *die;* **I hope it's not too much of an** ~: ich hoffe, es macht nicht zu viele Umstände

impossibility /ɪmpɒsɪ'bɪlɪtɪ/ *n.* **(a)** *no pl.* Unmöglichkeit, *die;* **(b)** **that's an absolute** ~: das ist völlig unmöglich *od.* ein Ding der Unmöglichkeit (ugs.)

impossible /ɪm'pɒsɪbl/ **1** *adj.* **(a)** unmöglich; **it is** ~ **for me to do it** es ist mir nicht möglich, es zu tun; **(b)** (not easy) schwer; (not easily believable) unmöglich (ugs.); **(c)** (coll.: intolerable) unmöglich (ugs.). **2** *n.* **the** ~: das Unmögliche; Unmögliches; **achieve the** ~: das Unmögliche erreichen

impostor /ɪm'pɒstə(r)/ *n.* Hochstapler, *der*/-staplerin, *die;* (swindler) Betrüger, *der*/Betrügerin, *die*

impotence /'ɪmpətəns/ *n., no pl.* **(a)** (powerlessness) Machtlosigkeit, *die;* **(b)** (sexual) Impotenz, *die*

impotent /'ɪmpətənt/ *adj.* **(a)** (powerless) machtlos; kraftlos ⟨*Argument*⟩; **be** ~ **to do sth.** nicht in der Lage sein, etw. zu tun; **(b)** (sexually) impotent

impound /ɪm'paʊnd/ *v.t.* **(a)** (shut up) einpferchen ⟨*Vieh*⟩; einsperren ⟨*streunende Hunde usw.*⟩; **(b)** (take possession of) beschlagnahmen; requirieren (Milit.)

impoverish /ɪm'pɒvərɪʃ/ *v.t.* **(a)** verarmen lassen; **be/ become** ~**ed** verarmt sein/verarmen; **(b)** (exhaust) auslaugen ⟨*Boden*⟩

impoverishment /ɪm'pɒvərɪʃmənt/ *n., no pl.* **(a)** (making poor) Verarmung, *die;* (being poor) Armut, *die;* **(b)** (of soil) (process) Auslaugung, *die;* (state) Ausgelaugtheit, *die*

impracticable /ɪm'præktɪkəbl/ *adj.* undurchführbar

imprecise /ɪmprɪ'saɪs/ *adj.,* **imprecisely** /ɪmprɪ'saɪslɪ/ *adv.* ungenau; unpräzise (geh.)

imprecision /ɪmprɪ'sɪʒn/ *n.* Ungenauigkeit, *die*

impregnable /ɪm'pregnəbl/ *adj.* uneinnehmbar ⟨*Festung, Bollwerk*⟩; einbruch[s]sicher ⟨*Tresorraum usw.*⟩; (fig.) unanfechtbar ⟨*Ruf, Tugend, Stellung*⟩

impregnate /'ɪmpregneɪt, ɪm'pregneɪt/ *v.t.* imprägnieren

impresario /ɪmprɪ'sɑːrɪəʊ/ *n., pl.* ~**s** Intendant, *der*/Intendantin, *die;* Impresario, *der* (veralt.)

impress /ɪm'pres/ *v.t.* **(a)** (apply) drücken; ~ **a pattern** *etc.* **on/in sth.** ein Muster *usw.* auf etw. (*Akk.*) aufdrücken/ in etw. (*Akk.*) eindrücken; **(b)** beeindrucken ⟨*Person*⟩; *abs.* Eindruck machen; ~ **sb. favourably/unfavourably** auf jmdn. einen günstigen/ungünstigen Eindruck machen; **(c)** ~ **sth. [up]on sb.** jmdm. etw. einprägen

impression /ɪm'preʃn/ *n.* **(a)** (mark) Abdruck, *der;* **(b)** (Printing) (quantity of copies) Auflage, *die;* (unaltered reprint) Nachdruck, *der;* **(c)** (effect on person) Eindruck, *der* (**of** von); (effect on inanimate things) Wirkung, *die;* **make an** ~ **on sb.** Eindruck auf jmdn. machen; **(d)** (impersonation) **do an** ~ **of sb.** jmdn. imitieren; **do** ~**s** andere Leute imitieren; **(e)** (notion) Eindruck, *der;* **it's my** ~ **that** …: ich habe den

Eindruck, dass …; **form an** ~ **of sb.** sich (*Dat.*) ein Bild von jmdm. machen; **give [sb.] the** ~ **that** …/**of being bored** [bei jmdm.] den Eindruck erwecken, als ob …/als ob man sich langweile; **be under the** ~ **that** …: der Auffassung *od.* Überzeugung sein, dass …; (less certain) den Eindruck haben, dass …

impressionable /ɪm'preʃənəbl/ *adj.* beeinflussbar; **have an** ~ **mind, be** ~: sich leicht beeinflussen lassen

impressionism /ɪm'preʃənɪzm/ *n., no pl.* Impressionismus, *der*

impressionist /ɪm'preʃənɪst/ *n.* Impressionist, *der*/Impressionistin, *die; attrib.* impressionistisch ⟨*Kunst usw.*⟩

impressive /ɪm'presɪv/ *adj.* beeindruckend; imponierend

imprint 1 /'ɪmprɪnt/ *n.* **(a)** Abdruck, *der;* **(b)** (fig.) Stempel, *der;* **leave one's** ~ **on sb.**/**sth.** jmdm./einer Sache seinen Stempel aufdrücken. **2** /ɪm'prɪnt/ *v.t.* **(a)** (stamp) aufdrucken; aufdrücken ⟨*Poststempel*⟩; (on metal) aufprägen; **(b)** (fix indelibly) **sth. is** ~**ed in** *or* **on sb.'s memory** etw. hat sich jmdm. [unauslöschlich] eingeprägt

imprison /ɪm'prɪzn/ *v.t.* in Haft nehmen; **be** ~**ed** sich in Haft befinden

imprisonment /ɪm'prɪznmənt/ *n.* Haft, *die;* **a long term** *or* **period of** ~: eine langjährige Haft- *od.* Freiheitsstrafe

improbability /ɪmprɒbə'bɪlɪtɪ/ *n.* Unwahrscheinlichkeit, *die*

improbable /ɪm'prɒbəbl/ *adj.* (not likely) unwahrscheinlich

impromptu /ɪm'prɒmptjuː/ **1** *adj.* improvisiert; **an** ~ **speech** eine Stegreifrede; **an** ~ **visit** ein Überraschungsbesuch. **2** *adv.* aus dem Stegreif

improper /ɪm'prɒpə(r)/ *adj.* **(a)** (wrong) unrichtig; ungeeignet ⟨*Werkzeug*⟩; **(b)** (unseemly) ungehörig; unpassend; (indecent) unanständig; **(c)** (not in accordance with rules of conduct) unangebracht; unzulässig ⟨*Gebühren*⟩

improperly /ɪm'prɒpəlɪ/ *adv.* **(a)** (wrongly) unrichtig; **use sth.** ~: etw. unsachgemäß gebrauchen; **(b)** (in unseemly fashion) unpassend; (indecently) unanständig

impropriety /ɪmprə'praɪətɪ/ *n.* **(a)** *no pl.* (unseemliness) Unpassende, *das;* (indecency) Unanständigkeit, *die;* **(b)** (instance of improper conduct) Unanständigkeit, *die;* **moral** ~: moralisches Fehlverhalten

improve /ɪm'pruːv/ **1** *v.i.* sich verbessern; besser werden; ⟨*Person, Wetter:*⟩ sich bessern; **he was ill, but he's improving now** er war krank, aber es geht ihm jetzt schon besser; **things are improving** es sieht schon besser aus. **2** *v.t.* verbessern; erhöhen, steigern ⟨*Produktion*⟩; ausbessern ⟨*Haus usw.*⟩; verschönern ⟨*öffentliche Anlage usw.*⟩; ~ **one's situation** sich verbessern. **3** *v. refl.* ~ **oneself** sich weiterbilden

~ **[up]on** *v.t.* überbieten ⟨*Rekord, Angebot*⟩; verbessern ⟨*Leistung*⟩

improvement /ɪm'pruːvmənt/ *n.* **(a)** *no pl.* Verbesserung, *die;* Besserung, *die;* (in trading) Steigerung, *die;* **there is need for** ~ **in your handwriting** deine Handschrift müsste besser werden; **(b)** (addition) Verbesserung, *die;* **make** ~**s to sth.** Verbesserungen an etw. (*Dat.*) vornehmen

improvise /'ɪmprəvaɪz/ *v.t.* improvisieren; aus dem Stegreif vortragen ⟨*Rede*⟩

imprudent /ɪm'pruːdənt/ *adj.* unklug; (showing rashness) unbesonnen

impudence /'ɪmpjʊdəns/ *n.* Unverschämtheit, *die;* (brazenness) Dreistigkeit, *die*

impudent /'ɪmpjʊdənt/ *adj.,* **impudently** /'ɪmpjʊdəntlɪ/ *adv.* unverschämt; (brazen) dreist

impugn /ɪm'pjuːn/ *v.t.* in Zweifel ziehen

impulse /'ɪmpʌls/ *n.* **(a)** (act of impelling) Stoß, *der;* Impuls, *der;* (fig.: motivation) Impuls, *der;* **give an** ~ **to sth.** einer Sache (*Dat.*) neue Impulse geben; **(b)** (mental incitement) Impuls, *der;* **be seized with an irresistible** ~ **to do sth.** von einem unwiderstehlichen Drang ergriffen werden, etw. zu tun; **from pure** ~: rein impulsiv; **act/do sth. on [an]** ~: impulsiv handeln/etw. tun '**impulse buying** *n.* Spontankäufe *Pl.*

impulsive /ɪm'pʌlsɪv/ *adj.* impulsiv

impulsively /ɪm'pʌlsɪvlɪ/ *adv.* impulsiv

impulsiveness /ɪm'pʌlsɪvnɪs/ *n.*, *no pl.* Impulsivität, *die*

impunity /ɪm'pju:nɪtɪ/ *n.*, *no pl.* **be able to do sth. with** ∼: etw. gefahrlos tun können; (*without being punished*) etw. ungestraft tun können

impure /ɪm'pjʊə(r)/ *adj.* (**a**) (lit. or fig.) unrein; (dirty) unsauber; schmutzig ‹*Wasser*›; (**b**) schmutzig ‹*Gedanke*›

impurity /ɪm'pjʊərɪtɪ/ *n.* (**a**) *no pl.* (lit. or fig.) Unreinheit, *die;* (being dirty) Unsauberkeit, *die;* (of water) Verschmutzung, *die;* (**b**) *in pl.* (dirt) Schmutz, *der;* (**c**) (foreign body) Fremdkörper, *der;* Fremdstoff, *der*

impute /ɪm'pju:t/ *v.t.* ∼ **sth. to sb./sth.** jmdm./einer Sache etw. zuschreiben; ∼ **bad intentions to sb.** jmdm. schlechte Absichten unterstellen

in /ɪn/ **1** *prep.* (**a**) (position; also fig.) in (+ *Dat.*); **in the fields** auf den Feldern; **a ride in a motor car** eine Autofahrt; **shot/wounded in the leg** ins Bein geschossen/am Bein verwundet; **in this heat** bei dieser Hitze; **the highest mountain in the world** der höchste Berg der Welt; (**b**) (wearing as dress) in (+ *Dat.*); (wearing as headgear) mit; **in brown shoes** mit braunen Schuhen; **a lady in black** eine Dame in Schwarz; (**c**) (with respect to) **two feet in diameter** mit einem Durchmesser von zwei Fuß; **a change in attitude** eine Änderung der Einstellung; *see also* **herself a; itself a;** (**d**) (as a proportionate part of) **eight dogs in ten** acht von zehn Hunden; *see also* **gradient;** (**e**) (as a member of) in (+ *Dat.*); **be in the Scouts** bei den Pfadfindern sein; **be employed in the Civil Service** als Beamter/Beamtin beschäftigt sein; (**f**) (as content of) **there are three feet in a yard** ein Yard hat drei Fuß; **what is there in this deal for me?** was springt für mich bei dem Geschäft heraus? (ugs.); **there is nothing/not much** *or* **little in it** (difference) da ist kein/kein großer Unterschied [zwischen ihnen]; **there is something in what you say** an dem, was Sie sagen, ist etwas dran (ugs.); (**g**) *expr. identity* in (+ *Dat.*); **have a faithful friend in sb.** an jmdm. einen treuen Freund haben; (**h**) (concerned with) in (+ *Dat.*); **what line of business are you in?** in welcher Branche sind Sie?; **he's in politics** er ist Politiker; **she's in insurance** sie ist in der Versicherungsbranche tätig; (**i**) **be [not] in it** (as competitor) [nicht] dabei od. im Rennen sein; (**j**) (with the means of; having as material or colour) **a message in code** eine verschlüsselte Nachricht; **in writing** schriftlich; **in this way** auf diese Weise; **in a few words** mit wenigen Worten; **a dress in velvet** ein Kleid aus Samt; **this sofa is also available in leather/blue** dieses Sofa gibt es auch in Leder/Blau; **write sth. in red** etw. in Rot schreiben; **draw in crayon/ink** *etc.* mit Kreide/Tinte *usw.* zeichnen; *see also* **English 2 a;** (**k**) (while, during) **in fog/rain** *etc.* bei Nebel/Regen *usw.;* **in the eighties/nineties** in den Achtzigern/Neunzigern; **4 o'clock in the morning/afternoon** 4 Uhr morgens/abends; **in 1990** [im Jahre] 1990; (**l**) (after a period of) in (+ *Dat.*); **in three minutes/years** in drei Minuten/Jahren; (**m**) (within the ability of) **have it in one [to do sth.]** fähig sein [, etw. zu tun]; **I didn't know you had it in you** das hätte ich dir nicht zugetraut; **there is no malice in him** er hat nichts Bösartiges an sich (*Dat.*); (**n**) in that insofern als; *see also* **far 1 d;** (**o**) **in doing this** (by so doing) indem jmd. das tut/tat; dadurch. **2** *adv.* (**a**) (inside) hinein‹*gehen usw.*›; (towards speaker) herein‹*kommen usw.*›; **is everyone in?** sind alle drin? (ugs.); '**In** „Einfahrt"/ „Eingang"; (**b**) (at home, work, etc.) **be in** da sein; **find sb. in** jmdn. antreffen; **ask sb. in** jmdn. hereinbitten; **he's been in and out all day** er war den ganzen Tag über mal da und mal nicht da; (**c**) (included) darin; drin (ugs.); **cost £50 all in** 50 Pfund kosten, alles inbegriffen; (**d**) (inward) innen; (**e**) (in fashion) in (ugs.); in Mode; (**f**) (elected) **be in** gewählt sein; (**g**) (having arrived) **be in** ‹*Zug, Schiff, Ware, Bewerbung:*› da sein; ‹*Ernte:*› eingebracht sein; (**h**) **sb. is in for sth.** (about to undergo sth.) jmdm. steht etw. bevor; (taking part in sth.) jmd. nimmt an etw. (*Dat.*) teil; **we're in for it now!** (coll.) jetzt blüht uns was! (ugs.); **have it in for**

sb. es auf jmdn. abgesehen haben (ugs.); (**i**) (coll.: as participant, accomplice, observer, etc.) **be in on the secret/discussion** in das Geheimnis eingeweiht sein/bei der Diskussion dabei sein; **be [well] in with sb.** mit jmdm. [gut] auskommen. **3** *attrib. adj.* (fashionable) Mode-; **the 'in crowd** die Clique, die gerade in ist (ugs.); '**in joke** Insiderwitz, *der.* **4** *n.* **know the ins and outs of a matter** sich in einer Sache genau auskennen

inability /ɪnə'bɪlɪtɪ/ *n.*, *no pl.* Unfähigkeit, *die*

inaccessibility /ɪnæksesɪ'bɪlɪtɪ/ *n.*, *no pl.* Unzugänglichkeit, *die*

inaccessible /ɪnæk'sesɪbl/ *adj.* unzugänglich

inaccuracy /ɪn'ækjʊrəsɪ/ *n.* (**a**) (incorrectness) Unrichtigkeit, *die;* (**b**) (imprecision) Ungenauigkeit, *die*

inaccurate /ɪn'ækjʊrət/ *adj.* (**a**) (incorrect) unrichtig; (**b**) (imprecise) ungenau

inaction /ɪn'ækʃn/ *n.*, *no pl.*, *no indef. art.* Untätigkeit, *die*

inactive /ɪn'æktɪv/ *adj.* (**a**) untätig; (**b**) (sluggish) träge

inactivity /ɪnæk'tɪvɪtɪ/ *n.*, *no pl.* (**a**) Untätigkeit, *die;* (**b**) (sluggishness) Trägheit, *die*

inadequacy /ɪn'ædɪkwəsɪ/ *n.* (**a**) Unzulänglichkeit, *die;* (**b**) (incompetence) mangelnde Eignung

inadequate /ɪn'ædɪkwət/ *adj.* (**a**) unzulänglich; **his response was** ∼ **[to the situation]** seine Antwort war [der Situation] nicht angemessen; **the resources are** ∼ **to his needs** die Mittel reichen für seine Bedürfnisse nicht aus; (**b**) (incompetent) ungeeignet; **feel** ∼: sich überfordert fühlen

inadmissible /ɪnəd'mɪsɪbl/ *adj.* unzulässig

inadvertent /ɪnəd'vɜ:tənt/ *adj.* ungewollt; versehentlich

inadvertently /ɪnəd'vɜ:təntlɪ/ *adv.* versehentlich

inadvisable /ɪnəd'vaɪzəbl/ *adj.* nicht ratsam; unratsam

inane /ɪ'neɪn/ *adj.* dümmlich

inanimate /ɪn'ænɪmət/ *adj.* unbelebt

inapplicable /ɪn'æplɪkəbl, ɪnə'plɪkəbl/ *adj.* nicht anwendbar (**to** auf + *Akk.*); **delete if** ∼: Unzutreffendes [bitte] streichen

inappropriate /ɪnə'prəʊprɪət/ *adj.* unpassend; **be** ∼ **for sth.** für etw. nicht geeignet sein; **be** ∼ **to the occasion** dem Anlass nicht angemessen sein

inapt /ɪn'æpt/ *adj.* unpassend

inarticulate /ɪnɑ:'tɪkjʊlət/ *adj.* (**a**) **she's rather/very** ∼: sie kann sich ziemlich/sehr schlecht ausdrücken; **a clever but** ∼ **mathematician** ein kluger Mathematiker, der sich aber nur schlecht ausdrücken kann; (**b**) (indistinct) unverständlich; inartikuliert (geh.)

inasmuch /ɪnəz'mʌtʃ/ *adv.* (formal) ∼ **as** insofern als; (because) da

inattention /ɪnə'tenʃn/ *n.*, *no pl.* Unaufmerksamkeit, *die* (**to** gegenüber)

inattentive /ɪnə'tentɪv/ *adj.* unaufmerksam (**to** gegenüber)

inaudible /ɪn'ɔ:dɪbl/ *adj.*, **inaudibly** /ɪn'ɔ:dɪblɪ/ *adv.* unhörbar

inaugural /ɪ'nɔ:gjʊrəl/ *adj.* (**a**) (first in series) Eröffnungs-; (**b**) (by person being inaugurated) ∼ **lecture** *or* **address** Antrittsrede, *die*

inaugurate /ɪ'nɔ:gjʊreɪt/ *v.t.* (**a**) (admit to office) in sein Amt einführen; (**b**) (begin) einführen; in Angriff nehmen ‹*Projekt*›

inauspicious /ɪnɔ:'spɪʃəs/ *adj.* (ominous) unheilverkündend; unheilvoll

'**inborn** *adj.* angeboren (**in** *Dat.*)

in'bred *adj.* (**a**) angeboren; (**b**) (impaired by inbreeding) **they are/have become** ∼: bei ihnen herrscht Inzucht

in'breeding *n.* Inzucht, *die*

'**inbuilt** *adj.* jmdm./einer Sache eigen

Inc. *abbr.* (Amer.) **Incorporated** e.G.

incalculable /ɪn'kælkjʊləbl/ *adj.* (**a**) (very great) unermesslich; (**b**) (unpredictable) unabsehbar

incantation /ɪnkæn'teɪʃn/ *n.* (**a**) (words) Zauberspruch, *der;* (**b**) (spell) Beschwörung, *die*

incapable /ɪn'keɪpəbl/ *adj.* (a) (lacking ability) **be ~ of doing sth.** außer Stande sein, etw. zu tun; **be ~ of sth.** zu etw. unfähig sein; (b) (incompetent) unfähig

incapacitate /ɪnkə'pæsɪteɪt/ *v.t.* unfähig machen; **physically ~d/~d by illness** körperlich/durch Krankheit behindert

incapacity /ɪnkə'pæsɪtɪ/ *n., no pl.* Unfähigkeit, *die* (for zu)

incarcerate /ɪn'kɑːsəreɪt/ *v.t.* einkerkern (geh.)

incarnate /ɪn'kɑːnət/ *adj.* **be the devil ~:** der leibhaftige Satan sein; **be beauty/wisdom** *etc.* **~:** die personifizierte Schönheit/Weisheit *usw.* sein

incarnation /ɪnkɑː'neɪʃn/ *n.* Inkarnation, *die*

incendiary /ɪn'sendɪərɪ/ *adj.* **~ attack** Brandstiftung, *die;* **~ device** Brandsatz, *der;* **~ bomb** Brandbombe, *die*

incense[1] /'ɪnsens/ *n.* Weihrauch, *der*

incense[2] /ɪn'sens/ *v.t.* erzürnen; erbosen; **be ~d at** *or* **by sth./with sb.** über etw./jmdn. erbost *od.* erzürnt sein

incentive /ɪn'sentɪv/ *n.* (a) (motivation) Anreiz, *der;* (b) (payment) finanzieller Anreiz

inception /ɪn'sepʃn/ *n.* Einführung, *die;* **from** *or* **since/at its ~:** von Beginn an/zu Beginn

incessant /ɪn'sesənt/ *adj.*, **incessantly** /ɪn'sesəntlɪ/ *adv.* unablässig; unaufhörlich

incest /'ɪnsest/ *n.* Inzest, *der;* Blutschande, *die*

incestuous /ɪn'sestjʊəs/ *adj.* (lit. or fig.) inzestuös

inch /ɪntʃ/ **1** *n.* (a) **▶ 850⌋, ▶ 904⌋** Inch, *der;* Zoll, *der* (veralt.); (b) (small amount) **~ by ~:** Zentimeter um Zentimeter; **by ~es** zentimeterweise; **not give** *or* **yield an ~:** keinen Fingerbreit nachgeben. **2** *v.t.* zentimeterweise bewegen; **~ one's way forward** sich Zoll für Zoll vorwärts bewegen. **3** *v.i.* sich zentimeterweise bewegen

incidence /'ɪnsɪdəns/ *n.* (a) (occurrence) Auftreten, *das;* Vorkommen, *das;* (b) (manner or range of occurrence) Häufigkeit, *die*

incident /'ɪnsɪdənt/ *n.* (a) (notable event) Vorfall, *der;* (minor occurrence) Begebenheit, *die;* Vorkommnis, *das;* (b) (clash) Zwischenfall, *der;* (c) (in play, novel, etc.) Episode, *die*

incidental /ɪnsɪ'dentl/ **1** *adj.* (casual) beiläufig ⟨*Art, Bemerkung*⟩; Neben⟨*ausgaben, -einnahmen*⟩. **2** *n., in pl.* Nebensächlichkeiten; (expenses) Nebenausgaben

incidentally /ɪnsɪ'dentəlɪ/ *adv.* (by the way) nebenbei [bemerkt]

inci'dental music *n.* Begleitmusik, *die*

'incident room *n.* [*temporäres*] *lokales Einsatzzentrum der Polizei*

incinerate /ɪn'sɪnəreɪt/ *v.t.* verbrennen

incinerator /ɪn'sɪnəreɪtə(r)/ *n.* Verbrennungsofen, *der;* (in garden) Abfallverbrenner, *der*

incipient /ɪn'sɪpɪənt/ *adj.* anfänglich; einsetzend ⟨*Schmerzen*⟩; aufkommend ⟨*Zweifel, Angst*⟩

incision /ɪn'sɪʒn/ *n.* (a) (cutting) Einschneiden, *das;* (b) (cut) Einschnitt, *der*

incisive /ɪn'saɪsɪv/ *adj.* schneidend ⟨*Ton*⟩; scharf ⟨*Verstand*⟩; scharfsinnig ⟨*Genie, Kritik, Frage, Bemerkung, Argument*⟩; präzise ⟨*Sprache, Stil*⟩

incisor /ɪn'saɪzə(r)/ *n.* (Anat., Zool.) Schneidezahn, *der*

incite /ɪn'saɪt/ *v.t.* anstiften; aufstacheln ⟨*Massen, Volk*⟩

incitement /ɪn'saɪtmənt/ *n.* (act) Anstiftung, *die;* (of masses, crowd) Aufstachelung, *die*

inclement /ɪn'klemənt/ *adj.* unfreundlich ⟨*Wetter*⟩

inclination /ɪnklɪ'neɪʃn/ *n.* (a) (slope) [Ab]hang, *der;* (of roof) Neigung, *die;* (b) (preference, desire) Neigung, *die* (**to, for** für); **my ~ is to let the matter rest** ich neige dazu, die Sache auf sich beruhen zu lassen; (c) (liking) **~ for sb.** Zuneigung für jmdn.

incline 1 /ɪn'klaɪn/ *v.t.* (a) (bend) neigen; (b) (dispose) veranlassen; **all her instincts ~d her to stay** alles in ihr drängte sie zu bleiben. **2** *v.i.* (a) (be disposed) neigen (**to[wards]** zu); **~ to believe that …:** geneigt sein zu glauben, dass …; (b) (lean) sich neigen. **3** /'ɪnklaɪn/ *n.* Steigung, *die*

inclined /ɪn'klaɪnd/ *adj.* geneigt; **be mathematically ~:** sich für Mathematik interessieren; **if you feel [so]**

~: wenn Sie Lust dazu haben; **he is that way ~:** er neigt dazu

include /ɪn'kluːd/ *v.t.* einschließen; (contain) enthalten; **his team ~s a number of people who …:** zu seiner Mannschaft gehören einige, die …; …, **[the] children ~d** …, [die] Kinder eingeschlossen; **does that ~ 'me?** gilt das auch für mich?; **your name is not ~d in the list** dein Name steht nicht auf der Liste; **have you ~d the full amount?** haben Sie den vollen Betrag einbezogen?; **~d in the price** im Preis einbegriffen

including /ɪn'kluːdɪŋ/ *prep.* einschließlich; **I make that ten ~ the captain** mit dem Kapitän sind das nach meiner Rechnung zehn; **up to and ~ the last financial year** bis einschließlich des letzten Geschäftsjahres; **~ VAT** inklusive MwSt.

inclusive /ɪn'kluːsɪv/ *adj.* (a) inklusive (bes. Kaufmannsspr.); einschließlich; **be ~ of sth.** etw. einschließen; **from 2 to 6 January ~:** vom 2. bis einschließlich 6. Januar; (b) (including everything) Pauschal-; Inklusiv-; **cost £50 ~:** 50 Pfund kosten, alles inbegriffen

incognito /ɪnkɒg'niːtəʊ/ **1** *adj., adv.* inkognito. **2** *n.* Inkognito, *das*

incoherent /ɪnkəʊ'hɪərənt/ *adj.* zusammenhanglos

income /'ɪnkəm/ *n.* Einkommen, *das;* **~s** (receipts) Einkünfte *Pl.;* **live within/beyond one's ~:** entsprechend seinen Verhältnissen/über seine Verhältnisse leben

income: ~ bracket *n.* Einkommensklasse, *die;* **~s policy** *n.* Einkommenspolitik, *die;* **~ support** *n.* (Brit.) zusätzliche Hilfe zum Lebensunterhalt; **~ tax** *n.* Einkommensteuer, *die;* (on wages, salary) Lohnsteuer, *die;* **~ tax return** Einkommensteuererklärung, *die/* Lohnsteuererklärung, *die*

'incoming *adj.* (a) (arriving) ankommend; einlaufend ⟨*Zug, Schiff*⟩; landend ⟨*Flugzeug*⟩; einfahrend ⟨*Zug*⟩; eingehend ⟨*Telefongespräch, Auftrag*⟩; **the ~ tide** die Flut; (b) (succeeding) neu ⟨*Vorsitzender, Präsident, Mieter, Regierung*⟩

incommunicado /ɪnkəmjuː'nɪkɑːdəʊ/ *pred. adj.* von der Außenwelt abgeschnitten; **hold sb. ~:** jmdn. ohne Verbindung zur Außenwelt halten

incomparable /ɪn'kɒmpərəbl/ *adj.*, **incomparably** /ɪn'kɒmpərəblɪ/ *adv.* unvergleichlich

incompatibility /ɪnkəmpætɪ'bɪlɪtɪ/ *n., no pl.* (a) (inability to harmonize) Unverträglichkeit, *die;* (b) (unsuitability for use together) Nichtübereinstimmung, *die*

incompatible /ɪnkəm'pætɪbl/ *adj.* (a) (unable to harmonize) unverträglich; **they were ~ and they separated** sie passten nicht zueinander und trennten sich; (b) (unsuitable for use together) unvereinbar; inkompatibel (Technik); (c) (inconsistent) unvereinbar

incompetence /ɪn'kɒmpɪtəns/, **incompetency** /ɪn'kɒmpɪtənsɪ/ *n.* Unfähigkeit, *die;* Unvermögen, *das*

incompetent /ɪn'kɒmpɪtənt/ **1** *adj.* unfähig; unzulänglich ⟨*Arbeit*⟩. **2** *n.* Unfähige, *der/die*

incomplete /ɪnkəm'pliːt/ *adj.*, **incompletely** /ɪnkəm'pliːtlɪ/ *adv.* unvollständig

incomprehensible /ɪnkɒmprɪ'hensɪbl/ *adj.* unbegreiflich; unverständlich ⟨*Sprache, Rede, Theorie, Argument*⟩

inconceivable /ɪnkən'siːvəbl/ *adj.*, **inconceivably** /ɪnkən'siːvəblɪ/ *adv.* unvorstellbar

inconclusive /ɪnkən'kluːsɪv/ *adj.* ergebnislos; nicht schlüssig ⟨*Beweis, Argument*⟩

incongruity /ɪnkɒŋ'gruːɪtɪ/ *n.* (a) *no pl.* (quality) Deplatziertheit, *die;* (b) (instance) Absurdität, *die*

incongruous /ɪn'kɒŋgrʊəs/ *adj.* (a) (inappropriate) unpassend; (b) (inharmonious) unvereinbar; nicht zusammenpassend ⟨*Farben, Kleidungsstücke*⟩

inconsequential /ɪnkɒnsɪ'kwenʃl/ *adj.* belanglos

inconsiderable /ɪnkən'sɪdərəbl/ *adj.* unbeträchtlich; unerheblich

inconsiderate /ɪnkən'sɪdərət/ *adj.* (a) (unkind) rücksichtslos; (b) (rash) unbedacht; unüberlegt

inconsistency /ɪnkən'sɪstənsɪ/ *n.* (a) (incompatibility, self-contradiction) Widersprüchlichkeit, *die* (with zu); (b) (illogicality) Inkonsequenz, *die;* (c) (irregularity) Unbeständigkeit, *die;* Inkonsistenz, *die* (geh.)

inconsistent /ɪnkən'sɪstənt/ *adj.* (a) (incompatible, self-contradictory) widersprüchlich; **be ~ with sth.** zu etw. im Widerspruch stehen; (b) (illogical) inkonsequent; (c) (irregular) unbeständig; inkonsistent (geh.)

inconsolable /ɪnkən'səʊləbl/ *adj.* untröstlich

inconspicuous /ɪnkən'spɪkjʊəs/ *adj.* unauffällig

incontestable /ɪnkən'testəbl/ *adj.* unbestreitbar; unwiderlegbar ‹*Beweis*›

incontinence /ɪn'kɒntɪnəns/ *n.* (Med.) Inkontinenz, *die*

incontinent /ɪn'kɒntɪmənt/ *adj.* (Med.) inkontinent; **be ~:** an Inkontinenz leiden

incontrovertible /ɪnkɒntrə'vɜːtɪbl/ *adj.* unbestreitbar; unwiderlegbar ‹*Beweis*›

inconvenience /ɪnkən'viːnɪəns/ **1** *n.* (a) *no pl.* (discomfort, disadvantage) Unannehmlichkeiten (**to** für); **go to a great deal of ~:** große Unannehmlichkeiten auf sich (*Akk.*) nehmen; (b) (instance) **if it's no ~:** wenn es keine Umstände macht. **2** *v.t.* Unannehmlichkeiten bereiten (+ *Dat.*); (disturb) stören

inconvenient /ɪnkən'viːnɪənt/ *adj.* unbequem; ungünstig ‹*Lage, Standort*›; unpraktisch ‹*Design, Konstruktion, Schnitt*›; **come at an ~ time** zu ungelegener Zeit kommen; **if it is not ~ [to you]** wenn es Ihnen recht ist

incorporate /ɪn'kɔːpəreɪt/ *v.t.* (include) aufnehmen (**in[to], with** in + *Akk.*)

incorporated /ɪn'kɔːpəreɪtɪd/ *adj.* eingetragen ‹*[Handels]gesellschaft*›

incorrect /ɪnkə'rekt/ *adj.* (a) unrichtig; inkorrekt; **be ~:** nicht stimmen; **you are ~ in believing that ...:** du irrst, wenn du glaubst, dass ...; (b) (improper) inkorrekt

incorrectly /ɪnkə'rektlɪ/ *adv.* (a) unrichtigerweise; falsch ‹*beantworten, aussprechen*›; (b) (improperly) inkorrekt

incorrigible /ɪn'kɒrɪdʒɪbl/ *adj.* unverbesserlich

increase 1 /ɪn'kriːs/ *v.i.* zunehmen; ‹*Schmerzen:*› stärker werden; ‹*Lärm:*› größer werden; ‹*Verkäufe, Preise, Nachfrage:*› steigen; **~ in weight/size/price** schwerer/größer/teurer werden; **~ in maturity/value/popularity** an Reife/Wert/Popularität (*Dat.*) gewinnen. **2** *v.t.* (a) (make greater) erhöhen; vermehren ‹*Besitz*›; (b) (intensify) verstärken; **~ one's efforts/commitment** sich mehr anstrengen/engagieren. **3** /'ɪnkriːs/ *n.* (a) (becoming greater) Zunahme, *die* (**in** *Gen.*); (in measurable amount) Anstieg, *der* (**in** *Gen.*); (deliberately caused) Steigerung, *die* (**in** *Gen.*); **~ in weight/size** Gewichtszunahme, *die*/Vergrößerung, *die*; **~ in popularity** Popularitätsgewinn, *der*; **be on the ~:** [ständig] zunehmen; (b) (by reproduction) Zunahme, *die*; Zuwachs, *der*; (c) (amount) Erhöhung, *die*; (of growth) Zuwachs, *der*

increasing /ɪn'kriːsɪŋ/ *adj.* steigend; wachsend; **an ~ number of people** mehr und mehr Menschen

increasingly /ɪn'kriːsɪŋlɪ/ *adv.* in zunehmendem Maße; **become ~ apparent** immer deutlicher werden

incredible /ɪn'kredɪbl/ *adj.* (a) (beyond belief) unglaublich; (b) (coll.) (remarkable) unglaublich (ugs.); (wonderful) toll (ugs.)

incredibly /ɪn'kredɪblɪ/ *adv.* (a) unglaublich; (b) (coll.: remarkably) unglaublich (ugs.); (unwahrscheinlich (ugs.); (c) *as sentence-modifier* es ist/war kaum zu glauben, aber ...

incredulity /ɪnkrɪ'djuːlɪtɪ/ *n., no pl.* Ungläubigkeit, *die*

incredulous /ɪn'kredjʊləs/ *adj.,* **incredulously** /ɪn'kredjʊləslɪ/ *adv.* ungläubig

increment /'ɪnkrɪmənt/ *n.* Erhöhung, *die;* (amount of growth) Zuwachs, *der*

incriminate /ɪn'krɪmɪneɪt/ *v.t.* belasten; **incriminating evidence** belastendes Material

incubate /'ɪnkjʊbeɪt/ *v.t.* bebrüten; (to hatching) ausbrüten

incubation /ɪnkjʊ'beɪʃn/ *n.* Inkubation, *die* (Biol.); Bebrütung, *die*

incubator /'ɪnkjʊbeɪtə(r)/ *n.* Inkubator, *der* (Biol., Med.); (for babies also) Brutkasten, *der*

inculcate /'ɪnkʌlkeɪt/ *v.t.* **~ sth. in[to] sb., ~ sb. with sth.** jmdm. etw. einpflanzen

incur /ɪn'kɜː(r)/ *v.t.,* **-rr-** sich (*Dat.*) zuziehen ‹*Unwillen, Ärger*›; **~ a loss** einen Verlust erleiden; **~ debts/expenses/risks** Schulden machen/Ausgaben haben/Risiken eingehen

incurable /ɪn'kjʊərəbl/ *adj.* (a) (Med.) unheilbar; (b) (fig.) unheilbar (ugs.); unstillbar ‹*Sehnsucht, Verlangen*›; unüberwindbar ‹*Zurückhaltung, Scheu*›

incursion /ɪn'kɜːʃn/ *n.* (invasion) Eindringen, *das;* (by sudden attack) Einfall, *der*

indebted /ɪn'detɪd/ *pred. adj.* **be/feel deeply ~ to sb.** tief in jmds. Schuld (*Dat.*) stehen (geh.); **he was ~ to a friend for this information** er verdankte einem Freund diese Information; **be [much] ~ to sb. for sth.** jmdm. für etw. [sehr] verbunden sein (geh.) *od.* zu Dank verpflichtet sein

indecency /ɪn'diːsənsɪ/ *n.* Unanständigkeit, *die*

indecent /ɪn'diːsənt/ *adj.* (a) (immodest, obscene) unanständig; *see also* **exposure a;** (b) (unseemly) ungehörig; **with ~ haste** mit unziemlicher Hast (geh.)

indecipherable /ɪndɪ'saɪfərəbl/ *adj.* unentzifferbar

indecision /ɪndɪ'sɪʒn/ *n., no pl.* Unentschlossenheit, *die*

indecisive /ɪndɪ'saɪsɪv/ *adj.* (a) (not conclusive) ergebnislos ‹*Streit, Diskussion*›; nichts entscheidend ‹*Krieg, Schlacht*›; (b) (hesitating) unentschlossen

indecisiveness /ɪndɪ'saɪsɪvnɪs/ *n., no pl.* (a) (inconclusiveness) Ergebnislosigkeit, *die;* (b) (hesitation) Unentschlossenheit, *die*

indeed /ɪn'diːd/ *adv.* (a) (in truth) in der Tat; tatsächlich; (b) *emphat.* **thank you very much ~:** haben Sie vielen herzlichen Dank; **it was very kind of you ~:** es war wirklich sehr freundlich von Ihnen; **~ it is** in der Tat; allerdings; **yes ~, it certainly is/I certainly did** *etc.* ja, das kann man wohl sagen; **no, ~:** nein, ganz bestimmt nicht; (c) (in fact) ja sogar; **if ~ such a thing is possible** wenn so etwas überhaupt möglich ist; **I feel, ~ I know, she will come** ich habe das Gefühl, [ja] ich weiß sogar, dass sie kommen wird; (d) (admittedly) zugegebenermaßen; zwar; (e) *interrog.* **~?** wirklich?; ist das wahr?; (f) *expr. irony, surprise, interest, etc.* **He expects to win — Does he ~!** Er glaubt, dass er gewinnt — Tatsächlich?; **I want a fortnight off work — [Do you] ~!** Ich möchte 14 Tage freihaben — Ach wirklich?

indefatigable /ɪndɪ'fætɪgəbl/ *adj.* unermüdlich

indefensible /ɪndɪ'fensɪbl/ *adj.* (a) (insecure) unhaltbar; (b) (untenable) unvertretbar; unhaltbar; (c) (intolerable) unverzeihlich

indefinable /ɪndɪ'faɪnəbl/ *adj.* undefinierbar

indefinite /ɪn'defɪnɪt/ *adj.* (a) (vague) unbestimmt; (b) (unlimited) unbegrenzt

indefinitely /ɪn'defɪnɪtlɪ/ *adv.* (a) (vaguely) unbestimmt; (b) (unlimitedly) unbegrenzt; **it can't go on ~:** es kann nicht endlos so weitergehen; **postponed ~:** auf unbestimmte Zeit verschoben

indelible /ɪn'delɪbl/ *adj.* unauslöschlich (auch fig.); nicht zu entfernen ‹*Fleck*›; **~ ink** Wäschetinte, *die;* **~ pencil** Kopierstift, *der;* Tintenstift, *der*

indelicate /ɪn'delɪkət/ *adj.* (coarse) ungehörig; (almost indecent) geschmacklos; (slightly tactless) nicht sehr feinfühlig

indemnify /ɪn'demnɪfaɪ/ *v.t.* (a) (protect) **~ sb. against sth.** jmdn. gegen etw. absichern; (b) (compensate) entschädigen

indemnity /ɪn'demnɪtɪ/ *n.* (a) (security) Absicherung, *die;* (b) (compensation) Entschädigung, *die*

indent /ɪn'dent/ *v.t.* (a) (make notches in) einkerben; (b) (form recesses in) einschneiden in (+ *Akk.*); (c) (from margin) einrücken

indentation /ɪnden'teɪʃn/ *n.* (a) (indenting, notch) Einkerbung, *die;* (b) (recess) Einschnitt, *der*

independence /ɪndɪ'pendəns/ *n.* Unabhängigkeit, *die*

Inde'pendence Day *n.* (Amer.) Unabhängigkeitstag, *der*

independent /ɪndɪ'pendənt/ **1** *adj.* (a) unabhängig; **~ income/means** eigenes Einkommen; (b) (not wanting obligations) selbstständig. **2** *n.* (Polit.) Unabhängige, *der/die*

independently /ɪndɪ'pendəntlɪ/ *adv.* unabhängig (**of** von); **they work ~:** sie arbeiten unabhängig voneinander

indescribable /ɪndɪ'skraɪbəbl/ *adj.* unbeschreiblich

indestructible /ɪndɪ'strʌktɪbl/ *adj.* unzerstörbar; unerschütterlich ‹*Glaube*›

indeterminate /ɪndɪ'tɜːmɪnət/ *adj.* (**a**) (not fixed, vague) unbestimmt ‹*Form, Menge*›; unklar ‹*Konzept, Bedeutung*›; (**b**) (left undecided) ergebnislos; offen ‹*Rechtsfrage*›

index /'ɪndeks/ **1** *n.* Index, *der;* Register, *das;* ~ **of sources** Quellenverzeichnis, *das.* **2** *v.t.* (**a**) (furnish with ~) mit einem Register *od.* Index versehen; (**b**) (enter in ~) ins Register aufnehmen

index: ~ **card** *n.* Karteikarte, *die;* ~ **finger** *n.* Zeigefinger, *der;* ~-**linked** *adj.* (Econ.) indexiert; dynamisch ‹*Rente*›

India /'ɪndɪə/ *pr. n.* Indien (*das*)

Indian /'ɪndɪən/ ▶947⎪ **1** *adj.* (**a**) indisch; (**b**) [American] ~: indianisch. **2** *n.* (**a**) Inder, *der*/Inderin, *die;* (**b**) [American] ~: Indianer, *der*/Indianerin, *die*

Indian: ~ **'ink** *n.* (Brit.) Tusche, *die;* ~ **'Ocean** *pr. n.* Indischer Ozean; ~ **'summer** *n.* Altweibersommer, *der;* Nachsommer, *der* (auch fig.)

'India rubber ⇨ **rubber¹** a, b

indicate /'ɪndɪkeɪt/ **1** *v.t.* (**a**) (be a sign of) erkennen lassen; (**b**) (state briefly) andeuten; ~ **the rough outlines of a project** ein Projekt kurz umreißen; (**c**) (mark, point out) anzeigen; (**d**) (suggest, make evident) zum Ausdruck bringen (**to** gegenüber). **2** *v.i.* blinken (bes. Verkehrsw.)

indication /ɪndɪ'keɪʃn/ *n.* [An]zeichen, *das* (**of** *Gen.*, für); **there is every/no ~ that ...:** alles/nichts weist darauf hin, dass ...; **first ~s are that ...:** die ersten Anzeichen deuten darauf hin, dass ...

indicator /'ɪndɪkeɪtə(r)/ *n.* (**a**) (instrument) Anzeiger, *der;* (**b**) (board) Anzeigetafel, *die;* (**c**) (on vehicle) Blinker, *der;* (**d**) (fig.: pointer) Indikator, *der* (bes. Wirtsch.)

indie /'ɪndɪ/ (coll.) **1** *adj.* Indie-‹*Gruppe, Szene, Charts etc.*›. **2** *n.*(record company) Indie-Label, *das;* (band) Indie-Band, *die*

indifference /ɪn'dɪfərəns/ *n., no pl.* (**a**) (unconcern) Gleichgültigkeit, *die* (**to[wards]** gegenüber); (**b**) (neutrality) Indifferenz, *die;* (**c**) (unimportance) **a matter of ~:** eine Belanglosigkeit; **this is a matter of complete ~ to** *or* **for him** das ist für ihn völlig belanglos

indifferent /ɪn'dɪfərənt/ *adj.* (**a**) (without concern or interest) gleichgültig; unbeteiligt ‹*Beobachter*›; (**b**) (not good) mittelmäßig; (fairly bad) mäßig; (neither good nor bad) durchschnittlich; **very ~:** schlecht

indigenous /ɪn'dɪdʒɪnəs/ *adj.* einheimisch; eingeboren ‹*Bevölkerung*›

indigestible /ɪndɪ'dʒestɪbl/ *adj.* (lit. or fig.) unverdaulich

indigestion /ɪndɪ'dʒestʃn/ *n., no pl., no indef. art.* Magenverstimmung, *die;* (chronic) Verdauungsstörungen

indignant /ɪn'dɪgnənt/ *adj.* entrüstet (**at, over, about** über + *Akk.*); indigniert ‹*Blick, Geste*›; **grow ~:** sich entrüsten; **it makes me ~:** es regt mich auf

indignation /ɪndɪg'neɪʃn/ *n., no pl.* Entrüstung, *die* (**about, at, against, over** über + *Akk.*)

indignity /ɪn'dɪgnɪtɪ/ *n.* Demütigung, *die;* **the ~ of my position** das Demütigende [an] meiner Situation

indigo /'ɪndɪgəʊ/ **1** *n., pl.* ~**s** (**a**) (dye) Indigo, *der od. das;* (**b**) (colour) ~ **[blue]** Indigoblau, *das.* **2** *adj.* ~ **[blue]** indigoblau

indirect /ɪndɪ'rekt, ɪndaɪ'rekt/ *adj.* indirekt; (long-winded) umständlich; **follow an ~ route** nicht den direkten Weg nehmen; **by ~ means** auf Umwegen (fig.)

indirectly /ɪndɪ'rektlɪ, ɪndaɪ'rektlɪ/ *adv.* indirekt; auf Umwegen ‹*hören, herausfinden*›

indirect: ~ **object** *n.* (Ling.) indirektes Objekt; (in German) Dativobjekt, *das;* ~ **speech** *n.* (Ling.) indirekte Rede

indiscreet /ɪndɪ'skriːt/ *adj.* indiskret; taktlos ‹*Benehmen*›

indiscretion /ɪndɪ'skreʃn/ *n.* (**a**) (conduct) Indiskretion, *die;* (tactlessness) Taktlosigkeit, *die;* (**b**) (imprudence) Unbedachtheit, *die;* (**c**) (action) Unbedachtsamkeit, *die;* (love affair)

Affäre, *die;* (**d**) (revelation of official secret etc.) Indiskretion, *die*

indiscriminate /ɪndɪ'skrɪmɪnət/ *adj.* (**a**) (undiscriminating) unkritisch; (**b**) (unrestrained, promiscuous) wahllos; willkürlich ‹*Anwendung*›

indispensable /ɪndɪ'spensəbl/ *adj.* unentbehrlich (**to** für); unabdingbar ‹*Voraussetzung*›

indisposed /ɪndɪ'spəʊzd/ *adj.* (unwell) unpässlich; indisponiert ‹*Sänger, Schauspieler*›; (**b**) (disinclined) **be ~ to do sth.** abgeneigt sein, etw. zu tun

indisposition /ɪndɪspə'zɪʃn/ *n.* (**a**) (ill health) Unpässlichkeit, *die;* (of singer, actor) Indisposition, *die;* (**b**) **an ~ to do sth.** eine Abneigung dagegen, etw. zu tun

indisputable /ɪndɪ'spjuːtəbl/ *adj.*, **indisputably** /ɪndɪ'spjuːtəblɪ/ *adv.* unbestreitbar

indistinct /ɪndɪ'stɪŋkt/ *adj.* undeutlich; (blurred) verschwommen

indistinguishable /ɪndɪ'stɪŋgwɪʃəbl/ *adj.* (**a**) (not distinguishable) nicht unterscheidbar; (**b**) (imperceptible) nicht erkennbar; nicht wahrnehmbar ‹*Geräusch*›

individual /ɪndɪ'vɪdjʊəl/ **1** *adj.* (**a**) (single) einzeln; (**b**) (special, personal) besonder... ‹*Vorteil, Merkmal*›; ~ **case** Einzelfall, *der;* (**c**) (intended for one) für eine [einzelne] Person bestimmt; (**d**) (distinctive) eigentümlich; individuell; (**e**) (characteristic) eigen; individuell. **2** *n.* (**a**) (one member) Einzelne, *der/die;* (animal) Einzeltier, *das;* ~**s** Einzelne; (**b**) (one being) Individuum, *das;* Einzelne, *der/die;* (**c**) (coll.: person) Individuum, *das* (abwertend)

individualist /ɪndɪ'vɪdjʊəlɪst/ *n.* Individualist, *der*/Individualistin, *die*

individuality /ɪndɪvɪdjʊ'ælɪtɪ/ *n., no pl.* eigene Persönlichkeit; Individualität, *die*

individually /ɪndɪ'vɪdjʊəlɪ/ *adv.* (**a**) (singly) einzeln; (**b**) (distinctively) individuell; (**c**) (personally) persönlich

indivisible /ɪndɪ'vɪzɪbl/ *adj.* (**a**) (not divisible) unteilbar; (**b**) (not distributable) nicht aufteilbar

indoctrinate /ɪn'dɒktrɪneɪt/ *v.t.* indoktrinieren (abwertend)

indolence /'ɪndələns/ *n., no pl.* Trägheit, *die*

indolent /'ɪndələnt/ *adj.* träge

Indonesia /ɪndə'niːzjə/ *pr. n.* Indonesien (*das*)

Indonesian /ɪndə'niːzjən/ ▶947⎪ **1** *adj.* indonesisch; **sb. is ~:** jmd. ist Indonesier/Indonesierin. **2** *n.* (person) Indonesier, *der*/Indonesierin, *die*

'indoor *adj.* ~ **swimming pool/sports** Hallenbad, *das*/ -sport, *der;* ~ **plants** Zimmerpflanzen; ~ **games** Spiele im Haus; (Sport) Hallenspiele

indoors /ɪn'dɔːz/ *adv.* drinnen; im Haus; **come/go ~:** nach drinnen *od.* ins Haus kommen/gehen

induce /ɪn'djuːs/ *v.t.* (**a**) (persuade) ~ **sb. to do sth.** jmdn. dazu bringen, etw. zu tun; (**b**) (bring about) hervorrufen; verursachen, führen zu ‹*Krankheit*›; (**c**) (Med.) einleiten ‹*Wehen, Geburt*›; herbeiführen ‹*Schlaf*›

inducement /ɪn'djuːsmənt/ *n.* (incentive) Anreiz, *der;* **as an added ~:** als besonderer Anreiz *od.* Ansporn

induction /ɪn'dʌkʃn/ *n.* (**a**) (formal introduction) Amtseinführung, *die;* (**b**) (initiation) Einführung, *die* (**into** in + *Akk.*); (**c**) (Med.) Einleitung, *die;* (**d**) (Electr., Phys., Math., Philos.) Induktion, *die*

indulge /ɪn'dʌldʒ/ **1** *v.t.* (**a**) (yield to) nachgeben (+ *Dat.*) ‹*Wunsch, Verlangen, Verlockung*›; frönen (geh.) (+ *Dat.*) ‹*Leidenschaft, Neigung*›; (**b**) (please) verwöhnen; ~ **sb. in sth.** jmdm. in etw. (*Dat.*) nachgeben; ~ **oneself in** schwelgen in (geh.) (+ *Dat.*). **2** *v.i.* (**a**) (allow oneself pleasure) ~ **in** frönen (geh.) (+ *Dat.*) ‹*Leidenschaft, Neigung*›; (**b**) (coll.: take alcoholic drink) sich (*Dat.*) einen genehmigen (ugs.)

indulgence /ɪn'dʌldʒəns/ *n.* (**a**) Nachsicht, *die;* (humouring) Nachgiebigkeit, *die* (**with** gegenüber); (**b**) **sb.'s ~ in sth.** jmds. Hang zu etw.; (**c**) (thing indulged in) Luxus, *der*

indulgent /ɪn'dʌldʒənt/ *adj.* nachsichtig (**with, to-[wards]** gegenüber)

industrial /ɪn'dʌstrɪəl/ *adj.* (**a**) industriell; betrieblich ‹*Ausbildung, Forschung*›; Arbeits‹*unfall, -medizin, -psychologie*›; (**b**) (intended for industry) Industrie‹*alkohol, -diamant usw.*›

industrial: ～ **'action** n. Arbeitskampfmaßnahmen Pl.; **take** ～ **action** in den Ausstand treten; ～ **disease** n. Berufskrankheit, die; ～ **di'spute** n. Arbeitskonflikt, der; ～ **'espionage** n. Industriespionage, die; ～ **estate** n. Industriegebiet, das; ～ **'injury** n. Arbeitsverletzung, die

industrialisation, industrialise ⇒ **industrializ-industrialist** /ɪn'dʌstrɪəlɪst/ n. Industrielle, der/die

industrialization /ɪndʌstrɪəlaɪ'zeɪʃn/ n. Industrialisierung, die

industrialize /ɪn'dʌstrɪəlaɪz/ v.i. & t. industrialisieren

industrial: ～ **re'lations** n. pl. Industrialrelations Pl. (Wirtsch.); Beziehungen zwischen Arbeitgebern und Gewerkschaften; **I** ～ **Revo'lution** n. (Hist.) industrielle Revolution; ～ **tribunal** n. Arbeitsgericht, das; ～ **un'rest** n. Unruhe in der Arbeitnehmerschaft; ～ **'waste** n. Industriemüll, der; ～**wastes** Industrieabfälle Pl.

industrious /ɪn'dʌstrɪəs/ adj. fleißig; (busy) emsig

industry /'ɪndəstrɪ/ n. (a) Industrie, die; **several industries** mehrere Industriezweige; (b) ⇒ **industrious:** Fleiß, der; Emsigkeit, die

inebriated /ɪ'ni:brɪeɪtɪd/ adj. (drunk) betrunken

inedible /ɪn'edɪbl/ adj. ungenießbar

ineffective /ɪnɪ'fektɪv/ adj. (a) unwirksam; ineffektiv; fruchtlos 〈Anstrengung, Versuch〉; wirkungslos 〈Argument〉; (b) (inefficient) untauglich

ineffectiveness /ɪnɪ'fektɪvnɪs/ n., no pl. ⇒ **ineffective:** Unwirksamkeit, die; Ineffizienz, die; Fruchtlosigkeit, die; Wirkungslosigkeit, die; Untauglichkeit, die

ineffectual /ɪnɪ'fektjʊəl/ adj. unwirksam; ineffektiv; fruchtlos 〈Versuch, Bemühung〉; ineffizient 〈Methode, Person〉

inefficiency /ɪnɪ'fɪʃənsɪ/ n. Ineffizienz, die; (incapability) Unfähigkeit, die

inefficient /ɪnɪ'fɪʃənt/ adj. ineffizient; (incapable) unfähig; **the worker/machine is** ～: der Arbeiter/die Maschine leistet nicht genug

inelegant /ɪn'elɪɡənt/ adj. (a) unelegant; schwerfällig 〈Bewegung, Gang〉; (b) (unrefined, unpolished) ungeschliffen (abwertend)

ineligible /ɪn'elɪdʒɪbl/ adj. ungeeignet; **be** ～ **for** nicht infrage kommen für 〈Beförderung, Position, Mannschaft〉; nicht berechtigt sein zu 〈Leistungen des Staats usw.〉

inept /ɪ'nept/ adj. (a) (unskilful, clumsy) unbeholfen; (b) (inappropriate) unpassend, unangebracht 〈Bemerkung, Eingreifen〉; (c) (foolish) albern

ineptitude /ɪ'neptɪtju:d/ n., no pl. (a) (unskilfulness, clumsiness) Unbeholfenheit, die; (b) (of remark, intervention) Unangebrachtheit, die; (c) (foolishness) Albernheit, die

inequality /ɪnɪ'kwɒlɪtɪ/ n. Ungleichheit, die

inequitable /ɪn'ekwɪtəbl/ adj. ungerecht

inert /ɪ'nɜ:t/ adj. (a) reglos; (sluggish) träge; (passive) untätig; (b) (Chem.: neutral) inert

inert 'gas n. (Chem.) Edelgas, das

inertia /ɪ'nɜ:ʃə, ɪ'nɜ:ʃɪə/ n. (also Phys.) Trägheit, die

i'nertia reel n. Aufrollautomatik, die; ～ **seat belt** Automatikgurt, der

inescapable /ɪnɪ'skeɪpəbl/ adj. unausweichlich 〈Logik, Schlussfolgerung〉

inessential /ɪnɪ'senʃl/ **1** adj. (not necessary) unwesentlich; (dispensable) entbehrlich. **2** n. Nebensächlichkeit, die

inevitability /ɪnevɪtə'bɪlɪtɪ/ n., no pl. Unvermeidlichkeit, die; (of fate, event) Unabwendbarkeit, die

inevitable /ɪn'evɪtəbl/ adj. unvermeidlich; unabwendbar 〈Ereignis, Krieg, Schicksal〉; zwangsläufig 〈Ergebnis, Folge〉; **bow to the** ～: sich in das Unvermeidliche fügen

inevitably /ɪn'evɪtəblɪ/ adv. zwangsläufig

inexact /ɪnɪɡ'zækt/ adj. ungenau

inexcusable /ɪnɪk'skju:zəbl/ adj. unverzeihlich; unentschuldbar

inexhaustible /ɪnɪɡ'zɔ:stɪbl/ adj. unerschöpflich 〈Reserven, Quelle, Energie〉; unverwüstlich 〈Person〉

inexorable /ɪn'eksərəbl/ adj. unerbittlich

inexpensive /ɪnɪk'spensɪv/ adj. preisgünstig; **the car is** ～ **to run** der Wagen ist sparsam im Verbrauch

inexperience /ɪnɪk'spɪərɪəns/ n. Unerfahrenheit, die; Mangel, der an Erfahrung

inexperienced /ɪnɪk'spɪərɪənst/ adj. unerfahren; ～ **in sth.** wenig vertraut mit etw.

inexpert /ɪn'ekspɜ:t/ adj. unerfahren; (unskilled) ungeschickt

inexplicable /ɪnek'splɪkəbl/ adj. unerklärlich

inexpressible /ɪnɪk'spresɪbl/ adj. unbeschreiblich

inextricable /ɪn'ekstrɪkəbl/ adj. unentwirrbar

infallibility /ɪnfælɪ'bɪlɪtɪ/ n., no pl. Unfehlbarkeit, die

infallible /ɪn'fælɪbl/ adj., **infallibly** /ɪn'fælɪblɪ/ adv. unfehlbar

infamous /'ɪnfəməs/ adj. (a) berüchtigt; (b) (wicked) infam; niederträchtig

infancy /'ɪnfənsɪ/ n. (a) frühe Kindheit; (b) (fig.: early state) Frühzeit, die; **be in its** ～: noch in den Anfängen od. Kinderschuhen stecken

infant /'ɪnfənt/ **1** n. kleines Kind. **2** adj. (a) kindlich; (b) (fig.: not developed) in den Anfängen steckend

infantile /'ɪnfəntaɪl/ adj. (a) (relating to infancy) kindlich; (b) (childish) kindisch (abwertend); infantil (abwertend)

infantry /'ɪnfəntrɪ/ n. constr. as sing. or pl. Infanterie, die

'infant school n. (Brit.) ≈ Vorschule, die; Grundschule für die ersten beiden Jahrgänge

infatuated /ɪn'fætjʊeɪtɪd/ adj. betört (geh.); verzaubert; **be** ～ **with sb./oneself** in jmdn./sich selbst vernarrt sein

infatuation /ɪnfætjʊ'eɪʃn/ n. Vernarrtheit, die (**with** in + Akk.)

infect /ɪn'fekt/ v.t. (a) (contaminate) verseuchen; (b) (affect with disease) infizieren (Med.) (**with** mit); **the wound became** ～**ed** die Wunde entzündete sich; (c) (with enthusiasm etc.) anstecken

infection /ɪn'fekʃn/ n. Infektion, die; **throat/ear/eye** ～: Hals-/Ohren-/Augenentzündung, die

infectious /ɪn'fekʃəs/ adj. (a) infektiös (Med.), ansteckend 〈Krankheit〉; **be** ～ 〈Person:〉 eine ansteckende Krankheit haben; ansteckend sein (ugs.); (b) (fig.) ansteckend 〈Heiterkeit, Begeisterung, Lachen〉

infer /ɪn'fɜ:(r)/ v.t., **-rr-** schließen (**from** aus); erschließen 〈Voraussetzung〉; gewinnen 〈Kenntnisse〉; ziehen 〈Schlussfolgerung〉

inference /'ɪnfərəns/ n. [Schluss]folgerung, die

inferior /ɪn'fɪərɪə(r)/ **1** adj. (of lower quality) minderwertig 〈Ware〉; minder... 〈Qualität〉; gering 〈Kenntnis〉; unterlegen 〈Gegner〉; ～ **to sth.** schlechter als etw.; **feel** ～: Minderwertigkeitsgefühle haben; **feel** ～ **to sb.** sich jmdm. gegenüber unterlegen fühlen. **2** n. Untergebene, der/die; **his social** ～**s** die gesellschaftlich unter ihm Stehenden

inferiority /ɪnfɪərɪ'ɒrɪtɪ/ n., no pl. Unterlegenheit, die (**to** gegenüber); (of goods) schlechtere Qualität

inferi'ority complex n. (Psych.) Minderwertigkeitskomplex, der

infernal /ɪn'fɜ:nl/ adj. (a) (of hell) höllisch; 〈Geister, Götter〉 der Unterwelt; (b) (hellish) teuflisch; (c) (coll.: detestable) verdammt (salopp)

inferno /ɪn'fɜ:nəʊ/ n., pl. ～**s** Inferno, das; **a blazing** ～: ein flammendes Inferno

infertile /ɪn'fɜ:taɪl/ adj. unfruchtbar

infertility /ɪnfɜ:'tɪlɪtɪ/ n., no pl. Unfruchtbarkeit, die

infest /ɪn'fest/ v.t. 〈Ungeziefer, Schädlinge:〉 befallen; 〈Unkraut:〉 überwuchern; (fig.) heimsuchen

infidelity /ɪnfɪ'delɪtɪ/ n. Untreue, die (**to** gegenüber)

'infighting n. interne Machtkämpfe

infiltrate /'ɪnfɪltreɪt/ **1** v.t. (a) (penetrate into) infiltrieren 〈feindliche Reihen〉; unterwandern 〈Partei, Organisation〉; (b) (cause to enter) einschleusen 〈Agenten〉; (esp. Biol., Med.: pass into, permeate) infiltrieren. **2** v.i. (a) (penetrate) einsickern (fig.); ～ **into** unterwandern 〈Partei, Organisation〉; infiltrieren 〈feindliche Reihen〉; (b) 〈Flüssigkeit:〉 eindringen

infiltrator /'ɪnfɪltreɪtə(r)/ n. Eindringling, der; (of party, organization) Unterwanderer, der

infinite /'ɪnfɪnɪt/ adj. (a) (endless) unendlich; (b) (very great) ungeheuer; unendlich groß

infinitesimal /ɪnfɪnɪ'tesɪml/ adj. (a) (Math.) infinitesimal; (b) (very small) äußerst gering; winzig ‹Menge›

infinitive /ɪn'fɪnɪtɪv/ n. (Ling.) Infinitiv, der

infinity /ɪn'fɪnɪtɪ/ n. Unendlichkeit, die; at ~ (Geom.) im Unendlichen ‹sich schneiden›; focus on ~ (Photog.) auf unendlich stellen

infirm /ɪn'fɜːm/ adj. (weak) gebrechlich; (irresolute) schwach

infirmary /ɪn'fɜːmərɪ/ n. Krankenhaus, das

inflame /ɪn'fleɪm/ v.t. (a) (excite) entflammen (geh.); (b) (aggravate) schüren ‹Feindschaft, Hass›; (c) (Med.) become/be ~d ‹Auge, Wunde:› sich entzünden/entzündet sein

inflammable /ɪn'flæməbl/ adj. (a) (easily set on fire) feuergefährlich; leicht entzündlich od. entflammbar; 'highly ~' „feuergefährlich"; (b) explosiv ‹Situation›

inflammation /ɪnflə'meɪʃn/ n. ▶865⟩ (Med.) Entzündung, die

inflammatory /ɪn'flæmətərɪ/ adj. (a) aufrührerisch; an ~ speech eine Hetzrede (abwertend); (b) (Med.) entzündlich

inflatable /ɪn'fleɪtəbl/ 1 adj. aufblasbar; ~ dinghy Schlauchboot, das. 2 n. (boat) Schlauchboot, das

inflate /ɪn'fleɪt/ v.t. (a) (distend) aufblasen; (with pump) aufpumpen; (b) (Econ.) in die Höhe treiben ‹Preise, Kosten›; inflationieren ‹Währung›; ~ the economy Inflationspolitik betreiben

inflated /ɪn'fleɪtɪd/ adj. (lit or fig.) aufgeblasen; geschwollen ‹Stil›; have an ~ opinion of oneself aufgeblasen sein (ugs. abwertend)

inflation /ɪn'fleɪʃn/ n. (a) Aufblasen, das; (with pump) Aufpumpen, das; (b) (Econ.) Inflation, die

inflationary /ɪn'fleɪʃənərɪ/ adj. (Econ.) inflationär

in'flation-proofed adj. mit Inflationsausgleich nachgestellt

inflect /ɪn'flekt/ v.t. flektieren; beugen

inflexible /ɪn'fleksɪbl/ adj. (a) (stiff) unbiegsam; (b) (obstinate) [geistig] unbeweglich ‹Person›; wenig flexibel ‹Einstellung, Meinung›

inflict /ɪn'flɪkt/ v.t. zufügen ‹Leid, Schmerzen›, beibringen ‹Wunde›, versetzen ‹Schlag› (on Dat.); ~ oneself or one's company on sb. sich jmdm. aufdrängen

'in-flight adj. Bord‹verpflegung, -programm›

influence /'ɪnfluəns/ 1 n. (also thing, person) Einfluss, der; exercise ~: Einfluss ausüben (over auf + Akk.); a person of ~: eine einflussreiche Persönlichkeit; be a bad/major ~ [on sb.] einen schlechten/bedeutenden Einfluss [auf jmdn.] ausüben; be under the ~ (coll.) betrunken sein. 2 v.t. beeinflussen; be too easily ~d sich zu leicht beeinflussen lassen

influential /ɪnflu'enʃl/ adj. einflussreich ‹Person›; be ~ in sb.'s decision/on sb.'s career jmdn. in seiner Entscheidung beeinflussen/jmds. Karriere beeinflussen

influenza /ɪnflu'enzə/ n. ▶865⟩ Grippe, die

influx /'ɪnflʌks/ n. Zustrom, der

info /'ɪnfəʊ/ n. (coll.) Infos Pl. (ugs.)

inform /ɪn'fɔːm/ 1 v.t. (a) informieren (of, about über + Akk.); I am pleased to ~ you that …: ich freue mich, Ihnen mitteilen zu können, dass …; keep sb./oneself ~ed jmdn./sich auf dem Laufenden halten; (b) (animate, inspire) durchdringen. 2 v.i. ~ against or on sb. jmdn. anzeigen od. (abwertend) denunzieren (to bei)

informal /ɪn'fɔːml/ adj. (a) (without formality) zwanglos; ungezwungen ‹Ton, Sprache›; leger ‹Kleidungsstück›; 'dress: ~' „keine festliche Garderobe"; (b) (unofficial) informell ‹Gespräch, Treffen›

informality /ɪnfɔː'mælɪtɪ/ n. no pl. Zwanglosigkeit, die; Ungezwungenheit, die

informant /ɪn'fɔːmənt/ n. Informant, der/Informantin, die; Gewährsmann, der

information /ɪnfə'meɪʃn/ n., no pl., no indef. art. Informationen Pl.; give ~ on sth. Auskunft über etw. (Akk.) erteilen; piece or bit of ~: Information, die; where can

we get hold of some ~? wo können wir Auskunft bekommen?; for your ~: zu Ihrer Information; (iron.) damit du Bescheid weißt

information: ~ bureau, ~ centre ns. Auskunftsbüro, das; ~ desk n. Informationsschalter, der; ~ highway n. (Computing) Datenautobahn, die; ~ pack n. Informationspaket, das; (folder etc.) Informationsmappe, die; (for journalists) Pressemappe, die; ~ retrieval n. (Computing) Retrieval, das; ~ retrieval system Retrievalsystem, das; ~ science n. Informatik, die; ~ scientist n. Informatiker, der/Informatikerin, die; ~ 'superhighway n. (Computing) Datenautobahn, die; Datensuperhighway, der; ~ system n. Informationssystem, das; management ~ system Managementinformationssystem, das; ~ technology n. Informationstechnologie, die; Informationstechnik, die

informative /ɪn'fɔːmətɪv/ adj. informativ; not very ~: nicht sehr aufschlussreich ‹Dokument, Schriftstück›

informed /ɪn'fɔːmd/ adj. informiert; fundiert ‹Schätzung›

informer /ɪn'fɔːmə(r)/ n. Denunziant, der/Denunziantin, die (abwertend); Informant, der/Informantin, die; police ~: Polizeispitzel, der (abwertend)

infra-red /ɪnfrə'red/ adj. (a) infrarot; (b) (using ~ radiation) Infrarot-

infrastructure /'ɪnfrəstrʌktʃə(r)/ n. Infrastruktur, die

infrequent /ɪn'friːkwənt/ adj. (a) (uncommon) selten; (b) (sparse) vereinzelt

infrequently /ɪn'friːkwəntlɪ/ adv. selten

infringe /ɪn'frɪndʒ/ 1 v.t. verstoßen gegen. 2 v.i. ~ [up]on verstoßen gegen ‹Recht, Gesetz usw.›

infringement /ɪn'frɪndʒmənt/ n. (a) (violation) Verstoß, der (of gegen); ~ of the contract Vertragsverletzung, die; Vertragsbruch, der; (b) (encroachment) Übergriff, der (on auf + Akk.)

infuriate /ɪn'fjʊərɪeɪt/ v.t. wütend machen; be ~d wütend sein (by über + Akk.)

infuriating /ɪn'fjʊərɪeɪtɪŋ/ adj. she is an ~ person sie kann einen zur Raserei bringen; it is ~ when/that …: es ist wahnsinnig ärgerlich, wenn/dass … (ugs.); ~ calmness/slowness aufreizende Gelassenheit/Langsamkeit

infuse /ɪn'fjuːz/ v.t. (a) (instil) ~ sth. into sb., ~ sb. with sth. jmdm. etw. einflößen; (b) (steep) aufgießen ‹Tee usw.›

infusion /ɪn'fjuːʒn/ n. (a) (Med.) Infusion, die; (b) (imparting) Einflößen, das; (c) (steeping) Aufgießen, das; (d) (liquid) Aufguss, der

ingenious /ɪn'dʒiːnɪəs/ adj. (a) (resourceful) einfallsreich; (skilful) geschickt; (b) (cleverly constructed) genial ‹Methode, Idee›; raffiniert ‹Spielzeug, Werkzeug, Maschine›

ingenuity /ɪndʒɪ'njuːɪtɪ/ n., no pl. (a) (resourcefulness) Einfallsreichtum, der; (skill) Geschicklichkeit, die; (b) (cleverness of construction) Genialität, die

ingot /'ɪŋgət/ n. Ingot, der (Metall.)

ingrained /'ɪŋgreɪnd, ɪn'greɪnd/ adj. (a) (embedded) hands ~ with dirt stark verschmutzte Hände; (b) (fig.) tief eingewurzelt ‹Vorurteil usw.›

ingratiate /ɪn'greɪʃɪeɪt/ v. refl. ~ oneself with sb. sich bei jmdm. einschmeicheln

ingratiating /ɪn'greɪʃɪeɪtɪŋ/ adj. schmeichlerisch

ingratitude /ɪn'grætɪtjuːd/ n., no pl. Undankbarkeit, die (to[wards] gegenüber)

ingredient /ɪn'griːdɪənt/ n. Zutat, die; the ~s of a successful marriage (fig.) die Voraussetzungen für eine gute Ehe

ingrowing /'ɪngrəʊɪŋ/ adj. eingewachsen ‹Zehennagel usw.›

inhabit /ɪn'hæbɪt/ v.t. bewohnen; the region was ~ed by penguins/the Celts in der Gegend lebten Pinguine/die Kelten

inhabitant /ɪn'hæbɪtənt/ n. Bewohner, der/Bewohnerin, die; (of village etc. also) Einwohner, der/Einwohnerin, die

inhale /ɪn'heɪl/ 1 v.t. (breathe in) einatmen; (take into the lungs) inhalieren (ugs.) ‹Zigarettenrauch usw.›; (Med.) inhalieren. 2 v.i. einatmen; (Med.) inhalieren; ‹Raucher:› inhalieren (ugs.)

inherent /ɪn'hɪərənt, ɪn'herənt/ *adj.* innewohnend (geh.); natürlich ‹*Anmut, Eleganz*›

inherently /ɪn'hɪərəntlɪ, ɪn'herəntlɪ/ *adv.* von Natur aus

inherit /ɪn'herɪt/ *v.t.* erben

inheritance /ɪn'herɪtəns/ *n.* (a) (what is inherited) Erbe, *das;* come into one's ∼: sein Erbe antreten; (b) *no pl.* (inheriting) Erbschaft, *die*

inhibit /ɪn'hɪbɪt/ *v.t.* hemmen; ∼ sb. from doing sth. jmdn. daran hindern, etw. zu tun

inhibited /ɪn'hɪbɪtɪd/ *adj.* gehemmt

inhibition /ɪnhɪ'bɪʃn/ *n.* (a) Unterdrückung, *die;* (b) (Psych.) Hemmung, *die;* (c) (coll.: emotional resistance) Hemmung, *die*

inhospitable /ɪnhɒ'spɪtəbl/ *adj.* (a) ungastlich ‹*Person, Verhalten*›; (b) unwirtlich ‹*Gegend, Klima*›

'in-house *adj.* hausintern

inhuman /ɪn'hju:mən/ *adj.* unmenschlich ‹*Tyrann, Grausamkeit, Strenge*›; inhuman ‹*Arbeitgeber, Verhalten*›

inhumane /ɪnhju:'meɪn/ *adj.* unmenschlich; inhuman (geh.); menschenunwürdig ‹*Zustände, Behandlung*›

inimical /ɪ'nɪmɪkl/ *adj.* (harmful) schädlich (to für)

inimitable /ɪ'nɪmɪtəbl/ *adj.* unnachahmlich ‹*Gabe, Fähigkeit*›; einzigartig ‹*Persönlichkeit*›

initial /ɪ'nɪʃl/ 1 *adj.* anfänglich; zu Anfang auftretend ‹*Symptome*›; Anfangs‹*stadium, -schwierigkeiten*›. 2 *n. esp. in pl.* Initiale, *die.* 3 *v.t.,* (Brit.) **-ll-** abzeichnen ‹*Scheck, Quittung*›; paraphieren ‹*Vertrag, Abkommen usw.*›

initial 'letter *n.* Anfangsbuchstabe, *der*

initially /ɪ'nɪʃəlɪ/ *adv.* anfangs; am od. zu Anfang

initiate 1 /ɪ'nɪʃɪeɪt/ *v.t.* (a) (admit) [feierlich] aufnehmen; initiieren (Soziol., Völkerk.); (introduce) einführen (into in + *Akk.*); ∼ sb. into sth. (into club, group, etc.) jmdn. in etw. (*Akk.*) aufnehmen; (into knowledge, mystery, etc.) jmdn. in etw. (*Akk.*) einweihen; (b) (begin) initiieren (geh.); in die Wege leiten ‹*Vorhaben*›; einleiten ‹*Verhandlungen, Reformen*›; eröffnen ‹*Diskussion, Verhandlung, Feindseligkeiten*›. 2 /ɪ'nɪʃɪət/ *n.* Eingeweihte, *der/die*

initiation /ɪnɪʃɪ'eɪʃn/ *n.* (a) (beginning) Initiierung, *die* (geh.); (of hostilities, discussion, negotiation) Eröffnung, *die;* (of reforms, negotiations) Einleitung, *die;* (b) (admission) Aufnahme, *die* (into in + *Akk.*); (introduction) Einführung, *die* (into in + *Akk.*); ∼ ceremony Aufnahmezeremonie, *die*

initiative /ɪ'nɪʃətɪv, ɪ'nɪʃɪətɪv/ *n.* (a) (power) the ∼ is ours/lies with them die Initiative liegt bei uns/ihnen; (b) *no pl., no indef. art.* (ability) Initiative, *die;* (c) (first step) Initiative, *die;* take the ∼: die Initiative ergreifen; on one's own ∼: aus eigener Initiative

inject /ɪn'dʒekt/ *v.t.* (a) [ein]spritzen; injizieren (Med.); (b) (put fluid into) ∼ a vein with sth. etw. in eine Vene spritzen *od.* (Med.) injizieren; (c) (administer sth. to) ∼ sb. with sth. jmdm. etw. spritzen *od.* (Med.) injizieren; ∼ sb. against smallpox jmdn. gegen Pocken impfen; (d) (fig.) pumpen ‹*Geld*›; ∼ new life into sth. einer Sache (*Dat.*) neues Leben geben

injection /ɪn'dʒekʃn/ *n.* (a) (injecting) Einspritzung, *die;* Injektion, *die* (Med.); (b) (liquid injected) Injektion, *die;* Injektionslösung, *die;* (c) (fig.) ∼ of money/capital Geldzuschuss, *der*

injudicious /ɪndʒu:'dɪʃəs/ *adj.* unklug, ungünstig ‹*Moment*›

injunction /ɪn'dʒʌŋkʃn/ *n.* (a) (order) Verfügung, *die;* (b) (Law) [richterliche] Verfügung

injure /'ɪndʒə(r)/ *v.t.* (a) (hurt) verletzen; (fig.) verletzen ‹*Stolz, Gefühle*›; kränken ‹*Person*›; (b) (impair) schaden (+ *Dat.*); schädigen ‹*Gesundheit*›

injured /'ɪndʒəd/ *adj.* (a) (hurt, lit. or fig.) verletzt; verwundet ‹*Soldat*›; the ∼: die Verletzten *Pl.*/Verwundeten *Pl.*; (b) (wronged) geschädigt; the ∼ party (Law) der/die Geschädigte; (c) (offended) gekränkt ‹*Stimme, Blick*›; verletzt, beleidigt ‹*Person*›

injurious /ɪn'dʒʊərɪəs/ *adj.* (a) (wrongful) ungerecht ‹*Behandlung*›; (b) (hurtful) schädlich; be ∼ to sb./sth. jmdm./einer Sache schaden

injury /'ɪndʒərɪ/ *n.* ([instance of] harm) Verletzung, *die* (to *Gen.*); (fig.) Kränkung, *die* (to *Gen.*); add insult to ∼: das

Ganze noch schlimmer machen; do sb./oneself an ∼: jmdm./sich weh tun

'injury time *n.* (Brit. Footb.) Nachspielzeit, *die;* be into/play ∼: nachspielen

injustice /ɪn'dʒʌstɪs/ *n.* Ungerechtigkeit, *die*

ink /ɪŋk/ 1 *n.* Tinte, *die;* (for stamp-pad) Farbe, *die;* (for drawing) Tusche, *die;* (in printing) Druckfarbe, *die;* (in duplicating, newsprint) Druckerschwärze, *die.* 2 *v.t.* (a) ∼ in mit Tinte/Tusche nachziehen; ∼ over mit Tusche übermalen ‹*Papier, Blatt*›; (b) (apply ink to) einfärben ‹*Druckform*›; mit Farbe schwärzen ‹*Stempel*›

'ink-jet printer *n.* Tintenstrahldrucker, *der*

inkling /'ɪŋklɪŋ/ *n.* Ahnung, *die;* I haven't an ∼: ich habe nicht die leiseste Ahnung *od.* (ugs.) keinen blassen Schimmer; have an ∼ of sth. etw. ahnen

inky /'ɪŋkɪ/ *adj.* (a) (covered with ink) tintenbeschmiert; tintig; (b) (black) tintenschwarz; tintig

inland 1 /'ɪnlənd, 'ɪnlænd/ *adj.* (a) (placed ∼) Binnen-; binnenländisch; (b) (carried on ∼) inländisch; Binnen‹*handel, -verkehr*›; Inlands‹*brief, -paket, -gebühren*›. 2 /ɪn'lænd/ *adv.* landeinwärts; im Landesinneren ‹*leben*›

inland: ∼ navi'gation *n.* Binnenschifffahrt, *die;* I∼ 'Revenue *n.* (Brit.) ≈ Finanzamt, *das;* ∼ 'sea *n.* Binnenmeer, *das*

'in-law *n., usu. in pl.* (coll.) angeheirateter Verwandter/angeheiratete Verwandte; ∼s (parents-in-law) Schwiegereltern

inlet /'ɪnlet, 'ɪnlɪt/ *n.* (a) [schmale] Bucht; (b) (opening) Einlassöffnung, *die*

in-liners /ɪn'laɪnəz/, **'in-line skates** *ns. pl.* Inliner, *Pl.;* Inlineskates, *Pl.*

'inmate *n.* (of hospital, prison, etc.) Insasse, *der*/Insassin, *die;* (of house) Bewohner, *der*/Bewohnerin, *die*

inn /ɪn/ *n.* (a) (hotel) Herberge, *die* (veralt.); Gasthof, *der;* (b) (pub) Wirtshaus, *das;* Gastwirtschaft, *die*

innards /'ɪnədz/ *n. pl.* (coll.) Eingeweide *Pl.;* (in animals for slaughter) Innereien *Pl.*

innate /ɪ'neɪt, 'ɪneɪt/ *adj.* (inborn) angeboren

inner /'ɪnə(r)/ *adj.* (a) inner...; Innen‹*hof, -tür, -fläche, -seite usw.*›; ∼ ear (Anat.) Innenohr, *das;* (b) (fig.) inner... ‹*Gefühl, Wesen, Zweifel, Ängste*›; verborgen ‹*Bedeutung*›

inner 'city *n.* Innenstadt, *die;* City, *die*

innermost /'ɪnəməʊst/ *adj.* innerst...; one's ∼ thoughts seine geheimsten Gedanken; in the ∼ depths of the forest im tiefsten Wald

'inner tube *n.* Schlauch, *der*

innings /'ɪnɪŋz/ *n., pl. same or* (coll.) ∼es (Cricket) Durchgang, *der;* Innings, *das* (fachspr.)

'innkeeper *n.* [Gast]wirt, *der*/-wirtin, *die*

innocence /'ɪnəsəns/ *n., no pl.* (a) Unschuld, *die;* (b) (freedom from cunning) Naivität, *die;* (c) (lack of knowledge) Unkenntnis, *die*

innocent /'ɪnəsənt/ 1 *adj.* (a) unschuldig (of an + *Dat.*); (b) (harmless) harmlos; (c) (naïve) unschuldig; he is ∼ about the ways of the world er ist völlig unerfahren; (d) (pretending to be guileless) arglos, unschuldig ‹*Blick, Erscheinung*›. 2 *n.* (innocent person) Unschuldige, *der/die*

innocuous /ɪ'nɒkjʊəs/ *adj.* (not injurious) unschädlich ‹*Tier, Mittel*›; (inoffensive) harmlos

innovate /'ɪnəveɪt/ *v.i.* Innovationen vornehmen

innovation /ɪnə'veɪʃn/ *n.* (a) (introduction of something new) Innovation, *die* (geh., fachspr.); (thing introduced) Neuerung, *die;* (b) (change) [Ver]änderung, *die;* Neuerung, *die;* Innovation, *die* (geh., fachspr.)

innuendo /ɪnju:'endəʊ/ *n., pl.* ∼es *or* ∼s versteckte Andeutung; Innuendo, *das* (geh.)

innumerable /ɪ'nju:mərəbl/ *adj.* unzählig; zahllos; (uncountable) unzählbar

innumerate /ɪ'nju:mərət/ *adj.* (Brit.) be ∼: nicht rechnen können

inoculate /ɪ'nɒkjʊleɪt/ *v.t.* impfen (against, for gegen)

inoculation /ɪnɒkjʊ'leɪʃn/ *n.* Impfung, *die;* give sb. an ∼: jmdn. impfen

inoffensive /ɪnəˈfensɪv/ adj. (a) (unoffending) harmlos; (b) (not objectionable) harmlos ‹Bemerkung›; unaufdringlich ‹Geruch, Art, Person›

inoperative /ɪnˈɒpərətɪv/ adj. ungültig; außer Kraft nicht attr.; **render sth. ~:** etw. außer Betrieb setzen

inopportune /ɪnˈɒpətjuːn/ adj. inopportun (geh.); unangebracht ‹Bemerkung›; ungelegen, unpassend ‹Augenblick, Besuch›

inordinate /ɪˈnɔːdɪnət/ adj. (immoderate) unmäßig; ungeheuer ‹Menge›; überzogen ‹Forderung›; **an ~ amount of work/money** ungeheuer viel Arbeit/eine Unmenge Geld

inorganic /ɪnɔːˈgænɪk/ adj. (Chem.) anorganisch

'in-patient n. stationär behandelter Patient/behandelte Patientin; **be an ~:** stationär behandelt werden

'input 1 n. (esp. Computing) Input, der od. das; (of capital) Investition, die; (of electricity) Energiezufuhr, die. **2** v.t., **-tt-, ~** or **~ted** eingeben ‹Daten, Programm›; zuführen ‹Strom, Energie›

'input data n. pl. Eingabedaten, Pl.; Rechnerdaten, Pl.

inquest /ˈɪnkwest, ˈɪŋkwest/ n. (legal inquiry) ~ [**into the causes of death**] gerichtliche Untersuchung der Todesursache

inquire /ɪnˈkwaɪə(r), ɪŋˈkwaɪə(r)/ **1** v.i. (a) (make search) Untersuchungen anstellen (**into** über + Akk.); **~ into a matter** eine Angelegenheit untersuchen; (b) (seek information) sich erkundigen (**about, after** nach, **of** bei). **2** v.t. sich erkundigen nach, fragen nach ‹Weg, Namen›

inquiring /ɪnˈkwaɪərɪŋ, ɪŋˈkwaɪərɪŋ/ adj. fragend; forschend ‹Geist›

inquiry /ɪnˈkwaɪərɪ, ɪŋˈkwaɪərɪ/ n. (a) (asking) Anfrage, die; **give sb. a look of ~:** jmdn. fragend ansehen; (b) (question) Erkundigung, die (**into** über + Akk.); **make inquiries** Erkundigungen einziehen; (c) (investigation) Untersuchung, die; **hold an ~:** eine Untersuchung durchführen (**into** Gen.)

inquiry: ~ desk, ~ office ns. Auskunft, die

inquisition /ɪnkwɪˈzɪʃn, ɪŋkwɪˈzɪʃn/ n. (a) (search) Nachforschung, die (**into** über + Akk.); (b) (judicial inquiry) gerichtliche Untersuchung; (fig. coll.) Verhör, das; (c) **I~** (Hist.) Inquisition, die

inquisitive /ɪnˈkwɪzɪtɪv, ɪŋˈkwɪzɪtɪv/ adj. (a) (unduly inquiring) neugierig; (b) (inquiring) wissbegierig

inquisitiveness /ɪnˈkwɪzɪtɪvnɪs, ɪŋˈkwɪzɪtɪvnɪs/ n., no pl. ⇒ **inquisitive:** Neugier[de], die; Wissbegier[de], die

'inroad n. (a) (intrusion) Eingriff, der (**on, into** in + Akk.); **make ~s into sb.'s savings** jmds. Ersparnisse angreifen; (b) (hostile incursion) Einfall, der (**into** in + Akk.); Überfall, der ([**up**]**on** auf + Akk.)

insane /ɪnˈseɪn/ adj. (a) geisteskrank; (b) (extremely foolish) wahnsinnig (ugs.); irrsinnig (ugs.)

insanitary /ɪnˈsænɪtərɪ/ adj. unhygienisch

insanity /ɪnˈsænɪtɪ/ n. (a) Geisteskrankheit, die; Wahnsinn, der; (b) (extreme folly) Irrsinn, der; (instance) Verrücktheit, die

insatiable /ɪnˈseɪʃəbl/ adj. unersättlich; unstillbar ‹Verlangen, Neugierde›

inscribe /ɪnˈskraɪb/ v.t. (a) (write) schreiben; (on ring etc.) eingravieren; (on stone, rock) einmeißeln; (b) mit einer Inschrift versehen ‹Denkmal, Grabstein›

inscription /ɪnˈskrɪpʃn/ n. (words inscribed) Inschrift, die; (on coin) Aufschrift, die

inscrutable /ɪnˈskruːtəbl/ adj. (mysterious) unergründlich; geheimnisvoll ‹Lächeln›; undurchdringlich ‹Miene›

insect /ˈɪnsekt/ n. Insekt, das; Kerbtier, das

'insect bite n. Insektenstich, der

'insecticide /ɪnˈsektɪsaɪd/ n. Insektizid, das

'insect repellent n. Insektenschutzmittel, das

insecure /ɪnsɪˈkjʊə(r)/ adj. (a) (unsafe) unsicher; (b) (not firm, liable to give way) nicht sicher; (c) (Psych.) unsicher; **feel ~:** sich nicht sicher fühlen

insecurity /ɪnsɪˈkjʊərɪtɪ/ n., no pl. (also Psych.) Unsicherheit, die

insensibility /ɪnsensɪˈbɪlɪtɪ/ n., no pl. (a) (lack of emotional feeling, indifference) Gefühllosigkeit, die (**to** gegenüber); (b)

(unconsciousness) Bewusstlosigkeit, die; (c) (lack of physical feeling) Unempfindlichkeit, die (**to** gegen)

insensible /ɪnˈsensɪbl/ adj. (a) (emotionless) gefühllos ‹Person, Art›; unempfindlich (**to** für); (b) (deprived of sensation) unempfindlich (**to** für); (c) (unconscious) bewusstlos; (d) (unaware) **be ~ of** or **to sth.** sich (Dat.) einer Sache (Gen.) nicht bewusst sein

insensitive /ɪnˈsensɪtɪv/ adj. (a) (lacking feeling) gefühllos ‹Person, Art›; (b) (unappreciative) unempfänglich (**to** für); (c) (not physically sensitive) unempfindlich (**to** gegen)

insensitiveness /ɪnˈsensɪtɪvnɪs/, **insensitivity** /ɪnsensɪˈtɪvɪtɪ/ ns., no pl. (a) (lack of feeling) Gefühllosigkeit, die (**to** gegenüber); (b) (unappreciativeness) Unempfindlichkeit, die (**to** für); (c) (lack of physical sensitiveness) Unempfindlichkeit, die (**to** gegen); ~ **to heat** Hitzeunempfindlichkeit, die

inseparable /ɪnˈsepərəbl/ adj. untrennbar; (fig.) unzertrennlich ‹Freunde, Zwillinge usw.›

insert 1 /ɪnˈsɜːt/ v.t. (a) einlegen ‹Film›; einwerfen ‹Münze›; einsetzen ‹Herzschrittmacher›; einstechen ‹Nadel›; ~ **a piece of paper into the typewriter** ein Blatt Papier in die Schreibmaschine einspannen; (b) (introduce into) einfügen ‹Wort, Satz usw.› (**in** in + Akk.); ~ **an advertisement in 'The Times'** eine Anzeige in die „Times" setzen; (c) (Computing) einfügen; ~ **key** Einfügetaste, die. **2** /ˈɪnsɜːt/ n. (in magazine) Beilage, die; (in book) Einlage, die; (printed in newspaper) Inserat, das

insertion /ɪnˈsɜːʃn/ n. (a) ⇒ **insert 1 a:** Einlegen, das; Einwerfen, das; Einsetzen, das; Einstechen, das; (b) (words etc. in a text) Einfügung, die; Beifügung, die; (in newspaper) Inserat, das

in-service 'training n. Fort- od. Weiterbildung, die [für Berufstätige]

inset /ˈɪnset/ n. (small map) Nebenkarte, die; (small photograph, diagram) Nebenbild, das

inshore /ˈɪnʃɔː/ adj. Küsten‹fischerei, -gewässer, -schifffahrt›

inside 1 /ˈɪnˈsaɪd, ˈɪnsaɪd/ n. (a) (internal side) Innenseite, die; **on the ~:** innen; **to/from the ~:** nach/von innen; **lock the door from the ~:** die Tür von innen abschließen; (b) (inner part) Innere, das; (c) **in** sing. or pl. (coll.: stomach and bowels) Eingeweide Pl.; Innere, das; (d) **the wind blew her umbrella ~ out** der Wind hat ihren Regenschirm umgestülpt; **turn a jacket ~ out** eine Jacke nach links wenden. **2** /ˈɪnsaɪd/ adj. inner...; Innen‹wand, -ansicht, -durchmesser›; (fig.) intern; **be on an ~ page** im Inneren [der Zeitung] stehen; **give the ~ story of sth.** etw. von innen beleuchten (fig.); ~ **information** interne Informationen; ~ **pocket** Innentasche, die; ~ **lane** Innenspur, die. **3** /ˈɪnsaɪd/ adv. (a) (on or in the ~) innen; (to the ~) nach innen hinein/herein; (indoors) drinnen; **come ~:** hereinkommen; **go ~:** [ins Haus] hineingehen; (b) (sl.: in prison) **be ~:** sitzen (ugs.); **put sb. ~:** jmdn. einlochen (salopp). **4** /ˈɪnsaɪd/ prep. (a) (on inner side of) [innen] in (+ Dat.); (with direction) in (+ Akk.) hinein; **sit/get ~ the house** im Haus sitzen/ins Haus hineinkommen; (b) (in less than) ~ **an hour** innerhalb [von] einer Stunde

inside-'leg adj. ~**-leg measurement** Schrittlänge, die

insider /ɪnˈsaɪdə(r)/ n. (within a society) Mitglied, das; Zugehörige, die/der; ~ **dealing** or **trading** (Stock Exch.) Insiderhandel, der

insidious /ɪnˈsɪdɪəs/ adj. heimtückisch

'insight n. Verständnis, das; (instance) Einblick, der (**into** in + Akk.); **gain an ~ into sth.** [einen] Einblick in etw. (Akk.) gewinnen od. bekommen

insignificant /ɪnsɪgˈnɪfɪkənt/ adj. (a) unbedeutend; geringfügig ‹Summe›; unbedeutend, geringfügig ‹Unterschied›; (b) (contemptible) unscheinbar ‹Person›

insincere /ɪnsɪnˈsɪə(r)/ adj. unaufrichtig; falsch ‹Lächeln›

insincerity /ɪnsɪnˈserɪtɪ/ n. Unaufrichtigkeit, die; (of smile) Falschheit, die

insinuate /ɪnˈsɪnjʊeɪt/ v.t. (a) (introduce) [auf geschickte Art] einflößen ‹Propaganda›; (b) (convey) andeuten (**to sb.** jmdm. gegenüber); unterstellen; **insinuating remarks** Andeutungen; Unterstellungen; (c) ~ **oneself into sb.'s favour** sich bei jmdm. einschmeicheln

insinuation /ɪnsɪnjʊ'eɪʃn/ n. Anspielung, die (about auf + Akk.)

insipid /ɪn'sɪpɪd/ adj. (a) fad[e] ‹Essen›; schal ‹Getränk›; (b) fad[e] (ugs.), geistlos ‹Person›; langweilig ‹Farbe, Musik›

insist /ɪn'sɪst/ 1 v.i. bestehen ([up]on auf + Dat.); ~ on doing sth. darauf bestehen, etw. zu tun; she ~s on her innocence sie behauptet beharrlich, unschuldig zu sein. 2 v.t. (a) ~ that …: darauf bestehen, dass …; (b) (maintain positively) they keep ~ing that …: sie beharren od. bestehen beharrlich darauf, dass …

insistence /ɪn'sɪstəns/ n., no pl. Bestehen, das (on auf + Dat.); I only came here at your ~: ich kam nur auf dein Drängen hierher

insistent /ɪn'sɪstənt/ adj. (a) beharrlich, hartnäckig ‹Person›; aufdringlich ‹Musik›; nachdrücklich ‹Forderung›; (b) ([annoyingly] persistent) penetrant (abwertend)

insole /'ɪnsəʊl/ n. Einlegesohle, die

insolence /'ɪnsələns/ n., no pl. Unverschämtheit, die; Frechheit, die

insolent /'ɪnsələnt/ adj., **insolently** /'ɪnsələntlɪ/ adv. (a) (insulting[ly]) unverschämt; frech; (b) (contemptuous[ly]) anmaßend; überheblich

insoluble /ɪn'sɒljʊbl/ adj. (a) unlösbar ‹Problem, Rätsel usw.›; (b) unlöslich ‹Substanz›; insolubel (Chem.) ‹Verbindung›

insolvency /ɪn'sɒlvənsɪ/ n. Insolvenz, die (bes. Wirtsch.); Zahlungsunfähigkeit, die

insolvent /ɪn'sɒlvənt/ adj. (unable to pay debts) insolvent (bes. Wirtsch.); zahlungsunfähig

insomnia /ɪn'sɒmnɪə/ n. Schlaflosigkeit, die

inspect /ɪn'spekt/ v.t. (a) (view closely) prüfend betrachten; (b) (examine officially) überprüfen; inspizieren, kontrollieren ‹Räumlichkeiten›

inspection /ɪn'spekʃn/ n. Überprüfung, die; (of premises) Kontrolle, die; Inspektion, die; present/submit sth. for ~: etw. zur Prüfung vorlegen

inspector /ɪn'spektə(r)/ n. (a) (official) (on bus, train, etc.) Kontrolleur, der/Kontrolleurin, die; (b) (Brit.: police officer) ≈ Polizeiinspektor, der

inspiration /ɪnspə'reɪʃn/ n. Inspiration, die (geh.); get one's ~ from sth. sich von etw. inspirieren lassen; sth. is an ~ to sb. etw. inspiriert jmdn.

inspire /ɪn'spaɪə(r)/ v.t. (a) inspirieren (geh.); in an ~d moment (coll.) in einem Augenblick der Erleuchtung; (b) (animate) inspirieren; anregen; (encourage) anspornen; ~d idea genialer Gedanke; ~d guess intuitiv richtige Vermutung; (c) (instil) einflößen ‹Mut, Angst, Respekt› (in Dat.); [er]wecken ‹Vertrauen, Gedanke, Hoffnung› (in + Dat.); hervorrufen ‹Hass, Abneigung› (in bei); (incite) anstiften; anzetteln (abwertend) ‹Unruhen usw.›

inspiring /ɪn'spaɪərɪŋ/ adj. inspirierend (geh.)

instability /ɪnstə'bɪlɪtɪ/ n. (mental, physical) Labilität, die; (inconstancy) Instabilität, die

install /ɪn'stɔːl/ v.t. (a) (establish) ~ oneself sich installieren; (in a house etc.) sich einrichten; (b) (set up for use) installieren ‹Heizung, Leitung›; anschließen ‹Telefon›; einbauen ‹Badezimmer›; aufstellen, anschließen ‹Herd›; (c) (place ceremonially) installieren (geh.); ~ sb. in an office/a post jmdn. in ein Amt einsetzen

installation /ɪnstə'leɪʃn/ n. (a) (in an office or post) Amtseinsetzung, die; (b) (setting up for use) Installation, die; (of bathroom etc.) Einbau, der; (of telephone, cooker) Anschluss, der; (c) (apparatus etc. installed) Anlage, die

instalment (Amer.: **installment**) /ɪn'stɔːlmənt/ n. (a) (part payment) Rate, die; pay by or in ~s in Raten od. ratenweise zahlen; (b) (of serial, novel) Fortsetzung, die; (of film, radio programme) Folge, die; (c) ~ plan (Amer.) Ratenzahlung, die; Teilzahlung, die; buy on an ~ plan auf Raten kaufen

instance /'ɪnstəns/ n. (a) (example) Beispiel, das (of für); as an ~ of …: als [ein] Beispiel für …; for ~: zum Beispiel; (b) (particular case) in your/this ~: in deinem/diesem Fall[e]; (c) in the first ~: zuerst od. zunächst einmal; (at the very beginning) gleich zu Anfang

instant /'ɪnstənt/ 1 adj. (a) (occurring immediately) unmittelbar; sofortig ‹Wirkung, Linderung, Ergebnis›; (b) ~ coffee/tea Instant- od. Pulverkaffee, der/Instanttee, der; ~ meal Fertiggericht, das. 2 n. Augenblick, der; come here this ~: komm sofort od. auf der Stelle her; the ~ he walked in at the door …: in dem Augenblick, als er hereintrat, …; in an ~: augenblicklich

instantaneous /ɪnstən'teɪnɪəs/ adj. unmittelbar; his reaction was ~: er reagierte sofort

instantly /'ɪnstəntlɪ/ adv. sofort

instead /ɪn'sted/ adv. stattdessen; ~ of doing sth. [an]statt etw. zu tun; ~ of sth. anstelle einer Sache (Gen.); I will go ~ of you ich gehe an deiner Stelle

'instep n. (a) (of foot) Spann, der; Fußrücken, der; (b) (of shoe) Blatt, das

instigate /'ɪnstɪgeɪt/ v.t. (a) (urge on) anstiften (to zu); (b) (bring about) initiieren (geh.) ‹Reformen, Projekt usw.›; anzetteln (abwertend) ‹Streik usw.›

instigation /ɪnstɪ'geɪʃn/ n. (a) (urging) Anstiftung, die; at sb.'s ~: auf jmds. Betreiben (Akk.); (b) (bringing about) Anzettelung, die (abwertend); (of reforms etc.) Initiierung, die (geh.)

instil (Amer.: **instill**) /ɪn'stɪl/ v.t., -ll- einflößen (in Dat.); einimpfen (in Dat.); beibringen ‹gutes Benehmen, Wissen› (in Dat.)

instinct /'ɪnstɪŋkt/ n. (a) Instinkt, der; ~ for survival, survival ~: Überlebenstrieb, der; (b) (intuition) Instinkt, der; instinktives Gefühl (for für); (unconscious skill) natürliche Begabung (for für); Sinn, der (for für)

instinctive /ɪn'stɪŋktɪv/ adj., **instinctively** /ɪn'stɪŋktɪvlɪ/ adv. instinktiv

institute /'ɪnstɪtjuːt/ 1 n. Institut, das. 2 v.t. einführen ‹Reform, Brauch, Beschränkung›; einleiten ‹Suche, Verfahren, Untersuchung›; gründen ‹Gesellschaft›; anstrengen ‹Prozess, Klage›; schaffen ‹Posten›

institution /ɪnstɪ'tjuːʃn/ n. (a) (instituting) Einführung, die; (b) (law, custom) Institution, die; (c) (coll.: familiar object) Institution, die; become an ~: zur Institution werden; (d) (institute) Heim, das; Anstalt, die

institutional /ɪnstɪ'tjuːʃənl/ adj. (a) (of, like, organized through institutions) institutionell (geh.); (b) (suggestive of typical charitable institutions) Heim-; Anstalts-

instruct /ɪn'strʌkt/ v.t. (a) (teach) unterrichten ‹Klasse, Fach›; (b) (direct, command) anweisen; die Anweisung erteilen (+ Dat.); (c) (inform) unterrichten; (d) (Law: appoint) beauftragen ‹Anwalt›

instruction /ɪn'strʌkʃn/ n. (a) (teaching) Unterricht, der; (b) esp. in pl. (direction, order) Anweisung, die; Instruktion, die; ~ manual/~s for use Gebrauchsanleitung, die; (for machine etc.) Betriebsanleitung, die

instructive /ɪn'strʌktɪv/ adj. aufschlussreich; instruktiv; lehrreich ‹Erfahrung, Buch›

instructor /ɪn'strʌktə(r)/ n. ▶887⟩ (a) Lehrer, der/ Lehrerin, die; (Mil.) Ausbilder, der; (b) (Amer. Univ.) Dozent, der/Dozentin, die

instrument /'ɪnstrʊmənt/ n. (also Mus.) Instrument, das; (person) Werkzeug, das

instrumental /ɪnstrʊ'mentl/ adj. (a) (serving as instrument or means) dienlich (to Dat.); förderlich (to Dat.); he was ~ in finding me a post er hat mir zu einer Stelle verholfen; (b) (Mus.) instrumental; Instrumental‹musik, -version, -nummer›

instrumentalist /ɪnstrʊ'mentəlɪst/ n. Instrumentalist, der/Instrumentalistin, die

'instrument panel n. Instrumentenbrett, das

insubordinate /ɪnsə'bɔːdɪnət/ adj. aufsässig; widersetzlich; (Mil.) ungehorsam

insubordination /ɪnsəbɔːdɪ'neɪʃn/ n., no pl. Aufsässigkeit, die; Widersetzlichkeit, die; (Mil.) Gehorsamsverweigerung, die

insubstantial /ɪnsəb'stænʃl/ adj. wenig substanziell (geh.); dürftig ‹Essen, Kleidung›; gering[fügig] ‹Menge, Betrag›

insufferable /ɪn'sʌfərəbl/ adj. (a) (unbearably arrogant) unausstehlich; (b) (intolerable) unerträglich

insufficient /ɪnsə'fɪʃənt/ *adj.* nicht genügend ⟨*Arbeit, Gründe, Geld*⟩; unzulänglich ⟨*Beweise*⟩; unzureichend ⟨*Versorgung, Beleuchtung*⟩; **give sb. ~ notice** jmdm. nicht rechtzeitig Bescheid geben

insular /'ɪnsjʊlə(r)/ *adj.* (a) (of an island) Insel-; insular (fachspr.); (b) (fig.) provinziell (abwertend)

insularity /ɪnsjʊ'lærɪtɪ/ *n.* Provinzialität, *die* (abwertend)

insulate /'ɪnsjʊleɪt/ *v.t.* (a) (isolate) isolieren (**against, from** gegen); (b) (detach from surroundings) isolieren (**from** von)

'insulating tape *n.* Isolierband, *das*

insulation /ɪnsjʊ'leɪʃn/ *n.* Isolierung, *die*

insulator /'ɪnsjʊleɪtə(r)/ *n.* Isolator, *der*

insulin /'ɪnsjʊlɪn/ *n.* (Med.) Insulin, *das*

insult 1 /'ɪnsʌlt/ *n.* Beleidigung, *die* (**to** *Gen.*); *see also* **injury. 2** /ɪn'sʌlt/ *v.t.* beleidigen

insulting /ɪn'sʌltɪŋ/ *adj.* beleidigend

insuperable /ɪn'su:pərəbl, ɪn'sju:pərəbl/ *adj.* unüberwindlich

insupportable /ɪnsə'pɔ:təbl/ *adj.* (that cannot be endured) unerträglich

insurance /ɪn'ʃʊərəns/ *n.* (a) (insuring) Versicherung, *die;* (fig.) Sicherheit, *die;* Gewähr, *die;* **take out ~ against/on sth.** eine Versicherung gegen etw. abschließen/etw. versichern lassen; **travel ~:** Reisegepäck- und -unfallversicherung, *die;* (b) (sum received) Versicherungssumme, *die;* (sum paid) Versicherungsbetrag, *der*

insurance: ~ agent *n.* ▶887│ Versicherungsvertreter, *der/*-vertreterin, *die;* **~ claim** *n.* Versicherungsanspruch, *der;* **make an ~ claim** eine Versicherung in Anspruch nehmen; **~ company** *n.* Versicherungsgesellschaft, *die;* **~ policy** *n.* Versicherungspolice, *die;* (fig.) Sicherheit, *die;* Gewähr, *die*

insure /ɪn'ʃʊə(r)/ *v.t.* (a) (secure payment to) versichern ⟨*Person*⟩ (**against** gegen); **~ [oneself] against sth.** sich gegen etw. versichern; (b) (secure payment for) ⟨*Versicherungsgesellschaft:*⟩ versichern; ⟨*Versicherungsnehmer:*⟩ versichern lassen ⟨*Gepäck, Gemälde usw.*⟩

insurgent /ɪn'sɜ:dʒənt/ **1** *attrib. adj.* aufständisch. **2** *n.* Aufständische, *der/die*

insurmountable /ɪnsə'maʊntəbl/ *adj.* unüberwindlich

insurrection /ɪnsə'rekʃn/ *n.* (uprising) Aufstand, *der*

intact /ɪn'tækt/ *adj.* (a) (entire) unbeschädigt; unversehrt; intakt ⟨*Uhr, Maschine usw.*⟩; (b) (unimpaired) unversehrt; **keep one's reputation ~:** sich (*Dat.*) einen guten Ruf bewahren; (c) (untouched) unberührt; unangetastet

'intake *n.* (a) (action) Aufnahme, *die;* **~ of breath** Atemholen, *das;* (b) (where water enters channel or pipe) Einströmungsöffnung, *die;* (where air or fuel enters engine) Ansaugöffnung, *die;* (c) (persons or things taken in) Neuzugänge; (amount taken in) aufgenommene Menge; **~ of calories** Kalorienzufuhr, *die*

intangible /ɪn'tændʒɪbl/ *adj.* (a) (that cannot be touched) nicht greifbar; (b) (that cannot be grasped mentally) unbestimmbar

integer /'ɪntɪdʒə(r)/ *n.* (Math.) ganze Zahl

integral /'ɪntɪgrl/ *adj.* (a) (of a whole) wesentlich, integral ⟨*Bestandteil*⟩; (b) (whole, complete) vollständig; vollkommen; (c) (forming a whole) ein Ganzes bildend; integrierend

integrate /'ɪntɪgreɪt/ *v.t.* (a) (combine into a whole; also Math.) integrieren; **an ~d Europe** ein vereintes Europa; (b) (into society) integrieren (**in** in + *Akk.*); (c) (open to all racial groups) **~ a school/college** eine Schule/ein College für alle Rassen zugänglich machen

integrated 'circuit *n.* (Electronics) integrierter Schaltkreis

integration /ɪntɪ'greɪʃn/ *n.* (a) (integrating; also Math.) Integration, *die;* (b) (ending of segregation) Integration, *die* (**into** in + *Akk.*); **racial ~:** Rassenintegration, *die*

integrity /ɪn'tegrɪtɪ/ *n.* (a) (uprightness, honesty) Redlichkeit, *die;* (of business, venture) Seriosität, *die;* (of style) Echtheit, *die;* Unverfälschtheit, *die;* (b) (wholeness) Einheit, *die;* **territorial ~:** territoriale Integrität

intellect /'ɪntəlekt/ *n.* (a) (faculty) Verstand, *der;* Intellekt, *der;* (b) (understanding) Intelligenz, *die;* **powers of ~:** Verstandeskräfte *Pl.*

intellectual /ɪntə'lektjʊəl/ **1** *adj.* (a) (of intellect) intellektuell; geistig ⟨*Klima, Interessen, Arbeit*⟩; abstrakt ⟨*Mitgefühl, Sympathie*⟩; (b) (possessing good understanding or intelligence) geistig anspruchsvoll ⟨*Person, Publikum*⟩. **2** *n.* Intellektuelle, *der/die*

intelligence /ɪn'telɪdʒəns/ *n.* (a) Intelligenz, *die;* **have the ~ to do sth.** so intelligent sein, etw. zu tun; (b) (information) Informationen *Pl.;* (news) Nachrichten *Pl.;* Meldungen *Pl.;* (c) ([persons employed in] collecting information) Nachrichtendienst, *der;* **military ~:** militärischer Geheimdienst

intelligence: ~ quotient *n.* Intelligenzquotient, *der;* **~ service** *n.* Nachrichtendienst, *der;* **~ test** *n.* Intelligenztest, *der*

intelligent /ɪn'telɪdʒent/ *adj.* intelligent; intelligent geschrieben, geistreich ⟨*Buch*⟩

intelligentsia /ɪntelɪ'dʒentsɪə/ *n.* Intelligentsia, *die* (geh.); Intelligenz, *die*

intelligible /ɪn'telɪdʒɪbl/ *adj.* verständlich (**to** für)

intemperate /ɪn'tempərət/ *adj.* (a) (immoderate) maßlos; überzogen, übertrieben ⟨*Verhalten, Bemerkung*⟩; unmäßig, maßlos ⟨*Verlangen, Appetit, Konsum*⟩; (b) (addicted to drinking) trunksüchtig

intend /ɪn'tend/ *v.t.* (a) (have as one's purpose) beabsichtigen; **~ doing sth.** *or* **to do sth.** beabsichtigen, etw. zu tun; **it isn't really what we ~ed** es ist eigentlich nicht das, was wir wollten; (b) (design, mean) **we ~ him to go** wir wollen, dass er geht; er soll gehen; **it was ~ed as a joke** das sollte ein Witz sein; **what do you ~ by that remark?** was willst du mit dieser Bemerkung sagen? *See also* **intended**

intended /ɪn'tendɪd/ **1** *adj.* beabsichtigt ⟨*Wirkung*⟩; erklärt ⟨*Ziel*⟩; absichtlich ⟨*Beleidigung*⟩; **be ~ for sb./sth.** für jmdn./etw. bestimmt *od.* gedacht sein. **2** *n.* (coll.) Zukünftige, *der/die* (ugs.)

intense /ɪn'tens/ *adj.*, **~r** /ɪn'tensə(r)/, **~st** /ɪn'tensɪst/ (a) intensiv; stark ⟨*Hitze, Belastung*⟩; stark, heftig ⟨*Schmerzen*⟩; kräftig, intensiv ⟨*Farbe*⟩; äußerst groß ⟨*Aufregung*⟩; ungeheuer ⟨*Kälte, Helligkeit*⟩; (b) (eager, ardent) eifrig, lebhaft ⟨*Diskussion*⟩; stark, ausgeprägt ⟨*Interesse*⟩; brennend, glühend ⟨*Verlangen*⟩; äußerst groß ⟨*Empörung, Aufregung, Betrübnis*⟩; tief ⟨*Gefühl*⟩; rasend ⟨*Hass, Eifersucht*⟩; (c) (with strong emotion) stark gefühlsbetont ⟨*Person, Brief*⟩; (earnest) ernst

intensely /ɪn'tenslɪ/ *adv.* äußerst ⟨*schwierig, verärgert, enttäuscht, kalt*⟩; ernsthaft, intensiv ⟨*studieren*⟩; intensiv ⟨*fühlen*⟩

intensifier /ɪn'tensɪfaɪə(r)/ *n.* (Ling.) intensivierendes Wort

intensify /ɪn'tensɪfaɪ/ **1** *v.t.* intensivieren. **2** *v.i.* zunehmen; ⟨*Hitze, Schmerzen:*⟩ stärker werden; ⟨*Kampf:*⟩ sich verschärfen

intensity /ɪn'tensɪtɪ/ *n.* Intensität, *die;* (of feeling also) Heftigkeit, *die*

intensive /ɪn'tensɪv/ *adj.* (a) (vigorous, thorough) intensiv; Intensiv⟨*kurs*⟩; (b) (Ling.) verstärkend; intensivierend; (c) (concentrated, directed to a single point or area) intensiv; heftig ⟨*Beschuss*⟩; gezielt ⟨*Entwicklung*⟩; (d) (Econ.) intensiv ⟨*Landwirtschaft*⟩; (e) *in comb.* **capital-~/labour-~:** kapital-/arbeitsintensiv

intensive 'care *n.* Intensivpflege, *die* (Med.); **be in ~:** auf der Intensivstation sein; **~ unit** Intensivstation, *die*

intent /ɪn'tent/ **1** *n.* Absicht, *die;* **by ~:** beabsichtigt; **with ~ to do sth.** (Law) in der Absicht *od.* mit dem Vorsatz, etw. zu tun; **to all ~s and purposes** im Grunde; praktisch; *see also* **loiter. 2** *adj.* (a) (resolved) erpicht, versessen (**[up]on** auf + *Akk.*); **be ~ on achieving sth.** etw. unbedingt erreichen wollen; (b) (attentively occupied) eifrig beschäftigt (**on** mit); **be ~ on one's work** auf seine Arbeit konzentriert sein; (c) (earnest, eager) aufmerksam; konzentriert; forschend ⟨*Blick*⟩

intention /ɪn'tenʃn/ n. (a) Absicht, die; Intention, die; it was my ～ to visit him ich hatte die Absicht od. beabsichtigte, ihn zu besuchen; **with the best of** ～s in der besten Absicht; **(b)** in pl. (coll.: in respect of marriage) [Heirats]absichten Pl.

intentional /ɪn'tenʃənl/ adj. absichtlich; vorsätzlich (bes. Rechtsspr.); **it wasn't** ～: es war keine Absicht

intentionally /ɪn'tenʃənlɪ/ adv. absichtlich; mit Absicht

intently /ɪn'tentlɪ/ adv. aufmerksam ‹zuhören, lesen, beobachten›

interact /ɪntər'ækt/ v.i. **(a)** ‹Ideen:› sich gegenseitig beeinflussen; ‹Chemikalien usw.:› aufeinander einwirken, miteinander reagieren; **(b)** (Sociol., Psych.) interagieren

interaction /ɪntər'ækʃn/ n. **(a)** gegenseitige Beeinflussung; (Chem., Phys.) Wechselwirkung, die; **(b)** (Sociol., Psych.) Interaktion, die

interactive /ɪntər'æktɪv/ adj. **(a)** (Chem.) miteinander reagierend; **(b)** (Sociol., Psych., Computing) interaktiv; ～ **television** interaktives Fernsehen

intercede /ɪntə'si:d/ v.i. sich einsetzen **(with** bei; **for, on behalf of** für)

intercept /ɪntə'sept/ v.t. **(a)** (seize) abfangen; **(b)** (check, stop) abwehren ‹Schlag, Angriff›; **(c)** (listen in to) abhören ‹Gespräch, Funkspruch›

interceptor /ɪntə'septə(r)/ n. (Air Force) Abfangjäger, der

interchange 1 /'ɪntətʃeɪndʒ/ n. **(a)** (reciprocal exchange) Austausch, der; **(b)** (road junction) [Autobahn]kreuz, das. **2** /ɪntə'tʃeɪndʒ/ v.t. **(a)** (exchange with each other) austauschen; **(b)** (put each in the other's place) [miteinander] vertauschen; **(c)** (alternate) wechseln

interchangeable /ɪntə'tʃeɪndʒəbl/ adj. austauschbar; synonym ‹Wörter, Ausdrücke›

inter-city /ɪntə'sɪtɪ/ adj. Intercity-; ～ **train** Intercity [-Zug], der

intercom /'ɪntəkɒm/ n. (coll.) Gegensprechanlage, die

interconnect /ɪntəkə'nekt/ **1** v.t. miteinander verbinden; zusammenschalten ‹Stromkreise, Verstärker, Lautsprecher›. **2** v.i. miteinander in Zusammenhang stehen; ～**ing rooms** miteinander verbundene Zimmer

intercontinental /ɪntəkɒntɪ'nentl/ adj. interkontinental; Interkontinental‹rakete, -reise, -flug›

intercourse /'ɪntəkɔ:s/ n., no pl. **(a)** (social communication) Umgang, der; **social** ～: gesellschaftlicher Verkehr; **(b)** (sexual ～) [Geschlechts]verkehr, der

interdependence /ɪntədɪ'pendəns/ n. gegenseitige Abhängigkeit; Interdependenz, die

interdependent /ɪntədɪ'pendənt/ adj. voneinander abhängig; interdependent

interest /'ɪntrəst, 'ɪntrɪst/ **1** n. **(a)** Interesse, das; Anliegen, das; **take** or **have an** ～ **in** sb./sth. sich für jmdn./ etw. interessieren; **[just] for** or **out of** ～: [nur] interessehalber; **with** ～: interessiert (see also **b**); **lose** ～ **in** sth. das Interesse an jmdm./etw. verlieren; ～ **in life/ food** Lust am Leben/Essen; **be of** ～: interessant od. von Interesse sein **(to** für); **this is of no** ～ **to me** das ist belanglos für mich; **act in one's own/sb.'s** ～**[s]** im eigenen/in jmds. Interesse handeln; **in the** ～**[s] of humanity** zum Wohle der Menschheit; **(b)** (thing in which one is concerned) Angelegenheit, die; Belange Pl.; **(c)** (Finance) Zinsen Pl.; at ～: gegen od. auf Zinsen; **with** ～ (fig.: with increased force etc.) überreichlich; doppelt und dreifach (ugs.) (see also **a**); **(d)** (financial stake) Beteiligung, die; Anteil, der; **declare an** ～: seine Interessen darlegen; **(e)** (legal concern) [Rechts]anspruch, der. **2** v.t. interessieren **(in** für); be ～**ed in** sb./sth. sich für jmdn./etw. interessieren; **sb. is** ～**ed by** sb./sth. jmd./etw. erregt jmds. Interesse; see also **interested**

interested /'ɪntrəstɪd, 'ɪntrɪstɪd/ adj. **(a)** (taking or showing interest) interessiert; **be** ～ **in music/football/sb.** sich für Musik/Fußball/jmdn. interessieren; **be** ～ **in doing sth.** sich dafür interessieren, etw. zu tun; **he is** ～ **in buying a car** er würde gern ein Auto kaufen; **not** ～ **in his work** nicht an seiner Arbeit interessiert; **(b)** (not impartial) voreingenommen

interest-free adj. unverzinslich ‹Schuldverschreibung›; zinsfrei ‹Darlehen›

interesting /'ɪntrəstɪŋ, 'ɪntrɪstɪŋ/ adj. interessant

interestingly /'ɪntrəstɪŋlɪ, 'ɪntrɪstɪŋlɪ/ adv. interessant; ～ **[enough]**, …: interessanterweise …

'**interest rate** n. Zinssatz, der; Zinsfuß, der

interface /'ɪntəfeɪs/ n. **(a)** (surface) Grenzfläche, die; **(b)** (Computing) Interface, der (fachspr.); Schnittstelle, die

interfere /ɪntə'fɪə(r)/ v.i. **(a)** (meddle) sich einmischen **(in** in + Akk.); ～ **with sth.** sich an etw. (Dat.) zu schaffen machen; **(b)** (come into opposition) in Konflikt geraten **(with** mit); ～ **with sth.** etw. beeinträchtigen; ～ **with sb.'s plans** jmds. Pläne durchkreuzen; **(c)** (Radio, Telev.) stören **(with** Akk.)

interference /ɪntə'fɪərəns/ n. **(a)** (interfering) Einmischung, die; **(b)** (Radio, Telev.) Störung, die

interim /'ɪntərɪm/ **1** n. **in the** ～: in der Zwischenzeit. **2** adj. **(a)** (intervening) dazwischenliegend; **(b)** (temporary, provisional) vorläufig ‹Vereinbarung, Bericht, Anordnung, Zustand, Maßnahme›; Zwischen‹lösung, -abkommen, -kredit›; Übergangs‹regierung, -regelung, -hilfe›

interior /ɪn'tɪərɪə(r)/ **1** adj. **(a)** inner…; Innen‹fläche, -einrichtung, -wand›; **(b)** (inland) im Landesinneren befindlich; **(c)** (internal, domestic) Inlands-. **2** n. **(a)** (inland region) [Landes]innere, das; **(b)** (～ part) Innere, das; **(c)** ([picture of] inside of building, room, etc.) Innere, das; (picture) Interieur, das; **(d)** (Cinemat.) Innenaufnahme, die

interject /ɪntə'dʒekt/ v.t. (interpose) einwerfen ‹Behauptung, Bemerkung, Frage›; ～ **remarks** Einwürfe od. Zwischenbemerkungen machen

interjection /ɪntə'dʒekʃn/ n. (exclamation) Ausruf, der; (Ling.) Interjektion, die

interlock /ɪntə'lɒk/ **1** v.i. sich ineinander haken; ‹Teile eines Puzzles:› sich zusammenfügen. **2** v.t. (lock together) zusammenfügen; verflechten ‹Fasern›

interloper /'ɪntələʊpə(r)/ n. Eindringling, der

interlude /'ɪntəlu:d, 'ɪntəlju:d/ n. **(a)** (Theatre: break) Pause, die; **(b)** (occurring in break) Zwischenspiel, das; Intermezzo, das; **musical** ～: musikalisches Zwischenspiel; **(c)** (intervening time) kurze Phase od. Periode; **(d)** (event interposed) Intermezzo, das

intermediary /ɪntə'mi:dɪərɪ/ n. Vermittler, der/Vermittlerin, die

intermediate /ɪntə'mi:dʒət/ **1** adj. **(a)** Zwischen-; **(b)** (Educ.) Mittel‹stufe, -schule›. **2** n. fortgeschrittener Anfänger

interminable /ɪn'tɜ:mɪnəbl/ adj. (lit. or fig.) endlos

intermingle /ɪntə'mɪŋgl/ **1** v.i. sich vermischen; ‹Personen:› miteinander in Kontakt treten. **2** v.t. vermischen

intermission /ɪntə'mɪʃn/ n. **(a)** (pause) Unterbrechung, die; **(b)** (period of inactivity) Pause, die

intermittent /ɪntə'mɪtənt/ adj. in Abständen auftretend ‹Signal, Fehler, Geräusch›; **be** ～: in Abständen auftreten; **there was** ～ **rain all day** es hat den ganzen Tag mit kurzen Unterbrechungen geregnet

intermittently /ɪntə'mɪtəntlɪ/ adv. in Abständen

intern /ɪn'tɜ:n/ v.t. gefangen halten; internieren ‹Kriegsgefangenen usw.›

internal /ɪn'tɜ:nl/ adj. **(a)** inner…; Innen‹winkel, -durchmesser, -fläche, -druck, -gewinde, -abmessungen›; **(b)** (Physiol.) inner… ‹Blutung, Sekretion, Verletzung›; **(c)** (intrinsic) inner… ‹Logik, Stimmigkeit›; **(d)** (within country) inner… ‹Angelegenheiten, Frieden, Probleme›; Binnen‹handel, -markt›; innenpolitisch ‹Angelegenheiten, Streitigkeiten, Probleme›; (within organization) [betriebs-/partei]intern ‹Auseinandersetzung, Post, Verfahren[sweise]›; inner[betrieblich-/kirchlich] -gewerkschaftlich usw.] ‹Streitigkeiten›; **(e)** (Med.) innerlich ‹Anwendung›; **(f)** (of the mind) inner… ‹Monolog, Regung, Widerstände, Groll›

internal: ～ '**clock** n. innere Uhr; ～**com'bustion engine** n. Verbrennungsmotor, der

internally /ɪn'tɜ:nəlɪ/ adv. innerlich; (within organization) [partei-/betriebs]intern

internal: ～ '**medicine** n. innere Medizin; **I**～ '**Revenue Service** n. (Amer.) ≈ Finanzamt, das

international /ɪntə'næʃənl/ **1** *adj.* international; ~ **travel** Auslandsreisen *Pl.;* ~ **team** (Sport) Nationalmannschaft, *die.* **2** *n.* **(a)** (Sport: contest) Länderkampf, *der;* (in team sports) Länderspiel, *das;* **(b)** (Sport: participant) Internationale, *der/die;* (in team sports) Nationalspieler, *der/* -spielerin, *die*

international: ~ call *n.* (Teleph.) Auslandsgespräch, *das;* ~ **date-line** ⇒ **date-line;** ~ **'law** *n.* Völkerrecht, *das;* **I~ 'Monetary Fund** *n.* internationaler Währungsfonds

Internet /'ɪntənet/ *n.* **the** ~ das Internet; **on the** ~: im Internet; ~ **connection** Internetanschluss, *der*

internment /ɪn'tɜ:nmənt/ *n.* Internierung, *die*

interplay /'ɪntəpleɪ/ *n.* **(a)** (interaction) Wechselwirkung, *die;* **(b)** (reciprocal action) Zusammenspiel, *das*

Interpol /'ɪntəpɒl/ *n.* Interpol, *die*

interpose /ɪntə'pəʊz/ **1** *v.t.* **(a)** (insert) dazwischenlegen; ~ **sth. between sb./sth. and sb./sth.** etw. zwischen jmdn./etw. und jmdn./etw. bringen; **(b)** einwerfen ⟨*Frage, Bemerkung*⟩. **2** *v.i.* [kurz] unterbrechen

interpret /ɪn'tɜ:prɪt/ **1** *v.t.* **(a)** interpretieren; deuten ⟨*Traum, Zeichen*⟩; **(b)** (between languages) dolmetschen; **(c)** (decipher) entziffern ⟨*Schrift, Inschrift*⟩. **2** *v.i.* dolmetschen

interpretation /ɪntɜ:prɪ'teɪʃn/ *n.* **(a)** Interpretation, *die;* (of dream, symptoms) Deutung, *die;* **(b)** (deciphering) Entzifferung, *die*

interpreter /ɪn'tɜ:prɪtə(r)/ *n.* **(a)** (between languages) Dolmetscher, *der/*Dolmetscherin, *die;* **(b)** (of dreams, hieroglyphics) Deuter, *der;* **(c)** (performer on stage etc.) Interpret, *der/* Interpretin, *die*

interrelated /ɪntərɪ'leɪtɪd/ *adj.* zusammenhängend ⟨*Tatsachen, Ereignisse, Themen*⟩; verwandt ⟨*Sprachen, Fachgebiete*⟩; **be** ~: zusammenhängen/verwandt sein

interrogate /ɪn'terəgeɪt/ *v.t.* vernehmen ⟨*Zeugen, Angeklagten*⟩; verhören ⟨*Angeklagten, Verdächtigen, Spion, Gefangenen*⟩; ausfragen ⟨*Freund, Kind usw.*⟩

interrogation /ɪnterə'geɪʃn/ *n.* (interrogating) Verhör, *das;* **under** ~: beim Verhör; **be under** ~: verhört werden

interrogative /ɪntə'rɒgətɪv/ *adj.* **(a)** (having question form) Frage-; fragend ⟨*Tonfall*⟩; **(b)** (Ling.) Interrogativ⟨*pronomen, -adverb, -form*⟩

interrupt /ɪntə'rʌpt/ **1** *v.t.* unterbrechen; ~ **sb.'s sleep** jmds. Schlaf stören; **don't** ~ **me when I'm busy** stör mich nicht, wenn ich zu tun habe. **2** *v.i.* stören; unterbrechen

interruption /ɪntə'rʌpʃn/ *n.* (of work etc.) Unterbrechung, *die;* Störung, *die;* (of peace, sleep) Störung, *die;* (of services) [zeitweiliger] Ausfall

intersect /ɪntə'sekt/ **1** *v.t.* **(a)** ⟨*Kanäle, Schluchten, [Quarz]adern:*⟩ durchziehen ⟨*Land, Boden*⟩; **(b)** (Geom.) schneiden. **2** *v.i.* **(a)** ⟨*Straßen:*⟩ sich kreuzen; **(b)** (Geom.) sich schneiden

intersection /ɪntə'sekʃn/ *n.* **(a)** (intersecting; road etc. junction) Kreuzung, *die;* **(b)** (Geom.) **[point of]** ~: Schnittpunkt, *der*

intersperse /ɪntə'spɜ:s/ *v.t.* **(a)** (scatter) [hier und da] einfügen; **(b) be** ~**d with** durchsetzt sein mit

intertwine /ɪntə'twaɪn/ **1** *v.t.* flechten **(in** in + Akk.). **2** *v.i.* sich [ineinander] verschlingen

interval /'ɪntəvl/ *n.* **(a)** (intervening space) Zwischenraum, *der;* (intervening time) [Zeit]abstand, *der;* **at** ~**s** in Abständen; **after an** ~ **of three years** nach [Ablauf von] drei Jahren; **(b)** (break; also Brit. Theatre etc.) Pause, *die;* **(c)** (period) Pause, *die*

intervene /ɪntə'vi:n/ *v.i.* **(a)** [vermittelnd] eingreifen **(in** in + Akk.); **if nothing** ~**s** wenn nichts dazwischenkommt; **(b) the intervening years** die dazwischenliegenden Jahre

intervention /ɪntə'venʃn/ *n.* Eingreifen, *das;* Intervention, *die* (bes. Politik)

interview /'ɪntəvju:/ **1** *n.* **(a)** (for job etc.) Vorstellungsgespräch, *das;* **(b)** (Journ., Radio, Telev.) Interview, *das.* **2** *v.t.* Vorstellungsgespräch[e] führen mit ⟨*Stellen-, Studienbewerber*⟩; interviewen ⟨*Politiker, Filmstar, Konsumenten usw.*⟩; vernehmen ⟨*Zeugen*⟩

interviewer /'ɪntəvju:ə(r)/ *n.* (reporter, pollster, etc.) Interviewer, *der/*Interviewerin, *die;* (for job etc.) Leiter/Leiterin des Vorstellungsgesprächs

intestate /ɪn'testət/ *adj.* Intestat⟨*erbe, -erbfolge, -nachlass*⟩; **die** ~: ohne Hinterlassung eines Testaments sterben

intestinal /ɪn'testɪnl/ *adj.* (Med.) Darm-; intestinal (fachspr.)

intestine /ɪn'testɪn/ *n. in sing. or pl.* ▶672│ Darm, *der;* Gedärme *Pl.*

intimacy /'ɪntɪməsɪ/ *n.* **(a)** (state) Vertrautheit, *die;* (close personal relationship) enges [Freundschafts]verhältnis; **(b)** (euphem.: sexual intercourse) Intimität, *die*

intimate 1 /'ɪntɪmət/ *adj.* **(a)** (close, closely acquainted) eng ⟨*Freund, Freundschaft, Beziehung, Verhältnis*⟩; vertraulich ⟨*Ton*⟩; **be on** ~ **terms with sb.** zu jmdm. ein enges od. vertrautes Verhältnis haben; **(b)** (euphem.: having sexual intercourse) intim ⟨*Beziehungen*⟩; **be/become** ~ **with sb.** mit jmdm. intim sein/werden; **(c)** (from close familiarity) ~ **knowledge of sth.** genaue od. intime Kenntnis einer Sache; **(d)** (closely personal) persönlich ⟨*Problem*⟩; privat ⟨*Angelegenheit, Gefühl, Dinge*⟩; geheim ⟨*Gedanken*⟩; (euphem.) Intim⟨*bereich, -spray*⟩. **2** /'ɪntɪmət/ *n.* (close friend) Vertraute, *der/die.* **3** /'ɪntɪmeɪt/ *v.t.* **(a)** ~ **sth. [to sb.]** (make known) [jmdm.] etw. mitteilen; (show clearly) [jmdm.] etw. deutlich machen od. zu verstehen geben; **(b)** (imply) andeuten

intimately /'ɪntɪmətlɪ/ *adv.* genau[estens] ⟨*kennen*⟩; bestens ⟨*vertraut*⟩; eng ⟨*verbinden*⟩

intimation /ɪntɪ'meɪʃn/ *n.* (hint) Andeutung, *die;* (of trouble, anger) Anzeichen, *das*

intimidate /ɪn'tɪmɪdeɪt/ *v.t.* einschüchtern

intimidation /ɪntɪmɪ'deɪʃn/ *n.* Einschüchterung, *die*

into /before vowel 'ɪntʊ, before consonant 'ɪntə/ *prep.* in (+ Akk.); (against) gegen; **I went out** ~ **the street** ich ging auf die Straße hinaus; **they disappeared** ~ **the night** sie verschwanden in die Nacht hinein; **4** ~ **20 = 5** 20 durch 4 = 5; **until well** ~ **this century** bis weit in unser Jahrhundert hinein; **translate sth.** ~ **English** etw. ins Englische übersetzen

intolerable /ɪn'tɒlərəbl/ *adj.* unerträglich; **it's** ~: es ist nicht auszuhalten

intolerance /ɪn'tɒlərəns/ *n., no pl.* Intoleranz, *die,* Unduldsamkeit, *die* **(of** gegenüber)

intolerant /ɪn'tɒlərənt/ *adj.* intolerant, unduldsam **(of** gegenüber)

intonation /ɪntə'neɪʃn/ *n.* Intonation, *die* (Sprachw.); Sprachmelodie, *die*

intoxicate /ɪn'tɒksɪkeɪt/ *v.t.* (make drunk) betrunken machen; **be/become** ~**d** betrunken sein/werden

intoxicating /ɪn'tɒksɪkeɪtɪŋ/ *adj.* berauschend ⟨*Wirkung, Schönheit*⟩; mitreißend ⟨*Worte, Rhythmus*⟩; ~ **liquors** alkoholische Getränke

intoxication /ɪntɒksɪ'keɪʃn/ *n.* Rausch, *der*

intractable /ɪn'træktəbl/ *adj.* widerspenstig ⟨*Verhalten, Kind, Tier*⟩; hartnäckig ⟨*Krankheit, Schmerzen, Problem*⟩

intransigence /ɪn'trænsɪdʒəns, ɪn'trænzɪdʒəns/ *n., no pl.* ⇒ **intransigent:** Kompromisslosigkeit, *die;* Unnachgiebigkeit, *die;* Intransigenz, *die* (geh.); Unerschütterlichkeit, *die*

intransigent /ɪn'trænsɪdʒənt, ɪn'trænzɪdʒənt/ *adj.* kompromisslos, unnachgiebig, (geh.) intransigent ⟨*Haltung, Einstellung*⟩; unerschütterlich ⟨*Wille, Grundsätze, Glaube*⟩

intra-uterine /ɪntrə'ju:təraɪn/ *adj.* (Med.) intrauterin; ~ **[contraceptive] device** Intrauterinpessar, *das*

'in-tray *n.* Ablage für Eingänge

intrepid /ɪn'trepɪd/ *adj.* unerschrocken

intricacy /'ɪntrɪkəsɪ/ *n.* **(a)** *no pl.* (quality) Kompliziertheit, *die;* **(b)** *in pl.* (things) Feinheiten *Pl.*

intricate /'ɪntrɪkət/ *adj.* verschlungen ⟨*Pfad, Windung*⟩; kompliziert ⟨*System, Muster, Werkstück, Aufgabe*⟩

intrigue /ɪn'tri:g/ *v.t.* faszinieren; **I'm** ~**d to find out what** ...: ich bin gespannt darauf, zu erfahren, was ... **2** *v.i.* ~ **against sb.** gegen jmdn. intrigieren; ~ **with sb.**

mit jmdm. Ränke schmieden *od.* Intrigen spinnen. **3** /ɪn 'triːg, 'ɪntriːg/ *n.* Intrige, *die*
intriguing /ɪn'triːgɪŋ/ *adj.*, **intriguingly** /ɪn'triːgɪŋlɪ/ *adv.* faszinierend
intrinsic /ɪn'trɪnsɪk, ɪn'trɪnzɪk/ *adj.* (inherent) innewohnend; inner… ⟨*Aufbau, Logik*⟩; (essential) wesentlich, (Philos.) essenziell ⟨*Eigenschaft, Bestandteil, Mangel*⟩; ∼ **value** innerer Wert; (of sth. concrete) Eigenwert, *der*
intro /'ɪntrəʊ/ *n., pl.* ∼**s** (coll.) (presentation) Vorstellung, *die*; (Mus.) Einleitung, *die;* Intro, *das* (fachspr.)
introduce /ɪntrə'djuːs/ *v.t.* (a) (bring in) [erstmals] einführen ⟨*Ware, Tier, Pflanze*⟩ (into in + *Akk.; from* … into von … nach); einleiten ⟨*Maßnahmen*⟩; einschleppen ⟨*Krankheit*⟩; (b) einführen ⟨*Katheter, Schlauch*⟩ (into in + *Akk.*); stecken ⟨*Schlüssel, Draht, Rohr, Schlauch*⟩ (into in + *Akk.*); (c) (bring into use) einführen ⟨*Neuerung, Verfahren, Brauch, Nomenklatur*⟩; aufbringen ⟨*Schlagwort*⟩; (d) (make known) vorstellen; einführen ⟨*Vortragenden*⟩; ∼ **oneself/sb. [to sb.]** sich/jmdn. [jmdm.] vorstellen; **I** ∼**d them to each other** ich machte sie miteinander bekannt; **I don't think we've been** ∼**d** ich glaube, wir kennen uns noch nicht; (e) (usher in, begin, precede) einleiten ⟨*Buch, Thema, Musikstück, Epoche*⟩; (f) (present) ankündigen ⟨*Programm, Darsteller*⟩; (g) (Parl.) einbringen ⟨*Antrag, Entwurf, Gesetz*⟩; einleiten ⟨*Reform*⟩
introduction /ɪntrə'dʌkʃn/ *n.* (a) (of methods, measures, process, machinery) Einführen, *das;* Einführung, *die;* (of rules) Aufstellung, *die;* (b) (formal presentation) Vorstellung, *die;* (into society) Einführung, *die;* (of reform) Einleiten, *das;* **do the** ∼**s** die Anwesenden miteinander bekannt machen; **letter of** ∼: Empfehlungsschreiben, *das;* (c) (preliminary matter) Einleitung, *die*
intro'duction agency *n.* Partnervermittlung[sagentur], *die;* **join an** ∼: sich bei einer Partnervermittlung registrieren lassen
introductory /ɪntrə'dʌktərɪ/ *adj.* einleitend; Einführungs⟨*kurs, -vortrag*⟩; Einleitungs⟨*kapitel, -rede*⟩
introspective /ɪntrə'spektɪv/ *adj.* in sich (*Akk.*) gerichtet; verinnerlicht; introspektiv (geh., Psych.)
introvert 1 /'ɪntrəvɜːt/ *n.* Introvertierte, *der/die;* introvertierter Mensch; **be an** ∼: introvertiert sein. **2** *adj.* introvertiert
introverted /ɪntrə'vɜːtɪd/ *adj.* introvertiert
intrude /ɪn'truːd/ **1** *v.i.* stören; ∼ **[up]on sb.'s grief/leisure time/privacy** jmdn. in seiner Trauer stören/ jmds. Freizeit beanspruchen/in jmds. Privatsphäre (*Akk.*) eindringen; ∼ **in[to] sb.'s affairs/conversation** sich in jmds. Angelegenheiten / Unterhaltung (*Akk*) einmischen. **2** *v.t.* aufdrängen (into, [up]on *Dat.*)
intruder /ɪn'truːdə(r)/ *n.* Eindringling, *der;* (Mil.) Intruder, *der*
in'truder alarm *n.* Einbruchmeldeanlage, *die*
intrusion /ɪn'truːʒn/ *n.* (a) (intruding) Störung, *die;* (b) (into building, country, etc.) [gewaltsames] Eindringen; (Mil.) Einmarsch, *der* (**into** in + *Akk.*); (c) (forcing oneself in) Einmischung, *die* (**upon** in + *Akk.*)
intrusive /ɪn'truːsɪv/ *adj.* aufdringlich ⟨*Person*⟩
intuition /ɪntjuːˈɪʃn/ *n.* Intuition, *die;* **have an** ∼ **that** …: eine Eingebung haben *od.* intuitiv spüren, dass …
intuitive /ɪn'tjuːɪtɪv/ *adj.* intuitiv; gefühlsmäßig ⟨*Ablehnung, Beurteilung*⟩; instinktiv ⟨*Annahme, Gefühl*⟩
inundate /'ɪnəndeɪt/ *v.t.* überschwemmen; ⟨*Meer:*⟩ überfluten; (fig.) (with inquiries, letters) überschwemmen; (with work, praise) überhäufen; ∼**d with tourists** von Touristen überlaufen
inure /ɪ'njʊə(r)/ *v.t.* gewöhnen (**to** an + *Akk.*); (toughen) abhärten (**to** gegen); **become** ∼**d to sth.** sich an etw. (*Akk.*) gewöhnen
invade /ɪn'veɪd/ *v.t.* (a) einfallen in ⟨*Gebiet, Staat*⟩; **Poland was** ∼**d by the Germans** die Deutschen marschierten in Polen (*Akk.*) ein; (b) (swarm into) ⟨*Touristen, Kinder:*⟩ überschwemmen; (c) (fig.) ⟨*unangenehmes Gefühl, Krankheit, Schwäche:*⟩ befallen; ⟨*Krankheit, Seuche, Unwetter:*⟩ heimsuchen; (d) (encroach upon) stören ⟨*Ruhe, Frieden*⟩; eindringen in (+ *Akk.*) ⟨*Bereich, Privatsphäre*⟩

invader /ɪn'veɪdə(r)/ *n.* Angreifer, *der;* Invasor, *der* (bes. Milit.)
invalid¹ 1 /'ɪnvəlɪd/ *n.* (Brit.) Kranke, *der/die;* (disabled person) Körperbehinderte, *der/die;* (from war injuries) Kriegsinvalide *der/*-invalidin, *die.* **2** *adj.* (Brit.) körperbehindert. **3** /'ɪnvəliːd, ɪnvə'liːd/ *v.t.* ∼ **home** *or* **out** als dienstuntauglich entlassen
invalid² /ɪn'vælɪd/ *adj.* nicht schlüssig ⟨*Argument, Behauptung, Folgerung, Theorie*⟩; nicht zulässig ⟨*Annahme*⟩; ungerechtfertigt ⟨*Forderung, Vorwurf*⟩; ungültig ⟨*Fahrkarte, Garantie, Vertrag, Testament, Ehe*⟩
invalidate /ɪn'vælɪdeɪt/ *v.t.* aufheben; widerlegen ⟨*Theorie, These, Behauptung*⟩
invalid /'ɪnvəlɪd/: ∼ **carriage** *n.* Kranken[fahr]stuhl, *der;* ∼ **chair** *n.* Rollstuhl, *der*
invaluable /ɪn'væljʊəbl/ *adj.* unbezahlbar; unersetzlich ⟨*Mitarbeiter, Person*⟩; unschätzbar ⟨*Dienst, Verdienst, Hilfe, Bedeutung*⟩; außerordentlich wichtig ⟨*Rolle, Funktion*⟩; außerordentlich wertvoll ⟨*Rat[schlag]*⟩
invariable /ɪn'veərɪəbl/ *adj.* (a) (fixed) unveränderlich ⟨*Wert, Einheit*⟩; (b) (always the same) [stets] gleich bleibend ⟨*Druck, Temperatur, Höflichkeit*⟩
invariably /ɪn'veərɪəblɪ/ *adv.* immer; ausnahmslos ⟨*falsch, richtig*⟩
invasion /ɪn'veɪʒn/ *n.* (a) (of troops, virus, locusts) Invasion, *die;* (of weeds etc.) massenweise Ausbreitung; (intrusion) [überfallartiges] Eindringen (**of** in + *Akk.*); **the** ∼ **of Belgium by German troops** der Einmarsch deutscher Truppen in Belgien; (b) (encroachment) ⇒ **invade d:** Störung, *die;* Eindringen, *das*
invective /ɪn'vektɪv/ *n.* (a) (abusive language) Beschimpfungen *Pl.;* (b) (violent attack in words) Schmähung, *die;* Invektive, *die* (geh.)
inveigh /ɪn'veɪ/ *v.i.* ∼ **against sb./sth.** über jmdn./etw. schimpfen *od.* sich empören
invent /ɪn'vent/ *v.t.* erfinden
invention /ɪn'venʃn/ *n.* (a) (thing invented, inventing) Erfindung, *die;* (concept) Idee, *die;* (b) (inventiveness) Erfindungsgabe, *die;* (c) (fictitious story) Erfindung, *die;* Lüge, *die*
inventive /ɪn'ventɪv/ *adj.* (a) schöpferisch ⟨*Person, Kraft, Geist, Begabung*⟩; fantasievoll ⟨*Künstler, Kind*⟩; (b) (produced with originality) originell; einfallsreich
inventor /ɪn'ventə(r)/ *n.* Erfinder, *der/*Erfinderin, *die*
inventory /'ɪnvəntərɪ/ *n.* (a) (list) Bestandsliste, *die;* **make** *or* **take an** ∼ **of sth.** von etw. ein Inventar aufstellen; (b) (stock) Lagerbestand, *der*
inverse /ɪn'vɜːs, 'ɪnvɜːs/ **1** *adj.* umgekehrt ⟨*Reihenfolge*⟩. **2** *n.* (opposite) Gegenteil, *das;* (inversion) Umkehrung, *die*
inversion /ɪn'vɜːʃn/ *n.* (a) (turning upside down) Umdrehen, *das;* (b) (reversal of role, relation) Umkehrung, *die;* (c) (Ling., Meteorol., Mus.) Inversion, *die*
invert /ɪn'vɜːt/ *v.t.* (a) (turn upside down) umstülpen; (b) umkehren ⟨*Wortstellung*⟩; vertauschen ⟨*Wörter*⟩
invertebrate /ɪn'vɜːtɪbrət, ɪn'vɜːtɪbreɪt/ (Zool.) **1** *adj.* wirbellos. **2** *n.* wirbelloses Tier
inverted /ɪn'vɜːtɪd/: ∼ **'commas** *n. pl.* (Brit.) Anführungszeichen *Pl.;* Gänsefüßchen *Pl.* (ugs.); ∼ **'snob** *n.* Edelproletarier, *der* (salopp); ∼ **'snobbery** *n.* Edelproletariertum, *das* (salopp)
invest /ɪn'vest/ **1** *v.t.* (a) (Finance) anlegen (**in** in + *Dat.*); investieren (**in** in + *Dat. od. Akk.*); ∼ **time and effort in sth.** Zeit und Mühe in etw. (*Akk.*) investieren; (b) ∼ **sb. with** jmdm. übertragen ⟨*Aufgabe, Amt, Leitung*⟩; jmdm. verleihen ⟨*Orden, Titel*⟩; (c) ∼ **sb. with sth.** einer Sache (*Dat.*) etw. verleihen. **2** *v.i.* investieren (**in** in + *Akk.*, **with** bei); ∼ **in sth.** (coll.: buy) sich (*Dat.*) etw. zulegen (ugs.)
investigate /ɪn'vestɪgeɪt/ **1** *v.t.* untersuchen; prüfen ⟨*Rechtsfrage, Material, Methode*⟩; ermitteln ⟨*Produktionskosten*⟩. **2** *v.i.* nachforschen; ⟨*Kripo, Staatsanwaltschaft:*⟩ ermitteln
investigation /ɪnvestɪ'geɪʃn/ *n.* ⇒ **investigate:** Untersuchung, *die;* Prüfung, *die;* Ermittlung, *die;* **sth. is under** ∼: etw. wird überprüft; **sb. is under** ∼: gegen jmdn. wird ermittelt

investigative /ɪn'vestɪgətɪv/ *adj.* detektivisch; **∼ journalism** Enthüllungsjournalismus, *der*

investigator /ɪn'vestɪgeɪtə(r)/ *n.* Ermittler, *der*/Ermittlerin, *die;* [**private**] **∼:** [Privat]detektiv, *der*/-detektivin, *die*

investiture /ɪn'vestɪtʃə(r)/ *n.* Investitur, *die*

investment /ɪn'vestmənt/ *n.* (**a**) (of money) Investition, *die* (auch fig.); Anlage, *die;* (fig.) Einsatz, *der;* Aufwand, *der; attrib.* Investitions-; Anlage-; **∼ of capital** Kapitalanlage, *die;* **∼ trust** Investmenttrust, *der;* Investmentgesellschaft, *die;* (**b**) (money invested) angelegtes Geld; (**c**) (property) Kapitalanlage, *die;* **be a good ∼** (fig.) sich bezahlt machen

investor /ɪn'vestə(r)/ *n.* Investor, *der*/Investorin, *die;* [Kapital]anleger, *der*/-anlegerin, *die;* **small ∼s** Kleinanleger

inveterate /ɪn'vetərət/ *adj.* (**a**) (deep-rooted) unüberwindbar ‹ *Vorurteil, Misstrauen* ›; unversöhnlich ‹ *Hass* ›; unverbesserlich ‹ *Faulheit usw.* ›; (**b**) (habitual) eingefleischt ‹ *Trinker, Raucher* ›; unverbesserlich ‹ *Lügner* ›

invidious /ɪn'vɪdɪəs/ *adj.* undankbar ‹ *Aufgabe* ›; unpassend, unfair ‹ *Vergleich, Bemerkung* ›

invigorate /ɪn'vɪgəreɪt/ *v.t.* (make vigorous) stärken; (physically) kräftigen

invincible /ɪn'vɪnsɪbl/ *adj.* unbesiegbar; unerschütterlich ‹ *Entschlossenheit, Mut* ›

inviolable /ɪn'vaɪələbl/ *adj.* unantastbar

inviolate /ɪn'vaɪələt/ *adj.* unversehrt; ungestört ‹ *Friede, Ruhe* ›; nicht verletzt ‹ *Abkommen* ›

invisibility /ɪnvɪzɪ'bɪlɪtɪ/ *n.* Unsichtbarkeit, *die*

invisible /ɪn'vɪzɪbl/ *adj.* (also Econ.) unsichtbar; (hidden because of fog etc.; too small) nicht sichtbar; **∼ mending** Kunststopfen, *das;* **∼ earnings** (Commerc.) unsichtbare Einkünfte

invitation /ɪnvɪ'teɪʃn/ *n.* (lit. or fig.) Einladung, *die;* **at sb.'s ∼:** auf jmds. Einladung; **an [open] ∼ to thieves** eine Aufforderung zum Diebstahl

invite /ɪn'vaɪt/ *v.t.* (**a**) (request to come) einladen; **before an ∼d audience** vor geladenen Gästen; (**b**) (request to do sth.) auffordern; **she ∼d him to accompany her** sie forderte ihn auf *od.* lud ihn ein, sie zu begleiten; (**c**) (bring on) herausfordern ‹ *Kritik, Verhängnis* ›; **you're inviting ridicule** du machst dich lächerlich *od.* zum Gespött

inviting /ɪn'vaɪtɪŋ/ *adj.* einladend; verlockend ‹ *Gedanke, Vorstellung, Aussicht* ›; freundlich ‹ *Klima* ›; ansprechend ‹ *Anblick* ›

invoice /'ɪnvɔɪs/ **1** *n.* (bill) Rechnung, *die;* (list) Lieferschein, *der.* **2** *v.t.* (**a**) (make ∼ for) eine Rechnung ausstellen für; (**b**) (send ∼ to) **∼ sb.** jmdm. eine Rechnung schicken; **∼ sb. for sth.** jmdm. etw. in Rechnung stellen

invoke /ɪn'vəʊk/ *v.t.* (**a**) (call on) anrufen; (**b**) (appeal to) sich berufen auf (+ *Akk.*); **∼ an example/sth. as an example** ein Beispiel/etw. als Beispiel anführen

involuntarily /ɪn'vɒləntərɪlɪ/ *adv.*, **involuntary** /ɪn'vɒləntərɪ/ *adj.* unwillkürlich

involve /ɪn'vɒlv/ *v.t.* (**a**) (implicate) verwickeln; (**b**) (draw in as a participant) **∼ sb. in a game/fight** jmdn. an einem Spiel beteiligen/in eine Schlägerei [mit] hineinziehen; **become** *or* **get ∼d in a fight** in eine Schlägerei verwickelt werden; **be ∼d in a project** (employed) an einem Projekt mitarbeiten; **get ∼d with sb.** sich mit jmdm. einlassen; (sexually, emotionally) eine Beziehung mit jmdm. anfangen; (**c**) (include) enthalten; (contain implicitly) beinhalten; (**d**) (be necessarily accompanied by) mit sich bringen; (require as accompaniment) erfordern; (cause, mean) bedeuten

involved /ɪn'vɒlvd/ *adj.* verwickelt; (complicated) kompliziert; (complex) komplex

involvement /ɪn'vɒlvmənt/ *n.* (**a**) **his ∼ in the company** seine Beteiligung an der Firma; **I don't know the extent of his ∼ in this affair** ich weiß nicht, inwieweit er mit dieser Sache zu tun hat; (**b**) (implication) **∼ in a conflict** Einmischung in einen Konflikt; **have an ∼ with sb.** (sexually) eine Affäre mit jmdm. haben

inward /'ɪnwəd/ **1** *adj.* (**a**) (situated within) inner...; (**b**) (mental, spiritual) inner... ‹ *Impuls, Regung, Friede, Kampf* ›; innerlich (geh.) ‹ *Leben* ›; (**c**) (directed inside) nach innen gehend; nach innen gerichtet. **2** *adv.* einwärts ‹ *gerichtet,*

gebogen ›; **open ∼:** nach innen öffnen; **an ∼-looking person** (fig.) ein in sich (*Akk.*) gekehrter Mensch

inwards /'ɪnwədz/ ⇒ **inward 2**

iodine /'aɪədiːn, 'aɪədɪn/ *n.* Jod, *das*

ion /'aɪən/ *n.* (Phys., Chem.) Ion, *das*

iota /aɪ'əʊtə/ *n.* Jota, *das* (geh.); **not an** *or* **one ∼:** nicht ein Jota (geh.); kein Jota (geh.); **there's not an ∼ of truth in that** daran ist nicht ein Fünkchen Wahrheit

IOU /aɪəʊ'juː/ *n.* Schuldschein, *der*

IPA *abbr.* **International Phonetic Alphabet/Association** IPA

IQ *abbr.* **intelligence quotient** IQ, *der;* **IQ-test** IQ-Test, *der*

IRA *abbr.* **Irish Republican Army** IRA, *die*

Iran /ɪ'rɑːn/ *pr. n.* Iran, *der*

Iranian /ɪ'reɪnɪən/ ▶ 897 |, ▶ 947 | **1** *adj.* iranisch; **sb. is ∼:** jmd. ist Iraner/Iranerin. **2** *n.* (**a**) (person) Iraner, *der*/Iranerin, *die;* (**b**) (Ling.) Iranisch, *das*

Iraq /ɪ'rɑːk/ *pr. n.* Irak, *der*

Iraqi /ɪ'rɑːkɪ/ ▶ 897 |, ▶ 947 | **1** *adj.* irakisch; **sb is ∼:** jmd. ist Iraker/Irakerin. **2** *n.* (**a**) (person) Iraker, *der*/Irakerin, *die;* (**b**) (Ling.) Irakisch, *das*

irascible /ɪ'ræsɪbl/ *adj.* (hot-tempered) aufbrausend; (irritable) reizbar

irate /aɪ'reɪt/ *adj.* wütend ‹ *Person, Menge* ›; erbost (geh.) ‹ *Person* ›

Ireland /'aɪələnd/ *pr. n.* [**Republic of**] **∼:** Irland (*das*)

iris /'aɪərɪs/ *n.* (**a**) (Anat.) Iris, *die;* Regenbogenhaut, *die;* (**b**) (Bot.) Iris, *die;* Schwertlilie, *die*

Irish /'aɪərɪʃ/ ▶ 897 |, ▶ 947 | **1** *adj.* irisch; **sb. is ∼:** jmd. ist Ire/Irin; **∼ joke** Irenwitz, *der.* **2** *n.* (**a**) (language) Irisch, *das; see also* **English 2 a;** (**b**) *constr. as pl.* **the ∼:** die Iren

Irish: ∼man /'aɪərɪʃmən/ *n., pl.* **∼men** /'aɪərɪʃmən/ Ire, *der;* **∼ Re'public** *pr. n.* Irische Republik; **∼ 'Sea** *pr. n.* Irische See; **∼woman** *n.* Irin, *die*

irk /ɜːk/ *v.t.* ärgern

irksome /'ɜːksəm/ *adj.* lästig

iron /'aɪən/ **1** *n.* (**a**) (metal) Eisen, *das;* **as hard as ∼:** eisenhart; **strike while the ∼ is hot** (prov.) das Eisen schmieden, solange es heiß ist (Spr.); (**b**) (tool) Eisen, *das;* **have several ∼s in the fire** mehrere Eisen im Feuer haben (ugs.); (**c**) (for smoothing) Bügeleisen, *das.* **2** *attrib. adj.* (**a**) (of iron) eisern; Eisen ‹ *platte usw.* ›; (**b**) (very robust) eisern ‹ *Konstitution* ›; (**c**) (unyielding) eisern; ehern (geh.) ‹ *Stoizismus* ›. **3** *v.t.* bügeln

∼ 'out *v.t.* herausbügeln ‹ *Falten* ›; (flatten) glätten ‹ *Papier* ›; (fig.) beseitigen ‹ *Kurve, Unregelmäßigkeit* ›; aus dem Weg räumen ‹ *Schwierigkeit, Problem* ›

Iron 'Curtain *n.* (fig.) Eiserner Vorhang

ironic /aɪ'rɒnɪk/, **ironical** /aɪ'rɒnɪkl/ *adjs.* ironisch; **it is ∼ that …:** es ist paradox, dass …

ironing /'aɪənɪŋ/ *n.* Bügeln, *das;* (things [to be] ironed) Bügelwäsche, *die;* **do the ∼:** bügeln

'ironing board *n.* Bügelbrett, *das*

ironmonger /'aɪənmʌŋgə(r)/ *n.* (Brit.) Eisenwarenhändler, *der*/-händlerin, *die; see also* **baker**

iron 'ore *n.* Eisenerz, *das*

irony /'aɪrənɪ/ *n.* Ironie, *die;* **the ∼ was that …:** die Ironie lag darin, dass …; das Ironische war, dass …

irradiate /ɪ'reɪdɪeɪt/ *v.t.* (Phys., Med., Gastr.) bestrahlen

irrational /ɪ'ræʃənl/ *adj.* (unreasonable) irrational (geh.); vernunftwidrig

irreconcilable /ɪ'rekənsaɪləbl/ *adj.* (**a**) (implacably hostile) unversöhnlich; (**b**) (incompatible) unvereinbar; unversöhnlich ‹ *Gegensätze* ›

irrecoverable /ɪrɪ'kʌvərəbl/ *adj.* unwiederbringlich verloren; endgültig ‹ *Verlust* ›

irrefutable /ɪ'refjʊtəbl, ɪrɪ'fjuːtəbl/ *adj.* unwiderlegbar

irregular /ɪ'regjʊlə(r)/ *adj.* (**a**) unkorrekt ‹ *Verhalten, Handlung usw.* ›; (**b**) (in duration, order, etc.) unregelmäßig; (**c**) (abnormal) sonderbar; eigenartig; (**d**) (not symmetrical) unregelmäßig; uneben ‹ *Oberfläche, Gelände* ›; (**e**) (Ling.) unregelmäßig

irregularity /ˌɪregjʊˈlærɪtɪ/ *n.* **(a)** (of behaviour, action) Unkorrektheit, *die;* (instance also) Unregelmäßigkeit, *die;* **(b)** (in duration, order, etc.) Unregelmäßigkeit, *die;* **(c)** (abnormality) Sonderbarkeit, *die,* Eigenartigkeit, *die;* **(d)** (lack of symmetry) Unregelmäßigkeit, *die;* (of surface) Unebenheit, *die*

irrelevant /ɪˈreləvənt/ *adj.* belanglos; irrelevant (geh.); **be ∼ to a subject** für ein Thema ohne Belang *od.* (geh.) irrelevant sein

irreparable /ɪˈrepərəbl/ *adj.* nicht wieder gutzumachend *nicht präd.;* irreparabel (geh., Med.)

irreplaceable /ɪrɪˈpleɪsəbl/ *adj.* **(a)** (not replaceable) nicht ersetzbar; **(b)** (of which the loss cannot be made good) unersetzlich

irrepressible /ɪrɪˈpresɪbl/ *adj.* nicht zu unterdrücken *nicht präd.;* unbezähmbar ‹*Neugier, Verlangen*›; unerschütterlich ‹*Optimismus*›; unbändig ‹*Freude, Entzücken*›; sonnig ‹*Gemüt*›; **he/she is ∼:** er/sie ist nicht unterzukriegen (ugs.)

irreproachable /ɪrɪˈprəʊtʃəbl/ *adj.* untadelig ‹*Charakter, Lebenswandel, Benehmen*›; unanfechtbar ‹*Ehrlichkeit*›; tadellos ‹*Kleidung, Manieren*›

irresistible /ɪrɪˈzɪstɪbl/ *adj.* unwiderstehlich; bestechend ‹*Argument*›

irresolute /ɪˈrezəluːt, ɪˈrezəljuːt/ *adj.* unentschlossen

irrespective /ɪrɪˈspektɪv/ *adj.* **∼ of** ungeachtet (+ *Gen.*); (independent of) unabhängig von

irresponsible /ɪrɪˈspɒnsɪbl/ *adj.* verantwortungslos ‹*Person*›; unverantwortlich ‹*Benehmen*›

irresponsibly /ɪrɪˈspɒnsɪblɪ/ *adv.* verantwortungslos; unverantwortlich

irretrievable /ɪrɪˈtriːvəbl/ *adj.* nicht mehr wiederzubekommen *nicht attr.;* (irreversible) endgültig ‹*Ruin, Verfall, Verlust*›; unheilbar ‹*Zerrüttung einer Ehe*›; ausweglos ‹*Situation*›

irreverent /ɪˈrevərənt/ *adj.* respektlos; (towards religious values or the dead) pietätlos (geh.)

irreversible /ɪrɪˈvɜːsɪbl/ *adj.* **(a)** (unalterable) unabänderlich, unumstößlich ‹*Entscheidung, Entschluss, Tatsache*›; unwiderruflich ‹*Entschluss, Entscheidung, Anordnung, Befehl usw.*›; **(b)** (not reversible) irreversibel (geh.) ‹*Vorgang*›; (inexorable) unaufhaltsam ‹*Entwicklung, Verfall*›

irrevocable /ɪˈrevəkəbl/ *adj.* unwiderruflich

irrigate /ˈɪrɪgeɪt/ *v.t.* bewässern

irrigation /ɪrɪˈgeɪʃn/ *n.* Bewässerung, *die*

irritability /ɪrɪtəˈbɪlɪtɪ/ *n.* ⇒ **irritable:** Reizbarkeit, *die;* Gereiztheit, *die*

irritable /ˈɪrɪtəbl/ *adj.* (quick to anger) reizbar; (temporarily) gereizt

irritant /ˈɪrɪtənt/ *n.* Reizstoff, *der*

irritate /ˈɪrɪteɪt/ *v.t.* **(a)** ärgern; **get ∼d** ärgerlich werden; **be ∼d by** *or* **feel ∼d at sth.** sich über etw. (*Akk.*) ärgern; **be ∼d with sb.** sich über jmdn. aufregen *od.* ärgern; **(b)** (Med.) reizen

irritating /ˈɪrɪteɪtɪŋ/ *adj.* lästig; **I find him ∼:** er geht mir auf die Nerven (ugs.)

irritation /ɪrɪˈteɪʃn/ *n.* **(a)** Ärger, *der;* [source *or* cause of] **∼:** Ärgernis, *das;* **(b)** (Med.) Reizung, *die*

is ⇒ **be**

Islam /ˈɪzlɑːm, ˈɪzlæm, ɪzˈlɑːm/ *n.* Islam, *der*

Islamic /ɪzˈlæmɪk/ *adj.* islamisch

island /ˈaɪlənd/ *n.* (lit. or fig.) Insel, *die; see also* **traffic island**

islander /ˈaɪləndə(r)/ *n.* Inselbewohner, *der*/-bewohnerin, *die*

island: ∼-hop *v.i.* go **∼ping** eine Islandhoppingtour machen; **∼-hopping** *n.; no pl.* Inselhopping, *das; attrib.* **an ∼-hopping holiday** eine Urlaubsreise von Insel zu Insel

isle /aɪl/ *n.* Insel, *die;* Eiland, *das* (dichter.); *see also* **British Isles**

Isle of Man /aɪl əv ˈmæn/ *pr. n.* Insel Man, *die*

isn't /ˈɪznt/ (coll.) = **is not;** ⇒ **be**

isobar /ˈaɪsəbɑː(r)/ *n.* (Meteorol., Phys.) Isobare, *die*

isolate /ˈaɪsəleɪt/ *v.t.* isolieren; (Electr.) vom Stromkreis trennen

isolated /ˈaɪsəleɪtɪd/ *adj.* **(a)** (single) einzeln; (occasional) vereinzelt; **∼ instances/cases** Einzelfälle; **(b)** (solitary) einsam; (remote) abgelegen (**from** von); (cut off) abgeschnitten (**from** von)

isolation /aɪsəˈleɪʃn/ *n.* **(a)** (act) Isolierung, *die;* Absonderung, *die;* **(b)** (state) Isoliertheit, *die;* Isolation, *die;* Abgeschnittenheit, *die;* (remoteness) Abgeschiedenheit, *die;* **examine/look at/treat sth. in ∼:** etw. isoliert *od.* gesondert betrachten; **∼ hospital** Infektionskrankenhaus, *das;* **∼ ward** Isolierstation, *die*

isosceles /aɪˈsɒsəliːz/ *adj.* (Geom.) gleichschenklig

isotope /ˈaɪsətəʊp/ *n.* Isotop, *das*

Israel /ˈɪzreɪl/ *pr. n.* Israel (*das*)

Israeli /ɪzˈreɪlɪ/ ▶947 **1** *adj.* israelisch. **2** *n.* Israeli, *der/die*

issue /ˈɪʃuː, ˈɪsjuː/ **1** *n.* **(a)** (point in question) Frage, *die;* contemporary **∼s** aktuelle Fragen *od.* Themen; **make an ∼ of sth.** etw. aufbauschen; **become an ∼:** zum Problem werden; **what is at ∼ here?** worum geht es [hier] eigentlich?; **evade** *or* **dodge the ∼:** ausweichen; **the point at ∼:** der strittige Punkt; worum es geht; **take ∼ with sb. over sth.** sich mit jmdm. auf eine Diskussion über etw. (*Akk.*) einlassen; **(b)** (giving out) Ausgabe, *die;* (of document) Ausstellung, *die;* (of shares) Emission, *die;* **date of ∼:** Ausgabedatum, *das;* (of document) Ausstellungsdatum, *das;* (of stamps) Ausgabetag, *der;* **(c)** (of magazine, journal, etc.) Ausgabe, *die;* **(d)** (total number of copies) Auflage, *die;* **(e)** (quantity of coins) Emissionszahl, *die;* (quantity of stamps) Auflage, *die;* **(f)** (result, outcome) Ergebnis, *das;* Ausgang, *der;* **decide the ∼:** den Ausschlag geben; **force the ∼:** eine Entscheidung erzwingen. **2** *v.t.* **(a)** (give out) ausgeben; ausstellen ‹*Pass, Visum, Lizenz, Zeugnis, Haft-, Durchsuchungsbefehl*›; erteilen ‹*Lizenz, Befehl*›; **∼ sb. with sth.** etw. an jmdn. austeilen; **(b)** (publish) herausgeben ‹*Publikation*›; herausbringen ‹*Publikation, Münze, Briefmarke*›; emittieren ‹*Wertpapiere*›; geben ‹*Warnung*›; **(c)** (supply) ausgeben (**to** an + *Akk.*); **∼ sb. with sth.** jmdn. mit etw. ausstatten; **be ∼d with sth.** etw. erhalten. **3** *v.i.* ‹*Personen:*› herausströmen (**from** aus); ‹*Gas, Flüssigkeit:*› austreten (**from** aus); ‹*Rauch:*› heraus-, hervorquellen (**from** aus); ‹*Ton, Geräusch:*› hervor-, herausdringen (**from** aus)

isthmus /ˈɪsməs, ˈɪsθməs/ *n.* (Geog.) Landenge, *die;* Isthmus, *der*

IT *abbr.* **information technology**

it /ɪt/ *pron.* **(a)** (the thing, animal, young child previously mentioned) er/sie/es; *as direct obj.* ihn/sie/es; *as indirect obj.* ihm/ihr/ihm; **behind/under it** dahinter/darunter; **(b)** (the person in question) **who is it?** wer ist da?; **it was the children** es waren die Kinder; **is it you, dad?** bist du es, Vater?; **(c)** *subj. of impers. v.* es; **it is snowing/warm** es schneit/ist warm; **it is winter/midnight/ten o'clock** es ist Winter/Mitternacht/zehn Uhr; **(d)** *anticipating subj. or obj.* es; **it is typical of her to do that** es ist typisch für sie, so etwas zu tun; **it is absurd talking** *or* **to talk like that** es ist absurd, so zu reden; **it was for our sake that he did it** um unseretwillen hat er es getan; **(e)** *as indef. obj.* es; **I can't cope with it any more** ich halte das nicht mehr länger aus; **have a hard time of it** eine schwere Zeit haben; **what is it?** was ist los?; was ist denn?; **(f)** (exactly what is needed) **That's it! That's exactly what I've been looking for** Das ist es! Genau das habe ich gesucht; **he thinks he's really 'it** er denkt, er ist der Größte (ugs.); **(g) that's 'it** (coll.) (that's the problem) das ist es [eben]; (that's the end) jetzt ist Schluss; (my patience is at an end) jetzt reicht's [mir]; (that's true) genau (ugs.); **this is 'it** (coll.) (the time for action) es ist soweit; (the real problem) das ist es [eben]. *See also* **its; itself**

Italian /ɪˈtæljən/ ▶897 , ▶947 **1** *adj.* italienisch; **sb. is ∼:** jmd. ist Italiener/Italienerin. **2** *n.* **(a)** (person) Italiener, *der*/Italienerin, *die;* **(b)** (language) Italienisch, *das; see also* **English 2 a**

italic /ɪˈtælɪk/ **1** *adj.* kursiv. **2** *n. in pl.* Kursivschrift, *die;* **in ∼s** kursiv

Italy /ˈɪtəlɪ/ *pr. n.* Italien (*das*)

itch /ɪtʃ/ **1** *n.* **(a)** Juckreiz, *der;* Jucken, *das;* **I have an ∼:** es juckt mich; **(b)** (restless desire) Drang, *der;* **I have an**

It

The tendency when translating *it* into German is to put **es** whatever it refers to. This is of course correct if *it* refers back to a neuter noun (**Brot, Messer, Auto** etc.). Remember the dative form is **ihm.**

Where's the knife? It's on the table	= Wo ist das Messer? Es liegt auf dem Tisch
The car is stuck. Can you give it a shove?	= Das Auto sitzt fest. Kannst du ihm einen Schubs geben?

The translation is also **es** where it stands for an idea which may be expressed in a whole sentence or clause (which is the case with actions, statements and impersonal subjects):

Who did it/said it?	= Wer hat es getan/gesagt?
It was very kind of you	= Es war sehr nett von Ihnen
It's true that I can't stand him	= Es stimmt, ich kann ihn nicht leiden

There are also impersonal verbs and constructions which always have *it* as the subject:

It's snowing/raining	= Es schneit/regnet
It was ten o'clock	= Es war zehn Uhr

But if *it* refers back to a noun which is masculine in German, it must be translated by **er** (or **ihn** if it is accusative and **ihm** in the dative):

The winter was over; it had been cold	= Der Winter war vorüber; er war kalt gewesen
That's my pencil — give it to me	= Das ist mein Bleistift — gib ihn mir
There's the river; the road follows it	= Dort ist der Fluss; die Straße folgt ihm

Similarly, if the noun referred to is feminine *it* must be translated by **sie** (or **ihr** in the dative):

The flower is wilting — it needs water/you must water it	= Die Blume ist welk — sie braucht Wasser/du musst sie begießen

He found a track and = Er fand eine Spur und
followed it   folgte ihr

There are some exceptions to this requirement for agreement, in particular when the noun referred to follows *it's* or *it was:*

It's a good film	= Es ist ein guter Film
It was a lovely evening	= Es war ein schöner Abend

In other cases, an expression with **es** may be seen as a set phrase which does not need to reflect the gender of the noun referred to. In the example with the pencil above, *give it to me* could also be translated by 'gibs her'.

After prepositions

Combinations such as *with it, from it, to it* etc. are translated by the prepositions with the prefix **da-** (**damit, davon, dazu** etc.). Prepositions beginning with a vowel insert an **r** (**daran, darauf, darunter, darüber** etc., in which the **a** is elided in colloquial speech to give **dran, drauf, drunter, drüber** etc.). This makes it possible to distinguish between a person and a thing in examples such as:

It suits him = Es passt zu ihm

and:

It goes well with it = Es passt dazu

Other examples:

I can't do anything with it	= Ich kann nichts damit anfangen
Don't lean on it!	= Lehn dich nicht daran!
Put something under it/ on top of it	= Leg etwas darunter *or* drunter/darauf *or* drauf

Sometimes the separable verb prefixes with **hin-** are sufficient:

It won't fit into it	= Es passt nicht hinein
Add sugar to it	= Geben Sie Zucker hinzu

~ to do it es juckt (ugs.) *od.* reizt mich, es zu tun. **2** *v.i.* (**a**) einen Juckreiz haben; **I'm ~ing** es juckt mich; **it ~es** es juckt; **my back ~es** mein Rücken juckt; es juckt mich am Rücken; (**b**) (feel a desire) **~** *or* **be ~ing to do sth.** darauf brennen, etw. zu tun; **~ for sth.** sich nach etw. sehnen; **he is ~ing for a fight** er ist nur darauf aus, sich zu prügeln

itchy /ˈɪtʃɪ/ *adj.* kratzig ‹*Socken, Laken*›; **be ~** ‹*Körperteil*:› jucken; **I've got ~ feet** (fig. coll.) mich hält es hier nicht länger; (by temperament) mich hält es nirgends lange

it'd /ˈɪtəd/ (coll.) (**a**) = **it had;** (**b**) = **it would**

item /ˈaɪtəm/ *n.* (**a**) Ding, *das;* Sache, *die;* (in shop, catalogue) Artikel, *der;* (in variety show, radio, TV) Nummer, *die;* (**b**) **~ [of news]** Nachricht, *die;* (**c**) (in account or bill) Posten, *der;* (in list, programme, agenda) Punkt, *der*

itemize (itemise) /ˈaɪtəmaɪz/ *v.t.* einzeln aufführen; spezifizieren ‹*Rechnung*›

itinerant /ɪˈtɪnərənt, aɪˈtɪnərənt/ **1** *adj.* reisend; umherziehend; Wander‹*prediger, -arbeiter*›. **2** *n.* Landfahrer, *der/* -fahrerin, *die*

itinerary /aɪˈtɪnərərɪ, ɪˈtɪnərərɪ/ *n.* [Reise]route, *die;* [Reise]weg, *der*

it'll /ˈɪtl/ (coll.) = **it will**

its /ɪts/ *poss. pron. attrib.* sein/ihr/sein; *see also* **her²**

it's /ɪts/ (**a**) = **it is;** (**b**) = **it has**

itself /ɪtˈself/ *pron.* (**a**) *emphat.* selbst; **by ~** (automatically) von selbst; (alone) allein; (taken in isolation) für sich; **in ~:** für sich genommen; **he is generosity ~:** er ist die Großzügigkeit in Person; (**b**) *refl.* sich; **the machine switches ~ off** die Maschine schaltet sich [von] selbst aus

ITV *abbr.* (Brit.) **Independent Television** *kommerzielles britisches Fernsehprogramm*

IUD *abbr.* **intrauterine device**

I've /aɪv/ = **I have**

ivory /ˈaɪvərɪ/ *n.* (**a**) (substance) Elfenbein, *das; attrib.* elfenbeinern; Elfenbein-; (**b**) (colour) Elfenbein, *das; attrib.* elfenbeinfarbig

ivory: I~ 'Coast *pr. n.* Elfenbeinküste, *die;* **~ 'tower** *n.* Elfenbeinturm, *der*

ivy /ˈaɪvɪ/ *n.* Efeu, *der*

'Ivy League *n.* (Amer.) *Eliteuniversitäten im Osten der USA*

J j

J, j /dʒeɪ/ *n., pl.* **Js** *or* **J's** J, j, *das*

jab /dʒæb/ **1** *v.t.,* **-bb-:** (**a**) (poke roughly, thrust abruptly) stoßen; (**b**) (stab) stechen. **2** *v.i.,* **-bb-: ~ at sb. [with sth.]** auf jmdn. [mit etw.] einhauen; (stab at) auf jmdn. [mit etw.] einstechen. **3** *n.* (**a**) (abrupt blow) Schlag, *der;* (with stick, elbow) Stoß, *der;* (with needle) Stich, *der;* (Boxing) Jab, *der;* (**b**) (Brit. coll.: hypodermic injection) Spritze, *die;* **give sb./oneself a ~:** jmdm./sich eine Spritze verpassen (ugs.)

jabber /ˈdʒæbə(r)/ **1** *v.i.* plappern (ugs.). **2** *v.t.* brabbeln (ugs.)

jack /dʒæk/ **1** *n.* (**a**) (Cards) Bube, *der;* (**b**) (for lifting vehicle wheel) Wagenheber, *der;* (**c**) (Bowls) Malkugel, *die.* **2** *v.t.* (**a**)

∼ **in** or **up** (Brit. coll.: abandon) [auf]stecken (ugs.); **(b)** ∼ **up** (lift) aufbocken ⟨ *Fahrzeug* ⟩; (fig. coll.: increase) was draufsatteln auf (+ *Akk.*) (ugs.)

jackass /'dʒækæs/ n. **(a)** (male ass) Eselhengst, der; **(b)** (stupid person) Esel, der (ugs.)

jackdaw /'dʒækdɔ:/ n. (Ornith.) Dohle, die

jacket /'dʒækɪt/ n. **(a)** Jacke, die; (of suit) Jackett, das; sports ∼: Sakko, der; ∼ **pocket** Jackentasche, die/Jacketttasche, die; **(b)** (round a boiler etc.) Mantel, der; **(c)** (of book) Schutzumschlag, der; **(d)** (of a potato) Schale, die; ∼ **potatoes** in der Schale gebackene Kartoffeln; **(e)** (Amer.) ⇒ **sleeve** b

jack: J∼ 'Frost n. Väterchen Frost (scherzh.); ∼**-in-the-box** n. Schachtelteufel, der; Kastenteufel, der; ∼**knife** v.i. the lorry ∼**-knifed** der Anhänger des Lastwagens stellte sich quer; ∼ **of 'all trades** n. Hansdampf [in allen Gassen]; ∼**pot** n. Jackpot, der; **hit the** ∼**pot** (fig.) das große Los ziehen; **J∼ Robinson** /dʒæk ˈrɔbɪnsn/ n. **before you could say J∼ Robinson** im Nu (ugs.)

jacuzzi, (Amer.: **P**) /dʒə'ku:zɪ/ n. ≈ Whirlpool, der

jade[1] /dʒeɪd/ v.t., esp. in p.p. (tire) ermüden; abstumpfen ⟨ *Geschmacksnerven* ⟩; **look** ∼**d** abgespannt od. erschöpft aussehen

jade[2] n. Jade, der od. die; (carvings) Jadearbeiten

jagged /'dʒægɪd/ adj. gezackt; ausgefranst ⟨ *Loch/Riß in Kleidungsstücken* ⟩; zerklüftet ⟨ *Küste* ⟩

jaguar /'dʒægjʊə(r)/ n. (Zool.) Jaguar, der

jail /dʒeɪl/ **1** n. (place) Gefängnis, das; (confinement) Haft, die; **in** ∼: im Gefängnis; **be sent to** ∼: ins Gefängnis kommen; **go to** ∼: ins Gefängnis kommen. **2** v.t. ins Gefängnis bringen

jail: ∼**bird** n. Knastbruder, der (ugs.); ∼**break** n. Gefängnisausbruch, der

jailer, jailor /'dʒeɪlə(r)/ n. Gefängniswärter, der/-wärterin, die

jalopy /dʒə'lɒpɪ/ n. (coll.) Klapperkiste, die (ugs.)

jam[1] /dʒæm/ **1** v.t., **-mm-: (a)** (squeeze and fix between two surfaces) einklemmen; ∼ **sth. into sth.** etw. in etw. (Akk.) zwängen; **(b)** (make immovable) blockieren; (fig.) lähmen; lahm legen; **(c)** (squeeze together in compact mass) stopfen (**into** in + Akk.); ∼ **together** zusammenpferchen ⟨ *Personen* ⟩; **(d)** (thrust into confined space) stopfen (**into** in + Akk.); stecken ⟨ *Schlüssel, Münze* ⟩ (**into** in + Akk.); **(e)** (block by crowding) blockieren; versperren, blockieren ⟨ *Eingang* ⟩; verstopfen, blockieren ⟨ *Rohr* ⟩; **the switchboard was** ∼**med with calls** sämtliche Leitungen waren durch Anrufe blockiert; **(f)** (Radio) stören. **2** v.i., **-mm-: (a)** (become tightly wedged) sich verklemmen; **(b)** (become unworkable) ⟨ *Maschine:* ⟩ klemmen. **3** n. **(a)** (crush, stoppage) Blockierung, die; Klemmen, das; **(b)** (crowded mass) Stau, der; **(c)** (coll.: dilemma) Klemme, die (ugs.); **be in a** ∼: in der Klemme stecken (ugs.)

∼ **'in** v.t. hineinzwängen; **we were** ∼**med in** wir waren eingepfercht

∼ **'on** v.t. ∼ **the brakes [full] on** [voll] auf die Bremse steigen (ugs.); eine Vollbremsung machen

∼ **'up** v.t. verstopfen ⟨ *Straße usw.* ⟩; lahmlegen ⟨ *System* ⟩; verklemmen ⟨ *Mechanismus* ⟩

jam[2] n. Marmelade, die; Konfitüre, die (bes. Kaufmannsspr.); **make** ∼: Marmelade einmachen; **sb. wants** ∼ **on it** (fig. coll.) jmdm. genügt etw. noch nicht

Jamaica /dʒə'meɪkə/ pr. n. Jamaika (das)

jamb /dʒæm/ n. (of doorway, window) Pfosten, der

'jam jar n. Marmeladenglas, das

jammy /'dʒæmɪ/ adj. (Brit. coll.: lucky) ∼ **beggar** Glückspilz, der (ugs.); **that was** ∼: das war Schwein (ugs.)

jam: ∼**-packed** adj. (coll.) knallvoll (ugs.), proppenvoll (ugs.) (**with** von); ∼ **session** n. (Jazz coll.) Jamsession, die; ∼ **'tart** n. Marmeladentörtchen, das

Jan. abbr. **January** Jan.

jangle /'dʒæŋgl/ **1** v.i. klimpern; ⟨ *Klingel:* ⟩ bimmeln. **2** v.t. rasseln mit; klimpern mit ⟨ *[Klein]geld* ⟩. **3** n. Geklapper, das; (of bell) Schrillen, das

janitor /'dʒænɪtə(r)/ n. **(a)** (doorkeeper) Portier, der; **(b)** (caretaker) Hausmeister, der

January /'dʒænjʊərɪ/ n. ▶ **738** Januar, der; see also **August**

Japan /dʒə'pæn/ n. Japan (das)

Japanese /dʒæpə'ni:z/ ▶ **897**, ▶ **947** **1** adj. japanisch; **sb. is** ∼: jmd. ist Japaner/Japanerin. **2** n., pl. same **(a)** (person) Japaner, der/ Japanerin, die; **(b)** (language) Japanisch, das

jape /dʒeɪp/ n. Scherz, der; Spaß, der; (practical joke) Streich, der

jar[1] /dʒɑ:(r)/ **1** n. **(a)** (harsh or grating sound) Quietschen, das; **(b)** (jolt) Stoß, der; (thrill of nerves, shock) Schlag, der. **2** v.i., **-rr-: (a)** (sound discordantly) quietschen; (rattle) ⟨ *Fenster:* ⟩ scheppern (ugs.); ∼ **on** or **against sth.** über etw. (Akk.) knirschen; **(b)** (have discordant or painful effect) ∼ [**up**]**on sb./sb.'s nerves** jmdm. auf die Nerven gehen; ∼ **on the ears** durch Mark und Bein gehen (ugs. scherzh.); **a** ∼**ring sound** ein Geräusch, das einem durch und durch geht. **3** v.t., **-rr-: (a)** (cause to vibrate) erschüttern; **(b)** (send shock through) ∼ **sb.'s nerves** jmdm. auf die Nerven gehen; ∼ **one's elbow** sich (Dat.) den Ellbogen anschlagen

jar[2] n. (vessel) Topf, der; (of glass) Glas, das; ∼ **of jam** etc. Topf/Glas Marmelade usw.

jargon /'dʒɑ:gən/ n. Jargon, der

jasmin[e] /'dʒæsmɪn, 'dʒæzmɪn/ n. Jasmin, der

jaundice /'dʒɔ:ndɪs/ **1** n. ▶ **865** (Med.) Gelbsucht, die. **2** v.t. usu. in p.p. (fig.: affect with bitterness) verbittern; ∼**d** verbittert; (cynical) zynisch; **with** [**a**] ∼**d eye** (enviously) neidvoll; mit Neid; **have a very** ∼**d view of life** dem Leben voller Verbitterung gegenüberstehen

jaunt /dʒɔ:nt/ n. Ausflug, der; **be off on/go for a** ∼: einen Ausflug machen

jaunty /'dʒɔ:ntɪ/ adj. unbeschwert; keck ⟨ *Hut* ⟩

Java /'dʒɑ:və/ pr. n. Java (das)

javelin /'dʒævəlɪn, 'dʒævlɪn/ n. **(a)** Speer, der; **(b)** (Sport: event) Speerwerfen, das

jaw /dʒɔ:/ n. **(a)** ▶ **672** (Anat.) Kiefer, der; **his** ∼ **dropped** er ließ die Kinnlade herunterfallen; **upper/lower** ∼: Ober-/Unterkiefer, der; **(b)** (of machine) [Klemm]backe, die; **(c)** in pl. (large dangerous mouth) Rachen, der; (fig.: of fate, death, etc.) Klauen

jawbone /'dʒɔ:bəʊn/ n. Kieferknochen, der

jay /dʒeɪ/ n. Eichelhäher, der

jay: ∼**walk** v.i. als Fußgänger im Straßenverkehr unachtsam sein; ∼**walker** n. im Straßenverkehr unachtsamer Fußgänger

jazz /dʒæz/ **1** n. Jazz, der; attrib. Jazz⟨ *musik, -musiker* ⟩; **and all that** ∼ (coll.) und der ganze Kram (ugs.). **2** v.t. ∼ **up** aufpeppen (ugs.); aufmotzen (ugs.)

'jazz band n. Jazzband, die

jealous /'dʒeləs/ adj. eifersüchtig (**of** auf + Akk.)

jealously /'dʒeləslɪ/ adv. eifersüchtig

jealousy /'dʒeləsɪ/ n. Eifersucht, die

jeans /dʒi:nz/ n. pl. Jeans Pl.; Jeans, die; **a pair of** ∼ ein Paar Jeans; eine Jeans

Jeep, (**P**) /dʒi:p/ n. Jeep Ⓦ, der

jeer /dʒɪə(r)/ **1** v.i. höhnen (geh.); ∼ **at sb.** jmdn. verhöhnen; ∼**ing** höhnisch johlend ⟨ *Menge, Mob* ⟩. **2** v.t. verhöhnen. **3** n. höhnisches Johlen; (remark) höhnische Bemerkung

Jehovah's 'Witness /dʒɪˈhəʊvəz 'wɪtnɪs/ n. (Relig.) Zeuge Jehovas

jell /dʒel/ v.i. (set as jelly) fest werden; gelieren

Jell-O (**P**), **jello** /'dʒeləʊ/ n. (esp. Amer.) Götterspeise, die

jelly /'dʒelɪ/ n. Gelee, das; (dessert) Götterspeise, die; **her legs felt like** ∼: sie hatte Pudding in den Knien (ugs.)

jelly: ∼ **baby** n. ≈ Gummibärchen, das; ∼**fish** n. Qualle, die

jemmy /'dʒemɪ/ n. (Brit.) Brecheisen, das

jeopardize (jeopardise) /'dʒepədaɪz/ v.t. gefährden

jeopardy /'dʒepədɪ/ n., no pl. Gefahr, die; **put sth./sb. in** ∼: etw. aufs Spiel setzen/jmdn. in Gefahr bringen; etw./jmdn. gefährden; **in** ∼: in Gefahr; gefährdet

jerk /dʒɜːk/ **1** *n.* **(a)** (sharp sudden pull) Ruck, *der;* **with a series of ~s** ruckartig; ruckend; **give sth. a ~:** einer Sache (*Dat.*) einen Ruck geben; **an etw.** (*Dat.*) rucken; **(b)** (involuntary movement) Zuckung, *die;* Zucken, *das.* **2** *v.t.* reißen an (+ *Dat.*) ⟨*Seil usw.*⟩; **~ sth. away/back** *etc.* etw. weg-/zurückreißen *usw.;* **~ sth. off/out of sth.** *etc.* etw. von etw. [herunter]reißen/aus etw. [heraus]reißen *usw.* **3** *v.i.* ruckeln; (move in a spasmodic manner) zucken

jerky /ˈdʒɜːkɪ/ *adj.* abgehackt, holprig ⟨*Art zu schreiben/sprechen*⟩; holprig ⟨*Busfahrt*⟩; holpernd ⟨*Fahrzeug*⟩; ruckartig ⟨*Bewegung*⟩

Jerry /ˈdʒerɪ/ *n.* (Brit. dated sl.) (soldier) Deutsche, *der*

'jerry-built *adj.* unsolide gebaut

jersey /ˈdʒɜːzɪ/ *n.* Pullover, *der;* (Sport) Trikot, *das;* Jersey, *das*

jest /dʒest/ **1** *n.* **(a)** (joke) Scherz, *der;* Witz, *der;* **(b)** *no pl.* (fun) Spaß, *der;* **in ~:** im Scherz. **2** *v.i.* scherzen; Witze machen

jester /ˈdʒestə(r)/ *n.* Spaßmacher, *der;* (at court) Hofnarr, *der;* (fool) Hanswurst, *der*

Jesuit /ˈdʒezjʊɪt/ *n.* Jesuit, *der*

Jesus /ˈdʒiːzəs/ **1** *pr. n.* Jesus (*der*). **2** *int.* (sl.) **~ [Christ]!** Herrgott noch mal! (ugs.)

jet¹ /dʒet/ **1** *n.* **(a)** (stream) Strahl, *der;* **~ of flame/steam/water** Feuer-/Dampf-/Wasserstrahl, *der;* **(b)** (spout, nozzle) Düse, *die;* **(c)** (aircraft) Düsenflugzeug, *das;* Jet, *der;* (engine) Düsentriebwerk, *das.* **2** *v.i.,* **-tt-:** **(a)** (spurt out) ⟨*Wasser:*⟩ herausschießen **(from** aus); ⟨*Gas, Dampf:*⟩ ausströmen **(from** aus); **(b)** (coll.: travel by **~** plane) jetten (ugs.)

jet² *n.* (Min.) Jett, *der od. das;* Gagat, *der*

jet: **~-black** *adj.* pechschwarz; kohlrabenschwarz; **~ engine** *n.* Düsen- *od.* Strahltriebwerk, *das;* **'fighter** *n.* Düsenjäger, *der;* **~foil** *n.* [Jetfoil-]Tragflügelboot, *das;* **~ lag** *n.* Jetlag, *der;* **~-lagged** *adj.* **sb. is ~-lagged** jmdm. macht die Zeitverschiebung zu schaffen; **~ plane** *n.* Düsenflugzeug, *das;* **~-propelled** *adj.* düsen- *od.* strahlgetrieben; mit Düsen- *od.* Strahlantrieb *nachgestellt*

jetsam /ˈdʒetsəm/ *n.* sinkendes Seewurfgut (Seew.); (on seashore) Strandgut, *das; see also* **flotsam**

jet: **~ set** *n.* Jetset, *der* **~-setter** *n.* Jetsetter, *der/* -setterin, *die;* **~ ski** *n.* Jetski, *der;* **~-ski** *v.i.* Jetski fahren

jettison /ˈdʒetɪsən/ *v.t.* **(a)** (from ship) über Bord werfen; (from aircraft) abwerfen ⟨*Ballast, Bombe*⟩; (discard) wegwerfen; **(b)** (fig.: abandon) aufgeben; über Bord werfen ⟨*Plan*⟩

jetty /ˈdʒetɪ/ *n.* **(a)** (protecting harbour or coast) [Hafen]mole, *die;* **(b)** (landing-pier) Landungsbrücke, *die*

Jew /dʒuː/ *n.* Jude, *der*/Jüdin, *die*

jewel /ˈdʒuːəl/ *n.* **(a)** (ornament) [kostbares] Schmuckstück; **~s** *collect.* Schmuck, *der;* Juwelen *Pl.;* **(b)** (precious stone) Juwel, *das od. der;* [wertvoller] Edelstein; (of watch) Stein, *der;* **(c)** (fig.) (person) Goldstück; ⟨*Juwel, das;* (thing) Kleinod, *das*

jeweller (*Amer.:* **jeweler**) /ˈdʒuːələ(r)/ *n.* ▶ 887 | Juwelier, *der*

jewellery (Brit.), **jewelry** /ˈdʒuːəlrɪ/ *n.* Schmuck, *der*

Jewess /ˈdʒuːɪs/ *n.* Jüdin, *die*

Jewish /ˈdʒuːɪʃ/ *adj.* jüdisch; **he/she is ~:** er ist Jude/sie ist Jüdin

jib¹ /dʒɪb/ *n.* **(a)** (Naut.) (on sailing ship) Stagsegel, *das* (Seew.); (on yacht or dinghy) Fock, *die* (Seew.); **(b)** (of crane) Ausleger, *der*

jib² *v.i.,* **-bb-:** **(a)** ⟨*Pferd usw.:*⟩ bocken; (because of fright) scheuen; **(b)** (fig.) sich sträuben; streiken (ugs.); **~ at sth./at doing sth.** sich gegen etw. sträuben/sich dagegen sträuben, etw. zu tun

jibe ⇒ **gibe**

jiff /dʒɪf/, **jiffy** /ˈdʒɪfɪ/ *ns.* (coll.) Augenblick, *der;* Moment, *der;* **in a ~:** sofort; gleich

'Jiffy bag, (P) *n.* gefütterte Versandtasche

jig /dʒɪɡ/ *n.* **(a)** (dance, music) Jig, *die;* **(b)** (appliance) Einspannvorrichtung, *die*

jiggle /ˈdʒɪɡl/ **1** *v.t.* rütteln an, wackeln an (+ *Dat.*). **2** *v.i.* rütteln; wackeln

'jigsaw *n.* **~ [puzzle]** Puzzle, *das*

jilt /dʒɪlt/ *v.t.* sitzen lassen (ugs.)

jingle /ˈdʒɪŋɡl/ **1** *n.* **(a)** Klingeln, *das;* Bimmeln, *das* (ugs.); (of cutlery, chains, spurs) Klirren, *das;* (of coins, keys) Geklimper, *das;* **(b)** (trivial verse) Wortgeklingel, *das* (abwertend); (Commerc.) Werbespruch, *der;* Jingle, *der* (Werbespr.). **2** *v.i.* ⟨*Metallgegenstände:*⟩ klimpern; ⟨*Kasse, Schelle:*⟩ klingeln; ⟨*Glöckchen:*⟩ bimmeln. **3** *v.t.* klingeln mit, (ugs.) bimmeln mit ⟨*Glöckchen*⟩; klimpern mit ⟨*Münzen, Schlüsseln, Armreifen*⟩

jingoism /ˈdʒɪŋɡəʊɪzm/ *n.,* *no pl.* Chauvinismus, *der* (abwertend); Hurrapatriotismus, *der* (ugs. abwertend)

jinx /dʒɪŋks/ **1** *n.* (coll.) Fluch, *der;* **there seemed to be a ~ on him** er schien vom Pech verfolgt zu sein. **2** *v.t.* verhexen

jitters /ˈdʒɪtəz/ *n. pl.* (coll.) großes Zittern; Bammel, *der* (salopp); **give sb. the ~:** jmdm. Schiss machen (salopp)

jittery /ˈdʒɪtərɪ/ *adj.* (nervous) nervös; (frightened) verängstigt

Jnr. *abbr.* **Junior** jr.; jun.

job /dʒɒb/ *n.* **(a)** (piece of work) **~ [of work]** Arbeit, *die;* **I have a little ~ for you** ich habe eine kleine Aufgabe *od.* einen kleinen Auftrag für dich; **do a ~ for sb.** für jmdn. etw. erledigen; **you're doing an excellent ~:** Sie machen das ausgezeichnet; **(b)** (position of employment) Stelle, *die;* Anstellung, *die;* Job, *der* (ugs.); **he is only doing his ~!** er tut schließlich nur seine Pflicht; **he knows his ~:** er versteht sein Handwerk; **~ vacancies** offene Stellen; (in newspaper) „Stellenangebote"; **have ~ security** einen sicheren Arbeitsplatz haben; **just the ~** (fig. coll.) genau das Richtige; die Sache (ugs.); **on the ~:** bei der Arbeit; **out of a ~:** arbeitslos; ohne Stellung; **(c)** (sl.: crime) [krummes] Ding (ugs.); **(d)** (result of work) Ergebnis, *das;* **make a [good] ~ of sth.** bei etw. gute Arbeit leisten; **(e)** (coll.: difficult task) [schönes] Stück Arbeit; **I had a [hard or tough] ~ convincing** *or* **to convince him** es war gar nicht so einfach für mich, ihn zu überzeugen; **(f)** (state of affairs) a bad **~:** eine schlimme *od.* üble Sache; **give sb./sth. up as a bad ~** ⇒ **give up 2 a; a good ~:** ein Glück; **we've finished, and a good ~ too!** wir sind fertig, zum Glück; **it's a good ~ he doesn't know about it!** nur gut, dass er nichts davon weiß!

job: **~ centre** *n.* (Brit.) Arbeitsvermittlungsstelle, *die;* **~ creation** *n.* Schaffung von Arbeitsplätzen; **~ description** *n.* Tätigkeitsbeschreibung, *die;* **~-hunting** *n.* Arbeitssuche, *die;* Stellensuche, *die*

jobless /ˈdʒɒblɪs/ *adj.* beschäftigungslos; arbeitslos

job: **~ lot** *n.* Partieware, *die* (Kaufmannsspr.); (fig.) Sammelsurium, *das* (abwertend); **~ satisfaction** *n.* satisfaction b; **~ security** *n.* Arbeitsplatzsicherheit, *die;* **there is no ~ security in this industry** in dieser Branche gibt es keine sicheren Arbeitsplätze; **~-sharing** *n.,* *no pl.* Jobsharing, *das;* Arbeitsplatzteilung, *die*

job-share **1** *n.* geteilter Arbeitsplatz; **look for a ~:** eine Jobsharing-Stelle suchen. **2** *v.t.* aufteilen ⟨*Arbeitsplatz*⟩. **3** *v.i.* sich (*Dat.*) einen Arbeitsplatz teilen (**with** mit)

jobsworth /ˈdʒɒbzwɜːθ/ *n.* (Brit. coll.) Beamtenseele, *die* (abwertend); sturer Bürokratentyp

jockey /ˈdʒɒkɪ/ **1** *n.* ▶ 887 | Jockei, *der;* Jockey, *der.* **2** *v.i.* rangeln (for um); **~ for position** (lit. or fig.) alles daransetzen, eine möglichst gute Position zu erringen

'jockey shorts *n. pl.* (Amer.) Unterhose, *die;* Unterhosen *Pl.*

jockstrap /ˈdʒɒkstræp/ *n.* [Sport]suspensorium, *das*

jocular /ˈdʒɒkjʊlə(r)/ *adj.* lustig, witzig ⟨*Bemerkung, Antwort*⟩; spaßig, scherzhaft ⟨*Person*⟩

jodhpurs /ˈdʒɒdpəz/ *n. pl.* Reithose, *die;* Jodhpur[hose], *die*

jog /dʒɒɡ/ **1** *v.t.,* **-gg-:** **(a)** (shake with push or jerk) rütteln; schütteln; **(b)** (nudge) [an]stoßen; **(c)** (stimulate) **~ sb.'s memory** jmds. Gedächtnis (*Dat.*) auf die Sprünge helfen. **2** *v.i.,* **-gg-:** **(a)** (move up and down) auf und ab hüpfen; **(b)** (move at ~trot) ⟨*Pferd:*⟩ [dahin]trotten; **(c)** (run at slow pace) [in mäßigem Tempo] laufen; traben (Sport); (for physical exercise) joggen; [einen] Dauerlauf machen. **3** *n.* **(a)** (shake, nudge) Stoß, *der;* Schubs, *der* (ugs.); **(b)** (slow walk or trot) (of

Jobs

What's your job?,	= Was machen Sie
What do you do	beruflich?, Was sind
[for a living]?	Sie von Beruf?
I work in a bank/in a	= Ich arbeite bei einer
bookshop	Bank/in einer
	Buchhandlung
He is in insurance/	= Er ist in der
in the city	Versicherungs-
	branche/in der City
	tätig
I am with a small	= Ich bin bei einem
company or *firm/a*	kleinen Unternehmen/
large combine or	einem großen
group/a multinational	Konzern/einem Multi
She owns/runs a small	= Sie hat/führt einen
business	kleinen Betrieb
My husband works for	= Mein Mann ist bei
or *is employed by*	derselben Firma
the same firm	angestellt
She works full time/	= Sie arbeitet ganztags or
part time	hat eine Ganztags-
	beschäftigung/ist als
	Teilzeitkraft angestellt
	or hat eine Teilzeit-
	beschäftigung
I work freelance/am	= Ich arbeite freiberuflich/
self-employed	bin selbständig

There is no article in German when giving someone's specific trade or profession. Also there are feminine forms for all nouns denoting professions, usually with the **-in** ending:

He's a baker	= Er ist Bäcker
She's a teacher	= Sie ist Lehrerin
George wants to be a	= George will System-
systems analyst	analytiker werden
Jane works as a	= Jane ist als Journalistin
journalist	tätig

However if an adjective is included, then there is an indefinite article as in English:

She is a good teacher	= Sie ist eine gute
	Lehrerin

Looking for a job

I'm looking for a job as	= Ich suche eine Stellung
a childminder	als Tagesmutter
I didn't find anything	= Ich habe in den
suitable in the	Stellenangeboten
situations vacant	nichts Geeignetes
	gefunden
I want to apply for	= Ich will mich um diese
this job	Stellung bewerben
A CV should be sent	= Der Bewerbung ist ein
with the application	Lebenslauf beizufügen
Could you come for an	= Könnten Sie bitte am
interview on March	24. März zu einem
24th?	Vorstellungsgespräch
	kommen?
What is the earliest you	= Wann könnten Sie
could start work?	frühestens anfangen?

---

horse) Trott, *der;* (of person for physical exercise) Dauerlauf, *der;* **go for a** ~: joggen gehen

jogger /'dʒɒɡə(r)/ *n.* Jogger, *der*/Joggerin, *die*

jogging /'dʒɒɡɪŋ/ *n.* Jogging, *das;* Joggen, *das*

'jogtrot *n.* (lit. or fig.) Trott, *der*

join /dʒɔɪn/ **1** *v.t.* **(a)** (put together, connect) verbinden (**to** mit); ~ **two things [together]** zwei Dinge miteinander verbinden; zwei Dinge zusammenfügen; ~ **hands** sich (*Dat.*) die Hände reichen; **(b)** (come into company of) sich gesellen zu; sich zugesellen (+ *Dat.*); (meet) treffen; (come with) mitkommen mit; sich anschließen (+ *Dat.*); **I'll ~ you in a minute** ich komme gleich nach; **may I ~ you** (at table) kann ich mich zu euch setzen?; **do ~ us for lunch** iss doch mit uns zu Mittag; **would you like to ~ me in a drink?** hast du Lust, ein Glas mit mir zu trinken?; **(c)** (become member of) eintreten in (+ *Akk.*) ⟨*Armee, Firma, Orden, Verein, Partei*⟩; beitreten (+ *Dat.*) ⟨*Verein, Partei, Orden*⟩; **(d)** (take one's place in) sich einreihen in (+ *Akk.*) ⟨*Umzug, Demonstrationszug*⟩; **(e)** ⟨*Fluss, Straße:*⟩ münden in (+ *Akk.*). **2** *v.i.* **(a)** (come together) ⟨*Flüsse:*⟩ sich vereinigen, zusammenfließen; ⟨*Straßen:*⟩ sich vereinigen, zusammenlaufen; ⟨*Grundstücke:*⟩ aneinander grenzen, aneinander stoßen; **(b)** (take part) ~ **with sb.** sich jmdm. anschließen. **3** *n.* Verbindung, *die;* (line) Nahtstelle, *die*

~ **in 1** /'-'-/ *v.i.* mitmachen (**with** bei); (in conversation) sich beteiligen (**with** an + *Dat.*); (in singing) einstimmen; mitsingen. **2** /'--/ *v.t.* mitmachen bei ⟨*Spiel, Spaß*⟩; sich beteiligen an (+ *Dat.*) ⟨*Spiel, Festlichkeiten, Gespräch*⟩; mitsingen ⟨*Refrain*⟩; sich anschließen (+ *Dat.*) ⟨*Demonstration, Umzug*⟩

~ **'up 1** *v.i.* **(a)** (Mil.) einrücken; Soldat werden; **(b)** ⟨*Straßen:*⟩ zusammenlaufen. **2** *v.t.* miteinander verbinden

joiner /'dʒɔɪnə(r)/ *n.* ▶ **887** | Tischler, *der*/Tischlerin, *die*

joinery /'dʒɔɪnərɪ/ *n., no pl.* **(a)** *no art.* (craft) Tischlerei, *die;* Tischlerhandwerk, *das;* **(b)** *no indef. art.* (products) Tischlerarbeiten

joint /dʒɔɪnt/ **1** *n.* **(a)** (place of joining) Verbindung, *die;* (line) Nahtstelle, *die;* (Building) Fuge, *die;* **(b)** ▶ **672** | (Anat., Mech. Engin., etc.) Gelenk, *das;* **(c) a ~ [of meat]** ein Stück Fleisch; (for roasting, roast) ein Braten; **a ~ of roast beef**

ein Rinderbraten; **(d)** (sl.) (place) Laden, *der;* (pub) Kaschemme, *die* (abwertend); **(e)** (sl.: marijuana cigarette) Joint, *der.* **2** *adj.* **(a)** (of two or more) gemeinsam ⟨*Anstrengung, Bericht, Besitz, Projekt, Ansicht, Konto*⟩; **(b)** Mit⟨*autor, -erbe, -besitzer*⟩

jointly /'dʒɔɪntlɪ/ *adv.* gemeinsam

joint: ~ **'stock** *n.* (Econ.) Gesellschafts- *od.* Aktienkapital, *das;* ~ **stock company** Aktiengesellschaft, *die;* ~ **'venture** *n.* (Commerc.) Jointventure, *das*

joist /dʒɔɪst/ *n.* (Building) Deckenbalken, *der;* (steel) [Decken]träger, *der*

joke /dʒəʊk/ **1** *n.* **(a)** Witz, *der;* Scherz, *der;* **sb.'s little** ~ (iron.) jmds. Scherzchen; ~ einen Scherz machen; **make a** ~: **do sth. for a** ~: etw. spaßeshalber *od.* zum Spaß tun; **tell a** ~: einen Witz erzählen; **have a** ~ **with sb.** mit jmdm. scherzen *od.* spaßen; **play a** ~ **on sb.** jmdm. einen Streich spielen; **he can/can't take a** ~: er versteht Spaß/ keinen Spaß; **the** ~ **was on him** er war der Narr; **this is getting beyond a** ~: da hört der Spaß auf; **this is no** ~: das ist nicht zum Lachen; **(b)** (ridiculous thing or circumstance) Witz, *der* (ugs.); (ridiculous person) Witzfigur, *die;* **treat sth. as a** ~: etw. nicht weiter ernst nehmen. **2** *v.i.* scherzen, Witze machen (**about** über + *Akk.*); **joking apart** Scherz *od.* Spaß beiseite!; **you have [got] to be joking!** (coll.) das soll wohl ein Witz sein!; mach keine Witze!

joker /'dʒəʊkə(r)/ *n.* **(a)** (person) Spaßvogel, *der;* Witzbold, *der* (ugs.); **(b)** (Cards) Joker, *der*

jolly /'dʒɒlɪ/ **1** *adj.* (cheerful) fröhlich; knallig ⟨*Farbe*⟩; (multicoloured) bunt. **2** *adv.* (Brit. coll.) ganz schön (ugs.); sehr ⟨*nett*⟩; ~ **good!** ausgezeichnet!; **I should** ~ **well think so!** das möchte ich auch meinen!

~ **a'long** *v.t.* bei Laune halten

jolt /dʒəʊlt/ **1** *v.t.* **(a)** (shake) ⟨*Fahrzeug:*⟩ durchrütteln, durchschütteln; ~ **sb./sth. out of/on to sth.** jmdn./etw. aus etw./auf etw. (*Akk.*) schleudern *od.* werfen; **(b)** (shock) aufschrecken; ~ **sb. into action** jmdn. auf Trab bringen (ugs.). **2** *v.i.* ⟨*Fahrzeug:*⟩ holpern, rütteln, rumpeln (ugs.). **3** *n.* **(a)** (jerk) Stoß, *der;* Ruck, *der;* **(b)** (fig.) (shock) Schock, *der;* Schreck, *der;* (surprise) Überraschung, *die*

Jordan /'dʒɔːdn/ *pr. n.* (a) ▶ 1048 ◄ (river) Jordan, *der;* (b) (country) Jordanien (*das*)

joss stick /'dʒɒsstɪk/ *n.* Räucherstäbchen, *das*

jostle /'dʒɒsl/ 1 *v.i.* ~ [against each other] aneinander stoßen. 2 *v.t.* stoßen

jot /dʒɒt/ *n.* [not] a ~: [k]ein bisschen ~ 'down *v.t.* [rasch] aufschreiben *od.* notieren

jotter /'dʒɒtə(r)/ *n.* (pad) Notizblock, *der;* (notebook) Notizbuch, *das*

jotting /'dʒɒtɪŋ/ *n.*, *usu. pl.* Notiz, *die*

journal /'dʒɜːnl/ *n.* (a) (newspaper) Zeitung, *die;* (periodical) Zeitschrift, *die;* **weekly** ~: Wochenzeitung, *die;* (b) (daily record of events) Tagebuch, *das*

journalism /'dʒɜːnəlɪzm/ *n.* Journalismus, *der*

journalist /'dʒɜːnəlɪst/ *n.* ▶ 887 ◄ Journalist, *der*/Journalistin, *die*

journalistic /dʒɜːnə'lɪstɪk/ *adj.* journalistisch ⟨*Stil*⟩

journey /'dʒɜːnɪ/ 1 *n.* Reise, *die;* (distance) Weg, *der;* a three-hour ~: eine dreistündige Fahrt; a ~ by car/train/ship eine Auto-/Bahn-/Schiffsreise; go on a ~: verreisen; eine Reise machen; go on a train/car ~: eine Reise mit dem Zug *od.* Zugreise/eine Reise mit dem Auto *od.* Autoreise machen; ~ through life Lebensreise, *die* (geh.). 2 *v.i.* (formal) fahren; ziehen

jovial /'dʒəʊvɪəl/ *adj.* (hearty) herzlich ⟨*Gruß*⟩; (merry) fröhlich ⟨*Ausdruck, Person*⟩

jowl /dʒaʊl/ *n.* (jaw) Unterkiefer, *der;* (lower part of face) Kinnbacken *Pl.;* (double chin) Doppelkinn, *das;* (flabby cheek) Hängebacke, *die;* cheek by ~: dicht nebeneinander

joy /dʒɔɪ/ *n.* (a) Freude, *die;* wish sb. ~: jmdm. viel Spaß *od.* Vergnügen wünschen; I wish you ~ of it (also iron.) ich wünsche dir viel Vergnügen damit; sing for/weep with ~: vor Freude (*Dat.*) singen/weinen; be full of the ~s of spring (fig. coll.) vor Freude ganz aus dem Häuschen sein (ugs.); it was a ~ to look at es war eine Augenweide; (b) *no pl., no art.* (coll.: success, satisfaction) Erfolg, *der;* he didn't get much ~ out of it es hat ihm nicht viel gebracht; any ~? Erfolg gehabt?; was erreicht? (ugs.)

joyful /'dʒɔɪfl/ *adj.* froh [gestimmt] ⟨*Person*⟩; froh ⟨*Gesicht*⟩; freudig ⟨*Blick, Ereignis, Umarmung, Gesang, Beifall*⟩; freudig, froh ⟨*Nachricht, Kunde*⟩; erfreulich ⟨*Nachricht, Ergebnis, Anblick*⟩

joyous /'dʒɔɪəs/ *adj.* freudig ⟨*Anlass, Ereignis*⟩; froh ⟨*Lachen, Herz*⟩; Freuden⟨*tag, -schrei*⟩

joy: ~ride *n.* (coll.) Spritztour [im gestohlenen Auto]; ~rider *n.* Autodieb (der den Wagen nur für eine Spritztour gestohlen hat); ~stick *n.* (a) (Aeronaut. coll.) Knüppel, *der;* (b) (on computer etc.) Hebel, *der;* Joystick, der (DV)

JP *abbr.* ▶ 887 ◄ Justice of the Peace

Jr. *abbr.* Junior jr.; jun.

jubilant /'dʒuːbɪlənt/ *adj.* jubelnd; freudestrahlend ⟨*Miene*⟩; be ~ ⟨*Person:*⟩ frohlocken

jubilation /dʒuːbɪ'leɪʃn/ *n.* Jubel, *der*

jubilee /'dʒuːbɪliː/ *n.* (anniversary) Jubiläum, *das*

judge /dʒʌdʒ/ 1 *n.* (a) ▶ 887 ◄ Richter, *der*/Richterin, *die;* (b) (in contest) Preisrichter, *der*/-richterin, *die;* (Sport) Kampfrichter, *der*/-richterin, *die;* Schiedsrichter, *der*/-richterin, *die;* (in dispute) Schiedsrichter, *der*/-richterin, *die;* (c) (fig.: connoisseur, critic) Kenner, *der*/Kennerin, *die;* ~ of character Menschenkenner, *der;* be a good ~ of sth. etw. gut beurteilen können; (d) (person who decides question) Schiedsrichter, *der;* be the ~ of sth. über etw. (*Akk.*) entscheiden. 2 *v.t.* (a) (pronounce sentence on) richten (geh.); ~ sb. (Law) jmds. Fall entscheiden; (b) (try) verhandeln ⟨*Fall*⟩; (c) (act as adjudicator of) Preisrichter/-richterin sein bei; (Sport) Schiedsrichter/-richterin sein bei; (d) (form opinion about) urteilen *od.* ein Urteil fällen über (+ *Akk.*); beurteilen; ~ sth. [to be] necessary etw. für *od.* als notwendig erachten; be good at judging distances gut Entfernungen schätzen können; (e) (decide) entscheiden ⟨*Angelegenheit, Frage*⟩. 3 *v.i.* (form a judgement) urteilen; to ~ by his size, …: der Größe nach zu urteilen, …; judging or to ~ by the look on his face …: nach dem Gesicht zu schließen, das er macht/machte, …; judging from what you say, …: nach dem, was du sagst, …; as far as I can ~, …: soweit ich es beurteilen kann, …

judgement, judgment /'dʒʌdʒmənt/ *n.* (a) Urteil, *das;* ~ was given in favour of/against sb. das Urteil fiel zu jmds. Gunsten/Ungunsten aus; pass [a] ~: ein Urteil abgeben (on über + *Akk.*); in *or* according to my ~: meines Erachtens; form a ~: sich (*Dat.*) ein Urteil *od.* eine Meinung bilden; against one's better ~: entgegen seiner besseren Einsicht; (b) (critical faculty) Urteilsfähigkeit, *die;* Urteilsvermögen, *das;* error of ~: Fehlurteil, *das;* Fehleinschätzung, *die;* I leave it to your ~: ich stelle das in Ihr Ermessen; use your own ~: verfahren Sie nach Ihrem Gutdünken; (c) (trial by God) day of ~, J~ Day Tag des Jüngsten Gerichts; the last ~: das Jüngste *od.* Letzte Gericht

judicial /dʒuː'dɪʃl/ *adj.* (a) gerichtlich; richterlich ⟨*Gewalt*⟩; ~ murder Justizmord, *der;* (b) (expressing judgement) kritisch

judiciary /dʒuː'dɪʃərɪ/ *n.* (Law) Richterschaft, *die*

judicious /dʒuː'dɪʃəs/ *adj.* (a) (discerning) klar blickend; (b) (sensible) besonnen

judiciously /dʒuː'dɪʃəslɪ/ *adv.* mit Bedacht

judo /'dʒuːdəʊ/ *n.*, *pl.* ~s Judo, *das*

jug /dʒʌg/ 1 *n.* (a) Krug, *der;* (with lid, water-~) Kanne, *die;* (small milk-~) Kännchen, *das;* a ~ of water ein Krug/eine Kanne Wasser; (b) (sl.: prison) Loch, *das* (salopp). 2 *v.t.* -gg- (Cookery) schmoren; ~ged hare Hasenpfeffer, *der*

juggernaut /'dʒʌgənɔːt/ *n.* (Brit.: lorry) schwerer Brummer (ugs.)

juggle /'dʒʌgl/ 1 *v.i.* (a) jonglieren; (perform conjuring tricks) zaubern; (b) ~ with (misrepresent) jonglieren mit ⟨*Fakten, Zahlen*⟩. 2 *v.t.* (lit., or fig.: manipulate) jonglieren [mit]

juggler /'dʒʌglə(r)/ *n.* Jongleur, *der*/Jongleuse, *die*

Jugoslav *etc.* ⇒ **Yugoslav** *etc.*

jugular /'dʒʌgjʊlə(r)/ *adj. & n.* (Anat.) ~ [vein] Jugularvene, *die* (fachspr.); Drosselvene, *die*

juice /dʒuːs/ *n.* (a) Saft, *der;* (b) (sl.) (electricity) Saft, *der* (salopp); (petrol) Sprit, *der* (ugs.)

juicy /'dʒuːsɪ/ *adj.* (a) saftig; (b) (coll.) (racy) saftig (ugs.) ⟨*Geschichte, Skandal*⟩; (suggestive) schlüpfrig; (profitable) fett (ugs.) ⟨*Vertrag, Geschäft usw.*⟩

ju-jitsu /dʒuː'dʒɪtsuː/ *n.* Jujutsu, *das;* Jiu-Jitsu, *das*

jukebox /'dʒuːkbɒks/ *n.* Jukebox, *die;* Musikbox, *die*

Jul. *abbr.* **July** Jul.

July /dʒʊ'laɪ/ *n.* ▶ 738 ◄ Juli, *der; see also* **August**

jumble /'dʒʌmbl/ 1 *v.t.* ~ up *or* together durcheinander bringen; durcheinander werfen. 2 *n.* (a) Wirrwarr, *der;* Gewirr, *das;* (muddle) Durcheinander, *das;* (b) *no pl., no indef. art.* (Brit.: articles for ~ sale) alte *od.* gebrauchte Sachen

'jumble sale *n.* (Brit.) Trödelmarkt, *der;* (for charity) Wohltätigkeitsbasar, *der*

jumbo /'dʒʌmbəʊ/ 1 *n.* (jet) Jumbo, *der.* 2 *adj.* ~[-sized] riesig; Riesen- (ugs.)

jumbo 'jet *n.* Jumbo-Jet, *der*

jump /dʒʌmp/ 1 *n.* (a) Sprung, *der;* always be one ~ ahead of sb. jmdm. immer um eine Nasenlänge voraus sein (ugs.); (b) (sudden transition) Sprung, *der;* sprunghafter Wechsel; (gap) Lücke, *die;* (c) (abrupt rise) sprunghafter Anstieg; ~ in value/temperature plötzliche Wertsteigerung/plötzlicher Temperaturanstieg; (d) (Parachuting) Absprung, *der.* 2 *v.i.* (a) springen; ⟨*Fallschirmspringer:*⟩ abspringen; ~ to one's feet/from one's seat aufspringen/vom Sitz aufspringen; (b) ~ to (reach overhastily) voreilig gelangen zu ⟨*Annahme, Lösung*⟩; ~ to conclusions voreilige Schlüsse ziehen; (c) (make sudden movement) springen; (start) zusammenzucken; ~ for joy einen Freudensprung/Freudensprünge machen; (d) (rise suddenly) ⟨*Kosten, Preise usw.:*⟩ sprunghaft steigen, in die Höhe schnellen; (e) ~ to it (coll.) zupacken; ~ to it! (coll.) mach/macht schon! 3 *v.t.* (a) springen über (+ *Akk.*); überspringen ⟨*Mauer, Zaun usw.*⟩; (b) (move to point beyond) überspringen; (c) (not stop at) überfahren ⟨*rote Ampel*⟩; ~ the lights bei Rot [durch]fahren; (d) ~ the rails *or* track ⟨*Zug:*⟩ entgleisen; (e) ~ ship ⟨*Seemann:*⟩ [unter Bruch des Heuervertrages vorzeitig] den Dienst quittieren; (f) ~ the queue (Brit.) sich vordrängeln; (g) (skip over) überspringen ⟨*Seite, Kapitel usw.*⟩; (h) (attack) herfallen über (+ *Akk.*)

~ **a'bout**, ~ **a'round** *v.i.* herumspringen (ugs.)

~ **at** *v.t.* (a) anspringen; (b) (fig.: accept eagerly) sofort [beim Schopf] ergreifen ‹*Gelegenheit*›; sofort zugreifen *od.* (ugs.) zuschlagen bei ‹*Angebot*›; sofort aufgreifen *od.* (ugs.) anspringen auf ‹*Vorschlag*›

~ **'in** *v.i.* reinspringen (ugs.)

~ **'off 1** *v.i.* abspringen. **2** *v.t.* ~ **off sth.** von etw. springen

~ **on 1** /-'-/ *v.i.* aufspringen; ~ **on to a bus/train** in einen Bus/Zug springen; ~ **on to one's bicycle/horse** sich aufs Fahrrad/Pferd schwingen. **2** /'--/ *v.t.* ~ **on a bus/train** in einen Bus/Zug springen; ~ **on one's bicycle** sich aufs Fahrrad schwingen

~ **'out** *v.i.* hinaus-/herausspringen; ~ **out of** springen aus

~ **'up** *v.i.* aufspringen (**from** von); ~ **up on to sth.** auf etw. (*Akk.*) springen

jumped-up /'dʒʌmptʌp/ *adj.* (coll.) emporgekommen

jumper /'dʒʌmpə(r)/ *n.* (a) Pullover, *der;* Pulli, *der* (ugs.); (b) (Amer.: pinafore dress) Trägerkleid, *das*

jump: ~ **jet** *n.* (Aeronaut.) Senkrechtstarter, *der;* ~ **leads** *n. pl.* (Brit. Motor Veh.) Starthilfekabel, *das;* ~ **start 1** *v.t.* ~**-start a car** einem Auto Starthilfe geben; (fig.) [wieder] in Gang bringen; [wieder] ankurbeln ‹*Wirtschaft, Industrie*›; **2** *n.* Start durch Starthilfe; (fig.) neuer Impuls *od.* Auftrieb; **the car needs a** ~**-start** das Auto braucht Starthilfe; **the economy received a** ~**-start** die Wirtschaft erfuhr [einen] neuen Aufschwung; ~**suit** *n.* Overall, *der*

jumpy /'dʒʌmpi/ *adj.* nervös; aufgeregt

Jun. *abbr.* (a) **June** Jun.; (b) **Junior** jun.

junction /'dʒʌŋkʃn/ *n.* (a) Verbindungspunkt, *der;* Verbindungsstelle, *die;* (b) (of railway lines, roads) ≈ Einmündung, *die;* (of motorway) Anschlussstelle, *die;* (crossroads) Kreuzung, *die*

'junction box *n.* (Electr.) Verteilerkasten, *der*

juncture /'dʒʌŋktʃə(r)/ *n.* **at this** ~: zu diesem Zeitpunkt

June /dʒuːn/ *n.* ▶ **738** Juni, *der; see also* **August**

jungle /'dʒʌŋgl/ *n.* Dschungel, *der* (auch fig.); Urwald, *der*

junior /'dʒuːnɪə(r)/ **1** *adj.* (a) (below a certain age) jünger; (b) (of lower rank) rangniedriger ‹*Person*›; einfach ‹*Angestellter*›; (c) appended to name (the younger) **Mr Smith J~:** Mr. Smith junior; (d) (Amer. Sch., Univ.) ~ **year** vorletztes Jahr vor der Abschlussprüfung. **2** *n.* (younger person) Jüngere, *der/die;* (person of lower rank) Untergebene, *der/die;* **be [six years] sb.'s** ~: [sechs Jahre] jünger sein als jmd.

junior: ~ **'minister** *n.* (Brit.) ≈ Ministerialdirektor, *der/-*direktorin, *die;* ~ **'partner** *n.* Juniorpartner, *der/-*partnerin, *die;* ~ **school** *n.* (Brit.) Grundschule, *die*

juniper /'dʒuːnɪpə(r)/ *n.* (Bot.) Wacholder, *der*

junk¹ /dʒʌŋk/ **1** *n.* (discarded material) Trödel, *der* (ugs.); Gerümpel, *das;* (trash) Plunder, *der* (ugs.); Ramsch, *der* (ugs.). **2** *v.t.* wegwerfen; ausmisten (ugs.); (fig.) aufgeben

junk² *n.* (ship) Dschunke, *die*

junk: ~ **food** *n.* minderwertige Kost; ~ **heap** *n.* (a) ⇨ **scrap heap**; (b) (sl.: old car etc.) Schrotthaufen, *der* (ugs.)

junkie /'dʒʌŋki/ *n.* (sl.) Junkie, *der* (Drogenjargon)

junk: ~ **mail** *n.* Postwurfsendungen *Pl.;* Reklame, *die;* ~ **shop** *n.* Trödelladen, *der* (ugs.)

junta /'dʒʌntə/ *n.* Junta, *die;* **military** ~: Militärjunta, *die*

Jupiter /'dʒuːpɪtə(r)/ *pr. n.* (a) (Astron.) Jupiter, *der;* (b) (Roman Mythol.) Jupiter (*der*)

jurisdiction /dʒʊərɪs'dɪkʃn/ *n.* (authority) Jurisdiktion, *die;* Gerichtsbarkeit, *die;* (extent) Zuständigkeit, *die;* **fall** *or* **come under** *or* **within the** ~ **of sth./sb.** in die Zuständigkeit *od.* den Zuständigkeitsbereich von etw./jmdm. fallen; **have** ~ **over sb./in a matter** für jmdn./in einer Angelegenheit zuständig sein

juror /'dʒʊərə(r)/ *n.* Geschworene, *der/die;* (in Germany, in some Austrian courts) Schöffe, *der/*Schöffin, *die*

jury /'dʒʊəri/ *n.* (a) (in court) **the** ~: die Geschworenen; (in Germany, in some Austrian courts) die Schöffen; **sit on the** ~:

auf der Geschworenen-/Schöffenbank sitzen; **do** ~ **service** das Amt eines Geschworenen/Schöffen ausüben; (b) (In competition) Jury, *die;* Preisgericht, *das*

'jury box *n.* Geschworenenbank, *die;* (in Germany, in some Austrian courts) Schöffenbank, *die*

just /dʒʌst/ **1** *adj.* (a) (morally right, deserved) gerecht; anständig, korrekt ‹*Verhalten, Benehmen*›; (b) (legally right) rechtmäßig; (c) (justified) berechtigt ‹*Angst, Zorn, Groll*›; (d) (right in amount) recht, richtig ‹*Proportion, Maß, Verhältnis*›. **2** *adv.* (a) (exactly) genau; ~ **then/enough** gerade da/genug; ~ **as** (exactly as, in the same way as) genauso wie; (when) gerade, als; ~ **as you like** ganz wie Sie wünschen; ~ **as good/tidy** *etc.* genauso gut/ordentlich *usw.;* **come** ~ **as you are** komm so, wie du bist; ~ **as fast as I can** so schnell, wie ich nur kann; **it'll** ~ **about be enough** (coll.) es wird in etwa reichen; **that is** ~ **'it** das ist es ja gerade; genau das ist es ja; **that's** ~ **like him** das ist typisch er *od.* für ihn; ~ **'so** (in an orderly manner) ordentlich; *expr. agreement* ganz recht; (b) (barely) gerade [eben]; (with very little time to spare) gerade [eben] noch; (no more than) nur; ~ **under £10** nicht ganz zehn Pfund; **it's** ~ **possible** das ist gerade noch möglich; **it's** ~ **after the traffic lights** es ist direkt hinter der Verkehrsampel; (c) (exactly or nearly now or then, in immediate past) gerade [eben]; [so]eben; (at this moment) gerade; **I have** ~ **seen him** (Brit.), **I** ~ **saw him** (Amer.) ich habe ihn gerade [eben] *od.* eben gesehen; ~ **now** (at this moment) [im Moment] gerade; (a little time ago) gerade eben; **not** ~ **now** im Moment nicht; (d) (coll.) (simply) einfach; (only) nur; *esp. with imperatives* mal [eben]; **I've come here** ~ **to see you** ich bin nur gekommen, um dich zu besuchen; ~ **anybody** irgendjemand; ~ **look at that!** guck dir das mal an!; **could you** ~ **turn round?** kannst du dich mal [eben] umdrehen?; ~ **come here a moment** komm [doch] mal einen Moment her; ~ **a moment, please** einen Moment mal; ~ **in case** für alle Fälle; (e) (coll.: positively) einfach; echt (ugs.); **that's** ~ **ridiculous/fantastic** das ist einfach lächerlich/fantastisch; (f) (quite) **not** ~ **yet** noch nicht ganz; **it is** ~ **as well that** ...: [es ist] nur gut *od.* es ist doch gut, dass ...; **you might** ~ **as well** ...: du könntest genauso gut ...; (g) (coll.: really, indeed) wirklich; echt (ugs.); **That's lovely. — Isn't it** ~? Das ist schön. — Ja, und wie; ~ **the same** (nevertheless) trotzdem; **that's** ~ **too bad** das ist Pech

justice /'dʒʌstɪs/ *n.* (a) Gerechtigkeit, *die;* **administer** ~: Recht sprechen; **poetic** ~: ausgleichende Gerechtigkeit; **do** ~ **to sth.** einer Sache (*Dat.*) gerecht werden; ~ **was done in the end** der Gerechtigkeit wurde schließlich Genüge getan; **do oneself** ~: sich richtig zur Geltung bringen; **in** ~ **to sb.** um jmdm. gerecht zu werden, with ~: mit Recht; (b) (judicial proceedings) **bring sb. to** ~: jmdn. vor Gericht bringen *od.* stellen; **let** ~ **take its course** der Gerechtigkeit ihren Lauf lassen; (c) ▶ **887** (magistrate) Schiedsrichter, *der/-*richterin, *die;* **J~ of the Peace** Friedensrichter, *der/-*richterin, *die*

justifiable /dʒʌstɪ'faɪəbl/ *adj.* berechtigt; gerechtfertigt ‹*Maßnahme, Handlung*›

justifiably /dʒʌstɪ'faɪəbli/ *adv.* zu Recht; berechtigterweise (Papierdt.)

justification /dʒʌstɪfɪ'keɪʃn/ *n.* Rechtfertigung, *die;* (condition of being justified) Berechtigung, *die;* **with some** ~: mit einigem Recht

justify /'dʒʌstɪfaɪ/ *v.t.* (a) (show justice of, vindicate) rechtfertigen; (demonstrate correctness of) belegen, beweisen ‹*Behauptung, Argument, Darstellung*›; (offer adequate grounds for) begründen ‹*Verhalten, Vorstellung, Behauptung*›; ~ **oneself/sth. to sb.** sich/etw. jmdm. gegenüber *od.* vor jmdm. rechtfertigen; **the end justifies the means** der Zweck heiligt die Mittel; **be justified in doing sth.** etw. zu Recht tun; (b) (Printing) ausschließen

just-in-'time *adj.* Just-in-Time-‹*Produktion, Lieferung usw.*›

jut /dʒʌt/ *v.i.* **-tt-:** ~ **[out]** [her]vorragen; herausragen

jute /dʒuːt/ *n.* Jute, *die*

juvenile /'dʒuːvənaɪl/ **1** *adj.* (a) jugendlich; (geh.) juvenil ‹*Geschmack, Einstellung*›; Jugend‹*literatur, -mode*›; ~ **crime** Jugendkriminalität, *die;* (b) (immature) kindisch (abwertend); infantil (abwertend). **2** *n.* Jugendliche, *der/die*

juvenile: ~ **court** n. (Law) Jugendgericht, das; ~ **de-'linquency** n. Jugendkriminalität, die; ~ **de'linquent** n. jugendlicher Straftäter/jugendliche Straftäterin; ~ **offender** n. jugendlicher Straftäter

juxtapose /dʒʌkstə'pəʊz/ v.t. nebeneinander stellen (**with,** to und)

juxtaposition /dʒʌkstəpə'zıʃn/ n. (action) Nebeneinanderstellung, die; (condition) Nebeneinander, das

Kk

K, k /keɪ/ n., pl. **Ks** or **K's** K, k, das

kale /keɪl/ n. (Bot.) [**curly**] ~: Grünkohl, der; Krauskohl, der

kaleidoscope /kə'laɪdəskəʊp/ n. (lit. or fig.) Kaleidoskop, das

Kampuchea /kæmpʊ'tʃiːə/ pr. n. Kampu[ts]chea (das)

kangaroo /kæŋgə'ruː/ n. Känguru, das

kangaroo 'court n. Femegericht, das; Feme, die

kaput /kæ'pʊt/ pred. adj. (coll.) kaputt (ugs.)

karaoke /kærr'əʊkɪ/ n., no pl., no indef. art. Karaoke, das; attrib. Karaoke-; ~ **machine** Karaokegerät, das

karate /kə'rɑːtɪ/ n., no pl., no indef. art. Karate, das

kayak /'kaɪæk/ n. Kajak, der

kebab /kɪ'bæb/ n. (Cookery) Kebab, der

keel /kiːl/ **1** n. (Naut.) Kiel, der; see also **even 1 b. 2** v.i. ~ **over** (a) (overturn) umstürzen; ⟨Schiff:⟩ kentern; (b) (fall) ⟨Person:⟩ umkippen

keen /kiːn/ adj. (a) (sharp) scharf ⟨Messer, Klinge, Schneide⟩; (b) (piercingly cold) scharf, schneidend ⟨Wind, Kälte⟩; (penetrating, strong) grell ⟨Licht⟩; durchdringend, stechend ⟨Geruch⟩; (c) (eager) begeistert, leidenschaftlich ⟨Fußballfan, Sportler⟩; ausgeprägt, lebhaft ⟨Interesse⟩; heftig ⟨Konkurrenz, Verlangen⟩; **be** ~ **to do sth.** darauf erpicht sein, etw. zu tun; **he's really** ~ **to win** er will unbedingt gewinnen; **be** ~ **on doing sth.** etw. gern[e] tun; **not be** ~ **on sth.** nicht gerade begeistert von etw. sein; **be** ~ **on sb.** scharf auf jmdn. sein (ugs.); (d) (highly sensitive) scharf ⟨Augen⟩; fein ⟨Sinne⟩; ausgeprägt ⟨Sinn für etw.⟩; (e) (intellectually sharp) scharf ⟨Verstand, Intellekt⟩; (f) (acute) heftig, stark ⟨Schmerzen, Qualen⟩; (g) (Brit.) niedrig, günstig ⟨Preis⟩

keenly /'kiːnlɪ/ adv. (a) (sharply) scharf ⟨geschliffen⟩; (b) (eagerly) eifrig ⟨arbeiten⟩; brennend ⟨interessiert sein⟩; (c) (piercingly) scharf ⟨ansehen⟩; (d) (acutely) **be** ~ **aware of sth.** sich (Dat.) einer Sache (Gen.) voll bewusst sein; **feel sth.** ~ etw. deutlich fühlen

keenness /'kiːnnɪs/ n., no pl. (a) (sharpness, coldness, acuteness of sense) Schärfe, die; (b) (eagerness) Eifer, der; (c) (of intellect) Schärfe, die

keep /kiːp/ **1** v.t., **kept** /kept/ (a) (observe) halten ⟨Versprechen, Schwur usw.⟩; einhalten ⟨Verabredung, Vereinbarung, Vertrag, Zeitplan⟩; (b) (guard) behüten, beschützen ⟨Person⟩; hüten ⟨Herde, Schafe⟩; schützen ⟨Stadt, Festung⟩; verwahren ⟨Wertgegenstände⟩; ~ **sb. safe** jmdn. beschützen; ~ **sth. locked away** etw. unter Verschluss halten od. aufbewahren; (c) (have charge of) aufbewahren; verwahren; (d) (retain possession of) behalten; (not lose or destroy) aufheben ⟨Quittung, Rechnung⟩; **you can** ~ **it** (coll.: I do not want it) das kannst du behalten od. dir an den Hut stecken (ugs.); (e) (maintain) unterhalten, instand halten ⟨Gebäude, Straße usw.⟩; pflegen ⟨Garten⟩; **neatly kept** gut gepflegt; (f) (carry on, manage) unterhalten, führen, betreiben ⟨Geschäft, Lokal, Bauernhof⟩; (g) halten ⟨Schweine, Bienen, Hund, Katze usw.⟩; sich (Dat.) halten ⟨Diener, Auto⟩; (h) führen ⟨Tagebuch, Liste usw.⟩; ~ **the books** die Bücher führen; (i) (provide for) versorgen, unterhalten ⟨Familie⟩; ~ **sb./oneself in cigarettes** etc. jmdn./sich mit Zigaretten usw. versorgen; (j) sich (Dat.) halten

⟨Geliebte, Mätresse usw.⟩; (k) (have on sale) führen ⟨Ware⟩; ~ **a stock of** etw. [am Lager] haben; (l) (maintain in quality, state, or position) halten ⟨Rhythmus⟩; ~ **sth. in one's head** etw. [im Kopf] behalten; sich (Dat.) etw. merken; ~ **sb. waiting** jmdn. warten lassen; ~ **the office running smoothly** dafür sorgen, dass im Büro alles reibungslos [ab]läuft; ~ **sb. alive** jmdn. am Leben halten; ~ **the traffic moving** den Verkehr in Fluss halten; ~ **sth. shut/tidy** etw. geschlossen/in Ordnung halten; (m) (detain) festhalten; **what kept you?** wo bleibst du denn?; **don't let me** ~ **you** lass dich [von mir] nicht aufhalten; ~ **sb. in prison** jmdn. in Haft halten; (n) (restrain, prevent) ~ **sb. from doing sth.** jmdn. davon abhalten od. daran hindern, etw. zu tun; **to** ~ **myself from falling** um nicht zu fallen; (o) (reserve) aufheben; aufsparen; ~ **a seat for sb.** jmdm. einen Platz freihalten; ~ **it for oneself** es für sich behalten; ~ **sth. for later** etc. sich (Dat.) etw. für später usw. aufheben od. aufsparen; (p) (conceal) ~ **sth. to oneself** etw. für sich behalten; ~ **sth. from sb.** jmdm. etw. verheimlichen. **2** v.i., **kept** (a) (remain in specified place, condition) bleiben; ~ **warm/clean** sich warm/sauber halten; **how are you** ~**ing?** (coll.) wie geht's [dir] denn so? (ugs.); **are you** ~**ing well?** geht's dir gut?; ~ **together** zusammenbleiben; (b) (continue in course, direction, or action) ~ [**to the**] **left/**[**to the**] **right/straight on** sich links/rechts halten/immer geradeaus fahren/gehen usw.; '~ **left**' (traffic sign) „links vorbeifahren"; ~ **behind me** halte dich od. bleib hinter mir; ~ **doing sth.** (not stop) etw. weiter tun; (repeatedly) etw. immer wieder tun; (constantly) etw. dauernd od. immer tun; ~ **talking/working** etc. **until …**: weiterreden/-arbeiten usw., bis …; (c) (remain good) ⟨Lebensmittel:⟩ sich halten; **what I have to say won't** ~: was ich zu sagen habe, ist eilig od. eilt. **3** n. (a) (maintenance) Unterhalt, der; **I get £100 a month and my** ~: ich bekomme 100 Pfund monatlich und Logis; **sth. doesn't earn its** ~: etw. zahlt sich nicht aus (ugs.); **you don't earn your** ~: du bist nichts als ein unnützer Esser; (b) **for** ~s (coll.) auf Dauer; (to be retained) zum Behalten; (c) (Hist.: tower) Bergfried, der

~ **'after** v.t. verfolgen; jagen; (fig.: chivvy) antreiben

~ **at** v.t. (work persistently) weitermachen mit; ~ **'at it!** nicht nachlassen!

~ **a'way 1** v.i. wegbleiben (ugs.) (**from** von); sich fernhalten (**from** von). **2** v.t. fernhalten (**from** von)

~ **'back 1** v.i. zurückbleiben; ~ **back!** bleib wo du bist!; ~ **back from sth.** von etw. wegbleiben (ugs.). **2** v.t. (a) (restrain) zurückhalten ⟨Menschenmenge, Tränen⟩; (b) (withhold) verschweigen ⟨Informationen, Tatsachen⟩ (**from** Dat.); einbehalten ⟨Geld, Zahlung⟩

~ **'down 1** v.i. unten bleiben. **2** v.t. (a) (oppress, suppress) unterdrücken ⟨Volk, Person⟩; **you can't** ~ **a good man down** (prov.) er/sie usw. lässt/lassen sich nicht unterkriegen (ugs.); (b) (prevent increase of) niedrig halten ⟨Steuern, Preise, Zinssatz, Ausgaben, usw.⟩; eindämmen ⟨Epidemie⟩; ~ **one's weight down** nicht zunehmen; ~ **the weeds down** dafür sorgen, dass das Unkraut nicht überhand nimmt; (c) (not raise) unten lassen ⟨Kopf⟩; ~ **your voice down** rede nicht so laut; (d) (not vomit) bei sich behalten ⟨Essen⟩

~ **from** v.t. ~ **from doing sth.** etw. nicht tun; (avoid doing) es vermeiden, etw. zu tun; **I couldn't** ~ **from smiling** ich musste einfach lächeln; see also ~ **1 n**

~ **'in 1** v.i. (remain in favour) ~ **in with sb.** sich mit jmdm. gut stellen; sich (Dat.) jmdn. warm halten (ugs.). **2** v.t. (a) unterdrücken ⟨Gefühle⟩; einziehen ⟨Bauch⟩; (b) (Sch.) nachsitzen lassen ⟨Schüler⟩; **be kept in** [**after school**] nachsitzen müssen

~ **'off 1** v.i. ⟨Person:⟩ wegbleiben; ⟨Regen, Sturm usw.:⟩ ausbleiben; '~ **off**' (on building site etc.) „Betreten verboten". **2** v.t. (a) fernhalten ⟨Person, Tier⟩; abhalten ⟨Sonne⟩; ~ **sb./sth. off sth.** jmdn./etw. von etw. fernhalten/abhalten; (b) (not go on) nicht betreten; '~ **off the grass**' „Betreten des Rasens verboten"; (c) (not touch) ~ **off my whisky!** Hände od. Finger weg von meinem Whisky!; (d) (not eat or drink) ~ **off chocolate/brandy** keine Schokolade essen/ keinen Brandy trinken; ~ **off the drink** keinen Alkohol od. (ugs.) nichts trinken; (e) (not mention) vermeiden ⟨Thema⟩

~ 'on 1 *v.i.* (a) (continue, persist) weitermachen (**with** *Akk.*); (b) (Brit.: talk tiresomely) ~ **on about sth.** immer wieder von etw. anfangen; ~ **on at sb. about sth.** jmdm. mit etw. ständig in den Ohren liegen (ugs.). 2 *v.t.* (a) ~ **on doing sth.** etw. [immer] weiter tun; (repeatedly) etw. immer wieder tun; (constantly) etw. dauernd *od.* immer tun; (b) weiterbeschäftigen, behalten ⟨*Angestellten*⟩; behalten ⟨*Wohnung, Auto*⟩; (c) anbehalten, anlassen ⟨*Kleid, Mantel*⟩; aufbehalten ⟨*Hut*⟩

~ 'out 1 *v.i.* draußen bleiben; '~ **out**„ "Zutritt verboten". 2 *v.t.* (a) (not let enter) nicht hereinlassen ⟨*Person, Tier*⟩; (b) abhalten ⟨*Kälte*⟩; abweisen ⟨*Nässe*⟩

~ 'out of *v.t.* (a) (stay outside) ~ **out of a room/an area/a country** ein Zimmer/eine Gegend nicht betreten/ nicht in ein Land reisen; (b) (avoid) ~ **out of danger** Gefahren meiden; sich nicht in Gefahr begeben; ~ **out of trouble** zurechtkommen; ~ **out of the rain/sun** *etc.* nicht in den Regen/die Sonne *usw.* gehen; ~ **out of sb.'s way** jmdm. aus dem Weg gehen; (c) (not let enter) nicht hereinlassen in (+ *Akk.*); (d) (cause to avoid) ~ **the dog out of my way** halte mir den Hund vom Leibe (ugs.)

~ **to** *v.t.* (a) (not leave) bleiben auf (+ *Dat.*) ⟨*Straße, Weg*⟩; ~ **to the left!** halte dich links!; bleib links!; (b) (follow, observe) sich halten an (+ *Akk.*) ⟨*Regeln, Muster, Gesetz, Diät, usw.*⟩; einhalten ⟨*Zeitplan*⟩; halten ⟨*Versprechen*⟩; ~ **to one's word** Wort halten; (c) ~ **[oneself] to oneself** für sich bleiben; **they** ~ **themselves to themselves** sie bleiben unter sich. *See also* ~ 2 **b**

~ 'up 1 *v.i.* (a) (proceed equally) ~ **up with sb./sth.** mit jmdm./etw. Schritt halten; ~ **up with the Joneses** mit den andern gleichziehen; (b) (maintain contact) ~ **up with sb.** mit jmdm. Kontakt halten; ~ **up with sth.** sich über etw. (*Akk.*) auf dem Laufenden halten. 2 *v.t.* (a) (prevent from falling) festhalten ⟨*Leiter, Zelt usw.*⟩; (b) (prevent from sinking) aufrechterhalten ⟨*Produktion, Standard usw.*⟩; auf gleichem Niveau halten ⟨*Preise, Löhne usw.*⟩; (c) (maintain) aufrechterhalten ⟨*Bräuche, Freundschaft, jmds. Moral*⟩; (keep in repair) instand *od.* (ugs.) in Schuss halten ⟨*Haus*⟩; (keep in proper condition) in Ordnung *od.* (ugs.) in Schuss halten ⟨*Garten*⟩; (d) (continue) weiterhin zahlen ⟨*Raten*⟩; ~ **one's courage/spirits up** den Mut nicht sinken lassen; ~ **one's strength up** sich bei Kräften halten; ~ **it up** weitermachen; ~ **it up!** weiter so!; **he'll never be able to** ~ **it up** er wird es nicht durchhalten [können]; (e) (prevent from going to bed) am Schlafengehen hindern; **they kept me up all night** sie haben mich die ganze Nacht nicht schlafen lassen

keeper /'ki:pə(r)/ *n.* ▶ 887 (a) ⇨ **gamekeeper**; (b) ⇨ **goalkeeper**; (a) (zoo-~) Tierwärter, *der*/-wärterin, *die*; (d) (custodian) Wärter, *der*/Wärterin, *die*

keep-'fit *n.* Fitnesstraining, *das*

keep-'fit class *n.* Fitnessgruppe, *die*; **go to** ~**es** zu Fitnessübungen gehen

keeping /'ki:pɪŋ/ *n., no pl.* (a) *no art.* **be in** ~ **with sth.** einer Sache (*Dat.*) entsprechen; (be suited to sth.) zu etw. passen; (b) (custody) **give sth. into sb.'s** ~: jmdm. etw. zur Aufbewahrung [über]geben

'keepsake *n.* Andenken, *das*

keg /keg/ *n.* (a) (barrel) [kleines] Fass; Fässchen, *das*; (b) *attrib.* ~ **beer** *aus luftdichten Metallbehältern gezapftes, mit Kohlensäure versetztes Bier;* ≈ Fassbier, *das*

ken /ken/ *n.* **this is beyond my** ~: das geht über meinen Horizont; (beyond range of knowledge) das übersteigt mein Wissen

kennel /'kenl/ *n.* (a) Hundehütte, *die*; (b) *in pl.* [**boarding**] ~**s** Hundepension, *die*; [**breeding**] ~**s** Zwinger, *der*

Kenya /'kenjə, 'ki:njə/ *pr. n.* Kenia (*das*)

Kenyan /'kenjən, 'ki:njən/ ▶ 947 1 *adj.* kenianisch; **sb. is** ~: jmd. ist Kenianer/Kenianerin. 2 *n.* Kenianer, *der*/ Kenianerin, *die*

kept ⇨ **keep** 1, 2

kerb /kɜ:b/ *n.* (Brit.) Bordstein, *der*

kerb: ~**-crawling** *n.* (Brit.) (langsames) Fahren auf dem Autostrich zur Kontaktaufnahme mit einer Prostituierten; ~**stone** *n.* (Brit.) Bordstein, *der*

kernel /'kɜ:nl/ *n.* (lit. or fig.) Kern, *der*; **a** ~ **of truth** ein Körnchen Wahrheit

kestrel /'kestrl/ *n.* (Ornith.) Turmfalke, *der*

ketchup /'ketʃʌp/ *n.* Ket[s]chup, *der od. das*

kettle /'ketl/ *n.* [Wasser]kessel, *der;* **a pretty** *or* **fine** ~ **of fish** (iron.) eine schöne Bescherung (ugs. iron.); **a different** ~ **of fish** eine ganz andere Sache

'kettledrum *n.* (Mus.) [Kessel]pauke, *die*

key /ki:/ 1 *n.* (a) (lit. or fig.) Schlüssel, *der;* **the** ~ **to success** der Schlüssel zum Erfolg; **the** ~ **to the mystery** des Rätsels Lösung; (b) (set of answers) [Lösungs]schlüssel, *der;* (to map etc.) Zeichenerklärung, *die;* (to cipher) Schlüssel, *der;* (c) (on piano, typewriter, etc.) Taste, *die;* (on wind instrument) Klappe, *die;* (d) (Mus.) Tonart, *die;* **sing/play in/off** ~: richtig/falsch singen/spielen. 2 *attrib. adj.* entscheidend; Schlüssel⟨*frage, -position, -rolle, -figur, -industrie*⟩. 3 *v.t.* (Computing) eintasten

~ **in** *v.t.* (Computing) eintasten

key: ~**board** 1 *n.* (of piano etc.) Klaviatur, *die;* (of typewriter etc.) Tastatur, *die;* 2 *v.t.* tasten; ~**boarder** *n.* Taster, *der*/Tasterin, *die;* ~**boarding** *n., no pl.* (Computing) Tasten, *das;* ~**boarding error** Tastfehler, *der*

keyed up /ki:d'ʌp/ *adj.* **be all** ~: ganz aufgeregt sein

key: ~**hole** *n.* Schlüsselloch, *das;* ~**hole surgery** *n.* Schlüssellochchirurgie, *die;* Knopflochchirurgie, *die;* ~**note** *n.* (a) (Mus.) Grundton, *der;* (b) (fig.) Grundgedanke, *der;* [Grund]tenor, *der;* ~**note speech** programmatische Rede; ~**ring** *n.* Schlüsselring, *der;* ~ **signature** *n.* (Mus.) Tonartvorzeichnung, *die;* ~**word** *n.* (key to cipher) Schlüsselwort, *das*

'keying *n., no pl.* ⇨ **keyboarding**

key: ~**pad** *n.* Tastenfeld, *das;* ~**stroke** *n.* (Computing) Anschlag, *der;*

kg. *abbr.* ▶ 1202 **kilogram[s]** kg

khaki /'kɑ:kɪ/ 1 *adj.* khakifarben. 2 *n.* (cloth) Khaki, *der*

kHz *abbr.* **kilohertz** kHz

kibbutz /kɪ'bʊts/ *n., pl.* **kibbutzim** /kɪbʊt'si:m/ Kibbuz, *der*

kick /kɪk/ 1 *n.* (a) [Fuß]tritt, *der;* (Footb.) Schuss, *der;* **give sb. a** ~: jmdm. einen Tritt geben *od.* versetzen; **give sth. a** ~: gegen etw. treten; **give sb. a** ~ **in the pants** (fig. coll.) jmdm. Feuer unterm Hintern machen (salopp); **a** ~ **in the teeth** (fig.) ein Schlag ins Gesicht; (b) (Sport: burst of speed) Spurt, *der;* (c) (coll.: sharp effect, thrill) Kitzel, *der;* (of wine) Feuer, *das;* **he gets a** ~ **out of it** er hat Spaß daran; es macht ihm Spaß; **do sth. for** ~**s** etw. zum Spaß tun; (d) (recoil of gun) Rückstoß, *der.* 2 *v.i.* (a) treten; ⟨*Pferd:*⟩ ausschlagen; ⟨*Baby:*⟩ strampeln; ⟨*Tänzer:*⟩ das Bein hochwerfen; ~ **at sth.** gegen etw. treten; (b) (show opposition) sich zur Wehr setzen (**at, against** gegen). 3 *v.t.* (a) einen Tritt geben (+ *Dat.*) ⟨*Person, Hund*⟩; treten gegen ⟨*Gegenstand*⟩; kicken (ugs.), schlagen, schießen ⟨*Ball*⟩; ~ **the door open/shut** die Tür auf-/zutreten; **he** ~**ed the ball straight at me** er kickte den Ball genau in meine Richtung; ~ **sb. in the teeth** (fig. coll.) jmdn. vor den Kopf stoßen; **I could** ~ **myself!** (coll.) ich könnte mir *od.* mich in den Hintern beißen (salopp); (b) (coll.: abandon) ablegen ⟨*schlechte Angewohnheit*⟩; aufgeben ⟨*Rauchen*⟩; ~ **the habit** es abstecken (ugs.)

~ **a'bout,** ~ **a'round** 1 *v.t.* (a) [in der Gegend] herumkicken (ugs.); (b) (treat badly) herumstoßen; schikanieren. 2 *v.i.* **be** ~**ing about** *or* **around** (coll.) (be present, alive) rumhängen (ugs.); (lie scattered) rumliegen (ugs.)

~ 'in *v.t.* (break, damage) eintreten

~ 'off 1 *v.t.* von sich schleudern ⟨*Kleidungsstück, Schuhe*⟩. 2 *v.i.* (Footb.) anstoßen ⟨*Spiel:*⟩ beginnen; (fig. coll.: start) anfangen

~ 'out *v.t.* (force to leave) hinauswerfen; rausschmeißen (ugs.); **get** ~**ed out** rausfliegen (ugs.); **get** ~**ed out of one's job** [aus der Stellung] fliegen (ugs.)

~ 'up *v.t.* (coll.: create) ~ **up a fuss/row** Krach schlagen/ anfangen (ugs.)

kick: ~**back** *n.* (coll.: bribe) Prozente (fig. ugs.); ~**-start** 1 *n.* (a) Kickstarter, *der;* (b) (fig.) [neuer] Auftrieb; 2 *v.t.* (a) [mit dem Kickstarter] starten; (b) (fig.) ankurbeln ⟨*Industrie, Wirtschaft*⟩; vorantreiben, forcieren ⟨*Friedensprozess, Entwicklung*⟩; ~**-start sb.'s career**

jmds. Karriere einen [neuen] Schub geben; **~-starter**
n. ⇨ **kick-start 1 a**

kid /kɪd/ **1** *n.* **(a)** (young goat) Kitz, *das;* Zickel, *das;* **(b)**
(leather) Ziegenleder, *das; attrib.* Ziegenleder-; **(c)** (coll.: child)
Kind, *das;* (Amer. coll.: young person) Jugendliche, *der/die;* Kid,
das (ugs.); **it's ~[s'] stuff** (coll.: easy) das ist ein Kinderspiel;
~ brother/sister (coll.) kleiner Bruder/kleine Schwester;
Brüderchen, *das*/Schwesterchen, *das.* **2** *v.t.* **-dd-** (coll.)
(hoax) anführen (ugs.); auf den Arm nehmen (ugs.); (deceive)
was vormachen (+ *Dat.*) (ugs.); (tease) aufziehen (ugs.); **~**
oneself sich (*Dat.*) was vormachen (ugs.). **3** *v.i.* **-dd-** (coll.)
be ~ding Spaß machen (ugs.); **you've got to be ~ding!**
das ist doch nicht dein Ernst!; **no ~ding** [ganz] im Ernst
od. ohne Scherz

kiddie /'kɪdɪ/ *n.* (coll.) Kindchen, *das*

kid 'glove *n.* Glacéhandschuh, *der;* **handle sb. with ~s**
(fig.) jmdn. mit Samt- *od.* Glacéhandschuhen anfassen (ugs.)

kidnap /'kɪdnæp/ *v.t.,* (Brit.) **-pp-** entführen ‹*Person*›; (to
obtain ransom) kidnappen; entführen

kidnapper /'kɪdnæpə(r)/ *n.* Entführer, *der*/Entführerin,
die; Kidnapper, *der*/Kidnapperin, *die*

kidney /'kɪdnɪ/ *n.* ▶ **672** (Anat., Gastr.) Niere, *die*

kidney: ~ bean *n.* Gartenbohne, *die;* (scarlet runner bean)
Feuerbohne, *die;* **~ failure** *n.* Nierenversagen, *das;* **~**
machine *n.* künstliche Niere

kill /kɪl/ **1** *v.t.* **(a)** töten; (deliberately) umbringen; ‹*Rauchen*
usw.›: tödliche Folgen haben für; **be ~ed in action** im
Kampf fallen; **shoot to ~:** gezielt schießen; **be ~ed in a**
car crash bei einem Autounfall ums Leben kommen; **the**
shock almost ~ed her sie wäre vor Schreck fast gestorben; **it won't ~ you** (iron.) es wird dich [schon] nicht
od. nicht gleich umbringen; **~ oneself** sich umbringen;
~ oneself laughing (fig.) sich totlachen; **(b)** (coll.: cause
severe pain to) **it is ~ing me** das bringt mich noch um; **my**
feet are ~ing me meine Füße tun wahnsinnig weh (ugs.);
(c) abtöten ‹*Krankheitserreger, Schmerz, Ungeziefer, Hefe*›;
absterben lassen ‹*Bäume, Pflanzen*›; totschlagen
‹*Geschmack*›; verderben ‹*Witz*›; [ab]töten ‹*Gefühl*›; zerstören ‹*Glauben*›; **(d) ~ time** sich (*Dat.*) die Zeit vertreiben; die Zeit totschlagen (abwertend); **(e)** (obtain meat from)
schlachten ‹*Tier*›; **(f)** (overwhelm) überwältigen; **dress to**
~: sich herausputzen. **2** *n.* (~ing of game) Abschuss, *der;*
(prey) Beute, *die;* **move in for the ~** ‹*Raubtier:*› die Beute
anschleichen, zum Sprung auf die Beute ansetzen; (fig.) zum
entscheidenden Schlag ausholen

~ 'off *v.t.* vernichten ‹*Feinde, Konkurrenz*›; abschlachten
‹*Vieh*›; sterben lassen ‹*Romanfigur usw.*›; vertilgen
‹*Unkraut*›; scheitern lassen ‹*Projekt*›

killer /'kɪlə(r)/ *n.* Mörder, *der*/Mörderin, *die;* (murderous
ruffian) Killer, *der* (salopp); **be a ~** ‹*Krankheit:*› tödlich sein;
attrib. **the ~ instinct** der Instinkt zum Töten; der Killer-
instinkt (Sportjargon)

'killer whale *n.* Mörderwal, *der*

killing /'kɪlɪŋ/ **1** *n.* **(a)** Töten, *das;* Tötung, *die;* **the ~ of**
the three children der Mord an den drei Kindern; **(b)**
(instance) Mord[fall], *der;* **(c)** (fig. coll.: great success) Coup, *der*
(ugs.); **make a ~** (make a great profit) einen [Mords]reibach
machen (ugs.). **2** *adj.* **(a)** tödlich; **(b)** (coll.: exhausting) mörderisch (ugs.); **(c)** (coll.: attractive, amusing, etc.) umwerfend

'killjoy *n.* Spielverderber, *der*/-verderberin, *die*

kiln /kɪln/ *n.* (for burning/drying) [Brenn-/Trocken]ofen, *der*

kilo /'kiːləʊ/ *n., pl.* **~s** ▶ **1202** Kilo, *das*

kilo- /'kɪlə/ *pref.* kilo-/Kilo-

'kilogram, 'kilogramme *n.* ▶ **1202** Kilogramm, *das*

kilometre (Brit.; Amer.: **kilometer**) /'kɪləmiːtə(r)** (Brit.),
kɪ'lɒmɪtə(r)/ *n.* ▶ **1102** Kilometer, *der*

'kilowatt *n.* (Electr., Phys.) Kilowatt, *das*

kilt /kɪlt/ *n.* Schottenrock, *der*

kilter /'kɪltə(r)/ *n.* **be out of ~:** nicht in Ordnung sein

kin /kɪn/ *n.* (ancestral stock) Geschlecht, *das;* (relatives) Verwandte; *see also* **kith; next 3 b**

kind[1] /kaɪnd/ *n.* **(a)** (class, sort) Art, *die;* **several ~s of**
apples mehrere Sorten Äpfel; **all ~s of things/excuses**
alles Mögliche/alle möglichen Ausreden; **no ... of any ~:**
keinerlei ...; **books of every ~:** Bücher aller Art; **be [of]**
the same ~: von derselben Sorte *od.* Art sein; **I know**
your ~: deine Sorte kenne ich; **something/nothing of**
the ~: so etwas Ähnliches/nichts dergleichen; **you'll do**
nothing of the ~! das kommt gar nicht in Frage!; **two**
of a ~: zwei gleiche; **what ~ is it?** was für einer/eine/
eins ist es?; **what ~ of [a] tree is this?** was für ein Baum
ist das?; **what ~ of people are they?** was für Leute sind
sie?; **what ~ of [a] fool do you take me for?** für wie
dumm hältst du mich?; **what ~ of [a] person do you**
think I am? für wen hältst du mich?; **the ~ of person**
we need der Typ, den wir brauchen; **they are the ~ of**
people who ...: sie gehören zu der Sorte von Leuten, die
...; das sind solche Leute, die ...; **this ~ of food/atmo-**
sphere diese Art *od.* solches Essen/solch *od.* so eine Stimmung; **these ~ of people/things** (coll.) solche Leute/
Sachen; **(b)** (implying vagueness) **a ~ of ...:** [so] eine Art ...;
~ of interesting/cute *etc.* (coll.) irgendwie interessant/
niedlich *usw.* (ugs.); **(c) in ~** (not in money) in Sachwerten;
pay in ~: in Naturalien zahlen/bezahlen; **pay back** *or*
repay sth. in ~ (fig.) etw. mit *od.* in gleicher Münze
zurückzahlen

kind[2] *adj.* (of gentle nature) liebenswürdig; (showing friendliness)
freundlich; (affectionate) lieb; **have a ~ heart** gutherzig
sein; **would you be so ~ as to do that?** wären Sie so
freundlich, das zu tun?; **be ~ to animals/children** gut
zu Tieren/Kindern sein; **oh, you 'are ~!** sehr nett *od.*
liebenswürdig von Ihnen; **how ~!** wie nett [von ihm/ihr/
Ihnen *usw.*]!

kindergarten /'kɪndəɡɑːtn/ *n.* Kindergarten, *der;* (forming part of a school) ≈ Vorklasse, *die*

kind-hearted /kaɪnd'hɑːtɪd/ *adj.* gutherzig; liebenswürdig ‹*Geste, Handlung*›

kindle /'kɪndl/ *v.t.* (light) anzünden, (geh.) entzünden ‹*Holz,*
Feuer›; entfachen (geh.) ‹*Flamme*›; wecken ‹*Interesse,*
Gefühl›

kindling /'kɪndlɪŋ/ *n., no pl., no indef. art.* Anmachholz,
das

kindly /'kaɪndlɪ/ **1** *adv.* **(a)** freundlich; nett; **..., she said**
~: ..., sagte sie freundlich; **(b)** *in polite request etc.* freundlicherweise; **(c) he didn't take at all ~ to the sugges-**
tion er konnte sich mit dem Vorschlag gar nicht recht
anfreunden; **(d) thank sb. ~:** jmdm. herzlich danken;
`thank you ~:` herzlichen Dank. **2** *adj.* freundlich; nett;
liebenswürdig; (kind-hearted) gütig; wohlwollend; gut ‹*Herz,*
Tat›

kindness /'kaɪndnɪs/ *n.* **(a)** *no pl.* (kind nature) Freundlichkeit, *die;* Liebenswürdigkeit, *die;* **do sth. out of ~:** etw.
aus Gefälligkeit tun; **out of the ~ of one's heart** aus
reiner Freundlichkeit; **(b)** (kind act) Gefälligkeit, *die;* **do sb.**
a ~: jmdm. eine Gefälligkeit erweisen *od.* einen Gefallen
tun

kindred /'kɪndrɪd/ **1** *n., no pl.* **(a)** (blood relationship) Blutsverwandtschaft, *die;* **(b)** (one's relatives) Verwandtschaft, *die;*
Verwandte. **2** *adj.* **(a)** (related by blood) blutsverwandt; **(b)**
(fig.: connected) verwandt

kindred 'spirit *n.* Gleichgesinnte, *der/die*

kinetic /kɪ'netɪk, kaɪ'netɪk/ *adj.* kinetisch

king /kɪŋ/ *n.* ▶ **1152** (also Chess, Cards) König, *der;* **live**
like a ~: leben wie ein Fürst; **a feast fit for a ~:** ein
königliches Mahl

kingdom /'kɪŋdəm/ *n.* **(a)** Königreich, *das;* **(b) the ~ of**
God das Reich Gottes; **the ~ of heaven** das Himmel-
reich; **wait till ~ come** (coll.) bis in alle Ewigkeit warten
(ugs.); **(c)** (province of nature) Reich, *das;* **animal ~:** Tier-
reich, *das*

'kingfisher /'kɪŋfɪʃə(r)/ *n.* (Ornith.) Eisvogel, *der*

kingly /'kɪŋlɪ/ *adj.* königlich

king: ~maker *n.* Königsmacher, *der;* **~pin** *n.* (lit.,
or fig.) Hauptstütze, *die;* **-size[d]** *adj.* extragroß; Kingsize-
‹*Zigaretten*›

kink /kɪŋk/ **1** *n.* **(a)** (in pipe, wire, etc.) Knick, *der;* (in hair,
wool) Welle, *die;* **(b)** (fig.: mental peculiarity) Tick, *der* (ugs.);
Spleen, *der.* **2** *v.i.* Knicke kriegen ‹*Haar:*› sich wellen. **3**
v.t. knicken

kinky /'kɪŋkɪ/ *adj.* (coll.: bizarre, perverted) spleenig; (sexually)
abartig

kinship /'kɪnʃɪp/ *n.* **(a)** (blood relationship) Blutsverwandt-schaft, *die;* **(b)** (similarity) Ähnlichkeit, *die;* (spiritual) Verwandtschaft, *die*

kinsman /'kɪnzmən/ *n., pl.* **kinsmen** /'kɪnzmən/ Verwandte, *der*

kinswoman /'kɪnzwʊmən/ *n.* Verwandte, *die*

kiosk /'kiːɒsk/ *n.* **(a)** Kiosk, *der;* **(b)** (public telephone booth) [Telefon]zelle, *die*

kip /kɪp/ (Brit. coll.) **1** *n.* (sleep) Schlaf, *der;* **have a** *or* **get some** ~: eine Runde pennen (salopp). **2** *v.i.,* **-pp-** pennen (salopp); ~ **down** sich hinhauen (salopp)

kipper /'kɪpə(r)/ *n.* Kipper, *der;* ≈ Bückling, *der*

kiss /kɪs/ **1** *n.* Kuss, *der;* **the** ~ **of death** der Todesstoß; **give sb. the** ~ **of life** (Brit.) jmdm. von Mund zu Mund beatmen. **2** *v.t.* küssen; ~ **sb. good night/goodbye** jmdm. einen Gutenacht-/Abschiedskuss geben. **3** *v.i.* sich küssen

kit /kɪt/ **1** *n.* **(a)** (personal equipment) Sachen (ugs.); **(b)** (Brit.: set of items) Set, *das;* **construction/self-assembly** ~: Bausatz, *der;* **repair** ~: Reparatursatz, *der;* Reparaturset, *das;* **(c)** (Brit.: clothing etc.) **sports** ~: Sportzeug, *das;* Sportsachen *Pl.;* **(d)** (Brit. Mil.) Ausrüstung, *die;* (pack) [Feld]gepäck, *das;* (uniform) Montur, *die.* **2** *v.t.,* **-tt-** (Brit.) ~ **out** *or* **up** (equip) ausrüsten; (give clothes or uniforms to) einkleiden

'kitbag *n.* Tornister, *der*

kitchen /'kɪtʃɪn/ *n.* Küche, *die; attrib.* Küchen-

kitchenette /kɪtʃɪ'net/ *n.* kleine Küche; (alcove) Kochnische, *die*

kitchen: ~ **'garden** *n.* Küchengarten, *der;* ~ **paper** *n.* Küchenkrepp, *der;* Küchentücher *Pl.;* ~ **roll** *n.* Küchenrolle, *die;* (kitchen paper) Küchenkrepp, *der;* ~ **'sink** *n.* [Küchen]ausguss, *der;* Spüle, *die;* **everything but the** ~ **sink** (fig.) der halbe Hausrat; ~ **unit** *n.* Küchenelement, *das;* ~ **units** Küchenmöbel *Pl.;* ~ **utensil** *n.* Küchengerät, *das;* ~ **ware** *n. no pl., no art.* Küchengeräte *Pl.*

kite /kaɪt/ *n.* **(a)** (toy) Drachen, *der;* **(b)** (Ornith.) Roter Milan

kith /kɪθ/ *n.* ~ **and kin** Freunde und Verwandte

kitten /'kɪtn/ *n.* **(a)** [Katzen]junge, *das;* Kätzchen, *das;* **the cat has had** ~s die Katze hat Junge bekommen; **(b)** (coll.) **have** ~s (be upset) Zustände kriegen (ugs.); **be having** ~s (be nervous) am Rotieren sein (ugs.)

kitty¹ /'kɪtɪ/ *n.* (kitten) Kätzchen, *das;* (child lang.) Miez[e], *die* (fam.)

kitty² *n.* **(a)** (Cards) [Spiel]kasse, *die;* **(b)** (joint fund) Kasse, *die*

'kiwi fruit /'kiːwiː fruːt/ *n.* Kiwi[frucht], *die*

kleptomania /kleptə'meɪnɪə/ *n., no pl.* (Psych.) Kleptomanie, *die*

knack /næk/ *n.* **(a)** (faculty) Talent, *das;* **have a** ~ **of doing sth.** das Talent haben, etw. zu tun; **get the** ~ **[of doing sth.]** den Bogen rauskriegen[, wie man etw. macht] (ugs.); **there's a [real]** ~ **in** *or* **to doing sth.** es gehört schon [einiges] Geschick dazu, etw. zu tun; **have lost the** ~: es nicht mehr zustande bringen *od.* (ugs.) hinkriegen; **(b)** (habit) **have a** ~ **of doing sth.** es [mit seltenem Talent] verstehen, etw. zu tun (iron.)

knacker /'nækə(r)/ *n.* (Brit.) Abdecker, *der*

knackered /'nækəd/ *adj.* (Brit. coll.) geschlaucht (ugs.)

knapsack /'næpsæk/ *n.* Rucksack, *der;* (Mil.) Tornister, *der*

knead /niːd/ *v.t.* kneten

knee /niː/ *n.* **▶ 672** Knie, *das;* **on one's** ~**s/on bended** ~**[s]** auf Knien; **be on one's** ~**s** knien; (fig.: be defeated) in die Knie gezwungen sein (geh.); **force sb. to his** ~**s** (fig.) jmdn. in die Knie zwingen (geh.); **go down on one's** ~**s** [to *or* before sb.] [vor jmdm.] auf die Knie sinken (geh.); **(b)** (of animal) Kniegelenk, *das*

knee: ~**cap** *n.* **▶ 672** (Anat.) Kniescheibe, *die;* ~**deep** *adj.* **(a)** knietief; **(b)** (fig.: deeply involved) **be** ~**-deep in sth.** bis über den Hals in etw. (*Dat.*) stecken (ugs.); ~**high** *adj.* kniehoch; ~**-jerk** *n.* Kniesehnenreflex, *der; attrib.* ~**-jerk reaction** (fig.) automatische Reaktion; ~ **joint** *n.* **▶ 672** Kniegelenk, *das*

kneel /niːl/ *v.i.,* **knelt** /nelt/ *or* (esp. Amer.) ~**ed** knien; ~ **down** niederknien; ~ **[down] to do sth.** niederknien *od.* sich [hin]knien, um etw. zu tun; ~ **to sb.** vor jmdm. [nieder]knien

'knee-length *adj.* knielang

knell /nel/ *n.* Glockengeläut, *das;* (at funeral) Totengeläut, *das*

knelt ⇒ **kneel**

knew ⇒ **know** 1

knickerbockers /'nɪkəbɒkəz/ *n. pl.* Knickerbocker *Pl.*

knickers /'nɪkəz/ *n. pl.* (Brit.: undergarment) [Damen]schlüpfer, *der*

knick-knack /'nɪknæk/ *n.* ~**s** Schnickschnack, *der* (ugs.)

knife /naɪf/ **1** *n., pl.* **knives** /naɪvz/ Messer, *das;* **put a** ~ **into sb.** jmdm. ein Messer zwischen die Rippen jagen; **turn** *or* **twist the** ~ **[in the wound]** (fig.) Salz in die Wunde streuen; **the knives are out [for sb.]** (fig.) das Messer wird [für jmdn.] gewetzt; *see also* **fork** 1 a. **2** *v.t.* (stab) einstechen auf (+ *Akk.*); (kill) erstechen

knife: ~**-edge** *n.* Schneide, *die;* **be [balanced] on a** ~**-edge** (fig.) auf des Messers Schneide stehen; ~**point** ⇒ **point** 1 b

knight /naɪt/ **1** *n.* **(a)** (Hist.) Ritter, *der;* **(b)** (Chess) Springer, *der.* **2** *v.t.* adeln; zum Ritter schlagen (hist.)

knighthood /'naɪthʊd/ *n.* (rank) Ritterwürde, *die;* **receive one's** ~: geadelt werden; in den Ritterstand erhoben werden (hist.)

knit /nɪt/ **1** *v.t.,* **-tt-,** **knitted** *or* (esp. fig.) **knit (a)** stricken ‹*Kleidungsstück usw.*›; **(b)** ~ **a stitch** eine [rechte] Masche stricken; ~ **2, purl 2** zwei rechts, zwei links [stricken]; **(c)** ~ **one's brow** die Stirn runzeln; **(d) tightly** ~ (fig.) festgefügt. **2** *v.i.* ‹*Knochenbruch:*› verheilen; ‹*Knochen:*› zusammenwachsen ~ **to'gether** *v.i.* ‹*Knochen:*› zusammenwachsen ‹*Knochenbruch:*› heilen, verheilen

knitting /'nɪtɪŋ/ *n., no pl., no indef. art.* Stricken, *das;* (work in process of being knitted) Strickarbeit, *die;* **do one's/ some** ~: stricken

knitting: ~ **machine** *n.* Strickmaschine, *die;* ~ **needle** *n.* Stricknadel, *die;* ~ **pattern** *n.* Strickmuster, *das*

'knitwear *n., no pl., no indef. art.* Strickwaren *Pl.*

knives *pl. of* **knife** 1

knob /nɒb/ *n.* **(a)** (protuberance) Verdickung, *die;* (on club, tree trunk, etc.) Knoten, *der;* **(b)** (on door, walking stick, etc.) Knauf, *der;* (on radio etc.) Knopf, *der*

knobbly /'nɒblɪ/ *adj.* knotig ‹*Finger, Stock*›; knorrig ‹*Baum*›

knock /nɒk/ **1** *v.t.* **(a)** (strike) (lightly) klopfen gegen *od.* an (+ *Akk.*); (forcefully) schlagen gegen *od.* an (+ *Akk.*); **(b)** (make by striking) schlagen; ~ **a hole in sth.** ein Loch in etw. (*Akk.*) schlagen; **(c)** (drive by striking) schlagen; ~ **sb.'s brains out** jmdm. den Schädel einschlagen; **I'd like to** ~ **their heads together** (lit.) ich könnte ihre Köpfe gegeneinander schlagen; (fig.: reprove them) ich möchte ihnen mal gehörig die Leviten lesen; **(d)** ~ **sb. on the head** jmdm. eins über *od.* auf den Schädel geben; ~ **sth. on the head** (fig.: put an end to) einer Sache (*Dat.*) ein Ende setzen; **(e)** (coll.: criticize) herziehen über (+ *Akk.*) (ugs.); **don't** ~ **it** halt dich zurück. **2** *v.i.* **(a)** (strike) (lightly) klopfen; (forcefully) schlagen; **(b)** (seek admittance) klopfen (at an + *Akk.*). **3** *n.* **(a)** (rap) Klopfen, *das;* **there was a** ~ **on** *or* **at the door** es klopfte an der Tür; **(b)** (blow) Schlag, *der;* (gentler) Stoß, *der;* **(c)** (fig.: blow of misfortune) [Schicksals]schlag, *der;* **take a** ~: einen Schlag erleiden

~ **a'bout 1** *v.t.* schlagen; verprügeln; **be** ~**ed about** Schläge *od.* Prügel einstecken müssen. **2** *v.i.* herumhängen (ugs.); ‹*Gegenstand:*› herumfliegen (ugs.); ~ **about with sb.** sich mit jmdm. herumtreiben (ugs.)

~ **a'round** ⇒ ~ **about**

~ **'back** *v.t.* (coll.) **(a)** (eat quickly) verputzen (ugs.); (drink quickly) hinunterkippen (ugs.); **(b)** (cost) ~ **sb. back a thousand** jmdn. um einen Tausender ärmer machen

~ **'down** v.t. (a) (strike to the ground) niederreißen, umstürzen ‹Zaun, Hindernis›; (with fist or weapon) niederschlagen; ‹Fahrer, Fahrzeug:› umfahren ‹Person›; (b) (demolish) abreißen; abbrechen; (c) (sell by auction) zuschlagen; ~ **sth. down to sb.** jmdm. etw. zuschlagen

~ **'off 1** v.t. (a) (coll.: leave off) aufhören mit; ~ **off work** Feierabend machen; ~ **it off!** (coll.) hör auf [damit]!; (b) (coll.) (produce rapidly) aus dem Ärmel schütteln (ugs.); (c) (deduct) ~ **five pounds off the price** es fünf Pfund billiger machen; (d) (sl.: steal) mitgehen lassen (ugs.); klauen (salopp); (e) (sl.: copulate with) bumsen (salopp). **2** v.i. (coll.) Feierabend machen; ~ **off for lunch** Mittag machen

~ **'out** v.t. (a) (make unconscious) bewusstlos umfallen lassen; (b) (Boxing) k.o. schlagen; (c) (fig.: defeat) be ~ed **out** ausscheiden od. (ugs.) rausfliegen; **they** ~ed us out of the Cup sie warfen uns aus dem Pokal; (d) (coll.: astonish) umhauen (salopp); (e) (coll.: exhaust) kaputtmachen (ugs.)

~ **'over** v.t. umstoßen; ‹Fahrer, Fahrzeug:› umfahren ‹Person›

~ **to'gether 1** v.t. zusammenzimmern (ugs.) ‹Hütte, Tisch, Bühne›; see also ~ **1 c. 2** v.i. **my knees were** ~ing **together** mir schlotterten die Knie

~ **'up** v.t. (a) (make hastily) [her]zaubern ‹Mahlzeit, Imbiss›; grob skizzieren ‹Plan›; (b) (score) erzielen; (c) (Brit.: awaken) durch Klopfen wecken; (unexpectedly) herausklopfen; (d) (exhaust) fertig machen (ugs.); **be** ~ed **up** fertig od. groggy sein (ugs.); (e) (sl.: make pregnant) dick machen (derb)

knock-down adj. (a) (low) ~-**down cost/prices** minimale Kosten/Schleuderpreise; (b) (minimum) Mindest‹preis, -gebot›

knocker /'nɒkə(r)/ n. (a) (on door) [Tür]klopfer, der; (b) (coll.: critic) Beckmesser, der

knocking-'off time n. (coll.) Feierabend, der

knock: ~-**kneed** /'nɒkni:d/ adj. x-beinig ‹Person›; ~ **'knees** n. pl. X-Beine Pl.; ~**out 1** n. (a) (blow) Knockout[schlag], der; K.-o.[-Schlag], der; (b) (competition) Ausscheidungs[wett]kampf, der; (c) (coll.: outstanding person or thing) **sb./sth. is a [real]** ~**out** jmd./etw. ist eine Wucht (salopp); **2** adj. (a) ~**out blow** K.-o.-Schlag, der; (b) Ausscheidungs‹spiel, -[wett]kampf, -runde›

knoll /nəʊl/ n. Anhöhe, die

knot /nɒt/ **1** n. (a) Knoten, der; **tie sb. [up] in** ~s (fig. coll.) jmdn. in Widersprüche verwickeln; (b) (in wood) Ast, der; (c) (speed unit) Knoten, der; **at a rate of** ~s (coll.) mit einem Affenzahn (salopp). **2** v.t., **-tt-:** (a) (tie) knoten ‹Seil, Faden usw.›; knoten ‹Schnürsenkel›; knoten, binden ‹Krawatte›; ~ **threads together** Fäden verknoten; ~ **a rope** Knoten in ein Seil machen; (b) (entangle) verfilzen; (c) **get** ~**ted!** (coll.) rutsch mir den Buckel runter! (ugs.)

knotty /'nɒtɪ/ adj. (fig.: puzzling) verwickelt

know /nəʊ/ **1** v.t., **knew** /nju:/, ~**n** /nəʊn/ (a) (recognize) erkennen (**by** an + Dat., **for** als + Akk.); (b) (be able to distinguish) ~ **sth. from sth.** etw. von etw. unterscheiden können; ~ **the difference between right and wrong** den Unterschied zwischen Gut und Böse kennen; **he wouldn't** ~ **the difference** er wüsste den Unterschied nicht; (c) (be aware of) wissen; kennen ‹Person›; **I** ~ **who she is** ich weiß, wer sie ist; **I** ~ **for a fact that** …: ich weiß ganz bestimmt, dass …; **it is** ~**n that** …: man weiß, dass …; es ist bekannt, dass …; ~ **sb./sth. to be** …: wissen, dass jmd./etw. … ist; **that's/that might be worth** ~**ing** das ist gut/wäre wichtig zu wissen; **he doesn't want to** ~: er will nichts davon wissen od. hören; **I 'knew it** ich hab's ja geahnt; **'I** ~ **what** ich weiß was (ugs.); **you** ~ (coll.: as reminder) weißt du [noch]; **you** ~ **something** or **what?** weißt du was? **you never** ~: man kann nie wissen (ugs.); **sb. has [never] been** ~**n to do sth.** jmd. hat bekanntlich [noch nie] etw. getan; **and he** ~s **it** und er weiß das auch; **don't 'I** ~ **it!** (coll.) das weiß ich nur zu gut; **before sb.** ~s **where he is** ehe jmd. sichs versieht; **what do you** ~ [**about that**]? (coll.: that is surprising) was sagst du dazu?; **sb. is not to** ~ (is not to be told) jmd. soll nichts wissen (**about**, of von); (has no way of learning) jmd. kann nicht wissen; **not** ~ **what hit one** (fig.) gar nicht begreifen, was geschehen ist; **that's all 'you** ~ [**about it**] das glaubst du vielleicht; **if you 'must** ~:

wenn du es unbedingt wissen willst; ~ **different** or **otherwise** es besser wissen; ~ **what's what** wissen, wie es in der Welt zugeht; **how should I** ~? woher soll ich das wissen?; **I might have** ~n das hätte ich mir denken können; **do you** ~, …: stell dir [mal] vor, …; (d) (have understanding of) können ‹ABC, Einmaleins, Deutsch usw.›; beherrschen ‹Grundlagen, Regeln›; sich auskennen mit ‹Gerät, Verfahren, Gesetz›; **do you** ~ **any German?** können Sie etwas Deutsch?; ~ **how to mend fuses** wissen, wie man Sicherungen repariert; ~ **how to drive a car** Auto fahren können; **he doesn't** ~ **much about computers** er hat nicht viel Ahnung von Computern; (e) (be acquainted with) kennen; **we have** ~n **each other for years** wir kennen uns [schon] seit Jahren; **you don't really** ~ **him** du kennst ihn nicht gut genug; **you** ~ **what he/it is** (is like) du kennst ja/du weißt ja, wie es ist; (f) (have experience of) erleben; erfahren; **he** ~s **no fear** er kennt keine Furcht; ~ **what it is to be hungry** wissen, was es heißt, Hunger zu haben. **2** n. (coll.) **be in the** ~: Bescheid wissen

~ **about** v.t. wissen über (+ Akk.); **oh, I didn't** ~ **about it/that** oh, das habe ich nicht gewusst; **did you** ~ **about your son's behaviour?** haben Sie gehört, wie sich Ihr Sohn benommen hat?; **I don't** ~ **about 'that** na, ich weiß nicht [so recht]

~ **of** v.t. wissen von ‹Plänen, Vorhaben›; kennen, wissen ‹Lokal, Geschäft›; ~ **of sb.** von jmdm. gehört haben; **not that I** ~ **of** nicht, dass ich wüsste

know: ~-**all** n. (derog.) Neunmalkluge, der/die (spöttisch); ~-**how** n., no pl., no indef. art. praktisches Wissen; (technical expertise) Know-how, das

knowing /'nəʊɪŋ/ adj. (a) (shrewd) verschmitzt ‹Blick, Lachen, Lächeln›; (indicating possession of inside information) vielsagend, wissend ‹Blick, Lächeln›; (b) (derog.: cunning) verschlagen (abwertend)

knowingly /'nəʊɪŋlɪ/ adv. (a) (intentionally) wissentlich ‹lügen, verletzen›; bewusst ‹planen›; (b) (in a shrewd manner) verschmitzt ‹lachen, blicken›; (indicating possession of inside information) vielsagend ‹lächeln, anblicken›

knowledge /'nɒlɪdʒ/ n., no pl. (a) (familiarity) Kenntnisse Pl. (**of** in + Dat.); **a** ~ **of this field** Kenntnisse auf diesem Gebiet; ~ **of human nature** Menschenkenntnis, die; (b) (awareness) Wissen, das; **have no** ~ **of sth.** nichts von etw. wissen; keine Kenntnis von etw. haben (geh.); **she had no** ~ **of it** sie wusste nichts davon; sie war völlig ahnungslos; **sth. came to my** ~: etw. ist mir zu Ohren gekommen; [**not**] **to my** etc. ~: meines usw. Wissens [nicht]; (c) (understanding) [**a**] ~ **of languages/French** Sprach-/Französischkenntnisse Pl.; **sb. with** [**a**] ~ **of computers** jmd., der sich mit Computern auskennt; (d) no art. (what is known) Wissen, das

knowledgeable /'nɒlɪdʒəbl/ adj. sachkundig; **be** ~ **about** or **on sth.** viel über etw. (Akk.) wissen

known /nəʊn/ **1** ⇒ **know** 1. **2** adj. bekannt; (generally recognized) anerkannt

knuckle /'nʌkl/ n. (a) ▶ 672 | (Anat.) [Finger]knöchel, der; (b) Hachse, die; ~ **of pork** Eisbein, das

~ **'down** v.i. ~ **down to sth.** sich hinter etw. (Akk.) klemmen (ugs.)

~ **'under** v.i. klein beigeben (**to** gegenüber)

'knuckleduster n. Schlagring, der

KO abbr. knockout K. o.

koala /kəʊ'ɑ:lə/ n. ~ [**bear**] (Zool.) Koala, der; Beutelbär, der

Koran /kɔ:'rɑ:n, kə'rɑ:n/ n. (Muslim Relig.) Koran, der

Korea /kə'rɪə/ pr. n. Korea (das)

Korean /kə'ri:ən/ ▶ 897 |, ▶ 947 | **1** adj. koreanisch; **sb. is** ~: jmd. ist Koreaner/Koreanerin. **2** n. (a) (person) Koreaner, der/Koreanerin, die; (b) (language) Koreanisch, das; see also **English** 2 a

kosher /'kəʊʃə(r), 'kɒʃə(r)/ adj. koscher

kowtow /kaʊ'taʊ/ v.i. ~ [**to sb./sth.**] [vor jmdm./etw.] [s]einen Kotau machen

Kraut /kraʊt/ n. & adj. (sl. derog.) angelsächsische abwertende Bez. für „Deutscher" und „deutsch"

Kremlin /ˈkremlɪn/ *n.* **the K~:** der Kreml
kudos /ˈkjuːdɒs/ *n., no pl., no indef. art.* (coll.) Prestige, *das*
kung fu /kʊŋˈfuː, kʌŋˈfuː/ *n.* Kung-Fu, *das*
Kurd /kɜːd/ *n.* Kurde, *der*/Kurdin, *die*
Kurdish ˈkɜːdɪʃ/ ▶ **897** , ▶ **947** **1** *adj.* kurdisch. **2** *n.* Kurdisch, *das*
Kurdistan /kɜːdɪˈstɑːn/ *pr. n.* Kurdistan (*das*)
Kuwait /kʊˈweɪt/ *pr. n.* Kuwait (*das*)
Kuwaiti /kʊˈweɪtɪ/ ▶ **947** **1** *adj.* kuwaitisch; **sb. is ~:** jmd. ist Kuwaiti. **2** *n.* Kuwaiti, *der/die*
kW *abbr.* **kilowatt[s]** kW

L l

L, l /el/ *n., pl.* **Ls** *or* **L's** L, l, *das*
L. *abbr.* **Lake**
£ *abbr.* **pound[s]** £; **cost £5** 5 £ *od.* Pfund kosten
l. *abbr.* (a) ▶ **1193** **litre[s]** l; (b) **left** l.; (c) **line** Z.
lab /læb/ *n.* (coll.) Labor, *das*
label /ˈleɪbl/ **1** *n.* (a) (slip) Schildchen, *das;* (on goods, bottles, jars, in clothes) Etikett, *das;* (tied/stuck to an object) Anhänger/ Aufkleber, *der;* (b) (on record) Label, *das;* (record company) Plattenfirma, *die;* (c) (fig.: classifying phrase) Etikett, *das;* **acquire the ~ of ...:** als ... etikettiert werden. **2** *v.t.,* (Brit.) **-ll-:** (a) (attach ~ to) etikettieren; (attach price tag to) auszeichnen ⟨*Waren*⟩; (write on) beschriften; (b) (fig.: classify) ~ **sb./sth. [as] sth.** jmdn./etw. als etw. etikettieren
labor (Amer.) ⇒ **labour**
laboratory /ləˈbɒrətərɪ/ *n.* Labor[atorium], *das*
labored, laborer (Amer.) ⇒ **labour-**
laborious /ləˈbɔːrɪəs/ *adj.* mühsam; mühevoll ⟨*Forschung, Aufgabe usw.*⟩; schwerfällig, umständlich ⟨*Stil*⟩
laboriously /ləˈbɔːrɪəslɪ/ *adv.* (with difficulty) mühevoll; ~ **slow** mühsam und schleppend
labour /ˈleɪbə(r)/ (Brit.) **1** *n.* (a) (task) Arbeit, *die;* **sth. is/ they did it as a ~ of love** etw. geschieht/sie taten es aus Liebe zur Sache; (b) (exertion) Mühe, *die;* (c) (work) Arbeit, *die;* **cost of ~:** Arbeitskosten *Pl.;* (d) (body of workers) Arbeiterschaft, *die;* **immigrant ~:** eingewanderte Arbeitskräfte; (e) **L~** (Polit.) die Labour Party; (f) (childbirth) Wehen *Pl.;* **be in ~:** in den Wehen liegen; **go into ~** Wehen bekommen. *See also* **intensive e. 2** *v.i.* (a) (work hard) hart arbeiten (**at, on** an + *Dat.*); (slave away) sich abmühen (**at, over** mit); (b) (strive) sich einsetzen (**for** für); (c) ~ **under a delusion** sich einer Täuschung (*Dat.*) hingeben. **3** *v.t.* (elaborate needlessly) ~ **the point** sich lange darüber verbreiten; **there's no need to ~ the point** du brauchst dich nicht lange darüber zu verbreiten
labour: ~ **camp** *n.* Arbeitslager, *das;* **L~ Day** *n.* Tag der Arbeit (in Amerika: erster Montag im September)
laboured /ˈleɪbəd/ *adj.* (Brit.) mühsam; schwerfällig ⟨*Stil*⟩; mühsam zusammengetragen ⟨*Argumente*⟩; **his breathing was ~:** er atmete schwer
labourer /ˈleɪbərə(r)/ *n.* ▶ **887** (Brit.) Arbeiter, *der*/Arbeiterin, *die*
labour: L~ Exchange *n.* (Brit. Hist./coll.) Arbeitsamt, *das;* ~ **force** *n.* Arbeitskräfte *Pl.;* ~ **market** *n.* Arbeitsmarkt, *der;* ~ **pains** *n. pl.* Wehenschmerzen *Pl.;* **L~ Party** *n.* (Polit.) Labour Party, *die;* ~ **relations** *n. pl.* Beziehungen zwischen Arbeitgebern und Arbeitnehmern; (within one company) Betriebsklima, *das;* ~**-saving** *adj.* arbeit[s]sparend ⟨*Methode, Vorrichtung*⟩
Labrador /ˈlæbrədɔː(r)/ *n.* ~ **[dog** *or* **retriever]** Labrador[hund], *der*
labyrinth /ˈlæbərɪnθ/ *n.* Labyrinth, *das*
lace /leɪs/ **1** *n.* (a) (for shoe) Schuhband, *das* (bes. südd.); Schnürsenkel, *der* (bes. nordd.); (b) (fabric) Spitze, *die; attrib.*

Spitzen-. **2** *v.t.* (a) (fasten) ~ **[up]** [zu]schnüren; (b) (pass through) [durch]ziehen; (c) ~ **sth. with alcohol** einen Schuss Alkohol in etw. (*Akk.*) geben; ~**d with brandy** mit einem Schuss Weinbrand; ~ **sb.'s drink** einen Schuss Alkohol/eine Droge in jmds. Getränk (*Akk.*) geben
lacerate /ˈlæsəreɪt/ *v.t.* aufreißen; **her arm was badly** ~**d** sie hatte tiefe Wunden am Arm
laceration /læsəˈreɪʃn/ *n.* Rißwunde, *die;* (from glass) Schnittwunde, *die*
'lace-up 1 *attrib. adj.* zum Schnüren *nachgestellt;* ~**-up boot** Schnürstiefel, *der.* **2** *n.* Schnürschuh/-stiefel, *der*
lack /læk/ **1** *n.* Mangel, *der* (**of** an + *Dat.*); ~ **of self-consciousness** Unbefangenheit, *die;* ~ **of work** Arbeitsmangel, *der;* **there is no ~ of it [for them]** es fehlt [ihnen] nicht daran; **for ~ of sth.** aus Mangel an etw. (*Dat.*); **for ~ of time** aus Zeitmangel. **2** *v.t.* **sb./sth.** ~**s sth.** jmdm./einer Sache fehlt es an etw. (*Dat.*); **sb.** ~**s the ability to do sth.** jmdm. fehlt die Fähigkeit, etw. zu tun; **what he ~s is ...:** woran es ihm fehlt, ist ...; ~ **content** inhaltsarm sein. **3** *v.i.* **I ~ for nothing** mir fehlt es an nichts
lackadaisical /lækəˈdeɪzɪkl/ *adj.* (unenthusiastic) gleichgültig; desinteressiert; (listless) lustlos
lackey /ˈlækɪ/ *n.* (a) (footman) Lakai, *der;* (b) (servant) Diener, *der*
lacking /ˈlækɪŋ/ *adj.* **be ~** ⟨*Geld, Ressourcen usw.:*⟩ fehlen; **he was found to be ~** (incapable) es erwies sich, dass er den Ansprüchen nicht genügte
'lacklustre *adj.* trüb; glanzlos ⟨*Augen*⟩; matt ⟨*Lächeln*⟩; langweilig ⟨*Aufführung, Party*⟩
laconic /ləˈkɒnɪk/ *adj.* (a) (concise) lakonisch; (b) wortkarg ⟨*Person, Naturell*⟩
lacquer /ˈlækə(r)/ **1** *n.* Lack, *der.* **2** *v.t.* lackieren; ~**ed wood** Lackholz, *das*
lacy /ˈleɪsɪ/ *adj.* Spitzen-; (of metalwork) spitzenartig; Filigran-
lad /læd/ *n.* (a) (boy) Junge, *der;* **young ~:** kleiner Junge; **when I was a ~:** als ich noch ein Junge war; **these are my ~s** das sind meine Jungen *od.* (ugs.) Jungs; (b) (man) Typ, *der;* **the ~s** die Jungs (ugs.); **he always goes out for a drink with the ~s** er geht immer mit seinen Kumpels einen trinken (ugs.); **my ~:** mein Junge (ugs.); (c) (spirited person) **be a bit of a ~:** kein Kind von Traurigkeit sein (ugs.); (one for the ladies) es mit den Mädchen/Frauen haben (ugs.)
ladder /ˈlædə(r)/ **1** *n.* (a) (lit. *or* fig.) Leiter, *die;* (fig.: means of advancement) Aufstiegsmöglichkeit, *die;* **have a foot on the ~:** die erste Sprosse auf der Leiter des Erfolgs erklommen haben (geh.); (b) (Brit.: in tights etc.) Laufmasche, *die.* **2** *v.i.* (Brit.) Laufmaschen/eine Laufmasche bekommen. **3** *v.t.* (Brit.) Laufmaschen/eine Laufmasche machen in (+ *Akk.*)
laddie /ˈlædɪ/ *n.* Jungchen, *das* (fam.); Bubi, *der* (bes. südd.)
laden /ˈleɪdn/ *adj.* beladen (**with** mit)
la-di-da /lɑːdɪˈdɑː/ *adj.* affektiert
ladies' /ˈleɪdɪz/: ~ **man** *n.* Frauenheld, *der;* ~ **room** *n.* Damentoilette, *die*
ladle /ˈleɪdl/ **1** *n.* Schöpfkelle, *die;* Schöpflöffel, *der.* **2** *v.t.* schöpfen
~ **'out** *v.t.* (lit. *or* fig.) austeilen
lady /ˈleɪdɪ/ *n.* (a) (lit.) Dame, *die;* (English, American, etc. also) Lady, *die;* ~**-in-waiting** (Brit.) Hofdame, *die;* **ladies' hairdresser** Damenfriseur, *der;* (b) 'Ladies' „Damen"; (c) *as form of address in sing.* (poet.) Herrin (veralt.); *in pl.* meine Damen; **Ladies and Gentlemen!** meine Damen und Herren!; (d) ▶ **1152** (Brit.) *as title* **L~:** Lady; **my ~:** My-lady; (e) (ruling woman) Herrin, *die;* ~ **of the house** Dame des Hauses; **Our L~** (Relig.) Unsere Liebe Frau; (f) *attrib.* (female) ~ **clerk** Angestellte, *die;* ~ **doctor** Ärztin, *die;* ~ **friend** Freundin, *die. See also* **first 2 a**
lady: ~**bird,** (Amer.) ~**bug** *ns.* (Zool.) Marienkäfer, *der;* ~**killer** *n.* (coll.) Herzensbrecher, *der;* ~**like** *adj.* damenhaft; **be ~like** sich wie eine Dame benehmen
ladyship /ˈleɪdɪʃɪp/ *n.* ▶ **1152** **her/your ~/their ~s** Ihre/Eure Ladyschaft/Ihre Ladyschaften
lady: ~**'s maid** *n.* [Kammer]zofe, *die;* ~**'s man** ⇒ **ladies' man**

lag¹ /læg/ **1** *v.i.*, **-gg-** (lit. or fig.) zurückbleiben; ∼ **behind sb./sth.** hinter jmdm./etw. bleiben. **2** *n.* (delay) Verzögerung, *die;* (falling behind) Zurückbleiben, *das*

lag² *v.t.*, **-gg-** (insulate) isolieren

lager /'lɑːgə(r)/ *n.* Lagerbier, *das;* **a small** ∼: ≈ ein kleines Helles

'lager lout *n.* Bier trinkender Rüpel

lagging¹ /'lægɪŋ/ *n.* **no** ∼! nicht zurückbleiben!

lagging² *n.* (insulation) Isolierung, *die*

lagoon /lə'guːn/ *n.* Lagune, *die*

laid ⇒ **lay²** 1

'laid-back *adj.* (coll.) gelassen

lain ⇒ **lie²** 2

lair /leə(r)/ *n.* (of wild animal) Unterschlupf, *der;* (fig.) (of bandits) Schlupfwinkel, *der;* (of children etc.) Versteck, *das*

laird /leəd/ *n.* (Scot.) Gutsbesitzer, *der*

laity /'leɪtɪ/ *n. pl.* Laien *Pl.*

lake /leɪk/ *n.* See, *der;* **the Great L**∼**s** die Großen Seen

lake: L∼ **Constance** /leɪk 'kɒnstəns/ *pr. n.* der Bodensee; **L**∼ **District, L**∼**land** /'leɪklənd/ *pr. ns.* (Brit.) Lake District, *der* (Seenlandschaft im Nordwesten Englands); **L**∼ **Lucerne** ⇒ **Lucerne;** ∼**side** *n.* Seeufer, *das;* **by the** ∼**side** am See[ufer]

lama /'lɑːmə/ *n.* Lama, *der*

lamb /læm/ **1** *n.* (a) Lamm, *das;* **as gentle/meek as a** ∼: sanft wie ein Lamm; **one may** *or* **might as well be hanged** *or* **hung for a sheep as [for] a** ∼ (fig.) darauf kommt es jetzt auch nicht mehr an; **like a** ∼ **[to the slaughter]** wie ein Lamm [zur Schlachtbank (geh.)]; (b) *no pl.* (flesh) Lamm[fleisch], *das.* **2** *v.i.* lammen; ∼**ing season** Lammzeit, *die*

lambaste /læm'beɪst/ (**lambast** /læm'bæst/) *v.t.* (coll.: thrash, lit. or fig.) fertig machen (ugs.)

lamb: ∼ **'chop** *n.* Lammkotelett, *das;* ∼ **'cutlet** *n.* Kammkotelett vom Lamm; ∼**skin** *n.* (with wool on) Lammfell, *das;* (as leather) Schafleder, *das;* ∼**swool** *n.* Lambswool, *die* (Textilw.)

lame /leɪm/ **1** *adj.* (a) (disabled) lahm; **go** ∼: lahm werden; **be** ∼ **in one's right leg** ein lahmes rechtes Bein haben; **the horse was** ∼ **in one leg** das Pferd lahmte auf einem Bein; (b) (fig.: unconvincing) lahm (ugs. abwertend). **2** *v.t.* lahm reiten ⟨*Pferd usw.*⟩; (fig.: hinder) lähmen ⟨*Person, Fähigkeiten, Kraft*⟩

lame 'duck *n.* (a) (incapable person) Versager, *der*/Versagerin, *die;* (b) (firm) zahlungsunfähige Firma

lameness /'leɪmnɪs/ *n.*, *no pl.* (lit.; also fig.: unconvincingness) Lahmheit, *die*

lament /lə'ment/ **1** *n.* (a) (expression of grief) Klage, *die* (for um); (b) (dirge) Klagegesang, *der.* **2** *v.t.* klagen über (+ *Akk.*) (geh.); klagen um (geh.) ⟨*Freund, Heimat, Glück*⟩; ∼ **that ...:** beklagen, dass ... **3** *v.i.* klagen (geh.); ∼ **over** *or* **for sth.** etw. beklagen (geh.); etw. beweinen; ∼ **over** *or* **for sb.** jmdn. beweinen

lamentable /'læməntəbl/ *adj.* beklagenswert; kläglich ⟨*Versuch, Leistung*⟩

lamentably /'læməntəblɪ/ *adv.* beklagenswert; kläglich ⟨*scheitern*⟩

lamentation /læmən'teɪʃn/ *n.* (a) *no pl., no art.* (lamenting) Wehklagen, *das* (geh.); (b) (lament) [Weh]klage, *die* (geh.)

laminated /'læmɪneɪtɪd/ *adj.* lamelliert (Technik); ∼ **glass** Verbundglas, *das*

lamp /læmp/ *n.* Lampe, *die;* (in street) [Straßen]laterne, *die;* [Straßen]lampe, *die;* (of vehicle) Licht, *das;* (car head∼) Scheinwerfer, *der*

'lamplight *n.* Lampenlicht, *das*

lampoon /læm'puːn/ **1** *n.* Spottschrift, *die;* Pasquill, *das* (geh.). **2** *v.t.* verhöhnen; verspotten

lamp: ∼**post** *n.* Laternenpfahl, *der;* (taller) Lichtmast, *der;* ∼**shade** *n.* Lampenschirm, *der;* ∼ **standard** *n.* Lichtmast, *der*

lance /lɑːns/ **1** *n.* (weapon) Lanze, *die.* **2** *v.t.* (Med.) mit der Lanzette öffnen

lance 'corporal *n.* ▶**1152** (Mil.) Obergefreite, *der*

land /lænd/ **1** *n.* (a) *no pl., no indef. art.* (solid part of the earth) Land, *das;* **by** ∼: auf dem Landweg; **on** ∼: zu Lande; (not in air) auf dem Boden; (not in or on water) an Land; (b) *no indef. art.* (expanse of country) Land, *das;* **see how the** ∼ **lies** (fig.) herausfinden, wie die Dinge liegen; *see also* **lie²** 1 a; (c) *no pl., no indef. art.* (ground for farming or building, property) Land, *das;* **work the** ∼: das Land bebauen; **live off the** ∼: sich von dem ernähren, was das Land hergibt; (d) (country) Land, *das;* **the greatest in the** ∼: der/die Größte im ganzen Land. **2** *v.t.* (a) (set ashore) [an]landen ⟨*Truppen, Passagiere, Waren, Fang*⟩; (b) (Aeronaut.) landen ⟨*[Wasser]flugzeug*⟩; (c) (bring into a situation) ∼ **oneself in trouble** sich in Schwierigkeiten bringen; (*Dat.*) Ärger einhandeln (ugs.); ∼ **sb. in [the thick of] it** jmdn. [ganz schön] reinreiten (salopp); (d) (deal) landen ⟨*Schlag*⟩; ∼ **sb. one** jmdm. einen Schlag verpassen (ugs.); (e) (burden) ∼ **sb. with sth.,** ∼ **sth. on sb.** jmdm. etw. aufhalsen (ugs.); **be** ∼**ed with sb./sth.** jmdn. auf dem Hals haben (ugs.)/etw. aufgehalst bekommen (ugs.); (f) ∼ **a fish** einen Fisch an Land ziehen; (g) (fig.: succeed in obtaining) an Land ziehen (ugs.). **3** *v.i.* (a) ⟨*Boot usw.*:⟩ anlegen, landen; ⟨*Passagier*:⟩ aussteigen (**from** aus); **we** ∼**ed at Dieppe** wir gingen in Dieppe an Land; (b) (Aeronaut.) landen; (on water) [auf dem Wasser] aufsetzen; **be about to** ∼: zur Landung angesetzt haben; gerade landen; (c) (alight) landen; ⟨*Ball*:⟩ aufkommen; ∼ **on one's feet** auf den Füßen landen; (fig.) [wieder] auf die Füße fallen

∼ **'back** *v.i.* wieder landen (ugs.)
∼ **'up** *v.i.* landen (ugs.)

'land agent *n.* ▶**887** Grundstücksmakler, *der*/-maklerin, *die*

'land breeze *n.* Landwind, *der*

landed /'lændɪd/ *adj.* ∼ **gentry/aristocracy** Landadel, *der*

'landfill *n.* (a) (material) Müll, *der;* Schutt, *der* (zur Geländeauffüllung); (b) (process) Geländeauffüllung, *die;* ∼ **site** (*mit Erde wieder aufgefüllte*) Müllgrube

landing /'lændɪŋ/ *n.* (a) (of ship) Landung, *die;* (b) (of aircraft) Landung, *die;* **emergency** ∼: Notlandung, *die;* (c) (place for disembarkation) Anlegestelle, *die;* (d) (between flights of stairs) Treppenabsatz, *der;* (passage) Treppenflur, *der*

landing: ∼**card** *n.* Landekarte, *die;* ∼ **craft** *n.* (Navy) Landungsboot, *das;* ∼ **gear** *n.* Fahrwerk, *das;* ∼ **stage** *n.* Landungssteg, *der;* Landungsbrücke, *die*

land: ∼**lady** *n.* (a) (of rented property) Vermieterin, *die;* (b) (of public house) [Gast]wirtin, *die;* (c) (of lodgings etc.) [Pensions]wirtin, *die;* ∼**locked** *adj.* vom Land eingeschlossen ⟨*Bucht, Hafen*⟩; ⟨*Staat*⟩ ohne Zugang zum Meer; ∼**lord** *n.* (a) (of rented property) Vermieter, *der;* [Haus]wirt, *der;* (b) (of public house) [Gast]wirt, *der;* (c) (of lodgings etc.) [Pensions]wirt, *der;* ∼**mark** *n.* (a) weithin sichtbares Erkennungszeichen; (Naut.) Landmarke, *die;* (b) (fig.) Markstein, *der;* **stand as a** ∼**mark** einen Meilenstein bedeuten; ∼ **mass** *n.* (Geog.) Landmasse, *die;* ∼**mine** *n.* (Mil.) Landmine, *die;* ∼**owner** *n.* [large *or* big] ∼**owner** [Groß]grundbesitzer, *der*/-besitzerin, *die*

landscape /'lændskeɪp, 'lænskeɪp/ **1** *n.* (a) Landschaft, *die;* (b) (picture) Landschaftsbild, *das;* Landschaft, *die.* **2** *v.t.* landschaftsgärtnerisch gestalten ⟨*Garten, Park*⟩

'landscape gardener *n.* ▶**887** Landschaftsgärtner, *der*/-gärtnerin, *die*

land: ∼**slide** *n.* (a) Erdrutsch, *der;* (b) (fig.: majority) Erdrutsch[wahl]sieg, *der; attrib.* **a** ∼**slide victory** ein Erdrutsch[wahl]sieg; ∼**slip** ⇒ ∼**slide a**

lane /leɪn/ *n.* (a) (in the country) Landsträßchen, *das;* (unmetalled) [Hecken]weg, *der;* (b) (in town) Gasse, *die;* (c) (part of road) [Fahr]spur, *die;* **slow** ∼ (in Britain) linke Spur; (on the continent) rechte Spur; **'get in** ∼" „bitte einordnen"; *see also* **fast lane;** (d) (for race) Bahn, *die*

language /'læŋgwɪdʒ/ *n.* (a) ▶**897** Sprache, *die;* **speak the same** ∼ (fig.) die gleiche Sprache sprechen; (b) *no pl., no art.* (words, wording) Sprache, *die;* **[style of]** ∼: [Sprach]stil, *der;* **use of** ∼: Sprachgebrauch, *der;* (c) (style) Ausdrucksweise, *die;* Sprache, *die; see also* **bad 1 d; strong language;** (d) (professional vocabulary) [Fach]sprache, *die;* (e) (Computing) Sprache, *die*

Languages

With the major European languages, the noun has the same form as the nationality adjective but with a capital, much as in English. All languages are neuter.

German is difficult to learn	= Deutsch ist schwer zu lernen
She writes faultless/ cultivated English	= Sie schreibt ein fehlerloses *or* perfektes Englisch/ ein gepflegtes Englisch
He speaks Spanish without an accent	= Er spricht akzentfrei Spanisch
My daughter speaks fluent Russian	= Meine Tochter spricht fließend Russisch

in with a language is usually **auf**:

Say it in German	= Sagen Sie es auf Deutsch

But **in** is also used, especially where there is an adjective:

a speech in fluent French	= eine Rede in fließendem Französisch
The brochure is in English and German	= Der Prospekt ist in Englisch und Deutsch

Furthermore when the features of a language are being discussed, **im** with the nominalized form of the adjective should be used:

In English there are fewer endings than in German	= Im Englischen gibt es weniger Endungen als im Deutschen

The adjective as a noun is also used in relation to translations:

a translation from German into English	= eine Übersetzung aus dem Deutschen ins Englische

There are however cases where the adverb is used, which is written with a small letter. This happens because the word or phrase in question answers the question *how*:

The speech was given in English	= Die Rede wurde englisch *or* auf Englisch gehalten
They spoke German (i.e. on this occasion, answering the question 'how did they speak?')	= Sie sprachen deutsch
They speak German (i.e. can speak it, answering the question 'what do they speak?')	= Sie sprechen Deutsch

language: ～ **laboratory** *n.* Sprachlabor, *das;* ～ **teacher** *n.* Sprachlehrer, *der*/-lehrerin, *die*

languid /'læŋgwɪd/ *adj.* (a) (sluggish) träge; (b) (inert) matt

languish /'læŋgwɪʃ/ *v.i.* (a) (lose vitality) ermatten (geh.); (b) (live wretchedly) ～ **under sth.** unter etw. *(Dat.)* schmachten (geh.); ～ **in prison** im Gefängnis schmachten (geh.); (c) (pine) ～ **for sth.** nach etw. schmachten (geh.)

languor /'læŋgə(r)/ *n.* ⇒ **languorous:** Mattigkeit, *die;* Trägheit, *die*

languorous /'læŋgərəs/ *adj.* (a) (faint) matt; (b) (inert) träge

lank /læŋk/ *adj.* (a) (tall) hager; (b) (limp) glatt herabhängend ‹*Haar*›

lanky /'læŋkɪ/ *adj.* schlaksig (ugs.); [dürr und] lang ‹*Arm, Bein*›

lantern /'læntən/ *n.* Laterne, *die*

lap[1] /læp/ *n.* (part of body) Schoß, *der;* **live in the ～ of luxury** (fig.) im Überfluss leben; **fall into sb.'s ～** (fig.) jmdm. in den Schoß fallen; *see also* **god a**

lap[2] **1** *n.* (Sport) Runde, *die;* **on the last ～** (fig. coll.) auf der Zielgeraden (fig.). **2** *v.t.,* **-pp-:** (a) (Sport) überrunden; (b) (cause to overlap) überlappen

lap[3] **1** *v.i.,* **-pp-** (drink) schlappen; schlecken. **2** *v.t.,* **-pp-:** (a) (drink) ～ **[up]** [auf]schlappen; [auf]schlecken; (b) ⇒ ～ **up b;** (c) ⇒ ～ **up c**
～ **'up** *v.t.* (a) (drink) ⇒ ～ **2 a;** (b) (consume greedily) hinunterschütten; (c) (fig.: receive eagerly) schlucken (ugs.); begierig aufnehmen ‹*Lob*›

laparoscopy /læpə'rɒskəpɪ/ *n.* (Med.) Laparoskopie, *die*

lapel /lə'pel/ *n.* Revers, *das od.* (österr.) *der*

Lapland /'læplænd/ *pr. n.* Lappland *(das)*

Lapp /læp/ ▶ 897|, ▶ 947| **1** *n.* Lappe, *der*/Lappin, *die.* **2** *adj.* (a) lappisch; lappländisch; (b) (of language) lappisch

lapse /læps/ **1** *n.* (a) (interval) **a/the ～ of …:** eine/die Zeitspanne von …; **a ～ in the conversation** eine Gesprächspause; (b) (mistake) Fehler, *der;* Lapsus, *der* (geh.); ～ **of memory** Gedächtnislücke, *die;* (c) (deviation) Verstoß, *der* (**from** gegen); **momentary ～ of concentration** momentane Konzentrationsschwäche. **2** *v.i.* (a) (fail) versagen; ～ **from sth.** etw. vermissen lassen; (b) (sink) ～ **into** verfallen in (+ *Akk.*); fallen in (+ *Akk.*) ‹*Schlaf, Koma*›; (c) (become void) ‹*Vertrag, Versicherungspolice usw.:*› ungültig werden ‹*Plan, Projekt:*› hinfällig werden; ‹*Anspruch:*› verfallen

lapsed /læpst/ *adj.* (a) abgefallen ‹*Christ, Katholik usw.*›; (b) abgelaufen, ungültig ‹*Pass, Führerschein, Versicherungspolice*›

'laptop 1 *adj.* Laptop‹*gerät, -PC*›. **2** *n.* Laptop, *der*

larceny /'lɑːsənɪ/ *n.* (Law) Diebstahl, *der*

larch /lɑːtʃ/ *n.* Lärche, *die*

lard /lɑːd/ *n.* Schweineschmalz, *das;* Schweinefett, *das*

larder /'lɑːdə(r)/ *n.* (room) Speisekammer, *die;* (cupboard) Speiseschrank, *der*

large /lɑːdʒ/ **1** *adj.* (a) groß; **a ～ lady** eine stattliche Dame; ～ **importer/user** Großimporteur, *der*/Großverbraucher, *der; see also* **life d;** (b) (comprehensive, broad) umfassend. **2** *n.* **at ～** (at liberty) frei; (not in prison etc.) auf freiem Fuß; in Freiheit; (as a body) insgesamt; **society at ～:** die Gesellschaft in ihrer Gesamtheit. **3** *adv.* ⇒ **by**[1] **2 c; loom**[2]**; write 2 d**

largely /'lɑːdʒlɪ/ *adv.* weitgehend

larger-than-'life *attrib. adj.* überlebensgroß

large: ～**-scale** *attrib. adj.* groß angelegt; ‹*Katastrophe*› großen Ausmaßes; ‹*Modell*› in großem Maßstab; ～**-scale manufacture** Massenproduktion, *die;* ～**size[d]** *adj.* groß

largish /'lɑːdʒɪʃ/ *adj.* ziemlich groß; recht stattlich ‹*Person*›

lark[1] /lɑːk/ *n.* (Ornith.) Lerche, *die;* **be up with the ～:** beim *od.* mit dem ersten Hahnenschrei aufstehen

lark[2] (coll.) **1** *n.* (a) (piece of fun) Jux, *der* (ugs.); **do sth. for a ～:** etw. aus Jux machen (ugs.); **what a ～!** das ist/war spitze! (ugs.); (b) (Brit.) (form of activity) Blödsinn, *der* (ugs.); (affair) Geschichte, *die* (ugs.). **2** *v.i.* ～ **[about** *or* **around]** herumalbern (ugs.)

larva /'lɑːvə/ *n., pl.* ～**e** /'lɑːviː/ Larve, *die*

laryngitis /lærɪn'dʒaɪtɪs/ *n.* ▶ 865| (Med.) Kehlkopfentzündung, *die*

larynx /'lærɪŋks/ *n., pl.* **larynges** /lə'rɪndʒiːz/ (Anat.) ▶ 672| Kehlkopf, *der;* Larynx, *der* (fachspr.)

lascivious /lə'sɪvɪəs/ *adj.* (a) (lustful) lüstern (geh.); (b) (inciting to lust) lasziv

laser /'leɪzə(r)/ *n.* Laser, *der*

laser: ～ **beam** *n.* Laserstrahl, *der;* ～**disc** *n.* Laserplatte, *die;* ～**-guided** *adj.* lasergesteuert; ～ **printer** *n.* Laserdrucker, *der*

lash /læʃ/ **1** *n.* **(a)** (stroke) [Peitschen]hieb, *der;* **(b)** (part of whip) *biegsamer Teil der Peitsche;* (whipcord) Peitschenschnur, *die;* (as punishment) **the ~:** die Peitsche; **(c)** (on eyelid) Wimper, *die.* **2** *v.i.* **(a)** (make violent movement) schlagen; *⟨Peitsche, Schlange:⟩* zuschlagen; **(b)** (strike) *⟨Welle, Regen:⟩* peitschen (**against** gegen, **on** auf + *Akk.*); *⟨Person:⟩* [mit der Peitsche] schlagen (**at** nach). **3** *v.t.* **(a)** (fasten) festbinden (**to** an + *Dat.*); **~ together** zusammenbinden; **(b)** (flog) mit der Peitsche schlagen; (as punishment) auspeitschen; **(c)** (move violently) schlagen mit; **(d)** (beat upon) peitschen; **the rain ~ed the windows/roof** der Regen peitschte gegen die Fenster/auf das Dach

~ 'down 1 *v.t.* festbinden; (Naut.) festzurren (bes. Seemannsspr.). **2** *v.i.* *⟨Regen:⟩* niederprasseln

~ 'out *v.i.* **(a)** (hit out) um sich schlagen; *⟨Pferd:⟩* ausschlagen; **~ out at sb.** nach jmdm. schlagen; (fig.) über jmdn. herziehen (ugs.); **(b) ~ out on sth.** (coll.: spend freely) sich (*Dat.*) etw. leisten *od.* gönnen

lashings /'læʃɪŋz/ *n. pl.* (large amounts) **~ of sth.** Unmengen *Pl.* von etw.

lass /læs/, **lassie** /'læsɪ/ *ns.* (Scot., N. Engl.) Mädchen, *das*

lasso /ləˈsuː, ˈlæsəʊ/ **1** *n., pl.* **~s** *or* **~es** Lasso, *das.* **2** *v.t.* mit dem Lasso fangen

last¹ /lɑːst/ **1** *adj.* ▶**739**] letzt...; **be ~ to arrive** als Letzter/Letzte ankommen; **for the [very] ~ time** zum [aller]letzten Mal; **who was ~?** wer war letzter?; **the ~ two** die letzten beiden; **he came ~:** er war Letzter; **second ~, ~ but one** vorletzt...; **~ but not least** last, not least; nicht zuletzt; **~ evening/night was windy** gestern Abend/gestern *od.* heute Nacht war es windig; **~ evening/week we were out** gestern Abend/letzte Woche waren wir aus; **that would be the '~ thing to do in this situation** das wäre das Letzte, was man in dieser Situation tun würde. **2** *adv.* **(a)** [ganz] zuletzt; als Letzter/Letzte *⟨sprechen, ankommen⟩*; **(b)** (on ~ previous occasion) das letzte Mal; zuletzt; **when did you ~ see him** *or* **see him ~?** wann hast du ihn zuletzt *od.* das letzte Mal gesehen? **3** *n.* **(a)** (mention, sight) **I shall never hear the ~ of it** das werde ich ständig zu hören bekommen; **you haven't heard the ~ of this matter** das letzte Wort in dieser Sache ist noch nicht gesprochen; **that was the ~ we ever saw of him** das war das letzte Mal, dass wir ihn gesehen haben; **(b)** (person or thing) Letzter...; **these ~:** Letztere; **I'm always the ~ to be told** ich bin immer der Letzte, der etwas erfährt; **she was the ~ to know about it** sie erfuhr es als Letzte; **(c)** (day, moment[s]) **to** *or* **till the ~:** bis zuletzt; *see also* **breathe 2 a; (d)** at [long] **~:** endlich; schließlich [doch noch]

last² *v.i.* **(a)** (continue) andauern; *⟨Wetter, Ärger:⟩* anhalten; **~ all night** die ganze Nacht dauern; **~ till** dauern bis; **~ from ... to ...:** von ... bis ... dauern; **built to ~:** dauerhaft gebaut; **it can't/won't ~:** das geht nicht mehr lange so; **it's too good to ~:** es ist zu schön, um von Dauer zu sein; **(b)** (manage to continue) es aushalten; **(c)** (suffice) reichen; **while stocks ~:** solange Vorrat reicht; **this knife will ~ [me] a lifetime** dies Messer hält mein ganzes Leben

last³ *n.* (for shoemaker) Leisten, *der*

'last-ditch *adj.* **~ attempt** letzter verzweifelter Versuch

lasting /'lɑːstɪŋ/ *adj.* (permanent) bleibend; dauerhaft *⟨Beziehung⟩*; nachhaltig *⟨Eindruck, Wirkung, Bedeutung⟩*; nicht nachlassend *⟨Interesse⟩*

lastly /'lɑːstlɪ/ *adv.* schließlich

last: ~-mentioned *attrib. adj.* letztgenannt; **~ 'minute** *n.* **at the ~ minute** in letzter Minute; **up to the ~ minute** bis zum letzten Augenblick; **~-minute** *attrib. adj.* in letzter Minute *nachgestellt;* **~ name** *n.* Zuname, *der;* Nachname, *der;* **L~ 'Supper** *n., no pl.* (Relig.) **the L~ Supper** das Abendmahl; **~ 'thing** *adv.* (coll.) als Letztes; **~ 'word** *n., no pl., no indef. art.* letztes Wort; **be the ~ word** (fig.) nicht zu überbieten sein (**in** an + *Dat.*); das Letzte sein (**in** an + *Dat.*)

lat. *abbr.* **latitude** Br.

latch /lætʃ/ *n.* **(a)** (bar) Riegel, *der;* **(b)** (spring-lock) Schnappschloss, *das;* **(c) on the ~** (with lock not in use) nur eingeklinkt

~ 'on to *v.t.* (coll.) **(a)** (attach oneself to) **~ on to sb.** sich an jmdn. hängen (ugs.); **(b)** (understand) kapieren (ugs.); **(c)** (be enthusiastic about) abfahren auf (+ *Akk.*) (salopp)

'latchkey *n.* Hausschlüssel, *der;* **~ child** (fig.) Schlüsselkind, *das*

late /leɪt/ **1** *adj.* **(a)** (after proper time) verspätet; **am I ~?** komme ich zu spät?; **be ~ for the train** den Zug verpassen; **the train is [ten minutes] ~:** der Zug hat [zehn Minuten] Verspätung; **spring is ~ this year** dieses Jahr haben wir einen späten Frühling; **~ riser** Spätaufsteher, *der/*-aufsteherin, *die;* **~ entry** verspätete Anmeldung; **~ shift** Spätschicht, *die;* **it is ~:** es ist [schon] spät; **have a ~ dinner** [erst] spät zu Abend essen; **~ summer** Spätsommer, *der;* **in ~ July** Ende Juli; **(b)** (deceased) verstorben; **(c)** (former) ehemalig; vormalig; **(d)** (recent) letzt...; **in ~ times** in letzter Zeit. *See also* **later; latest. 2** *adv.* **(a)** (after proper time) verspätet; **[too] ~:** zu spät; **they got home very ~:** sie kamen [erst] sehr spät nach Hause; **better ~ than never** lieber spät als gar nicht; **(b)** (far on in time) spät; **~ in August** Ende August; **~ last century** [gegen] Ende des letzten Jahrhunderts; **~ in life** erst im fortgeschrittenen Alter; **(c)** (at or till a ~ hour) spät; **be up/sit up ~:** bis spät in die Nacht *od.* lange aufbleiben; **work ~ at the office** [abends] lange im Büro arbeiten; **(d)** (formerly) **~ of ...:** ehemals wohnhaft in ...; ehemaliger Mitarbeiter *⟨einer Firma⟩;* **(e)** (at ~ stage) **she was seen as ~ as yesterday** sie wurde gestern noch gesehen; **[a bit] ~ in the day** (fig. coll.) reichlich spät. **3** *n.* **of ~:** in letzter Zeit

'latecomer *n.* Zuspätkommende, *der/die*

lately /'leɪtlɪ/ *adv.* in letzter Zeit; **till ~:** bis vor kurzem

lateness /'leɪtnɪs/ *n., no pl.* **(a)** (being after due time) Verspätung, *die;* **(b)** (being far on in time) **the ~ of the performance** der späte Beginn der Vorstellung; **the ~ of the hour** die späte *od.* vorgerückte Stunde

latent /'leɪtənt/ *adj.* latent [vorhanden]

later /'leɪtə(r)/ **1** *adv.* später; **~ on** später; **~ [on] the same day** im weiteren Verlauf des Tages; später am Tag; **see you ~:** bis nachher; bis später. **2** *adj.* später; (more recent) neuer; jünger; **at a ~ date** zu einem späteren Zeitpunkt; später

lateral /'lætərl/ *adj.* seitlich (**to** von); Seiten*⟨flügel, -ansicht⟩;* **~ thinker** Querdenker, *der;* **~ thinking** Querdenken, *das*

laterally /'lætərəlɪ/ *adv.* seitlich

latest /'leɪtɪst/ *adj.* **(a)** (modern) neu[e]st...; **the very ~ thing** das Allerneu[e]ste; **(b)** (most recent) letzt...; **have you heard the ~?** wissen Sie schon das Neu[e]ste?; **what's the ~?** was gibt's Neues?; **(c)** at [the] **~/the very ~:** spätestens/allerspätestens

latex /'leɪteks/ *n., pl.* **~es** *or* **latices** /'leɪtɪsiːz/ Latex, *der*

lath /lɑːθ/ *n., pl.* **~s** /lɑːθs, lɑːðz/ Latte, *die*

lathe /leɪð/ *n.* Drehbank, *die*

lather /'lɑːðə(r), 'læðə(r)/ **1** *n.* **(a)** (froth) [Seifen]schaum, *der;* **(b)** (sweat) Schweiß, *der;* **get [oneself] into a ~** [about sth.] (fig.) sich [über etw. (*Akk.*)] aufregen. **2** *v.t.* einschäumen; einseifen

Latin /'lætɪn/ **1** *adj.* **(a)** lateinisch; **(b)** (of Southern Europeans) romanisch; südländisch *⟨Temperament⟩.* **2** ▶**897**] *n.* Latein, *das; see also* **English 2 a**

Latin: ~ A'merica *pr. n.* Lateinamerika (*das*); **~ A'merican 1** *adj.* lateinamerikanisch; **2** *n.* Lateinamerikaner, *der/*Lateinamerikanerin, *die;* **~ Quarter** *n.* Quartier Latin, *das*

latitude /'lætɪtjuːd/ *n.* **(a)** (freedom) Freiheit, *die;* **(b)** (Geog.) [geographische] Breite; (of a place) Breite, *die;* **~s** (regions) Breiten *Pl.;* **~ 40° N.** 40° nördlicher Breite

latrine /ləˈtriːn/ *n.* Latrine, *die*

latter /'lætə(r)/ *attrib. adj.* **(a)** letzter...; **the ~:** der/die/das Letztere; *pl.* die Letzteren; **(b)** (later) letzt...; **the ~ half of the century** die zweite Hälfte des Jahrhunderts; **the ~ part of the year** die zweite Jahreshälfte

latterly /'lætəlı/ *adv.* in letzter Zeit

Latvia /'lætvıə/ *pr. n.* Lettland (*das*)

Latvian /'lætvıən/ **1** ▶ 897 , ▶ 947 *adj.* lettisch; **sb. is ~:** jmd. ist Lette/Lettin. **2** *n.* (a) (person) Lette, *der*/Lettin, *die;* (b) (language) Lettisch, *das; see also* **English 2 a**

laudable /'lɔːdəbl/ *adj.* lobenswert

laugh /lɑːf/ **1** *n.* Lachen, *das;* (loud and continuous) Gelächter, *das;* **have a [good] ~ about sth.** [herzlich] über etw. (*Akk.*) lachen; **give a loud ~:** laut auflachen; **this line always gets a ~:** diese Zeile bringt immer einen Lacher; **have the last ~:** derjenige sein, der zuletzt lacht (fig.); **he is always good for a ~:** bei ihm gibt es immer etwas zu lachen; **sb./sth. is a ~ a minute** bei jmdm./etw. muss man alle Augenblicke lachen; **for ~s** zum *od.* aus Spaß; **for a ~:** [so] zum Spaß. **2** *v.i.* lachen; **~ out loud** laut auflachen; **I ~ed till I cried** ich habe Tränen gelacht; **~ at sb./sth.** (in amusement) über jmdn./etw. lachen; (jeer) jmdn. auslachen/etw. verlachen; über jmdn./etw. lachen; **~ in sb.'s face** jmdm. ins Gesicht lachen; **he who ~s last ~s longest** (prov.) wer zuletzt lacht, lacht am besten (Spr.); **don't make me ~** (coll. iron.) dass ich nicht lache! **3** *v.t.* lachen; **~ oneself silly** sich krank- *od.* schieflachen (ugs.)

~ 'off *v.t.* mit einem Lachen abtun

laughable /'lɑːfəbl/ *adj.* lachhaft (abwertend); lächerlich

laughing /'lɑːfıŋ/ *n.* **be no ~ matter** nicht zum Lachen sein

'laughing gas *n.* Lachgas, *das*

laughingly /'lɑːfıŋlı/ *adv.* lachend; **what is ~ called …** (iron.) was sich … nennt (spött.)

'laughing stock *n.* **make sb. a ~, make a ~ of sb.** jmdn. zum Gespött machen

laughter /'lɑːftə(r)/ *n.* Lachen, *das;* (loud and continuous) Gelächter, *das*

launch[1] /lɔːntʃ/ **1** *v.t.* (a) zu Wasser lassen, aussetzen ‹*Rettungsboot, Segelboot*›; vom Stapel lassen ‹*neues Schiff*›; (propel) werfen, abschießen ‹*Harpune*›; schleudern ‹*Speer*›; abschießen ‹*Torpedo*›; **~ a rocket into space** eine Rakete ins All schießen; (b) (fig.) lancieren (bes. Wirtsch.); auf den Markt bringen ‹*Produkt*›; vorstellen ‹*Buch, Schallplatte, Sänger*›; auf die Bühne bringen ‹*Theaterstück*›; gründen ‹*Firma*›; **~ an attack** einen Angriff durchführen. **2** *v.i.* **~ into a song** ein Lied anstimmen; **~ into a long speech** eine lange Rede vom Stapel lassen (ugs.)

~ 'out *v.i.* (fig.) **~ out into films/a new career/on one's own** sich beim Film versuchen/beruflich etwas ganz Neues anfangen/sich selbstständig machen

launch[2] *n.* (boat) Barkasse, *die*

launching: ~ pad *n.* [Raketen]abschussrampe, *die;* **~ site** *n.* [Raketen]abschussbasis, *die*

'launch pad ⇒ **launching pad**

launder /'lɔːndə(r)/ *v.t.* (a) waschen und bügeln; (b) (fig.) waschen ‹*Geld*›

launderette /lɔːndə'ret/, **laundrette** /lɔːn'dret/, (Amer.) **laundromat** /'lɔːndrəmæt/ *ns.* Waschsalon, *der*

laundry /'lɔːndrı/ *n.* (a) (place) Wäscherei, *die;* (b) (clothes etc.) Wäsche, *die;* **do the ~:** Wäsche waschen

laurel /'lɒrl/ *n.* (emblem of victory) Lorbeer[kranz], *der;* **rest on one's ~s** (fig.) sich auf seinen Lorbeeren ausruhen (ugs.)

lav /læv/ *n.* (coll.) Klo, *das* (ugs.)

lava /'lɑːvə/ *n.* Lava, *die*

lavatory /'lævətrı/ *n.* Toilette, *die*

lavatory: ~ paper ⇒ **toilet paper; ~ seat** ⇒ **toilet seat**

lavender /'lævındə(r)/ *n.* (Bot.) Lavendel, *der*

lavish /'lævıʃ/ **1** *adj.* (generous) großzügig; überschwänglich ‹*Lob, Liebe*›; verschwenderisch ‹*Ausgaben*›; (abundant) üppig; **be ~ of** *od.* **with sth.** nicht mit etw. geizen; **be too ~ with sth.** mit etw. übertreiben. **2** *v.t.* **~ sth. on sb.** jmdn. mit etw. überhäufen *od.* überschütten

lavishly /'lævıʃlı/ *adv.* großzügig; verschwenderisch ‹*Geld ausgeben*›; herrschaftlich ‹*eingerichtet*›

law /lɔː/ *n.* (a) *no pl.* (body of established rules) Gesetz, *das;* Recht, *das;* **the ~ forbids/allows sth. to be done** nach dem Gesetz ist es verboten/erlaubt, etw. zu tun; **according to/under British** etc. **~:** nach britischem *usw.* Recht; **break the ~:** gegen das Gesetz verstoßen; **be against the ~:** gegen das Gesetz sein; **under the** *or* **by** *or* **in ~:** nach dem Gesetz; **be/become ~:** vorgeschrieben sein/ werden; **lay down the ~:** Vorschriften machen (**to** *Dat.*); **lay down the ~ on/about sth.** sich zum Experten für etw. aufschwingen; **~ enforcement** Durchführung der Gesetze/des Gesetzes; (b) *no pl., no indef. art.* (control through ~) Gesetz, *das;* **~ and order** Ruhe und Ordnung; **be above the ~:** über dem Gesetz stehen; **outside the ~:** außerhalb der Legalität; (c) (statute) Gesetz, *das;* **there ought to be a ~ against it/people like you** so etwas sollte/Leute wie du sollten verboten werden; **be a ~ unto oneself** machen, was man will; (d) *no pl., no indef. art.* (litigation) Rechtswesen, *das;* Gerichtswesen, *das;* **go to ~ [over sth.]** [wegen etw.] vor Gericht gehen; [wegen etw.] den Rechtsweg beschreiten; **have the ~ on sb.** (coll.) jmdm. die Polizei auf den Hals schicken (ugs.); jmdn. vor den Kadi schleppen (ugs.); **take the ~ into one's own hands** sich (*Dat.*) selbst Recht verschaffen; (e) *no pl., no indef. art.* (profession) **practise ~:** Jurist/Juristin sein; (f) *no pl., no art.* (Univ.: jurisprudence) Jura *o. Art.;* Rechtswissenschaft, *die; attrib.* Rechts-; **Faculty of Law** juristische Fakultät; **~ school** (Amer.) juristische Fakultät; (g) *no indef. art.* (branch of ~) **commercial ~:** Handelsrecht, *das;* (h) (Sci., Philos., etc.) Gesetz, *das;* **~ of nature, natural ~:** Naturgesetz, *das*

law: ~-abiding /'lɔːəbaıdıŋ/ *adj.* gesetzestreu; **~breaker** *n.* Gesetzesbrecher, *der*/-brecherin, *die;* Rechtsbrecher, *der*/-brecherin, *die;* **~court** *n.* Gerichtsgebäude, *das;* (room) Gerichtssaal, *der;* **~ firm** *n.* (Amer.) Anwaltskanzlei, *die*

lawful /'lɔːfl/ *adj.* rechtmäßig, legitim ‹*Besitzer, Erbe*›; legitim, ehelich ‹*Tochter, Sohn, Nachkomme*›; legal, gesetzmäßig ‹*Vorgehen, Maßnahme*›

lawfully /'lɔːfəlı/ *adv.* legal; auf legalem Weg[e] ‹*erwerben*›

lawless /'lɔːlıs/ *adj.* gesetzlos

lawn /lɔːn/ *n.* (grass) Rasen, *der;* **~s** Rasenflächen

lawn: ~mower *n.* Rasenmäher, *der;* **~ seed** *n.* Grassamen, *der;* **~ 'tennis** *n.* Rasentennis, *das*

'lawsuit *n.* Prozess, *der*

lawyer /'lɔːjə(r), 'lɔıə(r)/ *n.* ▶ 887 Rechtsanwalt, *der*/ Rechtsanwältin, *die*

lax /læks/ *adj.* lax; **be ~ about hygiene/paying the rent** etc. es mit der Hygiene/der Zahlung der Miete *usw.* nicht sehr genau nehmen

laxative /'læksətıv/ (Med.) **1** *adj.* abführend; Stuhlgang fördernd. **2** *n.* Abführmittel, *das;* Laxativ[um] *das* (fachspr.)

laxity /'læksıtı/, **laxness** /'læksnıs/ *ns.* Laxheit, *die*

lay[1] /leı/ *adj.* (a) (Relig.) laikal; Laien‹*bruder, -schwester, -predigt*›; (b) (inexpert) laienhaft

lay[2] **1** *v.t.,* **laid** /leıd/ (a) legen, [ver]legen ‹*Teppichboden, Rohr, Gleis, Steine, Kabel, Leitung*›; legen ‹*Parkett, Fliesen, Fundament*›; anlegen ‹*Straße, Gehsteig*›; *see also* **hand 1 a;** (b) (fig.) **~ one's case before sb.** jmdm. seinen Fall vortragen; **~ one's plans/ideas before sb.** jmdm. seine Pläne/Vorstellungen unterbreiten; *see also* **blame 2; open 1 d;** (c) (impose) auferlegen ‹*Verantwortung, Verpflichtung*› (**on** *Dat.*); **~ weight on sth.** Gewicht auf etw. (*Akk.*) legen; (d) (wager) **I'll ~ you five to one that …: ich wette mit dir fünf zu eins, dass … ~ a wager on sth.** eine Wette auf etw. (*Akk.*) abschließen; auf etw. (*Akk.*) wetten; (e) (prepare) **~ the table** den Tisch decken; **~ three places for lunch** drei Gedecke zum Mittagessen auflegen; **~ the breakfast things** den Frühstückstisch decken; (f) (Biol.) legen ‹*Ei*›; (g) (devise) schmieden ‹*Plan*›; bannen ‹*Geist, Gespenst*›; (h) (sl.: copulate with) **~ a woman** eine Frau vernaschen *od.* aufs Kreuz legen (salopp). **2** *n.* (sl.: sexual partner) **she's a good/an easy ~:** sie ist gut im Bett/ steigt mit jedem ins Bett (ugs.)

~ a'bout *v.t.* (coll.) **~ about sb.** auf jmdn. einschlagen; (scold) jmdn. ausschimpfen

~ a'side *v.t.* beiseite *od.* zur Seite legen, weglegen

⟨angefangene Arbeit⟩; beiseite od. auf die Seite legen ⟨Geld⟩

∼ **'by** v.t. beiseite od. auf die Seite legen; **have some money laid by** etwas [Geld] auf der hohen Kante haben (ugs.)

∼ **'down** v.t. (a) hinlegen; ∼ **sth. down on the table** etw. auf den Tisch legen; (b) (give up) niederlegen ⟨Amt, Waffen⟩; (deposit) hinterlegen ⟨Geld⟩; ∼ **down one's arms** sich ergeben; die Waffen strecken (geh.); ∼ **down one's life for sth./sb.** sein Leben für etw./jmdn. [hin]geben; (c) (formulate) festlegen ⟨Regeln, Richtlinien, Bedingungen⟩; aufstellen ⟨Grundsätze, Regeln, Norm⟩; festsetzen ⟨Preis⟩; (in a contract, constitution) verankern; niederlegen; see also **law a**

∼ **'in** v.t. einlagern; sich eindecken mit

∼ **into** v.t. (coll.) ∼ **into sb.** auf jmdn. losgehen; über jmdn. herfallen; (fig.) jmdn. zusammenstauchen (ugs.)

∼ **'off 1** v.t. (a) (from work) vorübergehend entlassen; (b) (coll.) (stop) ∼ **off it!** lass das!; hör auf damit!; (stop attacking, lit. or fig.) ∼ **off him!** lass ihn in Ruhe! **2** v.i. (coll.: stop) aufhören

∼ **'on** v.t. (a) (provide) sorgen für ⟨Getränke, Erfrischungen, Unterhaltung⟩; bereitstellen ⟨Transportmittel⟩; organisieren ⟨Theaterbesuch, Stadtrundfahrt⟩; anschließen ⟨Gas, Strom⟩; (b) (apply) auftragen ⟨Farbe usw.⟩; see also **trowel a**

∼ **'out** v.t. (a) (spread out) ausbreiten; (ready for use) zurechtlegen; ∼ **out sth. for sb. to see** etw. vor jmdm. ausbreiten; (b) (for burial) aufbahren; (c) (arrange) anlegen ⟨Garten, Park, Wege⟩; das Layout machen für ⟨Buch⟩; (d) (coll.: knock unconscious) ∼ **sb. out** jmdn. außer Gefecht setzen; (e) (spend) ausgeben

∼ **'up** v.t. (a) (store) lagern; **you're ∼ing up trouble/ problems for yourself [later on]** (fig.) du handelst dir [für später] nur Ärger/Schwierigkeiten ein; (b) (put out of service) [vorübergehend] aus dem Verkehr ziehen ⟨Fahrzeug⟩; **I was laid up in bed for a week** ich musste eine Woche das Bett hüten

lay³ ⇒ **lie² 2**

lay: ∼**about** n. (Brit.) Gammler, der (ugs. abwertend); Nichtstuer, der (abwertend); ∼**-by** n., pl. ∼**-bys** (Brit.) Parkbucht, die; Haltebucht, die

layer /'leɪə(r)/ n. Schicht, die; **several** ∼**s of paper** mehrere Lagen Papier

'layer cake n. Schichttorte, die

layette /leɪ'et/ n. [baby's] ∼: Babyausstattung, die

lay: ∼**man** /'leɪmən/ n., pl. ∼**men** /'leɪmən/ Laie, der; ∼**-off** n. (a) (temporary dismissal) vorübergehende Entlassung; (b) (Sport; coll.: break from work) Pause, die; ∼**out** n. (of house, office) Raumaufteilung, die; (of garden, park) Gestaltung, die; Anlage, die; (of book, magazine, advertisement) Gestaltung, die; Layout, das

laze /leɪz/ v.i. faulenzen; ∼ **around** or **about** herumfaulenzen (ugs.)

lazily /'leɪzɪlɪ/ adv. faul; (sluggishly) träge

laziness /'leɪzɪnɪs/ n., no pl. Faulheit, die; (sluggishness) Trägheit, die

lazy /'leɪzɪ/ adj. faul; träge ⟨Geste, Sprechweise⟩; träge fließend ⟨Fluss⟩; **have a** ∼ **day on the beach** einen Tag am Strand faulenzen

'lazybones n. sing. Faulpelz, der

lb. abbr. ▶ 1202 **pound[s]** ≈ Pfd.

LCD abbr. **liquid crystal display** LCD

L-driver /'eldraɪvə(r)/ (Brit.) ⇒ **learner driver**

lead¹ /led/ n. (a) (metal) Blei, das; **go down like a** ∼ **balloon** mit Pauken und Trompeten durchfallen (ugs.); ⟨Rede, Vorschlag usw.⟩ überhaupt nicht ankommen; (b) (in pencil) [Bleistift]mine, die

lead² /liːd/ **1** v.t., **led** /led/ (a) führen; ∼ **sb. by the hand** jmdn. an der Hand führen; ∼ **sb. by the nose** (fig.) jmdn. nach seiner Pfeife tanzen lassen; ∼ **sb. into trouble** (fig.) jmdm. Ärger einbringen; **this is** ∼**ing us nowhere** (fig.) das führt zu nichts; (fig.: influence, induce) ∼ **sb. to do sth.** jmdn. veranlassen, etw. zu tun; **be easily led** sich leicht beeinflussen lassen; **that** ∼**s me to believe that** …: das lässt mich glauben, dass …; **he led**

me to suppose/believe that …: er gab mir Grund zu der Annahme/er machte mich glauben, dass …; (c) führen ⟨Leben⟩; ∼ **a life of misery/a miserable existence** ein erbärmliches Dasein führen/eine kümmerliche Existenz fristen; (d) (be first in) anführen; ∼ **the world in electrical engineering** auf dem Gebiet der Elektrotechnik in der ganzen Welt führend sein; **Smith led Jones by several yards/seconds** (Sport) Smith hatte mehrere Yards/ Sekunden Vorsprung vor Jones; (e) (direct, be head of) anführen ⟨Bewegung, Abordnung⟩; leiten ⟨Diskussion, Veranstaltung, Ensemble⟩; ⟨Dirigent:⟩ leiten ⟨Orchester, Chor⟩; ⟨Konzertmeister:⟩ führen ⟨Orchester⟩; ∼ **a party** Vorsitzender/Vorsitzende einer Partei sein. **2** v.i., **led** (a) ⟨Straße usw., Tür:⟩ führen; ∼ **to the town/to the sea** zur Stadt/ans Meer führen; ∼ **to confusion** Verwirrung stiften; **one thing led to another** es kam eins zum anderen; (b) (be first) führen; (go in front) vorangehen; (fig.: be leader) an der Spitze stehen; ∼ **by 3 metres** mit 3 Metern in Führung liegen; 3 Meter Vorsprung haben; ∼ **in the race** das Rennen anführen. **3** n. (a) (precedent) Beispiel, das; (clue) Anhaltspunkt, der; **follow sb.'s** ∼, **take one's** ∼ **from sb.** jmds. Beispiel (Dat.) folgen; (b) (first place) Führung, die; **be in the** ∼: in Führung liegen; an der Spitze liegen; **move** or **go into the** ∼, **take the** ∼: sich an die Spitze setzen; in Führung gehen; (c) (amount, distance) Vorsprung, der; (d) (on dog etc.) Leine, die; **on a** ∼: an der Leine; **put a dog on the** ∼: einen Hund anleinen; (e) (Electr.) Kabel, die; Leitung, die; (f) (Theatre) Hauptrolle, die; (player) Hauptdarsteller, der/-darstellerin, die

∼ **a'way** v.t. abführen ⟨Gefangenen, Verbrecher⟩

∼ **'off 1** v.t. (a) (take away) abführen; (b) (begin) beginnen. **2** v.i. beginnen

∼ **'on 1** v.t. (a) (entice) ∼ **sb. on** jmdn. reizen; **he's** ∼**ing you on** er versucht, dich zu reizen; (b) (deceive) auf den Leim führen; **she's just** ∼**ing him on** sie hält ihn nur zum Narren; (c) (take further) **that** ∼**s me on to my next point** das bringt mich zu meinem nächsten Punkt. **2** v.i. (a) imper. (go first) ∼ **on!** geh vor!; (b) ∼**ing on from what you have just said,** …: um fortzufahren, was Sie eben sagten, …; ∼ **on to the next topic** etc. zum nächsten Thema usw. führen

∼ **'up to** v.t. [schließlich] führen zu; (aim at) hinauswollen auf (+ Akk.)

leaden /'lednʃ/ adj. (a) bleiern; (b) (fig.) bleiern ⟨Schlaf, Augenlider, Glieder⟩

leader /'liːdə(r)/ n. (a) Führer, der/Führerin, die; (of political party) Vorsitzende, der/die; (of gang, rebels) Anführer, der/ Anführerin, die; (of expedition, project) Leiter, der/Leiterin, die; (of deputation) Sprecher, der/Sprecherin, die; (of tribe) [Stammes]häuptling, der; Stammesführer, der; **the Egyptian/Labour** ∼: der ägyptische Präsident/der Vorsitzende der Labour Party; **union/the Labour** ∼**s** Gewerkschaftsvorsitzende Pl./die Führenden der Labour Party; **have the qualities of a** ∼: Führungsqualitäten haben; (b) (one who is first) **he is a** ∼ **in his field** er ist eine führende Kapazität auf seinem Gebiet; (in race etc.) **be the** ∼: in Führung liegen; (c) (Brit. Journ.) Leitartikel, der; (d) (Mus.) (leading performer) Leader, der/Leaderin, die; (Brit.: principal first violinist) Konzertmeister, der/-meisterin, die

leadership /'liːdəʃɪp/ n. (a) Führung, die; (capacity to lead) Führungseigenschaften Pl.; **under the** ∼ **of** unter [der] Führung von; (b) (leaders) Führung[sspitze], die; ∼ **of the party** Parteivorsitz, der

lead-free /'ledfriː/ adj. bleifrei

leading /'liːdɪŋ/ adj. führend; (in first position) ⟨Läufer, Pferd, Auto⟩ an der Spitze; ∼ **role** Hauptrolle, die; (fig.) führende Rolle

leading: ∼ **'article** n. (Brit. Journ.) Leitartikel, der; ∼ **'lady** n. Hauptdarstellerin, die; ∼ **'light** n. herausragende Persönlichkeit; (expert) führende Kapazität, die; ∼ **'man** n. Hauptdarsteller, der; ∼ **'question** n. Suggestivfrage, die

lead: ∼ **pencil** /led 'pensl/ n. Bleistift, der; ∼ **poisoning** /'ledpɔɪzənɪŋ/ n. Bleivergiftung, die; ∼ **story** /'liːd stɔːrɪ/ n. (Journ.) Titelgeschichte, die

leaf /liːf/ **1** n., pl. **leaves** /liːvz/ (a) Blatt, das; **shake like a** ∼: zittern wie Espenlaub; **be in** ∼: grün sein;

come into ~: grün werden; (b) (of paper) Blatt, *das;* a ~ of paper ein Blatt Papier; turn over a new ~ (fig.) einen neuen Anfang machen; sich ändern; *see also* book 1 a; (c) (of table) (hinged/sliding flap) Platte, *die;* (for inserting) Einlegebrett, *das.* 2 *v.i.* ~ through sth. etw. durchblättern; in etw. (*Dat.*) blättern

leaflet /'li:flɪt/ *n.* [Hand]zettel, *der;* (with instructions) Gebrauchsanweisung, *die;* (advertising) Reklamezettel, *der;* (political) Flugblatt, *das*

leafy /'li:fɪ/ *adj.* belaubt; a ~ country lane eine baumbestandene Landstraße

league /li:g/ *n.* (a) (agreement) Bündnis, *das;* Bund, *der;* (in history) Liga, *die;* be in ~ with sb. mit jmdm. im Bunde sein *od.* stehen; those two are in ~ [together] die beiden stecken unter einer Decke (ugs.); (b) (Sport) Liga, *die;* I am not in his ~, he is out of my ~ (fig.) ich komme nicht an ihn heran; be in the big ~ (fig.) es geschafft haben

league: ~ 'football *n.* Ligafußball, *der;* ~ game, ~ match *ns.* Ligaspiel, *das;* L~ of 'Nations *n.* (Hist.) Völkerbund, *der;* ~ table *n.* Tabelle, *die* (Sport)

leak /li:k/ 1 *n.* (a) (hole) Leck, *das;* (in roof, ceiling, tent) undichte Stelle; there's a ~ in the tank der Tank ist leck; der Tank hat ein Leck; spring a ~ ⟨*Schiff:*⟩ leckschlagen (Seemannsspr.); ⟨*Gas-, Flüssigkeitsbehälter:*⟩ ein Leck bekommen; stop the ~: das Leck abdichten *od.* stopfen; (b) (escaping fluid/gas) durch ein Leck austretende Flüssigkeit/ austretendes Gas; (c) (instance) a gas/oil ~, a ~ of gas/ oil ein Austreten von Gas/Öl; there has been a gas/oil ~: es ist Gas/Öl ausgetreten; (d) (fig.: of information) undichte Stelle; (e) (Electr.) Elektrizitätsverlust, *der;* (path or point) Fehlerstelle, *die.* 2 *v.t.* (a) austreten lassen; the pipe is ~ing water/gas aus dem lecken Rohr tritt Wasser/Gas aus; (b) (fig.: disclose) durchsickern lassen; ~ sth. to sb. jmdm. etw. zuspielen. 3 *v.i.* (a) (escape) austreten (from aus); (enter) eindringen (in in + *Akk.*); ⟨*Fass, Tank, Schiff:*⟩ lecken; ⟨*Rohr, Leitung, Dach:*⟩ undicht sein; ⟨*Gefäß, Füller:*⟩ auslaufen; the roof ~s es regnet durch das Dach; (c) (fig.) ~ [out] durchsickern

leakage /'li:kɪdʒ/ *n.* (a) Auslaufen, *das;* (of fluid, gas) Ausströmen, *das;* (fig.: of information) Durchsickern, *das;* (b) (substance, amount) the ~ is increasing das Leck wird größer; mop up the ~: das ausgelaufene Wasser *usw.* aufwischen

leaky /'li:kɪ/ *adj.* undicht; leck ⟨*Schiff, Boot, Tank*⟩

lean¹ /li:n/ 1 *adj.* (a) mager; hager ⟨*Person, Gesicht*⟩; we had a ~ time [of it] es ging uns sehr schlecht; (b) (Commerc.) schlank. 2 *n.* (meat) Magere, *das*

lean² 1 *v.i.,* ~ed /li:nd, lent/ *or* (Brit.) ~t /lent/ (a) sich beugen; ~ against the door sich gegen die Tür lehnen; ~ out of the window sich aus dem Fenster lehnen; ~ down/forward sich herab-/vorbeugen; ~ back sich zurücklehnen; (b) (support oneself) ~ against/on sth. sich gegen/an etw. (*Akk.*) lehnen; ~ on sth. (from above) sich auf etw. (*Akk.*) lehnen; ~ on sb.'s arm sich auf jmds. Arm (*Akk.*) stützen; (c) (be supported) lehnen (against an + *Dat.*); (d) (fig.: rely) ~ [up]on sb. auf jmdn. bauen; (e) (stand obliquely) sich neigen; (f) (fig.: tend) ~ to[wards] sth. zu etw. neigen. 2 *v.t.,* ~ed *or* (Brit.) ~t lehnen (against gegen *od.* an + *Akk.*). 3 *n.* Neigung, *die;* have a definite ~ to the right eine deutliche Neigung nach rechts aufweisen

~ over 1 /'---/ *v.t.* sich neigen über (+ *Akk.*). 2 /-'--/ *v.i.* ⟨*Person:*⟩ sich hinüberbeugen; (forwards) sich vorbeugen; *see also* backwards a

leaning /'li:nɪŋ/ *n.* Hang, *der;* Neigung, *die*

leanness /'li:nnɪs/ *n., no pl.* (of person, face) Hagerkeit, *die*

leant ⇒ lean² 1, 2

lean-to /'li:ntu:/ *n., pl.* ~s Anbau, *der*

leap /li:p/ 1 *v.i.,* ~ed /li:pt, lept/ *or* ~t /lept/ (a) springen; ⟨*Herz:*⟩ hüpfen; ~ to one's feet aufspringen; ~ out of/up from one's chair aus seinem Sessel/von seinem Stuhl aufspringen; ~ back in shock vor Entsetzen zurückspringen; (b) (fig.) ~ to sb.'s defence jmdm. beispringen (geh.); ~ at the chance die Gelegenheit beim Schopf packen. 2 *v.t.,* ~ed *or* ~t (jump over) überspringen; springen *od.* setzen über (+ *Akk.*). 3 *n.* Sprung, *der;* with *or* in one ~: mit einem Satz; by ~s and bounds (fig.)

mit Riesenschritten ⟨*vorangehen*⟩; sprunghaft ⟨*zunehmen*⟩; *see also* dark 2 b

'leapfrog 1 *n.* Bockspringen, *das.* 2 *v.i.,* -gg- Bockspringen machen; ~ over sb. einen Bocksprung über jmdn. machen. 3 *v.t.,* -gg- (fig.) überspringen

leapt ⇒ leap 1, 2

'leap year *n.* Schaltjahr, *das*

learn /lɜ:n/ 1 *v.t.,* learnt /lɜ:nt/ *or* learned /lɜ:nd, lɜ:nt/ (a) lernen; (with emphasis on completeness of result) erlernen; ~ sth. by *or* from experience etw. durch [die] *od.* aus der Erfahrung lernen; ~ sth. from sb./a book/ an example etw. von jmdm./aus einem Buch/am Beispiel lernen; I am ~ing [how] to play tennis ich lerne Tennis spielen; *see also* lesson b; rope e; (b) (find out) erfahren; lernen; (by oral information) hören; (by observation) erkennen; merken; (by thought) erkennen; (be informed of) erfahren; I ~ed from the newspaper that …: ich habe in der Zeitung gelesen *od.* aus der Zeitung erfahren, dass … 2 *v.i.,* learnt *or* learned (a) lernen; be slow to ~: langsam lernen; you'll soon ~: du wirst es bald lernen; will you never ~? du lernst es wohl nie!; some people never ~: mancher lernt's nie; ~ by one's mistakes aus seinen Fehlern lernen; ~ about sth. etwas über etw. (*Akk.*) lernen; (b) (get to know) erfahren (of von)

learned /'lɜ:nɪd/ *adj.* gelehrt; wissenschaftlich ⟨*Gesellschaft, Zeitschrift*⟩

learner /'lɜ:nə(r)/ *n.* Lernende, *der/die;* (beginner) Anfänger, *der/*Anfängerin, *die;* be a slow/quick ~: langsam/schnell lernen; the car is driven by a ~: ein Fahrschüler steuert den Wagen

learner 'driver *n.* (Brit.) Fahrschüler/-schülerin (der/die unter Aufsicht fährt)

learning /'lɜ:nɪŋ/ *n.* (scholarship) Wissen, *das;* (of person) Gelehrsamkeit, *die*

learning: ~ difficulties *n. pl.* Lernschwierigkeiten *Pl.;* ~ disabllity *n.* Lernbehinderung, *die*

learnt ⇒ learn

lease /li:s/ 1 *n.* (of land, business premises) Pachtvertrag, *der;* (of house, flat, office) Mietvertrag, *der;* be on [a] ~: gepachtet/gemietet sein; give sb./sth. a new ~ of life jmdm. Auftrieb geben/etw. wieder in Schuss bringen (ugs.). 2 *v.t.* (a) (grant ~ on) verpachten ⟨*Grundstück, Geschäft, Rechte*⟩; vermieten ⟨*Haus, Wohnung, Büro*⟩; (b) (take ~ on) pachten ⟨*Grundstück, Geschäft, Rechte*⟩; mieten ⟨*Haus, Wohnung, Büro*⟩; leasen ⟨*Auto*⟩

lease: ~back *n.* Verpachtung an den Verkäufer; ~hold ⇒ lease 2: 1 *n.* have the ~hold of *or* on sth. etw. gepachtet *od.* in Pacht/gemietet haben; 2 *adj.* gepachtet/gemietet; ~holder *n.* ⇒ lease 2: Pächter, *der/* Pächterin, *die;* Mieter, *der/*Mieterin, *die*

leash /li:ʃ/ ⇒ lead² 3 d

least /li:st/ 1 *adj.* (smallest) kleinst…; (in quantity) wenigst…; (in status) geringst…; that's the ~ of our problems das ist unser geringstes Problem; *see also* last¹ 1. 2 *n.* Geringste, *das;* the ~ I can do das Mindeste, was ich tun kann; the ~ he could do would be to apologize er könnte sich wenigstens entschuldigen; to say the ~ [of it] gelinde gesagt; at ~: wenigstens; (if nothing more; anyway) wenigstens; at the [very] ~: [aller]mindestens; not [in] the ~: nicht im Geringsten. 3 *adv.* am wenigsten; not ~ because …: nicht zuletzt deshalb, weil …; ~ of all am allerwenigsten; the ~ likely answer die unwahrscheinlichste Lösung

leather /'leðə(r)/ 1 *n.* Leder, *das;* (things made of ~) Lederwaren *Pl.* ⟨*jacke, -mantel, -handschuh*⟩

leathery /'leðərɪ/ *adj.* ledern

leave¹ /li:v/ *n., no pl.* (a) (permission) Erlaubnis, *die;* (official approval) Genehmigung, *die;* grant *or* give sb. ~ to do sth. jmdm. gestatten, etw. zu tun; be absent without ~: sich unerlaubt entfernt haben; get ~ from sb. to do sth. von jmdm. die Erlaubnis bekommen, etw. zu tun; by ~ of sb. mit jmds. Genehmigung; by your ~ (formal) mit Ihrer Erlaubnis; (b) (from duty or work) Urlaub, *der;* ~ [of absence] Beurlaubung, *die;* Urlaub, *der* (auch Mil.); go on ~: in Urlaub gehen; be on ~: Urlaub haben; in Urlaub sein; (c) take one's ~ (say farewell) sich verabschieden;

Abschied nehmen (geh.); **he must have taken** ~ **of his senses** er muss von Sinnen sein

leave² *v.t.*, **left** /left/ **(a)** (make or let remain, lit. or fig.) hinterlassen; **he left a message with me for Mary** er hat bei mir eine Nachricht für Mary hinterlassen; ~ **sb. to do sth.** es jmdm. überlassen, etw. zu tun; **6 from 10** ~**s 4** 10 weniger 6 ist 4; (in will) ~ **sb. sth.**, ~ **sth. to sb.** jmdm. etw. hinterlassen; **(b)** (by mistake) vergessen; **I left my gloves in your car** ich habe meine Handschuhe in deinem Auto liegen lassen *od.* vergessen; **(c) be left with** nicht loswerden 〈*Gefühl, Verdacht*〉; übrig behalten 〈*Geld*〉; zurückbleiben mit 〈*Schulden, Kind*〉; **I was left with the job of clearing up** es blieb mir überlassen, aufzuräumen; **(d)** (refrain from doing, using, etc., let remain undisturbed) stehen lassen 〈*Abwasch, Essen*〉; sich (*Dat.*) entgehen lassen 〈*Gelegenheit*〉; **(e)** (let remain in given state) lassen; ~ **the door open/the light on** die Tür offen lassen/das Licht anlassen; ~ **the book lying on the table** das Buch auf dem Tisch liegen lassen; ~ **sb. in the dark** (fig.) jmdn. im Dunkeln lassen; ~ **one's clothes all over the room** seine Kleider im ganzen Zimmer herumliegen lassen; ~ **sb. alone** (allow to be alone) jmdn. allein lassen; (stop bothering) jmdn. in Ruhe lassen; ~ **sth. alone** etw. in Ruhe lassen; ~ **it at that** (coll.) es dabei bewenden lassen; **(f)** (refer, entrust) ~ **sth. to sb./sth.** etw. jmdm./einer Sache überlassen; **I** ~ **the matter entirely in your hands** ich lege diese Angelegenheit ganz in Ihre Hand/Hände; ~ **it to me** lass mich nur machen; **(g)** (go away from) verlassen; ~ **home at 6 a.m.** um 6 Uhr früh von zu Hause weggehen/-fahren; **the plane** ~**s Bonn at 6 p.m.** das Flugzeug fliegt um 18 Uhr von Bonn ab; ~ **Bonn at 6 p.m.** (by car, in train) um 18 Uhr von Bonn abfahren; (by plane) um 18 Uhr in Bonn abfliegen; ~ **the road** (crash) von der Fahrbahn abkommen; ~ **the rails** *or* **tracks** entgleisen; **the train** ~**s the station** der Zug rollt aus dem Bahnhof; **I left her at the bus stop** (parted from) an der Bushaltestelle haben wir uns getrennt; (set down) ich habe sie an der Bushaltestelle abgesetzt; ~ **the table** vom Tisch aufstehen; *abs.* **the train** ~**s at 8.30 a.m.** der Zug fährt *od.* geht um 8.30 Uhr; ~ **for Paris** nach Paris fahren/fliegen; **it is time to** ~: wir müssen gehen *od.* aufbrechen; ~ **on the 8 a.m. train/flight** mit dem 8-Uhr-Zug fahren/ der Acht-Uhr-Maschine fliegen; **(h)** (quit permanently) verlassen; ~ **school** die Schule verlassen; (prematurely) von der Schule abgehen; ~ **work** aufhören zu arbeiten; **(i)** (desert) verlassen; ~ **sb. for another man/woman** jmdn. wegen eines anderen Mannes/einer anderen Frau verlassen; **he was left for dead** man ließ ihn zurück, weil man ihn für tot hielt

~ **a'side** *v.t.* beiseite lassen

~ **be'hind** *v.t.* **(a)** zurücklassen; **(b)** (by mistake) ⇒ ~ **b**

~ **'off** *v.t.* **(a)** (cease to wear) auslassen (ugs.); nicht anziehen; **(b)** (discontinue) aufhören mit; *abs.* aufhören; **has it left off raining?** hat es aufgehört zu regnen?

~ **'out** *v.t.* auslassen

~ **'over** *v.t.* **(a)** (Brit.: not deal with till later) zurückstellen; **(b) be left over** übrig [geblieben] sein

-leaved /li:vd/ *adj.* in comb. -blätt[e]rig

leaven /'levn/ *n.* Treibmittel, *das;* (fermenting dough) Sauerteig, *der*

Lebanon /'lebənən/ *pr. n.* **[the]** ~: [der] Libanon

lecherous /'letʃərəs/ *adj.* lüstern (geh.); geil (abwertend)

lechery /'letʃərɪ/ *n.* Wollust, *die* (geh.)

lectern /'lektən/ *n.* (for Bible etc.) Lektionar[ium], *das;* (for singers) Notenpult, *das*

lecture /'lektʃə(r)/ **1** *n.* **(a)** Vortrag, *der;* (Univ.) Vorlesung, *die;* **give [sb.] a** ~ **on sth.** [vor jmdm.] einen Vortrag/ eine Vorlesung über etw. (*Akk.*) halten; **(b)** (reprimand) Strafpredigt, *die* (ugs.); **give sb. a** ~: jmdm. eine Strafpredigt halten. **2** *v.i.* ~ **[to sb.] [on sth.]** [vor jmdm.] einen Vortrag/(Univ.) eine Vorlesung [über etw. (*Akk.*)] halten; (give ~s) [vor jmdm.] Vorträge/(Univ.) Vorlesungen [über etw. (*Akk.*)] halten. **3** *v.t.* (scold) ~ **sb.** jmdm. eine Strafpredigt halten (ugs.)

'lecture hall *n.* Hörsaal, *der*

lecturer /'lektʃərə(r)/ *n.* **(a)** Vortragende, *der/die;* **(b)** ▶ 887 (Univ.) Lehrbeauftragte, *der/die;* **senior** ~: Dozent,

der/Dozentin, *die;* **be a** ~ **in French** Dozent/Dozentin für Französisch sein

lecture: ~**-room** *n.* Vortragsraum, *der;* (Univ.) Vorlesungsraum, *der;* ~ **theatre** *n.* Hörsaal, *der*

led ⇒ **lead²** 1, 2

LED *abbr.* **light-emitting diode** LED

ledge /ledʒ/ *n.* **(a)** Vorsprung, *der;* Sims, *der od. das;* **(b)** (of rock) [schmaler] Vorsprung

ledger /'ledʒə(r)/ *n.* (Commerc.) Hauptbuch, *das*

lee /li:/ *n.* **(a)** (shelter) Schutz, *der;* **in/under the** ~ **of** im Schutz (+ *Gen.*); **(b)** ~ **[side]** (Naut.) Leeseite, *die*

leech /li:tʃ/ *n.* [Blut]egel, *der*

leek /li:k/ *n.* Porree, *der;* Lauch, *der;* (as Welsh emblem) Lauch, *der;* **I like** ~**s** ich mag Porree *od.* Lauch; **three** ~**s** drei Stangen Porree/Lauch

leer /lɪə(r)/ **1** *n.* [suggestive/sneering] ~: anzüglicher/ spöttischer Blick. **2** *v.i.* [anzüglich/spöttisch/(lustfully) begehrlich] blicken; ~ **at sb.** jmdm. einen anzüglichen/ spöttischen/begehrlichen [Seiten]blick zuwerfen

lees /li:z/ *n. pl.* Bodensatz, *der*

leeward /'li:wəd, (Naut.) 'lu:əd/ (esp. Naut.) **1** *adj.* to/on the ~ **side of the ship** nach/in Lee. **2** *n.* Leeseite, *die;* **to** ~: leewärts; nach Lee

'leeway *n.* **(a)** (Naut.) Leeweg, *der;* Abdrift, *die;* **(b)** (fig.) Spielraum, *der;* **allow** *or* **give sb.** ~: jmdm. Spielraum lassen

left¹ ⇒ **leave²**

left² /left/ ▶ 1199 **1** *adj.* **(a)** (opposite of right) link...; **on the** ~ **side** auf der linken Seite; links; *see also* **turn 1 c;** **(b) L**~ (Polit.) link... **2** *adv.* nach links; ~ **of the road** links von der Straße. **3** *n.* **(a)** (~-hand side) linke Seite; **move to the** ~: nach links rücken; **on** *or* **to the** ~ **[of sb./sth.]** links [von jmdm./etw.]; **on** *or* **to my** ~, **to the** ~ **of me** links von mir; **zu meiner Linken; drive on the** ~: links fahren; **(b)** (Polit.) **the L**~: die Linke; **be on the L**~ **of the Party** dem linken Flügel der Partei angehören; **(c)** (Boxing) Linke, *die;* **(d)** (in marching) ~, **right,** ~, **right,** ~, ... (Mil.) links, zwo, drei, vier, links, ...

left: ~ **'hand** *n.* **(a)** linke Hand; Linke, *die;* **(b)** (~ side) **on** *or* **at sb.'s** ~ **hand** zu jmds. Linken; links von jmdm.; ~**-hand** *adj.* link...; ~**-hand bend** Linkskurve, *die;* **on your** ~**-hand side you see** ...: links *od.* zur Linken sehen Sie ...; *see also* **drive 1 g;** ~**-handed** /'left'hæn dɪd/ **1** *adj.* **(a)** linkshändig; 〈*Werkzeug*〉 für Linkshänder; **be** ~**-handed** Linkshänder/Linkshänderin sein; **(b)** (turning to ~) linksgängig, linksdrehend 〈*Schraube, Gewinde*〉; **2** *adv.* linkshändig; mit der linken Hand; ~ **'luggage [office]** *n.* (Brit. Railw.) Gepäckaufbewahrung, *die;* ~**over** *attrib. adj.* übrig geblieben; ~**overs** *n. pl.* Reste; (fig.) Relikte; Überbleibsel (ugs.); ~ **'wing** *n.* linker Flügel; ~**wing** *adj.* **(a)** (Sport) Linksaußen〈*spieler, -position*〉; **(b)** (Polit.) link...; linksgerichtet; Links〈*intellektueller, -extremist, -radikalismus*〉; ~**-'winger** *n.* **(a)** (Sport) Linksaußen, *der;* **(b)** (Polit.) Angehöriger/Angehörige des linken Flügels

leg /leg/ **1** *n.* **(a)** ▶ 672 Bein, *das;* **upper/lower** ~: Ober-/Unterschenkel, *der;* **artificial** ~: Beinprothese, *die;* **wooden** ~: Holzbein, *das;* **as fast as my** ~**s would carry me** so schnell mich die Füße trugen; **give sb. a** ~ **up on to a horse/over the gate** jmdm. auf ein Pferd/ über das Gatter helfen; **be on one's last** ~**s** sich kaum noch auf den Beinen halten können; (be about to die) mit einem Fuß *od.* Bein im Grabe stehen; **the car is on its last** ~**s** das Auto macht es nicht mehr lange (ugs.); **pull sb.'s** ~ (fig.) jmdn. auf den Arm nehmen (ugs.); **not have a** ~ **to stand on** (fig.) nichts in der Hand haben (fig.); **stretch one's** ~**s** sich (*Dat.*) die Beine vertreten; **get one's** ~ **over** (sl.) einen wegstecken (ugs.); **(b)** (of table, chair, etc.) Bein, *das;* **(c)** trouser-~**s** Hosenbeine; **(d)** (Gastr.) Keule, *die;* ~ **of lamb/veal** Lamm-/Kalbskeule, *die;* **(e)** (of journey) Etappe, *die;* Teilstrecke, *die;* **(f)** (Sport coll.) Durchgang, *der;* (of relay race) Teilstrecke, *die.* **2** *v.t.*, **-gg-:** ~ **it** (coll.) die Beine in die Hand *od.* unter die Arme nehmen (ugs.)

legacy /'legəsɪ/ *n.* Vermächtnis, *das* (Rechtsspr.); Erbschaft, *die;* (fig.) Erbe, *das;* **leave sb. sth. as a** ~ (lit. or fig.) jmdm. etw. hinterlassen

legal /'li:gl/ *adj.* **(a)** (concerning the law) juristisch; Rechts‹*beratung, -berater, -streit, -schutz*›; gesetzlich ‹*Vertreter*›; rechtlich ‹*Gründe, Stellung*›; (of the law) Gerichts‹*kosten*›; **in ~ matters/affairs** in Rechtsfragen/-angelegenheiten; **seek ~ advice** sich juristisch beraten lassen; **he is a member of the ~ profession** er ist Jurist; **(b)** (required by law) gesetzlich vorgeschrieben ‹*Mindestalter, Zeitraum*›; gesetzlich ‹*Verpflichtung*›; gesetzlich verankert ‹*Recht*›; **(c)** (lawful) legal; rechtsgültig ‹*Vertrag, Testament*›; gesetzlich zulässig ‹*Grenze, Höchstwert*›; **it is ~/not ~ to do sth.** es ist rechtlich zulässig/gesetzlich verboten, etw. zu tun; **make sth. ~:** etw. legalisieren

legal: ~ 'action *n.* Gerichtsverfahren, *das;* Prozess, *der;* **take ~ action against sb.** gerichtlich gegen jmdn. vorgehen; **~ 'aid** *n.* ≈ Prozesskostenhilfe, *die*

legality /lɪ'gælɪtɪ/ *n.* Legalität, *die;* Rechtmäßigkeit, *die*

legalize /'li:gəlaɪz/ *v.t.* legalisieren

legally /'li:gəlɪ/ *adv.* rechtlich ‹*zulässig, verpflichtet, begründet, unhaltbar, möglich*›; gesetzlich ‹*verankert, verpflichtet*›; vor dem Gesetz ‹*verantwortlich*›; legal ‹*durchführen, abwickeln, erwerben*›; **~ valid/binding** rechtsgültig/-verbindlich; **be ~ entitled to sth.** einen Rechtsanspruch auf etw. (*Akk.*) haben

legation /lɪ'geɪʃn/ *n.* (Diplom.) Gesandtschaft, *die;* (residence also) Gesandtschaftsgebäude, *das*

legend /'ledʒənd/ *n.* Sage, *die;* (of life of saint etc.; unfounded belief) Legende, *die;* **~ has it that …:** es geht die Sage, dass …

legendary /'ledʒəndərɪ/ *adj.* **(a)** legendenhaft; (described in legend) legendär; sagenhaft; **(b)** (coll.: famous) sagenhaft (ugs.); legendär

-legged /legd, 'legɪd/ *adj. in comb.* -beinig; **two-~:** zweibeinig

leggy /'legɪ/ *adj.* langbeinig; hochbeinig; ‹*Junge, Fohlen*› mit [staksigen] langen Beinen

legibility /ledʒɪ'bɪlɪtɪ/ *n., no pl.* Leserlichkeit, *die*

legible /'ledʒɪbl/ *adj.* leserlich; **easily/scarcely ~:** leicht/kaum lesbar

legion /'li:dʒn/ *n.* Legion, *die*

legionnaire /li:dʒə'neə(r)/ *n.* Legionär, *der*

legislate /'ledʒɪsleɪt/ *v.i.* Gesetze verabschieden; **~ for/against sth.** Gesetze zum Schutz von/gegen etw. einbringen

legislation /ledʒɪs'leɪʃn/ *n.* **(a)** (laws) Gesetze; **(b)** (legislating) Gesetzgebung, *die*

legislative /'ledʒɪslətɪv/ *adj.* gesetzgebend; (created by legislature) gesetzgeberisch

legislator /'ledʒɪsleɪtə(r)/ *n.* Gesetzgeber, *der*

legislature /'ledʒɪsleɪtʃə(r)/ *n.* Legislative, *die*

legitimacy /lɪ'dʒɪtɪməsɪ/ *n., no pl.* **(a)** Rechtmäßigkeit, *die;* Legitimität, *die;* **(b)** (of child) Ehelichkeit, *die*

legitimate /lɪ'dʒɪtɪmət/ *adj.* **(a)** ehelich, legitim ‹*Kind*›; **(b)** (lawful) legitim; rechtmäßig ‹*Besitzer, Regierung*›; legal ‹*Vorgehen, Weg, Geschäft, Gewinn*›; **(c)** (valid) berechtigt; stichhaltig; legitim (geh.) ‹*Argument*›; ausreichend ‹*Entschuldigung*›; triftig ‹*Grund*›

legitimize (legitimise) /lɪ'dʒɪtɪmaɪz/ *v.t.* legitimieren; [durch Heirat] ehelich machen ‹*Kind*›

'legroom *n., no pl., no indef. art.* Beinfreiheit, *die*

leisure /'leʒə(r)/ *n.* Freizeit, *die;* (for relaxation) Muße, *die; attrib.* Freizeit‹*kleidung, -beschäftigung, -zentrum, -industrie*›; **a life/day of ~:** ein Leben/Tag der Muße (geh.); **do sth. at ~:** etw. in Ruhe tun; **do sth. at one's ~:** sich (*Dat.*) Zeit mit etw. lassen; **~ time or hours** Freizeit, *die*

leisurely /'leʒəlɪ/ **1** *adj.* gemächlich. **2** *adv.* langsam; ohne Hast

lemming /'lemɪŋ/ *n.* Lemming, *der*

lemon /'lemən/ *n.* **(a)** Zitrone, *die;* **(b)** (colour) Zitronengelb, *das*

lemonade /lemə'neɪd/ *n.* [Zitronen]limonade, *die*

lemon: ~ curd /lemən 'kɜ:d/ *n.* Zitronencreme, *die;* **~ juice** *n.* Zitronensaft, *der;* **~ 'sole** *n.* Seezunge, *die;* **~ yellow** *adj.* zitronengelb

lend /lend/ **1** *v.t.,* **lent** /lent/ **(a)** leihen; **~ sth. to sb.** jmdm. etw. leihen; **(b)** (give, impart) geben; zur Verfügung stellen ‹*Dienste*›; verleihen ‹*Würde, Glaubwürdigkeit, Zauber*›; **~ one's support to sth.** etw. unterstützen; **~ one's name/authority to sth.** seinen Namen/guten Namen für etw. hergeben. **2** *v. refl.,* **lent: the book ~s itself/does not ~ itself to use as a learning aid** das Buch eignet sich/eignet sich nicht als Lehrmittel; **the system ~s itself to manipulation** das System bietet sich zur Manipulation an

lender /'lendə(r)/ *n.* Verleiher, *der*/Verleiherin, *die*

length /leŋθ, leŋkθ/ *n.* **(a)** ▶ 904 (also Horseracing, Rowing, Fashion) Länge, *die;* **a road four miles in ~:** eine vier Meilen lange Straße; **be six feet** *etc.* **in ~:** sechs Fuß *usw.* lang sein; **the room is twice the ~ of yours** das Zimmer ist doppelt so lang wie deins; **travel the ~ and breadth of the British Isles** überall auf den Britischen Inseln herumreisen; **a list the ~ of my arm** (fig.) eine ellenlange Liste; **win by a ~:** mit einer Länge siegen; **(b)** (of time) Länge, *die;* **a short ~ of time** kurze Zeit; **the play was three hours in ~:** das Stück dauerte drei Stunden; **(c)** **at ~** (for a long time) lange; (eventually) schließlich; **at [great] ~** (in great detail) lang und breit; sehr ausführlich; **at some ~:** ziemlich ausführlich; **(d)** **go to any/great** *etc.* **~s** alles nur/alles Erdenkliche tun; **(e)** (piece of material) Länge, *die;* Stück, *das*

lengthen /'leŋθən, 'leŋkθən/ **1** *v.i.* länger werden. **2** *v.t.* verlängern; länger machen ‹*Kleid*›

lengthways /'leŋθweɪz, 'leŋkθweɪz/ *adv.* der Länge nach; längs

lengthwise /'leŋθwaɪz, 'leŋkθwaɪz/ ⇒ **lengthways**

lengthy /'leŋθɪ, 'leŋkθɪ/ *adj.* überlang

lenience /'li:nɪəns/, **leniency** /'li:nɪənsɪ/ *ns., no pl.* Nachsicht, *die;* Milde, *die;* **show ~:** Milde walten lassen; Nachsicht zeigen

lenient /'li:nɪənt/ *adj.* **(a)** (tolerant) nachsichtig; **(b)** (mild) mild ‹*Urteil, Strafe*›

lens /lenz/ *n.* **(a)** (Optics, Anat.) Linse, *die;* (in spectacles) Glas, *das;* **(b)** (Photog.) Objektiv, *das*

Lent /lent/ *n.* Fastenzeit, *die*

lent ⇒ **lend**

lentil /'lentɪl/ *n.* Linse, *die*

Leo /'li:əʊ/ *n., pl.* **~s** (Astrol., Astron.) der Löwe

leopard /'lepəd/ *n.* (Zool.) Leopard, *der*

leotard /'li:ɑ:d/ *n.* Turnanzug, *der*

leper /'lepə(r)/ *n.* Leprakranke, *der/die*

leprosy /'leprəsɪ/ *n.* (Med.) Lepra, *die*

lesbian /'lezbɪən/ **1** *n.* Lesbierin, *die.* **2** *adj.* lesbisch

lesion /'li:ʒn/ *n.* (Med.) Läsion, *die* (fachspr.); Verletzung, *die*

less /les/ **1** *adj.* weniger; **of ~ value/importance/account** *or* **note** weniger wertvoll/wichtig/bedeutend; **his chances are ~ than mine** seine Chancen sind geringer als meine; **for ~ time** kürzere Zeit; **the pain is getting ~:** der Schmerz lässt nach; **~ talking, please** etwas mehr Ruhe, bitte. **2** *adv.* weniger; **I think ~/no ~ of him after what he did** ich halte nicht mehr so viel/nicht weniger von ihm, seit er das getan hat; **~ and ~:** immer weniger; **~ and ~ [often]** immer seltener; **~ so** weniger; **the ~ so because …:** umso weniger, als *od.* weil …; **even** *or* **still/far** *or* **much ~:** noch/viel weniger. **3** *n., no pl.,* no indef. art. weniger; **~ and ~:** immer weniger; **the ~ said [about it] the better** je weniger man darüber sagt, umso besser; **in ~ than no time** (joc.) in Null Komma nichts (ugs.); **~ of that!** (coll.) Schluss damit!; **~ of your cheek!** (coll.) sei nicht so frech! **4** *prep.* (deducting) **ten ~ three is seven** zehn weniger drei ist sieben

lessee /le'si:/ *n.* ⇒ **lease 2:** Pächter, *der*/Pächterin, *die;* Mieter, *der*/Mieterin, *die*

lessen /'lesn/ **1** *v.t.* (reduce) verringern; lindern ‹*Schmerz*›. **2** *v.i.* (become less) sich verringern; ‹*Fieber:*› sinken, fallen; ‹*Schmerz:*› nachlassen

lesser /'lesə(r)/ *attrib. adj.* geringer…; weniger bedeutend… ‹*Schauspieler, Werk*›

lesson /'lesn/ *n.* **(a)** (class) [Unterrichts]stunde, *die;* (in textbook) Lektion, *die;* **I like her ~s** mir gefällt ihr Unterricht;

Length and width

	1 inch (in.)	= 25,4 mm (fünfundzwanzig Komma vier Millimeter)
12 inches	= 1 foot (ft)	= 30,48 cm (dreißig Komma vier acht Zentimeter)
3 feet	= 1 yard (yd)	= 0,914 m (null Komma neun eins vier Meter)
1,760 yards	= 1 mile	= 1,61 km (eins Komma sechs eins Kilometer)

What width/length is it? = Wie breit/lang ist es?
The room is 12 feet = Das Zimmer ist zwölf
[wide] by 15 feet [long] mal fünfzehn Fuß [groß]
A is the same length/ = A hat die gleiche
width as B Länge/Breite wie B
They are the same = Sie haben die gleiche
length or *are equal* Länge *or* sind gleich
in length lang
They are not the same = Sie sind nicht gleich
width or *are different* breit *or* sind
widths verschieden breit
a drive 100 metres = eine 100 Meter lange
long or *in length* Einfahrt
a plank five centimetres = ein fünf Zentimeter
wide or *in width* breites Brett
German usually puts such measurements before the
noun, with the adjective agreeing. However especially
if the measurement is more complicated it may also
come after:

a car 14 feet 2 inches = ein Auto von 4,32 Meter
long Länge
Note that the translations for *wide* and *width* are
nearly always **breit** and **Breite; weit** and **Weite** may
occasionally occur in relation to clothing, but mainly
in compounds such as **Hüftweite** (hip measurement)
and **Taillenweite** (waist measurement), or referring to
loose fit.

Material is sold in German-speaking countries *by the
metre* (**meterweise**):

three metres of = drei Meter Stoff zu
material at £3.50 3,50 Pfund das Meter
a metre
a four-metre length of = ein vier Meter langes
silk Stück Seide
two ten-foot lengths ≈ zwei drei Meter lange
of rope Stücke Seil
NB There is no translation of the English *of* after a
quantity.

---

give ∼s Privatstunden *od.* -unterricht geben; **give Italian** ∼s Italienischunterricht *od.* -stunden geben; **[give]**
∼s **in/on** Unterricht [erteilen] in (+ *Dat.*); **take piano**
∼s **with sb.** bei jmdm. Klavierstunden nehmen; **(b)** (fig.:
example, warning) Lektion, *die;* Lehre, *die;* **teach sb. a** ∼:
jmdm. eine Lektion erteilen; ⟨*Vorfall usw.*⟩ jmdm. eine
Lehre sein; **be a** ∼ **to sb.** jmdm. eine Lehre sein; **learn
one's** *or* **a** ∼ **from sth.** aus etw. eine Lehre ziehen; **I
have learnt my** ∼: das soll mir eine Lehre sein

lest /lest/ *conj.* (literary) damit ... nicht; **he ran away** ∼
he [should] be seen er rannte weg, um nicht gesehen zu
werden; **I was afraid** ∼ **he [should] come back before I was ready** ich fürchtete, dass er zurückkommen
würde, bevor ich fertig war

let[1] /let/ **1** *v.t.*, **-tt-, let (a)** (allow to) lassen; ∼ **sb. do sth.**
jmdn. etw. tun lassen; **don't** ∼ **things get you down/
worry you** lass dich nicht entmutigen/mach dir keine
Sorgen; **don't** ∼ **him upset you** reg dich seinetwegen
nicht auf; **I'll come if you will** ∼ **me** ich komme, wenn
ich darf; ∼ **sb./sth. alone** jmdn./etw. in Ruhe lassen; ∼
alone (far less) geschweige denn; ∼ **sb. be** jmdn. in Ruhe
od. Frieden lassen; ∼ **go [of] sth./sb.** etw./jmdn. loslassen; ∼ **sb. go** (from captivity) jmdn. freilassen; ∼ **go** (release hold) loslassen; (neglect) herunterkommen lassen
⟨*Haus*⟩; (∼ pass) durchgehen lassen ⟨*Bemerkung*⟩; ∼ **it go
[at that]** es dabei belassen *od.* bewenden lassen; ∼ **oneself go** (neglect oneself) sich vernachlässigen; (abandon self-
restraint) sich gehen lassen; ∼ **loose** lassen; **(b)** (cause to)
∼ **sb. know** jmdn. wissen lassen; ∼ **sb. think that** ...:
jmdn. in dem Glauben lassen, dass ...; **I will** ∼ **you know
as soon as** ...: ich gebe Ihnen Bescheid, sobald ...; **(c)**
(release) ablassen ⟨*Wasser*⟩ **(out of, from** aus); lassen
⟨*Luft*⟩ **(out of** aus); **(d)** (Brit.: rent out) vermieten ⟨*Haus,
Wohnung, Büro*⟩; verpachten ⟨*Gelände, Grundstück*⟩; **'to**
∼' „zu vermieten". **2** *v. aux.*, **-tt-, let (a)** *in exhortations*
lassen; ∼ **us suppose that** ...: nehmen wir [nur] einmal
an, dass ...; **Let's go to the cinema. — Yes,** ∼**'s/No,**
∼**'s not** *or* **don't** ∼**'s** Komm/Kommt, wir gehen ins Kino.
— Ja, gut/Nein, lieber nicht; **(b)** *in command, challenge*
lassen; ∼ **them come in** sie sollen hereinkommen;
lassen Sie sie herein; **never** ∼ **it be said that** ...: keiner
soll sagen, dass ...; **[just]** ∼ **him try!** das soll er [nur] mal
wagen! **3** *n.* (Brit.) **rent a flat on a short** ∼: eine
Wohnung für kurze Zeit mieten
∼ **'down** *v.t.* **(a)** (lower) herunter-/hinunterlassen; *see
also* **hair** b; **(b)** (deflate) die Luft [heraus]lassen aus; **(c)**

(Dressm.) auslassen ⟨*Saum, Ärmel, Kleid, Hose*⟩; **(d)** (disappoint, fail) im Stich lassen; **I** ∼ **myself down in the exam**
ich habe in der Prüfung enttäuschend abgeschnitten
∼ **'in** *v.t.* **(a)** (admit) herein-/hineinlassen; (fig.) die Tür
öffnen (+ *Dat.*); ∼ **oneself/sb. in** sich (*Dat.*) [die Tür]
aufschließen/jmdm. aufmachen; **my shoes are** ∼**ting in
water** meine Schuhe sind undicht; **(b)** (Dressm.) enger
machen; einnähen; **(c)** ∼ **oneself in for sth.** sich auf
etw. (*Akk.*) einlassen; **(d)** ∼ **sb. in on a secret/plan** *etc.*
jmdn. in ein Geheimnis/einen Plan *usw.* einweihen
∼ **into** *v.t.* **(a)** (admit into) lassen in (+ *Akk.*); **(b)** (fig.: acquaint with) ∼ **sb. into a secret** jmdn. in ein Geheimnis
einweihen
∼ **'off** *v.t.* **(a)** (excuse) laufen lassen (ugs.); (allow to go) gehen
lassen; ∼ **sb. off lightly/with a fine** jmdn. glimpflich/
mit einer Geldstrafe davonkommen lassen; ∼ **sb. off sth.**
jmdm. etw. erlassen; **(b)** abbrennen ⟨*Feuerwerk*⟩; **(c)** (allow
to escape) ablassen ⟨*Dampf, Flüssigkeit*⟩; **(d)** (allow to alight)
aussteigen lassen
∼ **'on** (coll.) **1** *v.i.* **don't** ∼ **on!** nichts verraten! **2** *v.t.* **(a)**
sb. ∼ **on to me that** ...: man hat mir gesteckt, dass ...
(ugs.); **(b)** (pretend) ∼ **on that** ...: so tun, als ob ... (ugs.)
∼ **'out** *v.t.* **(a)** (open door for) ∼ **sb./an animal out**
jmdn./ein Tier heraus-/hinauslassen; **Don't get up. I'll**
∼ **myself out** Bleiben Sie sitzen. Ich finde schon allein
hinaus; **(b)** (allow out) rauslassen (ugs.); gehen lassen; **(c)**
(emit) ausstoßen ⟨*Schrei*⟩; hören lassen ⟨*Lachen, Seufzer*⟩;
∼ **out a groan** aufstöhnen; **(d)** (reveal) verraten, ausplaudern ⟨*Geheimnis*⟩; ∼ **out that** ...: durchsickern lassen,
dass ...; **(e)** (Dressm.) auslassen; **(f)** (Brit.: rent out) ⇒ **let**[1] **1**
d; **(g)** (from duty) **On Saturday? That** ∼s **me out**
Samstag? Da falle ich schon mal aus
∼ **'through** *v.t.* durchlassen
∼ **'up** *v.i.* (coll.) nachlassen; **don't you ever** ∼ **up?** wirst
du überhaupt nicht müde?

let[2] *n.* **without** ∼ **[or hindrance]** (formal/Law) ohne jede
Behinderung
'let-down *n.* Enttäuschung, *die*
lethal /'liːθl/ *adj.* tödlich; (fig.) vernichtend
lethargic /lɪ'θɑːdʒɪk/ *adj.* träge; (apathetic) lethargisch;
(causing lethargy) träge machend
lethargy /'leθədʒɪ/ *n.* Trägheit, *die;* (apathy) Lethargie, *die*
letter /letə(r)/ *n.* **(a)** (written communication) Brief, *der* **(to
an** + *Akk.*); (official communication) Schreiben, *das;* **a** ∼ **of
appointment** eine [briefliche] Anstellungszusage; **(b)** (of
alphabet) Buchstabe, *der;* **write in capital/small** ∼s mit

Letter-writing

Addressing the envelope

German addresses look different.
Line 1: the person's basic title (*Mr* = Herrn*, *Mrs* or *Ms* = Frau, *Miss* = Fräulein), followed by any other title or rank (Professor, Major etc.), except Dr. and Dipl.-Ing. (Diplomingenieur) which precede the name on **Line 2.**
Line 3: the street, with the house number <u>after</u> it.
Line 4 has the place, preceded by the postcode (**die Postleitzahl**). Finally comes the country on **Line 5.**

Herrn* Professor	Frau	Fräulein
Manfred Bauer	Dr. Erika Engelsbach	Inge Walz
Fritz-Busch-Str. 48	Ahornweg 6	bei Wolf
D-86163 Augsburg-Hochzoll	A-4924 Waldzell	Hauptstr. 21
Germany	Austria	48637 Coesfeld

*There is an **n** after **Herr** in addresses (and only in addresses) because this is an accusative.

The Postleitzahl may be preceded by D for Germany, A for Austria or CH for Switzerland when writing from outside the country. A district of a large town will often be added after the name of the town and joined with a hyphen.

Writing to someone staying with a family or friend, use **bei** plus the surname, e.g. bei Wolf.

Writing to a firm, **Firma** may precede the name, The name of the department or person you want follows the firm's name (**z.H.** = **zu Händen**, 'for the attention of'). **Postfach** = P.O. Box. And in typed or printed business mail there is a blank line before the place.

Firma	Müller-Versand KG
Willi Müller	Verkaufsabteilung
z.H. Herrn Nesseldorn	Postfach 21 08 03
Endenicher Straße 218	
	20408 Hamburg
53121 Bonn	

The sender's address should also be given on the back of the envelope, preceded by **Abs.** or **Absender.**

Layout

There is usually no address at the top, just the name of the place and the date:

　　　　　　　　　　　　　　　　Rastatt, [den] 7.4.1997

Beginnings

Dear Hans	= Lieber Hans
Dear Karen	= Liebe Karen
Dear Hilde and Erwin	= Liebe Hilde, lieber Erwin
Dear Mr Engel/ Mrs Schulz	= *(personal letter)* Lieber Herr Engel/Liebe Frau Schulz; *(formal business letter)* Sehr geehrter Herr Engel/Sehr geehrte Frau Schulz
Dear Sir or Madam (formal)	= Sehr geehrte Damen und Herren

To someone with a title, omit the name:

Dear Professor Wolf	= Sehr geehrter Herr Professor/Sehr geehrte Frau Professor

An exception is the title **Doktor**, where the name is omitted when writing to a doctor of medicine but not when writing to someone who holds the academic title of **Doktor**.

All these greetings can either be followed by a comma, with the first line then starting with a small letter, or by an exclamation mark, with the first line starting with a capital. In the letter itself, **du, dein, ihr, euer** used to be written with a capital, but this is no longer necessary.

... and Endings

Informal:

Yours	= Herzliche Grüße
All my/our love	= Alles Liebe
With best wishes, Kind regards	= Mit herzlichen Grüßen

More formal, standard ending:

Yours sincerely or *(Amer.) truly*	= Mit freundlichen Grüßen

Formal business letter:

Yours faithfully	= Mit freundlichen Empfehlungen, Hochachtungsvoll

---

Groß-/Kleinbuchstaben schreiben; **have ~s after one's name** Ehrentitel/einen Ehrentitel haben; (**c**) (fig.) **to the ~:** buchstabengetreu; aufs Wort; **the ~ of the law** der Buchstabe des Gesetzes; (**d**) *in pl.* (literature) Literatur, *die;* **man of ~s** Homme de lettres, *der;* Literat, *der*

letter: ~ **bomb** *n.* Briefbombe, *die;* ~ **box** *n.* Briefkasten, *der;* **~head**, **~heading** *ns.* Briefpapier mit Briefkopf; (heading) Briefkopf, *der*

lettering /ˈletərɪŋ/ *n.* Typographie, *die;* (on book cover) Aufschrift, *die;* (carved) Inschrift, *die*

lettuce /ˈletɪs/ *n.* [Kopf]salat, *der*

leukaemia, (*Amer.*) **leukemia** /luːˈkiːmɪə/ *n.* ▶865 Leukämie, *die*

level /ˈlevl/ **1** *n.* (**a**) Höhe, *die;* (storey) Etage, *die;* (fig.: steady state) Niveau, *das;* (fig.: basis) Ebene, *die;* **the water rose to the ~ of the doorstep** das Wasser stieg bis zur Türschwelle; **be on a ~ [with sb./sth.]** sich auf gleicher *od.* einer Höhe [mit jmdm./etw.] befinden; (fig.) auf dem gleichen Niveau sein [wie jmd./etw.]; **on the ~** (fig. coll.) ehrlich; **find one's ~** (fig.) seinen Platz finden; (**b**) (height) **at waist/rooftop** *etc.* **~:** in Taillen-/Dachhöhe *usw.;* (**c**) (relative amount) **sugar/alcohol ~:** [Blut]zucker-/Alkoholspiegel, *der;* **noise ~:** Geräuschpegel, *der;* (**d**) (social, moral, or intellectual plane) Niveau, *das;* (degree of achievement etc.) Grad, *der* (**of** an + *Dat.*); **talks at the highest ~** [of government] Gespräche auf höchster [Regierungs]ebene; (**e**) (instrument to test horizontal) Wasserwaage, *die.* **2** *adj.* (**a**) waagerecht; flach 〈*Land*〉; eben 〈*Boden, Land*〉; **a ~**

spoonful of flour ein gestrichener Löffel Mehl; **the picture is not ~:** das Bild hängt nicht gerade; (**b**) (on a ~) **be ~ [with sth./sb.]** auf gleicher Höhe [mit etw./jmdm.] sein; (fig.) [mit etw./jmdm.] gleichauf liegen; **the two pictures are not ~:** die beiden Bilder hängen nicht gleich hoch; **draw/keep ~ with a rival** mit einem Gegner gleichziehen/auf gleicher Höhe bleiben; (**c**) (fig.: steady, even) ausgeglichen 〈*Leben, Temperament*〉; ausgewogen 〈*Stil*〉; **keep a ~ head** einen kühlen Kopf bewahren; (**d**) **do one's ~ best** (coll.) sein Möglichstes tun. **3** *v.t.,* (Brit.) **-ll-:** (**a**) (*make* ~ **2 a**) ebnen; (**b**) (aim) richten 〈*Blick, Gewehr, Rakete*〉 (**at, against** auf + *Akk.*); (fig.) richten 〈*Kritik usw.*〉 (**at, against** gegen); erheben 〈*Anklage, Vorwurf*〉 (**at, against** gegen); (**c**) (raze) dem Erdboden gleichmachen 〈*Stadt, Gebäude*〉

~ **'off 1** *v.t.* glatt machen. **2** *v.i.* (Aeronaut.) die Flughöhe beibehalten

~ **'out 1** *v.t.* einebnen. **2** *v.i.* (**a**) ⇒ ~ **off 2**; (**b**) (fig.) sich ausgleichen 〈*Preise, Markt*〉 sich beruhigen

level: ~ **'crossing** *n.* (Brit. Railw.) [schienengleicher] Bahnübergang; **~-'headed** *adj.* besonnen; **remain ~-headed** einen kühlen Kopf bewahren

lever /ˈliːvə(r)/ **1** *n.* (**a**) Hebel, *der;* (crowbar) Brechstange, *die;* (fig.) Druckmittel, *das.* **2** *v.t.* ~ **sth. open** etw. aufhebeln; ~ **sth. up** etw. hochhebeln

leverage /ˈliːvərɪdʒ/ *n.* (**a**) Hebelwirkung, *die;* (action of lever) Hebelkraft, *die;* (**b**) (fig.: influence) **give sb. [a lot of]** ~**:** jmds. Position [sehr] stärken

leveraged buyout /liːvərɪdʒd 'baɪaʊt/ *n.* Leveraged Buy-out, *das* (Wirtsch.)

levity /'levɪtɪ/ *n.* (**a**) (frivolity) Unernst, *der*

levy /'levɪ/ **1** *n.* (**a**) [Steuer]erhebung, *die;* (**b**) (tax) Steuer, *die.* **2** *v.t.* (exact) erheben ⟨ *Steuern, Beträge* ⟩; ~ **a fine on sb./a tax on sth.** jmdn. mit einer Geldstrafe/etw. mit einer Steuer belegen

lewd /ljuːd/ *adj.* geil (oft abwertend), lüstern (geh.) ⟨ *Person* ⟩; anzüglich ⟨ *Blick, Geste* ⟩; schlüpfrig, unanständig ⟨ *Lied, Witz* ⟩

lexicographer /leksɪ'kɒɡrəfə(r)/ *n.* ▶ 887 Lexikograf, *der*/Lexikografin, *die*

lexicography /leksɪ'kɒɡrəfɪ/ *n., no pl.* Lexikographie, *die*

lexicon /'leksɪkən/ *n.* Wörterbuch, *das;* Lexikon, *das* (veralt.)

liability /laɪə'bɪlɪtɪ/ *n.* (**a**) *no pl.* (legal obligation) Haftung, *die;* **limited** ~ (Brit.) beschränkte Haftung; ~ **to pay tax[es]** *or* **for taxation** Steuerpflicht, *die;* (**b**) *no pl.* (proneness to disease etc.) Anfälligkeit, *die* (**to** für); (**c**) (handicap) Belastung, *die* (**to** für)

liable /'laɪəbl/ *pred. adj.* (**a**) (legally bound) **be** ~ **for sth.** für etw. haftbar sein *od.* haften; **be** ~ **to pay tax[es]** steuerpflichtig sein; (**b**) (prone) **be** ~ **to sth.** ⟨ *Sache:* ⟩ leicht etw. haben; ⟨ *Person:* ⟩ zu etw. neigen; **be** ~ **to do sth.** ⟨ *Sache:* ⟩ leicht etw. tun; ⟨ *Person:* ⟩ dazu neigen, etw. zu tun; (**c**) (likely) **difficulties are** ~ **to occur** mit Schwierigkeiten muss man rechnen; **she is** ~ **to change her mind** es kann durchaus sein, dass sie ihre Meinung ändert; **it is** ~ **to be cold there** im Allgemeinen ist es dort kalt

liaise /lɪ'eɪz/ *v.i.* (coll.) eine Verbindung herstellen

liaison /lɪ'eɪzɒn/ *n.* (**a**) (cooperation) Zusammenarbeit, *die;* (connection) Verbindung, *die;* (**b**) (illicit relation) Verhältnis, *das;* Liaison, *die* (geh.)

liar /'laɪə(r)/ *n.* Lügner, *der*/Lügnerin, *die*

Lib /lɪb/ *abbr.* (**a**) **Liberal** Lib.; (**b**) (coll.) **liberation**

libel /'laɪbl/ **1** *n.* (schriftliche) Verleumdung. **2** *v.t.*, (Brit.) **-ll-** (schriftlich) verleumden

libellous (*Amer.:* **libelous**) /'laɪbələs/ *adj.* verleumderisch

liberal /'lɪbərl/ **1** *adj.* (**a**) (generous, abundant) großzügig; **a** ~ **amount of** reichlich; (**b**) (not strict) liberal; frei ⟨ *Auslegung* ⟩; (**c**) (open-minded; also Polit.) liberal; **the L**~ **Democrats** (Brit.) die Liberaldemokraten. **2** *n.* **L**~ (Polit.) Liberale, *der/die*

liberality /lɪbə'rælɪtɪ/ *n., no pl.* (generosity) Großzügigkeit, *die* (**to** gegenüber)

liberally /'lɪbərəlɪ/ *adv.* (generously) großzügig; (abundantly) reichlich

liberate /'lɪbəreɪt/ *v.t.* befreien (**from** aus)

liberation /lɪbə'reɪʃn/ *n.* Befreiung, *die* (**from** aus); *see also* **Women's Liberation**

liberator /'lɪbəreɪtə(r)/ *n.* Befreier, *der*/Befreierin, *die*

liberty /'lɪbətɪ/ *n.* Freiheit, *die;* **you are at** ~ **to come and go as you please** es steht Ihnen frei, zu kommen und zu gehen, wie Sie wollen; **be at** ~**:** auf freiem Fuß sein; **set sb. at** ~**:** jmdn. auf freien Fuß setzen; **take the** ~ **to do** *or* **of doing sth.** sich (*Dat.*) die Freiheit nehmen, etw. zu tun; **take liberties with sb.** sich (*Dat.*) Freiheiten gegen jmdn. herausnehmen (ugs.); **take liberties with sth.** mit etw. allzu frei umgehen

libido /lɪ'biːdəʊ/ *n.* (Psych.) Libido, *die*

Libra /'liːbrə, 'lɪbrə/ *n.* (Astrol., Astron.) die Waage

librarian /laɪ'breərɪən/ *n.* ▶ 887 Bibliothekar, *der*/Bibliothekarin, *die*

library /'laɪbrərɪ/ *n.* Bibliothek, *die;* Bücherei, *die;* **reference** ~**:** Präsenzbibliothek, *die;* **public** ~**:** öffentliche Bücherei

library: ~ **book** *n.* Buch aus der Bibliothek *od.* Bücherei; ~ **ticket** *n.* Lesekarte, *die*

libretto /lɪ'bretəʊ/ *n.*, *pl.* **libretti** /lɪ'bretiː/ *or* ~**s** Libretto, *das*

Libya /'lɪbɪə/ *pr. n.* Libyen (*das*)

Libyan /'lɪbɪən/ *adj.* libysch

lice *pl. of* **louse** a

licence /'laɪsəns/ **1** *n.* (**a**) (official permit) [behördliche] Genehmigung; Lizenz, *die;* Konzession, *die* (Amtsspr.); (driving-~) Führerschein, *der;* **gun** ~**:** Waffenschein, *der;* (**b**) ([excessive] liberty of action) [uneingeschränkte] Handlungsfreiheit; (**c**) (licentiousness) Unzüchtigkeit, *die;* Zügellosigkeit, *die;* (**d**) **poetic** ~**:** dichterische Freiheit. **2** *v.t.* ⇒ **license 1**

license /'laɪsəns/ **1** *v.t.* ermächtigen; ~**d** ⟨ *Händler, Makler, Buchmacher* ⟩ mit [einer] Lizenz; ~**d to sell alcoholic beverages** (formal) [für den Ausschank von alkoholischen Getränken] konzessioniert; **the restaurant is** ~**d to sell drinks** das Restaurant hat eine Schankerlaubnis *od.* -konzession; **licensing hours** (in public house) Ausschankzeiten; **licensing laws** Schankgesetze; ≈ Gaststättengesetz, *das;* ~**d premises** Gaststätte mit Schankerlaubnis; **get a car** ~**d, a car** ~**d** ≈ die Kfz-Steuer für ein Auto bezahlen. **2** *n.* (Amer.) ⇒ **licence 1**

licensee /laɪsən'siː/ *n.* Lizenzinhaber, *der;* Konzessionsinhaber, *der;* (of bar) Wirt, *der*/Wirtin, *die*

licentious /laɪ'senʃəs/ *adj.* zügellos, ausschweifend ⟨ *Leben, Person* ⟩; unzüchtig ⟨ *Benehmen* ⟩; freizügig ⟨ *Buch, Theaterstück* ⟩

lichen /'laɪkn, 'lɪtʃn/ *n.* Flechte, *die*

lick /lɪk/ **1** *v.t.* (**a**) lecken; ~ **a stamp** eine Briefmarke anlecken *od.* belecken; ~ **one's lips** (lit. *or* fig.) sich (*Dat.*) die Lippen lecken; ~ **sth./sb. into shape** (fig.) etw./jmdn. auf Vordermann bringen (ugs.); ~ **one's wounds** (lit. *or* fig.) seine Wunden lecken; (**b**) (play gently over) ⟨ *Flammen, Feuer:* ⟩ [empor]züngeln an (+ *Dat.*); (**c**) (coll.: beat) verdreschen (ugs.); (fig.) bewältigen, meistern ⟨ *Problem* ⟩; (in contest) eine Abfuhr erteilen (+ *Dat.*). **2** *n.* (**a**) (act) Lecken, *das;* **give a door a** ~ **of paint** eine Tür [oberflächlich] überstreichen; (**b**) (coll.: fast pace) **at a great** *or* **at full** ~**:** mit einem Affenzahn (ugs.)

~ **'off** *v.t.* ablecken

~ **'up** *v.t.* auflecken

lid /lɪd/ *n.* (**a**) Deckel, *der;* **take the** ~ **off sth.** (fig.) etw. aufdecken; **put the [tin]** ~ **on sth.** (Brit. coll.) (be the final blow) einer Sache (*Dat.*) die Krone aufsetzen; (put an end to) etw. stoppen; **keep the** ~ **on sth.** (coll.) (keep under control) etw. unter Kontrolle halten; (keep secret) etw. geheim halten *od.* abschirmen; (**b**) (eyelid) Lid, *das*

lie¹ /laɪ/ **1** *n.* (**a**) (false statement) Lüge, *die;* **tell** ~**s/a** ~**:** lügen; **no, I tell a** ~**,** ... (coll.) nein, nicht dass ich jetzt lüge, ... (ugs.); **white** ~**:** Notlüge, *die;* **give the** ~ **to sth.** etw. Lügen strafen; (**b**) (thing that deceives) [einzige] Lüge (fig.); Schwindel, *der* (abwertend). **2** *v.i.,* **lying** /'laɪɪŋ/ lügen; ~ **to sb.** jmdn. be- *od.* anlügen

lie² **1** *n.* (direction, position) Lage, *die;* **the** ~ **of the land** (Brit. fig.: state of affairs) die Lage der Dinge; die Sachlage. **2** *v.i.,* **lying** /'laɪɪŋ/, **lay** /leɪ/, **lain** /leɪn/ **(a)** liegen; (assume horizontal position) sich legen; **many obstacles** ~ **in the way of my success** (fig.) viele Hindernisse verstellen mir den Weg zum Erfolg; **she lay asleep/resting on the sofa** sie lag auf dem Sofa und schlief/ruhte sich aus; ~ **still/dying** still liegen/im Sterben liegen; (**b**) ~ **idle** ⟨ *Feld, Garten:* ⟩ brachliegen; ⟨ *Maschine, Fabrik:* ⟩ stillstehen; ⟨ *Gegenstand:* ⟩ [unbenutzt] herumstehen (ugs.); **let sth./things** ~**:** etw./die Dinge ruhen lassen; **how do things** ~**?** wie liegen die Dinge?; (**c**) (be buried) [begraben] liegen; (**d**) (be situated) liegen; **Austria** ~**s to the south of Germany** Österreich liegt südlich von Deutschland; (**e**) (be spread out to view) **the valley/plain/desert lay before us** vor uns lag das Tal/die Ebene/die Wüste; **a brilliant career lay before him** (fig.) eine glänzende Karriere lag vor ihm; (**f**) (Naut.) ~ **at anchor/in harbour** vor Anker/im Hafen liegen; (**g**) (fig.) ⟨ *Gegenstand:* ⟩ liegen; **her interest** ~**s in languages** ihr Interesse liegt auf sprachlichem Gebiet; **I will do everything that** ~**s in my power to help** ich werde alles tun, was in meiner Macht steht, um zu helfen

~ **a'bout,** ~ **a'round** *v.i.* herumliegen (ugs.)

~ **'back** *v.i.* (recline against sth.) sich zurücklegen; (in sitting position) sich zurücklehnen

~ **'down** *v.i.* sich hinlegen; **take sth. lying down** (fig.) etw. ruhig *od.* tatenlos hinnehmen

~ **'in** v.i. (Brit. coll.: stay in bed) liegen bleiben

~ **'up** v.i. (hide) sich versteckt halten

'lie detector n. Lügendetektor, der

'lie-in n. (Brit. coll.: extra time in bed) **have a** ~: [sich] ausschlafen

lieu /lju:, lu:/ n. **in** ~ **of** sth. anstelle einer Sache (Gen.); **get money/holiday in** ~: statt dessen Geld/Urlaub bekommen

lieutenant /lef'tenənt, ləf'tenənt/ n. ▶1152| **(a)** (Army) Oberleutnant, der; (Navy) Kapitänleutnant, der; **(b)** (Amer.: policeman) ≈ Polizeioberkommissar, der

life /laɪf/ n., pl. **lives** /laɪvz/ **(a)** Leben, das; **it is a matter of** ~ **and death** es geht [dabei] um Leben und Tod; (fig.: it is of vital importance) es ist äußerst wichtig (**to** für); **come to** ~ ⟨Bild, Statue:⟩ lebendig werden; **run** etc. **for one's** ~: um sein Leben rennen usw.; **I cannot for the** ~ **of me** ich kann beim besten Willen nicht; **lose one's** ~: sein Leben verlieren; **many lives were lost** viele Menschen kamen ums Leben; **without loss of** ~: ohne Todesopfer; ~ **is not worth living** das Leben ist nicht lebenswert; **marry early in** ~: früh heiraten; **late in** ~: erst im fortgeschrittenen Alter; **for** ~: lebenslänglich ⟨inhaftiert⟩; **he's doing** ~ (coll.) er sitzt lebenslänglich (ugs.); **get** ~ (coll.) lebenslänglich kriegen (ugs.); **expectation of** ~: Lebenserwartung, die; **get the fright/shock of one's** ~ (coll.) zu Tode erschrecken/den Schock seines Lebens bekommen (ugs.); **have the time of one's** ~: sich hervorragend amüsieren; **he will do anything for a quiet** ~: für ihn ist die Hauptsache, dass er seine Ruhe hat; **make** ~ **easy for oneself/sb.** es sich (Dat.)/jmdm. leicht machen; **make** ~ **difficult for oneself/sb.** sich (Dat.)/jmdm. das Leben schwer machen; **this is the** ~! expr. content so lässt sich's leben!; **that's** ~, ~**'s like that** so ist das Leben [nun mal]; **not on your** ~ (coll.) nie im Leben! (ugs.); **save one's/sb.'s** ~: sein Leben/jmdm. das Leben retten; **sth. is as much as sb.'s** ~ **is worth** mit etw. setzt jmd. sein Leben aufs Spiel; **take one's [own]** ~: sich (Dat.) das Leben nehmen; **take one's** ~ **in one's hands** sein Leben riskieren; **get a** ~ (coll.) was aus seinem Leben machen; **(b)** (energy, animation) Leben, das; **be the** ~ **and soul of the party** der Mittelpunkt der Party sein; **there is still** ~ **in sth.** in etw. (Dat.) steckt noch Leben; **(c)** (living things and their activity) Leben, das; **bird/insect** ~: die Vogelwelt/die Insekten; **(d)** (living form or model) **draw sb. from** ~: jmdn. nach dem Leben zeichnen; **as large as** ~ (~-size) lebensgroß; (in person) in voller Schönheit (ugs. scherzh.); **larger than** ~: überzeichnet; **true to** ~: wahrheitsgetreu; **(e)** (specific aspect) ⟨Privat-, Wirtschafts-, Dorf⟩leben, das; **in this** ~ (on earth) in diesem Leben; **the other** or **the future** or **the next** ~ (in heaven) das zukünftige Leben [nach dem Tode]; **eternal** or **everlasting** ~: ewiges Leben; **daily** ~: das Alltagsleben; **see** ~: etwas von der Welt sehen; **(f)** (of battery, lightbulb, etc.) Lebensdauer, die

life: ~**-and-death** adj. ⟨Kampf⟩ auf Leben und Tod; (fig.) überaus wichtig ⟨Frage, Brief⟩; ~**assurance** n. (Brit.) Lebensversicherung, die; ~**belt** n. Rettungsring, der; ~**blood** n. Blut, das; (fig.) Lebensnerv, der; ~**boat** n. Rettungsboot, das; ~**buoy** n. (ring-shaped) Rettungsring, der; ~**cycle** n. Lebenszyklus, der; ~**guard** n. **(a)** (soldiers) Leibwache, die; **(b)** ▶887| (expert swimmer) Rettungsschwimmer, der/-schwimmerin, die; ~ **'history** n. Lebensgeschichte, die; ~ **insurance** n. Lebensversicherung, die; ~**jacket** n. Schwimmweste, die

lifeless /'laɪflɪs/ adj. leblos; unbelebt ⟨Gegend, Planet⟩; (fig.) farblos ⟨Stimme, Rede, Aufführung⟩; ⟨Stadt⟩ ohne Leben

life: ~**like** adj. lebensecht; ~**line** n. **(a)** (rope) Rettungsleine, die; **(b)** (fig.) [lebenswichtige] Verbindung; (support) Rettungsanker, der; ~**long** adj. lebenslang; **sb.'s** ~**long friend** (future) jmds. Freund fürs Leben; (past) jmds. Freund seit der Kindheit; ~ **'member** n. Mitglied auf Lebenszeit; ~**raft** n. Rettungsfloß, das; ~**saving** n. Rettungsschwimmen, das; attrib. Rettungs⟨gerät, -technik⟩; lebensrettend ⟨Medikament⟩; ~ **sentence** n.

lebenslängliche Freiheitsstrafe; **get a** ~ **sentence** lebenslänglich bekommen; ~**-size**, ~**-sized** adj. lebensgroß; **in** Lebensgröße nachgestellt; ~**span** n. Lebenserwartung, die; (Biol.) Lebensdauer, die; ~ **story** n. Lebensgeschichte, die; ~**style** 1 **(a)** n. Lebensstil, der; **(b)** (Commerc.) Lifestyle, der. **2** adj. (Commerc.) Lifestyle-; ~**-support** n. ~**-support system** lebenserhaltende Apparate; ~**time** n. Lebenszeit, die; (Phys.) Lebensdauer, die; attrib. lebenslang; **once in a** ~**time** einmal im Leben; **during my** ~**time** während meines Lebens; **the chance of a** ~**time** eine einmalige Gelegenheit

lift /lɪft/ **1** v.t. **(a)** heben; (slightly) anheben; (fig.) erheben ⟨Seele, Gemüt, Geist⟩; ~ **sb.'s spirits** jmds. Stimmung heben; **(b)** (sl.: steal) klauen (salopp); **(c)** (sl.: plagiarize) abkupfern (salopp) (**from** aus); **(d)** (end) aufheben ⟨Verbot, Beschränkung, Blockade⟩. **2** v.i. **(a)** (disperse) sich auflösen; **(b)** (rise) ⟨Stimmung:⟩ sich aufhellen; ⟨Herz:⟩ höher schlagen. **3** n. **(a)** (ride in vehicle) Mitfahrgelegenheit, die; **get a** ~ [**with** or **from sb.**] [von jmdm.] mitgenommen werden; **give sb. a** ~: jmdn. mitnehmen; **would you like a** ~? möchtest du mitfahren?; **(b)** (Brit.: in building) Aufzug, der; Fahrstuhl, der; **(c)** (~ing) Heben, das

~ **'down** v.t. herunterheben

~ **off** v.t. & i. abheben

~ **'up** (raise) hochheben; (turn upwards) heben ⟨Kopf⟩

lift: ~ **attendant** n. (Brit.) Aufzugführer, der; ~**-off** n. (Astronaut.) Abheben, das

ligament /'lɪgəmənt/ n. (Anat.) Band, das; Ligament[um], das (fachspr.)

ligature /'lɪgətʃə(r)/ n. Bandage, die; (in surgery) Ligaturfaden, der

light¹ /laɪt/ **1** n. **(a)** Licht, das; **in a good** ~: bei gutem Licht; **be in sb.'s** ~: jmdm. im Licht sein; **at first** ~: bei Tagesanbruch; **while the** ~ **lasts** solange es [noch] hell ist; ~ **of day** (lit. or fig.) Tageslicht, das; **(b)** (electric lamp) Licht, das; (fitting) Lampe, die; **go out like a** ~ (fig.) sofort weg sein (ugs.); **(c)** (signal to ships) Leuchtfeuer, das; **(d)** in sing. or pl. (signal to traffic) Ampel, die; **at the third set of** ~s an der dritten Ampel; **(e)** (to ignite) Feuer, das; **have you got a** ~? haben Sie Feuer?; **put a/set** ~ **to sth.** etw. anzünden; **(f)** **throw** or **shed** ~ **[up]on sth.** Licht in etw. (Akk.) bringen; **bring sth. to** ~: etw. ans [Tages]licht bringen; see also **see 1 a**; **(g)** in pl. (beliefs, abilities) **according to one's** ~s nach bestem Wissen [und Gewissen]; **(h)** (aspect) **in that** ~: aus dieser Sicht; **seen in this** ~: so gesehen; **in the** ~ **of** (taking into consideration) angesichts (⟨ Gen ⟩; **show sb. in a bad** ~: ein schlechtes Licht auf jmdn. werfen; **put sb. in a good/bad** ~: jmdn. in einem guten/schlechten Licht erscheinen lassen. **2** adj. hell; ~**-blue/-brown** etc. hellblau/-braun usw. **3** v.t., **lit** /lɪt/ or ~**ed (a)** (ignite) anzünden; **(b)** (illuminate) erhellen; ~ **sb.'s/one's way** jmdn./sich leuchten. **4** v.i., **lit** or ~**ed** ⟨Feuer, Zigarette:⟩ brennen, sich anzünden lassen

~ **'up 1** v.i. **(a)** (become lit) erleuchtet werden; **(b)** (become bright) aufleuchten (**with** vor); **(c)** (begin to smoke a cigarette etc.) sich (Dat.) eine anstecken (ugs.). **2** v.t. **(a)** (illuminate) erleuchten; **(b)** (make bright) erhellen; **(c)** anzünden ⟨Zigarette usw.⟩

light² **1** adj. **(a)** leicht; **[for]** ~ **relief** [als] kleine Abwechslung; **be a** ~ **sleeper** einen leichten Schlaf haben; **(b)** (small in amount) gering; **traffic is** ~ **on these roads** auf diesen Straßen herrscht nur wenig Verkehr; **(c)** (not important) leicht; **make** ~ **of sth.** etw. bagatellisieren; **(d)** (nimble) leicht ⟨Schritt, Bewegungen⟩; **have** ~ **fingers** (steal) gern lange Finger machen (ugs.); **(e)** (easily borne) leicht ⟨Krankheit, Strafe⟩; gering ⟨Steuern⟩; mild ⟨Strafe⟩; **(f)** **with a** ~ **heart** (carefree) leichten od. frohen Herzens; **(g)** **feel** ~ **in the head** (giddy) leicht benommen sein. **2** adv. **travel** ~: mit wenig od. leichtem Gepäck reisen

light³ v.i., **lit** /lɪt/ or ~**ed** (come by chance) ~ **[up]on sth.** auf etw. (Akk.) kommen od. stoßen

light: ~ **'aircraft** n. Leichtflugzeug, das; ~**bulb** n. Glühbirne, die; ~**-coloured** adj. hell

lighted /'laɪtɪd/ adj. brennend ⟨Kerze, Zigarette⟩; angezündet ⟨Streichholz⟩; beleuchtet ⟨Zimmer, Pfad, Schild, Vitrine⟩

light-emitting 'diode /'daɪəʊd/ n. Leuchtdiode, *die*
lighten¹ /'laɪtn/ **1** v.t. **(a)** (make less heavy) leichter machen; **(b)** (make less oppressive) leichter machen ⟨*Arbeit, Aufgabe*⟩; erleichtern ⟨*Gewissen*⟩; ~ **sb.'s burden** jmdn. entlasten. **2** v.i. (become less heavy) leichter werden
lighten² **1** v.t. (make brighter) aufhellen; heller machen ⟨*Raum*⟩. **2** v.i. sich aufhellen
lighter /'laɪtə(r)/ n. (device) Feuerzeug, *das;* (in car) Zigarettenanzünder, *der*
light: ~**-fingered** /'laɪtfɪŋgəd/ adj. langfing[e]rig; ~**headed** /laɪt'hedɪd/ adj. leicht benommen; ~**hearted** /'laɪtɑːtɪd/ adj. **(a)** (gay, humorous) unbeschwert; heiter; **(b)** (optimistic, casual) unbekümmert; ~**house** n. Leuchtturm, *der;* ~**house keeper** n. Leuchtturmwärter, *der;* ~ **'industry** n. Leichtindustrie, *die*
lighting /'laɪtɪŋ/ n. Beleuchtung, *die*
lighting-'up time n. Zeit zum Einschalten der Beleuchtung
lightly /'laɪtlɪ/ adv. **(a)** (not heavily) leicht; **sleep** ~: einen leichten Schlaf haben; **(b)** (in a small degree) leicht; **(c)** (without serious consideration) leichtfertig; **(d)** (cheerfully, deprecatingly) leichthin; **not treat sth.** ~: etw. nicht auf die leichte Schulter nehmen; **take sth.** ~: etw. nicht [so] ernst nehmen; **(e)** (nimbly) behände; **(f) get off** ~ (not receive heavy penalty) glimpflich davonkommen; *see also* **let off a**
'lightmeter n. Lichtmesser, *der;* (exposure meter) Belichtungsmesser, *der*
lightness¹ /'laɪtnɪs/ n., *no pl.* **(a)** (having little weight, lit. or fig.) Leichtigkeit, *die;* **(b)** (of penalty, weather) Milde, *die;* **(c)** ~ **of heart/spirit** Heiterkeit/Unbekümmertheit, *die;* **(d)** (lack of concern) Leichtfertigkeit, *die;* **(e)** (agility of movement) Leichtigkeit, *die*
lightness² n. (brightness, paleness of colour) Helligkeit, *die*
lightning /'laɪtnɪŋ/ **1** n., *no pl., no indef. art.* Blitz, *der;* **flash of** ~: Blitz, *der;* **like** ~ (coll.) wie der Blitz (ugs.); **[as] quick as** ~ (coll.) schnell wie der Blitz (ugs.); ~ **never strikes twice [in the same place]** (prov.) der Blitz schlägt nie[mals] zweimal am selben Platz *od.* Ort ein. **2** adj. Blitz-; **with** ~ **speed** blitzschnell
'lightning conductor n. (lit. or fig.) Blitzableiter, *der*
light: ~**weight 1** adj. **(a)** leicht; **(b)** (fig.: of little consequence) unmaßgeblich; **2** n. (Boxing etc.) Leichtgewicht, *das;* (person also) Leichtgewichtler, *der;* (fig.) Leichtgewicht, *das* (fig.); ~ **year** n. Lichtjahr, *das*
lignite /'lɪgnaɪt/ n. Braunkohle, *die*
like¹ /laɪk/ **1** adj. **(a)** (resembling) wie; **your dress is** ~ **mine** dein Kleid ist so ähnlich wie meins; **your dress is very** ~ **mine** dein Kleid ist meinem sehr ähnlich; **in a case** ~ **that** in so einem Fall; **there was nothing** ~ **it** es gab nichts Vergleichbares; **what is sb./sth.** ~? wie ist jmd./etw.?; **what's he** ~ **to talk to?** wie redet es sich mit ihm?; **more** ~ **twelve** eher zwölf; **that's [a bit] more** ~ **it** (coll.: better) das ist schon [etwas] besser; (coll.: nearer the truth) das stimmt schon eher; **they are nothing** ~ **each other** sie sind sich (*Dat.*) nicht im Geringsten ähnlich; **nothing** ~ **as** *or* **so good/bad/easy** *usw.* **as** ...: bei weitem nicht so gut/schlecht/viele *usw.* wie ...; **(b)** (characteristic of) typisch für ⟨*dich, ihn usw.*⟩; **it's just** ~ **you to be late!** du musst natürlich wieder zu spät kommen!; **(c)** (similar) ähnlich; **be as** ~ **as two peas in a pod** sich (*Dat.*) gleichen wie ein Ei dem andern; ~ **father,** ~ **son** (prov.) der Apfel fällt nicht weit vom Stamm (Spr.). **2** prep. (in the manner of) wie; **[just]** ~ **that** [einfach] so. **3** conj. (coll.) **(a)** (in same or similar manner as) wie; **he is not shy** ~ **he used to be** er ist nicht mehr so schüchtern wie früher; **(b)** (coll.: for example) etwa; beispielsweise. **4** n. **(a)** (equal) his/her ~: seines-/ihresgleichen; **the** ~**s of me/you** (coll.) meines-/deinesgleichen; **(b)** (similar things) **the** ~: so etwas; **and the** ~: und dergleichen
like² **1** v.t. (be fond of, wish for) mögen; ~ **it or not** ob es dir/ihm *usw.* gefällt oder nicht; ~ **vegetables** Gemüse mögen; gern Gemüse essen; ~ **doing sth.** etw. gern tun; **would you** ~ **a drink/to borrow the book?** möchtest du etwas trinken/dir das Buch leihen?; **would you** ~ **me**

to do it? möchtest du, dass ich es tue?; **I'd** ~ **it back soon** ich hätte es gern bald zurück; **I didn't** ~ **to disturb you** ich wollte dich nicht stören; **I** ~ **'that!** (iron.) so was hab ich gern! (ugs. iron.); **how do you** ~ **it?** wie gefällt es dir?; **how does he** ~ **living in America?** wie gefällt es ihm in Amerika?; **how would you** ~ **an ice cream?** was hältst du von einem Eis?; **if you** ~ *expr. assent* wenn du willst *od.* möchtest; *expr. limited assent* wenn man so will. **2** n., *in pl.* ~**s and dislikes** Vorlieben und Abneigungen
likeable /'laɪkəbl/ adj. nett; sympathisch
likelihood /'laɪklɪhʊd/ n. Wahrscheinlichkeit, *die;* **what is the** ~ **of this happening?** wie wahrscheinlich ist es, dass dies geschieht?; **in all** ~: aller Wahrscheinlichkeit nach
likely /'laɪklɪ/ **1** adj. **(a)** (probable) wahrscheinlich; glaubhaft ⟨*Geschichte*⟩; voraussichtlich ⟨*Bedarf, Zukunft*⟩; **be the** ~ **reason/source** wahrscheinlich der Grund/die Ursache sein; **do you think it** ~? hältst du es für wahrscheinlich?; **is it** ~ **that he'd do that?** ist ihm so etwas zuzutrauen?; **[that's] a** ~ **story** (iron.) wer's glaubt, wird selig (ugs. scherzh.); **(b)** (to be expected) wahrscheinlich; **there are** ~ **to be [traffic] hold-ups** man muss mit [Verkehrs]staus rechnen; **they are [not]** ~ **to come** sie werden wohl [nicht] kommen; **is it** ~ **to rain tomorrow?** wird es morgen wohl regnen?; **this is not** ~ **to happen** es ist unwahrscheinlich, dass das geschieht; **the candidate most** ~ **to succeed** der Kandidat mit den größten Erfolgsaussichten; **(c)** (promising, apparently suitable) geeignet ⟨*Person, Ort, Methode, Weg*⟩; **we've looked in all the** ~ **places** wir haben an allen infrage kommenden Stellen gesucht. **2** adv. (probably) wahrscheinlich; **very** *or* **more than** *or* **quite** *or* **most** ~: höchstwahrscheinlich; sehr wahrscheinlich; **as** ~ **as not** höchstwahrscheinlich; **not** ~! (coll.) auf keinen Fall!
'like-minded adj. gleich gesinnt
liken /'laɪkn/ v.t. ~ **sth./sb. to sth./sb.** etw./jmdn. mit etw./jmdm. vergleichen
likeness /'laɪknɪs/ n. **(a)** (resemblance) Ähnlichkeit, *die* (to mit); **(b)** (guise) Aussehen, *das;* Gestalt, *die;* **(c)** (portrait) Bild, *das*
likewise /'laɪkwaɪz/ adv. ebenso; **do** ~: das Gleiche tun
liking /'laɪkɪŋ/ n. Vorliebe, *die;* **take a** ~ **to sb./sth.** an jmdm./etw. Gefallen finden; **sth. is [not] to sb.'s** ~: etw. ist [nicht] nach jmds. Geschmack
lilac /'laɪlək/ **1** n. **(a)** (Bot.) Flieder, *der;* **(b)** (colour) Zartlila, *das.* **2** adj. zartlila; fliederfarben
lilt /lɪlt/ n. (Scot./literary) schwingender Rhythmus
lily /'lɪlɪ/ n. Lilie, *die;* ~ **of the valley** Maiglöckchen, *das*
limb /lɪm/ n. **(a)** ▶ 672 (Anat.) Glied, *das;* ~**s** Glieder; Gliedmaßen; **a danger to life and** ~: eine Gefahr für Leib und Leben; **(b) be out on a** ~ (fig.) exponiert sein
limber up /lɪmbər'ʌp/ v.i. sich einlaufen/einspielen *usw.;* (loosen up) die Muskeln lockern
limbo /'lɪmbəʊ/ n., *pl.* ~**s (a)** (neglect, oblivion) Vergessenheit, *die;* **vanish into** ~: spurlos verschwinden; **(b) be in** ~ (be pending) in der Schwebe sein; (be abandoned) abgeschrieben sein
lime¹ /laɪm/ n. **[quick]**~: (ungelöschter) Kalk
lime² n. (fruit) Limone, *die*
lime³ ⇒ **lime tree**
lime: ~ **green 1** adj. [leuchtend] hellgrün; **2** n. Hellgrün, *das;* ~**light** n. (fig.: attention) **be in the** ~**light** im Rampenlicht [der Öffentlichkeit] stehen
limerick /'lɪmərɪk/ n. Limerick, *der*
lime: ~**stone** n. Kalkstein, *der;* ~ **tree** n. Linde, *die*
limit /'lɪmɪt/ **1** n. **(a)** *usu. in pl.* (boundary) Grenze, *die;* **(b)** (point or line that may not be passed) Limit, *das;* **set** *or* **put a** ~ **on sth.** etw. begrenzen *od.* beschränken; **be over the** ~ ⟨*Autofahrer:*⟩ zu viele Promille haben; ⟨*Reisender:*⟩ Übergepäck haben; **there is a** ~ **to what I can spend/do** ich kann nicht unbegrenzt Geld ausgeben/meine Möglichkeiten sind auch nur begrenzt; **there is a** ~ **to my patience** meine Geduld ist begrenzt; **lower/upper** ~: Untergrenze/Höchstgrenze, *die;* **without** ~: unbegrenzt; **within** ~**s** innerhalb gewisser Grenzen; **(c)** (coll.) **this is**

the ~! das ist [doch] die Höhe!; **he/she is the [very] ~:** er/sie ist [einfach] unmöglich (ugs.). **2** *v.t.* begrenzen (**to** auf + *Akk.*); einschränken ‹*Freiheit*›

limitation /lɪmɪˈteɪʃn/ *n.* (**a**) (act) Beschränkung, *die;* (of freedom) Einschränkung, *die;* (**b**) (condition) (of extent) Begrenzung, *die;* (of amount) Beschränkung, *die;* **know one's ~s** seine Grenzen kennen

limited /ˈlɪmɪtɪd/ *adj.* (**a**) (restricted) begrenzt; **~ company** (Brit.) Gesellschaft mit beschränkter Haftung; **~ edition** limitierte Auflage; (**b**) (intellectually narrow) beschränkt (abwertend)

limitless /ˈlɪmɪtlɪs/ *adj.* grenzenlos

limo /ˈlɪməʊ/ *n., pl.* **~s** (Amer. coll.) Limousine, *die*

limousine /ˈlɪmʊziːn/ *n.* Limousine, *die* (*mit Trennscheibe*)

limp¹ /lɪmp/ **1** *v.i.* (lit. or fig.) hinken; **the ship managed to ~ into port** das Schiff schaffte es mit Müh und Not in den Hafen. **2** *n.* Hinken, *das;* **walk with a ~:** hinken

limp² *adj.* (not stiff, lit. or fig.) schlaff; welk ‹*Blumen*›

limpet /ˈlɪmpɪt/ *n.* (Zool.) Napfschnecke, *die*

limpid /ˈlɪmpɪd/ *adj.* klar

linchpin /ˈlɪntʃpɪn/ *n.* (fig.: essential element) Kernstück, *das;* **he is the ~ of the company** mit ihm steht und fällt die Firma

line¹ /laɪn/ **1** *n.* (**a**) (string, cord, rope, etc.) Leine, *die;* [**fishing-**]**~:** [Angel]schnur, *die;* (**b**) (telephone or telegraph cable) Leitung, *die;* **our company has 20 ~s** unsere Firma hat 20 Anschlüsse; **get me a ~ to Washington** verbinden Sie mich mit Washington; **bad ~:** schlechte Verbindung; *see also* **hold²** 1 k; (**c**) (long mark; also Math., Phys.) Text, *die;* (less precise or shorter) Strich, *der;* (Telev.) Zeile, *die;* (**d**) *in pl.* (outline of car, ship, etc.) Linien *Pl.;* (**e**) (boundary) Linie, *die;* **lay sth. on the ~ [for sb.]** [jmdm.] etw. rundheraus sagen; **put oneself on the ~:** ein Risiko eingehen; (**f**) (row) Reihe, *die;* (Amer.: queue) Schlange, *die;* **~ of trees** Baumreihe, *die;* **bring sb. into ~:** dafür sorgen, dass jmd. nicht aus der Reihe tanzt (ugs.); **come *or* fall into ~:** sich in die Reihe stellen; ‹*Gruppe:*› sich in einer Reihe aufstellen; (fig.) nicht mehr aus der Reihe tanzen (ugs.); **be in ~ [with sth.]** [mit etw.] in einer Linie liegen; **be in ~ for promotion** Aussicht auf Beförderung haben; **be in/out of ~ with sth.** (fig.) mit etw. in/nicht in Einklang stehen; **somewhere along the ~:** irgendwann einmal; (**g**) (row of words on a page) Zeile, *die;* **~s** (actor's part) Text, *der;* **drop me a ~:** schreib mir ein paar Zeilen; **he gave the boy 100 ~s** (Sch.) er ließ den Jungen 100 Zeilen abschreiben; (**h**) (system of transport) Linie, *die;* [**shipping**] **~:** Schifffahrtslinie, *die;* (**i**) (series of persons or things) Reihe, *die;* (generations of family) Linie, *die;* **be third in ~ to the throne** dritter in der Thronfolge sein; (**j**) (direction, course) Richtung, *die;* **on the ~s of** nach Art (+ *Gen.*); **on similar ~s** auf ähnliche Art; **be on the right/wrong ~s** in die richtige/falsche Richtung gehen; **along *or* on the same ~s** in der gleichen Richtung; **be on the same ~s** die gleiche Richtung verfolgen; **~ of thought** Gedankengang, *der;* **take a strong ~ with sb.** jmdm. gegenüber bestimmt *od.* energisch auftreten; **~ of action** Vorgehensweise, *die;* (**k**) (Railw.) Bahnlinie, *die;* (track) Gleis, *das;* **the Waterloo ~, the ~ to Waterloo** die Linie nach Waterloo; **this is the end of the ~ [for you]** (fig.) dies ist das Aus [für dich]; (**l**) (field of activity) Branche, *die;* (academic) Fachrichtung, *die;* **what's your ~?** in welcher Branche sind Sie?/was ist Ihre Fachrichtung?; **he's in the building ~:** er ist in der Baubranche; **be in the ~ of duty/business** zu den Pflichten/zum Geschäft gehören; (**m**) (Commerc.: product) Artikel, *der;* Linie, *die* (fachspr.); (**n**) (Fashion) Linie, *die;* (**o**) (Mil.: series of defences) Linie, *die;* **enemy ~s** feindliche Stellungen *od.* Linien. **2** *v.t.* (**a**) (mark with ~s) linieren ‹*Papier*›; **a ~d face** ein faltiges Gesicht; (**b**) (stand at intervals along) säumen (geh.) ‹*Straße, Strecke*›

~ 'up 1 *v.t.* antreten lassen ‹*Gefangene, Soldaten usw.*›; [in einer Reihe] aufstellen ‹*Gegenstände*›; (fig.) **I've got a nice little job/a surprise ~d up for you** ich hab da eine nette kleine Beschäftigung/eine Überraschung für dich (ugs.). **2** *v.i.* ‹*Gefangene, Soldaten:*› antreten; ‹*Läufer:*› Aufstellung nehmen; (queue up) sich anstellen

line² *v.t.* füttern ‹*Kleidungsstück*›; auskleiden ‹*Magen, Nest*›; ausschlagen ‹*Schublade usw.*›; **~ one's pockets** (fig.) sich (*Dat.*) die Taschen füllen

lineage /ˈlɪnɪdʒ/ *n.* Abstammung, *die*

linear /ˈlɪnɪə(r)/ *adj.* linear

line: ~ dance 1 *n.* Linedance, *der;* **2** *v.i.* Linedance tanzen; **~ dancer** *n.* Linedance-Tänzer, *der*/Line-dance-Tänzerin, *die;* **~ dancing** *n.* Linedance-Tanzen, *das*

linen /ˈlɪnɪn/ **1** *n.* (**a**) Leinen, *das;* (**b**) (shirts, sheets, clothes, etc.) Wäsche, *die.* **2** *adj.* Leinen‹*faden, -bluse, -laken*›; Lein‹*tuch*›

linen: ~ basket *n.* (Brit.) Wäschekorb, *der;* **~ cupboard** *n.* Wäscheschrank, *der*

liner /ˈlaɪnə(r)/ *n.* (ship) Linienschiff, *das;* **ocean ~:** [Ozean-]Liner, *der*

linesman /ˈlaɪnzmən/ *n., pl.* **linesmen** /ˈlaɪnzmən/ (Sport) Linienrichter, *der*

'line-up *n.* Aufstellung, *die*

linger /ˈlɪŋɡə(r)/ *v.i.* (**a**) (remain, wait) verweilen (geh.); bleiben; (persist) fortbestehen; (**b**) (dwell) **~ over *or* up[on] a subject** etc. bei einem Thema *usw.* verweilen; **~ over a meal** lange beim Essen sitzen

lingerie /ˈlæʒəriː/ *n.* [**women's**] **~:** Damenunterwäsche, *die*

lingering /ˈlɪŋɡərɪŋ/ *adj.* anhaltend; verbleibend ‹*Zweifel*›; langwierig ‹*Krankheit*›; langsam ‹*Tod*›; nachklingend ‹*Melodie*›

lingo /ˈlɪŋɡəʊ/ *n., pl.* **~es** (**a**) (derog./joc.: language) Sprache, *die;* (**b**) (jargon) Fachjargon, *der*

linguist /ˈlɪŋɡwɪst/ *n.* (**a**) Sprachkundige, *der*/*die;* **she's a good ~:** sie kann mehrere Sprachen; (**b**) (philologist) Linguist, *der*/Linguistin, *die*

linguistic /lɪŋˈɡwɪstɪk/ *adj.* (of **~s**) linguistisch; sprachwissenschaftlich; (of language) sprachlich; Sprach-

linguistics /lɪŋˈɡwɪstɪks/ *n., no pl.* Linguistik, *die;* Sprachwissenschaft, *die*

liniment /ˈlɪnɪmənt/ *n.* Liniment, *das* (Med.); Einreib[e]mittel, *das*

lining /ˈlaɪnɪŋ/ *n.* (of clothes) Futter, *das;* (of stomach) Magenschleimhaut, *die;* (of objects, containers, machines, etc.) Auskleidung, *die*

link /lɪŋk/ **1** *n.* (**a**) (of chain) Glied, *das;* (**b**) (connecting part) Bindeglied, *das;* Verbindung, *die;* **road/rail ~:** Straßen-/Zugverbindung, *die;* **what is the ~ between these two?** was verbindet diese beiden?; **sever all ~s with sb.** alle Bindungen zu jmdm. lösen; (**c**) ⇒ **linkman a. 2** *v.t.* (**a**) (connect) verbinden; **how are these events ~ed?** was haben diese Ereignisse miteinander zu tun?; **~ sb. with sth.** jmdn. mit etw. in Verbindung bringen; (**b**) **~ hands** sich bei den Händen halten; **~ arms** sich unterhaken. **3** *v.i.* **~ together** sich zusammenfügen

~ 'up *v.t.* miteinander verbinden; ankoppeln ‹*Wagen, Raumschiff usw.*› (**to** an + *Akk.*); miteinander in Verbindung bringen ‹*Fakten usw.*›. **2** *v.i.* **~ up with sb.** sich mit jmdm. zusammentun *od.* zusammenschließen; **the spacecraft ~ed up** die Raumschiffe wurden angekoppelt; **this road ~s up with the M3** diese Straße mündet in die M3

linkage /ˈlɪŋkɪdʒ/ *n.* (**a**) Verbindung, *die;* (**b**) (system of links or bars) Gestänge, *das*

linkman *n.* (**a**) Verbindungsmann, *der;* (**b**) (Radio, Telev.) Moderator, *der*/Moderatorin, *die*

links /lɪŋks/ *sing. or pl.* [**golf**] **~:** Golfplatz, *der*

lino /ˈlaɪnəʊ/ *n., pl.* **~s** Linoleum, *das*

linoleum /lɪˈnəʊlɪəm/ *n.* Linoleum, *das*

linseed /ˈlɪnsiːd/ *n.* Leinsamen, *der*

linseed 'oil *n.* Leinöl, *das*

lint /lɪnt/ *n.* Mull, *der*

lintel /ˈlɪntl/ *n.* (Archit.) Sturz, *der*

lion /ˈlaɪən/ *n.* Löwe, *der;* **the ~'s share** der Löwenanteil

lioness /ˈlaɪənɪs/ *n.* Löwin, *die*

'lion tamer /ˈlaɪən teɪmə(r)/ *n.* Löwenbändiger, *der*

lip /lɪp/ *n.* (**a**) ▶ **672** Lippe, *die;* **lower/upper ~:** Unter-/Oberlippe, *die;* **bite one's ~** (lit. or fig.) sich (*Dat.*) auf die

Lippen beißen; **escape sb.'s** ∼**s** jmds. Lippen (Dat.) entschlüpfen; **lick one's** ∼**s** (lit. or fig.) sich (Dat.) die Lippen lecken; **not let a word pass one's** ∼**s** kein Wort über seine Lippen kommen lassen; **keep a stiff upper** ∼ (fig.) Haltung bewahren; **(b)** (of saucer, cup, crater) [Gieß]rand, der; (of jug) Schnabel, der; Tülle, die; **(c)** (coll.: impudence) **give sb. some** ∼: jmdm. gegenüber eine dicke Lippe riskieren (ugs.); **none of your** ∼! keine frechen Bemerkungen!

liposuction /'laɪpəʊsʌkʃn, 'lɪpəʊsʌkʃn/ **1** n. Fettabsaugung, die. **2** v.t. absaugen ⟨Fett⟩

lippy /'lɪpɪ/ adj. (coll.) frech; vorlaut

lip: ∼**-read 1** v.i. von den Lippen lesen; **2** v.t. **be able to** ∼**-read what sb. says** jmdm. von den Lippen ablesen können, was er/sie sagt; ∼**-reading** n. Lippenlesen, das; ∼**-service** n. **pay** or **give** ∼**-service to sth.** ein Lippenbekenntnis zu etw. ablegen; ∼**stick** n. Lippenstift, der

liquefy /'lɪkwɪfaɪ/ **1** v.t. verflüssigen. **2** v.i. sich verflüssigen

liqueur /lɪ'kjʊə(r)/ n. Likör, der

liquid /'lɪkwɪd/ **1** adj. **(a)** flüssig; **(b)** (Commerc.) liquid; ∼ **assets** flüssige Mittel. **2** n. Flüssigkeit, die

liquidate /'lɪkwɪdeɪt/ v.t. **(a)** (Commerc.) liquidieren; **(b)** (eliminate, kill) liquidieren; beseitigen

liquidation /lɪkwɪ'deɪʃn/ n. (Commerc.) Liquidation, die

liquid crystal dis'play n. Flüssigkeitskristallanzeige, die

liquidity /lɪ'kwɪdɪtɪ/ n., no pl. **(a)** flüssiger Zustand; **(b)** (Commerc.) Liquidität, die

liquidize /'lɪkwɪdaɪz/ v.t. auflösen; (Cookery) [im Mixer] pürieren

liquidizer /'lɪkwɪdaɪzə(r)/ n. Mixer, der

liquor /'lɪkə(r)/ n. (drink) Alkohol, der; Spirituosen Pl.; **be able to carry** or **hold one's** ∼: etwas vertragen können; **hard** or **strong** ∼: hochprozentiger Alkohol

liquorice /'lɪkərɪs/ n. (root) Süßholz, das; (preparation) Lakritze, die

'liquor store n. (Amer.) Spirituosenladen, der

Lisbon /'lɪzbən/ pr. n. ▶1159 Lissabon (das)

lisp /lɪsp/ **1** v.i. & t. lispeln. **2** n. Lispeln, das; **speak with a** ∼: lispeln; **have a bad** ∼: stark lispeln

lissom /'lɪsəm/ adj. geschmeidig

list[1] /lɪst/ **1** n. Liste, die; **shopping** ∼: Einkaufszettel, der. **2** v.t. aufführen; auflisten

list[2] (Naut.) **1** n. Schlagseite, die; **have a pronounced** ∼: deutlich Schlagseite haben. **2** v.i. Schlagseite haben

listen /'lɪsn/ v.i. zuhören; ∼ **to music/the radio** Musik/Radio hören; **just** ∼ **to the noise they are making!** hör dir bloß mal an, was sie für einen Lärm machen!; **they** ∼**ed to his words** sie hörten ihm zu; **you never** ∼ **to what I say** du hörst mir nie zu; ∼ **[out] for sth./sb.** auf etw. (Akk.) horchen/horchen, ob jmd. kommt; ∼ **to sth./sb.** (pay heed) auf etw./jmdn. hören; **he wouldn't** ∼ (heed) er wollte nicht hören

∼ **'in** v.i. **(a)** (Radio) hören (**on, to** Akk.); **(b)** (eavesdrop) mithören (**on, to** Akk.)

listener /'lɪsnə(r)/ n. **(a)** Zuhörer, der/Zuhörerin, die; **(b)** (Radio) Hörer, der/Hörerin, die

listless /'lɪstlɪs/ adj. lustlos

'list price n. Katalogpreis, der

lit /lɪt/ ⇒ **light**[1] 3, 4; **light**[3]

litany /'lɪtənɪ/ n. (lit. or fig.) Litanei, die

lite, Lite (P) /laɪt/ **1** adj. kalorienreduziert ⟨Bier, Käse etc.⟩. **2** n. Leichtbier, das

liter (Amer.) ⇒ **litre**

literacy /'lɪtərəsɪ/ n., no pl. Lese- und Schreibfertigkeit, die; **adult** ∼ **classes** Kurse für Analphabeten

literal /'lɪtərl/ adj. **(a)** wörtlich; **take sth. in a** ∼ **sense** etw. wörtlich nehmen; **(b)** (not exaggerated) buchstäblich; **the** ∼ **truth** die reine Wahrheit; **(c)** (coll.: with some exaggeration) wahr

literally /'lɪtərəlɪ/ adv. **(a)** wörtlich; **take sth./sb.** ∼: etw./was jmd. sagt, wörtlich nehmen; **(b)** (actually) buchstäblich; **(c)** (coll.: with some exaggeration) geradezu

literary /'lɪtərərɪ/ adj. literarisch; (not colloquial) gewählt

literary: ∼ **'agent** n. Literaturagent, der/-agentin, die; ∼ **'critic** n. Literaturkritiker, der/-kritikerin, die

literate /'lɪtərət/ adj. (able to read and write) des Lesens und Schreibens kundig; (educated) gebildet

literature /'lɪtərətʃə(r), 'lɪtrətʃə(r)/ n. **(a)** Literatur, die; **(b)** (writings on a subject) [Fach]literatur, die (**on** zu); **(c)** (coll.: printed matter) Literatur, die; Informationsmaterial, das

lithe /laɪð/ adj. geschmeidig

lithograph /'lɪθəɡrɑːf/ **1** n. Lithographie, die. **2** v.t. lithographieren

Lithuania /lɪθjʊ'eɪnɪə/ pr. n. Litauen (das)

Lithuanian /lɪθjʊ'eɪnɪən/ ▶897, ▶947 **1** adj. litauisch; **sb. is** ∼: jmd. ist Litauer/Litauerin. **2** n. **(a)** (person) Litauer, der/Litauerin, die; **(b)** (language) Litauisch, das; see also **English** 2 a

litigation /lɪtɪ'ɡeɪʃn/ n. Rechtsstreit, der; **in** ∼: rechtshängig

litmus /'lɪtməs/ n. Lackmus, das od. der

litre /'liːtə(r)/ n. (Brit.) ▶1193 Liter, der od. das

litter /'lɪtə(r)/ **1** n. **(a)** (rubbish) Abfall, der; Abfälle Pl.; **(b)** (for animals) Streu, die; **(c)** (young) Wurf, der. **2** v.t. verstreuen; **papers were** ∼**ed about the room** im Zimmer lagen überall Zeitungen herum

litter: ∼ **basket** n. Abfallkorb, der; ∼ **bin** n. Abfalleimer, der

little /'lɪtl/ **1** adj., ∼**r** /'lɪtlə(r)/, ∼**st** /'lɪtlɪst/ (Note: it is more common to use the compar. and superl. forms **smaller, smallest**) **(a)** (small) klein; ∼ **town/book/dog** kleine Stadt/kleines Buch/kleiner Hund; (showing affection or amusement) Städtchen, das/Büchlein, das/Hündchen, das; ∼ **toe** kleine Zehe; **you poor** ∼ **thing!** du armes kleines Ding!; **I know your** ∼ **ways** ich kenne deine Tricks; **(b)** (young) klein; **the** ∼ **ones** die Kleinen; **my** ∼ **sister** meine kleine Schwester; **(c)** (short) klein ⟨Person⟩; **a** ∼ **way** ein kleines od. kurzes Stück; **after a** ∼ **while** nach kurzer Zeit; **(d)** (not much) wenig; **you have** ∼ **time left** dir bleibt nicht mehr viel Zeit; **there is very** ∼ **tea left** es ist kaum noch Tee od. nur noch ganz wenig Tee da; **make a nice** ∼ **profit** (coll. iron.) einen hübschen Gewinn machen (ugs.); **a** ∼ **...** (a small quantity of) etwas ...; ein wenig od. bisschen ...; **no** ∼ **...:** nicht wenig ...; **(e)** (trivial) klein. **2** n. wenig; **but** ∼: nur wenig; ∼ **or nothing** kaum etwas; so gut wie nichts; **[do] not a** ∼: einiges [tun]; **not a** ∼ **angry** etc. ziemlich verärgert usw.; **there was** ∼ **we could do** wir konnten nur wenig tun; **a** ∼ (a small quantity) etwas; ein wenig od. bisschen; (somewhat) ein wenig; **think** ∼ **of sb.** gering von jmdm. denken; **a** ∼ **after eight** kurz nach acht; **we see very** ∼ **of one another** wir sehen sehr wenig voneinander; ∼ **by** ∼: nach und nach. **3** adv., **less** /les/, **least** /liːst/ **(a)** (not at all) **she** ∼ **thought that ...:** sie dachte nicht im Geringsten daran, dass ...; **he** ∼ **suspected/knew what ...:** er hatte nicht die geringste Ahnung/wusste überhaupt nicht, was ...; **(b)** (to only a small extent) ∼ **as he liked it** sowenig es ihm auch gefiel; **he writes** ∼ **now** er schreibt nur noch wenig; ∼ **more/less than ...:** kaum mehr/weniger als ...; **that is** ∼ **less than ...:** das grenzt schon an (+ Akk.) ...

little 'finger n. kleiner Finger; **twist sb. round one's** ∼: jmdn. um den [kleinen] Finger wickeln (ugs.)

liturgy /'lɪtədʒɪ/ n. Liturgie, die

live[1] /laɪv/ **1** adj. **(a)** attrib. (alive) lebend; **(b)** (Radio, Telev.) ∼ **performance** Live-Aufführung, die; ∼ **broadcast** Live-Sendung, die; Direktübertragung, die; **(c)** (topical) aktuell ⟨Thema, Frage⟩; **(d)** (Electr.) Strom führend; **(e)** (unexploded) scharf ⟨Munition usw.⟩; **(f)** (glowing) glühend ⟨Kohle⟩; **(g)** (joc.: actual) **real** ∼: richtig. **2** adv. (Radio, Telev.) live ⟨übertragen usw.⟩

live[2] /lɪv/ **1** v.i. **(a)** leben; ∼ **and let** ∼: leben und leben lassen; ∼ **by sth.** von etw. leben; **you'll** ∼ (iron.) du wirst's [schon] überleben (iron.); **as long as I** ∼ **I shall never ...:** mein Leben lang werde ich nicht ...; ∼ **to see** [mit]erleben; **she will** ∼ **to regret it** sie wird es noch bereuen; **you** ∼ **and learn** man lernt nie aus; ∼ **through sth.** etw. durchmachen (ugs.); (survive) etw. überleben; ∼ **to a**

ripe old age/to be a hundred ein hohes Alter erreichen/hundert Jahre alt werden; **long ~ the queen!** lang lebe die Königin!; **(b)** (make permanent home) wohnen; leben; **~ together** zusammenleben; **~ with sb.** mit jmdm. zusammenleben; **~ with sth.** (lit. or fig.) mit etw. leben. **2** *v.t.* leben; **~ it up** das Leben in vollen Zügen genießen; (have a good time) einen draufmachen (ugs.)

~ 'down *v.t.* Gras wachsen lassen über (+ *Akk.*); **he will never be able to ~ it down** das wird ihm ewig anhängen

~ 'in *v.i.* (Brit.) ⟨*Personal, Koch usw.:*⟩ im Haus wohnen; ⟨*Student, Krankenschwester:*⟩ im Wohnheim wohnen

~ on 1 /'--/ *v.t.* leben von. **2** /'-'-/ *v.i.* weiterleben

~ out 1 /-'-/ *v.i.* (Brit.) außerhalb wohnen. **2** /'--/ *v.t.* **(a)** (survive) überleben; **(b)** (complete, spend) verbringen; **they had ~d out their lives as fishermen** sie waren ihr Leben lang Fischer gewesen

~ 'up to *v.t.* gerecht werden (+ *Dat.*); **~ up to one's principles/faith** nach seinen Prinzipien/seinem Glauben leben; **~ up to one's reputation** seinem Ruf Ehre machen

livelihood /'laɪvlɪhʊd/ *n.* Lebensunterhalt, *der;* **gain** *or* **earn a ~ from sth.** sich (*Dat.*) seinen Lebensunterhalt mit etw. verdienen

liveliness /'laɪvlɪnɪs/ *n.,* *no pl.* Lebhaftigkeit, *die*

lively /'laɪvlɪ/ *adj.* **(a)** lebhaft; lebendig ⟨*Gegenwart*⟩; rege ⟨*Handel*⟩; **things start to get ~ at 9 a.m.** um 9 Uhr wird es lebhaft; **look ~** (coll.) sich ranhalten (ugs.); **(b)** (vivid) lebendig, anschaulich ⟨*Bericht, Schilderung*⟩; **(c)** (joc.: exciting, dangerous, difficult) **things were getting ~:** die Sache wurde gefährlich

liven ⇒ **~ up 1**

liven up /laɪvn 'ʌp/ **1** *v.t.* Leben bringen in (+ *Akk.*). **2** *v.i.* ⟨*Person:*⟩ aufleben; **things will ~ when …:** es wird Leben in die Bude kommen (ugs.), wenn …

liver /'lɪvə(r)/ *n.* ▶ 672 ◀ (Anat., Gastr.) Leber, *die*

liveried /'lɪvərɪd/ *adj.* livriert

liverish /'lɪvərɪʃ/ *adj.* **(a)** (unwell) unwohl; **(b)** (grumpy) mürrisch

liver: ~ salts *n. pl.* (Brit.) ≈ Magenmittel, *das;* **~ sausage** *n.* Leberwurst, *die*

livery /'lɪvərɪ/ *n.* Livree, *die*

live /laɪv/: **~stock** *n. pl.* Vieh, *das;* **~ 'wire** *n.* (Electr.) Strom führender Draht; (fig.) Energiebündel, *das* (ugs.)

livid /'lɪvɪd/ *adj.* **(a)** (bluish) bleigrau; **(b)** (Brit. coll.: furious) fuchtig (ugs.)

living /'lɪvɪŋ/ **1** *n.* **(a)** Leben, *das;* **(b)** (livelihood) Lebensunterhalt, *der;* **make a ~:** seinen Lebensunterhalt verdienen; **earn one's [own] ~:** sich (*Dat.*) seinen Lebensunterhalt [selbst] verdienen; **make one's ~ out of farming** von der Landwirtschaft leben; **make a good ~:** viel verdienen; **it's a ~** (joc.) man kann davon leben; **(c)** (way of life) Lebensstil, *der;* **good ~:** üppiges Leben; (pious) guter Lebenswandel; **high ~:** hoher Lebensstandard; **(d)** *constr. as pl.* **the ~:** die Lebenden; **be still/back in the land of the ~:** noch/wieder unter den Lebenden weilen. **2** *adj.* lebend; **~ things** Lebewesen; **within ~ memory** seit Menschengedenken

'living room *n.* Wohnzimmer, *das*

lizard /'lɪzəd/ *n.* Eidechse, *die*

llama /'lɑːmə/ *n.* Lama, *das*

lo /ləʊ/ *int.* **~ and behold** (joc.) sieh[e] da

load /ləʊd/ **1** *n.* **(a)** (burden, weight) Last, *die;* (amount carried) Ladung, *die;* **a ~ of hay** eine Ladung Heu; **barrow-~ of apples** Karre voll Äpfel; **a ~ of [old] rubbish** *or* **tripe** (fig. coll.) ein einziger Mist (ugs.); **talk a ~ of rubbish** eine Menge Blödsinn reden (ugs.); **what a ~ of rubbish!** was für ein Quatsch (ugs.) *od.* (ugs. abwertend) Schmarren!; **get a ~ of this!** (coll.) (listen) hör einmal gut *od.* genau zu! (ugs.); (look) guck mal genau hin! (ugs.); **(b)** (weight) Last, *die;* (Electr.) Belastung, *die;* **(c)** (fig.) Last, *die;* Bürde, *die* (geh.); **take a ~ off sb.'s mind** jmdm. eine Last von der Seele nehmen; **that's a ~ off my mind** damit fällt mir ein Stein vom Herzen; **(d)** *usu. in pl.* (coll.: plenty) **~s of** jede Menge *od.* massenhaft (ugs.) ⟨*Nahrungsmittel usw.*⟩. **2** *v.t.* **(a)** (put ~ on) beladen; **~ sb. with work** (fig.) jmdm. Arbeit auftragen

od. (ugs. abwertend) aufhalsen; **(b)** (put as ~) laden; **(c) the dice were ~ed against him** (fig.) er hatte schlechte Karten; **(d)** (charge) laden ⟨*Gewehr*⟩; **~ a camera** einen Film [in einen Fotoapparat] einlegen; **(e)** (insert) einlegen ⟨*Film, Tonband usw.*⟩ (into in + *Akk.*); laden ⟨*Datei, Dokument*⟩; **(f)** (strain) schwer belasten; **a table ~ed with food** ein mit Speisen beladener Tisch. **3** *v.i.* laden (**with** *Akk.*)

~ 'up *v.i.* laden (**with** *Akk.*)

loaded /'ləʊdɪd/ *adj.* **a ~ question** eine suggestive Frage; **be ~** (coll.: rich) [schwer] Kohle haben (salopp)

'loading bay *n.* Ladeplatz, *der*

loaf¹ /ləʊf/ *n., pl.* **loaves** /ləʊvz/ **(a)** Brot, *das;* [Brot]laib, *der;* **a ~ of bread** ein Laib Brot; **a brown/white ~:** ein dunkles Brot/Weißbrot; **half a ~ is better than no bread** *or* **none** (prov.) wenig ist besser als gar nichts; **(b)** (coll.: head) **use one's ~:** seinen Grips anstrengen (ugs.)

loaf² *v.i.* **~ round town/the house** in der Stadt/zu Hause herumlungern (ugs.)

loam /ləʊm/ *n.* (soil) Lehmboden, *der*

loan /ləʊn/ **1** *n.* **(a)** (thing lent) Leihgabe, *die;* **(b)** (lending) **let sb. have/give sb. the ~ of sth.** jmdm. etw. leihen; **be [out] on ~** ⟨*Buch, Schallplatte:*⟩ ausgeliehen sein; **have sth. on ~ [from sb.]** etw. [von jmdm.] geliehen haben; **(c)** (money lent) Darlehen, *das;* Kredit, *der;* (public ~) Anleihe, *die.* **2** *v.t.* **~ sth. to sb.** jmdm. etw. leihen; etw. an jmdn. verleihen

loan: ~ shark *n.* (coll.) Kredithai, *der* (ugs. abwertend); **~word** *n.* Lehnwort, *das*

loath /ləʊθ/ *pred. adj.* **be ~ to do sth.** etw. ungern tun

loathe /ləʊð/ *v.t.* verabscheuen; nicht ausstehen können; **he ~s eggs** er mag Eier überhaupt nicht

loathing /'ləʊðɪŋ/ *n.* Abscheu, *der* (**of, for** vor + *Dat.*); **have a ~ of sth.** Abscheu vor etw. (*Dat.*) haben; etw. verabscheuen

loathsome /'ləʊðsəm/ *adj.* abscheulich; widerlich; verhasst ⟨*Tätigkeit, Pflicht*⟩

loaves *pl. of* **loaf¹**

lob /lɒb/ *v.t.,* **-bb-** (in hohem Bogen werfen; (Tennis) lobben

lobby /'lɒbɪ/ **1** *n.* **(a)** (pressure group) Lobby, *die;* Interessenvertretung, *die;* **(b)** (of hotel) Eingangshalle, *die;* (of theatre) Foyer, *das.* **2** *v.t.* zu beeinflussen suchen ⟨*Abgeordnete*⟩. **3** *v.i.* seinen Einfluss geltend machen; **~ for/against sth.** sich für etw. einsetzen/gegen etw. wenden

lobe /ləʊb/ *n.* (ear~) Ohrläppchen, *das*

lobster /'lɒbstə(r)/ *n.* Hummer, *der*

'lobster pot *n.* Hummerkorb, *der*

local /'ləʊkl/ **1** *adj.* **(a)** lokal (bes. Zeitungsw.); Lokal⟨*teil, -nachrichten, -sender*⟩; Kommunal⟨*politiker, -wahl, -abgaben*⟩; (of this area) hiesig; (of that area) dortig; ortsansässig ⟨*Firma, Familie*⟩; ⟨*Wein, Produkt, Spezialität*⟩ [aus] der Gegend; **she's a ~ girl** sie ist von hier/dort; **~ resident** Anwohner, *der*/Anwohnerin, *die;* **~ bus** (serving immediate area) Nahverkehrsbus, *der;* **(b)** (Med.) lokal ⟨*Schmerzen, Entzündung*⟩; örtlich ⟨*Betäubung*⟩. **2** *n.* **(a)** (inhabitant) Einheimische, *der/die;* **(b)** (Brit. coll.: pub) [Stamm]kneipe, *die*

local: ~ anaes'thetic *n.* Lokalanästhetikum, *das* (Med.); **under a ~ anaesthetic** unter örtlicher Betäubung *od.* (Med.) Lokalanästhesie; **~ au'thority** *n.* (Brit.) Kommunalverwaltung, *die;* **~ call** *n.* (Teleph.) Ortsgespräch, *das;* Nahbereichsgespräch, *das* (fachspr.); **~ 'government** *n.* Kommunalverwaltung, *die;* **~ government elections/officials** Kommunalwahlen/-beamte

localise ⇒ **localize**

locality /lə'kælɪtɪ/ *n.* Ort, *der;* Gegend, *die*

localize /'ləʊkəlaɪz/ *v.t.* (restrict) eingrenzen (**to** auf + *Akk.*); lokalisieren (bes. Politik, Med.)

locally /'ləʊkəlɪ/ *adv.* im/am Ort; in der Gegend

locate /lə'keɪt/ *v.t.* **(a)** (position) platzieren; **be ~d** liegen; gelegen sein; **(b)** (determine position of) ausfindig machen; lokalisieren (fachspr.); orten (Flugw., Seew.)

location /lə'keɪʃn/ *n.* **(a)** (position) Lage, *die;* (place) Ort, *der;* (of ship, aircraft, police car) Position, *die;* (of person, building, etc.) Standort, *der;* **(b)** (positioning) Positionierung, *die;* **(c)**

(determination of position of) Lokalisierung, *die;* **(d)** (Cinemat.) Drehort, *der;* **be on ~:** bei Außenaufnahmen sein

loch /lɒx, lɒk/ *n.* (Scot.) See, *der;* (in Scotland) Loch, *der;* (arm of sea) Meeresarm, *der;* (in Scotland) Loch, *der*

lock¹ /lɒk/ *n.* (ringlet) Locke, *die*

lock² 1 *n.* **(a)** (of door etc.) Schloss, *das;* **under ~ and key** unter [strengem] Verschluss; **(b)** (on canal etc.) Schleuse, *die;* **(c)** (on wheel) Sperrvorrichtung, *die;* Sperre, *die;* **(d)** (Wrestling) Fesselgriff, *der;* Klammergriff, *der;* **(e)** ~, **stock, and barrel** (fig.) mit allem Drum und Dran (ugs.); **(f)** (Motor Veh.) Lenkeinschlag, *der.* 2 *v.t.* **(a)** (fasten) zuschließen; abschließen; ~ *or* **shut the stable door after the horse has bolted** (fig.) den Brunnen erst zudecken, wenn das Kind hineingefallen ist; **(b)** (shut) ~ **sb./sth. in sth.** jmdn./etw. in etw. (*Akk.*) [ein]schließen; ~ **sb./sth. out of sth.** jmdn./etw. aus etw. aussperren; **(c)** *in p.p.* (joined) **the wrestlers were ~ed in combat** die Ringer hielten sich im Fesselgriff. 3 *v.i.* ⟨*Tür, Kasten usw.*⟩ sich ab-/ zuschließen lassen

~ **a'way** *v.t.* einschließen; wegschließen; einsperren ⟨*Person, Tier*⟩

~ **'in** *v.t.* einschließen; (deliberately) einsperren ⟨*Person, Tier*⟩

~ **'out** *v.t.* **(a)** aussperren; ~ **oneself out** sich aussperren; **(b)** (Industry) aussperren ⟨*Arbeiter*⟩

~ **'up** 1 *v.i.* abschließen. 2 *v.t.* **(a)** abschließen ⟨*Haus, Tür*⟩; **(b)** (imprison) einsperren

locker /'lɒkə(r)/ *n.* Schließfach, *das*

locket /'lɒkɪt/ *n.* Medaillon, *das*

lock: ~ **gate** *n.* Schleusentor, *das;* ~**jaw** *n.* (Med.) Kieferklemme, *die;* (disease) Wundstarrkrampf, *der;* ~**keeper** *n.* Schleusenwärter, *der;* ~**out** *n.* Aussperrung, *die;* ~**smith** *n.* ▶ 887 Schlosser, *der;* ~**up** *attrib. adj.* (Brit.) ~**up shop/garage** Laden in einem Gebäude, in dem der Inhaber nicht wohnt/nicht unmittelbar bei der Wohnung gelegene Garage

locomotive /'ləʊkəməʊtɪv, ləʊkə'məʊtɪv/ *n.* Lokomotive, *die*

locust /'ləʊkəst/ *n.* [Wander]heuschrecke, *die*

lodge /lɒdʒ/ 1 *n.* **(a)** (cottage) Pförtner-/Gärtnerhaus, *das;* (Sport) [Jagd-/Ski]hütte, *die;* **(b)** (porter's room) [Pförtner]loge, *die;* **(c)** (of Freemasons) Loge, *die.* 2 *v.t.* **(a)** (deposit formally) einlegen ⟨*Beschwerde, Protest, Berufung usw.*⟩; (bring forward) erheben ⟨*Einspruch, Protest*⟩; einreichen ⟨*Klage*⟩; **(b)** (house) unterbringen; (receive as guest) beherbergen; bei sich unterbringen; **(c)** (leave) ~ **sth. with sb./in a bank** *etc.* etw. bei jmdm./in einer Bank *usw.* hinterlegen *od.* deponieren; **(d)** (put, fix) stecken; [hinein]stoßen ⟨*Schwert, Messer usw.*⟩; **be ~d in sth.** in etw. (*Dat.*) stecken; **become ~d in sth.** ⟨*Kugel, Messer*⟩ stecken bleiben in etw. (*Dat.*). 3 *v.i.* **(a)** (be paying guest) [zur Miete] wohnen; **(b)** (enter and remain) stecken bleiben (**in** in + *Dat.*)

lodger /'lɒdʒə(r)/ *n.* Untermieter, *der*/Untermieterin, *die*

lodging /'lɒdʒɪŋ/ *n.* **(a)** *usu. in pl.* (rented room) [möbliertes] Zimmer; **(b)** (accommodation) Unterkunft, *die;* **board** *or* **food and ~:** Unterkunft und Verpflegung

'lodging house *n.* Pension, *die*

loft /lɒft/ *n.* **(a)** (attic) [Dach]boden, *der;* **(b)** (over stable) Heuboden, *der*

lofty /'lɒftɪ/ *adj.* **(a)** (exalted, grandiose) hoch; hehr (geh.); hochfliegend ⟨*Ideen*⟩; hoch gesteckt ⟨*Ziele*⟩; **(b)** (high) hoch [aufragend] ⟨*Flug, Raum*⟩; **(c)** (haughty) hochmütig; überheblich

log¹ /lɒg/ 1 *n.* **(a)** (rough piece of timber) [geschlagener] Baumstamm; (part of tree trunk) Klotz, *der;* (as firewood) [Holz]scheit, *das;* **be as easy as falling off a ~:** kinderleicht sein; **sleep like a ~:** schlafen wie ein Klotz; **(b)** (Naut.) Logbuch, *das;* (Aeronaut.) Bordbuch, *das.* 2 *v.t.*, **-gg-** (record) Buch führen über (*Akk.*); (Naut.) ins Logbuch eintragen

~ **'in** ⇒ ~ **on**

~ **'off** *v.i.* (Computing) sich abmelden

~ **'on** *v.i.* (Computing) sich anmelden

~ **'out** ⇒ ~ **off**

log², **logarithm** /'lɒgərɪðm/ *n.* (Math.) Logarithmus, *der*

log: ~**book** *n.* **(a)** (Brit.: of car) Zulassung, *die;* **(b)** ⇒ **log¹** 1 b; ~ **'cabin** *n.* Blockhütte, *die;* ~**'fire** *n.* Holzfeuer, *das*

loggerheads /'lɒgəhedz/ *n. pl.* **be at ~ with sb.** mit jmdm. im Clinch liegen

logging /'lɒgɪŋ/ *n.*, *no pl.*, *no indef. art.* Holzeinschlag, *der* (Forstw.)

logic /'lɒdʒɪk/ *n.* Logik, *die*

logical /'lɒdʒɪkl/ *adj.* **(a)** logisch; **she has a ~ mind** sie denkt logisch; **(b)** (clear-thinking) logisch denkend; klar denkend

logically /'lɒdʒɪkəlɪ/ *adv.* logisch

logistic /lə'dʒɪstɪk/ *adj.* logistisch

logistics /lə'dʒɪstɪks/ *n. sing. or pl.* Logistik, *die*

'logjam *n.* Stau von treibendem Holz/Flößholz; **the talks failed to move** *or* **break the ~** (fig.) die Gespräche haben keinen Durchbruch gebracht

logo /'lɒgəʊ, 'ləʊgəʊ/ *n.*, *pl.* ~**s** Signet, *das;* Logo, *das*

loin /lɔɪn/ *n.* **(a)** *in pl.* (Anat.) Lende, *die;* **(b)** (meat) Lende, *die*

'loincloth *n.* Lendenschurz, *der*

loiter /'lɔɪtə(r)/ *v.i.* trödeln; bummeln; (linger suspiciously) herumlungern; ~ **with intent** sich mit gesetzwidriger Absicht herumtreiben

loll /lɒl/ *v.i.* **(a)** (lounge) sich lümmeln (ugs. abwertend); **(b)** (droop) ⟨*Zunge:*⟩ heraushängen; ⟨*Kopf:*⟩ hängen

lollipop /'lɒlɪpɒp/ *n.* Lutscher, *der*

lollipop: ~ **man/woman** *ns.* ▶ 887 (Brit. coll.) Mann/ Frau in der Funktion eines Schülerlotsen

lolly /'lɒlɪ/ *n.* **(a)** (Brit. coll.: lollipop) Lutscher, *der;* **ice[d] ~:** Eis am Stiel; **(b)** *no pl.*, *no indef. art.* (sl.: money) Kohle, *die* (salopp)

London /'lʌndən/ ▶ 1159 1 *pr. n.* London (*das*). 2 *attrib. adj.* Londoner

Londoner /'lʌndənə(r)/ *pr. n.* ▶ 1159 Londoner, *der*/ Londonerin, *die*

lone /ləʊn/ *attrib. adj.* (poet./rhet.: solitary) einsam

loneliness /'ləʊnlɪnɪs/ *n.*, *no pl.* Einsamkeit, *die*

lonely /'ləʊnlɪ/ *adj.* einsam

lone 'parent *n.* allein erziehender Elternteil; Alleinerziehende, *der/die;* **she/he is a ~ parent** sie/er ist allein erziehend

loner /'ləʊnə(r)/ *n.* Einzelgänger, *der*/-gängerin, *die*

lonesome /'ləʊnsəm/ *adj.* einsam

long¹ /lɒŋ/ 1 *adj.*, ~**er** /'lɒŋgə(r)/, ~**est** /'lɒŋgɪst/ **(a)** ▶ 904 lang; weit ⟨*Reise, Weg*⟩; **be ~ in the tooth** nicht mehr der/die Jüngste sein; **take a ~ view of sth.** etw. auf lange *od.* weite Sicht sehen; **two inches/weeks ~:** zwei Zoll/Wochen lang; **(b)** (elongated) länglich; schmal; **pull** *or* **make a ~ face** (fig.) ein langes Gesicht ziehen *od.* machen (ugs.); **(c)** (of extended duration) lang; ~ **service** (esp. Mil.) langjähriger Dienst; **in the '~ run** auf die Dauer; auf lange Sicht; **in the '~ term** auf lange Sicht; langfristig; **for a '~ time** lange; (still continuing) seit langem; **what a ~ time you've been away!** du warst aber lange [Zeit] fort!; ~ **time no see!** (coll.) lange nicht gesehen! (ugs.); **(d)** (tediously lengthy) lang[atmig]; weitschweifig; **(e)** (lasting) langjährig ⟨*Gewohnheit, Freundschaft*⟩; **(f)** klein, gering ⟨*Chance*⟩; **(g)** (seemingly more than stated) lang ⟨*Minute, Tag, Jahre usw.*⟩; **(h)** lang ⟨*Gedächtnis*⟩; **have a ~ memory for sth.** etw. nicht so schnell vergessen; **(i)** (consisting of many items) lang ⟨*Liste usw.*⟩; hoch ⟨*Zahl*⟩; **(j)** (Cards) ~ **suit** lange Farbe. 2 *n.* **(a)** (long interval) **take ~:** lange dauern; **for ~:** lange; (since ~ ago) seit langem; **before ~:** bald; **it is ~ since ...:** es ist lange her, dass ...; **(b)** **the ~ and the short of it is ...:** der langen Rede kurzer Sinn ist ... 3 *adv.*, ~**er**, ~**est** **(a)** lang[e]; **as** *or* **so ~ as** solange; **you should have finished ~ before now** du hättest schon längst *od.* viel früher fertig sein sollen; **I knew her ~ before I met you** ich kenne sie schon viel länger als dich; **not ~ before that** kurz davor *od.* zuvor; **not ~ before I ...:** kurz bevor ich ...; ~ **since** [schon] seit langem; **all day/night/summer ~:** den ganzen Tag/die ganze Nacht/den ganzen Sommer [über *od.* lang]; **I shan't**

be ~: ich bin gleich fertig; (departing) bis gleich!; **don't be** ~! beeil dich!; **sb. is** ~ **[in** or **about doing sth.]** jmd. braucht lange od. viel Zeit[, um etw. zu tun]; **much** ~**er** viel länger; **not wait any/much** ~**er** nicht mehr länger/ viel länger warten; **no** ~**er** nicht mehr; nicht länger ⟨warten usw.⟩; **(b) as** or **so** ~ **as** (provided that) solange; wenn

long² v.i. ~ **for sb./sth.** sich nach jmdm./etw. sehnen; ~ **for sb. to do sth.** sich ⟨Dat.⟩ [sehr] wünschen, dass jmd. etw. tut; ~ **to do sth.** sich danach sehnen, etw. zu tun

long. abbr. **longitude** Lg.

long: ~ **ago 1** n. längst vergangene Zeit[en]; **2** adj. längst vergangen; ~**-distance 1** /'---/ adj. Fern⟨gespräch, -verkehr usw.⟩; Langstrecken⟨lauf, -läufer, -flug usw.⟩; ~**-distance coach** Reise- od. Überlandbus, der; ~**-distance lorry driver** Fern[last]fahrer, der; **2** /'--'/ adv. **phone** ~**-distance** ein Ferngespräch führen; an die ~ **division** ⇒ **division** f; ~**-drawn[-out]** adj. langgezogen ⟨Schrei, Ton⟩; langatmig ⟨Erklärung, Diskussion⟩; ~ **drink** n. Longdrink, der

longevity /lɒn'dʒevɪtɪ/ n., no pl. Langlebigkeit, die

long: ~**-haired** adj. langhaarig; Langhaar⟨dackel, -katze⟩; ~**hand** n. Langschrift, die

longing /'lɒŋɪŋ/ **1** n. Verlangen, das; Sehnsucht, die; (craving) Gelüst, das (geh.). **2** adj. sehnsüchtig

longingly /'lɒŋɪŋlɪ/ adv. voll Sehnsucht; sehnsüchtig

longitude /'lɒŋɡɪtju:d/ n. (Geog.) [geographische] Länge; (of a place) Länge, die; ~ **40° E** 40° östlicher Länge

long: ~ **jump** n. (Brit. Sport) Weitsprung, der; ~**-legged** adj. langbeinig; ~**-lived** /'lɒŋlɪvd/ adj. (durable) andauernd; (having ~ life) langlebig; **be** ~**-lived** sehr alt werden; ~**-playing 'record** n. Langspielplatte, die; ~**-range** adj. (a) Langstrecken⟨flugzeug, -rakete usw.⟩; ⟨Geschütz⟩ mit großer Reichweite; **(b)** (relating to the future) langfristig; ~**-running** adj. anhaltend; Langzeit⟨versuch⟩; wochen-/monate-/jahrelang ⟨Debatte, Streit usw.⟩; lange laufend ⟨Theaterstück⟩; ~ **shot** n. **(a)** (wild guess) reine Spekulation; **(b) not by a** ~ **shot** bei weitem nicht; ~ **'sight** n. Weitsichtigkeit, die; **have** ~ **sight** weitsichtig sein; **(fig.)** weitblickend; voraussschauend; ~**-sighted** /lɒŋ'saɪtɪd/ adj. weitsichtig; **(fig.)** weitblickend; voraussschauend; ~**-sleeved** /'lɒŋsli:vd/ adj. langärmelig; ~**-standing** attrib. adj. seit langem bestehend; langjährig ⟨Freundschaft usw.⟩; alt ⟨Schulden, Freundschaft, Streit⟩; ~**-suffering** adj. schwer geprüft; (meek) geduldig; ~**-term** adj. langfristig; ~**-time** adj. seit langem bestehend; alt ⟨Zwist, Freund⟩; ~ **va'cation** n. (Brit.) Sommer[semester]ferien Pl.; ~ **wave** n. (Radio) Langwelle, die; ~**-wave** adj. (Radio) Langwellen-; ~**ways** adv. der Länge nach; längs; ~**-winded** /lɒŋ'wɪndɪd/ adj. langatmig; weitschweifig

loo /lu:/ n. (Brit. coll.) Klo, das (ugs. fam.); **go to/be on the** ~: aufs Klo gehen/auf dem Klo sein

look /lʊk/ **1** v.i. **(a)** sehen; gucken (ugs.); schauen (bes. südd., sonst geh.); ~ **before you leap** (prov.) erst wägen, dann wagen (Spr.); ~ **the other way** (fig.) die Augen verschließen; **not know which way to** ~! nicht wissen, wohin man sehen soll; **(b)** (search) nachsehen; **(c)** (face) zugewandt sein (to[wards] Dat.); **the room** ~**s on to the road/into the garden** das Zimmer liegt zur Straße/ zum Garten hin od. geht zur Straße/zum Garten; **(d)** (appear) aussehen; ~ **as if** [so] aussehen, als ob; ~ **well/ill** gut od. gesund/krank aussehen; ~ **like** aussehen wie; **(e)** (seem to be) **she** ~**s her age** man sieht ihr ihr Alter an; **you** ~ **yourself again** es scheint dir wieder gut zu gehen; **(f)** ~ **[here]!** (demanding attention) hören Sie/ hör zu!; (protesting) passen Sie/pass ja od. bloß auf!; ~ **sharp [about sth.]** (hurry up) sich [mit etw.] beeilen. **2** v.t. (ascertain by sight) nachsehen; in exclamation of surprise etc. sich ⟨Dat.⟩ ansehen; ~ **what you've done!** sieh [dir mal an], was du getan od. angerichtet hast!; ~ **who's here!** sieh mal, wer da od. gekommen ist! see also **dagger. 3** n. **(a)** Blick, der; **get a good** ~ **at sb.** jmdn. gut od. genau sehen [können]; **have** or **take a** ~ **at sb./sth.** sich ⟨Dat.⟩ jmdn./etw. ansehen; einen Blick auf jmdn./etw. werfen; **have a** ~ **at a town** sich ⟨Dat.⟩ eine Stadt ansehen; **let**

sb. have a ~ **at sth.** jmdn. etw. sehen lassen; **(b)** in sing. or pl. (person's appearance) Aussehen, das; (facial expression) [Gesichts]ausdruck, der; **from** or **by the** ~**[s] of sb.** von jmds. Aussehen zu schließen; **good** ~**s** gutes Aussehen; **have good** ~**s** gut aussehen; **(c)** (thing's appearance) Aussehen, das; (Fashion) Look, der; **have a neglected** ~: verwahrlost aussehen; **by the** ~**[s] of it** or **things** [so] wie es aussieht; **the house is empty, by the** ~ **of it** das Haus steht allem Anschein nach leer; **I don't like the** ~ **of this** das gefällt mir gar nicht

~ **a'bout 1** v.t. ~ **about one** sich umsehen od. umschauen. **2** v.i. sich umsehen

~ **'after** v.t. **(a)** (follow with one's eyes) nachsehen (+ Dat.); **(b)** (attend to) sich kümmern um; **(c)** (care for) sorgen für; ~ **after oneself** allein zurechtkommen; für sich selbst sorgen; ~ **'after yourself!** pass auf dich auf!

~ **a'head** v.i. **(a)** nach vorne sehen; **(b)** (fig.: plan for future) an die Zukunft denken; vorausschauen

~ **a'round** ⇒ ~ **about**

~ **at** v.t. **(a)** (regard) ansehen; ~ **at one's watch** auf seine Uhr sehen; **don't** ~ **at me like that!** sieh mich nicht so an!; **be good/not much to** ~ **at** nach etwas/nach nichts od. nicht nach viel aussehen (ugs.); **(b)** (examine) sich ⟨Dat.⟩ ansehen; **(c)** (consider) betrachten; in Betracht ziehen ⟨Angebot⟩

~ **a'way** v.i. weggucken (ugs.); wegsehen

~ **'back** v.i. **(a)** sich umsehen; (fig.: hesitate) zurückschauen; **he's never** ~**ed back since then** seitdem läuft bei ihm alles bestens; **(b)** (cast one's mind back) ~ **back [up]on** or **to sth.** an etw. ⟨Akk.⟩ zurückdenken

~ **'down [up]on** v.t. **(a)** herunter-/hinuntersehen, (ugs.) runtergucken auf (+ Akk.); **(b)** (fig.: despise) herabsehen auf (+ Akk.)

~ **for** v.t. **(a)** (expect) erwarten; **(b)** (seek) suchen nach; auf der Suche sein nach ⟨neuen Ideen⟩; ~ **for trouble** Streit suchen; (unintentionally) sich ⟨Dat.⟩ Ärger einhandeln

~ **'forward to** v.t. sich freuen auf (+ Akk.); ~ **forward to doing sth.** sich darauf freuen, etw. zu tun

~ **'in** v.i. hin-/hereinsehen; (visit) vorbeikommen (on bei)

~ **into** v.t. **(a)** sehen in (+ Akk.); **(b)** (fig.: investigate) [eingehend] untersuchen; prüfen ⟨Beschwerde⟩

~ **on 1** /'-'/ v.i. zusehen; zugucken (ugs.). **2** /'--'/ v.t. ~ **on sb. as a hero** etc. jmdn. als Held[en] usw. betrachten; ~ **on sb. with distrust/suspicion** jmdn. mit Misstrauen/ Argwohn betrachten

~ **'out 1** v.i. **(a)** hinaus-/heraussehen (**of** aus); rausgucken (ugs.); **(b)** (take care) aufpassen; **(c)** (have view) ~ **out on sth.** ⟨Zimmer, Wohnung usw.⟩ zu etw. gehen (ugs.), zu etw. hin liegen. **2** v.t. (Brit.) [her]aussuchen

~ **'out for** v.t. (be prepared for) aufpassen od. achten auf (+ Akk.); sich in Acht nehmen vor (+ Dat.) ⟨gefährliche Person, Sturm⟩; (keep watching for) Ausschau halten nach

~ **'out of** v.t. sehen od. (ugs.) gucken aus

~ **'over** v.t. **(a)** sehen über (+ Akk.) ⟨Mauer usw.⟩; überblicken ⟨Tal usw.⟩; **(b)** (survey) inspizieren, sich ⟨Dat.⟩ ansehen ⟨Haus, Anwesen⟩; **(c)** (scrutinize) mustern ⟨Person⟩; durchsehen ⟨Text⟩

~ **'round** v.i. sich umsehen; sich umgucken (ugs.)

~ **through** v.t. **(a)** ~ **through sth.** durch etw. [hindurch] sehen; **(b)** (inspect) durchsehen ⟨Papiere⟩; prüfen ⟨Antrag, Vorschlag, Aussage⟩; **(c)** (glance through) sich ⟨Dat.⟩ ansehen ⟨Buch, Notizen⟩; **(d)** ~ **straight 'through sb.** (fig.) durch jmdn. hindurchsehen

~ **to** v.t. **(a)** (rely on, count upon) ~ **to sb./sth. for sth.** etw. von jmdm./etw. erwarten; ~ **to sb./sth. to do sth.** von jmdm./etw. erwarten, dass er/es etw. tut; **(b)** (be careful about) sorgen für; (keep watch upon) aufpassen auf (+ Akk.)

~ **up 1** v.i. **(a)** aufblicken; **(b)** (improve) besser werden; ⟨Aktien, Chancen:⟩ steigen; **things are** ~**ing up** es geht bergauf; **business is** ~**ing up again** das Geschäft läuft wieder besser. **2** v.t. **(a)** (search for) nachschlagen ⟨Wort⟩; heraussuchen ⟨Telefonnummer, Zugverbindung usw.⟩; **(b)** (coll.: visit) ~ **sb. up** bei jmdm. reingucken (ugs.); **(c)** ~ **sb. up and down** jmdn. von Kopf bis Fuß mustern

~ **upon** ⇒ ~ **on 2**

~ **'up to** v.t. ~ **up to sb.** (lit. or fig.) zu jmdm. aufschauen od. aufsehen

'**lookalike** *n.* Doppelgänger, *der*/-gängerin, *die*

looker-'on /lʊkə(r)'ɒn/ *n.* Zuschauer, *der*/Zuschauerin, *die*

'**look-in** *n.* (opportunity) Chance, *die;* **we didn't get a ∼:** wir hatten überhaupt keine Chance

'**looking-glass** *n.* Spiegel, *der*

'**lookout** *n., pl.* ∼**s** (a) (keeping watch) (Naut.) Ausschauhalten, *das;* (guard) Wache, *die;* **keep a ∼** *or* **be on the ∼ [for sth./sb.]** (wanted) [nach etw./jmdn.] Ausschau halten; (not wanted) [auf etw./jmdn.] aufpassen; (b) (observation post) Ausguck, *der;* Beobachtungsstand, *der;* (c) (person) Wache, *die;* (Mil.) Wach[t]posten, *der;* Beobachtungsposten, *der;* (d) (esp. Brit. fig.: prospect) Aussichten; **that's a bad ∼:** das sind schlechte Aussichten; **it's a poor/bleak** *etc.* **∼ for sb./ sth.** es sieht schlecht/düster *usw.* aus für jmdn./etw.; (e) (concern) **that's his [own] ∼:** das ist [allein] sein Problem *od.* seine Sache

loom[1] /luːm/ *n.* (Weaving) Webstuhl, *der*

loom[2] *v.i.* sich [bedrohlich] abzeichnen; **∼ large** [bedrohlich] auftauchen; (fig.) eine große Rolle spielen

∼ 'up *v.i.* **∼ up [in front of sb.]** [unmittelbar] [vor jmdm.] auftauchen

loony /'luːnɪ/ (coll.) **1** *n.* Verrückte, *der/die* (ugs.). **2** *adj.* verrückt (ugs.); irr

loop /luːp/ **1** *n.* (a) Schleife, *die;* (b) (cord) Schlaufe, *die;* (c) (contraceptive coil) Spirale, *die.* **2** *v.t.* (a) (form into a ∼) zu einer Schlaufe/Öse formen; (b) (enclose) umschlingen; (c) (fasten) **∼ up/together** *etc.* mit einer Schlaufe hoch-/zusammenbinden *usw.;* (d) (Aeronaut.) **∼ the ∼:** einen Looping fliegen; loopen (fachspr.)

'**loophole** *n.* (fig.) Lücke, *die;* **∼ in the law** Gesetzeslücke, *die;* Lücke im Gesetz

loose /luːs/ **1** *adj.* (a) (unrestrained) freilaufend ⟨ *Tier* ⟩; (escaped) ausgebrochen; **set** *or* **turn ∼:** freilassen; (b) (not firm) locker ⟨ *Zahn, Schraube, Mutter, Knopf, Messerklinge* ⟩; **come/get/work ∼:** sich lockern; *see also* **screw 1 c**; (c) (not fixed) lose; (d) (not bound together) lose; offen ⟨ *Haar* ⟩; (e) (slack) locker; schlaff ⟨ *Haut, Gewebe usw.* ⟩; beweglich ⟨ *Glieder* ⟩; (f) (hanging free) lose; **be at a ∼ end** *or* (Amer.) **at ∼ ends** (fig.) beschäftigungslos sein; (not knowing what to do with oneself) nichts zu tun haben; nichts anzufangen wissen; (g) (inexact) ungenau; schief ⟨ *Vergleich* ⟩; frei ⟨ *Stil* ⟩; unsauber ⟨ *Denken* ⟩; (h) (morally lax) liederlich ⟨ *Leben[swandel], Person* ⟩; locker ⟨ *Moral, Lebenswandel* ⟩; **a ∼ woman** ein leichtes Mädchen. **2** *v.t.* (a) loslassen ⟨ *Hund usw.* ⟩; (b) (untie) lösen; aufmachen (ugs.); (c) **∼ [off]** abschießen ⟨ *Pfeil* ⟩; abfeuern ⟨ *Feuerwaffe, Salve* ⟩; abgeben ⟨ *Schuss, Salve* ⟩; (d) (relax) lockern; **∼ [one's] hold** loslassen

loose: ∼ 'change ⇒ **change 1 d**; **∼ 'cover** *n.* (Brit.) Überzug, *der;* Schoner, *der;* **∼-fitting** *adj.* bequem geschnitten; **∼-knit** *adj.* lose zusammenhängend ⟨ *Organisation, Gemeinschaft usw.* ⟩; **∼-leaf** *attrib. adj.* Loseblatt-; **∼-leaf file** Ringbuch, *das;* **∼-limbed** /'luːs lɪmd/ *adj.* gelenkig; geschmeidig; (gawky) schlaksig

loosely /'luːslɪ/ *adv.* (a) (not tightly) locker; lose; (b) (not strictly) locker ⟨ *gruppieren* ⟩; lose ⟨ *zusammenhängen* ⟩; frei ⟨ *übersetzen* ⟩; **∼ speaking** grob gesagt

loosen /'luːsn/ **1** *v.t.* (a) (make less tight etc.) lockern; (b) (fig.: relax) lockern ⟨ *Bestimmungen, Reglement usw.* ⟩; **∼ sb.'s tongue** (fig.) jmds. Zunge lösen. **2** *v.i.* (become looser) sich lockern

∼ up 1 /'---/ *v.t.* lockern ⟨ *Glieder, Muskeln* ⟩. **2** /-'-/ *v.i.* sich auflockern; (relax) auftauen

loot /luːt/ **1** *v.t.* (a) (plunder) plündern; (b) (carry off) rauben. **2** *n.* (a) [Kriegs]beute, *die;* (b) (sl.: money) Zaster, *der* (salopp); Knete, *die* (salopp)

looter /'luːtə(r)/ *n.* Plünderer, *der*

lop /lɒp/ *v.t.,* **∼ sth. [off** *or* **away]** etw. abhauen *od.* abhacken

lope /ləʊp/ *v.i.* ⟨ *Hase, Kaninchen:* ⟩ springen; ⟨ *Wolf, Fuchs:* ⟩ laufen; ⟨ *Person:* ⟩ beschwingten Schrittes gehen

lopsided /lɒp'saɪdɪd/ *adj.* schief; (fig.) einseitig

loquacious /lə'kweɪʃəs/ *adj.* redselig; schwatzhaft (abwertend)

lord /lɔːd/ **1** *n.* (a) (master) Herr, *der;* **∼ and master** (joc.) Herr und Gebieter *od.* Meister (scherzh.); (b) **L∼** (Relig.) Herr, *der;* **L∼ God [Almighty]** unser Herr[, der allmächtige Gott]; **the L∼ [God]** [Gott] der Herr; **the L∼'s Prayer** das Vaterunser; **L∼ only knows** (coll.) weiß der Himmel (ugs.); (c) ▶ **1152** (Brit.: nobleman, or as title) Lord, *der;* **the House of L∼s** (Brit.) das Oberhaus; *see also* **drunk 1**; (d) ▶ **1152** **My L∼** (Brit.) *form of address* (to earl, viscount) Graf; (to baron) Baron; (to bishop) Exzellenz; (to judge) /mlʌd/ Herr Richter. **2** *int.* (coll.) Gott!; **oh/good L∼!** du lieber Himmel *od.* Gott!; großer Gott! **3** *v.t.* **∼ it over sb.** bei jmdm. den großen Herrn/die große Dame spielen

lordship /'lɔːdʃɪp/ *n.* ▶ **1152** (title, estate) Lordschaft, *die;* **his/your ∼/their/your ∼s** seine/Eure Lordschaft/ihre/ Eure Lordschaften

lore /lɔː(r)/ *n.* Wissen, *das;* Kunde, *die;* (body of traditions) Überlieferung, *die;* (of a people, an area) Folklore, *die*

Lorraine /lɒ'reɪn/ *pr. n.* Lothringen (das)

lorry /'lɒrɪ/ *n.* (Brit.) Lastwagen, *der;* Lkw, *der;* Laster, *der* (ugs.); **it fell off the back of a ∼** (joc.) das ist mir/ihm *usw.* zugelaufen (ugs. scherzh.)

'**lorry driver** *n.* ▶ **887** (Brit.) Lastwagenfahrer, *der;* Lkw-Fahrer, *der*

lose /luːz/ **1** *v.t.,* **lost** /lɒst/ (a) verlieren; kommen um, verlieren ⟨ *Leben, Habe* ⟩; **sb. has nothing to ∼ [by doing sth.]** es kann jmdn. nicht schaden[, wenn er etw. tut]; **∼ one's way** sich verlaufen/verfahren; (b) (fail to maintain) verlieren; (become slow by) ⟨ *Uhr:* ⟩ nachgehen ⟨ *zwei Minuten täglich usw.* ⟩; (c) (waste) vertun ⟨ *Zeit* ⟩; (miss) versäumen, verpassen ⟨ *Zeitpunkt, Gelegenheit, Ereignis* ⟩; (d) (fail to obtain) nicht bekommen ⟨ *Preis, Vertrag usw.* ⟩; (fail to hear) nicht mitbekommen ⟨ *Teil einer Rede usw.* ⟩; (fail to catch) verpassen, versäumen ⟨ *Zug, Bus* ⟩; **the motion was lost** der Antrag kam nicht durch *od.* scheiterte; (e) (be defeated in) verlieren ⟨ *Kampf, Spiel, Wette, Prozess usw.* ⟩; (f) (cause loss of) **∼ sb. sth.** jmdn. um etw. bringen; **you['ve] lost me** (fig.) ich komme nicht mehr mit; (g) ▶ **1202** (get rid of) abschütteln ⟨ *Verfolger* ⟩; loswerden ⟨ *Erkältung* ⟩; **∼ weight** abnehmen. *See also* **lost. 2** *v.i.,* **lost** (a) (suffer loss) einen Verlust erleiden; (in business) Verlust machen (on bei); (in match, contest) verlieren; **∼ in freshness** an Frische verlieren; **you can't ∼** (coll.) du kannst nur profitieren *od.* gewinnen; (b) (become slow) ⟨ *Uhr:* ⟩ nachgehen

∼ 'out *v.i.* verdrängt werden (to von)

loser /'luːzə(r)/ *n.* Verlierer, *der*/Verliererin, *die;* (failure) Versager, *der*/Versagerin, *die*

loss /lɒs/ *n.* (a) (process) Verlust, *der* (of Gen.); (b) *in sing. or pl.* (what is lost) Verlust, *der;* **sell at a ∼:** mit Verlust verkaufen; *see also* **cut 1 j**; (c) (state) Verlust, *der;* **be no ∼ to sb.** für jmdn. kein Verlust sein; (d) **be at a ∼:** nicht [mehr] weiterwissen; **be at a ∼ what to do** nicht wissen, was zu tun ist; **be at a ∼ for words/an answer** um Worte/eine Antwort verlegen sein

'**loss-making** *adj.* mit Verlust arbeitend

lost /lɒst/ *adj.* (a) verloren; ausgestorben ⟨ *Kunst[fertigkeit]* ⟩; **get ∼** ⟨ *Person:* ⟩ sich verlaufen *od.* verirren/verfahren; **get ∼!** (sl.) verdufte! (salopp); **I'm ∼** (fig.) ich verstehe gar nichts mehr; **feel ∼ without sb./ sth.** (fig.) sich (*Dat.*) ohne jmdn./etw. hilflos vorkommen; *see also* **property a**; (b) (wasted) vertan ⟨ *Zeit, Gelegenheit* ⟩; verschwendet ⟨ *Zeit, Mühe* ⟩; verpasst, versäumt ⟨ *Gelegenheit* ⟩; (c) (not won) verloren; aussichtslos ⟨ *Sache* ⟩; *see also* **all 2 d**; **cause 1 c**; (d) **∼ in admiration** überwältigt; **be ∼ [up]on sb.** (unrecognized by) von jmdm. keine Anerkennung finden; von jmdm. nicht gewürdigt werden; **sarcasm was ∼ on him** mit Sarkasmus konnte er nichts anfangen

lot /lɒt/ *n.* (a) (method of choosing) Los, *das;* **by ∼:** durch das Los; (b) (destiny) Los, *das;* **fall to the ∼ of sb.** jmdm. bestimmt sein; (c) (item to be auctioned) Posten, *der;* (d) (set of persons) Haufen, *der;* **the ∼:** [sie] alle; **'our/'your/'their ∼** (coll.) wir/ihr/die; (e) (set of things) Menge, *die;* **divide sth. into five ∼s** etw. in fünf Stapel/Haufen *usw.* teilen; **that's the ∼** (coll.) das ist alles; das wär's (ugs.); (f) (coll.: large number or quantity) **∼s** *or* **a ∼ of money** *etc.* viel *od.* eine Menge Geld *usw.;* **∼s of books/coins** eine Menge Bücher/Münzen; **he has a ∼ to learn** er muss noch viel lernen; **have ~s to do** viel zu tun haben; **we have ~s of time** wir haben viel *od.* (ugs.) massenweise Zeit; **~s** *or* **a ~ better** viel besser; **like sth. a ~:** etw. sehr mögen; **(g)** (for choosing) Los, *das;* **draw/cast/throw ~s [for sth.]** das Los [über etw. (*Akk.*)] entscheiden lassen; [um etw.] losen; **cast/throw in one's ~ with sb.** sich mit jmdm. zusammentun; **draw ~s to determine sth.** etw. durch das Los entscheiden; **(h)** (plot of land) Gelände, *das;* Platz, *der;* (measured piece of land) Parzelle, *die*

lotion /'ləʊʃn/ *n.* Lotion, *die*

lottery /'lɒtərɪ/ *n.* Lotterie, *die;* (fig.) Glücksspiel, *das*

loud /laʊd/ **1** *adj.* **(a)** laut; schreiend ‹*Reklame*›; lautstark ‹*Protest, Kritik*›; **(b)** (flashy, conspicuous) aufdringlich; grell, schreiend ‹*Farbe*›. **2** *adv.* laut; **laugh out ~:** laut auflachen; **say sth. out ~:** etw. aussprechen; (fig.) etw. laut verkünden

loud hailer /'laʊd heɪlə(r)/ *n.* Megaphon, *das;* Flüstertüte, *die* (ugs. scherzh.)

loudly /'laʊdlɪ/ *adv.* **(a)** laut; **(b)** (flashily) aufdringlich

loud: **~mouth** *n.* Großmaul, *das;* **~-mouthed** /'laʊdmaʊðd/ *adj.* großmäulig (ugs. abwertend)

loudness /'laʊdnɪs/ *n., no pl.* **(a)** Lautstärke, *die;* **(b)** (flashiness) Aufdringlichkeit, *die*

loud'speaker *n.* Lautsprecher, *der*

lounge /laʊndʒ/ **1** *v.i.* **~ [about** *or* **around]** [faul] herumliegen/-sitzen/-stehen; [faul] herumhängen (ugs.); (in chair etc.) sich lümmeln (ugs.). **2** *n.* **(a)** (public room) Lounge, *die;* (in hotel) Lounge, *die;* [Hotel]halle, *die;* (at station) Wartesaal, *der;* (in theatre) Foyer, *das;* (at airport) Lounge, *die;* Wartehalle, *die;* **(b)** (sitting room) Wohnzimmer, *das;* **(c)** (Brit.: bar) **~ [bar]** ⇒ **saloon bar**

'lounge lizard *n.* (coll.) Salonlöwe, *der*

lounger /'laʊndʒə(r)/ *n.* **(a)** Nichtstuer, *der;* **(b)** (sunbed) Liege, *die*

lour /'laʊə(r)/ *v.i.* missmutig [drein]blicken; ein finsteres Gesicht machen; (fig.) ‹*Wolken, Gewitter:*› sich [bedrohlich] zusammenziehen; ‹*Himmel:*› sich [bedrohlich] verfinstern

louse /laʊs/ *n.* **(a)** *pl.* **lice** /laɪs/ Laus, *die;* **(b)** *pl.* **~s** (sl.: person) Ratte, *die* (derb)

lousy /'laʊzɪ/ *adj.* **(a)** (infested) verlaust; **(b)** (coll.: disgusting) ekelhaft; widerlich; (very poor) lausig (ugs.); mies (ugs.); **feel ~:** sich mies (ugs.) *od.* miserabel fühlen

lout /laʊt/ *n.* Rüpel, *der;* Flegel, *der;* (bumpkin) Tollpatsch, *der* (ugs.); Tölpel, *der*

louver, louvre /'luːvə(r)/ *n.* **~ window** Jalousiefenster, *das*

lovable /'lʌvəbl/ *adj.* liebenswert

love /lʌv/ **1** *n.* **(a)** (affection, sexual ~) Liebe, *die* (**for** zu); **in ~ [with]** verliebt [in (+ *Akk.*)]; **fall in ~ [with]** sich verlieben [in (+ *Akk.*)]; **make ~ to sb.** (have sex) mit jmdm. schlafen; jmdn. lieben; **for ~:** aus Liebe; (free) unentgeltlich; umsonst; (for pleasure) nur zum Vergnügen *od.* Spaß; **not for ~ or money** um nichts in der Welt; **[Happy Christmas,] ~ from Beth** (in letter) [fröhliche Weihnachten und] herzliche Grüße von Beth; **send one's ~ to sb.** jmdn. grüßen lassen; **Peter sends [you] his ~:** Peter lässt [dich] grüßen; **there is no ~ lost between them** sie sind sich (*Dat.*) nicht grün (ugs.); **(b)** (devotion) Liebe, *die* (**of, for, to**[**wards**] zu); **~ of life/eating/learning** Freude am Leben/Essen/Lernen; **for the ~ of God** um Gottes willen; **(c)** (sweetheart) Geliebte, *der/die;* Liebste, *der/die* (veralt.); **[my] ~** (coll.: form of address) [mein] Liebling *od.* Schatz; (to sb. less close) mein Lieber/meine Liebe; **(d)** (Tennis) **fifteen/thirty ~:** fünfzehn/dreißig null. **2** *v.t.* **(a)** lieben; **our/their ~d ones** unsere/ihre Lieben; **(b)** (like) **I'd ~ a cigarette** ich hätte sehr gerne eine Zigarette; **~ to do** *or* **doing sth.** etw. [leidenschaftlich] gern tun. **3** *v.i.* lieben

love: **~ affair** *n.* [Liebes]verhältnis, *das;* Liebschaft, *die;* **~-'hate** *adj.* von Hassliebe geprägt; **~ letter** *n.* Liebesbrief, *der;* **~ life** *n.* Liebesleben, *das*

lovely /'lʌvlɪ/ *adj.* **(a)** [wunder]schön; herrlich ‹*Tag, Essen*›; **(b)** (lovable) liebenswert; **(c)** (coll.: delightful) toll (ugs.); wunderbar; **~ and warm/cool** *etc.* (coll.) schön warm/kühl *usw.*

'lovemaking *n.* (sexual intercourse) körperliche Liebe

lover /'lʌvə(r)/ *n.* **(a)** Liebhaber, *der;* Geliebte, *der;* (woman) Geliebte, *die;* **be ~s** ein Liebespaar sein; **(b)** (person devoted to sth.) Liebhaber, *der*/Liebhaberin, *die;* Freund, *der*/Freundin, *die;* **~ of the arts** Kunstliebhaber, *der*/-liebhaberin, *die;* Kunstfreund, *der*/-freundin, *die;* **dog-~** Hundefreund, *der*/-freundin, *die*

love: **~sick** *adj.* an Liebeskummer leidend; liebeskrank (geh.); **~ song** *n.* Liebeslied, *das;* **~ story** *n.* Liebesgeschichte, *die*

loving /'lʌvɪŋ/ *adj.* **(a)** (affectionate) liebend; **(b)** (expressing love) liebevoll

lovingly /'lʌvɪŋlɪ/ *adv.* liebevoll; (painstakingly) mit viel Liebe

low¹ /ləʊ/ **1** *adj.* **(a)** ▶850◀ (not reaching far up) niedrig; niedrig, flach ‹*Absätze, Stirn*›; flach ‹*Relief*›; **(b)** (below normal level) niedrig; tief ‹*Flug*›; flach ‹*Welle*›; tief ausgeschnitten ‹*Kleid*›; tief ‹*Ausschnitt*›; **(c)** (not elevated) tief liegend ‹*Wiese, Grund, Land*›; tief hängend ‹*Wolke*›; tief stehend ‹*Gestirne*›; tief ‹*Verbeugung*›; **(d)** (inferior) niedrig; gering ‹*Intelligenz, Bildung*›; gewöhnlich ‹*Geschmack*›; **(e)** (not fair) gemein; **(f)** (Cards) niedrig; **(g)** (small in degree) niedrig; gering ‹*Silchtweite, Wert*›; **have a ~ opinion of sb./sth.** von jmdm./etw. keine hohe Meinung haben; **(h)** (in pitch) tief ‹*Ton, Stimme, Lage, Klang*›; (in loudness) leise ‹*Ton, Stimme*›; **(i)** (nearly gone) fast verbraucht *od.* aufgebraucht; **run ~:** allmählich ausgehen *od.* zu Ende gehen. *See also* **lower²** 1. **2** *adv.* **(a)** (in or to a ~ position) tief; niedrig, tief ‹*hängen*›; *see also* **high 2 a;** **(b)** (to a ~ level) **prices have gone too ~:** die Preise sind zu weit gefallen; **(c)** (not loudly) leise; **(d) lay sb. ~** (prostrate) jmdn. niederstrecken (geh.); **lie ~:** am Boden liegen; (hide) untertauchen. *See also* **lower²** 2. **3** *n.* **(a)** (Meteorol.) Tief, *das;* **(b)** Tiefstand, *der; see also* **all-time**

low² *v.i.* ‹*Kuh:*› muhen

low: **~-alcohol** *adj.* alkoholarm ‹*Getränk*›; **~brow** *adj.* (coll.) schlicht ‹*Person*›; [geistig] anspruchslos ‹*Buch, Programm*›; **~-budget** *adj.* Lowbudget-, Billig‹*film, -Produktion usw.*›; **~-calorie** *adj.* kalorienarm ‹*Kost, Getränk*›; **~-cost** *adj.* preiswert; **Low Countries** *pr. n. pl.* (Hist.) Niederlande *Pl.;* **~-cut** *adj.* [tief] ausgeschnitten ‹*Kleid*›; **~-down 1** *adj.* (coll.: mean) mies (ugs.); **2** *n.* (coll.) **give [sb.]/get the ~-down on sb./sth.** [jmdm.] sagen/rauskriegen, was es mit jmdm./etw. [wirklich] auf sich hat

lower¹ /'ləʊə(r)/ *v.t.* **(a)** (let down) herab-/hinablassen; einholen ‹*Flagge, Segel*›; **~ oneself into** hinuntersteigen in (+ *Akk.*) ‹*Kanalschacht, Keller*›; **~ oneself into a chair** sich in einen Sessel sinken lassen; **(b)** (reduce in height) senken ‹*Blick*›; niederschlagen ‹*Augen*›; absenken ‹*Zimmerdecke*›; auslassen ‹*Saum*›; **(c)** (lessen) senken ‹*Preis, Miete, Zins usw.*›; **(d)** (degrade) herabsetzen; **~ oneself to do sth.** sich so weit erniedrigen, etw. zu tun; **(e)** (weaken) schwächen; dämpfen ‹*Licht, Stimme, Lärm*›; **~ one's voice** leiser sprechen; die Stimme senken (geh.)

lower² **1** *compar. adj.* **(a)** unter... ‹*Nil, Themse usw., Atmosphäre*›; Unter‹*jura, -devon usw., -arm, -lippe usw.*›; Nieder‹*rhein, -kalifornien*›; **(b)** (in rank) unter...; **~ mammals/plants** niedere Säugetiere/Pflanzen; **the ~ orders/classes** die Unterschichten/die unteren Klassen. **2** *compar. adv.* tiefer ‹*sinken, hängen usw.*›

lower: **~ case** 1 *n.* Kleinbuchstaben *Pl.;* 2 *adj.* klein ‹*Buchstabe*›; **~ 'deck** *n.* (of ship) Unterdeck, *das;* (of bus) unteres Deck; **L~ 'Saxony** *pr. n.* Niedersachsen (*das*) ‹*sixth* (Brit.) ≈ Unterprima, *die*

low: **~-fat** *adj.* fettarm; **~-flying** *adj.* tief fliegend; **~-flying aircraft** Tiefflieger, *der;* **~-grade** *adj.* minderwertig; **~-income** *adj.* einkommenschwach; **~-income families** Familien mit niedrigem Einkommen; **a ~-income country** ein Land mit niedrigem Nationaleinkommen; **~-key** *adj.* zurückhaltend; unaufdringlich ‹*Beleuchtung, Unterhaltung usw.*›; **~land** *n.* 1 Tiefland, *das;* 2 *adj.* tiefländisch Tiefland‹*rasse, -farm*›; **~lights** *n. pl.* (in hair) dunkel getönte Strähnen *Pl.*

lowly /'ləʊlɪ/ *adj.* **(a)** (modest) bescheiden; **(b)** (not highly evolved) nieder...

low: ∼**-lying** *adj.* tief liegend; ∼**-paid** *adj.* niedrig bezahlt; ∼**-paid families** Familien mit geringem Einkommen; ∼ **point** *n.* Tiefpunkt, *der;* ∼**-powered** /ˈləʊ paʊəd/ *adj.* schwach ⟨*Motor, Glühbirne*⟩; ∼ **pressure** *n.* (Meteorol.) Tiefdruck, *der;* **an area of** ∼ **pressure** ein Tiefdruckgebiet; ∼ **season** *n.* Nebensaison, *die;* ∼**-'spirited** *adj.* niedergeschlagen; ∼**-tech** *adj.* Low-Tech-⟨*System, Ausrüstung etc.*⟩; ∼ **'tide** ⟹ **tide** 1 a; ∼ **'water** *n.* Niedrigwasser, *das;* ∼**-'water mark** *n.* Niedrigwassermarke, *die*

loyal /ˈlɔɪəl/ *adj.* (to person) treu; (to government etc.) treu [ergeben]; loyal

loyalty /ˈlɔɪəltɪ/ *n.* Treue, *die;* Loyalität, *die*

'loyalty card *n.* Treuekarte, *die (für Kunden)*

lozenge /ˈlɒzɪndʒ/ *n.* (a) (tablet) Pastille, *die;* (b) (diamond shape) Raute, *die;* Rhombus, *der*

LP *abbr.* **long-playing record** LP, *die*

'L-plate *n.* (Brit.) ʼLʼ-Schild, *das;* ≈ „Fahrschule"-Schild, *das*

LSD *abbr.* **lysergic acid diethylamide** LSD, *das*

Ltd. *abbr.* **Limited** GmbH; ... **Company** ∼**:** ...gesellschaft mbH

lubricant /ˈluːbrɪkənt/ *n.* Schmiermittel, *das*

lubricate /ˈluːbrɪkeɪt/ *v.t.* schmieren; einfetten ⟨*Haut*⟩

lubrication /luːbrɪˈkeɪʃn/ *n.* Schmierung, *die;* attrib. Schmier⟨*system, -vorrichtung*⟩

Lucerne /luːˈsɜːn/ *pr. n.* ▶ 1159 Luzern (*das*); **Lake** ∼**:** der Vierwaldstätter See

lucid /ˈluːsɪd/ *adj.* klar; [leicht] verständlich; einleuchtend ⟨*Argumentation*⟩; ∼ **interval** (period of sanity) lichter Augenblick

luck /lʌk/ *n.* (a) (good or ill fortune) Schicksal, *das;* **as** ∼ **would have it** wie das Schicksal es wollte; **good** ∼**:** Glück, *das;* **bad** ∼**:** Pech, *das;* **better** ∼ **next time** mehr Glück beim nächsten Mal; **good** ∼ **[to you]!** viel Glück!; alles Gute!; **good** ∼ **to him, I say** ich wünsche ihm viel Glück; (iron.) na, dann viel Glück!; **just my** ∼**:** typisch für mich; (b) (good fortune) Glück, *das;* **with [any]** ∼**:** mit ein bisschen *od.* etwas Glück; **do sth. for** ∼**:** etw. tun, damit es einem Glück bringen soll; **be in/out of** ∼**:** Glück/kein Glück haben; **no such** ∼**:** schön wär's

luckily /ˈlʌkɪlɪ/ *adv.* glücklicherweise; ∼ **for her** zu ihrem Glück

lucky /ˈlʌkɪ/ *adj.* (a) (favoured by chance) glücklich; **be** ∼ **[in love/at games]** Glück [in der Liebe/im Spiel] haben; **be** ∼ **enough to be rescued** das [große] Glück haben, gerettet zu werden; **Could you lend me £100? — 'You'll be** ∼**!** Könntest du mir 100 Pfund leihen? — So siehst du aus!; (b) (favouring sb. by chance) glücklich ⟨*Umstand, Zufall, Zusammentreffen usw.*⟩; *see also* **escape** 1 a; (c) (bringing good luck) Glücks⟨*zahl, -tag usw.*⟩; ∼ **charm** Glücksbringer, *der;* **be born under a** ∼ **star** ein Glückskind sein; **you can thank your** ∼ **stars** du kannst von Glück sagen

lucrative /ˈluːkrətɪv/ *adj.* einträglich; lukrativ

ludicrous /ˈluːdɪkrəs/ *adj.* lächerlich ⟨*Anblick, Lohn, Argument, Vorschlag, Idee*⟩; lachhaft ⟨*Angebot, Ausrede*⟩; **a** ∼ **speed** (low) eine lächerliche Geschwindigkeit; (high) eine haarsträubende Geschwindigkeit

ludo /ˈluːdəʊ/ *n., no pl., no art.* Mensch-ärgere-dich-nicht [-Spiel], *das*

lug /lʌg/ *v.t.,* **-gg-:** (a) (drag) schleppen; (b) (force) ∼ **sb. along** jmdn. mit herumschleppen (ugs.)

luggage /ˈlʌgɪdʒ/ *n.* Gepäck, *das*

luggage: ∼ **locker** *n.* [Gepäck]schließfach, *das;* ∼ **rack** *n.* Gepäckablage, *die;* ∼ **trolley** *n.* Kofferkuli, *der*

lugubrious /luːˈguːbrɪəs, lʊˈguːbrɪəs/ *adj.* (mournful) kummervoll; traurig; (dismal) düster

lukewarm /ˈluːkwɔːm, luːkˈwɔːm/ *adj.* (a) lauwarm; (b) (fig.) lau[warm]; halbherzig

lull /lʌl/ **1** *v.t.* (a) (soothe) lullen; (b) (fig.) einlullen; ∼ **sb. into a false sense of security** jmdn. in einer trügerischen Sicherheit wiegen. **2** *n.* Pause, *die;* **the** ∼ **before the storm** (fig.) die Ruhe vor dem Sturm

lullaby /ˈlʌləbaɪ/ *n.* Schlaflied, *das;* Wiegenlied, *das*

lumbago /lʌmˈbeɪgəʊ/ *n.* (Med.) Hexenschuss, *der;* Lumbago, *die* (fachspr.)

lumber¹ /ˈlʌmbə(r)/ *v.i.* ⟨*Person:*⟩ schwerfällig gehen; ⟨*Fahrzeug:*⟩ rumpeln

lumber² **1** *n.* (a) (furniture) Gerümpel, *das;* (b) (useless material) Kram, *der* (ugs. abwertend); Krempel, *der* (ugs. abwertend); (c) (Amer.: timber) [Bau]holz, *das.* **2** *v.t.* (fill up, encumber) voll stopfen (ugs.); überladen ⟨*Stil, Buch*⟩; ∼ **sb. with sth./sb.** jmdm. etw./jmdn. aufhalsen (ugs.); **get** ∼**ed with sth./sb.** etw./jmdn. aufgehalst kriegen (ugs.)

lumber: ∼**jack** *n.* ▶ 887 (Amer.) Holzfäller, *der;* ∼**room** *n.* Abstellkammer, *die;* Rumpelkammer, *die* (ugs.)

luminosity /luːmɪˈnɒsɪtɪ/ *n.* (also Astron.) Helligkeit, *die*

luminous /ˈluːmɪnəs/ *adj.* (a) (bright) hell ⟨*Feuer, Licht usw.*⟩; [hell] leuchtend; Leucht⟨*anzeige, -zeiger usw.*⟩; ∼ **paint** Leuchtfarbe, *die;* (b) (of light) Leucht⟨*kraft, -stärke usw.*⟩

lump¹ /lʌmp/ **1** *n.* (a) (shapeless mass) Klumpen, *der;* (of sugar, butter, etc.) Stück, *das;* (of wood) Klotz, *der;* (of dough) Kloß, *der;* (of bread) Brocken, *der;* **have/get a** ∼ **in one's throat** (fig.) einen Kloß im Hals haben (ugs.); (b) (swelling) Beule, *die;* (caused by cancer) Knoten, *der;* (c) (thickset person) Klotz, *der;* (d) **get payment in a** ∼**:** die gesamte Summe auf einmal erhalten. **2** *v.t.* (mass together) zusammentun; ∼ **sth. with sth.** etw. und etw. zusammentun; ∼ **sb./sth. with the rest** jmdn./etw. mit dem Rest in einen Topf werfen (ugs.)

∼ **to'gether** *v.t.* zusammenfassen

lump² *v.t.* (coll.) sich abfinden mit; **if you don't like it you can** ∼ **it** du musst dich wohl oder übel damit abfinden

lump: ∼ **'sugar** *n.* Würfelzucker, *der;* ∼ **'sum** *n.* (covering several items) Pauschalsumme, *die;* (paid at once) einmalige Pauschale

lumpy /ˈlʌmpɪ/ *adj.* klumpig ⟨*Brei, Lehm*⟩; ⟨*Kissen, Matratze*⟩ mit klumpiger Füllung

lunacy /ˈluːnəsɪ/ *n.* (a) (insanity) Wahnsinn, *der;* (b) (mad folly) Wahnsinn, *der* (ugs.); Irrsinn, *der*

lunar /ˈluːnə(r)/ *adj.* Mond-; lunar (fachspr.)

lunar e'clipse *n.* (Astron.) Mondfinsternis, *die*

lunatic /ˈluːnətɪk/ **1** *adj.* (a) (mad) wahnsinnig; irre (veralt.); *see also* **fringe** 1 c; (b) (foolish) wahnwitzig; Wahnsinns- (ugs.); idiotisch (ugs. abwertend). **2** *n.* Wahnsinnige, *der/die;* Irre, *der/die*

'lunatic asylum *n.* (Hist.) Irrenanstalt, *die* (veralt., ugs. abwertend)

lunch /lʌntʃ/ **1** *n.* Mittagessen, *das;* **have** *or* **eat [one's]** ∼**:** zu Mittag essen. **2** *v.i.* zu Mittag essen

lunch: ∼ **box** *n.* Lunchbox, *die;* ∼ **break** ⟹ **lunch hour**

luncheon /ˈlʌntʃən/ *n.* (formal) Mittagessen, *das*

luncheon: ∼ **meat** *n.* Frühstücksfleisch, *das;* ∼ **voucher** *n.* (Brit.) Essen[s]marke, *die*

lunch: ∼ **hour** *n.* Mittagspause, *die;* ∼**time** *n.* Mittagszeit, *die;* **at** ∼**time** mittags

lung /lʌŋ/ *n.* ▶ 672 Lunge, *die;* (right or left) Lungenflügel, *der;* ∼**s** *pl.* Lunge, *die;* **have good/weak** ∼**s** eine gute *od.* kräftige/schwache Lunge haben

'lung cancer *n.* ▶ 865 (Med.) Lungenkrebs, *der*

lunge /lʌndʒ/ **1** *n.* (a) (Sport) Ausfall, *der;* (b) (sudden forward movement) Sprung, *der* nach vorn. **2** *v.i.* (a) (Sport) einen Ausfall machen (at gegen); (b) ∼ **at sb. with a knife** jmdn. mit einem Messer angreifen

lupin /ˈluːpɪn/ *n.* [Edel]lupine, *die*

lurch¹ /lɜːtʃ/ *n.* **leave sb. in the** ∼**:** jmdn. im Stich lassen; jmdn. hängen lassen (ugs.)

lurch² **1** *n.* Rucken, *das;* (of ship) Schlingern, *das.* **2** *v.i.* rucken; ⟨*Betrunkener:*⟩ torkeln; ⟨*Schiff:*⟩ schlingern

lure /ljʊə(r), lʊə(r)/ **1** *v.t.* locken; ∼ **away from/out of/ into sth.** von etw. fortlocken/aus etw. [heraus]locken/in etw. (*Akk.*) [hinein]locken. **2** *n.* (Hunting) Lockvogel, *der;* (fig.) Lockmittel, *das*

lurid /'ljʊərɪd, 'lʊərɪd/ *adj.* **(a)** (ghastly) gespenstisch; (highly coloured) grell ‹*Licht, Schein, Himmel*›; **(b)** (fig.) (horrifying) grässlich; schaurig; (sensational) reißerisch (abwertend)

lurk /lɜ:k/ *v.i.* **(a)** lauern; ‹*Raubtier:*› auf der Lauer liegen; **(b)** (fig.) ~ **in sb.'s** *or* **at the back of sb.'s mind** ‹*Zweifel, Verdacht, Furcht:*› an jmdm. nagen

luscious /'lʌʃəs/ *adj.* **(a)** (sweet in taste or smell) köstlich [süß]; saftig [süß] ‹*Obst*›; **(b)** üppig ‹*Figur, Kurven*›; knackig (ugs.) ‹*Mädchen*›

lush /lʌʃ/ *adj.* saftig ‹*Wiese*›; grün ‹*Tal*›; üppig ‹*Vegetation*›

lust /lʌst/ **1** *n.* **(a)** (sexual drive) Sinnenlust, *die;* sinnliche Begierde; **(b)** (passionate desire) Gier, *die* (**for** nach). **2** *v.i.* ~ **after** [lustvoll] begehren (geh.); **he** ~**s after** …: es gelüstet ihn nach … (geh.)

lustful /'lʌstfl/ *adj.* lüstern (geh.)

lustily /'lʌstɪlɪ/ *adv.* kräftig; aus voller Kehle ‹*rufen, singen*›

lustre /'lʌstə(r)/ *n.* (Brit.) **(a)** Schimmer, *der;* [schimmernder] Glanz; **(b)** (fig.: splendour) Glanz, *der;* **add** ~ **to sth.** einer Sache (*Dat.*) Glanz verleihen

lusty /'lʌstɪ/ *adj.* **(a)** (healthy) gesund; (strong, powerful) kräftig; **(b)** (vigorous) herzhaft ‹*Applaus, Tritt*›; tüchtig, zupackend ‹*Arbeiter*›

lute /lu:t, lju:t/ *n.* (Mus.) Laute, *die*

Lutheran /'lu:θərən, 'lju:θərən/ **1** *adj.* lutherisch. **2** *n.* Lutheraner, *der*/Lutheranerin, *die*

luvvy (luvvie) /'lʌvɪ/ *n.* (coll. derog.) Luvvy, *der*/*die* (*affektierter Schickeriatyp, der seinesgleichen mit 'love' anredet*)

Luxembourg, Luxemburg /'lʌksəmbɜ:g/ *pr. n.* Luxemburg (*das*)

luxuriant /lʌg'zjʊərɪənt, lʌk'sjʊərɪənt/ *adj.* üppig ‹*Vegetation, Farbenpracht, Blattwerk*›; voll ‹*Haar*›

luxuriate /lʌg'zjʊərɪeɪt, lʌk'sjʊərɪeɪt/ *v.i.* ~ **in** sich aalen in (+ *Dat.*) ‹*Sonne, Bett usw.*›

luxurious /lʌg'zjʊərɪəs, lʌk'sjʊərɪəs/ *adj.* luxuriös

luxury /'lʌkʃərɪ/ **1** *n.* **(a)** Luxus, *der;* **live** *or* **lead a life of** ~: ein Leben im Luxus führen; *see also* **lap¹**; **(b)** (article) Luxusgegenstand, *der;* **luxuries** Luxus, *der;* **(c)** (sth. inessential) Luxus, *der.* **2** *attrib. adj.* Luxus-

LW *abbr.* (Radio) **long wave** LW

lying /'laɪɪŋ/ **1** *adj.* **(a)** (given to falsehood) verlogen; ~ **scoundrel** Lügenbold, *der;* **(b)** (false, untrue) lügnerisch; lügenhaft; erlogen ‹*Geschichte*›. **2** *n.* Lügen, *das;* **that would be** ~: das wäre gelogen. *See also* **lie¹ 2**

lymph /lɪmf/ *n.* Lymphe, *die* (fachspr.); Gewebsflüssigkeit, *die*

lynch /lɪntʃ/ *v.t.* lynchen

'lynch law *n.* Lynchjustiz, *die*

lynx /lɪŋks/ *n.* (Zool.) Luchs, *der*

lyre /'laɪə(r)/ *n.* (Mus.) Lyra, *die;* Leier, *die*

lyric /'lɪrɪk/ **1** *adj.* lyrisch; ~ **poet** Lyriker, *der*/Lyrikerin, *die;* ~ **poetry** Lyrik, *die.* **2** *n.* **(a)** (poem) lyrisches Gedicht; **(b)** *in pl.* (of song) Text, *der*

lyrical /'lɪrɪkl/ *adj.* **(a)** lyrisch; **(b)** (coll.: enthusiastic) gefühlvoll; **become** *or* **wax** ~ **about sth.** über etw. (*Akk.*) ins Schwärmen geraten

lyricism /'lɪrɪsɪzm/ *n.* Lyrismus, *der*

Mm

M, m /em/ *n., pl.* **Ms** *or* **M's** M, m, *das*

m. *abbr.* **(a)** male männl.; **(b)** masculine m.; **(c)** married verh.; **(d)** ▸ 756 |, ▸ 904 | metre[s] m; **(e)** ▸ 1193 | milli- m; **(f)** million[s] Mill.; **(g)** minute[s] Min.

MA *abbr.* **Master of Arts** M. A.; *see also* **B.Sc.**

ma /mɑ:/ *n.* (coll.) Mama, *die;* Mutti, *die* (fam.)

mac /mæk/ *n.* (Brit. coll.) Regenmantel, *der*

macabre /mə'kɑ:br/ *adj.* makaber

macaroni /mækə'rəʊnɪ/ *n.* Makkaroni Pl.

macaroni 'cheese *n.* (Brit.) Käsemakkaroni Pl.

macaroon /mækə'ru:n/ *n.* Makrone, *die*

mace¹ /meɪs/ *n.* **(a)** (Hist.: weapon) Keule, *die;* **(b)** (staff of office) Amtsstab, *der*

mace² *n.* (Bot., Cookery) Mazis, *der;* Muskatblüte, *die*

machete /mə'tʃetɪ, mə'ʃeɪtɪ/ *n.* Machete, *die;* Buschmesser, *das*

machiavellian /mækɪə'velɪən/ *adj.* machiavellistisch

machination /mækɪ'neɪʃn, mæʃɪ'neɪʃn/ *n.* Machenschaft, *die*

machine /mə'ʃi:n/ **1** *n.* **(a)** Maschine, *die;* **(b)** (bicycle) [Fahr]rad, *das;* (motorcycle) Maschine, *die* (ugs.); **(c)** (computer) Computer, *der;* **(d)** (fig.: person) Roboter, *der;* Maschine, *die;* **(e)** (system of organization) Apparat, *der.* **2** *v.t.* (make with ~) maschinell herstellen; (operate on with ~) maschinell bearbeiten ‹*Werkstück*›; (sew) mit *od.* auf der Maschine nähen

machine: ~ **code** *n.* (Computing) Maschinensprache, *die;* ~**-gun** *n.* Maschinengewehr, *das;* ~ **language** ⇒ ~ **code;** ~**-made** *adj.* maschinell hergestellt; ~**-minder** /mə'ʃi:nmaɪndə(r)/ *n.* Maschinenwärter, *der*/-wärterin, *die;* ~ **operator** *n.* ▸ 887 | Bediener, *der*/-bedienerin, *die;* ~**-pistol** *n.* Maschinenpistole, *die;* ~**-readable** *adj.* (Computing) maschinenlesbar

machinery /mə'ʃi:nərɪ/ *n.* **(a)** (machines) Maschinen Pl.; **(b)** (mechanism) Mechanismus, *der;* **(c)** (organized system) Maschinerie, *die*

machine: ~ **trans'lation** *n.* maschinelle Übersetzung; ~**-wash** *v.t.* in der Waschmaschine waschen; ~**-washable** *adj.* waschmaschinenfest

machinist /mə'ʃi:nɪst/ *n.* ▸ 887 | (who makes machinery) Maschinenbauer, *der;* (who controls machinery) Maschinist, *der*/Maschinistin, *die;* [sewing-]~: [Maschinen]näherin, *die*/-näher, *der*

machismo /mə'tʃɪzməʊ, mə'kɪzməʊ/ *n., no pl.* Machismo, *der;* Männlichkeitswahn, *der*

macho /'mætʃəʊ/ **1** *n., pl.* ~**s** Macho, der. **2** *adj.* Macho-; **he is really** ~: er ist wirklich ein Macho

mack /mæk/ ⇒ **mac**

mackerel /'mækərl/ *n., pl. same or* ~**s** (Zool.) Makrele, *die*

mackintosh /'mækɪntɒʃ/ *n.* Regenmantel, *der*

macro /'mækrəʊ/ *n.* (Computing) Makro, *das*

macro- /'mækrəʊ/ *in comb.* makro-/Makro-

macrobiotic /mækrəʊbar'ɒtɪk/ *adj.* makrobiotisch

macro: ~**economic** *adj.* makroökonomisch; ~**economics** *n.* Makroökonomie, *die*

macroscopic /mækrəʊ'skɒpɪk/ *adj.* makroskopisch

mad /mæd/ *adj.* **(a)** (insane) geisteskrank; irr ‹*Blick, Ausdruck*›; **you must be** ~! du bist wohl verrückt! (ugs.); **(b)** (frenzied) wahnsinnig; verrückt (ugs.); **it's one** ~ **rush** (coll.) es ist eine einzige Hetze; **drive sb.** ~: jmdn. um den Verstand bringen *od.* (ugs.) verrückt machen; **(c)** (foolish) verrückt (ugs.); **that was a** ~ **thing to do** das war eine Dummheit (ugs.) verrückt; **(d)** (very enthusiastic) **be/go** ~ **about** *or* **on sb./sth.** auf jmdn./etw. wild sein/werden (ugs.); **be** ~ **keen on sth.** (coll.) auf etw. (*Akk.*) ganz scharf *od.* wild sein (ugs.); **(e)** (coll.: annoyed) ~ [with *or* at sb.] sauer [auf jmdn.] (ugs.); **(f)** (with rabies) toll[wütig]; [run *etc.*]

like ~ (coll.) wie wild *od.* wie ein Wilder/eine Wilde (ugs.) [laufen *usw.*]

Madagascan /ˌmædəˈɡæskən/ ▶897], ▶947] **1** *adj.* madagassisch. **2** *n.* Madagasse, *der*/Madagassin, *die*

Madagascar /ˌmædəˈɡæskə(r)/ *pr. n.* Madagaskar (*das*)

madam /ˈmædəm/ *n.* ▶1184] **(a)** (formal address) gnädige Frau; **M~ Chairman** Frau Vorsitzende; **Dear M~** (in letter) Sehr verehrte gnädige Frau; **(b)** (euphem.: woman brothelkeeper) Bordellwirtin, *die;* Puffmutter, *die* (salopp); **(c)** (derog.: conceited, pert young woman) Kratzbürste, *die* (ugs. scherzh.)

ˈ**madcap 1** *adj.* unbesonnen. **2** *n.* Heißsporn, *der*

mad ˈcow disease *n.* (coll.) Rinderwahnsinn, *der*

madden /ˈmædn/ *v.t.* (irritate) [ver]ärgern

maddening /ˈmædənɪŋ/ *adj.* **(a)** (irritating, tending to infuriate) [äußerst] ärgerlich; **(b)** (tending to craze) unerträglich

made ⇒ **make 1, 2**

Madeira /məˈdɪərə/ **1** *n.* Madeira[wein], *der.* **2** *pr. n.* Madeira (*das*)

made-to-ˈmeasure *attrib. adj.* Maß-; **a ~ suit** ein Maßanzug *od.* maßgeschneiderter Anzug; *see also* **measure 1 a**

ˈ**made-up** *attrib. adj.* erfunden ⟨*Geschichte*⟩

ˈ**madhouse** *n.* Irrenanstalt, *die;* Irrenhaus, *das;* (fig.) Tollhaus, *das*

madly /ˈmædlɪ/ *adv.* **(a)** wie ein Verrückter/eine Verrückte (ugs.); **(b)** (coll.: passionately, extremely) wahnsinnig (ugs.)

madman /ˈmædmən/ *n., pl.* **madmen** /ˈmædmən/ Wahnsinnige, *der;* Irre, *der*

madness /ˈmædnɪs/ *n., no pl.* Wahnsinn, *der*

madonna /məˈdɒnə/ *n.* (Art, Relig.) Madonna, *die*

madrigal /ˈmædrɪɡl/ *n.* (Lit., Mus.) Madrigal, *das*

ˈ**madwoman** *n.* Wahnsinnige, *die;* Irre, *die*

maelstrom /ˈmeɪlstrəm/ *n.* (lit. or fig.) Ma[h]lstrom, *der;* Strudel, *der;* Sog, *der*

MAFF *abbr.* (Brit.) **Ministry of Agriculture, Fisheries, and Food** Landwirtschaftsministerium, *das*

Mafia /ˈmæfɪə/ *n.* Mafia, *die*

magazine /ˌmæɡəˈziːn/ *n.* **(a)** (periodical) Zeitschrift, *die;* (news ~, fashion ~, etc.) Magazin, *das;* **(b)** (Mil.: store) (for arms) Waffenkammer, *die;* (for ammunition) Munitionsdepot, *das;* (for explosives) Sprengstofflager, *das;* **(c)** (Arms, Photog.) Magazin, *das*

magenta /məˈdʒentə/ *n.* (colour) Magenta, *das*

maggot /ˈmæɡət/ *n.* Made, *die*

magic /ˈmædʒɪk/ **1** *n.* **(a)** (witchcraft, lit. or fig.) Magie, *die;* **do ~:** zaubern; **as if by ~:** wie durch Zauberei; **black ~:** schwarze Magie; **work like ~:** wie ein Wunder wirken; **(b)** (fig.: charm, enchantment) Zauber, *der.* **2** *adj.* **(a)** (of ~) magisch ⟨*Eigenschaft, Kraft*⟩; (resembling ~) zauberhaft; (used in ~) Zauber⟨*spruch, -trank, -wort, -bann*⟩; **(b)** (fig.: producing surprising results) wunderbar

magical /ˈmædʒɪkl/ *adj.* (of magic) magisch; (resembling magic) zauberhaft; **the effect was ~:** das wirkte [wahre] Wunder

magic ˈcarpet *n.* fliegender Teppich

magician /məˈdʒɪʃn/ *n.* (lit. or fig.) Magier, *der*/Magierin, *die;* (conjurer) Zauberer, *der*/Zauberin, *die;* **I'm not a ~:** ich kann doch nicht zaubern (ugs.)

magic ˈwand *n.* Zauberstab, *der*

magistrate /ˈmædʒɪstreɪt/ *n.* ▶887] Friedensrichter, *der*/Friedensrichterin, *die;* **~s' court** ≈ Schiedsgericht, *das*

magnanimous /mæɡˈnænɪməs/ *adj.,* **magnanimously** /mæɡˈnænɪməslɪ/ *adv.* großmütig (**towards** gegen)

magnate /ˈmæɡneɪt/ *n.* Magnat, *der*/Magnatin, *die*

magnesium /mæɡˈniːzɪəm/ *n.* (Chem.) Magnesium, *das*

magnet /ˈmæɡnɪt/ *n.* (lit. or fig.) Magnet, *der*

magnetic /mæɡˈnetɪk/ *adj.* (lit. or fig.) magnetisch; (fig.: very attractive) sehr anziehend, unwiderstehlich ⟨*Person*⟩

magnetic: ~ ˈdisc ⇒ **disc c; ~ ˈfield** *n.* (Phys.) Magnetfeld, *das;* **~ ˈpole** *n.* (Phys.) Magnetpol, *der;* (Geog.) magnetischer Pol; **~ ˈtape** *n.* Magnetband, *das*

magnetise ⇒ **magnetize**

magnetism /ˈmæɡnɪtɪzm/ *n.* **(a)** (force, lit. or fig.) Magnetismus, *der;* **(b)** (fig.: personal charm and attraction) Attraktivität, *die;* Anziehungskraft, *die*

magnetize /ˈmæɡnɪtaɪz/ *v.t.* magnetisieren; (fig.) in seinen Bann schlagen

magnification /ˌmæɡnɪfɪˈkeɪʃn/ *n.* Vergrößerung, *die*

magnificence /mæɡˈnɪfɪsəns/ *n., no pl.* (splendour) Prunk, *der;* Pracht, *die;* (grandeur) Stattlichkeit, *die;* Großartigkeit, *die;* (beauty) Herrlichkeit, *die;* (lavish display) Pracht, *die;* Üppigkeit, *die*

magnificent /mæɡˈnɪfɪsənt/ *adj.* **(a)** (stately, sumptuously constructed or adorned) prächtig; prachtvoll; (sumptuous) prunkvoll; grandios, großartig ⟨*Pracht, Herrlichkeit, Anblick*⟩; (beautiful) herrlich ⟨*Garten, Umgebung, Kleidung, Vorhang, Kunstwerk, Wetter, Gestalt*⟩; (lavish) üppig ⟨*Freigebigkeit, Mahl*⟩; **(b)** (coll.: fine, excellent) fabelhaft (ugs.)

magnify /ˈmæɡnɪfaɪ/ *v.t.* **(a)** vergrößern; **(b)** (exaggerate) aufbauschen; übertrieben darstellen ⟨*Gefahren*⟩

ˈ**magnifying glass** *n.* Lupe, *die;* Vergrößerungsglas, *das*

magnitude /ˈmæɡnɪtjuːd/ *n.* **(a)** (largeness, vastness) Ausmaß, *das;* (of explosion, earthquake) Stärke, *die;* **(b)** (size) Größe, *die;* **order of ~:** Größenordnung, *die;* **problems of this ~:** Probleme dieser Größenordnung; **(c)** (importance) Wichtigkeit, *die;* **(d)** (Astron.) Helligkeit, *die*

magpie /ˈmæɡpaɪ/ *n.* (Ornith.) Elster, *die*

mahogany /məˈhɒɡənɪ/ *n.* **(a)** (wood) Mahagoni[holz], *das; attrib.* Mahagoni-; **(b)** (tree) Mahagonibaum, *der;* **(c)** (colour) Mahagonibraun, *das*

maid /meɪd/ *n.* **(a)** (servant) Dienstmädchen, *das;* Dienstmagd, *die* (veralt.); **(b)** (young unmarried woman, virgin) Jungfrau, *die;* **(c)** (arch./poet./rhet.: young woman, girl) Maid, *die* (dichter. veralt.). *See also* **old maid**

maiden /ˈmeɪdn/ **1** *n.* Jungfrau, *die.* **2** *adj.* (first) **~ voyage/speech** Jungfernfahrt/-rede, *die*

maiden: ~head *n.* **(a)** (virginity) Jungfräulichkeit, *die;* **(b)** (Anat.) Jungfernhäutchen, *das;* **~ name** *n.* Mädchenname, *der*

maid: ~ of ˈhonour *n., pl.* **~s of honour (a)** (attendant of queen or princess) Hof- *od.* Ehrendame, *die;* **(b)** (Amer.: chief bridesmaid) Brautjungfer, *die;* **~servant** *n.* (arch.) Hausangestellte, *die;* Hausmädchen, *das*

mail /meɪl/ **1** *n.* **(a)** ⇒ **post²** 1; **(b)** (vehicle carrying ~) Postbeförderungsmittel, *das;* (train) Postzug, *der.* **2** *v.t.* ⇒ **post²** 2 a

mail: ~bag *n.* (postman's bag) Zustelltasche, *die;* (sack for transporting ~) Postsack, *der;* **~ bomb** *n.* (Amer.) Briefbombe, *die;* **~box** *n.* (Amer.) Briefkasten, *der;* (slot) Briefschlitz, *der*

mailing /ˈmeɪlɪŋ/: **~ address** *n.* Postanschrift, *die;* **~ list** *n.* Adressenliste, *die*

mail: ~man *n.* ▶887] (Amer.) Briefträger, *der;* Postbote, *der* (ugs.); **~ order** *n.* postalische Bestellung; Mailorder, *die* (Werbespr., Kaufmannsspr.); **by ~ order** durch Bestellung *od.* Mailorder; **~-order catalogue** *n.* Versandhauskatalog, *der* Poststelle, *die;* **~ shot** *n.* Versand, *der* von Werbeschriften; **~ train** *n.* Postzug, *der;* **~ van** *n.* (Railw.) Postwagen, *der;* Paketwagen, *der*

maim /meɪm/ *v.t.* (mutilate) verstümmeln; (cripple) zum Krüppel machen

main /meɪn/ **1** *n.* **(a)** (channel, pipe) Hauptleitung, *die;* **~s [system]** öffentliches Versorgungsnetz; (of electricity) Stromnetz, *das;* **turn the gas/water off at the ~[s]** den Haupthahn [für das Gas/Wasser] abstellen; **turn the electricity off at the ~s** [den Strom] am Hauptschalter abschalten; **(b)** **in the ~:** im Allgemeinen; im Großen und Ganzen. **2** *attrib. adj.* Haupt-; **the ~ doubt/principle** der entscheidende Zweifel/oberste Grundsatz; **the ~ thing is that ...:** die Hauptsache *od.* das Wichtigste ist, dass ...

main: ~ beam *n.* (Motor Veh.) **on ~ beam** aufgeblendet; **~ clause** *n.* (Ling.) Hauptsatz, *der;* **~ course** *n.* Hauptgang, *der;* Hauptgericht, *das;* **~frame** *n.* (Computing) Großrechner, *der;* **~land** /ˈmeɪnlənd/ *n.* Festland, *das;* **~ ˈline** *n.* (Railw.) Hauptstrecke, *die; attrib.* **~-line station/train** Fernbahnhof, *der*/-zug, *der*

mainly /'meɪnlɪ/ adv. hauptsächlich; in erster Linie; (for the most part) vorwiegend

main: ~ 'road n. Hauptstraße, die; ~spring n. Hauptfeder, die; (of clock, watch, etc.) also fig.) Triebfeder, die; ~stay n. (Naut.) Großstag, das; (fig.) [wichtigste] Stütze; ~stream n. (principal current) Hauptstrom, der; (fig.) Hauptrichtung, die; be in the ~stream der Hauptrichtung angehören; ~ street /Brit. -'-, Amer. '--/ n. Hauptstraße, die

maintain /meɪn'teɪn/ v.t. (a) (keep up) aufrechterhalten; bewahren ⟨Anschein, Haltung⟩; unterhalten ⟨Beziehungen, Briefwechsel⟩; [beibe]halten ⟨Preise, Geschwindigkeit⟩; wahren ⟨Rechte, Ruf⟩; (b) (provide for) ~ sb. für jmds. Unterhalt aufkommen; (c) (preserve) instand halten; warten ⟨Maschine, Gerät⟩; unterhalten ⟨Straße⟩; (d) (give aid to) unterstützen ⟨Partei, Wohlfahrtsorganisation, Sache⟩; (e) (assert as true) vertreten ⟨Meinung, Lehre⟩; beteuern ⟨Unschuld⟩; ~ that ...: behaupten, dass ...

maintenance /'meɪntənəns/ n. (a) ⇒ **maintain** a: Aufrechterhaltung, die; Bewahrung, die; Unterhaltung, die; [Beibe]halten, das; Wahrung, die; (b) (furnishing with means of subsistence) Unterhaltung, die; (c) (Law: money paid to support sb.) Unterhalt, der; (d) (preservation) Instandhaltung, die; (of machinery) Wartung, die

maintenance: ~-free adj. wartungsfrei; ~ **manual** n. Wartungsbuch, das

main 'verb n. Hauptverb, das

maison[n]ette /meɪzə'net/ n. [zweistöckige] Wohnung; Maison[n]ette, die

maize /meɪz/ n. Mais, der

majestic /mə'dʒestɪk/ adj. majestätisch; erhaben ⟨Erscheinung, Schönheit⟩; gemessen ⟨Auftreten, Schritt⟩; getragen ⟨Musik⟩; (stately) stattlich; (possessing grandeur) grandios

majesty /'mædʒɪstɪ/ n. ▶ 1152 Majestät, die; **Your/His/Her M~:** Eure/Seine/Ihre Majestät

major /'meɪdʒə(r)/ **1** adj. (a) attrib. (greater) größer...; ~ **part** Großteil, der; (b) attrib. (important) bedeutend...; (serious) schwer ⟨Unfall, Krankheit, Unglück, Unruhen⟩; größer... ⟨Krieg, Angriff, Durchbruch⟩; schwer, größer... ⟨Operation⟩; **of** ~ **interest/importance** von größerem Interesse/von größerer Bedeutung; ~ **road** (important) Hauptverkehrsstraße, die; (having priority) Vorfahrtsstraße, die; (c) (Mus.) Dur-; ~ **key/scale/chord** Durtonart, die/Durtonleiter, die/Durakkord, der; **C** ~: C-Dur; **in a** ~ **key** in Dur. **2** n. (a) (Mil.) Major, der; (b) (Amer. Univ.) Hauptfach, das. **3** v.i. (Amer. Univ.) ~ **in sth.** etwas als Hauptfach haben

majority /mə'dʒɒrɪtɪ/ n. (a) (greater number or part) Mehrheit, die; **the** ~ **of people think ...:** die meisten Menschen denken ...; **be in the** ~: in der Mehr- od. Überzahl sein; überwiegen; (b) (in vote) [Stimmen]mehrheit, die; Majorität, die

majority: ~ 'rule n. Mehrheitsregierung, die; ~ 'verdict n. Mehrheitsentscheid, der

make /meɪk/ **1** v.t., **made** /meɪd/ (a) (construct) machen, anfertigen (**of** aus); bauen ⟨Damm, Straße, Flugzeug, Geige⟩; anlegen ⟨See, Teich, Weg usw.⟩; zimmern ⟨Tisch, Regal⟩; basteln ⟨Spielzeug, Vogelhäuschen, Dekoration usw.⟩; nähen ⟨Kleider⟩; durchbrechen ⟨Türöffnung⟩; (manufacture) herstellen; (create) [er]schaffen ⟨Welt⟩; (prepare) zubereiten ⟨Mahlzeit⟩; machen ⟨Frühstück, Grog⟩; machen, kochen ⟨Kaffee, Tee, Marmelade⟩; backen ⟨Brot, Kuchen⟩; (compose, write) schreiben, verfassen ⟨Buch, Gedicht, Lied, Bericht⟩; machen ⟨Eintrag, Zeichen, Kopie, Zusammenfassung, Testament⟩; anfertigen ⟨Entwurf⟩; aufsetzen ⟨Bewerbung, Schreiben, Urkunde⟩; ~ **a film** einen Film drehen; ~ **a dress out of the material,** ~ **the material into a dress** aus dem Stoff ein Kleid machen; **a table made of wood/of the finest wood** ein Holztisch/ein Tisch aus feinstem Holz; **made in Germany** in Deutschland hergestellt; **show what one is made of** zeigen, was in einem steckt (ugs.); **be [simply] 'made of money,** (coll.) im Geld [nur so] schwimmen (ugs.); **be 'made for sth.** (fig.: ideally suited) wie geschaffen für etw./jmdn. sein; ~ **a bed** (for sleeping) ein Bett bauen (ugs.); ~ **the bed** (arrange after sleeping) das Bett machen; **have it made** (coll.) ausgesorgt haben (ugs.); (b) (combine into) sich verbinden zu;

bilden; **blue and yellow** ~ **green** aus Blau und Gelb wird Grün; (c) (cause to exist) machen ⟨Ärger, Schwierigkeiten, Lärm, Aufhebens⟩; ~ **enemies** sich (Dat.) Feinde machen od. schaffen; ~ **time for doing** or **to do sth.** sich (Dat.) die Zeit dazu nehmen, etw. zu tun; (d) (result in, amount to) machen ⟨Unterschied, Summe⟩; ergeben ⟨Resultat⟩; **two and two** ~ **four** zwei und zwei ist od. macht od. sind vier; **they** ~ **a handsome pair** sie geben ein hübsches Paar ab; **qualities that** ~ **a man** Eigenschaften, die einen Mann ausmachen; (e) (establish, enact) bilden ⟨Gegensatz⟩; treffen ⟨Unterscheidung, Übereinkommen⟩; ziehen ⟨Vergleich, Parallele⟩; erlassen ⟨Gesetz, Haftbefehl⟩; aufstellen ⟨Regeln, Behauptung⟩; stellen ⟨Forderung⟩; geben ⟨Bericht⟩; schließen ⟨Vertrag⟩; vornehmen ⟨Zahlung⟩; machen ⟨Geschäft, Vorschlag, Geständnis⟩; erheben ⟨Anschuldigung, Protest, Beschwerde⟩; (f) (cause to be or become) ~ **angry/happy/known** etc. wütend/glücklich/bekannt usw. machen; ~ **sb. captain** jmdn. zum Kapitän machen; ~ **a star of sb.** aus jmdm. einen Star machen; ~ **a friend of sb.** sich mit jmdm. anfreunden; ~ **oneself heard/respected** sich (Dat.) Gehör/Respekt verschaffen; ~ **oneself understood** sich verständlich machen; **shall we** ~ **it Tuesday then?** sagen wir also Dienstag?; **that** ~**s it one pound exactly** das macht genau ein Pfund; ~ **it a shorter journey by doing sth.** die Reise abkürzen, indem man etw. tut; (g) ~ **sb. do sth.** (cause) jmdn. dazu bringen, etw. zu tun; (compel) jmdn. zwingen, etw. zu tun; ~ **sb. repeat the sentence** jmdn. den Satz wiederholen lassen; **be made to do sth.** etw. tun müssen; (be compelled) gezwungen werden, etw. zu tun; ~ **oneself do sth.** sich überwinden, etw. zu tun; **what** ~**s you think that?** wie kommst du darauf?; (h) (form, be counted as) **this** ~**s the tenth time you've failed** das ist nun [schon] das zehnte Mal, dass du versagt hast; **will you** ~ **one of the party?** wirst du dabei od. (ugs.) mit von der Partie sein?; (i) (serve for) abgeben; **this story** ~**s good reading** diese Geschichte ist guter Lesestoff; (j) (become by development or training) **the site would** ~ **a good playground** der Platz würde einen guten Spielplatz abgeben; **he will** ~ **a good officer** aus ihm wird noch ein guter Offizier; (k) (gain, acquire, procure) machen ⟨Vermögen, Profit, Verlust⟩; machen (ugs.) ⟨Geld⟩; verdienen ⟨Lebensunterhalt⟩; sich (Dat.) erwerben ⟨Ruf⟩; (obtain as result) kommen zu od. auf, herausbekommen ⟨Ergebnis, Endsumme⟩; **how much did you** ~? wieviel hast du verdient?; **that** ~**s one pound exactly** das macht genau ein Pfund; (l) machen ⟨Geste, Bewegung, Verbeugung⟩; machen ⟨Reise, Besuch, Ausnahme, Fehler, Angebot, Entdeckung, Witz, Bemerkung⟩; begehen ⟨Irrtum⟩; vornehmen ⟨Änderung, Stornierung⟩; vorbringen ⟨Beschwerde⟩; tätigen, machen ⟨Einkäufe⟩; geben ⟨Versprechen, Kommentar⟩; halten ⟨Rede⟩; ziehen ⟨Vergleich⟩; durchführen, machen ⟨Experiment, Analyse, Inspektion⟩; (wage) führen ⟨Krieg⟩; (accomplish) schaffen ⟨Strecke pro Zeiteinheit⟩; (m) ~ **much of sth.** etw. betonen; ~ **little of sth.** (play sth. down) etw. herunterspielen; **they could** ~ **little of his letter** (understand) sie konnten mit seinem Brief nicht viel anfangen; **I don't know what to** ~ **of him/it** ich werde aus ihm/daraus nicht schlau od. klug; **what do you** ~ **of him?** was hältst du von ihm?; wie schätzt du ihn ein?; (n) (arrive at) erreichen ⟨Bestimmungsort⟩; (coll.: catch) [noch] kriegen (ugs.) ⟨Zug usw.⟩; ~ **it** (succeed in arriving) es schaffen; (o) **sth.** ~**s or breaks** or **mars sb.** etw. entscheidet über jmds. Glück oder Verderben (Akk.); ~ **sb.'s day** jmdm. einen glücklichen Tag machen; (p) (consider to be) **What do you** ~ **the time? — I** ~ **it five past eight** Wie spät hast du es od. ist es bei dir? — Auf meiner Uhr ist es fünf nach acht; (q) ~ 'do vorlieb nehmen; ~ 'do **with/without sth.** mit/ohne etw. auskommen. **2** v.i. (proceed) ~ **toward sth./sb.** auf etw./jmdn. zusteuern; (b) (act as if with intention) ~ **to do sth.** Anstalten machen, etw. zu tun; ~ **as if** or **as though to do sth.** so tun, als wolle man etw. tun. **3** n. (a) (kind of structure) Ausführung, die; (of clothes) Machart, die; (b) (type of manufacture) Fabrikat, das; (brand) Marke, die; ~ **of car** Automarke, die; (c) **on the** ~ (coll.: intent on gain) hinter dem Geld her (abwertend)

∼ for v.t. **(a)** (move towards) zusteuern auf (+ Akk.); zuhalten auf (+ Akk.); (rush towards) losgehen auf (+ Akk.); zustürzen auf (+ Akk.); ∼ **for home** heimwärts steuern; **(b)** (be conducive to) führen zu, herbeiführen ⟨gute Beziehungen, Erfolg, Zuversicht⟩

∼ 'off v.i. sich davonmachen

∼ 'off with v.t. ∼ **off with** sb./sth. sich mit jmdm./ etw. [auf und] davonmachen

∼ 'out 1 v.t. **(a)** (write) ausstellen ⟨Scheck, Dokument, Rechnung⟩; aufstellen ⟨Liste⟩; **(b)** (claim, assert) behaupten; **you ∼ me out to be a liar** du stellst mich als Lügner hin; **how do you ∼ that out?** wie kommst du darauf?; see also **case¹** d; **(c)** (understand) verstehen; **(d)** (manage to see or hear) ausmachen; (manage to read) entziffern; **(e)** (pretend) vorgeben. 2 v.i. (coll.: ∼ progress) zurechtkommen (**at** bei)

∼ 'over v.t. (transfer) übereignen, überschreiben ⟨Geld, Geschäft, Eigentum⟩ (**to** Dat.)

∼ 'up 1 v.t. **(a)** (replace) ausgleichen ⟨Fehlmenge, Verluste⟩; ∼ **up lost ground/time** Boden gut- od. wettmachen (ugs.)/den Zeitverlust aufholen; **(b)** (complete) komplett machen; **(c)** (prepare, arrange) zubereiten ⟨Arznei usw.⟩; (process material) verarbeiten (**into** zu); **(d)** (apply cosmetics to) schminken; ∼ **up one's face/eyes** sich schminken/sich (Dat.) die Augen schminken; **(e)** (assemble, compile) zusammenstellen; aufstellen ⟨Liste usw.⟩; bilden ⟨ein Ganzes⟩; **(f)** (invent) erfinden; sich (Dat.) ausdenken; **(g)** (reconcile) beilegen ⟨Streit, Meinungsverschiedenheit⟩; **(h)** (form, constitute) bilden; **be made up of …**: bestehen aus … 2 v.i. **(a)** (apply cosmetics etc.) sich schminken; **(b)** (be reconciled) sich wieder vertragen

∼ 'up for v.t. **(a)** (outweigh, compensate) wettmachen; **(b)** (∼ amends for) wieder gutmachen; **(c)** ∼ **up for lost time** Versäumtes nachholen od. (ugs.) wettmachen

∼ 'up to v.t. **(a)** (raise to, increase to) bringen auf (+ Akk.); **(b)** (coll.: act flirtatiously towards) sich heranmachen an (+ Akk.) (ugs.); **(c)** (coll.: give compensation to) ∼ **it/this up to sb.** jmdm. dafür entschädigen

'make-believe 1 n. **it's only ∼:** das ist bloß Fantasie. 2 adj. nicht echt; **a ∼ world/story** eine Scheinwelt/Fantasiegeschichte

maker /'meɪkə(r)/ n. **(a)** (manufacturer) Hersteller, der; **(b)** **M∼** (God) Schöpfer, der

make: ∼**shift** adj. behelfsmäßig; **a ∼shift shelter/ bridge** eine Behelfsunterkunft/-brücke; ∼**-up** n. **(a)** (Cosmetics) Make-up, das; (Theatre) Maske, die; **put on one's ∼-up** Make-up auflegen; sich schminken; (Theatre) Maske machen; attrib. ∼**-up bag** Kosmetiktasche, die; **(b)** (composition) Zusammensetzung, die; **(c)** (character, temperament) Veranlagung, die; **physical ∼-up** Konstitution, die

making /'meɪkɪŋ/ n. **(a)** (production) Herstellung, die; **in the ∼:** im Entstehen; im Werden; **be the ∼ of victory/ sb.'s career/sb.'s future** zum Sieg/zu jmds. Karriere führen/jmds. Zukunft sichern; **(b)** in pl. (qualities) Anlagen Pl.; Voraussetzungen Pl.; **have all the ∼s of sth.** alle Voraussetzungen für etw. haben; **have the ∼s of a leader** über Führerqualitäten verfügen; das Zeug zum Führer haben (ugs.)

maladjusted /mælə'dʒʌstɪd/ adj. (Psych., Sociol.) **[psychologically/socially] ∼:** verhaltensgestört

maladroit /mælə'drɔɪt, 'mælədrɔɪt/ adj. ungeschickt; taktlos ⟨Bemerkung⟩

malady /'mælədɪ/ n. Leiden, das; (fig.: of society, epoch) Übel, das

malaise /mæ'leɪz/ n. Unwohlsein, das; (feeling of uneasiness) Unbehagen, das

malaria /mə'leərɪə/ n. ▶865 Malaria, die

Malay /mə'leɪ/ ▶897, ▶947 1 adj. malaiisch; **sb. is ∼:** jmd. ist Malaie/Malaiin. 2 n. **(a)** (person) Malaie, der/Malaiin, die; **(b)** (language) Malaiisch, das; see also **English 2 a**

Malaya /mə'leɪə/ pr. n. Malaya (das)

Malayan /mə'leɪən/ ⇒ **Malay 1, 2 a**

Malaysia /mə'leɪzɪə/ pr. n. Malaysia (das)

Malaysian /mə'leɪzɪən/ ▶947 1 adj. malaysisch. 2 n. Malaysier, der/Malaysierin, die

male /meɪl/ 1 adj. männlich; Männer⟨stimme, -chor, -verein⟩; ∼ **child/dog/cat/doctor/nurse** Junge/Rüde/ Kater/Arzt/Krankenpfleger, der. 2 n. (person) Mann, der; (foetus, child) Junge, der; (animal) Männchen, das

'male-dominated adj. von Männern dominiert; **a ∼ field** eine Männerdomäne

malevolent /mə'levələnt/ adj. böse ⟨Macht, Tat⟩; übel wollend ⟨Gott⟩; boshaft, hämisch ⟨Gelächter⟩; böswillig ⟨Lüge⟩; boshaft ⟨Person⟩

malformed /mæl'fɔːmd/ adj. (Med.) missgebildet

malfunction /mæl'fʌŋkʃn/ 1 n. Störung, die; (Med.) Dysfunktion, die (fachspr.); Funktionsstörung, die. 2 v.i. ⟨Mechanismus, System, Gerät:⟩ nicht richtig funktionieren; ⟨Prozess, Vorgang:⟩ nicht richtig ablaufen

malice /'mælɪs/ n. Bosheit, die; Böswilligkeit, die; **bear ∼ to** or **towards** or **against sb.** jmdm. übel wollen

malicious /mə'lɪʃəs/ adj. **(a)** böse ⟨Klatsch, Tat, Person, Wort⟩; böswillig ⟨Gerücht, Lüge, Verleumdung⟩; boshaft ⟨Person⟩; hämisch ⟨Vergnügen, Freude⟩; **(b)** (Law) böswillig ⟨Sachbeschädigung, Verleumdung⟩

malign /mə'laɪn/ 1 v.t. (slander) verleumden; (speak ill of) schlechtmachen; ∼ **sb.'s character** jmdm. Übles nachsagen. 2 adj. **(a)** (injurious) böse ⟨Macht, Geist⟩; schlecht, unheilvoll ⟨Eigenschaft, Einfluss⟩; **(b)** (malevolent) böse ⟨Absicht⟩; niederträchtig ⟨Motiv⟩

malignant /mə'lɪgnənt/ adj. **(a)** (Med.) maligne (fachspr.), bösartig ⟨Krankheit, Geschwür⟩; ∼ **cancer** Karzinom, das (fachspr.); Krebs, der; **(b)** (harmful) böse ⟨Macht⟩; ungünstig ⟨Einfluss⟩; **(c)** (feeling or showing ill will) böse ⟨Geist, Zunge, Klatsch⟩

malinger /mə'lɪŋgə(r)/ v.i. simulieren

mall /mæl, mɔːl/ n. (esp. Amer.: shopping centre) Einkaufszentrum, das

malleable /'mælɪəbl/ adj. formbar ⟨Material, Person⟩

mallet /'mælɪt/ n. **(a)** (hammer) Holzhammer, der; Schlegel, der; (of stonemason) Klöpfel, der; (of carpenter) Klopfholz, das; **(b)** (Croquet) Hammer, der; (Polo) Schläger, der

malnutrition /mælnjuː'trɪʃn/ n. Unterernährung, die

malpractice /mæl'præktɪs/ n. (wrongdoing) Übeltat, die (geh.)

malt /mɔːlt, mɒlt/ 1 n. Malz, das. 2 v.t. mälzen ⟨Gerste⟩

Malta /'mɔːltə, 'mɒltə/ pr. n. Malta (das)

Maltese /mɔːl'tiːz, mɒl'tiːz/ ▶897, ▶947 1 adj. maltesisch; **sb. is ∼:** jmd. ist Malteser/Malteserin. 2 n., pl. same **(a)** (person) Malteser, der/Malteserin, die; **(b)** (language) Maltesisch (das)

maltreat /mæl'triːt/ v.t. misshandeln

maltreatment /mæl'triːtmənt/ n. Misshandlung, die

malt 'whisky n. Malzwhisky, der

mamma /'mæmə/ n. (coll./child lang.) Mama, die (fam.); Mami, die (fam.)

mammal /'mæml/ n. (Zool.) Säugetier, das; Säuger, der

mammography /mæ'mɒgrəfɪ/ n., no pl. (Med.) Mammographie, die

mammoth /'mæməθ/ 1 n. (Palaeont.) Mammut, das. 2 adj. Mammut-; gigantisch ⟨Vorhaben⟩

man /mæn/ 1 n., pl. **men** /men/ **(a)** no art., no pl. (human being, person) Mensch, der; (the human race) der Mensch; ∼ **is a political animal** der Mensch ist ein politisches Wesen; **what can a ∼ do?** was kann man tun?; **every ∼ for himself** rette sich, wer kann; **any ∼ who …:** wer …; **no ∼:** niemand; **[all] to a ∼:** ausnahmslos alle; **the ∼ in** or (Amer.) **on the street** der Mann auf der Straße; **the rights of ∼:** die Menschenrechte; **(b)** (adult male, individual male) Mann, der; **every ∼, woman, and child** ausnahmslos jeder od. alle; **the [very] ∼ for sth.** der richtige Mann od. der Richtige für etw.; **make a ∼ out of sb.** (fig.) einen Mann aus jmdm. machen; **a ∼ of property/great strength** ein vermögender/sehr kräftiger Mann; **men's clothing/outfitter** Herrenkleidung, die/ Herrenausstatter, der; **be ∼ enough to …:** Manns genug sein, um zu …; **sth. sorts out** or **separates the men from the boys** (coll.) an etw. (Dat.) zeigt sich, wer ein ganzer Kerl ist und wer nicht; **be one's own ∼:** seine eigenen Vorstellungen haben; **men's toilet** Herrentoilette, *die;* '**Men**' „Herren"; **my [good]** ∼: mein Guter; (**c**) (husband) Mann, *der;* **be** ∼ **and wife** verheiratet sein; (**d**) (Chess) Figur, *die;* (Draughts) Stein, *der;* (**e**) (coll.: as int. of surprise or impatience, as mode of address) Mensch! (salopp); (**f**) (type of ∼) Mann, *der;* Typ, *der;* **a** ∼ **of the people/world/of action** ein Mann des Volkes/von Welt/der Tat; (**g**) (∼ servant) Diener, *der.* **2** *v.t.,* **-nn-** bemannen ‹*Schiff, Spill*›; besetzen ‹*Büro, Stelle usw.*›; bedienen ‹*Telefon, Geschütz*›; ‹*Soldaten:*› Stellung beziehen in (+ *Dat.*) ‹*Festung*›; mit Personal besetzen ‹*Fabrik*›

manacle /ˈmænəkl/ **1** *n., usu. in pl.* [Hand]fessel, *die;* Kette, *die.* **2** *v.t.* Handfesseln anlegen (+ *Dat.*)

manage /ˈmænɪdʒ/ **1** *v.t.* (**a**) (handle, wield) handhaben ‹*Werkzeug, Segel, Boot*›; bedienen ‹*Schaltbrett*›; (**b**) (conduct, organize) durchführen ‹*Operation, Unternehmen*›; erledigen ‹*Angelegenheit*›; verwalten ‹*Geld, Grundstück*›; leiten ‹*Geschäft, Büro*›; führen ‹*Haushalt*›; (**c**) (Sport etc.: be manager of) managen, betreuen ‹*Team, Mannschaft*›; (**d**) (cope with) schaffen; **I couldn't** ∼ **another apple** (coll.) noch einen Apfel schaffe ich nicht; **we can** ∼ **another person in the car** einer hat noch Platz im Wagen; (**e**) (succeed in achieving) zustande bringen ‹*Lächeln*›; (**f**) (contrive) ∼ **to do sth.** (also iron.) es fertig bringen, etw. zu tun; **he** ∼**d to do it** es gelang ihm, es zu tun; **I'll** ∼ **it somehow** ich werde es schon irgendwie hinkriegen (ugs.). **2** *v.i.* zurechtkommen; ∼ **without sth.** ohne etw. auskommen; ∼ **on** zurecht- *od.* auskommen mit ‹*Geld, Einkommen*›; **I can** ∼: es geht; **can you** ∼? geht's?; geht es?

manageable /ˈmænɪdʒəbl/ *adj.* leicht frisierbar ‹*Haar*›; fügsam ‹*Person, Tier*›; überschaubar ‹*Größe, Menge*›; lenkbar ‹*Firma*›

management /ˈmænɪdʒmənt/ *n.* (**a**) Durchführung, *die;* (of a business) Leitung, *die;* Management, *das;* (of money) Verwaltung, *die;* (**b**) (managers) Leitung, *die;* Management, *das;* (of theatre etc.) Direktion, *die;* **the** ∼: die Geschäftsleitung

management: ∼ '**buyout** *n.* Management-Buy-out, *das;* ∼ **consultancy** *n.* Unternehmensberatung, *die;* ∼ **consultant** *n.* Unternehmensberater, *der*/-beraterin, *die*

manager /ˈmænɪdʒə(r)/ *n.* ▶ 887 (of branch of shop or bank) Filialleiter, *der*/-leiterin, *die;* (of football team) [Chef]trainer, *der*/-trainerin, *die;* (of tennis player, boxer, pop group) Manager, *der*/Managerin, *die;* (of restaurant, shop, hotel) Geschäftsführer, *der*/-führerin, *die;* (of estate, grounds) Verwalter, *der*/Verwalterin, *die;* (of department) Leiter, *der*/Leiterin, *die;* (of theatre) Direktor, *der*/Direktorin, *die*

manageress /ˈmænɪdʒəres, mænɪdʒəˈres/ *n.* (of restaurant, shop, hotel) Geschäftsführerin, *die; see also* **manager**

managerial /mænəˈdʒɪərɪəl/ *adj.* führend, leitend ‹*Stellung*›; geschäftlich ‹*Aspekt, Seite*›

managing /ˈmænɪdʒɪŋ/ *attrib. adj.* geschäftsführend; leitend; ∼ **director** Geschäftsführer, *der*

mandarin[1] /ˈmændərɪn/ *n.* ∼ [**orange**] Mandarine, *die*

mandarin[2] *n.* (**a**) **M**∼ (language) Hochchinesisch, *das;* (**b**) (party leader) Parteiboss, *der* (ugs.); [Partei]bonze, *der* (abwertend); (**c**) (bureaucrat) Bürokrat, *der*/Bürokratin, *die* (abwertend); Apparatschik, *der* (abwertend)

mandarine /ˈmændəri:n/ ⇒ **mandarin**[1]

mandate /ˈmændeɪt/ *n.* (also Polit.) Mandat, *das*

mandatory /ˈmændətərɪ/ *adj.* obligatorisch; **be** ∼: Pflicht *od.* obligatorisch sein

mandolin, mandoline /mændəˈlɪn/ *n.* (Mus.) Mandoline, *die*

mane /meɪn/ *n.* (lit. or fig.) Mähne, *die*

'**man-eating** *adj.* Menschen fressend ‹*Löwe, Tiger*›; **a** ∼ **shark** ein Menschenhai

maneuver (Amer.) ⇒ **manœuvre**

manful /ˈmænfl/ *adj.* mannhaft

manfully /ˈmænfəlɪ/ *adv.* mannhaft; wie ein Mann

manganese /ˈmæŋɡəni:z, mæŋɡəˈni:z/ *n.* (Chem.) Mangan, *das*

manger /ˈmeɪndʒə(r)/ *n.* Futtertrog, *der;* (Bibl.) Krippe, *die; see also* **dog 1 a**

mangle[1] /ˈmæŋɡl/ **1** *n.* Mangel, *die.* **2** *v.t.* mangeln ‹*Wäsche*›

mangle[2] *v.t.* verstümmeln, [übel] zurichten ‹*Person*›; demolieren ‹*Sache*›; verstümmeln, entstellen ‹*Zitat, Musikstück*›

mango /ˈmæŋɡəʊ/ *n., pl.* ∼**es** *or* ∼**s** (**a**) (tree) Mangobaum, *der;* (**b**) (fruit) Mango[frucht], *die*

mangrove /ˈmæŋɡrəʊv/ *n.* (Bot.) Mangrovebaum, *der*

mangy /ˈmeɪndʒɪ/ *adj.* (**a**) (Vet. Med.) räudig; (**b**) (shabby) schäbig ‹*Teppich, Decke, Stuhl*›

man: ∼**handle** *v.t.* (**a**) (move by human effort) von Hand bewegen ‹*Gegenstand*›; (**b**) (handle roughly) grob behandeln ‹*Person*›; ∼**hole** *n.* Mannloch, *das;* (in tank) Einstiegsluke, *die;* (to cables under pavement) Kabelschacht, *der*

manhood /ˈmænhʊd/ *n., no pl.* Mannesalter, *das;* (courage) Männlichkeit, *die*

man: ∼**-hour** *n.* Arbeitsstunde, *die;* ∼**hunt** *n.* Menschenjagd, *die;* (for criminal) Verbrecherjagd, *die*

mania /ˈmeɪnɪə/ *n.* (**a**) (madness) Wahnsinn, *der;* (**b**) (enthusiasm) Manie, *die;* ∼ **for detective novels** Leidenschaft für Krimis

maniac /ˈmeɪnɪæk/ **1** *adj.* wahnsinnig; krankhaft, (geh.) manisch ‹*Fantasie, Verlangen*›. **2** *n.* (**a**) (Psych.) Besessene, *der*/*die;* (madman/-woman) Wahnsinnige, *der*/*die;* (**b**) (person with passion for sth.) Fanatiker, *der*/Fanatikerin, *die*

manicure /ˈmænɪkjʊə(r)/ **1** *n.* Maniküre, *die;* **give sb. a** ∼: jmdn. maniküren. **2** *v.t.* maniküren

manifest /ˈmænɪfest/ **1** *adj.* offenkundig; offenbar ‹*Missverständnis*›; sichtbar ‹*Erfolg, Fortschritt*›; sichtlich ‹*Freude*›. **2** *v.t.* (**a**) (show, display) zeigen, bekunden (geh.) ‹*Interesse, Missfallen, Begeisterung, Zuneigung*›; (**b**) (reveal) offenbaren (meist geh.); ∼ **itself** ‹*Geist:*› erscheinen; ‹*Natur:*› sich offenbaren; ‹*Krankheit:*› manifest werden

manifestation /mænɪfeˈsteɪʃn/ *n.* (of ill will, favour, disapproval) Ausdruck, *der;* Bezeugung, *die;* (appearance) Erscheinung, *die; in pl.* Erscheinungsformen; (visible expression, sign) [An]zeichen, *das* (**of** von)

manifestly /ˈmænɪfestlɪ/ *adv.* offenkundig; **it is** ∼ **unjust that** …: es ist ganz offensichtlich ungerecht, dass …

manifesto /mænɪˈfestəʊ/ *n., pl.* ∼**s** Manifest, *das*

manifold /ˈmænɪfəʊld/ **1** *adj.* (literary) mannigfaltig (geh.); vielfältig. **2** (Mech. Engin.) Verteilerrohr, *das;* [**inlet**] ∼: [Ansaug]krümmer, *der;* [**exhaust**] ∼: [Auspuff]krümmer, *der*

manipulate /məˈnɪpjʊleɪt/ *v.t.* (**a**) (also Med.) manipulieren; ∼ **sb. into doing sth.** jmdn. dahin gehend manipulieren, dass er etw. tut; (**b**) (handle) handhaben

manipulation /mənɪpjʊˈleɪʃn/ *n.* (**a**) (also Med.) Manipulation, *die;* (**b**) (handling) Handhabung, *die*

manipulative /məˈnɪpjʊlətɪv/ *adj.* manipulativ

mankind /mænˈkaɪnd/ *n.* Menschheit, *die*

manly /ˈmænlɪ/ *adj.* männlich; (brave) mannhaft (geh.)

'**man-made** *adj.* künstlich ‹*See, Blumen, Schlucht*›; vom Menschen geschaffen ‹*Gesetze*›; (synthetic) Kunst‹*faser, -stoff*›

manned /mænd/ *adj.* bemannt ‹*Raumschiff usw.*›

mannequin /ˈmænɪkɪn/ *n.* (person) Mannequin, *das*

manner /ˈmænə(r)/ *n.* (**a**) (way, fashion) Art, *die;* Weise, *die;* (more emphatic) Art und Weise, *die; in this* ∼: auf diese Art und Weise; **he acted in such a** ∼ **as to offend her** er benahm sich so, dass sie beleidigt war; **in a** ∼ **of speaking** mehr oder weniger; (**b**) *no pl.* (bearing) Art, *die;* (towards others) Auftreten, *das;* (**c**) *in pl.* (social behaviour) Manieren *Pl.;* Benehmen, *das;* **teach sb. some** ∼**s** jmdm. Manieren beibringen; **that's good** ∼**s** das gehört sich so; **that's bad** ∼**s** das gehört sich nicht; das macht man nicht; (**d**) (artistic style) Stil, *der;* (**e**) (type) **all** ∼ **of things** alles Mögliche; *see also* **means c**

mannered /ˈmænəd/ *adj.* (**a**) (showing mannerism) maniériert; (**b**) *in comb.* … -∼: mit … Manieren *nachgestellt;* **be well-**∼/**bad-**∼: gute/schlechte Manieren haben

mannerism /ˈmænərɪzm/ *n.* (**a**) (addiction to a manner) Manieriertheit, *die;* (**b**) (trick of style) Manierismus, *der;* (**c**) (in behaviour) Eigenart, *die*

manœuvre /məˈnu:və(r)/ (Brit.) **1** *n.* (**a**) (Mil., Navy) Manöver, *das;* **be/go on** ∼**s** im Manöver sein/ins Manöver ziehen *od.* rücken; (**b**) (deceptive movement, scheme; also of vehicle, aircraft) Manöver, *das;* **room for** ~ (fig.) Spielraum, *der.* **2** *v.t.* (a) (Mil., Navy) führen; dirigieren; (b) (bring by ~s) manövrieren; bugsieren (ugs.) ⟨*Sperriges*⟩; ~ **sb./oneself/ sth. into a good position** (fig.) jmdn./sich/etw. in eine gute Position manövrieren; (c) (manipulate) beeinflussen; ~ **sb. into doing sth.** jmdn. dazu bringen, etw. zu tun. **3** *v.i.* (a) (Mil., Navy) [ein] Manöver durchführen; (b) (move, scheme) manövrieren; **room to** ~: Platz zum Manövrieren; (fig.) Spielraum, *der*

manor /'mænə(r)/ *n.* (a) (land) [Land]gut, *das;* **lord/lady of the** ~: Gutsherr, *der*/Gutsherrin, *die;* (b) (house) Herrenhaus, *das*

'**manor house** ⇒ manor b

'**manpower** *n.* (a) (available power) Arbeitspotenzial, *das;* (workers) Arbeitskräfte *Pl.;* (b) (Mil.) Stärke, *die*

mansion /'mænʃn/ *n.* Villa, *die;* (of lord) Herrenhaus, *das*

man: ~**-size,** ~**-sized** *adj.* (suitable for a man) ⟨*Mahlzeit, Steak*⟩ für einen [ganzen] Mann; (large) groß; ~**slaughter** *n.* (Law) Totschlag, *der*

mantel /'mæntl/**:** ~**piece** *n.* (a) (above fireplace) Kaminsims, *der od. das;* (b) (around fireplace) Kamineinfassung, *die;* ~**shelf** ⇒ ~**piece a**

mantle /'mæntl/ *n.* (cloak) Umhang, *der;* (fig.) Mantel, *der;* ~ **of snow** Schneedecke, *die*

'**man-to-man** *adj.* von Mann zu Mann *nachgestellt*

manual /'mænjʊəl/ **1** *adj.* (a) manuell; ~ **worker/ labourer** Handarbeiter/Schwerarbeiter, *der;* (b) (not automatic) handbetrieben; ⟨*Bedienung, Kontrolle, Schaltung*⟩ von Hand. **2** *n.* (handbook) Handbuch, *das*

manually /'mænjʊəlɪ/ *adv.* manuell; von Hand; mit der Hand

manufacture /mænjʊ'fæktʃə(r)/ **1** *n.* Herstellung, *die;* **articles of foreign/British** ~: ausländische/britische Erzeugnisse. **2** *v.t.* (Commerc.) herstellen; ~**d goods** Fertigprodukte

manufacturer /mænjʊ'fæktʃərə(r)/ *n.* Hersteller, *der;* '~'s **recommended [retail] price'** „unverbindliche Preisempfehlung"

manure /mə'njʊə(r)/ **1** *n.* (dung) Dung, *der;* (fertilizer) Dünger, *der.* **2** *v.t.* düngen

manuscript /'mænjʊskrɪpt/ *n.* (a) Handschrift, *die;* (b) (not yet printed) Manuskript, *das*

many /'menɪ/ **1** *adj.* (a) viele; *pred.* zahlreich; **how** ~ **people/books?** wie viele *od.* wieviel Leute/Bücher?; **there were as** ~ **as 50 of them** es waren mindestens *od.* bestimmt 50; **three accidents in as** ~ **days** drei Unfälle in ebenso vielen *od.* ebenso viel Tagen; **there were too** ~ **of them** es waren zu viele *od.* zu viel; **one is too** ~/**there is one too** ~: einer/eine/eins ist zu viel; **he's had one too** ~ (is drunk) er hat einen *od.* ein Glas zu viel getrunken; (b) ~ **a man** so mancher; manch einer. **2** *n.* viele [Leute]; ~ **of us** viele von uns; **a good/great** ~ [**of them/of the books**] eine Menge/eine ganze Reihe [von ihnen/der Bücher]

Maoist /'maʊɪst/ *n.* Maoist, *der; attrib.* maoistisch

Maori /'maʊrɪ/ **1** *n.* (a) (person) Maori, *der;* (b) ► 897| (language) Maori, *das.* **2** *adj.* maorisch

map /mæp/ **1** *n.* (a) [Land]karte, *die;* (street plan) Stadtplan, *der;* (b) (fig. coll.) **off the** ~: abgelegen; **wipe off the** ~: ausradieren; [**put sth./sb.**] **on the** ~: [etw./jmdn.] populär [machen]. **2** *v.t.,* -**pp-** (make ~ of) kartographieren; (make survey of) vermessen ~ '**out** *v.t.* im einzelnen festlegen

maple /'meɪpl/ *n.* Ahorn, *der*

'**maple leaf** *n.* Ahornblatt, *das*

'**map-maker** *n.* Kartograph, *der*/Kartographin, *die*

mar /mɑː(r)/ *v.t.,* -**rr-** verderben; entstellen ⟨*Aussehen*⟩; stören ⟨*Veranstaltung*⟩

Mar. *abbr.* **March** Mrz.

marathon /'mærəθən/ *n.* (a) (race) Marathon[lauf], *der; attrib.* Marathon⟨*läufer*⟩; (b) (fig.) Marathon, *der; attrib.* Marathon⟨*rede, -spiel, -sitzung*⟩

marauder /mə'rɔːdə(r)/ *n.* Plünderer, *der;* Marodeur, *der* (Soldatenspr.); (animal) Räuber, *der*

marble /'mɑːbl/ *n.* (a) (stone) Marmor, *der* (auch fig.); *attrib.* Marmor-; aus Marmor *nachgestellt;* (b) (toy) Murmel, *die;* [**game of**] ~**s** Murmelspiel, *das;* **play** ~**s** murmeln; [mit] Murmeln spielen; (c) *in pl.* **not have all** *or* **have lost one's** ~**s** (coll.) nicht alle Tassen im Schrank haben (ugs.)

March /mɑːtʃ/ *n.* ► 738| März, *der; see also* **August;** **hare 1**

march 1 *n.* (a) (Mil., Mus.; hike) Marsch, *der;* (gait) Marschschritt, *der;* **on the** ~: auf dem Marsch; ~ **past** Vorbeimarsch, *der;* Defilee, *das;* (b) (in protest) [**protest**] ~: Protestmarsch, *der;* (c) (progress of time, events, etc.) Gang, *der.* **2** *v.i.* (also Mil.) marschieren; (fig.) fortschreiten; **forward/quick** ~**!** vorwärts/im Eilschritt marsch!; ~**ing orders** Marschbefehl, *der;* **give sb. his/her** ~**ing orders** (fig. coll.) jmdn. den Laufpass geben (ugs.) ~ '**off 1** *v.i.* losmarschieren. **2** *v.t.* ⟨*Polizei usw.*⟩ abführen

marcher /'mɑːtʃə(r)/ *n.* [**protest**] ~: Demonstrant, *der*/ Demonstrantin, *die*

marchioness /mɑː.ʃə'nes/ *n.* Marquise, *die*

mare /meə(r)/ *n.* Stute, *die; see also* **shank**

margarine /mɑːdʒə'riːn, mɑːgə'riːn/, (coll.) **marge** /mɑːdʒ/ *ns.* Margarine, *die*

margin /'mɑːdʒɪn/ *n.* (a) (of page) Rand, *der;* **notes [written] in the** ~: Randbemerkungen; (b) (extra amount) Spielraum, *der;* **profit** ~: Gewinnspanne, *die;* **win by a narrow/wide** ~: knapp/mit großem Vorsprung gewinnen; ~ **of error** Spielraum für mögliche Fehler; (c) (edge) Rand, *der;* Saum, *der* (geh.)

marginal /'mɑːdʒɪnl/ *adj.* (a) (barely adequate, slight) geringfügig; unwesentlich; (b) (close to limit) marginal; (barely profitable) kaum rentabel; (c) knapp ⟨*Wahlergebnis*⟩; ~ **seat/ constituency** (Brit. Polit.) wackeliger (ugs.) *od.* nur mit knapper Mehrheit gehaltener Parlamentssitz/Wahlkreis; (d) (of or at the edge) Rand⟨*gebiet, -bereich usw.*⟩

marigold /'mærɪgəʊld/ *n.* Studentenblume, *die*

marijuana (marihuana) /mærɪ'hwɑːnə/ *n.* Marihuana, *das; attrib.* Marihuana⟨*zigarette*⟩

marina /mə'riːnə/ *n.* Marina, *die;* Jachthafen, *der*

marinade /mærɪ'neɪd/ **1** *n.* Marinade, *die.* **2** *v.t.* marinieren

marine /mə'riːn/ **1** *adj.* (a) (of the sea) Meeres-; (b) (of shipping) See⟨*versicherung, -recht usw.*⟩; (c) (for use at sea) Schiffs⟨*ausrüstung, -chronometer, -kessel, -turbine usw.*⟩. **2** *n.* (person) Marineinfanterist, *der;* **the M**~**s** die Marineinfanterie; die Marinetruppen; **tell that/it to the [horse]** ~**s** (coll.) das kannst du deiner Großmutter erzählen (ugs.)

mariner /'mærɪnə(r)/ *n.* Seemann, *der*

marionette /mærɪə'net/ *n.* Marionette, *die*

marital /'mærɪtl/ *adj.* ehelich ⟨*Rechte, Pflichten, Harmonie*⟩; Ehe⟨*beratung, -glück, -krach, -krise, -problem*⟩; ~ **status** Familienstand, *der*

maritime /'mærɪtaɪm/ *adj.* (a) (found near the sea) Küsten⟨*bewohner, -gebiet, -stadt, -provinz*⟩; (b) (connected with the sea) See⟨*recht, -versicherung, -volk, -wesen*⟩

marjoram /'mɑːdʒərəm/ *n.* (Bot., Cookery) Majoran, *der*

mark¹ /mɑːk/ **1** *n.* (a) (trace) Spur, *die;* (of finger, foot also) Abdruck, *der;* (stain etc.) Fleck, *der;* (scratch) Kratzer, *der;* **dirty** ~: Schmutzfleck, *der;* **leave one's/its** ~ **on sth.** (fig.) einer Sache (*Dat.*) seinen Stempel aufdrücken; **make one's/its** ~ (fig.) sich (*Dat.*) einen Namen machen; (b) (affixed sign, indication, symbol) Zeichen, *das;* (in trade names) Typ, *der* (Technik); **distinguishing** ~: Kennzeichen, *das;* **M**~ **2 version/model** Version/Modell 2; **have all the** ~**s of sth.** alle Anzeichen von etw. haben; **be a** ~ **of good taste/breeding** ein Zeichen guten Geschmacks/guter Erziehung sein; **sth. is the** ~ **of a good writer** an etw. (*Dat.*) erkennt man einen guten Schriftsteller; (c) (Sch.: grade) Zensur, *die;* Note, *die;* (Sch., Sport: unit of numerical award) Punkt, *der;* **get good/bad/35** ~**s in** *or* **for a subject** gute/schlechte Noten *od.* Zensuren/35 Punkte in einem Fach bekommen; (d) (line to indicate position) Markierung, *die;* (e.g. level) Marke, *die;* **reach the 15%** ~: die 15%- Marke erreichen; **around the 300** ~: ungefähr 300; (f) (Sport: starting position) Startlinie, *die;* **on your** ~**s!** [**get set! go!**] auf die Plätze! [Fertig! Los!]; **be quick/slow off the**

~: einen guten/schlechten Start haben; (fig.) fix (ugs.)/langsam sein; (**g**) (target, desired object) Ziel, *das;* **hit the ~** (fig.) ins Schwarze treffen; **be wide of the ~** (lit. or fig.) danebentreffen; **be close to the ~** (fig.) der Sache nahe kommen. **2** *v.t.* (**a**) (stain, dirty) Flecke[n] machen auf (+ *Dat.*); schmutzig machen; (scratch) zerkratzen; (**b**) (put distinguishing ~ on, signal) kennzeichnen, markieren (**with** mit); **the bottle was ~ed 'poison'** die Flasche trug die Aufschrift „Gift"; **~ an item with its price** eine Ware auszeichnen *od.* mit einem Preisschild versehen; **ceremonies to ~ the tenth anniversary** Feierlichkeiten aus Anlass des 10. Jahrestages; (**c**) (Sch.) (correct) korrigieren; (grade) benoten; zensieren; **~ an answer wrong** eine Antwort als falsch bewerten; (**d**) **~ time** (Mil.; also fig.) auf der Stelle treten; (**e**) (characterize) kennzeichnen; charakterisieren; (**f**) (heed) hören auf (+ *Akk.*) ⟨*Person, Wort*⟩; **[you] ~ my words** höre auf mich; eins kann ich dir sagen; (as a warning) lass dir das gesagt sein; (**g**) (Brit. Sport: keep close to) markieren (fachspr.), decken ⟨*Gegenspieler*⟩

~ 'down *v.t.* (**a**) (choose as victim, lit. or fig.) [sich (*Dat.*)] auswählen; ausersehen (geh.); (**b**) [im Preis] herabsetzen ⟨*Ware*⟩; herabsetzen ⟨*Preis*⟩

~ 'off *v.t.* abgrenzen (**from** von, gegen)

~ 'out *v.t.* (**a**) (trace out boundaries of) markieren ⟨*Spielfeld*⟩; (**b**) (destine) vorsehen; ⟨*Schicksal:*⟩ bestimmen, ausersehen

~ 'up *v.t.* [im Preis] heraufsetzen ⟨*Ware*⟩; heraufsetzen ⟨*Preis*⟩

mark² *n.* ▶ 938⌉ (monetary unit) Mark, *die*

marked /mɑːkt/ *adj.* (**a**) (noticeable) deutlich ⟨*Gegensatz, Unterschied, [Ver]besserung, Veränderung*⟩; ausgeprägt ⟨*Akzent, Merkmal, Neigung*⟩; (**b**) **be a ~ man** auf der schwarzen Liste stehen (ugs.)

markedly /'mɑːkɪdlɪ/ *adv.* eindeutig; deutlich

marker /'mɑːkə(r)/ *n.* Markierung, *die*

'marker pen *n.* Markierstift, *der*

market /'mɑːkɪt/ **1** *n.* (**a**) Markt, *der; attrib.* Markt⟨*händler, -stand*⟩; **at the ~:** auf dem Markt; **go to ~:** auf den Markt gehen; (**b**) (demand) Markt, *der;* (area of demand) Absatzmarkt, *der;* (persons) Abnehmer *Pl.;* (**c**) (conditions for buying and selling, trade) Markt, *der;* **be in the ~ for sth.** an etw. (*Dat.*) interessiert sein; **come on to the ~** ⟨*neue Produkte:*⟩ auf den Markt kommen; **put on the ~:** zum Verkauf anbieten ⟨*Haus*⟩. **2** *v.t.* vermarkten

market: **~ 'forces** *n. pl.* Kräfte *Pl.* des freien Marktes; **~ 'garden** *n.* (Brit.) Gartenbaubetrieb, *der;* **~ gardener** *n.* ▶ 887⌉ (Brit.) Gemüseanbauer, *der/*-anbauerin, *die*

marketing /'mɑːkɪtɪŋ/ *n.* (Econ.) Marketing, *das; attrib.* Marketing-

market: **~ 'leader** *n.* (company, brand) Marktführer, *der;* (product) meistverkauftes Produkt; **the company is the ~ leader in its field** die Firma ist marktführend auf ihrem Gebiet; **~ place** *n.* Marktplatz, *der;* (fig.) Markt, *der;* **~ 'research** *n.* Marktforschung, *die*

marking /'mɑːkɪŋ/ *n.* (**a**) (identification symbol) Markierung, *die;* Kennzeichen, *das;* (**b**) (on animal) Zeichnung, *die;* (**c**) (Sch.) (correcting) Korrektur, *die;* (grading) Benotung, *die;* Zensieren, *das*

'marking ink *n.* Wäschetinte, *die*

marksman /'mɑːksmən/ *n., pl.* **marksmen** /'mɑːksmən/ Scharfschütze, *der*

marksmanship /'mɑːksmənʃɪp/ *n., no pl.* Treffsicherheit, *die*

'mark-up *n.* (Commerc.) (**a**) (price increase) Preiserhöhung, *die;* (**b**) (amount added) Handelsspanne, *die* (Kaufmannsspr.)

marmalade /'mɑːməleɪd/ *n.* **[orange] ~:** Orangenmarmelade, *die;* **tangerine/lime ~:** Mandarinen-/Limonenmarmelade, *die*

maroon¹ /mə'ruːn/ **1** *adj.* kastanienbraun. **2** *n.* Kastanienbraun, *das*

maroon² *v.t.* (**a**) (Naut.: put ashore) aussetzen; (**b**) ⟨*Flut, Hochwasser:*⟩ von der Außenwelt abschneiden

marque /mɑːk/ *n.* Marke, *die;* (of cars also) Fabrikat, *das*

marquee /mɑː'kiː/ *n.* großes Zelt; (for public entertainment) Festzelt, *das*

marquess, marquis /'mɑːkwɪs/ *n.* Marquis, *der*

marriage /'mærɪdʒ/ *n.* (**a**) Ehe, *die* (**to** mit); **proposal** *or* **offer of ~:** Heiratsantrag, *der;* **related by ~:** verschwägert; **uncle/cousin by ~:** angeheirateter Onkel/Cousin; (**b**) (wedding) Hochzeit, *die;* (act of marrying) Heirat, *die;* (ceremony) Trauung, *die;* **~ ceremony** Trauzeremonie, *die;* Eheschließung, *die*

marriage: **~ bureau** *n.* Eheanbahnungs- *od.* Ehevermittlungsinstitut, *das;* **~ certificate** *n.* Trauschein, *der;* **~ 'guidance** *n.* Eheberatung, *die;* **~ vows** *n. pl.* Ehegelöbnis, *das* (geh.)

married /'mærɪd/ **1** *adj.* (**a**) verheiratet; **~ couple** Ehepaar, *das;* (**b**) (marital) ehelich ⟨*Leben, Liebe*⟩; Ehe⟨*leben, -name, -stand*⟩; **~ quarters** Verheiratetenquartiere *Pl.* **2** *n.* **young/newly ~s** Jungverheiratete *Pl.*

marrow /'mærəʊ/ *n.* (**a**) [vegetable] ~: Speisekürbis, *der;* (**b**) (Anat.) [Knochen]mark, *das;* **to the ~** (fig.) durch und durch; **be chilled to the ~** (fig.) völlig durchgefroren sein

marry /'mærɪ/ **1** *v.t.* (**a**) (take in marriage) heiraten; (**b**) (join in marriage) trauen; **they were** *or* **got married last summer** sie haben letzten Sommer geheiratet; (**c**) (give in marriage) verheiraten ⟨*Kind*⟩ (**to** mit); (**d**) (fig.: unite intimately) verquicken; eng miteinander verbinden. **2** *v.i.* heiraten; **~ into a [rich] family** in eine [reiche] Familie einheiraten

~ 'off *v.t.* verheiraten ⟨*Tochter*⟩ (**to** mit)

Mars /mɑːz/ *pr. n.* (**a**) (Astron.) Mars, *der;* (**b**) (Roman Mythol.) Mars (*der*)

marsh /mɑːʃ/ *n.* Sumpf, *der*

marshal /'mɑːʃl/ **1** *n.* (**a**) (officer of state) [Hof]marschall, *der;* (**b**) (officer in army) Marschall, *der;* (**c**) (Sport) Ordner, *der.* **2** *v.t.,* (Brit.) **-ll-** (arrange in order) aufstellen ⟨*Truppen*⟩; sich (*Dat.*) zurechtlegen ⟨*Argumente*⟩; ordnen ⟨*Fakten*⟩

'marshalling yard *n.* /'mɑːʃəlɪŋ jɑːd/ *n.* (Railw.) Rangierbahnhof, *der*

marsh: **~land** /'mɑːʃlənd/ *n.* Sumpfland, *das;* **~ mallow** /'mɑːʃ mæləʊ/ *n.* (**a**) (Bot.) Eibisch, *der;* (**b**) (confection) Marshmallow, *das;* süßer Speck; **~'mallow** *n.* (sweet) ≈ Mohrenkopf, *der*

marshy /'mɑːʃɪ/ *adj.* sumpfig; Sumpf⟨*boden, -gebiet, -land*⟩

marsupial /mɑː'sjuːpɪəl, mɑː'suːpɪəl/ (Zool.) **1** *adj.* Beutel⟨*tier, -frosch, -mulle*⟩. **2** *n.* Beuteltier, *das*

martial /'mɑːʃl/ *adj.* kriegerisch; *see also* **court martial**

martial: **~ 'arts** *n. pl.* (Sport) Kampfsportarten; **~ 'law** *n.* Kriegsrecht, *das*

martin /'mɑːtɪn/ *n.* (Ornith.) **[house-]~:** Mehlschwalbe, *die*

martyr /'mɑːtə(r)/ **1** *n.* (Relig.; also fig.) Märtyrer, *der/*Märtyrerin, *die;* **be a ~ to rheumatism** entsetzlich unter Rheumatismus leiden; **make a ~ of oneself** den Märtyrer/die Märtyrerin spielen. **2** *v.t.* (**a**) den Märtyrertod sterben lassen; **be ~ed** den Märtyrertod sterben; (**b**) (fig.: torment) martern (geh.)

martyrdom /'mɑːtədəm/ *n.* Martyrium, *das*

marvel /'mɑːvl/ **1** *n.* Wunder, *das; work* **~s** Wunder wirken; **be a ~ of patience** eine sagenhafte Geduld haben (ugs.). **2** *v.i.,* (Brit.) **-ll-** (literary) **~ at sth.** über etw. (*Akk.*) staunen

marvellous /'mɑːvələs/ *adj.,* **marvellously** /'mɑːvələslɪ/ *adv.* wunderbar

marvelous, marvelously (Amer.) ⇒ **marvell-**

Marxism /'mɑːksɪzm/ *n.* Marxismus, *der*

Marxist /'mɑːksɪst/ **1** *n.* Marxist, *der/*Marxistin, *die.* **2** *adj.* marxistisch

marzipan /'mɑːzɪpæn/ *n.* Marzipan, *das*

mascara /mæ'skɑːrə/ *n.* Mascara, *das*

mascot /'mæskɒt/ *n.* Maskottchen, *das*

masculine /'mæskjʊlɪn/ *adj.* (**a**) (of men) männlich; (**b**) (manly, manlike) maskulin; (**c**) (Ling.) männlich; maskulin (fachspr.)

masculinity /mæskjʊ'lɪnɪtɪ/ *n., no pl.* Männlichkeit, *die*

mash /mæʃ/ **1** *n.* (**a**) Brei, *der;* (**b**) (Brit. coll.: **~ed potatoes**) Kartoffelbrei, *der.* **2** *v.t.* zerdrücken; zerquetschen; **~ed potatoes** Kartoffelbrei, *der*

mask /mɑːsk/ **1** *n.* (also fig., Photog.) Maske, *die;* (worn by surgeon) Gesichtsmaske, *die;* Mundschutz, *der.* **2** *v.t.* **(a)** (cover with ⁓) maskieren; **(b)** (fig.: disguise, conceal) maskieren; ⟨*Wolken, Bäume:*⟩ verdecken; überdecken ⟨*Geschmack*⟩

'masking tape /'mɑːskɪŋ teɪp/ *n.* Abklebeband, *das*

masochism /'mæsəkɪzm/ *n.* Masochismus, *der*

masochist /'mæsəkɪst/ *n.* Masochist, *der*/Masochistin, *die*

masochistic /mæsə'kɪstɪk/ *adj.* masochistisch

mason /'meɪsn/ *n.* **(a)** ▶887⟩ (builder) Baumeister, *der;* Steinmetz, *der;* **(b)** M⁓ (Freemason) [Frei]maurer, *der*

masonry /'meɪsnrɪ/ *n.* **(a)** (stonework) Mauerwerk, *das;* **(b)** M⁓ (of Freemasons) [Frei]maurertum, *das*

masquerade /mæskə'reɪd, mɑːskə'reɪd/ **1** *n.* (lit. or fig.) Maskerade, *die.* **2** *v.i.* ⁓ **as sb./sth.** sich als jmd./etw. ausgeben

mass[1] /mæs/ *n.* (Eccl.) Messe, *die;* **say/hear** ⁓: die Messe lesen/hören; **go to** *or* **attend** ⁓: zur Messe gehen

mass[2] **1** *n.* **(a)** (solid body of matter) Brocken, *der;* (of dough, rubber) Klumpen, *der;* **(b)** (dense aggregation of objects) Masse, *die;* **a tangled** ⁓ **of threads** ein wirres Knäuel von Fäden; **(c)** (large number or amount of) **a** ⁓ **of …:** eine Unmenge von …; ⁓**es of …:** massenhaft … (ugs.); eine Masse … (ugs.); **(d)** (unbroken expanse) **a** ⁓ **of red** ein Meer von Rot; **be a** ⁓ **of bruises/mistakes** (coll.) voll blauer Flecken sein/von Fehlern nur so wimmeln; **(e)** (main portion) Masse, *die;* **the** ⁓**es** die breite Masse; die Massen; **(f)** (Phys.) Masse, *die;* **(g)** *attrib.* (for many people) Massen-. **2** *v.t.* **(a)** anhäufen; **(b)** (Mil.) massieren, zusammenziehen ⟨*Truppen*⟩. **3** *v.i.* sich ansammeln; ⟨*Truppen:*⟩ sich massieren, sich zusammenziehen; ⟨*Wolken:*⟩ sich zusammenziehen

massacre /'mæsəkə(r)/ **1** *n.* **(a)** (slaughter) Massaker, *das;* **(b)** (coll.: defeat) völlige Zerstörung. **2** *v.t.* massakrieren

massage /'mæsɑːʒ/ **1** *n.* Massage, *die;* ⁓ **parlour** (often euphem.) Massagesalon, *der.* **2** *v.t.* massieren

mass communi'cations *n. pl.* Massenkommunikation, *die*

masseur /mæ'sɜː(r)/ *n.* Masseur, *der*

masseuse /mæ'sɜːz/ *n.* Masseurin, *die;* Masseuse, *die* (oft verhüll.)

massive /'mæsɪv/ *adj.* (lit. or fig.) massiv; wuchtig ⟨*Statur, Stirn*⟩; gewaltig ⟨*Ausmaße, Aufgabe*⟩; enorm ⟨*Schulden, Vermögen*⟩

mass: ⁓ **market** *n.* Massenmarkt, *der;* ⁓**-market** *attrib. adj.* für den Massenmarkt *nachgestellt;* ⁓ **'media** *n. pl.* Massenmedien *Pl.;* ⁓ **'meeting** *n.* Massenversammlung, *die;* (Pol.) Massenkundgebung, *die;* (Industry) Belegschaftsversammlung, *die;* ⁓ **'murder** *n.* Massenmord, *der;* ⁓ **'murderer** *n.* Massenmörder, *der*/-mörderin, *die;* ⁓**-pro'duced** *adj.* serienmäßig produziert *od.* hergestellt; Massen⟨*artikel*⟩; ⁓ **pro'duction** *n.* Massenproduktion, *die*

mast /mɑːst/ *n.* (for sail, flag, aerial, etc.) Mast, *der;* **work** *or* **serve** *or* **sail before the** ⁓: als Matrose dienen

master /'mɑːstə(r)/ **1** *n.* **(a)** Herr, *der;* **be** ⁓ **of the situation/[the]** ⁓ **of one's fate** Herr der Lage/seines Schicksals sein; **be one's own** ⁓: sein eigener Herr sein; **(b)** (of animal, slave) Halter, *der;* (of dog) Herrchen, *das;* (of ship) Kapitän, *der;* **be** ⁓ **in one's own house** Herr im eigenen Hause sein; **(c)** (Sch.: teacher) Lehrer, *der;* **'French** ⁓: Französischlehrer, *der;* **(d)** (original of document, film, etc.) Original, *das;* **(e)** (expert, great artist) Meister, *der* (**at** in + *Dat.*); **be a** ⁓ **of sth.** etw. meisterhaft beherrschen; **(f)** (skilled workman) ⁓ **craftsman/carpenter** Handwerks-/Tischlermeister, *der;* **(g)** (Univ.) Magister, *der;* ⁓ **of Arts/Science** Magister Artium/rerum naturalium. **2** *adj.* Haupt⟨*strategie, -liste*⟩; ⁓ **bedroom** großes Schlafzimmer; ⁓ **tape/copy** Originalband, *das*/Original, *das;* ⁓ **plan** Gesamtplan, *der.* **3** *v.t.* **(a)** (learn) erlernen; **have** ⁓**ed a language/subject** eine Sprache/ein Fach beherrschen; **(b)** (overcome) meistern ⟨*Probleme usw.*⟩; besiegen ⟨*Feind*⟩; zügeln ⟨*Emotionen, Gefühle*⟩

masterful /'mɑːstəfl/ *adj.* **(a)** (imperious) herrisch ⟨*Haltung, Ton, Person*⟩; **(b)** (masterly) meisterhaft ⟨*Beherrschung, Fähigkeit*⟩

'master key *n.* General- *od.* Hauptschlüssel, *der*

masterly /'mɑːstəlɪ/ *adj.* meisterhaft

master: ⁓**mind 1** *n.* führender Kopf; **2** *v.t.* ⁓**mind the plot/conspiracy** *etc.* der Kopf des Komplotts/der Verschwörung *usw.* sein; ⁓**piece** *n.* (work of art) Meisterwerk, *das;* (production showing masterly skill) Meisterstück, *das;* ⁓ **stroke** *n.* Geniestreich, *der;* **be a** ⁓ **stroke** genial sein; ⁓ **switch** *n.* Hauptschalter, *der*

mastery /'mɑːstərɪ/ *n.* **(a)** (skill) Meisterschaft, *die;* **(b)** (knowledge) Beherrschung, *die* (**of** *Gen.*); **(c)** (upper hand) Oberhand, *die;* **(d)** (control) Herrschaft, *die* (**of** über + *Akk.*)

masticate /'mæstɪkeɪt/ *v.t.* zerkauen

mastiff /'mæstɪf/ *n.* (Zool.) Mastiff, *der*

masturbate /'mæstəbeɪt/ *v.i. & t.* masturbieren

masturbation /mæstə'beɪʃn/ *n.* Masturbation, *die*

mat /mæt/ *n.* **(a)** (on floor, Sport) Matte, *die;* **pull the** ⁓ **from under sb.'s feet** (fig.) jmdm. den Boden unter den Füßen wegziehen; **(b)** (to protect table etc.) Untersetzer, *der;* (as decorative support) Deckchen, *das*

match[1] /mætʃ/ **1** *n.* **(a)** (equal) Ebenbürtige, *der/die;* **be no** ⁓ **for sb.** sich mit jmdm. nicht messen können; **she is more than a** ⁓ **for him** sie ist ihm mehr als gewachsen; **find** *or* **meet one's** ⁓ (be defeated) seinen Meister finden; **(b)** (sb./sth. similar or appropriate) **be a [good** *etc.***]** ⁓ **for sth.** [gut *usw.*] zu etw. passen; **(c)** (Sport) Spiel, *das;* (Football, Tennis, etc. also) Match, *das;* (Boxing) Kampf, *der;* (Athletics) Wettkampf, *der;* **(d)** (marriage) Heirat, *die;* **make a good** ⁓: eine gute Partie machen. **2** *v.t.* **(a)** (equal) ⁓ **sb. at chess/in originality** es mit jmdm. im Schach/an Originalität (*Dat.*) aufnehmen [können]; **(b)** (pit) ⁓ **sb. with** *or* **against sb.** jmdn. jmdm. gegenüberstellen; **be** ⁓**ed against sb.** gegen jmdn. antreten; **(c)** **be well** ⁓**ed** ⟨*Mann u. Frau:*⟩ gut zusammenpassen; ⟨*Spieler, Mannschaften:*⟩ sich (*Dat.*) ebenbürtig sein; **(d)** (harmonize with) passen zu; ⁓ **each other exactly** genau zueinander passen. **3** *v.i.* (correspond) zusammenpassen; **with a scarf** *etc.* **to** ⁓: mit [dazu] passendem Schal *usw.*
⁓ **'up 1** *v.i.* **(a)** (correspond) zusammenpassen; **(b)** (be equal) ⁓ **up to sth.** einer Sache (*Dat.*) entsprechen. **2** *v.t.* aufeinander abstimmen ⟨*Farben usw.*⟩; passend zusammenfügen ⟨*Teile, Hälften*⟩

match[2] *n.* (for lighting) Streichholz, *das;* Zündholz, *das* (südd., österr.)

match: ⁓**box** *n.* Streichholzschachtel, *die;* ⁓**maker** *n.* Ehestifter, *der*/Ehestifterin, *die;* ⁓ **point** *n.* (Tennis etc.) Matchball, *der;* ⁓**stick** *n.* Streichholz, *das;* Zündholz, *das* (südd., österr.); ⁓**wood** *n.* **make** ⁓**wood of sth.**, **smash sth. to** ⁓**wood** Kleinholz aus etw. machen

mate[1] /meɪt/ **1** *n.* **(a)** Kumpel, *der* (ugs.); (friend also) Kamerad, *der*/Kameradin, *die;* **(b)** (Naut.: officer on merchant ship) ≈ Kapitänleutnant, *der;* **chief** *or* **first/second** ⁓: Erster/Zweiter Offizier; **(c)** (workman's assistant) Gehilfe, *der;* **(d)** (Zool.) (male) Männchen, *das;* (female) Weibchen, *das.* **2** *v.i.* (for breeding) sich paaren. **3** *v.t.* paaren ⟨*Tiere*⟩; ⁓ **a mare and** *or* **with a stallion** eine Stute von einem Hengst decken lassen

mate[2] (Chess) ⇨ **checkmate**

material /mə'tɪərɪəl/ **1** *adj.* **(a)** (physical) materiell; **(b)** (not spiritual) materiell (oft abwertend) ⟨*Person, Einstellung*⟩; **(c)** (relevant, important) wesentlich. **2** *n.* **(a)** (matter from which thing is made) Material, *das;* **(b)** *in sing. or pl.* (elements) Material, *das;* (for novel, sermon also) Stoff, *der;* **(c)** (cloth) Stoff, *der;* **(d)** *in pl.* **building/writing** ⁓**s** Bau-/Schreibmaterial, *das*

materialise ⇨ **materialize**

materialism /mə'tɪərɪəlɪzm/ *n., no pl.* Materialismus, *der*

materialistic /mətɪərɪə'lɪstɪk/ *adj.* materialistisch

materialize /mə'tɪərɪəlaɪz/ *v.i. & t.* **a)** ⟨*Hoffnung:*⟩ sich erfüllen; ⟨*Plan, Idee:*⟩ sich verwirklichen; ⟨*Treffen, Versammlung:*⟩ zustande kommen; **(b)** (come into view, appear) [plötzlich] auftauchen

maternal /mə'tɜːnl/ adj. **(a)** (motherly) mütterlich ‹Liebe, Sorge, Typ›; Mutter‹instinkt›; **(b)** (related) ‹Großeltern, Onkel, Tante› mütterlicherseits

maternity /mə'tɜːnɪtɪ/ n. (motherhood) Mutterschaft, die

maternity: ~ **allowance** n. Mutterschaftshilfe, die; ~ **benefit** n. Mutterschaftsgeld, das; ~ **dress** n. Umstandskleid, das; ~ **home**, ~ **hospital** ns. Entbindungsheim, das; ~ **leave** n. Mutterschaftsurlaub, der; ~ **pay** n. Mutterschaftsgeld, das; ~ **unit**, ~ **ward** ns. Entbindungsstation, die; ~ **wear** n. Umstandskleidung, die

matey /'meɪtɪ/ (Brit. coll.) adj., **matier** /'meɪtɪə(r)/, **matiest** /'meɪtɪɪst/ kameradschaftlich ‹Typ, Atmosphäre›

math /mæθ/ (Amer. coll.) ⇒ **maths**

mathematical /mæθɪ'mætɪkl/ adj. mathematisch

mathematician /mæθɪmə'tɪʃn/ n. ▶ 887 Mathematiker, der/Mathematikerin, die

mathematics /mæθɪ'mætɪks/ n., no pl. Mathematik, die; **pure/applied** ~: reine/angewandte Mathematik

maths /mæθs/ n. (Brit. coll.) Mathe, die (Schülerspr.)

matinée (Amer.: **matinee**) /'mætɪneɪ/ n. Matinee, die; Frühvorstellung, die; (in the afternoon) Nachmittagsvorstellung, die

matrices pl. of **matrix**

matriculate /mə'trɪkjʊleɪt/ (Univ.) **1** v.t. immatrikulieren (**in** an + Dat.). **2** v.i. sich immatrikulieren

matrimonial /mætrɪ'məʊnɪəl/ adj. Ehe-

matrimony /'mætrɪmənɪ/ n. **(a)** (marriage rite) Eheschließung, die; **(b)** (married state) Ehestand, der; **enter into** [holy] ~: in den [heiligen] Stand der Ehe treten (geh.)

matrix /'meɪtrɪks, 'mætrɪks/ n., pl. **matrices** /'meɪtrɪsiːz, 'mætrɪsiːz/ or ~es (Math., Geol.) Matrix, die

matron /'meɪtrən/ n. ▶ 887 (in school) ≈ Hausmutter, die; (in hospital) Oberin, die; Oberschwester, die

matt /mæt/ adj. matt

matted /'mætɪd/ adj. verfilzt

matter /'mætə(r)/ **1** n. **(a)** (affair) Angelegenheit, die; ~s die Dinge; **money** ~s Geldangelegenheiten od. -fragen; **raise an important** ~: einen wichtigen Punkt ansprechen; **that's another** or **a different** ~ **altogether** or **quite another** ~: das ist etwas ganz anderes; **and to make** ~s **worse** …: und was die Sache noch schlimmer macht/machte, …; **(b)** (cause, occasion) **a/no** ~ **for** or **of** …: ein/kein Grund od. Anlass zu …; **it's a** ~ **of complete indifference to me** es ist mir völlig gleichgültig; **(c)** (topic) Thema, das; Gegenstand, der; ~ **on the agenda** Punkt der Tagesordnung; **(d) a** ~ **of** … (something that amounts to) eine Frage (+ Gen.) …; eine Sache von …; **it's a** ~ **of taste/habit** das ist Geschmack- / Gewohnheitssache; **[only] a** ~ **of time** [nur noch] eine Frage der Zeit; **it's just a** ~ **of working harder** man muss sich ganz einfach [bei der Arbeit] mehr anstrengen; **in a** ~ **of minutes** in wenigen Minuten; **Do you know him?** — **Yes, as a** ~ **of fact, I do** Kennst du ihn? — Ja, ich kenne ihn tatsächlich; **(e) what's the** ~? was ist [los]?; **is something the** ~? stimmt irgendetwas nicht?; **is** [irgend]was (ugs.) ?; **(f) for that** ~: eigentlich; **(g) no** ~! [das] macht nichts!; **no** ~ **how/who/what/why** etc. ganz gleich od. egal (ugs.), wie/wer/was/warum usw.; **(h)** (material, as opposed to mind, spirit, etc.) Materie, die; **[in]organic/solid/vegetable** ~: [an]organische/feste/pflanzliche Stoffe. **2** v.i. etwas ausmachen; **what does it** ~? was macht das schon?; was macht's? (ugs.); **what** ~s **is that** …: worum es geht, ist …; **not** ~ **a damn** vollkommen egal sein; **[it] doesn't** ~: [das] macht nichts (ugs.); **it doesn't** ~ **how/when** etc. es ist einerlei, wie/wann usw.; **does it** ~ **to you if** …? macht es dir etwas aus, wenn …?; **the things which** ~ **in life** [das,] worauf es im Leben ankommt

matter-of-fact adj. sachlich; nüchtern

matting /'mætɪŋ/ n. **coconut/straw/reed** ~: Kokos-/ Stroh-/Schilfmatten

mattress /'mætrɪs/ n. Matratze, die

mature /mə'tjʊə(r)/ **1** adj., ~**r** /mə'tjʊərə(r)/, ~**st** /mə'tjʊərɪst/ reif; ausgereift ‹Plan, Methode, Stil, Käse›; durchgegoren ‹Wein›; ausgewachsen ‹Pflanze, Tier›; voll-

entwickelt ‹Zellen›; ~ **student** Spätstudierende, der/die. **2** v.t. reifen lassen ‹Frucht, Wein, Käse›. **3** v.i. **(a)** ‹Frucht, Wein, Käse usw.› reifen; **(b)** ‹Person:› reifen, reifer werden

maturity /mə'tjʊərɪtɪ/ n. Reife, die; **reach** ~, **come to** ~ ‹Person:› erwachsen werden; ‹Tier:› ausgewachsen sein

maudlin /'mɔːdlɪn/ adj. gefühlsselig

maul /mɔːl/ v.t. **(a)** ‹Tiger, Löwe, Bär usw.:› Pranken-/Tatzenhiebe versetzen (+ Dat.); (fig.) malträtieren; verreißen ‹Theaterstück, Buch›; ‹Boxer:› losgehen auf (+ Akk.) ‹Gegner›; **(b)** (fondle roughly) betatschen (ugs.)

mausoleum /mɔːsə'liːəm/ n. Mausoleum, das

mauve /məʊv/ adj. mauve

maverick /'mævərɪk/ n. Einzelgänger, der/Einzelgängerin, die

mawkish /'mɔːkɪʃ/ adj. rührselig

max. abbr. **maximum** (adj.) max., (n.) Max.

maxim /'mæksɪm/ n. Maxime, die

maximize (**maximise**) /'mæksɪmaɪz/ v.t. maximieren

maximum /'mæksɪməm/ **1** n., pl. **maxima** /'mæksɪmə/ Maximum, das. **2** adj. maximal; Maximal-; ~ **security prison** Hochsicherheitsgefängnis, das; ~ **temperatures today around** 20° Höchsttemperaturen am Tage um 20°

'maximum-security attrib. adj. Hochsicherheits-‹[gefängnis]trakt›

May /meɪ/ n. ▶ 738 Mai, der; see also **August**

may v. aux., only in pres. **may**, neg. (coll.) **mayn't** /meɪnt/, past **might** /maɪt/, neg. (coll.) **mightn't** /'maɪtnt/ ▶ 926 **(a)** expr. possibility können; **it** ~ **be true** das kann stimmen; **they** ~ **be related** es kann sein, dass sie verwandt sind; **he** ~ **have missed his train** vielleicht hat er seinen Zug verpasst; **it** ~ or **might rain** es könnte regnen; **they might decide to stay** womöglich beschließen sie zu bleiben; **he might have been right** vielleicht hat er [ja] recht gehabt; **it's not so bad as it might have been** es hätte schlimmer kommen können; **that** ~ **well be** das ist durchaus möglich; **you** ~ **well say so** so das kann man wohl sagen; **we** ~ or **might as well go** wir könnten eigentlich ebenso gut [auch] gehen; (we are not achieving anything here) dann können wir ja gehen; **be that as it** ~: wie dem auch sei; **(b)** expr. permission dürfen; **you** ~ **go now** du kannst od. darfst jetzt gehen; **if I** ~ **say so** …: wenn ich das sagen darf, …; ~ or **might I be permitted to** …? (formal) gestatten Sie, dass …?; ~ or **might I ask** (iron.) …, wenn ich [mal] fragen darf?; **(c)** expr. wish mögen; ~ **the best man win!** auf dass der Beste gewinnt!; **(d)** expr. request **you might at least try** [it] du könntest es wenigstens versuchen; **(e)** used concessively **he** ~ **be slow but he's accurate** mag od. kann sein, dass er langsam ist, aber dafür ist er auch genau; **(f)** in clauses so that **I** ~/ **might do sth.** damit ich etw. tun kann; **I hope he** ~ **succeed** ich hoffe, es gelingt ihm; **come what** ~, **whatever** ~ **happen** geschehe was will; was auch geschieht

maybe /'meɪbiː, 'meɪbɪ/ adv. vielleicht

'May Day n. der Erste Mai

'Mayday n. (distress signal) Mayday

mayhem /'meɪhem/ n. Chaos, das; **cause** or **create** ~: ein Chaos verursachen od. hervorrufen

mayn't /meɪnt/ (coll.) = **may not**; ⇒ **may**

mayonnaise /meɪə'neɪz/ n. Mayonnaise, die

mayor /meə(r)/ n. ▶ 887 Bürgermeister, der; **Lord M**~ (Brit.) Lord Mayor, der; ≈ Oberbürgermeister, der

mayoress /'meərɪs/ n. ▶ 887 (woman mayor) Bürgermeisterin, die; (mayor's wife) [Ehe]frau des Bürgermeisters

'maypole n. Maibaum, der

maze /meɪz/ n. (lit. or fig.) Labyrinth, das

MB abbr. **megabyte** MB

MBA abbr. **Master of Business Administration** Diplom in Betriebswirtschaft

MBE abbr. (Brit.) **Member [of the Order] of the British Empire** Träger des Ordens des British Empire 5. Klasse

Mbyte abbr. **megabyte** Mbyte; MByte

MC abbr. **(a) Master of Ceremonies; (b)** (Brit.) **Military Cross** militärisches Verdienstkreuz

McCoy /mə'kɔɪ/ n. **the real** ~ (coll.) der/die/das Echte; (not a fake or replica) das Original

May/might

Possibility

Where *may* simply means *can,* **können** is used in German:

These flowers may be grown in any soil	= Diese Blumen kann man in jeder Art Erde pflanzen

But where *may* in English is used to express degrees of possibility and uncertainty, there are a number of possible translations in German:

She may come (it's possible)	= Es kann sein *or* Es ist möglich, dass sie kommt
She may come (and on the other hand she may not)	= Vielleicht kommt sie (und vielleicht auch nicht)
She may or might come (a more distant possibility)	= Sie könnte kommen
She may (well) come (= there's a good possibility)	= Es kann schon sein *or* Es ist schon möglich, dass sie kommt
She may yet come	= Sie kann immerhin noch kommen; Es ist immerhin möglich, dass sie noch kommt

With *may have,* the perfect tense is applied to the verb governed and not to the translation of *may:*

I may have seen him	= Es kann sein *or* Es ist möglich, dass ich ihn gesehen habe
The train may have been late	= Vielleicht hat der Zug Verspätung gehabt
I might have said it (but I don't remember)	= Es könnte sein, dass ich es gesagt habe (aber ich weiß es nicht mehr)
She might have come if she had known	= Sie wäre vielleicht gekommen, wenn sie es gewusst hätte

However, where *might* is **könnte,** *might have* is **hätte ... können:**

It might have been worse (= could have been)	= Es hätte schlimmer sein können
You might have told me	= Du hättest es mir doch sagen können

Permission

This can always be translated by **dürfen:**

May I have the next dance?	= Darf ich [um den nächsten Tanz] bitten?
You may not smoke	= Sie dürfen nicht rauchen
Dear Bertie (if I may)	= Lieber Bertie (wenn ich dich so nennen darf)

MD *abbr.* **Doctor of Medicine** Dr. med.; *see also* **B. Sc.**

me /mɪ, *stressed* miː/ *pron.* mich; *as indirect object* mir; **bigger than/as big as me** größer als/so groß wie ich; **silly ~:** ich Dussel! (salopp); **who, me?** wer, ich?; **not me** ich/mich/mir nicht; **it's me** ich bin's

ME *abbr.* (Med.) **myalgic encephalomyelitis**

mead /miːd/ *n.* (drink) Met, *der*

meadow /'medəʊ/ *n.* Wiese, *die;* **in the ~:** auf der Wiese

meagre (*Amer.:* **meager**) /'miːɡə(r)/ *adj.* spärlich; dürftig (auch fig.); **a ~ attendance** eine geringe Teilnehmerzahl

meal¹ /miːl/ *n.* Mahlzeit, *die;* **stay for a ~:** zum Essen bleiben; **go out for a ~:** essen gehen; **make a ~ of sth.** (fig.) eine große Sache aus etw. machen

meal² *n.* (ground grain) Schrot[mehl], *das*

meal: **~ ticket** *n.* Essen[s]marke, *die;* (fig. coll.) melkende Kuh (ugs.); **~time** *n.* Essenszeit, *die;* **at ~times** während des Essens; bei Tisch

mealy-mouthed /'miːlɪmaʊðd/ *adj.* (derog.) unaufrichtig

mean¹ /miːn/ *n.* Mittelweg, *der;* Mitte, *die;* **a happy ~:** der goldene Mittelweg

mean² *adj.* **(a)** (niggardly) schäbig (abwertend); **(b)** (ignoble) schäbig (abwertend), gemein ‹Person, Verhalten, Gesinnung›; **(c)** (shabby) schäbig (abwertend) ‹Haus, Wohngegend›; armselig ‹Verhältnisse›; **be no ~ athlete/feat** kein schlechter Sportler/keine schlechte Leistung sein

mean³ *v.t.* **~t** /ment/ **(a)** (have as one's purpose) beabsichtigen; **~ well by** *or* **to** *or* **towards sb.** es gut mit jmdm. meinen; **I ~t him no harm** ich wollte ihm nichts Böses; **what do you ~ by [saying] that?** was willst du damit sagen?; **I ~t it** *or* **it was ~t as a joke** das sollte ein Scherz sein; **~ to do sth.** etw. tun wollen; **I ~ to be obeyed** ich verlange, dass man mir gehorcht; **I ~t to write, but forgot** ich hatte [fest] vor zu schreiben, aber habe es [dann] vergessen; **do you ~ to say that ...?** willst du damit sagen, dass ...?; **(b)** (design, destine) **these plates are ~t to be used** diese Teller sind zum Gebrauch bestimmt *od.* sind da, um benutzt zu werden; **I ~t it to be a surprise for him** es sollte eine Überraschung für ihn sein; **they are ~t for each other** sie sind füreinander bestimmt; **I ~t you to read the letter** ich wollte,

dass du den Brief liest; **be ~t to do sth.** etw. tun sollen; **(c)** (intend to convey, refer to) meinen; **if you know** *or* **see what I ~:** du verstehst, was ich meine?; **I really ~ it, I ~ what I say** ich meine das ernst; es ist mir Ernst damit; **(d)** (signify, entail, matter) bedeuten; **the name ~s/the instructions ~ nothing to me** der Name sagt mir nichts/ich kann mit der Anleitung nichts anfangen

meander /mɪ'ændə(r)/ *v.i.* **(a)** ‹Fluss:› sich schlängeln *od.* winden; **(b)** ‹Person:› schlendern

meaning /'miːnɪŋ/ *n.* Bedeutung, *die;* (of text etc., life) Sinn, *der;* **this sentence has no ~:** dieser Satz ergibt keinen Sinn; **if you get my ~:** du verstehst, was ich meine?; **what's the ~ of this?** was hat [denn] das zu bedeuten?

meaningful /'miːnɪŋfl/ *adj.* sinntragend ‹Wort, Einheit›; (fig.) bedeutungsvoll ‹Blick, Ergebnis, Folgerung›; sinnvoll ‹Leben, Aufgabe, Arbeit, Gespräch›

meanness /'miːnnɪs/ *n., no pl.* **(a)** (stinginess) Schäbigkeit, *die* (abwertend); **(b)** (baseness) Schäbigkeit, *die* (abwertend); Gemeinheit, *die;* **(c)** (shabbiness) ⇒ **mean² c:** Schäbigkeit, *die;* Armseligkeit, *die*

means /miːnz/ *n. pl.* **(a)** *usu. constr. as sing.* (way, method) Möglichkeit, *die;* [Art und] Weise, *die;* **by this ~:** hierdurch; auf diese Weise; **a ~ to an end** ein Mittel zum Zweck; **we have no ~ of doing this** wir haben keine Möglichkeit, dies zu tun; **~ of transport** Transportmittel, *das;* **(b)** (resources) Mittel *Pl.;* **live within/beyond one's ~:** seinen Verhältnissen entsprechend/über seine Verhältnisse leben; **(c)** **Will you help me? — By all ~:** Hilfst du mir? Selbstverständlich!; **by no [manner of] ~:** ganz und gar nicht; keineswegs; **by ~ of** durch; mit [Hilfe von]

'means test *n.* Überprüfung der Bedürftigkeit

meant ⇒ **mean³**

mean: **~time 1** *n.* **in the ~time** in der Zwischenzeit; inzwischen; **2** *adv.* inzwischen; **~while** *adv.* inzwischen

measles /'miːzlz/ *n., constr. as pl. or sing.* ▶865 (Med.) Masern *Pl.; see also* **German measles**

measly /'miːzlɪ/ *adj.* (coll. derog.) pop[e]lig (ugs. abwertend); **a ~ little portion** eine mickrige Portion (ugs. abwertend)

measure /'meʒə(r)/ **1** *n.* **(a)** Maß, *das;* **weights and ~s** Maße und Gewichte; **for good ~:** sicherheitshalber; (as an extra) zusätzlich; **give short/full ~** (in public house) zu wenig/vorschriftsmäßig ausschenken; **made to ~** *pred.*

(Brit., lit. or fig.) maßgeschneidert; **(b)** (degree) Menge, *die;* **in some ~:** in gewisser Hinsicht; **a ~ of freedom/responsibility** ein gewisses Maß an Freiheit/Verantwortung *(Dat.);* **(c)** (instrument or utensil for measuring) Maß, *das;* (for quantity also) Messglas, *das;* Messbecher, *der;* (for size also) Messstab, *der;* (fig.) Maßstab, *der;* **it gave us some ~ of the problems** das gab uns eine Vorstellung von den Problemen; **beyond [all] ~:** grenzenlos; über die *od.* alle Maßen *adv.;* **(d)** (Mus.: time) Takt, *der;* **(e)** (step, law) Maßnahme, *die;* (Law: bill) Gesetzesvorlage, *die;* **take ~s to stop/ensure sth.** Maßnahmen ergreifen *od.* treffen, um etw. zu unterbinden/sicherzustellen. **2** *v.t.* **(a)** messen ⟨*Größe, Menge usw.*⟩; ausmessen ⟨*Raum*⟩; **~ sb. for a suit** [bei] jmdm. Maß *od.* die Maße für einen Anzug nehmen; **(b)** (fig.: estimate) abschätzen; **(c)** (mark off) **~ sth. [off]** etw. abmessen. **3** *v.i.* **(a)** (have a given size) messen; **(b)** (take measurement[s]) Maß nehmen

~ 'out *v.t.* abmessen

~ 'up to *v.t.* entsprechen (+ *Dat.*) ⟨*Maßstäben, Erwartungen*⟩; gewachsen sein (+ *Dat.*) ⟨*Anforderungen*⟩

measured /'meʒəd/ *adj.* rhythmisch, gleichmäßig ⟨*Geräusch, Bewegung*⟩; gemessen ⟨*Schritt, Worte, Ausdrucksweise*⟩

measurement /'meʒəmənt/ *n.* **(a)** (act, result) Messung, *die;* **(b)** *in pl.* (dimensions) Maße *Pl.*

measuring /'meʒərɪŋ/**: ~ jug** *n.* Messbecher, *der;* **~ tape** *n.* Bandmaß, *das*

meat /mi:t/ *n.* **(a)** Fleisch, *das;* **(b)** (arch.: food) **one man's ~ is another man's poison** (prov.) was dem einen sin Uhl, ist dem andern sin Nachtigall (Spr.); **(c)** (fig.) Substanz, *die*

meat: ~ball *n.* Fleischkloß, *der;* Fleischklößchen, *das;* **~ loaf** *n.* Hackbraten, *der;* **~ 'pie** *n.* Fleischpastete, *die;* **~ safe** *n.* (Brit.) Fliegenschrank, *der*

meaty /'mi:tɪ/ *adj.* fleischig; ⟨*Gulasch usw.*⟩ mit reichlich Fleisch; **have a ~ taste** nach Fleisch schmecken

mechanic /mɪ'kænɪk/ *n.* ▶ 887 Mechaniker, *der*

mechanical /mɪ'kænɪkl/ *adj.* (lit. or fig.) mechanisch; **produced by ~ means** maschinell produziert

mechanical 'pencil *n.* (Amer.) Drehbleistift, *der*

mechanics /mɪ'kænɪks/ *n.*, *no pl.* **(a)** Mechanik, *die;* **(b)** *constr. as pl.* (means of construction or operation) Mechanismus, *der;* (of writing, painting, etc.) Technik, *die*

mechanise ⇒ **mechanize**

mechanism /'mekənɪzm/ *n.* Mechanismus, *der*

mechanize /'mekənaɪz/ *v.t.* **(a)** mechanisieren; **(b)** (Mil.) motorisieren

medal /'medl/ *n.* Medaille, *die;* (decoration) Orden, *der*

medalist (Amer.) ⇒ **medallist**

medallion /mɪ'dæljən/ *n.* (large medal) [große] Medaille

medallist /'medəlɪst/ *n.* Medaillengewinner, *der/*-gewinnerin, *die* (Sport)

meddle /'medl/ *v.i.* **~ with sth.** sich *(Dat.)* an etw. *(Dat.)* zu schaffen machen; **~ in sth.** sich in etw. *(Akk.)* einmischen

media /'mi:dɪə/ ⇒ **mass media; medium 1**

mediaeval ⇒ **medieval**

median strip /mi:dɪən 'strɪp/ *n.* (Amer.) Mittelstreifen, *der*

'media studies *n. sing.* Medienwissenschaft, *die;* (school subject) Medienkunde, *die*

mediate /'mi:dɪeɪt/ **1** *v.i.* vermitteln. **2** *v.t.* **(a)** (settle) vermitteln in (+ *Dat.*); **(b)** (bring about) vermitteln

mediator /'mi:dɪeɪtə(r)/ *n.* Vermittler, *der/*Vermittlerin, *die*

medic /'medɪk/ ⇒ **medico**

Medicaid /'medɪkeɪd/ *n.* (Amer.) [*bundes*]*staatliches Programm, das Unterstützungsbedürftigen Beihilfe zur Deckung von Arzt- und Heilmittelkosten gewährt*

medical /'medɪkl/ **1** *adj.* medizinisch; ärztlich ⟨*Behandlung*⟩; **~ ward** ≈ medizinische *od.* innere Abteilung. **2** *n.* (coll.) ⇒ **medical examination**

medical: ~ certificate *n.* Attest, *das;* **~ exami'nation** *n.* ärztliche Untersuchung; **~ insurance** *n.* Krankenversicherung, *die;* **have ~ insurance** krankenversichert sein; **~ prac'titioner** *n.* ▶ 887 praktischer

Arzt/praktische Ärztin; Arzt/Ärztin für Allgemeinmedizin; **~ school** *n.* medizinische Hochschule; (faculty) medizinische Fakultät; **~ student** *n.* Medizinstudent, *der/*-studentin, *die*

medicated /'medɪkeɪtɪd/ *adj.* **~ shampoo/soap** medizinisches Haarwaschmittel/medizinische Seife

medication /medɪ'keɪʃn/ *n.* **(a)** (treatment) Behandlung, *die;* Medikation, *die* (Med.); **(b)** (medicine) Medikament, *das*

medicinal /mɪ'dɪsɪnl/ *adj.* medizinisch; Arznei⟨*mittel, -kohle*⟩; **~ qualities** Heilkräfte

medicine /'medsən, 'medɪsɪn/ *n.* **(a)** *no pl., no art.* (science) Medizin, *die;* **(b)** (preparation) Medikament, *das;* Medizin, *die* (veralt.); **give sb. a dose** *or* **a taste of his/her own ~** (fig.) es jmdm. mit gleicher Münze heimzahlen

medicine: ~ chest *n.* Medikamentenschränkchen, *das;* (in home) Hausapotheke, *die;* **~ man** *n.* Medizinmann, *der*

medico /'medɪkəʊ/ *n., pl.* **~s** (coll.) **(a)** Doktor, *der* (ugs.); **(b)** (student) Mediziner, *der/*Medizinerin, *die* (ugs.)

medieval /medɪ'i:vl/ *adj.* (lit. or fig.) mittelalterlich; **the ~ period** das Mittelalter

mediocre /mi:dɪ'əʊkə(r)/ *adj.* mittelmäßig

mediocrity /mi:dɪ'ɒkrɪtɪ/ *n., no pl.* Mittelmäßigkeit, *die*

meditate /'medɪteɪt/ **1** *v.t.* (consider) denken an (+ *Akk.*); erwägen; (design) planen. **2** *v.i.* nachdenken, (esp. Relig.) meditieren ([up]on über + *Akk.*)

meditation /medɪ'teɪʃn/ *n.* **(a)** (act of meditating) Nachdenken, *das;* **(b)** (Relig.) Meditation, *die*

Mediterranean /medɪtə'reɪnɪən/ **1** *pr. n.* **the ~:** das Mittelmeer. **2** *adj.* mediterran (Geogr.); südländisch; **~ coast/countries** Mittelmeerküste, *die/*Mittelmeerländer *Pl.*

medium /'mi:dɪəm/ **1** *n., pl.* **media** /'mi:dɪə/ *or* **~s** **(a)** (substance) Medium, *das;* (fig.: environment) Umgebung, *die;* **(b)** (intermediate agency) Mittel, *das;* **by** *or* **through the ~ of** durch; **(c)** *pl.* **~s** (Spiritualism) Medium, *das;* **(d)** (means of communication or artistic expression) Medium, *das;* **(e)** *in pl.* **media** (means of mass communication) Medien *Pl.;* **(f)** (middle degree) Mittelweg, *der; see also* **happy a. 2** *adj.* mittler...; medium *nur präd.,* halb durchgebraten ⟨*Steak*⟩

medium: ~-dry *adj.* halbtrocken ⟨*Wein, Sherry*⟩; **~-size[d]** *adj.* mittelgroß; **~-sweet** *adj.* mittelsüß ⟨*Wein, Sherry*⟩; **~ term** ⇒ **term 1 d;** **~ wave** *n.* (Radio) Mittelwelle, *die*

medley /'medlɪ/ *n.* (forming a whole) buntes Gemisch; (collection of items) Sammelsurium, *das* (abwertend); (of colours) Kunterbunt, *das*

meek /mi:k/ *adj.* **(a)** (humble) sanftmütig; **(b)** (tamely submissive) zu nachgiebig

meet /mi:t/ **1** *v.t.,* **met** /met/ **(a)** (come face to face with or into the company of) treffen; **I have to ~ my boss at 11 a.m.** ich habe um 11 Uhr einen Termin beim Chef; **arrange to ~ sb.** sich mit jmdm. verabreden; **(b)** (go to place of arrival of) (meet) abholen; **I'll ~ your train** ich hole dich vom Zug ab; **~ sb. halfway** (fig.) jmdm. [auf halbem Wege] entgegenkommen; **(c)** (make the acquaintance of) kennen lernen; **I'd like you to ~ my wife** ich möchte Sie gern meiner Frau vorstellen *od.* mit meiner Frau bekannt machen; **pleased to ~ you** [sehr] angenehm; sehr erfreut; **(d)** (reach point of contact with) treffen auf (+ *Akk.*); **~ the eye/sb.'s eye[s]** sich den/jmds. Blicken darbieten; **~ the ear/sb.'s ears** das/jmds. Ohr treffen; **there's more to it than ~s the eye** da ist *od.* steckt mehr dahinter, als man zuerst denkt; **(e)** (experience) stoßen auf (+ *Akk.*) ⟨*Widerstand, Problem*⟩; ernten ⟨*Gelächter, Drohungen*⟩; **~ [one's] death** *or* **one's end/disaster/ one's fate** den Tod finden (geh.) /von einer Katastrophe/ seinem Schicksal ereilt werden (geh.); **(f)** (satisfy) entsprechen (+ *Dat.*) ⟨*Forderung, Wunsch*⟩; einhalten ⟨*Termin, Zeitplan*⟩; **(g)** (pay) decken ⟨*Kosten, Auslagen*⟩; bezahlen ⟨*Rechnung*⟩. **2** *v.i.,* **met** **(a)** (come face to face) (by chance) sich (*Dat.*) begegnen; (by arrangement) sich treffen; **we've met before** wir kennen uns bereits; **(b)** (assemble) ⟨*Komitee, Ausschuss usw.*⟩ tagen; **~ together** sich versammeln; **(c)** (come together) ⟨*Bahnlinien, Straßen usw.*⟩ aufeinander treffen; ⟨*Flüsse*⟩ zusammenfließen

~ **'up** *v.i.* sich treffen; ~ **up with sb.** (coll.) jmdn. treffen ~ **with** *v.t.* **(a)** (encounter) begegnen (+ *Dat.*); **(b)** (experience) haben ‹*Erfolg, Unfall*›; finden ‹*Zustimmung, Verständnis, Tod*›; stoßen auf (+ *Akk.*) ‹*Widerstand*›

meeting /'mi:tɪŋ/ *n.* **(a)** Begegnung, *die* (auch fig.); (by arrangement) Treffen, *das;* ~ **of minds** Verständigung, *die;* Annäherung der Standpunkte; **(b)** (assembly) Versammlung, *die;* (of committee, Cabinet, council, etc.) Sitzung, *die;* (social gathering) Treffen, *das;* **(c)** (Sport) Treffen, *das;* (Racing) Rennen, *das*

meeting: ~ **place** *n.* Treffpunkt, *der;* ~ **point** *n.* (of lines, roads) Schnittpunkt, *der;* (of rivers) Zusammenfluss, *der*

mega /'megə/ (coll.) **1** *adj.* **(a)** (enormous) Mega- (Jugendspr.); **(b)** (excellent) geil (Jugendspr.). **2** *adv.* äußerst; **be** ~ **rich** super- *od.* megareich (Jugendspr.) sein; **be** ~ **talented** höchst talentiert sein

mega- /'megə/ *pref.* mega-/Mega-

'megabyte *n.* (Computing) Megabyte, *das*

megalomania /megələ'meɪnɪə/ *n.* Größenwahn, *der;* Megalomanie, *die* (Psych.)

megalomaniac /megələ'meɪnɪæk/ **1** *n.* Größenwahnsinnige, *der/die;* Megalomane, *der/*Megalomanin, *die* (Psych.); **he's a** ~: er ist größenwahnsinnig; **2** *adj.* größenwahnsinnig; megaloman[isch] (Psych.)

'megaphone *n.* Megaphon, *das*

'megastar *n.* (coll.) Megastar, *der* (ugs.)

'megaton[ne] *n.* Megatonne, *die*

'megawatt *n.* Megawatt, *das*

melancholy /'melənkəlɪ/ **1** *n.* Melancholie, *die;* (pensive sadness) Schwermut, *die.* **2** *adj.* **(a)** (gloomy, expressing sadness) melancholisch; schwermütig; **(b)** (saddening) deprimierend

mêlée (*Amer.:* **melee**) /'meleɪ/ *n.* Handgemenge, *das*

mellow /'meləʊ/ **1** *adj.* **(a)** (softened by age or experience) abgeklärt; **(b)** (ripe, well-matured) reif; ausgereift ‹*Wein*›; **(c)** (genial) freundlich; **(d)** (full and soft) weich ‹*Stimme, Ton, Licht, Farben*›. **2** *v.t.* reifer machen ‹*Person*›; [aus]reifen lassen ‹*Wein*›. **3** *v.i.* ‹*Person, Obst, Wein:*› reifen ‹*Licht, Farbe:*› weicher werden

melodious /mɪ'ləʊdɪəs/ *adj.*, **melodiously** /mɪ'ləʊdɪəslɪ/ *adv.* melodisch

melodrama /'melədrɑːmə/ *n.* (lit. or fig.) Melodrama, *das*

melodramatic /melədrə'mætɪk/ *adj.* (lit. or fig.) melodramatisch

melody /'melədɪ/ *n.* **(a)** (pleasing sound) Gesang, *der;* **(b)** (tune) Melodie, *die*

melon /'melən/ *n.* Melone, *die*

melt /melt/ **1** *v.i.* **(a)** schmelzen; (dissolve) sich auflösen; ~ **in one's** *or* **the mouth** (coll.) auf der Zunge zergehen; *see also* **butter 1**; **(b)** (fig.: be softened) dahinschmelzen (geh.) **(at** bei); sich erweichen lassen **(at** durch). **2** *v.t.* **(a)** schmelzen ‹*Schnee, Eis, Metall*›; (Cookery) zerlassen ‹*Butter*›; **(b)** (fig.: make tender) erweichen ‹*Person, Herz*› ~ **a'way** *v.i.* ‹*Schnee, Eis:*› [weg]schmelzen; (fig.: dwindle away) ‹*Nebel, Dunst, Menschenmenge:*› sich auflösen; ‹*Verdacht, Mehrheit, Furcht:*› dahinschwinden (geh.) ~ **'down 1** *v.i.* schmelzen. **2** *v.t.* einschmelzen ‹*Metall, Glas*›

'meltdown *n.* Schmelzen, *das*

melting /'meltɪŋ/: ~ **point** *n.* Schmelzpunkt, *der;* ~ **pot** *n.* (fig.) Schmelztiegel, *der;* **be in the** ~ **pot** in rascher Veränderung begriffen sein

member /'membə(r)/ *n.* **(a)** Mitglied, *das; attrib.* Mitglieds‹*staat, -land*›; **be a** ~ **of the club** Mitglied des Vereins sein; ~ **of the expedition** Expeditionsteilnehmer, *der/*-teilnehmerin, *die;* ~ **of a/the family** Familienangehörige, *der/die;* **(b)** M~ **[of Parliament]** (Brit. Polit.) Abgeordnete [des Unterhauses], *der/die;* M~ **of Congress** (Amer. Polit.) Kongressabgeordnete, *der/die*

membership /'membəʃɪp/ *n.* **(a)** Mitgliedschaft, *die* (of in + *Dat.*); *attrib.* Mitglieds‹*karte, -ausweis, -beitrag*›; Mitglieder‹*liste, -verzeichnis*›; **(b)** (number of members) Mitgliederzahl, *die;* **(c)** (body of members) Mitglieder *Pl.*

membrane /'membreɪn/ *n.* (Biol.) Membran, *die*

memento /mɪ'mentəʊ/ *n., pl.* ~**es** *or* ~**s** Andenken, *das* (**of** an + *Akk.*)

memo /'meməʊ/ *n., pl.* ~**s** (coll.) ⇒ **memorandum** a, b

memoirs /'memwɑːz/ *n. pl.* Memoiren *Pl.*

memorable /'memərəbl/ *adj.* denkwürdig ‹*Ereignis, Gelegenheit, Tag*›; unvergesslich ‹*Film, Aufführung*›

memorandum /memə'rændəm/ *n., pl.* **memoranda** /memə'rændə/ *or* ~**s (a)** (note) Notiz, *die;* **(b)** (letter) Mitteilung, *die;* **(c)** (Diplom.) Memorandum, *das*

memorial /mɪ'mɔːrɪəl/ **1** *adj.* Gedenk‹*stein, -gottesdienst, -ausstellung*›. **2** *n.* Denkmal, *das* (**to** für)

memorize (**memorise**) /'meməraɪz/ *v.t.* sich (*Dat.*) merken *od.* einprägen; (learn by heart) auswendig lernen

memory /'memərɪ/ *n.* **(a)** Gedächtnis, *das;* **have a good/poor** ~ **for faces** ein gutes/schlechtes Personengedächtnis haben; **(b)** (recollection, person or thing remembered, act of remembering) Erinnerung, *die* (**of** an + *Akk.*); **have a vague** *or* **of sth.** sich nur ungenau an etw. (*Akk.*) erinnern; **it slipped** *or* **escaped my** ~: es ist mir entfallen; **from** ~: aus dem Gedächtnis *od.* Kopf; **in** ~ **of** zur Erinnerung an (+ *Akk.*); *attrib.* **a trip down** ~ **lane** eine Reise in die Vergangenheit; **(c)** (Computing) Speicher, *der*

'memory bank *n.* Speicherbank, *die*

men *pl. of* **man**

menace /'menɪs/ **1** *v.t.* bedrohen ‹*Person*›. **2** *n.* Plage, *die*

menacing /'menɪsɪŋ/ *adj.* drohend

mend /mend/ **1** *v.t.* **(a)** (repair) reparieren; ausbessern, flicken ‹*Kleidung, Fischernetz*›; kleben, kitten ‹*Glas, Porzellan, Sprung*›; beheben ‹*Schaden*›; beseitigen ‹*Riß*›; **(b)** (improve) ~ **one's ways** sich bessern; ~ **matters** die Sache bereinigen. **2** *v.i.* ▶ 865 | ‹*Knochen, Bein, Finger usw.:*› heilen; **has his leg** ~**ed yet?** ist sein Bein schon verheilt? **3** *n.* ▶ 865 | (in glass, china, etc.) Kleb[e]stelle, *die;* (in cloth) ausgebesserte Stelle; (repair) Ausbesserung, *die;* **be on the** ~ ‹*Person:*› auf dem Wege der Besserung sein

mendacious /men'deɪʃəs/ *adj.* unwahr ‹*Bericht, Behauptung, Darstellung*›; verlogen (abwertend) ‹*Person, Rede, Buch*›

'menfolk *n. pl.* Männer

menial /'mi:nɪəl/ *adj.* niedrig; untergeordnet ‹*Aufgabe*›

meningitis /menɪn'dʒaɪtɪs/ *n.* ▶ 865 | (Med.) Meningitis, *die* (fachspr.); Hirnhautentzündung, *die*

menopause /'menəpɔːz/ *n.* Wechseljahre *Pl.;* Klimakterium, *das* (fachspr.); **male** ~: Wechseljahre des Mannes

menstrual /'menstrʊəl/ *adj.* (Physiol.) menstrual (fachspr.); Menstruations-

menstruate /'menstrʊeɪt/ *v.i.* (Physiol.) menstruieren

menstruation /menstrʊ'eɪʃn/ *n.* (Physiol.) Menstruation, *die*

menswear /'menzweə(r)/ *n., no pl.* Herrenbekleidung, *die; attrib.* Herrenbekleidungs-

mental /'mentl/ *adj.* **(a)** geistig; seelisch ‹*Belastung, Labilität*›; Geistes‹*zustand, -störung, -verfassung*›; ~ **process** Denkprozess, -vorgang, *der;* **make a** ~ **note of sth.** sich (*Dat.*) etw. merken; **(b)** (Brit. coll.: mad) verrückt (salopp); bekloppt (salopp)

mental: ~ **age** *n.* geistiger Entwicklungsstand; Intelligenzalter, *das* (Psych.); ~ **a'rithmetic** *n.* Kopfrechnen, *das;* ~ **asylum** ⇒ **hospital;** ~ **'block** ⇒ **block 1 k;** ~ **'health** *n.* seelische Gesundheit; ~ **home** *n.* Nervenklinik, *die;* ~ **hospital** *n.* psychiatrische Klinik; Nervenklinik, *die;* ~ **'illness** *n.* Geisteskrankheit, *die*

mentality /men'tælɪtɪ/ *n.* Mentalität, *die*

mentally /'mentlɪ/ *adv.* **(a)** geistig; geistes‹*gestört, -krank*›; ~ **deficient** *or* **defective** schwachsinnig; **(b)** (inwardly) innerlich; im Geiste; im Kopf ‹*rechnen*›

mental: ~ **patient** *n.* Geisteskranke, *der/die;* ~ **re-ser'vation** *n.* geheimer Vorbehalt

menthol /'menθɒl/ *n.* Menthol, *das*

mention /'menʃn/ **1** *n.* Erwähnung, *die;* **there is a brief/no** ~ **of sth.** etw. wird kurz/nicht erwähnt; **get a** ~: erwähnt werden; **make [no]** ~ **of sth.** etw. [nicht]

erwähnen. **2** *v.t.* erwähnen (**to** gegenüber); ∼ **as the reason for sth.** als Grund für etw. nennen; **not to** ∼ ...: ganz zu schweigen von ...; **not to** ∼ **the fact that** ...: ganz abgesehen davon, dass ...; **Thank you very much.** — **Don't** ∼ **it** Vielen Dank. — Keine Ursache

mentor /'mentɔː(r)/ *n.* Mentor, *der*/Mentorin, *die*

menu /'menjuː/ *n.* **(a)** [Speise]karte, *die;* **(b)** (fig.: diet) Nahrung, *die;* **(c)** (Computing, Telev.) Menü, *das*

'**menu bar** *n.* (Computing) Menüleiste, *die*

MEP *abbr.* **Member of the European Parliament** MdEP

mercenary /'mɜːsɪnərɪ/ **1** *adj.* **(a)** gewinnsüchtig; **(b)** (hired) Söldner-. **2** *n.* Söldner, *der*

merchandise /'mɜːtʃəndaɪz/ *n., no pl., no indef. art.* [Handels]ware, *die*

merchant /'mɜːtʃənt/ *n.* Kaufmann, *der;* **corn-/timber**-∼: Getreide-/Holzhändler, *der*/-händlerin, *die*

merchant: ∼ '**bank** *n.* Handelsbank, *die;* ∼ '**banker** *n.* ▶ 887 ǀ Bankier, *der* (*bei einer Handelsbank*); ∼ **ma'rine** (Amer.), ∼ '**navy** (Brit.) *ns.* Handelsmarine, *die;* ∼ '**seaman** *n.* Matrose bei der Handelsmarine; ∼ **ship** *n.* Handelsschiff, *das*

merciful /'mɜːsɪfl/ *adj.* gnädig

mercifully /'mɜːsɪfəlɪ/ *adv.* gnädig; *as sentence-modifier* (fortunately) glücklicherweise

merciless /'mɜːsɪlɪs/ *adj.,* **mercilessly** /'mɜːsɪlɪslɪ/ *adv.* gnadenlos; unbarmherzig

mercury /'mɜːkjʊrɪ/ **1** *n.* Quecksilber, *das.* **2** *pr. n.* M∼ **(a)** (Astron.) Merkur, *der;* **(b)** (Roman Mythol.) Merkur (*der*)

mercy /'mɜːsɪ/ **1** *n.* **(a)** *no pl., no indef. art.* Erbarmen, *das* (on mit); **show sb.** [**no**] ∼: mit jmdm. [kein] Erbarmen haben; **God's great** ∼: Gottes große Barmherzigkeit; **be at the** ∼ **of sb./sth.** jmdm./einer Sache [auf Gedeih und Verderb] ausgeliefert sein; **(b)** (instance) glückliche Fügung; **we must be thankful or grateful for small mercies** (coll.) man darf [ja] nicht zu viel verlangen. **2** *attrib. adj.* Hilfs-, Rettungs〈*einsatz, -flug*〉; ∼ **killings** Fälle aktiver Sterbehilfe

mere /mɪə(r)/ *adj.* bloß; **he is a** ∼ **child** er ist nur ein Kind; ∼ **courage is not enough** Mut allein genügt nicht; **the** ∼**st hint/trace of sth.** die kleinste Andeutung/Spur von etw.

merely /'mɪəlɪ/ *adv.* bloß; lediglich; **not** ∼ ...: nicht bloß ...

merge /mɜːdʒ/ **1** *v.t.* **(a)** zusammenschließen 〈*Firmen, Unternehmen*〉 (**into** zu); zusammenlegen 〈*Anteile, Abteilungen*〉; **(b)** (blend gradually) verschmelzen (**with** mit). **2** *v.i.* **(a)** 〈*Firma, Unternehmen:*〉 sich zusammenschließen, fusionieren (**with** mit); 〈*Abteilung:*〉 zusammengelegt werden (**with** mit); **(b)** (blend gradually) 〈*Straße:*〉 zusammenlaufen (**with** mit); ∼ **into sth.** 〈*Farbe usw.:*〉 in etw. (*Akk.*) übergehen

merger /'mɜːdʒə(r)/ *n.* (of departments, parties) Zusammenschluss, *der;* Vereinigung, *die;* (of companies) Fusion, *die*

meridian /mə'rɪdɪən/ *n.* (Astron., Geog.) Meridian, *der*

meringue /mə'ræŋ/ *n.* Meringe, *die;* Baiser, *das*

merit /'merɪt/ **1** *n.* **(a)** *no pl.* (worth) Verdienst, *das;* **there is no** ∼ **in doing that** es ist nicht [sehr] sinnvoll, das zu tun; **(b)** (good feature) Vorzug, *der;* **on his/its** ∼**s** nach seinen Vorzügen; **(c)** *in pl.* (rights and wrongs) Für und Wider, *das.* **2** *v.t.* verdienen

'**merit award**, '**merit increase** *ns.* Leistungszulage, *die*

meritocracy /merɪ'tɒkrəsɪ/ *n.* Meritokratie, *die*

mermaid /'mɜːmeɪd/ *n.* Nixe, *die*

merrily /'merɪlɪ/ *adv.* munter

merriment /'merɪmənt/ *n., no pl.* Fröhlichkeit, *die;* **fall into fits of helpless** ∼: sich vor Lachen nicht mehr halten können

merry /'merɪ/ *adj.* **(a)** fröhlich; **a** ∼ **time was had by all** alle haben sich prächtig amüsiert; **the more the merrier** je mehr, desto besser; ∼ '**Christmas!** frohe *od.* fröhliche Weihnachten!; **(b)** (coll.: tipsy) beschwipst (ugs.)

merry: ∼-**go-round** *n.* Karussell, *das;* ∼**making** *n., no pl., no indef. art.* Feiern, *das;* **the sound of** ∼**making** fröhlicher Festlärm

mesh /meʃ/ **1** *n.* **(a)** Masche, *die;* **(b)** (netting; also fig.: network) Geflecht, *das;* **wire** ∼ [**fence**] Maschendraht[zaun], *der;* **(c)** *in pl.* (fig.: snare) Maschen. **2** *v.i.* **(a)** (Mech. Engin.) 〈*Zahnräder:*〉 ineinander greifen; ∼ **with** eingreifen in (*Akk.*); **(b)** (fig.: be harmonious) harmonieren (**with** mit)

mesmerize (**mesmerise**) /'mezməraɪz/ *v.t.* faszinieren; erstarren lassen 〈*Tier*〉

mess /mes/ *n.* **(a)** (dirty/untidy state) [**be**] **a** ∼ *or* **in a** ∼: schmutzig/unaufgeräumt [sein]; [**be**] **a complete** *or* **in an awful** ∼: in einem fürchterlichen Zustand [sein]; **what a** ∼! was für ein Dreck (ugs.)/Durcheinander!; **look a** ∼: schlimm aussehen; **your hair is a** ∼: dein Haar ist ganz durcheinander; **don't make too much** ∼: mach nicht zu viel Schmutz/Durcheinander; **leave a lot of** ∼ **behind one** (dirt) viel Schmutz hinterlassen; (untidiness) eine große Unordnung hinterlassen; **make a** ∼ **with sth.** mit etw. Schmutz machen; **(b)** (excreta) **dog's/cat's** ∼: Hunde-/Katzenkot, *der;* **make a** ∼ **on the carpet** auf den Teppich machen (ugs.); **(c)** (bad state) **be** [**in**] **a** ∼: sich in einem schlimmen Zustand befinden; 〈*Person:*〉 schlimm dran sein; **get into a** ∼: in Schwierigkeiten geraten; **make a** ∼ **of** verpfuschen (ugs.) 〈*Arbeit, Leben, Bericht, Vertrag*〉; durcheinander bringen 〈*Pläne*〉; **(d)** (eating place) Kantine, *die;* (for officers) Kasino, *das;* (on ship) Messe, *die;* **officers'** ∼: Offizierskasino, *das*/Offiziersmesse, *die*

∼ **a'bout,** ∼ **a'round 1** *v.i.* **(a)** (potter) herumwerken; (fool about) herumalbern; ∼ **about with cars** an Autos herumbasteln (ugs.); **(b)** (interfere) ∼ **about** *or* **around with** sich einmischen in (+ *Akk.*) 〈*Angelegenheit*〉; herumspielen an (+ *Dat.*) 〈*Mechanismus, Stromkabel usw.*〉. **2** *v.t.* ∼ **sb. about** *or* **around** mit jmdm. nach Belieben umspringen (abwertend)

∼ '**up** *v.t.* **(a)** (make dirty) schmutzig machen; (make untidy) in Unordnung bringen; **(b)** (bungle) verpfuschen; **(c)** (interfere with) durcheinander bringen 〈*Plan*〉

message /'mesɪdʒ/ *n.* Mitteilung, *die;* Nachricht, *die;* **send/take/leave a** ∼: eine Nachricht übermitteln/entgegennehmen/hinterlassen; **give sb. a** ∼: jmdm. etwas ausrichten; **can I take a** ∼? kann *od.* soll ich etwas ausrichten?; **get the** ∼ (fig. coll.) verstehen; es schnallen (salopp)

messenger /'mesɪndʒə(r)/ *n.* Bote, *der*/Botin, *die*

'**messenger boy** *n.* ▶ 887 ǀ Botenjunge, *der*

Messiah /mɪ'saɪə/ *n.* (lit. or fig.) Messias, *der*

Messrs /'mesəz/ *n. pl.* **(a)** (in name of firm) ≈ Fa.; **(b)** *pl. of* **Mr;** (in list of names) ∼ **A, B, and C** die Herren A, B und C

'**mess-up** *n.* Durcheinander, *das*

messy /'mesɪ/ *adj.* **(a)** (dirty) schmutzig; (untidy) unordentlich; **be a** ∼ **eater** sich beim Essen bekleckern; **(b)** (awkward) vertrackt (ugs.)

met ⇒ **meet**

metabolism /mɪ'tæbəlɪzm/ *n.* (Physiol.) Metabolismus, *der* (fachspr.); Stoffwechsel, *der*

metal /'metl/ **1** *n.* Metall, *das.* **2** *adj.* Metall-; **be** ∼: aus Metall sein. **3** *v.t.,* (Brit.) -**ll**- (Brit.: surface) schottern 〈*Straße*〉

'**metal-detector** *n.* Metallsuchgerät, *das*

metallic /mɪ'tælɪk/ *adj.* metallisch; Metall〈*salz, -oxid*〉; **have a** ∼ **taste** nach Metall schmecken

metallurgist /mɪ'tælədʒɪst, 'metəlɜːdʒɪst/ *n.* ▶ 887 ǀ Metallurg, *der*/Metallurgin, *die*

metallurgy /mɪ'tælədʒɪ, 'metəlɜːdʒɪ/ *n., no pl.* Metallurgie, *die*

metal: ∼ **polish** *n.* Metallputzmittel, *das;* ∼**work** *n., no pl.* **(a)** (activity) Metallbearbeitung, *die;* **(b)** (products) Metallarbeiten; **a piece of** ∼**work** eine Metallarbeit; ∼**worker** *n.* Metallarbeiter, *der*/-arbeiterin, *die*

metamorphic /metə'mɔːfɪk/ *adj.* (Geol.) metamorph 〈*Gestein*〉

metamorphose /metə'mɔːfəʊz/ *v.i.* sich verwandeln (**into** in + *Akk.*)

metamorphosis /metəˈmɔːfəsɪs, metəmɔːˈfəʊsɪs/ *n., pl.* **metamorphoses** /metəˈmɔːfəsiːz, metəmɔːˈfəʊsiːz/ Metamorphose, *die* (**into** in + *Akk.*)

metaphor /ˈmetəfə(r)/ *n.* (**a**) *no pl., no art.* (stylistic device) [**the use of**] ~: der Gebrauch von Metaphern; (**b**) (instance) Metapher, *die;* **mixed** ~: Bildbruch, *der*

metaphorical /metəˈfɒrɪkl/ *adj.,* **metaphorically** /metəˈfɒrɪkəlɪ/ *adv.* metaphorisch

metaphysical /metəˈfɪzɪkl/ *adj.* (Philos.) metaphysisch

metaphysics /metəˈfɪzɪks/ *n., no pl.* (Philos.) Metaphysik, *die*

mete /miːt/ *v.t.* (literary) ~ **out** zuteil werden lassen (geh.) 〈*Belohnung*〉 (**to** *Dat.*); auferlegen 〈*Strafe*〉 (**to** *Dat.*)

meteor /ˈmiːtɪə(r)/ *n.* (Astron.) Meteor, *der*

meteoric /miːtɪˈɒrɪk/ *adj.* (**a**) (Astron.) Meteor〈*schweif, -tätigkeit*〉; meteorisch; (**b**) (fig.) kometenhaft

meteorite /ˈmiːtɪəraɪt/ *n.* (Astron.) Meteorit, *der*

meteorological /miːtɪərəˈlɒdʒɪkl/ *adj.* meteorologisch 〈*Instrument*〉; Wetter〈*ballon, -bericht*〉; **M**~ **Office** (Brit.) Meteorologisches Amt; Wetteramt, *das*

meteorologist /miːtɪəˈrɒlədʒɪst/ *n.* ▶ 887 Meteorologe, *der*/Meteorologin, *die*

meteorology /miːtɪəˈrɒlədʒɪ/ *n., no pl.* Meteorologie, *die*

meter[1] /ˈmiːtə(r)/ **1** *n.* (**a**) Zähler, *der;* (taking coins) Münzzähler, *der;* (**b**) (parking-~) Parkuhr, *die.* **2** *v.t.* [mit einem Zähler] messen 〈[*Wasser-, Gas-, Strom*]*verbrauch*〉

meter[2] (Amer.) ⇨ **metre**[1, 2]

'meter maid *n.* (coll.) Politesse, *die*

methane /ˈmiːθeɪn, ˈmeθeɪn/ *n.* (Chem.) Methan, *das*

method /ˈmeθəd/ *n.* (**a**) (procedure) Methode, *die;* (process) Verfahren, *das;* (**b**) *no pl., no art.* (arrangement of ideas, orderliness) System, *das;* Systematik, *die;* **there's** ~ **in his madness** (fig. joc.) der Wahnsinn hat Methode

methodical /mɪˈθɒdɪkl/ *adj.* methodisch; systematisch; **be** ~: methodisch *od.* systematisch vorgehen

methodically /mɪˈθɒdɪkəlɪ/ *adv.* mit Methode; systematisch

Methodist /ˈmeθədɪst/ *n.* (Relig.) Methodist, *der*/Methodistin, *die; attrib.* Methodisten〈*kapelle, -gottesdienst, -pfarrer*〉

methodology /meθəˈdɒlədʒɪ/ *n.* (**a**) *no pl., no art.* (science of method) Methodik, *die;* Methodologie, *die;* (**b**) (methods used) Methodik, *die*

meths /meθs/ *n., no pl., no indef. art.* (Brit. coll.) [Brenn]spiritus, *der*

methylated spirit[s] /meθɪleɪtɪd ˈspɪrɪt(s)/ *n.* [*pl.*] Brennspiritus, *der;* vergällter *od.* denaturierter Alkohol (fachspr.)

meticulous /mɪˈtɪkjʊləs/ *adj.* (scrupulous) sorgfältig; (over-scrupulous) übergenau; **be** ~ **about sth.** es peinlich genau mit etw. nehmen

meticulously /mɪˈtɪkjʊləslɪ/ *adv.* (scrupulously) sorgfältig; (over-scrupulously) übergenau; ~ **clean** peinlich sauber

metre[1] /ˈmiːtə/ *n.* (Brit.: poetic rhythm) Metrum, *das*

metre[2] *n.* ▶ 904 (Brit.: unit) Meter, *der od. das;* **sell cloth by the** ~: Stoff meterweise verkaufen

metric /ˈmetrɪk/ *adj.* metrisch; ~ **system** metrisches System; **go** ~ (coll.) das metrische System einführen

metrical /ˈmetrɪkl/ *adj.* metrisch

metrication /metrɪˈkeɪʃn/ *n.* Umstellung auf das metrische System

metronome /ˈmetrənəʊm/ *n.* (Mus.) Metronom, *das*

metropolis /mɪˈtrɒpəlɪs/ *n.* (capital) Hauptstadt, *die;* (chief city) Metropole, *die*

metropolitan /metrəˈpɒlɪtən/ *adj.* ~ **New York/Tokyo** der Großraum New York/Tokio; ~ **London** Großlondon (*das*), die **M**~ **Police** die Londoner Polizei; ~ **borough/district** (Brit. Admin.) Gemeinde/Bezirk im Großraum einer Großstadt

mettle /ˈmetl/ *n.* (**a**) (quality of temperament) Wesensart, *die;* **show one's** ~: zeigen, aus welchem Holz man [geschnitzt] ist; (**b**) (spirit) Mut, *der;* **a man of** ~: ein mutiger Mann; **be on one's** ~: zeigen müssen, was man kann

mew /mjuː/ **1** *v.i.* 〈*Katze:*〉 miauen; 〈*Möwe:*〉 kreischen. **2** *n.* (of cat) Miauen, *das;* (of seagull) Kreischen, *das*

Mexican /ˈmeksɪkən/ ▶ 947 **1** *adj.*mexikanisch; **sb. is** ~: jmd. ist Mexikaner/Mexikanerin; ~ **wave** La-Ola [-Welle], *die.* **2** *n.* Mexikaner, *der*/Mexikanerin, *die*

Mexico /ˈmeksɪkəʊ/ *pr. n.* ▶ 1159 Mexiko (*das*); ~ **City** Mexiko [City] (*das*)

mg. *abbr.* **milligram[s]** mg

mi /miː/ ⇨ **me**[2]

miaow /mɪˈaʊ/ **1** *v.i.* miauen. **2** *n.* Miauen, *das*

mica /ˈmaɪkə/ *n.* (Min.) Glimmer, *der*

mice *pl. of* **mouse**

mickey /ˈmɪkɪ/ *n.* (Brit. coll.) **take the** ~ [**out of sb./sth.**] jmdn./etw. durch den Kakao ziehen (ugs.)

micro /ˈmaɪkrəʊ/ *n., pl.* ~**s** ⇨ **microcomputer**

micro- /ˈmaɪkrəʊ/ *in comb.* mikro-/Mikro-

microbe /ˈmaɪkrəʊb/ *n.* (Biol.) Mikrobe, *die*

micro: ~**bi'ology** *n.* Mikrobiologie, *die;* ~**brewery** *n.* Mikrobrauerei, *die;* ~**chip** *n.* [Mikro]chip, *der;* ~**computer** *n.* Mikrocomputer, *der;* ~**dot** *n.* Mikrat, *das;* ~**economic** *adj.* mikroökonomisch; ~**economics** *n.* Mikroökonomie, *die;* ~**fiche** *n., pl. same or* ~**fiches** Mikrofiche, *das od. der;* ~**film 1** *n.* Mikrofilm, *der;* **2** *v.t.* auf Mikrofilm (*Akk.*) aufnehmen; ~**light** [ˈaircraft] *n.* Ultraleichtflugzeug, *das*

micrometer /maɪˈkrɒmɪtə(r)/ *n.* (Mech. Engin.) [Fein]messschraube, *die*

micro-'organism *n.* Mikroorganismus, *der;* Kleinstlebewesen, *das*

microphone /ˈmaɪkrəfəʊn/ *n.* Mikrofon, *das*

micro'processor *n.* (Computing) Mikroprozessor, *der*

microscope /ˈmaɪkrəskəʊp/ *n.* Mikroskop, *das*

microscopic /maɪkrəˈskɒpɪk/ *adj.* (**a**) mikroskopisch; (**b**) (fig.: very small) winzig

micro: ~**surgery** *n.* (Med.) Mikrochirurgie, *die;* ~**wave 1** *n.* Mikrowelle, *die;* ~ [**oven**] Mikrowellenherd, *der;* **2** *v.t.* ~ **sth.** etw. in der Mikrowelle zubereiten; **a** ~**waved potato** eine Kartoffel aus der Mikrowelle

mid- /mɪd/ *in comb.* **in** ~-**air** in der Luft; ~-**air collision** Zusammenstoß in der Luft; **in** ~-**flight**-**sentence** mitten im Flug/Satz; [**in**] ~-**afternoon** [mitten] am Nachmittag; ~-**term elections** (Amer.) Kongress- und Kommunalwahlen in der Mitte der Amtszeit des Präsidenten; ~-**July** Mitte Juli; **the** ~-**60s** die Mitte der sechziger Jahre; **a man in his** ~-**fifties** ein Mittfünfziger; **be in one's** ~-**thirties** Mitte dreißig sein

midday /ˈmɪddeɪ, mɪdˈdeɪ/ *n.* ▶ 706 (**a**) (noon) zwölf Uhr; **round about** ~: um die Mittagszeit; (**b**) (middle of day) Mittag, *der; attrib.* Mittags-

middle /ˈmɪdl/ **1** *attrib. adj.* mittler...; **the** ~ **one** der/die/das mittlere; ~ **point** Mittelpunkt, *der.* **2** *n.* (**a**) Mitte, *die;* (central part) Mittelteil, *der;* **in the** ~ **of the room/the table** in der Mitte des Zimmers/des Tisches; (emphatic) mitten im Zimmer/auf dem Tisch; **right in the** ~ **of Manchester** genau im Zentrum von Manchester; **in the** ~ **of the forest** mitten im Wald; **fold sth. down the** ~: etw. in der Mitte falten; **in the** ~ **of the day** mittags; **in the** ~ **of the morning/afternoon** mitten am Vor-/Nachmittag; **in the** ~ **of the night/week** mitten in der Nacht/Woche; **be in the** ~ **of doing sth.** (fig.) gerade mitten dabei sein, etw. zu tun; (**b**) (waist) Taille, *die*

middle: ~ '**age** *n.* mittleres [Lebens]alter; ~-**aged** /ˈmɪdleɪdʒd/ *adj.* mittleren Alters *nachgestellt;* **M**~ '**Ages** *n. pl.* **the M**~ **Ages** das Mittelalter; ~**brow** *adj.* (coll.) für den [geistigen] Normalverbraucher *nachgestellt* (ugs.); ~ '**class** *n.* Mittelstand, *der;* ~-**class** *adj.* bürgerlich 〈*Vorort, Einstellung, Moral, Werte*〉; ~-**class people** Mittelständler; ~ '**course** *n.* Mittelweg, *der;* **M**~ '**East** *pr. n.* **the M**~ **East** der Nahe [und Mittlere] Osten; **M**~ '**Eastern** *adj.* nahöstlich; des Nahen Ostens *nachgestellt;* 〈*Person*〉 aus dem Nahen Osten; ~ **England** *n.* die konservative englische Mittelklasse *od.* -schicht; ~ **finger** *n.* Mittelfinger, *der;* ~**man** *n.* (Commerc.) Zwischenhändler, *der*/-händlerin, *die;* (fig.)

Vermittler, *der*/Vermittlerin, *die;* ~ **name** *n.* zweiter Vorname; ~**-of-the-'road** *adj.* gemäßigt; moderat; ~**-of-the-road politician/politics** Politiker/Politik der Mitte; ~ **school** *n.* (Brit.) Schule für 9- bis 13-jährige; ~**size[d]** *adj.* mittelgroß; ~ **'way** ⇨ ~ **course;** ~**weight** *n.* (Boxing etc.) Mittelgewicht, *das;* (person also) Mittelgewichtler, *der;* **M**~ **'West** *pr. n.* (Amer.) **the M**~ **West** der Mittlere Westen

middling /'mɪdlɪŋ/ **1** *adj.* (a) (second-rate) mittelmäßig; **(b)** (moderately good) **[fair to]** ~: ganz ordentlich (ugs.); [ganz] passabel; **(c)** (coll.: in fairly good health) mittelprächtig (ugs. scherzh.). **2** *adv.* recht; (only moderately) ganz

'midfield *n.* (Footb.) Mittelfeld, *das;* **play in** ~: im Mittelfeld spielen; *attrib.* ~ **player** Mittelfeldspieler, *der*

midget /'mɪdʒɪt/ **1** *n.* **(a)** (person) Liliputaner, *der*/Liliputanerin, *die;* Zwerg, *der*/Zwergin, *die;* **(b)** (thing) Zwerg, *der* (fig.); (animal) Zwergform, *die.* **2** *adj.* winzig; Mini‹*flugzeug, -U-Boot*›

Midland /'mɪdlənd/ **1** *n.* **the** ~**s** (Brit.) Mittelengland *das.* **2** *adj.* ~**[s]** (Brit.) in den Midlands *nachgestellt;* ‹*Dialekt*› der Midlands

'midnight *n.* ▶706 Mitternacht, *die; attrib.* Mitternachts‹*stunde, -messe, -zug*›; mitternächtlich ‹*Festgelage, Feiern*›

midnight 'sun *n.* Mitternachtssonne, *die*

'midpoint *n.* Mitte, *die*

midriff /'mɪdrɪf/ *n.* **the bulge below his** ~: die Wölbung seiner Taillengegend; **with bare** ~: nabelfrei

midst /mɪdst/ *n.* **in the** ~ **of sth.** mitten in einer Sache; **be in the** ~ **of doing sth.** gerade mitten dabei sein, etw. zu tun; **in our/their** ~: in unserer/ihrer Mitte

midsummer /'mɪdsʌmə(r), mɪd'sʌmə(r)/ *n.* die [Zeit der] Sommersonnenwende; **[on] M**~**['s] Day** [am] Johannistag

midway /'mɪdweɪ, mɪd'weɪ/ *adv.* auf halbem Weg[e] ‹*sich treffen, sich befinden*›; ~ **through sth.** (fig.) mitten in etw. (*Dat.*)

midwife /'mɪdwaɪf/ *n., pl.* **midwives** /'mɪdwaɪvz/ ▶887 Hebamme, *die*

midwifery /'mɪdwɪfrɪ, mɪd'wɪfərɪ/ *n., no pl., no art.* Geburtshilfe, *die*

mid'winter *n.* die [Zeit der] Wintersonnenwende; der Mittwinter

miff /mɪf/ *v.t.* (coll.) verärgern; **be** ~**ed** beleidigt *od.* (ugs.) eingeschnappt sein

might¹ ⇨ **may**

might² /maɪt/ *n.* **(a)** (force) Gewalt, *die;* (inner strength) Macht, *die;* **with all one's** ~: mit aller Kraft; **(b)** (power) Macht, *die;* ~ **is right** Macht geht vor Recht

might-have-been /'maɪtəvbiːn/ *n.* jemand, *der es zu etwas hätte bringen können;* **he is a** ~: er hat seine Chancen verpasst

mightily /'maɪtɪlɪ/ *adv.* (coll.: very) überaus; **be** ~ **amused** sich köstlich amüsieren

mightn't /'maɪtnt/ (coll.) = **might not;** ⇨ **may**

mighty /'maɪtɪ/ **1** *adj.* **(a)** (powerful) mächtig; gewaltig ‹*Krieger, Anstrengung*›; **how are the** ~ **fallen** welch tiefer Fall!; **(b)** (massive) gewaltig; **(c)** (coll.: great) riesig. *See also* **high 1 e. 2** *adv.* (coll.) verdammt (ugs.)

migraine /'miːgreɪn, 'maɪgreɪn/ *n.* (Med.) Migräne, *die*

migrant /'maɪgrənt/ **1** *adj.* **(a)** ~ **tribe** Nomadenstamm, *der;* ~ **worker** Wanderarbeiter, *der*/-arbeiterin, *die;* (in EC) Gastarbeiter, *der*/-arbeiterin, *die;* **(b)** ~ **bird/fish** Zugvogel, *der*/Wanderfisch, *der.* **2** *n.* **(a)** Auswanderer, *der*/Auswanderin, *die;* **(b)** (bird) Zugvogel, *der;* (fish) Wanderfisch, *der*

migrate /maɪ'greɪt/ *v.i.* **(a)** (from rural area to town) abwandern; (to another country) auswandern; (to another place of work) überwechseln; **(b)** ‹*Vogel:*› fortziehen; ‹*Fisch:*› wandern; ~ **to the south/sea** nach Süden ziehen/zum Meer wandern

migration /maɪ'greɪʃn/ *n.* **(a)** ⇨ **migrate a:** Abwandern, *das;* Auswandern, *das;* Überwechseln, *das;* **(b)** (of birds) Fortziehen, *das;* (of fish) Wandern, *das;* (instance) (of birds) Zug, *der;* (of fish) Wanderung, *die*

migratory /'maɪgrətərɪ, maɪ'greɪtərɪ/ *adj.* **(a)** ~ **tribe** Nomadenstamm, *der;* **(b)** ~ **bird/fish** Zugvogel, *der*/Wanderfisch, *der*

mike /maɪk/ *n.* (coll.) Mikro, *das*

Milan /mɪ'læn/ *pr. n.* ▶1159 Mailand (*das*)

mild /maɪld/ **1** *adj.* **(a)** sanft ‹*Person*›; mild ‹*Urteil, Bestrafung, Kritik*›; leicht ‹*Erkrankung, Gefühlsregung*›; gemäßigt ‹*Ausdrucksweise, Sprache*›; leicht ‹*Aufregung*› mild ‹*Wetter, Winter*›; mild, leicht ‹*Arzneimittel, Stimulans*›; **(b)** (not strong in taste) mild. **2** *n.* schwach gehopfte englische Biersorte

mildew /'mɪldjuː/ *n.* (on paper, cloth, wood) Schimmel, *der;* (on plant) Mehltau, *der*

mildly /'maɪldlɪ/ *adv.* **(a)** (gently) mild[e]; **(b)** (slightly) ein bisschen *od.* wenig ‹*enttäuscht, bestürzt, ermutigend, begeistert*›; **(c) to put it** ~: gelinde gesagt

mile /maɪl/ *n.* **(a)** ▶643, ▶756, ▶1102 Meile, *die;* ~ **after** *or* **upon** ~ *or* ~**s and** ~**s of sand/beaches** meilenweit Sand/Strände; ~**s per hour** Meilen pro Stunde; **not a million** ~**s from** (joc.) nicht allzu weit von; **go the extra** ~ (fig.) [noch] einen Schritt weiter gehen; **(b)** (fig. coll.: great amount) **win/miss by a** ~: haushoch gewinnen/meilenweit verfehlen; ~**s better/too big** tausendmal besser/viel zu groß; **be** ~**s ahead of sb.** jmdm. weit voraus sein; **sb. is** ~**s away** (in thought) jmd. ist mit seinen Gedanken ganz woanders; **(c)** (race) Meilenlauf, *der*

mileage /'maɪlɪdʒ/ *n.* **(a)** (number of miles) [Anzahl der] Meilen; **a low** ~ (on milometer) ein niedriger Meilenstand; **(b)** (number of miles per gallon) [Benzin]verbrauch, *der;* **what** ~ **do you get with your car?** wieviel verbraucht dein Auto?; **(c)** (fig.: benefit) Nutzen, *der;* **there is no** ~ **in the idea** dieser Vorschlag rentiert sich nicht

'milestone *n.* (lit. or fig.) Meilenstein, *der*

milieu /'miːljɜː, 'miːljɜː/ *n., pl.* ~**x** /'miːljɜːz, 'miːljɜːz/ *or* ~**s** Milieu, *das*

militancy /'mɪlɪtənsɪ/ *n., no pl.* Kampfbereitschaft, *die;* Militanz, *die*

militant /'mɪlɪtənt/ **1** *adj.* **(a)** (aggressively active) kämpferisch; militant; **(b)** (engaged in warfare) Krieg führend. **2** *n.* Militante, *der*/*die*

militarise ⇨ **militarize**

militarism /'mɪlɪtərɪzm/ *n.* Militarismus, *der*

militarize /'mɪlɪtəraɪz/ *v.t.* militarisieren

military /'mɪlɪtərɪ/ **1** *adj.* militärisch; Militär‹*regierung, -akademie, -uniform, -parade*›; ~ **service** Militärdienst, *der;* Wehrdienst, *der.* **2** *n., constr. as sing. or pl.* **the** ~: das Militär

militate /'mɪlɪteɪt/ *v.i.* ~ **against/in favour of sth.** [deutlich] gegen/für etw. sprechen; (have effect) sich zuungunsten/zugunsten einer Sache (*Gen.*) auswirken

militia /mɪ'lɪʃə/ *n.* Miliz, *die*

milk /mɪlk/ **1** *n.* Milch, *die;* **it's no use crying over spilt** ~ (prov.) [was] passiert ist[, ist] passiert. **2** *v.t.* (draw ~ from) melken; (fig.: get money out of) melken (salopp)

milk: ~ **bar** *n.* Milchbar, *die;* ~ **bottle** *n.* Milchflasche, *die;* ~ **'chocolate** *n.* Milchschokolade, *die;* ~**churn** *n.* Milchkanne, *die;* ~ **float** *n.* (Brit.) Milchwagen, *der;* ~ **jug** *n.* Milchkrug, *der;* (with tea, coffee, etc.) Milchkännchen, *das;* ~**maid** *n.* ▶887 Melkerin, *die;* ~**man** /'mɪlkmən/ *n., pl.* ~**men** /'mɪlkmən/ ▶887 Milchmann, *der;* ~ **powder** *n.* Milchpulver, *das;* ~**run** *n.* (fig.) [übliche] Tour; ~ **shake** *n.* Milchshake, *der;* ~ **tooth** *n.* Milchzahn, *der* ~ **train** *n.* Milchzug, *der;* **take the** ~ **train into London** (fig.) den ersten Zug nach London nehmen

milky /'mɪlkɪ/ *adj.* milchig; ~ **coffee** Milchkaffee, *der*

Milky 'Way *n.* Milchstraße, *die*

mill /mɪl/ **1** *n.* **(a)** Mühle, *die;* **(b)** (factory) Fabrik, *die;* (machine) Maschine, *die;* ~ **town** ≈ Textilstadt, *die.* **2** *v.t.* **(a)** mahlen ‹*Getreide*›; **(b)** fräsen ‹*Metallgegenstand*›; rändeln ‹*Münze*›

~ **a'bout** (Brit.), ~ **a'round** *v.i.* durcheinander laufen; **a mass of people** ~**ing about** *or* **around in the square** eine Menschenmenge, die sich hin und her über den Platz schiebt/schob

millennium /mɪ'lenɪəm/ n., pl. ∼s or **millennia** /mɪ'lenɪə/ (a) Jahrtausend, das; Millennium, das; (b) (Relig.) Tausendjähriges Reich; Millennium, das (fachspr.)

millepede /'mɪlɪpiːd/ n. (Zool.) Tausendfüß[l]er, der

miller /'mɪlə(r)/ n. ▶ 887 Müller, der

millet /'mɪlɪt/ n. (Bot.) Hirse, die

milli- /'mɪlɪ/ pref. milli-/Milli-

'milligram n. Milligramm, das

'millilitre (Brit.; Amer.: **milliliter**) n. ▶ 1193 Milliliter, der od. das

'millimetre (Brit.; Amer.: **millimeter**) ▶ 904 n. Millimeter, der

milliner /'mɪlɪnə(r)/ n. ▶ 887 Putzmacher, der/-macherin, die; Modist, der/Modistin, die

millinery /'mɪlɪnərɪ/ n., no pl. (a) (articles) Hüte; (b) (business) Hutmacherei, die

million /'mɪljən/ ▶ 956 1 adj. (a) a or one ∼: eine Million; **two/several** ∼: zwei/mehrere Millionen; **a** or **one** ∼ **and one** eine Million ein; **half a** ∼ eine halbe Million; (b) **a** ∼ **[and one]** (fig.: innumerable) tausend; **never in a** ∼ **years** nie im Leben (ugs.). 2 n. (a) Million, die; **a** or **one/two** ∼: eine Million/zwei Millionen; **in** or **by** ∼s millionenweise; **a** ∼ **and one** etc. eine Million einer/eine/eins; **the starving** ∼s die Millionen [von] Hungerleidenden; (b) (indefinite amount) **there were** ∼s of **people** eine Unmenge Leute waren da; **he is a man/she is one in a** ∼: so jemanden wie ihn/sie findet man nicht noch einmal

millionaire /mɪljə'neə(r)/ n. (lit. or fig.) Millionär, der/ Millionärin, die

millionth /'mɪljənθ/ ▶ 956 1 adj. millionst...; **a** ∼ **part** ein Millionstel. 2 n. (fraction) Millionstel, das

millipede ⇒ **millepede**

mill: ∼**-owner** n. Textilfabrikant, der; ∼**pond** n. **the sea was like a** ∼**pond** die See war ruhig wie ein Teich; ∼**-race** n. Mühlbach, der; ∼**stone** n. Mühlstein, der; **be a** ∼**stone round sb.'s neck** (fig.) jmdm. ein Klotz am Bein sein (ugs.); ∼**-wheel** n. Mühlrad, das

milometer /maɪ'lɒmɪtə(r)/ n. Meilenzähler, der

mime /maɪm/ 1 n. (a) (performance) Pantomime, die; (b) no pl., no art. (art) Pantomimik, die; Pantomime, die (ugs.). 2 v.i. pantomimisch agieren. 3 v.t. pantomimisch darstellen

mimic /'mɪmɪk/ 1 n. Imitator, der. 2 v.t., -ck-: (a) nachahmen; imitieren; (ridicule by imitating) parodieren; (b) (resemble closely) aussehen wie

mimicry /'mɪmɪkrɪ/ n., no pl. Nachahmen, das

Min. abbr. **Minister/Ministry** Min.

min. abbr. (a) **minute[s]** Min; (b) **minimum** (adj.) mind., (n.) Min.

minaret /'mɪnəret/ n. Minarett, das

mince /mɪns/ 1 n. Hackfleisch, das; Gehackte, das. 2 v.t. ∼ **beef** Rindfleisch durch den [Fleisch]wolf drehen; ∼**d meat** Hackfleisch, das; **not** ∼ **matters** die Dinge beim Namen nennen; **not** ∼ **one's words** kein Blatt vor den Mund nehmen. 3 v.i. trippeln

mince: ∼**meat** n. (a) Hackfleisch, das; Gehackte, das; **make** ∼**meat of sb.** (fig.) Hackfleisch aus jmdm. machen (ugs.); (b) (sweet) süße Pastetenfüllung aus Obst, Rosinen, Gewürzen, Nierenfett usw.; ∼ **'pie** n. mit süßem „mincemeat" gefüllte Pastete

mincer /'mɪnsə(r)/ n. Fleischwolf, der

mind /maɪnd/ 1 n. (a) (remembrance) **bear** or **keep sth. in** ∼: an etw. (Akk.) denken; etw. nicht vergessen; **have [it] in** ∼ **to do sth.** vorhaben, etw. zu tun; **bring sth. to** ∼: in Erinnerung rufen; **sth. comes into sb.'s** ∼: jmdm. fällt etw. ein; **it went out of my** ∼: ich habe es vergessen; es ist mir entfallen; **put sth./sb. out of one's** ∼: etw./jmdn. aus seinem Gedächtnis streichen; (b) (opinion) **give sb. a piece of one's** ∼: jmdm. gründlich die Meinung sagen; **in** or **to my** ∼: meiner Meinung od. Ansicht nach; **be of one** or **of the same** ∼, **be in one** ∼: einer Meinung sein; **be in two** ∼s **about sth.** [sich (Dat.)] unschlüssig über etw. (Akk.) sein; **change one's** ∼: seine Meinung ändern; **have a** ∼ **of one's own** seinen eigenen Kopf haben; **I have a good** ∼/**half a** ∼

to do that ich hätte große Lust/nicht übel Lust, das zu tun; **make up one's** ∼, **make one's** ∼ **up** sich entscheiden; **make up one's** ∼ **to do sth.** sich entschließen, etw. zu tun; **read sb.'s** ∼: jmds. Gedanken lesen; (c) (direction of thoughts) **his** ∼ **is on other things** er ist mit den Gedanken woanders; **give** or **put** or **turn one's** ∼ **to** sich konzentrieren auf (+ Akk.) ⟨Arbeit, Aufgabe, Angelegenheit⟩; **I have had sb./sth. on my** ∼: jmd./etw. hat mich beschäftigt; (worried) ich habe mir Sorgen wegen jmdm./etw. gemacht; **she has a lot of things on her** ∼: sie hat viele Sorgen; **sth. preys** or **weighs on sb.'s** ∼: etw. macht jmdm. zu schaffen; **take sb.'s** ∼ **off sth.** jmdn. von etw. ablenken; **keep one's** ∼ **on sth.** sich auf etw. (Akk.) konzentrieren; **close one's** ∼ **to sth.** sich einer Sache (Dat.) verschließen (geh.); (d) (way of thinking and feeling) Denkweise, die; **frame of** ∼: [seelische] Verfassung; **state of** ∼: [Geistes]zustand, der; **be in a frame of** ∼ **to do sth.** in der Verfassung sein, etw. zu tun; **have a logical** ∼: logisch denken; (e) (seat of consciousness, thought, volition) Geist, der; **it's all in the** ∼: es ist alles nur Einstellung; **in one's** ∼: im Stillen; **in my** ∼**'s eye** vor meinem geistigen Auge; im Geiste; **nothing could be further from my** ∼ **than** ...: nichts läge mir ferner, als ...; (f) (intellectual powers) Verstand, der; **have a very good** ∼: einen klaren od. scharfen Verstand haben; **great** ∼s **think alike** (joc.) große Geister denken [eben] gleich; (g) (normal mental faculties) Verstand, der; **lose** or **go out of one's** ∼: den Verstand verlieren; **be out of one's** ∼: den Verstand verloren haben; **in one's right** ∼: bei klarem Verstand. 2 v.t. (a) (heed) **don't** ∼ **what he says** gib nichts auf sein Gerede; ∼ **what I say** glaub mir; **let's do it, and never** ∼ **the expense** machen wir es doch, egal, was es kostet; (b) (concern oneself about) **he** ∼s **a lot what people think of him** es ist für ihn sehr wichtig, was die Leute von ihm denken; **I can't afford a bicycle, never** ∼ **a car** ich kann mir kein Fahrrad leisten, geschweige denn ein Auto; **never** ∼ **him/that** (don't be anxious) er/das kann dir doch egal sein (ugs.); **never** ∼ **how/where** ...: es tut nichts zur Sache, wie/wo ...; **don't** ∼ **me** nimm keine Rücksicht auf mich; (don't let my presence disturb you) lass dich [durch mich] nicht stören; (iron.) nimm bloß keine Rücksicht auf mich; ∼ **the doors!** Vorsicht an den Türen!; ∼ **one's P's and Q's** sich anständig benehmen; (c) usu. neg. or interrog. (object to) **did he** ∼ **being woken up?** hat es ihm was ausgemacht, aufgeweckt zu werden?; **would you** ∼ **opening the door?** würdest du bitte die Tür öffnen?; **do you** ∼ **my smoking?** stört es Sie od. haben Sie etwas dagegen, wenn ich rauche?; **I wouldn't** ∼ **a walk** ich hätte nichts gegen einen Spaziergang; (d) (remember and take care) ∼ **you don't leave anything behind** denk daran, nichts liegen lassen!; ∼ **how you go!** pass auf!; sei vorsichtig!; (as general farewell) machs gut! (ugs.); ∼ **you get this work done** sieh zu, dass du mit dieser Arbeit fertig wirst!; (e) (have charge of) aufpassen auf (+ Akk.); ∼ **the shop** or (Amer.) **the store** (fig.) sich um den Laden kümmern (ugs.). 3 v.i. (a) ∼! Vorsicht!; Achtung!; (b) usu. in imper. (take note) **follow the signposts,** ∼, **or** ...: denk daran und halte dich an die Wegweiser, sonst...; **I didn't know that,** ∼, **or** ...: das habe ich allerdings nicht gewusst, sonst ...; (c) (care, object) **do you '**∼**?** (may I?) hätten Sie etwas dagegen?; (please do not) ich muss doch sehr bitten; **he doesn't** ∼ **about your using the car** er hat nichts dagegen, wenn Sie den Wagen benutzen; **if you don't** ∼: wenn es dir recht ist; (d) (give heed) **never [you]** ∼ (it's not important) macht nichts; ist nicht schlimm; (it's none of your business) sei nicht so neugierig; **never** ∼: **I can do it** schon gut — das kann ich machen; **never** ∼ **about that now!** lass das jetzt mal [sein/liegen]!; **never** ∼ **about him — what happened to her?** er interessiert mich nicht — was ist ihr passiert?
∼ **'out** v.i. aufpassen (**for** auf + Akk.); ∼ **out!** Vorsicht!

mind-boggling /'maɪndbɒglɪŋ/ adj. (coll.) wahnsinnig (ugs.)

minded /'maɪndɪd/ adj. (a) (disposed) **be** ∼ **to do sth.** bereit od. (geh.) geneigt sein, etw. zu tun; (b) **mechanically** ∼: technisch veranlagt; **he is not in the least politically** ∼: er ist vollkommen unpolitisch

minder /'maɪndə(r)/ *n.* **(a)** (for child) **we need a ∼ for the child** wir brauchen jemanden, der auf das Kind aufpasst *od.* das Kind betreut; **(b)** (sl.: protector of criminal) Gorilla, *der* (salopp)

mindful /'maɪndfl/ *adj.* **be ∼ of sth.** (take into account) etw. bedenken *od.* berücksichtigen; (give attention to) an etw. *(Akk.)* denken

mindless /'maɪndlɪs/ *adj.* geistlos, (ugs.) hirnlos ⟨*Mensch*⟩; sinnlos ⟨*Handlung, Gewalt*⟩

mind: **∼-reader** ⇒ **thought-reader; ∼set** *n.* Denkart, *die*

mine¹ /maɪn/ **1** *n.* **(a)** (for coal) Bergwerk, *das;* (for metal, diamonds, etc.) Bergwerk, *das;* Mine, *die;* **go** *or* **work down the ∼:** unter Tage arbeiten; **(b)** (fig.: abundant source) unerschöpfliche Quelle; **he is a ∼ of useful facts/of information** von ihm kann man eine Menge Nützliches/eine Menge erfahren; **(c)** (explosive device) Mine, *die.* **2** *v.t.* **(a)** schürfen ⟨*Gold*⟩; abbauen, fördern ⟨*Erz, Kohle, Schiefer*⟩; **∼ an area for ore** etc. in einem Gebiet Erz *usw.* abbauen *od.* fördern; **(b)** (Mil.: lay ∼s in) verminen. **3** *v.i.* Bergbau betreiben; **∼ for** ⇒ **2a**

mine² *poss. pron.* **(a)** *pred.* meiner/meine/mein[e]s; der/die/das meinige (geh.); **you do your best and I'll do ∼:** du tust dein Bestes und ich auch; **those big feet of ∼:** meine großen Quanten (ugs.); *see also* **hers; (b)** *attrib.* (arch./poet.) mein

'minefield *n.* (lit. or fig.) Minenfeld, *das*

miner /'maɪnə(r)/ *n.* ▶887⟩ Bergmann, *der;* Kumpel, *der* (Bergmannsspr.)

mineral /'mɪnrl/ **1** *adj.* mineralisch; Mineral⟨*salz, -quelle*⟩. **2** *n.* **(a)** Mineral, *das;* **a country rich in ∼s** ein an Bodenschätzen reiches Land; **(b)** *esp. in pl.* (Brit.: soft drink) Erfrischungsgetränk, *das*

mineralogy /mɪnə'rælədʒɪ/ *n.* Mineralogie, *die*

mineral: **∼ oil** *n.* Mineralöl, *das;* **∼ water** *n.* Mineralwasser, *das*

minestrone /mɪnɪ'strəʊnɪ/ *n.* (Gastr.) Minestrone, *die*

mine: **∼sweeper** *n.* Minensuchboot, *das;* **∼worker** *n.* ▶887⟩ Bergmann, *der;* Kumpel, *der* (Bergmannsspr.)

mingle /'mɪŋgl/ **1** *v.t.* [ver]mischen. **2** *v.i.* sich [ver]mischen **(with** mit); **∼ with** *or* **among the crowds** sich unters Volk mischen

mingy /'mɪndʒɪ/ *adj.* (Brit. coll.) mick[e]rig (ugs.) ⟨*Gegenstand*⟩; knick[e]rig (ugs.) ⟨*Person*⟩; lumpig (ugs.) ⟨*Betrag*⟩

mini /'mɪnɪ/ *n.* (coll.) **(a)** (car) M∼, **(P)** Mini, *der;* **(b)** (skirt) Mini, *der* (ugs.)

mini- *in comb.* Mini-; Klein⟨*bus, -wagen, -taxi*⟩

miniature /'mɪnɪtʃə(r)/ **1** *n.* **(a)** (picture) Miniatur, *die;* **(b)** (small version) Miniaturausgabe, *die;* **in ∼:** im Kleinformat. **2** *adj.* **(a)** (small-scale) Miniatur-; **(b)** (smaller than normal) Mini- (ugs.); Kleinst-; **∼ poodle** Zwergpudel, *der;* **∼ golf** Minigolf, *das;* **∼ camera** Kleinstbildkamera, *die;* **∼ railway** Miniaturbahn, *die*

mini: **∼bus** *n.* Kleinbus, *der;* **∼cab** *n.* Kleintaxi, *das;* Minicar, *der;* **∼computer** *n.* Minicomputer, *der*

minim /'mɪnɪm/ *n.* (Brit. Mus.) halbe Note

minimal /'mɪnɪml/ *adj.,* **minimally** /'mɪnɪmlɪ/ *adv.* minimal

minimize (**minimise**) /'mɪnɪmaɪz/ *v.t.* **(a)** auf ein Mindestmaß reduzieren; **(b)** (understate) bagatellisieren; verharmlosen ⟨*Gefahr*⟩

minimum /'mɪnɪməm/ **1** *n., pl.* **minima** /'mɪnɪmə/ Minimum, *das* (**of** an + *Dat.*); **keep sth. to a ∼:** etw. so gering wie möglich halten; **a ∼ of £5** mindestens 5 Pfund; **at the ∼:** mindestens. **2** *attrib. adj.* Mindest-; **∼ temperatures tonight around 5°** nächtliche Tiefsttemperaturen um 5°; **∼ wage** Mindestlohn, *der*

minimum 'wage *n.* Mindestlohn, *der*

mining /'maɪnɪŋ/ *n.* Bergbau, *der; attrib.* Bergbau-; **∼ area** Bergbaugebiet, *das;* Revier, *das*

mining: **∼ engineer** *n.* ▶887⟩ Berg[bau]ingenieur, *der;* **∼ industry** *n.* Montanindustrie, *die;* Bergbau, *der;*

∼ town *n.* Bergbaustadt, *die;* **∼ village** *n.* Bergbaudorf, *das*

'mini-roundabout *n.* (Brit.) *sehr kleiner, oft nur aufs Pflaster aufgezeichneter Kreisverkehr*

'miniskirt *n.* Minirock, *der*

minister /'mɪnɪstə(r)/ **1** *n.* **(a)** ▶887⟩ (Polit.) Minister, *der*/Ministerin, *die;* **M∼ of State** (Brit.) ≈ Staatssekretär, *der*/-sekretärin, *die;* **(b)** (Eccl.) **∼** [of religion] Geistliche, *der*/*die;* Pfarrer, *der*/Pfarrerin, *die.* **2** *v.i.* **∼ to sb.'s wants/needs** jmds. Wünsche/Bedürfnisse befriedigen

ministerial /mɪnɪ'stɪərɪəl/ *adj.* (Polit.) Minister-; ministeriell

ministry /'mɪnɪstrɪ/ *n.* **(a)** (Government department or building) Ministerium, *das;* **∼ official** Ministerialbeamte, *der*/-beamtin, *die;* **(b)** (profession of clergyman) geistliches Amt; **go into** *or* **enter the ∼:** Geistlicher werden

mink /mɪŋk/ *n.* Nerz, *der; attrib.* **∼ coat** Nerzmantel, *der*

minnow /'mɪnəʊ/ *n.* (Zool.) Elritze, *die*

minor /'maɪnə(r)/ **1** *adj.* **(a)** (lesser) kleiner...; **(b)** (unimportant) weniger bedeutend; geringer ⟨*Bedeutung*⟩; leicht ⟨*Operation, Verletzung, Anfall*⟩; Neben⟨*figur, -rolle*⟩; **∼ matter** Nebensächlichkeit, *die;* **∼ road** kleine Straße; **(c)** (Mus.) Moll-; **∼ key/chord** Molltonart, *die*/Mollakkord, *der;* **A ∼:** a-Moll; **in a ∼ key** in Moll. **2** *n.* **(a)** (person) Minderjährige, *der*/*die;* **be a ∼:** minderjährig sein; **(b)** (Amer. Univ.) Nebenfach, *das.* **3** *v.i.* (Amer.) **∼ in sth.** etw. als Nebenfach haben

minority /maɪ'nɒrɪtɪ, mɪ'nɒrɪtɪ/ *n.* **(a)** Minderheit, *die;* Minorität, *die;* **in the ∼:** in der Minderheit; **(b)** *attrib.* Minderheits⟨*regierung, -bericht*⟩; **∼ group** Minderheit, *die;* Minorität, *die;* **∼ rights** Minderheitenrechte

minority 'rule *n.* Herrschaft einer/der Minderheit; **white ∼:** die Herrschaft der weißen Minderheit

minster /'mɪnstə(r)/ *n.* Münster, *das*

minstrel /'mɪnstrl/ *n.* Spielmann, *der;* fahrender Sänger

mint¹ /mɪnt/ **1** *n.* **(a)** (place) Münzanstalt, *die;* Münze, *die;* **(b)** (sum of money) **a ∼** [of money] eine schöne Stange Geld (ugs.). **2** *adj.* funkelnagelneu (ugs.); vorzüglich ⟨*Münze*⟩ (fachspr.); **in ∼ condition** ⟨*Auto, Bild usw.*⟩ in tadellosem Zustand. **3** *v.t.* (lit. or fig.) prägen

mint² *n.* **(a)** (plant) Minze, *die;* **(b)** (peppermint) Pfefferminz, *das; attrib.* Pfefferminz-

mint 'sauce *n.* Minzsoße, *die*

minuet /mɪnjʊ'et/ *n.* (Mus.) Menuett, *das*

minus /'maɪnəs/ **1** *prep.* **(a)** (with the subtraction of) minus; weniger; (without) ohne; abzüglich + *Gen.*); **(b)** ▶1141⟩ (below zero) minus; **∼ 20 degrees** 20 Grad Kälte *od.* minus 20 Grad; **(c)** (coll.: lacking) ohne. **2** *adj.* (Math.) negativ ⟨*Wert, Menge, Größe*⟩; Minus⟨*zeichen, -betrag*⟩. **3** *n.* (symbol) Minus[zeichen], *das*

minuscule /'mɪnəskju:l/ *adj.* winzig

minute¹ /'mɪnɪt/ **1** *n.* **(a)** ▶706⟩ Minute, *die;* (moment) Moment, *der;* Augenblick, *der;* **I expect him any ∼** [now] ich erwarte ihn jeden Augenblick; **for a ∼:** eine Minute/einen Moment [lang]; **in a ∼** (very soon) gleich; **come back this ∼!** komm sofort *od.* auf der Stelle zurück!; **at that very ∼:** genau in diesem Augenblick; **to the ∼:** auf die Minute; **up to the ∼:** hochaktuell; **the ∼** [that] I left in dem Augenblick, als ich wegging; **just a ∼!, wait a ∼!** (coll.) einen Augenblick!; (objecting) Augenblick mal! (ugs.); **be five ∼s' walk** [away] fünf Minuten zu Fuß entfernt sein; **(b)** (of angle) Minute, *die;* **(c)** *in pl.* (brief summary) Protokoll, *das;* **keep** *or* **take the ∼s** das Protokoll führen; **(d)** (official memorandum) Memorandum, *das.* **2** *v.t.* protokollieren ⟨*Vernehmung, Aussage*⟩; zu Protokoll nehmen ⟨*Bemerkung*⟩

minute² /maɪ'nju:t/ *adj.,* **∼r** /maɪ'nju:tə(r)/, **∼st** /maɪ'nju:tɪst/ **(a)** (tiny) winzig; **(b)** (precise) minuziös; exakt; **with ∼ care** mit peinlicher Sorgfalt

minute hand /'mɪnɪthænd/ *n.* Minutenzeiger, *der*

minutely /maɪ'nju:tlɪ/ *adv.* genauestens; sorgfältigst

minx /mɪŋks/ *n.* kleines Biest (ugs.)

miracle /'mɪrəkl/ *n.* Wunder, *das;* **perform** *or* **work ∼s** Wunder tun *od.* vollbringen; ⟨*Mittel, Behandlung usw.:*⟩

Wunder wirken; **economic** ∼: Wirtschaftswunder, *das;* **be a** ∼ **of ingenuity** ein Wunder an Genialität sein

miraculous /mɪˈrækjʊləs/ *adj.* **(a)** wunderbar; (having ∼ power) wunderkräftig; **(b)** (surprising) erstaunlich; unglaublich

miraculously /mɪˈrækjʊləslɪ/ *adv.* **(a)** auf wunderbare *od.* (geh.) wundersame Weise; ∼, **he escaped injury** wie durch ein Wunder blieb er unverletzt; **(b)** (surprisingly) erstaunlicherweise

mirage /ˈmɪrɑːʒ/ *n.* Fata Morgana, *die;* Luftspiegelung, *die;* (fig.) Illusion, *die*

mire /ˈmaɪə(r)/ *n.* Morast, *der*

mirror /ˈmɪrə(r)/ **1** *n.* (lit. or fig.) Spiegel, *der.* **2** *v.t.* (lit. or fig.) [wider]spiegeln

mirror 'image *n.* Spiegelbild, *das*

mirth /mɜːθ/ *n.* Fröhlichkeit, *die;* (laughter) Heiterkeit, *die*

misadventure /mɪsədˈventʃə(r)/ *n.* **(a)** Missgeschick, *das;* **(b)** (Law) **death by** ∼: Tod durch Unfall

misanthropist /mɪˈzænθrəpɪst/ *n.* Misanthrop, *der* (geh.); Menschenfeind, *der*

misapprehension /mɪsæprɪˈhenʃn/ *n.* Missverständnis, *das;* **be under a** ∼: einem Irrtum unterliegen; **have a lot of** ∼**s about sth.** völlig falsche Vorstellungen von etw. haben

misappropriate /mɪsəˈprəʊprɪeɪt/ *v.t.* unterschlagen, (Rechtsspr.) veruntreuen ⟨ *Geld usw.*⟩

misbehave /mɪsbɪˈheɪv/ *v.i. & refl.* sich schlecht benehmen

misbehaviour (*Amer.:* **misbehavior**) /mɪsbɪˈheɪvɪə(r)/ *n.* schlechtes Benehmen

miscalculate /mɪsˈkælkjʊleɪt/ *v.t.* falsch berechnen; (misjudge) falsch einschätzen; ∼ **the distance** sich bei der Entfernung verkalkulieren

miscalculation /mɪskælkjʊˈleɪʃn/ *n.* (arithmetical error) Rechenfehler, *der;* (misjudgement) Fehleinschätzung, *die*

miscarriage /mɪsˈkærɪdʒ/ *n.* **(a)** (Med.) Fehlgeburt, *die;* **(b)** (Law) ∼ **of justice** Justizirrtum, *der*

miscarry /mɪsˈkærɪ/ *v.i.* **(a)** (Med.) eine Fehlgeburt haben; **(b)** ⟨ *Plan, Vorhaben usw.*:⟩ fehlschlagen

miscellaneous /mɪsəˈleɪnɪəs/ *adj.* **(a)** (mixed) [kunter]-bunt ⟨ *[Menschen]menge, Sammlung*⟩; **(b)** *with pl. n.* (of various kinds) verschieden; verschiedenerlei

miscellany /mɪˈselənɪ/ *n.* (mixture) [bunte] Sammlung; [buntes] Gemisch

mischance /mɪsˈtʃɑːns/ *n.* (piece of bad luck) unglücklicher Zufall; **by a** *or* **some** ∼: durch einen unglücklichen Zufall

mischief /ˈmɪstʃɪf/ *n.* **(a)** Unsinn, *der;* Unfug, *der;* (pranks) [dumme] Streiche *Pl.;* (playful malice) Schalk, *der;* **be** *or* **get up to [some]** ∼: etwas anstellen; **keep out of** ∼: keinen Unfug machen; **(b)** (harm) Schaden, *der;* **do sb./oneself a** ∼ (coll.) jmdm./sich etwas antun; **(c)** (person) Schlawiner, *der* (ugs.)

'mischief-maker *n.* Böswillige, *der/die*

mischievous /ˈmɪstʃɪvəs/ *adj.* **(a)** spitzbübisch, schelmisch ⟨ *Blick, Gesichtsausdruck, Lächeln*⟩; ∼ **trick** Schabernack, *der;* **(b)** (malicious) boshaft ⟨ *Person*⟩; böse ⟨ *Absicht*⟩; **(c)** (harmful) bösartig ⟨ *Gerücht*⟩; böse ⟨ *Zeitungsartikel*⟩

misconceive /mɪskənˈsiːv/ *v.t.* **be** ∼**d** ⟨ *Projekt, Vorschlag, Aktion:*⟩ schlecht konzipiert sein

misconception /mɪskənˈsepʃn/ *n.* falsche Vorstellung (about von); **be [labouring] under a** ∼ **about sth.** sich (*Dat.*) eine falsche Vorstellung von etw. machen

misconduct /mɪsˈkɒndʌkt/ *n., no pl.* (improper conduct) unkorrektes Verhalten; (Sport) unsportliches *od.* unfaires Verhalten

misconstrue /mɪskənˈstruː/ *v.t.* missverstehen; ∼ **sb.'s meaning** jmdn. missverstehen

miscount /mɪsˈkaʊnt/ **1** *v.i.* sich verzählen; (when counting votes) falsch [aus]zählen. **2** *v.t.* falsch zählen

misdeed /mɪsˈdiːd/ *n.* **(a)** (evil deed) Missetat, *die* (geh. veralt.); **(b)** (crime) Verbrechen, *das*

misdemeanour (*Amer.:* **misdemeanor**) /mɪsdɪˈmiːnə(r)/ *n.* **(a)** Missetat, *die* (veralt., scherzh.); **(b)** (Law) Vergehen, *das*

misdirect /mɪsdɪˈrekt, mɪsdaɪˈrekt/ *v.t.* falsch einsetzen ⟨ *Energien*⟩; in die falsche Richtung schicken ⟨ *nach dem Weg Fragenden*⟩

miser /ˈmaɪzə(r)/ *n.* Geizhals, *der;* Geizkragen, *der* (ugs.)

miserable /ˈmɪzərəbl/ *adj.* **(a)** (unhappy) unglücklich; erbärmlich, elend ⟨ *Leben[sbedingungen]*⟩; **feel** ∼: sich elend fühlen; **(b)** (causing wretchedness) trostlos; trist ⟨ *Wetter, Urlaub*⟩; **(c)** (contemptible, mean) armselig; **a** ∼ **five pounds** klägliche *od.* (ugs.) miese fünf Pfund

miserably /ˈmɪzərəblɪ/ *adv.* **(a)** unglücklich; elend, jämmerlich ⟨ *leben, zugrunde gehen*⟩; ∼ **poor** bettelarm; **(b)** (meanly) miserabel, (ugs.) mies ⟨ *bezahlt*⟩; **(c)** kläglich, jämmerlich ⟨ *versagen*⟩; völlig, total ⟨ *verpfuscht, unzureichend*⟩

miserly /ˈmaɪzəlɪ/ *adj.* geizig; armselig ⟨ *Portion, Essen*⟩

misery /ˈmɪzərɪ/ *n.* **(a)** Elend, *das;* **make sb.'s life a** ∼: jmdm. das Leben zur Qual machen; **put an animal out of its** ∼: ein Tier von seinen Qualen erlösen; **put sb. out of his** ∼ (fig.) jmdn. nicht länger auf die Folter spannen; **miseries** Elend, *das;* Nöte *Pl.;* **(b)** (coll.: discontented person) ∼**[-guts]** Miesepeter, *der* (ugs. abwertend)

misfire /mɪsˈfaɪə(r)/ *v.i.* **(a)** ⟨ *Motor:*⟩ eine Fehlzündung/ Fehlzündungen haben; ⟨ *Kanone, Gewehr:*⟩ versagen, nicht losgehen; **(b)** ⟨ *Plan, Versuch:*⟩ fehlschlagen; ⟨ *Streich, Witz:*⟩ danebengehen

misfit /ˈmɪsfɪt/ *n.* (person) Außenseiter, *der/*Außenseiterin, *die*

misfortune /mɪsˈfɔːtʃən, mɪsˈfɔːtʃuːn/ *n.* **(a)** *no pl., no art.* (bad luck) Missgeschick, *das;* **suffer** ∼: [viel] Unglück haben; **(b)** (stroke of fate) Schicksalsschlag, *der;* (unlucky incident) Missgeschick, *das;* **it was his** ∼ *or* **he had the** ∼ **to …:** er hatte das Pech, zu …

misgiving /mɪsˈgɪvɪŋ/ *n.* Bedenken *Pl.;* Zweifel, *der;* **have some** ∼**s about sth.** wegen einer Sache Bedenken haben

misguided /mɪsˈgaɪdɪd/ *adj.* töricht ⟨ *Person*⟩; unangebracht ⟨ *Eifer*⟩; unsinnig ⟨ *Bemühung*⟩

mishandle /mɪsˈhændl/ *v.t.* **(a)** (deal with incorrectly) falsch behandeln ⟨ *Angelegenheit*⟩; schlecht verwalten ⟨ *Finanzen*⟩; **(b)** (handle roughly) misshandeln

mishap /ˈmɪshæp/ *n.* Missgeschick, *das;* **sb. suffers** *or* **meets with a** ∼: jmdm. passiert ein Missgeschick; **without further** ∼: ohne weitere Zwischenfälle

mishear /mɪsˈhɪə(r)/ **1** *v.i.,* **misheard** /mɪsˈhɜːd/ sich verhören. **2** *v.t.,* **misheard** falsch verstehen

mishit /mɪsˈhɪt/ *v.t.,* **-tt-,** **mishit** verschlagen ⟨ *Ball*⟩

mishmash /ˈmɪʃmæʃ/ *n.* Mischmasch, *der* (ugs.) (**of** aus)

misinform /mɪsɪnˈfɔːm/ *v.t.* falsch informieren

misinterpret /mɪsɪnˈtɜːprɪt/ *v.t.* **(a)** (interpret wrongly) fehlinterpretieren, falsch auslegen ⟨ *Text, Inschrift, Buch*⟩; **(b)** (make wrong inference from) falsch deuten; missdeuten

misinterpretation /mɪsɪntɜːprɪˈteɪʃn/ *n.* Fehlinterpretation, *die;* **be open to** ∼: leicht falsch ausgelegt werden können

misjudge /mɪsˈdʒʌdʒ/ *v.t.* falsch einschätzen; falsch beurteilen ⟨ *Person*⟩; ∼ **the height/distance** sich in der Höhe/Entfernung verschätzen

misjudgement, misjudgment /mɪsˈdʒʌdʒmənt/ *n.* Fehleinschätzung, *die;* (of person) falsche Beurteilung; (of distance, length, etc.) falsche Einschätzung

mislay /mɪsˈleɪ/ *v.t.,* **mislaid** /mɪsˈleɪd/ verlegen

mislead /mɪsˈliːd/ *v.t.,* **misled** /mɪsˈled/ irreführen; täuschen; ∼ **sb. about sth.** jmdm. ein falsches Bild von etw. vermitteln

misleading /mɪsˈliːdɪŋ/ *adj.* irreführend

mismanage /mɪsˈmænɪdʒ/ *v.t.* herunterwirtschaften ⟨ *Firma*⟩; schlecht führen ⟨ *Haushalt*⟩; schlecht handhaben *od.* abwickeln ⟨ *Angelegenheit, Projekt*⟩

mismanagement /mɪsˈmænɪdʒmənt/ *n.* Misswirtschaft, *die;* (of finances) schlechte Verwaltung; (of matters or affairs) schlechte Handhabung *od.* Abwicklung

misnomer /mɪsˈnəʊmə(r)/ *n.* unzutreffende Bezeichnung

misogynist /mɪˈsɒdʒɪnɪst/ *n.* Frauenhasser, *der*

misogyny /mɪˈsɒdʒɪnɪ/ *n.* Frauenhass, *der;* Misogynie, *die* (geh.)

misplace /mɪsˈpleɪs/ *v.t.* an die falsche Stelle stellen/ legen/setzen *usw.;* ～ **one's affection/confidence** seine Zuneigung/sein Vertrauen dem Falschen/der Falschen schenken; **be** ～**d** (inappropriate) unangebracht *od.* fehl am Platz sein

misprint /ˈmɪsprɪnt/ *n.* Druckfehler, *der*

mispronounce /mɪsprəˈnaʊns/ *v.t.* falsch aussprechen

misquote /mɪsˈkwəʊt/ *v.t.* falsch zitieren

misread /mɪsˈriːd/ *v.t.*, **misread** /mɪsˈred/ (read wrongly) falsch *od.* nicht richtig lesen ‹*Text, Wort, Schrift*›; (interpret wrongly) missdeuten ‹*Text, Absichten*›

misrepresent /mɪsreprɪˈzent/ *v.t.* falsch darstellen; verdrehen ‹*Tatsachen*›

Miss /mɪs/ *n.* ▶1152◀ (a) (title of unmarried woman) ～ **Brown** Frau Brown; Fräulein Brown (veralt.); (girl) Fräulein Brown; (b) (title of beauty queen) ～ **France** Miss Frankreich; (c) (as form of address to teacher etc.) Frau Schmidt *usw.*

miss 1 *n.* (a) (failure to hit or attain) Fehlschlag, *der;* (shot) Fehlschuss, *der;* (throw) Fehlwurf, *der;* **be a** ～: danebengehen (ugs.); **a** ～ **is as good as a mile** (prov.) fast getroffen ist auch daneben; (b) **give sb./sth. a** ～: sich (*Dat.*) jmdn./etw. schenken. **2** *v.t.* (a) (fail to hit, lit. or fig.) verfehlen; ～**ed!** nicht getroffen!; **the car just** ～**ed the tree** das Auto wäre um ein Haar gegen den Baum geprallt; (b) (fail to get) nicht bekommen; (fail to find or meet) verpassen; ～ **the goal** am Tor vorbeischießen; (c) (let slip) versäumen; ～ **an opportunity** sich (*Dat.*) eine Gelegenheit entgehen lassen; **it is too good to** ～ *or* **is not to be** ～**ed** das darf man sich (*Dat.*) [einfach] nicht entgehen lassen; (d) (fail to catch) versäumen, verpassen ‹*Bus, Zug, Flugzeug*›; ～ **the boat** *or* **bus** (fig.) den Anschluss verpassen (fig.); (e) (fail to take part in) versäumen; ～ **school** in der Schule fehlen; (f) (fail to see) übersehen; (fail to hear or understand) nicht mitbekommen; **you can't** ～ **it** es ist nicht zu übersehen; **he doesn't** ～ **much** ihm entgeht so schnell nichts; (g) (feel the absence of) vermissen; **she** ～**es him** er fehlt ihr; (h) (fail to keep or perform) versäumen ‹*Verabredung, Vorstellung*›. **3** *v.i.* (a) (not hit sth.) nicht treffen; (not catch sth.) danebengreifen; (b) ‹*Ball, Schuss usw.*› danebengehen; (c) ‹*Motor:*› aussetzen
～ **'out** 1 *v.t.* weglassen. **2** *v.i.* ～ **out on sth.** (coll.) sich (*Dat.*) etw. entgehen lassen

misshapen /mɪsˈʃeɪpn/ *adj.* missgebildet; missgestaltet

missile /ˈmɪsaɪl/ *n.* [Wurf]geschoss, *das;* (self-propelled) Missile, *das;* Flugkörper, *der*

missile: ～ **base** *n.* [Raketen]abschussbasis, *die;* ～ **launcher** *n.* [Raketen]abschussrampe, *die;* ～ **site** ⇒ ～ **base**

missing /ˈmɪsɪŋ/ *adj.* vermisst; fehlend ‹*Seite, Kapitel, Teil, Hinweis, Indiz*›; **be** ～ ‹*Kapitel, Wort, Seite:*› fehlen; ‹*Brille, Bleistift usw.:*› verschwunden sein; ‹*Person:*› vermisst werden; (not be present) nicht da sein; fehlen; **the jacket has two buttons** ～: an der Jacke fehlen zwei Knöpfe; **I am** ～ **£10** mir fehlen 10 Pfund; ～ **person** Vermisste, *der/die;* ～ **link** (Biol.) Missinglink, *das*

mission /ˈmɪʃn/ *n.* (a) (task) Mission, *die;* Auftrag, *der;* (b) (journey) Mission, *die;* **go/come on a** ～ **to do sth.** mit dem Auftrag reisen/kommen, etw. zu tun; (c) (planned operation) Einsatz, *der;* (d) (vocation) Mission, *die;* ～ **in life** Lebensaufgabe, *die;* (e) (missionary post) Mission[sstation], *die*

missionary /ˈmɪʃənəri/ 1 *adj.* missionarisch; Missions‹*station, -arbeit, -schrift*›. **2** *n.* ▶887◀ Missionar, *der*/Missionarin, *die*

'mission statement *n.* Unternehmensleitbild, *das*

missis /ˈmɪsɪz/, **'missis** /ˈmɪsɪz/ *n.* (sl./joc.: wife) **the** *or* **my/your** ～: die *od.* meine/deine Alte (salopp)

misspell /mɪsˈspel/ *v.t.*, *forms as* **spell¹** falsch schreiben

misspend /mɪsˈspend/ *v.t.*, *forms as* **spend** verschwenden; vergeuden

misstatement /mɪsˈsteɪtmənt/ *n.* falsche Darstellung

mist /mɪst/ *n.* (a) (fog) Nebel, *der;* (haze) Dunst, *der;* (on windscreen etc.) Beschlag, *der;* (b) **in the** ～**s of time** *or* **antiquity** (fig.) im Dunkel *od.* (geh.) Nebel der Vergangenheit; (c) (of spray, vapour, etc.) Wolke, *die*
～ **'over** *v.i.* [sich] beschlagen; **his eyes** ～**ed over**

Tränen verschleierten seinen Blick
～ **'up** *v.i.* [sich] beschlagen

mistakable /mɪˈsteɪkəbl/ *adj.* verwechselbar (**for** mit)

mistake /mɪˈsteɪk/ 1 *n.* Fehler, *der;* (misunderstanding) Missverständnis, *das;* **make a** ～: einen Fehler machen; (in thinking) sich irren; **there's some** ～! da liegt ein Irrtum *od.* Fehler vor!; **the** ～ **is mine** der Fehler liegt bei mir; **it is a** ～ **to assume that** …: es ist ein Irrtum anzunehmen, dass …; **by** ～: versehentlich; aus Versehen; **make no** ～ **about it,** …: täusch dich nicht, … **2** *v.t.*, *forms as* **take** 1 falsch verstehen; missverstehen; ～ **sth./sb. as meaning that** …: etw./jmdn. [fälschlicherweise] so verstehen, dass …; ～ **x for y** x mit y verwechseln; **there is no mistaking him** man kann ihn gar nicht verwechseln; ～ **sb.'s identity** jmdn. [mit jmd. anderem] verwechseln

mistaken /mɪˈsteɪkn/ *adj.* **be** ～: sich täuschen; ～ **kindness/zeal** unangebrachte Freundlichkeit/unangebrachter Eifer; **or** *or* **unless I'm very much** ～: wenn mich nicht alles täuscht; **a case of** ～ **identity** eine Verwechslung

mistakenly /mɪˈsteɪknli/ *adv.* irrtümlicherweise

mister /ˈmɪstə(r)/ *n.* (coll./joc.) **hey,** ～: he, Meister *od.* Chef (ugs.)

mistime /mɪsˈtaɪm/ *v.t.* einen ungünstigen Zeitpunkt wählen für; schlecht timen (bes. Sport)

mistletoe /ˈmɪsltəʊ/ *n.* Mistel, *die;* (sprig) Mistelzweig, *der*

mistook ⇒ **mistake** 2

mistranslate /mɪstrænsˈleɪt/ *v.t.* falsch übersetzen

mistranslation /mɪstrænsˈleɪʃn/ *n.* falsche Übersetzung; (error) Übersetzungsfehler, *der*

mistreat /mɪsˈtriːt/ *v.t.* schlecht behandeln; (violently) misshandeln

mistreatment /mɪsˈtriːtmənt/ *n.* schlechte Behandlung; (violent) Misshandlung, *die*

mistress /ˈmɪstrɪs/ *n.* (a) (of a household) Hausherrin, *die;* (b) (person in control, employer) Herrin, *die;* **she is her own** ～: sie ist ihr eigener Herr; **the dog's** ～: das Frauchen [des Hundes]; (c) (Brit. Sch.: teacher) Lehrerin, *die;* **'French** ～: Französischlehrerin, *die;* (d) (lover) Geliebte, *die*

mistrust /mɪsˈtrʌst/ 1 *v.t.* misstrauen (+ *Dat.*). **2** *n.*, no *pl.* Misstrauen, *das* (**of** gegenüber + *Dat.*)

mistrustful /mɪsˈtrʌstfl/ *adj.* misstrauisch; **be** ～ **of sb./sth.** jmdm./einer Sache gegenüber misstrauisch sein

misty /ˈmɪsti/ *adj.* neb[e]lig, dunstig ‹*Tag, Morgen*›; in Nebel *od.* Dunst gehüllt ‹*Berg, Hügel*›

misunderstand /mɪsʌndəˈstænd/ *v.t.*, *forms as* **understand** missverstehen; falsch verstehen; **don't** ～ **me** versteh mich nicht falsch

misunderstanding /mɪsʌndəˈstændɪŋ/ *n.* Missverständnis, *das;* **there has been a** ～: da liegt ein Missverständnis vor

misunderstood /mɪsʌndəˈstʊd/ *adj.* unverstanden; verkannt ‹*Künstler, Genie*›; **be** ～: kein Verständnis finden

misuse 1 /mɪsˈjuːz/ *v.t.* missbrauchen; zweckentfremden ‹*Werkzeug, Gelder*›; nichts Rechtes machen aus ‹*Gelegenheit, Talent*›. **2** /mɪsˈjuːs/ *n.* Missbrauch, *der;* (of funds) Zweckentfremdung, *die*

mite /maɪt/ *n.* (a) (Zool.) Milbe, *die;* (b) **the widow's** ～: das Scherflein der armen Witwe; (c) (small child) Würmchen, *das* (fam.); **poor little** ～: armes Kleines; (d) **a** ～ **too strong/outspoken** (coll.: somewhat) ein bisschen *od.* etwas zu stark/geradeheraus

miter (Amer.) ⇒ **mitre**

mitigate /ˈmɪtɪgeɪt/ *v.t.* (a) (alleviate) lindern; (b) (make less severe) mildern; **mitigating circumstances** mildernde Umstände

mitigation /mɪtɪˈgeɪʃn/ *n.* ⇒ **mitigate:** Linderung, *die;* Milderung, *die*

mitre /ˈmaɪtə(r)/ *n.* (Brit.) (a) (Eccl.) Mitra, *die;* (b) (joint) Gehrung, *die* (bes. Technik)

mitten /ˈmɪtn/ *n.* Fausthandschuh, *der;* Fäustling, *der;* (not covering fingers) fingerloser Handschuh

mix /mɪks/ 1 *v.t.* (a) (combine) [ver]mischen; vermengen; verrühren ‹*Zutaten*›; ～ **one's drinks** alles durcheinander trinken; (b) (prepare by ～ing) mischen, mixen

〈*Cocktail*〉; anrühren, ansetzen 〈*Lösung, Teig*〉; zubereiten 〈*Medikament*〉; **(c)** ~ **it [with sb.]** (coll.) sich [mit jmdm.] prügeln. **2** *v.i.* **(a)** (become ~ed) sich vermischen; **(b)** (be sociable) Umgang mit anderen [Menschen] haben; **(c)** (be compatible) zusammenpassen; 〈*Ideen*:〉 sich verbinden lassen. **3** *n.* **(a)** (coll.: mixture) Mischung, *die* **(of** aus); **(b)** (proportion) [Mischungs]verhältnis, *das;* **(c)** (ready ingredients) [gebrauchsfertige] Mischung; **[cake-]**~: Backmischung, *die*
~ **'in** *v.t.* einrühren
~ **'up** *v.t.* **(a)** vermischen; verrühren 〈*Zutaten*〉; **(b)** (make a muddle of) durcheinander bringen; (confuse one with another) verwechseln; **(c)** *in pass.* (involve) **be/get ~ed up in sth.** in etw. (*Akk.*) verwickelt sein/werden

mixed /mɪkst/ *adj.* **(a)** (diverse) unterschiedlich 〈*Reaktionen, Kritiken*〉; ~ **feelings** gemischte Gefühle, **(b)** gemischt 〈*Gesellschaft*〉; **a** ~ **bunch** ein bunt gemischter Haufen; **(c)** (for both sexes) gemischt

mixed: ~ **'bag** *n.* bunte Mischung; ~ **'blessing** *n.* **be a** ~ **blessing** nicht nur Vorteile haben; **children are a** ~ **blessing** Kinder sind kein reiner Segen; ~ **'company** *n.* **in** ~ **company** in Gesellschaft von Damen [und Kindern]; ~ **'grill** *n.* Mixed grill, *der* (Gastr.); gemischte Grillplatte; ~ **'metaphor** ⇒ **metaphor** b; ~ **'up** *adj.* (fig. coll.) verwirrt, konfus 〈*Person*〉; **be/feel very** ~ **up** völlig durcheinander sein; ~ **up kids** Jugendliche ohne [jeden] inneren Halt

mixer /'mɪksə(r)/ *n.* (for food) Mixer, *der;* (for concrete) Mischmaschine, *die*

mixture /'mɪkstʃə(r)/ *n.* **(a)** (mixing, being mixed) Mischen, *das;* (result) Mischung, *die* **(of** aus); **the** ~ **as before** (fig.) die altbekannte Mischung; **(b)** (Motor Veh.) Gemisch, *das*

'mix-up *n.* Durcheinander, *das;* (misunderstanding) Missverständnis, *das*

ml. *abbr.* ▶ 1193| **millilitre[s]** ml
mm. *abbr.* ▶ 904| **millimetre[s]** mm

mnemonic /nɪ'mɒnɪk/ *n.* Gedächtnishilfe, *die;* Eselsbrücke, *die* (ugs.)

moan /məʊn/ **1** *n.* **(a)** Stöhnen, *das;* **(b)** **have a** ~ (complain at length) jammern; (have a grievance) eine Beschwerde haben. **2** *v.i.* **(a)** stöhnen **(with** vor + *Dat.*); **(b)** (complain) jammern **(about** über + *Akk.*); ~ **at sb.** jmdm. etwas vorjammern. **3** *v.t.* stöhnen

moat /məʊt/ *n.* [Wasser]graben, *der;* **[castle]** ~: Burggraben, *der*

mob /mɒb/ **1** *n.* **(a)** (rabble) Mob, *der* (abwertend); Pöbel, *der* (abwertend); **(b)** (sl.: associated group) ~ **[of criminals]** Bande, *die* (abwertend); **Peter and his** ~: Peter und seine ganze Blase (salopp); ~ **law/rule** Gesetz/Herrschaft der Straße. **2** *v.t.,* **-bb-:** **(a)** (crowd round) belagern (ugs.) 〈*Schauspieler, Star*〉; **(b)** (attack) herfallen über (+ *Akk.*)

mobile /'məʊbaɪl/ *adj.* **(a)** (able to move easily) beweglich; (on wheels) fahrbar; **(b)** (accommodated in vehicle) mobil; fahrbar; ~ **library** Fahrbücherei, *die;* ~ **canteen** Kantine auf Rädern; **(c)** (in social status) mobil; **upwardly** ~: sozial aufsteigend; **be upwardly** ~: sozial aufsteigen; **downwardly** ~: im sozialen Abstieg begriffen; **be downwardly** ~: sich im sozialen Abstieg befinden

mobile: ~ **'home** *n.* transportable Wohneinheit; (caravan) Wohnwagen, *der;* ~ **'phone** *n.* Mobiltelefon, *das*

mobilisation, mobilise ⇒ **mobiliz-**

mobility /mə'bɪlɪtɪ/ *n.* **(a)** (ability to move) (of person) Beweglichkeit, *die;* (on wheels) Fahrbarkeit, *die;* **(b)** (in social status) Mobilität, *die*

mobilization /məʊbɪlaɪ'zeɪʃn/ *n.* **(a)** Mobilisierung, *die;* **(b)** (Mil.) Mobilmachung, *die*

mobilize /'məʊbɪlaɪz/ *v.t.* **(a)** mobilisieren; **(b)** (Mil.) mobil machen; *abs.* **make preparations to** ~: die Mobilmachung vorbereiten

moccasin /'mɒkəsɪn/ *n.* Mokassin, *der*

mock /mɒk/ **1** *v.t.* **(a)** (subject to ridicule) sich lustig machen über (+ *Akk.*); verspotten; **he was** ~ed man machte sich über ihn lustig; **(b)** (ridicule by imitation) ~ **sb./sth.** jmdn./ etw. nachmachen[, um sich über ihn/darüber lustig zu

machen]. **2** *v.i.* ~ **at sb./sth.** sich über jmdn./etw. mokieren *od.* lustig machen. **3** *attrib. adj.* gespielt 〈*Feierlichkeit, Bescheidenheit, Ernst*〉; Schein〈*kampf, -angriff*〉; ~ **Tudor style** Pseudotudorstil, *der;* ~ **examination** simulierte Prüfung; ~**-turtle soup** Mockturtlesuppe, *die* (Kochk.)

mockery /'mɒkərɪ/ *n.* **(a)** **be a** ~ **of justice/the truth** der Gerechtigkeit/Wahrheit (*Dat.*) hohnsprechen (geh.); **make a** ~ **of sth.** etw. zur Farce machen; **(b)** *no pl., no indef. art.* (derision) Spott, *der*

mocking /'mɒkɪŋ/ **1** *adj.* spöttisch. **2** *n.* Spott, *der*
'mockingbird *n.* Spottdrossel, *die*
'mock-up *n.* Modell, *das* [in Originalgröße]; (of book etc.) Layout, *das*

MOD *abbr.* (Brit.) **Ministry of Defence** Verteidigungsministerium, *das*

mod cons /mɒd 'kɒnz/ *n. pl.* (Brit. coll.) [moderner] Komfort; **have all** ~: mit allem Komfort *od.* (ugs.) allen Schikanen ausgestattet sein

mode /məʊd/ *n.* **(a)** (way in which thing is done) Art [und Weise], *die;* (method of procedure) Methode, *die;* (Computing) Betriebsart, *die;* ~ **of transport** Transportmittel, *das;* **(b)** (fashion) Mode, *die* (**for** Gen.)

model /'mɒdl/ **1** *n.* **(a)** Modell, *das;* **(b)** (perfect example) Muster, *das* (**of** an + *Dat.*); (to be imitated) Vorbild, *das;* **be a** ~ **of industry** ein Muster an Fleiß (*Dat.*) sein; **on the** ~ **of sth.** nach dem Vorbild einer Sache (*Gen.*); **(c)** ▶ 887| (Art) Modell, *das;* (Fashion) Modell, *das;* Mannequin, *das;* (male) Dressman, *der;* **photographer's** ~: Fotomodell, *das.* **2** *adj.* **(a)** (exemplary) vorbildlich; Muster- (oft iron.); **(b)** (miniature) Modell〈*stadt, -eisenbahn, -flugzeug*〉. **3** *v.t.,* (Brit.) **-ll-:** **(a)** modellieren; formen; ~ **sth. in clay** etw. in Ton modellieren; ~ **sth. after** *or* **[up]on sth.** etw. einer Sache (*Dat.*) nachbilden; **(b)** (Fashion) vorführen 〈*Kleid, Entwurf usw.*〉. **4** *v.i.,* (Brit.) **-ll-:** **(a)** (Fashion) als Mannequin *od.* Model arbeiten; 〈*Mann*:〉 als Dressman arbeiten; (Photog.) als [Foto]modell arbeiten; (Art) Modell stehen/sitzen; **(b)** ~ **in clay** *etc.* in Ton usw. modellieren

modelling (*Amer.:* **modeling**) /'mɒdəlɪŋ/ *n.* **(a)** *no art.* **do** ~ (Fashion) als Mannequin *od.* Model arbeiten; 〈*Mann:* 〉 als Dressman arbeiten; (Photog., Art) als Modell arbeiten; **(b)** *no indef. art.* (sculpturing) Modellieren, *das;* ~ **clay** Modellierton, *der*

modem /'məʊdem/ *n.* Modem, *der od. das*

moderate **1** /'mɒdərət/ *adj.* **(a)** gemäßigt 〈*Partei, Ansichten*〉; mäßig, maßvoll 〈*Person, bes. Trinker, Esser; Forderungen*〉; mäßig 〈*Begeisterung, Interesse*〉; **(b)** (fairly large or good) mittler... 〈*Größe, Menge, Wert*〉; **[only]** ~: mäßig 〈*Qualität, Ernte*〉; **(c)** (reasonable) angemessen, vernünftig 〈*Preis, Summe*〉; **(d)** mäßig 〈*Wind*〉. **2** /'mɒdərət/ *n.* Gemäßigte, *der/die.* **3** /'mɒdəreɪt/ *v.t.* mäßigen; zügeln 〈*Begeisterung*〉; mildern 〈*negativen Effekt*〉; ~ **one's demands** seine Forderungen einschränken. **4** /'mɒdəreɪt/ *v.i.* nachlassen

moderately /'mɒdərətlɪ/ *adv.* einigermaßen; mäßig 〈*begeistert, groß, begabt*〉; **be only** ~ **enthusiastic about sth.** sich nicht allzu sehr *od.* übermäßig für etw. begeistern

moderation /mɒdə'reɪʃn/ *n.* **(a)** (moderating) Mäßigung, *die;* **(b)** *no pl.* (moderateness) Mäßigkeit, *die;* **in** ~: mit *od.* in Maßen

modern /'mɒdn/ *adj.* modern; heutig 〈*Zeit[alter], Welt, Person*〉; ~ **jazz** Modern Jazz, *der;* **in** ~ **times** in der heutigen Zeit; ~ **history** neuere Geschichte; ~ **languages** neuere Sprachen; (subject of study) Neuphilologie, *die*

modernise ⇒ **modernize**
modernism /'mɒdənɪzm/ *n.* Modernismus, *der*
modernist /'mɒdənɪst/ *n.* Modernist, *der*/Modernistin, *die*
modernity /mə'dɜːnɪtɪ/ *n.* Modernität, *die*
modernize /'mɒdənaɪz/ *v.t.* modernisieren

modest /'mɒdɪst/ *adj.* bescheiden; vorsichtig 〈*Schätzung*〉; einfach, unauffällig 〈*Haus, Kleidung*〉; **have a** ~ **lifestyle** bescheiden *od.* einfach leben

modestly /'mɒdɪstlɪ/ adv. bescheiden; dezent, unauffällig ‹sich kleiden›

modesty /'mɒdɪstɪ/ n., no pl. Bescheidenheit, die; **in all ~:** bei aller Bescheidenheit

modification /mɒdɪfɪ'keɪʃn/ n. [Ab]änderung, die; Modifizierung, die

modifier /'mɒdɪfaɪə(r)/ n. (esp. Ling., Biol.) Modifikator, der

modify /'mɒdɪfaɪ/ v.t. (a) (make changes in) [ab-, ver]ändern; modifizieren; (b) (tone down) mäßigen; **~ one's position** in seiner Haltung gemäßigter werden

modular /'mɒdjʊlə(r)/ adj. aus Elementen [zusammengesetzt]; (in construction) aus Baueinheiten od. -elementen [zusammengesetzt]; **~ construction/design** Konstruktion/Entwurf nach dem Baukastensystem; **~ unit** [Bau-, Konstruktions]element, das

module /'mɒdjuːl/ n. (a) Bauelement, das; (Electronics) Modul, das; (b) (Educ.) Unterrichtseinheit, die; (c) (Astronaut.) **command ~:** Kommandoeinheit, die

mohair /'məʊheə(r)/ n. Mohair, der

moist /mɔɪst/ adj. feucht (**with** von)

moisten /'mɔɪsn/ v.t. anfeuchten; feucht machen; **~ one's lips** sich (Dat.) die Lippen [mit der Zunge] befeuchten

moisture /'mɔɪstʃə(r)/ n. Feuchtigkeit, die; **film of ~:** Feuchtigkeitsfilm, der

moisturizer (moisturiser) /'mɔɪstʃəraɪzə(r)/, **moisturizing cream** /'mɔɪstʃəraɪzɪŋ kriːm/ ns. Feuchtigkeitscreme, die

molar /'məʊlə(r)/ **1** n. Backenzahn, der; Molar[zahn], der (Anat.). **2** adj. **~ tooth** ⇒ **1**

molasses /mə'læsɪz/ n. Melasse, die

mold (Amer.) ⇒ **mould**[1, 2, 3]

molder, molding, moldy (Amer.) ⇒ **mould-**

mole[1] /məʊl/ n. (on skin) Leberfleck, der; (prominent) Muttermal, das

mole[2] n. (a) (animal) Maulwurf, der; (b) (coll.: spy) Maulwurf, der (ugs.)

molecular /mə'lekjʊlə(r)/ adj. (Phys., Chem.) molekular

molecule /'mɒlɪkjuːl, 'məʊlɪkjuːl/ n. (Phys., Chem.) Molekül, das

'molehill n. Maulwurfshügel, der; **make a mountain out of a ~** (fig.) aus einer Mücke einen Elefanten machen (ugs.)

molest /mə'lest/ v.t. belästigen; (sexually) [unsittlich] belästigen

moll /mɒl/ n. (coll.) Gangsterbraut, die

mollify /'mɒlɪfaɪ/ v.t. besänftigen; beschwichtigen

mollusc, (Amer.) **mollusk** /'mɒləsk/ n. (Zool.) Molluske, die (fachspr.); Weichtier, das

mollycoddle /'mɒlɪkɒdl/ v.t. [ver]hätscheln (oft abwertend)

molt (Amer.) ⇒ **moult**

molten /'məʊltn/ adj. geschmolzen; flüssig ‹Lava›

mom /mɒm/ (Amer. coll.) ⇒ **mum**[2]

moment /'məʊmənt/ n. (a) Moment, der; Augenblick, der; **barely a ~ had elapsed …:** es war kaum eine Minute vergangen …; **for a ~ or two** einen kurzen Augenblick; **for a few ~s** ein paar Augenblicke; **at any ~,** (coll.) **any ~:** jeden Augenblick od. Moment; **this is the ~!** dies ist der geeignete Augenblick!; **at the precise ~ she came in …:** genau in dem Augenblick, als sie hereintrat, …; **the ~ I get home** gleich od. sofort, wenn ich nach Hause komme; **one** or **just a** or **wait a ~!** einen Moment od. Augenblick!; **in a ~** (instantly) im Nu (ugs.); (very soon) sofort; gleich; **for a ~:** einen Moment [lang]; **not for a ~:** keinen Moment [lang]; **the ~ of truth** die Stunde der Wahrheit; **at the ~:** im Augenblick; momentan; **for the ~:** im od. für den Augenblick; vorläufig; **I shan't be a ~** (I'll be back very soon) ich bin sofort zurück; (I have very nearly finished) ich bin sofort soweit; **have you got a ~?** hast du mal einen Augenblick Zeit?; **be the man of the ~:** der Mann des Tages sein; **come here this ~!** komm sofort od. auf der Stelle her!; (b) (formal: importance) **of ~:** von Bedeutung; **of little/no ~:** von geringer/ohne Bedeutung; (c) (Phys.) Moment, das

momentarily /'məʊməntərɪlɪ/ adv. (a) (for a moment) einen Augenblick lang; (b) (Amer.) (at any moment) jeden Augenblick od. Moment; (in a few minutes) in wenigen Minuten

momentary /'məʊməntərɪ/ adj. kurz; **a ~ forgetfulness** ein Augenblick geistiger Abwesenheit

momentous /mə'mentəs/ adj. (important) bedeutsam; (of consequence) folgenschwer; von großer Tragweite nachgestellt

momentum /mə'mentəm/ n., pl. **momenta** /mə'mentə/ (a) (impetus) Schwung, der; **gather** or **gain ~:** schneller werden; (fig.) in Schwung kommen; (b) (Mech.) Impuls, der

mommy /'mɒmɪ/ (Amer. coll.) ⇒ **mummy**[2]

Mon. abbr. ▶ 739 | **Monday** Mo.

monarch /'mɒnək/ n. Monarch, der/Monarchin, die

monarchist /'mɒnəkɪst/ n. Monarchist, der/Monarchistin, die

monarchy /'mɒnəkɪ/ n. Monarchie, die

monastery /'mɒnəstrɪ/ n. [Mönchs]kloster, das

monastic /mə'næstɪk/ adj. mönchisch; (of monasteries) klösterlich; Kloster‹gebäude›

Monday /'mʌndeɪ, 'mʌndɪ/ ▶ 739 | **1** n. Montag, der. **2** adv. (coll.) **she comes ~s** sie kommt montags. See also **Friday**

monetarism /'mʌnɪtərɪzm/ n. (Econ.) Monetarismus, der

monetarist /'mʌnɪtərɪst/ **1** n. (Econ.) Monetarist, der/Monetaristin, die. **2** adj. monetaristisch

monetary /'mʌnɪtərɪ/ adj. (a) (of the currency in use) monetär; Währungs‹politik, -system›; (b) (of money) finanziell

money /'mʌnɪ/ n. ▶ 938 | (a) no pl. Geld, das; **your ~ or your life!** Geld oder Leben!; **be in the ~** (coll.) im Geld schwimmen (ugs.); **there is ~ in sth.** mit etw. kann man [viel] Geld verdienen; **~ for jam** or **old rope** (Brit. fig. coll.) leicht od. schnell verdientes Geld; **make ~** ‹Person.› [viel] Geld verdienen, (ugs.) [das große] Geld machen; **earn good ~:** gut verdienen; **~ talks** das Geld macht's (ugs.); **~ makes the world go round** Geld regiert die Welt; **put ~ into sth.** (Akk.) Geld in etw. investieren od. (ugs.) hineinstecken; **have ~ to burn** (fig. coll.) Geld wie Heu haben (ugs.); **[not] be made of ~** (fig. coll.) [k]ein Goldesel od. Krösus sein; **this would only be to throw good ~ after bad** das wäre nur rausgeschmissenes od. rausgeworfenes Geld (ugs.); **for 'my ~:** wenn man mich fragt; **the best that ~ can buy** das Beste, was es für Geld gibt; **~ can't buy happiness!** Geld allein macht nicht glücklich!; see also **big** 1 a; **love** 1 a; **make** 1 a; **run** 1 a; (b) pl. **~s** or **monies** /'mʌnɪz/ (sum of ~) Geld, das; [Geld]betrag, der

money: ~-back attrib. adj. **~-back guarantee** Geld-zurück-Garantie, die; **~-bag** n. Geldsack, der; **~ belt** n. Geldgürtel, der; **~ box** n. Sparbüchse, die; **~ changer** /'mʌnɪtʃeɪndʒə(r)/ n. ▶ 887 | Geldwechsler, der; **~-grubber** /'mʌnɪgrʌbə(r)/ n. (ugs.); **~-grubbing** 1 adj. geldgierig (abwertend); 2 n. Geldgier, die (abwertend); **~lender** n. ▶ 887 | Geldverleiher, der; **~maker** n. be a **~maker** ‹Projekt, Produkt, Film.› Geld bringen; **~making** adj. gewinnbringend, einträglich ‹Geschäft, Beschäftigung›; **~ market** n. Geldmarkt, der; **~ order** n. Zahlungsanweisung, die; (issued by Post Office) Postanweisung, die; **~-spinner** n. (Brit.) Verkaufsschlager, der; **~'s-worth** n. get or have one's **~'s-worth** etwas für sein Geld bekommen

Mongol /'mɒŋgl/ **1** n. (a) Mongole, der/Mongolin, die; (b) **m~** (Med.) Mongoloide, der/die; **she is a m~:** sie ist mongoloid. **2** adj. (a) mongolisch; (b) **m~** (Med.) mongoloid

Mongolia /mɒŋ'gəʊlɪə/ pr. n. Mongolei, die

Mongolian /mɒŋ'gəʊlɪən/ **1** adj. mongolisch. **2** n. (person) Mongole, der/Mongolin, die

mongoose /'mɒŋguːs/ n. (Zool.) Indischer Mungo

mongrel /'mʌŋgrəl, 'mɒŋgrəl/ n. **~ [dog]** Promenadenmischung, die (scherzh., auch abwertend)

monitor /'mɒnɪtə(r)/ **1** n. (a) (Sch.) Aufsichtsschüler, der/-schülerin, die; **pencil/milk ~:** Bleistift-/Milchwart, der; (b) (listener) Mithörer, der/Mithörerin, die; (c) (Mech. Engin., Phys., Med., Telev.) Monitor, der. **2** v.t. kontrollieren

Money

German money

90 pfennigs	= 90 Pf, 0,90 DM = neunzig Pfennig
one mark	= 1 DM = eine Mark
1 mark 90 [pfennigs]	= 1,90 DM = eine Mark neunzig, eine Mark und neunzig Pfennig
50 marks	= 50 DM = fünfzig Mark
1,000 marks	= 1 000 DM = [ein]tausend Mark
100 pfennigs make one mark	= 100 Pfennig sind eine Mark
a 20 mark note	= ein Zwanzigmarkschein or 20-Mark-Schein
a five mark piece	= ein Fünfmarkstück or 5-Mark-Stück
a 50 pfennig coin	= ein Fünfzigpfennigstück or 50-Pfennig-Stück

Although **DM** stands for "Deutsche Mark", this term is only occasionally used in full to denote the currency, and is not used when quoting amounts; however **D-Mark** will often be heard as a more specific alternative for the basic **Mark**. The abbreviation **DM** may also precede the number when prices are given in catalogues or advertisements, or is omitted altogether.

Note that there is a comma before the number of pfennigs, also that as with all denominations (not only marks and pfennigs) the plural form is the same as the singular when an amount is being quoted (and on most other occasions), although the form **Pfennige** will sometimes be heard.

Austrian and Swiss money

The Austrian unit of currency is the schilling (**Schilling**, abbreviation S, öS, or ATS), and the Swiss unit the Swiss franc (**Schweizer Franken**, abbreviation sfr or sFr). The abbreviations precede the number when prices are given in catalogues or advertisements, or are omitted, while in a text "Schilling" is usually written in full.

The Swiss franc is worth slightly more than the German mark, but there are about 7 Austrian schillings to one mark. In each case there are smaller denominations, with 100 centimes (**Rappen** in Swiss German) to the Swiss franc and 100 **Groschen** to the Austrian schilling. Not surprisingly one does not often see amounts in groschen, although some firms still quote prices such as "99,90".

Price including VAT 250 schillings	= Preis inkl. MWS S or öS 250,— = Preis inklusive Mehrwertsteuer 250 Schilling
Special offer 18 Swiss francs 90 centimes	= Sonderangebot sfr or sFr 18,90

British money

one penny	= 1p = ein Penny
five pence	= 5p = fünf Pence
one pound fifty [pence]	= £1.50 = ein Pfund fünfzig [Pence]

eight pounds	= £8.34
thirty-four pence	= acht Pfund vierunddreißig Pence
one thousand two hundred and fifty pounds or *twelve hundred and fifty pounds*	= £1 250 = [ein]tausendzweihundertfünfzig Pfund or zwölfhundertfünfzig Pfund
a five-pound note	= ein Fünfpfundschein
a pound coin	= ein Pfundstück
a 50 pence piece	= ein Fünfzigpencestück

American money

one cent	= 1c	= ein Cent
five cents	= 5c	= fünf Cent
one dollar	= $1 or $1.00	= ein Dollar
one dollar fifty	= $1.50	= ein Dollar fünfzig [Cent]
a ten dollar bill	= ein Zehndollarschein	
a dollar bill	= ein Dollarschein	
a dollar coin	= ein Dollarstück	
a dime, a ten cent piece	= ein Zehncentstück	
a quarter, a twenty-five cent piece	= ein Vierteldollarstück	

Other money phrases

What or *How much does it cost?*	= Was or Wie viel kostet das?
It costs just under/ just over £950	= Es kostet knapp 950/etwas über 950 Pfund
The potatoes are 30p a pound	= Die Kartoffeln kosten 30 Pence das Pfund
$100 in cash	= 100 Dollar in bar
Can I pay by cheque/ by credit card?	= Kann ich mit Scheck/mit Kreditkarte zahlen?
a cheque for £50	= ein Scheck über 50 Pfund
a dollar/sterling traveller's cheque or *(Amer.) traveler's check*	= ein Reisescheck in Dollar/Pfund [Sterling]
Can you change or *give me change for a 20 mark note?*	= Können Sie mir einen 20-Mark-Schein wechseln or auf einen 20-Mark-Schein herausgeben?
I want to change marks into dollars	= Ich will Mark in Dollar wechseln
Our pounds are hardly worth anything	= Unsere Pfunde sind kaum etwas wert

Notice again that the plural form of the various currencies is the same as the singular. The one exception is the use of the plural form with an ending in examples such as the last one (here "Pfunde" – one can also talk of "Schillinge" and "Franken", but marks are always **Mark**).

⟨*Strahlungsintensität*⟩; beobachten ⟨*Wetter, Flugzeug, Bewegung*⟩; abhören ⟨*Sendung, Telefongespräch*⟩

monk /mʌŋk/ *n.* Mönch, *der;* **order of** ~**s** Mönchsorden, *der*

monkey /'mʌŋkɪ/ *n.* **(a)** Affe, *der;* **make a** ~ **of sb.** (coll.) jmdn. zum Gespött machen; **(b)** (mischievous child) Schlingel, *der* (scherzh.)

monkey: ~ **business** *n.* (coll.) (mischief) Schabernack, *der;* (unlawful or unfair activities) krumme Touren *Pl.* (ugs.); ~**-nut** *n.* (Bot.) Erdnuss, *die;* ~ **wrench** *n.* Rollgabelschlüssel, *der* (fachspr.); Universalschraubenschlüssel, *der*

mono /'mɒnəʊ/ *adj.* Mono⟨*platte[nspieler], -wiedergabe*⟩

monochrome /'mɒnəkrəʊm/ **1** *n.* **in** ~: monochrom

(fachspr.); einfarbig; Schwarzweiß- (Ferns.). **2** *adj.* mono-chrom (fachspr.); einfarbig; Schwarzweiß- (Ferns.)

monocle /'mɒnəkl/ *n.* Monokel, *das;* Einglas, *das* (veralt.)

monogamy /mə'nɒgəmi/ *n.* Monogamie, *die;* Einehe, *die*

monogram /'mɒnəgræm/ *n.* Monogramm, *das*

monolingual /mɒnə'lɪŋgwəl/ *adj.* einsprachig

monolith /'mɒnəlɪθ/ *n.* (lit. or fig.) Monolith, *der*

monolithic /mɒnə'lɪθɪk/ *adj.* (lit. or fig.) monolithisch

monologue (*Amer.:* **monolog**) /'mɒnəlɒg/ *n.* (lit. or fig.) Monolog, *der*

monoplane /'mɒnəpleɪn/ *n.* (Aeronaut.) Eindecker, *der*

monopolize (**monopolise**) /mə'nɒpəlaɪz/ *v.t.* (Econ.) monopolisieren; (fig.) mit Beschlag belegen; ~ **the conversation** den/die anderen nicht zu Wort kommen lassen

monopoly /mə'nɒpəli/ *n.* (**a**) (Econ.) Monopol, *das* (**of** auf + *Dat.*); (exclusive possession) alleiniger Besitz; **you can't have a** ~ **of the car** du kannst das Auto nicht ständig mit Beschlag belegen; (**b**) (thing monopolized) Monopol, *das*

monorail /'mɒnəreɪl/ *n.* (**a**) (single rail) Einschienengleis, *das;* (**b**) (vehicle) Einschienenbahn, *die*

monosyllabic /mɒnəsɪ'læbɪk/ *adj.* einsilbig ‹Antwort, Person›

monosyllable /'mɒnəsɪləbl/ *n.* (**a**) einsilbiges Wort; (**b**) (Ling.) Einsilber, *der*

monotone /'mɒnətəʊn/ *n.* gleich bleibender Ton

monotonous /mə'nɒtənəs/ *adj.* eintönig; monoton

monotonously /mə'nɒtənəsli/ *adv.* eintönig

monotony /mə'nɒtəni/ *n.* Eintönigkeit, *die;* Monotonie, *die*

monsoon /mɒn'su:n/ *n.* (Geog.) (**a**) (wind) **summer** *or* **wet/dry** ~: Sommer-/Wintermonsun, *der;* (**b**) (season) Regenzeit, *die*

monster /'mɒnstə(r)/ **1** *n.* (**a**) (huge thing) Ungeheuer, *das;* Monster, *das;* (huge thing) Ungetüm, *das;* Monstrum, *das;* **what a** ~**!** (in surprise or admiration) das ist ja ungeheuer!; (**b**) (inhuman person) Unmensch, *der;* (iron.: naughty child) Monster, *das* (scherzh.). **2** *attrib. adj.* riesig

monstrosity /mɒn'strɒsɪti/ *n.* (**a**) (outrageous thing) Ungeheuerlichkeit, *die;* (**b**) (hideous building etc.) Ungetüm, *das;* (**c**) (creature) Ungeheuer, *das;* Monster, *das*

monstrous /'mɒnstrəs/ *adj.* (**a**) (huge) monströs (geh.); riesig ‹Lkw, Kuchen, Buch›; unnatürlich groß ‹Gemüse, Person, Baum, Pflanze›; (**b**) (outrageous) ungeheuerlich (abwertend) ‹Vorschlag, Vorstellung, Einstellung, Entscheidung›; (**c**) (atrocious) scheußlich; monströs

montage /mɒn'tɑːʒ/ *n.* (Photog., Art, Radio, Film) Montage, *die*

month /mʌnθ/ *n.* Monat, *der;* **last day of the** ~: Monatsletzte, *der;* **the** ~ **of January** der [Monat] Januar; **for a** ~**/several** ~**s** einen Monat [lang]/mehrere Monate [lang] *od.* monatelang; **for** ~**s** [**on end**] monatelang; **every six** ~**s** alle sechs Monate; halbjährlich; **once every** *or* **a** ~: einmal monatlich *od.* im Monat; **in a** ~**['s time**] in einem Monat; **take a** ~**'s holiday** [sich (*Dat.*)] einen Monat Urlaub nehmen; **£10** *a* **or** **per** ~: zehn Pfund im Monat; **a six-**~**[s]-old baby** ein sechs Monate altes *od.* sechsmonatiges Baby

monthly /'mʌnθli/ **1** *adj.* monatlich; Monats‹umsatz, -einkommen, -gehalt›; einmonatig ‹Abstand›; Monats‹zyklus, -karte›; **three-**~: dreimonatlich; vierteljährlich; **three-**~ **season ticket** Dreimonats- *od.* Vierteljahreskarte, *die.* **2** *adv.* [ein]monatlich; einmal im Monat. **3** *n.* (publication) Monatsschrift, *die*

monument /'mɒnjʊmənt/ *n.* (**a**) Denkmal, *das;* (**b**) (on grave) Grabmal, *das* (geh.)

monumental /mɒnjʊ'mentl/ *adj.* (**a**) (massive) gewaltig ‹Skulptur›; monumental ‹Plastik, Gemälde, Gebäude›; (**b**) (extremely great) kolossal (ugs.)

monumentally /mɒnjʊ'mentəli/ *adv.* enorm ‹stur, schlau, kreativ›; ~ **boring/stupid** sterbenslangweilig/strohdumm

moo /mu:/ **1** *n.* Muhen, *das.* **2** *v.i.* muhen

mooch /mu:tʃ/ *v.i.* (coll.) ~ **about** *or* **around/along** herumschleichen (ugs.) /zockeln (ugs.)

mood /mu:d/ *n.* (**a**) (state of mind) Stimmung, *die;* **there was a [general]** ~ **of optimism** es herrschte allgemeiner Optimismus; **be in a good/bad** ~**:** [bei] guter/schlechter Laune sein; **be in a cheerful** ~**:** froh gelaunt sein; **be in a serious/pensive** ~**:** ernst/nachdenklich gestimmt sein; **be in no** ~ **for joking** nicht zum Scherzen aufgelegt sein; **I'm not in the** ~**:** ich hab keine Lust dazu; (**b**) (fit of melancholy or bad temper) Verstimmung, *die;* schlechte Laune; **have one's** ~**s** [seine] Launen haben

moody /'mu:di/ *adj.* (**a**) (sullen) missmutig; verdrossen; (**b**) (subject to moods) launenhaft

moon /mu:n/ **1** *n.* Mond, *der;* **the** ~ **is full/waning/waxing** es ist Vollmond/abnehmender/zunehmender Mond; **be over the** ~ (fig. coll.) im siebten Himmel sein (ugs.); **promise sb. the** ~ (fig.) jmdm. das Blaue vom Himmel versprechen (ugs.). **2** *v.i.* (coll.) ~ **about** [**the house**] trübselig [im Haus] herumschleichen (ugs.)

moon: ~**beam** *n.* Mondstrahl, *der;* ~**beams** Mondschein, *der;* ~**light** **1** *n.* Mondlicht, *das;* Mondschein, *der;* **2** *v.i.* (coll.) nebenberuflich abends arbeiten; ~**lit** *adj.* mondbeschienen (geh.)

moor[1] /mʊə(r), mɔ:(r)/ *n.* (Geog.) [Hoch]moor, *das*

moor[2] /mʊə(r), mɔ:(r)/ *v.t.* festmachen; vertäuen. **2** *v.i.* festmachen

'moorhen *n.* (Ornith.) [Grünfüßiges] Teichhuhn

mooring /'mʊərɪŋ, 'mɔ:rɪŋ/ *n.* (**a**) usu. in pl. (means of attachment) Vertäuung, *die;* (**b**) usu. in pl. (place) ~[**s**] Anlegestelle, *die;* (**c**) (action of making fast) Vertäuung, *die*

moorland /'mʊələnd, 'mɔ:lənd/ *n.* (Geog.) Moorland, *das*

moose /mu:s/ *n., pl. same* (Zool.) Amerikanischer Elch

moot /mu:t/ *adj.* umstritten; offen ‹Frage›; strittig ‹Punkt›

mop /mɒp/ **1** *n.* (**a**) Mopp, *der;* (for washing up) ≈ Spülbürste, *die;* (**b**) ~ [**of hair**] Wuschelkopf, *der.* **2** *v.t.,* -**pp**-moppen ‹Fußboden›; (wipe) abwischen ‹Träne, Schweiß, Stirn›

~ **'up** *v.t.* (wipe up) aufwischen ‹Flüssigkeit›

mope /məʊp/ *v.i.* Trübsal blasen (ugs.); ~ **about** *or* **around** trübselig herumschleichen (ugs.)

moped /'məʊped/ *n.* Moped, *das*

moral /'mɒrl/ **1** *adj.* (**a**) moralisch; sittlich ‹Wert›; Moral‹begriff, -prinzip, -vorstellung›; Moral ‹philosoph[ie], -psychologie›; moralisch, sittlich ‹Verpflichtung, Pflicht›; **be under a** ~ **obligation** eine moralische *od.* sittliche Pflicht haben; (**b**) (virtuous) moralisch, sittlich ‹Leben, Person›. **2** *n.* Moral, *die;* **draw the** ~ **from sth.** die Lehre aus etw. ziehen; (**b**) *in pl.* (habits) Moral, *die*

morale /mə'rɑ:l/ *n.* Moral, *die;* **low/high**~: schlechte/gute Moral

mo'rale-booster *n.* be a work *or* act as a ~ **for sb.** jmds. Moral heben *od.* stärken

moralise ⇒ **moralize**

morality /mə'rælɪti/ *n.* (**a**) (conduct) Moral, *die;* Sittlichkeit, *die;* Moralität, *die* (geh.); (**b**) (particular system) Ethik, *die;* (**c**) (conformity to moral principles) Sittlichkeit, *die;* Moralität, *die* (geh.)

moralize /'mɒrəlaɪz/ *v.i.* moralisieren (geh.); moralische Betrachtungen anstellen ([**up**]**on** über + *Akk.*); **do stop moralizing!** hör auf mit deinen Moralpredigten!

morally /'mɒrəli/ *adv.* moralisch; (virtuously) moralisch einwandfrei

morass /mə'ræs/ *n.* Morast, *der* (auch fig.); **a** ~ **of paperwork** ein Wust von Papierkram (ugs.)

moratorium /mɒrə'tɔ:rɪəm/ *n., pl.* ~**s** *or* **moratoria** /mɒrə'tɔ:rɪə/ (**a**) [vorläufiger] Stopp (**on** für); (**b**) (authorized delay) Moratorium, *das*

morbid /'mɔ:bɪd/ *adj.* (**a**) krankhaft; makaber, (geh.) morbid ‹Freude, Faszination, Fantasie, Neigung›; (**b**) (coll.: melancholy) trübselig; (**c**) (Med.) krankhaft ‹Zustand, Veränderung›

more /mɔ:(r)/ **1** *adj.* (**a**) (additional) mehr; **would you like any** *or* **some/a few** ~? (apples, books, etc.) möchten Sie noch welche/ein paar?; **would you like any** *or* **some** ~ **apples?** möchten Sie noch Äpfel?; **would you like any** *or* **some/a little** ~? (tea, paper, etc.) möchten Sie noch etwas/ein wenig?; **would you like any** *or* **some ~ tea/ paper?** möchten Sie noch Tee/Papier?; **I haven't any ~ [apples/tea]** ich habe keine [Äpfel]/keinen [Tee] mehr; **~ and ~:** immer mehr; **many ~ things** noch viel mehr [Dinge]; **some ~ things** noch einige Dinge; **(b)** (greater in degree) größer; **~'s the pity** (coll.) leider!; **the ~ fool 'you** du bist vielleicht ein Dummkopf. **2** *n.*, *no pl.*, *no indef. art.* **(a)** (greater amount or number or thing) mehr; **~ and ~:** mehr und mehr; immer mehr; **six or ~:** mindestens sechs; **the ~ the merrier** ⇒ **merry a; (b)** (additional number or amount or thing) mehr; **what is ~ ...:** außerdem ...; **and ~:** mindestens *vorangestellt;* oder mehr; **there's no need to do/say [any] ~:** da braucht nichts weiter getan/gesagt zu werden; **(c) ~ than** (coll.: exceedingly) über‹*satt,* -glücklich, -froh›; hoch‹*erfreut, -willkommen*›. **3** *adv.* **(a)** mehr ‹*mögen, interessieren, gefallen, sich wünschen*›; *forming compar.* **a ~ interesting book** ein interessanteres Buch; **this book is ~ interesting** dieses Buch ist interessanter; **~ often** häufiger; **~ than anything [else]** vor allem; **(b)** (nearer, rather) eher; **~ ... than ...:** eher ... als ...; **~ dead than alive** mehr tot als lebendig; **(c)** (again) wieder; **never ~:** nie wieder *od.* mehr; **not any ~:** nicht einmal; **once ~:** noch einmal; **(d) ~ and ~ ...:** mehr und mehr *od.* immer mehr ...; *with adj. or adv.* immer ... (+ *Komp.*); **become ~ and ~ absurd** immer absurder werden; **(e) ~ or less** (fairly) mehr oder weniger; (approximately) annähernd; **(f) ~ so** noch mehr; **the ~ so because ...:** umso mehr, als *od.* weil ...

moreish /ˈmɔːrɪʃ/ *adj.* (coll.) lecker

moreover /mɔːˈrəʊvə(r)/ *adv.* und außerdem; zudem (geh.)

morgue /mɔːg/ ⇒ **mortuary**

moribund /ˈmɒrɪbʌnd/ *adj.* (fig.) dem Untergang geweiht

Mormon /ˈmɔːmən/ *n.* Mormone, *der*/Mormonin, *die*

morning /ˈmɔːnɪŋ/ *n.* ▶ **706**, ▶ **739** Morgen, *der;* (as opposed to afternoon) Vormittag, *der; attrib.* morgendlich; Morgen‹*kaffee, -spaziergang, -zeitung usw.*›; **this ~:** heute Morgen *od.* früh; **tomorrow ~:** morgen früh; **during the ~:** am Morgen/Vormittag; **[early] in the ~:** am [frühen] Morgen; (regularly) [früh] morgens; **at one** *etc.* **in the ~:** at one a.m. *etc.* ⇒ **a.m.; on Wednesday ~s** Mittwoch morgens; **Wednesday ~:** [am] Mittwochmorgen; [am] Mittwoch früh; **one ~:** eines Morgens; **~s, of a ~:** morgens; **in the ~** (coll.: next ~) morgen früh

morning: ~-'after pill *n.* Pille [für den Morgen] danach; **~ coat** *n.* Cut[away], *der;* **~ 'service** *n.* (Eccl.) Morgenandacht, *die;* (RC Ch.) Frühmesse, *die;* **~ sickness** *n.* morgendliche Übelkeit; **~ 'star** *n.* Morgenstern, *der*

Morocco /məˈrɒkəʊ/ *pr. n.* Marokko (*das*)

moron /ˈmɔːrɒn/ *n.* (coll.) Trottel, *der* (ugs. abwertend); Schwachkopf, *der* (ugs.)

morose /məˈrəʊs/ *adj.* verdrießlich

morphine /ˈmɔːfiːn/ *n.* Morphin, *das* (fachspr.); Morphium, *das*

morphing/ ˈmɔːfɪŋ/ *n.*, *no pl.* (Computing) Morphing, *das*

morris /ˈmɒrɪs/**: ~ dancer** *n.* Moriskentänzer, *der;* **~ dancing** *n.* Moriskentanzen, *das*

Morse /mɔːs/ *n.* Morseschrift, *die;* Morsezeichen *Pl.*

Morse 'code *n.* Morseschrift, *die;* Morsealphabet, *das*

morsel /ˈmɔːsl/ *n.* (of food) Bissen, *der;* Happen, *der*

mortal /ˈmɔːtl/ **1** *adj.* sterblich; (fatal, fought to the death, intense) tödlich **(to** für); **~ combat** ein Kampf auf Leben und Tod; **~ sin** Todsünde, *die;* **~ enemy** Todfeind, *der.* **2** *n.* Sterbliche, *der/die*

mortality /mɔːˈtælɪtɪ/ *n.* **(a)** Sterblichkeit, *die;* **(b)** (number of deaths) Sterblichkeit, *die;* Todesfälle *Pl.;* **(c) ~ [rate]** Sterblichkeitsrate, *die;* Sterbeziffer, *die*

mortally /ˈmɔːtəlɪ/ *adv.* **~ wounded** tödlich verletzt; **~ offended** zutiefst *od.* tödlich beleidigt

mortar /ˈmɔːtə(r)/ *n.* **(a)** (substance) Mörtel, *der;* **(b)** (vessel) Mörser, *der;* **(c)** (cannon) Minenwerfer, *der;* Mörser, *der*

'mortarboard *n.* (Univ.) *bei bestimmten Anlässen zum Talar getragene viereckige Kopfbedeckung der Studenten und*

Lehrer an britischen und amerikanischen Universitäten; ≈ Barett, *das*

mortgage /ˈmɔːgɪdʒ/ **1** *n.* Hypothek, *die; attrib.* Hypotheken-; **~ repayment** Hypothekenzahlung, *die.* **2** *v.t.* mit einer Hypothek belasten

mortice ⇒ **mortise**

mortician /mɔːˈtɪʃn/ *n.* ▶ **887** (Amer.) Leichenbestatter, *der*/-bestatterin, *die*

mortification /mɔːtɪfɪˈkeɪʃn/ *n.* (humiliation) Beschämung, *die*

mortify /ˈmɔːtɪfaɪ/ *v.t.* beschämen; **he felt mortified** er empfand es als beschämend

mortise /ˈmɔːtɪs/ *n.* **(a)** (Woodw.) Zapfenloch, *das;* **~ and tenon [joint]** Zapfenverbindung, *die;* Verzapfung, *die;* **(b)** *attrib.* **~ lock** Steckschloss, *das*

mortuary /ˈmɔːtjʊərɪ/ *n.* Leichenschauhaus, *das*

mosaic /məʊˈzeɪɪk/ *n.* (lit. or fig.) Mosaik, *das; attrib.* Mosaik-

Moscow /ˈmɒskəʊ/ ▶ **1159** **1** *pr. n.* Moskau (*das*). **2** *attrib. adj.* Moskauer

Moslem /ˈmɒzləm/ ⇒ **Muslim**

mosque /mɒsk/ *n.* Moschee, *die*

mosquito /mɒsˈkiːtəʊ/ *n.*, *pl.* **~es** Stechmücke, *die;* (in tropics) Moskito, *der;* **~ bite** Mücken-/Moskitostich, *der*

mos'quito net *n.* Moskitonetz, *das*

moss /mɒs/ *n.* Moos, *das*

mossy /ˈmɒsɪ/ *adj.* moosig; bemoost; moosbewachsen

most /məʊst/ **1** *adj.* (in greatest number, the majority of) die meisten; (in greatest amount) meist...; größt... ‹*Fähigkeit, Macht, Bedarf, Geduld, Lärm*›; **make the ~ mistakes/ noise** die meisten Fehler/den meisten *od.* größten Lärm machen; **~ people** die meisten Leute; **for the ~ part** größtenteils; zum größten Teil. **2** *n.* **(a)** (greatest amount) das meiste; **offer [the] ~ for it** das meiste *od.* am meisten dafür bieten; **pay the ~:** am meisten bezahlen; **(b)** (the greater part) **~ of the girls** die meisten Mädchen; **~ of his friends** die meisten seiner Freunde; **~ of the poem** der größte Teil des Gedichts; **~ of the time** die meiste Zeit; (on ~ occasions) meistens; **~ of what he said** das meiste von dem, was er sagte; **(c) make the ~ of sth., get the ~ out of sth.** etw. voll ausnützen; (represent at its best) das Beste aus etw. machen; **(d) at [the] ~:** höchstens; **at the very ~:** allerhöchstens. **3** *adv.* **(a)** (more than anything else) am meisten ‹*mögen, interessieren, gefallen, sich wünschen, verlangt*›; **~ of all** am allermeisten; **(b)** *forming superl.* **the ~ interesting book** das interessanteste Buch; **this book is the ~ interesting** dieses Buch ist das interessanteste; **~ often** am häufigsten; **(c)** (exceedingly) überaus; äußerst; **~ certainly** ohne jeden Zweifel

mostly /ˈməʊstlɪ/ *adv.* (most of the time) meistens; (mainly) größtenteils; hauptsächlich

MOT ⇒ **MOT test**

motel /məʊˈtel/ *n.* Motel, *das*

motet /məʊˈtet/ *n.* (Mus.) Motette, *die*

moth /mɒθ/ *n.* Nachtfalter, *der;* (in clothes) Motte, *die*

moth: ~ball **1** *n.* Mottenkugel, *die;* **in ~balls** (fig.: stored) eingemottet ‹*Kleider, Schiff, Waffen*›; beiseite geschoben ‹*Plan, Projekt*›; **2** *v.t.* einmotten ‹*Kleider, alte Sachen, Vorschlag, militärisches Gerät*›; beiseite schieben ‹*Plan, Projekt*›; **~-eaten** *adj.* von Motten zerfressen; (fig.) verstaubt; altmodisch ‹*Person*›

mother /ˈmʌðə(r)/ **1** *n.* Mutter, *die;* **she is a** *or* **the ~ of six [children]** sie ist Mutter von sechs Kindern; **like ~ used to make** ‹*Essen*› wie bei Muttern (ugs.); **M~ Superior** Äbtissin, *die;* **necessity is the ~ of invention** (prov.) Not macht erfinderisch (Spr.). **2** *v.t.* (overprotect) bemuttern

'mother country *n.* Mutterland, *das*

motherhood /ˈmʌðəhʊd/ *n.*, *no pl.* Mutterschaft, *die*

Mothering Sunday /ˈmʌðərɪŋ ˈsʌndɪ/ (Brit. Eccl.) ⇒ **Mother's Day**

mother: ~-in-law *n.*, *pl.* **~s-in-law** Schwiegermutter, *die;* **~land** *n.* Vaterland, *das*

motherly /ˈmʌðəlɪ/ *adj.* mütterlich; **~ love** Mutterliebe, *die*

mother: ~-of-'pearl *n.* Perlmutt, *das;* **M~'s Day** *n.* Muttertag, *der;* ~ **'tongue** *n.* Muttersprache, *die*

motif /məʊ'tiːf/ *n.* Motiv, *das*

motion /'məʊʃn/ **1** *n.* **(a)** (movement) Bewegung, *die;* Gang, *der;* **be in** ~: in Bewegung sein; sich bewegen; ⟨*Maschine:*⟩ laufen; ⟨*Fahrzeug:*⟩ fahren; **set** *or* **put sth. in** ~ (lit. *or* fig.) etw. in Bewegung *od.* Gang setzen; **(b)** (gesture) Bewegung, *die;* Wink, *der;* **(c)** (formal proposal; also Law) Antrag, *der;* **put forward** *or* **propose a** ~: einen Antrag stellen; **(d)** (of bowels) Stuhlgang, *der;* **have** *or* **make a** ~: Stuhlgang haben; **(e)** *in sing. or pl.* (faeces) Stuhl, *der;* **(f) go through the** ~**s of doing sth.** (coll.) (simulate) so tun, als ob man etw. täte; (do superficially) etw. pro forma tun; **go through the** ~**s** (coll.) (simulate) nur so tun; (do superficially) es nur pro forma tun. **2** *v.t.* ~ **sb. to do sth.** jmdm. bedeuten (geh.) *od.* winken, etw. zu tun. **3** *v.i.* winken; ~ **to sb. to come in** jmdn. hereinwinken; ~ **to sb. to do sth.** jmdm. bedeuten (geh.), etw. zu tun

motionless /'məʊʃnlɪs/ *adj.* reg[ungs]los; bewegungslos

'motion picture *n.* (esp. Amer.) Film, *der; attrib.* Film-

motivate /'məʊtɪveɪt/ *v.t.* motivieren

motivation /məʊtɪ'veɪʃn/ *n.* **(a)** (process) Motivierung, *die;* **(b)** (incentive) Motivation, *die* (**for** zu); **(c)** (condition) Motiviertheit, *die;* Motivation, *die*

motive /'məʊtɪv/ **1** *n.* Motiv, *das;* Beweggrund, *der;* **the** ~ **for the crime** das Tatmotiv; **do sth. from** ~**s of kindness** etw. aus Freundlichkeit tun. **2** *adj.* (moving to action) treibend ⟨*Geist, Kraft*⟩; (productive of motion) Antriebs-

motley /'mɒtlɪ/ *adj.* **(a)** [bunt]gescheckt; (multicoloured) [kunter]bunt; **(b)** (varied) bunt gemischt; bunt ⟨*Auswahl*⟩

motor /'məʊtə(r)/ **1** *n.* **(a)** Motor, *der;* **(b)** (Brit.: ~ car) Auto, *das.* **2** *adj.* **(a)** (driven by engine *or* ~) Motor⟨*schlitten, -mäher, -jacht usw.*⟩; **(b)** (of ~ vehicles) Kraftfahrzeug⟨*ersatzteile, -mechaniker, -verkehr*⟩. **3** *v.i.* (Brit.) [mit dem Auto] fahren

motor: ~**bike** (coll.) ⇒ ~ **cycle;** ~ **boat** *n.* Motorboot, *das;* ~ **car** *n.* (Brit.) Kraftfahrzeug, *das;* Automobil, *das* (geh.); ~ **caravan** *n.* (Brit.) Caravan, *der;* Omnibus, *der;* ~**cycle** *n.* Motorrad, *das;* Kraftrad, *das* (Amtsspr.); *attrib.* ~**cycle combination** (Brit.) Motorrad mit Beiwagen; ~**cyclist** *n.* Motorradfahrer, *der*/-fahrerin, *die;* ~ **home** *n.* Reisemobil, *das;* ~ **industry** *n.* Kraftfahrzeugindustrie, *die*

motoring /'məʊtərɪŋ/ *n.* (Brit.) Autofahren, *das;* **school of** ~: Fahrschule, *die; attrib.* ~ **offence** Verstoß gegen die [Straßen]verkehrsordnung; ~ **organisation** Automobilklub, *der*

motorise ⇒ **motorize**

motorist /'məʊtərɪst/ *n.* Autofahrer, *der*/-fahrerin, *die*

motorize /'məʊtəraɪz/ *v.t.* motorisieren

motor: ~ **racing** *n.* Autorennsport, *der;* ~ **scooter** ⇒ **scooter** b; ~ **show** *n.* Auto[mobil]ausstellung, *die;* ~ **trade** *n.* Kraftfahrzeughandel, *der;* ~ **vehicle** *n.* Kraftfahrzeug, *das;* ~**way** *n.* (Brit.) Autobahn, *die*

MO'T test *n.* (Brit.) ≈ TÜV, *der*

mottled /'mɒtld/ *adj.* gesprenkelt

motto /'mɒtəʊ/ *n., pl.* ~**es** *(a)* Motto, *das;* **my** ~ **is 'live and let live'** meine Devise ist „leben und leben lassen"; **(b)** (in cracker) Spruch, *der*

mould¹ /məʊld/ *n.* **(a)** (earth) Erde, *die;* **(b)** (upper soil) [Mutter]boden, *der*

mould² **1** *n.* **(a)** (hollow) Form, *die;* (Metallurgy) Kokille, *die;* (Plastics) Pressform, *die;* **(b)** (Cookery) [Kuchen-/Back-/Pudding]form, *die.* **2** *v.t.* formen (**out of, from** aus)

mould³ *n.* (Bot.) Schimmel, *der*

moulder /'məʊldə(r)/ *v.i.* ~ **[away]** (lit. *or* fig.) [ver]modern

moulding /'məʊldɪŋ/ *n.* **(a)** (process of forming, lit. *or* fig.) Formen, *das;* **(b)** (object) Formteil, *das* (**of, in** aus); Formling, *der* (fachspr.); (Archit.) Zierleiste, *die;* **(c)** (wooden strip) Leiste, *die*

mouldy /'məʊldɪ/ *adj.* (overgrown with mould) schimmlig ; **a** ~ **smell** ein Modergeruch; **go** ~: verschimmeln; schimmlig werden

moult /məʊlt/ **1** *v.t.* **(a)** (Ornith.) verlieren ⟨*Federn, Gefieder*⟩; **(b)** (Zool.) verlieren ⟨*Haar*⟩; abstreifen ⟨*Haut*⟩; abwerfen ⟨*Horn, Geweih*⟩. **2** *v.i.* ⟨*Vogel:*⟩ sich mausern; ⟨*Hund, Katze:*⟩ sich haaren

mound /maʊnd/ *n.* **(a)** (of earth) Hügel, *der;* (of stones) Steinhaufen, *der;* **burial** ~: Grabhügel, *der;* **(b)** (hillock) Anhöhe, *die;* **(c)** (heap) Haufen, *der*

mount /maʊnt/ **1** *n.* **(a)** (mountain) **M~ Vesuvius/Everest** der Vesuv/der Mount Everest; **(b)** (animal) Reittier, *das;* (horse) Pferd, *das;* **(c)** (of picture, photograph) Passepartout, *das;* **(d)** (for gem) Fassung, *die;* **(e)** (Philat.) [Klebe]falz, *der.* **2** *v.t.* **(a)** (ascend) hinaufsteigen ⟨*Treppe, Leiter, Stufe*⟩; steigen auf (+ *Akk.*) ⟨*Plattform, Kanzel*⟩; **(b)** (get on) steigen auf ⟨*Akk.*⟩ ⟨*Reittier, Fahrzeug*⟩; *abs.* aufsitzen; ~ **the pavement** auf den Bürgersteig fahren; **(c)** (place on support) montieren (**on** auf + *Akk.*); **(d)** (prepare) aufstellen ⟨*Maschine, Apparat*⟩; präparieren ⟨*Exemplar*⟩; in ein Album einkleben ⟨*Briefmarke*⟩; aufziehen ⟨*Bild usw.*⟩; einfassen ⟨*Edelstein usw.*⟩; **(e)** inszenieren ⟨*Stück, Show, Oper*⟩; organisieren ⟨*Festspiele, Ausstellung*⟩; **(f)** (carry out) durchführen ⟨*Angriff, Operation usw.*⟩. **3** ~ **[up]** (increase) steigen (**to** auf + *Akk.*); **it all** ~**s up** es summiert sich

mountain /'maʊntɪn/ *n.* **(a)** (lit. *or* fig.) Berg, *der;* **in the** ~**s** im Gebirge; **butter/grain** etc. ~ (fig.) Butter-/Getreideberg *usw., der;* **move** ~**s** (fig.) Berge versetzen; *see also* **molehill;** **(b)** *attrib.* Gebirgs-; ~ **bike** Mountainbike, *das;* Geländefahrrad, *das*

mountaineer /maʊntɪ'nɪə(r)/ *n.* Bergsteiger, *der*/ Bergsteigerin, *die*

mountaineering /maʊntɪ'nɪərɪŋ/ *n.* Bergsteigen, *das; attrib.* ~ **expedition** Bergpartie, *die*

mountainous /'maʊntɪnəs/ *adj.* **(a)** gebirgig; **(b)** (huge) riesig ⟨*Gegenstand, Welle*⟩

mountain: ~ **'range** *n.* Gebirgszug, *der;* ~ **'road** *n.* Gebirgsstraße, *die;* ~**side** *n.* [Berg][ab]hang, *der;* ~ **top** *n.* Berggipfel, *der*

mounted /'maʊntɪd/ *adj.* (on animal) beritten

Mountie /'maʊntɪ/ *n.* (coll.) Mountie, *der; berittener kanadischer Polizist*

mounting /'maʊntɪŋ/ *n.* **(a)** (of performance) Inszenierung, *die;* **(b)** (support) (Art: of drawing) Passepartout, *das;* (of engine, axle, etc.) Aufhängung, *die*

mourn /mɔːn/ **1** *v.i.* trauern; ~ **for** *or* **over** trauern um ⟨*Toten*⟩; nachtrauern (+ *Dat.*) ⟨*Jugend, Augenlicht, Haustier*⟩; betrauern ⟨*Verlust, Missgeschick*⟩. **2** *v.t.* betrauern; nachtrauern ⟨*etw. Verlorenem*⟩

mourner /'mɔːnə(r)/ *n.* Trauernde, *der*/*die*

mournful /'mɔːnfl/ *adj.* klagend ⟨*Stimme, Ton, Schrei, Geheul*⟩; trauervoll (geh.) ⟨*Person*⟩

mourning /'mɔːnɪŋ/ *n.* **(a)** (clothes) Trauer[kleidung], *die;* **be [dressed] in** *or* **wear/put on** *or* **go into** ~: Trauer tragen/anlegen; **(b)** (sorrowing, lamentation) Trauer, *die*

mouse /maʊs/ **1** *n., pl.* **mice** /maɪs/ **(a)** Maus, *die;* **as quiet as a** ~: ganz leise; mucksmäuschenstill (fam.) ⟨*dasitzen*⟩; **(b)** (fig.: timid person) Angsthase, *der* (ugs.); **(c)** (Computing) Maus, *die; attrib.* ~ **button** Maustaste, *die;* **2** *v.i.* mausen

mouse: ~**hole** *n.* Mauseloch, *das;* ~**trap** *n.* Mausefalle, *die*

mousse /muːs/ *n.* Mousse, *die*

moustache /mə'stɑːʃ/ *n.* Schnurrbart, *der*

mousy /'maʊsɪ/ *adj.* mattbraun ⟨*Haar*⟩

mouth 1 /maʊθ/ *n., pl.* ~**s** /maʊðz/ **(a)** ▶672 (of person) Mund, *der;* (of animal) Maul, *das;* **with one's** ~ **open** mit offenem Mund; **keep one's** ~ **shut** (fig. sl.) die *od.* seine Klappe halten (salopp); **put one's money where one's** ~ **is** (fig. coll.) seinen Worten Taten folgen lassen; **with one's** ~ **full** mit vollem Mund; **out of the** ~**s of babes [and sucklings]!** (fig.) Kindermund tut Wahrheit kund (Spr.); **have got many** ~**s to feed** viele hungrige Mäuler zu stopfen haben (ugs.); **take the words out of sb.'s** ~: jmdm. das Wort aus dem Mund *od.* von der Zunge nehmen; **(b)** (fig.) (entrance to harbour) [Hafen]einfahrt, *die;* (of valley, gorge, burrow, tunnel, cave) Eingang, *der;* (of bottle, cannon) Mündung, *die;* **(c)** ▶1048 (of river) Mündung, *die.* **2** /maʊð/

v.t. mit Lippenbewegungen sagen. **3** /maʊθ/ *v.i.* lautlos die Lippen bewegen

mouthful /'maʊθful/ *n.* **(a)** Bissen, *der;* (of drink) Schluck, *der;* a ~ **of soup/stew** ein Mund voll Suppe/Eintopf: **(b)** (sth. difficult to say) Zungenbrecher, *der* (ugs.)

mouth: ~ **organ** *n.* Mundharmonika, *die;* ~**piece** *n.* **(a)** (Mus., Med.) Mundstück, *das;* (of telephone) Sprechmuschel, *die;* **(b)** (speaker for others) Sprachrohr, *das;* ~**-to-** ~ **resusci'tation** *n.* Wiederbelebung durch Mund-zu-Mund-Beatmung; ~**wash** *n.* Mundwasser, *das;* ~**-watering** *adj.* lecker

movable /'muːvəbl/ *adj.* beweglich

move /muːv/ **1** *n.* **(a)** (change of residence) Umzug, *der;* (change of job) Wechsel, *der;* **(b)** (action taken) Schritt, *der;* (Footb. etc.) Spielzug, *der;* **(c)** (turn in game) Zug, *der;* (fig.) [Schach]zug, *der;* **make a** ~: ziehen; **it's your** ~: du bist am Zug; **(d)** **be on the** ~ (moving about) ⟨*Person:*⟩ unterwegs sein; **(e)** **make a** ~ (initiate action) etwas tun *od.* unternehmen; (coll.: leave, depart) losziehen (ugs.); **make the first** ~: den Anfang machen; **make no** ~: sich nicht rühren; **make no** ~ **to help sb.** keine Anstalten machen, jmdm. zu helfen; **(f)** **get a** ~ **on** (coll.) einen Zahn zulegen (ugs.); **get a** ~ **on!** (coll.) [mach] Tempo! (ugs.). **2** *v.t.* **(a)** (change position of) bewegen; wegräumen ⟨*Hindernis, Schutt*⟩; (transport) befördern; ~ **the chair over here** rück den Stuhl hier herüber!; ~ **sth. to a new position** etw. an einen neuen Platz bringen; ~ **house** umziehen; ~ **the luggage into the building** das Gepäck ins Gebäude hineinbringen; **not** ~ **a muscle** sich nicht rühren; **please** ~ **your head [to one side]** bitte tun Sie Ihren Kopf zur Seite; ~ **it!** (coll.), ~ **yourself!** (coll.) Beeilung! (ugs.); ~ **sb. to another department/job** jmdn. in eine andere Abteilung/Position versetzen; ~ **police/troops into an area** Polizeikräfte/Truppen in ein Gebiet schicken; **(b)** (in game) ziehen; **(c)** (affect) bewegen; berühren; ~ **sb. to laughter/anger** jmdn. zum Lachen bringen/jmds. Ärger erregen; ~ **sb. to tears** jmdn. zu Tränen rühren; ~ **sb. to pity** jmds. Mitleid erregen; **be** ~**d to pity** vor Mitleid gerührt sein; **be** ~**d by sth.** über etw. (*Akk.*) gerührt sein; **(d)** (prompt) ~ **sb. to do sth.** jmdn. dazu bewegen, etw. zu tun; **sb. is not to be** ~**d** jmd. lässt sich nicht erschüttern; **(e)** (propose) beantragen ⟨*Beendigung, Danksagung*⟩; stellen ⟨*Antrag*⟩; **(f)** (Commerc.: sell) absetzen. **3** *v.i.* **(a)** (go from place to place) sich bewegen; (by car, bus, train) fahren; (on foot) gehen; (coll.: start, leave) gehen; ⟨*Wolken:*⟩ ziehen (**across** über + *Akk.*); ~ **with the times** (fig.) mit der Zeit gehen; **get moving!** beeil dich!; **start to** ~ ⟨*Fahrzeug:*⟩ sich in Bewegung setzen; **nobody** ~**d** niemand rührte sich von der Stelle; **he has** ~**d to another department** er ist jetzt in einer anderen Abteilung; **Don't** ~. **I'll be back soon** Bleib hier *od.* Geh nicht weg. Ich bin gleich zurück; **(b)** (in games) ziehen; **(c)** (fig.: initiate action) handeln; aktiv werden; ~ **quickly to do sth.** schnell handeln und etw. tun; **(d)** (in certain circles, part of society, part of town) verkehren; **(e)** (change residence or accommodation) umziehen (**to** nach); (into flat etc.) einziehen (**into** in + *Akk.*); (out of town) wegziehen (**out of** aus); (out of flat etc.) ausziehen (**out of** aus); **I want to** ~ **to London** ich will nach London ziehen; **(f)** (change posture or state) sich bewegen; (in order to make oneself comfortable etc.) eine andere Haltung einnehmen; **don't** ~ **or I'll shoot** keine Bewegung, oder ich schieße; **(g)** (make progress) vorankommen; **get things moving** vorankommen; **things are moving now** jetzt geht es voran; ~ **towards** näher kommen (+ *Dat.*) ⟨*Einigung, Höhepunkt, Kompromiss*⟩; **(h)** (Commerc.: be sold) ⟨*Waren:*⟩ Absatz finden, sich absetzen lassen; **(i)** (coll.: go fast) **that car can really** ~: der Wagen ist enorm schnell (ugs.)

~ **a'bout 1** *v.i.* zugange sein; (travel) unterwegs sein. **2** *v.t.* herumräumen ⟨*Möbel, Bücher*⟩

~ **a'long 1** *v.i.* **(a)** gehen/fahren; **(b)** (make room) Platz machen; ~ **along, please!** gehen/fahren Sie bitte weiter! **2** *v.t.* zum Weitergehen/-fahren auffordern

~ **'in 1** *v.i.* **(a)** einziehen; (to start work) ⟨*Bauarbeiter:*⟩ kommen; **(b)** (come closer) ⟨*Truppen, Polizeikräfte:*⟩ anrücken; ~ **in on** ⟨*Truppen, Polizeikräfte:*⟩ vorrücken gegen. **2** *v.t.* einrücken lassen ⟨*Truppen, Polizeikräfte*⟩; hineinbringen ⟨*Gepäck, Ausrüstung*⟩

~ **'off** *v.i.* sich in Bewegung setzen

~ **'on 1** *v.i.* weitergehen/-fahren; ~ **on to another question** (fig.) zu einer anderen Frage übergehen. **2** *v.t.* zum Weitergehen/-fahren auffordern

~ **'out** *v.i.* ausziehen (**of** aus)

~ **'over** *v.i.* rücken

~ **'up** *v.i.* **(a)** (in queue, hierarchy) aufrücken ⟨*Fahrzeug:*⟩ vorfahren; **(b)** ⇒ ~ **over**

movement /'muːvmənt/ *n.* **(a)** Bewegung, *die;* (of people: towards city, country, etc.) [Ab]wanderung, *die;* (trend, tendency) Tendenz, *die;* a ~ **of the head/arm/leg** eine Kopf-/Arm-/Beinbewegung; **without** ~: bewegungslos; **(b)** *in pl.* Aktivitäten *Pl.;* **keep track of sb.'s** ~**s** jmdn. überwachen; **(c)** (Mus.) Satz, *der;* **(d)** (concerted action for purpose) Bewegung, *die;* **(e)** *in sing. or pl.* (Mech. esp. in clock, watch) Räderwerk, *das;* **(f)** (in price) Preisbewegung, *die*

movie /'muːvɪ/ *n.* (Amer. coll.) Film, *der; attrib.* Film-; **the** ~**s** (art form, cinema industry) **der** Film

movie-goer /'muːvɪɡəʊə(r)/ *n.* (Amer. coll.) Kinogänger, *der/*-gängerin, *die*

moving /'muːvɪŋ/ *adj.* **(a)** beweglich; **from a** ~ **car** ⟨*fallen, werfen, schießen*⟩ aus einem fahrenden Auto; **(b)** (affecting) ergreifend; bewegend

moving 'staircase ⇒ **escalator**

mow /məʊ/ *v.t., p.p.* **mown** /məʊn/ *or* **mowed** /məʊd/ mähen

~ **'down** *v.t.* niedermähen ⟨*Soldaten*⟩; überfahren ⟨*Fußgänger*⟩

mower /'məʊə(r)/ *n.* (for lawn) Rasenmäher, *der*

Mozambique /məʊzəm'biːk/ *pr. n.* Mosambik (*das*)

MP *abbr.* **Member of Parliament**

m.p.g. /empiː'dʒiː/ *abbr.* (Motor Veh.) **miles per gallon; do/get 34** ~ (Brit.) 8,3 l auf 100 km [ver]brauchen

m.p.h. /empiː'eɪtʃ/ *abbr.* ▶ **1102| miles per hour; we are driving at/doing 30** ~: wir fahren 50 [km/h]

Mr /'mɪstə(r)/ *n., pl.* **Messrs** /'mesəz/ ▶ **1152|** (title) Herr; (third person also) Hr.; (in an address) Herrn; **Messrs** Hrn.; (firm) Fa.

Mrs /'mɪsɪz/ *n., pl. same* ▶ **1152|** Frau; (third person also) Fr.

MS *abbr.* **(a)** **manuscript** Ms.; **(b)** (Med.) **multiple sclerosis** MS

Ms /mɪz/ *n., no pl.* ▶ **1152|** Frau

M.Sc. /emes'siː/ *abbr.* **Master of Science;** *see also* **B.Sc.**

Mt. *abbr.* **Mount;** ~ **Etna/Everest** der Ätna/der Mount Everest

much /mʌtʃ/ **1** *adj., more* /mɔː(r)/, *most* /məʊst/ **(a)** viel; groß ⟨*Erleichterung, Sorge, Dankbarkeit*⟩; **with** ~ **love** voller Liebe; **he never eats** ~ **breakfast/lunch** er isst nicht viel zum Frühstück/zu Mittag; **too** ~: zu viel *indekl.;* **(b)** **be a bit** ~ (coll.) ein bisschen zu viel sein; (fig.) ein bisschen zu weit gehen. **2** *n.; see also* **more 2; most 2**; *vieles;* **we don't see** ~ **of her any more** wir sehen sie kaum noch; **that doesn't come** *or* **amount to** ~: es kommt nicht viel dabei heraus; **he/this beer isn't up to** ~ (coll.) mit ihm/diesem Bier ist nicht viel los (ugs.); **spend** ~ **of the day/week doing sth.** den Großteil des Tages/der Woche damit verbringen, etw. zu tun; **they have done** ~ **to improve the situation** sie haben viel für die Verbesserung der Situation getan; **not be** ~ **of a cinema-goer** etc. (coll.) kein großer Kinogänger *usw.* sein (ugs.); **it isn't** ~ **of a bicycle** es ist kein besonders tolles Fahrrad (ugs.); **not be** ~ **to look at** nicht sehr ansehnlich sein; **it's as** ~ **as she can do to get up the stairs** sie kommt gerade noch die Treppe hinauf; **I expected/thought as** ~: das habe ich erwartet/mir gedacht; **you are as** ~ **to blame as he is** du bist ebenso sehr schuld wie er; **without so** ~ **as saying goodbye** ohne auch nur auf Wiedersehen zu sagen. **3** *adv.,* **more, most (a)** *modifying comparatives* viel ⟨*besser*⟩; ~ **more lively/happy/attractive** viel lebhafter/glücklicher/ attraktiver; **(b)** *modifying superlatives* mit Abstand ⟨*der/die/das beste, schlechteste, klügste usw.*⟩; **(c)** *modifying passive participles and predicative adjectives* sehr; **he is** ~ **improved** (in health) es geht ihm viel besser; **(d)** *modifying verbs* (greatly) sehr ⟨*lieben, mögen, genießen*⟩; (often) oft ⟨*sehen, treffen, besuchen*⟩; (frequently) viel; **I don't** ~ **like him** *or* **like him**

~: ich mag ihn nicht besonders; **not go** ~ **on sb./sth.** (coll.) nicht viel von jmdm./etw. halten; **it doesn't matter** ~: es ist nicht so wichtig; **I would** ~ **prefer to stay at home** ich würde viel lieber zu Hause bleiben; ~ **to my surprise/annoyance, I found that** …: zu meiner großen Überraschung/Verärgerung stellte ich fest, dass …; **(e)** (approximately) fast; **[pretty** or **very]** ~ **the same** fast [genau] der-/die-/dasselbe; **(f)** ~ **as** or **though** (although) sosehr … auch; ~ **as he disliked the idea** sosehr ihm die Idee auch missfiel; ~ **as I should like to go** so gern ich auch gehen würde

muck /mʌk/ n. **(a)** (farmyard manure) Mist, der; **(b)** (coll.: anything disgusting) Dreck, der (ugs.); (liquid) Brühe, die (ugs. abwertend); **covered in** ~: verdreckt (ugs.)
~ **a'bout,** ~ **a'round** (Brit. coll.) **1** v.i. **(a)** herumalbern (ugs.); **(b)** (tinker) herumfummeln (**with** an + Dat.). **2** v.t. ~ **sb. about** or **around** jmdn. verarschen (derb)
~ **'in** v.i. (coll.) mit zugreifen od. mit anpacken (**with** bei)
~ **'up** v.t. **(a)** (Brit. coll.: bungle) vermurksen, verbocken (ugs.); ~ **it up** Mist bauen (ugs.); **(b)** (make dirty) vollschmieren (ugs.); dreckig machen (ugs.); einsauen (derb); **(c)** (coll.: spoil) vermasseln (salopp)
muckraking /'mʌkreɪkɪŋ/ n. Skandalhascherei, die (abwertend)
mucky /'mʌkɪ/ adj. dreckig (ugs.)
mucus /'mju:kəs/ n. (Med., Bot., Zool.) Schleim, der
mud /mʌd/ n. **(a)** Schlamm, der; **be as clear as** ~ (joc. iron.) absolut unklar sein; **(b)** (fig.) **be dragged through the** ~: in den Schmutz gezogen werden; **his name is** ~ (coll.) er ist unten durch (ugs.) (**with** bei); **sling** or **throw** ~ **at sb.** (fig.) jmdn. mit Dreck (ugs.) od. Schmutz bewerfen
'mudbath n. (Med.; also fig.) Schlammbad, das
muddle /'mʌdl/ **1** n. Durcheinander, das; **the room is in a hopeless** ~: in dem Zimmer herrscht ein heilloses Durcheinander; **get sth. in a** ~: etw. in Unordnung bringen; etw. durcheinander bringen; **get in[to] a** ~: durcheinander kommen (ugs.). **2** v.t. ~ **[up]** durcheinander bringen; ~ **up** (mix up) verwechseln (**with** mit); be ~d **up** (out of order) durcheinander geraten sein
~ **a'long,** ~ **'on** v.i. vor sich (Akk.) hin wursteln (ugs.)
~ **'through** v.i. sich durchwursteln (ugs.)
muddled /'mʌdld/ adj. benebelt ⟨Person⟩; konfus ⟨Verhalten, Denken⟩; verworren ⟨Situation, Information, Ideen⟩
muddle-'headed adj. wirr
muddy /'mʌdɪ/ **1** adj. **(a)** schlammig; **get** or **become** ~: verschlammen; **(b)** (turbid, dull) trübe ⟨Flüssigkeit, Farbe⟩. **2** v.t. schmutzig machen; (make turbid) trüben ⟨Flüssigkeit⟩; ~ **the waters** (fig.) die Dinge [noch] undurchschaubarer od. verworrener machen; für zusätzliche Verwirrung sorgen
mud: ~**flap** n. (Motor Veh.) Schmutzfänger, der; ~**flat[s]** n. [pl.] (Geog.) Watt, das; ~**guard** n. Schutzblech, das; (of car) Kotflügel, der; ~**pack** n. Schlammpackung [für das Gesicht]; ~ **'pie** n. Kuchen (aus Sand usw.)
muesli /'mju:zlɪ/ n. Müsli, das
muff¹ /mʌf/ n. Muff, der
muff² v.t. **(a)** (bungle) verderben; verpatzen (ugs.); verhauen (ugs.) ⟨Examen⟩; **(b)** (Theatre) verpatzen (ugs.); ~ **a line** einen Patzer machen (ugs.)
muffin /'mʌfɪn/ n. Muffin, das
muffle /'mʌfl/ v.t. **(a)** (envelop) ~ **[up]** einhüllen; einmumme[l]n (ugs.); **(b)** dämpfen ⟨Geräusch⟩; [zur Schalldämpfung] umwickeln ⟨Ruder, Trommel, Glocke⟩
muffler /'mʌflə(r)/ n. **(a)** (wrap, scarf) Schal, der; **(b)** (Amer. Motor Veh.) Schalldämpfer, der
mug¹ /mʌg/ **1** n. **(a)** (vessel, contents) Becher, der (meist mit Henkel); (for beer etc.) Krug, der; **a** ~ **of milk** ein Becher Milch; **(b)** (sl.: face, mouth) Visage, die (salopp); Fresse, die (derb); **(c)** (Brit. coll.: simpleton) Schwachkopf, der (ugs.); **(d)** (Brit. coll.: gullible person) Trottel, der (ugs. abwertend); Doofi, der (ugs.); **that's a '**~**'s game** das ist doch Schwachsinn (ugs.). **2** v.t., **-gg-** (rob) überfallen und berauben

mug² (Brit. coll.: study) v.t., **-gg-:** ~ **up** büffeln (ugs.)
mugful /'mʌgfʊl/ (contents) ⇒ **mug¹ 1 a**
mugger /'mʌgə(r)/ n. Straßenräuber, der/Straßenräuberin, die
mugging /'mʌgɪŋ/ n. Straßenraub, der (**of** an + Dat.)
muggins /'mʌgɪnz/ n., pl. ~**es** or same (coll.) **(a)** (simpleton) Dummkopf, der (ugs.); Esel, der (ugs.); **(b)** (myself, stupidly) ich Dummkopf (ugs.)
muggy /'mʌgɪ/ adj. schwül; drückend ⟨Klima, Tag, Luft⟩
mulberry /'mʌlbərɪ/ n. **(a)** (fruit) Maulbeere, die; **(b)** (tree) Maulbeerbaum, der
mulch /mʌltʃ/ (Agric., Hort.) **1** n. Mulch, der. **2** v.t. mulchen
mule /mju:l/ n. Maultier, das; see also **obstinate; stubborn a**
mull¹ /mʌl/ v.t. ~ **over** nachdenken über (+ Akk.); (in conversation) diskutieren
mull² v.t. ~**ed wine** Glühwein, der
mullah /'mʊlə/ n. (Islam) Mullah, der
multi- /'mʌltɪ/ in comb. (several) mehr-/Mehr-; (many) viel-/Viel-; multi-/Multi-, poly-/Poly- (bes. mit Fremdwörtern)
multi: ~**coloured** (Brit.; Amer.: ~**colored**) adj. (with several colours) mehrfarbig, (with many colours) vielfarbig ⟨Gegenstand, Tier, Pflanze⟩; bunt ⟨Stoff, Kleid⟩; ~**cultural** adj. multikulturell
multifarious /mʌltɪ'feərɪəs/ adj. **(a)** (having great variety) vielgestaltig; **(b)** (many and various) mannigfach; vielfältig
multi: ~**gym** n. **(a)** (equipment) Multifunktionsfitnessgerät, das; **(b)** (room) Fitnessraum, der; ~**lateral** adj. mehrseitig; (Polit.) multilateral; ~**media** n. sing. Multimedia, das; attrib. Multimedia-; ~**millio'naire** n. Multimillionär, der/-millionärin, die; ~**'national** adj. **1** multinational; **2** n. multinationaler Konzern, der; Multi, der (ugs.)
multiple /'mʌltɪpl/ **1** adj. **(a)** (manifold) mehrfach; ~ **pile-up** Massenkarambolage, die; **(b)** (many and various) vielerlei; vielfältig. See also **sclerosis. 2** n. (Math.) Vielfache, das
multiple: ~**'choice** adj. Multiple-Choice-⟨Verfahren, Test, Frage⟩; ~ **'store** n. (Brit. Commerc.) Kettenladen, der
multiplex /'mʌltɪpleks/ **1** adj. Multiplex-⟨Kino, Filmtheater etc.⟩. **2** n. (Cinema) Multiplex[-Kino], das
multiplication /mʌltɪplɪ'keɪʃn/ n. (increase) Vervielfachung, die; (Math.) Multiplikation, die (fachspr.); Malnehmen, das; attrib. ~ **sign** Malzeichen, das; ~ **table** Multiplikationstabelle, die
multiplicity /mʌltɪ'plɪsɪtɪ/ n. Vielfalt, die (**of, in** an, von + Dat. Pl.); (great number) Vielzahl, die (**of** von, an + Dat.)
multiply /'mʌltɪplaɪ/ **1** v.t. **(a)** (Math., also abs.) multiplizieren (fachspr.), malnehmen (by mit); **(b)** (increase) vervielfachen. **2** v.i. (Biol.) sich vermehren; sich fortpflanzen
'multi-purpose adj. Mehrzweck-
multi'racial adj. mehrrassig; gemischtrassig
multi: ~**-storey** adj. mehrstöckig; mehrgeschossig; ~**-storey car park/block of flats** Parkhaus, das/Wohnhochhaus, das; ~**track** adj. mehrspurig; Mehrspur⟨aufnahme, -ton, -tonbandgerät⟩
multitude /'mʌltɪtju:d/ n. (crowd) Menge, die; (great number) Vielzahl, die
mum¹ /mʌm/ (coll.) **1** int. ~**'s the word** nicht weitersagen! **2 keep** ~: den Mund halten (ugs.)
mum² n. (Brit. coll.: mother) Mama, die (fam.)
mumble /'mʌmbl/ **1** v.i. nuscheln (ugs.). **2** v.t. nuscheln (ugs.)
mumbo-jumbo /mʌmbəʊ'dʒʌmbəʊ/ n., pl. ~**s** **(a)** (meaningless ritual) Brimborium, das (ugs.); Theater, das (ugs. abwertend); **(b)** (gibberish) Kauderwelsch, das
mummy¹ /'mʌmɪ/ n. Mumie, die
mummy² n. (Brit. coll.: mother) Mutti, die (fam.); Mami, die (fam.); Mama, die (fam.)
mumps /mʌmps/ n. sing. ▶ 865 (Med.) Mumps, der
munch /mʌntʃ/ **1** v.t. ~ **one's food** mampfen (salopp); schmatzend kauen. **2** v.i. mampfen (salopp)
mundane /mʌn'deɪn/ adj. **(a)** (dull) banal; **(b)** (worldly) weltlich

municipal /mjuːˈnɪsɪpl/ *adj.* gemeindlich; kommunal; Kommunal⟨*politik, -verwaltung*⟩; Gemeinde⟨*rat, -verwaltung*⟩

municipality /mjuːnɪsɪˈpælɪtɪ/ *n.* Gemeinde, *die*

munition /mjuːˈnɪʃn/ *n., usu. in pl.* Kriegsmaterial, *das;* ∼[s] **factory** Rüstungsbetrieb, *der*

mural /ˈmjʊərl/ *n.* Wandbild, *das;* (on ceiling) Deckengemälde, *das*

murder /ˈmɜːdə(r)/ **1** *n.* **(a)** (Law) Mord, *der* (**of** an + *Dat.*); ∼ **investigation** Ermittlungen *Pl.* in dem/einem Mordfall; ∼ **hunt** Fahndung nach dem/einem Mörder; **(b)** (fig.) **the exam/journey was** ∼**:** die Prüfung/Reise war der glatte *od.* reine Mord (ugs.). **2** *v.t.* **(a)** (kill unlawfully) ermorden; ∼ **sb. with a gun/knife** jmdn. erschießen/erstechen; **(b)** (kill inhumanly) umbringen; **(c)** (coll.: spoil) verhunzen (ugs.); **(d)** (coll.: defeat) fertig machen (ugs.)

murderer /ˈmɜːdərə(r)/ *n.* Mörder, *der*/Mörderin, *die*

murderous /ˈmɜːdərəs/ *adj.* tödlich; Mord⟨*absicht, -drohung*⟩; mörderisch (ugs.) ⟨*Fahrweise, Kampf, Bedingung*⟩

murk /mɜːk/ *n.* Dunkelheit, *die;* Nebelnacht, *die* (geh.)

murky /ˈmɜːkɪ/ *adj.* **(a)** (dark) düster; trüb ⟨*Tag, Wetter*⟩; **(b)** (dirty) schmutzig trüb ⟨*Wasser*⟩; **(c)** (fig.: obscure) dunkel; unergründlich ⟨*Geheimnis, Tiefen*⟩

murmur /ˈmɜːmə(r)/ **1** *n.* **(a)** (subdued sound) Rauschen, *das;* (of brook also) Murmeln, *das* (dichter.); **(b)** (expression of discontent) Murren, *das;* ∼ **of disagreement/impatience** ablehnendes/ungeduldiges Murren; **without a** ∼**:** ohne Murren; **(c)** (soft speech) Murmeln, *das;* ∼ **of approval/delight** beifälliges/freudiges Murmeln; **a** ∼ **of voices** ein Gemurmel. **2** *v.t.* murmeln. **3** *v.i.* ⟨*Person:*⟩ murmeln; (complain) murren (**against, at** über + *Akk.*)

muscle /ˈmʌsl/ **1** *n.* **(a)** ▶ 672 | Muskel, *der;* **not move a** ∼ (fig.) sich nicht rühren; **(b)** (tissue) Muskeln *Pl.;* **(c)** (muscular power) [Muskel-, Körper]kraft, *die;* Muskeln *Pl.;* (fig.: force, power, influence) Stärke, *die.* **2** *v.i.* ∼ **'in** (coll.) sich hineindrängen (**on in** + *Akk.*)

'muscleman *n.* Muskelmann, *der* (ugs.)

muscular /ˈmʌskjʊlə(r)/ *adj.* **(a)** (Med.) Muskel-; muskulär (fachspr.); **(b)** (sinewy) muskulös

muscular dystrophy /mʌskjʊlə ˈdɪstrəfɪ/ *n.* ▶ 865 | (Med.) Muskeldystrophie, *die*

muse /mjuːz/ (literary) *v.i.* grübeln; [nach]sinnen (geh.), sinnieren (**on, about, over** über + *Akk.*)

museum /mjuːˈziːəm/ *n.* Museum, *das;* ∼ **of art** Kunstmuseum, *das*

mu'seum piece *n.* **(a)** Museumsstück, *das;* **(b)** (joc. derog.) Museumsstück, *das* (ugs. iron.)

mush /mʌʃ/ *n.* **(a)** (soft pulp) Mus, *das;* Brei, *der;* **(b)** (coll.: weak sentimentality) Schmalz, *der* (ugs.)

mushroom /ˈmʌʃrʊm, ˈmʌʃruːm/ **1** *n.* Pilz, *der;* (edible) [Speise]pilz, *der;* (cultivated, esp. Agaricus campestris) Champignon, *der.* **2** *v.i.* (spring up) wie Pilze aus dem Boden schießen; **demand** ∼**ed overnight** die Nachfrage schoß über Nacht in die Höhe

'mushroom cloud *n.* Rauchpilz, *der;* (after nuclear explosion) Atompilz, *der*

mushy /ˈmʌʃɪ/ *adj.* **(a)** (soft) breiig; **(b)** (coll.: feebly sentimental) schmalzig (abwertend)

music /ˈmjuːzɪk/ *n.* **(a)** Musik, *die;* **make** ∼**:** Musik machen; musizieren; **piece of** ∼**:** Musikstück, *das;* Musik, *die;* **set** *or* **put sth. to** ∼**:** etw. vertonen *od.* in Musik setzen; **be** ∼ **to sb.'s ears** (fig. coll.) Musik in jmds. Ohren sein (ugs.); *see also* **face 2 c**; **(b)** (score) Noten *Pl.;* (as merchandise also) Musikalien *Pl.;* **sheet of** ∼**:** Notenblatt, *das*

musical /ˈmjuːzɪkl/ **1** *adj.* musikalisch; Musik⟨*instrument, -notation, -verein, -verständnis, -abend*⟩; Musik ⟨*film, -theater*⟩. **2** *n.* (Mus., Theatre) Musical, *das*

musical: ∼ **box** *n.* (Brit.) Spieldose, *die;* ∼ **'chairs** *n. sing.* Reise nach Jerusalem

musically /ˈmjuːzɪkəlɪ/ *adv.* musikalisch; (melodiously) melodisch; melodiös; ∼ **gifted** musikalisch [begabt]; musikbegabt

music: ∼ **centre** *n.* Kompaktanlage, *die;* ∼ **hall** *n.* (Brit.) Varietee, *das; attrib.* Varietee-

musician /mjuːˈzɪʃn/ *n.* ▶ 887 | Musiker, *der*/Musikerin, *die*

music: ∼ **lesson** *n.* Musikstunde, *die;* ∼ **stand** *n.* Notenständer, *der;* ∼ **stool** *n.* Klavierhocker, *der;* Klavierschemel, *der;* ∼**-teacher** *n.* Musiklehrer, *der*/-lehrerin, *die* ∼ **video** *n.* Musikvideo, *das*

musk /mʌsk/ *n.* **(a)** (substance) Moschus, *der;* **(b)** (odour) Moschusgeruch, *der*

musket /ˈmʌskɪt/ *n.* (Hist.) Muskete, *die*

musketeer /mʌskɪˈtɪə(r)/ *n.* (Hist.) Musketier, *der*

'muskrat *n.* **(a)** (Zool.) Bisamratte, *die;* **(b)** (fur) Bisam, *der*

musky /ˈmʌskɪ/ *adj.* moschusartig ⟨*Duft, Geruch, Geschmack*⟩; Moschus⟨*duft, -parfüm*⟩

Muslim /ˈmʊslɪm, ˈmʌzlɪm/ **1** *adj.* muslimisch (bes. fachspr.); moslemisch. **2** *n.* Muslim, *der*/Muslime, *die* (bes. fachspr.); Moslem, *der*/Moslime, *die*

muslin /ˈmʌzlɪn/ *n.* Musselin, *der*

musquash /ˈmʌskwɒʃ/ *n.* ⇒ **muskrat**

muss /mʌs/ *v.t.* (Amer. coll.) verstrubbeln (ugs.) ⟨*Haar, Frisur*⟩

∼ **'up** *v.t.* durcheinander bringen; verstrubbeln (ugs.) ⟨*Haar*⟩; zerknittern ⟨*Kleidung*⟩

mussel /ˈmʌsl/ *n.* Muschel, *die*

must /məst, *stressed* mʌst/ **1** *v. aux., only in pres. and past* **must**, neg. (coll.) **mustn't** /ˈmʌsnt/ **(a)** (have to) müssen; *with negative* dürfen; **you** ∼ **not/never do that** das darfst du nicht/nie tun; **you** ∼ **remember** ...**:** du darfst nicht vergessen, ...; du musst daran denken, ...; **you** ∼ **listen to me!** hör mir zu!; **you** ∼**n't do that again!** tu das [ja] nie wieder!; **I** ∼ **get back to the office** ich muss wieder ins Büro; ∼ **I?** muss das sein?; **I** ∼ **have a new dress** ich brauche ein neues Kleid; **if you '**∼ **know** wenn du es unbedingt wissen willst; **(b)** (ought to) müssen; *with negative* dürfen; **you** ∼ **think about it** du solltest [unbedingt] darüber nachdenken; **I** ∼ **not sit here drinking coffee** ich sollte *od.* dürfte eigentlich nicht hier sitzen und Kaffee trinken; **(c)** (be certain to) müssen; **you** ∼ **be tired** du musst müde sein; du bist bestimmt müde; **you** ∼ **be crazy** du bist wohl wahnsinnig!; **it** ∼ **be about 3 o'clock** es wird wohl *od.* dürfte *od.* müsste etwa 3 Uhr sein; **it** ∼ **have stopped raining by now** es dürfte *od.* müsste inzwischen aufgehört haben zu regnen; **there** ∼ **have been forty of them** (forty) es müssen vierzig gewesen sein; (probably about forty) es dürften etwa vierzig gewesen sein; **(d)** *expr. indignation or annoyance* **he** ∼ **come just when** ...**:** er muss/musste natürlich *od.* ausgerechnet kommen, wenn/als ... **2** *n.* (coll.) Muß, *das;* **be a** ∼ **for sb./sth.** ein Muß für jmdn./unerlässlich für etw. sein

mustache ⇒ **moustache**

mustang /ˈmʌstæŋ/ *n.* Mustang, *der*

mustard /ˈmʌstəd/ *n.* **(a)** Senf, *der;* ∼ **and cress** (Brit.) Senfkeimlinge und Kresse; **(b)** (colour) Senffarbe, *die; attrib.* senffarben

'mustard gas *n.* (Chem., Mil.) Senfgas, *das*

muster /ˈmʌstə(r)/ **1** *n.* (Mil.) Appell, *der;* **pass** ∼ (fig.) akzeptabel sein. **2** *v.t.* **(a)** (summon) versammeln; (Mil., Naut.) [zum Appell] antreten lassen; **(b)** (collect) zusammenbringen; zusammenziehen ⟨*Streitkräfte, Truppen*⟩; (raise) aufstellen ⟨*Armee*⟩; ausheben ⟨*Truppen*⟩; **(c)** (fig.: summon up) zusammennehmen ⟨*Kraft, Mut, Verstand*⟩; aufbringen ⟨*Unterstützung*⟩. **3** *v.i.* sich [ver]sammeln; ⟨*Truppen:*⟩ aufmarschieren; (for parade) antreten

∼ **'up** *v.t.* aufbringen ⟨*Unterstützung, Mut, Verständnis*⟩; ∼ **up all one's courage** seinen ganzen Mut zusammennehmen

mustiness /ˈmʌstɪnɪs/ *n., no pl.* (of smell, taste) Muffigkeit, *die*

mustn't /ˈmʌsnt/ (coll.) = **must not;** ⇒ **must 1**

musty /ˈmʌstɪ/ *adj.* **(a)** (smelling or tasting stale) muffig; **(b)** (mouldy) stockig; **(c)** (fig.) verstaubt

mutant /ˈmjuːtənt/ (Biol.) **1** *adj.* mutiert ⟨*Gen, Zelle, Stamm*⟩. **2** *n.* Mutante, *die*

mutate /mju:'teɪt/ (Biol.) **1** v.t. zur Mutation anregen; **be ∼d** mutieren. **2** v.i. mutieren

mutation /mju:'teɪʃn/ n. (Biol.) Mutation, die

mute /mju:t/ **1** adj. (dumb, silent; also Ling.) stumm; **be ∼ with rage/amazement** vor Zorn/Staunen kein Wort hervorbringen. **2** n. **(a)** (dumb person) Stumme, der/die; **(b)** (Mus.) Dämpfer, der

muted /'mju:tɪd/ adj. gedämpft; verhalten ⟨Kritik, Begeisterung⟩

mutilate /'mju:tɪleɪt/ v.t. (lit. or fig.) verstümmeln

mutilation /mju:tɪ'leɪʃn/ n. (lit. or fig.) Verstümmelung, die

mutineer /mju:tɪ'nɪə(r)/ n. Meuterer, der

mutinous /'mju:tɪnəs/ adj. rebellisch ⟨Geist, Person⟩; meuternd ⟨Mannschaft eines Schiffs, Truppen⟩

mutiny /'mju:tɪnɪ/ **1** n. Meuterei, die. **2** v.i. meutern

mutter /'mʌtə(r)/ **1** v.i. **(a)** murmeln; brummeln; **(b)** (grumble) murren (**at, about** über + Akk.). **2** v.t. murmeln. **3** n. Gemurmel, das

muttering /'mʌtərɪŋ/ n. **(a)** no pl. (low speech) Gemurmel, das; **(b)** ∼[s] (complaints) Gemurre, das

mutton /'mʌtn/ n. Hammelfleisch, das; Hammel, der; ∼ **dressed [up] as lamb** (coll. derog.) eine Alte, die auf jugendlich macht (ugs.)

mutual /'mju:tjʊəl/ adj. **(a)** gegenseitig; beiderseitig ⟨Einvernehmen, Vorteil, Bemühung⟩; wechselseitig ⟨Abhängigkeit⟩; **I can't bear you! — The feeling's ∼:** Ich kann dich nicht riechen! — Das beruht auf Gegenseitigkeit; **to our ∼ satisfaction/benefit** zu unser beider Zufriedenheit/Nutzen; **(b)** (coll.: shared) gemeinsam ⟨Interesse, Freund, Abneigung usw.⟩

mutually /'mju:tjʊəlɪ/ adv. **(a)** gegenseitig; **be ∼ exclusive** einander (geh.) od. sich [gegenseitig] ausschließen; ∼ **beneficial** für beide Seiten vorteilhaft; **(b)** (coll.: in common) gemeinsam

muzak /'mju:zæk/ n. (often derog.) Hintergrundmusik, die (ugs. abwertend)

muzzle /'mʌzl/ **1** n. **(a)** (of dog) Schnauze, die; (of horse, cattle) Maul, das; **(b)** (of gun) Mündung, die; **(c)** (put over animal's mouth) Maulkorb, der. **2** v.t. **(a)** einen Maulkorb umbinden (+ Dat.) ⟨Hund⟩; **(b)** (fig.) mundtot machen, einen Maulkorb anlegen (ugs.) (+ Dat.) ⟨Presse, Kritiker⟩; unterdrücken ⟨Protest⟩

muzzy /'mʌzɪ/ adj. **(a)** (mentally hazy, blurred) verschwommen; **(b)** (from intoxication) benebelt (**with** von)

MW abbr. (Radio) **medium wave** MW

my /maɪ/ poss. pron. attrib. mein; **my[, my]!, [my] oh my!** [ach du] meine Güte! (ugs.); see also **her²**

myalgic encephalomyelitis /maɪældʒɪk ensef əˌəʊmaɪə'laɪtɪs/ n. ▶ 865 | (Med.) myalgische Enzephalomyelitis

myopia /maɪ'əʊpɪə/ n. Kurzsichtigkeit, die (auch fig.); Myopie, die (fachspr.)

myopic /maɪ'ɒpɪk/ adj. (lit. or fig.) kurzsichtig

myriad /'mɪrɪəd/ (literary) **1** adj. unzählig; Myriaden von (geh.) ⟨Insekten, Sternen⟩. **2** n. Myriade, die (geh.)

myrrh /mɜ:(r)/ n. Myrrhe, die

myself /maɪ'self/ pron. **(a)** emphat. selbst; **I thought so ∼:** das habe ich auch gedacht; **[even] though/if I say it ∼:** wenn ich es auch selbst sage; **I am quite ∼ again** mir geht es wieder gut; **(b)** refl. mich/mir; **I washed ∼:** ich wusch mich; **I'm going to get ∼ a car** ich werde mir ein Auto zulegen. See also **herself**

mysterious /mɪ'stɪərɪəs/ adj. **(a)** mysteriös; rätselhaft; geheimnisvoll ⟨Fremder, Orient⟩; **(b)** (secretive) geheimnisvoll; **be very ∼ about sth.** ein großes Geheimnis aus etw. machen

mysteriously /mɪ'stɪərɪəslɪ/ adv. auf mysteriöse od. rätselhafte Weise; geheimnisvoll ⟨lächeln usw.⟩

mystery /'mɪstərɪ/ n. **(a)** Rätsel, das; **it's a ∼ to me why ...:** es ist mir ein Rätsel, warum ...; **(b)** (secrecy) Geheimnis, das; **shrouded in ∼:** geheimnisumwittert od. -umwoben (geh.); **there's no ∼ about it** das ist überhaupt kein Geheimnis

mystery: ∼ **tour,** ∼ **trip** ns. Fahrt ins Blaue (ugs.)

mystic /'mɪstɪk/ **1** adj. mystisch. **2** n. Mystiker, der/Mystikerin, die

mystical /'mɪstɪkl/ adj. mystisch

mysticism /'mɪstɪsɪzm/ n. Mystik, die; Mystizismus, der (geh.)

mystify /'mɪstɪfaɪ/ v.t. verwirren; **this mystifies me** das ist mir ein Rätsel od. rätselhaft

mystique /mɪ'sti:k/ n. geheimnisvoller Nimbus

myth /mɪθ/ n. Mythos, der; (rumour) Gerücht, das

mythical /'mɪθɪkl/ adj. **(a)** (based on myth) mythisch; ∼ **creatures** Sagengestalten; **(b)** (invented) fiktiv

mythological /mɪθə'lɒdʒɪkl/ adj. mythologisch

mythology /mɪ'θɒlədʒɪ/ n. Mythologie, die

myxomatosis /mɪksəmə'təʊsɪs/ n. (Vet. Med.) Myxomatose, die

Nn

N, n /en/ n., pl. **Ns** or **N's** N, n, das; **for the nth** /enθ/ **time** (coll.) zum x-ten Mal (ugs.)

N. abbr. ▶ 715 | **(a) north** N; **(b) northern** n.

n. abbr. **note** Anm.

NAAFI /'næfɪ/ abbr. (Brit.) **Navy, Army and Air Force Institutes** Kaufhaus für Angehörige der britischen Truppen

nab /næb/ v.t., **-bb-** (coll.) **(a)** (arrest) schnappen (ugs.); **(b)** (seize) sich (Dat.) schnappen; **(c)** (steal) klauen (salopp); krallen (salopp)

nadir /'neɪdɪə(r)/ n. Tief[st]punkt, der

nag¹ /næg/ **1** v.i., **-gg-** nörgeln (abwertend); ∼ **at sb.** an jmdm. herumnörgeln; ∼ **at sb. to do sth.** jmdm. zusetzen (ugs.), dass er etw. tut. **2** v.t., **-gg-** (scold) herumnörgeln an (+ Dat.) (abwertend); ∼ **sb. about sth./to do sth.** jmdm. wegen etw. zusetzen (ugs.) /jmdm. zusetzen (ugs.), dass er etw. tut

nag² /næg/ n. (coll.: horse) Gaul, der

nagging /'nægɪŋ/ **1** adj. **(a)** (annoying) nörglerisch (abwertend); **(b)** (persistent) quälend ⟨Angst, Sorge, Zweifel⟩; bohrend ⟨Schmerz⟩; **a ∼ conscience** [quälende] Gewissensbisse Pl. **2** n. Genörgel, das (abwertend)

nail /neɪl/ **1** n. **(a)** ▶ 672 | (on finger, toe) Nagel, der; **cut one's ∼s** sich (Dat.) die Nägel schneiden; **bite one's ∼s** an den Nägeln kauen; **(b)** (metal spike) Nagel, der; **be hard as ∼s** (fig.) steinhart sein; (fit) topfit sein; (unfeeling) knallhart sein (ugs.); **hit the [right] ∼ on the head** (fig.) den Nagel auf den Kopf treffen (ugs.); **be a ∼ in sb.'s/ sth.'s coffin** (fig.) ein Nagel zu jmds. Sarg/ein Sargnagel für etw. sein (ugs.); **on the ∼** (fig. coll.) pünktlich ⟨bezahlen, sein Geld kriegen⟩. **2** v.t. **(a)** nageln (**to** an + Akk.); ∼ **two planks together** zwei Bretter zusammennageln; **be ∼ed to the spot/ground** (fig.) wie angenagelt sein (ugs.); **(b)** (fig.: secure, catch, engage) an Land ziehen (ugs.) ⟨Vertrag, Auftrag⟩; **(c)** (fig.: expose) anprangern. See also **colour 1 g**

∼ **'down** v.t. festnageln; zunageln ⟨Kiste⟩

∼ **'up** v.t. **(a)** (close) vernageln; **(b)** (affix with ∼) annageln (**against** an + Akk.)

nail: ∼**-biting** /'neɪlbaɪtɪŋ/ adj. (fig.) bang ⟨Minuten, Schweigen, Sorge⟩; angstvoll ⟨Spannung⟩; spannungsgeladen ⟨Spiel, Film⟩; ∼ **brush** n. Nagelbürste, die; ∼ **clippers** n. pl. [pair of] ∼ **clippers** Nagelknipser, der; ∼ **file** n. Nagelfeile, die; ∼ **polish** n. Nagellack, der; ∼ **polish remover** Nagellackentferner, der; ∼ **scissors** n. pl. [pair of] ∼ **scissors** Nagelschere, die; ∼ **varnish** (Brit.) ⇒ ∼ **polish**

naïve, naive /naɪ'i:v, naɪ'i:v/ adj., **naïvely, naively** /naɪ'i:vlɪ, naɪ'i:vlɪ/ adv. naiv

naïvety, naivety /naɪ'i:vtɪ, naɪ'i:vtɪ/ n. Naivität, die

naked /'neɪkɪd/ adj. **(a)** nackt; **strip sb. ∼:** jmdn. nackt ausziehen; **(b)** nackt ⟨Glühbirne⟩; offen ⟨Licht, Flamme⟩; **(c)** (defenceless) wehrlos; **(d)** (plain) nackt ⟨Tatsache,

Wahrheit, Aggression, Gier, Ehrgeiz⟩; **visible to** *or* **with the ~ eye** mit bloßem Auge zu erkennen

name /neɪm/ **1** *n.* **(a)** Name, *der;* **what's your ~/the ~ of this place?** wie heißt du/dieser Ort?; **my ~ is Jack** ich heiße Jack; mein Name ist Jack; **no one of** *or* **by that ~:** niemand mit diesem Namen *od.* (geh.) dieses Namens; **last ~:** Zuname, *der,* Nachname, *der;* **the ~ of Edwards** der Name Edwards; **by ~:** namentlich ⟨*erwähnen, aufrufen usw.*⟩; **know sb. by ~/by ~ only** jmdn. mit Namen/nur dem Namen nach kennen; **that's the ~ of the game** (coll.) darum geht es; **put one's/sb.'s ~ down for sth.** sich/jmdn. für etw. vormerken lassen; **put one's/sb.'s ~ down on the waiting list** sich/jmdn. auf die Warteliste setzen lassen/jmdn. auf die Warteliste setzen; **without a penny to his ~:** ohne einen Pfennig in der Tasche; **in ~ [only]** [nur] auf dem Papier; **in all but ~:** im Grunde genommen; **(b)** (reputation) Ruf, *der;* **make a ~ for oneself** sich (*Dat.*) einen Namen machen; **make one's/sb.'s ~:** berühmt werden/jmdn. berühmt machen; **clear one's sb.'s ~:** seine/jmds. Unschuld beweisen; **(c) call sb. ~s** (abuse) jmdn. beschimpfen; **(d)** (famous person) Name, *der;* **many great** *or* **big ~s** viele namhafte Persönlichkeiten; viele Größen; **be a big ~:** einen großen Namen haben; **(e)** *attrib.* **~ brand** Markenartikel, *der.* **2** *v.t.* **(a)** (give ~ to) einen Namen geben (+ *Dat.*); **~ sb. John** jmdn. John nennen; **~ a ship 'Mary'** ein Schiff [auf den Namen] „Mary" taufen; **~ sb./sth. after** *or* (Amer.) **for sb.** jmdn./ etw. nach jmdm. benennen; **be ~d John** John heißen; **a man ~d Smith** ein Mann namens *od.* mit Namen Smith; **(b)** (call by right ~) benennen; **~ the capital of Zambia** nenne die Hauptstadt von Sambia; **(c)** (nominate) ernennen; **~ sb. [as] sth.** jmdn. zu etw. ernennen; **~ one's successor** seinen Nachfolger bestimmen; **he was ~d as the winner** ihm wurde der Sieg zuerkannt; **(d)** (mention) nennen; (specify) benennen; **~ names** Namen nennen; **~ the day** (choose wedding day) den Tag der Hochzeit festsetzen; **to ~ but a few** um nur einige zu nennen; **we were given champagne, oysters, you ~ it** wir kriegten Champagne, Austern, und, und, und

name: ~-calling *n.* Beschimpfungen *Pl.;* **~-dropping** *n.* Namedropping, *das; Nennung bedeutender Namen, um Eindruck zu machen*

nameless /ˈneɪmlɪs/ *adj.* **(a)** (having no name, anonymous) namenlos; **a person who shall remain ~:** eine Person, die ungenannt bleiben soll; **(b)** (abominable) unaussprechlich; unsäglich (geh.); **(c)** (inexpressible) unbeschreiblich

namely /ˈneɪmlɪ/ *adv.* nämlich

name: ~plate *n.* Namensschild, *das;* **~sake** *n.* Namensvetter, *der/*-schwester, *die*

nancy /ˈnænsɪ/ *n.* (sl.) **~ [boy]** Tunte, *die* (salopp)

nanny /ˈnænɪ/ *n.* **(a)** (Brit.: nursemaid) Kindermädchen, *das;* **(b)** (coll.: granny) Großmama, *die* (fam.); **(c)** ⇒ **nanny goat**

nanny: ~ goat *n.* Ziege, *die;* Geiß, *die* (südd., österr., schweiz., westmd.); **~ state** *n.* (derog.) Versorgungsstaat, *der*

nanotechnology /ˈnænəʊteknɒlədʒɪ/ *n.* Nanotechnologie, *die*

nap /næp/ **1** *n.* Schläfchen, *das* (ugs.); Nickerchen, *das* (fam.); **take** *or* **have a ~:** ein Schläfchen *od.* Nickerchen machen *od.* halten. **2** *v.i.* **-pp-** dösen (ugs.); **catch sb. ~ping** (fig.) jmdn. überrumpeln

napalm /ˈneɪpɑːm/ *n.* Napalm, *das*

nape /neɪp/ *n.* **~ [of the neck]** Nacken, *der;* Genick, *das*

napkin /ˈnæpkɪn/ *n.* **(a)** Serviette, *die;* **(b)** (waiter's) Serviertuch, *das*

'napkin ring *n.* Serviettenring, *der*

Naples /ˈneɪplz/ *pr. n.* ▶ 1159 | Neapel (*das*)

nappy /ˈnæpɪ/ *n.* (Brit.) Windel, *die*

narcissus /nɑːˈsɪsəs/ *n., pl.* **narcissi** /nɑːˈsɪsaɪ/ *or* **~es** (Bot.) Narzisse, *die*

narcotic /nɑːˈkɒtɪk/ **1** *n.* **(a)** (drug) Rauschgift, *das;* Betäubungsmittel, *das* (Rechtsw.); **(b)** (active ingredient) Betäubungsmittel, *das;* Narkotikum, *das* (Med.). **2** *adj.* narkotisch; **~ drug** Rauschgift, *das;* Betäubungsmittel, *das* (Rechtsw.)

nark /nɑːk/ (sl.) **1** *n.* (Brit.: informer) Spitzel, *der* (abwertend). **2** *v.t.* (annoy) stinken (+ *Dat.*) (salopp); **be ~ed [about sb./ at** *or* **about sth.]** [auf jmdn./über etw. (*Akk.*)] sauer sein (ugs.)

narrate /nəˈreɪt/ *v.t.* erzählen; schildern ⟨*Ereignisse*⟩; kommentieren ⟨*Film*⟩

narration /nəˈreɪʃn/ *n.* Erzählen, *das;* Erzählung, *die;* (of events) Schilderung, *die;* Schildern, *das*

narrative /ˈnærətɪv/ **1** *n.* **(a)** (tale, story) Geschichte, *die;* Erzählung, *die;* **(b)** *no pl.* **be written in ~:** in der Erzählform geschrieben sein. **2** *adj.* erzählend; Erzähl ⟨*kunst, -technik*⟩

narrator /nəˈreɪtə(r)/ *n.* Erzähler, *der/*Erzählerin, *die;* (of film) Kommentator, *der/*Kommentatorin, *die*

narrow /ˈnærəʊ/ **1** *adj.* **(a)** ▶ 904 | schmal; schmal geschnitten ⟨*Rock, Hose, Ärmel usw.*⟩; eng ⟨*Tal, Gasse*⟩; **(b)** (limited) eng; begrenzt, schmal ⟨*Auswahl*⟩; **(c)** (with little margin) knapp ⟨*Sieg, Führung, Mehrheit*⟩; **have a ~ escape** mit knapper Not entkommen (**from** *Dat.*); **(d)** (not tolerant) spießig (abwertend); engstirnig (abwertend); **(e)** (restricted) eng ⟨*Grenzen, Toleranzen*⟩; klein, begrenzt ⟨*Freundeskreis*⟩. **2** *v.i.* sich verschmälern; ⟨*Augen, Tal:*⟩ sich verengen; (fig.) [zusammen]schrumpfen; **the road ~s to one lane** die Straße wird einspurig; **'road ~s'** „Fahrbahnverengung". **3** *v.t.* verschmälern; (fig.) einengen; enger fassen ⟨*Definition*⟩; **~ one's eyes** die Augen zusammenkneifen

~ 'down 1 *v.t.* einengen, beschränken (**to** auf + *Akk.*). **2** *v.i.* sich reduzieren (**to** auf + *Akk.*); **the choice ~s down to two possibilities** es bleiben zwei Möglichkeiten [übrig]

narrow: ~ boat *n.* (Brit.) *besonders schmales Binnenschiff;* **~-gauge** *adj.* schmalspurig; Schmalspur-

narrowly /ˈnærəʊlɪ/ *adv.* **(a)** (with little width) schmal; **(b)** (only just) knapp; mit knapper Not ⟨*entkommen*⟩; **he ~ escaped being run over by a car** er wäre um ein Haar (ugs.) überfahren worden

narrow-'minded *adj.* engstirnig (abwertend)

NASA /ˈnæsə/ *abbr.* (Amer.) **National Aeronautics and Space Administration** NASA, *die*

nasal /ˈneɪzl/ *adj.* **(a)** (Anat.) Nasen-; **(b)** näselnd; **speak in a ~ voice** näseln

nastily /ˈnɑːstɪlɪ/ *adv.* **(a)** (disagreeably, unpleasantly) scheußlich; **(b)** (ill-naturedly) gemein; **behave ~:** hässlich sein; **(c)** (disgustingly) eklig; widerlich

nasturtium /nəˈstɜːʃəm/ *n.* Kapuzinerkresse, *die*

nasty /ˈnɑːstɪ/ *adj.* **(a)** (disagreeable, unpleasant) scheußlich ⟨*Geruch, Geschmack, Arznei, Essen, Wetter*⟩; gemein ⟨*Trick, Verhalten, Äußerung, Person*⟩; hässlich ⟨*Angewohnheit*⟩; **that was a ~ thing to say/do** das war gemein *od.* eine Gemeinheit; **a ~ bit** *or* **piece of work** (coll.) (man) ein fieser Kerl (ugs. abwertend); (woman) ein fieses Weibsstück (ugs. abwertend); **(b)** (ill-natured) böse; **be ~ to sb.** hässlich zu jmdm. sein; **(c)** (serious) übel; böse ⟨*Verletzung, Husten usw.*⟩; schlimm ⟨*Krankheit, Husten, Verletzung*⟩; **she had a ~ fall** sie ist übel *od.* böse gefallen; **(d)** (disgusting) eklig; widerlich

nation /ˈneɪʃn/ *n.* Nation, *die;* (people) Volk, *das;* **throughout the ~:** im ganzen Land

national /ˈnæʃənl/ **1** *adj.* national; National⟨*flagge, -denkmal, -held, -theater, -tanz, -gericht, -charakter*⟩; Landes⟨*durchschnitt, -sprache*⟩; Staats⟨*sicherheit, -symbol*⟩; überregional ⟨*Rundfunkstation, Zeitung*⟩; landesweit ⟨*Streik*⟩. **2** *n.* **(a)** (citizen) Staatsbürger, *der/*-bürgerin, *die;* **foreign ~:** Ausländer, *der/*Ausländerin, *die;* **(b)** *usu. in pl.* (newspaper) überregionale Zeitung

national: ~ 'anthem *n.* Nationalhymne, *die;* **~ call** *n.* (Brit. Teleph.) Inlandsgespräch, *das;* **~ 'costume** *n.* Nationaltracht, *die;* Landestracht, *die;* **N~ Cur'riculum** *n.* (Brit.) Nationales Curriculum; **N~ 'Debt** ⇒ **debt; ~ 'dress** ⇒ **~ costume; N~ 'Front** *n.* (Brit.) National Front, *die* (*britische Organisation mit extremen reaktionären Positionen z.B. in Bezug auf die Einwanderungspolitik*); (attrib.) National-Front-⟨*Mitglied, Slogan usw.*⟩; **'grid** *n.* (Brit. Electr.) nationales Verbundnetz; **N~ 'Health [Service]** *n.* (Brit.) *staatlicher Gesundheitsdienst;* attrib. **N~ Health doctor/patient/spectacles**

Nationalities

In English, words such as German, French, Italian etc. are both adjectives referring to the language and the people and nouns meaning a language or a person, and are always written with a capital. In German, the words **deutsch, französisch, italienisch** and so on are also used as both adjectives and nouns, with the differences that only the nouns are written with a capital, and the noun meaning a person is only in a few cases the same as the noun meaning a person (e.g. **ein Deutscher**), and then it has endings while that meaning a language usually does not (for full details of these see □ **Languages**).

Adjectives

Translating adjective plus noun combinations is straightforward (remembering the small letter for the adjective):

an Italian car	= ein italienisches Auto
the French government	= die französische Regierung
a German painter	= ein deutscher Maler/ eine deutsche Malerin

When referring to a unique national institution, the name of the country in the genitive is often preferred (just as one can also use *of* plus the name of the country in English):

the Indian capital = *the capital of India* = die Hauptstadt Indiens

When the adjective is predicative, i.e. standing on its own, and refers to a person or persons, the English nationality adjective will always be translated by the noun in German:

He is Italian	= Er ist Italiener
She is Indian	= Sie ist Inderin
The tourists are French	= Die Touristen sind Franzosen

Referring to a thing, German often prefers to avoid having the adjective standing on its own:

The car is Italian	= Es ist ein italienisches Auto, *rather than* Das Auto ist italienisch

Nouns

As in English, the nouns for people of different nationalities vary in form, but in German there are feminine forms in all cases ending in **-in**. A large number of them have the **-er** ending added to the word for the country for the masculine, and **-erin** for the feminine:

an Englishman/ Englishwoman	= ein Engländer/eine Engländerin
an Italian	= ein Italiener/eine Italienerin (*Italy* = Italien)
an Austrian	= ein Österreicher/eine Österreicherin (*Austria* = Österreich)
a Japanese	= ein Japaner/eine Japanerin

A number of these nouns end in **-e**, and this disappears when the feminine ending is added:

a Frenchman/ Frenchwoman	= ein Franzose/eine Französin
a Chinese	= ein Chinese/eine Chinesin
a Dane	= ein Däne/eine Dänin
a Russian	= ein Russe/eine Russin

The plural in these cases adds an **-n** (**Franzosen, Chinesen, Dänen, Russen**) to the masculine, and it is this masculine plural form that is used when referring to a group of mixed gender, or the whole nation:

the French	= die Franzosen
the English	= die Engländer

Last but not least, the noun for a German is the adjective as a noun:

a German	= ein Deutscher/eine Deutsche
the Germans	= die Deutschen
He was the only German	= Er war der einzige Deutsche
The prize was awarded to a German	= Der Preis wurde einem Deutschen verliehen

Phrases

She is Spanish by birth	= Sie ist von Geburt Spanierin *or* gebürtige Spanierin
He is of German extraction	= Er ist deutscher Abstammung
I come from the north of England	= Ich stamme *or* komme aus Nordengland
He's a Belgian national or citizen	= Er ist belgischer Staatsbürger
a naturalized Swiss citizen	= ein eingebürgerter *or* naturalisierter Schweizer/eine eingebürgerte *or* naturalisierte Schweizerin

---

≈ Kassenarzt, *der/*-patient, *der/*-brille, *die;* ~ **'holiday** *n.* Nationalfeiertag, *der;* (statutory holiday) gesetzlicher Feiertag; **N~ In'surance** *n.* (Brit.) Sozialversicherung, *die*
nationalisation, nationalise ⇒ **nationaliz-**
nationalism /'næʃənəlɪzm/ *n.* Nationalismus, *der;* (patriotism) nationale Gesinnung
nationalist /'næʃənəlɪst/ **1** *n.* Nationalist, *der/*Nationalistin, *die.* **2** *adj.* nationalistisch
nationalistic /næʃənə'lɪstɪk/ *adj.* (patriotic) nationalistisch
nationality /næʃə'nælɪtɪ/ *n.* **(a)** Staatsangehörigkeit, *die;* Nationalität, *die* (geh.); **be of** *or* **have British ~:** britischer Nationalität sein (geh.); die britische Staatsangehörigkeit haben; **what's his ~?** welche Staatsangehörigkeit hat er?; welcher Nationalität ist er? (geh.); **(b)** (ethnic group) Nationalität, *die;* Volksgruppe, *die*
nationalization /næʃənəlar'zeɪʃn/ *n.* Verstaatlichung, *die*
nationalize /'næʃənəlaɪz/ *v.t.* verstaatlichen
nationally /'næʃənəlɪ/ *adv.* als Nation; (throughout the nation) landesweit

national: ~ **'park** *n.* Nationalpark, *der;* ~ **'service** *n.* (Brit.) Wehrdienst, *der;* **do ~ service** seinen Wehrdienst ableisten; **N~ 'Socialist** *n.* Nationalsozialist, *der/*-sozialistin, *die; attrib.* nationalsozialistisch; **N~ 'Trust** *n.* (Brit.) *nationale Einrichtung für Naturschutz und Denkmalpflege;* **N~ Vo'cational Qualification** *n.* (Brit.) *staatliches Berufsausbildungsprogramm*
nation: ~ **state** *n.* Nationalstaat, *der;* ~**wide 1** /'---/ *adj.* landesweit; **2** /--'-/ *adv.* landesweit; im ganzen Land
native /'neɪtɪv/ **1** *n.* **(a)** (of specified place) **a ~ of Britain** ein gebürtiger Brite/eine gebürtige Britin; **(b)** (indigenous person) Eingeborene, *der/die;* **(c)** (local inhabitant) Einheimische, *der/die;* **the ~s** die Einheimischen; **(d)** (Zool., Bot.) **be a ~ of a place** in einem Ort beheimatet sein. **2** *adj.* **(a)** (indigenous) eingeboren; (local) einheimisch ‹*Pflanze, Tier*›; **be a ~ American** gebürtiger Amerikaner/gebürtige Amerikanerin sein; ~ **inhabitant** Eingeborene/ Einheimische, *der/die;* **(b)** (of one's birth) Geburts-, Heimat‹*land, -stadt*›; Mutter‹*sprache, -sprachler*›; **he's not a ~ speaker of English** Englisch ist nicht seine Muttersprache; **(c)** (innate) angeboren ‹*Qualitäten,*

Schläue); **(d)** (of the ∼s) Eingeborenen-; **go** ∼: die Lebensweise der Eingeborenen annehmen

nativity /nəˈtɪvɪtɪ/ *n.* **(a) the N∼ [of Christ]** die Geburt Christi; **(b)** (festival) **the N∼ of Christ** das Fest der Geburt Christi; **(c)** (picture) Geburt Christi

na'tivity play *n.* Krippenspiel, *das*

NATO, Nato /ˈneɪtəʊ/ *abbr.* **North Atlantic Treaty Organization** NATO, *die*

natter /ˈnætə(r)/ (Brit. coll.) **1** *v.i.* quatschen (ugs.); quasseln (ugs.) **2** *n.* **have a** ∼: quatschen (ugs.)

natty /ˈnætɪ/ *adj.* (coll.) schick, (ugs.) flott ⟨*Kleidung*[*sstück*]⟩; **be a** ∼ **dresser** immer schick *od.* flott angezogen sein

natural /ˈnætʃrəl/ **1** *adj.* **(a)** natürlich; Natur⟨*zustand, -begabung, -talent, -seide, -schwamm, -faser, -erscheinung*⟩; **the** ∼ **world** die Natur[welt]; **be a** ∼ **blonde** naturblondes Haar haben; **it is** ∼ **for dogs to fight** es ist natürlich, dass Hunde kämpfen; **die of** *or* **from** ∼ **causes** eines natürlichen Todes sterben; **have a** ∼ **tendency to** …: naturgemäß dazu neigen, … zu …; **(b)** (unaffected) natürlich ⟨*Art, Lächeln, Stil*⟩; **(c)** leiblich ⟨*Eltern, Kind usw.*⟩; natürlich (Rechtsspr. veralt.) ⟨*Kind*⟩. **2** *n.* (person) Naturtalent, *das;* **she's a** ∼ **for the part** die Rolle ist ihr auf den Leib geschrieben

natural: ∼ **'childbirth** *n.* natürliche Geburt; ∼ **'death** *n.* natürlicher Tod; ∼ **'gas** ⇒ **gas 1 a;** ∼ **'history** *n.* **(a)** (study) Naturkunde, *die; attrib.* Naturkunde-; naturkundlich ⟨*Museum*⟩; **(b)** (facts) Naturgeschichte, *die*

naturalisation, naturalise ⇒ **naturaliz-**

naturalist /ˈnætʃrəlɪst/ *n.* Naturforscher, *der/*-forscherin, *die*

naturalization /nætʃrəlaɪˈzeɪʃn/ *n.* (admitting as citizen) Einbürgerung, *die;* Naturalisierung, *die*

naturalize /ˈnætʃrəlaɪz/ *v.t.* **(a)** (admit as citizen) einbürgern; naturalisieren; **(b)** naturalisieren, einbürgern ⟨*Tiere, Pflanzen*⟩. **2** *v.i.* eingebürgert werden

naturally /ˈnætʃrəlɪ/ *adv.* **(a)** (by nature) von Natur aus ⟨*musikalisch, blass, fleißig usw.*⟩; (in a true-to-life way) naturgetreu; (with ease) natürlich; (in a natural manner) auf natürliche Weise; **it comes** ∼ **to her** es fällt ihr leicht; **lead** ∼ **to sth.** naturgemäß zu etw. führen; **(b)** (of course) natürlich

naturalness /ˈnætʃrəlnɪs/ *n.* Natürlichkeit, *die*

natural: ∼ **re'sources** *n. pl.* natürliche Ressourcen *Pl.;* Naturschätze *Pl.;* ∼ **'science** *n.* ∼ **science, the** ∼ **sciences** die Naturwissenschaften *Pl.;* ∼ **se'lection** *n.* (Biol.) natürliche Auslese

nature /ˈneɪtʃə(r)/ *n.* **(a)** Natur, *die;* **back to** ∼: zurück zur Natur; **paint from** ∼: nach der Natur malen; **(b)** (essential qualities) Beschaffenheit, *die;* **in the** ∼ **of things** naturgemäß; **(c)** (kind, sort) Art, *die;* **things of this** ∼: Derartiges; Dinge dieser Art; **it's in the** ∼ **of a command** es hat Befehlscharakter; **(d)** (character) [Wesens]art, *die;* Wesen, *das;* **have a happy** ∼: eine Frohnatur sein; **be of** *or* **have a placid** ∼: eine ruhige Art haben; **have a jealous** ∼: eifersüchtig sein; **it is not in her** ∼ **to lie** es ist nicht ihre Art zu lügen; **human** ∼: menschliche Natur; **it's only human** ∼ **to** …: es ist nur menschlich, … zu …

nature: ∼ **conservation** *n.* Naturschutz, *der;* ∼ **cure** *n.* Naturheilverfahren, *das;* ∼ **lover** *n.* Naturfreund, *der/*-freundin, *die;* ∼ **reserve** *n.* Naturschutzgebiet, *das;* ∼ **study** *n.* Naturkunde, *die;* ∼ **trail** *n.* Naturlehrpfad, *der*

naturism /ˈneɪtʃərɪzm/ *n.* (nudism) Naturismus, *der;* Freikörperkultur, *die*

naturist /ˈneɪtʃərɪst/ *n.* (nudist) Naturist, *der/*Naturistin, *die;* FKK-Anhänger, *der/*FKK-Anhängerin, *die*

naught /nɔːt/ *n.* (arch./dial.) **bring to** ∼: zunichte machen; **come to** ∼: zunichte werden

naughtiness /ˈnɔːtɪnɪs/ *n.* Ungezogenheit, *die;* Unartigkeit, *die*

naughty /ˈnɔːtɪ/ *adj.* **(a)** (disobedient) unartig; ungezogen; **you** ∼ **boy/dog** du böser Junge/Hund; **(b)** (indecent) unanständig

nausea /ˈnɔːzɪə, ˈnɔːsɪə/ *n.* **(a)** ▶865⌋ Übelkeit, *die;* **(b)** (fig.: disgust) Ekel, *der,* Abscheu, *der* **(with, at** vor + *Dat.*)

nauseate /ˈnɔːzɪeɪt, ˈnɔːsɪeɪt/ *v.t.* **(a)** ▶865⌋ ∼ **sb.** in jmdm. Übelkeit erregen; **the smell** ∼**d him** bei dem Geruch wurde ihm übel; **(b)** (fig.: disgust) anekeln; anwidern

nauseating /ˈnɔːzɪeɪtɪŋ, ˈnɔːsɪeɪtɪŋ/ *adj.* **(a)** Übelkeit verursachend *od.* erregend; **(b)** (fig.: disgusting) widerlich; Ekel erregend ⟨*Anblick, Geruch*⟩; ekelhaft ⟨*Person*⟩

nauseous /ˈnɔːzɪəs, ˈnɔːsɪəs/ *adj.* **(a)** ▶865⌋ **sb. is** *or* **feels** ∼: jmdm. ist übel; **(b)** (fig.: disgusting) widerlich

nautical /ˈnɔːtɪkl/ *adj.* nautisch; seemännisch ⟨*Ausdruck, Können*⟩; ∼ **map** Seekarte, *die*

naval /ˈneɪvl/ *adj.* Marine-; Flotten⟨*parade, -abkommen*⟩; See⟨*schlacht, -macht, -streitkräfte*⟩; ⟨*Überlegenheit*⟩ zur See; ∼ **ship** Kriegsschiff, *das*

naval: ∼ **base** *n.* Flottenstützpunkt, *der;* ∼ **officer** *n.* Marineoffizier, *der*

nave /neɪv/ *n.* (Archit.) [Mittel-, Haupt]schiff, *das*

navel /ˈneɪvl/ *n.* Nabel, *der*

navigable /ˈnævɪgəbl/ *adj.* (suitable for ships) schiffbar

navigate /ˈnævɪgeɪt/ **1** *v.t.* **(a)** (sail on) befahren ⟨*Kanal, Fluss, Gewässer*⟩; **(b)** navigieren ⟨*Schiff, Flugzeug*⟩. **2** *v.i.* **(a)** (in ship, aircraft) navigieren; **(b)** (assist driver) den Lotsen spielen (ugs.) (Rallyesport); **you drive, I'll** ∼: du fährst, und ich dirigiere *od.* lotse dich

navigation /nævɪˈgeɪʃn/ *n.* Navigation, *die;* (sailing on river etc.) Befahren, *das;* (assisting driver) Dirigieren, *das;* Lotsen, *das;* Franzen, *das* (Rallyesport)

navi'gation lights *n. pl.* (Naut.) Lichter; (Aeronaut.) Kennlichter

navigator /ˈnævɪgeɪtə(r)/ *n.* Navigator, *der/*Navigatorin, *die;* **his co-driver was acting as** ∼: sein Beifahrer dirigierte *od.* lotste ihn

navvy /ˈnævɪ/ *n.* (Brit.: labourer) Bau-/Straßenarbeiter, *der*

navy /ˈneɪvɪ/ *n.* **(a)** [Kriegs]marine, *die;* **(b)** ⇒ **navy blue**

navy: ∼ **'blue** *n.* Marineblau, *das;* ∼**-blue** *adj.* marineblau

Nazi /ˈnɑːtsɪ/ **1** *n.* **(a)** Nationalsozialist, *der/*-sozialistin, *die;* Nazi, *der;* **(b)** (fig. derog.) Faschist, *der/*Faschistin, *die;* Nazi, *der.* **2** *adj.* **(a)** nazistisch; Nazi-; **(b)** (fig. derog.) faschistisch; Nazi-

NB *abbr.* **nota bene** NB

NCO *abbr.* **non-commissioned officer** Uffz.

NE /ˈnɔːθiːst/ *abbr.* ▶715⌋ **north-east** NO

near /nɪə(r)/ **1** *adv.* **(a)** ▶756⌋ (at a short distance) nah[e]; **stand/live [quite]** ∼: [ganz] in der Nähe stehen/wohnen; **come** *or* **draw** ∼/∼**er** ⟨*Tag, Zeitpunkt:*⟩ nahen/näher rücken; **get** ∼**er together** näher zusammenrücken; ∼ **at hand** in Reichweite (*Dat.*); ⟨*Ort*⟩ ganz in der Nähe; **be** ∼ **at hand** ⟨*Ereignis:*⟩ nahe bevorstehen; **so** ∼ **and yet so far** so nah und doch so fern; **(b)** (closely) ∼ **to** = **2 a, b, c; we were** ∼ **to being drowned** wir wären fast *od.* beinah[e] ertrunken. **2** *prep.* **(a)** ▶756⌋ (in space) (position) nahe an/bei (+ *Dat.*); (motion) nahe an (+ *Akk.*); (fig.) nahe (geh.) *nachgestellt* (+ *Dat.*); in der Nähe (+ *Gen.*); **go** ∼ **the water's edge** nahe ans Ufer gehen; **keep** ∼ **me** halte dich *od.* bleib in meiner Nähe; ∼ **where** …: in der Nähe *od.* unweit der Stelle (*Gen.*), wo …; **move it** ∼**er her** rücke es näher zu ihr; **don't stand so** ∼ **the fire** geh nicht so nahe *od.* dicht an das Feuer; **when we got** ∼**er Oxford** als wir in die Nähe von Oxford kamen; **wait till we're** ∼**er home** warte, bis wir nicht mehr so weit von zu Hause weg sind; **don't come** ∼ **me** komm mir nicht zu nahe; **it's** ∼ **here** es ist hier in der Nähe; **the man** ∼/∼**est you** der Mann, der bei dir/der dir am nächsten steht; **(b)** (in quality) **nobody comes anywhere** ∼ **him at swimming** im Schwimmen kommt bei weitem keiner an ihn heran; **we're no** ∼**er solving the problem** wir sind der Lösung des Problems nicht näher gekommen; **(c)** (in time) **ask me again** ∼**er the time** frag mich, wenn der Zeitpunkt etwas näher gerückt ist, noch einmal; **it's drawing** ∼ **Christmas** es geht auf Weihnachten zu; **come back** ∼**er 8 o'clock** komm kurz vor 8 Uhr noch einmal zurück; ∼ **the end/the beginning of sth.** gegen Ende/zu Anfang einer Sache (*Gen.*); **(d)** *in comb.*

Beinahe‹*unfall*, *-zusammenstoß*, *-katastrophe*›; ∼-**hysterical** fast hysterisch; **be in a state of** ∼-**collapse** kurz vor dem Zusammenbruch stehen; **a** ∼-**miracle** fast *od.* beinahe ein Wunder. **3** *adj.* **(a)** (in space or time) nahe; **in the** ∼ **future** in nächster Zukunft; **the chair is** ∼**er** der Stuhl steht näher; **our** ∼**est neighbours** unsere nächsten Nachbarn; **(b)** (closely related) nahe ‹*Verwandte*›; eng ‹*Freund*›; ∼ **and dear** lieb und teuer; **(c)** (in nature) fast richtig ‹*Vermutung*›; groß ‹*Ähnlichkeit*›; **£30 or** ∼/ ∼**est offer** 30 Pfund oder nächstbestes Angebot; **this is the** ∼**est equivalent** dies entspricht dem am ehesten; **that's the** ∼**est you'll get to an answer** eine weitergehende Antwort wirst du nicht bekommen; ∼ **escape** Entkommen mit knapper Not; **round it up to the** ∼**est penny** runde es auf den nächsthöheren Pfennigbetrag; **be a** ∼ **miss** ‹*Schuss*, *Wurf:*› knapp danebengehen; **that was a** ∼ **miss** (escape) das war aber knapp!; **(d) the** ∼ **side** (Brit.) (travelling on the left/right) die linke/rechte Seite; **(e)** (direct) **4 miles by the** ∼**est road** 4 Meilen auf dem kürzesten Wege. **4** *v.t.* sich nähern (+ *Dat.*); **the building is** ∼**ing completion** das Gebäude steht kurz vor seiner Vollendung

'**nearby** *adj.* nahe gelegen

Near 'East ⇨ **Middle East**

nearly /'nɪəlɪ/ *adv.* ▶ **706**⏐ fast; **it** ∼ **fell over** es wäre fast umgefallen; **be** ∼ **in tears** den Tränen nahe sein; **it is** ∼ **six o'clock** es ist kurz vor sechs Uhr; **are you** ∼ **ready?** bist du bald fertig?; **not** ∼: nicht annähernd; bei weitem nicht

nearness /'nɪənɪs/ *n., no pl.* (proximity) Nähe, *die*

near: ∼-**sighted** *adj.* (Amer.) kurzsichtig; ∼ '**thing** *n.* **that was a** ∼ **thing!** das war knapp!

neat /niːt/ *adj.* **(a)** (tidy, clean) sauber, ordentlich ‹*Handschrift*, *Arbeit*›; gepflegt ‹*Haar*, *Person*›; **(b)** (undiluted) pur ‹*Getränk*›; **she drinks vodka** ∼: sie trinkt Wodka pur; **(c)** (smart) gepflegt ‹*Erscheinung*, *Kleidung*›; elegant, schick ‹*Anzug*, *Auto*›; **(d)** (deft) geschickt; raffiniert ‹*Trick*, *Plan*, *Lösung*, *Gerät*›; **make a** ∼ **job of sth.: repairing sth.** etw. sehr geschickt machen/reparieren

neatly /'niːtlɪ/ *adv.* **(a)** (tidily) ordentlich; [fein] säuberlich; **(b)** (smartly) gepflegt; ∼ **groomed** äußerst gepflegt; **(c)** (deftly) geschickt; auf raffinierte [Art und] Weise; **(d)** (briefly, clearly) prägnant; **a** ∼ **turned phrase** eine prägnante Formulierung

neatness /'niːtnɪs/ *n., no pl.* ⇒ **neat a, c, d:** Sauberkeit, *die;* Ordentlichkeit, *die;* Gepflegtheit, *die;* Eleganz, *die;* Geschicktheit, *die;* Raffiniertheit, *die*

nebula /'nɛbjʊlə/ *n., pl.* ∼**e** /'nɛbjʊliː/ *or* ∼**s** (Astron.) Nebel, *der*

nebulous /'nɛbjʊləs/ *adj.* (hazy) nebelhaft, (geh.) nebulös ‹*Vorstellung*, *Werte*›; unbestimmt, vage ‹*Angst*, *Hoffnung*›

necessarily /nɛsɪ'sɛrɪlɪ/ *adv.* notwendigerweise; zwangsläufig; **it is not** ∼ **true** es muss nicht [unbedingt] stimmen; **Do we have to do it?** — **Not** ∼: Müssen wir es tun? — Nicht unbedingt

necessary /'nɛsɪsərɪ/ **1** *adj.* **(a)** (indispensable) nötig; notwendig; unbedingt ‹*Erfordernis*›; **patience is** ∼ **for a teacher** ein Lehrer muss Geduld haben; **it is not** ∼ **for you to go** es ist nicht nötig *od.* notwendig, dass du gehst; **it may be** ∼ **for him to leave** vielleicht muss er gehen; **do no more than is** ∼: nur das Nötigste tun; **do everything** ∼ (that must be done) das Nötige *od.* Notwendige tun; **(b)** (inevitable) zwangsläufig ‹*Ergebnis*, *Folge*›; zwingend ‹*Schluss*›; **(c) a** ∼ **evil** ein notwendiges Übel. **2** *n.* **the necessaries of life** das Lebensnotwendige; **will you do the** ∼? kümmerst du dich drum?

necessitate /nɪ'sɛsɪteɪt/ *v.t.* erforderlich machen

necessity /nɪ'sɛsɪtɪ/ *n.* **(a)** (power of circumstances) Not, *die;* äußerer Zwang; **do sth. out of** *or* **from** ∼: etw. notgedrungen tun; **make a virtue of** ∼: aus der Not eine Tugend machen; **of** ∼: notwendigerweise; **(b)** (necessary thing) Notwendigkeit, *die;* **the necessities of life** das Lebensnotwendige; **(c)** (indispensability, imperative need) Notwendigkeit, *die;* **there is no** ∼ **for rudeness** es besteht keine Notwendigkeit, unhöflich zu sein; **in case of** ∼: nötigenfalls; **(d)** (want) Not, *die;* Bedürftigkeit, *die;* **be/live in** ∼: Not leiden

neck /nɛk/ **1** *n.* **(a)** ▶ **672**⏐ Hals, *der;* **be breathing down sb.'s** ∼ (fig.) (be close behind sb.) jmdm. im Nacken sitzen (ugs.); (watch sb. closely) jmdm. ständig auf die Finger sehen; **get it in the** ∼ (coll.) eins auf den Deckel kriegen (ugs.); **give sb./be a pain in the** ∼ (coll.) jmdm. auf die Nerven *od.* den Wecker gehen (ugs.); **break one's** ∼ (fig. coll.) sich (*Dat.*) den Hals brechen; **risk one's** ∼: Kopf und Kragen riskieren; **save one's** ∼: seinen Kopf retten; **be up to one's** ∼ **in work** (coll.) bis über den Hals in Arbeit stecken (ugs.); **be [in it] up to one's** ∼ (coll.) bis über den Hals drinstecken (ugs.); ∼ **and** ∼: Kopf an Kopf; **(b)** (length) Halslänge, *die;* (fig.) Nasenlänge, *die;* **(c)** (cut of meat) Hals, *der;* **(d)** (of garment) Kragen, *der;* **that dress has a high** ∼: das Kleid ist hochgeschlossen; **(e)** (narrow part) Hals, *der.* **2** *v.i.* (coll.) knutschen (ugs.)

necklace /'nɛklɪs/ *n.* [Hals]kette, *die;* (with jewels) Kollier, *das*

neck: ∼**line** *n.* [Hals]ausschnitt, *der;* ∼**tie** *n.* Krawatte, *die;* Binder, *der*

nectar /'nɛktə(r)/ *n.* (Bot.) Nektar, *der;* (delicious drink) Göttertrank, *der* (scherzh.)

nectarine /'nɛktərɪn, 'nɛktəriːn/ *n.* Nektarine, *die*

née (Amer.: **nee**) /neɪ/ *adj.* geborene

need /niːd/ **1** *n.* **(a)** *no pl.* Notwendigkeit, *die* (**for, of** *Gen.*); (demand) Bedarf, *der* (**for, of** an + *Dat.*); **as the** ∼ **arises** nach Bedarf; **if** ∼ **arise/be** nötigenfalls; falls nötig; **there's no** ∼ **for that** (as answer) [das ist] nicht nötig; **there's no** ∼ **to do sth.** es ist nicht nötig *od.* notwendig, etw. zu tun; **there is no** ∼ **to worry/get angry** es besteht kein Grund zur Sorge/sich zu ärgern; **be in** ∼ **of sth.** etw. brauchen *od.* nötig haben; **there is no** ∼ **for such behaviour** solch ein Verhalten ist unnötig; **there's no** ∼ **for you to apologize** du brauchst dich nicht zu entschuldigen; **feel the** ∼ **to do sth.** sich gezwungen *od.* genötigt sehen, etw. zu tun; **feel the** ∼ **to confide in sb.** das Bedürfnis haben, sich jmdm. anzuvertrauen; **be badly in** ∼ **of sth.** etw. dringend nötig haben; **be in** ∼ **of repair** reparaturbedürftig sein; **have** ∼ **of sb./sth.** jmdn./ etw. brauchen *od.* nötig haben; **(b)** *no pl.* (emergency) Not, *die;* **in case of** ∼: im Notfall; **in times of** ∼: in Notzeiten; **those in** ∼: die Notleidenden *od.* Bedürftigen; *see also* **friend a;** **(c)** (thing) Bedürfnis, *das.* **2** *v.t.* **(a)** (require) brauchen; **sth. that urgently** ∼**s doing** etw., was dringend gemacht werden muss; **much** ∼**ed** dringend notwendig; **that's all I** ∼**ed!** (iron.) auch das noch!; das hat mir gerade noch gefehlt!; **it** ∼**s a coat of paint** es muss gestrichen werden; ∼ **correction** berichtigt werden müssen. **(b)** *expr. necessity* müssen; **it needs/doesn't need to be done** es muss getan werden/es braucht nicht getan zu werden; **you don't need to do that** das brauchst du nicht zu tun; **I don't** ∼ **to be reminded** du brauchst/ihr braucht mich nicht daran zu erinnern; **it** ∼**ed doing** es musste getan werden; **he** ∼**s cheering up** er muss [ein bisschen] aufgeheitert werden; **you shouldn't** ∼ **to be told** das solltest *od.* müsstest du eigentlich wissen; **she** ∼**s everything [to be] explained to her** man muss ihr alles erklären; **you** ∼ **only ask** du brauchst nur zu fragen; **don't be away longer than you** ∼ **[be]** bleib nicht länger als nötig weg; **(c)** *pres.* **he** ∼, *neg.* ∼ **not** *or* (coll.) ∼**n't** /'niːdnt/ *expr. desirability* müssen; *with neg.* brauchen zu; ∼ **I say more?** muss ich noch mehr sagen?; **I** ∼ **hardly** *or* **hardly** ∼ **say that** …: ich brauche wohl kaum zu sagen, dass …; **he** ∼**n't be told** (let's keep it secret) das braucht er nicht zu wissen; **we** ∼**n't** *or* ∼ **not have done it, if** …: wir hätten es nicht zu tun brauchen, wenn …; **that** ∼ **not be the case** das muss nicht so sein *od.* der Fall sein

needle /'niːdl/ **1** *n.* Nadel, *die;* **it is like looking for a** ∼ **in a haystack** es ist, als wollte man eine Stecknadel in einem Heuhaufen finden; *see also* **pin 1 a. 2** *v.t.* (coll.) ärgern; nerven (ugs.); **what's needling him?** was fuchst ihn [denn so]? (ugs.)

needless /'niːdlɪs/ *adj.* unnötig; (senseless) sinnlos; ∼ **to say** *or* **add, he didn't do it** überflüssig zu sagen, dass er es nicht getan hat

needlessly /'niːdlɪslɪ/ *adv.* unnötigerweise; (senselessly) sinnlos '**needlework** *n.* Handarbeit, *die;* **do ~:** handarbeiten

needn't /'niːdnt/ (coll.) = **need not;** ⇒ **need 2 c**

needy /'niːdɪ/ *adj.* notleidend; bedürftig; **the ~:** die Notleidenden *od.* Bedürftigen *Pl.*

ne'er-do-well /'neədʊwel/ *n.* Tunichtgut, *der*

negation /nɪ'geɪʃn/ *n.* (Ling.) Negation, *die* (fachspr.); Verneinung, *die*

negative /'negətɪv/ **1** *adj.* (a) (also Math.) negativ; (b) (Ling.) verneint; Negations‹*partikel*›; (c) (Electr.) **~ pole/terminal** Minuspol, *der;* (d) (Photog.) negativ; Negativ-. **2** *n.* (a) (Photog.) Negativ, *das;* (b) (**~ statement**) negative Aussage; (answer) Nein, *das;* **be in the ~** ‹*Antwort:*› negativ *od.* „nein" sein

negative 'equity *n.* Negativwert, *der*

negatively /'negətɪvlɪ/ *adv.* (also Electr.) negativ

neglect /nɪ'glekt/ **1** *v.t.* vernachlässigen; versäumen ‹*Gelegenheit*›; unerledigt lassen, liegen lassen ‹*Korrespondenz, Arbeit*›; **she ~ed to write** sie hat es versäumt zu schreiben; **not ~ doing** *or* **to do sth.** es nicht versäumen, etw. zu tun. **2** *n.* (a) Vernachlässigung, *die;* **be in a state of ~** ‹*Gebäude:*› verwahrlost sein; **suffer from ~:** vernachlässigt werden; **~ of duty** Pflichtvergessenheit, *die;* (b) (negligence) Nachlässigkeit, *die;* Fahrlässigkeit, *die*

neglectful /nɪ'glektfl/ *adj.* (careless) gleichgültig (**of** gegenüber); **be ~** of sich nicht kümmern um

négligé, negligee /'neglɪʒeɪ/ *n.* Negligee, *das*

negligence /'neglɪdʒəns/ *n., no pl.* (carelessness) Nachlässigkeit, *die;* (Law, Insurance, etc.) Fahrlässigkeit, *die*

negligent /'neglɪdʒənt/ *adj.* nachlässig; **be ~ about sth.** sich um etw. nicht kümmern; **be ~ of one's duties/sb.** seine Pflichten/jmdn. vernachlässigen

negligible /'neglɪdʒɪbl/ *adj.* unerheblich

negotiable /nɪ'gəʊʃəbl/ *adj.* (a) (open to discussion) verhandlungsfähig ‹*Forderung, Bedingungen*›; (b) (that can be got past) zu bewältigen *nicht präd.;* zu bewältigen *nicht attr.;* passierbar ‹*Straße, Fluss*›

negotiate /nɪ'gəʊʃɪeɪt/ **1** *v.i.* verhandeln (**for, on, about** über + *Akk.*); **the negotiating table** der Verhandlungstisch. **2** *v.t.* (a) (arrange) aushandeln; (b) (get past) bewältigen; überwinden ‹*Hindernis*›; passieren ‹*Straße, Fluss*›; nehmen ‹*Kurve*›; (c) (Commerc.) (convert into cash) einlösen ‹*Scheck*›; (transfer) übertragen ‹*Wechsel, Papiere usw.*›

negotiation /nɪgəʊʃɪ'eɪʃn, nɪgəʊsɪ'eɪʃn/ *n.* (a) (discussion) Verhandlung, *die* (**for, about** über + *Akk.*); **by ~:** durch Verhandeln *od.* Verhandlungen; **enter into ~:** in Verhandlungen (*Akk.*) eintreten; **be a matter of ~:** Verhandlungssache sein; (b) *in pl.* (talks) Verhandlungen *Pl.*

negotiator /nɪ'gəʊʃɪeɪtə(r)/ *n.* Unterhändler, *der/*-händlerin, *die*

Negress /'niːgrɪs/ *n.* Negerin, *die*

Negro /'niːgrəʊ/ **1** *n., pl.* **~es** Neger, *der.* **2** *adj.* Neger-; **~ woman** Negerin, *die*

neigh /neɪ/ **1** *v.i.* wiehern. **2** *n.* Wiehern, *das*

neighbor etc. (Amer.) ⇒ **neighbour** etc.

neighbour /'neɪbə(r)/ *n.* Nachbar, *der/*Nachbarin, *die;* (at table) [Tisch]nachbar, *der/*[Tisch]nachbarin, *die;* (thing) der/die/das daneben; (building/country) Nachbargebäude/-land, *das;* **we're next-door ~s** wir wohnen Tür an Tür; **my next-door ~s** meine Nachbarn von nebenan

neighbourhood /'neɪbəhʊd/ *n.* (district) Gegend, *die;* (neighbours) Nachbarschaft, *die; attrib.* an der *od.* um die Ecke *nachgestellt* (ugs.); **your friendly ~ bobby** etc. (coll. joc.) der freundliche Polizist von nebenan; **the children from the ~:** die Kinder aus der Nachbarschaft; **it was [somewhere] in the ~ of £100** es waren [so] um [die] 100 Pfund

neighbouring /'neɪbərɪŋ/ *adj.* benachbart; Nachbar-; angrenzend ‹*Felder*›

neighbourly /'neɪbəlɪ/ *adj.* [gut]nachbarlich; (friendly) freundlich

neither /'naɪðə(r), niːðə(r)/ **1** *adj.* keiner/keine/keins der beiden; **in ~ case** in keinem Falle. **2** *pron.* keiner/keine/ keins von *od.* der beiden; **~ of them** keiner von *od.* der

beiden; **Which will you have? — N~:** Welches nehmen Sie? — Keins [von beiden]. **3** *adv.* (also not) auch nicht; **I'm not going — N~ am I** *or* (coll.) **Me ~:** Ich gehe nicht — Ich auch nicht; **if you don't go, ~ shall I** wenn du nicht gehst, gehe ich auch nicht. **4** *conj.* (not either, not on the one hand) weder; **~ … nor** weder … noch; **he ~ knows nor cares** weder weiß er es, noch will er es wissen; **he ~ ate, drank, nor smoked** er aß weder, noch trank, noch rauchte er

nelly /'nelɪ/ *n.* **not on your ~** (Brit. coll.) nie im Leben (ugs.)

neo- /'niːəʊ/ *in comb.* neo-/Neo-

neo'classical *adj.* klassizistisch

neolithic /niːə'lɪθɪk/ *adj.* (Archaeol.) neolithisch (fachspr.); jungsteinzeitlich

neologism /nɪ'ɒlədʒɪzm/ *n.* Neubildung, *die;* Neologismus, *der* (Sprachw.)

neon /'niːɒn/ *n.* (Chem.) Neon, *das*

neon: ~ 'light *n.* Neonlicht, *das;* (fitting) Neonlampe, *die; ~ 'sign* *n.* Neonreklame, *die*

Nepal /nɪ'pɔːl/ *pr. n.* Nepal (*das*)

nephew /'nevjuː, 'nefjuː/ *n.* Neffe, *der*

nepotism /'nepətɪzm/ *n.* Vetternwirtschaft, *die* (abwertend)

Neptune /'neptjuːn/ *pr. n.* (a) (Astron.) Neptun, *der;* (b) (Roman Mythol.) Neptun (*der*)

nerve /nɜːv/ **1** *n.* (a) Nerv, *der;* (b) *in pl.* (fig., of mental state) **be suffering from ~s** nervös sein; **get on sb.'s ~s** jmdm. auf die Nerven gehen *od.* fallen (ugs.); **~s of steel** Nerven wie Drahtseile (ugs.); (c) (coolness, boldness) Kaltblütigkeit, *die;* Mut, *der;* **not have the ~ for sth.** für *od.* zu etw. nicht die Nerven haben; **lose one's ~:** die Nerven verlieren; (d) (coll.: audacity) **what [a] ~!** [so eine] Frechheit!; **have the ~ to do sth.** den Nerv haben, etw. zu tun (ugs.); **he's got a ~:** der hat Nerven (ugs.). **2** *v.t.* (give strength or courage to) ermutigen; **~ oneself** seinen ganzen Mut zusammennehmen

nerve: ~ centre *n.* (fig.) Schaltzentrale, *die; ~ gas* *n.* Nervengas, *das; ~-racking* /'nɜːvrækɪŋ/ *adj.* nervenaufreibend

nervous /'nɜːvəs/ *adj.* (a) (Anat., Med.) Nerven-; **~ breakdown** Nervenzusammenbruch, *der;* (b) (having delicate nerves) nervös; **be a ~ wreck** mit den Nerven völlig am Ende sein; (c) (Brit.: timid) **be ~ of** *or* **about** Angst haben vor (+ *Dat.*); **be a ~ person** ängstlich sein

nervously /'nɜːvəslɪ/ *adv.* nervös

nervy /'nɜːvɪ/ *adj.* (a) (jerky, nervous) nervös; unruhig; (b) (Amer. coll.: impudent) unverschämt

nest /nest/ **1** *n.* (a) (of bird, animal, insect) Nest, *das;* (b) (fig.: retreat, shelter) Nest, *das* (fig.); Zufluchtsort, *der;* **leave the ~:** flügge werden; (c) **~ of tables** Satz Tische. **2** *v.i.* nisten. **3** *v.t.* (a) (place as in ~) einbetten; (b) (pack one inside the other) ineinander setzen ‹*Töpfe usw.*›

'**nest egg** *n.* (fig.) Notgroschen, *der*

nestle /'nesl/ *v.i.* (a) (settle oneself) sich kuscheln; (b) (press oneself affectionately) sich schmiegen (**to, up against** an + *Akk.*); (c) (lie half hidden) eingebettet sein

nestling /'nestlɪŋ/ *n.* Nestling, *der*

net¹ /net/ **1** *n.* (lit. or fig.) Netz, *das;* **the Net** (Computing) das Netz. **2** *v.t.,* **-tt-** [mit einem Netz] fangen ‹*Tier*›; einfangen ‹*Person*›

net² **1** *adj.* (a) (free from deduction) netto; Netto‹*einkommen,* -[*verkaufs*]*preis usw.*›; (b) (not subject to discount) **~ price** gebundener Preis; (c) (excluding weight of container etc.) netto; **~ weight** Nettogewicht, *das;* (d) (effective, ultimate) End‹*ergebnis,* -*effekt*›. **2** *v.t.,* **-tt-** (gain) netto einnehmen; (yield) netto einbringen

net: ~ball *n.* Korbball, *der; ~ 'curtain* *n.* Store [aus Gittertüll]; Tüllgardine, *die*

Netherlands /'neðələndz/ *pr. n. sing. or pl.* Niederlande *Pl.*

netiquette /'netɪket/ *n.* (Computing) Netiquette, *die;* **breaches of ~:** Verstöße gegen die Netiquette

net 'profit *n.* Reingewinn, *der*

nett ⇨ **net²**

netting /'netɪŋ/ *n.* ([piece of] net) Netz, *das;* **wire** ~: Drahtgeflecht, *das;* Maschendraht, *der*

nettle /'netl/ **1** *n.* Nessel, *die; see also* **grasp** 2 b. 2 *v.t.* reizen; aufbringen

'network *n.* **(a)** (of intersecting lines, electrical conductors) Netzwerk, *das;* **(b)** (of railways etc., persons, operations) Netz, *das;* **(c)** (of broadcasting stations) [Sender]netz, *das;* (company) Sender, *der;* **(d)** (Computing) Netzwerk, *das*

neuralgia /njʊəˈrældʒə/ *n.* ▶865 | (Med.) Neuralgie, *die* (fachspr.); Nervenschmerz, *der*

neurologist /njʊəˈrɒlədʒɪst/ *n.* Neurologe, *der*/Neurologin, *die;* Nervenarzt, *der*/-ärztin, *die*

neurology /njʊəˈrɒlədʒɪ/ *n.* Neurologie, *die*

neurosis /njʊəˈrəʊsɪs/ *n., pl.* **neuroses** /njʊəˈrəʊsiːz/ Neurose, *die*

neurotic /njʊəˈrɒtɪk/ **1** *adj.* **(a)** (suffering from neurosis) nervenkrank; **(b)** (of neurosis) neurotisch; **(c)** (coll.: unduly anxious) neurotisch; **don't get** ~ **about it** lass es nicht zu einer Neurose werden. **2** *n.* Neurotiker, *der*/Neurotikerin, *die*

neuter /'njuːtə(r)/ **1** *adj.* (Ling.) sächlich; neutral (fachspr.). **2** *v.t.* kastrieren

neutral /'njuːtrl/ **1** *adj.* neutral. **2** *n.* **(a)** Neutrale, *der*/ *die;* **(b)** (~ gear) Leerlauf, *der*

neutralise ⇨ **neutralize**

neutrality /njuːˈtrælɪtɪ/ *n.* Neutralität, *die*

neutralize /'njuːtrəlaɪz/ *v.t.* **(a)** (Chem.) neutralisieren; **(b)** (counteract) neutralisieren; entkräften ‹ *Argument* ›

neutron /'njuːtrɒn/ *n.* (Phys.) Neutron, *das*

neutron: ~ **bomb** *n.* Neutronenbombe, *die;* ~ **star** *n.* Neutronenstern, *der*

never /'nevə(r)/ *adv.* **(a)** nie; **the rain seemed as if it would** ~ **stop** der Regen schien gar nicht mehr aufhören zu wollen; **he** ~ **so much as apologized** er hat sich nicht einmal entschuldigt; ~, ~: nie, nie; niemals; **he was** ~ **one to do sth.** es war nicht seine Art, etw. zu tun; ~ **a** (not one) kein einziger/keine einzige/kein einziges; ~**-satisfied** unersättlich; ~**-ending** endlos; ~**-failing** unfehlbar; unerschöpflich ‹ *Quelle* ›; **(b)** (coll.) expr. *surprise* **you** ~ **believed that, did you?** du hast das doch wohl nicht geglaubt?; **well, I** ~ **[did]!** [na *od.* nein *od.* also] so was!; **He ate the whole turkey. — N**~! Er hat den ganzen Truthahn aufgegessen. — Nein!

never: ~-'~ *n.* (Brit. coll.) Abzahlungskauf, *der;* **on the** ~-~ **[system]** auf Stottern (ugs.); auf Raten; ~**the-'less** *adv.* trotzdem; nichtsdestoweniger

new /njuː/ **1** *adj.* neu; frisch ‹ *Brot, Gemüse* ›; neu ‹ *Kartoffeln* ›; neu, jung ‹ *Wein* ›; **as good as** ~: so gut wie neu; '~ **boy/girl** (lit. or fig.) Neuling, *der;* **that's a** ~ **one on me** (coll.) das ist mir neu; (of joke etc.) den habe ich noch nicht gehört; **visit** ~ **places** unbekannte Orte besuchen; **the** ~ **rich** die Neureichen *Pl.* (abwertend); **the** ~ **woman** (modern) die moderne Frau; die Frau von heute; **be like a** ~ **man/woman** wie neugeboren sein; **as** ~: neuwertig. **2** *adv.* (recently) vor kurzem; frisch ‹ *gebacken, gewaschen, geschnitten* ›; gerade erst ‹ *erblüht* ›

new: **N**~ **Age** *n.* Newage, *das; attrib.* Newage-; ~**born** *adj.* neugeboren; ~**comer** *n.* Neuankömmling, *der;* (one having no experience also) Neuling, *der* (**to** in + *Dat.*); ~**fangled** /'njuːˈfæŋgld/ *adj.* (derog.) neumodisch (abwertend); ~**found** *adj.* neu; ~**laid** *adj.* frisch [gelegt]

newly /'njuːlɪ/ *adv.* neu; ~ **married** seit kurzem verheiratet

'newly-wed *n.* Jungverheiratete, *der/die*

new: **N**~ **Man** *n.* der neue Mann; ~ '**moon** *n.* Neumond, *der*

news /njuːz/ *n., no pl.* **(a)** (new information) Nachricht, *die;* **be in the** *or* **make** ~: Schlagzeilen machen; **that's** ~ **to me** (coll.) das ist mir neu; **what's the latest** ~? was gibt es Neues?; **have you heard the** ~? hast du schon gehört?; weißt du schon das Neueste? (ugs.); **have you had any** ~ **of him?** hast du etwas von ihm gehört?; hast du

Nachricht von ihm?; **bad/good** ~: schlechte/gute Nachrichten; **(b)** (Radio, Telev.) Nachrichten *Pl.;* **the 10 o'clock** ~: die 10-Uhr-Nachrichten

news: ~**agent** *n.* ▶887 | Zeitungshändler, *der*/-händlerin, *die;* ~ **bulletin** *n.* Nachrichten *Pl.;* ~**caster** *n.* ▶887 | Nachrichtensprecher, *der*/ -sprecherin, *die;* ~**flash** *n.* Kurzmeldung, *die;* ~**group** *n.* (Computing) Newsgroup, *die;* ~ '**headline** *n.* Schlagzeile, *die;* ~**letter** *n.* Rundschreiben, *das;* ~**paper** /'njuːspeɪpə(r)/ *n.* **(a)** Zeitung, *die; attrib.* ~**paper boy/girl** Zeitungsausträger, *der*/-austrägerin, *die;* **(b)** (material) Zeitungspapier, *das;* ~**paperman** *n.* ▶887 | Zeitungsmann, *der* (ugs.); Journalist, *der;* ~**print** *n.* Zeitungspapier, *das;* ~**reader** *n.* ▶887 | Nachrichtensprecher, *der*/-sprecherin, *die;* ~**reel** *n.* Wochenschau, *die;* ~**room** *n.* Nachrichtenredaktion, *die;* ~-**sheet** *n.* Informationsblatt, *das;* ~-**stand** *n.* Zeitungskiosk, *der;* Zeitungsstand, *der;* ~ **summary** *n.* Kurznachrichten *Pl.;* ~**worthy** *adj.* [für die Medien] interessant; berichtenswert ‹ *Ereignis* ›

newsy /'njuːzɪ/ *adj.* (coll.) voller Neuigkeiten *nachgestellt*

newt /njuːt/ *n.* [Wasser]molch, *der*

New: ~ '**Testament** ⇨ **testament** a; **new** '**world** ⇨ **world** a; **new** '**year** *n.* ▶836 | Neujahr, *das;* **over the new year** über Neujahr; **a Happy** ~ **Year** ein glückliches *od.* gutes neues Jahr; **bring in the** ~ **Year** Silvester feiern; ~ '**Year's** (Amer.), ~ **Year's** '**Day** *ns.* Neujahrstag, *der;* ~ **Year's** '**Eve** *n.* Silvester, *der od. das;* Neujahrsabend, *der;* ~ **Zealand** /njuː ˈziːlənd/ **1** *pr. n.* Neuseeland (*das*); **2** *attrib. adj.* neuseeländisch; ~ **Zealander** /njuː ˈziːləndə(r)/ *n.* Neuseeländer, *der*/Neuseeländerin, *die*

next /nekst/ **1** *adj.* **(a)** (nearest) nächst...; **the seat** ~ **to me** der Platz neben mir; **the** ~ **room** das Nebenzimmer; **the** ~ **but one** der/die/das übernächste; ~ **to** (fig.: almost) fast; nahezu; **(b)** ▶738 | (in order) nächst...; **within the** ~ **few days** in den nächsten Tagen; ~ **month** nächsten Monat; **during the** ~ **year** während der nächsten zwölf Monate; **we'll come** ~ **May** wir kommen im Mai nächsten Jahres; **the** ~ **largest/larger** der/die/das nächstkleinere/nächstgrößere; **[the]** ~ **time** das nächste Mal; **the** ~ **best** der/die/das nächstbeste; **am I** ~? komme ich jetzt dran? **2** *adv.* (in the ~ place) als Nächstes; (on the ~ occasion) das nächste Mal; **whose name comes** ~? wessen Name kommt als Nächstes *od.* Nächster?; **it is my turn** ~: ich komme als nächster dran; **sit/stand** ~ **to sb.** neben jmdm. sitzen/stehen; **place sth.** ~ **to sb.**/ **sth.** etw. neben jmdn./etw. stellen; **come** ~ **to last** (in race) Zweitletzter/Zweitletzte werden; **come** ~ **to bottom** (in exam) der/die Zweitschlechteste sein. **3** *n.* **(a) from one day to the** ~: von einem Tag zum andern; **the week after** ~: [die] übernächste Woche; **(b)** (person) ~ **of kin** nächster/nächste Angehörige; ~ **please!** der nächste, bitte!

'next-door *adj.* gleich nebenan *nachgestellt*

NHS *abbr.* (Brit.) **National Health Service;** ~ **Trust** NHS-Trust, *der*

NI *abbr.* (Brit.) **National Insurance**

nib /nɪb/ *n.* Feder, *die*

nibble /'nɪbl/ **1** *v.t.* knabbern; ~ **off** abknabbern. **2** *v.i.* knabbern (**at, on** an + *Dat.*)

Nicaragua /nɪkəˈrægjuə/ *pr. n.* Nicaragua (*das*)

Nicaraguan /nɪkəˈrægjuən/ ▶947 | **1** *adj.* nicaraguanisch; **sb. is** ~: jmd. ist Nicaraguaner/Nicaraguanerin. **2** *n.* Nicaraguaner, *der*/Nicaraguanerin, *die*

nice /naɪs/ *adj.* **(a)** (pleasing) nett; angenehm ‹ *Stimme* ›; schön ‹ *Wetter* ›; (iron.: disgraceful, difficult) schön; sauber (iron.); **she has a** ~ **smile** sie lächelt so nett; **you're a** ~ **one, I must say** (iron.) du bist hier vielleicht einer; **be in a** ~ **mess** (iron.) in einem schönen Schlamassel sitzen (ugs.); ~ **work** saubere *od.* gute Arbeit; ~ **to meet you** freut mich, Sie kennen zu lernen; ~ **[and] warm/fast/high** schön warm/schnell/hoch; **a** ~ **long holiday** schöne lange Ferien; ~-**looking** hübsch; gut aussehend; hübsch ‹ *Person* ›; **(b)** (subtle) fein ‹ *Bedeutungsunterschied* ›

nicely /'naɪslɪ/ *adv.* (coll.) **(a)** (well) nett; gut ‹ *arbeiten, sich benehmen, platziert sein* ›; **(b)** (all right) gut; **he's got a new**

job and is doing very ~: er hat eine neue Arbeit und kommt prima (ugs.) damit zurecht; **that will do ~:** das reicht völlig

nicety /'naɪsɪtɪ/ n. **(a)** no pl. (punctiliousness) [peinliche] Genauigkeit; **(b)** no pl. (precision, accuracy) Feinheit, die; Genauigkeit, die; **to a ~:** perfekt ‹arrangieren›; sehr genau ‹schätzen›; **(c)** in pl. (minute distinctions) Feinheiten

niche /nɪtʃ, niːʃ/ n. **(a)** (in wall) Nische, die; **(b)** (fig.: suitable place) Platz, der

nick 1 n. **(a)** (notch) Kerbe, die; **(b)** (sl.: prison) Kittchen, das (ugs.); Knast, der (salopp); **(c)** (Brit. sl.: police station) Wache, die; Revier, das; **(d)** in **good/poor ~** (coll.) gut/nicht gut in Schuss (ugs.); **(e)** in **the ~ of time** gerade noch rechtzeitig. 2 v.t. **(a)** (make ~ in) einkerben ‹Holz›; **~ one's chin** sich am Kinn schneiden; **(b)** (Brit. coll.) (catch) schnappen (ugs.); (arrest) einlochen (salopp); **(c)** (Brit. coll.: steal) klauen (salopp); mitgehen lassen (ugs.)

nickel /'nɪkl/ n. **(a)** (metal) Nickel, das; **(b)** (US coin) Fünfcentstück, das

nickname /'nɪkneɪm/ 1 n. Spitzname, der; (affectionate) Koseform, die. 2 v.t. **~ sb. ...:** jmdm. den Spitznamen ... geben; jmdn. ... taufen

nicotine /'nɪkətiːn/ n. Nikotin, das

'nicotine patch n. Nikotinpflaster, das

niece /niːs/ n. Nichte, die

nifty /'nɪftɪ/ adj. (coll.) **(a)** klasse (ugs.); flott ‹Kleidung›; **(b)** (clever) geschickt; clever ‹Plan, Idee›

Nigeria /naɪ'dʒɪərɪə/ pr. n. Nigeria (das)

Nigerian /naɪ'dʒɪərɪən/ ▶947 1 adj. nigerianisch; **sb. is ~:** jmd. ist Nigerianer/Nigerianerin. 2 n. Nigerianer, der/Nigerianerin, die

niggardly /'nɪgədlɪ/ adj. **(a)** (miserly) knaus[e]rig (ugs.); **(b)** (given in small amounts) armselig, kümmerlich ‹Portion›

nigger /'nɪgə(r)/ n. (derog. offensive) Nigger, der (abwertend)

niggle /'nɪgl/ 1 v.i. (find fault pettily) [herum]nörgeln (ugs. abwertend) (**at** an + Dat.). 2 v.t. herumnörgeln an (+ Dat.)

niggling /'nɪglɪŋ/ adj. **(a)** (petty) belanglos; **(b)** (trivial) nichtssagend; oberflächlich ‹Kritik›; krittelig ‹Rezension, Rezensent›

nigh /naɪ/ adv. (arch./literary/dial.) nahe; **come** or **draw ~:** näherkommen ‹Tag, Zeitpunkt:›nahen; **it's ~ on impossible** es ist nahezu unmöglich

night /naɪt/ n. **(a)** ▶739 Nacht, die; (evening) Abend, der; **the following ~:** die Nacht/der Abend darauf; **the previous ~:** die vorausgegangene Nacht/der vorausgegangene Abend; **one ~ he came** eines Nachts/Abends kam er; **two ~s ago** vorgestern Nacht/Abend; **the other ~:** neulich abends/nachts; **far into the ~:** bis spät od. tief in die Nacht; **on Sunday ~:** Sonntagnacht/[am] Sonntag abend; **on Sunday ~s** sonntagabends; **[on] the ~ after/before** die Nacht danach/davor; **for the ~:** über Nacht; **late at ~:** spätabends; **take all ~** (fig.) den ganzen Abend brauchen; **at ~** (in the evening, at ~fall) abends; (during the ~) nachts; bei Nacht; **make a ~ of it** die Nacht durchfeiern; durchmachen (ugs.); **~ and day** Tag und Nacht; **as ~ follows day** so sicher wie das Amen in der Kirche; **a ~ off** eine Nacht/ein Abend frei; **have a ~ out** (festive evening) [abends] ausgehen; **spend the ~ with sb.** bei jmdm. übernachten; (implying sexual intimacy) die Nacht mit jmdm. verbringen; **stay the ~** or **over ~:** über Nacht bleiben; **(b)** (darkness, lit. or fig.) Nacht, die; **black as ~:** schwarz wie die Nacht; **(c)** (~fall) Einbruch der Dunkelheit; **(d)** (~'s sleep) **have a good/bad ~:** gut/schlecht schlafen; **have a sleepless ~:** eine schlaflose Nacht haben; **(e)** (evening of performance etc.) Abend, der; **opening ~:** Premiere, die; **(f)** attrib. Nacht-/Abend-

night: ~bird n. (person) Nachteule, die (ugs. scherzh.); **~cap** n. **(a)** Nachtmütze, die; (woman's) Nachthaube, die; **(b)** (drink) Schlaftrunk, der; **~clothes** n. pl. Nachtwäsche, die; **~club** n. Nachtklub, der; Nachtlokal, das; **~dress** n. Nachthemd, das; **~fall** n., no art. Einbruch der Dunkelheit; **at/after ~fall** bei/nach Einbruch der Dunkelheit; **~gown** n. Nachthemd, das

nightie /'naɪtɪ/ n. (coll.) Nachthemd, das

nightingale /'naɪtɪŋgeɪl/ n. Nachtigall, die

night: ~life n. Nachtleben, das; **~ light** n. Nachtlicht, das; **~-long** 1 adj. sich über die ganze Nacht hinziehend; 2 adv. die ganze Nacht [lang od. über]

nightly /'naɪtlɪ/ 1 adj. nächtlich/abendlich; (every night/ evening) allnächtlich/allabendlich. 2 adv. (every night) jede Nacht; (every evening) jeden Abend; **twice ~** (Theatre etc.) zweimal pro Abend

night: ~mare n. (lit. or fig.) Albtraum, der; **~ owl** n. (coll.: person) Nachteule, die (ugs. scherzh.); Nachtschwärmer, der (scherzh.); **~ safe** n. Nachttresor, der; **~ school** n. Abendschule, die; **~ shelter** n. Nachtasyl, das; **~ shift** n. Nachtschicht, die; **~-time** n., no indef. art. Nacht, die; **in the** or **at ~-time** nachts; **wait until ~-time** warten, bis es Nacht od. dunkel wird; **~'watchman** n. ▶887 Nachtwächter, der

nihilism /'naɪɪlɪzm, 'nɪhɪlɪzm/ n. Nihilismus, der

nil /nɪl/ n. **(a)** nichts; **his chances were ~:** seine Chancen waren gleich Null; **(b)** (Sport) null; **win one ~** or **by one goal to ~:** eins zu null gewinnen

Nile /naɪl/ pr. n. ▶1048 Nil, der

nimble /'nɪmbl/ adj. **(a)** (quick in movement) flink; behände; beweglich ‹Geist›; **(b)** (dextrous) geschickt

nimbly /'nɪmblɪ/ adv. flink ‹arbeiten, sich bewegen›

nincompoop /'nɪŋkəmpuːp/ n. Trottel, der (ugs. abwertend)

nine /naɪn/ ▶630, ▶706, ▶956 1 adj. neun; **~ times out of ten** (fig.: nearly always) in den weitaus meisten Fällen; **a ~ days' wonder** nur eine Eintagsfliege (ugs.); see also **eight 1. 2** n. Neun, die; **work from ~ to five** die übliche Arbeitszeit [von 9 bis 17 Uhr] haben; **dressed [up] to the ~s** sehr festlich gekleidet; **~-~-~, 999** (Brit.: emergency number) ≈ eins, eins, null; see also **eight 2 a, c, d**

nineteen /naɪn'tiːn/ ▶630, ▶706, ▶956 1 adj. neunzehn; see also **eight 1. 2** n. **(a)** Neunzehn, die; see also **eight 2 a; eighteen 2; (b)** talk ~ to the dozen (Brit.) wie ein Wasserfall reden (ugs.)

nineteenth /naɪn'tiːnθ/ ▶738, ▶956 1 adj. neunzehnt...; see also **eighth 1. 2** n. (fraction) Neunzehntel, das; see also **eighth 2**

ninetieth /'naɪntɪɪθ/ ▶956 1 adj. neunzigst...; see also **eighth 1. 2** n. (fraction) Neunzigstel, das; see also **eighth 2**

ninety /'naɪntɪ/ ▶630, ▶956 1 adj. neunzig; see also **eight 1. 2** n. Neunzig, die; see also **eight 2 a; eighty 2**

ninety: ~-'first etc. adj. ▶956 einundneunzigst... usw.; see also **eighth 1; ~-'one** etc. ▶956 1 adj. einundneunzig usw.; see also **eight 2 a; ~-nine times out of a hundred** (fig.: nearly always) so gut wie immer; see also **eight 1; 2** n. Einundneunzig usw., die; see also **eight 2 a**

ninth /naɪnθ/ ▶738, ▶956 1 adj. neunt...; see also **eighth 1. 2** n. (in sequence, rank) Neunte, der/die/das; (fraction) Neuntel, das; see also **eighth 2**

nip¹ /nɪp/ 1 v.t., **-pp-: (a)** (pinch) zwicken; **~ sb.'s toe/sb. on the leg** jmdm. od. jmdm. in den Zeh/jmdn. am Bein zwicken; **(b)** **~ off** abzwicken; (with scissors) abknipsen. See also **bud 1. 2** v.i., **-pp-** (Brit. coll.: step etc. quickly) **~ in** hinein-/hereinflitzen (ugs.); **~ out** hinaus-/herausflitzen (ugs.). 3 n. **(a)** (pinch, squeeze) Kniff, der; (bite) Biss, der; **(b)** (coldness of air) Kälte, die; **there's a ~ in the air** es ist frisch

nip² n. (of spirits etc.) Schlückchen, das

nipple /'nɪpl/ n. **(a)** (on breast) Brustwarze, die; **(b)** (of feeding bottle) Sauger, der

nippy /'nɪpɪ/ adj. (coll.) **(a)** (nimble) flink; spritzig ‹Auto›; **(b)** (cold) frisch; kühl

nit /nɪt/ n. **(a)** (egg) Nisse, die; **(b)** (coll.: stupid person) Dussel, der (ugs.); Blödmann, der (salopp)

nit: ~-pick v.i. kritteln (abwertend); **~-picking** adj. (coll.) kleinlich (abwertend)

nitric acid /'naɪtrɪk æsɪd/ n. (Chem.) Salpetersäure, die

nitrogen /'naɪtrədʒən/ n. Stickstoff, der

nitroglycerine /naɪtrəʊ'glɪsəriːn/ n. Nitroglyzerin, das

nitty-gritty /'nɪtɪ'grɪtɪ/ n. (coll.) **the ~ [of the matter]** der Kern [der Sache]; **get down to the ~:** zur Sache kommen

nitwit /'nɪtwɪt/ *n.* (coll.) Trottel, *der* (ugs.)

no /nəʊ/ **1** *adj.* **(a)** (not any) kein; **(b)** (not a) kein; (quite other than) alles andere als; **she is no beauty** sie ist keine Schönheit *od.* nicht gerade eine Schönheit; **you are no friend** du bist kein [wahrer] Freund; **(c)** (hardly any) **it's no distance from our house to the shopping centre** von unserem Haus ist es nicht weit bis zum Einkaufszentrum. **2** *adv.* **(a)** (by no amount) nicht; **no less [than]** nicht weniger [als]; **it is no different from before** es hat sich nichts geändert; **no more wine?** keinen Wein mehr?; **no more war!** nie wieder Krieg!; **(b)** (equivalent to negative sentence) nein; **say/answer 'no'** nein sagen/mit Nein antworten; **I won't take 'no' for an answer** ein Nein lasse ich nicht gelten. **3** *n.*, *pl.* **noes** /nəʊz/ Nein, *das;* (vote) Neinstimme, *die*

No. *abbr.* **number** Nr.

Noah's ark /nəʊəz 'ɑːk/ *n.* (Bibl.) die Arche Noah

nobble /'nɒbl/ *v.t.* (Brit. sl.) **(a)** (durch Spritzen o. ä.) langsam machen ‹*Rennpferd*›; **(b)** (durch Bestechung o. ä.) auf seine Seite ziehen ‹*Person*›

Nobel prize /nəʊbel 'praɪz/ *n.* Nobelpreis, *der*

nobility /nə'bɪlɪtɪ/ *n.* **(a)** *no pl.* (character) hohe Gesinnung; Adel, *der;* **(b)** (class) Adel, *der;* **many of the ~:** viele Adlige

noble /'nəʊbl/ **1** *adj.* **(a)** (by rank, title, or birth) ad[e]lig; **be of ~ birth** von adliger *od.* edler Geburt sein (geh.); adlig sein; **(b)** (of lofty character) edel ‹*Gedanken, Gefühle*›; **~ ideals** hohe Ideale; **(c)** (showing greatness of character) edel; hochherzig (geh.). **2** *n.* Adlige, *der/die*

noble: ~man /'nəʊblmən/ *n.*, *pl.* **~men** /'nəʊblmən/ Adlige, *der;* **~woman** *n.* Adlige, *die*

nobly /'nəʊblɪ/ *adv.* **(a)** (with noble spirit) edel[gesinnt]; **(b)** (generously) edelmütig (geh.)

nobody /'nəʊbədɪ/ *n. & pron.* niemand; keiner; (person of no importance) Niemand, *der*

no-'claim[s] bonus *n.* (Insurance) Schadenfreiheitsrabatt, *der*

nocturnal /nɒk'tɜːnl/ *adj.* nächtlich; nachtaktiv ‹*Tier*›; **~ animal/bird** Nachttier, *das/*-vogel, *der*

nocturne /'nɒktɜːn/ *n.* (Mus.) Nocturne, *das od. die*

nod /nɒd/ **1** *v.i.*, **-dd-: (a)** (as signal) nicken; **~ to sb.** jmdm. zunicken; **(b)** (in drowsiness) **she sat ~ding by the fire** sie war neben dem Kamin eingenickt (ugs.); **her head started to ~:** sie begann einzunicken (ugs.). **2** *v.t.*, **-dd-: (a)** (incline) **~ one's head [in greeting]** [zum Gruß] mit dem Kopf nicken; **(b)** (signify by ~) **~ approval** *or* **agreement** zustimmend nicken. **3** *n.* [Kopf]nicken, *das* **~ 'off** *v.i.* einnicken (ugs.)

node /nəʊd/ *n.* (Bot., Astron.) Knoten, *der*

no-'fly zone *n.* Flugverbotszone, *die*

no-'go *adj.* Sperr‹*gebiet, -zone*›

'no-good *adj.* (coll.) nichtsnutzig (abwertend)

no-hoper /nəʊ'həʊpə(r)/ *n.* absoluter Außenseiter; **be a ~:** keine Chance haben; **a team of ~s** eine völlig chancenlose Mannschaft

noise /nɔɪz/ *n.* **(a)** (loud outcry) Lärm, *der;* Krach, *der;* **don't make so much ~/such a loud ~:** sei nicht so laut/ mach nicht solchen Lärm *od.* Krach; **make a ~ about sth.** (fig.: complain) wegen etw. Krach machen *od.* schlagen (ugs.); **(b)** (any sound) Geräusch, *das;* (loud, harsh, unwanted) Lärm, *der;* **(c)** (Communications) Geräusch, *das;* (hissing) Rauschen, *das;* **(d) make ~s about doing sth.** davon reden, etw. tun zu wollen

noiseless /'nɔɪzlɪs/ *adj.*, **noiselessly** /'nɔɪzlɪslɪ/ *adv.* **(a)** (silent[ly]) lautlos; **(b)** (making no avoidable noise) geräuschlos

noise: ~ level *n.* Geräuschpegel, *der;* (of unpleasant noise) Lärmpegel, *der;* **~ pollution** *n.* Lärmbelastung, *die*

noisily /'nɔɪzɪlɪ/ *adv.* laut; lärmend ‹*spielen*›; geräuschvoll ‹*stolpern, schlürfen*›

noisy /'nɔɪzɪ/ *adj.* laut; lärmend; laut ‹*Menschenmasse, Kinder*›; lautstark ‹*Diskussion, Begrüßung*›; geräuschvoll ‹*Aufbruch, Ankunft*›

nomad /'nəʊmæd/ *n.* Nomade, *der;* **be a ~** (fig.) ein Nomadendasein führen

nomadic /nəʊ'mædɪk/ *adj.* nomadisch; **~ tribe** Nomadenstamm, *der*

'no man's land *n.* Niemandsland, *das*

nom de plume /nɒm də 'pluːm/ *n.*, *pl.* **noms de plume** /nɒm də 'pluːm/ Pseudonym, *das*

nomenclature /nə'menklətʃə(r)/ *n.* Nomenklatur, *die*

nominal /'nɒmɪnl/ *adj.* **(a)** (in name only) nominell; **(b)** (virtually nothing) äußerst gering; äußerst niedrig ‹*Preis, Miete*›

nominally /'nɒmɪnəlɪ/ *adv.* namentlich

nominate /'nɒmɪneɪt/ *v.t.* **(a)** (propose for election) nominieren; **(b)** (appoint to office) ernennen

nomination /nɒmɪ'neɪʃn/ *n.* **(a)** (appointment to office) Ernennung, *die;* **(b)** (proposal for election) Nominierung, *die*

nominative /'nɒmɪnətɪv/ (Ling.) **1** *adj.* Nominativ-; nominativisch; **~ case** Nominativ, *der.* **2** *n.* Nominativ, *der*

nominee /nɒmɪ'niː/ *n.* (candidate) Kandidat, *der/*Kandidatin, *die*

non- /nɒn/ *pref.* nicht-

non-ag'gression *n.* Gewaltverzicht, *der;* **~ pact** *or* **treaty** Nichtangriffspakt, *der*

non-alco'holic *adj.* alkoholfrei

non-a'ligned *adj.* blockfrei

nonchalant /'nɒnʃələnt/ *adj.* nonchalant (geh.); unbekümmert

non-'combatant **1** *n.* Nichtkämpfende, *der/die.* **2** *adj.* nicht am Kampf beteiligt

non-commissioned 'officer *n.* Unteroffizier, *der*

non-com'mittal /nɒnkə'mɪtl/ *adj.* unverbindlich

noncon'formist *n.* Nonkonformist, *der/*Nonkonformistin, *die*

non-co-oper'ation *n.* Verweigerung der Kooperation

non-denominational /nɒndɪnɒmɪ'neɪʃənl/ *adj.* konfessionslos

nondescript /'nɒndɪskrɪpt/ *adj.* unscheinbar; undefinierbar ‹*Farbe*›

none /nʌn/ **1** *pron.* kein...; **~ of them** keiner/keine/ keines von ihnen; **~ of this money is mine** von diesem Geld gehört mir nichts; **~ other than ...:** kein anderer/ keine andere als ... **2** *adv.* keineswegs; **I'm ~ the wiser now** jetzt bin ich um nichts klüger; **~ the less** nichtsdestoweniger

non'entity *n.* Nichts, *das*

'non-event *n.* Reinfall, *der* (ugs.); Enttäuschung, *die*

non-existence /nɒnɪg'zɪstənt/ *n.*, *no pl.* Nichtvorhandensein, *das*

non-existent /nɒnɪg'zɪstənt/ *adj.* nicht vorhanden

non-'fiction *n.* **~ [literature]** Sachliteratur, *die*

non-inter'ference, non-inter'vention *ns.*, *no pl.* Nichteinmischung, *die*

non-'iron *adj.* bügelfrei

non-'member *n.* Nichtmitglied, *das*

non-'nuclear *adj.* Nichtnuklear-; **~ weapons** konventionelle Waffen

no-'nonsense *adj.* nüchtern

non-'party *adj.* **(a)** (not attached to a party) parteilos; **(b)** (not related to a party) überparteilich

nonplus /nɒn'plʌs/ *v.t.*, **-ss-** verblüffen

non-'profit[-making] *adj.* nicht auf Gewinn ausgerichtet

non-'resident **1** *adj.* (residing elsewhere) nicht im Haus wohnend; (outside a country) nicht ansässig. **2** *n.* nicht im Haus Wohnende, *der/die;* (outside a country) Nichtansässige, *der/die;* **the bar is open to ~s** die Bar ist auch für Gäste geöffnet, die nicht im Hotel wohnen

non-re'turnable *adj.* Einweg‹*behälter, -flasche, -[ver]packung*›; nicht rückzahlbar ‹*Anzahlung*›

nonsense /'nɒnsəns/ **1** *n.* Unsinn, *der;* **piece of ~:** Firlefanz, *der* (ugs. abwertend); **talk ~:** Unsinn reden; **it's all a lot of ~:** das ist alles Unsinn; **make [a] ~ of sth.** etw. zur Farce machen; **make a ~ of a theory** eine Theorie in sich zusammenfallen lassen; **what's all this ~ about …?** was soll das [dumme] Gerede über (+ *Akk.*) …?; **stand no ~:** keinen Unfug dulden; **come along now, and no ~:** kommt jetzt, und mach keinen Unsinn. **2** *int.* Unsinn!

nonsensical /nɒnˈsensɪkl/ *adj.* unsinnig

non-'slip *adj.* rutschfest

non-'smoker *n.* **(a)** (person) Nichtraucher, *der*/Nichtraucherin, *die;* **(b)** (train compartment) Nichtraucherabteil, *das*

non-'starter *n.* **(a)** (Sport) Nichtstartende, *der*/*die;* **(b)** (fig. coll.) Reinfall, *der* (ugs.); (person) Blindgänger, *der* (fig. salopp)

non-'stick *adj.* **~ frying pan** *etc.* Bratpfanne *usw.* mit Antihaftbeschichtung

non-stop 1 /'--/ *adj.* durchgehend ‹*Zug, Busverbindung*›; Nonstop‹*flug, -revue*›. **2** /'-'-/ *adv.* ohne Unterbrechung ‹*tanzen, reden, reisen, senden*›; nonstop, im Nonstop ‹*fliegen, fahren*›

non-'violence *n., no pl.* Gewaltlosigkeit, *die*

non-'violent *adj.* gewaltlos

non-'white 1 *adj.* farbig. **2** *n.* Farbige, *der*/*die*

noodle /'nuːdl/ *n., usu. pl.* (pasta) Nudel, *die*

nook /nʊk/ *n.* Winkel, *der;* Ecke, *die;* **in every ~ and cranny** in allen Ecken und Winkeln

noon /nuːn/ *n.* ▶706 , ▶739 Mittag, *der;* zwölf Uhr [mittags]; **at/before ~:** um/vor zwölf [Uhr mittags]

'no one *pron.* **(a)** **~ of them** keiner/keine/keines von ihnen; **(b)** ⇒ **nobody**

noose /nuːs/ *n.* Schlinge, *die;* **put one's head in a ~** (fig.) den Kopf in die Schlinge stecken

nor /nə(r), *stressed* nɔː(r)/ *conj.* noch; **neither … ~ …, not … ~ …:** weder … noch …

norm /nɔːm/ *n.* Norm, *die*

normal /'nɔːml/ **1** *adj.* normal. **2** *n.* **(a)** (~ value) Normalwert, *der;* **(b)** (usual state) normaler Stand; **everything is back to** *or* **has returned to ~:** es hat sich wieder alles normalisiert; **his temperature is above ~:** er hat erhöhte Temperatur

normalise ⇒ **normalize**

normality /nɔːˈmælɪtɪ/ *n., no pl.* Normalität, *die*

normalize /'nɔːməlaɪz/ **1** *v.t.* normalisieren. **2** *v.i.* sich normalisieren

normally /'nɔːməlɪ/ *adv.* **(a)** (in normal way) normal; **(b)** (ordinarily) normalerweise

north /nɔːθ/ **1** *n.* **(a)** (direction) Norden, *der;* **the ~:** Nord (Met., Seew.); **in/to[wards]/from the ~:** im/nach/von Norden; **to the ~ of** nördlich von; nördlich (+ *Gen.*); **magnetic ~:** magnetischer Nordpol; **(b)** *usu.* **N~** (part lying to the ~) Norden, *der;* **from the N~:** aus dem Norden. **2** *adj.* nördlich; Nord‹*wind, -fenster, -küste, -grenze, -tor*›. **3** *adv.* nordwärts; nach Norden; **~ of** nördlich von; nördlich (+ *Gen.*)

north: N~ '**Africa** *pr. n.* Nordafrika (*das*); **N~ A'merica** *pr. n.* Nordamerika (*das*); **N~ A'merican 1** *adj.* nordamerikanisch; **2** *n.* Nordamerikaner, *der*/-amerikanerin, *die;* **~bound** *adj.* ▶715 ‹*Zug, Verkehr usw.*› in Richtung Norden; **~-'east** ▶715 **1** *n.* Nordosten, *der;* **2** *adj.* nordöstlich; Nordost‹*wind, -fenster, -küste*›; **3** *adv.* nordostwärts; nach Nordosten; **~-'eastern** *adj.* ▶715 nordöstlich

northerly /'nɔːðəlɪ/ ▶715 *adj.* **(a)** (in position or direction) nördlich; **in a ~ direction** nach Norden; **(b)** (from the north) ‹*Wind*› aus nördlichen Richtungen

northern /'nɔːðən/ *adj.* ▶715 nördlich; Nord‹*grenze, -hälfte, -seite*›

northerner /'nɔːðənə(r)/ *n.* (male) Nordengländer/-deutsche *usw., der;* (female) Nordengländerin/-deutsche *usw., die*

Northern: ~ 'Europe *pr. n.* Nordeuropa (*das*); **~ 'Ireland** *pr. n.* Nordirland (*das*); **n~ 'lights** *n. pl.* Nordlicht, *das*

northernmost /'nɔːðənməʊst/ *adj.* ▶715 nördlichst…

North: ~ 'German 1 *adj.* norddeutsch; **2** *n.* Norddeutsche, *der*/*die;* **~ 'Germany** *pr. n.* Norddeutschland (*das*); **~ Ko'rea** *pr. n.* Nordkorea (*das*); **~ of 'England** *pr. n.* Nordengland (*das*); *attrib.* nordenglisch; **~**

'**Pole** *pr. n.* Nordpol, *der;* **~ 'Sea** *pr. n.* Nordsee, *die; attrib.* **~ Sea gas/oil** Nordseegas/-öl, *das*

northward /'nɔːθwəd/ ▶715 **1** *adj.* nach Norden gerichtet; (situated towards the north) nördlich; **in a ~ direction** nach Norden; [in] Richtung Norden. **2** *adv.* nordwärts; **they are ~ bound** sie fahren nach *od.* [in] Richtung Norden

northwards /'nɔːθwədz/ *adv.* ▶715 nordwärts

north: ~-'west ▶715 **1** *n.* Nordwesten, *der;* **2** *adj.* nordwestlich; Nordwest‹*wind, -fenster, -küste*›; **3** *adv.* nordwestwärts; nach Nordwesten; **~-'western** *adj.* ▶715 nordwestlich

Norway /'nɔːweɪ/ *pr. n.* Norwegen (*das*)

Norwegian /nɔːˈwiːdʒn/ ▶897 , ▶947 **1** *adj.* norwegisch; **sb. is ~:** jmd. ist Norweger/Norwegerin. **2** *n.* **(a)** (person) Norweger, *der*/Norwegerin, *die;* **(b)** (language) Norwegisch, *das; see also* **English 2 a**

Nos. *abbr.* **numbers** Nrn.

nose /nəʊz/ **1** *n.* **(a)** ▶672 Nase, *die;* **[win] by a ~:** mit einer Nasenlänge [gewinnen]; **follow one's ~** (fig.) (be guided by instinct) seinem Instinkt folgen; (go forward) der Nase nachgehen; **get up sb.'s ~** (coll.: annoy sb.) jmdm. auf den Wecker gehen; **hold one's ~** (coll.) sich (*Dat.*) die Nase zuhalten; **pay through the ~:** tief in die Tasche greifen müssen (ugs.); **poke** *or* **thrust** *etc.* **one's ~ into sth.** (fig.) seine Nase in etw. (*Akk.*) stecken (fig. ugs.); **put sb.'s ~ out of joint** (fig. coll.) jmdn. vor den Kopf stoßen (ugs.); **rub sb.'s ~ in it** (fig.) es jmdm. ständig unter die Nase reiben (ugs.); **speak through one's ~:** näseln; durch die Nase sprechen; **turn up one's ~ at sth.** (fig.) die Nase über etw. (*Akk.*) rümpfen (fig. coll.); **under sb.'s ~** (fig. coll.) vor jmds. Augen (*Dat.*); **keep one's ~ out of sth.** (fig. coll.) sich aus etw. [he]raushalten; **keep your ~ out of this!** halt [du] dich da raus!; **(b)** (of ship, aircraft) Nase, *die.* **2** *v.t.* **(a)** (detect, smell out) **~ [out]** aufspüren; **(b) ~ one's way** sich (*Dat.*) vorsichtig seinen Weg bahnen. **3** *v.i.* (move) sich vorsichtig bewegen

~ about, ~ around *v.i.* (coll.) herumschnüffeln (ugs.)

~ out *v.t.* aufspüren

nose: ~bag *n.* Futterbeutel, *der;* **~bleed** *n.* Nasenbluten, *das;* **~dive 1** *n.* **(a)** Sturzflug, *der;* **(b)** (fig.) Einbruch, *der;* **take a ~dive** einen Einbruch erleben; **2** *v.i.* im Sturzflug hinuntergehen

nosey ⇒ **nosy**

nosh /nɒʃ/ *n.* (esp. Brit. sl.) (snack) Imbiss, *der;* (food) Futter, *das* (salopp)

no-'show *n.* (for a flight) No-show, *der* (fachspr.); **be a ~ at a dinner/at an event/on a flight/in a hotel** bei einem Abendessen/einer Veranstaltung nicht erscheinen/eine Flug-/Hotelreservierung nicht in Anspruch nehmen

'**nosh-up** *n.* (Brit. sl.) Essen, *das;* (good meal) Festessen, *das*

nostalgia /nɒˈstældʒə/ *n.* Nostalgie, *die;* **~ for sth.** Sehnsucht nach etw.

nostalgic /nɒˈstældʒɪk/ *adj.* nostalgisch

nostril /'nɒstrɪl/ *n.* Nasenloch, *das;* (of horse) Nüster, *die*

nosy /'nəʊzɪ/ *adj.* (coll . derog.) neugierig

Nosy Parker /ˈnəʊzɪ ˈpɑːkə(r)/ *n.* Schnüffler, *der*/Schnüfflerin, *die* (ugs. abwertend)

not /nɒt/ *adv.* **(a)** nicht; **he is ~ a doctor** er ist kein Arzt; **isn't she pretty?** ist sie nicht hübsch?; **(b)** *in ellipt. phrs.* nicht; **I hope ~:** hoffentlich nicht; **~ at all** überhaupt nicht; (in polite reply to thanks) keine Ursache; gern geschehen; **~ that** [I know of] nicht, dass [ich wüsste]; **(c)** *in emphat. phrs.* **~ … but …:** nicht …, sondern …; **~ a moment** nicht ein *od.* kein einziger Augenblick; **~ a thing** gar nichts; **~ a few/everybody** nicht wenige/jeder; **~ once** *or* **nor twice, but …:** nicht nur ein- oder zweimal, sondern …

notable /'nəʊtəbl/ *adj.* bemerkenswert; bedeutend, angesehen ‹*Person*›; **be ~ for sth.** für etw. bekannt sein

notably /'nəʊtəblɪ/ *adv.* besonders

notary /'nəʊtərɪ/ *n.* ▶887 **~ ['public]** Notar, *der*/Notarin, *die*

notation /nəʊˈteɪʃn/ *n.* (Math., Mus., Chem.) Notation, *die* (fachspr.); Notierung, *die*

notch /nɒtʃ/ **1** *n.* Kerbe, *die;* (in damaged blade) Scharte, *die;* (in belt) Loch, *das.* **2** *v.t.* kerben

∼ **'up** *v.t.* erreichen; aufstellen ‹*Rekord*›; erringen ‹*Sieg*›

note /nəʊt/ **1** *n.* **(a)** (Mus.) (sign) Note, *die;* (key of piano) Taste, *die;* (single sound) Ton, *der;* **strike the right** ∼ ‹*Sprecher, Redner, Brief:*› den richtigen Ton treffen; **hit the wrong** ∼: einen falschen Ton anschlagen; **(b)** (tone of expression) [Unter]ton, *der;* ∼ **of caution/anger** warnender/ärgerlicher [Unter]ton; **on a** ∼ **of optimism, on an optimistic** ∼: in optimistischem Ton; **his voice had a peevish** ∼: seine Stimme klang gereizt; **a festive** ∼, **a** ∼ **of festivity** eine festliche Note; **(c)** (jotting) Notiz, *die;* **take** *or* **make** ∼s sich (*Dat.*) Notizen machen; **take** *or* **make a** ∼ **of sth.** sich (*Dat.*) etw. notieren; **speak without** ∼s frei sprechen; **(d)** (annotation, foot∼) Anmerkung, *die;* **(e)** (short letter) [kurzer] Brief; **(f)** *no pl., no art.* (importance) Bedeutung, *die;* **person/sth. of** ∼: bedeutende Persönlichkeit/etw. Bedeutendes; **nothing of** ∼: nichts von Bedeutung; **be of** ∼: bedeutend sein; **(g)** *no pl., no art.* (attention) Beachtung, *die;* **worthy of** ∼: beachtenswert; **take** ∼ **of sth.** (heed) einer Sache (*Dat.*) Beachtung schenken; (notice) etw. zur Kenntnis nehmen. **2** *v.t.* **(a)** (pay attention to) beachten; **(b)** (notice) bemerken; **(c)** (set down) ∼ [**down**] [sich (*Dat.*)] notieren

note: ∼**book** *n.* **(a)** Notizbuch, *das;* (for lecture ∼s) Kollegheft, *das;* **(b)** ∼**book** [**computer**] Notebook, *das;* ∼**case** *n.* Brieftasche, *die*

noted /'nəʊtɪd/ *adj.* bekannt, berühmt (**for** für, wegen)

note: ∼**pad** *n.* Notizblock, *der;* ∼**paper** *n.* Briefpapier, *das;* ∼**worthy** *adj.* bemerkenswert

not-for-'profit *attrib. adj.* (Amer.) nicht profitorientiert; nicht gewinnorientiert

nothing /'nʌθɪŋ/ **1** *n.* **(a)** nichts; ∼ **interesting** nichts Interessantes; ∼ **much** nichts Besonderes; ∼ **more than** nur; ∼ **more,** ∼ **less** nicht mehr, nicht weniger; **I should like** ∼ **more than sth./to do sth.** ich würde etw. nur zu gern haben/tun; **next to** ∼: so gut wie nichts; **it's** ∼ **less than suicidal to do this** es ist reiner *od.* glatter Selbstmord, dies zu tun; ∼ **else than,** ∼ [**else**] **but** nur; **there was** ∼ [**else**] **for it but to do sth.** es blieb nichts anderes übrig, als etw. zu tun; **he is** ∼ **if not active** wenn er eins ist, dann [ist er] aktiv; **there is** ∼ **in it** (in race etc.) es ist noch nichts entschieden; (it is untrue) es ist nichts daran wahr; **there is** ∼ **'to it** es ist kinderleicht (fam.); ∼ **ventured** ∼ **gained** (prov.) wer nicht wagt, der nicht gewinnt (Spr.); £**300 is** ∼ **to him** 300 Pfund sind ein Klacks für ihn (ugs.); **have** [**got**] *or* **be** ∼ **to do with sb./sth.** (not concern) nichts zu tun haben mit jmdm./etw.; **have** ∼ **to do with sb./sth.** (avoid) jmdm./einer Sache aus dem Weg gehen; [**not**] **for** ∼: [nicht] umsonst; **count** *or* **go for** ∼ (be unappreciated) ‹*Person:*› nicht zählen; (be profitless) ‹*Arbeit, Bemühung:*› umsonst *od.* vergebens sein; **have** [**got**] ∼ **on sb./sth.** (be inferior to) nicht mit jmdm./etw. zu vergleichen sein; **have** [**got**] ∼ **on sb.** (know ∼ bad about) nichts gegen jmdn. in der Hand haben; **have** ∼ **'on** (be naked) nichts anhaben; (have no engagements) nichts vorhaben; **make** ∼ **of sth.** (make light of) keine große Sache aus etw. machen; (not understand) mit etw. nichts anfangen [können]; **it means** ∼ **to me** (is not understood) ich werde nicht klug daraus; (is not loved) es bedeutet mir nichts; **to say** ∼ **of** ganz zu schweigen von; **(b)** (zero) **multiply by** ∼: mit null multiplizieren; **(c)** (trifling event) Nichtigkeit, *die;* (trifling person) Nichts, *das;* Niemand, *der;* **soft** *or* **sweet** ∼s Zärtlichkeiten *Pl.* **2** *adv.* keineswegs; ∼ **near so bad as** …: nicht annähernd so schlecht wie …

notice /'nəʊtɪs/ **1** *n.* **(a)** Anschlag, *der;* Aushang, *der;* (in newspaper) Anzeige, *die;* **no-smoking** ∼: Rauchverbotsschild, *das;* **(b)** (warning) **give** [**sb.**] [**three days'**] ∼ **of** one's arrival [jmdm.] seine Ankunft [drei Tage vorher] mitteilen; **have** [**no**] ∼ [**of sth.**] [von etw.] [keine] Kenntnis haben; **at short/a moment's/ten minutes'** ∼: kurzfristig/von einem Augenblick zum andern/innerhalb von zehn Minuten; **(c)** (formal notification) Ankündigung, *die;* **until further** ∼: bis auf weiteres; ∼ **is given of sth.** etw. wird angekündigt; **(d)** (ending an agreement) Kündigung, *die;* **give sb. a month's** ∼: jmdm. mit einer Frist von einem Monat kündigen; **hand in one's** ∼, **give** ∼

(Brit.), **give one's** ∼ (Amer.) kündigen; **(e)** (attention) Beachtung, *die;* **bring sb./sth. to sb.'s** ∼: jmdn. auf jmdn./etw. aufmerksam machen; **it has come to my** ∼ **that** …: ich habe bemerkt *od.* mir ist aufgefallen, dass …; **take no** ∼ **of sb./sth.** (not observe) jmdn./etw. nicht bemerken; (disregard) keine Notiz von jmdm./etw. nehmen; **take** ∼ **of sb.:** sich nicht darum kümmern; **take** ∼ **of** wahrnehmen; hören auf ‹*Rat*›; zur Kenntnis nehmen ‹*Leistung*›; **(f)** (review) Besprechung, *die;* Rezension, *die.* **2** *v.t.* **(a)** (perceive, take notice of) bemerken; *abs.* **I pretended not to** ∼: ich tat so, als ob ich es nicht bemerkte; **(b)** (remark upon) erwähnen

noticeable /'nəʊtɪsəbl/ *adj.* (perceptible) wahrnehmbar ‹*Fleck, Schaden, Geruch*›; merklich ‹*Verbesserung*›; spürbar ‹*Mangel*›

noticeably /'nəʊtɪsəblɪ/ *adv.* sichtlich ‹*größer, kleiner*›; merklich ‹*verändern*›; spürbar ‹*kälter*›

'noticeboard *n.* (Brit.) Anschlagtafel, *die*

notification /nəʊtɪfɪ'keɪʃn/ *n.* Mitteilung, *die* (**of sb.** an jmdn.; **of sth.** über etw. (*Akk.*))

notify /'nəʊtɪfaɪ/ *v.t.* **(a)** (make known) ankündigen; **(b)** (inform) benachrichtigen (**of** über + *Akk.*)

notion /'nəʊʃn/ *n.* **(a)** Vorstellung, *die;* **not have the faintest/least** ∼ **of how/what** *etc.* nicht die blasseste/geringste Ahnung haben, wie/was *usw.;* **he has no** ∼ **of time** er hat kein Verhältnis zur Zeit; **(b)** (knack, inkling) **have no** ∼ **of sth.** keine Ahnung von etw. haben

notoriety /nəʊtə'raɪətɪ/ *n., no pl.* traurige Berühmtheit

notorious /nə'tɔːrɪəs/ *adj.* bekannt; (infamous) berüchtigt; notorisch ‹*Lügner*›; niederträchtig ‹*List*›; **be** *or* **have become** ∼ **for sth.** wegen *od.* für etw. bekannt/berüchtigt sein

notoriously /nə'tɔːrɪəslɪ/ *adv.* notorisch

notwithstanding /nɒtwɪθ'stændɪŋ, nɒtwɪð'stændɪŋ/ **1** *prep.* ungeachtet. **2** *adv.* dennoch; dessen ungeachtet. **3** *conj.* ∼ **that** …: ungeachtet dessen, dass …

nougat /'nuːgɑː/ *n.* Nougat, *das od. der*

nought /nɔːt/ *n.* ► **956**| Null, *die;* ∼**s and crosses** (Brit.) *Spiel, bei dem innerhalb eines Feldes von Kästchen Dreierreihen von Kreisen bzw. Kreuzen zu erzielen sind*

noun /naʊn/ *n.* (Ling.) Substantiv, *das;* Hauptwort, *das;* Nomen, *das* (fachspr.)

nourish /'nʌrɪʃ/ *v.t.* ernähren (**on** mit); (fig.) nähren (geh.)

nourishing /'nʌrɪʃɪŋ/ *adj.* nahrhaft

nourishment /'nʌrɪʃmənt/ *n.* (food) Nahrung, *die*

nous /naʊs/ *n.* (coll.) Grips, *der* (ugs.); **use a bit of** ∼: seinen Grips ein bisschen anstrengen

nouveau riche /nuːvəʊ 'riːʃ/ **1** *n., pl.* **nouveaux riches** /nuːvəʊ 'riːʃ/ Neureiche, *der/die.* **2** *adj.* neureich

Nov. *abbr.* **November** Nov.

novel /'nɒvl/ **1** *n.* Roman, *der.* **2** *adj.* neuartig

novelist /'nɒvəlɪst/ *n.* Romanautor, *der*/-autorin, *die*

novella /nə'velə/ *n.* Novelle, *die*

novelty /'nɒvltɪ/ *n.* **(a)** **be a/no** ∼: etwas/nichts Neues sein; **(b)** (newness) Neuheit, *die;* Neuartigkeit, *die;* **(c)** (gadget) Überraschung, *die*

November /nə'vembə(r)/ *n.* ► **738**| November, *der; see also* **August**

novice /'nɒvɪs/ *n.* **(a)** (Relig.) Novize, *der*/Novizin, *die;* **(b)** (beginner) Anfänger, *der*/Anfängerin, *die*

now /naʊ/ **1** *adv.* **(a)** jetzt; (nowadays) heutzutage; (immediately) [jetzt] sofort; (this time) [schon wieder]; **just** ∼ (very recently) gerade eben; (at this particular time) gerade jetzt; [**every**] ∼ **and then** *or* **again** hin und wieder; [**it's**] ∼ **or never!** jetzt oder nie!; **(b)** (not referring to time) **well** ∼: also; ∼, ∼: na, na; ∼, **what happened is this** …: also, passiert ist Folgendes: …; ∼ **then** na (ugs.); **quickly** ∼! nun aber schnell. **2** *conj.* ∼ [**that**] …: jetzt, wo *od.* da … **3** *n.* ∼ **is the time to do sth.** es ist jetzt an der Zeit, etw. zu tun; **before** ∼: früher; **up to** *or* **until** ∼: bis jetzt; **never before** ∼: noch nie; **by** ∼: inzwischen; **a week from** ∼: [heute] in einer Woche; **between** ∼ **and Friday** bis Freitag; **from** ∼ **on** von jetzt an; **as of** ∼: jetzt; **that's all for** ∼: das ist im Augenblick alles; **bye** *etc.* **for** ∼! (coll.) bis bald!

Numbers

Cardinal numbers = Kardinalzahlen

0 *(nought, zero)* = null
1 *(one)* = eins, ein...[1]
2 *(two)* = zwei
3 *(three)* = drei
4 *(four)* = vier
5 *(five)* = fünf
6 *(six)* = sechs
7 *(seven)* = sieben
8 *(eight)* = acht
9 *(nine)* = neun
10 *(ten)* = zehn
11 *(eleven)* = elf
12 *(twelve)* = zwölf
13 *(thirteen)* = dreizehn
14 *(fourteen)* = vierzehn
15 *(fifteen)* = fünfzehn
16 *(sixteen)* = sechzehn
17 *(seventeen)* = siebzehn
18 *(eighteen)* = achtzehn
19 *(nineteen)* = neunzehn
20 *(twenty)* = zwanzig
21 *(twenty-one)* = einundzwanzig
22 *(twenty-two)* = zweiundzwanzig
30 *(thirty)* = dreißig
40 *(forty)* = vierzig
50 *(fifty)* = fünfzig
60 *(sixty)* = sechzig
70 *(seventy)* = siebzig
80 *(eighty)* = achtzig
90 *(ninety)* = neunzig
100 *(a or one hundred)* = [ein]hundert
101 *(a or one hundred and one)* = [ein]hundert[und]ein[s][2]
555 *(five hundred and fifty-five)* = fünfhundert[und]fünfundfünfzig
1,000 *(a or one thousand)* = [ein]tausend[3]
1,001 *(a or one thousand and one)* = [ein]tausend[und]ein[s][2]
1,200 *(one thousand two hundred or twelve hundred)* = [ein]tausendzweihundert *or* zwölfhundert[4]
100,000 *(a or one hundred thousand)* = [ein]hunderttausend
1,000,000 *(a or one million)* = eine Million
3,536,000 *(three million five hundred and thirty-six thousand)* = drei Millionen fünfhundertsechsund-dreißigtausend
1,000,000,000 *(a or one billion, a or one thousand million)* = eine Milliarde
1,000,000,000,000 *(a or one trillion, a or one million million)* = eine Billion

[1] The form **eins** is used when the number appears on its own, e.g. when counting (eins, zwei, drei), calculating, giving times or scores (*a quarter to one* = Viertel vor eins, *to win one-nil* = eins zu null gewinnen) or quoting decimals (*O point one* = null Komma eins, *one point five* = eins Komma fünf).

Where the number comes before a noun, it is treated like an indefinite article and declined accordingly.

I would like one large knob and two small ones	= Ich möchte einen großen Knopf und zwei kleine
You mustn't use one new battery and three old ones	= Man darf nicht eine neue Batterie und drei alte verwenden

For other uses see the entry for *one*.

In larger numbers ending in **eins** it is not usually declined before a noun

201 days	= zweihundert[und]eins Tage

But note

A Thousand and one Nights =	Tausendundeine Nacht

[2] The bracketed **und** is usually included in numbers from 101 to 109, but omitted from 110 (hundertzehn) onwards when counting. The bracketed **ein** may be included for emphasis. For the use of the final **s** see the note on **eins** above.

[3] Where English style usually has a comma for thousands, Continental European usage has a space:

1,000 = 1 000; 5,500 = 5 500; 123,467 = 123 467; 6,327,456 = 6 327 456

[4] Note that in dates the **hundert** should not be omitted:

1895 = eighteen ninety-five =	achtzehnhundert-fünfundneunzig

Fractions = Brüche

½	ein halb	1½	ein[und]einhalb
¼	ein viertel	2¾	zwei[und]dreiviertel
⅓	ein drittel	5⅔	fünf[und]zweidrittel
⅛	ein achtel	8⅞	acht[und]siebenachtel

Fractions are formed in German by adding **-tel** to the number, except where the number ends in **t**, **d** or **g**. In these cases an **s** is inserted before the **-tel**:

ein hundertstel   ein tausendstel   ein zwanzigstel

The fractions are written as above with a small letter in a calculation or with units of measure, but when combined with other nouns they are written with a capital:

two thirds of the distance	= zwei Drittel des Weges

one eighth of the amount	= ein Achtel des Betrages

but:

an eighth of a litre	= ein achtel Liter, ein Achtelliter

Note that with measures, "of a" is not translated and the fraction is often written with the unit to form one word. Also with plural fractions the unit of measure is in the plural:

five eighths of a mile	= fünf achtel Meilen
six hundredths of a second	= sechs hundertstel Sekunden, sechs Hundertstelsekunden

▶

▶ **Numbers** continued

Ordinal numbers = Ordinalzahlen

1st (first) = 1. (erst...)[5]
2nd (second) = 2. (zweit...)
3rd (third) = 3. (dritt...)
4th (fourth) = 4. (viert...)
5th (fifth) = 5. (fünft...)
6th (sixth) = 6. (sechst...)
7th (seventh) = 7. (sieb[en]t...)
8th (eighth) = 8. (acht...)
9th (ninth) = 9. (neunt...)
10th (tenth) = 10. (zehnt...)
11th (eleventh) = 11. (elft...)
12th (twelfth) = 12. (zwölft...)
13th (thirteenth) = 13. (dreizehnt...)
14th (fourteenth) = 14. (vierzehnt...)
15th (fifteenth) = 15. (fünfzehnt...)
16th (sixteenth) = 16. (sechzehnt...)
17th (seventeenth) = 17. (siebzehnt...)
18th (eighteenth) = 18. (achtzehnt...)
19th (nineteenth) = 19. (neunzehnt...)
20th (twentieth) = 20. (zwanzigst...)
21st (twenty-first) = 21. (einundzwanzigst...)
22nd (twenty-second) = 22. (zweiundzwanzigst...)
30th (thirtieth) = 30. (dreißigst...)
40th (fortieth) = 40. (vierzigst...)
50th (fiftieth) = 50. (fünfzigst...)
60th (sixtieth) = 60. (sechzigst...)
70th (seventieth) = 70. (siebzigst...)
80th (eightieth) = 80. (achtzigst...)
90th (ninetieth) = 90. (neunzigst...)
100th ([one] hundredth) = 100. ([ein]hundertst...)
101st ([one] hundred and first) = 101. ([ein]hundert[und]erst...)
555th (five hundred and fifty-fifth) = 555. (fünfhundert[und]fünfundfünfzigst...)
1,000th ([one] thousandth) = 1 000. ([ein]tausendst...)
1,001st (one thousand and first) = 1 001. ([ein]tausend[und]erst...)
1,200th (one thousand two hundredth or twelve hundredth) = 1 200. ([ein]tausendzweihundertst... or zwölfhundertst...)
100,000th ([one] hundred thousandth) = 100 000. ([ein]hunderttausendst...)
1,000,000th ([one] millionth) = 1 000 000. (millionst...)
3,536,000th (three million five hundred and thirty-six thousandth) = 3 536 000. (drei Millionen fünfhundertsechsunddreißigtausendst...)
1,000,000,000th ([one] billionth, [one] thousand millionth) = 1 000 000 000. (milliardst...)
1,000,000,000,000th ([one] trillionth, [one] million millionth) = 1 000 000 000 000. (billionst...)

[5] Ordinal numbers are conjugated like adjectives:

the first time	= das erste Mal
her ninetieth birthday	= ihr neunzigster Geburtstag
at the tenth attempt	= beim zehnten Versuch
the end of his fifth symphony	= der Schluss seiner fünften Symphonie

For the use of ordinals in dates, *see* □ **Dates**

For order in races, note the following phrases:

He came (in) first	= Er kam als Erster ins Ziel
She finished third	= Sie ging als Dritte durchs Ziel *or* belegte den dritten Platz
I was sixth	= Ich wurde Sechster/Sechste

Decimal numbers = Dezimalzahlen

0.1	= 0,1 (null Komma eins)
0.015	= 0,015 (null Komma null eins fünf)
1.43	= 1,43 (eins Komma vier drei)
11.70	= 11,70 (elf Komma sieben null)
12.333 recurring	= 12,$\bar{3}$ (zwölf Komma Periode drei)

Calculations

7 + 3 = 10 (sieben plus drei ist [gleich] zehn)
10 − 3 = 7 (zehn minus drei ist [gleich] sieben)
10 x 3 = 30 (zehn mal *or* multipliziert mit drei ist [gleich] dreißig)
30 ÷ 3 = 10 (dreißig [dividiert *or* geteilt] durch drei ist [gleich] zehn)

Powers = Potenzen

3^2 = *three squared* = drei [im *or* zum] Quadrat, drei hoch zwei
3^3 = *three cubed* = drei hoch drei
3^{10} = *three to the power of ten* = drei hoch zehn
$\sqrt{25}$ = *the square root of twenty-five* = die [Quadrat]wurzel aus fünfundzwanzig

See also □ **Age**, **Area**, **the Clock**, **Distance**, **Height and Depth**, **Length and Width**, **Money**, **Temperature**, **Volume**, and **Weight**.

nowadays /'naʊədeɪz/ *adv.* heutzutage

nowhere /'nəʊweə(r)/ **1** *adv.* **(a)** (in no place) nirgends; nirgendwo; **(b)** (to no place) nirgendwohin; **(c)** ~ **near** (not even nearly) nicht annähernd. **2** *pron.* **come from** ~: wie aus dem Nichts auftauchen; **get** ~ (make no progress) nicht vorankommen; (have no success) nichts erreichen; **get sb.** ~: [jmdm.] nichts nützen

noxious /'nɒkʃəs/ *adj.* giftig

nozzle /'nɒzl/ *n.* Düse, *die*

NSPCC *abbr.* (Brit.) **National Society for the Prevention of Cruelty to Children** ≈ Kinderschutzbund, *der*

nth /enθ/ ⇒ **N, n**

nuance /'nju:ɑ̃s/ *n.* Nuance, *die*

nubile /'nju:baɪl/ *adj.* (sexy) sexy (ugs.); anziehend

nuclear /'nju:klɪə(r)/ *adj.* **(a)** Kern-; **(b)** (using ~ energy or weapons) Atom-; Kern〈*explosion, -technik*〉; atomar 〈*Antrieb, Gefechtskopf, Bedrohung, Gegenschlag, Wettrüsten*〉; nuklear 〈*Abschreckungspotenzial, Sprengkörper, Streitkräfte*〉; atomgetrieben 〈*Unterseeboot, Schiff*〉

nuclear: ~ **de'terrent** *n.* atomare *od.* nukleare Abschreckung; ~ **dis'armament** *n.* atomare *od.* nukleare Abrüstung; ~ **'energy** *n., no pl.* Atom- *od.* Kernenergie, *die;* ~ **'family** *n.* (Sociol.) Kernfamilie, *die;* ~ **'fission** *n.* Kernspaltung, *die;* ~**-free** *adj.* atomwaffenfrei 〈*Zone*〉; ~ **'physics** *n.* Kernphysik, *die;* ~ **'power** *n.* **(a)** Atom- *od.* Kernkraft, *die;* **(b)** (country) Atom- *od.* Nuklearmacht, *die;* ~ **'power station** *n.* Atom- *od.* Kernkraftwerk, *das;* ~ **'warfare** *n., no pl.* Atomkrieg, *der;* ~ **'waste** *n.* Atommüll, *der*

nuclei *pl. of* **nucleus**

nucleus /'nju:klɪəs/ *n., pl.* **nuclei** /'nju:klɪaɪ/ Kern, *der*

nude /nju:d/ **1** *adj.* nackt; ~ **figure** Akt, *der.* **2** *n.* **(a)** (Art: figure) Akt, *der;* **(b) in the** ~: nackt

nudge /nʌdʒ/ **1** *v.t.* (push gently) anstoßen. **2** *n.* Stoß, *der;* Puff, *der;* **give sb. a** ~: jmdn. anstoßen

nudist /'nju:dɪst/ *n.* Nudist, *der*/Nudistin, *die;* FKK-Anhänger, *der*/-Anhängerin, *die*

nudity /'nju:dɪtɪ/ *n.* Nacktheit, *die*

nugget /'nʌgɪt/ *n.* (Mining) Klumpen, *der;* (of gold) Goldklumpen, *der;* Nugget, *das*

nuisance /'nju:səns/ *n.* Ärgernis, *das;* Plage, *die;* **what a** ~! so etwas Dummes!; **make a** ~ **of oneself** lästig werden

null /nʌl/ *adj.* (Law) **declare sth.** ~ **[and void]** etw. für null und nichtig erklären

nullify /'nʌlɪfaɪ/ *v.t.* für null und nichtig *od.* rechtsungültig erklären 〈*Vertrag, Testament*〉

numb /nʌm/ **1** *adj.* (without sensation) gefühllos, taub (**with** vor + *Dat.*); (fig.: without emotion) benommen. **2** *v.t.* 〈*Kälte, Schock:*〉 gefühllos machen; 〈*Narkosemittel:*〉 betäuben

number /'nʌmbə(r)/ **1** *n.* ▶ **956** **(a)** (in series) Nummer, *die;* ~ **3 West Street** West Street [Nr.] 3; **the** ~ **of sb.'s car** jmds. Autonummer; **you've got the wrong** ~ (Teleph.) Sie sind falsch verbunden; **dial a wrong** ~: sich verwählen (ugs.); ~ **one** (oneself) man selbst; *attrib.* Nummer eins *nachgestellt;* Spitzen〈*position, -platz*〉; **take care of** *or* **look after** ~ **one** an sich (*Akk.*) selbst denken; **N**~ **Ten [Downing Street]** (Brit.) Amtssitz des britischen Premierministers/der britischen Premierministerin; **sb.'s** ~ **is up** (coll.) jmds. Stunde hat geschlagen; **(b)** (esp. Math.: numeral) Zahl, *die;* **(c)** (sum, total, quantity) [An]zahl, *die;* **a** ~ **of people/things** einige Leute/Dinge; **a** ~ **of times/on a** ~ **of occasions** mehrfach *od.* -mals; **a small** ~: eine geringe [An]zahl; **large** ~s eine große [An]zahl; **in [large** *or* **great]** ~s in großer Zahl; **in a small** ~ **of cases** in einigen wenigen Fällen; **any** ~: beliebig viele; **on any** ~ **of occasions** oft[mals]; **in** ~[s] zahlenmäßig 〈*überlegen sein, überwiegen*〉; **(d)** (person, song, turn, edition) Nummer, *die;* **(e)** (coll.: outfit) Kluft, *die;* **(f)** (company) **he was [one] of our** ~: er war einer von uns. **2** *v.t.* **(a)** (assign ~ to) beziffern; nummerieren; **(b)** (amount to, comprise) zählen; **the nominations** ~**ed ten in all** es wurden insgesamt zehn Kandidaten nominiert; **(c)** (include, regard as) zählen, rechnen (**among, with** zu); **(d) be** ~**ed** (be limited) begrenzt sein; **sb.'s days** *or* **years are** ~**ed** jmds. Tage sind gezählt

numberless /'nʌmbəlɪs/ *adj.* unzählig; zahllos

'number plate *n.* Nummernschild, *das*

numbness /'nʌmnɪs/ *n., no pl.* (caused by cold) Gefühllosigkeit, *die;* Taubheit, *die;* (caused by anaesthetic, sleeping pill) Betäubung, *die;* (fig.: stupor) Benommenheit, *die*

numeracy /'nju:mərəsɪ/ *n.* rechnerische Fähigkeiten *Pl.*

numeral /'nju:mrəl/ *n.* Ziffer, *die;* (word) Zahlwort, *das*

numerate /'nju:mərət/ *adj.* rechenkundig; **be** ~: rechnen können

numerator /'nju:məreɪtə(r)/ *n.* (Math.) Zähler, *der*

numerical /nju:'merɪkl/ *adj.* Zahlen〈*wert, -folge*〉; numerisch 〈*Reihenfolge, Stärke*〉; zahlenmäßig 〈*Überlegenheit*〉

numerous /'nju:mərəs/ *adj.* zahlreich

nun /nʌn/ *n.* Nonne, *die*

nunnery /'nʌnərɪ/ *n.* [Nonnen]kloster, *das*

nurse /nɜ:s/ **1** *n.* ▶ **887** Krankenschwester, *die;* **[male]** ~: Krankenpfleger, *der.* **2** *v.t.* **(a)** (act as ~ to) pflegen 〈*Kranke*〉; ~ **sb. back to health** jmdn. gesundpflegen; **(b)** (suckle) die Brust geben (+ *Dat.*), stillen 〈*Säugling*〉; **(c)** (cradle) vorsichtig halten; wiegen 〈*Baby*〉; **(d)** (treat carefully) ~ **gently/carefully** behutsam *od.* schonend umgehen mit. **3** *v.i.* **(a)** (act as wet-~) stillen; **(b)** (be a sick-~) Krankenschwester/-pfleger sein

'nursemaid *n.* (lit. or fig.) Kindermädchen, *das*

nursery /'nɜ:sərɪ/ *n.* **(a)** (room for children) Kinderzimmer, *das;* **(b)** (crèche) Kindertagesstätte, *die;* **(c)** ⇒ **nursery school;** **(d)** (Agric.) (for plants) Gärtnerei, *die;* (for trees) Baumschule, *die*

nursery: ~ **rhyme** *n.* Kinderreim, *der;* ~ **school** *n.* Kindergarten, *der;* ~**-school teacher** *n.* ▶ **887** (female) Kindergärtnerin, *die;* Erzieherin, *die;* (male) Erzieher, *der*

nursing /'nɜ:sɪŋ/ *n., no pl., no art.* ▶ **887** (profession) Krankenpflege, *die; attrib.* Pflege〈*personal, -beruf*〉

nursing: ~ **home** *n.* (Brit.) (for the aged, infirm) Pflegeheim, *das;* (for convalescents) Genesungsheim, *das;* (maternity hospital) Entbindungsheim, *das;* ~ **'mother** *n.* stillende Mutter

nurture /'nɜ:tʃə(r)/ *v.t.* **(a)** (rear) aufziehen; **(b)** (fig.) nähren (geh.)

nut /nʌt/ *n.* **(a)** Nuss, *die;* **be a hard** *or* **tough** ~ **[to crack]** 〈*Problem usw.*〉 eine harte Nuss sein (ugs.); **(b)** (Mech. Engin.) (Schrauben)mutter, *die;* ~**s and bolts** (fig.) praktische Grundlagen *Pl.*; **(c)** (coll.: head) Kürbis, *der* (salopp); **(d)** (crazy person) Verrückte, *der/die* (ugs.)

nut: ~**case** *n.* (coll.) Verrückte, *der/die* (ugs.); ~**crackers** *n. pl.* Nussknacker, *der*

nutmeg /'nʌtmeg/ *n.* Muskatnuss, *die;* Muskat, *der*

nutrient /'nju:trɪənt/ **1** *adj.* **(a)** (serving as nourishment) nahrhaft; **(b)** (providing nourishment) Ernährungs-; Nähr〈*salze, -lösung*〉. **2** *n.* Nährstoff, *der*

nutrition /nju:'trɪʃn/ *n.* (nourishment, diet) Ernährung, *die*

nutritious /nju:'trɪʃəs/ *adj.* nahrhaft

nuts /nʌts/ *pred. adj.* (coll.) verrückt (ugs.) (**about, on** nach)

'nutshell *n.* **(a)** Nussschale, *die;* **(b)** (fig.) **in a** ~: kurz gesagt

nutter /'nʌtə(r)/ *n.* (sl.) Verrückte, *der/die* (ugs.)

nutty /'nʌtɪ/ *adj.* **(a)** (in taste) nussig; **(b)** (coll.: crazy) verrückt (ugs.)

nuzzle /'nʌzl/ *v.i.* (nestle) sich kuscheln (**up to, at, against** an + *Akk.*)

NVQ *abbr.* (Brit.) **National Vocational Qualification**

NW *abbr.* /'nɔ:θwest/ ▶ **715** **north-west** NW

nylon /'naɪlɒn/ *n.* **(a)** *no pl.* (Textiles) Nylon, *das; attrib.* Nylon-; **(b)** *in pl.* (stockings) Nylonstrümpfe; Nylons (ugs.)

nymph /nɪmf/ *n.* Nymphe, *die*

nymphomaniac /nɪmfə'meɪnɪæk/ *n.* Nymphomanin, *die*

NZ *abbr.* **New Zealand**

O o

O, o /əʊ/ *n., pl.* **Os** *or* **O's** (a) (letter) O, o, *das;* (b) (zero) Null, *die*

oaf /əʊf/ *n., pl.* **~s** (a) (stupid person) Dummkopf, *der* (ugs.); (b) (awkward lout) Stoffel, *der* (ugs.)

oak /əʊk/ *n.* Eiche, *die; attrib.* Eichen⟨*wald, -möbel, -kiste, -blatt*⟩

'**oak tree** *n.* Eiche, *die*

OAP *abbr.* (Brit.) **old-age pensioner** Rentner, *der/* Rentnerin, *die;* **~ club** Seniorenklub, *der*

oar /ɔ:(r)/ *n.* Ruder, *das;* Riemen, *der* (Sport, Seemannsspr.); **put one's ~ in** (fig. coll.) seinen Senf dazugeben

oarsman /'ɔ:zmən/ *n., pl.* **oarsmen** /'ɔ:zmən/ Ruderer, *der*

oasis /əʊ'eɪsɪs/ *n., pl.* **oases** /əʊ'eɪsi:z/ (lit. or fig.) Oase, *die*

oast house /'əʊsthaʊs/ *n.* (Agric., Brewing) Hopfendarre, *die*

oat /əʊt/ *n.* **~s** Hafer, *der;* **rolled ~s** Haferflocken *Pl.;* **sow one's wild ~s** (fig.) sich (*Dat.*) die Hörner abstoßen (ugs.)

oath /əʊθ/ *n., pl.* **~s** /əʊðz/ (a) Eid, *der;* Schwur, *der;* **take** *or* **swear an ~** [**on sth.**] **that …:** einen Eid [auf etw. (*Akk.*)] schwören, dass …; (b) (Law) **swear** *or* **take the ~:** vereidigt werden; **on** *or* **under ~:** unter Eid; **put sb. on** *or* **under ~:** jmdn. vereidigen *od.* unter Eid nehmen; (c) (expletive) Fluch, *der*

'**oatmeal** *n.* Hafermehl, *das*

obdurate /'ɒbdjʊərət/ *adj.* (hardened) unerbittlich ⟨*Brutalität*⟩; verstockt ⟨*Herz, Sünder*⟩; (stubborn) verstockt; hartnäckig ⟨*Weigerung, Ablehnung*⟩

OBE *abbr.* (Brit.) **Officer [of the Order] of the British Empire**

obedience /ə'bi:dɪəns/ *n.* Gehorsam, *der;* **show ~:** gehorsam sein

obedient /ə'bi:dɪənt/ *adj.* gehorsam; (submissive) fügsam; **be ~ to sb./sth.** jmdm./einer Sache gehorchen

obelisk /'ɒbəlɪsk/ *n.* Obelisk, *der*

obese /əʊ'bi:s/ *adj.* fett (abwertend); fettleibig (bes. Med.)

obesity /əʊ'bi:sɪtɪ/ *n., no pl.* Fettheit, *die* (abwertend); Fettleibigkeit, *die* (bes. Med.)

obey /ə'beɪ/ **1** *v.t.* gehorchen (+ *Dat.*); ⟨*Kind, Hund:*⟩ folgen (+ *Dat.*), gehorchen (+ *Dat.*); sich halten an (+ *Akk.*) ⟨*Vorschrift, Regel*⟩; befolgen ⟨*Befehl*⟩. **2** *v.i.* gehorchen

obituary /ə'bɪtjʊərɪ/ **1** *n.* Nachruf, *der* (**to, of** auf + *Akk.*); (notice of death) Todesanzeige, *die.* **2** *adj.* **~ notice/ memoir** Todesanzeige, *die/*Nachruf, *der;* **the ~ page/ column** die Todesanzeigen

object 1 /'ɒbdʒɪkt/ *n.* (a) (thing) Gegenstand, *der;* (Philos.) Objekt, *das;* (b) (purpose) Ziel, *das;* **with this ~ in mind** *or* **view** mit diesem Ziel [vor Augen]; **with the ~ of doing sth.** in der Absicht, etw. zu tun; (c) (obstacle) **money/ time** *etc.* **is no ~:** Geld/Zeit *usw.* spielt keine Rolle; (d) (Ling.) Objekt, *das.* **2** /əb'dʒekt/ *v.i.* (a) (state objection) Einwände/einen Einwand erheben (**to** gegen); (protest) protestieren (**to** gegen); (b) (have objection or dislike) etwas dagegen haben; **~ to sb./sth.** etwas gegen jmdn./etw. haben; **if you don't ~:** wenn Sie nichts dagegen haben; **~ to sb.'s doing sth.** etwas dagegen haben, dass jmd. etw. tut; **I strongly ~ to this tone** ich verbitte mir diesen Ton. **3** *v.t.* /əb'dʒekt/ einwenden

objection /əb'dʒekʃn/ *n.* (a) Einwand, *der;* Einspruch, *der* (Amtsspr., Rechtsw.); **raise** *or* **make an ~** [**to sth.**] einen Einwand *od.* (Rechtsw.) Einspruch [gegen etw.] erheben; **make no ~ to sth.** nichts gegen etw. einzuwenden haben; (b) (feeling of opposition or dislike) Abneigung, *die;* **have an/no ~ to sb./sth.** etw./nichts gegen jmdn./etw. haben; **have an/no ~:** etwas/nichts dagegen haben

objectionable /əb'dʒekʃənəbl/ *adj.* unangenehm ⟨*Anblick, Geruch*⟩; anstößig ⟨*Wort, Benehmen*⟩; unausstehlich ⟨*Kind*⟩

objective /əb'dʒektɪv/ **1** *adj.* (unbiased) objektiv. **2** *n.* (goal) Ziel, *das*

objectively /əb'dʒektɪvlɪ/ *adv.* objektiv

objectivity /ɒbdʒɪk'tɪvɪtɪ/ *n., no pl.* Objektivität, *die*

'**object lesson** *n.* (warning) Denkzettel, *der;* (very clear example) Musterbeispiel, *das* (**in, on** für)

objector /əb'dʒektə(r)/ *n.* Gegner, *der/*Gegnerin, *die* (**to** Gen.)

obligation /ɒblɪ'geɪʃn/ *n.* Verpflichtung, *die;* (constraint) Zwang, *der;* **be under** *or* **have an/no ~ to do sth.** verpflichtet/nicht verpflichtet sein, etw. zu tun; **there's no ~ to buy** es besteht kein Kaufzwang

obligatory /ə'blɪgətərɪ/ *adj.* obligatorisch; **make sth. ~ for sb.** etw. für jmdn. vorschreiben; **it has become ~ to do sth.** es ist zur Pflicht geworden, etw. zu tun

oblige /ə'blaɪdʒ/ **1** *v.t.* (a) (be binding on) **~ sb. to do sth.** jmdm. vorschreiben, etw. zu tun; **one is ~d by law to do sth.** etw. ist gesetzlich vorgeschrieben; (b) (constrain, compel) zwingen, nötigen; **you are not ~d to answer these questions** Sie sind nicht verpflichtet, diese Fragen zu beantworten; **feel ~d to do sth.** sich verpflichtet fühlen, etw. zu tun; (c) (be kind to) **~ sb. by doing sth.** jmdm. den Gefallen tun und etw. tun; **~ sb. with sth.** (help out) jmdm. mit etw. aushelfen; **could you ~ me with a lift?** könnten Sie mich freundlicherweise mitnehmen?; (d) **~d** (bound by gratitude) **be much/greatly ~d to sb.** [**for sth.**] jmdm. [für etw.] sehr verbunden sein; **much ~d** besten Dank! **2** *v.i.* **be always ready to ~:** immer sehr gefällig sein; **anything to ~** (as answer) stets zu Diensten

obliging /ə'blaɪdʒɪŋ/ *adj.* entgegenkommend

oblique /ə'bli:k/ **1** *adj.* (a) (slanting) schief ⟨*Gerade, Winkel*⟩; (b) (fig.: indirect) indirekt ⟨*Bemerkung, Hinweis, Frage*⟩. **2** *n.* Schrägstrich, *der*

obliquely /ə'bli:klɪ/ *adv.* (a) (in a slanting direction) schräg; (b) (fig.: indirectly) indirekt ⟨*sich beziehen, antworten*⟩

obliterate /ə'blɪtəreɪt/ *v.t.* (a) auslöschen; (b) (fig.) verschleiern ⟨*Wahrheit*⟩; auslöschen ⟨*Erinnerung*⟩; zerstreuen ⟨*Bedenken*⟩

oblivion /ə'blɪvɪən/ *n., no pl.* (being forgotten) Vergessenheit, *die;* **sink** *or* **fall into ~:** in Vergessenheit geraten

oblivious /ə'blɪvɪəs/ *adj.* **be ~ to** *or* **of sth.** (be unconscious of) sich (*Dat.*) einer Sache (*Gen.*) nicht bewusst sein; (not notice) etw. nicht bemerken *od.* wahrnehmen

oblong /'ɒblɒŋ/ **1** *adj.* rechteckig. **2** *n.* Rechteck, *das*

obnoxious /əb'nɒkʃəs/ *adj.* widerlich (abwertend)

oboe /'əʊbəʊ/ *n.* (Mus.) Oboe, *die*

obscene /əb'si:n/ *adj.* obszön; (coll.: offensive) widerlich (abwertend); unanständig ⟨*Profit*⟩

obscenity /əb'senɪtɪ/ *n.* Obszönität, *die*

obscure /əb'skjʊə(r)/ **1** *adj.* (a) (unexplained) dunkel; **for some ~ reason** aus irgendeinem verborgenen Grund; (b) (hard to understand) schwer verständlich ⟨*Argument, Dichtung, Autor, Stil*⟩; unklar ⟨*Hinweis, Textstelle*⟩; (c) (unknown) unbekannt ⟨*Herkunft, Schriftsteller*⟩. **2** *v.t.* (a) (make indistinct) verdunkeln; (block) versperren ⟨*Aussicht*⟩; (conceal) ⟨*Nebel:*⟩ verhüllen; (b) (fig.) unverständlich machen

obscurity /əb'skjʊərɪtɪ/ *n., no pl.* (a) (being unknown or inconspicuous) Unbekanntheit, *die;* **sink into ~:** in Vergessenheit geraten; **in ~:** unbeachtet, unauffällig ⟨*leben*⟩; (b) (unintelligibleness, unintelligible thing) Unverständlichkeit, *die;* (c) *no pl.* (darkness) Dunkelheit, *die*

obsequious /əb'si:kwɪəs/ *adj.* unterwürfig (abwertend)

observance /əb'zɜ:vəns/ *n.* (a) *no pl.* (observing) Beachtung, *die;* (b) (Relig.) Regel, *die*

observant /əb'zɜ:vənt/ *adj.* aufmerksam; **how very ~ of you!** sehr scharf beobachtet!

observation /ɒbzə'veɪʃn/ *n.* (a) *no pl.* Beobachtung, *die;* **powers of ~:** Beobachtungsgabe, *die;* **be [kept] under ~:** beobachtet werden; (by police, detectives) observiert *od.*

überwacht werden; **(b)** (remark) Bemerkung, *die* (**on** über + *Akk.*); **make an ~ on sth.** sich zu etw. äußern

observatory /əb'zɜ:vətərɪ/ *n.* Observatorium, *das;* (Astron. also) Sternwarte, *die*

observe /əb'zɜ:v/ *v.t.* **(a)** (watch) beobachten; ⟨*Polizei, Detektiv:*⟩ observieren, überwachen; *abs.* aufpassen; (perceive) bemerken; **(b)** (abide by, keep) beachten; einlegen ⟨*Schweigeminute*⟩; halten ⟨*Gelübde*⟩; feiern ⟨*Weihnachten, Jahrestag usw.*⟩; **(c)** (say) bemerken

observer /əb'zɜ:və(r)/ *n.* Beobachter, *der*/Beobachterin, *die*

obsess /əb'ses/ *v.t.* **be/become ~ed with** *or* **by sb./sth.** von jmdm./etw. besessen sein/werden

obsession /əb'seʃn/ *n.* **(a)** (persistent idea) Zwangsvorstellung, *die;* **be/become an ~ with sb.** für jmdn. zur Sucht geworden sein/werden; **have an ~ with sb./sth.** von jmdm./etw. besessen sein; **have an ~ with sex** sexbesessen sein; **have an ~ with cleanliness/guns** einen Sauberheits-/Waffenfimmel haben; **have an ~ with detail** ein Kleinkrämer sein; **(b)** *no pl.* (Psych.: condition) Obsession, *die* (fachspr.); Besessenheit, *die*

obsessive /əb'sesɪv/ *adj.* zwanghaft; obsessiv (Psych.); **be ~ about sth.** von etw. besessen sein; **be an ~ eater** unter Esszwang leiden

obsolescence /ɒbsə'lesəns/ *n., no pl.* Veralten, *das;* **built-in** *or* **planned ~:** geplanter Verschleiß

obsolescent /ɒbsə'lesənt/ *adj.* veraltend

obsolete /'ɒbsəli:t/ *adj.* veraltet; **become/have become ~:** veralten/veraltet sein

obstacle /'ɒbstəkl/ *n.* Hindernis, *das* (**to** für); **put ~s in sb.'s path** (fig.) jmdm. Hindernisse *od.* Steine in den Weg legen

obstacle: ~ course *n.* Hindernisparcours, *der;* **~ race** *n.* Hindernisrennen, *das*

obstetrics /ɒb'stetrɪks/ *n., no pl.* (Med.) Obstetrik, *die* (fachspr.); Geburtshilfe, *die*

obstinacy /'ɒbstɪnəsɪ/ *n., no pl.* ⇨ **obstinate:** Starrsinn, *der;* Hartnäckigkeit, *die*

obstinate /'ɒbstɪnət/ *adj.* starrsinnig; (adhering to particular course of action) hartnäckig; **be as ~ as a mule** ein sturer Bock sein (ugs. abwertend)

obstruct /əb'strʌkt/ *v.t.* **(a)** (block) versperren; blockieren; (Med.) verstopfen; behindern ⟨*Verkehr*⟩; **~ sb.'s view** jmdm. die Sicht versperren; **(b)** (fig.: impede; also Sport) behindern

obstruction /əb'strʌkʃn/ *n.* **(a)** *no pl.* (blocking) Blockierung, *die;* (Med.) Verstopfung, *die;* (of progress; also Sport) Behinderung, *die;* **(b)** (obstacle) Hindernis, *das*

obstructive /əb'strʌktɪv/ *adj.* hinderlich; obstruktiv ⟨*Politik, Taktik*⟩; **be ~** ⟨*Person:*⟩ sich quer legen (ugs.)

obtain /əb'teɪn/ *v.t.* bekommen ⟨*Ware, Information, Hilfe*⟩; erreichen, erzielen ⟨*Resultat, Wirkung*⟩; erwerben, erlangen ⟨*akademischen Grad*⟩

obtainable /əb'teɪnəbl/ *adj.* erhältlich

obtrusive /əb'tru:sɪv/ *adj.* aufdringlich; (conspicuous) auffällig

obtuse /əb'tju:s/ *adj.* **(a)** (Geom.) stumpf ⟨*Winkel*⟩; **(b)** (stupid) einfältig; **he's being deliberately ~:** er stellt sich dumm

obvious /'ɒbvɪəs/ *adj.* offenkundig; (easily seen) augenfällig; sichtlich ⟨*Empfindung, innerer Zustand*⟩; plump ⟨*Trick, Mittel*⟩; **she was the ~ choice** es lag nahe, dass die Wahl auf sie fiel; **the answer is ~:** die Antwort liegt auf der Hand; **the ~ thing to do is …:** das Naheliegende ist …; **with the ~ exception of …:** natürlich mit Ausnahme von …; **be ~ [to sb.] that …:** [jmdm.] klar sein, dass …; **that's stating the ~:** das ist nichts Neues

obviously /'ɒbvɪəslɪ/ *adv.* offenkundig; sichtlich ⟨*enttäuschen, überraschen usw.*⟩; **~, we can't expect any help** es ist klar, dass wir keine Hilfe erwarten können

occasion /ə'keɪʒn/ **1** *n.* **(a)** (opportunity) Gelegenheit, *die;* **rise to the ~:** sich der Situation gewachsen zeigen; **(b)** (reason) Grund, *der* (**for** zu); (cause) Anlass, *der;* **should the ~ arise** falls sich die Gelegenheit ergibt; **be [an] ~ for celebration** ein Grund zum Feiern sein; **have ~ to do**

sth. [eine] Gelegenheit haben, etw. zu tun; **(c)** (point in time) Gelegenheit, *die;* **on several ~s** bei mehreren Gelegenheiten; **on that ~:** bei der Gelegenheit; damals; **on ~[s]** gelegentlich; **(d)** (special occurrence) Anlass, *der;* **it was quite an ~:** es war ein Ereignis; **on the ~ of** anlässlich (+ *Gen.*). **2** *v.t.* verursachen; erregen, Anlass geben zu ⟨*Besorgnis*⟩

occasional /ə'keɪʒənl/ *adj.* (happening irregularly) gelegentlich; vereinzelt ⟨*Regenschauer*⟩; **take an** *or* **the ~ break** gelegentlich eine Pause machen

occasionally /ə'keɪʒənəlɪ/ *adv.* gelegentlich; **[only] very ~:** gelegentlich einmal

oc'casional table *n.* Beistelltisch, *der*

occult /ɒ'kʌlt, 'ɒkʌlt/ *adj.* (mystical) okkult ⟨*Kunst, Wissenschaft*⟩; **the ~:** das Okkulte

occupant /'ɒkjʊpənt/ *n.* Bewohner, *der*/Bewohnerin, *die;* (of post) Inhaber, *der*/Inhaberin, *die;* (of car, bus, etc.) Insasse, *der*/Insassin, *die*

occupation /ɒkjʊ'peɪʃn/ *n.* **(a)** (of property) (tenure) Besitz, *der;* (occupancy) Bewohnung, *die;* **(b)** (Mil.) Okkupation, *die;* Besetzung, *die;* (period) Besatzungszeit, *die;* **(c)** (activity) Beschäftigung, *die;* (pastime) Zeitvertreib, *der;* **(d)** (profession) Beruf, *der;* **his ~ is civil engineering** er ist Bauingenieur [von Beruf]; **what's her ~?** was ist sie von Beruf?

occupational /ɒkjʊ'peɪʃnl/ *adj.* Berufs⟨*beratung, -risiko*⟩; betrieblich ⟨*Altersversorgung*⟩

occupational: ~ di'sease *n.* (also joc.) Berufskrankheit, *die;* **~ 'therapist** *n.* ▸ **887** │ Beschäftigungstherapeut, *der*/-therapeutin, *die;* **~ 'therapy** *n.* Beschäftigungstherapie, *die*

occupier /'ɒkjʊpaɪə(r)/ *n.* (Brit.) Besitzer, *der*/Besitzerin, *die;* (tenant) Bewohner, *der*/Bewohnerin, *die*

occupy /'ɒkjʊpaɪ/ *v.t.* **(a)** (Mil.; Polit. as demonstration) besetzen; **(b)** (reside in, be a tenant of) bewohnen; **(c)** (take up, fill) einnehmen; besetzen ⟨*Sitzplatz, Tisch*⟩; belegen ⟨*Zimmer*⟩; in Anspruch nehmen ⟨*Zeit, Aufmerksamkeit*⟩; **how did you ~ your time?** wie hast du die Zeit verbracht?; **(d)** (hold) innehaben ⟨*Stellung, Amt*⟩; **(e)** (busy, employ) beschäftigen; **~ oneself [with doing sth.]** sich [mit etw.] beschäftigen; **keep sb.['s mind] occupied** jmdn. [geistig] beschäftigen

occur /ə'kɜ:(r)/ *v.i.*, **-rr-:** **(a)** (be met with) vorkommen; ⟨*Gelegenheit, Schwierigkeit, Problem:*⟩ sich ergeben; **(b)** (happen) ⟨*Veränderung:*⟩ eintreten; ⟨*Unfall, Vorfall, Zwischenfall:*⟩ sich ereignen; **this must not ~ again** das darf nicht wieder vorkommen; **(c)** **~ to sb.** (be thought of) jmdm. einfallen; ⟨*Idee:*⟩ jmdm. kommen; **it never ~red to me** auf den Gedanken bin ich nie gekommen

occurrence /ə'kʌrəns/ *n.* **(a)** (incident) Ereignis, *das;* **(b)** (occurring) Vorkommen, *das;* **be of frequent ~:** häufig vorkommen

ocean /'əʊʃn/ *n.* Ozean, *der;* Meer, *das*

'ocean-going *adj.* Übersee-

oceanic /ˌəʊʃɪ'ænɪk, ˌəʊsɪ'ænɪk/ *adj.* ozeanisch; Meeres⟨*tier, -klima*⟩; See⟨*vogel, -klima*⟩

oceanography /ˌəʊʃə'nɒgrəfɪ/ *n.* Ozeanographie, *die;* Meereskunde, *die*

ochre (*Amer.:* **ocher**) /'əʊkə(r)/ *n.* Ocker, *der od.* das

o'clock /ə'klɒk/ *adv.* ▸ **706** │ **it is two/six ~:** es ist zwei/sechs Uhr; **at two/six ~:** um zwei/sechs Uhr; **six ~** *attrib.* Sechs-Uhr-⟨*Zug, Maschine, Nachrichten*⟩

Oct. *abbr.* **October** Okt.

octagon /'ɒktəgən/ *n.* (Geom.) Achteck, *das;* Oktogon, *das* (fachspr.)

octane /'ɒkteɪn/ *n.* Oktan, *das*

octave /'ɒktɪv/ *n.* (Mus.) Oktave, *die*

October /ɒk'təʊbə(r)/ *n.* ▸ **738** │ Oktober, *der; see also* **August**

octopus /'ɒktəpəs/ *n.* Krake, *der*

OD *abbr.* (esp. Amer. coll.) **1 overdose 1. 2 OD's, OD'd, ODing: overdose 3**

odd /ɒd/ *adj.* **(a)** (extraordinary) merkwürdig; (strange, eccentric) seltsam; **(b)** (surplus, spare) übrig ⟨*Stück*⟩; überzählig ⟨*Spieler*⟩; restlich, übrig ⟨*Silbergeld*⟩; **(c)** (additional) **1,000 and ~ pounds** etwas über 1 000 Pfund; **(d)** (occasional, random) gelegentlich; ~ **job**/~**-job man** Gelegenheitsarbeit, *die/*-arbeiter, *der;* **(e)** (one of pair or group) einzeln; ~ **socks/gloves** *etc.* nicht zusammengehörende Socken/Handschuhe *usw.;* **be the ~ man out** (extra person) überzählig sein; (thing) nicht dazu passen; **(f)** (uneven) ungerade ‹*Zahl, Seite, Hausnummer*›; **(g)** (plus something) **she must be forty ~:** sie muss etwas über vierzig sein; **twelve pounds ~:** etwas mehr als zwölf Pfund

oddity /'ɒdɪtɪ/ *n.* **(a)** (strangeness, peculiar trait) Eigentümlichkeit, *die;* **(b)** (person) Sonderling, *der;* **(c)** (object, event) Kuriosität, *die*

oddly /'ɒdlɪ/ *adv.* seltsam; merkwürdig; ~ **enough** seltsamer- *od.* merkwürdigerweise

oddment /'ɒdmənt/ *n.* **(a)** (left over) [Über]rest, *der;* (in sales) Reststück, *das;* **(b)** *in pl.* (odds and ends) Kleinigkeiten

oddness /'ɒdnɪs/ *n.*, *no pl.* Merkwürdigkeit, *die;* (strangeness) Seltsamkeit, *die*

'odd-numbered *adj.* ungerade

odds /ɒdz/ *n. pl.* **(a)** (Betting) Odds *pl.;* **the ~ were on Black Bess** Black Bess hatte die besten Chancen; **lay** *or* **give/take ~ of six to one in favour of/against sb./a horse** eine 6 : 1-Wette auf/gegen jmdn./ein Pferd anbieten/annehmen; **pay over the ~ for sth.** einen überhöhten Preis für etw. bezahlen; **(b)** (chances for or against) Möglichkeit, *die;* (chance for) Aussicht, *die;* Chance, *die;* [**the**] ~ **are that she did it** wahrscheinlich hat sie es getan; **the ~ are against/in favour of sb./sth.** jmds. Aussichten *od.* Chancen/die Aussichten *od.* Chancen für etw. sind gering/gut; **struggle against impossible ~:** völlig chancenlos kämpfen; **(c)** (balance of advantage) **against** [**all**] **the ~:** allen Widrigkeiten zum Trotz; **(d)** (difference) Unterschied, *der;* **it makes no/little ~** [**whether** ...] es ist völlig/ziemlich gleichgültig[, ob ...]; **what's the ~?** (coll.) was macht das schon?; **(e)** (variance) **be at ~ with sb. over sth.** mit jmdm. in etw. (*Dat.*) uneinig sein; **(f)** ~ **and ends** Kleinigkeiten *Pl.;* (of food) Reste *Pl.*

'odds-on *adj.* gut ‹*Chance, Aussicht*›; hoch, klar ‹*Favorit*›; **be ~** [**favourite**] **to win/for sth.** klarer *od.* hoher Favorit/Favorit für etw. sein

ode /əʊd/ *n.* Ode, *die* (**to** an + *Akk.*)

odious /'əʊdɪəs/ *adj.* widerwärtig

odor *etc.* (Amer.) ⇨ **odour** *etc.*

odour /'əʊdə(r)/ *n.* **(a)** (smell) Geruch, *der;* (fragrance) Duft, *der;* **(b)** (fig.) Note, *die;* **be in good/bad ~ with sb.** bei jmdm. in gutem/schlechtem Geruch stehen

odourless /'əʊdəlɪs/ *adj.* geruchlos

of /əv, *stressed* ɒv/ *prep.* **(a)** *indicating belonging, connection, possession* **articles of clothing** Kleidungsstücke; **the brother of her father** der Bruder ihres Vaters; **a friend of mine/the vicar's** ein Freund von mir/des Pfarrers; **that dog of yours** Ihr Hund da; **it's no business of theirs** es geht sie nichts an; **where's that pencil of mine?** wo ist mein Bleistift?; **(b)** *indicating starting point* von; **within a mile of the centre** nicht weiter als eine Meile vom Zentrum entfernt; **(c)** *indicating origin, cause* **it was clever of you to do that** es war klug von dir, das zu tun; **the approval of sb.** jmds. Zustimmung; **the works of Shakespeare** Shakespeares Werke; **(d)** *indicating material* aus; **be made of ...:** aus ... [hergestellt] sein; **(e)** *indicating closer definition, identity, or contents* **a pound of apples** ein Pfund Äpfel; **a glass of wine** ein Glas Wein; **a painting of the queen** ein Gemälde der Königin; **the city of Chicago** die Stadt Chicago; **increase of 10 %** Zuwachs/Erhöhung von zehn Prozent; **battle of Hastings** Schlacht von *od.* bei Hastings; **your letter of 2 January** Ihr Brief vom 2. Januar; **be of value/interest to** von Nutzen/von Interesse *od.* interessant sein für; **the whole of ...:** der/die/das ganze ...; **(f)** *indicating concern, reference* **do not speak of such things** sprich nicht von solchen Dingen; **inform sb. of sth.** jmdn. über etw. (*Akk.*) informieren; **well, what of it?** (asked as reply) na und?; **(g)** *indicating objective relation* **his love of his father** seine Liebe zu seinem Vater; **(h)** *indicating description, quality, condition* **a frown of disapproval** ein missbilligendes Stirnrunzeln; **work of authority** maßgebendes Werk; **a boy of 14 years** ein vierzehnjähriger Junge; **(i)** *indicating classification, selection*

von; **the five of us** wir fünf; **the five of us went there** wir sind zu fünft hingegangen; **he of all men** (most unsuitably) ausgerechnet er; (especially) gerade er; **here of all places** ausgerechnet hier; **of an evening** (coll.) abends

off /ɒf/ **1** *adv.* **(a)** (away, at or to a distance) **be a few miles ~:** wenige Meilen entfernt sein; **the lake is not far ~:** der See ist nicht weit [weg *od.* entfernt]; **Christmas is not far ~:** es ist nicht mehr lang bis Weihnachten; **some way ~:** in einiger Entfernung; **where are you ~ to?** wohin gehst du?; **I must be ~:** ich muss fort *od.* weg *od.* los; **I'm ~ now** ich gehe jetzt; ~ **we go!** (we are starting) los *od.* ab geht's!; (let us start) gehen/fahren wir!; **get the lid ~:** den Deckel abbekommen; **(b)** (not in good condition) mitgenommen; **the meat** *etc.* **is ~:** das Fleisch *usw.* ist schlecht [geworden]; **be a bit ~** (Brit. fig.) ein starkes Stück sein (ugs.); **(c)** **be ~** (switched or turned ~) ‹*Wasser, Gas, Strom:*› abgestellt sein; **the light/radio** *etc.* **is ~:** das Licht/Radio *usw.* ist aus; **put the light ~:** das Licht ausmachen; **is the gas tap ~?** ist der Gashahn zu?; **(d)** **be ~** (cancelled) abgesagt sein; ‹*Verlobung:*› [auf]gelöst sein; **is Sunday's picnic ~?** fällt das Picknick am Sonntag aus?; ~ **and on** immer mal wieder (ugs.); **(e)** (not at work) frei; **on my day ~:** an meinem freien Tag; **take/get/have a week** *etc.* **~:** eine Woche *usw.* Urlaub nehmen/bekommen/haben; **be ~ sick** wegen Krankheit fehlen; **(f)** (no longer available) **soup** *etc.* **is ~:** es gibt keine Suppe *usw.* mehr; **(g)** (situated as regards money etc.) **he is badly** *etc.* **~:** er ist schlecht *usw.* gestellt; **we'd be better ~ without him** ohne ihn wären wir besser dran; **there are many people worse ~ than you** vielen geht es schlechter als dir; **how are you ~ for food?** wieviel Essbares hast du noch?; **be badly ~ for sth.** mit etw. knapp sein. **2** *prep.* **(a)** (from) von; **cut a couple of slices ~ the loaf** einige Scheiben Brot abschneiden; **(b)** **be ~ school/work** in der Schule/am Arbeitsplatz fehlen; **(c)** (diverging from) **get ~ the subject** [vom Thema] abschweifen; **be ~ the point** nicht zur Sache gehören; **(d)** (designed not to cover) ~**-thc-shoulder** schulterfrei ‹*Kleid*›; **(e)** (having lost interest in) **be ~ sth.** etw. leid sein *od.* haben (ugs.); **be ~ one's food** keinen Appetit haben; **(f)** (leading from, not far from) **just ~ the square** ganz in der Nähe des Platzes; **a street ~ the main road** eine Straße, die von der Hauptstraße abgeht; **(g)** (to seaward of) vor (+ *Dat.*). **3** *adj.* **the ~ side** (Brit.) (when travelling on the left/right) die rechte/linke Seite

offal /'ɒfl/ *n.*, *no pl.* Innereien *Pl.*

off-: ~**beat** *adj.* **(a)** (Mus.) Off-Beat-; **(b)** (fig.: eccentric) unkonventionell ‹*Person, Lebensweise*›; außergewöhnlich ‹*Vorlesung, Kursus*›; ~**-'centre 1** *adj.* nicht zentriert, **2** *adv.* nicht [genau] in der Mitte; ~ **chance** ⇨ **chance 1 c;** ~ **'colour** *adj.* unwohl; **be** *or* **feel ~ colour** sich unwohl *od.* schlecht fühlen; ~**-day** *n.* schlechter Tag; ~**-duty** *attrib. adj.* Freizeit-; dienstfrei ‹*Zeit*›; ‹*Polizist usw.,*› der dienstfrei hat

offence /ə'fens/ *n.* (Brit.) **(a)** (hurting of sb.'s feelings) Kränkung, *die;* **I meant no ~:** ich wollte Sie/ihn *usw.* nicht kränken; **give ~:** Missfallen erregen; **take ~:** beleidigt *od.* verärgert sein; **no ~** (coll.) nichts für ungut; **(b)** (transgression) Verstoß, *der;* (crime) Delikt, *das;* Straftat, *die;* **criminal/petty ~:** strafbare Handlung/geringfügiges Vergehen

offend /ə'fend/ **1** *v.i.* verstoßen (**against** gegen). **2** *v.t.* ~ **sb.** bei jmdm. Anstoß erregen; (hurt feelings of) jmdn. kränken; ~ **the eye** das Auge beleidigen

offender /ə'fendə(r)/ *n.* (against law) Straffällige, *der/die;* Täter, *der/*Täterin, *die;* (against rule) Zuwiderhandelnde, *der/die*

offense (Amer.) ⇨ **offence**

offensive /ə'fensɪv/ **1** *adj.* **(a)** (aggressive) offensiv; Angriffs‹*waffe, -krieg*›; **(b)** (giving offence, insulting) ungehörig; (indecent) anstößig; ~ **language** Beschimpfungen; **(c)** (repulsive) widerlich; **be ~ to sb.** jmdm. zuwider sein; auf jmdn. abstoßend wirken. **2** *n.* (attack; also Sport) Offensive, *die;* Angriff, *der;* **take the ~** *or* **go on the ~:** in die *od.* zur Offensive übergehen; **be on the ~:** aggressiv sein

offer /'ɒfə(r)/ **1** *v.t.* anbieten; vorbringen ‹*Entschuldigung*›; bieten ‹*Chance*›; aussprechen ‹*Beileid*›; sagen ‹*Meinung*›; unterbreiten, machen ‹*Vorschläge*›;

have something to ∼**:** etwas zu bieten haben; **the job** ∼**s good prospects** der Arbeitsplatz hat Zukunft; ∼ **resistance** Widerstand leisten; ∼ **to do sth.** anbieten, etw. zu tun; ∼ **to help** seine Hilfe anbieten. **2** *n.* **(a)** Angebot, *das;* [**have/be**] **on** ∼**:** im Angebot [haben/sein]; **(b)** (marriage proposal) Antrag, *der*

offering /'ɒfərɪŋ/ *n.* Angebot, *das;* (to a deity) Opfer, *das*

offertory /'ɒfətərɪ/ *n.* (Eccl.) Kollekte, *die*

off'hand 1 *adv.* **(a)** (without preparation) auf Anhieb, aus der Hand (ugs.) ⟨*sagen, wissen*⟩; **(b)** (casually) leichthin. **2** *adj.* (casual) beiläufig; **be** ∼ **with sb.** zu jmdm. kurz angebunden sein

office /'ɒfɪs/ *n.* **(a)** Büro, *das;* **(b)** (branch of organization) Zweigstelle, *die;* **(c)** (position with duties) Amt, *das;* **be in/out of** ∼**:** im/nicht mehr im Amt sein; ⟨*Partei:*⟩ an der/nicht mehr an der Regierung sein; **hold** ∼**:** amtieren; **(d)** (government department) **Home O**∼ (Brit.) ≈ Innenministerium, *das;* **(e)** (Eccl.: service) Gottesdienst, *der;* **(f)** (kindness) [**good**] ∼**s** Hilfe, *die;* Unterstützung, *die*

office: ∼ **block** *n.* Bürogebäude, *das;* ∼ **hours** *n. pl.* Dienststunden *Pl.;* **after** ∼ **hours** nach Dienstschluss; ∼ **job** *n.* Bürotätigkeit, *die;* ∼ '**junior** *n.* Bürogehilfe, *der/*-gehilfin, *die*

officer /'ɒfɪsə(r)/ *n.* ▶ 887 | **(a)** (Army etc.) Offizier, *der;* **(b)** (official) Beamte, *der/*Beamtin, *die;* (of club etc.) Funktionär, *der/*Funktionärin, *die;* **(c)** (constable) Polizeibeamte, *der/*-beamtin, *die;* **yes,** ∼**:** jawohl, Herr Wachtmeister/Frau Wachtmeisterin

'**office worker** *n.* ▶ 887 | Büroangestellte, *der/die*

official /ə'fɪʃl/ **1** *adj.* **(a)** Amts⟨*pflicht, -robe, -person*⟩; **(b)** (derived from authority, formal) offiziell; amtlich ⟨*Verlautbarung*⟩; regulär ⟨*Streik*⟩; **is it** ∼ **yet?** (coll.) ist das schon amtlich? **2** *n.* Beamte, *der/*Beamtin, *die;* (party, union, or sports ∼) Funktionär, *der/*Funktionärin, *die*

officialdom /ə'fɪʃldəm/ *n., no pl., no art.* Beamtentum, *das*

officialese /əfɪʃə'li:z/ *n., no pl.* (derog.) Behördensprache, *die*

officially /ə'fɪʃəlɪ/ *adv.* offiziell

officiate /ə'fɪʃɪeɪt/ *v.i.* ∼ **as** ...: fungieren als ...; ∼ **at the service** den Gottesdienst abhalten; ∼ **at a wedding** eine Trauung vornehmen

officious /ə'fɪʃəs/ *adj.* übereifrig

offing /'ɒfɪŋ/ *n.* **be in the** ∼ (fig.) bevorstehen

off: ∼-'**key 1** *adj.* verstimmt; **2** *adv.* falsch ⟨*singen, spielen*⟩; ∼-**licence** *n.* (Brit.: premises) ≈ Wein- und Spirituosenladen, *der;* ∼-**line** (Computing) **1** ['--] *adj.* Offline-⟨*-gerät, -betrieb*⟩. **2** ['-'-] *adj.* offline; ∼-**load** *v.t.* abladen; ∼**load sth. on to sb.** (fig.: get rid of) etw. bei jmdm. loswerden; ∼-**peak** *attrib. adj.* **during** ∼-**peak hours** außerhalb der Spitzenlastzeiten; ∼-**peak electricity** Nachtstrom, *der;* ∼**print** *n.* Sonderdruck, *der;* ∼-**putting** /'ɒfpʊtɪŋ/ *adj.* (Brit. coll.) abstoßend ⟨*Gesicht, Äußeres, Weg*⟩; abschreckend ⟨*Umfang*⟩; ∼-**ramp** *n.* (Amer.) Abfahrt, *die;* ∼-**road** *attrib. adj.* Gelände-, Offroad⟨*fahrzeug, -fahrrad, -wagen, -fahrt, -einsatz*⟩; ∼-**road driving** Fahren im Gelände; ∼**set 1** /'--/ *n.* ∼**set** [**process**] (Printing) Offsetdruck, *der;* **2** [--, -'-] *v.t., forms as* **set 1:** ausgleichen; ∼**shoot** *n.* **(a)** (of plant) Spross, *der;* **(b)** (fig.: descendant) Spross, *der* (geh.); ∼**shore** *adj.* **(a)** (situated at sea) küstennah; **(b)** ablandig ⟨*Wind*⟩ (Seemannsspr.); ∼'**side** *adj.* (Sport) Abseits-; **be** ∼**side** abseits *od.* im Abseits sein; ∼**spring** *n., pl. same* (human) Nachkommenschaft, *die;* (of animal) Junge; ∼-'**stage** *adv.* in den Kulissen; **go** ∼-**stage** abgehen; ∼-**the-peg** *attrib. adj.* Konfektions-; von der Stange *nachgestellt;* ∼-**the-shoulder** *attrib. adj.* schulterfrei ⟨*Kleid, T-Shirt*⟩; ∼-**the-wall** *attrib. adj.* (esp. Amer. coll.) ausgeflippt (ugs.); ∼-'**white** *adj.* gebrochen weiß; (yellowish) vergilbt

often /'ɒfn, 'ɒftn/ *adv.* oft; **more** ∼**:** häufiger; **more** ∼ **than not** meistens; **every so** ∼**:** gelegentlich; **once too** ∼**:** einmal zu viel

ogle /'əʊgl/ *v.i.* gaffen (ugs. abwertend); ∼ **at sb.** jmdn. angaffen (ugs. abwertend)

ogre /'əʊgə(r)/ *n.* Oger, *der;* [menschenfressender] Riese

oh /əʊ/ *int.* oh; '**oh no** [**you don't**]! auf keinen Fall!; **oh** '**no!** na nein!; oje!; oh '**well** na ja (ugs.); tja (ugs.); '**oh yes** oh ja; **oh** '**yes?** ach ja?; **oh,** '**him**/'**that!** (coll.) ach, der/das!

ohm /əʊm/ *n.* (Electr.) Ohm, *das*

OHMS *abbr.* **on Her/His Majesty's Service**

oil /ɔɪl/ **1** *n.* **(a)** Öl, *das;* **strike** ∼ (lit.) auf Öl stoßen; (fig.) das große Los ziehen; **(b)** *in pl.* (paints) Ölfarben. **2** *v.t.* ölen

oil: ∼**can** *n.* Ölkanne, *die;* ∼ **colour** *n., usu. in pl.* Ölfarbe, *die;* ∼ **drum** *n.* Ölfass, *das;* ∼**field** *n.* Ölfeld, *das;* ∼-**fired** /'ɔɪlfaɪəd/ *adj.* ölgefeuert; ölbetrieben ⟨*Zentralheizung*⟩; ∼ **lamp** *n.* Öllampe, *die;* ∼ **painting** *n.* Ölgemälde, *das;* ∼ **rig** ⇒ **rig¹ 1 b**; ∼**skin** *n.* **(a)** (material) Öltuch, *das;* **(b)** (garment) **put on** ∼**skins/an** ∼**skin** Ölzeug anziehen; ∼ **slick** *n.* Ölteppich, *der;* ∼ **tanker** *n.* Öltanker, *der;* ∼ **well** *n.* Ölquelle, *die*

oily /'ɔɪlɪ/ *adj.* **(a)** ölig ⟨*Oberfläche, Hände, Lappen, Geschmack*⟩; Öl⟨*lache, -fleck*⟩; ölverschmiert ⟨*Gesicht, Hände*⟩; (containing oil) viel Öl enthaltend ⟨*Soße*⟩; fettig ⟨*Haut, Haar*⟩; **(b)** (fig.) schmierig (abwertend) ⟨*Kerl, Art*⟩; ölig ⟨*Lächeln, Stimme*⟩

ointment /'ɔɪntmənt/ *n.* Salbe, *die; see also* **fly¹**

OK /əʊ'keɪ/ (coll.) **1** *adj.* in Ordnung; okay (ugs.); [**it's**] **OK by me** mir ist es recht. **2** *adv.* gut; **be doing OK** seine Sache gut machen. **3** *int.* okay (ugs.); **OK?** [ist das] klar?; okay? **4** *n.* Zustimmung, *die;* Okay, *das* (ugs.). **5** *v.t.* (approve) zustimmen (+ *Dat.*); **be OK'd by sb.** von jmdm. das Okay bekommen

okay /əʊ'keɪ/ ⇒ **OK**

old /əʊld/ **1** *adj.* **(a)** ▶ 630 | alt; **he is** ∼ **enough to know better** aus diesem Alter ist er heraus; **he/she is** ∼ **enough to be your father/mother** er/sie könnte dein Vater/deine Mutter sein; **be/seem** ∼ **before one's time** frühzeitig gealtert sein/gealtert wirken; **be [more than] 30 years** ∼**:** [über] 30 Jahre alt sein; **at ten years** ∼**:** im Alter von 10 Jahren; mit 10 Jahren; **be an** ∼ **hand** ein alter Hase sein (ugs.); **in the** ∼ **days** früher; **be still working for the same** ∼ **firm** noch immer in derselben Firma arbeiten; **(b)** *in playful or friendly mention* alt (ugs.); **you lucky** ∼ **so-and-so!** du bist vielleicht ein alter Glückspilz!; **I saw** ∼ **George today** ich habe heute unsern Freund George getroffen; **good/dear** ∼ **Harry** (coll.) der gute alte Harry; **have a fine** ∼ **time** (coll.) sich köstlich amüsieren; **poor** ∼ **Jim/my poor** ∼ **arm** armer Jim/mein armer Arm (ugs.); **any** ∼ **thing** (coll.) irgendwas (ugs.); **any** ∼ **how** (coll.) irgendwie. **2** *n.* **(a)** the ∼ *constr. as pl.* (∼ people) alte Menschen; **(b)** **the knights of** ∼**:** die Ritter früherer Zeiten

old: ∼ '**age** *n., no pl.* [fortgeschrittenes] Alter; **in** ∼ **age** im [fortgeschrittenen] Alter; ∼-**age** *adj.* Alters⟨*rente, -ruhegeld, -versicherung*⟩; ∼-**age pensioner** Rentner, *der/*Rentnerin, *die;* ∼ **boy** *n.* (Sch.) ehemaliger Schüler; Ehemalige, *der*

olden /'əʊldn/ *adj.* (literary) **in [the]** ∼ **days** *or* **times** in alten Zeiten

old: ∼-**es'tablished** *adj.* alt ⟨*Tradition, Brauch*⟩; alteingesessen ⟨*Firma, Geschäft, Familie*⟩; ∼**fashioned** /əʊld'fæʃnd/ *adj.* altmodisch; ∼ **girl** *n.* (Sch.) ehemalige Schülerin; Ehemalige, *die;* ∼ '**hat** ⇒ **hat b**

oldish /'əʊldɪʃ/ *adj.* älter

old: ∼ '**maid** *n.* **(a)** (elderly spinster) alte Jungfer (abwertend); **(b)** (fig.: fussy, prim person) altjüngferliche Person; ∼ '**man** *n.* **(a)** (coll.: superior) **the** ∼ **man** der Alte (ugs.); **(b)** (coll.: father, husband) **the/one's** ∼ **man** der Alte/sein Alter (ugs.); ∼ '**master** *n.* (Art) alter Meister; ∼ '**people's home** *n.* Altenheim, *das;* Altersheim, *das;* ∼ '**soldier** *n.* alt[gedient]er Soldat; (fig.) alter Hase (ugs.); **Old 'Testament** ⇒ **testament a**; ∼-'**timer** *n.* (person with long experience) alter Hase (ugs.); Oldtimer, *der* (scherzh.); ∼-'**wives' tale** *n.* Ammenmärchen, *das;* Altweibermärchen, *das;* ∼ '**woman** *n.* **(a)** (fig.: fussy or timid person) altes Weib (abwertend); **(b)** (coll.: mother, wife) **the/one's** ∼ **woman** die/seine Alte (ugs.); ∼-'**world** *adj.* altertümlich; altväterisch ⟨*Höflichkeit, Benehmen*⟩

O level /əʊ levl/ *n.* (Brit. Sch. Hist.) Abschluss der Mittelstufe (*auch in der Erwachsenenbildung als Qualifikation*)

olive /'ɒlɪv/ **1** *n.* **(a)** (tree) Ölbaum, *der;* Olivenbaum, *der;* **(b)** (fruit) Olive, *die.* **2** *adj.* olivgrün

olive: ~ **branch** *n.* (fig.) Friedensangebot, *das;* **offer the** ~ **branch** ein Friedensangebots- *od.* Friedensangebot machen; ~**-green** *adj.* olivgrün; ~ **'oil** *n.* Olivenöl, *das*

Olympic /ə'lɪmpɪk/ *adj.* olympisch; ~ **Games** Olympische Spiele; ~ **champion** Olympiasieger, *der/*-siegerin, *die*

Olympics /ə'lɪmpɪks/ *n. pl.* Olympiade, *die;* Winter ~: Winterolympiade, *die*

ombudsman /'ɒmbʊdzmən/ *n., pl.* **ombudsmen** /'ɒmbʊdzmən/ Ombudsmann, *der*

omelette (omelet) /'ɒmlɪt/ *n.* (Gastr.) Omelett, *das*

omen /'əʊmən/ *n.* Omen, *das*

ominous /'ɒmɪnəs/ *adj.* (of evil omen) ominös; (worrying) beunruhigend

ominously /'ɒmɪnəslɪ/ *adv.* bedrohlich; beunruhigend ‹*still*›

omission /ə'mɪʃn/ *n.* **(a)** Auslassung, *die;* **(b)** (failure to act) Unterlassung, *die*

omit /ə'mɪt/ *v.t.,* -**tt-: (a)** (leave out) weglassen; **(b)** (not perform) versäumen; ~ **to do sth.** es versäumen, etw. zu tun

omnibus /'ɒmnɪbəs/ *n.* **(a)** (arch.) ⇒ **bus 1; (b)** (book) Sammelband, *der*

omnipotent /ɒm'nɪpətənt/ *adj.* allmächtig

omniscient /ɒm'nɪsɪənt, ɒm'nɪʃɪənt/ *adj.* allwissend

on /ɒn/ **1** *prep.* **(a)** (position) auf (+ *Dat.*); (direction) auf (+ *Akk.*); (attached to) an (+ *Dat./Akk.*); **put sth. on the table** etw. auf den Tisch legen *od.* stellen; **be on the table** auf dem Tisch sein; **write sth. on the wall** etw. an die Wand schreiben; **be hanging on the wall** an der Wand hängen; **have sth. on one** etw. bei sich (*Dat.*) haben; **on the bus/ train** im Bus/Zug sein; **be on the board/committee** im Vorstand/Ausschuss sein; **on Oxford 556767** unter der Nummer Oxford 55 67 67; **(b)** (with basis, motive, etc. of) **on the evidence** aufgrund des Beweismaterials; **on the assumption/hypothesis that** ...: angenommen, ...; **(c)** ▶706⌡, ▶739⌡ in expressions of time an ‹einem Abend, Tag usw.›; **on Sundays** sonntags; **it's just on nine** es ist gerade neun; **on [his] arrival** bei seiner Ankunft; **on entering the room** ...: beim Betreten des Zimmers ...; **on time or schedule** pünktlich; **(d)** expr. state etc. **be on heroin** heroinabhängig sein; **the drinks are on me** (coll.) die Getränke gehen auf mich; **be on £20,000 a year** 20 000 Pfund im Jahr kriegen *od.* haben; **(e)** (concerning, about) über (+ *Akk.*). **2** *adv.* **(a)** **have a hat on** einen Hut aufhaben; **your hat is on crooked** dein Hut sitzt schief; **the potatoes are on** die Kartoffeln sind aufgesetzt; **(b)** (in some direction) **face on** mit dem Gesicht voran; **on and on** immer weiter; **(c)** (switched or turned on) **the light/radio** etc. **is on** das Licht/Radio *usw.* ist an; **put the light on** das Licht anmachen; **is there a gas tap on?** ist ein Gashahn aufgedreht?; **(d)** (arranged) **is Sunday's picnic on?** findet das Picknick am Sonntag statt?; **I have nothing of importance on** ich habe nichts Wichtiges vor; **(e)** (being performed) **what's on at the cinema?** was gibt es *od.* was läuft im Kino?; **his play is currently on in London** sein Stück wird zur Zeit in London aufgeführt *od.* gespielt; **(f)** (on duty) **come/be on** seinen Dienst antreten/Dienst haben; **(g) sth. is on** (feasible) /**not on** etw. ist möglich/ausgeschlossen; **you're on!** (coll.: I agree) abgemacht!; (making bet) die Wette gilt!; **be on about sth.** (coll.) [dauernd] über jmdn./etw. sprechen; **what is he on about?** was will er [sagen]?; **be on at/keep on and on at sb.** (coll.) jmdm. in den Ohren/dauernd in den Ohren liegen (ugs.); **on to, onto** auf (+ *Akk.*); **be on to sth.** (have discovered sth.) etw. ausfindig gemacht haben.

once /wʌns/ **1** *adv.* **(a)** einmal; ~ **a week/month** einmal die Woche/im Monat; ~ **or twice** ein paar Mal; einige Male; ~ **again** *or* **more** noch einmal; ~ **[and] for all** ein für alle Male; **[every]** ~ **in a while** von Zeit zu Zeit; ~ **an X always an X** X bleibt X; *see also* **for 1** n; **(b)** (multiplied by one) ein mal; **(c)** (even for one or the first time) je[mals]; **never/not** ~: nicht ein einziges Mal; **(d)** (formerly) früher einmal; ~ **upon a time there lived a king** es war einmal ein König; **(e) at** ~ (immediately) sofort; sogleich; (at the same time) gleichzeitig; **all at** ~ (all together)

alle auf einmal; (without warning) mit einem Mal. **2** *conj.* sobald; ~ **past the fence we are safe** wenn wir [nur] den Zaun hinter uns bringen, sind wir in Sicherheit. **3** *n.* [just *or* only] **this** ~: [nur] dieses eine Mal

'once-over *n.* **give sb./sth. a/the** ~: jmdn./etw. kurz in Augenschein nehmen

'oncoming *adj.* entgegenkommend ‹*Fahrzeug, Verkehr*›

one /wʌn/ ▶630⌡, ▶706⌡, ▶956⌡ **1** *adj.* **(a)** attrib. ein; ~ **thing I must say** ein[e]s muss ich sagen; ~ **or two** (fig.: a few) ein paar; ~ **more** ...: noch ein ...; ~ **more time** noch einmal; **it's** ~ **[o'clock]** es ist eins *od.* ein Uhr; *see also* **eight 1; half 1 a, 3 b; quarter 1 a; (b)** attrib. (single, only) einzig; **the** ~ **thing** das Einzige; **any** ~: irgendein; **in any** ~ **day/year** an einem Tag/in einem Jahr; **at any** ~ **time** zur gleichen Zeit; (always) zu jeder Zeit; **no** ~: kein; **not** ~ **[little] bit** überhaupt nicht; **(c)** (identical, same) ein; ~ **and the same person/thing** ein und dieselbe Person/Sache; **at** ~ **and the same time** gleichzeitig; *see also* **all 2 a; (d)** pred. (united, unified) **we are** ~: wir sind uns einig; **be** ~ **as a family/nation** eine einige Familie/Nation sein; *see also* **with a; (e)** attrib. (a particular but undefined) **at** ~ **time** einmal; einst (geh.); ~ **morning/night** eines Morgens/Nachts; ~ **day** (on day specified) einmal; (at unspecified future date) eines Tages; ~ **day soon** bald einmal; ~ **day next week** irgendwann nächste Woche; ~ **Sunday** an einem Sonntag; **(f)** attrib. contrasted with 'other'/'another' ein; **for** ~ **thing** zum einen; **neither** ~ **thing nor the other** weder das eine noch das andere; *see also* **hand 1** n; **(g) in** ~ (coll.: at first attempt) auf Anhieb; **got it in** ~**!** (coll.) [du hast es] erraten! **2** *n.* **(a)** eins; **(b)** (number, symbol) Eins, *die; see also* **eight 2 a; (c)** (unit) **in** ~**s** einzeln; **two for the price of** ~: zwei zum Preis von einem. **3** *pron.* **(a)** ~ **of** ...: ein... (+ *Gen.*); ~ **of them/us** etc. einer von ihnen/uns usw.; **any** ~ **of them** jeder/jede/jedes von ihnen; **every** ~ **of them** jeder/jede/jedes [einzelne] von ihnen; **not** ~ **of them** keiner/keine/keines von ihnen; ~ **replacing n. implied or mentioned** ein...; **big** ~**s and little** ~**s** große und kleine; **the jacket is an old** ~: die Jacke ist [schon] alt; **the older/younger** ~: der/die/das ältere/jüngere; **this is the** ~ **I like** den/die/das mag ich; **my husband is the tall** ~ **over there** mein Mann ist der große da; **you are** *or* **were the** ~ **who insisted on going to Scotland** du warst der/diejenige, der/die unbedingt nach Schottland wollte; **this** ~: dieser/diese/dieses [da]; **that** ~: der/die/das [da]; **these** ~**s** *or* **those** ~**s?** (coll.) die [da] oder die [da]?; **these/those blue** etc. ~**s** diese/die blauen usw.; **which** ~**?** welcher/welche/welches?, **which** ~**s?** welche?; **not** ~: keiner/keine/keines; emphatic nicht einer/eine/eines; **all but** ~: alle außer einem/einer/einem; **the last house but** ~: das vorletzte Haus; **I for** ~: ich für mein[en] Teil; ~ **by** ~, ~ **after another** *or* **the other** einzeln; **love** ~ **another** sich *od.* (geh.) einander lieben; **be kind to** ~ **another** nett zueinander sein; **(c)** (contrasted with 'other'/'another') **[the]** ~ ... **the other** der/die/das eine ... der/die/das andere; **(d)** (person or creature of specified kind) **the little** ~: der/die/das Kleine; **our dear** *or* **loved** ~**s** unsere Lieben; **young** ~ (youngster) Kind, *das;* (young animal) Junge, *das;* **(e) [not]** ~ **who does** *or* **to do** *or* **for doing sth.** [nicht] der Typ, der etw. tut; **(f)** (representing people in general; also coll.: I, we) man; as indirect object einem; as direct object einen; ~**'s** sein; **wash** ~**'s hands** sich (*Dat.*) die Hände waschen; **(g)** (coll.: drink) **I'll have just a little** ~: ich trinke nur einen Kleinen (ugs.); **have** ~ **on me** ich geb dir einen aus; **(h)** (coll.: blow) **give sb.** ~ **on the head/nose** jmdm. eins über den Kopf/auf die Nase geben (ugs.)

one: ~**-armed** *adj.* einarmig; ~**-eyed** /'wʌnaɪd/ *adj.* einäugig; ~**-handed** /wʌnhændɪd/ **1** /'---/ *adj.* einhändig; **2** /-'--/ *adv.* mit einer Hand; ~**-legged** *adj.* einbeinig; ~**-man** *attrib. adj.* Einmann‹ *boot, -betrieb usw.*›; ~**-man band** Einmannkapelle, *die;* (fig.: firm etc.) Einmannbetrieb, *der;* ~**-night 'stand** *n.* (coll.) **(a)** (single performance) Einzelauftritt, *der;* **(b)** (sexual) [sexuelles] Abenteuer für eine Nacht; (partner) Mann/Frau für eine Nacht; ~**-off** (Brit.) **1** *n.* (article) Einzelstück, *das;* Einzelexemplar, *das;* (operation) einmalige Sache; **2** *adj.* einmalig ‹*Zahlung,*

Angebot, Produktion, Verkauf⟩; Einzel⟨*stück, -modell, -anfertigung*⟩; **~-parent family** *n.* Einelternfamilie, *die;* **~-piece** *adj.* einteilig; **~-room** *attrib. adj.* Einzimmer⟨*wohnung, -ap[p]art[e]ment*⟩; **a ~-room school/shack** eine aus einem [einzigen] Raum bestehende Schule/Hütte

onerous /'ɒnərəs, 'əʊnərəs/ *adj.* schwer

one: **~'self** *pron.* (a) *emphat.* selbst; **as old/rich as ~self** so alt/reich wie man selbst; **be ~self** man selbst sein; (b) *refl.* sich; *see also* **herself**; **~-sided** /'wʌnsaɪdɪd/ *adj.* einseitig; **~-time** *adj.* (a) (former) ehemalig; (b) (used once only) einmalig; **~-to-'~** *adj.* **~-to-~** relation/correspondence hundertprozentige Parallelität; **~-to-~ teaching** Einzelunterricht, *der;* **~-track** *adj.* eingleisig; **have a ~-track mind** (lack flexibility) eingleisig denken; (be obsessed by one subject) [immer] nur eins im Kopf haben; **~-'up** *pred. adj.* (coll.) **be ~-up** [on *or* over sb.] (fig.) [jmdm.] um eine Nasenlänge voraus sein; **~-way** *adj.* (a) in einer Richtung *nachgestellt;* Einbahn⟨*straße, -verkehr*⟩; (b) (single) einfach ⟨*Fahrpreis, Fahrkarte, Flug usw.*⟩

'ongoing *adj.* aktuell ⟨*Problem, Aktivitäten, Debatte*⟩; laufend ⟨*Forschung, Projekt*⟩; andauernd ⟨*Situation*⟩

onion /'ʌnjən/ *n.* Zwiebel, *die*

on-line (Computing) **1** ['--] *adj.* Online⟨*computer, -betrieb*⟩. **2** [-'-] *adv.* online

'onlooker *n.* Zuschauer, *der*/Zuschauerin, *die*

only /'əʊnlɪ/ **1** *attrib. adj.* (a) einzig...; **the ~ person** der/die Einzige; **my ~ regret is that** ...: ich bedaure nur, dass ...; **an ~ child** ein Einzelkind; **the ~ one/ones** der/die/das Einzige/die Einzigen; **the ~ thing** das Einzige; (b) (best by far) **the ~:** der/die/das einzig Wahre; **he/she is the ~ one for me** es gibt nur ihn für mich. **2** *adv.* (a) nur; **we had been waiting ~ 5 minutes when** ...: wir hatten erst 5 Minuten gewartet, als ...; **it's ~/~ just 6 o'clock** es ist erst 6 Uhr/gerade erst 6 Uhr vorbei; **I ~ wish I had known** wenn ich es doch nur gewusst hätte; **you ~ have** *or* **you have ~ to ask** *etc.* du brauchst nur zu fragen *usw.;* **you ~ live once** man lebt nur einmal; **~ if** nur [dann] ..., wenn; **he ~ just managed it/made it** er hat es gerade so/gerade noch geschafft; **not ~ ... but also** nicht nur ... sondern auch; *see also* **if 1 d**; (b) (no longer ago than) erst; **~ the other day/week** erst neulich *od.* kürzlich; **~ just** gerade erst; (c) (with no better result than) **~ to find/discover that** ...: nur, um zu entdecken, dass ...; (d) **~ too** [sogar] ausgesprochen ⟨*froh, begierig, bereitwillig*⟩; in context of undesirable circumstances viel zu; **be ~ too aware of sth.** sich (*Dat.*) einer Sache (*Gen.*) voll bewusst sein; **~ too well** nur zu gut ⟨*wissen, kennen, sich erinnern*⟩; gerne ⟨*mögen*⟩. **3** *conj.* (a) (but then) nur; (b) (were it not for the fact that) **~ [that]** I am/he is *etc.* ...: ich bin/er ist *usw.* nur ...

o.n.o. /əʊ en 'əʊ/ *abbr.* (Brit.) **or near offer** ≈ VHB

'on-off *adj.* **~ switch** Ein-aus-Schalter

onomatopoeia /ɒnəmætə'pi:ə/ *n.* (Ling.) Onomatopöie, *die*

on-screen 1 *adj.* (a) (Computing, TV) Bildschirm-; **~ editing** redaktionelle Bearbeitung am Bildschirm; (b) (Cinemat.) Leinwand-; **~ violence** Gewalt im Fernsehen/im Film; **her ~ daughter** ihre Filmtochter. **2** *adv.* (a) (Computing, TV) auf dem Bildschirm; (b) (Cinemat.) auf der Leinwand; **appear ~ simultaneously** gleichzeitig im Bild sein; **~ they were lovers** im Film waren sie ein Liebespaar

'onset *n.* (of storm) Einsetzen, *das;* (of winter) Einbruch, *der;* (of disease) Ausbruch, *der*

'onshore *adj.* auflandig (Seemannsspr.) ⟨*Wind*⟩

onslaught /'ɒnslɔːt/ *n.* [heftige] Attacke (fig.)

'on-target *attrib. adj.* **~ earnings** £50,000 Verdienst bei erfolgreicher Tätigkeit 50,000 Pfund

'on-the-job *attrib. adj.* berufsbegleitend ⟨*Unterricht, Fortbildungskurs usw.*⟩; **~ experience** Berufserfahrung, *die;* **~ training** Ausbildung am Arbeitsplatz

on-the-'spot *adj.* vor Ort *nachgestellt*

onto ⇒ **on 2 g**

onus /'əʊnəs/ *n.* Last, *die;* **the ~ is on him to do it** es ist seine Sache, es zu tun

onward[s] /'ɒnwəd(z)/ *adv.* (a) (in space) vorwärts; **from X ~:** von X an; (b) (in time) **from that day ~:** von diesem Tag an

onyx /'ɒnɪks/ *n.* (Min.) Onyx, *der*

ooze /u:z/ **1** *v.i.* (a) (percolate, exude) sickern (**from** aus); (more thickly) quellen (**from** aus); (b) (become moistened) triefen (**with** von, vor + *Dat.*). **2** *v.t.* (a) **~ [out]** triefen von *od.* vor (+ *Dat.*); (b) (fig.: radiate) ausstrahlen ⟨*Charme, Optimismus*⟩; ausströmen ⟨*Sarkasmus*⟩. **3** *n.* (mud) Schlick, *der*

opal /'əʊpl/ *n.* (Min.) Opal, *der*

opalescent /əʊpə'lesənt/ *adj.* schillernd; opalisierend

opaque /əʊ'peɪk/ *adj.* (a) (not transmitting light) lichtundurchlässig, opak (fachspr.); (b) (obscure) dunkel; unverständlich

OPEC /'əʊpek/ *abbr.* **Organization of Petroleum Exporting Countries** OPEC, *die*

open /'əʊpn/ **1** *adj.* (a) offen; **with the window ~:** bei geöffnetem Fenster; **be [wide/half] ~:** [weit/halb] offen stehen; **hold the door ~** [for sb.] [jmdm.] die Tür aufhalten; **push/pull/kick the door ~:** die Tür aufstoßen/aufziehen/eintreten; **force sth. ~:** etw. mit Gewalt öffnen; **with one's mouth ~:** mit offenem Mund; **have one's eyes ~:** die Augen offen haben; **[not] be able to keep one's eyes ~:** [nicht mehr] die Augen offenhalten können; *see also* **eye 1 a**; (b) (unconfined) offen ⟨*Gelände, Feuer*⟩; **on the ~ road** auf freier Strecke; **in the ~ air** im Freien; (c) (ready for business or use) **be ~** ⟨*Laden, Museum, Bank usw.*⟩; geöffnet sein; **'~'/'~ on Sundays'** „geöffnet"/„Sonntags geöffnet"; (d) (accessible) offen; öffentlich ⟨*Treffen, Rennen*⟩; (available) frei ⟨*Stelle*⟩; freibleibend ⟨*Angebot*⟩; **lay ~:** offen legen ⟨*Plan*⟩; **be ~ to the public** für die Öffentlichkeit zugänglich sein; **the offer remains ~ until the end of the month** das Angebot bleibt bestehen *od.* gilt noch bis Ende des Monats; **keep a position ~ for sb.** jmdm. eine Stelle freihalten; (e) **be ~ to** (exposed to) ausgesetzt sein (+ *Dat.*) ⟨*Wind, Sturm*⟩; (receptive to) offen sein für ⟨*Ratschlag, andere Meinung, Vorschlag*⟩; **I hope to sell it for £1,000, but I am ~ to offers** ich möchte es für 1 000 Pfund verkaufen, aber ich lasse mit mir handeln; **lay oneself [wide] ~ to criticism** *etc.* sich der Kritik *usw.* aussetzen; **be ~ to question/doubt/argument** fraglich/zweifelhaft/umstritten sein; (f) (undecided) offen; **have an ~ mind about** *or* **on sth.** einer Sache gegenüber aufgeschlossen sein; **with an ~ mind** aufgeschlossen; **leave sth. ~:** etw. offen lassen; (g) (undisguised, manifest) unverhohlen ⟨*Bewunderung, Hass*⟩; offen ⟨*Verachtung, Empörung, Widerstand*⟩; offensichtlich ⟨*Spaltung, Zwiespalt*⟩; **~ war/warfare** offener Krieg/Kampf; (h) (frank) offen ⟨*Wesen, Streit, Abstimmung, Gesicht*⟩; (not secret) öffentlich ⟨*Wahl*⟩; **be ~ [about sth./ with sb.]** [in Bezug auf etw. (*Akk.*)/gegenüber jmdm.] offen sein; (i) (expanded, unfolded) offen, geöffnet ⟨*Pore, Regenschirm*⟩; aufgeblüht ⟨*Blume, Knospe*⟩; aufgeschlagen ⟨*Zeitung, Landkarte, Stadtplan*⟩; **sth./sth. is an ~ book** [to sb.] (fig.) jmd./etw. ist ein aufgeschlagenes *od.* offenes Buch [für jmdn.]. **2** *n.* **in the ~** (outdoors) unter freiem Himmel; **[out] in the ~** (fig.) [öffentlich] bekannt; **come [out] into the ~** (fig.) (become obvious) herauskommen (ugs.); (speak out) offen sprechen; **bring sth. [out] into the ~** (fig.) etw. an die Öffentlichkeit bringen. **3** *v.t.* (a) öffnen; aufmachen (ugs.); **~ sth. with a key** etw. aufschließen; (b) (allow access to) **~ sth.** [to sb./sth.] etw. öffnen [für jmdn./etw.]; (fig.) [jmdm./einer Sache] etw. öffnen; **~ sth. to the public** etw. der Öffentlichkeit (*Dat.*) zugänglich machen; (c) (establish) eröffnen ⟨*Konferenz, Kampagne, Diskussion, Laden*⟩; beginnen ⟨*Verhandlungen, Krieg, Spiel*⟩; (declare ~) eröffnen ⟨*Gebäude usw.*⟩; **~ an account** ein Konto eröffnen; **~ fire** [on sb./sth.] das Feuer [auf jmdn./etw.] eröffnen; (d) (unfold, spread out) aufschlagen ⟨*Zeitung, Landkarte, Stadtplan, Buch*⟩; aufspannen, öffnen ⟨*Schirm*⟩; öffnen ⟨*Fallschirm, Poren*⟩; **~ one's arms [wide]** die *od.* seine Arme [weit] ausbreiten; (e) (reveal, expose) öffnen; **~s new horizons/a new world** (fig.) etw. eröffnet jmdm. neue Horizonte/eine neue Welt; (f) (make more receptive) **~ one's heart** *or* **mind to sb./sth.** sich jmdm./einer Sache öffnen; **~ sb.'s mind to sth.**

jmdm. etw. nahe bringen. **4** *v.i.* **(a)** sich öffnen; aufgehen; ⟨*Spalt, Kluft:*⟩ sich auftun; **'Doors ∼ at 7 p.m.'** „Einlass ab 19 Uhr"; **∼ inwards/outwards** nach innen/außen aufgehen; **the door would not ∼:** die Tür ging nicht auf *od,* ließ sich nicht öffnen; **his eyes ∼ed wide** er riss die Augen weit auf; **∼ into/on to sth.** zu etw. führen; **the kitchen ∼s into the living room** die Küche hat eine Tür zum Wohnzimmer; **(b)** (become ∼ to customers) öffnen; aufmachen (ugs.); (start trading etc.) eröffnet werden; **the shop does not ∼ on Sundays** der Laden ist sonntags geschlossen; **(c)** (make a start) beginnen; ⟨*Ausstellung:*⟩ eröffnet werden

∼ **'out 1** *v.t.* (unfold) auseinander falten. **2** *v.i.* **(a)** ⟨*Knospe:*⟩ sich öffnen; **(b)** (widen, expand) ∼ **out into sth.** sich zu etw. erweitern

∼ **'up 1** *v.t.* **(a)** aufmachen (ugs.); öffnen; aufschlagen ⟨*Buch*⟩; **(b)** (form or make by cutting etc.) machen ⟨*Loch, Riß*⟩; **(c)** (establish, make more accessible) eröffnen ⟨*Laden, Filiale*⟩; erschließen ⟨*neue Märkte usw.*⟩; ∼ **up a new world to sb.** jmdm. eine neue Welt erschließen. **2** *v.i.* **(a)** ⟨*Blüte, Knospe:*⟩ sich öffnen; **(b)** (be established) ⟨*Filiale:*⟩ eröffnet werden; ⟨*Firma:*⟩ sich niederlassen; **(c)** (appear, be revealed) entstehen; ⟨*Aussichten, Möglichkeiten:*⟩ sich eröffnen; ∼ **up before sb.** ⟨*Blick, Aussicht:*⟩ sich jmdm. bieten; ⟨*neue Welt:*⟩ sich vor jmdm. auftun; **(d)** (talk freely) gesprächig werden; ∼ **up to sb.** sich jmdm. anvertrauen

open: ∼**-air** *attrib. adj.* Openair-⟨*Konzert*⟩; Freiluft⟨*restaurant, -aktivitäten*⟩; Freilicht⟨*kino, -aufführung*⟩; ⟨*Ausstellung, Markt, Versammlung*⟩ im Freien *od.* unter freiem Himmel; ∼**-air [swimming-]pool** Freibad, *das;* ∼**-and-'shut case** *n.* (coll.) klarer Fall; ∼ **day** *n.* Tag der offenen Tür; ∼**-ended** /əʊpən'endɪd/ *adj.* (also fig.) unbefristet ⟨*Aufenthalt, Vertrag*⟩; Open-End-⟨*Diskussion, Debatte*⟩; offen ⟨*Frage*⟩

opener /'əʊpnə(r)/ *n.* Öffner, *der*

open: ∼**-handed** /əʊpn'hændɪd/ *adj.* freigebig; ∼**-'heart** *attrib. adj.* (Med.) am offenen Herzen *nachgestellt;* ∼**-hearted** /əʊpnhɑːtɪd/ *adj.* aufrichtig ⟨*Person, Mitgefühl*⟩; herzlich ⟨*Empfang*⟩

opening /'əʊpnɪŋ/ **1** *n.* **(a)** Öffnen, *das;* (becoming open) Sichöffnen, *das;* (of crack, gap, etc.) Entstehen, *das;* (of exhibition, new centre) Eröffnen, *das;* **hours or times of ∼:** Öffnungszeiten; **(b)** (establishment, inauguration, ceremony) Eröffnung, die; ∼ **of Parliament** Parlamentseröffnung, *die;* **(c)** (initial part) Anfang, *der;* **(d)** (gap, aperture) Öffnung, *die;* **(e)** (opportunity) Möglichkeit, *die;* (vacancy) freie *od.* offene Stelle; **give sb. an ∼ into sth.** ⟨*Person:*⟩ jmdm. den Einstieg in etw. (*Akk.*) ermöglichen; ⟨*Job:*⟩ für jmdn. ein Einstieg in etw. (*Akk.*) sein. **2** *adj.* einleitend; **the ∼ lines** (of play, poem, etc.) die ersten Zeilen; ∼ **night** (Theatre) Premiere, *die;* ∼ **move** (Chess) Eröffnung, *die*

opening: ∼ **ceremony** *n.* feierliche Eröffnung (**for** *Gen.*); ∼ **hours** *n. pl.* Öffnungszeiten *Pl.;* ∼ **time** *n.* **(a)** Öffnungszeit, *die;* **(b)** ∼ **times** ⇒ ∼ **hours**

openly /'əʊpnlɪ/ *adv.* **(a)** (publicly) in der Öffentlichkeit; öffentlich ⟨*zugeben, verurteilen, abstreiten*⟩; **quite ∼:** in aller Öffentlichkeit; **(b)** (frankly) offen

open: ∼ **'market** *n.* offener *od.* freier Markt; ∼**-minded** *adj.* aufgeschlossen (**about** für); ∼**-mouthed** /əʊpn'maʊðd/ *adj.* mit offenem Mund; ∼**-necked** /'əʊpnnekt/ *adj.* ⟨*Hemd, Bluse*⟩ mit offenem Kragen; ausgeschnitten ⟨*Kleid, Pullover*⟩

openness /'əʊpnnɪs/ *n., no pl.* **(a)** (receptiveness) Empfänglichkeit, *die;* **(b)** (frankness) Offenheit, *die*

open: ∼**-plan** *adj.* offen angelegt ⟨*Haus*⟩; ∼**-plan office** Großraumbüro, *das;* ∼ **'prison** *n.* offene Anstalt; ∼ **'sandwich** *n.* belegtes Brot; ∼ **season** *n.* (Brit.) Jagdzeit, *die;* (for fish) Fangzeit, *die;* **it is [the] ∼ season for** *or* **on sth.** (fig.) etw. ist an der Tagesordnung; ∼**-top** *attrib. adj.* offen; oben offen ⟨*Bus*⟩; **O∼ University** *pr. n.* (Brit.) **the O∼ University** die Open University (*britische Fernuniversität*); *attrib.* ⟨*Kurs*⟩ an der Fernuniversität; ⟨*akademischer Grad*⟩ der Fernuniversität

opera¹ /'ɒpərə/ *n.* **(a)** Oper, *die;* **(b)** *no pl.* **[the]** ∼**:** die Oper

opera² *pl. of* **opus**

opera: ∼ **glasses** *n. pl.* Opernglas, *das;* ∼ **house** *n.* Opernhaus, *das;* ∼ **singer** *n.* Opernsänger, *der/*-sängerin, *die*

operate /'ɒpəreɪt/ **1** *v.i.* **(a)** (be in action) in Betrieb sein; ⟨*Bus, Zug usw.:*⟩ verkehren; (have an effect) sich auswirken; **(b)** (function) arbeiten; **the torch ∼s on batteries** die Taschenlampe arbeitet mit Batterien; **(c)** (perform operation) operieren; arbeiten; ∼ **[on sb.]** (Med.) [jmdn.] operieren; **(d)** (exercise influence) ∼ **[up]on sb./sth.** auf jmdn./etw. einwirken; **(e)** (follow course of conduct) agieren; **(f)** (produce effect) wirken; **(g)** (Mil.) operieren. **2** *v.t.* bedienen ⟨*Maschine*⟩; fahren ⟨*Auto*⟩; betreiben ⟨*Unternehmen*⟩; unterhalten ⟨*Werk, Post, Busverbindung*⟩

'operating theatre *n.* (Brit. Med.) Operationssaal, *der*

operation /ɒpə'reɪʃn/ *n.* **(a)** (causing to work) (of machine) Bedienung, *die;* (of factory, mine, etc.) Betrieb, *der;* (of bus service etc.) Unterhaltung, *die;* **(b)** (way sth. works) Arbeitsweise, *die;* **(c)** (being operative) **come into ∼** ⟨*Gesetz, Gebühr usw.:*⟩ in Kraft treten; **be in ∼** ⟨*Maschine, Gerät usw.:*⟩ in Betrieb sein; ⟨*Service:*⟩ zur Verfügung stehen; ⟨*Gesetz:*⟩ in Kraft sein; **be out of ∼** ⟨*Maschine, Gerät usw.:*⟩ außer Betrieb sein; **(d)** (performance) Tätigkeit, *die;* **repeat the ∼:** das Ganze [noch einmal] wiederholen; **(e)** ▶ **865 |** (Med.) Operation, *die;* **have an ∼ [on one's foot]** [am Fuß] operiert werden; **(f)** (Mil.) Einsatz, *der*

operational /ɒpə'reɪʃənl/ *adj.* **(a)** Einsatz⟨*flugzeug, -breite*⟩; (Mil.) Einsatz-; **(b)** (esp. Mil.: ready to function) einsatzbereit

operative /'ɒpərətɪv/ **1** *adj.* **(a)** (in operation) **the law became ∼:** das Gesetz trat in Kraft; **the scheme is fully ∼:** das Programm läuft; **(b)** (most relevant) **the ∼ word is 'quietly'** die Betonung liegt auf „leise". **2** *n.* [Fach]arbeiter, *der/*-arbeiterin, *die*

operator /'ɒpəreɪtə(r)/ *n.* ▶ **887 |** **(a)** (worker) [Maschinen]bediener, *der/*-bedienerin, *die;* (of crane, excavator, etc.) Führer, *der;* **(b)** (Teleph.) (at exchange) Vermittlung, *die;* (at switchboard) Telefonist, *der/*Telefonistin, *die;* **(c)** (coll.: shrewd person) Schlitzohr, *das* (ugs.)

ophthalmic /ɒf'θælmɪk/ *adj.* Augen-

ophthalmic op'tician *n.* (Brit.) Augenoptiker, *der/*-optikerin, *die*

opinion /ə'pɪnjən/ *n.* **(a)** (belief, judgement) Meinung, *die* (**on** über + *Akk.*, zu); Ansicht, *die* (**on** von, zu, über + *Akk.*); **his ∼s on religion** seine Meinung dazu/seine Einstellung zur Religion; **in my ∼:** meiner Meinung nach; **be a matter of ∼:** Ansichtssache sein; **(b)** *no pl., no art.* (beliefs etc. of group) Meinung, *die* (**on** über + *Akk.*); **public ∼:** die öffentliche Meinung; **(c)** (estimate) **have a high/low ∼ of sb.** eine hohe/schlechte Meinung von jmdm. haben; **(d)** (formal statement of expert) Gutachten, *das;* **a second ∼:** die Meinung eines zweiten Sachverständigen

opinionated /ə'pɪnjəneɪtɪd/ *adj.* rechthaberisch

o'pinion poll *n.* Meinungsumfrage, *die*

opium /'əʊpɪəm/ *n.* Opium, *das*

opponent /ə'pəʊnənt/ *n.* Gegner, *der/*Gegnerin, *die*

opportune /'ɒpətjuːn/ *adj.* **(a)** (favourable) günstig; **(b)** (well-timed) zur rechten Zeit *nachgestellt*

opportunism /ɒpə'tjuːnɪzm/ *n., no pl.* Opportunismus, *der*

opportunist /ɒpə'tjuːnɪst/ *n.* Opportunist, *der/*Opportunistin, *die*

opportunity /ɒpə'tjuːnɪtɪ/ *n.* Gelegenheit, *die;* **have plenty of/little ∼ for doing** *or* **to do sth.** reichlich/wenig Gelegenheit haben, etw. zu tun

oppose /ə'pəʊz/ *v.t.* **(a)** (set oneself against) sich wenden gegen; **(b)** (place as obstacle) entgegenstellen (**to** *Dat.*); **(c)** (set as contrast) gegenüberstellen (**to, against** *Dat.*)

opposed /ə'pəʊzd/ *adj.* **(a)** (contrary) gegensätzlich; entgegengesetzt; **as ∼ to** im Gegensatz zu; **(b)** (hostile) **be ∼ to sth.** gegen etw. sein

opposite /'ɒpəzɪt/ **1** *adj.* **(a)** (on other or farther side) gegenüberliegend ⟨*Straßenseite, Ufer*⟩; entgegengesetzt ⟨*Ende*⟩; **(b)** (contrary) entgegengesetzt ⟨*Weg, Richtung*⟩; **(c)** (very different in character) entgegengesetzt, gegensätzlich

‹*Beschreibungen, Aussagen*›; **(d) the** ∼ **sex** das andere Geschlecht. **2** *n.* Gegenteil, *das* (**of** von); **be** ∼**s** einen Gegensatz bilden. **3** *adv.* gegenüber; **sit** ∼: auf der gegenüberliegenden Seite sitzen. **4** *prep.* gegenüber

opposite 'number *n.* (fig.) Pendant, *das*

opposition /ɒpə'zɪʃn/ *n.* **(a)** *no pl.* (antagonism) Opposition, *die;* (resistance) Widerstand, *der* (**to** gegen); **in** ∼ **to** entgegen (+ *Dat.*); **(b)** (Brit. Polit.) **the O**∼: die Opposition; [**be**] **in** ∼: in der Opposition [sein]; **(c)** (body of opponents) Gegner *Pl.;* **(d)** (contrast, antithesis) Gegensatz, *der* (**to** zu)

oppress /ə'pres/ *v.t.* **(a)** (govern cruelly) unterdrücken; **(b)** (fig.: weigh down) ‹*Gefühl:*› bedrücken; ‹*Hitze:*› schwer zu schaffen machen (+ *Dat.*)

oppression /ə'preʃn/ *n.* Unterdrückung, *die*

oppressive /ə'presɪv/ *adj.* **(a)** (tyrannical) repressiv; **(b)** (fig.: hard to endure) bedrückend ‹*Ängste, Atmosphäre*›; **(c)** (fig.: hot and close) drückend ‹*Wetter, Klima, Tag*›; **(d)** (fig.: burdensome) drückend ‹*Steuer*›; repressiv ‹*Gesetz, Beschränkung*›

opt /ɒpt/ *v.i.* sich entscheiden (**for** für); ∼ **to do sth.** sich dafür entscheiden, etw. zu tun; ∼ **out** (not join in) nicht mitmachen; (cease taking part) nicht länger mitmachen; ∼ **out of** nicht/nicht länger mitmachen bei

optic /'ɒptɪk/ *adj.* (Anat.) Seh-

optical /'ɒptɪkl/ *adj.* optisch; ∼ **'fibre** Lichtleitfaser, *die*

optician /ɒp'tɪʃn/ *n.* ▶ 887 | **(a)** (maker or seller of spectacles etc.) Optiker, *der*/Optikerin, *die;* **(b)** ⇒ **ophthalmic optician**

optics /'ɒptɪks/ *n., no pl.* Optik, *die*

optima *pl. of* **optimum**

optimal /'ɒptɪml/ ⇒ **optimum 2**

optimise ⇒ **optimize**

optimism /'ɒptɪmɪzm/ *n., no pl.* Optimismus, *der*

optimist /'ɒptɪmɪst/ *n.* Optimist, *der*/Optimistin, *die*

optimistic /ɒptɪ'mɪstɪk/ *adj.* optimistisch

optimize /'ɒptɪmaɪz/ *v.t.* optimieren

optimum /'ɒptɪməm/ **1** *n., pl.* **optima** /'ɒptɪmə/ Optimum, *das.* **2** *adj.* optimal

option /'ɒpʃn/ *n.* Wahl, *die;* (thing that may be chosen) Wahlmöglichkeit, *die;* (Brit. Univ., Sch.) Wahlfach, *das;* **I have no** ∼ **but to do sth.** mir bleibt nichts [anderes] übrig, als etw. zu tun; **keep** *or* **leave one's** ∼**s open** sich (*Dat.*) alle Möglichkeiten offenhalten

optional /'ɒpʃənl/ *adj.* nicht zwingend; ∼ **subject** Wahlfach, *das*

opulence /'ɒpjʊləns/ *n., no pl.* Wohlstand, *der*

opulent /'ɒpjʊlənt/ *adj.* wohlhabend ‹*Person, Aussehen*›; feudal ‹*Auto, Haus, Hotel usw.*›

opus /'əʊpəs, 'ɒpəs/ *n., pl.* **opera** /'ɒpərə/ (Mus.) Opus, *das*

or /ə(r), *stressed* ɔ:(r)/ *conj.* **(a)** oder; **he cannot read or write** er kann weder lesen noch schreiben; **without food or water** ohne Essen und Wasser; [**either**] ... **or** [**else**] ...: entweder ... oder [aber] ...; **(b)** *introducing synonym* oder [auch]; *introducing explanation* das heißt; **or rather** beziehungsweise; **(c)** *indicating uncertainty* oder; **15 or 20 minutes** 15 bis 20 Minuten; **in a day or two** in ein, zwei Tagen; **he must be ill or something** vielleicht ist er krank oder so (ugs.); **(d)** *expr. significant afterthought* oder; **he was obviously lying — or was he?** er hat ganz offensichtlich gelogen — oder [doch nicht]?

oracle /'ɒrəkl/ *n.* Orakel, *das*

oral /'ɔ:rl/ **1** *adj.* **(a)** (spoken) mündlich ‹*Prüfung, Vereinbarung*›; mündlich überliefert ‹*Tradition*›; **(b)** (Anat.) Mund‹*höhle, -schleimhaut*›. **2** *n.* (coll.: examination) **the** ∼[**s**] das Mündliche

orally /'ɔ:rəlɪ/ *adv.* **(a)** (in speech) mündlich; **(b)** (by mouth) oral; **take** ∼: einnehmen

orange /'ɒrɪndʒ/ **1** *n.* **(a)** Orange, *die;* Apfelsine, *die;* **(b)** (colour) ∼[**-colour**] Orange, *das.* **2** *adj.* orange[farben]; Orangen‹*geschmack*›

orange: ∼ **juice** *n.* Orangensaft, *der;* ∼ **peel** *n.* Orangenschale, *die;* ∼ **'squash** ⇒ **squash 3 a**

orang-utan /ɔ:ræŋʊ'tæn/ *n.* (Zool.) Orang-Utan, *der*

oration /ə'reɪʃn/ *n.* Rede, *die*

orator /'ɒrətə(r)/ *n.* Redner, *der*/Rednerin, *die*

oratorio /ɒrə'tɔ:rɪəʊ/ *n., pl.* ∼**s** (Mus.) Oratorium, *das*

oratory /'ɒrətərɪ/ *n., no pl.* **(a)** (art) Redekunst, *die;* **(b)** (rhetorical language) Rhetorik, *die*

orbit /'ɔ:bɪt/ **1** *n.* **(a)** (Astron.) [Umlauf]bahn, *die;* **(b)** (Astronaut.) Umlaufbahn, *die;* Orbit, *der;* **put/send into** ∼: in die Umlaufbahn bringen/schießen; **(c)** (fig.) Sphäre, *die.* **2** *v.i.* kreisen. **3** *v.t.* umkreisen

orchard /'ɔ:tʃəd/ *n.* Obstgarten, *der;* (commercial) Obstplantage, *die;* **cherry** ∼: Kirschgarten, *der*

orchestra /'ɔ:kɪstrə/ *n.* (Mus.) Orchester, *das*

orchestral /ɔ:'kestrl/ *adj.* Orchester-

orchestrate /'ɔ:kɪstreɪt/ *v.t.* (Mus.; also fig.) orchestrieren

orchestration /ɔ:kɪ'streɪʃn/ *n.* (Mus.) Orchesterbearbeitung, *die*

orchid /'ɔ:kɪd/ *n.* Orchidee, *die*

ordain /ɔ:'deɪn/ *v.t.* **(a)** (Eccl.) ordinieren; **(b)** (destine) bestimmen

ordeal /ɔ:'di:l/ *n.* Qual, *die* (**by** durch)

order /'ɔ:də(r)/ **1** *n.* **(a)** (sequence) Reihenfolge, *die;* **word** ∼: Wortstellung, *die;* **in** ∼ **of importance/size/age** nach Wichtigkeit/Größe/Alter; **put sth. in** ∼: etw. [in der richtigen Reihenfolge] ordnen; **keep sth. in** ∼: etw. in der richtigen Reihenfolge halten; **answer the questions in** ∼: die Fragen der Reihe nach beantworten; **out of** ∼: nicht in der richtigen Reihenfolge; **(b)** (normal state) Ordnung, *die;* **put** *or* **set sth./one's affairs in** ∼: Ordnung in etw. bringen/seine Angelegenheiten ordnen; **be/not be in** ∼: in Ordnung/nicht in Ordnung sein (ugs.); **be out of/ in** ∼ (not in/in working condition) nicht funktionieren/funktionieren; **'out of** ∼' „außer Betrieb"; **in good/bad** ∼: in gutem/schlechtem Zustand; **in working** ∼: betriebsfähig; **(c)** *in sing. and pl.* (command) Anweisung, *die;* Anordnung, *die;* (Mil.) Befehl, *der;* (Law) Beschluss, *der;* Verfügung, *die;* **my** ∼**s are to ...**, **I have** ∼**s to ...** ich habe Anweisung zu ...; **while following** ∼**s** bei Befolgung der Anweisung; **act on** ∼**s** auf Befehl handeln; ∼**s are** ∼**s** Befehl ist Befehl; **court** ∼: Gerichtsbeschluss, *der;* **by** ∼ **of** auf Anordnung (+ *Gen.*); **(d)** **in** ∼ **to do sth.** um etw. zu tun; **in** ∼ **that sb. should do sth.** damit jmd. etw. tut; **(e)** (Commerc.) Auftrag, *der* (**for** über + *Akk.*); Bestellung, *die* (**for** *Gen.*); Order, *die* (Kaufmannsspr.); (**to** waiter, ∼**ed goods**) Bestellung, *die;* **place an** ∼ [**with sb.**] [jmdm.] einen Auftrag erteilen; **have sth. on** ∼: etw. bestellt haben; **made to** ∼: nach Maß angefertigt, maßgeschneidert ‹*Kleidung*›; **(f)** (law-abiding state) **keep** ∼: Ordnung [be]wahren; *see also* **law b;** **(g)** (Eccl.) Orden, *der;* **holy** ∼**s** heilige Weihen; **(h) O**∼! **O**∼! zur Ordnung!; Ruhe bitte!; **call sb./the meeting to** ∼: jmdn./die Versammlung zur Ordnung rufen; **point of** ∼: Verfahrensfrage, *die;* **be in** ∼: zulässig sein; (fig.) ‹*Forderung:*› berechtigt sein; ‹*Drink, Erklärung:*› angebracht sein; **it is in** ∼ **for him to do that** (fig.) es ist in Ordnung, wenn er das tut (ugs.); **be out of** ∼ (unacceptable) gegen die Geschäftsordnung verstoßen; ‹*Verhalten, Handlung:*› unzulässig sein; **(i)** (kind, degree) Klasse, *die;* Art, *die;* (Finance) Order, *die;* [**banker's**] ∼: [Bank]anweisung, *die;* **'pay to the** ∼ **of ...'** „zahlbar an ..." (+ *Akk.*); **(k)** ∼ [**of magnitude**] Größenordnung, *die;* **of** *or* **in the** ∼ **of ...:** in der Größenordnung von ...; **a scoundrel of the first** ∼ (fig. coll.) ein Schurke ersten Ranges. **2** *v.t.* **(a)** (command) befehlen; anordnen; ‹*Richter:*› verfügen; verordnen ‹*Arznei, Ruhe usw.*›; ∼ **sb. to do sth.** jmdn. anweisen/(Mil.) jmdm. befehlen, etw. zu tun; ∼ **sth.** [**to be**] **done** anordnen, dass etw. getan wird; ∼ **sb. out of the house** jmdn. aus dem Haus weisen; **(b)** (direct the supply of) bestellen (**from** bei); ordern ‹*Kaufmannsspr.*›; ∼ **in advance** vorbestellen; **(c)** (arrange) ordnen

∼ **a'bout,** ∼ **a'round** *v.t.* (coll.) herumkommandieren

∼ **'off** *v.t.* (Sport) ∼ **sb. off** [**the field**] jmdn. vom Platz stellen

'order form *n.* Bestellformular, *das;* Bestellschein, *der*

orderly /'ɔ:dəlɪ/ **1** *adj.* friedlich ‹*Demonstration usw.*›; diszipliniert ‹*Menge*›; (methodical) methodisch; ordentlich ‹*Person*›; (tidy) ordentlich. **2** *n.* (Mil.) [Offiziers]bursche, *der*

ordinal /'ɔːdɪnl/ ▶956 (Math.) **1** *adj.* ~ **number** ⇒ 2. **2** *n.* Ordnungs-, Ordinalzahl, *die*

ordinance /'ɔːdɪnəns/ *n.* **(a)** (order, decree) Verordnung, *die;* **(b)** (enactment by local authority) Verfügung, *die;* Bestimmung, *die*

ordinarily /'ɔːdɪnərɪlɪ/ *adv.* normalerweise; gewöhnlich

ordinary /'ɔːdɪnərɪ/ *adj.* (regular, normal) normal ⟨*Gebrauch*⟩; üblich ⟨*Verfahren*⟩; (not exceptional) gewöhnlich; (average) durchschnittlich; **very** ~ (derog.) ziemlich mittelmäßig; ~ **tap water** normales *od.* gewöhnliches Leitungswasser; **out of the** ~: außergewöhnlich; ungewöhnlich; **something/nothing out of the** ~: etwas/ nichts Außergewöhnliches

ordinary level ⇒ **O level**

ordination /ɔːdɪ'neɪʃn/ *n.* (Eccl.) Ordination, *die;* Ordinierung, *die*

ordnance survey map /ɔːdnəns 'sɜːveɪ mæp/ *n.* (Brit.) amtliche topographische Karte

ore /ɔː(r)/ *n.* Erz, *das*

oregano /ɒrɪ'gɑːnəʊ/ *n., no pl.* (Cookery) Oregano, *der*

organ /'ɔːgən/ *n.* **(a)** (Mus.) Orgel, *die;* **(b)** (Biol.) Organ, *das;* **(c)** (medium of communication) Sprachrohr, *das;* (of political party etc.) Organ, *das*

'organ-grinder *n.* Drehorgelspieler, *der/*-spielerin, *die*

organic /ɔː'gænɪk/ *adj.* **(a)** (also Chem. Physiol.) organisch; **(b)** (without chemicals) biologisch, biodynamisch ⟨*Nahrungsmittel*⟩; biologisch-dynamisch ⟨*Ackerbau usw.*⟩

organisation, organise *etc.* ⇒ **organiz-**

organism /'ɔːgənɪzm/ *n.* (Biol.) Organismus, *der*

organist /'ɔːgənɪst/ *n.* Organist, *der/*Organistin, *die*

organization /ɔːgənaɪ'zeɪʃn/ *n.* **(a)** (organizing) Organisation, *die;* (of material) Ordnung, *die;* (of library) Anordnung, *die;* ~ **of time/work** Zeit-/Arbeitseinteilung, *die;* **(b)** (organized body, system) Organisation, *die*

organize /'ɔːgənaɪz/ *v.t.* **(a)** (give orderly structure to) ordnen; planen ⟨*Leben*⟩; einteilen ⟨*Arbeit, Zeit*⟩; (frame, establish) organisieren ⟨*Verein, Partei, Firma, Institution*⟩; **I must get** ~**d** (get ready) ich muss fertig werden; ~ **sb.** jmdn. an die Hand nehmen (fig.); **(b)** (arrange) organisieren; **can you** ~ **the catering?** kümmerst du dich um die Verpflegung?

organized /'ɔːgənaɪzd/ *adj.* organisiert; geregelt ⟨*Leben*⟩; ~ **crime** das organisierte Verbrechen; die organisierte Kriminalität

organizer /'ɔːgənaɪzə(r)/ *n.* Organisator, *der/*Organisatorin, *die;* (of event, festival) Veranstalter, *der/*Veranstalterin, *die*

orgasm /'ɔːgæzəm/ *n.* Orgasmus, *der;* Höhepunkt, *der* (auch fig.)

orgy /'ɔːdʒɪ/ *n.* Orgie, *die;* **drunken** ~: Orgie unter Alkoholeinfluss

orient **1** /'ɔːrɪənt/ *n.* **the O**~: der Orient. **2** /'ɔːrɪent, 'ɒrɪent/ *v.t.* (fig.) einweisen (**in** in + *Akk.*); ausrichten, abstellen (**towards** auf + *Akk.*) ⟨*Programm*⟩; ~ **oneself** sich orientieren *od.* zurechtfinden; **-**~**ed** -orientiert; **money-**~**ed** materiell orientiert

oriental /ɔːrɪ'entl, ɒrɪ'entl/ **1** *adj.* orientalisch. **2** *n.* Asiat, *der/*Asiatin, *die*

orientate /'ɒrɪənteɪt, 'ɔːrɪənteɪt/ ⇒ **orient 2**

orientation /ɒrɪən'teɪʃn, ɔːrɪən'teɪʃn/ *n.* Orientierung, *die*

orienteering /ɔːrɪən'tɪərɪŋ, ɒrɪən'tɪərɪŋ/ *n.* (Brit.) Orientierungsrennen, *das*

orifice /'ɒrɪfɪs/ *n.* Öffnung, *die*

origin /'ɒrɪdʒɪn/ *n.* (derivation) Abstammung, *die;* Herkunft, *die;* (beginnings) Anfänge *Pl.;* (of world etc.) Entstehung, *die;* (source) Ursprung, *der;* (of belief, rumour) Quelle, *die;* **be of humble** ~**, have humble** ~**s** bescheidener Herkunft sein; **country of** ~: Herkunftsland, *das;* **have its** ~ **in sth.** seinen Ursprung in etw. (*Dat.*) haben

original /ə'rɪdʒɪnl/ **1** *adj.* **(a)** (first, earliest) ursprünglich; **the** ~ **inhabitants** die Ureinwohner; **(b)** (primary) original; Original-; Ur⟨*text, -fassung*⟩; eigenständig ⟨*Forschung*⟩; (inventive) originell; (creative) schöpferisch; **an** ~ **painting** ein Original. **2** *n.* Original, *das*

originality /ərɪdʒɪ'nælɪtɪ/ *n.* Originalität, *die*

originally /ə'rɪdʒɪnəlɪ/ *adv.* **(a)** ursprünglich; **be** ~ **from** ...: [ursprünglich] aus ... stammen; **(b)** (in an original way) originell ⟨*schreiben usw.*⟩; **think** ~: originelle Gedanken haben

originate /ə'rɪdʒɪneɪt/ **1** *v.i.* ~ **from** entstehen aus; ~ **in** seinen Ursprung haben in (+ *Dat.*). **2** *v.t.* schaffen; hervorbringen; (discover) erfinden

origination /ərɪdʒɪ'neɪʃn/ *n.* Entstehung, *die*

originator /ə'rɪdʒɪneɪtə(r)/ *n.* Urheber, *der/*Urheberin, *die;* (inventor) Erfinder, *der/*Erfinderin, *die*

ornament **1** /'ɔːnəmənt/ *n.* Schmuck-, Ziergegenstand, *der.* **2** /'ɔːnəment/ *v.t.* verzieren

ornamental /ɔːnə'mentl/ *adj.* dekorativ; ornamental (bes. Kunst); Zier⟨*pflanze, -naht usw.*⟩; **purely** ~: nur zum Schmuck *od.* zur Zierde; rein dekorativ

ornamentation /ɔːnəmen'teɪʃn/ *n., no pl.* **(a)** (ornamenting) Ausschmückung, *die;* **(b)** (embellishment[s]) Verzierung, *die*

ornate /ɔː'neɪt/ *adj.* **(a)** (elaborately adorned) reich verziert; prunkvoll ⟨*Dekoration*⟩; **(b)** (style) blumig (abwertend); reich ausgeschmückt ⟨*Prosa*⟩

ornithology /ɔːnɪ'θɒlədʒɪ/ *n.* Ornithologie, *die;* Vogelkunde, *die*

orphan /'ɔːfn/ **1** *n.* Waise, *die;* Waisenkind, *das.* **2** *v.t.* **be** ~**ed** [zur] Waise werden

orphanage /'ɔːfənɪdʒ/ *n.* Waisenhaus, *das*

orthodox /'ɔːθədɒks/ *adj.* orthodox; (conservative) konventionell

orthodoxy /'ɔːθədɒksɪ/ *n.* Orthodoxie, *die*

orthopaedic, (Amer.) **orthopedic** /ɔːθə'piːdɪk/ *adj.* orthopädisch

oscillate /'ɒsɪleɪt/ *v.i.* **(a)** (swing like a pendulum) schwingen; oszillieren (fachspr.); **(b)** (fig.) schwanken

oscillation /ɒsɪ'leɪʃn/ *n.* **(a)** (action) ⇒ **oscillate:** Schwingen, *das*, Oszillieren, *das;* Schwanken, *das;* **(b)** (single ~) Schwingung, *die*

osmosis /ɒz'məʊsɪs/ *n., pl.* **osmoses** /ɒz'məʊsiːz/ Osmose, *die*

ossify /'ɒsɪfaɪ/ *v.i.* ossifizieren; verknöchern (auch fig.)

ostensible /ɒ'stensɪbl/ *adj.* vorgeschoben; Schein-

ostensibly /ɒ'stensɪblɪ/ *adv.* vorgeblich

ostentation /ɒsten'teɪʃn/ *n.* Ostentation, *die* (geh.); Prahlerei, *die* (abwertend); (showiness) Prunk, *der*

ostentatious /ɒsten'teɪʃəs/ *adj.* prunkhaft ⟨*Kleidung, Schmuck*⟩; prahlerisch ⟨*Art*⟩; auffällig großzügig ⟨*Spende*⟩; **be** ~ **about sth.** mit etw. prunken *od.* (ugs.) protzen

osteopath /'ɒstɪəpæθ/ *n.* ▶887 (Med.) Osteopath, *der/*Osteopathin, *die*

osteoporosis /ɒstɪəʊpə'rəʊsɪs/ *n., no pl.* ▶865 (Med.) Osteoporose, *die*

ostracise ⇒ **ostracize**

ostracism /'ɒstrəsɪzm/ *n.* Ächtung, *die*

ostracize /'ɒstrəsaɪz/ *v.t.* ächten

ostrich /'ɒstrɪtʃ/ *n.* Strauß, *der*

OTE *abbr.* **on-target earnings**

other /'ʌðə(r)/ **1** *adj.* **(a)** (not the same) ander...; **the** ~ **two/three** *etc.* (the remaining) die beiden/drei *usw.* anderen; **the** ~ **way round** *or* **about** gerade umgekehrt; ~ **people's property** fremdes Eigentum; **the** ~ **one** der/die/das andere; **there is no** ~ **way** es geht nicht anders; **I know of no** ~ **way of doing it** ich weiß nicht, wie ich es sonst machen soll; **some** ~ **time** ein andermal; **(b)** (further) **two** ~ **people/questions** noch zwei [andere *od.* weitere] Leute/Fragen; **one** ~ **thing** noch eins; **have you any** ~ **news/questions?** hast du noch weitere *od.* sonst noch Neuigkeiten/Fragen?; **(c)** ~ **than** (different from) anders als; (except) außer; **any person** ~ **than yourself** jeder außer dir; **(d)** **some writer/charity or** ~: irgendein Schriftsteller/Wohltätigkeitsverein; **some time/way or** ~: irgendwann/-wie; **something/somehow/somewhere/somebody or** ~: irgendetwas/-wie/-wo/-wer. **2** *n.* anderer/andere/anderes; **there are six** ~**s** es sind noch sechs andere da; **tell one from the** ~: sie auseinander halten; **one or ~ of you/them** irgendwer *od.* -einer/-eine von euch/ihnen; **any ~:** irgendein anderer/-eine andere/ -ein anderes; *see also* **each 2 b; a bit of the ~** (sl.) Sex, *der;* **have a bit of the ~** (sl.) es treiben (ugs.); **all he ever wants is a bit of the ~** (sl.) er will immer nur das eine. **3** *adv.* anders; **~ than that, no real news** abgesehen davon, keine echten Neuigkeiten

otherwise /'ʌðəwaɪz/ **1** *adv.* (a) (in a different way) anders; **think ~:** anders darüber denken; anderer Meinung sein; **be ~ engaged** anderweitige Verpflichtungen haben; **except where ~ stated** sofern nicht anders angegeben; **(b)** (or else) sonst; anderenfalls; **(c)** (in other respects) ansonsten (ugs.); im Übrigen. **2** *pred. adj.* anders

otter /'ɒtə(r)/ *n.* [Fisch]otter, *der*

OU *abbr.* (Brit.) **Open University**

ouch /aʊtʃ/ *int.* autsch

ought /ɔːt/ *v. aux., only in pres. and past* **ought**, *neg.* (coll.) **oughtn't** /'ɔːtnt/ (a) **I ~ to do/have done it** *expr. moral duty* ich müsste es tun/hätte es tun müssen; *expr. desirability* ich sollte es tun/hätte es tun sollen; **you ~ to see that film** sollte[s]t du diesen Film sehen; **she ~ to have been a teacher** sie hätte Lehrerin werden sollen; **~ not or ~n't you to have left by now?** müsstest du nicht schon weg sein?; **one ~ not to do it** man sollte es nicht tun; **he ~ to be hanged/in hospital** er gehört an den Galgen/ins Krankenhaus; **(b)** *expr. probability* **that ~ to be enough** das dürfte reichen; **he ~ to win** er müsste [eigentlich] gewinnen; **he ~ to have reached Paris by now** er müsste *od.* dürfte inzwischen in Paris [angekommen] sein

oughtn't /'ɔːtnt/ (coll.) = **ought not**

ounce /aʊns/ *n.* ▶ 1193 |, ▶ 1202 | (measure) Unze, *die;* (fig.) **not an ~ of common sense** kein Fünkchen Verstand; **there is not an ~ of truth in it** daran ist kein Körnchen Wahrheit

our /'aʊə(r)/ *poss. pron. attrib.* unser; **we have done ~ share** wir haben unseren Teil getan; **~ Joe** *etc.* (coll.) unser *od.* (ugs.) uns Joe *usw.; see also* **her²**

ours /'aʊəz/ *poss. pron. pred.* unserer/unsere/unseres; **that car is ~:** das ist unser Wagen; *see also* **hers**

ourselves /aʊə'selvz/ *pron.* (a) *emphat.* selbst; **(b)** *refl.* uns. *See also* **herself**

oust /aʊst/ *v.t.* (a) (expel, force out) **~ sb. from his job** jmdn. von seinem Arbeitsplatz vertreiben; **~ the president/government from power** den Präsidenten/die Regierung entmachten; **(b)** (force out and take place of) verdrängen; ablösen ‹*Regierung*›

out /aʊt/ **1** *adv.* (a) (away from place) **~ here/there** hier/ da draußen; **'Out'** „Ausfahrt"/„Ausgang" *od.* „Aus"; **be ~ in the garden** draußen im Garten sein; **what's it like ~?** wie ist es draußen?; **go ~ shopping** *etc.* einkaufen *usw.* gehen; **be ~** (not at home, not in one's office, etc.) nicht da sein; **go ~ in the evenings** abends aus- *od.* weggehen; **she was/stayed ~ all night** sie war/blieb eine/die ganze Nacht weg; **have a day ~ in London/at the beach** einen Tag in London/am Strand verbringen; **would you come ~ with me?** würdest du mit mir ausgehen?; **ten miles ~ from the harbour** 10 Meilen vom Hafen entfernt; **be ~ at sea** auf See sein; **the journey ~:** die Hinfahrt; **he is ~ in Africa** er ist in Afrika; **how long have you been living ~ here in Australia?** wie lange lebst du schon hier in Australien?; **(b)** **be ~** (asleep) weg sein (ugs.); (drunk) hinüber sein (ugs.); (unconscious) bewusstlos sein; (Boxing) aus sein; **(c)** (no longer burning) aus[gegangen]; **(d)** (in error) **be 3% ~ in one's calculations** sich um 3% verrechnet haben; **you're a long way ~:** du hast dich gewaltig geirrt; **this is £5 ~:** das stimmt um 5 Pfund nicht; **(e)** (not in fashion) passee (ugs.); out (ugs.); **(f)** (so as to be seen or heard) heraus; raus (ugs.); **there is a warrant ~ for his arrest** es liegt ein Haftbefehl gegen ihn vor; **say it ~ loud** es laut sagen; **~ with it!** heraus *od.* (ugs.) raus damit *od.* mit der Sprache!; **their secret is ~:** ihr Geheimnis ist bekannt geworden; **[the] truth will ~:** die Wahrheit wird herauskommen; **the moon is ~:** der Mond ist zu sehen; **is the evening paper ~ yet?** ist die Abendausgabe schon erschienen?; **the roses are just ~:** die Rosen fangen gerade an zu blühen; **that is the best**

car ~: das ist das beste Auto auf dem Markt; **(g) be ~ for sth./to do sth.** auf etw. (*Akk.*) aus sein/darauf aus sein, etw. zu tun; **be ~ for all one can get** alles haben wollen, was man bekommen kann; **be ~ for trouble** Streit suchen; **they're just ~ to make money** sie sind nur aufs Geld aus; **(h)** (to or at an end) **he had it finished before the day/month was ~:** er war noch am selben Tag/vor Ende des Monats damit fertig; **please hear me ~:** lass mich bitte ausreden; **Eggs? I'm afraid we're ~:** Eier? Die sind leider ausgegangen *od.* (ugs.) alle; **(i) an ~ and ~ scoundrel** ein Schurke durch und durch; **an ~ and ~ disgrace** eine ungeheure Schande. *See also* **out of. 2** *n.* (way of escape) Ausweg, *der* (fig.); (excuse) Alibi, *das*

out: **~back** *n.* (esp. Austral.) Hinterland, *das;* **~'bid** *v.t.,* **~bid** überbieten; **~board** *adj.* (Naut.) **~board motor** Außenbordmotor, *der;* **~break** *n.* Ausbruch, *der;* **at the ~break of war** bei Kriegsausbruch *od.* Ausbruch des Krieges; **an ~break of flu/smallpox** eine Grippe-/Pockenepidemie; **~building** *n.* Nebengebäude, *das;* **~burst** *n.* Ausbruch, *der;* **an ~burst of anger/temper** ein Zornesausbruch (geh.) *od.* Wutanfall; **~cast** *n.* Ausgestoßene, *der/die;* **a social ~cast** ein Geächteter/ eine Geächtete; ein Outcast (Soziol.); **~'class** *v.t.* überlegen sein (+ *Dat.*); **~come** *n.* Ergebnis, *das;* Resultat, *das;* **what was the ~come of your meeting?** was ist bei eurer Versammlung herausgekommen?; **~cry** *n., no pl.* (clamour) [Aufschrei der] Empörung; [Sturm der] Entrüstung; **a public/general ~cry about/against sth.** allgemeine Empörung *od.* Entrüstung über etw. (*Akk.*); **~'dated** *adj.* veraltet; überholt; antiquiert (abwertend) ‹*Ausdrucksweise*›; altmodisch ‹*Vorstellung, Kleidung*›; **~'distance** *v.t.* [weit] hinter sich (*Dat.*) lassen; überflügeln; **~'do** *v.t.,* **~doing** /aʊt'duːɪŋ/, **~did** /aʊt 'dɪd/, **~done** /aʊt'dʌn/ übertreffen, überbieten (**in** an + *Dat.*); **not to be ~done [by sb.]** um nicht zurückzustehen [hinter jmdm.]; **~door** *adj.* **~door shoes/ things** Straßenschuhe/-kleidung, *die;* **be an ~door type** gern und oft im Freien sein; **lead an ~door life** viel im Freien sein; **~door games/pursuits** Spiele/Beschäftigungen im Freien; **~door swimming pool** Freibad, *das;* **~'doors 1** *adv.* draußen; **go ~doors** nach draußen gehen; **2** *n.* **the [great] ~doors** die freie Natur

outer /'aʊtə(r)/ *adj.* äußer...; Außen‹*fläche, -seite, -wand, -tür, -hafen*›; **~ garments** Oberbekleidung, *die*

outer 'space *n.* Weltraum, *der;* All, *das*

out: **~fit** *n.* (a) (person's clothes) Kleider *Pl.;* (for fancy-dress party) Kostüm, *das;* **(b)** (complete equipment) Ausrüstung, *die;* Ausstattung, *die;* **(c)** (coll.: group of persons) Haufen, *der* (ugs.); (Mil.) Haufen, *der* (Soldatenspr.); Trupp, *der;* **(d)** (coll.: organization) Laden, *der* (ugs.); **~fitter** *n.* Ausrüster, *der*/Ausrüsterin, *die;* **~fitter** Camping-/Sportgeschäft, *das;* **~going 1** *adj.* (a) (retiring from office) [aus dem Amt] scheidend ‹*Regierung, Präsident, Ausschuss*›; **(b)** (friendly) kontaktfreudig ‹*Person*›; **you should be more ~going** du solltest mehr aus dir herausgehen; **(c)** (going ~) abgehend ‹*Zug, Schiff*›; ausziehend ‹*Mieter*›; **~going flights will be delayed** bei den Abflügen wird es zu Verzögerungen kommen; **2** *n.* in *pl.* (expenditure) Ausgaben *Pl.;* **~'grow** *v.t., forms as* **grow:** (a) (leave behind) entwachsen (+ *Dat.*); ablegen ‹*Interesse, Schüchternheit, Vorliebe*›; überwinden ‹*Ansicht, Schüchternheit*›; **we've ~grown all that** das alles haben wir hinter uns; **(b)** (become taller than) größer werden als; über den Kopf wachsen (+ *Dat.*) ‹*älterem Bruder usw.*›; (grow too big for) herauswachsen aus ‹*Kleidung*›; **~house** *n.* (building) Nebengebäude, *das*

outing /'aʊtɪŋ/ *n.* Ausflug, *der;* **school/day's ~:** Schul-/ Tagesausflug, *der;* **firm's/works ~:** Betriebsausflug, *der;* **go on an ~:** einen Ausflug machen

out: **~landish** /aʊt'lændɪʃ/ *adj.* (a) (looking or sounding foreign) fremdländisch; **(b)** (bizarre) ausgefallen; seltsam, sonderbar ‹*Benehmen*›; verschroben ‹*Ansichten*›; **~'last** *v.t.* überdauern; überleben ‹*Person, Jahrhundert*›; **~law 1** *n.* Bandit, *der*/Banditin, *die;* **2** *v.t.* (make illegal) verbieten ‹*Zeitung, Handlung*›; **~lay** *n.* **an ~lay** Ausgaben *Pl.* (**on** für); **initial ~lay** Anschaffungskosten *Pl.;* **~let** /'aʊt let, 'aʊtlɪt/ *n.* (a) Ablauf, -fluss, *der;* Auslauf, -lass, *der;* **(b)**

(fig.: vent) Ventil, *das;* **(c)** (Commerc.) (market) Absatzmarkt, *der;* (shop) Verkaufsstelle, *die;* ~**line 1** *n.* **(a)** *in sing. or pl.* (line[s]) Umriss, *der;* Kontur, *die;* Silhouette, *die;* **(b)** (short account) Grundriss, *der;* Grundzüge *Pl.;* (of topic) Übersicht, die (of über + *Akk.*); (rough draft) Entwurf, *der* (of, for *Gen. od.* zu); **2** *v.t.* **(a)** (draw ~line of) ~**line sth.** die Umrisse *od.* Konturen einer Sache zeichnen; **(b) the mountain was** ~**lined against the sky** die Umrisse *od.* Konturen des Berges zeichneten sich gegen den Himmel ab; **(c)** (describe in general terms) skizzieren, umreißen ⟨*Programm, Plan, Projekt*⟩; ~**live** /aʊt'lɪv/ *v.t.* überleben; **it's** ~**lived its usefulness** es ist unbrauchbar geworden; ~**look** *n.* **(a)** (prospect) Aussicht, *die* (over über + *Akk.*, on to auf + *Akk.*); (fig., Meteorol.) Aussichten *Pl.;* **(b)** (mental attitude) Haltung, *die* (on gegenüber); ~**look on life** Lebensauffassung, *die;* ~**lying** *adj.* abgelegen, entlegen ⟨*Gegend, Vorort, Dorf*⟩; ~**ma'nœuvre** *v.t.* überlisten ⟨*Truppen*⟩; ausstechen, ausmanövrieren ⟨*Rivalen*⟩; ~**moded** /aʊt'məʊdɪd/ *adj.* **(a)** (no longer in fashion) altmodisch; **(b)** (obsolete) veraltet; antiquiert (abwertend) ⟨*Ausdrucksweise*⟩; ~**'number** *v.t.* zahlenmäßig überlegen sein (+ *Dat.*); **they were** ~**numbered five to one** die anderen waren fünfmal so viele wie sie

'**out of** *prep.* **(a)** (from within) aus; **go** ~ **the door** zur Tür hinausgehen; **fall** ~ **sth.** aus etw. [heraus]fallen; **(b)** (not within) **be** ~ **the country** im Ausland sein; **be** ~ **town/the room** nicht in der Stadt/im Zimmer sein; **feel** ~ **it** *or* **things** sich ausgeschlossen *od.* nicht dazu gehörig fühlen; **I'm glad to be** ~ **it** ich bin froh, dass ich die Sache hinter mir habe; **be** ~ **the tournament** aus dem Turnier ausgeschieden sein; **(c)** (from among) **one** ~ **every three smokers** jeder dritte Raucher; **58** ~ **every 100** 58 von hundert; **pick one** ~ **the pile** einen/eine/eins aus dem Stapel herausgreifen; **eighth** ~ **ten** als Achter von zehn Teilnehmern *usw.;* **(d)** (beyond range of) außer ⟨*Reich-/Hörweite, Sicht, Kontrolle*⟩; **(e)** (from) aus; **get money** ~ **sb.** Geld aus jmdm. herausholen; **do well** ~ **sb./sth.** von jmdm./etw. profitieren; **(f)** (owing to) aus ⟨*Mitleid, Furcht, Neugier usw.*⟩; **(g)** (without) **be** ~ **luck** kein Glück haben; ~ **money** ohne Geld; **be** ~ **work** ohne Arbeit; arbeitslos; **we're** ~ **tea** der Tee ist uns ausgegangen; **(h)** (by use of) aus; **make a profit** ~ **sth.** mit etw. ein Geschäft machen; **made** ~ **silver** aus Silber; **(i)** (away from) von ... entfernt; **ten miles** ~ **London** 10 Meilen außerhalb von London; **(j)** (beyond) ⇒ **depth c; ordinary b**

out: ~**-of-court settlement** *n.* (Law) (agreement) außergerichtlicher Vergleich; außergerichtliche Einigung; (payment) Vergleichssumme, *die;* ~**-of-date** *attrib. adj.* (old, not relevant) veraltet; (old-fashioned) altmodisch; unmodern; antiquiert (abwertend) ⟨*Ausdrucksweise*⟩; (expired) ungültig, verfallen ⟨*Karte*⟩; ~**-of-the-way** *attrib. adj.* (remote) abgelegen; entlegen; (unusual) ausgefallen; ~**-of-work** *attrib. adj.* arbeitslos; ~**patient** *n.* ambulanter Patient/ambulante Patientin; ~**patients[' department]** Poliklinik, *die;* **be an** ~**patient** ambulant behandelt werden; ~**placement** /'aʊtpleɪsmənt/ *n., no pl.* (Commerc.) Outplacement, *das* (fachspr.) ~**'play** *v.t.* (Sport) besser spielen als; ~**post** *n.* Außenposten, *der;* (of civilization etc.; also Mil.) Vorposten, *der;* ~**put** *n.* **(a)** (amount) Output, *der* (fachspr.); Produktion, *die;* (of liquid, electricity, etc.) Leistung, *die;* **(b)** (Computing) Ausgabe, *die;* Output, *der* (fachspr.); **(c)** (Electr.) (energy) [Ausgangs]leistung, *die;* Output, *der* (fachspr.); (signal) Ausgangssignal, *das;* **2** *v.t.,* **-tt-,** ~**put** *or* ~**putted** /'aʊtpʊtɪd/ (Computing) ausgeben ⟨*Information*⟩

outrage 1 /'aʊtreɪdʒ/ *n.* (deed of violence, violation of rights) Verbrechen, *das;* (during war) Gräueltat, *die;* (against good taste or decency) grober *od.* krasser Verstoß; (upon dignity) krasse *od.* grobe Verletzung (**upon** *Gen.*); **be an** ~ **against good taste/decency** den guten Geschmack/Anstand in grober *od.* krasser Weise verletzen; **an** ~ **against humanity** ein Verbrechen gegen die Menschheit. **2** /'aʊtreɪdʒ, aʊt'reɪdʒ/ *v.t.* **(a)** empören; **be** ~**d at** *or* **by sth.** über etw. (*Akk.*) empört sein; **(b)** (infringe) in grober *od.* krasser Weise verstoßen gegen ⟨*Anstand, Moral*⟩

outrageous /aʊt'reɪdʒəs/ *adj.* **(a)** (immoderate) unverschämt (ugs.) ⟨*Forderung*⟩; unverschämt hoch ⟨*Preis, Summe*⟩; grell, schreiend ⟨*Farbe*⟩; zu auffällig ⟨*Kleidung*⟩;

maßlos ⟨*Übertreibung*⟩; **it's** ~**!** das ist unverschämt *od.* eine Unverschämtheit!; **(b)** (grossly cruel, offensive) ungeheuer ⟨*Grausamkeit*⟩; unverschämt ⟨*Lüge, Benehmen, Unterstellung*⟩; wüst ⟨*Schmähung*⟩; ungeheuerlich ⟨*Anklage*⟩; unerhört ⟨*Frechheit, Unhöflichkeit, Skandal*⟩; unflätig ⟨*Sprache*⟩

outrageously /aʊt'reɪdʒəslɪ/ *adv.* zu auffällig, aufdringlich ⟨*sich kleiden, schminken*⟩; maßlos ⟨*übertreiben*⟩; unverschämt, schamlos ⟨*lügen, sich benehmen*⟩; fürchterlich ⟨*fluchen*⟩

out: ~**rider** *n.* (motorcyclist) [motorcycle] ~**rider** Kradbegleiter, *der/*-begleiterin, *die;* ~**right 1** /-'-/ *adv.* **(a)** (altogether, entirely) ganz, komplett ⟨*kaufen, verkaufen*⟩; (instantaneously, on the spot) auf der Stelle; **pay for/purchase/buy sth.** ~**right** sofort den ganzen Preis für etw. bezahlen; **(b)** (openly) geradeheraus (ugs.), freiheraus, rundheraus ⟨*erzählen, sagen, lachen*⟩; **2** /'--/ *adj.* ausgemacht ⟨*Unsinn, Schlechtigkeit, Unehrlichkeit*⟩; rein, pur (ugs.) ⟨*Arroganz, Unverschämtheit, Irrtum, Egoismus, Unsinn*⟩; glatt (ugs.) ⟨*Ablehnung, Absage, Lüge*⟩; klar ⟨*Sieg, Niederlage, Sieger*⟩; ~**'run** *v.t.,* forms as **run 3: (a)** (run faster than) schneller laufen *od.* sein als; **(b)** (escape) entkommen (+ *Dat.*); ~**sell** *v.t.,* forms as **sell 1: (a)** (be sold in greater quantities than) sich besser verkaufen als; **(b)** (sell more than) mehr verkaufen als; ~**set** *n.* Anfang, *der;* Beginn, *der;* **at the** ~**set** zu Beginn *od.* Anfang; am Anfang; **from the** ~**set** von Anfang an; ~**'shine** *v.t.,* ~**shone** /aʊt'ʃɒn/ (fig.) in den Schatten stellen

outside 1 /-'-, '-/ *n.* **(a)** Außenseite, *die;* **on the** ~**:** außen; **to/from the** ~**:** nach/von außen; **overtake sb. on the** ~**:** jmdn. außen überholen; **(b)** (external appearance) Äußere, *das;* äußere Erscheinung; **(c) at the [very]** ~ (coll.) äußerstenfalls; höchstens. **2** /'--/ *adj.* **(a)** (of, on, nearer the ~) Außen⟨*wand, -mauer, -antenne, -toilette, -ansicht*⟩; ~ **lane** Überholspur, *die;* **(b)** (remote) **have only an** ~ **chance** nur eine sehr geringe Chance haben; **(c)** fremd ⟨*Hilfe*⟩; äußer... ⟨*Einfluss*⟩; Freizeit⟨*aktivitäten, -interessen*⟩; **(d)** (greatest possible) maximal, höchst... ⟨*Schätzung*⟩; **at an** ~ **estimate** maximal *od.* höchstens *od.* im Höchstfall. **3** /-'-/ *adv.* **(a)** (on the ~) draußen; (to the ~) nach draußen; **the world:** the ~ die Außenwelt; **(b)** ~ **of** ⇒ **4. 4** /-'-/ *prep.* **(a)** (on outer side of) außerhalb (+ *Gen.*); **(b)** (beyond) außerhalb (+ *Gen.*) ⟨*Reichweite, Festival, Familie*⟩; **it's** ~ **the terms of the agreement** es gehört nicht zu den Bedingungen der Abmachung; **(c)** (to the ~ of) aus ... hinaus; **go** ~ **the house** nach draußen gehen

outside 'broadcast *n.* (Brit.) Außenübertragung, *die*

outsider /aʊt'saɪdə(r)/ *n.* (Sport; also fig.) Außenseiter, *der*

out: ~**size** *adj.* überdimensional; ~**size clothes** Kleidung in Übergröße; ~**skirts** *n. pl.* Stadtrand, *der;* **the** ~**skirts of the city** die Außenbezirke der Stadt; ~**'smart** *v.t.* (coll.) reinlegen (ugs.); ~**source 1** *v.t.* extern vergeben ⟨*Arbeit, Aufträge*⟩; **2** *v.i.* Arbeiten/Aufträge extern vergeben; ~**sourcing** /aʊtˈsɔːsɪŋ/ *n., no pl.* Outsourcing, *das* (fachspr.); Fremdbezug, *der* (fachspr.); ~**'spoken** *adj.* freimütig ⟨*Person, Kritik, Bemerkung, Kommentar*⟩; ~**spread** *adj.* /'--, pred. -'-/ ausgebreitet; ~**'standing** *adj.* **(a)** (conspicuous) hervorstechend ⟨*Merkmal*⟩; **(b)** (exceptional) hervorragend ⟨*Leistung, Redner, Künstler, Dienst*⟩; überragend ⟨*Bedeutung*⟩; außergewöhnlich ⟨*Person, Mut, Fähigkeit, Geschick*⟩; **not be** ~**standing** nicht überragend sein; **of** ~**standing ability/skill** außergewöhnlich fähig/geschickt; **(c)** (not yet settled) ausstehend ⟨*Schuld, Verbindlichkeit, Geldsumme*⟩; offen, unbezahlt ⟨*Rechnung*⟩; unerledigt ⟨*Arbeit*⟩; ungelöst ⟨*Problem*⟩; **there's £5 still** ~**standing** es stehen noch 5 Pfund aus; ~**standingly** /aʊt'stændɪŋlɪ/ *adv.* außergewöhnlich ⟨*intelligent, gut, begabt*⟩; **not** ~**standingly** nicht besonders; **be** ~**standingly good at tennis** hervorragend Tennis spielen; ~**station** *n.* Außenposten, *der;* ~**'stay** *v.t.* (stay beyond) überziehen ⟨*Urlaub*⟩; ~**stretched** *adj.* ausgestreckt; (spread out) ausgebreitet; ~**'strip** *v.t.* **(a)** (pass in running) überholen; **(b)** (in competition) überflügeln; übersteigen ⟨*Einsicht, Ressourcen, Ersparnisse*⟩; ~**-tray** *n.* Ablage für Ausgänge; ~**'vote** *v.t.* überstimmen

outward /'aʊtwəd/ **1** adj. **(a)** (external, apparent) [rein] äußerlich; äußere ‹Erscheinung, Bedingung›; **with an ~ show of confidence** mit einem Anstrich von Selbstsicherheit; **(b)** (going out) Hin‹reise, -fracht›; **~ flow of money/traffic** Kapitalabfluss, der/abfließender Verkehr. **2** adv. nach außen ‹aufgehen, richten›

outwardly /'aʊtwədlɪ/ adv. nach außen hin ‹Gefühle zeigen›; öffentlich ‹Loyalität erklären›

outwards ⇨ **outward 2**

out: ~'weigh v.t. schwerer wiegen als; überwiegen ‹Nachteile›; **~'wit** v.t., **-tt-** überlisten

oval /'əʊvl/ **1** adj. oval. **2** n. Oval, das

ovary /'əʊvərɪ/ n. Ovarium, das; Eierstock, der; (Bot.) Ovarium, das; Fruchtknoten, der

ovation /əʊ'veɪʃn/ n. Ovation, die; begeisterter Beifall; **get an ~ for sth.** Ovationen od. begeisterten Beifall für etw. bekommen; **a standing ~:** stehende Ovationen

oven /'ʌvn/ n. [Back]ofen, der; **put sth. in the ~ for 40 minutes** etw. 40 Minuten backen; **it's like an ~ in here** hier ist es warm wie in einem Backofen

oven: ~-glove n. Topfhandschuh, der; **~proof** adj. feuerfest; **~-ready** adj. backfertig ‹Pommes frites, Pastete›; bratfertig ‹Geflügel›; **~ware** n., no pl. feuerfestes Geschirr

over /'əʊvə(r)/ **1** adv. **(a)** (outward and downward) hinüber; **(b)** (so as to cover surface) **draw/board/cover ~:** zuziehen/-nageln/-decken; **(c)** (with motion above sth.) **climb/look/jump ~:** hinüber- od. (ugs.) rüberklettern/-sehen/-springen; **(d)** (so as to reverse position etc.) herum; **switch ~:** umschalten ‹Programm, Sender›; **it rolled ~ and ~:** es rollte und rollte; **(e)** (across a space) hinüber; (towards speaker) herüber; **he swam ~ to us/the other side** er schwamm zu uns herüber/hinüber zur anderen Seite; **fly ~:** vorüberfliegen; **~ here/there** (direction) hier herüber/dort hinüber; (location) hier/dort; **they are ~ [here] for the day** sie sind einen Tag hier; **ask sb. ~ [for dinner]** jmdn. [zum Essen] einladen; **(f)** (Radio) [**come in, please,**] **~:** übernehmen Sie bitte; **~ and out** Ende; **(g)** (in excess etc.) **children of 12 and ~:** Kinder im Alter von zwölf Jahren und darüber; **be [left] ~:** übrig [geblieben] sein; **have ~:** übrig haben ‹Geld›; **9 into 28 goes 3 and 1 ~:** 28 geteilt durch neun ist gleich 3, Rest 1; **it's a bit ~** (in weight) es ist ein bisschen mehr; **(h)** (from beginning to end) von Anfang bis Ende; **say sth. twice ~:** etw. wiederholen od. zweimal sagen; **~ and ~ [again]** immer wieder; **several times ~:** mehrmals; **(i)** (at an end) vorbei; vorüber; **be ~:** vorbei sein; ‹Aufführung:› zu Ende sein; **get sth. ~ with** etw. hinter sich (Akk.) bringen; **be ~ and done with** erledigt sein; **(j) all ~** (completely finished) aus [und vorbei]; (in or on one's whole body etc.) überall; (in characteristic attitude) typisch; **I ache all ~:** mir tut alles weh; **be shaking all ~:** am ganzen Körper zittern; **embroidered all ~ with flowers** ganz mit Blumen bestickt; **that is him/sth. all ~:** das ist typisch für ihn/etw.; **(k)** (overleaf) umseitig; **see ~:** siehe Rückseite. **2** prep. **(a)** (above) (indicating position) über (+ Dat.); (indicating motion) über (+ Akk.); **(b)** (on) (indicating position) über (+ Dat.); (indicating motion) über (+ Akk.); **hit sb. ~ the head** jmdm. auf den Kopf schlagen; **carry a coat ~ one's arm** einen Mantel über dem Arm tragen; **(c)** (in or across every part of) [überall] in (+ Dat.); (to and fro upon) über (+ Akk.); (all through) durch; **all ~** (in or on all parts of) überall in (+ Dat.); **travel all ~ the country** das ganze Land bereisen; **all ~ Spain** überall in Spanien; **she spilt wine all ~ her skirt** sie hat sich (Dat.) Wein über den ganzen Rock geschüttet; **all ~ the world** in der ganzen Welt; **(d)** (round about) (indicating position) über (+ Dat.); (indicating motion) über (+ Akk.); **a sense of gloom hung ~ him** ihn umgab eine gedrückte Stimmung; **(e)** (on account of) wegen; **laugh ~ sth.** über etw. (Akk.) lachen; **(f)** (engaged with) bei; **take trouble ~ sth.** sich (Dat.) mit etw. Mühe geben; **be a long time ~ sth.** lange für etw. brauchen; **~ work/dinner/a cup of tea** bei der Arbeit/beim Essen/bei einer Tasse Tee; **(g)** (superior to, in charge of) über (+ Akk.); **have command/authority ~ sb.** Befehlsgewalt über jmdn./Weisungsbefugnis gegenüber jmdm. haben; **be ~ sb.** (in rank) über jmdm. stehen; **(h)** (beyond, more than) über (+ Akk.); **an increase ~ last**

year's total eine Zunahme gegenüber der letztjährigen Gesamtmenge; **it's been ~ a month since …:** es ist über einen Monat her, dass …; **~ and above** zusätzlich zu; **(i)** (in comparison with) **a decrease ~ last year** eine Abnahme gegenüber dem letzten Jahr; **(j)** (out and down from etc.) über (+ Akk.); **look ~ a wall** über eine Mauer sehen; **the window looks ~ the street** das Fenster geht zur Straße hinaus; **fall ~ a cliff** von einem Felsen stürzen; **(k)** (across) über (+ Akk.); **the pub ~ the road** die Wirtschaft auf der anderen Straßenseite od. gegenüber; **climb ~ the wall** über die Mauer steigen od. klettern; **be ~ the worst** das Schlimmste hinter sich (Dat.) od. überstanden haben; **be ~ an illness** eine Krankheit überstanden haben; **(l)** (throughout, during) über (+ Akk.); **stay ~ Christmas/the weekend/Wednesday** über Weihnachten/das Wochenende/bis Donnerstag bleiben; **~ the summer** den Sommer über; **~ the past years** in den letzten Jahren

over: ~-a'bundant adj. überreichlich; **~'act 1** v.t. übertrieben spielen ‹Rolle, Theaterstück›; chargieren ‹Nebenrolle›; **2** v.i. übertreiben; **~all 1** n. (a) (Brit.: garment) Arbeitsmantel, der; Arbeitskittel, der; **(b)** in pl. [**pair of**] **~alls** Overall, der; (with a bib and strap top) Latzhose, die; **2** adj. **(a)** (from end to end; total) Gesamt‹breite, -einsparung, -klassement, -abmessung›; **have an ~all majority** die absolute Mehrheit haben; **(b)** (general) allgemein ‹Verbesserung, Wirkung›; **3** /'---, --'-/ adv. (taken as a whole) im Großen und Ganzen; **~-'anxious** adj. übermäßig besorgt; **be ~-anxious to do sth.** etw. unbedingt tun wollen; **~'awe** v.t. Ehrfurcht einflößen (+ Dat.); ‹Waffe, Anzahl:› einschüchtern; **~'balance 1** v.i. ‹Person:› das Gleichgewicht verlieren, aus dem Gleichgewicht kommen; **2** v.t. aus dem Gleichgewicht bringen ‹Person›; **~'bearing** adj. herrisch; **~'bid** v.t., **~bid** überbieten ‹Händler, Gegner, Gebot›; **~board** adv. über Bord; **fall ~board** über Bord gehen; **go ~board** (fig. coll.) ausflippen (ugs.) (about wegen); **~'book** v.t. überbuchen; **~'burden** v.t. (fig.) überlasten ‹System, Person› (by mit); **~'careful** adj. übervorsichtig; **~'cast** adj. trübe ‹Wetter, Himmel, Tag›; bewölkt ‹Himmel, Nacht›; bedeckt, bezogen ‹Himmel›; **~'cautious** adj. übervorsichtig; **~'charge** v.t. **(a)** (charge beyond reasonable price) zu viel abnehmen od. abverlangen (+ Dat.); **(b)** (charge beyond right price) zu viel berechnen (+ Dat.); **~coat** n. Mantel, der; **~'come 1** v.t., forms as **come: (a)** (prevail ~) überwinden; bezwingen ‹Feind›; ablegen ‹Angewohnheit›; widerstehen (+ Dat.) ‹Versuchung›; ‹Schlaf:› übernommen, übermannen; ‹Dämpfe:› betäuben; **(b)** in p.p. (exhausted, affected) **he was ~come by grief/with emotion** Kummer/Rührung übermannte od. überwältigte ihn; **she was ~come by fear/shyness** Angst/Schüchternheit überkam od. überwältigte sie; **they were ~come with remorse** Reue befiel sie; **2** v.i., forms as **come** siegen; **~'confidence** n. übersteigertes Selbstvertrauen; **~'confident** adj. übertrieben zuversichtlich; **~'cooked** adj. verkocht; **~'critical** adj. zu kritisch; **be ~critical of sth.** etw. zu sehr kritisieren; **~'crowded** adj. überfüllt ‹Zug, Bus, Raum›; übervölkert ‹Stadt›; **~'crowding** n. (of train, bus, room) Überfüllung, die; (of city) Übervölkerung, die; **~'do** v.t., **~'doing** /əʊvə'du:ɪŋ/, **~'did** /əʊvə'dɪd/, **~'done** /əʊvə'dʌn/ **(a)** (carry to excess) übertreiben; **(b)** **~do it** or **things** (work too hard) sich übernehmen; (exaggerate) es übertreiben; **~'done** adj. **(a)** (exaggerated) übertrieben; **(b)** (cooked too much) verkocht; verbraten ‹Fleisch›; **~'dose 1** /'---/ n. Überdosis, die; **2** /-'-'-/ v.t. eine Überdosis geben (+ Dat.); **3** /'---/ v.i. eine Überdosis nehmen; **~dose on heroin/amphetamines** etc. eine Überdosis Heroin/Amphetamine nehmen; **~draft** n. Kontoüberziehung, die; **have an ~draft of £50 at the bank** sein Konto um 50 Pfund überzogen haben; **get/pay off an ~draft** einen Überziehungskredit erhalten/abbezahlen; **~'draw** v.t., forms as **draw 1** (Banking) überziehen ‹Konto›; **~'drawn** adj. überzogen ‹Konto›; **I am ~drawn [at the bank]** mein Konto ist überzogen; **~'dress** v.i. sich zu fein anziehen; **~'dressed** adj. zu fein angezogen; **~drive** n. (Motor Veh.) Overdrive, der; Schongang, der; **~'due** adj. überfällig; **the train is 15 minutes ~due** der Zug hat schon 15

Minuten Verspätung; ~'**eager** *adj.* übereifrig; **be** ~ **eager to do sth.** sich übereifrig bemühen, etw. zu tun; ~'**eat** *v.i.*, *forms as* **eat** zu viel essen; ~**eating** übermäßiges Essen; ~'**emphasize** *v.i.* überbetonen; ~**estimate** 1 /əʊvər'estɪmeɪt/ *v.t.* überschätzen; 2 /əʊvər'estɪmət/ *n.* zu hohe Schätzung; ~**ex'cite** *v.t.* zu sehr aufregen ‹*Patient*›; **become** ~**excited** ganz aufgeregt werden; ~**ex'ert** *v. refl.* sich überanstrengen; ~**ex'pose** *v.t.* (Photog.) überbelichten; ~'**feed** *v.t.*, *forms as* **feed** 1 überfüttern ‹*Tier*, (*fam.*) *Kind*›; ~'**fill** *v.t.* zu voll machen; ~**flow** 1 /-'-/ *v.t.* (a) (flow ~) laufen über (+ *Akk.*) ‹*Rand*›; (b) (flow ~ brim of) überlaufen aus ‹*Tank*›; **a river** ~**flowing its banks** ein Fluss, der über die Ufer tritt; (c) (extend beyond limits of) ‹*Menge*, *Personen:*› nicht genug Platz finden in (+ *Dat.*); (d) (flood) überschwemmen ‹*Feld*›; 2 /-'-/ *v.i.* (a) (flow ~ edge or limit) überlaufen; **be filled/full to** ~**flowing** ‹*Raum:*› überfüllt sein; ‹*Flüssigkeitsbehälter:*› zum Überlaufen voll sein; (b) (fig.) ‹*Herz*, *Person:*› überfließen (geh.), überströmen (**with** vor + *Dat.*); 3 /'---/ *n.* (a) (what flows ~, lit. or fig.) **the** ~**flow** was übergelaufen ist; ~**flow of population** Bevölkerungsüberschuss, *der;* (b) (outlet) ~**flow** [**pipe**] Überlauf, *der;* ~'**fly** *v.t.*, *forms as* **fly²** 2: (a) (fly ~) überfliegen; (b) (fly beyond) hinausschießen über (+ *Akk.*) ‹*Landebahn*›; ~'**full** *adj.* zu voll; übervoll; ~'**generous** *adj.* zu *od.* übertrieben großzügig ‹*Person*›; reichlich groß ‹*Portion*›; ~**grown** *adj.* (a) überwachsen, überwuchert ‹*Beet*› (**with** von); (b) **he acts like an** ~**grown schoolboy** er führt sich auf wie ein großes Kind; ~**hang** 1 /-'-/ *v.t.*, ~**hung** /əʊvə'hʌŋ/ ‹*Felsen*, *Stockwerk:*› hinausragen über (+ *Akk.*); 2 /'---/ *n.* Überhang, *der;* ~**hanging** *adj.* überhängend; ~'**hasty** *adj.* vorschnell, übereilt ‹*Urteil*, *Entschluss*, *Antwort*›; ~**haul** 1 /-'-/ *v.t.* (a) überholen ‹*Auto*, *Schiff*, *Maschine*, *Motor*›; überprüfen ‹*System*›; (b) (~take) überholen ‹*Fahrzeug*, *Person*›; 2 /'---/ *n.* Überholung, *die;* **need an** ~**haul** ‹*Maschine:*› überholt werden müssen; ‹*System:*› überarbeitet werden müssen; ~**head** 1 /-'-/ *adv.* **high** ~**head** hoch oben; **hear a sound** ~**head** ein Geräusch über sich (*Dat.*) hören; 2 /'---/ *adj.* (a) ~**head wires** Hochleitung, *die;* ~**head cable** Luftkabel, *das;* ~**head projector** Overheadprojektor, *der;* (b) ~**head expenses/charges/costs** (Commerc.) Gemeinkosten *Pl.;* 3 /'---/ *n.* ~**heads**, (Amer.) ~**head** (Commerc.) Gemeinkosten *Pl.;* ~'**hear** *v.t.*, *forms as* **hear** 1 (accidentally) zufällig [mit]hören, mitbekommen ‹*Unterhaltung*, *Bemerkung*›; (intentionally) belauschen ‹*Gespräch*, *Personen*›; ~'**heat** *v.t.* überhitzen ‹*Motor*, *Metall usw.*›; ~-**in'dulge** 1 *v.t.* zu sehr frönen (geh.) (+ *Dat.*) ‹*Appetit*›; ~**indulge oneself** sich allzu sehr gehen lassen; 2 *v.i.* es übertreiben; ~-**in'dulgence** *n.* übermäßiger Genuss (**in** von); ~-**indulgence in drink/drugs** übermäßiges Trinken/übermäßiger Drogengenuss

overjoyed /əʊvə'dʒɔɪd/ *adj.* überglücklich (**at** über + *Akk.*)

over: ~**kill** *n.* (Mil.) Overkill, *das od. der;* **be** ~**kill** (fig.) zu viel des Guten sein; ~**land** 1 /-'-/ *adv.* auf dem Landweg; 2 /'---/ *adj.* **by the** ~**land route** auf dem Landweg; ~**land transport/journey** Beförderung/Reise auf dem Landweg; ~**lap** 1 /-'-/ *v.t.* überlappen ‹*Fläche*, *Dachziegel*›; sich überschneiden mit ‹*Aufgabe*, *Datum*›; 2 /-'-/ *v.i.* ‹*Flächen*, *Dachziegel:*› sich überlappen; ‹*Aufgaben*, *Daten:*› sich überschneiden; ‹*Bretter:*› teilweise übereinander liegen; 3 /'---/ *n.* Überlappung, *die;* (of dates or tasks; between subjects, periods, etc.) Überschneidung, *die;* ~**lay** 1 /-'-/ *v.t.*, *forms as* **lay²** 1 (cover) bedecken; 2 /'---/ *n.* (a) (cover) Überzug, *der;* (b) (transparent sheet) Auflegefolie, *die;* ~**leaf** *adv.* auf der Rückseite; **see diagram** ~**leaf** siehe das umseitige Diagramm; ~**load** 1 /-'-/ *v.t.* überladen (auch fig.), überlasten ‹*Stromkreis*, *Lautsprecher usw.*›; überbelasten ‹*Maschine*, *Motor*, *Mechanismus usw.*›; 2 /'---/ *n.* (Electr.) Überlastung, *die;* ~'**look** *v.t.* (a) (have view of) ‹*Hotel*, *Zimmer*, *Haus:*› Aussicht haben *od.* bieten auf (+ *Akk.*); **house** ~**looking the lake** Haus mit Blick auf den See; (b) (not see, ignore) übersehen; (allow to go unpunished) hinwegsehen über (+ *Akk.*) ‹*Vergehen*, *Beleidigung*›; ~'**man** *v.t.* überbesetzen; ~'**manning** *n.* [personelle] Überbesetzung; ~-'**modest** *adj.* zu bescheiden; ~'**much** 1 *adj.* allzu viel; 2 *adv.* allzusehr

overnight 1 /-'-/ *adv.* (also fig.: suddenly) über Nacht; **stay** ~ **in a hotel** in einem Hotel übernachten. 2 /'---/ *adj.* (a) ~ **train/bus** Nachtzug, *der*/Nachtbus, *der;* ~ **stay** Übernachtung, *die;* (b) (fig.: sudden) **be an** ~ **success** über Nacht Erfolg haben

overnight: ~ **bag** *n.* [kleine] Reisetasche; ~ **case** *n.* Handköfferchen, *das*

over: ~**pass** ⇒ flyover; ~'**pay** *v.t.*, *forms as* **pay** 2 überbezahlen; ~'**payment** *n.* Überbezahlung, *die;* ~'**populated** *adj.* überbevölkert; ~'**power** *v.t.* überwältigen; ~**powering** /əʊvə'paʊərɪŋ/ *adj.* überwältigend; durchdringend ‹*Geruch*›; **the heat was** ~**powering** die Hitze war unerträglich; ~**priced** /əʊvə'praɪst/ *adj.* zu teuer; ~**pro'tective** *adj.* überfürsorglich (**towards** gegenüber); ~'**qualified** *adj.* überqualifiziert; ~'**rate** *v.t.* überschätzen; **be** ~**rated** überschätzt werden ‹*Buch*, *Film:*› überbewertet werden; ~'**reach** *v. refl.* sich übernehmen; ~**re'act** *v.i.* unangemessen heftig reagieren (**to** auf + *Akk.*); ~**re'action** *n.* Überreaktion, *die* (**to** auf + *Akk.*); ~**ride** 1 /-'-/ *v.t.*, *forms as* **ride** 3 sich hinwegsetzen über (+ *Akk.*); 2 /'---/ *n.* [**manual**] ~**ride** Automatikabschaltung, *die;* ~'**riding** *adj.* vorrangig; ~'**ripe** *adj.* überreif; ~'**rule** *v.t.* aufheben ‹*Entscheidung*›; zurückweisen ‹*Einwand*, *Appell*, *Forderung*, *Argument*›; ~**rule sb.** jmds. Vorschlag ablehnen; ~'**run** *v.t.*, *forms as* **run** 3: **be** ~**run with** überlaufen sein von ‹*Touristen*›; überwuchert sein von ‹*Unkraut*›; (b) (Mil.) einfallen in (+ *Akk.*) ‹*Land*›; überrennen ‹*Stellungen*›; (c) (exceed) ~**run its allotted time** ‹*Programm*, *Treffen*, *Diskussion:*› länger als vorgesehen dauern; ~**run** [**one's time**] ‹*Dozent*, *Redner:*› überziehen; ~**seas** 1 /-'-/ *adv.* in Übersee ‹*leben*, *sein*, *sich niederlassen*›; nach Übersee ‹*gehen*›; 2 /'---/ *adj.* (a) (across the sea) Übersee‹*postgebühren*, *-handel*, *-telefonat*›; (b) (foreign) Auslands‹*hilfe*, *-zulage*, *-ausgabe*, *-nachrichten*›; ausländisch ‹*Student*›; ~**seas visitors** Besucher aus dem Ausland; ~'**see** *v.t.*, *forms as* **see** 1 überwachen; (manage) leiten ‹*Abteilung*›; ~'**sensitive** *adj.* überempfindlich; ~'**shadow** *v.t.* (lit. or fig.) überschatten; ~'**shoot** *v.t.*, *forms as* **shoot** 2 vorbeifahren an (+ *Akk.*) ‹*Abzweigung*›; ~**shoot the mark** (fig.) über das Ziel hinausschießen; ~**shoot** [**the runway**] ‹*Pilot*, *Flugzeug:*› zu weit kommen; ~**sight** *n.* Versehen, *das;* **by or through an** ~**sight** versehentlich; aus Versehen; ~'**simplify** *v.t.* zu stark vereinfachen; ~'**sleep** *v.i.*, *forms as* **sleep** 2 verschlafen; ~'**spend** *v.i.*, *forms as* **spend** zu viel [Geld] ausgeben; ~**spend by £100** 100 Pfund zu viel ausgeben; ~**spill** *n.* Bevölkerungsüberschuss, *der; attrib.* Satelliten‹*stadt*, *-siedlung*›; ~'**staff** *v.t.* überbesetzen; ~'**state** *v.t.* übertrieben darstellen; ~'**stay** *v.t.* überziehen ‹*Urlaub*›; ~'**step** *v.t.* überschreiten; ~**step the mark** (fig.) ‹ zu weit gehen; ~'**stretch** *v.t.* überdehnen; (fig.) überfordern

overt /'əʊvət, əʊ'vɜːt/ *adj.* unverhohlen

over: ~'**take** *v.t.* (a) also *abs.* (esp. Brit.: pass) überholen; '**no** ~**taking**' (Brit.) „Überholen verboten"; (b) (catch up) einholen; (c) (fig.) **be** ~**taken by events** ‹*Plan:*› von den Ereignissen überholt werden; ~'**tax** *v.t.* (a) (demand too much tax from) überbesteuern; (b) (strain) überstrapazieren, überfordern ‹*Verstand*, *Geduld*›; ~**tax one's strength** sich übernehmen; ~-**the-top** *adj.* übertrieben; ~**throw** 1 /-'-/ *v.t.*, *forms as* **throw** 1 stürzen ‹*Regierung*, *Regime usw.*›; (defeat) schlagen, besiegen ‹*Feind*›; 2 /'---/ *n.* (removal from power) Sturz, *der;* ~**time** 1 *n.* Überstunden; **work ten hours'/put in a lot of** ~**time** zehn/eine Menge Überstunden machen; **be on** ~**time** Überstunden machen; 2 *adv.* **work** ~**time** Überstunden machen; ~'**tire** *v.t.* übermüden; ~**tone** *n.* (fig.: implication) Unterton, *der*

overture /'əʊvətjʊə(r)/ *n.* (a) (Mus.) Ouvertüre, *die;* (b) (formal proposal or offer) Angebot, *das*

over: ~'**turn** 1 *v.t.* (a) (upset) umstoßen; (b) (~throw) umstürzen ‹*bestehende Ordnung*, *Vorstellung*, *Prinzip*›; stürzen ‹*Regierung*›; 2 *v.i.* ‹*Auto*, *Boot*, *Kutsche:*› umkippen; ‹*Boot:*› kentern; ~**use** /əʊvə'juːz/ *v.t.* zu oft verwenden; ~'**value** *v.t.* überbewerten

overweening /əʊvə'wiːnɪŋ/ *adj.* maßlos ‹*Ehrgeiz, Gier, Stolz*›

'overweight *adj.* ▶ 1202| (a) übergewichtig ‹*Person*›; **be [12 pounds]** ∼: [12 Pfund] Übergewicht haben; (b) **be** ∼ ‹*Gegenstand:*› zu schwer sein

overwhelm /əʊvə'welm/ *v.t.* (lit. or fig.) überwältigen; **be** ∼**ed with work** die Arbeit kaum bewältigen können

overwhelming /əʊvə'welmɪŋ/ *adj.* überwältigend; unbändig ‹*Wut, Kraft, Verlangen, Zorn*›; unermesslich ‹*Leid, Kummer*›; **against** ∼ **odds** entgegen aller Wahrscheinlichkeit

over: ∼**'work 1** *v.t.* (a) (cause to work too hard) mit Arbeit überlasten; (b) (fig.) überstrapazieren ‹*Metapher, Wort usw.*›; **2** *v.i.* sich überarbeiten; **3** *n.* [Arbeits]überlastung, *die;* ∼**'wrought** *adj.* überreizt; ∼**'zealous** *adj.* übereifrig

owe /əʊ/ *v.t.,* **owing** /'əʊɪŋ/ (a) schulden; ∼ **sb. sth.** jmdm. etw. schulden; ∼ **it to sb. to do sth.** es jmdm. schuldig sein, etw. zu tun; **I** ∼ **you an explanation** ich bin dir eine Erklärung schuldig; **you** ∼ **it to yourself to take a break** du musst dir einfach eine Pause gönnen; **can I** ∼ **you the rest?** kann ich dir den Rest schuldig bleiben?; ∼ **[sb.] for sth.** [jmdm.] etw. bezahlen müssen; **I [still]** ∼ **you for the ticket** du kriegst von mir noch das Geld für die Karte (ugs.); (b) (feel gratitude for, be indebted for) verdanken; ∼ **sth. to sb.** jmdm. etw. verdanken

owing /'əʊɪŋ/ *pred. adj.* ausstehend; **be** ∼ ausstehen

'owing to *prep.* wegen; ∼ **unfortunate circumstances** auf Grund unglücklicher Umstände

owl /aʊl/ *n.* Eule, *die*

own /əʊn/ **1** *adj.* eigen; **with one's** ∼ **eyes** mit eigenen Augen; **speak from one's** ∼ **experience** aus eigener Erfahrung sprechen; **this is all my** ∼ **work** das habe ich alles selbst gemacht; **do one's** ∼ **cooking/housework** selbst kochen/die Hausarbeit selbst machen; **make one's** ∼ **clothes** seine Kleidung selbst schneidern; **a house/ ideas** *etc.* **of one's** ∼: ein eigenes Haus/eigene Ideen *usw.;* **have nothing of one's** ∼: kein persönliches Eigentum haben; **have enough problems of one's** ∼: selbst genug Probleme haben; **for reasons of his** ∼ ...: aus nur ihm selbst bekannten Gründen ...; **that's where he/ it comes into his/its** ∼ (fig.) da kommt er/es voll zur Geltung; **on one's/its** ∼ (alone) allein; **he's in a class of his** ∼ (fig.) er ist eine Klasse für sich; *see also* **get back 2 c; hold 1 j; man 1 b. 2** *v.t.* besitzen; **be** ∼**ed by sb.** jmdm. gehören; **be privately** ∼**ed** sich in Privatbesitz befinden; **they behaved as if they** ∼**ed the place** sie benahmen sich, als ob der Laden ihnen gehörte (ugs.)

∼ **'up** *v.i.* (coll.) ‹*Schuldiger, Täter:*› gestehen; ∼ **up to sth.** etw. [ein]gestehen *od.* zugeben; ∼ **up to having done sth.** [ein]gestehen *od.* zugeben, dass man etw. getan hat

'own-brand, 'own-label 1 *attrib. adjs.* Eigenmarken-. **2** *n.* Hausmarke, *die*

owned /əʊnd/ *adj.* **publicly** ∼: gemeinde-/staatseigen; **privately** ∼: in Privatbesitz *nachgestellt*

owner /'əʊnə(r)/ *n.* Besitzer, *der*/Besitzerin, *die;* Eigentümer, *der*/Eigentümerin, *die;* (of car also) Halter, *der*/Halterin, *die;* (of shop, hotel, firm, etc.) Inhaber, *der*/Inhaberin, *die;* **at** ∼**'s risk** auf eigene Gefahr

ownership /'əʊnəʃɪp/ *n., no pl.* Besitz, *der;* **be under new** ∼ ‹*Firma, Laden, Restaurant:*› einen neuen Inhaber/ eine neue Inhaberin haben

own 'goal *n.* (lit. or fig.) Eigentor, *das*

ox /ɒks/ *n., pl.* **oxen** /'ɒksn/ Ochse, *der*

oxidation /ɒksɪ'deɪʃn/ *n.* (Chem.) Oxidation, *die*

oxide /'ɒksaɪd/ *n.* (Chem.) Oxid, *das*

oxidize (oxidise) /'ɒksɪdaɪz/ *v.t. & i.* (Chem.) oxidieren

oxyacetylene /ɒksɪə'setɪliːn/ *adj.* ∼ **welding** Autogenschweißen, *das;* ∼ **torch** Schweißbrenner, *der*

oxygen /'ɒksɪdʒən/ *n.* (Chem.) Sauerstoff, *der*

oyster /'ɔɪstə(r)/ *n.* Auster, *die;* **the world's his** ∼ (fig.) ihm liegt die Welt zu Füßen

oz. *abbr.* ▶ 1193|, ▶ 1202| **ounce[s]**

ozone /'əʊzəʊn/ *n.* Ozon, *das*

ozone: ∼ **depletion** *n.* Ozonabbau, *der;* ∼**friendly** *adj.* ozonsicher; (not using CFCs) FCKW-frei; ∼ **layer** *n.* Ozonschicht, *die;* **the hole in the** ∼ **layer** das Ozonloch (ugs.)

P p

P, p /piː/ *n., pl.* **Ps** *or* **P's** P, p, *das; see also* **mind 2 b**

p. *abbr.* (a) **page** S.; (b) [piː] ▶ 938| (Brit.) **penny/pence** p; (c) (Mus.) **piano** p

PA *abbr.* (a) ▶ 887| **personal assistant** pers. Ass.; (b) **public address: PA [system]** LS-Anlage, *die*

p.a. *abbr.* **per annum** p.a.

pace /peɪs/ **1** *n.* (a) (step, distance) Schritt, *der;* (b) (speed) Tempo, *das;* **slacken/quicken one's** ∼ (walking) seinen Schritt verlangsamen/beschleunigen; **at a steady/good** ∼: in gleichmäßigem/zügigem Tempo; **set the** ∼: das Tempo angeben *od.* bestimmen; **keep** ∼ **[with sb./sth.]** [mit jmdm./etw.] Schritt halten; **stay** *or* **stand the** ∼, **stay** *or* **keep with the** ∼ (Sport) das Tempo durchhalten; (c) **put sb./a horse through his/its** ∼**s** (fig.) jmdn./ein Pferd zeigen lassen, was er/es kann; **show one's** ∼**s** zeigen, was man kann. **2** *v.i.* schreiten (geh.); [gemessenen Schrittes] gehen; ∼ **up and down [the platform/ room]** [auf dem Bahnsteig/im Zimmer] auf und ab gehen *od.* marschieren. **3** *v.t.* (a) auf- und abgehen in (+ *Dat.*); (b) (set the ∼ for) Schrittmacher sein für

'pacemaker *n.* (a) (Sport) Schrittmacher, *der*/-macherin, *die;* (b) (Med.) [Herz]schrittmacher, *der*

pacific /pə'sɪfɪk/ **1** *adj.* (Geog.) Pazifik‹*küste, -insel*›; **P**∼ **Ocean** Pazifischer *od.* Stiller Ozean. **2** *n.* **the P**∼: der Pazifik

pacifism /'pæsɪfɪzm/ *n., no pl., no art.* Pazifismus, *der*

pacifist /'pæsɪfɪst/ *n.* Pazifist, *der*/Pazifistin, *die*

pacify /'pæsɪfaɪ/ *v.t.* besänftigen; beruhigen ‹*weinendes Kind*›

pack /pæk/ **1** *n.* (a) (bundle) Bündel, *das;* (Mil.) Tornister, *der;* (rucksack) Rucksack, *der;* (b) (derog.) (people) Bande, *die;* **a** ∼ **of lies/nonsense** ein Sack voll Lügen/eine Menge Unsinn; **what a** ∼ **of lies!** alles erlogen!; (c) (Brit.) ∼ **[of cards]** [Karten]spiel, *das;* (d) (wolves, wild dogs) Rudel, *das;* (hounds) Meute, *die;* (e) (Cub Scouts, Brownies) Gruppe, *die;* (f) (packet, set) Schachtel, *die;* Packung, *die;* ∼ **of ten** Zehnerpackung, *die;* Zehnerpack, *der.* **2** *v.t.* (a) (put into container) einpacken; ∼ **sth. into sth.** etw. in etw. (*Akk.*) packen; (b) (fill) packen; ∼ **one's bags** seine Koffer packen; (c) (cram) voll stopfen (ugs.); füllen ‹*Raum, Stadion usw.*›; (d) (wrap) verpacken (**in** in + *Dat. od. Akk.*); ∼**ed in** verpackt in (+ *Dat.*); (e) (coll.) tragen, dabeihaben ‹*Waffe*›; (f) ∼ **[quite] a punch** (coll.) ganz schön zuschlagen können (ugs.). **3** *v.i.* packen; **send sb.** ∼**ing** (fig.) jmdn. rausschmeißen (ugs.)

∼ **a'way** *v.t.* wegpacken

∼ **'in** *v.t.* (a) (coll.) (give up) aufstecken (ugs.); aufhören mit ‹*Arbeit, Spiel*›; ∼ **it in!** hör [doch] auf damit! (b) (find time for) hineinpacken

∼ **into** *v.t.* sich drängen in (+ *Akk.*); **we all** ∼**ed into the car** wir quetschten uns alle in das Auto (ugs.)

∼ **'off** *v.t.* (send away) wegschicken

∼ **'up 1** *v.t.* (a) (package) zusammenpacken ‹*Sachen, Werkzeug*›; packen ‹*Paket*›; (b) (coll.: stop) aufhören *od.* (ugs.) Schluss machen mit; ∼ **up work** Feierabend machen. **2** *v.i.* (coll.) (a) (give up) aufhören; Schluss machen (ugs.); (b) (break down) den Geist aufgeben (ugs.)

package /'pækɪdʒ/ **1** n. **(a)** (bundle; fig. coll.: transaction) Paket, das; **(b)** (container) Verpackung, die. **2** v.t. (lit. or fig.) verpacken

package: ~ **deal** n. Paket, das; ~ **holiday,** ~ **tour** ns. Pauschalreise, die

packaging /'pækɪdʒɪŋ/ n. Verpackung, die

packed /pækt/ adj. **(a)** gepackt ‹Kiste, Koffer›; ~ **meal/lunch** Esspaket, das/Lunchpaket, das; **(b)** (crowded) [über]voll ‹Theater, Kino, Halle›; ~ **out** (coll.) gerammelt voll (ugs.)

packet /'pækɪt/ n. **(a)** (package) Päckchen, das; (box) Schachtel, die; **a** ~ **of cigarettes** eine Schachtel/ein Päckchen Zigaretten; **(b)** (coll.: large sum of money) Haufen Geld (ugs.); **cost/earn a** ~**:** ein Heidengeld kosten (ugs.)/ein Schweinegeld verdienen (ugs.)

packing /'pækɪŋ/ n. **(a)** (packaging) (material) Verpackungsmaterial, das; (action) Verpacken, das; **including postage and** ~**:** einschließlich Porto und Verpackung; **(b)** **do one's** ~**:** packen

'**packing case** n. [Pack]kiste, die

pact /pækt/ n. Pakt, der; **make a** ~ **with sb.** einen Pakt mit jmdm. schließen

pad[1] /pæd/ **1** n. **(a)** (cushioning material) Polster, das; (to protect wound) Kompresse, die; (Sport) (on leg) Beinschützer, der; (on knee) Knieschützer, der; **(b)** (block of paper) Block, der; **a** ~ **of notepaper, a [writing]**~**:** ein Schreibblock; **(c)** (launching surface) Abschussrampe, die; **(d)** (coll.: house, flat) Bude, die (ugs.). **2** v.t., **-dd-: (a)** polstern ‹Jacke, Schulter, Stuhl›; **(b)** (fig.: lengthen unnecessarily) auswalzen (ugs.) ‹Brief, Aufsatz usw.› **(with** durch)
~ '**out** ⇒ **pad**[1] **2**

pad[2] v.t. & i., **-dd-** (walk) (in socks, slippers, etc.) tappen; (along path etc.) trotten

padded /'pædɪd/ adj. gepolstert; ~ '**cell** Gummizelle, die; ~ **envelope** wattierter Umschlag

padding /'pædɪŋ/ n. **(a)** Polsterung, die; **(b)** (fig.: superfluous matter) Füllsel, das

paddle[1] /'pædl/ **1** n. (oar) Paddel, das; (with one oar) Stechpaddel, das. **2** v.t. & i. (in canoe) paddeln

paddle[2] **1** v.i. (with feet) planschen. **2** n. **have a/go for a** ~**:** ein bisschen planschen/planschen gehen

paddle: ~ **boat,** ~ **steamer** ns. [Schaufel]raddampfer, der; ~ **wheel** n. Schaufelrad, das

'**paddling pool** n. Planschbecken, das

paddock /'pædək/ n. **(a)** Koppel, die; **(b)** (Horse racing) Sattelplatz, der

paddy /'pædɪ/, '**paddy field** ns. Reisfeld, das

'**padlock 1** n. Vorhängeschloss, das. **2** v.t. [mit einem Vorhängeschloss] verschließen

paediatric /piːdɪ'ætrɪk/ adj. (Med.) pädiatrisch; Kinder‹schwester, -station›

pagan /'peɪgən/ **1** n. Heide, der/Heidin, die. **2** adj. heidnisch

page[1] /peɪdʒ/ **1** n. ~**[-boy]** Page, der. **2** v.t. & i. ~ **[for] sb.** (over loudspeaker) jmdn. ausrufen; (by pager) jmdn. anpiepen (ugs.)

page[2] n. Seite, die; (leaf, sheet of paper) Blatt, das; **front/sports/fashion** ~**:** erste Seite/Sport-/Modeseite, die; **turn to the next** ~**:** umblättern

pageant /'pædʒənt/ n. **(a)** (spectacle) Schauspiel, das; **(b)** (play) **historical** ~**:** Historienspiel, das

pageantry /'pædʒəntrɪ/ n. Prachtentfaltung, die; Prunk, der

page: ~**-boy** n. **(a)** ⇒ **page**[1] **1; (b)** (hairstyle) Pagenkopf, der; ~ **break** n. (Computing) Seitenumbruch, der; ~ **number** n. Seitenzahl, die

pager /'peɪdʒə(r)/ n. Piepser, der (ugs.)

pagoda /pə'gəʊdə/ n. Pagode, die

paid /peɪd/ **1** ⇒ **pay 2, 3. 2** adj. bezahlt ‹Urlaub, Arbeit›; **put** ~ **to** (Brit. fig. coll.) zunichte machen ‹Hoffnung, Plan, Aussichten›; kurzen Prozess machen mit (ugs.) ‹Person›

'**paid-up** adj. bezahlt; **[fully]** ~ **member** Mitglied, das alle Beträge bezahlt hat; (fig.) überzeugtes Mitglied

pail /peɪl/ n. Eimer, der

pain /peɪn/ **1** n. **(a)** ▶865 | no indef. art. (suffering) Schmerzen; (mental ~) Qualen; **feel [some]** ~**, be in** ~**:** Schmerzen haben; **cause sb.** ~ (lit. or fig.) jmdm. wehtun; **(b)** ▶865 | (instance of suffering) Schmerz, der; **I have a** ~ **in my shoulder/knee/stomach** meine Schulter/mein Knie/Magen tut weh; **be a** ~ **in the neck** ⇒ **neck 1 a; (c)** (coll.: nuisance) Plage, die; (sb./sth. getting on one's nerves) Nervensäge, die (ugs.); **(d)** in pl. (trouble taken) Mühe, die; Anstrengung, die; **take** ~**s** sich (Dat.) Mühe geben (over mit, bei); **be at** ~**s to do sth.** sich sehr bemühen od. sich (Dat.) große Mühe geben, etw. zu tun; **he got nothing for all his** ~**s** seine ganze Mühe war umsonst; **(e)** (Law) **on** or **under** ~ **of death** bei Todesstrafe. **2** v.t. schmerzen

pained /peɪnd/ adj. gequält

painful /'peɪnfl/ adj. **(a)** (causing pain) schmerzhaft ‹Krankheit, Operation, Wunde›; **be/become** ~ ‹Körperteil:› weh tun od. schmerzen; **suffer from a** ~ **shoulder** Schmerzen in der Schulter haben; **(b)** (distressing) schmerzlich ‹Gedanke, Erinnerung›; traurig ‹Pflicht›; **it was** ~ **to watch him** es tat weh, ihm zuzusehen

painfully /'peɪnfəlɪ/ adv. **(a)** (with great pain) unter großen Schmerzen; **(b)** (fig.) (excessively) über die Maßen (geh.); (laboriously) quälend ‹langsam›; ~ **obvious** nur zu offensichtlich

'**painkiller** n. schmerzstillendes Mittel; Schmerzmittel, das (ugs.)

painless /'peɪnlɪs/ adj. schmerzlos; (fig.: not causing problems) unproblematisch

painstaking /'peɪnzteɪkɪŋ/ adj. gewissenhaft; **it is** ~ **work** es ist eine mühsame Arbeit; **with** ~ **care** mit äußerster Sorgfalt

paint /peɪnt/ **1** n. **(a)** Farbe, die; (on car) Lack, der; **(b)** (joc.: cosmetic) Schminke, die. **2** v.t. **(a)** (cover, colour) [an]streichen; ~ **the town red** (fig. coll.) auf die Pauke hauen (ugs.); **(b)** (make picture of, make by ~ing) malen; **the picture was** ~**ed by R.** das Bild ist von R.; **(c)** (adorn with ~ing) bemalen ‹Wand, Vase, Decke›; **(d)** ~ **a glowing/gloomy picture of sth.** (fig.) etw. in leuchtenden/düsteren Farben malen od. schildern; **(e)** (apply cosmetic to) schminken ‹Augen, Gesicht, Lippen›; lackieren ‹Nägel›

paint: ~**box** n. Malkasten, der; ~**brush** n. Pinsel, der

painter /'peɪntə(r)/ n. ▶887 | **(a)** (artist) Maler, der/Malerin, die; **(b)** **[house-]**~**:** Maler, der/Malerin, die; Anstreicher, der/Anstreicherin, die

painting /'peɪntɪŋ/ n. **(a)** no pl., no indef. art. (art) Malerei, die; **(b)** (picture) Gemälde, das; Bild, das

'**paint stripper** n. Abbeizmittel, das; **hot-air** ~ **stripper** Heißluftpistole, die (zum Entfernen alter Farbe)

pair /peə(r)/ **1** n. **(a)** (set of two) Paar, das; **a** ~ **of gloves/socks/shoes** etc. ein Paar Handschuhe/Socken/Schuhe usw.; **a** or **one** ~ **of hands/eyes** zwei Hände/Augen; **in** ~**s** paarweise; **the** ~ **of them** die beiden; **(b)** (single article) **a** ~ **of pyjamas/scissors** etc. ein Schlafanzug/eine Schere usw.; **a** ~ **of trousers/jeans** eine Hose/Jeans; ein Paar Hosen/Jeans; **(c)** (married couple) [Ehe]paar, das; (mated animals) Paar, das; Pärchen, das; **(d)** (Cards) Pärchen, das. **2** v.t. paaren; [paarweise] zusammenstellen
~ '**off 1** v.t. zu Paaren od. paarweise zusammenstellen; **she was** ~**ed off with Alan** sie bekam Alan als Partner. **2** v.i. Zweiergruppen bilden

pajamas /pə'dʒɑːməz/ (Amer.) ⇒ **pyjamas**

Pakistan /pɑːkɪ'stɑːn/ pr. n. Pakistan (das)

Pakistani /pɑːkɪ'stɑːnɪ/ ▶947 | **1** adj. pakistanisch; **sb. is** ~**:** jmd. ist Pakistani. **2** n. Pakistani, der/die; Pakistaner, der/Pakistanerin, die

pal /pæl/ n. (coll.) Kumpel, der (ugs.)

palace /'pælɪs/ n. Palast, der

palatable /'pælətəbl/ adj. **(a)** genießbar; trinkbar ‹Wein›; (pleasant) wohlschmeckend ‹Speise›; **(b)** (fig.) annehmbar, akzeptabel ‹Gesetz, Erhöhung, Aufführung›

palate /'pælət/ n. (Anat.) Gaumen, der

palatial /pə'leɪʃl/ adj. palastartig

palaver /pə'lɑːvə(r)/ n. (coll.: fuss) Umstand, der; Theater, das (ugs.)

pale¹ /peɪl/ *n.* **be beyond the ～** ‹*Verhalten, Benehmen:*› unmöglich sein; **regard sb. as beyond the ～:** jmdn. indiskutabel finden

pale² **1** *adj.* **(a)** blass, (esp. in illness) fahl, (nearly white) bleich ‹*Gesichtsfarbe, Haut, Gesicht, Aussehen*›; **go ～:** blass/ bleich werden; **his face was ～:** er war blass/bleich; **(b)** (light in colour) von blasser Farbe *nachgestellt;* blass ‹*Farbe*›; **a ～ blue/red dress** ein blassblaues/-rotes Kleid. **2** *v.i.* bleich/blass werden **(at** bei); **～ into insignificance** völlig bedeutungslos werden

paleness /ˈpeɪlnɪs/ *n., no pl.* (of person) Blässe, *die*

Palestine /ˈpælɪstaɪn/ *pr. n.* Palästina *(das)*

Palestinian /pælɪˈstɪnɪən/ ▶947┃ **1** *adj.* palästinensisch; **sb. is ～:** jmd. ist Palästinenser/Palästinenserin. **2** *n.* Palästinenser, *der*/Palästinenserin, *die*

palette /ˈpælɪt/ *n.* Palette, *die*

palisade /pælɪˈseɪd/ *n.* Palisade, *die;* Palisadenzaun, *der*

pall¹ /pɔːl/ *n.* **(a)** (over coffin) Sargtuch, *das;* **(b)** (fig.) Schleier, *der*

pall² *v.i.* **～ [on sb.]** [jmdm.] langweilig werden

'pall-bearer *n.* Sargträger, *der*/-trägerin, *die*

pallet /ˈpælɪt/ *n.* (platform) Palette, *die*

palliative /ˈpælɪətɪv/ *n.* (Med.) Palliativ[um], *das* (fachspr.); Linderungsmittel, *das*

pallid /ˈpælɪd/ *adj.* **(a)** ⇒ **pale²** 1 a; **(b)** matt, blass ‹*Farbe*›

pallor /ˈpælə(r)/ *n.* Blässe, *die;* Fahlheit, *die*

palm¹ /pɑːm/ *n.* (tree) Palme, *die;* **～ [branch]** (also Eccl.) Palmzweig, *der*

palm² *n.* ▶672┃ Handteller, *der;* Handfläche, *die;* **have sth. in the ～ of one's hand** (fig.) etw. in der Hand haben **～ 'off** *v.t.* **～ sth. off on sb., ～ sb. off with sth.** jmdm. etw. andrehen (ugs.)

palmist /ˈpɑːmɪst/ *n.* Handleser, *der*/-leserin, *die*

palmistry /ˈpɑːmɪstrɪ/ *n., no pl.* Handlesekunst, *die*

palm: **P～ 'Sunday** *n.* (Eccl.) Palmsonntag, *der;* **～top** *n.* **～top [computer]** Palmtop, *der;* **～ tree** *n.* Palme, *die*

palpable /ˈpælpəbl/ *adj.* offenkundig ‹*Lüge, Unwissenheit, Absurdität*›

palpitate /ˈpælpɪteɪt/ *v.i.* (pulsate) ‹*Herz:*› palpitieren (fachspr.), pochen, hämmern; (tremble) zittern **(with** vor + *Dat.)*

palpitations /pælpɪˈteɪʃnz/ *n. pl.* (Med.) Palpitation, *die* (fachspr.); Herzklopfen, *das*

paltry /ˈpɔːltrɪ, ˈpɒltrɪ/ *adj.* schäbig; armselig ‹*Auswahl*›; (trivial) belanglos

pampas /ˈpæmpəs/ *n. pl.* (Geog.) Pampas *Pl.*

'pampas grass *n.* Pampasgras, *das*

pamper /ˈpæmpə(r)/ *v.t.* verhätscheln; **～ oneself** sich verwöhnen

pamphlet /ˈpæmflɪt/ *n.* (leaflet) Prospekt, *der;* (esp. Polit.) Flugblatt, *das;* (booklet) Broschüre, *die*

pan¹ /pæn/ *n.* **(a)** [Koch]topf, *der;* (for frying) Pfanne, *die;* **pots and ～s** Kochtöpfe; **(b)** (of scales) Schale, *die;* **(c)** (Brit.: of WC) **[lavatory] ～:** Toilettenschüssel, *die* **～ 'out** *v.i.* (progress) sich entwickeln

pan² (Cinemat., Telev.) **1** *v.t.* **-nn-** schwenken. **2** *v.i.* **-nn-** schwenken **(to** auf + *Akk.*); **～ning shot** Schwenk, *der*

pan- /pæn/ *in comb.* pan-, Pan-

panacea /pænəˈsɪːə/ *n.* Allheilmittel, *das*

panache /pəˈnæʃ/ *n.* Schwung, *der;* Elan, *der*

Panama /pæˈnɑː/ **1** *pr. n.* Panama *(das)*. **2** *n.* **p～ [hat]** Panamahut, *der*

Panama Ca'nal *pr. n.* Panamakanal, *der*

Panamanian /pænəˈmeɪnɪən/ ▶947┃ **1** *adj.* panamaisch. **2** *n.* Panamaer, *der*/Panamaerin, *die*

pancake /ˈpænkeɪk/ *n.* Pfannkuchen, *der*

Pancake Day *n.* (Brit.) Fastnachtsdienstag, *der*

pancreas /ˈpæŋkrɪəs/ *n.* (Anat.) Bauchspeicheldrüse, *die;* Pankreas, *das* (fachspr.)

panda /ˈpændə/ *n.* (Zool.) Panda, *der*

pandemonium /pændɪˈməʊnɪəm/ *n.* Chaos, *das;* (uproar) Tumult, *der*

pander /ˈpændə(r)/ *v.i.* **～ to** allzu sehr entgegenkommen (+ *Dat.*) ‹*Person, Geschmack, Instinkt*›

p. & p. *abbr.* (Brit.) **postage and packing** Porto und Verpackung

pane /peɪn/ *n.* Scheibe, *die;* **window-～/～ of glass** Fenster-/Glasscheibe, *die*

panel /ˈpænl/ *n.* **(a)** (of door, wall, etc.) Paneel, *das;* **(b)** (esp. Telev., Radio, etc.) (quiz team) Rateteam, *das;* (in public discussion) Podium, *das;* **(c)** (advisory body) Gremium, *das;* Kommission, *die;* **～ of experts** Expertengremium, *das;* **(d)** (Dressmaking) Einsatz, *der*

'panel game *n.* Ratespiel, *das*

paneling, panelist (Amer.) ⇒ **panell-**

panelling /ˈpænəlɪŋ/ *n.* Täfelung, *die*

panellist /ˈpænəlɪst/ *n.* (Telev., Radio) (on quiz programme) Mitglied des Rateteams; (on discussion panel) Diskussionsteilnehmer, *der*/-teilnehmerin, *die*

'pan-fry *v.t.* [in der Pfanne] braten

pang /pæŋ/ *n.* **(a)** (of pain) Stich, *der;* **(b)** feel **～s of conscience/guilt** Gewissensbisse haben; **feel ～s of remorse** bittere Reue empfinden

panic /ˈpænɪk/ **1** *n.* Panik, *die;* **be in a [state of] ～:** von Panik erfasst sein; **hit the ～ button** (fig. coll.) Alarm schlagen; **(～)** durchdrehen (ugs.). **2** *v.i.,* **-ck-** in Panik *(Akk.)* geraten; **don't ～!** nur keine Panik! **3** *v.t.,* **-ck-** in Panik versetzen; **～ sb. into doing sth.** jmdn. so in Panik versetzen, dass er etw. tut

'panic attack *n.* Angstanfall, *der;* Anfall von Panik; **she suffers from ～s** sie leidet an Angstzuständen

panicky /ˈpænɪkɪ/ *adj.* von Panik bestimmt ‹*Verhalten, Handeln, Rede*›; **be ～:** in Panik sein

panic: **～ stations** *n. pl.* (fig. coll.) **be at ～ stations** am Rotieren sein (ugs.) **(about** wegen); **～-stricken, ～-struck** *adjs.* von Panik erfasst *od.* ergriffen

panorama /pænəˈrɑːmə/ *n.* Panorama, *das;* (fig.: survey) Überblick, *der* **(of** über + *Akk.*)

panoramic /pænəˈræmɪk/ *adj.* Panorama-

'pan-pipes *n. pl.* (Mus.) Panflöte, *die*

pansy /ˈpænzɪ/ *n.* **(a)** (Bot.) Stiefmütterchen, *das;* **(b)** (coll.: effeminate man) Tunte, *die* (ugs.)

pant /pænt/ *v.i.* keuchen; ‹*Hund:*› hecheln **～ for** *v.t.* ringen nach ‹*Luft, Atem*›; schnappen nach ‹*Luft*›

pantechnicon /pænˈteknɪkən/ *n.* **～ [van]** (Brit.) Möbelwagen, *der*

panther /ˈpænθə(r)/ *n.* (Zool.) **(a)** Panther, *der;* **(b)** (Amer.: puma) Puma, *der;* Berglöwe, *der*

panties /ˈpæntɪz/ *n. pl.* (coll.) **[pair of] ～:** Schlüpfer, *der*

pantomime /ˈpæntəmaɪm/ *n.* **(a)** (Brit.) Märchenspiel im Varieteestil, *das* um Weihnachten aufgeführt wird; **(b)** (gestures) Pantomime, *die*

pantry /ˈpæntrɪ/ *n.* Speisekammer, *die*

pants /pænts/ *n. pl.* **(a)** (esp. Amer. coll.: trousers) **[pair of] ～:** Hose, *die;* **catch sb. with his ～ down** (fig. coll.) jmdn. unvorbereitet treffen; **(b)** (Brit. coll.: underpants) Unterhose, *die*

papacy /ˈpeɪpəsɪ/ *n.* **(a)** *no pl.* (office) Papat, *der;* **(b)** (tenure) Amtszeit als Papst; **(c)** *no pl.* (papal system) Papsttum, *das*

papal /ˈpeɪpl/ *adj.* päpstlich

paper /ˈpeɪpə(r)/ **1** *n.* **(a)** (material) Papier, *das;* **put sth. down on ～:** etw. schriftlich festhalten *od.* niederlegen; **it looks all right on ～** (in theory) auf dem Papier sieht es ganz gut aus; **put pen to ～:** zur Feder greifen; **the treaty etc. isn't worth the ～ it's written on** (coll.) der Vertrag *usw.* ist nicht das Papier wert, auf dem er geschrieben steht; **(b)** *in pl.* (documents) Dokumente; Unterlagen *Pl.;* (to prove identity etc.) Papiere *Pl.;* **(c)** (in examination) (Univ.) Klausur, *die;* (Sch.) Arbeit, *die;* **(d)** (newspaper) Zeitung, *die;* **daily/weekly ～:** Tages-/Wochenzeitung, *die;* **(e)** (wallpaper) Tapete, *die;* **(f)** (wrapper) Stück Papier, *das;* **don't scatter the ～s all over the floor** wirf das Papier nicht überall auf den Boden; **(g)** (learned article) Referat, *das;* (shorter) Paper, *das.* **2** *adj.* **(a)** (made of ～) aus Papier *nachgestellt;* Papier‹*mütze, -taschentuch*›; **(b)** (theoretical) nominell ‹*zahlenmäßige Stärke, Profit*›. **3** *v.t.* tapezieren

∼ '**over** *v.t.* [mit Tapete] überkleben; ∼ **over the cracks** (fig.: cover up mistakes/differences) die Fehler/Differenzen übertünchen

paper: ∼**back** *n.* Paperback, *das;* (pocket-size) Taschenbuch, *das;* ∼ '**bag** *n.* Papiertüte, *die;* ∼ **boy** *n.* Zeitungsjunge, *der;* ∼**chase** *n.* Schnitzeljagd, *die;* ∼ **clip** *n.* Büroklammer, *die;* (larger) Aktenklammer, *die;* ∼ '**cup** *n.* Pappbecher, *der;* ∼ **girl** *n.* Zeitungsausträgerin, *die;* ∼ '**handkerchief** *n.* Papiertaschentuch, *das;* ∼**knife** *n.* Brieföffner, *der*

paperless /ˈpeɪpəlɪs/ *adj.* papierlos ‹*Transaktionen, System*›; **the** ∼ **office** das papierlose Büro

paper: ∼ **mill** *n.* Papierfabrik *od.* -mühle, *die;* ∼ **money** *n.* Papiergeld, *das;* ∼ '**napkin** *n.* Papierserviette, *die;* ∼ '**plate** *n.* Pappteller, *der;* ∼ **round** *n.* Zeitungenaustragen, *das;* **have/do a** ∼**-round** Zeitungen austragen; ∼ **servi'ette** ⇒ ∼ **napkin;** ∼ **shop** *n.* Zeitungsgeschäft, *das;* ∼**-thin** *adj.* (lit. or fig.) hauchdünn; ∼ '**towel** *n.* Papierhandtuch, *das;* ∼**weight** *n.* Briefbeschwerer, *der;* ∼**work** *n.* Schreibarbeit, *die*

papier mâché /ˈpæpjeɪ ˈmæʃeɪ/ *n.* Papiermaschee, *das;* Pappmaschee, *das*

papist /ˈpeɪpɪst/ *n.* (Relig. derog.) Papist, *der*/Papistin, *die*

paprika /ˈpæprɪkə, pəˈpriːkə/ *n.* (a) ⇒ **pepper 1 b;** (b) (Cookery: condiment) Paprika, *der*

par /pɑː(r)/ *n.* (a) (average) **above/below** ∼**:** über/unter dem Durchschnitt; **feel rather below** ∼**, not feel up to** ∼ (fig.) nicht ganz auf dem Posten *od.* Damm sein (ugs.); (b) (equality) **be on a** ∼**:** vergleichbar sein; **be on a** ∼ **with sb./sth.** jmdm./einer Sache gleichkommen; (c) (Golf) Par, *das;* **that's about** ∼ **for the course** (fig. coll.) das ist so das Übliche

parable /ˈpærəbl/ *n.* Gleichnis, *das;* Parabel, *die* (bes. Literaturw.)

parabola /pəˈræbələ/ *n.* (Geom.) Parabel, *die*

parachute /ˈpærəʃuːt/ **1** *n.* (a) Fallschirm, *der;* (b) (to brake aircraft etc.) Bremsfallschirm, *der.* **2** *v.t.* [mit dem Fallschirm] absetzen ‹*Person*› (**into** über + *Dat.*); mit dem Fallschirm abwerfen ‹*Vorräte*›. **3** *v.i.* [mit dem Fallschirm] abspringen (**into** über + *Dat.*)

parachutist /ˈpærəʃuːtɪst/ *n.* [**sports**] ∼**:** Fallschirmspringer, *der*/-springerin, *die*

parade /pəˈreɪd/ **1** *n.* (a) (display) Zurschaustellung, *die;* **make a** ∼ **of** zur Schau stellen ‹*Tugend, Eigenschaft*›; (b) (Mil.: muster) Appell, *der;* **on** ∼**:** beim Appell; (c) (procession) Umzug, *der;* (of troops) Parade, *die;* (d) (succession) Reihe, *die.* **2** *v.t.* (a) (display) zur Schau stellen; vorzeigen ‹*Person*› (**before** bei); (b) (march through) ∼ **the streets** durch die Straßen marschieren. **3** *v.i.* paradieren; ‹*Demonstranten:*› marschieren

pa'rade ground *n.* Exerzierplatz, *der*

paradise /ˈpærədaɪs/ *n.* Paradies, *das*

paradox /ˈpærədɒks/ *n.* Paradox[on], *das*

paradoxical /pærəˈdɒksɪkl/ *adj.* paradox

paraffin /ˈpærəfɪn/ *n.* (a) (Chem.) Paraffin, *das;* (b) (Brit.: fuel) Petroleum, *das*

paraffin: ∼ **stove** *n.* Petroleumkocher, *der;* (for heating) Petroleumofen, *der;* ∼ **wax** *n.* Paraffin[wachs], *das*

paragliding /ˈpærəɡlaɪdɪŋ/ *n.*, no *pl.* Paragliding, *das;* Gleitschirmfliegen, *das*

paragon /ˈpærəɡən/ *n.* Muster, *das* (**of** an + *Dat.*); ∼ **of virtue** Tugendheld, *der*

paragraph /ˈpærəɡrɑːf/ *n.* (a) (section of text) Absatz, *der;* (b) (subsection of law etc.) Paragraph, *der*

parakeet /ˈpærəkiːt/ *n.* (Ornith.) Sittich, *der*

parallel /ˈpærəlel/ **1** *adj.* (a) parallel; **the railway ran** ∼ **to the river** die Bahnlinie verlief parallel zum Fluss; ∼ **bars** (Gymnastics) Barren, *der;* (b) (fig.: similar) vergleichbar; **be** ∼**:** sich (*Dat.*) [genau] entsprechen. **2** *n.* (a) Parallele, *die;* **this has no** ∼**:** dazu gibt es keine Parallele; **there is a** ∼ **between x and y** es gibt eine Parallelität zwischen x und y; (b) (Electr.) **in** ∼**:** parallel; (c) (Geog.) ∼ [**of latitude**] Breitenkreis, *der;* **the 42nd** ∼**:** der 42. Breitengrad. **3** *v.t.* gleichkommen (+ *Dat.*)

parallelogram /pærəˈleləɡræm/ *n.* (Geom.) Parallelogramm, *das*

parallel 'processing *n.* (Computing) Parallelverarbeitung, *die*

paralyse /ˈpærəlaɪz/ *v.t.* lähmen; **he is** ∼**d in both legs** seine beiden Beine sind gelähmt; (fig.) lahmlegen ‹*Verkehr, Industrie*›; **be** ∼**d with fright** vor Schreck wie gelähmt sein

paralysis /pəˈrælɪsɪs/ *n.*, *pl.* **paralyses** /pəˈrælɪsiːz/ Lähmung, *die;* (fig., of industry, traffic) Lahmlegung, *die*

paralytic /pærəˈlɪtɪk/ *n.* Gelähmte, *der*/*die*

paralyze (Amer.) ⇒ **paralyse**

paramedic /pærəˈmedɪk/ *n.* medizinische Hilfskraft; (ambulance-worker) Sanitäter, *der*/Sanitäterin, *die*

parameter /pəˈræmɪtə(r)/ (a) (defining feature) Faktor, *der;* (b) (Math.) Parameter, *der*

paramilitary /pærəˈmɪlɪtərɪ/ *adj.* paramilitärisch

paramount /ˈpærəmaʊnt/ *adj.* höchst... ‹*Macht, Autorität, Wichtigkeit*›; Haupt‹*gesichtspunkt, -überlegung*›

paranoia /pærəˈnɔɪə/ *n.* (a) (disorder) Paranoia, *die* (Med.); (b) (tendency) [**feeling of**] ∼**:** krankhaftes Misstrauen

paranormal /pærəˈnɔːml/ *adj.* paranormal; übersinnlich

parapet /ˈpærəpɪt, ˈpærəpet/ *n.* (low wall or barrier) Brüstung, *die*

paraphernalia /pærəfəˈneɪlɪə/ *n. sing.* (a) (belongings) Utensilien *Pl.;* (b) (of justice, power) Instrumentarium, *das* (geh.); Apparat, *der;* **the whole** ∼ (coll.) alles, was so dazugehört (ugs.)

paraphrase /ˈpærəfreɪz/ **1** *n.* Umschreibung, *die.* **2** *v.t.* umschreiben

paraplegia /pærəˈpliːdʒɪə/ *n.* (Med.) Paraplegie, *die* (fachspr.); ≈ Querschnittslähmung, *die*

paraplegic /pærəˈpliːdʒɪk/ (Med.) **1** *adj.* doppelseitig gelähmt; paraplegisch (fachspr.). **2** *n.* doppelseitig Gelähmter/Gelähmte; Paraplegiker, *der*/Paraplegikerin, *die* (fachspr.)

parasailing /ˈpærəseɪlɪŋ/ *n.*, no *pl.* Parasailing, *das*

parascending /ˈpærəsendɪŋ/ *n.*, no *pl.* (a) ⇒ **parasailing;** (b) ⇒ **paragliding**

parasite /ˈpærəsaɪt/ *n.* (Biol.: also fig. derog.) Schmarotzer, *der;* Parasit, *der*

parasitic /pærəˈsɪtɪk/ *adj.* (a) (Biol.) parasitisch; parasitär ‹*Pilz*›; **be** ∼ **on** schmarotzen an (+ *Dat.*); (b) (fig.) schmarotzerisch

parasol /ˈpærəsɒl/ *n.* Sonnenschirm, *der*

paratrooper /ˈpærətruːpə(r)/ *n.* (Mil.) Fallschirmjäger, *der*

paratroops /ˈpærətruːps/ *n. pl.* (Mil.) Fallschirmjäger *Pl.*

parboil /ˈpɑːbɔɪl/ *v.t.* ankochen

parcel /ˈpɑːsl/ *n.* (a) (package) Paket, *das;* **send/receive sth. by** ∼ **post** etw. mit der Paketpost schicken/bekommen; (b) **a** ∼ **of land** ein Stück Land

∼ '**out** *v.t.* aufteilen ‹*Land*›

∼ '**up** *v.t.* einwickeln

'**parcel bomb** *n.* Paketbombe, *die*

parched /pɑːtʃt/ *adj.* ausgedörrt ‹*Kehle, Land, Boden*›; trocken ‹*Lippen*›

parchment /ˈpɑːtʃmənt/ *n.* Pergament, *das*

pardon /ˈpɑːdn/ **1** *n.* (a) (forgiveness) Vergebung, *die* (geh.); Verzeihung, *die;* **beg sb.'s** ∼**:** jmdm. um Entschuldigung *od.* (geh.) Verzeihung bitten; **I beg your** ∼**:** entschuldigen *od.* verzeihen Sie bitte; (please repeat) wie bitte? (auch iron.); **beg** ∼ (coll.) Entschuldigung; Verzeihung; ∼**?** (coll.) bitte?; ∼**!** (coll.) Entschuldigung!; (c) (Law) [**free**] ∼**:** Begnadigung, *die.* **2** *v.t.* (a) (forgive) ∼ **sb.** [**for**] **sth.** jmdm. etw. verzeihen; (b) (excuse) entschuldigen; ∼ **my saying so, but** ...**:** entschuldigen Sie bitte, dass ich es so ausdrücke, aber...; ∼ '**me!** Entschuldigung!; ∼'**me?** (Amer.) wie bitte?; (c) (Law) begnadigen

pare /peə(r)/ *v.t.* (a) (trim) schneiden ‹*Finger-, Zehennägel*›; (b) (peel) schälen ‹*Apfel, Kartoffel*›

∼ '**down** *v.t.* reduzieren ‹*Kosten etc.*›

parent /ˈpeərənt/ *n.* Elternteil, *der;* ∼**s** Eltern *Pl.;* attrib. Stamm‹*firma, -organisation*›

parentage /ˈpeərəntɪdʒ/ *n.* (lit. or fig.) Herkunft, *die*
parental /pəˈrentl/ *adj.* elterlich ⟨*Gewalt*⟩; Eltern⟨*pflicht, -haus*⟩
parenthesis /pəˈrenθɪsɪs/ *n., pl.* **parentheses** /pəˈrenθɪsiːz/ (a) (bracket) runde Klammer; Parenthese, *die* (fachspr.); (b) (word, clause, sentence) Parenthese, *die* (geh.); Einschub, *der*
parenthetic /pærənˈθetɪk/, **parenthetical** /pærənˈθe tɪkl/ *adj.* eingeschoben; parenthetisch (fachspr.)
parenthood /ˈpeərənthʊd/ *n.*, *no pl.* Elternschaft, *die*
'parents' evening *n.* Elternabend, *der*
parent-'teacher association *n.* Eltern-Lehrer-Vertretung, *die*
Paris /ˈpærɪs/ *pr. n.* ▶ **1159**] Paris (*das*)
parish /ˈpærɪʃ/ *n.* Gemeinde, *die*
parish: ~ **'church** *n.* Pfarrkirche, *die;* ~ **'council** *n.* (Brit.) Gemeinderat, *der*
parishioner /pəˈrɪʃənə(r)/ *n.* Gemeinde[mit]glied, *das*
parish: ~ **'priest** *n.* Gemeindepfarrer, *der;* ~ **'register** *n.* Kirchenbuch, *das*
Parisian /pəˈrɪzɪən/ ▶ **1159**] **1** *n.* Pariser, *der*/Pariserin, *die.* **2** *adj.* Pariser
parity /ˈpærɪtɪ/ *n.* (a) (equality) Parität, *die* (geh.); Gleichheit, *die;* (b) (Commerc.) Parität, *die;* **the ~ of sterling against the dollar** die Pfund-Dollar-Parität
park /pɑːk/ **1** *n.* (a) Park, *der;* (land kept in natural state) Natur[schutz]park, *der;* (b) (sports ground) Sportplatz, *der;* (stadium) Stadion, *das;* (Baseball, Footb.) Spielfeld, *das;* (c) **amusement** ~: Vergnügungspark, *der.* **2** *v.i.* parken; **find somewhere to** ~: einen Parkplatz finden. **3** *v.t.* (a) (place, leave) abstellen ⟨*Fahrzeug*⟩; parken ⟨*Kfz*⟩; (b) (coll.: leave, put) deponieren ⟨*scherzh.*⟩; ~ **oneself [down]** (coll.) sich [hin]pflanzen (ugs.)
parka /ˈpɑːkə/ *n.* Parka, *der*
park-and-'ride *n.* Park-and-ride-System, *das;* (place) Park-and-ride-Platz, *der*
parking /ˈpɑːkɪŋ/ *n.*, *no pl., no indef. art.* Parken, *das;* 'No ~' „Parken verboten"
parking: ~ **attendant** *n.* ▶ **887**] Parkplatzwächter *der*/-wächterin, *die;* ~ **bay** *n.* Stellplatz, *der;* ~ **light** *n.* Parklicht, *das;* Parkleuchte, *die;* ~ **lot** *n.* (Amer.) Parkplatz, *der;* ~ **meter** *n.* Parkuhr, *die;* ~ **space** *n.* (a) *no pl.* Parkraum, *der;* (b) (single space) Platz zum Parken; Parkplatz, *der;* ~ **ticket** *n.* Strafzettel [für falsches Parken]
park: ~**keeper** *n.* ▶ **887**] Parkwärter, *der*/-wärterin, *die;* ~**land** *n.* Parklandschaft, *die*
parlance /ˈpɑːləns/ *n.* **in common/legal/modern** ~: im allgemeinen/juristischen/modernen Sprachgebrauch
parliament /ˈpɑːləmənt/ *n.* Parlament, *das;* **[Houses of] P~** (Brit.) Parlament, *das*
parliamentary /pɑːləˈmentərɪ/ *adj.* parlamentarisch; Parlaments⟨*geschäfte, -reform*⟩
parlour (*Brit.; Amer.:* **parlor**) /ˈpɑːlə(r)/ *n.* (dated: sitting room) Wohnzimmer, *das;* gute Stube (veralt.)
Parmesan /ˈpɑːmɪzæn, pɑːmɪˈzæn/ *adj., n.* **[cheese]** Parmesan[käse], *der*
parochial /pəˈrəʊkɪəl/ *adj.* (a) (narrow) krähwinklig (abwertend); eng ⟨*Horizont*⟩; **be ~ in one's outlook** einen engen Horizont haben; (b) (Eccl.) Gemeinde-
parody /ˈpærədɪ/ **1** *n.* (a) (humorous imitation) Parodie, *die* (of auf + *Akk.*); (b) (feeble imitation) Abklatsch, *der* (abwertend); (of justice) Verhöhnung, *die.* **2** *v.t.* parodieren
parole /pəˈrəʊl/ **1** *n.* (conditional release) bedingter Straferlass (Rechtsw.); **he was released** *or* **let out on** ~/**he is on** ~: er wurde auf Bewährung entlassen. **2** *v.t.* (Law) ~ **sb.** jmdm. seine Strafe bedingt erlassen
paroxysm /ˈpærəksɪzm/ *n.* Krampf, *der;* (fit, convulsion) Anfall, *der* (**of** von); ~ **of rage/laughter** Wut-/Lachanfall, *der*
parquet /ˈpɑːkɪ, ˈpɑːkeɪ/ *n.* ~ **[flooring]** Parkett, *das;* ~ **floor** Parkettfußboden, *der*
parrot /ˈpærət/ **1** *n.* Papagei, *der;* **I was as sick as a** ~ (sl.) mir war zum Kotzen zumute (salopp). **2** *v.t.* nachplappern (abwertend); ~ **sb.** jmdm. alles nachplappern

'parrot-fashion *adv.* papageienhaft, wie ein Papagei ⟨*wiederholen*⟩
parry /ˈpærɪ/ *v.t.* (Boxing) abwehren ⟨*Faustschlag*⟩; (Fencing; also fig.) parieren ⟨*Fechthieb, Frage*⟩
parsimonious /pɑːsɪˈməʊnɪəs/ *adj.* sparsam; (niggardly) geizig
parsley /ˈpɑːslɪ/ *n., no pl., no indef. art.* Petersilie, *die*
parsnip /ˈpɑːsnɪp/ *n.* Gemeiner Pastinak, *der;* Pastinake, *die*
parson /ˈpɑːsn/ *n.* (vicar, rector) Pfarrer, *der;* (coll.: any clergyman) Geistliche, *der*
parsonage /ˈpɑːsənɪdʒ/ *n.* Pfarrhaus, *das*
part /pɑːt/ **1** *n.* (a) Teil, *der;* **four-~:** vierteilig ⟨*Serie*⟩; **the hottest ~ of the day** die heißesten Stunden des Tages; **accept ~ of the blame** die Schuld teilweise mit übernehmen; **for the most ~:** größtenteils; zum größten Teil; **in ~:** teilweise; **in large ~:** groß[en]teils; **in ~s** zum Teil; ~ **and parcel** wesentlicher Bestandteil; **the funny ~ of it was that he ...:** das Komische daran war, dass er ...; **it's [all]** ~ **of the fun/job** *etc.* das gehört [mit] dazu; **be** *or* **form** ~ **of sth.** zu etw. gehören; (b) (of machine or other apparatus) [Einzel]teil, *das;* (c) (share) Anteil, *der;* **I want no** ~ **in this** ich möchte damit nichts zu tun haben; (d) (duty) Aufgabe, *die;* **do one's** ~: seinen Teil od. das Seine tun; (e) (Theatre: character, words) Rolle, *die;* **dress the** ~ (fig.) die angemessene Kleidung tragen; **play a [great/considerable]** ~ (contribute) eine [wichtige] Rolle spielen; (f) (Mus.) Part, *der;* Partie, *die;* Stimme, *die;* (g) *usu. in pl.* (region) Gegend, *die;* (of continent, world) Teil, *der;* **I am a stranger in these** ~s ich kenne mich hier nicht aus; (h) (side) Partei, *die;* **take sb.'s** ~: jmds. od. für jmdn. Partei ergreifen; **for my** ~: für mein[en] Teil; **on my/ your** *etc.* ~: meiner-/deinerseits *usw.;* (i) *pl.* (abilities) **a man of [many]** ~s ein [vielseitig] begabter od. befähigter Mann; (j) (Ling.) ~ **of speech** Wortart od. -klasse, *die;* (k) **take [no]** ~ **[in sth.]** sich [an etw. (*Dat.*)] [nicht] beteiligen; (l) **take sth. in good** ~: etw. nicht übel nehmen. **2** *adv.* teils. **3** *v.t.* (a) (divide into ~s) teilen; scheiteln ⟨*Haar*⟩; (b) (separate) trennen. **4** *v.i.* ⟨*Menge:*⟩ eine Gasse bilden; ⟨*Wolken:*⟩ sich teilen; ⟨*Vorhang:*⟩ sich öffnen; ⟨*Seil, Tau, Kette:*⟩ reißen; ⟨*Lippen:*⟩ sich öffnen; ⟨*Wege, Personen:*⟩ sich trennen; ~ **from sb./sth.** sich von jmdm./etw. trennen; ~ **with** sich trennen von ⟨*Besitz, Geld*⟩
partake /pɑːˈteɪk/ *v.i., forms as* **take 2** (formal) ~ **of** (eat) zu sich nehmen ⟨*Kost, Mahlzeit*⟩
partaken ⇒ **partake**
part-ex'change *n.* **accept sth. in** ~ **for sth.** etw. für etw. in Zahlung nehmen; **sell sth. in** ~: etw. in Zahlung geben
partial /ˈpɑːʃl/ *adj.* (a) (biased, unfair) voreingenommen; parteiisch ⟨*Urteil*⟩; (b) **be/not be** ~ **to sb./sth.** (like/dislike) eine Schwäche/keine besondere Vorliebe für jmdn./ etw. haben; (c) (incomplete) partiell ⟨*Lähmung, Sonnen-, Mondfinsternis*⟩; teilweise ⟨*Verlust, Misserfolg*⟩
partiality /pɑːʃɪˈælɪtɪ/ *n.* (a) (fondness) Vorliebe, *die;* (b) (bias) Voreingenommenheit, *die*
partially /ˈpɑːʃəlɪ/ *adv.* zum Teil; teilweise
participant /pɑːˈtɪsɪpənt/ *n.* Beteiligte, *der*/*die* (**in** an + *Dat.*); (in arranged event) Teilnehmer, *der*/Teilnehmerin, *die* (**in** an + *Dat.*)
participate /pɑːˈtɪsɪpeɪt/ *v.i.* (be actively involved) sich beteiligen (**in** an + *Dat.*); (in arranged event) teilnehmen (**in** an + *Dat.*)
participation /pɑːtɪsɪˈpeɪʃn/ *n.* Beteiligung, *die* (**in** an + *Dat.*); (in arranged event) Teilnahme, *die* (**in** bei, an + *Dat.*)
participle /ˈpɑːtɪsɪpl/ *n.* (Ling.) Partizip, *das;* **present/ past** ~: Partizip Präsens/Perfekt
particle /ˈpɑːtɪkl/ *n.* (a) (tiny portion; also Phys.) Teilchen, *das;* (of sand) Körnchen, *das;* (b) (fig.) (of sense, truth) Fünkchen, *das;* (c) (Ling.) Partikel, *die*
particoloured (*Brit.; Amer.:* **particolored**) /pɑː tɪˈkʌləd/ *adj.* bunt
particular /pɑːˈtɪkjʊlə(r)/ **1** *adj.* (a) (special) besonder...; **which** ~ **place do you have in mind?** an welchen Ort denkst du speziell?; **here in** ~: besonders hier; **nothing/ anything [in]** ~: nichts/irgendetwas Besonderes; **in his**

~ case in seinem [besonderen] Fall; **(b)** (fussy, fastidious) genau; eigen (landsch.); **I am not ~:** es ist mir gleich; **be ~ about sth.** es mit etw. genau nehmen. **2** *n.* **(a)** *in pl.* (details) Einzelheiten; Details; (of person) Personalien *Pl.;* (of incident) nähere Umstände; **(b)** (detail) Einzelheit, *die;* Detail, *das*

particularly /pə'tɪkjʊləlɪ/ *adv.* **(a)** (especially) besonders; **(b)** (specifically) speziell; insbesondere

parting /'pɑ:tɪŋ/ **1** *n.* **(a)** (leave-taking) **[final]** ~: Trennung, *die;* Abschied, *der;* **(b)** (Brit.: in hair) Scheitel, *der;* **(c)** ~ **of the ways** (fig.: critical point) Scheideweg, *der;* **we came to a ~ of the ways** (fig.) unsere Wege trennten sich. **2** *attrib. adj.* Abschieds-; ~ **shot** Schlussbemerkung, *die*

partisan /'pɑ:tɪzæn/ **1** *n.* (Mil.) Partisan, *der*/Partisanin, *die.* **2** *adj.* **(a)** (often derog.: biased) voreingenommen, parteiisch ⟨Ansatz, Urteil, Versuch⟩; Partei⟨politik, -geist⟩; **(b)** (Mil.) Partisanen-

partition /pɑ:'tɪʃn/ **1** *n.* **(a)** (Polit.) Teilung, *die;* **(b)** (room divider) Trennwand, *die;* **(c)** (section of hall or library) Abteilung, *die;* Bereich, *der.* **2** *v.t.* **(a)** (divide) aufteilen ⟨Land, Zimmer⟩; **(b)** (Polit.) teilen ⟨Land⟩
~ **'off** *v.t.* abteilen ⟨Teil, Raum⟩

partly /'pɑ:tlɪ/ *adv.* zum Teil; teilweise

partner /'pɑ:tnə(r)/ **1** *n.* Partner, *der*/Partnerin, *die;* ~ **in crime** Komplize, *der*/Komplizin, *die* (abwertend); **be a ~ in a firm** Teilhaber/-haberin einer Firma sein. **2** *v.t.* **(a)** (make a ~) ~ **sb. with sb.** jmdn. mit jmdm. zusammenbringen; **(b)** (be ~ of) ~ **sb.** jmds. Partner/Partnerin sein; ~ **sb. at tennis/in the dance** mit jmdm. Tennis spielen/tanzen

partnership /'pɑ:tnəʃɪp/ *n.* **(a)** (association) Partnerschaft, *die;* **(b)** (Commerc.) **business ~:** [Personen]gesellschaft, *die;* **go or enter into ~ with sb.** mit jmdm. eine [Personen]gesellschaft gründen

partook ⇒ **partake**

part 'payment *n.* **(a)** ⇒ **part exchange**; **(b)** (sum) Anzahlung, *die*

partridge /'pɑ:trɪdʒ/ *n., pl. same or* ~**s** Rebhuhn, *das*

part: ~**-time 1** /'--/ *adj.* Teilzeit⟨arbeit, -arbeiter⟩; **he is only** ~**-time** er ist nur eine Teilzeitkraft; **2** /-'-/ *adv.* stundenweise, halbtags ⟨arbeiten, studieren⟩; **work** ~**-time** als Teilzeitkraft beschäftigt sein; ~**-way** *adv.* **we were** ~**-way through the tunnel** wir hatten ein Stück des Tunnels hinter uns; **go** ~**-way towards meeting sb.'s demands** Forderungen ⟨Dat.⟩ teilweise od. halbwegs entsprechen; ~**-way through her speech** mitten in ihrer Rede

party /'pɑ:tɪ/ *n.* **(a)** (group united in a cause etc.; Polit., Law) Partei, *die; attrib.* Partei⟨apparat, -versammlung, -mitglied, -politik, -politiker usw.⟩; **opposing ~:** Gegenpartei, *die;* **(b)** (group) Gruppe, *die;* **a ~ of tourists** eine Touristengruppe; **(c)** (social gathering) Party, *die;* Fete, *die* (ugs.); (more formal) Gesellschaft, *die;* **office ~:** Betriebsfest, *das;* **throw a ~** (coll.) eine Party schmeißen (ugs.); **(d)** (participant) Beteiligte, *der/die;* **be [a] ~ in or to sth.** sich an etw. ⟨Dat.⟩ beteiligen; **parties to an agreement/a dispute** Parteien bei einem Abkommen/streitende Parteien

party: ~ **line** *n.* **(a)** /'---/ (Teleph.) Gemeinschaftsanschluss, *der;* Sammelanschluss, *der;* **(b)** /--'-/ (Polit.) Parteilinie, *die;* ~ **piece** *n.* **this song was my ~ piece** dieses Lied musste ich auf jeder Gesellschaft zum Besten geben; ~ **po'litical** *adj.* parteipolitisch ⟨Propaganda, Sendung, Ziele, Fragen etc.⟩; ~ **political broadcast** parteipolitische Sendung; **a Labour ~ political broadcast** eine Sendung der Labour Party; ~ **'politics** *n.* Parteipolitik, *die;* ~ **wall** *n.* Mauer zum Nachbargrundstück/-gebäude

pass /pɑ:s/ **1** *n.* **(a)** (passing of an examination) bestandene Prüfung; **get a ~ in maths** die Mathematikprüfung bestehen; **'~'** (mark or grade) Ausreichend, *das;* **(b)** (written permission) Ausweis, *der;* (for going into or out of a place also) Passierschein, *der;* (Mil.: for leave) Urlaubsschein, *der;* (for free transportation) Freifahrschein, *der;* (for free admission) Freikarte, *die;* **(c)** (critical position) Notlage, *die;* **things have come to a pretty ~ [when ...]** es muss schon weit gekommen sein[, wenn ...]; **(d)** (Football) Pass, *der* (fachspr.); Ballabgabe, *die;* (Fencing) Ausfall, *der;* **make a ~ to a player** [den Ball] zu einem Spieler passen (fachspr.) *od.*

abgeben; **(e) make a ~ at sb.** (fig. coll.: amorously) jmdn. anmachen (ugs.); **(f)** (in mountains) Pass, *der.* **2** *v.i.* **(a)** (move onward) ⟨Prozession:⟩ ziehen; ⟨Wasser:⟩ fließen; ⟨Gas:⟩ strömen; (fig.) ⟨Redner:⟩ übergehen (**to** zu); ~ **further along** *or* **down the bus, please!** bitte weiter durchgehen!; **(b)** (go) passieren; ⟨Zug, Reisender:⟩ fahren (**through** durch); ~ **over** (in plane) überfliegen ⟨Ort⟩; **let sb. ~:** jmdn. durchlassen *od.* passieren lassen; **(c)** (be transported, lit. or fig.) kommen; ~ **into history/oblivion** in die Geschichte eingehen/in Vergessenheit geraten; **the title/property ~es to sb.** der Titel/Besitz geht auf jmdn. über; **(d)** (change) wechseln; ~ **from one state to another** von einem Zustand in einen anderen übergehen; **(e)** (go by) ⟨Fußgänger:⟩ vorbeigehen; ⟨Fahrer, Fahrzeug:⟩ vorbeifahren; ⟨Prozession:⟩ vorbeiziehen; ⟨Zeit, Sekunde:⟩ vergehen; (by chance) ⟨Person, Fahrzeug:⟩ vorbeikommen; **let sb./a car ~:** jmdn./ein Auto vorbeilassen (ugs.); **(f)** (be accepted as adequate) durchgehen; hingehen; **let it/the matter ~:** es/die Sache durch- *od.* hingehen lassen; **(g)** (come to an end) vorbeigehen; ⟨Fieber:⟩ zurückgehen; ⟨Ärger, Zorn, Sturm:⟩ sich legen; ⟨Gewitter, Unwetter:⟩ vorüberziehen; **(h)** (happen) passieren; (between persons) vorfallen; **(i)** (be accepted) durchgehen (**as** als, **for** für); **(j)** (satisfy examiner) bestehen; **(k)** (Cards) passen; **[I] ~!** [ich] passe! **3** *v.t.* **(a)** (move past) ⟨Fußgänger:⟩ vorbeigehen an (+ Dat.); ⟨Fahrer, Fahrzeug:⟩ vorbeifahren an (+ Dat.); ⟨Prozession:⟩ vorbeiziehen an (+ Dat.); **(b)** (overtake) vorbeifahren an (+ Dat.) ⟨Fahrzeug, Person⟩; **(c)** (cross) überschreiten ⟨Schwelle, feindliche Linien, Grenze, Marke⟩; **(d)** (reach standard in) bestehen ⟨Prüfung⟩; **(e)** (approve) verabschieden ⟨Gesetzentwurf⟩; annehmen ⟨Vorschlag⟩; ⟨Zensor:⟩ bestehen ⟨Film, Buch, Theaterstück⟩; bestehen lassen ⟨Prüfungskandidaten⟩; **(f)** (be too great for) überschreiten, übersteigen ⟨Auffassungsgabe, Verständnis⟩; **(g)** (move) bringen; ~ **a thread through the eye of a needle** einen Faden durch ein Nadelöhr ziehen *od.* führen; **(h)** (Footb. etc.) abgeben (**to** an + Akk.); **(i)** (spend) verbringen ⟨Leben, Zeit, Tag⟩; **(j)** (hand) ~ **sb. sth.** jmdm. etw. reichen *od.* geben; **would you ~ the salt, please?** gibst *od.* reichst du mir bitte das Salz?; **(k)** (utter) fällen, verkünden ⟨Urteil⟩; machen ⟨Bemerkung⟩; **(l)** (discharge) lassen ⟨Wasser⟩
~ **a'way 1** *v.i.* (euphem.: die) die Augen schließen *od.* zumachen (verhüll.). **2** *v.t.* verbringen ⟨Zeit[raum], Abend⟩
~ **by 1** /'--/ *v.t.* **(a)** (go past) ⟨Fußgänger:⟩ vorbeigehen an (+ Dat.); ⟨Fahrer, Fahrzeug:⟩ vorbeifahren an (+ Dat.); ⟨Prozession:⟩ vorbeiziehen an (+ Dat.); **(b)** (omit, disregard) übergehen. **2** /'-'-/ *v.i.* ⟨Fußgänger:⟩ vorbeigehen; ⟨Fahrer, Fahrzeug:⟩ vorbeifahren; ⟨Prozession:⟩ vorbeiziehen
~ **'down ⇒ hand down a**
~ **for** *v.t.* durchgehen für
~ **'off 1** *v.t.* (represent falsely) ausgeben (**as, for** als); als echt ausgeben ⟨Fälschung⟩. **2** *v.i.* **(a)** (disappear gradually) ⟨Schock, Schmerz, Hochstimmung:⟩ abklingen; **(b)** (take place) verlaufen
~ **'on 1** *v.i.* **(a)** (proceed) fortfahren; ~ **on to sth.** zu etw. übergehen; **(b)** (euphem.: die) die Augen schließen (verhüll.). **2** *v.t.* weitergeben (**to** an + Akk.)
~ **'out** *v.i.* **(a)** (faint) umkippen (ugs.); **(b)** (complete military training) seine militärische Ausbildung abschließen
~ **'over** *v.t.* übergehen
~ **'through** *v.i.* durchreisen; **be just ~ing through** nur auf der Durchreise sein
~ **'up** *v.t.* sich ⟨Dat.⟩ entgehen lassen ⟨Gelegenheit⟩; ablehnen ⟨Angebot, Einladung⟩

passable /'pɑ:səbl/ *adj.* **(a)** (acceptable) passabel; **(b)** passierbar, befahrbar ⟨Straße⟩

passage /'pæsɪdʒ/ *n.* **(a)** (going by, through, etc.) (of river) Überquerung, *die;* (of time) [Ab-, Ver]lauf, *der;* (of seasons) Wechsel, *der;* **(b)** (transition) Übergang, *der;* **(c)** (voyage) Überfahrt, *die;* **(d)** Gang, *der;* (corridor) Korridor, *der;* (between houses) Durchgang, *der;* (in shopping precinct) Passage, *die;* **(e)** *no art., no pl.* (liberty or right to pass through) Durchreise, *die;* **(f)** (right to travel) Passage, *die;* **work one's ~:** seine Überfahrt abarbeiten; **(g)** (part of book etc.) Passage, *die;* **(h)** (Mus.) Passage, *die;* Stelle, *die;* **(i)** (of a bill into law) parlamentarische Behandlung; (final) Annahme, *die;* Verabschiedung, *die;* **(j)** (Anat.) **urinary ~:** Harntrakt, *der;* **air ~s** Luft- *od.* Atemwege '**passageway** *n*. Gang, *der;* (between houses) Durchgang, *der*

pass: ∼**book** *n*. Sparbuch, *das;* ∼ **degree** *n*. (Brit. Univ.) **get a** ∼ **degree** ein Examen ohne Prädikat bestehen

passenger /'pæsɪndʒə(r)/ *n*. **(a)** (on ship) Passagier, *der;* (on plane) Passagier, *der;* Fluggast, *der;* (on train) Reisende, *der/die;* (on bus, in taxi) Fahrgast, *der;* (in car, on motorcycle) Mitfahrer, *der/*Mitfahrerin, *die;* (in front seat of car) Beifahrer, *der/*Beifahrerin, *die;* **(b)** (coll.: ineffective member) *Mensch, der von den anderen mit durchgeschleppt wird* (ugs.)

passenger: ∼ **aircraft** *n*. Passagierflugzeug, *das;* ∼ **door** *n*. Beifahrertür, *die;* ∼ **list** *n*. Passagierliste, *die;* ∼ **lounge** *n*. Warteraum, *der;* ∼ **seat** *n*. Beifahrersitz, *der;* ∼ **service** *n*. (train) Personenzugverbindung, *die;* (ferry) Personenfährverbindung, *die;* **all** ∼ **services out of London Victoria Station** alle Personenzüge ab London Victoria Station; ∼ **train** *n*. Zug im Personenverkehr

passer-by /pɑːsə'baɪ/ *n*. Passant, *der/*Passantin, *die*

passing /'pɑːsɪŋ/ **1** *n*. (of time, years) Lauf, *der;* (of winter) Vorübergehen, *das;* (of old year) Ausklang, *der;* (death) Ende, *das;* **in** ∼**:** beiläufig ⟨*bemerken usw.*⟩; flüchtig ⟨*begrüßen*⟩. **2** *adj*. **(a)** (going past) vorbeifahrend ⟨*Zug, Auto*⟩; vorbeikommend ⟨*Person*⟩; vorbeiziehend ⟨*Schatten*⟩; **(b)** (fleeting) flüchtig ⟨*Blick*⟩; vorübergehend ⟨*Mode, Laune, Interesse*⟩; **(c)** (superficial) flüchtig ⟨*Bekanntschaft*⟩; schnell vorübergehend ⟨*Empfindung*⟩

'**passing place** *n*. Ausweichstelle, *die*

passion /'pæʃn/ *n*. **(a)** Leidenschaft, *die;* **he has a** ∼ **for steam engines** Dampfloks sind seine Leidenschaft; er hat eine Passion für Dampfloks; **(b) P**∼ (Relig., Mus.) Passion, *die*

passionate /'pæʃənət/ *adj*. leidenschaftlich; **have a** ∼ **belief in sth.** mit unbeirrbarem Eifer von etw. überzeugt sein

passion: ∼ **flower** *n*. (Bot.) Passionsblume, *die;* ∼ **fruit** *n*. Passionsfrucht, *die*

passive /'pæsɪv/ **1** *adj*. **(a)** passiv; widerspruchslos ⟨*Hinnahme, Annahme*⟩; ∼ **smoking** passives Rauchen; **(b)** (Ling.) Passiv-; passivisch. **2** *n*. (Ling.) Passiv, *das*

passiveness /'pæsɪvnɪs/, **passivity** /pæ'sɪvɪtɪ/ *ns.*, *no pl*. Passivität, *die*

pass: ∼**-mark** *n*. Mindestpunktzahl, *die;* **P**∼**over** *n*. Passah, *das*

'**passport** *n*. **(a)** [Reise]pass, *der; attrib*. Pass-; **(b)** (fig.) Schlüssel, *der* (**to** zu)

'**password** *n*. **(a)** Parole, *die;* Losung, *die;* **(b)** (Computing) Passwort, *das*

past /pɑːst/ **1** *adj*. **(a)** *pred*. (over) vorbei; vorüber; **(b)** *attrib*. (previous) früher; vergangen; früher, ehemalig ⟨*Präsident, Vorsitzende usw.*⟩; **(c)** (just gone by) letzt...; vergangen; **in the** ∼ **few days** während der letzten Tage; **the** ∼ **hour** die letzte *od*. vergangene Stunde; **(d)** (Ling.) ∼ **tense** Vergangenheit, *die; see also* **participle**. **2** *n*. **(a)** Vergangenheit, *die;* (that which happened in the ∼) Vergangene, *das;* Gewesene, *das;* **in the** ∼**:** früher; in der Vergangenheit ⟨*leben*⟩; **be a thing of the** ∼**:** der Vergangenheit ⟨*Dat*.⟩ angehören; **(b)** (Ling.) Vergangenheit, *die*. **3** *prep*. **(a)** ▶**706]** (beyond in time) nach; (beyond in place) hinter (+ *Dat*.); **half** ∼ **three** halb vier; **five [minutes]** ∼ **two** fünf [Minuten] nach zwei; **it's** ∼ **midnight** es ist schon nach Mitternacht *od*. Mitternacht vorbei; **he is** ∼ **sixty** er ist über sechzig; **walk** ∼ **sb./sth.** an jmdm./etw. vorüber- *od*. vorbeigehen; **(b)** (not capable of) **he is** ∼ **help/caring** ihm ist nicht mehr zu helfen/es kümmert ihn nicht mehr; **be/ be getting** ∼ **it** (coll.) [ein bisschen] zu alt sein/allmählich zu alt werden; **I wouldn't put it** ∼ **her to do that** ich würde es ihr schon zutrauen, dass sie das tut. **4** *adv*. vorbei; vorüber; **hurry** ∼**:** vorüber- *od*. vorbeieilen

pasta /'pæstə, 'pɑːstə/ *n*. Nudeln *Pl.;* Teigwaren *Pl.*

paste /peɪst/ **1** *n*. **(a)** Brei, *der;* **mix into a smooth/ thick** ∼**:** zu einem lockeren/dicken Brei anrühren; zu einem glatten/festen Teig anrühren ⟨*Backmischung*⟩; **(b)** (glue) Kleister, *der;* **(c)** (of meat, fish, etc.) Paste, *die;* **(d)** *no pl., no indef. art*. (imitation gems) Strass, *der;* Similisteine *Pl*. **2** *v.t*. **(a)** (fasten with glue) kleben; ∼ **sth. down/into sth.**

etw. ankleben/in etw. (*Akk*.) einkleben; **(b)** (Computing) einfügen (**into** in + *Akk*.); *see also* **cut**

'**pasteboard** *n*. Pappe, *die;* Karton, *der*

pastel /'pæstl/ **1** *n*. **(a)** (crayon) Pastellstift, *der;* Pastellkreide, *die;* **(b)** (drawing) Pastellzeichnung, *die*. **2** *adj*. pastellen; pastellfarben; Pastell⟨*farben, -töne, -zeichnung, -bild*⟩

pasteurize (pasteurise) /'pæstʃəraɪz, 'pɑːstʃəraɪz/ *v.t*. pasteurisieren

pastille /'pæstɪl/ *n*. Pastille, *die*

pastime /'pɑːstaɪm/ *n*. Zeitvertreib, *der;* (person's specific ∼) Hobby, *das;* **national** ∼**:** Nationalsport, *der* (auch iron.)

past '**master** *n*. (fig.) Meister, *der*

pastor /'pɑːstə(r)/ *n*. Pfarrer, *der/*Pfarrerin, *die;* Pastor, *der/*Pastorin, *die*

pastoral /'pɑːstərl/ *adj*. **(a)** Weide-; ländlich ⟨*Reiz, Idylle, Umgebung*⟩; **(b)** (Lit., Art, Mus.) pastoral; **(c)** (Eccl.) pastoral; des Pfarrers *nachgestellt;* seelsorgerisch ⟨*Pflicht, Aufgabe, Leitung, Aktivitäten*⟩

pastry /'peɪstrɪ/ *n*. **(a)** (flour paste) Teig, *der;* **(b)** (article of food) Gebäckstück, *das;* **(c) pastries** collect. [Fein]gebäck, *das*

pasture /'pɑːstʃə(r)/ *n*. **(a)** (grass) Futter, *das;* Gras, *das;* **(b)** (land) Weideland, *das;* (piece of land) Weide, *die;* **(c)** (fig.) **in search of** ∼**s new** auf der Suche nach etwas Neuem

'**pastureland** *n*. Weideland, *das*

pasty[1] /'pæstɪ/ *n*. Pastete, *die*

pasty[2] /'peɪstɪ/ *adj*. **(a)** teigig; zähflüssig; **(b)** ⇒ **pastyfaced**

pasty-faced /'peɪstɪfeɪst/ *adj*. mit teigigem Gesicht *nachgestellt;* **be** ∼**:** ein teigiges Gesicht haben

pat[1] /pæt/ **1** *n*. **(a)** (stroke, tap) Klaps, *der;* leichter Schlag; **give sb./a dog a** ∼**:** jmdn./einen Hund tätscheln; **give sb./a dog a** ∼ **on the head** jmdm./einem Hund den Kopf tätscheln; **a** ∼ **on the back** (fig.) eine Anerkennung; **give oneself/sb. a** ∼ **on the back** (fig.) sich (*Dat*.) [selbst] auf die Schulter klopfen/jmdm. einige anerkennende Worte sagen; **(b)** (of butter) Stückchen, *das;* (of mud, clay) Klümpchen, *das*. **2** *v.t.*, **-tt-: (a)** (strike gently) leicht klopfen auf (+ *Akk*.); tätscheln, (once) einen Klaps geben (+ *Dat*.) ⟨*Person, Hund, Pferd*⟩; ∼ **sb. on the back** (fig.) jmdm. auf die Schulter klopfen; **(b)** (flatten) festklopfen ⟨*Sand*⟩; andrücken ⟨*Haare*⟩

pat[2] **1** *adv*. (ready, prepared) **have sth. off** ∼**:** etw. parat haben; **know sth. off** ∼**:** etw. aus dem Effeff können *od*. beherrschen (ugs.). **2** *adj*. (ready) allzu schlagfertig ⟨*Antwort*⟩

patch /pætʃ/ **1** *n*. **(a)** Stelle, *die;* **a** ∼ **of blue sky** ein Stückchen blauer Himmel; **there were still** ∼**es of snow** es lag vereinzelt *od*. hier und da noch Schnee; **the dog had a black** ∼ **on its ear** der Hund hatte einen schwarzen Fleck am Ohr; **fog** ∼**es** Nebelfelder; **in** ∼**es** stellenweise; **go through** *or* **strike a bad/good** ∼ (Brit.) eine Pech-/Glückssträhne haben; **(b)** (on worn garment) Flicken, *der;* **be not a** ∼ **on sth.** (fig. coll.) nichts gegen etw. sein; **(c)** (on eye) Augenklappe, *die;* **(d)** (piece of ground) Stück Land, *das;* **potato** ∼**:** Kartoffelacker, *der;* (in garden) Kartoffelbeet, *das;* **(e)** (area patrolled by police; also fig.) Revier, *das*. **2** *v.t.* (apply ∼ to) flicken

∼ '**up** *v.t.* reparieren; zusammenflicken ⟨*Segel, Buch*⟩; notdürftig verbinden ⟨*Wunde*⟩; zusammenflicken (scherzh.) ⟨*Verletzten*⟩; (fig.) beilegen ⟨*Streit, Differenzen*⟩; kitten ⟨*Ehe, Freundschaft*⟩

'**patchwork** *n*. Patchwork, *das;* (fig.) **a** ∼ **of fields** ein bunter Teppich von Feldern

patchy /'pætʃɪ/ *adj*. uneinheitlich ⟨*Qualität*⟩; ungleichmäßig, unterschiedlich ⟨*Arbeit, Aufführung, Ausstoß*⟩; fleckig ⟨*Anstrich*⟩; sehr lückenhaft ⟨*Wissen*⟩; in der Qualität unterschiedlich ⟨*Film, Buch, Theaterstück*⟩

pâté /'pæteɪ/ *n*. Pastete, *die;* ∼ **de foie gras** /'pæteɪ, 'pɑːteɪ də fwɑ: 'grɑ:/ Gänseleberpastete, *die*

patent /'peɪtənt, 'pætənt/ **1** *adj*. **(a)** patentiert; ∼ **medicine** Markenmedizin, *die;* ∼ **remedy** Spezial- *od*. Patentrezept, *das;* **(b)** (obvious) offenkundig; offensichtlich. **2**

n. Patent, *das;* ~ **applied for** *or* **pending** Patent angemeldet. **3** *v.t.* patentieren lassen; **sth. has been** ~**ed** etw. ist patentrechtlich geschützt

patent 'leather *n.* Lackleder, *das;* ~ **shoes** Lackschuhe

patently /'peɪtəntlɪ, 'pætəntlɪ/ *adv.* offenkundig; offensichtlich; ~ **obvious** ganz offenkundig *od.* offensichtlich

paternal /pə'tɜːnl/ *adj.* **(a)** (fatherly) väterlich; **(b)** (related) ‹Großeltern, Onkel, Tante› väterlicherseits

paternity /pə'tɜːnɪtɪ/ *n.* Vaterschaft, *die*

paternity: ~ **leave** *n.* Vaterschaftsurlaub, *der;* ~ **suit** *n.* Vaterschaftsklage, *die*

path /pɑːθ/ *n., pl.* ~**s** /pɑːðz/ **(a)** (way) Weg, *der;* Pfad, *der;* (made by walking) Trampelpfad, *der;* **keep to the** ~**:** auf dem Weg bleiben; **(b)** (of rocket, missile, etc.) Bahn, *die;* (of tornado) Weg, *der;* **(c)** (fig.: course of action) Weg, *der;* **the** ~ **to salvation/of virtue** der Weg des Heils/der Pfad der Tugend

pathetic /pə'θetɪk/ *adj.* **(a)** (pitiful) Mitleid erregend; herzergreifend; **be a** ~ **sight** ein Bild des Jammers bieten; **(b)** (full of pathos) pathetisch; **(c)** (contemptible) armselig ‹Entschuldigung›; erbärmlich ‹Darbietung, Rede, Person, Leistung›; **you're/it's** ~**:** du bist ein hoffnungsloser Fall/ es ist wirklich ein schwaches Bild (ugs.)

pathetically /pə'θetɪkəlɪ/ *adv.* **(a)** (pitifully) Mitleid erregend; herzergreifend ‹flehen›; **(b)** (contemptibly) erbärmlich; erschreckend ‹wenig›

pathological /pæθə'lɒdʒɪkl/ *adj.* **(a)** pathologisch; Pathologie-; **(b)** (fig.: obsessive) krankhaft; pathologisch

pathologist /pə'θɒlədʒɪst/ *n.* ▶ **887** ▏ Pathologe, *der*/Pathologin, *die*

pathology /pə'θɒlədʒɪ/ *n.* (science) Pathologie, *die*

pathos /'peɪθɒs/ *n.* Pathos, *das*

'pathway *n.* **(a)** ⇒ **path** a; **(b)** (Physiol.) Bahn, *die;* Leitung, *die*

patience /'peɪʃəns/ *n.* **(a)** *no pl., no art.* Geduld, *die;* (perseverance) Ausdauer, *die;* Beharrlichkeit, *die;* (forbearance) Langmut, *die;* **with** ~**:** geduldig; **have endless** ~**:** eine Engelsgeduld haben; **lose [one's]** ~ **[with sth./sb.]** [mit etw./jmdm.] die Geduld verlieren; **I lost my** ~**:** mir riss der Geduldsfaden (ugs.) *od.* die Geduld; ~ **is a virtue** Geduld ist eine Tugend; **(b)** (Brit. Cards) Patience, *die*

patient /'peɪʃənt/ **1** *adj.* geduldig; (forbearing) langmütig; (persevering) beharrlich; **please be** ~**:** bitte hab Geduld; **remain** ~**:** sich in Geduld fassen. **2** *n.* ▶ **865** ▏ Patient, *der*/ Patientin, *die*

patiently /'peɪʃəntlɪ/ *adv.* geduldig; mit Geduld

patina /'pætɪnə/ *n.* (on bronze) Patina, *die;* (on woodwork) Altersglanz, *der*

patio /'pætɪəʊ/ *n., pl.* ~**s** Veranda, *die;* Terrasse, *die*

patriarch /'peɪtrɪɑːk/ *n.* Patriarch, *der;* (of tribe) Stammesoberhaupt, *das*

patriarchal /peɪtrɪ'ɑːkl/ *adj.* patriarchalisch

patriot /'pætrɪət, 'peɪtrɪət/ *n.* Patriot, *der*/Patriotin, *die*

patriotic /pætrɪ'ɒtɪk, peɪtrɪ'ɒtɪk/ *adj.* patriotisch

patriotism /'pætrɪətɪzm, 'peɪtrɪətɪzm/ *n.* Patriotismus, *der*

patrol /pə'trəʊl/ **1** *n.* **(a)** (of police) Streife, *die;* (of watchman) Runde, *die;* (of aircraft, ship; also Mil.) Patrouille, *die;* **be on** *or* **keep** ~ ‹Soldat, Wächter:› patrouillieren; **(b)** (person, group) (Police) Streife, *die;* (Mil.) Patrouille, *die;* **police** ~**:** Polizeistreife, *die;* **(c)** (troops) Spähtrupp, *der;* Spähpatrouille, *die*. **2** *v.i.,* **-ll-** patrouillieren; ‹Polizei:› Streife laufen/fahren; ‹Wachmann:› seine Runde[n] machen; ‹Flugzeug:› Patrouille fliegen. **3** *v.t.,* **-ll-** patrouillieren durch (+ *Akk.*); abpatrouillieren ‹Straßen, Mauer, Gegend, Lager›; patrouillieren vor (+ *Dat.*) ‹Küste, Grenze›; ‹Polizei:› Streife laufen/fahren in (+ *Dat.*) ‹Straßen, Stadtteil›; ‹Wachmann:› seine Runde[n] machen in (+ *Dat.*)

patrol: ~ **boat** *n.* Patrouillenboot, *das;* ~ **car** *n.* Streifenwagen, *der;* ~**man** /pə'trəʊlmən/ *n., pl.* **-men** /pə'trəʊlmən/ (Amer.) [Streifen]polizist, *der*

patron /'peɪtrən/ *n.* **(a)** (supporter) Gönner, *der*/Gönnerin, *die;* (of institution, campaign) Schirmherr, *der*/Schirmherrin, *die;* ~ **of the arts** Kunstmäzen, *der;* **(b)** (customer) (of shop)

Kunde, *der*/Kundin, *die;* (of restaurant, hotel) Gast, *der;* (of theatre, cinema) Besucher, *der*/Besucherin, *die;* **(c)** ~ **[saint]** Schutzheilige, *der/die*

patronage /'pætrənɪdʒ/ *n.* (support) Gönnerschaft, *die;* Unterstützung, *die;* (for campaign, institution) Schirmherrschaft, *die*

patronise, patronising ⇒ **patroniz-**

patronize /'pætrənaɪz/ *v.t.* **(a)** (frequent) besuchen; **(b)** (support) fördern; unterstützen; **(c)** (condescend to) ~ **sb.** jmdn. von oben herab *od.* herablassend behandeln

patronizing /'pætrənaɪzɪŋ/ *adj.* gönnerhaft; herablassend

patter /'pætə(r)/ **1** *n.* **(a)** (of rain) Prasseln, *das;* (of feet) Trappeln, *das;* Getrappel, *das;* **(b)** (of salesman or comedian) Sprüche *Pl.;* **sales** ~**:** Vertretersprüche *Pl.* **2** *v.i.* **(a)** ‹Regen, Hagel:› prasseln; ‹Schritte:› trappeln; **(b)** (run) trippeln

pattern /'pætən/ **1** *n.* **(a)** (design) Muster, *das;* (on carpet, wallpaper, cloth, etc. also) Dessin, *das;* **(b)** (form, order) Muster, *das;* Schema, *das;* **follow a** ~**:** einem regelmäßigen Muster *od.* Schema folgen; **behaviour** ~**:** Verhaltensmuster, *das;* ~ **of thought** Denkmuster, *das;* Denkschema, *das;* ~ **of events** Ereignisfolge; **(c)** (model) Vorlage, *die;* (for sewing) Schnittmuster, *das;* Schnitt, *der;* (for knitting) Strickanleitung, *die;* Strickmuster, *das;* **follow a** ~**:** nach einer Vorlage arbeiten; (knitting) nach einem Strickmuster stricken; **a democracy on the British** ~**:** eine Demokratie nach britischem Muster. **2** *v.t.* (model) gestalten; ~ **sth. after/ on sth.** etw. einer Sache (*Dat.*) nachbilden

paucity /'pɔːsɪtɪ/ *n.* (formal) Mangel, *der* (**of** an + *Dat.*)

paunch /pɔːntʃ/ *n.* Bauch, *der;* Wanst, *der* (salopp abwertend)

pauper /'pɔːpə(r)/ *n.* Arme, *der/die*

pause /pɔːz/ **1** *n.* Pause, *die;* **without [a]** ~**:** ohne Pause; **an anxious** ~**:** ängstliches Schweigen; **give sb.** ~**:** jmdn. zu denken geben. **2** *v.i.* eine Pause machen; eine Pause einlegen; ‹Redner:› innehalten; (hesitate) zögern; ~ **for reflection/thought** in Ruhe überlegen; ~ **for a rest** eine Erholungspause *od.* Ruhepause einlegen

pave /peɪv/ *v.t.* pflastern; ~ **the way for** *or* **to sth.** (fig.) einer Sache (*Dat.*) den Weg ebnen

pavement /'peɪvmənt/ *n.* **(a)** (Brit.: for pedestrians) Bürgersteig, *der;* Gehsteig, *der;* **(b)** (Amer.: roadway) Fahrbahn, *die*

'pavement café *n.* Straßencafé, *das*

pavilion /pə'vɪljən/ *n.* **(a)** Pavillon, *der;* **(b)** (Brit. Sport) Klubhaus, *das*

paw /pɔː/ **1** *n.* **(a)** Pfote, *die;* (of bear, lion, tiger) Pranke, *die;* **(b)** (coll. derog.: hand) Pfote, *die* (ugs. abwertend); **keep your** ~**s off!** Pfoten weg! **2** *v.t.* **(a)** ‹Hund, Wolf:› mit der Pfote/ den Pfoten berühren; ‹Bär, Löwe, Tiger:› mit der Pranke/ den Pranken berühren; (playfully) tätscheln; ~ **the ground** scharren; **(b)** (coll. derog.: fondle) befummeln (ugs.). **3** *v.i.* scharren; ~ **at** mit der Pfote/den Pfoten *usw.* berühren

pawn¹ /pɔːn/ *n.* **(a)** (Chess) Bauer, *der;* **(b)** (fig.) Schachfigur, *die*

pawn² **1** *n.* Pfand, *das;* **in** ~**:** verpfändet; versetzt. **2** *v.t.* verpfänden; versetzen

pawn: ~**broker** *n.* ▶ **887** ▏ Pfandleiher, *der*/-leiherin, *die;* ~**shop** *n.* Leihhaus, *das;* Pfandleihe, *die*

pay /peɪ/ **1** *n., no pl., no indef. art.* (wages) Lohn, *der;* (salary) Gehalt, *das;* (of soldier) Sold, *der;* **the** ~ **is good** die Bezahlung ist gut; **be in the** ~ **of sb./sth.** für jmdn./etw. arbeiten. **2** *v.t.,* **paid** /peɪd/ **(a)** (give money to) bezahlen; **(b)** belohnen; **I paid him for the tickets** ich habe ihm das Geld für die Karten gegeben; ~ **sb. to do sth.** jmdn. dafür bezahlen, dass er etw. tut; **(b)** (hand over) zahlen; (~ back) zurückzahlen; (in instalments) abbezahlen; ~ **the bill** Rechnung bezahlen; ~ **sb.'s expenses** (reimburse) jmds. Auslagen erstatten; ~ **sb. £10** jmdm. 10 Pfund zahlen; ~ **£10 for sth.** 10 Pfund für etw. [be]zahlen; ~ **sth. into a bank account** etw. auf ein Konto ein[be]zahlen; **(c)** (yield) einbringen, abwerfen ‹Dividende *usw.*›; **this job** ~**s very little** diese Arbeit bringt sehr wenig ein; **(d)** (be profitable to) **it would** ~ **her to do that** (fig.) es würde ihr nichts schaden *od.* es würde sich für sie bezahlt machen, das zu tun; **(e)** ~ **the price** den Preis zahlen; **it's too high a**

price to ∼: das ist ein zu hoher Preis. **3** *v.i.*, **paid** (a) zahlen; ∼ **for sth./sb.** etw./für jmdn. bezahlen; **sth.** ∼**s for itself** etw. macht sich bezahlt; **has this been paid for?** ist das schon bezahlt?; **(b)** (yield) sich lohnen; sich auszahlen; ⟨*Geschäft:*⟩ rentabel sein; **it** ∼**s to be careful** es lohnt sich, vorsichtig zu sein; **(c)** (fig.: suffer) büßen müssen; **if you do this you'll have to** ∼ **for it later** wenn du das tust, wirst du später dafür büßen müssen
∼ **'back** *v.t.* **(a)** zurückzahlen; **I'll** ∼ **you back later** ich gebe dir das Geld später zurück; **(b)** (fig.) erwidern ⟨*Kompliment*⟩; sich revanchieren für ⟨*Beleidigung, Untreue*⟩; **I'll** ∼ **him back** ich werde es ihm heimzahlen
∼ **'in** *v.t. & i.* einzahlen
∼ **'off 1** *v.t.* auszahlen ⟨*Arbeiter*⟩; abbezahlen ⟨*Schulden*⟩; ablösen ⟨*Hypothek*⟩; befriedigen ⟨*Gläubiger*⟩; (fig.) abgelten ⟨*Verpflichtung*⟩. **2** *v.i.* (coll.) sich auszahlen; sich bezahlt machen
∼ **'out 1** *v.t.* **(a)** auszahlen; (spend) ausgeben; ∼ **out large sums on sth.** hohe Beträge für etw. ausgeben; **(b)** (Naut.) ablaufen lassen ⟨*Seil, Tau*⟩; **(c)** (coll.: punish) ∼ **sb. out for sth.** jmdm. etw. heimzahlen. **2** *v.i.* bezahlen
∼ **'up 1** *v.t.* zurückzahlen ⟨*Schulden*⟩. **2** *v.i.* zahlen
payable /'peɪəbl/ *adj.* zahlbar; **be** ∼ **to sb.** jmdm. *od.* an jmdn. zu zahlen sein; **make a cheque** ∼ **to the Post Office/to sb.** einen Scheck auf die Post/auf jmds. Namen ausstellen

pay: ∼**-as-you-'earn** *attrib. adj.* (Brit.) ∼**-as-you-earn system/method** Quellenabzugsverfahren, *das;* ∼**-as-you-earn tax system** Steuersystem, bei dem die Lohnsteuer direkt einbehalten wird; ∼ **award** *n.* Gehaltserhöhung, *die;* ∼ **bed** *n.* Privatbett, *das;* ∼ **claim** *n.* Lohnforderung, *die/*Gehaltsforderung, *die;* ∼ **day** *n.* Zahltag, *der;* ∼ **dirt** *n.* (Amer.) abbauwürdiges Erzlager; **hit** ∼ **dirt** (fig.) einen Volltreffer landen (fig. ugs.)
PAYE *abbr.* (Brit.) **pay-as-you-earn**
payee /peɪ'iː/ *n.* Zahlungsempfänger, *der/*-empfängerin, *die*
pay: ∼ **envelope** (Amer.) ⇒ **pay packet;** ∼ **increase** ⇒ **pay rise**
paying: ∼ **'guest** *n.* zahlender Gast; ∼**-'in slip** *n.* (Brit. Banking) Einzahlungsschein, *der*
'payload *n.* Nutzlast, *die*
payment /'peɪmənt/ *n.* **(a)** (act) Zahlung, *die;* (paying back) Rückzahlung, *die;* (in instalments) Abzahlung, *die;* **in** ∼ **[for sth.]** als Bezahlung [für etw.]; **on** ∼ **of ...:** gegen Zahlung von ...; **(b)** (amount) Zahlung, *die;* **make a** ∼: eine Zahlung leisten; **by monthly** ∼**s** auf Monatsraten
pay: ∼ **negotiations** *n. pl.* Tarifverhandlungen *Pl.;* ∼**-off** *n.* (coll.) (return) Lohn, *der;* (punishment) Quittung, *die;* (bribe) Schmiergeld, *das* (ugs. abwertend); ∼ **packet** *n.* (Brit.) Lohntüte, *die;* ∼ **phone** *n.* Münzfernsprecher, *der;* ∼ **rise** *n.* Lohnerhöhung, *die/*Gehaltserhöhung, *die;* ∼**roll** *n.* Lohnliste, *die;* **have 200 workers/people on the** ∼**roll** 200 Arbeiter beschäftigen/Beschäftigte haben; **be on sb.'s** ∼**roll** für jmdn. *od.* bei jmdm. arbeiten; ∼ **round** *n.* Tarifrunde, *die;* ∼**slip** *n.* Lohnstreifen, *der/*Gehaltszettel, *der;* ∼ **station** (Amer.) ⇒ ∼ **phone;** ∼ **talks** *n. pl.* Tarifverhandlungen *Pl.*
PC *abbr.* **(a)** ▶ 1152❘ (Brit.) **police constable** Wachtm.; **(b) personal computer** PC; **(c) politically correct** politisch korrekt
PE *abbr.* **physical education**
pea /piː/ *n.* Erbse, *die;* **they are as like as two** ∼**s [in a pod]** sie gleichen sich (*Dat.*) *od.* einander wie ein Ei dem anderen
peace /piːs/ *n.* **(a)** (freedom from war) Frieden, *der;* **maintain/restore** ∼: den Frieden bewahren/wiederherstellen; ∼ **talks/treaty** Friedensgespräche *Pl./*Friedensvertrag, *der;* **make** ∼ **[with sb.]** [mit jmdm.] Frieden schließen; **(b)** (freedom from civil disorder) Ruhe und Ordnung, *die;* (absence of discord) Frieden, *der;* **in** ∼ **[and harmony]** in [Frieden und] Eintracht; **restore** ∼: Ruhe und Ordnung wiederherstellen; **bind sb. over to keep the** ∼: jmdn. verwarnen, die öffentliche Ordnung zu wahren; **be at** ∼ **[with sb./sth.]** [mit jmdm./etw.] in Frieden leben; **be at** ∼ **with oneself** mit sich selbst im Reinen sein; **make [one's]** ∼ **[with sb.]** sich [mit jmdm.] aussöhnen; **hold**

one's ∼: schweigen; **(c)** (tranquillity) Ruhe, *die;* **in** ∼: in Ruhe; **leave sb. in** ∼: jmdn. in Frieden *od.* in Ruhe lassen; **give sb. no** ∼: jmdm. keine Ruhe lassen; ∼ **and quiet** Ruhe und Frieden; **(d)** (mental state) Ruhe, *die;* **find** ∼: Frieden finden; ∼ **of mind** Seelenfrieden, *der;* innere Ruhe; **I shall have no** ∼ **of mind until I know it** ich werde keine ruhige Minute haben, bis ich es weiß
peaceable /'piːsəbl/ *adj.* (not quarrelsome) friedfertig; friedliebend ⟨*Volk*⟩; (calm) friedlich
peaceably /'piːsəblɪ/ *adv.* (amicably) friedlich
'peace dividend *n.* Friedensdividende, *die*
peaceful /'piːsfl/ *adj.* friedlich; friedfertig ⟨*Person, Volk*⟩; ruhig ⟨*Augenblick*⟩
peacefully /'piːsfəlɪ/ *adv.* friedlich; **die** ∼: sanft entschlafen
peace: ∼**keeper** *n.* Friedenswächter, *der;* ∼**keeping 1** *adj.* ⟨*Maßnahmen, Operationen*⟩ zur Friedenssicherung; ∼**keeping force** Friedenstruppe, *die;* **2** *n.* Friedenssicherung, *die;* ∼**-loving** *adj.* friedliebend; ∼**maker** *n.* Friedensstifter, *der/*-stifterin, *die;* ∼**-offer** *n.* Friedensangebot, *das;* ∼**-offering** *n.* Friedensangebot, *das;* (fig.) Versöhnungsgeschenk, *das;* ∼ **process** *n.* Friedensprozess, *der;* ∼**time** *n.* Friedenszeiten *Pl.; attrib.* Friedens⟨*produktion, -wirtschaft, -stärke*⟩
peach /piːtʃ/ *n.* **(a)** Pfirsich, *der;* **(b)** (coll.) **sb./sth. is a** ∼: jmd./etw. ist spitze *od.* klasse (ugs.); **(c)** (colour) Pfirsichton, *der*
'peach tree *n.* Pfirsichbaum, *der*
'peacock *n.* Pfau, *der;* Pfauhahn, *der;* **proud/vain as a** ∼: stolz/eitel wie ein Pfau
'pea-green *adj.* erbsengrün; maigrün
peak /piːk/ **1** *n.* **(a)** (of cap) Schirm, *der;* **(b)** (of mountain) Gipfel, *der;* (of wave) Kamm, *der;* Krone, *die;* **(c)** (highest point) Höhepunkt, *der;* **be at/be past its** ∼: den Höhepunkt erreicht haben/den Höhepunkt überschritten haben. **2** *attrib. adj.* Höchst-, Spitzen⟨*preise, -werte*⟩; ∼ **listening/ viewing period** Hauptsendezeit, *die.* **3** *v.i.* seinen Höhepunkt erreichen
peaked /piːkt/ *adj.* ∼ **cap** Schirmmütze, *die*
peak: ∼**-hour** *attrib. adj.* ∼**-hour travel** Fahren während der Hauptverkehrszeit; ∼**-hour traffic** Stoßverkehr, *der;* ∼ **season** *n.* Hochsaison, *die*
peaky /'piːkɪ/ *adj.* kränklich; **look** ∼: angeschlagen aussehen
peal /piːl/ **1** *n.* **(a)** (ringing) Geläut[e], *das;* Läuten, *das;* ∼ **of bells** Glockengeläut[e], *das;* **(b)** (set of bells) Glockenspiel, *das;* **(c) a** ∼ **of laughter** schallendes Gelächter; **a** ∼ **of thunder** ein Donnerschlag. **2** *v.i.* ⟨*Glocken:*⟩ läuten
peanut /'piːnʌt/ *n.* Erdnuss, *die;* ∼ **butter** Erdnussbutter, *die;* ∼**s** (coll.) (trivial thing) nichts ein Klacks (ugs.); (money) ein paar Kröten (salopp); **this is** ∼**s compared to ...:** das ist ein Klacks gegen ...; **work for** ∼**s** für ein Butterbrot arbeiten (ugs.)
pear /peə(r)/ *n.* Birne, *die*
pearl /pɜːl/ *n.* Perle, *die;* **[string of]** ∼**s** (necklace) Perlenkette, *die;* ∼ **of wisdom** (often iron.) Weisheit, *die*
pearl: ∼ **'barley** *n.* Perlengraupen *Pl.;* ∼**-diver** *n.* Perlentaucher, *der/*-taucherin, *die;* ∼**-grey** *adj.* perlgrau; ∼**-oyster** *n.* Perlmuschel, *die*
pearly /'pɜːlɪ/ *adj.* perlmuttern ⟨*Glanz, Schimmer*⟩
'pear tree *n.* Birnbaum, *der*
peasant /'pezənt/ *n.* **(a)** [armer] Bauer, *der;* Landarbeiter, *der;* ∼ **farmer** Bauer, *der;* ∼ **woman** Bauersfrau, *die;* **(b)** (coll. derog.) (stupid person) Bauer, *der* (ugs. abwertend); (lower-class person) Plebejer, *der* (abwertend)
peasantry /'pezəntrɪ/ *n.* Bauernschaft, *die*
pease pudding /piːz'pʊdɪŋ/ *n.* Erbsenpudding, *der*
pea: ∼**-shooter** /'piːʃuːtə(r)/ *n.* Pusterohr, *das;* ∼ **'soup** *n.* Erbsensuppe, *die*
peat /piːt/ *n.* **(a)** (substance) Torf, *der;* **(b)** (piece) Torfstück, *das*
pebble /'pebl/ *n.* Kiesel[stein], *der;* **he is/you are not the only** ∼ **on the beach** es gibt noch andere

pebbly /'peblɪ/ adj. steinig

peck /pek/ **1** v.t. **(a)** hacken; picken ‹ Körner ›; **the bird ~ed my finger** der Vogel pickte mir od. mich in den Finger; **(b)** (kiss) flüchtig küssen. **2** v.i. picken (**at** nach); **~ at one's food** in seinem Essen herumstochern. **3** n. **(a) the hen gave its chick a ~:** die Henne pickte od. hackte nach ihrem Küken; **(b)** (kiss) flüchtiger Kuss; Küsschen, das

'pecking order n. Hackordnung, die

peckish /'pekɪʃ/ adj. (coll.) hungrig; **feel/get ~:** Hunger haben/bekommen

pectin /'pektɪn/ n. (Chem.) Pektin, das

peculiar /pɪ'kju:lɪə(r)/ adj. **(a)** (strange) seltsam; eigenartig; sonderbar; **I feel [slightly] ~:** mir ist [etwas] komisch; **(b)** (especial) **be of ~ interest [to sb.]** [für jmdn.] von besonderem Interesse sein; **(c)** (belonging exclusively) eigentümlich (**to** Dat.); **this bird is ~ to South Africa** dieser Vogel kommt nur in Südafrika vor

peculiarity /pɪkju:lɪ'ærɪtɪ/ n. **(a)** no pl., no indef. art. (unusualness) Ausgefallenheit, die; (of behaviour, speech) Sonderbarkeit, die; **(b)** (odd trait) Eigentümlichkeit, die; **(c)** (distinguishing characteristic) [charakteristisches] Merkmal; (special characteristic) Besonderheit, die

peculiarly /pɪ'kju:lɪəlɪ/ adv. **(a)** (strangely) seltsam; eigenartig; sonderbar; **(b)** (especially) besonders; **(c)** (in a way that is one's own) **be something ~ British** etwas rein Britisches sein

pedagogic[al] /pedə'ɡɒɡɪk(l), pedə'ɡɒdʒɪk(l)/ adj. (of pedagogy) pädagogisch

pedagogy /'pedəɡɒdʒɪ/ n. Pädagogik, die

pedal /'pedl/ **1** n. Pedal, das. **2** v.i., (Brit.) **-ll-: (a)** (work cycle ~s) **~ [away]** in die Pedale treten; strampeln (ugs.); **(b)** (ride) [mit dem Fahrrad] fahren; radeln (ugs.); **~ by/off** vorbeiradeln/losradeln (ugs.)

'pedal bin n. Treteimer, der

pedalo /'pedələʊ/ n., pl. **~s** Tretboot, das

pedant /'pedənt/ n. Pedant, der/Pedantin, die (abwertend)

pedantic /pɪ'dæntɪk/ adj. pedantisch (abwertend)

pedantry /'pedəntrɪ/ n. Pedanterie, die

peddle /'pedl/ v.t. auf der Straße verkaufen; (from door to door) hausieren mit; handeln mit, (ugs.) dealen mit ‹ Drogen, Rauschgift ›

peddler /'pedlə(r)/ ⇒ **pedlar**

pederast /'pedəræst/ n. Päderast, der

pedestal /'pedɪstl/ n. Sockel, der; **put sb./sth. on a ~** (fig.) jmdn./etw. in den Himmel heben (ugs.)

pedestrian /pɪ'destrɪən/ **1** adj. (uninspired) trocken; langweilig. **2** n. Fußgänger, der/-gängerin, die

pedestrian: ~ **'crossing** n. Fußgängerüberweg, der; ~ **'precinct** ⇒ **precinct a**

pedestrianize (pedestrianise) /pɪ'destrɪənaɪz/ v.t. zur Fußgängerzone machen

pediatric (Amer.) ⇒ **paediatric**

pedicure /'pedɪkjʊə(r)/ n. Pediküre, die; **give sb. a ~:** jmdn. pediküren

pedigree /'pedɪɡrɪ/ **1** n. **(a)** Stammbaum, der; Ahnentafel, die (geh.); (of animal) Stammbaum, der; **(b)** no pl., no art. (ancient descent) **have ~, be a man/woman of ~:** von berühmten Ahnen abstammen. **2** adj. (with recorded line of descent) mit Stammbaum nachgestellt

pedlar /'pedlə(r)/ n. Straßenhändler, der/-händlerin, die; (from door to door) Hausierer, der/Hausiererin, die; (selling drugs) Rauschgifthändler, der/-händlerin, die; Dealer, der/Dealerin, die (ugs.)

pee /pi:/ (coll.) **1** v.i. pinkeln (salopp); Pipi machen (Kinderspr.). **2** n. **(a) need/have a ~:** pinkeln müssen/pinkeln (salopp); **I must go for a ~:** ich muss mal eben pinkeln (salopp); **(b)** (urine) Pipi, das (Kinderspr.)

peek /pi:k/ **1** v.i. gucken (ugs.); **no ~ing!** nicht gucken!; **~ at sb./sth.** zu jmdm./etw. hingucken. **2** n. (quick) kurzer Blick; (sly) verstohlener Blick; **have a ~ through the keyhole** durch das Schlüsselloch gucken (ugs.); **take a quick ~ at sb.** kurz zu jmdm. hingucken

peel /pi:l/ **1** v.t. schälen; **~ the shell off an egg/the skin off a banana** ein Ei/eine Banane schälen; see also

eye 1 a. 2 v.i. ‹ Person, Haut: › sich schälen; ‹ Rinde, Borke: › sich lösen; ‹ Farbe: › abblättern. **3** n. Schale, die **~ a'way 1** v.t. abschälen. **2** v.i. **(a)** ‹ Haut: › sich schälen od. (bes. nordd.) pellen; ‹ Rinde, Borke: › sich lösen; ‹ Farbe: › abblättern; **(b)** (veer away) ausscheren **~ 'back** v.t. halb abziehen ‹ Kabelmantel, Bananenschale › **~ 'off 1** v.t. abschälen; abstreifen, ausziehen ‹ Kleider ›. **2** v.i. **(a)** ⇒ **~ away 2 a; (b)** (veer away) ausscheren; **(c)** (coll.: undress) sich ausziehen

peeler /'pi:lə(r)/ n. Schäler, der; Schälmesser, das

peeling /'pi:lɪŋ/ n. Stück Schale; **~s** Schalen

peep¹ /pi:p/ **1** v.i. ‹ Maus, Vogel: › piep[s]en; (squeal) quieken. **2** n. (shrill sound) Piepsen, das; (coll.: slight utterance) Piep[s], der (ugs.); **one ~ out of you and ...:** ein Pieps [von dir], und ...

peep² **1** v.i. **(a)** (look through narrow aperture) gucken (ugs.); **(b)** (look furtively) verstohlen gucken; **~ round** sich umgucken; **no ~ing!** nicht gucken!; **(c)** (come into view) **~ out** [he]rausgucken; (fig.: show itself) zum Vorschein kommen. **2** n. kurzer Blick; **take a ~ through the curtain** durch die Gardine spähen

'peephole n. Guckloch, das

peeping Tom /pi:pɪŋ 'tɒm/ n. Spanner, der (ugs.); Voyeur, der

peer¹ /pɪə(r)/ n. **(a)** (Brit.: member of nobility) **~ [of the realm]** Peer, der; **(b)** (equal in standing) Gleichgestellte, der/die; **among her social ~s** unter ihresgleichen

peer² v.i. (look searchingly) forschend schauen; (look with difficulty) angestrengt schauen; **~ at sth./sb.** (searchingly) [sich (Dat.)] etw. genau ansehen/jmdn. forschend od. prüfend ansehen; (with difficulty) [sich (Dat.)] etw. angestrengt ansehen/ jmdn. angestrengt ansehen; **~ into the distance** in die Ferne spähen

peerage /'pɪərɪdʒ/ n. **(a)** no pl. (body of peers) **the ~:** die Peers; **be raised to the ~:** in den Adelsstand erhoben werden; **(b)** (rank of peer) Peerswürde, die

'peer group n. Peer-Group, die (Psych., Soziol.)

peerless /'pɪəlɪs/ adj. beispiellos

'peer pressure n. Gruppenzwang, der

peeved /pi:vd/ adj. (coll.) sauer (ugs.); **be/get ~ with sb.** auf jmdn. sauer sein/werden; **be ~ at/get ~ about sth.** über etw. (Akk.) sauer sein/wegen etw. sauer werden

peevish /'pi:vɪʃ/ adj. (querulous) nörgelig (abwertend); quengelig (ugs.) ‹ Kind ›; (showing vexation) gereizt

peewit /'pi:wɪt/ n. (Ornith.) Kiebitz, der

peg /peɡ/ **1** n. (for holding together parts of framework) Stift, der; (for tying things to) Pflock, der; (for hanging things on) Haken, der; (clothes ~) Wäscheklammer, die; (for holding tent-ropes) Hering, der; (Mus.: for adjusting strings) Wirbel, der; **off the ~** (Brit.: ready-made) von der Stange (ugs.); **take sb. down a ~ [or two]** (fig.) jmdm. einen Dämpfer aufsetzen od. geben; **a ~ to hang sth. on** (fig.) ein Aufhänger für etw. **2** v.t., **-gg-: (a)** (fix with ~) mit Stiften/Pflöcken befestigen; **(b)** (Econ.: stabilize) stabilisieren; (support) stützen; (freeze) einfrieren; **~ wages/prices/exchange rates** Löhne/Preise/Wechselkurse stabil halten **~ a'way** v.i. schuften (ugs.); **[keep] ~[ging] away with sth.** nicht lockerlassen mit etw. (ugs.) **~ 'out 1** v.t. **(a)** (spread out and secure) ausspannen ‹ Felle etc. ›; (Brit.) [draußen] aufhängen ‹ Wäsche ›; **(b)** (mark) abstecken ‹ Gebiet, Fläche ›. **2** v.i. (coll.) (faint) zusammenklappen (ugs.); (die) den Löffel abgeben (salopp)

pejorative /pɪ'dʒɒrətɪv/ **1** adj. pejorativ (Sprachw.); abwertend. **2** n. Pejorativum, das (Sprachw.)

Pekingese (Pekinese) /pi:kɪ'ni:z/ n., pl. same **~ [dog]** Pekinese, der

pelican /'pelɪkən/ n. (Ornith.) Pelikan, der

'pelican crossing n. (Brit.) Ampelübergang, der

pellet /'pelɪt/ n. **(a)** (small ball) Kügelchen, das; (mass of food) Pellet, das (fachspr.); **(b)** (small shot) Schrot, der od. das

pell-mell /pel'mel/ adv. **(a)** (in disorder) durcheinander; **(b)** (headlong) Hals über Kopf

pelmet /'pelmɪt/ n. (of wood) Blende, die; (of fabric) Schabracke, die

pelt¹ /pelt/ n. (of sheep or goat) Fell, das; (of fur-bearing animal) [Roh]fell, das

pelt² v.t. (lit. or fig.) ~ **sb. with sth.** jmdn. mit etw. bewerfen; ~ **sb. with questions** jmdn. mit Fragen überschütten. **2** v.i. (a) ⟨Regen:⟩ prasseln; **it was ~ing down [with rain]** es goss wie aus Kübeln (ugs.); **(b)** (run fast) rasen (ugs.); pesen (ugs.). **3** n. **[at] full ~:** mit Karacho (ugs.)

pelvic /'pelvɪk/ adj. (Anat.) Becken-

pelvis /'pelvɪs/ n., pl. **pelves** /'pelviːz/ or ~**es** ▶ 672 | (Anat.) Becken, das

pen¹ /pen/ **1** n. Pferch, der. **2** v.t., **-nn-:** (a) (shut up in ~) einpferchen; **(b)** ~ **sb. in a corner** jmdn. in eine Ecke drängen

~ **'in** v.t. (a) einpferchen; **(b)** (fig.: restrict) einengen

pen² **1** n. (a) (for writing) Federhalter, der; (fountain ~) Füller, der; (ball ~) Kugelschreiber, der; Kuli, der (ugs.); (felt-tip ~) Filzstift, der; (ball ~ or felt-tip ~) Stift, der; **the ~ is mightier than the sword** (prov.) die Feder ist mächtiger als das Schwert; see also **paper 1 a; (b)** (quill-feather) Feder, die. **2** v.t., **-nn-** niederschreiben; ~ **a letter to/a note for sb.** jmdm. einen Brief/ein paar Worte schreiben

penal /'piːnl/ adj. (a) (of punishment) Straf-; ~ **reform** Strafvollzugsreform, die; **(b)** (punishable) strafbar ⟨Handlung, Tat⟩; ~ **offence** Straftat, die; **(c)** ~ **colony** or **settlement** Strafkolonie, die

penalize (penalise) /'piːnəlaɪz/ v.t. bestrafen; (Sport) eine Strafe verhängen gegen

penalty /'penltɪ/ n. (a) (punishment) Strafe, die; **the ~ for this offence is imprisonment/a fine** auf dieses Delikt steht Gefängnis/eine Geldstrafe; **pay the ~/the ~ for sth.** (lit. or fig.) dafür/für etw. büßen; **on** or **under ~ of £200/of instant dismissal** bei einer Geldstrafe von 200 Pfund/unter Androhung (Dat.) der sofortigen Entlassung; **(b)** (disadvantage) Preis, der; **(c)** (Sport) (Golf) ~ **[stroke]** Strafschlag, der; (Footb., Rugby) ⇒ **penalty kick**

penalty: ~ **goal** n. (Rugby) durch einen Straftritt erzieltes Tor; ~ **kick** n. (Footb.) Strafstoß, der; Elfmeter, der; (Rugby) Straftritt, der

penance /'penəns/ n., no pl., no art. Buße, die; **act of ~:** Bußübung, die; **undergo/do ~:** büßen/Buße tun

pence ⇒ **penny**

penchant /'pɑ̃ʃɑ̃/ n. Schwäche, die, Vorliebe, die (**for** für)

pencil /'pensɪl/ **1** n. (a) Bleistift, der; (coloured) Rot-/Bunt- od. Farbstift, der; **write in ~:** mit Bleistift schreiben; **a ~ drawing, a drawing in ~:** eine Bleistiftzeichnung; **(b)** (cosmetic) Stift, der. **2** v.t., (Brit.) **-ll-:** (a) (mark) mit Bleistift/Farbstift markieren; **(b)** (sketch) mit Bleistift zeichnen od. skizzieren; **(c)** (write with ~) mit einem Bleistift/Farbstift schreiben

~ **'in** v.t. (a) (shade with ~) mit Bleistift [aus]schraffieren; **(b)** (note or arrange provisionally) vorläufig notieren

pencil: ~ **case** n. Griffelkasten, der; (made of a soft material) Federmäppchen, das; ~ **sharpener** n. Bleistiftspitzer, der

pendant /'pendənt/ n. Anhänger, der

pending /'pendɪŋ/ **1** adj. (a) (undecided) unentschieden ⟨Angelegenheit, Sache⟩; anhängig (Rechtsspr.), schwebend (Rechtsspr.), noch schweben ⟨Sache, Angelegenheit:⟩ noch unentschieden sein od. in der Schwebe sein; ⟨Entscheidung, Probleme:⟩ noch anstehen; **(b)** (about to come into existence) bevorstehend ⟨Krieg⟩; **patent ~:** Patent angemeldet. **2** prep. (until) ~ **his return** bis zu seiner Rückkehr; ~ **full discussion of the matter** bis die Angelegenheit ausdiskutiert ist

'pending tray n. Ablage für noch Unerledigtes

pendulum /'pendjʊləm/ n. Pendel, das

penetrate /'penɪtreɪt/ **1** v.t. (a) (find access into) eindringen in (+ Akk.); (pass through) durchdringen; **(b)** (permeate) dringen in (+ Akk.); (fig.) durchdringen; ⟨Spion:⟩ sich einschleusen in (+ Akk.). **2** v.i. (a) (make a way) ~ **into/ to sth.** in etw. (Akk.) eindringen/zu etw. vordringen; ~ **through sth.** durch etw. hindurch dringen; **the cold ~d through the whole house** die Kälte durchdrang das

ganze Haus; **(b)** (be understood or realized) **my hint did not ~:** mein Wink wurde nicht verstanden

penetrating /'penɪtreɪtɪŋ/ adj. (a) (easily heard) durchdringend; (keenly felt) durchdringend ⟨Kälte⟩; beißend ⟨Wind⟩ **(b)** scharf ⟨Verstand⟩; scharfsinnig ⟨Bemerkung, Kommentar, Studie⟩; scharf ⟨Beobachtung⟩; durchdringend ⟨Blick⟩

penetration /penɪ'treɪʃn/ n. (a) Eindringen, das (**of** in + Akk.); (act of passing through) Durchdringen, das; **(b)** no pl. (fig.: discernment) Scharfsinn, der; **(c)** (act of permeating) Durchdringen, das; (infiltration) Infiltration, die; Unterwanderung, die; **(d)** (seeing into sth.) Durchdringen, das

'penfriend n. Brieffreund, der/-freundin, die

penguin /'peŋgwɪn/ n. Pinguin, der

penicillin /penɪ'sɪlɪn/ n. (Med.) Penizillin, das

peninsula /pɪ'nɪnsjʊlə/ n. Halbinsel, die

penis /'piːnɪs/ n., pl. ~**es** or **penes** /'piːniːz/ ▶ 672 | (Anat.) Penis, der

penitence /'penɪtəns/ n., no pl. Reue, die

penitent /'penɪtənt/ **1** adj. reuevoll (geh.); reuig (geh.) ⟨Sünder⟩; **be ~:** bereuen. **2** n. Büßer, der/Büßerin, die (Rel.)

penitentiary /penɪ'tenʃərɪ/ n. (Amer.) Straf[vollzugs]anstalt, die

pen: ~**knife** n. Taschenmesser, das; ~**name** n. Schriftstellername, der

pennant /'penənt/ n. (Naut.: tapering flag) Stander, der

penniless /'penɪlɪs/ adj. **be ~:** keinen Pfennig Geld haben; (fig.: be poor) mittellos sein

penny /'penɪ/ n., pl. usu. **pennies** /'penɪz/ (for separate coins), **pence** /pens/ (for sum of money) (a) ▶ 938 | (British coin, monetary unit) Penny, der; **fifty pence** fünfzig Pence; **two/ five/ten/twenty/fifty pence [piece]** Zwei-/Fünf-/Zehn-/ Zwanzig-/Fünfzigpencestück, das od. -münze, die; see also **halfpenny; (b) keep turning up like a bad ~** (coll.) immer wieder auftauchen; **the ~ has dropped** (fig. coll.) der Groschen ist gefallen (ugs.); **in for a ~, in for a pound** (prov.) wennschon, dennschon (ugs.); **a pretty ~** (coll.) eine hübsche od. schöne Stange Geld (ugs.); **take care of the pence** or **pennies, and the pounds will look after themselves** (prov.) spare im Kleinen, dann hast du im Großen; **a ~ for your thoughts** (coll.) woran denkst du [gerade]?; **sth. is two** or **ten a ~:** etw. gibt es wie Sand am Meer (ugs.)

penny: ~ **'farthing [bicycle]** n. (Brit. coll) Hochrad, das; ~**-pinching** /'penɪpɪntʃɪŋ/ **1** n., no pl., no indef. art. Pfennigfuchserei, die (ugs.); **2** adj. knaus[e]rig (ugs. abwertend)

pen: ~**-pusher** n. (coll.) Büromensch, der; (male) Bürohengst, der (ugs. abwertend); ~**-pushing** n., no pl., no indef. art. (coll.) Schreibkram, der (ugs. abwertend)

pension /'penʃn/ n. Rente, die; (payment to retired civil servant also) Pension, die; **retire on a ~:** in od. auf Rente gehen (ugs.); ⟨Beamter:⟩ in Pension gehen; **be on a ~:** eine Rente beziehen; ~ **fund** Rentenfonds, der; ~ **book** ≈ Rentenausweis, der; ~ **rights** Renten- od. Pensionsansprüche; ~ **scheme** Rentenversicherung, die

~ **'off** v.t. (discharge) berenten (Amtsspr.); auf Rente setzen (ugs.); pensionieren ⟨Lehrer, Beamten⟩

pensionable /'penʃənəbl/ adj. **reach ~ age** das Rentenalter erreichen; (as civil servant) das Pensionsalter erreichen; ~ **salary/earnings** rentenfähiges Gehalt/ rentenfähiger Verdienst

pensioner /'penʃənə(r)/ n. Rentner, der/Rentnerin, die; (retired civil servant also) Pensionär, der/Pensionärin, die

pensive /'pensɪv/ adj. (a) (plunged in thought) nachdenklich; **(b)** (sorrowfully thoughtful) schwermütig

pent /pent/ adj. ~ **in** or **up** eingedämmt ⟨Fluss⟩; angestaut ⟨Wut, Ärger⟩; see also **pent-up**

pentagon /'pentəgən/ n. (a) (Geom.) Fünfeck, das; Pentagon, das (fachspr.); **(b) the P~** (Amer. Polit.) das Pentagon

pentathlon /pen'tæθlən/ n. (Sport) Fünfkampf, der

Pentecost /'pentɪkɒst/ n. (Relig.) Pfingsten, das; Pfingstfest, das

pent: ~**house** n. Penthaus, das; Penthouse, das; ~-**up** attrib. adj. angestaut ‹Ärger, Wut›; verhalten ‹Freude›; unterdrückt ‹Sehnsucht, Gefühle›

penultimate /pe'nʌltɪmət/ adj. vorletzt...

penury /'penjʊərɪ/ n., no pl. Armut, die; Not, die

peony /'pi:ənɪ/ n. (Bot.) Pfingstrose, die; Päonie, die

people /'pi:pl/ **1** n. (a) (persons composing nation, community, etc.) Volk, das; (b) constr. as pl. (persons forming class etc.) Leute Pl.; Menschen; **city/country** ~ (inhabitants) Stadt-/Landbewohner; (who prefer the city/the country) Stadt-/Landmenschen; **village** ~: Dorfbewohner; **local** ~: Einheimische; **working** ~: arbeitende Menschen; **coloured/white** ~: Farbige/Weiße; (c) constr. as pl. (persons not of nobility) **the** ~: das [gemeine] Volk; (d) constr. as pl. (persons in general) Menschen; Leute Pl.; (as opposed to animals) Menschen; ~ **say he's very rich** die Leute sagen od. man sagt od. es heißt, dass er sehr reich sei; **a crowd of** ~: eine Menschenmenge; **'some** ~ (certain persons, usu. with whom the speaker disagrees) gewisse Leute; (you) manche Leute; **some '**~**!** Leute gibt es!; **honestly, some '**~**!** also wirklich!; **what do you** ~ **think?** was denkt ihr [denn]?; **you of 'all** ~ **ought** ...: gerade du solltest ... **2** v.t. bevölkern

peopled /'pi:pld/ adj. bevölkert

People's Re'public n. (Polit.) Volksrepublik, die; **the** ~ **of China** die Volksrepublik China

pep /pep/ (coll.) **1** n., no pl., no indef. art. Schwung, der; Pep, der (salopp). **2** v.t., **-pp-:** ~ **[up]** aufpeppen (ugs.)

PEP /pep/ abbr. (Brit.) **personal equity plan**

pepper /'pepə(r)/ **1** n. (a) Pfeffer, der; (b) (vegetable) Paprikaschote, die; **red/yellow/green** ~: roter/gelber/grüner Paprika. **2** v.t. (a) (sprinkle with ~) pfeffern; (b) (pelt with missiles) bombardieren (ugs., auch fig.)

pepper: ~**corn** n. Pfefferkorn, das; ~ **mill** n. Pfeffermühle, die; ~**mint** n. (a) (plant) Pfefferminze, die; (b) (sweet) Pfefferminz, das; ~ **pot** n. Pfefferstreuer, der

peppery /'pepərɪ/ adj. pfeff[e]rig; (spicy) scharf; (fig.: pungent) scharf

pep: ~ **pill** n. (coll.) Peppille, die (ugs.); Aufputschtablette, die; ~ **talk** n. (coll.) Aufmunterung, die; **give sb. a** ~ **talk** jmdm. ein paar aufmunternde Worte sagen

per /pɜ(r), stressed pɜ:(r)/ prep. (a) (by means of) per ‹Post, Bahn, Schiff, Bote›; durch ‹Spediteur, Herrn X.›; (b) (according to) **[as]** ~ **sth.** wie in etw. (Dat.) angegeben; laut ‹Anweisung, Preisliste›; (c) ▶ **1102**] (for each) pro; **£50** ~ **week** 50 Pfund in der Woche od. pro Woche; **fifty kilometres** ~ **hour** fünfzig Kilometer in der od. pro Stunde; **get 11 francs** ~ **pound** 11 Francs für ein Pfund bekommen

perambulator /pə'ræmbjʊleɪtə(r)/ (Brit. formal) ⇒ **pram**

per annum /pər 'ænəm/ adv. im Jahr; pro Jahr (bes. Kaufmannsspr., ugs.)

perceive /pə'si:v/ v.t. (a) (with the mind) spüren; bemerken; (b) (through the senses) wahrnehmen; **we** ~**d a figure in the distance** wir erblickten in der Ferne eine Gestalt; (c) (regard mentally in a certain way) wahrnehmen; ~**d** vermeintlich ‹Bedrohung, Gefahr, Wert›

per cent (Brit.; Amer.: **percent**) /pə 'sent/ **1** adv. **ninety** ~ **effective** zu 90 Prozent wirksam; see also **hundred 1** c. **2** adj. **a 5** ~ **increase** ein Zuwachs von 5 Prozent; ein fünfprozentiger Zuwachs. **3** n. (a) ⇒ **percentage;** (b) (hundredth) Prozent, das

percentage /pə'sentɪdʒ/ n. (a) (rate or proportion per cent) Prozentsatz, der; **a high** ~ **of alcohol** ein hoher Alkoholgehalt; **what** ~ **of 48 is 11?** wie viel Prozent von 48 sind 11?; (b) (proportion) [prozentualer] Anteil

per'centage sign n. Prozentzeichen, das

perceptible /pə'septɪbl/ adj. wahrnehmbar; **be quite** ~: ganz offensichtlich sein

perceptibly /pə'septɪblɪ/ adv. sichtlich; sichtbar, merklich ‹schrumpfen, welken›

perception /pə'sepʃn/ n. (a) (act) Wahrnehmung, die; (result) Erkenntnis, die; **have keen** ~**s** ein stark ausgeprägtes Wahrnehmungsvermögen haben; (b) no pl. (faculty) Wahrnehmungsvermögen, das; (c) (intuitive recognition) Gespür, das (**of** für); (instance) Erfassen, das

perceptive /pə'septɪv/ adj. (a) (discerning) scharf ‹Auge›; fein ‹Gehör, Nase, Geruchssinn›; scharfsinnig ‹Person›; (b) (having intuitive recognition or insight) einfühlsam ‹Person, Zeitungsartikel, Bemerkung›

perceptively /pə'septɪvlɪ/ adv. (a) (discerningly) mit scharfer Wahrnehmung; (b) (with intuitive recognition or insight) einfühlsam

perch¹ /pɜ:tʃ/ n., pl. same or ~**es** (Zool.) Flussbarsch, der

perch² **1** n. (a) (horizontal bar) Sitzstange, die; (for hens) Hühnerstange, die; (b) (place to sit) Sitzplatz, der. **2** v.i. (a) (alight) sich niederlassen; (b) (be supported) sitzen. **3** v.t. setzen/stellen/legen; **be** ~**ed** ‹Vogel:› sitzen; **stand** ~**ed on a cliff** hoch auf einer Klippe stehen; **a village** ~**ed on a hill** ein hoch oben auf einem Berg gelegenes Dorf

percolate /'pɜ:kəleɪt/ **1** v.i. (a) (ooze) ~ **through sth.** durch etw. [durch]sickern; (b) (fig.: spread gradually) vordringen; (c) ‹Kaffee:› durchlaufen. **2** v.t. (a) (permeate) sickern durch ‹Gestein›; (b) (fig.: penetrate) dringen in (+ Akk.) ‹Bewusstsein›; (c) [mit der Kaffeemaschine] machen ‹Kaffee›

percolator /'pɜ:kəleɪtə(r)/ n. Kaffeemaschine, die

percussion /pə'kʌʃn/ n. (Mus.) (group of instruments) Schlagzeug, das; ~ **instrument** Schlaginstrument, das

peregrine /'perɪgrɪn/ n. ~ **[falcon]** (Ornith.) Wanderfalke, der

peremptory /pə'remptərɪ, 'perɪmptərɪ/ adj. (admitting no contradiction) kategorisch; (imperious) herrisch; gebieterisch (geh.)

perennial /pə'renjəl/ **1** adj. (a) (lasting all year) ganzjährig; (b) (lasting indefinitely) immer während; ewig ‹Jugend, Mythos, Suche›; ungelöst ‹Problem›; (c) (Bot.) ausdauernd. **2** n. (Bot.) ausdauernde Pflanze

perestroika /perɪ'strɔɪkə/ n. Perestroika, die

perfect 1 /'pɜ:fɪkt/ adj. (a) (complete) vollkommen; umfassend ‹Kenntnisse, Wissen›; (b) (faultless) vollkommen; perfekt ‹Englisch, Technik, Timing›; tadellos ‹Zustand›; [absolut] gelungen ‹Aufführung›; lupenrein ‹Diamant›; see also **practice¹ a;** (c) (very satisfactory) herrlich; wunderbar; (d) (exact) perfekt; getreu ‹Ebenbild, Abbild›; (fully what the name implies) perfekt ‹Gentleman, Gastgeberin›; (e) (absolute) **a** ~ **stranger** ein völlig Fremder; **he is a** ~ **stranger to me** er ist mir völlig unbekannt; **he is a** ~ **angel** (coll.)/**charmer** er ist wirklich ein Engel/charmant; **I have a** ~ **right to stay** ich habe eindeutig od. durchaus das Recht zu bleiben; (f) (coll.: unmitigated) absolut; **look a** ~ **fright/mess** wirklich zum Weglaufen/absolut verboten aussehen (ugs.). **2** /pə'fekt/ v.t. vervollkommnen; perfektionieren

perfection /pə'fekʃn/ n., no pl. (a) (making perfect) Vervollkommnung, die; Perfektionierung, die; (b) (faultlessness) Vollkommenheit, die; Perfektion, die; **to** ~: perfekt; **it/he succeeded to** ~: es war ein voller Erfolg/er war absolut erfolgreich; (c) (perfect person or thing) **be** ~: perfekt sein

perfectionism /pə'fekʃənɪzm/ n., no pl. Perfektionismus, der

perfectionist /pə'fekʃənɪst/ n. Perfektionist, der/Perfektionistin, die

perfectly /'pɜ:fɪktlɪ/ adv. (a) (completely) vollkommen; völlig; **I understand that** ~: ich verstehe das vollkommen; **be** ~ **entitled to do sth.** durchaus berechtigt sein, etw. zu tun; (b) (faultlessly) perfekt; tadellos ‹sich verhalten›; (c) (exactly) vollkommen; exakt, genau ‹vorhersagbar›; (d) (coll.: to an unmitigated extent) furchtbar (ugs.) ‹schrecklich, schlimm, ekelhaft›

perfidious /pə'fɪdɪəs/ adj. perfid (geh.)

perforate /'pɜ:fəreɪt/ v.t. (a) (make hole[s] through) perforieren; (b) (make an opening into) durchlöchern

perforation /pɜ:fə'reɪʃn/ n. (a) (action of perforating) Perforierung, die; (b) (hole) Loch, das; ~**s** (line of holes esp. in paper) Perforation, die; (in sheets of stamps) Zähnung, die; Perforation, die

perform /pə'fɔ:m/ **1** v.t. ausführen ‹Befehl, Arbeit›; erfüllen ‹Bitte, Wunsch, Pflicht, Aufgabe›; vollbringen ‹[Helden]tat, Leistung›; durchführen ‹Operation, Experiment›; ausfüllen ‹Funktion›; vollbringen ‹Wunder›; vorführen, zeigen ‹Trick›; vollziehen ‹Trauung, Taufe,

Riten); aufführen ⟨*Theaterstück*⟩; vortragen, vorsingen ⟨*Lied*⟩; vorspielen, vortragen ⟨*Sonate usw.*⟩. **2** *v.i.* **(a)** eine Vorführung geben; (sing) singen; (play) spielen; ⟨*Zauberer:*⟩ Zaubertricks ausführen *od.* vorführen; **he ~ed very well** seine Darbietung war sehr gut; **she ~ed skilfully on the flute/piano** sie spielte mit großer Könnerschaft Flöte/ Klavier; **(b)** (Theatre) auftreten; **he ~ed very well** sein Auftritt war sehr gut; **(c)** (execute tricks) ⟨*Tier:*⟩ Kunststücke zeigen *od.* vorführen; **train an animal to ~:** einem Tier Kunststücke beibringen; **(d)** (work, function) ⟨*Auto:*⟩ laufen, fahren; **he ~ed all right/well [in the exam]** er machte seine Sache [in der Prüfung] ordentlich/gut

performance /pə'fɔ:məns/ *n.* **(a)** (fulfilment) (of duty, task) Erfüllung, *die;* (of command) Ausführung, *die;* **(b)** (carrying out) Durchführung, *die;* **(c)** (notable feat) Leistung, *die;* **put up a good ~:** eine gute Leistung zeigen; **(d)** (performing of play etc.) Vorstellung, *die;* **her ~ as Desdemona** ihre Darstellung der Desdemona; **the ~ of a play/opera** die Aufführung eines Theaterstücks/einer Oper; **give a ~ of a symphony/play** eine Sinfonie/ein Stück spielen *od.* aufführen; **(e)** (achievement under test) Leistung, *die;* **athletic ~:** die Leistung eines Sportlers; **the car has good ~:** der Wagen bringt viel Leistung; **(f)** (coll.: difficult procedure) Theater, *das* (ugs., abwertend); Umstand, *die*

performance: **~ art** *n.* Performance-Art, *die;* **~ artist** *n.* Performancekünstler, *der*/-künstlerin, *die*

performer /pə'fɔ:mə(r)/ *n.* Künstler, *der*/Künstlerin, *die*

performing 'arts *n. pl.* darstellende Künste

perfume 1 /'pɜ:fju:m/ *n.* **(a)** (sweet smell) Duft, *der;* **(b)** (fluid) Parfüm, *das.* **2** /pə'fju:m, 'pɜ:fju:m/ *v.t.* (give sweet scent to) mit Wohlgeruch erfüllen; (impregnate with sweet smell) parfümieren

perfunctory /pə'fʌŋktərɪ/ *adj.* (done for duty's sake only) pflichtschuldig; flüchtig ⟨*Erkundigung, Bemerkung*⟩; (superficial) oberflächlich ⟨*Arbeit, Überprüfung*⟩

perhaps /pə'hæps, præps/ *adv.* vielleicht; **I'll go out, ~:** ich gehe vielleicht aus; **~ so** [das] mag [ja] sein; **~ not** (maybe this is or will not be the case) vielleicht auch nicht; (it might be best not to do this) vielleicht lieber nicht

peril /'perɪl/ *n.* Gefahr, *die;* **be in deadly ~:** in Lebensgefahr sein; **do sth. at one's ~** (accepting risk of injury) etw. auf eigene Gefahr tun

perilous /'perələs/ *adj.* gefahrvoll; **be ~:** gefährlich sein

perilously /'perələslɪ/ *adv.* gefährlich; **~ ill** todkrank

perimeter /pə'rɪmɪtə(r)/ *n.* **(a)** (outer boundary) [äußere] Begrenzung; Grenze, *die;* **at the ~ of the racetrack** am Rande der Rennbahn; **(b)** (length of outline) Umfang, *der*

period /'pɪərɪəd/ **1** *n.* **(a)** (distinct portion of history or life) Periode, *die;* Zeit, *die;* **~s of history** geschichtliche Perioden; **at a later ~ of her life** zu einem späteren Zeitpunkt ihres Lebens; **the Classical / Romantic / Renaissance ~:** die Klassik/Romantik/Renaissance; **of the ~** (of the time under discussion) der damaligen Zeit; **(b)** (any portion of time) Zeitraum, *der;* Zeitspanne, *die;* **over a ~ [of time]** über einen längeren Zeitraum; **within the agreed ~:** innerhalb der vereinbarten Frist; **showers and bright ~s** (Meteorol.) Schauer und Aufheiterungen; **(c)** (Sch.) Stunde, *die;* **have two chemistry ~s** zwei Stunden Chemie haben; **a free ~:** eine Freistunde; **(d)** (occurrence of menstruation) Periode, *die;* Regel[blutung], *die;* **have her/a ~:** ihre Periode *od.* Regel *od.* (ugs. verhüll.) Tage haben; **(e)** (punctuation mark) Punkt, *der;* **(f)** (appended to statement) **we can't pay higher wages, ~:** wir können keine höheren Löhne zahlen, da ist nichts zu machen; **(g)** (Geol.) Periode, *die.* **2** *adj.* zeitgenössisch ⟨*Tracht, Kostüm*⟩; Zeit⟨*roman, -stück*⟩; antik ⟨*Möbel*⟩

periodic /pɪərɪ'ɒdɪk/ *adj.* periodisch *od.* regelmäßig [auftretend *od.* wiederkehrend]; (intermittent) gelegentlich [auftretend]; vereinzelt ⟨*Regenschauer*⟩

periodical /pɪərɪ'ɒdɪkl/ **1** *adj.* ⇒ **periodic. 2** *n.* Zeitschrift, *die;* **weekly/monthly/quarterly ~:** Wochenzeitschrift/Monatsschrift/Vierteljahresschrift, *die*

periodically /pɪərɪ'ɒdɪkəlɪ/ *adv.* (at regular intervals) regelmäßig; (intermittently) gelegentlich

periodic 'table *n.* (Chem.) Periodensystem, *das*

peripatetic /perɪpə'tetɪk/ *adj.* **~ teacher** Lehrer, *der*/ Lehrerin, *die an mehreren Schulen unterrichtet*

peripheral /pə'rɪfərl/ **1** *adj.* **(a)** (of the periphery) ⟨*Parkraum*⟩ in Randlage; **~ road** Ringstraße, *die;* **(b)** (of minor importance) peripher (geh.); marginal (geh.); Rand⟨*problem, -erscheinung, -figur, -bemerkung*⟩; **(c)** (Computing) peripher. **2** *n.* (Computing) Peripheriegerät, *das*

periphery /pə'rɪfərɪ/ *n.* **(a)** ⇒ **circumference; (b)** (external boundary) Begrenzung, *die;* (of surface) Außenfläche, *die;* **(c)** (outer region) Peripherie, *die* (geh.); Rand, *der*

periscope /'perɪskəʊp/ *n.* Periskop, *das*

perish /'perɪʃ/ **1** *v.i.* **(a)** ⟨*Person:*⟩ umkommen; ⟨*Volk, Rasse, Kultur:*⟩ untergehen; ⟨*Kraft, Energie:*⟩ versiegen; ⟨*Pflanze:*⟩ eingehen; **~ the thought!** Gott behüte *od.* bewahre!; **(b)** (rot) verderben ⟨*Fresken, Gemälde:*⟩ verblassen; ⟨*Gummi:*⟩ altern. **2** *v.t.* **(a) we were ~ed [with cold]** wir waren ganz durchgefroren; **(b)** (cause to rot) [schneller] altern lassen ⟨*Gummi*⟩; angreifen ⟨*Reifen*⟩

perishable /'perɪʃəbl/ **1** *adj.* [leicht] verderblich ⟨*Lebensmittel, Waren*⟩. **2** *n. in pl.* leicht verderbliche Güter *od.* Waren

perishing /'perɪʃɪŋ/ (coll.) **1** *adj.* **(a)** mörderisch ⟨*Wind, Kälte*⟩; **it's/I'm ~:** es ist bitterkalt/ich komme um vor Kälte (ugs.); **(b)** (Brit.: confounded) elend; **that child is a ~ nuisance** das Kind kann einem den Nerv töten (ugs.). **2** *adv.* mörderisch ⟨*kalt*⟩

perjure /'pɜ:dʒə(r)/ *v. refl.* (swear to false statement) einen Meineid leisten; (Law: give false evidence under oath) [unter Eid] falsch aussagen

perjury /'pɜ:dʒərɪ/ *n.* (swearing to false statement) Meineid, *der;* (Law: giving false evidence) eidliche Falschaussage; **commit ~:** einen Meineid leisten/sich der eidlichen Falschaussage schuldig machen

perk¹ /pɜ:k/ (coll.) **1** *v.i.* **~ up** munter werden. **2** *v.t.* **(a) ~ up** (restore liveliness of) aufmuntern; **(b) ~ up** (raise briskly) aufstellen ⟨*Schwanz, Ohren*⟩; heben ⟨*Kopf*⟩

perk² *n.* (Brit. coll.: benefit) [Sonder]vergünstigung, *die*

perky /'pɜ:kɪ/ *adj.* **(a)** (lively) lebhaft; munter; **(b)** (self-confident) keck; selbstbewusst

perm /pɜ:m/ **1** *n.* (permanent wave) Dauerwelle, *die.* **2** *v.t.* **have one's hair ~ed** sich (*Dat.*) eine Dauerwelle machen lassen; **have ~ed hair** eine Dauerwelle haben

permanence /'pɜ:mənəns/ *n., no pl.* Dauerhaftigkeit, *die*

permanency /'pɜ:mənənsɪ/ *n.* **(a)** *no pl.* ⇒ **permanence; (b)** (condition) Dauerzustand, *der;* (job) Dauerstellung, *die*

permanent /'pɜ:mənənt/ *adj.* fest ⟨*Sitz, Bestandteil, Mitglied*⟩; beständig, ewig ⟨*Werte*⟩; ständig ⟨*Plage, Meckern, Adresse, Kampf*⟩; Dauer⟨*gast, -stellung, -visum*⟩; bleibend ⟨*Folge, Schaden*⟩; **of ~ value** von bleibendem Wert; **sb./sth. is a ~ fixture** jmd./etw. gehört zum Inventar; **be employed on a ~ basis** fest angestellt sein

permanently /'pɜ:mənəntlɪ/ *adv.* dauernd; auf Dauer ⟨*verhindern, bleiben*⟩; fest ⟨*anstellen, einstellen*⟩; (repeatedly) ständig; dauernd; **they live in France ~** now sie leben jetzt ganz (ugs.) *od.* ständig in Frankreich; **she was ~ disabled in the accident** sie hat bei dem Unfall eine bleibende Behinderung davongetragen

permeable /'pɜ:mɪəbl/ *adj.* durchlässig

permeate /'pɜ:mɪeɪt/ **1** *v.t.* (get into) dringen in (+ *Akk.*); (pass through) dringen durch; **be ~d with or by sth.** (fig.) von etw. durchdrungen sein. **2** *v.i.* **~ through** etw. durchdringen; **~ through to sb.** zu jmdm. durchdringen

permissible /pə'mɪsɪbl/ *adj.* zulässig; **be ~ to or for sb.** jmdm. erlaubt sein

permission /pə'mɪʃn/ *n., no indef. art.* Erlaubnis, *die;* (given by official body) Genehmigung, *die;* **ask [sb.'s] ~:** [jmdn.] um Erlaubnis bitten; **who gave you ~ to do this?** wer hat dir erlaubt, das zu tun?; **with your ~:** wenn Sie gestatten; mit Ihrer Erlaubnis; **written ~:** eine schriftliche Genehmigung

permissive /pə'mɪsɪv/ *adj.* (tolerant) tolerant; großzügig; (in relation to moral matters) freizügig; permissiv (geh.); **the ~ society** die permissive Gesellschaft

permit 1 /pə'mɪt/ *v.t.,* **-tt-** zulassen ⟨*Berufung, Einspruch usw.*⟩; **~ sb. sth.** jmdm. etw. erlauben *od.* (geh.) gestatten. **2** *v.i.,* **-tt-** **(a)** (give opportunity) es zulassen; **weather ~ting**

bei entsprechendem Wetter; **(b)** (admit) ∼ **of sth.** etw. erlauben *od.* gestatten; **not** ∼ **of sth.** etw. verbieten. **3** /ˈpɜːmɪt/ *n.* Genehmigung, *die;* (for entering premises) Passierschein, *der*

permutation /pɜːmjʊˈteɪʃn/ *n.* **(a)** (varying of order) Umstellung, *die;* **(b)** (result of variation of order) Anordnung, *die;* (of series of items) Reihenfolge, *die;* Permutation, *die* (Math.)

pernicious /pəˈnɪʃəs/ *adj.* verderblich; bösartig ⟨*Krankheit, Person*⟩; schlimm, übel ⟨*Angewohnheit*⟩

pernickety /pəˈnɪkɪtɪ/ *adj.* (coll.) pingelig (ugs.) **(about in** Bezug auf + *Akk.*)

peroxide /pəˈrɒksaɪd/ *n.* **(a)** (Chem.) Peroxid, *das;* **(b)** [hydrogen] ∼: Wasserstoffperoxid, *das;* ∼ **blonde** Wasserstoffblondine, *die*

perpendicular /pɜːpənˈdɪkjʊlə(r)/ **1** *adj.* **(a)** senkrecht; lotrecht; **(b)** (very steep) [fast] senkrecht ⟨*Aufstieg, Abstieg*⟩; senkrecht abfallend/aufragend ⟨*Kliff, Felswand usw.*⟩; ∼ **drop/slope/rock face** Steilabfall, *der/* -hang, *der/*-wand, *die;* **(c)** (Geom.) senkrecht **(to** zu); **two** ∼ **planes/ lines** zwei zueinander senkrechte Ebenen/Linien. **2** *n.* Senkrechte, *die* **(to** zu); Lot, *das* **(to** auf + *Dat.*); **be [slightly] out of [the]** ∼: [etwas] aus dem Lot sein

perpetrate /ˈpɜːpɪtreɪt/ *v.t.* begehen; anrichten ⟨*Schaden*⟩; verüben ⟨*Gemetzel, Gräuel*⟩

perpetrator /ˈpɜːpɪtreɪtə(r)/ *n.* [Übel]täter, *der/*-täterin, *die;* **be the** ∼ **of a crime/fraud/atrocity** ein Verbrechen/einen Betrug begangen haben/eine Gräueltat verübt haben

perpetual /pəˈpetjʊəl/ *adj.* **(a)** (eternal) ewig; **(b)** (continuous) ständig; **(c)** (repeated) ständig; [an]dauernd; **(d)** (applicable or valid for ever) immer während; ewig

perpetually /pəˈpetjʊəlɪ/ *adv.* **(a)** (eternally) ewig; **(b)** (continuously) ständig; **(c)** (repeatedly) ständig; [an]dauernd

perpetual 'motion *n., no pl., no art.* ewige Bewegung

perpetuate /pəˈpetjʊeɪt/ *v.t.* **(a)** (preserve from oblivion) lebendig erhalten ⟨*Andenken*⟩; unsterblich machen ⟨*Namen*⟩; aufrechterhalten ⟨*Tradition*⟩; **(b)** (make perpetual) aufrechterhalten; erhalten ⟨*Art, Macht*⟩

perpetuity /pɜːpɪˈtjuːɪtɪ/ *n., no pl., no indef. art.* ewiger Bestand; **in** *or* **to** *or* **for** ∼: für alle Ewigkeit *od.* alle Zeiten

perplex /pəˈpleks/ *v.t.* verwirren

perplexed /pəˈplekst/ *adj.* (bewildered) verwirrt; (puzzled) ratlos

perplexity /pəˈpleksɪtɪ/ *n. no pl.* (bewilderment) Verwirrung, *die;* (puzzlement) Ratlosigkeit, *die*

persecute /ˈpɜːsɪkjuːt/ *v.t.* **(a)** verfolgen; **(b)** (harass, worry) plagen; zusetzen (+ *Dat.*)

persecution /pɜːsɪˈkjuːʃn/ *n.* **(a)** Verfolgung, *die;* **(b)** (harassment) Plagerei, *die*

perseverance /pɜːsɪˈvɪərəns/ *n.* Beharrlichkeit, *die;* Ausdauer, *die*

persevere /pɜːsɪˈvɪə(r)/ *v.i.* ausharren; ∼ **with** *or* **at** *or* **in th.** bei etw. dabeibleiben; ∼ **in doing sth.** darauf beharren, etw. zu tun

Persia /ˈpɜːʃə/ *pr. n.* (Hist.) Persien *(das)*

Persian /ˈpɜːʃn/ **1** *adj.* persisch. **2** *n.* **(a)** (person) Perser, *der/*Perserin, *die;* **(b)** ▶ 897 (language) Persisch, *das;* see also **English 2** a; **(c)** ⇒ **Persian cat**

Persian: ∼ **'carpet** *n.* Perser[teppich], *der;* ∼ **'cat** *n.* Perserkatze, *die*

persist /pəˈsɪst/ *v.i.* **(a)** (continue firmly) beharrlich sein Ziel verfolgen; nicht nachgeben; ∼ **in sth.** an etw. (*Dat.*) [beharrlich] festhalten; ∼ **in doing sth.** etw. weiterhin [beharrlich] tun; **(b)** (continue in existence) anhalten

persistence /pəˈsɪstəns/ *n., no pl.* **(a)** (continuance in particular course) Hartnäckigkeit, *die;* Beharrlichkeit, *die;* **(b)** (quality of perseverance) Ausdauer, *die;* Zähigkeit, *die;* **(c)** (continued existence) Fortbestehen, *das*

persistent /pəˈsɪstənt/ *adj.* **(a)** (continuing firmly or obstinately) hartnäckig; **(b)** (constantly repeated) dauernd; hartnäckig ⟨*Gerüchte*⟩; nicht nachlassend ⟨*Anstrengung, Bemühung*⟩; ∼ **showers** anhaltende Schauertätigkeit; **(c)** (enduring) anhaltend

person /ˈpɜːsn/ *n.* **(a)** Mensch, *der;* Person, *die* (oft abwertend); **a rich/sick/unemployed** ∼: ein Reicher/ Kranker/Arbeitsloser/eine Reiche *usw.;* **the first** ∼ **to leave was** ...: der/die Erste, der/die wegging, war ...; **what sort of** ∼ **do you think I am?** wofür halten Sie mich eigentlich?; **in the** ∼ **of sb.** in jmdm. *od.* jmds. Person; **in** ∼ (personally) persönlich; selbst; **(b)** (living body) Körper, *der;* (appearance) [äußere] Erscheinung; Äußere, *das;* **(c)** (Ling.) Person, *die;* **first/second/third** ∼: erste/ zweite/dritte Person

personable /ˈpɜːsənəbl/ *adj.* sympathisch

personage /ˈpɜːsənɪdʒ/ *n.* **(a)** (person of rank) Persönlichkeit, *die;* **(b)** (person not known to speaker) Person, *die*

personal /ˈpɜːsənl/ *adj.* persönlich; Privat⟨*angelegenheit, -leben*⟩; ⟨*Sache*⟩ jmdm. persönlich gehören; ∼ **appearance** äußere Erscheinung; ∼ **hygiene** Körperpflege, *die;* ∼ **call** (Brit. Teleph.) Anruf mit Voranmeldung; ∼ **stereo** Walkman, *der;* **pay sb. a** ∼ **call** jmdn. privat aufsuchen; **it's nothing** ∼**, but** ...: nimm es bitte nicht persönlich, aber ...

personal: ∼ **ad** *n.* Privatanzeige, *die;* (seeking friendship, romance) Kontaktanzeige, *die;* ∼ **as'sistant** *n.* ▶ 887 persönlicher Referent/persönliche Referentin; ∼ **column** *n.* Rubrik für private [Klein]anzeigen; ∼ **com'puter** *n.* Personalcomputer, *der;* ∼ **'equity plan** *n.* (Brit.) *persönlicher Vermögensplan auf Aktienbasis;* ∼ **identifi'cation number** *n.* persönliche Identifikationsnummer

personalise ⇒ **personalize**

personality /pɜːsəˈnælɪtɪ/ *n.* Persönlichkeit, *die;* **have a strong** ∼, (coll.) **have lots of** ∼: eine starke Persönlichkeit sein *od.* haben

personalize /ˈpɜːsənəlaɪz/ *v.t.* **(a)** (make personal) persönlich gestalten; eine persönliche Note geben (+ *Dat.*); (mark with owner's name etc.) als persönliches Eigentum kennzeichnen; **(b)** (personify) personifizieren

'personal loan *n.* Privatdarlehen, *das;* Privatkredit, *der*

personally /ˈpɜːsənəlɪ/ *adv.* persönlich; ∼**, I see no objection** ich persönlich sehe keine Einwände

personal: ∼ **'organizer** *n.* Terminplaner, *der;* ∼ **'pension plan** *n.* persönlicher Renten[vorsorge]plan; persönliche Rentenvorsorge; ∼ **'property** *n.* persönliches Eigentum; ∼ **'service** *n.* individueller Service; **get** ∼ **service** individuell *od.* persönlich bedient werden

personification /pəsɒnɪfɪˈkeɪʃn/ *n.* Verkörperung, *die;* **be the [very]** ∼ **of kindness** die Freundlichkeit selbst *od.* in Person sein

personify /pəˈsɒnɪfaɪ/ *v.t.* verkörpern; **be kindness personified,** ∼ **kindness** die Freundlichkeit in Person sein

personnel /pɜːsəˈnel/ *n.* **(a)** *constr. as sing. or pl.* ▶ 887 Belegschaft, *die;* (of shop, restaurant, etc.) Personal, *das; attrib.* Personal-; **military** ∼: Militärangehörige; ∼ **manager** Personalchef, *der/*-chefin, *die;* ∼ **officer** Personalsachbearbeiter, *der/*-sachbearbeiterin, *die;* **(b)** *no pl., no art.* (department of firm) Personalabteilung, *die*

person-to-'person *adj.* (Amer. Teleph.) ∼ **call** Anruf mit Voranmeldung

perspective /pəˈspektɪv/ *n.* **(a)** Perspektive, *die;* (fig.) Blickwinkel, *der;* **throw sth. into** ∼: etw. ins rechte Licht rücken; **put a different** ∼ **on events** ein neues Licht auf die Ereignisse werfen; **[do] keep things in** ∼: das darfst du nicht so eng sehen; (don't get too excited) bleib mal auf dem Teppich; **(b)** (view) Aussicht, *die;* (fig.: mental view) Ausblick, *der*

Perspex, (P) /ˈpɜːspeks/ *n.* Plexiglas ℗, *das*

perspicacious /pɜːspɪˈkeɪʃəs/ *adj.* scharfsinnig

perspiration /pɜːspɪˈreɪʃn/ *n.* **(a)** Schweiß, *der;* **(b)** (action of perspiring) Schwitzen, *das*

perspire /pəˈspaɪə(r)/ *v.i.* schwitzen; transpirieren (geh.)

persuadable /pəˈsweɪdəbl/ *adj.* leicht zu überreden; **be easily** ∼: sich leicht überreden lassen

persuade /pə'sweɪd/ v.t. (a) (cause to have belief) überzeugen (of von); ~ **oneself of sth.** sich (Dat.) etw. einreden; ~ **oneself [that]** ...: sich (Dat.) einreden, dass ...; (b) (induce) überreden; ~ **sb. into/out of doing sth.** jmdn. [dazu] überreden, etw. zu tun/nicht zu tun

persuasion /pə'sweɪʒn/ n. (a) (action of persuading) Überzeugung, die; (persuasiveness) Überzeugungskraft, die; **it didn't take much ~:** es brauchte nicht viel Überredungskunst; **he didn't need much ~ [to have another drink]** man brauchte ihn nicht lange dazu überreden[, noch etwas zu trinken]; (b) (belief) Überzeugung, die; (c) (religious belief) Glaubensrichtung, die; (sect) Glaubensgemeinschaft, die

persuasive /pə'sweɪsɪv/ adj., **persuasively** /pə'sweɪsɪvlɪ/ adv. überzeugend

persuasiveness /pə'sweɪsɪvnɪs/ n., no pl. Überzeugungskraft, die

pert /pɜːt/ adj. (a) (saucy, impudent) unverschämt; frech; (b) (neat) keck ⟨Hut, Anzug usw.⟩; hübsch ⟨Körper, Nase, Hinterteil⟩

pertain /pə'teɪn/ v.i. (a) (belong as part) ~ **to** [dazu]gehören zu; (b) (be relevant) ⟨Kriterien usw.⟩ gelten; ~ **to** von Bedeutung sein für; (c) (have reference) ~ **to sth.** etw. betreffen; mit etw. zu tun haben

pertinence /'pɜːtɪnəns/ n., no pl. Relevanz, die

pertinent /'pɜːtɪnənt/ adj. relevant (**to** für)

perturb /pə'tɜːb/ v.t. beunruhigen

Peru /pə'ruː/ pr. n. Peru (das)

perusal /pə'ruːzl/ n. Lektüre, die; (of documents) sorgfältiges Studium, das; (fig.: action of examining) (of documents) sorgfältige Durchsicht; **give sth. a careful ~:** etw. genau durchlesen od. studieren

peruse /pə'ruːz/ v.t. genau durchlesen; (fig.: examine) untersuchen

Peruvian /pə'ruːvɪən/ ▶947 1 adj. peruanisch. 2 n. Peruaner, der/Peruanerin, die

pervade /pə'veɪd/ v.t. (a) (spread throughout) durchdringen; **be ~d with** or **by** durchdrungen sein von; (b) (be rife among) ⟨Ansicht:⟩ weit verbreitet sein in (+ Dat.)

pervasive /pə'veɪsɪv/ adj. (pervading) durchdringend ⟨Geruch, Feuchtigkeit, Kälte⟩; weit verbreitet ⟨Ansicht⟩; sich ausbreitend ⟨Gefühl⟩; (able to pervade) alles durchdringend

perverse /pə'vɜːs/ adj. (a) (persistent in error) uneinsichtig, verstockt ⟨Person⟩; borniert ⟨Person, Argument⟩; (b) (unreasonable) verrückt

perversely /pə'vɜːslɪ/ adv. uneinsichtig; verstockt

perversion /pə'vɜːʃn/ n. (a) (turning aside from proper use) Missbrauch, der; (misconstruction) Pervertierung, die; (of words, statement) Verdrehung, die; (leading astray) Verführung, die; (b) (perverted form of sth.) Pervertierung, die; (c) (sexual) Perversion, die

perversity /pə'vɜːsɪtɪ/ n. (persistence in error) Uneinsichtigkeit, die; Verstocktheit, die

pervert 1 /pə'vɜːt/ v.t. (a) (turn aside from proper use or nature) pervertieren (geh.); beugen ⟨Recht⟩; untergraben ⟨Staatsform, Demokratie⟩; ~ **[the course of] justice** die Justiz behindern; (b) (misconstrue) verfälschen; (c) (lead astray) verderben. 2 /'pɜːvɜːt/ n. Perverse, der/die

perverted /pə'vɜːtɪd/ adj. (turned aside from proper use) pervertiert (geh.); (b) (misconstrued) verdreht; (c) (led astray) schlecht; verdorben; (d) (sexually) pervers

pesky /'peskɪ/ adj. (Amer. coll.) verdammt (ugs.)

pessimism /'pesɪmɪzm/ n., no pl. Pessimismus, der

pessimist /'pesɪmɪst/ n. Pessimist, der/Pessimistin, die

pessimistic /pesɪ'mɪstɪk/ adj., **pessimistically** /pesɪ'mɪstɪkəlɪ/ adv. pessimistisch

pest /pest/ n. (troublesome thing) Ärgernis, das; Plage, die; (troublesome person) Nervensäge, die (ugs.); (destructive animal) Schädling, der; ~**s** (insects) Schädlinge; Ungeziefer, das

pester /'pestə(r)/ v.t. belästigen; nerven (ugs.); ~ **sb. for sth.** jmdm. wegen etw. in den Ohren liegen; ~ **sb. to do sth.** jmdm. in den Ohren liegen, etw. zu tun; ~ **sb. for money** jmdn. [um Geld] anbetteln

pesticide /'pestɪsaɪd/ n. Pestizid, das

pestilential /pestɪ'lenʃl/ adj. (a) (fig. coll.: troublesome) ungaussehlich; (b) (pernicious) verderblich

pestle /'pesl/ n. Stößel, der; Pistill, das (fachspr.)

pet /pet/ 1 n. (a) (tame animal) Haustier, das; (b) (darling, favourite) Liebling, der; (sweet person; also as term of endearment) Schatz, der; **teacher's ~** (derog.) Liebling des Lehrers/der Lehrerin. 2 adj. (a) (kept as ~) zahm; (b) (of or for ~ animals) Haustier-; (c) (favourite) Lieblings-; **sth./sb. is sb.'s ~ aversion** or **hate** jmd. kann etw./jmdn. auf den Tod nicht ausstehen (ugs.); (d) (expressing fondness) Kose⟨form, -name⟩. 3 v.t., **-tt-:** (a) (treat as favourite) bevorzugen; verwöhnen; (indulge) verhätscheln; (b) (fondle) streicheln; liebkosen. 4 v.i., **-tt-** knutschen (ugs.); zärtlich sein (verhüll.)

petal /'petl/ n. Blütenblatt, das

petard /pɪ'taːd/ n. (Hist.) Petarde, die; see also **hoist** 3

peter /'piːtə(r)/ v.i. ~ **out** [allmählich] zu Ende gehen; ⟨Wasserlauf:⟩ versickern; ⟨Weg:⟩ sich verlieren; ⟨Briefwechsel:⟩ versanden; ⟨Angriff:⟩ sich totlaufen

'pet food n. Tierfutter, das

petit bourgeois /pətɪ 'bʊəʒwaː/ n., pl. **petits bourgois** /pətɪ 'bʊəʒwaː/ (usu. derog.) Kleinbürger, der; attrib. Kleinbürger-; kleinbürgerlich

petite /pə'tiːt/ adj. fem. zierlich

petition /pə'tɪʃn/ 1 n. (a) (formal written supplication) Petition, die; Eingabe, die; **get together** or **up a ~ for/against sth.** Unterschriften für/gegen etw. sammeln; (b) (Law) [förmlicher] Antrag; (for divorce) Klage, die. 2 v.t. eine Eingabe richten an (+ Akk.); ~ **sb. for sth.** jmdn. um etw. ersuchen. 3 v.i. ~ **for** ersuchen um (geh.); (present ~ for) eine Unterschriftenliste einreichen für; ~ **for divorce** die Scheidung einreichen

petrel /'petrl/ n. (Ornith.) Sturmvogel, der

petrify /'petrɪfaɪ/ 1 v.t. (a) (change into stone) versteinern lassen; **become petrified** versteinern; (b) (fig.) erstarren lassen; **be petrified with fear/shock** starr vor Angst/ Schrecken sein; **be petrified by sb./sth.** vor jmdm./etw. erstarren. 2 v.i. (turn to stone) versteinern; (fig.) erstarren

petrochemical /petrəʊ'kemɪkl/ n. Petrochemikalie, die

petrodollar /'petrəʊdɒlə(r)/ n. Petrodollar, der

petrol /'petrl/ n. (Brit.) Benzin, das; **fill up with ~:** tanken

petrol: ~ **bomb** n. (Brit.) Benzinbombe, die; ~ **can** n. (Brit.) Benzinkanister, der; ~ **cap** n. (Brit.) Tankverschluss, der; ~ **engine** n. Benzinmotor, der

petroleum /pɪ'trəʊlɪəm/ n. Erdöl, das

petroleum 'jelly n. Vaseline, die

petrol: ~ **gauge** n. (Brit.) Benzinuhr, die; ~ **pump** n. (Brit.) (a) (in ~-station) Zapfsäule, die; (b) (in car, aircraft, etc.) Benzin- od. Kraftstoffpumpe, die; ~ **station** n. (Brit.) Tankstelle, die; ~ **tank** n. (Brit.) (in car, aircraft, etc.) Benzintank, der; ~ **tanker** n. (Brit.) Benzintankwagen, der

'pet shop n. Tierhandlung, die

petticoat /'petɪkəʊt/ n. Unterrock, der

petty /'petɪ/ adj. (a) (trivial) belanglos ⟨Detail, Sorgen⟩; kleinlich ⟨Einwand, Vorschrift⟩; (b) (minor) Klein⟨staat, -unternehmer. -landwirt⟩; klein ⟨Geschäftsmann⟩; Duodez-⟨fürst, -fürstentum, -staat⟩; ~ **criminal** Kleinkriminelle, der/die; ~ **theft** Bagatelldiebstahl, der; ~ **thief** kleiner Dieb/kleine Diebin; (c) (small-minded) kleinlich; kleinkariert

petty: ~ **'cash** n. kleine Kasse; Portokasse, die; ~-**minded** adj. ⇒ **small-minded;** ~ **'officer** n. (Navy) ≈ [Ober]maat, der

petulant /'petjʊlənt/ adj. bockig

petunia /pɪ'tjuːnɪə/ n. (Bot.) Petunie, die

pew /pjuː/ n. (a) (Eccl.) Kirchenbank, die; (b) (coll.: seat) [Sitz]platz, der; **have** or **take a ~:** sich platzen (ugs. scherzh.)

pewter /'pjuːtə(r)/ n., no pl., no indef. art. (substance, vessels) Pewter, der; [Hart]zinn, das

PG abbr. (Brit. Cinemat.) **Parental Guidance** ≈ bedingt jugendfrei

PGCE abbr. (Brit.) **Postgraduate Certificate in Education**

phallic /'fælɪk/ adj. phallisch; ~ **symbol** Phallussymbol, das

phantom /'fæntəm/ **1** n. Phantom, das. **2** adj. Phantom-

Pharaoh /'feərəʊ/ n. Pharao, der

pharmaceutical /fɑːmə'sjuːtɪkl/ **1** adj. pharmazeutisch; Pharma‹industrie, -konzern, -hersteller›; ~ **chemist** Arzneimittelchemiker, der/-chemikerin, die. **2** n. in pl. Pharmaka

pharmacist /'fɑːməsɪst/ n. ▶887┃ Apotheker, der/Apothekerin, die; (in research) Pharmazeut, der/Pharmazeutin, die

pharmacology /fɑːmə'kɒlədʒɪ/ n. Pharmakologie, die

pharmacy /'fɑːməsɪ/ n. (a) no pl., no art. (preparation of drugs) Pharmazie, die; (b) (dispensary) Apotheke, die

phase /feɪz/ **1** n. Phase, die; (of project, construction, history also) Abschnitt, der; (of illness, development also) Stadium, das; **it's only** or **just a** ~ [**he's/she's going through**] das gibt sich [mit der Zeit] wieder (ugs.). **2** v.t. stufenweise durchführen
~ **'in** v.t. stufenweise einführen
~ **'out** v.t. (a) (eliminate gradually) nach und nach auflösen ‹Abteilung›; allmählich abschaffen ‹Verfahrensweise, Methode›; (b) (discontinue production of) [langsam] auslaufen lassen

Ph.D. /piːeɪtʃ'diː/ abbr. **Doctor of Philosophy** Dr. phil.

pheasant /'fezənt/ n. Fasan, der

phenomenal /fɪ'nɒmɪnl/ adj. (remarkable) phänomenal; sagenhaft (ugs.); unwahrscheinlich (ugs.) ‹Spektakel, Radau›

phenomenon /fɪ'nɒmɪnən/ n., pl. **phenomena** /fɪ'nɒmɪnə/ Phänomen, das

phew /fjuː/ int. puh

phial /'faɪəl/ n. [Medizin]fläschchen, das; Phiole, die

philanderer /fɪ'lændərə(r)/ n. Schürzenjäger, der (spött.)

philanthropic /fɪlən'θrɒpɪk/ adj. philanthropisch (geh.); menschenfreundlich; Wohltätigkeits‹organisation, -verein usw.›

philanthropist /fɪ'lænθrəpɪst/ n. Philanthrop, der/Philanthropin, die (geh.); Menschenfreund, der/Menschenfreundin, die

philanthropy /fɪ'lænθrəpɪ/ n. Philanthropie, die (geh.)

philately /fɪ'lætəlɪ/ n. Philatelie, die; Briefmarkenkunde, die

philharmonic /fɪlhɑː'mɒnɪk, fɪlɑː'mɒnɪk/ **1** adj. philharmonisch. **2** n. Philharmonie, die

Philippines /'fɪlɪpiːnz/ pr. n. pl. Philippinen Pl.

philistine /'fɪlɪstaɪn/ n. (uncultured person) [Kultur]-banause, der/-banausin, die

Phillips /'fɪlɪps/ n. ~ **screw,** (P) Kreuz[schlitz]schraube, die; ~ **screwdriver,** (P) Kreuz[schlitz]schraubenzieher, der

philology /fɪ'lɒlədʒɪ/ n. [historische] Sprachwissenschaft

philosopher /fɪ'lɒsəfə(r)/ n. Philosoph, der/Philosophin, die

philosophic /fɪlə'sɒfɪk/, **philosophical** /fɪlə'sɒfɪkl/ adjs. (a) philosophisch; (b) (resigned, calm) abgeklärt; gelassen

philosophize (philosophise) /fɪ'lɒsəfaɪz/ v.i. philosophieren (about, on über + Akk.)

philosophy /fɪ'lɒsəfɪ/ n. Philosophie, die

phlegm /flem/ n., no pl., no indef. art. (a) (Physiol.) Schleim, der; Mucus, der (Med.); (b) (coolness) stoische Ruhe; Gleichmut, der; (c) (stolidness) Phlegma, das

phlegmatic /fleg'mætɪk/ adj. (a) (cool) gleichmütig; (b) (stolid) phlegmatisch

phobia /'fəʊbɪə/ n. Phobie, die (Psychol.); [krankhafte] Angst

phobic /'fəʊbɪk/ adj. phobisch; **be** ~ **about sth.** eine Phobie (bildungsspr.) od. krankhafte Angst vor etw. haben

phoenix /'fiːnɪks/ n. (Mythol.) Phönix, der

phone /fəʊn/ (coll.) **1** n. Telefon, das; **pick up/put down the** ~: [den Hörer] abnehmen/auflegen; **by** ~: telefonisch; **speak to sb. by** ~ or **on the** ~: mit jmdm. telefonieren. **2** v.i. anrufen; **can we** ~ **from here?** können wir

von hier aus telefonieren? **3** v.t. anrufen; ~ **the office/home** im Büro/zu Hause anrufen
~ **'back** v.t. & i. (make a return ~ call [to]) zurückrufen; (make a further ~ call [to]) wieder od. nochmals anrufen
~ **'in 1** v.i. anrufen. **2** v.t. telefonisch mitteilen od. durchgeben
~ **'up** v.t. & i. anrufen

phone: ~ **book** n. Telefonbuch, das; ~ **booth** n. Telefonzelle, die; ~ **box** n. Telefonzelle, die; ~ **call** n. Anruf, der; see also **telephone call;** ~ **card** n. Telefonkarte, die; ~-**in** n. ~-in [**programme**] (Radio) Hörersendung, die; (Telev.) Sendung mit Zuschaueranrufen; ~ **number** n. Telefonnummer, die; ~**tapping** n. Anzapfen von Telefonleitungen

phonetic /fə'netɪk/ adj. phonetisch

phonetics /fə'netɪks/ n. (a) no pl. Phonetik, die; (b) no pl. (phonetic script) phonetische Umschrift; (c) constr. as pl. phonetische Angaben

phoney /'fəʊnɪ/ (coll.) **1** adj., **phonier** /'fəʊnɪə(r)/, **phoniest** /'fəʊnɪɪst/ (a) (sham) falsch; gefälscht ‹Brief, Dokument›; (b) (fictitious) falsch ‹Name›; erfunden ‹Geschichte›; (c) (fraudulent) Schein‹firma, -geschäft, -krieg›; falsch, scheinbar ‹Doktor, Diplomat, Geschäftsmann›. **2** n. (a) (person) Blender, der/Blenderin, die; **this doctor is just a** ~: dieser Arzt ist ein Scharlatan; (b) (sham) Fälschung, die

phonograph /'fəʊnəgrɑːf/ (Amer.) ⇒ **gramophone**

phony ⇒ **phoney**

phosphate /'fɒsfeɪt/ n. (Chem.) Phosphat, das

phosphorescence /fɒsfə'resns/ n. Phosphoreszenz, die

phosphorescent /fɒsfə'resnt/ adj. phosphoreszierend

phosphorus /'fɒsfərəs/ n. (Chem.) Phosphor, der

photo /'fəʊtəʊ/ n., pl. ~**s** Foto, das; see also **photograph 1**

photo: ~ **album** n. Fotoalbum, das; ~**call** n. (Brit.) Fototermin, der; ~**copier** n. Fotokopiergerät, das; ~**copy 1** n. Fotokopie, die **2** v.t. fotokopieren; ~**fit** n. Phantombild, das

photogenic /fəʊtə'dʒenɪk, fəʊtə'dʒiːnɪk/ adj. fotogen

photograph /'fəʊtəgrɑːf/ **1** n. Fotografie, die; Foto, das; **take a** ~ [**of sb./sth.**] [jmdn./etw.] fotografieren; ein Foto [von jmdm./etw.] machen. **2** v.t. & i. fotografieren

'photograph album n. Fotoalbum, das

photographer /fə'tɒgrəfə(r)/ n. ▶887┃ Fotograf, der/Fotografin, die

photographic /fəʊtə'græfɪk/ adj. fotografisch; Foto‹ausrüstung, -club, -ausstellung›

photography /fə'tɒgrəfɪ/ n., no pl., no indef. art. Fotografie, die

photo: ~ **opportunity** n. (a) ⇒ **photocall;** (b) (Brit.: opportunity for a good photograph) [Foto]motiv, das; ~**'sensitive** adj. lichtempfindlich; ~ **session,** ~ **shoot** ns. Shooting, das; ~**'synthesis** n. (Bot.) Photosynthese, die

phrase /freɪz/ **1** n. (a) (Ling.) (idiomatic expression) idiomatische Wendung; [Rede]wendung, die; **set** ~: feste [Rede]-wendung; **noun/verb** ~: Nominal-/Verbalphrase, die; (b) (brief expression) kurze Formel; see also **turn 1 j. 2** v.t. (a) (express in words) formulieren; (b) (Mus.) phrasieren

'phrase book n. Sprachführer, der

phraseology /freɪzɪ'ɒlədʒɪ/ n. Ausdrucksweise, die; (technical terms) Terminologie, die

physical /'fɪzɪkl/ **1** adj. (a) (material) physisch ‹Gewalt›; stofflich, dinglich ‹Welt, Universum›; (b) (of physics) physikalisch; **it's a** ~ **impossibility** (fig.) es ist absolut unmöglich; (c) (bodily) körperlich; physisch; **you need to take more** ~ **exercise** du brauchst mehr Bewegung; (d) (carnal, sensual) körperlich ‹Liebe›; sinnlich ‹Person, Ausstrahlung›. **2** n. ärztliche [Vorsorge]untersuchung; (for joining the army) Musterung, die

physical: ~ **edu'cation** n. Sport, der; Leibesübungen Pl. (Amtsspr.); ~ **'jerks** n. pl. (coll.) Gymnastikübungen Pl.

physically /'fɪzɪkəlɪ/ *adv.* (a) (in accordance with physical laws) physikalisch; ~ **impossible** (fig.) absolut unmöglich; (b) (relating to the body) körperlich; physisch; **be ~ sick** einen physischen Ekel empfinden; ~ **disabled** körperbehindert

physician /fɪ'zɪʃn/ *n.* ▶ 887 | Arzt, *der*/Ärztin, *die*

physicist /'fɪzɪsɪst/ *n.* ▶ 887 | Physiker, *der*/Physikerin, *die*

physics /'fɪzɪks/ *n., no pl.* Physik, *die*

physiological /fɪzɪə'lɒdʒɪkl/ *adj.* physiologisch

physiology /fɪzɪ'ɒlədʒɪ/ *n.* Physiologie, *die*

physiotherapist /fɪzɪəʊ'θerəpɪst/ *n.* ▶ 887 | Physiotherapeut, *der*/-therapeutin, *die*

physiotherapy /fɪzɪəʊ'θerəpɪ/ *n.* Physiotherapie, *die*

physique /fɪ'ziːk/ *n.* Körperbau, *der*

pianist /'piːənɪst/ *n.* Pianist, *der*/Pianistin, *die*

piano /pɪ'ænəʊ/ *n., pl.* ~**s** (Mus.) (upright) Klavier, *das;* (grand) Flügel, *der; attrib.* Klavier-; **play the ~:** Klavier spielen

piano-ac'cordion *n.* Akkordeon, *das*

piano /pɪ'ænəʊ/**:** ~ **music** *n.* Klaviermusik, *die;* (score) Klaviernoten *Pl.;* ~ **player** *n.* Klavierspieler, *der*/-spielerin, *die;* ~ **stool** *n.* Klavierschemel, *der;* ~**-tuner** *n.* Klavierstimmer, *der*/-stimmerin, *die*

piccolo /'pɪkələʊ/ *n., pl.* ~**s** (Mus.) Pikkoloflöte, *die;* Pikkolo, *das*

pick[1] /pɪk/ *n.* (a) (for breaking up hard ground, rocks, etc.) Spitzhacke, *die;* (for breaking up ice) [Eis]pickel, *der;* (b) ⇒ **toothpick;** (c) (Mus.) Plektrum, *das*

pick[2] **1** *n.* (a) (choice) Wahl, *die;* **take your ~:** du hast die Wahl; **she had the ~ of several jobs** sie konnte zwischen mehreren Jobs [aus]wählen; **have [the] first ~ of sth.** als Erster aus etw. auswählen dürfen; (b) (best part) Elite, *die;* **the ~ of the fruit** *etc.* die besten Früchte *usw.* **2** *v.t.* (a) pflücken ‹*Blumen*›; [ab]ernten, [ab]pflücken ‹*Äpfel, Trauben usw.*›; (b) (select) auswählen; aufstellen ‹*Mannschaft*›; ~ **the** *or* **a winner/the winning horse** auf den Sieger/das richtige *od.* siegreiche Pferd setzen; ~ **one's way** sich (*Dat.*) vorsichtig [s]einen Weg suchen; ~ **and choose** sich (*Dat.*) aussuchen; ~ **one's time [for sth.]** den Zeitpunkt [für etw.] festlegen; (c) (clear of flesh) ~ **the bones [clean]** ‹*Hund:*› die Knochen [sauber] abnagen; (d) ~ **sb.'s brains [about sth.]** jmdn. [über etw. (*Akk.*)] ausfragen *od.* (ugs.) ausquetschen; (e) ~ **one's nose/teeth** in der Nase bohren/in den Zähnen [herum]stochern; (f) ~ **sb.'s pocket** jmdn. bestehlen; **he had his pocket ~ed** er wurde von einem Taschendieb bestohlen; (g) ~ **a lock** ein Schloss knacken (salopp); (h) ~ **to pieces** (fig.: criticize) kein gutes Haar lassen an (+ *Dat.*) (ugs.). **3** *v.i.* ~ **and choose [too much]** [zu] wählerisch sein

~ **at** *v.t.* (a) herumstochern in (+ *Dat.*) ‹*Essen*›; (b) herumspielen an (+ *Dat.*) ‹*Pickel*›

~ **off** *v.t.* (a) /'--/ abzupfen, ablesen ‹*Haare, Fusseln*›; (b) /-'-/ (shoot one by one) [einzeln] abschießen

~ **on** *v.t.* (victimize) es abgesehen haben auf (+ *Akk.*); **why ~ on me every time?** warum immer gerade *od.* ausgerechnet ich?; ~ **on someone your own size!** leg dich doch wenigstens mit einem Gleichstarken an! (ugs.)

~ **'out** *v.t.* (a) (choose) auswählen; (for oneself) sich (*Dat.*) aussuchen ‹*Kleid, Blume*›; (b) (distinguish) ausmachen, entdecken ‹*Detail, jmds. Gesicht in der Menge*›; ~ **out sth. from sth.** etw. von etw. unterscheiden

~ **up 1** /'--/ *v.t.* (a) (take up) [in die Hand] nehmen ‹*Brief, Buch usw.*›; hochnehmen ‹*Baby*›; [wieder] aufnehmen ‹*Handarbeit*›; aufnehmen ‹*Masche*›; auffinden ‹*Fehler*›; (after dropping) aufheben ‹*Masche*›; ~ **sth. up from the table** etw. vom Tisch nehmen; ~ **a child up in one's arms** ein Kind auf den Arm nehmen; ~ **up the telephone** den [Telefon]hörer abnehmen; ~ **up the pieces** (lit. *or* fig.) die Scherben aufsammeln; (b) (collect) mitnehmen; (by arrangement) abholen (at, from von); (obtain) ~ **up sth. on the way home** etw. auf dem Nachhauseweg abholen; (become infected by) sich (*Dat.*) einfangen *od.* holen (ugs.) ‹*Virus, Grippe*›; (d) (take on board) ‹*Bus, Autofahrer:*› mitnehmen; ~ **sb. up at** *or* **from the station** jmdn. vom

Bahnhof abholen; (e) (rescue from the sea) [aus Seenot] bergen; (f) (coll.: earn) einstreichen (ugs.); (g) (coll.: make acquaintance of) aufreißen (ugs.); (h) (find and arrest) festnehmen; (i) (receive) empfangen ‹*Signal, Funkspruch usw.*›; (j) (obtain casually) sich (*Dat.*) aneignen; bekommen ‹*Sache*›; ~ **up languages easily** mühelos Sprachen lernen; (k) (obtain) auftreiben (ugs.); (l) (resume) wieder aufnehmen ‹*Erzählung, Gespräch*›; (m) (regain) wieder finden ‹*Spur, Fährte*›; wieder aufnehmen ‹*Witterung*›; (n) (pay) ~ **up the bill** *etc.* **for sth.** die Kosten *od.* die Rechnung *usw.* für etw. übernehmen. **2** /-'-/ *v.i.* ‹*Gesundheitszustand, Befinden, Stimmung, Laune, Wetter:*› sich bessern; ‹*Person:*› sich erholen; ‹*Markt, Geschäft:*› sich erholen *od.* beleben; ‹*Gewinne:*› steigen, zunehmen. **3** *v. refl.* ~ **oneself up** wieder aufstehen; (fig.) sich aufrappeln (ugs.)

'pickaxe (*Amer.:* **'pickax**) ⇒ **pick**[1] **a**

picket /'pɪkɪt/ **1** *n.* (a) (Industry) Streikposten, *der;* **mount a ~ [at** *or* **on a gate]** [an einem Tor] Streikposten aufstellen; (b) (pointed stake) Pfahl, *der.* **2** *v.t.* Streikposten aufstellen vor (+ *Dat.*) ‹*Fabrik, Büro usw.*›. **3** *v.i.* Streikposten stehen

'picket line *n.* Streikpostenkette, *die*

pickings /'pɪkɪŋz/ *n. pl.* (gleanings) Reste *Pl.;* (things stolen) [Aus]beute, *die;* (yield) Ausbeute, *die;* **it's easy ~:** das ist ein einträgliches Geschäft

pickle /'pɪkl/ **1** *n.* (a) (brine) Salzlake, *die;* (vinegar solution) Marinade, *die;* (b) *usu. in pl.* (food) [Mixed] Pickles *Pl.;* (c) (coll.: predicament) **be in a ~:** in der Klemme sitzen (ugs.); **get into a ~:** in die Klemme geraten (ugs.). **2** *v.t.* [in Essig *od.* sauer] einlegen ‹*Gurken, Zwiebeln, Eier*›; marinieren ‹*Hering*›

pick: ~**-me-up** *n.* Stärkungsmittel, *das;* **the holiday was a real ~-me-up** der Urlaub hat mir richtig gut getan; ~**pocket** *n.* Taschendieb, *der*/-diebin, *die;* ~**-up** *n.* (a) (truck) ~**-up** [**truck**/**van**] Kleinlastwagen, *der;* (b) (of record player, guitar) Tonabnehmer, *der;* (c) (coll.: person) Zufallsbekanntschaft, *die;* ~**-up point** *n.* (a) (for person) Zusteigepunkt, *der;* (b) (for goods) Warenausgabe, *die*

picnic /'pɪknɪk/ **1** *n.* (a) Picknick, *das;* **go for** *or* **on a ~:** ein Picknick machen; picknicken gehen; **have a ~:** ein Picknick machen; picknicken; (b) (coll.: easy task) Kinderspiel, *das;* **be no ~:** kein Zuckerlecken *od.* Honig[sch]lecken sein. **2** *v.i.*, **-ck-** picknicken; Picknick machen

picnic: ~ **'lunch** *n.* (a) Picknick, *das* (als Mittagessen); (b) (packed up) Lunchpaket, *das;* ~ **site** *n.* Picknickplatz, *der*

pictorial /pɪk'tɔːrɪəl/ *adj.* illustriert ‹*Bericht, Zeitschrift, Wochenmagazin*›; bildlich ‹*Darstellung*›

picture /'pɪktʃə(r)/ **1** *n.* (a) Bild, *das;* (b) (portrait) Porträt, *das;* (photograph) Porträtfoto, *das;* **have one's ~ painted** sich malen *od.* portraitieren lassen; (c) (mental image) Vorstellung, *die;* Bild, *das;* **get a ~ of sth.** sich (*Dat.*) von etw. ein Bild machen; **give a ~ of sth.** von etw. einen Eindruck vermitteln; **present a sorry ~** (fig.) ein trauriges *od.* jämmerliches Bild abgeben; **look the [very] ~ of health/innocence** wie das blühende Leben aussehen/ein Bild des Jammers sein/wie die Unschuld in Person aussehen; **get the ~** (coll.) verstehen[, worum es geht]; **I'm beginning to get the ~:** langsam *od.* allmählich verstehe *od.* (ugs.) kapiere ich; [**do you**] **get the ~?** verstehst du?; **put sb. in the ~:** jmdn. ins Bild setzen; **be in the ~** (be aware) im Bilde sein; **keep sb. in the ~:** jmdn. auf dem Laufenden halten; **come** *or* **enter into the ~:** [dabei] eine Rolle spielen; (d) (film) Film, *der;* (e) *in pl.* (Brit.: cinema) Kino, *das;* **go to the ~s** ins Kino gehen; **what's on at the ~s?** was gibt's *od.* läuft im Kino?; (f) (delightful object) **be a ~:** wunderschön *od.* (ugs.) ein Gedicht sein; **her face was a ~:** ihr Gesicht sprach Bände; **she looked a ~:** sie sah bildschön aus. **2** *v.t.* (a) (represent) abbilden; (b) (imagine) ~ [**to oneself**] sich (*Dat.*) vorstellen

picture: ~ **book 1** *n.* Bilderbuch, *das;* **2** *adj.* Bilderbuch-; ~ **frame** *n.* Bilderrahmen, *der;* ~ **gallery** *n.* Gemäldegalerie, *die;* ~ **hook** *n.* Bilderhaken, *der;* ~ **'postcard** *n.* Ansichtskarte, *die;* ~ **rail** *n.* Bilderleiste, *die*

picturesque /ˌpɪktʃə'resk/ *adj.* malerisch; pittoresk (geh.); (vivid) anschaulich, bildhaft ‹*Beschreibung, Erzählung*›

piddle /'pɪdl/ (coll.) **1** *v.i.* Pipi machen (Kinderspr.); pinkeln (ugs.). **2** *n.* **(a)** have a/do one's ~: Pipi machen (Kinderspr.); pinkeln (ugs.); **(b)** (urine) Pipi, *das* (Kinderspr.)

pidgin /'pɪdʒɪn/ *n.* Pidgin, *das*

pidgin 'English *n.* Pidgin-Englisch, *das*

pie /paɪ/ *n.* (of meat, fish, etc.) Pastete, *die;* (of fruit etc.) ≈ Obstkuchen, *der;* **as sweet/nice** etc. **as** ~ (coll.) superfreundlich (ugs.); **as easy as** ~ (coll.) kinderleicht (ugs.); **have a finger in every** ~ (coll.) überall die Finger drin haben (ugs.); **that's all just** ~ **in the sky** (coll.) das sind alles nur Luftschlösser

piece /piːs/ **1** *n.* **(a)** Stück, *das;* (of broken glass or pottery) Scherbe, *die;* (of jigsaw puzzle, crashed aircraft, etc.) Teil, *der;* (Amer.: distance) [kleines] Stück; **a** ~ **of meat** ein Stück Fleisch; **[all] in one** ~: unbeschädigt; (fig.) heil; wohlbehalten; **in** ~s (broken) kaputt (ugs.); zerbrochen; (taken apart) [in Einzelteile] zerlegt; **break into** ~s, **fall to** ~s zerbrechen; kaputtgehen (ugs.); **go [all] to** ~s (fig.) [völlig] die Fassung verlieren; **[all] of a** ~: aus einem Guss; **say one's** ~ (fig.) sagen, was man zu sagen hat; **(b)** (part of set) ~ **of furniture/clothing/luggage** Möbel-/Kleidungs-/Gepäckstück, *das;* **a three-/four-**~ **suite** eine drei-/vierteilige Sitzgarnitur; **(c)** (enclosed area) **a** ~ **of land/property** ein Stück Land/Grundstück; **(d)** (example) ~ **of luck** Glücksfall, *der;* **a fine** ~ **of pottery** eine sehr schöne Töpferarbeit; **fine** ~ **of work** hervorragende Arbeit; **he's an unpleasant** ~ **of work** (fig.) er ist ein unangenehmer Vertreter (ugs.); **(e)** (item) ~ **of news/gossip/information** Nachricht, *die*/Klatsch, *der*/Information, *die;* **(f)** (Chess) Figur, *die;* (Draughts, Backgammon, etc.) Stein, *der;* **(g)** ▶ **938** (coin) **gold** ~: Goldstück, *das;* **a 10p** ~: ein 10-Pence-Stück; eine 10-Pence-Münze; **(h)** (article in newspaper, magazine, etc.) Beitrag, *der;* **(i)** (literary or musical composition) Stück, *das;* ~ **of music** Musikstück, *das.* **2** *v.t.* ~ **together** (lit. or fig.) zusammenfügen **(from** aus)

'piecemeal *adv., adj.* stückweise

piece: ~**-rate** *n.* Akkordsatz, *der;* ~**work** *n., no pl.* Akkordarbeit, *die*

pie: ~ **chart** *n.* Kreisdiagramm, *das;* ~ **dish** *n.* Pastetenform, *die;* ~**-eyed** *adj.* (coll.) sternhagelvoll (ugs.)

pier /pɪə(r)/ *n.* Pier, *der od.* (Seemannsspr.) *die*

pierce /pɪəs/ *v.t.* **(a)** (prick) durchbohren, durchstechen ‹*Hülle, Verkleidung, Ohrläppchen*›; (penetrate) sich bohren in, [ein]dringen in (+ Akk.) ‹*Körper, Fleisch, Herz*›; **have one's ears** ~d ʒich (Dat.) Löcher in die Ohrläppchen machen od. stechen lassen; **(b)** (fig.) **the cold** ~d **him to the bone** die Kälte drang ihm bis ins Mark; **a scream** ~d **the night/silence** ein Schrei gellte durch die Nacht/ zerriss die Stille

piercing /'pɪəsɪŋ/ *adj.* durchdringend ‹*Stimme, Schrei, Blick*›; schneidend ‹*Sarkasmus, Kälte*›

piety /'paɪətɪ/ *n., no pl.* Frömmigkeit, *die*

piffling /'pɪflɪŋ/ *adj.* (coll.) lächerlich

pig /pɪɡ/ *n.* **(a)** Schwein, *das;* ~s **might fly** (iron.) da müsste schon ein Wunder geschehen; **buy a** ~ **in a poke** (fig.) die Katze im Sack kaufen; **(b)** (coll.) (greedy person) Vielfraß, *der* (ugs.); (dirty person) Ferkel, *das* (ugs.); (unpleasant person) Schwein, *das* (derb); **make a** ~ **of oneself** (overeat) sich (Dat.) den Bauch od. Wanst vollschlagen (salopp)

pigeon¹ /'pɪdʒɪn/ *n.* Taube, *die*

pigeon² *n.* (coll.: business) **be sb.'s** ~: jmdn. angehen; **that's not my** ~: das ist nicht mein Bier (ugs.)

pigeon: ~ **fancier** *n.* Taubenfreund, *der*/-freundin, *die;* ~**-hole 1** *n.* [Ablage]fach, *das;* (for letters) Postfach, *das;* **put people in** ~**-holes** (fig.) Menschen in Schubladen einordnen; **2** *v.t.* **(a)** (deposit) [in die Fächer] sortieren; **(b)** (categorize) einordnen; ~**-toed 1** *adj.* **be** ~**-toed** mit einwärts gerichteten Füßen gehen; **2** *adv.* mit einwärts gerichteten Füßen

piggy /'pɪɡɪ**:** ~**back** *n.* **give sb. a** ~back jmdn. huckepack nehmen od. tragen; ~ **bank** *n.* Sparschwein[chen], *das;* ~**-in-the-middle** *n.* **(a)** (game) Schweinchen in der Mitte; **(b)** (fig.: person) **I don't**

want to be *or* **play** ~**-in-the-middle** ich möchte nicht zwischen die Fronten geraten

pig: ~**'headed** *adj.* dickschädelig (ugs.); stur; ~**-iron** *n.* Roheisen, *das*

piglet /'pɪɡlɪt/ *n.* Ferkel, *das*

pigment /'pɪɡmənt/ **1** *n.* Pigment, *das.* **2** *v.t.* pigmentieren

pigmentation /ˌpɪɡmən'teɪʃn/ *n.* Pigmentierung, *die*

pigmy ⇒ **pygmy**

pig: ~**'s 'ear** *n.* (Brit. coll.) **make a** ~'s ear of sth. etw. verpfuschen *od.* (ugs.) vermurksen; ~**skin** *n.* (leather) Schweinsleder, *das;* ~**sty** *n.* (lit. or fig.) Schweinestall, *der;* ~**swill** *n.* Schweinefutter, *das;* (fig. coll.: food) Schweinefraß, *der* (derb); ~**tail** *n.* (plaited) Zopf, *der;* ~**tails** (worn loose, at either side of head) Rattenschwänzchen *Pl.* (ugs.)

pike¹ /paɪk/ *n., pl.* same (Zool.) Hecht, *der*

pike² *n.* (Arms Hist.) Pike, *die;* Spieß, *der*

'pikestaff *n.* **plain as a** ~: sonnenklar (ugs.)

pilchard /'pɪltʃəd/ *n.* Sardine, *die*

pile¹ /paɪl/ **1** *n.* **(a)** (heap) (of dishes, plates) Stapel, *der;* (of paper, books, letters) Stoß, *der;* (of clothes) Haufen, *der;* **(b)** (coll.: large quantity) Masse, *die* (ugs.); Haufen, *der* (ugs.); **a** ~ **of troubles/letters** eine od. jede Menge Sorgen/Briefe; **(c)** (coll.: fortune) **make a** *or* **one's** ~: ein Vermögen machen. **2** *v.t.* **(a)** (load) [voll] beladen; **(b)** (heap up) aufstapeln ‹*Holz, Steine*›; aufhäufen ‹*Abfall, Schnee*›; **(c)** ~ **furniture into a van** etc. Möbel in einen Lieferwagen usw. laden

~ **'in** *v.i.* (get in) (seen from outside) hineindrängen; (seen from inside) hereindrängen; ~ **in!** [kommt] nur od. immer herein!; quetscht euch rein! (ugs.)

~ **into** *v.t.* drängen in (+ Akk.) ‹*Stadion, Halle*›; drängen auf (+ Akk.) ‹*Platz, Wiese*›; sich zwängen in (+ Akk.) ‹*Auto, Zimmer, Zugabteil, Telefonzelle*›

~ **on to** *v.t.* **(a)** ~ **logs on to the fire** Holzscheite auf das Feuer legen; **he** ~d **food on to my plate** er häufte mir Essen auf den Teller; ~ **work on to sb.** (fig.) jmdm. Arbeit aufbürden; **(b)** (enter) drängen in (+ Akk.) ‹*Bus usw.*›

~ **'out** *v.i.* nach draußen strömen *od.* drängen

~ **'up 1** *v.i.* **(a)** (accumulate) ‹*Waren, Post, Aufträge, Arbeit, Schnee:*› sich auftürmen; ‹*Verkehr:*› sich stauen; ‹*Schulden:*› sich vermehren; ‹*Verdacht, Eindruck, Beweise:*› sich verdichten; **(b)** (crash) aufeinander auffahren. **2** *v.t.* aufstapeln ‹*Steine, Bücher usw.*›; auftürmen ‹*Haar, Frisur*›; aufhäufen ‹*Abfall, Schnee*›; (fig.) zusammentragen ‹*Beweise usw.*›; ~ **up debts** sich immer mehr verschulden

pile² *n.* (soft surface) Flor, *der*

pile³ *n.* (stake) Pfahl, *der*

'piledriver *n.* [Pfahl]ramme, *die*

piles /paɪlz/ *n. pl.* (Med.) Hämorrhoiden *Pl.*

'pile-up *n.* Massenkarambolage, *die*

pilfer /'pɪlfə(r)/ *v.t.* stehlen; klauen (ugs.)

pilgrim /'pɪlɡrɪm/ *n.* Pilger, *der*/Pilgerin, *die;* Wallfahrer, *der*/Wallfahrerin, *die*

pilgrimage /'pɪlɡrɪmɪdʒ/ *n.* Pilgerfahrt, *die;* Wallfahrt, *die*

pill /pɪl/ *n.* **(a)** Tablette, *die;* Pille, *die* (ugs.); **be on** ~s Tabletten einnehmen müssen; **(b)** (coll.: contraceptive) **the** ~ *or* **P**~: die Pille (ugs.); **be on the** ~: die Pille nehmen (ugs.); **(c)** (fig.: unpleasant thing) **swallow the** ~: die [bittere] Pille schlucken (ugs.); **sweeten the** ~: die bittere Pille versüßen (ugs.); **be a bitter** ~ **[to swallow]** eine bittere Pille *od.* bitter sein

pillage /'pɪlɪdʒ/ **1** *n.* Plünderung, *die.* **2** *v.t.* [aus]plündern

pillar /'pɪlə(r)/ *n.* **(a)** (vertical support) Säule, *die;* **from** ~ **to post** (fig.) hin und her; **(b)** (fig.: supporter) Stütze, *die*

'pillar box *n.* (Brit.) Briefkasten, *der; attrib.* ~ **red** knallrot (ugs.)

pillion /'pɪljən/ *n.* Soziussitz, *der;* Beifahrersitz, *der;* **ride** ~: als Beifahrer/Beifahrerin *od.* auf dem Soziussitz mitfahren

pillory /'pɪlərɪ/ **1** *v.t.* (lit. or fig.) an den Pranger stellen. **2** *n.* (Hist.) Pranger, *der*

pillow /'pɪləʊ/ n. [Kopf]kissen, das

pillow: ~**case,** ~**slip** ns. [Kopf]kissenbezug, der

pilot /'paɪlət/ 1 n. ▶ 887 (a) (Aeronaut.) Pilot, der/Pilotin, die; (b) (Naut.; also fig.: guide) Lotse, der. 2 adj. Pilot⟨programm, -studie, -projekt usw.⟩. 3 v.t. (a) (Aeronaut.) fliegen; (b) (Naut.; also fig.: guide) lotsen

pilot: ~ **boat** n. Lotsenboot, das; ~ **light** n. (a) (gas burner) Zündflamme, die; (b) (electric light) Kontrolllampe, die

pimento /pɪ'mentəʊ/ n., pl. ~**s** (berry) Piment, der od. das

pimp /pɪmp/ n. Zuhälter, der

pimple /'pɪmpl/ n. Pickel, der; Pustel, die; **he/his face had come out in** ~**s** er hat Pickel/Pickel im Gesicht bekommen

pimply /'pɪmplɪ/ adj. pick[e]lig

PIN /pɪn/ abbr. ~ **[number]** ⇒ **personal identification number**

pin 1 n. (a) Stecknadel, die; **you could have heard a** ~ **drop** man hätte eine Stecknadel fallen hören können; **as clean as a new** ~: blitzblank (ugs.); ~**s and needles** (fig.) Kribbeln, das; **I had** ~**s and needles in my legs** (fig.) meine Beine kribbelten; (b) (peg) Stift, der; (c) (Electr.) Kontaktstift, der; **a two-/three-**~ **plug** ein zwei-/dreipoliger Stecker; (d) **for two** ~**s I'd resign** es fehlt nicht mehr viel, dann kündige ich. 2 v.t., **-nn-**: (a) nageln ⟨Knochen, Bein, Hüfte⟩; ~ **a badge to one's lapel** sich (Dat.) ein Abzeichen ans Revers heften od. stecken; ~ **a notice on the board** einen Zettel ans schwarze Brett hängen od. (ugs.) pinnen; ~ **together** mit einer Stecknadel zusammenhalten; (Dressm.) zusammenstecken; (b) (fig.) ~ **one's ears back** die Ohren spitzen (ugs.); ~ **one's hopes on sb./sth.** seine [ganze] Hoffnung auf jmdn./etw. setzen; ~ **the blame for sth. on sb.** jmdm. die Schuld an etw. (Dat.) zuschieben; (c) (seize and hold fast) ~ **sb. against the wall** jmdn. an die Wand drängen; ~ **sb. to the ground** jmdn. auf den Boden drücken

~ **'down** v.t. (a) (fig.: bind) festlegen, festnageln (**to** or **on** auf + Akk.); **he's a difficult man to** ~ **down** man kann ihn nur schwer dazu bringen, sich [auf etwas] festzulegen; (b) (trap) festhalten; ~ **sb. down [to the ground]** jmdn. auf den Boden drücken; (c) (define exactly) ~ **sth. down in words** into. in Worte fassen; **I can't quite** ~ **it down** ich kann es nicht richtig ausmachen

~ **'up** v.t. aufhängen ⟨Bild, Foto⟩; anschlagen ⟨Bekanntmachung, Hinweis, Liste⟩; aufstecken, hochstecken ⟨Haar, Frisur⟩; heften ⟨Saum, Naht⟩

pinafore /'pɪnəfɔː(r)/ n. Schürze, die (mit Oberteil)

'pinball n. Flippern, das

pincers /'pɪnsəz/ n. pl. (a) **[pair of]** ~: Beiß- od. Kneifzange, die; (b) (of crab etc.) Schere, die

pinch /pɪntʃ/ 1 n. (a) (squeezing) Kniff, der; **give sb. a** ~: jmdn. kneifen; **give sb. a** ~ **on the arm/cheek** etc. jmdn. od. jmdm. in den Arm/die Backe usw. kneifen; (b) (fig.) **feel the** ~: knapp bei Kasse sein (ugs.); **the firm is feeling the** ~: der Firma geht es finanziell nicht gut; **at a** ~: zur Not; **if it comes to the** ~: wenn es zum Äußersten kommt; (c) (small amount) Prise, die. 2 v.t. (a) (grip tightly) kneifen; ~ **sb.'s cheek/bottom** jmdn. in die Wange/den Hintern (ugs.) kneifen; **I had to** ~ **myself** ich musste mich erst mal in den Arm kneifen (ugs.); (b) (esp. Brit. coll.: steal) klauen (salopp); (c) (coll.: arrest) sich (Dat.) schnappen (ugs.); **get** ~**ed** geschnappt werden (ugs.). 3 v.i. (a) ⟨Schuh:⟩ drücken; (b) (be niggardly) knausern (ugs.) (**on** mit)

'pincushion n. Nadelkissen, das

pine¹ /paɪn/ n. (a) (tree) Kiefer, die; (b) (wood) Kiefernholz, das

pine² v.i. (a) (languish) sich [vor Kummer] verzehren (geh.) (**over, about** wegen); (b) (long eagerly) ~ **for sb./sth.** sich nach jmdm./etw. sehnen od. (geh.) verzehren

~ **a'way** v.i. dahinkümmern

pineapple /'paɪnæpl/ n. Ananas, die

pine: ~ **cone** n. Kiefernzapfen, der; ~**-needle** n. Kiefernnadel, die; ~ **tree** n. Kiefer, die

ping-pong (Amer.: **Ping-Pong, P**) /'pɪŋpɒŋ/ n. Tischtennis, das

ping-pong: ~ **ball** n. Tischtennisball, der; Pingpongball, der (ugs. veralt.); ~ **table** n. Tischtennisplatte, die

pinion /'pɪnjən/ n. (cogwheel) Ritzel, das (Technik); kleines Zahnrad

pink /pɪŋk/ 1 n. (a) Rosa, das; (b) **in the** ~ **of condition** in hervorragendem Zustand; **be in the** ~ (coll.) kerngesund sein; (c) (Bot.) [Garten]nelke, die. 2 adj. rosa ⟨Kleid, Wand⟩; rosig, rosarot ⟨Himmel, Gesicht, Haut, Wangen⟩

pinkie /'pɪŋkɪ/ n. (Amer., Scot.) kleiner Finger

pinking /'pɪŋkɪŋ/: ~ **scissors,** ~ **shears** ns. pl. **[pair of]** ~ **scissors** or **shears** Zackenschere, die

'pin money n. (for private expenditure) Taschengeld, das; (coll.: small sum) Taschen- od. Trinkgeld, das (ugs.)

pinnacle /'pɪnəkl/ n. (a) (Archit.) Fiale, die; (b) (natural peak) Gipfel, der; (c) (fig.: climax) Höhepunkt, der; Gipfel, der

pinny /'pɪnɪ/ n. (child lang./coll.) Schürze, die

pin: ~**point** v.t. (locate, define) genau bestimmen; (determine) genau festlegen; ~**prick** n. Nadelstich, der; (fig.) [harmlose] Stichelei; ~**stripe** n. Nadelstreifen, der; (suit) Nadelstreifenanzug, der; attrib. Nadelstreifen⟨anzug, -kostüm⟩

pint /paɪnt/ n. ▶ 1193 (a) (one-eighth of a gallon) Pint, das; ≈ halber Liter; (b) (Brit.: quantity of liquid) Pint, das; **a** ~ **of milk/beer** ≈ ein halber Liter Milch/Bier; **have a** ~: ein Bier trinken

'pin-up n. (a) (picture) (of beautiful girl) Pin-up[-Foto], das; (esp. of sports, film or pop star) Starfoto, das; (b) (beautiful girl in photograph) Pin-up-Girl, das

pioneer /paɪə'nɪə(r)/ 1 n. Pionier, der; (fig. also) Wegbereiter, der/Wegbereiterin, die. 2 v.t. Pionierarbeit leisten für ⟨Entwicklung, Technologie, Nutzung⟩

pious /'paɪəs/ adj. (a) (devout) fromm; (b) (hypocritically virtuous) heuchlerisch; scheinheilig

pip¹ /pɪp/ n. (seed) Kern, der

pip² n. (a) (on cards, dominoes, etc.) Auge, das; Punkt, der; (b) (Brit. Mil.) Stern, der; (c) (on radar screen) Echosignal, das

pip³ n. (Brit.: sound) [kurzer] Piepston; (time signal also) Zeitzeichen, das; **when the** ~**s go** (during telephone call) wenn die Piepstöne anzeigen, dass eine neue Münze eingeworfen werden muss

pip⁴ n. (coll.) **give sb. the** ~: jmdn. auf den Wecker gehen (ugs.)

pip⁵ v.t., **-pp-** (Brit.) (defeat) besiegen; schlagen; ~ **sb. at the post** (coll.) jmdn. im Ziel abfangen; (fig.) jmdn. im letzten Moment ausbooten (ugs.)

pipe /paɪp/ 1 n. (a) (tube) Rohr, das; (b) (Mus.) Pfeife, die; (flute) Flöte, die; (in organ) [Orgel]pfeife, die; (c) in pl. (bagpipes) Dudelsack, der; (d) **[tobacco-]**~: [Tabaks]pfeife, die; **put that in your** ~ **and smoke it** schreib dir das hinter die Ohren (ugs.). 2 v.t. (a) (convey by ~) [durch ein Rohr/durch Rohre] leiten; **be** ~**d** ⟨Öl, Wasser:⟩ [durch eine Rohrleitung] fließen; ⟨Gas:⟩ [durch eine Rohrleitung] strömen; (b) ~**d music** Hintergrundmusik, die; (c) (utter shrilly) ⟨Vogel:⟩ piepsen, pfeifen; ⟨Kind:⟩ piepsen; (d) (Cookery) spritzen. 3 v.i. (a) (whistle) pfeifen; (b) ⟨Stimme:⟩ hell klingen, schrillen; ⟨Person:⟩ piepsen, mit heller od. schriller Stimme sprechen; ⟨Vogel:⟩ pfeifen, piepsen

~ **'down** v.i. (coll.: be less noisy) ruhig sein

~ **'up** v.i. (begin to speak) sich vernehmen lassen

pipe: ~**-cleaner** n. Pfeifenreiniger, der; ~ **dream** n. Wunschtraum, der; ~**line** n. Pipeline, die; **in the** ~**line** (fig.) in Vorbereitung

piper /'paɪpə(r)/ n. (a) Pfeifer, der/Pfeiferin, die; **he who pays the** ~ **calls the tune** (prov.) wes Brot ich ess', des Lied ich sing' (Spr.); (b) (bagpiper) Dudelsackspieler, der/-spielerin, die

pipette /pɪ'pet/ n. (Chem.) Pipette, die

piping /'paɪpɪŋ/ n. (a) (system of pipes) Rohrleitungssystem, das; (quantity of pipes) Rohrmaterial, das; (c) (Sewing) Paspel, die; (d) (Cookery) Spritzgussverzierung, die

piping 'hot adj. kochendheiß

piquancy /'piːkənsɪ/ n. (a) (sharpness) Würze, die; (b) (fig.) Pikanterie, die (geh.)

piquant /'piːkənt, 'piːkɑːnt/ adj. (lit. or fig.) pikant

pique /piːk/ **1** v.t. **(a)** (irritate) verärgern; **be ~d at sb./ sth.** über jmdn./etw. verärgert sein; **(b)** (wound the pride of) kränken; **be ~d at sth.** wegen etw. gekränkt sein. **2** n. **in a [fit of] ~:** verstimmt; eingeschnappt (ugs.)

piracy /'paɪrəsɪ/ n. Seeräuberei, die; Piraterie, die; (fig.) Piraterie, die

piranha /pɪˈrɑːnə, pɪˈrɑːnjə/ n. (Zool.) Piranha, der

pirate /'paɪrət/ **1** n. **(a)** Pirat, der; Seeräuber, der; (fig.) Schwindler, der; **(b)** (Radio) [Rundfunk]pirat, der; attrib. **~ radio station** Piratensender, der. **2** v.t. ausplündern ‹Schiff›; rauben ‹Waren usw.›; (fig.) illegal nachdrucken ‹Buch›; illegal pressen ‹Schallplatte›; illegal vervielfältigen ‹Videoband›; **~d edition** Raubdruck, der

pirouette /pɪrʊˈet/ **1** n. Pirouette, die. **2** v.i. pirouettieren

Pisces /'paɪsiːz/ n., pl. same (Astrol., Astron.) Fische Pl.

piss /pɪs/ (coarse) **1** n. **(a)** (urine) Pisse, die (derb); **(b)** have **a/go for a ~:** pissen/pissen gehen (derb). **2** v.i. pissen (derb)

~ 'off (Brit. sl.) **1** v.i. sich verpissen (salopp). **2** v.t. ankotzen (derb)

pissed /pɪst/ adj. (sl.) voll (salopp); besoffen (derb)

pissed 'off adj. (sl.) stocksauer (salopp) (**with** auf + Akk.); **get ~ [with sb./sth.]** langsam die Schnauze voll haben [von jmdm./etw.] (salopp)

'piss-up n. (sl.) Sauferei, die (salopp)

pistachio /pɪˈstɑːʃɪəʊ/ n., pl. **~s** Pistazie, die

pistil /'pɪstɪl/ n. (Bot.) Stempel, der

pistol /'pɪstl/ n. Pistole, die; **hold a ~ to sb.'s head** jmdm. die Pistole an die Schläfe od. den Kopf setzen; (fig.) jmdm. die Pistole auf die Brust setzen

'pistol shot n. Pistolenschuss, der

piston /'pɪstn/ n. Kolben, der

piston: ~ engine n. Kolbenmotor, der; **~ rod** n. Kolbenstange, die; Pleuelstange, die

pit /pɪt/ **1** n. **(a)** (hole, mine) Grube, die; (natural) Vertiefung, die; (as trap) Fallgrube, die; **[work] down the ~:** unter Tage [arbeiten] (Bergmannsspr.); **(b) ~ of the stomach** Magengrube, die; **(c)** (Brit. Theatre) (for audience) Parkett, das; **(d)** (Motor racing) Box, die. **2** v.t., **-tt-: (a)** (set to fight) kämpfen lassen; **(b)** (fig.: match) **~ sth. against sth.** etw. gegen etw. einsetzen; **~ one's wits/skill** etc. **against sth.** seinen Verstand/sein Können usw. an etw. (Dat.) messen; **(c)** be **~ted** (have **~s**) voller Vertiefungen sein

'pit-bull terrier n. Pitbullterrier, der

pitch¹ /pɪtʃ/ **1** n. **(a)** (Brit.: usual place) [Stand]platz, der; (stand) Stand, der; (Sport: playing area) Feld, das; Platz, der; **(b)** (Mus.) Tonhöhe, die; (of voice) Stimmlage, die; (of instrument) Tonlage, die; **(c)** (slope) Neigung, die; **(d)** (fig.: degree, intensity) **reach such a ~ that …:** sich so zuspitzen, dass… **2** v.t. **(a)** (erect) aufschlagen ‹Zelt›; **~ camp** ein/das Lager aufschlagen; **(b)** (throw) werfen; **the horse ~ed its rider over its head** das Pferd warf den Reiter vornüber; **~ sb. out of sth.** jmdn. aus etw. hinauswerfen; **(c)** (Mus.) anstimmen ‹Melodie›; stimmen ‹Instrument›; **(d)** (fig.) **~ a programme at a particular level** ein Programm auf ein bestimmtes Niveau abstimmen; **our expectations were ~ed too high** unsere Erwartungen waren zu hoch gesteckt; **(e) ~ed battle** offene [Feld]schlacht. **3** v.i. (fall) [kopfüber] stürzen ‹Schiff, Fahrzeug, Flugzeug›; mit einem Ruck nach vorn kippen; (repeatedly) ‹Schiff:› stampfen; **~ forward** vornüberstürzen

~ 'in v.i. (coll.) loslegen (ugs.); (begin) sich daranmachen (ugs.); **~ in [and or to help]** zupacken (ugs.) [und helfen]; mit anpacken

~ into v.t. (coll.) herfallen über (+ Akk.); sich hermachen über (+ Akk.) (ugs.) ‹Essen›

pitch² n. (substance) Pech, das; **as black as ~:** pechschwarz

pitch: ~-'black adj. pechschwarz; stockdunkel (ugs.); **~-'dark** adj. stockdunkel (ugs.); pechfinster; **~-'darkness** n. tiefste Finsternis

pitched 'roof n. schräges Dach

pitcher¹ /'pɪtʃə(r)/ n. [Henkel]krug, der

pitcher² n. (Baseball) Werfer, der; Pitcher, der

'pitchfork 1 n. (for hay) Heugabel, die; (for manure) Mistgabel, die. **2** v.t. gabeln; **~ sb. into sth.** (fig.) jmdn. in etw. ‹Akk.› katapultieren

piteous /'pɪtɪəs/ adj. erbärmlich; (causing pity) mitleiderregend; kläglich ‹Schrei›

'pitfall n. Fallstrick, der; (risk) Gefahr, die

pith /pɪθ/ n. **(a)** (in plant) Mark, das; (of orange etc.) weiße Haut; **(b)** (fig.: essential part) Kern, der

'pithead n. ≈ Zechengelände, das

pithy /'pɪθɪ/ adj. **(a)** markhaltig; reich an Mark nicht attr.; ‹Orange usw.› mit dicker weißer Haut; **(b)** (fig.: full of meaning) prägnant

pitiable /'pɪtɪəbl/ ⇒ **pitiful**

pitiful /'pɪtɪfl/ adj. **(a)** Mitleid erregend; **(b)** (contemptible) jämmerlich (abwertend)

pitifully /'pɪtɪfəlɪ/ adv. erbärmlich; jämmerlich

pitiless /'pɪtɪlɪs/ adj., **pitilessly** /'pɪtɪlɪslɪ/ adv. unbarmherzig (auch fig.); erbarmungslos

pittance /'pɪtəns/ n. Hungerlohn, der (abwertend); (small allowance) [magere] Beihilfe

pity /'pɪtɪ/ **1** n. **(a)** (sorrow) Mitleid, das; Mitgefühl, das; **feel ~ for sb.** Mitgefühl für jmdn. od. mit jmdm. empfinden; **have/take ~ on sb.** Erbarmen mit jmdm. haben; **for ~'s sake!** um Gottes od. Himmels willen!; **(b)** (cause for regret) **[what a] ~!** [wie] schade!; **it's a ~ about sb./sth.** es ist ein Jammer mit jmdm./etw. (ugs.); **the ~ of it is [that] …:** das Traurige daran ist, dass …; **more's the ~:** leider! **2** v.t. bedauern; bemitleiden; **I ~ you** (also contemptuously) du tust mir Leid

pitying /'pɪtɪɪŋ/ adj., **pityingly** /'pɪtɪɪŋlɪ/ adv. mitleidig

pivot /'pɪvət/ **1** n. **(a)** [Dreh]zapfen, der; **(b)** (fig.) [Drehund] Angelpunkt, der; (crucial point) springender Punkt. **2** v.i. sich drehen; **~ on sth.** (fig.) von etw. abhängen

pivotal /'pɪvətl/ adj. (fig.: crucial) zentral; **~ figure** Schlüsselfigur, die

pixel /'pɪksl/ n. Pixel, das

pixie /'pɪksɪ/ n. Kobold, der

pizza /'piːtsə/ n. Pizza, die

pl. abbr. **plural** Pl.

placard /'plækɑːd/ n. Plakat, das

placate /plə'keɪt/ v.t. beschwichtigen, besänftigen ‹Person›

place /pleɪs/ **1** n. **(a)** Ort, der; (spot) Stelle, die; Platz, der; **I left it in a safe ~:** ich habe es an einem sicheren Ort gelassen; **it was still in the same ~:** es war noch an derselben Stelle od. am selben Platz; **a ~ in the queue** ein Platz in der Schlange; **all over the ~:** überall; (coll.: in a mess) ganz durcheinander (ugs.); **from ~ to ~:** von Ort zu Ort; **in ~s** hier und da; (in parts) stellenweise; **find a ~ in sth.** (be included) in etw. (Akk.) eingehen; see also **take 1** d; **(b)** (fig.: rank, position) Stellung, die; **put sb. in his ~:** jmdn. in seine Schranken weisen; **know one's ~:** wissen, was sich für einen gehört; **it's not my ~ to do that** es kommt mir nicht zu, das zu tun; **(c)** (building or area for specific purpose) **a [good] ~ to park/to eat** ein [guter] Platz zum Parken/eine [gute] Stelle zum Halten; **do you know a good/cheap ~ to eat?** weißt du, wo man gut/billig essen kann?; **~ of residence** Wohnort, der; **~ of work** Arbeitsplatz, der; Arbeitsstätte, die; **~ of worship** Andachtsort, der; **(d)** (country, town) Ort, der; **Paris/Italy is a great ~:** Paris ist eine tolle Stadt/Italien ist ein tolles Land (ugs.); **~ of birth** Geburtsort, der; **'go ~s** (coll.) herumkommen (ugs.); (fig.) es [im Leben] zu was bringen (ugs.); **(e)** (coll.: premises) Bude, die (ugs.); (hotel, restaurant, etc.) Laden, der (ugs.); **she is at his/John's ~:** sie ist bei ihm/John; **[shall we go to] your ~ or mine?** [gehen wir] zu dir oder zu mir?; **(f)** (seat etc.) [Sitz]platz, der; **change ~s [with sb.]** [mit jmdm.] die Plätze tauschen; (fig.) [mit jmdm.] tauschen; **lay a/another ~:** ein/noch ein Gedeck auflegen; **is this anyone's ~?** ist dieser Platz noch frei?; **(g)** (in book etc.) Stelle, die; **lose one's ~:** die Seite verschlagen od. verblättern; (on page) nicht mehr wissen, an welcher Stelle man ist; **(h)**

(step, stage) **in the first** ∼: zuerst; **why didn't you say so in the first** ∼? warum hast du das nicht gleich gesagt?; **in the first/second/third** *etc.* ∼: erstens/zweitens/drittens *usw.;* **(i)** (proper ∼) Platz, *der;* **everything fell into** ∼ (fig.) alles wurde klar; **a woman's** ∼ **is in the home** eine Frau gehört ins Haus; **the clamp is properly in** ∼: die Klammer sitzt richtig; **into** ∼: fest⟨*nageln, -schrauben, -kleben*⟩; **out of** ∼: nicht am richtigen Platz; (several things) in Unordnung; (fig.) fehl am Platz; **take the** ∼ **of sb.** jmds. Platz einnehmen; **(j)** (position in competition) Platz, *der;* **take first/second** *etc.* ∼: den ersten/zweiten *usw.* Platz belegen; **(k)** (job, position, etc.) Stelle, *die;* (as pupil; in team, crew) Platz, *der;* **(l)** (personal situation) **what would you do in my** ∼? was würden Sie an meiner Stelle tun?; **put yourself in my** ∼: versetzen Sie sich in meine Lage. **2** *v.t.* **(a)** (put) (vertically) stellen; (horizontally) legen; ∼ **in position** richtig hinstellen/hinlegen; ∼ **an announcement/advertisement in a paper** eine Anzeige/ein Inserat in eine Zeitung setzen; ∼ **a bet** auf ein Pferd wetten; **(b)** (fig.) ∼ **one's trust in sb./sth.** sein Vertrauen auf *od.* in jmdn./etw. setzen; **he** ∼**s happiness above all other things** Glück steht für ihn an erster Stelle; **(c)** *in p.p.* (situated) gelegen; **a badly** ∼**d window** ein Fenster an einer ungünstigen Stelle; **we are well** ∼**d for buses/shops** *etc.* wir haben es nicht weit zur Bushaltestelle/zum Einkaufen *usw.;* **how are you** ∼**d for time/money?** (coll.) wie steht's mit deiner Zeit/deinem Geld?; **(d)** (find situation or home for) unterbringen **(with** bei); ∼ **sb. under sb.'s care** jmdn. in jmds. Obhut geben; **(e)** (class, identify) einordnen; einstufen; **I've seen him before but I can't** ∼ **him** ich habe ihn schon einmal gesehen, aber ich weiß nicht, wo ich ihn unterbringen soll; **be** ∼**d second in the race** den zweiten Platz belegen

place: ∼ **card** *n.* Tischkarte, *die;* ∼ **mat** *n.* Set, *der od. das;* ∼ **name** *n.* Ortsname, *der*

placenta /pləˈsentə/ *n., pl.* ∼**e** /pləˈsentiː/ *or* ∼**s** (Anat., Zool.) Plazenta, *die* (fachspr.); Mutterkuchen, *der*

placid /ˈplæsɪd/ *adj.* ruhig, gelassen ⟨*Person*⟩; ruhig ⟨*Wasser, Wesensart*⟩; (peaceable) friedlich, friedfertig ⟨*Person*⟩

plagiarise ⇒ **plagiarize**

plagiarism /ˈpleɪdʒərɪzm/ *n.* Plagiat, *das*

plagiarize /ˈpleɪdʒəraɪz/ *v.t.* plagiieren

plague /pleɪɡ/ **1** *n.* **(a)** (esp. Hist.: epidemic) Seuche, *die;* **the** ∼ (bubonic) die Pest; **avoid/hate sb./sth. like the** ∼: jmdn./etw. wie die Pest meiden/hassen; **(b)** (infestation) ∼ **of rats** Rattenplage, *die.* **2** *v.t.* **(a)** (afflict) plagen; quälen; ∼**d with** *or* **by sth.** von etw. geplagt; **(b)** (bother) ∼ **sb.** **[with sth.]** jmdm. [mit etw.] auf die Nerven gehen (ugs.)

plaice /pleɪs/ *n., pl. same* (Zool.) Scholle, *die*

plaid /plæd/ **1** *n.* Plaid, *das od. der.* **2** *adj.* [bunt]kariert

plain /pleɪn/ **1** *adj.* **(a)** (clear) klar; (obvious) offensichtlich; **make sth.** ∼ **[to sb.]** [jmdm.] etw. klarmachen; **make it** ∼ **that …:** klarstellen, dass …; **the reason is** ∼ **[to see]** der Grund liegt auf der Hand; *see also* **English 2 a; pikestaff; (b)** (frank, straightforward) ehrlich; offen; schlicht ⟨*Wahrheit*⟩; **be** ∼ **with sb.** mit jmdm. *od.* jmdm. gegenüber offen sein; **be [all]** ∼ **sailing** (fig.) [ganz] einfach sein; **(c)** (unsophisticated) einfach; schlicht ⟨*Kleidung, Frisur*⟩; klar ⟨*Wasser*⟩; einfach, bescheiden ⟨*Lebensstil*⟩; (not plain) unliniert ⟨*Papier*⟩; (not patterned) ⟨*Stoff*⟩ ohne Muster; **(d)** (unattractive) wenig attraktiv ⟨*Mädchen*⟩; **(e)** (sheer) rein; **that's** ∼ **bad manners** das ist einfach schlechtes Benehmen. **2** *adv.* **(a)** (clearly) deutlich; **(b)** (simply) einfach. **3** *n.* **(a)** Ebene, *die;* **(b)** (Knitting) rechte Masche

plain: ∼ **'chocolate** *n.* halbbittere Schokolade; ∼ **'clothes** *n. pl.* **in** ∼ **clothes** in Zivil

plainly /ˈpleɪnlɪ/ *adv.* **(a)** (clearly) deutlich; verständlich ⟨*erklären*⟩; **(b)** (obviously) offensichtlich; (undoubtedly) eindeutig; **(c)** (frankly) offen; **(d)** (simply, unpretentiously) einfach; schlicht

plainness /ˈpleɪnnɪs/ *n., no pl.* **(a)** (clearness) Klarheit, *die;* **(b)** (frankness) Offenheit, *die;* **(c)** (simplicity) Schlichtheit, *die;* **(d)** (ugliness) Unattraktivität, *die;* Unansehnlichkeit, *die*

plain-'spoken *adj.* freimütig

plaintiff /ˈpleɪntɪf/ *n.* (Law) Kläger, *der*/Klägerin, *die*

plaintive /ˈpleɪntɪv/ *adj.* klagend; traurig, leidend ⟨*Blick*⟩

plait /plæt/ **1** *n.* (of hair) Zopf, *der;* (of straw, ribbon, etc.) geflochtenes Band. **2** *v.t.* flechten

plan /plæn/ **1** *n.* Plan, *der;* (for story etc.) Konzept, *das;* Entwurf, *der;* (intention) Absicht, *die;* ∼ **of action** Aktionsprogramm, *das;* **have great** ∼**s for sb.** große Pläne mit jmdm. haben; **what are your** ∼**s for tomorrow?** was hast du morgen vor?; **[go] according to** ∼: nach Plan [gehen]; planmäßig [verlaufen *od.* laufen]. **2** *v.t.,* **-nn-** planen; (design) entwerfen ⟨*Gebäude, Maschine*⟩; ∼ **to do sth.** planen *od.* vorhaben, etw. zu tun. **3** *v.i.,* **-nn-** planen; ∼ **for sth.** Pläne für etw. machen; ∼ **on doing sth.** (coll.) vorhaben, etw. zu tun

plane¹ /pleɪn/ *n.* ∼ **[tree]** Platane, *die*

plane² **1** *n.* (tool) Hobel, *der.* **2** *v.t.* hobeln

plane³ *n.* **(a)** (Geom.) Ebene, *die;* (flat surface) Fläche, *die;* **(b)** (fig.) Ebene, *die;* (moral, intellectual) Niveau, *das;* **(c)** (aircraft) Flugzeug, *das;* Maschine, *die* (ugs.)

planet /ˈplænɪt/ *n.* Planet, *der*

planetarium /plænɪˈteərɪəm/ *n., pl.* ∼**s** *or* **planetaria** /plænɪˈteərɪə/ Planetarium, *das*

plank /plæŋk/ *n.* (piece of timber) Brett, *das;* (thicker) Bohle, *die;* (on ship) Planke, *die;* **be as thick as two [short]** ∼**s** (coll.) dumm wie Bohnenstroh sein (ugs.)

plankton /ˈplæŋktn/ *n.* (Biol.) Plankton, *das*

planner /ˈplænə(r)/ *n.* Planer, *der*/Planerin, *die*

planning /ˈplænɪŋ/ *n.* Planen, *das;* Planung, *die;* **at the** ∼ **stage** im Planungsstadium; ∼ **permission** Baugenehmigung, *die*

plant /plɑːnt/ **1** *n.* **(a)** (Bot.) Pflanze, *die;* **(b)** (machinery) *no indef. art.* Maschinen *Pl.;* (single complex) Anlage, *die;* **(c)** (factory) Fabrik, *die;* Werk, *das;* **(d)** (coll.: undercover agent) Spitzel, *der;* **(e)** (coll.: thing concealed) Untergeschobene, *das.* **2** *v.t.* **(a)** pflanzen; aussäen ⟨*Samen*⟩; anlegen ⟨*Garten usw.*⟩; anpflanzen ⟨*Beet*⟩; bepflanzen ⟨*Land*⟩; ∼ **a field with barley** auf einem Feld Gerste anpflanzen; **(b)** (fix) setzen; ∼ **oneself** sich hinstellen *od.* (ugs.) aufpflanzen; **(c)** (in mind) ∼ **an idea** *etc.* **in sb.'s mind/in sb.** jmdm. eine Idee *usw.* einimpfen (ugs.) *od.* (geh.) einpflanzen; **(d)** (coll.: conceal) anbringen ⟨*Wanze*⟩; legen ⟨*Bombe*⟩; ∼ **sth. on sb.** jmdm. etw. unterschieben; **(e)** (station as spy etc.) einschmuggeln

∼ **'out** *v.t.* auspflanzen ⟨*Setzlinge*⟩

plantation /plænˈteɪʃn, plɑːnˈteɪʃn/ *n.* **(a)** (estate) Pflanzung, *die;* Plantage, *die;* **(b)** (group of plants) Anpflanzung, *die*

planter /ˈplɑːntə(r)/ *n.* **(a)** Pflanzer, *der*/Pflanzerin, *die;* **(b)** (container) Pflanzgefäß, *das*

plant: ∼ **food** *n.* Pflanzennahrung, *die;* (naturally occurring) Nährstoffe *Pl.;* ∼ **hire** *n.* Baumaschinenverleih, *der;* ∼ **life** *n.* pflanzliches Leben; (all plant species) Pflanzenwelt, *die*

plaque /plɑːk, plæk/ *n.* **(a)** (ornamental tablet) [Schmuck]platte, *die;* (commemorating sb.) [Gedenk]tafel, *die;* Plakette, *die* (Kunstwiss.); **(b)** (Dent.) Plaque, *die* (fachspr.); [weißer] Zahnbelag

plasma /ˈplæzmə/ *n.* Plasma, *das*

plaster /ˈplɑːstə(r)/ **1** *n.* **(a)** (for walls etc.) [Ver]putz, *der;* **(b)** ∼ **[of Paris]** Gips, *der;* **have one's leg in** ∼: ein Gipsbein *od.* sein Bein in Gips haben; **put sb.'s leg in** ∼: jmds. Bein in Gips legen; **(c)** ⇒ **sticking plaster. 2** *v.t.* **(a)** verputzen ⟨*Wand*⟩; vergipsen, zugipsen ⟨*Loch, Riß*⟩; **(b)** (daub) ∼ **sth. on sth.** etw. dick auf etw. (*Akk.*) auftragen; ∼**ed with mud** mit Schlamm bedeckt; **(c)** (stick on) kleistern (ugs.) ⟨*Plakate, Briefmarken*⟩ **(on** auf + *Akk.*)

plaster: ∼**board** *n.* Gipsplatte, *die;* ∼ **cast** *n.* **(a)** (model in plaster) Gipsabguss *od.* -abdruck, *der;* **(b)** (Med.) Gipsverband, *der*

plastered /ˈplɑːstəd/ *pred. adj.* (sl.: drunk) voll (salopp); **get** ∼: sich voll laufen lassen (salopp)

plasterer /ˈplɑːstərə(r)/ *n.* ▶ 887 Gipser, *der*

plastic /ˈplæstɪk/ **1** *n.* **(a)** Plastik, *das;* Kunststoff, *der; in pl., attrib.* Plastik-; Kunststoff-; **(b)** (coll.: credit cards etc.)

Plastikgeld, *das.* **2** *adj.* **(a)** (made of ~) aus Plastik *od.* Kunststoff *nachgestellt;* ~ **bag** Plastiktüte, *die;* ~ **money** Plastikgeld, *das;* **(b)** (produced by moulding) plastisch; **(c)** (malleable, lit. or fig.) formbar; bildbar; **(d)** ▶ **887|** the ~ **arts** die Plastik; (including painting etc.) die bildende Kunst; ~ **surgeon** Facharzt für plastische Chirurgie; ~ **surgery** plastische Chirurgie

plastic 'bullet *n.* Plastikgeschoss, *das*

Plasticine, (P) /'plæstɪsiːn/ *n.* Plastilin, *das*

plate /pleɪt/ **1** *n.* **(a)** (for food) Teller, *der;* (large ~ for serving food) Platte, *die;* **a** ~ **of soup/sandwiches** ein Teller Suppe/belegte Brote *od.* mit belegten Broten; **have sth. handed to one on a** ~ (fig. coll.) etw. auf silbernem Tablett serviert bekommen (fig.); **have a lot on one's** ~ (fig. coll.) viel am Hals *od.* um die Ohren haben (ugs.); **(b)** (metal ~ with name etc.) Schild, *das;* **[number]** ~: Nummernschild, *das;* **(c)** *no pl., no indef. art.* (Brit.: tableware) [Tafel]silber, *das;* **(d)** (for engraving, printing) Platte, *die;* (impression) Stich, *der;* (illustration) [Bild]tafel, *die;* **(e)** (Dent.) Gaumenplatte, *die;* (coll.: denture) [Zahn]prothese, *die;* Gebiss, *das.* **2** *v.t.* **(a)** (coat) plattieren; ~ **sth. [with gold/silver/chromium]** etw. vergolden/versilbern/verchromen; **(b)** panzern ‹*Schiff*›

plateau /'plætəʊ/ *n., pl.* ~**x** /'plætəʊz/ *or* ~**s** Hochebene, *die;* Plateau, *das*

plateful /'pleɪtfʊl/ *n.* Teller, *der;* **a** ~ **of rice** ein Teller [voll] Reis; **I've already had two** ~**s** ich habe schon zwei Teller voll gegessen; **I've had a** ~ (fig. coll.) ich habe die Nase voll davon (ugs.)

plate: ~ **'glass** *n.* Flachglas, *das;* ~ **rack** *n.* (Brit.) Abtropfständer, *der;* Geschirrablage, *die*

platform /'plætfɔːm/ *n.* **(a)** (Brit. Railw.) Bahnsteig, *der;* **the train leaves from/will arrive at** ~ **4** der Zug fährt von Gleis 4 ab/in Gleis 4 ein; **(b)** (stage) Podium, *das;* **(c)** (Polit.) Wahlplattform, *die*

'platform ticket *n.* (Brit.) Bahnsteigkarte, *die*

plating /'pleɪtɪŋ/ *n.* (process) Plattierung, *die;* (coat) Plattierung, *die;* Auflage, *die*

platinum /'plætɪnəm/ *n.* Platin, *das*

platinum 'blonde 1 *n.* Platinblonde, *die.* **2** *adj.* platinblond

platitude /'plætɪtjuːd/ *n.* **(a)** (trite remark) Plattitüde, *die* (geh.); Gemeinplatz, *der;* **(b)** *no pl.* (triteness) Banalität, *die*

platonic /pləˈtɒnɪk/ *adj.* platonisch ‹*Liebe, Freundschaft*›

platoon /pləˈtuːn/ *n.* (Mil.) Zug, *der*

plausible /'plɔːzɪbl/ *adj.* plausibel; einleuchtend; glaubwürdig ‹*Person*›

play /pleɪ/ **1** *n.* **(a)** (Theatre) [Theater]stück, *das;* **put on a** ~: ein Stück aufführen; **(b)** (recreation) Spielen, *das;* Spiel, *das;* **at** ~: beim Spielen; **say/do sth. in** ~: etw. aus *od.* im *od.* zum Spaß sagen/tun; ~ **[up]on words** Wortspiel, *das;* **(c)** (Sport) Spiel, *das;* (Amer.: manœuvre) Spielzug, *der;* **a good piece of** ~: ein guter Spielzug; **be in/out of** ~ ‹*Ball:*› im Spiel/aus [dem Spiel] sein; **make a** ~ **for sb./ sth.** (fig. coll.) hinter jmdm./etw. her sein (ugs.); es auf jmdn./ etw. abgesehen haben; **(d) come into** ~, **be brought** *or* **called into** ~: ins Spiel kommen; **make [great]** ~ **with sth.** viel Wesen um etw. machen; **(e)** (freedom of movement) Spiel, *das* (Technik); (fig.) Spielraum, *der;* **give full** ~ **to one's emotions/imagination** *etc.* (fig.) seinen Gefühlen/ seiner Fantasie *usw.* freien Lauf lassen; **(f)** (rapid movement) **the** ~ **of light on water** das Spiel des Lichts auf Wasser. **2** *v.i.* **(a)** spielen; ~ **for money** um Geld spielen; **have no one to** ~ **with** niemanden zum Spielen haben; ~ **[up]on words** Wortspiele/ein Wortspiel machen; **not have much time to** ~ **with** (coll.) zeitlich nicht viel Spielraum haben; ~ **into sb.'s hands** (fig.) jmdm. in die Hand *od.* Hände arbeiten; ~ **safe** sichergehen; auf Nummer Sicher gehen (ugs.); ~ **for time** Zeit gewinnen wollen; **(b)** (Mus.) spielen (**on** auf + *Dat.*). **3** *v.t.* **(a)** (Mus.: perform on) spielen; ~ **the violin** *etc.* Geige *usw.* spielen; ~ **sth. on the piano** *etc.* etw. auf dem Klavier *usw.* spielen; ~ **sth. by ear** etw. nach dem Gehör spielen; ~ **it by ear** (fig.) es dem Augenblick/der Situation überlassen; **(b)** spielen ‹*Grammophon, Tonbandgerät*›; abspielen ‹*Schallplatte, Tonband*›; spielen lassen ‹*Radio*›; **(c)** (Theatre; also fig.) spielen; ~ **a town**

in einer Stadt spielen; ~ **the fool/innocent** den Clown/ Unschuldigen spielen; **(d)** (execute, practise) ~ **a trick/joke on sb.** jmdn. hereinlegen (ugs.) /jmdm. einen Streich spielen; **(e)** (Sport, Cards) spielen ‹*Fußball, Karten, Schach usw.*›; spielen *od.* antreten gegen ‹*Mannschaft, Gegner*›; ~ **a match** einen Wettkampf bestreiten; (in team games) ein Spiel machen; **he** ~**ed me at chess/squash** er war im Schach/Squash mein Gegner; ~ **it safe** auf Nummer Sicher gehen; **(f)** (Sport) ausführen ‹*Schlag*›; (Cricket etc.) schlagen ‹*Ball*›; **(g)** (Cards) spielen; ~ **one's cards right** (fig.) es richtig anfassen (fig.); **(h)** (coll.: gamble on) ~ **the market** spekulieren (**in** mit *od. Wirtsch.* in + *Dat.*)

~ **a'bout** ⇒ ~ **around**

~ **a'long** *v.i.* mitspielen

~ **a'round** *v.i.* (coll.) spielen; ~ **around with sb./sb.'s affections/sth.** mit jmdm./jmds. Zuneigung spielen/mit etw. herumspielen (ugs.)

~ **at** *v.t.* spielen; **what do you think you're** ~**ing at?** was soll denn das?

~ **'back** *v.t.* abspielen ‹*Tonband, Aufnahme*›

~ **'down** *v.t.* herunterspielen

~ **'off 1** *v.i.* zum Entscheidungsspiel antreten. **2** *v.t.* ausspielen; ~ **one person/firm** *etc.* **off against another** eine Person/Firma *usw.* gegen eine andere ausspielen

~ **on** ⇒ ~ **upon**

~ **'up** (coll.) **1** *v.i.* ‹*Kinder:*› nichts als Ärger machen; ‹*Auto:*› verrückt spielen; ‹*Rücken, Bein usw.:*› Schwierigkeiten machen. **2** *v.t.* (annoy, torment) ärgern; ‹*Krankheit:*› zu schaffen machen (+ *Dat.*)

~ **upon** *v.t.* sich (*Dat.*) zunutze machen ‹*Gefühle, Ängste usw.*›; ~ **upon sb.'s sympathies** auf jmds. Mitgefühl (*Akk.*) spekulieren (ugs.)

play: ~**-acting** *n.* (fig.) Theater, *das* (ugs.); ~**back** *n.* Wiedergabe, *die;* ~**boy** *n.* Playboy, *der*

played 'out *adj.* verbraucht; erschöpft ‹*Person, Tier*›; **this idea is** ~: diese Idee hat sich überlebt

player /'pleɪə(r)/ *n.* **(a)** Spieler, *der*/Spielerin, *die;* **(b)** (Mus.) Musiker, *der*/Musikerin, *die;* **(c)** (actor) Schauspieler, *der*/Schauspielerin, *die*

playful /'pleɪfl/ *adj.* **(a)** (fond of playing) spielerisch; (frolicsome) verspielt; **(b)** (teasing) neckisch; (joking) scherzhaft

play: ~**goer** *n.* Theaterbesucher, *der*/-besucherin, *die;* ~**ground** *n.* Spielplatz, *der;* (Sch.) Schulhof, *der;* ~**group** *n.* Spielgruppe, *die;* ~**house** *n.* **(a)** (theatre) Schauspielhaus, *das;* **(b)** (toy house) Spielhaus, *das*

playing: ~ **card** *n.* Spielkarte, *die;* ~ **field** *n.* Sportplatz, *der;* **they are not competing on a level** ~ **field** (fig.) zwischen ihnen besteht keine Chancengleichheit

play: ~**mate** *n.* Spielkamerad, *der*/Spielkameradin, *die;* ~**-off** *n.* Entscheidungsspiel, *das;* ~**pen** *n.* Laufgitter, *das;* Laufstall, *der;* ~**school** *n.* Kindergarten, *der;* ~**thing** *n.* (lit. or fig.) Spielzeug, *das;* ~**time** *n.* Zeit zum Spielen; ~**wright** /'pleɪraɪt/ *n.* Dramatiker, *der*/ Dramatikerin, *die;* Stückeschreiber, *der*/-schreiberin, *die*

PLC, plc *abbr.* (Brit.) **public limited company** ≈ GmbH

plea /pliː/ *n.* **(a)** (appeal, entreaty) Appell, *der* (**for** zu); **make a** ~ **for sth.** zu etw. aufrufen; **(b)** (Law) Verteidigungsrede, *die*

plead /pliːd/ **1** *v.i.* ~**ed** *or* (esp. Amer., Scot., dial.) **pled** /pled/ **(a)** (make appeal) inständig bitten (**for** um); (imploringly) flehen (**for** um); ~ **with sb. for sth./to do sth.** jmdn. inständig um etw. bitten/jmdn. inständig [darum] bitten, etw. zu tun; (imploringly) jmdn. um etw. anflehen/jmdn. anflehen, etw. zu tun; **(b)** (Law: put forward plea; also fig.) plädieren; (Law) **how do you** ~? bekennen Sie sich schuldig? **2** *v.t.* ~**ed** *or* (esp. Amer., Scot., dial.) **pled (a)** (beg) inständig bitten; (imploringly) flehen; **(b)** (Law: offer in mitigation) sich berufen auf (+ *Akk.*); geltend machen; (as excuse) sich entschuldigen mit; ~ **guilty/not guilty** (lit. or fig.) sich schuldig/nicht schuldig bekennen; **(c)** (present in court) ~ **sb.'s case** *or* ~ **the case for sb.** jmds. Sache vor Gericht vertreten

pleading /'pliːdɪŋ/ *adj.* flehend

pleasant /'plezənt/ *adj.*, ~**er** /'plezəntə(r)/, ~**est** /'plezəntɪst/ angenehm; schön ‹*Tag, Zeit*›; nett ‹*Gesicht, Lächeln*›

pleasantry /'plezəntrɪ/ *n.* (agreeable remark) Nettigkeit, *die;* (humorous remark) Scherz, *der*

please /pli:z/ **1** *v.t.* **(a)** (give pleasure to) gefallen (+ *Dat.*); Freude machen (+ *Dat.*); **there's no pleasing her** man kann ihr nichts *od.* es ihr nicht recht machen; **she's easy to ~** *or* **easily ~d/hard to ~:** sie ist leicht/nicht leicht zufrieden zu stellen; **~ oneself** tun, was man will; **~ yourself** ganz wie du willst; **(b)** ([may it] be the will of) gefallen; **~ God** das gebe Gott; so Gott will. **2** *v.i.* **(a)** (think fit) **they come and go as they ~:** sie kommen und gehen, wie es ihnen gefällt; **do as one ~s** tun, was man will; **(b)** (give pleasure) gefallen; **anxious** *or* **eager to ~:** bemüht, gefällig zu sein; **(c) if you ~:** bitte schön; (iron.: believe it or not) stell dir vor. **3** *int.* bitte; **may I have the bill, ~?** kann ich bitte zahlen?; **~ do!** aber bitte *od.* gern!; **~ don't** bitte nicht

pleased /pli:zd/ *adj.* (satisfied) zufrieden (**by** mit); (glad, happy) erfreut (**by** über + *Akk.*); **be ~ at** *or* **about sth.** sich über etw. (*Akk.*) freuen; **be ~ with sth./sb.** mit etw./ jmdm. zufrieden sein; **be ~ to do sth.** sich freuen, etw. zu tun; *see also* **meet¹ 1 c**

pleasing /'pli:zɪŋ/ *adj.* gefällig; ansprechend; nett 〈*Ausblick*〉

pleasurable /'pleʒərəbl/ *adj.,* **pleasurably** /'pleʒəblɪ/ *adv.* angenehm

pleasure /'pleʒə(r)/ *n.* **(a)** (feeling of joy) Freude, *die;* (sensuous enjoyment) Vergnügen, *das;* **sth. gives sb. ~:** etw. macht jmdm. Freude; **get a lot of ~ from** *or* **out of sb./sth.** viel Freude *od.* Spaß an jmdm./etw. haben; **(b)** (gratification) **have the ~ of doing sth.** das Vergnügen haben, etw. zu tun; **may I have the ~ [of the next dance]?** darf ich [Sie um den nächsten Tanz] bitten?; **take [a] ~ in** Vergnügen finden *od.* Spaß haben an (+ *Dat.*); **it's a ~:** gern geschehen; es war mir ein Vergnügen; **it gives me great ~ to inform you that ...** (formal) ich freue mich, Ihnen mitteilen zu können, dass ...; **with ~:** mit Vergnügen; gern[e]

pleasure: ~ boat *n.* Vergnügungsboot, *das;* **~ cruise** *n.* Vergnügungsfahrt, *die*

pleat /pli:t/ **1** *n.* Falte, *die.* **2** *v.t.* in Falten legen; fälteln

pleated /'pli:tɪd/ *adj.* gefältelt; Falten〈*rock*〉

plectrum /'plektrəm/ *n., pl.* **plectra** /'plektrə/ *or* **~s** (Mus.) Plektrum, *das*

pled ⇒ **plead**

pledge /pledʒ/ **1** *n.* **(a)** (promise, vow) Versprechen, *das;* Gelöbnis, *das* (geh.); **take** *or* **sign the ~** (coll.) sich zur Abstinenz verpflichten; **(b)** (as security) Pfand, *das;* Sicherheit, *die.* **2** *v.t.* **(a)** (promise solemnly) versprechen; geloben 〈*Treue*〉; **(b)** (bind by promise) verpflichten; **(c)** (deposit, pawn) verpfänden (**to** *Dat.*)

plenary /'pli:nərɪ/ *adj.* Plenar〈*sitzung*〉; Voll〈*versammlung*〉

plenipotentiary /plenɪpə'tenʃərɪ/ **1** *adj.* (invested with full power) [general]bevollmächtigt 〈*Gesandte*〉. **2** *n.* [General]bevollmächtigte, *der/die*

plentiful /'plentɪfl/ *adj.* reichlich; häufig 〈*Element, Rohstoff*〉; **be ~** *or* **in ~ supply** reichlich vorhanden sein

plenty /'plentɪ/ **1** *n., no pl.* **~ of** viel; eine Menge; (coll.: enough) genug; **have you all got ~ of meat?** habt ihr alle reichlich Fleisch?; **we gave him ~ of warning** wir haben ihn früh genug gewarnt. **2** *adj.* (coll.) reichlich vorhanden. **3** *adv.* (coll.) **it's ~ large enough** es ist groß genug; **there's ~ more where this/those** *etc.* **came from** es ist noch genug da (ugs.)

pleurisy /'plʊərɪsɪ/ *n.* ▶ 865 (Med.) Pleuritis, *die* (fachspr.); Brustfellentzündung, *die*

pliable /'plaɪəbl/ *adj.* biegsam; geschmeidig 〈*Ton, Leder*〉; (fig.) nachgiebig 〈*Charakter*〉

pliers /'plaɪəz/ *n. pl.* **[pair of] ~:** Zange, *die*

plight /plaɪt/ *n.* Notlage, *die;* **hopeless/miserable ~:** trostloser/jämmerlicher Zustand

plimsoll /'plɪmsl/ *n.* (Brit.) Turnschuh, *der*

plinth /plɪnθ/ *n.* (for vase, statue, etc.; of wall) Sockel, *der*

plod /plɒd/ *v.i.,* **-dd-** trotten; **~ along** dahintrotten; **~ [on] through the snow** [weiter] durch den Schnee stapfen

~ a'way *v.i.* (fig.) sich abmühen

~ 'on *v.i.* (fig.) sich weiterkämpfen

plodder /'plɒdə(r)/ *n.* **he is a ~:** er arbeitet schwerfällig; (Sch.) er ist ein bisschen langsam

plonk¹ /plɒŋk/ *v.t.* (coll.) **~ sth. [down]** etw. hinknallen (ugs.)

plonk² *n.* (coll.: wine) [billiger] Wein

plop /plɒp/ **1** *v.i.,* **-pp-** plumpsen (ugs.); 〈*Regen:*〉 klatschen, platschen. **2** *v.t.,* **-pp-** plumpsen lassen (ugs.). **3** *n.* Plumpsen, *das;* **with a ~:** mit einem Plumps. **4** *adv.* plumps

plot /plɒt/ **1** *n.* **(a)** (conspiracy) Komplott, *das;* Verschwörung, *die;* **(b)** (of play, film, novel) Handlung, *die;* **(c)** (of ground) Stück Land; **vegetable ~:** Gemüsebeet, *das;* **building ~:** Baugrundstück, *das.* **2** *v.t.* **(a)** (plan secretly) [heimlich] planen; **~ treason** auf Verrat sinnen (geh.); **(b)** (make plan or map of) kartieren, kartographieren 〈*Gebiet usw.*〉; (make by ~ting) zeichnen 〈*Karte, Plan*〉; **(c)** (mark on map, diagram) **~ [down]** eintragen; einzeichnen. **3** *v.i.,* **-tt-:** **~ against sb.** sich gegen jmdn. verschwören

plotter /'plɒtə(r)/ *n.* Verschwörer, *der*/Verschwörerin, *die*

plough /plaʊ/ **1** *n.* (Agric.) Pflug, *der;* **the P~** (Astron.) der Große Wagen *od.* Bär. **2** *v.t.* **(a)** pflügen; **~ furrows** Furchen ziehen *od.* pflügen; **(b)** (fig.) 〈*Schiff:*〉 [durch]pflügen 〈*Wasserfläche*〉

~ 'back *v.t.* **(a)** unterpflügen; **(b)** (Finance) reinvestieren; **~ profits** *etc.* **back into the business** *etc.* Gewinne *usw.* wieder in die Firma *usw.* stecken

~ through *v.t.* (advance laboriously in) sich kämpfen durch; (move violently through) rasen durch

~ 'up *v.t.* auspflügen 〈*Kartoffeln, Rüben usw.*〉; zerpflügen 〈*Boden*〉

ploughman /'plaʊmən/ *n., pl.* **ploughmen** /'plaʊmən/ Pflüger, *der;* **~'s [lunch]** (Brit.) *Imbiss aus Käse, Brot und Mixed Pickles*

plow (Amer./arch.) ⇒ **plough**

ploy /plɔɪ/ *n.* Trick, *der*

pluck /plʌk/ **1** *v.t.* **(a)** (pull off, pick) pflücken 〈*Blumen, Obst*〉; **~ [out]** auszupfen 〈*Federn, Haare*〉; **(b)** (pull at, twitch) zupfen (+ *Dat.*); zupfen 〈*Saite, Gitarre*〉; **(c)** (strip of feathers) rupfen. **2** *v.i.* **~ at sth.** an etw. (*Dat.*) zupfen. **3** *n.* Mut, *der;* Schneid, *der* (ugs.)

~ 'up *v.t.* **~ up [one's] courage** all seinen Mut zusammennehmen

pluckily /'plʌkɪlɪ/ *adv.,* **plucky** /'plʌkɪ/ *adj.* tapfer

plug /plʌg/ **1** *n.* **(a)** (filling hole) Pfropfen, *der;* (in cask) Spund, *der;* Zapfen, *der;* (stopper for basin, vessel, etc.) Stöpsel, *der;* **(b)** (Electr.) Stecker, *der;* **(c)** (coll.: piece of good publicity) **give sth. a ~:** Werbung für etw. machen. **2** *v.t.,* **-gg-: (a) ~ [up]** zustopfen, verstopfen 〈*Loch usw.*〉; **(b)** (coll.: advertise) Schleichwerbung machen für; (by presenting sth. repeatedly) pushen (ugs.)

~ a'way *v.i.* (coll.) vor sich hin schuften (ugs.); **~ away at sth.** sich mit etw. abschuften (ugs.)

~ 'in *v.t.* anschließen; **is it ~ged in?** ist der Stecker in der Steckdose *od.* (ugs.) drin?

plug: ~hole *n.* Abfluss, *der;* **~-in** *adj.* anschließbar

plum /plʌm/ *n.* **(a)** (fruit) Pflaume, *die;* **(b)** (fig.) Leckerbissen, *der; attrib.* **a ~ job/position** ein Traumjob (ugs.)

plumage /'plu:mɪdʒ/ *n.* Gefieder, *das*

plumb¹ /plʌm/ **1** *v.t.* (sound, measure) [aus]loten; **~ the depths of loneliness/sorrow** die tiefsten Tiefen der Einsamkeit/Trauer erleben. **2** *adv.* **(a)** (vertically) senkrecht; lotrecht; **(b)** (fig.: exactly) genau. **3** *n.* Lot, *das;* **out of ~:** außer Lot

plumb² *v.t.* **~ in** (connect) fest anschließen

plumber /'plʌmə(r)/ *n.* Klempner, *der;* Installateur, *der*

plumbing /'plʌmɪŋ/ *n.* **(a)** (plumber's work) Klempnerarbeiten *Pl.;* Installationsarbeiten *Pl.;* **(b)** (water pipes) Wasserrohre; Wasserleitungen

'plumb line *n.* Lot, *das*

plume /plu:m/ *n.* **(a)** (feather) Feder, *die;* (ornamental bunch) Federbusch, *der;* **(b) ~ of smoke/steam** Rauchwolke *od.* -fahne, *die*/Dampfwolke, *die*

plummet /'plʌmɪt/ *v.i.* stürzen

plump /plʌmp/ *adj.* mollig; rundlich; stämmig ‹*Arme, Beine*›; fleischig ‹*Brathuhn usw.*›; ~ **cheeks** Pausbacken *Pl.* (fam.)

~ **for** *v.t.* (a) (Brit.: vote for) stimmen für; (b) (choose) sich entscheiden für

~ **'up** *v.t.* aufschütteln ‹*Kissen*›; (fatten up) mästen

plunder /'plʌndə(r)/ **1** *v.t.* [aus]plündern ‹*Gebäude, Gebiet*›; ausplündern ‹*Person*›; rauben ‹*Sache*›. **2** *n.* (a) (action) Plünderung, *die;* (spoil, booty) Beute, *die;* (b) (coll.: profit) Profit, *der*

plunge /plʌndʒ/ **1** *v.t.* (a) (thrust violently) stecken; (into liquid) tauchen; (b) (fig.) ~**d in thought** in Gedanken versunken; **be ~d into darkness** in Dunkelheit getaucht sein (geh.). **2** *v.i.* (a) ~ **into sth.** (lit. or fig.) in etw. (*Akk.*) stürzen; (b) (descend suddenly) ‹*Straße usw.*› steil abfallen; **plunging neckline** tiefer Ausschnitt. **3** *n.* Sprung, *der;* **take the** ~ (fig. coll.) den Sprung wagen

plunger /'plʌndʒə(r)/ *n.* (a) (part of mechanism) [Tauch]kolben, *der;* Plunger[kolben], *der;* (b) (rubber suction cup) Stampfer, *der*

pluperfect /plu:'pɜ:fɪkt/ (Ling.) **1** *n.* Plusquamperfekt, *das.* **2** *adj.* ~ **tense** Plusquamperfekt, *das*

plural /'plʊərl/ (Ling.) **1** *adj.* pluralisch; Plural-; ~ **noun** Substantiv im Plural; **third person** ~: dritte Person Plural. **2** *n.* Mehrzahl, *die;* Plural, *der*

plurality /plʊə'rælɪtɪ/ *n.* (a) (being plural) Pluralität, *die;* (b) (large number) Vielzahl, *die*

plus /plʌs/ **1** *prep.* (a) (with the addition of) plus (+ *Dat.*); (and also) und [zusätzlich]; (b) (above zero) plus; ~ **ten degrees** plus zehn Grad; zehn Grad plus. **2** *adj.* (a) (additional, extra) zusätzlich; (b) (at least) **fifteen** *etc.* ~: über fünfzehn *usw.;* (c) (Math.: positive) positiv ‹*Wert, Menge, Größe*›. **3** *n.* (a) (symbol) Plus[zeichen], *das;* (b) (additional quantity) Plus, *das;* (c) (advantage) Pluspunkt, *der.* **4** *conj.* (coll.) und außerdem

plush /plʌʃ/ **1** *n.* Plüsch, *der.* **2** *adj.* Plüsch-; plüschen; (coll.: luxurious) feudal (ugs.)

Pluto /'plu:təʊ/ *n.* (a) (Astron.) Pluto, *der;* (b) (Roman Mythol.) Pluto, (*der*)

plutonium /plu:'təʊnɪəm/ *n.* (Chem.) Plutonium, *das*

ply[1] /plaɪ/ **1** *v.t.* (a) (use, wield) gebrauchen; führen; (b) (work at) nachgehen (+ *Dat.*) ‹*Handwerk, Arbeit*›; (c) (supply) ~ **sb. with sth.** jmdn. mit etw. versorgen; (d) (assail) überhäufen; (e) (sail over) befahren. **2** *v.i.* (a) (go to and fro) ~ **between** zwischen ‹*Orten*› [hin- und her]pendeln; (operate on regular services) zwischen ‹*Orten*› verkehren; (b) (attend regularly for custom) seine Dienste anbieten; ~ **for customers/hire** auf Kundschaft warten

ply[2] *n.* (a) (of yarn, wool, etc.) [Einzel]faden, *der;* (of rope, cord, etc.) Strang, *der;* (of plywood, cloth, etc.) Lage, *die;* Schicht, *die; see also* **three-ply; two-ply;** (b) ⇒ **plywood**

'plywood *n.* Sperrholz, *das*

PM *abbr.* **Prime Minister**

p.m. /pi:'em/ *adv.* ▶ **706** nachmittags; **one** ~: ein Uhr mittags; **six/eleven** ~: sechs/elf Uhr abends

PMT *abbr.* **premenstrual tension**

pneumatic /nju:'mætɪk/ *adj.* pneumatisch; mit Druckluft betrieben *od.* arbeitend ‹*Maschine*›

pneumatic 'drill *n.* Pressluftbohrer, *der*

pneumonia /nju:'məʊnɪə/ *n.* ▶ **865** Lungenentzündung, *die;* Pneumonie, *die* (Med.)

PO *abbr.* (a) **postal order** PA; (b) **Post Office** PA

poach[1] /pəʊtʃ/ **1** *v.t.* (a) (catch illegally) wildern; illegal fangen ‹*Fische*›; (b) (obtain unfairly) stehlen, (ugs.) klauen ‹*Idee*›. **2** *v.i.* (a) (catch animals illegally) wildern; (b) (encroach) ~ **on sb.'s territory** jmdm. ins Handwerk pfuschen

poach[2] *v.t.* (Cookery) pochieren ‹*Ei*›; dünsten, pochieren ‹*Fisch, Fleisch, Gemüse*›; ~**ed eggs** pochierte *od.* verlorene Eier

poacher /'pəʊtʃə(r)/ *n.* Wilderer, *der;* Wilddieb, *der*

PO box ⇒ **post-office box**

pocket /'pɒkɪt/ **1** *n.* (a) Tasche, *die;* (in suitcase etc.) Seitentasche, *die;* (in handbag) [Seiten]fach, *das;* (Billiards etc.) Loch, *das;* Tasche, *die;* **be in sb.'s** ~ (fig.) von jmdm. abhängig sein; (b) (fig.: financial resources) **it is beyond my** ~: es

übersteigt meine finanziellen Möglichkeiten; **put one's hand in one's** ~: in die Tasche greifen (ugs.); **be in** ~: Geld verdient haben; **be out of** ~ (have lost money) draufgelegt haben (ugs.); zugesetzt haben; (c) (Mil.) ~ **of resistance** Widerstandsnest, *das.* **2** *adj.* Taschen‹*rechner, -uhr, -ausgabe*›. **3** *v.t.* (a) (put in one's ~) einstecken; (b) (steal) in die eigene Tasche stecken (ugs.)

pocket: ~**book** *n.* (a) (wallet) Brieftasche, *die;* (b) (notebook) Notizbuch, *das;* (c) (Amer.: paperback) Taschenbuch, *das;* (d) (Amer.: handbag) Handtasche, *die;* ~ **'handkerchief** *n.* Taschentuch, *das;* ~ **knife** *n.* Taschenmesser, *das;* ~ **money** *n.* Taschengeld, *das;* ~**-size[d]** *adj.* (a) im Taschenformat *nachgestellt;* (b) (fig.: small scale) im [Westen]taschenformat *nachgestellt* (ugs. scherzh.)

pock: ~**-mark** *n.* (a) (Med.) Pockennarbe, *die;* (b) Delle, *die;* (from bullet) Einschuss, *der;* ~**-marked** *adj.* (a) pockennarbig ‹*Gesicht, Haut*›; (b) **a wall** ~**-marked with bullets** eine mit Einschüssen übersäte Wand

pod /pɒd/ *n.* (a) (seed case) Hülse, *die;* (of pea) Schote, *die;* (b) (in aircraft etc.) (for engine) Gondel, *die;* (for fuel) Außentank, *der*

podgy /'pɒdʒɪ/ *adj.* dicklich; pummelig (ugs.), rundlich (fam.), mollig ‹*Frau*›; pausbäckig, (fam.) rundlich ‹*Gesicht*›

podium /'pəʊdɪəm/ *n., pl.* **podia** /'pəʊdɪə/ *or* **-s** Podium, *das*

poem /'pəʊɪm/ *n.* Gedicht, *das*

poet /'pəʊɪt/ *n.* Dichter, *der;* Poet, *der* (geh.)

poetess /'pəʊɪtes/ *n.* Dichterin, *die;* Poetin, *die* (geh.)

poetic /pəʊ'etɪk/ *adj.,* **poetically** /pəʊ'etɪkəlɪ/ *adv.* dichterisch; poetisch (geh.); *see also* **justice** a; **licence 1 d**

poetry /'pəʊɪtrɪ/ *n.* [Vers]dichtung, *die;* Lyrik, *die;* ~ **reading** ≈ Dichterlesung, *die*

po-faced /'pəʊfeɪst/ *adj.* mit unbewegter Miene *nachgestellt*

poignancy /'pɔɪnjənsɪ/ *n., no pl.* [schmerzliche] Intensität; (of words, wit, etc.) Schärfe, *die*

poignant /'pɔɪnjənt/ *adj.* tief ‹*Bedauern, Trauer*›; überwältigend ‹*Schönheit*›; (causing sympathy) ergreifend, herzzerreißend ‹*Anblick, Geschichte*›

point /pɔɪnt/ **1** *n.* (a) (tiny mark, dot) Punkt, *der;* **nought** ~ **two** Null Komma zwei; (b) (sharp end of tool, weapon, pencil, etc.) Spitze, *die;* **come to a [sharp]** ~: spitz zulaufen; **at gun-~/knife-~:** mit vorgehaltener [Schuss]waffe/ vorgehaltenem Messer; **not to put too fine a** ~ **on it** (fig.) um nichts zu beschönigen; (c) (single item) Punkt, *der;* **agree on a** ~: in einem Punkt *od.* einer Frage übereinstimmen; **be a** ~ **of honour with sb.** für jmdn. [eine] Ehrensache sein; (d) (unit of scoring) Punkt, *der;* **score** ~s **off sb.** (fig.) jmdn. an die Wand spielen; (e) (stage, degree) **things have reached a** ~ **where** *or* **come to such a** ~ **that** …: die Sache ist dahin *od.* so weit gediehen, dass …; (negatively) es ist so weit gekommen, dass …; **up to a** ~: bis zu einem gewissen Grad; **beyond a certain** ~: über einen bestimmten Punkt hinaus; **she was abrupt to the** ~ **of rudeness** sie war in einer Weise barsch, die schon an Unverschämtheit grenzte; (f) (moment) Zeitpunkt, *der;* **be at/on the** ~ **of sth.** kurz vor etw. (*Dat.*) sein; einer Sache (*Dat.*) nahe sein; **be on the** ~ **of doing sth.** im Begriff sein, etw. zu tun; etw. gerade tun wollen; (g) (distinctive trait) Seite, *die;* **best/strong** ~: starke Seite, *die;* **getting up early has its** ~s frühes Aufstehen hat auch seine Vorzüge; **the** ~ (essential thing) das Entscheidende; (thing to be discussed) **that is just the** ~ *or* **the whole** ~: das ist genau der springende Punkt; **come to** *or* **get to the** ~: zur Sache *od.* zum Thema kommen; **keep** *or* **stick to the** ~: beim Thema bleiben; **be beside the** ~: unerheblich sein; keine Rolle spielen; ~ **taken** habe verstanden; **carry** *or* **make one's** ~: sich durchsetzen; **a case in** ~: ein typisches Beispiel; **make a** ~ **of doing sth.** [großen] Wert darauf legen, etw. zu tun; **make** *or* **prove a** ~: etw. beweisen; **to the** ~: sachbezogen; **more to the** ~: wichtiger; **you have a** ~ **there** da hast du recht; da ist [et]was dran (ugs.); (i) (tip) Spitze, *die;* (Boxing) Kinnspitze, *die;* Kinn, *das;* (Ballet) Spitze, *die;* (j) (of story, joke, remark) Pointe, *die;* (pungency, effect) (of literary work) Eindringlichkeit, *die;* (of remark) Durchschlagskraft, *die;* **(k)** (purpose, value) Zweck, *der;* Sinn, *der;* **there's no ~ in protesting** es hat keinen Sinn *od.* Zweck zu protestieren; **(l)** (precise place, spot) Punkt, *der;* Stelle, *die;* (Geom.) Punkt, *der;* **~ of contact** Berührungspunkt, *der;* **~ of no return** Punkt, an dem es kein Zurück mehr gibt; **~ of view** (fig.) Standpunkt, *der;* **(m)** (Brit.) [**power** *or* **electric**] **~:** Steckdose, *die;* **(n)** *usu. in pl.* (Brit. Railw.) Weiche, *die;* **(o)** *usu. in pl.* (Motor Veh.: contact device) Kontakt, *der;* **(p)** (unit in competition, rationing, stocks, shares, etc.) Punkt, *der;* **prices/the cost of living went up three ~s** die Preise/Lebenshaltungskosten sind um drei [Prozent]punkte gestiegen; **(q)** (on compass) Strich, *der.* **2** *v.i.* **(a)** zeigen, weisen, *‹Person auch:›* deuten **(to, at** auf + *Akk.***); she ~ed through the window** sie zeigte aus dem Fenster; **the compass needle ~ed to the north** die Kompassnadel zeigte *od.* wies nach Norden; **(b) ~ towards** *or* **to** (fig.) [hin]deuten *od.* hinweisen auf (+ *Akk.*). **3** *v.t.* **(a)** (direct) richten *‹Waffe, Kamera›* **(at** auf + *Akk.***); ~ one's finger at sth./sb.** mit dem Finger auf etw./jmdn. deuten *od.* zeigen *od.* weisen; **(b)** (Building) aus-, verfugen *‹Mauer, Steine›*

~ 'out *v.t.* hinweisen auf (+ *Akk.***); ~ sth./sb. out to sb.** jmdn. auf etw./jmdn. hinweisen *od.* aufmerksam machen; **he ~ed out the house** er zeigte das Haus; **he ~ed out my mistake** er zeigte mir meinen Fehler an

point-'blank 1 *adj.* (direct, lit. or fig.) direkt; glatt *‹Weigerung›;* **~ shot** Schuss aus kürzester Entfernung; **~ range** kürzeste Entfernung. **2** *adv.* **(a)** (at very close range) aus kürzester Entfernung *‹schießen›;* **(b)** (in direct line) direkt; (fig.: directly) rundheraus, (ugs.) geradeheraus *‹fragen, sagen›*

pointed /'pɔɪntɪd/ *adj.* **(a)** spitz; **~ arch** Spitzbogen, *der;* **(b)** (fig.) (sharply expressed) unmissverständlich; deutlich; (ostentatious) demonstrativ

pointer /'pɔɪntə(r)/ *n.* **(a)** (indicator) Zeiger, *der;* (rod) Zeigestock, *der;* **(b) ~ [dog]** Pointer, *der;* englischer Vorstehhund

pointless /'pɔɪntlɪs/ *adj.* (without purpose, useless) sinnlos; (without force, meaningless) belanglos *‹Bemerkung, Geschichte›*

poise /pɔɪz/ **1** *n.* (composure) Haltung, *die;* (self-confidence) Selbstsicherheit, *die;* Selbstvertrauen, *das.* **2** *v.t.* **(a)** *in p.p.* **sit ~d on the edge of one's chair** auf der Stuhlkante balancieren; **be ~d for action** einsatzbereit sein; *see also* **poised; (b)** (balance) balancieren

poised /pɔɪzd/ *adj.* selbstsicher; *see also* **poise 2 a**

poison /'pɔɪzn/ **1** *n.* (lit. or fig.) Gift, *das;* **hate sb./sth. like ~:** jmdn./etw. wie die Pest hassen. **2** *v.t.* **(a)** vergiften; (contaminate) verseuchen *‹Boden, Luft, Wasser›;* verpesten (abwertend) *‹Luft›;* **(b)** (fig.) vergiften *‹Gedanken, Seele›;* zerstören, ruinieren *‹Ehe, Leben›;* vergällen *‹Freude›;* **~ sb.'s mind** jmdn. verderben *od.* (geh.) korrumpieren

poison 'gas *n.* Giftgas, *das*

poisoning /'pɔɪzənɪŋ/ *n.* Vergiftung, *die;* (contamination) Verseuchung, *die*

poisonous /'pɔɪzənəs/ *adj.* **(a)** giftig; tödlich *‹Dosis›;* **(b)** (fig.) verderblich *‹Lehre, Wirkung›;* giftig *‹Blick, Zunge›*

poke 1 *v.t.* **(a) ~ sth. [with sth.]** [mit etw.] gegen etw. stoßen; **~ sth. into sth.** etw. in etw. (*Akk.*) stoßen; **~ the fire** das Feuer schüren; **he accidentally ~d me in the eye** er stieß mir versehentlich ins Auge; **(b)** (thrust forward) stecken *‹Kopf›;* **~ one's head round the corner/door** um die Ecke gucken (ugs.) /den Kopf in die Türöffnung stecken; **(c)** (pierce) bohren. **2** *v.i.* **(a)** (in pond, at food, among rubbish) [herum]stochern **(at, in, among** in + *Dat.***); ~ at sth. with a stick** *etc.* mit einem Stock *usw.* nach etw. stoßen; **(b)** (thrust itself) sich schieben; **his elbows were poking through the sleeves** seine Ärmel hatten Löcher, aus denen die Ellbogen hervorguckten; **(c)** (pry) schnüffeln (ugs. abwertend). **3** *n.* (thrust) Stoß, *der;* **give sb. a ~ [in the ribs]** jmdm. einen [Rippen]stoß versetzen *od.* geben; **give the fire a ~:** das Feuer [an]schüren

~ a'bout, ~ a'round *v.i.* herumschnüffeln (ugs. abwertend)

.**poker¹** /'pəʊkə(r)/ *n.* Schürstange, *die;* Schüreisen, *das*

poker² *n.* (Cards) Poker, *das od. der*

'**poker-faced** *adj.* mit unbewegter Miene *nachgestellt*

poky /'pəʊkɪ/ *adj.* winzig; **it's so ~ in here** es ist so eng hier drinnen

Poland /'pəʊlənd/ *pr. n.* Polen (*das*)

polar /'pəʊlə(r)/ *adj.* **(a)** (of pole) polar *‹Kaltluft, Gewässer›;* Polar*‹eis, -gebiet, -fuchs›;* **(b)** (Magn.) polar; **(c)** (directly opposite) [diametral] entgegengesetzt

polar 'bear *n.* Eisbär, *der*

polarisation, polarise ⇒ **polariz-**

polarity /pə'lærɪtɪ/ *n.* **(a)** (Magn.) Polung, *die;* Polarität, *die;* **(b)** (fig.: contrary qualities) Gegensatz, *der*

polarization /ˌpəʊlərɑɪ'zeɪʃn/ *n.* (Phys.) Polarisation, *die;* (fig.) Polarisierung, *die*

polarize /'pəʊlərɑɪz/ **1** *v.t.* spalten; polarisieren (geh.). **2** *v.i.* sich [auf]spalten

Polaroid, (P) /'pəʊlərɔɪd/ *n.* **~ [camera]** Polaroidkamera,ⓦ *die*

pole² *n.* (Astron., Geog., Magn., Electr., fig.) Pol, *der;* **they are ~s apart** zwischen ihnen liegen Welten

Pole /pəʊl/ *n.* ▶ **947** Pole, *der*/Polin, *die*

pole¹ *n.* **(a)** (support) Stange, *die;* **drive sb. up the ~** (Brit. coll.) jmdn. zum Wahnsinn treiben (ugs.); **climb the greasy ~** (fig.) sich hocharbeiten; **(b)** (for propelling boat) Stake, *die* (nordd.)

'**polecat** *n.* (Zool.) **(a)** (Brit.) Iltis, *der;* **(b)** (Amer.) ⇒ **skunk**

polemic /pə'lemɪk/ **1** *adj.* polemisch. **2** *n.* (discussion) Polemik, *die;* (written also) Streitschrift, *die*

pole: ~ star *n.* (Astron.) Polarstern, *der;* **~ vault** *n.* Stabhochsprung, *der;* **~-vaulter** *n.* Stabhochspringer, *der/*-springerin, *die;* **~-vaulting** *n.* Stabhochsprung, *der;* Stabhochspringen, *das*

police /pə'li:s/ **1** *n. pl.* **(a)** Polizei, *die;* attrib. Polizei*‹wagen, -hund, -schutz, -eskorte, -staat›;* **be in the ~:** bei der Polizei sein; **(b)** (members) Polizisten *Pl.;* Polizeibeamte *Pl.;* attrib. Polizei-; **the ~ are on his trail** die Polizei ist ihm auf der Spur; **help the ~ with their enquiries** von der Polizei vernommen werden. **2** *v.t.* [polizeilich] überwachen *‹Gebiet, Verkehr, Fußballspiel›;* kontrollieren *‹Gebiet, Grenze, Gewässer›;* Polizeibeamte einsetzen in (+ *Dat.*) *‹Gebiet, Stadt usw.›*

police: ~ constable *n.* ▶ **887** Polizist, *der/*Polizistin, *die;* (rank) Polizeihauptwachtmeister, *der;* **~ force** *n.* Polizeitruppe, *die;* **the ~ force** die Polizei; **~man** /pə'li:smən/ *n., pl.* **~men** /pə'li:smən/ ▶ **887** Polizist, *der;* Polizeibeamte, *der;* **~ officer** *n.* ▶ **887** Polizeibeamte, *der/*-beamtin, *die;* **~ state** *n.* Polizeistaat, *der;* **~ station** *n.* Polizeiwache, *die;* Polizeirevier, *das;* **~woman** *n.* ▶ **887** Polizistin, *die;* Polizeibeamtin, *die*

policy¹ /'pɒlɪsɪ/ *n.* (method) Handlungsweise, *die;* Vorgehensweise, *die;* (overall plan) Politik, *die;* **~ on immigration** Einwanderungspolitik, *die;* **it's bad ~ to ...:** es ist unvernünftig, zu ...

policy² *n.* (Insurance) Police, *die;* Versicherungsschein, *der*

polio /'pəʊlɪəʊ/ *n., no pl., no art.* ▶ **865** Polio, *die;* [spinale] Kinderlähmung

Polish /'pəʊlɪʃ/ ▶ **897**, ▶ **947** **1** *adj.* polnisch; **sb. is ~:** jmd. ist Pole/Polin. **2** *n.* Polnisch, *das; see also* **English 2 a**

polish /'pɒlɪʃ/ **1** *v.t.* **(a)** (make smooth) polieren; bohnern *‹Fußboden›;* putzen *‹Schuhe›;* **(b)** (fig.) ausfeilen *‹Text, Theorie, Technik, Stil›;* polieren *‹Text›;* **~ed** geschliffen *‹Stil, Manieren›;* ausgefeilt *‹Technik, Taktik, Plan, Satz›.* **2** *n.* **(a)** (smoothness) Glanz, *der;* **a table with a high ~:** ein auf Hochglanz polierter Tisch; **(b)** (substance) Poliermittel, *das;* Politur, *die;* **(c)** (fig.) Geschliffenheit, *die;* Schliff, *der;* **(d)** (action) **give sth. a ~:** etw. polieren; **give the shoes a ~:** die Schuhe putzen

~ 'off *v.t.* (coll.) **(a)** (consume) verdrücken (ugs.); wegputzen (ugs.) *‹Essen›;* aussüffeln (ugs.) *‹Getränk›;* **(b)** (complete quickly) durchziehen (ugs.)

~ 'up *v.t.* **(a)** (make shiny) polieren; **(b)** (improve) ausfeilen *‹Stil, Technik›;* aufpolieren *‹[Sprach]kenntnisse›*

polite /pə'laɪt/ adj., ~**r** /pə'laɪtə(r)/, ~**st** /pə'laɪtɪst/ höflich; **be** ~ **about her dress** mach ihr ein paar Komplimente zu Ihrem Kleid

politeness /pə'laɪtnɪs/ n., no pl. Höflichkeit, die

politic /'pɒlɪtɪk/ adj. klug ‹Person, Handlung›; opportun (geh.) ‹Handlung›; **it's not** ~ **to do sth.** es ist unklug od. nicht ratsam, etw. zu tun

political /pə'lɪtɪkl/ adj. politisch

political: ~ **a'sylum** ⇒ **asylum;** ~ **'prisoner** n. politischer Gefangener/politische Gefangene

politically /pə'lɪtɪkəlɪ/ adv. politisch; **be** ~ **aware** or **conscious** politisches Bewusstsein haben; ~ **correct** politisch korrekt

politician /pɒlɪ'tɪʃn/ n. ▶ 887 Politiker, der/Politikerin, die

politics /'pɒlɪtɪks/ n., no pl. **(a)** no art. (political administration) Politik, die; (Univ.: subject) Politik[wissenschaft], die; Politologie, die; **(b)** no art., constr. as sing. or pl. (political affairs) Politik, die; **interested/involved in** ~: politisch interessiert/engagiert; **enter** ~: in die Politik gehen; **(c)** as pl. (political principles) Politik, die; (of individual) politische Einstellung; **what are his** ~? wo steht er politisch?; **practical** ~: Realpolitik, die

polka /'pɒlkə, 'pəʊlkə/ n. Polka, die

'polka dot n. [großer] Tupfen

poll /pəʊl/ **1** n. **(a)** (voting) Abstimmung, die; (to elect sb.) Wahl, die; (result of vote) Abstimmungsergebnis, das/Wahlergebnis, das; (number of votes) Wahlbeteiligung, die; **take a** ~: abstimmen lassen; eine Abstimmung durchführen; **at the** ~[s] bei den Wahlen; **go to the** ~: seine Stimme abgeben; zur Wahl gehen; **a heavy/light** or **low** ~: eine starke/geringe od. niedrige Wahlbeteiligung; **(b)** (survey of opinion) Umfrage, die. **2** v.t. **(a)** (take vote[s] of) abstimmen/ wählen lassen; **(b)** (take opinion of) befragen; (take survey of) [demoskopisch] erforschen; **(c)** (obtain in ~) erhalten ‹Stimmen›

pollen /'pɒlən/ n. (Bot.) Pollen, der; Blütenstaub, der

'pollen count n. Pollenmenge, die

pollinate /'pɒlɪneɪt/ v.t. (Bot.) bestäuben

pollination /pɒlɪ'neɪʃn/ n. (Bot.) Bestäubung, die

polling /'pəʊlɪŋ/**:** ~ **booth** n. Wahlkabine, die; ~ **station** n. (Brit.) Wahllokal, das

pollster /'pɒlstə(r)/ n. Meinungsforscher, der/-forscherin, die

'poll tax n. Kopfsteuer, die

pollutant /pə'lu:tənt/ n. [Umwelt]schadstoff, der

pollute /pə'lu:t/ v.t. **(a)** (contaminate) verschmutzen, verunreinigen ‹Luft, Boden, Wasser›; verpesten (abwertend) ‹Luft›; **(b)** (make foul) verseuchen

pollution /pə'lu:ʃn/ n. **(a)** (contamination) [Umwelt]verschmutzung, die; **water** ~: Gewässerverschmutzung, die; **(b)** (polluting substance[s]) Verunreinigungen; Schadstoffe

polo /'pəʊləʊ/ n., no pl. Polo, das

'polo neck n. Rollkragen, der; ~[**ed**] attrib. Rollkragen-

poltergeist /'pɒltəgaɪst/ n. Klopfgeist, der; Poltergeist, der

poly /'pɒlɪ/ n., pl. ~**s** (coll.) Polytechnikum, das; ≈ TH, die

polyester /pɒlɪ'estə(r)/ n. Polyester, der

polygamy /pə'lɪgəmɪ/ n. Polygamie, die (geh., fachspr.); Mehrehe, die; Vielehe, die

polyglot /'pɒlɪglɒt/ **1** adj. **(a)** polyglott (geh., fachspr.); mehrsprachig; **(b)** (speaking several languages) polyglott (geh.). **2** n. Polyglotte, der/die (geh.)

polygon /'pɒlɪgən/ n. (Geom.) Vieleck, das; Polygon, das (fachspr.)

polymer /'pɒlɪmə(r)/ n. (Chem.) Polymer[e], das

polyp /'pɒlɪp/ n. (Zool., Med.) Polyp, der

polystyrene /pɒlɪ'staɪri:n/ n. Polystyrol, das; ~ **foam** Styropor ⓦ, das

polytechnic /pɒlɪ'teknɪk/ n. (Brit.) ≈ Technische Hochschule od. Universität

polythene /'pɒlɪθi:n/ n. Polyäthylen, das; Polyethylen, das (fachspr.); (coll.: plastic) Plastik, das; ~ **bag/sheet** Plastikbeutel, der/-folie, die

polyunsaturated /pɒlɪʌn'sætʃəreɪtɪd/ adj. mehrfach ungesättigt

polyunsaturates /pɒlɪʌn'sætjʊrəts/ pl. n. mehrfach ungesättigte Fettsäuren

pomegranate /'pɒmɪgrænɪt/ n. Granatapfel, der

pommel /'pʌml, 'pɒml/ n. **(a)** (on sword) [Schwert]knauf, der; **(b)** (on saddle) Sattelknopf, der

'pommel horse n. Seitpferd, das

pommy (**pommie**) /'pɒmɪ/ n. (Austral. and NZ sl. derog.) Brite, der/Britin, die

pomp /pɒmp/ n. Pomp, der (abwertend); Prunk, der; ~ **and circumstance** festliches Gepränge (geh.)

pom-pom /'pɒmpɒm/, **pompon** /'pɒmpɒn/ n. (tuft) Pompon, der; ~ **hat** Pudelmütze, die

pompous /'pɒmpəs/ adj. (self-important) großspurig; aufgeblasen; geschwollen (abwertend); gespreizt (abwertend) ‹Sprache›

ponce /pɒns/ n. (Brit. sl.) **(a)** (pimp) Zuhälter, der; **(b)** (derog.: homosexual) Schwule, der (ugs.); Homo, der (ugs.)

~ **a'bout,** ~ **a'round** v.i. (derog.) herumtänzeln (ugs.)

pond /pɒnd/ n. Teich, der

ponder /'pɒndə(r)/ **1** v.t. nachdenken über (+ Akk.) ‹Frage, Problem, Ereignis›; bedenken ‹Folgen›; abwägen ‹Vorteile, Worte›. **2** v.i. nachdenken (**over, on** über + Akk.)

ponderous /'pɒndərəs/ adj. **(a)** (heavy) schwer; **(b)** (unwieldy, laborious) schwerfällig; umständlich ‹Ausdrucksweise›

pong /pɒŋ/ (Brit. coll.) **1** n. Mief, der (ugs. abwertend). **2** v.i. miefen (ugs. abwertend)

pontiff /'pɒntɪf/ n. Papst, der

pontificate /pɒn'tɪfɪkeɪt/ v.i. dozieren

pontoon¹ /pɒn'tu:n/ n. **(a)** (boat) Ponton, der; Prahm, der; **(b)** (support) Ponton, der

pontoon² n. (Brit. Cards) Siebzehnundvier, das

pontoon 'bridge n. Pontonbrücke, die

pony /'pəʊnɪ/ n. Pony, das; see also **shank a**

pony: ~**tail** n. Pferdeschwanz, der; ~**-trekking** /'pəʊnɪtrekɪŋ/ n. (Brit.) Ponyreiten, das

poodle /'pu:dl/ n. Pudel, der; **be sb.'s** ~ (fig.) immer nach jmds. Pfeife tanzen

poof /puf/ n. (Brit. sl. derog.), **poofter** /'pʊftə(r)/ n. (Austral. sl. derog.) Schwule, der (ugs.); Schwuchtel, die (salopp abwertend); Tunte, die (salopp abwertend)

pooh /pu:/ int. **(a)** expr. disgust bah; bäh; pfui [Teufel]; **(b)** expr. disdain pah

pooh-'pooh v.t. [als läppisch] abtun

pool¹ /pu:l/ n. **(a)** (permanent) Tümpel, der; **(b)** (temporary) Pfütze, die; Lache, die; ~ **of blood** Blutlache, die; **(c)** (swimming ~) Schwimmbecken, das; (public swimming ~) Schwimmbad, das; (in house or garden) [Swimming]pool, der

pool² **1** n. **(a)** (Gambling) [gemeinsame Spiel]kasse; **the** ~**s** (Brit.) das Toto; **do the** ~**s** Toto spielen; **win the** ~**s** im Toto gewinnen; **(b)** (common supply) Fonds, der; Topf, der; **a** [**great**] ~ **of experience** ein [großer] Fundus von od. an Erfahrung; **(c)** (game) Pool[billard], das. **2** v.t. zusammenlegen ‹Geld, Ersparnisse, Mittel, Besitz›; bündeln ‹Anstrengungen›; **they** ~**ed their experience** sie nutzten ihre Erfahrung gemeinsam

poor /pʊə(r)/ **1** adj. **(a)** arm; **(b)** (inadequate) schlecht; schwach ‹Rede, Spiel, Leistung, Gesundheit›; dürftig ‹Essen, Kleidung, Unterkunft, Entschuldigung›; **of** ~ **quality** minderer Qualität; **be** ~ **at maths** etc. schlecht od. schwach in Mathematik usw. sein; **sb. is** ~ **at games** Ballspiele liegen jmdm. nicht; **(c)** (paltry) schwach ‹Trost›; schlecht ‹Aussichten, Situation›; (disgusting) mies (ugs. abwertend); **that's pretty** ~! das ist reichlich dürftig od. (ugs.) ganz schön schwach; **(d)** (unfortunate) arm (auch iron.); ~ **you!** du Armer/Arme!; du Ärmster/Ärmste!; **(e)** (infertile) karg, schlecht ‹Boden, Land›; **(f)** (spiritless, pathetic) arm ‹Teufel, Dummkopf›; armselig, (abwertend) elend ‹Kreatur, Stümper›; **(g)** (deficient) arm (**in** an + Dat.); ~ **in content/ ideas/vitamins** inhalts-/ideen-/vitaminarm; **(h)** **take a** ~ **view of** nicht [sehr] viel halten von; für gering halten ‹Aussichten, Chancen›. **2** n. pl. **the** ~: die Armen Pl.

poorly /'pʊəlɪ/ **1** *adv.* **(a)** (scantily) schlecht; unzureichend; **(b)** (badly) schlecht; unbeholfen ‹*schreiben, sprechen*›; **he did ~ in his exams** er hat bei seinen Prüfungen schlecht abgeschnitten; **(c)** (meanly) schlecht ‹*leben*›. **2** *pred. adj.* schlecht ‹*aussehen, sich fühlen*›; **he has been ~ lately** ihm geht es in letzter Zeit schlecht

'**poor:** **~ man's** *attrib. adj.* (coll.) des kleinen Mannes *nachgestellt;* **~ re'lation** *n.* arme Verwandte, *der/die;* (fig.) Stiefkind, *das;* **be the ~ relation** (fig.) im Vergleich zu etw. schlecht abschneiden

pop¹ /pɒp/ **1** *v.i.,* **-pp-:** **(a)** (make sound) ‹*Korken:*› knallen; ‹*Schote, Samenkapsel:*› aufplatzen, aufspringen; (fig.) **his eyes ~ped** with amazement er guckte wie ein Auto (ugs.); **(b)** (coll.: move, go quickly) **let's ~ round to Fred's** komm, wir gehen mal eben *od.* schnell bei Fred vorbei (ugs.); **~ down to London** mal eben *od.* schnell nach London fahren; **you must ~ round and see us** du musst mal vorbeikommen und uns besuchen *od.* musst mal bei uns reingucken (ugs.). **2** *v.t.,* **-pp-:** **(a)** (coll.: put) **~ the meat in the fridge** das Fleisch in den Kühlschrank tun; **~ a peanut into one's mouth** [sich (*Dat.*)] eine Erdnuss in den Mund stecken; **~ one's head in at the door** den Kopf zur Tür reinstecken; **(b)** (cause to burst) enthülsen ‹*Erbsen, Bohnen*›; platzen *od.* (ugs.) knallen lassen ‹*Luftballon*›; zerknallen ‹*Papiertüte*›; **(c)** **~ the question [to sb.]** (coll.) jmdm. einen [Heirats]antrag machen. **3** *n.* **(a)** (sound) Knall, *der;* Knallen, *das;* **(b)** (coll.: drink) Sprudel, *der;* (flavoured) Brause, *die* (ugs.). **4** *adv.* **go ~:** knallen; peng machen (ugs.)

~ 'off *v.i.* **(a)** (coll.: die) abnibbeln (ugs., bes. nordd.); den Löffel weglegen *od.* abgeben (salopp); **(b)** (move or go away) ‹*Person:*› verschwinden, (ugs.) abdampfen

~ 'out *v.i.* hervorschießen aus; **~ out for a newspaper/to the shops** schnell *od.* eben mal eine Zeitung holen gehen/einkaufen gehen (ugs.); **he's just ~ped out for a moment** er ist nur mal kurz weggegangen (ugs.)

~ 'out of *v.t.* hervorschieben; **~ one's head out of the window** den Kopf zum Fenster herausstrecken; **sb.'s eyes nearly** *or* **almost ~ out of his head** (coll.) (with surprise) jmdm. fallen fast die Augen aus dem Kopf; (with excitement) jmd. (bes. Kind) macht große Augen

~ 'up *v.i.* **(a)** (fig.: appear) auftauchen; **(b)** (rise up) sich aufstellen; (spring up) hochspringen

pop² (coll.) **1** *n.* (popular music) Popmusik, *die;* Pop, *der.* **2** *adj.* Pop‹*star, -musik usw.*›

pop³ *n.* (Amer. coll.: father) Pa[pa], *der* (fam.)

pop: **~ art** *n.,* *no pl., no indef. art.* Pop-Art, *die;* attrib. Pop-Art-; **~ concert** *n.* Popkonzert, *das;* **~corn** *n.* Popcorn, *das*

pope /pəʊp/ *n.* Papst, *der/*Päpstin, *die*

pop: **~-eyed** *adj.* (coll.) großäugig; **they were ~-eyed with amazement** sie staunten Bauklötze (salopp); **~ festival** *n.* Popfestival, *das;* **~ group** *n.* Popgruppe, *die;* **~gun** *n.* Spielzeuggewehr, *das/*Spielzeugpistole, *die*

poplar /'pɒplə(r)/ *n.* Pappel, *die*

poplin /'pɒplɪn/ *n.* (Textiles) Popelin, *der;* Popeline, *der od. die*

'**pop music** *n.* Popmusik, *die*

popper /'pɒpə(r)/ *n.* (Brit. coll.) Druckknopf, *der*

poppy /'pɒpɪ/ *n.* **(a)** (Bot.) Mohn, *der;* **opium ~:** Schlafmohn, *der;* **(b)** (Brit.: emblem) [künstliche] Mohnblume (als Zeichen des Gedenkens am 'Poppy Day')

'**Poppy Day** (Brit.) ⇒ **Remembrance Day**

Popsicle, (P) /'pɒpsɪkl/ *n.* (Amer.) Eis am Stiel

pop: **~ singer** *n.* Popsänger, *der/*-sängerin, *die;* Schlagersänger, *der/*-sängerin, *die;* **~ song** *n.* Popsong, *der;* Schlager, *der;* **~ star** *n.* Popstar, *der;* Schlagerstar, *der*

popular /'pɒpjʊlə(r)/ *adj.* **(a)** (well liked) beliebt; populär ‹*Entscheidung, Maßnahme*›; **he was a very ~ choice** mit ihm hatte man sich für einen sehr beliebten *od.* populären Mann entschieden; **be ~ with sb.** bei jmdm. beliebt sein; **(b)** (suited to the public) volkstümlich; populär (geh.); **~ newspaper** Massenblatt, *das;* **(c)** (prevalent) landläufig; allgemein ‹*Unzufriedenheit*›; **(d)** (of the people) Volks-; verbreitet ‹*Aberglaube, Irrtum, Meinung*›; allgemein ‹*Wahl, Zustimmung, Unterstützung*›; **by ~ request** auf allgemeinen Wunsch

popularise ⇒ **popularize**

popularity /pɒpjʊ'lærɪtɪ/ *n., no pl.* Popularität, *die;* Beliebtheit, *die;* (of decision, measure) Popularität, *die*

popularize /'pɒpjʊləraɪz/ *v.t.* **(a)** (make popular) populär machen; **(b)** (make known) bekannt machen; **(c)** (make understandable) breiteren Kreisen zugänglich machen

popularly /'pɒpjʊləlɪ/ *adv.* **(a)** (generally) allgemein; landläufig; **it is ~ believed that ...:** es ist ein im Volk verbreiteter Glaube, dass ...; **(b)** (for the people) volkstümlich; [all]gemein verständlich

popular 'music *n.* Unterhaltungsmusik, *die*

populate /'pɒpjʊleɪt/ *v.t.* bevölkern ‹*Land, Gebiet*›; bewohnen ‹*Insel, Gebiet*›; **heavily** *or* **densely/sparsely ~d** dicht/dünn besiedelt ‹*Land, Gebiet usw.*›; dicht/dünn bevölkert ‹*Stadt*›

population /pɒpjʊ'leɪʃn/ *n.* Bevölkerung, *die;* **Britain has a ~ of 56 million** Großbritannien hat 56 Millionen Einwohner

popu'lation explosion *n.* Bevölkerungsexplosion, *die*

populous /'pɒpjʊləs/ *adj.* dicht bevölkert

'**pop-up** *adj.* Stehauf‹*buch, -illustration*›; **~ toaster** Toaster mit Auswerfmechanismus; **~ menu** (Computing) Pop-up-Menü, *das*

porcelain /'pɔːslɪn/ *n.* Porzellan, *das; attrib.* Porzellan-

porch /pɔːtʃ/ *n.* Vordach, *das;* (with side walls) Vorbau, *der;* (enclosed) Windfang, *der;* (of church etc.) Vorhalle, *die*

porcupine /'pɔːkjʊpaɪn/ *n.* (Zool.) Stachelschwein, *das*

pore¹ /pɔː(r)/ *n.* Pore, *die*

pore² *v.i.* **~ over sth.** etw. [genau] studieren; (think deeply) **~ over** *or* **on sth.** über etw. (*Akk.*) [gründlich] nachdenken

pork /pɔːk/ *n.* Schweinefleisch, *das; attrib.* Schweine-; Schweins- (bes. südd.)

pork: **~ 'chop** *n.* Schweinekotelett, *das;* **~ 'pie** *n.* Schweinepastete, *die;* **~ 'sausage** *n.* Schweinswürstchen, *das*

porn /pɔːn/ *n., no pl.* (coll.) Pornographie, *die;* Pornos (ugs.)

pornographic /pɔːnə'græfɪk/ *adj.* pornographisch; Porno- (ugs.)

pornography /pɔː'nɒgrəfɪ/ *n.* Pornographie, *die*

porous /'pɔːrəs/ *adj.* porös ‹*Fels, Gestein, Stoff*›

porpoise /'pɔːpəs/ *n.* (Zool.) Schweinswal, *der*

porridge /'pɒrɪdʒ/ *n., no pl.* (food) Porridge, *der;* [Hafer]brei, *der*

port¹ /pɔːt/ **1** *n.* **(a)** (harbour) Hafen, *der;* **come** *or* **put into ~:** [in den Hafen] einlaufen; **leave ~:** [aus dem Hafen] auslaufen; **reach ~:** den Hafen erreichen; **any ~ in a storm** (fig. coll.) ≈ in der Not frisst der Teufel Fliegen (ugs.); **~ of call** Anlaufhafen, *der;* (fig.) Ziel, *das;* **(b)** (town) Hafenstadt, *die;* Hafen, *der;* **(c)** (Naut., Aeronaut.: left side) Backbord, *das;* **land to ~!** Land an Backbord! **2** *adj.* (Naut., Aeronaut.: left) Backbord-; backbordseitig; **on the ~ bow/quarter** Backbord voraus/Backbord achteraus

port² *n.* (wine) Portwein, *der;* Port, *der* (ugs.)

portable /'pɔːtəbl/ **1** *adj.* tragbar. **2** *n.* (television) Portable, *der;* (radio) Portable, *der;* Koffergerät, *das;* (typewriter) Portable, *die;* Koffermaschine, *die*

porter¹ /'pɔːtə(r)/ *n.* ▶ 887 (Brit.: doorman) Pförtner, *der;* (of hotel etc.) Portier, *der*

porter² *n.* **(a)** (luggage-handler) [Gepäck]träger, *der/*-trägerin, *die;* (in hotel) Hausdiener, *der;* **(b)** (Amer., Ir./Hist.: beer) Porter, *der od. das*

portfolio /pɔːt'fəʊlɪəʊ/ *n., pl.* **~s** **(a)** (list) Portefeuille, *das;* **(b)** (Polit.) Geschäftsbereich, *der;* Portefeuille, *das* (geh.); **(c)** (case, contents) Mappe, *die*

porthole /'pɔːθəʊl/ *n.* (Naut.) Seitenfenster, *das;* (round) Bullauge, *das*

portion /'pɔːʃn/ *n.* **(a)** (part) Teil, *der;* (of ticket) Abschnitt, *der;* (of inheritance) Anteil, *der;* **(b)** (amount of food) Portion, *die*

~ 'out *v.t.* aufteilen (**among, between** unter + *Akk.*)

portly /'pɔːtlɪ/ *adj.* beleibt; korpulent

portmanteau /pɔːt'mæntəʊ/ *n., pl.* ~s *or* ~x /pɔːt'mæntəʊz/ Reisekoffer, *der*

portrait /'pɔːtrɪt/ *n.* Porträt, *das;* Bildnis, *das* (geh.); *attrib.* Porträt-; **have one's ~ painted** sich porträtieren lassen

portray /pɔː'treɪ/ *v.t.* (a) (describe) darstellen; schildern; (b) (make likeness of) porträtieren ‹*Person*›; ‹*Schauspieler:*› darstellen ‹*Rolle, Person*›

Portugal /'pɔːtjʊɡl/ *pr. n.* Portugal (*das*)

Portuguese /pɔːtjʊ'ɡiːz/ ▶897 , ▶947 **1** *adj.* portugiesisch; **sb. is ~:** jmd. ist Portugiese/Portugiesin. **2** *n., pl. same* (a) (person) Portugiese, *der*/Portugiesin, *die;* (b) (language) Portugiesisch, *das; see also* **English 2 a**

pose /pəʊz/ **1** *v.t.* (a) (be cause of) aufwerfen ‹*Frage, Problem*›; darstellen ‹*Bedrohung, Problem*›; bedeuten ‹*Bedrohung*›; mit sich bringen ‹*Schwierigkeiten*›; (b) (propound) vorbringen; aufstellen ‹*Theorie*›; (c) (place) Aufstellung nehmen lassen; posieren lassen ‹*Modell*›. **2** *v.i.* (a) (assume attitude) posieren; (fig.) sich geziert benehmen (abwertend); (b) **~ as** sich geben als; **he likes to ~ as an expert** er spielt gern den Experten. **3** *n.* Haltung, *die;* Pose, *die;* (fig.) Pose, *die;* Gehabe, *das* (abwertend); **strike a ~:** eine Pose einnehmen

poser /'pəʊzə(r)/ *n.* (question) knifflige Frage; (problem) schwieriges Problem; **that's a real ~:** das ist eine harte Nuss (ugs.)

posh /pɒʃ/ **1** *adj.* (coll.) vornehm; nobel (spött.); stinkvornehm (salopp); **the ~ people** die Schickeria (ugs.). **2** *adv.* **talk ~** hochgestochen reden/mit vornehmem Akzent sprechen

position /pə'zɪʃn/ **1** *n.* (a) (place occupied) Platz, *der;* (of player in team; of plane, ship, etc.) Position, *die;* (of hands of clock, words, stars) Stellung, *die;* (of building) Lage, *die;* (of river) [Ver]lauf, *der;* **find one's ~ on a map** seinen Standort auf einer Karte finden; **take [up] one's ~** seinen Platz einnehmen; **after the second lap he was in fourth ~:** nach der zweiten Runde lag er an vierter Stelle; **he finished in second ~:** er belegte den zweiten Platz; (b) (proper place) **be in/out of ~:** an seinem Platz/nicht an seinem Platz sein; (c) (Mil.) Stellung, *die;* (d) (fig.: mental attitude) Standpunkt, *der;* Haltung, *die;* **take up a ~ on sth.** einen Standpunkt *od.* eine Haltung zu etw. einnehmen; (e) (fig.: situation) **be in a good ~ [financially]** [finanziell] gut gestellt sein *od.* dastehen; **be in a ~ of strength** eine starke Position haben; **put yourself in my ~!** versetz dich [einmal] in meine Lage!; **be in a ~ to do sth.** in der Lage sein, etw. zu tun; (f) (rank) Stellung, *die;* Position, *die;* (g) (employment) [Arbeits]stelle, *die;* Stellung, *die;* **the ~ of assistant manager** die Stelle *od.* Position des stellvertretenden Geschäftsführers; **~ of trust** Vertrauensstellung, *die;* Vertrauensposten, *der;* (h) (posture) Haltung, *die;* (during sexual intercourse) Stellung, *die;* Position, *die;* **in a reclining ~:** zurückgelehnt. **2** *v.t.* (a) (place) aufstellen, postieren ‹*Polizisten, Wachen*›; **~ oneself near the exit** sich in die Nähe des Ausgangs stellen/setzen; ‹*Wache, Posten usw.:*› sich in der Nähe des Ausgangs aufstellen; (b) (Mil.: station) stationieren

positive /'pɒzɪtɪv/ *adj.* (a) (definite) eindeutig; entschieden ‹*Weigerung*›; positiv ‹*Recht*›; **in a ~ tone of voice** in bestimmtem *od.* entschiedenem Ton; (b) (convinced) sicher; **Are you sure? — P~!** Bist du sicher? — Absolut [sicher]!; **I'm ~ of it** ich bin [mir] [dessen] ganz sicher; (c) (affirmative) positiv; (d) (optimistic) positiv; (e) (showing presence of sth.) positiv ‹*Ergebnis, Befund, Test*›; (f) (constructive) konstruktiv ‹*Kritik, Vorschlag*›; positiv ‹*Philosophie, Erfahrung, Denken*›; (g) (Math.) positiv; (h) (Electr.) positiv ‹*Elektrode, Platte, Ladung, Ion*›; (i) *as intensifier* (coll.) echt; **it would be a ~ miracle** es wäre ein echtes Wunder *od.* (ugs.) echt ein Wunder

positively /'pɒzɪtɪvlɪ/ *adv.* (a) (constructively) konstruktiv ‹*kritisieren*›; positiv ‹*denken*›; (b) (distinct) sicher; (c) (definitely) eindeutig, entschieden ‹*sich weigern*›; (d) *as intensifier* (coll.) echt (ugs.); **it's ~ marvellous that …:** es ist echt spitze, dass …

'positive vetting *n., no indef. art.* (Brit.) Sicherheitsüberprüfung, *die*

posse /'pɒsɪ/ *n.* (a) (Amer.: force with legal authority) [Polizei]trupp, *der;* [Polizei]aufgebot, *das;* (b) (crowd) Schar, *die*

possess /pə'zes/ *v.t.* (a) (own) besitzen; (b) (have as faculty or quality) haben; (c) (dominate) ‹*Furcht usw.:*› ergreifen, Besitz nehmen von ‹*Person*›; **what ~ed you/him?** (coll.) was ist in dich/ihn gefahren?

possessed /pə'zest/ *adj.* (dominated) besessen; **like one ~:** wie ein Besessener/eine Besessene

possession /pə'zeʃn/ *n.* (a) (thing possessed) Besitz, *der;* **some of my ~s** einige meiner Sachen; (b) *in pl.* (property) Besitz, *der;* (territory) Besitzungen; (c) (controlling) Besitz *od.* (Mil.) einnehmen ‹*Festung, Stadt usw.*›; besetzen ‹*Gebiet*›; (d) (possessing) Besitz, *der;* **be in ~ of sth.** im Besitz einer Sache (Gen.) sein; **come into** *or* **get ~ of sth.** in den Besitz einer Sache (Gen.) gelangen; **in full ~ of one's senses** im Vollbesitz seiner geistigen Kräfte; **be in full ~ of the facts** voll im Bilde sein; **have sth. in one's ~:** im Besitz einer Sache (Gen.) sein; **take ~ of** in Besitz nehmen; beziehen ‹*Haus, Wohnung*›; **in ~** (Sport) im Ballbesitz

possessive /pə'zesɪv/ *adj.* (a) (jealously retaining possession) besitzergreifend; **be ~ about sth.** etw. eifersüchtig hüten; **be ~ about** *or* **towards sb.** an jmdm. Besitzansprüche stellen; (b) (Ling.) possessiv; **~ adjective** Possessivadjektiv, *das;* **~ pronoun** Possessivpronomen, *das*

pos'sessive case *n.* Possessiv[us], *der*

possessor /pə'zesə(r)/ *n.* Besitzer, *der*/Besitzerin, *die*

possibility /pɒsɪ'bɪlɪtɪ/ *n.* (a) Möglichkeit, *die;* **there's no ~ of his coming/agreeing** es ist ausgeschlossen, dass er kommt/zustimmt; **there's not much ~ of success** die Erfolgschancen sind nicht groß; **it's a distinct ~ that …:** es ist gut möglich, dass …; (b) *in pl.* (potential) Möglichkeiten *Pl.;* **the house/subject has possibilities** aus dem Haus/Thema lässt sich etwas machen

possible /'pɒsɪbl/ **1** *adj.* (a) möglich; **if ~:** wenn *od.* falls möglich; wenn es geht; **as … as ~:** so … wie möglich; möglichst …; **all the assistance ~:** alle denkbare Unterstützung; **they made it ~ for me to be here** sie haben es mir ermöglicht, hier zu sein; **would it be ~ for me to …?** könnte ich vielleicht …?; **for ~ emergencies** für eventuelle Notfälle; **I'll do everything ~ to help you** ich werde mein Möglichstes tun, um dir zu helfen; **we will help as far as ~:** wir werden helfen, soweit wir können; (b) (likely) [durchaus *od.* gut] möglich; (c) (acceptable) möglich; **there's no ~ excuse for it** dafür gibt es keine Entschuldigung; **the only ~ man for the position** der einzige Mann, der für die Stellung infrage kommt. **2** *n.* Anwärter, *der*/Anwärterin, *die;* Kandidat, *der*/Kandidatin, *die*

possibly /'pɒsɪblɪ/ *adv.* (a) (by possible means) **I cannot ~ commit myself** ich kann mich unmöglich festlegen; **how can I ~?** wie könnte ich?; **they did all they ~ could** sie haben alles Menschenmögliche getan; **as often as I ~ can** sooft ich irgend kann; (b) (perhaps) möglicherweise; vielleicht; **Do you think …? — P~:** Glaubst du …? — Möglich[erweise] *od.* Vielleicht

post¹ /pəʊst/ **1** *n.* (a) (as support) Pfosten, *der;* (b) (stake) Pfahl, *der;* **deaf as a ~** (coll.) stocktaub (ugs.); *see also* **pillar a;** (c) (Racing) (starting/finishing ~) Start-/Zielpfosten, *der;* **be left at the ~:** [hoffnungslos] abgehängt werden (ugs.); weit zurückbleiben; **the 'first past the ~' system** das Mehrheitswahlsystem; *see also* **pip⁵;** (d) (Sport: of goal) Pfosten, *der.* **2** *v.t.* (a) (stick up) anschlagen, ankleben ‹*Plakat, Aufruf, Notiz, Zettel*›; (b) (make known) [öffentlich] anschlagen *od.* bekannt geben; **~ [as] missing** als vermisst melden

~ 'up *v.t.* anschlagen; ankleben; **~ up a notice** einen Anschlag machen

post² **1** *n.* (a) (Brit.: one dispatch of letters) Postausgang, *der;* **by return of ~:** postwendend; (b) (Brit.: one collection of letters) [Briefkasten]leerung, *die;* (c) (Brit.: one delivery of letters) Post[zustellung], *die;* **in the ~:** bei der Post (*see also* **d**); **the ~ has come** die Post ist da *od.* ist schon gekommen; **sort the ~:** die Posteingänge sortieren; **is there any ~ for me?** habe ich Post?; (d) *no pl., no indef. art.* (Brit.: official conveying) Post, *die;* **by ~:** mit der Post; per Post; **in the ~:** in der Post (*see also* **c**); (e) (~ office) Post, *die;* (~box) Briefkasten, *der;* **take sth. to the ~:** etw. zur Post bringen/(to ∼box) etw. einwerfen *od.* in den Briefkasten werfen. **2** *v.t.* **(a)** (dispatch) abschicken; ∼ **sb. sth.** jmdm. etw. schicken; **(b)** (fig. coll.) **keep sb. ∼ed** [**about** *or* **on sth.**] jmdn. [über etw. (*Akk.*)] auf dem Laufenden halten

post³ 1 *n.* **(a)** (job) Stelle, *die;* Posten, *der;* **a teaching ∼:** eine Stelle als Lehrer *od.* Lehrerstelle; **a diplomatic ∼:** ein diplomatischer Posten; **(b)** (Mil.: place of duty) Posten, *der;* (fig.) Platz, *der;* Posten, *der;* **take up one's ∼** (fig.) seinen Platz einnehmen; **last/first ∼** (Brit. Mil.) letzter/erster Zapfenstreich. **2** *v.t.* **(a)** (place) postieren; aufstellen; **(b)** (appoint) einsetzen; **be ∼ed to an embassy** an eine Botschaft versetzt werden

post- /pəʊst/ *pref.* nach-/Nach-; post-/Post- (mit Fremdwörtern)

postage /'pəʊstɪdʒ/ *n.* Porto, *das*

'postage stamp *n.* Briefmarke, *die*

postal /'pəʊstl/ *adj.* Post-; postalisch 〈*Aufgabe, Einrichtung*〉; (by post) per Post *nachgestellt*

postal: ∼ **district** *n.* Zustellbezirk, *der;* ∼ **order** *n.* ≈ Postanweisung, *die;* ∼ **vote** *n.* Briefwahl, *die*

post: ∼**bag** (Brit.) ⇒ **mailbag;** ∼**box** *n.* (Brit.) Briefkasten, *der;* ∼**card** *n.* Postkarte, *die;* ∼**code** *n.* (Brit.) Postleitzahl, *die*

post'date *v.t.* **(a)** (give later date to) vordatieren; **(b)** (belong to later date than) späteren *od.* jüngeren Datums sein als (+ *Nom.*)

poster /'pəʊstə(r)/ *n.* **(a)** (placard) Plakat, *das;* (notice) Anschlag, *der;* **(b)** (printed picture) Plakat, *das;* Poster, *das*

poste restante /pəʊst re'stɑ̃t/ *n.* Abteilung/Schalter für postlagernde Sendungen; **write to sb [at the] ∼ in Rome** jmdm. postlagernd nach Rom schreiben

posterior /pɒ'stɪərɪə(r)/ *n.* (joc.) Hinterteil, *das* (ugs.)

posterity /pɒ'sterɪtɪ/ *n., no pl., no art.* die Nachwelt; **go down to ∼ [as sth.]** [als etw.] in die Geschichte eingehen

post-'free (Brit.) *adj., adv.* portofrei

post'graduate **1** *adj.* Graduierten-; 〈*College, Studiengang*〉 für Graduierte; ∼ **student** Graduierte, *der/die.* **2** *n.* Graduierte, *der/die*

post'haste *adv.* schnellstens

posthumous /'pɒstjʊməs/ *adj.* **(a)** nachgelassen, (geh.) postum 〈*Buch usw.*〉; **(b)** (occurring after death) nachträglich; post[h]um (geh.); ∼ **fame** Nachruhm, *der*

post: ∼**man** /'pəʊstmən/, *pl.* ∼**men** /'pəʊstmən/ *n.* ▶ **887** Briefträger, *der;* Postbote, *der* (ugs.); ∼**mark** **1** *n.* Poststempel, *der;* **2** *v.t.* abstempeln; **the letter was ∼marked 'Brighton'** der Brief war in Brighton abgestempelt; ∼**master** *n.* ▶ **887** Postamtvorsteher, *der;* Postmeister, *der* (veralt.)

postmortem /pəʊst'mɔːtəm/ **1** *adv.* nach dem Tode; post mortem (fachspr.). **2** *adj.* nach dem Tode eintretend; ∼ **examination** Leichenschau, *die;* (with dissection) Obduktion, *die.* **3** *n.* **(a)** (examination) Obduktion, *die;* **(b)** (fig.) nachträgliche Bewertung

postnatal /pəʊst'neɪtl/ *adj.* nach der Geburt *nachgestellt;* postnatal (fachspr.)

post: ∼ **office** *n.* **(a)** (organization) **the P∼ Office** die Post; **(b)** (place) Postamt, *das;* Post, *die;* ∼**-office box** *n.* Postfach, *das;* ∼**paid** **1** /'--/ *adj.* frankiert; freigemacht; **2** /-'-/ *adv.* portofrei

postpone /pəʊst'pəʊn, pə'spəʊn/ *v.t.* verschieben; (for an indefinite period) aufschieben; ∼ **sth. until next week** etw. auf nächste Woche verschieben

postponement /pəʊst'pəʊnmənt, pə'spəʊnmənt/ *n.* Verschiebung, *die;* (for an indefinite period) Aufschub, *der*

postpositive /pəʊst'pɒzɪtɪv/ *adj.* (Ling.) nachgestellt; postpositiv (fachspr.)

'post room *n.* Poststelle, die

postscript /'pəʊstskrɪpt, 'pəʊskrɪpt/ *n.* Nachschrift, *die;* Postskript, *das;* (fig.) Nachtrag, *der*

postulate 1 /'pɒstjʊleɪt/ *v.t.* **(a)** (claim as true, existent, necessary) postulieren; ausgehen von; (depend on) voraussetzen; (put forward) aufstellen 〈*Theorie*〉. **2** /'pɒstjʊlət/ *n.* **(a)** (fundamental condition) Postulat, *das* (geh.); (prerequisite) Voraussetzung, *die;* Postulat, *das* (geh.)

posture /'pɒstʃə(r)/ **1** *n.* (relative position) [Körper]haltung, *die;* (fig.: mental, political, military) Haltung, *die.* **2** *v.i.* posieren; (strike a pose) sich in Positur werfen (ugs., leicht spött.)

'post-war *adj.* Nachkriegs-; der Nachkriegszeit *nachgestellt*

posy /'pəʊzɪ/ *n.* Sträußchen, *das*

pot¹ /pɒt/ **1** *n.* **(a)** (cooking vessel) [Koch]topf, *der;* **go to ∼** (coll.) den Bach runtergehen (ugs.); **(b)** (container, contents) Topf, *der;* (tea∼, coffee-∼) Kanne, *die;* **a ∼ of tea** eine Kanne Tee; (in café etc.) ein Kännchen Tee; **(c)** (sl.: prize) Preis, *der;* (coll.: large sum) **a ∼ of/∼s of** massenweise; jede Menge. **2** *v.t.,* **-tt-:** **(a)** (put in container[s]) in einen Topf/in Töpfe füllen; **(b)** (put in plant ∼) ∼ **[up]** eintopfen; ∼ **out** austopfen; **(c)** (kill) abschießen; abknallen (ugs. abwertend); **(d)** (Brit. Billiards, Snooker) einlochen

pot² *n.* (sl.: marijuana) Pot, *das* (Jargon)

potash /'pɒtæʃ/ *n.* Kaliumkarbonat, *das;* Pottasche, *die* (veralt.)

potassium /pə'tæsɪəm/ *n.* (Chem.) Kalium, *das*

potato /pə'teɪtəʊ/ *n., pl.* ∼**es** Kartoffel, *die;* **a hot ∼** (fig. coll.) ein heißes Eisen (ugs.)

potato 'salad *n.* Kartoffelsalat, *der*

'potbelly *n.* Schmerbauch, *der* (ugs.); Wampe, *die* (ugs. abwertend); (from malnutrition) Blähbauch, *der*

potency /'pəʊtənsɪ/ *n.* **(a)** (of drug) Wirksamkeit, *die;* (of alcoholic drink) Stärke, *die;* (Mil.) Schlagkraft, *die;* (of reason, argument) Gewichtigkeit, *die;* (influence) Einfluss, *der;* Potenz, *die* (geh.); **(b)** (of male) [sexual] ∼: [sexuelle] Potenz

potent /'pəʊtənt/ *adj.* **(a)** [hoch]wirksam 〈*Droge*〉; stark 〈*Schnaps usw.*〉; schlagkräftig 〈*Waffe*〉; gewichtig, schwerwiegend 〈*Grund, Argument*〉; wichtig, entscheidend 〈*Faktor*〉; stark 〈*Motiv*〉; (influential) einflussreich; potent (geh.); **(b)** (sexually) potent 〈*Mann*〉

potential /pə'tenʃl/ **1** *adj.* potenziell (geh.); möglich. **2** *n.* Potenzial, *das* (geh.); Möglichkeiten *Pl.;* ∼ **for growth/development** Wachstums-/Entwicklungspotenzial, *das;* **realize/reach one's ∼:** seine Möglichkeiten ausschöpfen

pot: ∼**hole** **1** *n.* **(a)** (in road) Schlagloch, *das;* **(b)** (deep cave) [tiefe] Höhle; **2** *v.i.* Höhlen erkunden; ∼**holer** /'pɒthəʊlə(r)/ *n.* [Hobby]höhlenforscher, *der/*-forscherin, *die;* ∼**holing** /'pɒthəʊlɪŋ/ *n.* Erkundung von Höhlen

potion /'pəʊʃn/ *n.* Trank, *der*

pot'luck *n.* **take ∼:** sich überraschen lassen

potpourri /pəʊpʊə'riː, pəʊ'pʊərɪ/ *n.* Duftmischung, *die*

pot: ∼ **roast** *n.* Schmorbraten, *der;* ∼**shot** *n.* **(a)** (random shot); **take a ∼shot [at sb./sth.]** aufs Geratewohl [auf jmdn./etw.] schießen; **(b)** (fig.: critical remark) Attacke, *die*

potted /'pɒtɪd/ *adj.* **(a)** (preserved) eingemacht; ∼ **meat/fish** Fleisch-/Fischkonserven *Pl.;* **(b)** (planted) Topf-; **(c)** (abridged) kurz gefasst

potter¹ /'pɒtə(r)/ *n.* ▶ **887** Töpfer, *der/*Töpferin, *die*

potter² *v.i.* **(a)** [he]rumwerkeln (ugs.); ∼ **round the shops** durch die Geschäfte bummeln

∼ **a'bout,** ∼ **a'round** *v.i.* herumwerkeln (ugs.) (**with** an + *Dat.*)

potter's 'wheel *n.* Töpferscheibe, *die*

pottery /'pɒtərɪ/ *n.* **(a)** *no pl., no indef. art.* (vessels) Töpferware, *die;* Keramik, *die; attrib.* Ton-; Keramik-; **(b)** (workshop, craft) Töpferei, *die*

'potting compost *n.* Blumenerde, *die*

potty¹ /'pɒtɪ/ *adj.* (Brit. coll.: crazy) verrückt (ugs.) (**about, on** nach)

potty² *n.* (Brit. coll.) Töpfchen, *das*

'potty-train *v.t.* ∼ **a baby** ein Baby an den Topf *od.* ans Töpfchen gewöhnen; **the baby is ∼ed** das Baby ist sauber *od.* geht aufs Töpfchen

pouch /paʊtʃ/ *n.* **(a)** (small bag) Tasche, *die;* Täschchen, *das;* **(b)** (under eye) [Tränen]sack, *der;* **(c)** (ammunition bag) [Patronen]tasche, *die;* **(d)** (Zool.) (of marsupial) Beutel, *der*

pouffe /puːf/ *n.* (cushion) Sitzpolster, *der;* Puff, *der*

poultry /'pəʊltrɪ/ *n.* **(a)** *constr. as pl.* (birds) Geflügel, *das;* **(b)** *no pl., no indef. art.* (as food) Geflügel, *das*

pounce /paʊns/ **1** *v.i.* **(a)** sich auf sein Opfer stürzen; 〈*Raubvogel:*〉 herabstoßen auf (+ *Akk.*); **(b)** (fig.) ∼

[up]on/at sich stürzen auf (+ *Akk.*). **2** *n.* Sprung, *der;* Satz, *der*

pound¹ /paʊnd/ *n.* **(a)** ►1202│ (unit of weight) [britisches] Pfund (453,6 Gramm); **two ~s of apples** 2 Pfund Äpfel; **by the ~:** pfundweise; **(b)** ►938│ (unit of currency) Pfund, *das;* **five-~ note** Fünfpfundnote, *die;* Fünfpfundschein, *der*

pound² *n.* (enclosure) Pferch, *der;* (for stray dogs) Zwinger [für eingefangene Hunde]; (for cars) Abstellplatz [für polizeilich abgeschleppte Fahrzeuge]

pound³ 1 *v.t.* **(a)** (crush) zerstoßen; **(b)** (thump) einschlagen auf (+ *Akk.*) ⟨*Person*⟩; klopfen ⟨*Fleisch*⟩; ⟨*Sturm:*⟩ heimsuchen ⟨*Gebiet, Insel*⟩; ⟨*Wellen:*⟩ klatschen auf (+ *Akk.*) ⟨*Strand, Ufer*⟩, gegen *od.* an (+ *Akk.*) ⟨*Felsen, Schiff*⟩; ⟨*Geschütz:*⟩ unter Beschuss (*Akk.*) nehmen ⟨*Ziel*⟩; ⟨*Bombenflugzeug:*⟩ bombardieren ⟨*Ziel*⟩; **(c)** (knock) **~ to pieces** ⟨*Wellen:*⟩ zertrümmern, zerschmettern ⟨*Schiff*⟩; ⟨*Geschütz, Bomben:*⟩ in Trümmer legen ⟨*Stadt, Mauern*⟩; **(d)** (compress) **~ [down]** feststampfen ⟨*Erde, Boden*⟩. **2** *v.i.* **(a)** (make one's way heavily) stampfen; **(b)** (beat rapidly) ⟨*Herz:*⟩ heftig schlagen *od.* klopfen *od.* (geh.) pochen

pounding /ˈpaʊndɪŋ/ *n.* **(a)** (striking) (of hammer etc.) Schlagen, *das;* Klopfen, *das;* (of artillery) [schwerer] Beschuss; (of waves) Klatschen, *das;* **(b)** (of hooves, footsteps) Stampfen, *das;* **(c)** (beating) (of heart) Klopfen, *das;* Pochen, *das* (geh.); (of music, drums) Dröhnen, *das*

pour /pɔː(r)/ **1** *v.t.* gießen, schütten ⟨*Flüssigkeit*⟩; schütten ⟨*Sand, Kies, Getreide usw.*⟩; (into drinking vessel) einschenken; eingießen; (fig.) pumpen ⟨*Geld, Geschosse*⟩; **~ scorn** *or* **ridicule on sb./sth.** jmdn. mit Spott übergießen *od.* überschütten/über etw. (*Akk.*) spotten. **2** *v.i.* **(a)** (flow) strömen; ⟨*Rauch:*⟩ hervorquellen (**from** aus); **sweat was ~ing off the runners** den Läufern lief der Schweiß in Strömen herunter; **~ [with rain]** in Strömen regnen; [in Strömen] gießen (ugs.); **it never rains but it ~s** (fig.) da kommt aber auch alles zusammen; **(b)** (fig.) strömen; **~ in** herein-/hineinströmen; **~ out** heraus-/hinausströmen; **letters/protests ~ed in** eine Flut von Briefen/Protesten brach herein

~ 'down *v.i.* it's **~ing down** es gießt [in Strömen] (ugs.)

~ 'forth 1 *v.t.* von sich geben; ausschütten ⟨*Kummer*⟩; erzählen ⟨*Geschichte*⟩. **2** *v.i.* ⟨*Gesang, Musik usw.:*⟩ ertönen, erklingen; ⟨*Menge, Personen:*⟩ herausströmen

~ 'off *v.t.* abgießen

~ 'out 1 *v.t.* eingießen, einschenken ⟨*Getränk*⟩; **~ out one's woes** *or* **troubles/heart to sb.** jmdm. seinen Kummer/sein Herz ausschütten. **2** *v.i.* ⇒ **~ 2 b**

pouring /ˈpɔːrɪŋ/ *adj.* **(a)** strömend ⟨*Regen*⟩; **a ~ wet day** ein völlig verregneter Tag; **(b)** (for dispensing) Gieß-

pout /paʊt/ **1** *v.i.* **~ing lips** Schmolllippen *Pl.* **2** *v.t.* aufwerfen, schürzen ⟨*Lippen*⟩. **3** *n.* Schmollmund, *der*

poverty /ˈpɒvətɪ/ *n.* **(a)** Armut, *die;* **be reduced to ~:** verarmt sein; **(b)** (fig.: deficiency) Armut, *die* (**in** an + *Dat.*); **~ of ideas** Ideenarmut, *die;* **~ of imagination/intellect** Fantasielosigkeit, *die*

poverty: ~ line *n.* Armutsgrenze, *die;* **~-stricken** *adj.* Not leidend; verarmt; (fig.) armselig; kümmerlich; **~ trap** *n.* Armutsfalle, *die;* (soziale Situation, in der die Aufnahme einer Erwerbstätigkeit für die Betroffenen zu einer Verschlechterung seiner wirtschaftlichen Lage führen kann, weil er durch sie seinen Anspruch auf staatliche Sozialhilfe verlieren würde)

POW *abbr.* **prisoner of war**

powder /ˈpaʊdə(r)/ **1** *n.* **(a)** Pulver, *das;* **(b)** (cosmetic) Puder, *der.* **2** *v.t.* **(a)** pudern; **I'll just go and ~ my nose** (euphem.) ich muss [nur] mal verschwinden (ugs. verhüll.); **(b)** (reduce to ~) pulverisieren; zu Pulver verarbeiten ⟨*Milch, Eier*⟩; **~ed milk** Milchpulver, *das;* Trockenmilch, *die*

'powder compact ⇒ **compact²** a

powdering /ˈpaʊdərɪŋ/ *n.* [Ein]pudern, *das;* **a ~ of snow** eine dünne Schicht Schnee

powder: ~ keg *n.* (lit. *or* fig.) Pulverfass, *das;* **~-puff** *n.* Puderquaste, *die;* **~ room** *n.* [Damen]toilette, *die*

powdery /ˈpaʊdərɪ/ *adj.* **(a)** (like powder) pulv[e]rig; (in powder form) pulverförmig; (finer) pud[e]rig/puderförmig; **(b)** (crumbly) bröckelig; bröselig

power /ˈpaʊə(r)/ **1** *n.* **(a)** (ability) Kraft, *die;* **do all in one's ~ to help sb.** alles in seiner Macht *od.* seinen Kräften Stehende tun, um jmdm. zu helfen; **(b)** (faculty) Fähigkeit, *die;* Vermögen, *das* (geh.); (talent) Begabung, *die;* Talent, *das;* **psychic ~s** übersinnliche Kräfte; **~s of persuasion** Überredungskünste; **(c)** (vigour, intensity) (of sun's rays) Kraft, *die;* (of sermon, performance) Eindringlichkeit, *die;* (solidity, physical strength) Kraft, *die;* (of a blow) Wucht, *die;* **(d)** (authority) Macht, *die,* Herrschaft, *die* (**over** über + *Akk.*); **she was in his ~:** sie war in seiner Gewalt; **(e)** (personal ascendancy) **[exercise/get] ~:** Einfluss [ausüben/gewinnen] (**over** auf + *Akk.*); **(f)** (political or social ascendancy) Macht, *die;* **hold ~:** an der Macht sein; **come into ~:** an die Macht kommen; **balance of ~:** Kräftegleichgewicht, *das;* **hold the balance of ~:** das Zünglein an der Waage sein; **(g)** (authorization) Vollmacht, *die;* **(h)** (influential person) Autorität, *die;* (influential thing) Machtfaktor, *der;* **be the ~ behind the throne** (Polit.) die graue Eminenz sein; **the ~s that be** die maßgeblichen Stellen; die da oben (ugs.); **(i)** (State) Macht, *die;* **(j)** (coll.: large amount) Menge, *die* (ugs.); **do sb. a ~ of good** jmdm. außerordentlich gut tun; **(k)** (Math.) Potenz, *die;* **3 to the ~ of 4** 3 hoch 4; **(l)** (mechanical, electrical) Kraft, *die;* (electric current) Strom, *der;* (of loudspeaker, engine, etc.) Leistung, *die;* **(m)** (deity) Macht, *die;* **the ~s of darkness** die Mächte der Finsternis. **2** *v.t.* ⟨*Treibstoff, Dampf, Strom, Gas:*⟩ antreiben; ⟨*Batterie:*⟩ mit Energie versehen *od.* versorgen

power: ~-assisted *adj.* **~-assisted steering/brakes** Servolenkung, *die/*-bremsen *Pl.;* **~ boat** *n.* Motorboot, *das;* **~ cut** *n.* Stromsperre, *die;* Stromabschaltung, *die;* (failure) Stromausfall, *der;* **~ dressing** *n.:* das Tragen betont streng wirkender Kleidung; **~ drill** *n.* elektrische Bohrmaschine; **~ failure** *n.* Stromausfall, *der*

powerful /ˈpaʊəfl/ *adj.* **(a)** (strong) stark; kräftig ⟨*Tritt, Schlag, Tier, Geruch, Körperbau*⟩; heftig ⟨*Gefühl, Empfindung*⟩; hell, strahlend ⟨*Licht*⟩; scharf ⟨*Verstand, Geist*⟩; überzeugend ⟨*Redner, Schauspieler*⟩; eindringlich ⟨*Buch, Rede*⟩; beeindruckend ⟨*Film, Darstellung*⟩; **(b)** (influential); mächtig ⟨*Clique, Person, Herrscher*⟩; wesentlich ⟨*Faktor*⟩

'powerhouse *n.* **(a)** ⇒ **power station**; **(b)** (fig.) treibende Kraft

powerless /ˈpaʊəlɪs/ *adj.* machtlos; **be ~ to do sth.** nicht die Macht haben, etw. zu tun

power: ~ line *n.* Stromleitung, *die;* **overhead ~ line** Freileitung, *die;* **~ plant** *n.* **(a)** ⇒ **power station**; **(b)** (engine) Triebwerk, *das;* **~ point** *n.* (Brit.) Steckdose, *die;* **~ saw** *n.* Motorsäge, *die;* **~ station** *n.* Kraftwerk, *das;* Elektrizitätswerk, *das;* **~ steering** *n.* Servolenkung, *die*

pox /pɒks/ *n.* **(a)** (disease with pocks) Pocken *Pl.;* Blattern *Pl.* (veralt.); **(b)** (coll.: syphilis) Syphilis, *die;* Syph, *die od. der* (salopp)

p.p. /piːˈpiː/ *abbr.* **by proxy** pp[a].

pp. *abbr.* **pages**

PR *abbr.* **(a)** **proportional representation**; **(b)** **public relations** PR; Public Relations; **PR man** Werbefachmann, *der;* PR-Mann, *der*

practicable /ˈpræktɪkəbl/ *adj.* (feasible) durchführbar ⟨*Projekt, Idee, Plan*⟩; praktikabel ⟨*Lösung, Plan*⟩

practical /ˈpræktɪkl/ *adj.* **(a)** praktisch; **(b)** (inclined to action) praktisch veranlagt ⟨*Person*⟩; **have a ~ approach/mind** praktisch an die Dinge herangehen; **(c)** (virtual) tatsächlich ⟨*Freiheit, Organisator*⟩; **(d)** (feasible) möglich ⟨*Alternative*⟩; praktikabel ⟨*Alternative, Möglichkeit*⟩

practicality /præktɪˈkælɪtɪ/ *n.* **(a)** *no pl.* (of plan) Durchführbarkeit, *die;* (of person) praktische Veranlagung; **(b)** *in pl.* (practical details) **the practicalities of the situation are that …:** die Situation sieht praktisch so aus, dass …

practical 'joke *n.* Streich, *der;* **play ~s on sb.** jmdm. Streiche spielen

practical 'joker *n.* Witzbold, *der*

practically /ˈpræktɪkəlɪ/ *adv.* **(a)** (almost) praktisch (ugs.); so gut wie; beinahe; **(b)** (in a practical manner) praktisch

practice¹ /ˈpræktɪs/ *n.* **(a)** (repeated exercise) Praxis, *die;* Übung, *die;* **put in** *or* **do some/a lot of ~:** üben/viel üben; ∼ **makes perfect** (prov.) Übung macht den Meister; **be out of** ∼, **not be in** ∼: außer Übung sein; **(b)** (spell) Übungen *PL.;* **piano** ∼: Klavierüben, *das;* **(c)** (work or business of doctor, lawyer, etc.) Praxis, *die; see also* **general practice;** **(d)** (habitual action) übliche Praxis; Gewohnheit, *die;* ∼ **shows that** …: die Erfahrung zeigt *od.* lehrt, dass …; **good** ∼ (sound procedure) gutes Vorgehen; **(e)** (action) Praxis, *die;* **in** ∼: in der Praxis; in Wirklichkeit; **put sth. into** ∼: etw. in die Praxis umsetzen; **(f)** (custom) Gewohnheit, *die;* **regular** ∼: Brauch, *der*

practice², **practiced**, **practicing** (Amer.) ⇒ **practis-**

practise /'præktɪs/ **1** *v.t.* **(a)** (apply) anwenden; praktizieren; **(b)** (be engaged in) ausüben ‹*Beruf, Tätigkeit, Religion*›; ∼ **medicine** [als Arzt] praktizieren; **(c)** (exercise oneself in) trainieren in (+ *Dat.*) ‹*Sportart*›; ∼ **the piano/flute** Klavier/Flöte üben. **2** *v.i.* üben

practised /'præktɪst/ *adj.* geübt ‹*Person, Auge, Blick*›; erfahren, versiert, routiniert ‹*Person*›; **with** [a] ∼ **eye** mit geübtem Blick

practising /'præktɪsɪŋ/ *adj.* praktizierend ‹*Arzt, Katholik, Anglikaner usw.*›; ∼ **homosexual** aktiv Homosexueller

practitioner /præk'tɪʃənə(r)/ *n.* Fachmann, *der;* Praktiker, *der*/Praktikerin, *die;* ∼ **of the law, legal** ∼: Anwalt, *der*/Anwältin, *die; see also* **general practitioner; medical practitioner**

pragmatic /præg'mætɪk/ *adj.* pragmatisch

Prague /prɑːg/ *pr. n.* ▶ **1159**┘ Prag (*das*)

prairie /'preərɪ/ *n.* Grasland, *das;* Grassteppe, *die;* (in North America) Prärie, *die*

praise /preɪz/ **1** *v.t.* **(a)** (commend) loben; (more strongly) rühmen; ∼ **sb. for doing sth.** jmdn. dafür loben, dass er etw. tut/getan hat; **(b)** (glorify) preisen (geh.), (dichter.) lobpreisen ‹*Gott*›. **2** *n.* **(a)** (approval) Lob, *das;* **win high** ∼: großes *od.* hohes Lob erhalten *od.* ernten; **sing one's own/sb.'s** ∼**s** ein Loblied auf sich/jmdn. singen; **(b)** (worship) Lobpreisung, *die* (dichter.)

praiseworthy /'preɪzwɜːði/ *adj.* lobenswert; löblich (oft iron.)

pram /præm/ *n.* (Brit.) Kinderwagen, *der;* (for dolls) Puppenwagen, *der*

prance /prɑːns/ *v.i.* **(a)** ‹*Pferd:*› tänzeln; **(b)** (fig.) stolzieren; ‹*Tänzer:*› tänzeln; ∼ **about** or **around** ‹*Kind, Tänzer:*› herumhüpfen

prank /præŋk/ *n.* Streich, *der;* Schabernack, *der;* **play a** ∼ **on sb.** jmdm. einen Streich *od.* Schabernack spielen

prattle /'prætl/ **1** *v.i.* ‹*Kleinkind:*› plappern (ugs.); schwafeln (ugs. abwertend). **2** *n.* Geplapper, *das* (ugs.); Geschwafel, *das* (ugs. abwertend)

prawn /prɔːn/ *n.* Garnele, *die*

pray /preɪ/ **1** *v.i.* beten (**for** um); **let us** ∼: lasset uns beten; ∼ **to God for help** Gott um Hilfe anflehen. **2** *v.t.* **(a)** (beseech) anflehen, flehen zu ‹*Gott, Heiligen, Jungfrau Maria*› (**for** um); **(b)** (∼ to) beten zu; **(c)** (ellipt.: I ask) bitte

prayer /preə(r)/ *n.* **(a)** Gebet, *das;* **offer** ∼**s for** beten für; **say one's** ∼**s** beten; **(b)** *no pl., no art.* (praying) Beten, *das;* **(c)** (entreaty) inständige *od.* eindringliche Bitte

'prayerbook *n.* Gebetbuch, *das*

preach /priːtʃ/ **1** *v.i.* predigen (**to** zu, vor + *Dat.*; **on** über + *Akk.*); (fig.) eine Predigt halten (ugs.); ∼ **to the converted** (fig.) offene Türen einrennen (ugs.). **2** *v.t.* **(a)** halten ‹*Predigt, Ansprache*›; predigen ‹*Evangelium, Botschaft*›; verkündigen ‹*Glauben, Lehre*›; **(b)** (advocate) predigen (ugs.); **practice what one** ∼**es** (fig.) was man [anderen] predigt, selbst auch tun

preacher /'priːtʃə(r)/ *n.* Prediger, *der*/Predigerin, *die*

preamble /priː'æmbl/ *n.* **(a)** Vorbemerkung, *die;* Einleitung, *die;* (to a book) Geleitwort, *das;* **(b)** (Law) Präambel, *die*

pre-arrange /priːə'reɪndʒ/ *v.t.* vorher absprechen; vorher ausmachen *od.* verabreden ‹*Treffpunkt, Zeichen*›

precarious /prɪ'keərɪəs/ *adj.* **(a)** (uncertain) labil, prekär ‹*Gleichgewicht, Situation*›; unsicher ‹*Friede*›; **make a** ∼ **living** eine unsichere Existenz haben; **(b)** (insecure) gefährlich ‹*Weg, Pfad*›; riskant, gefährlich ‹*Balanceakt, Leben*›; instabil (geh.) ‹*Bauwerk*›; unsicher ‹*Koalition*›

precaution /prɪ'kɔːʃn/ *n.* Vorsichts-, Schutzmaßnahme, *die;* **take** ∼**s against sth.** Vorsichts- *od.* Schutzmaßnahmen gegen etw. treffen; **do sth. as a** ∼: vorsichts- *od.* sicherheitshalber etw. tun

precautionary /prɪ'kɔːʃənərɪ/ *adj.* vorsorglich; vorbeugend; prophylaktisch (geh., Med.); **as a** ∼ **measure** vorsichts- *od.* sicherheitshalber

precede /prɪ'siːd/ *v.t.* **(a)** (in rank) rangieren vor (+ *Dat.*); (in importance) wichtiger sein als; Vorrang haben vor (+ *Dat.*); **(b)** (in order or time) vorangehen (+ *Dat.*); (in vehicle) voranfahren (+ *Dat.*); (in time also) vorausgehen (+ *Dat.*); **(c)** (preface, introduce) ∼ **X with Y** X (*Dat.*) Y vorausschicken *od.* voranstellen

precedence /'presɪdəns/ *n., no pl.* Priorität, *die* (geh.) (**over** vor + *Dat.*, gegenüber); Vorrang, *der* (**over** vor + *Dat.*)

precedent /'presɪdənt/ *n.* Präzedenzfall, *der;* **set** or **create a** ∼: ein Präzedenzfall schaffen

precept /'priːsept/ *n.* Grundsatz, *der;* Prinzip, *das*

precinct /'priːsɪŋkt/ *n.* **(a)** (traffic-free area) [**pedestrian**] ∼: Fußgängerzone, *die;* [**shopping**] ∼: für den Verkehr weitgehend gesperrtes Einkaufsviertel; **(b)** (enclosed area) Bereich, *der;* Bezirk, *der*

precious /'preʃəs/ **1** *adj.* **(a)** (costly) wertvoll, kostbar ‹*Schmuckstück*›; Edel‹*metall, -stein*›; **(b)** (highly valued) wertvoll, kostbar ‹*Zeit, Eigenschaft*›; **(c)** (beloved) teuer (geh.); lieb; **(d)** (affected) affektiert; **(e)** (coll.: considerable) beträchtlich; erheblich. **2** *adv.* (coll.) herzlich ‹*wenig, wenige*›

precipice /'presɪpɪs/ *n.* Abgrund, *der*

precipitate **1** /prɪ'sɪpɪtət/ *adj.* eilig ‹*Flucht*›; hastig ‹*Abreise*›; übereilt, überstürzt ‹*Tat, Entschluss, Maßnahme*›; groß, fliegend ‹*Eile*›. **2** /prɪ'sɪpɪteɪt/ *v.t.* **(a)** (throw down) hinunterschleudern; **(b)** (hasten) beschleunigen; (trigger) auslösen

precipitation /prɪsɪpɪ'teɪʃn/ *n.* (Meteorol.) Niederschlag, *der*

precipitous /prɪ'sɪpɪtəs/ *adj.* **(a)** (very steep) sehr steil ‹*Schlucht, Abhang, Treppe, Weg*›; schroff ‹*Abhang, Felswand*›; ∼ **slope/drop** Steilhang, *der*/[steiler] Absturz; **(b)** ⇒ **precipitate 1**

précis /'preɪsiː/ **1** *n., pl. same* /'preɪsiːz/ Inhaltsangabe, *die;* Zusammenfassung, *die.* **2** *v.t.* zusammenfassen

precise /prɪ'saɪs/ *adj.* genau; präzise; fein ‹*Instrument*›; groß ‹*Genauigkeit*›; förmlich ‹*Art*›; **be [more]** ∼: sich präzise[r] ausdrücken; **what are your** ∼ **intentions?** was hast du vor?; …, **to be** ∼: …, um genau zu sein; …, genauer gesagt; **at that** ∼ **moment** genau in dem Augenblick

precisely /prɪ'saɪslɪ/ *adv.* genau; präzise ‹*antworten*›; **speak** ∼: sich präzise ausdrücken; **that is** ∼ **what/why** …: genau das/deswegen …; **what** ∼ **do you want/ mean?** was willst/meinst du eigentlich genau?; **at** ∼ **1.30, at 1.30** ∼: Punkt 1 Uhr 30

precision /prɪ'sɪʒn/ *n., no pl.* Genauigkeit, *die; attrib.* a ∼ **landing** eine Präzisionslandung

precision 'instrument *n.* Präzisions[mess]gerät, *das;* Feinmessgerät, *das*

preclude /prɪ'kluːd/ *v.t.* ausschließen ‹*Zweifel*›; ∼ **sb. from a duty/taking part** jmdn. von einer Pflicht entbinden/von der Teilnahme ausschließen

precocious /prɪ'kəʊʃəs/ *adj.* frühreif ‹*Kind, Jugendlicher, Genie*›; altklug ‹*Äußerung*›

preconceived /priːkən'siːvd/ *adj.* vorgefasst ‹*Ansicht, Vorstellung*›

preconception /priːkən'sepʃn/ *n.* vorgefasste Meinung (**of** über + *Akk.*)

precondition /priːkən'dɪʃn/ *n.* Vorbedingung, *die* (**of** für)

pre-cooked /priː'kʊkt/ *adj.* vorgekocht

precursor /priː'kɜːsə(r)/ *n.* **(a)** (of revolution, movement, etc.) Wegbereiter, *der*/-bereiterin, *die;* **(b)** (predecessor) Vorgänger, *der*/-gängerin, *die*

pre-date /priː'deɪt/ *v.t.* ∼ **sth.** ‹*Ereignis:*› einer Sache (*Dat.*) vorausgehen; ‹*Sache:*› aus der Zeit vor etw. (*Dat.*) stammen

predator /'predətə(r)/ *n.* Raubtier, *das;* (fish) Raubfisch, *der*

predatory /'predətərı/ *adj.* räuberisch; ~ **animal** Raubtier, *das*

predecessor /'pri:dısesə(r)/ *n.* **(a)** (former holder of position) Vorgänger, *der*/-gängerin, *die;* **(b)** (preceding thing) Vorläufer, *der*

predestination /pri:destı'neıʃn/ *n., no pl.* Vorherbestimmung, *die*

predestine /pri:'destın/ *v.t.* von vornherein bestimmen (**to** zu)

predetermine /pri:dı'tɜ:mın/ *v.t.* im Voraus *od.* von vornherein bestimmen; ‹*Gott, Schicksal:*› vorherbestimmen

predicament /prı'dıkəmənt/ *n.* Dilemma, *das;* Zwangslage, *die*

predicate /'predıkət/ *n.* (Ling.) Prädikat, *das*

predicative /prı'dıkətıv/ *adj.* (Ling.) prädikativ

predict /prı'dıkt/ *v.t.* voraus-, vorhersagen; prophezeien; voraus-, vorhersehen ‹*Folgen*›

predictable /prı'dıktəbl/ *adj.* voraus-, vorhersagbar; voraus-, vorhersehbar ‹*Folgen, Reaktion, Ereignis*›; berechenbar ‹*Person*›

predictably /prı'dıktəblı/ *adv.* wie voraus- *od.* vorherzusehen war

prediction /prı'dıkʃn/ *n.* Voraus-, Vorhersage, *die*

predilection /pri:dı'lekʃn/ *n.* Vorliebe, *die* (**for** für)

predispose /pri:dı'spəʊz/ *v.t.* **be** ~**d to do sth.** (be willing to do sth.) geneigt sein, etw. zu tun; (tend to do sth.) dazu neigen, etw. zu tun; ~ **sb. in favour of sb./sth.** jmdn. für jmdn./etw. einnehmen

predisposition /pri:dıspə'zıʃn/ *n.* Neigung, *die* (**to** zu)

predominance /prı'domınəns/ *n.* **(a)** (control) Vorherrschaft, *die* (**over** über + *Akk.*); **(b)** (majority) Überzahl, *die* (**of** von)

predominant /prı'domınənt/ *adj.* **(a)** (having more power) dominierend; **(b)** (prevailing) vorherrschend

predominantly /prı'domınəntlı/ *adv.* überwiegend

predominate /prı'domıneıt/ *v.i.* (be more powerful) dominierend sein; (be more important) vorherrschen; überwiegen; (be more numerous) in der Überzahl sein

pre-eminence /pri:'emınəns/ *n., no pl.* Vorrangstellung, *die;* **her** ~ **in this field** ihre herausragende Stellung auf diesem Gebiet

pre-eminent /pri:'emınənt/ *adj.* herausragend; **be** ~: eine herausragende Stellung einnehmen

pre-eminently /pri:'emınəntlı/ *adv.* herausragend; (mainly) vor allem; in erster Linie

pre-empt /pri:'empt/ *v.t.* (forestall) zuvorkommen (+ *Dat.*)

pre-emptive /pri:'emptıv/ *adj.* (Mil.) Präventiv‹*krieg, -maßnahme, -schlag*›

preen /pri:n/ **1** *v.t.* ‹*Vogel:*› putzen ‹*Federn, Gefieder*›. **2** *v. refl.* ‹*Vogel:*› sich putzen; ‹*Person:*› sich herausputzen

prefab /'pri:fæb/ *n.* (coll.) (house) Fertighaus, *das;* (building) Fertigbau, *der*

prefabricate /pri:'fæbrıkeıt/ *v.t.* vorfertigen

prefabricated *adj.* /pri:'fæbrıkeıtıd/ vorgefertigt; ~ **house/building** Fertighaus, *das*/Fertigbau, *der*

preface /'prefəs/ **1** *n.* Vorwort, *das* (**to** *Gen.*). **2** *v.t.* (introduce) einleiten

prefect /'pri:fekt/ *n.* (Sch.) *die Aufsicht führender älterer Schüler*/*führende ältere Schülerin*

prefer /prı'fɜ:(r)/ *v.t.*, **-rr-:** **(a)** (like better) vorziehen; ~ **to do sth.** etw. lieber tun; es vorziehen, etw. zu tun; ~ **sth. to sth.** etw. einer Sache (*Dat.*) vorziehen; **I** ~ **skiing to skating** ich fahre lieber Ski als Schlittschuh; **I** ~ **not to talk about it** darüber möchte ich lieber nicht sprechen; **I should** ~ **to wait** ich würde lieber warten; **he** ~**s blondes** er bevorzugt Blondinen; **I** ~ **water to wine** ich trinke lieber Wasser als Wein; **(b)** (submit) erheben ‹*Anklage, Anschuldigungen*› (**against** gegen, **for** wegen)

preferable /'prefərəbl/ *adj.* vorzuziehen *präd.;* vorzuziehend *attr.;* besser (**to** als); **the cold was** ~ **to the smoke** die Kälte war noch erträglicher als der Rauch

preferably /'prefərəblı/ *adv.* am besten; (as best liked) am liebsten; **a piano,** ~ **not too expensive** ein möglichst nicht zu teures Klavier; **Wine or beer?** — **Wine,** ~! Wein oder Bier? — Lieber Wein!

preference /'prefərəns/ *n.* **(a)** (greater liking) Vorliebe, *die;* **for** ~ ⇒ **preferably; have a** ~ **for sth.** [over sth.] etw. [einer Sache (*Dat.*)] vorziehen; **do sth. in** ~ **to sth. else** etw. lieber als etw. anderes tun; **(b)** (thing preferred) **what are your** ~**s?** was wäre dir am liebsten?; **I have no** ~: mir ist alles gleich recht; **(c)** (favouring of one person or country) Präferenzbehandlung, *die;* **give [one's]** ~ **to sb.** jmdn. bevorzugen; **give sb.** ~ **over others** jmdm. anderen gegenüber Vergünstigungen einräumen; **(d)** *attrib.* (Brit. Finance) Vorzugs-, Prioritäts‹*obligation, -aktie*›

preferential /prefə'renʃl/ *adj.* bevorzugt ‹*Behandlung*›; bevorrechtigt ‹*Ansprache, Stellung*›; **give sb.** ~ **treatment** jmdn. bevorzugt behandeln

prefix (Ling.) **1** /'pri:fıks, prı:'fıks/ *v.t.* als Präfix setzen (**to** vor + *Akk.*). **2** /'pri:fıks/ *n.* Präfix, *das;* Vorsilbe, *die*

pregnancy /'pregnənsı/ *n.* (of woman) Schwangerschaft, *die;* (of animal) Trächtigkeit, *die*

'pregnancy test *n.* Schwangerschaftstest, *der*

pregnant /'pregnənt/ *adj.* **(a)** schwanger ‹*Frau*›; trächtig ‹*Tier*›; **she is** ~ **with her second child** sie erwartet ihr zweites Kind; **be six months** ~: im siebten Monat schwanger sein; **(b)** (fig.: momentous) bedeutungsschwer (geh.); ~ **with meaning** bedeutungsschwanger

preheat /pri:'hi:t/ *v.t.* vorheizen ‹*Backofen*›; vorher erwärmen ‹*Gas, Werkzeug*›

prehensile /prı'hensaıl/ *adj.* (Zool.) Greif‹*-fuß, -schwanz*›

prehistoric /pri:hı'stɒrık/ *adj.* **(a)** vorgeschichtlich; prähistorisch; **(b)** (coll.) (ancient) uralt (ugs.); (out of date) vorsintflutlich (ugs.)

prehistory /pri:'hıstərı/ *n.* Vorgeschichte, *die*

prejudge /pri:'dʒʌdʒ/ *v.t.* **(a)** (form premature opinion about) vorschnell *od.* voreilig urteilen über (+ *Akk.*); **(b)** (judge before trial) im Voraus beurteilen, vorverurteilen ‹*Person*›; im Voraus entscheiden ‹*Fall*›

prejudice /'predʒʊdıs/ **1** *n.* **(a)** (bias) Vorurteil, *das;* **colour** ~: Vorurteil aufgrund der Hautfarbe; **overcome** ~: Vorurteile ablegen; **(b)** (injury) Schaden, *der;* Nachteil, *der;* **without** ~ (Law) unbeschadet aller Rechte. **2** *v.t.* **(a)** (bias) beeinflussen; ~ **sb. in sb.'s favour/against sb.** jmdn. für/gegen jmdn. einnehmen; **(b)** (injure) beeinträchtigen

prejudiced /'predʒʊdıst/ *adj.* voreingenommen (**about** gegenüber, **against** gegen); **be racially** ~: Rassenvorurteile haben

prejudicial /predʒʊ'dıʃl/ *adj.* abträglich (geh.) (**to** *Dat.*); nachteilig (**to** für); **be** ~ **to** beeinträchtigen ‹*Anspruch, Chance, Recht*›; schaden (+ *Dat.*) ‹*Interesse*›

prelate /'prelət/ *n.* Prälat, *der*

prelim /'pri:lım/ *n.* (coll.: exam) Vorprüfung, *die*

preliminary /prı'lımınərı/ **1** *adj.* Vor-; vorbereitend ‹*Forschung, Maßnahme*›; einleitend ‹*Kapitel, Vertragsbestimmungen*›; ~ **inquiry/search** erste Nachforschung/Suche. **2** *n., usu. in pl.* **preliminaries** Präliminarien *Pl.;* (Sports) Ausscheidungskämpfe *Pl.;* **as a** ~ **to sth.** (as a preparation) als Vorbereitung auf etw. (*Akk.*); **just a** ~: nur ein Vorspiel (**to** zu); **without any further preliminaries** ohne [weitere] Umschweife

prelude /'prelju:d/ *n.* **(a)** (introduction) Anfang, *der* (**to** *Gen.*); Auftakt, *der* (**to** zu); **(b)** (of play) Vorspiel, *das* (**to** zu); **(c)** (Mus.) Präludium, *das;* Vorspiel, *das*

premarital /pri:'mærıtl/ *adj.* vorehelich; ~ **sex** Geschlechtsverkehr vor der Ehe

premature /'premətjʊə(r)/ *adj.* **(a)** (hasty) voreilig, übereilt ‹*Entscheidung, Handeln*›; **(b)** (early) früh-, vorzeitig ‹*Altern, Ankunft, Haarausfall*›; verfrüht ‹*Bericht, Eile, Furcht*›; ~ **baby** Frühgeburt, *die;* **the baby was five weeks** ~: das Baby wurde fünf Wochen zu früh geboren

prematurely /'premətjʊəlı/ *adv.* (early) vorzeitig; zu früh ‹*geboren werden*›; (hastily) voreilig, übereilt ‹*entscheiden, handeln*›

premeditated /pri:'medıteıtıd/ *adj.* vorsätzlich

premenstrual /pri:'menstrʊəl/ *adj.* (Med.) prämenstruell; ~ **tension** prämenstruelle Spannung

premier /'premɪə(r)/ *n.* Premier[minister], *der*/Premierministerin, *die*

première /'premjeə(r)/ *n.* (of production) Premiere, *die;* Erstaufführung, *die;* (of work) Uraufführung, *die*

premise /'premɪs/ *n.* (a) *in pl.* (building) Gebäude, *das;* (buildings and land of factory or school) Gelände, *das;* (rooms) Räumlichkeiten *Pl.;* **on the ~s** hier/dort; (of public house, restaurant, etc.) im Lokal; (b) ⇒ **premiss**

premiss /'premɪs/ *n.* (Logic) Prämisse, *die*

premium /'priːmɪəm/ *n.* (a) (Insurance) Prämie, *die;* (b) (reward) Preis, *der;* Prämie, *die;* **put a ~ on sth.** (attach special value to) etw. [hoch ein]schätzen; (c) (St. Exch.) Agio, *das;* Aufgeld, *das;* **be at a ~:** über pari stehen; (fig.: be highly valued) sehr gefragt sein

'Premium Bond *n.* (Brit.) Prämienanleihe, *die;* Losanleihe, *die*

premonition /premə'nɪʃn/ *n.* (a) (forewarning) Vorwarnung, *die;* (b) (presentiment) Vorahnung, *die;* **feel/have a ~ of sth.** eine Vorahnung von etw. haben

preoccupation /prɪɒkjʊ'peɪʃn/ *n.* Sorge, *die* (**with** um); **first** *or* **greatest** *or* **main ~:** Hauptanliegen, *das;* Hauptsorge, *die*

preoccupied /prɪ'ɒkjʊpaɪd/ *adj.* (lost in thought) gedankenverloren; (concerned) besorgt (**with** um); (absorbed) beschäftigt (**with** mit)

preoccupy /prɪ'ɒkjʊpaɪ/ *v.t.* beschäftigen

prep /prep/ *n.* (Brit. Sch. coll.) [Haus-, Schul]aufgaben *Pl.*

pre-packaged /priː'pækɪdʒd/, **pre-packed** /priː'pækt/ *adjs.* abgepackt

prepaid ⇒ **prepay**

preparation /prepə'reɪʃn/ *n.* (a) Vorbereitung, *die;* **be in ~** ⟨*Publikation:*⟩ in Vorbereitung sein; **in ~ for the new baby/term** als Vorbereitung auf das neue Baby/Semester; (b) *in pl.* (things done to get ready) Vorbereitungen *Pl.* (for für); **~s for war/the wedding** Kriegs-/Hochzeitsvorbereitungen; **make ~s for sth.** Vorbereitungen für etw. treffen; (c) (Chem., Med., Pharm.) Präparat, *das*

preparatory /prɪ'pærətərɪ/ **1** *adj.* vorbereitend ⟨*Schritt, Maßnahme*⟩; Vor⟨*ermittlung, -untersuchung*⟩; **~ work** Vorarbeiten *Pl.* **2** *adv.* **~ to sth.** vor etw. (*Dat.*); **~ to doing sth.** bevor man etw. tut

pre'paratory school *n.* (a) (Brit. Sch.) *für die Aufnahme an einer Public School vorbereitende Privatschule;* (b) (Amer. Univ.) *meist private, für die Aufnahme an einem College vorbereitende Schule*

prepare /prɪ'peə(r)/ **1** *v.t.* (a) (make ready) vorbereiten; entwerfen, ausarbeiten ⟨*Plan, Rede*⟩; herrichten (ugs.), fertig machen ⟨*Gästezimmer*⟩; (make mentally ready, equip with necessary knowledge) vorbereiten ⟨*Person* (for auf + *Akk.*); **~ oneself for a shock/the worst** sich auf einen Schock/das Schlimmste gefasst machen; **be ~d for anything** auf alles gefasst sein; **be ~d to do sth.** (be willing) bereit sein, etw. zu tun; (b) (make) herstellen ⟨*Chemikalie, Metall usw.*⟩; zubereiten ⟨*Essen*⟩. **2** *v.i.* sich vorbereiten (**for** auf + *Akk.*); **~ for battle/war** ⟨*Land:*⟩ zum Kampf/Krieg rüsten; **~ to do sth.** sich bereit machen, etw. zu tun

prepay /priː'peɪ/ *v.t.*, **prepaid** /priː'peɪd/ im Voraus [be]zahlen; (pay postage on) frankieren, freimachen ⟨*Brief, Paket usw.*⟩; **prepaid envelope** frankierter Umschlag; Freiumschlag, *der*

preponderance /prɪ'pɒndərəns/ *n.* Überlegenheit, *die* (**over** über + *Akk.*, gegenüber); Übergewicht, *das*

preposition /prepə'zɪʃn/ *n.* (Ling.) Präposition, *die;* Verhältniswort, *das*

prepositional /prepə'zɪʃənl/ *adj.* (Ling.) präpositional; Präpositional⟨*attribut, -fall, -objekt*⟩

prepossessing /priːpə'zesɪŋ/ *adj.* einnehmend, anziehend ⟨*Äußeres, Erscheinung, Person, Lächeln usw.*⟩

preposterous /prɪ'pɒstərəs/ *adj.* absurd; grotesk ⟨*Äußeres, Kleidung*⟩

'pre-program *v.t.*, **-mm-** [vor]programmieren

'prep school (coll.) ⇒ **preparatory school**

prerequisite /priː'rekwɪzɪt/ **1** *n.* [Grund]voraussetzung, *die.* **2** *adj.* unbedingt erforderlich

prerogative /prɪ'rɒɡətɪv/ *n.* Privileg, *das;* Vorrecht, *das*

Presbyterian /prezbɪ'tɪərɪən/ **1** *adj.* presbyterianisch. **2** *n.* Presbyterianer, *der*/Presbyterianerin, *die*

preschool /'priːskuːl/ *adj.* Vorschul-; **~ years** Vorschulalter, *das*

prescribe /prɪ'skraɪb/ *v.t.* (a) (impose) vorschreiben; (b) (Med.; also fig.) verschreiben; verordnen

prescription /prɪ'skrɪpʃn/ *n.* (a) (prescribing) Anordnung, *die;* Vorschreiben, *das;* (b) (Med.) Rezept, *das;* (medicine) [verordnete *od.* verschriebene] Medizin; Verordnung, *die* (fachspr.); **be available only on ~:** nur auf Rezept zu bekommen sein

pre'scription charge *n.* Rezeptgebühr, *die*

prescriptive /prɪ'skrɪptɪv/ *adj.* (Ling.) präskriptiv

presence /'prezns/ *n.* (a) (being present) (of person) Gegenwart, *die;* Anwesenheit, *die;* (of things) Vorhandensein, *das;* **in the ~ of his friends** in Gegenwart *od.* Anwesenheit seiner Freunde; **make one's ~ felt** sich bemerkbar machen; (b) (bearing) Auftreten, *das;* (c) (being represented) Präsenz, *die;* **police ~:** Polizeipräsenz, *die;* (d) **~ of mind** Geistesgegenwart, *die*

present¹ /'preznt/ **1** *adj.* (a) anwesend, (geh.) zugegen (at bei); **~ in the air/water/in large amounts** in der Luft/im Wasser/in großen Mengen vorhanden sein; **all ~ and correct** (joc.) alle sind da; **all those ~:** alle Anwesenden; **~ company excepted** Anwesende ausgenommen; (b) (being dealt with) betreffend; **in the ~ case** im vorliegenden Fall; (c) (existing now) gegenwärtig; jetzig, derzeitig ⟨*Bischof, Chef usw.*⟩; (d) (Ling.) **~ tense** Präsens, *das;* Gegenwart, *die; see also* **participle. 2** *n.* (a) **the ~:** die Gegenwart; **up to the ~:** bis jetzt; bisher; **at ~:** zur Zeit; **for the ~:** vorläufig; (b) (Ling.) Präsens, *das;* Gegenwart, *die*

present² **1** /'preznt/ *n.* (gift) Geschenk, *das;* **parting ~:** Abschiedsgeschenk, *das;* **make a ~ of sth. to sb.**, **make sb. a ~ of sth.** jmdm. etw. zum Geschenk machen; *see also* **give 1 b. 2** /prɪ'zent/ *v.t.* (a) schenken; überreichen ⟨*Preis, Medaille*⟩; **~ sth. to sb.** *or* **sb. with sth.** jmdm. etw. schenken *od.* zum Geschenk machen; **~ sb. with difficulties/a problem** jmdn. vor Schwierigkeiten/ein Problem stellen; **he was ~ed with an opportunity that ...:** ihm bot sich eine Gelegenheit, die ...; (b) (deliver) überreichen ⟨*Gesuch*⟩ (**to** bei); vorlegen ⟨*Scheck, Bericht, Rechnung*⟩ (**to** *Dat.*); **~ one's case** seinen Fall darlegen; (c) (exhibit) zeigen ⟨*Schwierigkeit*⟩; aufweisen ⟨*Aspekt*⟩; (d) (introduce) vorstellen (**to** *Dat.*); (e) (to the public) geben, aufführen ⟨*Theaterstück*⟩; zeigen ⟨*Film*⟩; moderieren ⟨*Sendung*⟩; bringen ⟨*Fernsehserie, Schauspieler in einer Rolle*⟩; vorstellen ⟨*Produkt usw.*⟩; vorstellen ⟨*Abhandlung*⟩; (f) **~ arms!** (Mil.) präsentiert das Gewehr! **3** *v. refl.* ⟨*Problem:*⟩ auftreten; ⟨*Möglichkeit:*⟩ sich ergeben; **~ oneself for interview/an examination** zu einem Gespräch/einer Prüfung erscheinen

presentable /prɪ'zentəbl/ *adj.* ansehnlich; **the flat is not very ~ at the moment** die Wohnung ist im Augenblick nicht besonders präsentabel; **make oneself/sth. ~:** sich/etw. zurechtmachen; **I'm not ~:** ich kann mich so nicht zeigen

presentation /prezn'teɪʃn/ *n.* (a) (giving) Schenkung, *die;* (of prize, medal, gift) Überreichung, *die;* (b) (ceremony) Verleihung, *die;* **~ of the awards/medals** Preis-/Ordensverleihung, *die;* (c) (delivering) (of petition) Überreichung, *die;* (of cheque, report, account) Vorlage, *die;* (of case, position, thesis) Darlegung, *die;* **on ~ of** gegen Vorlage (+ *Gen.*); (d) (exhibition) Darstellung, *die;* (e) (Theatre, Radio, Telev.) Darbietung, *die;* (Theatre also) Inszenierung, *die;* (Radio, Telev. also) Moderation, *die;* (f) (introduction) Vorstellung, *die*

presen'tation skills *n. pl.* Präsentationsfähigkeiten *Pl.*

present-'day *adj.* heutig; zeitgemäß ⟨*Einstellungen, Ansichten*⟩

presenter /prɪ'zentə(r)/ *n.* ▶ 887 | (Radio, Telev.) Moderator, *der*/Moderatorin, *die*

presentiment /prɪ'zentɪmənt/ *n.* Vorahnung, *die;* **have a ~ that ...:** vorausahnen, dass ...

presently /'prezntlɪ/ *adv.* (a) (soon) bald; (b) (Amer., Scot.: now) zur Zeit; derzeit

preservation /prezə'veɪʃn/ *n., no pl.* **(a)** (action) Erhaltung, *die;* (of leather, wood, etc.) Konservierung, *die;* **(b)** (state) Erhaltungszustand, *der*

preservative /prɪ'zɜːvətɪv/ *n.* Konservierungsmittel, *das*

preserve /prɪ'zɜːv/ **1** *n.* **(a)** *in sing. or pl.* (fruit) Eingemachte, *das;* **strawberry/quince** ∼s eingemachte Erdbeeren/Quitten; **(b)** (jam) Konfitüre, *die;* **(c)** (fig.: special sphere) Domäne, *die* (geh.); **(d)** **wildlife/game** ∼: Tierschutzgebiet, *das*/Wildpark *der.* **2** *v.t.* **(a)** (keep safe) schützen **(from** *or* + *Dat.*); ∼ **sth. from destruction** etw. vor der Zerstörung bewahren; **(b)** (maintain) aufrechterhalten ⟨*Disziplin*⟩; bewahren ⟨*Sehfähigkeit, Brauch, Würde*⟩; behalten ⟨*Stellung*⟩; wahren ⟨*Anschein, Reputation*⟩; ∼ **the peace** den Frieden bewahren *od.* erhalten; **(c)** (retain) speichern ⟨*Hitze*⟩; bewahren ⟨*Haltung, Distanz, Humor*⟩; **(d)** (prepare, keep from decay) konservieren; (bottle) einmachen ⟨*Obst, Gemüse*⟩; **(e)** (keep alive) erhalten; (fig.) bewahren ⟨*Erinnerung, Andenken*⟩; **Heaven** ∼ **us!** [Gott] bewahre!; **(f)** (care for and protect) hegen ⟨*Tierart, Wald*⟩; unter Schutz stellen ⟨*Gewässer, Gebiet*⟩

pre-set /priː'set/ *v.t., forms as* **set 1** vorher einstellen

'**pre-shrunk** *adj.* vorgeschrumpft, vorgewaschen ⟨*Jeans usw.*⟩

preside /prɪ'zaɪd/ *v.i.* **(a)** (at meeting etc.) den Vorsitz haben **(at** bei); präsidieren, vorsitzen **(over** *Dat.*); **(b)** (exercise control) ∼ **over** leiten ⟨*Abteilung, Organisation, Programm*⟩

presidency /'prezɪdənsɪ/ *n.* **(a)** Präsidentschaft, *die;* **(b)** (of society, legislative body) Vorsitz, *der;* **(c)** (Univ., esp. Amer.) Präsidentschaft, *die;* Rektorat, *das*

president /'prezɪdənt/ *n.* ▶**887** **(a)** Präsident, *der*/Präsidentin, *die;* **(b)** (of society, council, legislative body) Vorsitzende, *der/die;* **(c)** (Univ., esp. Amer.) Präsident, *der*/Präsidentin, *die;* Rektor, *der*/Rektorin, *die*

presidential /prezɪ'denʃl/ *adj.* Präsidenten-; ∼ **campaign** Präsidentschaftswahlkampf, *der*

press¹ /pres/ **1** *n.* **(a)** (newspapers etc.) Presse, *die; attrib.* Presse-; der Presse *nachgestellt;* **get/have a good/bad** ∼ (fig.) eine gute/schlechte Presse bekommen/haben; **(b)** = **printing press; (c)** (printing house) Druckerei, *die;* **at** *or* **in** [**the**] ∼: im Druck; **send to** [**the**] ∼: in Druck geben; **go to** [**the**] ∼: in Druck gehen; **(d)** (publishing firm) Verlag, *der;* **(e)** (for flattening, compressing, etc.) Presse, *die;* (for sports racket) Spanner, *der;* **(f)** (crowd) Menge, *die;* **(g)** (∼ing) Druck, *der;* **give sth. a** ∼: etw. drücken. **2** *v.t.* **(a)** drücken; pressen; drücken auf (+ *Akk.*) ⟨*Klingel, Knopf*⟩; treten auf (+ *Akk.*) ⟨*Gas-, Brems-, Kupplungspedal usw.*⟩; ∼ **the trigger** abdrücken; **(b)** (urge) drängen ⟨*Person*⟩; (force) aufdrängen [**up**]**on** *Dat.*); (insist on) nachdrücklich vorbringen ⟨*Forderung, Argument, Vorschlag*⟩; ∼ **sb. for an answer** jmdn. zu einer Antwort drängen; **he did not** ∼ **the point** er ließ die Sache auf sich beruhen; **(c)** (compress) pressen; auspressen ⟨*Orangen, Saft*⟩; keltern ⟨*Trauben, Äpfel*⟩; (iron) bügeln; **(e)** **be** ∼**ed for space/time/money** (have barely enough) zu wenig Platz/Zeit/Geld haben. **3** *v.i.* **(a)** (exert pressure) drücken; **the child** ∼**ed against the railings** das Kind drückte sich gegen das Geländer; **(b)** (be urgent) drängen; **time/sth.** ∼**es** die Zeit drängt/etw. eilt *od.* ist dringend; **(c)** (make demand) ∼ **for sth.** auf etw. (*Akk.*) drängen

∼ **a'head,** ∼ **'on** *v.i.* (continue activity) [zügig] weitermachen; (continue travelling) [zügig] weitergehen/-fahren; ∼ **on with one's work** sich mit der Arbeit ranhalten (ugs.)

∼ '**out** *v.t.* auspressen; (out of cardboard) herausdrücken

press² *v.t.* ∼ **into service/use** in Dienst nehmen; einsetzen

press: ∼-**button** ⇒ **push-button;** ∼ **conference** *n.* Pressekonferenz, *die;* ∼ **coverage** *n.* Berichterstattung in der Presse; ∼ **gallery** *n.* Pressetribüne, *die;* ∼-**gang 1** *n.* (Hist.) Pressgang, *der* (veralt.). **2** *v.t.* (Hist.) pressen; zwangsrekrutieren

pressing /'presɪŋ/ *adj.* **(a)** (urgent) dringend; **(b)** (persistent) dringlich; nachdrücklich

press: ∼ **release** *n.* Presseinformation, *die;* ∼ **report** *n.* Pressebericht, *der;* ∼ **stud** *n.* (Brit.) Druckknopf, *der;* ∼-**up** *n.* Liegestütz, *der*

pressure /'preʃə(r)/ **1** *n.* **(a)** (exertion of force, amount) Druck, *der;* **apply firm** ∼ **to the joint** die Verbindung fest zusammendrücken; **atmospheric** ∼: Luftdruck, *der;* **(b)** (oppression) Last, *die;* Belastung, *die;* **mental** ∼: psychische Belastung; **(c)** (trouble) Druck, *der;* ∼**s at** [**one's**] **work** berufliche Belastungen; **(d)** (urgency) Druck, *der;* (of affairs) Dringlichkeit, *die;* **(e)** (constraint) Druck, *der;* Zwang, *der;* **put** ∼ **on sb.** jmdn. unter Druck setzen; **be under a lot of** ∼ **to do sth.** stark unter Druck gesetzt werden, etw. zu tun. *See also* **high pressure; low pressure. 2** *v.t.* ∼ **sb. into doing sth.** jmdn. [dazu] drängen, etw. zu tun

pressure: ∼ **cooker** *n.* Schnellkochtopf, *der;* ∼ **gauge** *n.* (Motor Veh.) Druckluftmesser, *der;* ∼ **group** *n.* Pressuregroup, *die*

pressurize (pressurise) /'preʃəraɪz/ *v.t.* **(a)** ⇒ **pressure 2; (b)** (maintain normal pressure in) druckfest machen, auf Normaldruck halten ⟨*Flugzeugkabine*⟩; ∼**d cabin** Druckkabine, *die*

prestige /pre'stiːʒ/ **1** *n.* Prestige, *das;* Renommee, *das.* **2** *adj.* renommiert; Nobel⟨*hotel, -gegend*⟩; ∼ **value** Prestigewert, *der*

prestigious /pre'stɪdʒəs/ *adj.* angesehen

presto /'prestəʊ/ ⇒ **hey**

presumably /prɪ'zjuːməblɪ/ *adv.* vermutlich; ∼ **he knows what he is doing** er wird schon wissen, was er tut

presume /prɪ'zjuːm/ **1** *v.t.* **(a)** (venture) ∼ **to do sth.** sich (*Dat.*) anmaßen, etw. zu tun; (take the liberty) sich (*Dat.*) erlauben, etw. zu tun; **(b)** (suppose) annehmen; **be** ∼**d innocent** als unschuldig gelten *od.* angesehen werden; **missing** ∼**d dead** vermisst, wahrscheinlich *od.* mutmaßlich tot. **2** *v.i.* sich (*Dat.*) anmaßen; ∼ [**up**]**on sth.** etw. ausnützen

presumption /prɪ'zʌmpʃn/ *n.* **(a)** (arrogance) Anmaßung, *die;* Vermessenheit, *die;* **have the** ∼ **to do sth.** die Vermessenheit besitzen, etw. zu tun; sich (*Dat.*) anmaßen, etw. zu tun; **(b)** (assumption) Annahme, *die;* Vermutung, *die*

presumptuous /prɪ'zʌmptjʊəs/ *adj.* anmaßend; überheblich; (impertinent) aufdringlich

presumptuously /prɪ'zʌmptjʊəslɪ/ *adv.* überheblich; (impertinently) aufdringlich

presuppose /priːsə'pəʊz/ *v.t.* (assume, imply) voraussetzen

pre-tax /'priːtæks/ *adj.* vor Steuern *nachgestellt;* ∼ **profits** Gewinn vor Steuern

pre-teen /'priːtiːn/ *adj.* ≈ zehn- bis zwölfjährig

pretence /prɪ'tens/ *n.* (Brit.) **(a)** (pretext) Vorwand, *der;* **under** [**the**] ∼ **of helping** unter dem Vorwand zu helfen; *see also* **false pretences; (b)** *no art.* (make-believe, insincere behaviour) Verstellung, *die;* **(c)** (piece of insincere behaviour) **it is all** *or* **just a** ∼: das ist alles nicht echt; **(d)** (affectation) Affektiertheit, *die* (abwertend); Unnatürlichkeit, *die;* **(e)** (claim) Anspruch, *der;* **make the/no** ∼ **of** *or* **to sth.** Anspruch/keinen Anspruch auf etw. (*Akk.*) erheben

pretend /prɪ'tend/ **1** *v.t.* **(a)** (vorgeben); **she** ∼**ed to be asleep** sie tat, als ob sie schlief[e]; **(b)** (imagine in play) ∼ **to be sth.** so tun, als ob man etw. sei; **(c)** (profess falsely) vortäuschen; (say falsely) vorgeben, fälschlich beteuern (**to** gegenüber); **(d)** (claim) **not** ∼ **to do sth.** nicht behaupten wollen, etw. zu tun. **2** *v.i.* sich verstellen; **she's only** ∼**ing** sie tut nur so

pretense (Amer.) ⇒ **pretence**

pretension /prɪ'tenʃn/ *n.* **(a)** (claim) Anspruch, *der;* **have/make** ∼**s to great wisdom** vorgeben *od.* den Anspruch erheben, sehr klug zu sein; **(b)** (justifiable claim) Anspruch, *der* (**to** auf + *Akk.*); **people with** ∼**s to taste** Menschen, die Geschmack für sich in Anspruch nehmen können; **(c)** (pretentiousness) Überheblichkeit, *die;* Anmaßung, *die;* (of things: ostentation) Protzigkeit, *die*

pretentious /prɪ'tenʃəs/ *adj.* **(a)** hochgestochen; wichtigtuerisch ⟨*Person*⟩; **(b)** (ostentatious) protzig; großspurig ⟨*Person, Verhalten, Art*⟩

pretext /'priːtekst/ *n.* Vorwand, *der;* Ausrede, *die;* [**up**]**on** *or* **under the** ∼ **of doing sth.** unter dem Vorwand *od.*

mit der Entschuldigung, etw. tun zu wollen; **on the slightest** ~: mit *od.* unter dem fadenscheinigsten Vorwand

prettily /'prɪtɪlɪ/ *adv.* hübsch; sehr schön ⟨*singen, tanzen*⟩

pretty /'prɪtɪ/ **1** *adj.* **(a)** (attractive) hübsch; nett ⟨*Art*⟩; niedlich ⟨*Geschichte, Liedchen*⟩; **she's not just a ~ face!** sie ist nicht nur hübsch[, sie kann auch was]!; **as ~ as a picture** bildhübsch; **not a ~ sight** (iron.) kein schöner Anblick; **(b)** (iron.) hübsch, schön (ugs. iron.). **2** *adv.* ziemlich; **I am ~ well** es geht mir ganz gut; **we have ~ nearly finished** wir sind so gut wie fertig; **be ~ well over/exhausted** so gut wie vorbei/erschöpft sein; ~ **much the same** ziemlich unverändert; **be sitting ~** (coll.) sein Schäfchen im Trockenen haben (ugs.)

pretzel /'pretsl/ *n.* Brezel, *die*

prevail /prɪ'veɪl/ *v.i.* **(a)** (gain mastery) siegen, die Oberhand gewinnen (**against, over** über + *Akk.*); ~ **[up]on sb. to do sth.** jmdn. dazu bewegen, etw. zu tun; **(b)** (predominate) ⟨*Zustand, Bedingung:*⟩ vorherrschen; **(c)** (be current) herrschen

prevailing /prɪ'veɪlɪŋ/ *adj.* **(a)** (common) [vor]herrschend; aktuell ⟨*Mode*⟩; **(b)** (most frequent) **the ~ wind is from the West** der Wind kommt vorwiegend von Westen

prevalence /'prevələns/ *n., no pl.* Vorherrschen, *das;* (of crime, corruption, etc.) Überhandnehmen, *das;* (of disease, malnutrition, etc.) weite Verbreitung

prevalent /'prevələnt/ *adj.* **(a)** (existing) herrschend; weit verbreitet ⟨*Krankheit*⟩; aktuell ⟨*Trend*⟩; **(b)** (predominant) vorherrschend; **be/become ~:** vorherrschen/sich durchsetzen

prevaricate /prɪ'værɪkeɪt/ *v.i.* Ausflüchte machen (**over** wegen)

prevarication /prɪværɪ'keɪʃn/ *n.* (prevaricating) Ausflüchte *Pl.*

prevent /prɪ'vent/ *v.t.* (hinder) verhindern; verhüten; (forestall) vorbeugen; verhüten; ~ **sb. from doing sth.,** **sb.'s doing sth.,** (coll.) ~ **sb. doing sth.** jmdn. daran hindern *od.* davon abhalten, etw. zu tun; **there is nothing to ~ me** nichts hindert mich daran; ~ **sb. from coming** jmdn. am Kommen hindern; **catch sb.'s arm to ~ him [from] falling** jmdn. am Arm fassen, damit er nicht fällt

prevention /prɪ'venʃn/ *n.* Verhinderung, *die;* Verhütung, *die;* (forestalling) Vorbeugung, *die;* Verhütung, *die;* ~ **is better than cure** (prov.) Vorbeugen ist besser als Heilen (Spr.)

preventive /prɪ'ventɪv/ *adj.* vorbeugend; präventiv (geh.); Präventiv⟨*maßnahme, -krieg*⟩

preview /'pri:vju:/ **1** *n.* (of film, play) Voraufführung, *die;* (of exhibition) Vernissage, *die* (geh.). **2** *v.t.* eine Vorschau sehen von ⟨*Film*⟩

previous /'pri:vɪəs/ **1** *adj.* **(a)** (coming before) früher ⟨*Anstellung, Gelegenheit*⟩; ⟨*Tag, Morgen, Abend, Nacht*⟩ vorher; vorig ⟨*Besitzer, Wohnsitz*⟩; **the ~ page** die Seite davor; **(b)** (prior) ~ **to** vor (+ *Dat.*). **2** *adv.* ~ **to** vor (+ *Dat.*); ~ **to being a nurse, she was …:** bevor sie Krankenschwester wurde, war sie …

previously /'pri:vɪəslɪ/ *adv.* vorher; **two years ~:** zwei Jahre zuvor

pre-war /'pri:wɔː(r)/ *adj.* Vorkriegs-; **these houses are all ~:** diese Häuser stammen alle aus der Zeit vor dem Krieg

prey /preɪ/ **1** *n., pl. same* **(a)** (animal[s]) Beute, *die;* Beutetier, *das;* **beast/bird of ~:** Raubtier, *das/*-vogel, *der;* **(b)** (victim) Beute, *die* (geh.); Opfer, *das.* **2** *v.i.* ~ **[up]on** ⟨*Raubtier, Raubvogel:*⟩ schlagen; (plunder) ausplündern ⟨*Person*⟩; (exploit) ausnutzen; ~ **[up]on sb.'s mind** jmdm. keine Ruhe lassen; ⟨*Kummer, Angst:*⟩ an jmdm. nagen

price /praɪs/ **1** *n.* **(a)** (money etc.) Preis, *der;* **the ~ of wheat/a pint** der Weizenpreis/der Preis für ein Bier; **what is the ~ of this?** was kostet das?; **at a ~ of** zum Preis von; **sth. goes up/down in ~:** der Preis von etw. steigt/fällt; etw. steigt/fällt im Preis; **at a ~:** zum entsprechenden Preis; **(b)** (betting odds) Eventualquote, *die;* **(c)** (value) **be beyond ~:** [mit Geld] nicht zu bezahlen sein; **(d)** (fig.) Preis, *der;* **he succeeded, but at a great ~:** er hatte Erfolg, musste aber einen hohen Preis dafür bezahlen; **at/not at any ~:** um jeden/keinen Preis; **at the**

~ **of ruining his marriage** auf Kosten seiner Ehe; **what ~ …?** (Brit. coll.) (what is the chance of …) wie wär's mit …?; (… has failed) wie steht's jetzt mit …? *See also* **pay 2 e. 2** *v.t.* (fix ~ of) kalkulieren ⟨*Ware*⟩; (label with ~) auszeichnen

price: ~ **cut** *n.* Preissenkung, *die;* ~**-cutting** *n.* Preisschleuderei, *die;* ~**-fixing** *n.* Preisabsprache, *die;* ~ **freeze** *n.* Preisstopp, *der*

priceless /'praɪslɪs/ *adj.* **(a)** (invaluable) unbezahlbar; unschätzbar ⟨*Gut*⟩; **(b)** (coll.: amusing) köstlich

price: ~ **list** *n.* Preisliste, *die;* ~ **range** *n.* Preisspanne, *die;* ~ **rise** *n.* Preisanstieg, *der* (**on** bei); ~ **tag** *n.* Preisschild, *das;* ~ **war** *n.* Preiskrieg, *der*

pricey /'praɪsɪ/ *adj.,* **pricier** /'praɪsɪə(r)/, **priciest** /'praɪsɪɪst/ (Brit. coll.) teuer

prick /prɪk/ **1** *v.t.* stechen; stechen in ⟨*Ballon*⟩; aufstechen ⟨*Blase*⟩; **he ~ed his finger with the needle** er stach sich (*Dat.*) mit der Nadel in den Finger. **2** *v.i.* stechen. **3** *n.* **(a)** (pain) [little] ~: [leichter] Stich; **(b)** (coarse: penis) Schwanz, *der* (derb)

~ **up 1** *v.t.* aufrichten ⟨*Ohren*⟩; ~ **up one's/its ears** (listen) die Ohren spitzen. **2** *v.i.* ⟨*Ohren:*⟩ sich aufrichten

prickle /'prɪkl/ **1** *n.* **(a)** (thorn) Dorn, *der;* **(b)** (Zool., Bot.) Stachel, *der.* **2** *v.i.* kratzen

prickly /'prɪklɪ/ *adj.* **(a)** (with prickles) ⇒ **prickle 1:** dornig; stachelig; **be ~** ⟨*Pflanze:*⟩ Dornen/Stacheln haben; **(b)** (fig.) empfindlich

pricy ⇒ **pricey**

pride /praɪd/ **1** *n.* **(a)** Stolz, *der;* (arrogance) Hochmut, *der;* **take or have ~ of place** die Spitzenstellung einnehmen; (in collection etc.) das Glanzstück sein; **take [a] ~ in sb./ sth.** auf jmdn./etw. stolz sein; **(b)** (object, best one) Stolz, *der;* **sb.'s ~ and joy** jmds. ganzer Stolz; **give sth. ~ of place** einer Sache einen Ehrenplatz einräumen; **(c)** (of lions) Rudel, *das.* **2** *v. refl.* ~ **oneself [up]on sth.** (congratulate oneself) auf etw. (*Akk.*) stolz sein

priest /pri:st/ *n.* Priester, *der; see also* **high priest**

priestess /'pri:stɪs/ *n.* Priesterin, *die*

priesthood /'pri:sthʊd/ *n.* (office) geistliches Amt; (order of priests; priests) Geistlichkeit, *die;* **go into the ~:** Priester werden

priestly /'pri:stlɪ/ *adj.* priesterlich; Priester⟨*kaste, -rolle*⟩

prig /prɪg/ *n.* Tugendbold, *der* (ugs., iron.)

priggish /'prɪgɪʃ/ *adj.* übertrieben tugendhaft

prim /prɪm/ *adj.* **(a)** spröde, steif ⟨*Person*⟩; ~ **and proper** etepetete (ugs.); **(b)** (prudish) zimperlich; prüde

prima facie /praɪmə 'feɪʃɪ/ **1** *adv.* auf den ersten Blick. **2** *adj.* glaubhaft klingend; ~ **evidence** (Law) Anscheinsbeweis, *der*

primarily /'praɪmərɪlɪ/ *adv.* in erster Linie

primary /'praɪmərɪ/ **1** *adj.* **(a)** (first) primär (geh.); grundlegend; ~ **source** Primärquelle, *die* (geh.); **(b)** (chief) Haupt⟨*rolle, -sorge, -ziel, -zweck*⟩; **of ~ importance** von höchster Bedeutung. **2** *n.* (Amer.: election) Vorwahl, *die*

primary: ~ **colour** ⇒ **colour 1 a;** ~ **edu'cation** *n.* Grundschulerziehung, *die;* ~ **e'lection** *n.* (Amer.) Vorwahl, *die;* ~ **school** *n.* ▶ **887 |** Grundschule, *die;* attrib. ~**-school teacher** Grundschullehrer, *der/*-lehrerin, *die*

primate /'praɪmeɪt/ *n.* **(a)** (Eccl.) Primas, *der;* **(b)** (Zool.) Primat, *der*

prime¹ /praɪm/ **1** *n.* **(a)** (Höhepunkt, *der;* Krönung, *die;* **in the ~ of life/youth** in der Blüte seiner/ihrer Jahre/ der Jugend (geh.); **be in/past one's ~:** in den besten Jahren sein/die besten Jahre überschritten haben; **(b)** (Math.) Primzahl, *die.* **2** *adj.* **(a)** (chief) Haupt-; hauptsächlich; ~ **motive** Hauptmotiv, *das;* **be of ~ importance** von höchster Wichtigkeit sein; **(b)** (excellent) erstklassig; vortrefflich ⟨*Beispiel*⟩; ⟨*Fleisch*⟩ erster Güteklasse; **in ~ condition** ⟨*Sportler, Tier*⟩ in bester Verfassung; voll ausgereift ⟨*Obst*⟩

prime² *v.t.* **(a)** (equip) vorbereiten; ~ **sb. with information/advice** jmdm. instruieren/jmdm. Ratschläge erteilen; **well ~d** gut vorbereitet; **(b)** grundieren ⟨*Wand, Decke*⟩; **(c)** füllen ⟨*Pumpe*⟩; **(d)** schärfen ⟨*Sprengkörper*⟩

prime: ~ **'minister** *n.* ▶ **887 |** Premierminister, *der/* -ministerin, *die;* ~ **'number** *n.* (Math.) Primzahl, *die*

primer¹ /'praɪmə(r)/ n. (book) Fibel, *die*

primer² n. **(a)** (explosive) Zündvorrichtung, *die;* **(b)** (paint etc.) Grundierlack, *der*

'prime time n. Hauptsendezeit, *die;* ∼-**time** TV Hauptsendezeit im Fernsehen

primeval /praɪ'miːvl/ adj. urzeitlich; Ur‹*zeiten, -wälder*›

primitive /'prɪmɪtɪv/ adj. primitiv; (prehistoric) urzeitlich ‹*Mensch*›; frühzeitlich ‹*Ackerbau, Technik*›

primitively /'prɪmɪtɪvlɪ/ adv. primitiv

primrose /'prɪmrəʊz/ n. **(a)** (Bot.) gelbe Schlüsselblume; **(b)** (colour) schlüsselblumengelb

primula /'prɪmjʊlə/ n. (Bot.) Primel, *die*

Primus, (P) /'praɪməs/ n. ∼ **[stove]** Primuskocher, *der*

prince /prɪns/ n. **(a)** ▶ 1152 | (member of royal family) Prinz, *der;* **(b)** (rhet.: sovereign ruler) Fürst, *der;* Monarch, *der*

Prince: ∼ **'Charming** n. (fig.) Märchenprinz, *der;* **p**∼ **'consort** n. Prinzgemahl, *der*

princely /'prɪnslɪ/ adj. (lit. or fig.) fürstlich; ∼ **houses** Fürstenhäuser

Prince 'Regent n. Prinzregent, *der*

princess /'prɪnses, prɪn'ses/ n. ▶ 1152 | **(a)** Prinzessin, *die;* **(b)** (wife of prince) Fürstin, *die*

princess 'royal n. [*Titel für*] *älteste Tochter eines Monarchen*

principal /'prɪnsɪpl/ **1** adj. **(a)** Haupt-; (most important) wichtigst...; bedeutendst...; **the** ∼ **cause of lung cancer** die häufigste Ursache für Lungenkrebs; **(b)** (Mus.) ∼ **horn/bassoon** etc. erstes Horn/Fagott usw. **2** n. **(a)** (head of school or college) Rektor, *der*/Rektorin, *die;* **(b)** (Finance) (invested) Kapitalbetrag, *der;* (lent) Kreditsumme, *die*

principality /prɪnsɪ'pælɪtɪ/ n. Fürstentum, *das;* **the P**∼ (Brit.) Wales (*das*)

principally /'prɪnsɪpəlɪ/ adv. in erster Linie

principle /'prɪnsɪpl/ n. **(a)** Prinzip, *das;* **on the** ∼ **that** ...: nach dem Grundsatz, dass ...; **be based on the** ∼ **that** ...: auf dem Grundsatz basieren, dass ...; **basic** ∼: Grundprinzip, *das;* **go back to first** ∼s zu den Grundlagen zurückgehen; **in** ∼: im Prinzip; **it's the** ∼ [**of the thing**] es geht [dabei] ums Prinzip; **a man of high** ∼ or **strong** ∼s ein Mann von od. mit hohen Prinzipien; **a matter of** ∼: eine Prinzipfrage; **do sth. on** ∼ or **as a matter of** ∼: etw. prinzipiell od. aus Prinzip tun; **(b)** (Phys.) Lehrsatz, *der*

print /prɪnt/ **1** n. **(a)** (impression) Abdruck, *der;* (finger∼) Fingerabdruck, *der;* **(b)** (∼ed lettering) Gedruckte, *das;* (typeface) Druck, *der;* **clear/large** ∼: deutlicher/großer Druck; **editions in large** ∼: Großdruckbucher; *see also* **small print;** **(c)** (published or ∼ed state) **be in/out of** ∼ ‹*Buch:*› erhältlich/vergriffen sein; **(d)** (∼ed picture or design) Druck, *der;* **(e)** (Photog.) Abzug, *der;* (Cinemat.) Kopie, *die;* **(f)** (Textiles) (cloth with design) bedruckter Stoff. **2** v.t. **(a)** drucken ‹*Buch, Zeitschrift, Geldschein usw.*›; **(b)** (write) in Druckschrift schreiben; **(c)** (cause to be published) veröffentlichen ‹*Artikel, Roman, Ansichten usw.*›; **(d)** (Photog.) abziehen; (Cinemat.) kopieren; **(e)** (Textiles) bedrucken ‹*Stoff*›

∼ **'out** v.t. (Computing) ausdrucken

printable /'prɪntəbl/ adj. druckbar; **what he replied is not** ∼ (fig.) was er geantwortet hat, kann man [hier] nicht wiederholen

printed /'prɪntɪd/ adj. **(a)** (Printing) gedruckt; ∼ **characters** or **letters** Druckbuchstaben; **on the** ∼ **page** gedruckt; **(b)** (written like print) in Druckschrift; **(c)** (published) veröffentlicht ‹*Artikel, Roman, Ansichten usw.*›; **(d)** (Textiles) bedruckt ‹*Stoff*›

printed: ∼ **'circuit** n. (Electronics) gedruckte Schaltung; ∼ **matter** n., *no pl., no indef. art.* Gedruckte, *das*

printer /'prɪntə(r)/ n. **(a)** (Printing) (worker) Drucker, *der*/ Druckerin, *die;* firm of printers Druckerei, *die;* **send sth. off to the** ∼**'s** etw. in die Druckerei schicken; **(b)** (Computing) Drucker, *der*

printer: ∼**'s 'error** n. Druckfehler, *der;* ∼**'s 'ink** n. Druckfarbe, *die*

printing /'prɪntɪŋ/ n. **(a)** Drucken, *das;* [the] ∼ **[trade]** das Druckgewerbe; **(b)** (writing like print) Druckschrift, *die;* **(c)** (edition) Auflage, *die*

printing: ∼ **error** n. Druckfehler, *der;* ∼ **ink** n. Druckfarbe, *die;* ∼ **press** n. Druckerpresse, *die*

'printout n. (Computing) Ausdruck, *der*

prior /'praɪə(r)/ **1** adj. vorherig ‹*Warnung, Zustimmung, Vereinbarung usw.*›; früher ‹*Verabredung, Ehe*›; Vor‹*geschichte, -kenntnis*›; **have a** or **the** ∼ **claim to sth.** ältere Rechte an etw. (Dat.) od. auf etw. (Akk.) haben. **2** adv. ∼ **to** vor (+ Dat.); ∼ **to doing sth.** bevor man etw. tut/tat; ∼ **to that** vorher. **3** n. (Eccl.) Prior, *der*

prioritize (prioritise) /praɪ'ɒrɪtaɪz/ v.t. nach Vordringlichkeit ordnen

priority /praɪ'ɒrɪtɪ/ n. **(a)** (precedence) Vorrang, *der; attrib.* vorrangig; **have** or **take** ∼: Vorrang haben (**over** vor + Dat.); **have** ∼ (on road) Vorfahrt haben; **give** ∼ **to sth./ sth.** jmdn./einer Sache den Vorrang geben; **give top** ∼ **to sth.** einer Sache (Dat.) höchste Priorität einräumen; **be listed in order of** ∼: der Vorrangigkeit nach aufgeführt sein; **(b)** (matter) vordringliche Angelegenheit; **our first** ∼ **is to** ...: zuallererst müssen wir ...; **be high/low on the list of priorities** oben/unten auf der Prioritätenliste stehen; **get one's priorities right/wrong** seine Prioritäten richtig/falsch setzen

priory /'praɪərɪ/ n. (Eccl.) Priorat, *das*

prise ⇒ **prize²**

prism /'prɪzm/ n. Prisma, *das*

prison /'prɪzn/ n. **(a)** (lit. or fig.) Gefängnis, *das; attrib.* Gefängnis-; **(b)** *no pl., no art.* (custody) Haft, *die;* **in** ∼: im Gefängnis; **go to** ∼: ins Gefängnis gehen; **send sb. to** ∼: jmdn. ins Gefängnis schicken; **escape from** ∼: aus dem Gefängnis ausbrechen; **let sb. out of** ∼: jmdn. aus der Haft entlassen

'prison camp n. Gefangenenlager, *das*

prisoner /'prɪznə(r)/ n. **(a)** (lit. or fig.) Gefangene, *der/die;* (accused person) Angeklagte, *der/die;* **take/hold** or **keep sb.** ∼: jmdn. gefangen nehmen/halten

prisoner of 'war n. Kriegsgefangene, *der/die;* **prisoner-of-war camp** [Kriegs]gefangenenlager, *das*

prison: ∼ **'guard** n. ▶ 887 | Gefängniswärter, *der*/-wärterin, *die;* ∼ **service** n. Strafvollzugsbehörde, *die;* ∼ **'visitor** n. ≈ Gefangenenfürsorger, *der*/-fürsorgerin, *die*

pristine /'prɪstiːn, 'prɪstaɪn/ adj. unberührt; ursprünglich ‹*Glanz, Weiße, Schönheit*›; **in** ∼ **condition** in tadellosem Zustand

privacy /'prɪvəsɪ, 'praɪvəsɪ/ n. **(a)** (seclusion) Zurückgezogenheit, *die;* **in the** ∼ **of one's [own] home** in den eigenen vier Wänden (ugs.); **invasion of** ∼**/sb.'s** ∼: Eindringen in die/jmds. Privatsphäre; **allow sb. no** ∼: jmdm. kein Privatleben erlauben; **(b)** (confidentiality) **in the strictest** ∼: unter strengster Geheimhaltung

private /'praɪvɪt/ **1** adj. **(a)** (outside State system) privat; Privat‹*unterricht, -schule, -industrie, -klinik, -patient, -station usw.*›; **a doctor working in** ∼ **medicine** ein Arzt, der Privatpatienten hat; **have a** ∼ **education** auf eine Privatschule gehen; **(b)** (belonging to individual, not public, not business) persönlich ‹*Dinge*›; nichtöffentlich ‹*Versammlung, Sitzung*›; privat ‹*Telefongespräch, Schriftverkehr*›; Privat‹*eigentum, -wagen, -flugzeug, -strand, -parkplatz, -leben, -konto*›; '∼' (on door) „Privat"; (in public building) „kein Zutritt"; (on ∼ land) „Betreten verboten"; **for [one's own]** ∼ **use** für den persönlichen Gebrauch; **(c)** (personal, affecting individual) persönlich ‹*Meinung, Interesse, Überzeugung, Rache*›; privat ‹*Vereinbarung, Zweck*›; **(d)** (not for public disclosure) geheim ‹*Verhandlung, Geschäft, Tränen*›; still ‹*Gebet, Nachdenken, Grübeln*›; persönlich ‹*Gründe*›; (confidential) vertraulich; **have a** ∼ **word with sb.** jmdn. unter vier Augen sprechen; **(e)** (secluded) still ‹*Ort*›; (undisturbed) ungestört; **(f)** (not in public office) ∼ **citizen** or **individual** Privatperson, *die.* **2** n. **(a)** (Brit. Mil.) einfacher Soldat; **(b) in** ∼: privat; in kleinem Kreis ‹*feiern*›; (confidentially) ganz im Vertrauen; **speak to sb. in** ∼: jmdn. unter vier Augen sprechen; **(c)** *in pl.* (coll.: genitals) Geschlechtsteile *Pl.*

private: ∼ **de'tective** n. ▶ 887 | [Privat]detektiv, *der*/-detektivin, *die;* ∼ **'enterprise** n. (Commerc.) das freie od. private Unternehmertum; ∼ **'eye** (coll.) ⇒ ∼ **detective**

privately /'praɪvətlɪ/ adv. privat ‹erziehen, zugeben›; vertraulich ‹jmdn. sprechen›; insgeheim ‹denken, glauben›; **study** ~: private Studien betreiben; ~ **owned** in Privatbesitz

private: ~ **'parts** n. pl. Geschlechtsteile Pl.; ~ **'practice** n. Privatpraxis, die; **he is in** ~ **practice** er hat eine Privatpraxis; ~ **sector** n. **the** ~ **sector [of industry]** die Privatwirtschaft

privation /praɪ'veɪʃn/ n. (lack of comforts) Not, die; **suffer many** ~s viele Entbehrungen erleiden

privatisation, privatise ⇒ **privatiz-**

privatization /praɪvətaɪ'zeɪʃn/ n. (Econ.) Privatisierung, die

privatize /'praɪvətaɪz/ v.t. (Econ.) privatisieren

privet /'prɪvɪt/ n. (Bot.) Liguster, der

privilege /'prɪvɪlɪdʒ/ n. (a) (right, immunity) Privileg, das; collect. Privilegien Pl.; (b) (special benefit) Sonderrecht, das; (honour) Ehre, die; **it was a** ~ **to listen to him** es war ein besonderes Vergnügen, ihm zuzuhören

privileged /'prɪvɪlɪdʒd/ adj. privilegiert; **the** ~ **few** die kleine Gruppe von Privilegierten; **sb. is** ~ **to do sth.** jmd. hat die Ehre, etw. zu tun; **be in a** ~ **position** eine bevorzugte Position innehaben

privy /'prɪvɪ/ adj. **be** ~ **to sth.** in etw. (Akk.) eingeweiht sein

Privy: ~ **'Council** n. (Brit.) Geheimer [Staats]rat; **p~ 'counsellor** (p~ **'councillor**) n. (Brit.) Geheimer Rat

prize[1] /praɪz/ **1** n. (a) (reward, money) Preis, der; **win** or **take first** ~: den ersten Preis gewinnen; (b) (in lottery) Gewinn, der; **win sth. as a** ~: etw. gewinnen; (c) (fig.: something worth striving for) Lohn, der; **glittering** ~s verlockender Lohn. **2** v.t. (value) ~ **sth. [highly]** etw. hoch schätzen; **sb.'s most** ~d **possessions** jmds. wertvollster Besitz. **3** attrib. adj. (a) (~-winning) preisgekrönt; (b) (awarded as ~) ~ **medal/trophy** Siegesmedaille, die/Siegestrophäe, die; (c) (iron.) ~ **idiot** Vollidiot, der/-idiotin, die (ugs.); ~ **example** Musterbeispiel, das (iron.)

prize[2] v.t. (force) ~ **[open]** aufstemmen; ~ **the lid off a crate** eine Kiste aufstemmen; ~ **information/a secret out of sb.** Informationen/ein Geheimnis aus jmdm. herauspressen

prize: ~**fight** n. (Boxing) Preisboxkampf, der; ~**fighter** n. (Boxing) Preisboxer, der; ~**giving** n. (Sch.) Preisverleihung, die; ~ **money** n. Geldpreis, der; (Sport) Preisgeld, das; ~**winner** n. Preisträger, der/ -trägerin, die; (in lottery) Gewinner, der/Gewinnerin, die; ~**winning** adj. preisgekrönt; (in lottery) Gewinner-

pro[1] /prəʊ/ **1** n. in pl. **the** ~s **and cons** das Pro und Kontra. **2** adv. ~ **and con** pro und kontra. **3** prep. für

pro[2] **1** n. (Sport & Theatre coll.) Profi, der. **2** adj. Profi-

pro-[3] pref. pro-; ~-**Communist** prokommunistisch

'proactive adj. aktiv ‹Haltung, Rolle›; **be** ~ ‹Person:› [selbst] die Initiative ergreifen; Eigeninitiative zeigen

probability /prɒbə'bɪlɪtɪ/ n. (a) (likelihood; also Math.) Wahrscheinlichkeit, die; **in all** ~: aller Wahrscheinlichkeit nach; **there is little/a strong** ~ **that** …: die Wahrscheinlichkeit, dass …, ist gering/groß; (b) (likely event) **the** ~ **is that** …: es ist zu erwarten, dass …; **war is becoming a** ~: der Ausbruch eines Krieges wird immer wahrscheinlicher

probable /'prɒbəbl/ adj. wahrscheinlich; **highly** ~: höchstwahrscheinlich; **another wet summer looks** ~: es sieht ganz nach einem weiteren verregneten Sommer aus

probably /'prɒbəblɪ/ adv. wahrscheinlich

probate /'prəʊbeɪt/ n. (Law) gerichtliche Testamentsbestätigung

probation /prə'beɪʃn/ n. (a) Probezeit, die; **be on** ~: Probezeit haben; (b) (Law) Bewährung, die; **be on** ~: auf Bewährung sein

probationary /prə'beɪʃənərɪ/ adj. Probe-; ~ **period** Probezeit, die

pro'bation officer n. ▶887 Bewährungshelfer, der/ -helferin, die

probe /prəʊb/ **1** n. (a) (investigation) Untersuchung, die (into Gen.); (b) (Med., Electronics, Astron.) Sonde, die. **2** v.t. (a) (investigate) erforschen; untersuchen; (b) (reach deeply into) gründlich erforschen ‹Kontinent, Weltall›. **3** v.i. (a) (make investigation) forschen; ~ **into a matter** einer Angelegenheit (Dat.) auf den Grund gehen; (b) (reach deeply) vordringen (**into** in + Akk.)

probing /'prəʊbɪŋ/ adj. (penetrating) gründlich; durchdringend ‹Blick›; ~ **question** Testfrage, die

probity /'prəʊbɪtɪ/ n., no pl. Rechtschaffenheit, die

problem /'prɒbləm/ n. (a) (difficult matter) Problem, das; attrib. Problem‹gebiet, -fall, -kind, -familie›; **I find it a** ~ **to start** or **have a** ~ **[in] starting the car** ich habe Probleme, das Auto anzulassen; **[I see] no** ~ (coll.) kein Problem; **what's the** ~? (coll.) wo fehlt's denn?; **the** ~ **about** or **with sb./sth.** das Problem mit jmdm./bei etw.; **the Northern Ireland** ~: die Nordirlandfrage; **he has a drink** ~: er hat ein Alkoholproblem; **that presents a** ~: das ist ein Problem; (b) (puzzle) Rätsel, das

problematic /prɒblə'mætɪk/, **problematical** /prɒblə'mætɪkl/ adjs. problematisch; (doubtful) fragwürdig

procedure /prə'siːdjə(r)/ n. (a) (particular course of action) Verfahren, das; Prozedur, die (meist abwertend); (b) (way of doing sth.) Verfahrensweise, die; **what is the normal** ~? wie wird das normalerweise gehandhabt?

proceed /prə'siːd/ v.i. (formal) (a) (go) (on foot) gehen; (as or by vehicle) fahren; (on horseback) reiten; (after interruption) weitergehen/-fahren/-reiten; ~ **to business** sich geschäftlichen Dingen zuwenden; ~ **to the next item on the agenda** zum nächsten Punkt der Tagesordnung übergehen; (b) (begin and carry on) beginnen; (after interruption) fortfahren; ~ **to talk/eat** etc. (begin and carry on) beginnen, zu sprechen/essen usw.; (after interruption) weitersprechen/ -essen usw.; ~ **in** or **with sth.** (begin) [mit] etw. beginnen; (continue) etw. fortsetzen; (c) (adopt course) vorgehen; ~ **discreetly with sth.** etw. diskret behandeln; (d) (be carried on) ‹Rennen:› verlaufen; (be under way) ‹Verfahren:› laufen; (be continued after interruption) fortgesetzt werden; (e) (originate) ~ **from** (issue from) kommen von; (be caused by) herrühren von

~ **against** v.t. (Law) gerichtlich vorgehen gegen

proceeding /prə'siːdɪŋ/ n. (a) (action) Vorgehensweise, die; (b) in pl. (events) Vorgänge; **I'll go along to watch the** ~s ich geh mal gucken, was da läuft; (c) in pl. (Law) Verfahren, das; **legal** ~s Gerichtsverfahren, das; **start/ take [legal]** ~s gerichtlich vorgehen (**against** gegen); (d) in pl. (report) Tätigkeitsbericht, der; (of single meeting) Protokoll, das

proceeds /'prəʊsiːdz/ n. pl. Erlös, der (**from** aus)

process[1] /'prəʊses/ **1** n. (a) (of time or history) Lauf, der; **he learnt a lot in the** ~: er lernte eine Menge dabei; **be in the** ~ **of doing sth.** gerade etw. tun; **be in** ~: in Gang sein; (b) (proceeding) Vorgang, der; Prozedur, die; **the democratic** ~: das demokratische Verfahren; (c) (method) Verfahren, das; see also **elimination a**; (d) (natural operation) Prozess, der; Vorgang, der; ~ **of evolution** Evolutionsprozess, der. **2** v.t. verarbeiten ‹Rohstoff, Signal, Daten›; bearbeiten ‹Antrag, Akte, Darlehen›; (for conservation) behandeln ‹Leder, Lebensmittel›; (Photog.) entwickeln ‹Film›

process[2] /prə'ses/ v.i. marschieren

'process cheese (Amer.), **'processed cheese** ns. Schmelzkäse, der

processer ⇒ **processor**

procession /prə'seʃn/ n. (a) (Zug, der; (religious) Prozession, die; (festive) Umzug, der; **go/march/move** etc. **in** ~: ziehen; **funeral** ~: Trauerzug, der; (b) (fig.: series) Reihe, die

processor /'prəʊsesə(r)/ n. (machine) Prozessor, der

proclaim /prə'kleɪm/ v.t. (a) erklären ‹Absicht›; geltend machen ‹Recht, Anspruch›; (declare officially) verkünden ‹Amnestie›; ausrufen ‹Republik›; ~ **oneself King** jmdn./sich zum König ausrufen; ~ **a country [to be] a republic** in einem Land die Republik ausrufen; (b) (reveal) verraten; ~ **sb./sth. [to be] sth.** verraten, dass jmd./etw. etw. ist

proclamation /prɒklə'meɪʃn/ *n.* (**a**) (act of proclaiming) Verkündung, *die;* Proklamation, *die* (geh.); (of sovereign) Ausrufung, *die;* (**b**) (notice) Bekanntmachung, *die;* (edict, decree) Erlass, *der*

proclivity /prə'klɪvɪtɪ/ *n.* Neigung, *die;* **have a ~/proclivities for sth.** einen Hang zu etw. haben

procrastinate /prə'kræstɪneɪt/ *v.i.* zaudern (geh.); **~ in doing sth.** es hinauszögern, etw. zu tun

procrastination /prəkræstɪ'neɪʃn/ *n.* Saumseligkeit, *die* (geh.)

procure /prə'kjʊə(r)/ **1** *v.t.* (**a**) (obtain) beschaffen; **~ for sb./oneself** jmdm./sich verschaffen ⟨*Arbeit, Unterkunft, Respekt, Reichtum*⟩; jmdm./sich beschaffen ⟨*Arbeit, Ware*⟩; (**b**) (bring about) herbeiführen ⟨*Ergebnis, Wechsel, Frieden*⟩; bewirken ⟨*Freilassung*⟩; (**c**) (for sex) beschaffen. **2** *v.i.* Kuppelei betreiben; **procuring** Kuppelei, *die*

procurement /prə'kjʊəmənt/ *n.* ⇒ **procure 1**: Beschaffung, *die;* Herbeiführung, *die;* Bewirkung, *die*

prod 1 *v.t.*, **-dd-**: (**a**) (poke) stupsen (ugs.); stoßen mit ⟨*Stock, Finger usw.*⟩; **he ~ded the map with his finger** er stieß mit dem Finger auf die Karte; **~ sb. gently** jmdn. anstupsen *od.* leicht anstoßen; (**b**) (fig.: rouse) antreiben; nachhelfen (+ *Dat.*) ⟨*Gedächtnis*⟩; **~ sb. into doing sth.** jmdn. drängen, etw. zu tun. **2** *v.i.*, **-dd-** stochern. **3** *n.* Stupser, *der;* **a ~ in the/my** *etc.* **ribs** ein Rippenstoß; **give sb. a ~:** jmdm. einen Stupser geben; (fig.) jmdn. auf Touren bringen

~ at *v.t.* anstupsen

prodigal /'prɒdɪgl/ *adj.* verschwenderisch

prodigal 'son *n.* (Bibl.; also fig. iron.) verlorener Sohn

prodigious /prə'dɪdʒəs/ *adj.* ungeheuer; unglaublich ⟨*Lügner, Dummkopf*⟩; wunderbar ⟨*Ereignis, Taten*⟩; außerordentlich ⟨*Begabung, Können*⟩; gewaltig ⟨*Fortschritt, Kraft, Energie*⟩

prodigy /'prɒdɪdʒɪ/ *n.* (**a**) (gifted person) [außergewöhnliches] Talent; **musical ~:** musikalisches Wunderkind; *see also* **child prodigy;** (**b**) (marvel) Wunder, *das*

produce 1 /'prɒdjuːs/ *n.* Produkte *Pl.;* Erzeugnisse *Pl.;* **'~ of Spain** „spanisches Erzeugnis". **2** /prə'djuːs/ *v.t.* (**a**) (bring forward) erbringen ⟨*Beweis*⟩; vorlegen ⟨*Beweismaterial*⟩; beibringen ⟨*Zeugen*⟩; geben ⟨*Erklärung*⟩; vorzeigen ⟨*Pass, Fahrkarte, Papiere*⟩; herausholen ⟨*Brieftasche, Portemonnaie, Pistole*⟩; **~ sth. from one's pocket** etw. aus der Tasche ziehen; **he ~d a few coins from his pocket** er holte einige Münzen aus seiner Tasche; **she ~d a gun from her pocket** sie zog einen Revolver aus ihrer Tasche; (**b**) (produzieren ⟨*Show, Film*⟩; inszenieren ⟨*Theaterstück, Hörspiel, Fernsehspiel*⟩; herausgeben ⟨*Schallplatte, Buch*⟩; **well-~d** gut gemacht ⟨*Film, Theaterstück, Programm*⟩; (**c**) (manufacture) herstellen; zubereiten ⟨*Mahlzeit*⟩; (in nature; Agric.) produzieren; (**d**) (create) schreiben ⟨*Roman, Gedichte, Artikel, Aufsatz, Symphonie*⟩; schaffen ⟨*Gemälde, Skulptur, Meisterwerk*⟩; aufstellen ⟨*Theorie*⟩; (**e**) (cause) hervorrufen; bewirken ⟨*Änderung*⟩; (**f**) (bring into being) erzeugen; führen zu ⟨*Situation, Lage, Zustände*⟩; (**g**) (yield) erzeugen ⟨*Ware, Produkt*⟩; geben ⟨*Milch*⟩; tragen ⟨*Wolle*⟩; liefern ⟨*Ernte*⟩; fördern ⟨*Metall, Kohle*⟩; abwerfen ⟨*Ertrag, Gewinn*⟩; hervorbringen ⟨*Dichter, Denker, Künstler*⟩; führen zu ⟨*Resultat*⟩; (**h**) (bear) gebären ⟨*Säugetier:*⟩ werfen ⟨*Vogel, Reptil:*⟩ legen ⟨*Eier*⟩; ⟨*Fisch, Insekt:*⟩ legen ⟨*Eier*⟩; ⟨*Baum, Blume:*⟩ tragen ⟨*Früchte, Blüten*⟩; entwickeln ⟨*Triebe*⟩; bilden ⟨*Keime*⟩

producer /prə'djuːsə(r)/ *n.* ▶ **887** (**a**) (Cinemat., Theatre, Radio, Telev., Econ.) Produzent, *der*/Produzentin, *die;* (**b**) (Brit. Theatre/Radio/Telev.) Regisseur, *der*/Regisseurin, *die*

product /'prɒdʌkt/ *n.* (**a**) (thing produced) Produkt, *das;* (of industrial process) Erzeugnis, *das;* (of art or intellect) Werk, *das;* **carbon dioxide is a ~ of respiration** Kohlendioxid entsteht bei der Atmung; (**b**) (result) Folge, *die;* (**c**) (Math.) Produkt, *das* (**of** aus). *See also* **gross¹ 1 d**

production /prə'dʌkʃn/ *n.* (**a**) (bringing forward) (of evidence) Erbringung, *die;* (in physical form) Vorlage, *die;* (of witness) Beibringung, *die;* (of passport etc.) Vorzeigen, *das;* **on ~ of your passport** gegen Vorlage Ihres Passes; (**b**) (public presentation) (Cinemat.) Produktion, *die;* (Theatre) Inszenierung,

die; (of record, book) Herausgabe, *die;* (**c**) (action of making) Produktion, *die;* (manufacturing) Herstellung, *die;* (thing produced) Produkt, *das;* **be in/go into ~:** in Produktion sein/gehen; **be** *or* **have gone out of ~:** nicht mehr hergestellt werden; *see also* **mass production;** (**d**) (thing created) Werk, *das;* (Brit. Theatre: show produced) Inszenierung, *die;* (**e**) (causing) Hervorrufen, *das;* (**f**) (bringing into being) Hervorbringung, *die;* (**g**) (process of yielding) Produktion, *die;* (Mining) Förderung, *die;* **the mine has ceased ~:** das Bergwerk hat die Förderung eingestellt; (**h**) (yield) Ertrag, *der;* [**the**] **annual/total ~ from the mine** die jährliche/gesamte Förderleistung des Bergwerks

pro'duction line *n.* Fertigungsstraße, *die*

productive /prə'dʌktɪv/ *adj.* (**a**) (producing) **be ~** ⟨*Fabrik:*⟩ produzieren; (**b**) (producing abundantly) ertragreich ⟨*Land, Boden, Obstbaum, Mine*⟩; leistungsfähig ⟨*Betrieb, Bauernhof*⟩; produktiv ⟨*Künstler, Komponist, Schriftsteller, Geist*⟩; (**c**) (yielding favourable results) fruchtbar ⟨*Gespräch, Verhandlungen, Forschungsarbeit*⟩

productivity /prɒdʌk'tɪvɪtɪ/ *n.* Produktivität, *die;* **~ agreement** *or* **deal** Produktivitätsvereinbarung, *die;* **~ bonus** Leistungszulage, *die*

Prof. /prɒf/ *abbr.* ▶ **1152** | **Professor** Prof.

profane /prə'feɪn/ **1** *adj.* (**a**) (irreligious) gotteslästerlich; (**b**) (irreverent) respektlos ⟨*Bemerkung, Person*⟩; profan ⟨*Humor, Sprache*⟩; (**c**) (secular) weltlich; profan. **2** *v.t.* entweihen

profanity /prə'fænɪtɪ/ *n.* (**a**) (irreligiousness, irreligious act) Gotteslästerung, *die;* (**b**) (irreverent behaviour, act, or utterance) Respektlosigkeit, *die*

profess /prə'fes/ *v.t.* (**a**) (declare openly) bekunden ⟨*Vorliebe, Abneigung, Interesse*⟩; **~ to be/do sth.** erklären, etw. zu sein/tun; (**b**) (claim) vorgeben; geltend machen ⟨*Recht, Anspruch*⟩; **~ to be/do sth.** behaupten, etw. zu sein/tun; (**c**) (affirm faith in) sich bekennen zu

professed /prə'fest/ *adj.* (**a**) (self-acknowledged) erklärt ⟨*Marxist, Bewunderer, Absicht*⟩; **be a ~ Christian** ein bekennender Christ sein; (**b**) (alleged) angeblich

profession /prə'feʃn/ *n.* (**a**) Beruf, *der;* **what is your ~?** was sind Sie von Beruf?; **take up/go into** *or* **enter a ~:** einen Beruf ergreifen/in einen Beruf gehen; **she is in the legal ~:** sie ist Juristin; **be a pilot by ~:** von Beruf Pilot sein; **the [learned] ~s** Theologie, Jura und Medizin; (**b**) (body of people) Berufsstand, *der;* (**c**) (declaration) **~ of friendship/sympathy** Freundschafts-/Sympathiebekundung, *die;* (**d**) (Relig.: affirmation of faith) Bekenntnis, *das* (**of** zu)

professional /prə'feʃənl/ **1** *adj.* (**a**) (of profession) Berufs⟨*ausbildung, -leben*⟩; beruflich ⟨*Qualifikation, Laufbahn, Tätigkeit, Stolz, Ansehen*⟩; **~ body** Berufsorganisation, *die;* **~ advice** fachmännischer Rat; **~ standards** Leistungsniveau, *das;* (**b**) (worthy of profession) (in technical expertise) fachmännisch; (in attitude) professionell; (in experience) routiniert; (**c**) (engaged in profession) **~ people** Angehörige hoch qualifizierter Berufe; **'apartment to let to ~ woman'** „Wohnung an berufstätige Dame zu vermieten"; **the ~ class[es]** die gehobenen Berufe; (**d**) (by profession) gelernt; (not amateur) Berufs⟨*musiker, -sportler, -soldat, -fotograf*⟩; Profi⟨*sportler*⟩; (**e**) (paid) Profi⟨*sport, -boxen, -fußball, -tennis*⟩; **go** *or* **turn ~:** Profi werden; **be in the ~ army** Berufssoldat sein; **be in the ~ theatre/on the ~ stage** beruflich am Theater/als Schauspieler arbeiten. **2** *n.* (trained person, lit. or fig.) Fachmann, *der*/Fachfrau, *die;* (nonamateur; also Sport, Theatre) Profi, *der*

professionalism /prə'feʃənəlɪzm/ *n.*, *no pl.* (**a**) (of work) fachmännische Ausführung; (attitude) professionelle Einstellung; (**b**) (paid participation) Profitum, *das*

professionally /prə'feʃənəlɪ/ *adv.* (**a**) (in professional capacity) geschäftlich ⟨*beraten, besuchen, konsultieren*⟩; beruflich ⟨*erfolgreich*⟩; (in manner worthy of profession) professionell; **be ~ trained/qualified** eine Berufsausbildung/abgeschlossene Berufsausbildung haben; (**b**) (as paid work) berufsmäßig; **she plays tennis/the piano ~:** sie ist Tennisprofi/von Beruf Pianistin; (**c**) (by professional) fachmännisch ⟨*leiten, betreiben*⟩; von einem Fachmann/von Fachleuten ⟨*erledigen lassen*⟩

professor /prə'fesə(r)/ *n.* ▶887 (a) (Univ.: holder of chair) Professor, *der*/Professorin, *die* (**of** für); (**b**) (Amer.: teacher at university) Dozent, *der*/Dozentin, *die*

proffer /'prɒfə(r)/ *v.t.* (literary) darbieten ⟨*Hand, Geschenk*⟩; anbieten ⟨*Frieden, Hilfe, Arm, Freundschaft*⟩; aussprechen ⟨*Dank*⟩; vorbringen ⟨*Vorschlag*⟩

proficiency /prə'fɪʃənsɪ/ *n.* Können, *das;* **degree** *or* **standard of** ∼: Fertigkeit, *die;*

pro'ficiency test *n.* Leistungstest, *der*

proficient /prə'fɪʃənt/ *adj.* fähig; gut ⟨*Pianist, Reiter, Skiläufer usw.*⟩; geschickt ⟨*Radfahrer, Handwerker, Lügner*⟩; **be** ∼ **at** *or* **in maths/French** viel von Mathematik verstehen/gute Französischkenntnisse haben

profile /'prəʊfaɪl/ *n.* (**a**) (side aspect) Profil, *das;* **in** ∼: im Profil; (**b**) (representation) Profilbild, *das;* (outline) Umriss, *der;* (**c**) (biographical sketch) Porträt, *das* (**of, on** *Gen.*); (**d**) (fig.) **keep** *or* **maintain a low** ∼: sich zurückhalten

profit /'prɒfɪt/ **1** *n.* (**a**) (Commerc.) Gewinn, *der;* Profit, *der;* **at a** ∼: mit Gewinn ⟨*verkaufen*⟩; **make a** ∼ **from** *or* **out of sth.** mit etw. Geld verdienen; **make [a few pence]** ∼ **on sth.** [ein paar Pfennige] an etw. (*Dat.*) verdienen; **show a** ∼: einen Gewinn verzeichnen; **yield a** ∼: Gewinn abwerfen; ∼**-and-loss account** Gewinn-und-Verlust-Rechnung, *die;* (**b**) (advantage) Nutzen, *der;* **there is no** ∼ **in sth.** etw. ist zwecklos. **2** *v.t.* ∼ **sb.** für jmdn. von Nutzen sein; **it did not** ∼ **them in the end** es hat ihnen letztes Endes gar nichts gebracht. **3** *v.i.* profitieren

∼ **by** *v.t.* profitieren von; Nutzen ziehen aus ⟨*Fehler, Erfahrung*⟩

∼ **from** *v.t.* profitieren von ⟨*Reise, Studium, Ratschlag*⟩; nutzen ⟨*Gelegenheit*⟩

profitability /prɒfɪtə'bɪlɪtɪ/ *n., no pl.* Rentabilität, *die*

profitable /'prɒfɪtəbl/ *adj.* (**a**) (lucrative) rentabel; einträglich; (**b**) (beneficial) lohnend ⟨*Unternehmung, Zeitvertreib, Kauf*⟩; nützlich ⟨*Studium, Diskussion, Verhandlung, Nachforschungen*⟩

profiteer /prɒfɪ'tɪə(r)/ **1** *n.* Profitmacher, *der*/-macherin, *die.* **2** *v.i.* sich bereichern

profiteering /prɒfɪ'tɪərɪŋ/ *n.* Wucher, *der*

profit: ∼**-making** *adj.* gewinnorientiert; ∼ **margin** *n.* Gewinnspanne, *die;* ∼**-sharing** *n.* Gewinnbeteiligung, *die; attrib.* Gewinnbeteiligungs-

profligate /'prɒflɪgət/ *adj.* (**a**) (extravagant) verschwenderisch; (**b**) (dissipated) ausschweifend ⟨*Person*⟩

pro forma 'invoice *n.* (Commerc.) Pro-Forma-Rechnung, *die*

profound /prə'faʊnd/ *adj.,* ∼**er** /prə'faʊndə(r)/, ∼**est** /prə'faʊndɪst/ (**a**) (extreme) tief; nachhaltig ⟨*Wirkung, Einfluss, Eindruck*⟩; tief greifend ⟨*Wandel, Veränderung*⟩; lebhaft ⟨*Interesse*⟩; tief empfunden ⟨*Beileid, Mitgefühl*⟩; tiefsitzend ⟨*Angst, Misstrauen*⟩; völlig ⟨*Unwissenheit*⟩; hochgradig ⟨*Schwerhörigkeit*⟩; **it is a matter of** ∼ **indifference to me** es ist mir völlig gleichgültig; (**b**) (penetrating) tief; profund (geh.) ⟨*Wissen, Erkenntnis, Werk, Kenner*⟩; tiefgründig ⟨*Untersuchung, Abhandlung, Betrachtung*⟩; tief schürfend ⟨*Essay, Analyse, Forscher*⟩; tiefsinnig ⟨*Gedicht, Buch, Schriftsteller*⟩; scharfsinnig ⟨*Denker, Forscher*⟩

profoundly /prə'faʊndlɪ/ *adv.* zutiefst; stark ⟨*beeinflusst, mitgenommen*⟩; hochgradig ⟨*schwerhörig*⟩; ungemein ⟨*scharfsinnig, beschlagen, feinfühlig*⟩; **I am** ∼ **indifferent about it** es ist mir völlig gleichgültig

profundity /prə'fʌndɪtɪ/ *n.* (**a**) *no pl.* (extremeness) Tiefe, *die;* (of joy, sorrow, concern, change) [großes] Ausmaß; (**b**) *no pl.* (depth of intellect) Tiefsinnigkeit, *die;* (of analysis, book) Tiefe, *die*

profuse /prə'fju:s/ *adj.* (abundant) verschwenderisch ⟨*Fülle, Üppigkeit, Vielfalt*⟩; groß ⟨*Dankbarkeit*⟩; überschwänglich ⟨*Entschuldigung, Lob*⟩; ∼ **bleeding** starke Blutung

profusely /prə'fju:slɪ/ *adv.* (abundantly) massenhaft ⟨*wachsen, vorkommen*⟩; heftig ⟨*bluten, erröten, schwitzen*⟩; überaus ⟨*dankbar*⟩; überschwänglich ⟨*sich entschuldigen*⟩

profusion /prə'fju:ʒn/ *n.* ungeheure *od.* überwältigende Menge; **in** ∼: in Hülle und Fülle

prognosis /prɒg'nəʊsɪs/ *n., pl.* **prognoses** /prɒg'nəʊsi:z/ (**a**) (Med.) Prognose, *die;* (**b**) (prediction) Vorhersage, *die;* Prognose, *die;* **give** *or* **make a** ∼ **of sth.** einen Ausblick auf etw. (*Akk.*) geben

program /'prəʊgræm/ **1** *n.* (**a**) (Amer.) ⇒ **programme 1**; (**b**) (Computing, Electronics) Programm, *das.* **2** *v.t.,* **-mm-:** (**a**) (Amer.) ⇒ **programme 2**; (**b**) (Computing, Electronics) programmieren; ∼**ming language** Programmiersprache, *die*

programer (Amer.) ⇒ **programmer**

programme /'prəʊgræm/ **1** *n.* (**a**) ([notice of] events) Programm, *das;* **the evening's** ∼: das Abendprogramm; **what is the** ∼ **for today?** was steht heute auf dem Programm?; **my** ∼ **for today** mein [heutiges] Tagesprogramm; (**b**) (Radio, Telev.) (presentation) Sendung, *die;* (Radio: service) Sender, *der;* Programm, *das;* (**c**) (plan, instructions for machine) Programm, *das;* **a** ∼ **of study** ein Studienprogramm. **2** *v.t.* (**a**) (make ∼ for) ein Programm zusammenstellen für; (**b**) **the tumble-drier can be** ∼**d to operate for between 10 and 60 minutes** der Trockner kann auf 10–60 Minuten Betriebszeit eingestellt werden; (**c**) ⇒ **program 2 b**

programmer /'prəʊgræmə(r)/ *n.* ▶887 (Computing, Electronics: operator) Programmierer, *der*/Programmiererin, *die*

progress 1 /'prəʊgres/ *n.* (**a**) *no pl., no indef. art.* (onward movement) [Vorwärts]bewegung, *die;* **our** ∼ **has been slow** wir sind nur langsam vorangekommen; **make** ∼: vorankommen; **in** ∼: im Gange; (**b**) *no pl., no indef. art.* (advance) Fortschritt, *der;* ∼ **of science/civilization** wissenschaftlicher/kultureller Fortschritt; **make** ∼: vorankommen; ⟨*Student, Patient:*⟩ Fortschritte machen; **make good** ∼ **[towards recovery]** ⟨*Patient:*⟩ sich gut erholen; **some** ∼ **was made** es wurden einige Fortschritte erzielt. **2** /prə'gres/ *v.i.* (**a**) (move forward) vorankommen; (**b**) (be carried on, develop) Fortschritte machen; ∼ **towards sth.** einer Sache (*Dat.*) näherkommen. **3** /'prəʊgres/ *v.t.* vorantreiben

progression /prə'greʃn/ *n.* (**a**) (development) Fortschritt, *der* (**in** bei); (**b**) (succession) Folge, *die;* (**c**) (Math.) Reihe, *die*

progressive /prə'gresɪv/ **1** *adj.* (**a**) (gradual) fortschreitend ⟨*Verbesserung, Verschlechterung*⟩; schrittweise ⟨*Reform*⟩; allmählich ⟨*Veränderung, Herannahen, Fortschreiten, Prozess, Besserung*⟩; (**b**) (worsening) schlimmer werdend; (Med.) progressiv; (**c**) (favouring reform; in culture) fortschrittlich; progressiv; (**d**) (Taxation) gestaffelt; progressiv (fachspr.); ∼ **tax** Progressivsteuer, *die.* **2** *n.* Progressive, *der*/*die*

progressively /prə'gresɪvlɪ/ *adv.* (continuously) immer ⟨*weiter, schlechter*⟩; (gradually) stetig; Schritt für Schritt ⟨*reformieren*⟩; (successively) [chronologisch] fortschreitend; **move** ∼ **towards sth.** sich immer weiter auf etw. (*Akk.*) zubewegen

'progress report *n.* Tätigkeitsbericht, *der;* (fig.: news) Lagebericht, *der*

prohibit /prə'hɪbɪt/ *v.t.* (**a**) (forbid) verbieten; ∼ **sb.'s doing sth.,** ∼ **sb. from doing sth.** jmdm. verbieten, etw. zu tun; (**b**) (prevent) verhindern; ∼ **sb.'s doing sth.,** ∼ **sb. from doing sth.** jmdn. daran hindern, etw. zu tun

prohibition /prəʊhɪ'bɪʃn, prəʊɪ'bɪʃn/ *n.* (**a**) (edict) [gesetzliches] Verbot (**against** *Gen.*); (**b**) *no pl., no art.* (Amer. Hist.) [gesetzliches] Alkoholverbot; **P**∼ (1920–33) die Prohibition

prohibitive /prə'hɪbɪtɪv/ *adj.* unerschwinglich ⟨*Preis, Miete*⟩; untragbar ⟨*Kosten*⟩

prohibitively /prə'hɪbɪtɪvlɪ/ *adv.* unerschwinglich ⟨*hoch, teuer*⟩

project 1 /'prɒdʒekt/ *n.* (**a**) (plan) Plan, *der;* (**b**) (enterprise) Projekt, *das;* ∼ **manager** Projektmanager, *der*/-managerin, *die;* Projektleiter, *der*/-leiterin, *die.* **2** /prə'dʒekt/ *v.t.* (**a**) werfen ⟨*Schatten, Schein, Licht*⟩; senden ⟨*Strahl*⟩; (Cinemat.) projizieren; (**b**) (make known) vermitteln; ∼ **one's own personality** seine eigene Person in den Vordergrund stellen; (**c**) (plan) planen; (**d**) (extrapolate) übertragen (**to** auf + *Akk.*). **3** /prə'dʒekt/ *v.i.* (jut out) ⟨*Felsen:*⟩ vorspringen; ⟨*Zähne, Brauen:*⟩ vorstehen; ∼ **over the street** ⟨*Balkon:*⟩ über die Straße ragen. **4** *v. refl.* (transport oneself) ∼ **oneself into sth.** sich in etw. (*Akk.*) [hinein]versetzen

projectile /prə'dʒektaɪl/ n. Geschoss, das; Projektil, das (Waffent.)

projection /prə'dʒekʃn/ n. (a) (protruding thing) Vorsprung, der; (b) (making of visible image) Projektion, die; (of film) Vorführung, die; (c) (thing planned) Plan, der; (d) (extrapolation) Übertragung, die; Hochrechnung, die (Statistik); (estimate of future possibilities) Voraussage, die (of über + Akk.)

projectionist /prə'dʒekʃənɪst/ n. ▶ 887 | (Cinemat.) Filmvorführer, der/-vorführerin, die

pro'jection room n. (Cinemat.) Vorführraum, der

projector /prə'dʒektə(r)/ n. Projektor, der

proletarian /prəʊlɪ'teərɪən/ 1 adj. proletarisch. 2 n. Proletarier, der/Proletarierin, die

proletariat /prəʊlɪ'teərɪət/ n. Proletariat, das

'pro-life adj. Lebensschutz-; a ~ movement/position eine Pro-Leben-Bewegung; a ~ activist ein aktiver Befürworter des Rechts auf Leben

proliferate /prə'lɪfəreɪt/ v.i. (a) (Biol.) sich stark vermehren; (Med.) proliferieren (fachspr.); wuchern; (b) (increase, lit. or fig.) sich ausbreiten

proliferation /prəlɪfə'reɪʃn/ n. (a) (Biol.) starke Vermehrung; (Med.) Proliferation, die (fachspr.); Wucherung, die; (b) (increase, lit. or fig.) starke Zunahme; (of nuclear weapons) Proliferation, die

prolific /prə'lɪfɪk/ adj. (a) (fertile) fruchtbar; (b) (productive) produktiv

prologue (Amer.: **prolog**) /'prəʊlɒg/ n. (a) (introduction) Prolog, der (to zu); (b) (fig.) Vorspiel, das (to zu)

prolong /prə'lɒŋ/ v.t. verlängern; ~ the agony (fig. coll.) die Qual [unnötig] in die Länge ziehen

prolongation /prəʊlɒŋ'geɪʃn/ n. Verlängerung, die

prolonged /prə'lɒŋd/ adj. lang; lang anhaltend ‹Beifall›; langgezogen ‹Schrei›

promenade /prɒmə'nɑːd/ 1 n. (walkway) Promenade, die; (Brit.: at seaside) [Strand]promenade, die. 2 v.i. promenieren (geh.)

promenade: ~ **concert** n. Promenadenkonzert, das; ~ **deck** n. (Naut.) Promenadendeck, das

prominence /'prɒmɪnəns/ n. (a) (conspicuousness) Auffälligkeit, die; (b) (distinction) Bekanntheit, die; come into or rise to ~: bekannt werden; give ~ to sth. etw. in den Vordergrund stellen; (c) (projecting part) Vorsprung, der

prominent /'prɒmɪnənt/ adj. (a) (conspicuous) auffallend; (b) (foremost) herausragend; become very ~: sehr bekannt werden; he was a ~ in politics er war ein prominenter Politiker; (c) (projecting) vorspringend; vorstehend ‹Backenknochen, Brauen›

prominently /'prɒmɪnəntlɪ/ adv. (a) (conspicuously) auffallend; (b) (in forefront) in einer führenden Rolle; he figured ~ in the case er spielte in dem Fall eine wichtige Rolle

promiscuity /prɒmɪ'skjuːɪtɪ/ n., no pl. (in sexual relations) Promiskuität, die (geh.)

promiscuous /prə'mɪskjʊəs/ adj. (in sexual relations) promiskuitiv; be ~ ‹Person:› den [Sexual]partner/die [Sexual]partnerin häufig wechseln; a ~ man ein Mann, der häufig die Partnerin wechselt

promiscuously /prə'mɪskjʊəslɪ/ adv. (in sexual relations) promiskuitiv

promise /'prɒmɪs/ 1 n. (a) (assurance) Versprechen, das; sb.'s ~s jmds. Versprechungen; give or make a ~ [to sb.] [jmdm.] ein Versprechen geben; I'm not making any ~s ich kann nichts versprechen; give or make a ~ of sth. [to sb.] [jmdm.] etw. versprechen; it's a ~: ganz bestimmt; (b) (guarantee) Zusicherung, die; (c) (fig.: reason for expectation) Hoffnung, die; a painter of or with ~: ein vielversprechender Maler; ~ of sth. Aussicht auf etw. (Akk.); show [great] ~: zu großen Hoffnungen berechtigen. 2 v.t. (a) (give assurance of) versprechen; ~ sth. to sb., ~ sb. sth. jmdm. etw. versprechen; (b) (fig.: give reason for expectation of) verheißen (geh.); ~ sb. sth. jmdm. etw. in Aussicht stellen; (c) ~ oneself sth./that one will do sth.'s sich (Dat.) etw. vornehmen/sich vornehmen, etw. zu tun. 3 v.i. (a) ~ well or favourably [for the future]

vielversprechend [für die Zukunft] sein; (b) (give assurances) Versprechungen machen; I can't ~: ich kann es nicht versprechen

promising /'prɒmɪsɪŋ/ adj. vielversprechend

promontory /'prɒməntərɪ/ n. Vorgebirge, das

promote /prə'məʊt/ v.t. (a) (to more senior job) befördern; (b) (encourage) fördern; (c) (publicize) Werbung machen für; (d) (Footb.) be ~d aufsteigen

promoter /prə'məʊtə(r)/ n. (a) (who organizes and finances event) Veranstalter, der/Veranstalterin, die; (of ballet tour, pop festival, boxing match, cycle race also) Promoter, der; (b) (publicizer) Promoter, der/Promoterin, die

promotion /prə'məʊʃn/ n. (a) (to more senior job) Beförderung, die; win or gain ~: befördert werden; ~ to [the rank of] sergeant etc. Beförderung zum Unteroffizier usw.; (b) (furtherance) Förderung, die; (c) (Sport, Theatre: event) Veranstaltung, die; (d) (publicization) Werbung, die; (instance) Werbekampagne, die; sales ~: Werbung, die; (e) (Footb.) Aufstieg, der; be sure of ~: mit Sicherheit aufsteigen

promotional /prə'məʊʃənl/ adj. Werbe‹kampagne, -broschüre, -strategie usw.›

prompt /prɒmpt/ 1 adj. (a) (ready to act) bereitwillig; be ~ in doing sth. or to do sth. etw. unverzüglich tun; (b) (done readily) sofortig; her ~ answer/reaction ihre prompte Antwort/Reaktion; take ~ action sofort handeln; make a ~ decision sich sofort entschließen; (c) (punctual) pünktlich. 2 adv. pünktlich; at 6 o'clock ~: Punkt 6 Uhr. 3 v.t. (a) (incite) veranlassen; ~ sb. to sth./to do sth. jmdn. zu etw. veranlassen/dazu veranlassen, etw. zu tun; (b) (supply with words; also Theatre) soufflieren (+ Dat.); (supply with answers) vorsagen (+ Dat.); (give suggestion to) weiterhelfen (+ Dat.); (c) (inspire) hervorrufen ‹Kritik, Eifersucht usw.›; provozieren ‹Antwort›. 4 n. (Computing) Bereitschaftsmeldung, die; Prompt, der (fachspr.)

prompter /'prɒmptə(r)/ n. (Theatre) Souffleur, der/Souffleuse, die

prompting /'prɒmptɪŋ/ n. (a) he never needs ~: man muss ihn nicht zweimal bitten; (b) (Theatre) Soufflieren, das

promptly /'prɒmptlɪ/ adv. (a) (quickly) prompt; he ~ went and did the opposite (iron.) er hat natürlich prompt [genau] das Gegenteil getan; (b) (punctually) pünktlich; at 8 o'clock ~, ~ at 8 o'clock Punkt 8 Uhr; pünktlich um 8 Uhr

prone /prəʊn/ adj. (a) (liable) be ~ to anfällig sein für ‹Krankheiten, Depressionen›; neigen zu ‹Faulheit, Meditation›; be ~ to do sth. dazu neigen, etw. zu tun; (b) (down-facing) assume a ~ position on the floor sich in Bauchlage auf den Boden legen

prong /prɒŋ/ n. (of fork) Zinke, die

-pronged /prɒŋd/ adj. in comb. -zinkig; three-~ attack (Mil.; also fig.) Angriff von drei Seiten

pronoun /'prəʊnaʊn/ n. (Ling.) (word replacing noun) Pronomen, das; Fürwort, das; (pronominal adjective) Pronominaladjektiv, das

pronounce /prə'naʊns/ 1 v.t. (a) (declare formally) verkünden; ~ judgement das Urteil verkünden; ~ judgement on sb./sth. über jmdn./etw. das Urteil sprechen; ~ sb./sth. [to be] sth. jmdn./etw. für etw. erklären; ~ sb. fit for work jmdn. für arbeitsfähig erklären; (b) (declare as opinion) erklären für; he ~d himself disgusted with it er erklärte, er sei empört darüber; (c) (speak) aussprechen ‹Wort, Buchstaben usw.›; the h is not ~d das h wird nicht gesprochen. 2 v.i. ~ on sth. zu etw. Stellung nehmen; ~ for or in favour of/against sth. sich für/gegen etw. aussprechen

pronounced /prə'naʊnst/ adj. (a) (declared) erklärt; ausgesprochen ‹Gegner, Autorität›; (b) (marked) ausgeprägt; walk with or have a ~ limp stark hinken

pronouncement /prə'naʊnsmənt/ n. Erklärung, die; make a ~ [about sth.] eine Erklärung [zu etw.] abgeben

pronto /'prɒntəʊ/ adv. (coll.) dalli (ugs.); and [do it] ~! aber [ein bisschen] dalli! (ugs.)

pronunciation /prənʌnsɪ'eɪʃn/ n. Aussprache, die; what is the ~ of this word? wie wird dieses Wort ausgesprochen?

proof /pruːf/ **1** *n.* (a) (fact, evidence) Beweis, *der;* **very good** ∼: sehr gute Beweise; ∼ **positive** eindeutige Beweise; (b) *no pl., no indef. art.* (Law) Beweismaterial, *das;* (c) *no pl.* (proving) **in** ∼ **of** zum Beweis (+ *Gen.*); (d) *no pl.* (test, trial) Beweis, *der;* **put a theory to the** ∼: eine Theorie unter Beweis stellen; **the** ∼ **of the pudding is in the eating** (prov.) Probieren geht über Studieren (Spr.); (e) *no pl., no art.* (standard of strength) Proof *o. Art.;* **100** ∼ (Brit.), **128** ∼ (Amer.) 64 Vol.-% Alkohol; (f) (Printing) Abzug, *der.* **2** *adj.* (a) (impervious) **be** ∼ **against sth.** unempfindlich gegen etw. sein; (fig.) gegen etw. immun sein; (b) *in comb.* 〈*kugel-, bruch-, einbruch-, diebes-, idioten*〉sicher; 〈*schall-, wasser*〉dicht; **flame-**∼: nicht brennbar; (c) hochprozentig 〈*Alkohol*〉; **this liqueur is 67.4°** (Brit.) *or* (Amer.) **76.8°** ∼: dieser Likör hat 38,4 Vol.-% Alkohol. **3** *v.t.* (Printing) (take ∼ of) andrucken; (∼-read) Korrektur lesen

proof: ∼-**read** *v.t.* (Printing) Korrektur lesen; ∼-**reader** *n.* ▶ 887 (Printing) Korrektor, *der*/Korrektorin, *die;* ∼-**reading** *n.* (Printing) Korrekturlesen, *das*

prop /prɒp/ **1** *n.* (support, lit. or fig.) Stütze, *die;* (Mining) Strebe, *die.* **2** *v.t.,* -**pp-:** (a) (support) stützen; **the ladder was** ∼**ped against the house** die Leiter war gegen das Haus gelehnt; (b) (fig.) ⇒ ∼ **up b**

∼ '**up** *v.t.* (a) (support) stützen; ∼ **oneself up on one's elbows** sich auf die Ellbogen stützen; (b) (fig.) aufrichten 〈*Person*〉; vor dem Konkurs bewahren 〈*Firma*〉; stützen 〈*Regierung, Währung*〉

propaganda /prɒpə'gændə/ *n., no pl., no indef. art.* Propaganda, *die*

propagate /'prɒpəgeɪt/ **1** *v.t.* (a) (Hort., Bacteriol.) vermehren (**from, by** durch); (Breeding, Zool.) züchten; (b) (spread) verbreiten; (c) (Phys.) **be** ∼**d** sich fortpflanzen. **2** *v.i.* (a) (Bot., Zool., Bacteriol.) sich vermehren; (b) (spread, extend, travel) sich ausbreiten

propagation /prɒpə'geɪʃn/ *n.* (a) (Hort., Breeding, Bacteriol.: causing to propagate) Züchtung, *die;* (b) (Bot., Zool., Bacteriol.: reproduction) Vermehrung, *die;* (c) (spreading) Verbreitung, *die;* (d) (Phys.) Fortpflanzung, *die*

propagator /'prɒpəgeɪtə(r)/ *n.* (Hort.: device) [beheizbare] Saatkiste

propane /'prəʊpeɪn/ *n.* (Chem.) Propan, *das*

propel /prə'pel/ *v.t.,* -**ll-** (lit. or fig.) antreiben

propeller /prə'pelə(r)/ *n.* Propeller, *der*

pro'peller shaft *n.* (Motor Veh.) Kardanwelle, *die*

propelling 'pencil *n.* (Brit.) Drehbleistift, *der*

propensity /prə'pensɪtɪ/ *n.* Neigung, *die;* [**have] a** ∼ **to** *or* **towards sth.** einen Hang zu etw. [haben]; **have a** ∼ **to do sth.** *or* **for doing sth.** dazu neigen, etw. zu tun

proper /'prɒpə(r)/ **1** *adj.* (a) (accurate) richtig; wahrheitsgetreu 〈*Bericht*〉; zutreffend 〈*Beschreibung*〉; eigentlich 〈*Wortbedeutung*〉; ursprünglich 〈*Fassung*〉; **in the** ∼ **sense** im wahrsten Sinne des Wortes; (b) (*postpos.* (strictly so called) im engeren Sinn *nachgestellt;* **in London** ∼: in London selbst; (c) (genuine) echt; richtig 〈*Wirbelsturm, Schauspieler*〉; (d) (satisfactory) richtig; zufrieden stellend 〈*Antwort*〉; hinreichend 〈*Grund*〉; (e) (suitable) angemessen; (morally fitting) gebührend; **do sth. the** ∼ **way** etw. richtig machen; **we must do the** ∼ **thing by him** wir müssen ihn fair behandeln; **do as you think** ∼: tu, was du für richtig hältst; (f) (conventionally acceptable) gehörig; **it would not be** ∼ **for me to** …: es gehört sich nicht, dass ich …; (g) (conventional, prim) förmlich; (h) *attrib.* (coll.: thorough) richtig; **she gave him a** ∼ **hiding** sie gab ihm eine ordentliche Tracht Prügel; **you gave me a** ∼ **turn** du hast mir einen ganz schönen Schrecken eingejagt. **2** *adv.* (coll.) **good and** ∼: gehörig; nach Strich und Faden (ugs.)

properly /'prɒpəlɪ/ *adv.* (a) richtig; (rightly) zu Recht; (with decency) anständig; ∼ **speaking** genaugenommen; **I'm not** ∼ **authorized to do it** ich bin eigentlich nicht dazu berechtigt; (b) (primly) förmlich; (c) (coll.: thoroughly) total (ugs.)

proper 'name, proper 'noun *ns.* (Ling.) Eigenname, *der*

property /'prɒpətɪ/ *n.* (a) (possession[s], ownership) Eigentum, *das;* **lost** ∼: Fundsachen *Pl.;* **lost** ∼ **[department**

or **office]** Fundbüro, *das;* (b) (estate) Besitz, *der;* Immobilie, *die* (fachspr.); ∼ **in London is expensive** die Immobilienpreise in London sind hoch; (c) (attribute) Eigenschaft, *die;* (effect, special power) Wirkung, *die;* (d) (Cinemat., Theatre) Requisit, *das*

'**property tax** *n.* Vermögenssteuer, *die*

prophecy /'prɒfɪsɪ/ *n.* (a) (prediction) Vorhersage, *die;* (b) (prophetic utterance) Prophezeiung, *die;* (c) (prophetic faculty) [**the power** *or* **gift of]** ∼: die Gabe der Prophetie (geh.)

prophesy /'prɒfɪsaɪ/ **1** *v.t.* (a) (predict) vorhersagen; (fig.) prophezeien 〈*Unglück*〉; (as fortune-teller) weissagen. **2** *v.i.* (a) (foretell future) Vorhersagen machen; (b) (speak as prophet) Prophezeiungen machen

prophet /'prɒfɪt/ *n.* (lit. or fig.) Prophet, *der*

prophetess /'prɒfɪtɪs/ *n.* Prophetin, *die*

prophetic /prə'fetɪk/ *adj.* prophetisch

propitious /prə'pɪʃəs/ *adj.* (a) (auspicious) verheißungsvoll; (b) (favouring) günstig; ∼ **for** *or* **to sth.** günstig für etw.; ∼ **for** *or* **to doing sth.** dafür geeignet, etw. zu tun

proponent /prə'pəʊnənt/ *n.* Befürworter, *der*/Befürworterin, *die*

proportion /prə'pɔːʃn/ **1** *n.* (a) (portion) Teil, *der;* (in recipe) Menge, *die;* **the** ∼ **of deaths is high** der Anteil der Todesfälle ist hoch; **what** ∼ **of candidates pass the exam?** wie groß ist der Anteil der erfolgreichen Prüfungskandidaten?; (b) (ratio) Verhältnis, *das;* **the** ∼ **of sth. to sth.** das Verhältnis von etw. zu etw.; **the high** ∼ **of imports to exports** der hohe Anteil der Importe im Vergleich zu den Exporten; **in** ∼ **[to sth.]** [einer Sache (*Dat.*)] entsprechend; (correct relation) Proportion, *die;* (fig.) Ausgewogenheit, *die;* **sense of** ∼: Sinn für Proportionen; **be in** ∼ **[to** *or* **with sth.]** (lit. or fig.) im richtigen Verhältnis [zu *od.* mit etw.] stehen; **try to keep things in** ∼ (fig.) versuchen Sie, die Dinge im richtigen Licht zu sehen; **be out of** ∼**/all** *or* **any** ∼ **[to** *or* **with sth.]** (lit. or fig.) in keinem/keinerlei Verhältnis zu etw. stehen; **get things out of** ∼ (fig.) die Dinge zu wichtig nehmen; (worry unnecessarily) sich (*Dat.*) zu viele Sorgen machen; **in** *pl.* (size) Dimension, *die;* (e) (Math.) Proportion, *die;* **in direct/inverse** ∼: direkt/umgekehrt proportional. **2** *v.t.* (make proportionate) proportionieren; ∼ **sth. to sth.** etw. einer Sache (*Dat.*) anpassen; *see also* **proportioned**

proportional /prə'pɔːʃənl/ *adj.* (a) (in proportion) entsprechend; **be** ∼ **to sth.** einer Sache (*Dat.*) entsprechen; (b) (in correct relation) ausgewogen; **be** ∼ **to sth.** (lit. or fig.) einer Sache (*Dat.*) entsprechen; (c) (Math.) **be directly/indirectly** ∼ **to sth.** einer Sache (*Dat.*) direkt/umgekehrt proportional sein

proportionally /prə'pɔːʃənəlɪ/ *adv.* (a) (in proportion) [dem]entsprechend; (b) (in correct relation) proportional gesehen; **correspond/not correspond** ∼ **to sth.** im richtigen/in keinem Verhältnis zu etw. stehen

proportional represen'tation *n.* (Polit.) Verhältniswahlsystem, *das*

proportionate /prə'pɔːʃənət/ *adj.* (a) (in proportion) entsprechend; ∼ **to sth.** proportional zu etw.; (b) (in correct relation) ausgewogen; ∼ **to sth.** einer Sache (*Dat.*) entsprechend

proportioned /prə'pɔːʃnd/ *adj.* proportioniert; **well-/ill-**∼: wohlproportioniert/schlecht proportioniert

proposal /prə'pəʊzl/ *n.* (a) (thing proposed) Vorschlag, *der;* (offer) Angebot, *das;* **make a** ∼ **for doing sth.** *or* **to do sth.** einen Vorschlag machen, etw. zu tun; **his** ∼ **for improving the system** sein Vorschlag zur Verbesserung des Systems; **draw up** ∼**s/a** ∼: Pläne/einen Plan aufstellen; (b) ∼ **[of marriage]** [Heirats]antrag, *der*

propose /prə'pəʊz/ **1** *v.t.* (a) (put forward for consideration) vorschlagen; ∼ **sth. to sb.** jmdm. etw. vorschlagen; ∼ **marriage [to sb.]** [jmdm.] einen Heiratsantrag machen; (b) (nominate) ∼ **sb. as/for sth.** jmdn. als/für etw. vorschlagen; (c) (intend) ∼ **doing** *or* **to do sth.** beabsichtigen, etw. zu tun; (d) (set up as aim) planen. *See also* **toast 1 b. 2** *v.i.* (offer marriage) ∼ **[to sb.]** jmdm. einen Heiratsantrag machen

proposition /prɒpə'zɪʃn/ **1** *n.* (a) (proposal) Vorschlag, *der;* **make** *or* **put a** ∼ **to sb.** jmdm. einen Vorschlag machen; **(b)** (statement) Aussage, *die;* **(c)** (coll.: undertaking, problem) Sache, *die* (ugs.); **paying** ∼: lohnendes Geschäft; **(d)** (Logic) Satz, *der;* Proposition, *die* (fachspr.). **2** *v.t.* (coll.) jmdn. anmachen (ugs.)

propound /prə'paʊnd/ *v.t.* darlegen; ∼ **a question** eine Frage aufwerfen

proprietary /prə'praɪətərɪ/ *adj.* **(a)** Eigentums‹*rechte, -ansprüche usw.*›; **(b)** (patented) Marken-; ∼ **brand** *or* **make of washing powder** Markenwaschmittel, *das*

proprietary: ∼ **'medicine** *n.* Markenmedikament, *das;* ∼ **'name,** ∼ **'term** *ns.* (Commerc.) Markenname, *der*

proprietor /prə'praɪətə(r)/ *n.* Inhaber, *der*/Inhaberin, *die;* (of newspaper) Besitzer, *der*/Besitzerin, *die*

propriety /prə'praɪətɪ/ *n.* **(a)** *no pl.* (decency) Anstand, *der;* **with** ∼: anständig; **breach of** ∼: Verstoß gegen die guten Sitten; **(b)** *no pl.* (accuracy) Richtigkeit, *die;* **with perfect** ∼: völlig zu Recht

propulsion /prə'pʌlʃn/ *n.* Antrieb, *der;* (driving force, lit. or fig.) Antriebskraft, *die*

prosaic /prə'zeɪɪk, prəʊ'zeɪɪk/ *adj.* prosaisch (geh.); nüchtern

proscribe /prə'skraɪb/ *v.t.* **(a)** (exile) verbannen; (fig.) ächten; **(b)** (prohibit) verbieten

prose /prəʊz/ *n.* **(a)** Prosa, *die; attrib.* Prosa‹*werk, -stil*›; **(b)** (Sch., Univ.) ∼ **[translation]** Übersetzung in die Fremdsprache

prosecute /'prɒsɪkjuːt/ **1** *v.t.* **(a)** (Law) strafrechtlich verfolgen; ∼ **sb. for sth./doing sth.** jmdn. wegen etw. strafrechtlich verfolgen/jmdn. strafrechtlich verfolgen, weil er etw. tut/getan hat; **(b)** (pursue) verfolgen; **(c)** (carry on) ausüben. **2** *v.i.* Anzeige erstatten

prosecution /prɒsɪ'kjuːʃn/ *n.* **(a)** (Law) (bringing to trial) [strafrechtliche] Verfolgung; (court procedure) Anklage, *die;* **start a** ∼ **against sb.** Anklage gegen jmdn. erheben; **(b)** (Law: prosecuting party) Anklage[vertretung], *die;* **the [case for the]** ∼: die Anklage; **witness for the** ∼, ∼ **witness** Zeuge/Zeugin der Anklage; ∼ **lawyer** Staatsanwalt, *der/* -anwältin, *die;* **(c)** (pursuing) Verfolgung, *die;* (carrying on) Ausübung, *die*

prosecutor /'prɒsɪkjuːtə(r)/ *n.* (Law) Ankläger, *der/*Anklägerin, *die;* **public** ∼ ≈ Generalstaatsanwalt, *der/*-anwältin, *die*

prosody /'prɒsədɪ/ *n.* Verslehre, *die*

prospect 1 /'prɒspekt/ *n.* **(a)** (extensive view) Aussicht, *die* (**of** auf + *Akk.*); (spectacle) Anblick, *der;* **(b)** (expectation) Erwartung, *die* (**of** hinsichtlich); **[at the]** ∼ **of sth./doing sth.** (mental picture, likelihood) [bei der] Aussicht auf etw. (*Akk.*) /[darauf], etw. zu tun; **have the** ∼ **of sth., have sth. in** ∼: etw. in Aussicht haben; **(c)** *in pl.* (hope of success) Zukunftsaussichten; **a man with [good]** ∼s ein Mann mit Zukunft; **a job with no** ∼s eine Stelle ohne Zukunft; **sb.'s** ∼s **of sth./doing sth.** jmds. Chancen auf etw. (*Akk.*) /darauf, etw. zu tun; **the** ∼s **for sb./sth.** die Aussichten für jmdn./etw.; **(d)** (possible customer) [möglicher] Kunde/[mögliche] Kundin; **be a good** ∼ **for a race/the job** bei einem Rennen gute Chancen haben/ein aussichtsreicher Kandidat für den Job sein. **2** /prə'spekt/ *v.i.* (explore for mineral) prospektieren (Bergw.); nach Bodenschätzen suchen; (fig.) Ausschau halten (**for** nach); ∼ **for gold** nach Gold suchen

prospective /prə'spektɪv/ *adj.* (expected) voraussichtlich; zukünftig ‹*Erbe, Braut*›; potenziell ‹*Käufer, Kandidat*›

prospector /prə'spektə(r)/ *n.* Prospektor, *der* (Bergw.); (for gold) Goldsucher, *der*

prospectus /prə'spektəs/ *n.* **(a)** (of enterprise) Prospekt, *der* (Wirtsch.); **(b)** (of book) Prospekt, *der;* **(c)** (Brit. Univ.) Studienführer, *der*

prosper /'prɒspə(r)/ *v.i.* gedeihen; ‹*Geschäft:*› florieren; ‹*Kunst usw.:*› eine Blütezeit erleben; ‹*Berufstätiger:*› Erfolg haben

prosperity /prɒ'sperɪtɪ/ *n., no pl.* Wohlstand, *der*

prosperous /'prɒspərəs/ *adj.* (flourishing) wohlhabend; gut gehend, florierend ‹*Unternehmen*›; (blessed with good fortune) erfolgreich; ∼ **years/time** Jahre/Zeit des Wohlstands

prostate /'prɒsteɪt/ *n.* ∼ **[gland]** (Anat., Zool.) Prostata, *die;* Vorsteherdrüse, *die*

prostitute /'prɒstɪtjuːt/ **1** *n.* **(a)** (woman) Prostituierte, *die;* **(b)** (man) Strichjunge, *der* (salopp). **2** *v.t.* zur Prostitution anbieten; (fig.) prostituieren ‹*Talent, Integrität*›; ∼ **oneself** (lit. or fig.) sich prostituieren

prostitution /prɒstɪ'tjuːʃn/ *n.* (lit. or fig.) Prostitution, *die*

prostrate 1 /'prɒstreɪt/ *adj.* **(a)** [auf dem Bauch] ausgestreckt; **(b)** (exhausted) erschöpft; **be** ∼ **with fever** vom Fieber geschwächt sein. **2** /prɒ'streɪt, prə'streɪt/ *v.t.* **(a)** (lay flat) zu Boden werfen ‹*Person*›; **(b)** (overcome emotionally) übermannen; **(c)** (exhaust) erschöpfen; **be** ∼**d by exhaustion** vor Erschöpfung ganz kraftlos sein. **3** *v. refl.* (throw oneself down) ∼ **oneself [at sth./before sb.]** sich [vor etw./jmdn.] niederwerfen; ∼ **oneself at sb.'s feet** sich jmdm. zu Füßen werfen; ∼ **oneself [before sb.]** (humble oneself) sich [vor jmdm.] demütigen

protagonist /prəʊ'tægənɪst/ *n.* **(a)** (advocate) Vorkämpfer, *der/*Vorkämpferin, *die;* **(b)** (Lit./Theatre: chief character) Protagonist, *der/*Protagonistin, *die;* (fig.) Hauptakteur, *der/*-akteurin, *die*

protect /prə'tekt/ *v.t.* **(a)** (defend) schützen (**from** vor + *Dat.,* **against** gegen); ∼**ed by law** gesetzlich geschützt; ∼ **sb. against** *or* **from himself/herself** jmdn. vor sich (*Dat.*) selbst schützen; ∼ **one's/sb.'s interests** seine/jmds. Interessen wahren; **(b)** (preserve) unter [Natur]schutz stellen ‹*Pflanze, Tier, Gebiet*›; ∼**ed plants/animals** geschützte Pflanzen/Tiere; **(c)** (give legal immunity to) schützen; **the law** ∼**s foreign diplomats** ausländische Diplomaten genießen den Schutz der Immunität; **(d)** (Econ.) durch Protektionismus schützen

protected 'species *n.* geschützte Art

protection /prə'tekʃn/ *n.* **(a)** Schutz, *der* (**from** vor + *Dat.,* **against** gegen); **under the** ∼ **of sb./sth.** unter jmds. Schutz/dem Schutz einer Sache (*Gen.*); **[under] police** ∼: [unter] Polizeischutz; **(b)** (immunity from molestation) Schutz, *der;* (money paid) Schutzgeld, *das;* **(c)** (of wildlife etc.) Schutz, *der;* **(d)** (legal immunity) Immunität, *die;* **(e)** (Econ.) Schutz, *der;* (system) Protektionismus, *der*

protection: ∼ **money** *n.* Schutzgeld, *das;* ∼ **racket** *n.* Erpresserorganisation, *die;* **run a** ∼ **racket** die Erpressung von Schutzgeldern organisieren

protective /prə'tektɪv/ *adj.* (protecting) schützend; Schutz‹*hülle, -anstrich, -vorrichtung, -maske*›; **be** ∼ **towards sb.** fürsorglich gegenüber jmdm. sein; ∼ **instinct** Beschützerinstinkt, *der;* ∼ **clothing** Schutzkleidung, *die*

protective: ∼ **ar'rest,** ∼ **'custody** *ns.* Schutzgewahrsam, *der* (Amtsspr.), Schutzhaft, *die*

protector /prə'tektə(r)/ *n.* **(a)** (person) Beschützer, *der/* Beschützerin, *die;* **(b)** (thing) Schutz, *der; in comb.* -schutz, *der*

protégé /'prɒteʒeɪ/ *n.* Protegé, *der* (geh.); Schützling, *der*

protégée /'prɒteʒeɪ/ *n.* Schützling, *die*

protein /'prəʊtiːn/ *n.* (Chem.) Protein, *das* (fachspr.); Eiweiß, *das;* **a high-**∼ **diet** eine eiweißreiche Kost

protest 1 /'prəʊtest/ *n.* **(a)** (remonstrance) Beschwerde, *die;* (Sport) Protest, *der;* **make** *or* **lodge a** ∼ **[against sb./sth.]** eine Beschwerde [gegen jmdn./etw.] einreichen; **(b)** (show of unwillingness, gesture of disapproval) ∼**[s]** Protest, *der;* **under** ∼: unter Protest; **in** ∼ **[against sth.]** aus Protest [gegen etw.]; **(c)** *no pl., no art.* (dissent) Protest, *der;* **the right of** ∼: das Recht zu protestieren. **2** /prə'test/ *v.t.* **(a)** (affirm) beteuern; **(b)** (Amer.: object to) protestieren gegen. **3** /prə'test/ *v.i.* protestieren; (make written or formal ∼) Protest einlegen (**to** bei); ∼ **about sb./sth.** gegen jmdn./etw. protestieren; ∼ **against being/doing sth.** dagegen protestieren, dass man etw. ist/tut

Protestant /'prɒtɪstənt/ (Relig.) **1** *n.* Protestant, *der/*Protestantin, *die;* Evangelische, *der/die.* **2** *adj.* protestantisch; evangelisch

Protestantism /'prɒtɪstəntɪzm/ *n., no pl., no art.* (Relig.) Protestantismus, *der*

protestation /prɒtɪ'steɪʃn/ *n.* **(a)** (affirmation) Beteuerung, *die;* **(b)** (protest) Protest, *der*

protester /prə'testə(r)/ *n.* (dissenter) Protestierende, *der/ die;* (at demonstration) Demonstrant, *der/*Demonstrantin, *die*

protest /'prəʊtest/**:** ~ **march** n. Protestmarsch, der; ~ **marcher** ⇒ marcher; ~ **song** n. Protestsong, der; ~ **vote** n. Proteststimme, die

protocol /'prəʊtəkɒl/ n. Protokoll, das

proton /'prəʊtɒn/ n. (Phys.) Proton, das

prototype /'prəʊtətaɪp/ n. Prototyp, der; **a** ~ **aeroplane/machine** der Prototyp eines Flugzeugs/einer Maschine

protract /prə'trækt/ v.t. verlängern; ~ed länger ⟨Diskussion, Krankheit, Besuch⟩

protractor /prə'træktə(r)/ n. (Geom.) Winkelmesser, der

protrude /prə'truːd/ **1** v.i. herausragen (**from** aus); ⟨Zähne:⟩ vorstehen; ~ **above/beneath/from behind** sth. etw. überragen/unter/hinter etw. (Dat.) hervorragen; ~ **beyond sth.** über etw. (Akk.) hinausragen. **2** v.t. ausstrecken ⟨Fühler⟩; vorstülpen ⟨Lippen⟩

protrusion /prə'truːʒn/ n. (projecting thing) Vorsprung, der

protuberance /prə'tjuːbərəns/ n. (thing) Auswuchs, der

protuberant /prə'tjuːbərənt/ adj. vorstehend; hervortretend ⟨Augen⟩

proud /praʊd/ **1** adj. (a) stolz; **it made me [feel] really** ~: es erfüllte mich mit Stolz; ~ **to do sth.** or **to be doing sth.** stolz darauf, etw. zu tun; ~ **of sb./sth./doing sth.** stolz auf jmdn./etw./darauf, etw. zu tun; **he is far too** ~ **of himself/his house** er bildet sich (Dat.) zu viel ein/ zu viel auf sein Haus ein; (**b**) (arrogant) hochmütig; stolz ⟨Tier⟩; **I'm not too** ~ **to scrub floors** ich bin mir nicht zu gut zum Fußbodenschrubben. **2** adv. (Brit. coll.) **do sb.** ~ (treat generously) jmdn. verwöhnen; (honour greatly) jmdm. eine Ehrung bereiten; **do oneself** ~: sich (Dat.) etwas Gutes tun

proudly /'praʊdlɪ/ adv. (a) stolz; (b) (arrogantly) hochmütig

prove /pruːv/ **1** v.t., p.p. ~**d** or (esp. Amer., Scot., literary) ~**n** /'pruːvn/ beweisen; nachweisen ⟨Identität⟩; ~ **one's ability** sein Können unter Beweis stellen; **his guilt/innocence was** ~**d, he was** ~**d** [to be] **guilty/innocent** er wurde überführt/seine Unschuld wurde bewiesen; ~ **sb. right/wrong** ⟨Ereignis:⟩ jmdm. Recht/Unrecht geben; **be** ~**d wrong** or **to be false** ⟨Theorie, System:⟩ widerlegt werden; ~ **sth. to be true** beweisen, dass etw. wahr ist; ~ **one's/sb.'s case** or **point** beweisen, dass man Recht hat/jmdm. Recht geben; **it was** ~**d that** …: es stellte sich heraus od. erwies od. zeigte sich, dass … **2** v. refl. ~ **oneself** sich bewähren; ~ **oneself intelligent/a good player** sich als intelligent/als [ein] guter Spieler erweisen. **3** v.i. (be found to be) sich erweisen als; ~ [to be] **unnecessary/interesting/a failure** sich als unnötig/interessant/ [ein] Fehlschlag erweisen

Provence /prɒ'vɑ̃s/ pr. n. die Provence

proverb /'prɒvɜːb/ n. Sprichwort, das; **be a** ~ (fig.) ⟨Eigenschaft:⟩ sprichwörtlich sein

proverbial /prə'vɜːbɪəl/ adj., **proverbially** /prə'vɜːbɪəlɪ/ adv. sprichwörtlich

provide /prə'vaɪd/ v.t. (a) (supply) besorgen; sorgen für; liefern ⟨Beweis⟩; bereitstellen ⟨Dienst, Geld⟩; **instructions are** ~**d with every machine** mit jeder Maschine wird eine Anleitung mitgeliefert; ~ **homes/materials/a car for sb.** jmdm. Unterkünfte/Materialien/ein Auto [zur Verfügung] stellen; ~ **sb. with money** jmdn. unterhalten; (for journey etc.) jmdm. Geld zur Verfügung stellen; **be** [well] ~**d with sth.** mit etw. [wohl]versorgt od. [wohl]versehen sein; ~ **oneself with sth.** sich (Dat.) etw. besorgen; (b) (stipulate) ⟨Vertrag, Gesetz:⟩ vorsehen; (c) **providing that** ⇒ **provided**

~ **for** v.t. (a) (make provision for) vorsorgen für; Vorsorge treffen für; ⟨Plan, Gesetz:⟩ vorsehen ⟨Maßnahmen, Steuern⟩; ⟨Schätzung:⟩ berücksichtigen ⟨Inflation⟩; (b) (maintain) sorgen für, versorgen ⟨Familie, Kind⟩

provided /prə'vaɪdɪd/ conj. ~ [that] …: vorausgesetzt, [dass] …

providence /'prɒvɪdəns/ n. (a) [divine] ~: die [göttliche] Vorsehung; (b) P~ (God) der Himmel

providential /prɒvɪ'denʃl/ adj. (opportune) **it was** ~ **that** …: es war ein Glück, dass …

provider /prə'vaɪdə(r)/ n. (breadwinner) Ernährer, der/Ernährerin, die; Versorger, der/Versorgerin, die

province /'prɒvɪns/ n. (a) (administrative area) Provinz, die; (b) **the** ~**s** (regions outside capital) die Provinz (oft abwertend); (c) (sphere of action) [Arbeits-, Tätigkeits-, Wirkungs]bereich, der; [Arbeits-, Tätigkeits]gebiet, das; (area of responsibility) Zuständigkeitsbereich, der; **that is not my** ~: da kenne ich mich nicht aus; (not my responsibility) dafür bin ich nicht zuständig

provincial /prə'vɪnʃl/ **1** adj. Provinz-; (of the provinces) Provinz-; (typical of the provinces) provinziell. **2** n. Provinzler, der/Provinzlerin, die (abwertend)

provision /prə'vɪʒn/ n. (a) (providing) Bereitstellung, die; **as a** or **by way of** ~ **against** …: zum Schutz gegen …; ~ **of medical care** medizinische Versorgung; **make** ~ **for** vorsorgen od. Vorsorge treffen für ⟨Notfall⟩; berücksichtigen ⟨Inflation⟩; **make** ~ **for sb. in one's will** jmdn. in seinem Testament bedenken; **make** ~ **against sth.** Vorkehrungen zum Schutz gegen etw. treffen; (b) (amount available) Vorrat, der; (c) in pl. (food) Lebensmittel; (for expedition also) Proviant, der; **stock up with** ~**s** Lebensmittelvorräte anlegen; (d) (legal statement) Verordnung, die; (clause) Bestimmung, die

provisional /prə'vɪʒənl/ **1** adj. vorläufig; provisorisch; ~ **arrangement** Provisorium, das. **2** n. in pl. **the P**~**s** die provisorische IRA

provisional: P~ **IR'A** n. provisorische IRA; ~ **licence** n. vorläufige Fahrerlaubnis

provisionally /prə'vɪʒənəlɪ/ adv. vorläufig; provisorisch

proviso /prə'vaɪzəʊ/ n., pl. ~**s** Vorbehalt, der

provocation /prɒvə'keɪʃn/ n. Provokation, die; Herausforderung, die; **be under severe** ~: stark provoziert werden; **he loses his temper at** or **on the slightest** or **smallest** ~: er verliert die Beherrschung beim geringsten Anlass

provocative /prə'vɒkətɪv/ adj. provozierend; herausfordernd; (sexually) aufreizend; **his actions were felt to be** ~: seine Aktionen wurden als Provokation empfunden

provoke /prə'vəʊk/ v.t. (a) (annoy, incite) provozieren ⟨Person⟩; reizen ⟨Person, Tier⟩; (sexually) aufreizen; **be easily** ~**d** leicht reizbar sein; sich leicht provozieren lassen; ~ **sb. to anger/fury** jmdn. in Wut (Akk.) /zur Raserei bringen; ~ **sb. into doing sth.** jmdn. so sehr provozieren od. reizen, dass er etw. tut; **he was finally** ~**d into taking action** er ließ sich schließlich dazu hinreißen od. provozieren, etwas zu unternehmen; (b) (give rise to) hervorrufen; erregen ⟨Ärger, Neugier, Zorn⟩; auslösen ⟨Kontroverse, Krise⟩; herausfordern ⟨Widerstand⟩; verursachen ⟨Zwischenfall⟩; Anlass geben zu ⟨Klagen, Kritik⟩

provoking /prə'vəʊkɪŋ/ adj. provozierend; herausfordernd; **his behaviour/refusal was** [very] ~: sein Benehmen/seine Weigerung war eine [große] Provokation

prow /praʊ/ n. (Naut.) Bug, der

prowess /'praʊɪs/ n. (a) (valour) Tapferkeit, die; (b) (skill) Fähigkeiten; Können, das; ~ **at sports** [große] Sportlichkeit; **sexual** ~: sexuelle Leistungsfähigkeit

prowl /praʊl/ **1** v.i. streifen; ~ **about/around sth.** etw. durchstreifen. **2** v.t. durchstreifen. **3** n. Streifzug, der; **be on the** ~: auf einem Streifzug sein

prowler /'praʊlə(r)/ n. **the police have warned of** ~**s in the area** die Polizei warnt vor verdächtigen Personen, die in der Gegend herumstreifen

proximity /prɒk'sɪmɪtɪ/ n., no pl. Nähe, die (**to** zu)

proxy /'prɒksɪ/ n. (a) (agency, document) Vollmacht, die; Bevollmächtigung, die; **by** ~: durch einen Bevollmächtigten/eine Bevollmächtigte; see also **stand 1 g**; (b) (person) Bevollmächtigte, der/die; (vote) durch einen Bevollmächtigten/eine Bevollmächtigte abgegebene Stimme; **make sb. one's** ~: jmdn. bevollmächtigen

prude /pruːd/ n. prüder Mensch

prudence /'pruːdəns/ n., no pl. Besonnenheit, die; Überlegtheit, die; **act with** ~: besonnen od. überlegt handeln

prudent /'pruːdənt/ adj. (a) (careful) besonnen ⟨Person⟩; besonnen, überlegt ⟨Verhalten⟩; (b) (circumspect) vorsichtig; **think it more** ~ **to do sth.** es für klüger halten, etw. zu tun

prudish /'pru:dɪʃ/ *adj.* prüde
prune¹ /pru:n/ *n.* (a) (fruit) [**dried**] ∼: Back- *od.* Dörrpflaume, *die;* (b) (coll.: simpleton) Trottel, *der* (ugs. abwertend)
prune² *v.t.* (a) (trim) [be]schneiden; ∼ **back** zurückschneiden; (b) (lop off) ∼ [**away/off**] ab- *od.* wegschneiden; ∼ [**out**] herausschneiden; (c) (fig.: reduce) reduzieren; ∼ **back** Abstriche machen an (+ *Dat.*) ⟨Projekt⟩
pruning shears /'pru:nɪŋ ʃɪəz/ *n. pl.* Gartenschere, *die;* Rosenschere, *die*
pry /praɪ/ *v.i.* neugierig sein
∼ **a'bout** *v.i.* herumschnüffeln (ugs. abwertend) *od.* -spionieren
∼ **into** *v.t.* seine Nase stecken in (+ *Akk.*) (ugs.) ⟨Angelegenheit⟩
prying /'praɪɪŋ/ *adj.* neugierig
PS *abbr.* **postscript** PS
psalm /sɑːm/ *n.* (Eccl.) Psalm, *der*
pseud /sju:d/ (coll.) **1** *adj.* (a) (pretentious) pseudointellektuell; (b) ⇒ **pseudo 1 a. 2** *n.* ⇒ **pseudo 2**
pseudo /'sju:dəʊ/ **1** *adj.* (a) (sham, spurious) unecht; (b) (insincere) verlogen. **2** *n., pl.* ∼**s** (a) (pretentious person) Möchtegern, *der* (ugs. spött.); (b) (insincere person) Heuchler, *der/* Heuchlerin, *die*
pseudo- *in comb.* pseudo-/Pseudo- (fachspr., geh.)
pseudonym /'sju:dənɪm/ *n.* Pseudonym, *das*
psst, pst /pst/ *int.* st
psych /saɪk/ *v.t.* (coll.) ∼ **sb. out** jmdn. durchschauen; ∼ **sb./oneself up** jmdn./sich einstimmen
psyche /'saɪkɪ/ *n.* Psyche, *die*
psychiatric /saɪkɪ'ætrɪk/ *adj.* psychiatrisch
psychiatrist /saɪ'kaɪətrɪst/ *n.* ▶887| Psychiater, *der/* Psychiaterin, *die*
psychiatry /saɪ'kaɪətrɪ/ *n.* Psychiatrie, *die*
psychic /'saɪkɪk/ *adj.* (having occult powers) **be** ∼: übernatürliche Fähigkeiten haben; **you must be** ∼ (fig.) du kannst wohl Gedanken lesen
psycho /'saɪkəʊ/ (coll.) **1** *adj.* verrückt (ugs.). **2** *n., pl.* ∼**s** Verrückte, *der/die* (ugs.)
psycho'analyse *v.t.* psychoanalysieren (fachspr.); psychoanalytisch behandeln
psychoa'nalysis *n.* Psychoanalyse, *die*
psycho'analyst *n.* ▶887| Psychoanalytiker, *der/*-analytikerin, *die*
psychological /saɪkə'lɒdʒɪkl/ *adj.* (a) (of the mind) psychisch ⟨Problem⟩; psychologisch ⟨Wirkung, Druck⟩; (b) (of psychology) psychologisch
psychological 'warfare *n.* psychologische Kriegsführung
psychologist /saɪ'kɒlədʒɪst/ *n.* ▶887| (also fig.) Psychologe, *der/*Psychologin, *die*
psychology /saɪ'kɒlədʒɪ/ *n.* (a) Psychologie, *die;* (b) (coll.: characteristics) Psychologie, *die* (ugs.)
psychopath /'saɪkəpæθ/ *n.* Psychopath, *der/*Psychopathin, *die*
psychosis /saɪ'kəʊsɪs/ *n., pl.* **psychoses** /saɪ'kəʊsi:z/ Psychose, *die*
psychosomatic /saɪkəʊsə'mætɪk/ *adj.* (Med.) psychosomatisch
psychotherapist /saɪkəʊ'θerəpɪst/ *n.* Psychotherapeut, *der/*-therapeutin, *die*
psycho'therapy *n., no pl.* (Med.) Psychotherapie, *die*
PTO *abbr.* **please turn over** b.w.
pub /pʌb/ *n.* (Brit.) Kneipe, *die* (ugs.); (esp. in British Isles) Pub, *das; attrib.* Kneipen-
'pub crawl *n.* (Brit. coll.) Zechtour, *die;* Bierreise, *die* (ugs. scherzh.); **go on a** ∼: eine Zechtour machen
puberty /'pju:bətɪ/ *n., no pl., no art.* Pubertät, *die;* **at** ∼: in *od.* während der Pubertät
pubic /'pju:bɪk/ *adj.* (Anat.) Scham-
public /'pʌblɪk/ **1** *adj.* öffentlich; ∼ **assembly** Volksversammlung, *die;* **a** ∼ **danger/service** eine Gefahr für die/ ein Dienst an der Allgemeinheit; **be a matter of** ∼

knowledge allgemein bekannt sein; **in the** ∼ **eye** im Blickpunkt der Öffentlichkeit; **make sth.** ∼: etw. publik (geh.) *od.* bekannt machen. **2** *n., no pl.; constr. as sing. or pl.* (a) (the people) Öffentlichkeit, *die;* Allgemeinheit, *die;* **the general** ∼: die Allgemeinheit; die breite Öffentlichkeit; **member of the** ∼: Bürger, *der/*Bürgerin, *die;* **be open to the** ∼: für den Publikumsverkehr geöffnet sein; (b) (section of community) Publikum, *das;* (author's readers also) Leserschaft, *die;* **the reading** ∼: das Lesepublikum; (c) **in** ∼ (publicly) öffentlich; (openly) offen; **behave oneself in** ∼: sich in der Öffentlichkeit benehmen
public-ad'dress system *n.* Lautsprecheranlage, *die*
publican /'pʌblɪkən/ *n.* ▶887| (Brit.) [Gast]wirt, *der/*-wirtin, *die*
publication /pʌblɪ'keɪʃn/ *n.* (issuing of book etc.; book etc. issued) Veröffentlichung, *die;* Publikation, *die;* **the magazine is a weekly** ∼: die Zeitschrift erscheint wöchentlich
public: ∼ **'bar** *n.* (Brit.) ≈ Ausschank, *der;* ∼ **'company** *n.* (Brit. Econ.) Aktiengesellschaft, *die;* ∼ **convenience** ⇒ **convenience e;** ∼ **'figure** *n.* Persönlichkeit des öffentlichen Lebens; ∼ **'footpath** *n.* öffentlicher Fußweg; ∼ **'health** *n.* [öffentliches] Gesundheitswesen; ∼ **'holiday** *n.* gesetzlicher Feiertag; ∼ **'house** *n.* (Brit.) Gastwirtschaft, *die;* Gaststätte, *die;* ∼ **'interest** *n.* Interesse der Allgemeinheit
publicise ⇒ **publicize**
publicity /pʌb'lɪsɪtɪ/ *n., no pl., no indef. art.* (a) Publicity, *die;* (advertising) Werbung, *die;* ∼ **campaign** Werbekampagne, *die;* ∼ **material** Werbematerial, *das;* (b) (attention) Publicity, *die;* Publizität, *die* (geh.); **attract** ∼ ⟨Vorfall:⟩ Aufsehen erregen
pub'licity agent *n.* ▶887| Publicitymanager, *der/* -managerin, *die*
publicize /'pʌblɪsaɪz/ *v.t.* publik machen ⟨Ungerechtigkeit⟩; werben für, Reklame machen für ⟨Produkt, Veranstaltung⟩; **well-**∼**d** ausreichend publik gemacht
public: ∼ **'library** *n.* öffentliche Bücherei; ∼ **limited 'company** *n.* (Brit.) ≈ Aktiengesellschaft, *die*
publicly /'pʌblɪklɪ/ *adv.* (a) (in public) öffentlich; (b) (by the public) mit öffentlichen Geldern ⟨finanzieren, subventionieren⟩; ∼ **owned** staatseigen; staatlich
public: ∼ **'nuisance** *n.* (Law) Störung der öffentlichen [Sicherheit und] Ordnung; ∼ **o'pinion** ⇒ **opinion b;** ∼ **'ownership** *n., no pl.* Staatseigentum, *das* (**of an** + *Dat.*); Gemeineigentum, *das* (**of an** + *Dat.*); **be taken into** ∼ **ownership** verstaatlicht werden; ∼ **property** *n.* Staatsbesitz, *der;* **sth. is** ∼ **property** (fig.) etw. ist allgemein bekannt; ∼ **'prosecutor** *n.* ▶887| (Law) Staatsanwalt, *der/*-anwältin, *die;* ∼ **'purse** ⇒ **purse 1;** ∼ **re'lations** *n. pl., constr. as sing. or pl.* Public Relations *Pl.;* Öffentlichkeitsarbeit, *die; attrib.* Public-Relations- ⟨-Abteilung, -Berater⟩; ∼ **relations officer** Öffentlichkeitsreferent, *der/*-referentin, *die;* ∼ **school** *n.* (a) (Brit.) Privatschule, *die; attrib.* Privatschul-; (b) (Scot., Amer.: school run by ∼ authorities) staatliche *od.* öffentliche Schule; ∼**-'spirited** *adj.* von Gemeinsinn zeugend ⟨Verhalten⟩; **be a** ∼**-spirited person** Gemeinsinn haben; ∼ **'transport** *n.* öffentlicher Personenverkehr; **travel by** ∼ **transport** mit öffentlichen Verkehrsmitteln fahren; ∼ **u'tility** *n.* öffentlicher Versorgungsbetrieb
publish /'pʌblɪʃ/ *v.t.* (a) ⟨Verleger, Verlag:⟩ verlegen ⟨Buch, Zeitschrift, Musik usw.⟩; ⟨Autor:⟩ veröffentlichen ⟨Text⟩; **the book has been** ∼**ed by a British company** das Buch ist in *od.* bei einem britischen Verlag erschienen; (b) (announce publicly) verkünden; (read out) verlesen ⟨Aufgebot⟩; (c) (make generally known) publik machen ⟨Ergebnisse, Einzelheiten⟩
publisher /'pʌblɪʃə(r)/ *n.* ▶887| Verleger, *der/*Verlegerin, *die;* ∼[s] (company) Verlag, *der;* ∼**s of children's books** Kinderbuchverlag, *der;* **music/scientific/magazine** ∼**s** Musikverlag, *der/*wissenschaftlicher Verlag/ Zeitschriftenverlag, *der*
publishing /'pʌblɪʃɪŋ/ *n., no pl., no art.* Verlagswesen, *das; attrib.* Verlags-; ∼ **firm/company** Verlag, *der*

'publishing house *n.* Verlag, *der*

puce /pjuːs/ **1** *n.* Flohbraun, *das.* **2** *adj.* flohbraun; **go ~ in the face** puterrot werden

puck /pʌk/ *n.* (Ice Hockey) Puck, *der*

pucker /'pʌkə(r)/ **1** *v.t.* **~ [up]** runzeln ‹*Brauen, Stirn*›; krausen, krausziehen ‹*Stirn*›; kräuseln ‹*Lippen*›; (sewing) kräuseln ‹*Stoff*›. **2** *v.i.* **~ [up]** ‹*Gesicht:*› sich in Falten legen; ‹*Stoff:*› sich kräuseln

pud /pʊd/ (coll.) ⇒ **pudding**

pudding /'pʊdɪŋ/ *n.* **(a)** Pudding, *der;* **(b)** (dessert) süße Nachspeise

pudding: ~ basin, ~ bowl *ns.* Puddingform, *die*

puddle /'pʌdl/ *n.* Pfütze, *die*

puerile /'pjʊəraɪl/ *adj.* kindisch (abwertend); infantil (abwertend)

Puerto Rican /pwɜːtəʊ 'riːkən/ [▶ 947] **1** *adj.* puertoricanisch. **2** *n.* Puertoricaner, *der*/Puertoricanerin, *die*

Puerto Rico /pwɜːtəʊ 'riːkəʊ/ *pr. n.* Puerto Rico (*das*)

puff /pʌf/ **1** *n.* **(a)** Stoß, *der;* **~ of breath/wind** Atem-/Windstoß, *der;* **(b)** (sound of escaping vapour) Zischen, *das;* **(c)** (quantity) **~ of smoke** Rauchstoß, *der;* **~ of steam** Dampfwolke, *die;* **(d)** (pastry) Blätterteigteilchen, *das;* **(e) sb. runs out of ~** (lit. or fig. coll.) jmdm. geht die Puste aus (ugs.). **2** *v.i.* **(a)** ‹*Blasebalg:*› blasen; **~ [and blow]** pusten (ugs.) *od.* schnaufen [und keuchen]; **(b)** (**~** cigarette smoke etc.) paffen (ugs.) (**at** an + *Dat.*); **(c)** (move with **~**ing) ‹*Person:*› keuchen; ‹*Zug, Lokomotive, Dampfer:*› schnaufend fahren. **3** *v.t.* **(a)** (blow) pusten (ugs.), blasen ‹*Rauch*›; stäuben ‹*Puder*›; **(b)** (smoke in **~**s) paffen (ugs.); **(c)** (put out of breath) ⇒ **~ out 1 b; (d)** (utter pantingly) keuchen

~ 'out *v.t.* **(a)** (inflate) ‹*Wind:*› blähen, bauschen ‹*Segel*›; **(b)** (put out of breath) außer Puste (salopp) *od.* Atem bringen ‹*Person*›; **be ~ed out** außer Puste (salopp) *od.* Atem sein

~ 'up *v.t.* **(a)** (inflate) aufblasen; aufpusten (ugs.); **(b) be ~ed up** (proud) aufgeblasen sein

puffin /'pʌfɪn/ *n.* (Ornith.) Papageientaucher, *der*

'puffin crossing *n.* (Brit.) Fußgängerüberweg mit elektronisch gesteuerter Ampel

puff: ~ 'pastry *n.* (Cookery) Blätterteig, *der;* **~ 'sleeve** *n.* Puffärmel, *der*

puffy /'pʌfɪ/ *adj.* verschwollen

pug /pʌg/ *n.* **~[-dog]** Mops, *der*

pugnacious /pʌg'neɪʃəs/ *adj.* (literary) kampflustig

'pug-nosed *adj.* stumpfnasig

puke /pjuːk/ (coarse) **1** *v.i.* kotzen (salopp). **2** *v.t.* **~ up** auskotzen (salopp); ausspucken (ugs.). **3** *n.* Kotze, *die* (salopp)

pull /pʊl/ **1** *v.t.* **(a)** (draw, tug) ziehen an (+ *Dat.*); ziehen ‹*Hebel*›; **~ aside** beiseite ziehen; **~ sb.'s** *or* **sb. by the hair/ears/sleeve** jmdn. an den Haaren/Ohren/am Ärmel ziehen; **~ shut** zuziehen ‹*Tür*›; **~ sth. over one's ears/head** sich ‹*Dat.*› etw. über die Ohren/den Kopf ziehen; **~ the other one** *or* **leg[, it's got bells on]** (fig. coll.) das kannst du einem anderen erzählen; **(b)** (fig.: criticize severely) zerpflücken ‹*Argument, Artikel*›; **(c)** (extract) [heraus]ziehen; [heraus]ziehen ‹*Zahn*›; zapfen ‹*Bier*›; **(c)** (coll.: accomplish) bringen (ugs.); **a stunt** *or* **trick** etwas Wahnsinniges tun; **(d) ~ a knife/gun on sb.** ein Messer/eine Pistole ziehen und jmdn. damit bedrohen; **(e) not ~ one's punches** (fig.) nicht zimperlich sein. **2** *v.i.* **(a)** ziehen; **'P~'** „Ziehen"; **(b) ~ [to the left/right]** ‹*Auto, Boot:*› [nach links/rechts] ziehen; **(c)** (pluck) **~** ziehen an (+ *Dat.*); **~ at sb.'s sleeve** jmdn. am Ärmel ziehen. **3** *n.* **(a)** Zug, *der;* Ziehen, *das;* (of conflicting emotions) Widerstreit, *der;* **give a ~ at sth.** an etw. ‹*Dat.*› ziehen; **(b)** *no pl.* (influence) Einfluss, *der* (**with** auf + *Akk.*, bei)

~ a'head *v.i.* in Führung gehen; **~ ahead of** sich setzen vor (+ *Akk.*)

~ a'part 1 *v.t.* **(a)** (take to pieces) auseinander nehmen; zerlegen; **(b)** (fig.: criticize severely) zerpflücken ‹*Interpretation, Argumentation usw.*›; verreißen ‹*Buch, [literarisches] Werk*›

~ a'way 1 *v.t.* wegziehen. **2** *v.i.* anfahren; (with effort) anziehen

~ 'back 1 *v.i.* **(a)** (retreat) zurücktreten; ‹*Truppen:*› sich zurückziehen; **(b)** (Sport) [wieder]aufholen (**to** bis auf +

Akk.). **2** *v.t.* **(a)** zurückziehen; **(b)** (Sport) aufholen

~ 'down *v.t.* **(a)** herunterziehen; **(b)** (demolish) abreißen; **(c)** (make less) drücken ‹*Preis*›; (weaken) mitnehmen ‹*Person*›

~ 'in 1 *v.t.* **(a)** hereinziehen; zurückziehen ‹*Beine*›; **(b)** (attract) anziehen; **(c)** (coll.: detain in custody) einkassieren (salopp); kassieren (ugs.). **2** *v.i.* **(a)** ‹*Zug:*› einfahren; **(b)** (move to side of road) an die Seite fahren; (stop) anhalten; **~ in to the side of the road** an den Straßenrand fahren

~ into *v.t.* **(a)** ‹*Zug:*› einfahren in (+ *Akk.*); **(b)** (move off road into) fahren in (+ *Akk.*)

~ 'off *v.t.* **(a)** (remove) abziehen; (violently) abreißen; ausziehen ‹*Kleidungsstück, Handschuhe*›; **(b)** (accomplish) an Land ziehen (ugs.) ‹*Geschäft, Knüller*›

~ 'on *v.t.* [sich (*Dat.*)] an- *od.* überziehen; (in a hurry) sich werfen in (+ *Akk.*)

~ 'out 1 *v.t.* **(a)** (extract) herausziehen; [heraus]ziehen ‹*Zahn*›; **(b)** (take out of pocket etc.) aus der Tasche ziehen; herausziehen ‹*Messer, Pistole*›; [heraus]ziehen, (scherzh.) zücken ‹*Brieftasche*›; **(c)** (withdraw) abziehen ‹*Truppen*›; herausnehmen ‹*Spieler, Mannschaft*›. **2** *v.i.* **(a)** (depart) ‹*Zug:*› abfahren; **~ out of the station** aus dem Bahnhof ausfahren; **(b)** (away from roadside) ausscheren; **(c)** (withdraw) ‹*Truppen:*› abziehen (**of** aus); (from deal, project, competition, etc.) aussteigen (ugs.) (**of** aus)

~ 'over ⇒ **~ in 2 b**

~ 'through *v.i.* ‹*Patient:*› durchkommen

~ to'gether 1 *v.i.* **~ in einem** *od.* am selben Strang ziehen. **2** *v. refl.* sich zusammennehmen

~ 'up 1 *v.t.* **(a)** hochziehen; **(b) ~ up a chair** einen Stuhl heranziehen; **(c)** [he]rausziehen ‹*Unkraut, Pflanze usw.*›; (violently) [he]rausreißen; **(d)** (stop) anhalten, zum Stehen bringen ‹*Auto*›; **(e)** (reprimand) zurechtweisen; rügen. **2** *v.i.* **(a)** (stop) anhalten; **(b)** (improve) sich verbessern. **3** *v. refl.* sich hocharbeiten

'pull-down menu *n.* (Computing) Pull-down-Menü, *das* (fachspr.)

pulley /'pʊlɪ/ *n.* Rolle, *die;* **set of ~s** (tackle) Flaschenzug, *der*

Pullman /'pʊlmən/ *n.* **~ [car** *or* **coach]** Pullman[wagen], *der*

'pull-out *n.* **(a)** (folding portion of book etc.) ausfaltbarer Teil; (detachable section) heraustrennbarer Teil; **(b)** (withdrawal) Abzug, *der*

pullover /'pʊləʊvə(r)/ *n.* Pullover, *der;* Pulli, *der* (ugs.)

pulp /pʌlp/ **1** *n.* **(a)** (of fruit) Fruchtfleisch, *das;* **(b)** (soft mass) Brei, *der;* **beat sb. to a ~:** jmdn. zu Brei schlagen (salopp). **2** *v.t.* zerdrücken, zerstampfen ‹*Rübe*›; einstampfen ‹*Druckerzeugnis*›

pulpit /'pʊlpɪt/ *n.* (Eccl.) Kanzel, *die*

pulsate /pʌl'seɪt, 'pʌlseɪt/ *v.i.* **(a)** (beat, throb) pulsieren; ‹*Herz:*› schlagen; (fig. literary) pulsieren; **(b)** (fig.: vibrate) schwingen

pulse¹ /pʌls/ **1** *n.* **(a)** (lit. or fig.) Puls, *der;* (single beat) Pulsschlag, *der;* **have/keep one's finger on the ~ of sth.** die Hand am Puls einer Sache (*Gen.*) haben/auf dem Laufenden über etw. (*Akk.*) bleiben; **(b)** (rhythmical recurrence) Rhythmus, *der;* **(c)** (Electronics) Impuls, *der.* **2** *v.i.* ⇒ **pulsate**

pulse² *n.* (variety of edible seed) Hülsenfrucht, *die*

'pulse rate *n.* Pulsfrequenz, *die;* **push up sb's ~:** jmds. Puls hochtreiben

pulverize (pulverise) /'pʌlvəraɪz/ *v.t.* **(a)** (to powder or dust) pulverisieren; **(b)** (fig.: crush) abservieren (Sport) ‹*Gegner*›; **I'll ~ you!** ich schlag dich zu Brei! (derb)

puma /'pjuːmə/ *n.* (Zool.) Puma, *der*

pumice /'pʌmɪs/ *n.* (Min.) **~ [stone]** Bimsstein, *der*

pummel /'pʌml/ *v.t.,* (Brit.) **-ll-** einschlagen auf (+ *Akk.*)

pump /pʌmp/ **1** *n.* (machine; also fig.) Pumpe, *die.* **2** *v.i.* pumpen. **3** *v.t.* **(a)** pumpen; **~ bullets into sth.** Kugeln in etw. (*Akk.*) jagen (ugs.); **(b) ~ sth. dry** etw. leer pumpen; **~ sb. for information** Auskünfte aus jmdm. herausholen; **(c) ~ up** (inflate) aufpumpen ‹*Reifen, Fahrrad*›

pumpkin /'pʌmpkɪn/ n. (Bot.) Kürbis, der; attrib. Kürbis-
pun /pʌn/ n. Wortspiel, das
punch² n. (drink) Punsch, der
Punch /pʌntʃ/ n. Punch, der; Hanswurst, der; ~ **and
Judy show** Kasperletheater, das; **be as pleased as** ~:
sich freuen wie ein Schneekönig (ugs.)
punch¹ 1 v.t. **(a)** (strike with fist) boxen; **(b)** (pierce, open up)
lochen; ~ **a hole** ein Loch stanzen; ~ **a hole/holes in**
sth. etw. lochen. **2** n. **(a)** (blow) Faustschlag, der; **(b)** (coll.:
vigour) Pep, der (ugs.); **(c)** (device for making holes) (in leather,
tickets) Lochzange, die; (in paper) Locher, der. See also **pack
2 f; pull 1 e**
punch: ~**ball** n. (Brit.) (ball) Punchingball, der; (bag)
Sandsack, der; ~**bowl** n. Bowlengefäß, das; Bowle, die;
~ **card** n. (Computing) Lochkarte, die; ~**-drunk** adj. (fig.)
benommen
punched /pʌntʃt/: ~ **card**, ~ **tape** ⇒ **punch
card,** ~**tape**
'punching bag (Amer.) ⇒ **punchball**
punch: ~ **line** n. Pointe, die; ~ **tape** n. (Computing)
Lochstreifen, der; ~**-up** n. (Brit. coll.) (fist-fight, brawl) Prügelei, die
punctilious /pʌŋk'tɪlɪəs/ adj. [peinlich] korrekt; peinlich ⟨Genauigkeit⟩
punctual /'pʌŋktjʊəl/ adj. pünktlich
punctuality /pʌŋktjʊ'ælɪtɪ/ n., no pl. Pünktlichkeit, die
punctuate /'pʌŋktjʊeɪt/ v.t. interpunktieren (fachspr.);
mit Satzzeichen versehen; (fig.: interrupt) unterbrechen (**with**
durch)
punctuation /pʌŋktjʊ'eɪʃn/ n., no pl. Interpunktion, die
(fachspr.); Zeichensetzung, die
punctu'ation mark n. Satzzeichen, das
puncture /'pʌŋktʃə(r)/ 1 n. **(a)** (flat tyre) Reifenpanne, die;
Platte, der (ugs.); **(b)** (hole) Loch, das; (in skin) Einstich, der;
~ [**repair**] **kit** Flickzeug, das; Pannenset, das. **2** v.t.
durchstechen; (fig.) verletzen ⟨Wurde⟩; **be** ~**d** ⟨Reifen:⟩ ein
Loch haben, platt sein; ⟨Haut:⟩ einen Einstich aufweisen.
3 v.i. ⟨Reifen:⟩ ein Loch bekommen, platt werden
pundit /'pʌndɪt/ n. Experte, der/Expertin, die
pungent /'pʌndʒənt/ adj. **(a)** beißend, ätzend ⟨Rauch,
Dämpfe⟩; scharf ⟨Soße, Gewürz usw.⟩; stechend riechend
⟨Gas⟩; **(b)** (fig.: biting) beißend; ätzend
punish /'pʌnɪʃ/ v.t. **(a)** bestrafen ⟨Person, Tat⟩; strafen
(geh.) ⟨Person⟩; **(b)** (Boxing coll.) schwer zusetzen (+ Dat.);
(c) (coll.: tax) auf eine harte Probe stellen; **(d)** (coll.: put under
stress) strapazieren ⟨Nerven, Bauwerk⟩
punishable /'pʌnɪʃəbl/ adj. strafbar; **it is a** ~ **offence
to** ...: es ist strafbar, ... zu ...; **be** ~ **by sth.** mit etw.
bestraft werden
punishing /'pʌnɪʃɪŋ/ adj. **(a)** (Boxing coll.) mörderisch
⟨Haken⟩; **(b)** (Sport coll.) tödlich (Sportjargon) ⟨Schuss, Schlag,
Volley⟩; **(c)** (coll.: taxing) mörderisch (ugs.) ⟨Rennen, Zeitplan,
Kurs⟩
punishment /'pʌnɪʃmənt/ n. **(a)** no pl. (punishing) Bestrafung, die; **(b)** (penalty) Strafe, die; **(c)** (coll.: rough treatment)
take a lot of ~: ganz schön getriezt od. gezwiebelt
werden (ugs). See also **take 1 w**
punitive /'pju:nɪtɪv/ adj. **(a)** (penal) Straf-; **(b)** (severe)
[allzu] rigoros ⟨finanzielle Maßnahmen, Besteuerung⟩; unzumutbar ⟨Steuersatz⟩
punk /pʌŋk/ n. **(a)** (Amer. sl.: worthless person) Dreckskerl,
der (salopp); **(b)** (Amer. coll.: young ruffian) Rabauke, der (ugs.);
(c) (admirer of a ~ rock) Punk, der; (performer of ~ rock)
Punk[rock]er, der/-[rock]erin, die; **(d)** (music) ⇒ ~ **rock**
punk 'rock n. Punkrock, der
punnet /'pʌnɪt/ n. (Brit.) Körbchen, das
punt /pʌnt/ 1 n. Stechkahn, der. **2** v.t. **(a)** (propel) staken
⟨Boot⟩; **(b)** (convey) in einem Stechkahn fahren ⟨Person⟩.
3 v.i. staken
punter /'pʌntə(r)/ n. (coll.) **(a)** (gambler) Zocker, der/Zo-
ckerin, die (salopp); **(b)** (client of prostitute) Freier, der (verhüll.);
(c) the ~**s** (customers) die Leutchen (ugs.)
puny /'pju:nɪ/ adj. **(a)** (undersized) zu klein ⟨Baby, Junge⟩;
(b) (feeble) gering ⟨Kraft⟩; schwach ⟨Waffe, Person⟩; **(c)**
(petty) belanglos, unerheblich ⟨Leistung, Einwand⟩

pup /pʌp/ n. **(a)** (young dog or wolf) Welpe, der; **(b)** (young
animal) Junge, das
pupa /'pju:pə/ n., pl. ~**e** /'pju:pi:/ (Zool.) Puppe, die
pupate /pju:'peɪt/ v.i. (Zool.) sich verpuppen
pupil /'pju:pɪl/ n. **(a)** (schoolchild, disciple) Schüler, der/Schü-
lerin, die; **(b)** (Anat.) Pupille, die
puppet /'pʌpɪt/ n. Puppe, die; (marionette; also fig.) Marionette, die; attrib. Marionetten⟨regime, -regierung⟩
'puppet show n. Puppenspiel, das; (with marionettes) Ma-
rionettenspiel, das
puppy /'pʌpɪ/ n. Hundejunge, das; Welpe, der
'puppy fat n., no pl. (Brit.) Babyspeck, der
purchase /'pɜ:tʃəs/ 1 n. **(a)** (buying) Kauf, der; **make several** ~**s/a** ~: Verschiedenes/etwas kaufen; **(b)** (thing
bought) Kauf, der; **(c)** no pl. (hold) Halt, der; (leverage) Hebelwirkung, die; Hebelkraft, die; **get a** ~: guten od. festen
Halt finden. **2** v.t. **(a)** kaufen; erwerben (geh.); **purchasing
power** Kaufkraft, die; **(b)** (acquire) erkaufen
'purchase price n. Kaufpreis, der
purchaser /'pɜ:tʃəsə(r)/ n. Käufer, der/Käuferin, die
'purchasing power n. Kaufkraft, die
pure /pjʊə(r)/ adj. (lit. or fig.) rein; **it is madness** ~ **and
simple** es ist schlicht od. ganz einfach Wahnsinn
pure: ~**-blooded** adj. reinblütig; ~**-bred** adj. reinrassig
purée /'pjʊəreɪ/ 1 n. Püree, das; **tomato** ~: Tomatenmark, das. **2** v.t. pürieren
purely /'pjʊəlɪ/ adv. **(a)** (solely) rein; **(b)** (merely) lediglich
purgative /'pɜ:gətɪv/ n. (medicine) [starkes] Abführmittel
purgatory /'pɜ:gətərɪ/ n. (Relig.) Fegefeuer, das; **it was** ~
(fig.) es war eine Strafe od. die Hölle
purge /pɜ:dʒ/ 1 v.t. **(a)** (cleanse) reinigen (**of** von); **(b)** (remove) entfernen; ~ **away** or **out** beseitigen; **(c)** (rid) säubern ⟨Partei⟩ (**of** von); (remove) entfernen ⟨Person⟩; **(d)**
(Med.) abführen lassen ⟨Patienten⟩. **2** n. (clearance) Säuberung[saktion], die; (Polit.) Säuberung, die
purification /pjʊərɪfɪ'keɪʃn/ n. **(a)** Reinigung, die; **(b)**
(spiritual cleansing) Läuterung, die
purifier /'pjʊərɪfaɪə(r)/ n. (machine) Reinigungsapparat,
der; Reinigungsanlage, die
purify /'pjʊərɪfaɪ/ v.t. **(a)** (make pure or clear) reinigen; **(b)**
(spiritually) reinigen; läutern
purist /'pjʊərɪst/ n. Purist, der/Puristin, die
puritan, (Hist.) **Puritan** /'pjʊərɪtn/ 1 n. Puritaner, der/
Puritanerin, die. **2** adj. puritanisch
puritanical /pjʊərɪ'tænɪkl/ adj. puritanisch
purity /'pjʊərɪtɪ/ n., no pl. **(a)** Reinheit, die; **(b)** (chastity)
Keuschheit, die
purl /pɜ:l/ 1 n. linke Masche. **2** v.t. ~ **three** [**stitches**]
drei linke Maschen stricken; see also **knit 1 b**
purple /'pɜ:pl/ 1 adj. lila; violett; (fig.) überfrachtet, überladen ⟨Prosa⟩; **his face went** ~ **with rage** vor Zorn bekam er ein hochrotes Gesicht. **2** n. Lila, das; Violett, das
purport 1 /pə'pɔ:t/ v.t. ~ **to do sth.** (profess) [von sich]
behaupten, etw. zu tun; (be intended to seem) den Anschein
erwecken sollen, etw. zu tun; **a letter** ~**ing to be written by the president** ein angeblich vom Präsidenten
geschriebener Brief. **2** /'pɜ:pɔ:t/ n. Inhalt, der
purpose /'pɜ:pəs/ n. **(a)** (object) Zweck, der; (intention) Absicht, die; **what is the** ~ **of doing that?** was hat es für
einen Zweck, das zu tun?; **you must have had some**
~ **in mind** du musst irgendetwas damit bezweckt haben;
answer or **suit sb.'s** ~: jmds. Zwecken dienen od. entsprechen; **for a** ~: zu einem bestimmten Zweck; **for the**
~ **of discussing sth.** um etw. zu besprechen; **on** ~: mit
Absicht; absichtlich; **for** ~**s of** zum Zwecke (+ Gen.); **(b)**
(effect) **to no** ~: ohne Erfolg; **to some/good** ~: mit eini-
gem/gutem Erfolg; **(c)** (determination) Entschlossenheit, die;
have a ~ **in life** in seinem Leben einen Sinn sehen; **(d)**
(intention to act) Absicht, die
'purpose-built adj. [eigens] zu diesem Zweck errichtet
⟨Gebäude⟩; [eigens] zu diesem Zweck hergestellt, speziell
angefertigt ⟨Gerät, Bauteil⟩
purposeful /'pɜ:pəsfl/ adj. **(a)** zielstrebig; (with specific
aim) entschlossen; **(b)** (with intention) absichtsvoll

purposely /'pɜːpəslɪ/ *adv.* absichtlich; mit Absicht

purr /pɜː(r)/ **1** *v.i.* schnurren; (fig.: be in satisfied mood) strahlen. **2** *v.t.* durch Schnurren zum Ausdruck bringen; (fig.) säuseln. **3** *n.* Schnurren, *das*

purse /pɜːs/ **1** *n.* (lit. or fig.) Portemonnaie, *das;* Geldbeutel, *der* (bes. südd.); **the public ~**: die Staatskasse. **2** *v.t.* kräuseln, schürzen ‹*Lippen*›

purser /'pɜːsə(r)/ *n.* ▶ 887 Zahlmeister, *der/*-meisterin, *die*

'purse-strings *n. pl.* Schnüre *od.* Bänder [zum Verschließen des Geldbeutels]; **hold the ~** (fig.) über das Geld bestimmen

pursue /pə'sjuː/ *v.t.* **(a)** (literary: chase, lit. or fig.) verfolgen; **(b)** (seek after) streben nach; suchen nach; verfolgen ‹*Ziel*›; **(c)** (look into) nachgehen (+ *Dat.*); **(d)** (engage in) betreiben; **(e)** (carry out) durchführen ‹*Plan*›

pursuer /pə'sjuːə(r)/ *n.* Verfolger, *der/*Verfolgerin, *die*

pursuit /pə'sjuːt, pə'suːt/ *n.* **(a)** (pursuing) (of person, animal, aim) Verfolgung, *die;* (of knowledge, truth, etc.) Streben, *das* (**of** nach); (of pleasure) Jagd, *die* (**of** nach); **in ~ of** auf der Jagd nach ‹*Wild, Dieb usw.*›; in Ausführung (+ *Gen.*) ‹*Beschäftigung, Tätigkeit, Hobby*›; **with the police in [full] ~:** mit der Polizei [dicht] auf den Fersen; **in hot ~:** dicht auf den Fersen (ugs.); **(b)** (pastime) Beschäftigung, *die;* Betätigung, *die*

purveyor /pə'veɪə(r)/ *n.* Lieferant, *der/*Lieferantin, *die*

pus /pʌs/ *n., no indef. art.* (Med.) Eiter, *der*

push /pʊʃ/ **1** *v.t.* **(a)** schieben; (make fall) stoßen; schubsen (ugs.); **don't ~ me like that!** schieb *od.* drängel [doch] nicht so!; **~ a car** (to start the engine) ein Auto anschieben; **~ the door to/open** die Tür zu-/aufstoßen; **she ~ed the door instead of pulling** sie drückte gegen die Tür, statt zu ziehen; **the policemen ~ed the crowd back** die Polizisten drängten die Menge zurück; **~ sth. up the hill** etw. den Berg hinaufschieben; **~ one's way through/into/on to** *etc.* **sth.** sich (*Dat.*) einen Weg durch/in/auf usw. etw. (*Akk.*) bahnen; **(b)** (fig.: impel) drängen; **~ sb. into doing sth.** jmdn. dahin bringen, dass er etw. tut; **(c)** (tax) **~ sb. [hard]** jmdn. [stark] fordern; **~ sb. too hard/too far** jmdn. überfordern; **he ~es himself very hard** er verlangt sich (*Dat.*) sehr viel ab; **be ~ed for sth.** (coll.: find it difficult to provide sth.) mit etw. knapp sein; **be ~ed for money** *or* **cash** knapp bei Kasse sein (ugs.); **be ~ed to do sth.** (coll.) Mühe haben, etw. zu tun; **~ one's luck** (coll.) übermütig werden; **(d)** (press for sale of) die Werbetrommel rühren für; pushen (Werbejargon); **(e)** (sell illegally, esp. drugs) dealen; pushen (Drogenjargon); **(f)** (advance) **~ sth. a step/stage further** etw. einen Schritt vorantreiben; **not ~ the point** die Sache auf sich beruhen lassen; **~ sth. too far** mit etw. zu weit gehen; **~ things to extremes** die Dinge *od.* es zum Äußersten *od.* auf die Spitze treiben; **(g)** (coll.) **be ~ing sixty** *etc.* auf die sechzig *usw.* zugehen. **2** *v.i.* **(a)** schieben; (in queue) drängeln; (at door) drücken; **'P~'** (on door etc.) „Drücken"; **~ and shove** schubsen und drängeln; **~ at sth.** gegen etw. drücken; **(b)** (make demands) **~ for sth.** etw. fordern; **(c)** (make one's way) **he ~ed between us** er drängte sich zwischen uns; **~ through the crowd** sich durch die Menge drängeln; **~ past** *or* **by sb.** sich an jmdn. vorbeidrängeln *od.* -drücken; **(d)** (assert oneself for one's advancement) sich in den Vordergrund spielen. **3** *n.* **(a)** Stoß, *der;* Schubs, *der* (ugs.); **give sth. a ~:** etw. schieben *od.* stoßen; **give sb. a ~:** jmdm. einen Schubs geben (ugs.); jmdm. einen Stoß versetzen; **My car won't start; can you give me a ~?** Mein Auto springt nicht an. Kannst du mich anschieben?; **(b)** (effort) Anstrengungen *Pl.;* (Mil.: attack) Vorstoß, *der;* Offensive, *die;* **(c)** (determination) Tatkraft, *die;* Initiative, *die;* **(d)** (crisis) **when it comes/came to the ~,** (Amer. coll.) **when ~ comes/came to shove** wenn es ernst wird/als es ernst wurde; **at a ~:** wenn es sein muss; **(e)** (Brit. coll.: dismissal) **get the ~:** rausfliegen (ugs.); **give sb. the ~:** jmdn. rausschmeißen (ugs.)

~ a'bout *v.t.* herumschieben; (bully) herumkommandieren

~ a'head *v.i.* ‹*Armee:*› [weiter] vorstoßen; (with plans etc.) weitermachen; **~ ahead with sth.** etw. vorantreiben

~ a'round ⇒ **~ about**

~ a'side *v.t.* (lit. or fig.) beiseite schieben

~ a'way *v.t.* wegschieben

~ 'forward 1 *v.i.* ⇒ **~ ahead. 2** *v.t.* vorschieben; (Mil.) vorstoßen; **~ oneself forward** sich in den Vordergrund schieben

~ in /-'-/ **1** *v.t.* eindrücken; (make fall into the water) hineinstoßen. **2** /'--/ *v.i.* sich hineindrängen

~ 'off 1 *v.i.* **(a)** (Boating) abstoßen; **(b)** (coll.: leave) abhauen (salopp); abschieben (salopp). **2** *v.t.* **(a)** abdrücken ‹*Deckel, Verschluss usw.*›; **(b)** (Boating) abstoßen

~ 'on 1 *v.i.* ⇒ **~ ahead. 2** *v.t.* draufdrücken ‹*Deckel, Verschluss usw.*›

~ 'out *v.t.* hinausschieben

~ 'out of *v.t.* (force to leave) hinausdrängen aus

~ 'over *v.t.* (make fall) umstoßen

~ 'through *v.t.* (fig.) durchpeitschen (ugs.) ‹*Gesetzesvorlage*›; durchdrücken (ugs.) ‹*Vorschlag*›

~ 'up *v.t.* hochschieben; (fig.) hochtreiben

push: **~-bike** *n.* (Brit. coll.) Fahrrad, *das;* **~-button 1** *adj.* Drucktasten‹*telefon, -radio*›; **2** *n.* [Druck]knopf, *der;* Drucktaste, *die;* **~-chair** *n.* (Brit.) Sportwagen, *der*

pusher /'pʊʃə(r)/ *n.* **(a)** (seller of drugs) Dealer, *der* (Drogenjargon); Pusher, *der* (Drogenjargon); **(b)** (pushy person) Streber, *der/*Streberin, *die* (abwertend)

push: **~over** *n.* (coll.) Kinderspiel, *das;* **he'll be a ~over for her** sie steckt ihn [glatt] in die Tasche (ugs.); **~-start 1** *n.* Schubstart, *der;* **give sb. a ~-start** jmdn. anschieben; **2** *v.t.* anschieben

'push-up (Amer.) ⇒ **press-up**

pushy /'pʊʃɪ/ *adj.* (coll.) [übermäßig] ehrgeizig ‹*Person*›

puss /pʊs/ *n.* (coll.) Mieze, *die* (fam.)

pussy /'pʊsɪ/ *n.* (child lang.: cat) Miezekatze, *die* (fam.); Muschi, *die* (Kinderspr.)

pussy: **~ cat** ⇒ **pussy;** **~foot** *v.i.* [herum]schleichen; (act cautiously) überängstlich sein; **~ willow** *n.* Salweide, *die*

put /pʊt/ **1** *v.t.,* **-tt-,** **put** **(a)** (place) tun; (vertically) stellen; (horizontally) legen; (through or into narrow opening) stecken; **~ plates on the table** Teller auf den Tisch stellen; **~ clean sheets on the bed** das Bett frisch beziehen; **don't ~ your elbows on the table** lass deine Ellbogen vom Tisch; **I ~ my hand on his shoulder** ich legte meine Hand auf seine Schulter; **~ a stamp on the letter** eine Briefmarke auf den Brief kleben; **~ salt on one's food** Salz auf sein Essen tun *od.* streuen; **~ some more coal on the fire** Kohle nachlegen; **~ the letter in an envelope/the letter box** den Brief in einen Umschlag/in den Briefkasten stecken; **~ sth. in one's pocket** etw. in die Tasche stecken; **~ one's hands in one's pockets** die Hände in die Taschen stecken; **~ sugar in one's tea** sich (*Dat.*) Zucker in den Tee tun; **~ petrol in the tank** Benzin in den Tank tun *od.* füllen; **~ the car in[to] the garage** das Auto in die Garage stellen; **~ the cork in the bottle** die Flasche mit dem Korken verschließen; **~ the plug in the socket** den Stecker in die Steckdose stecken; **~ the ball into the net/over the bar** den Ball ins Netz befördern *od.* setzen/über die Latte befördern; **~ one's arm round sb.'s waist** den Arm um jmds. Taille legen; **~ a bandage round one's wrist** sich (*Dat.*) einen Verband ums Handgelenk legen; **~ one's hands over one's eyes** sich (*Dat.*) die Hände auf die Augen legen; **~ one's finger to one's lips** den *od.* seinen Finger auf die Lippen legen; **~ the boxes one on top of the other** die Kisten übereinander stellen; **~ the jacket on its hanger** die Jacke auf den Bügel tun *od.* hängen; **where shall I ~ it?** wohin soll ich es tun (ugs.) /stellen/legen *usw.*?; wo soll ich es hintun (ugs.) /-stellen/-legen *usw.*?; **~ sb. into a taxi** jmdn. in ein Taxi setzen; **we ~ our guest in Peter's room** wir haben unseren Gast in Peters Zimmer (*Dat.*) untergebracht; **~ the baby in the pram** das Baby in den Kinderwagen legen *od.* (ugs.) stecken; **not know where to ~ oneself** (fig.) sehr verlegen sein/werden; **~ it there!** (coll.) lass mich deine Hand schütteln!; **(b)** (cause to enter) stoßen; **~ a satellite into orbit** einen Satelliten in eine Umlaufbahn bringen; **(c)** (bring into specified state) setzen; **~ through Parliament** im Parlament durchbringen ‹*Gesetzentwurf usw.*›; **be ~ in a difficult** *etc.* **position** in eine schwierige *usw.* Lage geraten; **be ~ into power**

an die Macht kommen; ∼ **sb. on the committee** jmdn. in den Ausschuss schicken; ∼ **sth. above** *or* **before sth.** (fig.) einer Sache (*Dat.*) den Vorrang vor etw. (*Dat.*) geben; **be** ∼ **out of order** kaputtgehen (ugs.); ∼ **sb. on to sth.** (fig.) jmdn. auf etw. (*Akk.*) hinweisen *od.* aufmerksam machen; ∼ **sb. on to a job** (assign) jmdn. eine Arbeit zuweisen; **(d)** (impose) ∼ **a limit/an interpretation on sth.** etw. begrenzen *od.* beschränken/interpretieren; **(e)** (submit) unterbreiten (**to** *Dat.*) ⟨*Vorschlag, Plan usw.*⟩; ∼ **the situation to sb.** jmdm. die Situation darstellen; ∼ **sth. to the vote** über etw. (*Akk.*) abstimmen lassen; **(f)** (cause to go or do) ∼ **sb. to work** jmdn. arbeiten lassen; **be** ∼ **out of the game by an injury** wegen einer Verletzung nicht mehr spielen können; ∼ **sb. on antibiotics** jmdn. auf Antibiotika setzen; ∼ **sb. on the stage** jmdn. zur Bühne schicken; **(g)** (express) ausdrücken; **let's** ∼ **it like this:** …: sagen wir so: …; **that's one way of** ∼**ting it** (also iron.) so kann man es [natürlich] auch ausdrücken; **(h)** (render) ∼ **sth. into English** etw. ins Englische übertragen *od.* übersetzen; ∼ **sth. into words** etw. in Worte fassen; **(i)** (write) schreiben; ∼ **one's name on the list** seinen Namen auf die Liste setzen; ∼ **a tick in the box** ein Häkchen in das Kästchen machen; ∼ **one's signature to sth.** seine Unterschrift unter etw. (*Akk.*) setzen; ∼ **sth. on the bill** etw. auf die Rechnung setzen; ∼ **sth. on the list** (fig.) sich (*Dat.*) etw. [fest] vornehmen; etw. vormerken; **(j)** (imagine) ∼ **oneself in sb.'s place** *or* **situation** sich in jmds. Lage versetzen; **(k)** (invest) ∼ **money** *etc.* **into sth.** Geld *usw.* in etw. (*Akk.*) stecken; ∼ **work/time/ effort into sth.** Arbeit/Zeit/Energie in etw. (*Akk.*) stecken; **(l)** (stake) setzen (**on** auf + *Akk.*); ∼ **money on a horse/on sth. happening** auf ein Pferd setzen/darauf wetten, dass etw. passiert; **(m)** (estimate) ∼ **sb./sth. at** jmdn./etw. schätzen auf (+ *Akk.*); **(n)** (subject) ∼ **sb. to** jmdm. ⟨*Unkosten, Mühe, Umstände*⟩ verursachen *od.* machen; **(o)** (Athletics) throw ⟨stoßen ⟨*Kugel*⟩; ∼ **the shot** kugelstoßen. **2** *v.i.*, **-tt-**, **put** (Naut.) ∼ **[out] to sea** In See stechen; ∼ **into port** [in den Hafen] einlaufen

∼ **a'bout 1** *v.t.* (circulate) verbreiten; in Umlauf bringen; **it was** ∼ **about that** …: man munkelte (ugs.) *od.* es hieß, dass … **2** *v.i.* (Naut.) den Kurs ändern

∼ **a'cross** *v.t.* **(a)** (communicate) vermitteln (**to** *Dat.*); **(b)** (make acceptable) ankommen mit; (make effective) durchsetzen; ∼ **sth. across to sb.** mit etw. bei jmdm. ankommen/etw. bei jmdm. durchsetzen

∼ **a'side** *v.t.* **(a)** (disregard) absehen von; ∼**ting aside the fact that** …: wenn man von der Tatsache *od.* davon absieht, dass …; **(b)** (save) beiseite legen

∼ **a'way** *v.t.* **(a)** wegräumen; reinstellen ⟨*Auto*⟩; (in file) abheften; **(b)** (save) beiseite legen; **(c)** (coll.) (eat) verdrücken (ugs.); (drink) runterkippen (ugs.); **(d)** (coll.: confine) einsperren (ugs.)

∼ **'back** *v.t.* **(a)** ∼ **the book back** das Buch zurücktun; ∼ **the book back on the shelf** das Buch wieder ins Regal stellen; **(b)** ∼ **the clock back [one hour]** die Uhr [eine Stunde] zurückstellen; *see also* **clock 1 a**; **(c)** (delay) zurückwerfen; **(d)** (postpone) verschieben

∼ **'by** *v.t.* beiseite legen; **I've got a few hundred pounds** ∼ **by** ich habe ein paar hundert Pfund auf der hohen Kante (ugs.)

∼ **'down 1** *v.t.* **(a)** (set down) (vertically) hinstellen; (horizontally) hinlegen; auflegen ⟨*Hörer*⟩; ∼ **sth. down on sth.** etw. auf etw. (*Akk.*) stellen/legen; ∼ **down a deposit** eine Anzahlung machen; **(b)** (suppress) niederwerfen, -schlagen ⟨*Revolte, Rebellion, Aufruhr*⟩; **(c)** (humiliate) herabsetzen; (snub) eine Abfuhr erteilen (+ *Dat.*); **(d)** (kill painlessly) töten; **(e)** (write) notieren; aufschreiben; ∼ **sth. down in writing** etw. schriftlich niederlegen; ∼ **sb.'s name down on a list** jmdn. *od.* jmds. Namen auf eine Liste setzen; ∼ **sb. down for** für jmdn. reservieren ⟨*Lose*⟩; jmdn. notieren für ⟨*Dienst, Arbeit*⟩; jmdn. anmelden bei ⟨*Schule, Verein usw.*⟩; **(f)** (fig.: classify) ∼ **sb./sth. down as** …: jmdn./etw. halten für *od.* einschätzen als …; **(g)** (attribute) ∼ **sth. down to sth.** etw. auf etw. (*Akk.*) zurückführen; **(h)** (cease to read) weglegen, aus der Hand legen ⟨*Buch*⟩. *See also* **down³ 1 f. 2** *v.i.* (Aeronaut.) niedergehen

∼ **'forward** *v.t.* **(a)** (propose) aufwarten mit; **several theories have been** ∼ **forward to account for this**

darüber gibt es verschiedene Theorien; **(b)** (nominate) vorschlagen; **(c)** ∼ **the clock forward [one hour]** die Uhr [eine Stunde] vorstellen

∼ **'in 1** *v.t.* **(a)** (install) einbauen; **(b)** (elect) an die Regierung *od.* Macht bringen; **(c)** (enter) melden ⟨*Person*⟩; **(d)** (submit) stellen ⟨*Forderung, Antrag*⟩; einreichen ⟨*Bewerbung, Antrag*⟩; ∼ **in a claim for damages** eine Schadensersatzforderung stellen; ∼ **in a plea of not guilty** sich nicht schuldig bekennen; **(e)** (devote) aufwenden ⟨*Mühe, Kraft*⟩; (perform) einlegen ⟨*Sonderschicht, Überstunden*⟩; (coll.: spend) einschieben ⟨*eine Stunde usw.*⟩; **(f)** (interpose) einwerfen ⟨*Bemerkung*⟩. **2** *v.i.* ∼ **in for** sich bewerben um ⟨*Stellung, Posten, Vorsitz*⟩; beantragen ⟨*Urlaub, Versetzung*⟩

∼ **'off** *v.t.* **(a)** (postpone) verschieben (**until** auf + *Akk.*); (postpone engagement with) vertrösten (**until** auf + *Akk.*); **can't you** ∼ **her off?** kannst du ihr nicht [erst einmal] absagen?; **(b)** (switch off) ausmachen; **(c)** (repel) abstoßen; **don't be** ∼ **off by his rudeness** lass dich von seiner Grobheit nicht abschrecken; ∼ **sb. off sth.** jmdm. etw. verleiden; **(d)** (distract) stören; **(e)** (fob off) abspeisen; **(f)** (dissuade) ∼ **sb. off doing sth.** jmdn. davon abbringen, etw. zu tun

∼ **'on** *v.t.* **(a)** anziehen ⟨*Kleidung, Hose usw.*⟩; aufsetzen ⟨*Hut, Brille*⟩; draufsetzen, (ugs.) draufmachen ⟨*Deckel, Verschluss usw.*⟩; (fig.) aufsetzen ⟨*Miene, Lächeln, Gesicht*⟩; ∼ **it on** (coll.) [nur] Schau machen (ugs.); **his modesty is all** ∼ **on** seine Bescheidenheit ist nur gespielt *od.* (ugs.) ist reine Schau; **(b)** (switch or turn on) anmachen ⟨*Radio, Motor, Heizung, Licht usw.*⟩; (cause to heat up) aufsetzen ⟨*Wasser, Essen, Kessel, Topf*⟩; (fig.: apply) ausüben ⟨*Druck*⟩; **(c)** ▶ **1202** (gain) ∼ **on weight/two pounds** zunehmen/zwei Pfund zunehmen; **(d)** (add) ∼ **on speed** beschleunigen; ∼ **8p on [to] the price** den Preis um 8 Pence erhöhen; **(e)** (stage) spielen ⟨*Stück*⟩; zeigen ⟨*Show, Film*⟩; veranstalten ⟨*Ausstellung*⟩; *see also* **act 1 e**; **(f)** (arrange) einsetzen ⟨*Sonderzug, -bus*⟩; **(g)** ⇒ ∼ **forward c**; **(h)** (coll.: tease) veräppeln (ugs.)

∼ **'out** *v.t.* **(a)** rausbringen; ∼ **one's hand out** die Hand ausstrecken; *see also* **tongue a**; **(b)** (extinguish) ausmachen ⟨*Licht, Lampe*⟩; löschen ⟨*Feuer, Brand*⟩; **(c)** (issue) [he]rausgeben ⟨*Buch, Zeitschrift, Broschüre, Anweisung, Erlass*⟩; abgeben ⟨*Stellungnahme, Erklärung*⟩; (broadcast) senden; **(d)** (annoy) verärgern; **be** ∼ **out** verärgert *od.* entrüstet sein; **(e)** (inconvenience) in Verlegenheit bringen; ∼ **oneself out to do sth.** die Mühe auf sich (*Akk.*) nehmen, etw. zu tun; **(f)** (make inaccurate) verfälschen ⟨*Ergebnis, Berechnung*⟩; **(g)** (dislocate) verrenken; ausrenken ⟨*Schulter*⟩

▶ ∼ **'over** ⇒ ∼ **across**

∼ **'through** *v.t.* **(a)** (carry out) durchführen ⟨*Plan, Programm, Kampagne, Sanierung*⟩; durchbringen ⟨*Gesetz, Vorschlag*⟩; (complete) zum Abschluss bringen, abschließen ⟨*Geschäft usw.*⟩; **(b)** (Teleph.) verbinden (**to** mit); durchstellen ⟨*Gespräch*⟩ (**to** zu). *See also* ∼ **1 c**

∼ **to'gether** *v.t.* zusammensetzen ⟨*Bauteile, Scherben, Steine, Einzelteile, Maschine usw.*⟩; ordnen ⟨*Gedanken*⟩; erstellen, ausarbeiten ⟨*Begründung, Argumentation*⟩

∼ **'up 1** *v.t.* **(a)** heben ⟨*Hand*⟩; (erect) errichten ⟨*Gebäude, Denkmal, Gerüst, Zaun usw.*⟩; bauen ⟨*Haus*⟩; aufstellen ⟨*Denkmal, Gerüst, Leinwand, Zelt*⟩; aufbauen ⟨*Zelt, Verteidigungsanlagen*⟩; anbringen ⟨*Schild, Notiz usw.*⟩ (**on** an + *Dat.*); (fig.) aufbauen ⟨*Fassade*⟩; abziehen ⟨*Schau*⟩; **(b)** (display) anschlagen; aushängen; **(c)** (offer as defence) hochnehmen ⟨*Fäuste*⟩; leisten ⟨*Widerstand, Gegenwehr*⟩; ∼ **up a struggle** sich wehren *od.* zur Wehr setzen; **(d)** (present for consideration) einreichen ⟨*Petition, Gesuch, Vorschlag*⟩; (nominate) aufstellen; ∼ **sb. up for election** jmdn. als Kandidaten aufstellen; **(e)** (incite) ∼ **sb. up to sth.** jmdn. zu etw. anstiften; **(f)** (accommodate) unterbringen; **(g)** (increase) [he]raufsetzen, anheben ⟨*Preis, Miete, Steuer, Zins*⟩; **(h)** ∼ **sth. up for sale** etw. zum Verkauf anbieten. **2** *v.i.* **(a)** (be candidate) kandidieren; sich aufstellen lassen; **(b)** (lodge) übernachten; sich einquartieren

∼ **upon** *v.t.* ausnutzen

∼ **'up with** *v.t.* sich (*Dat.*) gefallen *od.* bieten lassen ⟨*Beleidigung, Benehmen, Unhöflichkeit*⟩; sich abfinden mit

⟨*Lärm, Elend, Ärger, Bedingungen*⟩; sich abgeben mit ⟨*Person*⟩

'put-down *n.* Herabsetzung, *die;* (snub) Abfuhr, *die*

putrefaction /pjuːtrɪˈfækʃn/ *n., no pl., no indef. art.* Zersetzung, *die*

putrefy /ˈpjuːtrɪfaɪ/ *v.i.* sich zersetzen

putrid /ˈpjuːtrɪd/ *adj.* (a) (rotten) faul; **become** ∼: sich zersetzen; (b) (of putrefaction) faulig; ∼ **smell** Fäulnisgeruch, *der*

putt /pʌt/ (Golf) **1** *v.i. & t.* putten. **2** *n.* Putt, *der*

putter /ˈpʌtə(r)/ (Golf) Putter, *der*

putting green /ˈpʌtɪŋ griːn/ *n.* (a) (area of grass) Grün, *das;* (b) (golf-course) *kleiner Golfplatz nur zum Putten*

putty /ˈpʌtɪ/ **1** *n.* Kitt, *der.* **2** *v.t.* (fix with ∼) einkitten ⟨*Fensterscheibe*⟩; (fill with ∼) auskitten ⟨*Risse*⟩

'put-up *adj.* **a** ∼ **thing/job** eine abgekartete Sache/ein abgekartetes Spiel (ugs.)

puzzle /ˈpʌzl/ **1** *n.* (a) (problem) Rätsel, *das;* (toy) Geduldsspiel, *das;* (b) (enigma) Rätsel, *das;* **be a** ∼ **to sb.** jmdm. ein Rätsel sein; **be a** ∼: rätselhaft sein. **2** *v.t.* rätselhaft *od.* ein Rätsel sein (+ *Dat.*). **3** *v.i.* ∼ **over** *or* **about sth.** sich (*Dat.*) über etw. (*Akk.*) den Kopf zerbrechen ∼ **'out** *v.t.* herausfinden; ∼ **out an answer to a question** eine Antwort auf eine Frage finden

puzzled /ˈpʌzld/ *adj.* ratlos

puzzlement /ˈpʌzlmənt/ *n., no pl.* Verwirrung, *die*

puzzling /ˈpʌzlɪŋ/ *adj.* rätselhaft

PVC *abbr.* **polyvinyl chloride** PVC, *das*

pygmy /ˈpɪɡmɪ/ *n.* (a) Pygmäe, *der;* (b) (dwarf; also fig.) Zwerg, *der*/Zwergin, *die*

pyjamas /pɪˈdʒɑːməz/ *n. pl.* **[pair of]** ∼: Schlafanzug, *der;* Pyjama, *der*

pylon /ˈpaɪlən/ *n.* Mast, *der*

pyramid /ˈpɪrəmɪd/ *n.* Pyramide, *die*

'pyramid selling *n., no pl.* Pyramidenverkauf, *der* (*Verkauf von Vertriebsrechten nach dem Schneeballsystem*)

pyre /ˈpaɪə(r)/ *n.* Scheiterhaufen, *der*

Pyrenees /pɪrəˈniːz/ *pr. n. pl.* **the** ∼: die Pyrenäen

Pyrex, (P) /ˈpaɪreks/ *n.* ≈ Jenaer Glas, *das* (Ⓦ); *attrib.* ∼ **dish** feuerfeste Glasschüssel

pyrotechnics /paɪərəʊˈtekaɪks/ *n. pl.* Feuerwerk, *das;* (fig.) Brillanz, *die*

python /ˈpaɪθən/ *n.* Python[schlange], *die*

....

Q q

....

Q, q /kjuː/ *n., pl.* **Qs** *or* **Q's** Q, q, *das; see also* **mind 2 b**

qr. *abbr.* **quarter[s]** qr.

quack¹ /kwæk/ **1** *v.i.* ⟨*Ente:*⟩ quaken. **2** *n.* Quaken, *das*

quack² (derog.) **1** *n.* Quacksalber, *der* (abwertend). **2** *attrib. adj.* (a) ∼ **doctor** Quacksalber, *der;* (b) Quacksalber⟨*kur, -tropfen, -pillen*⟩ (abwertend)

quad /kwɒd/ *n.* (coll.) (a) (quadrangle) Innenhof, *der;* (b) (quadruplet) Vierling, *der*

'quad bike *n.* Quad, *das*

quadrangle /ˈkwɒdræŋɡl/ *n.* (enclosed court) [viereckiger] Innenhof; (with buildings) Block, *der;* Karree, *das*

quadraphonic /kwɒdrəˈfɒnɪk/ *adj.* quadrophon; Quadro⟨*anlage, -sound usw.*⟩

quadratic /kwəˈdrætɪk/ *adj.* (Math.) quadratisch

quadrilateral /kwɒdrɪˈlætərl/ *n.* (Geom.) Viereck, *das*

quadruped /ˈkwɒdruped/ *n.* Vierfüßler, *der*

quadruple /ˈkwɒdrʊpl/ **1** *adj.* (a) vierfach; (b) (four times) viermal. **2** *v.t.* vervierfachen ⟨*Einkommen, Produktion, Profit*⟩. **3** *v.i.* sich vervierfachen

quadruplet /ˈkwɒdruplɪt, kwɒˈdruːplɪt/ *n.* Vierling, *der*

quagmire /ˈkwæɡmaɪə(r), kwɒɡmaɪə(r)/ *n.* Sumpf, *der;* Morast, *der;* (fig.: complex or difficult situation) Sumpf, *der*

quail¹ /kweɪl/ *n., pl. same or* ∼**s** (Ornith.) Wachtel, *die*

quail² *v.i.* ⟨*Person:*⟩ [ver]zagen, den Mut sinken lassen; ∼ **at the prospect of sth.** bei der Aussicht auf etw. (*Akk.*) verzagen

quaint /kweɪnt/ *adj.* drollig; putzig (ugs.) ⟨*Häuschen, Einrichtung*⟩; malerisch, pittoresk ⟨*Ort*⟩; (odd, strange) kurios, seltsam ⟨*Bräuche, Anblick, Begebenheit*⟩

quake /kweɪk/ **1** *n.* (coll.) [Erd]beben, *das.* **2** *v.i.* beben; ⟨*Sumpfboden:*⟩ schwingen; ∼ **with fear/fright** vor Angst/Schreck zittern *od.* beben

Quaker /ˈkweɪkə(r)/ *n.* Quäker, *der*/Quäkerin, *die*

qualification /kwɒlɪfɪˈkeɪʃn/ *n.* (a) (ability) Qualifikation, *die;* (condition to be fulfilled) Voraussetzung, *die;* **secretarial** ∼**s** Ausbildung als Sekretärin; (b) (limitation) Vorbehalt, *der;* **without** ∼: vorbehaltlos; ohne Vorbehalt

qualified /ˈkwɒlɪfaɪd/ *adj.* (a) qualifiziert; (by training) ausgebildet; **be** ∼ **for a job/to vote** die Qualifikation für eine Stelle besitzen/wahlberechtigt sein; **you are better** ∼ **to judge that** du kannst das besser beurteilen; (b) (restricted) nicht uneingeschränkt; **a** ∼ **success** kein voller Erfolg; ∼ **approval/reply** Zustimmung/Antwort unter Vorbehalt; ∼ **acceptance** bedingte Annahme

qualifier /ˈkwɒlɪfaɪə(r)/ *n.* (a) (restriction) Einschränkung, *die* (**of, on** *Gen.*); (b) (person) **be among the** ∼**s** zu denen gehören, die sich qualifiziert haben; (c) (Sport: match) Qualifikationsspiel, *das*

qualify /ˈkwɒlɪfaɪ/ **1** *v.t.* (a) (make competent, make officially entitled) befähigen (**for** zu); (b) (modify) einschränken; modifizieren ⟨*Meinung, Feststellung*⟩. **2** *v.i.* (a) ∼ **in law/medicine** seinen [Studien]abschluss in Jura/Medizin machen; ∼ **as a doctor/lawyer** sein Examen als Arzt/Anwalt machen; (b) (fulfil a condition) infrage kommen (**for** für); ∼ **for admission to a university/club** die Aufnahmebedingungen einer Universität/eines Vereins erfüllen; ∼ **for membership** die Bedingungen für die Mitgliedschaft erfüllen; (c) (Sport) sich qualifizieren

qualifying /ˈkwɒlɪfaɪɪŋ/ *adj.* (a) ∼ **statement** einschränkende Aussage; (b) (Sport) ∼ **match** Qualifikationsspiel, *das;* ∼ **round/heat** Ausscheidungs- *od.* Qualifikationsrunde, *die;* (c) ∼ **examination** Zulassungsprüfung, *die*

qualitative /ˈkwɒlɪtətɪv/ *adj.* qualitativ

quality /ˈkwɒlɪtɪ/ **1** *n.* (a) Qualität, *die; of good/poor etc.* ∼: von guter/schlechter *usw.* Qualität; **of the best** ∼: bester Qualität; (b) (characteristic) Eigenschaft, *die;* **possess the qualities of a ruler/leader** eine Führernatur sein; (c) (of sound, voice) Klang, *der.* **2** *adj.* (a) (excellent) Qualitäts-; (b) (maintaining ∼) Qualitäts⟨*prüfung, -kontrolle*⟩; (denoting ∼) Güte⟨*grad, -klasse, -zeichen*⟩

quality: ∼ **control** *n.* Qualitätskontrolle, *die;* ∼ **controller** *n.* ▶ 887⌐ Qualitätsprüfer, *der*/-prüferin, *die;* ∼ **time** *n.:* ganz dem Miteinander gewidmete Zeit; **spend** ∼ **time with sb.** einen Teil seiner Zeit ganz jmdm. widmen

qualm /kwɑːm, kwɔːm/ *n.* (a) (sudden misgiving) ungutes Gefühl; (b) (scruple) Bedenken, *das* (*meist Pl.*) (**over, about** gegen); **he had no** ∼**s about borrowing money** er hatte keine Bedenken, sich (*Dat.*) Geld zu leihen

quandary /ˈkwɒndərɪ/ *n.* Dilemma, *das;* **this demand put him in a** ∼: diese Forderung brachte ihn in eine verzwickte Lage; **he was in a** ∼ **about what to do next** er wusste nicht, was er als Nächstes tun sollte

quango /ˈkwæŋɡəʊ/ *n., pl.* ∼**s** (Brit.) halböffentliche Verwaltungseinrichtung

quantify /ˈkwɒntɪfaɪ/ *v.t.* quantifizieren

quantitative /ˈkwɒntɪtətɪv/ *adj.* quantitativ

quantity /ˈkwɒntɪtɪ/ *n.* (a) Quantität, *die;* (b) (amount, sum) Menge, *die;* (c) (large amount) [Un]menge, *die;* (d) (Math.) Größe, *die;* **an unknown** ∼ (fig.) eine unbekannte Größe

'quantity surveyor *n.* ▶ 887⌐ Baukostenkalkulator, *der*/-kalkulatorin, *die*

quantum /ˈkwɒntəm/ *n., pl.* **quanta** /ˈkwɒntə/ (Phys.) Quant, *das*

quantum: ~ **jump**, ~ **leap** *ns.* (Phys.: also fig.) Quantensprung, *der;* ~ **theory** *n.* (Phys.) Quantentheorie, *die*

quarantine /'kwɒrənti:n/ **1** *n.* Quarantäne, *die;* **be in** ~: unter Quarantäne stehen. **2** *v.t.* unter Quarantäne stellen

quarrel /'kwɒrl/ **1** *n.* (a) Streit, *der;* **have a** ~ **with sb.** [about/over sth.] sich mit jmdm. [über etw. (*Akk.*) *od.* wegen etw./um etw.] streiten; **let's not have a** ~ **about it** wir wollen uns nicht darüber streiten; **pick a** ~ [with **sb. over sth.**] [mit jmdm. wegen etw.] Streit anfangen; **(b)** (cause of complaint) Einwand, *der* (with gegen); **I have no** ~ **with you** ich habe nichts gegen dich. **2** *v.i.,* (Brit.) **-ll-:** (a) [sich] streiten (over um; about über + *Akk.,* wegen); ~ **with each other** [sich] [miteinander] streiten; (fall out, dispute) sich [zer]streiten (**over** um; **about** über + *Akk.,* wegen); **(b)** (find fault) etwas auszusetzen haben (with an + *Dat.*); **I really can't** ~ **with that** daran habe ich wirklich nichts auszusetzen

quarrelsome /'kwɒrlsəm/ *adj.* streitsüchtig

quarry[1] /'kwɒrɪ/ **1** *n.* Steinbruch, *der;* **marble** ~: Marmorbruch, *der.* **2** *v.t.* brechen

quarry[2] *n.* (prey) Beute, *die;* (fig.) Opfer, *das*

quart /kwɔ:t/ *n.* ▶ **1193** Quart, *das*

quarter /'kwɔ:tə(r)/ **1** *n.* (a) ▶ **956** Viertel, *das;* **a** *or* **one** ~ **of** ein Viertel (+ *Gen.*); **divide/cut sth. into** ~**s** etw. in vier Teile teilen/schneiden; etw. vierteln; **six and a** ~: sechseinviertel; **an hour and a** ~: eineinviertel Stunden; **a** ~ [of a pound] of cheese ein Viertel[pfund] Käse; **a** ~ **of a mile/an hour** eine Viertelmeile/-stunde; **(b)** (of year) Quartal, *das;* Vierteljahr, *das;* (c) ▶ **706** (point of time) [a] ~ **to/past six** Viertel vor/nach sechs; drei Viertel sechs/Viertel sieben (landsch.); **there are buses at** ~ **to and** ~ **past [the hour]** es fahren Busse um viertel vor und viertel nach jeder vollen Stunde; **(d)** (direction) Richtung, *die;* **blow from all** ~**s** 〈*Wind:*〉 aus allen Richtungen wehen; **(e)** (source of supply or help) Seite, *die;* **(f)** (area of town) [Stadt]viertel, *das;* Quartier, *das;* **in some** ~**s** (fig.) in gewissen Kreisen; **(g)** *in pl.* (lodgings) Quartier, *das* (bes. Milit.); Unterkunft, *die;* **(h)** (Brit.: measure) (of volume) Quarter, *der;* (of weight) ≈ Viertelzentner, *der;* **(i)** (Amer.) (school term) Vierteljahr, *das;* (university term) halbes Semester; **(j)** (Astron.) Viertel, *das;* **(k)** (mercy) **give no** ~ **to sb.** jmdm. keinen Pardon (veralt.) gewähren *od.* geben; **(l)** ▶ **938** (Amer.: amount, coin) Vierteldollar, *der;* 25-Cent-Stück, *das.* **2** *v.t.* (a) (divide) vierteln; durch vier teilen 〈*Zahl, Summe*〉; **(b)** (lodge) einquartieren 〈*Soldaten*〉

quarter: ~**back** *n.* (Amer. Football) Quarterback, *der;* ~**deck** *n.* (Naut.) Quarterdeck, *das;* ~**final** *n.* Viertelfinale, *das;* ~**light** *n.* (Brit. Motor Veh.) ausstellbares Fondfenster

quarterly /'kwɔ:təlɪ/ **1** *adj.* vierteljährlich. **2** *n.* Vierteljahr[e]sschrift, *die.* **3** *adv.* vierteljährlich; alle Vierteljahre

quarter: ~**master** *n.* (a) (Naut.) Quartermeister, *der;* **(b)** (Mil.) Quartiermeister, *der* (veralt.); ~ **note** (Amer. Mus.) ⇒ **crotchet**

quartet, quartette /kwɔ:'tet/ *n.* (also Mus.) Quartett, *das*

quarto /'kwɔ:təʊ/ *n., pl.* ~**s** (a) (book) Quartband, *der;* **(b)** (size) Quart[format], *das;* ~ **paper** Papier im Quartformat

quartz /kwɔ:ts/ *n.* Quarz, *der;* ~ **clock/watch** Quarzuhr, *die*

quasar /'kweɪsɑ:(r), 'kweɪzɑ:(r)/ *n.* (Astron.) Quasar, *der*

quash /kwɒʃ/ *v.t.* (a) (annul, make void) aufheben 〈*Urteil, Entscheidung*〉; zurückweisen 〈*Einspruch, Klage*〉; **(b)** (suppress, crush) unterdrücken 〈*Opposition*〉; niederschlagen 〈*Aufstand, Generalstreik*〉

quasi- /'kweɪzaɪ, 'kwɑ:zɪ/ *pref.* (a) (not real, seeming) Schein-; **(b)** (half-) Quasi-; quasi-

quaver /'kweɪvə(r)/ **1** *n.* (a) (Brit. Mus.) Achtelnote, *die;* **(b)** (in speech) Zittern, *das;* Beben, *das* (geh.). **2** *v.i.* (vibrate, tremble) zittern

quay /ki:/, **'quayside** *ns.* Kai, *der;* Kaje, *die* (nordd.)

queasy /'kwi:zɪ/ *adj.* unwohl; (uneasy) mulmig (ugs.); **a** ~ **feeling** ein Gefühl der Übelkeit

queen /kwi:n/ *n.* (a) ▶ **1152** (also bee, wasp, ant) Königin, *die;* **(b)** (Chess, Cards) Dame, *die*

queen: ~ **'bee** *n.* Bienenkönigin, *die;* ~ **'mother** *n.* Königinmutter, *die*

queer /'kwɪə(r)/ **1** *adj.* (a) (strange) sonderbar; seltsam; (eccentric) komisch; verschroben; **a** ~ **feeling** ein komisches Gefühl; **(b)** (shady, suspect) merkwürdig; seltsam; **(c)** (out of sorts, faint) unwohl; **I feel** ~: mir ist komisch *od.* (ugs.) flau; **(d)** (sl. derog.: homosexual) schwul (ugs.). **2** *n.* (sl. derog.: homosexual) Schwule, *der* (ugs.). **3** *v.t.* (coll.: spoil) vermasseln (salopp); ~ **the pitch for sb.**, ~ **sb.'s pitch** jmdm. einen Strich durch die Rechnung machen

quell /kwel/ *v.t.* (literary) niederschlagen 〈*Aufstand, Rebellion*〉; zügeln 〈*Leidenschaft, Furcht*〉; überwinden 〈*Ängste, Befürchtungen*〉

quench /kwentʃ/ *v.t.* (a) (extinguish) löschen; (fig.) auslöschen (geh.); **(b)** (satisfy) ~ **one's thirst** seinen Durst löschen *od.* stillen

querulous /'kwerʊləs/ *adj.* gereizt; (by nature) reizbar

query /'kwɪərɪ/ **1** *n.* (a) (question) Frage, *die;* **put/raise a** ~: eine Frage stellen/aufwerfen; **(b)** (question mark) Fragezeichen, *das.* **2** *v.t.* (a) (call in question) infrage stellen 〈*Anweisung, Glaubwürdigkeit, Ergebnis usw.*〉; beanstanden 〈*Rechnung, Kontoauszug*〉; **(b)** (ask, inquire) ~ **whether/if …:** fragen, ob …

quest /kwest/ *n.* Suche, *die* (**for** nach); (for happiness, riches, etc.) Streben, *das* (**for** nach); **in** ~ **of sth.** auf der Suche nach etw.

question /'kwestʃn/ **1** *n.* (a) Frage, *die;* **ask sb. a** ~: jmdm. eine Frage stellen; **put a** ~ **to sb.** an jmdn. eine Frage richten; **don't ask so many** ~**s!** frag nicht soviel!; **ask** ~**s** Fragen stellen; **and no** ~**s asked** ohne dass groß gefragt wird/worden ist (ugs.); **(b)** (doubt, objection) Zweifel, *der* (**about** an + *Dat.*); **there is no** ~ **about sth.** es besteht kein Zweifel an etw. (*Dat.*); **there is no** ~ **[but] that …:** es besteht kein Zweifel, dass …; **accept/follow sth. without** ~: etwas kritiklos akzeptieren/befolgen; **not be in** ~: außer [allem] Zweifel stehen; **beyond all** *or* **without** ~: zweifellos; ohne Frage *od.* Zweifel; **(c)** (problem, concern, subject) Frage, *die;* **sth./it is only a** ~ **of time** etw./es ist [nur] eine Frage der Zeit; **it is [only] a** ~ **of doing sth.** es geht [nur] darum, etw. zu tun; **there is no** ~ **of his doing that** es kann keine Rede davon sein, dass er das tut; **the** ~ **of sth. arises** es erhebt sich die Frage von etw.; **the person/thing in** ~: die fragliche *od.* betreffende Person/Sache; **sth./it is out of the** ~: etw./es ist ausgeschlossen; etw./es kommt nicht infrage (ugs.); **the** ~ **is whether …:** es geht darum, ob …; **that is not the** ~: darum geht es nicht; **put the** ~: zur Abstimmung aufrufen (**to** *Akk.*). **2** *v.t.* (a) befragen; 〈*Polizei, Gericht usw.:*〉 vernehmen; **(b)** (throw doubt upon, raise objections to) bezweifeln; **her goodwill cannot be** ~**ed** an ihrem guten Willen kann nicht gezweifelt werden

questionable /'kwestʃənəbl/ *adj.* fragwürdig

questioning /'kwestʃənɪŋ/ **1** *adj.* fragend. **2** *n.* Fragen, *das;* (at examination) Befragung, *die;* (by police etc.) Vernehmung, *die*

question: ~ **mark** *n.* (lit. or fig.) Fragezeichen, *das;* ~ **master** *n.* Quizmaster, *der*

questionnaire /kwestʃə'neə(r)/ *n.* Fragebogen, *der*

queue /kju:/ **1** *n.* Schlange, *die;* **a** ~ **of people/cars** eine Menschen-/Autoschlange; **stand** *or* **wait in a** ~: Schlange stehen; anstehen; **join the** ~: sich anstellen. **2** *v.i.* ~ **[up]** Schlange stehen; anstehen; (join ~) sich anstellen; ~ **for a bus** an der Bushaltestelle Schlange stehen

queue: ~**-jumper** *n.* (Brit.) jmd., *der sich vordrängt;* ~**-jumping** *n.* (Brit.) Vordrängen, *das;* Vordrängeln, *das*

quibble /'kwɪbl/ **1** *n.* (a) (argument) spitzfindiges Argument; **(b)** (petty objection) Spitzfindigkeit, *die.* **2** *v.i.* streiten; ~ **over** *or* **about sth.** über etw. (*Akk.*) streiten

quiche /ki:ʃ/ *n.* Quiche, *die*

quick /kwɪk/ **1** *adj.* (a) schnell; kurz 〈*Rede, Zusammenfassung, Pause*〉; flüchtig 〈*Kuss, Blick usw.*〉; **it's** ~**er by train** mit dem Zug geht es schneller; **'that was/'you were** ~! das ging aber schnell!; **could I have a** ~ **word with you?** kann ich Sie kurz einmal sprechen?; **be** ~! mach schnell! (ugs.); beeil[e] dich!; **(b)** (prompt to act or understand) schnell 〈*Person*〉; wach 〈*Verstand*〉; aufgeweckt 〈*Kind*〉; **he**

is very ~: er ist sehr schnell von Begriff (ugs.); **be ~ to do sth.** etw. schnell tun; **be ~ to take offence** schnell *od.* leicht beleidigt sein; **she is ~ to criticize** mit Kritik ist sie schnell bei der Hand; **[have] a ~ temper** ein aufbrausendes Wesen [haben]. **2** *adv.* schnell; **~!** [mach] schnell! **3** *n.* empfindliches Fleisch; **bite one's nails to the ~:** die Nägel bis zum Fleisch abkauen; **be cut to the ~** (fig.) tief getroffen *od.* verletzt sein

quicken /'kwɪkn/ **1** *v.t.* (make quicker) beschleunigen. **2** *v.i.* (become quicker) sich beschleunigen; schneller werden

quickie /'kwɪkɪ/ *n.* (coll.) (drink) Schluck auf die Schnelle (ugs.); (sexual intercourse) eine Nummer auf die Schnelle (salopp)

'quicklime *n.* ungelöschter Kalk

quickly /'kwɪklɪ/ *adv.* schnell

quickness /'kwɪknɪs/ *n., no pl.* **(a)** (speed) Schnelligkeit, *die;* **(b)** (acuteness of perception) Schärfe, *die;* **~ of the mind** schnelle Auffassungsgabe

quick: ~sand *n.* Treibsand, *der;* **~silver** *n.* Quecksilber, *das;* **~ step** *n.* (Dancing) Quickstep, *der;* **~-tempered** *adj.* hitzig; **be ~-tempered** leicht aufbrausen; **~-witted** *adj.* geistesgegenwärtig; schlagfertig ‹Antwort›

quid /kwɪd/ *n.* (Brit. coll.) *pl. same* (one pound) Pfund, *das;* **fifty ~:** fünfzig Kugeln (salopp)

quiet /'kwaɪət/ **1** *adj.,* **~er** /'kwaɪətə(r)/, **~est** /'kwaɪətɪst/ **(a)** (silent) still; (not loud) leise ‹Schritte, Musik, Stimme, Motor, Fahrzeug›; **be ~!** (coll.) sei still *od.* ruhig!; **~!** Ruhe!; **keep ~:** still sein; **keep sth. ~, keep ~ about sth.** (fig.) etw. geheimhalten; **(b)** (peaceful, not busy) ruhig; **(c)** (gentle) sanft; (peaceful) ruhig ‹Kind, Person›; **(d)** (not overt, disguised) versteckt; heimlich ‹Groll›; **have a ~ word with sb.** mit jmdm. unter vier Augen reden; **on the ~:** still und heimlich; **(e)** (not formal) zwanglos; klein ‹Feier›; **(f)** (not showy) dezent ‹Farben, Muster›; schlicht ‹Eleganz, Stil›. **2** *n.* Ruhe, *die;* (silence, stillness) Stille, *die.* **3** *v.t.* ⇒ **quieten**

quieten /'kwaɪətn/ (Brit.) *v.t.* **(a)** beruhigen; zur Ruhe bringen ‹Kind, Schulklasse›; **(b)** zerstreuen ‹Bedenken, Angst, Verdacht›

~ 'down 1 *v.t.* ⇒ **~ a. 2** *v.i.* sich beruhigen

quietly /'kwaɪətlɪ/ *adv.* **(a)** (silently) still; (not loudly) leise; **(b)** (peacefully, tranquilly) ruhig; **be ~ drinking one's tea** in [aller] Ruhe seinen Tee trinken; **(c)** (gently) sanft; **be ~ spoken** eine ruhige Art zu sprechen haben; **(d)** (not overtly) insgeheim; **they settled the affair ~:** sie haben die Angelegenheit unter sich (*Dat.*) ausgemacht; **(e)** (not formally) zwanglos; **get married ~:** im kleinen Rahmen heiraten; **(f)** (not showily) dezent; schlicht

quietness /'kwaɪətnɪs/ *n., no pl.* **(a)** (absence of noise) Stille, *die;* (of reply) Ruhe, *die;* (of car, engine) Geräuscharmut, *die;* (of footsteps) Geräusch-, Lautlosigkeit, *die;* **(b)** (peacefulness) Ruhe, *die*

quill /kwɪl/ *n.* **(a)** ⇒ **quill-feather; (b)** ⇒ **quill pen; (c)** (stem of feather) [Feder]kiel, *der;* **(d)** (of porcupine) Stachel, *der*

quill: ~-feather *n.* Kielfeder, *die;* **~ pen** *n.* [Feder]kiel, *der*

quilt /kwɪlt/ **1** *n.* Schlafdecke, *die;* **continental ~:** Steppdecke, *die.* **2** *v.t.* **(a)** (cover with padded material) wattieren; **(b)** (join like ~) steppen

quin /kwɪn/ *n.* (coll.) Fünfling, *der*

quince /kwɪns/ *n.* **(a)** (fruit) Quitte, *die;* **(b)** (tree) Quittenbaum, *der*

quinine /'kwɪniːn, kwɪ'niːn/ *n.* Chinin, *das*

quintessence /kwɪn'tesəns/ *n.* (most perfect form) Quintessenz, *die;* (embodiment) Inbegriff, *der*

quintet, quintette /kwɪn'tet/ *n.* (also Mus.) Quintett, *das*

quintuplet /'kwɪntjʊplɪt, kwɪn'tjuːplɪt/ *n.* Fünfling, *der*

quip /kwɪp/ **1** *n.* Witzelei, *die.* **2** *v.i.,* **-pp-** witzeln (**at** über + *Akk.*)

quirk /kwɜːk/ *n.* Marotte, *die;* **[by a] ~ of nature/fate** [durch eine] Laune der Natur/des Schicksals

quirky /'kwɜːkɪ/ *adj.* schrullig (ugs.)

quit /kwɪt/ **1** *pred. adj.* **be ~ of sb./sth.** jmds./einer Sache ledig sein (geh.). **2** *v.t.,* **-tt-,** (Amer.) **quit (a)** (give up)

aufgeben; (cease, stop) aufhören mit; **~ doing sth.** aufhören, etw. zu tun; **(b)** (depart from) verlassen; (leave occupied premises) ausziehen aus; *abs.* ausziehen; **they were given** *or* **had notice to ~** [**the flat** *etc.*] ihnen wurde [die Wohnung *usw.*] gekündigt; **(c)** *also abs.* (from job) kündigen

quite /kwaɪt/ *adv.* **(a)** (entirely) ganz; völlig; vollkommen; gänzlich ‹unnötig›; fest ‹entschlossen›; **not ~** (almost) nicht ganz; (noticeably not) nicht gerade; **I'm sorry — That's ~ all right** Entschuldigung — Schon gut; In Ordnung; **not ~ five o'clock** noch nicht ganz fünf Uhr; **I don't need any help; I'm ~ all right, thank you** danke, es geht schon, ich komme allein zurecht; **I ~ agree/understand** ganz meine Meinung/ich verstehe schon; **~ [so]!** [ja,] genau *od.* richtig!; **that is ~ a different matter** das ist etwas ganz anderes; **~ another story/case** eine ganz andere Geschichte/ein ganz anderer Fall; **(b)** (somewhat, to some extent) ziemlich; recht; ganz ‹gern›; **it was ~ an effort** es war ziemlich *od.* recht anstrengend; **that is ~ a shock/surprise** das ist ein ziemlicher Schock/eine ziemliche Überraschung; **I'd ~ like to talk to him** ich würde ganz gern mit ihm sprechen; **~ a few** ziemlich viele

quits /kwɪts/ *pred. adj.* **be ~ [with sb.]** [mit jmdm.] quitt sein (ugs.); **call it ~** ‹Einzelperson:› zustimmen *od.* Ruhe geben; ‹mehrere Personen:› sich vertragen; **let's call it ~!** wollen wir die Sache auf sich beruhen lassen!; (nothing owed) sagen wir, wir sind quitt; *see also* **double 3 c**

quiver¹ /'kwɪvə(r)/ **1** *v.i.* zittern (**with** vor + *Dat.*); ‹Stimme, Lippen:› beben (geh.); ‹Lid:› zucken. **2** *n.* Zittern, *das;* (of lips, voice also) Beben, *das* (geh.); (of eyelid) Zucken, *das*

quiver² *n.* (for arrows) Köcher, *der*

quiz /kwɪz/ **1** *n., pl.* **~zes (a)** (Radio, Telev., etc.) Quiz, *das;* **(b)** (questionnaire, test) Prüfung, *die;* (for pupils) Aufgabe, *die.* **2** *v.t.,* **-zz-** ausfragen (**about** nach etw., **about sb.** über jmdn.); ‹Polizei:› verhören, vernehmen ‹Verdächtige›

quiz: ~master *n.* (Radio, Telev.) Quizmaster, *der;* Spielleiter, *der;* **~ programme, ~ show** *ns.* (Radio, Telev.) Quizsendung, *die*

quizzical /'kwɪzɪkl/ *adj.* fragend ‹Blick, Miene›; (mocking) spöttisch ‹Lächeln›

quoit /kɔɪt/ *n.* (Games) [Gummi]ring, *der*

quoits /kɔɪts/ *n., no pl.* (Games) Ringtennis, *das*

quorate /'kwɔːrət/ *adj.* beschlussfähig

quorum /'kwɔːrəm/ *n.* Quorum, *das*

quota /'kwəʊtə/ *n.* **(a)** (share) Anteil, *der;* **(b)** (quantity of goods to be produced) Produktionsmindestquote, *die;* (of work) [Arbeits]pensum, *das;* **(c)** (maximum number) Höchstquote, *die;* (of immigrants/students permitted) maximale Einwanderungs-/Zulassungsquote

quotation /kwəʊ'teɪʃn/ *n.* **(a)** Zitieren, *das;* (passage) Zitat, *das;* **(b)** (amount stated as current price) [Börsen]kurs, *der;* [Börsen-, Kurs]notierung, *die;* **(c)** (estimate) Kosten[vor]anschlag, *der*

quo'tation marks *n. pl.* Anführungszeichen *Pl.*

quote /kwəʊt/ **1** *v.t.* **(a)** *also abs.* zitieren (**from** aus); zitieren aus ‹Buch, Text, Übersetzung›; (appeal to) sich berufen auf (+ *Akk.*) ‹Person, Buch, Text, Quelle›; (mention) anführen ‹Vorkommnis, Beispiel›; **he is ~d as saying that ...:** er soll gesagt haben, dass ...; ..., **and I ~, ...:** ich zitiere, ...; **(b)** (state price of) angeben, nennen ‹Preis›; **~ sb. a price** jmdm. einen Preis nennen; **(c)** (St. Exch.) notieren ‹Aktie›; **(d)** (enclose in quotation marks) in Anführungszeichen (*Akk.*) setzen; ..., **~, ...: ...,** Zitat, ... **2** *n.* (coll.) **(a)** (passage) Zitat, *das;* **(b)** (commercial quotation) Kosten[vor]anschlag, *der;* **(c)** *usu. in pl.* (quotation mark) Anführungszeichen, *das;* Gänsefüßchen, *das* (ugs.)

quotient /'kwəʊʃnt/ *n.* (Math.) Quotient, *der*

Rr

R, r /ɑ:(r)/ n., pl. Rs or R's R, r, das; the three Rs Lesen, Schreiben und Rechnen
R. abbr. (a) ▶ 1048┃ River Fl.; R. Thames die Themse; (b) Regina/Rex Königin, die/König, der
r. abbr. right re.
rabbi /'ræbaɪ/ n. Rabbi[ner], der; (as title) Rabbi, der
rabbit /'ræbɪt/ n. Kaninchen, das
rabbit: ~ burrow, ~ hole ns. Kaninchenbau, der; ~ hutch n. (lit. or fig. joc.) Kaninchenstall, der; ~ warren n. Kaninchengehege, das; (fig.) Labyrinth, das
rabble /'ræbl/ n. Mob, der (abwertend); Pöbel, der (abwertend)
rabid /'ræbɪd/ adj. (a) ([Vet.] Med.) tollwütig ‹ Tier, Person›; (b) (furious, violent) wild ‹ Hass, Wut›; (extreme) fanatisch
rabies /'reɪbi:z/ n. ▶ 865┃ ([Vet.] Med.) Tollwut, die
RAC abbr. (Brit.) Royal Automobile Club Königlicher Britischer Automobilklub
raccoon ⇨ racoon
race[1] /reɪs/ 1 n. (a) Rennen, das; have a ~ [with or against sb.] mit jmdm. um die Wette laufen/schwimmen usw.; 100 metres ~: 100-m-Rennen/-Schwimmen, das; (b) in pl. (series) (for horses) Pferderennen, das; (for dogs) Hunderennen, das; (c) (fig.) a ~ against time ein Wettlauf mit der Zeit. 2 v.i. (a) (in swimming, running, sailing, etc.) um die Wette schwimmen/laufen/segeln usw. (with, against mit); ~ against time (fig.) gegen die Uhr od. Zeit arbeiten; (b) (go at full or excessive speed) ‹Motor:› durchdrehen; ‹Puls:› jagen, rasen; (c) (rush) sich sehr beeilen; hetzen; (on foot also) rennen; jagen; ~ after sb. jmdm. hinterherhetzen; ~ to finish sth. sich beeilen, um etw. fertigzukriegen (ugs.); ~ ahead with sth. (hurry) etw. im Eiltempo vorantreiben (ugs.); (make rapid progress) bei etw. mit Riesenschritten vorankommen (ugs.). 3 v.t. (in swimming, riding, walking, running, etc.) um die Wette schwimmen/reiten/gehen/laufen usw. mit; I'll ~ you ich mache mit dir einen Wettlauf
race[2] n. (Anthrop., Biol.) Rasse, die; the human ~: die Menschheit
race: ~course n. Rennbahn, die; ~ hatred n. Rassenhass, der; ~horse n. Rennpferd, das; ~ relations n. pl. Beziehung zwischen den Rassen; ~track n. Rennbahn, die
racial /'reɪʃl/ adj. Rassen‹ diskriminierung, -konflikt, -gleichheit, -vorurteil›; rassisch ‹ Gruppe, Minderheit›; ~ harmony Eintracht unter den Rassen
racialism /'reɪʃəlɪzm/ n., no pl. Rassismus, der
racialist /'reɪʃəlɪst/ 1 n. Rassist, der/Rassistin, die. 2 adj. rassistisch
racing /'reɪsɪŋ/ n., no pl., no indef. art. (a) (profession, sport) Rennsport, der; (with horses) Pferdesport, der; (b) (races) Rennen Pl.
racing: ~ bicycle n. Rennrad, das; ~ car n. Rennwagen, der; ~ driver n. Rennfahrer, der/-fahrerin, die
racism /'reɪsɪzm/ n. Rassismus, der
racist /'reɪsɪst/ 1 n. Rassist, der/Rassistin, die. 2 adj. rassistisch
rack /ræk/ 1 n. (a) (for luggage in bus, train, etc.) Ablage, die; (for pipes, hats, toast, plates) Ständer, der; (on bicycle, motorcycle) Gepäckträger, der; (on car) Dachgepäckträger, der; (b) (instrument of torture) Folter[bank], die; be on the ~ (lit. or fig.) Folterqualen leiden. 2 v.t. (a) (lit. or fig.: torture) quälen; plagen; be ~ed by or with pain etc. von Schmerzen usw. gequält und geplagt werden; (b) ~ one's brain[s] (fig.) sich (Dat.) den Kopf zerbrechen (ugs.) (for über + Akk.)
racket[1] /'rækɪt/ n. (Sport) Schläger, der; (Tennis also) Racket, das
racket[2] n. (a) (disturbance, uproar) Lärm, der; Krach, der; make a ~: Krach od. Lärm machen; (b) (dishonest scheme) Schwindelgeschäft, das (ugs.)

racketeer /rækɪ'tɪə(r)/ n. Ganove, der; (profiteer) Wucherer, der
racking /'rækɪŋ/ attrib. adj. quälend
raconteur /rækɒn'tɜ:(r)/ n. Geschichten-, Anekdotenerzähler, der/-erzählerin, die
racoon /rə'ku:n/ n. (Zool.) Waschbär, der
racquet ⇨ racket[1]
racy /'reɪsɪ/ adj. flott (ugs.), schwungvoll ‹ Erzählweise, Stil, Sprache›; schwungvoll ‹ Rede›; saftig (ugs.) ‹ Humor›
radar /'reɪdɑː(r)/ n. Radar, das od. der
radar: ~ operator n. Radartechniker, der/-technikerin, die; ~ screen n. Radarschirm, der; ~ trap n. Radarfalle, die (ugs.)
radial /'reɪdɪəl/ 1 adj. (a) (arranged like rays) strahlenförmig angeordnet; strahlenförmig ‹ Muster›; (b) ~ wheel Radialrad, das. 2 n. Radial-, Gürtelreifen, der
'radial[-ply] tyre n. Radial-, Gürtelreifen, der
radiance /'reɪdɪəns/, radiancy /'reɪdɪənsɪ/ n. Leuchten, das; (of sun, stars, lamp; also fig.) Strahlen, das
radiant /'reɪdɪənt/ adj. (a) strahlend, leuchtend ‹ Himmelskörper, Dämmerung›; leuchtend ‹ Lichtstrahl›; (b) (fig.) strahlend; fröhlich ‹ Stimmung›; be ~ ‹ Person, Augen:› strahlen (with vor + Dat.)
radiate /'reɪdɪeɪt/ 1 v.i. (a) ‹ Sonne, Sterne:› scheinen, strahlen; ‹ Hitze, Wärme:› ausstrahlen; ‹ Schein, Radiowellen:› ausgesendet werden, ausgehen (from von); (b) (from central point) strahlenförmig ausgehen (from von). 2 v.t. (a) verbreiten, ausstrahlen ‹ Licht, Wärme, Klang›; aussenden ‹ Strahlen, Wellen›; (b) ausstrahlen ‹ Glück, Liebe, Gesundheit, Fröhlichkeit›
radiation /reɪdɪ'eɪʃn/ n. (a) (emission of energy) Emission, die; (of signals) Ausstrahlung, die; (b) (energy transmitted) Strahlung, die; contaminated by ~: strahlenverseucht; (c) attrib. Strahlen‹ therapie, -krankheit, -dosis usw.›; Strahlungs‹ intensität, -messgerät, -niveau usw.›
radiator /'reɪdɪeɪtə(r)/ n. (a) (for heating a room) Heizkörper, der; Radiator, der; (portable) Heizgerät, das; (b) (for cooling engine) Kühler, der
radical /'rædɪkl/ 1 adj. (a) (thorough, drastic; also Polit.) radikal; drastisch, radikal ‹ Maßnahme›; umwälzend ‹ Auswirkungen›; durchgreifend ‹ Umstrukturierung, Veränderung usw.›; a ~ cure eine Radikalkur; (b) (progressive, unorthodox) radikal; revolutionär ‹ Stil, Design, Sprachgebrauch›; (c) (inherent, fundamental) grundlegend ‹ Fehler, Unterschied›. 2 n. (Polit.) Radikale, der/die
radically /'rædɪkəlɪ/ adv. (a) (thoroughly, drastically; Polit.) radikal; (b) (originally, basically) prinzipiell; (c) (inherently, fundamentally) von Grund auf
radio /'reɪdɪəʊ/ 1 n., pl. ~s (a) no pl., no indef. art. Funk, der; (for private communication) Sprechfunk, der; over the/by ~: über/per Funk; (b) no pl., no indef. art. (Broadcasting) Rundfunk, der; Hörfunk, der; listen to the ~: Radio hören; on the ~: im Radio od. Rundfunk; (c) (apparatus) Radio, das. 2 attrib. adj. Rundfunk-; Radio‹ welle, -teleskop›; Funk‹ mast, -turm, -frequenz, -taxi, -telefon›; ~ drama or play Hörspiel, das. 3 v.t. funken ‹ Meldung, Nachricht›. 4 v.i. funken; eine Funkmeldung übermitteln
radio: ~'active adj. radioaktiv; ~ac'tivity n. Radioaktivität, die; ~ beacon n. Funkfeuer, das; ~carbon dating n. Radiokarbondatierung, die; ~ cas'sette player n. Kassettenradio, das; Radio mit Kassetteitil; ~-controlled adj. funkgesteuert
radiography /reɪdɪ'ɒgrəfɪ/ n. Radiographie, die; Röntgenographie, die
'radio ham n. Funkamateur, der/-amateurin, die
radiology /reɪdɪ'ɒlədʒɪ/ n., no pl. Radiologie, die; Röntgenologie, die
radish /'rædɪʃ/ n. Rettich, der; (small, red) Radieschen, das
radium /'reɪdɪəm/ n. (Chem.) Radium, das
radius /'reɪdɪəs/ n., pl. radii /'reɪdɪaɪ/ or ~es (Math.) Radius, der; (fig.) Umkreis, der; within a ~ of 20 miles im Umkreis von 20 Meilen

radon /'reɪdɒn/ n. (Chem.) Radon, das
RAF /ɑ:rer'ef, (coll.) ræf/ abbr. **Royal Air Force**
raffia /'ræfɪə/ n. Raphia-, Raffiabast, der
raffle /'ræfl/ **1** n. Tombola, die; ∼ **ticket** Los, das. **2** v.t. ∼ **[off]** verlosen
raft /rɑ:ft/ n. Floß, das
rafter /'rɑ:ftə(r)/ n. (Building) Sparren, der
rag¹ /ræg/ n. **(a)** [Stoff]fetzen, der; [Stoff]lappen, der; **[all] in** ∼s [ganz] zerrissen; **sb. loses his** ∼ (coll.) jmdm. reißt die Geduld; **(b)** in pl. (old and torn clothes) Lumpen Pl.; **[dressed] in** ∼s **[and tatters]** abgerissen; **go from** ∼s **to riches** vom armen Schlucker zum Millionär/zur Millionärin werden; **(c)** (derog.: newspaper) Käseblatt, das (salopp abwertend)
rag² **1** v.t., **-gg-** (tease, play jokes on) aufziehen; necken. **2** n. **(a)** (Brit. Univ.) spaßige studentische [Wohltätigkeits]veranstaltung; **(b)** (prank) Ulk, der; Streich, der
ragamuffin /'rægəmʌfɪn/ n. [zerlumptes] Gassenkind
rag: ∼-**and**-**'bone man** n. (Brit.) Lumpensammler, der; ∼**bag** n. (fig.: collection) Sammelsurium, das (abwertend); ∼ **doll** n. Stoffpuppe, die
rage /reɪdʒ/ **1** n. **(a)** (violent anger) Wut, die; **(fit of anger)** Wutausbruch, der; **be in/fly into a** ∼: in Wut od. (ugs.) Rage sein/geraten; **in a fit of** ∼: in einem Anfall von Wut; **(b)** (vehement desire or passion) Besessenheit, die; **sth. is [all] the** ∼: etw. ist [ganz] groß in Mode. **2** v.i. **(a)** (rave) toben; ∼ **at** or **against sth./sb.** gegen etw./jmdn. wüten od. (ugs.) wettern; **(b)** (be violent, operate unchecked) toben; ⟨Krankheit:⟩ wüten
ragged /'rægɪd/ adj. **(a)** zerrissen; kaputt (ugs.); ausgefranst ⟨Saum, Manschetten⟩; **(b)** (rough, shaggy) zottig ⟨Bart⟩; **(c)** (jagged) zerklüftet ⟨Felsen, Küste, Klippe⟩; (in tattered clothes) abgerissen; zerlumpt
'rag trade n. (coll.) Modebranche, die (ugs.)
raid /reɪd/ **1** n. **(a)** Einfall, der; Überfall, der; (Mil.) Überraschungsangriff der; **(b)** (by police) Razzia, die **(on** in + Dat.). **2** v.t. ⟨Polizei:⟩ eine Razzia machen auf (+ Akk.); ⟨Bande/Räuber/Soldaten:⟩ überfallen ⟨Bank/Viehherde/Land⟩; ⟨Trupp, Kommando:⟩ stürmen ⟨feindliche Stellung⟩; ∼ **the larder** (joc.) die Speisekammer plündern (scherzh.)
raider /'reɪdə(r)/ n. (on bank, farm) Räuber, der/Räuberin, die; (looter) Plünderer, der/Plünderin, die; (burglar) Einbrecher, der/Einbrecherin, die
rail¹ /reɪl/ n. **(a)** (for clothes, curtains) [Kleider-, Gardinen]stange, die; (as part of fence) (wooden) Latte, die; (metal) Stange, die; (on ship) Reling, die; (as protection against contact) Barriere, die; (Railw.: of track) Schiene, die; **go off the** ∼s (lit.) entgleisen; (fig.: depart from what is accepted) auf die schiefe Bahn geraten; **(c)** (∼way) [Eisen]bahn, die; attrib. Bahn-; **by** ∼: mit der Bahn; mit dem Zug
rail² v.i. ∼ **at/against sb./sth.** auf/über jmdn./etw. schimpfen
railing /'reɪlɪŋ/ n. (round garden, park) Zaun, der; (on sides of staircase) Geländer, das
rail: ∼**road 1** n. (Amer.) ⇒ **railway; 2** v.t. (send or push through in haste) ∼**road sb. into doing sth.** jmdn. dazu antreiben, etw. zu tun; ∼**road a bill through parliament** einen Gesetzentwurf im Parlament durchpeitschen (ugs.); ∼ **strike** n. Eisenbahnerstrik, der; **R**∼**track** n., no pl., no art. (Brit.) Betreibergesellschaft des britischen Schienennetzes
railway /'reɪlweɪ/ n. **(a)** (track) Bahnlinie, die; Bahnstrecke, die; **(b)** (system) [Eisen]bahn, die; **work on the** ∼: bei der Bahn arbeiten
railway: ∼ **carriage** n. Eisenbahnwagen, der; ∼ **crossing** n. Bahnübergang, der; ∼ **engine** n. Lokomotive, die; ∼ **line** n. [Eisen]bahnlinie, die; [Eisen]bahnstrecke, die; ∼**man** /'reɪlweɪmən/ n., pl. ∼**men** /'reɪlweɪmən/ ▶ 887| Eisenbahner, der; ∼ **station** n. Bahnhof, der; (smaller) [Eisen]bahnstation, die; ∼ **worker** n. ▶ 887| Bahnarbeiter, der
rain /reɪn/ **1** n. **(a)** Regen, der; **it looks like** ∼: es sieht nach Regen aus; **come** ∼ **or shine** (fig.) unter allen Umständen; **(b)** (fig.: of arrows, blows, etc.) Hagel, der; **(c)** in pl. (falls of ∼) **the** ∼**s** die Regenzeit. **2** v.i. impers. **it is** ∼**ing** es regnet; **it is starting to** ∼: es fängt an zu regnen. **3** v.t. prasseln od. hageln lassen ⟨Schläge, Hiebe⟩
∼ **'down** v.i. ⟨Schläge, Steine, Flüche usw.:⟩ niederprasseln; ⟨Schüsse, Kugeln usw.:⟩ niederhageln
∼ **'off,** (Amer.) ∼ **'out** v.t. **be** ∼**ed off** or **out** (be terminated) wegen Regen abgebrochen werden; (be cancelled) wegen Regen ausfallen
rainbow /'reɪnbəʊ/ **1** n. Regenbogen, der; **all the colours of the** ∼: alle Regenbogenfarben. **2** adj. Regenbogen⟨farben, -streifen⟩; regenbogenfarbig, -farben ⟨Kleid, Blumen⟩
'rainbow coalition n. Regenbogenkoalition, die
rain: ∼ **check** n. (Amer. fig.) **take a** ∼ **check on sth.** auf etw. (Akk.) später wieder zurückkommen; ∼**coat** n. Regenmantel, der; ∼**drop** n. Regentropfen, der; ∼**fall** n. (shower) [Regen]schauer, der; (quantity) Niederschlag, der; ∼**forest** n. Regenwald, der; ∼**proof 1** adj. regendicht; wasserdicht; **2** v.t. apprettieren; ∼**water** n. Regenwasser, das
rainy /'reɪnɪ/ adj. regnerisch ⟨Tag, Wetter⟩; regenreich ⟨Klima, Gebiet, Sommer, Winter⟩; ∼ **season** Regenzeit, die; **keep sth. for a** ∼ **day** (fig.) sich (Dat.) etw. für schlechte Zeiten aufheben
raise /reɪz/ v.t. **(a)** (lift up) heben; erhöhen ⟨Pulsfrequenz, Temperatur, Miete, Gehalt, Kosten⟩; hochziehen ⟨Rollladen, Fahne, Schultern⟩; aufziehen ⟨Vorhang⟩; hochheben ⟨Koffer, Arm, Hand⟩; ∼ **one's eyes to heaven** die Augen zum Himmel erheben (geh.); ∼ **one's glass to sb.** das Glas auf jmdn. erheben; ∼ **one's voice** die Stimme heben; **they** ∼**d their voices** (in anger) sie od. ihre Stimmen wurden lauter; **war** ∼**d its [ugly] head** der Krieg erhob sein [hässliches] Haupt; **(b)** (set upright, cause to stand up) aufrichten; erheben ⟨Banner⟩; aufstellen ⟨Fahnenstange, Zaun, Gerüst⟩; **be** ∼**d from the dead** von den Toten [auf]erweckt werden; ∼ **sb.'s spirits** jmds. Stimmung heben; **(c)** (build up, construct) errichten ⟨Gebäude, Statue⟩; erheben ⟨Forderungen, Einwände⟩; entstehen lassen ⟨Vorurteile⟩; (introduce) aufwerfen ⟨Frage⟩; zur Sprache bringen, anschneiden ⟨Thema, Problem⟩; (utter) erschallen lassen ⟨Ruf, Schrei⟩; **(d)** (grow, breed, rear) anbauen ⟨Gemüse, Getreide⟩; aufziehen ⟨Vieh, [Haus]tiere⟩; großziehen ⟨Familie, Kinder⟩; **(e)** (bring together, procure) aufbringen ⟨Geld, Betrag, Summe⟩; aufstellen ⟨Armee, Flotte, Truppen⟩; aufnehmen ⟨Hypothek, Kredit⟩; **(f)** (end, cause to end) aufheben, beenden ⟨Belagerung, Blockade⟩; (remove) aufheben ⟨Embargo, Verbot⟩; **(g)** ∼ **[merry] hell** (coll.) Krach schlagen (ugs.) **(over** wegen); **(h)** (Math.) ∼ **to the fourth power** in die 4. Potenz erheben
raisin /'reɪzn/ n. Rosine, die
rake¹ /reɪk/ **1** n. (Hort.) Rechen, der (bes. südd. u. md.); Harke, die (bes. nordd.). **2** v.t. **(a)** harken ⟨Laub, Erde, Fußboden, Kies, Oberfläche⟩; **(b)** ∼ **the fire** die Asche entfernen; **(c)** (with eyes/shots) bestreichen
∼ **'in** v.t. (coll.) scheffeln (ugs.) ⟨Geld⟩
∼ **over** v.t. **(a)** harken; **(b)** (fig.) wieder ausgraben
∼ **'up** v.t. **(a)** zusammenharken; **(b)** (fig.) wieder ausgraben
rake² n. (person) Lebemann, der
'rake-off n. (coll.) [Gewinn]anteil, der
rakish /'reɪkɪʃ/ adj. (jaunty) flott; kess; **wear one's hat at a** ∼ **angle** seinen Hut frech od. keck aufgesetzt haben
rally /'rælɪ/ **1** v.i. **(a)** (come together) sich versammeln; ∼ **to the support of** or **the defence of,** ∼ **behind** or **to sb.** (fig.) sich hinter jmdn. stellen; **(b)** (regain health) sich wieder [ein wenig] erholen; **(c)** (reassemble) sich [wieder] sammeln; **(d)** (increase in value after fall) ⟨Aktie, Kurs:⟩ wieder anziehen, sich wieder erholen. **2** v.t. **(a)** (reassemble) wieder zusammenrufen; **(b)** (bring together) einigen ⟨Partei, Kräfte⟩; sammeln ⟨Anhänger⟩; **(c)** (rouse) aufmuntern; (revive) ∼ **one's strength** seine [ganze] Kraft zusammennehmen. **3** n. **(a)** (mass meeting) Versammlung, die; **peace** ∼**:** Friedenskundgebung, die; **(b)** (competition) [motor] ∼**:** Rallye, die; **(c)** (Tennis) Ballwechsel, der
RAM /ræm/ abbr. (Computing) **random access memory** RAM
ram /ræm/ **1** n. **(a)** (Zool.) Schafbock, der; Widder, der; **(b)** ⇒ **battering ram; (c)** (hydraulic lifting-machine) hydraulischer Widder. **2** v.t., **-mm-:** **(a)** (force) stopfen; ∼ **a post**

into the ground einen Pfosten in die Erde rammen; ∼ **sth. in** etw. hinein rammen; ∼ **sth. home to sb.** jmdm. etw. deutlich vor Augen führen; **(b)** (collide with) rammen ⟨*Fahrzeug, Pfosten*⟩; **(c)** ∼ **[down]** (beat down) feststampfen ⟨*Erde, Ton, Kies*⟩

ramble /'ræmbl/ **1** *n.* [**nature**] ∼: Wanderung, *die*. **2** *v.i.* **(a)** (walk) umherstreifen (**through, in** in + *Dat.*); **(b)** (in talk) zusammenhangloses Zeug reden (abwertend); **keep rambling on about sth.** sich endlos über etw. (*Akk.*) auslassen

rambler /'ræmblə(r)/ *n.* **(a)** Wanderer, *der*/Wanderin, *die;* **(b)** (Bot.) Kletterrose, *die*

rambling /'ræmblɪŋ/ **1** *n.* Wandern, *das*. **2** *adj.* **(a)** (irregularly arranged) verschachtelt; verwinkelt ⟨*Straßen*⟩; **(b)** (incoherent) unzusammenhängend ⟨*Erklärung, Brief*⟩; zerstreut ⟨*Professor*⟩; **(c)** ∼ **rose** Kletterrose, *die*

ramifications /ræmɪfɪ'keɪʃnz/ *n.* Auswirkungen *Pl.*

rammer /'ræmə(r)/ *n.* Stampfer, *der*

ramp /ræmp/ *n.* **(a)** (slope) Rampe, *die;* **'beware** or **caution, ∼!'** „Vorsicht, unebene Fahrbahn!"; **(b)** (Aeronaut.) Gangway, *die*

rampage 1 /'ræmpeɪdʒ/ *n.* Randale, *die* (ugs.); **be/go on the ∼** (coll.) ⟨*Rowdys:*⟩ randalieren; ⟨*verärgerte Person:*⟩ toben. **2** /'ræm'peɪdʒ/ *v.i.* ⟨*Rowdys:*⟩ randalieren; ∼ **about** ⟨*verärgerte Person:*⟩ toben

rampant /'ræmpənt/ *adj.* zügellos ⟨*Gewalt, Rassismus*⟩; steil ansteigend ⟨*Inflation*⟩; üppig ⟨*Wachstum*⟩

rampart /'ræmpɑːt/ *n.* **(a)** (walk) Wehrgang, *der;* **(b)** (protective barrier) Wall, *der*

ram: ∼ **raid 1** *v.t.* [durch Rammen mit einem Fahrzeug] einbrechen in (+ *Akk.*); **2** *n.* [durch Rammen eines Gebäudes verübter] Einbruch; ∼**-raider** *n.* Einbrecher, der sich durch Einrammen, bes. eines Schaufensters, mit einem Fahrzeug Zutritt verschafft; ∼**rod** *n.* Ladestock, *der;* **as straight** or **stiff as a** ∼**rod** (fig. coll.) so steif, als ob man einen Besenstiel verschluckt hätte; stocksteif; ∼**shackle** *adj.* klapprig ⟨*Auto*⟩; verkommen ⟨*Gebäude*⟩

ran ⇒ **run 2, 3**

ranch /rɑːntʃ/ *n.* Ranch, *die;* [**mink/poultry**] ∼: [Nerz-/Geflügel]farm, *die*

rancher /'rɑːntʃə(r)/ *n.* Rancher, *der*/Rancherin, *die*

rancid /'rænsɪd/ *adj.* ranzig

rancour (*Brit.; Amer.:* **rancor**) /'ræŋkə(r)/ *n.* [tiefe] Verbitterung

R&B *abbr.* **rhythm and blues** R&B

R&D *abbr.* **research and development** F&E

random /'rændəm/ **1** *n.* **at** ∼: wahllos; willkürlich; (aimlessly) ziellos; **choose at** ∼: aufs Geratewohl wählen. **2** *adj.* **(a)** (unsystematic) willkürlich ⟨*Auswahl*⟩; **make a** ∼ **guess** raten aufs Geratewohl; **(b)** (Statistics) Zufalls-

random 'access memory *n.* (Computing) Schreib-Lese-Speicher, *der*

randy /'rændɪ/ *adj.* geil; scharf (ugs.); **feel** ∼: geil sein

rang ⇒ **ring² 2, 3**

range /reɪndʒ/ **1** *n.* **(a)** (row) ∼ **of mountains** Bergkette, *die;* **(b)** (of subjects, interests, topics) Palette, *die;* (of musical instrument) Tonumfang, *der;* (of knowledge, voice) Umfang, *der;* (of income, department, possibility) Bereich, *der;* **sth. is out of** or **beyond sb's** ∼ (lit. or fig.) etw. ist außerhalb jmds. Reichweite; **(c)** (of telescope, missile, aircraft, etc.) Reichweite, *die;* (distance between gun and target) Schussweite, *die;* **flying** ∼: Flugbereich, *der;* **at a** ∼ **of 200 metres** auf eine Entfernung von 200 Metern; **up to a** ∼ **of 5 miles** bis zu einem Umkreis von 5 Meilen; **shoot at close** or **short/long** ∼: aus kurzer/großer Entfernung schießen; **experience sth. at close** ∼: etw. in unmittelbarer Nähe erleben; **(d)** (series, selection) Kollektion, *die;* **(e)** [**shooting**] ∼: Schießstand, *der;* (at funfair) Schießbude, *die;* **(f)** (testing site) Versuchsgelände, *das;* **(g)** (grazing ground) Weide[fläche], *die.* **2** *v.i.* **(a)** (vary within limits) ⟨*Preise, Temperaturen:*⟩ schwanken, sich bewegen (**from ... to** zwischen [+ *Dat.*] ... und); **they** ∼ **in age from 3 to 12** sie sind zwischen 3 und 12 Jahre alt; **(b)** (extend) ⟨*Klippen, Gipfel, Häuser:*⟩ sich hinziehen; **(c)** (roam) umherziehen (**around, about** in + *Dat.*); (fig.) ⟨*Gedanken:*⟩ umherschweifen; **the discussion** ∼**d over** ...: die Diskussion erstreckte sich auf

(+ *Akk.*) ... **3** *v.t.* (arrange) aufreihen ⟨*Bücher, Tische*⟩; ∼ **oneself against sb./sth.** (fig.) sich gegen jmdn./etw. zusammenschließen

'rangefinder *n.* Entfernungsmesser, *der*

ranger /'reɪndʒə(r)/ *n.* **(a)** (keeper) Aufseher, *der*/Aufseherin, *die;* (of forest) Förster, *der*/Försterin, *die;* **(b)** (Amer.: law officer) Ranger, *der; Angehöriger der berittenen Polizeitruppe*

rank¹ /ræŋk/ **1** *n.* **(a)** (position in hierarchy) Rang, *der;* (Mil. also) Dienstgrad, *der;* **be above/below sb. in** ∼: einen höheren/niedrigeren Rang/Dienstgrad als jmd. haben; **(b)** (social position) [soziale] Stellung; **people of all** ∼**s** Menschen aus allen [Gesellschafts]schichten; **(c)** (row) Reihe, *die;* **(d)** (Brit.: taxi stand) [Taxen]stand, *der;* **(e)** (line of soldiers) Reihe, *die;* **the** ∼**s** (enlisted men) die Mannschaften und Unteroffiziere; **the** ∼ **and file** die Mannschaften und Unteroffiziere; (fig.) die breite Masse; **close** [**our/their**] ∼**s** die Reihen schließen; (fig.) sich zusammenschließen; **rise from the** ∼**s** sich [aus dem Mannschaftsstand] zum Offizier hochdienen; (fig.) sich hocharbeiten. **2** *v.t.* (classify) ∼ **among** or **with** zählen od. rechnen zu; ∼ **sth. highly** etw. hoch einstufen. **3** *v.i.* ∼ **among** or **with** gehören od. zählen zu; ∼ **above/next to sb.** rangmäßig über/direkt unter jmdm. stehen

rank² *adj.* **(a)** (complete) blank ⟨*Unsinn, Frechheit*⟩; krass ⟨*Außenseiter, Illoyalität*⟩; **(b)** (stinking) stinkend; **(c)** (rampant) ∼ **weeds** [wild] wucherndes Unkraut

rankings /'ræŋkɪŋz/ *n. pl.* (Sport) Rangliste, *die*

rankle /'ræŋkl/ *v.i.* **sth.** ∼**s** [**with sb.**] etw. wurmt jmdn. (ugs.)

ransack /'rænsæk/ *v.t.* **(a)** (search) durchsuchen (**for** nach); **(b)** (pillage) plündern

ransom /'rænsəm/ **1** *n.* ∼ [**money**] Lösegeld, *das;* **hold to** ∼: als Geisel festhalten; (fig.) erpressen, unter Druck (*Akk.*) setzen ⟨*Regierung*⟩. **2** *v.t.* **(a)** (obtain release of) Lösegeld bezahlen für; auslösen; **(b)** (hold to ∼) als Geisel festhalten

'ransom note *n.* Erpresserbrief, *der*

rant /rænt/ *v.i.* ∼ [**and rave**] wettern (ugs.) (**about** über + *Akk.*); ∼ **at** anschnauzen (ugs.)

rap /ræp/ **1** *n.* **(a)** (sharp knock) [energisches] Klopfen; **there was a** ∼ **on** or **at the door** es klopfte [laut]; **give sb. a** ∼ **on** or **over the knuckles** jmdm. auf die Finger schlagen; (fig.) jmdm. auf die Finger klopfen; **(b)** (coll.: blame) **take the** ∼ [**for sth.**] [für etw.] den Kopf hinhalten (ugs.). **2** *v.t.*, **-pp-** (strike smartly) klopfen; ∼ **sb. on the knuckles** jmdm. auf die Finger klopfen. **3** *v.i.*, **-pp-** klopfen (**on an** + *Akk.*); ∼ **on the table** auf den Tisch klopfen

∼ **'out** *v.t.* ausstoßen ⟨*Befehl, Fluch*⟩; ∼ **out a message** melden

rapacious /rə'peɪʃəs/ *adj.* (greedy) habgierig

rape¹ /reɪp/ **1** *n.* Vergewaltigung, *die* (auch fig.); Notzucht, *die* (Rechtsspr.). **2** *v.t.* vergewaltigen; notzüchtigen (Rechtsspr.)

rape² *n.* (Bot., Agric.) Raps, *der*

rapid /'ræpɪd/ **1** *adj.* schnell ⟨*Bewegung, Wachstum, Puls*⟩; rasch ⟨*Folge, Bewegung, Fortschritt, Ausbreitung, Änderung*⟩; rapide ⟨*Niedergang*⟩; steil ⟨*Abstieg*⟩; reißend ⟨*Gewässer, Strömung*⟩; stark ⟨*Gefälle, Strömung*⟩; **there has been a** ∼ **decline** es ging rapide abwärts. **2** *n. in pl.* Stromschnellen *Pl.*

rapidity /rə'pɪdɪtɪ/ *n., no pl.* Schnelligkeit, *die*

rapier /'reɪpɪə(r)/ *n.* (Fencing) Rapier, *das*

rapist /'reɪpɪst/ *n.* Vergewaltiger, *der*

rapport /rə'pɔː(r)/ *n.* [harmonisches] Verhältnis; **have a great** ∼ **with sb.** ein ausgezeichnetes Verhältnis zu jmdm. haben; **establish a** ∼ **with sb.** eine Beziehung zu jmdm. aufbauen

rapt /ræpt/ *adj.* gespannt ⟨*Aufmerksamkeit, Miene*⟩; **in** ∼ **contemplation** in Betrachtungen versunken

rapture /'ræptʃə(r)/ *n.* **(a)** (ecstatic delight) [**state of**] ∼: Verzückung, *die;* **(b)** *in pl.* **be in** ∼**s** entzückt sein (**over, about** über + *Akk.*); **go into** ∼**s** [überschwänglich] schwärmen (**over, about** von)

rapturous /'ræptʃərəs/ *adj.* begeistert ⟨*Applaus, Menge, Willkommen*⟩; verzückt ⟨*Miene*⟩

rare¹ /reə(r)/ *adj.* (a) (uncommon) selten; **it's ~ for him to do that** es kommt selten vor, dass er das tut; (b) (thin) dünn ⟨*Luft, Atmosphäre*⟩

rare² *adj.* (Cookery) englisch gebraten; nur schwach gebraten

rarebit /'reəbɪt/ ⇒ **Welsh rarebit**

rarefied /'reərɪfaɪd/ *adj.* dünn ⟨*Luft*⟩; (fig.) exklusiv

rarely /'reəlɪ/ *adv.* selten

raring /'reərɪŋ/ *adj.* (coll.) **be ~ to go** kaum abwarten können, bis es losgeht

rarity /'reərɪtɪ/ *n.* Seltenheit, *die;* Rarität, *die;* **be an object of great ~:** eine große Seltenheit sein

rascal /'rɑːskl/ *n.* (a) (dishonest person) Schuft, *der;* (b) (joc.: mischievous person) Schlingel, *der* (scherzh.); Spitzbube, *der* (scherzh.)

rash¹ /ræʃ/ *n.* (Med.) [Haut]ausschlag, *der;* **develop a *or* break out *or* come out in a ~:** einen Ausschlag bekommen

rash² *adj.* voreilig ⟨*Urteil, Entscheidung, Entschluss*⟩; überstürzt ⟨*Versprechungen, Handlung, Erklärung*⟩; ungestüm ⟨*Person*⟩

rasher /'ræʃə(r)/ *n.* **~ [of bacon]** Speckscheibe, *die*

rasp /rɑːsp/ **1** *n.* (a) (tool) Raspel, *die;* (b) (sound) (of metal on wood) schneidendes Geräusch; (of breathing) Rasseln, *das.* **2** *v.t.* (a) (scrape with ~) raspeln ⟨*Blech, Kante*⟩; (b) (say gratingly) schnarren

raspberry /'rɑːzbərɪ/ *n.* (a) Himbeere, *die; attrib.* Himbeer⟨*marmelade, -torte, -rosa, -eis*⟩; (b) (coll.: rude noise) **blow a ~:** verächtlich prusten

rasping /'rɑːspɪŋ/ *adj.* krächzend ⟨*Husten, Stimme*⟩; rasselnd ⟨*Geräusch*⟩

rat /ræt/ *n.* (a) Ratte, *die;* **brown *or* sewer ~:** Wanderratte, *die;* **smell a ~** (fig. coll.) Lunte *od.* den Braten riechen (ugs.); (b) (coll. derog.: unpleasant person) Ratte, *die* (derb)

'rat-arsed /'rætɑːst/ *adj.* (Brit. sl.) stockbesoffen (derb); stinkbesoffen (derb)

ratchet /'rætʃɪt/ *n.* (Mech. Engin.) (set of teeth) Zahnkranz, *der;* **~ [wheel]** Klinkenrad, *das*

'ratchet screwdriver *n.* Drillschraubenzieher, *der*

rate /reɪt/ **1** *n.* (a) (proportion) Rate, *die;* **increase at a ~ of 50 a week** [um] 50 pro Woche anwachsen; **~ of inflation/absentee ~:** Inflations-/Abwesenheitsrate, *die;* (b) (tariff) Satz, *der;* **interest/ taxation ~, ~ of interest/ taxation** Zins-/Steuersatz, *der;* (c) (amount of money) Gebühr, *die;* **~ [of pay]** Lohnsatz, *der;* **letter/parcel ~:** Briefporto, *das*/Paketgebühr, *die;* **at reduced ~:** gebührenermäßigt ⟨*Drucksache*⟩; (d) (speed) Geschwindigkeit, *die;* Tempo, *das;* **at a *or* the ~ of 50 mph** mit [einer Geschwindigkeit von] 80 km/h; **at a good/fast/dangerous ~:** zügig/mit hoher Geschwindigkeit/gefährlich schnell; (e) (Brit.: local authority levy) **[local *or* council] ~s** Gemeindeabgaben; (f) (coll.) **at any ~** (at least) zumindest, wenigstens; (whatever happens) auf jeden Fall; **at this ~ we won't get any work done** so kriegen wir gar nichts fertig (ugs.); **at the ~ you're going, ...** (fig.) wenn du so weitermachst, ... **2** *v.t.* (a) (estimate worth of) schätzen ⟨*Vermögen*⟩; einschätzen ⟨*Intelligenz, Leistung, Fähigkeit*⟩; **~ sb./sth. highly** jmdn./etw. hoch einschätzen; (b) (consider) betrachten; rechnen (**among** zu); **be ~d the top tennis player in Europe** als der beste Tennisspieler Europas gelten; (c) (Brit.: value) **the house is ~d at £100 a year** die Grundlage für die Berechnung der Gemeindeabgaben für das Haus beträgt 100 Pfund pro Jahr; (d) (merit) verdienen ⟨*Auszeichnung, Erwähnung*⟩. **3** *v.i.* zählen (**among** zu); **~ as** gelten als

rateable /'reɪtəbl/ *adj.* (Brit.) **~ value** steuerbarer Wert

ratepayer /'reɪtpeɪə(r)/ *n.* (Brit.) Realsteuerpflichtige, *der/ die;* ≈ Steuerzahler, *der*/-zahlerin, *die*

rather /'rɑːðə(r)/ *adv.* (a) (by preference) lieber; **he wanted to appear witty ~ than brainy** er wollte lieber geistreich als klug erscheinen; **~ than accept bribes, he decided to resign** ehe er sich bestechen ließ, trat er lieber zurück; (b) (somewhat) ziemlich ⟨*gut, gelangweilt, unvorsichtig, nett, warm*⟩; **I ~ think that ...:** ich bin ziemlich sicher, dass ...; **be ~ better/more complicated than**

expected um einiges besser/komplizierter sein als erwartet; **it is ~ too early** ich fürchte, es ist zu früh; **it looks ~ like a banana** es sieht ungefähr wie eine Banane aus; **I ~ like beans/him** ich esse Bohnen ganz gern/ich mag ihn recht gern; (c) (more truly) vielmehr; **or ~:** beziehungsweise; [oder] genauer gesagt; **he was careless ~ than wicked** er war eher nachlässig als böswillig

ratify /'rætɪfaɪ/ *v.t.* ratifizieren ⟨*völkerrechtlichen Vertrag*⟩; bestätigen ⟨*Ernennung*⟩; sanktionieren ⟨*Vertrag, Gesetzentwurf*⟩

rating /'reɪtɪŋ/ *n.* (a) (estimated standing) Einschätzung, *die;* (b) (Radio, Telev.) **[popularity] ~:** Einschaltquote, *die;* **be high/low in the ~s** eine hohe/niedrige Einschaltquote haben; (c) (Navy: rank) Dienstgrad, *der;* (d) (Brit. Navy: sailor) [naval] **~:** Mannschaftsdienstgrad, *der*

ratio /'reɪʃɪəʊ/ *n., pl.* **~s** Verhältnis, *das;* **in a *or* the ~ of 1 to 5** im Verhältnis 1 : 5; **in direct ~ to *or* with** im gleichen Verhältnis wie; **the teacher-student ~:** das Verhältnis von Lehrern zu Schülern; **what is the ~ of men to women?** wie hoch ist der Männeranteil im Vergleich zu dem der Frauen?

ration /'ræʃn/ **1** *n.* (a) (daily food allowance) [Tages]ration, *die;* **put sb. on short ~s** jmdn. auf halbe Ration setzen (ugs.); (b) (fixed allowance of food etc. for civilians) **~[s]** Ration, *die* (of an + *Dat.*); **petrol/meat ~:** Benzin-/Fleischration, *die.* **2** *v.t.* rationieren ⟨*Benzin, Autos*⟩; Rationen zuteilen (+ *Dat.*) ⟨*Person*⟩; **be ~ed to one glass of spirits per day** nur ein Glas Alkohol pro Tag trinken dürfen **~ 'out** *v.t.* zuteilen (**to** *Dat.*); in Rationen austeilen (**to** an + *Akk.*)

rational /'ræʃnl/ *adj.* (having reason) rational, vernunftbegabt ⟨*Wesen*⟩; (sensible) vernünftig ⟨*Person, Art, Politik usw.*⟩

rationale /ræʃə'nɑːl/ *n.* (a) (statement of reasons) rationale Erklärung (**of** für); (b) (fundamental reason) logische Grundlage

rationalisation, rationalise ⇒ **rationaliz-**

rationalization /ræʃənəlaɪ'zeɪʃn/ *n.* (Econ., Psych.) Rationalisierung, *die*

rationalize /'ræʃənəlaɪz/ **1** *v.t.* (Econ., Psych.) rationalisieren. **2** *v.i.* Scheinbegründungen finden

ration: ~ book *n.* Bezugsscheinheft, *das;* **~ card, ~ coupon** *ns.* Bezugsschein, *der*

rationing /'ræʃənɪŋ/ *n.* Rationierung, *die*

rat: ~ poison *n.* Rattengift, *das;* **~ race** *n.* erbarmungsloser Konkurrenzkampf

'ratted /'rætɪd/ *adj.* ⇒ **rat-arsed**

rattle /'rætl/ **1** *v.i.* (a) (clatter) ⟨*Fenster, Maschinenteil, Schlüssel:*⟩ klappern; ⟨*Hagel:*⟩ prasseln; ⟨*Flaschen:*⟩ klirren; ⟨*Kette:*⟩ rasseln; ⟨*Münzen:*⟩ klingen; **~ at the door** an der Tür rütteln; (b) (move) ⟨*Zug, Bus:*⟩ rattern; ⟨*Kutsche:*⟩ rumpeln. **2** *v.t.* (a) (make ~) klappern mit ⟨*Würfel, Geschirr, Dose, Münzen, Schlüsselbund*⟩; klirren lassen ⟨*Fenster[scheiben]*⟩; rasseln mit ⟨*Kette*⟩; (b) (coll.: disconcert) **~ sb., get sb. ~d** jmdn. durcheinander bringen; **don't get ~d!** reg dich nicht auf! **3** *n.* (a) (of baby; Mus.) Rassel, *die;* (of sports fan) Ratsche, *die;* (b) (sound) Klappern, *das;* (of hail) Prasseln, *das;* (of drums) Schnarren, *das;* (of machine gun) Rattern, *das;* (of chains) Rasseln, *das* **~ 'off** *v.t.* (coll.) herunterrasseln (ugs.). **~ 'on** *v.i.* (coll.) plappern (ugs.)

'rattlesnake *n.* Klapperschlange, *die*

ratty /'rætɪ/ *adj.* (coll.: irritable) gereizt

raucous /'rɔːkəs/ *adj.* rau ⟨*Stimme, Lachen*⟩

raunchy /'rɔːntʃɪ/ *adj.* (suggestive) scharf (salopp)

ravage /'rævɪdʒ/ **1** *v.t.* heimsuchen ⟨*Gebiet, Stadt*⟩; so gut wie vernichten ⟨*Ernte*⟩; schwer zeichnen ⟨*Gesichtszüge*⟩. **2** *n. in pl.* verheerende Wirkung; **the ~s of time/war** die Zeichen der Zeit/die Wunden des Krieges

rave /reɪv/ **1** *v.i.* (a) (talk wildly) irrereden; **~ at** [wüst] beschimpfen; (b) (speak with admiration) schwärmen (**about, over** von). **2** *v.t.* (coll.) [hellauf] begeistert ⟨*Kritik*⟩. **3** *n.* (coll.: dancing party) Rave, *der od. das*

raven /'reɪvn/ *n.* Rabe, *der;* Kolkrabe, *der* (Zool.)

ravenous /'rævənəs/ *adj.* ausgehungert; **I'm ~:** ich habe einen Bärenhunger (ugs.)

'rave-up *n.* (Brit. coll.) Rave, *der od. das*

ravine /rə'viːn/ *n.* Schlucht, *die;* (made by river also) Klamm, *die*

raving /'reɪvɪŋ/ **1** *n. in pl.* irres Gerede. **2** *adj.* **(a)** (talking madly) irreredend ‹*Wahnsinniger, Idiot*›; **(b)** (outstanding) fantastisch (ugs.) ‹*Erfolg*›. **3** *adv.* **be ~ mad** (stupid) völlig verrückt sein (ugs.)

ravishing /'rævɪʃɪŋ/ *adj.* bildschön ‹*Anblick, Person*›; hinreißend ‹*Schönheit*›

raw /rɔː/ **1** *adj.* **(a)** (uncooked) roh; **(b)** (inexperienced) unerfahren; blutig ‹*Anfänger*›; *see also* **recruit 1 a, c; (c)** (stripped of skin) roh ‹*Fleisch*›; offen ‹*Wunde*›; (sore) wund ‹*Füße*›; **touch** *or* **hit a ~ nerve** einen wunden Punkt *od.* eine empfindliche Stelle treffen; **(d)** (chilly) nasskalt; **(e)** (untreated) Roh‹*-haut, -holz, -seide, -zucker, -erz, -leder*›; (undiluted) rein ‹*Alkohol*›; **(f)** (fig.: unpolished) grob; **(g)** (Statistics) unaufbereitet. **2** *n.* **nature in the ~:** unverfälschte Natur; **touch sb. on the ~** (Brit. coll.) jmdn. an [s]einer verwundbaren Stelle treffen

raw ma'terial *n.* Rohstoff, *der*

ray¹ /reɪ/ *n.* **(a)** (lit. or fig.) Strahl, *der;* **~ of sunshine/ light** Sonnen-/Lichtstrahl, *der;* **~ of hope** Hoffnungsstrahl, *der;* **(b)** *in pl.* (radiation) Strahlen; Strahlung, *die*

ray² *n.* (fish) Rochen, *der*

rayon /'reɪɒn/ *n.* (Textiles) Reyon, *das od. der; attrib.* Reyon‹*kleid, -hemd*›

raze /reɪz/ *v.t.* **~ to the ground** dem Erdboden gleichmachen

razor /'reɪzə(r)/ *n.* Rasiermesser, *das;* [**electric**] **~:** [elektrischer] Rasierapparat; [Elektro- *od.* Trocken]rasierer, *der* (ugs.)

razor: ~ blade *n.* Rasierklinge, *die;* **~ edge** *n.* Rasierschneide, *die;* **be** *or* **stand on a ~ edge** *or* **~'s edge** (fig.) sich auf einer Gratwanderung befinden; **~sharp** *adj.* sehr scharf ‹*Messer*›; (fig.) messerscharf ‹*Verstand, Intellekt*›; scharfsinnig ‹*Person*›

RC *abbr.* **Roman Catholic** r.-k.; röm.-kath.

Rd. *abbr.* **road** Str.

RE *abbr.* (Brit.) **Religious Education** Religionslehre, *die*

re /riː/ *prep.* (coll.) über (+ *Akk.*)

're /ə(r)/ (coll.) **= are; ⇒ be**

reach /riːtʃ/ **1** *v.t.* **(a)** (arrive at) erreichen; ankommen *od.* eintreffen in (+ *Dat.*) ‹*Stadt, Land*›; erzielen ‹*Übereinstimmung, Übereinkunft*›; kommen zu ‹*Entscheidung, Entschluss; Ausgang, Eingang*›; **be easily ~ed** leicht erreichbar *od.* zu erreichen sein (**by** mit); **not a sound ~ed our ears** kein Laut drang an unsere Ohren; **have you ~ed page 45 yet?** bist du schon auf Seite 45 [angelangt]?; **you can ~ her at this number/ by radio** du kannst sie unter dieser Nummer/über Funk erreichen; **(b)** (extend to) ‹*Straße:*› führen bis zu; ‹*Leiter, Haar:*› reichen bis zu; **(c)** (pass) **~ me that book** reich mir das Buch herüber. **2** *v.i.* **(a)** (stretch out hand) **~ for sth.** nach etw. greifen; **how high can you ~?** wie hoch kannst du langen?; **(b)** (be long/tall enough) **sth. will/won't ~:** etw. ist/ist nicht lang genug; **he can't ~ up to the top shelf** er kann das oberste Regal nicht [mit der Hand] erreichen; **will it ~ as far as …?** wird es bis zu … reichen? **can you ~?** kannst *od.* kommst du dran? (ugs.); **(c)** (go as far as) ‹*Wasser, Gebäude, Besitz:*› reichen ([**up**] **to** bis [hinauf] zu). **3** *n.* **(a)** (extent of ~ing) Reichweite, *die;* **be within easy ~ [of a place]** (von einem Ort aus) leicht erreichbar sein; **be above sb.'s ~:** zu hoch für jmdn. sein; **keep sth. out of ~ of sb.** etw. unerreichbar für jmdn. aufbewahren; **keep sth. within easy ~:** etw. in greifbarer Nähe aufbewahren; **be within/beyond the ~ of sb.** in/außer jmds. Reichweite sein; (fig.) für jmdn. im/ nicht im Bereich des Möglichen liegen; (financially) für jmdn. erschwinglich/unerschwinglich sein; **(b)** (expanse) Abschnitt, *der*

~ 'down 1 *v.i.* den Arm nach unten ausstrecken; **~ down to sb.** (be long enough) bis zu jmdm. [hinunter]reichen. **2** *v.t.* hinunterreichen; (to receiving speaker) herunterreichen

~ 'out 1 *v.t.* (stretch out) ausstrecken ‹*Fuß, Bein, Hand, Arm*› (**for** nach). **2** *v.i.* die Hand ausstrecken (**for** nach); **~ out for, ~ out to grasp** ‹*Person, Hand:*› greifen nach

reachable /'riːtʃəbl/ *adj.* erreichbar

react /rɪ'ækt/ *v.i.* **(a)** (respond) reagieren (**to** auf + *Akk.*); **(b)** (act in opposition) sich widersetzen (**against** *Dat.*); **(c)** (Chem., Phys.) reagieren

reaction /rɪ'ækʃn/ *n.* Reaktion, *die* (**to** auf + *Akk.*); **~ against sth.** Widerstand gegen etw.; **action and ~:** Wirkung und Gegenwirkung; **what was his ~?** wie hat er reagiert?; **there was a favourable ~ to the proposal** der Vorschlag ist positiv aufgenommen worden

reactionary /rɪ'ækʃənərɪ/ (Polit.) **1** *adj.* reaktionär. **2** *n.* Reaktionär, *der*/Reaktionärin, *die*

reactor /rɪ'æktə(r)/ *n.* [**nuclear**] **~:** Kernreaktor, *der*

read /riːd/ **1** *v.t.,* **read** /red/ **(a)** lesen; **~ sb. sth., ~ sth. to sb.** jmdm. etwas vorlesen; *see also* **take 1 u; (b)** (show a reading of) anzeigen; **(c)** (interpret) deuten; **~ sb.'s hand** jmdm. aus der Hand lesen; **~ sb.'s mind** *or* **thoughts** jmds. Gedanken lesen; **~ sth. into sth.** etw. in etw. (*Akk.*) hineinlesen; **(d)** (Brit. Univ.: study) studieren. **2** *v.i.,* **read** /red/ **(a)** lesen; **~ to sb.** jmdm. vorlesen; **(b)** (convey meaning) lauten; **the contract ~s as follows** der Vertrag hat folgenden Wortlaut; **(c)** (affect reader) sich lesen. **3** *n.* **(a)** **have a quiet ~:** in Ruhe lesen; **(b)** (Brit. coll.: reading matter) **be a good ~:** sich gut lesen. **4** /red/ *adj.* **widely** *or* **deeply ~:** sehr belesen ‹*Person*›; **the most widely ~ book/author** das meistgelesene Buch/der meistgelesene Autor

~ 'back *v.t.* wiederholen; noch einmal vorlesen

~ 'off *v.t.* durchlesen; (from meter, board) ablesen ‹*Zahl, Stand*›

~ 'out *v.t.* laut vorlesen

~ 'over, ~ 'through *v.t.* durchlesen

~ 'up *v.t.* sich informieren (**on** über + *Akk.*)

readable /'riːdəbl/ *adj.* **(a)** (pleasant to read) lesenswert; **(b)** (legible) leserlich

readdress /riːə'dres/ *v.t.* umadressieren

reader /'riːdə(r)/ *n.* **(a)** Leser, *der*/Leserin, *die;* **be a slow/good/great ~ [of sth.]** [etw.] langsam/gut/gern lesen; **(b)** (who reads aloud) Vorlesende, *der/die;* **(c)** (textbook) Lehrbuch, *das;* (to learn to read, containing original texts) Lesebuch, *das;* **(d)** (Brit. Univ.) ≈ Assistenzprofessor, *der*/-professorin, *die* (**in** für)

readership /'riːdəʃɪp/ *n.* (number or type of readers) Leserschaft, *die;* Leserkreis, *der;* **what is the ~ of the paper?** wie groß ist die Leserschaft der Zeitung?

readily /'redɪlɪ/ *adv.* **(a)** (willingly) bereitwillig; **(b)** (without difficulty) ohne weiteres

readiness /'redɪnɪs/ *n.,* no pl. Bereitschaft, *die;* **~ to learn** Lernbereitschaft, *die;* **have/be in ~ [for sth.]** [für etw.] bereithalten/bereit sein

reading /'riːdɪŋ/ *n.* **(a)** Lesen, *das;* **(b)** (matter to be read) Lektüre, *die;* **make interesting/be good/dull ~:** interessant/gut/langweilig zu lesen sein; **(c)** (figure shown) Anzeige, *die;* **(d)** (recital) Lesung, *die* (**from** aus); **(e)** (interpretation) [Aus]deutung, *die;* **(f)** (Parl.) [**first/second/ third**] **~:** [erste/zweite/dritte] Lesung

reading: ~ glasses *n. pl.* Lesebrille, *die;* **~ knowledge** *n.* **have a ~ knowledge of a language** Texte in einer Sprache lesen können; **~ lamp, ~ light** *ns.* Leselampe, *die;* **~ list** *n.* Literaturliste, *die;* **~ matter** *n., no pl., no indef. art.* Lesestoff, *der;* Lektüre, *die;* **~ room** *n.* Lesesaal, *der*

readjust /riːə'dʒʌst/ **1** *v.t.* neu einstellen. **2** *v.i.* **~ to** sich wieder gewöhnen an (+ *Akk.*) ‹*Leben*›

read: ~-only memory *n.* (Computing) Fest[wert]speicher, *der;* **~out** *n.* (Computing) Ausgabe, *die*

ready /'redɪ/ **1** *adj.* **(a)** (prepared) fertig; **be ~ to do sth.** bereit sein, etw. zu tun; **I'm not ~ to go to the cinema yet** ich kann jetzt noch nicht ins Kino gehen; **the troops are ~ to march/for battle** die Truppen sind marsch-/ gefechtsbereit; **be ~ for work/school** zur Arbeit/für die Schule bereit sein; (about to leave) für die Arbeit/Schule fertig sein; **be ~ to leave** aufbruchsbereit sein; **be ~ for sb.** bereit sein, sich jmdm. zu stellen; **be ~ for anything** auf alles vorbereitet sein; **get ~ to go** sich zum Aufbruch bereit machen; **~, set** *or* **steady, go!** Achtung, fertig, los!; **(b)** (willing) bereit; **(c)** (prompt) schnell; **have ~, be ~ with**

parat haben, nicht verlegen sein um ⟨*Antwort, Ausrede, Vorschlag*⟩; **(d)** (likely) im Begriff; **be ~ to cry** den Tränen nahe sein; **(e)** (within reach) griffbereit ⟨*Fahrkarte, Taschenlampe, Waffe*⟩; **have your tickets ~!** halten Sie Ihre Fahrkarten bitte bereit! **2** *adv.* fertig; **~ cooked** vorgekocht. **3** *n.* **at the ~:** schussbereit, im Anschlag ⟨*Schusswaffe*⟩

ready: ~ 'cash ⇒ **~ money; ~-cooked** *adj.* vorgekocht; **~-cooked meal** Fertiggericht, *das;* Fertigmahlzeit, *die;* **~-'made** *adj.* (a) Konfektions⟨*anzug, -kleidung*⟩; **~-made curtains** Fertiggardinen; **(b)** (fig.) vorgefertigt; **~ 'money** *n.* **(a)** (cash) Bargeld, *das;* **(b)** (immediate payment) **for ~ money** gegen bar; **~ reckoner** /redɪ 'rekənə(r)/ *n.* Berechnungstabelle, *die;* (for conversion) Umrechnungstabelle, *die;* **~-to-eat** *adj.* Fertig⟨*mahlzeit, -dessert*⟩; **~-to-serve** *adj.* tischfertig; **~-to-'wear** *adj.* Konfektions⟨*anzug, -kleidung*⟩

reaffirm /riːəˈfɜːm/ *v.t.* [erneut] bekräftigen

reafforest /riːəˈfɒrɪst/ (Brit.) ⇒ **reforest**

reafforestation /riːəfɒrɪˈsteɪʃn/ (Brit.) ⇒ **reforestation**

real /rɪəl/ *adj.* **(a)** (actually existing) real ⟨*Gestalt, Ereignis, Lebewesen*⟩; wirklich ⟨*Macht*⟩; **(b)** (genuine) echt ⟨*Interesse, Gold, Seide*⟩; **(c)** (true) wahr ⟨*Grund, Freund, Name, Glück*⟩; echt ⟨*Mitleid, Vergnügen, Sieg*⟩; **the ~ thing** (genuine article) der/die/das Echte; **be [not] the ~ thing** [un]echt sein; **(d)** (Econ.) real; Real-; **in ~ terms** real ⟨*sinken, steigen*⟩; **(e)** **be for ~** (coll.) echt sein; ⟨*Angebot, Drohung:*⟩ ernst gemeint sein

real: ~ 'ale *n.* (Brit.) echtes Ale; **~ 'coffee** *n.* Bohnenkaffee, *der;* **~ e'state** *n.* (Law) Immobilien *Pl.*

realisation, realise ⇒ **realiz-**

realism /ˈrɪəlɪzm/ *n.* Realismus, *der*

realist /ˈrɪəlɪst/ *n.* Realist, *der*/Realistin, *die*

realistic /rɪəˈlɪstɪk/ *adj.* realistisch; **be ~ about sth.** etw. realistisch sehen

reality /rɪˈælɪtɪ/ *n.* **(a)** *no pl.* Realität, *die;* **bring sb. back to ~:** jmdn. in die Realität zurückholen; **in ~:** in Wirklichkeit; **(b)** *no pl.* (resemblance to original) Naturtreue, *die*

realization /rɪəlaɪˈzeɪʃn/ *n.* **(a)** (understanding) Erkenntnis, *die;* **(b)** (becoming real) Verwirklichung, *die;* **(c)** (Finance: act of selling) Realisierung, *die*

realize /ˈrɪəlaɪz/ *v.t.* **(a)** (be aware of) bemerken; realisieren; erkennen ⟨*Fehler*⟩; **~ [that]** ...: merken, dass ...; **I didn't ~** (abs.) ich habe es nicht gewusst/(had not noticed) bemerkt; **(b)** (make happen) verwirklichen; **(c)** (Finance: sell for cash) realisieren (fachspr.); in Geld (*Akk.*) umsetzen; **(d)** (fetch as price or profit) erbringen ⟨*Summe, Gewinn, Preis*⟩

real: ~ 'life *n.* das wirkliche Leben; die Realität; **~ life** *attrib. adj.* real

really /ˈrɪəlɪ/ *adv.* wirklich; **I don't ~/~ don't know what to do now** ich weiß eigentlich/wirklich nicht, was ich jetzt tun soll; **not ~:** eigentlich nicht; **that's not ~ a problem** das ist eigentlich kein Problem; **[well,] ~!** [also] so was!; **~?** wirklich?; tatsächlich?

realm /relm/ *n.* [König]reich, *das;* **be within/beyond the ~s of possibility** im/nicht im Bereich des Möglichen liegen

real time *n.* (Computing) Realzeit, *die;* Echtzeit, *die*

reap /riːp/ *v.t.* **(a)** (cut) schneiden ⟨*Getreide*⟩; **(b)** (gather in) einfahren ⟨*Getreide, Ernte*⟩; **(c)** (fig.) ernten ⟨*Ruhm, Lob*⟩; erhalten ⟨*Belohnung*⟩; erzielen ⟨*Gewinn*⟩

reappear /riːəˈpɪə(r)/ *v.i.* wieder auftauchen; (come back) [wieder] zurückkommen

reappearance /riːəˈpɪərəns/ *n.* Wiederauftauchen, *das*

reappraisal /riːəˈpreɪzl/ *n.* Neubewertung, *die*

reappraise /riːəˈpreɪz/ *v.t.* neu bewerten

rear¹ /rɪə(r)/ **1** *n.* **(a)** (back part) hinterer Teil; **at** *or* (Amer.) **in the ~** of im hinteren Teil (+ *Gen.*); **(b)** (back) Rückseite, *die;* **be in** *or* **bring up the ~** den Schluss bilden; **to the ~ of the house there is** ...: hinter dem Haus ist ...; **go round to the ~ of the house** hinter das Haus gehen; **(c)** (Mil.) rückwärtiger Teil; **(d)** (coll.: buttocks) Hintern, *der*

(ugs.). **2** *adj.* hinter ... ⟨*Eingang, Tür, Blinklicht*⟩; Hinter⟨*achse, -rad*⟩

rear² **1** *v.t.* **(a)** großziehen ⟨*Kind, Familie*⟩; halten ⟨*Vieh*⟩; hegen ⟨*Wild*⟩; **(b)** (lift up) heben ⟨*Kopf*⟩; **~ its ugly head** (fig.) seine hässliche Fratze zeigen. **2** *v.i.* ⟨*Pferd:*⟩ sich aufbäumen

rear: ~ 'door *n.* (Motor Veh.) Fondtür, *die;* Hintertür, *die;* **~guard** *n.* (Mil.) Nachhut, *die;* **~ light** *n.* Rücklicht, *das*

rearm /riːˈɑːm/ **1** *v.i.* wieder aufrüsten. **2** *v.t.* wieder aufrüsten ⟨*Land*⟩; wiederbewaffnen/(give more modern arms to) neu bewaffnen *od.* ausrüsten ⟨*Truppen*⟩

rearmament /riːˈɑːməmənt/ *n.* Wiederbewaffnung, *die;* (of country also) Wiederaufrüstung, *die*

rearrange /riːəˈreɪndʒ/ *v.t.* umräumen ⟨*Möbel, Zimmer*⟩; verlegen ⟨*Treffen, Spiel*⟩ (**for** auf + *Akk.*); ändern ⟨*Anordnung, Programm*⟩

rearrangement /riːəˈreɪndʒmənt/ *n.* ⇒ **rearrange:** Umräumen, *das;* Verlegung, *die;* Änderung, *die*

rear: ~-view 'mirror *n.* Rückspiegel, *der;* **~-wheel drive** **1** *n.* Hinterradantrieb, *der;* Heckantrieb, *der;* **2** *adj.* a **~-wheel drive vehicle** ein Fahrzeug mit Hinterrad- *od.* Heckantrieb; **the car is ~-wheel drive** das Auto hat Hinterrad- *od.* Heckantrieb

reason /ˈriːzn/ **1** *n.* **(a)** (cause) Grund, *der;* **there is [no/every] ~ to assume** *or* **believe that** ...: es besteht [kein/ein guter] Grund zu der Annahme, dass ...; **have no ~ to complain** *or* **for complain** sich nicht beklagen können; **for that [very] ~:** aus [eben] diesem Grund; **no particular ~** (as answer) einfach so; **all the more ~ for doing sth.** ein Grund mehr, etw. zu tun; **for no obvious ~:** aus keinem ersichtlichen Grund; **for the [simple] ~ that** ...: [einfach,] weil ...; **by ~ of** wegen; aufgrund; **with ~:** aus gutem Grund; **(b)** *no pl., no art.* (power to understand; sense; Philos.) Vernunft, *die;* (sanity) gesunder Verstand; **lose one's ~:** den Verstand verlieren; **you can have anything within ~:** du kannst alles haben, solange es im Rahmen bleibt; **stand to ~:** unzweifelhaft sein; **not listen to ~:** sich (*Dat.*) nichts sagen lassen; **see ~:** zur Einsicht kommen. **2** *v.i.* **(a)** schlussfolgern (**from** aus); **(b)** **~ with** diskutieren mit (**about, on** über + *Akk.*); **you can't ~ with her** mit ihr kann man nicht vernünftig reden. **3** *v.t.* schlussfolgern; **ours not to ~ why** es ist nicht unsere Sache, nach dem Warum zu fragen

~ 'out *v.t.* sich (*Dat.*) überlegen

reasonable /ˈriːzənbl/ *adj.* **(a)** vernünftig; angemessen, vernünftig ⟨*Forderung*⟩; **(b)** (inexpensive) günstig; **it's a ~ price** das ist ein vernünftiger Preis; **(c)** (fair) passabel ⟨*Leistung, Wein*⟩; **(d)** (within limits) realistisch ⟨*Chancen, Angebot*⟩

reasonably /ˈriːzənblɪ/ *adv.* **(a)** (within reason) vernünftig; **(b)** (moderately) **~ priced** preisgünstig; **(c)** (rather) ganz ⟨*gut*⟩; ziemlich ⟨*gesund*⟩

reasoned /ˈriːznd/ *adj.* durchdacht

reasoning /ˈriːzənɪŋ/ *n.* logisches Denken; (argumentation) Argumentation, *die*

reassurance /riːəˈʃʊərəns/ *n.* **(a)** (calming) **give sb. ~:** jmdn. beruhigen; **(b)** (confirmation in opinion) Bestätigung, *die;* **in pl.** [wiederholte] Versicherungen

reassure /riːəˈʃʊə(r)/ *v.t.* **(a)** (calm fears of) beruhigen; **(b)** (confirm in opinion) bestätigen

reassuring /riːəˈʃʊərɪŋ/ *adj.* beruhigend

rebate¹ /ˈriːbeɪt/ *n.* **(a)** (refund) Rückzahlung, *die;* **(b)** (discount) Rabatt, *der* (**on** auf + *Akk.*)

rebate² *n.* (groove) Falz, *der;* (to receive edge of door or window) Anschlag, *der*

rebel **1** /ˈrebl/ *n.* Rebell, *der*/Rebellin, *die.* **2** *attrib. adj.* **(a)** (of rebels) Rebellen-; **(b)** (refusing obedience to ruler) rebellisch; aufständisch. **3** /rɪˈbel/ *v.i.*, **-ll-** rebellieren

rebellion /rɪˈbeljən/ *n.* Rebellion, *die;* **rise [up] in ~:** rebellieren

rebellious /rɪˈbeljəs/ *adj.* (defiant) rebellisch; aufsässig

rebirth /riːˈbɜːθ/ *n.* **(a)** Wiedergeburt, *die;* **(b)** (revival) Wiederaufleben, *das*

reboot /riː'buːt/ *v.t.* (Computing) neu booten

reborn /riː'bɔːn/ *adj.* wieder geboren; **be ∼:** wieder geboren werden

rebound 1 /rɪ'baʊnd/ *v.i.* (a) (spring back) abprallen (**from** von); (b) (have adverse effect) zurückfallen (**upon** auf + *Akk.*). **2** /'riːbaʊnd/ *n.* (a) (recoil) Abprall, *der;* (b) (fig.: emotional reaction) **marry sb. on the ∼:** in seiner Enttäuschung jmdn. heiraten

rebuff /rɪ'bʌf/ **1** *n.* [schroffe] Abweisung; **be met with a ∼:** auf Ablehnung stoßen. **2** *v.t.* [schroff] zurückweisen

rebuild /riː'bɪld/ *v.t.*, **rebuilt** /riː'bɪlt/ (lit. or fig.) wieder aufbauen; (make extensive changes to) umbauen

rebuke /rɪ'bjuːk/ **1** *v.t.* tadeln, rügen (**for** wegen); **∼ sb. for doing sth.** jmdn. zurechtweisen, weil er etwas tut/ getan hat. **2** *n.* Rüge, *die;* Zurechtweisung, *die*

rebut /rɪ'bʌt/ *v.t.*, **-tt-** (formal) widerlegen

rebuttal /rɪ'bʌtl/ *n.* (Law) Widerlegung, *die*

recalcitrant /rɪ'kælsɪtrənt/ *adj.* aufsässig ⟨*Person*⟩

recall 1 /rɪ'kɔːl/ *v.t.* (a) (remember) sich erinnern an (+ *Akk.*); (b) (serve as reminder of) erinnern an (+ *Akk.*); **∼ sth. to sb.** jmdn. an etw. (*Akk.*) erinnern; (c) (summon back) zurückrufen ⟨*Soldat, fehlerhaftes Produkt*⟩; zurückfordern ⟨*Buch*⟩; (d) abberufen ⟨*Botschafter, Delegation*⟩ (**from** aus). **2** /rɪ'kɔːl, 'riːkɔːl/ *n.* (a) (ability to remember) [**powers of**] **∼:** Erinnerungsvermögen, *das;* Gedächtnis, *das;* (b) (possibility of annulling) **beyond** *or* **past ∼:** unwiderruflich; (c) (summons back) Rückruf, *der;* (to active duty) Wiedereinberufung, *die*

recant /riː'kænt/ **1** *v.i.* [öffentlich] widerrufen. **2** *v.t.* widerrufen

recap /'riːkæp/ (coll.) **1** *v.t. & i.*, **-pp-** rekapitulieren; kurz zusammenfassen. **2** *n.* Zusammenfassung, *die*

recapitulate /riːkə'pɪtjʊleɪt/ *v.t. & i.* rekapitulieren; kurz zusammenfassen

recapitulation /riːkəpɪtjʊ'leɪʃn/ *n.* Zusammenfassung, *die*

recapture /riː'kæptʃə(r)/ *v.t.* (a) (capture again) wieder ergreifen ⟨*Gefangenen*⟩; wieder einfangen ⟨*Tier*⟩; zurückerobern ⟨*Stadt*⟩; (b) (recreate) wieder lebendig werden lassen ⟨*Atmosphäre*⟩

recede /rɪ'siːd/ *v.i.* (a) ⟨*Hochwasser, Flut:*⟩ zurückgehen; ⟨*Küste:*⟩ zurückweichen; **his hair is beginning to ∼:** er bekommt eine Stirnglatze; (b) (be left at increasing distance) ∼ [**into the distance**] in der Ferne verschwinden

receding /rɪ'siːdɪŋ/ *adj.* fliehend ⟨*Kinn, Stirn*⟩; zurückgehend ⟨*Flut, Hochwasser*⟩

receipt /rɪ'siːt/ *n.* (a) (receiving) Empfang, *der;* **please acknowledge ∼ of this letter/order** bestätigen Sie bitte den Empfang dieses Briefes/dieser Bestellung; **be in ∼ of** (formal) erhalten haben ⟨*Brief*⟩; (b) (written acknowledgement) Empfangsbestätigung, *die;* Quittung, *die;* (c) *in pl.* (amount received) Einnahmen (**from** aus)

receive /rɪ'siːv/ *v.t.* (a) (get) erhalten; beziehen ⟨*Gehalt, Rente*⟩; verliehen bekommen ⟨*akademischer Grad*⟩; '**payment ∼d with thanks**' „Betrag dankend erhalten"; **∼d a lot of attention/sympathy [from him]** es wurde ihr [von ihm] viel Aufmerksamkeit/Verständnis entgegengebracht; **∼ [fatal] injuries** [tödlich] verletzt werden; **∼ 30 days [imprisonment]** 30 Tage Gefängnis bekommen; **∼ the sacraments/holy communion** (Relig.) das Abendmahl/die heilige Kommunion empfangen; (b) (accept) entgegennehmen ⟨*Bukett, Lieferung*⟩; (submit to) über sich (*Akk.*) ergehen lassen; **be convicted for receiving [stolen goods]** (Law) der Hehlerei überführt werden; (c) (serve as receptacle for) aufnehmen; (d) (greet) reagieren auf (*Akk.*), aufnehmen ⟨*Angebot, Nachricht, Theaterstück, Roman*⟩; empfangen ⟨*Person*⟩; (e) (entertain) empfangen ⟨*Botschafter, Delegation, Nachbarn, Gast*⟩; (f) (Radio, Telev.) empfangen ⟨*Sender, Signal*⟩; **are you receiving me?** können Sie mich hören?

receiver /rɪ'siːvə(r)/ *n.* (a) Empfänger, *der*/Empfängerin, *die;* (b) (Teleph.) [Telefon]hörer, *der;* (c) (Radio, Telev.) Empfänger, *der;* Receiver, *der* (Technik); (d) [**official**] ∼ (Law: for property of bankrupt) [gerichtlich bestellter/bestellte] Konkursverwalter/-verwalterin, *der*/*die;* (e) (of stolen goods) Hehler, *der*/Hehlerin, *die*

recent /'riːsənt/ *adj.* (a) (not long past) jüngst ⟨*Ereignisse, Wahlen, Vergangenheit usw.*⟩; **the ∼ closure of the factory** die kürzlich erfolgte Schließung der Fabrik; **at our ∼ meeting** als wir uns kürzlich *od.* vor kurzem trafen; **a ∼/more ∼ survey** eine neuere Untersuchung; **at our most ∼ meeting** bei unserer letzten Begegnung; (b) (not long established) Neu⟨*auflage, -anschaffung, -erscheinung*⟩

recently /'riːsəntlɪ/ *adv.* (a short time ago) neulich; kürzlich; vor kurzem; (in the recent past) in der letzten Zeit; **until ∼/until quite ∼:** bis vor kurzem/bis vor ganz kurzer Zeit; **∼ we've been following a different policy** seit kurzem verfolgen wir eine andere Politik; **as ∼ as last year** (last year still) noch letztes Jahr; **as ∼ as this morning** (not until this morning) [gerade] erst heute Morgen

receptacle /rɪ'septəkl/ *n.* Behälter, *der;* Gefäß, *das*

reception /rɪ'sepʃn/ *n.* (a) (welcome) (of person) Empfang, *der;* Aufnahme, *die;* (of play, speech) Aufnahme, *die;* **meet with a cool ∼:** kühl aufgenommen werden; **give sb. a warm ∼:** jmdn. herzlich empfangen; (b) (party) Empfang, *der;* **hold** *or* **give a ∼:** einen Empfang geben; (c) *no art.* (Brit.: foyer) die Rezeption; (d) *no art.* (Radio, Telev.) der Empfang

reception: ∼ class *n.* (Brit.) Vorschulklasse, *die;* Anfängerklasse, *die;* **∼ committee** *n.* Empfangskomitee, *das;* **∼ desk** *n.* Rezeption, *die*

receptionist /rɪ'sepʃənɪst/ *n.* ▶ **887**⟩ (in hotel) Empfangschef, *der*/-dame, *die;* (at doctor's, dentist's) Sprechstundenhilfe, *die;* (with firm) Empfangssekretärin, *die*

re'ception room *n.* Wohnzimmer, *das*

receptive /rɪ'septɪv/ *adj.* aufgeschlossen, empfänglich (**to** für); **have a ∼ mind** aufgeschlossen sein

recess /rɪ'ses, 'riːses/ *n.* (a) (alcove) Nische, *die;* (b) (Brit. Parl.; Amer.: short vacation) Ferien *Pl.;* (Amer. Sch.: between classes) Pause, *die*

recession /rɪ'seʃn/ *n.* (a) (Econ.: decline) Rezession, *die;* (b) (receding) Zurückgehen, *das*

recharge /riː'tʃɑːdʒ/ *v.t.* aufladen ⟨*Batterie*⟩; nachladen ⟨*Waffe*⟩

rechargeable /riː'tʃɑːdʒəbl/ *adj.* wiederaufladbar

recipe /'resɪpɪ/ *n.* (lit. or fig.) Rezept, *das;* **∼ for success** Erfolgsrezept, *das;* **it's a ∼ for disaster** damit ist die Katastrophe vorprogrammiert

recipient /rɪ'sɪpɪənt/ *n.* Empfänger, *der*/Empfängerin, *die*

reciprocal /rɪ'sɪprəkl/ *adj.* gegenseitig ⟨*Abkommen, Zuneigung, Hilfe*⟩

reciprocate /rɪ'sɪprəkeɪt/ **1** *v.t.* austauschen ⟨*Versprechen*⟩; erwidern ⟨*Gruß, Lächeln, Abneigung, Annäherungsversuch*⟩; sich revanchieren für ⟨*Hilfe*⟩. **2** *v.i.* (respond) sich revanchieren

recital /rɪ'saɪtl/ *n.* (a) (performance) [Solisten]konzert, *das;* (of literature also) Rezitation, *die;* (b) (detailed account) Schilderung, *die*

recitation /resɪ'teɪʃn/ *n.* Rezitation, *die*

recite /rɪ'saɪt/ **1** *v.t.* (a) (speak from memory) rezitieren ⟨*Passage, Gedicht*⟩; (b) (give list of) aufzählen. **2** *v.i.* rezitieren

reckless /'reklɪs/ *adj.* unbesonnen; rücksichtslos ⟨*Fahrweise*⟩; tollkühn ⟨*Fluchtversuch*⟩

reckon /'rekn/ **1** *v.t.* (a) (work out) ausrechnen ⟨*Kosten, Lohn, Ausgaben*⟩; bestimmen ⟨*Position*⟩; (b) (conclude) schätzen; **I ∼ you're lucky to be alive** ich glaube, du kannst von Glück sagen, dass du noch lebst!; **I ∼ to arrive** *or* **I shall arrive there by 8.30** ich nehme an, dass ich [spätestens] halb neun dort bin; **I usually ∼ to arrive there by 8.30** in der Regel bin ich [spätestens] halb neun dort; (c) (consider) halten (**as** für); **be ∼ed as** *or* **to be sth.** als etw. gelten; (d) (arrive at as total) kommen auf (+ *Akk.*). **2** *v.i.* rechnen

∼ 'in *v.t.* [mit] einrechnen

∼ on ⇒ **∼ upon**

∼ 'up 1 *v.t.* zusammenzählen. **2** *v.i.* **∼ up with sb.** mit jmdm. abrechnen

∼ upon *v.t.* (a) (rely on) zählen auf (+ *Akk.*); (b) (expect) rechnen mit

∼ with *v.i.* (a) (take into account) rechnen mit ⟨*Hindernis,*

Möglichkeit); **he is a man to be ~ed with** er ist ein Mann, den man nicht unterschätzen sollte; **(b)** (deal with) abrechnen mit

~ without *v.i.* nicht rechnen mit

reckoning /'rɛknɪŋ/ *n.* **(a)** (calculation) Berechnung, *die;* **by my ~:** nach meiner Rechnung; **day of ~** (fig.) Tag der Abrechnung; (moment of truth) Stunde der Wahrheit; **be [wildly] out in one's ~:** sich [gehörig] verrechnet haben; **(b)** (bill) Rechnung, *die*

reclaim /rɪ'kleɪm/ **1** *v.t.* **(a)** urbar machen (*Land, Wüste*); **~ land from the sea** dem Meer Land abgewinnen; **(b)** (for reuse) zur Wiederverwertung sammeln; wieder verwenden (*Rohstoff*). **2** *n.* **be past** *or* **beyond ~:** unwiederbringlich verloren sein

reclamation /rɛklə'meɪʃn/ *n.* Urbarmachung, *die;* **land ~:** Landgewinnung, *die*

recline /rɪ'klaɪn/ **1** *v.i.* **(a)** (lean back) sich zurücklehnen; **the chair ~s** die Rückenlehne des Sessels lässt sich [nach hinten] verstellen; **reclining seat** (in car) Liegesitz, *der;* **(b)** (be lying down) liegen. **2** *v.t.* [nach hinten] lehnen

recluse /rɪ'klu:s/ *n.* Einsiedler, *der*/Einsiedlerin, *die*

recognisable, recognise ⇒ **recogniz-**

recognition /rɛkəg'nɪʃn/ *n.* **(a)** *no pl., no art.* Wiedererkennen, *das;* **he's changed beyond all ~:** er ist nicht mehr wiederzuerkennen; **(b)** (acceptance, acknowledgement) Anerkennung, *die;* **achieve/receive ~:** Anerkennung finden; **in ~ of** als Anerkennung für

recognizable /'rɛkəgnaɪzəbl/ *adj.* erkennbar; deutlich (*Unterschied*); **be ~:** wiederzuerkennen sein

recognize /'rɛkəgnaɪz/ *v.t.* **(a)** (know again) wiedererkennen (**by** an + *Dat.*, **from** durch); **(b)** (acknowledge) erkennen; anerkennen (*Gültigkeit, Land, Methode, Leistung, Bedeutung, Dienst*); **be ~d as** angesehen werden *od.* gelten als; **(c)** (admit) zugeben; **(d)** (identify nature of) erkennen; **~ sb. to be a fraud** erkennen, dass jmd. ein Betrüger ist

recoil 1 /rɪ'kɔɪl/ *v.i.* **(a)** (shrink back) zurückfahren; **~ from an idea** vor einem Gedanken zurückschrecken; **(b)** (*Waffe*) einen Rückstoß haben. **2** /'ri:kɔɪl/ *n.* Rückstoß, *der*

recollect /rɛkə'lɛkt/ *v.t.* sich erinnern an (+ *Akk.*); **~ meeting sb.** sich daran erinnern, jmdn. getroffen zu haben

recollection /rɛkə'lɛkʃn/ *n.* Erinnerung, *die;* **have a/ no ~ of sth.** sich an etw. (*Akk.*) erinnern/nicht erinnern können

recommend /rɛkə'mɛnd/ *v.t.* **(a)** empfehlen; **~ sb. to do sth.** jmdm. empfehlen, etw. zu tun; **(b)** (make acceptable) sprechen für; **the plan has little/nothing to ~ it** es spricht wenig/nichts für den Plan

recommendation /rɛkəmɛn'deɪʃn/ *n.* Empfehlung, *die;* **on sb.'s ~:** auf jmds. Empfehlung (*Akk.*)

recompense /'rɛkəmpɛns/ (formal) **1** *v.t.* **(a)** (reward) belohnen; **(b)** (make amends to) entschädigen. **2** *n., no art., no pl.* **(a)** (reward) Anerkennung, *die;* **(b)** (compensation) Entschädigung, *die*

reconcile /'rɛkənsaɪl/ *v.t.* **(a)** (restore to friendship) versöhnen; **become ~d** sich versöhnen; **(b)** (resign oneself) **~ oneself** *or* **become/be ~d to sth.** sich mit etw. versöhnen; **(c)** (make compatible) in Einklang bringen (*Vorstellungen, Überzeugungen*); (show to be compatible) miteinander vereinen; **(d)** (settle) beilegen (*Meinungsverschiedenheit*)

reconciliation /rɛkənsɪlɪ'eɪʃn/ *n.* **(a)** (restoring to friendship) Versöhnung, *die;* **(b)** (making compatible) Harmonisierung, *die*

recondition /ri:kən'dɪʃn/ *v.t.* [general]überholen; **~ed engine** Austauschmotor, *der*

reconnaissance /rɪ'kɒnɪsəns/ *n., no pl., no def. art.* (Mil.) Aufklärung, *die;* (of area) Erkundung, *die;* **the plane was on ~:** das Flugzeug war auf einem Aufklärungsflug; *attrib.* **~ aircraft** Aufklärungsflugzeug, *das*

reconnoitre (*Brit.; Amer.:* **reconnoiter**) /rɛkə'nɔɪtə(r)/ **1** *v.t.* (esp. Mil.) auskundschaften; erkunden (*Gelände*); (fig.) erkunden. **2** *v.i.* (esp. Mil.) auf Erkundung [aus]gehen; (fig.) sich umsehen

reconsider /ri:kən'sɪdə(r)/ *v.t.* [noch einmal] überdenken; **~ a case** einen Fall von neuem aufrollen; *abs.* **there is still time to ~:** du kannst es dir/wir können es uns *usw.* immer noch überlegen

reconstruct /ri:kən'strʌkt/ *v.t.* (build again) wieder aufbauen (*Stadt, Gebäude*); neu errichten (*Gerüst*); rekonstruieren (*Anlage*); (fig.) rekonstruieren

reconstruction /ri:kən'strʌkʃn/ *n.* **(a)** (process) Wiederaufbau, *der;* **(b)** (thing reconstructed) Rekonstruktion, *die*

record 1 /rɪ'kɔ:d/ *v.t.* **(a)** aufzeichnen; **~ a new CD** eine neue CD aufnehmen; **~ sth. in a book/painting** etw. in einem Buch/auf einem Gemälde festhalten; **(b)** (register officially) dokumentieren; protokollieren (*Verhandlung*). **2** *v.i.* aufzeichnen; (on tape) Tonbandaufnahmen/eine Tonbandaufnahme machen. **3** /'rɛkɔ:d/ *n.* **(a)** **be on ~** (*Prozess, Verhandlung, Besprechung*) protokolliert sein; **there is no such case on ~:** ein solcher Fall ist nicht dokumentiert; **it is on ~ that ...:** es ist dokumentiert, dass ...; **have sth. on ~:** etw. dokumentiert haben; **put sth. on ~:** etw. schriftlich festhalten; **(b)** (report) Protokoll, *das;* (Law: official report) [Gerichts]akte, *die;* **(c)** (document) Dokument, *das;* (piece of evidence) Zeugnis, *das;* Beleg, *der;* **medical ~s** medizinische Unterlagen; **for the ~:** für das Protokoll; **just for the ~:** der Vollständigkeit halber; (iron.) nur der Ordnung halber; **[strictly] off the ~:** [ganz] inoffiziell; **get** *or* **keep** *or* **put** *or* **set the ~ straight** keine Missverständnisse aufkommen lassen; **(d)** (recorded disc) [Schall]platte, *die;* **(e)** (facts of sb.'s/sth.'s past) Ruf, *der;* **have a good ~ [of achievements]** gute Leistungen vorweisen können; **have a [criminal/police] ~:** vorbestraft sein; **(f)** (best performance) Rekord, *der;* **set a ~:** einen Rekord aufstellen; **break** *or* **beat the ~:** den Rekord brechen. **4** *attrib. adj.* Rekord-

record: ~-breaking *adj.* Rekord-; **~ deck** *n.* Plattenspieler, *der*

recorded /rɪ'kɔ:dɪd/ *adj.* aufgezeichnet (*Film, Konzert, Rede*); überliefert (*Ereignis, Geschichte*); bespielt (*Band*); **~ music** Musikaufnahmen

recorded de'livery *n.* (Brit. Post) eingeschriebene Sendung (ohne Versicherung)

recorder /rɪ'kɔ:də(r)/ *n.* **(a)** (instrument/apparatus) Aufzeichnungsgerät, *das;* **(b)** ⇒ **tape recorder; (c)** (Mus.) Blockflöte, *die*

'record holder *n.* (Sport) Rekordhalter, *der*/-halterin, *die*

recording /rɪ'kɔ:dɪŋ/ *n.* (what is recorded) Aufnahme, *die;* (to be heard or seen later) Aufzeichnung, *die*

recording: ~ head *n.* Aufnahmekopf, *der;* **~ session** *n.* Aufnahme, *die;* **~ studio** *n.* Tonstudio, *das*

record /'rɛkɔ:d/: **~ library** *n.* Phonothek, *die;* **~ player** *n.* Plattenspieler, *der;* **~ sleeve** *n.* Plattenhülle, *die;* Plattencover, *das;* **~ token** *n.* [Schall]plattengutschein, *der*

recount /rɪ'kaʊnt/ *v.t.* (tell) erzählen

re-count 1 /ri:'kaʊnt/ *v.t.* (count again) [noch einmal] nachzählen. **2** /'ri:kaʊnt/ *n.* Nachzählung, *die;* **have a ~:** nachzählen

recoup /rɪ'ku:p/ *v.t.* (regain) ausgleichen (*Verlust*); [wieder] hereinbekommen (*[Geld]einsatz*)

recourse /rɪ'kɔ:s/ *n.* **(a)** (resort) Zuflucht nahme, *die;* **have ~ to sb./sth.** bei jmdm./zu etw. Zuflucht nehmen; **(b)** (person or thing resorted to) Zuflucht, *die*

recover /rɪ'kʌvə(r)/ **1** *v.t.* **(a)** (regain) zurückerobern; (find again) wieder finden (*Verlorenes, Fährte, Spur*); **(c)** (retrieve) zurückbekommen; bergen (*Wrack*); **(d)** (make up for) aufholen (*verlorene Zeit*); **(e)** (acquire again) wiedergewinnen (*Vertrauen*); wieder finden (*Gleichgewicht, innere Ruhe usw.*); **~ consciousness** das Bewusstsein wiedererlangen; **~ one's senses** (lit. or fig.) wieder zur Besinnung kommen; **~ one's sight** sein Sehvermögen wiedergewinnen; **~ one's breath** wieder zu Atem kommen; **(f)** (reclaim) **~ land from the sea** dem Meer Land abgewinnen; **~ metal from scrap** Metall aus Schrott gewinnen; **(g)** (Law) erheben (*Steuer, Abgabe*); erhalten (*Schadenersatz, Schmerzensgeld*). **2** *v.i.* ▶865| **~ from sth.** sich von etw. [wieder] erholen; **how long will it take**

him to ∾? wann wird er wieder gesund sein?; **be [completely** *or* **fully]** ∾**ed** [völlig] wiederhergestellt sein

re-cover /riː'kʌvə(r)/ *v.t.* neu beziehen ⟨ *Sessel, Schirm usw.* ⟩

recovery /rɪ'kʌvərɪ/ *n.* **(a)** ▶ 865] (after illness) Erholung, *die;* **make a quick/good** ∾: sich schnell/gut erholen; **he is past** ∾: für ihn gibt es keine Hoffnung mehr; **(b)** (of sth. lost) Wiederfinden, *das;* **(c)** (of raw materials) Rückgewinnung, *die*

re'covery vehicle *n.* Bergungsfahrzeug, *das*

recreate /riːkrɪ'eɪt/ *v.t.* **(a)** (create over again) [wieder] neu [er]schaffen; wider aufleben lassen ⟨ *Industrie* ⟩; **(b)** (simulate, re-enact) nachempfinden, nachbilden ⟨ *Kunstwerk, Gegenstand* ⟩; reproduzieren (geh.) ⟨ *Atmosphäre, Klänge* ⟩; nachstellen ⟨ *Szene* ⟩

recreation /rekrɪ'eɪʃn/ *n.* (means of entertainment) Freizeitbeschäftigung, *die;* Hobby, *das;* **for** *or* **as a** ∾: zur Freizeitbeschäftigung *od.* Entspannung

recreational /rekrɪ'eɪʃənl/ *adj.* Freizeit⟨ *wert, -möglichkeiten, -gelände* ⟩; Erholungs⟨ *gebiet* ⟩; ∾ **drug** Freizeitdroge, *die;* Droge zum Entspannen; ∾ **vehicle** (Amer.) Wohnmobil, *das*

recreation: ∾ **centre** *n.* Freizeitzentrum, *das;* ∾ **ground** *n.* Freizeitgelände, *das*

recrimination /rɪkrɪmɪ'neɪʃn/ *n.* Gegenbeschuldigung, *die;* (counter-accusation) **[mutual]** ∾s [gegenseitige] Beschuldigungen

recruit /rɪ'kruːt/ **1** *n.* **(a)** (Mil.) Rekrut, *der;* **a raw** ∾: ein frisch Eingezogener; **(b)** (new member) neues Mitglied; **(c)** **[raw]** ∾ (fig.: novice) blutiger Anfänger. **2** *v.t.* **(a)** (Mil.: enlist) anwerben; (into society, party, etc.) werben ⟨ *Mitglied* ⟩; **(b)** (select for appointment) neu einstellen

recruitment /rɪ'kruːtmənt/ *n.* **(a)** (Mil.) Anwerbung, *die;* (for membership) ∾ **of members** Mitgliederwerbung, *die;* **(b)** (process of selecting for appointment) Neueinstellung, *die*

recta *pl. of* **rectum**

rectangle /'rektæŋgl/ *n.* Rechteck, *das*

rectangular /rek'tæŋgjʊlə(r)/ *adj.* rechteckig

rectify /'rektɪfaɪ/ *v.t.* korrigieren ⟨ *Fehler, Berechnung, Kurs* ⟩; richtig stellen ⟨ *Bemerkung, Sachverhalt* ⟩; Abhilfe schaffen (+ *Dat.*) ⟨ *Mangel, Missstand* ⟩

rector /'rektə(r)/ *n.* **(a)** Pfarrer, *der;* **(b)** (Univ.) Rektor, *der*/Rektorin, *die*

rectory /'rektərɪ/ *n.* Pfarrhaus, *das*

rectum /'rektəm/ *n., pl.* ∾s *or* **recta** /'rektə/ (Anat.) Mastdarm, *der;* Rektum, *das* (fachspr.)

recuperate /rɪ'kjuːpəreɪt/ **1** *v.i.* sich erholen. **2** *v.t.* wiederherstellen ⟨ *Gesundheit* ⟩

recuperation /rɪkjuːpə'reɪʃn/ *n.* Erholung, *die*

recur /rɪ'kɜː(r)/ *v.i.,* **-rr-:** **(a)** sich wiederholen; ⟨ *Krankheit, Beschwerden usw.* ⟩ wiederkehren; ⟨ *Problem, Symptom* ⟩ wieder auftreten; **(b)** (return to one's mind) ⟨ *Gedanke, Furcht, Gefühl* ⟩ wiederkehren; **(c)** (Math.) **2.3** ∾**ring** 2 Komma 3 Periode

recurrence /rɪ'kʌrəns/ *n.* Wiederholung, *die;* (of illness, complaint) Wiederkehr, *die;* (of problem, symptom) Wiederauftreten, *das*

recurrent /rɪ'kʌrənt/ *adj.* immer wiederkehrend; wiederholt ⟨ *Hinweis, Bezugnahme* ⟩

recyclable /riː'saɪkləbl/ *adj.* recycelbar

recycle /riː'saɪkl/ *v.t.* **(a)** (reuse) wieder verwerten ⟨ *Papier, Glas, Abfall* ⟩; (convert) wieder aufbereiten ⟨ *Metall, Brauchwasser, Abfall* ⟩

recycling /riː'saɪklɪŋ/ *n.* Recycling, *das;* Wiederaufbereitung, *die;* ∾ **plant** Recyclingwerk, *das*

red /red/ **1** *adj.* **(a)** rot; Rot⟨ *wild, -buche* ⟩; rot glühend ⟨ *Feuer, Lava usw.* ⟩; **go** ∾ **with shame** rot vor Scham werden; **go** ∾ **in the face** rot werden; **as** ∾ **as a beetroot** puterrot; rot wie eine Tomate (ugs. scherzh.); **her eyes were** ∾ **with crying** sie hatte rot geweinte Augen; *see also* **paint** 2 a; *see* 2 a; **(b) Red** (communist) rot, kommunistisch ⟨ *Soldat, Propaganda* ⟩; **the Red Army** die Rote Armee. **2** *n.* **(a)** (colour, traffic light) Rot, *das;* **underline sth. in** ∾: etw. rot unterstreichen; **(b)** (debt) **[be] in the** ∾: in den roten Zahlen [sein]; **(c) Red** (communist) Rote, *der*/*die*

red: ∾-**blooded** /'redblʌdɪd/ *adj.* heißblütig; ∾**brick** *adj.* (Brit.) weniger traditionsreich ⟨ *Universität* ⟩; ∾ '**carpet** *n.* (lit. *or* fig.) roter Teppich; ∾ **card** *n.* (Footb.) rote Karte; **he was shown the** ∾ **card** er bekam die rote Karte; **Red 'Cross** *n.* Rotes Kreuz; ∾'**currant** *n.* [rote] Johannisbeere

redden /'redn/ **1** *v.i.* ⟨ *Gesicht, Himmel:* ⟩ sich röten; ⟨ *Person:* ⟩ rot werden, erröten; ⟨ *Blätter, Wasser:* ⟩ sich rot färben. **2** *v.t.* rot färben; röten (geh.)

reddish /'redɪʃ/ *adj.* rötlich

redecorate /riː'dekəreɪt/ *v.t.* renovieren; (with wallpaper) neu tapezieren; (with paint) neu streichen

redeem /rɪ'diːm/ *v.t.* **(a)** (regain) wiederherstellen ⟨ *Ehre, Gesundheit* ⟩; wiedergewinnen ⟨ *Position* ⟩; **(b)** (buy back) tilgen ⟨ *Hypothek* ⟩; [wieder] einlösen ⟨ *Pfand* ⟩; abzahlen ⟨ *Grundstück* ⟩; **(c)** (convert) einlösen ⟨ *Gutschein, Coupon* ⟩; **(d)** (make amends for) ausgleichen, wettmachen ⟨ *Fehler, Schuld usw.* ⟩; **he has one** ∾**ing feature** man muss ihm eins zugute halten; **(e)** (repay) abzahlen ⟨ *Schuld, Kredit* ⟩; **(f)** (save) retten; **(g)** ∾ **oneself** sich freikaufen

Redeemer /rɪ'diːmə(r)/ *n.* (Relig.) Erlöser, *der;* Heiland, *der*

redemption /rɪ'dempʃn/ *n.* **(a)** (of pawned goods) Einlösen, *das;* Rückkauf, *der;* **(b)** (of tokens, trading stamps, stocks, etc.) Einlösen, *das;* **(c)** (of mortgage, debt) Tilgung, *die;* (of land) Abzahlung, *die;* **(d)** (of person, country) Befreiung, *die;* **he's past** *or* **beyond** ∾: für ihn gibt es keine Rettung mehr; **(e)** (deliverance from sin) Erlösung, *die*

redeploy /riːdɪ'plɔɪ/ *v.t.* umstationieren ⟨ *Truppen, Raketen* ⟩; woanders einsetzen ⟨ *Arbeitskräfte* ⟩

red: ∾-**eyed** *adj.* **be** ∾-**eyed** /'redaɪd/ rote Augen haben; ∾-**faced** /'redfeɪst/ *adj.* rotgesichtig; **be** ∾-**faced** (with rage/embarrassment) ein [hoch]rotes Gesicht haben/vor Verlegenheit rot werden; ∾-**haired** *adj.* rothaarig; ∾-'**handed** *adj.* **catch sb.** ∾-**handed** jmdn. auf frischer Tat ertappen; ∾-**head** *n.* Rotschopf, *der* (ugs.); Rothaarige, *der/die;* ∾-**headed** *adj.* rothaarig; ∾-'**herring** *n.* (fig.) Ablenkungsmanöver, *das;* (in thriller, historical research) falsche Fährte; ∾-**hot** *adj.* **(a)** [rot]glühend; **(b)** (fig.) glühend ⟨ *Anhänger, Gläubiger* ⟩; heiß ⟨ *Blondine, Thema, Musik* ⟩; brandaktuell ⟨ *Nachricht* ⟩

redial **1** /riː'daɪəl/ *v.t.* noch einmal wählen ⟨ *Telefonnummer* ⟩; *abs.* noch einmal wählen; **to** ∾, **just press the button** zur Wahlwiederholung einfach die Taste drücken. **2** /'riːdaɪəl/ *n.* Wahlwiederholung, *die;* **last number** ∾: Wahlwiederholung, *die;* ∾ **button** Wahlwiederholungstaste, *die*

redid ⇒ **redo**

Red 'Indian (Brit.) **1** *n.* Indianer, *der*/Indianerin, *die.* **2** *adj.* Indianer-

redirect /riːdaɪ'rekt, riːdɪ'rekt/ *v.t.* nachsenden ⟨ *Post, Brief usw.* ⟩; umleiten ⟨ *Verkehr* ⟩; weiterleiten (**to** an + *Akk.*) ⟨ *Anfrage* ⟩

rediscover /riːdɪ'skʌvə(r)/ *v.t.* wieder entdecken

redistribute /riːdɪ'strɪbjuːt/ *v.t.* umverteilen

red: ∾-'**letter day** *n.* (memorable day) im Kalender rot anzustreichender Tag; großer Tag; ∾ '**light** *n.* **(a)** [rotes] Warnlicht; (of traffic lights) rote [Verkehrs]ampel; **(b)** (fig.) Warnzeichen, *das;* ∾-'**light district** *n.* Amüsierviertel, *das;* Strich, *der* (salopp); ∾-**neck** *n.* (Amer.) armer weißer Landbewohner aus den Südstaaten; (derog.) weißer Rassist *od.* Reaktionär

redness /'rednɪs/ *n., no pl.* (of face, skin, eyes, sky) Röte, *die;* (of blood, fire, rose, dress, light) rote Farbe

redo /riː'duː/ *v.t.,* **redoes** /riː'dʌz/, **redoing** /riː'duːɪŋ/, **redid** /riː'dɪd/, **redone** /riː'dʌn/ (do again) wiederholen ⟨ *Prüfung, Spiel, Test* ⟩; neu frisieren ⟨ *Haare* ⟩; erneuern ⟨ *Make-up, Lidschatten* ⟩; noch einmal machen ⟨ *Bett, Hausaufgabe* ⟩; überarbeiten ⟨ *Aufsatz, Überarbeitung, Komposition* ⟩

redone ⇒ **redo**

redouble /riː'dʌbl/ **1** *v.t.* verdoppeln. **2** *v.i.* sich verdoppeln

redoubtable /rɪ'daʊtəbl/ *adj.* Ehrfurcht gebietend ⟨ *Person* ⟩; gewaltig ⟨ *Aufgabe, Pflicht usw.* ⟩; gefürchtet ⟨ *Gegner, Krieger* ⟩

red: ~ **'pepper** *n.* (a) ⇒ **cayenne;** (b) (vegetable) ⇒ **pepper 1 b;** ~ **'rag** *n.* (fig.) rotes Tuch (to für); **be like a ~ rag to a bull [to sb.]** wie ein rotes Tuch [auf jmdn.] wirken

redress /rɪ'dres/ **1** *n.* (reparation, correction) Entschädigung, *die;* **seek** ~ **for sth.** eine Entschädigung für etw. verlangen; **seek [legal]** ~**:** auf Schadenersatz klagen; **have no** ~**:** keine Entschädigung erhalten; (Law) keinen Rechtsanspruch auf Entschädigung haben. **2** *v.t.* (a) (adjust again) ins Gleichgewicht bringen; ~ **the balance** das Gleichgewicht wiederherstellen; (b) (set right, rectify) wieder gutmachen ‹ *Unrecht* ›; ausgleichen ‹ *Ungerechtigkeiten* ›; abhelfen (+ *Dat.*) ‹ *Beschwerden, Missbrauch* ›

Red 'Sea *pr. n.* Rote Meer, *das*

red: ~**skin** ⇒ **Red Indian 1;** ~ **'squirrel** *n.* Eichhörnchen, *das;* ~ **'tape** *n.* (fig.) [unnötige] Bürokratie

reduce /rɪ'dju:s/ *v.t.* (a) (diminish) senken ‹ *Preis, Gebühr, Fieber, Aufwendungen, Blutdruck usw.* ›; verbilligen ‹ *Ware* ›; reduzieren ‹ *Geschwindigkeit, Gewicht, Anzahl, Menge, Preis* ›; **at** ~**d prices** zu herabgesetzten Preisen; (b) ~ **to despair/silence/tears** in Verzweiflung stürzen/verstummen lassen/zum Weinen bringen; ~ **sb. to begging** jmdn. an den Bettelstab bringen; **be** ~**d to starvation** hungern müssen

reduction /rɪ'dʌkʃn/ *n.* (a) (amount, process) (in price, costs, wages, rates, speed, etc.) Senkung, *die* (**in** *Gen.*); (in numbers, output, etc.) Verringerung, *die* (**in** *Gen.*); **in prices/wages** Preis-/Lohnsenkung, *die;* **there is a** ~ **on all furniture** alle Möbel sind im Preis heruntergesetzt; **a** ~ **of £10** ein Preisnachlass von 10 Pfund; (b) (smaller copy) Verkleinerung, *die*

redundancy /rɪ'dʌndənsɪ/ *n.* (a) (Brit.) Arbeitslosigkeit, *die;* **redundancies** Entlassungen; **take** *or* **accept voluntary** ~**:** seiner betriebsbedingten Kündigung zustimmen; (b) (being more than needed) Überfluss, *der*

re'dundancy payment *n.* Abfindung, *die*

redundant /rɪ'dʌndənt/ *adj.* (a) (Brit.: now unemployed) arbeitslos; **be made** *or* **become** ~**:** den Arbeitsplatz verlieren; **make** ~**:** entlassen; (b) (more than needed) überflüssig

red 'wine *n.* Rotwein, *der*

reed /ri:d/ *n.* (a) (Bot.) Schilf[rohr], *das;* Ried, *das;* (b) (Mus.: part of instrument) Rohrblatt, *das*

'reed instrument *n.* (Mus.) Rohrblattinstrument, *das*

re-educate /ri:'edjʊkeɪt/ *v.t.* umerziehen

re-education /ri:edjʊ'keɪʃn/ *n., no pl.* Umerziehung, *die*

reef /ri:f/ *n.* (ridge) Riff, *das*

'reef knot *n.* Kreuzknoten, *der*

reek /ri:k/ **1** *n.* Geruch, *der;* Gestank, *der* (abwertend). **2** *v.i.* riechen, (abwertend) stinken (**of** nach)

reel /ri:l/ **1** *n.* (a) (roller, cylinder) ‹ *Papier-, Schlauch-, Garn-, Angel* ›rolle, *die;* ‹ *Film-, Tonband-, Garn* ›spule, *die;* (b) (quantity) Rolle, *die;* (c) (dance, music) Reel, *der.* **2** *v.t.* ~ **[up]** (wind on) aufspulen. **3** *v.i.* (a) (be in a whirl) sich drehen; **his head was** ~**ing** in seinem Kopf drehte sich alles; (b) (sway) torkeln; (fig.: be shaken) taumeln

~ **'in** *v.t.* an Land ziehen ‹ *Fisch* ›

~ **'off** *v.t.* (say rapidly) herunterleiern (ugs. abwertend), hersagen ‹ *Geschichte* ›; (without apparent effort) abspulen (ugs.) ‹ *Gedicht, Namen, Einzelheiten* ›

re-elect /ri:ɪ'lekt/ *v.t.* wieder wählen

re-election /ri:ɪ'lekʃn/ *n.* Wiederwahl, *die*

re-enact /ri:ɪ'nækt/ *v.t.* nachspielen ‹ *Szene, Schlacht* ›; ~ **a crime** den Hergang eines Verbrechens nachspielen

re-enter /ri:'entə(r)/ **1** *v.i.* wieder eintreten; (b) (for race, exam, etc.) wieder antreten. **2** *v.t.* wieder betreten ‹ *Raum, Gebäude* ›; wieder eintreffen in (+ *Dat.*) ‹ *Ortschaft* ›; wieder einreisen in (+ *Akk.*) ‹ *Land* ›; wieder eintreten in (+ *Akk.*) ‹ *Erdatmosphäre* ›

re-entry /ri:'entrɪ/ *n.* Wiedereintreten, *das;* (into country) Wiedereinreise, *die;* (of spacecraft) Wiedereintritt, *der*

ref /ref/ *n.* (Sport coll.) Schiri, *der* (Sportjargon); (Boxing) Ringrichter, *der*

ref. *abbr.* **our/your** ~**:** unser/Ihr Zeichen

refashion /ri:'fæʃn/ *v.t.* umgestalten

refectory /rɪ'fektərɪ/ *n.* Mensa, *die*

refer /rɪ'fɜ:(r)/ **1** *v.i.,* **-rr-:** (a) ~ **to** (allude to) sich beziehen auf (+ *Akk.*) ‹ *Buch, Person usw.* ›; (speak of) sprechen von ‹ *Person, Problem, Ereignis usw.* ›; (b) ~ **to** (apply to, relate to) betreffen; ‹ *Beschreibung:* › sich beziehen auf (+ *Akk.*); **does that remark** ~ **to me?** gilt diese Bemerkung mir?; (c) ~ **to** (consult, cite as proof) konsultieren (geh.); nachsehen in (+ *Dat.*). **2** *v.t.,* **-rr-** (send on to) ~ **sb./sth. to sb./sth.** jmdn./etw. an jmdn./auf etw. (*Akk.*) verweisen; ~ **a patient to a specialist** einen Patienten an einen Facharzt überweisen; ~ **sb. to a paragraph/ an article** jmdn. auf einen Absatz/Artikel aufmerksam machen

referee /refə'ri:/ **1** *n.* (a) ▶ 887 | (Sport: umpire) Schiedsrichter, *der*/-richterin, *die;* (Boxing) Ringrichter, *der;* (Wrestling) Kampfrichter, *der;* (b) (Brit.) ⇒ **reference e;** (c) (person who assesses) Gutachter, *der*/Gutachterin, *die.* **2** *v.t.* (Sport: umpire) als Schiedsrichter/-richterin leiten; ~ **a football game** ein Fußballspiel pfeifen *od.* leiten. **3** *v.i.* (Sport: umpire) Schiedsrichter/-richterin sein

reference /'refrəns/ *n.* (a) (allusion) Hinweis, *der* (**to** auf + *Akk.*); **make [several]** ~**[s] to sth.** sich [mehrfach] auf etw. (*Akk.*) beziehen; **make no** ~ **to sth.** etw. nicht ansprechen; (b) (note directing reader) Verweis, *der* (**to** auf + *Akk.*); (c) (cited book, passage) Quellenangabe, *die;* (d) (testimonial) Zeugnis, *das;* Referenz, *die;* **character** ~**:** persönliche Referenzen; **give sb. a good** ~**:** jmdm. ein gutes Zeugnis ausstellen; (e) (person willing to testify) Referenz, *die;* **quote sb. as one's** ~**:** jmdn. als Referenz angeben; (f) (act of referring) Konsultation, *die* (**to** *Gen.*) (geh.); ~ **to a dictionary/map** Nachschlagen in einem Wörterbuch/ Nachsehen auf einer Karte; **work of** ~**:** Nachschlagewerk, *das*

reference: ~ **book** *n.* Nachschlagewerk, *das;* ~ **mark** *n.* Verweiszeichen, *das;* ~ **number** *n.* [Kenn]nummer, *die;* ~ **point** *n.* Bezugspunkt, *der*

referendum /refə'rendəm/ *n.,* pl. ~**s** *or* **referenda** /refə'rendə/ Volksentscheid, *der;* Referendum, *das*

refill 1 /ri:'fɪl/ *v.t.* nachfüllen ‹ *Glas, Feuerzeug* ›; neu füllen ‹ *Kissen* ›; mit einer neuen Füllung versehen ‹ *Zahn* ›; ~ **the glasses** nachschenken. **2** /'ri:fɪl/ *n.* (a) (cartridge) [Nachfüll]patrone, *die;* (for ball pen) Ersatzmine, *die;* (b) **can I have a** ~? (coll.) gießt du mir noch einmal nach?

refine /rɪ'faɪn/ **1** *v.t.* (a) (purify) raffinieren; (b) (make cultured) kultivieren; (c) (improve) verbessern; verfeinern ‹ *Stil, Technik* ›. **2** *v.i.* (a) (become pure) rein werden; (b) (become more cultured) sich verfeinern

refined /rɪ'faɪnd/ *adj.* (a) (purified) raffiniert; Fein‹ *kupfer, -silber usw.* ›; ~ **sugar** [Zucker]raffinade, *die;* (b) (cultured) kultiviert

refinement /rɪ'faɪnmənt/ *n.* (a) (purifying) Raffination, *die;* (b) (fineness of feeling, elegance) Kultiviertheit, *die;* (c) (improvement) Verbesserung, *die;* Weiterentwicklung, *die* ([**up**]**on** *Gen.*)

refinery /rɪ'faɪnərɪ/ *n.* Raffinerie, *die*

refit 1 /ri:'fɪt/ *v.t.,* **-tt-** überholen; reparieren; (equip with new things) neu ausstatten. **2** (renew supplies or equipment) sich neu ausrüsten. **3** /'ri:fɪt/ *n.* Überholung, *die;* (with supplies or equipment) Neuausstattung, *die*

reflate /ri:'fleɪt/ *v.t.* (Econ.) ankurbeln ‹ *Wirtschaft, Konjunktur* ›

reflation /ri:'fleɪʃn/ *n.* (Econ.) Reflation, *die*

reflect /rɪ'flekt/ **1** *v.t.* (a) (throw back) reflektieren; (b) (reproduce) spiegeln; (fig.) widerspiegeln ‹ *Ansichten, Gefühle, Werte* ›; **be** ~**ed** sich spiegeln; (c) (contemplate) nachdenken über (+ *Akk.*). **2** *v.i.* (meditate) nachdenken

~ **[up]on** *v.t.* (consider, contemplate) nachdenken über (+ *Akk.*) abwägen ‹ *Konsequenzen* ›

reflection /rɪ'flekʃn/ *n.* (a) (of light etc.) Reflexion, *die;* (by surface of water etc.) Spiegelung, *die;* (b) (reflected light, heat, or colour) Reflexion, *die;* (image, lit. or fig.) Spiegelbild, *das;* (c) (meditation, consideration) Nachdenken, *das* (**upon** über + *Akk.*); **be lost in** ~**:** in Gedanken versunken sein; **on** ~**:** bei weiterem Nachdenken; **on** ~**, I think …:** wenn ich mir das recht überlege, [so] glaube ich ...; **(d)** (remark) Reflexion, die (geh.), Betrachtung, *die* (**on** über + *Akk.*)

reflective /rɪˈflektɪv/ *adj.* **(a)** reflektierend; **be ~:** reflektieren; **(b)** (thoughtful) nachdenklich

reflector /rɪˈflektə(r)/ *n.* **(a)** Rückstrahler, *der;* **(b)** (telescope) Reflektor, *der*

reflex /ˈriːfleks/ **1** *n.* (Physiol.) Reflex, *der.* **2** *adj.* (by reflection) Reflex-

reflex: ~ action *n.* (Physiol.) Reflexhandlung, *die;* **~ camera** *n.* (Photog.) Spiegelreflexkamera, *die*

reflexive /rɪˈfleksɪv/ *adj.* (Ling.) reflexiv

reflex reˈaction *n.* (Physiol.; also fig.) Reflexreaktion, *die*

refloat /riːˈfləʊt/ *v.t.* [wieder] flottmachen ⟨*Schiff*⟩; (fig.) wieder flüssig machen (ugs.)

reforest /riːˈfɒrɪst/ *v.t.* wieder aufforsten

reforestation /riːfɒrɪˈsteɪʃn/ *n.*, *no pl.* Wiederaufforstung, *die*

reform /rɪˈfɔːm/ **1** *v.t.* **(a)** (make better) bessern ⟨*Person*⟩; reformieren ⟨*Institution*⟩; **(b)** (abolish) **~ sth.** mit etw. aufräumen. **2** *v.i.* sich bessern. **3** *n.* (of person) Besserung, *die;* (in a system) Reform, *die* (**in** *Gen.*)

re-form /riːˈfɔːm/ **1** *v.t.* neu gründen ⟨*Gesellschaft usw.*⟩. **2** *v.i.* sich neu bilden; ⟨*Band, Gesellschaft:*⟩ neu gegründet werden

reformation /refəˈmeɪʃn/ *n.* (of person, character) Wandlung, *die* (**in** + *Gen.*); **the R~** (Hist.) die Reformation

reformed /rɪˈfɔːmd/ *adj.* gewandelt; **he's a ~ character** er hat sich positiv verändert

reformer /rɪˈfɔːmə(r)/ *n.* [**political**] **~:** Reformpolitiker, *der/*-politikerin, *die*

refraction /rɪˈfrækʃn/ *n.* (Phys.) Brechung, *die*

refractor /rɪˈfræktə(r)/ *n.* (telescope) Refraktor, *der*

refractory /rɪˈfræktərɪ/ *adj.* **(a)** (stubborn) störrisch; widerspenstig; **(b)** (heat-resistant) hitzebeständig

refrain[1] /rɪˈfreɪn/ *n.* Refrain, *der*

refrain[2] *v.i.* **~ from doing sth.** es unterlassen, etw. zu tun; ʻ**please ~ from smoking**ʼ „bitte nicht rauchen"; **he ~ed from comment** er enthielt sich jeden Kommentars (geh.)

refresh /rɪˈfreʃ/ *v.t.* **(a)** erfrischen; (with food and/or drink) stärken; **~ oneself** (with rest) sich ausruhen; (with food and/or drink) sich stärken; **(b)** auffrischen ⟨*Wissen*⟩; **let me ~ your memory** lassen Sie mich Ihrem Gedächtnis nachhelfen

refreshing /rɪˈfreʃɪŋ/ *adj.* **(a)** wohltuend ⟨*Abwechslung, Ruhe*⟩; erfrischend ⟨*Brise, Schlaf, Getränk*⟩; **(b)** (interesting) erfrischend

refreshment /rɪˈfreʃmənt/ *n.* Erfrischung, *die*

refreshment: ~ room *n.* Imbissstube, *die;* **~ stall** *n.* Erfrischungsstand, *der*

refrigerate /rɪˈfrɪdʒəreɪt/ *v.t.* **(a)** kühl lagern ⟨*Lebensmittel*⟩; **(b)** (chill) kühlen; (freeze) einfrieren; **(c)** (make cool) abkühlen ⟨*Luft*⟩

refrigeration /rɪfrɪdʒəˈreɪʃn/ *n.* kühle Lagerung; (chilling) Kühlung, *die;* (freezing) Einfrieren, *das*

refrigerator /rɪˈfrɪdʒəreɪtə(r)/ *n.* Kühlschrank, *der*

refuel /riːˈfjuːəl/, (Brit.) **-ll-: 1** *v.t.* auftanken. **2** *v.i.* [auf]tanken

refuge /ˈrefjuːdʒ/ *n.* Zuflucht, *die;* **take ~ in** Schutz *od.* Zuflucht suchen in (+ *Dat.*) (**from** vor + *Dat.*); **women's ~:** Frauenhaus, *das*

refugee /refjʊˈdʒiː/ *n.* Flüchtling, *der;* **economic ~:** Wirtschaftsflüchtling, *der*

refuˈgee camp *n.* Flüchtlingslager, *das*

refund 1 /riːˈfʌnd/ *v.t.* (pay back) zurückzahlen ⟨*Geld, Schulden*⟩; erstatten ⟨*Kosten*⟩. **2** /ˈriːfʌnd/ *n.* Rückzahlung, *die;* (of expenses) [Rück]erstattung, *die;* **obtain a ~ of sth.** etw. zurückbekommen

refurbish /riːˈfɜːbɪʃ/ *v.t.* renovieren ⟨*Haus*⟩; aufarbeiten ⟨*Kleidung*⟩; aufpolieren ⟨*Möbel*⟩

refusal /rɪˈfjuːzl/ *n.* Ablehnung, *die;* (after a period of time) Absage, *die;* (of admittance, entry, permission) Verweigerung, *die;* **~ to do sth.** Weigerung, etw. zu tun; **have/get [the]**

first ~ on sth. das Vorkaufsrecht für etw. haben/eingeräumt bekommen

refuse[1] /rɪˈfjuːz/ **1** *v.t.* **(a)** ablehnen; abweisen ⟨*Heiratsantrag*⟩; verweigern ⟨*Nahrung, Befehl, Bewilligung, Zutritt, Einreise, Erlaubnis*⟩; **~ sb. admittance/ entry/permission** jmdm. den Zutritt/die Einreise/die Erlaubnis verweigern; **~ to do sth.** sich weigern, etw. zu tun; **(b)** (not oblige) abweisen ⟨*Person*⟩; **(c)** ⟨*Pferd:*⟩ verweigern ⟨*Hindernis*⟩. **2** *v.i.* **(a)** ablehnen; (after request) sich weigern; **(b)** ⟨*Pferd:*⟩ verweigern

refuse[2] /ˈrefjuːs/ *n.* Müll, *der;* Abfall, *der*

refuse /ˈrefjuːs/: ~ collection *n.* Müllabfuhr, *die;* **~ collector** *n.* ▶ 887 | Müllwerker, *der;* **~ disposal** *n.* Abfallbeseitigung, *die;* **~ heap** *n.* Müllhaufen, *der*

refute /rɪˈfjuːt/ *v.t.* widerlegen

regain /rɪˈgeɪn/ *v.t.* zurückgewinnen ⟨*Zuversicht, Vertrauen, Augenlicht*⟩; zurückerobern ⟨*Gebiet*⟩; **~ control of sth.** etw. wieder unter Kontrolle bringen; *see also* **consciousness a**

regal /ˈriːgl/ *adj.* **(a)** (magnificent, stately) majestätisch ⟨*Person, Baum, Art, Tier, Würde*⟩; groß ⟨*Luxus*⟩; **(b)** (royal) königlich

regale /rɪˈgeɪl/ *v.t.* (entertain) verwöhnen (**with, on** mit); **~ sb. with stories** jmdn. mit Geschichten unterhalten

regalia /rɪˈgeɪlɪə/ *n. pl.* **(a)** (of royalty) Krönungsinsignien *Pl.;* **(b)** (of order) Ordensinsignien *Pl.*

regard /rɪˈgɑːd/ **1** *v.t.* **(a)** (gaze upon) betrachten; **(b)** (give heed to) beachten ⟨*jmds. Worte, Rat*⟩; Rücksicht nehmen auf (+ *Akk.*) ⟨*Wunsch, Gesundheit, jmds. Recht*⟩; **(c)** (fig.: look upon) betrachten; **~ sb. kindly/warmly** jmdm. freundlich gesinnt/herzlich zugetan sein; **~ sb. with envy/scorn** neidisch auf jmdn. sein/jmdn. verachten; **~ sb. as a friend/fool** jmdn. als Freund betrachten/für einen Dummkopf halten; **be ~ed as** gelten als; **~ sth. as wrong** etw. für falsch halten; **(d)** (concern, have relation to) betreffen; berücksichtigen ⟨*Tatsachen*⟩; **as ~s sb./sth., ~ing sb./sth.** was jmdn./etw. angeht *od.* betrifft. **2** *n.* **(a)** (attention) Beachtung, *die;* **pay ~ to/have ~ to or for sb./ sth.** jmdn./etw. Beachtung schenken; **without ~ to** ohne Rücksicht auf (+ *Akk.*); **(b)** (esteem, kindly feeling) Achtung, *die;* **hold sb./sth. in high/low ~, have or show a high/low ~ for sb./sth.** jmdn./etw. sehr schätzen/geringschätzen; **(c)** *in pl.* Grüße; **send one's ~s** grüßen lassen; **give her my ~s** grüße sie von mir; **with kind[est] ~s** mit herzlich[st]en Grüßen; **(d)** (relation, respect) Beziehung, *die;* **in this ~:** in dieser Beziehung *od.* Hinsicht; **in** *or* **with ~ to sb./sth.** in Bezug auf jmdn./etw.

regarding /rɪˈgɑːdɪŋ/ ⇒ **regard 1 d**

regardless /rɪˈgɑːdlɪs/ **1** *adj.* **~ of sth.** ungeachtet *od.* trotz einer Sache (*Gen.*); **~ of the cost** ohne Rücksicht auf die Kosten. **2** *adv.* trotzdem; **carry on ~:** trotzdem weitermachen

regatta /rɪˈgætə/ *n.* Regatta, *die*

regenerate /rɪˈdʒenəreɪt/ *v.t.* **(a)** (generate again, recreate) regenerieren (bes. Chemie, Biol.); **(b)** (improve, reform) erneuern ⟨*Kirche, Gesellschaft*⟩; **feel ~d** sich wie neu geboren fühlen

regeneration /rɪdʒenəˈreɪʃn/ *n.* **(a)** (re-creation) Neuentstehung, *die;* (fig.: revival, renaissance) Wiederbelebung, *die;* (of church, society) Erneuerung, *die;* **(b)** (Biol.: regrowth) Regeneration, *die* (fachspr.); Neubildung, *die*

regent /ˈriːdʒənt/ *n.* Regent, *der/*Regentin, *die*

reggae /ˈregeɪ/ *n.* (Mus.) Reggae, *der*

regime, régime /reɪˈʒiːm/ *n.* (system) [Regierungs]system, *das;* (derog.) Regime, *das;* (fig.) bestehende Ordnung

regiment 1 /ˈredʒɪmənt/ *n.* **(a)** (Mil.: organizational unit) Regiment, *das;* **parachute ~:** Luftlanderegiment, *das;* **(b)** (Mil.: operational unit) Abteilung, *die;* **tank ~:** Panzerabteilung, *die.* **2** /ˈredʒɪmənt, ˈredʒɪment/ *v.t.* (organize) reglementieren

regimental /redʒɪˈmentl/ (Mil.) *adj.* Regiments⟨*kleidung, -vorräte*⟩

regimentation /redʒɪmenˈteɪʃn, redʒɪmenˈteɪʃn/ *n.* Reglementierung, *die*

region /'riːdʒn/ n. (a) (area) Gebiet, das; (b) (administrative division) Bezirk, der; **administrative** ∼: Verwaltungsbezirk, der; **Strathclyde R**∼: Bezirk Strathclyde; (c) (fig.: sphere) Bereich, der; Gebiet, das; **in the** ∼ **of two tons** ungefähr zwei Tonnen

regional /'riːdʒənl/ adj. regional ⟨System, Akzent, Förderung⟩; Regional⟨planung, -fernsehen, -programm⟩

register /'redʒɪstə(r)/ **1** n. (book, list) Register, das; (at school) Klassenbuch, das; **parish/hotel/marriage** ∼: Kirchen-/Fremden-/Heiratsbuch, das; ∼ **of births, deaths and marriages** Personenstandsbuch, das; **medical** ∼: Ärzteregister, das; **electoral** ∼: Wählerverzeichnis, das. **2** v.t. (a) (set down) schriftlich festhalten ⟨Name, Zahl, Detail⟩; (b) (enter) registrieren ⟨Geburt, Heirat, Todesfall, Patent⟩; (cause to be entered) registrieren lassen; eintragen ⟨Warenzeichen, Firma, Verein⟩; anmelden ⟨Auto, Patent⟩; abs. (at hotel) sich ins Fremdenbuch eintragen; ∼ **[oneself] with the police** sich polizeilich anmelden; (c) (enrol) anmelden; (Univ.) einschreiben; immatrikulieren; (as voter) eintragen (**on** in + Akk.) ⟨Person⟩; abs. (as student) sich einschreiben od. immatrikulieren; (in list of voters) sich ins Wählerverzeichnis eintragen lassen; (d) (Post) eingeschrieben versenden; **have sth.** ∼**ed** etw. einschreiben lassen; (e) zum Ausdruck bringen ⟨Entsetzen, Überraschung⟩; ∼ **a protest** Protest anmelden. **3** v.i. (make impression) einen Eindruck machen (**on**, **with** auf+ Akk.); **it didn't** ∼ **with him** er hat das nicht registriert

registered /'redʒɪstəd/ adj. [ins Standesregister] eingetragen ⟨Taufe, Heirat⟩; [ins Handelsregister] eingetragen ⟨Firma⟩; eingeschrieben, immatrikuliert ⟨Student⟩; eingeschrieben ⟨Brief, Post, Päckchen⟩; ∼ **disabled** ≈ Behinderter/Behinderte mit Schwerbehindertenausweis; ∼ **trade mark** eingetragenes Warenzeichen; **by** ∼ **post** per Einschreiben

registrar /'redʒɪstrɑː(r)/ n. ▶887◀ (a) (Univ.) ≈ Kanzler, der/Kanzlerin, die; (public official) Standesbeamte, der/-beamtin, die; (b) (Med.) Arzt/Ärztin in der klinischen Fachausbildung

registration /redʒɪ'streɪʃn/ n. (act of registering) Registrierung, die; (enrolment) Anmeldung, die; (of students) Einschreibung, die; Immatrikulation, die; (of voters) Eintragung ins Wählerverzeichnis

registration: ∼ **document** n. (Brit.) Kraftfahrzeugbrief, der; ∼ **number** n. (Motor Veh.) amtliches od. polizeiliches Kennzeichen; ∼ **plate** n. (Motor Veh.) Nummernschild, das

registry /'redʒɪstrɪ/ n. ∼ **[office]** Standesamt, das; attrib. standesamtlich ⟨Trauung⟩; **be married in a** ∼ **[office]** sich standesamtlich trauen lassen

regret /rɪ'gret/ **1** v.t., **-tt-:** (a) (feel sorrow for loss of) nachtrauern (+ Dat.); (b) ▶639◀ (be sorry for) bedauern; ∼ **having done sth.** es bedauern, dass man etw. getan hat; **it is to be** ∼**ted that …:** es ist bedauerlich, dass …; **I** ∼ **to say that …:** ich muss leider sagen, dass … **2** n. ▶639◀ Bedauern, das; **much to my** ∼: zu meinem großen Bedauern; **have no** ∼**s** nichts bereuen; **send one's** ∼**s** (polite refusal) sich entschuldigen lassen

regretfully /rɪ'gretfəlɪ/ adv. mit Bedauern

regrettable /rɪ'gretəbl/ adj. bedauerlich

regrettably /rɪ'gretəblɪ/ adv. bedauerlicherweise; bedauerlich ⟨teuer⟩

regroup /riː'gruːp/ **1** v.t. (a) umgruppieren; (b) (Mil.: reorganize) neu formieren ⟨Truppen⟩. **2** v.i. (a) (form a new group) sich neu gruppieren; (b) (Mil.) sich neu formieren

regular /'regjʊlə(r)/ **1** adj. (a) (recurring uniformly, habitual) regelmäßig; geregelt ⟨Arbeit⟩; fest ⟨Anstellung, Reihenfolge⟩; ∼ **customer** Stammkunde, der/-kundin, die; **our** ∼ **postman** unser [gewohnter] Briefträger; **get** ∼ **work** ⟨Freiberufler:⟩ regelmäßig Aufträge bekommen; **have** or **lead a** ∼ **life** ein geregeltes Leben führen; (b) (evenly arranged, symmetrical) regelmäßig; (c) (properly qualified) ausgebildet; ∼ **soldiers** Berufssoldaten; (d) (Ling.) regelmäßig; (e) (coll.: thorough) richtig (ugs.). **2** n. (a) (coll.: ∼ customer, visitor, etc.) Stammkunde, der/-kundin, die; (in pub) Stammgast, der; (b) (soldier) Berufssoldat, der

regularise ⇒ **regularize**

regularity /regjʊ'lærɪtɪ/ n. Regelmäßigkeit, die

regularize /'regjʊləraɪz/ v.t. (a) (make regular) regeln; (by law) gesetzlich regeln od. festlegen; (b) (make steady) stabilisieren ⟨Atmung, Puls, Spannung⟩

regularly /'regjʊləlɪ/ adv. (a) (at fixed times) regelmäßig; (constantly) ständig; (b) (steadily) gleichmäßig; (c) (symmetrically) regelmäßig ⟨bauen, anlegen⟩

regulate /'regjʊleɪt/ v.t. (a) (control) regeln; (subject to restriction) begrenzen; (b) ˙(adjust) regulieren; einstellen ⟨Apparat, Maschine⟩; [richtig ein]stellen ⟨Uhr⟩

regulation /regjʊ'leɪʃn/ n. (a) (regulating) Regelung, die; (of quantity, speed) Regulierung, die; (of machine) Einstellen, das; (b) (rule) Vorschrift, die; **be against** ∼**s** vorschriftswidrig sein; (c) attrib. vorschriftsmäßig ⟨Kleidung⟩

regulator /'regjʊleɪtə(r)/ n. (device) Regler, der; (of clock, watch) Gangregler, der

regulatory /'regjʊlətərɪ/ adj. regulativ (geh.); ∼ **body/ authority** Aufsichtsgremium, das/-behörde, die

rehabilitate /riːhə'bɪlɪteɪt/ v.t. rehabilitieren; ∼ **[back into society]** wieder [in die Gesellschaft] eingliedern

rehabilitation /riːhəbɪlɪ'teɪʃn/ n. Rehabilitation, die; ∼ **[in society]** Wiedereingliederung [in die Gesellschaft]

rehash 1 /riː'hæʃ/ v.t. aufwärmen. **2** /'riːhæʃ/ n. (restatement) Aufguss, der (abwertend)

rehearsal /rɪ'hɜːsl/ n. (Theatre, Mus., etc.) Probe, die; see also **dress rehearsal**

rehearse /rɪ'hɜːs/ v.t. (Theatre, Mus., etc.) proben

reheat /riː'hiːt/ v.t. wieder erwärmen; aufwärmen ⟨Essen⟩

rehouse /riː'haʊz/ v.t. umquartieren

reign /reɪn/ **1** n. Herrschaft, die; (of monarch also) Regentschaft, die; **in the** ∼ **of King Charles** während der Regentschaft König Karls. **2** v.i. (a) (hold office) herrschen (**over** über + Akk.); ∼**ing champion** amtierender Meister/amtierende Meisterin; (b) (prevail) herrschen

reimburse /riːɪm'bɜːs/ v.t. zurück]erstatten ⟨[Un]kosten, Spesen⟩; entschädigen ⟨Person⟩; ∼ **sb. for** jmdm. [zurück]erstatten ⟨[Un]kosten, Spesen⟩; jmdm. ersetzen ⟨Verlust⟩

reimbursement /riːɪm'bɜːsmənt/ n. Rückzahlung, die; (of expenses) Erstattung, die

rein /reɪn/ n. (a) Zügel, der; **keep a child on** ∼**s** ein Kind am Laufgurt führen; (b) (fig.) Zügel, der; **hold the** ∼**s** die Zügel in der Hand haben; **keep a tight** ∼ **on** an der Kandare halten ⟨Person⟩; im Zaum halten ⟨Gefühle⟩; see also **free 1 a**

∼ **'in** v.t. (check, lit. or fig.) zügeln

reincarnation /riːɪnkɑː'neɪʃn/ n. (Relig.) Reinkarnation, die; Wiedergeburt, die

reindeer /'reɪndɪə(r)/ n., pl. same Ren[tier], das

reinforce /riːɪn'fɔːs/ v.t. verstärken ⟨Truppen, Festung, Stoff⟩; erhöhen ⟨Anzahl⟩; untermauern ⟨Argument⟩; bestätigen ⟨Behauptung⟩; ∼ **sb.'s opinion** jmdn. in seiner Meinung bestärken; ∼**d concrete** Stahlbeton, der

reinforcement /riːɪn'fɔːsmənt/ n. (a) Verstärkung, die; (of numbers) Zunahme, die; (of argument) Untermauerung, die; (b) ∼**[s]** (additional men etc.) Verstärkung, die

reinstate /riːɪn'steɪt/ v.t. (in job) wieder einstellen

reinterpret /riːɪn'tɜːprɪt/ v.t. (interpret afresh) noch einmal interpretieren; (give different interpretation) neu interpretieren

reinvest /riːɪn'vest/ v.t. reinvestieren (fachspr.); wieder anlegen ⟨Kapital⟩

reissue /riː'ɪʃuː, riː'ɪsjuː/ **1** v.t. neu herausbringen. **2** n. Neuauflage, die

reiterate /riː'ɪtəreɪt/ v.t. wiederholen

reject 1 /rɪ'dʒekt/ v.t. (a) ablehnen; abweisen ⟨Freier⟩; zurückweisen ⟨Bitte, Annäherungsversuch⟩; (b) (Med.) nicht vertragen ⟨Nahrung, Medizin⟩; abstoßen ⟨Transplantat⟩. **2** /'riːdʒekt/ n. (thing) Ausschuss, der

rejection /rɪ'dʒekʃn/ n. (a) ⇒ **reject 1 a:** Ablehnung, die; Abweisung, die; Zurückweisung, die; **parental** ∼: Ablehnung durch die Eltern; (b) (Med.) Abstoßung, die

rejoice /rɪ'dʒɔɪs/ v.i. (a) (feel great joy) sich freuen (**over, at** über + Akk.); (b) (make merry) feiern

rejoicing /rɪˈdʒɔɪsɪŋ/ n. (a) [sounds of] ∼: Jubel, der; (b) in pl. (celebrations) Feier, die

rejoin¹ /rɪˈdʒɔɪn/ v.t. (reply) erwidern (to auf + Akk.)

rejoin² /riːˈdʒɔɪn/ v.t. (a) (join again) wieder stoßen zu ⟨Regiment⟩; wieder eintreten in (+ Akk.) ⟨Partei, Verein⟩; ∼ one's ship wieder an Bord gehen; (b) ⟨Verkehrsteilnehmer:⟩ wieder kommen auf (+ Akk.) ⟨Straße, Autobahn⟩; ⟨Straße:⟩ wieder [ein]münden in (+ Akk.) ⟨Straße, Autobahn⟩

rejoinder /rɪˈdʒɔɪndə(r)/ n. Erwiderung, die (to auf + Akk.)

rejuvenate /rɪˈdʒuːvəneɪt/ v.t. verjüngen ⟨Person, Haut⟩

rekindle /riːˈkɪndl/ v.t. (a) (relight) wieder anfachen; (b) (fig.: reawaken) wieder entfachen ⟨Liebe, Leidenschaft⟩; wieder aufleben lassen ⟨Sehnsucht, Verlangen, Hoffnung⟩

relapse /rɪˈlæps/ 1 v.i. ⟨Kranker:⟩ einen Rückfall bekommen; ∼ into zurückfallen in (+ Akk.) ⟨Götzendienst, Barbarei⟩; ∼ into silence/lethargy wieder in Schweigen/Lethargie verfallen. 2 n. Rückfall, der (into in + Akk.)

relate /rɪˈleɪt/ 1 v.t. (a) (tell) erzählen ⟨Geschichte⟩; erzählen von ⟨Abenteuer⟩; (b) (bring into relation) in Zusammenhang bringen (to, with mit); (c) (establish relation or connection between) einen Zusammenhang herstellen zwischen. 2 v.i. (a) ∼ to (have reference) ⟨Behauptung, Frage, Angelegenheit:⟩ in Zusammenhang stehen mit; betreffen ⟨Person⟩; (b) ∼ to (feel involved or connected with) eine Beziehung haben zu

related /rɪˈleɪtɪd/ adj. (a) (by kinship or marriage) verwandt (to mit); ∼ by marriage verschwägert; (b) (connected) miteinander in Zusammenhang stehend; verwandt ⟨Sprache, Begriff, Spezies, Fach⟩

relation /rɪˈleɪʃn/ n. (a) (connection) Beziehung, die; Zusammenhang, der (of ... and zwischen ... und); be out of all ∼ to in keinem Verhältnis stehen zu ⟨Kosten, geleisteter Arbeit⟩; in or with ∼ to in Bezug auf (+ Akk.); see also bear² 1 c; (b) in pl. (dealings) (with parents, police) Verhältnis, das (with zu); (with country) Beziehungen (with zu, mit); (sexual intercourse) intime Beziehungen (with zu); (c) (kin, relative) Verwandte, der/die; what ∼ is he to you? wie ist er mit dir verwandt?; is she any ∼ [to you]? ist sie mit dir verwandt?

relationship /rɪˈleɪʃnʃɪp/ n. (a) (mutual tie) Beziehung, die (with zu); have a good/bad ∼ with sb. zu jmdm. ein gutes/schlechtes Verhältnis haben; doctor-patient ∼: Verhältnis zwischen Arzt und Patient; (b) (kinship) Verwandtschaftsverhältnis, das; (c) (connection) Beziehung, die; (d) (sexual) Verhältnis, das

relative /ˈrelətɪv/ 1 n. Verwandte, der/die. 2 adj. relativ; (comparative) jeweilig; the ∼ costs of a and b die Kostenrelation zwischen a und b; with ∼ calmness relativ gelassen; be ∼ to sth. sich nach etw. richten; a large population ∼ to the town's size eine im Verhältnis zur Größe der Stadt beachtliche Einwohnerzahl

relative 'clause n. (Ling.) Relativsatz, der

relatively /ˈrelətɪvlɪ/ adv. relativ; verhältnismäßig

relative 'pronoun n. (Ling.) Relativpronomen, das

relativity /reləˈtɪvɪtɪ/ n. (Phys.) Relativität, die; ∼ theory, the theory of ∼: die Relativitätstheorie

relax /rɪˈlæks/ 1 v.t. (a) (make less tense) entspannen ⟨Muskel, Körper[teil]⟩; lockern ⟨Muskel, Feder, Griff⟩; (fig.) lockern; (b) (make less strict) lockern ⟨Gesetz, Disziplin, Sitten⟩; (c) (slacken) nachlassen in (+ Dat.) ⟨Bemühungen, Aufmerksamkeit⟩; verlangsamen ⟨Tempo⟩. 2 v.i. (a) (become less tense) sich entspannen; (b) (slacken) nachlassen (in in + Dat.); (c) (become less stern) sich mäßigen (in in + Dat.); (d) (cease effort) sich entspannen; ausspannen; (stop worrying, calm down) sich beruhigen

relaxation /riːlækˈseɪʃn/ n. (a) (recreation) Freizeitbeschäftigung, die; play tennis as a ∼: zur Entspannung Tennis spielen; (b) (cessation of effort) Erholung, die (from von); (c) (reduction of tension; lit. or fig.) Lockerung, die

relaxed /rɪˈlækst/ adj. (a) (informal, not anxious) entspannt, gelöst ⟨Atmosphäre, Lächeln, Gefühl, Person⟩; (b) (not strict or exact) gelockert ⟨Regel, Beschränkung⟩

relaxing /rɪˈlæksɪŋ/ adj. entspannend; erholsam; have a ∼ bath zur Entspannung ein Bad nehmen

relay 1 /ˈriːleɪ/ n. (a) (gang) Schicht, die; work in ∼s schichtweise arbeiten; (b) (race) Staffel, die; (c) (Electr.) Relais, das; (d) (Radio, Telev.) radio ∼: Richtfunkverbindung, die; ∼ station Relaisstation, die; (e) (transmission) Übertragung, die. 2 /riːˈleɪ/ v.t. (a) (pass on) weiterleiten; ∼ a message to sb. that ...: jmdm. ausrichten od. mitteilen, dass ...; (b) (Radio, Telev., Teleph.) übertragen

'relay race n. (Running) Staffellauf, der; (Swimming) Staffelschwimmen, das

release /rɪˈliːs/ 1 v.t. (a) (free) freilassen ⟨Tier, Häftling, Sklaven⟩; (from jail) entlassen (from aus); (from bondage, trap) befreien (from aus); (from pain) erlösen (from von); (from promise, obligation, vow) entbinden (from von); (b) (let go, let fall) loslassen; lösen ⟨Handbremse⟩; ausklinken ⟨Bombe⟩; ∼ one's hold or grip on sth. etw. loslassen; (c) (make known) veröffentlichen ⟨Erklärung, Nachricht⟩; (issue) herausbringen ⟨Film, Schallplatte, Produkt⟩. 2 n. (a) (act of freeing) ⇒ 1a: Freilassung, die; Entlassung, die; Befreiung, die; Erlösung, die; Entbindung, die; (b) (of published item) Veröffentlichung, die; when does the film go out on general ∼? wann kommt der Film in die Kinos?; a new ∼ by Bob Dylan eine neue Platte od. eine Neuveröffentlichung von Bob Dylan; (c) (handle, lever, button) Auslöser, der

relegate /ˈrelɪgeɪt/ v.t. (a) ∼ sb. to the position or status of ...: jmdn. zu ... degradieren; (b) (Sport) absteigen lassen; be ∼d absteigen (to in + Akk.)

relegation /relɪˈgeɪʃn/ n. (a) Degradierung, die; her ∼ to the position of ...: ihre Degradierung zu ...; (b) (Sport) Abstieg, der

relent /rɪˈlent/ v.i. sich erweichen lassen; (yield to compassion) Mitleid zeigen; ⟨Wetter:⟩ besser werden

relentless /rɪˈlentlɪs/ adj. unerbittlich; schonungslos ⟨Kritik, Heftigkeit⟩

relevance /ˈrelɪvəns/ n. Relevanz, die (to für)

relevant /ˈrelɪvənt/ adj. relevant (to für); wichtig ⟨Information, Dokument⟩; entsprechend ⟨Formular⟩

reliability /rɪlaɪəˈbɪlɪtɪ/ n., no pl. Zuverlässigkeit, die

reliable /rɪˈlaɪəbl/ adj. zuverlässig

reliably /rɪˈlaɪəblɪ/ adv. zuverlässig; I am ∼ informed that ...: ich habe aus zuverlässiger Quelle erfahren, dass ...

reliance /rɪˈlaɪəns/ n. (trust, confidence) Vertrauen, das (in in zu, on auf + Akk.)

reliant /rɪˈlaɪənt/ adj. be ∼ on sb./sth. auf jmdn./etw. angewiesen sein

relic /ˈrelɪk/ n. (a) (Relig.) Reliquie, die; (b) (surviving trace) Überbleibsel, das (ugs.); Relikt, das

relief¹ /rɪˈliːf/ n. (a) (alleviation, deliverance) Erleichterung, die; give or bring [sb.] ∼ [from pain] [jmdm.] [Schmerz]linderung verschaffen; breathe or heave a sigh of ∼: erleichtert aufatmen; what a ∼!, that's a ∼! da bin ich aber erleichtert!; (b) (assistance) Hilfe, die; (financial state assistance) Sozialhilfe, die; attrib. Hilfs⟨fond, -organisation, -komitee⟩; (c) (replacement of person) Ablösung, die; attrib. ∼ driver ablösender Fahrer

relief² n. (a) (Art) works in ∼: Reliefarbeiten; high/low ∼: Hoch-/Flachrelief, das; (b) (sculpture) Relief, das; (c) stand out in strong ∼ against sth. sich scharf gegen etw. abheben; (fig.) in krassem Gegensatz zu etw. stehen

relief: ∼ agency n. Hilfsorganisation, die; Hilfswerk, das; ∼ bus n. Entlastungsbus, der; (as replacement) Ersatzbus, der; ∼ map n. Reliefkarte, die; ∼ road n. Entlastungsstraße, die; ∼ supplies n. pl. Hilfsgüter, Pl.; ∼ worker n. Helfer, der/Helferin, die

relieve /rɪˈliːv/ v.t. (a) (lessen, mitigate) lindern; verringern ⟨Dampfdruck, Anspannung⟩; unterbrechen ⟨Eintönigkeit⟩; erleichtern ⟨Gewissen⟩; (remove) abbauen ⟨Anspannung⟩; stillen ⟨Schmerzen⟩; (remove or lessen monotony of) auflockern; I am ∼d to hear that ...: es erleichtert mich zu hören, dass ...; (b) (release from duty) ablösen ⟨Wache, Truppen⟩; (c) ∼ sb. (of task, duty) jmdn. entbinden ⟨of responsibility, load⟩ jmdm. abnehmen (of Akk.); (from debt) jmdm. erlassen (from Akk.); (of burden, duty; from sorrow, worry) jmdn. befreien (of, from von); (d) ∼ oneself (empty the bladder or bowels) sich erleichtern (verhüll.); (**e**) (release from a post) entbinden (**of, from** von); (dismiss) entheben (geh.) (**of, from** *Gen.*)

religion /rɪˈlɪdʒn/ *n.* Religion, *die;* **freedom of ∼:** Glaubensfreiheit, *die;* **what is your ∼?** welcher Religion gehörst du an?

religious /rɪˈlɪdʒəs/ *adj.* (**a**) (pious) religiös; fromm; (**b**) (concerned with religion) Glaubens⟨*freiheit, -eifer*⟩; Religions⟨*freiheit, -unterricht, -kenntnisse*⟩; religiös ⟨*Überzeugung, Zentrum*⟩; (**c**) (of monastic order) religiös ⟨*Orden*⟩; **∼ community** Ordensgemeinschaft, *die;* (**d**) (scrupulous) peinlich ⟨*Sorgfalt, Genauigkeit*⟩

religiously /rɪˈlɪdʒəslɪ/ *adv.* (**a**) (piously, reverently) inbrünstig ⟨*beten*⟩; ehrfürchtig ⟨*verehren, niederknien*⟩; (**b**) (conscientiously) gewissenhaft ⟨*durchsehen, verbessern*⟩; peinlich genau ⟨*sauber machen, verbessern*⟩

relinquish /rɪˈlɪŋkwɪʃ/ *v.t.* (**a**) (give up, abandon) aufgeben; ablassen von ⟨*Glaube*⟩; verzichten auf (+ *Akk.*) ⟨*Recht, Anspruch, Macht*⟩; aufgeben ⟨*Anspruch, Stelle, Arbeit, Besitz*⟩; **∼ the right/** one's **claim to sth.** auf sein Recht/ seinen Anspruch auf etw. (*Akk.*) verzichten; (**b**) **∼** one's **hold** *or* **grip on sb./sth.** jmdn./etw. loslassen

relish /ˈrelɪʃ/ **1** *n.* (**a**) (liking) Vorliebe, *die;* **do sth. with** [**great**] **∼:** etw. mit [großem] Genuss tun; **he takes** [**great**] **∼ in doing sth.** es bereitet ihm [große] Freude, etw. zu tun; (**b**) (condiment) Relish, *das* (Kochk.). **2** *v.t.* genießen; reizvoll finden ⟨*Gedanke, Vorstellung*⟩

reload /riːˈləʊd/ *v.t.* nachladen ⟨*Schusswaffe*⟩; **∼ the camera** einen neuen Film einlegen

relocate /riːləˈkeɪt/ *v.t.* verlegen ⟨*Fabrik, Büro*⟩

relocation /riːləˈkeɪʃn/ *n.* (of factory, office) Verlegung, *die;* (of employee) Versetzung, *die;* **∼ expenses** Umzugskosten *Pl.*

reluctance /rɪˈlʌktəns/ *n., no pl.* Widerwille, *der;* Abneigung, *die;* **have a** [**great**] **∼ to do sth.** etw. nur mit Widerwillen tun

reluctant /rɪˈlʌktənt/ *adj.* unwillig; **be ∼ to do sth.** etw. nur ungern *od.* widerstrebend tun

rely /rɪˈlaɪ/ *v.i.* (**a**) (have trust) sich verlassen ([**up**]**on** auf + *Akk.*); (**b**) (be dependent) angewiesen sein ([**up**]**on** auf + *Akk.*); [**have to**] **∼ on sb. to help** darauf angewiesen sein, dass jmd. hilft

remain /rɪˈmeɪn/ *v.i.* (**a**) (be left over) übrig bleiben; **all that ∼ed for me to do was to …:** ich musste *od.* brauchte nur noch …; **nothing ∼s but to thank you all** es bleibt mir nur, Ihnen allen zu danken; (**b**) (stay) bleiben; **∼ behind** noch dableiben; **∼ in sb.'s memory** jmdm. im Gedächtnis bleiben; (**c**) (continue to be) bleiben; **it ∼s to be seen** das bleibt abzuwarten *od.* wird sich zeigen; **the fact ∼s that …:** das ändert nichts an der Tatsache *od.* daran, dass …

remainder /rɪˈmeɪndə(r)/ *n.* (**a**) (sb. or sth. left over; also Math.) Rest, *der;* (**b**) (remaining stock) Restposten, *der*

remaining /rɪˈmeɪnɪŋ/ *adj.* restlich; übrig; **spend** one's **∼ years …:** seinen Lebensabend … verbringen

remains /rɪˈmeɪnz/ *n. pl.* (**a**) (leftover part) Reste; (**b**) (corpse) sterbliche [Über]reste (verhüll.); (**c**) (relics) Relikte; Reste; **Roman ∼:** Relikte aus der Römerzeit

remake /ˈriːmeɪk/ *n.* (Cinemat.) Remake, *das* (fachspr.); Neuverfilmung, *die*

remand /rɪˈmɑːnd/ **1** *v.t.* **∼ sb.** [**in custody**] jmdn. in Untersuchungshaft behalten; **be ∼ed in custody/on bail** in Untersuchungshaft bleiben müssen/gegen Kaution aus der Untersuchungshaft entlassen werden. **2** *n.* [**period of**] **∼:** Untersuchungshaft, *die;* **place** *or* **put sb. on ∼:** jmdn. in Untersuchungshaft nehmen; **be on ∼:** in Untersuchungshaft sein; **be held on ∼:** in Untersuchungshaft bleiben müssen; **∼ prisoner** Untersuchungsgefangene, *der/die*

re'mand centre *n.* (Brit.) *Untersuchungsgefängnis für jugendliche Straftäter zwischen 14 und 21 Jahren*

remark /rɪˈmɑːk/ **1** *v.t.* bemerken (**to** gegenüber). **2** *v.i.* eine Bemerkung machen ([**up**]**on** zu, über + *Akk.*). **3** *n.* (comment) Bemerkung, *die* (**on** über + *Akk.*); **make a ∼:** eine Bemerkung machen (**about, at** über + *Akk.*).

remarkable /rɪˈmɑːkəbl/ *adj.* (**a**) (notable) bemerkenswert; (**b**) (extraordinary) außergewöhnlich

remarkably /rɪˈmɑːkəblɪ/ *adv.* (**a**) (notably) bemerkenswert; (**b**) (exceptionally) außergewöhnlich

remarry /riːˈmærɪ/ *v.i.* & *t.* wieder heiraten

remedial /rɪˈmiːdɪəl/ *adj.* (**a**) (affording a remedy) Heil⟨*behandlung, -wirkung*⟩; (intended to remedy deficiency etc.) rehabilitierend ⟨*Maßnahme*⟩; **take ∼ action** Hilfsmaßnahmen ergreifen; (**b**) (Educ.) Förder-; **classes in ∼ reading** Förderunterricht im Lesen

remedy /ˈremɪdɪ/ **1** *n.* (**a**) (cure) [Heil]mittel, *das* (**for** gegen); **cough/herbal ∼:** Husten-/Kräutermittel, *das;* **cold/flu ∼:** Mittel gegen Erkältung/Grippe; (**b**) (means of counteracting) [Gegen]mittel, *das* (**for** gegen). **2** *v.t.* beheben ⟨*Sprachfehler, Problem*⟩; ausgleichen ⟨*Kurzsichtigkeit*⟩; retten ⟨*Situation*⟩; **the situation cannot be remedied** die Situation ist nicht zu retten

remember /rɪˈmembə(r)/ *v.t.* (**a**) (keep in memory) denken an (+ *Akk.*); (bring to mind) sich erinnern an (+ *Akk.*); **don't you ∼ me?** erinnern Sie sich nicht an mich?; **∼ who/ where you are!** vergiss nicht, wer/wo du bist; **I can't ∼ the word I want** das Wort, das ich brauche, fällt mir gerade nicht ein; **I ∼ed to bring the book** ich habe daran gedacht, das Buch mitzubringen; **I can never ∼ her name** ich kann mir ihren Namen einfach nicht merken; **if I ∼ correctly** (abs.) wenn ich mich recht erinnere; **an evening to ∼:** ein unvergesslicher Abend; (**b**) (convey greetings from) grüßen; **∼ me to them** grüße sie von mir; **she asked to be ∼ed to you** sie lässt dich grüßen

remembrance /rɪˈmembrəns/ *n.* Gedenken, *das;* **in ∼ of sb.** zu jmds. Gedächtnis; zum Gedenken an jmdn.

Remembrance: ∼ Day, ∼ Sunday *ns.* (Brit.) ≈ Volkstrauertag, *der*

remind /rɪˈmaɪnd/ *v.t.* erinnern (**of** an + *Akk.*); **∼ sb. to do sth.** jmdn. daran erinnern, etw. zu tun; **that ∼s me, …:** dabei fällt mir ein, …; **you are ∼ed that …:** beachten Sie bitte, dass …

reminder /rɪˈmaɪndə(r)/ *n.* Erinnerung, *die* (**of** an + *Akk.*); (mnemonic) Gedächtnishilfe *od.* -stütze, *die;* **give sb. a ∼ that …:** jmdn. daran erinnern, dass …; **serve as/be a ∼ of sth.** an etw. (*Akk.*) erinnern

reminisce /remɪˈnɪs/ *v.i.* sich in Erinnerungen (*Dat.*) ergehen (**about** an + *Akk.*)

reminiscence /remɪˈnɪsəns/ *n.* Erinnerung, *die* (**of** an + *Akk.*)

reminiscent /remɪˈnɪsənt/ *adj.* **∼ of sth.** an etw. (*Akk.*) erinnernd; **be ∼ of sth.** an etw. (*Akk.*) erinnern

remiss /rɪˈmɪs/ *adj.* nachlässig (**of** von)

remission /rɪˈmɪʃn/ *n.* (**a**) (of sins) Vergebung, *die;* (**b**) (of debt, punishment) Erlass, *der;* (**c**) (prison sentence) Straferlass, *der;* **he gained one year's ∼:** ihm ist ein Jahr erlassen worden; (**d**) (Med.) Remission, *die;* **go into ∼:** remittieren

remit /rɪˈmɪt/ *v.t.,* **-tt-:** (**a**) (pardon) vergeben ⟨*Sünde, Beleidigung usw.*⟩; (**b**) (cancel) erlassen ⟨*Steuer, Gebühr usw.*⟩; (**c**) (send) überweisen ⟨*Geld*⟩

remittance /rɪˈmɪtəns/ *n.* Überweisung, *die*

remnant /ˈremnənt/ *n.* Rest, *der;* (trace) Überrest, *der*

remould (Amer.) ⇒ **remould**

remonstrance /rɪˈmɒnstrəns/ *n.* Protest, *der* (**with, against** gegen)

remonstrate /ˈremənstreɪt/ *v.i.* protestieren (**against** gegen); **∼ with sb.** jmdm. Vorhaltungen machen (**on** wegen)

remorse /rɪˈmɔːs/ *n.* Reue, *die* (**for, about** über + *Akk.*); **without ∼** (merciless) erbarmungslos

remorseful /rɪˈmɔːsfl/ *adj.* reuig; reuevoll (geh.)

remorseless /rɪˈmɔːslɪs/ *adj.* (**a**) (merciless) erbarmungslos ⟨*Grausamkeit, Barbarei*⟩; (**b**) (relentless) unerbittlich ⟨*Schicksal, Logik*⟩

remote /rɪˈməʊt/ *adj.,* **∼r** /rɪˈməʊtə(r)/, **∼st** /rɪˈməʊtɪst/ (**a**) (far apart) entfernt; (**b**) (far off) fern ⟨*Vergangenheit, Zukunft, Zeit*⟩; früh ⟨*Altertum*⟩; abgelegen, (geh.) entlegen ⟨*Ort, Gebiet*⟩; **∼ from** (lit. or fig.) weit entfernt von; (**c**) (not closely related) entfernt, weitläufig ⟨*Vorfahr, Nachkomme, Verwandte*⟩; (**d**) (slight) gering ⟨*Chance, Möglichkeit*⟩

remote: ~ **con'trol** *n.* (of vehicle) Fernlenkung, *die;* Fernsteuerung, *die;* (of apparatus) Fernbedienung, *die;* ~-**control[led]** *adj.* ferngesteuert; ferngelenkt; fernbedient ‹*Anlage*›

remotely /rɪˈməʊtlɪ/ *adv.* (a) (distantly) entfernt, weitläufig ‹*verwandt*›; (b) (slightly) **they are not [even]** ~ **alike** sie haben [aber auch] nicht die entfernteste Ähnlichkeit [miteinander]; **it is** ~ **conceivable that** …: es ist nicht völlig auszuschließen, dass …

remould 1 /ˈriːməʊld/ *v.t.* (refashion) ummodeln, umgestalten (**into** zu); (Motor Veh.) runderneuern ‹*Reifen*›. 2 /ˈriːməʊld/ *n.* (Motor Veh.) runderneuerter Reifen

remount /riːˈmaʊnt/ *v.i.* (on horse) wieder aufsitzen; (on bicycle) wieder aufs Fahrrad steigen

removable /rɪˈmuːvəbl/ *adj.* abnehmbar; entfernbar ‹*Fleck, Trennwand*›; herausnehmbar ‹*Futter*›

removal /rɪˈmuːvl/ *n.* (a) (taking away) Entfernung, *die;* (of traces) Beseitigung, *die;* (b) (dismissal) Entlassung, *die;* **the minister's** ~ **from office** die Entfernung des Ministers aus dem Amt; (c) ⇨ **remove** 1 c: Beseitigung, *die;* Vertreibung, *die;* Zerstreuung, *die;* (d) (transfer of furniture) Umzug, *der;* 'Smith & Co., R~s' „Smith & Co., Spedition"

removal: ~ **firm** *n.* Spedition, *die;* ~ **man** *n.* Möbelpacker, *der;* ~ **van** *n.* Möbelwagen, *der*

remove /rɪˈmuːv/ 1 *v.t.* (a) (take away) entfernen; streichen ‹*Buchpassage*›; wegnehmen, wegräumen ‹*Papiere, Ordner usw.*›; abräumen ‹*Geschirr*›; beseitigen ‹*Spur*›; (take off) abnehmen; ausziehen ‹*Kleidungsstück*›; **she** ~**d her/the child's coat** sie legte ihren Mantel ab/sie zog dem Kind den Mantel aus; ~ **one's make-up** sich abschminken; **the parents** ~**d the child from the school** die Eltern nahmen das Kind von der Schule; (b) (dismiss) entlassen; ~ **sb. from office/his post** jmdn. aus dem Amt/von seinem Posten entfernen; (c) (eradicate) beseitigen ‹*Gefahr, Hindernis, Problem, Zweifel*›; vertreiben ‹*Angst*›; zerstreuen ‹*Verdacht, Befürchtungen*›; (d) *in p.p.* (remote) **be entirely** ~ **from politics/everyday life** gar nichts mit Politik zu tun haben/völlig lebensfremd sein. 2 *v.i.* (formal) [um]ziehen. 3 *n.* **be but one** ~ **from** nur noch einen Schritt entfernt sein von; **at one** ~: auf Distanz (**from** gegenüber)

remover /rɪˈmuːvə(r)/ *n.* (a) (of paint/varnish/hair/rust) Farb-/Lack-/Haar-/Rostentferner, *der;* (b) (removal man) Möbelpacker, *der*

remuneration /rɪmjuːnəˈreɪʃn/ *n.* Bezahlung, *die;* Entlohnung, *die;* (reward) Belohnung, *die*

Renaissance /rəˈneɪsəns, rɪˈneɪsəns/ *n., no pl.* (Hist.) Renaissance, *die*

rename /riːˈneɪm/ *v.t.* umbenennen; umtaufen ‹*Schiff*›

render /ˈrendə(r)/ *v.t.* (a) (show, give) leisten ‹*Gehorsam, Hilfe*›; erweisen ‹*Ehre, Achtung, Respekt, Dienst*›; bieten, gewähren ‹*Schutz*›; ~ **a service to sb.**, ~ **sb. a service** jmdm. einen Dienst erweisen; (b) (pay) entrichten ‹*Tribut, Steuern, Abgaben*›; (c) (represent, reproduce) wiedergeben; spielen ‹*Musik, Szene*›; (translate) übersetzen (**by** mit); ~ **a text into another language** einen Text in eine andere Sprache übertragen

rendering /ˈrendərɪŋ/ *n.* ⇨ **render** c: Wiedergabe, *die;* Spielen, *das;* Übersetzung, *die;* Übertragung, *die*

rendezvous /ˈrɒndɪvuː, ˈrɒndeɪvuː/ *n., pl. same* /ˈrɒndɪvuːz, ˈrɒndeɪvuːz/ (a) (meeting place) Treffpunkt, *der;* (b) (meeting) Rendezvous, *das* (veralt.); Verabredung, *die;* (c) (Astronaut.) Rendezvous, *das*

rendition /renˈdɪʃn/ *n.* ⇨ **rendering**

renegade /ˈrenɪgeɪd/ 1 *n.* Abtrünnige, *der/die.* 2 *adj.* abtrünnig

renew /rɪˈnjuː/ *v.t.* (a) (restore, regenerate, recover) erneuern; wieder wecken *od.* wachrufen ‹*Gefühle*›; wiederherstellen ‹*Kraft*›; (b) (replace) erneuern; auffüllen ‹*Vorrat*›; ausbessern ‹*Kleidungsstück*›; (c) (begin again) erneuern ‹*Bekanntschaft*›; fortsetzen ‹*Angriff, Bemühungen*›; (d) (repeat) wiederholen ‹*Aussage, Beschuldigung*›; (e) (extend) erneuern, verlängern ‹*Vertrag, Genehmigung, Ausweis etc.*›; ~ **a library book** ‹*Bibliothekar/Benutzer:*› ein Buch [aus der Bücherei] verlängern/verlängern lassen

renewable /rɪˈnjuːəbl/ *adj.* regenerationsfähig ‹*Energiequelle*›; verlängerbar ‹*Vertrag, Genehmigung, Ausweis*›

renewal /rɪˈnjuːəl/ *n.* Erneuerung, *die;* (of contract, passport etc. also) Verlängerung, *die;* (of attack) Wiederaufnahme, *die;* (of library book) Verlängerung der Leihfrist

renounce /rɪˈnaʊns/ *v.t.* (a) (abandon) verzichten auf (+ *Akk.*); (b) (refuse to recognize) aufkündigen ‹*Vertrag, Freundschaft*›; aufgeben ‹*Grundsatz, Plan, Versuch*›; verstoßen ‹*Person*›; ~ **the devil/one's faith** dem Teufel/seinem Glauben abschwören

renovate /ˈrenəveɪt/ *v.t.* renovieren ‹*Gebäude*›; restaurieren ‹*Möbel, Gemälde*›

renovation /renəˈveɪʃn/ *n.* Renovierung, *die;* (of furniture etc.) Restaurierung, *die*

renown /rɪˈnaʊn/ *n.* Renommee, *das;* Ansehen, *das;* **of [great]** ~: von hohem Ansehen

renowned /rɪˈnaʊnd/ *adj.* berühmt (**for** wegen, für)

rent /rent/ 1 *n.* (for house, flat, etc.) Miete, *die;* (for land) Pacht, *die.* 2 *v.t.* (a) (use) mieten ‹*Haus, Wohnung usw.*›; pachten ‹*Land*›; mieten ‹*Auto, Gerät*›; (b) (let) vermieten ‹*Haus, Wohnung, Auto etc.*› (**to** *Dat.*, an + *Akk.*); verpachten ‹*Land*› (**to** *Dat.*, an + *Akk.*)
  ~ **'out** ⇨ **rent** 2 b

'rent-a-crowd *n.* bestellter Haufen; (claque) Claque, *die*

rental /ˈrentl/ *n.* (a) (from houses etc.) Miete, *die;* (from land) Pacht, *die;* (b) ⇨ **rent** 2: Mietung, *die;* Pachtung, *die;* (letting) Vermietung, *die;* Verpachtung, *die;* **car** ~: Autoverleih, *der*

rent: ~**-a-mob** *n.* bestellter Haufen von Randalierern; ~**-a-van** *attrib. adj.* ~**-a-van business/company/ service** Transportervermietung, *die*

rent: ~**-controlled** *adj.* mietpreisgebunden; ~**-free** *adj.* mietfrei; ~ **rebate** *n.* Mietermäßigung, *die*

renunciation /rɪnʌnsɪˈeɪʃn/ *n.* (a) ⇨ **renounce** 1 a, b: Verzicht, *der;* Aufkündigung, *die;* Aufgabe, *die;* Verstoßung, *die;* (b) (self-denial) Selbstverleugnung, *die*

reopen /riːˈəʊpn/ 1 *v.t.* (a) (open again) wieder öffnen; wieder aufmachen; wieder eröffnen ‹*Geschäft, Lokal usw.*›; (b) (return to) wieder aufnehmen ‹*Diskussion, Verhandlung, Feindseligkeiten*›; wieder aufnehmen, wieder aufrollen ‹*Fall*›; zurückkommen auf (+ *Akk.*) ‹*Angelegenheit*›. 2 *v.i.* ‹*Geschäft, Lokal usw.*› wieder öffnen; wieder eröffnet werden; ‹*Verhandlungen, Unterricht:*› wieder beginnen

reorder /riːˈɔːdə(r)/ *v.t.* (a) (Commerc.: order again) nachbestellen ‹*Ware*›; (after theft, loss) neu bestellen, (b) (rearrange) umordnen

reorganisation, reorganise ⇨ **reorganiz-**

reorganization /riːɔːgənaɪˈzeɪʃn/ *n.* Umorganisation, *die;* (of time, work) Neueinteilung, *die;* (of text) Neugliederung, *die*

reorganize /riːˈɔːgənaɪz/ *v.t.* umorganisieren; neu einteilen ‹*Zeit, Arbeit*›; neu gliedern ‹*Aufsatz, Referat*›

reorient /riːˈɔːrɪent/, **reorientate** /riːˈɔːrɪenteɪt/ *v.t.* neu ausrichten; ~ **sb.** jmdm. eine neue Orientierung geben

reorientation /riːɔːrɪənˈteɪʃn/ *n.* Neuorientierung, *die*

rep¹ /rep/ *n.* ▶ 887 | (coll.: representative) Vertreter, *der*/Vertreterin, *die*

rep² *n.* (Theatre coll.) Repertoiretheater, *das;* **be in** ~: an einem Repertoiretheater spielen

repaid ⇨ **repay**

repaint /riːˈpeɪnt/ *v.t.* neu streichen ‹*Gebäude, Wand, Tür usw.*›; neu lackieren ‹*Auto*›

repair /rɪˈpeə(r)/ 1 *v.t.* (a) (restore, mend) reparieren; ausbessern ‹*Kleidung, Straße*›; (b) (remedy) wieder gutmachen ‹*Schaden, Fehler*›; beheben ‹*Schaden, Mangel*›. 2 *n.* (a) (restoring, renovation) Reparatur, *die;* **be beyond** ~: sich nicht mehr reparieren lassen; **be in need of** ~: reparaturbedürftig sein; (b) *no pl., no art.* (condition) **be in good/ bad** ~: in gutem/schlechtem Zustand sein

repairable /rɪˈpeərəbl/ *adj.* reparabel

reparation /repəˈreɪʃn/ *n.* (a) (making amends) Wiedergutmachung, *die;* (b) (compensation) Entschädigung, *die;* ~**s** (for war damage) Reparationen; **make ~ [for sth.]** [für etw.] Ersatz leisten

repartee /repɑːˈtiː/ *n.* **(a)** (skill in making retorts) Schlagfertigkeit, *die;* **be good at ~:** schlagfertig sein; **(b)** (conversation) von [Geist und] Schlagfertigkeit sprühende Unterhaltung

repatriate /riːˈpætrɪeɪt/ *v.t.* repatriieren

repatriation /riːpætrɪˈeɪʃn/ *n.* Repatriierung, *die*

repay /riːˈpeɪ/ **1** *v.t.*, **repaid** /riːˈpeɪd/ **(a)** (pay back) zurückzahlen ‹*Schulden usw.*›; erstatten ‹*Spesen*›; **(b)** (return) erwidern ‹*Besuch, Freundlichkeit*›; **(c)** (give in recompense) **~ sb. for sth.** jmdm. etw. vergelten. **2** *v.i.*, **repaid** Rückzahlungen leisten

repayable /riːˈpeɪəbl/ *adj.* rückzahlbar

repayment /riːˈpeɪmənt/ *n.* **(a)** (paying back) Rückzahlung, *die;* **(b)** (reward) Lohn, *der* **(for** für)

repeal /rɪˈpiːl/ **1** *v.t.* aufheben ‹*Gesetz, Erlass usw.*›. **2** *n.* Aufhebung, *die*

repeat /rɪˈpiːt/ **1** *n.* **(a)** Wiederholung, *die;* (Radio, TV also) Wiederholungssendung, *die;* **do a ~ of sth.** etw. wiederholen; **(b)** (Commerc.) Nachbestellung, *die.* **2** *v.t.* **(a)** (say, do, broadcast again) wiederholen; **please ~ after me: ...:** sprich/sprecht/sprechen Sie mir bitte nach: ...; **(b)** (recite) aufsagen ‹*Gedicht, Strophe, Text*›; **(c)** (report) weitererzählen (**to** *Dat.*). **3** *v.i.* (Math.: recur) ‹*Zahl:*› periodisch sein

repeat: ~ ˈorder *n.* (Commerc.) Nachbestellung, *die;* **~ perˈformance** *n.* Wiederholungsvorstellung, *die* (Theater)

repel /rɪˈpel/ *v.t.*, **-ll-: (a)** (drive back) abwehren ‹*Feind, Annäherungsversuch usw.*›; abstoßen ‹*Feuchtigkeit, elektrische Ladung, Magnetpol*›; **(b)** (be repulsive to) abstoßen

repellent /rɪˈpelənt/ *adj.* **(a)** (repugnant) abstoßend; **(b)** (repelling) **water-~:** Wasser abstoßend

repent /rɪˈpent/ *v.i.* bereuen (**of** *Akk.*)

repentance /rɪˈpentəns/ *n.* Reue, *die*

repentant /rɪˈpentənt/ *adj.* reuig; reuevoll (geh.); reumütig (öfter scherzh.)

repercussion /riːpəˈkʌʃn/ *n. usu. in pl.* Auswirkung, *die* (**[up]on** auf + *Akk.*)

repertoire /ˈrepətwɑː(r)/ *n.* (Mus., Theatre) Repertoire, *das* (**of** an + *Dat.*, von)

repertory /ˈrepətrɪ/ *n.* **(a)** ⇒ **repertoire;** **(b)** (Theatre) Repertoiretheater, *das*

ˈrepertory company *n.* Repertoiretheater, *das*

repetition /repɪˈtɪʃn/ *n.* Wiederholung, *die*

repetitious /repɪˈtɪʃəs/ *adj.* sich immer wiederholend *attr.*

repetitive /rɪˈpetɪtɪv/ *adj.* eintönig; **sth. is ~:** etw. bietet keine Abwechslung

repetitive ˈstrain injury *n.* chronisches Überlastungssyndrom

rephrase /riːˈfreɪz/ *v.t.* umformulieren; **I'll ~ that** ich will es anders ausdrücken

replace /rɪˈpleɪs/ *v.t.* **(a)** (vertically) zurückstellen; (horizontally) zurücklegen; wieder einordnen ‹*Karteikarte*›; [wieder] auflegen ‹*Telefonhörer*›; **(b)** (take place of, provide substitute for) ersetzen; **~ A with** *or* **by B** A durch B ersetzen; **(c)** (renew) ersetzen ‹*Gestohlenes usw.*›; austauschen, auswechseln ‹*Maschinen[teile] usw.*›

replacement /rɪˈpleɪsmənt/ *n.* **(a)** ⇒ **replace a:** Zurückstellen, *das;* Zurücklegen, *das;* Wiedereinordnen, *das;* Auflegen, *das;* **(b)** (provision of substitute for) Ersatz, *der;* Ersetzen, *das; attrib.* Ersatz-; **(c)** (substitute) Ersatz, *der;* **~ [part]** Ersatzteil, *das*

replay 1 /riːˈpleɪ/ *v.t.* wiederholen ‹*Spiel*›; nochmals abspielen ‹*Tonband usw.*›. **2** /ˈriːpleɪ/ *n.* Wiederholung, *die;* (match) Wiederholungsspiel, *das*

replenish /rɪˈplenɪʃ/ *v.t.* [wieder] auffüllen

replete /rɪˈpliːt/ *adj.* (filled) reich (**with** an + *Dat.*)

replica /ˈreplɪkə/ *n.* Nachbildung, *die;* (of work of art) Kopie, *die*

reply /rɪˈplaɪ/ **1** *v.i.* **~ [to sb./sth.]** [jmdm./auf etw. (*Akk.*)] antworten. **2** *v.t.* **~ that ...:** antworten, dass ... **3** *n.* Antwort, *die* (**to** auf + *Akk.*); **in/by way of ~:** als

Antwort; **in ~ to your letter** in Beantwortung Ihres Schreibens (Amtsspr.)

report /rɪˈpɔːt/ **1** *v.t.* **(a)** (relate) berichten/(in writing) einen Bericht schreiben über (+ *Akk.*) ‹*Ereignis usw.*›; (state formally also) melden; **sb. is/was ~ed to be ...:** jmd. soll ... sein/gewesen sein; **~ sb. missing** jmdn. als vermisst melden; **(b)** (repeat) übermitteln (**to** *Dat.*) ‹*Botschaft*›; wiedergeben (**to** *Dat.*) ‹*Worte, Sinn*›; **he is ~ed as having said that ...:** er soll gesagt haben, dass ...; **(c)** (name or notify to authorities) melden (**to** *Dat.*); (for prosecution) anzeigen (**to** bei). **2** *v.i.* **(a)** Bericht erstatten (**on** über + *Akk.*); berichten (**on** über + *Akk.*); (Radio, Telev.) **[this is]** John Tally **~ing [from Delhi]** John Tally berichtet [aus Delhi]; **(b)** (present oneself) sich melden (**to** bei); **~ for duty** sich zum Dienst melden; **~ sick** sich krankmelden; **(c)** (be responsible) **~ to sb.** jmdm. unterstehen. **3** *n.* **(a)** (account) Bericht, *der* (**on, about** über + *Akk.*); (in newspaper etc. also) Reportage, *die* (**on** über + *Akk.*); **make a ~:** einen Bericht abfassen; **(b)** (Sch.) Zeugnis, *das;* **(c)** (sound) Knall, *der;* **(d)** (rumour) Gerücht, *das*

~ ˈback *v.i.* **(a)** (present oneself again) sich zurückmelden (**for** zu); **(b)** (give a ~) Bericht erstatten (**to** *Dat.*)

reˈport card *n.* (Amer.) Zeugnis, *das*

reported ˈspeech *n.* (Ling.) indirekte Rede

reporter /rɪˈpɔːtə(r)/ *n.* **▶ 887⎮** (Radio, Telev., Journ.) Reporter, *der*/Reporterin, *die;* Berichterstatter, *der*/-erstatterin, *die*

repose /rɪˈpəʊz/ (literary) **1** *n.* (rest, respite) Ruhe, *die.* **2** *v.i.* (lie) ruhen

reprehensible /reprɪˈhensɪbl/ *adj.* tadelnswert; sträflich

represent /reprɪˈzent/ *v.t.* **(a)** (symbolize) verkörpern; **(b)** (denote, depict, present) darstellen (**as** als); (Theatre also) spielen; **(c)** (correspond to) entsprechen (+ *Dat.*); **(d)** (be specimen of, act for) vertreten

representation /reprɪzenˈteɪʃn/ *n.* **(a)** (depicting, image) Darstellung, *die;* **(b)** (acting for sb.) Vertretung, *die;* **(c)** (protest) Protest, *der;* **make ~s to sb.** bei jmdm. Protest einlegen

representative /reprɪˈzentətɪv/ **1** *n.* **(a) ▶ 887⎮** (member, agent, deputy) Vertreter, *der*/Vertreterin, *die;* (firm's agent, deputy also) Repräsentant, *der*/Repräsentantin, *die;* **(b) R~** (Amer. Polit.) Abgeordneter/Abgeordnete im Repräsentantenhaus; **House of R~s** Repräsentantenhaus, *das.* **2** *adj.* **(a)** (typical) repräsentativ (**of** für); **(b)** (consisting of deputies) Abgeordneten‹*versammlung, -kammer usw.*›; **(c)** (Polit.: based on representation) repräsentativ; Repräsentativ‹*system, -verfassung*›; **(d) be ~ of** (portray) darstellen; (symbolize) symbolisieren; ‹*Person:*› verkörpern

repress /rɪˈpres/ *v.t.* **(a)** unterdrücken ‹*Aufruhr, Gefühle, Lachen usw.*›; **(b)** (Psych.) verdrängen ‹*Gefühle*› (**from** aus)

repressed /rɪˈprest/ *adj.* unterdrückt; (Psych.) verdrängt

repression /rɪˈpreʃn/ *n.* Unterdrückung, *die;* (Psych.) Verdrängung, *die*

repressive /rɪˈpresɪv/ *adj.* repressiv

reprieve /rɪˈpriːv/ **1** *v.t.* **~ sb.** (postpone execution) jmdm. Strafaufschub gewähren; (remit execution) jmdn. begnadigen; (fig.) verschonen. **2** *n.* Strafaufschub, *der* (**of** für); Begnadigung, *die;* (fig.) Gnadenfrist, *die*

reprimand /ˈreprɪmɑːnd/ **1** *n.* Tadel, *der;* Verweis, *der.* **2** *v.t.* tadeln; einen Verweis erteilen (+ *Dat.*)

reprint 1 /riːˈprɪnt/ *v.t.* **(a)** (print again) wieder abdrucken; **(b)** (make ~ of) nachdrucken. **2** /ˈriːprɪnt/ *n.* (book ~ed) Nachdruck, *der*

reprisal /rɪˈpraɪzl/ *n.* Vergeltungsakt, *der* (**for** gegen)

reproach /rɪˈprəʊtʃ/ **1** *v.t.* **~ sb.** jmdm. Vorwürfe machen; **~ sb. with** *or* **for sth.** jmdm. etw. vorwerfen *od.* zum Vorwurf machen; **have nothing to ~ oneself for** *or* **with** sich (*Dat.*) nichts vorzuwerfen haben. **2** *n.* **(a)** (rebuke) Vorwurf, *der;* **be above** *or* **beyond ~:** über jeden Vorwurf erhaben sein; **look of ~:** vorwurfsvoller Blick; **(b)** (disgrace) Schande, *die* (**to** für)

reproachful /rɪˈprəʊtʃfl/ *adj.* vorwurfsvoll

reprobate /ˈreprəbeɪt/ *n.* Halunke, *der*

reprocess /riːˈprəʊses/ *v.t.* wieder aufbereiten

reproduce /riːprəˈdjuːs/ **1** *v.t.* wiedergeben; reproduzieren (Druckw.) ‹*Bilder usw.*›. **2** *v.i.* (multiply) sich fortpflanzen; sich vermehren

reproduction /riːprəˈdʌkʃn/ *n.* **(a)** Wiedergabe, *die;* Reproduktion, *die* (Druckw.); ~ **of sound** Tonwiedergabe, *die;* **(b)** (producing offspring) Fortpflanzung, *die;* **(c)** (copy) Reproduktion, *die; attrib.* ~ **furniture** Stilmöbel *Pl.*

reproof /rɪˈpruːf/ *n.* Tadel, *der*

reprove /rɪˈpruːv/ *v.t.* tadeln ‹*Verhalten usw.*›; tadeln, zurechtweisen ‹*Person*›

reptile /ˈreptaɪl/ *n.* Reptil, *das;* Kriechtier, *das*

reptilian /repˈtɪljən/ *adj.* reptilartig; (of reptile) Reptilien‹*knochen, -schädel*›

republic /rɪˈpʌblɪk/ *n.* Republik, *die*

republican /rɪˈpʌblɪkən/ **1** *adj.* **(a)** republikanisch; **(b)** (Amer. Polit.) **R~ Party** Republikanische Partei. **2** *n.* **R~** (Amer. Polit.) Republikaner, *der*/Republikanerin, *die*

repudiate /rɪˈpjuːdɪeɪt/ *v.t.* **(a)** (deny) zurückweisen ‹*Anschuldigung usw.*›; (reject) nicht anerkennen ‹*Autorität, Vertrag usw.*›; **(b)** (disown) verstoßen ‹*Person*›

repugnance /rɪˈpʌgnəns/ *n.* Abscheu, *der* (**to[wards]** vor + *Dat.*)

repugnant /rɪˈpʌgnənt/ *adj.* widerlich; abstoßend; **be ~ to sb.** jmdm. widerlich sein

repulse /rɪˈpʌls/ *v.t.* (lit. or fig.) abwehren

repulsion /rɪˈpʌlʃn/ *n.* **(a)** (disgust) Widerwille, *der* (**towards** gegen); **(b)** (Phys.) Repulsion, *die*

repulsive /rɪˈpʌlsɪv/ *adj.* (disgusting) abstoßend; widerwärtig

reputable /ˈrepjʊtəbl/ *adj.* angesehen ‹*Person, Familie, Beruf, Zeitung usw.*›; anständig ‹*Verhalten*›; seriös ‹*Firma*›

reputation /repjʊˈteɪʃn/ *n.* **(a)** Ruf, *der;* **have a ~ for doing/being sth.** in dem Ruf stehen, etw. zu tun/sein; **what sort of ~ do they have?** wie ist ihr Ruf?; **(b)** (good name) Name, *der;* **(c)** (bad name) schlechter Ruf

repute /rɪˈpjuːt/ **1** *v.t. in pass.* **be ~d [to be] sth.** als etw. gelten; **she is ~d to have/make …:** man sagt, dass sie … hat/macht. **2** *n.* Ruf, *der;* Ansehen, *das;* **hold sb./ sth. in high ~:** von jmdm./etw. eine hohe Meinung haben; jmdn./etw. hoch schätzen (geh.)

reputedly /rɪˈpjuːtɪdlɪ/ *adv.* angeblich; vermeintlich

request /rɪˈkwest/ **1** *v.t.* bitten; ~ **sth. of** *or* **from sb.** jmdn. um etw. bitten; ~ **a record** einen Plattenwunsch äußern; ~ **sb. to do sth.** jmdn. [darum] bitten, etw. zu tun; **'You are ~ed not to smoke'** „Bitte nicht rauchen". **2** *n.* Bitte, *die* (**for** um); **at sb.'s ~:** auf jmds. Bitte *od.* Wunsch (*Akk.*) [hin]; **I have one ~ to make of you** ich habe eine Bitte an Sie; **by** *or* **on ~:** auf Wunsch; **record ~s** (Radio) Plattenwünsche *Pl.*

re'quest stop *n.* (Brit.) Bedarfshaltestelle, *die*

requiem /ˈrekwɪem/ *n.* Requiem, *das*

require /rɪˈkwaɪə(r)/ *v.t.* **(a)** (need, wish to have) brauchen; benötigen; erfordern ‹*Tun, Verhalten*›; **a catalogue/ guide is available if ~d** bei Bedarf ist ein Katalog erhältlich/auf Wunsch steht ein Führer zur Verfügung; **is there anything else you ~?** brauchen/(want) wünschen Sie außerdem noch etwas?; **(b)** (order, demand) verlangen (**of** von); ~ **sb. to do sth.**, ~ **of sb. that he does sth.** von jmdm. verlangen, dass er etw. tut; **be ~d to do sth.** etw. tun müssen *od.* sollen

requirement /rɪˈkwaɪəmənt/ *n.* **(a)** (need) Bedarf, *der;* **meet the ~s** den Bedarf decken; **meet sb.'s ~s** jmds. Wünschen entsprechen; **(b)** (condition) Erfordernis, *das;* (for a job) Voraussetzung, *die;* **fulfil sb.'s ~s** jmds. Anforderungen (*Dat.*) genügen

requisite /ˈrekwɪzɪt/ **1** *adj.* notwendig (**to, for** für). **2** *n.* **toilet/travel ~s** Toiletten-/Reiseartikel *Pl.*

requisition /rekwɪˈzɪʃn/ **1** *n.* **(a)** (esp. Law: demand) Aufforderung, *die;* **(b)** (order for sth.) Anforderung, *die* (**for** *Gen.*); (by force if necessary) Beschlagnahmung, *die* (**for** *Gen.*). **2** *v.t.* anfordern; (by force if necessary) beschlagnahmen

reran ⇒ **rerun 1**

reread /riːˈriːd/ *v.t.*, **reread** /riːˈred/ wieder *od.* nochmals lesen

re-route /riːˈruːt/ *v.t.*, **~ing** umleiten

rerun 1 /riːˈrʌn/ *v.t.*, *forms as* **run 3** wiederholen ‹*Rennen*›; wieder auf- *od.* vorführen ‹*Film*›; wieder abspielen ‹*Tonband*›. **2** /ˈriːrʌn/ *n.* ⇒ **1:** Wiederholung, *die;* Wiederaufführung, *die*

resale /riːˈseɪl/ *n.* Weiterverkauf, *der* (Wirtsch.) (**to** an + *Akk.*); **'not for ~'** 'nicht zum Wiederverkauf bestimmt'; (on free samples) 'unverkäufliches Muster'; ~ **price maintenance** Preisbindung, *die*

resat ⇒ **resit 1**

reschedule /riːˈʃedjuːl, riːˈskedjuːl/ *v.t.* zeitlich neu festlegen ‹*Veranstaltung, Flug, Programm usw.*›; **the flight will be ~d for 5 o'clock** der Flug wird auf 5 Uhr verlegt

rescind /rɪˈsɪnd/ *v.t.* für ungültig erklären

rescue /ˈreskjuː/ **1** *v.t.* retten (**from** aus); (set free) befreien (**from** aus); ~ **sb. from drowning** jmdn. vorm Ertrinken retten. **2** *n.* ⇒ **1:** Rettung, *die;* Befreiung, *die; attrib.* Rettungs‹*dienst, -versuch, -mannschaft, -aktion*›; **go/come to the/sb.'s ~:** jmdm. zu Hilfe kommen

rescuer /ˈreskjuːə(r)/ *n.* Retter, *der*/Retterin, *die*

'rescue worker *n.* [Einsatz]helfer, *der*/-helferin, *die*

research /rɪˈsɜːtʃ, ˈriːsɜːtʃ/ **1** *n.* **(a)** (scientific study) Forschung, *die* (**into, on** über + *Akk.*); **do ~ in biochemistry** auf dem Gebiet der Biochemie forschen; **piece of ~:** Forschungsarbeit, *die;* (investigation) Untersuchung, *die;* **(b)** (inquiry) Nachforschung, *die* (**into** über + *Akk.*). **2** *v.i.* forschen; ~ **into sth.** etw. erforschen *od.* untersuchen; (esp. Univ.) über etw. (*Akk.*) forschen. **3** *v.t.* erforschen; untersuchen; recherchieren ‹*Buch usw.*›

research assistant /-ˈ—, -ˈ—/ *n.* **▶ 887|** wissenschaftlicher Assistent/wissenschaftliche Assistentin

researcher /rɪˈsɜːtʃə(r)/ *n.* **▶ 887|** Forscher, *der*/Forscherin, *die*

research: ~ **fellowship** *n.* Forschungsstipendium, *das;* ~ **student** *n.* ≈ Doktorand, *der*/Doktorandin, *die;* ~ **worker** *n.* mit Nachforschungen beauftragte Person; ≈ Rechercheur, *der*/Rechercheurin, *die*

reselect /riːsɪˈlekt/ *v.t.* (Parl.) wieder aufstellen ‹*Abgeordneten*›

resemblance /rɪˈzembləns/ *n.* Ähnlichkeit, *die* (**to** mit, **between** zwischen + *Dat.*); **bear a faint/strong/no ~ to …:** eine geringe/starke/keine Ähnlichkeit mit … haben

resemble /rɪˈzembl/ *v.t.* ähneln, gleichen (+ *Dat.*)

resent /rɪˈzent/ *v.t.* übel nehmen; **she ~ed his success** sie missgönnte ihm seinen Erfolg; **she ~ed his having won** sie ärgerte sich darüber, dass er gewonnen hatte

resentful /rɪˈzentfl/ *adj.* übelnehmerisch, nachtragend ‹*Person, Art, Verhalten*›; grollend (geh.) ‹*Blick*›; **feel ~ about sth.** etw. übel nehmen; **be ~ of sb.'s success** jmdm. seinen Erfolg missgönnen

resentment /rɪˈzentmənt/ *n.*, *no pl.* Groll, *der* (geh.); **feel ~ towards** *or* **against sb.** einen Groll auf jmdn. haben

reservation /rezəˈveɪʃn/ *n.* **(a)** Reservierung, *die;* [seat] ~**:** [Platz]reservierung, *die;* **(b)** (doubt, objection) Vorbehalt, *der* (**about** gegen); Bedenken (**about** bezüglich + *Gen.*); **without ~:** ohne Vorbehalt; vorbehaltlos; **with ~s** mit [gewissen] Vorbehalten; **(c)** ⇒ **central reservation**

reserve /rɪˈzɜːv/ **1** *v.t.* **(a)** (secure) reservieren lassen ‹*Tisch, Platz, Zimmer*›; (set aside) reservieren; ~ **the right to do sth.** sich (*Dat.*) [das Recht] vorbehalten, etw. zu tun; **all rights ~d** alle Rechte vorbehalten; **(b)** *in pass.* (be kept) **be ~d for sb.** ‹*Funktion, Tätigkeit:*› jmdm. vorbehalten sein; **(c)** (postpone) ~ **judgement** sein Urteil aufschieben. **2** *n.* **(a)** (extra amount) Reserve, *die* (**of** an + *Dat.*); (Banking also) Rücklage, *die;* ~**s of energy/strength** Energie-/Kraftreserven; **keep sth. in ~:** etw. in Reserve halten; (**in** *sing. or pl.* (Mil.) (troops) Reserve, *die;* **(c)** (Sport) Reservespieler, *der*/-spielerin, *die;* **the R~s** die Reserve; **(d)** (restriction) Vorbehalt, *der;* **without ~:** ohne Vorbehalt; vorbehaltlos; **(e)** (reticence) Reserve, *die;* Zurückhaltung, *die*

reserved /rɪˈzɜːvd/ adj. (a) (reticent) reserviert; zurückhaltend; (b) (booked) reserviert

reservist /rɪˈzɜːvɪst/ n. (Mil.) Reservist, der

reservoir /ˈrezəvwɑː(r)/ n. (a) ([artificial] lake) Reservoir, das; (b) (container) Behälter, der; Speicher, der

resettle /riːˈsetl/ v.t. umsiedeln ‹Flüchtlinge usw.› (in in + Akk.)

reshape /riːˈʃeɪp/ v.t. (a) (give new form to) umgestalten; umstellen ‹Politik›; (b) (remould) umformen

reshuffle /riːˈʃʌfl/ 1 v.t. (a) (reorganize) umbilden ‹Kabinett usw.›; (b) (Cards) neu mischen. 2 n. Umbildung, die; ‹Cabinet ∼: Kabinettsumbildung, die

reside /rɪˈzaɪd/ v.i. (formal) (a) (dwell) wohnen; wohnhaft sein (Amtsspr.); ‹Monarch, Präsident usw.:› residieren; (b) (be vested, present) liegen (in bei)

residence /ˈrezɪdəns/ n. (a) (abode) Wohnsitz, der; (house) Wohnhaus, das; (mansion) Villa, die; (of a head of state or church, an ambassador) Residenz, die; **the President's official ∼:** der offizielle Wohnsitz des Präsidenten; (b) (residing) Aufenthalt, der; **take up ∼ in Rome** seinen Wohnsitz in Rom nehmen; **be in ∼** ‹König, Präsident usw.:› [an seinem offiziellen Wohnsitz] anwesend sein

'residence permit n. Aufenthaltsgenehmigung, die

resident /ˈrezɪdənt/ 1 adj. (a) (residing) wohnhaft; **he is ∼ in England** er hat seinen Wohnsitz in England; (b) (living in) im Haus wohnend ‹Haushälterin›; Anstalts‹arzt, -geistlicher›. 2 n. (inhabitant) Bewohner, der/Bewohnerin, die; (in a town etc. also) Einwohner, der/Einwohnerin, die; (at hotel) Hotelgast, der; **'access/parking for ∼s only'** „Anlieger frei"/„Parken nur für Anwohner"

residential /rezɪˈdenʃl/ adj. (a) Wohn‹gebiet, -siedlung, -straße›; (b) **∼ course** Kurs, dessen Teilnehmer am Ort wohnen

residual /rɪˈzɪdjʊəl/ adj. zurückgeblieben; noch vorhanden

residue /ˈrezɪdjuː/ n. (a) (remainder) Rest, der; (b) (Chem.) Rückstand, der

resign /rɪˈzaɪn/ 1 v.t. (hand over) zurücktreten von ‹Amt›; verzichten auf (+ Akk.) ‹Recht, Anspruch›; **∼ one's job/ post** seine Stelle/Stellung kündigen. 2 v. refl. **∼ oneself to sth.** sich mit etw. abfinden. 3 v.i. ‹Arbeitnehmer:› kündigen; ‹Regierungsbeamter:› zurücktreten (from von); ‹Vorsitzender:› zurücktreten, sein Amt niederlegen

resignation /rezɪɡˈneɪʃn/ n. (a) ⇒ **resign 3:** Kündigung, die; Rücktritt, der; **give in** or **tender one's ∼:** seine Kündigung/seinen Rücktritt einreichen; (b) (being resigned) Ergebenheit, die (**to** in + Akk.)

resigned /rɪˈzaɪnd/ adj. resigniert; **be ∼ to sth.** sich mit etw. abgefunden haben

resilience /rɪˈzɪliəns/ n., no pl. (a) (elasticity) Elastizität, die; (b) (fig.) Unverwüstlichkeit, die

resilient /rɪˈzɪliənt/ adj. (a) (elastic) elastisch; (b) (fig.) unverwüstlich; **be ∼:** sich nicht [so leicht] unterkriegen lassen

resin /ˈrezɪn/ n. (Bot.) Harz, das

resist /rɪˈzɪst/ 1 v.t. (a) (withstand action of) standhalten (+ Dat.) ‹Frost, Hitze, Feuchtigkeit usw.›; (b) (oppose, repel) sich widersetzen (+ Dat.) ‹Maßnahme, Festnahme, Plan usw.›; widerstehen (+ Dat.) ‹Versuchung, jmds. Charme›; Widerstand leisten gegen ‹Angriff, Feind›; sich wehren gegen ‹Veränderung, Einfluss›. 2 v.i. ⇒ **1b:** sich widersetzen; widerstehen; Widerstand leisten; sich wehren

resistance /rɪˈzɪstəns/ n. (a) (resisting, opposing force) Widerstand, der (**to** gegen); **make** or **offer no ∼ [to sb./ sth.]** [jmdm./einer Sache] keinen Widerstand leisten; (b) (Biol., Med.) Widerstandskraft, die (**to** gegen); (c) (against occupation) Widerstand, der

resistance: ∼ fighter n. Widerstandskämpfer, der/ -kämpferin, die; **∼ movement** n. Widerstandsbewegung, die

resistant /rɪˈzɪstənt/ adj. (a) (having power to resist) widerstandsfähig (**to** gegen); **heat-/water-/rust-∼:** hitze-/ wasser-/rostbeständig; (b) (Med., Biol.) resistent (**to** gegen)

resit 1 /riːˈsɪt/ v.t., **-tt-, resat** /riːˈsæt/ wiederholen ‹Prüfung›. 2 /ˈriːsɪt/ n. Wiederholungsprüfung, die

reskill /riːˈskɪl/ v.t. fort- od. weiterbilden; umschulen ‹Arbeitslose›

resolute /ˈrezəluːt/ adj. resolut, energisch ‹Person›; entschlossen ‹Tat›; entschieden ‹Antwort, Weigerung›

resolution /rezəˈluːʃn/ n. (a) (decision) Entschließung, die; (Polit. also) Resolution, die; (b) (resolve) Vorsatz, der; **make a ∼:** einen Vorsatz fassen; **make a ∼ to do sth.** den Vorsatz fassen, etw. zu tun; **New Year['s] ∼s** gute Vorsätze fürs neue Jahr; (c) no pl. (firmness) Entschlossenheit, die; (d) no pl. (solving) ⇒ **resolve 1 a, b:** Beseitigung, die; Ausräumung, die; Lösung, die

resolve /rɪˈzɒlv/ 1 v.t. (a) (dispel) beseitigen, ausräumen ‹Schwierigkeit, Zweifel, Unklarheit›; (b) (explain) lösen ‹Problem, Rätsel›; (c) (decide) beschließen; (d) (settle) beilegen ‹Streit›; klären ‹Streitpunkt›; regeln ‹Angelegenheit›. 2 v.i. (decide) **∼ [up]on sth./doing sth.** sich zu etw. entschließen/sich [dazu] entschließen, etw. zu tun. 3 n. Vorsatz, der; **make a ∼ to do sth.** den Vorsatz fassen, etw. zu tun

resolved /rɪˈzɒlvd/ pred. adj. **∼ [to do sth.]** entschlossen[, etw. zu tun]

resonance /ˈrezənəns/ n. Resonanz, die; (of voice) voller Klang, (fig.) Widerhall, der

resonant /ˈrezənənt/ adj. (a) hallend ‹Echo, Ton, Klang›; volltönend ‹Stimme›; (b) ‹Raum, Körper:› mit viel Resonanz

resort /rɪˈzɔːt/ 1 n. (a) (resource, recourse) Ausweg, der; **you were my last ∼:** du warst meine letzte Rettung (ugs.); **as a last ∼:** als letzter Ausweg; (b) (place frequented) Aufenthalt[sort], der; **[holiday] ∼:** Urlaubsort, der; **ski/health ∼:** Skiurlaubs-/Kurort, der; **seaside ∼:** Seebad, das. 2 v.i. **∼ to sth./sb.** zu etw. greifen/sich an jmdn. wenden (**for** um); **∼ to violence** Gewalt anwenden; **∼ to stealing/shouting** etc. sich aufs Stehlen/Schreien usw. verlegen

resound /rɪˈzaʊnd/ v.i. (a) (ring) widerhallen (**with** von); (b) (produce echo) hallen

resounding /rɪˈzaʊndɪŋ/ adj. hallend ‹Lärm, Schreie›; schallend ‹Gelächter, Stimme›; überwältigend ‹Sieg, Erfolg›; gewaltig ‹Niederlage, Misserfolg›

resource /rɪˈsɔːs/ n. (a) usu. in pl. (stock) Mittel Pl.; Ressource, die; **financial/mineral ∼s** Geldmittel Pl./ Bodenschätze Pl.; (b) usu. pl. (Amer.: asset) Aktivposten, der; (c) (expedient) Ausweg, der; **be left to one's own ∼s** sich (Dat.) selbst überlassen sein; see also **throw 1 b**

resourceful /rɪˈsɔːsfl/ adj. findig ‹Person›; einfallsreich ‹Plan›

respect /rɪˈspekt/ 1 n. (a) (esteem) Respekt, der (**for** vor + Dat.); Achtung, die (**for** vor + Dat.); **show ∼ for sb./ sth.** Respekt vor jmdm./etw. zeigen; **hold sb. in [high** or **great] ∼:** jmdn. [sehr] achten; **treat sb./sth. with ∼:** jmdm./etw. mit Respekt od. Achtung begegnen/etw. mit Vorsicht behandeln; **with [all due] ∼, …:** bei allem Respekt, …; (b) (consideration) Rücksicht, die (**for** auf + Akk.); (c) (aspect) Beziehung, die; Hinsicht, die; **in all/many/ some ∼s** in jeder/vieler/mancher Beziehung od. Hinsicht; (d) (reference) Bezug, der; **with ∼ to …:** in Bezug auf … (Akk.); was … [an]betrifft; (e) in pl. **pay one's ∼s to sb.** (formal) jmdm. seine Aufwartung machen (veralt.). 2 v.t. respektieren; achten; **∼ sb.'s feelings** auf jmds. Gefühle Rücksicht nehmen

respectability /rɪspektəˈbɪlɪtɪ/ n., no pl. ⇒ **respectable a:** Ansehen, das; Ehrbarkeit, die (geh.)

respectable /rɪˈspektəbl/ adj. (a) (of good character) angesehen ‹Bürger usw.›; ehrenwert ‹Motive›; (decent) ehrbar (geh.) ‹Leute, Kaufmann, Hausfrau›; (b) (presentable) anständig, respektabel ‹Beschäftigung usw.›; vornehm, gut ‹Adresse›; ordentlich, (that one can be seen in) vorzeigbar (ugs.) ‹Kleidung›; (c) (considerable) beachtlich ‹Summe›

respectably /rɪˈspektəblɪ/ adv. anständig ‹sich benehmen›; ordentlich ‹gekleidet›

respectful /rɪˈspektfl/ adj. respektvoll (**to[wards]** gegenüber)

respecting /rɪˈspektɪŋ/ *prep.* bezüglich; hinsichtlich

respective /rɪˈspektɪv/ *adj.* jeweilig

respectively /rɪˈspektɪvlɪ/ *adv.* beziehungsweise, *usu. abbr.* bzw.; **he and I contributed £10 and £1 ~:** er und ich steuerten 10 bzw. 1 Pfund bei

respiration /respɪˈreɪʃn/ *n.* (one breath) Atemzug, *der;* (breathing) Atmung, *die*

respirator /ˈrespɪreɪtə(r)/ *n.* (a) (protecting device) Atemschutzgerät, *das;* (b) (Med.) Respirator, *der*

respiratory /ˈrespərətərɪ, rɪˈspɪrətərɪ/ *adj.* Atem⟨geräusch, -wege⟩; Atmungs⟨system, -organ⟩

respite /ˈrespaɪt/ *n.* (a) (delay) Aufschub, *der;* (b) (interval of relief) Ruhepause, *die;* **without ~:** ohne Pause *od.* Unterbrechung

resplendent /rɪˈsplendənt/ *adj.* prächtig

respond /rɪˈspɒnd/ **1** *v.i.* (a) (answer) antworten (**to** auf + *Akk.*); **~ to sb.'s greeting** jmds. Gruß erwidern; (b) (react) reagieren (**to** auf + *Akk.*); ⟨*Patient, Bremsen, Lenkung usw.*⟩ ansprechen (**to** auf + *Akk.*); **they ~ed very generously to this appeal** der Aufruf fand bei ihnen ein großes Echo. **2** *v.t.* antworten; erwidern

response /rɪˈspɒns/ *n.* (a) (answer) Antwort, *die* (**to** auf + *Akk.*); **in ~ [to]** als Antwort [auf (+ *Akk.*)]; **in ~ to your letter** in Beantwortung Ihres Schreibens (Papierdt.); **make no ~:** (b) (reaction) Reaktion, *die;* **make no ~ to sth.** auf etw. (*Akk.*) nicht reagieren

responsibility /rɪspɒnsɪˈbɪlɪtɪ/ *n.* (a) *no pl., no indef. art.* (being responsible) Verantwortung, *die;* **take** *or* **accept/ claim [full] ~ [for sth.]** die [volle] Verantwortung [für etw.] übernehmen; **do sth. on one's own ~:** etw. in eigener Verantwortung tun; (at one's own risk) etw. auf eigene Verantwortung tun; (b) (duty) Verpflichtung, *die;* **that's 'your ~:** dafür bist du verantwortlich

responsible /rɪˈspɒnsɪbl/ *adj.* (a) verantwortlich (**for** für); **hold sb. ~ for sth.** jmdn. für etw. verantwortlich machen; **be ~ to sb. [for sth.]** jmdm. gegenüber [für etw.] verantwortlich sein; **be ~ for sth.** ⟨*Person:*⟩ für etw. verantwortlich sein; ⟨*Sache:*⟩ die Ursache für etw. sein; (b) verantwortlich, verantwortungsvoll ⟨*Stellung, Tätigkeit, Aufgabe*⟩; (c) (trustworthy) verantwortungsvoll, verantwortungsbewusst ⟨*Person*⟩

responsive /rɪˈspɒnsɪv/ *adj.* aufgeschlossen ⟨*Person*⟩; **be ~ to sth.** auf etw. (*Akk.*) reagieren

respray **1** /riːˈspreɪ/ *v.t.* neu spritzen ⟨*Auto*⟩. **2** /ˈriːspreɪ/ *n.* neue Lackierung; **give the car a ~:** den Wagen neu spritzen

rest¹ /rest/ **1** *v.i.* (a) (lie, lit. or fig.) ruhen; **~ on** ruhen auf (+ *Dat.*); (fig.) ⟨*Argumentation:*⟩ sich stützen auf (+ *Akk.*); ⟨*Ruf:*⟩ beruhen auf (+ *Dat.*); **~ against sth.** an etw. (*Dat.*) lehnen, (b) (take repose) ruhen; sich ausruhen (**from** von); (pause) eine Pause machen *od.* einlegen; **I won't ~ until …:** ich werde nicht ruhen noch rasten, bis …; **tell sb. to ~** ⟨*Arzt:*⟩ jmdm. Ruhe verordnen; (c) (be left) **let the matter ~:** die Sache ruhen lassen; **~ assured that …:** seien Sie versichert, dass …; (d) **~ with sb.** ⟨*Verantwortung, Entscheidung, Schuld:*⟩ bei jmdm. liegen. **2** *v.t.* (a) (place for support) **~ sth. against sth.** etw. an etw. (*Akk.*) lehnen; **~ sth. on sth.** (lit. or fig.) etw. auf etw. (*Akk.*) stützen; (b) (give relief to) ausruhen lassen ⟨*Pferd, Körperteil:*⟩; ausruhen ⟨*Augen*⟩; schonen ⟨*Stimme, Körperteil*⟩. **3** *n.* (a) (repose) Ruhe, *die;* **get a good night's ~:** sich ordentlich ausschlafen; **be at ~** (euphem.: be dead) ruhen (geh.); **lay to ~** (euphem.: bury) zur letzten Ruhe betten (geh. verhüll.); (b) (freedom from exertion) Ruhe[pause], *die;* Erholung, *die* (**from** von); **take a ~:** sich ausruhen (**from** von); **tell sb. to take a ~** ⟨*Arzt:*⟩ jmdm. Ruhe verordnen; **set sb.'s mind at ~:** jmdn. beruhigen (**about** hinsichtlich); (c) (pause) **have** *or* **take a ~:** [eine] Pause machen; **give sb./ sth. a ~:** ausruhen lassen ⟨*Person, Nutztier*⟩; (fig.) ruhen lassen ⟨*Thema, Angelegenheit*⟩; **give it a ~!** (coll.) hör jetzt mal auf damit!; (d) (stationary position) **at ~:** in Ruhe; **come to ~:** zum Stehen kommen; (have final position) landen; (e) (Mus.) Pause, *die*

rest² *n.* (remainder) **the ~:** der Rest; **we'll do the ~:** alles Übrige erledigen wir; **the ~ of her clothes** ihre übrigen Kleider; **she's no different from the ~:** sie ist nicht

besser als die anderen; **and [all] the ~ of it** und so weiter; **for the ~:** im Übrigen; sonst

restart /riːˈstɑːt/ *v.t.* (a) (start again) wieder anstellen ⟨*Maschine*⟩; wieder anlassen ⟨*Auto, Motor*⟩; (b) (resume) wieder aufnehmen ⟨*Verhandlungen, Berufstätigkeit*⟩; fortsetzen ⟨*Spiel*⟩; neu starten ⟨*Rennen*⟩

restate /riːˈsteɪt/ *v.t.* (express again) noch einmal darlegen; (express differently) anders darlegen

restaurant /ˈrestərɔ̃, ˈrestərɒnt/ *n.* Restaurant, *das*

'restaurant car *n.* (Brit. Railw.) Speisewagen, *der*

rest: **~-cure** *n.* (Med.) Erholungskur, *die;* **~ day** *n.* Ruhetag, *der*

rested /ˈrestɪd/ *adj.* ausgeruht

restful /ˈrestfl/ *adj.* (a) (free from disturbance) ruhig ⟨*Tag, Woche, Ort*⟩; (b) (conducive to rest) beruhigend

'rest home *n.* Pflegeheim, *das*

restive /ˈrestɪv/ *adj.* (a) (restless) unruhig; (b) (unmanageable) aufsässig ⟨*Einwohner, Bevölkerung*⟩

restless /ˈrestlɪs/ *adj.* unruhig ⟨*Nacht, Schlaf, Bewegung*⟩; ruhelos ⟨*Person, Sehnsucht*⟩

restock /riːˈstɒk/ *v.t.* (a) **~ a shop** das Lager eines Geschäfts wieder auffüllen; (b) wieder besetzen ⟨*Fluss, Teich*⟩

restoration /restəˈreɪʃn/ *n.* (a) (restoring) (of peace, health) Wiederherstellung, *die;* (of a work of art, building, etc.) Restaurierung, *die;* Restauration, *die* (fachspr.); (b) (giving back) Rückgabe, *die;* (c) (re-establishment) Wiedereinführung, *die;* **the R~** (Brit. Hist.) die Restauration

restorative /rɪˈstɔːrətɪv/ *adj.* stärkend; aufbauend

restore /rɪˈstɔː(r)/ *v.t.* (a) (bring to original state) restaurieren ⟨*Bauwerk, Kunstwerk usw.*⟩; konjizieren ⟨*Text, Satz*⟩ (Literaturw.); **~ sb. to health** jmds. Gesundheit wiederherstellen; **his strength was ~d** er kam wieder zu Kräften; (b) (give back) zurückgeben; (c) (reinstate) wieder einsetzen (**to** in + *Akk.*); **~ sb. to power** jmdn. wieder an die Macht bringen; (d) (re-establish) wiederherstellen ⟨*Ordnung, Ruhe, Vertrauen*⟩

restorer /rɪˈstɔːrə(r)/ *n.* (Art, Archit.: person) Restaurator, *der*/Restauratorin, *die*

restrain /rɪˈstreɪn/ *v.t.* zurückhalten ⟨*Gefühl, Lachen, Drang, Person*⟩; bändigen ⟨*unartiges Kind, Tier*⟩; **~ sb./ oneself from doing sth.** jmdn. davon abhalten/sich zurückhalten, etw. zu tun; **~ yourself!** beherrsch dich!

restrained /rɪˈstreɪnd/ *adj.* zurückhaltend ⟨*Wesen, Kritik*⟩; verhalten ⟨*Blick, Geste, Gefühl*⟩; beherrscht ⟨*Reaktion, Worte*⟩

restraint /rɪˈstreɪnt/ *n.* (a) (restriction) Einschränkung, *die;* **without ~:** ungehindert; (b) (reserve) Zurückhaltung, *die;* (c) (moderation) Unaufdringlichkeit, *die;* (self-control) Selbstbeherrschung, *die;* **without ~:** ungehemmt

restrict /rɪˈstrɪkt/ *v.t.* beschränken (**to** auf + *Akk.*); ⟨*Kleidung:*⟩ beengen, einengen

restricted /rɪˈstrɪktɪd/ *adj.* (a) (limited) beschränkt; begrenzt; **~ diet** Diät, *die;* (b) (subject to restriction) Sperr⟨gebiet⟩; begrenzt ⟨*Zulassung, Aufnahme, Anwendbarkeit*⟩; **be ~ to doing sth.** sich darauf beschränken müssen, etw. zu tun

restricted 'area *n.* (a) Sperrgebiet, *das;* (b) (Brit.: with speed limit) *Gebiet mit Geschwindigkeitsbeschränkung*

restriction /rɪˈstrɪkʃn/ *n.* Beschränkung, *die;* Einschränkung, *die* (**on** *Gen.*); **without ~:** ohne Einschränkung; **put** *or* **place** *or* **impose ~s on sth.** etw. einschränken; **speed/weight ~** Geschwindigkeits-/Gewichtsbeschränkung, *die*

restrictive /rɪˈstrɪktɪv/ *adj.* restriktiv; einschränkend *nicht präd.*

'restroom *n.* (esp. Amer.) Toilette, *die*

restructure /riːˈstrʌktʃə(r)/ *v.t.* umstrukturieren

restyle /riːˈstaɪl/ *v.t.* neu stylen

result /rɪˈzʌlt/ **1** *v.i.* (a) (follow) **~ from sth.** die Folge einer Sache ⟨*Gen.*⟩ sein; von etw. herrühren; (future) aus etw. resultieren; (b) (end) **~ in sth.** in etw. (*Dat.*) resultieren; zu etw. führen; **the game ~ed in a draw** das Spiel endete mit einem Unentschieden; **~ in sb.'s doing sth.** zur

Folge haben, dass jmd. etw. tut. **2** *n.* Ergebnis, *das;* Resultat, *das;* **be the** ~ **of sth.** die Folge einer Sache (*Gen.*) sein; **as a** ~ **[of this]** infolgedessen; **without** ~: ergebnislos

resultant /rɪ'zʌltənt/ *attrib. adj.* daraus resultierend

resume /rɪ'zju:m/ **1** *v.t.* (a) (begin again) wieder aufnehmen; fortsetzen ‹*Reise*›; (b) (get back) wieder-, zurückgewinnen; wieder übernehmen ‹*Kommando*›. **2** *v.i.* weitermachen; ‹*Parlament:*› die Sitzung fortsetzen; ‹*Unterricht:*› wieder beginnen

résumé /'rezʊmeɪ/ *n.* (summary) Zusammenfassung, *die*

resumption /rɪ'zʌmpʃn/ *n.* (a) ⇨ **resume 1 a:** Wiederaufnahme, *die;* Fortsetzung, *die;* (b) ⇨ **resume 1 b:** Wieder-, Zurückgewinnung, *die;* Wiederübernahme, *die*

resurface /ri:'sɜ:fɪs/ **1** *v.t.* ~ **a road** den Belag einer Straße erneuern. **2** *v.i.* (lit. or fig.) wieder auftauchen

resurrection /rezə'rekʃn/ *n.* (Relig.) Auferstehung, *die;* **the R**~: die Auferstehung Christi

resuscitate /rɪ'sʌsɪteɪt/ *v.t.* (lit. or fig.) wieder beleben

retail /'ri:teɪl/ **1** *n.* Einzelhandel, *der.* **2** *adj.* Einzel- ‹*handel*›; Einzelhandels‹*geschäft, -preis*›; [End]verkaufs‹*preis*›. **3** *adv.* **buy/sell** ~: en détail kaufen/verkaufen (Kaufmannsspr.). **4** *v.t.* (sell) [im Einzelhandel] verkaufen. **5** *v.i.* im Einzelhandel verkauft werden (**at, for** für)

retailer /'ri:teɪlə(r)/ *n.* Einzelhändler, *der/*-händlerin, *die*

retail 'price index *n.* (Brit.) Preisindex des Einzelhandels

retain /rɪ'teɪn/ *v.t.* (a) (keep) behalten; sich (*Dat.*) bewahren ‹*Witz, Fähigkeit*›; ein-, zurückbehalten ‹*Gelder*›; gespeichert lassen ‹*Information*›; ~ **power** ‹*Partei:*› an der Macht bleiben; ~ **control [of sth.]** die Kontrolle [über etw. (*Akk.*)] behalten; (b) (keep in place) ‹*Damm:*› stauen/‹*Deich:*› zurückhalten/‹*Gefäß:*› halten ‹*Wasser*›; ~ **sth. in position** etw. in der richtigen Position halten; (c) (secure services of) beauftragen ‹*Anwalt*›; (d) (not forget) behalten, sich (*Dat.*) merken ‹*Gedanke, Tatsache*›

retainer /rɪ'teɪnə(r)/ *n.* (fee) Honorarvorschuss, *der*

retake /ri:'teɪk/ *v.t., forms as* **take 1, 2:** (a) (recapture) wieder einnehmen ‹*Stadt, Festung*›; (b) (take again) wiederholen ‹*Prüfung, Strafstoß*›

retaliate /rɪ'tælɪeɪt/ *v.i.* Vergeltung üben (**against** an + *Dat.*); ‹*Truppen:*› zurückschlagen; kontern (**against** *Akk.*) ‹*Maßnahme, Kritik*›

retaliation /rɪtælɪ'eɪʃn/ *n.* (in war, fight) Vergeltung, *die;* Gegenschlag, *der;* (in argument etc.) Konter, *der* (ugs.); Konterschlag, *der;* **in** ~ **for** als Vergeltung für

retard /rɪ'tɑːd/ *v.t.* verzögern; retardieren (bes. Physiol., Psych.)

retarded /rɪ'tɑːdɪd/ *adj.* (Psychol.) **[mentally]** ~: [geistig] zurückgeblieben

retch /retʃ/ **1** *v.i.* würgen. **2** *n.* Würgen, *das*

retell /ri:'tel/ *v.t.*, **retold** /ri:'təʊld/ nacherzählen; (tell again) noch einmal erzählen

retentive /rɪ'tentɪv/ *adj.* gut ‹*Gedächtnis*›

reticence /'retɪsəns/ *n., no pl.* Zurückhaltung, *die*

reticent /'retɪsənt/ *adj.* zurückhaltend (**on, about** in Bezug auf + *Akk.*)

retina /'retɪnə/ *n., pl.* ~**s** *or* ~**e** /'retɪmi:/ (Anat.) Retina, *die* (fachspr.); Netzhaut, *die*

retinue /'retɪnju:/ *n.* Gefolge, *das*

retire /rɪ'taɪə(r)/ **1** *v.i.* (a) (give up work or position) ausscheiden (**from** aus); ‹*Angestellter, Arbeiter:*› in Rente gehen; ‹*Beamter, Militär:*› in Pension *od.* den Ruhestand gehen; ‹*Selbstständiger:*› sich zur Ruhe setzen; (b) (withdraw) sich zurückziehen (**to** in + *Akk.*); (Sport) aufgeben; ~ **[to bed]** sich [zum Schlafen] zurückziehen. **2** *v.t.* aus Altersgründen entlassen; pensionieren, in den Ruhestand versetzen ‹*Beamten, Militär*›

retired /rɪ'taɪəd/ *adj.* aus dem Berufsleben ausgeschieden ‹*Angestellter, Arbeiter, Selbstständiger*›; ‹*Beamter, Soldat:*› im Ruhestand, pensioniert; **be** ~: nicht mehr arbeiten; ‹*Angestellter, Arbeiter:*› Rentner/Rentnerin *od.* in Rente sein; ‹*Beamter, Soldat:*› im Ruhestand *od.* pensioniert sein

retirement /rɪ'taɪəmənt/ *n.* (a) (leaving work) Ausscheiden aus dem Arbeitsleben; (b) *no art.* (period) Ruhestand, *der;* **take early** ~ ‹*Selbstständiger:*› sich vorzeitig zur Ruhe setzen; ‹*Angestellter, Arbeiter:*› vorzeitig in Rente gehen; ‹*Beamter, Militär:*› sich vorzeitig pensionieren lassen; (c) (withdrawing) Rückzug, *der* (**to, into** in + *Akk.*)

retirement: ~ **age** *n.* Altersgrenze, *die;* (of employees also) Rentenalter, *das;* ~ **home** *n.* (a) (house, flat) Altersod. Ruhesitz, *der;* (b) (institution) Alters- *od.* Altenheim, *das;* ~ **pension** *n.* (for employees) [Alters]rente, *die;* (for civil servants, servicemen) Pension, *die*

retiring /rɪ'taɪərɪŋ/ *adj.* (shy) zurückhaltend

retiring age /rɪ'taɪrɪŋ/ ⇨ **retirement age**

retold ⇨ **retell**

retook ⇨ **retake**

retort[1] /rɪ'tɔ:t/ **1** *n.* Entgegnung, *die,* Erwiderung, *die* (**to** auf + *Akk.*). **2** *v.t.* entgegnen. **3** *v.i.* scharf antworten

retort[2] *n.* (Chem., Industry) Retorte, *die*

retrace /rɪ'treɪs/ *v.t.* (a) (trace back) zurückverfolgen; (b) (trace again) nachvollziehen ‹*Entwicklung*›; (c) (go back over) zurückgehen; ~ **one's steps** denselben Weg noch einmal zurückgehen

retract /rɪ'trækt/ **1** *v.t.* (a) (withdraw) zurücknehmen; (b) (Aeronaut.) einziehen, einfahren ‹*Fahrgestell*›; (c) (draw back) zurückziehen; einziehen ‹*Fühler, Krallen*›. **2** *v.i.* (a) (Aeronaut.) ‹*Fahrgestell:*› einziehbar *od.* einfahrbar sein; (b) (be drawn back) ‹*Fühler, Krallen:*› eingezogen werden

retraction /rɪ'trækʃn/ *n.* (withdrawing) Zurücknahme, *die*

retrain /ri:'treɪn/ **1** *v.i.* [sich] umschulen [lassen]. **2** *v.t.* umschulen ‹*Person*›

retread /'ri:tred/ *n.* (Motor Veh.) runderneuerter Reifen

retreat /rɪ'tri:t/ **1** *n.* (a) (withdrawal; also Mil. or fig.) Rückzug, *der;* **beat a** ~: den Rückzug antreten; (fig.) das Feld räumen; (b) (place of seclusion) Zuflucht, *die;* Zufluchtsort, *der;* (hiding place also) Unterschlupf, *der.* **2** *v.i.* (withdraw; also Mil. or fig.) sich zurückziehen; (in fear) zurückweichen; ~ **within oneself** sich in sich (*Akk.*) selbst zurückziehen

retrench /rɪ'trentʃ/ **1** *v.t.* senken ‹*Ausgaben, Lohn*›. **2** *v.i.* sich einschränken

retrial /ri:'traɪəl/ *n.* (Law) Wiederaufnahmeverfahren, *das*

retribution /retrɪ'bju:ʃn/ *n.* Vergeltung, *die;* **in** ~ **for** zur Vergeltung für

retrieval /rɪ'tri:vl/ *n.* (a) (setting right) (of situation) Rettung, *die;* (of mistake) Wiedergutmachung, *die;* **beyond** *or* **past** ~: hoffnungslos; (b) (rescue) Rettung, *die;* (from wreckage) Bergung, *die;* (c) (recovery) (of letter) Zurückholen, *das;* (of ball) Wiederholen, *das;* (d) (Computing) Wiederauffinden, *das*

retrieve /rɪ'tri:v/ *v.t.* (a) (set right) wieder gutmachen ‹*Fehler*›; retten ‹*Situation*›; (b) (rescue) retten (**from** aus); (from wreckage) bergen (**from** aus); (c) (recover) zurückholen ‹*Brief*›; wiederholen ‹*Ball*›; wiederbekommen ‹*Geld*›; (d) (Computing) wieder auffinden ‹*Information*›; (e) (fetch) ‹*Hund:*› apportieren

retriever /rɪ'tri:və(r)/ *n.* Apportierhund, *der;* (breed) Retriever, *der*

retrograde /'retrəgreɪd/ *adj.* rückschrittlich ‹*Idee, Politik, Maßnahme*›; ~ **step** (fig.) Rückschritt, *der*

retro-rocket /'retrəʊrɒkɪt/ *n.* (Astronaut.) Bremsrakete, *die*

retrospect /'retrəspekt/ *n.* **in** ~: im Nachhinein

retrospective /retrə'spektɪv/ *adj.* (a) retrospektiv (geh.); **take a** ~ **look at sth.** Rückschau auf etw. (*Akk.*) halten (geh.); (b) (applying to the past) rückwirkend ‹*Lohnerhöhung, Gesetz, Vertragsänderung*›

retrospectively /retrə'spektɪvlɪ/ *adv.* (so as to apply to the past) rückwirkend

retrovirus /'retrəʊvaɪrəs/ *n.* Retrovirus, *das od. der*

return /rɪ'tɜ:n/ **1** *v.i.* (a) (come back) zurückkommen; zurückkehren (geh.); (go back) zurückgehen; zurückkehren (geh.); (go back by vehicle) zurückfahren; zurückkehren (geh.); ~ **home** wieder nach Hause kommen/gehen/fahren; zurückkehren; ~ **to work** (after holiday or strike) die Arbeit wieder aufnehmen; (b) (revert) ~ **to a subject** auf ein

Thema zurückkommen. **2** *v.t.* **(a)** (bring back) zurückbringen; zurückgeben ⟨*geliehenen/gestohlenen Gegenstand, gekaufte Ware*⟩; [wieder] zurückschicken ⟨*unzustellbaren Brief*⟩; (hand back, refuse) zurückweisen ⟨*Scheck*⟩; ~ed with thanks mit Dank zurück; '~ to sender' (on letter) „zurück an Absender"; **(b)** (restore) ~ sth. to its original state *or* condition etw. wieder in seinen ursprünglichen Zustand versetzen; **(c)** (yield) abwerfen ⟨*Gewinn*⟩; **(d)** (give back sth. similar) erwidern ⟨*Besuch, Gruß, Liebe, Gewehrfeuer*⟩; sich revanchieren für (ugs.) ⟨*Freundlichkeit, Gefallen*⟩; zurückgeben ⟨*Schlag*⟩; **(e)** (elect) wählen ⟨*Kandidaten*⟩; ~ sb. to Parliament jmdn. ins Parlament wählen; **(f)** (Sport) zurückschlagen ⟨*Ball*⟩; (throw back) zurückwerfen; **(g)** (answer) erwidern; entgegnen; **(h)** (declare) ~ a verdict of guilty/not guilty ⟨*Geschworene:*⟩ auf „schuldig"/„nicht schuldig" erkennen. **3** *n.* **(a)** ▶**836**┃ (coming back) Rückkehr, *die;* (to home) Heimkehr, *die;* ~ to health Genesung, *die* (geh.); many happy ~s [of the day]! herzlichen Glückwunsch [zum Geburtstag]!; **(b)** by ~ [of post] postwendend; **(c)** (ticket) Rückfahrkarte, *die;* single or ~? einfach oder hin und zurück?; **(d)** (proceeds) ~[s] Ertrag, Gewinn, *der* (on, from aus); ~ on capital Kapitalgewinn, *der;* **(e)** (bringing back) Zurückbringen, *das;* (of property, goods, book) Rückgabe, *die* (to an + *Akk.*); **(f)** (giving back of sth. similar) Erwiderung, *die;* receive/get sth. in ~ [for sth.] etw. [für etw.] bekommen

returnable /rɪˈtɜːnəbl/ *adj.* Mehrweg⟨*behälter, -flasche usw.*⟩; rückzahlbar ⟨*Gebühr, Kaution*⟩

return: ~ 'fare *n.* Preis für eine Rückfahrkarte/(for flight) einen Rückflugschein; what is the ~ fare? wieviel kostet eine Rückfahrkarte/ein Rückflugschein?; ~ 'flight *n.* Rückflug, *der;* (both ways) Hin- und Rückflug, *der*

re'turning officer *n.* (Brit. Parl.) Wahlleiter, *der/*-leiterin, *die*

return: ~ 'journey *n.* Rückreise, *die;* Rückfahrt, *die;* (both ways) Hin- und Rückfahrt, *die;* ~ 'match *n.* Rückspiel, *das;* ~ 'ticket *n.* (Brit.) Rückfahrkarte, *die;* (for flight) Rückflugschein, *der;* ~ trip *n.* **(a)** (trip back) Rückweg, *der;* Rückfahrt, *die;* **(b)** (trip out and back) Hin- und Rückfahrt, *die;* Hin- und Rückreise, *die;* (by plane) Hin- und Rückflug, *der;* ~ visit *n.* **(a)** (further visit) nochmaliger Besuch; make a ~ visit to a place einen Ort noch einmal besuchen; **(b)** (visit in reciprocation) Gegenbesuch, *der*

retype /riːˈtaɪp/ *v.t.* neu tippen

reunification /riːjuːnɪfɪˈkeɪʃn/ *n.* Wiedervereinigung, *die*

reunion /riːˈjuːnjən/ *n.* **(a)** (gathering) Treffen, *das;* **(b)** (reuniting) Wiedersehen, *das;* **(c)** (reunited state) Wiedervereinigung, *die*

reunite /riːjuːˈnaɪt/ **1** *v.t.* wieder zusammenführen; a ~d Germany ein wieder vereinigtes Deutschland. **2** *v.i.* sich wieder zusammenschließen

reusable /riːˈjuːzəbl/ *adj.* wiederverwendbar

reuse /riːˈjuːz/ *v.t.* wieder verwenden

Rev. /ˈrevərənd, (coll.) rev/ *abbr.* ▶**1152**┃ Reverend Rev.

rev /rev/ (coll.) **1** *n., usu. in pl.* Umdrehung, *die;* Tour, *die* (Technikjargon). **2** *v.i.,* -vv- mit hoher Drehzahl *od.* hochtourig laufen. **3** *v.t.,* -vv- hochdrehen (Technikjargon); (noisily) aufheulen lassen ⟨*Motor:*⟩

~ 'up *v.i.* ⟨*Motor:*⟩ hochgejagt werden (Technikjargon). **2** *v.t.* hochjagen (Technikjargon); aufheulen lassen ⟨*Motor[rad]*⟩

revaluation /riːvæljuˈeɪʃn/ *n.* (Econ.) Aufwertung, *die*

revalue /riːˈvæljuː/ *v.t.* (Econ.) aufwerten ⟨*Währung*⟩

revamp /riːˈvæmp/ (coll.) *v.t.* renovieren ⟨*Zimmer, Gebäude*⟩; [wieder] aufmöbeln *od.* aufpolieren ⟨*Schrank, Auto usw.*⟩; neu bearbeiten ⟨*Stück, Musical usw.*⟩

reveal /rɪˈviːl/ *v.t.* enthüllen (geh.); verraten; offenbaren (geh., Theol.), [offen] zeigen ⟨*Gefühle:*⟩ be ~ed ⟨*Wahrheit:*⟩ ans Licht kommen; ~ one's identity seine Identität preisgeben (geh.); ~ sb. to be sth. jmdn. als etw. enthüllen (geh.)

revealing /rɪˈviːlɪŋ/ *adj.* aufschlussreich ⟨*Darstellung, Dokument*⟩; verräterisch ⟨*Bemerkung, Versprecher*⟩; offenherzig (scherzh.) ⟨*Kleid, Bluse usw.*⟩

reveille /rɪˈvælɪ/ *n.* (Mil.) Wecksignal, *das*

revel /ˈrevl/ **1** *v.i.,* (Brit.) **-ll-** **(a)** (take delight) genießen (in *Akk.*); ~ in doing sth. es [richtig] genießen, etw. zu tun;

(b) (carouse) feiern. **2** *n. usu pl.* Feiern, *das;* Feierei, *die* (ugs.)

revelation /revəˈleɪʃn/ *n.* **(a)** Enthüllung, *die;* be a ~: einem die Augen öffnen; be a ~ to sb. jmdm. die Augen öffnen; **(b)** (Relig.) Offenbarung, *die*

reveller /ˈrevələ(r)/ *n.* Feiernde, *der/die*

revelry /ˈrevlrɪ/ *n.* Feiern, *das;* Feierei, *die* (ugs.)

revenge /rɪˈvendʒ/ **1** *v.t.* rächen ⟨*Person, Tat*⟩; sich rächen für ⟨*Tat*⟩; ~ oneself *or* be ~d [on sb.] [for sth.] sich [für etw.] [an jmdm.] rächen. **2** *n.* Rache, *die;* [desire for] ~ Rachsucht, *die* (geh.); take ~ *or* have one's ~ [on sb.] [for sth.] Rache [an jmdm.] [für etw.] nehmen *od.* (geh.) üben; in ~ for sth. als Rache für etw.

revenue /ˈrevənjuː/ *n.* **(a)** (State's income) [national/ state] ~: Staatseinnahmen *Pl.;* öffentliche Einnahmen *Pl.;* **(b)** ~[s] (income) Einnahmen *Pl.;* Einkünfte *Pl.*

reverberate /rɪˈvɜːbəreɪt/ *v.i.* ⟨*Geräusch, Musik:*⟩ widerhallen

reverberation /rɪvɜːbəˈreɪʃn/ *n.* ~[s] Widerhall, *der*

revere /rɪˈvɪə(r)/ *v.t.* verehren

reverence /ˈrevərəns/ *n.* (revering) Verehrung, *die;* Ehrfurcht, *die*

reverend /ˈrevərənd/ **1** *adj.* ▶**1152**┃ ehrwürdig; the R~ John Wilson Hochwürden John Wilson. **2** *n.* (coll.) Pfarrer, *der*

reverent /ˈrevərənt/ *adj.* ehrfürchtig

reverie /ˈrevərɪ/ *n.* Träumerei, *die;* fall into a ~: in Träumereien (*Akk.*) versinken

reversal /rɪˈvɜːsl/ *n.* Umkehrung, *die*

reverse /rɪˈvɜːs/ **1** *adj.* entgegengesetzt ⟨*Richtung*⟩; Rück⟨*seite*⟩; umgekehrt ⟨*Reihenfolge*⟩. **2** *n.* **(a)** (contrary) Gegenteil, *das;* quite the ~! ganz im Gegenteil!; **(b)** (Motor Veh.) Rückwärtsgang, *der;* in ~: im Rückwärtsgang; put the car into ~, go into ~: den Rückwärtsgang einlegen; **(c)** (defeat) Rückschlag, *der.* **3** *v.t.* **(a)** (turn around) umkehren ⟨*Reihenfolge, Wortstellung, Bewegung, Richtung*⟩; grundlegend revidieren ⟨*Politik*⟩; ~ the charge[s] (Brit.) ein R-Gespräch anmelden; **(b)** (cause to move backwards) zurücksetzen; **(c)** (revoke) aufheben ⟨*Urteil, Anordnung*⟩; rückgängig machen ⟨*Maßnahme*⟩. **4** *v.i.* zurücksetzen; rückwärts fahren

reverse: ~-charge *adj.* (Brit.) make a ~-charge call ein R-Gespräch führen; ~ 'gear *n.* (Motor Veh.) Rückwärtsgang, *der; see also* gear 1 a

reversible /rɪˈvɜːsɪbl/ *adj.* **(a)** umkehrbar, (fachspr.) reversibel ⟨*Vorgang*⟩; (capable of being revoked) aufhebbar ⟨*Entscheidung, Anordnung*⟩; **(b)** (having two usable sides) beidseitig verwendbar ⟨*Stoff*⟩; beidseitig tragbar ⟨*Kleidungsstück*⟩

re'versing light *n.* Rückfahrscheinwerfer, *der*

revert /rɪˈvɜːt/ *v.i.* **(a)** (recur, return) zurückkommen (to auf + *Akk.*), wieder aufgreifen (to *Akk.*) ⟨*Thema, Angelegenheit, Frage*⟩; ⟨*Gedanken:*⟩ zurückkehren (geh.) (to zu); to ~ to …: um wieder auf … (*Akk.*) zurückzukommen; **(b)** (Law) ⟨*Eigentum:*⟩ zurückfallen (Rechtsspr.) heimfallen (to an + *Akk.*)

review /rɪˈvjuː/ **1** *n.* **(a)** (survey) Übersicht, *die* (of über + *Akk.*); (of past events) Rückschau, *die* (of auf + *Akk.*); be a ~ of sth. einen Überblick *od.* eine Übersicht über etw. (*Akk.*) geben; **(b)** (re-examination) [nochmalige] Überprüfung; (of salary) Revision, *die;* be under ~ ⟨*Vereinbarung, Lage:*⟩ nochmals geprüft werden; **(c)** (of book, play, etc.) Besprechung, *die;* Kritik, *die;* Rezension, *die;* **(d)** (periodical) Zeitschrift, *die;* **(e)** (Mil.) Inspektion, *die.* **2** *v.t.* **(a)** (survey) untersuchen; prüfen; **(b)** (re-examine) überprüfen; **(c)** (Mil.) inspizieren; mustern; **(d)** (write a criticism of) besprechen; rezensieren; **(e)** (Law) überprüfen

revile /rɪˈvaɪl/ *v.t.* schmähen (geh.)

revise /rɪˈvaɪz/ *v.t.* **(a)** (amend) revidieren ⟨*Urteil, Gesetz, Vorschlag*⟩; **(b)** (check over) durchsehen ⟨*Manuskript, Text, Notizen*⟩; **(c)** (reread) noch einmal durchlesen ⟨*Notizen*⟩; *abs.* lernen; ~ one's maths Mathe (ugs.) wiederholen

revision /rɪˈvɪʒn/ *n.* **(a)** (amending) Revision, *die;* in need of ~: revisionsbedürftig; **(b)** (checking over) Durchsicht, *die;* **(c)** (amended version) [Neu]bearbeitung, *die;* überarbeitete *od.* revidierte Fassung; **(d)** (rereading) Wiederholung, *die*

revisit /riːˈvɪzɪt/ *v.t.* wieder besuchen
revitalize (**revitalise**) /riːˈvaɪtəlaɪz/ *v.t.* neu beleben
revival /rɪˈvaɪvl/ *n.* (**a**) (making active again) Wieder- *od.* Neubelebung, *die;* (**b**) (Theatre) Wiederaufführung, *die;* Revival, *das;* (**c**) (Relig.: awakening) Erweckung, *die;* (**d**) (restoration) Wiederherstellung, *die;* Regenerierung, *die* (geh.); (to consciousness or life; also fig.) Wiederbelebung, *die*
revive /rɪˈvaɪv/ **1** *v.i.* (**a**) (come back to consciousness) wieder zu sich kommen; (**b**) (be revitalized) wieder aufleben; zu neuem Leben erwachen; ⟨*Geschäft:*⟩ sich wieder beleben. **2** *v.t.* (**a**) (restore to consciousness) wieder beleben; (**b**) (restore to healthy state) wieder auf die Beine bringen ⟨*Person*⟩; (strengthen, reawaken) wieder wecken ⟨*Wunsch, Interesse, Ehrgeiz*⟩; ~ **sb.'s hopes** jmdn. neue Hoffnung schöpfen lassen; (**c**) (make active again) wieder aufleben lassen; (**d**) (Theatre) wieder auf die Bühne bringen
revoke /rɪˈvəʊk/ *v.t.* aufheben ⟨*Erlass, Privileg, Entscheidung*⟩; zurückziehen ⟨*Auftrag*⟩; widerrufen ⟨*Befehl, Erlaubnis, Genehmigung*⟩; zurücknehmen ⟨*Versprechen*⟩
revolt /rɪˈvəʊlt/ **1** *v.i.* (**a**) (rebel) revoltieren, aufbegehren (geh.) (**against** gegen); (**b**) (feel revulsion) sich sträuben (**at, against, from** gegen). **2** *v.t.* mit Abscheu erfüllen. **3** *n.* (rebelling) Aufruhr, *der;* Rebellion, *die;* (rising) Revolte, *die* (auch fig.); Aufstand, *der;* **be** *or* **rise in** ~: revoltieren; aufbegehren (geh.)
revolting /rɪˈvəʊltɪŋ/ *adj.* (repulsive) abscheulich; scheußlich ⟨*Gedanke, Wetter*⟩; widerlich ⟨*Person*⟩
revolution /revəˈluːʃn/ *n.* (**a**) (lit. or fig.) Revolution, *die;* (**b**) (single turn) Umdrehung, *die;* **number of** ~**s** Drehzahl, *die*
revolutionary /revəˈluːʃənərɪ/ **1** *adj.* (**a**) (Polit.) revolutionär; (**b**) (involving great changes) revolutionär; umwälzend; (pioneering) bahnbrechend. **2** *n.* Revolutionär, *der*/Revolutionärin, *die*
revolutionize (**revolutionise**) /revəˈluːʃənaɪz/ *v.t.* grundlegend verändern; revolutionieren ⟨*Gesellschaft, Technik*⟩
revolve /rɪˈvɒlv/ **1** *v.t.* drehen. **2** *v.i.* sich drehen (**round, about, on** um); **everything** ~**s around her** sie ist der Mittelpunkt[, um den sich alles dreht]
revolver /rɪˈvɒlvə(r)/ *n.* [Trommel]revolver, *der*
revolving /rɪˈvɒlvɪŋ/ *attrib. adj.* drehbar; Dreh⟨*stuhl, -bühne, -tür*⟩
revue /rɪˈvjuː/ *n.* Kabarett, *das;* (musical show) Revue, *die*
revulsion /rɪˈvʌlʃn/ *n.* (feeling) Abscheu, *der* (**at** vor + *Dat.,* gegen)
reward /rɪˈwɔːd/ **1** *n.* Belohnung, *die;* (for kindness) Dank, *der;* Lohn, *der;* (recognition of merit etc.) Auszeichnung, *die;* **offer a** ~ **of** £100 100 Pfund Belohnung aussetzen. **2** *v.t.* belohnen
rewarding /rɪˈwɔːdɪŋ/ *adj.* lohnend ⟨*Zeitvertreib, Beschäftigung*⟩; **be** ~/**financially** ~: sich lohnen/einträglich sein
rewind /riːˈwaɪnd/ *v.t.,* **rewound** /riːˈwaʊnd/ (**a**) (wind again) wieder aufziehen ⟨*Uhr*⟩; (**b**) (wind back) zurückspulen ⟨*Film, Band*⟩
'rewind button *n.* (on camera) Rückspulknopf, *der;* (on tape recorder etc.) Rücklauftaste, *die*
rewire /riːˈwaɪə(r)/ *v.t.* mit neuen Leitungen versehen
reword /riːˈwɜːd/ *v.t.* umformulieren; neu formulieren
rewrite /riːˈraɪt/ *v.t.,* **rewrote** /riːˈrəʊt/, **rewritten** /riːˈrɪtn/ (write again) noch einmal [neu] schreiben; (write differently) umschreiben
rhapsody /ˈræpsədɪ/ *n.* (**a**) (Mus.) Rhapsodie, *die;* (**b**) (ecstatic utterance) Schwärmerei, *die*
rhesus /ˈriːsəs/: ~ **factor** *n.* (Med.) Rhesusfaktor, *der;* ~ **monkey** *n.* Rhesusaffe, *der*
rhetoric /ˈretərɪk/ *n.* (**a**) [art of] ~: Redekunst, *die;* Rhetorik, *die;* (**b**) (derog.) Phrasen (abwertend)
rhetorical /rɪˈtɒrɪkl/ *adj.* (**a**) rhetorisch ⟨*Frage, Diskurs*⟩; (**b**) (derog.) phrasenhaft (abwertend)
rheumatic /ruːˈmætɪk/ ▶ 865 **1** *adj.* rheumatisch. **2** *n.* (**a**) *in pl.* (coll.) Rheuma, *das* (ugs.); (**b**) (person) Rheumatiker, *der*/Rheumatikerin, *die;* Rheumakranke, *der/die*

rheumatism /ˈruːmətɪzm/ *n.* ▶ 865 (Med.) Rheumatismus, *der;* Rheuma, *das* (ugs.)
rheumatoid arthritis /ruːmətɔɪd ɑːˈθraɪtɪs/ *n.* ▶ 865 (Med.) chronischer Gelenkrheumatismus
Rhine /raɪn/ *pr. n.* ▶ 1048 Rhein, *der*
rhino /ˈraɪnəʊ/ *n., pl. same or* ~**s** (coll.), **rhinoceros** /raɪˈnɒsərəs/ *n., pl. same or* ~**es** Nashorn, *das;* Rhinozeros, *das*
rhododendron /rəʊdəˈdendrən/ *n.* (Bot.) Rhododendron, *der;* Alpenrose, *die*
rhubarb /ˈruːbɑːb/ *n.* Rhabarber, *der*
rhyme /raɪm/ **1** *n.* (**a**) Reim, *der;* **without** ~ **or reason** ohne Sinn und Verstand; (**b**) (short poem) Reim, *der;* (rhyming verse) gereimte Verse; (**c**) (rhyming word) Reimwort, *das.* **2** *v.i.* sich reimen (**with** auf + *Akk.*). **3** *v.t.* reimen
rhythm /ˈrɪðm/ *n.* Rhythmus, *der*
rhythmic /ˈrɪðmɪk/, **rhythmical** /ˈrɪðmɪkl/ *adj.* rhythmisch; gleichmäßig
rhythmic gym'nastics *n.* rhythmische Sportgymnastik
'rhythm method *n.* (of contraception) Knaus-Ogino-Methode, *die*
rib /rɪb/ **1** *n.* (**a**) ▶ 672 (Anat.) Rippe, *die;* (**b**) ~[**s**] (joint of meat) Rippenstück, *das;* (**c**) (supporting piece) (of insect's wing) Ader, *die;* (of feather) Kiel, *der;* Schaft, *der;* (of leaf, in knitting) Rippe, *die.* **2** *v.t.,* **-bb-** (coll.) aufziehen (ugs.)
ribald /ˈrɪbəld/ *adj.* zotig; schmutzig ⟨*Lachen*⟩; unanständig ⟨*Ausdrücke*⟩; (irreverent) anzüglich
ribbon /ˈrɪbn/ *n.* (**a**) (band for hair, dress, etc.) Band, *das;* (on typewriter) [Farb]band, *das;* (on medal) [Ordens]band, *das;* (**b**) (fig.: strip) Streifen, *der*
'ribbon development *n.* Bandbebauung, *die*
'ribcage *n.* (Anat.) Brustkorb, *der*
rice /raɪs/ *n.* Reis, *der*
rice: ~-**paper** *n.* Reispapier, *das;* ~ **'pudding** *n.* Reispudding, *der*
rich /rɪtʃ/ **1** *adj.* (**a**) (wealthy) reich; (**b**) (having great resources) reich (**in** an + *Dat.*); (fertile) fruchtbar ⟨*Land, Boden*⟩; **oil-**~: ölreich; ~ **in vitamins**/**lime** vitamin-/kalkreich; (**c**) (splendid) prachtvoll; prächtig; reich ⟨*Ausstattung*⟩; (**d**) (containing much fat, oil, eggs, etc.) gehaltvoll; (indigestible) schwer ⟨*Essen*⟩; (**e**) (deep, full) voll[tönend] ⟨*Stimme*⟩; voll ⟨*Ton*⟩; satt ⟨*Farbe, Farbton*⟩; voll ⟨*Geschmack*⟩; (**f**) (valuable) reich (geh.) ⟨*Geschenke, Opfergaben*⟩; (**g**) (amusing) köstlich; **that's** ~! köstlich!; (iron.) das ist stark! (ugs.). **2** *n. pl.* **the** ~: die Reichen
riches /ˈrɪtʃɪz/ *n. pl.* Reichtum, *der*
richly /ˈrɪtʃlɪ/ *adv.* (**a**) (splendidly) reich; üppig ⟨*ausgestattet*⟩; prächtig ⟨*gekleidet*⟩; ~ **ornamented** reichverziert; (**b**) (fully) voll und ganz; ~ **deserved** wohlverdient
richness /ˈrɪtʃnɪs/ *n., no pl.* (**a**) (elaborateness) Pracht, *die;* Prächtigkeit, *die;* (**b**) (of food) Reichhaltigkeit, *die;* (**c**) (fullness) (of voice) voller Klang; (of colour) Sattheit, *die;* (**d**) (great resources) Reichtum, *der* (**in** an + *Dat.*); (of soil) Fruchtbarkeit, *die*
rickets /ˈrɪkɪts/ *n., constr. as sing. or pl.* ▶ 865 (Med.) Rachitis, *die*
rickety /ˈrɪkɪtɪ/ *adj.* wack[e]lig ⟨*Tisch, Stuhl usw.*⟩; klapp[e]rig ⟨*Auto*⟩
rickshaw /ˈrɪkʃɔː/ *n.* Rikscha, *die*
ricochet /ˈrɪkəʃeɪ/ **1** *n.* (**a**) Abprallen, *das;* (**b**) (hit) Abpraller, *der.* **2** *v.i.,* ~**ed** /ˈrɪkəʃeɪd/ abprallen (**off** von)
rid /rɪd/ *v.t.,* **-dd-, rid:** ~ **sth. of sth.** etw. von etw. befreien; ~ **oneself of sb.**/**sth.** sich von jmdm./etw. befreien; sich jmds./einer Sache entledigen (geh.); **be** ~ **of sb.**/**sth.** jmdn./etw. los sein (ugs.); **get** ~ **of sb.**/**sth.** jmdn./etw. loswerden
riddance /ˈrɪdəns/ *n.* **good** ~ [**to bad rubbish**]! zum Glück *od.* Gott sei Dank ist er/es *usw.* weg!
ridden ⇒ ride 2, 3
riddle¹ /ˈrɪdl/ *n.* Rätsel, *das;* **tell sb. a** ~: jmdm. ein Rätsel aufgeben

riddle² *v.t.* (fill with holes) durchlöchern; ~d **with bullets** von Kugeln durchsiebt; ~d **with corruption** (fig.) von Korruption durchsetzt

ride /raɪd/ **1** *n.* **(a)** (journey) (on horseback) [Aus]ritt, *der;* (in vehicle, at fair) Fahrt, *die;* ~ **in a train/coach** Zug-/Busfahrt, *die;* **go for a** ~: ausreiten; **go for a [bi]cycle** ~: Rad fahren; (longer distance) eine Radtour machen; **go for a** ~ **[in the car]** [mit dem Auto] wegfahren; **have a** ~ **in a train/taxi/on the merry-go-round** mit dem Zug/Taxi/Karussell fahren; **give sb. a** ~: jmdn. mitnehmen; **take sb. for a** ~: jmdn. spazieren fahren; (fig. coll.: deceive) jmdn. reinlegen (ugs.); **(b)** (quality of ~) Fahrkomfort, *der.* **2** *v.i.*, **rode** /rəʊd/, **ridden** /'rɪdn/ **(a)** (travel) (on horse) reiten; (on bicycle, in vehicle; Amer.: in elevator) fahren; ~ **to town on one's bike/in one's car/on the train** mit dem Rad/Auto/Zug in die Stadt fahren; **(b)** (float) ~ **at anchor** vor Anker liegen *od.* (Seemannsspr.) reiten; **(c)** (be carried) reiten; rittlings sitzen; **'X ~s again'** (fig.) „X ist wieder da"; **be riding high** (fig.) Oberwasser haben (ugs.); **let sth.** ~ (fig.) etw. auf sich beruhen lassen. **3** *v.t.*, **rode**, **ridden (a)** (~ on) reiten ⟨*Pferd usw.*⟩; fahren mit ⟨*Fahrrad*⟩; **learn to** ~ **a bicycle** Rad fahren lernen; **(b)** (traverse) (on horseback) reiten; (on cycle) fahren

~ **a'way**, ~ **'off** *v.i.* wegreiten/wegfahren

~ **'out** *v.t.* abreiten (Seemannsspr.) ⟨*Sturm*⟩; (fig.) überstehen

~ **'up** *v.i.* **(a)** ~ **up [to sth.]** ⟨*Reiter:*⟩ an etw. (*Akk.*) heranreiten; ⟨*Fahrer:*⟩ an etw. (*Akk.*) heranfahren; **(b) the skirt rode up over her knees** (fig.) der Rock rutschte über ihr Knie

rider /'raɪdə(r)/ *n.* **(a)** Reiter, *der*/Reiterin, *die;* (of cycle, motorcycle) Fahrer, *der*/Fahrerin, *die;* **(b)** (addition) Zusatz, *der;* **add a** ~: einen Zusatz machen

ridge /rɪdʒ/ *n.* **(a)** (of roof) First, *der;* (of nose) Rücken, *der;* **(b)** (long hilltop) Grat, *der;* Kamm, *der;* ~ **of mountains** Gebirgskamm, *der;* **(c)** (Meteorol.) ~ **[of high pressure]** lang gestrecktes Hoch

ridge tent *n.* Hauszelt, *das*

ridicule /'rɪdɪkjuːl/ **1** *n.* Spott, *der;* **hold sb./sth. up to** ~: jmdn./etw. der Lächerlichkeit preisgeben. **2** *v.t.* verspotten; spotten über (+ *Akk.*)

ridiculous /rɪ'dɪkjʊləs/ *adj.* lächerlich; **don't be** ~! sei nicht albern!; **make oneself [look]** ~: sich lächerlich machen

riding /'raɪdɪŋ/ *n.* Reiten, *das*

riding: ~ **breeches** *n. pl.* Reithose, *die;* ~ **lesson** *n.* Reitstunde, *die;* ~ **school** *n.* Reitschule, *die*

rife /raɪf/ *pred. adj.* (widespread) weit verbreitet; **rumours were** ~: es gingen Gerüchte um

riff-raff /'rɪfræf/ *n.* Gesindel, *das*

rifle /'raɪfl/ **1** *n.* Gewehr, *das;* (hunting ~) Büchse, *die.* **2** *v.t.* (ransack) durchwühlen; (pillage) plündern. **3** *v.i.* ~ **through sth.** etw. durchwühlen

rifle: ~ **range** *n.* Schießstand, *der;* Schießplatz, *der;* ~ **shot** *n.* Gewehrschuss, *der*

rift /rɪft/ *n.* **(a)** (dispute) Unstimmigkeit, *die;* **(b)** (cleft) Spalte, *die*

rig¹ /rɪg/ **1** *n.* **(a)** (Naut.) Takelung, *die;* **(b)** (for oil well) [Öl]förderturm, *der;* (offshore) Förderinsel, *die;* **drilling** ~: Bohrturm, *der;* (offshore) Bohrinsel, *die.* **2** *v.t.*, **-gg-** (Naut.) auftakeln

~ **'out** *v.t.* ausstaffieren

~ **'up** *v.t.* aufbauen

rig² *v.t.*, **-gg-** (falsify) fälschen ⟨*Wahl*⟩; verfälschen, (geh.) manipulieren ⟨[*Wahl*]*ergebnis*⟩

rigging /'rɪgɪŋ/ *n.* (Naut.) Takelung, *die*

right /raɪt/ **1** *adj.* **(a)** (just, morally good) richtig; **it is only** ~ **[and proper] to do sth./that sb. should do sth.** es ist nur recht und billig, etw. zu tun/dass jmd. etw. tut; **(b)** (correct, true) richtig; ~ **enough** völlig richtig; **you're [quite]** ~: du hast [völlig] recht; **too** ~! (coll.) allerdings!; **how** ~ **you are!** wie recht du hast!; **be** ~ **in sth.** Recht mit etw. haben; **let's get it** ~ **this time!** machen wir es diesmal besser!; **is that clock** ~? geht die Uhr da richtig?; **have you got the** ~ **fare?** haben Sie das Fahrgeld passend?; **put** *or* **set** ~: richtig stellen ⟨*Irrtum*⟩; wieder gutmachen ⟨*Unrecht*⟩; berichtigen ⟨*Fehler*⟩; bereinigen

⟨*Missverständnis*⟩; wieder in Ordnung bringen ⟨*Situation, Angelegenheit, Gerät*⟩; **put** *or* **set sb.** ~: jmdn. berichtigen *od.* korrigieren; ~ **[you are]!**, (Brit.) ~ **oh!** (coll.) okay! (ugs.); **alles klar!** (ugs.); **that's** ~: ja[wohl]; **so ist es; is that** ~? stimmt das?; (indeed) aha!; **[am I]** ~? nicht [wahr]?; **oder [nicht]?** (ugs.); *see also* **all** 3; **(c)** (preferable, most suitable) richtig; recht; **do sth. the** ~ **way** etw. richtig machen; **say/do the** ~ **thing** das Richtige sagen/tun; **(d)** (sound, sane) richtig; **not be quite** ~ **in the head** nicht ganz richtig [im Kopf] sein; **as** ~ **as rain** (coll.) (in health) gesund wie ein Fisch im Wasser; (satisfactory) in bester Ordnung; **put sb.** ~ (restore to health) jmdn. [wieder] auf die Beine bringen; *see also* **mind** 1 g; **(e) you're a** ~ **one!** (coll.) du bist mir der/die Richtige!; **(f)** ▶ **1199** (opposite of left) recht…; **on the** ~ **side** auf der rechten Seite; rechts; *see also* **turn** 1 c; **be sb.'s** ~ **arm** (fig.) jmds. rechte Hand sein; **(g)** R~ (Polit.) recht… *See also* **right side. 2** *v.t.* **(a)** (correct) berichtigen; richtig stellen; **(b)** (restore to upright position) [wieder] aufrichten ⟨*Boot usw.:*⟩ ~ **itself** sich [von selbst] [wieder] aufrichten; (fig.: come to proper state) ⟨*Mangel:*⟩ sich [von selbst] geben. **3** *n.* **(a)** (fair claim, authority) Recht, *das;* Anrecht, *das;* **have a/no** ~ **to sth.** ein/kein Anrecht *od.* Recht auf etw. (*Akk.*) haben; **have a** *or* **the/no** ~ **to do sth.** das/kein Recht haben, etw. zu tun; **by** ~ *of* auf Grund (+ *Gen.*); **belong to sb. as** *of or* **by** ~: jmds. rechtmäßiges Eigentum sein; **what** ~ **has he [got] to do that?** mit welchem Recht tut er das?; **in one's own** ~: aus eigenem Recht; **the** ~ **to work/life** das Recht auf Arbeit/Leben; ~ **of way** (~ to pass across) Wegerecht, *das;* (path) öffentlicher Weg; (precedence) Vorfahrtsrecht, *das;* **who has the** ~ **of way?** wer hat Vorfahrt?; **be within one's** ~**s to do sth.** etw. mit [Fug und] Recht tun können; **(b)** (what is just) Recht, *das;* ~ **is on our side** das Recht ist auf unserer Seite; **by** ~[s] von Rechts wegen; **do** ~: sich richtig verhalten; richtig handeln; **do** ~ **to do sth.** recht daran tun, etw. zu tun; **in the** ~: im Recht; **(c)** ▶ **1199** (~-hand side) rechte Seite; **move to the** ~: nach rechts rücken; **on** *or* **to the** ~ **[of sb./sth.]** rechts [von jmdm./etw.]; **on** *or* **to my** ~, **to the** ~ **of me** rechts von mir; zu meiner Rechten; **drive on the** ~: rechts fahren; **(d)** (Polit.) **the R**~: die Rechte; **be on the R**~ **of the party** dem rechten Flügel der Partei angehören; **(e)** *in pl.* (proper state) **set** *or* **put sth. to** ~**s** etw. in Ordnung bringen; **(f)** (in marching) ⇒ **left² 3** d; **(g)** (Boxing) Rechte, *die.* **4** *adv.* **(a)** (properly, correctly, justly) richtig ⟨*machen, raten, halten*⟩; **go** ~ (succeed) klappen (ugs.); **nothing is going** ~ **for me today** bei mir klappt heute nichts (ugs.); **(b)** ▶ **1199** (to the side opposite left) nach rechts; ~ **of the road** rechts von der Straße; **(c)** (all the way) bis ganz; (completely) ganz; völlig; ~ **through the summer** den ganzen Sommer hindurch; ~ **round the house** ums ganze Haus [herum]; **rotten** ~ **through** durch und durch verfault; **(d)** (exactly) genau; ~ **in the middle of sth.** mitten in etw. (*Dat./Akk.*); ~ **now** im Moment; jetzt sofort, gleich ⟨*handeln:*⟩; ~ **at the beginning** gleich am Anfang; ~ **on!** (coll.) (approving) recht so!; so ist's recht!; (agreeing) genau!; ganz recht!; **(e)** (straight) direkt; genau; **go** ~ **on [the way one is going]** [weiter] geradeaus gehen *od.* fahren; **(f)** (coll.: immediately) ~ **[away/off]** sofort; gleich; **(g)** (arch./dial.: very) sehr

right: ~ **angle** *n.* rechter Winkel, *der;* **at** ~ **angles to …:** rechtwinklig zu …; im rechten Winkel zu …; ~**-angled** *adj.* rechtwinklig

righteous /'raɪtʃəs/ *adj.* **(a)** (upright) rechtschaffen, (bibl.) gerecht ⟨*Person*⟩; gerecht ⟨*Gott*⟩; **(b)** (morally justifiable) gerecht ⟨*Sache, Zorn*⟩

rightful /'raɪtfl/ *adj.* **(a)** (fair) gerecht ⟨*Sache, Strafe*⟩; berechtigt ⟨*Forderung, Anspruch*⟩; **(b)** (entitled) rechtmäßig ⟨*Besitzer, Herrscher, Erbe, Anteil*⟩

right: ~ **'hand** *n.* **(a)** rechte Hand; Rechte, *die;* **(b)** (~ side) **on** *or* **at sb.'s** ~ **hand** zu jmds. Rechten; rechts von jmdm.; ~**-hand** *adj.* recht…; ~**-hand bend** Rechtskurve, *die; see also* **drive 1** g; ~**-handed** /raɪt'hæn dɪd/ **1** *adj.* **(a)** rechtshändig; ⟨*Werkzeug*⟩ für Rechtshänder; **be** ~**-handed** ⟨*Person:*⟩ Rechtshänder/Rechtshänderin sein; **(b)** (turning to ~) rechtsgängig, rechtsdrehend ⟨*Schraube, Gewinde*⟩; **2** *adv.* rechtshändig; mit der rechten Hand; ~**-hand 'man** *n.* (chief assistant) rechte Hand

rightly /'raɪtlɪ/ *adv.* (a) (fairly, correctly) richtig; **do ~:** richtig handeln; ..., **and ~ so** ..., und zwar zu Recht; **~ or wrongly,** ...: ob es nun richtig ist/war oder nicht, ...; (b) (fitly) zu Recht

right-'minded *adj.* gerecht denkend

righto /'raɪtəʊ, raɪ'təʊ/ *int.* (Brit.) okay (ugs.); alles klar (ugs.)

right: **~ side** *n.* (a) (of fabric) Oberseite, *die;* (b) **be on the ~ side of fifty** noch keine fünfzig sein; **[the] ~ side out/up** richtig herum; **~ 'wing** *n.* rechter Flügel; **~-wing** *adj.* (a) (Sport) Rechtsaußen⟨*spieler, -position*⟩; (b) (Polit.) recht...; rechtsgerichtet; Rechts⟨*intellektueller, -extremist, -radikalismus*⟩; **~-winger** *n.* (a) (Sport) Rechtsaußen, *der;* (b) (Polit.) Angehöriger/Angehörige des rechten Flügels

right-to-'life *attrib. adj.* Recht-auf-Leben-; **~ advocate** Befürworter des Rechts auf Leben

rigid /'rɪdʒɪd/ *adj.* (a) starr; (stiff) steif; (hard) hart; (firm) fest; (b) (fig.: harsh, inflexible) streng ⟨*Person*⟩; unbeugsam ⟨*Haltung, System*⟩

rigidity /rɪ'dʒɪdɪtɪ/ *n., no pl.* ⇒ **rigid:** (a) Starrheit, *die;* Steifheit, *die;* Härte, *die;* Festigkeit, *die;* (b) Strenge, *die*

rigidly /'rɪdʒɪdlɪ/ *adv.* (a) starr; (b) (harshly, inflexibly) [allzu] streng; peinlich ⟨*korrekt*⟩; rigoros ⟨*beschränken*⟩

rigmarole /'rɪɡmərəʊl/ *n.* (derog.) (a) (long story) langatmiges Geschwafel (ugs. abwertend); Zirkus, *der* (ugs. abwertend); (b) (complex procedure) Zirkus, *der* (ugs. abwertend)

rigor (Amer.) ⇒ **rigour**

rigor mortis /rɪɡə 'mɔːtɪs/ *n.* (Med.) Totenstarre, *die;* Rigor mortis, *der* (fachspr.)

rigorous /'rɪɡərəs/ *adj.* (a) (strict) streng; rigoros ⟨*Methode, Maßnahme, Beschränkung, Strenge*⟩; (b) (marked by extremes) hart ⟨*Leben, Bedingungen*⟩; (c) (precise) peinlich ⟨*Genauigkeit, Beachtung*⟩; exakt ⟨*Analyse*⟩; streng ⟨*Beurteilung, Maßstab*⟩; schlüssig ⟨*Argumentation*⟩

rigour /'rɪɡə(r)/ *n.* (Brit.) (a) (strictness) Strenge, *die;* (b) (of life, conditions, etc.) Härte, *die;* Strenge, *die;* **the ~s of sth.** die Unbilden (geh.) einer Sache (Gen.); (c) (precision) Stringenz, *die* (geh.); (of argument) Schlüssigkeit, *die*

rile /raɪl/ *v.t.* (coll.) ärgern; **get/feel ~d** sich ärgern

rim /rɪm/ *n.* Rand, *der;* (of wheel) Felge, *die*

rimless /'rɪmlɪs/ *adj.* randlos

rind /raɪnd/ *n.* (of fruit) Schale, *die;* (of cheese) Rinde, *die;* (of bacon) Schwarte, *die*

ring¹ /rɪŋ/ **1** *n.* (a) Ring, *der;* (b) (Horseracing, Boxing) Ring, *der;* (in circus) Manege, *die;* (c) (group) Ring, *der;* (gang) Bande, *die;* (controlling prices) Kartell, *das;* (d) (circle) Kreis, *der;* **make** *or* **run ~s [a]round sb.** (fig.) jmdm. in die Tasche stecken (ugs.). **2** *v.t.* (a) (surround) umringen; einkreisen ⟨*Wort, Buchstaben usw.*⟩; (b) (Brit.: put ~ on leg of) beringen ⟨*Vogel*⟩

ring² **1** *n.* (a) (act of sounding bell) Läuten, *das;* Klingeln, *das;* **there's a ~ at the door** es hat geklingelt; **give two ~s** zweimal läuten *od.* klingeln; (b) (Brit. coll.: telephone call) Anruf, *der;* **give sb. a ~:** jmdn. anrufen; (c) (resonance; fig.: impression) Klang, *der;* (fig.) **have the ~ of truth** glaubhaft klingen. **2** *v.i.,* **rang** /ræŋ/, **rung** /rʌŋ/ (a) (sound clearly) [er]schallen; ⟨*Hammer:*⟩ [er]dröhnen; (b) (be sounded) ⟨*Glocke, Klingel, Telefon:*⟩ läuten; ⟨*Kasse, Telefon, Wecker:*⟩ klingeln; **the doorbell rang** die Türklingel ging; es klingelte; (c) (~ bell) läuten (**for** nach); **please ~ for attention** bitte läuten; (d) (Brit.: make telephone call) anrufen; (e) (resound) **~ in sb.'s ears** jmdm. in den Ohren klingen; **~ true/false** (fig.) glaubhaft/unglaubhaft klingen; (f) (hum) summen; (loudly) dröhnen; **my ears are ~ing** mir dröhnen die Ohren. **3** *v.t.,* **rang, rung** (a) läuten ⟨*Glocke*⟩; **~ the [door]bell** läuten; klingeln; **it ~s a bell** (fig. coll.) es kommt mir [irgendwie] bekannt vor; (b) (Brit.: telephone) anrufen

~ 'back *v.t. & i.* (Brit.) (a) (again) wieder anrufen; (b) (in return) zurückrufen

~ 'in *v.i.* (Brit.) anrufen

~ 'off *v.i.* (Brit.) auflegen; abhängen

~ 'out **1** *v.i.* ertönen. **2** *v.t.* ausläuten

~ round (Brit.) **1** /-'-/ *v.i.* herumtelefonieren. **2** /'--/ *v.t.* herumtelefonieren bei

~ 'up *v.t.* (a) (Brit.: telephone) anrufen; (b) (record on cash register) [ein]tippen; bongen (ugs.)

ring: **~-a-~-o'-roses** *n.* Ringelreihen, *der;* **~ binder** *n.* Ringbuch, *das*

ringed /rɪŋd/ *adj.* beringt

ring: **~-fence** *v.t.* [ab]sichern ⟨*Gelder*⟩; **~ finger** *n.* Ringfinger, *der*

ringing /'rɪŋɪŋ/ **1** *adj.* (clear and full) schallend ⟨*Stimme, Gelächter*⟩; (sonorous) klangvoll, volltönend ⟨*Stimme, Lachen, Lied*⟩; (resounding) dröhnend ⟨*Schlag*⟩. **2** *n.* (a) (sounding, sound) Läuten, *das;* (b) (Brit. Teleph.) **~ tone** Freiton, *der*

'ringleader *n.* Anführer, *der*/Anführerin, *die*

ringlet /'rɪŋlɪt/ *n.* [Ringel]löckchen, *das*

ring: **~master** *n.* Dresseur, *der;* **~-pull** *adj.* **~-pull can** Aufreißdose, *die;* Ring-Pull-Dose, *die;* **~ road** *n.* Ringstraße, *die*

rink /rɪŋk/ *n.* (for ice-skating) Eisbahn, *die;* (for roller skating) Rollschuhbahn, *die*

rinse /rɪns/ **1** *v.t.* (a) (wash out) ausspülen ⟨*Mund, Gefäß usw.*⟩; (b) (put through water) [aus]spülen ⟨*Wäsche usw.*⟩; abspülen ⟨*Hände, Geschirr*⟩. **2** *n.* (rinsing) Spülen, *das;* Spülung, *die*

~ a'way *v.t.* wegspülen

~ 'out *v.t.* (a) (wash with clean water) ausspülen ⟨*Wäsche, Mund, Behälter*⟩; (b) (remove by washing) [her]ausspülen

'rinse aid *n.* Klarspülmittel, *das*

riot /'raɪət/ **1** *n.* (a) (violent disturbance) Aufruhr, *der;* **~s** Unruhen *Pl.;* Aufstand, *der;* (b) (noisy or uncontrolled behaviour) Krawall, *der;* Tumult, *der;* **run ~:** randalieren; **let one's imagination run ~:** seiner Fantasie freien Lauf lassen; (c) (coll.: amusing thing or person) **be a ~:** zum Piepen sein (ugs.). **2** *v.i.* einen Aufstand machen

'riot act *n.* **read sb. the ~** (fig. coll.) jmdm. die Leviten lesen

rioter /'raɪətə(r)/ *n.* Aufrührer, *der*

'riot gear *n.* (*bei Krawallen von Polizeibeamten getragene*) Schutzkleidung *od.* -ausrüstung

riotous /'raɪətəs/ *adj.* (a) (turbulent) aufrührerisch ⟨*Menge*⟩; tumultartig ⟨*Vorgang*⟩; (b) (dissolute) ausschweifend; (c) (unrestrained) wild

riotously /'raɪətəslɪ/ *adv.* **~ funny** (coll.) urkomisch; zum Schreien *präd.* (ugs.)

riot: **~ police** *n.* Bereitschaftspolizei, *die;* **~ shield** *n.* Schutzschild, *der;* **~ squad** *n.* Einsatzkommando, *das od.* -truppe, *die* (der Bereitschaftspolizei)

RIP *abbr.* **rest in peace** R.I.P.

rip /rɪp/ **1** *n.* (tear) Riß, *der.* **2** *v.t.,* **-pp-:** (a) (make tear in) zerreißen; **~ open** aufreißen; (with knife) aufschlitzen; **~ one's dress on sth.** sich (Dat.) an etw. (Dat.) das Kleid einreißen; (b) (make by tearing) reißen ⟨*Loch*⟩. **3** *v.i.,* **-pp-:** (a) (split) [ein]reißen; (b) **let ~** (coll.) loslegen (ugs.)

~ a'part *v.t.* (tear apart) auseinander reißen; zerreißen; (destroy) demolieren

~ into *v.t.* (fig.: attack verbally) jmdm. ins Gesicht springen (ugs.)

~ 'off *v.t.* (a) (remove from) reißen von; (remove) abreißen; herunterreißen ⟨*Maske, Kleidungsstück*⟩; (b) (coll.: defraud) übers Ohr hauen (ugs.); bescheißen (derb)

~ 'out *v.t.* herausreißen (**of** aus)

~ 'up *v.t.* zerreißen; kaputtreißen (ugs.); **~ up an agreement** (fig.) aus einer Vereinbarung einfach wieder aussteigen (ugs.)

'ripcord *n.* Reißleine, *die*

ripe /raɪp/ *adj.* reif (**for** zu); ausgereift ⟨*Käse, Wein, Plan*⟩; **the time is ~ for doing sth.** es ist an der Zeit, etw. zu tun; **~ old age** hohes Alter

ripen /'raɪpn/ **1** *v.t.* zur Reife bringen; (fig.) reifen lassen (geh.). **2** *v.i.* (lit. or fig.) reifen; **~ into sth.** (fig.) zu etw. reifen (geh.)

'rip-off *n.* (coll.) Nepp, *der* (ugs. abwertend)

riposte /rɪ'pɒst/ **1** *n.* (retort) [rasche] Entgegnung *od.* (geh.) Replik. **2** *v.i.* (retort) [rasch] antworten

ripple /'rɪpl/ **1** *n.* kleine Welle; **a ~ of applause** kurzer Beifall. **2** *v.i.* (a) ⟨*See:*⟩ sich kräuseln; ⟨*Welle:*⟩ plätschern; (b) (sound) erklingen. **3** *v.t.* kräuseln

'rip-roaring *adj.* wahnsinnig (ugs.); Wahnsinns- (ugs.)

rise /raɪz/ **1** *n.* **(a)** (going up) (of sun etc.) Aufgang, *der;* (Theatre: of curtain) Aufgehen, *das;* (advancement) Aufstieg, *der;* **(b)** (emergence) Aufkommen, *das;* **(c)** (increase) (in value, price, cost) Steigerung, *die;* (St. Exch.: in shares) Hausse, *die;* (in population, temperature) Zunahme, *die;* **(d)** (Brit.) **[pay]** ~ (in wages) Lohnerhöhung, *die;* (in salary) Gehaltserhöhung, *die;* **(e)** (hill) Anhöhe, *die;* Erhebung, *die;* **(f)** (origin) Ursprung, *der;* **give** ~ **to** führen zu; 〈*Ereignis:*〉 Anlass geben zu 〈*Spekulation*〉; **(g) get** *or* **take a** ~ **out of sb.** (fig.: make fun of) sich über jmdn. lustig machen. **2** *v.i.,* **rose** /rəʊz/, **risen** /'rɪzn/ **(a)** (go up) aufsteigen; ~ **[up] into the air** 〈*Rauch:*〉 aufsteigen, in die Höhe steigen; 〈*Ballon, Vogel, Flugzeug:*〉 sich in die Luft erheben; **(b)** (come up) 〈*Sonne, Mond:*〉 aufgehen; 〈*Blase:*〉 aufsteigen; **(c)** (reach higher level) steigen; 〈*Stimme:*〉 höher werden; **(d)** (extend upward) aufragen; sich erheben; 〈*Weg, Straße:*〉 ansteigen; ~ **to 2,000 metres** 〈*Berg:*〉 2 000 Meter hoch aufragen; **(e)** (advance) 〈*Person:*〉 aufsteigen, aufrücken; ~ **to be the director** zum Direktor aufsteigen; ~ **in the world** voran- *od.* weiterkommen; **(f)** (increase) steigen; 〈*Stimme:*〉 lauter werden; 〈*Wind, Sturm:*〉 auffrischen, stärker werden; **(g)** (Cookery) 〈*Teig, Kuchen:*〉 aufgehen; **(h)** 〈*Stimmung, Moral:*〉 steigen; **(i)** (come to surface) 〈*Fisch:*〉 steigen; ~ **to the bait** (fig.) sich ködern lassen (ugs.); **(j)** (Theatre) 〈*Vorhang:*〉 aufgehen, sich heben; **(k)** (rebel, cease to be quiet) 〈*Person:*〉 aufbegehren (geh.), sich erheben; **(l)** (get up) ~ **[to one's feet]** aufstehen; ~ **on its hind legs** 〈*Pferd:*〉 steigen; **(m)** (adjourn) 〈*Parlament:*〉 in die Ferien gehen, die Sitzungsperiode beenden; (end a session) die Sitzung beenden; **(n)** (come to life again) auferstehen; **(o)** ▶1048 (have origin) 〈*Fluss:*〉 entspringen

~ **to** ⇨ **occasion 1 a**

~ **'up** *v.i.* **(a)** (get up) aufstehen; sich erheben; **(b)** (advance) aufsteigen; (in level) ansteigen; **(c)** (rebel) ~ **up [in revolt]** aufbegehren (geh.); sich erheben; **(d)** 〈*Berg:*〉 aufragen; ~ **up to 2,000 metres** 2 000 Meter hoch aufragen

riser /'raɪzə(r)/ *n.* **early** ~: Frühaufsteher, *der*/Frühaufsteherin, *die;* **late** ~: Spätaufsteher, *der*/Spätaufsteherin, *die*

rising /'raɪzɪŋ/ **1** *n.* **(a)** (of sun, moon, star) Aufgang, *der;* **(b)** (getting up) Aufstehen, *das;* **(c)** (revolt) Aufstand, *der.* **2** *adj.* **(a)** aufgehend 〈Sonne, Mond, Stern〉; **(b)** (increasing) steigend 〈Kosten, Temperatur〉; (fig.) wachsend 〈Entrüstung, Wut, Ärger, Bedeutung〉; **(c)** steigend 〈Wasser, Flut〉; **(d) the** ~ **generation** die heranwachsende Generation; **(e)** (advancing in standing) aufstrebend; **(f)** (sloping upwards) ansteigend

rising 'damp *n.* aufsteigende Feuchtigkeit

risk /rɪsk/ **1** *n.* **(a)** (hazard) Gefahr, *die;* (chance taken) Risiko, *das;* **there is a/no** ~ **of sb.'s doing sth.** *or* **that sb. will do sth.** es besteht die/keine Gefahr, dass jmd. etw. tut; **at one's own** ~: auf eigene Gefahr *od.* eigenes Risiko; **put at** ~: gefährden; in Gefahr bringen; **run the** ~ **of doing sth.** Gefahr laufen, etw. zu tun; (knowingly) es riskieren, etw. zu tun; **take the** ~ **of doing sth.** es riskieren, etw. zu tun; das Risiko eingehen, etw. zu tun; **(b)** (Insurance) **he is a poor/good** ~: bei ihm ist das Risiko groß/gering. **2** *v.t.* riskieren; wagen 〈Sprung, Kampf〉; **you'll** ~ **losing your job** du riskierst es, deinen Job zu verlieren; **I'll** ~ **it!** ich lasse es drauf ankommen; ich riskiere es; ~ **one's life** sein Leben riskieren; (thoughtlessly) sein Leben aufs Spiel setzen

risky /'rɪskɪ/ *adj.* gefährlich; riskant, gewagt 〈Experiment, Unternehmen, Projekt〉

risqué /'rɪskeɪ/ *adj.* gewagt; nicht ganz salonfähig

rissole /'rɪsəʊl/ *n.* Rissole, *die*

rite /raɪt/ *n.* Ritus, *der*

ritual /'rɪtʃʊəl/ **1** *adj.* rituell; Ritual〈mord, -tötung〉. **2** *n.* (act) Ritual, *das*

rival /'raɪvl/ **1** *n.* **(a)** (competitor) Rivale, *der*/Rivalin, *die;* ~**s in love** Nebenbuhler *Pl.;* **business** ~**s** Konkurrenten, *Pl.;* **(b)** (equal) **have no** ~/~**s** seines-/ihresgleichen suchen; **without** ~ **[s]** konkurrenzlos. **2** *v.t.,* (Brit.) **-ll-** gleichkommen (+ *Dat.*); nicht nachstehen (+ *Dat.*). **3** *adj.* rivalisierend 〈Gruppen〉; konkurrierend 〈Forderungen〉; Konkurrenz〈unternehmen usw.〉

rivalry /'raɪvlrɪ/ *n.* Rivalität, *die* (geh.); **business** ~: Wettbewerb, *der*

river /'rɪvə(r)/ *n.* **(a)** ▶1048 Fluss, *der;* (large) Strom, *der;* **the** ~ **Thames** (Brit.), **the Thames** ~ (Amer.) die Themse; **sell sb. down the** ~ (fig. coll.) jmdn. verschaukeln (ugs.); **(b)** (fig.) Strom, *der*

river: ~ **bank** *n.* Flussufer, *das;* ~ **bed** *n.* Flussbett, *das;* ~ **police** *n. pl.* Wasser[schutz]polizei, *die;* ~**side** **1** *n.* Flussufer, *das;* **on** *or* **by the** ~**side** am Fluss; **2** *attrib. adj.* am Fluss gelegen; am Fluss *nachgestellt*

rivet /'rɪvɪt/ **1** *n.* Niete, *die;* Niet, *der od. das* (Technik). **2** *v.t.* **(a)** [ver]nieten; ~ **sth. together** etw. zusammennieten; **(b)** (fig.: hold firmly) fesseln 〈Person, Aufmerksamkeit, Blick〉; **be** ~**ed to the spot** wie angenagelt [da]stehen (ugs.)

riveting /'rɪvɪtɪŋ/ *adj.* fesselnd

RN *abbr.* (Brit.) **Royal Navy** Königl. Mar.

RNLI *abbr.* (Brit.) **Royal National Lifeboat Institution** *Königliches Institut für Rettungsboote*

road /rəʊd/ *n.* **(a)** Straße, *die;* **the Birmingham/London** ~: die Straße nach Birmingham/London; (name of ~/ street) **London/Shelley R**~: Londoner Straße/Shelleystraße; '~ **up**' „Straßenarbeiten"; **across** *or* **over the** ~ **[from us]** [bei uns *od.* (geh.) uns (*Dat.*)] gegenüber; **by** ~ (by car/bus) per Auto/Bus; (by lorry/truck) per Lkw; **off the** ~ (being repaired) in der Werkstatt; in Reparatur; **one for the** ~ (coll.) ein Glas zum Abschied; **be on the** ~: auf Reisen *od.* unterwegs sein; 〈Theaterensemble usw.:〉 auf Tournee *od.* (ugs.) Tour (*Dat.*) sein; **put a vehicle on the** ~: ein Fahrzeug in Betrieb nehmen; **(b)** (means of access) Weg, *der;* **set sb. on the** ~ **to ruin** jmdn. ins Verderben führen; **be on the right** ~: auf dem richtigen Weg sein; **end of the** ~ (destination) Ziel, *das;* (limit) Ende, *das;* **(c)** (one's way) Weg, *der;* **get in sb.'s** ~ (coll.) jmdm. in die Quere kommen (ugs.); **get out of my** ~! (coll.) geh mir aus dem Weg!; **(d)** (Amer.) ⇨ **railway; (e)** (Mining) Strecke, *die;* **(f)** *usu. in pl.* (Naut.) Reede, *die*

road: ~ **accident** *n.* Verkehrsunfall, *der;* ~ **atlas** *n.* Autoatlas, *der;* ~**block** *n.* Straßensperre, *die;* ~ **haulage** *n.* Gütertransport auf der Straße; ~ **hog** *n.* Verkehrsrowdy, *der* (abwertend); ~**holding** *n.* (Brit. Motor Veh.) Straßenlage, *die;* ~ **hump** *n.* ⇨ **speed hump;** ~ **manager** *n.* ▶887 Roadmanager, *der;* ~ **map** *n.* Straßenkarte, *die;* ~ **rage** *n.:* häufig zu gewalttätigen Ausbrüchen führende Wut eines Autofahrers; ~ **safety** *n.* Verkehrssicherheit, *die;* ~ **sense** *n.* Gespür für Verkehrssituationen; ~**show** *n.* (promotional) [Werbe]tour der; Roadshow, *die;* (political) [Wahlkampf]tour, *die;* '**Radio One R**~**show**' 'Radio One unterwegs *od.* vor Ort'; ~**side** **1** *n.* Straßenrand, *der;* **at** *or* **by/along the** ~**side** am Straßenrand; an/entlang der Straße; **2** *adj.* 〈Gasthaus usw.〉 am Straßenrand, an der Straße; ~ **sign** *n.* Straßenschild, *das* (ugs.); Verkehrszeichen, *das;* ~ **sweeper** *n.* ▶887 Straßenkehrer, *der/* -kehrerin, *die* (bes. südd.); Straßenfeger, *der/*-fegerin, *die* (bes. nordd.); ~ **tax** *n.* (Brit.) Kraftfahrzeugsteuer, *die;* Kfz-Steuer, *die;* ~ **test** *n.* Fahrtest, *der;* ~-**test** *v.t.* einem Fahrtest unterziehen; ~ **transport** *n.* Personen- und Güterbeförderung auf der Straße; ~ **user** *n.* Verkehrsteilnehmer, *der/*-teilnehmerin, *die;* ~**way** *n.* Fahrbahn, *die;* ~**works** *n. pl.* Straßenbauarbeiten *Pl.;* '~**works**' „Baustelle"; ~**worthy** *adj.* fahrtüchtig 〈Fahrzeug〉

roam /rəʊm/ **1** *v.i.* umherstreifen; herumstreifen (ugs.); 〈Nomade:〉 wandern; (stray) 〈Tier:〉 streunen. **2** *v.t.* streifen durch; durchstreifen (geh.).

~ **a'bout,** ~ **a'round** **1** *v.i.* herumstreifen (ugs.); umherstreifen. **2** *v.t.* herumstreifen in (+ *Dat.*) (ugs.); durchstreifen (geh.)

roar /rɔː(r)/ **1** *n.* (of wild beast) Brüllen, *das;* Gebrüll, *das;* (of water, applause) Tosen, *das;* Getose, *das;* (of avalanche, guns) Donner, *der;* (of machine, traffic) Dröhnen, *das;* Getöse, *das;* ~**s/a** ~ **[of laughter]** dröhnendes *od.* brüllendes Gelächter. **2** *v.i.* **(a)** (cry loudly) brüllen (**with** vor + *Dat.*); ~ **[with laughter]** [vor Lachen] brüllen; **(b)** 〈Motor:〉 dröhnen; 〈Artillerie:〉 donnern; (blaze up) 〈Feuer:〉 bullern (ugs.). **3** *v.t.* brüllen

Rivers

German has two words for *river*. The usual one is **der Fluss**, which applies to any river, while **der Strom** is only used for a really large river such as the Rhine (**der Rhein**), the Danube (**die Donau**), the Volga (**die Wolga**), the Zambezi (**der Sambesi**), the Amazon (**der Amazonas**), and so on. Most rivers are masculine, but there are quite a number of exceptions (including of course the two already mentioned). All French rivers are feminine for a start, since they are feminine in French. The following German and most Austrian rivers are also feminine:

die Weser, die Elbe, die Saar, die Mosel, die Ruhr, die Isar, die Spree, die Havel, die Oder, die Neiße; (and in Austria) die Salzach, die Enns, die Etsch, die Drau and many others.

In addition there are a couple of rivers in neighbouring countries:

die Maas, die Amstel in Holland;

die Moldau (the Vltava) in the Czech Republic;

die Weichsel (the Vistula) in Poland.

Virtually all rivers in the rest of the world are masculine, with the one exception of the Thames (die Themse).

German does not insert a word for river before the name as does English:

the river Main = der Main
the river Seine = die Seine

When rivers occur in place names, the preposition used is **an**. Such mentions often distinguish between places with the same name:

Frankfurt am Main ↔ Frankfurt an der Oder
Linz am Rhein ↔ Linz an der Donau

am can be abbreviated as **a.** and **an der** as **a.d.**, and the names of the rivers can be reduced to the initial letter where these are familiar, giving e.g.

Frankfurt a.M. ↔ Frankfurt a.d.O.
Bruck a.d. Mur

Some river phrases

to go upstream/ downstream or *up/ down the river*	= flussaufwärts/ flussabwärts fahren
to go up/down the Rhine	= rheinaufwärts/ rheinabwärts fahren

Similar adverbs can be formed with the name of any river (**donauaufwärts, themseabwärts** etc.).

a house by or *on the river*	= ein Haus am Fluss
on the right bank of the Weser	= am rechten Weserufer
He was carried along by the current	= Er wurde von der Strömung mitgerissen
The river is in flood or *in full spate*	= Der Fluss führt Hochwasser
The river is very low	= Der Fluss führt sehr wenig Wasser
The Rhine rises in Switzerland and flows into the North Sea	= Der Rhein entspringt in der Schweiz und mündet in die Nordsee
The ship sank in the mouth of the Elbe or *the Elbe estuary*	= Das Schiff ist in der Elbmündung gesunken

roaring /'rɔːrɪŋ/ **1** *adj.* **(a)** dröhnend ‹*Motor, Donner*›; tosend ‹*Meer*›; brüllend ‹*Löwe*›; **(b)** (blazing loudly) bullernd (ugs.) ‹*Feuer*›; **(c)** (riotous) **a ~ success** ein Bombenerfolg (ugs.); **the ~ twenties** die wilden zwanziger Jahre; die Roaring Twenties; **(d)** (brisk) **do a ~ trade** ein Bombengeschäft machen. **2** *adv.* **~ drunk** sternhagelvoll (salopp)

roast /rəʊst/ **1** *v.t.* braten; rösten ‹*Kaffeebohnen, Erdnüsse, Mandeln, Kastanien*›. **2** *attrib. adj.* gebraten ‹*Fleisch, Ente usw.*›; Brat‹*hähnchen, -kartoffeln*›; **eat ~ duck/pork/beef** Enten-/ Schweine-/ Rinderbraten essen; **~ beef** (sirloin) Roastbeef, *das.* **3** *n.* Braten, *der*

rob /rɒb/ *v.t.*, **-bb-** ausrauben ‹*Bank, Safe, Kasse*›; berauben ‹*Person*›; *abs.* rauben; **~ sb. of sth.** jmdm. etw. rauben *od.* stehlen; (deprive of what is due) jmdm. um etw. bringen *od.* betrügen; (withhold sth. from) jmdm. etw. vorenthalten; **be ~bed** bestohlen werden; (by force) beraubt werden

robber /'rɒbə(r)/ *n.* Räuber, *der*/Räuberin, *die*

robbery /'rɒbərɪ/ *n.* Raub, *der*; **robberies** Raubüberfälle

robe /rəʊb/ *n.* **(a)** (ceremonial garment) Gewand, *das* (geh.); (of judge, vicar) Talar, *der*; **~ of office** Amtstracht, *die*; **(b)** (long garment) [langes Über]gewand; **(c)** (dressing gown) Morgenrock, *der*; **beach ~** Bademantel, *der*

robin /'rɒbɪn/ *n.* (Ornith.) **~ [redbreast]** Rotkehlchen, *das*

robot /'rəʊbɒt/ *n.* Roboter, *der*

robust /rəʊ'bʌst/ *adj.* robust ‹*Person, Gesundheit*›; kräftig ‹*Person, Gestalt, Körperbau*›; widerstandsfähig ‹*Pflanze*›; robust ‹*Fahrzeug, Maschine, Möbel*›; stabil ‹*Haus*›

rock¹ /rɒk/ *n.* **(a)** (piece of ~) Fels, *der;* **be as solid as a ~** (fig.) absolut zuverlässig sein; **(b)** (large ~, hill) Felsen, *der;* Fels, *der* (geh.); **(c)** (substance) Fels, *der;* (esp. Geol.) Gestein, *das;* **(d)** (boulder) Felsbrocken, *der;* (Amer.: stone) Stein, *der;* Steinbrocken, *der;* **'danger, falling ~s'** „Achtung *od.* Vorsicht, Steinschlag!"; „Steinschlaggefahr!"; **be caught between a ~ and a hard place** in einer Zwickmühle stizen (ugs.); **(e)** *no pl., no indef. art.* (hard sweet) **stick**

of ~: Zuckerstange, *die;* **(f)** (fig.: support) Stütze, *die;* Rückhalt, *der;* (of society) Fundament, *das;* **(g) be on the ~s** (fig. coll.: have failed) ‹*Ehe, Firma:*› kaputt sein (ugs.); **(h) on the ~s** (with ice cubes) mit Eis *od.* on the rocks

rock² **1** *v.t.* **(a)** (move to and fro) wiegen; (in cradle) schaukeln; wiegen; **(b)** (shake) erschüttern; (fig.) erschüttern ‹*Person*›; **~ the boat** (fig. coll.) Trouble machen (ugs.). **2** *v.i.* **(a)** (move to and fro) sich wiegen; schaukeln; **(b)** (sway) schwanken; wanken; **(c)** (dance) **~ and roll** Rock and Roll tanzen. **3** *n.* (music) Rock, *der;* *attrib.* Rock-; **~ and** or **'n' roll** [music] Rock and Roll, *der;* Rock 'n' Roll, *der*

rock: **~-'bottom** (coll.) **1** *adj.* **~-bottom prices** Schleuderpreise (ugs.); **2** *n.* **reach** or **touch ~-bottom** ‹*Handel, Währung, Preis usw.:*› in den Keller fallen *od.* sinken (ugs.); **her spirits reached ~-bottom** ihre Stimmung war auf dem Tiefpunkt [angelangt]; **~-climber** *n.* Kletterer, *der*/Kletterin, *die;* **~-climbing** *n.* [Fels]klettern, *das*

rocker /'rɒkə(r)/ *n.* **(a)** (Brit.: gang member) Rocker, *der;* **(b) be off one's ~** (fig. coll.) übergeschnappt *od.* durchgedreht sein (ugs.)

rockery /'rɒkərɪ/ *n.* Steingarten, *der*

rocket /'rɒkɪt/ **1** *n.* **(a)** Rakete, *die;* **(b)** (Brit. coll.: reprimand) **give sb. a ~:** jmdm. eine Zigarre verpassen (ugs.). **2** *v.i.* ‹*Preise:*› in die Höhe schnellen

rocket: **~ engine** *n.* Raketentriebwerk, *das;* **~ flight** *n.* Raketenflug, *der;* **~ launcher** *n.* Raketenwerfer, *der;* **~-powered, ~-propelled** *adjs.* raketengetrieben

rock: **~ face** *n.* Felswand, *die;* **~fall** *n.* Steinschlag, *der;* **~ formation** *n.* Gesteinsformation, *die;* **~ garden** *n.* Steingarten, *der;* **~-hard** *adj.* steinhart

Rockies /'rɒkɪz/ *pr. n. pl.* **the ~:** die Rocky Mountains

rocking: **~ chair** *n.* Schaukelstuhl, *der;* **~ horse** *n.* Schaukelpferd, *das*

rock: **~like** *adj.* felsartig; felsenfest ‹*Glaube usw.*›; **~ plant** *n.* Felsenpflanze, *die;* (Hort.) Steingartengewächs, *das*

rocky /'rɒkɪ/ *adj.* (**a**) (coll.: unsteady) wackelig (ugs.); (**b**) (full or consisting of rocks) felsig; (**c**) **the R~ Mountains** ⇒ **Rockies**

rococo /rə'kəʊkəʊ/ *adj.* Rokoko-

rod /rɒd/ *n.* (**a**) Stange, *die;* (**b**) (shorter) Stab, *der;* (**c**) (for punishing) Stock, *der;* Rute, *die;* **rule with a ~ of iron** (fig.) mit eiserner Faust *od.* Rute regieren; **spare the ~ and spoil the child** wer die Rute schont, verdirbt das Kind

rode ⇒ **ride** 2, 3

rodent /'rəʊdənt/ *n.* Nagetier, *das*

rodeo /'rəʊdɪəʊ, rə'deɪəʊ/ *n., pl.* **~s** Rodeo, *der od. das*

roe¹ /rəʊ/ *n.* (of fish) [**hard**] **~:** Rogen, *der;* [**soft**] **~:** Milch, *die*

roe² *n.* (deer) Reh, *das*

roe: ~buck *n.* Rehbock, *der;* **~-deer** *n.* Reh, *das*

roger /'rɒdʒə(r)/ *int.* (message received) verstanden

rogue /rəʊg/ *n.* (**a**) Gauner, *der* (abwertend); **~s' gallery** (Police) Verbrecheralbum, *das;* (**b**) (joc.: mischievous child) Spitzbube, *der* (scherzh.); (**c**) (dangerous animal) ~ [**buffalo/ elephant** *etc.*] bösartiger Einzelgänger

roguish /'rəʊgɪʃ/ *adj.* (**a**) gaunerhaft; (**b**) (mischievous) spitzbübisch

role, rôle /rəʊl/ *n.* Rolle, *die*

role: ~ model *n.* Leitbild, *das;* **~-playing** *n.* Rollenspiel, *das;* Rollenverhalten, *das;* **~ reversal** *n.* Rollentausch, *der*

roll¹ /rəʊl/ *n.* (**a**) Rolle, *die;* (of cloth, tobacco, etc.) Ballen, *der;* (of fat on body) Wulst, *der;* **~ of film** Rolle Film; (**b**) (of bread etc.) [**bread**] **~:** Brötchen, *das;* **egg/ham ~:** Eier-/ Schinkenbrötchen, *das;* (**c**) (document) [Schrift]rolle, *die;* (**d**) (register, catalogue) Liste, *die;* Verzeichnis, *das;* **~ of honour** Gedenktafel [für die Gefallenen] (*der;* (**e**) (Mil., Sch.: list of names) Liste, *die;* **schools with falling ~s** Schulen mit sinkenden Schülerzahlen; **call the ~:** die Anwesenheit feststellen; (**f**) **be on a ~** (coll.) eine Glückssträhne haben

roll² 1 *n.* (**a**) (of drum) Wirbel, *der;* (of thunder) Rollen, *das;* (**b**) (motion) Rollen, *das;* (**c**) (single movement) Rolle, *die;* (of dice) Wurf, *der.* 2 *v.t.* (**a**) (move, send) rollen; (between surfaces) drehen; (**b**) (shape by ~ing) rollen; **~ a cigarette** eine Zigarette rollen *od.* drehen; **~ one's own** [selbst] drehen; **~ snow/wool into a ball** einen Schneeball formen/Wolle zu einem Knäuel aufwickeln; [**all**] **~ed into one** (fig.) in einem; **~ oneself/itself into a ball** sich zusammenrollen; (**c**) (flatten) walzen (*Rasen, Metall usw.*); ausrollen (*Teig*); (**d**) **~ one's eyes** die Augen rollen; (**e**) **~ one's r's** das r rollen. 3 *v.i.* (**a**) (move by turning over) rollen; **heads will ~** (fig.) es werden Köpfe rollen; (**b**) (operate) (*Maschine:*) laufen; (*Presse:*) sich drehen; (on wheels) rollen; (**c**) (wallow, sway, walk) sich wälzen; (**d**) (Naut.) (*Schiff:*) rollen, schlingern; (**e**) (revolve) (*Augen:*) sich [ver]drehen; (**f**) (flow, go forward) sich wälzen (fig.); (*Wolken:*) ziehen; (*Tränen:*) rollen; (**g**) (*Donner:*) rollen; (*Trommel:*) dröhnen

~ a'bout *v.i.* herumrollen; (*Schiff:*) schlingern, rollen; (*Kind, Hund usw.:*) sich wälzen; **be ~ing about with laughter** sich vor Lachen wälzen

~ a'way 1 *v.i.* (*Ball:*) wegrollen; (*Nebel, Wolken:*) sich verziehen. 2 *v.t.* wegrollen

~ 'back *v.t.* (**a**) zurückrollen; (**b**) (cause to retreat) zurückschlagen (*Feinde, Truppen*)

~ 'by *v.i.* vorbeirollen; (*Zeit:*) vergehen; **the years ~ed by** die Jahre zogen ins Land

~ 'in *v.i.* (coll.) (*Briefe, Geschenke, Geldbeträge:*) eingehen; **~ in an hour late** mit einer Stunde Verspätung aufkreuzen (salopp)

~ 'on 1 *v.t.* mit einer Rolle auftragen (*Farbe:*). 2 *v.i.* (**a**) (pass by) (*Jahre:*) vergehen; (**b**) (Brit. coll.) **~ on Saturday!** wenn doch schon Samstag wäre!

~ 'out 1 *v.t.* (make flat and smooth) auswalzen (*Metall*); ausrollen (*Teig, Teppich*); (**b**) (bring out) herausbringen. 2 *v.i.* heraus-/hinausrollen

~ 'over 1 *v.i.* (*Person:*) sich umdrehen, (to make room) sich zur Seite rollen; **~ over [and over]** (*Auto:*) sich [immer wieder] überschlagen; **the dog ~ed over on to its back** der Hund rollte sich auf den Rücken. 2 *v.t.* herumdrehen; (with effort) herumwälzen

~ 'up 1 *v.t.* aufrollen (*Teppich, Maßband*); zusammenrollen (*Regenschirm, Landkarte, Dokument usw.*); hochkrempeln (*Hose*); *see also* **sleeve a.** 2 *v.i.* (**a**) (curl up) sich zusammenrollen; (**b**) (arrive) aufkreuzen (salopp); **~ up!** hereinspaziert!

roll: ~ bar *n.* (Motor Veh.) Überrollbügel, *der;* **~-call** *n.* Aufrufen aller Namen; (Mil.) Zählappell, *der*

roller /'rəʊlə(r)/ *n.* (**a**) (heavy, for pressing, smoothing road, lawn, etc.) Walze, *die;* (smaller, for towel, painting, pastry) Rolle, *die;* (**b**) (for hair) Lockenwickler, *der;* **put one's hair in ~s** sich (*Dat.*) die Haare aufdrehen

roller: R~blade (P) *n.* Rollerblade, *der;* [**a pair of**] **R~blades** [ein Paar] Rollerblades; **~blade** *v.i.* Rollerblades fahren; **~ blind** *n.* Rouleau, *das;* Rollo, *das;* **~ coaster** *n.* Achterbahn, *die;* **~ skate** 1 *n.* Rollschuh, *der;* 2 *v.i.* Rollschuh laufen; **~ skating** *n.* Rollschuhlaufen, *das; attrib.* **~ skating rink** Rollschuhbahn, *die;* **~ towel** *n.: auf einer Rolle hängendes endloses Handtuch*

'roll film *n.* Rollfilm, *der*

rolling /'rəʊlɪŋ/ *adj.* (**a**) (moving from side to side) rollend (*Augen*); schwankend (*Gang*); schlingernd (*Schiff*); (**b**) (undulating) wogend (*See*); wellig (*Gelände*); **~ hills** sanfte Hügel

rolling: ~ mill *n.* Walzwerk, *das;* **~ pin** *n.* (Cookery) Teigrolle, *die;* Nudelholz, *das;* **~ stock** *n.* (Brit. Railw.) Fahrzeugbestand, *der;* rollendes Material (fachspr.); **~ 'stone** *n.* (fig.) unsteter Mensch; **a ~ stone gathers no moss** (prov.) wer ein unstetes Leben führt, bringt es zu nichts

roll: ~over *n.* (von Auslosung zu Auslosung) aufgestockter Jackpot; **~-up** (Brit. coll.), **~-your-own** (esp. Amer. coll.) *ns.* Selbstgedrehte, *die*

ROM /rɒm/ *abbr.* (Computing) read-only memory ROM

Roman /'rəʊmən/ 1 *n.* Römer, *der/*Römerin, *die.* 2 *adj.* römisch; **~ road** Römerstraße, *die*

Roman: ~ 'alphabet *n.* lateinisches Alphabet; **~ 'Catholic** 1 *adj.* römisch-katholisch; 2 *n.* Katholik, *der/* Katholikin, *die;* **sb. is a ~ Catholic** jmd. ist römisch-katholisch

romance /rəʊ'mæns/ 1 *n.* (**a**) (love affair) Romanze, *die;* (**b**) (love story) [romantische] Liebesgeschichte; (**c**) (romantic quality) Romantik, *die;* (**d**) (Lit.) (medieval tale) Romanze, *die;* (improbable tale) fantastische Geschichte; (**e**) (make-believe) Fantasterei, *die;* (**f**) **R~** (Ling.) Romanisch, *das.* 2 *adj.* **R~** (Ling.) romanisch; **R~ languages and literature** (subject) Romanistik, *die*

Romanesque /rəʊmə'nesk/ (Art, Archit.) *n.* 1 Romanik, *die.* 2 *adj.* romanisch

Romania /rəʊ'meɪnɪə/ *pr. n.* Rumänien (*das*)

Romanian /rəʊ'meɪnɪən/ **▶ 897**, **▶ 947** 1 *adj.* rumänisch; **sb. is ~:** jmd. ist Rumäne/Rumänin. 2 *n.* (**a**) (person) Rumäne, *der/*Rumänin, *die;* (**b**) (language) Rumänisch, *das; see also* **English** 2 a

Roman 'numeral *n.* römische Ziffer

romantic /rəʊ'mæntɪk/ 1 *adj.* (**a**) (emotional) romantisch; **~ fiction** (love stories) Liebesromane; (**b**) **R~** (Lit., Art) romantisch; *der* Romantik *nachgestellt.* 2 *n.* **R~** (Lit., Art, Mus.) Romantiker, *der/*Romantikerin, *die*

romanticise ⇒ **romanticize**

Romanticism /rəʊ'mæntɪsɪzm/ *n.* (Lit., Art, Mus.) Romantik, *die*

romanticize /rəʊ'mæntɪsaɪz/ *v.t.* romantisieren

Romany /'rəʊmənɪ/ 1 *n.* (**a**) (gypsy) Rom, *der;* **the Romanies** die Roma; (**b**) **▶ 897** (language) Romani, *das.* 2 *adj.* (**a**) Roma-; (**b**) (Ling.) Romani-

Rome /rəʊm/ *pr. n.* **▶ 1159** Rom (*das*); **~ was not built in a day** (prov.) Rom ist nicht an einem Tag erbaut worden (Spr.)

romp /rɒmp/ 1 *v.i.* (**a**) [herum]tollen; (**b**) (coll.: win, succeed, etc. easily) **~ home** *or* **in** spielend gewinnen; **~ through** sth. etw. spielend schaffen. 2 *n.* Tollerei, *die;* **have a ~:** [herum]tollen

roof /ru:f/ 1 *n.* (**a**) Dach, *das;* **under one ~:** unter einem Dach; **have a ~ over one's head** ein Dach über dem

Kopf haben; **go through the** ~ ⟨*Preise:*⟩ krass in die Höhe steigen; **sb. goes through** *or* **hits the** ~ (fig. coll.) jmd. geht an die Decke (ugs.); **(b)** (Anat.) ~ **of the mouth** Gaumen, *der.* **2** *v.t.* bedachen; ~ **in** *or* **over** überdachen

roofless /ˈruːflɪs/ *adj.* dachlos

roof: ~**-rack** *n.* Dachgepäckträger, *der;* ~**top** *n.* Dach, *das;* **shout sth. from the** ~**tops** (fig.) etw. in die Welt hinausrufen

rook¹ /rʊk/ **1** *n.* (Ornith.) Saatkrähe, *die.* **2** *v.t.* (charge extortionately) neppen (ugs. abwertend)

rook² *n.* (Chess) Turm, *der*

rookery /ˈrʊkərɪ/ *n.* Saatkrähenkolonie, *die*

rookie /ˈrʊkɪ/ *n.* **(a)** (Mil. sl.) Rekrut, *der*/Rekrutin, *die;* **(b)** (Amer.: new member etc.) Neuling, *der*

room /ruːm, rʊm/ *n.* **(a)** (in building) Zimmer, *das;* (esp. without furniture) Raum, *der;* (large ~, for function) Saal, *der;* **leave the** ~ (coll.: go to lavatory) austreten (ugs.); **(b)** *no pl., no indef. art.* (space) Platz, *der;* **give sb.** ~: jmdm. Platz machen; **give sb.** ~ **to do sth.** (fig.) jmdm. die Freiheit lassen, etw. zu tun; **make** ~ **[for sb./sth.]** [jmdm./einer Sache] Platz machen; **(c)** (scope) **there is still** ~ **for improvement in his work** seine Arbeit ist noch verbesserungsfähig; *see also* **manœuvre 1 b, 3 b; (d)** *in pl.* (apartments, lodgings) Wohnung, *die;* '~**s to let**' „Zimmer zu vermieten". *See also* **cat a**

-roomed /rʊmd/ *adj. in comb.* **a three-**~ **flat** eine Dreizimmerwohnung; **a one-**~/**four-**~ **building** ein Haus mit einem Zimmer/vier Zimmern

room: ~**-mate** *n.* Zimmergenosse, *der*/-genossin, *die;* Stubenkamerad, *der* (Milit.); ~ **service** *n.* Zimmerservice, *der;* ~ **temperature** *n.* Zimmertemperatur, *die*

roomy /ˈruːmɪ/ *adj.* geräumig

roost /ruːst/ **1** *n.* Schlafplatz, *der;* (perch) [Sitz]stange, *die;* **come home to** ~ (fig.) jmdm. heimgezahlt werden; *see also* **rule 2 b. 2** *v.i.* ⟨*Vogel:*⟩ sich [zum Schlafen] niederlassen

rooster /ˈruːstə(r)/ *n.* (Amer.) Hahn, *der*

root¹ /ruːt/ **1** *n.* **(a)** Wurzel, *die;* **pull sth. up by the** ~**s** etw. mit den Wurzeln ausreißen; (fig.) etw. mit der Wurzel ausrotten; **put down** ~**s/strike** *or* **take** ~ (lit. or fig.) Wurzeln schlagen; **have** ~**s** verwurzelt sein; **(b)** (source) Wurzel, *die;* (basis) Grundlage, *die;* **have its** ~**s in** ... einer Sache (*Dat.*) entspringen; **get at** *or* **to the** ~**[s] of things** den Dingen auf den Grund kommen; **be at the** ~ **of the matter** der Kern der Sache sein. **2** *v.t.* **(a)** **a plant firmly** eine Pflanze fest einpflanzen; **have** ~**ed itself in sth.** (fig.) in etw. (*Dat.*) verwurzelt sein; **stand** ~**ed to the spot** wie angewurzelt dastehen. **3** *v.i.* ⟨*Pflanze:*⟩ wurzeln, anwachsen

~ **'out** *v.t.* ausrotten; ausmerzen

root² *v.i.* **(a)** (turn up ground) wühlen (**for** nach); **(b)** (coll.) ~ **for** (cheer) anfeuern; (wish for success of) Stimmung machen für

'**root crop[s]** *n.* [*pl.*] Hackfrüchte *Pl.*

rooted /ˈruːtɪd/ *adj.* eingewurzelt

rootless /ˈruːtlɪs/ *adj.* wurzellos

rope /rəʊp/ *n.* **(a)** (cord) Seil, *das;* Tau, *das;* **(b)** (Amer.: lasso) Lasso, *das;* (c) (for hanging sb.) **the** ~: der Strang; (fig.: death penalty) die Todesstrafe; **(d)** *in pl.* (Boxing) **the** ~**s** die Seile; **be on the** ~**s** (lit. or fig.) in den Seilen hängen; **(e)** *in pl.* **learn the** ~**s** lernen, sich zurechtzufinden; (at work) sich einarbeiten; **know the** ~**s** sich auskennen; **show sb. the** ~**s** jmdn. mit allem vertraut machen

~ **'in** *v.t.* **(a)** mit einem Seil/mit Seilen absperren ⟨*Gebiet*⟩; **(b)** (fig.) einspannen (ugs.); **how did you get** ~**d in to that?** warum hast du dich dazu breitschlagen lassen? (ugs.)

~ **'off** *v.t.* [mit einem Seil/mit Seilen] absperren

~ **to'gether** *v.t.* (Mount.) aneinander seilen

rope: ~ **'ladder** *n.* Strickleiter, *die;* ~**way** *n.* Seilbahn, *die*

ropy /ˈrəʊpɪ/ *adj.* (coll.) (poor) schäbig; (in a bad state) mitgenommen; **you look a bit** ~: du siehst ziemlich kaputt aus

rosary /ˈrəʊzərɪ/ *n.* (Relig.) Rosenkranz, *der*

rose¹ /rəʊz/ **1** *n.* **(a)** (plant, flower) Rose, *die;* **no bed of** ~**s** (fig.) kein Honigschlecken; **it's not all** ~**s** es ist nicht alles

[so] rosig; **everything's [coming up]** ~**s** alles ist bestens; **(b)** (colour) Rosa, *das.* **2** *adj.* rosa[farben]

rose² ⇒ **rise 2**

rose: ~ **bed** *n.* Rosenbeet, *das;* ~**bud** *n.* Rosenknospe, *die;* ~ **bush** *n.* Rosenstrauch, *der;* ~**-coloured** *adj.* (lit. or fig.) rosarot; **see things through** ~**-coloured spectacles** die Dinge durch eine rosarote Brille sehen; ~**-hip** *n.* (Bot.) Hagebutte, *die;* ~**-hip tea** Hagebuttentee, *der*

rosemary /ˈrəʊzmərɪ/ *n.* (Bot.) Rosmarin, *der*

rose: ~ **petal** *n.* Rosen[blüten]blatt, *das;* ~**-tinted** ⇒ **rose-coloured**

rosette /rəʊˈzet/ *n.* Rosette, *die*

roster /ˈrɒstə(r)/ *n.* Dienstplan, *der*

rostrum /ˈrɒstrəm/ *n., pl.* **rostra** /ˈrɒstrə/ *or* ~**s** (platform) Podium, *das;* (desk) Rednerpult, *das*

rosy /ˈrəʊzɪ/ *adj.* **(a)** rosig; **(b)** (fig.) rosig ⟨*Zukunft, Aussichten*⟩; **paint a** ~ **picture of sth.** etw. in den rosigsten Farben schildern

rot /rɒt/ **1** *n.* **(a)** ⇒ **2a:** Verrottung, *die;* Fäulnis, *die;* Verwesung, *die;* (fig.: deterioration) Verfall, *der;* **stop the** ~ (fig.) dem Verfall Einhalt gebieten; **the** ~ **has set in** (fig.) der Verfall hat eingesetzt; *see also* **dry rot; (b)** (coll.: nonsense) Quark, *der* (salopp); ~**!** Blödsinn! (ugs.). **2** *v.i.,* **-tt-: (a)** (decay) verrotten; ⟨*Fleisch, Gemüse, Obst:*⟩ verfaulen; ⟨*Leiche:*⟩ verwesen; ⟨*Holz:*⟩ faulen; ⟨*Zähne:*⟩ schlecht werden; **(b)** (fig.: go to ruin) verrotten. **3** *v.t.,* **-tt-** verrotten lassen; verfaulen lassen ⟨*Fleisch, Gemüse, Obst*⟩; faulen lassen ⟨*Holz*⟩; verwesen lassen ⟨*Leiche*⟩; zerstören ⟨*Zähne*⟩

~ **a'way** *v.i.* verfaulen; ⟨*Leiche:*⟩ verwesen; ⟨*Holz:*⟩ faulen

rota /ˈrəʊtə/ *n.* (Brit.) **(a)** (order of rotation) Turnus, *der;* **(b)** (list of persons) [Arbeits]plan, *der*

rotary /ˈrəʊtərɪ/ *adj.* **(a)** (acting by rotation) rotierend; Rotations-; ~ **engine** Drehkolbenmotor, *der;* **(b)** R~: Rotarier-; R~ **Club** Rotary-Club, *der*

rotate /rəʊˈteɪt/ **1** *v.i.* (revolve) rotieren; sich drehen; ~ **on an axis** sich um eine Achse drehen. **2** *v.t.* **(a)** (cause to revolve) in Rotation versetzen; **(b)** (alternate) abwechselnd erledigen ⟨*Aufgaben*⟩; abwechselnd erfüllen ⟨*Pflichten*⟩; ~ **[the] crops** Fruchtwechselwirtschaft betreiben

rotation /rəʊˈteɪʃn/ *n.* **(a)** Rotation, *die,* Drehung, *die* (**about** um); **(b)** (succession) turnusmäßiger Wechsel; (in political office) Rotation, *die;* ~ **of crops** Fruchtfolge, *die;* **by** ~: im Turnus

rote /rəʊt/ *n.* **by** ~: auswendig ⟨*lernen, aufsagen*⟩

rotisserie /rəʊˈtɪsərɪ/ *n.* **(a)** (restaurant) Rotisserie, *die;* **(b)** (appliance) Grill, *der*

rotor /ˈrəʊtə(r)/ *n.* Rotor, *der* (Technik)

rotten /ˈrɒtn/ **1** *adj.,* ~**er** /ˈrɒtənə(r)/, ~**est** /ˈrɒtənɪst/ **(a)** (decayed) verrottet; verwest ⟨*Leiche*⟩; verrottet ⟨*Holz*⟩; verfault ⟨*Obst, Gemüse, Fleisch*⟩; faul ⟨*Ei, Zähne*⟩; (rusted) verrostet; ~ **to the core** (fig.) verdorben bis ins Mark; völlig verrottet ⟨*System, Gesellschaft*⟩; **(b)** (corrupt) verdorben; verkommen; **(c)** (coll.: bad) mies (ugs.); **feel** ~ (ill) sich mies fühlen (ugs.); (have a bad conscience) ein schlechtes Gewissen haben; ~ **luck** saumäßiges Pech (salopp). **2** *adv.* (coll.) saumäßig (salopp); **hurt/stink something** ~: saumäßig weh tun/stinken (salopp); **spoilt** ~: ganz schön verwöhnt (ugs.)

rotund /rəʊˈtʌnd/ *adj.* **(a)** (round) rund; **(b)** (plump) rundlich

rouble /ˈruːbl/ *n.* Rubel, *der*

rouge /ruːʒ/ *n.* (cosmetic powder) Rouge, *das*

rough /rʌf/ **1** *adj.* **(a)** (coarse, uneven) rau; holp[e]rig ⟨*Straße usw.*⟩; uneben ⟨*Gelände*⟩; aufgewühlt ⟨*Wasser*⟩; **(b)** (violent) rau, roh ⟨*Person, Worte, Behandlung, Benehmen*⟩; rau ⟨*Gegend*⟩; **(c)** (harsh to the senses) rau; kratzig ⟨*Geschmack, Getränk*⟩; ~ **cider** saurer Apfelwein; **(d)** (trying) hart; **this is** ~ **on him** das ist hart für ihn; **have a** ~ **time** es schwer haben; **give sb. a** ~ **time** es jmdm. schwer machen; **(e)** (fig.: lacking finish, polish) derb; rau ⟨*Empfang*⟩; unbeholfen ⟨*Stil*⟩; unbeholfen ⟨*Benehmen, Sprache*⟩; **he has a few** ~ **edges** (fig.) er ist ein wenig ungeschliffen; **(f)** (rudimentary) primitiv ⟨*Unterkunft, Leben*⟩; (approximate) grob ⟨*Skizze, Schätzung, Einteilung,*

Übersetzung⟩; vag[e] ⟨*Vorstellung*⟩; ~ **notes** stichwort-artige Notizen; ~ **draft** Rohentwurf, *der;* ~ **paper/note-book** Konzeptpapier, *das*/Kladde, *die;* **(g)** (coll.: ill) angeschlagen (ugs.). **2** *n.* **(a)** (Golf) Rough, *das;* **(b) take the** ~ **with the smooth** die Dinge nehmen, wie sie kommen; **(c)** (unfinished state) **[be] in** ~: [sich] im Rohzustand [be-finden]. **3** *adv.* rau ⟨*spielen*⟩; scharf ⟨*reiten*⟩; **sleep** ~: im Freien schlafen. **4** *v.t.* ~ **it** primitiv leben

~ **'out** *v.t.* [grob] entwerfen

~ **'up** *v.t.* (coll.: deal roughly with) anrempeln (ugs.)

roughage /'rʌfɪdʒ/ *n.* Ballaststoffe *Pl.* (Med.)

rough: ~**-and-ready** *adj.* **(a)** (not elaborate) proviso-risch; skizzenhaft ⟨*Beschreibung*⟩; behelfsmäßig ⟨*Hütte, Methode*⟩; **(b)** (not refined) raubeinig (ugs.) ⟨*Person*⟩; ~**and-'tumble** *n.* [wildes] Handgemenge; [wilde] Rau-ferei; ~ **'copy** *n.* **(a)** (original draft) [erster] Entwurf; Kon-zept, *das;* **(b)** (simplified copy) grobe Skizze; ~ **'diamond** *n.* (fig.) ungehobelter, aber guter Mensch; **he's a [bit of a]** ~ **diamond** er ist rau, aber herzlich

roughen /'rʌfn/ **1** *v.t.* aufrauen ⟨*Oberfläche*⟩; rau machen ⟨*Hände*⟩. **2** *v.i.* rau werden

rough: ~ **house** *n.* (coll.) Keilerei, *die* (ugs.); ~ **'jus-tice** *n.* ziemlich willkürliche Urteile; ~ **'luck** *n.* Pech, *das*

roughly /'rʌflɪ/ *adv.* **(a)** (violently) roh; grob; **(b)** (crudely) leidlich; grob ⟨*skizzieren, bearbeiten, bauen*⟩; **(c)** (approx-imately) ungefähr; grob ⟨*schätzen*⟩

roughness /'rʌfnɪs/ *n.* **(a)** *no pl.* Rauheit, *die;* (uneven-ness) Unebenheit, *die;* **(b)** *no pl.* (sharpness) (of wine, fruit juice) Säure, *die;* (of voice) Rauheit, *die;* **(c)** *no pl.* (violence) Rohheit, *die;* **the** ~ **of the area** die Häufigkeit von Gewalttaten in der Gegend; **(d)** (rough place or part) unausgefeilte Stelle

rough: ~ **shod** *adj.* **ride** ~**shod over sb./sth.** jmdn./etw. mit Füßen treten; ~ **stuff** *n.* (coll.) Zoff, *der* (salopp)

roulette /ru:'let/ *n.* Roulette, *das*

round /raʊnd/ **1** *adj.* rund; rundlich ⟨*Arme*⟩; ~ **cheeks** Pausbacken *Pl.* (fam.); **in** ~ **figures, it will cost £1,000** rund gerechnet wird es 1 000 Pfund kosten. **2** *n.* **(a)** (re-curring series) Serie, *die;* **the daily** ~: der Alltag; **(b)** (charge of ammunition) Ladung, *die;* **50** ~**s [of am-munition]** 50 Schuss Munition; **fire five** ~**s** fünf Schüsse abfeuern; **(c)** (division of game or contest) Runde, *die;* **(d)** (burst) ~ **of applause** Beifallssturm, *der;* ~**s of cheers** Hoch-rufe; **(e)** ~ **[of drinks]** Runde, *die;* **(f)** (regular calls) Runde, *die;* **Tour,** *die;* **the doctor is on her** ~ **at present** Frau Doktor macht gerade Hausbesuche; **go** [ɒn] *or* **make one's** ~**s** ⟨*Posten, Wächter usw.:*⟩ seine Runde machen *od.* gehen; ⟨*Krankenhausarzt:*⟩ Visite machen; **do** *or* **go the** ~**s** ⟨*Person, Gerücht usw.:*⟩ die Runde machen (ugs.); **(g)** (Golf) Runde, *die;* **a** ~ **of golf** eine Runde Golf; **(h)** (slice) ~ **of bread/toast** eine Scheibe Brot/Toast. **3** *adv.* **(a)** all **the year** ~: das ganze Jahr hindurch; **the third time** ~: beim dritten Mal; **have a wall all** ~: von einer Mauer eingeschlossen sein; **have a look** ~: sich umsehen; **(b)** (in girth) **be [all of] ten feet** ~: einen Umfang von [mindes-tens] zehn Fuß haben; **(c)** (from one point, place, person, etc. to another) **he asked** ~ **among his friends** er fragte seine Freunde; **(d)** (by indirect way) herum; **walk** ~: außen herum gehen; **go a the long way** ~: einen weiten Umweg machen; **(e)** (here) hier; (there) dort; **I'll go** ~ **tomorrow** ich gehe morgen hin; **call** ~ **any time!** kommen Sie doch jederzeit vorbei!; **ask sb.** ~ **[for a drink]** jmdn. [zu ei-nem Gläschen *u.ä.*] einladen; *see also* **clock 1 a.** **4** *prep.* **(a)** um [... herum]; **a tour** ~ **the world** eine Welt-reise; **travel** ~ **England** durch England reisen; **she had a blanket** ~ **her** sie hatte eine Decke um sich ge-schlungen; **right** ~ **the lake** um den ganzen See herum; **be** ~ **the back of the house** hinter dem Haus sein; **run** ~ **the streets** durch die Straßen rennen; **walk** *etc.* ~ **and** ~ **sth.** immer wieder um etw. herumgehen *usw.;* **we looked** ~ **the shops** wir sahen uns in den Geschäften um; **(b)** (in various directions from) um [... herum]; rund um ⟨*einen Ort*⟩; **look** ~ **one** um sich schauen; **do you live** ~ **here?** wohnst du [hier] in der Nähe?; **if you're ever**

~ **this way** wenn du hier in der Nähe bist. **5** *v.t.* **(a)** (give ~ **shape to)** rund machen; runden ⟨*Lippen, Rücken*⟩; **(b)** (state as ~ number) runden **(to auf** + *Akk.*); **(c)** (go ~) um-fahren/umgehen *usw.;* ~ **a bend** um eine Kurve fahren/gehen/kommen *usw.*

~ **'down** *v.t.* abrunden ⟨*Zahl*⟩ **(to auf** + *Akk.*)

~ **'off** *v.t.* (also fig.: complete) abrunden

~ **on** *v.t.* anfahren

~ **'up** *v.t.* **(a)** (gather, collect together) verhaften ⟨*Verdächtige*⟩; zusammentreiben ⟨*Vieh*⟩; beschaffen, (ugs.) auftreiben ⟨*Geld*⟩; **(b)** (to ~ figure) aufrunden **(to auf** + *Akk.*)

round: ~ **a'bout 1** *adv.* **(a)** (on all sides) ringsum; **the villages** ~ **about** die umliegenden Dörfer; **(b)** (indirectly) auf Umwegen; **(c)** (approximately) rund; ~ **about 2,500 people** um die *od.* rund 2 500 Leute; **2** *prep.* rund um; ~**about 1** *n.* **(a)** (Brit.: road junction) Verkehrskreisel, *der;* **(b)** (Brit.: merry-go-round) Karussell, *das;* **it's swings and** ~**abouts** es gleicht sich aus; **2** *adj.* **(a)** (meandering) **a [very]** ~**about way** ein [sehr] umständlicher Weg; **the taxi went a** ~**about way** das Taxi machte einen Umweg; **(b)** (fig.: indirect) umständlich

rounders /'raʊndəz/ *n. sing.* (Brit.) Rounders, *das;* Rund-ball, *das* (dem Baseball ähnliches Spiel)

round: ~**-eyed** /'raʊndaɪd/ *adj.* mit großen Augen *nachgestellt;* **be** ~**-eyed with amazement** große Augen machen; ~**-faced** /'raʊndfeɪst/ *adj.* pausbäckig (fam.); **R**~**head** *n.* (Brit. Hist.) Rundkopf, *der*

roundly /'raʊndlɪ/ *adv.* entschieden

roundness /'raʊndnɪs/ *n., no pl.* Rundheit, *die;* (of figure) Rundlichkeit, *die*

round: ~ **'number** *n.* runde Zahl; ~**-shoul-dered** /raʊnd'ʃəʊldəd/ *adj.* ⟨*Person*⟩ mit einem Rund-rücken; **be** ~**-shouldered** einen Rundrücken haben; ~**-the-'clock** *adj.* rund um die Uhr *nachgestellt;* ~**-the-world** *attrib. adj.* ~**-the-world flight/cruise** *etc.* Flug/Kreuzfahrt *usw.* um die [ganze] Welt; ~**-the-world voy-age/trip** Weltreise, *die;* ~**-the-world yachtsman/yachtswoman** Weltumsegler, *der*/Weltumseglerin, *die;* ~**-the-world** **'trip** *n.* **(a)** Rundreise, *die;* **(b)** (Amer.: return trip) Hin- und Rückfahrt, *die;* ~**-up** *n.* **(a)** (gathering-in) (of persons) Ein-fangen, *das;* (arrest) Verhaftung, *die;* (of animals) Zusammen-treiben, *das;* **(b)** (summary) Zusammenfassung, *die*

rouse /raʊz/ *v.t.* **(a)** (awaken, lit. or fig.) wecken **(from** aus); ~ **oneself** aufwachen; (overcome indolence) sich aufraffen; ~ **sb./oneself to action** jmdn. zur Tat anstacheln/sich zur Tat aufraffen; **(b)** (provoke) reizen; **he is terrible when** ~**d** er ist furchtbar, wenn man ihn reizt; ~ **sb. to anger** jmdn. in Wut bringen; **(c)** (cause) wecken; hervorrufen, auslösen ⟨*Empörung, Beschuldigungen*⟩

rousing /'raʊzɪŋ/ *adj.* mitreißend ⟨*Lied*⟩; leidenschaftlich ⟨*Rede*⟩; stürmisch ⟨*Beifall*⟩

rout[1] /raʊt/ **1** *n.* (disorderly retreat) [wilde] Flucht; (disastrous defeat) verheerende Niederlage; **put to** ~: in die Flucht schlagen. **2** *v.t.* aufreiben ⟨*Feind, Truppen*⟩; vernichtend schlagen ⟨*Gegner*⟩

rout[2] *v.i.* (root) wühlen

~ **'out** *v.t.* herausjagen; ~ **sb. out of sth.** jmdn. aus etw. jagen

route /ru:t, *Mil. also:* raʊt/ **1** *n.* (course) Route, *die;* Weg, *der;* **shipping** ~: Schifffahrtsstraße, *die.* **2** *v.t.,* ~**ing** fahren lassen ⟨*Fahrzeug*⟩; führen ⟨*Linie*⟩; **the train is** ~**d through** *or* **via Crewe** der Zug fährt über Crewe

'route march *n.* (Mil.) Übungsmarsch, *der*

routine /ru:'ti:n/ **1** *n.* **(a)** (regular procedure; Computing) Rou-tine, *die;* **(b)** (coll.) (set speech) Platte, *die* (ugs.); (formula) Spruch, *der;* **(c)** (Theatre) Nummer, *die;* (Dancing, Skating) Fi-gur, *die;* (Gymnastics) Übung, *die.* **2** *adj.* routinemäßig; Routine⟨*arbeit, -untersuchung usw.*⟩

rove /raʊv/ **1** *v.i.* ziehen ⟨*Blick:*⟩ schweifen (geh.); ~ [about] herumziehen; **have a roving eye** den Frauen/Männern schöne Augen machen. **2** *v.t.* streifen durch; durchstreifen (geh.); ⟨*Blick:*⟩ durchschweifen ⟨*Raum*⟩

row[1] /raʊ/ (coll.) **1** *n.* **(a)** (noise) Krach, *der;* **make a** ~: Krach machen; (protest) Rabatz machen (ugs.); **(b)** (quarrel) Krach, *der* (ugs.); **have/start a** ~: Krach haben/anfangen (ugs.). **2** *v.i.* sich streiten

row² /rəʊ/ n. (a) Reihe, die; **in a ~:** in einer Reihe; (coll.: in succession) nacheinander; (b) (line of numbers etc.) Zeile, die; (c) (terrace) ~ **[of houses]** [Häuser]zeile, die; [Häuser]reihe, die

row³ /rəʊ/ **1** v.i. rudern. **2** v.t. rudern; ~ **sb. across** jmdn. hinüberrudern. **3** n. **go for a ~:** rudern gehen

rowan /ˈrəʊən/ n. ~**[-tree]** Eberesche, die

rowboat /ˈrəʊbəʊt/ n. (Amer.) Ruderboot, das

rowdy /ˈraʊdɪ/ **1** adj. rowdyhaft (abwertend); ~ **adolescents** jugendliche Rowdys (abwertend); ~ **scenes** tumultartige Szenen; **the party was ~:** auf der Party ging es laut zu. **2** n. Krawallmacher, der; Rabauke, der

rowing /ˈrəʊɪŋ/ n., no pl. Rudern, das

rowing: ~ **boat** n. (Brit.) Ruderboot, das; ~ **club** n. Ruderklub, der

royal /ˈrɔɪəl/ **1** adj. königlich. **2** n. (coll.) Mitglied der königlichen Familie; **the ~s** die königliche Familie

royal: R~ '**Air Force** n. (Brit.) Königliche Luftwaffe; ~ '**blue** n. (Brit.) Königsblau, das; ~ '**family** n. königliche Familie

royalist /ˈrɔɪəlɪst/ n. Royalist, der/Royalistin, die; attrib. Royalisten-; royalistisch

Royal 'Navy n. (Brit.) Königliche Kriegsmarine

royalty /ˈrɔɪəltɪ/ n. (a) (payment) Tantieme, die (**on** für); (b) collect. (royal persons) Mitglieder des Königshauses; (c) no pl., no art. (member of royal family) ein Mitglied der königlichen Familie

RPI abbr. (Brit.) **retail price index**

r.p.m. /ɑːpiːˈem/ abbr. **revolutions per minute** U.p.M.

RSI abbr. **repetitive strain injury**

RSPCA abbr. (Brit.) **Royal Society for the Prevention of Cruelty to Animals** britischer Tierschutzverein

rub /rʌb/ **1** v.t., **-bb-:** reiben (**on, against** an + Dat.); (with ointment etc.) einreiben; (to remove dirt etc.) abreiben; (to dry) trockenreiben; (with sandpaper) [ab]schmirgeln; ~ **sth. off** sth. etw. von etw. reiben; ~ **one's hands** sich (Dat.) die Hände reiben; ~ **shoulders** or **elbows with sb.** (fig.) Tuchfühlung mit jmdm. haben; ~ **two things together** zwei Dinge aneinander reiben; ~ **sth. through a sieve** etw. durch ein Sieb streichen. **2** v.i., **-bb-:** (a) (exercise friction) reiben (**[up]on, against** an + Dat.); (b) (get frayed) sich abreiben. **3** n. Reiben, das; **give it a quick ~:** reib es kurz ab; **there's the ~** (fig.) da liegt der Haken [dabei] (ugs.)

~ '**down** v.t. (a) (prepare) abschmirgeln; (b) (dry) abreiben

~ '**in** v.t. einreiben; **there's no need to** or **don't ~ it in** (fig.) reib es mir nicht [dauernd] unter die Nase (ugs.)

~ '**off** v.t. wegreiben; wegwischen. **2** v.i. (lit. or fig.) abfärben (**on** auf + Akk.)

~ '**out 1** v.t. ausreiben; (from paper) ausradieren. **2** v.i. sich ausreiben/(from paper) sich ausradieren lassen

~ '**up** v.t. (a) (polish) blank reiben; wienern (ugs.); (b) ~ **sb. up the wrong way** (fig.) jmdm. auf den Schlips treten (ugs.)

rubber¹ /ˈrʌbə(r)/ n. (a) Gummi, das od. der; attrib. Gummi-; (b) (eraser) Radiergummi, der

rubber² n. (Cards) Robber, der

rubber: ~ '**band** n. Gummiband, das; ~ '**bullet** n. Gummigeschoss, das; ~ '**cheque** n. (coll.) ungedeckter Scheck; ~ '**glove** n. Gummihandschuh, der; ~**neck** (Amer.) **1** n. Gaffer, der/Gafferin, die (abwertend); **2** v.i. gaffen (abwertend); ~ **plant** n. (Bot.) Gummibaum, der; ~ '**stamp** n. Gummistempel, der; ~**-'stamp** v.t. (fig.: approve) absegnen (ugs. scherzh.)

rubbery /ˈrʌbərɪ/ adj. gummiartig; (tough) zäh; **be tough and ~:** zäh wie Gummi sein

rubbish /ˈrʌbɪʃ/ **1** n., no pl., no indef. art. (a) (refuse) Abfall, der; Abfälle; (to be collected and dumped) Müll, der; (b) (worthless material) Plunder, der (ugs. abwertend); **be ~:** nichts taugen; (nonsense) Quatsch, der (ugs.); Blödsinn, der (ugs.); **what ~!** was für ein Quatsch od. Schmarren! **2** int. Quatsch (ugs. abwertend)

rubbish: ~ **bin** n. Abfall-/Mülleimer, der; (in factory) Abfall-/Mülltonne, die; ~ **chute** n. Müllschlucker, der;

~ **dump** n. Müllkippe, die; ~ **heap** n. Müllhaufen, der; (in garden) Abfallhaufen, der; ~ **tip** n. Müllabladeplatz, der

rubbishy /ˈrʌbɪʃɪ/ adj. mies (ugs.); ~ **newspaper** Käseblatt, das (salopp abwertend)

rubble /ˈrʌbl/ n. (from damaged building) Trümmer Pl.; (Geol. also) Schutt, der; **reduce sth. to ~:** etw. in Schutt und Asche legen

ruby /ˈruːbɪ/ **1** n. (a) (precious stone) Rubin, der; (b) (colour) Rubinrot, das. **2** adj. (a) (red) rubinfarben; rubinrot; (b) Rubin⟨ring, -brosche usw.⟩

ruby: ~**-red** adj. rubinrot; ~ '**wedding** n. Rubinhochzeit, die

RUC abbr. **Royal Ulster Constabulary** nordirische Polizei

ruck /rʌk/, (Brit.) **ruckle** /ˈrʌkl/ **1** n. (crease) Falte, die. **2** v.i. ~ **up** hochrutschen

rucksack /ˈrʌksæk, ˈrʊksæk/ n. Rucksack, der

ruckus /ˈrʌkəs/ n., **ructions** /ˈrʌkʃnz/ n. pl. (coll.) Rabatz, der (ugs.)

rudder /ˈrʌdə(r)/ n. Ruder, das

ruddy /ˈrʌdɪ/ adj. (a) (reddish) rötlich; (b) (Brit. sl. euphem.: bloody) verdammt (salopp)

rude /ruːd/ adj. (a) (impolite) unhöflich; (stronger) rüde; **say ~ things** or **be ~ about sb.** in ungehöriger Weise von jmdm. sprechen; **be ~ to sb.** zu jmdm. grob unhöflich sein/jmdn. rüde behandeln; (b) (abrupt) unsanft; ~ **awakening** böses od. (geh.) jähes Erwachen; (c) (obscene) unanständig

rudeness /ˈruːdnɪs/ n., no pl. (bad manners) ungehöriges od. rüdes Benehmen

rudimentary /ruːdɪˈmentərɪ/ adj. (elementary) elementar; primitiv ⟨Gebäude⟩; ~ **knowledge** Grundkenntnisse Pl.

rudiments /ˈruːdɪmənts/ n. pl. (a) (first principles) Grundzüge Pl.; Grundlagen Pl.; (b) (imperfect beginning) [erster] Ansatz

rueful /ˈruːfl/ adj., **ruefully** /ˈruːfəlɪ/ adv. reumütig; reuig

ruff /rʌf/ n. Halskrause, die

ruffian /ˈrʌfɪən/ n. Rohling, der (abwertend); **gang of ~s** Schlägerbande, die

ruffle /ˈrʌfl/ **1** v.t. (a) (disturb smoothness of) kräuseln; ~ **sb.'s hair** jmdm. durch die Haare fahren; (b) (upset) aus der Fassung bringen; **be easily ~d** leicht aus der Fassung geraten. **2** n. (frill) Rüsche, die

~ '**up** v.t. sträuben ⟨Gefieder⟩

rug /rʌg/ n. (a) (for floor) [kleiner, dicker] Teppich; **Persian ~:** Perserbrücke, die; **pull the ~ [out] from under sb.** (fig.) jmdm. den Boden unter den Füßen wegziehen; (b) (wrap, blanket) [dicke] Wolldecke

Rugby /ˈrʌgbɪ/ n. Rugby, das

Rugby: ~ **ball** n. Rugbyball, der; ~ **tackle** n. tiefes Fassen (Rugby); **the policeman brought him down with a ~ tackle** der Polizist warf sich auf ihn und riss ihn zu Boden

rugged /ˈrʌgɪd/ adj. (a) (sturdy) robust; (b) (involving hardship) rau ⟨Test⟩; (c) (unpolished) rau; **with ~ good looks** gut aussehend mit markanten Gesichtszügen; (d) (uneven) zerklüftet; unwegsam ⟨Land, Anstieg⟩; zerfurcht ⟨Gesicht⟩

rugger /ˈrʌgə(r)/ n. (Brit. coll.) Rugby, das

ruin /ˈruːɪn/ **1** n. (a) no pl., no indef. art. (decay) Verfall, der; **go to** or **fall into rack and ~** ⟨Gebäude:⟩ völlig verfallen; ⟨Garten:⟩ völlig verwahrlosen; (b) no pl., no indef. art. (downfall) Ruin, der; ~ **stared her in the face** sie stand vor dem Ruin; (c) in sing. or pl. (remains) Ruine, die; **in ~s** in Trümmern; (d) (cause of ~) Ruin, der; Untergang, der; **you'll be the ~ of me** du ruinierst mich [noch]. **2** v.t. ruinieren; verderben ⟨Urlaub, Abend⟩; zunichte machen ⟨Aussichten, Möglichkeiten usw.⟩

ruined /ˈruːɪnd/ adj. (a) (reduced to ruins) verfallen; ~ **town** Ruinenstadt, die; **a ~ castle/palace/church** eine Burg-/Palast-/Kirchenruine; (b) (brought to ruin) ruiniert; (c) (spoilt) verdorben

ruinous /ˈruːməs/ adj. ruinös; katastrophal ⟨Wirkung⟩; **be ~ to sb./sth.** jmdn./etw. ruinieren

rule /ruːl/ **1** *n.* **(a)** (principle) Regel, *die;* **the** ~**s of the game** (lit. or fig.) die Spielregeln; **stick to** *or* **play by the** ~**s** (lit. or fig.) sich an die Spielregeln halten; ~**s and regulations** Regeln und Vorschriften; **be against the** ~**s** regelwidrig sein; (fig.) gegen die Spielregeln verstoßen; **as a** ~: in der Regel; ~ **of thumb** Faustregel, *die;* **(b)** (custom) Regel, *die;* **the** ~ **of the house is that** ...: in diesem Haus ist es üblich, dass ...; **(c)** *no pl.* (government) Herrschaft, *die* (**over** über + *Akk.*); **the** ~ **of law** die Autorität des Gesetzes; **(d)** (graduated measure) Maß, *das;* (tape) Bandmaß, *das;* (folding) Zollstock, *der.* **2** *v.t.* **(a)** (control) beherrschen; **(b)** (be the ruler of) regieren; ⟨*Monarch, Diktator usw.*:⟩ herrschen über (+ *Akk.*); ~ **the roost [in the house]** Herr im Hause sein; **(c)** (give as decision) entscheiden; ~ **a motion out of order** einen Antrag nicht zulassen; **(d)** (draw) ziehen ⟨*Linie*⟩; (draw lines on) linieren ⟨*Papier*⟩. **3** *v.i.* **(a)** (govern) herrschen; **(b)** (decide, declare formally) entscheiden (**against** gegen; **in favour of** für); ~ **on a matter** in einer Sache entscheiden

~ **'off 1** *v.t.* mit einem Strich abtrennen. **2** *v.i.* einen Schlussstrich ziehen

~ **'out** *v.t.* **(a)** (exclude, eliminate) ausschließen; **(b)** (prevent) unmöglich machen

ruled /ruːld/ *adj.* liniert ⟨*Papier*⟩

ruler /'ruːlə(r)/ *n.* **(a)** (person) Herrscher, *der*/Herrscherin, *die;* **(b)** (for drawing or measuring) Lineal, *das*

ruling /'ruːlɪŋ/ **1** *n.* (decision) Entscheidung, *die.* **2** *adj.* **(a)** (predominating) herrschend ⟨*Meinung*⟩; vorherrschend ⟨*Charakterzug*⟩; **(b)** (governing, reigning) herrschend ⟨*Klasse*⟩; regierend ⟨*Partei*⟩; amtierend ⟨*Regierung*⟩

rum /rʌm/ *n.* Rum, *der*

rumble¹ /'rʌmbl/ **1** *n.* Grollen, *das;* (of heavy vehicle) Rumpeln, *das* (ugs.). **2** *v.i.* **(a)** grollen; ⟨*Magen*:⟩ knurren; **(b)** (go with rumbling noise) rumpeln (ugs.)

rumble² *v.t.* (coll.: understand) spitzkriegen (ugs.) ⟨*Sache*⟩; auf die Schliche kommen (+ *Dat.*) ⟨*Person*⟩

'rumble strip *n.* Signalschwelle, *die;* akustische Schwelle

ruminate /'ruːmɪneɪt/ *v.i.* **(a)** ~ **over** *or* **about** *or* **on sth.** über etw. (*Akk.*) nachsinnen (geh.) *od.* grübeln; **(b)** (Zool.) wiederkäuen

rummage /'rʌmɪdʒ/ **1** *v.i.* wühlen (ugs.); kramen (ugs.); ~ **about** *or* **around** herumkramen (ugs.). **2** *n.* **have a** ~ **through sth.** etw. durchwühlen *od.* durchstöbern

'rummage sale (esp. Amer.) ⇒ **jumble sale**

rummy /'rʌmɪ/ *n.* (Cards) Rommé, *das*

rumour (Brit.; Amer.: **rumor**) /'ruːmə(r)/ **1** *n.* (unverified story) Gerücht, *das;* **there is a** ~ **that** *or* ~ **has it that** ...: es geht das Gerücht, dass ... **2** *v.t.* **sb. is** ~**ed to have done sth., it is** ~**ed that sb. has done sth.** man munkelt (ugs.) *od.* es geht das Gerücht, dass jmd. etw. getan hat

rump /rʌmp/ *n.* **(a)** (buttocks) Hinterteil, *das* (ugs.); **(b)** (remnant) Rest, *der*

'rump steak *n.* Rumpsteak, *das*

rumpus /'rʌmpəs/ *n., no pl.* (coll.) Krach, *der* (ugs.); Spektakel, *der* (ugs.); **kick up** *or* **make a** ~: einen Spektakel veranstalten (ugs.)

'rumpus room *n.* (Amer.) Spielzimmer, *das*

run /rʌn/ **1** *n.* **(a)** Lauf, *der;* **go for a** ~ **before breakfast** vor dem Frühstück einen Lauf machen; **make a late** ~ (Sport or fig.) zum Endspurt ansetzen; **come towards sb./start off at a** ~: jmdm. entgegenlaufen/losrennen; **I've had a good** ~ **for my money** ich bin auf meine Kosten gekommen; **on the** ~: auf der Flucht; **(b)** (trip in vehicle) Fahrt, *die;* (for pleasure) Ausflug, *der;* **on the** ~ **down to Cornwall** auf der Fahrt nach Cornwall; **go for a** ~ **[in the car]** einen [Auto]ausflug machen; **(c) she has had a long** ~ **of success** sie war lange [Zeit] erfolgreich; **have a long** ~ ⟨*Stück, Show*:⟩ viele Aufführungen erleben; **(d)** (succession) Serie, *die;* (cards) Sequenz, *die;* **a** ~ **of victories** eine Siegesserie; **(e)** (tendency) Ablauf, *der;* **the general** ~ **of things/events** der Lauf der Dinge/der Gang der Ereignisse; **(f)** (regular route) Strecke, *die;* **(g)** (Cricket, Baseball) Lauf, *der;* Run, *der;* **(h)** (quantity produced) (of book) Auflage, *die;* **production** ~: Ausstoß, *der* (Wirtsch.); **(i)** (demand) Run, *der* (**on** auf + *Akk.*); **(j) the** ~**s** (coll.: diarrhoea) Durchmarsch, *der* (salopp); **(k)** (unrestricted use) **give**

sb. the ~ **of sth.** jmdm. etw. zu seiner freien Verfügung überlassen; **have the** ~ **of sth.** etw. zu seiner freien Verfügung haben; **(l)** (animal enclosure) Auslauf, *der.* **2** *v.i.*, **-nn-, ran** /ræn/, **run (a)** laufen; (fast also) rennen; ~ **for the bus** laufen *od.* rennen, um den Bus zu kriegen (ugs.); ~ **to help sb.** jmdm. zu Hilfe eilen; **(b)** (compete) laufen; **(c)** (hurry) laufen; **don't** ~ **to me when things go wrong** komm mir nicht angelaufen, wenn etwas schief geht (ugs.); ~ **to meet sb.** jmdm. entgegenlaufen; **(d)** (roll) laufen; ⟨*Ball, Kugel*:⟩ rollen, laufen; **(e)** (slide) laufen; ⟨*Schlitten,* [*Schiebe*]*tür*:⟩ gleiten; **(f)** (revolve) ⟨*Rad, Maschine*:⟩ laufen; **(g)** (flee) davonlaufen; **(h)** (operate on a schedule) fahren; ~ **between two places** ⟨*Zug, Bus*:⟩ zwischen zwei Orten verkehren; **the train is** ~**ning late** der Zug hat Verspätung; **the train doesn't** ~ **on Sundays** der Zug verkehrt nicht an Sonntagen; **(i)** (pass cursorily) ~ **through** überfliegen ⟨*Text*⟩; ~ **through one's head** *or* **mind** ⟨*Gedanken, Ideen*:⟩ einem durch den Kopf gehen; ~ **through the various possibilities** die verschiedenen Möglichkeiten durchspielen; **(j)** (flow) laufen; ⟨*Fluss*:⟩ fließen; ~ **dry** ⟨*Fluss*:⟩ austrocknen; ⟨*Quelle*:⟩ versiegen; ~ **low** *or* **short** knapp werden; ausgehen; **(k)** (be current) ⟨*Vertrag, Theaterstück*:⟩ laufen; **(l)** (be present) ~ **through sth.** sich durch etw. ziehen; ~ **in the family** ⟨*Eigenschaft, Begabung*:⟩ in der Familie liegen; **(m)** (function) laufen; **keep/leave the engine** ~**ning** den Motor laufen lassen/nicht abstellen; **the machine** ~**s on batteries/oil** *etc.* die Maschine läuft mit Batterien/Öl *usw.;* **(n)** (have a course) ⟨*Straße, Bahnlinie*:⟩ verlaufen; **(o)** (have wording) lauten; ⟨*Geschichte*:⟩ gehen (fig.); **(p)** (have certain level) **inflation is** ~**ning at 15 %** die Inflationsrate beläuft sich auf *od.* beträgt 15 %; **(q)** (seek election) kandidieren; ~ **for mayor** für das Amt des Bürgermeisters kandidieren; **(r)** (spread quickly) **a shiver ran down my spine** ein Schau[d]er (geh.) lief mir den Rücken hinunter; **(s)** (spread undesirably) ⟨*Butter, Eis*:⟩ zerlaufen; (in washing) ⟨*Farben*:⟩ auslaufen; **(t)** (ladder) ⟨*Strumpf*:⟩ Laufmaschen bekommen. **3** *v.t.*, **-nn-, ran, run (a)** (cause to move) laufen lassen; (drive) fahren; ~ **one's hand/fingers through/along** *or* **over sth.** mit der Hand/den Fingern durch etw. fahren/über etw. (*Akk.*) streichen; ~ **an** *or* **one's eye along** *or* **down** *or* **over sth.** (fig.) etw. überfliegen; **(b)** (cause to flow) [ein]laufen lassen; ~ **a bath** ein Bad einlaufen lassen; **(c)** (organize, manage) führen, leiten ⟨*Geschäft usw.*⟩; durchführen ⟨*Experiment*⟩; veranstalten ⟨*Wettbewerb*⟩; führen ⟨*Leben*⟩; **(d)** (operate) bedienen ⟨*Maschine*⟩; verkehren lassen ⟨*Verkehrsmittel*⟩; einsetzen ⟨*Sonderbus, -zug*⟩; laufen lassen ⟨*Motor*⟩; abspielen ⟨*Tonband*⟩; ~ **forward/back** vorwärts-/zurückspulen ⟨*Film, Tonband*⟩; **(e)** (own and use) sich (*Dat.*) halten ⟨*Auto*⟩; **this car is expensive to** ~: dieses Auto ist im Unterhalt sehr teuer; ~ **a car with defective brakes** ein Auto mit defekten Bremsen fahren; **(f)** (take for journey) fahren; **I'll** ~ **you into town** ich fahre *od.* bringe dich in die Stadt; **(g)** (pursue) jagen; ~ **sb. hard** *or* **close** jmdm. auf den Fersen sein *od.* sitzen (ugs.); **be** ~ **off one's feet** alle Hände voll zu tun haben (ugs.); (in business) Hochbetrieb haben (ugs.); *see also* **earth 1 d;** **(h)** (complete) laufen ⟨*Rennen, Marathon, Strecke*⟩; ~ **messages/errands** Botengänge machen; **(i)** ~ **a fever/a temperature** Fieber/erhöhte Temperatur haben; **(j)** (publish) bringen (ugs.) ⟨*Bericht, Artikel usw.*⟩

~ **a'bout** *v.i.* **(a)** (bustle) hin- und herlaufen; **(b)** (play without restraint) herumtollen; herumspringen (ugs.)

~ **a'cross** *v.t.* ~ **across sb.** jmdn. treffen; jmdm. über den Weg laufen; ~ **across sth.** auf etw. (*Akk.*) stoßen

~ **after** *v.t.* hinterherlaufen (+ *Dat.*)

~ **a'long** *v.i.* (coll.: depart) sich trollen (ugs.)

~ **a'round 1** *v.i.* **(a)** ~ **around with sb.** sich mit jmdm. herumtreiben; **(b)** ⇒ **run about a;** **(c)** ⇒ **run about b. 2** *v.t.* herumfahren

~ **a'way** *v.i.* **(a)** (flee) weglaufen; fortlaufen; **(b)** (abscond) ~ **away [from home/from the children's home]** [von zu Hause/aus dem Kinderheim] weglaufen; **(c)** (elope) ~ **away with sb./together** mit jmdm./zusammen durchbrennen (ugs.); **(d)** (bolt) ⟨*Pferd*:⟩ durchgehen; **(e)** ⟨*Wasser*:⟩ ablaufen

~ **a'way with** *v.t.* **(a)** (coll.: steal) abhauen mit (salopp);

(b) (fig.: win) ~ **away with the top prize/all the trophies** den ersten Preis/alle Trophäen erringen; (c) (fig.: be misled by) **don't ~ away with the idea that …:** glaub bloß nicht, dass …; **he let his imagination/enthusiasm ~ away with him** seine Fantasie/Begeisterung ist mit ihm durchgegangen

~ **'down 1** v.t. (a) (collide with) überfahren; (b) (criticize) heruntermachen (ugs.); herabsetzen; (c) (cause to diminish) abbauen; verringern ‹*Produktion*›; (d) (cause to lose power) leer machen ‹*Batterie*›. **2** v.i. (a) hin-/herunterlaufen/-rennen/-fahren; (b) (decline) sich verringern; (c) (lose power) ausgehen; ‹*Batterie*:› leer werden; ‹*Uhr, Spielzeug*:› ablaufen

~ **'in** v.t. (a) (prepare for use) einfahren ‹*Auto*›; sich einlaufen lassen ‹*Maschine*›; (b) (coll.: arrest) hoppnehmen (salopp)

~ **into** v.t. (a) ~ **into a telegraph pole/tree** gegen einen Telegrafenmast/Baum fahren; (b) (cause to collide with) ~ **one's car into a tree** seinen Wagen gegen einen Baum fahren; (c) (fig.: meet) ~ **into sb.** jmdm. in die Arme laufen (ugs.); (d) (be faced with) stoßen auf (+ Akk.) ‹*Schwierigkeiten, Widerstand, Probleme usw.*›; (e) (enter) geraten in (+ Akk.) ‹*Sturm, schlechtes Wetter, Schulden*›; **his debts ~ into thousands** seine Schulden gehen in die Tausende

~ **'off 1** v.i. ⇒ ~ **away a, c. 2** v.t. (a) (compose rapidly) hinwerfen ‹*ein paar Zeilen, Verse, Notizen*›; zu Papier bringen ‹*Brief*›; (b) (produce on machine) abziehen ‹*Kopien, Handzettel usw.*›; (c) (cause to drain away) ablaufen lassen

~ **'off with** v.t. (a) (coll.: steal) abhauen mit (salopp); (b) = ~ **away with** ⇒ ~ **away c;** (c) ⇒ ~ **away with b**

~ **'on** v.i. weitergehen; ‹*Krankheit*:› fortschreiten

~ **'out** v.i. (a) hin-/herauslaufen/-rennen; (b) (become exhausted) ‹*Vorräte, Bestände*:› zu Ende gehen; ‹*Geduld*:› sich erschöpfen; **we have ~ out** wir haben keinen/keine/keines mehr; (sold everything) wir sind ausverkauft; (c) (expire) ‹*Vertrag*:› ablaufen

~ **'out of** v.t. sb. ~s **out of** sth. jmdm. geht etw. aus; **I'm ~ning out of patience** meine Geduld geht zu Ende; **we're ~ning out of time** uns wird die Zeit allmählich knapp

~ **over 1** /'---/ v.t. (knock down) überfahren. **2** /-'--/ v.i. überlaufen

~ **through** v.t. (a) /'--/ abspielen ‹*Tonband, Film*›; (b) /'--/ (rehearse) durchspielen ‹*Theaterstück*›; (c) /-'-/ (pierce right through) ~ **sb. through with** sth. jmdn. mit etw. durchbohren. *See also* ~ **2 i, l**

~ **to** v.t. (a) (amount to) umfassen; ‹*Geldsumme, Kosten*:› sich belaufen auf (+ Akk.); (b) (be sufficient for) **sth. will ~ to** sth. etw. reicht für etw.; (c) (afford) **sb. can ~ to** sth. jmd. kann sich (Dat.) etw. leisten

~ **'up 1** v.i. hinlaufen; **come ~ning up** herangelaufen kommen. **2** v.t. (a) (hoist) hissen ‹*Fahne*›; (b) (make quickly) rasch nähen ‹*Kleidungsstück*›; (c) (allow to accumulate) ~ **up debts** Schulden zusammenkommen lassen

~ **'up against** v.t. stoßen auf (+ Akk.) ‹*Probleme, Widerstand usw.*›

run: ~**-around** n. (coll.) **give sb. the ~-around** jmdn. an der Nase herumführen (ugs.); ~**away 1** n. Ausreißer, der/Ausreißerin, die (ugs.); **2** attrib. adj. (a) (out of control) durchgegangen ‹*Pferd*›; außer Kontrolle geraten ‹*Fahrzeug, Preise*›; (fig.) galoppierend ‹*Inflation*›; (b) (outstanding) überwältigend ‹*Erfolg*›; triumphal ‹*Sieg*›; ~**down** /-'-/ n. (coll.: briefing) Übersicht, die (on über + Akk.); **2** /-'-/ adj. (tired) mitgenommen

rung¹ /rʌŋ/ n. (of ladder) Sprosse, die

rung² ⇒ **ring² 2, 3**

runner /'rʌnə(r)/ n. (a) Läufer, der/Läuferin, die; (b) (horse in race) **eight ~s were in the race** acht Pferde liefen beim Rennen; (c) (messenger) Bote, der; (d) curtain ~: Gardinenröllchen, das; (e) (part on which sth. slides) Kufe, die; (groove) Laufschiene, die; (f) (carpet) Läufer, der; (g) **do a ~** (Brit. sl.) abhauen (salopp); türmen (salopp)

runner: ~ **bean** n. (Brit.) Stangenbohne, die; ~**-'up** n. Zweite, der/die; **the ~s-up** die Platzierten

running /'rʌnɪŋ/ **1** n. (a) (management) Leitung, die; (b) (action) Laufen, das; (jogging) Jogging, das; **make the ~** (in

competition) an der Spitze liegen; (fig.: have the initiative) den Ton angeben; **in/out of the ~:** im/aus dem Rennen; (c) (of engine, machine) Laufen, das. **2** adj. (a) (continuous) ständig; fortlaufend ‹*Erklärungen*›; **have** or **fight a ~ battle** (fig.) ständig im Streit liegen; (b) (in succession) hintereinander; **win for the third year ~:** schon drei Jahre hintereinander gewinnen

running: ~ **'commentary** n. (Broadcasting; also fig.) Livekommentar, der; ~ **costs** n. pl. Betriebskosten Pl.; ~ **'jump** n. **you can [go and] take a ~ jump** (fig. coll.) du kannst mir den Buckel herunterrutschen (ugs.); ~ **mate** n. (Amer.) Mitkandidat, der/Mitkandidatin, die [als Vizepräsidentschaftskandidat]; ~ **re'pairs** n. pl. laufende Reparaturen; ~ **shoe** n. Rennschuh, der; ~ **shorts** n. pl. Sporthose, die; ~ **'sore** n. nässende Wunde; (fig.) schwärende Wunde; ~ **'total** n. fortlaufende Summe; ~ **'water** n. (a) (in stream) fließendes Gewässer; (b) (available through pipe) fließendes Wasser

runny /'rʌnɪ/ adj. (a) (secreting mucus) laufend ‹*Nase*›; (b) (excessively liquid) zerlaufend; zu dünn ‹*Farbe, Marmelade*›

run: ~**-of-the-'mill** adj. ganz gewöhnlich; ~**-through** n. (a) (cursory reading) **give a text a [quick] ~-through** einen Text [kurz] überfliegen; (b) (rapid summary) Überblick, der (of über + Akk.); (c) (rehearsal) Durchlaufprobe, die; ~**-up** n. (a) (approach to an event) **during** or **in the ~-up to an event** im Vorfeld (fig.) eines Ereignisses; (b) (Sport) Anlauf, der; **take a ~-up** Anlauf nehmen

runway /'rʌnweɪ/ n. (for take-off) Startbahn, die; (for landing) Landebahn, die

rupture /'rʌptʃə(r)/ **1** n. (a) (lit. or fig.) Bruch, der; (b) (Med.) Ruptur, die. **2** v.t. (a) (burst) aufreißen; **a ~d appendix/spleen** ein geplatzter Blinddarm/eine gerissene Milz; (b) ~ **oneself** sich (Dat.) einen Bruch zuziehen od. heben

rural /'rʊərl/ adj. ländlich; ~ **life** Landleben, das

ruse /ruːz/ n. List, die

rush¹ /rʌʃ/ n. (Bot.) Binse, die

rush² **1** n. (a) (rapid moving forward) **make a ~ for** sth. sich auf etw. (Akk.) stürzen; **the holiday ~:** der [hektische] Urlaubsverkehr; (b) (hurry) Eile, die; **what's all the ~?** wozu diese Hast?; **be in a [great] ~:** in [großer] Eile sein; es [sehr] eilig haben; (c) (surging) Anwandlung, die (of von); **a ~ of blood [to the head]** (fig. coll.) eine [plötzliche] Anwandlung; (d) (period of great activity) Hochbetrieb, der; **there is a ~ on** es herrscht Hochbetrieb (ugs.); **a ~ of new orders** eine Flut von neuen Aufträgen; (e) (heavy demand) Ansturm, der (for, on auf + Akk.). **2** v.t. (a) (convey rapidly) ~ **sb./sth. somewhere** jmdn./etw. auf schnellstem Wege irgendwohin bringen; ~ **through Parliament** im Parlament durchpeitschen (ugs. abwertend) ‹*Gesetz*›; **be ~ed** (have to hurry) in Eile sein; (b) (cause to act hastily) ~ **sb. into doing sth.** jmdn. dazu drängen, etw. zu tun; **she hates to be ~ed** sie kann es nicht ausstehen, wenn sie sich [ab]hetzen muss; (c) (perform quickly) auf die Schnelle erledigen; (perform too quickly) ~ **it** zu schnell machen; (d) (Mil. or fig.: charge) stürmen; überrumpeln ‹*feindliche Gruppe*›. **3** v.i. (a) (move quickly) eilen; ‹*Hund, Pferd*:› laufen; **she ~ed into the room** sie stürzte ins Zimmer; ~ **through Customs/the exit** durch den Zoll/Ausgang stürmen; (b) (hurry unduly) sich zu sehr beeilen; **don't ~!** nur keine Eile!; (c) (flow rapidly) stürzen; ~ **past** vorbeistürzen; **the blood ~ed to his face** das Blut schoß ihm ins Gesicht

~ **a'bout,** ~ **a'round** v.i. herumhetzen

~ **into** v.t. ~ **into sth.** (enter) hin-/hereinstürzen; (fig.) sich in etw. (Akk.) stürzen; etw. überstürzt tun

~ **'up** v.i. angestürzt kommen

rush: ~ **hour** n. Stoßzeit, die; attrib. ~ **hour traffic** Berufsverkehr, der; ~ **job** n. eilige Arbeit; ~ **mat** n. Binsenmatte, die; ~ **order** n. Eilauftrag, der; dringende Bestellung

rusk /rʌsk/ n. Zwieback, der

russet /'rʌsɪt/ **1** n. (reddish-brown) Rotbraun, das. **2** adj. rotbraun

Russia /'rʌʃə/ *pr. n.* Russland (*das*)

Russian /'rʌʃn/ ▶897▮, ▶947▮ **1** *adj.* russisch; **sb. is ~:** jmd. ist Russe/Russin. **2** *n.* **(a)** (person) Russe, *der*/ Russin, *die;* **(b)** (language) Russisch, *das; see also* **English 2 a**

'Russian Federation *pr. n.* Russiche Föderation

rust /rʌst/ **1** *n., no pl., no indef. art.* Rost, *der.* **2** *v.i.* rosten. **3** *v.t.* [ver]rosten lassen
~ 'through *v.i.* durchrosten

'Rust Belt *n.* (esp. Amer. coll.) Rostgürtel, *der;* **a ~ town** eine Stadt im Rostgürtel

rustic /'rʌstɪk/ *adj.* **(a)** (of the country) ländlich; **(b)** (unrefined) bäurisch (abwertend); **(c)** (roughly built) rustikal ‹ *Mobiliar* ›

rustle /'rʌsl/ **1** *n.* Rascheln, *das.* **2** *v.i.* rascheln. **3** *v.t.* **(a)** rascheln lassen; rascheln mit ‹ *Papieren* ›; **(b)** (Amer.: steal) stehlen
~ 'up *v.t.* (coll.: produce) auftreiben (ugs.); zusammenzaubern (fig.) ‹ *Mahlzeit* ›

rustler /'rʌslə(r)/ *n.* (Amer.) Viehdieb, *der*

'rustproof 1 *adj.* rostfrei. **2** *v.t.* rostfrei *od.* rostbeständig machen

rusty /'rʌstɪ/ *adj.* **(a)** (rusted) rostig; **(b)** (fig.: impaired by neglect) eingerostet; **I am a bit ~:** ich bin ein bisschen aus der Übung

rut¹ /rʌt/ *n.* **(a)** (track) Spurrille, *die;* **(b)** (fig.: established procedure) **get into a ~:** in einen gewissen Trott verfallen; **be in a ~:** aus dem [Alltags]trott nicht mehr herauskommen

rut² *n.* (sexual excitement) Brunst, *die;* (of roe-deer, stag, etc.) Brunft, *die* (Jägersprache)

ruthless /'ru:θlɪs/ *adj.,* **ruthlessly** /'ru:θlɪslɪ/ *adv.* rücksichtslos

rutted /'rʌtɪd/ *adj.* zerfurcht

RV *abbr.* (Amer.) **recreational vehicle**

rye /raɪ/ *n.* **(a)** (cereal) Roggen, *der;* **(b)** **~ [whisky]** Roggenwhisky, *der;* Rye, *der*

'rye bread *n.* Roggenbrot, *das*

....

S s

....

S, s /es/ *n., pl.* **Ss** *or* **S's** /'esɪs/ S, s, *das*

S. *abbr.* **(a)** ▶715▮ **south** S; **(b)** ▶715▮ **southern** s.; **(c) Saint** St.

s. *abbr.* **second[s]** Sek.

sabbath /'sæbəθ/ *n.* **(a)** (Jewish) Sabbat, *der;* **(b)** (Christian) Sonntag, *der*

sabbatical /sə'bætɪkl/ **1** *adj.* **~ term/year** Forschungssemester/-jahr, *das.* **2** *n.* Forschungsurlaub, *der*

saber (Amer.) ⇒ **sabre**

sable /'seɪbl/ *n.* (Zool., also fur) Zobel, *der*

sabotage /'sæbətɑːʒ/ **1** *n.* (lit. or fig.) Sabotage, *die;* **act of ~:** Sabotageakt, *der.* **2** *v.t.* einen Sabotageakt verüben auf (+ *Akk.*); (fig.) sabotieren ‹ *Pläne usw.* ›

saboteur /sæbə'tɜː(r)/ *n.* Saboteur, *der*

sabre /'seɪbə(r)/ *n.* (Brit.) Säbel, *der*

'sabre-rattling 1 *n.* Säbelrasseln, *das* (abwertend). **2** *adj.* säbelrasselnd (abwertend)

saccharin /'sækərɪn/ *n.* Saccharin, *das*

sachet /'sæʃeɪ/ *n.* **(a)** (small packet) (for shampoo etc.) Beutel, *der;* (cushion-shaped) Kissen, *das;* **(b)** (bag for scenting clothes) Duftkissen

sack¹ /sæk/ **1** *n.* **(a)** Sack, *der;* **a ~ of potatoes** ein Sack Kartoffeln; **(b)** (coll.: dismissal) Rausschmiss, *der* (ugs.); **get the ~:** rausgeschmissen werden (ugs.); **give sb. the ~:** jmdn. rausschmeißen (ugs.); **(c)** **hit the ~** (coll.) sich in die Falle hauen (salopp). **2** *v.t.* (coll.: dismiss) rausschmeißen (ugs.) **(for** wegen)

sack² *v.t.* (loot) plündern. **2** *n.* Plünderung, *die*

sacking /'sækɪŋ/ *n.* (coll.: dismissal) Rausschmiss, *der* (ugs.)

'sack race *n.* Sackhüpfen, *das*

sacrament /'sækrəmənt/ *n.* Sakrament, *das;* **the Holy S~** (in the Eucharist) das Allerheiligste

sacred /'seɪkrɪd/ *adj.* heilig; geheiligt ‹ *Tradition* ›; geistlich ‹ *Musik, Dichtung* ›; **is nothing ~?** (iron.) scheut man denn vor nichts mehr zurück?

sacred 'cow *n.* (lit. or fig.) heilige Kuh

sacrifice /'sækrɪfaɪs/ **1** *n.* **(a)** (giving up valued thing) Opferung, *die;* (of principles) Preisgabe, *die;* (of pride, possessions) Aufgabe, *die;* **make ~s** Opfer bringen; **(b)** (offering to deity) Opfer, *das;* **(c)** (Games: deliberate incurring of loss) Opfern, *das.* **2** *v.t.* (give up, offer as **~**) opfern; **~ oneself/sth. to sth.** sich/etw. einer Sache (*Dat.*) opfern

sacrificial /sækrɪ'fɪʃl/ *adj.* Opfer-

sacrilege /'sækrɪlɪdʒ/ *n., no pl.* **[act of] ~:** Sakrileg, *das*

sacrilegious /sækrɪ'lɪdʒəs/ *adj.* sakrilegisch; (fig.) frevelhaft

sacrosanct /'sækrəsæŋkt/ *adj.* (lit. or fig.) sakrosankt

sad /sæd/ *adj.* **(a)** (sorrowful) traurig **(at, about** über + *Akk.*); **feel ~, be in a ~ mood** traurig sein; **(b)** (causing grief) traurig; schmerzlich ‹ *Tod, Verlust* ›; **~ to say, ...:** bedauerlicherweise ...; leider ...; **(c)** (derog./joc.: deplorably bad) traurig

SAD *abbr.* **seasonal affective disorder**

sadden /'sædn/ *v.t.* traurig stimmen; **be deeply ~ed** tieftraurig sein; **I was ~ed to see that ...:** es betrübte mich, zu sehen, dass ...

saddle /'sædl/ **1** *n.* **(a)** (seat for rider) Sattel, *der;* **be in the ~** (fig.) das Heft in der Hand haben (geh.); **(b)** (ridge between summits) [Berg]sattel, *der.* **2** *v.t.* **(a)** satteln ‹ *Pferd usw.* ›; **(b)** (fig.) **~ sb. with sth.** jmdm. etw. aufbürden (geh.)

saddle: ~bag *n.* Satteltasche, *die;* **~ sore** *n.* Sattelwunde, *die;* **~-sore** *adj.* **be ~-sore** wund vom Reiten/Rad fahren sein

sadism /'seɪdɪzm/ *n.* Sadismus, *der*

sadist /'seɪdɪst/ *n.* Sadist, *der*/Sadistin, *die*

sadistic /sə'dɪstɪk/ *adj.,* **sadistically** /sə'dɪstɪkəlɪ/ *adv.* sadistisch

sadly /'sædlɪ/ *adv.* **(a)** (with sorrow) traurig; **(b)** (unfortunately) leider; **(c)** (deplorably) erbärmlich (abwertend)

sadness /'sædnɪs/ *n., no pl.* Traurigkeit, *die* **(at, about** über + *Akk.*)

sadomasochism /seɪdəʊ'mæsəkɪzm/ *n.* Sadomasochismus, *der*

sadomasochist /seɪdəʊ'mæsəkɪst/ *n.* Sadomasochist, *der*/Sadomasochistin, *die*

s.a.e. /eseɪ'iː/ *abbr.* **stamped addressed envelope** adressierter Freiumschlag

safari /sə'fɑːrɪ/ *n.* Safari, *die;* **be/go on ~:** auf Safari sein/gehen

sa'fari park *n.* Safaripark, *der*

safe /seɪf/ **1** *n.* Safe, *der;* Geldschrank, *der.* **2** *adj.* **(a)** (out of danger) sicher **(from** vor + *Dat.*); **he's ~:** er ist in Sicherheit; **make sth. ~ from sth.** etw. gegen etw. sichern; **~ and sound** sicher und wohlbehalten; **(b)** (free from danger) ungefährlich; sicher ‹ *Ort, Hafen* ›; **better ~ than sorry** Vorsicht ist besser als Nachsicht (ugs.); **wish sb. a ~ journey** jmdm. eine gute Reise wünschen; **is the car ~ to drive?** ist der Wagen verkehrssicher?; **to be on the ~ side** zur Sicherheit; **(c)** (unlikely to produce controversy) sicher; bewährt (iron.) ‹ *Klischee* ›; **it is ~ to say [that ...]** man kann mit einiger Sicherheit sagen[, dass ...]; **(d)** (reliable) sicher ‹ *Methode, Investition, Stelle* ›; **~ is my liegend** ‹ *Vermutung* ›; **(e)** (secure) **your secrets will be ~ with me** deine Geheimnisse sind bei mir gut aufgehoben. *See also* **play 2 a, 3 e**

safe: ~ 'bet *n.* **it is a ~ bet he will be there** man kann darauf wetten, dass er dort ist; **~-breaker** *n.* Geldschrankknacker, *der* (ugs.); **~ 'conduct** *n.* freies *od.* sicheres Geleit; **~ de'posit** *n.* Tresor, *der; attrib.* **~-deposit box** (at the bank) Banksafe, *der;* **~guard 1** *n.* Schutz, *der;* **2** *v.t.* schützen; **~guard sb.'s future/ interests** jmds. Zukunft sichern/Interessen wahren;

~ **haven** *n.* (a) (safe place) Zuflucht, *die;* Zufluchtsort, *der;* (b) (Polit.: protected zone) Schutzzone, *die;* ~ **house** *n.* geheimer Unterschlupf (*von Terroristen, Agenten usw.*); ~ **'keeping** *n.* sichere Obhut (geh.); (of thing) [sichere] Aufbewahrung

safely /'seɪflɪ/ *adv.* (a) (without harm) sicher; **did the parcel arrive** ~? ist das Paket heil angekommen?; (b) (securely) sicher; **be** ~ **behind bars** [in sicherem Gewahrsam] hinter Schloss und Riegel sein; (c) (with certainty) **one can** ~ **say** [that] **she will come** man kann mit ziemlicher Sicherheit sagen, dass sie kommt

safe 'sex *n.* Safer Sex, *der;* sicherer Sex

safety /'seɪftɪ/ *n.* (a) (being out of danger) Sicherheit, *die;* (b) (lack of danger) Ungefährlichkeit, *die;* (of a machine) Betriebssicherheit, *die;* **there is** ~ **in numbers** zu mehreren ist man sicherer; **a** ~ **first policy** eine Politik der Vorsicht; (c) *attrib.* Sicherheits‹*netz, -kette, -faktor, -maßnahmen, -vorrichtungen, -lampe*›

safety: ~ **belt** *n.* Sicherheitsgurt, *der;* ~ **catch** *n.* (of door) Sicherheitsverriegelung, *die;* (of gun) Sicherungshebel, *der;* ~ **helmet** *n.* Schutzhelm, *der;* ~ **margin** *n.* Spielraum, *der;* ~ **match** *n.* Sicherheitszündholz, *das;* ~ **pin** *n.* Sicherheitsnadel, *die;* ~ **razor** *n.* Rasierapparat, *der;* ~ **valve** *n.* Sicherheitsventil, *das* (Technik); (fig.) Ventil, *das* (fig.)

'safe zone *n.* (Polit.) Schutzzone, *die*

saffron /'sæfrən/ **1** *n.* Safran, *der.* **2** *adj.* safrangelb

sag /sæg/ **1** *v.i.,* **-gg-:** (a) (have downward bulge) durchhängen; (b) (sink) sich senken; absacken (ugs.); ‹*Gebäude:*› [in sich (*Akk.*)] zusammensacken (ugs.); ‹*Schultern:*› herabhängen; ‹*Brüste:*› hängen; (fig.: decline) ‹*Mut, Stimmung:*› sinken. **2** *n.* (a) (amount that rope etc. ~s) Durchhang, *der;* (b) (sinking) **there was a** ~ **in the seat** der Sitz war durchgesessen

saga /'sɑːgə/ *n.* (a) (story of adventure) Heldenepos, *das* (fig.); (medieval narrative) Saga, *die* (Literaturw.); (b) (coll.: long involved story) [ganzer] Roman (fig.)

sagacious /sə'geɪʃəs/ *adj.* klug

sage¹ /seɪdʒ/ *n.* (Bot.) Salbei, *der od. die*

sage² **1** *n.* Weise, *der.* **2** *adj.* weise

Sagittarius /sædʒɪ'teərɪəs/ *n.* (Astrol., Astron.) der Schütze

sago /'seɪgəʊ/ *n., pl.* ~**s** Sago, *der*

Sahara /sə'hɑːrə/ *pr. n.* **the** ~ **[Desert]** die [Wüste] Sahara

said ⇨ **say 1**

sail /seɪl/ **1** *n.* (a) (voyage in ~ing vessel) Segelfahrt, *die;* **go for a** ~: eine Segelfahrt machen; **set** ~ (begin voyage) losfahren (**for** nach); (b) (piece of canvas) Segel, *das.* **2** *v.i.* (a) (travel on water) fahren; (in ~ing boat) segeln; (b) (start voyage) auslaufen (**for** nach); in See stechen; (c) (glide in air) segeln; (d) (fig.: be thrown) segeln (ugs.); (e) (move smoothly) gleiten; (f) (fig. coll.: pass easily) ~ **through an examination** eine Prüfung spielend schaffen. **3** *v.t.* (a) steuern ‹*Boot, Schiff*›; segeln mit ‹*Segeljacht, -schiff*›; (b) (travel across) durchfahren, befahren ‹*Meer*›

sail: ~**board** *n.* Surfbrett, *das* (*zum Windsurfen*); ~**boarding** ⇨ **windsurfing;** ~**boat** *n.* (Amer.) Segelboot, *das*

sailing /'seɪlɪŋ/ *n.* (a) (handling a boat) Segeln, *das;* (b) (departure from a port) Abfahrt, *die;* **there are regular** ~**s from here across to the island** von hier fahren regelmäßig Schiffe hinüber zur Insel

sailing: ~ **boat** *n.* Segelboot, *das;* ~ **ship,** ~ **vessel** *ns.* Segelschiff, *das*

sailor /'seɪlə(r)/ *n.* Seemann, *der;* (in navy) Matrose, *der;* **be a good/ bad** ~ (not get seasick/get seasick) seefest/nicht seefest sein

saint 1 /sənt/ *adj.* **S**~ **Michael/Helena** der heilige Michael/die heilige Helena; Sankt Michael/Helena; ~ **Michael's [Church]** die Michaelskirche. **2** /seɪnt/ *n.* Heilige, *der/die;* **make** *or* **declare sb. a** ~ (RC Ch.) jmdn. heilig sprechen; **be as patient as a** ~: eine Engelsgeduld haben

saintly /'seɪntlɪ/ *adj.* heilig

sake¹ /seɪk/ *n.* **for the** ~ **of** um … (*Gen.*) willen; **for my** *etc.* ~: um meinetwillen *usw.;* mir *usw.* zuliebe; **for your/**

its own ~: um deiner/seiner selbst willen; **for the** ~ **of a few pounds** wegen ein paar Pfund; **for Christ's** *or* **God's** *or* **goodness'** *or* **Heaven's** *or* (coll.) Pete's ~: um Gottes *od.* Himmels willen; **for old times'** ~: um der schönen Erinnerung willen

sake² /'sɑːkɪ/ *n.* (drink) Sake, *der*

salacious /sə'leɪʃəs/ *adj.* (a) (lustful) lüstern; (b) (inciting sexual desire) pornographisch

salad /'sæləd/ *n.* Salat, *der*

salad: ~ **cream** *n.* ≈ Mayonnaise, *die;* ~ **dressing** *n.* Dressing, *das;* Salatsoße, *die;* ~ **servers** /'sælədsɜːvəz/ *n. pl.* Salatbesteck, *das*

salami /sə'lɑːmɪ/ *n.* Salami, *die*

salaried /'sælərɪd/ *adj.* (a) (receiving salary) Gehalt beziehend; ~ **employee** Angestellte, *der/die;* (b) ~ **post** Stelle mit festem Gehalt

salary /'sælərɪ/ *n.* Gehalt, *das; attrib.* ~ **increase** Gehaltserhöhung, *die*

sale /seɪl/ *n.* (a) (selling) Verkauf, *der;* [up] for ~: zu verkaufen; **put up** *or* **offer for** ~: zum Verkauf anbieten; **on** ~ **at your chemist's** in Ihrer Apotheke erhältlich; **offer** *etc.* **sth. on a** ~ *or* **return basis** etw. auf Kommissionsbasis anbieten *usw.;* (b) (instance of selling) Verkauf, *der;* (c) *in pl., no art.* (amount sold) Verkaufszahlen *Pl.* (**of** für); Absatz, *der;* (d) (disposal at reduced prices) Ausverkauf, *der;* **clearance/end-of-season** ~: Räumungs-/Schlussverkauf, *der*

saleable /'seɪləbl/ *adj.* verkäuflich; **be [highly]** ~: sich [gut] verkaufen lassen

'saleroom *n.* (Brit.) Auktionsraum, *der*

sales: ~ **assistant** (Brit.), ~ **clerk** (Amer.) *ns.* ▶ 887 | Verkäufer, *der/*Verkäuferin, *die;* ~ **department** *n.* Verkaufsabteilung, *die;* ~**girl,** ~ **lady** *ns.* ▶ 887 | Verkäuferin, *die;* ~**man** /'seɪlzmən/ *n., pl.* ~**men** /'seɪlzmən/ ▶ 887 | Verkäufer, *der;* ~ **manager** *n.* ▶ 887 | Verkaufsleiter, *der/*-leiterin, *die;* Salesmanager, *der;* ~ **patter,** ~ **pitch** *ns.* Verkaufsargumentation, *die;* ~ **rep** (coll.), ~ **representative** *ns.* ▶ 887 | [Handels]vertreter, *der/*-vertreterin, *die;* ~ **talk** ⇨ ~ **patter;** ~**woman** *n.* ▶ 887 | Verkäuferin, *die*

salient /'seɪlɪənt/ *adj.* (striking) auffallend; ins Auge springend; hervorstechend ‹*Charakterzug*›; **the** ~ **points of a speech** die herausragenden Punkte einer Rede

saline /'seɪlaɪn/ *adj.* salzig

saliva /sə'laɪvə/ *n.* Speichel, *der*

salivate /'sælɪveɪt/ *v.i.* speicheln

sallow /'sæləʊ/ *adj.* blassgelb

sally *n.* (a) (Mil.: sortie) Ausfall, *der;* (b) (excursion) Ausflug, *der*

salmon /'sæmən/ **1** *n., pl. same* Lachs, *der.* **2** *adj.* (colour) lachsfarben; lachsrosa ‹*Farbton*›

salmonella /sælmə'nelə/ *n.* ▶ 865 | Salmonelle, *die;* ~ **poisoning** Salmonellenvergiftung, *die*

'salmon pink 1 *n.* lachsrosa Farbton. **2** *adj.* lachsfarben

salon /'sælɒ/ *n.* Salon, *der*

saloon /sə'luːn/ *n.* (a) (public room in ship, hotel, etc.) Salon, *der;* **dining** ~: Speisesaal, *der;* (b) (Brit.: motor car) Limousine, *die;* (c) (Amer.: bar) Saloon, *der*

saloon: ~ **bar** *n.* (Brit.) *separater Teil eines Pubs mit mehr Komfort;* ~ **'car** ⇨ **saloon b**

SALT /sɔːlt, sɒlt/ *abbr.* **Strategic Arms Limitation Talks/Treaty** SALT

salt 1 *n.* (a) (for food etc.; also Chem.) [common] ~: [Koch]salz, *das;* **rub** ~ **in[to] the wound** (fig.) Salz in die Wunde streuen; **take sth. with a grain** *or* **pinch of** ~ (fig.) etw. cum grano salis (geh.) *od.* nicht ganz wörtlich nehmen; **be the** ~ **of the earth** (fig.) anständig und rechtschaffen sein; (b) *in pl.* (medicine) Salz, *das;* **like a dose of** ~**s** (coll.) in null Komma nichts (ugs.). **2** *adj.* (a) (containing or tasting of ~) salzig; (preserved with ~) gepökelt ‹*Fleisch*›; gesalzen ‹*Butter*›; (b) (bitter) salzig ‹*Tränen*›. **3** *v.t.* (add ~ to) salzen; (fig.) würzen

~ **a'way** *v.t.* (coll.) auf die hohe Kante legen (ugs.)

salt: ~ **cellar** *n.* (open) Salzfass, *das;* (sprinkler) Salzstreuer, *der;* ~ **spoon** *n.* Salzlöffelchen, *das;* ~ **'water** *n.* Salzwasser, *das;* ~**-water** *adj.* Salzwasser-

salty /'sɔːltɪ, 'sɒltɪ/ *adj.* salzig

salubrious /sə'luːbrɪəs/ *adj.* gesund; **not a very** ~ **area** (fig.) ein etwas zweifelhaftes Viertel

salutary /'sæljʊtərɪ/ *adj.* heilsam ‹*Wirkung, Einfluss, Schock*›

salute /sə'luːt/ **1** *v.t.* **(a)** (Mil., Navy) ~ **sb.** jmdn. [militärisch] grüßen; (fig.: pay tribute to) sich vor jmdm. verneigen; **(b)** (greet) grüßen. **2** *v.i.* (Mil., Navy) [militärisch] grüßen. **3** *n.* (Mil., Navy) Salut, *der;* militärischer Gruß; **fire a seven-gun** ~: sieben Schuss Salut abfeuern

salvage /'sælvɪdʒ/ **1** *n.* **(a)** (rescue of property) Bergung, *die; attrib.* Bergungs‹*arbeiten, -aktion*›; **(b)** (rescued property) Bergegut, *das;* (for recycling) Sammelgut, *das.* **2** *v.t.* **(a)** (rescue) bergen; retten (auch fig.) **(from** von); **(b)** (save for recycling) für die Wiederverwendung sammeln

salvation /sæl'veɪʃn/ *n.* **(a)** *no art.* (Relig.) Erlösung, *die;* **(b)** (means of preservation) Rettung, *die*

Salvation 'Army *n.* Heilsarmee, *die*

salvo /'sælvəʊ/ *n., pl.* ~**es** *or* ~**s** (of guns) Salve, *die*

Samaritan /sə'mærɪtən/ *n.* **good** ~: [barmherziger] Samariter; **the** ~**s** (organization) ≈ die Telefonseelsorge

same /seɪm/ **1** *adj.* **the** ~: der/die/das gleiche; **the** ~ **[thing]** (identical) der-/die-/dasselbe; **the** ~ **afternoon/evening** (of ~ day) schon am Nachmittag/Abend; **she seemed just the** ~ **[as ever] to me** sie schien mir unverändert *od.* immer noch die Alte; **one and the** ~ **person/man** ein und dieselbe Person/ein und derselbe Mann; **the very** ~: genau der/die/das; ebenderselbe/-dieselbe/ -dasselbe; **much the** ~ **as** fast genauso wie. **2** *pron.* **the** ~, (coll.) ~ **(the** ~ **thing)** der-/die-/dasselbe; **they look [exactly] the** ~: sie sehen gleich aus; **more of the** ~: noch mehr davon; **and the** ~ **to you!** (also iron.) danke gleichfalls; **[the]** ~ **again** das gleiche noch einmal; **I feel bored — S**~ **here** (coll.) Ich langweile mich — Dito. **3** *adv.* **[the]** ~ **as you do** genau wie du; **the** ~ **as before** genau wie vorher; **all** *or* **just the** ~: trotzdem; nichtsdestototrotz (ugs., oft scherzh.); **think the** ~ **of/feel the** ~ **towards** dasselbe halten von/empfinden für

sameness /'seɪmnɪs/ *n., no pl.* Gleichheit, *die*

Samoa /sə'məʊə/ *pr. n.* Samoa (*das*)

sample /'sɑːmpl/ **1** *n.* **(a)** (representative portion) Auswahl, *die;* (in opinion research, statistics) Querschnitt, *der;* Sample, *das;* **(b)** (example) [Muster]beispiel, *das;* (specimen) Probe, *die;* **[commercial]** ≈ Muster, *das; attrib.* Probe ‹*exemplar, -seite*›. **2** *v.t.* probieren; ~ **the pleasures of country life** die Freuden des Landlebens kosten (geh.)

sanatorium /sænə'tɔːrɪəm/ *n., pl.* ~**s** *or* **sanatoria** /sænə'tɔːrɪə/ (clinic) Sanatorium, *das*

sanctify /'sæŋktɪfaɪ/ *v.t.* **(a)** heiligen; **(b)** (consecrate) weihen; heiligen (bes. bibl.)

sanctimonious /sæŋktɪ'məʊnɪəs/ *adj.,* **sanctimoniously** /sæŋktɪ'məʊnɪəslɪ/ *adv.* scheinheilig

sanction /'sæŋkʃn/ **1** *n.* **(a)** (official approval) Sanktion, *die;* **give one's** ~ **to sth.** seine Erlaubnis für etw. geben; **(b)** (Polit.: penalty; Law: punishment) Sanktion, *die.* **2** *v.t.* sanktionieren

sanctity /'sæŋktɪtɪ/ *n., no pl.* Heiligkeit, *die*

sanctuary /'sæŋktʃʊərɪ/ *n.* **(a)** (holy place) Heiligtum, *das;* **(b)** (part of church) Altarraum, *der;* **(c)** (place of refuge) Zufluchtsort, *der;* **(d)** (for animals or plants) Naturschutzgebiet, *das;* **(e) take** ~**:** Zuflucht suchen

sand /sænd/ **1** *n.* **(a)** Sand, *der;* **have** *or* **keep** *or* **bury one's head in the** ~ (fig.) den Kopf in den Sand stecken; **(b)** *in pl.* (expanse) Sandbank, *die;* (beach) Sandstrand, *der.* **2** *v.t.* **(a)** (sprinkle) ~ **the road** die Straße mit Sand streuen; **(b)** (polish) ~ **sth. down** etw. [ab]schmirgeln

sandal /'sændl/ *n.* Sandale, *die*

sand: ~**bag** *n.* Sandsack, *der;* ~**bank** *n.* Sandbank, *die;* ~**blast** *v.t.* sandstrahlen (Technik); ~**box** *n.* (Amer.) Sandkasten, *der;* ~**boy** *n.* **be happy as a** ~**boy** glücklich und zufrieden sein; ~**castle** *n.* Sandburg, *die;* ~ **dune** *n.* Düne, *die*

sander /'sændə(r)/ *n.* Sandpapierschleifmaschine, *die*

sand: ~**paper 1** *n.* Sandpapier, *das;* **2** *v.t.* [mit Sandpapier] [ab]schmirgeln; ~**pit** *n.* Sandkasten, *der;* ~**stone** *n.* Sandstein, *der;* ~**storm** *n.* Sandsturm, *der;* ~ **trap** *n.* (Amer. Golf) Bunker, *der*

sandwich /'sændwɪdʒ, 'sændwɪtʃ/ **1** *n.* Sandwich, *der od. das;* ≈ [zusammengeklapptes] belegtes Brot; **cheese** ~: Käsebrot, *das.* **2** *v.t.* einschieben **(between** zwischen + *Akk.;* **into** in + *Akk.*); **be** ~**ed between other people/cars** zwischen andere Personen gequetscht werden/Autos eingeklemmt sein

'sandwich course *n.* Ausbildung mit abwechselnd theoretischem und praktischem Unterricht

sandy /'sændɪ/ *adj.* **(a)** sandig; Sand ‹*boden, -strand*›; **(b)** (yellowish-red) rotblond ‹*Haar*›

sane /seɪn/ *adj.* **(a)** geistig gesund; **(b)** (sensible) vernünftig

sang ⇒ **sing**

sanguine /'sæŋgwɪn/ *adj.* (confident) zuversichtlich **(about** was … betrifft); heiter ‹*Temperament*›

sanitary /'sænɪtərɪ/ *adj.* sanitär ‹*Verhältnisse, Anlagen*›; gesundheitlich ‹*Gesichtspunkt, Problem*›; Gesundheits‐ ‹*behörde*›; hygienisch ‹*Küche, Krankenhaus, Gewohnheit*›

sanitary: ~ **napkin** (Amer.), ~ **towel** (Brit.) *ns.* Damenbinde, *die*

sanitation /sænɪ'teɪʃn/ *n., no pl.* **(a)** (drainage, refuse disposal) Kanalisation und Abfallbeseitigung; **(b)** (hygiene) Hygiene, *die*

sanity /'sænɪtɪ/ *n.* **(a)** (mental health) geistige Gesundheit; **lose one's** ~: den Verstand verlieren; **fear for/doubt sb.'s** ~: um jmds. Zurechnungsfähigkeit fürchten/an jmds. Verstand (*Dat.*) zweifeln; **(b)** (good sense) Vernünftigkeit, *die;* **restore** ~ **to the proceedings** die Veranstaltung wieder in vernünftige Bahnen lenken

sank ⇒ **sink 2, 3**

Santa /'sæntə/ (coll.), **Santa Claus** /'sæntə klɔːz/ *n.* Weihnachtsmann, *der*

sap /sæp/ **1** *n.* Saft, *der;* (fig.: vital spirit) belebende Kraft. **2** *v.t.,* **-pp-** (fig.: exhaust vigour of) zehren an (+ *Dat.*)

sapling /'sæplɪŋ/ *n.* junger Baum

sapper /'sæpə(r)/ *n.* (Brit. Mil.) Pionier, *der*

sapphire /'sæfaɪə(r)/ *n.* Saphir, *der; attrib.* ~ **blue** saphirblau; ~ **ring** Saphirring, *der*

sarcasm /'sɑːkæzm/ *n.* Sarkasmus, *der*

sarcastic /sɑː'kæstɪk/ *adj.,* **sarcastically** /sɑː'kæstɪkəlɪ/ *adv.* sarkastisch

sardine /sɑː'diːn/ *n.* (Zool.) Sardine, *die;* (Gastr.) [Öl]sardine, *die;* **like** ~**s** (fig.) wie die Ölsardinen

Sardinia /sɑː'dɪnɪə/ *pr. n.* Sardinien (*das*)

Sardinian /sɑː'dɪnɪən/ **▶ 897 , ▶ 947** **1** *n.* **(a)** (person) Sarde, *der*/Sardin, *die;* Sardinier, *der*/Sardinierin, *die;* **(b)** (language) Sardisch, *das.* **2** *adj.* sardisch

sardonic /sɑː'dɒnɪk/ *adj.* höhnisch ‹*Bemerkung*›; sardonisch ‹*Lachen, Lächeln*›

sari /'sɑːrɪ/ *n.* Sari, *der*

sarong /sə'rɒŋ/ *n.* Sarong, *der*

sash[1] /sæʃ/ *n.* Schärpe, *die*

sash[2] *n.* **(a)** (of window) Fensterrahmen, *der;* **(b)** (window) Schiebefenster, *das*

sash 'window *n.* Schiebefenster, *das*

sassy /'sæsɪ/ *adj.* (Amer. coll.) **(a)** (cheeky) frech; **(b)** (stylish) schick

sat ⇒ **sit**

Sat. *abbr.* **▶ 739 | Saturday** Sa.

Satan /'seɪtən/ *pr. n.* Satan, *der*

satanic /sə'tænɪk/ *adj.* satanisch; teuflisch

satchel /'sætʃl/ *n.* [Schul]ranzen, *der*

sate /seɪt/ *v.t.* (literary) **(a)** (gratify) stillen ‹*Hunger, Verlangen*›; zufrieden stellen ‹*Person*›; **(b)** (cloy) übersättigen ‹*Lust, Verlangen*›; **become** ~**d with/be** ~**d by sth.** einer Sache (*Gen.*) überdrüssig werden/sein

satellite /'sætəlaɪt/ *n.* (Astronaut., Astron.; also country) Satellit, *der;* **by** ~**:** über Satellit

satellite: ~ **'broadcasting** n., no pl., no art. Satellitenfunk, der; ~ **dish** n. Parabolantenne, die; ~ **town** n. Satelliten- od. Trabantenstadt, die

satiate /'seɪʃɪeɪt/ ⇒ **sate**

satin /'sætɪn/ 1 n. Satin, der. 2 attrib. adj. (a) (made of ~) Satin-; (b) (like ~) seidig

satire /'sætaɪə(r)/ n. Satire, die (on auf + Akk.)

satirical /sə'tɪrɪkl/ adj., **satirically** /sə'tɪrɪkəlɪ/ adv. satirisch

satirise ⇒ **satirize**

satirist /'sætɪrɪst/ n. Satiriker, der/Satirikerin, die

satirize /'sætɪraɪz/ v.t. (a) (write satire on) satirisch darstellen; (b) (describe satirically) ⟨Buch, Film usw.:⟩ eine Satire sein auf (+ Akk.)

satisfaction /sætɪs'fækʃn/ n. (a) no pl. (act) Befriedigung, die; (b) no pl. (feeling of gratification) Befriedigung, die (at, with über + Akk.); Genugtuung, die (at, with über + Akk.); **job** ~: Befriedigung in der Arbeit; **what** ~ **can it give you?** was befriedigt dich daran?; (c) no pl. (gratified state) **meet with sb.'s** or **give sb. [complete]** ~: jmdn. [in jeder Weise] zufriedenstellen; **to sb.'s** ~, **to the** ~ **of sb.** zu jmds. Zufriedenheit; (d) (instance of gratification) Befriedigung, die; **it is a great** ~ **to me that** …: es erfüllt mich mit großer Befriedigung, dass …; **have the** ~ **of doing sth.** das Vergnügen haben, etw. zu tun

satisfactory /sætɪs'fæktərɪ/ adj. zufriedenstellend; angemessen ⟨Bezahlung⟩; '~' (as school mark) „ausreichend"

satisfied /'sætɪsfaɪd/ adj. (a) (contented) zufrieden; **be** ~ **with doing sth.** sich damit begnügen, etw. zu tun; (b) (convinced) überzeugt (of von); **be** ~ **that** …: [davon] überzeugt sein, dass …

satisfy /'sætɪsfaɪ/ v.t. (a) (content) befriedigen; zufrieden stellen ⟨Kunden, Publikum⟩; entsprechen (+ Dat.) ⟨Vorliebe, Empfinden, Meinung, Zeitgeist⟩; erfüllen ⟨Hoffnung, Erwartung⟩; (b) (rid of want) befriedigen; (put an end to) stillen ⟨Hunger, Durst⟩; (make replete) sättigen; (c) (convince) ~ **sb. [of sth.]** jmdn. [von etw.] überzeugen; ~ **oneself of** or **as to** sich überzeugen von ⟨Wahrheit, Ehrlichkeit⟩; sich (Dat.) Gewissheit verschaffen über (+ Akk.) ⟨Motiv⟩; (d) (adequately deal with) ausräumen ⟨Einwand, Zweifel⟩; erfüllen ⟨Bitte, Forderung, Bedingung⟩; (e) (fulfil) erfüllen ⟨Vertrag, Verpflichtung, Forderung⟩

satisfying /'sætɪsfaɪɪŋ/ adj. befriedigend; zufriedenstellend ⟨Antwort, Lösung, Leistung⟩

satsuma /sæt'su:mə/ n. Satsuma, die

saturate /'sætʃəreɪt, 'sætjʊəreɪt/ v.t. (a) (soak) durchnässen; [mit Feuchtigkeit durch]tränken ⟨Boden, Erde⟩; (b) (fill to capacity) auslasten; sättigen ⟨Markt⟩; (c) (Phys., Chem.) sättigen

saturated /'sætʃəreɪtɪd, 'sætjʊəreɪtɪd/ adj. (a) (soaked) durchnässt; völlig nass ⟨Boden⟩; (b) (imbued) durchdrungen (with, in von); (c) (filled to capacity) ausgelastet; gesättigt ⟨Markt⟩; (d) (Phys., Chem.) gesättigt ⟨Lösung, Verbindung, Fett⟩

saturation point /sætʃə'reɪʃn pɔɪnt, sætjʊ'reɪʃn pɔɪnt/ n. (limit of capacity) [Ober]grenze, die; (of market; Phys.) Sättigungspunkt, der

Saturday /'sætədeɪ, 'sætədɪ/ ▶ 739 1 n. Samstag, der. 2 adv. (coll.) **he comes** ~**s** er kommt samstags. See also **Friday**

Saturn /'sætən/ pr. n. (a) (Astron.) Saturn, der; (b) (Roman Mythol.) Saturn (der)

sauce /sɔ:s/ 1 n. (a) (Cookery) Soße, die; (b) (impudence) Frechheit, die. 2 v.t. (coll.) frech sein zu

sauce: ~**-boat** n. Sauciere, die; ~**pan** n. Kochtopf, der; (with straight handle) [Stiel]kasserolle, die

saucer /'sɔ:sə(r)/ n. Untertasse, die; **their eyes were like** ~**s** (fig.) sie machten große Augen (ugs.)

saucy /'sɔ:sɪ/ adj. (a) (rude) frech; (b) (pert, jaunty) keck

Saudi Arabia /saʊdɪ ə'reɪbɪə/ pr. n. Saudi-Arabien (das)

Saudi-Arabian /saʊdɪə'reɪbɪən/ 1 adj. saudiarabisch. 2 n. Saudi[araber], der/-araberin, die

sauna /'sɔ:nə/ n. Sauna, die; **have** or **take a** ~: saunieren; ein Saunabad nehmen

saunter /'sɔ:ntə(r)/ 1 v.i. schlendern. 2 n. (stroll) Bummel, der (ugs.); (leisurely pace) Schlenderschritt, der

sausage /'sɒsɪdʒ/ n. Wurst, die; (smaller) Würstchen, das; **not a** ~ (fig. coll.) gar nix (ugs.)

sausage: ~ **dog** n. (Brit. coll.) Dackel, der; ~ **meat** n. Wurstmasse, die; ~ **'roll** n. Blätterteig mit Wurstfüllung

sauté /'səʊteɪ/ (Cookery) 1 adj. sautiert (fachspr.); kurz [an]gebraten; ~ **potatoes** ≈ Bratkartoffeln. 2 n. Sauté, das. 3 v.t., ~**d** or ~**ed** /'səʊteɪd/ sautieren (fachspr.); kurz [an]braten

savage /'sævɪdʒ/ 1 adj. (a) (uncivilized) primitiv; wild ⟨Volksstamm⟩; unzivilisiert ⟨Land⟩; (b) (fierce) brutal; wild ⟨Tier⟩; scharf ⟨Hund⟩; jähzornig ⟨Temperament⟩; **make a** ~ **attack on sb.** brutal über jmdn. herfallen; (fig.) jmdn. schonungslos angreifen. 2 n. (a) (uncivilized person) Wilde, der/die (veralt.); (b) (barbarous or uncultured person) Barbar, der/Barbarin, die (abwertend). 3 v.t. ⟨Hund:⟩ anfallen ⟨Kind usw.⟩

savagery /'sævɪdʒrɪ/ n., no pl. (ferocity) Brutalität, die

savannah (savanna) /sə'vænə/ n. (Geog.) Savanne, die

save /seɪv/ 1 v.t. (a) (rescue) retten (from vor + Dat.); **please,** ~ **me!** bitte helfen Sie mir!; ~ **sb. from the clutches of the enemy/from making a mistake** jmdn. aus den Klauen des Feindes retten/davor bewahren, dass er einen Fehler macht; ~ **oneself from falling** sich [beim Hinfallen] fangen; ~ **the day** die Situation retten; **sb. can't do sth. to** ~ **his/her life** jmd. kann etw. [ganz] einfach nicht tun; (b) (keep undamaged) schonen ⟨Kleidung, Möbelstück⟩; (c) **God** ~ **the King/Queen** etc. Gott behüte od. beschütze den König/die Königin usw.; (d) (Theol.) retten ⟨Sünder, Seele, Menschen⟩; **be past saving** nicht mehr zu retten sein; (e) (put aside) aufheben; sparen ⟨Geld⟩; sammeln ⟨Rabattmarken, Briefmarken⟩; (conserve) sparsam umgehen mit ⟨Geldmitteln, Kräften, Wasser⟩; ~ **money for a rainy day** (fig.) einen Notgroschen zurücklegen; ~ **oneself** sich schonen; seine Kräfte sparen; ~ **one's breath** sich (Dat.) seine Worte sparen; ~ **a seat for sb.** jmdm. einen Platz freihalten; (f) (make unnecessary) sparen ⟨Geld, Zeit, Energie⟩; ~ **sb./oneself sth.** jmdm./sich etw. ersparen; ~ **sb./oneself doing sth.** or **having to do sth.** es jmdm./sich ersparen, etw. tun zu müssen; (g) (avoid losing) nicht verlieren ⟨Satz, Karte, Stich⟩; (Sport) abwehren ⟨Schuss, Ball⟩; verhindern ⟨Tor⟩; (h) (Computing) speichern; sichern; ~ **sth. on a disc** etw. auf einer Diskette abspeichern. 2 v.i. (a) (put money by) sparen; ~ **with a building society** bei einer Bausparkasse sparen; (b) (avoid waste) sparen (on Akk.); ~ **on food** am Essen sparen; (c) (Sport) ⟨Torwart:⟩ halten. 3 n. (Sport) Abwehr, die; Parade, die (fachspr.); **make a** ~ ⟨Torwart:⟩ halten. 4 prep. (arch./poet./rhet.) mit Ausnahme (+ Gen.); ~ **for sth.** von etw. abgesehen

~ **'up** 1 v.t. sparen; sammeln ⟨Marken, Gutscheine usw.⟩. 2 v.i. sparen (**for** für, auf + Akk.)

save-as-you-'earn n. (Brit.) Sparen durch regelmäßige Abbuchung eines bestimmten Betrages vom Lohn-/Gehaltskonto

saveloy /'sævəlɔɪ/ Zervelatwurst, die

saver /'seɪvə(r)/ n. (a) (of money) Sparer, der/Sparerin, die; (b) in comb. (device) **sth. is a time-**~**/labour-**~**/ money-**~: etw. spart Zeit/Arbeit/Geld

saving /'seɪvɪŋ/ 1 n. (a) in pl. (money saved) Ersparnisse Pl.; **have money put by in** ~**s** Geld zurückgelegt haben; (b) (rescue; also Theol.) Rettung, die; (c) (instance of economy) Ersparnis, die. 2 adj. in comb. ⟨kosten-, benzin⟩sparend. 3 prep. bis auf (+ Akk.)

saving 'grace n. versöhnender Zug

'savings bank n. Sparkasse, die

saviour (Amer.: **savior**) /'seɪvjə(r)/ n. (a) Retter, der/ Retterin, die; (b) (Relig.) **our/the S**~: unser/der Heiland

savor, savory (Amer.) ⇒ **savour, savoury**

savour /'seɪvə(r)/ (Brit.) 1 n. (a) (flavour) Geschmack, der; (fig.) Charakter, der; (b) (trace) **a** ~ **of sth.** ein Hauch od. Anflug von etw.; (c) (enjoyable quality) Reiz, der. 2 v.t. (lit. or fig., literary) genießen

savoury /'seɪvərɪ/ (Brit.) 1 adj. (a) (not sweet) pikant; (having salt flavour) salzig; (b) (appetizing) appetitanregend. 2 n. [pikantes] Häppchen

saw¹ /sɔ:/ **1** *n.* Säge, *die.* **2** *v.t., p.p.* **∼n** /sɔ:n/ *or* **∼ed** [zer]sägen; (make with ∼) sägen; **∼ in half** in der Mitte durchsägen. **3** *v.i., p.p.* **∼n** *or* **∼ed** sägen; **∼ through sth.** *etw.* durchsägen
∼ **'down** *v.t.* umsägen ‹*Baum*›
∼ **'off** *v.t.* absägen
∼ **'up** *v.t.* zersägen (**into** in + *Akk.*)
saw² ⇒ **see**
saw: **∼dust** *n.* Sägemehl, *das;* **∼mill** *n.* Sägemühle, *die*
'sawn-off *adj.* (Brit.) abgesägt; ‹*Gewehr*› mit abgesägtem Lauf
Saxon /'sæksn/ **1** *n.* **(a)** Sachse, *der/*Sächsin, *die;* **(b)** (Ling.) Sächsisch, *das.* **2** *adj.* **(a)** sächsisch; **(b)** (Ling.) sächsisch
Saxony /'sæksənɪ/ *pr. n.* Sachsen (*das*)
saxophone /'sæksəfəʊn/ *n.* (Mus.) Saxophon, *das*
saxophonist /sæk'sɒfənɪst/ *n.* Saxophonist, *der/*Saxophonistin, *die*
say /seɪ/ **1** *v.t., pres. t.* **he ∼s** /sez/, *p.t. & p.p.* **said** /sed/ **(a)** sagen; **∼ sth. out loud** etw. aussprechen *od.* laut sagen; **he said something about going out** er hat etwas von Ausgehen gesagt; **what more can I ∼?** was soll ich da noch [groß] sagen?; **it ∼s a lot** *or* **much** *or* **something for sb./sth. that** ...: es spricht sehr für jmdn./ etw., dass ...; **have a lot/not much to ∼ for oneself** viel reden/nicht viel von sich geben; **to ∼ nothing of** (quite apart from) ganz zu schweigen von; mal ganz abgesehen von; **that is to ∼:** das heißt; **having said that, that said** (nevertheless) abgesehen davon; **when all is said and done** letzten Endes; **you can ∼ 'that again, you 'said it** (coll.) das kannst du laut sagen (ugs.); **you don't '∼ [so]** (coll.) was du nicht sagst (ugs.); **∼s 'you** (coll.) wer's glaubt, wird selig (ugs. scherzh.); **I'll ∼ [it is]!** (coll.: it certainly is) und wie!; **don't let** *or* **never let it be said [that]** ...: niemand soll sagen können, [dass] ...; **I can't ∼ [that] I like cats/the idea** ich kann nicht gerade sagen *od.* behaupten, dass ich Katzen mag/die Idee gut finde; **[well,] I 'must ∼:** also, ich muss schon sagen; **I should ∼ so/not** ich glaube schon/nicht; (emphatic) bestimmt/bestimmt nicht; **what have you got to ∼ for yourself?** was haben Sie zu Ihren Gunsten zu sagen?; **there's something to be said on both sides/either side** man kann für beide Seiten/jede Seite Argumente anführen; **I can't ∼ fairer than that** ein besseres Angebot kann ich nicht machen; **and so ∼ all of us** der Meinung sind wir auch; **what do** *or* **would you ∼ to sb./sth.?** (think about) was hältst du von jmdm./ etw.?; was würdest du zu jmdm./etw. sagen?; **what I'm trying to ∼ is this** was ich sagen will, ist folgendes; **∼ nothing to sb.** (fig.) ‹*Musik, Kunst:*› jmdm. nichts bedeuten; **which/that is not ∼ing much** *or* **a lot** was nicht viel heißen will/das will nicht viel heißen; **(b)** (recite, repeat, speak words of) sprechen ‹*Gebet, Text*›; aufsagen ‹*Einmaleins, Gedicht*›; **(c)** (have specified wording or reading) sagen; ‹*Zeitung:*› schreiben; ‹*Uhr:*› zeigen ‹*Uhrzeit*›; **the Bible ∼s** *or* **it ∼s in the Bible [that]** ...: in der Bibel heißt es, dass ...; **a sign ∼ing** ...: ein Schild mit der Aufschrift ...; **what does it ∼ here?** was steht hier?; **(d)** *in pass.* **she is said to be clever/have done it** man sagt, sie sei klug/habe es getan. **2** *v.i., forms as* **1: (a)** (speak) sagen; **I ∼!** (Brit.) (seeking attention) Entschuldigung!; (admiring) Donnerwetter!; **(b)** *in imper.* (Amer.) Mensch! **3** *n.* **(a)** (share in decision) **have a** *or* **some ∼:** ein Mitspracherecht haben (**in** bei); **have no ∼:** nichts zu sagen haben; **(b)** (power of decision) **the [final] ∼:** das letzte Wort (**in** bei); **(c)** (what one has to ∼) **have one's ∼:** seine Meinung sagen; (chance to speak) **get one's** *or* **have a ∼:** zu Wort kommen
SAYE *abbr.* (Brit.) **save-as-you-earn**
saying /'seɪɪŋ/ *n.* **(a)** (maxim) Redensart, *die;* **there is a ∼ that** ...: wie es [im Sprichwort/in der Maxime] heißt, ...; **as the ∼ goes** wie es so schön heißt; **(b)** (remark) Ausspruch, *der;* **(c) there is no ∼ what/why** ...: man kann nicht sagen, was/warum ...; **go without ∼:** sich von selbst verstehen
'say-so *n.* **(a)** (power of decision) **on/without sb.'s ∼:** auf/ ohne jmds. Anweisung (*Akk.*); **(b)** (assertion) **I won't believe it just on your ∼:** das glaube ich dir nicht einfach so

scab /skæb/ *n.* **(a)** (over wound or sore) [Wund]schorf, *der;* **(b)** *no pl.* (skin disease) Räude, *die;* **(c)** (derog.: strike-breaker) Streikbrecher, *der/-*brecherin, *die*
scabbard /'skæbəd/ *n.* Scheide, *die*
scaffold /'skæfəld/ *n.* (for execution) Schafott, *das;* **go to the ∼:** aufs Schafott kommen
scaffolding /'skæfəldɪŋ/ *n., no pl.* Gerüst, *das;* (materials) Gerüstmaterial, *das;* **be surrounded by ∼:** eingerüstet sein (Bauw.)
scald /skɔ:ld, skɒld/ **1** *n.* Verbrühung, *die.* **2** *v.t.* **(a)** verbrühen; **∼ oneself** *or* **one's skin** sich verbrühen; **∼ing hot** brühheiß; **(b)** (Cookery) erhitzen ‹*Milch*›; **(c)** (clean with boiling water) auskochen
scale¹ /skeɪl/ *n.* **(a)** (of fish, reptile) Schuppe, *die;* **(b)** *no pl.* (deposit) (in kettles, boilers, etc.) Kesselstein, *der;* (on teeth) Zahnstein, *der*
scale² *n.* **(a)** *in sing. or pl.* (weighing instrument) **∼[s]** Waage, *die;* **a pair** *or* **set of ∼s** eine Waage; **bathroom/kitchen ∼[s]** Personen-/Küchenwaage, *die;* **the ∼s are evenly balanced** (fig.) die Chancen sind ausgewogen; **(b)** (dish of balance) Waagschale, *die;* **tip** *or* **turn the ∼[s]** (fig.) den Ausschlag geben
scale³ **1** *n.* **(a)** (series of degrees) Skala, *die;* **the social ∼:** die gesellschaftliche Stufenleiter; **(b)** (Mus.) Tonleiter, *die;* **(c)** (dimensions) Ausmaß, *das;* **on a grand ∼:** im großen Stil; **on a commercial ∼:** gewerbsmäßig; **plan on a large ∼:** in großem Rahmen planen; **on an international ∼:** auf internationaler Ebene; ‹*Katastrophe*› von internationalem Ausmaß; **(d)** (ratio of reduction) Maßstab, *der; attrib.* maßstab[s]gerecht ‹*Modell, Zeichnung*›; **a map with a ∼ of 1 : 250,000** eine Karte im Maßstab 1 : 250 000; **to ∼:** maßstab[s]gerecht; **be out of ∼:** im Maßstab nicht passen (**with** zu); **(e)** (indication) (on map, plan) Maßstab, *der;* (on thermometer, ruler, exposure meter) [Anzeige]skala, *die;* (instrument) Messstab, *der.* **2** *v.t.* **(a)** (climb, clamber up) ersteigen ‹*Festung, Mauer, Leiter, Gipfel*›; erklettern ‹*Felswand, Leiter, Gipfel*›; **(b)** [ab]stufen, staffeln ‹*Fahrpreise*›; maßstab[s]gerecht anfertigen ‹*Zeichnung*›; **∼ production to demand** die Produktion an die Nachfrage anpassen
∼ **'down** *v.t.* [entsprechend] drosseln ‹*Produktion*›; [entsprechende] Abstriche machen an (+ *Dat.*) ‹*Ideen*›; **we ∼d down our plans** wir haben bei unseren Planungen Abstriche gemacht
∼ **'up** *v.t.* [entsprechend] vergrößern ‹*Umfang, Ausmaß*›; hochfahren ‹*Produktion, Plan*›; **we ∼d up our plans** wir haben im größeren Maßstab neu geplant
scallop /'skæləp, 'skɒləp/ *n.* **(a)** *tn pl.* (ornamental edging) Feston, *das;* Bogenkante, *die;* **(b)** (Zool.) Kammmuschel, *die;* (Gastr.) Jakobsmuschel, *die*
scalp /skælp/ **1** *n.* **(a)** ▶672◀ Kopfhaut, *die;* **(b)** (war trophy) Skalp, *der;* (fig.) Trophäe, *die;* **be after sb.'s ∼** (fig.) jmdm. an den Kragen wollen. **2** *v.t.* skalpieren
scalpel /'skælpl/ *n.* (Med.) Skalpell, *das*
scaly /'skeɪlɪ/ *adj.* schuppig
scam /skæm/ *n.* (Amer. coll.) Masche, *die* (ugs.)
scamp /skæmp/ *n.* (coll./joc.) Spitzbube, *der* (abwertend/fam.)
scamper /'skæmpə(r)/ *v.i.* ‹*Person:*› flitzen; ‹*Tier:*› huschen; (hop) hoppeln; **∼ down the stairs** die Treppe hinunterflitzen
scampi /'skæmpɪ/ *n. pl.* Scampi *Pl.*
scan /skæn/ **1** *v.t.,* **-nn-: (a)** (examine intensely) [genau] studieren; (search thoroughly, lit. or fig.) absuchen (**for** nach); **(b)** (look over cursorily) flüchtig ansehen; überfliegen ‹*Zeitung, Liste usw.*› (**for** auf der Suche nach); **(c)** (Tech.) [mittels Strahlen] abtasten ‹*Luftraum*›; ‹*Flugsicherung:*› [mittels Radar] überwachen ‹*Luftraum*›; **(d)** (Med.) szintigraphisch untersuchen ‹*Körper, Organ*›. **2** *v.i.,* **-nn-** ‹*Vers[zeile]:*› das richtige Versmaß haben. **3** *n.* **(a)** (thorough search) Absuchen, *das;* **(b)** (quick look) [**cursory**] **∼:** flüchtiger Blick; **(c)** (examination by beam) Durchleuchtung, *die;* **(d)** (Med.) szintigraphische Untersuchung; **body-/brain-∼:** Ganzkörper-/Gehirnscan, *der*
scandal /'skændl/ *n.* **(a)** Skandal, *der* (**about/of** um); (story) Skandalgeschichte, *die;* **cause** *or* **create a ∼:** einen Skandal verursachen; **(b)** (outrage) Empörung, *die;* **(c)** *no*

art. (damage to reputation) Schande, *die;* **be untouched by ~:** einen makellosen Ruf haben; **(d)** (malicious gossip) Klatsch, *der* (ugs.); (in newspapers etc.) Skandalgeschichten *Pl.*

scandalize (scandalise) /'skændəlaɪz/ *v.t.* schockieren

scandalous /'skændələs/ *adj.* skandalös; schockierend ‹*Bemerkung*›; Skandal ‹*blatt, -geschichte, -bericht*›; **how ~!** unerhört!

Scandinavia /skændɪ'neɪvɪə/ *pr. n.* Skandinavien (*das*)

Scandinavian /skændɪ'neɪvɪən/ ‹▶947▶ **1** *adj.* skandinavisch; **sb. is ~:** jmd. ist Skandinavier/Skandinavierin. **2** *n.* **(a)** (person) Skandinavier, *der*/Skandinavierin, *die;* **(b)** (Ling.) skandinavische Sprachen

scanner /'skænə(r)/ *n.* **(a)** (to detect radioactivity) Geigerzähler, *der;* **(b)** (radar aerial) Radarantenne, *die;* **(c)** (Med.) [Szinti]scanner, *der*

scant /skænt/ *adj.* (literary) karg (geh.) ‹*Lob, Lohn*›; wenig ‹*Rücksicht*›; **pay sb./sth. ~ attention** jmdn./etw. kaum beachten

scantily /'skæntɪlɪ/ *adv.* kärglich; spärlich ‹*bekleidet*›

scanty /'skæntɪ/ *adj.* spärlich; knapp ‹*Bikini*›; nur wenig ‹*Vergnügen, Spaß*›

scapegoat /'skeɪpgəʊt/ *n.* Sündenbock, *der;* **make sb. a ~:** jmdn. zum Sündenbock machen

scar /skɑː(r)/ **1** *n.* (lit. or fig.) Narbe, *die;* **bear the ~s of sth.** (fig.) von etw. gezeichnet sein. **2** *v.t.,* **-rr-: ~ sb./sb.'s face** bei jmdm./in jmds. Gesicht (*Dat.*) Narben hinterlassen; **~ sb. for life** (fig.) jmdn. für sein ganzes Leben zeichnen

scarce /skeəs/ *adj.* **(a)** (insufficient) knapp; **(b)** (rare) selten; **make oneself ~** (coll.) sich aus dem Staub machen (ugs.)

scarcely /'skeəslɪ/ *adv.* kaum; **there was ~ a drop of wine left** es war fast kein Tropfen Wein mehr da; **~ [ever]** kaum [jemals]; **it is ~ likely** es ist wenig wahrscheinlich

scarcity /'skeəsɪtɪ/ *n.* **(a)** (short supply) Knappheit, *die* (of an + *Dat.*); **~ of teachers** Lehrermangel, *der;* **food ~:** Lebensmittelknappheit, *die;* **(b)** *no pl.* (rareness) Seltenheit, *die*

scare /skeə(r)/ **1** *n.* **(a)** (sensation of fear) Schreck[en], *der;* **give sb. a ~:** jmdm. einen Schreck[en] einjagen; **(b)** (general alarm; panic) [allgemeine] Hysterie; **bomb ~:** Bombendrohung, *die; attrib.* **~ story** Schauergeschichte, *die.* **2** *v.t.* **(a)** (frighten) Angst machen (+ *Dat.*); (startle) erschrecken; **~ sb. into doing sth.** jmdn. dazu bringen, etw. [aus Angst] zu tun; **horror films ~ the pants off me** (coll.) bei Horrorfilmen habe ich immer eine wahnsinnige Angst (ugs.); **(b)** (drive away) verscheuchen ‹*Vögel*›. **3** *v.i.* erschrecken (**at** bei); **~ easily** sich leicht erschrecken lassen

~ a'way, ~ 'off *v.t.* verscheuchen

'scarecrow *n.* (lit. or fig.) Vogelscheuche, *die*

scared /skeəd/ *adj.* verängstigt ‹*Gesicht, Stimme*›; **be/feel [very] ~:** [große] Angst haben; **be ~ of sb./sth.** vor jmdm./etw. Angst haben; **be ~ of doing/to do sth.** sich nicht [ge]trauen, etw. zu tun

scaremonger /'skeəmʌŋgə(r)/ *n.* Panikmacher, *der/* -macherin, *die* (abwertend)

scaremongering /'skeəmʌŋgərɪŋ/ *n., no pl.* Panikmache, *die*

scarf /skɑːf/ *n., pl.* **~s** or **scarves** /skɑːvz/ Schal, *der;* (triangular/square piece of fine material) Halstuch, *das;* (worn over hair) Kopftuch, *das;* (worn over shoulders) Schultertuch, *das*

scarlet /'skɑːlɪt/ **1** *n.* Scharlach, *der;* Scharlachrot, *das.* **2** *adj.* scharlachrot; **I turned ~:** ich wurde puterrot

scarlet 'fever *n.* ‹▶865▶ (Med.) Scharlach, *der*

scarper /'skɑːpə(r)/ *v.i.* (Brit. sl.) abhauen (salopp); sich aus dem Staub machen (ugs.)

scarves ⇒ **scarf**

scary /'skeərɪ/ *adj.* (coll.: frightening) Furcht erregend ‹*Anblick*›; schaurig ‹*Film, Geschichte*›; Angst einflößend ‹*Person, Gesicht*›; **it was ~ to listen to** beim Zuhören konnte man richtig Angst kriegen (ugs.)

scathing /'skeɪðɪŋ/ *adj.* beißend ‹*Spott, Kritik*›; scharf ‹*Angriff*›; bissig ‹*Person, Humor, Bemerkung*›; **be ~ about sth.** etw. heruntermachen

scatter /'skætə(r)/ **1** *v.t.* **(a)** vertreiben; zerstreuen, auseinander treiben ‹*Menge*›; **(b)** (distribute irregularly) verstreuen; ausstreuen ‹*Samen*›. **2** *v.i.* sich auflösen; ‹*Menge:*› sich zerstreuen; (in fear) auseinander stieben

scatter: ~brain *n.* zerstreuter Mensch; Schussel, *der* (ugs.); **~brained** /'skætəbreɪnd/ *adj.* zerstreut; schusselig (ugs.)

scattered /'skætəd/ *adj.* verstreut; vereinzelt ‹*Fälle, Anzeichen, Regenschauer*›; **thinly ~ population** verstreut lebende Bevölkerung

scatty /'skætɪ/ *adj.* (Brit. coll.) dusslig (salopp); **drive sb. ~:** jmdn. verrückt machen (ugs.)

scavenge /'skævɪndʒ/ **1** *v.t.* **(a)** sich (*Dat.*) holen; **(b)** (search) durchstöbern (**for** nach); absuchen ‹*Strand*›; fleddern ‹*Leiche*›. **2** *v.i.* **~ for sth.** nach etw. suchen

scavenger /'skævɪndʒə(r)/ *n.* (animal) Aasfresser, *der;* (fig. derog.: person) Aasgeier, *der* (ugs. abwertend)

scenario /sɪ'nɑːrɪəʊ, sɪ'neərɪəʊ/ *n., pl.* **~s** (also fig.) Szenario, *das*

scene /siːn/ *n.* **(a)** (place of event) Schauplatz, *der;* (in novel, play, etc.) Ort der Handlung; **~ of the crime** Ort des Verbrechens; Tatort, *der;* **(b)** (portion of play, film, or book) Szene, *die;* (division of act) Auftritt, *der;* **love/trial ~:** Liebes-/Gerichtsszene, *die;* **(c)** (display of passion, anger, jealousy) Szene, *die;* **create** or **make a ~:** eine Szene machen; **(d)** (view) Anblick, *der;* (as depicted) Aussicht, *die;* **change of ~:** Tapetenwechsel, *der* (ugs.); **(e)** (place of action) Ort des Geschehens; **arrive** or **come on the ~:** auftauchen; **(f)** (field of action) **the political/drug/artistic ~:** die politische/ Drogen-/Kunstszene; **the social ~:** das gesellschaftliche Leben; **(g)** (coll.: area of interest) **what's your ~?** worauf stehst du? (ugs.); **that's not my ~:** das ist nicht mein Fall (ugs.); **(h)** (Theatre: set) Bühnenbild, *das;* **behind the ~s** (lit. or fig.) hinter den Kulissen; **set the ~ [for sb.]** (fig.) [jmdm.] die Ausgangssituation darlegen

scenery /'siːnərɪ/ *n., no pl.* **(a)** (Theatre) Bühnenbild, *das;* **(b)** (landscape) Landschaft, *die;* (picturesque) [malerische] Landschaft; **change of ~:** Tapetenwechsel, *der* (ugs.)

scenic /'siːnɪk/ *adj.* (with fine natural scenery) landschaftlich schön; **a ~ drive** eine Fahrt durch schöne Landschaft; **~ railway** Berg-und-Tal-Bahn, *die*

scent /sent/ **1** *n.* **(a)** (smell) Duft, *der;* (fig.) [Vor]ahnung, *die;* **catch the ~ of sth.** den Duft von etw. in die Nase bekommen; **(b)** (Hunting; also fig.: trail) Fährte, *die;* **be on the ~ of sb./sth.** (fig.) jmdm./einer Sache auf der Spur sein; **put** or **throw sb. off the ~** (fig.) jmdn. auf eine falsche Fährte bringen; **(c)** (Brit.: perfume) Parfüm, *das;* **(d)** (sense of smell) Geruchssinn, *der;* (fig.: power to detect) Spürsinn, *der.* **2** *v.t.* **(a)** (lit. or fig.) wittern; **(b)** (apply perfume to) parfümieren

scented /'sentɪd/ *adj.* **(a)** (having smell) duftend; **be ~** ‹*Blume:*› duften; **(b)** (perfumed) parfümiert

scepter (Amer.) ⇒ **sceptre**

sceptic /'skeptɪk/ *n.* Skeptiker, *der*/Skeptikerin, *die;* (with religious doubts) [Glaubens]zweifler, *der*/-zweiflerin, *die*

sceptical /'skeptɪkl/ *adj.* skeptisch; **be ~ about** or **of sb./sth.** jmdm./einer Sache skeptisch gegenüberstehen

scepticism /'skeptɪsɪzm/ *n.* Skepsis, *die;* (Philos.) Skeptizismus, *der;* (religious doubt) Glaubenszweifel *Pl.*

sceptre /'septə(r)/ *n.* (Brit.; lit. or fig.) Zepter, *das*

schedule /'ʃedjuːl, 'skedjuːl/ **1** *n.* **(a)** (list) Tabelle, *die;* (for event, festival) Programm, *das;* **(b)** (plan of procedure) Zeitplan, *der;* **we are working to a tight ~:** unsere Termine sind sehr eng; **(c)** (set of tasks) Terminplan, *der;* Programm, *das;* **work/study ~:** Arbeits-/Studienplan, *der;* **(d)** (tabulated statement) Aufstellung, *die;* **(e)** (time stated in plan) **on ~:** programmgemäß; **arrive on ~:** pünktlich ankommen. **2** *v.t.* **(a)** (make plan of) zeitlich planen; **be ~d for Thursday** für Donnerstag geplant sein; **(b)** (make timetable of) einen Fahrplan aufstellen für; (include in timetable) in den Fahrplan aufnehmen

scheduled /'ʃedjuːld, 'skedjuːld/ *adj.* (according to timetable) [fahr]planmäßig ‹*Zug, Halt*›; flugplanmäßig ‹*Zwischenlandung*›; **~ flight** Linienflug, *der*

schematic /skɪˈmætɪk, skiːˈmætɪk/ *adj.* schematisch

scheme /skiːm/ **1** *n.* **(a)** (arrangement) Anordnung, *die;* **(b)** (table of classification, outline) Schema, *das;* **(c)** (plan) Programm, *das;* (project) Projekt, *das;* **pension ~:** Rentenversicherung, *die;* **(d)** (dishonest plan) Intrige, *die.* **2** *v.i.* Pläne schmieden

scheming /ˈskiːmɪŋ/ **1** *n., no pl., no indef. art.* Winkelzüge *Pl.;* Machenschaften *Pl.* **2** *adj.* intrigant

schizophrenia /skɪtsəˈfriːnɪə/ *n.* (Psych.) Schizophrenie, *die*

schizophrenic /skɪtsəˈfrenɪk, skɪtsəˈfriːnɪk/ (Psych.; also fig. coll.) **1** *adj.* schizophren. **2** *n.* Schizophrene, *der/die*

scholar /ˈskɒlə(r)/ *n.* **(a)** (learned person) Gelehrte, *der/die;* **literary ~:** Literaturwissenschaftler *der/*-wissenschaftlerin, *die;* **Shakespeare[an] ~:** Shakespeare-Forscher, *der/*-Forscherin, *die;* **(b)** (one who learns) Schüler, *der/* Schülerin, *die;* **(c)** (holder of scholarship) Stipendiat, *der/* Stipendiatin, *die*

scholarly /ˈskɒləlɪ/ *adj.* wissenschaftlich; (having much learning) gelehrt

scholarship /ˈskɒləʃɪp/ *n.* **(a)** (payment for education) Stipendium, *das;* **(b)** *no pl.* (scholarly work) Gelehrsamkeit, *die* (geh.); (methods) Wissenschaftlichkeit, *die;* **(c)** *no pl.* (body of learning) **literary/linguistic/historical ~:** Literatur-/ Sprach-/Geschichtswissenschaft, *die*

school[1] /skuːl/ **1** *n.* **(a)** Schule, *die;* (Amer.: university, college) Hochschule, *die; attrib.* Schul-; **be at or in ~:** in der Schule sein; (attend ~) zur Schule gehen; **to/from ~:** zur/ von *od.* aus der Schule; **go to ~:** zur Schule gehen; **have time off ~:** schulfrei haben; **there will be no ~ today** heute ist keine Schule; **(b)** *attrib.* Schul ‹*aufsatz, -bus, -jahr, -system*›; **~ holidays** Schulferien *Pl.;* **~ exchange** Schüleraustausch, *der;* **the ~ term** die Schulzeit; **(c)** (disciples) Schule, *die;* **~ of thought** Lehrmeinung, *die;* **(d)** (Brit.: group of gamblers) Runde, *die.* **2** *v.t.* (train) erziehen; dressieren ‹*Pferd*›; **~ sb. in sth.** jmdn. in etw. (*Akk.*) unterweisen (geh.)

school[2] *n.* (of fish) Schwarm, *der;* Schule, *die* (Zool.)

school: ~ age *n.* Schulalter, *das;* **children of ~ age** Kinder im schulpflichtigen Alter; **~boy** *n.* Schüler, *der;* (with reference to behaviour) Schuljunge, *der;* **~child** *n.* Schulkind, *das;* **~days** *n. pl.* Schulzeit, *die;* **~ friend** *n.* Schulfreund, *der/*-freundin, *die;* **~girl** *n.* Schülerin, *die;* (with reference to behaviour) Schulmädchen, *das*

schooling /ˈskuːlɪŋ/ *n.* Schulbildung, *die;* **he has had little ~:** er hat keine richtige Schulbildung gehabt

school: ~ leaver /ˈskuːlliːvə(r)/ *n.* (Brit.) Schulabgänger, *der/*-abgängerin, *die;* **~-leaving age** *n.* (Brit.) Schulabgangsalter, *das;* **~master** *n.* ▶887⟩ Lehrer, *der;* **~mistress** *n.* ▶887⟩ Lehrerin, *die;* **~room** *n.* Schulzimmer, *das;* **~teacher** *n.* ▶887⟩ Lehrer, *der/*Lehrerin, *die;* **~ work** *n.* Schularbeiten *Pl.*

schooner /ˈskuːnə(r)/ *n.* **(a)** (Naut.) Schoner, *der;* **(b)** (Brit.: sherry glass) [hohes] Sherryglas

sciatica /saɪˈætɪkə/ *n.* ▶865⟩ (Med.) Ischias, *die* (fachspr. der od. das)

science /ˈsaɪəns/ *n.* **(a)** *no pl., no art.* Wissenschaft, *die;* **applied/pure ~:** angewandte/reine Wissenschaft; **(b)** (branch of knowledge) Wissenschaft, *die;* **(c)** **[natural] ~:** Naturwissenschaften; *attrib.* naturwissenschaftlich ‹*Buch, Labor*›; **(d)** (technique, expert's skill) Kunst, *die*

science: ~ 'fiction *n.* Sciencefiction, *die;* **~ park** *n.* Technologiepark, *der*

scientific /saɪənˈtɪfɪk/ *adj.* **(a)** wissenschaftlich; (of natural science) naturwissenschaftlich; **(b)** (using technical skill) technisch gut ‹*Boxer, Schauspieler, Tennis*›

scientist /ˈsaɪəntɪst/ *n.* ▶887⟩ Wissenschaftler, *der/*Wissenschaftlerin, *die;* (in physical or natural science) Naturwissenschaftler, *der/*-wissenschaftlerin, *die;* **biological/social/ computer ~s** Biologen/Soziologen/Informatiker *Pl.*

sci-fi /ˈsaɪfaɪ/ *n.* (coll.) Sciencefiction, *die*

Scillies /ˈsɪlɪz/, **Scilly Isles** /ˈsɪlɪ aɪlz/ *pr. n. pl.* Scilly-Inseln *Pl.*

scimitar /ˈsɪmɪtə(r)/ *n.* Krummsäbel, *der*

scintillating /ˈsɪntɪleɪtɪŋ/ *adj.* (fig.) geistsprühend

scissors /ˈsɪzəz/ *n. pl.* **[pair of] ~:** Schere, *die;* **be a ~- and-paste job** ‹*Buch, Werk:*› [aus anderen Werken] zusammengeschrieben sein

'scissors kick *n.* (Swimming) Scherenschlag, *der*

sclerosis /sklɪəˈrəʊsɪs/ *n., pl.* **scleroses** /sklɪəˈrəʊsiːz/ (Med.) Sklerose, *die;* **disseminated** *or* **multiple ~:** multiple Sklerose

scoff[1] /skɒf/ *v.i.* (mock) spotten; **~ing remarks** spöttische Bemerkungen; **~ at sb./sth.** sich über jmdn./etw. lustig machen

scoff[2] (sl.) **1** *v.t.* (eat greedily) verschlingen. **2** *v.i.* sich [(*Dat.*) den Bauch] vollschlagen (salopp)

scold /skəʊld/ **1** *v.t.* schelten (geh.); ausschimpfen **(for** wegen); **she ~ed him for coming late** sie schimpfte ihn aus *od.* schalt ihn, weil er zu spät kam. **2** *v.i.* schimpfen; **~ing wife** zänkische Ehefrau

scolding /ˈskəʊldɪŋ/ *n.* Schimpfen, *das;* (instance) Schelte, *die* (geh.); Schimpfe, *die* (ugs.); **get a ~:** ausgeschimpft werden

scone /skɒn, skəʊn/ *n.: weicher, oft zum Tee gegessener kleiner Kuchen*

scoop /skuːp/ **1** *n.* **(a)** (shovel) Schaufel, *die;* **(b)** (ladle, ladleful) Schöpflöffel, *der;* (Schöpf]kelle, *die;* **(c)** (for ice cream, mashed potatoes) Portionierer, *der;* (of ice cream) Kugel, *die;* **(d)** (Journ.) Knüller, *der* (ugs.); Scoop, *der* (fachspr.). **2** *v.t.* **(a)** (lift) schaufeln ‹*Kohlen, Schnee*›; (with ladle) schöpfen ‹*Flüssigkeit, Schaum*›; **(b)** (secure) erzielen ‹*Gewinn*›; hereinholen (ugs.) ‹*Auftrag*›; (in a lottery, bet) gewinnen ‹*Vermögen*›; **(c)** (Journ.) ausstechen

~ 'out *v.t.* **(a)** (hollow out) aushöhlen; schaufeln ‹*Loch, Graben*›; **(b)** (remove) [her]ausschöpfen ‹*Flüssigkeit*›; auslöffeln ‹*Fruchtfleisch*›; (with a knife) herausschneiden ‹*Fruchtfleisch, Gehäuse*›; (excavate) ausbaggern ‹*Erde*›

~ 'up *v.t.* schöpfen ‹*Wasser, Suppe*›; schaufeln ‹*Erde*›; aufschaufeln ‹*Kohlen, Kies*›

scoot /skuːt/ *v.i.* (coll.) rasen; (to escape) die Kurve kratzen (ugs.)

scooter /ˈskuːtə(r)/ *n.* **(a)** (toy) Roller, *der;* **(b)** **[motor] ~:** [Motor]roller, *der*

scope /skəʊp/ *n., no indef. art.* **(a)** Bereich, *der;* (of person's activities) Betätigungsfeld, *das;* (of person's job) Aufgabenbereich, *der;* (of department etc.) Zuständigkeitsbereich, *der;* Zuständigkeit, *die;* (of discussion, meeting, negotiations, investigations, etc.) Rahmen, *der;* **that is a subject beyond my ~:** das fällt nicht in meine Sparte; (beyond my grasp) das ist mir zu hoch; **(b)** (opportunity) Entfaltungsmöglichkeiten *Pl.;* **give ample ~ for new ideas** weiten Raum für neue Ideen bieten

scorch /skɔːtʃ/ **1** *v.t.* verbrennen; versengen. **2** *v.i.* versengt werden; verbrennen. **3** *n.* versengte Stelle; Brandfleck, *der*

scorcher /ˈskɔːtʃə(r)/ *n.* (Brit. coll.: hot day) **what a ~!** ist das eine Affenhitze heute!

scorching /ˈskɔːtʃɪŋ/ *adj.* glühend heiß; sengend, glühend ‹*Hitze*›

score /skɔː(r)/ **1** *n.* **(a)** (points) [Spiel]stand, *der;* (made by one player) Punktzahl, *die;* **What's the ~?** — The **~ was 4–1 at half-time** Wie steht es? — Der Halbzeitstand war 4 : 1; **final ~:** Endstand, *der;* **keep [the] ~:** zählen; **know the ~** (fig. coll.) wissen, was Sache ist *od.* was läuft (salopp); **(b)** (Mus.) Partitur, *die;* (Film) [Film]musik, *die;* **(c)** *pl.* **~ or ~s** (group of 20) zwanzig; **(d)** *in pl.* (great numbers) **~s [and ~s] of** zig (ugs.); Dutzende [von]; **~s of times** zigmal (ugs.); **(e)** (notch) Kerbe, *die;* (weal) Striemen, *der;* **(f) pay off** *or* **settle an old ~** (fig.) eine alte Rechnung begleichen; **(g)** (reason) Grund, *der;* **on that ~:** was das betrifft *od.* angeht; diesbezüglich. **2** *v.t.* **(a)** (win) erzielen ‹*Erfolg, Punkt, Treffer usw.*›; **~ a direct hit on sth.** ‹*Person:*› einen Volltreffer landen; ‹*Bombe:*› etw. voll treffen; **they ~d a success** sie konnten einen Erfolg [für sich] verbuchen; **~ a goal** ein Tor schießen/werfen; **(b)** (make notch/notches in) einkerben; **(c)** (be worth) zählen; **(d)** (Mus.) setzen; (orchestrate) orchestrieren ‹*Musikstück*›. **3** *v.i.* **(a)** (make ~) Punkte/einen Punkt erzielen *od.* (ugs.) machen;

punkten (bes. Boxen); (~ goal/goals) ein Tor/Tore schießen/ werfen; ~ **high** *or* **well** (in test etc.) eine hohe Punktzahl erreichen *od.* erzielen; **(b)** (keep ~) aufschreiben; anschreiben; **(c)** (secure advantage) die besseren Karten haben **(over** gegenüber, im Vergleich zu)

~ **'out,** ~ **'through** *v.t.* durchstreichen; ausstreichen

score: ~**board** *n.* Anzeigetafel, *die;* ~**card** *n.* (Sport) Anschreibekarte, *die;* (Golf) Scorekarte, *die*

scorer /'skɔːrə(r)/ *n.* **(a)** (recorder of score) Anschreiber, *der/*Anschreiberin, *die;* **(b)** (Footb.) Torschütze, *der/*-schützin, *die*

scorn /skɔːn/ **1** *n., no pl., no indef. art.* Verachtung, *die;* **with** ~: mit *od.* voll[er] Verachtung; verachtungsvoll. **2** *v.t.* **(a)** (hold in contempt) verachten; **(b)** (refuse) in den Wind schlagen ‹*Rat*›; ausschlagen ‹*Angebot*›; ~ **doing** *or* **to do sth.** es für unter seiner Würde halten, etw. zu tun

scornful /'skɔːnfl/ *adj.* verächtlich ‹*Lächeln, Blick*›; **be** ~ **of sth.** für etw. nur Verachtung haben

Scorpio /'skɔːpɪəʊ/ *n.* (Astrol., Astron.) der Skorpion

scorpion /'skɔːpɪən/ *n.* (Zool.) Skorpion, *der*

Scot /skɒt/ *n.* ▶ 947 Schotte, *der/*Schottin, *die*

Scotch /skɒtʃ/ **1** *adj.* **(a)** (of Scotland) ⇒ **Scottish; (b)** (Ling.) ⇒ **Scots 1 b. 2** *n.* **(a)** (whisky) Scotch, *der;* schottischer Whisky; **(b)** (Ling.) ⇒ **Scots 2; (c)** *constr. as pl.* **the** ~: die Schotten

scotch *v.t.* **(a)** (frustrate) zunichte machen ‹*Plan*›; **(b)** (put an end to) den Boden entziehen (+ *Dat.*) ‹*Gerücht*›

Scotch: ~ **'egg** *n.* (Gastr.) *hart gekochtes Ei in Wurstbrät;* ~ **'mist** *n.* dichter Nieselregen; ~ **tape,** **(P)** *n.* (Amer.) Klebeband, *der;* ≈ Tesafilm, *der* Ⓦ; ~ **'terrier** *n.* Scotch[terrier], *der;* ~ **'whisky** *n.* schottischer Whisky

scot-'free *pred. adj.* ungeschoren; **get off/go/escape** ~: ungeschoren davonkommen

Scotland /'skɒtlənd/ *pr. n.* Schottland (*das*)

Scots /skɒts/ **1** *adj.* **(a)** (esp. Scot.) ⇒ **Scottish; (b)** (Ling.) schottisch. **2** *n.* (dialect) Schottisch, *das*

Scots: ~**man** /'skɒtsmən/ *n., pl.* ~**men** /'skɒtsmən/ Schotte, *der;* ~**woman** *n.* Schottin, *die*

Scottish /'skɒtɪʃ/ *adj.* ▶ 947 schottisch

scoundrel /'skaʊndrl/ *n.* Schuft, *der* (abwertend); (villain) Schurke, *der* (abwertend)

scour[1] /skaʊə(r)/ *v.t.* **(a)** scheuern ‹*Topf, Metall*›; ~ **out** ausscheuern ‹*Topf*›; **(b)** (clear out) ~ **[out]** durchspülen ‹*Rohr*›; **(c)** (remove by rubbing) [ab]scheuern

scour[2] *v.t.* (search) durchkämmen **(for** nach)

scourer /'skaʊərə(r)/ *n.* Topfreiniger, *der;* Topfkratzer, *der*

scourge /skɜːdʒ/ **1** *n.* (lit. *or* fig.) Geißel, *die.* **2** *v.t.* **(a)** (whip) geißeln; **(b)** (afflict) heimsuchen

scout /skaʊt/ **1** *n.* **(a)** **[Boy] S**~: Pfadfinder, *der;* **(b)** (Mil. etc.: sent to get information) Späher, *der/* Späherin, *die;* Kundschafter, *der/* Kundschafterin, *die.* **2** *v.i.* auf Erkundung gehen; ~ **for sb./sth.** nach jmdm./etw. Ausschau halten; **be** ~**ing for talent** auf Talentsuche sein

~ **a'bout,** ~ **a'round** *v.i.* sich umsehen **(for** nach)

'scout leader *n.* Pfadfinderführer, *der*

scowl /skaʊl/ **1** *v.i.* ein mürrisches Gesicht machen; ~ **at sb.** jmdn. mürrisch ansehen. **2** *n.* mürrischer [Gesichts]ausdruck

scrabble /skræbl/ **1** *v.i.* ‹*Maus, Hund:*› scharren, kratzen. **2** *n.* **S**~, **(P)** Scrabble, *das*

scram /skræm/ *v.i.,* **-mm-** (coll.) abhauen (salopp); verschwinden (ugs.)

scramble /'skræmbl/ **1** *v.i.* **(a)** (clamber) klettern; kraxeln (ugs.); **(b)** (move hastily) hasten (geh.); rennen (ugs.); ~ **for sth.** um etw. rangeln; ‹*Kinder:*› sich um etw. balgen; **(c)** (Air Force) [im Alarmfalle] aufsteigen. **2** *v.t.* **(a)** (Cookery) ~ **some eggs** Rührei[er] machen; *see also* **scrambled egg; (b)** (Teleph., Radio) verschlüsseln; **(c)** (mix together) [ver] mischen; **(d)** ~ **the ball away** (Footb.) den Ball [irgendwie] wegschlagen. **3** *n.* **(a)** (struggle) Gerangel, *das* **(for** um); **(b)** (climb) Kletterpartie, *die* (ugs.)

scrambled egg /skræmbld 'eg/ *n.* (Gastr.) Rührei, *das*

scrap[1] /skræp/ **1** *n.* **(a)** (fragment) (of paper, conversation) Fetzen, *der;* (of food) Bissen, *der;* ~ **of paper** Stück Papier; (small, torn) Papierfetzen, *der;* **(b)** *in pl.* (odds and ends) (of food) Reste *Pl.;* (of language) Brocken *Pl.;* **a few** ~**s of information/news** ein paar bruchstückhafte Informationen/Nachrichten; **(c)** (smallest amount) **not a** ~ **of** kein bisschen; (of sympathy, truth also) nicht ein Fünkchen; **not a** ~ **of evidence** nicht die Spur eines Beweises; **(d)** *no pl., no indef. art.* (waste metal) Schrott, *der; attrib.* ~ **metal** Schrott, *der;* Altmetall, *das;* **(e)** *no pl., no indef. art.* (rubbish) Abfall, *der;* **they are** ~: das ist Abfall *od.* sind Abfälle. **2** *v.t.,* **-pp-** wegwerfen; wegschmeißen (ugs.); (send for ~) verschrotten; (fig.) aufgeben ‹*Plan, Projekt usw.*›; **you can** ~ **that idea right away** die Idee kannst du gleich vergessen (ugs.)

scrap[2] (coll.) **1** *n.* (fight) Rauferei, *die;* Klopperei, *die* (ugs.). **2** *v.i.,* **-pp-** sich raufen **(with** mit)

'scrapbook *n.* [Sammel]album, *das*

scrape /skreɪp/ **1** *v.t.* **(a)** (make smooth) schaben ‹*Häute, Möhren, Kartoffeln usw.*›; abziehen ‹*Holz*›; (damage) verkratzen, verschrammen ‹*Fußboden, Auto*›; schürfen ‹*Körperteil*›; **(b)** (remove) [ab]schaben, [ab]kratzen ‹*Farbe, Schmutz, Rost*› **(off, from** von); **(c)** (draw along) schleifen; **(d)** (remove dirt from) abstreifen ‹*Schuhe, Stiefel*›; **(e)** (draw back) straff kämmen ‹*Haar*›; **(f)** (excavate) scharren ‹*Loch*›; **(g)** (accumulate by care with money) ~ **together/up** (raise) zusammenkratzen (ugs.); (save up) zusammensparen; **(h)** ~ **together/up** (amass by scraping) zusammenscharren ‹*Sand, Kies*›; **(i)** (leave no food on or in) abkratzen ‹*Teller*›; auskratzen ‹*Schüssel*›. *See also* **barrel a. 2** *v.i.* **(a)** (make with scraping sound) schleifen; **(b)** (rub) streifen **(against, over** *Akk.*); **(c)** ~ **past each other** ‹*Autos:*› haarscharf aneinander vorbeifahren; **(d) bow and** ~: katzbuckeln (abwertend). *See also* **scrimp. 3** *n.* **(a)** (act, sound) Kratzen, *das* **(against** an + *Dat.*); Schaben, *das* **(against** an + *Dat.*); **(b)** (predicament) Schwulitäten *Pl.* (ugs.); **be in a/get into a** ~: in Schwulitäten sein/kommen; **get sb. out of a** ~: jmdm. aus der Bredouille *od.* Patsche helfen (ugs.); **(c)** (~d place) Kratzer, *der* (ugs.); Schramme, *die*

~ **a'long** *v.i.* (fig.) sich über Wasser halten **(on** mit)

~ **a'way** *v.t.* abkratzen; abschaben

~ **'by** ⇒ ~ **along**

~ **'out** *v.t.* **(a)** (excavate) buddeln (ugs.); scharren; **(b)** (clean) auskratzen; ausschaben

~ **through 1** /'--/ *v.t.* **(a)** sich zwängen durch; **(b)** (fig.: just succeed in passing) mit Hängen und Würgen kommen durch ‹*Prüfung*›. **2** /'-'-/ *v.i.* **(a)** sich durchzwängen; **(b)** (fig.: just succeed in passing examination) mit Hängen und Würgen durchkommen

scraper /'skreɪpə(r)/ *n.* **(a)** (for shoes) Kratzeisen, *das;* (grid) Abtreter, *der;* Abstreifer, *der;* **(b)** (hand tool, kitchen utensil) Schaber, *der;* (for clearing snow) Schneescharre, *die;* (decorator's) Spachtel, *der;* (for removing ice from car windows) [Eis]kratzer, *der*

scrap: ~ **heap** *n.* Schrotthaufen, *der* ~ **merchant** *n.* ▶ 887 Schrotthändler, *der/*-händlerin, *die;* ~ **'paper** *n.* Schmierpapier, *das*

scrappy /'skræpɪ/ *adj.* **(a)** (not complete) lückenhaft ‹*Bericht, Bildung usw.*›; **(b)** (made up of bits or scraps) zusammengestoppelt (abwertend)

'scrapyard *n.* Schrottplatz, *der;* **be sent to the** ~: verschrottet werden

scratch /skrætʃ/ **1** *v.t.* **(a)** (score surface of) zerkratzen; verkratzen; (score skin of) kratzen; ~ **the surface [of sth.]** ‹*Geschoss usw.:*› [etw.] streifen; **he has only** ~**ed the surface [of the problem]** er hat das Problem nur oberflächlich gestreift; **(b)** (get ~ed) ~ **oneself/one's hands** *etc.* sich schrammen/sich ‹*Dat.*› die Hände *usw.* zerkratzen *od.* [zer]schrammen *od.* ritzen; **(c)** (scrape without marking) kratzen; kratzen an (+ *Dat.*) ‹*Insektenstich usw.*›; ~ **oneself/one's arm** *etc.* sich kratzen/sich ‹*Dat.*› den Arm *usw. od.* am Arm *usw.* kratzen; *abs.* ‹*Person:*› sich kratzen; ~ **one's head** sich am Kopf kratzen; ~ **one's head [over sth.]** (ugs. ‹*Dat.*›) den Kopf über etw. ‹*Akk.*› zerbrechen; **you** ~ **my back and I'll** ~ **yours** (fig. coll.) eine Hand wäscht die andere (Spr.); **(d)** (form) kratzen, ritzen ‹*Buchstaben etc.*›; kratzen, scharren ‹*Loch*› **(in** in + *Akk.*);

~ **a living** sich schlecht und recht ernähren (**from** von); (**e**) (erase from list) streichen (**from** aus); (withdraw from competition) von der Starter- od. Teilnehmerliste streichen ⟨*Rennpferd, Athleten*⟩. **2** *v.i.* (**a**) kratzen; (**b**) (scrape) ⟨*Huhn:*⟩ kratzen, scharren. **3** *n.* (**a**) (mark, wound; coll.: trifling wound) Kratzer, *der* (ugs.); Schramme, *die;* (**b**) (sound) Kratzen, *das* (**at** an + *Dat.*); Kratzgeräusch, *das;* (**c**) **have a [good]** ~**:** sich [ordentlich] kratzen; (**d**) **start from** ~ (fig.) bei Null anfangen (ugs.); **be up to** ~ ⟨*Arbeit, Leistung:*⟩ nichts zu wünschen übrig lassen; ⟨*Person:*⟩ in Form *od.* (ugs.) auf Zack sein; **bring sth. up to** ~**:** etw. auf Vordermann (scherz.) bringen. **4** *adj.* (collected haphazardly) bunt zusammengewürfelt

~ **a'bout**, ~ **a'round** *v.i.* scharren; (fig.: search) suchen (**for** nach)

~ **'off** *v.t.* abkratzen

~ **'out** *v.t.* (**a**) (score out) aus-, durchstreichen ⟨*Name, Wort*⟩; (**b**) (gouge out) auskratzen ⟨*Auge*⟩

'scratch card *n.* Rubbellos, *das;* ~ **game** Rubbellos-Gewinnspiel, *das*

scratchy /ˈskrætʃɪ/ *adj.* (**a**) kratzig [klingend] ⟨*Schallplatte*⟩; (**b**) kratzig ⟨*Wolle, Kleidungsstück*⟩

scrawl /skrɔːl/ **1** *v.t.* hinkritzeln; ~ **sth. on sth.** etw. auf etw. (*Akk.*) kritzeln. **2** *v.i.* kritzeln. **3** *n.* (piece of writing) Gekritzel, *das;* (handwriting) Klaue, *die* (salopp abwertend)

~ **'out** *v.t.* wegstreichen ⟨*Wort*⟩

scrawny /ˈskrɔːnɪ/ *adj.* (derog.) hager, dürr ⟨*Hals, Person*⟩; mager ⟨*Vieh*⟩

scream /skriːm/ **1** *v.i.* (**a**) schreien (**with** vor + *Dat.*); ~ **at sb.** jmdn. anschreien; (**b**) ⟨*Vogel, Affe:*⟩ schreien; ⟨*Sirene, Triebwerk:*⟩ heulen; ⟨*Reifen:*⟩ quietschen; ⟨*Säge:*⟩ kreischen. **2** *v.t.* schreien. **3** *n.* (**a**) Schrei, *der;* (of siren or jet engine) Heulen, *das;* ~**s of laughter/pain** gellendes Gelächter/Schmerzensschreie; (**b**) (coll.: comical person or thing) **be a** ~**:** zum Schreien sein (ugs.)

scree /skriː/ *n.* ~**[s]** (stones) Schutt, *der;* Geröll, *das;* Schotter, *der*

screech /skriːtʃ/ **1** *v.i.* ⟨*Kind, Eule:*⟩ kreischen, schreien; ⟨*Bremsen:*⟩ quietschen, kreischen; ~ **to a halt, come to a** ~**ing** halt ⟨*Auto:*⟩ quietschend *od.* kreischend zum Stehen kommen. **2** *v.t.* kreischen. **3** *n.* (cry) Schrei, *der;* Kreischen, *das;* **give a** ~ **of laughter** gellend auflachen

screen /skriːn/ **1** *n.* (**a**) (partition) Trennwand, *die;* (piece of furniture) Wandschirm, *der;* (**b**) (sth. that conceals from view) Sichtschutz, *der;* (of trees, persons, fog) Wand, *die;* (of persons) Mauer, *die;* (of secrecy) Wand, *die;* Mauer, *die;* (**c**) (on which pictures are projected) Leinwand, *die;* (of computer, TV) Bildschirm, *der;* (radar ~) [Radar]schirm, *der;* ~ (Cinemat.) die Leinwand; (**d**) (Phys.) [Schutz]schirm, *der;* (Electr.) Abschirmung, *die;* (**e**) (Motor Veh.) ⇒ **windscreen;** (**f**) (Amer.: netting to exclude insects) Fliegendraht, *der;* Fliegengitter, *das.* **2** *v.t.* (**a**) (shelter) schützen (**from** vor + *Dat.*); (conceal) verdecken; ~ **one's eyes from the sun** seine Augen vor der Sonne schützen *od.* (geh.) gegen die Sonne beschirmen; ~ **sth. from sb.** etw. jmds. Blicken entziehen; (**b**) (show) vorführen, zeigen ⟨*Dias, Film*⟩; (**c**) (check) (for disease) untersuchen (**for** auf + *Akk.*); (for loyalty etc.) unter die Lupe nehmen

~ **'off** *v.t.* abteilen ⟨*Teil eines Raumes*⟩; [mit einem Wandschirm] abtrennen ⟨*Bett*⟩

screening /ˈskriːnɪŋ/ *n.* (**a**) (in cinema) Vorführung, *die;* (on TV) Sendung, *die;* Ausstrahlung, *die;* (**b**) (Med.) Untersuchung, *die;* **mass** ~ Reihenuntersuchung, *die*

screen: ~**play** *n.* (Cinemat.) Drehbuch, *das;* ~ **printing** *n.* (Textiles) Siebdruck, *der* ~ **saver** *n.* (Computing) Bildschirmschoner, *der*

screw /skruː/ **1** *n.* (**a**) Schraube, *die;* **he has a** ~ **loose** (coll. joc.) bei ihm ist eine Schraube locker *od.* lose (salopp); **put the** ~**[s] on sb.** (fig. coll.) jmdm. [die] Daumenschrauben anlegen (ugs.); (**b**) (Naut., Aeronaut.) Schraube, *die;* (**c**) (sl.: prison warder) Wachtel, *die* (salopp); (**d**) (coarse: copulation) Fick, *der* (vulg.); Nummer, *die* (derb); (partner in copulation) Ficker, *der*/Fickerin, *die* (vulg.); **have a** ~**:** ficken (vulg.); vögeln (vulg.). **2** *v.t.* (**a**) (fasten) schrauben (**to** an + *Akk.*); ~ **down** festschrauben; **have one's head** ~**ed on [straight** or **the right way** or **properly]** (coll.) ein vernünftiger Mensch sein; (**b**) (turn) schrauben

⟨*Schraubverschluss usw.*⟩; ~ **a piece of paper into a ball** ein Stück Papier zu einer Kugel zusammendrehen; (**c**) (sl.: extort) [raus]quetschen (salopp) ⟨*Geld, Geständnis*⟩ (**out of** aus); (**d**) (coarse: copulate with) ⟨*Mann:*⟩ ficken (vulg.), vögeln (vulg.); ⟨*Frau:*⟩ ficken mit (vulg.), vögeln mit (vulg.); ~ **you!** (sl.) leck mich am Arsch! (salopp); ~ **you and your …!** (sl.) leck mich am Arsch mit deinem/deiner/deinen …! **3** *v.i.* (**a**) (revolve) sich schrauben lassen; sich drehen lassen; (**b**) (coarse: copulate) ficken (vulg.); vögeln (vulg.)

~ **'up** *v.t.* (**a**) (crumple up) zusammenknüllen ⟨*Blatt Papier*⟩; (**b**) verziehen ⟨*Gesicht*⟩; zusammenkneifen ⟨*Augen, Mund*⟩; (**c**) (sl.: bungle) vermurksen (ugs.); vermasseln (salopp); ~ **it/things up** Mist bauen (salopp); (**d**) ~ **up one's courage** sich (*Dat.*) ein Herz fassen

screw: ~**ball** (Amer. sl.) **1** *n.* Spinner, *der*/Spinnerin, *die* (ugs. abwertend); **2** *adj.* spleenig; ~ **cap** *n.* Schraubdeckel, *der;* Schraubverschluss, *der;* ~**driver** *n.* Schraubenzieher, *der*

'screwed-up *adj.* (fig. coll.) neurotisch

screw top ⇒ **screw cap**

screwy /ˈskruːɪ/ *adj.* (coll.: eccentric) spinnig (ugs. abwertend)

scribble /ˈskrɪbl/ **1** *v.t.* (**a**) (write hastily) hinkritzeln ⟨*Zeilen, Nachricht*⟩; (**b**) (draw carelessly or meaninglessly) kritzeln ⟨*Skizze, Muster*⟩. **2** *v.i.* kritzeln. **3** *n.* Gekritzel, *das* (abwertend)

scribbler /ˈskrɪblə(r)/ *n.* (joc. derog.) Schreiberling, *der* (abwertend); (of poems also) Dichterling, *der* (abwertend)

scribe /skraɪb/ *n.* (**a**) (producer of manuscripts) Schreiber, *der;* Skriptor, *der;* (copyist) Abschreiber, *der;* Kopist, *der;* (**b**) (Bibl.: theologian) Schriftgelehrte, *der*

scrimmage /ˈskrɪmɪdʒ/ *n.* Gerangel, *das*

scrimp /skrɪmp/ *v.i.* knausern (ugs.); knapsen (ugs.); ~ **and save** or **scrape** knapsen und knausern (ugs.)

script /skrɪpt/ *n.* (**a**) (handwriting) Handschrift, *die;* (**b**) (of play) Regiebuch, *das;* (of film) [Dreh]buch, *das;* Skript, *das* (fachspr.); (**c**) (for broadcaster) Skript, *das;* Manuskript, *das;* (**d**) (system of writing) Schrift, *die*

scripture /ˈskrɪptʃə(r)/ *n.* (**a**) (Relig.: sacred book) heilige Schrift; **[Holy] S**~, **the [Holy] S**~**s** (Christian Relig.) die [Heilige] Schrift; *attrib.* Bibel ⟨*text, -stunde*⟩; (**b**) *no pl., no art.* (Sch.) Religion, *die*

'scriptwriter *n.* **▶ 887** (of film) Drehbuchautor, *der*/-autorin, *die*

scroll /skrəʊl/ **1** *n.* (**a**) (roll) Rolle, *die;* (**b**) (Archit.) Volute, *die;* Schnecke, *die.* **2** *v.t.* (Computing) verschieben; scrollen (fachspr.)

scrollable /ˈskrəʊləbl/ *adj.* (Computing) scrollbar

'scroll bar *n.* Rollbalken, *der*

scrounge /skraʊndʒ/ (coll.) **1** *v.t.* schnorren (ugs.) (**off, from** von); ~ **things** schnorren. **2** *v.i.* schnorren (ugs.) (**from** bei)

scrounger /ˈskraʊndʒə(r)/ *n.* (coll.) Schnorrer, *der*/Schnorrerin, *die* (ugs. abwertend)

scrub[1] /skrʌb/ **1** *v.t.,* **-bb-:** (**a**) (rub) schrubben (ugs.); scheuern; (**b**) (coll.: cancel, scrap) zurücknehmen ⟨*Befehl*⟩; sausen lassen, schießen lassen (salopp) ⟨*Plan, Projekt*⟩; wegschmeißen (ugs.) ⟨*Brief*⟩. **2** *v.i.,* **-bb-** schrubben (ugs.); scheuern. **3** *n.* **give sth. a** ~**:** etw. schrubben (ugs.) *od.* scheuern

scrub[2] *n.* (brushwood) Buschwerk, *das;* Strauchwerk, *das;* Gesträuch, *das;* (area of brushwood) Buschland, *das*

scrubber /ˈskrʌbə(r)/ *n.* (sl.: immoral woman) Flittchen, *das* (ugs. abwertend); Nutte, *die* (abwertend)

'scrubbing-brush, (Amer.) **'scrub-brush** *ns.* Scheuerbürste, *die*

scrubby /ˈskrʌbɪ/ *adj.* (**a**) (bristly) stoppelig ⟨*Kinn*⟩; stachelig, borstig ⟨*Bart*⟩; (**b**) (stunted) krüppelhaft ⟨*Büsche, Sträucher*⟩

scruff[1] /skrʌf/ *n.* **by the** ~ **of the neck** beim *od.* am Genick

scruff[2] *n.* (Brit. coll.) (man) vergammelter Typ (ugs.); (woman, girl) Schlampe, *die* (abwertend)

scruffy /ˈskrʌfɪ/ *adj.* vergammelt (ugs.); heruntergekommen ⟨*Gegend, Haus*⟩

scrum /skrʌm/ n. (Rugby) Gedränge, das

scrumptious /'skrʌmʃəs/ adj. (coll.) lecker ‹Essen›

scruple /'skru:pl/ n., usu. pl. Skrupel, der; Bedenken, das; **a person with no** ∿s ein gewissen- od. skrupelloser Mensch; **have no** ∿s **about doing sth.** keine Bedenken od. Skrupel haben, etw. zu tun

scrupulous /'skru:pjʊləs/ adj. gewissenhaft ‹Person›; unbedingt ‹Ehrlichkeit›; peinlich ‹Sorgfalt›; **pay** ∿ **attention to sth.** peinlich auf etw. (Akk.) achten

scrupulously /'skru:pjʊləslɪ/ adv. peinlich ‹sauber, genau›; ∿ **honest** auf unbedingte Ehrlichkeit bedacht

scrutinize (scrutinise) /'skru:tɪnaɪz/ v.t. [genau] untersuchen ‹Gegenstand, Forschungsgegenstand›; [über]prüfen ‹Rechnung, Pass, Fahrkarte›; mustern ‹Miene, Person›

scrutiny /'skru:tɪnɪ/ n. (critical gaze) prüfender Blick; (close examination) (of recruit) Musterung, die; (of bill, passport) [Über]prüfung, die; **bear** ∿: einer [genauen] Prüfung standhalten

scuba /'sku:bə, 'skju:bə/ n. (Sport) Regenerationstauchgerät, das; ∿ **diving** Gerätetauchen, das; ∿ **equipment** [Geräte]tauchausrüstung, die

scuff /skʌf/ 1 v.t. (a) (graze) streifen; ∿ **one's shoe against sth.** etw. mit dem Schuh streifen; (b) (mark by grazing) verkratzen, verschrammen ‹Schuhe, Fußboden›. 2 n. Kratzer, der; Kratzspur, die; Schramme, die

scuffle /'skʌfl/ 1 n. Handgreiflichkeiten Pl.; Tätlichkeiten Pl.; **a** ∿ **broke out** es kam zu Handgreiflichkeiten od. Tätlichkeiten. 2 v.i. handgreiflich od. tätlich werden (**with** gegen)

scull /skʌl/ 1 n. (oar) Skull, das. 2 v.t. skullen; rudern. 3 v.i. skullen

scullery /'skʌlərɪ/ n. Spülküche, die

sculpt /skʌlpt/ v.t. & i. (coll.) bildhauern (ugs.)

sculptor /'skʌlptə(r)/ n. Bildhauer, der/-hauerin, die

sculptress /'skʌlptrɪs/ n. Bildhauerin, die

sculpture /'skʌlptʃə(r)/ 1 n. (a) (art) Bildhauerei, die; (b) (piece of work) Skulptur, die; Plastik, die; (pieces collectively) Skulpturen; Plastiken. 2 v.t. (a) (represent) skulpt[ur]ieren (geh.); bildhauerisch darstellen; (b) (shape) formen (**into** zu)

scum /skʌm/ n. (a) Schmutzschicht, die; (film) Schmutzfilm, der; **a ring of** ∿ **around the bath** ein Schmutzrand in der Badewanne; (b) no pl., no indef. art. (fig. derog.) Abschaum, der (abwertend); Auswurf, der (abwertend); **the** ∿ **of the earth/of humanity** der Abschaum der Menschheit

'scumbag n. (sl. derog.) Schwein, das (salopp)

scupper /'skʌpə(r)/ v.t. (a) (Brit. coll.) über den Haufen werfen (ugs.) ‹Plan›; **we're** ∿ed **if the police arrive** wenn die Polizei kommt, sind wir erledigt; (b) (sink) versenken ‹Schiff›

scurrilous /'skʌrɪləs/ adj. niederträchtig

scurry /'skʌrɪ/ v.i. huschen; flitzen (ugs.)

scurvy /'skɜ:vɪ/ n. (Med.) Skorbut, der

scuttle¹ /'skʌtl/ n. (coalbox) Kohlenfüller, der

scuttle² (Naut.) v.t. versenken

scuttle³ v.i. (scurry) rennen; flitzen (ugs.); ‹Maus, Krabbe:› huschen; **she** ∿d **off** sie huschte davon

scythe /saɪð/ 1 n. Sense, die. 2 v.t. [mit der Sense] mähen

SDI abbr. **strategic defence initiative** SDI

SDLP abbr. **Social Democratic and Labour Party** sozialistische Partei Nordirlands

SDP abbr. (Hist.) **Social Democratic Party**

SE /saʊθ'i:st/ abbr. ▶ 715 **south-east** SO

sea /si:/ (a) Meer, das; **the** ∿: das Meer; die See; **by** ∿: mit dem Schiff; **by the** ∿: am Meer; **at** ∿: auf See (Dat.); **be all at** ∿ (fig.) nicht mehr weiter wissen; **go to** ∿: in See stechen; (become sailor) zur See gehen (ugs.); **put [out] to** ∿: in See (Akk.) gehen od. stechen; auslaufen; (b) (specific tract of water) Meer, das; **the seven** ∿s (literary/poet.) die sieben [Welt]meere; (c) (freshwater lake) See, der; (d) in sing. or pl. (state of ∿) See, die; (wave) Welle, die; Woge, die (geh.); See, die (Seemannsspr.); (f) attrib. (of or on the ∿) Meer, das; (of drink) Strom, der; (f) attrib. (of or on the ∿) See ‹wasser, -schlacht, -karte, -wind›; Meer ‹ungeheuer, -wasser, -salz usw.›; Meeres ‹grund, -küste usw.›; (in names of marine fauna or flora) See ‹maus, -anemone, -löwe usw.›; Meer ‹brasse, -neunauge usw.›

sea: ∿ **'air** n. Seeluft, die; ∿ **a'nemone** n. (Zool.) Seeanemone, die; Seerose, die; ∿**'bed** n. Meeresboden der; Meeresgrund, der; ∿**bird** n. Seevogel, der; ∿ **breeze** n. (Meteorol.) Seewind, der; Seebrise, die; ∿**faring** /'si:feərɪŋ/ adj. ∿**faring man** Seemann, der; ∿**faring nation** Seefahrernation, die; seefahrende Nation; ∿**food** n. Meeresfrüchte Pl.; attrib. Fisch ‹restaurant›; ∿**front** n. unmittelbar am Meer gelegene Straße[n] einer Seestadt; **a walk along the** ∿**front** ein Spaziergang am Wasser od. auf der Uferpromenade; ∿**going** adj. (for crossing ∿) seegehend; ∿-**going yacht** Hochseejacht, die; ∿-**green 1** /-'-/ n. Seegrün, das; Meergrün, das; 2 /'-/ adj. seegrün; meergrün; ∿**gull** n. [See]möwe, die; ∿ **horse** n. (Zool.) Seepferdchen, das

seal¹ /si:l/ n. (Zool.) Robbe, die; [**common**] ∿: [Gemeiner] Seehund

seal² 1 n. (a) (piece of wax, lead, etc., stamp, impression) Siegel, das; (lead ∿ also) Plombe, die; (stamp also) Siegelstempel, der; Petschaft, das; (impression also) Siegelabdruck, der; (b) **set the** ∿ **on** (fig.) zementieren (+ Akk.); **gain the** ∿ **of respectability** sich (Dat.) großes Ansehen erwerben; **have the** ∿ **of official approval** offiziell gebilligt werden; (c) (to close aperture) Abdichtung, die. 2 v.t. (a) (stamp with ∿, affix ∿ to) siegeln ‹Dokument›; (fasten with ∿) verplomben, plombieren ‹Tür, Stromzähler›; (b) (close securely) abdichten ‹Behälter, Rohr usw.›; zukleben ‹Umschlag, Paket›; [zum Verschließen der Poren] kurz anbraten ‹Fleisch›; **my lips are** ∿ed (fig.) meine Lippen sind versiegelt; (c) (stop up) verschließen; abdichten ‹Leck›; verschmieren ‹Riß›; (d) (decide) besiegeln ‹Geschäft, Abmachung, jmds. Schicksal›

∿ **'in** v.t. bewahren ‹Geschmack›; am Austreten hindern ‹Fleischsaft›

∿ **'off** v.t. abriegeln

∿ **'up** ⇒ ∿ **2 b, c**

sealant /'si:lənt/ n. Dichtungsmaterial, das

sea: ∿ **legs** n. pl. Seebeine Pl. (Seemannsspr.); **get** or **find one's** ∿ **legs** sich (Dat.) Seebeine wachsen lassen (Seemannsspr.); ∿ **level** n. Meeresspiegel, der (fachspr.); **200 metres above/below** ∿ **level** 200 Meter über/unter dem Meeresspiegel od. über/unter Meereshöhe od. (fachspr.) Normalnull; **at** ∿ **level** auf Meereshöhe (Dat.)

'sealing wax n. Siegellack, der; Siegelwachs, das

'sea lion n. (Zool.) Seelöwe, der

seam /si:m/ n. (a) (line of joining) Naht, die; **come apart at the** ∿s aus den Nähten gehen; (fig. coll.: fail) zusammenbrechen; **burst at the** ∿s (fig.) aus den od. allen Nähten platzen (ugs.); (b) (fissure) Spalt, der; Spalte, die; (c) (Mining) Flöz, das; (Geol.: stratum) Schicht, die

seaman /'si:mən/ n., pl. **seamen** /'si:mən/ (a) (sailor) Matrose, der; (b) (expert in navigation etc.) Seemann, der

seamanship /'si:mənʃɪp/ n., no pl. seemännisches Geschick; Seemannschaft, die (fachspr.)

'sea-mark n. (Naut.) Seezeichen, das

seamed /si:md/ adj. ∿ **stockings** Strümpfe mit Naht

'sea mist n. Küstennebel, der

seamless /'si:mlɪs/ adj. nahtlos

seamstress /'semstrɪs/ n. Näherin, die

seamy /'si:mɪ/ adj. **the** ∿ **side** [**of life** etc.] (fig.) Schattenseite[n] [des Lebens usw.]

seance /'seɪəns/, **séance** /'seɪɑ̃s/ n. Séance, die (fachspr.); spiritistische Sitzung

sea: ∿**plane** n. Wasserflugzeug, das; ∿**port** n. Seehafen, der; ∿ **power** n. Seemacht, die

sear /sɪə(r)/ v.t. verbrennen; versengen

search /sɜ:tʃ/ 1 v.t. durchsuchen (**for** nach); absuchen ‹Gebiet, Fläche› (**for** nach); prüfend od. musternd blicken in (+ Akk.) ‹Gesicht›; (fig.: probe) erforschen ‹Herz, Gewissen›; suchen in (+ Dat.), durchstöbern (ugs.) ‹Gedächtnis› (**for** nach); ∿ **me!** (coll.) keine Ahnung! 2 v.i. suchen. 3 n. Suche, die (for nach); (of building, room, etc.) Durchsuchung, die; **make a** ∿ **for** suchen nach ‹Waffen, Drogen, Diebesgut›; **in** ∿ **of sb./sth.** auf der Suche nach jmdm./etw.

∿ **for** v.t. suchen [nach]

Seasons

In German, the seasons are always written with an article, whether there is one in English or not:

in spring, in the spring = im Frühling *or* Frühjahr
in summer, in the summer = im Sommer
in autumn, in the autumn (esp. Brit.)
in the fall (Amer.) } = im Herbst
in winter, in the winter = im Winter

All four words for the seasons in German are masculine, with the exception of the alternative term for *spring*, **das Frühjahr**. Generally this refers simply to the time of year, whereas **der Frühling** has all the connotations of rebirth etc. associated with spring, while also being the term used in astronomical contexts (there is even a third term, **der Lenz**, which occurs only in poetry).

Spring came early = Der Frühling ist früh eingetroffen
in early/late spring = zu Anfang/Ende des Frühjahrs
It's going to be a hard winter = Der Winter wird hart werden
He is staying [for] the whole summer = Er bleibt den ganzen Sommer
It lasted all summer or *throughout the summer* = Es dauerte den ganzen Sommer
She was here last winter = Sie war letzten Winter hier
They are coming this/ next autumn = Sie kommen diesen/ nächsten Herbst

Seasonal adjectives

The four adjectives in German derived from the names of the seasons are **frühlingshaft**, **sommerlich**, **herbstlich** and **winterlich**. They have the sense "typical or appropriate for the season", like the English *springlike*, *summery*, *autumnal* and *wintry* respectively, although they will also equate to some attributive uses of the noun.

winter clothing = *(worn in winter)* Winterkleidung; *(warm and thus suitable for winter)* winterliche Kleidung
summer clothing = *(worn in summer)* Sommerkleidung; *(light and thus suitable for summer)* sommerliche Kleidung
winter/summer temperatures = winterliche/sommerliche Temperaturen
a winter landscape = *(seen in winter)* eine Winterlandschaft; *(typical of winter, wintry)* eine winterliche Landschaft

---

~ 'out *v.t.* heraussuchen; aufspüren ‹*Person mit unbekanntem Aufenthalt*›
~ through *v.t.* durchsuchen; durchsehen ‹*Buch*›
'search engine *n.* (Computing) Suchmaschine, *die;* Suchroboter, *der*
searching /'sɜːtʃɪŋ/ *adj.* prüfend, forschend ‹*Blick*›; bohrend ‹*Frage*›; (thorough) eingehend ‹*Untersuchung*›
search: ~light *n.* **(a)** (lamp) Suchscheinwerfer, *der;* **(b)** (beam of light) Scheinwerferlicht, *das* (auch fig.); (fig.) Rampenlicht, *das;* **~ party** *n.* Suchtrupp, *der;* Suchmannschaft, *die;* **~ warrant** *n.* (Law) Durchsuchungsbefehl, *der*
scaring /'sɪərɪŋ/ *adj.* sengend ‹*Hitze*›; brennend ‹*Schmerz*›
sea: ~ salt *n.* Meersalz, *das;* Seesalz, *das;* **~scape** /'siːskeɪp/ *n.* (Art: picture) Seestück, *das;* Marine, *die;* **S~ Scout** *n.* (Brit.) Seepfadfinder, *der/*-pfadfinderin, *die;* **~shell** *n.* Muschel[schale], *die;* **~shore** *n.* (land near ~) [Meeres]küste, *die;* (beach) Strand, *der;* **walk along the ~shore** am Meer/Strand entlanggehen; **~sick** *adj.* seekrank; **~sickness** *n.*, *no pl.* Seekrankheit, *die;* **~side** *n.*, *no pl.* [Meeres]küste, *die;* **at** *or* **by/to the ~side** am/ans/Meer; an der/an die See; *attrib.* **~side town** Seestadt, *die*
season /'siːzn/ **1** *n.* **(a)** (time of the year) Jahreszeit, *die;* **dry/rainy ~:** Trocken-/Regenzeit, *die;* **(b)** (time of breeding) (for mammals) Tragezeit, *die;* (for birds) Brutzeit, *die;* (time of flourishing) Blüte[zeit], *die;* (time when animal is hunted) Jagdzeit, *die;* **nesting ~:** Nistzeit, *die;* Brut[zeit], *die; see also* **close season; open season; (c)** (time devoted to specified, social activity) Saison, *die;* **harvest/opera ~:** Erntezeit, *die/* Opernsaison, *die;* **football ~:** Fußballsaison, *die;* **holiday** *or* (Amer.) **vacation ~:** Urlaubszeit, *die;* Ferienzeit, *die;* **tourist ~:** Touristensaison, *die;* Reisezeit, *die;* **'the ~'s greetings'** „ein frohes Weihnachtsfest und ein glückliches neues Jahr"; **(d)** **raspberries are in/out of** *or* **not in ~:** jetzt ist die/nicht die Saison *od.* Zeit für Himbeeren; **(e)** (ticket) ⇒ **season ticket; (f)** (Theatre, Cinemat.) Spielzeit, *die. See also* **high season; low season; silly 1 a. 2** *v.t.* **(a)** (lit. or fig.) würzen ‹*Fleisch, Rede*›; **(b)** (mature) ablagern lassen ‹*Holz*›; **~ed** erfahren ‹*Wahlkämpfer, Soldat, Reisender*›

seasonable /'siːzənbl/ *adj.* der Jahreszeit gemäß
seasonal /'siːzənl/ *adj.* Saison ‹*arbeit, -geschäft*›; saisonabhängig ‹*Preise*›
seasonal af'fective disorder /'siːzənl ə'fektɪv dɪsɔː: də(r)/ *n.* saisonabhängige Depression; Winterdepression, *die*
seasoning /'siːzənɪŋ/ *n.* **(a)** (Cookery) Gewürze *Pl.;* Würze, *die;* **(b)** (fig.) Würze, *die*
'season ticket *n.* Dauerkarte, *die;* (for one year/month) Jahres-/Monatskarte, *die*
seat /siːt/ **1** *n.* **(a)** (thing for sitting on) Sitzgelegenheit, *die;* (in vehicle, cinema, etc.) Sitz, *der;* (of toilet) [Klosett]brille, *die* (ugs.); **(b)** (place) Platz, *der;* (in vehicle) [Sitz]platz, *der;* **have** *or* **take a ~:** sich [hin]setzen; Platz nehmen (geh.); **take one's ~ at table** sich zu Tisch setzen; **(c)** (part of chair) Sitzfläche, *die;* **(d)** (buttocks) Gesäß, *das;* (of trousers) Sitz, *der;* Hosenboden, *der;* **by the ~ of one's pants** (coll. fig.) nach Gefühl; **(e)** (site) Sitz, *der;* (of disease also) Herd, *der* (Med.); (of learning) Stätte, *die* (geh.); (of trouble) Quelle, *die;* **the ~ of the fire** der Brandherd, **(f)** (right to sit in Parliament etc.) Sitz, *der;* Mandat, *das;* **be elected to a ~ in Parliament** ins Parlament gewählt werden. **2** *v.t.* **(a)** (cause to sit) setzen; (accommodate at table etc.) unterbringen; (ask to sit) ‹*Platzanweiser:*› einen Platz anweisen (+ *Dat.*); **~ oneself** sich setzen; **(b)** (have ~s for) Sitzplätze bieten (+ *Dat.*); **~ 500 people** 500 Sitzplätze haben; **the car ~s five comfortably** in dem Auto haben fünf Personen bequem Platz
'seat belt *n.* (Motor Veh., Aeronaut.) Sicherheitsgurt, *der;* **fasten one's ~:** sich anschnallen; den Gurt anlegen; **wear a ~:** angeschnallt sein; (during journey) angeschnallt fahren
seated /'siːtɪd/ *adj.* sitzend; **remain ~:** sitzen bleiben; **be ~** (formal) Platz nehmen (geh.)
-seater /'siːtə(r)/ *adj. in comb.* -sitzig; **two-~ [car]** Zweisitzer, *der*
seating /'siːtɪŋ/ *n.*, *no pl.*, *no indef. art.* **(a)** (seats) Sitzplätze *Pl.;* Sitzgelegenheiten *Pl.;* **(b)** *attrib.* Sitz ‹*ordnung, -plan*›; **the ~ arrangements** die Sitzordnung
sea: ~ urchin *n.* (Zool.) Seeigel, *der;* **~ wall** *n.* Strandmauer, *die;* (dike) Deich, *der*

seaward /'si:wəd/ **1** *adj.* seewärtig ‹*Kurs, Wind*›. **2** *adv.* seewärts; nach See zu

sea: ∼ **water** *n.* Meerwasser, *das;* Seewasser, *das;* ∼**weed** *n.* [See]tang, *der;* ∼**worthy** *adj.* seetüchtig

sec /sek/ (coll.) ⇒ **second¹** 2 b

Sec. *abbr.* **Secretary** Sekr.

sec. *abbr.* **second[s]** Sek.

secateurs /sekə'tɜ:z, 'sekətɜ:z/ *n. pl.* (Brit.) Gartenschere, *die;* Rosenschere, *die*

secede /sɪ'si:d/ *v.i.* (Polit./Eccl./formal) sich abspalten (**from** von)

secession /sɪ'seʃn/ *n.* (Polit./Eccl./formal) Abspaltung, *die*

secluded /sɪ'klu:dɪd/ *adj.* **(a)** (hidden from view) versteckt; (somewhat isolated) abgelegen; **(b)** (solitary) zurückgezogen ‹*Leben*›

seclusion /sɪ'klu:ʒn/ *n., no pl.* **(a)** (keeping from company) Absonderung, *die;* (being kept from company) Abgesondertheit, *die;* **(b)** (privacy of life) Zurückgezogenheit, *die;* **(c)** (remoteness) Abgelegenheit, *die*

second¹ /'sekənd/ ▶956⌋ **1** *adj.* zweit...; zweitwichtigst... ‹*Stadt, Hafen usw.*›; ∼ **largest/highest** etc. zweitgrößt.../-höchst... *usw.;* **every** ∼ **week** jede zweite Woche; ∼ **to none** unübertroffen. **2** *n.* **(a)** ▶706⌋ (unit of time or angle) Sekunde, *die;* **(b)** (coll.: moment) Sekunde, *die* (ugs.); **wait a few** ∼**s** einen Moment warten; **in a** ∼ (immediately) sofort (ugs.); (very quickly) im Nu (ugs.); **just a** ∼**!** (coll.) einen Moment!; **(c)** (additional person or thing) **a** ∼: noch einer/eine/ eins; **(d) the** ∼ (in sequence, rank) der/die/das Zweite; **be the** ∼ **to arrive** als Zweiter/Zweite ankommen; **(e)** (in duel, boxing) Sekundant, *der*/Sekundantin, *die;* **(f)** *in pl.* (helping of food) zweite Portion; **(∼ course)** zweiter Gang; **(g)** ▶738⌋ (day) **the** ∼ **of May** der zweite Mai; **the** ∼ **[of the month]** der Zweite [des Monats]; **(h)** *in pl.* (goods of ∼ quality) Waren zweiter Wahl; **(i)** (Brit. Univ.) ≈ Gut, *das;* ≈ Zwei, *die*. **3** *v.t.* (support) unterstützen ‹*Antrag, Nominierung*›; **I'll** ∼ **that!** (coll.) dem schließe ich mich an!

second² /sɪ'kɒnd/ *v.t.* (transfer) vorübergehend versetzen

secondary /'sekəndərɪ/ *adj.* **(a)** (of less importance) zweitrangig; sekundär (geh.); Neben ‹*akzent, -sache*›; (derived from sth. primary) weiterverarbeitend ‹*Industrie*›; ∼ **literature** Sekundärliteratur, *die;* **be** ∼ **to sth.** einer Sache (*Dat.*) untergeordnet sein; **(b)** (indirectly caused) sekundär (geh., Med./Biol.)

secondary: ∼ **education** *n.* höhere Schule; (result) höhere Schulbildung; ∼ **'modern [school]** *n.* (Brit. Hist.) ≈ Mittelschule, *die* (veralt.); Realschule, *die;* ∼ **school** *n.* höhere *od.* weiterführende Schule

second: ∼**-best 1** /'---/ *adj.* zweitbest...; **2** /--'-/ *adv.* **come off** ∼**-best** den Kürzeren ziehen (ugs.); **3** /--'-/ *n., no pl.* Zweitbeste, *der/die/das;* ∼ **'childhood** ⇒ **childhood;** ∼ **'class** *n.* **(a)** zweite Kategorie; **(b)** (Transport, Post) zweite Klasse; **(c)** (Brit. Univ.) ≈ Gut, *das;* Zwei, *die;* ∼**-class 1** /'---/ *adj.* **(a)** (of lower class) zweiter Klasse *nachgestellt;* Zweiter-Klasse- ‹*Fahrkarte, Abteil, Passagier, Post, Brief usw.*›; ∼**-class stamp** Briefmarke für einen Zweiter-Klasse-Brief; **(b)** (of inferior class) zweitklassig (abwertend); ∼**-class citizen** Bürger zweiter Klasse; **2** /--'-/ *adv.* zweiter Klasse ‹*fahren*›; **send a letter** ∼**-class** einen Brief mit Zweiter-Klasse-Post schicken; ∼ **'cousin** ⇒ **cousin**

seconder /'sekəndə(r)/ *n.* Befürworter, *der*/-worterin, *die*

second: ∼ **gear** *n., no pl.* (Motor Veh.) zweiter Gang; *see also* **gear** 1 a; ∼ **hand** *n.* (Horol.) Sekundenzeiger, *der;* ∼**-hand 1** /'---/ *adj.* **(a)** gebraucht ‹*Kleidung, Auto usw.*›; antiquarisch ‹*Buch*›; ∼**-hand car** Gebrauchtwagen, *der;* **(b)** (selling used goods) Gebrauchtwaren-; Secondhand ‹*laden*›; **(c)** (obtained from sb. else) ‹*Nachrichten, Bericht*› aus zweiter Hand; **2** /--'-/ *adv.* aus zweiter Hand (auch fig.); ∼ **'home** *n.* Zweitwohnung, *die;* (holiday house) Ferienhaus, *das*

secondly /'sekəndlɪ/ *adv.* zweitens

secondment /sɪ'kɒndmənt/ *n.* (Brit.) **(a)** (of official) vorübergehende Versetzung; **(b)** (Mil.) Abstellung, *die*

second: ∼ **name** *n.* Nachname, *der;* Zuname, *der;* ∼ **'nature** *n., no pl., no art.* (coll.) zweite Natur; **become/**

be ∼ **nature to sb.** jmdm. zur zweiten Natur werden/ geworden sein; jmdm. in Fleisch und Blut (*Akk.*) übergehen/übergegangen sein; ∼**'rate** *adj.* zweitklassig; ∼**s hand** ⇒ **hand;** ∼ **sight** ⇒ **sight** 1 a; ∼ **'thoughts** *n. pl.* **have** ∼ **thoughts** es sich (*Dat.*) anders überlegen (**about** mit); **we've had** ∼ **thoughts about buying the house** wir wollen das Haus nun doch nicht kaufen; **but on** ∼ **thoughts I think I will** wenn ich mir's [noch mal] überlege, werde ich es doch tun

secrecy /'si:krɪsɪ/ *n.* **(a)** (keeping of secret) Geheimhaltung, *die;* **with great** ∼**:** in aller Heimlichkeit *od.* ganz im geheimen; **(b)** (secretiveness) Heimlichtuerei, *die* (abwertend); **(c)** (unrevealed state) Heimlichkeit, *die;* **in** ∼**:** im geheimen

secret /'si:krɪt/ **1** *adj.* **(a)** (kept private) geheim; Geheim ‹*fach, -tür, -abkommen, -kode*›; **keep sth.** ∼**:** etw. geheimhalten (**from** vor + *Dat.*); **(b)** (acting in ∼) heimlich ‹*Trinker, Liebhaber, Bewunderer*›. **2** *n.* **(a)** Geheimnis, *das;* **make no** ∼ **of sth.** kein Geheimnis aus etw. machen; (not conceal feelings, opinion) kein[en] Hehl aus etw. machen; **keep** ∼**s/a** ∼**:** schweigen (fig.); den Mund halten (ugs.); **can you keep a** ∼**?** kannst du schweigen?; **keep** ∼**s from sb.** Geheimnisse vor jmdm. haben; **be in the** ∼**:** eingeweiht sein; **open** ∼**:** offenes Geheimnis; **(b)** in ∼**:** im Geheimen; heimlich

secret 'agent *n.* Geheimagent, *der*/-agentin, *die*

secretarial /sekrə'teərɪəl/ *adj.* Sekretariats ‹*personal*›; Sekretärinnen ‹*kursus, -tätigkeit*›; ‹*Arbeit*› als Sekretärin

secretariat /sekrə'teərɪət/ *n.* Sekretariat, *das*

secretary /'sekrətərɪ/ *n.* ▶887⌋ Sekretär, *der*/Sekretärin, *die;* (of company) Schriftführer, *der*/-führerin, *die*

Secretary: ∼**-'General** *n., pl.* **Secretaries-General** Generalsekretär, *der*/-sekretärin, *die;* ∼ **of 'State** *n.* **(a)** (Brit. Polit.) Minister, *der*/Ministerin, *die;* **(b)** (Amer. Polit.) Außenminister, *der*/-ministerin, *die*

secret 'ballot *n.* geheime Abstimmung

secrete /sɪ'kri:t/ *v.t.* **(a)** (Physiol.) absondern; **(b)** (formal/ literary: hide) verbergen

secretion /sɪ'kri:ʃn/ *n.* **(a)** (Physiol.) Absonderung, *die;* (substance also) Sekret, *das* (fachspr.); **(b)** (formal/literary: concealing) Verbergen, *das*

secretive /'si:krɪtɪv/ *adj.* verschlossen ‹*Person*›; geheimnisvoll ‹*Lächeln*›; **be** ∼**:** heimlich tun (abwertend), geheimnisvoll tun (**about** mit); **she was being very** ∼ **about something** sie versuchte, irgendetwas zu verheimlichen

secretly /'si:krɪtlɪ/ *adv.* heimlich; insgeheim ‹*etw. glauben*›

Secret: ∼ **Po'lice** *n.* Geheimpolizei, *die;* ∼ **'Service** *n.* Geheimdienst, *der;* **s**∼ **so'ciety** *n.* Geheimbund, *der*

sect /sekt/ *n.* Sekte, *die*

sectarian /sek'teərɪən/ *adj.* konfessionell; konfessionell motiviert ‹*Handlungen*›; konfessionell ausgerichtet ‹*Erziehung*›; Konfessions ‹*krieg, -streit*›

section /'sekʃn/ *n.* **(a)** (part cut off) Abschnitt, *der;* Stück, *das;* (part of divided whole) Teil, *der;* (of railway track) Teilstück, *das;* [Strecken]abschnitt, *der;* **(b)** (of firm) Abteilung, *die;* (of organization etc.) Sektion, *die;* (of orchestra or band) Gruppe, *die;* **(c)** (component part) [Einzel]teil, *das;* [Bau]element, *das;* **(d)** (of chapter, book) Abschnitt, *der;* (of statute, act) Paragraph, *der;* **(e)** (part of community) Gruppe, *die*

sectional /'sekʃənl/ *adj.* Gruppen‹*interessen*›; partikular ‹*Interessen*›; ‹*Auseinandersetzung*› zwischen den Bevölkerungsgruppen

sector /'sektə(r)/ *n.* **(a)** Sektor, *der;* **the leisure/industrial** ∼**:** der Freizeitsektor/der Bereich der Industrie; **(b)** (Mil.: area) Kampfabschnitt, *der;* Gefechtsabschnitt, *der*

secular /'sekjʊlə(r)/ *adj.* säkular (geh.); weltlich ‹*Angelegenheit, Schule, Musik, Gericht*›

secure /sɪ'kjʊə(r)/ **1** *adj.* **(a)** (safe) sicher; ∼ **against burglars/fire** gegen Einbruch/Feuer geschützt; einbruch-/feuersicher; **make sth.** ∼ **from attack/enemies** etw. gegen Angriffe/Feinde sichern; **(b)** (firmly fastened) fest; **be** ∼ ‹*Ladung:*› gesichert sein; ‹*Riegel, Tür:*› fest zu sein; ‹*Tür:*› ver- *od.* zugeriegelt sein; ‹*Schraube:*› fest sein *od.* sitzen; **make sth.** ∼**:** etw. sichern; **(c)** (untroubled) sicher, gesichert ⟨*Existenz*⟩; **feel ∼:** sich sicher *od.* geborgen fühlen; **∼ in the knowledge that …:** in dem sicheren Bewusstsein, dass … **2** *v.t.* **(a)** (obtain) sichern **(for** *Dat.*); beschaffen ⟨*Auftrag*⟩ **(for** *Dat.*); (for oneself) sich (*Dat.*) sichern; **(b)** (confine) fesseln ⟨*Gefangenen*⟩; (in container) einschließen ⟨*Wertsachen*⟩; (fasten firmly) sichern, fest zumachen ⟨*Fenster, Tür*⟩; festmachen ⟨*Boot*⟩ **(to** an + *Dat.*); **(c)** (guarantee) absichern ⟨*Darlehen*⟩

securely /sɪˈkjʊəlɪ/ *adv.* **(a)** (firmly) fest ⟨*verriegeln, zumachen*⟩; sicher ⟨*befestigen*⟩; **(b)** (safely) sicher ⟨*untergebracht sein*⟩

security /sɪˈkjʊərɪtɪ/ *n.* **(a)** (safety) Sicherheit, *die;* ∼ **[measures]** Sicherheitsmaßnahmen *Pl.;* **national** ∼: nationale Sicherheit, *die;* **(b)** (thing that guarantees) Sicherheit, *die;* Gewähr, *die;* **(c)** *usu. in pl.* (Finance) Wertpapier, *das;* **securities** Wertpapiere; **(d) emotional** ∼: emotionale Sicherheit; **he needs the** ∼ **of a good home** er braucht die Geborgenheit eines guten Zuhauses

security: ∼ **check** *n.* Sicherheitskontrolle, *die;* **S**∼ **Council** *n.* (Polit.) Sicherheitsrat, *der;* ∼ **forces** *n. pl.* Sicherheitskräfte *Pl.;* ∼ **guard** *n.* ▶ 887 Wächter, *der/* Wächterin, *die;* ∼ **officer** *n.* ▶ 887 Sicherheitsbeauftragte, *der/die;* ∼ **risk** *n.* Sicherheitsrisiko, *das;* ∼ **van** *n.* gepanzerter Transporter; (for transporting money) Geldtransporter, *der*

sedan /sɪˈdæn/ *n.* **(a)** (Hist.: chair) Sänfte, *die;* **(b)** (Amer. Motor Veh.) Limousine, *die*

se'dan chair ⇨ **sedan** a

sedate /sɪˈdeɪt/ **1** *adj.* bedächtig; gesetzt ⟨*alte Dame*⟩; ruhig ⟨*Kind*⟩; gemächlich ⟨*Tempo, Leben, Auto*⟩. **2** *v.t.* (Med.) sedieren (fachspr.); ruhig stellen

sedation /sɪˈdeɪʃn/ *n.* (Med.) Sedation, *die* (fachspr.); Ruhigstellung, *die*

sedative /ˈsedətɪv/ **1** *n.* (Med.) Sedativum, *das* (fachspr.); Beruhigungsmittel, *das.* **2** *adj.* **(a)** (Med.) sedativ (fachspr.); **(b)** (fig.: calming) beruhigend ⟨*Wirkung*⟩

sedentary /ˈsedəntərɪ/ *adj.* sitzend ⟨*Haltung, Lebensweise, Tätigkeit*⟩; **lead a** ∼ **life** eine sitzende Lebensweise haben

sediment /ˈsedɪmənt/ *n.* **(a)** (matter) Ablagerung, *die;* Ablagerungen *Pl.;* **(b)** (lees) Bodensatz, *der;* (of wine also) Depot, *das* (fachspr.)

sedition /sɪˈdɪʃn/ *n.* Aufruhr, *der*

seditious /sɪˈdɪʃəs/ *adj.* aufrührerisch; staatsgefährdend ⟨*Delikt*⟩

seduce /sɪˈdjuːs/ *v.t.* **(a)** (sexually) verführen; **(b)** (lead astray) verführen; (distract) ablenken **(away from** von); ∼ **sb. into doing sth.** jmdn. dazu verführen *od.* verleiten, etw. zu tun

seducer /sɪˈdjuːsə(r)/ *n.* Verführer, *der*

seduction /sɪˈdʌkʃn/ *n.* **(a)** (sexual) Verführung, *die;* **(b)** (leading astray) Verführung, *die* **(into** zu)

seductive /sɪˈdʌktɪv/ *adj.* verführerisch; verlockend ⟨*Angebot*⟩

see /siː/ **1** *v.t.,* **saw** /sɔː/, **seen** /siːn/ **(a)** sehen; **let sb.** ∼ **sth.** (show) jmdm. etw. zeigen; **let me** ∼: lass mich mal sehen; **I saw her fall** *or* **falling** ich habe sie fallen sehen; **he was** ∼**n to leave** *or* ∼**n leaving the building** er ist beim Verlassen des Gebäudes gesehen worden; **I'll believe it when I** ∼ **it** das will ich erst mal sehen; **they saw it happen** sie haben gesehen, wie es passiert ist; **can you** ∼ **that house over there?** siehst du das Haus da drüben?; **be worth** ∼**ing** sehenswert sein; sich lohnen (ugs.); ∼ **the light** (fig.: undergo conversion) das Licht schauen (geh.); **I saw the light** (I realized my error etc.) mir ging ein Licht auf (ugs.); ∼ **things** Halluzinationen haben; **I must be** ∼**ing things** (joc.) ich glaub', ich seh' nicht richtig; ∼ **the sights/town** sich (*Dat.*) die Sehenswürdigkeiten/ Stadt ansehen; ∼ **one's way [clear] to do** *or* **to doing sth.** es einrichten, etw. zu tun; **(b)** (watch) sehen; **let's** ∼ **a film** sehen wir uns (*Dat.*) einen Film an!; **(c)** (meet [with]) sehen; treffen; (meet socially) zusammenkommen mit; sich treffen mit; **I'll** ∼ **you there/at 5** wir sehen uns dort/um 5; ∼ **you!** (coll.), **[I'll] be** ∼**ing you!** (coll.) bis bald! (ugs.); ∼ **you on Saturday/soon** bis Samstag/bald; *see also* **long**[1] **1** c; **(d)** (speak to) sprechen ⟨*Person*⟩ **(about** wegen);

(pay visit to) gehen zu, (geh.) aufsuchen ⟨*Arzt, Anwalt usw.*⟩; (receive) empfangen; **the doctor will** ∼ **you now** Herr/ Frau Doktor lässt bitten; **whom would you like to** ∼**?** wen möchten Sie sprechen?; zu wem möchten Sie?; **(e)** (discern mentally) sehen; **I** ∼ **it all!** jetzt ist mir alles klar; **I can** ∼ **it's difficult for you** ich verstehe, dass es nicht leicht für dich ist; **I** ∼ **what you mean** ich verstehe [, was du meinst]; ∼ **what I mean?** siehst du?; **I saw that it was a mistake** mir war klar, dass es ein Fehler war; **I don't** ∼ **the point of it** ich sehe keinen Sinn darin; **he didn't** ∼ **the joke** er fand es [gar] nicht lustig; (did not understand) er hat den Witz nicht verstanden; **I can't think what she** ∼**s in him** ich weiß nicht, was sie an ihm findet; **(f)** (consider) sehen; **let me** ∼ **what I can do** [ich will] mal sehen, was ich tun kann; **(g)** (foresee) sehen; **I can** ∼ **I'm going to be busy** ich sehe [es] schon [kommen], dass ich beschäftigt sein werde; **I can** ∼ **it won't be easy** ich sehe schon, dass es nicht einfach sein wird; **(h)** (find out) feststellen; (by looking) nachsehen; **that remains to be** ∼**n** das wird man sehen; ∼ **if you can read this** guck mal, ob du das hier lesen kannst (ugs.); **(i)** (take view of) sehen; betrachten; ∼ **things as sb. does** jmds. Ansichten teilen; **try to** ∼ **it my way** versuche es doch mal aus meiner Sicht zu sehen; **as I** ∼ **it** meines Erachtens; **(j)** (learn) sehen; **I** ∼ **from your letter that …:** ich entnehme Ihrem Brief, dass …; **(k)** (make sure) ∼ **[that] …:** zusehen *od.* darauf achten, dass …; **(l)** *usu. in imper.* (look at) einsehen ⟨*Buch*⟩; ∼ **below/p. 15** siehe unten/S. 15; **(m)** (experience, be witness of) erleben; **live to** ∼ **sth.** etw. miterleben; **now I've** ∼**n everything!** (iron.) hat man so etwas schon erlebt *od.* gesehen!; **we shall** ∼: wir werden [ja/schon] sehen; **he will not** *or* **never** ∼ **50 again** er ist [bestimmt] über 50; **(n)** (imagine) sich (*Dat.*) vorstellen; ∼ **sb./oneself doing sth.** sich vorstellen, dass jmd./man etw. tut; **I can** ∼ **it now** – … ich sehe es schon bildhaft vor mir – …; **(o)** (watch) mit ansehen; zusehen bei; **[stand by and]** ∼ **sb. doing sth.** [tatenlos] zusehen *od.* es [tatenlos] mit ansehen, wie jmd. etw. tut; **(p)** (escort) begleiten, bringen **(to** [bis] zu); **(q)** (consent willingly to) einsehen; **not** ∼ **oneself doing sth.** es nicht einsehen, dass man etw. tut. **2** *v.i.,* **saw, seen (a)** (discern objects) sehen; ∼ **for yourself!** sieh doch selbst!; **as far as the eye can** ∼: soweit das Auge reicht; ∼ **red** rotsehen (ugs.); **(b)** (make sure) nachsehen; **(c)** (reflect) überlegen; **let me** ∼: lass mich überlegen; warte mal ['n Moment] (ugs.); **(d) I** ∼ ich verstehe; aha (ugs.); ach so (ugs.); **you** ∼ weißt du/wisst ihr/wissen Sie; **there you are, you** ∼! Siehst du? Ich hab's doch gesagt!; **as far as I can** ∼: soweit ich das *od.* es beurteilen kann ∼ **about** *v.t.* sich kümmern um; **I've come to** ∼ **about the room/cooker** ich komme wegen des Zimmers/des Herdes

∼ **into** *v.t.* **(a)** (gain view into) [hinein]sehen in (+ *Akk.*); [rein]gucken (ugs.) in (+ *Akk.*); **(b)** (fig.: investigate) nachgehen, auf den Grund gehen (+ *Dat.*) ⟨*Angelegenheit, Klage*⟩

∼ **'off** *v.t.* **(a)** (say farewell to) verabschieden; **(b)** (chase away) vertreiben

∼ **'out 1** *v.i.* hinaussehen; rausgucken (ugs.). **2** *v.t.* **(a)** (remain till end of) ⟨*Zuschauer:*⟩ sich (*Dat.*) zu Ende ansehen ⟨*Spiel*⟩; ableisten ⟨*Amtsperiode*⟩; ⟨*Patient:*⟩ überleben ⟨*Zeitraum*⟩; **(b)** (escort from premises) hinausbegleiten **(of** aus); ∼ **oneself out** allein hinausfinden

∼ **over,** ∼ **round** *v.t.* besichtigen

∼ **through** *v.t.* **(a)** /'–/ hindurchsehen durch; durchgucken (ugs.) durch; (fig.) durchschauen; **(b)** /-'-/ (not abandon) zu Ende *od.* zum Abschluss bringen; **(c)** /-'-/ (be sufficient for) ∼ **sb. through** jmdm. reichen

∼ **to** *v.t.* sich kümmern um; **I'll** ∼ **to that** dafür werde ich sorgen; ∼ **to it that …:** dafür sorgen, dass …

seed /siːd/ **1** *n.* **(a)** (grain) Samen, *der;* Samenkorn, *das;* (of grape etc.) Kern, *der;* (for birds) Korn, *das;* (fig no pl., no indef. art.) ⟨∼s collectively) Samen[körner] *Pl.;* (for sowing) Saatgut, *das;* Saat, *die;* **grass** ∼: Grassamen *Pl.;* **go** *or* **run to** ∼: Samen bilden; ⟨*Salat:*⟩ [in Samen] schießen; (fig.) herunterkommen (ugs.); **(c)** (fig.: beginning) Saat, *die;* **sow [the]** ∼**s of doubt/discord** Zweifel aufkommen lassen/Zwietracht säen; **(d)** (Sport coll.) gesetzter Spieler/gesetzte Spielerin. **2** *v.t.* **(a)** (place ∼s in) besäen; **(b)** (Sport) setzen ⟨*Spieler*⟩; **be**

~ed **number one** als Nummer eins gesetzt werden/sein; **(c)** (lit. or fig.: sprinkle [as] with ~) besäen. **3** v.i. (produce ~s) Samen bilden

seed: ~**bed** n. **(a)** (Hort.) [Saat]beet, das; **(b)** (fig.: place of development) Grundlage, die; ~ **cake** n. Kümmelkuchen, der; ~**corn** n. Saatgetreide, das; Saatkorn, das

seedless /'si:dlɪs/ adj. kernlos

seedling /'si:dlɪŋ/ n. Sämling, der

seedy /'si:dɪ/ adj. **(a)** (coll.: unwell) **feel** ~: sich [leicht] angeschlagen fühlen; **(b)** (shabby) schäbig, (ugs. abwertend) vergammelt ‹Aussehen, Kleidung›; heruntergekommen ‹Stadtteil›; **(c)** (disreputable) zweifelhaft ‹Person›

seeing /'si:ɪŋ/ **1** conj. ~ [that] …: da …; wo … (ugs.). **2** n. ~ **is believing** so was glaubt man erst, wenn man es gesehen hat

seek /si:k/ v.t., **sought** /sɔ:t/ **(a)** suchen; anstreben ‹Posten, Amt›; sich bemühen um ‹Anerkennung, Freundschaft, Interview, Einstellung›; (try to reach) aufsuchen; **(b)** (literary/formal: attempt) suchen (geh.); versuchen; ~ **to do sth.** suchen, etw. zu tun (geh.)

~ **after** v.t. suchen nach; **be much sought after** sehr gesucht sein

~ **for** v.t. suchen nach

~ '**out** v.t. ausfindig machen ‹Sache, Ort›; aufsuchen, kommen zu ‹Personen›

seem /si:m/ v.i. **(a)** (appear [to be]) scheinen; **you** ~ **tired** du wirkst müde; **she** ~**s nice** sie scheint nett zu sein; **it's not quite what it** ~**s** es ist nicht ganz das, was es [zunächst] zu sein scheint; **it** ~**s like only yesterday** es ist, als wäre es erst gestern gewesen; **he** ~**s certain to win** es sieht ganz so aus, als würde er gewinnen; **what** ~**s to be the trouble?** wo fehlt's denn? **I** ~ **to recall having seen him before** ich glaube mich zu erinnern, ihn schon einmal gesehen zu haben; **it** ~**s [that]** …: anscheinend …; **it would** ~ **to be** …: es scheint ja wohl … zu sein; **so it** ~**s** or **would** ~: so will es scheinen; **(b) sb. can't** ~ **to do sth.** (coll.) jmd. scheint etw. nicht tun zu können; **she doesn't** ~ **to notice such things** (coll.) so was merkt sie irgendwie nicht (ugs.)

seeming /'si:mɪŋ/ adj. scheinbar

seemingly /'si:mɪŋlɪ/ adv. **(a)** (evidently) offensichtlich; **(b)** (to outward appearance) scheinbar

seemly /'si:mlɪ/ adj. anständig; **it isn't** ~ **to praise oneself** es gehört sich nicht, sich selbst zu loben

seen ⇒ **see**

seep /si:p/ v.i. ~ **[away]** [ab]sickern; ~ **in through sth.** durch etw. hineinsickern; ~ **out of sth.** aus etw. heraussickern

seer /sɪə(r)/ n. (prophet) Seher, der/Seherin, die

'**see-saw 1** n. **(a)** (plank) Wippe, die; **(b)** no art. (game) Wippen, das; **(c)** (fig.: contest) Auf und Ab, das. **2** v.i. ‹Weg, Straße:› auf und ab führen; ‹Deck:› [auf und ab] schaukeln

seethe /si:ð/ v.i. **(a)** (surge) ‹Wellen, Meer:› branden; ‹Straßen usw.:› wimmeln **(with** von); (bubble or foam as if boiling) schäumen; **(b)** (fig.: be agitated) ~ **[with anger/inwardly]** vor Wut/innerlich schäumen

'**see-through** adj. durchsichtig

segment /'segmənt/ n. (of orange, pineapple) Scheibe, die; (of cake, pear) Stück, das; (of worm, skull, limb) Segment, das; (of economy, market) Bereich, der

segregate /'segrɪgeɪt/ v.t. **(a)** trennen; isolieren ‹Kranke›; aussondern ‹Forschungsgebiet›; **(b)** (racially) segregieren (geh.); absondern

segregation /segrɪ'geɪʃn/ n., no pl. **(a)** Trennung, die; **(b)** [**racial**] ~: Rassentrennung, die

seismic /'saɪzmɪk/ adj. seismisch

seize /si:z/ v.t. **(a)** ergreifen; ~ **power** die Macht ergreifen; ~ **sb. by the arm/collar/shoulder** jmdn. am Arm/ Kragen/an der Schulter packen; ~ **the opportunity** or **occasion/moment [to do sth.]** die Gelegenheit ergreifen/den günstigen Augenblick nutzen [und etw. tun]; ~ **any/a** or **the chance [to do sth.]** jede/die Gelegenheit nutzen[, um etw. zu tun]; **be** ~**d with remorse/panic** von Gewissensbissen geplagt/von Panik ergriffen werden; **(b)** (capture) gefangen nehmen ‹Person›; kapern ‹Schiff›; mit Gewalt übernehmen ‹Flugzeug, Gebäude›; einnehmen

‹Festung, Brücke›; **(c)** (confiscate) beschlagnahmen

~ **on** v.t. sich (Dat.) vornehmen ‹Einzelheit, Aspekt, Schwachpunkt›; aufgreifen ‹Idee, Vorschlag›; ergreifen ‹Chance›

~ '**up** v.i. sich festfressen; ‹Verkehr:› zusammenbrechen, zum Erliegen kommen

~ **upon** ⇒ ~ **on**

seizure /'si:ʒə(r)/ n. **(a)** (capturing) Gefangennahme, die; (of ship) Kapern, das; (of aircraft, building) Übernahme, die; (of fortress, bridge) Einnahme, die; ~ **of power** Machtergreifung, die; **(b)** (confiscation) Beschlagnahme, die; **(c)** (Med.: attack) Anfall, der

seldom /'seldəm/ adv. selten; ~ **or never** so gut wie nie; ~, **if ever** fast nie; äußerst selten

select /sɪ'lekt/ **1** adj. **(a)** (carefully chosen) ausgewählt; **(b)** (exclusive) exklusiv. **2** v.t. auswählen; ~ **one's own apples** sich (Dat.) die Äpfel selbst aussuchen

select com'mittee n. Sonderkommission, die

selection /sɪ'lekʃn/ n. **(a)** (what is selected [from]) Auswahl, die (**of** an + Dat., **from** aus); (person) Wahl, die; **a** ~ **from** … (Mus.) eine Auswahl aus …; **make a** ~ (one) eine Wahl treffen; (several) eine Auswahl treffen; ~**s from the best writers** ausgewählte Werke der besten Schriftsteller; **(b)** (act of choosing) [Aus]wahl, die; ~ **committee** Auswahlkomitee, das; **(c)** (being chosen) Wahl, die; **his** ~ **as president** seine Wahl zum Präsidenten

selective /sɪ'lektɪv/ adj. (using selection) selektiv; (careful in one's choice) wählerisch

selectively /sɪ'lektɪvlɪ/ adv. selektiv; **shop** ~: gezielt einkaufen

selector /sɪ'lektə(r)/ n. **(a)** (person who selects team) Mannschaftsaufsteller, der/-aufstellerin, die; **(b)** (knob) Schaltknopf, der; (switch) Wahlschalter, der

self /self/ n., pl. **selves** /selvz/ (person's essence) Selbst, das (geh.); Ich, das; **be your usual** ~: seien Sie [einfach] Sie selbst; **be back to one's former** or **old** ~ **[again]** wieder der/die Alte sein; **one's better** ~: sein besseres Ich

self- in comb. selbst-/Selbst-

self: ~-**absorbed** adj. mit sich selbst beschäftigt; ~-**ab'sorption** n. Mit-sich-selbst-beschäftigt-Sein, das; ~-**ad'dressed** adj. a ~-**addressed envelope** ein adressierter Rückumschlag; ~-**ad'hesive** adj. selbstklebend; ~-**ap'pointed** adj. selbst ernannt; ~-**as'surance** n., no pl. Selbstbewusstsein, das; Selbstsicherheit, die; ~-**as'sured** adj. selbstsicher; selbstbewusst; ~**a'wareness** n. Selbsterkenntnis, die; ~-'**catering 1** adj. mit Selbstversorgung nachgestellt; **2** n. Selbstversorgung, die; ~-**con'fessed** adj. erklärt; ~-'**confidence** n., no pl. Selbstvertrauen, das; ~-'**confident** adj., ~-'**confidently** adv. selbstsicher; ~-'**conscious** adj. **(a)** (ill at ease) unsicher; **(b)** (deliberate) reflektiert ‹Prosa, Stil›; ~-'**consciousness** n. **(a)** Unsicherheit, die; **(b)** (deliberateness) Reflektiertheit, die; ~-**con'tained** adj. **(a)** (not dependent) selbstgenügsam; **(b)** (Brit.: complete in itself) abgeschlossen ‹Wohnung›; ~-**contra'dictory** adj. mit sich selbst im Widerspruch stehend; ~-**con'trol** n., no pl. Selbstbeherrschung, die; ~-**con'trolled** adj. beherrscht; ~-'**critical** adj. selbstkritisch; ~-**de'ception** n. Selbsttäuschung, die; ~-**de'feating** adj. unsinnig; zwecklos; ~-**de'fence** n., no pl., no indef. art. Notwehr, die; Selbstverteidigung, die; **in** ~-**defence** aus od. in Notwehr; ~-**de'lusion** n. Selbsttäuschung, die; ~-**deprecating** /self 'deprɪkeɪtɪŋ/ adj. bescheiden; ~-**de'structive** adj. selbstzerstörerisch; ~-'**discipline** n., no pl. Selbstdisziplin, die; ~-**drive** adj. ~-**drive hire [company]** Autovermietung, die; ~-**drive vehicle** Mietwagen, der; ~-**ef'facing** adj. zurückhaltend; ~-**em'ployed** adj. selbstständig; ~-**employed man/woman** Selbstständige, der/die; ~-**e'steem** n. Selbstachtung, die; ~-'**evident** adj., ~-'**evidently** adv. offenkundig; ~-**ex'planatory** adj. ohne weiteres verständlich; **be** ~-**explanatory** für sich selbst sprechen; ~-**ex'pression** n., no pl., no indef. art. Selbstdarstellung, die; ~-**ful'filling** adj. zur eigenen Bestätigung mit beitragend; ~-**fulfilling prophecy** zur Bestätigung ihrer selbst mitbeitragende Voraussage; Selffulfilling Prophecy, die

(Soziol.); **~-'governing** *adj.* selbstverwaltet; **~-'help** *n., no pl.* Selbsthilfe, *die;* **~-im'portance** *n., no pl.* Selbstgefälligkeit, *die;* (arrogant and pompous bearing) Selbstherrlichkeit, *die;* **~-im'portant** *adj.* selbstgefällig; (arrogant and pompous) selbstherrlich; **~-im'posed** *adj.* selbst auferlegt; **~-in'dulgence** *n.* Maßlosigkeit, *die;* **~-in'dulgent** *adj.* maßlos; **~-in'flicted** *adj.* selbst beigebracht ⟨*Wunde*⟩; selbst auferlegt ⟨*Strafe*⟩; **~-'interest** *n.* Eigeninteresse, *das*

selfish /'selfɪʃ/ *adj.* egoistisch; selbstsüchtig

selfishness /'selfɪʃnɪs/ *n., no pl.* Egoismus, *der;* Selbstsucht, *die*

selfless /'selflɪs/ *adj.* selbstlos

self: ~-'loading *adj.* mit Selbstladevorrichtung *nachgestellt;* **~-'loathing** *n.* Selbstverachtung, *die;* **be consumed by deep ~-loathing** eine tiefe Abscheu gegen sich selbst empfinden; **~-'locking** *adj.* selbstschließend; **~-made** *adj.* selbst gemacht; **a ~-made man** ein Selfmademan; **she is a ~-made woman** sie hat sich aus eigener Kraft hochgearbeitet; **~-'mockery** *n.* Selbstverspottung, *die;* **~-'mocking** *adj.* selbstspöttisch; **~-'motivated** *adj.* von sich aus motiviert; selbstmotiviert ⟨*Lernen*⟩; **~-moti'vation** *n.* Motiviertheit, *die;* [innere] Motivation; **~-ob'sessed** *adj.* ich-besessen; **~-o'pinionated** *adj.* (a) (conceited) eingebildet; von sich eingenommen; **(b)** (obstinate) starrköpfig, rechthaberisch; **~-'pity** *n., no pl.* Selbstmitleid, *das;* **~-'pitying** *adj.* selbstmitleidig; **~-'portrait** *n.* Selbstporträt, *das;* **~-pos'sessed** *adj.* selbstbeherrscht; **~-preser'vation** *n., no pl., no indef. art.* Selbsterhaltung, *die;* **~-'raising flour** *n.* (Brit.) mit Backpulver versetztes Mehl; **~-re'liant** *adj.* selbstbewusst; selbstsicher; **~-re'spect** *n., no pl.* Selbstachtung, *die;* **~-re'specting** *adj.* mit Selbstachtung *nachgestellt;* **no ~-respecting person ...:** niemand, der etwas auf sich hält, ...; **~-re'straint** *n., no pl.* Selbstbeherrschung, *die;* **~-'righteous** *adj.* selbstgerecht; **~-'righteousness** *n., no pl.* Selbstgerechtigkeit, *die;* **~-'sacrifice** *n.* Selbstaufopferung, *die;* **~-'sacrificing** *adj.* [sich] aufopfernd ⟨*Mutter, Vater*⟩; aufopfernd ⟨*Liebe*⟩; **~-same** *adj.* **the ~same** der-/die-/dasselbe; **~-'satisfied** *adj.* selbstzufrieden; (smug) selbstgefällig; **~-'seeking** *adj.* selbstsüchtig; **~-'service** *n.* Selbstbedienung, *die; attrib.* Selbstbedienungs-; **~-styled** *adj.* selbst ernannt; **~-suf'ficiency** *n.* Unabhängigkeit, *die;* (of country) Autarkie, *die;* **~-suf'ficient** *adj.* (independent) unabhängig; autark ⟨*Land*⟩; selb[st]ständig ⟨*Person*⟩; **~-sup'porting** *adj.* sich selbst tragend ⟨*Unternehmen, Verein*⟩; finanziell unabhängig ⟨*Person*⟩; **the club is ~-supporting** der Verein trägt sich selbst; **~-'tapping** *adj.* selbstschneidend ⟨*Schraube*⟩; **~-'taught** *adj.* autodidaktisch; selbst erlernt ⟨*Fertigkeiten*⟩; **~-taught person** Autodidakt, *der*/Autodidaktin, *die;* **she is ~-taught** sie ist Autodidaktin; **~-'will** *n., no pl.* Eigensinn, *der;* **~-willed** /self'wɪld/ *adj.* eigensinnig

sell /sel/ 1 *v.t.,* **sold** /səʊld/ (a) verkaufen; **the shop ~s groceries** in dem Laden gibt es Lebensmittel [zu kaufen]; **~ sth. to sb., ~ sb. sth.** jmdm. etw. verkaufen; **~ by ...** (on package) ≈ mindestens haltbar bis ...; **(b)** (betray) verraten; **(c)** (offer dishonourably) verkaufen; verhökern (ugs. abwertend); **~ oneself/one's soul** sich/seine Seele verkaufen (**to** *Dat.*); **(d)** (coll.: cheat, disappoint) verraten; anschmieren (salopp); **I've been sold!, sold again!** ich bin [wieder] der/die Dumme (ugs.); **(e)** (gain acceptance for) **~ sb. as ...:** jmdn. als ... verkaufen (ugs.); **~ sth. to sb.** jmdn. für etw. gewinnen; **~ sb. the idea of doing sth.** jmdn. für den Gedanken gewinnen, etw. zu tun; **(f) ~ sb. on sth.** (coll.: make enthusiastic) jmdn. für etw. begeistern *od.* erwärmen; **be sold on sth.** (coll.) von etw. begeistert sein. 2 *v.i.,* **sold** (a) sich verkaufen [lassen]; ⟨*Person:*⟩ verkaufen; **the book sold 5,000 copies in a week** in einer Woche wurden 5 000 Exemplare des Buches verkauft; **(b) ~ at** *or* **for** kosten. *See also* **river** 1 a

~ 'off *v.t.* verkaufen; abstoßen ⟨*Anteile, Aktien*⟩

~ 'out 1 *v.t.* (a) ausverkaufen; **the play/performance was sold out** das Stück/die Aufführung war ausverkauft; **(b)** (coll.: betray) verpfeifen (ugs.). 2 *v.i.* (a) **we have** *or* **are sold out** wir sind ausverkauft; **(b)** (coll.: betray one's cause)

~ out to sb./sth. zu jmdm./etw. überlaufen

~ 'out of *v.t.* **we have** *or* **are sold out of sth.** etw. ist ausverkauft

~ 'up *v.t.* (Brit.) verkaufen; *abs.* sein Hab und Gut verkaufen

'sell-by date *n.* ≈ Mindesthaltbarkeitsdatum, *das*

seller /'selə(r)/ *n.* (a) Verkäufer, *der*/Verkäuferin, *die;* **a ~'s** *or* **~s' market** ein Verkäufermarkt; **(b)** (product) **be a slow/bad ~:** sich nur langsam/schlecht verkaufen; **be a good ~:** sich gut verkaufen

selling /'selɪŋ/ *n.* (a) (act, occupation) Verkaufen, *das;* **(b)** (salesmanship) Verkauf, *der*

selling: ~ point *n.* **a** [good] **~ point** ein Verkaufsargument; (fig.) ein Pluspunkt; **~ price** *n.* Verkaufspreis, *der*

Sellotape, (P) /'seləʊteɪp/ *n., no pl., no indef. art.* Klebeband, *der;* ≈ Tesafilm, *der* Ⓦ

sellotape *v.t.* mit Klebeband kleben

'sell-out *n.* (a) (event) **be a ~:** ausverkauft sein; **(b)** (coll.: betrayal) Verrat, *der*

selves *pl. of* **self**

semantic /sɪ'mæntɪk/ *adj.* semantisch

semantics /sɪ'mæntɪks/ *n., no pl.* Semantik, *die*

semaphore /'seməfɔː(r)/ 1 *n.* (system) Winken, *das.* 2 *v.i.* **~ to sb.** jmdm. ein Winksignal übermitteln

semblance /'sembləns/ *n.* Anschein, *der;* **without a ~ of regret/a smile** ohne das geringste Zeichen von Bedauern/den Anflug eines Lächelns; **bring some ~ of order to sth.** wenigstens den Anschein von Ordnung in etw. (*Akk.*) bringen

semen /'siːmen/ *n.* (Physiol.) Samen, *der;* Sperma, *das*

semester /sɪ'mestə(r)/ *n.* (Univ.) Semester, *das*

semi /'semɪ/ *n.* (Brit. coll.: house) Doppelhaushälfte, *die*

semi- *in comb.* halb-/Halb-

semi: ~-bold *adj.* (Printing) halbfett; **~breve** *n.* (Brit. Mus.) ganze Note; **~circle** *n.* Halbkreis, *der;* **~circular** *adj.* halbkreisförmig; **~'colon** *n.* Semikolon, *das;* **~conductor** *n.* (Phys.) Halbleiter, *der;* **~'conscious** *adj.* halb bewusstlos; **~-de'tached** 1 *adj.* **the house is ~-detached** es ist eine Doppelhaushälfte; **a ~-detached house** eine Doppelhaushälfte; 2 *n.* (Brit.: house) Doppelhaushälfte, *die;* **~-'final** *n.* Halbfinale, *das;* **in the ~-finals** im Halbfinale; **~-'finalist** *n.* Halbfinalteilnehmer, *der*/-teilnehmerin, *die;* Halbfinalist, *der*/-finalistin, *die;* **~-literate** *adj.* **be ~-literate** kaum lesen und schreiben können

seminal /'semɪnl/ *adj.* (strongly influencing later developments) schöpferisch

seminar /'semɪnɑː(r)/ *n.* Seminar, *das*

semi: ~-precious *adj.* **~-precious stone** Halbedelstein, *der;* **~quaver** *n.* (Brit. Mus.) Sechzehntelnote, *die;* **~-skilled** *adj.* angelernt; **~-skimmed** 1 *adj.* teilentrahmt; 2 *n.* teilentrahmte Milch; **~tone** *n.* (Mus.) Halbton, *der*

semolina /semə'liːnə/ *n.* Grieß, *der*

Sen. *abbr.* **(a) Senator** Sen.; **(b) Senior** sen.

senate /'senət/ *n.* Senat, *der*

senator /'senətə(r)/ *n.* ▶ 1152 | Senator, *der*/Senatorin, *die*

send /send/ *v.t.,* **sent** /sent/ **(a)** (cause to go) schicken; senden (geh.); **~ sb. to boarding school/university** jmdn. ins Internat/auf die Universität schicken; **~ sb. on a course/tour** jmdn. in einen Kurs/auf eine Tour schicken; **she ~s her best wishes/love** sie lässt grüßen/ herzlich grüßen; **~** [sb.] **apologies/congratulations** sich [bei jmdm.] entschuldigen lassen/[jmdm.] seine Glückwünsche übermitteln; **~ sb. home/to bed** jmdn. nach Hause/ins Bett schicken; *see also* **word** 1 f; **(b)** (propel) **~ a rocket into space** eine Rakete in den Weltraum schießen; **~ up clouds of dust** Staubwolken aufwirbeln; **~ sb. sprawling/reeling** jmdn. zu Boden strecken/ins Wanken bringen; *see also* **fly²** 1 c; **(c) ~ sb. mad** *or* **crazy** jmdn. verrückt machen (ugs.); **~ sb. to sleep** jmdn. zum Einschlafen bringen

~ a'head *v.t.* vorausschicken

~ a'way 1 *v.t.* wegschicken. 2 *v.i.* **~ away [to sb.] for**

sth. etw. [bei jmdm.] anfordern

~ 'back v.t. (a) (return) zurückschicken; (b) (because of dissatisfaction) zurückgehen lassen ‹ Speise, Getränk ›; (by post) zurückschicken ‹ Ware ›

~ 'down v.t. [hinunter]schicken

~ for v.t. (a) (tell to come) holen lassen; rufen ‹ Polizei, Arzt, Krankenwagen ›; (b) (order from elsewhere) anfordern

~ 'in v.t. einschicken

~ 'off 1 v.t. (a) (dispatch) abschicken ‹ Sache ›; losschicken (ugs.) ‹ Person ›; (b) (bid farewell to) verabschieden; (c) (Sport) vom Platz stellen (**for** wegen). **2** v.i. **~ off for sth.** [to sb.] etw. [von jmdm.] anfordern

~ 'on v.t. (a) (forward) nachsenden ‹ Post ›; (b) **~ sb. on [ahead]** jmdn. vorausschicken; (c) (Sport) **~ a player on** einen Spieler einsetzen

~ 'out 1 v.t. (a) (issue) verschicken; (b) (emit) aussenden ‹ Hilferuf, Nachricht ›; abgeben ‹ Hitze ›; senden ‹ Lichtstrahlen ›; ausstoßen ‹ Rauch ›; (c) (dispatch) schicken; **~ sb. out for sth.** jmdn. schicken, um etw. zu besorgen; (d) (order to leave) hinausschicken. **2** v.i. **~ out for sth.** etw. besorgen od. holen lassen

~ 'up v.t. (a) (Brit. coll.: parody) parodieren; (b) (cause to rise) steigen lassen ‹ Ballon ›; hochtreiben ‹ Preis, Kosten, Temperatur ›; **~ sb.'s temperature up** (fig. joc.) jmdn. zum Kochen bringen (ugs.)

sender /'sendə(r)/ n. (of goods) Lieferant, der/Lieferantin, die; (of letter) Absender, der/Absenderin, die

send: ~-off n. Verabschiedung, die; **~-up** n. (Brit. coll.: parody) Parodie, die; **do a ~-up** parody of sb./sth. jmdn./etw. parodieren

senile /'si:naıl/ adj. senil; (physically) altersschwach

senility /sɪ'nɪlɪtɪ/ n., no pl. Senilität, die; (physical infirmity) Altersschwäche, die

senior /'si:nıə(r)/ **1** adj. (a) (older) älter; **be ~ to sb.** älter als jmd. sein; (b) (of higher rank) höher ‹ Rang, Beamter, Stellung ›; leitend ‹ Angestellter, Stellung ›; (longest-serving) ältest ...; **someone ~:** jemand in höherer Stellung; **be ~ to sb.** eine höhere Stellung als jmd. haben; **~ manager** obere Führungskraft; **~ management** oberer Führungskreis; (c) appended to name (the elder) **Mr Smith S~:** Mr. Smith senior; (d) (Amer. Sch., Univ.) **~ class** Abschlussklasse, die; **~ year** letztes Jahr vor der Abschlussprüfung. **2** n. (older person) Ältere, der/die; (person of higher rank) Vorgesetzte, der/die; **be sb.'s ~ [by six years]** or **[six years] sb.'s ~:** [sechs Jahre] älter als jmd. sein

senior 'citizen n. Senior, der/Seniorin, die

seniority /si:nɪ'ɒrɪtɪ/ n. (a) (superior age) Alter, das; (b) (priority in length of service) höheres Dienstalter; (c) (superior rank) höherer Rang

senior: ~ 'officer n. höherer Beamter/höhere Beamtin; (Mil.) ranghöchster Offizier; **~ 'partner** n. Seniorpartner, der/-partnerin, die; **~ school** (Brit.) ⇒ **secondary school**

sensation /sen'seɪʃn/ n. (a) (feeling) Gefühl, das; **~ of giddiness** Schwindelgefühl, das; **have a ~ of falling** das Gefühl haben zu fallen; (b) (person, event) Sensation, die; **a great ~:** ein großes Ereignis; (c) (excitement) Aufsehen, das

sensational /sen'seɪʃənl/ adj. (a) (spectacular) Aufsehen erregend; sensationell; (b) (provocative) reißerisch (abwertend); Sensations‹ blatt, -presse ›; (c) (phenomenal) phänomenal

sensationalise ⇒ **sensationalize**

sensationalism /sen'seɪʃənəlɪzm/ n. Sensationshascherei, die (abwertend); [desire for] **~:** Sensationsgier, die (abwertend)

sensationalist /sen'seɪʃənəlɪst/ adj. sensationslüstern (abwertend); sensationsgeil (ugs. abwertend); Sensations‹ blatt, -presse, usw. ›; **~ nonsense** um der Sensation willen verbreiteter Unsinn

sensationalize /sen'seɪʃənəlaɪz/ v.t. **~ sth.** etw. zur Sensation aufbauschen

sense /sens/ **1** n. (a) (faculty of perception) Sinn, der; **~ of smell/touch/taste** Geruchs-/Tast-/Geschmackssinn, der; **come to one's ~s** das Bewusstsein wiedererlangen; (b) in pl. (normal state of mind) Verstand, der; **have taken leave**

of one's **~s** den Verstand verloren haben; **come to one's ~s** zur Vernunft kommen; **bring sb. to his ~s** jmdn. zur Vernunft od. Besinnung bringen; (c) (consciousness) Gefühl, das; **~ of responsibility/guilt** Verantwortungs-/Schuldgefühl, das; **out of a ~ of duty** aus Pflichtgefühl; (d) (practical wisdom) Verstand, der; **there's a lot of ~ in what he's saying** was er sagt, klingt sehr vernünftig; **have the ~ to do sth.** so vernünftig sein, etw. zu tun; **what is the ~ of** or **in doing that?** was hat man davon od. wozu soll es gut sein, das zu tun?; **talk ~:** vernünftig reden; **now you are talking ~:** jetzt wirst du vernünftig; **see ~:** zur Vernunft kommen; **make sb. see ~:** jmdn. zur Vernunft bringen; see also **common sense; good 1** l; (e) (meaning) Sinn, der; (of word) Bedeutung, die; **in the strict** or **literal ~:** im strengen od. wörtlichen Sinn; **in every ~ [of the word]** in jeder Hinsicht; **in some ~:** irgendwie; **in a** or **one ~:** in gewisser Hinsicht od. Weise; **make ~:** einen Sinn ergeben; **her arguments do not make ~ to me** ihre Argumente leuchten mir nicht ein; **it does not make ~ to do that** es ist Unsinn od. unvernünftig, das zu tun; **it makes [a lot of] ~** (is [very] reasonable) es ist [sehr] sinnvoll; **it all makes ~ to me now** jetzt verstehe ich alles; **it just doesn't make ~:** es ergibt einfach keinen Sinn; **make ~ of sth.** etw. verstehen. **2** v.t. spüren; ‹ Tier: › wittern

senseless /'senslɪs/ adj. (a) (unconscious) bewusstlos; (b) (foolish) unvernünftig; dumm; (c) (purposeless) unsinnig ‹ Argument ›; sinnlos ‹ Diskussion, Vergeudung ›

sensibilities /sensɪ'bɪlɪtɪz/ n. pl. (susceptibility) Empfindlichkeit, die; **her ~ are easily wounded** sie ist sehr schnell gekränkt

sensible /'sensɪbl/ adj. (a) (reasonable) vernünftig; (b) (practical) praktisch; zweckmäßig; fest ‹ Schuhe ›

sensibly /'sensɪblɪ/ adv. (a) (reasonably) vernünftig; besonnen; **~ enough, he refused** er war so vernünftig abzulehnen; (b) (practically) zweckmäßig

sensitise ⇒ **sensitize**

sensitive /'sensɪtɪv/ adj. (a) (responsive) empfindlich (**to** gegen); **~ to light** lichtempfindlich; (b) (easily upset) empfindlich; sensibel; **be ~ to sth.** empfindlich auf etw. (Akk.) reagieren; **sb. is ~ about sth.** etw. ist bei jmdm. ein wunder Punkt; (c) heikel ‹ Thema, Diskussion ›; (d) (perceptive) einfühlsam

sensitivity /sensɪ'tɪvɪtɪ/ n. ⇒ **sensitive:** Empfindlichkeit, die; Sensibilität, die; Heikelkeit, die; Einfühlsamkeit, die; **~ to light** Lichtempfindlichkeit, die

sensitize /'sensɪtaɪz/ v.t. sensibilisieren (**to** für)

sensor /'sensə(r)/ n. Sensor, der

sensory /'sensərɪ/ adj. sensorisch; Sinnes‹ wahrnehmung, -organ ›

sensual /'sensjʊəl, 'senʃʊəl/ adj. sinnlich; lustvoll ‹ Leben ›; Sinnen ‹ freude, -genuss ›

sensuous /'sensjʊəs/ adj. sinnlich

sent ⇒ **send**

sentence /'sentəns/ **1** n. (a) (decision of lawcourt) [Straf]urteil, das; (fig.) Strafe, die; **pass ~ [on sb.]** [jmdm.] das Urteil verkünden; **be under ~ of death** zum Tode verurteilt sein; (b) (Ling.) Satz, der. **2** v.t. (lit. or fig.) verurteilen (**to** zu)

'sentence-modifier n. (Ling.) Satzpartikel, die

sentiment /'sentɪmənt/ n. (a) (mental feeling) Gefühl, das; (b) (emotion conveyed in art) Empfindung, die; (c) no pl. (emotional weakness) Sentimentalität, die

sentimental /sentɪ'mentl/ adj. sentimental; **sth. has ~ value [for sb.]** jmd. hängt an etw. (Dat.); **for ~ reasons** aus Sentimentalität

sentinel /'sentɪnl/ n. (lit. or fig.) Wache, die

sentry /'sentrɪ/ n. (lit. or fig.) Wache, die

'sentry box n. Wachhäuschen, das

separable /'sepərəbl/ adj. (a) trennbar; zerlegbar ‹ Werkzeug, Gerät ›; (b) (Ling.) trennbar

separate 1 /'sepərət/ adj. verschieden ‹ Fragen, Probleme ›; getrennt ‹ Konten, Betten ›; gesondert ‹ Teil ›; separat ‹ Eingang, Toilette, Blatt Papier, Abteil ›; Sonder‹ vereinbarung ›; (one's own, individual) eigen ‹ Zimmer, Identität, Organisation ›; **lead ~ lives** getrennt leben; **go ~**

ways getrennte Wege gehen; **keep two things** ~: zwei Dinge auseinander halten; **keep issue A** ~ **from issue B** Frage A und Frage B getrennt behandeln. **2** /'separeɪt/ *v.t.* trennen; **they are** ~**d** (no longer live together) sie leben getrennt. **3** /'separeɪt/ *v.i.* (a) (disperse) sich trennen; (b) ⟨*Ehepaar:*⟩ sich trennen

separately /'separətlɪ/ *adv.* getrennt

separates /'separəts/ *n. pl.* (Fashion) Separates *Pl.*; einzelne Kleidungsstücke [, die man kombinieren kann]

separation /sepə'reɪʃn/ *n.* Trennung, *die*

separatist /'separətɪst/ *n.* Separatist, *der*/Separatistin, *die; attrib.* ~ **movement** Separatistenbewegung, *die*

sepia /'si:pɪə/ *n.* (a) (pigment) Sepia, *die;* (b) (colour) Sepia-braun, *das*

Sept. *abbr.* **September** Sept.

September /sep'tembə(r)/ *n.* ▶**738**| September, *der; see also* **August**

septic /'septɪk/ *adj.* septisch

septic 'tank *n.* Faulraum, *der*

sepulchre (*Amer.:* **sepulcher**) /'seplkə(r)/ *n.* Grab, *das*

sequel /'si:kwl/ *n.* (a) (consequence, result) Folge, *die* (**to** von); (b) (continuation) Fortsetzung, *die;* **there was a tragic** ~: es gab ein tragisches Nachspiel

sequence /'si:kwəns/ *n.* (a) (succession) Reihenfolge, *die;* **rapid/logical** ~: rasche/logische Abfolge; (b) (part of film) Sequenz, *die*

sequestered /sɪ'kwestəd/ *adj.* abgelegen; ⟨*Leben*⟩ in Abgeschiedenheit

sequin /'si:kwɪn/ *n.* Paillette, *die*

Serb /sɜ:b/ ⇒ **Serbian**

Serbia /'sɜ:bɪə/ *pr. n.* Serbien (*das*)

Serbian /'sɜ:brən/ ▶**897**|, ▶**947**| **1** *adj.* serbisch; **sb. is** ~: jmd. ist Serbe/Serbin. **2** *n.* (a) (language) Serbisch, *das;* (b) (person) Serbe, *der*/Serbin, *die; see also* **English 2 a**

Serbo-Croat /sɜ:bəʊ'krəʊæt/, **Serbo-Croatian** /sɜ:bəʊkrəʊ'eɪʃn/ ▶**947**| **1** *adj.* serbokroatisch. **2** *n.* Serbokroatisch, *das; see also* **English 2 a**

serenade /serə'neɪd/ **1** *n.* (song) Ständchen, *das;* (orchestral work) Serenade, *die* **2** *v.t.* ~ **sb.** jmdm. ein Ständchen bringen

serene /sɪ'ri:n/ *adj.,* ~**r** /sɪ'ri:nə(r)/, ~**st** /sɪ'ri:nɪst/ (a) (placid) ruhig; gelassen; (b) (calm) klar ⟨*Wetter, Himmel*⟩; (unruffled) unbewegt ⟨*See, Wasser usw.*⟩

serenity /sɪ'renɪtɪ, sə'renɪtɪ/ *n., no pl.* (a) (placidity) Gelassenheit, *die;* (b) (of clear weather) Klarheit, *die*

serge /sɜ:dʒ/ *n.* (Textiles) Serge, *die*

sergeant /'sɑ:dʒənt/ *n.* ▶**1152**| (a) (Mil.) Unteroffizier, *der;* (b) (police officer) ≈ Polizeimeister, *der*

sergeant 'major *n.* ▶**1152**| ≈ [Ober]stabsfeldwebel, *der*

serial /'sɪərɪəl/ *n.* Fortsetzungsgeschichte, *die;* (on radio, television) Serie, *die*

serialize /'sɪərɪəlaɪz/ *v.t.* in Fortsetzungen veröffentlichen; (on radio, television) in Fortsetzungen *od.* als Serie senden

serial 'killer *n.* Serienmörder, *der*/-mörderin, *die*

serial: ~ **mo'nogamy** *n.* serielle Monogamie; ~ **number** *n.* Seriennummer, *die*

series /'sɪərɪ:z, 'sɪərɪz/ *n., pl.* same (a) (sequence) Reihe, *die;* **a** ~ **of events/misfortunes** eine Folge von Ereignissen/Missgeschicken; (b) (set of successive issues) Serie, *die;* **radio/TV** ~: Hörfunkreihe/Fernsehserie, *die;* ~ **of programmes** Sendereihe, *die;* (c) (set of books) Reihe, *die;* (d) (group of stamps, games, etc.) Serie, *die;* (e) (Electr.) **in** ~: in Reihe

serious /'sɪərɪəs/ *adj.* (a) (earnest) ernst; ~ **music** ernste Musik; **a** ~ **play** ein ernstes Stück; (b) (important, grave) ernst ⟨*Angelegenheit, Lage, Problem, Zustand*⟩; ernsthaft ⟨*Frage, Einwand, Kandidat*⟩; gravierend ⟨*Änderung*⟩; schwer ⟨*Krankheit, Unfall, Fehler, Verstoß, Niederlage*⟩; ernst zu nehmend ⟨*Rivale*⟩; ernstlich ⟨*Gefahr, Bedrohung*⟩; bedenklich ⟨*Verschlechterung, Mangel*⟩; schwerwiegend ⟨*Vorwurf*⟩; **things are/sth. is getting** ~: die Lage spitzt sich zu/etw. nimmt ernste Ausmaße an; **there is a** ~ **danger that …**: es besteht ernste Gefahr, dass …; (c) (in earnest) **are you** ~? ist das dein Ernst?; **be**

~ **about sth./doing sth.** etw. ernst nehmen/ernsthaft tun wollen; **is he** ~ **about her?** meint er es ernst mit ihr?

seriously /'sɪərɪəslɪ/ *adv.* (a) (earnestly) ernst[haft]; **quite** ~, …: ganz im Ernst, …; **take sth./sb.** ~: etw./jmdn. ernst nehmen; (b) (severely) ernstlich; schwer ⟨*verletzt*⟩

seriousness /'sɪərɪəsnɪs/ *n., no pl.* (a) (earnestness) Ernst, *der;* Ernsthaftigkeit, *die;* **in all** ~: ganz im Ernst; (b) (gravity) Schwere, *die;* (of situation) Ernst, *der*

sermon /'sɜ:mən/ *n.* (Relig.) Predigt, *die;* **give a** ~: eine Predigt halten

serpent /'sɜ:pənt/ *n.* (a) (snake) Schlange, *die;* (b) (fig.: treacherous person) falsche Schlange

SERPS /sɜ:ps/ *abbr.* (Brit.) **State earnings-related pension scheme** staatliche einkommensbezogene Rentenversicherung

serrated /se'reɪtɪd/ *adj.* gezackt; ~ **knife** Sägemesser, *das*

serum /'sɪərəm/ *n., pl.* **sera** /'sɪərə/ *or* ~**s** (Physiol.) Serum, *das*

servant /'sɜ:vənt/ *n.* Diener, *der*/Dienerin, *die;* (female also) Dienstmädchen, *das;* **keep** *or* **have** ~**s** Bedienstete haben

'servant girl *n.* Dienstmädchen, *das*

serve /sɜ:v/ **1** *v.t.* (a) (work for) dienen (+ *Dat.*); (b) (be useful to) dienlich sein (+ *Dat.*); **this car** ~**d us well** dieses Auto hat uns gute Dienste getan; **if my memory** ~**s me right** wenn mich mein Gedächtnis nicht täuscht; (c) (meet needs of) nutzen (+ *Dat.*); ~ **a/no purpose** einen Zweck erfüllen/keinen Zweck haben; ~ **its purpose** *or* **turn** seinen Zweck erfüllen; (d) (go through period of) durchlaufen ⟨*Lehre*⟩; absitzen, verbüßen ⟨*Haftstrafe*⟩; ~ **[one's] time** (undergo apprenticeship) seine Lehrzeit durchmachen; (undergo imprisonment) seine Zeit absitzen; (e) (dish up) servieren; (pour out) einschenken (**to** *Dat.*); **dinner is** ~**d** das Essen ist aufgetragen; (f) (render obedience to) dienen (+ *Dat.*) ⟨*Gott, König, Land*⟩; (g) (attend) bedienen; **are you being** ~**d?** werden Sie schon bedient?; (h) (supply) versorgen; ~**s three** (in recipe) für drei Personen *od.* Portionen; (i) (provide with food) bedienen; (j) (make legal delivery of) zustellen; ~ **a summons on sb.** jmdn. vorladen; **he has been** ~**d notice to quit** ihm ist gekündigt worden; (k) (Tennis etc.) aufschlagen; ~ **an ace** ein Ass schlagen; (l) ~**[s]** *or* **it** ~**s him right!** (coll.) [das] geschieht ihm recht! **2** *v.i.* (a) (do service) dienen; ~ **as chairman** das Amt des Vorsitzenden innehaben; ~ **on a jury** Geschworener/Geschworene sein; (b) (be employed; be soldier etc.) dienen; (c) (be of use) ~ **to do sth.** dazu dienen, etw. zu tun; ~ **to show sth.** etw. zeigen; ~ **for** *or* **as** dienen als; (d) (~ food) **shall I** ~? soll ich auftragen?; (e) (attend in shop etc.) bedienen; (f) (Eccl.) ministrieren; (g) (Tennis etc.) aufschlagen; **it's your turn to** ~: du hast Aufschlag. **3** *n.* ⇒ **service 1 h**

serve 'up *v.t.* (a) (put before eaters) servieren; (b) (offer for consideration) auftischen (ugs.)

server /'sɜ:və(r)/ *n.* (Computing) Server, *der*

service /'sɜ:vɪs/ **1** *n.* (a) (doing of work for employer etc.) Dienst, *der;* **give good** ~: gute Dienste leisten; **do** ~ **as sth.** als etw. dienen; **he died in the** ~ **of his country** er starb in Pflichterfüllung für sein Vaterland; (b) (sth. done to help others) **do sb. a** ~: jmdm. einen guten Dienst erweisen; ~**s** Dienste; (Commerc.) Dienstleistungen; **[in recognition of her]** ~**s to the hospital/state** [in Anerkennung ihrer] Verdienste um das Krankenhaus/den Staat; (c) (Eccl.) Gottesdienst, *der;* (d) (act of attending to customer) Service, *der;* (in shop, garage, etc.) Bedienung, *die;* (e) (system of transport) Verbindung, *die;* **there is no bus** ~ **on Sundays** sonntags verkehren keine Busse; **the number 325 bus** ~: die Buslinie Nr. 325; (f) (provision of maintenance) **[after-sale** *or* **follow-up]** ~: Kundendienst, *der;* **take one's car in for a** ~: sein Auto zur Inspektion bringen; (g) *no pl., no art.* (operation) Betrieb, *der;* **bring into** ~: in Betrieb nehmen; **out of** ~: außer Betrieb; **take out of** ~: außer Betrieb setzen; **go** *or* **come into** ~: in Betrieb genommen werden; (h) (Tennis etc.) Aufschlag, *der;* **whose** ~ **is it?** wer hat Aufschlag?; (i) (crockery set) Service, *das;* **dessert/tea** ~: Dessert-/Tee-Service, *das;* (j) (assistance) **can I be of** ~ **[to you]?** kann ich Ihnen behilflich sein?;

(k) (person's behalf) **in his** ∼: in seinem Auftrag; **I'm at your** ∼: ich stehe zu Ihren Diensten; **(l) the consular** ∼: der Konsulatsdienst; **BBC World S**∼: BBC Weltsender; **public** ∼: öffentlicher Dienst; **(m)** *in pl.* (Brit.: electricity, gas, water) Versorgungseinrichtungen; **(n)** (Mil.) **the** [**armed** *or* **fighting**] ∼**s** die Streitkräfte; **in the** ∼**s** beim Militär; **(o)** (being servant) **be in/go into** ∼: in Stellung sein/gehen (veralt.) **(with** bei). **2** *v.t.* **(a)** (provide maintenance for) warten ⟨*Wagen, Waschmaschine, Heizung*⟩; **take one's car to be** ∼**d** sein Auto zur Inspektion bringen; **(b)** (pay interest on) Zinsen zahlen für ⟨*Schulden*⟩

serviceable /'sɜːvɪsəbl/ *adj.* **(a)** (useful) nützlich; **(b)** (durable) haltbar

service: ∼ **area** *n.* (for motorists' needs) Raststätte, *die;* ∼ **charge** *n.* (in restaurant) Bedienungsgeld, *das;* (of bank) Bearbeitungsgebühr, *die;* ∼ **industry** *n.* Dienstleistungsindustrie, *die;* ∼**man** *n.* (in armed services) Militärangehörige, *der;* ∼ **station** *n.* Tankstelle, *die*

serviette /sɜːvɪ'et/ *n.* (Brit.) Serviette, *die*

servile /'sɜːvaɪl/ *adj.* unterwürfig; erbärmlich ⟨*Furcht, Unterwürfigkeit*⟩

serving /'sɜːvɪŋ/ *n.* Portion, *die*

serving: ∼ **dish** *n.* Servierschüssel, *die;* ∼ **hatch** *n.* Durchreiche, *die;* ∼ **spoon** *n.* Vorlegelöffel, *der*

servitude /'sɜːvɪtjuːd/ *n., no pl.* (lit. or fig.) Knechtschaft, *die*

session /'seʃn/ *n.* **(a)** (meeting) Sitzung, *die;* discussion ∼: Diskussionsrunde, *die;* **be in** ∼: tagen; **(b)** (period spent) Sitzung, *die;* (by several people) Treffen, *das;* **recording** ∼: Aufnahme, *die*

set /set/ **1** *v.t.* **-tt-, set (a)** (put) (horizontally) legen; (vertically) stellen; ∼ **sb. ashore** jmdn. an Land setzen; ∼ **the proposals before the board** (fig.) dem Vorstand die Vorschläge unterbreiten *od.* vorlegen; ∼ **sth. against sth.** (balance) etw. einer Sache (*Dat.*) gegenüberstellen; **(b)** (apply) setzen; ∼ **pen to paper** etwas zu Papier bringen; ∼ **a match to sth.** ein Streichholz an etw. (*Akk.*) halten; **(c)** (adjust) einstellen (**at** auf + *Akk.*); aufstellen ⟨*Falle*⟩; stellen ⟨*Uhr*⟩; ∼ **the alarm for 5.30 a.m.** den Wecker auf 5.30 Uhr stellen; **(d) be** ∼ (have location of action) ⟨*Buch, Film:*⟩ spielen; ∼ **a book/film in Australia** ein Buch/einen Film in Australien spielen lassen; **(e)** (specify) festlegen ⟨*Bedingungen*⟩; festsetzen ⟨*Termin, Ort usw.*⟩ (**for** auf + *Akk.*); ∼ **the interest rate at 10 %** die Zinsen auf 10 % festsetzen; ∼ **limits** Grenzen setzen; **(f)** (bring into specified state) ∼ **sth./things right** *or* **in order** etw./die Dinge in Ordnung bringen; ∼ **sb. laughing** jmdn. zum Lachen bringen; ∼ **a dog barking** einen Hund anschlagen lassen; ∼ **sb. thinking that** …: jmdn. auf den Gedanken bringen, dass …; **the news** ∼ **me thinking** die Nachricht machte mich nachdenklich; **(g)** (put forward) stellen ⟨*Frage, Aufgabe*⟩; aufgeben ⟨*Hausaufgabe*⟩; vorschreiben ⟨*Textbuch, Lektüre*⟩; (compose) zusammenstellen ⟨*Rätsel, Fragen*⟩; ∼ **sb. a task/problem** jmdm. eine Aufgabe stellen/jmdn. vor ein Problem stellen; ∼ [**sb./oneself**] **a target** /jmdm./sich] ein Ziel setzen; **(h)** (turn to solid) fest werden lassen; **is the jelly** ∼ **yet?** ist das Gelee schon fest?; **(i)** (lay for meal) decken ⟨*Tisch*⟩; auflegen ⟨*Gedeck*⟩; **(j)** (establish) aufstellen ⟨*Rekord, Richtlinien*⟩; **(k)** (Med.: put into place) [ein]richten; einrenken ⟨*verrenktes Gelenk*⟩; **(l)** (fix) legen ⟨*Haare*⟩; ∼ **eyes on sb./sth.** jmdn./etw. sehen; **(m)** (Printing) setzen; **(n)** ∼ **sb. in charge of sth.** jmdn. mit etw. betrauen; ∼ **a dog on sb.** einen Hund auf jmdn. hetzen; ∼ **the police after sb.** die Polizei auf jmdn. hetzen; ∼ **sb. against sb.** jmdn. gegen jmdn. aufbringen; **(o) be** ∼ **on a hill** ⟨*Haus:*⟩ auf einem Hügel stehen. **2** *v.i.* **-tt-, set (a)** (solidify) fest werden; **has the jelly** ∼ **yet?** ist das Gelee schon fest?; **(b)** (go down) ⟨*Sonne, Mond:*⟩ untergehen. **3** *n.* **(a)** (group) Satz, *der;* ∼ [**of two**] Paar, *das;* **a** ∼ **of chairs** eine Sitzgruppe; **a complete** ∼ **of Dickens' novels** eine Gesamtausgabe der Romane von Dickens; **chess** ∼: Schachspiel, *das;* **(b)** ⇒ **service 1 i;** **(c)** (section of society) Kreis, *der;* **racing** ∼: Rennsportfreunde *od.* -fans; **the fast** ∼: die Lebewelt; **(d)** (Math.) Menge, *die;* **(e)** ∼ [**of teeth**] Gebiss, *das;* **(f)** (radio or TV receiver) Gerät, *das;* Apparat, *der;* **(g)** (Tennis) Satz, *der;* **(h)** (of hair) Frisieren, *das;* Einlegen, *das;* **(i)** (Theatre, Cinemat.:

built-up scenery) Szenenaufbau, *der;* Dekoration, *die;* **(j)** (acting area for film) **on the** ∼ bei den Dreharbeiten. **4** *adj.* **(a)** (fixed) starr ⟨*Linie, Gewohnheit, Blick, Lächeln*⟩; fest ⟨*Absichten, Zielvorstellungen, Zeitpunkt*⟩; **be** ∼ **in one's ways** *or* **habits** in seinen Gewohnheiten festgefahren sein; **deep-**∼ **eyes** tief liegende Augen; **(b)** (assigned for study) vorgeschrieben ⟨*Buch, Text*⟩; **be a** ∼ **book** Pflichtlektüre sein; **(c)** (according to fixed menu) ∼ **meal** *or* **menu** Menü, *das;* **(d)** (ready) **sth. is** ∼ **to increase** etw. wird bald steigen; **be/get** ∼ **for sth.** zu etw. bereit sein/sich zu etw. fertig machen; **be/get** ∼ **to leave** bereit sein/sich fertig machen zum Aufbruch; **all** ∼**?** (coll.) alles klar *od.* fertig?; **be all** ∼ **to do sth.** bereit sein, etw. zu tun; **(e)** (determined) **be** ∼ **on sth./doing sth.** zu etw. entschlossen sein/entschlossen sein, etw. zu tun; **be** [**dead**] ∼ **against sth.** [absolut] gegen etw. sein

∼ **about** *v.t.* **(a)** (begin purposefully) ∼ **about sth.** sich an etw. (*Akk.*) machen; etw. in Angriff nehmen; ∼ **about doing sth.** sich daranmachen, etw. zu tun; **(b)** (coll.: attack) herfallen über (+ *Akk.*)

∼ **a'part** *v.t.* **(a)** (reserve) reservieren; einplanen ⟨*Zeit*⟩; **(b)** (make different) abheben (**from** von)

∼ **a'side** *v.t.* **(a)** (put to one side) beiseite legen ⟨*Buch, Zeitung, Strickzeug*⟩; beiseite stellen ⟨*Stuhl, Glas usw.*⟩; unterbrechen ⟨*Arbeit, Tätigkeit*⟩; außer Acht lassen ⟨*Frage*⟩; (postpone) aufschieben ⟨*Arbeit*⟩; **(b)** (cancel) aufheben ⟨*Urteil, Entscheidung*⟩; **(c)** (pay no attention to) außer acht lassen ⟨*Unterschiede, Formalitäten*⟩; **(d)** (reserve) aufheben ⟨*Essen, Zutaten*⟩; einplanen ⟨*Minute, Zeit*⟩; beiseite legen ⟨*Geld*⟩; (save for customer) zurücklegen ⟨*Ware*⟩

∼ '**back** *v.t.* **(a)** (hinder progress of) behindern ⟨*Fortschritt*⟩; aufhalten ⟨*Entwicklung*⟩; zurückwerfen ⟨*Projekt, Programm*⟩; **(b)** (coll.: be an expense to) ∼ **sb. back a fair amount** jmdn. eine hübsche Summe kosten; **(c)** (place at a distance) zurücksetzen; **the house is** ∼ **back some distance from the road** das Haus steht in einiger Entfernung von der Straße; **(d)** (postpone) verschieben ⟨*Termin*⟩ (**to** auf + *Akk.*)

∼ '**by** ⇒ ∼ **aside a, d**

∼ '**down** *v.t.* **(a)** absetzen ⟨*Fahrgast, Ladung*⟩; **the bus will** ∼ **you down there** du kannst dort aus dem Bus aussteigen; **(b)** (record on paper) niederschreiben; **(c)** (place on surface) absetzen; abstellen

∼ '**forth 1** *v.i.* (begin journey) aufbrechen; ∼ **forth on a journey** eine Reise antreten. **2** *v.t.* (present) darstellen ⟨*Zahlen, Kosten*⟩; darlegen ⟨*Programm, Ziel, Politik*⟩

∼ '**in** *v.i.* ⟨*Dunkelheit, Regen, Reaktion, Verfall:*⟩ einsetzen

∼ '**off 1** *v.i.* (begin journey) aufbrechen; (start to move) loslaufen; ⟨*Zug:*⟩ losfahren; ∼ **off for work** sich auf den Weg zur Arbeit machen. **2** *v.t.* **(a)** (show to advantage) hervorheben; **(b)** (start) führen zu; auslösen ⟨*Reaktion, Alarmanlage*⟩; **(c)** (cause to explode) explodieren lassen; abbrennen ⟨*Feuerwerk*⟩; **(d)** (counterbalance) ausgleichen; ∼ **sth. off against sth.** etw. einer Sache (*Dat.*) gegenüberstellen

∼ **on** *v.t.* (attack) überfallen

∼ '**out 1** *v.i.* **(a)** (begin journey) aufbrechen; **(b)** ∼ **out to do sth.** sich (*Dat.*) vornehmen, etw. zu tun. **2** *v.t.* **(a)** (present) darlegen ⟨*Gedanke, Argument*⟩; auslegen ⟨*Waren*⟩; ausbreiten ⟨*Geschenke*⟩; aufstellen ⟨*Schachfiguren*⟩; **(b)** (state, specify) darlegen ⟨*Bedingungen, Einwände, Vorschriften*⟩

∼ '**to** *v.i.* **(a)** (begin vigorously) sich daranmachen; **(b)** (begin to fight) loslegen (ugs.)

∼ '**up 1** *v.t.* **(a)** (erect) errichten ⟨*Straßensperre, Denkmal*⟩; aufstellen ⟨*Kamera*⟩; aufbauen ⟨*Zelt, Spieltisch*⟩; **(b)** (establish) bilden ⟨*Regierung usw.*⟩; gründen ⟨*Gesellschaft, Organisation, Orden*⟩; aufbauen ⟨*Kontrollsystem, Verteidigung*⟩; einleiten ⟨*Untersuchung*⟩; einrichten ⟨*Büro*⟩; ∼ **oneself up in business** ein Geschäft aufmachen; ∼ **sb. up in business** jmdm. die Gründung eines eigenen Geschäfts ermöglichen; **(c)** (begin to utter) anstimmen; **the class** ∼ **up such a din** die Klasse veranstaltete einen solchen Lärm; **(d)** (coll.: make stronger) stärken; **a good breakfast should** ∼ **you up for the day** ein gutes Frühstück gibt dir Kraft für den ganzen Tag; **(e)** (achieve) aufstellen ⟨*Rekord, Zeit*⟩; **(f)** (provide adequately) ∼ **sb. up with sth.** jmdn. mit etw. versorgen; **(g)** (place in view) anbringen ⟨*Schild, Warnung*⟩; **(h)** (prepare) vorbereiten ⟨*Experiment*⟩; betriebsbereit machen ⟨*Maschine*⟩. **2** *v.i.* ∼ **up in business** ein Geschäft aufmachen; ∼ **up as a dentist** sich als Zahnarzt niederlassen

set: ∼**back** *n.* Rückschlag, *der;* Niederlage, *die;* ∼ **phrase** *n.* feste Wendung; Phrase, *die;* ∼ **'piece** *n.* (Footb.) Standardsituation, *die;* ∼ **point** *n.* (Tennis etc.) Satzball, *der*

settee /se'ti:/ *n.* Sofa, *das*

setting /'setɪŋ/ *n.* **(a)** (Mus.) Vertonung, *die;* **(b)** (frame for jewel) Fassung, *die;* **(c)** (surroundings) Rahmen, *der;* (of novel etc.) Schauplatz, *der;* **(d)** (plates and cutlery) Gedeck, *das*

settle /'setl/ **1** *v.t.* **(a)** (place) (horizontally) [sorgfältig] legen; (vertically) [sorgfältig] stellen; (at an angle) [sorgfältig] lehnen; **he** ∼**d himself comfortably on the couch** er machte es sich (*Dat.*) auf der Couch bequem; **(b)** (establish) (in house or business) · unterbringen; (in country or colony) ansiedeln ⟨*Volk*⟩; **(c)** (determine, resolve) aushandeln, sich einigen auf ⟨*Preis*⟩; beilegen ⟨*Streit, Konflikt, Meinungsverschiedenheit*⟩; beseitigen, ausräumen ⟨*Zweifel, Bedenken*⟩; entscheiden ⟨*Frage, Spiel*⟩; regeln, in Ordnung bringen ⟨*Angelegenheit*⟩; **nothing has been** ∼**d as yet** es ist noch nichts entschieden; **that** ∼**s it** dann ist ja alles klar (ugs.); *expr.* **exasperation** jetzt reicht's! (ugs.); ∼ **a case out of court** sich außergerichtlich vergleichen; ∼ **one's affairs** seine Angelegenheiten in Ordnung bringen; seinen Nachlass regeln; **(d)** (deal with, dispose of) fertig werden mit; **(e)** bezahlen, (geh.) ausgleichen ⟨*Rechnung, Betrag*⟩; erfüllen ⟨*Forderung, Anspruch*⟩; ausgleichen ⟨*Konto*⟩; **(f)** (cause to sink) sich absetzen lassen ⟨*Bodensatz, Sand, Sediment*⟩; **a shower will** ∼ **the dust** ein Schauer wird den Staub binden; **(g)** (calm) beruhigen ⟨*Nerven, Magen*⟩; **(h)** (colonize) besiedeln; **(i)** (bestow) ∼ **money/property on sb.** jmdm. Geld/Besitz übereignen. **2** *v.i.* **(a)** (become established) sich niederlassen; (as colonist) sich ansiedeln; **(b)** (end dispute) sich einigen; **(c)** (pay what is owed) abrechnen; **(d)** (in chair etc.) sich niederlassen; (to work etc.) sich konzentrieren **(to auf** ⊦ *Akk.*); (into way of life etc.) sich gewöhnen **(into an** + *Akk.*); **the snow/dust** ∼**d on the ground** der Schnee blieb liegen/der Staub setzte sich [am Boden] ab; **darkness/silence/fog** ∼**d over the village** Dunkelheit/Stille/Nebel legte od. senkte sich über das Dorf; **(e)** (subside) ⟨*Haus, Fundament, Boden:*⟩ sich senken; ⟨*Sediment:*⟩ sich ablagern; **(f)** (be digested) ⟨*Essen:*⟩ sich setzen; (become calm) ⟨*Magen:*⟩ sich beruhigen; **(g)** (become clear) ⟨*Wein, Bier:*⟩ sich klären

∼ **'back** *v.i.* **(a)** (relax) sich zurücklehnen **(in** in + *Dat.*); **(b)** ∼ **back into one's routine** sich wieder in die Alltagsroutine hineinfinden

∼ **'down** **1** *v.i.* **(a)** (make oneself comfortable) sich niederlassen **(in** in + *Dat.*); ∼ **down for the night** sich schlafen od. zur Ruhe legen; **(b)** (become established in a town or house) sesshaft od. heimisch werden; ∼ **down in a job** (find permanent work) eine feste Anstellung finden; (get used to a job) sich einarbeiten; **(c)** (marry) **it's about time he** ∼**d down** er sollte allmählich häuslich werden [und heiraten]; **(d)** (calm down) ⟨*Person:*⟩ sich beruhigen; ⟨*Lärm, Aufregung:*⟩ sich legen; ∼ **down to work** richtig mit der Arbeit anfangen. **2** *v.t.* **(a)** (make comfortable) ∼ **oneself down** sich [gemütlich] hinsetzen; ∼ **the baby down for the night/ to sleep** das Baby schlafen legen; **(b)** (calm down) beruhigen

∼ **for** *v.t.* **(a)** (agree to) sich zufrieden geben mit; **(b)** (decide on) sich entscheiden für

∼ **'in** *v.i.* (in new home) sich einleben; (in new job or school) sich eingewöhnen

∼ **on** *v.t.* **(a)** (decide on) sich entscheiden für; **(b)** (agree on) sich einigen auf (+ *Akk.*).

∼ **'up** *v.i.* abrechnen; ∼ **up with the waiter** beim Kellner bezahlen

∼ **with** *v.t.* ∼ **with sb.** (pay agreed amount to sb.) jmdm. eine Abfindung zahlen; (pay all the money owed to sb.) bei jmdm. seine Rechnung begleichen

settled /'setld/ *adj.* vorausbestimmt ⟨*Zukunft*⟩; beständig ⟨*Wetter*⟩; geregelt ⟨*Lebensweise*⟩; **I don't feel** ∼ **in this house/job** ich kann mich in diesem Haus nicht heimisch fühlen/in diese Arbeit nicht hineinfinden

settlement /'setlmənt/ *n.* **(a)** Entscheidung, *die;* (of price) Einigung, *die;* (of argument, conflict, etc.) Beilegung, *die;* (of

problem) Lösung, *die;* (of question) Klärung, *die;* (of affairs) Regelung, *die;* (of court case) Vergleich, *der;* **reach a** ∼**:** zu einer Einigung kommen; **reach a** ∼ **out of court** sich außergerichtlich vergleichen; **(b)** (of bill, account, etc.) Bezahlung, *die;* Begleichung, *die;* **(c)** (Law: bestowal) Zuwendung, *die;* (in will) Legat, *das* (fachspr.); Vermächtnis, *das;* **(d)** (colony) Siedlung, *die;* (colonization) Besiedlung, *die*

settler /'setlə(r)/ *n.* Siedler, *der*/Siedlerin, *die*

set: ∼**-to** /'setu:/ *n., pl.* ∼**-tos** Streit, *der;* ∼**-tos** Streitereien; (with fists) Prügeleien; **have a** ∼**-to** Streit haben; (with fists) sich prügeln; ∼**-up** *n.* (coll.) **(a)** (organization) System, *das;* (structure) Aufbau, *der;* **(b)** (situation) Zustand, *der;* **what's the** ∼**-up here?** wie läuft das hier? (ugs.)

seven /'sevn/ ▶630⏌, ▶706⏌, ▶956⏌ **1** *adj.* sieben; *see also* **eight 1**. **2** *n.* Sieben, *die; see also* **eight 2** a, c, d

seventeen /sevn'ti:n/ ▶630⏌, ▶706⏌, ▶956⏌ **1** *adj.* siebzehn; *see also* **eight 1**. **2** *n.* Siebzehn, *die; see also* **eight 2** a; **eighteen 2**

seventeenth /sevn'ti:nθ/ ▶738⏌, ▶956⏌ **1** *adj.* siebzehnt...; *see also* **eighth 1**. **2** *n.* (fraction) Siebzehntel, *das; see also* **eighth 2**

seventh /'sevnθ/ ▶738⏌, ▶956⏌ **1** *adj.* sieb[en]t...; *see also* **eighth 1**. **2** *n.* ▶956⏌ (in sequence, rank) Sieb[en]te, *der/ die/das;* (fraction) Sieb[en]tel, *das; see also* **eighth 2**

seventieth /'sevntɪθ/ ▶956⏌ **1** *adj.* siebzigst...; *see also* **eighth 1**. **2** *n.* (fraction) Siebzigstel, *das; see also* **eighth 2**

seventy /'sevntɪ/ ▶630⏌, ▶956⏌ **1** *adj.* siebzig; *see also* **eight 1**. **2** *n.* Siebzig, *die; see also* **eight 2** a; **eighty 2**

seventy: ∼**-eight** *n.* (record) Achtundsiebziger[platte], *die;* ∼**-first** *etc. adj.* ▶956⏌ einundsiebzigst... *usw.; see also* **eight 1**; ∼**-one** *etc.* ▶956⏌ **1** *adj.* einundsiebzig *usw.; see also* **eight 1**; **2** *n.* Einundsiebzig *usw., die; see also* **eight 2** a

sever /'sevə(r)/ *v.t.* **(a)** (cut) durchtrennen; (fig.: break off) abbrechen ⟨*Beziehungen, Verbindung*⟩; **(b)** (separate with force) abtrennen; (with axe etc.) abhacken

several /'sevrl/ **1** *adv.* **(a)** (a few) mehrere; einige; ∼ **times** mehrmals; mehrere od. einige Male; ∼ **more copies** noch einige Exemplare mehr; **(b)** (separate, diverse) verschieden. **2** *pron.* einige; ∼ **of us** einige von uns; ∼ **of the buildings** einige od. mehrere [der] Gebäude

severance /'sevərəns/ *n.* (of diplomatic relations) Abbruch, *der;* (of communications) Unterbrechung, *die; attrib.* ∼ **pay** Abfindung, *die*

severe /sɪ'vɪə(r)/ *adj.,* ∼**r** /sɪ'vɪərə(r)/, ∼**st** /sɪ'vɪərɪst/ **(a)** (strict) streng; hart ⟨*Urteil, Strafe, Kritik*⟩; **be** ∼ **on** *or* **with sb.** streng mit jmdm. sein od. umgehen; **(b)** (violent, extreme) streng ⟨*Frost, Winter*⟩; schwer ⟨*Sturm, Dürre, Verlust, Behinderung, Verletzung*⟩; rau ⟨*Wetter*⟩; heftig ⟨*Anfall, Schmerz*⟩; **(c)** (making great demands) hart ⟨*Test, Prüfung, Konkurrenz*⟩; **(d)** (serious, not slight) bedrohlich ⟨*Mangel, Knappheit*⟩; heftig, stark ⟨*Blutung*⟩; schwer ⟨*Krankheit*⟩; **(e)** (unadorned) streng ⟨*Stil, Schönheit, Dekor*⟩

severely /sɪ'vɪəlɪ/ *adv.* hart; hart, streng ⟨*bestrafen*⟩; schwer ⟨*verletzt, behindert*⟩; **be** ∼ **critical of sth.** etw. scharf kritisieren

severity /sɪ'verɪtɪ/ *n.* Strenge, *die;* (of drought, shortage) großes Ausmaß; (of criticism) Schärfe, *die*

sew /səʊ/ **1** *v.t., p.p.* ∼**n** /səʊn/ *or* ∼**ed** /səʊd/ nähen; ∼ **together** zusammennähen ⟨*Stoff, Leder usw.*⟩. **2** *v.i., p.p.* ∼**n** *or* ∼**ed** nähen

∼ **'on** *v.t.* annähen ⟨*Knopf*⟩; aufnähen ⟨*Abzeichen, Band*⟩

∼ **'up** *v.t.* **(a)** nähen ⟨*Saum, Naht, Wunde*⟩; **they** ∼**ed me up after the operation** (coll.) nach der Operation haben sie mich wieder zugenäht; **(b)** (Brit. fig. coll.: settle, arrange) **be** ∼ **up** unter Dach und Fach sein; (completely organized) durchorganisiert sein

sewage /'sju:ɪdʒ, 'su:ɪdʒ/ *n.* Abwasser, *das*

sewage: ∼ **disposal** *n.* Abwasserbeseitigung, *die;* ∼ **farm** *n.,* ∼ **works** *n. sing., pl. same* Kläranlage, *die*

sewer /'sju:ə(r), 'su:ə(r)/ *n.* (tunnel) Abwasserkanal, *der;* (pipe) Abwasserleitung, *die*

sewerage /'sju:ərɪdʒ, 'su:ərɪdʒ/ *n.* **(a)** (system of sewers) Kanalisation, *die;* **(b)** *no pl.* (removal of sewage) Abwasserbeseitigung, *die;* **(c)** (sewage) Abwasser, *das*

sewing /'səʊɪŋ/ *n.* Näharbeit, *die*

sewing: ∼ **basket** *n.* Nähkorb, *der;* ∼ **machine** *n.* Nähmaschine, *die*

sewn ⇨ **sew**

sex /seks/ **1** *n.* **(a)** Geschlecht, *das;* **what** ∼ **is the baby/ puppy?** welches Geschlecht hat das Baby/der Welpe?; **(b)** (sexuality; coll.: intercourse) Sex, *der* (ugs.); **have** ∼ **with sb.** (coll.) mit jmdm. schlafen (verhüll.); Sex mit jmdm. haben (salopp). **2** *attrib. adj.* Geschlechts⟨*organ, -trieb*⟩; Sexual- ⟨*verbrechen, -trieb, -instinkt*⟩

sex: ∼ **act** *n.* Geschlechtsakt, *der;* ∼ **appeal** *n.* Sexappeal, *der;* ∼ **change** *n.* Geschlechtsumwandlung, *die;* ∼ **change operation** *n.* operative Geschlechtsumwandlung; ∼ **discrimination** *n.* sexuelle Diskriminierung; ∼ **education** *n.* Sexualerziehung, *die*

sexily /'seksɪlɪ/ *adv.* aufreizend, (ugs.) sexy ⟨*sprechen, lächeln*⟩

sexism /'seksɪzm/ *n., no pl.* Sexismus, *der*

sexist /'seksɪst/ **1** *n.* Sexist, *der*/Sexistin, *die.* **2** *adj.* sexistisch

sex: ∼ **life** *n.* Geschlechtsleben, *das;* ∼ **maniac** *n.* Triebverbrecher, *der;* ∼ **offender** *n.* Sexual[straf]täter, *der*/-täterin, *die;* ∼ **symbol** *n.* Sexidol, *das*

sexual /'seksjʊəl, 'sekʃʊəl/ *adj.* sexuell; geschlechtlich, sexuell ⟨*Anziehung, Erregung, Verlangen, Diskriminierung*⟩; ∼ **maturity/behaviour** Geschlechtsreife, *die*/Sexualverhalten, *das*

sexual: ∼ **abuse** *n.* sexueller Missbrauch; **suffer** ∼ **abuse** sexuell missbraucht werden; ∼ **harassment** *n.* sexuelle Belästigung; ∼ **'intercourse** *n., no pl., no indef. art.* Geschlechtsverkehr, *der*

sexuality /seksjʊ'ælɪtɪ, sekʃʊ'ælɪtɪ/ *n., no pl.* Sexualität, *die*

sexually /'seksjʊəlɪ, 'sekʃʊəlɪ/ *adv.* **(a)** sexuell; ∼ **mature** geschlechtsreif; ∼ **transmitted disease** durch Geschlechtsverkehr übertragbare Krankheit; Geschlechtskrankheit, *die;* **(b)** (Biol.) geschlechtlich

sexy /'seksɪ/ *adj.* sexy (ugs.); erotisch ⟨*Film, Buch*⟩

Seychelles /ser'ʃelz/ *pr. n.* Seychellen *Pl.*

shabbily /'ʃæbɪlɪ/ *adv.,* **shabby** /'ʃæbɪ/ *adj.* schäbig

shack /ʃæk/ **1** *n.* Hütte, *die.* **2** *v.i.* (coll.) ∼ **up with sb.** mit jmdm. zusammenziehen

shackle /'ʃækl/ **1** *n., usu. in pl.* (lit. or fig.) Fessel, *die.* **2** *v.t.* (lit. or fig.) anketten (**to an** + *Akk.*)

shade /ʃeɪd/ **1** *n.* **(a)** Schatten, *der;* **put sb./sth. in[to] the** ∼ (fig.) jmdn./etw. in den Schatten stellen; **38 [°C] in the** ∼**:** 38° im Schatten; **(b)** (colour) Ton, *der;* (fig.) Schattierung, *die;* **various** ∼**s of purple** verschiedene Violetttöne; ∼**s of meaning** Bedeutungsnuancen *od.* -schattierungen; **(c)** (small amount) Spur, *die;* **(d)** (eye-shield) [Augen]schirm, *der;* (lamp∼) [Lampen]schirm, *der;* **(e)** *in pl.* (coll: sunglasses) Sonnenbrille, *die.* **2** *v.t.* **(a)** (screen) beschatten (geh.); Schatten geben (+ *Dat.*); **be** ∼**d from the sun** vor Sonneneinstrahlung geschützt sein; ∼ **one's eyes with one's hand** die Hand schützend über die Augen halten; **(b)** abdunkeln ⟨*Fenster, Lampe, Licht*⟩. **3** *v.i.* (lit. or fig.) übergehen (**into** in + *Akk.*) ∼ **'in** *v.t.* [ab]schattieren

shading /'ʃeɪdɪŋ/ *n.* Schattierung, *die;* (protection from light) Lichtschutz, *der*

shadow /'ʃædəʊ/ **1** *n.* **(a)** Schatten, *der;* **cast a** ∼ **over** (lit. or fig.) einen Schatten werfen auf (+ *Akk.*); **be in sb.'s** ∼ (fig.) in jmds. Schatten stehen; **be afraid of one's own** ∼ (fig.) sich vor seinem eigenen Schatten fürchten; **(b)** (slightest trace) **without a** ∼ **of doubt** ohne den Schatten eines Zweifels; **catch at** *or* **chase after** ∼**s** einem Phantom *od.* (geh.) Schatten nachjagen; **(c)** (ghost, lit. or fig.) Schatten, *der;* **(d)** S∼ *attrib.* (Brit. Polit.) ⟨*Minister, Kanzler*⟩ im Schattenkabinett; S∼ **Cabinet** Schattenkabinett, *das.* **2** *v.t.* **(a)** (darken) überschatten; **(b)** (follow secretly) beschatten

shadowy /'ʃædəʊɪ/ *adj.* **(a)** (not distinct) schattenhaft; schemenhaft (geh.); **(b)** (full of shade) schattig

shady /'ʃeɪdɪ/ *adj.* **(a)** (giving shade) schattenspendend (geh.); (situated in shade) schattig; **(b)** (disreputable) zwielichtig

shaft /ʃɑːft/ *n.* **(a)** (of tool, golf club, spear) Schaft, *der;* **(b)** (Mech. Engin.) Welle, *die;* **(c)** (of cart or carriage) Deichsel, *die;* **(d)** (of mine, lift, etc.) Schacht, *der*

shaggy /'ʃægɪ/ *adj.* **(a)** (hairy) zottelig; **(b)** (unkempt) struppig

shaggy-'dog story *n.* endlos langer Witz ohne richtige Pointe

Shah /ʃɑː/ *n.* Schah, *der*

shake /ʃeɪk/ **1** *n.* Schütteln, *das;* **give sb./sth. a** ∼**:** jmdn./etw. schütteln; **with a** ∼ **of the head** mit einem Kopfschütteln; **be no great** ∼**s** (coll.) nicht gerade unwerfend sein (ugs.). **2** *v.t.,* **shook** /ʃʊk/, **shaken** /'ʃeɪkn/ *or* (arch./coll.) **shook** **(a)** (move violently) schütteln; **the dog shook itself** der Hund schüttelte sich; **be** ∼**n to pieces** völlig durchgeschüttelt werden; ∼ **one's fist/a stick at sb.** jmdm. mit der Faust/einem Stock drohen; '∼ **[well] before using'** „vor Gebrauch [gut] schütteln!"; ∼ **hands** sich (*Dat.*) *od.* einander die Hand geben *od.* schütteln; ∼ **sb. by the hand** jmdm. die Hand schütteln *od.* drücken; **(b)** (cause to tremble) erschüttern ⟨*Gebäude usw.*⟩; ∼ **one's head [over sth.]** [über etw. (*Akk.*)] den Kopf schütteln; **(c)** (weaken) erschüttern; ∼ **sb.'s faith in sth./sb.** jmds. Glauben an etw./jmdn. erschüttern; **(d)** (agitate) erschüttern; **she was badly** ∼**n by the news of his death** die Nachricht von seinem Tod erschütterte sie sehr; **he failed his exam — that shook him!** er hat die Prüfung nicht bestanden — das war ein Schock für ihn!; ∼ **sb.'s composure** jmdn. aus dem Gleichgewicht bringen. **3** *v.i.,* **shook**, **shaken** *or* (arch./coll.) **shook** **(a)** (tremble) wackeln; ⟨*Boden, Stimme:*⟩ beben; ⟨*Hand:*⟩ zittern; ∼ **[all over] with cold/ fear** [am ganzen Leib] vor Kälte/Angst schlottern; ∼ **like a leaf** wie Espenlaub zittern; ∼ **with emotion** vor Erregung beben; ∼ **in one's shoes** (coll.) vor Angst schlottern; **(b)** (coll.: ∼ **hands**) sich (*Dat.*) die Hand geben; **let's** ∼ **on it!** schlag ein!; Hand drauf!

∼ **'off** *v.t.* (lit. or fig.) abschütteln

∼ **'out** *v.t.* ausschütteln; (spread out) ausbreiten

∼ **'up** *v.t.* **(a)** (mix) schütteln; **(b)** aufschütteln ⟨*Kissen*⟩; **(c)** (upset) einen Schrecken einjagen (+ *Dat.*); **she felt pretty** ∼**n up** sie hatte einen ziemlichen Schrecken bekommen; **(d)** (rouse to activity) aufrütteln; **(e)** (coll.: reorganize) umkrempeln (ugs.)

shaken ⇨ **shake 2, 3**

'shake-up *n.* (coll.: reorganization) **give sth. a [good]** ∼**:** etw. [total] umkrempeln (ugs.); **sth. needs a** ∼**:** etw. muss [mal] umgekrempelt werden (ugs.)

shaky /'ʃeɪkɪ/ *adj.* **(a)** (unsteady) wack[el]ig ⟨*Möbelstück, Leiter*⟩; zittrig ⟨*Hand, Stimme, Bewegung, Greis*⟩; **feel** ∼**:** sich zittrig fühlen; **be** ∼ **on one's legs** wacklig auf den Beinen sein (ugs.); **(b)** (unreliable) **his German is rather** ∼**:** sein Deutsch steht auf wack[el]igen Füßen (ugs.)

shall /ʃl, *stressed* ʃæl/ *v. aux. only in pres.* **shall**, *neg.* (coll.) **shan't** /ʃɑːnt/, *past* **should** /ʃəd, *stressed* ʃʊd/, *neg.* (coll.) **shouldn't** /'ʃʊdnt/ **(a)** *expr. simple future* werden; **(b)** **should** *expr. conditional* würde/würdest/würden/würdet; **I should have been killed if I had let go** ich wäre getötet worden, wenn ich losgelassen hätte; **(c)** *expr. command* **the committee** ∼ **not be disturbed** der Ausschuss darf nicht gestört werden; **(d)** *expr. will or intention* **what** ∼ **we do?** was sollen wir tun?; **let's go in,** ∼ **we?** gehen wir doch hinein, oder?; **I'll buy six,** ∼ **I?** ich kaufe 6 [Stück], ja?; **you** ∼ **pay for this!** das sollst du mir büßen!; **we should be safe now** jetzt dürften wir in Sicherheit sein; **he shouldn't do things like that!** er sollte so etwas nicht tun!; **oh, you shouldn't have!** *expr. gratitude* das wäre doch nicht nötig gewesen!; **you should be more careful** du solltest vorsichtiger *od.* sorgfältiger sein; **(e)** *in conditional clause* **if we should be defeated** falls wir unterliegen [sollten]; **I should hope so** ich hoffe es; (indignant) das möchte ich hoffen!; **(f)** *in tentative assertion* **I should like to disagree with you on that point** in dem Punkt *od.* da möchte ich dir widersprechen; **I should say it is time we went home** ich würde sagen *od.* ich glaube, es ist Zeit, dass wir nach Hause gehen

shallot /ʃə'lɒt/ *n.* Schalotte, *die*

shallow /'ʃæləʊ/ *adj.* ▶ **1048**] seicht ⟨*Wasser, Fluss*⟩; flach ⟨*Schüssel, Teller, Wasser*⟩; (fig.) seicht (abwertend)

‹*Unterhaltung, Gerede*›; flach (abwertend) ‹*Person, Denker, Geist*›; platt (abwertend) ‹*Argument, Verallgemeinerung*›

sham /ʃæm/ **1** *adj.* unecht; imitiert ‹*Leder, Holz, Pelz, Stein*›. **2** *n.* (pretence) Heuchelei, *die;* (person) Heuchler, *der/* Heuchlerin, *die;* **their marriage is only a ∼:** ihre Ehe besteht nur auf dem Papier. **3** *v.t.* **-mm-** vortäuschen; simulieren; **∼ dead/ill** sich tot/krank stellen. **4** *v.i.* **-mm-** simulieren; sich verstellen

shamble /ˈʃæmbl/ **1** *v.i.* schlurfen. **2** *n.* Schlurfen, *das*

shambles /ˈʃæmblz/ *n. sing.* (coll.: mess) Chaos, *das;* **the house/room was a ∼:** das Haus/Zimmer glich einem Schlachtfeld; **the economy is in a ∼:** in der Wirtschaft herrschen chaotische Zustände

shame /ʃeɪm/ **1** *n.* (a) Scham, *die;* **feel ∼/no ∼ for what one did** sich schämen/sich nicht schämen für das, was man getan hat; **hang one's head in** *or* **for ∼:** beschämt den Kopf senken; **blush with ∼:** vor Scham erröten; **have no [sense of] ∼:** kein[erlei] Schamgefühl besitzen; **have you no ∼?** schämst du dich nicht?; **to my ∼ I must confess …:** ich muss zu meiner Schande gestehen …; (b) (state of disgrace) Schande, *die;* **∼ on you!** du solltest dich schämen; **put sb./sth. to ∼:** jmdn. beschämen/etw. in den Schatten stellen; (c) **what a ∼!** (bad luck) so ein Pech!; (pity) wie schade!; **it is a crying** *or* **terrible** *or* **great ∼:** es ist eine wahre Schande. **2** *v.t.* beschämen; **∼ sb. into doing/out of doing sth.** jmdn. dazu bringen, dass er sich schämt und etw. tut/nicht tut

'shamefaced *adj.* betreten; **have a ∼ look, look ∼:** betreten dreinblicken

shameful /ˈʃeɪmfl/ *adj.* beschämend

shameless /ˈʃeɪmlɪs/ *adj.* schamlos

shampoo /ʃæmˈpuː/ **1** *v.t.* schamponieren ‹*Haar, Teppich, Polster*›. **2** *n.* Shampon, *das;* Schampoo, *das;* **carpet ∼:** Teppichschaum, *der;* **have a ∼ and set** sich (*Dat.*) die Haare waschen und [ein]legen lassen; **give one's hair a ∼:** sich (*Dat.*) die Haare waschen

shamrock /ˈʃæmrɒk/ *n.* Klee, *der;* (emblem of Ireland) Shamrock, *der*

shandy /ˈʃændɪ/ *n.* Bier mit Limonade; Radler, *der* (bes. südd.)

shank /ʃæŋk/ *n.* (a) (of person) Unterschenkel, *der;* [**go] on S∼s's mare** *or* **pony** auf Schusters Rappen [reisen] (scherzh.); (b) (of horse) Vordermittelfuß, *der*

shan't /ʃɑːnt/ (coll.) = **shall not**

shanty[1] /ˈʃæntɪ/ *n.* (hut) [armselige] Hütte

shanty[2] *n.* (song) Shanty, *das;* Seemannslied, *das*

'shanty town *n.* Elendsviertel, *das*

shape /ʃeɪp/ **1** *v.t.* (a) (create, form) formen; bearbeiten ‹*Holz, Stein*› (**into** zu); (b) (adapt, direct) prägen, formen ‹*Charakter, Person*›; [entscheidend] beeinflussen ‹*Gang der Geschichte, Leben, Zukunft, Gesellschaft*›. **2** *v.i.* sich entwickeln. **3** *n.* (a) (external form, outline) Form, *die;* **spherical/rectangular in ∼:** kugelförmig/rechteckig; **take ∼:** ‹*Konstruktion, Skulptur*› Gestalt annehmen (see also **c**); (b) (appearance) Gestalt, *die;* **in the ∼ of a woman** in Gestalt einer Frau; (c) (specific form) Form, *die;* Gestalt, *die;* **take ∼:** ‹*Plan, Vorhaben*› Gestalt *od.* feste Formen annehmen (*see also* **a**)**; get one's ideas into ∼:** seine Gedanken sammeln; **lick** *or* **knock sth. into ∼:** etw. auf Vordermann bringen (ugs.); **in all ∼s and sizes, in every ∼ and size** in allen Formen und Größen; **the ∼ of things to come** die Dinge, die da kommen sollen/sollten; (d) (condition) Form, *die* (bes. Sport); **do yoga to keep in ∼:** Yoga machen, um in Form zu bleiben; **be in good/bad ∼:** gut/schlecht in Form sein; (e) (person seen, ghost) Gestalt, *die*

∼ 'up *v.i.* sich entwickeln; **how's the new editor shaping up?** wie macht sich der neue Redakteur?

shaped /ʃeɪpt/ *adj.* geformt; **be ∼ like a pear** die Form einer Birne haben

shapeless /ˈʃeɪplɪs/ *adj.* formlos; unförmig ‹*Kleid, Person*›

shapely /ˈʃeɪplɪ/ *adj.* wohlgeformt ‹*Beine, Busen*›; gut ‹*Figur*›

share /ʃeə(r)/ **1** *n.* (a) (portion) Teil, *der od. das;* (part one is entitled to) [fair] **∼:** Anteil, *der;* **he had a large ∼ in bringing it about** er hatte großen Anteil daran, dass es

zustande kam; **pay one's ∼ of the bill** seinen Teil der Rechnung bezahlen; **have a ∼ in the profits** am Gewinn beteiligt sein; **do more than one's [fair] ∼ of the work** mehr als seinen Teil zur Arbeit beitragen; **each had his ∼ of the cake** jeder bekam seinen Teil vom Kuchen ab; **have more than one's [fair] ∼ of the blame/attention** mehr Schuld zugewiesen bekommen/mehr Beachtung finden, als man verdient; **she had her ∼ of luck/bad luck** sie hat aber auch Glück/Pech gehabt; **take one's ∼ of the responsibility** seinen Teil Verantwortung tragen; **take one's ∼ of the blame** seinen Teil Schuld auf sich (*Akk.*) nehmen; **go ∼s** teilen; **it was ∼ and ∼ alike** es wurde brüderlich geteilt; (b) (part-ownership of property) [Geschäfts]anteil, *der;* (part of company's capital) Aktie, *die;* **hold ∼s in a company** (Brit.) Anteile *od.* Aktien einer Gesellschaft besitzen. **2** *v.t.* teilen; gemeinsam tragen ‹*Verantwortung*›; **∼ the same birthday/surname** am selben Tag Geburtstag/denselben Nachnamen haben. **3** *v.i.* **∼ in** teilnehmen an (+ *Dat.*); beteiligt sein an (+ *Dat.*) ‹*Gewinn, Planung*›; teilen ‹*Freude, Erfahrung*›

∼ 'out *v.t.* aufteilen (**among** unter + *Akk.*)

share: ∼ certificate *n.* Aktienurkunde, *die;* **∼holder** *n.* Aktionär, *der/*Aktionärin, *die;* **∼-out** *n.* Aufteilung, *die;* **∼ware** *n., no pl.* (Computing) Shareware, *die*

shark /ʃɑːk/ *n.* (a) Hai[fisch], *der;* (b) (fig.: swindler) gerissener Geschäftemacher; **property ∼:** Grundstückshai, *der* (ugs. abwertend); *see also* **loan shark**

sharp /ʃɑːp/ **1** *adj.* (a) (with fine edge) scharf; (with fine point) spitz ‹*Nadel, Bleistift, Giebel, Gipfel*›; (b) (clear-cut) scharf ‹*Umriss, Kontrast, Bild, Gesichtszüge, Linie*›; deutlich ‹*Unterscheidung*›; präzise ‹*Eindruck*›; (c) (abrupt, angular) scharf ‹*Kurve, Winkel*›; steil, schroff ‹*Abhang*›; stark ‹*Gefälle*›; **a ∼ rise/fall in prices** ein jäher Preisanstieg/Preissturz; (d) (intense) groß ‹*Appetit, Hunger[gefühl]*›; (acid, pungent) scharf ‹*Würze, Geschmack, Sauce, Käse*›; sauer ‹*Apfel*›; herb ‹*Wein*›; (shrill, piercing) schrill ‹*Schrei, Pfiff*›; (biting) scharf ‹*Wind, Frost, Luft*›; (sudden, severe) heftig ‹*Schmerz, Anfall, Krampf, Kampf*›; (harsh, acrimonious) scharf ‹*Protest, Tadel, Ton, Stimme, Zunge, Worte*›; **a short ∼ struggle** ein kurzer, heftiger Kampf; (e) (acute, quick) scharf ‹*Augen, Verstand, Gehör, Ohr, Beobachtungsgabe, Intelligenz, Geruchssinn*›; aufgeweckt ‹*Kind*›; scharfsinnig ‹*Bemerkung*›; begabt ‹*Schüler, Student*›; **that was pretty ∼!** das war ganz schön clever!; **keep a ∼ lookout for the police!** halt die Augen offen, falls die Polizei kommt!; (f) (derog.: artful, dishonest, quick to take advantage) gerissen; (g) (Mus.) [um einen Halbton] erhöht ‹*Note*›; **F/G/C** *etc.* **∼:** fis, Fis/gis, Gis/cis, Cis *usw.,* *das.* **2** *adv.* (a) (punctually) **at six o'clock ∼:** Punkt sechs Uhr; (b) (suddenly) scharf ‹*bremsen*›; plötzlich ‹*anhalten*›; **turn ∼ right** scharf nach rechts abbiegen; (c) **look ∼!** halt dich ran! (ugs.); (d) (Mus.) zu hoch ‹*singen, spielen*›. **3** *n.* (Mus.) erhöhter Ton; (symbol) Kreuz, *das;* Erhöhungszeichen, *das*

sharpen /ˈʃɑːpn/ *v.t.* schärfen (auch fig.); [an]spitzen ‹*Bleistift*›; (fig.) anregen ‹*Appetit*›

sharpener /ˈʃɑːpnə(r)/ *n.* (for pencil) Bleistiftspitzer, *der;* Spitzer, *der* (ugs.); (for tools) Abziehstein, *der;* Schleifstein, *der*

sharp-eyed /ˈʃɑːpaɪd/ *adj.* scharfäugig; **be ∼:** scharfe Augen haben

sharpish /ˈʃɑːpɪʃ/ *adv.* (coll.) (quickly) rasch; (promptly) unverzüglich; sofort

sharply /ˈʃɑːplɪ/ *adv.* (a) (acutely) spitz; **∼ angled** spitzwinklig; (b) (clearly) scharf ‹*voneinander unterschieden, kontrastierend, umrissen*›; (c) (abruptly) scharf ‹*bremsen, abbiegen*›; steil, schroff ‹*abfallen*›; (d) (acidly) scharf ‹*gewürzt*›; (harshly) in scharfem Ton ‹*antworten*›; **∼ worded letter** Brief in scharfem Ton; (e) (quickly) schnell, rasch ‹*denken, handeln*›

sharp: ∼shooter *n.* Scharfschütze, *der;* **∼-witted** /ˈʃɑːpwɪtɪd/ *adj.* scharfsinnig

shatter /ˈʃætə(r)/ **1** *v.t.* (a) (smash) zertrümmern; (b) (destroy) zerschlagen ‹*Hoffnungen*›; (c) (coll.: greatly upset) schwer mitnehmen. **2** *v.i.* zerbrechen; zerspringen

shattered /'ʃætəd/ *adj.* **(a)** zerbrochen, zersprungen ⟨*Scheibe, Glas, Fenster*⟩; (fig.) zerstört ⟨*Hoffnungen*⟩; zerrüttet ⟨*Nerven*⟩; **(b)** (coll.: greatly upset) **she was ~ by the news** die Nachricht hat sie schwer mitgenommen; **I'm ~!** ich bin ganz erschüttert!; **(c)** (Brit. coll.: exhausted) **I'm ~:** ich bin [völlig] kaputt (ugs.)

shattering /'ʃætərɪŋ/ *adj.* **(a)** (ruinously destructive) verheerend ⟨*Wirkung, Explosion*⟩; vernichtend ⟨*Schlag, Niederlage*⟩; **(b)** (coll.: very upsetting) erschütternd

shave /ʃeɪv/ **1** *v.t.* **(a)** rasieren; abrasieren ⟨*Haare*⟩; **he ~d his beard** er hat sich ⟨*Dat.*⟩ den Bart abrasiert; **(b)** (graze) ⟨*Auto:*⟩ streifen. **2** *v.i.* **(a)** sich rasieren; **(b)** (scrape) **~ past sth.** etw. [leicht] streifen. **3** *n.* **(a)** Rasur, *die;* **have** *or* **get a ~:** sich rasieren; **a clean** *or* **close ~:** eine Glattrasur; **(b)** close ~ (fig.) ⇒ **close 1 f**
~ 'off *v.t.* abrasieren ⟨*Bart, Haare*⟩

shaven /'ʃeɪvn/ *adj.* rasiert; [kahl]geschoren ⟨*Kopf*⟩

shaver /'ʃeɪvə(r)/ *n.* Rasierapparat, *der;* Rasierer, *der* (ugs.)

'shaver point *n.* Anschluss *od.* Steckdose für den Rasierapparat

shaving /'ʃeɪvɪŋ/ *n.* **(a)** (action) Rasieren, *das;* **(b)** *in pl.* (of wood, metal, etc.) Späne *Pl.*

shaving: **~-brush** *n.* Rasierpinsel, *der;* **~-cream** *n.* Rasiercreme, *die;* **~-foam** *n.* Rasierschaum, *der*

shawl /ʃɔːl/ *n.* Schultertuch, *das*

she /ʃɪ, stressed ʃiː/ *pron.* sie; *referring to personified things or animals which correspond to German masculines/neuters* er/es; **it was ~** (formal) sie war es; *see also* **her**[1, 2]; **hers; herself**

she- /ʃiː/ *in comb.* weiblich; **~-ass/-bear** Eselin, *die*/Bärin, *die*

sheaf /ʃiːf/ *n., pl.* **sheaves** /ʃiːvz/ (of corn etc.) Garbe, *die;* (of paper, arrows, etc.) Bündel, *das*

shear /ʃɪə(r)/ *v.t., p.p.* **shorn** /ʃɔːn/ *or* **~ed** (clip) scheren
~ 'off 1 *v.t.* abtrennen. **2** *v.i.* abscheren (Technik)

shears /ʃɪəz/ *n. pl.* **[pair of]** ~ (große) Schere, *die;* **garden ~:** Heckenschere, *die*

sheath /ʃiːθ/ *n., pl.* **~s** /ʃiːðz, ʃiːθs/ **(a)** (for sword etc.) Scheide, *die;* **(b)** (condom) Gummischutz, *der;* **(c)** (Electr.) Mantel, *der*

'sheath knife *n.* Fahrtenmesser, *das*

sheaves *pl. of* **sheaf**

shebang /ʃɪ'bæŋ/ *n.* (Amer. sl.) **the whole ~:** der ganze Kram (ugs.); **who runs the whole ~?** wer ist der Boss vom Ganzen? (ugs.)

shed[1] /ʃed/ *v.t.*, **-dd-**, **shed (a)** (part with) verlieren; abwerfen, verlieren ⟨*Laub, Geweih*⟩; abstreifen ⟨*Haut, Hülle, Badehose*⟩; ausziehen ⟨*Kleidung*⟩; **the snake is ~ding its skin** die Schlange häutet sich; **you should ~ a few pounds** du solltest ein paar Pfund abspecken (salopp); **(b)** vergießen ⟨*Blut, Tränen*⟩; **don't ~ any tears over him** seinetwegen solltest du keine Tränen vergießen; **(c)** (dispense) verbreiten ⟨*Wärme, Licht*⟩; *see also* **light**[1] **1 f**; **(d)** (fig.: cast off) abschütteln ⟨*Sorgen, Bürde*⟩

shed[2] *n.* Schuppen, *der*

she'd /ʃid, stressed ʃiːd/ **(a)** = **she had; (b)** = **she would**

sheen /ʃiːn/ *n.* Glanz, *der*

sheep /ʃiːp/ *n., pl.* **same** Schaf, *das;* **separate the ~ from the goats** (fig.) die Böcke von den Schafen trennen; **count ~** (fig.) Schäfchen zählen (fam.); **follow sb. like ~:** jmdm. wie eine Schafherde folgen

'sheepdog *n.* Hütehund, *der;* Schäferhund, *der;* **Old English S~:** Bobtail, *der*

sheepish /'ʃiːpɪʃ/ *adj.* (awkwardly self-conscious) verlegen; (embarrassed) kleinlaut; **he felt a bit ~** (foolish) es war ihm ein bisschen peinlich

sheep shearer /'ʃiːp ʃɪərə(r)/ *n.* ▶ 887 Schafscherer, *der*

'sheepskin *n.* Schaffell, *das; attrib.* ~ **[jacket]** Schaffelljacke, *die*

sheer /ʃɪə(r)/ *adj.* **(a)** *attrib.* (mere, absolute) rein; blank ⟨*Unsinn, Gewalt*⟩; **by ~ chance** rein zufällig; **the ~ insolence of it!** so eine Frechheit!; **only by ~ hard work** nur durch harte Arbeit; **(b)** (perpendicular) schroff ⟨*Felsen,*

Abfall⟩; steil ⟨*Felsen, Abfall, Aufstieg*⟩; **(c)** (finely woven) hauchfein

sheet /ʃiːt/ *n.* **(a)** Laken, *das;* (for covering mattress) Betttuch, *das;* Laken, *das;* **put clean ~s on the bed** das Bett frisch beziehen; **between the ~s** (in bed) im Bett; **(b)** (of thin metal, plastic) Folie, *die;* (of iron, tin) Blech, *das;* (of glass, of thicker metal, plastic) Platte, *die;* (of stamps) Bogen, *der;* (of paper) Bogen, *der;* Blatt, *das;* **a ~ of paper** ein Papierbogen; ein Bogen *od.* Blatt Papier; **start with/have a clean ~** (fig.) ganz neu beginnen/eine reine Weste haben (ugs.); *attrib.* **~ glass/metal/iron** Flachglas, *das*/Blech, *das*/Eisenblech, *das;* **(c)** (wide expanse) ⟨*Eis-, Lava-, Nebel*⟩decke, *die;* **a huge ~ of flame** ein Flammenmeer; **the rain was coming down in ~s** es regnete in Strömen

sheet: ~ **lightning** *n.* (Meteorol.) Flächenblitz, *der;* ~ **music** *n.* Notenblätter

sheik, sheikh /ʃeɪk, ʃiːk/ *ns.* Scheich, *der*

shelf /ʃelf/ *n., pl.* **shelves** /ʃelvz/ (flat board) Brett, *das;* Bord, *das;* (compartment) Fach, *das;* (set of shelves) Regal, *das;* ~ **of books** Bücherbrett, *das;* **be left on the ~** (fig.) sitzengeblieben sein (ugs.); **be put on the ~** (fig.) aufs Abstellgleis geschoben werden (ugs.)

shelf: ~-**life** *n.* Lagerfähigkeit, *die;* ~ **mark** *n.* Standortnummer, *die;* ~ **room,** ~ **space** *ns.* Stellfläche [im Regal]; **give sth.** ~ **room** *or* ~ **space** sich ⟨*Dat.*⟩ etw. ins Regal stellen

shell /ʃel/ **1** *n.* **(a)** (casing) Schale, *die;* (of turtle, tortoise) Panzer, *der;* (of snail) Haus, *das;* (of pea) Schote, *die;* Hülse, *die;* **collect ~s on the beach** am Strand Muscheln sammeln; **come out of one's ~** (fig.) aus sich herausgehen; **retire** *or* **go into one's ~** (fig.) sich in sein Schneckenhaus zurückziehen; **(b)** (pastry case) Teighülle, *die;* **(c)** (Mil.: bomb) Granate, *die;* **(d)** (of unfinished building) Rohbau, *der;* (of ruined building) Ruine, *die;* (Motor Veh.) Aufbau, *der;* Karosserie, *die;* (after fire, at breaker's, etc.) [Karosserie]gerippe, *das.* **2** *v.t.* **(a)** (take out of ~) schälen; knacken, schälen ⟨*Nuss*⟩; enthülsen, (nordd.) palen ⟨*Erbsen*⟩; **(b)** (Mil.) [mit Artillerie] beschießen
~ **'out** *v.t. & i.* (coll.) blechen (ugs.) (**on** für)

she'll /ʃɪl, stressed ʃiːl/ = **she will**

shell: ~**fish** *n., pl.* **same (a)** Schal[en]tier, *das;* (oyster, clam) Muschel, *die;* (crustacean) Krebstier, *das;* **(b)** *in pl.* (Gastr.) Meeresfrüchte *Pl.;* ~**-shock** *n.* (Psych.) Kriegsneurose, *die;* ~**-shocked** *adj.* **be ~-shocked** eine Kriegsneurose haben; (fig.) niedergeschmettert sein; ~ **suit** *n.* Trilobalanzug, *der*

shelter /'ʃeltə(r)/ **1** *n.* **(a)** (shield) Schutz, *der* (**against** vor + *Dat.*, gegen); **bomb** *or* **air-raid ~:** Luftschutzraum, *der;* **get under ~:** sich unterstellen; **(b)** *no pl.* (place of safety) Zuflucht, *die;* **we needed food and ~:** wir brauchten etwas zu essen und eine Unterkunft; (esp. Amer.) **look for ~ for the night** eine Unterkunft für die Nacht suchen; **offer** *or* **give sb.** ~, **provide** ~ **for sb.** jmdm. Zuflucht gewähren *od.* bieten; **take** ~ **[from a storm]** [vor einem Sturm] Schutz suchen; **seek/reach** ~ **:** Schutz *od.* Zuflucht suchen/finden. **2** *v.t.* schützen (**from** vor + *Dat.*); Unterschlupf gewähren (+ *Dat.*) ⟨*Flüchtling*⟩; ~ **sb. from blame/harm** jmdn. decken/gegen alle Gefahren schützen. **3** *v.i.* Schutz *od.* Zuflucht suchen (**from** vor + *Dat.*); **this is a good place to ~:** hier ist man gut geschützt

sheltered /'ʃeltəd/ *adj.* geschützt ⟨*Platz, Tal*⟩; behütet ⟨*Leben*⟩

shelve /ʃelv/ **1** *v.t.* (put on ~s) ins Regal stellen; (fig.) (abandon) ad acta *od.* (ugs.) zu den Akten legen; (defer) auf Eis legen (ugs.). **2** *v.i.* ~ **away/off/out into** ⟨*Berg, Boden, Ebene:*⟩ abfallen nach

shelves *pl. of* **shelf**

shepherd /'ʃepəd/ **1** *n.* ▶ 887 Schäfer, *der;* Schafhirt, *der.* **2** *v.t.* hüten; (fig.) führen

shepherdess /'ʃepədɪs/ *n.* ▶ 887 Schäferin, *die;* Schafhirtin, *die*

shepherd's 'pie *n.* (Gastr.) Auflauf aus Hackfleisch mit einer Schicht Kartoffelbrei darüber

sherbet /'ʃɜːbət/ *n.* **(a)** (fruit juice; also Amer.: water ice) Sorbet[t], *der od. das;* **(b)** (effervescent drink) Brauselimonade, *die;* (powder) Brausepulver, *das*

sheriff /'ʃerɪf/ n. Sheriff, der

sherry /'ʃerɪ/ n. Sherry, der

she's /ʃɪz, stressed ʃiːz/ (a) = **she is**; (b) = **she has**

Shetland Islands /'ʃetlənd aɪləndz/ pr. n. pl. Shetlandinseln Pl.; Shetlands Pl.

Shetland 'pony n. Shetlandpony, das

Shetlands /'ʃetləndz/ pr. n. pl. Shetlands Pl.

shield /ʃiːld/ **1** n. (a) (piece of armour) Schild, der; (b) (in machinery etc.) Schutz, der; **radiation** ~: Strahlenschutz, der; (c) (fig.: person or thing that protects) Schild, der (geh.); (d) (Sport: trophy) Trophäe, die (in Form eines Schildes). **2** v.t. (a) (protect) schützen (**from** vor + Dat.); (b) (conceal) decken ‹Schuldigen›; ~ **sb. from the truth** die Wahrheit von jmdm. fernhalten

shier, shiest ⇒ **shy¹ 1**

shift /ʃɪft/ **1** v.t. (a) (move) verrücken, umstellen ‹Möbel›; wegnehmen ‹Arm, Hand, Fuß›; wegräumen ‹Schutt›; entfernen ‹Schmutz, Fleck›; (to another floor, room, or place) verlegen ‹Büro, Patienten, Schauplatz›; ~ **one's weight to the other foot** sein Gewicht auf den anderen Fuß verlagern; ~ **the responsibility/blame on to sb.** (fig.) die Verantwortung/Schuld auf jmdn. schieben; (b) (Amer. Motor Veh.) ~ **gears** schalten. **2** v.i. (a) ‹Wind:› drehen (**to** nach); ‹Ladung:› verrutschen; ~ **uneasily in one's chair** unruhig auf dem Stuhl hin und her rutschen; (b) (manage) ~ **for oneself** selbst für sich sorgen; (c) (coll.: move quickly) rasen; **this new Porsche really** ~s der neue Porsche geht ab wie eine Rakete (ugs.); (d) (Amer. Motor Veh.: change gear) schalten; ~ **down into second gear** in den zweiten Gang runterschalten (ugs.). **3** n. (a) **a** ~ **in emphasis** eine Verlagerung des Akzents; **a** ~ **in values/public opinion** ein Wandel der Wertvorstellungen/ein Umschwung der öffentlichen Meinung; **a** ~ **towards/away from liberalism** eine Hinwendung zum/Abwendung vom Liberalismus; (b) (for work) Schicht, die; **eight-hour/late** ~: Achtstunden-/Spätschicht, die; **do** or **work the late** ~: Spätschicht haben; **work in** ~s Schichtarbeit machen; (c) **make** ~ **with/without sth.** sich (Dat.) mit/ ohne etw. behelfen; (d) (of typewriter) Umschaltung, die; (e) (Amer. Motor Veh.: gear change) Schaltung, die

shift: ~ **key** n. Umschalttaste, die; Umschalter, der; ~ **work** n. Schichtarbeit, die

shifty /'ʃɪftɪ/ adj. verschlagen (abwertend)

shilling /'ʃɪlɪŋ/ n. (Hist.) Shilling, der

shilly-shally /'ʃɪlɪʃælɪ/ v.i. zaudern; **stop** ~**ing!** entschließ dich endlich!

shimmer /'ʃɪmə(r)/ **1** v.i. schimmern. **2** n. Schimmer, der

shin /ʃɪn/ **1** n. ▶ 672 Schienbein, das. **2** v.i., **-nn-:** ~ **up/ down a tree** etc. einen Baum usw. hinauf-/hinunterklettern

'shin bone n. ▶ 672 Schienbein, das

shindig /'ʃɪndɪɡ/ n. (coll.) (a) ⇒ **shindy**; (b) (party) Fete, die (ugs.)

shindy /'ʃɪndɪ/ n. (brawl) Rauferei, die; (row) Streit, der; (noise) Krach, der

shine /ʃaɪn/ **1** v.i. (a) ‹Lampe, Licht, Stern:› leuchten; ‹Sonne:› scheinen; (reflect light) glänzen; ‹Mond:› scheinen; **his face shone with happiness/excitement** (fig.) er strahlte vor Glück/sein Gesicht glühte vor Aufregung; (b) (fig.: be brilliant) glänzen; **a shining example/ light** ein leuchtendes Beispiel/eine Leuchte; ~ **at sport** im Sport glänzen. **2** v.t. (a) p.t. & p.p. **shone** leuchten lassen; ~ **a light on sth./in sb.'s eyes** etw. anleuchten/ jmdm. in die Augen leuchten; (b) p.t. & p.p. ~**d** (clean and polish) putzen; (make shiny) polieren. **3** n., no pl. (a) (brightness) Schein, der; Licht, das; (b) (polish) Glanz, der; **have a** ~ ‹Oberfläche:› glänzen; **take the** ~ **off sth.** (fig.: spoil sth.) einen Schatten auf etw. (Akk.) werfen; (c) **take a** ~ **to sb./sth.** (coll.) Gefallen an jmdm./etw. finden

shingle /'ʃɪŋɡl/ n., no pl., no indef. art. (pebbles) Kies, der

shingles /'ʃɪŋɡlz/ n. sing. ▶ 865 (Med.) Gürtelrose, die

shin: ~**guard**, ~**pad** ns. Schienbeinschutz, der

shiny /'ʃaɪnɪ/ adj. glänzend

ship /ʃɪp/ **1** n. Schiff, das; **run a tight** ~ (fig.) ein strenges Regiment führen. **2** v.t., **-pp-** (take on board) einschiffen, an

Bord bringen ‹Vorräte, Ladung, Passagiere›; (transport by sea) verschiffen ‹Auto, Truppen›; (send by train, road, or air) verschicken, versenden ‹Waren›

~ **'out** v.t. verschiffen ‹Ladung, Güter›

ship: ~**builder** n. ▶ 887 Schiff[s]bauer, der; ~ **building** n., no pl., no indef. art. Schiffbau, der

shipment /'ʃɪpmənt/ n. (a) Versand, der; (by sea) Verschiffung, die; (b) (amount) Sendung, die

'shipowner n. Schiffseigentümer, der/-eigentümerin, die; (of several ships) Reeder, der/Reederin, die

shipper /'ʃɪpə(r)/ n. (merchant) Spediteur, der/Spediteurin, die; (company) Spedition, die

shipping /'ʃɪpɪŋ/ n. (a) no pl., no indef. art. (ships) Schiffe Pl.; (traffic) Schifffahrt, die; Schiffsverkehr, der; **all** ~: alle Schiffe/der ganze Schiffsverkehr; **closed to** ~: für Schiffe/für die Schifffahrt gesperrt; (b) (transporting) Versand, der

'shipping forecast n. Seewetterbericht, der

ship: ~**shape** pred. adj. in bester Ordnung; **get sth.** ~**shape** etw. in Ordnung bringen; ~**wreck 1** n. (lit. or fig.) Schiffbruch, der; **2** v.t. **be** ~**wrecked** Schiffbruch erleiden; (fig.: be ruined) ‹Hoffnung:› sich zerschlagen haben; ‹Karriere:› gescheitert sein; ~**yard** n. [Schiffs]werft, die

shire /'ʃaɪə(r)/ n. (county) Grafschaft, die

'shire-horse n. bes. in Mittelengland gezüchtetes schweres Zugpferd

shirk /ʃɜːk/ v.t. sich entziehen (+ Dat.) ‹Pflicht, Verantwortung›; ~ **one's job/doing sth.** sich vor der Arbeit drücken/sich davor drücken (ugs.), etw. zu tun

shirker /'ʃɜːkə(r)/ n. Drückeberger, der (ugs. abwertend)

shirt /ʃɜːt/ n. [**man's**] ~: [Herren- od. Ober]hemd, das; [**woman's** or **lady's**] ~: Hemdbluse, die; **sports/rugby/ football** ~: Trikot/Rugby-/Fußballtrikot, das; **keep your** ~ **on!** (fig. coll.) [nur] ruhig Blut! (ugs.)

'shirtsleeve n. Hemdsärmel, der; **work in one's** ~s in Hemdsärmeln arbeiten

shit /ʃɪt/ (coarse) **1** v.i., **-tt-**, **shitted** or **shit** or **shat** /ʃæt/ scheißen (derb); ~ **in one's pants** sich (Dat.) in die Hose[n] scheißen. **2** v. refl., **-tt-**, **shitted** or **shit** or **shat** sich (Dat.) in die Hose[n] scheißen (derb). **3** int. Scheiße (derb). **4** n. (a) (excrement) Scheiße, die (derb); **have** (Brit.) or (Amer.) **take a** ~: scheißen (derb); (b) (person) Scheißkerl, der; (nonsense) Scheiß, der (salopp abwertend); **don't give me that** ~: erzähl mir nicht so einen Scheiß! (salopp); **I don't give a** ~ [**about it**] das ist mir scheißegal (salopp); **be up** ~ **creek** [**without a paddle**] (fig.) bis zum Hals in der Scheiße stecken (derb)

shiver /'ʃɪvə(r)/ **1** v.i. (tremble) zittern (**with** vor + Dat.). **2** n. (trembling, lit. or fig.) Schau[d]er, der (geh.); ~ **of cold/ fear** Kälte-/Angstschauer, der; **send** ~**s** or **a** ~ **up** or [**up and**] **down sb.'s back** or **spine** jmdm. [einen] Schauder über den Rücken jagen; **give sb. the** ~**s** (fig.) jmdn. schaudern lassen

shivery /'ʃɪvərɪ/ adj. verfroren ‹Person›

shoal /ʃəʊl/ n. (of fish) Schwarm, der

shock /ʃɒk/ **1** n. (a) Schock, der; **I got the** ~ **of my life** ich erschrak zu Tode; **come as a** ~ **to sb.** ein Schock für jmdn. sein; **give sb. a** ~: jmdm. einen Schock versetzen; **he's in for a** [**nasty**] ~! er wird eine böse Überraschung erleben!; (b) (violent impact) Erschütterung, die (of durch); (c) (Electr.) Schlag, der; (d) (Med.) Schock, der; **be in** [**a state of**] ~: unter Schock[wirkung] stehen; [**electric**] ~: Elektroschock, der. **2** v.t. (a) ~ **sb.** [**deeply**] ein [schwerer] Schock für jmdn. sein; (b) (scandalize) schockieren; **I'm not easily** ~**ed** mich schockiert so leicht nichts; **be** ~**ed by sth.** über etw. (Akk.) schockiert sein

shock absorber /'ʃɒk əbzɔːbə(r)/ n. Stoßdämpfer, der

shocking /'ʃɒkɪŋ/ adj. (a) schockierend; (b) (coll.: very bad) fürchterlich (ugs.); **what a** ~ **thing to say!** wie kann man nur so etwas sagen! (ugs.)

shock: ~ **jock** n. (coll.) Skandal-DJ, der; ~**proof** adj. stoßfest ‹Uhr, Kiste›; erschütterungsfest ‹Gebäude›; ~ **therapy**, ~ **treatment** ns. (Med.) Schocktherapie, die; Schockbehandlung, die

shod ⇒ shoe 2

shoddy /'ʃɒdɪ/ *adj.* schäbig (abwertend); (poorly done, poor in quality) minderwertig ⟨*Arbeit, Stoff, Artikel*⟩

shoe /ʃuː/ **1** *n.* (a) Schuh, *der;* **I shouldn't like to be in his ~s** (fig.) ich möchte nicht in seiner Haut stecken (ugs.); **put oneself into sb.'s ~s** (fig.) sich in jmds. Lage (*Akk.*) versetzen; **sb. shakes in his ~s** jmdm. schlottern die Knie; (b) (of horse) [Huf]eisen, *das.* **2** *v.t.*, **~ing** /'ʃuːɪŋ/, **shod** /ʃɒd/ beschlagen ⟨*Pferd*⟩

shoe: **~ bar** *n.* Schnellschusterei, *die;* **~horn** *n.* Schuhlöffel, *der;* **~lace** *n.* Schnürsenkel, *der;* Schuhband, *das;* **~maker** *n.* ▶ 887 | Schuhmacher, *der;* Schuster, *der;* **~making** *n., no pl.* Schuhmacherei, *die;* **~ polish** *n.* Schuhcreme, *die;* **~ shop** *n.* Schuhgeschäft, *das;* **~string** *n.* (a) ⇒ **~-lace;** (b) (coll.: small amount) **on a ~string** mit ganz wenig Geld; *attrib.* **~string budget** ein minimaler Etat

shone ⇒ shine 1, 2

shoo /ʃuː/ **1** *int.* sch. **2** *v.t.* scheuchen; **~ away** fort- *od.* wegscheuchen

shook ⇒ shake 2, 3

shoot /ʃuːt/ **1** *v.i.*, **shot** /ʃɒt/ (a) schießen (**at** auf + *Akk.*); **~ to kill** ⟨*Polizei:*⟩ scharf schießen; (b) (move rapidly) schießen (ugs.); **~ past sb./down the stairs** an jmdm. vorbeischießen/die Treppe hinunterschießen (ugs.); **pain shot through/up his arm** ein Schmerz schoss durch seinen Arm/seinen Arm hinauf; (c) (Bot.) austreiben; (d) (Sport) schießen. **2** *v.t.*, **shot** (a) (wound) anschießen; (kill) erschießen; (hunt) schießen; **~ sb. dead** jmdn. erschießen *od.* (ugs.) totschießen; **you'll get shot for this** (fig.) du kannst dein Testament machen (ugs.); **he ought to be shot** (fig.) der gehört aufgehängt (ugs.); **~ oneself in the foot** (fig. coll.) sich (*Dat.*) selbst ein Bein stellen; **stop ~ing oneself in the foot** aufhören, sich selbst Knüppel zwischen die Beine zu werfen; (b) schießen mit ⟨*Bogen, Munition, Pistole*⟩; abschießen ⟨*Pfeil, Kugel*⟩ (**at** auf + *Akk.*); (c) (sl.: inject) schießen (Drogenjargon) ⟨*Heroin, Kokain*⟩; (d) (send out) zuwerfen ⟨*Lächeln, Blick*⟩ (**at** *Dat.*); [aus]treiben ⟨*Knospen, Schösslinge*⟩; (e) (Sport) schießen ⟨*Tor, Ball, Puck*⟩; (Basketball) werfen ⟨*Korb*⟩; (f) (push, slide) vorschieben ⟨*Riegel*⟩; (g) (Cinemat.) drehen ⟨*Film, Szene*⟩; (h) (pass swiftly over, under, etc.) durchfahren ⟨*Stromschnelle*⟩; unterfahren ⟨*Brücke*⟩; **~ the lights** (coll.) eine rote Ampel überfahren. **3** *n.* (a) (Bot.) Trieb, *der;* (b) ⟨*ing* party, expedition, practice, scene) Jagd, *die;* **the whole [bang] ~** (coll.) der ganze Kram *od.* Krempel (ugs. abwertend)

~ a'head *v.i.* vorpreschen; **~ ahead of sb.** jmdm. blitzschnell hinter sich (*Dat.*) lassen

~ 'down *v.t.* niederschießen ⟨*Person*⟩; abschießen ⟨*Flugzeug*⟩; (fig.) entkräften ⟨*Argument*⟩

~ 'off *v.i.* losschießen (ugs.); **~ one's mouth off** (sl.) das Maul aufreißen (derb.)

~ 'out 1 *v.i.* hervorschießen; **the dog shot out of the gate** der Hund schoss aus dem Tor heraus (ugs.). **2** *v.t.* herausschleudern; **~ it out** (coll.) sich auslichten

~ 'up *v.i.* (a) in die Höhe schießen; ⟨*Preise, Temperatur, Kosten, Pulsfrequenz:*⟩ in die Höhe schnellen; (b) (coll.: inject drug) sich (*Dat.*) einen Schuss setzen (ugs.)

shooting /'ʃuːtɪŋ/ *n.* (a) Schießerei, *die;* **two more ~s were reported** Meldungen zufolge wurden erneut zwei Menschen von Schüssen getroffen; (b) (Sport) Schießen, *das;* **rifle ~** Gewehrschießen, *das;* (c) (Hunting) **go ~:** auf die Jagd gehen; (d) (Cinemat.) Dreharbeiten *Pl.*

shooting: **~ gallery** *n.* Schießstand, *der;* (at funfair) Schießbude, *die;* **~ match** *n.* (a) Wettschießen, *das;* (b) **the whole ~ match** (coll.) der ganze Kram *od.* Krempel (ugs. abwertend); **~ range** *n.* Schießstand, *der;* **~ 'star** *n.* Sternschnuppe, *die*

'shoot-out *n.* Schießerei, *die*

shop /ʃɒp/ **1** *n.* (a) (premises) Laden, *der;* Geschäft, *das;* **go to the ~s** einkaufen gehen; **keep a ~:** einen Laden *od.* ein Geschäft haben; **keep [the] ~ for sb.** jmdn. im Laden *od.* Geschäft vertreten; **all over the ~** (fig. coll.) überall; (b) (business) **set up ~:** ein Geschäft eröffnen; (as a lawyer, dentist, etc.) eine Praxis aufmachen; **shut up ~:** das Geschäft schließen; **talk ~:** fachsimpeln (ugs.); (c) (workshop) Werkstatt, *die.* **2** *v.i.*, **-pp-** einkaufen; **go ~ping** einkaufen

gehen; **~** *or* **go ~ping for shoes** Schuhe kaufen gehen. **3** *v.t.*, **-pp-** (Brit. sl.) verpfeifen

~ a'round *v.i.* sich umsehen (**for** nach)

shopaholic /ˈʃɒpəhɒlɪk/ *n.* Kaufsüchtige, *der/die*

shop: **~ assistant** *n.* ▶ 887 | (Brit.) Verkäufer, *der/* Verkäuferin, *die;* **~ 'floor** *n.* (a) (place) Produktion, *die* (ugs.); (b) (workers) **the ~ floor** die Arbeiter; *attrib.* Arbeiter-; **~keeper** *n.* ▶ 887 | Ladenbesitzer, *der/*-besitzerin, *die;* **~lifter** /ˈʃɒplɪftə(r)/ *n.* Ladendieb, *der/*-diebin, *die;* **~lifting** *n., no pl., no indef. art.* Ladendiebstahl, *der;* **~owner** ⇒ **~keeper**

shopper /ˈʃɒpə(r)/ *n.* (a) (person) Käufer, *der/*Käuferin, *die;* (b) (wheeled bag) Einkaufsroller, *der*

shopping /ˈʃɒpɪŋ/ *n., no pl., no indef. art.* (a) (buying goods) Einkaufen, *das;* **do the ~:** einkaufen/[seine] Einkäufe machen; (b) (items bought) Einkäufe *Pl.*

shopping: **~ bag** *n.* Einkaufstasche, *die;* **~ basket** *n.* Einkaufskorb, *der;* **~ centre** *n.* Einkaufszentrum, *das;* **~ list** *n.* Einkaufszettel, *der;* (fig.) Wunschliste, *die;* **~ mall** *n.* Einkaufszentrum, *das;* **~ precinct** *n.* Einkaufs- *od.* Geschäftsviertel, *das;* **~ street** *n.* Geschäftsstraße, *die;* **~ trolley** *n.* Einkaufswagen, *der*

shop: **~-soiled** *adj.* (Brit.) (slightly damaged) leicht beschädigt; (slightly dirty) angeschmutzt; **~ steward** *n.* ▶ 887 | [gewerkschaftlicher] Vertrauensmann/[gewerkschaftliche] Vertrauensfrau; **~ 'window** *n.* Schaufenster, *das*

shore¹ /ʃɔː(r)/ *n.* Ufer, *das;* (coast) Küste, *die;* (beach) Strand, *der;* **on the ~:** am Ufer/an der Küste/am Strand; **on the ~[s] of Lake Garda** am Ufer des Gardasees; **off ~:** vor der Küste; **be on ~** ⟨*Seemann:*⟩ an Land sein

shore² *v.t.* (support) abstützen ⟨*Tunnel*⟩

~ 'up *v.t.* (support) abstützen ⟨*Mauer, Haus*⟩; (fig.) stützen ⟨*Preis, Währung, Wirtschaft*⟩

shorn ⇒ shear

short /ʃɔːt/ **1** *adj.* (a) kurz; **a ~ time** *or* **while ago/ later** vor kurzem/kurze Zeit später; **for a ~ time** *or* **while** eine kleine Weile; ein [kleines] Weilchen; **a ~ time before he left** kurz bevor er ging; **a ~ time** *or* **while before/after sth.** kurz vor/nach etw. (*Dat.*); **in a ~ time** *or* **while** (soon) bald; in Kürze; **within a ~ [space of] time** innerhalb kurzer Zeit; **in the ~ run** *or* **term** kurzfristig; kurzzeitig; **wear one's hair/skirts ~:** seine Haare kurz tragen/kurze Röcke tragen; (b) (not tall) klein ⟨*Person, Wuchs*⟩; niedrig ⟨*Gebäude, Baum, Schornstein*⟩; (c) (not far-reaching) kurz ⟨*Wurf, Schuss, Gedächtnis*⟩; (d) (deficient, scanty) knapp; **be in ~ supply** knapp sein; **good doctors are in ~ supply** gute Ärzte sind rar *od.* (ugs.) sind Mangelware; **be [far/not far] ~ of a record** einen Rekord [bei weitem] nicht erreichen/[knapp] verfehlen; **sb./sth. is so much/so many ~:** jmdm./einer Sache fehlt soundsoviel/fehlen soundsoviele; **sb. is ~ of sth.** jmdm. fehlt es an etw. (*Dat.*); **time is getting/is ~:** die Zeit wird/ist knapp; **keep sb. ~ [of sth.]** jmdn. [mit etw.] kurz halten; **[have to] go ~ [of sth.]** [an etw. (*Dat.*)] Mangel leiden [müssen]; **she is ~ of milk today** sie hat heute nicht genug Milch; **the firm is ~ of staff** die Firma hat zu wenig Arbeitskräfte; **be ~ [of cash]** knapp [bei Kasse] sein (ugs.); **he is just ~ of six feet/not far ~ of 60** er ist knapp sechs Fuß [groß]/sechzig [Jahre alt]; **it is nothing ~ of miraculous** es ist ein ausgesprochenes Wunder; (e) (brief, concise) kurz; **a ~ history of Wales** eine kurz gefasste Geschichte von Wales; **the ~ answer is …:** um es kurz zu machen die Antwort ist …; **~ and sweet** (iron.) kurz und schmerzlos (ugs.); **in ~, …:** kurz, … ; (f) (curt, uncivil) kurz angebunden; barsch; (g) (Cookery) mürbe ⟨*Teig*⟩; (h) **sell oneself ~** (fig.) sein Licht unter den Scheffel stellen; **sell sb./sth. ~** (fig.) jmdn./etw. unterschätzen. **2** *adv.* (a) (abruptly) plötzlich; **stop ~:** plötzlich abbrechen; ⟨*Musik, Gespräch:*⟩ jäh (geh.) abbrechen; **stop ~ at sth.** über etw. (*Akk.*) nicht hinausgehen; **stop sb. ~:** jmdn. ins Wort fallen; **pull up ~:** plötzlich anhalten; **bring** *or* **pull sb. up ~:** jmdn. stutzen lassen; (b) (curtly) kurz angebunden; barsch; (c) (before the expected place or time) **jump/land ~:** zu kurz springen/zu früh landen (ugs.); **~ of sth.** vor etw. (*Dat.*); **stop ~ of the line** vor der Linie stehen-/liegenbleiben; **the bomb dropped ~ [of its target]** die Bombe fiel vor das Ziel;

fall *or* **come [far/considerably]** ∿ **of sth.** etw. [bei weitem] nicht erreichen; **stop** ∿ **of sth.** (fig.) vor etw. zurückschrecken; **stop** ∿ **of doing sth.** davor zurückschrecken, etw. zu tun; **(d) nothing** ∿ **of a catastrophe/miracle can** …: nur eine Katastrophe/ein Wunder kann …; ∿ **of locking him in, how can I keep him from going out?** wie kann ich ihn daran hindern auszugehen — es sei denn ich schlösse ihn ein? **3** *n.* **(a)** (Electr. coll.) Kurze, *der* (ugs.); **(b)** (coll.: drink) Schnaps, *der* (ugs.). **4** *v.t.* (Electr. coll.) kurzschließen. **5** *v.i.* (Electr. coll.) einen Kurzschluss kriegen (ugs.).

shortage /'ʃɔːtɪdʒ/ *n.* Mangel, *der* (**of** an + *Dat.*); ∿ **of fruit/teachers** Obstknappheit, *die*/Lehrermangel, *der*

short: ∿**bread**, ∿**cake** *ns.* Shortbread, *das;* Keks *aus Butterteig;* ∿**change** *v.t.* zu wenig [Wechselgeld] herausgeben (+ *Dat.*); (fig.) übers Ohr hauen (ugs.); ∿ **'circuit** *n.* (Electr.) Kurzschluss, *der;* ∿**'circuit** (Electr.) **1** *v.t.* kurzschließen; **2** *v.i.* umgehen; **2** *v.i.* einen Kurzschluss bekommen; ∿**coming** *n., usu. in pl.* Unzulänglichkeit, *die;* ∿ **'cut** *n.* Abkürzung, *die;* **take a** ∿ **cut** (lit. or fig.) eine Abkürzung machen; **be a** ∿ **cut to sth.** (fig.) den Weg zu etw. abkürzen; ∿ **division** ⇒ **division f;** ∿ **'drink** *n.* hochprozentiges Getränk

shorten /'ʃɔːtn/ **1** *v.i.* (become shorter) kürzer werden. **2** *v.t.* (make shorter) kürzen; (curtail) verkürzen ⟨*Besuch, Wartezeit, Inkubationszeit*⟩

short: ∿**fall** *n.* Fehlmenge, *die;* (in budget, financial resources) Defizit, *das;* ∿**haired** *adj.* kurzhaarig; ∿**hand** *n.* Kurzschrift, *die;* Stenografie, *die;* **write** ∿**hand** stenografieren; **that's** ∿**hand for** … (fig.) das ist eine Kurzformel für …; *see also* **typist**

shortish /'ʃɔːtɪʃ/ *adj.* ziemlich kurz; ziemlich klein ⟨*Person*⟩

short: ∿**-legged** *adj.* kurzbeinig; ∿**list** *n.* (Brit.) engere Auswahl; **be on/put sb. on the** ∿**list** in der engeren Auswahl sein/jmdn. in die engere Auswahl nehmen; ∿**list** *v.t.* in die engere Auswahl nehmen; ∿**-lived** /'ʃɔːtlɪvd/ *adj.* kurzlebig

shortly /'ʃɔːtlɪ/ *adv.* **(a)** (soon) in Kürze; gleich (ugs.); ∿ **before/after sth.** kurz vor/nach etw.; **(b)** (briefly) kurz; **(c)** (curtly) kurz angebunden; in barschem Ton

shortness /'ʃɔːtnɪs/ *n., no pl.* **(a)** Kürze, *die;* **(b)** (of person) Kleinheit, *die;* geringe Körpergröße; **(c)** (scarcity, lack) Knappheit, *die* (**of** an + *Dat.*); **(d)** (curtness) Barschheit, *die*

'short: ∿ **'pastry** *n.* (Cookery) Mürbeteig, *der;* ∿**range** *adj.* **(a)** Kurzstrecken ⟨*flugzeug, -rakete usw.*⟩; **(b)** (relating to ∿ future period) kurzfristig

shorts /ʃɔːts/ *n. pl.* **(a)** (trousers) kurze Hose[n]; Shorts *Pl.;* (in sports) Sporthose, *die;* **(b)** (Amer.: underpants) Unterhose, *die*

short: ∿ **'sight** *n., no pl., no art.* Kurzsichtigkeit, *die;* **have** ∿ **sight** kurzsichtig sein; ∿**-sighted** /'ʃɔːt'saɪtɪd/ *adj.* (lit. or fig.) kurzsichtig; ∿**-sleeved** /'ʃɔːtsliːvd/ *adj.* kurzärm[el]ig; ∿**-staffed** /'ʃɔːt'staːft/ *adj.* **be [very]** ∿**staffed** [viel] zu wenig Personal haben; ∿ **'story** *n.* (Lit.) Shortstory *n.;* Kurzgeschichte, *die;* ∿ **'temper** *n.* **have a** ∿ **temper** aufbrausend *od.* cholerisch sein; ∿**'tempered** *adj.* aufbrausend; cholerisch; ∿**term** *adj.* kurzfristig; (provisional) vorläufig ⟨*Lösung, Antwort*⟩; ∿ **'wave** *n.* (Radio) Kurzwelle, *die;* ∿**-wave** *adj.* (Radio) Kurzwellen-

shot /ʃɒt/ **1** *n.* **(a)** (discharge of gun) Schuss, *der;* (firing of rocket) Abschuss, *der;* **Start**, *der;* **fire a** ∿ **[at sb./sth.]** einen Schuss [auf jmdn./etw.] abgeben; **like a** ∿ (fig.) wie der Blitz (ugs.); **I'd do it like a** ∿: ich würde es auf der Stelle tun; **have a** ∿ **at sth./at doing sth.** (fig.) etw. versuchen/versuchen, etw. zu tun; *see also* **dark 2 b; long shot; (b)** (Athletics) Kugel, *die;* **put the** ∿: die Kugel stoßen; kugelstoßen; **[putting] the** ∿: Kugelstoßen, *das;* **(c)** (Sport: stroke, kick, throw, Archery, Shooting) Schuss, *der;* **(d)** (Photog.) Aufnahme, *die;* (Cinemat.) Einstellung, *die;* **do** *or* **film interior/location** ∿s (Cinemat.) Innenaufnahmen machen/am Originalschauplatz drehen; **(e)** (injection) Spritze, *die;* (of drug) Schuss, *der* (Jargon); **be a** ∿ **in the arm for sb./sth.** (fig.) jmdm./einer Sache Aufschwung geben. **2** ⇒ **shoot 1, 2. 3** *adj.* **be/get** ∿ **of sb./sth.** (coll.) jmdn./etw. los sein/loswerden

shot: ∿**gun** *n.* [Schrot]flinte, *die;* ∿**gun wedding/marriage** (fig. coll.) Mussheirat/Mussehe, *die* (ugs.); **ride** ∿**gun** zur Bewachung als Beifahrer mitfahren; ∿**-put** *n., no pl., no indef. art.* (Athletics) Kugelstoßen, *das;* ∿**putter** /'ʃɒtpʊtə(r)/ *n.* (Athletics) Kugelstoßer, *der*/-stoßerin, *die*

should ▶ 1080 ◀ ⇒ **shall**

shoulder /'ʃəʊldə(r)/ **1** *n.* **(a)** ▶ 672 ◀ Schulter, *die;* ∿ **to** ∿ (lit. or fig.) Schulter an Schulter; **straight from the** ∿ (fig.) unverblümt; **cry on sb.'s** ∿ (fig.) sich bei jmdm. ausweinen; **give sb. the cold** '∿: jmdn. schneiden; **(b)** *in pl.* (upper part of back) Schultern *Pl.;* (of garment) Schulterpartie, *die;* **lie** *or* **rest/fall on sb.'s** ∿s (fig.) auf jmds. Schultern (*Dat.*) lasten/jmdm. aufgebürdet werden; **he has broad** ∿s (fig.: is able to take responsibility) er hat einen breiten Rücken; **(c)** (Anat.) ∿ **joint** Schultergelenk, *das;* **(d)** (Gastr.) Bug, *der;* Schulter, *die;* ∿ **of lamb** Lammschulter, *die;* **(e)** (Road Constr.) Randstreifen, *der;* Seitenstreifen, *der; see also* **hard shoulder. 2** *v.t.* **(a)** (push with ∿) rempeln; ∿ **one's way through the crowd** sich rempelnd einen Weg durch die Menge bahnen; **(b)** (take on one's ∿s) schultern; (fig.) übernehmen ⟨*Verantwortung, Aufgabe*⟩

∿ **a'side** *v.t.* beiseite rempeln; (fig.) beiseite schieben

shoulder: ∿ **bag** *n.* Umhängetasche, *die;* ∿ **blade** *n.* Schulterblatt, *das;* ∿ **strap** *n.* **(a)** (on ∿ of garment) Schulterklappe, *die;* **(b)** (on bag) Tragriemen, *der;* (suspending a garment) Träger, *der*

shouldn't /'ʃʊdnt/ (coll.) = **should not;** ⇒ **shall**

shout /ʃaʊt/ **1** *n.* Ruf, *der;* (inarticulate) Schrei, *der;* **warning** ∿, ∿ **of alarm** Warnruf, *der*/-schrei, *der;* ∿ **of joy/ rage** Freuden-/ Wutschrei, *der;* ∿ **of encouragement/ approval** Anfeuerungs-/Beifallsruf, *der.* **2** *v.i.* schreien; ∿ **with laughter/pain** vor Lachen/Schmerzen schreien; ∿ **with** *or* **for joy** vor Freude schreien; ∿ **at sb.** (abusively) jmdn. anschreien; ∿ **for sb./sth.** nach jmdm./etw. schreien; ∿ **for help** um Hilfe schreien *od.* rufen. **3** *v.t.* schreien; ∿ **abuse** pöbeln; ∿ **abuse at sb.** jmdn. anpöbeln. ∿ **'down** *v.t.* ∿ **sb. down** (prevent from being heard) jmdn. niederschreien

∿ **'out 1** *v.i.* aufschreien. **2** *v.t.* [laut] rufen

shouting /'ʃaʊtɪŋ/ *n.* (act) Schreien, *das;* (shouts) Geschrei, *das;* **it's all over but** *or* **bar the** ∿ (fig.) das Rennen ist im Grunde schon gelaufen (ugs.)

shove /ʃʌv/ **1** *n.* Stoß, *der.* **2** *v.t.* **(a)** stoßen; schubsen (ugs.); **(b)** (use force to propel) schieben; **(c)** (coll.: put) tun. **3** *v.i.* drängen; drängeln (ugs.); ∿ **through the crowd** (coll.) sich durch die Menge drängeln (ugs.). See also **push 2 a, 3 d**

∿ **a'way** *v.t.* (coll.) wegschubsen (ugs.)

shovel /'ʃʌvl/ **1** *n.* Schaufel, *die;* (machine) Bagger, *der.* **2** *v.t.,* (Brit.) **-ll-: (a)** schaufeln; **(b)** (fig.) ∿ **food into one's mouth** Essen in sich (*Akk.*) reinschaufeln *od.* -stopfen

shovelful /'ʃʌvlfʊl/ *n.* **a** ∿ **of earth** *etc.* eine Schaufel Erde *usw.*

show /ʃəʊ/ **1** *n.* **(a)** (display) Pracht, *die;* **a** ∿ **of flowers/ colour** eine Blumen-/Farbenpracht; ∿ **of force/ strength** *etc.* Demonstration der Macht/Stärke *usw.;* **be on** ∿: ausgestellt sein; **put sth. on** ∿: etw. ausstellen; **(b)** (exhibition) Ausstellung, *die;* Schau, *die;* **dog** ∿: Hundeschau, *die;* **(c)** (entertainment, performance) Show, *die;* (Theatre) Vorstellung, *die;* (Radio, Telev.) [Unterhaltungs]sendung, *die; see also* **steal 1 a; (d)** (coll.: effort) **it's a poor** ∿: das ist ein schwaches Bild; **put up a good/poor** ∿: eine gute/ schlechte Figur machen; **good** ∿! gut [gemacht]!; **(e)** (coll.: undertaking, business) **it's his** ∿: er ist der Boss (ugs.); **run the** ∿: der Boss sein (ugs.); **take the [whole]** ∿ **away** alles ausquatschen (salopp); **(f)** (outward appearance) Anschein, *der;* **make a great** ∿ **of friendliness** ungeheuer freundlich tun; **make** *or* **put on a [great]** ∿ **of doing sth.** sich (*Dat.*) [angestrengt] den Anschein geben, etw. zu tun; **be for** ∿: reine Angeberei sein (ugs.); **do sth. just for** ∿: etw. nur aus Prestigegründen tun. **2** *v.t., p.p.* ∿**ed** /ʃəʊn/ *or* ∿**ed** **(a)** (allow or cause to be seen) zeigen; vorzeigen ⟨*Pass, Fahrschein usw.*⟩; ∿ **sb. sth.,** ∿ **sth. to sb.** jmdm. etw. zeigen; **have nothing/something to** ∿ **for it** [dabei] nichts/etwas zum Vorzeigen haben; **that dress**

Should

Conditional

In the first person singular and plural, *should* is used for *would* to form the conditional, and so is translated by the conditional in German:

I should be surprised if he wins	= Es würde mich wundern, wenn er gewänne
I should have gone if I had been invited	= Ich wäre gegangen, wenn ich eingeladen gewesen wäre
I should have thought it was obvious	= Ich hätte gedacht, es liegt auf der Hand
We should welcome more opportunity for contact	= Wir würden es begrüßen, wenn wir mehr Kontakt- möglichkeiten hätten
We should like to help you	= Wir möchten Ihnen helfen

Where *should* occurs in the conditional clause (with any person), the translation is **sollte**, **sollten** etc., and like the English *should* this can stand at the beginning of the clause:

If they should be delayed or *Should they be delayed, ...*	= Falls sie aufgehalten werden sollten or Sollten sie aufgehalten werden, ...
Should he turn up after all, let me know	= Sollte er doch noch auftauchen, sagen Sie mir Bescheid

Meaning *ought to*

In most cases expressing obligation, this is also translated by **sollte** (and **hätte sollen** in the past):

You should tell her	= Du solltest es ihr sagen
They shouldn't really be here	= Eigentlich sollten or dürften sie nicht hier sein
We should have gone earlier	= Wir hätten früher hingehen sollen

He shouldn't have come	= Er hätte nicht kommen sollen

Note that unlike *should*, **sollte** does not normally stand on its own:

I don't think you should	= Ich finde, du solltest es nicht tun

With an impersonal subject, **müsste** is used.

It should be banned	= Das müsste man verbieten

Also expressing a surmise or estimate, **dürfte** or **müsste** can be used:

They should be there by now	= Jetzt dürften or müssten sie dort angekommen sein
That should be enough	= Das dürfte or müsste genügen
That should have been enough	= Das hätte genügen müssen

After that

In clauses beginning with *that* preceded by an adjective, the *should* is not translated:

It is strange that he should never have told you	= Es ist seltsam, dass er es dir nie gesagt hat
It is important that they should be warned	= Es ist wichtig, dass sie gewarnt werden

Much the same applies to clauses with *in order that* or *so that*:

She gave me a cushion in order that or *so that I should sit more comfortably*	= Sie gab mir ein Kissen, damit ich bequemer saß
In order that they should all be able to hear, I used a megaphone	= Damit sie alle hören konnten, verwendete ich ein Megaphon

---

~**s your petticoat** bei diesem Kleid sieht man deinen Unterrock; **this material does not** ~ **the dirt** auf diesem Material sieht man den Schmutz nicht; *see also* **colour 1 e; sign 1 e; (b)** (manifest, give evidence of) zeigen; beweisen ‹*Mut, Entschlossenheit, Urteilsvermögen usw.*›; ~ **hesitation** zaudern; **he is** ~**ing his age** man sieht ihm sein Alter an; **(c)** ~ **[sb.] kindness/mercy** freundlich [zu jmdm.] sein/Erbarmen [mit jmdm.] haben; ~ **mercy on** or **to sb.** Erbarmen mit jmdm. haben; **(d)** (indicate) zeigen ‹*Gefühl, Freude usw.*›; ‹*Thermometer, Uhr usw.*› anzeigen; **as** ~**n in the illustration** wie die Abbildung zeigt; **frontiers are** ~**n by blue lines and towns are** ~**n in red** Grenzen sind durch blaue Linien und Städte sind rot gekennzeichnet; **the accounts** ~ **a profit** die Bücher weisen einen Gewinn aus; **the firm** ~**s a profit/loss** die Firma macht Gewinn/Verlust; **(e)** (demonstrate, prove) zeigen; ~ **sb. that ...:** jmdm. beweisen, dass ...; **it all/just goes to** ~ **that ...:** das beweist nur, dass ...; **it all goes to** ~, **doesn't it?** das beweist es doch, oder?; **I'll** ~ **you/him** *etc.!* ich werd's dir/ihm *usw.* schon zeigen!; ~ **sb. who's boss** jmdm. zeigen, wer das Sagen hat; **(f)** (conduct) führen; ~ **sb. over** or **round the house/to his place** jmdn. durchs Haus/an seinen Platz führen. **3** *v.i., p.p.* ~**n** or ~**ed (a)** (be visible) sichtbar od. zu sehen sein; **he was angry/bored, and it** ~**ed** er war wütend/langweilte sich, und man sah es [ihm an]; **his age is beginning to** ~: man sieht ihm sein Alter allmählich an; **(b)** (be ~n) ‹*Film:*› laufen; ‹*Künstler:*› ausstellen; **'Gandhi' — now** ~**ing in the West End** „Gandhi" — Jetzt im West End; **(c)** (make sth. known) **time will** ~: man wird es [ja] sehen
~ **'in** *v.t.* hineinführen/hereinführen
~ **'off 1** *v.t.* **(a)** (display) ~ **sth./sb. off** etw./jmdn. vorführen od. vorzeigen; (in order to impress) mit etw./jmdm.

prahlen od. (ugs.) angeben; **(b)** (display to advantage) zur Geltung bringen. **2** *v.i.* angeben (ugs.); prahlen
~ **'out** *v.t.* hinausführen
~ **'round** *v.t.* herumführen
~ **'through** *v.i.* durchscheinen
~ **'up 1** *v.t.* **(a)** (make visible) deutlich sichtbar machen; aufdecken ‹*Betrug*›; **(b)** (coll.: embarrass) blamieren. **2** *v.i.* **(a)** (be easily visible) [deutlich] zu sehen od. erkennen sein; (fig.) sich zeigen; **(b)** (coll.: arrive) sich blicken lassen (ugs.); auftauchen

show: ~**biz** /ˈʃəʊbɪz/ (coll.), ~ **business** *ns.*, *no pl.*, *no art.* Schaugeschäft, *das;* Showbusiness, *das.* Vitrine, *die;* Schaukasten, *der;* (fig.) Schaufenster, *das;* ~**down** *n.* (fig.) Kraftprobe, *die;* **have a** ~**down [with sb.]** sich [mit jmdm.] auseinander setzen

shower /ˈʃaʊə(r)/ **1** *n.* **(a)** Schauer, *der;* ~ **of rain/sleet/hail** Regen- / Schneeregen- / Hagelschauer, *der;* **a** ~ **of confetti/sparks/stones** ein Konfettiregen/Funkenregen/Steinhagel; **(b)** (for washing) Dusche, *die; attrib.* Dusch-; **have** or **take a [cold/quick]** ~: [kalt/schnell] duschen; **be under the** ~: unter der Dusche stehen; **(c)** (Amer.: party) ~ **[party]** Geschenkparty, *die (für eine Braut, bei der sie Aussteuergegenstände geschenkt bekommt).* **2** *v.t.* **(a)** ~ **sth. over** or **on sb.,** ~ **sb. with sth.** jmdm. mit etw. überschütten; **(b)** (fig.: lavish) ~ **sth. [up]on sb.,** ~ **sb. with sth.** jmdm. mit etw. überhäufen. **3** *v.i.* **(a)** (fall in ~s) ‹*Wasser, Konfetti:*› auf jmdn. herabregnen; ‹*Steine, Verwünschungen:*› auf jmdn. niederhageln; **(b)** (have a ~) duschen

'shower: ~ **curtain** *n.* Duschvorhang, *der;* ~ **gel** *n.* Duschgel, *das;* ~**proof** *adj.* [bedingt] regendicht

showery /'ʃaʊərɪ/ *adj.* it is ∼: es gibt immer wieder kurze Schauer; **a cold and** ∼ **day** ein kalter Tag mit häufigen Schauern

show: ∼**girl** *n.* Showgirl, *das;* ∼**ground** *n.* Ausstellungsgelände, *das;* ∼ **house** *n.* Musterhaus, *das*

showing /'ʃəʊɪŋ/ *n.* **(a)** (of film) Vorführung, *die;* (of television programme) Sendung, *die;* **(b)** (evidence) **on this** ∼: demnach; **on any** ∼: wie man es auch [dreht und] wendet; **(c)** (quality of performance) Leistung, *die;* **make a good/poor** *etc.* ∼: eine gute/schwache *usw.* Leistung zeigen; **on this** ∼: bei dieser Leistung

show: ∼**jumper** *n.* (Sport) **(a)** (person) Springreiter, *der/*-reiterin, *die;* **(b)** (horse) Springpferd, *das;* ∼**jumping** *n.* (Sport) Springreiten, *das;* ∼**man** /'ʃəʊmən/ *n., pl.* ∼**men** /'ʃəʊmən/ **(a)** (proprietor of fairground booth etc.) Schausteller, *der;* **(b)** (effective presenter) Showman, *der*

shown ⇨ show 2, 3

show: ∼**-off** *n.* (coll.) Angeber, *der/*Angeberin, *die* (ugs.); **don't be such a** ∼**-off** gib nicht so an!; ∼**piece** *n.* (of exhibition, collection) Schaustück, *das;* (highlight) Paradestück, *das;* ∼**place** *n.* Attraktion, *die;* ∼**room** *n.* Ausstellungsraum, *der;* ∼ **trial** *n.* Schauprozess, *der*

showy /'ʃəʊɪ/ *adj.* **(a)** (gaudy, ostentatious) protzig (ugs.); **(b)** (striking) prächtig ⟨*Farben*⟩; [farben]prächtig ⟨*Blumen*⟩

shrank ⇨ shrink

shrapnel *n.* /'ʃræpnl/ *n.* (Mil.: fragments) Bombensplitter *Pl.;* Granatsplitter *Pl.*

shred /ʃred/ *n.* Fetzen, *der;* **not a** ∼ **of evidence** keine Spur eines Beweises; **tear** *etc.* **sth. to** ∼**s** etw. in Fetzen reißen *usw.;* **tear a theory/an argument to** ∼**s** eine Theorie/eine Argumentation zerpflücken; **our clothes were in** ∼**s** unsere Kleidung war zerfetzt

shrew /ʃru:/ *n.* **(a)** (Zool.) Spitzmaus, *die;* **(b)** (woman) Beißzange, *die* (salopp)

shrewd /ʃru:d/ *adj.* scharfsinnig ⟨*Person*⟩; klug ⟨*Entscheidung, Investition, Schritt, Geschäftsmann*⟩; genau ⟨*Schätzung, Einschätzung*⟩; treffsicher ⟨*Urteilsvermögen*⟩

shriek /ʃri:k/ 1 *n.* [Auf]schrei, *der;* **give a** ∼: [auf]schreien; **give a** ∼ **of horror/fear** *etc.* einen Schrei des Entsetzens/der Angst *usw.* ausstoßen. 2 *v.i.* [auf]schreien; ∼ **with horror/fear** *etc.* vor Entsetzen/Angst *usw.* [auf]schreien

shrift /ʃrɪft/ *n.* **give sb. short** ∼: jmdn. kurz abfertigen (ugs.); **get short** ∼ **[from sb.]** [von jmdm.] kurz abgefertigt werden (ugs.)

shrill /ʃrɪl/ *adj.,* **shrilly** /'ʃrɪlɪ/ *adv.* schrill

shrimp /ʃrɪmp/ *n., pl.* ∼**s** *or* ∼: (Zool.) Garnele, *die;* Krabbe, *die* (ugs.); (Gastr.) Krabbe, *die; attrib.* Garnelen-/Krabben-

shrine /ʃraɪn/ *n.* Heiligtum, *das;* (tomb) Grab, *das;* (casket) Schrein, *der* (veralt.); (casket holding sacred relics) Reliquienschrein, *der*

shrink /ʃrɪŋk/ 1 *v.i.,* **shrank** /ʃræŋk/, **shrunk** /ʃrʌŋk/ **(a)** (grow smaller) schrumpfen ⟨*Person:*⟩ kleiner werden; ⟨*Kleidung, Stoff:*⟩ einlaufen; ⟨*Holz:*⟩ sich zusammenziehen; ⟨*Handel, Einkünfte:*⟩ zurückgehen; **(b)** (recoil) sich zusammenkauern; ∼ **from sb./sth.** vor jmdm. zurückweichen/ vor etw. (*Dat.*) zurückschrecken; ∼ **from doing sth.** sich scheuen, etw. zu tun. 2 *v.t.,* **shrank, shrunk** sich zusammenziehen lassen ⟨*Holz*⟩; einlaufen lassen ⟨*Textilien*⟩

∼ **a'way** *v.i.* **(a)** (recoil) zurückweichen (**from** vor + *Dat.*); **(b)** (grow smaller) zusammenschrumpfen

∼ **'back** *v.i.* zurückweichen (**from** vor + *Dat.*); ∼ **back from sth./doing sth.** (fig.) vor etw. (*Dat.*) zurückschrecken/sich scheuen, etw. zu tun

shrinkage /'ʃrɪŋkɪdʒ/ *n.* **(a)** (act) (of clothing, material) Einlaufen, *das;* (of income, trade, etc.) Rückgang, *der;* **(b)** (degree) Schrumpfung, *die*

shrink: ∼**-proof,** ∼**-resistant** *adjs.* schrumpffrei; ∼**-wrap** *v.t.* in einer Schrumpffolie verpacken

shrivel /'ʃrɪvl/ 1 *v.t.,* **-ll-,** (Brit.) **-ll-** [**up**] runzlig machen ⟨*Haut, Gesicht*⟩; welk werden lassen ⟨*Pflanze, Blume*⟩. 2 *v.i.,* (Brit.) **-ll-** ∼ [**up**] verschrumpeln; ⟨*Haut, Gesicht:*⟩ runzlig werden; ⟨*Pflanze, Blume:*⟩ welk werden; ⟨*Ballon:*⟩ zusammenschrumpfen

shroud /ʃraʊd/ 1 *n.* **(a)** Leichentuch, *das* (veralt.); **(b)** (fig.: of fog, mystery, etc.) Schleier, *der.* 2 *v.t.* einhüllen; ∼ **sth. in sth.** etw. in etw. (*Akk.*) hüllen

Shrove Tuesday /ʃrəʊv 'tju:zdeɪ, ʃrəʊv 'tju:zdɪ/ *n.* Fastnachtsdienstag, *der*

shrub /ʃrʌb/ *n.* Strauch, *der*

shrubbery /'ʃrʌbərɪ/ *n.* **(a)** Gesträuch, *das;* **(b)** (shrubs collectively) Sträucher

shrug /ʃrʌg/ 1 *n.* ∼ **[of one's** *or* **the shoulders]** Achselzucken, *das;* **give a** ∼ **[of one's** *or* **the shoulders]** die od. mit den Achseln zucken. 2 *v.t. & i.,* **-gg-:** ∼ **[one's shoulders]** die od. mit den Achseln zucken

∼ **'off** *v.t.* in den Wind schlagen; ∼ **sth. off as unimportant** etw. als unwichtig abtun

shrunk ⇨ shrink

shrunken /'ʃrʌŋkn/ *adj.* verhutzelt (ugs.) ⟨*Person*⟩; schrumpelig, verschrumpelt ⟨*Äpfel*⟩; ∼ **head** Schrumpfkopf, *der*

shudder /'ʃʌdə(r)/ 1 *v.i.* **(a)** (shiver) zittern (**with** vor + *Dat.*); **sb.** ∼**s to think of sth.** jmdn. schaudert bei dem Gedanken an etw. (*Akk.*); **(b)** (vibrate) zittern; ∼ **to a halt** zitternd zum Stehen kommen. 2 *n.* **(a)** (shivering) Zittern, *das;* Schauder, *der;* **sb. has/ gets the** ∼**s** (coll.) jmdn. schaudert; **it gives me the** ∼**s to think of it** (coll.) mich schaudert, wenn ich daran denke; **(b)** (vibration) Zittern, *das*

shuffle /'ʃʌfl/ 1 *n.* **(a)** Schlurfen, *das;* **walk with a** ∼: schlurfend gehen; schlurfen; **(b)** (Cards) Mischen, *das;* **give the cards a [good]** ∼: die Karten [gut] mischen; **(c)** (fig.: change) Umbildung, *die;* **cabinet** ∼: Kabinettsumbildung, *die.* 2 *v.t.* **(a)** (rearrange) umbilden ⟨*Kabinett*⟩; neu verteilen ⟨*Aufgaben*⟩; sortieren ⟨*Schriftstücke usw.*⟩; (mix up) durcheinander bringen; **(b)** (Cards) mischen; **(c) he** ∼**s his feet when he walks** er schlurft beim Gehen. 3 *v.i.* **(a)** (Cards) mischen; **(b)** (move, walk) schlurfen; **(c)** (shift one's position) herumrutschen

shun /ʃʌn/ *v.t.,* **-nn-** meiden

shunt /ʃʌnt/ *v.t.* (Railw.) rangieren; ∼ **[off]** (fig.) abschieben

shush /ʃʊʃ/ 1 *int.* ⇨ hush 3. 2 *v.t.* zum Schweigen bringen

shut /ʃʌt/ 1 *v.t.,* **-tt-, shut (a)** zumachen; schließen; ∼ **sth. to sb./sth.** etw. für jmdn./etw. schließen; ∼ **a road to traffic** eine Straße für den Verkehr sperren; ∼ **the door on sb.** jmdm. die Tür vor der Nase zuschlagen (ugs.); ∼ **the door on sth.** (fig.) die Möglichkeit einer Sache (*Gen.*) verbauen; ∼ **one's eyes to sth.** (fig.) seine Augen vor etw. (*Dat.*) verschließen; (choose to ignore sth.) über etw. (*Akk.*) hinwegsehen; ∼ **one's ears to sth.** (fig.) die Ohren vor etw. (*Dat.*) verschließen; ∼ *or* **lock the stable door after the horse has bolted** ⇨ lock[?] 2 a; **(b)** (confine) ∼ **sb./an animal in[to] sth.** jmdn./ein Tier in etw. (*Akk.*) sperren; ∼ **oneself in[to] a room** sich in einem Zimmer einschließen; **(c)** (exclude) ∼ **sb./an animal out of sth.** jmdn./ein Tier aus etw. aussperren; **(d)** (trap) ∼ **one's finger/coat in a door** sich ⟨*Dat.*⟩ den Finger/Mantel in einer Tür einklemmen; **(e)** (fold up) schließen, zumachen ⟨*Buch, Hand*⟩; zusammenklappen ⟨*Klappmesser, Fächer*⟩. 2 *v.i.,* **-tt-, shut** schließen; ⟨*Laden:*⟩ schließen, zumachen; ⟨*Blüte:*⟩ sich schließen; **the door/case won't** ∼: die Tür/ der Koffer geht nicht zu od. schließt nicht; **the door** ∼ **on/after him** die Tür schloss sich vor/hinter ihm. 3 *adj.* zu; geschlossen; **we are** ∼ **on Saturdays/for lunch** wir haben samstags/über Mittag geschlossen od. zu; **keep sth.** ∼: etw. geschlossen halten od. zu lassen

∼ **a'way** *v.t.* wegschließen; **keep sth.** ∼ **away safely** etw. unter sicherem Verschluss halten

∼ **'down** 1 *v.t.* **(a)** schließen, zumachen ⟨*Deckel, Fenster*⟩; **(b)** (end operation of) stilllegen; abschalten ⟨*Kernreaktor*⟩; einstellen ⟨*Aktivitäten*⟩; (Radio, Telev.) einstellen ⟨*Sendebetrieb*⟩. 2 *v.i.* (cease working) ⟨*Laden, Fabrik:*⟩ geschlossen werden; ⟨*Zeitung, Sendebetrieb:*⟩ eingestellt werden

∼ **'in** *v.t.* **(a)** (keep in) einschließen; **(b)** (encircle) umschließen; **feel** ∼ **in** sich eingeschlossen fühlen

∼ **'off** *v.t.* **(a)** (stop) unterbrechen ⟨*Strom, Fluss*⟩; abstellen ⟨*Motor, Maschine, Gerät*⟩; **(b)** (isolate) absperren; ∼ **sb. off from sb./sth.** jmdn. von jmdm./etw. abschneiden;

~ **oneself off from sb./sth.** sich gegen jmdn./etw. abkapseln
~ **'out** *v.t.* aussperren; versperren ⟨*Aussicht*⟩; (exclude from view) verdecken; (prevent) ausschließen ⟨*Gefahr, Möglichkeit*⟩; **the tree ~s out the light** der Baum nimmt das Licht weg
~ **'up 1** *v.t.* (a) (close) abschließen; zuschließen; ~ **up** [**the/one's**] **house** das/sein Haus [sicher] abschließen; *see also* **shop 1 b;** (b) (put away) einschließen ⟨*Dokumente, Wertsachen usw.*⟩; einsperren ⟨*Tier, Person*⟩; ~ **sth. up in sth.** etw. in etw. (*Akk.*) schließen; ~ **sb. up in an asylum** jmdn. in eine Anstalt sperren; (c) (reduce to silence) zum Schweigen bringen. **2** *v.i.* (coll.: be quiet) den Mund halten (ugs.); ~ **up!** halt den Mund! (ugs.)
'shut-eye *n.* (coll.) **get** *or* **have some** *or* **a bit of ~:** ein Nickerchen halten (fam.)

shutter /'ʃʌtə(r)/ *n.* (a) Laden, *der;* (of window) Fensterladen, *der;* **put up the ~s** (fig.: cease business) zumachen; schließen; (b) (Photog.) Verschluss, *der;* ~ **release** Auslöser, *der;* ~ **speed** Verschlusszeit, *die*

shuttle /'ʃʌtl/ **1** *n.* (a) (in loom, sewing machine) Schiffchen, *das;* (b) (Transport) (service) Pendelverkehr, *der;* (bus) Pendelbus, *der;* (aircraft) Pendelmaschine, *die;* (train) Pendelzug, *der; see also* **space shuttle. 2** *v.t.* ~ **sth. backwards and forwards** etw. hin und her schicken; ~ **passengers about** Passagiere hin und her fahren. **3** *v.i.* pendeln
shuttle: ~**cock** *n.* Federball, *der;* ~ **service** *n.* Pendelverkehr, *der*

shy[1] /ʃaɪ/ **1** *adj.,* ~**er** *or* **shier** /'ʃaɪə(r)/, ~**est** *or* **shiest** /'ʃaɪɪst/ scheu; (diffident) schüchtern; **don't be ~:** sei nicht [so] schüchtern!; **feel ~ about doing sth.** sich genieren, etw. zu tun; **be ~ of doing sth.** Hemmungen haben, etw. zu tun. **2** *v.i.* scheuen (**at** vor + *Dat.*)
~ **a'way** *v.i.* ~ **away from sth.** ⟨*Pferd:*⟩ vor etw. (*Dat.*) scheuen; ~ **away from sth./doing sth.** (fig.) etw. scheuen/sich scheuen, etw. zu tun
shy[2] *v.t.* (throw) ~ **sth. at sth./sb.** etw. auf etw./jmdn. schmeißen (ugs.). **2** *v.i.* schmeißen (ugs.) (**at** nach)
shyly /'ʃaɪlɪ/ *adv.* scheu; (diffidently) schüchtern
shyness /'ʃaɪnɪs/ *n., no pl.* Scheuheit, *die;* (diffidence) Schüchternheit, *die*

Siamese /saɪə'miːz/ **1** *adj.* siamesisch. **2** *n., pl. same* (Zool.) Siamese, *der*
Siamese: ~ **'cat** *n.* Siamkatze, *die;* ~ **'twins** *n. pl.* siamesische Zwillinge
Siberia /saɪ'bɪərɪə/ *pr. n.* Sibirien (*das*)
sibling /'sɪblɪŋ/ *n.* (male) Bruder, *der;* (female) Schwester, *die; in pl.* Geschwister *Pl.*
sic /sɪk/ *adv.* sic
Sicily /'sɪsɪlɪ/ *pr. n.* Sizilien (*das*)

sick /sɪk/ **▶ 865 | 1** *adj.* (a) (ill) krank; **be ~ with sth.** etw. haben; **go ~, fall ~** *or* (coll.) **take ~:** krank werden; **be off ~:** krank [gemeldet] sein; **sb. is ~ at** *or* **to his/her stomach** (Amer.) jmdm. ist [es] schlecht *od.* übel; (b) (Brit.: vomiting or about to vomit) **be ~:** sich erbrechen; **be ~ over sb./sth.** sich über jmdn./etw. erbrechen; **I think I'm going to be ~:** ich glaube, ich muss [mich er]brechen; **a ~ feeling** ein Übelkeitsgefühl; **sb. gets/feels ~:** jmdm. wird/ist [es] übel *od.* schlecht; **he felt ~ with fear** ihm war vor Angst [ganz] übel; **sth. makes sb. ~:** von etw. wird [es] jmdm. schlecht *od.* übel (*see also* **d**)*;* (c) (sickly) elend ⟨*Aussehen*⟩; leidend ⟨*Blick*⟩; (d) (fig.) **worried ~:** krank vor Sorgen; **be/get ~ of sb./sth.** jmdn./etw. satt haben/allmählich satt haben; **be ~ and tired** *or* ~ **to death of sb./sth.** (coll.) von jmdm./etw. die Nase [gestrichen] voll haben (ugs.); **be ~ of the sight/sound of sb./sth.** (coll.) jmdn./etw. nicht mehr sehen/hören können; **be ~ of doing sth.** es satt haben, etw. zu tun; **make sb. ~** (disgust) jmdn. anekeln; (coll.: make envious) jmdn. ganz neidisch machen (*see also* **b**)*;* (e) (deranged) pervers; (morally corrupt) krank ⟨*Gesellschaft*⟩; (morbid) makaber ⟨*Witz, Humor, Fantasie*⟩. **2** *n. pl.* **the ~:** die Kranken
sick: ~**bay** ⇒ **bay**[2] **b;** ~**bed** *n.* Krankenbett, *das;* ~ **'building syndrome** *n.* Sickbuildingsyndrom, *das.*

sicken /'sɪkn/ **1** *v.i.* (a) (become ill) krank werden; **be ~ing for something/the measles** (Brit.) krank werden *od.* (ugs.) etwas ausbrüten/[die] Masern bekommen; (b) (feel nausea or disgust) ~ **at sth.** sich vor etw. (*Dat.*) ekeln; ~ **of sth./of doing sth.** einer Sache (*Gen.*) überdrüssig sein/ es überdrüssig sein, etw. zu tun. **2** *v.t.* (a) **sth. ~s sb.** bei etw. wird jmdm. übel; (b) (disgust) anwidern
sickening /'sɪknɪŋ/ *adj.* (a) ekelerregend; widerlich ⟨*Anblick, Geruch*⟩; (b) (coll.: infuriating) unerträglich; **it's really ~:** es kann einen krank machen
sickle /'sɪkl/ *n.* Sichel, *die*
sick: ~ **leave** *n.* Urlaub wegen Krankheit, *der;* **be on ~ leave** ≈ krank geschrieben sein; ~ **list** *n.* Liste der Kranken, *die;* **on the ~ list** krank [gemeldet/geschrieben]
sickly /'sɪklɪ/ *adj.* (a) (ailing) kränklich; (b) (weak, faint) schwach; matt ⟨*Lächeln*⟩; kraftlos ⟨*Sonne*⟩; fahl ⟨*Licht*⟩; blass ⟨*Hautfarbe, Gesicht*⟩; (c) (nauseating) ekelhaft; widerlich; (mawkish) süßlich
sickness /'sɪknɪs/ *n.* **▶ 865 |** (a) (being ill) Krankheit, *die;* (b) (disease; also fig.) Krankheit, *die;* (c) (nausea) Übelkeit, *die;* (vomiting) Erbrechen, *das*
sick: ~ **pay** *n.* Entgeltfortzahlung im Krankheitsfalle; (paid by insurance) Krankengeld, *das;* ~**room** *n.* Krankenzimmer, *das*

side /saɪd/ **1** *n.* (a) (also Geom.) Seite, *die;* **this ~ up** oben; **lie on its ~:** auf der Seite liegen; **on both ~s** auf beiden Seiten; (b) (of animal or person) Seite, *die;* **sleep on one's right/left ~:** auf der rechten/linken Seite schlafen; ~ **of mutton/beef/pork** Hammel-/Rinder-/Schweinehälfte, *die;* ~ **of bacon** Speckseite, *die;* **split one's ~s** [**laughing**] (fig.) vor Lachen platzen; **walk/stand ~ by ~:** nebeneinander gehen/stehen; **work/fight** *etc.* ~ **by ~** [**with sb.**] Seite an Seite [mit jmdm.] arbeiten/kämpfen *usw.;* (c) (part away from the centre) Seite, *die;* **the eastern ~ of the town** der Ostteil der Stadt; **the ~s of sb.'s mouth** jmds. Mundwinkel; **right**[**-hand**]/**left**[**-hand**] ~: rechte/linke Seite; **on the right**[**-hand**]/**left**[**-hand**] ~ **of the road** auf der rechten/linken Straßenseite; **from ~ to ~** (right across) quer hinüber; (alternately each way) von einer Seite auf die andere *od.* zur anderen; **to one ~:** zur Seite; **on one ~:** an der Seite; **stand on** *or* **to one ~:** an *od.* auf der Seite stehen; **on the ~** (fig.: in addition to regular work or income) nebenbei; nebenher; (*space beside person or thing*) Seite, *die;* **at** *or* **by sb.'s ~:** an jmds. Seite (*Dat.*); neben jmdm.; **at** *or* **by the ~ of the car** beim *od.* am Auto; **at** *or* **by the ~ of the road/lake/grave** an der Straße/am See/ am Grab; **on all ~s** *or* **every ~:** von allen Seiten ⟨*umzingelt, kritisiert*⟩; (e) (in relation to dividing line) Seite, *die;* [**on**] **either ~ of** beiderseits, auf beiden Seiten (+ *Gen.*); [**to** *or* **on**] **one ~ of** neben (+ *Dat.*); **this/the other ~ of** (with regard to space) diesseits/ jenseits (+ *Gen.*); (with regard to time) vor/nach (+ *Dat.*); **he is this ~ of fifty** er ist unter fünfzig; *see also* **right side; wrong side;** (f) (aspect) Seite, *die;* **there are two ~s to every question** alles hat seine zwei Seiten; **look on the bright/gloomy ~** [**of things**] die Dinge von der angenehmen/düsteren Seite sehen; **be on the high/expensive** *etc.* ~: [etwas] hoch/ teuer *usw.* sein; (g) (opposing group or position) Seite, *die;* Partei, *die;* (Sport: team) Mannschaft, *die;* **put sb.'s ~:** jmds. Seite vertreten; **be on the winning ~** (fig.) auf der Seite der Gewinner stehen; **let the ~ down** (fig.) versagen; **change ~s** zur anderen Seite überwechseln; **time is on sb.'s ~:** die Zeit arbeitet für jmdn.; **take sb.'s ~:** sich auf jmds. Seite stellen; **take ~s** [**with/against sb.**] [für/ gegen jmdn.] Partei ergreifen; (h) (of family) Seite, *die;* **on one's/sb.'s father's/mother's ~:** väterlicher-/mütterlicherseits. **2** *v.i.* ~ **with sb.** sich auf jmds. Seite (*Akk.*) stellen; ~ **against sb.** sich gegen jmdn. stellen. **3** *adj.* seitlich; Seiten-
side: ~**board** *n.* Anrichte, *die;* ~**boards** (coll.), ~**burns** *ns. pl.* (a) (hair on cheeks) Backenbart, *der;* (b) (hair in front of the ears) Koteletten *Pl.;* ~**car** *n.* Beiwagen, *der;* ~ **dish** *n.* Beilage, *die;* ~ **door** *n.* Seitentür, *die;* ~ **effect** *n.* Nebenwirkung, *die;* ~ **entrance** *n.* Seiteneingang, *der;* ~ **exit** *n.* Seitenausgang, *der;* ~ **glance** *n.* (lit. or fig.) Seitenblick, *der* (**at** auf + *Akk.*); ~**kick** *n.*

(coll.) Kumpan, *der;* ~**light** *n.* (Motor Veh.) Begrenzungsleuchte, *die;* **drive on** ~**lights** mit Standlicht fahren; ~**line** *n.* (**a**) (goods) Nebensortiment, *das;* (**b**) (occupation) Nebenbeschäftigung, *die;* (**c**) *in pl.* (Sport) Begrenzungslinien; **on the** ~**lines** (outside play area/track etc.) am Spielfeldrand/am Rande der Bahn *usw.;* **remain on the** ~**lines** (fig.) sich [aus allem] heraushalten; ~ **road** *n.* Seitenstraße, *die;* ~**-saddle 1** *n.* Damensattel, *der;* **2** *adv.* **ride** ~**-saddle** im Damensattel reiten; ~ **salad** *n.* Salat [als Beilage]; ~**show** *n.* Nebenattraktion, *die;* ~**-splitting** *adj.* zwerchfellerschütternd; ~**step 1** *n.* Schritt zur Seite, *der;* **2** *v.t.* (lit. or fig.) ausweichen (+ *Dat.*); ~ **street** *n.* Seitenstraße, *die;* ~ **table** *n.* Beistelltisch, *der;* ~**track** *v.t.* **get** ~**tracked** abgelenkt werden; ~**walk** (Amer.) ⇒ **pavement a;** ~**ways** /'saɪdweɪz/ **1** *adv.* seitwärts; **look at sb./sth.** ~**ways** jmdn./etw. von der Seite ansehen; **2** *adj.* seitlich; ~**-whiskers** *n. pl.* Backenbart, *der;* ~ **wind** *n.* Seitenwind, *der*

siding /'saɪdɪŋ/ *n.* (Railw.) Abstellgleis, *das;* Rangiergleis, *das*

sidle /'saɪdl/ *v.i.* schleichen; ~ **up to sb.** [sich] zu jmdm. schleichen

siege /siːdʒ/ *n.* (Mil.) Belagerung, *die;* (by police) Umstellung, *die;* **be under** ~ (lit. or fig.) belagert sein; (by police) umstellt sein; **lay** ~ **to sth.** (lit. or fig.) etw. belagern

siesta /sɪ'esta/ *n.* Siesta, *die;* **have** *or* **take a** ~: [eine] Siesta halten *od.* machen

sieve /sɪv/ **1** *n.* Sieb, *das;* **have a head** *or* **memory like a** ~ (coll.) ein Gedächtnis wie ein Sieb haben (ugs.). **2** *v.t.* sieben

sift /sɪft/ **1** *v.t.* sieben; (fig.: examine closely) unter die Lupe nehmen; ~ **sth. from sth.** etw. von etw. trennen. **2** *v.i.* ~ **through** durchsehen ⟨*Briefe, Dokumente usw.*⟩; durchsuchen ⟨*Trümmer, Asche, Habseligkeiten usw.*⟩ ~ **'out** *v.t.* (lit. or fig.) aussieben; ~ **out sth. from sth.** etw. aus etw. heraussieben; (fig.) etw. von etw. trennen

sigh /saɪ/ **1** *n.* Seufzer, *der;* **give** *or* **breathe** *or* **utter** *or* **heave a** ~: einen Seufzer ausstoßen *od.* tun; ~ **of relief/contentment** Seufzer der Erleichterung/Zufriedenheit. **2** *v.i.* seufzen; ~ **with relief/contentment** *etc.* vor Erleichterung/Zufriedenheit *usw. od.* erleichtert/zufrieden *usw.* seufzen; ~ **for sth./sb.** (fig.) sich nach etw./jmdm. sehnen. **3** *v.t.* seufzen

sight /saɪt/ **1** *n.* (**a**) (faculty) Sehvermögen, *das;* **loss of** ~: Verlust des Sehvermögens; **second** ~: das Zweite Gesicht; **near** ~ ⇒ **short sight; by** ~: mit dem Gesichtssinn *od.* den Augen; **know sb. by** ~: jmdn. vom Sehen kennen; *see also* **long sight; short sight;** (**b**) (act of seeing) Anblick, *der;* **at [the]** ~ **of sb./blood** bei jmds. Anblick/beim Anblick von Blut; **catch** ~ **of sb./sth.** (lit. or fig.) jmdn./etw. erblicken; **lose** ~ **of sb./sth.** (lit. or fig.) jmdn./etw. aus dem Auge *od.* den Augen verlieren; **play sth. at** ~: etw. vom Blatt spielen; **shoot sb. at** *or* **on** ~: jmdn. gleich [bei seinem Erscheinen] erschießen; **at first** ~: auf den ersten Blick; **love at first** ~: Liebe auf den ersten Blick; (**c**) (spectacle) Anblick, *der;* **be a sorry** ~: einen traurigen Anblick *od.* ein trauriges Bild bieten; **it is a** ~ **to see** *or* **to behold** *or* **worth seeing** das muss man gesehen haben; **a** ~ **for sore eyes** eine Augenweide; **be/look a [real]** ~ (coll.) (amusing) [vollkommen] unmöglich aussehen (ugs.); (horrible) böse *od.* schlimm aussehen; (**d**) *in pl.* (noteworthy features) Sehenswürdigkeiten *Pl.;* **see the** ~**s** sich (*Dat.*) die Sehenswürdigkeiten ansehen; (**e**) (range) Sichtweite, *die;* **in** ~ (lit. or fig.) in Sicht; **come into** ~: in Sicht kommen; **keep sb./sth. in** ~ (lit. or fig.) jmdn./etw. im Auge behalten; **within** *or* **in** ~ **of sb./sth.** (able to see) in jmds. Sichtweite (*Dat.*)/in Sichtweite einer Sache; **out of sb.'s** ~: außerhalb jmds. Sichtweite; **be out of** ~: außer Sicht sein; (coll.: be excellent) wahnsinnig sein (ugs.); **keep** *or* **stay out of [sb.'s]** ~: sich [von jmdm.] nicht sehen lassen; **keep sb./sth. out of** ~: jmdn./etw. niemanden sehen lassen; **keep sth./sb. out of sb.'s** ~: jmdn. etw./jmdn. nicht sehen lassen; **not let sb./sth. out of one's** ~: jmdn./etw. nicht aus den Augen lassen; **out of** ~, **out of mind** (prov.) aus den Augen, aus dem Sinn; (**f**) (device for aiming) Visier, *das;* ~**s** Visiervorrichtung, *die;* **set/have [set] one's** ~**s on sth.** (fig.) etw. anpeilen; **set**

one's ~**s [too] high** (fig.) seine Ziele [zu] hoch stecken; **lower/raise one's** ~**s** (fig.) zurückstecken/sich (*Dat.*) ein höheres Ziel setzen. **2** *v.t.* sichten ⟨*Land, Schiff, Flugzeug, Wrack*⟩; sehen ⟨*Entflohenen, Vermissten*⟩; antreffen ⟨*seltenes Tier, seltene Pflanze*⟩

sighted /'saɪtɪd/ *adj.* sehend; **partially** ~: [hochgradig] sehbehindert

sight: ~**-read** *v.t. & i.* (Mus.) ⟨*Pianist usw.:*⟩ vom Blatt spielen; ⟨*Sänger:*⟩ vom Blatt singen; ~**seeing** *n.* Sightseeing, *das* (Touristikjargon); **go** ~**seeing** Besichtigungen machen; ~**seer** /'saɪtsiːə(r)/ *n.* Tourist(, *der die Sehenswürdigkeiten besichtigt*)

sign /saɪn/ **1** *n.* (**a**) (symbol, gesture, signal, mark) Zeichen, *das;* (**b**) (Astrol.) ~ **[of the zodiac]** [Tierkreis]zeichen, *das;* Sternzeichen, *das;* **what** ~ **are you?** welches Tierkreiszeichen *od.* Sternzeichen bist du?; **sb.'s birth** ~: jmds. Tierkreiszeichen; (**c**) (notice) Schild, *das;* **[direction]** ~: Wegweiser, *der;* **[advertising]** ~: Reklameschild, *das;* Reklame, *die;* (illuminated, flashing) Leuchtreklame, *die;* **danger** ~ (lit. or fig.) Gefahrenzeichen, *das;* (**d**) (outside shop etc.) ⇒ **signboard;** (**e**) (indication) Zeichen, *das;* (of future event) Anzeichen, *das;* **there is little/no/every** ~ **of sth./that** ...: wenig/nichts/alles deutet auf etw. (*Akk.*) hin *od.* deutet darauf hin, dass ...; **show [no]** ~**s of fatigue/strain/improvement** *etc.* [keine] Anzeichen der Müdigkeit/Anstrengung / Besserung *usw.* zeigen *od.* erkennen lassen; **the carpet showed little/ some** ~**[s] of wear** der Teppich wirkte kaum/etwas abgenutzt; **as a** ~ **of** als Zeichen (+ *Gen.*); **do sth. as a** ~ **of sth.** etw. zum Zeichen einer Sache (*Gen.*) tun; **at the first** *or* **slightest** ~ **of sth.** schon beim geringsten Anzeichen von etw.; **there was no** ~ **of him/the car anywhere** er/der Wagen war nirgends zu sehen; **there was no** ~ **of life** keine Menschenseele war zu sehen; ~ **of the times** Zeichen der Zeit. **2** *v.t.* (**a**) (write one's name etc. on) unterschreiben; ⟨*Künstler, Autor:*⟩ signieren ⟨*Werk*⟩; (**b**) ~ **one's name** [mit seinem Namen] unterschreiben; ~ **oneself R. A. Smith** mit R. A. Smith unterschreiben. **3** *v.i.* (write one's name) unterschreiben; ~ **for sth.** (acknowledge receipt of sth.) den Empfang einer Sache (*Gen.*) bestätigen

~ **a'way** *v.t.* abtreten ⟨*Eigentum*⟩; verzichten auf ⟨*Recht, Freiheit usw.*⟩

~ **'off 1** *v.i.* (**a**) (cease employment) kündigen; (**b**) (at end of shift etc.) sich [zum Feierabend *usw.*] abmelden; (**c**) (Radio) sich verabschieden. **2** *v.t.* kündigen

~ **'on 1** *v.t.* einstellen ⟨*Arbeiter*⟩; verpflichten ⟨*Fußballspieler*⟩; anwerben ⟨*Soldaten*⟩; anheuern, anmustern ⟨*Seeleute*⟩. **2** *v.i.* (**a**) sich verpflichten (**with** bei); (**b**) ~ **on [for the dole]** sich arbeitslos melden; stempeln gehen (ugs. veralt.)

~ **'out 1** *v.t.* ~ **books out from the library** Bücher als [aus der Bibliothek] entliehen eintragen. **2** *v.i.* sich [schriftlich] abmelden; ⟨*Hotelgast:*⟩ abreisen

~ **'over** *v.t.* überschreiben ⟨*Immobilien*⟩; übertragen ⟨*Rechte*⟩

~ **'up 1** *v.t.* (engage) [vertraglich] verpflichten; einstellen ⟨*Arbeiter*⟩; aufnehmen ⟨*Mitglied*⟩; einschreiben ⟨*Kursteilnehmer*⟩. **2** *v.i.* sich [vertraglich] verpflichten (**with** bei); (join a course etc.) sich einschreiben

signal /'sɪgnl/ **1** *n.* Signal, *das;* **a** ~ **for sth./to sb.** ein Zeichen zu etw./für jmdn.; **at a** ~ **from the headmaster** auf ein Zeichen des Direktors; **the** ~ **was against us/at red** (Railw.) das Signal zeigte „halt"/stand auf Rot; **hand** ~**s** (Motor Veh.) Handzeichen; **radio** ~ (message) Funkspruch, *der.* **2** *v.i.,* (Brit.) **-ll-** signalisieren; Signale geben; ⟨*Kraftfahrer:*⟩ blinken; (using hand etc. ~s) anzeigen; ~ **for assistance** ein Hilfesignal geben; ~ **to sb.** [to do sth.] jmdn. ein Zeichen geben[, etw. zu tun]. **3** *v.t.,* (Brit.) **-ll-:** (**a**) (lit. or fig.) signalisieren; ~ **sb.** [to do sth.] jmdn. ein Zeichen geben[, etw. zu tun]; **the driver** ~**led that he was turning right** der Fahrer zeigte an, dass er [nach] rechts abbiegen wollte; (**b**) (Radio etc.) funken; [über Funk] durchgeben. **4** *adj.* außergewöhnlich

signal: ~ **box** *n.* (Railw.) Stellwerk, *das;* ~**man** /'sɪgnlmən/ *n., pl.* ~**men** /'sɪgnlmən/ ▶ 887 | (Brit. Railw.) Stellwerkswärter, *der*

signatory /'sɪgnətərɪ/ *n.* (person) Unterzeichner, *der;* (party) vertragschließende Partei; (state) Signatarstaat, *der*

signature /'sɪɡnətʃə(r)/ *n.* **(a)** Unterschrift, *die;* (on painting) Signatur, *die;* **put one's ~ to sth.** seine Unterschrift unter etw. (*Akk.*) setzen; **(b)** (Mus.) ⇒ **key signature; time signature**

'**signature tune** *n.* (Radio, Telev.) Erkennungsmelodie, *die*

'**signboard** *n.* Schild, *das;* (advertising) Reklameschild, *das*

signet ring /'sɪɡnɪt rɪŋ/ *n.* Siegelring, *der*

significance /sɪɡ'nɪfɪkəns/ *n.* (meaning, importance) Bedeutung, *die;* **be of [no] ~:** [nicht] von Bedeutung sein; **a matter of great/little/no ~:** eine [sehr] wichtige/ziemlich unwichtige/völlig unwichtige Angelegenheit

significant /sɪɡ'nɪfɪkənt/ *adj.* **(a)** (noteworthy, important) bedeutend; **(b)** (full of meaning) bedeutsam

significantly /sɪɡ'nɪfɪkəntli/ *adv.* **(a)** (meaningfully) bedeutungsvoll; *as sentence-modifier* ~ **[enough]** bedeutsamerweise; **(b)** (notably) bedeutend; signifikant (geh., fachspr.)

signify /'sɪɡnɪfaɪ/ *v.t.* **(a)** (indicate, mean) bedeuten; **(b)** (communicate, make known) kundtun (geh.); zum Ausdruck bringen

sign: ~ **language** *n.* Zeichensprache, *die;* ~**post** **1** *n.* (lit. or fig.) Wegweiser, *der;* **2** *v.t.* ausschildern ‹*Route, Umleitungsstrecke usw.*›; mit Wegweisern versehen ‹*Straße*›; ~**writer** *n.* Schildermaler, *der*

silage /'saɪlɪdʒ/ *n.* (Agric.) Silage, *die;* Gärfutter, *das*

silence /'saɪləns/ **1** *n.* Schweigen, *das;* (keeping a secret) Verschwiegenheit, *die;* (taciturnity) Schweigsamkeit, *die;* (stillness) Stille, *die;* **there was ~:** es herrschte Schweigen/ Stille; ~! Ruhe!; **in ~:** schweigend; **call for ~:** um Ruhe bitten; **keep ~** (lit. or fig.) schweigen; **break the ~:** die Stille unterbrechen; (be the first to speak) das Schweigen brechen; **break one's ~** (lit. or fig.) sein Schweigen brechen; **a minute's ~:** eine Schweigeminute. **2** *v.t.* zum Schweigen bringen ‹*Zweifel, Ängste, Proteste*›; mundtot machen ‹*Gegner, Zeugen*›

silencer /'saɪlənsə(r)/ *n.* (Brit. Motor Veh., Arms) Schalldämpfer, *der*

silent /'saɪlənt/ *adj.* **(a)** (noiseless) unhörbar; (still) still; **be ~** (say nothing) schweigen; (be still) still sein; (not be working) ‹*Maschine:*› stillstehen; ‹*Waffen:*› schweigen; **fall ~:** verstummen; **keep *or* remain ~** (lit. or fig.) schweigen; ‹*jmd., der verhört wird:*› beharrlich schweigen; **(b)** (taciturn) schweigsam; **(c)** (Ling.) stumm; **(d)** (Cinemat.) ~ **film** Stummfilm, *der*

silently /'saɪləntli/ *adv.* schweigend; stumm ‹*weinen, beten*›; (noiselessly) lautlos

silent ma'jority *n.* schweigende Mehrheit

Silesia /saɪ'liːʃə/ *pr. n.* Schlesien (*das*)

Silesian /saɪ'liːʃn/ **1** *adj.* schlesisch. **2** *n.* **(a)** (person) Schlesier, *der*/Schlesierin, *die;* **(b)** (dialect) Schlesisch, *das*

silhouette /sɪlu'et/ **1** *n.* **(a)** (picture) Schattenriss, *der;* **(b)** (appearance against the light) Silhouette, *die.* **2** *v.t.* **be ~d against sth.** sich als Silhouette gegen etw. abheben

silicon /'sɪlɪkən/ *n.* (Chem.) Silicium, *das;* Silizium, *das;* ~ **chip** Siliciumchip, *der;* Siliziumchip, *der*

silicone /'sɪlɪkəʊn/ *n.* (Chem.) Silikon, *das;* ~ **[breast] implant** Silikon[brust]implantat, *das*

silk /sɪlk/ **1** *n.* **(a)** Seide, *die;* **take ~** (Brit. Law) Kronanwalt werden; **(b)** *in pl.* (garments) seidene Kleider *od.* Kleidungsstücke; **(c)** (of spider etc.) [Spinnen]faden, *der;* **(d)** (Brit. Law coll.) Kronanwalt, *der.* **2** *attrib. adj.* seiden; Seiden-

silken /'sɪlkn/ *adj.* seiden; Seiden-

silk: ~**-screen printing** ⇒ **screen printing;** ~**worm** *n.* (Zool.) Seidenraupe, *die*

silky /'sɪlki/ *adj.* seidig

sill /sɪl/ *n.* (of door) [Tür]schwelle, *die;* (of window) Fensterbank, *die*

silliness /'sɪlɪnɪs/ *n., no pl.* Dummheit, *die;* Blödheit, *die* (ugs.)

silly /'sɪli/ **1** *adj.* dumm; blöd[e] (ugs.); (imprudent, unwise) töricht; unklug; (childish) albern; **the ~ season** (Journ.) die Sauregurkenzeit; **a ~ thing** (a foolish action) etwas Dummes *od.* (ugs.) Blödes; (a trivial matter) eine blödsinnige Kleinigkeit (ugs.); **it/that was a ~ thing to do** es/das war dumm *od.* (ugs.) blöd; **I was scared ~** (coll.) mir rutschte das Herz in

die Hose (ugs.). **2** *n.* (coll.) Dummchen, *das;* Dummerchen, *das* (fam.)

silly billy /'sɪlɪbɪli/ *n.* (coll.) Kindskopf, *der*

silo /'saɪləʊ/ *n., pl.* ~**s** (Agric.) Silo, *der;* **(b)** (Mil.) **[missile]** ~**:** [Raketen]silo, *der*

silt /sɪlt/ **1** *n.* Schlamm, *der;* Schlick, *der.* **2** *v.t.* ~ **up** verschlämmen. **3** *v.i.* ~ **up** verschlammen

silver /'sɪlvə(r)/ **1** *n.* **(a)** *no pl., no indef. art.* Silber, *das;* **(b)** (colour, medal, vessels, cutlery) Silber, *das;* (cutlery of other material) Besteck, *das;* **(c)** *no pl., no indef. art.* (coins) Silbermünzen *Pl.;* Silber, *das* (ugs.). **2** *attrib. adj.* silbern; Silber ‹*pokal, -münze*›; *see also* **spoon. 3** *v.t.* (coat with ~) versilbern; (coat with amalgam) verspiegeln ‹*Glas*›

silver: ~ '**birch** *n.* (Bot.) Weißbirke, *die;* ~**-coloured** *adj.* silberfarben; silberfarbig; ~**-haired** *adj.* silberhaarig (geh.); ~ '**medal** *n.* Silbermedaille, *die;* ~ '**medallist** *n.* Silbermedaillengewinner, *der*/-gewinnerin, *die;* ~ '**paper** *n.* Silberpapier, *das;* ~ '**plate** *n., no pl., no indef. art.* versilberte Ware; (coating) Silberauflage, *die;* ~**smith** *n.* ▸ 887 ‖ Silberschmied, *der*/-schmiedin, *die;* ~**ware** *n., no pl.* Silber, *das;* ~ '**wedding** *n.* Silberhochzeit, *die;* silberne Hochzeit

silvery /'sɪlvəri/ *adj.* (silver-coloured) silbrig; (clear-sounding) silbern (dichter.); silbrig (geh.)

similar /'sɪmɪlə(r)/ *adj.* ähnlich (**to** Dat.); **some flour and a ~ amount of sugar** etwas Mehl und ungefähr die gleiche Menge Zucker; **of ~ size/colour** *etc.* von ähnlicher Größe/Farbe *usw.;* **be ~ in size/appearance** *etc.* **[to sb./sth.]** eine ähnliche Größe/ein ähnliches Aussehen haben [wie jmd./etw.]; **look/taste/smell** *etc.* ~ **[to sth.]** ähnlich aussehen/schmecken/riechen *usw.* [wie etw.]; **the two brothers look very ~:** die beiden Brüder sehen sich (*Dat.*) sehr ähnlich

similarity /sɪmɪ'lærɪti/ *n.* Ähnlichkeit, *die* (**to** mit)

similarly /'sɪmɪləli/ *adv.* ähnlich; (to the same degree) ebenso; *as sentence-modifier* ebenso gut

simile /'sɪmɪli/ *n.* (Lit.) Vergleich, *der*

simmer /'sɪmə(r)/ **1** *v.i.* **(a)** (Cookery) ‹*Flüssigkeit:*› sieden; **allow the fish to ~ for ten minutes** den Fisch zehn Minuten ziehen lassen; **(b)** (fig.) gären; **let things ~:** die Dinge sich entwickeln lassen; ~ **with rage/excitement** eine Wut haben/innerlich ganz aufgeregt sein. **2** *v.t.* (Cookery) köcheln lassen ‹*Suppe, Soße usw.*›; ziehen lassen ‹*Fisch, Klöße usw.*›

~ '**down** *v.i.* sich abregen (ugs.)

simper /'sɪmpə(r)/ *v.i.* affektiert *od.* gekünstelt lächeln

simple /'sɪmpl/ *adj.* **(a)** (not compound, not complicated) einfach; (not elaborate) schlicht ‹*Mobiliar, Schönheit, Kunstwerk, Kleidung*›; **the ~ life** das einfache Leben; **(b)** (unqualified, absolute) einfach; simpel; **it was a ~ misunderstanding** es war [ganz] einfach ein Missverständnis; **it is a ~ fact that ...:** es ist [ganz] einfach eine Tatsache *od.* eine simple Tatsache, dass ...; **(c)** (easy) einfach; **it's [not] as ~ as that** so einfach ist das [nicht]; **(d)** (unsophisticated) schlicht; (foolish) dumm; einfältig

'**simple-minded** *adj.* **(a)** (unsophisticated) schlicht; **(b)** (feeble-minded) debil

simpleton /'sɪmpltən/ *n.* Einfaltspinsel, *der* (ugs.)

simplicity /sɪm'plɪsɪti/ *n., no pl.* Einfachheit, *die;* (unpretentiousness, lack of sophistication) Schlichtheit, *die*

simplification /sɪmplɪfɪ'keɪʃn/ *n.* Vereinfachung, *die*

simplify /'sɪmplɪfaɪ/ *v.t.* vereinfachen; ~ **matters** die Sache vereinfachen

simplistic /sɪm'plɪstɪk/ *adj.* [all]zu simpel

simply /'sɪmpli/ *adv.* **(a)** (in an uncomplicated manner) einfach; (in an unsophisticated manner) schlicht; **live/eat ~:** einfach leben/essen; **(b)** (absolutely) einfach; **(c)** (categorically, without good reason, without asking) einfach; (merely) nur; **it ~ isn't true** es ist einfach nicht wahr; **you ~ must see that film** du musst den Film einfach sehen; **I was ~ trying to help** ich wollte nur helfen; **quite ~:** ganz einfach; ~ **because ...:** einfach weil ...

simulate /'sɪmjʊleɪt/ *v.t.* **(a)** (feign) vortäuschen; heucheln ‹*Reue, Entrüstung, Begeisterung*›; simulieren, vortäuschen ‹*Krankheit*›; **(b)** (mimic) nachahmen; **(c)** simulieren ‹*Bedingungen, Wetter, Umwelt usw.*›

Since

As a preposition

The translation of *since* is not a problem — it is always **seit** — but it is important to note that the tense of the verb is often different in German. Whereas English uses the perfect and particularly the perfect continuous *(have been ...ing)*, German uses the present:

I have been waiting since 8 o'clock	= Ich warte [schon] seit 8 Uhr
He has lived here since his childhood	= Er wohnt seit seiner Kindheit hier

Similarly an English verb in the past continuous is translated by a German verb in the imperfect:

I had been waiting since 8 o'clock	= Ich wartete [schon] seit 8 Uhr

Particularly with **warten, schon** is often added to stress the length of time.

However in the negative and in other cases where there is no sense of a continuous process the same tense is used in both languages:

We haven't seen her since the wedding	= Wir haben sie seit der Hochzeit nicht gesehen
I hadn't been there since 1980	= Ich war seit 1980 nicht [mehr] dort gewesen

In such cases, **mehr** is often added for emphasis.

I have only seen her once since the wedding	= Ich habe sie seit der Hochzeit nur einmal gesehen

As an adverb

This is simply the phrase *since then* (= **seitdem**) minus the *then:*

I haven't seen her since	= Ich habe sie seitdem nicht gesehen

It often has the sense of *in the meantime* and can be translated by **inzwischen:**

We have since got to know them better	= Wir haben sie inzwischen näher kennen gelernt

As a conjunction
In time expressions

As in the case of the preposition, the English perfect continuous describing a continuous process is translated by the German present:

since she has been living in Germany	= seit sie in Deutschland wohnt
since they had been in London	= seit sie in London waren

Referring to the time since a specific event, a different construction is used:

How long is it since he left?	= Wie lange ist es her, dass er weggezogen ist?
It's a year since he left	= Es ist ein Jahr her, dass er weggezogen ist

Meaning because

In the sense of *because, since* is translated by **da:**

Since she was ill, I had to do it	= Da sie krank war, musste ich es tun

---

simulated /'sımjʊleıtıd/ *adj.* **(a)** (feigned) vorgetäuscht; geheuchelt; **(b)** (artificial) imitiert ‹ *Leder, Pelz usw.*›; **(c)** simuliert ‹ *Bedingungen, Wetter, Umwelt usw.*›

simulator /'sımjʊleıtə(r)/ *n.* Simulator, *der*

simultaneous /sıml'teıniəs/ *adj.* gleichzeitig (**with** mit); simultan (fachspr., geh.); **be** ~**:** gleichzeitig/simultan erfolgen

simultaneous interpre'tation *n.* Simultandolmetschen, *das*

simultaneously /sıml'teıniəslı/ *adv.* gleichzeitig

sin /sın/ **1** *n.* Sünde, *die;* **live in** ~ (coll.) in Sünde leben (veralt., scherzh.); [**as**] **miserable as** ~**:** todunglücklich; **for my** ~**s** (joc.) um meiner Missetaten willen (scherzh.). **2** *v.i.* **-nn-** sündigen; ~ **against sb./God** an jmdm./Gott *od.* gegen jmdn./Gott sündigen

since /sıns/ **1** *adv.* seitdem; **he has** ~ **remarried, he has remarried** ~**:** er hat inzwischen wieder geheiratet; **long** ~**:** vor langer Zeit; **not long** ~**:** vor nicht allzu langer Zeit; **he is long** ~ **dead** er ist seit langem tot. **2** *prep.* seit; ~ **seeing you ...:** seit ich dich gesehen habe; ~ **then/that time** seitdem; inzwischen; ~ **when?** seit wann? **3** *conj.* **(a)** seit; **it is a long time/so long/not so long** ~ **...:** es ist lange/so lange/gar nicht lange her, dass ...; **how long is it** ~ **he left you?** wie lange ist es her, dass er dich verlassen hat?; **(b)** (seeing that, as) da

sincere /sın'sıə(r)/ *adj.*, ~**r** /sın'sıərə(r)/, ~**st** /sın'sıə rıst/ aufrichtig; herzlich ‹ *Grüße, Glückwünsche usw.*›; wahr ‹ *Freund* ›

sincerely /sın'sıəlı/ *adv.* aufrichtig; **yours** ~ (in letter) mit freundlichen Grüßen

sincerity /sın'serıtı/ *n., no pl.* Aufrichtigkeit, *die*

sine /saın/ *n.* (Math.) Sinus, *der*

sinecure /'sınıkjʊə(r), 'saınıkjʊə(r)/ *n.* Pfründe, *die*

sinew /'sınju:/ *n.* (Anat.) Sehne, *die*

sinewy /'sınju:ı/ *adj.* sehnig; (fig.: vigorous) kraftvoll

sinful /'sınfl/ *adj.* sündig; (reprehensible) sündhaft; **it is** ~ **to ...:** es ist eine Sünde, ... zu ...

sing /sıŋ/ **1** *v.i.,* **sang** /sæŋ/, **sung** /sʌŋ/ singen; (fig.) ‹ *Kessel, Wind:*› singen. **2** *v.t.,* **sang, sung** singen; ~ **sb. a song** *or* **a song for sb.** jmdm. ein Lied vorsingen; ~ **sb. to sleep** jmdn. in den Schlaf singen

~ **a'long** *v.i.* mitsingen

~ **'out 1** *v.i.* **(a)** (~ loudly) [laut *od.* aus voller Kehle] singen; **(b)** (call out) [laut] rufen; ~ **out for sb./sth.** nach jmdm./etw. rufen. **2** *v.t.* rufen; schreien

~ **'up** *v.i.* lauter singen

Singapore /sıŋə'pɔ:(r)/ *pr. n.* Singapur (*das*)

singe /sındʒ/ **1** *v.t.,* ~**ing** ansengen; versengen. **2** *v.i.,* ~**ing** [ver]sengen

singer /'sıŋə(r)/ *n.* Sänger, *der*/Sängerin, *die*

singing /'sıŋıŋ/ *n., no pl.* (lit. or fig.: of kettle, wind) Singen, *das;* **the** ~ **of the birds** der Gesang der Vögel

single /'sıŋgl/ **1** *adj.* **(a)** einfach; einzig ‹ *Ziel, Hoffnung* ›; (for one person) Einzel‹ *bett, -zimmer* ›; einfach ‹ *Größe* ›; (without the other one of a pair) einzeln; **speak with a** ~ **voice** (fig.) mit einer Stimme sprechen; ~ **sheet** Betttuch für ein Einzelbett; ~ **ticket** (Brit.) einfache Fahrkarte; ~ **fare** (Brit.) Preis für [die] einfache Fahrt; **(b)** (one by itself) einzig; (isolated) einzeln; **one** ~ **...:** ein einziger/eine einzige/ein einziges ...; **at a** *or* **one** ~ **blow** *or* **stroke** mit einem Schlag; **(c)** (unmarried) ledig; **a** ~ **man/woman/**~ **people** ein Lediger/eine Ledige/Ledige; ~ **parent** allein erziehender Elternteil; ~ **mother** allein erziehende *od.* stehende Mutter; **(d)** (separate, individual) einzeln; **every** ~ **one** jeder/jede/jedes Einzelne; **every** ~ **time/day** aber auch jedesmal/jeden Tag; **not a** ~ **one** kein Einziger/keine Einzige/kein Einziges; **not a** ~ **word** kein einziges Wort; **not/never for a** ~ **minute** *or* **moment** keinen [einzigen] Augenblick [lang]. **2** *n.* **(a)** (Brit.: ticket) einfache Fahrkarte; [**a**] ~**/two** ~**s to Manchester, please** einmal/zweimal einfach nach Manchester, bitte; **(b)** (record) Single, *die;* **(c)** in *pl.* (Golf) Single, *das;* (Tennis) Einzel, *das;* **men's/women's** *or* **ladies'** ~**s** Herren-/Dameneinzel, *das*

~ **out** *v.t.* aussondern; (be distinctive quality of) auszeichnen (**from** vor + *Dat.*); ∼ **sb./sth. out as/for sth.** jmdn./etw. als etw./für etw. auswählen; ∼ **sb. out for promotion/ special attention** jmdn. für eine Beförderung vorsehen/ sich mit jmdm. besonders befassen

single: ∼ **cream** *n.* [einfache] Sahne; ∼ **currency** *n.* Einheitswährung, *die;* ∼**-decker 1** *n.* be a ∼-decker ⟨*Bus, Straßenbahn:*⟩ nur ein Deck haben; **2** *adj.* ∼**-decker bus/tram** Bus/Straßenbahn mit [nur] einem Deck; ∼ **[European] market** *n.* [europäischer] Binnenmarkt; ∼**-handed 1** /'----/ *adj.* Einhand⟨*segeln, -segler*⟩; **his** ∼**-handed efforts to get a new hospital** seine einsamen Bemühungen um ein neues Krankenhaus; **2** /-'--/ *adv.* allein; **sail round the world** ∼**-handed** als Einhandsegler um die Welt fahren; ∼**-lens 'reflex [camera]** *n.* (Photog.) einäugige Spiegelreflexkamera; ∼**-line** *adj.* einspurig; ∼**-minded** *adj.* zielstrebig

singleness /'sɪŋglnɪs/ *n., no pl.* ∼ **of purpose** Zielstrebigkeit, *die*

'**singles bar** *n.* Singlekneipe, *die*

'**single-sex** *adj.* ∼ **school** reine Mädchen-/Jungenschule; ∼ **accommodation** nach Geschlecht getrennte Unterbringung

singlet /'sɪŋglɪt/ *n.* (Brit.) (vest) Unterhemd, *das;* (Sport) Trikot, *das*

singly /'sɪŋglɪ/ *adv.* (a) einzeln; (b) (by oneself) allein

'**singsong** *n.* (Brit.) **have a** ∼: gemeinsam singen

singular /'sɪŋgjʊlə(r)/ **1** *adj.* (a) (Ling.) singularisch; Singular-; ∼ **noun** Substantiv im Singular; **first person** ∼: erste Person Singular; (b) (individual) einzeln; (unique) einmalig; einzigartig; (c) (extraordinary) einmalig; einzigartig. **2** *n.* (Ling.) Einzahl, *die;* Singular, *der*

singularity /sɪŋgjʊ'lærɪtɪ/ *n., no pl.* Eigenartigkeit, *die;* Sonderbarkeit, *die*

singularly /'sɪŋgjʊləlɪ/ *adv.* (extraordinarily) außerordentlich; einmalig ⟨*schön*⟩; (strangely) seltsam

sinister /'sɪnɪstə(r)/ *adj.* (a) (of evil omen) unheilverkündend; (b) (suggestive of malice) finster; (wicked) übel

sink /sɪŋk/ **1** *n.* Spülbecken, *das;* Spüle, *die;* **pour sth. down the** ∼: etw. in den Ausguss schütten. **2** *v.i.*, sank /sæŋk/ *or* sunk /sʌŋk/, sunk (a) sinken; **leave sb. to** ∼ **or swim** (fig.) jmdn. seinem Schicksal überlassen; (b) ∼ **into** (become immersed in) sinken in (+ *Akk.*); versinken in (+ *Dat.*); (penetrate) eindringen in (+ *Akk.*); (fig.: be absorbed into) dringen in (+ *Akk.*) ⟨*Bewusstsein*⟩; ∼ **into an armchair/the cushions** in einen Sessel/die Kissen sinken; ∼ **into a deep sleep/a coma** in einen tiefen Schlaf/in ein Koma sinken (geh.); **be sunk in thought/despair** in Gedanken/in Verzweiflung (*Akk.*) versunken sein; (c) (come to lower level or pitch) sinken; (fig.: fail) ⟨*Moral, Hoffnung:*⟩ sinken; **sb.'s heart** ∼**s/spirits** ∼: jmds. Stimmung sinkt; ∼ **to one's knees** auf die *od.* seine Knie sinken; (d) (fall) ⟨*Preis, Temperatur, Währung, Produktion usw.:*⟩ sinken; ∼ **in value** im Wert sinken. **3** *v.t.*, **sank** *or* **sunk**, **sunk** (a) versenken; (cause failure of) zunichte machen; **be sunk** (fig. coll.: have failed) aufgeschmissen sein (ugs.); ∼ **one's differences** seine Streitigkeiten begraben; (b) (lower) senken; (Golf) ins Loch schlagen ⟨*Ball*⟩; (c) (dig) niederbringen; (recess) versenken; (embed) stoßen ⟨*Schwert, Messer*⟩; graben (geh.) ⟨*Zähne, Klauen*⟩

∼ '**in** *v.i.* (a) (become immersed) einsinken; (penetrate) eindringen; (b) (fig.: be absorbed into the mind) jmdm. ins Bewusstsein dringen; ⟨*Warnung, Lektion:*⟩ verstanden werden

sinking /'sɪŋkɪŋ/ **1** *adj.* (a) sinkend; (b) (declining) untergehend ⟨*Sonne*⟩; (c) (falling in value) sinkend; (d) **with a** ∼ **heart** (fig.) beklommen; resigniert. **2** *n.* (a) (of ship) (deliberate) Versenkung, *die;* (accidental) Sinken, *das;* Untergang, *der;* (of well) Niederbringung, *die;* (b) *attrib.* **a** ∼ **feeling** (fig.) ein flaues Gefühl [im Magen]

'**sink unit** *n.* Spüle, *die*

sinner /'sɪnə(r)/ *n.* Sünder, *der*/Sünderin, *die*

sinuous /'sɪnjʊəs/ *adj.* (winding) sich schlängelnd ⟨*Schlange*⟩; (lithe) geschmeidig ⟨*Körper, Bewegungen*⟩

sinus /'saɪnəs/ *n.* (Anat.) Sinus, *der* (fachspr.)

sip /sɪp/ **1** *v.t.*, **-pp-:** ∼ **[up]** schlürfen. **2** *v.i.*, **-pp-:** ∼ **at/ from sth.** an etw. (*Dat.*) nippen. **3** *n.* Schlückchen, *das*

siphon /'saɪfn/ **1** *n.* Siphon, *der.* **2** *v.t.* [durch einen Saugheber] laufen lassen; ∼ **sth. from a tank** etw. [mit einem Saugheber] aus einem Tank ablassen

∼ '**off** *v.t.* [mit einem Saugheber] ablassen; (fig.: transfer) abzweigen

sir /sɜː(r)/ *n.* ▶ **1152** | (a) (formal address) der Herr; (to teacher) Herr Meier/Schmidt *usw.;* **no** '∼! keinesfalls!; von wegen! (ugs.); **yes** '∼! allerdings!; **Sir!** (Mil.) Herr Oberst/Leutnant *usw.*!; (yes) jawohl, Herr Oberst/Leutnant *usw.*!; (b) (in letter) **Dear Sirs** Sehr geehrte [Damen und] Herren; **Dear Sir or Madam** Sehr geehrte Damen und Herren; (c) **Sir** /sə(r)/ (title of knight etc.) Sir

sire /'saɪə(r)/ **1** *n.* Vatertier, *das.* **2** *v.t.* zeugen

siren /'saɪrən/ *n.* (a) Sirene, *die;* (b) (temptress) Sirene, *die* (geh.)

sirloin /'sɜːlɔɪn/ *n.* (a) (Brit.: upper part of loin of beef) Roastbeef, *das;* **a** ∼ **of beef** ein Stück Roastbeef; ∼ **steak** Rumpsteak, *das;* (b) (Amer.) Rumpsteak, *das*

sisal /'saɪsl/ *n.* (fibre) Sisal, *der*

sissy /'sɪsɪ/ **1** *n.* Waschlappen, *der* (ugs. abwertend). **2** *adj.* feige

sister /'sɪstə(r)/ *n.* (a) Schwester, *die;* (b) (fellow member of trade union) Kollegin, *die;* (c) (Brit.: senior nurse) Oberschwester, *die*

'**sister-in-law** *n., pl.* **sisters-in-law** Schwägerin, *die*

sisterly /'sɪstəlɪ/ *adj.* schwesterlich

sit /sɪt/ **1** *v.i.*, **-tt-**, **sat** /sæt/ (a) (become seated) sich setzen; ∼ **on** *or* **in a chair/in an armchair** sich auf einen Stuhl/in einen Sessel setzen; ∼ **by** *or* **with sb.** sich zu jmdm. setzen; ∼ **over there!** setz dich dort drüben hin!; (b) (be seated) sitzen; **don't just** ∼ **there!** sitz nicht einfach rum! (ugs.); ∼ **in judgement on** *or* **over sb./sth.** über jmdn./etw. zu Gericht sitzen; ∼ **still!** sitz ruhig *od.* still!; ∼ **tight** (coll.) ruhig sitzen bleiben; (fig.: stay in hiding) sich nicht fortrühren; (c) ∼ **for one's portrait** Porträt sitzen; (d) (take a test) ∼ **for sth.** die Prüfung für etw. machen; (e) (be in session) tagen; (f) (be on perch or nest) sitzen. **2** *v.t.*, **-tt-**, **sat** (a) (cause to be seated, place) setzen; (b) (Brit.) ∼ **an examination** eine Prüfung machen

∼ **a'bout**, ∼ **a'round** *v.i.* herumsitzen (ugs.)

∼ '**back** *v.i.* (a) sich zurücklehnen; (b) (fig.: do nothing) sich im Sessel zurücklehnen (fig.)

∼ '**down** *v.i.* (a) (become seated) sich setzen (**on/in** auf/ in + *Akk.*); (b) (be seated) sitzen; **take sth.** ∼**ting down** (fig.) etw. auf sich (*Dat.*) sitzen lassen. **2** *v.t.* ∼ **sb. down** (invite to ∼) jmdn. Platz nehmen lassen; (help to ∼) jmdm. helfen, sich zu setzen

∼ '**in** *v.i.* (a) (occupy place as protest) ein Sit-in veranstalten; (b) ∼ **in on** (be present at) teilnehmen an (+ *Dat.*); dabei sein bei

∼ **on** *v.t.* (a) (serve as member of) sitzen in (+ *Dat.*) ⟨*Ausschuss usw.*⟩; (b) (coll.: delay) in der Schublade liegen lassen (fig. ugs.); auf die lange Bank schieben (ugs.) ⟨*Entscheidung*⟩; (c) (coll.: repress) unterdrücken; (d) (fig.: hold on to) festhalten

∼ '**up 1** *v.i.* (a) (rise) sich aufsetzen; (b) (be sitting erect) [aufrecht] sitzen; (c) (not slouch) gerade sitzen; ∼ **up straight!** sitz gerade!; ∼ **up [and take notice]** (fig. coll.) aufhorchen; (d) (delay going to bed) aufbleiben; ∼ **up [waiting] for sb.** aufbleiben und auf jmdn. warten; ∼ **up with sb.** bei jmdm. Nachtwache halten. **2** *v.t.* aufsetzen

∼ **upon** ⇨ ∼ **on**

sitcom /'sɪtkɒm/ (coll.) ⇨ **situation comedy**

'**sit-down 1** *n.* **have a** ∼: sich setzen. **2** *adj.* ∼ **demonstration** Sitzblockade, *die;* ∼ **strike** Sitzstreik, *der*

site /saɪt/ **1** *n.* (a) (land) Grundstück, *das;* (b) (location) Sitz, *der;* (of new factory etc.) Standort, *der.* **2** *v.t.* (locate) stationieren ⟨*Raketen*⟩; ∼ **a factory in London** London als Standort einer Fabrik wählen; **be** ∼**d** gelegen sein

'**sit-in** *n.* Sit-in, *das*

siting /'saɪtɪŋ/ *n.* Standortwahl, *die* (**of** für); (position) Lage, *die;* (of missiles) Stationierung, *die*

sitter /'sɪtə(r)/ *n.* (artist's model) Modell, *das*

sitting /'sɪtɪŋ/ *n.* Sitzung, *die;* **in one** *or* **at a** ∼ (fig.) in einem Zug[e]

sitting: ∼ **'duck** n. (fig.) leichtes Ziel; ∼ **room** n. Wohnzimmer, das; ∼ **'target** ⇒ ∼ **duck;** ∼ **'tenant** n. **he is/was the** ∼ **tenant** er ist/war der jetzige/damalige Mieter; **there is a** ∼ **tenant** es ist ein Mieter vorhanden

situate /'sɪtjʊeɪt/ v.t. legen

situated /'sɪtjʊeɪtɪd/ adj. **(a)** gelegen; **be** ∼**:** liegen; **a badly** ∼ **house** ein Haus in schlechter od. ungünstiger Lage; **(b) be well/badly** ∼ **financially** finanziell gut/ schlecht gestellt sein

situation /sɪtjʊ'eɪʃn/ n. **(a)** (location) Lage, die; **(b)** (circumstances) Situation, die; **be in the happy** ∼ **of being able to do sth.** in der glücklichen Lage sein, etw. tun zu können; **what's the** ∼**?** wie steht's?; **(c)** (job) Stelle, die

situation 'comedy n. Situationskomödie, die (Serie von Radio- oder Fernsehkomödien mit unverbundenen Episoden bei gleichbleibenden Rollen)

six /sɪks/ ▶ 630⎜, ▶ 706⎜, ▶ 956⎜ **1** adj. sechs; **be** ∼ **feet** or **foot under** (coll.) unter der Erde liegen; **it is** ∼ **of one and half-a-dozen of the other** (coll.) das ist Jacke wie Hose (ugs.); see also **eight 1. 2** n. Sechs, die; **be at** ∼**es and sevens** sich in einem heillosen Durcheinander befinden; (on an issue or matter) heillos zerstritten sein (**on** über + Akk.); see also **eight 2 a, c, d; hit 1 i**

six: ∼**-footer** /sɪks'fʊtə(r)/ n. (person) Zwei-Meter-Mann, der/-Frau, die; ∼**-pack** n. Sechserpack, der; ∼**pence** /'sɪkspəns/ n. (Brit. Hist.: coin) Sixpence, der; ∼**-shooter** n. sechsschüssiger Revolver

sixteen /sɪks'tiːn, 'sɪkstiːn/ ▶ 630⎜, ▶ 706⎜, ▶ 956⎜ **1** adj. sechzehn; see also **eight 1. 2** n. Sechzehn, die; see also **eight 2 a; eighteen 2**

sixteenth /sɪks'tiːnθ/ ▶ 738⎜, ▶ 956⎜ **1** adj. sechzehnt...; see also **eighth 1. 2** n. (fraction) Sechzehntel, das; see also **eighth 2**

six'teenth note n. (Amer. Mus.) Sechzehntelnote, die

sixth /sɪksθ/ ▶ 738⎜, ▶ 956⎜ **1** adj. sechst...; see also **eighth 1. 2** n. (in sequence, rank) Sechste, der/die/das; (fraction) Sechstel, das; see also **eighth 2**

sixth: ∼ **form** n. (Brit. Sch.) ≈ zwölfte/dreizehnte Klasse; ∼ **form college** n. (Brit. Sch.) ≈ Oberstufenzentrum, das; College, das nur Schüler der zwölften/dreizehnten Klasse aufnimmt; ∼**-former** n. (Brit. Sch.) Schüler/Schülerin der zwölften/dreizehnten Klasse; ∼ **sense** n. sechster Sinn

sixtieth /'sɪkstɪɪθ/ ▶ 956⎜ **1** adj. sechzigst...; see also **eighth 1. 2** n. (fraction) Sechzigstel, das; see also **eighth 2**

sixty /'sɪkstɪ/ ▶ 630⎜, ▶ 956⎜ **1** adj. sechzig; see also **eight 1. 2** n. Sechzig, die; see also **eight 2 a; eighty 2**

sixty: ∼**-'first** etc. adj. ▶ 956⎜ einundsechzigst... usw.; see also **eighth 1;** ∼**-'one** etc. ▶ 956⎜ **1** adj. einundsechzig usw.; see also **eight 1; 2** n. Einundsechzig usw., die; see also **eight 2 a**

size¹ /saɪz/ n. **(a)** Größe, die; (fig. of problem, project) Umfang, der; Ausmaß, das; **reach full** ∼**:** auswachsen; **be quite a** ∼**:** ziemlich groß sein; **be twice the** ∼ **of sth.** zweimal so groß wie etw. sein; **who can afford a car that** ∼**?** wer kann sich (Dat.) einen so großen Wagen leisten?; **what** ∼ **[of] box do you want?** welche Größe soll die [gewünschte] Schachtel haben?; **be small in** ∼**:** klein sein; **be the** ∼ **of sth.** so groß wie etw. sein; **that's [about] the** ∼ **of it** (fig. coll.) so sieht die Sache aus (ugs.); **try sth. for** ∼**:** etw. [wegen der Größe] anprobieren; (fig.) es einmal mit etw. versuchen; **what** ∼**?** wie groß?; **(b)** (graded class) Größe, die; (of paper) Format, das; **collar/waist** ∼**:** Kragen-/Taillenweite, die; **take a** ∼ **7 shoe, take** ∼ **7 in shoes** Schuhgröße 7 haben
∼ **'up** v.t. taxieren ‹Lage›

size² n. Leim, der; (for textiles) Schlichte, die

sizeable /'saɪzəbl/ adj. ziemlich groß; beträchtlich ‹Summe, Wissen, Einfluss, Unterschied›; ansehnlich ‹Betrag›

sizzle /'sɪzl/ **1** v.i. zischen. **2** n. Zischen, das

skate¹ /skeɪt/ n. (Zool.) Rochen, der

skate² **1** n. (ice-∼) Schlittschuh, der; (roller ∼) Rollschuh, der; **get one's** ∼**s on** (Brit. fig. coll.) sich beeilen. **2** v.i. (ice-∼) Schlittschuh laufen; (roller ∼) Rollschuh laufen; ∼ **on**

thin ice (fig.) sich auf dünnem Eis bewegen; (put oneself in danger) sich auf dünnes Eis begeben
∼ **over,** ∼ **round** v.t. (fig.) (avoid) hinweggehen über (+ Akk.) ‹Frage, Problem›; (touch lightly on) [nur] streifen

skate: ∼**board 1** n. Skateboard, das; Rollerbrett, das; **2** v.i. Skateboard fahren; ∼**boarding** n., no pl. Skateboardfahren, das

skater /'skeɪtə(r)/ n. (ice-∼) Eisläufer, der/-läuferin, die; (roller ∼) Rollschuhläufer, der/-läuferin, die

skating /'skeɪtɪŋ/ n., no pl. (ice-∼) Schlittschuhlaufen, das; (roller ∼) Rollschuhlaufen, das

'skating rink n. **(a)** (ice) Eisbahn, die; Eisfläche, die; **(b)** (for roller skating) Rollschuhbahn, die

skeleton /'skelɪtn/ n. Skelett, das; Gerippe, das; **have a** ∼ **in the cupboard** (Brit.) or (Amer.) **closet** (fig.) eine Leiche im Keller haben (ugs.)

skeleton: ∼ **crew** n. Stammbesatzung, die; ∼ **key** n. Dietrich, der; ∼ **service** n. **provide a** ∼ **service** den Betrieb notdürftig aufrechterhalten; **there were buses running, but it was only a** ∼ **service** es fuhren zwar Busse, aber nur einige wenige; ∼ **staff** n. Minimalbesetzung, die

skeptic etc. (Amer.) ⇒ **sceptic** etc.

sketch /sketʃ/ **1** n. **(a)** (drawing) Skizze, die; **do** or **make a** ∼**:** eine Skizze anfertigen; **(b)** (play) Sketch, der; **(c)** (Lit.) Skizze, die. **2** v.t. (lit. or fig.) skizzieren
∼ **'in** v.t. **(a)** (draw) einzeichnen; **(b)** (fig.: outline) skizzieren
∼ **'out** v.t. (lit. or fig.) [in groben Umrissen] skizzieren

sketch: ∼**book** n. Skizzenbuch, das; ∼ **map** n. Faustskizze, die; ∼ **pad** n. Skizzenblock, der

sketchy /'sketʃɪ/ adj. **(a)** skizzenhaft; (fig.: incomplete) lückenhaft ‹Information, Bericht›; **(c)** (inadequate) unzureichend

skew /skjuː/ **1** adj. schräg; schief ‹Gesicht›. **2** n. **on the** ∼**:** schräg ‹überqueren›; schief ‹tragen, aufsetzen›; **the picture is [hanging] on the** ∼**:** das Bild hängt schief. **3** v.i. ∼ **round** sich drehen

skewer /'skjuːə(r)/ **1** n. [Brat]spieß, der. **2** v.t. aufspießen

skew-'whiff (Brit. coll.) ⇒ **askew**

ski /skiː/ **1** n. **(a)** Ski, der; **(b)** (on vehicle) Kufe, die. **2** v.i. Ski laufen od. fahren

'ski boot n. Skistiefel, der

skid /skɪd/ **1** v.i. **-dd-:** **(a)** schlittern; (from one side to the other; spinning round) schleudern; **(b)** (on road) rutschen. **2** n. **(a)** Schlittern/Schleudern, das; **go into a** ∼**:** ins Schlittern/Schleudern geraten; **(b)** (Aeronaut.) Gleitkufe, die

skid: ∼ **marks** n. pl. Schleuderspur, die; ∼ **row** /skɪd 'rəʊ/ n. (Amer.) Pennerviertel, das (salopp abwertend); **end up on** ∼ **row** (coll.) als Penner enden (salopp abwertend)

skier /'skiːə(r)/ n. Skiläufer, der/-läuferin, die; Skifahrer, der/-fahrerin, die

skiing /'skiːɪŋ/ n., no pl. Skilaufen, das; Skifahren, das; (Sport) Skisport, der

ski: ∼ **jump** n. **(a)** (slope) Sprungschanze, die; **(b)** (leap) Skisprung, der; ∼ **jumper** n. Skispringer, der/-springerin, die; ∼ **jumping** n., no pl. Skispringen, das

skilful /'skɪlfl/ adj. **(a)** (having skill) geschickt; gewandt ‹Redner›; gut ‹Beobachter, Lehrer›; **(b)** (well executed) geschickt; kunstvoll ‹Gemälde, Plastik, Roman, Komposition›; (expert) fachgerecht ‹Beurteilung›

skilfully /'skɪlfəlɪ/ adv. ⇒ **skilful b:** geschickt; kunstvoll; fachgerecht; kunstgerecht

'ski lift n. Skilift, der

skill /skɪl/ n. **(a)** (expertness) Geschick, das, Fertigkeit, die (**at, in** in + Dat.); (of artist) Können, das; **(b)** (technique) Fertigkeit, die; (of weaving, bricklaying) Technik, die; Kunst, die; **(c)** in pl. (abilities) Fähigkeiten; **office** ∼**s** Büroerfahrung, die; **language** ∼**s** Sprachkenntnisse Pl.

skilled /skɪld/ adj. **(a)** ⇒ **skilful a;** **(b)** (requiring skill) qualifiziert ‹Arbeit, Tätigkeit›; ∼ **trade** Ausbildungsberuf, der; **(c)** (trained) ausgebildet; (experienced) erfahren; **be** ∼ **in diplomacy/sewing** ein guter Diplomat sein/gut nähen können

skillful, skillfully (Amer.) ⇒ **skilful, skilfully**

skim /skɪm/ **1** v.t., **-mm-:** **(a)** (remove) abschöpfen; abrahmen ‹Milch›; **(b)** (touch in passing) streifen; **(c)** (pass closely over) ∼ **sth.** dicht über etw. (*Akk.*) fliegen; (**d**) (scan briefly) ⇒ ∼ **through. 2** *v.i.*, **-mm-** segeln

∼ **'off** *v.t.* (**a**) abschöpfen; (**b**) (fig.) ⇒ **cream off**

∼ **through** *v.t.* überfliegen 〈*Buch, Zeitung*〉

skimmed 'milk, skim 'milk *n.* entrahmte Milch

skimp /skɪmp/ **1** *v.t.* sparen an (+ *Dat.*); **he did the work badly,** ∼**ing it** er schluderte bei seiner Arbeit (ugs.). **2** *v.i.* sparen (**with, on** an + *Dat.*); **he had to** ∼ **on food/clothes** er musste am Essen/an der Kleidung sparen

skimpy /'skɪmpɪ/ *adj.* sparsam; karg 〈*Mahl*〉; kärglich 〈*Leben*〉; winzig 〈*Badeanzug*〉; [zu] knapp 〈*Anzug*〉; spärlich 〈*Wissen*〉

skin /skɪn/ **1** *n.* (**a**) ▶ **672** Haut, *die;* **be all** *or* **just** ∼ **and bone** (fig.) nur Haut und Knochen sein (ugs.); **be soaked** *or* **wet to the** ∼: bis auf die Haut durchnässt sein; **by** *or* **with the** ∼ **of one's teeth** mit knapper Not; **get under sb.'s** ∼ (fig. coll.) (irritate sb.) jmdm. auf die Nerven gehen *od.* fallen (ugs.); (fascinate enchant sb.) jmdm. unter die Haut gehen (ugs.); **have a thick/thin** ∼ (fig.) ein dickes Fell haben (ugs.) /dünnhäutig sein; **jump out of one's** ∼ (fig.) aus dem Häuschen geraten (ugs.); **save one's** ∼ (fig.) seine Haut retten (ugs.); **it's no** ∼ **off my/his** *etc.* **nose** (coll.) das braucht mich/ihn *usw.* nicht zu jucken (ugs.); (**b**) (hide) Haut, *die;* (**c**) (fur) Fell, *das;* (**d**) (peel) Schale, *die;* (of onion, peach also) Haut, *die;* (**e**) (sausage-casing) Haut, *die;* (**f**) (on milk) Haut, *die.* **2** *v.t.*, **-nn-** häuten; schälen 〈*Frucht*〉; ∼ **sb. alive** (fig. coll.) Hackfleisch aus jmdm. machen (ugs.). *see also* **eye 1 a**

skin: ∼ **cancer** *n.* ▶ **865** Hautkrebs, *der;* ∼ **cream** *n.* Hautcreme, *die;* ∼**'deep** *adj.* (fig.) oberflächlich; *see also* **beauty a;** ∼ **diver** *n.* Taucher, *der*/Taucherin, *die;* ∼ **diving** *n., no pl.* Tauchen, *das;* ∼**flint** *n.* Geizhals, *der* (abwertend)

skinful /'skɪnfʊl/ *n.* (coll.) **have had a** ∼: voll sein (salopp)

skin: ∼ **graft** *n.* Hauttransplantation, *die;* ∼**head** *n.* (Brit.) Skinhead, *der*

skinny /'skɪnɪ/ *adj.* mager

skint /skɪnt/ *adj.* (Brit. coll.) bankrott; **be** ∼: blank *od.* pleite sein (ugs.)

'skintight *adj.* hauteng

skip¹ /skɪp/ **1** *v.i.*, **-pp-:** (**a**) hüpfen; (**b**) (use skipping rope) seilspringen; (**c**) (change quickly) springen (fig.); (**d**) (make omissions) überspringen. **2** *v.t.*, **-pp-:** (**a**) (omit) überspringen; (in mentioning names) übergehen; **my heart** ∼**ped a beat** (fig.) mir stockte das Herz; (**b**) (coll.: miss) schwänzen (ugs.) 〈*Schule usw.*〉; liegen lassen 〈*Hausarbeit*〉; ∼ **breakfast/lunch** *etc.* das Frühstück/Mittagessen *usw.* auslassen. **3** *n.* Hüpfer, *der;* Hopser, *der* (ugs.)

∼ **a'bout,** ∼ **a'round** *v.i.* (**a**) herumhüpfen; (**b**) **he did not stay with his subject but** ∼**ped about** er hielt sich nicht an sein Thema, sondern sprang von einem Gegenstand zum anderen *od.* nächsten

∼ **over** ⇒ ∼ **2 a**

∼ **through** *v.t.* (**a**) ⇒ **skim through;** (**b**) (make short work of) [rasch] durchziehen (ugs.); herunterschnurren (ugs.) 〈*Vorlesung*〉

skip² *n.* (Building) Container, *der*

ski: ∼ **pass** *n.* Skipass, *der;* ∼ **pole** *n.* Skistock, *der*

skipper /'skɪpə(r)/ *n.* (**a**) (Naut.) Kapitän, *der;* (of yacht) Skipper, *der* (Seglerjargon); (**b**) (Aeronaut.) [Flug]kapitän, *der;* (**c**) (Sport) [Mannschafts]kapitän, *der*

'skipping rope (Brit.), **'skip-rope** (Amer.) *ns.* Sprungseil, *das;* Springseil, *das*

'ski resort *n.* Skiurlaubsort, *der*

skirmish /'skɜːmɪʃ/ *n.* (**a**) (fight) Rangelei, *die* (ugs.); (of troops, armies) Gefecht, *das* (Milit.); (**b**) (fig.: argument) Auseinandersetzung, *die*

skirt /skɜːt/ **1** *n.* Rock, *der.* **2** *v.t.* herumgehen um. **3** *v.i.* ∼ **along sth.** an etw. (*Dat.*) entlanggehen/-fahren/-reiten *usw.*

∼ **round** *v.t.* herumgehen um; (fig.) umgehen; ausweichen (+ *Dat.*)

skirting /'skɜːtɪŋ/ *n.* ∼**[board]** (Brit.) Fußleiste, *die*

ski: ∼ **run** *n.* Skihang, *der;* (prepared) [Ski]piste, *die;* ∼ **stick** *n.* Skistock, *der*

skit /skɪt/ *n.* parodistischer Sketch (**on** über + *Akk.*)

skittish /'skɪtɪʃ/ *adj.* (**a**) (nervous) nervös 〈*Pferd*〉; (inclined to shy) schreckhaft 〈*Pferd*〉; (**b**) (lively) ausgelassen; aufgekratzt (ugs.)

skittle /'skɪtl/ *n.* (**a**) Kegel, *der;* (**b**) *in pl., constr. as sing.* (game) Kegeln, *das*

skive /skaɪv/ *v.i.* (Brit. coll.) sich drücken (ugs.)

∼ **'off** (Brit. coll.) **1** *v.i.* sich verdrücken (ugs.). **2** *v.t.* schwänzen (ugs.)

skulk /skʌlk/ *v.i.* (**a**) (lurk) lauern; (**b**) (move stealthily) schleichen

∼ **'off** *v.i.* sich fortschleichen

skull /skʌl/ *n.* (**a**) (Anat.) Schädel, *der;* (**b**) (as object) Totenschädel, *der;* (representation) Totenkopf, *der*

skull and crossbones /skʌl ən 'krɒsbəʊnz/ *n.* Totenkopf, *der (mit gekreuzten Knochen);* (flag) Totenkopfflagge, *die*

skunk /skʌŋk/ *n.* (Zool.) Stinktier, *das*

sky /skaɪ/ *n.* Himmel, *der;* **in the** ∼**:** am Himmel; **praise sb./sth. to the skies** jmdn./etw. in den Himmel heben (ugs.); **the** ∼**'s the limit** (fig.) da gibt es [praktisch] keine Grenze

sky: ∼**-blue 1** *adj.* himmelblau; **2** *n.* Himmelblau, *das;* ∼**diver** *n.* Fallschirmspringer, *der*/-springerin, *die;* ∼**diving** *n.* Fallschirmspringen, *das* (als Sport); Fallschirmsport, *der;* ∼**-high 1** *adj.* himmelhoch; astronomisch (ugs.) 〈*Preise usw.*〉; **2** *adv.* hoch in die Luft 〈*werfen, steigen usw.*〉; **go** ∼**-high** 〈*Preise usw.:*〉 in astronomische Höhen klettern (ugs.); ∼**lark 1** *n.* (Ornith.) [Feld]lerche, *die;* **2** *v.i.* ∼**lark [about** *or* **around]** herumalbern (ugs.); ∼**light** *n.* Dachfenster, *das;* ∼**line** *n.* Silhouette, *die;* (characteristic of certain town) Skyline, *die;* ∼**scraper** *n.* Wolkenkratzer, *der*

slab /slæb/ *n.* (**a**) (flat stone etc.) Platte, *die;* (**b**) (thick slice) [dicke] Scheibe; (of cake) [dickes] Stück; (of chocolate, toffee) Tafel, *die*

slack /slæk/ **1** *adj.* (**a**) (lax) nachlässig; schlampig (ugs. abwertend); **be** ∼ **about** *or* **in** *or* **with sth.** in Bezug auf etw. (*Akk.*) nachlässig sein; (**b**) (loose) schlaff; locker 〈*Verband, Strumpfband*〉; (**c**) (sluggish) schlaff; schwach 〈*Wind, Flut*〉; (**d**) (Commerc.: not busy) flau. **2** *n.* **there's too much** ∼ **in the rope** das Seil ist zu locker *od.* nicht straff genug; **take in** *or* **up the** ∼**:** das Seil/die Schnur *usw.* straffen. **3** *v.i.* (coll.) bummeln (ugs.)

slacken /'slækn/ **1** *v.i.* (**a**) (loosen) sich lockern; 〈*Seil:*〉 schlaff werden; (**b**) (diminish) nachlassen; 〈*Geschwindigkeit:*〉 sich verringern; 〈*Schritt:*〉 sich verlangsamen. **2** *v.t.* (**a**) (loosen) lockern; (**b**) (diminish) verringern; verlangsamen 〈*Schritt*〉

∼ **'off 1** *v.i.* (**a**) (loosen) ⇒ ∼ **1 a;** (**b**) (diminish) ⇒ ∼ **1 b;** (**c**) (relax) es etwas langsamer angehen lassen (ugs.). **2** *v.t.* (**a**) (loosen) ⇒ ∼ **2 a;** (**b**) (diminish) ⇒ ∼ **2 b**

slacker /'slækə(r)/ *n.* (coll. derog.) (**a**) Faulenzer, *der;* (**b**) (Amer.: young adult) Hänger, *der* (ugs.); Durchhänger, *der* (ugs.)

slackness /'slæknɪs/ *n., no pl.* (**a**) (negligence) Nachlässigkeit, *die;* (**b**) (idleness) Bummelei, *die* (ugs.); (**c**) (looseness) Schlaffheit, *die;* (**d**) (of market, trade) Flaute, *die*

slacks /slæks/ *n. pl.* **[pair of]** ∼**:** lange Hose; Slacks *Pl.* (Mode)

slag /slæg/ *n.* (Metallurgy) Schlacke, *die*

'slag heap *n.* (Mining) Schlackenhalde, *die*

slain ⇒ **slay a**

slake /sleɪk/ *v.t.* stillen

slalom /'slɑːləm/ *n.* (Skiing) Slalom, *der*

slam¹ /slæm/ **1** *v.t.*, **-mm-:** (**a**) (shut) zuschlagen; zuknallen (ugs.); ∼ **the door in sb.'s face** jmdm. die Tür vor der Nase zuschlagen; (**b**) (put violently) knallen (ugs.); ∼ **one's foot on the brake** (coll.) auf die Bremse steigen (ugs.). **2** *v.i.*, **-mm-:** (**a**) zuschlagen; zuknallen (ugs.); (**b**) (move violently) stürmen; **the car** ∼**med against** *or* **into the wall** das Auto knallte (ugs.) gegen die Mauer. **3** *n.* Knall, *der*

∼ **'on** *v.t.* (coll.) ∼ **on the brakes** auf die Bremse latschen (salopp)

slam² *n.* (a) (Cards) Schlemm, *der;* **grand** ∼: großer Schlemm; (b) (Sport) **achieve the grand** ∼: alle [wichtigen] Meistertitel gewinnen; (Tennis) den Grand Slam gewinnen

slander /'slɑːndə(r)/ **1** *n.* Verleumdung, *die* (**on** *Gen.*). **2** *v.t.* verleumden; schädigen ‹*Ruf*›

slanderous /'slɑːndərəs/ *adj.* verleumderisch

slang /slæŋ/ *n.* Slang, *der;* ‹*Theater-, Soldaten-, Juristen*›jargon, *der; attrib.* Slang ‹*wort, -ausdruck*›

'slanging match *n.* gegenseitige [lautstarke] Beschimpfung

slangy /'slæŋɪ/ *adj.* Slang ‹*ausdruck, -wort*›; salopp ‹*Wortwahl, Redeweise*›

slant /slɑːnt/ **1** *v.i.* (*Fläche:*) sich neigen; (*Linie:*) schräg verlaufen. **2** *v.t.* (a) abschrägen; schräg zeichnen ‹*Linie*›. (b) (fig.: bias) [so] hinbiegen (ugs.) ‹*Meldung, Bemerkung*›. **3** *n.* (a) Schräge, *die;* **be on a** *or* **the** ∼: schräg sein; (b) (fig.: bias) Tendenz, *die;* Färbung, *die;* **have a left-wing** ∼ ‹*Bericht:*› links gefärbt sein

slanted /'slɑːntɪd/ *adj.* (fig.) gefärbt; **a** ∼ **question** eine Suggestivfrage

slanting /'slɑːntɪŋ/ *adj.* schräg

slap /slæp/ **1** *v.t.*, **-pp-:** (a) schlagen; ∼ **sb. on the face/ arm/hand** jmdm. ins Gesicht/auf den Arm/auf die Hand schlagen; ∼ **sb.'s face** *or* **sb. in** *or* **on the face** jmdn. ohrfeigen; ∼ **sb. on the back** jmdm. auf die Schulter klopfen; **she deserves to be** ∼**ped on the back** (fig.) sie verdient Beifall; Hut ab vor ihr! (ugs.); (b) (put forcefully) knallen (ugs.); ∼ **a fine on sb.** (fig.) jmdm. eine Geldstrafe aufbrummen (ugs.). **2** *v.i.*, **-pp-** schlagen; klatschen. **3** *n.* Schlag, *der;* **give sb. a** ∼: jmdn. [mit der flachen Hand] schlagen; **a** ∼ **in the face** (lit. or fig.) ein Schlag ins Gesicht; **give sb. a** ∼ **on the back** (lit. or fig.) jmdm. auf die Schulter klopfen; **a** ∼ **on the back for sb./sth.** (fig.) eine Anerkennung für jmdn./etw. **4** *adv.* voll; **run** ∼ **into sb.** (lit. or fig.) mit jmdm. zusammenprallen; ∼ **in the eye/face** *etc.* jmdm. mit voller Wucht ins Auge/Gesicht *usw.* treffen; ∼ **in the middle** genau in der Mitte

∼ **'down** *v.t.* (a) (lay forcefully) hinknallen (ugs.); ∼ **sth. down on the table** etw. auf etw. (*Akk.*) knallen (ugs.); (b) (coll.: reprimand) ∼ **sb. down** jmdm. eins auf den Deckel geben (ugs.); **be** ∼ **ped down** eins auf den Deckel kriegen (ugs.)

∼ **'on** *v.t.* (a) (coll.: apply hastily) draufklatschen (ugs.) ‹*Farbe, Make-up*›; zuschnappen lassen ‹*Handschellen*›; (b) (coll.: impose) draufschlagen (ugs.). *See also* ∼ **1 a**

slap: ∼ **bang** *adv.* **the table was** ∼ **bang in the middle of the room** der Tisch stand einfach mitten im Zimmer; ∼**dash 1** *adv.* ruck, zuck (ugs.); **2** *adj.* schludrig (ugs. abwertend); **in a** ∼**dash fashion** schludrig; **her essay is** ∼**dash** ihr Aufsatz ist hingeschludert (ugs. abwertend); **be** ∼**dash in one's work** bei der Arbeit schludern (ugs. abwertend); ∼**-happy** *adj.* (coll.: cheerfully casual) unbekümmert; ∼**-up** *attrib. adj.* (coll.) ‹*Essen, Diner*› mit allen Schikanen (ugs.)

slash /slæʃ/ **1** *v.i.* ∼ **at sb./sth. with a knife** auf jmdn./ etw. mit einem Messer losgehen. **2** *v.t.* (a) (make gashes in) aufschlitzen; (b) (fig.: reduce sharply) [drastisch] reduzieren; [drastisch] kürzen ‹*Etat, Gehalt, Umfang*›; ∼ **costs by one million** die Kosten um eine Million reduzieren. **3** *n.* (a) (∼ing stroke) Hieb, *der;* (b) (wound) Schnitt, *der*

slat /slæt/ *n.* Leiste, *die;* (of wood in bedstead, fence) Latte, *die;* (in Venetian blind) Lamelle, *die*

slate /sleɪt/ **1** *n.* (a) (Geol.) Schiefer, *der;* (b) (Building) Schieferplatte, *die;* (c) (writing surface) Schiefertafel, *die;* **put sth. on the** ∼ (Brit. coll.) etw. anschreiben (ugs.); **wipe the** ∼ **clean** (fig.) einen Schlussstrich ziehen. **2** *attrib. adj.* Schiefer-. **3** *v.t.* (Brit. coll.: criticize) in der Luft zerreißen (ugs.) (**for** wegen)

slate: ∼**-coloured** *adj.* schieferfarben; ∼**-grey 1** *n.* Schiefergrau, *das;* **2** *adj.* schiefergrau

slaughter /'slɔːtə(r)/ **1** *n.* (a) (killing for food) Schlachten, *das;* Schlachtung, *die; see also* **lamb 1 a**; (b) (massacre) Abschlachten, *das;* (in battle) Gemetzel, *das.* **2** *v.t.* (a) (kill for food) schlachten; (b) (massacre) abschlachten; niedermetzeln (abwertend); (c) (coll.: defeat) fertig machen (salopp); (d) (coll.: severely criticize) verreißen

'slaughterhouse ⇒ **abattoir**

Slav /slɑːv/ *n.* Slawe, *der*/Slawin, *die*

slave /sleɪv/ **1** *n.* (a) Sklave, *der*/Sklavin, *die;* (b) (fig.) **be a** ∼ **of** *or* **to sth.** Sklave von etw. sein; **be a** ∼ **to sb.** jmdm. verfallen sein. **2** *v.i.* ∼ [**away**] schuften (ugs.); sich abplagen *od.* (salopp) abrackern (**at** mit); ∼ **over a hot stove all day** den ganzen Tag am Herd stehen (ugs.)

slave: ∼**-driver** *n.* (a) Sklavenaufseher, *der;* (b) (fig.) Sklaventreiber, *der*/-treiberin, *die* (abwertend); ∼ **'labour** *n.* Sklavenarbeit, *die;* (fig.) Ausbeutung, *die*

slavery /'sleɪvərɪ/ *n., no pl.* (a) Sklaverei, *die;* (b) (drudgery) Sklavenarbeit, *die;* Sklaverei, *die*

slavish /'sleɪvɪʃ/ *adj.* sklavisch

Slavonic /sləˈvɒnɪk/ **1** *adj.* slawisch. **2** *n.* Slawisch, *das*

slay /sleɪ/ *v.t.* (a) **slew** /sluː/, **slain** /sleɪn/ (literary) ermorden; (with sword, club also) erschlagen; (b) ∼**ed**, ∼**ed** (coll.: amuse greatly) **he/his jokes** ∼**ed me** über ihn/seine Witze habe ich mich totgelacht (ugs.)

sleaze /sliːz/ *n., no pl.* (derog.) Korruption, *die*

'sleazebag, **'sleazeball** *ns.* (sl. derog.) Drecksack, *der* (derb abwertend)

sleazy /'sliːzɪ/ *adj.* schäbig (abwertend); heruntergekommen (ugs.) ‹*Person*›; (disreputable) anrüchig

sled /sled/ (Amer.), **sledge** /sledʒ/ *ns.* Schlitten, *der*

'sledgehammer *n.* Vorschlaghammer, *der;* [**take/use**] **a** ∼ **to crack a nut** (coll.) mit Kanonen auf Spatzen schießen

sleek /sliːk/ *adj.* (a) (glossy) seidig ‹*Fell, Haar, Pelz*›; ‹*Tier*› mit seidigem Fell; (b) **the** ∼ **lines of the car** die schnittige Form des Wagens

sleep /sliːp/ **1** *n.* Schlaf, *der;* **get some** ∼: schlafen; **get/ go to** ∼: einschlafen; **go to** ∼**!** schlaf jetzt!; **not lose [any]** ∼ **over sth.** (fig.) wegen etw. keine schlaflose Nacht haben; **put an animal to** ∼ (euphem.) ein Tier einschläfern; **talk in one's** ∼: im Schlaf sprechen; **walk in one's** ∼: schlafwandeln; **I can/could do it in my** ∼ (fig.) ich kann/könnte es im Schlaf; **get** *or* **have a good night's** ∼: [sich] gründlich ausschlafen; **have a** ∼: schlafen. **2** *v.i.*, **slept** /slept/ schlafen; ∼ **late** lange schlafen; ausschlafen; ∼ **like a log** *or* **top** wie ein Stein schlafen (ugs.); ∼ **tight!** (coll.) schlaf gut! **3** *v.t.*, **slept** schlafen lassen; **the hotel** ∼**s 80** das Hotel hat 80 Betten

∼ **a'round** *v.i.* (coll.) herumschlafen (ugs.)

∼ **'in** *v.i.* im Bett bleiben

∼ **'off** *v.t.* ausschlafen; ∼ **it off** seinen Rausch ausschlafen

∼ **on 1** *v.i.* /-'-/ weiterschlafen. **2** *v.t.* /'--/ überschlafen

∼ **through** *v.t.* ∼ **through the noise/alarm** trotz des Lärms/Weckerklingelns [weiter]schlafen

∼ **together** *v.i.* (coll. euphem.) miteinander schlafen

∼ **with** *v.t.* ∼ **with sb.** (coll. euphem.) mit jmdm. schlafen

sleeper /'sliːpə(r)/ *n.* (a) Schläfer, *der;* **be a heavy/light** ∼: einen tiefen/leichten Schlaf haben; (b) (Brit. Railw.: support) Schwelle, *die;* (c) (Railw.) (coach) Schlafwagen, *der;* (berth) Schlafwagenplatz, *der;* (overnight train) [**night**] ∼: Nachtzug mit Schlafwagen

sleeping /'sliːpɪŋ/ *adj.* (lit. or fig.) schlafend; **let** ∼ **dogs lie** (fig.) keine schlafenden Hunde wecken

sleeping: ∼ **bag** *n.* Schlafsack, *der;* ∼ **car** *n.* (Railw.) Schlafwagen, *der;* ∼ **'partner** *n.* (Commerc.) stiller Teilhaber; ∼ **pill**, ∼ **tablet** *ns.* Schlaftablette, *die;* ∼ **policeman** *n.* (Brit.) Bodenschwelle, *die*

sleepless /'sliːplɪs/ *adj.* schlaflos

sleep: ∼**walk** *v.i.* schlafwandeln; ∼**walker** *n.* Schlafwandler, *der*/-wandlerin, *die*

sleepy /'sliːpɪ/ *adj.* (a) (drowsy) schläfrig; (b) (sluggish) schwerfällig; (unobservant) schlafmützig (ugs. abwertend); (c) (peaceful) verschlafen ‹*Dorf, Stadt usw.*›

sleet /sliːt/ **1** *n., no indef. art.* Schneeregen, *der.* **2** *v.i. impers.* **it was** ∼**ing** es gab Schneeregen

sleeve /sliːv/ *n.* (a) Ärmel, *der;* **have sth. up one's** ∼ (fig.) etw. in petto haben (ugs.); **roll up one's** ∼**s** (lit. or fig.) die Ärmel hochkrempeln (ugs.); (b) (record cover) Hülle, *die*

sleeveless /'sliːvlɪs/ *adj.* ärmellos

sleigh /sleɪ/ *n.* Schlitten, *der*

'sleigh ride *n.* Schlittenfahrt, *die*

sleight of hand /slaɪt əv 'hænd/ *n.* Fingerfertigkeit, *die*

slender /'slendə(r)/ *adj.* **(a)** (slim) schlank; schmal ‹*Buch, Band*›; **(b)** (meagre) mager ‹*Einkommen, Kost*›; gering ‹*Chance, Mittel, Vorräte, Hoffnung, Kenntnis*›; schwach ‹*Entschuldigung, Argument, Grund*›

slept ⇒ **sleep 2**

sleuth /sluːθ/ *n.* Detektiv, *der*

slew¹ /sluː/ **1** *v.i.* ~ **to the side/left** sich [schnell] seitwärts/nach links drehen; ‹*Kran:*› seitwärts/nach links schwenken. **2** *v.t.* schwenken ‹*Kran*›

slew² ⇒ **slay a**

slice /slaɪs/ **1** *n.* **(a)** (cut portion) Scheibe, *die;* (of apple, melon, peach, apricot, cake, pie) Stück, *das;* **a** ~ **of life** ein Ausschnitt aus dem Leben; *see also* **cake 1 a;** **(b)** (share) Teil, *der;* (allotted part of profits, money) Anteil, *der;* **(c)** (utensil) [Braten]wender, *der.* **2** *v.t.* **(a)** in Scheiben schneiden; in Stücke schneiden ‹*Bohnen, Apfel, Pfirsich, Kuchen usw.*›; **(b)** (Golf) slicen; (Tennis) unterschneiden; slicen. **3** *v.i.* schneiden; ~ **through** durchschneiden; durchpflügen ‹*Wellen, Meer*›
~ **'off** *v.t.* abschneiden
~ **'up** *v.t.* aufschneiden; (fig.: divide) aufteilen

sliced /slaɪst/ *adj.* (cut into slices) aufgeschnitten; klein geschnitten ‹*Gemüse*›; ~ **bread** Schnittbrot, *das;* **the greatest thing since** ~ **bread** (coll. joc.) der/die/das Größte seit der Erfindung der Bratkartoffel (ugs. scherzh.)

slick /slɪk/ **1** *adj.* (coll.) **(a)** (dextrous) professionell; **(b)** (pretentiously dextrous) clever (ugs.). **2** *n.* **[oil]** ~: Ölteppich, *der*

slid ⇒ **slide 1, 2**

slide /slaɪd/ **1** *v.i.,* **slid** /slɪd/ **(a)** rutschen ‹*Kolben, Schublade, Feder:*› gleiten; ~ **down sth.** etw. hinunterrutschen; **(b)** (glide over ice) schlittern; **(c)** (move smoothly) gleiten; **(d)** (fig.: take its own course) **let sth./things** ~: etw./die Dinge schleifen lassen (fig.). **2** *v.t.,* **slid (a)** schieben; **(b)** (place unobtrusively) gleiten lassen. **3** *n.* **(a)** [Photog.] Dia [positiv], *das;* **(b)** (chute) (in children's playground) Rutschbahn, *die;* (for goods etc.) Rutsche, *die;* **(c)** ⇒ **hairslide; (d)** (fig.: decline) **the** ~ **in the value of the pound** das Abgleiten des Pfundes; **(e)** (for microscope) Objektträger, *der*

slide: ~ **film** *n.* (Photog.) Diafilm, *der;* ~ **projector** *n.* Diaprojektor, *der;* ~**-rule** *n.* (Math.) Rechenschieber, *der*

sliding /'slaɪdɪŋ/**:** ~ **'door** *n.* Schiebetür, *die;* ~ **'roof** *n.* Schiebedach, *das;* ~ **'scale** *n.* ~ scale [of fees] gleitende [Gebühren]skala; ~ **seat** *n.* (Rowing) Rollsitz, *der*

slight /slaɪt/ **1** *adj.* **(a)** leicht; schwach ‹*Hoffnung, Aussichten, Wirkung*›; gedämpft ‹*Optimismus*›; gering ‹*Bedeutung*›; **the** ~**est thing makes her nervous** die kleinste Kleinigkeit macht sie nervös; **(b)** (scanty) oberflächlich; **(c)** (slender) zierlich; (weedy) schmächtig; (flimsy) zerbrechlich; **(d) not in the** ~**est** nicht im geringsten; **not the** ~**est** …: nicht der/die/das geringste …; **I haven't the** ~**est idea** ich habe nicht die leiseste Ahnung. **2** *v.t.* (disparage) herabsetzen; (be discourteous or disrespectful to) brüskieren; (ignore) ignorieren. **3** *n.* (on sb.'s character, reputation, good name) Verunglimpfung, *die* (**on** Gen.); (on sb.'s abilities) Herabsetzung, *die* (**on** Gen.); (lack of courtesy) Affront, *der* (**on** gegen)

slightly /'slaɪtlɪ/ *adv.* **(a)** ein bisschen; leicht ‹*verletzen, riechen nach, ansteigen*›; flüchtig ‹*jmdn. kennen*›; oberflächlich ‹*etw. kennen*›; **(b)** ~ **built** (slender) zierlich; (weedy) schmächtig

slim /slɪm/ **1** *adj.* **(a)** schlank; schmal ‹*Band, Buch*›; **(b)** (meagre) mager; schwach ‹*Entschuldigung, Aussicht, Hoffnung*›; gering ‹*Gewinn, Chancen*›. **2** *v.i.,* **-mm-** abnehmen. **3** *v.t.,* **-mm-** schlanker machen; (fig.: decrease) kürzen ‹*Budget*›; verschlanken (Jargon) ‹*Produktion*›
~ **'down 1** *v.i.* abnehmen; schlanker werden. **2** *v.t.* ⇒ ~ **3**

slime /slaɪm/ *n.* Schlick, *der;* (mucus, viscous matter) Schleim, *der*

'slimline *adj.* schlank; schlank geschnitten ‹*Kleid*›; kalorienarm ‹*Lebensmittel*›

slimmer /'slɪmə(r)/ *n.* (Brit.) jmd., der etwas für die schlanke Linie tut

slimming /'slɪmɪŋ/ **1** *n.* **(a)** Abnehmen, *das; attrib.* Schlankheits-; **(b)** (fig.: reduction of budget) Kürzung, *die.* **2** *adj.* schlank machend ‹*Lebensmittel*›; **be** ~: schlank machen

slimy /'slaɪmɪ/ *adj.* schleimig; schlickig ‹*Schlamm*›

sling /slɪŋ/ **1** *n.* **(a)** (weapon) Schleuder, *die;* **(b)** (Med.) Schlinge, *die;* **(c)** (carrying belt) Tragriemen, *der;* (for carrying babies) Tragehöschen, *das.* **2** *v.t.,* **slung** /slʌŋ/ **(a)** (hurl from ~) schleudern; **(b)** (coll.: throw) schmeißen (ugs.); **she slung him his coat** sie schmiss ihm seinen Mantel zu (ugs.)
~ **a'way** *v.t.* (coll.) wegschmeißen (ugs.)
~ **'out** *v.t.* (coll.) **(a)** (throw out) ~ **sb. out** jmdn. rausschmeißen (ugs.); **(b)** ⇒ ~ **away**

'slingshot (Amer.) ⇒ **catapult 1**

slink /slɪŋk/ *v.i.,* **slunk** /slʌŋk/ schleichen
~ **a'way,** ~ **off** *v.i.* davonschleichen; sich fortstehlen

slinky /'slɪŋkɪ/ *adj.* aufreizend; hauteng ‹*Kleidung*›

slip /slɪp/ **1** *v.i.,* **-pp-: (a)** (slide) rutschen; ‹*Messer:*› abrutschen; (and fall) ausrutschen; **(b)** (escape) schlüpfen; **let a chance/opportunity** ~: sich (Dat.) eine Chance/Gelegenheit entgehen lassen; **let [it]** ~ **that** …: verraten, dass …; **(c)** (go) ~ **to the butcher's** [rasch] zum Fleischer rüberspringen (ugs.); ~ **from the room** aus dem Zimmer schlüpfen; **(d)** (move smoothly) gleiten; **everything** ~**ped into place** (fig.) alles fügte sich zusammen; **(e)** (make mistake) einen [Flüchtigkeits]fehler machen; **(f)** (deteriorate) nachlassen ‹*Moral, Niveau, Ansehen:*› sinken. **2** *v.t.,* **-pp-: (a)** stecken; ~ **the dress over one's head** das Kleid über den Kopf streifen; ~ **sb. sth.** jmdm. etw. zustecken; **(b)** (escape from) entwischen (+ Dat.); **the dog** ~**ped its collar** der Hund streifte sein Halsband ab; **the boat** ~**ped its mooring** das Boot löste sich aus seiner Verankerung; ~ **sb.'s attention** jmds. Aufmerksamkeit (Dat.) entgehen; ~ **sb.'s memory** or **mind** jmdm. entfallen; **(c)** (release) loslassen. **3** *n.* **(a)** (fall) **after his** ~: nachdem er ausgerutscht [und gestürzt] war; **a** ~ **on these steps could be nasty** auf diesen Stufen auszurutschen könnte schlimme Folgen haben; **(b)** (mistake) Versehen, *das;* Ausrutscher, *der* (ugs.); **a** ~ **of the tongue/pen** ein Versprecher/Schreibfehler; **make a** ~: einen Fehler machen; **(c)** (underwear) Unterrock, *der;* **(d)** (pillowcase) [Kopf]kissenbezug, *der;* **(e)** (strip) ~ **of metal/plastic** Metall-/Plastikstreifen, *der;* **(f)** (piece of paper) ‹*Einzahlungs-, Wett*›schein, *der;* ~ **[of paper]** Zettel, *der;* **(g) give sb. the** ~ (escape) jmdm. entwischen (ugs.); (avoid) jmdm. ausweichen; **(h) a** ~ **of a girl** ein zierliches Mädchen
~ **a'cross** *v.i.* rüberspringen (ugs.)
~ **a'way** *v.i.* **(a)** ‹*Person:*› sich fortschleichen; **(b)** (pass quickly) ‹*Zeit, Tage, Wochen usw.:*› verfliegen
~ **'back** *v.i.* zurückschleichen; (very quickly) zurücksausen; ~ **back into unconsciousness** wieder das Bewusstsein verlieren
~ **be'hind** *v.i.* zurückfallen; (with one's work) in Rückstand geraten
~ **'by** *v.i.* **(a)** (pass unnoticed) vorbeischleichen; ‹*Fehler:*› durchrutschen (ugs.); **(b)** ⇒ ~ **away b**
~ **'down** *v.i.* runterrutschen (ugs.); ‹*Getränk:*› die Kehle runterlaufen (ugs.)
~ **'in 1** *v.i.* sich hineinschleichen; (enter briefly) [kurz] reinkommen (ugs.); (enter unnoticed) ‹*Fehler:*› sich einschleichen. **2** *v.t.* einfließen lassen ‹*Bemerkung*›
~ **into** *v.t.* **(a)** (put on) schlüpfen in (+ Akk.) ‹*Kleidungsstück*›; **(b)** (lapse into) verfallen in (+ Akk.)
~ **'off 1** *v.i.* **(a)** (slide down) runterrutschen (ugs.); **(b)** ⇒ ~ **away a. 2** *v.t.* abstreifen ‹*Schmuck, Bezug, Handschuh*›; schlüpfen aus ‹*Kleid, Hose, Schuh*›; ausziehen ‹*Strumpf, Handschuh*›
~ **'on** *v.t.* überstreifen ‹*Bezug, Handschuh, Ring*›; schlüpfen in (+ Akk.) ‹*Kleid, Hose, Schuh*›; anziehen ‹*Strumpf, Handschuh*›; anlegen ‹*Schmuck*›
~ **'out** *v.i.* **(a)** (leave) sich hinausschleichen; ~ **out to the butcher's** zum Fleischer rüberspringen (ugs.); **(b)** (be revealed) **it** ~**ped out** es ist mir/dir/ihm usw. herausgerutscht
~ **'over** *v.i.* **(a)** (fall) ausrutschen; **(b)** ⇒ ~ **across**

~ **'past** ⇒ ~ **by**
~ **'through** *v.i.* durchschlüpfen; ⟨*Fehler:*⟩ durchrutschen (ugs.)
~ **'up** *v.i.* (coll.) einen Schnitzer machen (ugs.) (**on, over** bei)
slip: ~ **case** *n.* Schuber, *der;* ~ **cover** *n.* (for unused furniture) Schutzüberzug, *der;* ~**-knot** *n.* (easily undone knot) Slipstek, *der;* ~**-on** 1 *adj.* ~**-on** shoes Slipper; 2 *n.* (shoe) Slipper, *der*
slipper /'slɪpə(r)/ *n.* Hausschuh, *der*
slippery /'slɪpərɪ/ *adj.* (a) schlüpfrig; glitschig; **be on a** ~ **path** *or* **slope** (fig.) auf einem verhängnisvollen Weg sein; (b) (elusive) schlüpfrig; glitschig; wendig ⟨*Spieler*⟩; (shifty) aalglatt (abwertend); **he is a** ~ **customer** er ist aalglatt (abwertend); (c) (fig.: delicate) heikel ⟨*Thema, Fall*⟩
slippy /'slɪpɪ/ (coll.) ⇒ **slippery a**
slip: ~ **road** *n.* (Brit.) (for approach) Zufahrtsstraße, *die;* (to motorway) Auffahrt, *die;* (for leaving) Ausfahrt, *die;* ~**shod** *adj.* schlampig (ugs. abwertend); (fig.: careless, unsystematic) schludrig (ugs. abwertend); ~**stream** *n.* (a) (of car, motorcycle) Fahrtwind, *der;* (Racing) Windschatten, *der;* (b) (of propeller) Propellerwind, *der;* (of ship; also Brit. fig.) Kielwasser, *das;* ~**way** *n.* (Shipb.) Helling, *die od. der*
slit /slɪt/ 1 *n.* Schlitz, *der.* 2 *v.t.*, **-tt-, slit** aufschlitzen; ~ **sb.'s throat** jmdm. die Kehle durchschneiden
slither /'slɪðə(r)/ *v.i.* rutschen; (on ice, polished floor also) schlittern
sliver /'slɪvə(r)/ *n.* (a) (thin slice of food) dünne Scheibe; (b) (splinter) Splitter, *der;* ~ **of wood/glass/bone** Holz-/Glas-/Knochensplitter, *der*
slob /slɒb/ *n.* (coll.) Schwein, *das* (derb); **lazy** ~: fauler Sack (salopp abwertend); **fat** ~: Fettsack, *der* (salopp abwertend)
slobber /'slɒbə(r)/ *v.i.* sabbern (ugs.); ~ **over sb./sth.** jmdn./etw. besabbern; (fig.) von jmdm./etw. schwärmen
sloe /sləʊ/ *n.* (Bot.) Schlehe, *die*
slog /slɒg/ 1 *v.t.*, **-gg-** dreschen (ugs.) ⟨*Ball*⟩; (in boxing, fight) voll treffen. 2 *v.i.*, **-gg-:** (a) (hit) draufschlagen (ugs.); (b) (fig.: work doggedly) sich abplagen; schuften (ugs.); (for school, exams) büffeln (ugs.); (c) (walk doggedly) sich schleppen. 3 *n.* (a) (hit) [wuchtiger] Schlag; **give sb./sth. a** ~: jmdm./einer Sache einen wuchtigen Schlag versetzen; (b) (hard work) Plackerei, *die* (ugs.).
~ **at** *v.t.* (a) (hit) ~ **at sb./sth.** auf jmdn./etw. eindreschen (ugs.); (b) (work hard at) sich abplagen mit
~ **a'way** *v.i.* sich abplagen (**at** mit)
~ **'out** *v.t.* (coll.) ~ **it out** es [bis zum Ende] durchstehen; ~ **one's guts out** sich kaputtarbeiten (ugs.)
slogan /'sləʊgən/ *n.* (a) (striking phrase) Slogan, *der;* (advertising ~) Werbeslogan, *der;* Werbespruch, *der;* (b) (motto) Wahlspruch, *der;* (in political campaign) [Wahl]slogan, *der*
slogger /'slɒgə(r)/ *n.* (a) (hitter) **be a [real]** ~: immer nur draufschlagen (ugs.); (b) (hard worker) Arbeitstier, *das* (fig.)
slop /slɒp/ 1 *v.i.*, **-pp-** schwappen (**out of, from** aus). 2 *v.t.*, **-pp-** schwappen; (intentionally) kippen; klatschen (ugs.) ⟨*Farbe an die Wand*⟩
~ **a'bout** *v.i.* ~ **a'round** *v.i.* herumschwappen (ugs.)
~ **'over** *v.i.* (splash over) überschwappen
slope /sləʊp/ 1 *n.* (a) (slant) Neigung, *die;* (of river) Gefälle, *das;* **the roof was at a** ~ **of** 45° das Dach hatte eine Neigung von 45°; **be on a** *or* **the** ~: geneigt sein; (b) (slanting ground) Hang, *der;* (c) (Skiing) Piste, *die.* 2 *v.i.* (slant) sich neigen; ⟨*Wand, Mauer:*⟩ schief sein; ⟨*Boden, Garten:*⟩ abschüssig sein; ~ **upwards/downwards** ⟨*Straße:*⟩ ansteigen/abfallen
~ **a'way** *v.i.* abfallen
~ **down** *v.i.* sich hinabneigen
~ **'off** *v.i.* (coll.) sich verdrücken (ugs.)
sloppy /'slɒpɪ/ *adj.* (a) (careless) schlud[e]rig (ugs. abwertend); (b) (untidy) unordentlich; schlampig (ugs. abwertend)
slosh /slɒʃ/ 1 *v.i.* platschen (ugs.); ⟨*Flüssigkeit:*⟩ schwappen. 2 *v.t.* (coll.: pour clumsily) schwappen
slot /slɒt/ 1 *n.* (a) (hole) Schlitz, *der;* (b) (groove) Nut, *die;* (c) (coll.: position) Platz, *der;* (d) (coll.: in schedule) Termin, *der;* (Radio, Telev.) Sendezeit, *die.* 2 *v.t.*, **-tt-:** ~ **sth. into place/ sth.** etw. einfügen/in etw. (*Akk.*) einfügen. 3 *v.i.*, **-tt-:** ~

into place/sth. (lit. or fig.) sich einfügen/in etw. (*Akk.*) einfügen; **everything** ~**ted into place** (fig.) alles fügte sich zusammen
~ **'in** 1 *v.t.* einfügen. 2 *v.i.* (lit. or fig.) sich einfügen
~ **to'gether** 1 *v.t.* zusammenfügen. 2 *v.i.* (lit. or fig.) sich zusammenfügen
sloth /sləʊθ/ *n.* (a) *no pl.* (lethargy) Trägheit, *die;* (b) (Zool.) Faultier, *das*
slothful /'sləʊθfl/ *adj.* träge; schwerfällig ⟨*Anstrengungen, Versuche*⟩
'slot machine *n.* (a) (vending machine) Automat, *der;* (b) (Amer.) ⇒ **fruit machine**
slouch /slaʊtʃ/ 1 *n.* (a) (posture) schlaffe Haltung; (b) (coll.: lazy person) Faulpelz, *der;* **be no** ~ **at sth.** etwas loshaben in etw. (*Dat.*). 2 *v.i.* (a) sich schlecht halten; **don't** ~**!** halte dich gerade!; (b) (be ungainly) sich herumflegeln (ugs. abwertend)
Slovak /'sləʊvæk/ ▶ 897 |, ▶ 947 | 1 *adj.* slowakisch; **sb. is** ~: jmd. ist Slowake/Slowakin. 2 *n.* (a) (person) Slowake, *der*/Slowakin, *die;* (b) (language) Slowakisch, *das; see also* **English 2 a**
Slovakia /slə'vɑːkɪə/ *pr. n.* Slowakei, *die*
Slovene /'sləʊviːn/ ▶ 897 |, ▶ 947 | 1 *adj.* slowenisch; **sb. is** ~: jmd. ist Slowene/Slowenin. 2 *n.* (a) (person) Slowene, *der*/Slowenin, *die;* (b) (language) Slowenisch, *das; see also* **English 2a**
Slovenia /slə'viːnɪə/ *pr. n.* Slowenien (*das*)
Slovenian /slə'viːnɪən/ ⇒ **Slovene**
slovenly /'slʌvnlɪ/ *adj.* schlampig (ugs.); schlud[e]rig (ugs.)
slow /sləʊ/ 1 *adj.* (a) langsam; ~ **but sure** langsam, aber zuverlässig; (b) (gradual) langsam; langwierig ⟨*Suche, Arbeit*⟩; **get off to a** ~ **start** beim Start langsam wegkommen; ⟨*Aufruf, Produkt:*⟩ zunächst nur wenig Anklang finden; **make** ~ **progress** [**in** *or* **at** *or* **with sth.**] nur langsam [mit etw.] vorankommen; (c) **be** ~ [**by ten minutes**], **be** [**ten minutes**] ~ ⟨*Uhr:*⟩ [zehn Minuten] nachgehen; (d) (preventing quick motion) nur langsam befahrbar ⟨*Strecke, Straße, Belag*⟩; (e) (tardy) [**not**] **be** ~ **to do sth.** [nicht] zögern, etw. zu tun; (f) (not easily roused) **be** ~ **to anger/to take offence** sich nicht leicht ärgern/beleidigen lassen; (g) (dull-witted) schwerfällig; langsam; *see also* **uptake;** (h) (burning feebly) schwach; **in a** ~ **oven** bei schwacher Hitze [im Backofen]; (i) (uninteresting) langweilig; (j) (Commerc.) flau ⟨*Geschäft*⟩. 2 *adv.* langsam; '~' „langsam fahren!"; **go** ~: langsam fahren; (Brit. Industry) langsam arbeiten. 3 *v.i.* langsamer werden; ~ **to a halt** anhalten; ⟨*Zug:*⟩ zum Stehen kommen. 4 *v.t.* ~ **a train/car** die Geschwindigkeit eines Zuges/Wagens verringern
~ **'down** 1 *v.i.* (a) langsamer werden; seine Geschwindigkeit verringern; (in working/speaking) langsamer arbeiten/sprechen; ⟨*Produktion, Geburten-/Sterbeziffer, Inflation[srate]:*⟩ sinken; (b) (reduce pace of living) langsamer machen (ugs.). 2 *v.t.* verlangsamen; **the driver** ~**ed the car/train down** der Autofahrer/Lokomotivführer fuhr langsamer
~ **'up** ⇒ ~ **down**
slow: ~**coach** *n.* Trödler, *der*/Trödlerin, *die* (ugs. abwertend); ~**down** *n.* Verlangsamung, *die* (**in** *Gen.*); (in birth, death, inflation rate, output, production, number) Sinken, *das* (**in** *Gen.*)
slowly /'sləʊlɪ/ *adv.* langsam; ~ **but surely** langsam, aber sicher
slow: ~ **'motion** *n.* (Cinemat.) Zeitlupe, *die;* **in** ~ **motion** in Zeitlupe; *attrib.* ~ **motion replay** Zeitlupenwiederholung, *die;* ~**-moving** *adj.* sich langsam fortbewegend
slowness /'sləʊnɪs/ *n., no pl.* (a) Langsamkeit, *die;* (b) (gradualness) Langsamkeit, *die;* (of search, work) Langwierigkeit, *die;* (c) (slackness) Zögern, *das; his* ~ **to react** *or* **in reacting** sein zögerndes Reagieren; (d) (stupidity) Schwerfälligkeit, *die;* ~ [**of comprehension/mind/wit**] Begriffsstutzigkeit, *die* (abwertend); (e) (dullness) Langweiligkeit, *die*
slow: ~**-witted** /sləʊ'wɪtɪd/ *adj.* [geistig] schwerfällig; ~**-worm** *n.* (Zool.) Blindschleiche, *die*

SLR *abbr.* (Photog.) **single-lens reflex**

sludge /slʌdʒ/ *n.* **(a)** (mud) Matsch, *der* (ugs.); Schlamm, *der;* **(b)** (sediment) [schlammiger] Bodensatz

slug[1] /slʌg/ *n.* **(a)** (Zool.) Nacktschnecke, *die;* **(b)** (bullet) [rohe] Gewehrkugel; **(c)** (Amer.: tot of liquor) **a ~ of whisky/rum** *etc.* ein Schluck Whisky/Rum *usw.*

slug[2] (Amer.: hit) **1** *v.t.* **-gg-** niederschlagen. **2** *n.* [harter] Schlag

sluggish /'slʌgɪʃ/ *adj.* träge; schleppend ⟨*Gang, Schritt*⟩; schwerfällig ⟨*Reaktion, Vorstellungskraft*⟩; (Commerc.) flau; schleppend ⟨*Nachfrage, Geschäftsgang*⟩

sluice /slu:s/ **1** *n.* (Hydraulic Engin.) Schütz, *das.* **2** *v.t.* ~ **[down]** (with hose) abspritzen; (with bucket) übergießen

slum /slʌm/ **1** *n.* Slum, *der;* (single house or apartment) Elendsquartier, *das.* **2** *v.t.* **-mm-:** ~ **it** wie arme Leute leben; (fig.) sich unters [gemeine] Volk mischen

slumber /'slʌmbə(r)/ (poet./rhet.) **1** *n.* (lit. or fig.) ~**[s]** Schlummer, *der* (geh.); **fall into a light/long ~:** in leichten/tiefen Schlummer sinken. **2** *v.i.* (lit. or fig.) schlummern (geh.)

slump /slʌmp/ **1** *n.* Sturz, *der* (fig.); (in demand, investment, sales, production) starker Rückgang (**in** *Gen.*); (economic depression) Depression, *die* (Wirtsch.); (in morale, support, popularity) Nachlassen, *das* (**in** *Gen.*). **2** *v.i.* **(a)** (Commerc.) stark zurückgehen; ⟨*Preise, Kurse:*⟩ stürzen (fig.); **(b)** (be diminished) ⟨*Popularität, Moral, Unterstützung usw.:*⟩ nachlassen; **(c)** (collapse) fallen; **they found him ~ed over the table** sie fanden ihn über dem Tisch zusammengesunken

slung ⇨ **sling 2**

slunk ⇨ **slink**

slur /slɜ:(r)/ **1** *v.t.* **-rr-:** ~ **one's words/speech** undeutlich sprechen; ~**red speech** undeutliche Aussprache. **2** *n.* (insult) Beleidigung, *die* (**on** für); **cast a ~ on sb./sth.** jmdn./etw. verunglimpfen (geh.); **it's a ~ on his reputation** es schmälert seinen Ruf

slurp /slɜ:p/ (coll.) **1** *v.t.* ~ **[up]** schlürfen. **2** *n.* Schlürfen, *das*

slush /slʌʃ/ *n.* **(a)** (thawing snow) Schneematsch, *der;* **(b)** (fig. derog.: sentiment) sentimentaler Kitsch

'slush fund *n.* Fonds für Bestechungsgelder

slushy /'slʌʃɪ/ *adj.* **(a)** (wet) matschig; **(b)** (derog.: sloppy) sentimental

slut /slʌt/ *n.* Schlampe, *die* (ugs. abwertend)

sly /slaɪ/ **1** *adj.* **(a)** (crafty) schlau; gerissen (ugs.) ⟨*Geschäftsmann, Schachzug, Trick*⟩; verschlagen (abwertend) ⟨*Blick*⟩; **he is a ~ one** *or* **customer** das ist ein ganz Gerissener *od.* Schlauer (ugs.); **(b)** (secretive) heimlichtuerisch; verschlagen (abwertend) ⟨*Rivale*⟩; **(c)** (knowing) vielsagend ⟨*Blick, Lächeln*⟩. **2** *n.* **on the ~:** heimlich

smack[1] /smæk/ **1** *n.* **(a)** (sound) Klatsch, *der;* **(b)** (blow) Schlag, *der;* (on child's bottom) Klaps, *der* (ugs.). **2** *v.t.* **(a)** (slap) [mit der flachen Hand] schlagen; (lightly) einen Klaps (ugs.) geben (+ *Dat.*); ~ **sb.'s face/bottom/hand** jmdn. ohrfeigen/jmdm. eins hintendrauf geben (ugs.) /jmdm. eins auf die Hand geben (ugs.); **(b)** ~ **one's lips** [mit den Lippen] schmatzen. **3** *v.i.* ~ **into the net/wall** ins Netz/gegen die Mauer knallen (ugs.). **4** *adv.* **(a)** (coll.: with a ~) **go ~ into a lamp-post** gegen einen Laternenpfahl knallen (ugs.); **(b)** (exactly) direkt

smack[2] *v.i.* ~ **of** schmecken nach; (fig.) riechen nach (ugs.)

small /smɔ:l/ **1** *adj.* **(a)** ▶ 850 ◀ (in size) klein; gering ⟨*Wirkung, Appetit, Fähigkeit*⟩; schmal ⟨*Taille, Handgelenk*⟩; dünn ⟨*Stimme*⟩; **it's a ~ world** die Welt ist klein; **(b)** *attrib.* (~-scale) klein; Klein ⟨*aktionär, -sparer, -händler, -betrieb, -bauer*⟩; (young, not fully grown) klein; **(d)** (of the ~er kind) klein; ~ **letter** Kleinbuchstabe, *der;* **feel ~** (fig.) sich (*Dat.*) ganz klein vorkommen; **make sb. feel/look ~** (fig.) jmdn. beschämen/ein schlechtes Licht auf jmdn. werfen; **(e)** (not much) wenig; **demand for/interest in the product was ~:** die Nachfrage nach/das Interesse an dem Produkt war gering; **[it's] ~ wonder** [es ist] kein Wunder; **(f)** (trifling) gering; **we have a few ~ matters/points/problems to clear up before …:** es sind noch ein paar Kleinigkeiten zu klären, bevor …; **(g)** (minor) unbedeutend; **great and ~:** hoch und niedrig; **(h)**

(petty) kleinlich (abwertend); **have a ~ mind** ein Kleinkrämer sein (abwertend). **2** *n.* (Anat.) ~ **of the back** Kreuz, *das.* **3** *adv.* klein

small: ~ **'ad** *n.* (coll.) Kleinanzeige, *die;* ~ **'change** *n., no pl., no indef. art.* Kleingeld, *das;* ~**holder** *n.* (Brit. Agric.) Kleinbauer, *der/*-bäuerin, *die;* ~**holding** *n.* (Brit. Agric.) landwirtschaftlicher Kleinbetrieb

smallish /'smɔ:lɪʃ/ *adj.* ziemlich klein/gering; ziemlich schmal ⟨*Taille*⟩

small: ~**-'minded** *adj.* kleinlich; engstirnig, kleingeistig ⟨*Einstellung*⟩; ~**pox** *n.* ▶ 865 ◀ (Med.) Pocken *Pl.;* ~ **'print** *n.* (lit. or fig.) Kleingedruckte, *das;* ~**-scale** *attrib. adj.* in kleinem Maßstab *nachgestellt;* klein ⟨*Konflikt, Unternehmer*⟩; Klein ⟨*betrieb, -bauer, -gärtner*⟩; ~ **'screen** *n.* (Telev.) **on the ~ screen** im Fernsehen; ~**-size[d]** *adj.* klein; ~ **talk** *n.* leichte Unterhaltung; (at parties) Smalltalk, *der;* **make ~ talk [with sb.]** [mit jmdm.] Konversation machen; ~**-time** *attrib. adj.* (coll.) Schmalspur- (ugs. abwertend); ~**-time crook** kleiner Ganove (ugs. abwertend)

smarmy /'smɑ:mɪ/ *adj.* kriecherisch, schmeichlerisch ⟨*Stimme*⟩

smart /smɑ:t/ **1** *adj.* **(a)** (clever) clever; (ingenious) raffiniert; (accomplished) hervorragend; **(b)** (neat) schick; schön ⟨*Haus, Garten, Auto*⟩; **(c)** *attrib.* (fashionable) elegant; smart; **the ~ set** die elegante Welt; die Schickeria; **(d)** (vigorous) hart ⟨*Schlag, Gefecht*⟩; scharf ⟨*Zurechtweisung, Schritt*⟩; **(e)** (prompt) flink; **look ~:** sich beeilen. **2** *v.i.* schmerzen; ~ **under sth.** (fig.) unter etw. (*Dat.*) leiden

smart: ~ **alec[k]** /smɑ:t 'ælɪk/ (coll. derog.) **1** *n.* Besserwisser, *der* (abwertend); **2** *attrib. adj.* neunmalklug; besserwisserisch (abwertend); ~**-arse**, (Amer.) **'smart-ass** *n.* (sl.) Klugscheißer, *der* (salopp abwertend); ~ **bomb** *n.* intelligente Bombe; ~ **card** *n.* Chipkarte, *die;* ~ **drug** *n.* Nootropikum, *das* (fachspr.); ~ **money** *n.* **the ~ money is on …** Experten setzen auf …

smarten /'smɑ:tn/ **1** *v.t.* **(a)** (make spruce) herrichten; **he ~ed his hair/clothes** er brachte sein Haar/seine Kleidung in Ordnung (ugs.); ~ **oneself** (tidy up) sich zurechtmachen; (dress up) sich herrichten; (improve appearance in general) auf sein Äußeres achten; **(b)** (accelerate) ~ **one's pace** seinen Schritt/seine Schritte beschleunigen. **2** *v.i.* **the pace ~ed** das Tempo beschleunigte sich

~ **'up 1** *v.t.* **(a)** ⇨ **~ 1 a;** **(b)** (fig.) ~ **up one's ideas** sich am Riemen reißen (ugs.). **2** *v.i.* (tidy up) sich zurechtmachen; (improve appearance in general) auf sein Äußeres achten

smartly /'smɑ:tlɪ/ *adv.* **(a)** (cleverly) clever; **(b)** (neatly) schmuck ⟨[an]gestrichen⟩; smart, flott ⟨gekleidet, geschnitten⟩; **(c)** (fashionably) vornehm; **(d)** (vigorously) hart; (sharply) scharf ⟨zurechtweisen⟩; hart ⟨anpacken⟩; **(e)** (promptly) sofort; auf der Stelle

smartness /'smɑ:tnɪs/ *n., no pl.* **(a)** (cleverness) Cleverness, *die;* **(b)** (neatness) Gepflegtheit, *die;* ~ **[of appearance]** ansprechendes Äußeres

smash /smæʃ/ **1** *v.t.* **(a)** (break) zerschlagen; ~ **sth. to pieces** etw. zerschmettern; **(b)** (defeat) zerschlagen ⟨*Rebellion, Revolution, Opposition*⟩; zerschmettern ⟨*Feind*⟩; (in games) vernichtend schlagen; klar verbessern ⟨*Rekord*⟩; **(c)** (hit hard) ~ **sb. in the face/mouth** jmdm. [hart] ins Gesicht/auf den Mund schlagen; **(d)** (Tennis) schmettern; **(e)** (propel forcefully) schmettern; **he ~ed the car into a wall** er knallte (ugs.) mit dem Wagen gegen eine Mauer. **2** *v.i.* **(a)** (shatter) zerbrechen; **(b)** (crash) krachen; **the cars ~ed into each other** die Wagen krachten zusammen (salopp). **3** *n.* **(a)** (sound) Krachen, *das;* (of glass) Klirren, *das;* **(b)** (collision) ⇨ **smash-up**

~ **'down** *v.t.* einschlagen ⟨*Tür*⟩
~ **'in** *v.t.* zerschmettern; eindrücken ⟨*Rippen, Motorhaube, Kotflügel*⟩; einschlagen ⟨*Fenster, Tür, Schädel*⟩; ~ **sb.'s face in** (coll.) jmdm. die Fresse polieren (derb)
~ **'up 1** *v.t.* zertrümmern. **2** *v.i.* zerschellen; ⟨*Auto:*⟩ zertrümmert werden

smash-and-'grab [raid] *n.* (coll.) Schaufenstereinbruch, *der*

smasher /'smæʃə(r)/ *n.* (coll.) **be a ~:** [ganz] große Klasse sein (ugs.)

smash 'hit *n.* (coll.) (film, play) Kassenschlager, *der* (ugs.); (song, record) Riesenhit, *der* (ugs.)

smashing /'smæʃɪŋ/ *adj.* (coll.) toll (ugs.); klasse (ugs.)

'smash-up *n.* schwerer Zusammenstoß

smatter /'smætə(r)/, **smattering** /'smætərɪŋ/ *ns.* oberflächliche Kenntnisse; (feeble) Halbwissen, *das* (abwertend); **have a ~ of German** ein paar Brocken Deutsch können

smear /smɪə(r)/ **1** *v.t.* **(a)** (daub) beschmieren; (put on or over) schmieren; **~ cream/ointment over one's body/face** sich (*Dat.*) den Körper/das Gesicht mit Creme/Salbe einreiben; **~ed with blood** blutbeschmiert *od.* -verschmiert; **(b)** (smudge) verwischen; verschmieren; **(c)** (fig.: defame) in den Schmutz ziehen. **2** *n.* **(a)** (blotch) [Schmutz]fleck, *der;* **(b)** (fig.: defamation) **a ~ on him/ his [good] name** eine Beschmutzung seiner Person/seines [guten] Namens

smear: ~ campaign *n.* Schmutzkampagne, *die;* **~ tactics** *n. pl.* schmutzige Mittel; **~ test** *n.* (Med.) Abstrich, *der*

smell /smel/ **1** *n.* **(a)** *no pl., no art.* **have a good/bad sense of ~:** einen guten/schlechten Geruchssinn haben; **(b)** (odour) Geruch, *der* (of nach); (pleasant also) Duft, *der* (of nach); **a ~ of burning/gas** ein Brand-/ Gasgeruch; **there was a ~ of coffee** es duftete nach Kaffee; **sth. has a nice/strong** *etc.* **~ [to it]** etw. riecht angenehm/stark *usu.;* **(c)** (stink) Gestank, *der.* **2** *v.t.* **smelt** /smelt/ *or* **~ed (a)** (perceive) riechen; (fig.) wittern; **I can ~ burning/gas** es riecht brandig/nach Gas; **I could ~ trouble** (fig.) es roch nach Ärger; **(b)** (inhale ~ of) riechen an (+ *Dat.*). **3** *v.i.,* **smelt** *or* **~ed (a)** (emit ~) riechen; (pleasantly also) duften; **(b)** (recall ~; fig.: suggest) **~ of sth.** nach etw. riechen; **(c)** (stink) riechen; **his breath ~s** er riecht aus dem Mund

~ 'out *v.t.* (lit. or fig.) aufspüren

smelling salts /'smelɪŋ sɔːlts, 'smelɪŋ sɒlts/ *n. pl.* Riechsalz, *das*

smelly /'smelɪ/ *adj.* stinkend (abwertend); **be ~:** stinken (abwertend)

smelt¹ /smelt/ *v.t.* (Metallurgy) **(a)** (melt) verhütten ⟨*Erz*⟩; **(b)** (refine) erschmelzen ⟨*Metall*⟩

smelt² ⇒ **smell** 2, 3

smile /smaɪl/ **1** *n.* Lächeln, *das;* **a ~ of joy/satisfaction** ein freudiges/befriedigtes Lächeln; **be all ~s** über das ganze Gesicht strahlen; **break into a ~:** [plötzlich] zu lächeln beginnen; **give sb. a ~:** jmdn. anlächeln; **raise a few ~s** zum Lächeln anregen; **take that ~ off your face!** hör auf zu grinsen!; **with ~** in einem Lächeln [auf den Lippen]; lächelnd. **2** *v.i.* lächeln; **make sb. ~:** jmdn. zum Lachen bringen; **keep smiling** (fig.: not despair) das Lachen nicht verlernen (fig.); **keep smiling!** Kopf hoch!; **~ at sth.** (lit. or fig.) über etw. (*Akk.*) lächeln; **~ with delight/pleasure** vor Freude strahlen; **Fortune ~d on us** das Glück lachte uns (veralt.)

smirk /smɜːk/ **1** *v.i.* grinsen. **2** *n.* Grinsen, *das*

smite /smaɪt/ **1** *v.t.,* **smote** /sməʊt/, **smitten** /'smɪtn/ **(a)** (arch./literary: strike) schlagen (**on** auf, an + *Akk.*); **(b)** (afflict) **be smitten by** *or* **with desire/terror/the plague** von Verlangen/Schrecken ergriffen/mit der Pest geschlagen sein (geh.); **be smitten by** *or* **with sb.'s/sb.'s charms** jmdm./jmds. Zauber erlegen sein

smith /smɪθ/ *n.* ▶ 887 | Schmied, *der*

smithy /'smɪðɪ/ *n.* Schmiede, *die*

smitten ⇒ **smite**

smock /smɒk/ *n.* [Arbeits]kittel, *der*

smog /smɒg/ *n.* Smog, *der*

smoke /sməʊk/ **1** *n.* **(a)** Rauch, *der;* **go up in ~:** in Rauch [und Flammen] aufgehen; (fig.) in Rauch aufgehen; **[there is] no ~ without fire** (prov.) kein Rauch ohne Flamme (Spr.); **(b)** (act of smoking tobacco) **a ~ would be nice just now** jetzt würde ich gern eine rauchen. **2** *v.i.* **(a)** (~ tobacco) rauchen; **~ like a chimney** rauchen wie ein Schlot (ugs.); **(b)** (emit ~) rauchen; (burn imperfectly) qualmen; (emit vapour) dampfen. **3** *v.t.* **(a)** rauchen; **(b)** (darken) schwärzen ⟨*Glas*⟩; ⟨*Petroleumlampe:*⟩ verräuchern ⟨*Wand, Decke*⟩; **(c)** räuchern ⟨*Fleisch, Fisch*⟩

~ 'out *v.t.* ausräuchern; (fig.: discover) aufspüren ⟨*Verbrecher*⟩

'smoke bomb *n.* Rauchbombe, *die*

smoked /sməʊkt/ *adj.* (Cookery) geräuchert

'smoke detector *n.* Rauchmelder, *der*

smokeless /'sməʊklɪs/ *adj.* rauchlos; rauchfrei ⟨*Zone*⟩

smoker /'sməʊkə(r)/ *n.* **(a)** Raucher, *der*/Raucherin, *die;* **be a heavy ~:** ein starker Raucher/eine starke Raucherin sein; **(b)** ⇒ **smoking compartment**

smoke: ~screen *n.* [künstliche] Nebelwand, *die;* (fig.) Vernebelung, *die* (**for** *Gen.*); **~ signal** *n.* Rauchzeichen, *das;* Rauchsignal, *das*

smoking /'sməʊkɪŋ/ *n.* **(a)** (act) Rauchen, *das;* '**no ~**' „Rauchen verboten"; **(b)** *no art.* (seating area) **[do you want to sit in] ~ or non-~?** [möchten Sie für] Raucher oder Nichtraucher?

'smoking compartment *n.* (Railw.) Raucherabteil, *das*

smoky /'sməʊkɪ/ *adj.* (emitting smoke) rauchend; qualmend; (smoke-filled, smoke-stained) verräuchert; (coloured or tasting like smoke) rauchig

smolder (Amer.) ⇒ **smoulder**

smooth /smuːð/ **1** *adj.* **(a)** (even) glatt; eben ⟨*Straße, Weg*⟩; **as ~ as glass/silk** spiegelglatt/glatt wie Seide; **be worn ~** ⟨*Treppenstufe:*⟩ abgetreten sein; ⟨*Reifen:*⟩ abgefahren sein; ⟨*Fels, Stein:*⟩ glatt geschliffen sein; **this razor gives a ~ shave** dieser Rasierapparat rasiert glatt; **(b)** (mild) weich; **as ~ as velvet** (fig.) samtweich; **(c)** (fluent) flüssig; geschliffen ⟨*Stil, Diktion*⟩; **(d)** (not jerky) geschmeidig ⟨*Bewegung*⟩; ruhig ⟨*Fahrt, Flug, Lauf einer Maschine, Bewegung, Atmung*⟩; weich ⟨*Start, Landung, Autofahren, Schalten*⟩; **(e)** (without problems) reibungslos; **the changeover was fairly ~:** der Wechsel ging ziemlich reibungslos vonstatten; **(f)** (derog.: suave) glatt; (~-tongued) glattzüngig (geh. abwertend); **he is a ~ operator** er ist gewieft; **(g)** (coll.: elegant) schick; **(h)** (skilful) geschickt; souverän. **2** *v.t.* **(a)** glätten; glatt streichen, ebnen ⟨*Stoff, Tuch, Papier*⟩; glatt streichen ⟨*Haar*⟩; (with sandpaper) glatt schleifen, glätten ⟨*Holz*⟩; (fig.: soothe) besänftigen

~ 'down *v.t.* glatt streichen ⟨*Haar*⟩; (fig.) schlichten ⟨*Streit*⟩

smoothly /'smuːðlɪ/ *adv.* **(a)** (evenly) glatt; **(b)** (not jerkily) geschmeidig ⟨*sich bewegen*⟩; reibungslos ⟨*funktionieren*⟩; ruhig ⟨*atmen, fließen, fahren*⟩; weich ⟨*starten, landen, schalten*⟩; **a ~ running engine** (Motor Veh.) ein rund laufender Motor; **(c)** (without problems) reibungslos; glatt; **(d)** (derog.: suavely) aalglatt (abwertend); glattzüngig (geh. abwertend) ⟨*sprechen*⟩; **(e)** (coll.: elegantly) schick; **(f)** (skilfully) geschickt; souverän

smoothness /'smuːðnɪs/ *n., no pl.* **(a)** (evenness) Glätte, *die;* **(b)** (mildness) Weichheit, *die;* **(c)** (of movement) Geschmeidigkeit, *die;* (of machine operation, breathing) Gleichmäßigkeit, *die;* **(d)** (lack of problems) Reibungslosigkeit, *die;* **(e)** (derog.: suavity) Glätte, *die* (abwertend); **(f)** (coll.: elegance) Schick, *der;* **(g)** (skill) Geschicklichkeit, *die;* Souveränität, *die*

smote ⇒ **smite**

smother /'smʌðə(r)/ *v.t.* **(a)** (stifle, extinguish) ersticken; **(b)** (overwhelm) überschütten (**with, in** mit); **~ sb. with kisses** jmdn. mit seinen Küssen [fast] ersticken; **(c)** (fig.: suppress) unterdrücken ⟨*Kichern, Gähnen, Wahrheit*⟩; ersticken ⟨*Kritik, Gerücht, Schluchzen, Gelächter, Schreie*⟩; dämpfen ⟨*Lärm*⟩

smoulder /'sməʊldə(r)/ *v.i.* schwelen; **(a)** ⟨*Feuer:*⟩ schwelen; **(b)** (fig.) ⟨*Hass, Rebellion:*⟩ schwelen ⟨*Liebe:*⟩ glimmen (geh.); **she was ~ing with rage** Zorn schwelte in ihr

smudge /smʌdʒ/ **1** *v.t.* **(a)** (blur) verwischen; **(b)** (smear) schmieren; **(c)** (make smear on) verschmieren. **2** *v.i.* ⟨*Füller, Tinte, Farbe:*⟩ schmieren. **3** *n.* **(a)** (smear) Fleck, *der;* (fig.) Schandfleck, *der;* **(b)** (blur) Schmierage, *die* (ugs.)

smug /smʌg/ *adj.* selbstgefällig (abwertend)

smuggle /'smʌgl/ *v.t.* schmuggeln

~ 'in *v.t.* einschmuggeln; hinein-/hereinschmuggeln ⟨*Person*⟩

~ 'out *v.t.* hinaus-/herausschmuggeln

smuggler /'smʌglə(r)/ *n.* Schmuggler, *der*/Schmugglerin, *die*

smuggling /'smʌglɪŋ/ *n.* Schmuggel, *der;* Schmuggeln, *das*

smut /smʌt/ *n.* Rußflocke, *die;* (smudge) Rußfleck, *der*

smutty /'smʌtɪ/ *adj.* (a) (dirty) verschmutzt; (b) (lewd) schmutzig (abwertend)

snack /snæk/ *n.* Imbiss, *der;* Snack, *der;* **have a [quick] ~:** [rasch] eine Kleinigkeit essen (ugs.)

'snack bar *n.* Schnellimbiss, *der;* Snackbar, *die*

snag /snæg/ **1** *n.* (a) (jagged point) Zacke, *die;* (b) (problem) Haken, *der;* **what's the ~?** wo klemmt es [denn]? (ugs.); **hit a ~, run up against a ~:** auf ein Problem *od.* eine Schwierigkeit stoßen; **there's a ~ in it** die Sache hat einen Haken. **2** *v.t.,* **-gg-:** I've ~ged my coat mein Mantel hat sich verfangen

snail /sneɪl/ *n.* Schnecke, *die;* **at [a] ~'s pace** im Schneckentempo (ugs.)

'snail mail *n.* (sl. joc.) Schneckenpost, *die*

snake /sneɪk/ *n.* (a) Schlange, *die;* (b) (derog.) **~ [in the grass]** (woman) [falsche] Schlange; (man) falscher Kerl *od.* (ugs.) Hund

snake: ~bite *n.* Schlangenbiss, *der;* **~ charmer** /'sneɪktʃaːmə(r)/ *n.* Schlangenbeschwörer, *der;* **~skin** *n.* Schlangenleder, *das*

snap /snæp/ **1** *v.t.,* **-pp-:** (a) (break) zerbrechen; **~ sth. in two** *or* **in half** etw. in zwei Stücke brechen; (b) **~ one's fingers** mit den Fingern schnalzen; (c) (move with snapping sound) **~ sth. home** *or* **into place** etw. einrasten *od.* einschnappen lassen; **~ shut** zuschnappen lassen ‹Portemonnaie, Schloss›; zuklappen ‹Buch, Zigarettendose, Etui›; (d) (take photograph of) knipsen; (e) (say in sharp manner) fauchen; (speak crisply or curtly) bellen. **2** *v.i.,* **-pp-:** (a) (break) brechen; (b) (fig.: give way under strain) ausrasten (ugs.); **my patience has finally ~ped** nun ist mir der Geduldsfaden aber gerissen; (c) (make as if to bite) [zu]schnappen; (d) (move smartly) **~ into action** loslegen (ugs.); **~ to attention** strammstehen; (e) **~ shut** zuschnappen; ‹Kiefer:› zusammenklappen; ‹Mund:› zuklappen; (f) (speak sharply) fauchen. **3** *n.* (a) (sound) Knacken, *das;* (b) (Photog.) Schnappschuss, *der;* (c) (Brit. Cards) Schnippschnapp[schnurr], *das.* **4** *attrib. adj.* (spontaneous) spontan. **5** *int.* (Brit. Cards) schnapp

~ at *v.t.* (a) (bite) **~ at sb./sth.** nach jmdm./etw. schnappen; **~ at sb.'s heels** jmdm. auf den Fersen sein; (b) (speak sharply to) anfauchen (ugs.)

~ 'off 1 *v.i.* abbrechen; abknicken ‹Zweig, Antenne›. **2** *v.t.* (a) (break) abbrechen; (b) (bite) abbeißen; **~ sb.'s head off** (fig.) jmdm. den Kopf abreißen (fig.)

~ 'out *v.t.* bellen ‹Befehl, Anweisung›

~ 'out of *v.t.* abwerfen; sich befreien von ‹Gefühl, Stimmung, Komplex›; **~ out of it!** (coll.) hör auf damit!; (wake up) wach auf!

~ 'up *v.t.* (a) (pick up) [sich *(Dat.)*] schnappen; (b) (fig. coll.: seize) [sich *(Dat.)*] schnappen (ugs.); **~ up a bargain/an offer** bei einem Angebot [sofort] zugreifen *od.* (salopp) zuschlagen; **the tickets were ~ped up immediately** die Karten waren sofort weg

'snapdragon *n.* (Bot.) Löwenmäulchen, *das*

snappy /'snæpɪ/ *adj.* (a) (lively) lebhaft; (b) (smart) schick; **be a ~ dresser** sich flott *od.* schick kleiden; (c) (coll.) **look ~!, make it ~!** ein bisschen dalli! (ugs.)

'snapshot *n.* (Photog.) Schnappschuss, *der*

snare /sneə(r)/ **1** *n.* (a) (trap) Schlinge, *die;* Falle, *die* (auch fig.); (b) (temptation) Fallstrick, *der.* **2** *v.t.* [mit einer Schlinge] fangen ‹Tier›

snarl¹ /snaːl/ **1** *v.i.* (a) (growl) ‹Hund:› knurren; (b) (speak) knurren. **2** *n.* Knurren, *das*

snarl² **1** *n.* (tangle) Knoten, *der.* **2** *v.t.* verheddern (ugs.). **3** *v.i.* sich verheddern (ugs.)

~ 'up 1 *v.t.* (confuse) durcheinander bringen; (bring to a halt) zum Erliegen bringen; **get ~ed up in the traffic** im Verkehr stecken bleiben. **2** *v.i.* ‹Verkehr:› stocken; ‹Wolle:› sich verheddern (ugs.)

'snarl-up *n.* Stau, *der;* Stockung, *die*

snatch /snætʃ/ **1** *v.t.* (a) (grab) schnappen; **~ a bite to eat** [schnell] einen Bissen zu sich nehmen; **~ a rest** sich *(Dat.)* eine Ruhepause verschaffen; **~ some sleep** ein bisschen schlafen (ugs.); (very abruptly) etw. von etw. reißen; **~ sth. from sth.** etw. schnell von etw. nehmen; (very abruptly) etw. von etw. reißen; **~ sth. from**

sb. jmdm. etw. wegreißen; (b) (steal) klauen (ugs.); (kidnap) kidnappen. **2** *v.i.* einfach zugreifen. **3** *n.* (a) **make a ~ at sb./sth.** nach jmdm./etw. schnappen; (b) (Brit. sl.: robbery) Raub, *der;* (c) (sl.: kidnap) Kidnapping, *das;* (d) (fragment) **~es of talk/conversation** Gesprächsfetzen *Pl. od.* -brocken *Pl.*

~ a'way *v.t.* [schnell] wegziehen **(from** *Dat.*); **~ sth. away from sb.** jmdm. etw. wegreißen

~ 'up *v.t.* [sich *(Dat.)*] schnappen

sneak /sniːk/ **1** *v.t.* (a) (take) stibitzen (fam.); (b) (fig.) **~ a look at sb./sth.** nach jmdm./etw. schielen; (c) (bring) **~ sth./sb. into a place** etw./jmdn. in einen Ort schmuggeln. **2** *v.i.* (a) (Brit. Sch. sl.: tell tales) petzen (Schülerspr.); (b) (move furtively) schleichen. **3** *attrib. adj.* (a) (without warning) **~ attack/raid** Überraschungsangriff, *der;* (b) **a ~ preview of the film** eine inoffizielle Vorpremiere des Films. **4** *n.* (Brit. Sch. sl.) Petze, *die* (Schülerspr.)

~ a'way *v.i.* [sich] fortschleichen; sich davonmachen

~ 'in 1 *v.i.* (a) (enter stealthily) sich hineinschleichen; (fig.) sich einschleichen; (b) (win narrowly) knapp siegen. **2** *v.t.* (bring in) einschmuggeln (ugs.)

~ 'out *v.i.* [sich] hinausschleichen

~ 'out of (Amer.: avoid) **~ out of sth./doing sth.** sich vor etw. *(Dat.)* drücken (ugs.) /sich davor drücken (ugs.), etw. zu tun

sneaking /'sniːkɪŋ/ *attrib. adj.* heimlich; leise ‹Verdacht›

'sneak thief *n.* Einschleichdieb, *der*

sneaky /'sniːkɪ/ *adj.* (a) (underhand) hinterhältig; (b) **have a ~ feeling that …:** so ein leises Gefühl haben, dass …

sneer /snɪə(r)/ *v.i.* (a) (smile scornfully) spöttisch *od.* höhnisch lächeln/grinsen; hohnlächeln; (b) (speak scornfully) höhnen (geh.); spotten

~ at *v.t.* (a) (smile scornfully at) höhnisch anlächeln/angrinsen; (b) (express scorn for) verhöhnen (geh.); spotten über (+ *Akk.*)

sneeze /sniːz/ **1** *v.i.* niesen; **not to be ~d at** (fig. coll.) nicht zu verachten (ugs.). **2** *n.* Niesen, *das*

snide /snaɪd/ *adj.* abfällig

sniff /snɪf/ **1** *n.* Schnüffeln, *das;* Schnuppern, *das;* (with running nose, while crying) Schniefen, *das;* (contemptuous) Naserümpfen, *das;* **have a ~ at sth.** an etw. *(Dat.)* riechen *od.* schnuppern. **2** *v.i.* schniefen; die Nase hochziehen; (to detect a smell) schnuppern; (to express contempt) die Nase rümpfen. **3** *v.t.* (smell) riechen *od.* schnuppern an (+ *Dat.*) ‹Essen, Getränk, Blume, Parfüm, Wein›

~ at *v.t.* (a) schnuppern *od.* riechen an (+ *Dat.*) ‹Blume, Essen›; (b) (show contempt for) die Nase rümpfen über (+ *Akk.*); **not to be ~ed at** (fig. coll.) nicht zu verachten (ugs.)

sniffer dog /'snɪfə dɒg/ *n.* Spürhund, *der*

snigger /'snɪgə(r)/ **1** *v.i.* [boshaft] kichern. **2** *n.* [boshaftes] Kichern

snip /snɪp/ **1** *v.t.,* **-pp-** schnippeln (ugs.), schneiden ‹Loch›; schnippeln (ugs.) *od.* schneiden an (+ *Dat.*) ‹Tuch, Haaren, Hecke›; (cut off) abschnippeln (ugs.); abschneiden. **2** *v.i.,* **-pp-** schnippeln (ugs.); schneiden. **3** *n.* (a) (Brit. coll.: good bargain) Schnäppchen, *das* (ugs.); (b) (cut) Schnitt, *der;* Schnipser, *der* (ugs.)

snipe /snaɪp/ *v.i.* (Mil.) aus dem Hinterhalt schießen

~ at *v.t.* (a) (Mil.) aus dem Hinterhalt beschießen; (b) (fig.: make snide comments about) anschießen (ugs.)

sniper /'snaɪpə(r)/ *n.* Heckenschütze, *der*/-schützin, *die;* **~ fire** Gewehrfeuer von Heckenschützen

snippet /'snɪpɪt/ *n.* (a) (piece) Schnipsel, *der od. das;* (b) (of information in newspaper) Notiz, *die;* (of knowledge) Bruchstück, *das;* (from a book) Passage, *die;* (of conversation) Gesprächsfetzen, *der;* **useful ~s of information** nützliche Hinweise *Pl.*

snivel /'snɪvl/ *v.i.,* (Brit.) **-ll-** (sniff, sob) schniefen; schnüffeln (ugs.)

snob /snɒb/ *n.* Snob, *der; attrib.* **~ appeal** *or* **value** Snob-Appeal, *der*

snobbery /'snɒbərɪ/ *n.* Snobismus, *der*

snobbish /'snɒbɪʃ/ *adj.* snobistisch

snooker /'snuːkə(r)/ *n., no pl., no indef. art.* Snooker [Pool], *das;* Taschenbillard, *das*

snoop /snuːp/ (coll.) *v.i.* schnüffeln (ugs.); ∼ **about** *or* **around** herumschnüffeln (ugs.)

snooper /ˈsnuːpə(r)/ *n.* (coll.) Schnüffler, *der*/Schnüfflerin, *die* (ugs.)

snootily /ˈsnuːtɪlɪ/ *adv.*, **snooty** /ˈsnuːtɪ/ *adj.* (coll.) hochnäsig (ugs.)

snooze /snuːz/ (coll.) **1** *v.i.* dösen (ugs.). **2** *n.* Nickerchen, *das* (fam.); **have a** ∼: ein Nickerchen machen

'snooze button *n.* Schlummertaste, *die*

snore /snɔː(r)/ **1** *v.i.* schnarchen. **2** *n.* Schnarcher, *der* (ugs.); ∼s Schnarchen, *das*

snorkel /ˈsnɔːkl/ **1** *n.* Schnorchel, *der.* **2** *v.i.*, (Brit.) **-ll-** schnorcheln

snort /snɔːt/ **1** *v.i.* schnauben (**with, in** vor + *Dat.*); ∼ **with laughter** vor Lachen prusten. **2** *v.t.* schnauben. **3** *n.* Schnauben, *das;* **with a** ∼ **of rage** wutschnaubend

snot /snɒt/ *n.* (sl.) Rotz, *der* (derb)

snotty /ˈsnɒtɪ/ *adj.* (coll.) (a) ⇒ **snooty;** (b) (running with nasal mucus) rotznäsig (salopp); ∼ **child/nose** Rotznase, *die;* ∼ **handkerchief** Rotzfahne, *die* (salopp)

snout /snaʊt/ *n.* (nose) Schnauze, *die;* (of pig, anteater) Rüssel, *der*

snow /snəʊ/ **1** *n.* (a) *no indef. art.* Schnee, *der;* (b) *in pl.* (falls) Schneefälle *Pl.;* (c) (on TV screen etc.) Schnee, *der.* **2** *v.i. impers.* it ∼s **or is** ∼**ing** es schneit

∼ **'in** *v.t.* **they are** ∼**ed in** sie sind eingeschneit

∼ **'under** *v.t.* **be** ∼**ed under** (with work) erdrückt werden; (with presents, letters) überschüttet werden

snow: ∼**ball 1** *n.* Schneeball, *der; attrib.* **have a** ∼**ball effect** eine Kettenreaktion auslösen; **2** *v.i.* (a) Schneebälle werfen; (b) (fig.: increase greatly) lawinenartig zunehmen; ∼ **blindness** *n.* Schneeblindheit, *die;* ∼**board** *n.* Snowboard, *das;* ∼**boarding** *n.* Snowboardfahren, *das;* ∼**bound** *adj.* eingeschneit; ∼**covered** *adj.* schneebedeckt; ∼**drift** *n.* Schneeverwehung, *die;* Schneewehe, *die;* ∼**drop** *n.* Schneeglöckchen, *das;* ∼**fall** *n.* Schneefall, *der;* ∼**flake** *n.* Schneeflocke, *die;* ∼**man** *n.* Schneemann, *der;* ∼**plough** *n.* Schneepflug, *der;* ∼**storm** *n.* Schneesturm, *der;* ∼**white** *adj.* schneeweiß

snowy /ˈsnəʊɪ/ *adj.* (a) schneereich ⟨*Gegend, Monat*⟩; schneebedeckt ⟨*Berge*⟩; (b) (white) schneeweiß

SNP *abbr.* **Scottish National Party** Schottische Nationalpartei

snub /snʌb/ **1** *v.t.*, **-bb-** (a) (rebuff) brüskieren; vor den Kopf stoßen; (b) (reprove) zurechtweisen; (insult) beleidigen; (c) (reject) ablehnen. **2** *n.* Abfuhr, *die*

snub: ∼ **'nose** *n.* Stupsnase, *die;* ∼**-nosed** /ˈsnʌbnəʊzd/ *adj.* stupsnasig

snuff[1] /snʌf/ *n.* Schnupftabak, *der;* **take a pinch of** ∼: eine Prise schnupfen

snuff[2] *v.t.* beschneiden, putzen ⟨*Kerze*⟩; ∼ **it** (sl.: die) ins Gras beißen (salopp)

∼ **'out** *v.t.* (a) (extinguish) löschen ⟨*Kerze*⟩; (b) (fig.: put an end to) zerstören; zunichte machen ⟨*Hoffnung*⟩

snuffle /ˈsnʌfl/ *v.i.* (sniff) schnüffeln (**at** an + *Dat.*); (with cold, after crying) schniefen

snug /snʌg/ *adj.* (a) (cosy) gemütlich, behaglich ⟨*Haus, Zimmer, Bett*⟩; (warm) mollig warm ⟨*Zimmer, Mantel, Bett*⟩; (b) (sheltered) geschützt; (c) (close-fitting) **be a** ∼ **fit** genau passen; ⟨*Kleidung:*⟩ wie angegossen passen

so /səʊ/ **1** *adv.* (a) (by that amount) so; **as winter draws near, so it gets darker** je näher der Winter rückt, desto dunkler wird es; **as fast as the water poured in, so we bailed it out** in dem Maße, wie das Wasser eindrang, schöpften wir es heraus; so ... as so ...; **there is nothing so fine as** ...: es gibt nichts Schöneres als ...; **not so [very] difficult/easy** *etc.* nicht so schwer/leicht *usw.;* **so beautiful a present** so ein schönes Geschenk; ein so schönes Geschenk; **so far** bis hierher; (until now) bisher; bis jetzt; (to such a distance) so weit; **and so on [and so forth]** und so weiter [und so fort]; **so long!** bis dann *od.* nachher! (ugs.); **so many** so viele; (unspecified number) soundso viele; **so much** so viel; (unspecified amount) soundso viel; **the villages are all so much alike** die Dörfer gleichen sich alle so sehr; **so much for him/his plans** (that is all) das wärs,

was ihn/seine Pläne angeht; **so much for my hopes** und ich habe mir solche Hoffnungen gemacht; **so much the better** um so besser; **not so much** ... **as** weniger ... als [eher]; **not so much as** (not even) [noch] nicht einmal; (b) (in that manner) so; **so be it** einverstanden; **this being so** da dem so ist (geh.); **it so happened that he was not there** er war [zufällig] gerade nicht da; (c) (to such a degree) so; **this answer so provoked him that** ...: diese Antwort provozierte ihn so *od.* derart, dass ...; **so much so that** ...: so sehr, dass ...; das geht/ging so weit, dass ...; (d) (with the intent) **so as to** um ... zu; ∼ **[that]** damit; (e) (emphatically) so; **I'm so glad/tired!** ich bin ja so froh/müde!; **so kind of you!** wirklich nett von Ihnen!; **so sorry!** (coll.) Entschuldigung!; Verzeihung!; (f) (indeed) **a rainbow! — So it is!** Es ist ein Regenbogen! — Ja, wirklich!; **you said it was good, and so it was** du sagtest, es sei gut, und so war es auch; **is that so?** so? (ugs.); wirklich?; **and so he did** und das machte/tat er [dann] auch; **it may be so, possibly so** [das ist] möglich; (g) (likewise) **so am/have/would/could/will/do I** ich auch; (h) (thus) so; **and so it was that** ...: so geschah es, dass ...; **not so!** nein, nein! (i) *pron.* **he suggested that I should take the train, and if I had done so,** ...: er riet mir, den Zug zu nehmen, und wenn ich es getan hätte, ...; **I'm afraid so** leider ja; ich fürchte schon; **the teacher said so** der Lehrer hat es gesagt; **I suppose so** ich nehme an (ugs.); *expr. reluctant agreement* wenn es sein muss; *granting grudging permission* von mir aus; **I told you** so ich habe es dir [doch] gesagt; **he is a man of the world, so to say** *or* **speak** er ist sozusagen ein Mann von Welt; **it will take a week or so** es wird so ungefähr (ugs.) *od.* etwa eine Woche dauern; **there were twenty or so people** es waren so (ugs.) um die zwanzig Leute da; **very much so** in der Tat; allerdings. **2** *conj.* (therefore) daher; so **'that's what he meant** das hat er also gemeint; **so what is the answer?** wie lautet also die Antwort?; so **'there you are!** da bist du also!; **so there you 'are!** ich habe also Recht!; **so that's 'that** (coll.) (it's done) [al]so, das wars (ugs.); (it's over) das wars also (ugs.); (everything has been taken care of) das wärs dann (ugs.); so **'there!** [und] fertig!; [und damit] basta! (ugs.); **so you see** ...: du siehst also ...; **so?** na und?

soak /səʊk/ **1** *v.t.* (a) (steep) einweichen ⟨*Wäsche in Lauge*⟩; eintauchen ⟨*Brot in Milch*⟩; ∼ **oneself in the sun** sich in der Sonne aalen (ugs.); (b) (wet) nass machen; durchnässen; durchtränken ⟨*Erde*⟩; ∼ **sb. from head to foot** jmdn. von Kopf bis Fuß durchnässen; **a rag** ∼**ed in petrol** ein mit Benzin getränkter Lappen; ∼**ed in sweat** schweißgebadet. **2** *v.i.* (a) (steep) **put sth. in sth. to** ∼: etw. in etw. (*Dat.*) einweichen; **lie** ∼**ing in the bath** ⟨*Person:*⟩ sich im Bad durchweichen lassen; (b) (drain) ⟨*Feuchtigkeit, Nässe:*⟩ sickern; ∼ **away** wegsickern. **3** *n.* **give sth. a [good]** ∼: etw. [gründlich] einweichen

∼ **'in** *v.i.* (a) (seep in) einsickern; eindringen; (b) (fig.) **let the atmosphere** ∼ **in** die Atmosphäre auf sich (*Akk.*) einwirken lassen

∼ **into** *v.t.* sickern in (+ *Akk.*); ⟨*Tinte usw.:*⟩ einziehen in (+ *Akk.*)

∼ **through 1** *v.t.* (a) /ˈ-/ (penetrate) ⟨*Flüssigkeit, Strahlen:*⟩ dringen durch; ⟨*Regenwasser, Blut:*⟩ sickern durch; (b) /-ˈ-/ (drench) durchnässen. **2** *v.i.* /-ˈ-/ durchdringen

∼ **'up** *v.t.* (a) (absorb) aufsaugen; ∼ **up the sunshine** in der Sonne baden; (b) (fig.) aufnehmen ⟨*Atmosphäre*⟩; aufnehmen, in sich (*Akk.*) aufsaugen ⟨*Wissen usw.*⟩

soaking /ˈsəʊkɪŋ/ **1** *n.* (drenching) **need a [good]** ∼ ⟨*Garten:*⟩ [gut] gewässert werden müssen; **get a** ∼: eine Dusche abbekommen; **give sb./sth. a** ∼: jmdn./etw. nass machen. **2** *adv.* ∼ **wet** völlig durchnässt; klatsch- *od.* patschnass (ugs.). **3** *adj.* (a) (drenched) nass [bis auf die Haut]; patschnass (ugs.); **be** ∼ ⟨*Kleidung:*⟩ völlig durchnässt sein; (b) (saturating) alles durchnässend ⟨*Strom, Regen*⟩

'so-and-so *n., pl.* ∼**'s** (a) (person not named) [Herr/Frau] Soundso; (thing not named) Dings, *das;* (b) (coll.: contemptible person) Biest, *das* (ugs.)

soap /səʊp/ *n., no indef. art.* (a) Seife, *die;* **a bar** *or* **tablet of** ∼: ein Stück Seife; (b) (coll.) ⇒ **soap opera**

soap: ~**box** n. (a) (packing-box) Seifenschachtel, die; (b) (stand) ≈ Apfelsinenkiste, die; **get on one's** ~**box** (fig.) laut seine Meinung äußern; Volksreden halten; (c) (cart) Seifenkiste, die; ~ **bubble** n. Seifenblase, die; ~ **dish** n. Seifenschale, die; ~ **flakes** n. pl. Seifenflocken Pl.; ~ **opera** n. (Telev., Radio) Seifenoper, die (ugs.); ~ **powder** n. Seifenpulver, das; ~**suds** n. pl. Seifenschaum, der

soapy /'səʊpɪ/ adj. seifig; ~ **water** Seifenlauge, die

soar /sɔː(r)/ v.i. (a) (fly up) aufsteigen; (hover in the air) segeln; (b) (extend) ~ **into the sky** in den Himmel ragen; (c) (fig.: rise rapidly) steil ansteigen ⟨Preise, Kosten usw.⟩; in die Höhe schießen (ugs.); **my hopes have** ~**ed again** ich schöpfe wieder große Hoffnung

soaring /'sɔːrɪŋ/ attrib. adj. (a) (flying) segelnd; [hoch am Himmel] schwebend; (b) (fig.: rising rapidly) sprunghaft ansteigend; galoppierend ⟨Preise, Inflation, Kosten⟩

sob /sɒb/ **1** v.i., **-bb-** schluchzen (**with** vor + Dat.). **2** v.t., **-bb-** schluchzen. **3** n. Schluchzer, der
~ **'out** v.t. schluchzen; ~ **one's heart out** bitterlich weinen

sober /'səʊbə(r)/ adj. (a) (not drunk) nüchtern; **as** ~ **as a judge** stocknüchtern; (b) (moderate) solide; (c) (solemn) ernst
~ **'down** v.i. ruhig werden; **he has** ~**ed down a lot** er ist wesentlich vernünftiger geworden
~ **'up 1** v.i. nüchtern werden; ausnüchtern. **2** v.t. ausnüchtern

sobering /'səʊbərɪŋ/ adj. ernüchternd

sobriety /sə'braɪətɪ/ n., no pl., no indef. art. (a) (not being drunk) Nüchternheit, die; (b) (moderation) Bescheidenheit, die

so-called /'səʊkɔːld/ adj. so genannt; (alleged) angeblich

soccer /'sɒkə(r)/ n. (coll.) Fußball, der

sociable /'səʊʃəbl/ adj. gesellig; **he did it just to be** ~: er hat es nur getan, um nicht ungesellig zu sein

social /'səʊʃl/ adj. (a) sozial; gesellschaftlich; ~ **welfare** Fürsorge, die; (b) (of ~ life) gesellschaftlich; gesellig ⟨Abend, Beisammensein⟩; ~ **behaviour** Benehmen in Gesellschaft

social: ~ **'chapter** n. (Polit.) Sozialprotokoll, das; ~ **'class** n. Gesellschaftsschicht, die; [Gesellschafts]klasse, die; ~ **'climber** n. Emporkömmling, der (abwertend); [sozialer] Aufsteiger (ugs.); ~ **club** n. Klub für geselliges Beisammensein; ~ **'conscience** n. soziales Gewissen; S~ **'Democrat** n. (Polit.) Sozialdemokrat, der/-demokratin, die; S~ **Demo'cratic Party** n. (Brit. Polit. Hist.) Sozialdemokratische Partei; ~ **'history** n. Sozialgeschichte, die

socialise ⇒ socialize

socialism /'səʊʃəlɪzm/ n. Sozialismus, der

socialist /'səʊʃəlɪst/ **1** n. Sozialist, der/Sozialistin, die. **2** adj. sozialistisch

socialize /'səʊʃəlaɪz/ v.i. geselligen Umgang pflegen; ~ **with sb.** (chat) sich mit jmdm. unterhalten

'social life n. gesellschaftliches Leben; **a place with plenty of** ~: ein Ort, wo etwas los ist (ugs.); **not have much** ~ ⟨Person:⟩ nicht viel ausgehen

socially /'səʊʃəlɪ/ adv. **meet** ~: sich privat treffen; ~ **deprived** sozial benachteiligt

social: ~ **'science** n. Sozialwissenschaften Pl.; Gesellschaftswissenschaften Pl.; ~ **se'curity** n. soziale Sicherheit; ~ **'services** n. pl. Sozialdienste Pl.; ~ **studies** n. (Educ.) Gemeinschaftskunde, die; ~ **system** n. Gesellschaftssystem, das; ~ **work** n. Sozialarbeit, die; ~ **worker** n. ▶887 Sozialarbeiter, der/-arbeiterin, die

society /sə'saɪətɪ/ **1** n. (a) Gesellschaft, die; **high** ~: Highsociety, die; (b) (club, association) Verein, der; (Commerc.) Gesellschaft, die; (group of persons with common beliefs, aims, interests, etc.) Gemeinschaft, die. **2** attrib. adj. (a) (of high ~) Gesellschafts-; [High-]Society-; **she is a** ~ **hostess** sie gibt Feste für die [gehobene] Gesellschaft; (b) (of club or association) Vereins-, Klub ⟨vorsitzender, -treffen, -ausflug usw.⟩

sociological /səʊsɪə'lɒdʒɪkl/ adj. soziologisch

sociologist /səʊsɪ'ɒlədʒɪst/ n. ▶887 Soziologe, der/Soziologin, die

sociology /səʊsɪ'ɒlədʒɪ/ n. Soziologie, die

sock¹ /sɒk/ n., pl. ~**s or** (Commerc./coll.) **sox** /sɒks/ Socke, die; Socken, der (südd., österr., schweiz.); (ankle ~, esp. for children also) Söckchen, das; **pull one's** ~**s up** (Brit. fig. coll.) sich am Riemen reißen (ugs.); **put a** ~ **in it!** (Brit. sl.) halt die Klappe! (salopp)

sock² v.t. (coll.: hit) schlagen; hauen (ugs.)

socket /'sɒkɪt/ n. (a) (Anat.) (of eye) Höhle, die; (of joint) Pfanne, die; (b) (Electr.) Steckdose, die; (receiving a bulb) Fassung, die; (c) (for attachment) Fassung, die

sod¹ /sɒd/ n. (turf) Sode, die

sod² (sl.) **1** n. (bastard, swine) Sau, die (derb); **the poor old** ~: das arme Schwein (salopp); **that's** ~**'s law**, ~**'s law was proved right** (coll.) es musste ja so kommen. **2** v.t., **-dd-:** ~ **that/you!** verdammter Mist/scher dich zum Teufel! (ugs.)
~ **'off** v.i. imper. (sl.) verpiss dich (derb)

soda /'səʊdə/ n. (a) (sodium compound) Soda, die od. das; (b) (drink) Soda[wasser], das; **whisky and** ~: Whisky mit Soda

'soda water n. Soda[wasser], das

sodden /'sɒdn/ adj. durchnässt (**with** von)

sodium /'səʊdɪəm/ n. (Chem.) Natrium, das

sodium 'chloride n. (Chem.) Natriumchlorid, das

sodomy /'sɒdəmɪ/ n. Analverkehr, der

sofa /'səʊfə/ n. Sofa, das; attrib. ~ **bed** Bettcouch, die

soft /sɒft/ adj. (a) weich; zart, weich ⟨Haut⟩; **the ground is** ~: der Boden ist aufgeweicht; (Sport) der Boden ist schwer; **as** ~ **as butter** weich wie Butter; butterweich; ~ **ice cream** Soft-Eis, das; ~ **toys** Stofftiere; (b) (mild) sanft; mild ⟨Klima⟩; zart ⟨Duft⟩; (c) (affectionate) **have a** ~ **spot for sb./sth.** eine Vorliebe od. Schwäche für jmdn./etw. haben; (d) (delicate) sanft ⟨Augen⟩; weich ⟨Farbe, Licht⟩; (e) (quiet) leise; sanft; (f) (gentle) sanft; **be** ~ **on or with sb.** (coll.: be unusually lenient with) mit jmdm. sanft umgehen; (g) (coll.: easy) bequem, (ugs.) locker ⟨Job, Leben⟩; **have a** ~ **job** eine ruhige Kugel schieben (ugs.); (h) (compliant) nachgiebig; (i) (too indulgent) zu nachsichtig; zu lasch (ugs.)

soft: ~**-boiled** adj. weich gekocht ⟨Ei⟩; ~**-centred** adj. ⟨Praline usw.⟩ mit weicher Füllung; ~ **copy** n. (Computing) Softcopy, die; ~ **currency** n. (Econ.) weiche Währung; ~ **drink** n. alkoholfreies Getränk; ~ **drug** n. weiche Droge

soften /'sɒfn/ **1** v.i. weicher werden. **2** v.t. weich klopfen ⟨Fleisch⟩; aufweichen ⟨Boden⟩; dämpfen ⟨Beleuchtung⟩; mildern ⟨Farbe, Farbton⟩; enthärten ⟨Wasser⟩; ~ **the blow** (fig.) den Schock mildern
~ **'up** v.t. weichklopfen (ugs.) ⟨Boxgegner⟩; aufweichen ⟨Verteidigungsanlagen⟩; (verbally) milder stimmen

softener /'sɒfnə(r)/ n. (a) (for water) [Wasser]enthärter, der; (b) (for fabrics) Weichspülmittel, das; Weichspüler, der

soft: ~ **fruit** n. Beerenobst, das; ~**-hearted** /sɒft'hɑːtɪd/ adj. weichherzig

softie ⇒ softy

softly /'sɒftlɪ/ adv. (a) (quietly) leise ⟨sprechen, singen, gehen⟩; (b) (gently) sanft; **speak** ~: mit sanfter Stimme sprechen

softness /'sɒftnɪs/ n., no pl. ⇒ soft 1: (a) Weichheit, die; Zartheit, die; (b) Sanftheit, die; Milde, die; Zartheit, die; (c) (delicacy) Sanftheit, die; Weichheit, die; (d) (of voice, music, etc.) Gedämpftheit, die; (e) (gentleness) Sanftheit, die; (f) (leniency) Nachsichtigkeit, die; Laschheit, die (ugs.)

soft: ~ **option** n. einfacherer Weg; ~**-'pedal** v.i. (tone down) herunterspielen; ~ **'porn** (coll.), ~ **por'nography** ns. Softpornographie, die; ~ **'sell** n. give sb. the ~ **sell** jmdn. auf die sanfte Tour (ugs.) zum Kauf zu bewegen versuchen; ~ **'soap** n. (a) (cleanser) Schmierseife, die; (b) (fig.: flattery) Schmeichelei, die; **use** ~ **soap** schmeicheln; schöntun (ugs.); ~**-'soap** v.t. ~**-soap sb.** jmdm. Honig um den Bart schmieren (ugs.); ~**-spoken** adj. leise sprechend ⟨Person⟩; **be** ~**-spoken** leise sprechen; ~ **top** n. (a) (roof) Stoffverdeck, das; **folding** ~ **top** Faltverdeck, das; (b) (car) Cabrio, das; Kabrio, das; ~ **'toy** n. Stoffspielzeug, das; (toy animal) Stofftier, das; ~**ware** n., no pl., no indef. art. (Computing)

Software, *die;* **~wood** *n.* Weichholz, *das; attrib.* Weich-holz-

softy /'sɒftɪ/ *n.* (a) (coll.: weakling) Weichling, *der;* Wasch-lappen, *der* (ugs.); (b) (sentimental person) **be a ~:** senti-mental sein

soggy /'sɒgɪ/ *adj.* aufgeweicht ‹*Boden*›; durchnässt ‹*Kleider*›; matschig ‹*Salat*›; nicht durchgebacken, (landsch.) glitschig ‹*Brot, Kuchen*›

soil¹ /sɔɪl/ *n.* (a) (earth) Erde, *die;* Boden, *der;* (b) (ground) Boden, *der;* **on British/foreign ~:** auf britischem Boden/im Ausland *od.* (geh.) in der Fremde

soil² *v.t.* (lit. or fig.) beschmutzen

soiled /sɔɪld/ *adj.* schmutzig ‹*Wäsche, Windel*›; gebraucht ‹*Damenbinde*›

sojourn /'sɒdʒən/ (literary) **1** *v.i.* verweilen (geh.); weilen (geh.) (**at** in + *Dat.*). **2** *n.* Aufenthalt, *der*

solace /'sɒləs/ *n.* Trost, *der;* **take** *or* **find ~ in sth.** Trost in etw. (*Dat.*) finden; sich mit etw. trösten; **turn to sb./sth. for ~:** bei jmdm./etw. Trost suchen

solar /'səʊlə(r)/ *adj.* Sonnen-

solar: ~ cell *n.* Sonnenzelle, *die;* Solarzelle, *die;* **~ e'clipse** *n.* (Astron.) Sonnenfinsternis, *die;* **~ energy** *n.* Solarenergie, *die;* Sonnenenergie, *die*

solarium /sə'leərɪəm/ *n., pl.* **solaria** /sə'leərɪə/ So-larium, *das*

solar: ~ plexus /səʊlə 'pleksəs/ *n.* (Anat.) Solarplexus, *der;* Sonnengeflecht, *das;* **~ 'power** *n.* Sonnenenergie, *die;* **~powered** *adj.* mit Sonnenenergie betrieben; **~ system** *n.* (Astron.) Sonnensystem, *das*

sold ⇒ **sell**

solder /'səʊldə(r), 'sɒldə(r)/ **1** *n.* Lot, *das* (Technik). **2** *v.t.* löten

'soldering iron *n.* Lötkolben, *der*

soldier /'səʊldʒə(r)/ *n.* ▶ 887 | Soldat, *der;* **~ of fortune** Glücksritter, *der* (abwertend); (mercenary) Söldner, *der* **~ 'on** *v.i.* (coll.) weitermachen

sole¹ /səʊl/ **1** *n.* (Anat.; of shoe) Sohle, *die.* **2** *v.t.* [be]sohlen

sole² *n.* (fish) Seezunge, *die*

sole³ *adj.* einzig; alleinig ‹*Verantwortung, Erbe, Recht*›; Allein‹*erbe, -eigentümer*›; **he is the ~ judge of whether ...:** or allein urteilt darüber, ob .../entscheidet, ob ...

solely /'səʊllɪ/ *adv.* einzig und allein; ausschließlich; **~ because ...:** nur [deswegen], weil ...; einzig und allein, weil ...

solemn /'sɒləm/ *adj.* feierlich; ernst ‹*Anlass, Gespräch*›

solemnity /sə'lemnɪtɪ/ *n.* (a) no pl. Feierlichkeit, *die;* (b) (rite) Feierlichkeit, *die*

solenoid /'sɒlənɔɪd/ *n.* Zylinderspule, *die;* (converting energy) Magnetspule, *die*

solicit /sə'lɪsɪt/ **1** *v.t.* (a) (appeal for) werben um ‹*Wählerstimmen, Unterstützung*›; (b) (appeal to) **~ sb. for sth.** bei jmdm. um etw. werben; (c) (make sexual offer to) **~ sb.** sich jmdm. anbieten. **2** *v.i.* (make request) **~ for sth.** um etw. bitten *od.* (geh.) ersuchen; (in a petition) etw. [mit einer Eingabe] fordern; (b) (Commerc.) **~ for sth.** um etw. werben; (c) (offer illicit sex) **~ [for custom]** sich anbieten

solicitor /sə'lɪsɪtə(r)/ *n.* ▶ 887 | (Brit.: lawyer) Rechtsanwalt, *der/*-anwältin, *die* (*der/die nicht vor höheren Gerichten auf-tritt*)

solicitous /sə'lɪsɪtəs/ *adj.* (a) (eager) **be ~ of sth.** um etw. bemüht sein; **be ~ to do sth.** [darum] bemüht sein, etw. zu tun; (b) (anxious) besorgt; **~ about sb./sth.** um jmdn./etw. besorgt

solid /'sɒlɪd/ *adj.* (a) (rigid) fest; **freeze/be frozen ~:** [fest] gefrieren/gefroren sein; **set ~:** fest werden; (b) (of the same substance all through) massiv; **~ silver** massives Silber; **~ gold** reines Gold; **~ tyre** Vollgummireifen, *der;* **be packed ~** (coll.) gerammelt voll sein (ugs.); (c) (well-built) stabil; solide gebaut ‹*Haus, Mauer usw.*›; **have a ~ majority** (Polit.) eine solide Mehrheit haben; (d) (reliable) verlässlich, zuverlässig ‹*Freund, Helfer, Verbündeter*›; ‹*Stütze*›; (e) (complete) ganz; **a good ~ meal** eine kräftige Mahlzeit; (f) (sound) stichhaltig ‹*Argument, Grund*›; solide ‹*Arbeiter, Finanzlage, Firma*›; solide, gediegen ‹*Komfort,*

Grundlage›; **(g)** (Geom.: having three dimensions) dreidimen-sional; räumlich. **2** *n.* (a) (substance) fester Körper; (b) *in pl.* (food) feste Nahrung

solidarity /sɒlɪ'dærɪtɪ/ *n., no pl.* Solidarität, *die*

solid 'fuel *n.* fester Brennstoff

solidify /sə'lɪdɪfaɪ/ **1** *v.t.* verfestigen. **2** *v.i.* (become solid) hart *od.* fest werden; erstarren; ‹*Flüssigkeit, Lava:*› erstar-ren

solidity /sə'lɪdɪtɪ/ *n., no pl.* ⇒ **solid 1:** (a) Festigkeit, *die;* (b) Massivität, *die;* (c) Stabilität, *die;* (d) (of reasons, argu-ment) Stichhaltigkeit, *die*

solidly /'sɒlɪdlɪ/ *adv.* (a) (firmly) stabil; (b) (compactly) **a ~ built person** ein kräftig gebauter Mensch; (c) (ceaselessly) pausenlos; (d) (wholeheartedly) **be ~ behind sb./sth.** un-eingeschränkt hinter jmdm./einer Sache stehen

'solid-state *adj.* (Phys.) Festkörper ‹*physik, -geräte, -schaltung*›

soliloquy /sə'lɪləkwɪ/ *n.* Monolog, *der;* (talking to oneself) Selbstgespräch, *das*

solitaire /sɒlɪ'teə(r)/ *n.* (a) (gem) Solitär, *der;* (b) (ring) Solitärring, *der;* (c) (game) Solitär, *das*

solitary /'sɒlɪtərɪ/ *adj.* einsam; **a ~ existence/life** ein Einsiedlerdasein/-leben; **~ confinement** Einzelhaft, *die*

solitude /'sɒlɪtjuːd/ *n.* Einsamkeit, *die*

solo /'səʊləʊ/ **1** *n., pl.* **~s** (a) (Mus.) Solo, *das;* (b) (Cards) **~ [whist]** Solo[-whist], *das.* **2** *adj.* (a) (Mus.) Solo‹*spiel, -part, -tanz, -instrument*›; (b) (unaccompanied) **~ flight** Alleinflug, *der.* **3** *adv.* (unaccompanied) solo ‹*singen, spielen, tanzen usw.*›; **go/fly ~** (Aeronaut.) einen Alleinflug machen

soloist /'səʊləʊɪst/ *n.* (Mus.) Solist, *der/*Solistin, *die*

solstice /'sɒlstɪs/ *n.* Sonnenwende, *die;* **summer/win-ter ~:** Sommer-/Wintersonnenwende, *die*

soluble /'sɒljʊbl/ *adj.* (a) (esp. Chem.) löslich; solubel (fachspr.); **~ in water, water-~:** wasserlöslich; (b) (solv-able) lösbar

solution /sə'luːʃn, sə'ljuːʃn/ *n.* (a) (esp. Chem.) Lösung, *die;* (b) ([result of] solving) Lösung, *die* (**to** *Gen.*); **find a ~ to sth.** eine Lösung für etw. finden; etw. lösen

solve /sɒlv/ *v.t.* lösen

solvent /'sɒlvənt/ **1** *adj.* (a) (Chem.: dissolving) lösend; (b) (Finance) solvent. **2** *n.* (Chem.) Lösungsmittel, *das* (**of, for** für); **~ abuse** Missbrauch von Lösungsmitteln als Rauschmittel

sombre (*Amer.:* **somber**) /'sɒmbə(r)/ *adj.* dunkel; düster ‹*Atmosphäre, Stimmung*›

some /səm, *stressed* sʌm/ **1** *adj.* (a) (one or other) [irgend]-ein; **~ fool** irgendein Dummkopf (ugs.); **~ day** eines Tages; **~ shop/book or other** irgendein Laden/Buch; **~ person or other** irgendjemand; irgendwer; (b) (a consider-able quantity of) einig...; etlich... (ugs. verstärkend); **speak at ~ length/wait for ~ time** ziemlich lang[e] sprechen/warten; **~ time/weeks/days/years ago** vor einiger Zeit/vor einigen Wochen/Tagen/Jahren; **~ time soon** bald [einmal]; (c) (a small quantity of) ein bisschen; **would you like ~ wine?** möchten Sie [etwas] Wein?; **do ~ shopping/reading** einkaufen/lesen; (d) (to a certain extent) **~ guide** eine gewisse Orientierungshilfe; **that is ~ proof** das ist [doch] gewissermaßen ein Beweis; (e) **this is ~ war/poem/car!** (coll.) das ist vielleicht ein Krieg/Gedicht/Wagen! (ugs.); (f) (approximately) etwa; ungefähr. **2** *pron.* einig...; **she only ate ~ of it** sie hat es nur teilweise aufgegessen; (~ **of her ideas are good** sie hat einige gute Ideen; **~ of the greatest music** einige der größten Werke der Musik; **~ say ...:** manche sagen ...; **~ ...,** **others ...:** manche ..., andere ...; die einen ..., andere ...; ... **and then ~:** und noch einige/einiges mehr. **3** *adv.* (coll.: in ~ degree) ein bisschen; etwas; **~ more** noch ein bisschen

somebody /'sʌmbədɪ/ *n. & pron.* jemand; **~ or other** irgendjemand; (important person) **be ~:** jemand *od.* etwas sein

'somehow *adv.* **~ [or other]** irgendwie

someone /'sʌmwən, *stressed* 'sʌmwʌn/ *pron.* ⇒ **some-body**

'someplace (Amer. coll.) ⇨ **somewhere**

somersault /'sʌməsɔːlt, 'sʌməsɒlt/ **1** *n.* Purzelbaum, *der* (ugs.); Salto, *der* (Sport); **turn a ~:** einen Purzelbaum schlagen (ugs.); einen Salto springen (Sport); **the car ~ed [into a ditch]** das Auto überschlug sich [und landete in einem Graben]. **2** *v.i.* einen Purzelbaum schlagen (ugs.); einen Salto springen (Sport)

'something *n. & pron.* **(a)** (some thing) etwas; **~ new/ old/good/bad** etwas Neues/Altes/Gutes/Schlechtes; **(b)** (some unspecified thing) [irgend] etwas; **~ or other** irgendetwas; **(c)** (some quantity of a thing) etwas; **there is ~ in what you say** was du sagst, hat etwas für sich; an dem, was du sagst, ist etwas dran (ugs.); **he has ~ about him** er hat etwas Besonderes an sich (*Dat.*); **(d)** (impressive or important thing, person, etc.) **the party was quite ~:** die Party war spitze (ugs.); **(e) or ~** ⇨ **or¹ c; (f) ~ like** etwa wie; **that's ~ like it** das ist schon besser; **(g) ~ of an expert/a specialist** so etwas wie ein Fachmann/Spezialist; **see ~ of sb.** jmdn. sehen

'sometime 1 *adj.* ehemalig. **2** *adv.* irgendwann

'sometimes *adv.* manchmal; **~ ..., at other times ...:** manchmal ..., manchmal ...

'somewhat *adv.* (rather) irgendwie; ziemlich

'somewhere 1 *adv.* **(a)** (in a place) irgendwo; **~ about** *or* **around thirty [years old]** [so (ugs.)] um die dreißig [Jahre alt]; **~ between five and ten** [so (ugs.)] zwischen fünf und zehn; **(b)** (to a place) irgendwohin; **get ~** (coll.) (in life) es zu etwas bringen; (in a task) weiterkommen. **2** *n.* **look for ~ to stay** sich nach einer Unterkunft umsehen; **she prefers ~ hot for her holidays** in den Ferien fährt sie am liebsten irgendwohin, wo es heiß ist

son /sʌn/ *n.* Sohn, *der;* (as address) **[my] ~:** mein Sohn; **~ and heir** Sohn und Erbe; **the Son [of God]** (Relig.) der Sohn [Gottes]

sonar /'səʊnɑː(r)/ *n.* Sonar, *der*

sonata /sə'nɑːtə/ *n.* (Mus.) Sonate, *die*

song /sɒŋ/ *n.* **(a)** Lied, *das;* (esp. political ballad, pop ~) Song, *der;* **(b)** *no pl.* (singing) Gesang, *der;* **on ~** (fig. coll.) in Spitzenform; **break** *or* **burst into ~:** ein Lied anstimmen; **for a ~:** für einen Apfel und ein Ei (ugs.); **a ~ and dance** (Brit. coll.: fuss; Amer. coll.: rigmarole) viel *od.* großes Trara (ugs.); **(c)** (bird cry) Gesang, *der;* (of cuckoo) Ruf, *der*

song: ~bird *n.* Singvogel, *der;* **~book** *n.* Liederbuch, *das;* **~writer** *n.* Songschreiber, *der*/-schreiberin, *die*

sonic /'sɒnɪk/ *attrib. adj.* Schall-

sonic 'boom *n.* Überschallknall, *der*

'son-in-law *n., pl.* **sons-in-law** Schwiegersohn, *der*

sonnet /'sɒnɪt/ *n.* Sonett, *das*

sonny /'sʌnɪ/ *n.* (coll.) Kleiner (*der*); kleiner Mann (ugs.)

sonorous /'sɒnərəs/ *adj.* volltönend; sonor ⟨Stimme⟩; klangvoll ⟨*Instrument, Sprache*⟩

soon /suːn/ **(a)** bald; (quickly) schnell; **(b)** (early) früh; **how ~ will it be ready?** wann ist es denn fertig?; **none too ~:** keinen Augenblick zu früh; **no ~er said than done** gesagt, getan; **~er said than done** leichter gesagt als getan; **no ~er had I arrived than ...:** kaum war ich angekommen, da ...; **~er or later** früher oder später; **the ~er [...] the better** (coll.) je früher *od.* eher [...], desto besser; **(c) we'll set off just as ~ as he arrives** sobald er ankommt, machen wir uns auf den Weg; **as ~ as possible** so bald wie möglich; **(d)** (willingly) **just as ~ [as ...]** genauso gern [wie ...]; **she would ~er die than ...:** sie würde lieber sterben, als ...; **they would kill you as ~ as look at you** (coll.) sie würden dich auf der Stelle umbringen; **~er you than me** lieber du als ich

soot /sʊt/ *n.* Ruß, *der*

soothe /suːð/ *v.t.* **(a)** (calm) beruhigen; beschwichtigen ⟨*Gefühle*⟩; **(b)** (make less severe) mildern; lindern ⟨*Schmerz*⟩

soothing /'suːðɪŋ/ *adj.* beruhigend; wohltuend ⟨*Bad, Creme, Massage*⟩

sooty /'sʊtɪ/ *adj.* verrußt; rußig

sop /sɒp/ **1** *n.* **(a)** (piece of bread) Stück eingeweichtes Brot; **(b)** (fig.) Beschwichtigungsmittel, *das.* **2** *v.i.,* **-pp-: be ~ping [wet]** völlig durchnässt sein

sophisticated /sə'fɪstɪkeɪtɪd/ *adj.* **(a)** (cultured) kultiviert; gepflegt ⟨*Restaurant, Küche*⟩; anspruchsvoll ⟨*Roman, Autor, Unterhaltung, Stil*⟩; **(b)** (elaborate) ausgeklügelt ⟨*Autozubehör*⟩; differenziert, subtil ⟨*Argument, System, Ansatz*⟩; hoch entwickelt ⟨*Technik, Elektronik, Software, Geräte*⟩

sophistication /səfɪstɪ'keɪʃn/ *n.* **(a)** (refinement) Kultiviertheit, *die;* (of argument) Differenziertheit, *die;* (of style, manner) Subtilität, *die;* **(b)** (advanced methods, state) hoher Entwicklungsstand [der Technik]; **era of technical ~:** Zeitalter hoch entwickelter Technik

sophomore /'sɒfəmɔː(r)/ *n.* (Amer. Sch./Univ.) Student/Studentin einer Highschool bzw. Universität im zweiten Studienjahr

soporific /sɒpə'rɪfɪk/ *adj.* schläfrig ⟨*Person*⟩; einschläfernd ⟨*Wirkung, Rede*⟩

soppy /'sɒpɪ/ *adj.* (Brit. coll.: sentimental) rührselig; sentimental ⟨*Person*⟩

soprano /sə'prɑːnəʊ/ *n., pl.* **~s** *or* **soprani** /sə'prɑːniː/ (Mus.) (voice, singer, part) Sopran, *der;* (female singer also) Sopranistin, *die*

sorcerer /'sɔːsərə(r)/ *n.* Zauberer, *der*

sorcery /'sɔːsərɪ/ *n.* Zauberei, *die*

sordid /'sɔːdɪd/ *adj.* **(a)** (base) dreckig (abwertend); unehrenhaft, unlauter ⟨*Motiv*⟩; unerfreulich ⟨*Detail, Geschichte*⟩; (greedy) schmutzig ⟨*Geschäft*⟩; **(b)** (squalid) schmutzig; schäbig ⟨*Wohnung, Verhältnisse*⟩; heruntergekommen ⟨*Stadtviertel*⟩

sore /sɔː(r)/ **1** *adj.* **(a)** weh; (inflamed or injured) wund; **sb. has a ~ back/foot/arm** *etc.* jmdm. tut der Rücken/Fuß/ Arm *usw.* weh; **~ point** *or* **spot** (fig.) wunder Punkt; **(b)** (irritated) verärgert; sauer (ugs.). **2** *n.* wunde Stelle

sorely /'sɔːlɪ/ *adv.* sehr; dringend ⟨*nötig, benötigt*⟩; **be ~ in need of sth.** etw. dringend brauchen; **~ tempted** stark versucht

soreness /'sɔːnɪs/ *n.* Schmerz, *der*

sorrow /'sɒrəʊ/ *n.* **(a)** Kummer, *der;* Leid, *das;* **feel [great] ~ that ...:** es [sehr] bedauern, dass ...; **cause sb. [great] ~:** jmdm. [großen] Kummer bereiten; **(b)** (misfortune) Sorge, *die;* **he has had many ~s** er hat viel [Schweres] durchgemacht; *see also* **drown 2 b**

sorrowful /'sɒrəʊfl, 'sɒrəfl/ *adj.* betrübt ⟨*Person*⟩; traurig ⟨*Anlass, Lächeln, Herz*⟩

sorry /'sɒrɪ/ *adj.* ▶ **639| sb. is ~ to do sth.** jmdm. tut es leid, etw. tun zu müssen; **I am ~ to disappoint you** ich muss dich leider enttäuschen; **sb. is ~ that ...:** es tut jmdm. leid, dass ...; **sb. is ~ about sth.** jmdm. tut etw. leid; **~, but ...** (coll.) tut mir leid, aber ...; **I'm ~** (won't change my mind) tut mir leid; **~ I'm late** (coll.) Entschuldigung, dass ich zu spät komme; **I'm ~ to say** leider; **I can't say [that] I'm ~!** ich bin nicht gerade traurig darüber; **sb. is** *or* **feels ~ for sb./sth.** jmd. tut jmdm. leid/ jmd. bedauert etw.; **you'll be ~:** das wird dir noch leid tun; **feel ~ for oneself** (coll.) sich selbst bemitleiden; sich (*Dat.*) leid tun; **~!** Entschuldigung!; **~?** wie bitte?; **~ about that!** (coll.) tut mir leid!

sort /sɔːt/ **1** *n.* **(a)** Art, *die;* (type) Sorte, *die;* **cakes of several ~s** verschiedene Kuchensorten; **a new ~ of bicycle** ein neuartiges Fahrrad; **people of every/that ~:** Menschen jeden/diesen Schlages; **it takes all ~s [to make a world]** (coll.) es gibt so'ne und solche (ugs.); **all ~s of ...:** alle möglichen ...; **support sb. in all ~s of ways** jmdn. auf vielerlei Art und Weise unterstützen; **she is just/not my ~:** sie ist genau/nicht mein Typ (ugs.); **what ~ of [a] person do you think I am?** für wen hältst du mich?; **you'll do nothing of the ~:** das kommt gar nicht in Frage; **~ of** (coll.) irgendwie; (more or less) mehr oder weniger; (to some extent) ziemlich (ugs.); **nothing of the ~:** nichts dergleichen; **or something of the ~:** oder so [etwas ähnliches] (ugs.); **he is a doctor/footballer of a ~** *or* **of ~s** (derog.) er nennt sich Arzt/Fußballspieler; **we don't mix with people of that ~:** mit solchen Leuten wollen wir nichts zu tun haben; **he/she is a good ~** (coll.) er/sie ist schon in Ordnung (ugs.); **(b) be out of ~s** nicht in Form sein; (be irritable) schlecht gelaunt sein. **2** *v.t.* sortieren

~ **'out** *v.t.* (a) (arrange) sortieren; (b) (settle) klären; schlichten ‹*Streit*›; beenden ‹*Verwirrung*›; **it will** ~ **itself out** es wird schon in Ordnung kommen; (c) (organize) durchorganisieren; auf Vordermann bringen (ugs.); **things have** ~**ed themselves out** die Dinge haben sich eingerenkt; (d) (coll.: punish) ~ **sb. out** jmdm. zeigen, wo's langgeht (ugs.); (e) (select) aussuchen; wählen

'sort code *n.* (Banking) Bankleitzahl, *die*

sortie /'sɔːtiː, 'sɔːtɪ/ *n.* (Mil.; also fig.) (a) Ausfall, *der;* (b) (flight) Einsatz, *der*

SOS /esəʊ'es/ *n.* SOS, *das*

'so so, **'so-so** *adj., adv.* so lala (ugs.)

soufflé /'suːfleɪ/ *n.* (Gastr.) Soufflé, *das;* ~ **dish** Soufflé-form, *die*

sought ⇒ **seek**

soul /səʊl/ *n.* (a) Seele, *die;* **sell one's** ~ **for sth.** (fig.) seine Seele für etw. verkaufen; **bare one's** ~ **to sb.** jmdm. sein Herz ausschütten; (b) (person) Seele, *die; not a* ~**:** keine Menschenseele; **the poor little** ~**:** das arme kleine Ding

'soul-destroying *adj.* (a) (boring) nervtötend; geisttötend; (b) (depressing) deprimierend

soulful /'səʊlfl/ *adj.* gefühlvoll; (sad) schwermütig

soul: ~**mate** *n.* Seelenverwandte, *der/die;* ~-**searching** *n.* Gewissenskampf, *der*

sound¹ /saʊnd/ *1 adj.* (a) (healthy) gesund; intakt ‹*Gebäude, Mauerwerk*›; gut ‹*Frucht, Obst, Holz, Boden*›; **of** ~ **mind** im Vollbesitz der geistigen Kräfte; **the building was structurally** ~**:** das Gebäude hatte eine gesunde Bausubstanz; (b) (well-founded) vernünftig ‹*Argument, Rat*›; klug ‹*Wahl*›; **it makes** ~ **sense** es ist sehr vernünftig; (c) (Finance: secure) gesund, solide ‹*Basis*›; klug ‹*Investition*›; (d) (competent, reliable) solide ‹*Spieler*›; **have a** ~ **character** charakterfest sein; (e) (undisturbed) tief, gesund ‹*Schlaf*›; (f) (thorough) gehörig (ugs.) ‹*Niederlage, Tracht Prügel*›; gekonnt ‹*Leistung*›. *2 adv.* fest, tief ‹*schlafen*›

sound² *1 n.* (a) (Phys.) Schall, *der;* (b) (noise) Laut, *der;* (of wind, sea, car, footsteps, breaking glass or twigs) Geräusch, *das;* (of voices, laughter, bell) Klang, *der;* **do sth. without a** ~**:** etw. lautlos tun; (c) (Radio, Telev., Cinemat.) Ton, *der;* **loss of** ~**:** Tonausfall, *der;* (d) (music) Klang, *der;* (e) (Phonet.: articulation) Laut, *der;* (f) (fig.: impression) **I like the** ~ **of your plan** ich finde, Ihr Plan hört sich gut an; **I don't like the** ~ **of this** das hört sich nicht gut an. *2 v.i.* (a) (seem) klingen; **it** ~**s as if** .../**like** ...**:** es klingt, als .../wie ...; **it** ~**s to me from what you have said that** ...**:** was du gesagt hast, klingt für mich so, als ...; **that** ~**s [like] a good idea to me** ich finde, die Idee hört sich gut an; ~**s good to me!** klingt gut! (ugs.); gute Idee! (ugs.); (b) (emit ~) [er]tönen. *3 v.t.* (a) (cause to emit ~) ertönen lassen; ~ **the trumpet** trompeten; in die Trompete blasen; (b) (utter) ~ **a note of caution** zur Vorsicht mahnen; (c) (pronounce) aussprechen

~ **'off** *v.i.* tönen (ugs.), schwadronieren (**on, about** von)

sound³ *n.* (strait) Sund, *der;* Meerenge, *die*

sound⁴ *v.t.* (a) (Naut.: fathom) ausloten; sondieren; (b) (fig.: test) ⇒ ~ **out**

~ **'out** *v.t.* ausfragen ‹*Person*›; sondieren (geh.), herausbekommen ‹*Sache*›; ~ **sb. out on sth.** bei jmdm. wegen etw. vorfühlen

sound: ~ **barrier** *n.* Schallmauer, *die;* ~ **bite** *n.* kurzes, prägnantes Zitat; ~ **broadcasting** *n.* Hörfunk, *der;* ~ **card** *n.* (Computing) Soundkarte, *die;* ~ **effect** *n.* Geräuscheffekt, *der;* ~ **engineer** *n.* ▶ 887 (Radio, Telev., Cinemat.) Toningenieur, *der/*-ingenieurin, *die*

sounding /'saʊndɪŋ/ *n.* (a) (Naut.: measurement) Lotung, *die;* **take** ~**s** Lotungen vornehmen; loten; (b) (fig.) Sondierung, *die* (geh.); **carry out** ~**s of public opinion/of interested parties** die öffentliche Meinung sondieren/ mit den Beteiligten Sondierungsgespräche führen

soundless /'saʊndlɪs/ *adj.* lautlos; stumm; tonlos ‹*Sprache, Gebet*›

soundly /'saʊndlɪ/ *adv.* (a) (solidly) stabil, solide ‹*bauen*›; (b) (well) vernünftig ‹*argumentieren, urteilen, investieren*›;

(c) (deeply) tief, fest ‹*schlafen*›; (d) (thoroughly) ordentlich (ugs.) ‹*verhauen*›; vernichtend ‹*schlagen, besiegen*›

soundness /'saʊndnɪs/ *n., no pl.* (a) (of mind, body) Gesundheit, *die;* (of construction, structure) Solidität, *die;* (b) (of argument) Stichhaltigkeit, *die;* (of policy, views) Vernünftigkeit, *die;* (c) (of sleep) Tiefe, *die;* (d) (competence, reliability) Solidität, *die;* (e) (solvency) wirtschaftliche Gesundheit; Solvenz, *die*

sound: ~**proof** *1 adj.* schalldicht; *2 v.t.* schalldicht machen; ~ **recorder** *n.* Tonaufnahmegerät, *das;* ~ **system** *n.* Tonanlage, *die;* ~**track** *n.* (Cinemat.) Soundtrack, *der;* ~ **wave** *n.* (Phys.) Schallwelle, *die*

soup /suːp/ *n.* Suppe, *die;* **be/land in the** ~ (fig. coll.) in der Patsche sitzen/landen (ugs.)

souped-up /'suːptʌp/ *attrib. adj.* (Motor Veh. coll.) frisiert (ugs.)

soup: ~ **plate** *n.* Suppenteller, *der;* ~ **spoon** *n.* Suppenlöffel, *der*

sour /saʊə(r)/ *1 adj.* (a) (having acid taste) sauer; (b) (morose) griesgrämig (abwertend); säuerlich ‹*Blick*›; (c) (unpleasant) bitter; **when things go** ~**:** wenn man *od.* einem alles leid wird. *2 v.t.* (a) versauern lassen; sauer machen; (b) (fig.: spoil) verbauen ‹*Karriere*›; trüben ‹*Beziehung*›; (c) (fig.: make gloomy) verbittern. *3 v.i.* ‹*Beziehungen:*› sich trüben

source /sɔːs/ *n.* Quelle, *die;* ~ **of income/infection** Einkommensquelle, *die/*Infektionsherd, *der;* **locate the** ~ **of a leak** (lit. or fig.) feststellen, wo eine undichte Stelle ist; **the whole thing is a** ~ **of some embarrassment to us** das Ganze ist für uns ziemlich unangenehm; **at** ~**:** an der Quelle

'sourpuss *n.* (coll.) (male) Miesepeter, der (ugs.); (female) miesepetrige Ziege (ugs.)

souse /saʊs/ *v.t.* eintauchen

south /saʊθ/ ▶ 715 *1 n.* (a) (direction) Süden, *der;* **the** ~**:** Süd (Met., Seew.); **in/to[wards]/from the** ~**:** im/nach/von Süden; **to the** ~ **of** südlich von; südlich (+ *Gen.*); (b) *usu.* **S~** (part lying to the ~) Süden, *der; from the* **S~:** aus dem Süden. *2 adj.* südlich; Süd ‹*küste, -wind, -grenze, -tor*›. *3 adv.* südwärts; nach Süden; ~ **of** südlich von; südlich (+ *Gen.*)

South: ~ **'Africa** *pr. n.* Südafrika (*das*); ~ **'African** *1 adj.* südafrikanisch; *2 n.* Südafrikaner, *der/*-afrikanerin, *die;* ~ **A'merica** *pr. n.* Südamerika (*das*); ~ **A'merican** *1 adj.* südamerikanisch; *2 n.* Südamerikaner, *der/* -amerikanerin, *die*

south: ~**bound** *adj.* ▶ 715 ‹*Zug, Verkehr usw.*› in Richtung Süden; ~-**'east** ▶ 715 *1 n.* Südosten, *der; 2 adj.* südöstlich; Südost ‹*wind, -küste*›; *3 adv.* südostwärts; nach Südosten; ~-**'eastern** *adj.* ▶ 715 südöstlich

southerly /'sʌðəlɪ/ ▶ 715 *adj.* (a) (in position or direction) südlich; **in a** ~ **direction** nach Süden; (b) (from the south) ‹*Wind*› aus südlichen Richtungen

southern /'sʌðən/ ▶ 715 *adj.* südlich; Süd ‹*grenze, -hälfte, -seite*›; südländisch ‹*Temperament*›; ~ **Spain** Südspanien; das südliche Spanien; ~ **Africa** das südliche Afrika

southerner /'sʌðənə(r)/ *n.* (male) Südengländer/-franzose/-italiener *usw.*, *der;* (female) Südengländerin/-französin/-italienerin *usw.*, *die*

Southern 'Europe *pr. n.* Südeuropa, (*das*)

southernmost /'sʌðənməʊst/ *adj.* ▶ 715 südlichst...

South: ~ **'German** *1 adj.* süddeutsch; *2 n.* Süddeutsche, *der/die;* ~ **'Germany** *pr. n.* Süddeutschland (*das*); ~ **Ko'rea** *pr. n.* Südkorea (*das*); ~ **of 'England** *pr. n.* Südengland (*das*); *attrib.* südenglisch; ~ **'Pole** *pr. n.* Südpol, *der;* ~ **'Seas** *pr. n. pl.* Südsee, *die*

southward /'saʊθwəd/ *1 adj.* nach Süden gerichtet; (situated towards the south) südlich; **in a** ~ **direction** nach Süden; [in] Richtung Süden. *2 adv.* südwärts; **they are** ~ **bound** sie fahren nach *od.* [in] Richtung Süden

southwards /'saʊθwədz/ *adv.* ▶ 715 südwärts

south: ~-**'west** ▶ 715 *1 n.* Südwesten, *der; 2 adj.* südwestlich; Südwest ‹*wind, -küste*›; *3 adv.* südwestwärts; nach Südwesten; **S~West 'Africa** *pr. n.* Südwestafrika, (*das*); ~-**'western** *adj.* ▶ 715 südwestlich

souvenir /suːvəˈnɪə(r)/ *n.* (of holiday) Andenken, *das;* Souvenir, *das* (**of** aus); (of wedding day, one's youth, etc.) Andenken, *das* (**of** an + *Akk.*)

sou'wester /saʊˈwestə(r)/ *n.* (**a**) (hat) Südwester, *der;* (**b**) (coat) Ölhaut, *die*

sovereign /ˈsɒvrɪn/ *n.* (**a**) (ruler) Souverän, *der;* (**b**) (Brit. Hist.: coin) Sovereign, *der;* 20-Shilling-Münze, *die*

sovereignty /ˈsɒvrɪntɪ/ *n.* Souveränität, *die;* Oberhoheit, *die*

Soviet /ˈsəʊvɪət, ˈsɒvɪət/ (Hist.) **1** *adj.* sowjetisch; Sowjet ‹*bürger, -literatur, -kultur, -ideologie*›. **2** *n.* Sowjet, *der*

Soviet 'Union *pr. n.* (Hist.) Sowjetunion, *die*

sow¹ /səʊ/ *v.t., p.p.* **sown** /səʊn/ *or* ∼**ed** /səʊd/ (**a**) (plant) [aus]säen; (**b**) (plant with seed) einsäen, besäen ‹*Feld, Boden*›; (**c**) (cover thickly) spicken (ugs.)

sow² /saʊ/ *n.* (female pig) Sau, *die*

sown ⇒ **sow¹**

soya [bean] /ˈsɔɪə (biːn)/, **soy bean** /ˈsɔɪ biːn/ *ns.* (**a**) (plant) Soja[bohne], *die;* (**b**) (seed) Sojabohne, *die*

soy sauce /ˈsɔɪ sɔːs/ *n.* Sojasoße, *die*

sozzled /ˈsɒzld/ *adj.* (coll.) voll (ugs.)

spa /spaː/ *n.* (**a**) (place) Bad, *das;* Badeort, *der;* (**b**) (spring) Mineralquelle, *die*

space /speɪs/ **1** *n.* (**a**) (place) Raum, *der;* **stare into** ∼: in die Luft *od.* ins Leere starren; (**b**) (interval between points) Platz, *der;* **clear a** ∼: Platz schaffen; (**c**) (area on page) Platz, *der;* (**d**) **the wide open** ∼**s** das weite, flache Land; (**e**) (Astron.) Weltraum, *der; see also* **outer space**; (**f**) (blank between words) Zwischenraum, *der;* (**g**) (interval of time) Zeitraum, *der;* **in the** ∼ **of a minute/an hour** *etc.* innerhalb einer Minute/Stunde *usw.* **2** *v.t.* **the posts are** ∼**d at intervals of one metre** die Pfosten sind im Abstand von einem Meter aufgestellt

∼ **'out** *v.t.* verteilen

space: ∼ **age** *n.* [Welt]raumzeitalter, *das;* Zeitalter der Raumfahrt,; ∼ **bar** *n.* Leertaste, *die;* ∼**craft** *n.* Raumfahrzeug, *das;* (unmanned) Raumsonde, *die;* ∼ **flight** *n.* (**a**) (a journey through ∼) [Welt]raumflug, *der;* (**b**) ⇒ ∼ **travel;** ∼**heater** *n.* Heizgerät, *das;* ∼**man** *n.* Raumfahrer, *der/*-fahrerin, *die;* ∼**-saving** *adj.* Platz sparend; ∼**ship** *n.* Raumschiff, *das;* ∼ **shuttle** *n.* Raumfähre, *die;* Raumtransporter, *der;* ∼ **station** *n.* [Welt]raumstation, *die;* ∼**suit** *n.* Raumanzug, *der;* ∼ **travel** *n.* Raumfahrt, *die;* ∼ **walk** *n.* Spaziergang im All

spacing /ˈspeɪsɪŋ/ *n.* Zwischenraum, *der;* (Printing) Sperrungen; Spationierung, *die* (Druckw.); **single/double** ∼ (on typewriter) einfacher/doppelter Zeilenabstand

spacious /ˈspeɪʃəs/ *adj.* (**a**) (vast in area) weitläufig ‹*Garten, Park, Ländereien*›; (**b**) (roomy) geräumig ‹*Raum*›; breit ‹*Straße*›

spade /speɪd/ *n.* (**a**) Spaten, *der;* **call a** ∼ **a** ∼: das Kind beim [rechten] Namen nennen (ugs.); **in** ∼**s** (coll.) in höchstem Maße; **have sth. in** ∼**s** etw. in höchstem Maße haben *od.* besitzen; **pay sb. back in** ∼**s** es jmdm. doppelt heimzahlen; (**b**) (Cards) Pik, *das; see also* **club 1 d**

'spadework *n.* (preliminary work) Vorarbeit, *die*

spaghetti /spəˈgetɪ/ *n.* Spaghetti *Pl.*

Spain /speɪn/ *pr. n.* Spanien (*das*)

Spam, (P) /spæm/ *n.* Frühstücksfleisch, *das*

span¹ /spæn/ **1** *n.* (**a**) (full extent) Spanne, *die;* ∼ **of life/time** Lebens-/Zeitspanne, *die;* (**b**) (of bridge) Spannweite, *die.* **2** *v.t.,* **-nn-** überspannen ‹*Fluss*›; umfassen ‹*Zeitraum*›

span² ⇒ **spick**

spangle /ˈspæŋgl/ **1** *n.* ⇒ **sequin. 2** *v.t.* ∼**d with stars/buttercups** von glitzernden Sternen/mit leuchtenden Butterblumen übersät

Spaniard /ˈspænjəd/ *n.* ▶947⫞ Spanier, *der/*Spanierin, *die*

spaniel /ˈspænjəl/ *n.* Spaniel, *der*

Spanish /ˈspænɪʃ/ ▶897⫞, ▶947⫞ **1** *adj.* spanisch; **sb. is** ∼: jmd. ist Spanier/Spanierin. **2** *n.* (**a**) (language) Spanisch, *das; see also* **English 2 a;** (**b**) *constr. as pl.* (people) Spanier

spank /spæŋk/ **1** *n.* ≈ Klaps, *der* (ugs.). **2** *v.t.* ∼ **sb.** jmdm. den Hintern versohlen (ugs.); **get** ∼**ed** den Hintern voll kriegen (ugs.)

spanking /ˈspæŋkɪŋ/ *n.* Tracht Prügel, *die* (ugs.)

spanner /ˈspænə(r)/ *n.* (Brit.) Schraubenschlüssel, *der;* **put** *or* **throw a** ∼ **in the works** (fig.) Sand ins Getriebe streuen

spar¹ /spaː(r)/ *v.i.,* **-rr-** (Boxing) sparren

spar² *n.* (pole) Rundholz, *das;* Spiere, *die* (Seemannsspr.)

spare /speə(r)/ **1** *adj.* (**a**) (not in use) übrig; ∼ **time/moment** Freizeit, *die/*freier Augenblick; **there is one** ∼ **seat** ein Platz ist noch frei; **are there any** ∼ **tickets for Friday?** gibt es noch Karten für Freitag?; (**b**) (for use when needed) zusätzlich, Extra ‹*bett, -tasse*›; ∼ **room** Gästezimmer, *das;* **go** ∼ (Brit. coll.: be very angry) durchdrehen (salopp). **2** *n.* (spare part) Ersatzteil, *das;* (spare tyre) Ersatzreifen, *der.* **3** *v.t.* (**a**) (do without) entbehren; **can you** ∼ **me a moment?** hast du einen Augenblick Zeit für mich?; **we arrived with ten minutes to** ∼: wir kamen zehn Minuten früher an; (**b**) (not inflict on) ∼ **sb. sth.** jmdm. etw. ersparen; (**c**) (not hurt) [ver]schonen; (**d**) (fail to use) **not** ∼ **any expense/pains** *or* **efforts** keine Kosten/Mühe scheuen; **no expense** ∼**d** an nichts gespart. *See also* **rod c**

spare: ∼ **'part** *n.* Ersatzteil, *das;* ∼ **'tyre** *n.* (**a**) Ersatzreifen, *der;* (**b**) (Brit. fig. coll.) Rettungsring, *der* (ugs.); ∼ **'wheel** *n.* Ersatzrad, *die*

sparing /ˈspeərɪŋ/ *adj.* sparsam; **be** ∼ **of sth./in the use of sth.** mit etw. sparsam umgehen

spark /spaːk/ **1** *n.* (**a**) Funke, *der;* **the** ∼**s [begin to] fly** (fig.) es funkt (ugs.); **a** ∼ **of generosity/decency** (fig.) ein Funke[n] Großzügigkeit/Anstand; (**b**) (in sparking plug) Zündfunke[n], *der* (Kfz-W.); (**c**) **a bright** ∼ (clever person; also iron.) ein schlauer Kopf. **2** *v.t.* ⇒ ∼ **off**

∼ **'off** *v.t.* (**a**) (cause to explode) zünden; (**b**) (fig.: start) auslösen

'sparking plug *n.* (Brit. Motor Veh.) Zündkerze, *die*

sparkle /ˈspaːkl/ **1** *v.i.* (**a**) (flash) ‹*Tautropfen:*› glitzern; ‹*Augen:*› funkeln, sprühen; (**b**) (perform brilliantly) glänzen; (**c**) (be lively) sprühen (**with** vor + *Dat.*). **2** *n.* Glitzern, *das;* Funkeln, *das*

sparkler /ˈspaːklə(r)/ *n.* Wunderkerze, *die*

sparkling /ˈspaːklɪŋ/ *adj.* (**a**) (flashing) glitzernd ‹*Stein, Diamant*›; (**b**) (bright) funkelnd ‹*Augen*›; (**c**) (brilliant) glänzend ‹*Schauspiel, Aufführung, Rede*›

sparkling 'wine *n.* Schaumwein, *der*

'spark plug ⇒ **sparking plug**

'sparring partner *n.* (Boxing) Sparringspartner, *der*

sparrow /ˈspærəʊ/ *n.* Sperling, *der;* Spatz, *der*

sparse /spaːs/ *adj.* spärlich; dünn ‹*Besiedlung*›

Spartan /ˈspaːtn/ **1** *adj.* spartanisch. **2** *n.* Spartaner, *der/*Spartanerin, *die*

spasm /ˈspæzm/ *n.* (**a**) Krampf, *der;* Spasmus, *der* (Med.); (**b**) (convulsive movement) Anfall, *der;* (**c**) (coll.) **a** ∼ **of activity** plötzliche fieberhafte Aktivität

spasmodic /spæzˈmɒdɪk/ *adj.* (**a**) (marked by spasms) krampfartig; (**b**) (intermittent) sporadisch ‹*Anwachsen, Bemühungen*›

spastic /ˈspæstɪk/ (Med.) **1** *n.* Spastiker, *der/*Spastikerin, *die.* **2** *adj.* spastisch [gelähmt]

spat ⇒ **spit¹ 1, 2**

spate /speɪt/ *n.* (**a**) (flood) **the river/waterfall is in [full]** ∼: der Fluss/Wasserfall führt Hochwasser; (**b**) (fig.: large amount) **a** ∼ **of sth.** eine Flut von etw.; **a** ∼ **of burglaries** eine Einbruchsserie

spatial /ˈspeɪʃl/ *adj.* räumlich

spatter /ˈspætə(r)/ *v.t.* spritzen; ∼ **sb./sth. with sth.** jmdn./etw. mit etw. bespritzen

spatula /ˈspætjʊlə/ *n.* Spachtel, *die*

spawn /spɔːn/ (Zool.) **1** *v.t.* ablegen ‹*Eier*›; (fig.) hervorbringen. **2** *v.i.* laichen. **3** *n., constr. as sing. or pl.* Laich, *der*

spay /speɪ/ *v.t.* sterilisieren ‹*Katze, Hündin*›

speak /spiːk/ **1** *v.i.,* **spoke** /spəʊk/, **spoken** /ˈspəʊkn/ (**a**) sprechen; ∼ **[with sb.] on** *or* **about sth.** [mit jmdm.] über etwas (*Akk.*) sprechen; ∼ **for/against sth.** sich für/

gegen etw. aussprechen; **sth. ~s well for sb.** etw. spricht
für jmdn.; **(b)** (on telephone) **Is Mr Grant there? —
S~ing!** Ist Mister Grant da? — Am Apparat!; **Mr Grant
~ing** (when connected to caller) Grant hier; hier ist Grant;
who is ~ing, please? wer ist am Apparat, bitte?; mit
wem spreche ich, bitte? **2** *v.t.*, **spoke, spoken (a)** (utter)
sprechen ‹*Satz, Wort, Sprache*›; **(b)** (make known) sagen
‹*Wahrheit*›; **~ one's opinion/mind** seine Meinung
sagen/sagen, was man denkt; **(c)** (convey without words) **sth.
~s volumes** etw. spricht Bände
~ for *v.t.* sprechen für; **~ for yourself!** das ist [nur]
deine Meinung!; **~ for itself/themselves** für sich selbst
sprechen; **sth. is spoken for** (reserved) etw. ist schon vergeben
~ of *v.t.* sprechen von; **~ing of Mary** da wir gerade von
Mary sprechen; apropos Mary; **nothing to ~ of** nichts
Besonderes *od.* Nennenswertes
~ 'out *v.i.* seine Meinung sagen; **~ out against sth.**
sich gegen etw. aussprechen
~ to *v.t.* **(a)** (address) sprechen mit; reden mit; **I know
him to ~ to** ich kenne ihn [nur] flüchtig; **(b)** (request action
from) **~ to sb. about sth.** mit jmdm. wegen einer Sache
od. über etw. (*Akk.*) sprechen; **(c)** (coll.: reprove) **~ to sb.**
sich mit jmdm. unterhalten (verhüllend)
~ 'up *v.i.* **(a)** (~ more loudly) lauter sprechen; **(b)** ⇒ ~
out
speaker /'spiːkə(r)/ *n.* **(a)** (in public) Redner, *der*/Rednerin,
die; **(b)** (of a language) Sprecher, *der*/Sprecherin, *die;* **be a
French ~, be a ~ of French** Französisch sprechen; **(c)
S~** (Polit.) Sprecher, *der;* ≈ Parlamentspräsident, *der;* **(d)**
⇒ **loudspeaker**
speaking /'spiːkɪŋ/ **1** *n.* (talking) Sprechen, *das;* **a good
~ voice** eine gute Sprechstimme; **not be on ~ terms
with sb.** nicht [mehr] mit jmdm. reden; **~ clock** (Brit.)
telefonische Zeitansage. **2** *adv.* **strictly/roughly/generally/legally ~:** genaugenommen/grob gesagt/im allgemeinen/aus juristischer Sicht
spear /spɪə(r)/ **1** *n.* Speer, *der.* **2** *v.t.* aufspießen
spear: ~head 1 *n.* (fig.) Speerspitze, *die;* (Mil.) Angriffsspitze, *die;* **2** *v.t.* (fig.) **~head sth.** etw. anführen;
~mint *n.* Grüne Minze
special /'speʃl/ *adj.* speziell; besonder ...; Sonder
‹*korrespondent, -zug, -mission usw.*›; **nobody ~:** niemand
Besonderer; **a ~ occasion** ein besonderer Anlass
special: S~ Branch *n.* (Brit. Police) *Abteilung der britischen Polizei, deren Aufgabe die Wahrung der inneren Sicherheit ist;* ≈ Sicherheitsdienst, *der;* **~ 'case** *n.*
Sonderfall, *der;* **~ correspondent** *n.* Sonderkorrespondent, *der*/-korrespondentin, *die;* Sonderberichterstatter, *der*/-berichterstatterin, *die;* **~ de'livery** *n.* (Post)
Eilzustellung, *die;* **~ e'dition** *n.* Sonderausgabe, *die;* **~
effects** *n. pl.* (Cinemat.) Special effects *Pl.* (fachspr.);
Spezialeffekte
specialise ⇒ **specialize**
specialist /'speʃəlɪst/ *n.* **(a)** Spezialist, *der*/Spezialistin,
die (**in** für); Fachmann, *der*/Fachfrau, *die* (**in** für); **~
knowledge** Fachwissen, *das;* **(b)** (Med.) Facharzt, *der*/-ärztin, *die*
speciality /speʃɪ'ælɪtɪ/ *n.* Spezialität, *die*
specialization /speʃəlaɪ'zeɪʃn/ *n.* Spezialisierung, *die*
specialize /'speʃəlaɪz/ *v.i.* sich spezialisieren (**in** auf +
Akk.)
specialized /'speʃəlaɪzd/ *adj.* **(a)** (requiring detailed knowledge) speziell; Spezial‹*kenntnisse, -gebiet*›; **(b)** (concentrating
on small area) spezialisiert
specially /'speʃəlɪ/ *adv.* **(a)** speziell; **make sth. ~:** etw.
speziell *od.* extra anfertigen; **~ made/chosen for me**
eigens für mich gemacht/ausgewählt; **a ~ made
wheelchair/lift** ein spezieller Rollstuhl/Lift; **(b)** (especially) besonders
special: ~ 'needs *n.* **children with ~ needs, ~
needs children** Kinder, die besonders betreut werden
müssen; **~ 'offer** *n.* Sonderangebot, *die;* **on ~ offer** im
Sonderangebot; **~ school** *n.* Sonderschule, *die*
specialty /'speʃltɪ/ (esp. Amer.) ⇒ **speciality**
species /'spiːʃiːz/ *n., pl. same* **(a)** (Biol.) Spezies, *die*
(fachspr.); Art, *die;* **(b)** (sort) Art, *die*

specific /spɪ'sɪfɪk/ *adj.* deutlich, klar ‹*Aussage*›; bestimmt ‹*Ziel, Grund*›; **make a ~ request** einen bestimmten Wunsch äußern; **could you be more ~?**
kannst du dich genauer ausdrücken?
specifically /spɪ'sɪfɪkəlɪ/ *adv.* ausdrücklich; eigens; extra (ugs.)
specification /spesɪfɪ'keɪʃn/ *n.* **(a)** *often pl.* (details) technische Daten; (instructions) Konstruktionsplan, *der;* (for building) Baubeschreibung, *die;* **(b)** (specifying) Spezifizierung, *die*
(geh.); **(c)** [**patent**] **~:** Patentschrift, *die*
specify /'spesɪfaɪ/ *v.t.* ausdrücklich sagen; ausdrücklich
nennen ‹*Namen*›; **as specified above** wie oben aufgeführt; **unless otherwise specified** wenn nicht anders angegeben
specimen /'spesɪmən/ *n.* **(a)** (example) Exemplar, *das;* **a
~ of his handwriting** eine Schriftprobe von ihm; **~ signature** Unterschriftsprobe, *die;* **(b)** (sample) Probe, *die;* **a
~ of his urine was required** es wurde eine Urinprobe
von ihm benötigt; **(c)** (coll./derog.: type) Marke, *die* (salopp)
specious /'spiːʃəs/ *adj.* **a ~ argument** ein nur scheinbar treffendes Argument; **a ~ pretence/appearance of
honesty** ein Anschein von Ehrlichkeit
speck /spek/ *n.* **(a)** (spot) Fleck, *der;* (of paint also) Spritzer,
der; **(b)** (particle) Teilchen, *das;* **~ of soot/dust** Rußflocke,
die/Staubkörnchen, *das*
specs /speks/ *n. pl.* (coll.: spectacles) Brille, *die*
spectacle /'spektəkl/ *n.* **(a)** *in pl.* [**pair of**] **~s** Brille,
die; **(b)** (public show) Spektakel, *das;* **(c)** (object of attention)
Anblick, *der;* Schauspiel, *das;* **make a ~ of oneself** sich
unmöglich aufführen
'spectacle case *n.* Brillenetui, *das*
spectacular /spek'tækjʊlə(r)/ **1** *adj.* spektakulär. **2** *n.*
Spektakel, *das*
spectator /spek'teɪtə(r)/ *n.* Zuschauer, *der*/Zuschauerin,
die
spec'tator sport *n.* Publikumssport, *der*
specter (Amer.) ⇒ **spectre**
spectra *pl. of* **spectrum**
spectral /'spektrl/ *adj.* (Phys.) spektral
spectre /'spektə(r)/ *n.* (Brit.) **(a)** (apparition) Gespenst, *das;*
(b) (disturbing image) Schreckgespenst, *das*
spectrum /'spektrəm/ *n., pl.* **spectra** /'spektrə/ Spektrum, *das;* **~ of opinion** Meinungsspektrum, *das*
speculate /'spekjʊleɪt/ *v.i.* spekulieren (**about, on** über
+ *Akk.*); Vermutungen *od.* Spekulationen anstellen
(**about, on** über + *Akk.*); **~ on the Stock Exchange/
in rubber** an der Börse/mit *od.* (Wirtsch. Jargon) in Gummi
spekulieren
speculation /spekjʊ'leɪʃn/ *n.* Spekulation, *die* (**over**
über + *Akk.*)
speculative /'spekjʊlətɪv/ *adj.* spekulativ
speculator /'spekjʊleɪtə(r)/ *n.* Spekulant, *der*/Spekulantin, *die*
sped ⇒ **speed** 2, 3
speech /spiːtʃ/ *n.* **(a)** (public address) Rede, *die;* **make** *or*
deliver *or* **give a ~:** eine Rede halten; **(b)** (faculty of speaking) Sprache, *die;* **(c)** (act of speaking) Sprechen, *das;* Sprache,
die; **(d)** (manner of speaking) Sprache, *die;* Sprechweise, *die;*
his ~ was slurred er sprach undeutlich
speech: ~ day *n.* (Brit. Sch.) jährliches Schulfest; **~
defect** *n.* Sprachfehler, *der*
speechless /'spiːtʃlɪs/ *adj.* sprachlos (**with** vor + *Dat.*)
speed /spiːd/ **1** *n.* **(a)** ▶ **1102** Geschwindigkeit, *die;* **at**
full *or* **top ~:** mit Höchstgeschwindigkeit; mit Vollgas
(ugs.); **pick up ~:** schneller werden; **at a ~ of eighty
miles an hour** mit einer Geschwindigkeit von achtzig
Meilen in der Stunde; **at ~:** mit hoher Geschwindigkeit; **(b)** (gear) Gang, *der;* **a five-~ gearbox** eine 5-Gang-
Schaltung; **(c)** (Photog.) (of film etc.) Lichtempfindlichkeit,
die; (of lens) [**shutter**] **~:** Belichtungszeit, *die.* **2** *v.i.*, **sped**
/sped/ *or* **~ed (a)** (go fast) schnell fahren; rasen (ugs.); **(b)**
p.t. & p.p. **~ed** (go too fast) zu schnell fahren; rasen (ugs.).
3 *v.t.*, **sped** *or* **~ed: ~ sb. on his/her way** jmdn. verabschieden
~ 'off *v.i.* davonbrausen

Speed

In Germany, as in the rest of continental Europe, the speed of road, rail and air traffic is measured in kilometres per hour, for which kph is the usual British abbreviation, and km/h the abbreviation used on the continent and now also found in some English-language publications:

100 kph = 62.14 mph 100 mph ≈ 160 kph
50 mph ≈ 80 kph

... miles per hour	= ... Meilen in der or pro Stunde
... kilometres per hour	= ... Kilometer in der or pro Stunde, Stunden-kilometer (coll.)
100 miles per hour (mph)	≈ 160 Kilometer in der or pro Stunde (km/h)
How fast was the car going?, What speed was the car doing?	= Wie schnell or Mit welcher Geschwindig-keit fuhr der Wagen?
He was driving flat out/ at full speed/at 50 miles per hour	≈ Er fuhr mit Vollgas/mit Höchstgeschwindigkeit/ mit 80 Kilometern pro Stunde
It was going at or doing 75 [miles per hour]	≈ Es fuhr mit 120 Stundenkilometern or (coll.) Sachen
The car's top speed is 125 [mph]	≈ Die Höchstgeschwindig-keit des Autos liegt bei 200 km/h, Das Auto fährt 200 Kilometer Spitze (coll.)

You were exceeding the speed limit	= Sie haben das Tempolimit überschritten
They were tearing along/going at a crazy speed	= Sie rasten dahin/ fuhren mit rasender Geschwindigkeit or in rasendem Tempo
We had to go at a crawl/were reduced to a crawl	= Wir mussten im Kriechtempo fahren/ kamen nur im Kriechtempo vorwärts

Speed of light and sound

The speed of sound is 330 metres per second	= Die Schallgeschwin-digkeit beträgt 330 Meter pro Sekunde (m/s)
to break the sound barrier	= die Schallmauer durchbrechen
The speed of light is 186,300 miles per second	= Die Lichtgeschwindigkeit beträgt 300 000 Kilometer pro Sekunde (km/s)
at or with the speed of light	= mit Lichtgeschwindigkeit

∼ **'up 1** v.t., ∼**ed up** beschleunigen; ∼ **up the work** die Arbeit vorantreiben; (one's own work) sich mit der Arbeit beeilen. **2** v.i., ∼**ed up** sich beeilen

speed: ∼**boat** n. Rennboot, das; ∼ **bump** n. Bodenschwelle, die; ∼ **camera** n. Geschwindigkeits-überwachungskamera, die; **be caught by a** ∼ **camera** bei einer Geschwindigkeitskontrolle geblitzt werden; ∼ **hump** ⇒ ∼ **bump**

speeding /'spiːdɪŋ/ n. (going too fast) zu schnelles Fahren; Rasen, das (ugs. abwertend); (exceeding speed limit) Geschwin-digkeitsüberschreitung, die (Verkehrsw.)

'**speed limit** n. Tempolimit, das; Geschwindig-keitsbeschränkung, die (Verkehrsw.)

speedometer /spiː'dɒmɪtə(r)/ n. Tachometer, der od. das

speed: ∼ **trap** n. Geschwindigkeitskontrolle, die; (with radar) Radarfalle, die (ugs.); ∼**way** n. (a) (motorcycle racing) Speedwayrennen, das; (b) (racetrack) Speedwaybahn, die

speedy /'spiːdɪ/ adj. schnell; umgehend, prompt ⟨Antwort⟩

spell[1] /spel/ **1** v.t., ∼**ed** or (Brit.) **spelt** /spelt/ (a) schreiben; (aloud) buchstabieren; (b) (form) **what do these letters/what does b-a-t** ∼? welches Wort ergeben diese Buchstaben/die Buchstaben b-a-t?; (c) (fig.: have as result) bedeuten; **that** ∼**s trouble** das bedeutet nichts Gutes. **2** v.i., ∼**ed** or (Brit.) **spelt** (say) buchstabieren; (write) richtig schreiben; **he can't** ∼: er kann keine Rechtschreibung (ugs.)

∼ '**out**, ∼ '**over** v.t. (a) (read letter by letter) [langsam] buchstabieren; (b) (fig.: explain precisely) genau erklären; genau darlegen

spell[2] n. Weile, die; **a** ∼ **of overseas service** eine Zeit lang Dienst in Übersee; **on Sunday it will be cloudy with some sunny** ∼**s** am Sonntag wolkig mit sonnigen Abschnitten; **a cold** ∼: eine Kälteperiode; **a long** ∼ **when ...:** eine lange Zeit, während der ...

spell[3] n. (a) (words used as a charm) Zauberspruch, der; **cast a** ∼ **over** or **on sb./sth., put a** ∼ **on sb./sth.:** jmdn./ etw. verzaubern; (b) (fascination) Zauber, der; **break the** ∼: den Bann brechen; **be under a** ∼: unter einem Bann stehen

spell: ∼**bound** adj. verzaubert; **he can hold his readers** ∼: er kann seine Leser in seinem Bann halten; ∼ **checker** ⇒ **spelling checker**

spelling /'spelɪŋ/ n. (a) Rechtschreibung, die; (b) (sequence of letters) Schreibweise, die

spelling: ∼ **bee** n. Rechtschreib[e]wettbewerb, der; ∼ **checker** n. (Computing) Rechtschreibprogramm, das; ∼ **mistake** n. Rechtschreibfehler, der

spelt ⇒ **spell**[1]

spend /spend/ v.t., **spent** /spent/ (a) (pay out) ausgeben; ∼ **money like water** or (coll.) as if it's going out of fashion sein od. das Geld mit beiden Händen ausgeben od. hinaus-werfen (ugs.); **it was money well spent** es hat sich ausge-zahlt; ∼ **a penny** (fig. coll.) mal verschwinden [müssen] (ugs.); (b) (use) aufwenden (**on** für)

'**spending money** n. (a) (Amer.) ⇒ **pocket money;** (b) (Brit.: sum intended for spending) verfügbares Geld

'**spendthrift** n. Verschwender, der/Verschwenderin, die

spent 1 ⇒ **spend. 2** adj. (a) (used up) verbraucht; ∼ **cartridge** leere Geschosshülse; (b) (drained of energy) er-schöpft; ausgelaugt; **a** ∼ **force** (fig.) eine Kraft, die sich erschöpft hat

sperm /spɜːm/ n., pl. ∼**s** or **same** (Biol.) (semen) Sperma, das

sperm: ∼ **bank** n. Samenbank, die; ∼ **count** n. Spermienzahl, die; ∼ **whale** n. Pottwal, der

spermicidal /spɜːmɪ'saɪdl/ adj. spermizid (Med.)

spermicide /'spɜːmɪsaɪd/ n. Spermizid, das (Med.)

spew /spjuː/ **1** v.t. spucken. **2** v.i. sich ergießen

∼ '**out 1** v.t. erbrechen, [aus]spucken ⟨Gegessenes⟩; ⟨Vul-kan:⟩ spucken, speien ⟨Lava⟩. **2** v.i. sich ergießen (**of, from** aus)

SPF abbr. **sun protection factor** LSF

sphere /sfɪə(r)/ n. (a) (field of action) Bereich, der; Sphäre, die (geh.); **be distinguished in many** ∼**s** sich auf vielen Gebieten ausgezeichnet haben; **that's outside my** ∼: das gehört nicht zu meinem Tätigkeitsbereich; ∼ **of influence** Einflussbereich, der; (b) (Geom.) Kugel, die

spherical /'sferɪkl/ adj. kugelförmig

spice /spaɪs/ **1** n. (a) Gewürz, das; (collectively) Gewürze Pl.; attrib. Gewürz-; (b) (fig.: excitement) Würze, die; **the** ∼ **of life** die Würze des Lebens. **2** v.t. würzen

spick /spɪk/ *adj.* ～ **and span** blitzblank *od.* -sauber (ugs.)

spicy /'spaɪsɪ/ *adj.* pikant; würzig

spider /'spaɪdə(r)/ *n.* Spinne, *die*

'spider's web (*Amer.:* **'spider web**) *n.* Spinnennetz, *das;* (fig.) Netz, *das*

spidery /'spaɪdərɪ/ *adj.* spinnenförmig; krakelig (ugs.) 〈*Schrift*〉

spike /spaɪk/ **1** *n.* **(a)** Stachel, *der;* (of running shoe) Spike, *der;* **(b)** *in pl.* (shoes) Spikes *Pl.* **2** *v.t.* **(a)** ～ **sb.'s guns** (fig.) jmdm. einen Strich durch die Rechnung machen (ugs.); **(b)** (coll.: add spirits or drugs to) **sb.** ～**d his drink** jmd. hat ihm etwas in seinen Drink getan

spiky /'spaɪkɪ/ *adj.* **(a)** (like a spike) spitz [zulaufend]; stachelig 〈*Haare*〉; **(b)** (having spikes) stach[e]lig

spill /spɪl/ **1** *v.t.,* **spilt** /spɪlt/ *or* ～**ed (a)** verschütten 〈*Flüssigkeit*〉; ～ **sth. on sth.** etw. auf etw. (*Akk.*) schütten; **(b)** (coll.: divulge) ausquatschen (salopp); ～ **the beans [to sb.]** [jmdm. gegenüber] aus der Schule plaudern; **not** ～ **the beans [to sb.]** [jmdm. gegenüber] dichthalten (ugs.). *See also* **milk** 1. **2** *v.i.,* **spilt** *or* ～**ed** überlaufen. **3** *n.* (fall) Sturz, *der*

～ **'over** *v.i.* überlaufen; (fig.) überquellen; 〈*Unruhen:*〉 sich ausbreiten

spillage /'spɪlɪdʒ/ *n.* **(a)** (act) Verschütten, *das;* ～ **of oil** (from tanker) das Auslaufen von Öl; **(b)** (quantity) Verschüttete, *das*

spilt ⇒ **spill** 1, 2

spin /spɪn/ **1** *v.t.,* **-nn-, spun** /spʌn/ **(a)** spinnen; ～ **a yarn** (fig.) ein Garn spinnen (bes. Seemannsspr.); fabulieren; **(b)** (in washing machine etc.) schleudern; **(c)** (cause to whirl round) [schnell] drehen; wirbeln [lassen]; ～ **a coin** eine Münze kreiseln lassen; (toss) eine Münze werfen. **2** *v.i.,* **-nn-, spun** sich drehen; **my head is** ～**ning** (fig.) (from noise) mir brummt der Schädel (ugs.); (from many impressions) mir schwirrt der Kopf. **3** *n.* **(a)** (whirl) **give sth. a** ～: etw. in Drehung versetzen; **(b)** (Aeronaut.) Trudeln, *das;* **(c)** (Sport: revolving motion) Effet, *der;* Spin, *der;* **(d)** (outing) **go for a** ～: einen Ausflug machen; **a** ～ **in the car** eine Spritztour mit dem Auto

～ **'out** *v.t.* **(a)** (prolong) in die Länge ziehen; **(b)** (use sparingly) ～ **one's money out until pay day** sein Geld bis zum Zahltag strecken

～ **'round 1** *v.i.* sich drehen; 〈*Person:*〉 sich [schnell] umdrehen. **2** *v.t.* [schnell] drehen

spinach /'spɪnɪdʒ/ *n.* Spinat, *der*

spinal /'spaɪnl/ *adj.* (Anat.) Wirbelsäulen-; Rückgrat[s]-

spinal: ～ **'column** *n.* Wirbelsäule, *die;* ～ **'cord** *n.* Rückenmark, *das*

spindle /'spɪndl/ *n.* Spindel, *die*

spindly /'spɪndlɪ/ *adj.* spindeldürr 〈*Person, Beine, Arme*〉

spin: ～ **doctor** *n.* (coll.) Spin-Doktor, *der;* ～**-'drier** *n.* Wäscheschleuder, *die;* Trockenschleuder, *die*

spin-'dry *v.t.* schleudern

spine /spaɪn/ *n.* **(a)** ▶ 672 (backbone) Wirbelsäule, *die;* **(b)** (Bot., Zool.) Stachel, *der;* **(c)** (of book) Buchrücken, *der*

spine: ～**-chiller** *n.* Schocker, *der* (ugs.); ～**-chilling** *adj.* gruselig

spineless /'spaɪnlɪs/ *adj.* (fig.) rückgratlos

spinney /'spɪnɪ/ *n.* (Brit.) Gehölz, *das*

spinning: ～ **top** *n.* Kreisel, *der;* ～ **wheel** *n.* Spinnrad, *das*

'spin-off *n.* Nebenprodukt, *das*

spinster /'spɪnstə(r)/ *n.* **(a)** ledige Frau; Junggesellin, *die;* **(b)** (derog.: old maid) alte Jungfer (abwertend)

spiny /'spaɪnɪ/ *adj.* dornig; stachelig

spiral /'spaɪrl/ **1** *adj.* spiralförmig; spiralig; ～ **spring** Spiralfeder, *die.* **2** *n.* Spirale, *die;* **the** ～ **of rising prices and wages** die Lohn-Preis-Spirale. **3** *v.i.* (Brit.) **-ll-** 〈*Weg:*〉 sich hochwinden; 〈*Kosten, Profite:*〉 in die Höhe klettern; 〈*Rauch:*〉 in einer Spirale aufsteigen

spiral 'staircase *n.* Wendeltreppe, *die*

spire /spaɪə(r)/ *n.* Turmspitze, *die*

spirit /'spɪrɪt/ **1** *n.* **(a)** *in pl.* (distilled liquor) Spirituosen *Pl.;* **(b)** (mental attitude) Geisteshaltung, *die;* **in the right/wrong**

～: mit der richtigen/falschen Einstellung; **take sth. in the wrong** ～: etw. falsch auffassen; **take sth. in the** ～ **in which it is meant** etw. so auffassen, wie es gemeint ist; **enter into the** ～ **of sth.** innerlich bei einer Sache [beteiligt] sein *od.* dabei sein; **(c)** (courage) Mut, *der;* **(d)** (vital principle, soul, inner qualities) Geist, *der;* **in** ～: innerlich; im Geiste; **be with sb. in** ～: in Gedanken *od.* im Geist[e] bei jmdm. sein; **(e)** (real meaning) Geist, *der;* Sinn, *der;* **(f)** (mental tendency) Geist, *der;* (mood) Stimmung, *die;* **the** ～ **of the age** *or* **times** der Zeitgeist; **(g)** *in pl.* (state of mind) Stimmung, *die;* gute Laune; **in poor** *or* **low** ～**s** niedergedrückt; **(h)** (liquid obtained by distillation) Spiritus, *der;* (purified alcohol) reiner Alkohol. **2** *v.t.* ～ **away,** ～ **off** verschwinden lassen

spirited /'spɪrɪtɪd/ *adj.* **(a)** beherzt 〈*Angriff, Versuch, Antwort, Verteidigung*〉; lebhaft 〈*Antwort*〉; **(b)** **low-/proud-**～: niedergedrückt/stolz; **high-**～: ausgelassen; temperamentvoll 〈*Pferd*〉; **mean-**～: gemein

'spirit level *n.* Wasserwaage, *die*

spiritual /'spɪrɪtʃʊəl/ **1** *adj.* spirituell (geh.); **his** ～ **home** seine geistige Heimat. **2** *n.* [Negro] ～: [Negro] Spiritual, *das*

spiritualism /'spɪrɪtʃʊəlɪzm/ *n.* Spiritismus, *der*

spiritualist /'spɪrɪtʃʊəlɪst/ *n.* Spiritist, *der*/Spiritistin, *die*

spit¹ /spɪt/ **1** *v.i.,* **-tt-, spat** /spæt/ *or* **spit (a)** spucken; **he spat in his enemy's face** er spuckte seinem Feind ins Gesicht; **(b)** (make angry noise) fauchen; ～ **at sb.** jmdn. anfauchen; **(c)** (rain lightly) ～ **[down]** tröpfeln (ugs.). **2** *v.t.,* **-tt-, spat** *or* **spit (a)** spucken; **(b)** (fig.: utter angrily) ～ **defiance at sb.** jmdn. trotzig anfauchen. **3** *n.* Spucke, *die;* ～ **and polish** (cleaning work) Putzen und Reinigen; Wienern, *das*

～ **'out** *v.t.* ausspucken; **she spat out the words** sie spuckte die Worte nur so aus; ～ **it out!** (fig. coll.) spuck es aus! (ugs.)

spit² *n.* **(a)** (point of land) Halbinsel, *die;* **(b)** (reef) Riff, *das;* (shoal) Untiefe, *die;* (sandbank) Sandbank, *die;* **(c)** (for roasting meat) Spieß, *der*

spite /spaɪt/ **1** *n.* **(a)** (malice) Boshaftigkeit, *die;* **(b)** **in** ～ **of** trotz; **in** ～ **of oneself** obwohl man es eigentlich nicht will. **2** *v.t.* ärgern; **cut off one's nose to** ～ **one's face** sich (*Dat. od. Akk.*) ins eigene Fleisch schneiden

spiteful /'spaɪtfl/ *adj.,* **spitefully** /'spaɪtfəlɪ/ *adv.* boshaft; gehässig (abwertend)

spitting 'image *n.* **be the** ～ **of sb.** jmdm. wie aus dem Gesicht geschnitten sein

spittle /'spɪtl/ *n.* Spucke, *die;* Speichel, *der*

spiv /spɪv/ *n.* (Brit. sl.) **(a)** (person living by his wits) smarter kleiner Geschäftemacher; **(b)** (black-market dealer) Schwarzhändler, *der;* Schieber, *der* (ugs.)

splash /splæʃ/ **1** *v.t.* **(a)** spritzen; ～ **sb./sth. with sth.** jmdn./etw. mit etw. bespritzen; **(b)** (Journ.) als Aufmacher bringen 〈*Story usw.*〉. **2** *v.i.* **(a)** (fly about in drops) spritzen; **(b)** (cause liquid to fly about) [umher]spritzen; **(c)** (move with ～ing) platschen (ugs.). **3** *n.* **(a)** Spritzen, *das;* **hit the water with a** ～: ins Wasser platschen (ugs.); **make a [big]** ～ (fig.) Furore machen; **(b)** (liquid) Spritzer, *der;* **(c)** (noise) Plätschern, *das*

～ **a'bout** *v.i.* herumspritzen (ugs.); [herum]planschen

～ **'out** *v.i.* (coll.) ～ **out on sth.** für etw. unbekümmert Geld ausgeben

splay /spleɪ/ **1** *v.t.* **(a)** (spread) ～ **[out]** spreizen; **(b)** (construct with divergent sides) ausschrägen. **2** *v.i.* 〈*Linien:*〉 [schräg] auseinander laufen; 〈*Tischbeine, Stuhlbeine:*〉 schräg nach außen gehen; 〈*Finger, Zehen:*〉 gespreizt sein

spleen /spliːn/ *n.* ▶ 672 Milz, *die*

splendid /'splendɪd/ *adj.* (excellent, outstanding) großartig; (beautiful) herrlich; (sumptuous, magnificent) prächtig

splendour (*Brit.; Amer.:* **splendor**) /'splendə(r)/ *n.* **(a)** (magnificence) Pracht, *die;* **(b)** (brightness) Glanz, *der*

splice /splaɪs/ *v.t.* **(a)** (join ends of by interweaving) verspleißen (Seemannsspr.); **(b)** (join in overlapping position) [an den Enden überlappend] zusammenfügen; zusammenkleben 〈*Filmstreifen usw.*〉

splint /splɪnt/ *n.* Schiene, *die;* **put sb.'s arm in a** ∼: jmds. Arm schienen

splinter /'splɪntə(r)/ *n.* Splitter, *der*

'splinter group *n.* Splittergruppe, *die*

split /splɪt/ **1** *n.* **(a)** (tear) Riß, *der;* **(b)** (division into parts) [Auf]teilung, *die;* **(c)** (fig.: rift) Spaltung, *die;* **a** ∼ **between Moscow and her allies** ein Bruch zwischen Moskau und seinen Verbündeten; **(d)** (Gymnastics, Skating) **the** ∼**s** *or* (Amer.) ∼: Spagat, *der od. das;* **do the** ∼**s** Spagat machen. **2** *adj.* gespalten; **be** ∼ **on a question** [sich (*Dat.*)] in einer Frage uneins sein. **3** *v.t.,* **-tt-, split (a)** (tear) zerreißen; **(b)** (divide) teilen; spalten ‹*Holz*›; ∼ **persons/ things into groups** Personen/Dinge in Gruppen (*Akk.*) aufteilen *od.* einteilen; ∼ **the difference** sich in der Mitte treffen; ∼ **hairs** (fig.) Haare spalten; **(c)** (divide into disagreeing parties) spalten; **(d)** (remove by breaking) ∼ **[off** *or* **away]** abbrechen. **4** *v.i.,* **-tt-, split (a)** (break into parts) ‹*Holz*:› splittern; ‹*Stoff, Seil*:› reißen; **(b)** (divide into parts) sich teilen; ‹*Gruppe*:› sich spalten; ‹*zwei Personen*:› sich trennen; **(c)** (be removed by breaking) ∼ **from** absplittern von; ∼ **apart** zersplittern; **(d)** (sl.: depart) abhauen (ugs.)
∼ **a'way** *v.i.* absplittern; ∼ **away from** absplittern von; ‹*Parteiflügel, Gruppierung*:› sich abspalten von
∼ **'off 1** *v.t.* abspalten. **2** *v.i.* ⇒ ∼ **away**
∼ **on** *v.t.* (coll.) ∼ **on sb.** [**to sb.**] jmdn. [bei jmdm.] verpfeifen (ugs.)
∼ **'open 1** *v.i.* aufbrechen. **2** *v.t.* öffnen ‹*Nuss, Schote*›; **he** ∼ **his head open** er hat sich (*Dat.*) den Kopf aufgeschlagen
∼ **'up 1** *v.t.* aufteilen. **2** *v.i.* (coll.) sich trennen; ∼ **up with sb.** sich von jmdm. trennen; mit jmdm. Schluss machen (ugs.)

split: ∼ **in'finitive** *n.* (Ling.) *Konstruktion im Englischen, bei der zwischen 'to' und Infinitiv ein Adverb eingeschoben wird;* ∼**-level** *adj.* mit Zwischengeschoss; auf zwei Ebenen; ∼ **perso'nality** *n.* gespaltene Persönlichkeit (Psych.); ∼ **'second** *n.* **in a** ∼ **second** im Bruchteil einer Sekunde; ∼**-second timing** [zeitliche] Abstimmung auf die Sekunde genau

splitting /'splɪtɪŋ/ *adj.* **a** ∼ **headache** rasende Kopfschmerzen

splutter /'splʌtə(r)/ **1** *v.i.* ‹*Feuer, Gaslampe*:› flackern; ‹*Fett*:› spritzen; ‹*Person*:› prusten; ‹*Motor*:› stottern; ∼ **with rage/indignation** vor Wut/Entrüstung schnauben. **2** *v.t.* stottern ‹*Worte*›

spoil /spɔɪl/ **1** *v.t.,* ∼**t** /spɔɪlt/ *or* ∼**ed (a)** (impair) verderben; ruinieren ‹*Leben*›; **the news** ∼**t his dinner/ evening** die Nachricht verdarb ihm das Essen/den Abend; ∼**t ballot papers** ungültige Stimmzettel; **(b)** (injure character of) verderben (geh.); verziehen ‹*Kind*›; ∼ **sb. for sth.** jmdn. für etw. zu anspruchsvoll machen; **(c)** (pamper) verwöhnen; **be** ∼**t for choice** die Qual der Wahl haben. **2** *v.i.,* ∼**t** *or* ∼**ed (a)** (go bad) verderben; **(b) be** ∼**ing for a fight/for trouble** Streit/Ärger suchen. **3** *n.* (plunder) ∼**[s]** Beute, *die*

spoiler /'spɔɪlə(r)/ *n.* (of car, aircraft) Spoiler, *der;* (of glider) Bremsklappe, *die*

'spoilsport *n.* Spielverderber, *der*/-verderberin, *die*

spoilt 1 ⇒ **spoil 1, 2. 2** *adj.* verzogen ‹*Kind*›

spoke[1] /spəʊk/ *n.* Speiche, *die;* **put a** ∼ **in sb.'s wheel** (fig.) jmdm. einen Knüppel zwischen die Beine werfen

spoke[2]**, spoken** ⇒ **speak**

spokesman /'spəʊksmən/ *n., pl.* **spokesmen** /'spəʊksmən/ Sprecher, *der*

spokesperson /'spəʊkspɜːsn/ *n.* Sprecher, *der*/Sprecherin, *die*

spokeswoman /'spəʊkswʊmən/ *n.* Sprecherin, *die*

sponge /spʌndʒ/ **1** *n.* **(a)** Schwamm, *der;* **(b)** ⇒ **sponge cake; sponge pudding. 2** *v.t.* **(a)** ⇒ **cadge 1; (b)** (wipe) mit einem Schwamm waschen
∼ **off** *v.t.* **(a)** /-'-/ (wipe off) mit einem Schwamm abwischen; (wash off) mit einem Schwamm abwaschen; **(b)** /'--/ ⇒ ∼ **on**
∼ **on** *v.t.* ∼ **on sb.** bei *od.* von jmdm. schnorren

sponge: ∼ **bag** *n.* (Brit.) Kulturbeutel, *der;* ∼ **cake** *n.* Biskuitkuchen, *der;* ∼ **'pudding** *n.* Schwammpudding, *der* (Kochk.)

sponger /'spʌndʒə(r)/ *n.* Schmarotzer, *der*/Schmarotzerin, *die;* Schnorrer, *der*/Schnorrerin, *die*

spongy /'spʌndʒɪ/ *adj.* schwammig

sponsor /'spɒnsə(r)/ **1** *n.* Sponsor, *der.* **2** *v.t.* **(a)** sponsern ‹*Wohlfahrtsverband, Teilnehmer, Programm, Veranstaltung*›; **(b)** (support in election) unterstützen ‹*Kandidaten*›; ∼ **sb.** jmds. Kandidatur unterstützen

sponsored /'spɒnsəd/ *adj.* gesponsert; finanziell gefördert; ∼ **run** *als Wohltätigkeitsveranstaltung durchgeführter Dauerlauf* mit gesponserten Teilnehmern

sponsorship /'spɒnsəʃɪp/ *n.* **(a)** (financial support) Sponsorschaft, *die;* **(b)** (support of candidate) Unterstützung, *die;* **the party's** ∼ **of sb.** die Unterstützung von jmds. Kandidatur durch die Partei

spontaneous /spɒn'teɪnɪəs/ *adj.* spontan; **make a** ∼ **offer of sth.** spontan etw. anbieten

spontaneous com'bustion *n.* Selbstentzündung, *die*

spoof /spuːf/ (coll.) *n.* Veralberung, *die* **(of, on** von); Parodie, *die* **(of, on** auf + *Akk.*)

spook /spuːk/ *n.* (joc.) Geist, *der;* Gespenst, *das*

spooky /'spuːkɪ/ *adj.* gespenstisch

spool /spuːl/ *n.* Spule, *die*

spoon /spuːn/ *n.* Löffel, *der;* **be born with a silver** ∼ **in one's mouth** mit einem goldenen *od.* silbernen Löffel im Mund geboren werden

spoonerism /'spuːnərɪzm/ *n.* witziges Vertauschen der Anfangsbuchstaben o. Ä. von zwei oder mehr Wörtern (*wie bei „Leichenzehrer" für „Zeichenlehrer"*)

'spoon-feed *v.t.* mit dem Löffel füttern; ∼ **sb.** (fig.) jmdm. alles vorkauen (ugs.)

spoonful /'spuːnfʊl/ *n.* **a** ∼ **of sugar** ein Löffel [voll] Zucker

sporadic /spə'rædɪk/ *adj.* sporadisch; vereinzelt ‹*Schauer, Schüsse*›

spore /spɔː(r)/ *n.* Spore, *die*

sport /spɔːt/ **1** *n.* **(a)** (pastime) Sport, *der;* ∼**s** Sportarten; **team/winter/water/indoor** ∼: Mannschafts-/Winter-/Wasser-/Hallensport, *der;* **(b)** *no pl., no art.* (collectively) Sport, *der;* **go in for** ∼, **do** ∼: Sport treiben; **(c)** *in pl.* (Brit.) **[athletic]** ∼**s** Athletik, *die;* **S**∼**s Day** (Sch.) Sportfest, *das;* **(d)** *no pl., no art.* (dated: fun) Spaß, *der;* **do/say sth. in** ∼: etw. im *od.* zum Scherz tun/sagen; **(e)** (coll.: easygoing person) **be a [real]** ∼: ein prima Kerl sein (ugs.); [schwer] in Ordnung sein (ugs.); **be a** ∼! sei kein Spielverderber!; **Aunt Joan is a real** ∼: Tante Joan ist echt (ugs.) in Ordnung; **be a good/bad** ∼ (in games) ein guter/schlechter Verlierer sein. **2** *v.t.* stolz tragen ‹*Kleidungsstück*›

sporting /'spɔːtɪŋ/ *adj.* **(a)** (interested in sport) sportlich; **(b)** (generous) großzügig; (fair) fair; anständig; **give sb. a** ∼ **chance** jmdm. eine [faire] Chance geben; **(c)** (relating to sport) Sport-

sports: ∼ **bra** *n.* Sport-BH, *der;* ∼ **car** *n.* Sportwagen, *der;* ∼ **centre** *n.* Sportzentrum, *das;* ∼ **channel** *n.* Sportkanal, *der;* ∼ **complex** *n.* Sportzentrum, *das;* ∼ **field** *n.* Sportplatz, *der;* ∼ **hall** *n.* Sporthalle, *die;* ∼ **jacket** *n.* sportlicher Sakko; ∼**man** /'spɔːtsmən/ *n., pl.* ∼**men** /'spɔːtsmən/ Sportler, *der*

sportsmanship /'spɔːtsmənʃɪp/ *n., no pl.* **(a)** (fairness) [sportliche] Fairness; **(b)** (skill) sportliche Leistung

sports: ∼ **programme** *n.* (Radio, Telev.) Sportsendung, *die;* ∼**wear** *n., no pl.* Sport[be]kleidung, *die;* ∼**woman** *n.* Sportlerin, *die*

sporty /'spɔːtɪ/ *adj.* **(a)** (coll.: sport-loving) sportlich; **the whole family is** ∼: die ganze Familie ist sportbegeistert; **(b)** (jaunty) sportlich ‹*Aussehen*›; **wear one's hat at a** ∼ **angle** seinen Hut flott aufgesetzt haben

spot /spɒt/ **1** *n.* **(a)** (precise place) Stelle, *die;* **on this** ∼: an dieser Stelle; **on the** ∼ (fig.) (instantly) auf der Stelle; **be on the** ∼ (be present) zur Stelle sein; **be in/get into/get out of a [tight]** ∼ (fig. coll.) in der Klemme sitzen/sich aus einer brenzligen Lage befreien (ugs.); **put sb. on the** ∼ (fig. coll.: cause difficulties for sb.) jmdn. in Verlegenheit bringen; **(b)** (inhabited place) Ort, *der;*

a nice ~ **on the Moselle** ein hübscher Flecken an der Mosel; (c) (suitable area) Platz, *der;* **holiday/sun** ~: Ferienort, *der/*Ferienort [mit Sonnengarantie]; **picnic** ~: Picknickplatz, *der;* **hit the high** ~s (coll.) groß ausgehen; (d) (dot) Tupfen, *der;* Tupfer, *der;* (larger) Flecken, *der;* **knock** ~s **off sb.** (fig. coll.) jmdn. in die Pfanne hauen (ugs.); **see** ~s **before one's eyes** Sterne sehen (ugs.); (e) (stain) ~ [of blood/ grease/ink] [Blut-/Fett-/Tinten]fleck, *der;* (f) (Brit. coll.: small amount) **do a** ~ **of work/sewing** ein bisschen arbeiten/nähen; **how about a** ~ **of lunch?** wie wärs mit einem Bissen zu Mittag?; **have** *or* **be in a** ~ **of bother** *or* **trouble** etwas Ärger haben; (g) (drop) **a** ~ *or* **a few** ~s **of rain** ein paar Regentropfen; (h) (area on body) [Körper]stelle, *die;* **have a weak** ~ (fig.) eine Schwachstelle haben; *see also* **sore 1 a;** (i) (Telev. coll.: position in programme) Sendezeit, *die;* **the 7 o'clock** ~: das Siebenuhrprogramm; (j) (Med.) Pickel, *der;* **heat** ~: Hitzebläschen, *das;* **break out in** ~s einen Ausschlag bekommen; (k) (on dice, dominoes) Punkt, *der;* (l) (spotlight) Spot, *der.* **2** *v.t.,* **-tt-:** (a) (detect) entdecken; identifizieren ‹*Verbrecher*›; erkennen ‹*Gefahr*›; (b) (take note of) erkennen ‹*Flugzeugtyp, Vogel, Talent*›; **go train-/plane-**~**ting** Zug-/Flugzeugtypen bestimmen; (c) (coll.: pick out) tippen auf (+ *Akk.*) ‹*Sieger, Gewinner usw.*›; (d) (stain) beflecken; (with ink or paint) beklecksen; (with mud) beschmutzen

spot: ~ '**check** *n.* (test made immediately) sofortige Überprüfung (**on** *Gen.*); (test made on randomly selected subject) Stichprobe, *die;* ~**-check** *v.t.* stichprobenweise überprüfen; ~**lamp** *n. see* **spotlight** (a), (b)

spotless /'spɒtlɪs/ *adj.* (a) (immaculate) **her house is absolutely** ~: ihr Haus ist makellos sauber; (b) (fig.: blameless) mustergültig; untadelig ‹*Charakter*›

spot: ~**light 1** *n.* (a) (Theatre) [Bühnen]scheinwerfer, *der;* (b) (Motor Veh.) Weitstrahler, *der;* (c) (fig.: attention) **be in the** ~**light** im Rampenlicht [der Öffentlichkeit] stehen; **keep out of the** ~**light** sich von der Öffentlichkeit fernhalten; **2** *v.t.,* ~**lighted** *or* ~**lit** (a) (Theatre) [mit dem Scheinwerfer] anstrahlen; (b) (fig.: highlight) in den Blickpunkt der Öffentlichkeit bringen; ~ '**on** (coll.) **1** *adj.* goldrichtig (ugs.); **I was** ~ **on** ich lag genau richtig (ugs.); **your estimate was** ~ **on** mit deiner Schätzung hast du ins Schwarze getroffen; **2** *adv.* haargenau (ugs.)

spotted /'spɒtɪd/ *adj.* (a) gepunktet; (b) (Zool.) ~ **woodpecker/hyena** Buntspecht, *der/*Tüpfelhyäne, *die*

spotty /'spɒtɪ/ *adj.* (a) (spotted) gefleckt; (stained) fleckig; (b) (pimply) picklig; **be** ~: viele Pickel haben

spouse /spaʊz, spaʊs/ *n.* [Ehe]gatte, *der/*-gattin, *die;* (joc.) Angetraute, *der/die;* Gemahl, *der/*Gemahlin, *die*

spout /spaʊt/ **1** *n.* Schnabel, *der;* (of water pump) [Auslauf]rohr, *das;* (of tap) Ausflussrohr, *das;* **be up the** ~ (coll.: ruined) im Eimer sein (ugs.). **2** *v.t.* (a) (discharge) ausstoßen ‹*Wasser, Lava, Öl*›; (b) (declaim) deklamieren ‹*Verse*›; (rattle off) herunterrasseln (ugs.) ‹*Zahlen, Fakten usw.*›; ~ **nonsense** Unsinn verzapfen (ugs.). **3** *v.i.* (a) (gush) schießen (**from** aus); (b) (declaim) schwadronieren (abwertend); schwafeln (ugs. abwertend)

~ '**out** *v.i.* herausströmen; ~ **out of sth.** aus etw. strömen

sprain /spreɪn/ ▶865 **1** *v.t.* verstauchen; ~ **one's ankle/wrist** sich (*Dat.*) den Knöchel/das Handgelenk verstauchen. **2** *n.* Verstauchung, *die*

sprang ⇒ **spring 2, 3**

sprawl /sprɔːl/ **1** *n.* (a) (slump) **lie in a** ~: ausgestreckt [da]liegen; (b) (straggle) verstreute Ansammlung. **2** *v.i.* (a) (spread oneself) sich ausstrecken; (b) (fall) der Länge nach hinfallen; (c) (straggle) sich ausbreiten

sprawling /'sprɔːlɪŋ/ *attrib. adj.* (a) (extended) ausgestreckt [liegend]; (b) (falling) der Länge nach hinfallend; (c) (straggling) verstreut liegend ‹*Gebäude*›; wuchernd ‹*Großstadt*›

spray¹ /spreɪ/ *n.* (a) (bouquet) Strauß, *der;* (b) (branch) Zweig, *der;* (of palm or fern) Wedel, *der*

spray² /spreɪ/ **1** *v.t.* (a) (in a stream) spritzen; (in a mist) sprühen ‹*Parfum, Farbe, Spray*›; lackieren ‹*Auto*›; **they** ~**ed the general's car with bullets** sie durchsiebten den Wagen des Generals mit Kugeln; (b) (treat) besprühen ‹*Haar, Haut, Pflanze*›; spritzen ‹*Nutzpflanzen*›. **2** *v.i.* spritzen. **3** *n.* (a) (drops) Sprühnebel, *der;* (b) (liquid) Spray, *der od. das;* (c) (container) Spraydose, *die;* (in gardening) Spritze, *die;* **hair/throat** ~: Haar-/Rachenspray, *der od. das*

~ **on** [**to**] *v.t.* ~ **sth. on** [**to**] **sth.** etw. mit etw. besprühen

'spray can *n.* Spraydose, *die*

spread /spred/ **1** *v.t.,* **spread** (a) ausbreiten ‹*Tuch, Landkarte*› (**on** auf + *Dat.*); streichen ‹*Butter, Farbe, Marmelade*›; (b) (cover) ~ **a roll with marmalade/butter** ein Brötchen mit Marmelade/Butter bestreichen; **the sofa was** ~ **with a blanket** auf dem Sofa lag eine Decke [ausgebreitet]; (c) (fig.: display) **a magnificent view was** ~ **before us** uns (*Dat.*) bot sich eine herrliche Aussicht; (d) (extend range of) verbreiten; (e) (distribute) verteilen; (untidily) verstreuen; streuen ‹*Dünger*›; verbreiten ‹*Zerstörung, Angst, Niedergeschlagenheit*›; (f) (make known) verbreiten; ~ **the word** (tell news) es weitersagen; (g) (separate) ausbreiten ‹*Arme*›. **2** *v.i.* **spread** (a) sich ausbreiten; **a smile** ~ **across** *or* **over his face** ein Lächeln breitete sich (geh.) über sein Gesicht; **margarine** ~s **easily** Margarine lässt sich leicht streichen; ~ **like wildfire** sich in *od.* mit Windeseile verbreiten; (b) (scatter, disperse) sich verteilen; **the odour** ~s **through the room** der Geruch breitet sich im ganzen Zimmer aus; (c) (circulate) ‹*Neuigkeiten, Gerücht, Kenntnis usw.*› sich verbreiten. **3** *n.* (a) (expanse) Fläche, *die;* (b) (span) (of tree) Kronendurchmesser, *der;* (of wings) Spann[weite], *die;* (c) (breadth) **have a wide** ~ ‹*Interessen, Ansichten*› breit gefächert sein; (d) (extension) Verbreitung, *die;* (of city, urbanization, poverty) Ausbreitung, *die;* (e) (diffusion) Ausbreitung, *die;* (of learning, knowledge) Verbreitung, *die;* Vermittlung, *die;* (f) (distribution) Verteilung, *die;* (g) (coll.: meal) Festessen, *das;* (h) (paste) Brotaufstrich, *der;* ‹*Rindfleisch-, Lachs*›paste, *die;* ‹*Käse-, Erdnuss-, Schokoladen*›krem, *die*

~ **a'bout,** ~ **a'round** *v.t.* (a) verbreiten ‹*Neuigkeiten, Gerücht usw.*›; (b) (strew) verstreuen

~ '**out 1** *v.t.* (a) (extend) ausbreiten ‹*Arme*›; (b) (space out) verteilen ‹*Soldaten, Tänzer, Pfosten*›; legen ‹*Karten*›; ausbreiten ‹*Papiere*›. **2** *v.i.* sich verteilen; ‹*Soldaten*› ausschwärmen

'spreadsheet *n.* (Computing) Arbeitsblatt, *das*

spree /spriː/ *n.* (a) (spending ~) Einkaufsorgie, *die* (ugs.); **go on a shopping** ~: ganz groß einkaufen gehen; (b) **be/go out on the** ~ (coll.) einen draufmachen (ugs.)

'spree killer *n.* Amokläufer, *der/*-läuferin, *die*

sprig /sprɪg/ *n.* Zweig, *der*

sprightly /'spraɪtlɪ/ *adj.* munter

spring /sprɪŋ/ **1** *n.* (a) ▶1065 (season) Frühling, *der;* **in** ~ **1969, in the** ~ **of 1969** im Frühjahr 1969; **in early/late** ~: zu Anfang/Ende des Frühjahrs; **last/next** ~: letzten/nächsten Frühling; **in** [**the**] ~: im Frühling *od.* Frühjahr; (b) (source, lit. or fig.) Quelle, *die;* (c) (Mech.) Feder, *die;* ~s (vehicle suspension) Federung, *die;* (d) (jump) Sprung, *der;* **make a** ~ **at sb./at an animal** sich auf jmdn./ein Tier stürzen; (e) (elasticity) Elastizität, *die;* **walk with a** ~ **in one's step** mit beschwingten Schritten gehen. **2** *v.i.,* **sprang** /spræŋ/ *or* (Amer.) **sprung** /sprʌŋ/, **sprung** (a) (jump) springen; ~ [**up**] **from sth.** von etw. aufspringen; ~ **to one's feet** aufspringen; ~ **to sb.'s assistance/defence** jmdm. beispringen; (b) (arise) entspringen (**from** *Dat.*); ‹*Saat, Hoffnung*› keimen; ~ **to fame** über Nacht bekannt werden; ~ **to mind** jmdm. einfallen; (c) (recoil) ~ **back into position** zurückschnellen; ~ **to** *or* **shut** ‹*Tür, Falle, Deckel*› zuschnappen. **3** *v.t.,* **sprang** *or* (Amer.) **sprung**, **sprung** (a) (make known suddenly) ~ **a new idea on sb.** jmdn. mit einer neuen Idee überfallen; ~ **a surprise on sb.** jmdn. überraschen; (b) aufspringen lassen ‹*Schloss*›; zuschnappen lassen ‹*Falle*›; (c) (coll.: set free) herausholen (**from** aus)

~ '**back** *v.i.* zurückschnellen

~ '**from** *v.t.* (a) (appear from) [plötzlich] herkommen; (originate from) herrühren von; ‹*Person*› abstammen von

~ '**up** *v.i.* ‹*Wind, Zweifel*› aufkommen; ‹*Gebäude*› aus dem Boden wachsen; ‹*Pflanze*› aus dem Boden schießen; ‹*Organisation, Freundschaft*› entstehen

spring: ∼ '**binder** n. Klemmmappe, die; ∼**board** n. (Sport; also fig.) Sprungbrett, das; (in circus) Schleuderbrett, das; ∼ '**chicken** n. (a) (fowl) junges Hähnchen; (b) (fig.: person) be no ∼ **chicken** nicht mehr der/die Jüngste sein (ugs.); ∼-'**clean** 1 n. [großer] Hausputz; (in spring) Frühjahrsputz, der; 2 v.t. ∼-**clean** [the whole house] [großen] Hausputz/Frühjahrsputz machen; ∼-**loaded** adj. mit Sprungfeder nachgestellt; ∼ '**onion** n. Frühlingszwiebel, die; ∼ '**tide** n. Springflut, die; ∼**time** n. Frühling, der

springy /'sprɪŋɪ/ adj. elastisch; federnd ⟨Schritt, Brett, Boden⟩

sprinkle /'sprɪŋkl/ v.t. streuen; sprengen ⟨Flüssigkeit⟩; ∼ sth. over/on sth. etw. über/auf etw. (Akk.) streuen/ sprengen; ∼ sth. with sth. etw. mit etw. bestreuen/besprengen

sprinkler /'sprɪŋklə(r)/ n. (a) (Hort.: for watering) Sprinkler, der; (Agric.) Regner, der; (b) (fire extinguisher) ∼s, ∼ system Sprinkleranlage, die

sprinkling /'sprɪŋklɪŋ/ n. a ∼ of snow/sugar/dust eine dünne Schneedecke / Zucker- / Staubschicht; there was only a ∼ of holidaymakers on the beach nur ein paar vereinzelte Urlauber waren am Strand

sprint /sprɪnt/ 1 v.t. & i. rennen; sprinten (bes. Sport); spurten (bes. Sport). 2 n. Sprint, der (bes. Sport); the hundred-metres ∼ der Hundertmeterlauf

sprinter /'sprɪntə(r)/ n. Sprinter, der/Sprinterin, die

spritzer /'sprɪtsə(r)/ n. (Amer.) Schorle, die

sprocket /'sprɒkɪt/ n. (Mech. Engin.) Zahn, der

'**sprocket-wheel** n. (Mech. Engin.) [Ketten]zahnrad, das

sprout /spraʊt/ 1 n. (a) in pl. (coll.) ⇒ **Brussels sprouts;** (b) (Bot.) ⇒ **shoot** 3 a. 2 v.i. (a) (lit. or fig.) sprießen (geh.); (b) (grow) emporschießen; (c) (fig.) ⟨Gebäude:⟩ wie Pilze aus dem Boden schießen. 3 v.t. [aus]treiben ⟨Blüten, Knospen⟩; sich (Dat.) wachsen lassen ⟨Bart⟩

spruce /spruːs/ 1 adj. gepflegt; look ∼: adrett aussehen. 2 n. (Bot.) Fichte, die. 3 v.t. ∼ up verschönern; ∼ the house up das [ganze] Haus aufräumen und putzen; get ∼d up sich feinmachen (ugs.)

sprung /sprʌŋ/ 1 ⇒ **spring** 2, 3. 2 attrib. adj. gefedert

spry /spraɪ/ adj. rege

spud /spʌd/ n. (Brit. coll.: potato) Kartoffel, die

spun ⇒ **spin** 1, 2

spur /spɜː(r)/ 1 n. (a) Sporn, der; (b) (fig.: stimulus) Ansporn, der (to für); on the ∼ of the moment ganz spontan. 2 v.t., -rr-: (a) die Sporen geben (+ Dat.) ⟨Pferd⟩; (b) (fig.: incite) anspornen; ∼ sb. [on] to sth./to do sth. jmdn. zu etw. anspornen/anspornen, etw. zu tun; (c) (fig.: stimulate) hervorrufen; in Gang setzen ⟨Aktivität⟩; erregen ⟨Interesse⟩

spurious /'spjʊərɪəs/ adj. unaufrichtig ⟨Charakter, Verhalten⟩; gespielt ⟨Gefühl, Interesse⟩; zweifelhaft ⟨Anspruch, Vergnügen⟩; falsch ⟨Name, Münze⟩

spurn /spɜːn/ v.t. zurückweisen; abweisen; ausschlagen ⟨Angebot, Gelegenheit⟩

spurt[1] /spɜːt/ 1 n. Spurt, der (bes. Sport); final ∼: Endspurt, der; there was a ∼ of activity es brach kurzzeitig lebhafte Aktivität aus; in a sudden ∼ of energy in einem plötzlichen Anfall von Energie; put on a ∼: einen Spurt einlegen. 2 v.i. spurten (bes. Sport)

spurt[2] 1 v.i. ∼ out [from or of] herausspritzen [aus]; ∼ from spritzen aus. 2 v.t. the wound ∼ed blood aus der Wunde spritzte Blut. 3 n. Strahl, der

spy /spaɪ/ 1 n. (a) (secret agent) Spion, der/Spionin, die; (b) (watcher) Spion, der/Spionin, die; Schnüffler, der/Schnüfflerin, die (abwertend); ∼ in the sky/cab (coll.) Spionagesatellit, der/Fahrt[en]schreiber, der. 2 v.t. (literary) ausmachen. 3 v.i. (watch closely) [herum]spionieren; (practise espionage) Spionage treiben; ∼ on sb./a country jmdn. nachspionieren/gegen ein Land spionieren

∼ '**out** v.t. aufspüren; ausspionieren ⟨Feind, feindliche Stellung⟩; ∼ out the land (lit. or fig.) die Lage erkunden

spy: ∼-**ring** n. Spionagering, der; ∼ **satellite** n. Spionagesatellit, der

sq., Sq. abbr. **square, Square**

squabble /'skwɒbl/ 1 n. Streit, der; petty ∼s kleine Streitereien; have a ∼ [with sb. about sth.] sich [mit jmdm. wegen einer Sache] streiten. 2 v.i. sich zanken (over, about wegen)

squad /skwɒd/ n. (a) (Mil.) Gruppe, die; Trupp, der; (b) (group) Mannschaft, die; (c) (Police) **Drug/Fraud S∼:** Rauschgift-/Betrugsdezernat, das; ∼ **car** (Amer.) Einsatzwagen, der

squadron /'skwɒdrən/ n. (a) (Mil.) (of tanks) Bataillon, das; (of cavalry) Schwadron, die; (b) (Navy) Geschwader, das; (c) (Air Force) Staffel, die

squalid /'skwɒlɪd/ adj. (a) (dirty) [abstoßend] schmutzig; (b) (poor) schäbig; armselig; (c) (fig.: sordid) abstoßend

squall /skwɔːl/ n. (gust) Bö, die

squalor /'skwɒlə(r)/ n., no pl. Schmutz, der; live in ∼: in Schmutz und Elend leben

squander /'skwɒndə(r)/ v.t. vergeuden ⟨Talent, Zeit, Geld⟩; verschleudern ⟨Ersparnisse, Vermögen⟩; nicht nutzen ⟨Chance, Gelegenheit⟩

square /skweə(r)/ 1 n. (a) (Geom.) Quadrat, das; (b) (object, arrangement) Quadrat, das; **carpet** ∼: Teppichfliese, die; (c) (on board in game) Feld, das; **be or go back to** ∼ **one** (fig. coll.) wieder von vorn anfangen müssen; (d) (open area) Platz, der; (e) (scarf) [quadratisches] Tuch; **silk** ∼: Seidentuch, das; (f) (Mil.: drill area) Kasernenhof, der; (g) (Math.: product) Quadrat, das; (h) (coll.: old-fashioned person) Spießer, der/Spießerin, die (abwertend). 2 adj. (a) quadratisch; (b) ▶643⏐ a ∼ **foot/mile/metre** etc. ein Quadratfuß/eine Quadratmeile/ein Quadratmeter usw.; a foot ∼: ein Fuß im Quadrat; (c) (right-angled) rechtwink[e]lig; ∼ with or to im rechten Winkel zu; (d) (stocky) gedrungen ⟨Statur, Gestalt⟩; (e) (in outline) rechteckig; eckig ⟨Schultern, Kinn⟩; (f) (quits) quitt (ugs.); be [all] ∼: [völlig] quitt sein (ugs.); ⟨Spieler:⟩ gleich stehen; ⟨Spiel:⟩ unentschieden stehen. 3 adv. breit ⟨sitzen⟩; put sth. ∼ in the middle of sth. etw. mitten auf etw. (Akk.) stellen; the ball hit him ∼ on the head der Ball traf ihn genau am Kopf. 4 v.t. (a) (make right-angled) rechtwinklig machen; vierkantig zuschneiden ⟨Holz⟩; (b) (place ∼ly) ∼ one's shoulders seine Schultern straffen; (c) (divide into ∼s) in Karos einteilen; ∼d paper kariertes Papier; (d) ▶956⏐ (Math.: multiply) quadrieren; 3 ∼d is 9 3 [im] Quadrat ist 9; 3 hoch 2 ist 9; (e) (reconcile) ∼ sth. with sth. etw. mit etw. in Einklang bringen; (f) ∼ it with sb. (coll.: get sb.'s approval) es mit jmdm. klären; (g) (Sport) ∼ the match gleichziehen. 5 v.i. (be consistent) übereinstimmen; sth. does not ∼ with sth. etw. steht nicht im Einklang mit etw.; it just does not ∼: hier stimmt doch etwas nicht ∼ '**up** v.i. (settle up) abrechnen

square: ∼ '**brackets** n. pl. eckige Klammern; '**deal** n. faires Geschäft; get a ∼ **deal** kein schlechtes Geschäft machen

squarely /'skweəlɪ/ adv. fest ⟨ansehen⟩; genau ⟨treffen⟩; aufrecht ⟨sitzen⟩

square: ∼ '**meal** n. anständige Mahlzeit (ugs.); ∼ '**root** n. (Math.) Quadratwurzel, die; ∼-**root sign** [Quadrat]wurzelzeichen, das

squash[1] /skwɒʃ/ 1 v.t. (a) (crush) zerquetschen; ∼ sth. flat etw. platt drücken; (b) (compress) pressen; ∼ in/up eindrücken/zusammendrücken ⟨Gegenstand⟩; ∼ sb./sth. into sth. jmdn./etw. in etw. (Akk.) [hinein]zwängen; (c) (put down) niederschlagen ⟨Aufstand⟩; zunichte machen ⟨Hoffnung, Traum⟩; (d) (coll.: dismiss) ablehnen ⟨Vorschlag, Plan⟩; (e) (coll.: silence) zum Schweigen bringen. 2 v.i. sich quetschen; ∼ in sich hineinquetschen; we ∼ed up wir drängten uns zusammen 3 n. (a) (Brit.: drink) Fruchtsaftgetränk, das; **orange/lemon** ∼: Orangen- / Limonensaftgetränk, das; (b) (Sport) ∼ [**rackets**] Squash, das

squash[2] n. (gourd) [Speise]kürbis, der

squat /skwɒt/ 1 v.i., -tt-: (a) (crouch) hocken; (crouch down) sich hocken; (b) (coll.: sit) sitzen; (sit down) sich setzen; (c) (coll.: occupy property) (house) eine Hausbesetzung machen; (land) eine Landbesetzung machen; ∼ in a house/on land ein Haus besetzen/Land besetzen. 2 adj. rundlich; untersetzt

∼ '**down** v.i. sich [nieder]hocken; (on seat) sich hinsetzen

squatter /'skwɒtə(r)/ *n.* (illegal occupier) Besetzer, *der*/Besetzerin, *die;* (of house also) Hausbesetzer, *der*/-besetzerin, *die*

squaw /skwɔː/ *n.* Squaw, *die*

squawk /skwɔːk/ **1** *v.i.* ⟨*Hahn, Krähe, Rabe:*⟩ krähen; ⟨*Huhn:*⟩ kreischen; (complain) ⟨*Person:*⟩ keifen (abwertend). **2** *n.* ∼[s] (of crow, cockerel, raven) Krähen, *das;* (of hen) Kreischen, *das*

squeak /skwiːk/ **1** *n.* **(a)** (of animal) Quieken, *das;* **(b)** (of hinge, door, brake, shoe, etc.) Quietschen, *das;* **(c)** (coll.: escape) **have a narrow** ∼: gerade noch [mit dem Leben] davonkommen. **2** *v.i.* **(a)** ⟨*Tier:*⟩ quieken; **(b)** ⟨*Scharnier, Tür, Bremse, Schuh usw.:*⟩ quietschen

squeaky /'skwiːkɪ/ *adj.* quietschend; schrill ⟨*Stimme*⟩; **be** ∼ **clean** blitzsauber sein (ugs.); (fig.) eine blütenweiße Weste haben (fig. ugs.)

squeal /skwiːl/ *v.i.* **(a)** ∼ **with pain/in fear** ⟨*Person:*⟩ vor Schmerz/Angst aufschreien; ⟨*Tier:*⟩ vor Schmerz/Angst laut quieken; ∼ **with laughter/in excitement** vor Lachen/Aufregung kreischen; **(b)** ⟨*Bremsen, Räder:*⟩ kreischen ⟨*Reifen:*⟩ quietschen; **(c)** (coll.: protest) ∼ **[in protest]** lauthals protestieren. **2** *v.t.* kreischen. **3** *n.* Kreischen, *das;* (of tyres) Quietschen, *das;* (of animal) Quieken, *das*

squeamish /'skwiːmɪʃ/ *adj.* **be** ∼: zartbesaitet sein; **this film is not for the** ∼: dieser Film ist nichts für zarte Gemüter

squeegee /skwiː'dʒiː/ *n.* (for floor) [Boden]wischer, *der;* (for window) [Fenster]wischer, *der*

squeeze /skwiːz/ **1** *n.* **(a)** (pressing) Druck, *der;* **it only takes a gentle** ∼: man braucht nur leicht zu drücken; **give sth. a [small]** ∼: etw. [leicht] drücken; **(b)** (small quantity) **a** ∼ **of juice/washing-up liquid** ein Spritzer Saft/Spülmittel; **(c)** (crush) Gedränge, *das.* **2** *v.t.* **(a)** (press) drücken; drücken auf (+ *Akk.*) ⟨*Tube, Plastikflasche:*⟩ kneten ⟨*Ton, Knetmasse:*⟩; ausdrücken ⟨*Schwamm, Wäsche, Pickel*⟩; (to get juice) auspressen ⟨*Früchte, Obst*⟩; ∼ **sb.'s hand** jmdm. die Hand drücken; ∼ **the trigger** auf den Abzug drücken; **(b)** (extract) drücken (**out of** aus); ∼ **out sth.** etw. herausdrücken; **(c)** (force) zwängen; ∼ **one's way past/into/out of sth.** sich an etw. (*Dat.*) vorbei-/in etw. (*Akk.*) hinein-/aus etw. herauszwängen; **(d)** (fig. coll.) ∼ **sth. from sb.** etw. aus jmdm. herauspressen. **3** *v.i.* ∼ **past sb./sth.** sich an jmdm./etw. vorbeidrängen; ∼ **between two persons** sich zwischen zwei Personen (*Dat.*) durchdrängen; ∼ **together** sich zusammendrängen. ∼ **'in 1** *v.t.* **(a)** reinquetschen; **(b)** (fig.: fit in) einschieben. **2** *v.i.* sich hineinzwängen

squelch /skweltʃ/ *v.i.* **(a)** (make sucking sound) quatschen (ugs.); **(b)** (go over wet ground) patschen

squib /skwɪb/ *n.* (firework) Knallfrosch, *der;* **damp** ∼ (fig.) Reinfall, *der*

squid /skwɪd/ *n.* (Zool., Gastr.) Kalmar, *der*

squidgy /'skwɪdʒɪ/ *adj.* (Brit. coll.) durchweicht; matschig (ugs.)

squiggle /'skwɪgl/ *n.* Schnörkel, *der*

squint /skwɪnt/ **1** *n.* **(a)** (Med.) Schielen, *das;* **have a** ∼: schielen; **(b)** (stealthy look) Schielen, *das* (ugs.); **(c)** (coll.: glance) kurzer Blick; **have or take a** ∼ **at** einen Blick werfen auf (+ *Akk.*); überfliegen ⟨*Text, Zeitung*⟩. **2** *v.i.* **(a)** (Med.) schielen; **(b)** (with half-closed eyes) blinzeln; die Augen zusammenkneifen; **(c)** (obliquely) ∼ **through a gap** durch eine Lücke lugen; **(d)** (coll.: glance) ∼ **at** einen [kurzen] Blick werfen auf (+ *Akk.*); überfliegen ⟨*Zeitung, Text*⟩

squire /'skwaɪə(r)/ *n.* (country gentleman) Squire, *der;* ≈ Gutsherr, *der*

squirm /skwɜːm/ *v.i.* **(a)** ⇒ **wriggle 1;** **(b)** (fig.: show unease) sich winden (**with** vor)

squirrel /'skwɪrl/ *n.* (Zool.) Eichhörnchen, *das*

squirt /skwɜːt/ **1** *v.t.* spritzen; sprühen ⟨*Spray, Puder*⟩; ∼ **sth. at sb.** jmdn. mit etw. bespritzen/besprühen; ∼ **sb. in the eye/face [with sth.]** jmdm. [etw.] ins Auge/Gesicht spritzen/sprühen; ∼ **oneself with water/deodorant** sich mit Wasser besprühen/mit Deodorant besprühen. **2** *v.i.* spritzen. **3** *n.* Spritzer, *der*

Sr. *abbr.* **Senior** sen.

Sri Lanka /sriː 'læŋkə/ *pr. n.* Sri Lanka (*das*)

Sri Lankan /sriː 'læŋkən/ **1** *adj.* srilankisch. **2** *n.* Srilanker, *der*/Srilankerin, *die*

SRN *abbr.* **State Registered Nurse** staatl. gepr. Krankenschwester/-pfleger

St *abbr.* **Saint** St.

St. *abbr.* **Street** Str.

st. *abbr.* **▶ 1202」** (Brit.: unit of weight) **stone**

stab /stæb/ **1** *v.t.,* **-bb-** stechen; ∼ **sb. in the chest** jmdm. in die Brust stechen. **2** *v.i.,* **-bb-: (a)** (pierce) stechen; **(b)** (thrust) zustechen; ∼ **at sb.** nach jmdm. stechen. **3** *n.* **(a)** (act) Stich, *der;* **(b)** (coll.: attempt) **make or have a** ∼ **[at it]** [es] probieren

stabbing /'stæbɪŋ/ **1** *n.* Messerstecherei, *die.* **2** *attrib. adj.* stechend ⟨*Schmerz*⟩

stability /stə'bɪlɪtɪ/ *n., no pl.* Stabilität, *die*

stabilize /'steɪbɪlaɪz/ **1** *v.t.* stabilisieren. **2** *v.i.* sich stabilisieren

stable /'steɪbl/ **1** *adj.* **(a)** (steady) stabil; **a** ∼ **family background** geordnete Familienverhältnisse; **(b)** (resolute) gefestigt ⟨*Person, Charakter*⟩. **2** *n.* Stall, *der.* **3** *v.t.* (put in ∼) in den Stall bringen; (keep in ∼) **the pony was** ∼**d at a nearby farm** das Pony war im Stall eines nahe gelegenen Bauernhofes untergebracht

staccato /stə'kɑːtəʊ/ (Mus.) **1** *adj.* staccato gesetzt; (fig.) abgehackt ⟨*Sprache*⟩. **2** *adv.* staccato

stack /stæk/ **1** *n.* **(a)** (of hay etc.) Schober, *der* (südd., österr.); Feim, *der* (nordd., md.); **(b)** (pile) Stoß, *der;* Stapel, *der;* **place sth. in** ∼s etw. [auf]stapeln; **(c)** (coll.: large amount) Haufen, *der* (ugs.); **a** ∼ **of work/money** ein Haufen Arbeit/Geld; **have a** ∼ **of things to do** einen Haufen zu tun haben (ugs.); **(d)** **[chimney-]**∼**:** Schornstein, *der.* **2** *v.t.* **(a)** (pile) ∼ **[up]** [auf]stapeln; ∼ **logs in a pile** Holz zu einem Stoß aufschichten; **(b)** (arrange fraudulently) ∼ **the cards** beim Mischen betrügen; **the odds** *or* **cards** *or* **chips are** ∼**ed against sb.** (fig.) jmd. hat schlechte Karten (fig. ugs.). ∼ **'up** ⇒ ∼ **2 a**

stadium /'steɪdɪəm/ *n.* Stadion, *das*

staff /stɑːf/ **1** *n.* **(a)** (stick) Stock, *der;* **(b)** *constr. as pl.* (personnel) Personal, *das;* **editorial** ∼**:** Redaktion, *die;* **the** ∼ **of the firm** die Betriebsangehörigen; die Belegschaft [der Firma]; **(c)** *constr. as pl.* (of school) Lehrerkollegium, *das;* Lehrkörper, *der* (Amtsspr.); (of university or college) Dozentenschaft, *die;* **(d)** *pl.* **staves** /steɪvz/ (Mus.) Liniensystem, *das.* **2** *v.t.* mit Personal ausstatten

staff: ∼ **meeting** *n.* (Sch.) [Lehrer]konferenz, *die;* ∼ **nurse** *n.* (Brit.) Zweitschwester, *die*/Krankenpfleger in der Stellung einer Zweitschwester; ∼**room** *n.* (Sch.) Lehrerzimmer, *das*

stag /stæg/ *n.* Hirsch, *der*

stage /steɪdʒ/ **1** *n.* **(a)** (Theatre) Bühne, *die;* **down/up** ∼ (position) vorne/hinten auf der Bühne; (direction) nach vorn/nach hinten; **(b)** (fig.) **the** ∼: das Theater; **go on the** ∼: zur Bühne *od.* zum Theater gehen; **(c)** (part of process) Stadium, *das;* Phase, *die;* **be at a late/critical** ∼: sich in einer späten/kritischen Phase befinden; **at this** ∼: in diesem Stadium; **do sth. in** *or* **by** ∼s etw. abschnittsweise *od.* nach und nach tun; **in the final** ∼s in der Schlussphase; **(d)** (raised platform) Gerüst, *das;* **(e)** (of microscope) Mikroskoptisch, *der;* **(f)** (fig.: scene) Bühne, *die;* **set the** ∼ **for sb./sth.** jmdm. den Weg ebnen/etw. in die Wege leiten; **(g)** (distance) Etappe, *die.* **2** *v.t.* **(a)** (present) inszenieren; **(b)** (arrange) veranstalten ⟨*Wettkampf, Ausstellung*⟩; ausrichten ⟨*Veranstaltung*⟩; organisieren ⟨*Streik*⟩; bewerkstelligen ⟨*Rückzug*⟩

stage: ∼**coach** *n.* Postkutsche, *die;* ∼ **'door** *n.* (Theatre) Bühneneingang, *der;* ∼ **fright** *n.* (Theatre) Lampenfieber, *das;* ∼**-manage** *v.t.* **(a)** (Theatre) als Inspizient/Inspizientin mitwirken bei ⟨*Inszenierung*⟩; **(b)** (fig.) veranstalten; inszenieren ⟨*Revolte usw.*⟩; ∼**-manager** *n.* **▶ 887」** (Theatre) Inspizient, *der*/Inspizientin, *die;* ∼**-struck** *adj.* theaterbesessen; ∼ **whisper** *n.* Beiseitesprechen, *das;* **in a** ∼ **whisper** beiseite

stagger /'stægə(r)/ **1** *v.i.* schwanken; torkeln (ugs.). **2** *v.t.* **(a)** (astonish) die Sprache verschlagen (+ *Dat.*); **(b)** versetzt anordnen; ∼**ed junction** versetzt angelegte Kreuzung

staggering /'stægərɪŋ/ adj. erschütternd 〈Schlag, Schock, Verlust〉; Schwindel erregend 〈Höhe, Menge〉; folgenschwer 〈Auswirkung, Bedeutung〉; zutiefst beunruhigend 〈Nachricht〉

stagnant /'stægnənt/ adj. **(a)** (motionless) stehend 〈Gewässer〉; **the water is** ~: das Wasser steht; **(b)** (fig.: lifeless) abgestumpft 〈Geist, Seele〉; stagnierend 〈Wirtschaft〉; dumpf 〈Leben〉; **the economy is** ~: die Wirtschaft stagniert

stagnate /stæg'neɪt/ v.i. **(a)** 〈Wasser usw.:〉 abstehen; **(b)** (fig.) 〈Wirtschaft, Geschäft:〉 stagnieren; 〈Geist:〉 in Lethargie verfallen; 〈Person:〉 abstumpfen

stagnation /stæg'neɪʃn/ n., no pl. **(a)** (of water etc.) Stehen, das; **(b)** (fig.) Stagnation, die

'stag night n. Zechabend des Bräutigams mit seinen Freunden kurz vor seiner Hochzeit

staid /steɪd/ adj. **(a)** (steady, sedate) gesetzt; **(b)** (serious) bieder

stain /steɪn/ **1** v.t. **(a)** (discolour) verfärben; (make ~s on) Flecken hinterlassen auf (+ Dat.); **(b)** (fig.: damage) beflecken; besudeln (geh. abwertend); **(c)** (colour) färben; beizen 〈Holz〉. **2** n. **(a)** (discoloration) Fleck, der; **(b)** (fig.: blemish) Schandfleck, der

stained 'glass n. farbiges Glas; Farbglas, das; ~ '**window** Fenster mit Glasmalerei

stainless /'steɪnlɪs/ adj. (non-rusting) rostfrei

stainless 'steel n. Edelstahl, der

'stain remover n. Fleckentferner, der

stair /steə(r)/ n. ~**s** or (arch./Scot.) same Treppe, die

stair: ~ **carpet** ⇒ **carpet 1 a;** ~**case** n. Treppenhaus, das; (one flight) Treppe, die; **on the** ~**case** auf der Treppe; ~**way** n. **(a)** (access via ~s) Treppenaufgang, der; **(b)** (~-case) Treppe, die; ~**well** n. Treppenhaus, das

stake /steɪk/ **1** n. **(a)** (pointed stick) Pfahl, der; **(b)** (wager) Einsatz, der; **be at** ~: auf dem Spiel stehen. **2** v.t. **(a)** (secure) [an einem Pfahl/an Pfählen] anbinden; **(b)** (wager) setzen (on auf + Akk.); **(c)** (risk) aufs Spiel setzen (on für) ~ '**out** v.t. **(a)** (mark out) mit Pfählen begrenzen; **(b)** (fig.: claim) beanspruchen; **(c)** (Amer. coll.: observe) überwachen

stalactite /'stæləktaɪt/ n. (Geol.) Stalaktit, der

stalagmite /'stæləgmaɪt/ n. (Geol.) Stalagmit, der

stale /steɪl/ adj. alt; muffig; abgestanden 〈Luft〉; alt[backen] 〈Brot〉; schal 〈Bier, Wein usw.〉; (fig.) abgedroschen 〈Witz, Trick〉; überholt 〈Nachricht〉

'stalemate n. (Chess; also fig.) Patt, das

stalk¹ /stɔːk/ v.t. **(a)** sich heranpirschen an (+ Akk.); **(b)** (follow obsessively) ~ **sb.** jmdm. nachstellen

stalk² n. (Bot.) (main stem) Stängel, der; (of leaf, flower, fruit) Stiel, der

stalker /'stɔːkə(r)/ n. [lästiger] Verfolger

stall¹ /stɔːl/ **1** n. **(a)** Stand, der; **(b)** (for horse) Box, die; (for cow) Stand, der; **(c)** (Eccl.: seat) Stuhl, der; **the choir** ~**s** das Chorgestühl; **(d)** in pl. (Brit. Theatre: seats) **[front]** ~**s** Parkett, das. **2** v.t. abwürgen (ugs.) 〈Motor〉. **3** v.i. 〈Motor:〉 stehen bleiben

stall² **1** v.i. ausweichen. **2** v.t. blockieren 〈Gesetz, Fortschritt〉; aufhalten 〈Feind, Fortschritt〉

stallion /'stæljən/ n. Hengst, der

stalwart /'stɔːlwət/ adj. **(a)** (sturdy) stämmig; **(b)** attrib. (fig.: determined) entschieden; entschlossen 〈Kämpfer〉; (loyal) treu; getreu (geh.)

stamen /'steɪmen, 'steɪmən/ n. (Bot.) Staubblatt, das

stamina /'stæmɪnə/ n. **(a)** (physical staying power) Ausdauer, die; **(b)** (endurance) Durchhaltevermögen, das

stammer /'stæmə(r)/ **1** v.i. stottern. **2** v.t. stammeln. **3** n. Stottern, das

stamp /stæmp/ **1** v.t. **(a)** (impress, imprint sth. on) [ab]stempeln; ~ **sth. on sth.** etw. auf etw. (Akk.) [auf]stempeln; **(b)** ~ **one's foot/feet** mit dem Fuß/den Füßen stampfen; ~ **the floor** or **ground [in anger/with rage]** [ärgerlich/wütend] auf den Boden stampfen; **(c)** (put postage on) frankieren; freimachen (Postw.); ~**ed addressed envelope** frankierter Rückumschlag; **(d)** (mentally) **become** or **be** ~**ed on sb.['s memory** or **mind]** sich jmdm. fest

einprägen. **2** v.i. aufstampfen. **3** n. **(a)** Marke, die; (postage ~) Briefmarke, die; **(b)** (instrument for ~ing, mark) Stempel, der; **(c)** (fig.: characteristic) **bear the** ~ **of genius/greatness** Genialität/Größe erkennen lassen

~ **on** v.t. **(a)** zertreten 〈Insekt, Dose〉; zertrampeln 〈Blumen〉; ~ **on sb.'s foot** jmdm. auf den Fuß treten; **(b)** (suppress) durchgreifen gegen. See also ~ **1 a, d**

~ '**out** v.t. **(a)** (eliminate) ausmerzen; ersticken 〈Aufstand, Feuer〉; niederwalzen 〈Opposition, Widerstand〉; **(b)** (cut out) [aus]stanzen

stamp: ~ **album** n. Briefmarkenalbum, das; ~**-collecting** n. Briefmarkensammeln, das; ~ **collection** n. Briefmarkensammlung, die; ~ **collector** n. Briefmarkensammler, der/-sammlerin, die

stampede /stæm'piːd/ n. Stampede, die

'stamp machine n. Briefmarkenautomat, der

stanch /staːntʃ, stɔːntʃ/ v.t. **(a)** (stop flow of) stillen 〈Blut〉; **(b)** (stop flow from) abbinden 〈Wunde〉

stand /stænd/ **1** v.i., **stood** /stʊd/ **(a)** stehen; ~ **in a line** or **row** sich in einer Reihe aufstellen; (be ~ing) in einer Reihe stehen; **we stood talking** wir standen da und unterhielten uns; **(b)** (have height) **he** ~**s six feet tall/the tree** ~**s 30 feet high** er ist sechs Fuß groß/der Baum ist 30 Fuß hoch; **(c)** (be at level) 〈Aktien, Währung, Thermometer:〉 stehen (at auf + Dat.); 〈Fonds:〉 sich belaufen (at auf + Akk.); 〈Absatz, Export usw.:〉 liegen (at bei); **(d)** (hold good) bestehen bleiben; **my offer/promise still** ~**s** mein Angebot/Versprechen gilt nach wie vor; **(e)** (find oneself, be) ~ **convicted of treachery** wegen Verrats verurteilt sein; **as it** ~**s, as things** ~: wie die Dinge [jetzt] liegen; **the law as it** ~**s** das bestehende od. gültige Recht; **I'd like to know where I** ~ (fig.) ich möchte wissen, wo ich dran bin; ~ **in need of sth.** einer Sache (Gen.) dringend bedürfen; **(f)** (be candidate) kandidieren (**for** für); ~ **in an election** bei einer Wahl kandidieren; ~ **as a Liberal Democrat/Conservative** für die Liberaldemokraten/Konservativen kandidieren; ~ **for Parliament** (Brit.) für einen Parlamentssitz kandidieren; **(g)** ~ **proxy for sb.** jmdn. vertreten; **(h)** (place oneself) sich stellen; ~ **in the way of sth.** (fig.) einer Sache (Dat.) im Weg stehen; **[not]** ~ **in sb.'s way** (fig.) jmdm. [keine] Steine in den Weg legen; **(i)** (be likely) ~ **to win** or **gain/lose sth.** etw. gewinnen/verlieren können. **2** v.t., **stood** **(a)** (set in position) stellen; ~ **sth. on end/upside down** etw. hochkant/auf den Kopf stellen; **(b)** (endure) ertragen; vertragen 〈Klima〉; **I can't** ~ **the heat/noise** ich halte die Hitze/den Lärm nicht aus; **I cannot** ~ **[the sight of] him/her** ich kann ihn/sie nicht ausstehen; **he can't** ~ **the pressure/strain/stress** er ist dem Druck/den Strapazen/dem Stress nicht gewachsen; **I can't** ~ **it any longer!** ich halte es nicht mehr aus!; see also **time 1 a; (c)** (undergo) ausgesetzt sein (+ Dat.); ~ **trial [for sth.]** [wegen etw.] vor Gericht stehen; **(d)** (buy) ~ **sb. sth.** jmdm. etw. ausgeben od. spendieren (ugs.). **3** n. **(a)** (support) Ständer, der; **(b)** (stall; at exhibition) Stand, der; **(c)** (raised structure, grand~) Tribüne, die; **(d)** (resistance) Widerstand, der; **take** or **make a** ~ (fig.) klar Position beziehen (**for/against/on** für/gegen/zu); **(e)** (~ing place for taxi, bus, etc.) Stand, der

~ **a'bout,** ~ **a'round** v.i. herumstehen

~ **a'side** v.i. zur Seite treten; Platz machen

~ '**back** v.i. **(a)** ~ **[well] back [from sth.]** [ein gutes Stück] [von etw.] entfernt stehen; **(b)** ⇒ ~ **aside; (c)** (fig.: distance oneself) zurücktreten; **(d)** (fig.: withdraw) ~ **back from sth.** sich aus einer Sache heraushalten

~ **between** v.t. **sth.** ~**s between sb. and sth.** (fig.) etw. steht jmdm. bei etw. im Wege

~ **by 1** /-'-/ v.i. **(a)** (remain apart) abseits stehen; **(b)** (be near) daneben stehen; **(c)** (be ready) sich zur Verfügung halten. **2** /'--/ v.t. **(a)** (support) ~ **by sb./one another** jmdm./sich [gegenseitig] od. (geh.) einander beistehen; **(b)** (adhere to) ~ **by sth.** zu etw. stehen; ~ **by the terms of a contract** einen Vertrag einhalten; ~ **by a promise** ein Versprechen halten

~ '**down** v.i. (withdraw, retire) verzichten; ~ **down in favour of a person** zugunsten einer Person (Gen.) zurücktreten

~ **for** v.t. **(a)** (signify) bedeuten; **(b)** (coll.: tolerate) sich bieten lassen

~ **'in** *v.i.* (deputize) aushelfen; ~ **in for sb.** für jmdn. einspringen

~ **'out** *v.i.* **(a)** (be prominent) herausragen; ~ **out against** *or* **in contrast to sth.** sich gegen etw. abheben; ~ **out a mile** nicht zu übersehen sein; ⟨*Grund, Antwort:*⟩ [klar] auf der Hand liegen; **(b)** (be outstanding) herausragen (**from** aus)

~ **over** *v.t.* beaufsichtigen

~ **to'gether** *v.i.* zusammenstehen; (for a photograph) sich [gemeinsam] aufstellen; (fig.) zusammenhalten

~ **'up 1** *v.i.* **(a)** (rise) aufstehen; **(b)** (be upright) stehen; ~ **up straight** sich aufrecht hinstellen; **(c)** (be valid) gelten; Gültigkeit haben; **(d)** ~ **up well [in comparison with sb./sth.]** [im Vergleich zu jmdm./etw.] gut abschneiden. **2** *v.t.* **(a)** (put upright) aufstellen; [wieder] hinstellen ⟨*Fahrrad, Stuhl usw.*⟩; **(b)** (coll.: fail to keep date with) ~ **sb. up** jmdn. versetzen (ugs.)

~ **'up for** *v.t.* ~ **up for sb./sth.** für jmdn./etw. Partei ergreifen; sich für jmdn./etw. stark machen

~ **'up to** *v.t.* **(a)** (face steadfastly) ~ **up to sb.** sich jmdm. entgegenstellen; jmdm. die Stirn bieten; ~ **up to sth.** sich einer Sache (*Dat.*) stellen; **(b)** (survive intact under) ~ **up to sth.** einer Sache (*Dat.*) standhalten; ~ **up to wear and tear** eine starke Beanspruchung aushalten

stand-a'lone *adj.* (Computing) selbstständig

standard /'stændəd/ **1** *n.* **(a)** (norm) Maßstab, *der;* **safety** ~**s** Sicherheitsnormen; **above/below/up to** ~: überdurchschnittlich [gut]/unter dem Durchschnitt/der Norm entsprechend; **(b)** (degree) Niveau, *das;* **set a high/low** ~ **in** *or* **of sth.** hohe/niedrige Ansprüche an etw. (*Akk.*) stellen; ~ **of living** Lebensstandard, *der;* **(c)** *in pl.* (moral principles) Prinzipien; **(d)** (flag) Standarte, *die.* **2** *adj.* **(a)** (conforming to ~) Standard-; (used as reference) Normal-; **(b)** (widely used) normal; **be** ~ **procedure** Vorschrift sein; **be fitted with sth. as** ~: serienmäßig mit etw. ausgerüstet sein; **a** ~ **letter** ein Schemabrief (Bürow.); **be** ~ **practice** allgemein üblich sein

standard: ~**-bearer** *n.* **(a)** (Mil.: flag-bearer) Standartenträger, *der;* **(b)** (fig.: leader) Vorkämpfer, *der*/-kämpferin, *die;* **S**~ **'English** *n.* Standardenglisch, *das*

standardize (standardise) /'stændədaɪz/ *v.t.* standardisieren

'standard lamp *n.* (Brit.) Stehlampe, *die*

'standby 1 *n., pl.* ~**s (a)** (reserve) [**act**] **as a** ~: als Ersatz [bereitstehen]; **be on** ~ ⟨*Polizei, Feuerwehr, Truppen:*⟩ einsatzbereit sein; **(b)** (resource) Rückhalt, *der;* **sth. is a good** ~: auf etw. (*Akk.*) kann man jederzeit zurückgreifen. **2** *attrib. adj.* Ersatz-; ~ **ticket/passenger** Stand-by-Ticket, *das*/-Passagier, *der*

'stand-in 1 *n.* Ersatz, *der;* (in theatre, film) Ersatzdarsteller, *der*/-darstellerin, *die.* **2** *attrib. adj.* Ersatz-

standing /'stændɪŋ/ **1** *n.* **(a)** (repute) Ansehen, *das;* **be of** *or* **have [a] high** ~: ein hohes Ansehen genießen; **what is his** ~? welchen Rang bekleidet er?; **(b)** (service) **be an MP of twenty years'** ~: seit zwanzig Jahren [ununterbrochen] dem Parlament angehören; **(c)** (duration) **of long/short** ~: von langer/kurzer Dauer. **2** *adj.* **(a)** (erect) stehend; **after the storm there was scarcely a tree still** ~: nach dem Sturm stand kaum mehr ein Baum; **leave sb.** ~ (lit. or fig.: progress much faster) jmdn. weit hinter sich (*Dat.*) lassen; **(b)** *attrib.* (established) fest ⟨*Regel, Brauch*⟩; **he has a** ~ **excuse** er bringt immer die gleiche Entschuldigung; **(c)** *attrib.* (permanent) stehend ⟨*Heer*⟩

standing: ~ **com'mittee** *n.* ständiger Ausschuss; ~ **'order** *n.* Dauerauftrag, *der;* (for regular supply) Abonnement, *das;* ~ **o'vation** *n.* stehende Ovation (geh.); ~ **room** *n., no pl., no indef. art.* Stehplätze

stand-offish /stænd'ɒfɪʃ/ *adj.* reserviert

stand: ~**pipe** *n.* (for water supply) Standrohr, *das;* ~**point** *n.* **(a)** (observation point) Standort, *der;* **(b)** (fig.: viewpoint) Standpunkt, *der;* ~**still** *n.* Stillstand, *der;* **be at a** ~**still** stillstehen; **come to a** ~**still** zum Stehen kommen; ⟨*Verhandlungen:*⟩ zum Stillstand kommen; **the traffic/production came to a** ~**still** der Verkehr/die Produktion kam zum Erliegen; **bring to a** ~**still** zum Stehen bringen; zum Erliegen bringen ⟨*Produktion*⟩; ~**up** *adj.* ~**-up fight** Schlägerei, *die*

stank ⇒ **stink 1**

stanza /'stænzə/ *n.* (Pros.) Strophe, *die*

staple[1] /'steɪpl/ **1** *n.* (for fastening paper) [Heft]klammer, *die.* **2** *v.t.* heften (**on to** an + *Akk.*)

staple[2] *attrib. adj.* **(a)** (principal) Grund-; **(b)** (Commerc.: important) grundlegend

stapler /'steɪplə(r)/ *n.* [Draht]hefter, *der*

star /stɑː(r)/ **1** *n.* **(a)** Stern, *der;* **three/four** ~ **hotel** Drei-/Vier-Sterne-Hotel, *das;* **two/four** ~ [**petrol**] Normal-/Super[benzin], *das;* **the S**~**s and Stripes** (Amer.) das Sternenbanner; **(b)** (prominent person) Star, *der;* **(c)** (asterisk) Stern, *der;* Sternchen, *das;* **(d)** (Astrol.) Stern, *der;* **read one's/the** ~**s** sein/das Horoskop lesen. **2** *attrib. adj.* Star-; ~ **pupil** bester Schüler/beste Schülerin; ~ **turn** *or* **attraction** Hauptattraktion, *die.* **3** *v.t.,* **-rr-** (feature as ~) ~**ring Humphrey Bogart and Lauren Bacall** mit Humphrey Bogart und Lauren Bacall in den Hauptrollen. **4** *v.i.,* **-rr-:** ~ **in a film/play/TV series** in einem Film/einem Stück/einer Fernsehserie die Hauptrolle spielen

starboard /'stɑːbəd/ (Naut., Aeronaut.) **1** *n.* Steuerbord, *das;* **land to** ~! Land an Steuerbord! **2** *adj.* steuerbord-; steuerbordseitig; **on the** ~ **bow/quarter** Steuerbord voraus/achteraus

starch /stɑːtʃ/ **1** *n.* Stärke, *die.* **2** *v.t.* stärken

starchy /'stɑːtʃɪ/ *adj.* **(a)** stärkehaltig ⟨*Nahrungsmittel*⟩; **(b)** (fig.: prim) steif

stardom /'stɑːdəm/ *n.* Starruhm, *der*

stare /steə(r)/ **1** *v.i.* **(a)** (gaze) starren; ~ **in surprise/amazement** überrascht/erstaunt starren; ~ **at sb./sth.** jmdn./etw. anstarren; **(b)** (have fixed gaze) starr blicken. **2** *v.t.* ~ **sb. in the face** jmdn. [feindselig] fixieren; (fig.) jmdm. ins Auge springen; **ruin was staring him in the face** ihm drohte der Ruin. **3** *n.* Starren, *das;* **fix sb. with a [curious/malevolent]** ~: jmdn. [neugierig/böse] anstarren

~ **'down,** ~ **'out** *v.t.* ~ **sb. down** *or* **out** jmdn. so lange anstarren, bis er/sie die Augen abwendet

'starfish *n.* Seestern, *der*

staring /'steərɪŋ/ *attrib. adj.* starrend ⟨*Augen*⟩; **with** ~ **eyes** mit starrem Blick; **be stark** ~ **mad** (fig. coll.) völlig verrückt sein (ugs.)

stark /stɑːk/ **1** *adj.* **(a)** (bleak) öde; spröde ⟨*Schönheit, Dichtung*⟩; **(b)** (obvious) scharf umrissen; nackt ⟨*Wahrheit*⟩; scharf ⟨*Kontrast, Umriss*⟩; krass ⟨*Unterschied, Gegensatz, Realismus*⟩; **(c)** (extreme) schier ⟨*Entsetzen, Dummheit*⟩; nackt ⟨*Armut, Angst*⟩. **2** *adv.* völlig; ~ **naked** splitternackt (ugs.); *see also* **staring**

'starlight *n., no pl.* Sternenlicht, *das*

starling /'stɑːlɪŋ/ *n.* (Ornith.) [Gemeiner] Star

'starlit *adj.* sternhell

starry /'stɑːrɪ/ *adj.* sternklar ⟨*Himmel, Nacht*⟩; sternenübersät ⟨*Himmel*⟩

'starry-eyed *adj.* blauäugig (fig.)

'star-studded *adj.* ⟨*Show, Film, Besetzung*⟩ mit großem Staraufgebot

start /stɑːt/ **1** *v.i.* **(a)** (begin) anfangen; beginnen (oft geh.); ~ **on sth.** etw. beginnen; ~ **with sth./sb.** bei od. mit etw./jmdm. anfangen; **prices** ~ **at ten dollars** die Preise beginnen bei zehn Dollar; ~ **at the beginning** am Anfang beginnen; **to** ~ **with** zuerst *od.* zunächst einmal; ~**ing from next month** ab nächsten Monat; **(b)** (set out) aufbrechen; **(c)** (make sudden movement) aufschrecken; ~ **with pain/surprise** vor Schmerz/Überraschung auffahren; ~ **from one's chair** von seinem Stuhl hochfahren; **(d)** (begin to function) anlaufen ⟨*Auto, Motor usw.*⟩. **2** *v.t.* **(a)** (begin) beginnen [mit]; ~ **school** in die Schule kommen; ~ **work** mit der Arbeit beginnen (**on** an + *Dat.*); (after leaving school) zu arbeiten anfangen; ~ **doing** *or* **to do sth.** [damit] anfangen, etw. zu tun; **(b)** (cause) auslösen; anfangen ⟨*Streit, Schlägerei*⟩; legen ⟨*Brand*⟩; (accidentally) verursachen ⟨*Brand*⟩; **(c)** (set up) ins Leben rufen ⟨*Organisation, Projekt*⟩; aufmachen ⟨*Laden, Geschäft*⟩; gründen ⟨*Verein, Firma, Zeitung*⟩; **(d)** (switch on) einschalten; starten, anlassen ⟨*Motor, Auto*⟩; **(e)** ~ **sb. doing sth.** jmdn. anfangen lassen, etw. zu tun; ~ **sb. drinking/coughing/laughing** jmdn. zum Trinken/

Husten/Lachen bringen; ~ **sb. on a diet** jmdn. auf Diät (*Akk.*) setzen; ~ **sb. in business/a trade** jmdm. die Gründung eines Geschäfts ermöglichen/jmdn. in ein Handwerk einführen; (**f**) (Sport) ~ **a race** ein Rennen starten; ~ **a football match** ein Fußballspiel anpfeifen. **3** *n.* (**a**) Anfang, *der;* Beginn, *der;* (of race) Start, *der;* **from the ~:** von Anfang an; **from ~ to finish** von Anfang bis Ende; **at the ~:** am Anfang; **at the ~ of the war/day** bei Kriegsbeginn/zum Tagesanfang; **make a ~:** anfangen (**on, with** mit); (on journey) aufbrechen; **get off to** *or* **make a good/slow/poor ~:** einen guten/langsamen/ schlechten Start haben; **for a ~** (coll.) zunächst einmal; (**b**) (Sport: ~ing-place) Start, *der;* (**c**) (Sport: advantage) Vorsprung, *der;* **give sb.** [a] **60 metres ~:** jmdm. eine Vorgabe von 60 Metern geben; **have a ~ over** *or* **on sb./sth.** (fig.) einen Vorsprung vor jmdm./etw. haben; (**d**) (jump) **she remembered** *or* **realized with a ~ that ...:** sie schreckte zusammen, als ihr einfiel, dass ...; **give sb.** [a] **~:** jmdm. einen Schreck einjagen

~ **'off 1** *v.i.* (**a**) ⇒ **set off 1;** (**b**) (coll.: begin action) ~ **off by showing sth.** zu Beginn etw. zeigen; (**c**) ~ **off with** *or* **on sth.** (begin on) mit etw. beginnen. **2** *v.t.* (**a**) ~ **sb. off on a task/job** jmdn. in eine Aufgabe/Arbeit einweisen; (**b**) ⇒ **set off 2 b**
~ **'out** *v.i.* (**a**) ⇒ **set out 1;** (**b**) ⇒ **set off 1**
~ **'up 1** *v.i.* (**a**) ⇒ **jump up;** (**b**) (be set going) starten; (*Motor:*) anspringen; (**c**) (begin to work) ~ **up in engineering/insurance** als Ingenieur/in der Versicherungsbranche anfangen. **2** *v.t.* (**a**) beginnen 〈*Gespräch*〉; gründen 〈*Geschäft, Firma*〉; schließen 〈*Freundschaft*〉; (**b**) starten 〈*Fahrzeug, Motor*〉

starter /'sta:tə(r)/ *n.* (**a**) (Sport: signaller) Starter, *der;* (**b**) (Sport: entrant) Starter, *der*/Starterin, *die;* (horse) startendes Pferd; (**c**) (Motor Veh.) ~ [**motor**] Anlasser, *der;* (**d**) (initial action) Anfang, *der;* **as a ~:** zuerst; (**e**) (hors d'œuvre etc.) Vorspeise, *die*

starting: ~ **block** *n.* (Athletics) Startblock, *der;* ~ **line** *n.* Startlinie, *die;* ~ **point** *n.* (lit. or fig.) Ausgangspunkt, *der;* (for solving a problem) Ansatzpunkt, *der;* ~ **salary** *n.* Anfangsgehalt, *das;* (for civil servants also) Eingangsbesoldung, *die*

startle /'sta:tl/ *v.t.* erschrecken; **be ~d by sth.** über etw. (*Akk.*) erschrecken

startling /'sta:tlıŋ/ *adj.* erstaunlich; überraschend 〈*Nachricht*〉

starvation /sta:'veıʃn/ *n.* Verhungern, *das;* **die of** *or* **from/suffer from ~:** verhungern/hungern *od.* Hunger leiden; **be** *or* **live on a ~ diet** fast am Verhungern sein; ~ **wages** Hungerlohn, *der*

starve /sta:v/ **1** *v.i.* (**a**) (die of hunger) ~ [**to death**] verhungern; (**b**) (suffer hunger) hungern; (**c**) **be starving** (coll.: feel hungry) am Verhungern sein (ugs.). **2** *v.t.* (**a**) (kill by starving) ~ **sb.** [**to death**] jmdn. verhungern lassen; (**b**) (deprive of food) hungern lassen; (**c**) (deprive) **we were ~d of knowledge** uns (*Dat.*) wurde [viel] Wissen vorenthalten; **feel ~d of affection** unter einem Mangel an Zuneigung leiden
~ **'out** *v.t.* aushungern

'star wars *n. pl.* Krieg der Sterne

state /steıt/ **1** *n.* (**a**) (condition) Zustand, *der;* ~ **of the economy** Wirtschaftslage, *die;* **the ~ of play** (Sport) der Spielstand; **the ~ of play in the negotiations/debate** (fig.) der [gegenwärtige] Stand der Verhandlungen/Debatte; **the ~ of things in general** die allgemeine Lage; **the ~ of the nation** die Lage der Nation; **a ~ of war exists** es herrscht Kriegszustand; **be in a ~ of excitement/ sadness/anxiety** aufgeregt/traurig/ängstlich sein; (**b**) (mess) **what a ~ you're in!** wie siehst du denn aus!; (**c**) (anxiety) **be in a ~** (be in a panic) aufgeregt sein; (be excited) ganz aus dem Häuschen sein (ugs.); **get into a ~** (coll.) Zustände kriegen (ugs.); **don't get into a ~!** reg dich nicht auf! (ugs.); (**d**) (nation) Staat, *der;* [**affairs**] **of S~:** Staats[geschäfte]; (**e**) (federal ~) (of Germany, Austria) Land, *das;* (of America) Staat, *der;* **the** [**United**] **S~s** *sing.* die [Vereinigten] Staaten; (**f**) **S~** (civil government) Staat, *der;* (**g**) (pomp) Prunk, *der;* **in ~:** in vollem Staat; **lie in ~:** aufgebahrt sein. **2** *attrib. adj.* (**a**) (of nation or federal ~) staatlich;

Staats〈*bank, -sicherheit, -geheimnis, -dienst*〉; ~ **education** staatliches Erziehungswesen; (**b**) (ceremonial) Staats-. **3** *v.t.* (**a**) (express) erklären; (fully or clearly) darlegen; äußern 〈*Meinung*〉; angeben 〈*Alter usw.*〉; **'please ~ full particulars'** „bitte genaue Angaben machen"; (**b**) (specify) festlegen; **at ~d intervals** in genau festgelegten Abständen

'State Department *n.* (Amer. Polit.) Außenministerium, *das*

stateless /'steıtlıs/ *adj.* staatenlos; ~ **person** Staatenlose, *der/die*

stately /'steıtlı/ *adj.* majestätisch; stattlich 〈*Körperbau, Erscheinung, Gebäude*〉; hochtrabend 〈*Stil*〉; feierlich 〈*Prozession*〉; **at a ~ pace** gemessenen Schrittes

stately 'home *n.* (Brit.) Herrensitz, *der;* (grander) Schloss, *das*

statement /'steıtmənt/ *n.* (**a**) (stating, account, thing stated) Aussage, *die;* (declaration) Erklärung, *die;* (allegation) Behauptung, *die;* **make a ~** 〈*Zeuge:*〉 eine Aussage machen; 〈*Politiker:*〉 eine Erklärung abgeben (**on** zu); (**b**) (Finance: report) [**bank**] ~**:** Kontoauszug, *der*

state: ~**-of-the-'art** *adj.* auf dem neuesten Stand der Technik *nachgestellt;* ~**-owned** *adj.* staatlich; in Staatsbesitz *nachgestellt;* **S~ school** *n.* (Brit.) staatliche Schule; **S~side** *adv.* (Amer. coll.) **be/work/travel S~side** in den Staaten (ugs.) sein/arbeiten/in die Staaten (ugs.) reisen

statesman /'steıtsmən/ *n., pl.* **statesmen** /'steıtsmən/ Staatsmann, *der*

static /'stætık/ **1** *adj.* (**a**) (Phys.) statisch; (**b**) (not moving) statisch; (not changing) konstant 〈*Umweltbedingungen*〉. **2** *n.* (atmospherics) atmosphärische Störungen

station /'steıʃn/ **1** *n.* (**a**) (position) Position, *die;* (**b**) (establishment) Station, *die;* (**c**) ⇒ **railway station;** (**d**) (status) Rang, *der.* **2** *v.t.* (**a**) (assign position to) stationieren; abstellen 〈*Auto*〉; aufstellen 〈*Wache*〉; (**b**) (place) stellen; ~ **oneself** sich aufstellen

stationary /'steıʃənərı/ *adj.* (**a**) (not moving) stehend; **be ~:** stehen; **the traffic was ~:** der Verkehr war zum Erliegen gekommen; (**b**) (fixed) stationär

stationer /'steıʃənə(r)/ *n.* ▶ **887** Schreibwarenhändler, *der*/-händlerin, *die;* ~**'s** [**shop**] Schreibwarengeschäft, *das*

stationery /'steıʃənərı/ *n.* (**a**) (writing materials) Schreibwaren *Pl.;* (**b**) (writing paper) Briefpapier, *das*

station: ~**master** *n.* ▶ **887** (Railw.) Stationsvorsteher, *der*/-vorsteherin, *die;* ~ **wagon** *n.* (Amer.) Kombi[wagen], *der*

statistical /stə'tıstıkl/ *attrib. adj.,* **statistically** /stə'tıstıkəlı/ *adv.* statistisch

statistician /stætɪ'stıʃn/ *n.* Statistiker, *der*/Statistikerin, *die*

statistics /stə'tıstıks/ *n.* (**a**) *as pl.* (facts) Statistik, *die;* (**b**) *no pl.* (science) Statistik, *die*

statue /'stætʃu:, 'stætju:/ *n.* Statue, *die*

statuette /stætʃu'et, stætju'et/ *n.* Statuette, *die*

stature /'stætʃə(r)/ *n.* (**a**) (body height) Statur, *die;* (**b**) (fig.: standing) Format, *das;* **a person of** [**some**] ~**:** eine [recht] bedeutende Persönlichkeit

status /'steıtəs/ *n.* (**a**) (position) Rang, *der;* **rise in ~:** an Ansehen gewinnen; **social ~:** (gesellschaftlicher) Status; **equality of ~** [**with sb.**] Gleichstellung [mit jmdm.]; **financial ~:** finanzielle *od.* wirtschaftliche Lage; (**b**) (superior position) Status, *der*

status: ~ **quo** /steıtəs 'kwəʊ/ *n.* Status quo, *der;* ~ **symbol** *n.* Statussymbol, *das*

statute /'stætju:t/ *n.* (**a**) (Law) Gesetz, *das;* **by ~:** per Gesetz; (**b**) *in pl.* (rules) Statut, *das;* Satzung, *die*

'statute book *n.* (Law) Gesetzbuch, *das*

statutory /'stætjʊtərı/ *adj.* (**a**) (Law) gesetzlich 〈*Feiertag, Bestimmung, Erfordernis, Erbe*〉; gesetzlich vorgeschrieben 〈*Strafe*〉; gesetzlich festgeschrieben 〈*Löhne, Zinssatz*〉; gesetzlich festgelegt 〈*Voraussetzung, Sätze, Zeit*〉; ~ **law** kodifiziertes Recht; ~ **rights** [gesetzliche] Rechte; (**b**) (relating to the statutes of an institution) Satzungs〈*bestimmungen*〉; von der Satzung vorgesehen 〈*Geldbuße usw.*〉

staunch¹ /stɔːntʃ, stɑːntʃ/ *adj.* treu ‹*Freund, Anhänger*›; streitbar ‹*Kämpfer, Anhänger*›; überzeugt ‹*Katholik, Demokrat usw.*›; unerschütterlich ‹*Mut, Hingabe, Glaube*›; standhaft ‹*Herz*›

staunch² ⇨ **stanch**

stave /steɪv/ **1** *n.* (Mus.) ⇨ **staff 1 d. 2** *v.t.,* **~d** *or* **stove** /stəʊv/ ein Loch schlagen in (+ *Akk.*)

~ 'in *v.t.* (crush) eindrücken ‹*Karosserie, Tür, Rippen*›; einschlagen ‹*Kopf, Kiste*›; (break hole in) ein Loch schlagen in (+ *Akk.*)

~ 'off *v.t.,* **~d** off abwenden; abwehren ‹*Angriff*›; verhindern ‹*Krankheit*›; stillen ‹*Hunger, Durst*›

stay /steɪ/ **1** *n.* (a) Aufenthalt, *der;* (visit) Besuch, *der;* **during her ~ with us** während sie bei uns zu Besuch war; **come/go for a short ~ with sb.** jmdn. kurz besuchen; **have a week's ~ in London** eine Woche in London verbringen; **(b)** (Law) **~ [of execution]** Aussetzung [der Vollstreckung], *die;* (fig.) Galgenfrist, *die.* **2** *v.i.* (a) (remain) bleiben; **be here to ~, have come to ~:** sich fest eingebürgert haben; ‹*Arbeitslosigkeit, Inflation:*› zum Dauerzustand geworden sein; ‹*Modeartikel:*› in Mode bleiben; **~ for** *or* **to dinner/for the party** zum Essen/zur Party bleiben; **~ put** (coll.) ‹*Ball, Haar:*› liegen bleiben; ‹*Hut:*› fest sitzen; ‹*Bild:*› hängen bleiben; ‹*Person:*› bleiben[, wo man ist]; **(b)** (dwell temporarily) wohnen; **~ abroad** im Ausland leben; **~ the night in a hotel** die Nacht in einem Hotel verbringen; **~ at sb.'s** *or* **with sb. for the weekend** das Wochenende bei jmdm. verbringen; **(c)** (Sport) durchhalten. **3** *v.t.* (a) (literary: stop) **~ sb.'s hand** (fig.) jmdn. zurückhalten; **(b)** (endure) **~ the course** *or* **distance** die [ganze] Strecke durchhalten; (fig.) durchhalten

~ a'way *v.i.* (a) (not attend) **~ away [from sth.]** [von etw.] wegbleiben; [einer Sache (*Dat.*)] fernbleiben; **~ away from school/a meeting** nicht zur Schule/zu einem Treffen gehen/kommen; **(b)** (~ distant) **he ~ed well away from the wall** er hielt sich ein gutes Stück von der Wand entfernt

~ 'back *v.i.* (a) (not approach) zurückbleiben; **(b)** ⇨ **~ behind**

~ be'hind *v.i.* zurückbleiben; **have to ~ behind [after school]** nachsitzen müssen

~ 'down *v.i.* (a) (remain lowered) unten bleiben; **(b)** (not increase) stabil bleiben; **(c)** (Educ.: not go to higher form) sitzen bleiben (ugs.)

~ 'in *v.i.* (a) (remain in position) halten; **will these creases ~ in?** bleiben diese Falten [drin (ugs.)]?; **this passage [of the book] should ~ in** diese Passage sollte nicht gestrichen werden; **(b)** (remain at home) zu Hause bleiben

~ off *v.t.* **~ off the bottle/off drugs** die Finger vom Alkohol/von Drogen lassen (ugs.)

~ 'on *v.i.* (a) (remain in place) ‹*Hut, Perücke, Kopftuch:*› sitzen bleiben; ‹*falsche Wimpern, Aufkleber:*› haften; ‹*Deckel, Rad:*› halten; **(b)** (remain in operation) angeschaltet bleiben; anbleiben (ugs.); **(c)** (remain present) noch [da]bleiben; **~ on at school** auf der Schule bleiben; **~ on as chairman** Vorsitzender bleiben

~ 'out *v.i.* (a) (not go home) wegbleiben (ugs.); nicht nach Hause kommen/gehen; **don't ~ out late!** komm nicht zu spät nach Hause!; **(b)** (remain outside) draußen bleiben; **(c)** (fig.) **~ out of sb.'s way** jmdm. aus dem Wege gehen; **(d)** (remain on strike) **~ out [on strike]** im Ausstand bleiben

~ 'up *v.i.* (a) (not go to bed) aufbleiben; **(b)** (remain in position) ‹*Pfosten, Plakat:*› stehen bleiben; ‹*Plakat:*› hängen bleiben; ‹*Flugzeug, Haare:*› oben bleiben

'stay-at-home 1 *n.* häuslicher Mensch. **2** *attrib. adj.* häuslich

'staying power *n.* Durchhaltevermögen, *das*

STD *abbr.* (Brit. Teleph.) **subscriber trunk dialling** Selbstwählfernverkehr, *der;* **~ code** Vorwahl[nummer], *die*

stead /sted/ *n., no pl., no art.* (a) **in sb.'s ~:** an jmds. Stelle; **(b) stand sb. in good ~:** jmdm. zustatten kommen; **that car has stood her in good ~:** dieser Wagen hat ihr gute Dienste geleistet

steadfast /'stedfɑːst/ *adj.* standhaft; zuverlässig ‹*Freund*›; fest ‹*Entschluss*›; unverwandt ‹*Blick*›; unerschütterlich ‹*Glaube*›; unverbrüchlich (geh.) ‹*Freundschaft, Treue*›

steadily /'stedɪlɪ/ *adv.* (a) (stably) fest; festen Schrittes ‹*gehen*›; sicher ‹*Rad fahren*›; **(b)** (without faltering) fest ‹[an]blicken›; **(c)** (continuously) stetig; ohne Unterbrechung ‹*arbeiten, marschieren*›; **it was raining ~:** es hat ununterbrochen geregnet; **progress ~:** stetige Fortschritte machen; **(d)** (firmly) standhaft ‹*sich weigern*›; fest ‹*glauben*›; **(e)** (reliably) zuverlässig

steady /'stedɪ/ **1** *adj.* (a) (stable) stabil; (not wobbling) standfest; **as ~ as a rock** völlig standfest ‹*Leiter, Tisch*›; völlig stabil ‹*Boot*›; ganz ruhig ‹*Hand*›; **be ~ on one's feet** *or* **legs/bicycle** sicher auf den Beinen sein/sicher auf seinem Fahrrad fahren; **hold** *or* **keep the ladder ~:** die Leiter festhalten; **~ as she goes!** (coll.) immer so weiter!; **(b)** (still) ruhig; **turn a ~ gaze** *or* **look on sb.** jmdn. fest ansehen; **(c)** (regular, constant) stetig; gleichmäßig ‹*Tempo*›, stabil ‹*Preis, Lohn*›; gleich bleibend ‹*Temperatur*›; beständig ‹*Klima, Summen, Lärm*›; **we had ~ rain/drizzle** wir hatten Dauerregen/es nieselte [bei uns] ständig; **~!** Vorsicht!; (to dog, horse) ruhig!; **~ on!** langsam! (ugs.); **(d)** (invariable) unerschütterlich; beständig ‹*Wesensart*›; standhaft ‹*Weigerung*›; fest ‹*Charakter, Glaube*›; **(e)** (enduring) **a ~ job** eine feste Stelle; **a ~ boyfriend/girlfriend** ein fester Freund/eine feste Freundin (ugs.). **2** *v.t.* festhalten ‹*Leiter*›; beruhigen ‹*Pferd, Nerven*›; ruhig halten ‹*Boot, Flugzeug*›; **she steadied herself against the table/with a stick** sie hielt sich am Tisch fest/stützte sich mit einem Stock. **3** *v.i.* ‹*Preise:*› sich stabilisieren; ‹*Geschwindigkeit:*› sich mäßigen. **4** *adv.* **go ~ with sb.** mit ihr. vorsichtig sein; **go ~ with sb.** (coll.) mit jmdm. gehen (ugs.)

steak /steɪk/ *n.* Steak, *das;* (of ham, bacon, gammon, salmon, etc.) Scheibe, *die;* **a chicken/turkey/veal ~:** ein Hähnchen-/Puten-/Kalbsschnitzel; **~ and kidney pie** Rindfleisch-Nieren-Pastete, *die*

steal /stiːl/ **1** *v.t.,* **stole** /stəʊl/, **stolen** /'stəʊln/ (a) stehlen (**from** *Dat.*); **~ sb.'s boyfriend/girlfriend** jmdm. den Freund/die Freundin ausspannen (ugs.); **she was the star of the play, but the little dog stole the show** (fig.) sie war der Star des Stückes, aber der kleine Hund stahl ihr die Schau; **~ the show** die Hauptattraktion sein; **a newcomer stole the show** ein Newcomer war der Star [des Abends]; **~ the show from sb.** jmdm. die Schau stehlen *od.* den Rang ablaufen; **(b)** (get slyly) rauben (geh. scherz.) ‹*Kuss, Umarmung*›; entlocken ‹*Worte, Interview*›; sich (*Dat.*) genehmigen (ugs. scherz.) ‹*Nickerchen*›; **~ a glance [at sb./sth.]** jmdm. einen verstohlenen Blick zuwerfen/einen verstohlenen Blick auf etw. (*Akk.*) werfen; **(c)** (fig.: win) **she stole my heart** sie eroberte mein Herz. **2** *v.i.,* **stole, stolen** (a) stehlen; **~ from sb.** jmdn. bestehlen; **~ from the till/supermarket** aus der Kasse/im Supermarkt stehlen; **(b)** (move furtively) sich stehlen; **~ in/out/up** sich hinein-/hinaus-/hinaufstehlen; **~ up [on sb./sth.]** sich [an jmdn./etw.] heranschleichen

~ a'way *v.i.* sich fortstehlen

stealth /stelθ/ *n.* Heimlichkeit, *die;* **by ~:** heimlich

stealthy /'stelθɪ/ *adj.* heimlich; verstohlen ‹*Blick, Bewegung, Tun*›

steam /stiːm/ **1** *n., no pl., no indef. art.* Dampf, *der;* **the window was covered with ~:** das Fenster war beschlagen; **get up ~:** Dampf aufmachen; **let off ~** Dampf ablassen (ugs.); **run out of ~:** keinen Dampf mehr haben; (fig.) den Schwung verlieren; **under one's own ~** (fig.) aus eigener Kraft. **2** *v.t.* (a) (Cookery) dämpfen; dünsten; **~ed pudding** gedämpfter Pudding; **(b) ~ open an envelope** einen Umschlag mit [heißem] Wasserdampf öffnen. **3** *v.i.* dampfen; **~ing hot** dampfend heiß

~ 'up 1 *v.t.* (a) beschlagen lassen; **be ~ed up** beschlagen sein; **(b)** (fig. coll.) **be/get [all] ~ed up [total]** ausrasten (ugs.) **2** *v.i.* beschlagen

steam: ~boat *n.* Dampfschiff, *das;* **~ engine** *n.* (a) (Railw.) Dampflok[omotive], *die;* **(b)** (stationary engine) Dampf[kraft]maschine, *die*

steamer /'stiːmə(r)/ *n.* (a) (Naut.) Dampfer, *der;* **(b)** (Cookery) Dämpfer, *der*

steam: ~ iron *n.* Dampfbügeleisen, *das;* **~roller 1** *n.* Dampfwalze, *die;* **2** *v.t.* [mit der Dampfwalze] walzen; **~ship** *n.* Dampfschiff, *das;* **~ train** *n.* Dampfzug, *der*

steamy /ˈstiːmɪ/ *adj.* (a) dunstig; feucht ⟨*Hitze*⟩; beschlagen ⟨*Glas*⟩; (b) (coll.: erotic) heiß

steel /stiːl/ 1 *n.* Stahl, *der;* **as hard as** ∼: stahlhart. 2 *attrib. adj.* stählern; Stahl ⟨*helm, -block, -platte*⟩. 3 *v.t.* ∼ **oneself for/against sth.** sich für/gegen etw. wappnen (geh.); ∼ **oneself to do sth.** allen Mut zusammennehmen, um etw. zu tun

steel: ∼ **'band** *n.* (Mus.) Steelband, *die;* ∼ **gui'tar** *n.* (Mus.) Hawaiigitarre, *die;* ∼ **industry** *n.* Stahlindustrie, *die;* ∼**worker** *n.* ▶ 887 Stahlarbeiter, *der/*-arbeiterin, *die;* ∼**works** *n. sing., pl. same* Stahlwerk, *das*

steely /ˈstiːlɪ/ *adj.* (a) (strong) stählern; (b) (resolute) eisern; (c) (severe) steinern

steep[1] /stiːp/ *adj.* (a) steil; (b) (rapid) stark ⟨*Preissenkung*⟩; steil ⟨*Preisanstieg*⟩; (c) (coll.: excessive) happig (ugs.); **the bill is [a bit]** ∼: die Rechnung ist [ziemlich] gesalzen (ugs.); **be a bit** ∼: ein bisschen zu weit gehen

steep[2] *v.t.* (a) (soak) einweichen; (b) (bathe) baden

steeped /stiːpt/ *adj.* durchdrungen (**in** von); **a place** ∼ **in history/tradition** ein geschichtsträchtiger/von der Tradition durchdrungener Ort

steepen /ˈstiːpn/ *v.i.* steil[er] werden

steeple /ˈstiːpl/ *n.* Kirchturm, *der*

steeple: ∼**chase** *n.* (Sport) (a) (horse-race) Steeplechase, *die;* Hindernisrennen, *das;* (b) (Athletics) Hindernislauf, *der;* ∼**jack** *n.* ▶ 887 Arbeiter, *der/*Arbeiterin, *die.* Reparaturarbeiten an Kaminen, Kirchtürmen usw. ausführt

steeply /ˈstiːplɪ/ *adv.* steil ⟨*ansteigen, abfallen*⟩

steer[1] /stɪə(r)/ 1 *v.t.* (a) steuern; lenken; **this car is easy to** ∼: dieser Wagen ist leicht lenkbar; (b) (direct) ∼ **a** *or* **one's way through …:** steuern durch …; ∼ **a** *or* **one's course for a place** auf einen Ort zusteuern; (in ship, plane, etc.) Kurs auf einen Ort nehmen; (c) (guide movement of) führen, lotsen ⟨*Person*⟩; ∼ **sb./the conversation towards/away from a subject** jmdn./das Gespräch auf ein Thema lenken/von einem Thema ablenken. 2 *v.i.* steuern; ∼ **clear of sb./sth.** (fig. coll.) jmdm./einer Sache aus dem Weg[e] gehen; ∼ **for sth.** etw. ansteuern

steer[2] *n.* (Zool.) junger Ochse

steering /ˈstɪərɪŋ/ *n.* (a) (Motor Veh.) Lenkung, *die;* (b) (Naut.) Ruder, *das;* Steuerung, *die*

steering: ∼ **column** *n.* (Motor Veh.) Lenksäule, *die;* ∼ **committee** *n.* Lenkungsausschuss, *der;* ∼ **lock** *n.* (Motor Veh.) Lenkradschloss, *das;* ∼ **wheel** *n.* (a) (Motor Veh.) Lenkrad, *das;* (b) (Naut.) Steuerrad, *das*

stem[1] /stem/ 1 *n.* (a) (Bot.) (of tree, shrub) Stamm, *der;* (of flower, leaf, fruit) Stiel, *der;* (b) (of glass) Stiel, *der;* (c) (of tobacco pipe) Pfeifenrohr, *das;* (d) (Ling.) Stamm, *der.* 2 *v.i.* **-mm-:** ∼ **from sth.** auf etw. (*Akk.*) zurückzuführen sein

stem[2] *v.t.* **-mm-** (check, dam up) aufhalten; eindämmen ⟨*Flut*⟩; stillen ⟨*Blutung, Wunde*⟩; (fig.) Einhalt gebieten (+ *Dat.*) (geh.); stoppen ⟨*Redefluss*⟩

stench /stentʃ/ *n.* Gestank, *der* (abwertend)

stencil /ˈstensl/ 1 *n.* (a) ∼ **[-plate]** Schablone, *die;* (b) (for duplicating) Matrize, *die;* (c) (∼led pattern/lettering) schabloniertes Muster/schablonierte Schrift. 2 *v.t.*, (Brit.) **-ll-** mit einer Schablone zeichnen; schablonieren

step /step/ 1 *n.* (a) (movement, distance) Schritt, *der;* **at every** ∼: mit jedem Schritt; **watch sb.'s every** ∼ (fig.) jmdn. auf Schritt und Tritt überwachen; **take a** ∼ **towards/away from sb.** einen Schritt auf jmdn. zugehen/von jmdm. wegtreten; **take a** ∼ **back/sideways/forward** einen Schritt zurücktreten/zur Seite treten/nach vorn treten; **a** ∼ **forward/back** (fig.) ein Schritt nach vorn/zurück; **a** ∼ **in the right/wrong direction** (fig.) ein Schritt in die richtige/falsche Richtung; **mind** *or* **watch your** ∼! (lit. or fig.) pass auf!; **I can't walk another** ∼: ich kann keinen Schritt mehr gehen; (b) (stair) Stufe, *die;* (on vehicle) Tritt, *die;* **a flight of** ∼**s** eine Treppe; **[pair of]** ∼**s** (ladder) Stehleiter, *die;* (small) Trittleiter, *die;* **(c)** **follow** *or* **walk in sb.'s** ∼**s** (fig.) in jmds. Fußstapfen treten; (d) (short distance) **it's only a** ∼ **to my house** es sind nur ein paar Schritte bis zu mir; (e) **be in** ∼: im Schritt sein; (with music, in dancing) im Takt sein; **be in/out of** ∼ **with sth.** (fig.) mit etw. Schritt/nicht Schritt halten; **be out of** ∼: aus dem Schritt geraten sein; (with music, in dancing) nicht im

Takt sein; (f) (action) Schritt, *der;* **take** ∼**s to do sth.** Schritte unternehmen, um etw. zu tun; (g) ∼ **by** ∼: Schritt für Schritt; **what is the next** ∼? wie geht es weiter?; (h) (grade) Stufe, *die.* 2 *v.i.* **-pp-** treten; ∼ **lightly** *or* **softly** leise auftreten; ∼ **inside** eintreten; **please** ∼ **inside for a moment** kommen Sie bitte auf einen Augenblick herein; ∼ **into sb.'s shoes** (fig.) an jmds. Stelle treten; ∼ **on sth.** (on the ground) auf etw. (*Akk.*) treten; **on [to]** steigen auf (+ *Akk.*); steigen in (+ *Akk.*) ⟨*Fahrzeug, Flugzeug*⟩; ∼ **on it** (coll.) auf die Tube drücken (ugs.); ∼ **on sb.'s toes** (lit. or fig.) jmdm. auf die Füße treten; ∼ **out of one's dress/trousers** aus seinem Kleid/seiner Hose steigen (ugs.); ∼ **over sb./sth.** über jmdn./etw. steigen

∼ **a'side** *v.i.* (a) zur Seite treten; (b) (fig.: resign) seine Stellung räumen

∼ **'back** *v.i.* zurücktreten; ∼ **back in fright/surprise** vor Schreck/Überraschung [einen Schritt] zurückweichen

∼ **'down** *v.i.* (a) ∼ **down from the train/into the boat** aus dem Zug/in das Boot steigen; (b) (fig.) ⇒ **stand down**

∼ **'forward** *v.i.* (a) [einen Schritt] vortreten; (b) (fig.: present oneself) sich melden; **would somebody like to** ∼ **forward and help with the trick?** würde jemand gern nach vorn kommen und bei dem Trick assistieren?

∼ **'in** *v.i.* (a) eintreten; (into vehicle) einsteigen; (into pool) hineinsteigen; (b) (fig.) (take sb.'s place) einspringen; (intervene) eingreifen

∼ **'off** 1 *v.i.* (from vehicle) aussteigen; (from a height) hinabspringen. 2 *v.t.* (get off) steigen aus ⟨*Fahrzeug*⟩; treten von ⟨*Bürgersteig*⟩

∼ **'out** *v.i.* hinausgehen; **the car/boat stopped and she** ∼**ped out** der Wagen/das Boot hielt an und sie stieg aus

∼ **'up** 1 *v.i.* (a) (ascend) hinaufsteigen; ∼ **up into** [ein]-steigen in (+ *Akk.*) ⟨*Fahrzeug*⟩; ∼ **up on to** steigen auf (+ *Akk.*) ⟨*Podest, Tisch*⟩; (b) (approach) ∼ **right up!** treten Sie näher!; ∼ **up to sb.** zu jmdm. treten; (c) (increase) zunehmen. 2 *v.t.* erhöhen; intensivieren ⟨*Wahlkampf*⟩; verstärken ⟨*Anstrengungen*⟩; verschärfen ⟨*Sicherheitsmaßnahmen, Streik*⟩

step: ∼ **aerobics** *n.* Step-Aerobic, *das;* ∼**brother** *n.* Stiefbruder, *der;* ∼**child** *n.* Stiefkind, *das;* ∼**daughter** *n.* Stieftochter, *die;* ∼**father** *n.* Stiefvater, *der;* ∼**ladder** *n.* Stehleiter, *die;* ∼**mother** *n.* Stiefmutter, *die*

steppe /step/ *n.* (Geog.) Steppe, *die*

'stepping stone *n.* Trittstein, *der;* (fig.) Sprungbrett, *das* (**to** für, in)

step: ∼**sister** *n.* Stiefschwester, *die;* ∼**son** *n.* Stiefsohn, *der*

stereo /ˈsterɪəʊ/ 1 *n., pl.* ∼**s** (a) (equipment) Stereoanlage, *die;* (b) *no pl.* (sound reproduction) Stereo, *das.* 2 *adj.* stereo; Stereo ⟨*effekt, -aufnahme, -platte*⟩

stereophonic /sterɪəˈfɒnɪk/ *adj.* stereophon

stereoscopic /sterɪəˈskɒpɪk/ *adj.* stereoskopisch

stereotype /ˈsterɪətaɪp/ 1 *n.* Stereotyp, *das* (Psych.); Klischee, *das.* 2 *v.t.* in ein Klischee zwängen; ∼**d** stereotyp ⟨*Redensart, Frage, Vorstellung*⟩; klischeehaft ⟨*Sprache, Denkweise*⟩

sterile /ˈsteraɪl/ *adj.* (a) (germ-free) steril; (b) (barren, lit. or fig.) steril; (fig.) nutzlos ⟨*Tätigkeit*⟩; fruchtlos ⟨*Diskussion, Gespräch*⟩

sterilize (sterilise) /ˈsterɪlaɪz/ *v.t.* sterilisieren

sterling /ˈstɜːlɪŋ/ 1 *n., no pl., no indef. art.* ▶ 938 Sterling, *der;* **five pounds** ∼: fünf Pfund Sterling; **in** ∼: in Pfund [Sterling]. 2 *attrib. adj.* (a) ∼ **silver** Sterlingsilber, *das;* (b) (fig.) gediegen; **do** ∼ **work** erstklassige Arbeit leisten

stern[1] /stɜːn/ *adj.* streng; hart ⟨*Strafe*⟩; ernst ⟨*Warnung*⟩

stern[2] *n.* (Naut.) Heck, *das*

sternly /ˈstɜːnlɪ/ *adv.* streng; ernsthaft ⟨*warnen*⟩; in strengem Ton ⟨*sprechen*⟩

steroid /'stɪərɔɪd, 'sterɔɪd/ *n.* (Chem.) Steroid, *das*
stet /stet/ (Printing) *v.i. imper.* bleibt
stethoscope /'steθəskəʊp/ *n.* (Med.) Stethoskop, *das*
Stetson, P /'stetsn/ *n.* Stetson[hut], *der*
stevedore /'sti:vədɔ:(r)/ *n.* ▶ 887 | (Naut.) Schauermann, *der*
stew /stju:/ **1** *n.* (Gastr.) Eintopf, *der;* **Irish** ~: Irish-Stew, *das.* **2** *v.t.* (Cookery) schmoren [lassen]; ~ **apples/plums** Apfel-/Pflaumenkompott kochen. **3** *v.i.* (Cookery) schmoren; ⟨*Obst:*⟩ gedünstet werden; ~ **[in one's own juice]** (fig.) [im eigenen Saft] schmoren (ugs.)
steward /'stju:əd/ *n.* ▶ 887 | **(a)** (on ship, plane) Steward, *der;* **(b)** (at public meeting, ball, etc.) Ordner, *der*/Ordnerin, *die;* ~**s** (of race) Rennleitung, *die;* **(c)** (estate manager) Verwalter, *der*/Verwalterin, *die*
stewardess /'stju:ədɪs/ *n.* ▶ 887 | Stewardess, *die*
'stewing steak *n.*, *no pl.*, *no indef. art.* [Rinder]schmorfleisch, *das*
stick /stɪk/ **1** *v.t.*, **stuck** /stʌk/ **(a)** (thrust point of) stecken; ~ **sth. in[to] sth.** mit etw. in etw. (*Akk.*) stechen; **get stuck into sb./sth./a meal** (coll.: begin action) jmdm. eine Abreibung verpassen/sich in etw. (*Akk.*) reinknien/tüchtig reinhauen (salopp); **(b)** (impale) spießen; ~ **sth. [up]on sth.** etw. auf etw. (*Akk.*) [auf]spießen; **(c)** (coll.: put) stecken; **he stuck a feather in his hat** er steckte sich (*Dat.*) eine Feder an den Hut; ~ **a picture on the wall/a vase on the shelf** ein Bild an die Wand hängen/eine Vase aufs Regal stellen; ~ **sth. in the kitchen** etw. in die Küche tun (ugs.); ~ **one on sb.** (sl.: hit) jmdm. eine langen (ugs.); **you know where you can** ~ **that!**, **[you can]** ~ **it!** (sl.) das kannst du dir sonst wohin stecken!; **(d)** (with glue etc.) kleben; **(e)** (make immobile) **the car is stuck in the mud** das Auto ist im Schlamm stecken geblieben; **the door is stuck** die Tür klemmt [fest]; **(f)** (puzzle) **be stuck for an answer/for ideas** um eine Antwort/um Ideen verlegen sein; **Can you help me with this problem? I'm stuck** Kannst du mir bei diesem Problem helfen? Ich komme nicht weiter; **(g)** (cover) ~ **sth. with pins/needles** Stecknadeln/Nadeln in etw. (*Akk.*) stecken; **(h)** (Brit. coll.: tolerate) ~ **it** durchhalten; **she can't** ~ **him** sie kann ihn nicht riechen (salopp); **(i)** (coll.) **be stuck with sth.** (have to accept) sich mit etw. herumschlagen müssen (ugs.); **be stuck with sb.** jmdn. am *od.* auf dem Hals haben (ugs.). **2** *v.i.*, **stuck (a)** (be fixed by point) stecken; **(b)** (adhere) kleben; ~ **to sth.** an etw. (*Dat.*) kleben; ~ **in the/sb.'s mind** (fig.) im/jmdm. im Gedächtnis haften bleiben; **(c)** (become immobile) ⟨*Auto, Räder:*⟩ stecken bleiben; ⟨*Schublade, Tür, Griff, Bremse:*⟩ klemmen; ⟨*Schlüssel:*⟩ feststecken; ~ **fast** ⟨*Auto, Rad:*⟩ feststecken; ⟨*Reißverschluss, Tür, Schublade:*⟩ festklemmen; **the record is stuck** die Platte ist hängen geblieben; **(d)** (protrude) **a letter stuck from his pocket** ein Brief schaute ihm aus der Tasche. **3** *n.* **(a)** ([cut] shoot of tree, piece of wood; also for punishment) Stock, *der;* (staff) [Holz]stab, *der;* (walking-~) Spazierstock, *der;* (for handicapped person) Krückstock, *der;* **(b)** (Hockey etc.) Schläger, *der;* **(c)** (long piece) **a** ~ **of chalk/shavingsoap** ein Stück Kreide/Rasierseife; **a** ~ **of rock/celery/rhubarb** eine Zuckerstange/eine Stange Sellerie/Rhabarber; **(d)** *no pl.*, *no art.* (coll.: criticism) **get** *or* **take [some]** ~: viel einstecken müssen; **give sb. [some]** ~: jmdn. zusammenstauchen (ugs.).
~ **a'bout,** ~ **a'round** *v.i.* (coll.) dableiben; (wait) warten
~ **at** *v.t.* ~ **at one's books/studying** fleißig Bücher wälzen/studieren; ~ **'at it** (coll.) dranbleiben (ugs.)
~ **by** *v.t.* (fig.) stehen zu
~ **'down** *v.t.* festkleben; zukleben ⟨*Umschlag*⟩
~ **'in** *v.t.* **(a)** (jab in) hineinstechen ⟨*Spritze, Nadel*⟩; anstecken ⟨*Hutnadel*⟩; **(b)** (glue in) einkleben; **(c)** (coll.: put in) hineinstecken
~ **'on 1** *v.t.* **(a)** (glue on) aufkleben ⟨*Briefmarke, Etikett*⟩; ankleben ⟨*Tapete*⟩; **(b)** (attach by pin etc.) anstecken. **2** *v.i.* kleben[bleiben]
~ **'out 1** *v.t.* **(a)** herausstrecken ⟨*Brust, Zunge*⟩; ausstrecken ⟨*Arm, Bein*⟩; **(b)** ~ **it out** (coll.) durchhalten; ausharren. **2** *v.i.* **(a)** (project) ⟨*Brust, Bauch:*⟩ vorstehen; ⟨*steifes Kleid:*⟩ abstehen; ⟨*Nagel, Ast:*⟩ herausstehen; **his ears** ~ **out** er hat abstehende Ohren; **(b)** (fig.: be obvious) sich abheben; ~ **out a mile** (coll.) [klar] auf der Hand

liegen; ~ **out like a sore thumb** (coll.) ins Auge springen
~ **to** *v.t.* **(a)** (be faithful to) halten zu ⟨*Person*⟩; halten ⟨*Versprechen*⟩; bleiben bei ⟨*Entscheidung, Meinung*⟩; treu bleiben (+ *Dat.*) ⟨*Idealen, Grundsätzen*⟩; **(b)** (not deviate from) sich halten an (+ *Akk.*) ⟨*Plan, Text, Original*⟩; bleiben an (+ *Dat.*) ⟨*Arbeit*⟩; bleiben bei ⟨*Wahrheit, Thema*⟩; ~ **to business** bei der Sache bleiben; ~ **to the point** beim Thema bleiben
~ **to'gether 1** *v.t.* zusammenkleben. **2** *v.i.* **(a)** (adhere together) zusammenkleben; **(b)** (fig.: remain united) zusammenhalten
~ **'up 1** *v.t.* **(a)** (seal) zukleben; **(b)** (coll.: put up, raise) strecken, recken ⟨*Kopf, Hals*⟩; anschlagen ⟨*Bekanntmachung, Poster*⟩; aufschlagen ⟨*Zelt*⟩; hinbauen, -setzen ⟨*Häuser*⟩; raufsetzen (ugs.) ⟨*Preise*⟩; ~ **up one's hand** die Hand heben; ~ **'em up!** (coll.) Pfoten hoch! (salopp); **(c)** (coll.: rob) ausrauben; **(d) stuck up** (conceited) eingebildet. **2** *v.i.* **(a)** ⟨*Haar, Kragen:*⟩ hochstehen; ⟨*Nagel, Pflasterstein:*⟩ hervorstehen; **(b)** ~ **up for sb./sth.** für jmdn./etw. eintreten; ~ **up for yourself!** setz dich zur Wehr!
~ **with** *v.t.* (coll.) **(a)** (keep contact with) ~ **with the leaders** sich an der Spitze halten (bes. Sport); ~ **'with it!** bleib dran! (ugs.); **(b)** (remain faithful to) bleiben bei ⟨*Gruppe, Partei*⟩; halten zu ⟨*Freund*⟩
sticker /'stɪkə(r)/ *n.* Aufkleber, *der*
'sticking plaster *n.* (Med.) Heftpflaster, *das*
'stick-in-the-mud 1 *n.* (person lacking initiative) Trantüte, *die* (ugs. abwertend); (unprogressive person) Spießer, *der* (abwertend). **2** *adj.* (lacking in initiative) schlafmützig (ugs. abwertend); (unprogressive) spießig (abwertend)
stickleback /'stɪklbæk/ *n.* (Zool.) Stichling, *der*
stickler /'stɪklə(r)/ *n.* **be a** ~ **for tidiness/authority** es mit der Sauberkeit sehr genau nehmen/in puncto Autorität keinen Spaß verstehen
stick: ~**-on** *adj.* selbstklebend; ~**-up** *n.* (coll.) bewaffneter Raubüberfall
sticky /'stɪkɪ/ *adj.* **1 (a)** klebrig; feucht ⟨*Farbe, gestrichener/gewaschener Gegenstand*⟩; zäh ⟨*Teig, Brei, Mischung*⟩; ~ **label** Aufkleber, *der;* ~ **tape** Klebstreifen, *der;* **(b)** (humid) schwül ⟨*Klima, Luft*⟩; feucht ⟨*Haut*⟩; **(c)** (coll.: unpleasant) vertrackt (ugs.); heikel; **a** ~ **situation** eine brenzlige Lage. **2** *n.* (coll.) Post-it, *das* (ugs.)
stiff /stɪf/ *adj.* **1 (a)** (rigid) steif; hart ⟨*Bürste, Stock*⟩; **be frozen** ~: steif vor Kälte sein; ⟨*Wäsche, Körper[teile]:*⟩ steif gefroren sein; **(b)** (intense, severe) hartnäckig; schroff ⟨*Absage*⟩; kräftig ⟨*Standpauke*⟩; ~ **competition** scharfe Konkurrenz, **(c)** (formal) steif, förmlich ⟨*Brief, Stil*⟩; **(d)** (difficult) hart ⟨*Test*⟩; schwer ⟨*Frage, Prüfung*⟩; steil ⟨*Abstieg, Anstieg*⟩; **be** ~ **going** (fig. coll.) harte Arbeit sein; **(e)** stark, (Seemannsspr.) steif ⟨*Wind, Brise*⟩; **(f)** (not bending, not working freely, aching) steif ⟨*Gelenk, Gliedmaßen, Nacken, Person*⟩; schwergängig ⟨*Angel, Kolben, Gelenk*⟩; **(g)** (coll.: excessive) saftig (ugs.) ⟨*Preis, Strafe*⟩; **(h)** (strong) steif (ugs.) ⟨*Drink*⟩; stark ⟨*Dosis, Medizin*⟩; **(i)** (thick) zäh[flüssig]; **(j)** (coll.) **be bored/scared/worried** ~: sich zu Tode langweilen/eine wahnsinnige Angst haben (ugs.) /sich (*Dat.*) furchtbare (ugs.) Sorgen machen
stiffen /'stɪfn/ **1** *v.t.* **(a)** steif machen; stärken ⟨*Kragen*⟩; versteifen ⟨*Material*⟩; zäh[flüssig] machen ⟨*Paste, Teig*⟩; **(b)** (fig.: bolster) verstärken ⟨*Widerstand*⟩; stärken ⟨*Moral, Entschlossenheit*⟩. **2** *v.i.* **(a)** ⟨*Person:*⟩ erstarren; **(b)** ⟨*Wind, Brise:*⟩ steifer werden (Seemannsspr.), auffrischen; **(c)** (become thicker) ⟨*Teig:*⟩ steifer werden; ⟨*Mischung:*⟩ zäher werden; **(d)** (fig.: become more resolute) sich verstärken
stiffness /'stɪfnɪs/ *n.*, *no pl.* **(a)** (rigidity, formality) Steifheit, *die;* (of letter, language) Förmlichkeit, *die;* **(b)** (intensity) Härte, *die;* **(c)** (difficulty) Schwierigkeit, *die;* **(d)** (of wind) Stärke, *die;* Steifheit, *die* (Seemannsspr.); **(e)** (lack of suppleness) Steifheit, *die;* (of hinge, piston) geringe Beweglichkeit, *die;* **(f)** (coll.: excessiveness) (of punishment) Strenge, *die;* (of demand, price) Überzogenheit, *die;* **(g)** (thick consistency) Zähheit, *die*
stifle /'staɪfl/ **1** *v.t.* ersticken; (fig.: suppress) unterdrücken; ersticken ⟨*Widerstand, Aufstand, Schrei*⟩; **we were** ~**d by the heat** wir erstickten fast vor Hitze. **2** *v.i.* ersticken
stifling /'staɪflɪŋ/ *adj.* stickig; drückend ⟨*Hitze*⟩; (fig.) einengend ⟨*Atmosphäre*⟩; erdrückend ⟨*Einfluss, Herrschaft*⟩

stigma /'stɪgmə/ *n.* Stigma, *das* (geh.); Makel, *der* (geh.)

stile /staɪl/ *n.* Zauntritt, *der;* Trittleiter, *die*

stiletto /stɪ'letəʊ/ *n., pl.* ~s *or* ~es (a) (dagger) Stilett, *das;* (b) ~ [heel] Stöckelabsatz, *der*

still¹ /stɪl/ **1** *adj.* (a) *pred.* still; **be** ~: [still] stehen; ⟨*Fahne:*⟩ sich nicht bewegen; ⟨*Hand:*⟩ ruhig sein; **hold** *or* **keep sth.** ~: etw. ruhig halten; **hold** *or* **keep a ladder/ horse** ~: eine Leiter/ein Pferd festhalten; **hold** ~! halt still!; **keep** *or* **stay** ~: stillhalten; (not change posture) ruhig bleiben; ⟨*Pferd:*⟩ stillstehen; ⟨*Gegenstand:*⟩ liegen bleiben; **sit** ~: stillsitzen; **stand** ~: stillstehen; ⟨*Uhr:*⟩ stehen; ⟨*Arbeit:*⟩ ruhen; (stop) stehen bleiben; (b) (calm) ruhig; (c) (without sound) still; ruhig; (d) (not sparkling) nicht moussierend ⟨*Wein*⟩; still ⟨*Mineralwasser*⟩; (e) (hushed) leise. **2** *adv.* (a) (without change) noch; *expr. surprise or annoyance* immer noch; **drink your tea while it is** ~ **hot** trink deinen Tee, solange er [noch] heiß ist; (b) (nevertheless) trotzdem; ~, **what can you do about it?** aber was kann man dagegen tun?; (c) *with comparative* (even) noch; **become fatter** ~ *or* ~ **fatter** noch *od.* immer dicker werden; **better/worse** ~ *as sentence-modifier* besser/ schlimmer noch. **3** *n.* (Photog.) Fotografie, *die*

still² *n.* Destillierapparat, *der*

still: ~**born** *adj.* tot geboren; **the child was** ~**born** das Kind war eine Totgeburt *od.* kam tot zur Welt; ~ **life** *n., pl.* ~ **lifes** *or* ~ **lives** (Art) Stillleben, *das*

stillness /'stɪlnɪs/ *n., no pl.* (a) (motionlessness) Bewegungslosigkeit, *die;* (b) (quietness) Stille, *die*

stilt /stɪlt/ *n.* Stelze, *die*

stilted /'stɪltɪd/ *adj.* gestelzt; gespreizt

stimulant /'stɪmjʊlənt/ **1** *attrib. adj.* (Med.) stimulierend. **2** *n.* (lit. *or* fig.) Stimulans, *das;* Anregungsmittel, *das*

stimulate /'stɪmjʊleɪt/ *v.t.* (a) anregen; stimulieren (geh.); beleben ⟨*Körper*⟩; (sexually) erregen; (b) (fig.) anregen ⟨*Geist, Diskussion, Appetit*⟩; hervorrufen ⟨*Reaktion*⟩; wecken ⟨*Interesse, Neugier*⟩; beleben ⟨*Wirtschaft, Wachstum, Markt, Absatz*⟩

stimulation /stɪmjʊ'leɪʃn/ *n.* (a) Anregung, *die;* Stimulierung, *die* (geh.); (sexual) Erregung, *die;* (b) (fig.) Anregung, *die;* (of reaction) Hervorrufen, *das;* (of interest, curiosity) Wecken, *das;* (of economy, market, growth, sales) Belebung, *die*

stimulus /'stɪmjʊləs/ *n., pl.* **stimuli** /'stɪmjʊlaɪ/ (a) (spur) Ansporn, *der* (**to** zu); (b) (rousing effect) Anregung, *die*

sting /stɪŋ/ **1** *n.* (a) (wounding) Stich, *der;* (by jellyfish, nettles) Verbrennung, *die;* (b) (pain) Stechen, *das;* stechender Schmerz; (from ointment, cane, whip, wind, rash) Brennen, *das;* **a** ~ **in the tail** (fig.) ein Pferdefuß; **take the** ~ **out of sth.** (fig.) einer Sache (*Dat.*) den Stachel nehmen (geh.); (c) (Zool.) [Gift]stachel, *der;* (d) (fraud) Ding, *das* (ugs.); (police operation) Operation, *die.* **2** *v.t.,* **stung** /stʌŋ/ (a) (wound) stechen; **a bee stung [him on] his arm** eine Biene stach ihm in den Arm; **a jellyfish stung me/my leg** ich habe mich/mein Bein an einer Qualle verbrannt; (b) (cause pain to) **the smoke/the wind stung my eyes** der Rauch/der Wind brannte mir in den Augen; (c) (hurt mentally) tief treffen; [zutiefst] verletzen; ~**ing** scharf ⟨*Vorwürfe, Anklagen, Kritik*⟩; (d) (incite) ~ **sb. into sth./doing sth.** jmdn. zu etw. anstacheln/dazu anstacheln, etw. zu tun; (e) (sl.: swindle) übers Ohr hauen (ugs.). **3** *v.i.,* **stung** (a) (feel pain) brennen; (b) (have ~) stechen

'stinging nettle *n.* (Bot.) Brennnessel, *die*

'stingray *n.* (Zool.) Stechrochen, *der*

stingy /'stɪndʒɪ/ *adj.* geizig; knaus[e]rig (ugs.); kümmerlich ⟨*Spende, Portion, Mahlzeit*⟩

stink /stɪŋk/ **1** *v.i.,* **stank** /stæŋk/ *or* **stunk** /stʌŋk/, **stunk** (a) stinken (**of** nach); (fig.) ⟨*Angelegenheit, Korruption:*⟩ zum Himmel stinken; (b) (fig.: be repulsive) **sth.** ~**s** an etw. (+ *Dat.*) stinkt etwas (ugs.). **2** *n.* (a) (bad smell) Gestank, *der;* (b) (coll.: fuss) Stunk, *der* (ugs.); **kick up** *or* **raise a** ~ **about sth.** wegen etw. Stunk machen (ugs.).

'stink bomb *n.* Stinkbombe, *die*

stint /stɪnt/ **1** *v.t.* kurz halten; ~ **oneself [of sth.]** sich [mit etw.] einschränken. **2** *v.i.* ~ **on sth.** an etw. (*Dat.*) sparen. **3** *n.* (a) (allotted amount) [Arbeits]pensum, *das;* **each of us did a** ~ **at the wheel** jeder von uns saß eine Zeit

lang am Steuer; (b) (limitation) **without** ~: uneingeschränkt

stipulate /'stɪpjʊleɪt/ (demand) fordern; verlangen; (lay down) festlegen; (insist on) sich (*Dat.*) ausbedingen

stipulation /stɪpjʊ'leɪʃn/ *n.* (a) (condition) Bedingung, *die;* **on** *or* **with the** ~ **that** ...: unter der Bedingung, dass ...; (b) (act) ⇒ **stipulate:** Forderung, *die;* Festlegung, *die;* Ausbedingung, *die*

stir /stɜː(r)/ **1** *v.t.,* **-rr-:** (a) (mix) rühren; umrühren ⟨*Tee, Kaffee*⟩; ~ **sth. into sth.** etw. in etw. (*Akk.*) [ein]rühren; (b) (move) bewegen; (c) (fig.: arouse) bewegen; wecken ⟨*Neugier, Interesse, Gefühle, Fantasie*⟩. **2** *v.i.,* **-rr-** (move) sich rühren; (in sleep, breeze) sich bewegen; **without** ~**ring** regungslos. **3** *n., no pl.* Aufregung, *die;* (bustle, activity) Betriebsamkeit, *die;* **cause** *or* **create a [big** *or* **great]** ~: [großes] Aufsehen erregen

~ **'in** *v.t.* einrühren

~ **'up** *v.t.* (a) (disturb) aufrühren; (b) (fig.: arouse, provoke) wecken ⟨*Neugier, Interesse, Leidenschaft*⟩; aufrütteln ⟨*Anhänger, Gefolgsleute*⟩; entfachen ⟨*Liebe, Hass, Streit, Zorn, Revolution*⟩; schüren ⟨*Hass, Feindseligkeit*⟩

'stir-fry *v.t.* (Cookery) unter Rühren schnell braten

stirring /'stɜːrɪŋ/ *adj.* bewegend ⟨*Musik, Theaterstück, Poesie*⟩; spannend ⟨*Roman, Geschichte*⟩; mitreißend ⟨*Auftritt, Rede, Marsch*⟩; bewegt ⟨*Zeiten*⟩

stirrup /'stɪrəp/ *n.* (Riding) Steigbügel, *der*

stitch /stɪtʃ/ **1** *n.* (a) (Sewing: pass of needle) Stich, *der;* (b) (result of needle movement) (Knitting, Crocheting) Masche, *die;* (Sewing, Embroidery) Stich, *der;* **drop a** ~ (Knitting) eine Masche fallen lassen; (c) (coll.: piece of clothing) **not have a** ~ **on** splitter[faser]nackt (ugs.) sein; (d) (pain) [have] **a** ~ **[in the side]** Seitenstechen [haben]; (e) (coll.) **be in** ~**es** sich kugeln vor Lachen (ugs.); (f) (Med.: to sew up wound) Stich, *der;* ~**es** Naht, *die;* **he had his** ~**es taken out** ihm wurden die Fäden gezogen. **2** *v.t.* nähen; (Embroidery) sticken. **3** *v.i.* nähen; (Embroidery) sticken

~ **'on** *v.t.* annähen ⟨*Knopf*⟩; aufnähen ⟨*Flicken, Borte*⟩

~ **'up** *v.t.* (disturb) aufrühren; zusammennähen ⟨*Stoffteile*⟩; vernähen ⟨*Loch, Riß, Wunde*⟩

stoat /stəʊt/ *n.* Hermelin, *das*

stock /stɒk/ **1** *n.* (a) (origin, family, breed) Abstammung, *die;* **be** *or* **come of farming/French** ~: bäuerlicher/französischer Herkunft sein; (b) (supply, store) Vorrat, *der;* (in shop etc.) Warenbestand, *der;* **our** ~**s of food/sherry** unsere Lebensmittelvorräte *Pl.* unser Vorrat an Sherry (*Dat.*); **be in** ~/**out of** ~: vorrätig/nicht vorrätig sein; **have sth. in** ~: etw. auf *od.* (Kaufmannsspr.) am Lager haben; **keep sth. in** ~: etw. führen; **take** ~: Inventur machen; (fig.) Bilanz ziehen; **take** ~ **of sth.** (fig.) über etw. (*Akk.*) Bilanz ziehen; **take** ~ **of one's situation/prospects** seine Situation/seine Zukunftsaussichten bestimmen; (c) (Cookery) Brühe, *die;* (d) (Finance) Wertpapiere *Pl.;* (shares) Aktien *Pl.;* **sb.'s** ~ **is high/low** (fig.) jmds. Aktien stehen gut/schlecht (fig.); (e) (Hort.) Stamm, *der;* (for grafting) Unterlage, *die;* (f) (handle) Griff, *der;* (of gun) Schaft, *der;* (g) (Agric.) Vieh, *das;* (h) (raw material) [Roh]material, *das;* **[film]** ~: Filmmaterial, *das.* **2** *v.t.* (a) (supply with) ~ beliefern; ~ **a pond/ river/lake with fish** einen Teich/Fluss/See mit Fischen besetzen; (b) (Commerc.: keep in ~) auf *od.* (Kaufmannsspr.) am Lager haben; führen. **3** *attrib. adj.* (a) (Commerc.) vorrätig; **a** ~ **size/model** eine Standardgröße/ein Standardmodell; (b) (fig.: trite, unoriginal) abgedroschen (ugs.); ~ **character** Standardrolle, *die*

~ **'up** **1** *v.i.* ~ **up [with sth.]** sich (*Dat.*) einen Vorrat an etw. (*Dat.*) anlegen; ~ **up on sth.** seine Vorräte an etw. (*Dat.*) auffüllen. **2** *v.t.* auffüllen; mit Fischen besetzen ⟨*Teich, Fluss, See*⟩

stockade /stɒ'keɪd/ *n.* Palisade, *die*

stock: ~**broker** *n.* ▶ 887 | (Finance) Effektenmakler, *der/*-maklerin, *die;* ~**broking** /'stɒkbrəʊkɪŋ/ *n., no pl.* (Finance) Effektenhandel, *der;* ~ **cube** *n.* (Cookery) Brühwürfel, *der;* ~ **exchange** *n.* (Finance) Börse, *die;* **the S**~ **Exchange** (Brit.) die [Londoner] Börse

stocking /'stɒkɪŋ/ *n.* Strumpf, *der;* **in one's** ~**[ed]** feet in Strümpfen; **hang up one's** ~: den Strumpf für den Weihnachtsmann aufhängen

stocking: ∿ **filler** (Brit.), ∿ **stuffer** (Amer.) *ns.* (a) *kleines Geschenk, das in den für den Weihnachtsmann aufgehängten Strumpf gesteckt wird;* (b) zusätzliche Kleinigkeit (*als Weihnachtsgeschenk*)

stock-in-'trade *n.* Inventar, *das;* (workman's tools) Handwerkszeug, *das;* (fig.: resource) [festes] Repertoire; **be the** ∿ **of sb.** zu jmds. festem Repertoire gehören

stockist /'stɒkɪst/ *n.* (Brit. Commerc.) Fachhändler/-händlerin [mit größerem Warenlager]

stock: ∿ **market** *n.* (Finance) (a) ⇒ **stock exchange;** (b) (trading) Börsengeschäft, *das;* ∿**pile** 1 *n.* Vorrat, *der;* (of weapons) Arsenal, *das;* 2 *v.t.* horten; anhäufen ⟨*Waffen*⟩; ∿**pot** *n.* (Cookery) Suppentopf, *der;* ∿**room** *n.* Lager, *das;* ∿-'**still** *pred. adj.* bewegungslos; **stand** ∿-**still** regungslos [da]stehen; ∿**taking** *n.* (Commerc.) Inventur, *die;* **closed for** ∿**taking** wegen Inventur geschlossen

stocky /'stɒkɪ/ *adj.* stämmig

stockyard /'stɒkjɑːd/ *n.* Viehhof, *der*

stodgy /'stɒdʒɪ/ *adj.* pappig [und schwer verdaulich] ⟨*Essen*⟩

stoic /'stəʊɪk/ 1 *n.* (a) S∿ (Philos.) Stoiker, *der;* (b) (impassive person) Stoiker, *der*/Stoikerin, *die.* 2 *adj.* (a) S∿ (Philos.) stoisch; (b) stoisch ⟨*Person, Ablehnung, Antwort usw.*⟩

stoical /'stəʊɪkl/ *adj.* stoisch

stoke /stəʊk/ *v.t.* heizen ⟨*Ofen, Kessel*⟩; unterhalten ⟨*Feuer*⟩

∿ '**up** 1 *v.t.* aufheizen ⟨*Kessel, Ofen, Dampfmaschine*⟩. 2 *v.i.* (coll.: feed oneself) sich voll stopfen (ugs.)

stoker /'stəʊkə(r)/ *n.* ▶ 887 | Heizer, *der*/Heizerin, *die*

stole ⇒ **steal**

stolen /'stəʊln/ 1 ⇒ **steal.** 2 *attrib. adj.* heimlich ⟨*Vergnügen, Kuss*⟩; verstohlen ⟨*Blick*⟩; ∿ **goods** Diebesgut, *das;* **receiver of** ∿ **goods** Hehler, *der*/Hehlerin, *die*

stolid /'stɒlɪd/ *adj.* stur (ugs.); unbeirrbar ⟨*Entschlossenheit*⟩; hartnäckig ⟨*Schweigen, Weigerung, Gleichgültigkeit*⟩

stomach /'stʌmək/ 1 *n.* (a) ▶ 672 | (Anat., Zool.) Magen, *der;* **on an empty** ∿: mit leerem Magen ⟨*arbeiten, fahren, weggehen*⟩; auf nüchternen Magen ⟨*Alkohol trinken, Medizin einnehmen*⟩; **on a full** ∿: mit vollem Magen; **turn sb.'s** ∿: jmdm. den Magen umdrehen (ugs.); (b) (abdomen, paunch) Bauch, *der;* **have a pain in one's** ∿: Bauchschmerzen haben; (c) **have the/no** ∿ **[for sth.]** (wish/not wish to eat) Appetit/keinen Appetit [auf etw. (*Akk.*)] haben; (fig.: courage) Mut/keinen Mut [zu etw.] haben. 2 *v.t.* (a) (eat, drink) herunterbekommen (ugs.); (keep down) bei sich behalten; (b) (fig.: tolerate) ausstehen; akzeptieren ⟨*Vorstellung, Vorgehen, Rat*⟩

stomach: ∿-**ache** *n.* ▶ 865 | Magenschmerzen *Pl.;* **have a** ∿-**ache** Magenschmerzen haben; ∿ **upset** *n.* ▶ 865 | Magenverstimmung, *die*

stone /stəʊn/ 1 *n.* (a) (also Med., Bot.) Stein, *der;* [as] **hard as** [a] ∿: steinhart; **throw** ∿s/a ∿ **at sb.** jmdn. mit Steinen bewerfen/einen Stein auf jmdn. werfen; **only a** ∿'s **throw [away]** (fig.) nur einen Steinwurf weit entfernt; **leave no** ∿ **unturned** (fig.) Himmel und Hölle in Bewegung setzen; **sink like a** ∿: wie ein Stein untergehen; **the lift dropped like a** ∿: der Aufzug fiel wie ein Stein in die Tiefe; **be written** *or* **carved** *or* **set in** ∿: (fig.) unverrückbar sein; (b) (gem) [Edel]stein, *der;* (c) *pl. same* ▶ 1202 | (Brit.: weight unit) Gewicht von 6,35 kg. 2 *adj.* steinern; Stein⟨*hütte, -kreuz, -mauer, -brücke*⟩. 3 *v.t.* (a) mit Steinen bewerfen; ∿ **me!,** ∿ **the crows!** (coll.) mich laust der Affe! (ugs.); (b) (remove stone from) entsteinen ⟨*Obst*⟩

stone: S∿ **Age** *n.* (Archaeol.) Steinzeit, *die; attrib.* Steinzeit-; ∿-**cold** 1 *adj.* eiskalt; 2 *adv.* ∿-**cold sober** stocknüchtern

stoned /stəʊnd/ *adj.* (coll.) stoned (Drogenjargon); (drunk) voll zu (salopp)

stone: ∿-'**dead** *pred. adj.* mausetot (fam.); **kill sth.** ∿-**dead** (fig.) etw. völlig zunichte machen; ∿-'**deaf** *adj.* stocktaub (ugs.); ∿'**wall** (Brit.) 1 *v.i.* mauern (fig.); 2 *v.t.* ∿**wall sth.** bei etw. mauern; ∿**walling** /'stəʊnwɔːlɪŋ/ *n.* (Brit.) ∿**walling [tactics]** Hinhaltetaktik, *die;* ∿**ware** *n., no pl.* Steingut, *das; attrib.* ⟨*Krug, Vase*⟩ aus Steingut;

∿**washed** *adj.* mit Steinen ausgewaschen; stonewashed (fachspr.)

stony /'stəʊnɪ/ *adj.* (a) (full of stones) steinig; (b) (like stone) steinartig; (c) (hostile) steinern (geh.) ⟨*Blick, Miene*⟩; frostig ⟨*Person, Empfang, Schweigen*⟩

stood ⇒ **stand** 1, 2

stool /stuːl/ *n.* Hocker, *der;* **fall between two** ∿s (fig.) sich zwischen zwei Stühle setzen

stoop /stuːp/ 1 *v.i.* (a) ∿ **[down]** sich bücken; ∿ **over sth.** sich über etw. (*Akk.*) beugen; **he'd** ∿ **to anything to get his way** (fig.) ihm ist jedes Mittel recht[, um sein Ziel zu erreichen]; ∿ **to do sth.** (fig.) sich dazu erniedrigen, etw. zu tun; (b) (have ∿) gebeugt gehen. 2 *v.t.* beugen; ∿**ed with old age** vom Alter gebeugt. 3 *n.* gebeugte Haltung; **have a/walk with a** ∿: einen krummen Rücken haben/gebeugt gehen

stop /stɒp/ 1 *v.t.,* -**pp-:** (a) (not let move further) anhalten ⟨*Person, Fahrzeug*⟩; aufhalten ⟨*Fortschritt, Verkehr, Feind*⟩; verstummen lassen (geh.) ⟨*Gerücht, Geschichte, Lüge*⟩; ⟨*Tormann:*⟩ halten ⟨*Ball*⟩; **she** ∿**ped her car** sie hielt an; ∿ **thief!** haltet den Dieb!; **there's no** ∿**ping sb.** jmd. lässt sich nicht aufhalten; (b) (not let continue) unterbrechen ⟨*Redner, Spiel, Gespräch, Vorstellung*⟩; beenden ⟨*Krieg, Gespräch, Treffen, Spiel, Versuch, Arbeit*⟩; stillen ⟨*Blutung*⟩; stoppen ⟨*Produktion, Uhr, Streik, Inflation*⟩; einstellen ⟨*Handel, Zahlung, Lieferung, Besuche, Subskriptionen, Bemühungen*⟩; abstellen ⟨*Strom, Gas, Wasser, Missstände*⟩; beseitigen ⟨*Schmerz*⟩; ∿ **that/that nonsense/that noise!** hör damit/mit diesem Unsinn/diesem Lärm auf!; **bad light** ∿**ped play** (Sport) das Spiel wurde wegen schlechter Lichtverhältnisse abgebrochen; ∿ **the show** (fig.) Furore machen; **just you try and** ∿ **me!** versuch doch, mich daran zu hindern!; ∿ **smoking/crying** aufhören zu rauchen/weinen; **never** ∿ **doing sth.** etw. unaufhörlich tun; ∿ **it!** hör auf [damit]!; (in more peremptory tone) Schluss damit!; ∿ **oneself** sich zurückhalten; **I couldn't** ∿ **myself** ich konnte nicht anders; (c) (not let happen) verhindern ⟨*Verbrechen, Unfall*⟩; **he tried to** ∿ **us parking** er versuchte uns am Parken zu hindern; **he phoned his mother to** ∿ **her [from] worrying** er rief seine Mutter an, damit sie sich keine Sorgen machte; ∿ **sth. [from] happening** verhindern, dass etw. geschieht; (d) (cause to cease working) abstellen ⟨*Maschine usw.*⟩; ⟨*Streikende:*⟩ stilllegen ⟨*Betrieb*⟩; (e) (block up) zustopfen ⟨*Loch, Öffnung, Riß, Ohren*⟩; verschließen ⟨*Wasserhahn, Rohr, Schlauch, Flasche*⟩; (f) (withhold) streichen; ∿ **[payment of] a cheque** einen Scheck sperren lassen. 2 *v.i.,* -**pp-:** (a) (not extend further) aufhören; ⟨*Straße, Treppe:*⟩ enden; ⟨*Ton:*⟩ verstummen; ⟨*Ärger:*⟩ verfliegen; ⟨*Schmerz:*⟩ abklingen; ⟨*Zahlungen, Lieferungen:*⟩ eingestellt werden; (b) (not move or operate further) ⟨*Fahrzeug, Fahrer:*⟩ halten; ⟨*Maschine, Motor:*⟩ stillstehen; ⟨*Uhr, Fußgänger, Herz:*⟩ stehen bleiben; **he** ∿**ped in the middle of the sentence** er unterbrach sich mitten im Satz; **he never** ∿**s to think [before he acts]** er denkt nie nach [bevor er handelt]; ∿! halt!; ∿ **at nothing** vor nichts zurückschrecken; ∿ **dead** plötzlich stehen bleiben; ⟨*Redner:*⟩ abbrechen. (c) (coll.: stay) bleiben; ∿ **at a hotel/at a friend's house/with sb.** in einem Hotel/im Hause eines Freundes/bei jmdm. wohnen. 3 *n.* (a) (halt) Halt, *der;* **there will be two** ∿s **for coffee on the way** es wird unterwegs zweimal zum Kaffeetrinken angehalten; **this train goes to London with only two** ∿s dieser Zug fährt mit nur zwei Zwischenhalten nach London; **bring to a** ∿: zum Stehen bringen ⟨*Fahrzeug*⟩; zum Erliegen bringen ⟨*Verkehr*⟩; unterbrechen ⟨*Arbeit, Diskussion, Treffen*⟩; **come to a** ∿: stehen bleiben; ⟨*Fahrzeug:*⟩ zum Stehen kommen; ⟨*Gespräch:*⟩ abbrechen; ⟨*Arbeit, Verkehr:*⟩ zum Erliegen kommen; ⟨*Vorlesung:*⟩ abgebrochen werden; **make a** ∿ **at** *or* **in a place** in einem Ort Halt machen; **put a** ∿ **to** abstellen ⟨*Missstände, Unsinn*⟩; unterbinden ⟨*Versuche*⟩; aus der Welt schaffen ⟨*Gerücht*⟩; **put a** ∿ **on a cheque** einen Scheck sperren lassen; **without a** ∿: ohne Halt ⟨*fahren, fliegen*⟩; ohne anzuhalten ⟨*gehen, laufen*⟩; ununterbrochen ⟨*arbeiten, reden*⟩; (b) (place) Haltestelle, *die;* **the ship's first** ∿ **is Cairo** der erste Hafen, den das Schiff anläuft, ist Kairo; **the plane's first** ∿ **is Frankfurt** die erste Zwischenlandung des Flugzeuges ist in Frankfurt; (c) (Brit.: punctuation mark) Satzzeichen, *das; see also* **full stop a; (d)** (in telegram) stop

~ **be'hind** (coll.) ⇒ **stay behind**

~ **'by** (Amer.) **1** *v.i.* vorbeischauen (ugs.). **2** *v.t.* ~ **by sb.'s house** *or* **place [and have a drink]** bei jmdm. [auf einen Drink] vorbeischauen (ugs.)

~ **'off** *v.i.* einen Zwischenaufenthalt einlegen

~ **'out** *v.i.* (coll.) **(a)** draußen bleiben; **(b)** (remain on strike) ⟨*Arbeiter:*⟩ weiterstreiken (ugs.)

~ **'over** *v.i.* einen Zwischenaufenthalt machen; (remain for the night) übernachten (**at** bei)

~ **'up 1** *v.t.* ~ ⇒ **1 e. 2** *v.i.* (coll.) ⇒ **stay up a**

stop: ~**cock** *n.* Abstellhahn, *der;* Absperrhahn, *der* (Technik); ~**gap** *n.* Notbehelf, *der;* (scheme, measure, plan, person) Notlösung, *die; attrib.* behelfsmäßig; **a** ~**gap measure** eine Behelfsmaßnahme; ~**'go** *n.* (Brit.) Hin und Her, *das;* (boom and recession) Auf und Ab, *das;* ~ **light** *n.* **(a)** (red traffic light) rotes Licht; **(b)** (Motor Veh.) Bremslicht, *das;* ~**over** *n.* Stopover, *der;* Zwischenaufenthalt, *der;* (of aircraft) Zwischenlandung, *die*

stoppage /'stɒpɪdʒ/ *n.* **(a)** (halt) Stillstand, *der;* (strike) Streik, *der;* **(b)** (cancellation) Sperrung, *die;* (of delivery) Einstellung, *die;* **(c)** (deduction) Abzug, *der*

stopper /'stɒpə(r)/ **1** *n.* Stöpsel, *der;* Pfropfen, *der.* **2** *v.t.* zustöpseln

stop: ~ **press** *n.* (Brit. Journ.) letzte Meldung/Meldungen; ~ **sign** *n.* Stoppschild, *das;* ~ **signal** *n.* Haltesignal, *das;* ~**watch** *n.* Stoppuhr, *die*

storage /'stɔːrɪdʒ/ *n., no pl., no indef. art.* (storing) Lagerung, *die;* (of furniture) Einlagerung, *die;* (of films, books, documents) Aufbewahrung, *die;* (of data, water, electricity) Speicherung, *die*

storage: ~ **capacity** *n.* (Computing) Speicherkapazität, *die;* ~ **device** *n.* (Computing) Speichermedium, *das;* Datenträger, *der;* ~ **heater** *n.* [Nacht]speicherofen, *der;* ~ **space** *n.* Lagerraum, *der;* (in house) Platz [zum Aufbewahren]; ~ **tank** *n.* Sammelbehälter, *der*

store /stɔː(r)/ **1** *n.* **(a)** (Amer.: shop) Laden, *der;* **(b)** *in sing. or pl.* (Brit.: large general shop) Kaufhaus, *das;* **(c)** (warehouse) Lager, *das;* (for valuables) Depot, *das;* (for books, films, documents) Magazin, *das;* **put sth. in** ~: etw. [bei einer Spedition] einlagern; **(d)** (stock) Vorrat, *der* (**of** an + *Dat.*); **get in** *or* **lay in a** ~ **of sth.** einen Vorrat an etw. (*Dat.*) anlegen; **be** *or* **lie in** ~ **for sb.** jmdn. erwarten; **have a surprise in** ~ **for sb.** eine Überraschung für jmdn. [auf Lager] haben; **who knows what the future has in** ~? wer weiß, was die Zukunft mit sich bringt?; **(e)** *in pl.* (supplies) Vorräte; **the** ~**s** (place) das [Vorrats]lager; **(f)** **lay** *or* **put** *or* **set [great]** ~ **by** *or* **on sth.** [großen] Wert auf etw. (*Akk.*) legen. **2** *v.t.* **(a)** (put in ~) einlagern; speichern ⟨*Getreide, Energie, Wissen*⟩; einspeichern ⟨*Daten*⟩; ablegen ⟨*Papiere, Dokumente*⟩; **(b)** (leave for storage) unterbringen; **(c)** (hold) aufnehmen; speichern ⟨*Energie, Daten*⟩

~ **a'way** *v.t.* lagern; ablegen ⟨*Akten*⟩; ~ **things away in a trunk/at a friend's house** Sachen in einer Truhe verstauen/bei einem Freund aufbewahren

~ **'up** *v.t.* speichern; ~ **up provisions/food/nuts** sich (*Dat.*) Vorräte / Lebensmittelvorräte / einen Vorrat an Nüssen anlegen; **you're only storing up trouble for yourself** du handelst dir nur immer mehr Schwierigkeiten ein

store: ~ **detective** *n.* ▶ 887 Kaufhausdetektiv, *der;* ~**house** *n.* Lager[haus], *das;* **sb. is a** ~**house of knowledge/information** [about angling] jmd. ist ein wandelndes Lexikon[, was das Angeln betrifft]; **the book is a real** ~**house of facts [about Germany]** das Buch ist eine wahre Fundgrube [für jeden, der sich über Deutschland orientieren will]; ~**keeper** *n.* ▶ 887 **(a)** (in charge of ~s) Lagerist, *der*/Lageristin, *die;* (Mil.) Verwalter der Materialausgabe; **(b)** (Amer.: shopkeeper) Besitzer eines Einzelhandelsgeschäftes; ~**room** *n.* Lagerraum, *der*

storey /'stɔːrɪ/ *n.* Stockwerk, *das;* Geschoss, *das;* **a five-**~ **house** ein fünfgeschossiges Haus; **third-**~ **window** Fenster im zweiten Stock[werk]

stork /stɔːk/ *n.* Storch, *der*

storm /stɔːm/ **1** *n.* **(a)** Unwetter, *das;* (thunder~) Gewitter, *das;* **the night of the** ~: die Sturmnacht; **a** ~ **in a teacup** (fig.) ein Sturm im Wasserglas; **(b)** (fig.: dispute) Sturm

der Entrüstung; **(c)** (fig.: outburst) (of applause, protest, indignation, criticism) Sturm, *der;* (of abuse) Flut, *die;* **(d)** (Mil.: attack) Sturm, *der;* **take sb./sth. by** ~: jmdn. überrumpeln/etw. im Sturm nehmen. **2** *v.i.* **(a)** stürmen; **he** ~**ed in** er kam hereingestürmt; **(b)** (talk violently) toben; ~ **at sb.** jmdn. andonnern (ugs.). **3** *v.t.* (Mil.) stürmen

storm: ~ **cloud** *n.* (Meteorol.) Gewitterwolke, *die;* ~ **damage** *n.* Sturmschaden, *der* (*meist Pl.*)

stormy /'stɔːmɪ/ *adj.* **(a)** stürmisch; hitzig ⟨*Auseinandersetzung*⟩; **(b)** (indicating storms) auf Sturm hindeutend; **be** *or* **look** ~: nach Sturm aussehen

story¹ /'stɔːrɪ/ *n.* **(a)** (account of events) Geschichte, *die;* **give the** ~ **of sth.** etw. schildern *od.* darstellen; **it is quite another** ~ **now** (fig.) jetzt sieht alles ganz anders aus; **the [old,] old** ~**, the same old** ~ (fig.) das alte Lied (ugs.); **tall** ~: unglaubliche Geschichte; **that's [a bit of] a tall** ~! das ist ein bisschen dick aufgetragen! (ugs.); **that's a different** ~ (fig.) das ist etwas ganz anderes; **that's his** ~ **[and he's sticking to it]** er bleibt bei dem, was er gesagt hat; **that's only 'half the** ~: das ist noch nicht alles; **the** ~ **goes that …:** man erzählt sich, dass …; **that's not the whole** ~: das ist noch nicht alles; **to cut** *or* **make a long** ~ **short,** …: kurz [gesagt], …; **(b)** (narrative) Geschichte, *die;* **that's the** ~ **of my life!** (fig.) das ist mein ewiges Problem!; **(c)** (news item) Bericht, *der;* Story, *die* (ugs.); **(d)** (plot) Story, *die;* **(e)** (set of [interesting] facts) **the objects in the room have a** ~: die Gegenstände in dem Zimmer haben ihre eigene Geschichte; **(f)** (coll./child lang.: lie) Märchen, *das;* **tell stories** Märchen erzählen

story² (Amer.) ⇒ **storey**

story: ~ **book 1** *n.* Geschichtenbuch, *das;* (with fairy tales) Märchenbuch, *das;* **2** *attrib. adj.* Bilderbuch-; ~**book world** Märchenwelt, *die;* ~**teller** *n.* **(a)** (narrator) [Geschichten]erzähler, *der*/-erzählerin, *die;* **(b)** (writer) Erzähler, *der*/Erzählerin, *die;* **(c)** (raconteur) Anekdotenerzähler, *der*/-erzählerin, *die;* **she's a wonderful** ~**teller** sie kann wundervoll erzählen

stout /staʊt/ **1** *adj.* **(a)** (strong) fest; stabil ⟨*Boot, Werkzeug, Messer, Zaun*⟩; dick ⟨*Tür, Mauer, Damm, Stock, Papier*⟩; robust ⟨*Material, Kleidung*⟩; stark ⟨*Seil, Abwehr*⟩; kräftig ⟨*Pflanze, Pferd, Pfeiler*⟩; **(b)** (fat) beleibt; **(c)** (brave, staunch) unverzagt; heftig ⟨*Widerstand, Opposition*⟩; entschieden ⟨*Ablehnung*⟩; stark ⟨*Gegner*⟩; fest ⟨*Glaube*⟩; **a** ~ **heart** ein festes Herz. **2** *n.* (drink) Stout, *der*

stout-hearted /'staʊthɑːtɪd/ *adj.* beherzt; unerschrocken

stoutly /'staʊtlɪ/ *adv.* **(a)** (strongly) stabil ⟨*gebaut, gezimmert*⟩; ~ **made** solide, robust ⟨*Schuhwerk*⟩; stark ⟨*Seil*⟩; ~ **built** stämmig; kräftig ⟨*Tier*⟩; stabil ⟨*Haus, Zaun, Tor*⟩; dick ⟨*Tür, Mauer*⟩; **(b)** (staunchly) beherzt; hartnäckig ⟨*behaupten, ablehnen, widerstehen*⟩; fest ⟨*glauben*⟩

stove¹ /staʊv/ *n.* Ofen, *der;* (for cooking) Herd, *der;* **electric** ~: Elektroherd, *der*

stove² ⇒ **stave 2**

stow /staʊ/ *v.t.* **(a)** (put into place) packen (**into** in + *Akk.*); verstauen (**into** in + *Dat.*); (Naut.) stauen; **(b)** (fill) voll packen; voll stopfen (ugs.); (Naut.) befrachten

~ **a'way 1** *v.t.* verwahren. **2** *v.i.* als blinder Passagier reisen

'stowaway *n.* blinder Passagier

straddle /'strædl/ *v.t.* ~ *or* **sit straddling a fence/chair** rittlings auf einem Zaun/Stuhl sitzen; ~ *or* **stand straddling a ditch** mit gespreizten Beinen über einem Graben stehen; **his legs** ~**d the chair/brook** er saß rittlings auf dem Stuhl/stand mit gespreizten Beinen über dem Bach; **their farm** ~**s the border** ihre Farm liegt beiderseits der Grenze; **the bridge** ~**s the river/road** die Brücke überspannt den Fluss/die Straße

straggle /'strægl/ *v.i.* **(a)** (trail) ~ **[along] behind the others** den anderen hinterherzockeln (ugs.); **(b)** (spread in irregular way) ⟨*Dorf, Stadt:*⟩ sich ausbreiten; ⟨*Häuser, Bäume:*⟩ verstreut stehen; **(c)** (grow untidily) ⟨*Pflanze:*⟩ wuchern; ⟨*Haar, Bart:*⟩ zottig wachsen

straggler /'stræglə(r)/ *n.* Nachzügler, *der*

straggling /'stræglɪŋ/ *adj.* **(a)** (trailing) nachzockelnd (ugs.); **(b)** (irregular) verstreut ⟨*Häuser*⟩; ungeordnet ⟨*Reihe*⟩;

unregelmäßig ⟨*Baumreihe, Schrift*⟩; weiträumig angelegt ⟨*Stadt, Gebäude*⟩; **(c)** (long and untidy) wuchernd; zottig ⟨*Haar, Bart*⟩

straggly /'stræglɪ/ ⇒ **straggling** c

straight /streɪt/ **1** *adj.* **(a)** gerade; aufrecht ⟨*Haltung*⟩; glatt ⟨*Haar*⟩; **in a** ∼ **line** in gerader Linie; **(b)** (not having been bent) ausgestreckt ⟨*Arm, Bein*⟩; durchgedrückt ⟨*Knie*⟩; **(c)** (not misshapen) gerade ⟨*Bein*⟩; **(d)** (Fashion) gerade geschnitten; **(e)** (undiluted, unmodified) unvermischt; **have** *or* **drink whisky/gin** ∼: Whisky/Gin pur trinken; **a** ∼ **choice** eine klare Wahl; **(f)** (successive) fortlaufend; **win in** ∼ **sets** (Tennis) ohne Satzverlust gewinnen; **the team had ten** ∼ **wins** die Mannschaft hat zehn Spiele hintereinander gewonnen; ∼ **As** (Amer.) lauter Einsen; **(g)** (undeviating) direkt ⟨*Blick, Schlag, Schuss, Pass, Ball, Weg*⟩; **(h)** (candid) geradlinig ⟨*Person*⟩; ehrlich ⟨*Antwort*⟩; klar ⟨*Abfuhr, Weigerung, Verurteilung*⟩; unmissverständlich ⟨*Rat*⟩; ∼ **dealings/speaking** direkte Verhandlungen/unverblümte Sprache; **a** ∼ **answer to a** ∼ **question** eine klare Antwort auf eine klare Frage; **he did some** ∼ **talking with her** er sprach sich mit ihr offen aus; **be** ∼ **with sb.** zu jmdm. offen sein; **(i)** (Theatre) ernst; (not avant-garde) konventionell; **(j)** (in good order, not askew) **the accounts are** ∼: die Bücher sind in Ordnung; **the picture is** ∼: das Bild hängt gerade; **is my hair/tie** ∼? sitzt meine Frisur/Krawatte [richtig]?; **is my hat [on]** ∼? sitzt mein Hut [richtig]?; **put** ∼: gerade ziehen ⟨*Krawatte*⟩; gerade aufsetzen ⟨*Hut*⟩; gerade hängen ⟨*Bild*⟩; aufräumen ⟨*Zimmer, Sachen*⟩; richtig stellen ⟨*Fehler, Missverständnis*⟩; **put things** ∼: alles in Ordnung bringen; **put things** ∼ **with sb.** mit jmdm. alles klären; **get sth.** ∼ (fig.) etw. genau *od.* richtig verstehen; **let's get it** *or* **things** *or* **the facts** ∼: wir sollten alles genau klären; **get this** ∼! merk dir das [ein für allemal]!; **put sb.** ∼: jmdm. aufklären; **put** *or* **set the record** ∼: die Sache *od.* das richtig stellen. **2** *adv.* **(a)** (in a ∼ line) gerade; **she came** ∼ **at me** sie kam geradewegs auf mich zu; ∼ **opposite** genau gegenüber; **head** ∼ **for the wall** genau auf die Mauer zusteuern; **go** ∼ (fig.: give up crime) ein bürgerliches Leben führen; **(b)** ▶ **1199** (directly) geradewegs; ∼ **after** sofort nach; **come** ∼ **to the point** direkt *od.* gleich zur Sache kommen; **look sb.** ∼ **in the eye** jmdm. direkt in die Augen blicken; ∼ **ahead** *or* **on** immer geradeaus; **they went** ∼ **ahead and did it** sie taten es sofort; **(c)** (honestly, frankly) aufrichtig; **give it to me** ∼: sei ganz offen zu mir!; **he came** ∼ **out with it** er sagte es ohne Umschweife; **I told him** ∼ **[out] that** ...: ich sagte [es] ihm ins Gesicht, dass ...; **play** ∼ **with sb.** mit jmdm. ein ehrliches Spiel spielen; **(d)** (upright) gerade ⟨*sitzen, stehen, wachsen*⟩; **(e)** (accurately) zielsicher; **he can't shoot [very]** ∼: er ist nicht [sehr] zielsicher; **(f)** (clearly) klar ⟨*sehen, denken*⟩. **3** *n.* (∼ stretch) gerade Strecke; (Sport) Gerade, *die;* **final** *or* **home** *or* **finishing** ∼ (Sport; also fig.) Zielgerade, *die*

straight a'way *adv.* (coll.) sofort; gleich

straighten /'streɪtn/ **1** *v.t.* **(a)** gerade ziehen ⟨*Kabel, Teppich, Seil*⟩; gerade biegen ⟨*Draht*⟩; glätten ⟨*Falte, Kleidung, Haare*⟩; gerade halten ⟨*Rücken*⟩; strecken ⟨*Beine, Arme*⟩; gerade hängen ⟨*Bild*⟩; **(b)** (put in order) aufräumen; einrichten ⟨*neue Wohnung*⟩; in Ordnung bringen ⟨*Geschäftsbücher, Finanzen*⟩. **2** *v.i.* gerade werden

∼ **'out 1** *v.t.* **(a)** geradebiegen ⟨*Draht*⟩; gerade ziehen ⟨*Seil, Kabel*⟩; glätten ⟨*Decke, Teppich*⟩; begradigen ⟨*Fluss, Straße*⟩; **(b)** (put in order, clear up) klären; aus der Welt schaffen ⟨*Missverständnis, Meinungsverschiedenheit*⟩; in Ordnung bringen ⟨*Angelegenheit*⟩; berichtigen ⟨*Fehler*⟩. **2** *v.i.* gerade werden

∼ **'up 1** *v.t.* ≈ **tidy up 2. 2** *v.i.* sich aufrichten

straight: ∼ **'face** *n.* unbewegtes Gesicht; **with a** ∼ **face** ohne eine Miene zu verziehen; **keep a** ∼ **face** keine Miene verziehen; ∼**-faced** /'streɪtfeɪst/ *adj.* mit unbewegter Miene *nachgestellt;* **be** ∼**-faced** keine Miene verziehen; ∼**'forward** *adj.* **(a)** (frank) freimütig; geradlinig ⟨*Politik*⟩; schlicht ⟨*Stil, Sprache, Erzählung, Bericht*⟩; klar ⟨*Anweisung, Vorstellungen*⟩; **have a** ∼**forward approach to a problem** ein Problem direkt angehen; **(b)** (simple) einfach; eindeutig ⟨*Lage*⟩; ∼ **'off** *adv.* (coll.) schlankweg (ugs.)

strain¹ /streɪn/ **1** *n.* **(a)** (pull) Belastung, *die;* (on rope) Spannung, *die;* **put a** ∼ **on sb./sth.** jmdn./etw. belasten; **(b)** (extreme physical or mental tension) Stress, *der;* **feel the** ∼: die Anstrengung spüren; **stand** *or* **take the** ∼: die Belastung *od.* den Stress aushalten; **place sb. under [a] great** ∼: jmdn. einer starken Belastung aussetzen; **be under [a great deal of]** ∼: unter großem Stress stehen; **(c)** (person, thing) **be a** ∼ **on sb./sth.** jmdn./etw. belasten; eine Belastung für jmdn. sein; **find sth. a** ∼: etw. als Belastung empfinden; **(d)** (injury) (muscular) Zerrung, *die;* (over-∼ on heart, back, etc.) Überanstrengung, *die;* **(e)** *in sing. or pl.* (burst of music) Klänge; (burst of poetry) Vers, *der;* Zeile, *die.* **2** *v.t.* **(a)** (overexert) überanstrengen; zerren ⟨*Muskel*⟩; überbeanspruchen ⟨*Geduld, Loyalität usw.*⟩; **(b)** (stretch tightly) [fest] spannen; **(c)** (exert to maximum) ∼ **oneself/sb./sth.** das Letzte aus sich/jmdm./etw. herausholen; ∼ **one's ears/ eyes/voice** seine Ohren/Augen/Stimme anstrengen; ∼ **oneself to do sth.** sich nach Kräften bemühen, etw. zu tun; **(d)** (use beyond proper limits) verzerren ⟨*Wahrheit, Lehre, Tatsachen*⟩; überbeanspruchen ⟨*Geduld, Wohlwollen*⟩; **(e)** (filter) durchseihen; seihen **(through** durch); ∼ **[the water from] the vegetables** das Gemüse abgießen. **3** *v.i.* (strive intensely) sich anstrengen; ∼ **at sth.** an etw. (*Dat.*) zerren; ∼ **at the leash** an der Leine zerren; (fig.) es kaum erwarten können; ∼ **after sth.** sich mit aller Gewalt um etw. bemühen

∼ **a'way,** ∼ **'off** *v.t.* abseihen; abgießen ⟨*Wasser*⟩

∼ **'out** *v.t.* [her]ausfiltern

strain² *n.* **(a)** (breed) Rasse, *die;* (of plants) Sorte, *die;* (of virus) Art, *die;* **(b)** *no pl.* (tendency) Neigung, *die* **(of** zu); Hang, *der* (**of** zu); **a cruel** ∼: ein grausamer Zug

strained /streɪnd/ *adj.* gezwungen ⟨*Lächeln*⟩; künstlich ⟨*Humor, Witz*⟩; gewagt ⟨*Interpretation*⟩; ∼ **relations** gespannte Beziehungen

strainer /'streɪnə(r)/ *n.* Sieb, *das*

strait /streɪt/ *n.* **(a)** *in sing. or pl.* (Geog.) [Wasser]straße, *die;* Meerenge, *die;* **(b)** *in pl.* (bad situation) Schwierigkeiten

strait: ∼**jacket** *n.* (lit. or fig.) Zwangsjacke, *die;* ∼**-laced** /streɪt'leɪst/ *adj.* (fig.) puritanisch

strand¹ /strænd/ *n.* (thread) Faden, *der;* (of wire) Litze, *die* (Elektrot.); (of rope) Strang, *der;* (of beads, pearls, flowers, etc.) Kette, *die;* (of hair) Strähne, *die*

strand² *v.t.* **(a)** (leave behind) trocken setzen; **be [left]** ∼**ed** (fig.) seinem Schicksal überlassen sein; (be stuck) festsitzen; **the strike left them** ∼**ed in England** wegen des Streiks saßen sie in England fest; **(b)** (wash ashore) an Land spülen ⟨*Leiche, Wrackteile*⟩; (run aground) auf Grund setzen ⟨*Schiff*⟩

strange /streɪndʒ/ *adj.* **(a)** (peculiar) seltsam; sonderbar; merkwürdig; **feel [very]** ∼: sich [ganz] komisch fühlen; **it feels** ∼ **to do sth.** es ist ein merkwürdiges *od.* komisches Gefühl, wenn man etw. tut; ∼ **to say** seltsamerweise; **(b)** (alien, unfamiliar) fremd; ∼ **to sb.** jmdm. fremd; **(c)** (unaccustomed) ∼ **to sth.** nicht vertraut mit etw.; **feel** ∼: sich nicht zu Hause fühlen

strangely /'streɪndʒlɪ/ *adv.* seltsam; merkwürdig; ∼ **enough,** ...: seltsamerweise ...

stranger /'streɪndʒə(r)/ *n.* **(a)** (foreigner, unknown person) Fremde, *der/die;* **he is a/no** ∼ **to me** er ist mir nicht bekannt/ist mir bekannt; **hello,** ∼: hallo, lange nicht gesehen; **(b)** (one lacking certain experience) **be a/no** ∼ **to sth.** etw. nicht gewöhnt/etw. gewöhnt sein; **he is no** ∼ **to this sort of work** diese Arbeit ist ihm nicht fremd; **he is a** ∼ **here/to the town** er ist hier/in der Stadt fremd; **be a/no** ∼ **to Oxford** Oxford gar nicht/[recht gut] kennen

strangle /'stræŋgl/ *v.t.* erdrosseln; erwürgen

'stranglehold *n.* (lit. or fig.) Würgegriff, *der;* **have a** ∼ **on sb./sth.** jmdn./etw. im Würgegriff haben

strangulation /stræŋgjʊ'leɪʃn/ *n.* Erdrosseln, *das;* Erwürgen, *das*

strap /stræp/ **1** *n.* **(a)** (leather strip) Riemen, *der;* (textile strip) Band, *das;* (shoulder-∼) Träger, *der;* (to grasp in vehicle) Halteriemen, *der.* **2** *v.t.,* **-pp-:** ∼ **[into position/down]** festschnallen; ∼ **oneself in** sich anschnallen

∼ **'up** *v.t.* zuschnallen

'straphanger *n.* stehender Fahrgast
strapless /'stræplɪs/ *adj.* trägerlos
strapping /'stræpɪŋ/ *adj.* stramm
Strasburg /'stræzbɜːg/ *pr. n.* ▶ 1159 Straßburg (*das*)
strata *pl. of* stratum
stratagem /'strætədʒəm/ *n.* (trick) [Kriegs]list, *die*
strategic /strə'tiːdʒɪk/ *adj.* (a) strategisch; (b) (of great military importance) strategisch wichtig; (necessary to plan) bedeutsam ⟨Element, Faktor⟩
strategist /'strætɪdʒɪst/ *n.* Stratege, *der*/Strategin, *die*
strategy /'strætɪdʒɪ/ *n.* Strategie, *die;* (fig. also) Taktik, *die;* it was bad ∼ (fig.) es war taktisch *od.* strategisch unklug
stratosphere /'strætəsfɪə(r)/ *n.* Stratosphäre, *die*
stratum /'strɑːtəm/ *n., pl.* **strata** /'strɑːtə/ Schicht, *die*
straw /strɔː/ *n.* (a) *no pl.* (stalks of grain) Stroh, *das;* (b) (single stalk) Strohhalm, *der;* **clutch** *or* **grasp at** ∼s (fig. coll.) sich an einen Strohhalm klammern; **be the last** ∼, **be the** ∼ **that broke the camel's back** (coll.) das Fass zum Überlaufen bringen; **that's the last** *or* **final** ∼: jetzt reicht's aber; **draw** ∼s **[for sth.]** Hölzchen [um etw.] ziehen; **pick the short** ∼ (fig.) das schlechtere Los ziehen; (c) **[drinking-]**∼: Trinkhalm, *der;* Strohhalm, *der*
strawberry /'strɔːbərɪ/ *n.* Erdbeere, *die*
straw: ∼ **boss** *n.* (Amer.) Vorarbeiter, *der;* ∼**-coloured** *adj.* strohgelb; ∼ **'hat** *n.* Strohhut, *der*
stray /streɪ/ **1** *n.* (a) (wander) streunen; (fig.: in thought etc.) abschweifen (**into** in + *Akk.*); ∼ **[away] from** sich absondern von; **the child had** ∼**ed from his parents** das Kind war seinen Eltern weggelaufen; ∼ **into enemy territory** sich auf feindliches Gebiet verirren; (b) (deviate) abweichen (**from** von); **have** ∼**ed** sich verirrt haben; ∼ **from the point/from** *or* **off the road** vom Thema/von der Straße abkommen. **2** *n.* (animal) streunendes Tier; (without owner) herrenloses Tier. **3** *adj.* (a) streunend; (without owner) herrenlos; (out of proper place) verirrt; (b) (occasional, isolated) vereinzelt
streak /striːk/ **1** *n.* (a) (narrow line) Streifen, *der;* (in hair) Strähne, *die;* ∼ **of lightning** Blitzstrahl, *der;* **like a** ∼ **[of lightning]** [schnell] wie der Blitz (ugs.); wie ein geölter Blitz (ugs.); (b) (fig.: element) **have a jealous/cruel** ∼: zur Eifersucht/Grausamkeit neigen; **have a** ∼ **of meanness/jealousy** eine geizige/eifersüchtige Ader haben; (c) (fig.: spell) ∼ **of good/bad luck, lucky/unlucky** ∼: Glücks-/Pechsträhne, *die;* **be on a** ∼ **have a winning/losing** ∼: eine Glücks-/Pechsträhne haben. **2** *v.t.* streifen; ∼ **sth. with green** etw. mit grünen Streifen versehen; **hair** ∼**ed with grey** Haar mit grauen Strähnen; ∼**ed with paint/mud** farb-/tränenverschmiert/dreckbeschmiert. **3** *v.i.* (a) (move rapidly) flitzen (ugs.); (b) (coll.: run naked) blitzen (ugs.); flitzen (ugs.)
streaker /'striːkə(r)/ *n.* (coll.) Blitzer, *der*/Blitzerin, *die* (ugs.); Flitzer, *der*/Flitzerin, *die* (ugs.)
streaky /'striːkɪ/ *adj.* streifig; gestreift ⟨Muster, Fell⟩
streaky 'bacon *n.* durchwachsener Speck
stream /striːm/ **1** *n.* (a) (of flowing water) Wasserlauf, *der;* (brook) Bach, *der;* (b) (flow, large quantity) Strom, *der;* (of abuse, excuses, words) Schwall, *der;* ∼s *or* a ∼ **of applications** eine Flut von Bewerbungen; **in** ∼s in Strömen; **the children rushed in** ∼s/**in a** ∼ **through the school gates** die Kinder strömten durch die Schultore; (c) (current) Strömung, *die;* (fig.) Trend, *der;* **against/with the** ∼ **of sth.** (fig.) gegen den/mit dem Strom einer Sache; **go against/with the** ∼ ⟨Person:⟩ gegen den/mit dem Strom schwimmen; (d) (Brit. Educ.) Parallelzug, *der;* (e) **be/go on** ∼ (Industry) in Betrieb sein/den Betrieb aufnehmen. **2** *v.i.* (a) (flow) strömen; ⟨Sonnenlicht:⟩ fluten; **tears** ∼**ed down her face** Tränen strömten ihr über das Gesicht; (b) **my eyes** ∼**ed** mir tränten die Augen. **3** *v.t.* **his nose was** ∼**ing blood** Blut floss ihm aus der Nase
∼ **'in** *v.i.* hereinströmen/hineinströmen
∼ **'out** *v.i.* herausströmen/hinausströmen
∼ **'past** *v.i.* vorbeiströmen
∼ **'through** *v.i.* hindurchströmen
streamer /'striːmə(r)/ *n.* Band, *das;* (of paper) Luftschlange, *die*

'streamline *v.t.* (a) [eine] Stromlinienform geben (+ *Dat.*); **be** ∼**d** eine Stromlinienform haben; (b) (simplify) rationalisieren; (reduce) einschränken
street /striːt/ *n.* Straße, *die;* **in** (Brit.) *or* **on** ... **Street** in der ...straße; **in the** ∼: auf der Straße; **be on the** ∼**[s]** (be published) ⟨Zeitung:⟩ draußen sein; (have no place to live) auf der Straße liegen (ugs.); **keep the youngsters off the** ∼s dafür sorgen, dass sich die Jugendlichen nicht auf der Straße herumtreiben; ∼s **ahead [of sb./sth.]** (coll.) um Längen besser [als jmd./etw.] (ugs.); **be [right] up sb.'s** ∼ (coll.) jmds. Fall sein (ugs.)
street: ∼**ball** *n.* Streetball, *der;* ∼**car** *n.* (Amer.) Straßenbahn, *die;* Tram, *die* (südd., österr., schweiz.); ∼ **cred** /strɪ:t kred/ (coll.), ∼ **credibility** *n.* glaubwürdiges Image als junger modebewusster Städter; ∼ **crime** *n., no pl., no indef. art.* Straßenkriminalität, *die;* ∼ **door** *n.* [vordere] Haustür; ∼ **furniture** *n.:* Gegenstände wie Straßenlaternen, Abfallkörbe, Telefonzellen, Verkehrszeichen usw.; ∼ **lamp,** ∼ **light** *ns.* Straßenlaterne, *die;* ∼ **lighting** *n.* Straßenbeleuchtung, *die;* ∼ **map** *n.* Stadtplan, *der;* ∼ **market** *n.* Markt, *der;* ∼ **plan** ⇒ **map;** ∼ **sweeper** *n.* (a) ▶ 887 (person) Straßenfeger, *der*/-fegerin, *die* (bes. nordd.); Straßenkehrer, *der*/-kehrerin, *die* (bes. südd.); (b) (machine) Kehrmaschine, *die;* (vehicle) Straßenkehrmaschine, *die;* ∼ **value** *n.* Straßenverkaufswert, *der;* ∼ **vendor** *n.* ▶ 887 Straßenhändler, *der*/-händlerin, *die;* ∼**wise** *adj.* (coll.) **be** ∼**wise** wissen, wos langgeht (ugs.)
strength /streŋθ/ *n.* (a) Stärke, *die;* (speed) Kraft, *die;* (of argument) [Überzeugungs]kraft, *die;* (of poison, medicine) Wirksamkeit, *die;* (of legal evidence) [Beweis]kraft, *die;* (resistance of material, building, etc.) Stabilität, *die;* **not know one's own** ∼: nicht wissen, wie stark man ist; **give sb.** ∼ jmdm. stärken; jmdm. Kraft geben; **go from** ∼ **to** ∼: immer erfolgreicher werden; **on the** ∼ **of sth./that** aufgrund einer Sache (Gen.) /dessen; (b) (proportion present) Stärke, *die;* (full complement) **be below** ∼/**up to** ∼: weniger als/ etwa die volle Stärke haben; **in [full]** ∼: in voller Stärke; **the police were there in** ∼: ein starkes Polizeiaufgebot war da
strengthen /'streŋθən/ **1** *v.t.* (give power to) stärken; (reinforce, intensify, increase in number) verstärken; erhöhen ⟨Anteil⟩; (make more effective) unterstützen; ∼ **sb.'s resolve** jmdn. in seinem Entschluss bestärken; ∼ **sb.'s hand** (fig.) jmds. Position stärken. **2** *v.i.* stärker werden
strenuous /'strenjʊəs/ *adj.* (a) (energetic) energisch; gewaltig ⟨Anstrengung⟩; (b) (requiring exertion) anstrengend
stress /stres/ **1** *n.* (a) (strain) Stress, *der;* **be under** ∼: unter Stress (*Dat.*) stehen; (b) (emphasis) Betonung, *die;* Nachdruck, *der;* **lay** *or* **place** *or* **put [a]** ∼ **on sth.** auf etw. (*Akk.*) Wert *od.* Gewicht legen; (c) (accentuation) Betonung, *die;* **put the/a** ∼ **on sth.** etw. betonen. **2** *v.t.* (a) (emphasize) betonen; Wert legen auf (+ *Akk.*) ⟨richtige Ernährung, gutes Benehmen, Sport usw.⟩; ∼ **[the point] that** ...: darauf hinweisen, dass ...; (b) (Ling.) betonen ⟨Silbe, Vokal usw.⟩
'stressed out *adj.* (coll.) [völlig] gestresst; **be** ∼ **by sb.**/**sth.** von jmdm./etw. [völlig] gestresst sein; **get** ∼: [völlig] gestresst werden
stressful /'stresfl/ *adj.* anstrengend; stressig (ugs.)
stress: ∼ **mark** *n.* Betonungszeichen, *das;* ∼**-related** *adj.* stressbedingt
stretch /stretʃ/ **1** *v.t.* (a) (lengthen, extend) strecken ⟨Arm, Hand⟩; recken ⟨Hals⟩; dehnen ⟨Gummiband⟩; (spread) ausbreiten ⟨Decke⟩; (tighten) spannen; **he lay** ∼**ed out on the ground** er lag ausgestreckt auf dem Boden; ∼ **one's legs** (by walking) sich (*Dat.*) die Beine vertreten; (b) (widen) dehnen; ∼ **[out of shape]** ausweiten ⟨Schuhe, Jacke⟩; (c) (fig.: make the most of) ausschöpfen ⟨Reserve⟩; fordern ⟨Person, Begabung⟩; (d) (fig.: extend beyond proper limit) überschreiten ⟨Befugnis, Grenzen des Anstands⟩; strapazieren (ugs.) ⟨Geduld⟩; es nicht so genau nehmen mit ⟨Gesetz, Bestimmung, Begriff, Grundsätzen⟩; ∼ **a point** großzügig sein; ∼ **the truth** ⟨Aussage:⟩ nicht ganz der Wahrheit entsprechen; **he's certainly** ∼**ing the truth there** er nimmt es hier mit der Wahrheit nicht so genau; **we're a bit** ∼**ed at the moment** wir sind zur Zeit ziemlich überlastet; ∼ **it/things** den Bogen überspannen. **2**

v.i. **(a)** (extend in length) sich dehnen; ⟨*Person, Tier:*⟩ sich strecken; **(b)** (have specified length) sich ausdehnen; ∼ **from A to B** sich von A bis B erstrecken; **(c)** ∼ **to sth.** (be sufficient for) für etw. reichen; **could you** ∼ **to £10?** hast du vielleicht sogar 10 Pfund? **3** *v. refl.* sich strecken. **4** *n.* **(a)** (lengthening, drawing out) **have a** ∼: sich strecken; **give sth. a** ∼: etw. dehnen; **(b)** (exertion) **by no** ∼ **of the imagination** auch mit viel Fantasie nicht; **at a** ∼ (fig.) wenn es sein muss (*see also* **b**)*;* **at full** ∼: auf Hochtouren; **(c)** (expanse, length) Abschnitt, *der;* **a** ∼ **of road/open country** ein Stück Straße/freies Gelände; **(d)** (period) **for a** ∼: eine Zeit lang; **a four-hour** ∼: eine [Zeit]spanne von vier Stunden; **at a** ∼: ohne Unterbrechung (*see also* **b**). **5** *adj.* dehnbar; Stretch⟨*hose, -gewebe*⟩

∼ **'out 1** *v.t.* **(a)** [aus]strecken ⟨*Arm, Bein*⟩; ausbreiten ⟨*Decke*⟩; auseinander ziehen ⟨*Seil*⟩; ∼ **oneself out** sich [lang] ausstrecken; **(b)** (eke out) ∼ **sth. out** mit etw. reichen. **2** *v.i.* **(a)** (∼ one's hands out, lit. or fig.) die Hände ausstrecken (**to** nach); **(b)** (extend) sich ausdehnen

stretcher /'stretʃə(r)/ *n.* (for carrying a person) [Trag]bahre, *die*

'stretcher-bearer *n.* [Kranken]träger, *der*

strew /struː/ *v.t., p.p.* ∼**ed** /struːd/ *or* ∼**n** /struːn/ **(a)** (scatter) streuen ⟨*Blumen, Sand usw.*⟩; **clothes were** ∼**n about the room** Kleider lagen im ganzen Zimmer verstreut herum; **(b)** (cover, lit. or fig.) bestreuen; **the grass was** ∼**n with litter** [überall] auf dem Gras war Abfall verstreut

stricken /'strɪkn/ *adj.* (afflicted) heimgesucht; havariert ⟨*Schiff, Flugzeug*⟩; (showing affliction) schmerzerfüllt; **be** ∼ **with fever** von Fieber geschüttelt werden; ∼ **with fear/grief** angsterfüllt/grambebeugt

strict /strɪkt/ *adj.* **(a)** (firm) streng; strenggläubig ⟨*Katholik, Moslem usw.*⟩; **in** ∼ **confidence** streng vertraulich; **(b)** (precise) streng; genau ⟨*Übersetzung*⟩; **in the** ∼ **sense [of the word]** im strengen Sinn[e] [des Wortes]

strictly /'strɪktlɪ/ *adv.* streng; ∼ **no smoking** Rauchen streng[stens] verboten; ∼ **[speaking]** streng genommen

strictness /'strɪktnɪs/ *n., no pl.* **(a)** (firmness) Strenge, *die;* **(b)** (precision) Genauigkeit, *die*

stricture /'strɪktʃə(r)/ *n. usu. in pl.* (critical remark) ∼**[s]** [scharfe *od.* heftige] Kritik

stride /straɪd/ **1** *n.* Schritt, *der;* **make** ∼**s [towards sth.]** (fig.) [in Richtung auf etw. (*Akk.*)] Fortschritte machen; **get into one's** ∼: seinen Rhythmus finden; (fig.) in Fahrt *od.* Schwung kommen; **put sb. off his** ∼ (fig.) jmdn. aus dem Konzept bringen; **take sth. in one's** ∼ (fig.) mit etw. gut fertig werden. **2** *v.t.,* **strode** /strəʊd/ **stridden** /'strɪdn/ [mit großen Schritten] gehen; (solemnly) schreiten (geh.)

∼ **'out** *v.i.* ausschreiten (geh.)

strident /'straɪdənt/ *adj.* schrill ⟨*Stimme, Blech[bläser]*⟩; (fig.) grell ⟨*Farbe*⟩; schrill ⟨*Protest, Ton*⟩

strife /straɪf/ *n., no pl., no indef. art.* Streit, *der*

strike /straɪk/ **1** *n.* **(a)** (Industry) Streik, *der;* Ausstand, *der;* **be on/go [out]** *or* **come out on** ∼: in den Streik getreten sein/in den Streik treten; **(b)** (Finance, Mining, Oil Industry) Treffer, *der* (fig. ugs.); **make a** ∼: sein Glück machen; (Mining) fündig werden; **(c)** (sudden success) **[lucky]** ∼: Glückstreffer, *der;* **(d)** (act of hitting) Schlag, *der;* **(e)** (Mil.) Angriff, *der* (at auf + *Akk.*). **2** *v.t.,* **struck** /strʌk/ **struck** *or* (arch.) **stricken** /'strɪkn/ **(a)** (hit) schlagen ⟨*Schlag, Geschoss:*⟩ treffen ⟨*Ziel*⟩; ⟨*Blitz:*⟩ [ein]schlagen in (+ *Akk.*); treffen; (afflict) treffen ⟨*Epidemie, Seuche, Katastrophe usw.*⟩; heimsuchen; ∼ **one's head on** *or* **against the wall** mit dem Kopf gegen die Wand schlagen; **the car struck a pedestrian** das Auto erfasste einen Fußgänger; **the ship struck the rocks** das Schiff lief auf die Felsen; **(b)** (delete) streichen (**from, off** aus); **(c)** (deliver) ∼ **two punches** zweimal zuschlagen; ∼ **sb. a blow** jmdm. einen Schlag versetzen; **who struck [the] first blow?** wer hat zuerst geschlagen?; ∼ **a blow against sb./against** *or* **to sth.** (fig.) jmdm./einer Sache einen Schlag versetzen; ∼ **a blow for sth.** (fig.) eine Lanze für etw. brechen; **(d)** (produce by hitting flint) schlagen ⟨*Funken*⟩; (ignite) anzünden ⟨*Streichholz*⟩; **(e)** (chime) schlagen; **(f)** (Mus.) anschlagen ⟨*Töne auf dem Klavier*⟩; anzupfen, anreißen ⟨*Töne auf der*

Gitarre⟩; (fig.) anschlagen ⟨*Ton*⟩; **(g)** (impress) beeindrucken; ∼ **sb. as [being] silly** jmdm. dumm zu sein scheinen *od.* dumm erscheinen; **it** ∼**s sb. that** ...: es scheint jmdm., dass...; **how does it** ∼ **you?** was hältst du davon?; **(h)** (occur to) einfallen (+ *Dat.*); **(i)** (cause to become) **a heart attack struck him dead** er erlag einem Herzanfall; **be struck blind/dumb** erblinden/verstummen; **(j)** (attack) überfallen; (Mil.) angreifen; **(k)** (encounter) begegnen (+ *Dat.*); **(l)** (Mining) stoßen auf (+ *Akk.*); ∼ **gold** auf Gold stoßen; (fig.) einen Glückstreffer landen (ugs.) **(in** mit); **(m)** (reach) stoßen auf (+ *Akk.*) ⟨*Hauptstraße, Weg, Fluss*⟩; **(n)** (adopt) einnehmen ⟨[*Geistes*]*haltung*⟩; **(o)** (take down) einholen ⟨*Segel, Flagge*⟩; abbrechen ⟨*Zelt, Lager*⟩. **3** *v.i.,* **struck, struck** *or* (arch.) **stricken (a)** (deliver a blow) zuschlagen; ⟨*Pfeil:*⟩ treffen; ⟨*Blitz:*⟩ einschlagen; ⟨*Unheil, Katastrophe, Krise, Leid:*⟩ hereinbrechen (geh.); (collide) zusammenstoßen; (hit) schlagen (**against** gegen, **[up]on** auf + *Akk.*); **(b)** (ignite) zünden; **(c)** (chime) schlagen; **(d)** (Industry) streiken; **(e)** (attack; also Mil.) zuschlagen (fig.); **(f)** (make a find) (Mining) fündig werden; ∼ **lucky** Glück haben; **(g)** (direct course) ∼ **south** *etc.* sich nach Süden *usw.* wenden

∼ **at** *v.t.* schlagen nach; (fig.) einen Schlag versetzen (+ *Dat.*); rütteln an (+ *Dat.*) ⟨*Grundfesten*⟩

∼ **'back** (lit. or fig.) zurückschlagen; ∼ **back at sb./sth.** sich gegen jmdn./etw. zur Wehr setzen

∼ **'down** *v.t.* niederschlagen; (fig.) niederwerfen (geh.)

∼ **'off** *v.t.* **(a)** (remove) abschlagen; **(b)** (remove from membership) streichen ⟨*Namen*⟩; (from professional body) die Zulassung *od.* Approbation entziehen (+ *Dat.*)

∼ **'out 1** *v.t.* (delete) streichen. **2** *v.i.* **(a)** (hit out) zuschlagen; ∼ **out at sb./sth.** nach jmdm./etw. schlagen; (fig.) jmdn./etw. scharf angreifen; **(b)** (set out, lit. or fig.) aufbrechen; ∼ **out in a new direction** (fig.) etwas Neues anfangen

∼ **through** *v.t.* durchstreichen

∼ **up** *v.t.* **(a)** (start) beginnen ⟨*Unterhaltung*⟩; anknüpfen ⟨*Bekanntschaft*⟩; schließen ⟨*Freundschaft*⟩; **(b)** (begin to play) anstimmen

strike: ∼ **action** *n.* Streikaktionen; ∼ **ballot** *n.* Urabstimmung, *die;* ∼ **benefit** ⇒ ∼ **pay;** ∼**breaker** *n.* Streikbrecher, *der/-*brecherin, *die;* ∼ **force** ⇒ **striking force;** ∼ **pay** *n.* Streikgeld, *das*

striker /'straɪkə(r)/ *n.* **(a)** (worker on strike) Streikende, *der/ die;* **(b)** (Footb.) Stürmer, *der/*Stürmerin, *die*

striking /'straɪkɪŋ/ *adj.* auffallend; erstaunlich ⟨*Ähnlichkeit, Unterschied*⟩; bemerkenswert ⟨*Idee*⟩; schlagend ⟨*Beispiel*⟩

striking: ∼ **distance** *n.* Reichweite, *die;* **within easy** ∼ **distance of a town** (fig.) in unmittelbarer Nähe einer Stadt; ∼ **force** *n.* (Mil., Police) Einsatzkommando, *das*

string /strɪŋ/ **1** *n.* **(a)** (thin cord) Schnur, *die;* (to tie up parcels etc. also) Bindfaden, *der;* (ribbon) Band, *das;* **how long is a piece of** ∼? (fig.) wie weit ist der Himmel?; **[have/keep sb.] on a** ∼: [jmdn.] an der Leine (ugs.) *od.* am Gängelband [haben/halten]; **pull [a few** *or* **some]** ∼**s** (fig.) seine Beziehungen spielen lassen; **there are** ∼**s attached** (fig.) es sind Bedingungen/es ist eine Bedingung damit verknüpft; **without** ∼**s, with no** ∼**s attached** ohne Bedingung[en]; **(b)** (of bow) Sehne, *die;* (of racket, musical instrument) Saite, *die;* **have another** ∼ **to one's bow** (fig.) noch ein Eisen im Feuer haben (ugs.); **(c)** *in pl.* (Mus.) (instruments) Streichinstrumente *Pl.;* (players) Streicher *Pl.;* ∼ **quartet/orchestra** Streichquartett/-orchester, *das;* **(d)** (series, sequence) Kette, *die;* (procession) Zug, *der.* **2** *v.t.,* **strung** /strʌŋ/ **(a)** bespannen ⟨*Tennisschläger, Bogen, Gitarre usw.*⟩; **(b)** (thread) auffädeln; aufziehen

∼ **a'long** (coll.) **1** *v.i.* sich anschließen; ∼ **along with sb.** mit jmdm. mitgehen; (have relationship) mit jmdm. gehen (ugs.). **2** *v.t.* (deceive) an der Nase herumführen (ugs.)

∼ **'out** *v.t.* verstreuen. **2** *v.i.* (in space) sich verteilen

∼ **to'gether** *v.t.* (on a thread) auffädeln; aufziehen; (by tying) zusammenbinden; miteinander verknüpfen ⟨*Worte*⟩

∼ **'up** *v.t.* **(a)** (hang up) aufhängen ⟨*Lampions, Papiergirlanden*⟩; **(b)** (coll.: kill by hanging) aufhängen (ugs.); **(c)** (make tense) **strung up** angespannt

string: ∼ **'bag** *n.* [Einkaufs]netz, *das;* ∼ **band** *n.* (Mus.) Streichorchester, *das*

stringed /strɪŋd/ *attrib. adj.* (Mus.) Saiten-

stringent /'strɪndʒənt/ *adj.* **(a)** (strict) streng ⟨*Bestimmung, Gesetz, Maßnahme, Test*⟩; **(b)** (tight) angespannt ⟨*Finanzlage*⟩

string 'vest *n.* Netzhemd, *das*

stringy /'strɪŋɪ/ *adj.* **(a)** (fibrous) faserig; **(b)** (resembling string) dünn ⟨*Haar*⟩; faserig ⟨*Gewebe*⟩

strip¹ /strɪp/ **1** *v.t.*, **-pp-:** **(a)** ausziehen ⟨*Person*⟩; leerräumen, ausräumen ⟨*Haus, Schrank, Regal*⟩; abziehen ⟨*Bett*⟩; entrinden ⟨*Baum*⟩; abbeizen ⟨*Möbel, Türen*⟩; ausschlachten, (dismantle) auseinander nehmen ⟨*Maschine, Auto*⟩; **∼ped to the waist** mit nacktem Oberkörper; **∼ sb. of sth.** jmdn. einer Sache (*Gen.*) berauben (geh.); **∼ sb. of his rank/title/medals/decorations/office** jmdm. seinen Rang/Titel/seine Medaillen/Auszeichnungen aberkennen/jmdn. seines Amtes entkleiden (geh.); **∼ the walls** die Tapeten entfernen; **(b)** (remove) entfernen (**from, off** von); abziehen ⟨*Laken*⟩; abstreifen ⟨*Hülle*⟩. **2** *v.i.*, **-pp-** sich ausziehen; **∼ to the waist/[down] to one's underwear** den Oberkörper freimachen/sich bis auf die Unterwäsche ausziehen

∼ 'down 1 *v.t.* **(a)** (dismantle) auseinander nehmen; **(b)** (undress) ausziehen. **2** *v.i.* sich ausziehen

∼ 'off 1 *v.t.* **(a)** abreißen; abschälen ⟨*Rinde*⟩; abziehen ⟨*Tapete*⟩; **∼ sth. off sth.** etw. von etw. abreißen/abschälen/abziehen; **(b)** ausziehen ⟨*Kleidung*⟩. **2** *v.i.* sich ausziehen

strip² *n.* **(a)** (narrow piece) Streifen, *der;* **a ∼ of land** ein schmales Stück *od.* Streifen Land; **tear sb. off a ∼, tear a ∼ off sb.** (Brit. coll.) jmdm. den Marsch blasen (ugs.); **(b)** ⇨ **strip cartoon**

'strip cartoon *n.* Comic[strip], *der*

stripe /straɪp/ *n.* **(a)** Streifen, *der;* **(b)** (Mil.) [Ärmel]streifen, *der.* See also **star 1 a**

striped /straɪpt/ *adj.* gestreift; Streifen ⟨*muster*⟩

strip: ∼ light *n.* Neonröhre, *die;* **∼ lighting** *n.* Neonbeleuchtung, *die;* Neonlicht, *das*

stripling /'strɪplɪŋ/ *n.* Jüngelchen, *das*

'stripped pine *n.* abgebeizte Kiefer

stripper /'strɪpə(r)/ *n.* **(a)** (solvent) Farbentferner, *der;* (for wallpaper) Tapetenlöser, *der;* (tool) Kratzer, *der;* **(b)** ▶887⃒ (striptease performer) Stripper, *der/*Stripperin, *die* (ugs.)

strip: ∼ show *n.* Strip-Show, *die;* **∼'tease** *n.* Striptease, *der*

stripy /'straɪpɪ/ *adj.* gestreift ⟨*Fell, Blazer*⟩; Streifen ⟨*muster, -stoff*⟩

strive /straɪv/ *v.i.*, **strove** /strəʊv/, **striven** /'strɪvn/ **(a)** (endeavour) sich bemühen; **∼ to do sth.** bestrebt sein (geh.) *od.* sich bemühen, etw. zu tun; **∼ after** *or* **for sth.** nach etw. streben; **(b)** (contend) kämpfen (**for** um)

strobe /strəʊb/ *n.* (coll.) Stroboskoplicht, *das*

strode ⇨ **stride 2**

stroke¹ /strəʊk/ *n.* **(a)** (act of striking) Hieb, *der;* Schlag, *der;* (of sword, axe) Hieb, *der;* **finishing ∼** (lit. or fig.) Todesstoß, *der;* **(b)** (Med.) Schlaganfall, *der;* **paralytic/apoplectic ∼:** paralytischer/apoplektischer Anfall; **(c)** (sudden impact) **∼ of lightning** Blitzschlag, *der;* **by a ∼ of fate/fortune** durch eine Fügung des Schicksals/einen [glücklichen] Zufall; **∼ of [good] luck** Glücksfall, *der;* **have a ∼ of bad/[good] luck** Pech/Glück haben; **(d)** (single effort) Streich, *der;* (skilful effort) Schachzug, *der;* **at a** *or* **one ∼:** auf einen Schlag *od.* Streich; **not do a ∼ [of work]** keinen [Hand]schlag tun; **∼ of genius** genialer Einfall; **(e)** (of pendulum, heart, wings, oar) Schlag, *der;* (in swimming) Zug, *der;* **(f)** (Billiards etc.) Stoß, *der;* (Tennis, Cricket, Golf, Rowing) Schlag, *der;* **(g)** (mark, line) Strich, *der;* (of handwriting; also fig.: detail) Zug, *der;* (symbol /) Schrägstrich, *der;* **(h)** (sound of clock) Schlag, *der;* **on the ∼ of nine** Punkt neun [Uhr]

stroke² *v.t.* streicheln; **∼ sth. over/across sth.** mit etw. über etw. (*Akk.*) streichen; **∼ sth. back** etw. zurückstreichen. **2** *n.* **give sb./sth. a ∼:** jmdn./etw. streicheln

stroll /strəʊl/ **1** *v.i.* (saunter) spazieren gehen; **∼ into sth.** in etw. (*Akk.*) schlendern. **2** *n.* Spaziergang, *der;* **go for a ∼:** einen Spaziergang machen

∼ a'long *v.i.* daherspazieren *od.* -schlendern

∼'on *v.i.* weiterschlendern

stroller /'strəʊlə(r)/ *n.* (pushchair) Sportwagen, *der*

strong /strɒŋ/ **1** *adj.*, **∼er** /'strɒŋɡə(r)/, **∼est** /'strɒŋɡɪst/ **(a)** (resistant) stark; gefestigt ⟨*Ehe*⟩; stabil ⟨*Möbel*⟩; solide, fest ⟨*Fundament, Schuhe*⟩; streng ⟨*Vorschriften, Vorkehrungen*⟩; robust ⟨*Konstitution, Magen, Stoff, Porzellan*⟩; **you have to have a ∼ stomach** (fig.) man muss einiges vertragen können; **(b)** (powerful) stark, kräftig ⟨*Person, Tier*⟩; kräftig ⟨*Arme, Beine, Muskeln, Tritt, Schlag, Zähne*⟩; stark ⟨*Linse, Brille, Strom, Magnet*⟩; gut ⟨*Augen*⟩; **as ∼ as a horse** *or* **an ox** (fig.) bärenstark (ugs.); **a man of ∼ character** ein charakterstarker Mann; **(c)** (effective) stark ⟨*Regierung, Herrscher, Wille*⟩; streng ⟨*Disziplin, Lehrer*⟩; gut ⟨*Gedächtnis, Schüler*⟩; fähig ⟨*Redner, Mathematiker*⟩; (formidable) stark ⟨*Gegner, Kombination*⟩; aussichtsreich ⟨*Kandidat*⟩; (powerful in resources) reich ⟨*Nation, Land*⟩; leistungsfähig ⟨*Wirtschaft*⟩; stark ⟨*Besetzung, Delegation, Truppe, Kontingent usw.*⟩; **sb.'s ∼ point** jmds. Stärke; **(d)** (convincing) gut, handfest ⟨*Grund, Beispiel, Argument*⟩; **there is a ∼ possibility that …:** es ist sehr wahrscheinlich, dass …; **(e)** (vigorous, moving forcefully) stark; voll ⟨*Unterstützung*⟩; fest ⟨*Überzeugung*⟩; kraftvoll ⟨*Stil*⟩; (fervent) glühend ⟨*Anhänger, Verfechter einer Sache*⟩; **take ∼ measures/action** energisch vorgehen; **(f)** (affecting the senses) stark; kräftig, stark ⟨*Geruch, Geschmack, Stimme*⟩; markant ⟨*Gesichtszüge*⟩; (pungent) streng ⟨*Geruch, Geschmack*⟩; kräftig ⟨*Käse*⟩; **(g)** (concentrated) stark; kräftig ⟨*Farbe*⟩; **I need a ∼ drink** ich muss mir erst mal einen genehmigen (ugs.); **(h)** (emphatic) stark ⟨*Ausdruck, Protest*⟩; heftig ⟨*Worte, Wortwechsel*⟩. **2** *adv.* stark; **sb. is going ∼:** es geht jmdm. gut; **they are still going ∼** (after years of marriage) mit ihnen geht es noch immer gut; (after hours of work) sie sind noch immer eifrig dabei

strong: ∼ 'arm *n.*, no pl. Muskelkraft, *die; attrib.* **∼-arm methods** brutale Methoden; **∼ box** *n.* Kassette, *die;* **∼hold** *n.* Festung, *die;* (fig.) Hochburg, *die;* **∼'language** *n.*, no pl., no indef. art. derbe Ausdrucksweise; **use ∼ language** sich derb ausdrücken

strongly /'strɒŋlɪ/ *adv.* **(a)** stark; fest ⟨*etabliert*⟩; solide ⟨*gearbeitet*⟩; **∼ built** solide gebaut; (in body) kräftig gebaut; **(b)** (powerfully) stark; **(c)** (convincingly) überzeugend ⟨*darlegen*⟩; **(d)** (vigorously) energisch ⟨*protestieren, bestreiten*⟩; nachdrücklich ⟨*unterstützen*⟩; dringend ⟨*raten*⟩; fest ⟨*glauben*⟩; **I feel ∼ about it** es ist mir sehr ernst damit; es liegt mir sehr am Herzen; **I ∼ suspect that …:** ich habe den starken Verdacht, dass …

strong: ∼man *n.* Muskelmann, *der* (ugs.); **∼-'minded** *adj.* [seelisch] robust; (determined) willensstark; **∼ point** *n.* (fortified position) Stützpunkt, *der; see also* **∼ 1 c; ∼room** *n.* Tresorraum, *der;* Stahlkammer, *die*

strontium /'strɒntɪəm/ *n.* (Chem.) Strontium, *das*

stroppy /'strɒpɪ/ *adj.* (Brit. coll.) pampig (salopp)

strove ⇨ **strive**

struck ⇨ **strike 2, 3**

structural /'strʌktʃərl/ *adj.* baulich; Bau ⟨*material*⟩; tragend ⟨*Wand, Säule, Balken*⟩; Konstruktions ⟨*fehler*⟩

structure /'strʌktʃə(r)/ **1** *n.* **(a)** Struktur, *die;* Aufbau, *der;* (Mus.) Kompositionsweise, *die;* (manner of construction) Bauweise, *die;* Struktur, *die;* **(b)** (something constructed) Konstruktion, *die;* (building) Bauwerk, *das;* (complex whole; also Biol.) Struktur, *die.* **2** *v.t.* strukturieren; regeln ⟨*Leben*⟩; aufbauen ⟨*literarisches Werk*⟩; (construct) konstruieren; bauen

struggle /'strʌɡl/ **1** *v.i.* **(a)** (try with difficulty) kämpfen; **∼ to do sth.** sich abmühen, etw. zu tun; **∼ for a place/a better world** um einen Platz/für eine bessere Welt kämpfen; **∼ against** *or* **with sb./sth.** mit jmdn./etw. *od.* gegen jmdn./etw. kämpfen; **∼ with sth.** (try to cope) sich mit etw. quälen; mit etw. kämpfen; **(b)** (proceed with difficulty) sich quälen; (into tight dress, through narrow opening) sich zwängen; **I ∼d past** ich kämpfte mich vorbei; **(c)** (physically) kämpfen; (resist) sich wehren; **∼ free** freikommen; sich befreien; **(d)** (be in difficulties) kämpfen (fig.); **after three laps I was struggling** nach drei Runden hatte ich zu kämpfen. **2** *n.* (exertion) Mühe, *die;* **with a ∼:** mit Mühe; **it was a long ∼:** es kostete viel Mühe; **have a [hard] ∼ to do sth.** [große] Mühe haben, etw. zu tun; **the ∼ for freedom** der Kampf für die Freiheit; **(b)** (physical fight) Kampf, *der;*

the ~ **against** or **with sb./sth.** der Kampf gegen od. mit jmdm./etw.; **the ~ for influence/power** der Kampf um Einfluss/die Macht; **surrender without a ~:** kampflos aufgeben

strum /strʌm/ 1 v.i., **-mm-** klimpern (ugs.) (**on** auf + Dat.). 2 v.t., **-mm-** klimpern (ugs.) auf (+ Dat.)

strung ⇒ **string 2**

strut¹ /strʌt/ 1 v.i., **-tt-** (walk) stolzieren. 2 n. stolzierender Gang

strut² n. (support) Strebe, die

stub /stʌb/ 1 n. (a) (short remaining portion) Stummel, der; (of cigarette) Kippe, die; ~ **of pencil** Bleistiftstummel, der; (b) (counterfoil) Abschnitt, der; (of ticket) Abriss, der. 2 v.t., **-bb-:** (a) ~ **one's toe [against** or **on sth.]** sich (Dat.) den Zeh [an etw. (Dat.)] stoßen; (b) ausdrücken ⟨Zigarette usw.⟩; (with one's foot) austreten ⟨Zigarette usw.⟩
~ **'out** v.t. ausdrücken

stubble /'stʌbl/ n., no pl. Stoppeln Pl.

stubborn /'stʌbən/ adj. (a) (obstinate) starrköpfig (abwertend); dickköpfig (ugs.); störrisch ⟨Tier, Gesicht, Haltung⟩; hartnäckig ⟨Vorurteil⟩; **be ~ in insisting on sth.** stur (ugs. abwertend) auf etw. (Dat.) beharren; [**as**] ~ **as a mule** störrisch wie ein Maulesel (ugs.); (b) (resolute) hartnäckig; fest ⟨Mut, Entschlossenheit, Treue⟩; (c) (intractable) störrisch (fig.); vertrackt (ugs.) ⟨Problem⟩

stubbornness /'stʌbənnɪs/ n., no pl. (a) (obstinacy) Starrköpfigkeit, die; (b) (resolution, intractability) Hartnäckigkeit, die

stucco /'stʌkəʊ/ n., pl. ~**es** (fine plaster) Stuck, der; (coarse plaster) Putz, der

stuck ⇒ **stick 1, 2**

'stuck up ⇒ **stick up 1 d**

stud¹ /stʌd/ 1 n. (a) (nail) Beschlagnagel, der; (on clothes) Niete, die; (on boot) Stollen, der; (marker in road) Nagel, der (Verkehrsw.); (b) (for ear) Ohrstecker, der. 2 v.t., **-dd-** (set with ~s) beschlagen; (be scattered over) verstreut sein über (+ Akk.); ~**ded with flowers/stars** etc. mit Blumen/ Sternen usw. übersät

stud² n. (a) (Breeding) Gestüt, das; (b) (stallion) Zuchthengst, der

student /'stju:dənt/ n. Student, der/Studentin, die; (in school or training establishment) Schüler, der/Schülerin, die; **be a ~ of sth.** etw. studieren; ~ **of medicine** Student/Studentin der Medizin; Medizinstudent, der/-studentin, die; attrib. ~ **days** Studenten-/Schulzeit, die; ~ **driver** (Amer.) Fahrschüler, der/-schülerin, die; ~ **nurse** Lernschwester, die/Pflegeschüler, der; **be a ~ doctor/teacher** ein medizinisches Praktikum/Schulpraktikum machen

'stud farm n. Gestüt, das

studied /'stʌdɪd/ adj. (a) (thoughtful) [wohl]überlegt; (b) (intentional) gewollt; gesucht ⟨Stil, Ausdrucksweise⟩

studio /'stju:dɪəʊ/ n., pl. ~**s** (a) (photographer's or painter's workroom) Atelier, das; (workshop for the performing arts) Studio, das; (b) (Cinemat., Radio, Telev.) Studio, das

studio: ~ **apartment** (Amer.), ~ **flat** (Brit.) ns. Einzimmerwohnung, die

studious /'stju:dɪəs/ adj. (assiduous in study) lerneifrig; gelehrt ⟨Beschäftigung, Buch, Aussehen, Atmosphäre⟩

study /'stʌdɪ/ 1 n. (a) Studium, das; Lernen, das; **the ~ of mathematics/law** das Studium der Mathematik/der Rechtswissenschaft; [**books on**] **African/Social Studies** (Educ./Univ.) [Bücher zur] Afrikanistik/Sozialwissenschaft; **graduate studies** (Educ./Univ.) Graduiertenstudium, das; (b) (piece of work) **a ~ of** or **on sth.** eine Studie über etw. (Akk.); **studies are being carried out** zur Zeit werden Untersuchungen durchgeführt; (c) **a ~ in sth.** ein Musterbeispiel (fig.) für etw.; **his face was a ~!** sein Gesicht war sehenswert!; (d) (Art) Studie, die; (Mus.) Etüde, die; Übung, die; (Lit., Theatre) Studie, die (**in**, **of** über + Akk.); (e) (room) Arbeitszimmer, das. 2 v.t. (a) studieren; (at school) lernen; (b) (scrutinize) studieren; (c) (read attentively) studieren ⟨Fahrplan⟩; sich (Dat.) [sorgfältig] durchlesen ⟨Prüfungsfragen, Bericht⟩. 3 v.i. lernen; (at university) studieren; ~ **to be a doctor/teach French** Medizin studieren/Französisch für das Lehramt studieren

stuff /stʌf/ 1 n. (a) no pl., no indef. art. (material[s]) Zeug, das (ugs.); **be made of sterner ~:** aus härterem Stoff gemacht sein (fig.); **the ~ that dreams/heroes are made of** der Stoff, aus dem die Träume sind/Helden gemacht sind (fig.); **plastic is useful ~:** Plastik ist eine nützliche Sache; (b) no pl., no indef. art. (activity, knowledge) **do painting** or **drawing,** ~ **like that** malen oder zeichnen oder so was (ugs.); **do one's ~** (coll.) seine Sache machen; **know one's ~** (coll.: be knowledgeable) sich auskennen; (know one's job) seine Sache verstehen; **that's the ~!** (coll.) so ist's richtig! 2 v.t. (a) stopfen; zustopfen ⟨Loch, Ohren⟩; (in taxidermy) ausstopfen; (Cookery) füllen; ~ **sth. with** or **full of sth.** etw. mit etw. voll stopfen (ugs.); [**go and**] **get** ~**ed!** (sl.) hau ab! (ugs.); ~ **oneself** (sl.) sich voll stopfen (ugs.); ~ **one's face** (sl.) sich (Dat.) den Bauch voll stopfen (ugs.); ~ **ballot boxes** (Amer.: insert bogus votes) Stimmen fälschen; (b) (sl.) ~ **him!** zum Teufel mit ihm!; ~ **it!** Scheiß drauf! (derb); **he can ~ it!** er kann mich mal! (derb). 3 v.i. sich voll stopfen (ugs.)

stuffing /'stʌfɪŋ/ n. (a) (material) Füllmaterial, das; **a ~ of horsehair** eine Füllung aus Roßhaar; **knock the ~ out of sb.** (fig. coll.) jmdn. umhauen (ugs.); (b) (Cookery) Füllung, die

stuffy /'stʌfɪ/ adj. (a) (stifling) stickig ⟨Zimmer, Atmosphäre⟩; (b) (congested) verstopft; (c) (coll.: prim) spießig ⟨about gegenüber⟩

stultify /'stʌltɪfaɪ/ v.t. lähmen; **have a ~ing effect on sth.** sich lähmend auf etw. (Akk.) auswirken; ~**ing boredom/monotony** lähmende Langeweile/Monotonie

stumble /'stʌmbl/ v.i. (a) stolpern (**over** über + Akk.); (b) (falter) stocken; ~ **over sth./through life** über etw. (Akk.) /durchs Leben stolpern; (c) ~ **across** or [**up**]**on sb./sth.** (find by chance) über jmdn. stolpern (fig. ugs.)/auf etw. (Akk.) stoßen

stumbling block /'stʌmblɪŋblɒk/ n. Stolperstein, der

stump /stʌmp/ 1 n. (a) (of tree, branch, tooth) Stumpf, der; (of cigar, pencil, limb, tail, etc.) Stummel, der; (b) (Cricket) Stab, der. 2 v.t. (confound) verwirren; durcheinander bringen; **be** ~**ed** ratlos sein; **be** ~**ed for an answer** um eine Antwort verlegen sein. 3 v.i. (walk stiffly) stapfen; (walk noisily) trampeln

stumpy /'stʌmpɪ/ adj. gedrungen; ~ **tail** Stummelschwanz, der

stun /stʌn/ v.t., **-nn-:** (a) (knock senseless) betäuben; **be** ~**ned** (unconscious) bewusstlos sein; (dazed) benommen sein; (b) (fig.) **be** ~**ned at** or **by sth.** von etw. wie betäubt sein

stung ⇒ **sting 2, 3**

stunk ⇒ **stink 1**

stunning /'stʌnɪŋ/ adj. (coll.) (a) (splendid) hinreißend; umwerfend (ugs.); (b) (causing insensibility) wuchtig ⟨Schlag⟩; (c) (shocking) bestürzend ⟨Nachricht⟩; (amazing) sensationell

stunt¹ /stʌnt/ v.t. hemmen, beeinträchtigen ⟨Wachstum, Entwicklung⟩; ~**ed trees** verkümmerte Bäume

stunt² n. halsbrecherisches Kunststück; (Cinemat.) Stunt, der; (Advertising) [Werbe]gag, der

stupefying /'stju:pɪfaɪɪŋ/ adj. die Sinne betäubend ⟨Hitze⟩; stumpfsinnig ⟨Arbeit⟩; (fig.: astonishing) unfassbar

stupendous /stju:'pendəs/ adj. gewaltig; außergewöhnlich ⟨Schönheit, Intelligenz, Talent⟩; großartig ⟨Urlaub, Schauspieler⟩

stupid /'stju:pɪd/ adj., ~**er** /'stju:pɪdə(r)/, ~**est** /'stju:pɪdɪst/ (slow-witted, unintelligent) dumm; einfältig ⟨Person, Aussehen⟩; (ridiculous) lächerlich; (pointless) dumm (ugs.) ⟨Witz, Geschichte, Gedanke⟩; expr. rejection or irritation blöd (ugs.); **it would be ~ to do sth.** es wäre töricht, etw. zu tun

stupidity /stju:'pɪdɪtɪ/ n. Dummheit, die; (of action also) Torheit, die

stupidly /'stju:pɪdlɪ/ adv. dumm; ~ [**enough**], **I have …:** dummerweise habe ich …

stupor /'stju:pə(r)/ n. Benommenheit, die; **in a drunken ~:** sinnlos betrunken

sturdy /'stɜ:dɪ/ adj. (robust) stabil ⟨Haus, Stuhl, Schiff⟩; kräftig ⟨Rasse, Pflanze, Pferd, Kind⟩; kräftig [gebaut] ⟨Person⟩; (thickset) stämmig ⟨Person⟩; (strong) stämmig

⟨*Beine, Arme*⟩; (sound) solide; (resolute) stark ⟨*Gegner, Verfechter, Widerstand*⟩

sturgeon /'stɜːdʒən/ *n.* Stör, *der*

stutter /'stʌtə(r)/ **1** *v.i.* stottern; ⟨*Gewehr:*⟩ tacken. **2** *n.* Stottern, *das;* **have a bad ∼:** stark stottern

sty¹ /staɪ/ ⇒ **pigsty**

sty², **stye** /staɪ/ *n.* (Med.) Gerstenkorn, *das*

style /staɪl/ **1** *n.* (a) Stil, *der;* (in conversation) Ton, *der;* (in performance) Art, *die;* (of habitual behaviour) Art, *die;* **that's the ∼!** so ist es richtig!; **be bad** *or* **not good ∼:** schlechter *od.* kein guter Stil sein; **it's not my ∼ [to do that]** das ist nicht mein Stil; **dress in the latest/modern ∼:** sich nach der neuesten/neuen Mode kleiden; **cook in the French ∼:** französisch kochen; **(b)** (superior way of living, behaving, etc.) Stil, *der;* **in ∼:** stilvoll; (on a grand scale) im großen Stil; **in the grand ∼:** im großen Stil; **(c)** (sort) Art, *die;* **∼ of music** Musikrichtung, *die;* **(d)** (pattern) Art, *die;* (of clothes) Machart, *die;* (hair-∼) Frisur, *die.* **2** *v.t.* (design) entwerfen; **elegantly ∼d clothes** elegant geschnittene Kleidung

styli *pl. of* **stylus**

stylish /'staɪlɪʃ/ *adj.* stilvoll; elegant ⟨*Kleidung, Auto, Hotel, Person*⟩

stylist /'staɪlɪst/ *n.* ▶ 887 ◀ Designer, *der*/Designerin, *die;* (hair-∼) Haarstilist, *der*/-stilistin, *die*

stylistic /staɪ'lɪstɪk/ *adj.* stilistisch; Stil ⟨*mittel, -merkmale*⟩

stylus /'staɪləs/ *n., pl.* **styli** /'staɪlaɪ/ *or* **∼es** (of record player) [Abtast]nadel, *die*

styptic /'stɪptɪk/ *adj.* blutstillend

suave /swɑːv/ *adj.* gewandt

sub /sʌb/ *n.* (coll.) **(a)** (membership fee) Mitgliedsbeitrag, *der;* **(b)** (esp. Sport: substitute) Ersatz, *der;* **(c)** ⇒ **sub-editor**

sub- *pref.* unter-; (mit Fremdwörtern meist) sub-

'subcommittee *n.* Unterausschuss, *der*

sub'conscious (Psych.) **1** *adj.* unterbewusst; **∼ mind** Unterbewusstsein, *das.* **2** *n.* Unterbewusstsein, *das*

sub'consciously *adv.* (Psych.) unterbewusst

'subcontinent *n.* (Geog.) Subkontinent, *der*

subcon'tract 1 *v.t.* (accept under secondary contract) als Subunternehmer übernehmen; (offer under secondary contract) an Subunternehmer/an einen Subunternehmer vergeben; **∼ a job to sb.** eine Arbeit an jmdn. [in einem Untervertrag] vergeben. **2** *v.i.* (accept secondary contract) als Subunternehmer arbeiten; (offer secondary contract) Aufträge an Subunternehmer/an einen Subunternehmer vergeben

'subcontractor *n.* ▶ 887 ◀ Subunternehmer, *der*/-unternehmerin, *die*

'subdirectory *n.* (Computing) Unterverzeichnis, *das*

subdivide /'sʌbdɪvaɪd, sʌbdɪ'vaɪd/ **1** *v.t.* (further divide) erneut teilen; (divide into parts) unterteilen. **2** *v.i.* **∼ into sth.** sich in etw. (*Akk.*) teilen

subdivision /'sʌbdɪvɪʒn, sʌbdɪ'vɪʒn/ *n.* (subdividing) erneute Teilung; (subordinate division) Unterabteilung, *die;* **∼ [of sth.] into sth.** Unterteilung [einer Sache (*Gen.*)] in etw. (*Akk.*)

subdue /səb'djuː/ *v.t.* (conquer) besiegen; unterwerfen; (bring under control) bändigen ⟨*Kind, Tier*⟩; ruhig stellen ⟨*Patienten*⟩; unter Kontrolle bringen ⟨*Demonstranten usw.*⟩; bezähmen ⟨*Gefühle, zornige Person*⟩; (reduce in intensity) dämpfen ⟨*Zorn, Heftigkeit, gute Laune, Lärm, Licht*⟩; abkühlen (fig.) ⟨*Leidenschaft*⟩; verblassen lassen ⟨*Farben*⟩

subdued /səb'djuːd/ *adj.* gedämpft; **he seemed rather ∼:** er schien ziemlich gedämpfter Stimmung zu sein

sub-'editor *n.* (Journ., Publishing) **(a)** (assistant editor) Mitherausgeber, *der*/Mitherausgeberin, *die;* **(b)** (Brit.: one who prepares material) Redaktionsassistent, *der*/-assistentin, *die*

'subgroup *n.* Untergruppe, *die*

'subheading *n.* **(a)** (subordinate division) Unterabschnitt, *der;* **(b)** (subordinate title) Untertitel, *der*

sub'human *adj.* unmenschlich

subject 1 /'sʌbdʒɪkt/ *n.* **(a)** (citizen) Staatsbürger, *der*/-bürgerin, *die;* (in relation to monarch) Untertan, *der*/Untertanin, *die;* **(b)** (topic) Thema, *das;* (department of study) Fach,

das; (area of knowledge) Fach[gebiet], *das;* (Art) Motiv, *das;* (Mus.) Thema, *das;* **be the ∼ of an investigation** Gegenstand einer Untersuchung sein; **on the ∼ of money** über das Thema Geld ⟨*reden usw.*⟩; beim Thema Geld ⟨*sein, bleiben*⟩; **change the ∼:** das Thema wechseln; **(c) be a ∼ for sth.** (cause sth.) zu etw. Anlass geben; **(d)** (Ling., Logic, Philos.) Subjekt, *das.* **2** /'sʌbdʒɪkt/ *adj.* **(a)** (conditional) **be ∼ to sth.** von etw. abhängig sein *od.* abhängen; **sth. is ∼ to alteration** etw. kann geändert werden; **(b)** (prone) **be ∼ to sth.** anfällig sein für ⟨*Krankheit*⟩; neigen zu ⟨*Melancholie*⟩; **(c)** (dependent) abhängig; **∼ to** (dependent on) untertan (+ *Dat.*) ⟨*König usw.*⟩; unterworfen (+ *Dat.*) ⟨*Verfassung, Gesetz, Krone*⟩; untergeben (+ *Dat.*) ⟨*Dienstherrn*⟩. **3** /'sʌbdʒɪkt/ *adv.* **∼ to sth.** vorbehaltlich einer Sache (*Gen.*). **4** /səb'dʒekt/ *v.t.* **(a)** (subjugate, make submissive) unterwerfen (**to** *Dat.*); **(b)** (expose) **∼ sb./sth. to sth.** jmdn./etw. einer Sache (*Dat.*) aussetzen; **∼ sb. to torture** jmdn. der Folter unterwerfen; **∼ sth. to chemical analysis** etw. einer chemischen Analyse unterziehen

subjective /səb'dʒektɪv/ *adj.* **(a)** subjektiv; **(b)** (Ling.) Subjekt-

'subject matter *n., no pl., no indef. art.* Gegenstand, *der*

subjugate /'sʌbdʒʊgeɪt/ *v.t.* unterjochen (**to** unter + *Akk.*)

subjunctive /səb'dʒʌŋktɪv/ (Ling.) **1** *adj.* konjunktivisch; Konjunktiv-; **∼ mood** Konjunktiv, *der.* **2** *n.* Konjunktiv, *der;* **past/present ∼:** Konjunktiv II *od.* Präteritum/Konjunktiv I *od.* Präsens

sub'let *v.t.,* **-tt-,** **sublet** untervermieten

sublime /sə'blaɪm/ *adj.,* **∼r** /sə'blaɪmə(r)/, **∼st** /sə'blaɪmɪst/ (exalted) erhaben; (iron.) vollendet (fig. iron.) ⟨*Chaos*⟩

subliminal /sʌb'lɪmɪnl/ *adj.* **∼ advertising** unterschwellige Werbung

sub-ma'chine gun *n.* Maschinenpistole, *die*

submarine /'sʌbməriːn, sʌbmə'riːn/ **1** *n.* Unterseeboot, *das;* U-Boot, *das.* **2** *adj.* Unterwasser-; unterseeisch (Geol.)

submerge /səb'mɜːdʒ/ **1** *v.t.* **(a)** (place under water) **∼ sth. [in the water]** etw. eintauchen *od.* ins Wasser tauchen; **(b)** (inundate) ⟨*Wasser:*⟩ überschwemmen; **be ∼d in water** unter Wasser stehen. **2** *v.i.* abtauchen (Seemannsspr.)

submission /səb'mɪʃn/ *n.* **(a)** (surrender) Unterwerfung, *die* (**to** unter + *Akk.*); **force/frighten sb. into ∼:** jmdn. zwingen, sich zu unterwerfen/jmdm. durch Einschüchterung seinen Willen aufzwingen; **(b)** *no pl., no art.* (meekness) Unterwerfung, *die;* **(c)** (presentation) Einreichung, *die* (**to** bei); (thing put forward) Einsendung, *die;* (by witness) Aussage, *die*

submissive /səb'mɪsɪv/ *adj.* gehorsam; unterwürfig (abwertend); **be ∼ to sb./sth.** sich jmdn./einer Sache unterwerfen

submit /səb'mɪt/ **1** *v.t.,* **-tt-:** **(a)** (present) einreichen; vorbringen ⟨*Vorschlag*⟩; abgeben ⟨[*Doktor*]*arbeit usw.*⟩; **∼ sth. to sb.** jmdm. etw. vorlegen; **∼ sth. to scrutiny/investigation** etw. einer Prüfung/Untersuchung unterziehen; **∼ one's entry/answer to a competition** seine Teilnehmerkarte/Lösung für ein Preisausschreiben einsenden; **∼ that …** (suggest, argue) behaupten, dass …; **(b)** (surrender) **∼ oneself to sb./sth.** sich jmdm./einer Sache unterwerfen; **(c)** (subject) **∼ sth. to heat** etw. der Hitze (*Dat.*) aussetzen; **∼ oneself to sth.** sich einer Sache (*Dat.*) unterziehen. **2** *v.i.,* **-tt-:** **(a)** (surrender) aufgeben; sich unterwerfen (**to** *Dat.*); **(b)** (defer) **∼ to sb./sth.** sich jmdm./einer Sache beugen; **(c)** (agree to undergo) **∼ to sth.** sich einer Sache (*Dat.*) aussetzen

sub'normal *adj.* unterdurchschnittlich; subnormal (Med.)

subordinate 1 /sə'bɔːdɪnət/ *adj.* (inferior) untergeordnet; (lower-ranking) rangniedriger; (secondary) zweitrangig; **be ∼ to sb./sth.** jmdm./einer Sache untergeordnet sein. **2** /sə'bɔːdɪnət/ *n.* Untergebene, *der/die.* **3** /sə'bɔːdɪneɪt/ *v.t.* (render subject) unterordnen (**to** *Dat.*)

'subroutine *n.* (Computing) Unterprogramm, *das;* Subroutine, *die*

subscribe /səb'skraɪb/ **1** *v.t.* ([promise to] contribute) ～ sth. zusichern, etw. zu spenden; **be ～d** als Spende zugesichert worden sein. **2** *v.i.* **(a)** (express support) ～ **to sth.** sich einer Sache (*Dat.*) anschließen; **(b)** ([promise to] make contribution) ～ **to** *or* **for sth.** eine Spende für etw. zusichern

subscriber /səb'skraɪbə(r)/ *n.* **(a)** (one who assents) Befürworter, *der*/Befürworterin, *die* (**to** *Gen.*); **(b)** (contributor) Spender, *der*/Spenderin, *die* (**of, to** für); (to a newspaper etc.) Abonnent, *der*/ Abonnentin, *die* (**to** *Gen.*); **(c)** (Teleph.) Fernsprechkunde, *der*/-kundin, *die*

subscription /səb'skrɪpʃn/ *n.* **(a)** (thing subscribed) Spendenbeitrag, *der* (**to** für); (membership fee) Mitgliedsbeitrag, *der* (**to** für); (prepayment for newspaper etc.) Abonnement, *das* (**to** *Gen.*); **[buy] by ～:** im Abonnement [beziehen]; **(b)** (act of subscribing money) Spende, *die;* **[be built] by ～:** mit Spenden [gebaut werden]

'subsection *n.* Unterabschnitt, *der*

subsequent /'sʌbsɪkwənt/ *adj.* folgend; nachfolgend 〈*Kind*〉; später 〈*Gelegenheit*〉; ～ **events** spätere *od.* die folgenden Ereignisse

subservient /səb'sɜ:vɪənt/ *adj.* **(a)** (merely instrumental) dienend; **be ～ to sb./sth.** jmdm./einer Sache dienen; **(b)** (subordinate) untergeordnet (**to** *Dat.*); **(c)** (obsequious) unterwürfig; servil (abwertend)

subside /səb'saɪd/ *v.i.* **(a)** (sink to lower level) 〈*Wasser, Flut, Fluss:*〉 sinken; 〈*Boden, Haus:*〉 sich senken; 〈*Schwellung:*〉 zurückgehen; **(b)** (abate) nachlassen; ～ **into** verfallen in (+ *Akk.*) 〈*Untätigkeit, Schweigen usw.*〉

subsidence /'sʌbsɪdəns/ *n.* **(a)** (sinking) (of ground, structure) Senkung, *die;* (of liquid) Sinken, *das;* **(b)** (abatement) Nachlassen, *das*

subsidiary /səb'sɪdɪərɪ/ **1** *adj.* **(a)** (auxiliary) unterstützend; subsidiär (fachspr.); untergeordnet 〈*Funktion, Stellung*〉; Neben 〈*fach, -aspekt*〉; ～ **to sth.** einer Sache (*Dat.*) untergeordnet; (secondary) gegenüber einer Sache (*Dat.*) zweitrangig; **(b)** (Commerc.) ～ **company** ➝ **2. 2** *n.* (Commerc.) Tochtergesellschaft, *die*

subsidize (**subsidise**) /'sʌbsɪdaɪz/ *v.t.* subventionieren; finanziell unterstützen 〈*Person*〉

subsidy /'sʌbsɪdɪ/ *n.* Subvention, *die;* **receive a ～:** subventioniert werden

subsist /səb'sɪst/ *v.i.* (keep oneself alive) existieren; ～ **on sth.** von etw. leben

subsistence /səb'sɪstəns/ *n.* **(a)** (subsisting) [Über]leben, *das;* **be enough for a bare ～:** gerade genug zum [Über]leben sein; 〈*Einkommen:*〉 das Existenzminimum sein; **(b)** **[means of] ～:** Lebensgrundlage, *die*

subsistence: ～ allowance *n.* Außendienstzulage, *die;* ～ **level** *n.* Existenzminimum, *das;* **live at ～ level** gerade genug zum Leben haben

sub'sonic *adj.* Unterschall-

substance /'sʌbstəns/ *n.* **(a)** Stoff, *der;* Substanz, *die;* **(b)** *no pl.* (solidity) Substanz, *die;* **(c)** *no pl.* (content) (of book etc.) Inhalt, *der;* **there is no ～ in his claim/the rumour** seine Behauptung/das Gerücht entbehrt jeder Grundlage; **(d)** *no pl.* (essence) Kern, *der;* **in ～:** im Wesentlichen

'substance abuse *n.* Drogen- und Genussmittelmissbrauch, *der*

sub'standard *adj.* **(a)** unzulänglich; **the printing/recording was ～:** der Druck/die Aufnahme war nicht zufriedenstellend; **(b)** (Ling.) nicht standardsprachlich

substantial /səb'stænʃl/ *adj.* **(a)** (considerable) beträchtlich; erheblich 〈*Zugeständnis, Verbesserung*〉; größer... 〈*Darlehen*〉; **(b)** gehaltvoll 〈*Essen, Nahrung*〉; **(c)** (solid in structure) solide, stabil 〈*Möbel*〉; solide 〈*Haus*〉; kräftig 〈*Körperbau*〉; wesentlich 〈*Unterschied, Argument*〉

substantially /səb'stænʃəlɪ/ *adv.* **(a)** (considerably) wesentlich; **(b)** (solidly) ～ **built** solide gebaut 〈*Haus usw.*〉; kräftig gebaut 〈*Person*〉; **(c)** (essentially) im Wesentlichen; ～ **free from sth.** weitgehend frei von etw.

substitute /'sʌbstɪtju:t/ **1** *n.* **(a)** ～[**s**] Ersatz, *der;* ～**s for rubber** Ersatzstoffe für Gummi; **coffee ～:** Kaffee-Ersatz, *der;* **there is no ～ for real ale/hard work** es geht nichts über das echte englische Bier/über harte Arbeit; **(b)** (Sport) Ersatzspieler, *der*/-spielerin, *die.* **2** *adj.* Ersatz-; **a ～ teacher/secretary** *etc.* eine Vertretung. **3** *v.t.*

～ **A for B** B durch A ersetzen; ～ **oil for butter** statt Butter Öl nehmen; ～ **a striker for a midfield player** einen Mittelfeldspieler gegen einen Stürmer auswechseln *od.* austauschen. **4** *v.i.* ～ **for sb.** jmdn. vertreten; für jmdn. einspringen; (Sport) für jmdn. ins Spiel kommen

substitution /sʌbstɪ'tju:ʃn/ *n.* Ersetzung, *die;* (Sport) Spielerwechsel, *der;* ～ **of A for B** Verwendung von A statt B; **make a ～** (Sport) [einen Spieler] auswechseln

'subtenant *n.* Untermieter, *der*/-mieterin, *die;* (of land, farm, shop) Unterpächter, *der*/-pächterin, *die*

subterranean /sʌbtə'reɪnɪən/ *adj.* unterirdisch

'subtitle 1 *n.* Untertitel, *der.* **2** *v.t.* untertiteln; **the book is ～d ...:** das Buch hat den Untertitel ...

subtle /'sʌtl/ *adj.,* ～**r** /'sʌtlə(r)/, ～**st** /'sʌtlɪst/ **(a)** zart 〈*Duft, Dunst, Parfüm*〉; fein 〈*Geschmack, Aroma*〉; **(b)** (elusive) subtil (geh.); fein 〈*Unterschied*〉; unaufdringlich 〈*Charme*〉; **(c)** (refined) fein 〈*Ironie, Humor*〉; zart 〈*Hinweis*〉; subtil (geh.) 〈*Scherz*〉; **(d)** (perceptive) feinsinnig 〈*Beobachter, Kritiker*〉; fein 〈*Intellekt*〉

subtlety /'sʌtltɪ/ *n., no pl.* ⇨ **subtle:** Zartheit, *die;* Feinheit, *die;* Subtilität, *die* (geh.)

subtly /'sʌtlɪ/ *adv.* auf subtile Weise (geh.); zart 〈*hinweisen auf, andeuten*〉; ～ **flavoured/perfumed** von feinem Geschmack *nachgestellt*/zart duftend

'subtotal *n.* Zwischensumme, *die*

subtract /səb'trækt/ *v.t.* abziehen (**from** von); subtrahieren (**from** von)

subtraction /səb'trækʃn/ *n.* Subtraktion, *die*

sub'tropical *adj.* subtropisch

suburb /'sʌbɜ:b/ *n.* Vorort, *der;* **live in the ～s** am Stadtrand leben

suburban /sə'bɜ:bən/ *adj.* **(a)** (of suburbs) Vorort-; 〈*Leben, Haus*〉 am Stadtrand; ～ **spread** *or* **sprawl** eintönige, endlose Vororte; **(b)** (derog.: limited in outlook) spießig (abwertend)

suburbia /sə'bɜ:bɪə/ *n.* (derog.) die [eintönigen] Vororte

subversive /səb'vɜ:sɪv/ **1** *adj.* subversiv. **2** *n.* Subversive, *der/die*

subvert /səb'vɜ:t/ *v.t.* stürzen 〈*Monarchie, Regierung*〉; unterminieren 〈*Moral, Loyalität*〉; [zur Illoyalität] aufstacheln 〈*Person*〉

'subway *n.* **(a)** (passage) Unterführung, *die;* **(b)** (Amer.: railway) Untergrundbahn, *die;* U-Bahn, *die* (ugs.)

sub-'zero *adj.* ▶ **1141** ～ **temperatures/conditions** Temperaturen unter Null

succeed /sək'si:d/ **1** *v.i.* **(a)** (achieve aim) Erfolg haben; **sb. ～s in sth.** jmdm. gelingt etw.; jmd. schafft etw.; **sb. ～s in doing sth.** es gelingt jmdm., etw. zu tun; ～ **in business/college** geschäftlich/im Studium erfolgreich sein; **I ～ed in passing the test** ich habe die Prüfung mit Erfolg *od.* erfolgreich abgelegt; **the plan did not ～:** der Plan ist gescheitert; **(b)** (come next) die Nachfolge antreten; ～ **to an office/the throne** die Nachfolge in einem Amt/die Thronfolge antreten; ～ **to a title/an estate** einen Titel/ein Gut erben. **2** *v.t.* ablösen 〈*Monarchen, Beamten*〉; ～ **sb. [in a post]** jmds. Nachfolge [in einem Amt] antreten

success /sək'ses/ *n.* ▶ **836** Erfolg, *der;* **meet with ～:** Erfolg haben; erfolgreich sein; **make a ～ of sth.** bei etw. Erfolg haben

successful /sək'sesfl/ *adj.* erfolgreich; **be ～ in sth./doing sth.** Erfolg bei etw. haben/dabei haben, etw. zu tun; **she made a ～ attempt on the record** der Rekordversuch ist ihr gelungen

successfully /sək'sesfəlɪ/ *adv.* erfolgreich

succession /sək'seʃn/ *n.* **(a)** Folge, *die;* **four games/years** *etc.* **in ～:** vier Spiele/Jahre *usw.* hintereinander; **in close ～** (in space) dicht hintereinander; (in time) kurz hintereinander; **(b)** (series) Serie, *die;* **a ～ of losses/visitors** eine Verlust-/Besucherserie; **(c)** (right of succeeding to the throne etc.) Erbfolge, *die;* **he is second in ～:** er ist Zweiter in der Erbfolge; **in ～ to his uncle** als Nachfolger seines Onkels

successive /sək'sesɪv/ *adj.* aufeinander folgend; **five ～ games/jobs** fünf Spiele/Stellungen hintereinander

successively /sək'sesɪvlɪ/ *adv.* hintereinander

successor /sək'sesə(r)/ *n.* Nachfolger, *der*/Nachfolgerin, *die;* **sb.'s** ~, **the** ~ **to sb.** jmds. Nachfolger; **the** ~ **to the throne** der Nachfolger auf dem Thron

suc'cess story *n.* Erfolgsstory, *die* (ugs.)

succinct /sək'sɪŋkt/ *adj.* (terse) knapp; (clear, to the point) prägnant

succinctly /sək'sɪŋktlɪ/ *adv.* (tersely) in knappen Worten; (clearly) prägnant

succinctness /sək'sɪŋktnɪs/ *n., no pl.* (terseness) Knappheit, *die;* (clarity) Prägnanz, *die*

succulent /'sʌkjʊlənt/ **1** *adj.* (a) saftig ‹*Pfirsich, Steak usw.*›; (b) (Bot.) sukkulent; fleischig; ~ **plants** Sukkulenten. **2** *n.* (Bot.) Sukkulente, *die;* Fettpflanze, *die*

succumb /sə'kʌm/ *v.i.* (a) (be forced to give way) unterliegen; ~ **to sth.** einer Sache (*Dat.*) erliegen; ~ **to temptation** der Versuchung erliegen; ~ **to pressure** dem Druck nachgeben; (b) (die) ~ **[to one's illness/wounds** *etc.*] seiner Krankheit/seinen Verletzungen *usw.* erliegen

such /sʌtʃ/ **1** *adj., no compar. or superl.* (a) (of that kind) solch ...; ~ **a person** solch *od.* (ugs.) so ein Mensch; ein solcher Mensch; ~ **a book** solch *od.* (ugs.) so ein Buch; ein solches Buch; ~ **people** solche Leute; ~ **things** so etwas; **symphonies and other** ~ **compositions** Sinfonien und andere Kompositionen dieser Art; **or some** ~ **thing** oder so etwas; oder etwas in der Art; **I said no** ~ **thing** ich habe nichts dergleichen gesagt; **you'll do no** ~ **thing** das wirst du nicht tun; **there is no** ~ **bird** solch einen *od.* einen solchen Vogel gibt es nicht; **experiences** ~ **as these** solche *od.* derartige Erfahrungen; **there is no** ~ **thing as a unicorn** Einhörner gibt es gar nicht; ~ **writers as Eliot and Fry** Schriftsteller wie Eliot und Fry; **I will take** ~ **steps as I think necessary** ich werde die Schritte unternehmen, die ich für notwendig halte; **at** ~ **a time** zu einer solchen Zeit; **at** ~ **a moment as this** in einem Augenblick wie diesem; (disapproving) gerade jetzt; **in** ~ **a case** in einem solchen *od.* (ugs.) so einem Fall; **for** *or* **on** ~ **an occasion** zu einem solchen Anlass; ~ **a one as he/she is impossible to replace** jemand wie er/sie ist unersetzlich; (b) (so great) solch ...; derartig; **I got** ~ **a fright that** ...: ich bekam einen derartigen *od.* (ugs.) so einen Schrecken, dass ...; ~ **was the force of the explosion that** ...: die Explosion war so stark, dass ...; **to** ~ **an extent** dermaßen; (c) *with adj.* so; ~ **a big house** ein so großes Haus; **she has** ~ **lovely blue eyes** sie hat so schöne blaue Augen; ~ **a long time** so lange. **2** *pron.* **as** ~: als solcher/solche/solches; (strictly speaking) im Grunde genommen; an sich; ~ **is life** so ist das Leben; ~ **as** wie [zum Beispiel]

such-and-such /'sʌtʃənsʌtʃ/ **1** *adj.* **in** ~ **a place at** ~ **a time** an dem und dem Ort um die und die Zeit; **Mr** ~: Herr Sowieso. **2** *pron.* der und der/die und die/das und das

suchlike /'sʌtʃlaɪk/ *pron.* (coll.) derlei

suck /sʌk/ **1** *v.t.* saugen (**out of** aus); lutschen ‹*Bonbon*›; ~ **one's thumb** am Daumen lutschen. **2** *v.i.* (a) ‹*Baby:*› saugen; ~ **at sth.** an etw. (*Dat.*) saugen; ~ **at a lollipop** an einem Lutscher lecken; (b) sth. ~s (esp. Amer. sl.) etw. ist scheiße (derb)

~ **'down** *v.t.* hinunterziehen; ‹*Strudel:*› in die Tiefe ziehen

~ **'in** *v.t.* einsaugen; ‹*Strudel:*› in die Tiefe ziehen

~ **'under** *v.t.* in die Tiefe ziehen

~ **'up 1** *v.t.* aufsaugen ‹*Staub, Feuchtigkeit*›; (with a straw) einsaugen. **2** *v.i.* ~ **up to sb.** (coll.) jmdm. in den Hintern kriechen (salopp)

sucker /'sʌkə(r)/ *n.* (a) (suction pad) Saugfuß, *der;* (Zool.) Saugnapf, *der;* (b) (one attracted) **be a** ~ **for sb./sth.** eine Schwäche für jmdn./etw. haben; (c) (coll.: dupe) Dumme, *der/die;* **poor** ~: armer Trottel

suckle /'sʌkl/ **1** *v.t.* säugen. **2** *v.i.* [an der Brust] trinken

suction /'sʌkʃn/ *n.* (a) (sucking) Absaugen, *das;* (force) Saugwirkung, *die;* (b) (of air, currents, etc.) Sog, *der*

Sudan /suː'dɑːn/ *pr. n.* **[the]** ~: [der] Sudan

sudden /'sʌdn/ **1** *adj.* (a) (unexpected) plötzlich; **I had a** ~ **thought** auf einmal *od.* plötzlich fiel mir etwas ein; (b) (abrupt, without warning) jäh ‹*Abgrund, Übergang, Ruck*›;

there was a ~ **bend in the road** plötzlich machte die Straße eine Biegung. **2** *n.* **all of a** ~: plötzlich

sudden 'death *attrib. adj.* (Sport coll.) **a** ~ **play-off** ein Stichentscheid; (Footb.: using penalties) ein Elfmeterschießen

suddenly /'sʌdnlɪ/ *adv.* plötzlich

suddenness /'sʌdnɪs/ *n., no pl.* Plötzlichkeit, *die*

suds /sʌdz/ *n. pl.* **[soap]**~: [Seifen]lauge, *die;* (froth) Schaum, *der*

sue /suː, sjuː/ (Law) **1** *v.t.* verklagen (**for** auf + *Akk.*). **2** *v.i.* klagen (**for** auf + *Akk.*)

suede /sweɪd/ *n.* Wildleder, *das*

suet /'suːɪt, 'sjuːɪt/ *n.* Talg, *der*

Suez /'suːɪz, 'sjuːɪz/ *pr. n.* Suez (*das*); ~ **Canal** Suez-Kanal, *der*

suffer /'sʌfə(r)/ **1** *v.t.* (a) (undergo) erleiden ‹*Verlust, Unrecht, Schmerz, Niederlage*›; durchmachen, erleben ‹*Schweres, Kummer*›; dulden ‹*Unverschämtheit*›; **the dollar** ~**ed further losses against the yen** der Dollar musste weitere Einbußen gegenüber dem Yen hinnehmen; (b) (tolerate) dulden; **not** ~ **fools gladly** mit dummen Leuten keine Geduld haben. **2** *v.i.* leiden; ~ **for sth.** (for a cause) für etw. leiden; (to make amends) für etw. büßen

~ **from** *v.t.* leiden unter (+ *Dat.*); leiden an (+ *Dat.*) ‹*Krankheit*›; ~ **from shock** unter Schock[wirkung] stehen; ~ **from faulty planning** an falscher Planung kranken

sufferance /'sʌfərəns/ *n.* Duldung, *die;* **he remains here on** ~ **only** er ist hier bloß geduldet

sufferer /'sʌfərə(r)/ *n.* Betroffene, *der/die;* (from disease) Leidende, *der/die*

suffering /'sʌfərɪŋ/ *n.* Leiden, *das;* **her** ~s **are now at an end** sie hat jetzt ausgelitten (geh.)

suffice /sə'faɪs/ **1** *v.i.* genügen; ~ **it to say:** ...: nur so viel sei gesagt: ... **2** *v.t.* genügen (+ *Dat.*); reichen für

sufficiency /sə'fɪʃnsɪ/ *n., no pl.* Zulänglichkeit, *die*

sufficient /sə'fɪʃnt/ *adj.* genug; ~ **money/food** genug Geld/genug zu essen; **be** ~: genügen; ~ **reason** Grund genug; **have you had** ~? (food, drink) haben Sie schon genug?

sufficiently /sə'fɪʃntlɪ/ *adv.* genug; (adequately) ausreichend; ~ **large** groß genug; **a** ~ **large number** eine genügend große Zahl

suffix /'sʌfɪks/ *n.* (Ling.) Suffix, *das* (fachspr.); Nachsilbe, *die*

suffocate /'sʌfəkeɪt/ **1** *v.t.* ersticken; **he was** ~**d by the smoke** der Rauch erstickte ihn; er erstickte an dem Rauch. **2** *v.i.* ersticken

suffocation /sʌfə'keɪʃn/ *n.* Erstickung, *die;* **a feeling of** ~: das Gefühl, zu ersticken

suffrage /'sʌfrɪdʒ/ *n.* Wahlrecht, *das;* **female** ~: das Frauenwahlrecht

suffragette /sʌfrə'dʒet/ *n.* (Hist.) Frauenrechtlerin, *die;* Suffragette, *die*

sugar /'ʃʊgə(r)/ **1** *n.* Zucker, *der;* **two** ~s, **please** (spoonfuls) zwei Löffel Zucker, bitte; (lumps) zwei Stück Zucker, bitte. **2** *v.t.* zuckern; (fig.) versüßen

sugar: ~ **basin** ⇒ ~-**bowl;** ~ **beet** *n.* Zuckerrübe, *die;* ~ **bowl** *n.* Zuckerschale, *die;* (covered) Zuckerdose, *die;* ~ **cane** *n.* Zuckerrohr, *das;* ~-**coated** *adj.* gezuckert; mit Zucker überzogen ‹*Dragee usw.*›; ~ **lump** *n.* Zuckerstück, *das;* (when counted) Stück Zucker, *das*

sugary /'ʃʊgərɪ/ *adj.* süß; (fig.) süßlich ‹*Lächeln, Stimme, Musik*›

suggest /sə'dʒest/ **1** *v.t.* (a) (propose) vorschlagen; ~ **sth. to sb.** jmdm. etw. vorschlagen; **he** ~**ed going to the cinema** er schlug vor, ins Kino zu gehen; (b) (assert) **are you trying to** ~ **that he is lying?** wollen Sie damit sagen, dass er lügt?; **he** ~**ed that the calculation was incorrect** er sagte, die Rechnung sei falsch; **I** ~ **that** ... (Law) ich unterstelle, dass ...; (c) (make one think of) suggerieren; ‹*Symptome, Tatsachen:*› schließen lassen auf (+ *Akk.*). **2** *v. refl.* ~ **itself [to sb.]** ‹*Möglichkeiten, Ausweg:*› sich [jmdm.] anbieten; ‹*Gedanke:*› sich [jmdm.] aufdrängen

suggestion /sə'dʒestʃn/ *n.* (a) Vorschlag, *der;* **at** *or* **on sb.'s** ~: auf jmds. Vorschlag (*Akk.*); (b) (insinuation) Andeutungen *Pl.;* **there is no** ~ **that he cooperated with the**

kidnappers niemand unterstellt, dass er mit den Entführern zusammengearbeitet hat; **what a ∼!** wie kann man so etwas nur sagen!; **(c)** (fig.: trace) Spur, *die*

suggestive /sə'dʒestɪv/ *adj.* **(a)** suggestiv (geh.); **be ∼ of sth.** auf etw. (*Akk.*) schließen lassen; **(b)** (risqué) anzüglich; gewagt; zweideutig ‹ *Scherze, Lieder* ›

suicidal /su:ɪ'saɪdl, sju:ɪ'saɪdl/ *adj.* **(a)** selbstmörderisch ‹ *Akt, Absicht* ›; suizidal (fachspr.) ‹ *Verhalten, Patient* ›; **∼ tendencies** eine Neigung zum Selbstmord; **I felt** *or* **was quite ∼:** ich hätte mich am liebsten gleich umgebracht; **(b)** (dangerous) selbstmörderisch ‹ *Fahrweise, Verhalten usw.* ›

suicide /'su:ɪsaɪd, 'sju:ɪsaɪd/ *n.* Selbstmord, *der* (auch fig.); Suizid, *der* (fachspr.)

suicide: **∼ attempt** *n.* Selbstmordversuch, *der;* **∼ pact** *n.* Selbstmordpakt, *der*

suit /su:t, sju:t/ **1** *n.* **(a)** (for men) Anzug, *der;* (for women) Kostüm, *das;* **a three-piece ∼:** ein dreiteiliger Anzug; ein Dreiteiler; **buy [oneself] a new ∼ of clothes** sich neu einkleiden; **(b)** (Law) **∼ [at law]** Prozess, *der;* [Gerichts]verfahren, *das;* **(c)** (Cards) Farbe, *die;* **follow ∼:** Farbe bedienen; (fig.) das Gleiche tun. **2** *v.t.* **(a)** anpassen (to *Dat.*); **(b) be ∼ed [to sth./one another]** [zu etw./zueinander] passen; **he is not at all ∼ed to marriage** er eignet sich überhaupt nicht für die Ehe; **they are ill/well ∼ed** sie passen schlecht/gut zueinander; **(c)** (satisfy needs of) passen (+ *Dat.*); recht sein (+ *Dat.*); **does the climate ∼ you/your health?** bekommt Ihnen das Klima?; **dried fruit/asparagus does not ∼ me** ich vertrage kein Trockenobst/keinen Spargel; **(d)** (go well with) passen zu; **does this hat ∼ me?** steht mir dieser Hut?; **black ∼s her** Schwarz steht ihr gut. **3** *v. refl.* **∼ oneself** tun, was man will; **∼ yourself!** [ganz] wie du willst!

suitability /su:tə'bɪlɪtɪ, sju:tə'bɪlɪtɪ/ *n., no pl.* Eignung, *die* (**for** für); (of clothing, remark; for an occasion) Angemessenheit, *die* (**for** für); **his ∼ as a teacher** seine Eignung zum *od.* als Lehrer

suitable /'su:təbl, 'sju:təbl/ *adj.* geeignet; (for an occasion) angemessen ‹ *Kleidung* ›; angebracht ‹ *Bemerkung* ›; (matching, convenient) passend; **this girlfriend is not ∼ for him** diese Freundin passt nicht zu ihm; **Monday is the most ∼ day [for me]** Montag passt [mir] am besten

suitably /'su:təblɪ, 'sju:təblɪ/ *adv.* angemessen; gehörig ‹ *entrüstet* ›; gebührend ‹ *beeindruckt* ›; entsprechend ‹ *gekleidet* ›

'suitcase *n.* Koffer, *der;* **live out of a ∼:** aus dem Koffer leben

suite /swi:t/ *n.* **(a)** (of furniture) Garnitur, *die;* **three-piece ∼:** Polstergarnitur, *die;* **bedroom ∼:** Schlafzimmereinrichtung, *die;* **(b)** (of rooms) Suite, *die;* **(c)** (Mus.) Suite, *die*

suitor /'su:tə(r), 'sju:tə(r)/ *n.* Freier, *der*

sulfate, sulfide, sulfur, sulfuric (Amer.) ⇒ **sulph-**

sulk /sʌlk/ **1** *n., usu. in pl.* **have a ∼** *or* **the ∼s, be in** *or* **have a fit of the ∼s** eingeschnappt sein (ugs.); schmollen. **2** *v.i.* schmollen

sulky /'sʌlkɪ/ *adj.* schmollend; eingeschnappt (ugs.)

sullen /'sʌlən/ *adj.* mürrisch; verdrießlich; (fig.) düster ‹ *Himmel* ›

sully /'sʌlɪ/ *v.t.* (formal) besudeln (geh.)

sulphate /'sʌlfeɪt/ *n.* Sulfat, *das*

sulphide /'sʌlfaɪd/ *n.* Sulfid, *das*

sulphur /'sʌlfə(r)/ *n.* Schwefel, *der*

sulphuric /sʌl'fjʊərɪk/ *adj.* **∼ acid** Schwefelsäure, *die*

sultan /'sʌltən/ *n.* Sultan, *der*

sultana /sʌl'tɑːnə/ *n.* (raisin) Sultanine, *die*

sultry /'sʌltrɪ/ *adj.* schwül ‹ *Wetter, Tag, Atmosphäre* ›; (fig.: sensual) sinnlich; schwül ‹ *Schönheit* ›

sum /sʌm/ **1** *n.* **(a)** (total amount, lit. or fig.) Summe, *die* (of aus); **∼ [total]** Ergebnis, *das; that was the ∼ total of our achievements* *or* **of what we achieved** das war alles, was wir erreicht haben; **(b)** (amount of money) Summe, *die;* **a cheque for this ∼:** ein Scheck über diesen Betrag; **(c)** (Arithmetic) Rechenaufgabe, *die;* **do ∼s** rechnen; **she is good at ∼s** sie kann gut rechnen; sie ist gut im Rechnen. **2** *v.t.,* **-mm-** addieren

∼ 'up 1 *v.t.* **(a)** zusammenfassen; **(b)** (Brit.: assess) einschätzen; **this ∼med him up perfectly** damit war er treffend charakterisiert. **2** *v.i.* ein Fazit ziehen; ‹ *Richter:* › resümieren; **in ∼ming up, I should like to …:** zusammenfassend möchte ich …

summarily /'sʌmərɪlɪ/ *adv.* **(a)** (shortly) knapp; **(b)** (without formalities or delay) summarisch; **∼ dismissed** fristlos entlassen; **∼ convicted** (Law) im summarischen Verfahren verurteilt

summarize (**summarise**) /'sʌməraɪz/ *v.t.* zusammenfassen

summary /'sʌmərɪ/ **1** *adj.* **(a)** knapp; **(b)** (without formalities or delay) summarisch; fristlos ‹ *Entlassung* ›; **∼ justice** Schnelljustiz, *die.* **2** *n.* Zusammenfassung, *die*

summer /'sʌmə(r)/ **▶ 1065** **1** *n.* Sommer, *der;* **in [the] ∼:** im Sommer; **in early/late ∼:** im Früh-/Spätsommer; **last/next ∼:** letzten/nächsten Sommer; **a ∼'s day/night** ein Sommertag/eine Sommernacht; **in the ∼ of 1983,** in **∼ 1983** im Sommer 1983; **two ∼s ago we went to France** im Sommer vor zwei Jahren waren wir in Frankreich. **2** *attrib. adj.* Sommer-

summer: **∼ house** *n.* [Garten]laube, *die;* **∼ school** *n.* Sommerkurs, *der;* **∼ term** *n.* Sommerhalbjahr, *das;* **S∼ Time** *n.* (Brit.: system) die Sommerzeit; **∼time** *n.* (season) Sommer, *der;* **in [the] ∼time** im Sommer

summery /'sʌmərɪ/ *adj.* sommerlich

summing-'up *n.* Zusammenfassung, *die*

summit /'sʌmɪt/ *n.* **(a)** (peak, lit. or fig.) Gipfel, *der;* **(b)** (discussion) Gipfel, *der;* **∼ conference/meeting** Gipfelkonferenz, *die/*-treffen, *das*

summon /'sʌmən/ *v.t.* **(a)** (call upon) rufen (**to** zu); holen ‹ *Hilfe* ›; zusammenrufen ‹ *Aktionäre* ›; **(b)** (call by authority) zu sich zitieren; einberufen ‹ *Parlament* ›; **(c)** (Law: to court) vorladen ‹ *Angeklagten, Zeugen* ›

∼ 'up *v.t.* aufbringen ‹ *Mut, Kräfte, Energie, Begeisterung* ›

summons /'sʌmənz/ *n.* (Law) Vorladung, *die;* **serve a ∼ on sb.** jmdm. eine Vorladung zustellen

sump /sʌmp/ *n.* (Brit. Motor Veh.) Ölwanne, *die*

sumptuous /'sʌmptjʊəs/ *adj.* üppig; luxuriös ‹ *Einband, Möbel, Kleidung* ›

sun /sʌn/ *n.* Sonne, *die;* **catch the ∼** (be in a sunny position) viel Sonne abbekommen; (get ∼burnt) einen Sonnenbrand bekommen; **a touch of the ∼:** ein leichter Sonnenstich; **under the ∼** (fig.) auf der Welt. **2** *v. refl.,* **-nn-** sich sonnen

Sun. *abbr.* **▶ 739** **Sunday** So.

sun: **∼bathe** *v.i.* sonnenbaden; **∼bather** *n.* Sonnenbadende, *der/die;* **∼bathing** *n.* Sonnenbaden, *das;* **∼beam** *n.* Sonnenstrahl, *der;* **∼bed** *n.* (with UV lamp) Sonnenbank, *die;* (in garden etc.) Gartenliege, *die;* **∼blind** *n.* Markise, *die;* **∼block** *n.* [starkes] Sonnenschutzmittel; **∼burn** *n.* Sonnenbrand, *der;* **∼burnt** *adj.* **(a)** (suffering from ∼burn) **be ∼burnt** einen Sonnenbrand haben; **have a ∼burnt back/face** einen Sonnenbrand auf dem Rücken/im Gesicht haben; **get badly ∼burnt** einen schlimmen Sonnenbrand bekommen; **(b)** (tanned) sonnenverbrannt ‹ *Person, Gesicht usw.* ›

sundae /'sʌndeɪ, 'sʌndɪ/ *n.* [ice cream] **∼:** Eisbecher, *der*

Sunday /'sʌndeɪ, 'sʌndɪ/ **▶ 739** **1** *n.* Sonntag, *der;* **∼ opening** die sonntägliche Öffnung (of von); **∼ opening is allowed** es darf [auch] sonntags geöffnet werden; **∼ trading** sonntägliche Ladenöffnung. **2** *adv.* (coll.) **she comes ∼s** sie kommt sonntags. *See also* **Friday**

'Sunday school *n.* Sonntagsschule, *die*

sun: **∼dial** *n.* Sonnenuhr, *die;* **∼down** ⇒ **sunset**

sundry /'sʌndrɪ/ **1** *adj.* verschieden; **∼ articles** verschiedene *od.* diverse Artikel. **2** *n. in pl.* Verschiedenes; Diverses; *see also* **all 2 a**

'sunflower *n.* Sonnenblume, *die;* **∼ seeds** Sonnenblumenkerne

sung ⇒ **sing**

sun: **∼glasses** *n. pl.* Sonnenbrille, *die;* **∼hat** *n.* Sonnenhut, *der*

sunk ⇒ sink 2, 3

sunken /'sʌŋkn/ *adj.* versunken ‹*Schatz*›; gesunken ‹*Schiff*›; eingefallen ‹*Augen, Wangen*›; tieferliegend ‹*Garten, Zimmer*›; in den Boden eingelassen ‹*Badewanne*›

'sunlamp *n.* Höhensonne, *die*

sunless /'sʌnlɪs/ *adj.* ‹*Ecke, Stelle, Tal*› wo die Sonne nie hinkommt; trübe ‹*Tag*›

sun: ∼**light** *n.* Sonnenlicht, *das;* ∼**lit** *adj.* sonnenbeschienen ‹*Landschaft*›; sonnig ‹*Zimmer, Garten*›; ∼ **lounge** *n.* Veranda, *die*

sunny /'sʌnɪ/ **(a)** sonnig; ∼ **intervals** Aufheiterungen; **the** ∼ **side of the house/street** die Sonnenseite des Hauses/der Straße; ∼ **side up** ‹*Spiegelei*› mit dem Gelben nach oben; **(b)** (cheery) fröhlich ‹*Wesen, Lächeln*›

sun: ∼ **protection factor** *n.* Lichtschutzfaktor, *der;* ∼**ray** *n.* Sonnenstrahl, *der;* ∼**rise** *n.* Sonnenaufgang, *der;* **at** ∼**rise** bei Sonnenaufgang; *attrib.* ∼**rise industry** Zukunftsindustrie, *die;* ∼**roof** *n.* (Motor Veh.) Schiebedach, *das;* ∼**set** *n.* Sonnenuntergang, *der;* **at** ∼**set** bei Sonnenuntergang; ∼**shade** *n.* Sonnenschirm, *der;* (awning) Markise, *die;* ∼**shine** *n.* Sonnenschein, *der;* ∼**shine roof** ⇒ sunroof; ∼**stroke** *n.* Sonnenstich, *der;* **suffer from/get** ∼**stroke** einen Sonnenstich haben/bekommen; ∼**tan** *n.* [Sonnen]bräune, *die;* **get a** ∼**tan** braun werden; ∼**tan lotion** *n.* Sonnencreme, *die;* ∼**tanned** *adj.* braun[gebrannt]; sonnengebräunt (geh.); ∼**tan oil** *n.* Sonnenöl, *das;* ∼**trap** *n.* sonniges Plätzchen; ∼**up** (Amer.) ⇒ ∼**rise**

super /'su:pə(r)/ *adj.* (Brit. coll.) super (ugs.)

superannuation /su:pərænjʊ'eɪʃn/ *n.* **(a)** ∼ [contribution/payment] Beitrag zur Rentenversicherung; **(b)** (pension) Rente, *die*

superb /sʊ'pɜ:b/ *adj.* einzigartig; erstklassig ‹*Essen, Zustand*›

'superbug *n.* (resistant strain of bacteria) multiresistenter Erreger

supercilious /su:pə'sɪlɪəs/ *adj.* hochnäsig

supercomputer /'su:pəkəmpju:tə(r)/ *n.* Supercomputer, *der*

superficial /su:pə'fɪʃl/ *adj.* (also fig.) oberflächlich; leicht ‹*Änderung, Schaden*›; äußerlich ‹*Ähnlichkeit*›

superficially /su:pə'fɪʃəlɪ/ *adv.* an der Oberfläche; oberflächlich ‹*ein Thema behandeln*›; äußerlich ‹*ähnlich sein*›

superfluous /sʊ'pɜ:flʊəs/ *adj.* überflüssig

superglue /'su:pəglu:/ *n.* Sekundenkleber, *der*

supergrass /'su:pəgrɑ:s/ *n.* Superspitzel, *der* (abwertend)

superhighway /'su:pəhaɪweɪ/ *n.* **(a)** (Amer.) Autobahn, *die;* **(b)** (Computing) Datenautobahn, *die*

superhuman /su:pə'hju:mən/ *adj.* übermenschlich

superimpose /su:pərɪm'pəʊz/ *v.t.* aufbringen ‹*Schicht usw.*›; aufkopieren ‹*Bild*›

superintend /su:pərɪn'tend/ *v.t.* überwachen; beaufsichtigen

superintendent /su:pərɪn'tendənt/ *n.* ▶1152 (Brit. Police) Kommissar, *der*/Kommissarin, *die;* (Amer. Police) [Polizei]präsident, *der*/-präsidentin, *die*

superior /su:'pɪərɪə/, sju:'pɪərɪə(r)/ **1** *adj.* **(a)** (of higher quality) besonders gut ‹*Restaurant, Qualität, Stoff*›; überlegen ‹*handwerkliches Können, Technik, Intelligenz*›; **(b)** (having higher rank) höher... ‹*Stellung, Rang, Gericht*›; **be** ∼ **to sb.** einen höheren Rang als jmd. haben. **2** *n.* **(a)** (sb. higher in rank) Vorgesetzte, *der/die;* **(b)** (sb. better) Überlegene, *der/die*

superiority /su:pɪərɪ'ɒrɪtɪ, sju:pɪərɪ'ɒrɪtɪ/ *n.* Überlegenheit, *die* **(to** über + *Akk.*); (of goods) besondere Qualität

superlative /su:'pɜ:lətɪv/ **1** *adj.* **(a)** unübertrefflich; **(b)** (Ling.) superlativisch; **a** ∼ **adjective/adverb** ein Adjektiv/Adverb im Superlativ. **2** *n.* (Ling.) Superlativ, *der*

supermarket /'su:pəmɑ:kɪt/ *n.* Supermarkt, *der*

'supermodel *n.* Supermodel, *das*

supernatural /su:pə'nætʃərl/ *adj.* übernatürlich

superpower /'su:pəpaʊə(r)/ *n.* (Polit.) Supermacht, *die*

superscript /'su:pəskrɪpt/ **1** *n.* hochgestelltes Zeichen. **2** *adj.* hochgestellt

supersede /su:pə'si:d/ *v.t.* ablösen **(by durch); old** ∼**d ideas** alte, überholte Vorstellungen

supersonic /su:pə'sɒnɪk/ *adj.* Überschall-; **go** ∼**:** die Schallmauer durchbrechen

superstar /'su:pəstɑ:(r)/ *n.* Superstar, *der*

superstition /su:pə'stɪʃn/ *n.* (lit. or fig.) Aberglaube, *der;* ∼**s** abergläubische Vorstellungen

superstitious /su:pə'stɪʃəs/ *adj.* abergläubisch

superstore /'su:pəstɔ:(r)/ *n.* Großmarkt, *der*

superstructure /'su:pəstrʌktʃə(r)/ *n.* **(a)** Aufbau, *der;* **(b)** (Sociol.) Überbau, *der*

supertanker /'su:pətæŋkə(r)/ *n.* Supertanker, *der*

super un'leaded **1** *adj.* ∼ **petrol** Superbleifrei, *das.* **2** *n.* Superbleifrei, *das*

supervise /'su:pəvaɪz/ *v.t.* beaufsichtigen

supervision /su:pə'vɪʒn/ *n.* Aufsicht, *die*

supervisor /'su:pəvaɪzə(r)/ *n.* ▶887 Aufseher, *der*/Aufseherin, *die;* (for Ph.D. thesis) Doktorvater, *der;* **office** ∼**:** Bürovorsteher, *der*/-vorsteherin, *die*

supervisory /'su:pəvaɪzərɪ/ *adj.* Aufsichts-

supper /'sʌpə(r)/ *n.* Abendessen, *das;* (simpler meal) Abendbrot, *das;* **have or eat [one's]** ∼**:** zu Abend essen; **be at or eating or having [one's]** ∼**:** beim Abendessen/Abendbrot sein; **The Last S**∼**:** das [letzte] Abendmahl

'suppertime *n.* Abendbrotzeit, *die;* **it's** ∼**:** es ist Zeit zum Abendessen

supplant /sə'plɑ:nt/ *v.t.* ablösen, ersetzen **(by durch);** ausstechen ‹*Widersacher, Rivalen*›

supple /'sʌpl/ *adj.* geschmeidig

supplement **1** /'sʌplɪmənt/ *n.* **(a)** Ergänzung, *die* **(to +** *Gen.*); (addition) Zusatz, *der;* **(b)** (of book) Nachtrag, *der;* (separate volume) Supplement, *das;* Nachtragsband, *der;* (of newspaper) Beilage, *die;* **(c)** (to fare etc.) Zuschlag, *der.* **2** /'sʌplɪment/ *v.t.* ergänzen

supplementary /sʌplɪ'mentərɪ/ *adj.* zusätzlich; Zusatz‹*rente, -frage*›; ∼ **fare/charge** Zuschlag, *der*

supplier /sə'plaɪə(r)/ *n.* (Commerc.) Lieferant, *der*/Lieferantin, *die*

supply /sə'plaɪ/ **1** *v.t.* **(a)** liefern ‹*Waren usw.*›; sorgen für ‹*Unterkunft*›; zur Verfügung stellen ‹*Lehrmittel, Arbeitskleidung usw.*›; beliefern ‹*Kunden, Geschäft*›; versorgen ‹*System*›; ∼ **sth. to sb.,** ∼ **sb. with sth.** jmdn. mit etw. versorgen/(Commerc.) beliefern; **(b)** (make good) erfüllen ‹*Nachfrage, Bedarf*›; abhelfen **(+** *Dat.*) ‹*Mangel*›. **2** *n.* **(a)** (stock) Vorräte *Pl.;* **a large** ∼ **of food** große Lebensmittelvorräte; **military/medical supplies** militärischer/medizinischer Nachschub; ∼ **and demand** (Econ.) Angebot und Nachfrage; **(b)** (provision) Versorgung, *die* **(of mit); their gas** ∼ **was cut off** ihnen ist das Gas abgestellt worden; **the blood** ∼ **to the brain** die Versorgung des Gehirns mit Blut; **(c)** ∼ **[teacher]** Vertretung, *die.* **3** *attrib.* Versorgungs‹*schiff, -netz, -basis, -lager usw.*›; ∼ **lines** Nachschubwege

support /sə'pɔ:t/ **1** *v.t.* **(a)** (hold up) stützen ‹*Mauer, Verletzten*›; (bear weight of) tragen ‹*Dach*›; **(b)** (give strength to) stärken; **(c)** unterstützen ‹*Politik, Verein*›; (Footb.) ∼ **Spurs** Spurs-Fan sein; **(d)** (give money to) unterstützen; spenden für; **(e)** (provide for) ernähren ‹*Familie, sich selbst*›; **(f)** (bring facts to confirm) stützen ‹*Theorie, Anspruch, Behauptung*›; (speak in favour of) befürworten ‹*Streik, Maßnahme*›. **2** *n.* **(a)** Unterstützung, *die;* **give** ∼ **to sb./sth.** jmdn./etw. unterstützen; **in** ∼**:** zur Unterstützung; **speak in** ∼ **of sb./sth.** jmdn. unterstützen/etw. befürworten; **(b)** (sb./sth. that** ∼**s)** Stütze, *die;* **hold on to sb./ sth. for** ∼**:** sich an jmdm./etw. festhalten

supporter /sə'pɔ:tə(r)/ *n.* Anhänger, *der*/Anhängerin, *die;* **a football** ∼**:** ein Fußballfan; ∼**s of a strike** Befürworter eines Streiks

sup'porters' club *n.* (Sport) Fanclub, *der*

supporting /sə'pɔːtɪŋ/ *adj.* (Cinemat., Theatre) ~ **rolc** Nebenrolle, *die;* ~ **actor/actress** Schauspieler/-spielerin in einer Nebenrolle; ~ **film** Vorfilm, *der*

supportive /sə'pɔːtɪv/ *adj.* hilfreich; **be very** ~ **[to sb.]** [jmdm.] eine große Hilfe *od.* Stütze sein

suppose /sə'pəʊz/ *v.t.* **(a)** (assume) annehmen; ~ *or* **supposing [that] he** ...: angenommen, [dass] er ...; **always supposing that** ...: immer vorausgesetzt, dass ...; ~ **we wait until tomorrow** wir könnten eigentlich bis morgen warten; **(b)** (presume) vermuten; **I** ~**d she was in Glasgow** ich vermutete sie in Glasgow; **I don't** ~ **you have an onion to spare?** Sie haben wohl nicht zufällig eine Zwiebel übrig?; **we're not going to manage it, are we? — I** ~ **not** wir werden es wohl nicht schaffen — ich glaube kaum; **I** ~ **so** ich nehme es an; (doubtfully) ja, vermutlich; (more confidently) ich glaube schon; **(c) be** ~**d to do/be sth.** (be generally believed to do/be sth.) etw. tun/sein sollen; **cats are** ~**d to have nine lives** Katzen sollen angeblich neun Leben haben; **(d)** (allow) **you are not** ~**d to do that** das darfst du nicht; **I'm not** ~**d to be here** ich dürfte eigentlich gar nicht hier sein; **(e)** (presuppose) voraussetzen

supposedly /sə'pəʊzɪdlɪ/ *adv.* angeblich

supposition /sʌpə'zɪʃn/ *n.* Annahme, *die;* Vermutung, *die;* **be based on** ~: auf Annahmen *od.* Vermutungen beruhen

suppress /sə'pres/ *v.t.* unterdrücken

suppression /sə'preʃn/ *n.* Unterdrückung, *die*

supremacy /suː'preməsɪ, sjuː'preməsɪ/ *n., no pl.* **(a)** (supreme authority) Souveränität, *die;* **(b)** (superiority) Überlegenheit, *die*

supreme /suː'priːm, sjuː'priːm/ *adj.* höchst...

Supt. *abbr.* **Superintendent**

surcharge /'sɜːtʃɑːdʒ/ *n.* Zuschlag, *der*

sure /ʃʊə(r)/ **1** *adj.* **(a)** (confident) sicher; **be** ~ **of sth.** sich (*Dat.*) einer Sache (*Gen.*) sicher sein; ~ **of oneself** selbstsicher; **don't be too** ~: da wäre ich mir nicht so sicher; **(b)** (safe) sicher; **be on** ~**r ground** (lit. or fig.) sich auf festerem Boden befinden; **(c)** (certain) sicher; **you're** ~ **to be welcome** Sie werden ganz sicher *od.* bestimmt willkommen sein; **it's** ~ **to rain** es wird bestimmt regnen; **don't worry, it's** ~ **to turn out well** keine Sorge, es wird schon alles gut gehen; **he is** ~ **to ask questions about the incident** er wird auf jeden Fall Fragen zu dem Vorfall stellen; **(d)** (undoubtedly true) sicher; **to be** ~ *expr. concession* natürlich; *expr. surprise* wirklich!; tatsächlich!; **for** ~ (coll.: without doubt) auf jeden Fall; **(e) make** ~ **[of sth.]** sich [einer Sache] vergewissern; (check) [etw.] nachprüfen; **you'd better make** ~ **of a seat** *or* **that you have a seat** du solltest dir einen Platz sichern; **make** *or* **be** ~ **you do it, be** ~ **to do it** (do not fail to do it) sieh zu, dass du es tust; (do not forget) vergiss nicht, es zu tun; **be** ~ **you finish the work by tomorrow** machen Sie die Arbeit auf jeden Fall bis morgen fertig; **(f)** (reliable) sicher ‹*Zeichen*›; zuverlässig ‹*Freund, Tote, Heilmittel*›; **a** ~ **winner** ein todsicherer Tipp (ugs.). **2** *adv.* **(a) as** ~ **as** ~ **can be** (coll.) so sicher wie das Amen in der Kirche; **as** ~ **as I'm standing here** so wahr ich hier stehe; ~ **enough** tatsächlich; **(b)** (Amer. coll.: certainly) wirklich; echt (ugs.). **3** *int.* ~!, ~ **thing!** (Amer.) na klar! (ugs.)

sure: ~**-fire** *attrib. adj.* (Amer. coll.) todsicher; ~**-footed** /'ʃʊəfʊtɪd/ *adj.* (lit. or fig.) trittsicher

surely /'ʃʊəlɪ/ **1** *adv.* **(a)** *as sentence-modifier* doch; ~ **we've met before?** wir kennen uns doch, oder?; ~ **you are not going out in this snowstorm?** du willst doch wohl in dem Schneesturm nicht rausgehen?; **(b)** (steadily) sicher; **slowly but** ~: langsam, aber sicher; **(c)** (certainly) sicherlich; **the plan will** ~ **fail** der Plan wird garantiert scheitern. **2** *int.* (Amer.) natürlich; selbstverständlich

surf /sɜːf/ **1** *n.* Brandung, *die.* **2** *v.i.* (Computing) surfen; (TV) zappen. **3** *v.t.* (Computing, TV) ~ **the Internet** im Internet surfen; ~ **the channels** sich durch die Kanäle zappen

surface /'sɜːfɪs/ **1** *n.* **(a)** *no pl.* Oberfläche, *die;* **outer** ~: Außenfläche, *die;* **the earth's** ~: die Erdoberfläche; **the**

~ **of the lake** die Seeoberfläche; **on the** ~: an der Oberfläche; (Mining) über Tage; **(b)** (outward appearance) Oberfläche, *die;* **on the** ~: oberflächlich betrachtet; **come to the** ~: an die Oberfläche kommen; ‹*Taucher, Unterseeboot:*› auftauchen; (fig.) ans Licht kommen (fig.). **2** *v.i.* auftauchen; (fig.) hochkommen

surface: ~ **area** *n.* Oberfläche, *die;* ~ **mail** *n.* gewöhnliche Post (*die auf dem Land- bzw. Seeweg befördert wird*)

'surfboard *n.* Surfbrett, *das*

surfeit /'sɜːfɪt/ *n.* Übermaß, *das*

surfer /'sɜːfə(r)/ *n.* Surfer, *der*/Surferin, *die*

surfing /'sɜːfɪŋ/ *n.* Surfen, *das*

surge /sɜːdʒ/ **1** *v.i.* ‹*Wellen:*› branden; ‹*Fluten, Menschenmenge:*› sich wälzen; ‹*elektrischer Strom:*› ansteigen; **the crowd** ~**d forward** die Menschenmenge drängte sich nach vorn. **2** *n.* **(a)** (of the sea) Branden, *das;* **(b)** (of crowd) Sichwälzen, *das;* (of electric current) Anstieg, *der* ~ **'up** *v.i.* aufsteigen; ‹*Gefühl:*› aufwallen

surgeon /'sɜːdʒən/ *n.* ▶ **887|** Chirurg, *der*/Chirurgin, *die*

surgery /'sɜːdʒərɪ/ *n.* **(a)** *no pl., no indef. art.* Chirurgie, *die;* **need** ~: operiert werden müssen; **undergo** ~: sich einer Operation (*Dat.*) unterziehen; **(b)** (Brit.: place) Praxis, *die;* **doctor's/dental** ~: Arzt-/Zahnarztpraxis, *die;* **(c)** (Brit.: time; session) Sprechstunde, *die;* **when is his** ~? wann hat er Sprechstunde?; **hold a** ~ (Brit. coll.) ‹*Abgeordneter, Anwalt usw.:*› eine Sprechstunde abhalten

surgical /'sɜːdʒɪkl/ *adj.* chirurgisch; ~ **treatment** Operation, *die*/Operationen

surly /'sɜːlɪ/ *adj.* mürrisch; verdrießlich

surmise /sə'maɪz/ **1** *n.* Vermutung, *die;* Mutmaßung, *die.* **2** *v.t.* mutmaßen

surmount /sə'maʊnt/ *v.t.* überwinden ‹*Hindernis, Schwierigkeiten*›

surname /'sɜːneɪm/ *n.* Nachname, *der;* Zuname, *der*

surpass /sə'pɑːs/ *v.t.* übertreffen (**in** an + *Dat.*); ~ **oneself** sich selbst übertreffen; **sth.** ~**es [sb.'s] comprehension** etw. ist [jmdm.] unbegreiflich

surplice /'sɜːplɪs/ *n.* (Eccl.) Chorhemd, *das*

surplus /'sɜːpləs/ **1** *n.* Überschuss, *der* (**of** an + *Dat.*); **army** ~ **store/boots** Laden für Restbestände/Schuhe aus Restbeständen der Armee. **2** *adj.* überschüssig; **be** ~ **to sb.'s requirements** von jmdm. nicht benötigt werden; ~ **stocks** Überschüsse *Pl.*

surprise /sə'praɪz/ **1** *n.* **(a)** Überraschung, *die;* **take sb. by** ~: jmdn. überrumpeln; **give sb. a** ~: jmdn. erschrecken; **to my great** ~, **much to my** ~: zu meiner großen Überraschung; sehr zu meiner Überraschung; **it came as a** ~ **to us** es war für uns eine Überraschung; ~, ~! (iron.) sieh mal einer an! (spött.); **(b)** *attrib.* überraschend, unerwartet ‹*Besuch*›; **a** ~ **attack/defeat** ein Überraschungsangriff/eine überraschende Niederlage; **it's to be a** ~ **party** die Party soll eine Überraschung sein. **2** *v.t.* überraschen; überrumpeln ‹*Feind*›; **I shouldn't be** ~**d if** ...: es würde mich nicht wundern, wenn ...; **be** ~**d at sb./sth.** sich über jmdn./etw. wundern

surprising /sə'praɪzɪŋ/ *adj.* überraschend; **it's hardly** ~ **that** ...: es ist kaum verwunderlich, dass ...

surprisingly /sə'praɪzɪŋlɪ/ *adv.* überraschend; ~ **[enough], he was** ...: überraschenderweise war er ...

surreal /sə'riːəl/ *adj.* surrealistisch

surrealism /sə'riːəlɪzm/ *n., no pl.* Surrealismus, *der*

surrealist /sə'riːəlɪst/ **1** *n.* Surrealist, *der*/Surrealistin, *die.* **2** *adj.* surrealistisch

surrender /sə'rendə(r)/ **1** *n.* **(a)** (submitting to enemy) Kapitulation, *die;* **(b)** (giving up possession) Aufgabe, *die;* (of insurance policy) Rückkauf, *der;* (of firearms) Abgabe, *die.* **2** *v.i.* kapitulieren; ~ **to despair** sich der Verzweiflung überlassen. **3** *v.t.* (give up possession of) aufgeben; preisgeben ‹*Freiheit, Privileg*›; niederlegen ‹*Amt*›; abgeben, aushändigen ‹*Wertgegenstände*›. **4** *v. refl.* sich hingeben (**to** + *Dat.*)

surreptitious /sʌrəp'tɪʃəs/ *adj.* heimlich; verstohlen ‹*Blick*›

surrogate /'sʌrəgət/ n. (substitute) Ersatz, der

surrogate 'mother n. Leihmutter, die

surround /sə'raʊnd/ v.t. (a) (come or be all round) umringen; ⟨Truppen, Heer:⟩ umzingeln ⟨Stadt, Feind⟩; (b) (enclose, encircle) umgeben; **be ∼ed by** or **with sth.** von etw. umgeben sein

surrounding /sə'raʊndɪŋ/ adj. umliegend ⟨Dörfer⟩; ∼ **area** Umgebung, die; **the** ∼ **countryside** die [Landschaft in der] Umgebung

surroundings /sə'raʊndɪŋz/ n. pl. Umgebung, die

surtax /'sɜːtæks/ n. Ergänzungsabgabe od. -steuer, die

surveillance /sə'veɪləns/ n. Überwachung, die; **keep sb. under** ∼: jmdn. überwachen; **be under** ∼: überwacht werden

survey 1 /sə'veɪ/ v.t. (a) (take general view of) betrachten; (from high point) überblicken ⟨Landschaft, Umgebung⟩; (b) (examine) inspizieren ⟨Gebäude usw.⟩; (c) (assess) bewerten ⟨Situation, Problem usw.⟩. 2 /'sɜːveɪ/ n. (a) (general view, critical inspection) Überblick, der (of über + Akk.); (b) (by opinion poll) Umfrage, die; (by research) Untersuchung, die; **conduct a** ∼ **into sth.** eine Umfrage zu etw. veranstalten/etw. untersuchen; (c) (Surv.) Vermessung, die; (d) (building inspection) Inspektion, die

surveying /sə'veɪɪŋ/ n. (a) Landvermessung, die; (b) (Constr.) Abstecken, das

surveyor /sə'veɪə(r)/ n. ▶ 887 | (a) (of building) Gutachter, der/Gutachterin, die; (b) (of land) Landvermesser, der/-vermesserin, die

survival /sə'vaɪvl/ n., no pl. Überleben, das; (of tradition) Fortbestand, der; (of building) Erhaltung, die; **fight for** ∼: Existenzkampf, der; **the** ∼ **of the fittest** (Biol.) [das] Überleben der Stärkeren

survive /sə'vaɪv/ 1 v.t. überleben. 2 v.i. ⟨Person:⟩ überleben; ⟨Schriften, Gebäude, Traditionen:⟩ erhalten bleiben

survivor /sə'vaɪvə(r)/ n. Überlebende, der/die; **he's a** ∼: er ist nicht unterzukriegen

susceptibility /səseptɪ'bɪlɪtɪ/ n. (to flattery, persuasion, etc.) Empfänglichkeit, die (to für); (to illness, injury, etc.) Anfälligkeit, die (to für)

susceptible /sə'septɪbl/ adj. (a) (sensitive) (to flattery, persuasion, etc.) empfänglich (to für); (to illness, injury, etc.) anfällig (to für); (b) (easily influenced) empfindsam; beeindruckbar

suspect 1 /sə'spekt/ v.t. (a) (imagine to be likely) vermuten; ∼ **the worst** das Schlimmste befürchten; ∼ **sb. to be sth.,** ∼ **that sb. is sth.** glauben od. vermuten, dass jmd. etw. ist; (b) (mentally accuse) verdächtigen; ∼ **sb. of sth./ of doing sth.** jmdn. einer Sache verdächtigen/jmdn. verdächtigen, etw. zu tun; ∼**ed of drug-trafficking** des Drogenhandels verdächtig; (c) (mistrust) bezweifeln ⟨Echtheit⟩; ∼ **sb.'s motives** jmds. Beweggründen mit Argwohn gegenüberstehen. 2 /'sʌspekt/ adj. fragwürdig; suspekt (geh.); verdächtig ⟨Stoff, Paket, Fahrzeug⟩. 3 /'sʌspekt/ n. Verdächtige, der/die; **a murder** ∼: ein Mordverdächtiger/ eine Mordverdächtige

suspected /sə'spektɪd/ adj. verdächtig; ∼ **smallpox cases,** ∼ **cases of smallpox** Fälle mit Verdacht auf Pocken

suspend /sə'spend/ v.t. (a) (hang up) [auf]hängen; **be** ∼**ed [from sth.]** [von etw.] [herab]hängen; (b) (stop, defer) suspendieren ⟨Rechte⟩; [vorübergehend] einstellen ⟨Zugverkehr, Kampfhandlungen⟩; ∼ **judgement** sich des Urteils enthalten; (c) (remove from work etc.) ausschließen (**from** von); sperren ⟨Sportler⟩; vom Unterricht ausschließen ⟨Schüler⟩; ∼ **sb. from duty [pending an inquiry]** jmdn. [während einer schwebenden Untersuchung] vom Dienst suspendieren

suspended 'sentence n. (Law) Strafe mit Bewährung; **he was given a two-year** ∼: er erhielt zwei Jahre Haft auf Bewährung

suspender belt /sə'spendə belt/ n. (Brit.) Strumpfbandgürtel, der

suspenders /sə'spendəz/ n. pl. (a) (Brit.: for stockings) Strumpfbänder od. -halter Pl.; (b) (Amer.: for trousers) Hosenträger Pl.

suspense /sə'spens/ n. Spannung, die; **the** ∼ **is killing me** (joc.) ich bin gespannt wie ein Regenschirm (ugs. scherzh.); **keep sb. in** ∼: jmdn. auf die Folter spannen

suspension /sə'spenʃn/ n. (a) (action of debarring) Ausschluss, der; (from office) Suspendierung, die; (Sport) Sperrung, die; **be under** ∼ ⟨Schüler:⟩ [zeitweilig] vom Unterricht ausgeschlossen sein; ⟨Sportler:⟩ [zeitweilig] gesperrt sein; (b) (temporary cessation) Suspendierung, die; (of train service, hostilities) [vorübergehende] Einstellung; (c) (Motor Veh.) Federung, die

su'spension bridge n. Hängebrücke, die

suspicion /sə'spɪʃn/ n. (a) (uneasy feeling) Misstrauen, das (of gegenüber); (more specific) Verdacht, der; (unconfirmed belief) Ahnung, die; Verdacht, der; **have a** ∼ **that** ...: er Verdacht haben, dass ...; **I have my** ∼**s about him** er kommt mir verdächtig vor; (b) (suspecting) Verdacht, der (of auf + Akk.); **on** ∼ **of theft/murder** etc. wegen Verdachts auf Diebstahl/Mordverdachts usw.; **lay oneself open to** ∼: sich verdächtig machen; **be under** ∼: verdächtigt werden

suspicious /sə'spɪʃəs/ adj. (a) (tending to suspect) misstrauisch (of gegenüber); **be** ∼ **of sb./sth.** jmdm./einer Sache misstrauen; (b) (arousing suspicion) verdächtig

suspiciously /sə'spɪʃəslɪ/ adv. (a) (as to arouse suspicion) verdächtig; **look** ∼ **like sth.** verdächtig nach etw. aussehen; (b) (warily) misstrauisch

suss out /sʌs 'aʊt/ v.t. (Brit. sl.) checken (ugs.); spannen (ugs.)

sustain /sə'steɪn/ v.t. (a) (withstand) widerstehen (+ Dat.) ⟨Druck⟩; standhalten (+ Dat.) ⟨Angriff⟩; tragen ⟨Gewicht⟩; (b) (support, uphold) aufrechterhalten; ∼ **an objection** einem Einwand stattgeben; (c) (suffer) erleiden ⟨Niederlage, Verlust, Verletzung⟩; ∼ **damage** Schaden nehmen; (d) (maintain) bestreiten ⟨Unterhaltung⟩; bewahren ⟨Interesse⟩

sustainable /sʌ'steɪnəbl/ adj. (Ecology) nachhaltig

sustained /sə'steɪnd/ adj. (prolonged) länger ...; anhaltend ⟨Beifall⟩; ausdauernd ⟨Anstrengung⟩

sustenance /'sʌstɪnəns/ n. (a) (nourishment, food) Nahrung, die; (b) (nourishing quality) Nährwert, der

SW abbr. (a) /saʊθ'west/ ▶ 715 | **south-west** SW; (b) (Radio) **short wave** KW

swab /swɒb/ n. (a) (Med.: absorbent pad) Tupfer, der; (b) (Med.: specimen) Abstrich, der

Swabia /'sweɪbɪə/ pr. n. Schwaben (das)

swagger /'swægə(r)/ 1 v.i. (a) (walk with a ∼) großspurig stolzieren; (b) (boast) angeben (ugs.). 2 n. ∼ 1: (a) großspuriges Stolzieren; (b) Angeberei, die (ugs.)

Swahili /swɑː'hiːlɪ, swə'hiːlɪ/ 1 adj. Swahili-. 2 n. ▶ 897 | Swahili, das; see also **English** 2 a

swallow[1] /'swɒləʊ/ 1 v.t. (a) schlucken; (by mistake) verschlucken ⟨Fischgräte; fig.: Wort, Silbe⟩; ∼ **the bait** (fig.) den Köder schlucken (ugs.); (b) (repress) hinunterschlucken (ugs.) ⟨Stolz, Ärger⟩; ∼ **one's words** [demütig] zurücknehmen, was man gesagt hat; (c) (believe) schlucken (ugs.), glauben ⟨Geschichte, Erklärung⟩; (d) (put up with) schlucken (ugs.) ⟨Beleidigung, Unrecht⟩. 2 v.i. schlucken. ∼ **'up** v.t. (a) (make disappear) verschlucken; schlucken ⟨kleinere Betriebe, Gebiete⟩; **I wished the earth would** ∼ **me up** ich wäre am liebsten vor Scham in den Boden versunken; (b) (exhaust, consume) auffressen; verschlingen ⟨große Summen⟩

swallow[2] n. (Ornith.) Schwalbe, die

swam ⇒ **swim** 1, 2

swamp /swɒmp/ 1 n. Sumpf, der. 2 v.t. (a) (flood) überschwemmen; (b) (overwhelm) **be** ∼**ed with letters/ applications/work** mit Briefen/Bewerbungen überschwemmt werden/bis über den Hals in Arbeit stecken (ugs.)

swampy /'swɒmpɪ/ adj. sumpfig

swan /swɒn/ n. Schwan, der

swank /swæŋk/ v.i. (coll.) angeben (ugs.) (**about** mit)

swanky /'swæŋkɪ/ adj. (coll.) protzig (ugs.)

'swansong n. (fig.) Schwanengesang, der

swap /swɒp/ 1 v.t. **-pp-** tauschen (**for** gegen); austauschen ⟨Erfahrungen, Erinnerungen⟩; ∼ **places [with**

sb.] [mit jmdm.] den Platz od. die Plätze tauschen. **2** v.i., **-pp-** tauschen. **3** n. Tausch, der; **do a** ~ **[with sb.]** [mit jmdm.] tauschen

swarm /swɔːm/ **1** n. (a) Schwarm, der; ~ **[of bees]** Bienenschwarm, der; (b) in pl. (great numbers) ~s **of tourists/children** Scharen von Touristen/Kindern. **2** v.i. (a) (move in a ~) schwärmen; (b) (teem) wimmeln (**with** von)

swarthy /'swɔːðɪ/ adj. dunkel ‹Gesichtsfarbe›; dunkelhäutig ‹Person›

swastika /'swɒstɪkə/ n. (of Nazis) Hakenkreuz, das

swat /swɒt/ v.t., **-tt-** totschlagen ‹Fliege, Wespe›

swathe /sweɪð/ v.t. [ein]hüllen

swatter /'swɒtə(r)/ n. Klatsche, die

sway /sweɪ/ **1** v.i. (hin und her) schwanken; (gently) sich wiegen. **2** v.t. (a) wiegen ‹Kopf, Hüften, Zweig, Wipfel›; hin und her schwanken lassen ‹Baum, Mast, Antenne›; (b) (have influence over) beeinflussen; (persuade) überreden. **3** n. Herrschaft, die; **have sb. under one's** ~, **hold** ~ **over sb.** über jmdn. herrschen

swear /sweə(r)/ **1** v.t., **swore** /swɔː(r)/, **sworn** /swɔːn/ (a) schwören ‹Eid usw.›; **I could have sworn [that] it was him** ich hätte schwören können, dass er es war; (b) (administer oath to) vereidigen ‹Zeugen›; ~ **sb. to secrecy** jmdn. auf Geheimhaltung einschwören. **2** v.i., **swore**, **sworn** (a) (use ~-words) fluchen; (b) ~ **to sth.** (be certain of) etw. beschwören; einen Eid auf etw. (Akk.) ablegen; **I wouldn't like to** ~ **to it** (coll.) ich will es nicht beschwören; (c) (take oath) schwören, einen Eid ablegen (**on** auf + Akk.)

~ **at** v.t. beschimpfen

~ **by** v.t. (coll.: have confidence in) schwören auf (+ Akk.)

~ **in** v.t. vereidigen ‹Geschworenen, Zeugen›

'**swear word** n. Kraftausdruck, der; Fluch, der; **use** ~s fluchen

sweat /swet/ **1** n. (a) Schweiß, der; **in** or **by the** ~ **of one's brow** im Schweiße seines Angesichts; **I came** or **broke out in a** ~: mir brach der [Angst]schweiß aus; **don't get in such a** ~! reg dich nicht so auf!; (b) (drudgery) Plagerei, die; Plackerei, die (ugs.); **no** ~! (coll.) kein Problem! (ugs.). **2** v.i., ~**ed** or (Amer.) ~: (a) (perspire) schwitzen; ~ **like a pig** (coll.) schwitzen wie die Sau (salopp); ~ **with fear** vor Angst schwitzen; (b) (fig.: suffer) **he made me sit outside** ~**ing** er ließ mich draußen sitzen und schmoren (ugs.); (c) (drudge) sich placken (ugs.). **3** v.t. (a) ~ **blood** (fig.) Blut und Wasser schwitzen (ugs.); (b) ~ **it out** (coll.) durchhalten; ausharren

'**sweatband** n. Schweißband, das

sweated labour /swetɪd 'leɪbə(r)/ n. unterbezahlte [Schwer]arbeit

sweater /'swetə(r)/ n. Pullover, der

sweat: ~**shirt** n. Sweatshirt, das; ~**shop** n. ausbeuterische [kleine] Klitsche (ugs.)

sweaty /'swetɪ/ adj. schweißig; schweißnass

Swede /swiːd/ n. ▶947 Schwede, der/Schwedin, die

swede n. Kohlrübe, die

Sweden /'swiːdn/ pr. n. Schweden (das)

Swedish /'swiːdɪʃ/, ▶897, ▶947 **1** adj. schwedisch; **sb. is** ~: jmd. ist Schwede/Schwedin. **2** n. Schwedisch, das; see also **English 2 a**

sweep /swiːp/ **1** v.t., **swept** /swept/ (a) fegen (bes. nordd.); kehren (bes. südd.); ~ **the board**, ~ **all before one** (fig.: win all awards) auf der ganzen Linie siegen; (b) (move with force) fegen; **the current swept the logs along** die Strömung riss die Hölzer mit; (c) (traverse swiftly) ~ **the hillside/plain** ‹Wind:› über die Hügel/Ebene fegen; ~ **the country** ‹Epidemie, Mode:› das Land überrollen; ‹Feuer:› durch das Land fegen. **2** v.i., **swept** (a) (clean) fegen (bes. nordd.); kehren (bes. südd.); (b) (go fast, in stately manner) ‹Vogel:› gleiten; ‹Person, Auto:› rauschen; ‹Wind usw.:› fegen; (c) (extend) sich erstrecken; **the road** ~s **to the left** die Straße macht einen großen Bogen nach links; **his glance swept from left to right** sein Blick glitt von links nach rechts. **3** n. (a) (cleaning) **give sth. a** ~: etw. fegen (bes. nordd.); etw. kehren (bes. südd.); **make a clean** ~ (fig.: get rid of everything) gründlich aufräumen; (b) ⇒ **chimney sweep**; (c) (coll.) ⇒ **sweepstake**; (d) (motion

of arm) ausholende Bewegung; (e) (stretch) **a wide/an open** ~ **of country** ein weiter Landstrich; (f) (curve of road, river) Bogen, der; **the wide** ~ **of the bay** die geschwungene Kurve der Bucht

~ **a'side** v.t. (a) (dismiss) beiseite schieben ‹Einwand, Zweifel›; (b) (push aside) wegfegen; beiseite fegen

~ **a'way** v.t. fortreißen; (fig.) hinwegfegen (geh.) ‹Traditionen›; (abolish) aufräumen mit ‹Privilegien, Korruption›

~ '**by** v.i. vorbeirauschen

~ '**down** v.i. **the hills** ~ **down to the sea** die Berge fallen in sanftem Bogen zum Meer hinab

~ '**in** v.i. (enter majestically) einziehen

~ '**out** v.t. ausfegen (bes. nordd.); auskehren (bes. südd.)

~ '**up 1** v.t. zusammenfegen (bes. nordd.); zusammenkehren (bes. südd.). **2** v.i. angerauscht kommen

sweeper /'swiːpə(r)/ n. [**road**] ~ (person) Straßenfeger, der (bes. nordd.); Straßenkehrer, der (bes. südd.); (machine) Straßenkehrmaschine, die

sweeping /'swiːpɪŋ/ adj. (a) (without limitations) pauschal; (b) (far-reaching) weit reichend ‹Einsparung›; umfassend ‹Reform›; durchschlagend ‹Sieg, Erfolg›; umwälzend ‹Veränderung›

'**sweepstake** n. (a) (race, contest) Sweepstake[rennen], das; (b) (lottery) Pferdetoto, bei dem sich die Gewinnsumme aus den Einsätzen zusammensetzt

sweet /swiːt/ **1** adj. (a) (to taste) süß; ~ **tea** gesüßter Tee; **have a** ~ **tooth** gern Süßes mögen; (b) (lovely) süß; reizend ‹Wesen, Gesicht, Mädchen, Kleid›; ~ **dreams!** träum[e]/träumt süß!; **how** ~ **of you!** wie nett od. lieb von dir!; **go one's own** ~ **way** machen, was einem passt; (c) (fragrant) süß; frisch ‹Atem›; (d) (musical) süß (geh.); lieblich ‹Stimme, Musik, Klang›. **2** n. (a) (Brit.: piece of confectionery) Bonbon, das od. der; (with chocolate, fudge, etc.) Süßigkeit, die; (b) (Brit.: dessert) Nachtisch, der; Dessert, das; **for** ~: zum Nachtisch od. Dessert

sweet: ~**-and-'sour** attrib. adj. süßsauer; ~**corn** n. Zuckermais, der

sweeten /'swiːtn/ v.t. (a) (add sugar etc. to) süßen; (b) (add fragrance to) süß machen; versüßen; (remove bad smell of) reinigen ‹Luft, Atem›; (c) (make agreeable) versüßen ‹Leben, Abend›; milde stimmen ‹Person›

sweetener /'swiːtnə(r)/ n. (a) Süßstoff, der; (b) (bribe) kleine Aufmerksamkeit (iron.)

'**sweetheart** n. (a) Schatz, der; Liebling, der

sweetie /'swiːtɪ/ (Brit. child lang.) ⇒ **sweet 2 a**; (b) (person) Schatz, der

sweetness /'swiːtnɪs/ n., no pl. (a) Süße, die; (b) (fragrance) süßer Duft; (c) (melodiousness) Süße, die (geh.)

sweet: ~ '**pea** n. (Bot.) Wicke, die; ~**shop** n. (Brit.) Süßwarengeschäft, das; ~**smelling** adj. süß [duftend]; ~**-tempered** /'swiːttempəd/ adj. sanftmütig

swell /swel/ **1** v.t., ~**ed, swollen** /'swəʊln/ or ~**ed** (a) (increase in size, height) anschwellen lassen; aufquellen lassen ‹Holz›; (b) (increase amount of) anschwellen lassen; vergrößern; ~ **the ranks [of participants]** die Zahl der Teilnehmer vergrößern; (c) blähen ‹Segel›. **2** v.i., ~**ed, swollen** or ~**ed** (a) (expand) ‹Körperteil:› anschwellen; ‹Segel:› sich blähen; ‹Material:› aufquellen; (b) (increase in amount) ‹Anzahl:› zunehmen; (c) (become louder) anschwellen ([in]to zu). **3** n. (of sea) Dünung, die

swelling /'swelɪŋ/ **1** n. Schwellung, die (Med.). **2** adj. (growing larger, louder) anschwellend

swelter /'sweltə(r)/ v.i. [vor Hitze] [fast] vergehen; ~ **in the heat** in der Hitze schmoren (ugs.); ~**ing** glühend heiß ‹Tag, Wetter›; ~**ing heat** Bruthitze, die

swept ⇒ **sweep 1, 2**

swerve /swɜːv/ **1** v.i. (deviate) einen Bogen od. (ugs.) Schlenker machen; ~ **to the right/left** nach rechts/links [aus]schwenken. **2** n. (divergence from course) Bogen, der; Schlenker, der (ugs.)

swift /swɪft/ **1** adj. schnell; flink, schnell ‹Bewegung›; ~ **action** rasches Handeln; ~ **retribution** prompte Bestrafung. **2** n. (Ornith.) Mauersegler, der

swiftly /'swɪftlɪ/ adv. schnell; (soon) bald

swiftness /'swɪftnɪs/ n. Schnelligkeit, die; ~ of action schnelles od. rasches Handeln

swig /swɪg/ (coll.) **1** v.t., **-gg-** schlucken (ugs.); [herunter]-kippen (ugs.). **2** v.i., **-gg-** [hastig] trinken. **3** n. Schluck, der; **have/take a ~ [of beer** etc.] einen tüchtigen Schluck [Bier usw.] trinken/nehmen

swill /swɪl/ **1** v.t. **(a)** (rinse) ~ **[out]** [aus]spülen; **(b)** (derog.: drink greedily) hinunterspülen (ugs.). **2** n. give sth. a ~ [out]/down etw. [aus]spülen/abspülen

swim /swɪm/ **1** v.i., **-mm-, swam** /swæm/, **swum** /swʌm/ **(a)** schwimmen; ~ **with/against the tide/stream** (fig.) mit dem/gegen den Strom schwimmen; **(b)** (fig.: be flooded, overflow) ~ **with** or **in sth.** in etw. (Dat.) schwimmen; **the deck was ~ming with water** das Deck stand unter Wasser; **(c)** (appear to whirl) ~ **[before sb.'s eyes]** [vor jmds. Augen] verschwimmen; **(d)** (have dizzy sensation) **my head was ~ming** mir war schwindelig. See also **sink** 2 a. **2** v.t., **-mm-, swam, swum** schwimmen ⟨Strecke⟩; durchschwimmen ⟨Fluss, See⟩. **3** n. **(a)** have a/go for a ~: schwimmen/schwimmen gehen; **(b)** be in the ~ [of things] mitten im Geschehen sein

swimmer /'swɪmə(r)/ n. Schwimmer, der/Schwimmerin, die; **be a good/poor ~:** gut/schlecht schwimmen können

swimming /'swɪmɪŋ/ n. Schwimmen, das

swimming: ~ **baths** n. pl. Schwimmbad, das; ~ **costume** n. Badeanzug, der; ~ **lesson** n. Schwimmstunde, die; ~ **lessons** Schwimmunterricht, der; ~ **pool** n. Schwimmbecken, das; (in house or garden) Swimmingpool, der; (building) Schwimmbad, das; ~ **trunks** n. pl. Badehose, die

'swimsuit n. Badeanzug, der

swindle /'swɪndl/ **1** v.t. betrügen; ~ **sb. out of sth.** jmdn. um etw. betrügen; (take by persuasion) jmdm. etw. abschwindeln. **2** n. Schwindel, der; Betrug, der

swindler /'swɪndlə(r)/ n. Schwindler, der/Schwindlerin, die

swine /swaɪn/ n., pl. same **(a)** (Amer./formal/Zool.) Schwein, das; **(b)** (derog.: contemptible person) Schwein, das (abwertend)

swing /swɪŋ/ **1** n. **(a)** (apparatus) Schaukel, die; **(b)** (spell of ~ing) Schaukeln, das; **(c)** (Sport: strike, blow) Schlag, der; (Boxing) Schwinger, der; (Golf) Schwung, der; **take a ~ at sb./sth.** zum Schlag gegen jmdn./auf etw. (Akk.) ausholen; **(d)** (of suspended object) Schwingen, das; **in full ~** (fig.) in vollem Gang[e]; **(e)** (steady movement) Rhythmus, der; **the party went with a ~:** auf der Party herrschte eine tolle Stimmung (ugs.); **get into/be in the ~ of things** or **it** richtig reinkommen/richtig drin sein (ugs.); **(f)** (Mus.) Swing, der; **(g)** (shift) Schwankung, die; (of public opinion) Wende, die; (amount of change in votes) Abwanderung, die. **2** v.i., swung / swʌŋ/ **(a)** (turn on axis, sway) schwingen; (in wind) schaukeln; ~ **open** ⟨Tür:⟩ aufgehen; **(b)** (go in sweeping curve) schwenken; ~ **from sb.'s arm/a tree** an jmds. Arm/einem Baum schwingen (geh.) od. baumeln; **(c)** ~ **into action** (fig.) loslegen (ugs.); **(d)** (move oneself by ~ing) sich schwingen; **the car swung out of the drive** der Wagen schwenkte aus der Einfahrt; **(e)** (sl.: be executed by hanging) baumeln (salopp); **he'll ~ for it** dafür wird er baumeln. **3** v.t., swung **(a)** schwingen; (rock) schaukeln; ~ **sth. round and round** etw. kreisen od. im Kreise wirbeln lassen; **(b)** (cause to face in another direction) schwenken; **he swung the car off the road/into the road** er schwenkte [mit dem Auto] von der Straße ab/in die Straße ein; **(c)** (have influence on) umschlagen lassen ⟨öffentliche Meinung⟩; ~ **the elections** den Ausgang der Wahlen entscheiden; **what swung it for me ...:** was für mich den Ausschlag gab ... ~ **'round** v.i. sich schnell umdrehen (**on** nach); (in surprise) herumfahren

swing: ~**bin** n. Schwingdeckel[müll]eimer, der; Mülleimer mit Schwingdeckel; ~**bridge** n. Drehbrücke, die; ~**'door** n. Pendeltür, die

swingeing /'swɪndʒɪŋ/ adj. (Brit.) hart ⟨Schlag⟩; (fig.) drastisch ⟨Kürzung, Maßnahme⟩; scharf ⟨Attacke⟩

swinging /'swɪŋɪŋ/ adj. **(a)** schwingend; **(b)** (rhythmical) [stark] rhythmisch; **(c)** (coll.: lively) wild (ugs.); swingend (ugs.)

swipe /swaɪp/ (coll.) **1** v.i. ~ **at** eindreschen auf (+ Akk.) (ugs.). **2** v.t. **(a)** (hit hard) knallen (ugs.); **(b)** (coll.: steal) klauen (ugs.); **(c)** ~ **the card through the swipe reader** die Karte durch das [Karten]lesegerät ziehen. **3** n. **(a)** take a wild ~ at sth. wild auf etw. (Akk.) losschlagen; **(b)** (device) [Karten]lesegerät, das

'swipe card n. Magnetkarte, die

swirl /swɜːl/ **1** v.i. wirbeln. **2** v.t. umherwirbeln. **3** n. (spiralling shape) Spirale, die

swish /swɪʃ/ **1** v.t. schlagen mit ⟨Schwanz⟩; sausen lassen ⟨Stock⟩. **2** v.i. zischen. **3** n. Zischen, das. **4** adj. (coll.) schick (ugs.)

Swiss /swɪs/ ▶ 947 **1** adj. Schweizer; schweizerisch; **sb. is ~:** jmd. ist Schweizer/Schweizerin. **2** n. Schweizer, der/Schweizerin, die; **the ~** pl. die Schweizer

Swiss: ~ **'German 1** adj. schweizerdeutsch; **2** n. Schweizerdeutsch, das; ~ **'roll** n. Biskuitrolle, die

switch /swɪtʃ/ **1** n. **(a)** (esp. Electr.) Schalter, der; **(b)** (Amer. Railw.) Weiche, die; **(c)** (change with another) Wechsel, der; **(d)** (flexible shoot, whip) Gerte, die. **2** v.t. **(a)** (change) ~ **sth. [over] to sth.** etw. auf etw. (Akk.) umstellen od. (Electr.) umschalten; ~ **the conversation to another topic** das Gespräch auf ein anderes Thema lenken; **(b)** (exchange) tauschen. **3** v.i. wechseln; ~ **[over] to sth.** auf etw. (Akk.) umstellen od. (Electr.) umschalten

~ **a'round 1** v.t. umstellen ⟨Möbel, Dienstplan⟩. **2** v.i. [die Stellung] wechseln

~ **'off** v.t. & i. ausschalten; (also fig. coll.) abschalten

~ **'on** v.t. einschalten; anschalten. **2** v.i. sich anschalten

~ **'over 1** v.t. ⇒ ~ 2 a. **2** v.i. ⇒ ~ 3

~ **'round** ⇒ ~ around

~ **'through** v.t. durchstellen ⟨Telefongespräch, Anrufer⟩

switch: ~**back** n. (roller coaster) Achterbahn, die; ~**board** n. ▶ 887 (Teleph.) [Telefon]zentrale, die; Vermittlung, die; ~**board operator** Telefonist, der/Telefonistin, die

Switzerland /'swɪtsələnd/ pr. n. die Schweiz

swivel /'swɪvl/ **1** n. Drehgelenk, das. **2** v.i., (Brit.) **-ll-** sich drehen. **3** v.t., (Brit.) **-ll-** drehen

'swivel chair n. Drehstuhl, der

swollen /'swəʊlən/ **1** ⇒ swell 1, 2. **2** adj. geschwollen; angeschwollen ⟨Fluss⟩; **have a ~ head** (fig.) sehr eingebildet od. von sich eingenommen sein

'swollen-headed adj. eingebildet

swoon /swuːn/ (literary) **1** v.i. **(a)** (faint) ohnmächtig werden; **(b)** (go into ecstasies) ~ **over sb./sth.** von jmdm./etw. schwärmen. **2** n. Ohnmacht, die

swoop /swuːp/ **1** n. **(a)** (downward plunge) Sturzflug, der; **(b)** (coll.: raid) Razzia, die. **2** v.i. (plunge suddenly) herabstoßen; (pounce) ~ **on sb.** sich auf jmdn. stürzen; (to attack) gegen jmdn. einen Schlag führen; **the police ~ed on several addresses** die Polizei führte in mehreren Wohnungen Razzien durch

swop ⇒ swap

sword /sɔːd/ n. Schwert, das

'swordfish n. Schwertfisch, der

swore ⇒ swear

sworn /swɔːn/ **1** ⇒ swear. **2** attrib. adj. **(a)** (bound by an oath) verschworen ⟨Freund⟩; ~ **enemy** Todfeind, der; **(b)** (certified by oath) beeidigt; ~ **evidence** Aussage unter Eid; ~ **affidavit/statement** eidesstattliche Versicherung/eidliche Erklärung

swot /swɒt/ (Brit. coll.) **1** n. Streber, der/Streberin, die (abwertend). **2** v.i., **-tt-** büffeln (ugs.). ~ **up** v.t. büffeln (ugs.)

swum ⇒ swim 1, 2

swung ⇒ swing 2, 3

'swung dash n. Tilde, die

sycamore /'sɪkəmɔː(r)/ n. Bergahorn, der; (Amer.: plane tree) Platane, die

sycophant /'sɪkəfænt/ n. Kriecher, der; Schranze, die

sycophantic /sɪkə'fæntɪk/ adj. sykophantisch (bildungsspr., veralt.); kriecherisch (abwertend)

syllable /'sɪləbl/ *n.* (lit. or fig.) Silbe, *die;* **in words of one ∼** (fig.) mit [sehr] einfachen Worten

syllabus /'sɪləbəs/ *n., pl.* **∼es** *or* **syllabi** /'sɪləbaɪ/ Lehrplan, *der;* (for exam) Studienplan, *der*

symbiosis /sɪmbɪ'əʊsɪs/ *n., pl.* **symbioses** /sɪmbɪ'əʊsiːz/ (Biol.; also fig.) Symbiose, *die*

symbiotic /sɪmbɪ'ɒtɪk/ *adj.* symbiotisch

symbol /'sɪmbl/ *n.* Symbol, *das* (**of** für)

symbolic /sɪm'bɒlɪk/, **symbolical** /sɪm'bɒlɪkl/ *adj.* symbolisch

symbolise ⇒ **symbolize**

symbolism /'sɪmbəlɪzm/ *n.* Symbolik, *die*

symbolize /'sɪmbəlaɪz/ *v.t.* symbolisieren

symmetrical /sɪ'metrɪkl/ *adj.*, **symmetrically** /sɪ'metrɪkəlɪ/ *adv.* symmetrisch

symmetry /'sɪmɪtrɪ/ *n.* Symmetrie, *die*

sympathetic /sɪmpə'θetɪk/ *adj.* (**a**) (showing pity) mitfühlend; (understanding) verständnisvoll; (**b**) (favourably inclined) wohlgesinnt; geneigt ‹*Leser*›; **be ∼ to a cause/to new ideas** einer Sache wohlwollend gegenüberstehen/für neue Ideen empfänglich *od.* zugänglich sein; **give sb. a ∼ hearing** ein offenes Ohr für jmdn. haben; **he is not at all ∼ to this idea** er ist von dieser Idee ganz und gar nicht angetan

sympathise, sympathiser ⇒ **sympathiz-**

sympathize /'sɪmpəθaɪz/ *v.i.* (**a**) (feel or express sympathy) **∼ with sb.** mit jmdm. [mit]fühlen *od.* Mitleid haben; (by speaking) sein Mitgefühl mit jmdm. äußern; **I do ∼:** es tut mir wirklich leid; (**b**) **∼ with** (have understanding for) Verständnis haben für ‹*jmds. Not, Denkweise usw.*›; (Polit.: share ideas of) sympathisieren mit ‹*Partei usw.*›

sympathizer /'sɪmpəθaɪzə(r)/ *n.* Sympathisant, *der*/ Sympathisantin, *die*

sympathy /'sɪmpəθɪ/ *n.* (**a**) (sharing feelings of another) Mitgefühl, *das;* **in deepest ∼:** mit aufrichtigem Beileid; (**b**) (agreement in opinion or emotion) Sympathie, *die;* **my sympathies are with Schmidt** ich bin auf Schmidts Seite; **be in/out of ∼ with sth.** mit etw. sympathisieren/ nicht sympathisieren; **come out** *or* **strike in ∼ with sb.** mit jmdm. in einen Sympathiestreik treten

'sympathy strike *n.* Sympathiestreik, *der*

symphonic /sɪm'fɒnɪk/ *adj.* sinfonisch; symphonisch

symphony /'sɪmfənɪ/ *n.* Sinfonie, *die*

'symphony orchestra *n.* Sinfonieorchester, *das*

symposium /sɪm'pəʊzɪəm/ *n., pl.* **symposia** /sɪm'pəʊzɪə/ Symposion, *das;* Symposium, *das*

symptom /'sɪmptəm/ *n.* (Med.; also fig.) Symptom, *das*

symptomatic /sɪmptə'mætɪk/ *adj.* (Med.; also fig.) symptomatisch (**of** für)

synagogue (*Amer.:* **synagog**) /'sɪnəgɒg/ *n.* Synagoge, *die*

sync, synch /sɪŋk/ *n.* (coll.) **in/out of ∼:** synchron/ nicht synchron

synchromesh /'sɪŋkrəmeʃ/ *n.* (Motor Veh.) **∼** [gearbox] Synchrongetriebe, *das;* **there is ∼ on all gears** alle Gänge sind synchronisiert

synchronize (synchronise) /'sɪŋkrənaɪz/ *v.t.* (**a**) synchronisieren ‹*Vorgänge, Maschinen, Bild und Ton*›; (**b**) (set to same time) gleichstellen ‹*Uhren*›; **we'd better ∼ [our] watches** wir sollten Uhrenvergleich machen

syndicate /'sɪndɪkət/ *n.* (**a**) (for business, in organized crime) Syndikat, *das;* (**b**) (in newspapers) *Presseagentur, die Beiträge ankauft und an eine od. mehrere Zeitungen vertreibt*

syndrome /'sɪndrəʊm/ *n.* (Med.; also fig.) Syndrom, *das*

synod /'sɪnəd/ *n.* Synode, *die*

synonym /'sɪnənɪm/ *n.* (Ling.) Synonym, *das*

synonymous /sɪ'nɒnɪməs/ *adj.* (**a**) (Ling.) synonym (**with** mit); (**b**) **∼ with** (fig.: suggestive of, linked with) gleichbedeutend mit

synonymy /sɪ'nɒnəmɪ/ *n.* (Ling.) Synonymie, *die*

synopsis /sɪ'nɒpsɪs/ *n., pl.* **synopses** /sɪ'nɒpsiːz/ Inhaltsangabe, *die*

syntactic /sɪn'tæktɪk/ *adj.* (Ling.) syntaktisch

syntax /'sɪntæks/ *n.* (Ling.) Syntax, *die*

synthesis /'sɪnθɪsɪs/ *n., pl.* **syntheses** /'sɪnθɪsiːz/ Synthese, *die*

synthesise, synthesiser ⇒ **synthesiz-**

synthesize /'sɪnθɪsaɪz/ *v.t.* (**a**) (form into a whole) zur Synthese bringen; (**b**) (Chem.) synthetisieren; (**c**) (Electronics) **∼ speech** Sprache elektronisch generieren

synthesizer /'sɪnθɪsaɪzə(r)/ *n.* (Mus.) Synthesizer, *der*

synthetic /sɪn'θetɪk/ **1** *adj.* synthetisch. **2** *n.* Kunststoff, *der;* **∼s** (Textiles) Synthetics

syphilis /'sɪfɪlɪs/ *n.* (Med.) Syphilis, *die*

syphon ⇒ **siphon**

Syria /'sɪrɪə/ *pr. n.* Syrien (*das*)

Syrian /'sɪrɪən/ ▶ 947 **1** *adj.* syrisch; **sb. is ∼:** jmd. ist Syrer/Syrerin. **2** *n.* Syrer, *der*/Syrerin, *die*

syringe /sɪ'rɪndʒ/ **1** *n.* Spritze, *die; see also* **hypodermic 1. 2** *v.t.* spritzen; ausspritzen ‹*Ohr*›

syrup /'sɪrəp/ *n.* Sirup, *der;* **cough ∼:** Hustensaft, *der*

system /'sɪstəm/ *n.* (**a**) (lit. or fig.) System, *das;* (of roads, railways also) Netz, *das;* **root ∼** (Bot.) Wurzelgeflecht, *das;* (**b**) (Anat., Zool.: body) Körper, *der;* (part) **digestive/muscular/nervous ∼:** Verdauungsapparat, *der*/Muskulatur, *die*/Nervensystem, *das;* **get sth. out of one's ∼** (fig.) etw. loswerden; (by talking) sich (*Dat.*) etw. von der Seele reden

systematic /sɪstə'mætɪk/ *adj.*, **systematically** /sɪstə'mætɪkəlɪ/ *adv.* systematisch

systematize (systematise) /'sɪstəmətaɪz/ *v.t.* systematisieren (**into** zu)

'system disk *n.* (Computing) Systemdiskette, *die*

systemic /sɪ'stemɪk/ *adj.* (Biol.) systemisch

'systems analyst *n.* ▶ 887 Systemanalytiker, *der*/ -analytikerin, *die*

·····································

·····································

T, t /tiː/ *n., pl.* **Ts** *or* **T's** T, t, *das;* **to a T** ganz genau; haargenau; **T-junction** Einmündung, *die* (*in eine Vorfahrtsstraße*); **T-bone steak** T-bone-Steak, *das;* **T-shirt** T-shirt, *das*

ta /tɑː/ *int.* (Brit. coll.) danke

tab¹ /tæb/ *n.* (**a**) (projecting flap) Zunge, *die;* (label) Schildchen, *das;* (on clothing) Etikett, *das;* (with name) Namensschild, *das;* (on file [card]) Reiter, *der;* (**b**) (Amer. coll.: bill) Rechnung, *die;* **pick up the ∼:** die Zeche bezahlen; (**c**) **keep ∼s** *or* **a ∼ on sb./sth.** (watch) jmdn./etw. [genau] beobachten

tab² ⇒ **tabulator**

tabby /'tæbɪ/ *n.* (**a**) **∼** [cat] Tigerkatze, *die;* (**b**) (female cat) [weibliche] Katze; Kätzin, *die*

table /'teɪbl/ **1** *n.* (**a**) Tisch, *der;* **at ∼:** bei Tisch; **sit down at ∼:** sich zu Tisch setzen; **after two whiskies he was under the ∼** (coll.) nach zwei Whisky lag er unter dem Tisch (ugs.); **drink sb. under the ∼:** jmdn. unter den Tisch trinken (ugs.); **get sb./get round the ∼:** jmdn. an einen Tisch bringen/sich an einen Tisch setzen; **turn the ∼s [on sb.]** (fig.) [jmdm. gegenüber] den Spieß umdrehen *od.* umkehren; *see also* **lay² 1 e;** (**b**) (list) Tabelle, *die;* **∼ of contents** Inhaltsverzeichnis, *das;* **learn one's ∼s** das Einmaleins lernen; **say one's nine times ∼:** die Neunerreihe aufsagen. **2** *v.t.* einbringen; auf den Tisch legen (ugs.)

tableau /'tæbləʊ/ *n., pl.* **∼x** /'tæbləʊz/ (lit. or fig.) Tableau, *das*

table: ∼cloth *n.* Tischdecke, *die;* Tischtuch, *das;* **∼ knife** *n.* Messer, *das;* **∼ lamp** *n.* Tischlampe, *die;* **∼ manners** *n. pl.* Tischmanieren *Pl.;* **∼-mat** *n.* Set, *das;*

∼ salt *n.* Tafelsalz, *das;* **∼spoon** *n.* Servierlöffel, *der;* **∼spoonful** *n.* Servierlöffel, *der;* **a ∼spoonful** ein Servierlöffel [voll]

tablet /'tæblɪt/ *n.* **(a)** (pill) Tablette, *die;* **(b)** (of soap) Stück, *das;* **(c)** (stone slab) Tafel, *die*

table: **∼ tennis** *n.* (Sport) Tischtennis, *das;* **∼ tennis bat** Tischtennisschläger, *der;* **∼ware** *n.*, *no pl.* Geschirr, Besteck und Gläser; **∼ wine** *n.* Tischwein, *der*

tabloid /'tæblɔɪd/ *n.* (kleinformatige, bebilderte) Boulevardzeitung; **the ∼s** (derog.) die Boulevardpresse

taboo, tabu /tə'buː/ **1** *n.* Tabu, *das.* **2** *adj.* tabuisiert; Tabu⟨*wort*⟩; **be ∼:** tabu sein

tabulate /'tæbjʊleɪt/ *v.t.* tabellarisch darstellen; tabellarisieren

tabulation /tæbjʊ'leɪʃn/ *n.* tabellarische Aufstellung; Tabellarisierung, *die*

tabulator /'tæbjʊleɪtə(r)/ *n.* Tabulator, *der*

tachograph /'tækəɡrɑːf/ *n.* (Motor Veh.) Fahrt[en]schreiber, *der*

tacit /'tæsɪt/ *adj.*, **tacitly** /'tæsɪtlɪ/ *adv.* stillschweigend

taciturn /'tæsɪtɜːn/ *adj.* schweigsam; wortkarg

tack /tæk/ **1** *n.* **(a)** (small nail) kleiner Nagel; **(b)** (temporary stitch) Heftstich, *der;* **(c)** (Naut.: direction of vessel; also fig.) Kurs, *der;* **on the right/wrong ∼** (fig.) auf dem richtigen/falschen Weg *od.* Kurs; **change one's ∼, try another ∼** (fig.) einen anderen Kurs einschlagen. **2** *v.t.* **(a)** (stitch loosely) heften; **(b)** (nail) festnageln. **3** *v.i.* (Naut.) kreuzen ∼ **'on** *v.t.* anhängen (**to** an + *Akk.*)

tackle /'tækl/ **1** *v.t.* angehen, in Angriff nehmen ⟨*Problem usw.*⟩; **∼ sb. about/on/over sth.** jmdn. auf etw. (*Akk.*) ansprechen; (ask for sth.) jmdn. um etw. angehen; **(b)** (Sport) angreifen ⟨*Spieler*⟩; (Amer. Footb.; Rugby) fassen. **2** *n.* **(a)** (equipment) Ausrüstung, *die;* **(b)** (Sport) Angriff, *der;* (sliding ∼) Tackling, *das;* (Amer. Footb.; Rugby) Fassen und Halten

tacky /'tækɪ/ *adj.* (sticky) klebrig

tact /tækt/ *n.* Takt, *der;* **he has no ∼:** er hat kein Taktgefühl

tactful /'tæktfl/ *adj.*, **tactfully** /'tæktfəlɪ/ *adv.* taktvoll

tactic /'tæktɪk/ *n.* Taktik, *die*

tactical /'tæktɪkl/ *adj.* taktisch ⟨*Fehler, Manöver, Rückzug*⟩; **∼ voting** taktische Stimmabgabe

tactician /tæk'tɪʃn/ *n.* Taktiker, *der*/Taktikerin, *die*

tactics /'tæktɪks/ *n. pl.* Taktik, *die*

tactless /'tæktlɪs/ *adj.* taktlos

tactlessly /'tæktlɪslɪ/ *adv.* taktlos; *as sentence-modifier* taktloserweise

tadpole /'tædpəʊl/ *n.* Kaulquappe, *die*

tag¹ /tæɡ/ **1** *n.* **(a)** (label) Schild, *das;* (on clothes) Etikett, *das;* (on animal's ear) Ohrmarke, *die;* **(b)** (electronic device) (on person) elektronische Fessel; (on goods) Sicherungsetikett, *das;* **(c)** (loop) Schlaufe, *die;* **(d)** (stock phrase) Zitat, *das;* geflügeltes Wort. **2** *v.t.* **-gg-** **(a)** (attach) anhängen (**to** an + *Akk.*); **∼ together** aneinander hängen; zusammenheften ⟨*Blätter*⟩; **(b)** (with electronic device) ∼ sb. etw. mit einem Sicherungsetikett versehen; **∼ sb.** jmdm. eine elektronische Fessel anlegen. **3** *v.i.*, **-gg-:** **∼ behind** [nach]folgen; **∼ after sb.** hinter jmdm. hertrotteln (ugs.) ∼ **a'long** *v.i.* hinterherlaufen; **do you mind if I ∼ along?** darf ich mich anschließen? ∼ **'on** *v.t.* anhängen (**to** an + *Akk.*)

tag² *n.* (game) Fangen, *das*

tag 'question *n.* (Ling.) (*auf eine bestätigende Antwort zielendes*) Frageanhängsel, *das*

tail /teɪl/ **1** *n.* **(a)** Schwanz, *der;* **(b)** (fig.) **have sb./sth. on one's ∼** (coll.) jmdn./etw. auf den Fersen haben (ugs.); **be/keep on sb.'s ∼** (coll.) jmdm. auf den Fersen sein/ bleiben (ugs.); **with one's ∼ between one's legs** mit eingezogenem Schwanz (ugs.); **sb. has his ∼ up** jmd. ist übermütig; **turn ∼** [and run] Fersengeld geben; (in die Flucht ergreifen); **(c)** (of comet) Schweif, *der;* **(d)** [shirt-]∼: Hemdzipfel, *der* (ugs.); **(e)** (of man's coat) Schoß, *der;* **(f)** *in pl.* (man's evening dress) Frack, *der;* **(g)** *in pl.* (on coin) ∼s [**it is**] Zahl; *see also* **head 1 e. 2** *v.t.* (coll.: follow) beschatten

∼ 'away ⇒ **∼ off**

∼ 'back *v.i.* sich stauen

∼ 'off *v.i.* **(a)** (decrease) zurückgehen; **(b)** (fade into silence) verstummen

tail: **∼back** *n.* (Brit.) Rückstau, *der;* **∼board** *n.* hintere Bordwand; **∼ coat** *n.* Frack, *der;* **∼-end** *n.* (hindmost end) Schwanz, *der;* (fig.) Ende, *das;* **∼gate** *n.* (Motor Veh.) Heckklappe, *die;* **∼ lamp** (esp. Amer.), **∼ light** *ns.* Rück- *od.* Schlusslicht, *das*

tailor /'teɪlə(r)/ **1** *n.* ▶887 Schneider, *der*/Schneiderin, *die; see also* **baker. 2** *v.t.* **(a)** schneidern; **(b)** (fig.) **∼ed to** *or* **for sb./sth.** für jmdn./etw. maßgeschneidert; **∼ed to sb.'s needs** auf jmds. Bedürfnisse zugeschnitten

'tailor-made *adj.* (lit. or fig.) maßgeschneidert

tail: **∼plane** *n.* (Aeronaut.) Höhenleitwerk, *das;* **∼spin** *n.* **(a)** (of aircraft) Trudeln, *das;* **(b)** (fig.: state of panic) **send sb./go into a ∼spin** jmdn. in Panik versetzen/zu rotieren anfangen (ugs.); **∼ wind** *n.* Rückenwind, *der*

taint /teɪnt/ **1** *n.* Makel, *der.* **2** *v.t.* verderben; beflecken ⟨*Ruf*⟩; **be ∼ed with sth.** mit etw. behaftet sein (geh.)

Taiwan /taɪ'wɑːn/ *pr. n.* Taiwan (*das*)

take /teɪk/ **1** *v.t.*, **took** /tʊk/, **taken** /'teɪkn/ **(a)** (get hold of, grasp, seize) nehmen; **∼ sb.'s arm** jmds. Arm nehmen; **∼ sb. by the hand/arm** jmdn. bei der Hand/am Arm nehmen; **(b)** (capture) einnehmen ⟨*Stadt, Festung*⟩ machen ⟨*Gefangenen*⟩; (chess) schlagen; nehmen; **(c)** (gain, earn) ⟨*Laden:*⟩ einbringen ⟨*Film, Stück:*⟩ einspielen; (win) gewinnen ⟨*Satz, Spiel, Preis, Titel*⟩; erzielen ⟨*Punkte*⟩; (Cards) machen ⟨*Stich*⟩; **∼ first/second** *etc.* **place** den ersten/ zweiten *usw.* Platz belegen; (fig.) an erster/zweiter *usw.* Stelle kommen; **∼ the biscuit** (Brit. coll.) *or* (coll.) cake (fig.) alle/alles übertreffen; **(d)** (assume possession of) nehmen; **(∼ away with one)** mitnehmen; (steal) mitnehmen (verhüll.); (obtain by purchase) kaufen, (by rent) mieten ⟨*Auto, Wohnung, Haus*⟩; nehmen ⟨*Klavier-, Deutsch-, Fahrstunden*⟩; mitmachen ⟨*Tanzkurs*⟩; (buy regularly) nehmen; lesen ⟨*Zeitung, Zeitschrift*⟩; (subscribe to) beziehen; (obtain) erwerben ⟨*akademischen Grad*⟩; (form a relationship with) sich ⟨*Dat.*⟩ nehmen ⟨*Frau, Geliebten usw.*⟩; **that woman took my purse** die Frau hat mir meinen Geldbeutel gestohlen; **he took his degree at Sussex University** er hat sein Examen an der Universität von Sussex gemacht; **∼ place** stattfinden; (spontaneously) sich ereignen; ⟨*Wandlung:*⟩ sich vollziehen; **I'll ∼ this handbag/the curry, please** ich nehme diese Handtasche/das Curry; **who has ∼n my pencil?** wer hat meinen Bleistift weggenommen?; **(e)** (avail oneself of, use) nehmen; machen ⟨*Pause, Ferien, Nickerchen*⟩; nehmen ⟨*Beispiel, Zitat usw.*⟩ (**from** aus); **∼ the opportunity to do/of doing sth.** die Gelegenheit dazu benutzen, etw. zu tun; **∼ the car/bus into town** mit dem Auto/Bus in die Stadt fahren; **∼ two eggs** *etc.* (in recipe) man nehme zwei Eier *usw.;* **∼ all the time you want** nimm dir ruhig Zeit; [**let's**] **∼ a more recent example/my sister** [**for example**] nehmen wir ein Beispiel neueren Datums/einmal meine Schwester; **(f)** (carry, guide, convey) bringen; **∼ sb.'s shoes to the mender['s]/sb.'s coat to the cleaner's** jmds. Schuhe zum Schuster/jmds. Mantel in die Reinigung bringen; **∼ a message to sb.** jmdm. eine Nachricht überbringen; **∼ sb. to school/hospital** jmdn. zur Schule/ins Krankenhaus bringen; **∼ sb. to visit sb.** jmdn. zu Besuch bei jmdm. mitnehmen; **∼ sb. to the zoo/cinema/to dinner** mit jmdm. in den Zoo/ins Kino/ zum Abendessen gehen; **∼ sb. into one's home/house** jmdn. bei sich aufnehmen; **the road ∼s you/the story ∼s us to London** die Straße führt nach/die Erzählung führt uns nach London; **his ability will ∼ him far/to the top** mit seinen Fähigkeiten wird er es weit bringen/ wird er ganz nach oben kommen; **∼ sb./sth. with one** jmdn./etw. mitnehmen; **∼ home** mit nach Hause nehmen; (earn) nach Hause bringen ⟨*Geld*⟩; (accompany) nach Hause bringen *od.* begleiten; (to meet one's parents etc.) mit nach Hause bringen; **∼ sb. through/over sth.** (fig.) mit jmdm. etw. durchgehen; **∼ in hand** (begin) in Angriff nehmen; (assume responsibility for) sich kümmern um; **∼ sb. into partnership [with one]/into the business** jmdn. zu seinem Teilhaber machen/in sein Geschäft aufnehmen; **∼ a stick** *etc.* **to sb.** den Stock *usw.* bei jmdm. gebrauchen;

∼ **sth. to pieces** *or* **bits** etw. auseinander nehmen; **you can/can't ∼ sb. anywhere** (fig. coll.) man kann jmdn. überallhin/nirgendwohin mitnehmen; **you can't ∼ it 'with you** (coll.) man kann es ja nicht mitnehmen; **(g)** (remove) nehmen; (deduct) abziehen; ∼ **sth./sb. from sb.** jmdm. etw./jmdn. wegnehmen; **I took the parcel from her** ich nahm ihr das Paket ab; ∼ **all the fun/hard work out of sth.** einem alle Freude an etw. *(Dat.)* nehmen/einem die schwere Arbeit bei etw. ersparen; **(h) sb. ∼s courage from sb.** etw. macht jmdm. Mut; *see also* **heart a; (i) be ∼n ill** *or* (coll.) **sick** krank werden; **(j)** (make) machen ⟨*Foto, Kopie*⟩; (photograph) aufnehmen; **(k)** (perform, execute) aufnehmen ⟨*Brief, Diktat*⟩; machen ⟨*Prüfung, Sprung, Spaziergang, Reise, Umfrage*⟩; durchführen ⟨*Befragung, Volkszählung*⟩; ablegen ⟨*Gelübde, Eid*⟩; übernehmen ⟨*Rolle, Part*⟩; treffen ⟨*Entscheidung*⟩; ∼ **a fall/tumble** stürzen/straucheln; ∼ **a step forward/backward** einen Schritt vor-/zurücktreten; ∼ **a turn for the better/ worse** eine Wende zum Besseren/Schlechteren nehmen; **(l)** (negotiate) nehmen ⟨*Zaun, Mauer, Hürde, Kurve, Hindernis*⟩; **(m)** (conduct) halten ⟨*Gottesdienst, Andacht, Unterricht*⟩; **Ms X ∼s us for maths** in Mathe haben wir Frau X; **(n)** (be taught) ∼ **Latin at school** in der Schule Latein haben; **(o)** (consume) trinken ⟨*Tee, Kaffee, Kognak usw.*⟩; nehmen ⟨*Zucker, Milch, Überdosis, Tabletten, Medizin*⟩; ∼ **sugar in one's tea** den Tee mit Zucker trinken; **what can I ∼ for a cold?** was kann ich gegen eine Erkältung nehmen?; **to be ∼n three times a day** dreimal täglich einzunehmen; **not to be ∼n [internally]** nicht zur innerlichen Anwendung; **(p)** (occupy) einnehmen ⟨*Sitz im Parlament*⟩; übernehmen, antreten ⟨*Amt*⟩; ∼ **sb.'s seat** auf jmds. Platz setzen; **is that/this seat ∼n?** ist da/hier noch frei?; **(q)** (need, require) brauchen ⟨*Platz, Zeit*⟩; haben ⟨*Kleider-, Schuhgröße usw.*⟩; (Ling.) haben ⟨*Objekt, Plural-s*⟩; gebraucht werden mit ⟨*Kasus*⟩; **this verb ∼s 'sein'** dieses Verb wird mit „sein" konjugiert; **the wound will ∼ some time to heal** es braucht einige Zeit, bis die Wunde geheilt ist; **the ticket machine ∼s 20p and 50p coins** der Fahrkartenautomat nimmt 20-Pence- und 50-Pence-Stücke; **as long as it ∼s** so lange wie nötig; **sth. ∼s an hour/a year/all day** etw. dauert eine Stunde ein Jahr/einen ganzen Tag; **it ∼s an hour** *etc.* **to do sth.** es dauert eine Stunde *usw.*, [um] etw. zu tun; **sb. ∼s** *or* **it ∼s sb. a long time/an hour** *etc.* **to do sth.** jmd. braucht lange/eine Stunde *usw.*, um etw. zu tun; **what took you so long?** was hast du denn so lange gemacht?; ∼ **a lot of work/effort/courage** viel Arbeit/ Mühe/Mut kosten; **have [got] what it ∼s** das Zeug dazu haben; **it will ∼ [quite] a lot of explaining** es wird schwer zu erklären sein; **that story of his ∼s some believing** die Geschichte, die er da erzählt, ist kaum zu glauben; **it ∼s a thief to know a thief** nur ein Dieb kennt eine Dieb; **it ∼s all sorts [to make a world]** es gibt solche und solche; **(r)** (contain, hold) fassen; (support) tragen; **(s)** ▶**1141|** (ascertain and record) notieren ⟨*Namen, Adresse, Autonummer usw.*⟩; fühlen ⟨*Puls*⟩; messen ⟨*Temperatur, Größe usw.*⟩; ∼ **the minutes of a meeting** bei einer Sitzung [das] Protokoll führen; **(t)** (apprehend, grasp) ∼ **sb.'s meaning/drift** verstehen, was jmd. meint; ∼ **sth.'s point** jmds. Standpunkt verstehen; ∼ **it [that] ...: annehmen, [dass] ...; can I ∼ it that ...?** kann ich davon ausgehen, dass ...?; ∼ **sth. to mean sth.** etw. so verstehen, dass ...; **what do you ∼ that to mean?** wie verstehen Sie das?; ∼ **sth. as settled/as a compliment/refusal** etw. als erledigt betrachten/als eine Ablehnung/ein Kompliment auffassen; ∼ **sb./sth. for/to be sth.** jmdn./etw. für etw. halten; **what do you ∼ me for?** wofür halten Sie mich?; **(u)** (treat or react to in a specified manner) aufnehmen; ∼ **sth. like a man** etw. wie ein Mann nehmen; ∼ **sth. well/badly/hard** etw. gut/schlecht/nur schwer verkraften; **sb. ∼s sth. very badly/hard** etw. trifft jmdn. sehr; ∼ **sth. calmly** *or* **coolly** etw. gelassen [auf- *od.* hin]nehmen; ∼ **sth. as read** etw. als bekannt voraussetzen; **you can/may ∼ it as read that ...:** du kannst sicher sein, dass ...; **taking it all in all, taking one thing with another** alles in allem; **(v)** (accept) annehmen; ∼ **money** *etc.* **[from sb./for sth.]** Geld *usw.* [von jmdm./für etw.] [an]nehmen; **will you ∼ £500 for the**

car? wollen Sie den Wagen für 500 Pfund verkaufen?; **[you can] ∼ it or leave it** entweder du bist damit einverstanden, oder du lässt es bleiben; ∼ **the hint** den Wink verstehen; ∼ **sb.'s word for it** sich auf jmdn. *od.* jmds. Wort[e] verlassen; **you don't have to ∼ my word for it** du brauchst es mir nicht zu glauben; ∼ **things as they come,** ∼ **it as it comes** es nehmen, wie es kommt; **(w)** (receive, submit to) einstecken [müssen] ⟨*Schlag, Tritt, Stoß*⟩; (Boxing) nehmen [müssen] ⟨*Schlag*⟩; (endure, tolerate) aushalten; vertragen ⟨*Klima, Alkohol, Kaffee, Knoblauch*⟩; verwinden ⟨*Schock*⟩; (put up with) sich *(Dat.)* gefallen lassen [müssen] ⟨*Kritik, Grobheit*⟩; ∼ **one's punishment bravely** seine Strafe tapfer ertragen; ∼ **no nonsense** sich *(Dat.)* nichts bieten lassen; ∼ **'that!** nimm das!; ∼ **it** (coll.) es verkraften; (referring to criticism, abuse) damit fertigwerden; **(x)** (adopt, choose) ergreifen ⟨*Maßnahmen*⟩; unternehmen ⟨*Schritte*⟩; einschlagen ⟨*Weg*⟩; sich entschließen zu ⟨*Schritt, Handlungsweise*⟩; ∼ **the wrong road** die falsche Straße nehmen; ∼ **a firm** *etc.* **stand [with sb./on** *or* **over sth.]** jmdm. gegenüber/hinsichtlich einer Sache nicht nachgeben; ∼ **the easy way out** die einfachste Lösung wählen; **(y)** (receive, accommodate) [an]nehmen ⟨*Bewerber, Schüler*⟩; aufnehmen ⟨*Gäste*⟩; **the city ∼s its name from its founder** die Stadt ist nach ihrem Gründer benannt; **(z)** (swindle) **he was ∼n for £500 by the conman** (coll.) der Schwindler hat ihm 500 Pfund abgeknöpft (ugs.); **(aa) be ∼n with sb./sth.** von jmdm./etw. angetan sein. **2** *v.i.*, **took, taken (a)** (be successful, effective) ⟨*Transplantat:*⟩ vom Körper angenommen werden; ⟨*Impfung:*⟩ anschlagen; ⟨*Pfropfreis:*⟩ anwachsen; ⟨*Sämling, Pflanze:*⟩ angehen; ⟨*Feuer:*⟩ zu brennen beginnen; ⟨*Fisch:*⟩ [an]beißen; **(b)** (detract) ∼ **from sth.** etw. schmälern. **3** *n.* (Telev., Cinemat.) Einstellung, *die*; Take, *der od. das* (fachspr.)

∼ **after** *v.t.* ∼ **after sb.** (resemble) jmdm. ähnlich sein; (∼ as one's example) es jmdm. gleichtun

∼ **a'long** *v.t.* mitnehmen

∼ **a'part** ⇒ **apart b**

∼ **a'round** *v.t.* **(a)** (∼ with one) überallhin mitnehmen; **(b)** (show around) herumführen

∼ **a'side** ⇒ **aside 1**

∼ **a'way** *v.t.* **(a)** (remove) wegnehmen; (to a distance) mitnehmen; ∼ **sth. away from sb.** jmdm. etw. abnehmen; ∼ **sb.'s licence/passport away** jmdm. den Führerschein/Pass abnehmen; **to ∼ away** ⟨*Pizza, Snack usw.*⟩ zum Mitnehmen; ∼ **away sb.'s rights/privileges/freedom** jmdm. seine Rechte/Privilegien/die Freiheit nehmen; ∼ **sb. away** jmdn. wegbringen; ⟨*Polizei:*⟩ jmdn. abführen; ∼ **him away!** schafft ihn fort!; hinweg mit ihm! (geh.); **a child away from its parents/home/from school** ein Kind den Eltern wegnehmen/aus seiner häuslichen Umgebung herausreißen/aus der Schule nehmen; **(b)** (Math.: deduct) abziehen

∼ **a'way from** *v.t.* schmälern

∼ **'back** *v.t.* **(a)** (retract, have back) zurücknehmen; wieder einstellen ⟨*Arbeitnehmer*⟩; wieder [bei sich] aufnehmen ⟨*Ehepartner*⟩; (reclaim) sich *(Dat.)* wiedergeben lassen; **(b)** (return) zurückbringen; (∼ somewhere again) wieder bringen ⟨*Person*⟩; (carry or convey back) wieder mitnehmen; **that ∼s me back [to my childhood]** das weckt bei mir [Kindheits]erinnerungen

∼ **'down** *v.t.* **(a)** (carry or lead down) hinunterbringen; **this path ∼s you down to the harbour** auf diesem Weg kommen Sie zum Hafen [hinunter]; **(b)** (lower or lift down) abnehmen ⟨*Bild, Ankündigung, Weihnachtsschmuck*⟩; einholen ⟨*Fahne*⟩; herunterziehen, herunterlassen ⟨*Hose*⟩; ∼ **a box down from a shelf** eine Schachtel von einem Regal herunternehmen; **(c)** (dismantle) abreißen; abbauen ⟨*Gerüst, Zelt*⟩; **(d)** (write down) aufnehmen ⟨*Brief, Personalien*⟩; aufschreiben ⟨*Autonummer*⟩; mitschreiben ⟨*Vortrag*⟩

∼ **'in** *v.t.* **(a)** (convey to a place) hinbringen; (conduct) hineinführen ⟨*Gast*⟩; (coll.: ∼ for repair or service) wegbringen (ugs.) ⟨*Auto, Gerät usw.*⟩; ∼ **sb. in [in the car]** jmdn. [mit dem Auto] reinfahren (ugs.); **I took the car in** ich fuhr mit dem Auto rein (ugs.); **(b)** (bring indoors) hereinholen; **(c)** (receive, admit) aufnehmen; (for payment) vermieten an (+ *Akk.*); [auf]nehmen ⟨[*Kur*]*gäste*⟩; ∼ **in lodgers** ⟨*Haus-,*

Wohnungseigentümer:⟩ Zimmer vermieten; **(d)** (make narrower) enger machen ⟨*Kleidungsstück*⟩; **(e)** (include, comprise) einbeziehen; **(f)** (coll.: visit) mitnehmen (ugs.); **our tour took in most of the main sights** auf unserer Rundfahrt haben wir die wichtigsten Sehenswürdigkeiten besichtigt; **(g)** (understand, grasp) begreifen; überblicken, erfassen ⟨*Lage*⟩; **(h)** (observe) erfassen; (watch, listen to) mitbekommen; **(i)** (deceive) einwickeln (salopp); **be** ∼**n in [by sb./sth.]** sich [von jmdm./durch etw.] einwickeln lassen (salopp)

∼ **'off 1** *v.t.* **(a)** abnehmen ⟨*Deckel, Hut, Bild, Hörer, Tischtuch, Verband*⟩; ausziehen ⟨*Schuhe, Handschuhe*⟩; ablegen ⟨*Hut, Mantel, Schmuck*⟩; ∼ **the cover off a pillow/ bed** ein Kissen abziehen/ein Bett abdecken; ∼ **a parcel off sb.** jmdm. ein Paket abnehmen; ∼ **your hands off me!** fass mich nicht an!; **(b)** (transfer from) übernehmen ⟨*Passagiere, Besatzung, Fracht*⟩; ∼ **sb. off sth.** jmdm. von etw. holen; (withdraw from job, assignment, etc.) jmdm. etw. entziehen; ∼ **sth. off a list/the menu** etw. von einer Liste streichen/von der Speisekarte nehmen; ∼ **a train/ bus off a route** einen Zug/Bus vom Fahrplan streichen; **(c)** (cut off) abtrennen; (with saw) absägen; (with knife, scissors, etc.) abschneiden; (amputate) amputieren; **(d)** (lead, conduct) ∼ **sb. off to hospital/prison** jmdn. ins Krankenhaus/Gefängnis bringen; **(e)** (deduct) abziehen; ∼ **sth. off sth.** etw. von etw. abziehen; ∼ **£10 off the price** den Preis um zehn Pfund reduzieren; **(f)** ∼ **off weight/a few pounds** (lose weight) abnehmen/einige Pfund abnehmen; **(g)** (have free) ∼ **a day** *etc.* **off** sich (*Dat.*) einen Tag *usw.* frei nehmen (ugs.); ∼ **time off [work** *or* **from work]** sich (*Dat.*) frei nehmen; **(h)** (mimic) nachmachen (ugs.). **2** *v.i.* **(a)** (Aeronaut.) starten; **(b)** (Sport) ⟨*Springer, Pferd:*⟩ abspringen

∼ **'on** *v.t.* **(a)** (undertake) übernehmen; annehmen ⟨*Herausforderung, Wette usw.*⟩; auf sich (*Akk.*) nehmen ⟨*Bürde*⟩; (accept responsibility for) sich einlassen auf (+ *Akk.*) ⟨*Person*⟩; sich (*Dat.*) aufbürden *od.* aufladen ⟨*Sache*⟩; **(b)** (enrol, employ) einstellen; aufnehmen ⟨*Schüler, Studenten*⟩; annehmen ⟨*Privatschüler*⟩; **(c)** (acquire, assume) annehmen ⟨*Farbe, Form, Ausdruck, Ausmaße*⟩; erhalten ⟨*Bedeutung*⟩; **(d)** (accept as opponent) sich auf eine Auseinandersetzung einlassen mit; es aufnehmen mit; den Kampf aufnehmen mit ⟨*Regierung, Gesetz*⟩; **(e)** (∼ on board) aufnehmen

∼ **'out** *v.t.* **(a)** (remove) herausnehmen; ziehen ⟨*Zahn*⟩; ∼ **sth. out of sth.,** ∼ **out sth. from sth.** etw. aus etw. [heraus]nehmen; ∼ **it/a lot out of sb.** (fig.) jmdn. mitnehmen/sehr mitnehmen; **(b)** (destroy) zerstören; (fig.) (Footb. etc.) ausschalten; (kill) töten; **(c)** (withdraw) abheben ⟨*Geld*⟩; **(d)** (deduct) abziehen **(of** von); **(e)** (go out with) ∼ **sb. out** mit jmdm. ausgehen; ∼ **sb. out for a walk/drive** mit jmdm. einen Spaziergang/eine Spazierfahrt machen; ∼ **sb. out to** *or* **for lunch/out to the cinema** jmdn. zum Mittagessen/ins Kino einladen; ∼ **the dog out [for a walk]** den Hund ausführen; **(f)** (get issued) erwerben; erhalten; abschließen ⟨*Versicherung*⟩; ausleihen ⟨*Bücher*⟩; aufgeben ⟨*Anzeige*⟩; ∼ **out a subscription to sth.** etw. abonnieren; **(g)** ∼ **it/sth. out on sb./sth.** seine Wut/ etw. an jmdm./etw. auslassen

∼ **'over 1** *v.t.* **(a)** (assume control of) übernehmen; ∼ **sth. over from sb.** etw. von jmdm. übernehmen; ∼ **sb./sth. over** (fig.) von jmdm./etw. Besitz ergreifen; (carry or transport over) ∼ **sb./sth. over to sb./sb.'s flat/Guildford** jmdn./etw. zu jmdm./in jmds. Wohnung/nach Guildford bringen *od.* (ugs.) rüberbringen. **2** *v.i.* übernehmen; ⟨*Manager, Firmenleiter:*⟩ die Geschäfte übernehmen; ⟨*Regierung, Präsident:*⟩ die Amtsgeschäfte übernehmen; ⟨*Beifahrer:*⟩ das Steuer übernehmen; **the night nurse** ∼**s over at 10 p.m.** um zehn Uhr [abends] tritt die Nachtschwester ihren Dienst an

∼ **'round** *v.t.* **(a)** (carry, deliver) vorbeibringen; **(b)** (show around) [herum]führen; ∼ **sb. round the factory** jmdn. durch die Fabrik führen

∼ **to** *v.i.* **(a)** (get into habit of) ∼ **to doing sth.** anfangen, etw. zu tun; es sich (*Dat.*) angewöhnen, etw. zu tun; ∼ **to drugs/gambling/crime** zu Drogen greifen/dem Spiel/ der Kriminalität verfallen; **(b)** (escape to) sich flüchten in (+ *Akk.*); **(c)** (develop a liking for) sich hingezogen fühlen zu ⟨*Person*⟩; sich erwärmen für ⟨*Sache*⟩; (adapt oneself to) sich gewöhnen an (+ *Akk.*)

∼ **'up 1** *v.t.* **(a)** (lift up) hochheben; (pick up) aufheben; aufnehmen ⟨*Staub, Partikel*⟩; herausnehmen ⟨*Pflanzen*⟩; herausreißen ⟨*Schienenstrang, Dielen*⟩; aufreißen ⟨*Straße*⟩; **(b)** (move up) weiter nach oben rücken; (shorten) kürzer machen; **(c)** (carry or lead up) ∼ **sb./sth. up** jmdn./ etw. hinaufbringen (to zu); ∼ **sth. up to sb.** jmdm. etw. hinaufbringen; **(d)** (absorb) aufnehmen; **(e)** (wind up) aufwickeln; **(f)** (occupy, engage) beanspruchen; **I'm sorry to have** ∼**n up so much of your time** es tut mir Leid, Ihre Zeit so lange in Anspruch genommen zu haben; **(g)** ergreifen ⟨*Beruf*⟩; anfangen ⟨*Jogging, Tennis, Schach, Gitarre*⟩; ∼ **up a musical instrument** ein Instrument zu spielen beginnen; ∼ **up German/a hobby** anfangen, Deutsch zu lernen/sich (*Dat.*) ein Hobby zulegen; **(h)** (start, adopt) aufnehmen ⟨*Arbeit, Kampf*⟩; antreten ⟨*Stelle*⟩; übernehmen ⟨*Pflicht, Funktion*⟩; einnehmen ⟨*Haltung, Position*⟩; eintreten für, sich einsetzen für ⟨*Sache*⟩; ∼ **up a/one's position** ⟨*Polizeiposten, Politiker:*⟩ Position beziehen; **(i)** (accept) annehmen; aufnehmen ⟨*Idee, Vorschlag, Kredit, Geld*⟩; kaufen ⟨*Aktien*⟩; **(j)** (raise, pursue further) aufgreifen; ∼ **sth. up with sb.** sich in einer Sache an jmdn. wenden; **(k)** ∼ **sb. up [on sth.]** (accept) jmdn. [in Bezug auf etw. (*Akk.*)] beim Wort nehmen. **2** *v.i.* **(a)** (coll.: become friendly) ∼ **up with sb.** sich mit jmdm. einlassen; **(b)** ∼ **up where sb./sth. has left off** da einsetzen, wo jmd./ etw. aufgehört hat

∼ **upon** *v.t.* ∼ **upon oneself** auf sich (*Akk.*) nehmen ⟨*Aufgabe, Pflicht, Verantwortung*⟩; ∼ **it upon oneself to do sth.** es auf sich (*Akk.*) nehmen, etw. zu tun; (in an interfering way) sich (*Dat.*) herausnehmen (ugs.), etw. zu tun

take: ∼**away** *n.* (restaurant) Restaurant mit Straßenverkauf; (meal) Essen zum Mitnehmen; *attrib.* ⟨*Restaurant*⟩ mit Straßenverkauf; ⟨*Essen, Mahlzeit*⟩ zum Mitnehmen; ∼**-home** *attrib. adj.* ∼**-home pay/wages** Nettolohn, *der*

taken ⇒ **take 1, 2**

take: ∼**-off** *n.* **(a)** (Sport) Absprung, *der;* **(b)** (Aeronaut.) Start, *der;* Take-off, *das* (fachspr.); **(c)** (coll.: caricature) Parodie, *die;* ∼**out** (Amer.) ⇒ **takeaway;** ∼**-over** *n.* (Commerc.) Übernahme, *die;* ∼**-over bid** Übernahmeangebot, *das*

taker /'teɪkə(r)/ *n.* **there were no** ∼**s [for the offer]** niemand hat [das Angebot] angenommen

taking /'teɪkɪŋ/ *n.* **(a)** *in pl.* (amount taken) Einnahmen; **(b)** (seizure) Einnahme, *die;* **(c)** **they are yours/his** *etc.* **for the** ∼: du kannst/er kann *usw.* sie haben; **victory was his for the** ∼: sein Sieg war so gut wie sicher

talc /tælk/ *n.* Talkum, *das*

talcum /'tælkəm/ *n.* Talkumpuder, *der;* Talkum, *das;* (as cosmetic) ∼ **[powder]** Körperpuder, *der*

tale /teɪl/ *n.* **(a)** (story) Erzählung, *die;* Geschichte, *die* (**of** von, **about** über + *Akk.*); **(b)** (piece of gossip) Geschichte, *die* (ugs.)

talent /'tælənt/ *n.* **(a)** (ability) Talent, *das;* **have [great/no** *etc.*] ∼ **[for sth.]** [viel/kein *usw.*] Talent [zu *od.* für etw.] haben; **have a** ∼ **for music** musikalisches Talent haben; **have a [great]** ∼ **for doing sth.** das Talent haben, etw. zu tun; **(b)** (people with ability) Talente; Begabungen

talented /'tæləntɪd/ *adj.* talentiert

talk /tɔːk/ **1** *n.* **(a)** (discussion) Gespräch, *das;* **have a** ∼ **[with sb.] [about sth.]** [mit jmdm.] [über etw. (*Akk.*)] reden *od.* sprechen; **have a long** ∼ **on the phone** lange miteinander telefonieren; **could I have a** ∼ **with you?** könnte ich Sie einmal sprechen?; **have** *or* **hold** ∼**s [with sb.]** [mit jmdm.] Gespräche führen; **(b)** (speech, lecture) Vortrag, *der;* **give a** ∼**/a series of** ∼**s [on sth./sb.]** einen Vortrag/eine Vortragsreihe [über etw./jmdn.] halten; **(c)** *no pl.* (form of communication) Sprache, *die;* **(d)** *no pl.* (talking) Gerede, *das* (abwertend); **there's too much** ∼ **[of ...]** es wird zu viel [von ...] geredet; **be the** ∼ **of the town/ neighbourhood** *etc.* Stadtgespräch/das Thema in der Nachbarschaft *usw.* sein. **2** *v.i.* **(a)** (speak) sprechen, reden **(with, to** mit); (lecture) sprechen; (converse) sich unterhalten; (have ∼s) Gespräche führen; (gossip) reden; **be** ∼**ing in German** deutsch sprechen; **love to hear oneself** ∼: sich gern reden hören; **we must** ∼: wir müssen miteinander reden; ∼ **on the phone** telefonieren; **keep sb.** ∼**ing** jmdn. in ein [längeres] Gespräch verwickeln; **now**

you're ~ing! (coll.) das hört sich schon besser an; **that's no way to ~/~ to your uncle** das darfst du nicht sagen/so darfst du aber nicht mit deinem Onkel reden!; **it's easy for you/him** etc. **to ~:** du hast/er hat usw. gut reden; **look who's ~ing** (iron.) das musst du gerade sagen; **you can** (iron.) or can't **~!** sei du nur ganz still!; **could·I ~ to you for a moment?** könnte ich Sie einen Augenblick sprechen?; **get ~ing [to sb.]** [mit jmdm.] ins Gespräch kommen; **~ to oneself** Selbstgespräche führen; **~ of** or **about sb./sth.** über jmdn./etw. reden; **everyone's ~ing about him/his divorce** er/seine Scheidung ist in aller Munde; **~ of** or **about doing sth.** davon reden, etw. zu tun; **[not] know what one is ~ing about** [gar nicht] wissen, wovon man redet; **[not] know what sb. is ~ing about** [nicht] wissen, was jmd. meint od. wovon jmd. spricht; **~ing of holidays** etc. da wir [gerade] vom Urlaub usw. sprechen; **(b)** (have power of speech) sprechen; **(c)** (betray secrets) reden; **make sb. ~:** jmdn. zum Reden bringen. **3** v.t. **(a)** (utter, express) **~ [a load of] nonsense** [eine Menge] Unsinn od. (ugs.) Stuss reden; **(b)** (discuss) **~ politics/music** etc. über Politik/Musik usw. reden; **(c)** (use) sprechen ‹Sprache, Dialekt usw.›; **(d)** **~ oneself hoarse** sich heiser reden; **~ oneself** or **one's way out of trouble** sich aus Schwierigkeiten herausreden; **~ sb. into/out of sth.** jmdn. zu etw. überreden/jmdm. etw. ausreden

~ 'down 1 v.t. (silence) in Grund und Boden reden. **2** v.i. **~ down to sb.** von oben herab od. herablassend mit jmdm. reden

~ 'over v.t. **(a)** **~ sth. over [with sb.]** etw. [mit jmdm.] besprechen; **(b)** (persuade) **~ sb. over** jmdn. überreden

~ 'round v.t. **(a)** (persuade) **~ sb. round** jmdn. überreden; **(b)** (skirt) **~ round sth.** um etw. herumreden (ugs.)

~ 'through v.t. **~ sb. through sth.** etw. mit jmdm. durchgehen od. durchsprechen; **~ sth. through** etw. durchsprechen

talkative /'tɔ:kətɪv/ adj. gesprächig; geschwätzig (abwertend)

'talked-of attrib. adj. much **~:** viel diskutiert ‹Buch, Stück, Projekt›; **a much ~ actor/artist** ein Schauspieler/Künstler, der in aller Munde ist

talker /'tɔ:kə(r)/ n. **(a)** Redner, der/Rednerin, die; **(b)** (one who talks but does not act) Schwätzer, der/Schwätzerin, die

talking /'tɔ:kɪŋ/ **1** n. Reden, das; **do [all] the ~:** das Gespräch dominieren; **let me do the ~:** überlass lieber mir das Reden. **2** adj. sprechend

talking: ~ point n. Gesprächsthema, das; **~ shop** n. (derog.) Quasselbude, die (ugs. abwertend); **~-to** /'tɔ:k-ɪntu:/ n. (coll.) Standpauke, die (ugs.); **give sb. a good ~-to** jmdm. eine ordentliche Standpauke halten (ugs.)

'talk show n. Talk-Show, die

tall /tɔ:l/ adj. **(a)** ▶ 850 hoch; groß ‹Person, Tier›; **grow ~:** groß werden; wachsen; **(b)** (coll.: excessive) **a ~ tale** eine unglaubwürdige Geschichte; **that's a ~ order** das ist ziemlich viel verlangt; see also **story**[1] **a**

'tallboy n. Doppelkommode, die; Tallboy, der

tallow /'tæləʊ/ n. Talg, der

tally /'tælɪ/ **1** n. (record) **sb.'s ~ is 18 goals** jmd. kann 18 Tore für sich verbuchen; **keep a [daily] ~ of sth.** [täglich] über etw. (Akk.) Buch führen. **2** v.i. übereinstimmen

talon /'tælən/ n. Klaue, die; **~s** (fig.: long fingernails) Krallen (ugs. abwertend)

tambourine /tæmbə'ri:n/ n. (Mus.) Tamburin, das

tame /teɪm/ **1** adj. **(a)** zahm; (joc.) hauseigen ‹Anarchist, Genie usw.›; **grow/become ~:** zahm werden; **(b)** (spiritless) lahm (ugs.), lustlos ‹Einwilligung, Anerkennung, Kampagne, Versuch›; zahm (ugs.) ‹Besprechung, Kritik›; **(c)** (dull) wenig aufregend; lasch ‹Stil›. **2** v.t. (lit. or fig.) zähmen

tamper /'tæmpə(r)/ v.i. **~ with** sich (Dat.) zu schaffen machen an (+ Dat.)

tampon /'tæmpɒn/ n. Tampon, der

tan /tæn/ **1** v.t., **-nn-: (a)** gerben; **(b)** (bronze) ‹Sonne:› bräunen; ‹Person:› braun werden lassen ‹Körperteil›; **(c)** (sl.: beat) das Fell gerben (salopp) (+ Dat.). **2** v.i., **-nn-** braun werden. **3** n. **(a)** (colour) Gelbbraun, das; **(b)** (sun-~)

Bräune, die; **have/get a ~:** braun sein/werden. **4** adj. gelbbraun

tandem /'tændəm/ n. Tandem, das; **~ bicycle** Tandem, das; **coupled/harnessed in ~:** hintereinander gekoppelt/-gespannt

tang /tæŋ/ n. (taste/smell) [sharp] **~:** scharfer Geschmack/Geruch; **[spicy/salty] ~:** würziger/salziger Geschmack/Geruch

tangent /'tændʒənt/ n. (Math.) Tangente, die; **go** or **fly off at a ~** (fig.) plötzlich vom Thema abschweifen

tangerine /tændʒə'ri:n/ n. **(a)** (fruit) **~ [orange]** Tangerine, die; **(b)** (colour) Orangerot, das

tangible /'tændʒɪbl/ adj. **(a)** (perceptible by touch) fühlbar; **(b)** (fig.: real, definite) greifbar; spürbar, merklich ‹Unterschied, Verbesserung›; handfest ‹Beweis›

tangle /'tæŋgl/ **1** n. Gewirr, das; (in hair) Verfilzung, die; (fig.: dispute) Auseinandersetzung, die; **be in a ~:** sich verheddert haben (ugs.); ‹Haar:› sich verfilzt haben; (fig.) ‹Angelegenheiten:› in Unordnung (Dat.) sein; ‹Person:› verwirrt sein. **2** v.t. verheddern (ugs.); verfilzen ‹Haar›

~ 'up v.t. verheddern (ugs.); verfilzen ‹Haar›; **become** or **get ~d up** sich verheddern (ugs.)

~ with v.t. (coll.) **~ with sb.** sich mit jmdm. anlegen

tangled /'tæŋgld/ adj. verheddert (ugs.); verfilzt ‹Haar›; (confused, complicated) verworren; verwickelt ‹Angelegenheit›

tango /'tæŋgəʊ/ n., pl. **~s** Tango, der

tangy /'tæŋɪ/ adj. scharf; (spicy) würzig; (salty) salzig

tank /tæŋk/ n. **(a)** Tank, der; (for fish etc.) Aquarium, das; (for rainwater) Auffangbecken, das; **fill the ~** (with petrol) volltanken; **(b)** (Mil.) Panzer, der

~ 'up v.i. (get fuel) auftanken. **2** v.t. auftanken; **get ~ed up** (coll.: drunk) sich volltanken (salopp)

tankard /'tæŋkəd/ n. Krug, der; **a ~ of beer** etc. ein Krug Bier usw.

tanker /'tæŋkə(r)/ n. (ship) Tanker, der; Tankschiff, das; (vehicle) Tank[last]wagen, der

tanned /tænd/ adj. braun gebrannt

tanner /'tænə(r)/ n. (person) Gerber, der/Gerberin, die

tannery /'tænərɪ/ n. Gerberei, die

Tannoy, (P) /'tænɔɪ/ n. Lautsprecher, der; **over** or **on the ~:** über Lautsprecher

tantalise, tantalising ⇒ **tantaliz-**

tantalize /'tæntəlaɪz/ v.t. reizen; (tease also) zappeln lassen (ugs.); (with promises) [falsche] Hoffnungen wecken bei

tantalizing /'tæntəlaɪzɪŋ/ adj. verlockend; **a ~ puzzle** ein Rätsel, das einen nicht loslässt

tantamount /'tæntəmaʊnt/ pred. adj. **be ~ to sth.** gleichbedeutend mit etw. sein; einer Sache (Dat.) gleichkommen

tantrum /'tæntrəm/ n. Wutanfall, der; (of child) Trotzanfall, der; **be in a ~:** einen Wutanfall/Trotzanfall haben; **get into/throw a ~:** einen Wutanfall/Trotzanfall bekommen

Tanzania /tænzə'ni:ə/ pr. n. Tansania (das)

tap[1] /tæp/ **1** n. **(a)** Hahn, der; (on barrel, cask) [Zapf]hahn, der; **hot/cold[-water] ~:** Warm-/Kaltwasserhahn, der; **on ~:** vom Fass nachgestellt; **be on ~** (fig.) zur Verfügung stehen; **have on ~** (fig.) zur Verfügung haben ‹Geld, Mittel›; an der Hand haben ‹Experten›; **(b)** (plug) Zapfen, der; Spund, der. **2** v.t., **-pp-: (a)** (make use of) erschließen ‹Reserven, Ressourcen, Bezirk, Markt, Land, Einnahmequelle›; **(b)** (Teleph.: intercept) abhören; anzapfen (ugs.)

tap[2] **1** v.t., **-pp-** (strike lightly) klopfen an (+ Akk.); (on upper surface) klopfen auf (+ Akk.); **~ one's fingers on the table** (repeatedly) mit den Fingern auf den Tisch trommeln; **~ one's foot** mit dem Fuß auf den Boden klopfen; **~ one's foot to the music** mit dem Fuß den Takt schlagen; **~ sb. on the shoulder** jmdm. auf die Schulter klopfen/ (more lightly) tippen. **2** v.i., **-pp-: ~ at/on sth.** an etw. (Akk.) klopfen; (on upper surface) auf etw. (Akk.) klopfen. **3** n. Klopfen, das; (given to naughty child) Klaps, der (ugs.); **there was a ~ at/on the door** es klopfte an die Tür; **I felt a ~ on my shoulder** jemand klopfte/(more lightly) tippte mir auf die Schulter

~ **'in** *v.t.* einklopfen ‹*Nagel usw.*›
~ **'out** *v.t.* (a) (knock out) ausklopfen ‹*Pfeife*›; herausklopfen ‹*Nagel, Keil*›; (b) klopfen ‹*Rhythmus, Takt*›; (in Morse) morsen ‹*Nachricht*›; (on typewriter) tippen (ugs.)
tap: ~**-dance 1** *n.* Stepp[tanz], *der;* **2** *v.i.* Stepp tanzen; steppen; ~**-dancer** *n.* Stepptänzer, *der/*-tänzerin, *die;* ~**-dancing** *n.* Stepptanz, *der;* Steppen, *das*
tape /teɪp/ **1** *n.* (a) Band, *das;* **adhesive**/(coll.) **sticky** ~: Klebstreifen, *der;* Klebeband, *das;* (b) (Sport) Zielband, *das;* (c) (for recording) [Ton]band, *das* (of mit); **[have sth.] on** ~: [etw.] auf Band (*Dat.*) [haben]; **put/record sth. on** ~, **make a** ~ **of sth.** etw. auf Band (*Akk.*) aufnehmen; **blank** ~: unbespieltes Band; (d) **[paper]** ~: Papierstreifen, *der;* (punched with holes) Lochstreifen, *der.* **2** *v.t.* (a) (record on ~) [auf Band (*Akk.*)] aufnehmen; (b) (bind with ~) [mit Klebeband *od.* Klebstreifen] zukleben ‹*Paket*›; kleben ‹*Einband, eingerissene Seite*›; (c) **have got sb./sth.** ~**d** (coll.) jmdn. durchschaut haben/etw. im Griff *od.* unter Kontrolle haben
~ **to'gether** *v.t.* [mit Klebeband] zusammenkleben
~ **'up** *v.t.* [mit Klebeband] zukleben; [mit Klebeband] zusammenkleben ‹*zerrissene Seite, zerbrochene Pfeife usw.*›
tape: ~ **cassette** *n.* Tonbandkassette, *die;* ~ **deck** *n.* Tapedeck, *das;* ~**-measure** *n.* Bandmaß, *das;* (for measuring garments etc.) [Zenti]metermaß, *das;* ~**-player** *n.* Tonband[wiedergabe]gerät, *das*
taper /'teɪpə(r)/ **1** *v.t.* sich verjüngen lassen; ~ **[to a point]** spitz zulaufen lassen; **be** ~**ed** sich verjüngen; (to a point) spitz zulaufen. **2** *v.i.* sich verjüngen; ~ **[to a point]** spitz zulaufen. **3** *n.* **[wax]** ~: Wachsstock, *der*
~ **away** ⇒ ~ **off** 2
~ **'off 1** *v.t.* ⇒ ~ **1. 2** *v.i.* (a) ⇒ ~ **2;** (b) (fig.: decrease gradually) zurückgehen
tape: ~**-record** /'teɪprɪkɔːd/ *v.t.* [auf Tonband (*Akk.*)] aufnehmen *od.* aufzeichnen; ~ **recorder** *n.* Tonbandgerät, *das;* ~ **recording** *n.* Tonbandaufnahme, *die*
tapered /'teɪpəd/, **tapering** /'teɪpərɪŋ/ *adjs.* sich verjüngend; (to a point) spitz zulaufend
tapestry /'tæpɪstrɪ/ *n.* Gobelingewebe, *das;* (wall hanging) Bildteppich, *der;* Tapisserie, *die*
'tapeworm *n.* Bandwurm, *der*
tapioca /tæpɪ'əʊkə/ *n.* Tapioka, *die*
'tap water *n.* Leitungswasser, *das*
tar /tɑː(r)/ **1** *n.* Teer, *der;* **high-**~**/low-**~ **cigarette** Zigarette mit hohem/niedrigem Teergehalt. **2** *v.t.,* **-rr-** teeren; **they are** ~**red with the same brush** *or* **stick** (fig.) der eine ist ~t nicht besser als der andere
tardy /'tɑːdɪ/ *adj.* (a) (slow) [zögernd] langsam; (b) (late) spät; (too late) zu spät
target /'tɑːgɪt/ **1** *n.* (a) (lit. or fig.) Ziel, *das;* **hit/miss the/one's/its** ~: [das Ziel] treffen/das Ziel verfehlen; **set oneself a** ~ (fig.) sich (*Dat.*) ein Ziel setzen *od.* stecken; **set oneself a** ~ **of £5,000** sich (*Dat.*) 5 000 Pfund zum Ziel setzen; **set sb. a** ~ **of six months** jmdm. eine Frist von sechs Monaten setzen; **reach one's** ~ (fig.) sein Ziel erreichen; **be on/off** *or* **not on** ~ ‹*Geschoss, Schuss:*› treffen/danebengehen; **be on** ~ (fig.) ‹*Sparer, Sammler:*› auf dem Wege dahin sein[, sein Ziel zu erreichen]; **be on** ~ **for sth.** (lit. or fig.) auf etw. (*Akk.*) zusteuern; **be above/below** ~ (fig.) das Ziel über-/unterschritten haben; (b) (Sport) Zielscheibe, *die.* **2** *v.t.* (a) (Mil.) angreifen; (b) (fig.) zielen auf ‹*Käufergruppe*›; **be** ~**ed on sth.** auf etw. (*Akk.*) gerichtet sein; **be** ~**ed on** *or* **at sth.** (fig.) auf etw. (*Akk.*) abzielen
'target practice *n., no art.* Schießübungen *Pl.*
tariff /'tærɪf/ *n.* (a) (tax) Zoll, *der;* (table or scale of customs duties) Zolltarif, *der;* **[import]** ~: Einfuhr- *od.* Importzoll, *der;* (b) (list of charges) Tarif, *der*
Tarmac, tarmac /'tɑːmæk/ **1** *n.* (P) (a) Makadam, *der* (Bauw.); (b) (at airport) Rollbahn, *die.* **2** *v.t.* **-ck-** makadamisieren (Bauw.)
tarnish /'tɑːnɪʃ/ **1** *v.t.* stumpf werden lassen ‹*Metall*›; (fig.) beflecken ‹*Ruf, Namen*›. **2** *v.i.* ‹*Metall:*› stumpf werden, anlaufen. **3** *n.* (discolouring film) Beschlag, *der;* Überzug, *der*
tarnished /'tɑːnɪʃt/ *adj.* stumpf ‹*Metall*›; (fig.) befleckt ‹*Ruf, Name, Image*›

tarpaulin /tɑː'pɔːlɪn/ *n.* Persenning, *die*
tarry /'tɑːrɪ/ *adj.* teerig; teerverschmiert ‹*Hand, Kleidung*›
tart¹ /tɑːt/ *adj.* herb; sauer ‹*Obst usw.*›; (fig.) scharfzüngig
tart² *n.* (a) (Brit.) (filled pie) ≈ Obstkuchen, *der;* (small pastry) Obsttörtchen, *das;* **jam** ~: Marmeladentörtchen, *das;* (b) (sl.: prostitute) Nutte, *die* (salopp)
~ **'up** *v.t.* (Brit. coll.) ~ **oneself up, get** ~**ed up** sich auftakeln (ugs.); ~ **a pub/restaurant up** (fig.) eine Kneipe/ein Lokal aufmotzen (ugs.)
tartan /'tɑːtən/ **1** *n.* Schotten[stoff], *der;* (pattern) **the Stewart** ~: der Stewart (Textilw.); *das Schottenmuster des Stewart-Clans.* **2** *adj.* (a) Schotten‹*rock, -jacke*›; ~ **plaid/rug** Tartan, *der;* (b) **T**~ **track** (P) Tartanbahn, *die*
tartare /'tɑːtɑː(r)/ *adj.* ~ **sauce, sauce** ~ ⇒ **tartar sauce**
tartar sauce /tɑːtə'sɔːs/ *n.* (Gastr.) Remoulade[nsoße], *die*
task /tɑːsk/ *n.* Aufgabe, *die;* **set sb. the** ~ **of doing sth.** jmdm. auftragen, etw. zu tun; **set oneself the** ~ **of doing sth.** es sich (*Dat.*) zur Aufgabe machen, etw. zu tun; **carry out/perform a** ~: eine Aufgabe erfüllen; **take sb. to** ~: jmdm. eine Lektion erteilen
task: ~ **force,** ~ **group** *ns.* (sent out) Sonderkommando, *das;* (set up) Sonderkommission, *die;* ~**master** *n.* **a hard** ~**master** ein strenger Vorgesetzter; (teacher) ein strenger Lehrmeister
Tasmania /tæz'meɪnɪə/ *pr. n.* Tasmanien (*das*)
tassel /'tæsl/ *n.* Quaste, *die*
taste /teɪst/ **1** *v.t.* (a) schmecken; (try a little) probieren; kosten; (b) (recognize flavour of) [heraus]schmecken; (c) (fig.: experience) kosten (geh.) ‹*Macht, Freiheit, [Miss]erfolg, Glück, Niederlage*›. **2** *v.i.* (a) (have sense of flavour) schmecken; (b) (have certain flavour) schmecken (of nach); **not** ~ **of anything** nach nichts schmecken. **3** *n.* (a) (flavour) Geschmack, *der;* **to** ~: nach Geschmack ‹*verdünnen*›; **this dish has no** ~: dieses Gericht schmeckt nach nichts; **there's a** ~ **of garlic in sth.** etw. schmeckt nach Knoblauch; **leave a nasty/bad** *etc.* ~ **in the mouth** (lit. or fig.) einen unangenehmen/üblen *usw.* Nachgeschmack hinterlassen; (b) (sense) **[sense of]** ~: Geschmack[ssinn], *der;* (c) (discernment) Geschmack, *der;* ~ **in art/music** Kunst-/Musikgeschmack, *der;* **have good** ~ **in clothes** sich geschmackvoll kleiden; **it would be bad** ~ **to do that** es wäre geschmacklos, das zu tun; **in good/bad** ~: geschmackvoll/geschmacklos; (d) (sample, lit. or fig.) Kostprobe, *die;* **have a** ~ **of** probieren ‹*Speise, Getränk*›; kennen lernen ‹*Freiheit, jmds. Jähzorn, Arroganz*›; **give sb. a** ~ **of sth.** (lit. or fig.) jmdm. eine Kostprobe einer Sache (*Gen.*) geben; (e) (liking) Geschmack, *der* (**in** für); **have a/no** ~ **for sth.** an etw. (*Dat.*) Geschmack/keinen Geschmack finden; **have expensive** ~**s in clothes** *etc.* eine Vorliebe für teure Kleidung *usw.* haben; **be/not be to sb.'s** ~: nach jmds./nicht nach jmds. Geschmack sein
'taste bud *n.* Geschmacksknospe, *die*
tasteful /'teɪstfl/ *adj.,* **tastefully** /'teɪstfəlɪ/ *adv.* geschmackvoll
tasteless /'teɪstlɪs/ *adj.* geschmacklos
taster /'teɪstə(r)/ *n.* (a) Verkoster, *der/*Verkosterin, *die;* (b) (sample) **a** ~ **for** *or* **of sth.** ein [kleiner] Vorgeschmack *od.* eine [kleine] Kostprobe von etw.
tasty /'teɪstɪ/ *adj.* lecker
tat ⇒ **tit²**
ta-ta /tæ'tɑː/ *int.* (coll.) tschüs (ugs.)
tattered /'tætəd/ *adj.* zerlumpt ‹*Kleidung, Person*›; zerrissen ‹*Segel*›; zerfleddert ‹*Buch, Zeitschrift*›; (fig.) ramponiert (ugs.) ‹*Ruf*›
tatters /'tætəz/ *n. pl.* Fetzen; **be in** ~: in Fetzen sein; (fig.) ‹*Karriere, Leben:*› ruiniert sein
tattoo /tə'tuː/ **1** *v.t.* tätowieren; ~ **sth. on sb.'s arm** jmdm. etw. auf den Arm tätowieren. **2** *n.* Tätowierung, *die*
tattooed /tə'tuːd/ *adj.* tätowiert
tatty /'tætɪ/ *adj.* (coll.) schäbig (abwertend); zerfleddert ‹*Zeitschrift, Buch*›; (inferior) mies (ugs.) ‹*Publikation, Firma*›; (threadbare) billig ‹*Ausrede*›

taught ⇨ **teach**

taunt /tɔːnt/ **1** *v.t.* verspotten (**about** wegen); ∼ *sb.* **with being a weakling** jmdn. als Schwächling verspotten. **2** *n.* spöttische Bemerkung

taunting /ˈtɔːntɪŋ/ *n.* Spott, *der*

Taurus /ˈtɔːrəs/ *n.* (Astrol., Astron.) der Stier

taut /tɔːt/ *adj.* **(a)** (tight) straff ‹*Seil, Kabel, Saite*›; gespannt ‹*Muskel*›; **(b)** (fig.: tense) angespannt ‹*Nerven, Ausdruck*›; **(c)** (fig.: concise) knapp ‹*Stil*›

tautology /tɔːˈtɒlədʒɪ/ *n.* Tautologie, *die*

tavern /ˈtævən/ *n.* (literary) Schenke, *die*

tawdry /ˈtɔːdrɪ/ *adj.* billig und geschmacklos; (fig.) zweifelhaft

tawny /ˈtɔːnɪ/ *adj.* gelbbraun

tax /tæks/ **1** *n.* **(a)** Steuer, *die;* **pay 20 % in** ∼ [**on** sth.] 20 % Steuern [für etw.] zahlen; **before/after** ∼: vor Steuern/nach Abzug der Steuern; **free of** ∼: steuerfrei; (after ∼, ∼ paid) nach Abzug der Steuern; netto; **(b)** (fig.: burden) Belastung, *die* (**on** für). **2** *v.t.* **(a)** (impose ∼ on) besteuern; (pay ∼ on) versteuern ‹*Einkommen*›; **(b)** (make demands on) strapazieren ‹*Mittel, Kräfte, Geduld usw.*›; **(c)** (accuse) beschuldigen, bezichtigen (**with** Gen.)

taxable /ˈtæksəbl/ *adj.* steuerpflichtig

'tax allowance *n.* Steuerfreibetrag, *der*

taxation /tækˈseɪʃn/ *n.* (imposition of taxes) Besteuerung, *die;* (taxes payable) Steuern *Pl.*

tax: ∼ **avoidance** *n.* Steuerminderung, *die;* ∼ **bill** *n.* Steuerbescheid, *der;* (amount) Steuerschuld, *die;* ∼ **bracket** *n.* Stufe im Steuertarif; ∼ **collector** *n.* Finanzbeamte, *der*/-beamtin, *die;* ∼**-deductible** *adj.* steuerabzugsfähig; [steuerlich] absetzbar; ∼ **demand** *n.* Steuerforderung, *die;* ∼ **disc** *n.* Steuerplakette, *die;* ∼ **dodge** *n.* Steuertrick, *der;* ∼ **dodger** *n.* Steuerbetrüger, *der*/-betrügerin, *die;* ∼ **evasion** *n.* Steuerhinterziehung, *die;* ∼ **exile** *n.* **(a)** (person) Steuerflüchtling, *der;* **(b)** (place) Steueroase, *die* (ugs.); ∼**-free 1** *adj.* steuerfrei; (after payment of ∼) Netto-; ∼**-free allowance** Steuerfreibetrag, *der;* **2** *adv.* steuerfrei; (after payment of ∼) netto; ∼ **haven** *n.* Steueroase, *die* (ugs.)

taxi /ˈtæksɪ/ **1** *n.* Taxi, *das;* **go by** ∼: mit dem Taxi fahren. **2** *v.i.,* ∼**ing** or **taxying** /ˈtæksɪɪŋ/ (Aeronaut.) ‹*Flugzeug:*› rollen

'taxicab ⇨ **taxi 1**

taxidermist /ˈtæksɪdɜːmɪst/ ▶ **887** | *n.* Präparator, *der*/ Präparatorin, *die*

'taxi driver *n.* ▶ **887** | Taxifahrer, *der*/-fahrerin, *die*

'tax incentive *n.* steuerlicher Anreiz

taxing /ˈtæksɪŋ/ *adj.* strapaziös, anstrengend ‹*Arbeit, Rolle, Reise*›; schwierig ‹*Problem*›

'tax inspector *n.* ▶ **887** | Steuerinspektor, *der*/-inspektorin, *die*

taxi: ∼ **rank** (Brit.), (Amer.) ∼ **stand** *ns.* Taxistand, *der*

tax: ∼**man** *n.* (coll.) Finanzbeamte, *der*/-beamtin, *die;* **a letter from the** ∼**man** ein Brief vom Finanzamt; ∼ **office** *n.* Finanzamt, *das;* ∼**payer** *n.* Steuerzahler, *der*/-zahlerin, *die;* ∼**paying** *attrib. adj.* Steuern zahlend...; ∼ **return** *n.* Steuererklärung, *die*

TB *abbr.* **tuberculosis** Tb, *die*

tbsp. *abbr., pl. same or* **tbsps. tablespoon** Essl.; EL

tea /tiː/ *n.* **(a)** Tee, *der;* [**not**] **be sb.'s cup of** ∼ (fig. coll.) [nicht] jmds. Fall sein (ugs.); **(b)** (meal) [**high**] ∼: Abendessen, *das;* **afternoon** ∼: [Nachmittags]tee, *der*

tea: ∼ **bag** *n.* Teebeutel, *der;* ∼ **break** *n.* (Brit.) Teepause, *die;* ∼ **caddy** *n.* Teebüchse, *die;* ∼**cake** *n.* **(a)** (Brit.: sweet bread bun) ≈ Rosinenbrötchen, *das;* **(b)** (Amer.: sweet cake) Keks, *der;* ∼**cakes** Teegebäck, *das*

teach /tiːtʃ/ **1** *v.t.,* **taught** /tɔːt/ unterrichten; (at university) lehren; ∼ **music** *etc.* **to sb.,** ∼ **sb. music** *etc.* jmdn. in Musik *usw.* unterrichten; ∼ **oneself** sich (*Dat.*) selbst beibringen; ∼ **sb./oneself/an animal sth.** jmdm./sich/ einem Tier etw. beibringen; ∼ **sb./oneself/an animal to do sth.** jmdm./sich/einem Tier beibringen, etw. zu tun; ∼ **sb. to ride/to play the piano** jmdm. das Reiten/Klavierspielen beibringen; **I'll/that'll** ∼ **you** *etc.* **to do that!** (coll. iron.) ich werde/das wird dich *usw.* lehren, das zu tun! (iron.); **that'll** ∼ **him/you** *etc.!* (coll. iron.) das hat

er/hast du *usw.* nun davon! (iron.); ∼ *sb.* **how/that** ...: jmdm. beibringen, wie/dass ...; ‹*Bibel, Erfahrung:*› jmdn. lehren, wie/dass ... **2** *v.i.,* **taught** unterrichten

teacher /ˈtiːtʃə(r)/ *n.* ▶ **887** | Lehrer, *der*/Lehrerin, *die;* **she's a university/evening class** ∼: sie lehrt an der Universität/unterrichtet an der Abendschule; **kindergarten** ∼: ≈ Vorschullehrer, *der*/-lehrerin, *die;* **geography/music** ∼: Geographie-/Musiklehrer, *der*/ Geographie-/Musiklehrerin, *die*

'teacher training college *n.* ≈ pädagogische Hochschule

'tea chest *n.* Teekiste, *die*

teaching /ˈtiːtʃɪŋ/ *n.* **(a)** (act) Unterrichten, *das* (**of** von); **the** ∼ **of languages, language** ∼: der Sprachunterricht; **(b)** *no pl., no art.* (profession) Lehrberuf, *der*

teaching: ∼ **aid** *n.* Lehr- od. Unterrichtsmittel, *das;* ∼ **hospital** *n.* Ausbildungskrankenhaus, *das;* ∼ **practice** *n.* ≈ Schulpraktikum, *das*

tea: ∼ **cloth** *n.* (for drying) Geschirrtuch, *das;* ∼ **cosy** *n.* Teewärmer, *der;* ∼**cup** *n.* Teetasse, *die;* ∼**cupful** *n.* Tasse, *die;* **a** ∼**cupful of flour** eine Tasse Mehl

teak /tiːk/ *n.* Teak[holz], *das; attrib.* Teak[holz]‹*öl, -furnier, -möbel*›

tea: ∼**kettle** *n.* Teekessel, *der;* ∼ **lady** *n.* Frau, die in einer Firma, Behörde o. ä. den Pausentee usw. zubereitet; ∼ **leaf** *n.* Teeblatt, *das*

team /tiːm/ *n.* **(a)** (group) Team, *das;* (Sport also) Mannschaft, *die;* **a football/cricket** ∼: eine Fußball-/Kricketmannschaft; **a** ∼ **of scientists** eine Gruppe *od.* ein Team von Wissenschaftlern; **make a good** ∼: ein gutes Team *od.* Gespann sein; **work as a** ∼: im Team zusammenarbeiten; **(b)** (draught animals) Gespann, *das*

∼ **'up 1** *v.t.* zusammenbringen. **2** *v.i.* sich zusammentun (ugs.)

'tea maker *n.* (device) Teemaschine, *die*

team: ∼ **effort** *n.* Team- *od.* Gemeinschaftsarbeit, *die;* **a great** ∼ **effort** eine großartige Gemeinschaftsleistung; ∼ **game** *n.* Mannschaftsspiel, *das;* ∼ **leader** *n.* Gruppenleiter, *der*/-leiterin, *die;* ∼**-mate** *n.* Mannschaftskamerad, *der*/-kameradin, *die;* ∼ **member** *n.* Mitglied des Teams/der Mannschaft/der Gruppe; ∼ **'spirit** *n.* Teamgeist, *der;* (Sport also) Mannschaftsgeist, *der*

teamster /ˈtiːmstə(r)/ *n.* (Amer.) Lkw-Fahrer, *der*/-Fahrerin, *die*

'teamwork *n.* Teamarbeit, *die*

tea: ∼ **party** *n.* Teegesellschaft, *die;* ∼**pot** *n.* Teekanne, *die*

tear[1] /teə(r)/ **1** *n.* Riß, *der; see also* **wear 1 a. 2** *v.t.,* **tore** /tɔː(r)/, **torn** /tɔːn/ **(a)** (rip, lit. or fig.) zerreißen; (pull apart) auseinander reißen; (damage) aufreißen; ∼ **open** aufreißen ‹*Brief, Schachtel, Paket*›; ∼ **one's dress [on a nail]** sich (*Dat.*) das Kleid [an einem Nagel] aufreißen; ∼ **a hole/gash in sth.** ein Loch/eine klaffende Wunde in etw. (*Akk.*) reißen; ∼ **sth. in half** *or* **in two** etw. entzweireißen; ∼ **to shreds** *or* **pieces** (lit.) zerfetzen; in Stücke reißen ‹*Flagge, Kleidung, Person*›; ∼ **to shreds** (fig.) (destroy) ruinieren ‹*Ruf, Leumund*›; zerrütten ‹*Nerven*›; zunichte machen ‹*Argument, Alibi*›; auseinander nehmen (salopp) ‹*Mannschaft*›; (criticize) verreißen (ugs.); **a country torn by war** ein durch Krieg zerrissenes Land; **be torn between two things/people/between x and y** zwischen zwei Dingen/Personen/x und y hin- und hergerissen sein; **that's torn it** (Brit. fig. coll.) das hat alles vermasselt (salopp); **(b)** (remove with force) reißen; ∼ **sth. out of** *or* **from sb.'s hands** jmdm. etw. aus der Hand reißen; ∼ **one's hair** (fig.) sich (*Dat.*) die Haare raufen (ugs.). **3** *v.i.,* **tore, torn** **(a)** (rip) [zer]reißen; **it** ∼**s along the perforation** es lässt sich entlang der Perforation abreißen; ∼ **in half** *or* **in two** entzweireißen; durchreißen; **(b)** ▶ **1102** | (move hurriedly) rasen (ugs.); ∼ **past** vorbeirasen (ugs.); ∼ **along the street** die Straße hinunterrasen (ugs.); ∼ **off** losrasen (ugs.)

∼ **apart** *v.t.* (lit. or fig.) auseinander reißen; (coll.: criticize) zerreißen (ugs.)

∼ **at** *v.t.* zerren an (+ *Dat.*)

∼ **a'way** *v.t.* wegreißen; abreißen ‹*Tapete, Verpackung*›;

~ **sb./oneself away [from sb./sth.]** (fig.) jmdn./sich [von jmdm./etw.] loseisen (ugs.); ~ **oneself away [from a sight/book]** (fig.) sich [von einem Anblick/Buch] losreißen ~ **'down** *v.t.* herunterreißen; niederreißen ‹*Zaun, Mauer*›; abreißen ‹*Gebäude*› ~ **into** *v.t.* ‹*Geschoss:*› ein Loch reißen in (+ *Akk.*); ‹*Säge:*› sich [hinein]fressen in (+ *Akk.*); ‹*Raubtier:*› zerfleischen; (fig.: tell off, criticize) heftig angreifen ~ **'off** *v.t.* abreißen; *see also* ~ **3 b** ~ **'out** *v.t.* herausreißen; ausreißen ‹*Baum*›; *see also* ~ **2 b** ~ **'up** *v.t.* **(a)** (remove) aufreißen ‹*Straße, Bürgersteig*›; herausreißen ‹*Zaun, Pflanze*›; ausreißen ‹*Baum*›; **(b)** (destroy) zerreißen; (fig.) für null und nichtig erklären ‹*Vertrag, Abkommen*›

tear² /tɪə(r)/ *n.* Träne, *die;* **there were** ~**s in her eyes** sie hatte *od.* ihr standen Tränen in den Augen; **with** ~**s in one's eyes** mit Tränen in den Augen; **burst into** ~**s** in Tränen ausbrechen; **move sb. to** ~**s** jmdn. zu Tränen rühren; **bore sb. to** ~**s** jmdn. zu Tode langweilen; **be in** ~**s** in Tränen aufgelöst sein; **end in** ~**s** böse enden *od.* ausgehen; ein böses *od.* schlimmes Ende nehmen

tearaway /'teərəweɪ/ *n.* Rabauke, *der* (ugs.)

teardrop /'tɪədrɒp/ *n.* Träne, *die*

tearful /'tɪəfl/ *adj.* (crying) weinend; tränenreich ‹*Versöhnung, Abschied, Anlass*›; **she was looking very** ~: sie sah sehr verweint aus; (about to cry) sie schien den Tränen nahe

tear gas /'tɪəgæs/ *n.* Tränengas, *das*

tearing /'teərɪŋ/ *adj.* **(a)** reißend ‹*Geräusch*›; **(b)** (coll.: violent) rasend; **be in a** ~ **hurry** schrecklich in Eile sein

tear-jerker /'tɪə dʒɜːkə(r)/ *n.* (coll.) Schnulze, *die* (ugs. abwertend); **this film is a real** ~: in diesem Film wird kräftig auf die Tränendrüsen gedrückt

tear-off /'teərɒf/ *attrib. adj.* ~ **calendar** Abreißkalender, *der*

tea: ~**room** *n.* Teestube, *die;* ≈ Café, *das;* ~ **rose** *n.* Teerose, *die*

tease /tiːz/ **1** *v.t.* necken; ~ **sb. [about sth.]** jmdn. [mit etw.] aufziehen (ugs.); jmdn. [wegen etw.] verspotten; **he's only teasing you** er macht nur Spaß (ugs.); **stop teasing the dog** hör auf, den Hund zu ärgern. **2** *v.i.* seine Späße machen; **I'm only teasing** ich mache nur Spaß

teasel /'tiːzl/ *n.* (Bot.) Karde, *die*

teaser /'tiːzə(r)/ *n.* (coll.: puzzle) **brain-**~: Denk[sport]aufgabe, *die;* **be a [real]** ~ (fig.) eine harte Nuss sein (ugs.)

tea: ~ **service,** ~**set** *ns.* Tee-Service, *das;* ~ **shop** (Brit.) ⇒ tearoom

teasing /'tiːzɪŋ/ *adj.* neckend

tea: ~**spoon** *n.* Teelöffel, *der;* ~**spoonful** *n.* Teelöffel, *der;* **a** ~**spoonful** ein Teelöffel [voll]; ~**strainer** *n.* Teesieb, *das*

teat /tiːt/ *n.* **(a)** (nipple) Zitze, *die;* **(b)** (of rubber or plastic) Sauger, *der*

tea: ~ **table** *n.* Teetisch, *der;* ~ **things** *n. pl.* (coll.) Teegeschirr, *das;* ~**time** *n.* Teezeit, *die;* ~ **towel** *n.* Geschirrtuch, *das;* ~ **trolley,** (Amer.) ~ **wagon** *ns.* Teewagen, *der*

teazel, teazle /'tiːzl/ ⇒ teasel

'techie *n.* (coll.) Technikfreak, *der;* (computer expert) Computerfreak, *der*

technical /'teknɪkl/ *adj.* **(a)** technisch ‹*Problem, Detail, Daten, Fortschritt*›; (of particular science, art, etc.) fachlich; Fach‹*kenntnis, -sprache, -begriff, -wörterbuch*›; (of the execution of a work of art) technisch ‹*Fertigkeit, Schwierigkeit*›; ~ **expertise/expert** Sachkenntnis, *die*/Fachmann, *der;* ~ **college/school** Fachhochschule, *die*/Fachschule, *die;* **explain sth. without being or getting too** ~: etw. erklären, ohne sich zu fachsprachlich auszudrücken; ~ **hitch** technisches Problem; ~ **term** Fachbegriff, *der;* Fachausdruck, *der;* Fachterminus, *der;* **for** ~ **reasons** aus technischen Gründen; **(b)** (Law) formaljuristisch; **(c)** ~ **knockout** (Boxing) technischer K.o.

technical 'drawing *n., no pl., no art.* (Brit.) technisches Zeichnen

technicality /teknɪ'kælɪtɪ/ *n.* (technical expression) Fachausdruck, *der;* (technical distinction) technisches Detail; (technical point) technische Frage; **be acquitted on a** ~ (Law) aufgrund eines Formfehlers freigesprochen werden

technician /tek'nɪʃn/ *n.* ► **887**⌋ Techniker, *der*/Technikerin, *die*

technique /tek'niːk/ *n.* Technik, *die;* (procedure) Methode, *die*

technological /teknə'lɒdʒɪkl/ *adj.* ⇒ **technology:** technisch; technologisch

technologist /tek'nɒlədʒɪst/ *n.* ► **887**⌋ Technologe, *der*/ Technologin, *die;* ‹*Lebensmittel-, Erdöl-*›techniker, *der*/ -technikerin, *die*

technology /tek'nɒlədʒɪ/ *n.* Technik, *die;* (application of science) Technologie, *die;* **science and** ~: Wissenschaft und Technik; **college of** ~: Fachhochschule für Technik

technophobe /'teknəʊfəʊb/ *n.* Mensch mit einer Technikphobie; **be a** ~: eine Technikphobie haben

technophobia /teknəʊ'fəʊbɪə/ *n., no pl.* Technikphobie, *die;* **suffer from** ~: eine Technikphobie haben

teddy /'tedɪ/ *n.* ~ **[bear]** Teddy[bär], *der*

tedious /'tiːdɪəs/ *adj.* langwierig ‹*Reise, Arbeit*›; (uninteresting) langweilig

tedium /'tiːdɪəm/ *n.* (of journey) Langwierigkeit, *die;* (of waiting) Langweiligkeit, *die*

tee /tiː/ *n.* (Golf) Tee, *das* ~ **'off** *v.i.* (Golf) abschlagen

teem /tiːm/ *v.i.* wimmeln (**with** von)

teenage /'tiːneɪdʒ/, **teenaged** /'tiːneɪdʒd/ *attrib. adjs* im Teenageralter *nachgestellt*

teenager /'tiːneɪdʒə(r)/ *n.* ► **630**⌋ Teenager, *der;* (loosely) Jugendliche, *der/die*

teens /tiːnz/ *n. pl.* ► **630**⌋ Teenagerjahre; **be out of/in one's** ~: aus den Teenagerjahren heraus sein/in den Teenagerjahren sein

'tee shirt *n.* T-shirt, *das*

teeter /'tiːtə(r)/ *v.i.* wanken; ~ **on the edge** *or* **brink of sth.** schwankend am Rande einer Sache (*Gen.*) stehen; (fig.) am Rande einer Sache stehen

teeth *pl. of* tooth

teething troubles /'tiːðɪŋ trʌblz/ *n. pl.* Beschwerden während des Zahnens; **have** ~ (fig.) ‹*Person, Vorhaben:*› Anfangsschwierigkeiten haben; ‹*Maschine usw.:*› Kinderkrankheiten haben

teetotal /tiː'təʊtl/ *adj.* abstinent lebend; alkoholfrei ‹*Restaurant, Hotel, Feier*›; **sb. is** ~: jmd. ist Abstinenzler/ Abstinenzlerin

teetotaller /tiː'təʊtələ(r)/ *n.* Abstinenzler, *der*/Abstinenzlerin, *die*

TEFL /'tefl/ *abbr.* **teaching of English as a foreign language**

Tel., tel. *abbr.* **telephone** Tel.

telebanking /'telɪbæŋkɪŋ/ *n.* Telebanking, *das*

telecommunication /telɪkəmjuːnɪ'keɪʃn/ *n.* **(a)** (long-distance communication) Fernmeldeverkehr, *der; attrib.* Fernmelde-; **(b)** *in pl.* (science) Fernmelde- *od.* Nachrichtentechnik, *die; attrib.* Fernmelde- *od.* Nachrichten‹*techniker, -satellit*›

telecommute /'telɪkəmjuːt/ *v.i.* Telearbeit verrichten

telecommuter /'telɪkəmjuːtə(r)/ *n.* Telearbeiter, *der*/ -arbeiterin, *die*

telecommuting /'telɪkəmjuːtɪŋ/ *n.* Telearbeit, *die*

teleconference /'telɪkɒnfərəns/ *n.* Telekonferenz, *die*

telecottage /'telɪkɒtɪdʒ/ *n.: jedermann zugängliche Einrichtung, die bes. Telearbeitern Zugang zu einem ans Internet angeschlossenen Computer bietet*

telegram /'telɪgræm/ *n.* Telegramm, *das;* **by** ~: telegrafisch

telegraph /'telɪgrɑːf/ *n.* Telegraf, *der; attrib.* Telegrafen-; ~ **pole** Telegrafenmast, *der*

telemarketing /'telɪmɑːkɪtɪŋ/ *n., no pl.* Telefonmarketing, *das*

telepathic /telɪ'pæθɪk/ *adj.* telepathisch; **be** ~: telepathische Fähigkeiten haben

telepathy /tɪˈlepəθɪ/ n. Telepathie, *die*

telephone /ˈtelɪfəʊn/ **1** n. Telefon, *das; attrib.* Telefon-; **[public]** ~: öffentlicher Fernsprecher (Amtsspr.); [öffentliches] Telefon; **answer the** ~: Anrufe entgegennehmen; (on one occasion) ans Telefon gehen; (speak) sich melden; **by** ~: telefonisch; **over** *or* **on the** ~: am Telefon; **speak** *or* **talk to sb. on the** *or* **by** ~: mit jmdm. telefonieren; **be on the** ~ (be connected to the system) Telefon haben; (be speaking) telefonieren (**to** mit); **it's your sister on the** ~: deine Schwester ist am Apparat; **get on the** ~ **to sb.** jmdn. anrufen; **get sb. on the** ~: jmdn. telefonisch erreichen; **be wanted on the** ~: am Telefon verlangt werden; *attrib.* ~ **answering machine** Anrufbeantworter, *der.* **2** *v.t.* telefonisch übermitteln ⟨*Nachricht, Ergebnis usw.*⟩ (**to** *Dat.*); ~ **the office/**~ **home** im Büro/zu Hause anrufen. **3** *v.i.* anrufen; ~ **for a taxi/the doctor** nach einem Taxi/dem Arzt telefonieren; **can we** ~ **from here?** können wir von hier aus telefonieren?

telephone: ~ **'answering machine** n. Anrufbeantworter, *der;* ~ **banking** n. Telefonbanking, *das;* ~ **book** n. Telefonbuch, *das;* ~ **booth,** (Brit.) ~ **box** ns. Telefonzelle, *die;* ~ **call** n. Telefonanruf, *der;* Telefongespräch, *das;* **make a** ~ **call** ein Telefongespräch führen; **have** *or* **receive a** ~ **call** einen Anruf erhalten; **there was a** ~ **call for you** es hat jemand für Sie angerufen; **international** ~ **call** Auslandsgespräch, *das;* ~ **directory** n. Telefonverzeichnis, *das;* Telefonbuch, *das;* ~ **exchange** n. Fernmeldeamt, *das;* ~ **kiosk** n. Telefonzelle, *die;* ~ **line** n. Telefonleitung, *die;* ~ **message** n. telefonische Nachricht; ~ **number** n. Telefonnummer, *die;* ~ **operator** n. ▶ 887 | Telefonist, *der*/Telefonistin, *die;* ~ **receiver** n. Telefonhörer, *der*

telephoto /ˈtelɪˈfəʊtəʊ/ *adj.* (Photog.) telefotografisch; ~ **lens** Teleobjektiv, *das*

teleprinter /ˈtelɪprɪntə(r)/ n. Fernschreiber, *der*

'telesales n. pl. Telefonverkauf, *der;* Verkauf per Telefon

telescope /ˈtelɪskəʊp/ **1** n. Teleskop, *das;* Fernrohr, *das.* **2** *v.t.* zusammenschieben ⟨*Antenne, Rohr*⟩; ineinander schieben ⟨*Abschnitte, Waggons*⟩; (fig.) komprimieren (**into** zu)

telescopic /telɪˈskɒpɪk/ *adj.* (collapsible) ausziehbar; Teleskop⟨*antenne, -mast*⟩; ~ **umbrella** Taschenschirm, *der*

teleshopping /ˈtelɪʃɒpɪŋ/ n., no pl. Teleshopping, *das*

teletext /ˈtelɪtekst/ n. Teletext, *der*

televise /ˈtelɪvaɪz/ *v.t.* im Fernsehen senden *od.* übertragen

television /ˈtelɪvɪʒn, telɪˈvɪʒn/ n. **(a)** no pl., no art. das Fernsehen; **colour/black and white** ~: das Farb- / Schwarzweißfernsehen; **we have ten hours of** ~ **a day** bei uns gibt es täglich 10 Stunden Fernsehprogramm; **live** ~: Live-Sendungen [im Fernsehen]; **on** ~: im Fernsehen; **what's on** ~? was läuft *od.* gibt's im Fernsehen?; **watch** ~: fernsehen; **(b)** (~ set) Fernsehapparat, *der;* Fernseher, *der* (ugs.); **portable** ~: tragbares Fernsehgerät

television: ~ **advertising** n. Fernsehwerbung, *die;* ~ **aerial** n. Fernsehantenne, *die;* ~ **camera** n. Fernsehkamera, *die;* ~ **channel** n. [Fernseh]kanal, *der;* ~ **licence** n. (Brit.) Fernsehgenehmigung, *die* (die jährlich gegen Zahlung der Gebühren erneuert wird); *attrib.* ~ **licence fee** Fernsehgebühren *Pl.;* ~ **lounge** n. Fernsehraum, *der;* ~ **personality** n. Fernsehgröße, *die* (ugs.); ~ **programme** n. Fernsehsendung, *die;* (sequence) Fernsehprogramm, *das;* **my favourite** ~ **programme** meine Lieblingssendung im Fernsehen; ~ **screen** n. Bildschirm, *der;* ~ **serial** n. Fernsehserie, *die;* ~ **set** n. Fernsehgerät, *das;* ~ **studio** n. Fernsehstudio, *das;* ~ **viewer** n. Fernsehzuschauer, *der*/-zuschauerin, *die*

telework /ˈtelɪwɜːk/ *v.i.* Telearbeit verrichten

teleworker /ˈtelɪwɜːkə(r)/ n. Telearbeiter, *der*/-arbeiterin, *die*

teleworking /ˈtelɪwɜːkɪŋ/ n., no pl. Telearbeit, *die*

Telex, telex /ˈteleks/ **1** n. Telex, *das;* **by** ~: über Telex. **2** *v.t.* ein Telex schicken (+ *Dat.*) ⟨*Person, Firma*⟩; telexen ⟨*Nachricht*⟩

tell /tel/ **1** *v.t.*, **told** /təʊld/ **(a)** (make known) sagen ⟨*Name, Adresse, Alter*⟩; (give account of) erzählen ⟨*Neuigkeit, Sorgen*⟩; anvertrauen ⟨*Geheimnis*⟩; ~ **sb. sth.** *or* **sth. to sb.** jmdm. etw. sagen/erzählen/anvertrauen; ~ **sb. the way to the station** jmdm. den Weg zum Bahnhof beschreiben; ~ **sb. the time** jmdm. sagen, wie spät es ist; jmdm. die Uhrzeit sagen; ~ **all** auspacken (ugs.); ~ **sb. [something] about sb./sth.** jmdm. [etwas] von jmdm./ etw. erzählen; ~ **sb. nothing/all about what happened** jmdm. nichts davon/alles erzählen, was passiert ist; **will you** ~ **him [that] I will come?** sag ihm bitte, dass ich kommen werde; **they** ~ **me/us [that]** ... (according to them) man sagt, dass ...; **I'll** ~ **you what I'll do** weißt du, was ich machen werde?; ~ **everyone/**(coll.) **the world** [that/how *etc.*] jedem/(ugs.) aller Welt erzählen[, dass/wie *usw.*]; **I cannot** ~ **you how** ... (cannot express how ...) ich kann dir gar nicht sagen, wie ...; **I couldn't** ~ **you** (I don't know) das kann ich nicht sagen; **I can** ~ **you,** ... (I can assure you) ich kann dir sagen, ...; ... , **I can** ~ **you** ... ; das kann ich dir sagen; **you can't** ~ **me [that]** ... (it can't be true that ...) du kannst mir doch nicht erzählen, dass ...; **you can't** ~ **him anything** (he won't accept advice) er lässt sich (*Dat.*) ja nichts sagen; (he is well-informed) ihm kannst du nichts erzählen; **let me** ~ **you** (let me assure you) ... , das kann ich dir sagen; **let me** ~ **you that** ...: ich kann dir versichern, dass ...; ... , **I** ~ **you** *or* **I'm** ~**ing you** ..., das sage ich dir; **you're** ~**ing 'me!** (coll.) wem sagst du das! (ugs.); **I don't need to** ~ **you [that]** ...: ich brauche dir wohl nicht extra zu sagen, dass ...; **be told sth. by sb.** etw. von jmdm. erfahren; **I was told that** ...: mir wurde gesagt, dass ...; **so I've been told** (I know that) [das] habe ich schon gehört; ... **or so I've been/I'm told** ... , wie ich gehört habe/höre; **no, don't** ~ **me, let me guess** [nein], sags nicht, lass mich raten; **don't** ~ **me [that]** ... (expressing incredulity, dismay, etc.) jetzt sag bloß nicht, [dass] ...; **you aren't trying** *or* **don't mean to** ~ **me [that]** ...? du wirst doch nicht sagen wollen, dass ...?; **(b)** (relate, lit. or fig.) erzählen; **sth.** ~**s its own story** *or* **tale** (needs no comment) etw. spricht für sich selbst; ~ **a different story** *or* **tale** (reveal the truth) eine andere Sprache sprechen (fig.); **live** *or* **survive to** ~ **the tale** überleben; ~ **tales [about sb.]** (gossip; reveal secret) [über jmdn.] tratschen (ugs. abwertend); ~ **tales [to sb.]** (report) andere/ einen anderen [bei jmdm.] anschwärzen; [bei jmdm.] petzen (Schülerspr. abwertend); ~ **tales** (tell) Lügengeschichten erzählen; **(c)** (instruct) sagen; ~ **sb. [not] to do sth.** jmdm. sagen, dass er etw. [nicht] tun soll; jmdm. sagen, er soll[e] etw. [nicht] tun; ~ **sb. what to do** jmdm. sagen, was er tun soll, *do as* or *what I* ~ *you* tu, was ich dir sage; **do as you are told** tu, was man dir sagt; **(d)** (determine) feststellen; (see, recognize) erkennen (**by** an + *Dat.*); (with reference to the future) [vorher]sagen; ~ **the difference [between** ...] den Unterschied [zwischen ...] erkennen *od.* feststellen; **it's impossible/difficult to** ~ **[if/what** *etc.*] es ist unmöglich/schwer zu sagen[, ob/was *usw.*]; **it's easy to** ~ **whether** ...: es lässt sich leicht sagen, ob ...; **you never can** ~ **how/what** *etc.* man weiß nie, wie/was *usw.;* **(e)** (distinguish) unterscheiden; **(f)** (utter) sagen; **(g) all told** insgesamt. **2** *v.i.*, **told** (a) (determine) **how can you** ~? wie kann man das feststellen *od.* wissen?; **it's difficult** *or* **hard to** ~: das ist schwer zu sagen; **how can one** ~?, **how can** *or* **do you** ~? woran kann man das erkennen?; **as far as one/I can** ~, ...: wie es aussieht, ...; **you never can** ~: man kann nie wissen; **who can** ~? wer kann das sagen *od.* will das wissen?; **(b)** (give information) erzählen (**of, about**) von); (give evidence) ~ **of sth.** etw. Zeugnis geben *od.* ablegen; **(c)** (reveal secret) es verraten; **time [alone] will** ~: das wird sich [erst noch] zeigen; **(d)** (produce an effect) sich auswirken; ⟨*Wort, Fausthieb, Schuss:*⟩ sitzen; ~ **in favour of sb.** *or* **in sb.'s favour** sich zu jmds. Gunsten auswirken; ~ **against sb./sth.** sich nachteilig für jmdn./auf etw. (*Akk.*) auswirken

~ **a'part** *v.t.* auseinander halten

~ **'off** *v.t.* (coll.: scold) ~ **sb. off [for sth.]** jmdn. [für *od.* wegen etw.] ausschimpfen

~ **on** *v.t.* **(a)** (affect) ~ **on sb./sth.** sich bei jmdm. bemerkbar machen/sich [nachteilig] auf etw. (*Akk.*) auswirken; **(b)** (coll.: inform against) ~ **on sb.** jmdn. verpetzen (Schülerspr. abwertend)

teller /'telə(r)/ *n.* (a) (in bank) ⇒ **cashier;** (b) (counter of votes) Stimmenzähler, *der*/-zählerin, *die*

telling /'telɪŋ/ 1 *adj.* (effective, striking) schlagend ‹*Argument, Antwort*›; wirkungsvoll ‹*Worte, Phrase, Stil*›; ∼ **blow** (Boxing) Wirkungstreffer, *der;* (fig.) empfindlicher Schlag; **with** ∼ **effect** mit durchschlagender Wirkung. 2 *n.* Erzählen, *das;* **he did not need any** ∼, **he needed no** ∼: dazu brauchte man ihn nicht lange *od.* eigens aufzufordern; **that would be** ∼: damit würde ich ein Geheimnis verraten; **there's no** ∼ **what/how** ...: man weiß nie, was/wie ...

telling-'off *n.* (coll.) Standpauke, *die* (ugs.); **give sb. a** ∼: jmdn. ausschimpfen (**for** wegen); **get a** ∼: Schimpfe kriegen (ugs.)

'tell-tale *n.* Klatschmaul, *das* (ugs. abwertend); Petze, *die* (Schülerspr. abwertend); *attrib.* vielsagend ‹*Blick, Lächeln*›; verräterisch ‹*Röte, Fleck, Glanz, Zucken, Zeichen*›

telly /'telɪ/ *n.* (Brit. coll.) Fernseher, *der* (ugs.); Glotze, *die* (salopp); **watch** ∼: Fernsehen gucken (ugs.); **what's on [the]** ∼? was kommt im Fernsehen?

temp /temp/ (Brit. coll.) 1 *n.* Zeitarbeitskraft, *die.* 2 *v.i.* Zeitarbeit machen

temper /'tempə(r)/ 1 *n.* (a) (disposition) Naturell, *das;* **be in a good/bad** ∼: gute/schlechte Laune haben; gut/schlecht gelaunt sein; **be in a foul** *or* **filthy** ∼: eine miese Laune haben (ugs.); **keep/lose one's** ∼: sich beherrschen/die Beherrschung verlieren; **lose one's** ∼ **with sb.** die Beherrschung bei jmdm. verlieren; **control one's** ∼: sich beherrschen; (b) (anger) **fit/outburst of** ∼: Wutanfall, *der*/-ausbruch, *der;* **have a** ∼: jähzornig sein; **be in/get into a** ∼: wütend sein/werden (**over** wegen). 2 *v.t.* mäßigen; mildern ‹*Trostlosigkeit, Strenge, Kritik*›

temperament /'temprəmənt/ *n.* (nature) Veranlagung, *die;* Natur, *die;* (disposition) Temperament, *das;* **have an artistic** ∼: künstlerisch veranlagt sein

temperamental /temprə'mentl/ *adj.* launisch (abwertend); launenhaft; **be a bit** ∼ (fig. coll.) ‹*Auto, Maschine:*› seine Mucken haben (ugs.)

temperance /'tempərəns/ *n.* (a) (moderation) Mäßigung, *die;* (in one's eating, drinking) Mäßigkeit, *die;* (b) (total abstinence) Abstinenz, *die*

temperate /'tempərət/ *adj.* gemäßigt

temperature /'temprɪtʃə(r)/ *n.* ▶ 1141 (a) Temperatur, *die;* **what is the** ∼? wie viel Grad sind es?; **the** ∼ **is below/above** ...: die Temperatur liegt unter/über ... (*Dat.*); **at high/low** ∼s bei hohen/niedrigen Temperaturen; (b) (Med.) Temperatur, *die;* **have** *or* **run a** ∼ (coll.) Temperatur *od.* Fieber haben; **have a slight/high** ∼: leichtes/hohes Fieber haben; **take sb.'s** ∼: bei jmdm. Fieber messen

template /'templɪt/ *n.* Schablone, *die*

temple¹ /'templ/ *n.* Tempel, *der*

temple² *n.* ▶ 672 (Anat.) Schläfe, *die*

tempo /'tempəʊ/ *n., pl.* ∼s *or* **tempi** /'tempiː/ (a) (fig.: pace) **the** ∼ **of life in the town** der Rhythmus der Stadt; **the campaign** ∼ **stepped up** der Wahlkampf ging in die heiße Phase über; (b) (Mus.: speed) Tempo, *das*

temporal /'tempərl/ *adj.* (of this life) irdisch; (secular) weltlich

temporarily /'tempərərɪlɪ/ *adv.* vorübergehend

temporary /'tempərərɪ/ 1 *adj.* vorübergehend; provisorisch ‹*Gebäude, Büro*›; ∼ **worker** Aushilfe, *die;* ∼ **job** Aushilfstätigkeit, *die.* 2 *n.* Aushilfe, *die;* Aushilfskraft, *die*

temporize (**temporise**) /'tempəraɪz/ *v.i.* (a) (adopt indecisive policy) sich nicht festlegen; (b) (act so as to gain time) sich abwartend verhalten

tempt /tempt/ *v.t.* (a) (attract) ∼ **sb. out/into the town** jmdn. hinauslocken/in die Stadt locken; ∼ **sb. to do sth.** in jmdm. den Wunsch wecken, etw. zu tun; (b) (cause to have strong urge) ∼ **sb. to do sth.** jmdn. geneigt machen, etw. zu tun; **be** ∼**ed to do sth.** versucht sein, etw. zu tun; (c) (entice) verführen; **be** ∼**ed into doing sth.** sich dazu verleiten lassen, etw. zu tun; ∼ **sb. away from sth.** jmdn. von etw. weglocken; **don't** ∼ **me!** verleite mich nicht!; (d) (provoke) herausfordern; ∼ **fate** *or* **providence** das Schicksal herausfordern

temptation /temp'teɪʃn/ *n.* (a) *no pl.* (attracting) Verlockung, *die;* (being attracted) Versuchung, *die;* (enticing) Verführung, *die* (**into** zu); (being enticed) Versuchung, *die* (geh.); **feel a** ∼ **to do sth.** versucht sein, etw. zu tun; **give in to** [**the**] ∼: der Versuchung erliegen; (b) (thing) Verlockung, *die* (**to** zu)

tempting /'temptɪŋ/ *adj.* verlockend; verführerisch

ten /ten/ ▶ 630 | , ▶ 706 | , ▶ 956 | 1 *adj.* zehn; *see also* **eight** 1. 2 *n.* (a) (number, symbol) Zehn, *die;* (b) (set of ∼) Zehnerpackung, *die;* (c) **bet sb.** ∼ **to one that** ... (fig.) jede Wette halten, dass ... (ugs.). *See also* **eight** 2 a, c, d

tenable /'tenəbl/ *adj.* (a) haltbar; (fig.) haltbar ‹*Theorie, Annahme*›; vertretbar ‹*Standpunkt*›; (b) ∼ **for five years** auf fünf Jahre befristet ‹*Arbeitsverhältnis, Stelle*›

tenacious /tɪ'neɪʃəs/ *adj.* (a) (holding fast) hartnäckig haftend ‹*Dornen, Samen*›; (b) (resolute) hartnäckig; **be** ∼: sich hartnäckig halten

tenacity /tɪ'næsɪtɪ/ *n., no pl.* Hartnäckigkeit, *die*

tenancy /'tenənsɪ/ *n.* (a) (of flat, residential building) Mietverhältnis, *das;* (of farm, shop) Pachtverhältnis, *das;* **have** ∼ **of a flat** eine Wohnung gemietet haben; (b) (period) Mietdauer, *die*

tenant /'tenənt/ *n.* (a) (of flat, residential building) Mieter, *der*/Mieterin, *die;* (of farm, shop) Pächter, *der*/Pächterin, *die;* (b) (occupant) Bewohner, *der*/Bewohnerin, *die*

tend¹ /tend/ *v.i.* ∼ **to do sth.** dazu neigen *od.* tendieren, etw. zu tun; ∼ **to sth.** zu etw. neigen; **it** ∼s **to get quite cold there at nights** es wird dort nachts oft sehr kalt; **he** ∼s **to get upset if** ...: er regt sich leicht auf, wenn ...; **this** ∼s **to suggest that** ...: dies deutet darauf hin, dass ...

tend² *v.t.* sich kümmern um; hüten ‹*Schafe*›; bedienen ‹*Maschine*›; **rice has to be** ∼**ed carefully** Reis erfordert sorgfältige Pflege

tendency /'tendənsɪ/ *n.* (inclination) Tendenz, *die;* **have a** ∼ **to do sth.** dazu neigen, etw. zu tun; **there is a** ∼ **for everyone to get complacent** die Leute neigen dazu, selbstzufrieden zu werden

tendentious /ten'denʃəs/ *adj.* tendenziös

tender¹ /'tendə(r)/ *adj.* (a) (not tough) zart; (b) (sensitive) empfindlich; ∼ **spot** (fig.) wunder Punkt; (c) (loving) zärtlich; liebevoll; (d) **be of** ∼ **age** *or* **years** noch sehr jung sein; **at a** ∼ **age** in jungen Jahren; **at the** ∼ **age of twelve** im zarten Alter von zwölf Jahren

tender² *n.* (Naut.) Tender, *der*

tender³ 1 *v.t.* (a) (present) einreichen ‹*Rücktritt*›; vorbringen ‹*Entschuldigung*›; (b) (offer as payment) anbieten; **please** ∼ **exact fare** bitte den genauen Betrag bereithalten. 2 *v.i.* ∼ **for sth.** ein Angebot für etw. einreichen. 3 *n.* Angebot, *das;* **put in a** ∼: ein Angebot einreichen; **put sth. out to** ∼: etw. ausschreiben

tender-hearted /'tendəhɑːtɪd/ *adj.* weichherzig

tenderize (**tenderise**) /'tendəraɪz/ *v.t.* (Cookery) zart machen; (by beating) weich klopfen

tenderly /'tendəlɪ/ *adv.* (a) (gently) behutsam ‹*behandeln*›; (b) (lovingly) zärtlich

tenderness /'tendənɪs/ *n., no pl.* (a) (of meat etc.) Zartheit, *die;* (b) (loving quality) Zärtlichkeit, *die;* (c) (delicacy) Empfindlichkeit, *die*

tendon /'tendən/ *n.* (Anat.) Sehne, *die;* **Achilles** ∼: Achillessehne, *die*

tendril /'tendrɪl/ *n.* Ranke, *die*

tenement /'tenɪmənt/ *n.* (a) (Scot.: house containing several dwellings) Mietshaus, *das;* Mietskaserne, *die* (abwertend); (b) (Amer.: house containing several apartments) ∼ [**house**] Mietshaus, *das*

Tenerife /tenə'riːf/ *pr. n.* Teneriffa (*das*)

tenet /'tenɪt/ *n.* Grundsatz, *der*

ten-gallon 'hat *n.* Cowboyhut, *der*

tenner /'tenə(r)/ *n.* (coll.) (Brit.) Zehnpfundschein, *der;* Zehner, *der* (ugs.); (Amer.) Zehndollarschein, *der;* Zehner, *der* (ugs.)

tennis /'tenɪs/ *n., no pl.* Tennis, *das*

tennis: ∼ **ball** *n.* Tennisball, *der;* ∼ **club** *n.* Tennisverein, *der;* ∼ **court** *n.* (for lawn ∼) Tennisplatz, *der;* (for

Temperature

Temperatures in Germany, as in the rest of continental Europe, are always quoted using the centigrade scale only. To convert from Fahrenheit to centigrade (or Celsius which is the term used in Germany), deduct 32 from the number of degrees, divide by 9 and multiply by 5. The table below shows the main equivalents.

Fahrenheit (°F)		Celsius (°C)	
Boiling point	212	100	Siedepunkt
	194	90	
	176	80	
	158	70	
	140	60	
	122	50	
	104	40	
Body temperature	98.4	37	Körpertemperatur
	86	30	
	68	20	
	50	10	
Freezing point	32	0	Gefrierpunkt
	14	− 10	
	0	− 17,8	
Absolute zero	− 459.67	− 273,15	absoluter Nullpunkt

Weather

What's the temperature? = Wie viel Grad sind es?

The outside temperature is 20 degrees [centigrade] or 68 degrees Fahrenheit = Die Außentemperatur beträgt 20 Grad [Celsius]

Maximum temperature 27 degrees or (esp. Amer.) Highs around 80 degrees = Höchsttemperaturen um 27 Grad

Temperatures falling to 10 degrees or (esp. Amer.) Lows around 50 degrees = Tiefsttemperaturen um 10 Grad

temperatures around freezing = Temperaturen um den Gefrierpunkt

ten degrees below freezing = zehn Grad unter Null

− 15°C (minus fifteen degrees centigrade) = − 15° [C] (minus fünfzehn Grad [Celsius])

The temperature is above/below freezing = Die Temperatur liegt über/unter dem Gefrierpunkt *or* Nullpunkt

It's the same temperature in Berlin = In Berlin herrscht die gleiche Temperatur

People

She has a [slight] temperature, Her temperature is above normal = Sie hat [leicht] erhöhte Temperatur

He has a high temperature/a temperature of 40 [centigrade] or 104 [Fahrenheit] = Er hat [hohes] Fieber/ 40 Grad Fieber

What is your temperature? = Wie hoch ist *or* Was ist Ihre Temperatur?

My temperature is normal = Ich habe kein Fieber

She took his temperature = Sie hat bei ihm Fieber gemessen *or* hat seine Temperatur gemessen

Things

What temperature does water boil at? = Bei welcher Temperatur kocht Wasser?

Water boils at 100°C = Wasser kocht bei 100°C

What is the temperature of the wine? = Welche Temperatur hat der Wein?

The wine must be the right temperature = Der Wein muss die richtige Temperatur haben

A is the same temperature as B = A hat die gleiche Temperatur wie B

indoor ∼) Tennishalle, *die;* ∼ **'elbow** *n., no pl., no art.* (Med.) Tennisell[en]bogen, *der;* ∼ **match** *n.* Tennismatch, *das;* Tennisspiel, *das;* ∼ **player** *n.* Tennisspieler, *der/* -spielerin, *die;* ∼ **racket** *n.* Tennisschläger, *der*

tenon /'tenən/ *n.* (Woodw.) Zapfen, *der; see also* **mortise a**

tenor /'tenə(r)/ *n.* **(a)** (Mus.: voice, singer, part) Tenor, *der;* ∼ **voice** Tenorstimme, *die;* **(b)** (of argument, speech) T̄enor, *der*

tenpenny /'tenpənɪ/ *adj.* für zehn Pence *nachgestellt*

tenpenny 'piece *n.* (Brit.) Zehnpencemünze, *die*

tenpin bowling /tenpɪn 'bəʊlɪŋ/ *n.* Bowling, *das*

tense¹ /tens/ *n.* (Ling.) Zeit, *die;* **in the present/future** *etc.* ∼: im Präsens/Futur *usw.*

tense² **1** *adj.* **(a)** (taut; showing nervous tension) gespannt; **a** ∼ **silence** eine [an]gespannte Stille; **(b)** (causing nervous tension) spannungsgeladen. **2** *v.i.* **sb.** ∼**s** jmds. Muskeln spannen sich an. **3** *v.t.* anspannen

∼ **'up** *v.i.* ⟨Muskeln:⟩ sich anspannen; ⟨Person:⟩ sich verkrampfen

tension /'tenʃn/ *n.* **(a)** (latent hostility) Spannung, *die;* ∼ **between the police and the people is on the increase** die Spannungen zwischen Polizei und Bevölkerung wachsen; **there is a lot of** ∼ **between them** zwischen ihnen herrscht ein gespanntes Verhältnis; **racial** ∼: Rassenspannungen *Pl.;* **(b)** (mental strain) Anspannung, *die;* **(c)** *no pl.* (of violin string, tennis racket) Spannung, *die*

tent /tent/ *n.* Zelt, *das*

tentacle /'tentəkl/ *n.* (Zool., Bot.) Tentakel, *der od. das*

tentative /'tentətɪv/ *adj.* **(a)** (not definite) vorläufig; **make a** ∼ **suggestion** einen Vorschlag in den Raum stellen; **say a** ∼ **'yes'** vorläufig „ja" sagen; **(b)** (hesitant) zaghaft

tentatively /'tentətɪvlɪ/ *adv.* **(a)** (not definitely) vorläufig; **(b)** (hesitantly) zaghaft

tenterhooks /'tentəhʊks/ *n. pl.* **be on** ∼: [wie] auf glühenden Kohlen sitzen; **keep sb. on** ∼: jmdn. auf die Folter spannen

tenth /tenθ/ ▶738▶, ▶956▶ **1** *adj.* zehnt...; *see also* **eighth 1. 2** *n.* (in sequence, rank) Zehnte, *der/die/das;* (fraction) Zehntel, *das; see also* **eighth 2**

tent: ∼ **peg** *n.* Zeltpflock, *der;* Hering, *der;* ∼ **pole** *n.* Zeltstange, *die*

tenuous /'tenjʊəs/ *adj.* dünn ⟨Faden⟩; zart ⟨Spinnwebe⟩; (fig.) dünn ⟨Atmosphäre⟩; dürftig ⟨Argument⟩; unbegründet ⟨Anspruch⟩

tenure /'tenjə(r)/ *n.* **(a)** (right, title) Besitztitel, *der;* **(b)** (possession) Besitz, *der;* **(c)** (period) ∼ **[of office]** Amtszeit, *die;* **(d)** (permanent appointment) Dauerstellung, *die*

tepid /'tepɪd/ *adj.* lauwarm

term /tɜːm/ **1** *n.* **(a)** (word expressing definite concept) [Fach]begriff, *der;* **legal/medical** ∼: juristischer/medizinischer Fachausdruck; ∼ **of reproach** Vorwurf, *der;* **in** ∼**s of money/politics** unter finanziellem/politischem Aspekt; **(b)** *in pl.* (conditions) Bedingungen; **he does everything on his own** ∼**s** er tut alles, wie er es für richtig hält; **come to** *or* **make** ∼**s [with sb.]** sich [mit jmdm.] einigen; **come to** ∼**s [with each other]** sich einigen; **come to** ∼**s with sth.** (be able to accept sth.) mit etw. zurechtkommen; (resign oneself to sth.) sich mit etw. abfinden; ∼ **of reference** (Brit.) Aufgabenbereich, *der;* **(c)** *in pl.* (charges) Konditionen; **their** ∼**s are …:** sie verlangen …; **hire purchase on easy** ∼**s** Ratenkauf zu günstigen Bedingungen; **(d)** **in the short/long/medium** ∼: kurz-/

lang-/mittelfristig; **(e)** (Sch.) Halbjahr, *das;* (Univ.: one of two/ three/four divisions per year) Semester, *das*/Trimester, *das*/ Quartal, *das;* **during ~:** während des Halbjahres/Semesters *usw.;* **out of ~:** in den Ferien; **end of ~:** Halbjahres-/Semesterende *usw.;* **(f)** (limited period) Zeitraum, *der;* (period of tenure) ~ **[of office]** Amtszeit, *die;* **(g)** (period of imprisonment) Haftzeit, *die;* **(h)** *in pl.* (mode of expression) Worte; **praise in the highest ~s** in den höchsten Tönen loben; **(i)** *in pl.* (relations) **be on good/poor/friendly ~s with sb.** mit jmdm. auf gutem/schlechtem/freundschaftlichem Fuß stehen. **2** *v.t.* nennen

terminal /'tɜ:mnl/ **1** *n.* **(a)** (Electr.) Anschluss, *der;* (of battery) Pol, *der;* **(b)** (for train or bus) Bahnhof, *der;* (for airline passengers) Terminal, *der od. das;* **(c)** (Teleph., Computing) Terminal, *das.* **2** *adj.* **(a)** End⟨*bahnhof, -station*⟩; **(b)** (Med.) unheilbar; **have a ~ illness** unheilbar krank sein; **a ~ case** ein hoffnungsloser Fall

terminate /'tɜ:mneɪt/ **1** *v.t.* **(a)** beenden; **the contract was ~d** der Vertrag wurde gelöst; **(b)** (Med.) unterbrechen ⟨*Schwangerschaft*⟩. **2** *v.i.* enden; ⟨*Vertrag:*⟩ ablaufen

termination /tɜ:mɪ'neɪʃn/ *n.* **(a)** *no pl.* (coming to an end) Ende, *das;* (of lease) Ablauf, *der;* **(b)** *no pl.* (bringing to an end) Beendigung, *die;* (of a marriage) Auflösung, *die;* **(c)** (Med.) Schwangerschaftsabbruch, *der*

terminology /tɜ:mɪ'nɒlədʒɪ/ *n.* Terminologie, *die*

terminus /'tɜ:mɪnəs/ *n., pl.* **~es** *or* **termini** /'tɜ:mɪnaɪ/ (of bus, train, etc.) Endstation, *die*

termite /'tɜ:maɪt/ *n.* (Zool.) Termite, *die*

tern /tɜ:n/ *n.* (Ornith.) Seeschwalbe, *die*

terrace /'terəs, 'terɪs/ *n.* **(a)** (row of houses) Häuserreihe, *die;* **(b)** (adjacent to house; Agric.: on hillside) Terrasse, *die;* **(c)** *in pl.* (Footb.) Ränge *Pl.*

terraced house /'terəshaus, 'terɪshaus/, **'terrace house** *ns.* Reihenhaus, *das*

terracotta /terə'kɒtə/ *n., no pl., no indef. art.* Terrakotta, *die*

terra firma /terə 'fɜ:mə/ *n., no pl., no art.* fester Boden

terrain /te'reɪn/ *n.* Gelände, *das;* Terrain, *das* (bes. Milit.)

terrapin /'terəpɪn/ *n.* (Zool.) Sumpfschildkröte, *die*

terrestrial /tə'restrɪəl, tɪ'restrɪəl/ *adj.* terrestrisch; Erd⟨*satellit, -bevölkerung*⟩

terrible /'terɪbl/ *adj.* **(a)** (coll.: very great or bad) schrecklich (ugs.); fürchterlich (ugs.); **I feel ~ about doing it** es tut mir schrecklich leid, es zu tun; **(b)** (coll.: incompetent) schlecht; **be ~ at maths/tennis/carpentry** in Mathe schlecht sein/schlecht Tennis spielen/ein schlechter Tischler sein; **(c)** (causing terror) furchtbar

terribly /'terɪblɪ/ *adv.* **(a)** (coll.: very) unheimlich (ugs.); furchtbar (ugs.); **(b)** (coll.: appallingly) furchtbar (ugs.); **(c)** (coll.: incompetently) schlecht; **(d)** (fearfully) auf erschreckende Weise

terrier /'terɪə(r)/ *n.* Terrier, *der*

terrific /tə'rɪfɪk/ *adj.* (coll.) **(a)** (great, intense) irrsinnig (ugs.); Wahnsinns- (ugs.); unwahrscheinlich (ugs.); **(b)** (magnificent) sagenhaft (ugs.); **(c)** (highly expert) klasse (ugs.); toll (ugs.); **be ~ at sth.** in etw. (Dat.) Spitze sein (ugs.); **a ~ singer** ein Spitzensänger/eine Spitzensängerin (ugs.)

terrify /'terɪfaɪ/ *v.t.* **(a)** (fill with terror) Angst machen (+ Dat.); **terrified** verängstigt; **(b)** (coll.: make very anxious) Angst machen (+ Dat.); **be terrified that ...:** Angst haben, dass ...; **(c)** (scare) Angst einjagen (+ Dat.)

terrifying /'terɪfaɪɪŋ/ *adj.* **(a)** (causing terror) entsetzlich ⟨*Erlebnis, Film, Buch, Theaterstück*⟩; erschreckend ⟨*Klarheit, Gedanke*⟩; Furcht erregend ⟨*Anblick*⟩; beängstigend ⟨*Geschwindigkeit, Neigungswinkel*⟩; **(b)** (formidable) Furcht erregend; beängstigend ⟨*Gelehrsamkeit, Intensität*⟩

territorial /terɪ'tɔ:rɪəl/ *adj.* territorial; Gebiets- ⟨*anspruch, -hoheit usw.*⟩; Hoheits⟨*gebiet*⟩

territorial: T~ 'Army *n.* (Brit. Mil.) Territorialarmee, *die;* **~ 'waters** *n. pl.* Hoheitsgewässer *Pl.*

territory /'terɪtərɪ/ *n.* **(a)** (Polit.) Staatsgebiet, *das;* Hoheitsgebiet, *das;* **(b)** (fig.: area of knowledge or action) Gebiet, *das;* **(c)** (of commercial traveller etc.) Bezirk, *der;* **(d)** (large tract of land) Region, *die;* Gebiet, *das*

terror /'terə(r)/ *n.* **(a)** (extreme fear) [panische] Angst; **in ~:** in panischer Angst; **(b)** (person or thing causing ~)

Schrecken, *der;* **(c)** **[holy]** ~ (troublesome person) Plage, *die*

terrorise ⇒ **terrorize**

terrorism /'terərɪzm/ *n.* Terrorismus, *der;* (terrorist acts) Terror, *der;* **acts of ~:** Terrorakte

terrorist /'terərɪst/ *n.* Terrorist, *der*/Terroristin, *die; attrib.* Terror⟨*gruppe, -organisation*⟩

terrorize /'terəraɪz/ *v.t.* **(a)** (frighten) in [Angst und] Schrecken versetzen; **(b)** (coerce by terrorism) terrorisieren; (intimidate) durch Terror[akte] einschüchtern

terror: ~-stricken, ~-struck *adjs.* zu Tode erschrocken

terse /tɜ:s/ *adj.* **(a)** (concise) kurz und bündig; **(b)** (curt) knapp

tertiary /'tɜ:ʃərɪ/ *adj.* (of third order or rank) tertiär

Terylene, (P) /'terɪli:n/ *n.* Terylen, *das* ⓦ

test /test/ **1** *n.* **(a)** (examination) (Sch.) Klassenarbeit, *die;* (Univ.) Klausur, *die;* (short examination) Test, *der;* **put sb./sth. to the ~:** jmdn./etw. erproben; **(b)** (critical inspection, analysis) Test, *der;* **(c)** (basis for evaluation) Prüfstein, *der;* **(d)** (Cricket) Testmatch, *das.* **2** *v.t.* **(a)** (examine, analyse) untersuchen ⟨*Wasser, Gehör, Augen*⟩; testen ⟨*Gehör, Augen*⟩; prüfen ⟨*Schüler*⟩; überprüfen ⟨*Hypothese, Aussage, Leitungen*⟩; **~ sb. for Aids** jmdn. auf Aids untersuchen; **(b)** (try severely) auf die Probe stellen **~ out** *v.t.* ausprobieren ⟨*neue Produkte*⟩ (on an + Dat.); erproben ⟨*Theorie, Idee*⟩

testament /'testəmənt/ *n.* **(a)** **Old/New T~** (Bibl.) Altes/Neues Testament; **(b)** ⇒ **will²** **1 b**

test: ~ ban treaty *n.* [Atom]teststopp-Abkommen, *das;* **~ card** *n.* (Telev.) Testbild, *das;* **~ 'case** *n.* (Law) Musterprozess, *der;* **~ drive** *n.* Probefahrt, *die;* **~-drive** *v.t.* Probe fahren

tester /'testə(r)/ *n.* Prüfer, *der*/Prüferin, *die;* (device) Prüfgerät, *das*

test: ~ flight *n.* Testflug, *der;* Erprobungsflug, *der;* **~-fly** *v.t.* Probe fliegen

testicle /'testɪkl/ *n.* ▶672| (Anat., Zool.) Testikel, *der* (fachspr.); Hoden, *der*

testify /'testɪfaɪ/ **1** *v.i.* **(a)** **~ to sth.** etw. bezeugen; **~ to sb.'s high intelligence** jmdm. große Intelligenz bescheinigen; **(b)** (Law) **~ against sb./before sth.** gegen jmdn./vor etw. (Dat.) aussagen. **2** *v.t.* **(a)** (declare) bestätigen; **(b)** (be evidence of) beweisen

testimonial /testɪ'məʊnɪəl/ *n.* (certificate of character) Zeugnis, *das;* (recommendation) Referenz, *die*

testimony /'testɪmənɪ/ *n.* **(a)** (witness) Aussage, *die;* **(b)** (Law) [Zeugen]aussage, *die;* **(c)** *no pl.* (statements) Angaben

test: ~ match *n.* (Sport) Testmatch, *das;* **~ paper** *n.* **(a)** (Educ.) Übungsarbeit, *die;* (Univ.) Übungsklausur, *die;* **(b)** (Chem.) Indikatorpapier, *das;* **~ piece** *n.* Pflicht[übung], *die;* (Mus.) Pflichtstück, *das;* **~ pilot** *n.* (Aeronaut.) Testpilot, *der*/-pilotin, *die;* **~ run** *n.* Testfahrt, *die;* Probefahrt, *die;* (of engine) Testlauf, *der;* Probelauf, *der;* **~ tube** *n.* (Chem., Biol.) Reagenzglas, *das; attrib.* **~ tube baby** (coll.) Retortenbaby, *das* (ugs.)

testy /'testɪ/ *adj.* leicht reizbar ⟨*Person*⟩; gereizt ⟨*Antwort*⟩

tetanus /'tetənəs/ *n.* ▶865| (Med.) Tetanus, *der* (fachspr.); [Wund]starrkrampf, *der*

tetchy /'tetʃɪ/ *adj.* leicht reizbar; (on single occasion) gereizt

tête-à-tête /teɪtɑ:'teɪt/ *n.* Tête-à-tête, *das* (veralt.); Gespräch unter vier Augen

tether /'teðə(r)/ **1** *n.* (chain) Kette, *die;* (rope) Strick, *der;* **be at the end of one's ~:** am Ende [seiner Kraft] sein. **2** *v.t.* anbinden (**to** an)

Teutonic /tju:'tɒnɪk/ *adj.* **(a)** (Germanic) germanisch; **(b)** (with Germanic characteristics) teutonisch (abwertend, auch scherzh.)

text /tekst/ *n.* **(a)** Text, *der;* **they couldn't agree on the ~ of the agreement** sie konnten sich über den Wortlaut des Vertrages nicht einigen; **(b)** (passage of Scripture) Bibelstelle, *die*

'textbook *n.* (Educ.) Lehrbuch, *das*

textile /'tekstaɪl/ *n.* Stoff, *der;* ∼s Textilien *Pl.*

'text processing *n.* Textverarbeitung, *die*

textual /'tekstjʊəl/ *adj.* textlich

texture /'tekstʃə(r)/ *n.* (a) Beschaffenheit, *die;* (of fabric, material) Struktur, *die;* (of food) Konsistenz, *die;* **have a smooth** ∼: sich glatt anfühlen; (b) (of prose, music, etc.) Textur, *die* (geh.)

Th. *abbr.* **Thursday** Do.

Thai /taɪ/ **1** *adj.* thailändisch. **2** *n.* (a) *pl.* ∼s *or* same Thai, *der/die;* Thailänder, *der*/Thailänderin, *die;* (b) ▶ 897] (language) Thai, *das*

Thailand /'taɪlænd/ *pr. n.* Thailand (*das*)

Thames /temz/ *pr. n.* ▶ 1048] Themse, *die*

than /ðən, *stressed* ðæn/ *conj.* (a) (in comparison) als; **I know you better** ∼ **[I do] him** ich kenne dich besser als ihn; **I know you better** ∼ **he [does]** ich kenne dich besser als er; **you are taller** ∼ **he [is]** *or* (coll.) him du bist größer als er; (b) (introducing statement of difference) als

thank /θæŋk/ *v.t.* ∼ **sb. [for sth.]** jmdm. [für etw.] danken; sich bei jmdm. [für etw.] bedanken; **have sb./sth. to** ∼ **for sth.** jmdm./einer Sache etw. zu verdanken haben; **have [only] oneself to** ∼ **for sth.** etw. sich (*Dat.*) selbst zuzuschreiben haben; **he won't** ∼ **you for that** (iron.) er wird dir dafür nicht gerade dankbar sein; ∼ **God** *or* **goodness** *or* **heaven[s]** Gott sei Dank; **[I]** ∼ **you** danke; (slightly formal) vielen Dank; **no,** ∼ **you** nein, danke; **yes,** ∼ **you** ja, bitte; danke, ja; ∼ **you very much [indeed]** vielen herzlichen Dank; ∼**ing 'you** (coll.) danke; ∼ **you for nothing!** (iron.) danke bestens!; **I will** ∼ **you to do as you are told** (iron.) ich wäre dir sehr verbunden, wenn du tätest, was man dir sagt

thankful /'θæŋkfl/ *adj.* dankbar; **I am just** ∼ **that it's all over** ich bin nur froh, dass das jetzt alles vorüber ist

thankfully /'θæŋkfəlɪ/ *adv.* (a) (gratefully) dankbar; (b) (as sentence-modifier: fortunately) glücklicherweise

thankless /'θæŋklɪs/ *adj.* undankbar ⟨*Aufgabe, Person*⟩

thanks /θæŋks/ *n. pl.* (a) (gratitude) Dank, *der;* **accept sth. with** ∼: etw. dankend annehmen; **that's all the** ∼ **one gets** das ist nun der Dank dafür!; **give** ∼ **[to God]** dem Herrn danken; ∼ **to** (with the help of) dank; (on account of the bad influence of) wegen; ∼ **to you** dank deiner; (reproachfully) deinetwegen; **it is small** *or* **no** ∼ **to him that we won** ihm haben wir es jedenfalls nicht zu verdanken, dass wir gewonnen haben; (b) (as formula expressing gratitude) danke; **no,** ∼: nein, danke; **yes,** ∼: ja, bitte; ∼ **awfully** *or* **a lot** *or* **very much, many** ∼ (coll.) vielen *od.* tausend Dank

Thanksgiving /'θæŋksgɪvɪŋ/ *n.* ∼ **[Day]** (Amer.) [amerikanisches] Erntedankfest; Thanksgiving Day, *der*

'thank-you *n.* (coll.) Dankeschön, *das;* **a warm** *or* **hearty** ∼: ein herzliches Dankeschön; *attrib.* ∼ **letter** Dankbrief, *der;* **give sb. a** ∼ **present** jmdm. zum Dank etwas schenken

that 1 /ðæt/ *adj., pl.* **those** /ðəʊz/ (a) dieser/diese/dieses; (b) *expr. strong feeling* der/die/das; **never will I forget** ∼ **day** den Tag werde ich nie vergessen; (c) (coupled or contrasted with 'this') das/dieses [da]. **2** /ðæt/ *pron., pl.* **those** (a) der/die/das; **who is** ∼ **in the garden?** wer ist das [da] im Garten?; **what bird is** ∼**?** was für ein Vogel ist das?; **I know all** ∼: ich weiß das alles; **and [all]** ∼: und so weiter; **like** ∼: (of the kind or in the way mentioned, or ∼ character) so; **[just] like '**∼ (without effort, thought) einfach so; **don't be like** ∼**!** sei doch nicht so; **don't talk like** ∼: hör auf, so zu reden; **he is 'like** ∼: so ist er eben; ∼ **is [to say]** introducing explanation das heißt; introducing reservation das heißt; genauer gesagt; **if they'd have me,** ∼ **is** das heißt, wenn sie mich nehmen; '∼**'s more like it** (of suggestion, news) das sieht schon besser aus an; (of action, work) das sieht schon besser aus; ∼**'s right!** *expr. approval* gut *od.* recht so; (iron.) nur so weiter!; (coll.: expr. assent) jawohl; ∼**'s a good** *etc.* **boy/girl** das ist lieb [von dir, mein Junge/Mädchen]; (with request) sei so lieb *usw.;* ∼ **will do** das reicht; **sb./sth. is not as ... as all '**∼ (coll.) so ... ist jmd./etw. nun auch wieder nicht; **[so]** ∼**'s '**∼ (it's finished) so, das wär's; (it's settled) so ist es nun mal; **you are not**

going to the party, and ∼**'s '**∼**!** du gehst nicht zu der Party, und damit Schluss!; (b) (Brit.: person spoken to) **who is** ∼**?** wer ist da?; (behind wall etc.) wer ist denn da?; (on telephone) wer ist am Apparat?; **who was** ∼**?** wer war das? **3** /ðət/ *rel. pron., pl.* same der/die/das; **the people** ∼ **you got it from** die Leute, von denen du es bekommen hast; **the box** ∼ **you put the apples in** die Kiste, in die du die Äpfel getan hast; **is he the man** ∼ **you saw last night?** ist das der Mann, den Sie gestern Abend gesehen haben?; **everyone** ∼ **I know** jeder, den ich kenne; **this is all [the money]** ∼ **I have** das ist alles [Geld], was ich habe. **4** /ðət/ *adv.* (coll.) so; **he may be daft, but he's not [all] '**∼ **daft** er mag ja blöd sein, aber so blöd [ist er] auch wieder nicht. **5** /ðət/ *rel. adv.* der/die/das; **at the speed** ∼ **he was going** bei der Geschwindigkeit, die er hatte; **the day** ∼ **I first met her** der Tag, an dem ich sie zum ersten Mal sah. **6** /ðət, *stressed* ðæt/ *conj.* (a) *introducing statement; expr. result, reason or cause* dass; (b) *expr. purpose* **[in order]** ∼: damit

thatch /θætʃ/ **1** *n.* (of straw) Strohdach, *das;* (of reeds) Schilf- *od.* Reetdach, *das;* (of palm-leaves) Palmblattdach, *das;* (material) Stroh, *das*/Schilf, *das*/Palmblätter; (roofing) Dachbedeckung, *die.* **2** *v.t.* mit Stroh/Schilf/Palmblättern decken

thatched /θætʃt/ *adj.* strohgedeckt/schilf- *od.* reetgedeckt; gedeckt ⟨*Dach*⟩; Stroh-/Schilf- *od.* Reet⟨*dach*⟩

Thatcherism /'θætʃərɪzm/ *n.* (Polit.) Thatcherismus, *der*

thaw /θɔː/ **1** *n.* (a) (warmth) Tauwetter, *das;* (b) (act of ∼ing) after the ∼: nachdem es getaut hat/hatte; (c) (fig.) Tauwetter, *das;* Tauwetterperiode, *die.* **2** *v.i.* (a) (melt) auftauen; (b) (become warm enough to melt ice etc.) tauen; (c) (fig.: become less aloof or hostile) auftauen. **3** *v.t.* (a) (cause to melt) auftauen; (b) (fig.: cause to be less aloof or hostile) auftauen; entspannen ⟨*Atmosphäre*⟩

∼ **'out** ⇒ ∼ **2, 3**

the /*before vowel* ðɪ, *before consonant* ðə, *when stressed* ðiː/ **1** *def. art.* der/die/das; **all** ∼ **doors** alle Türen; **play** ∼ **piano** Klavier spielen; **if you want a quick survey, this is** ∼ **book** für einen raschen Überblick ist dies das richtige Buch; **it's** *or* **there's only** ∼ **one** es ist nur die-ser/diese/dieses eine; **he lives in** ∼ **district** er wohnt in dieser Gegend; **£5** ∼ **square metre/**∼ **gallon/**∼ **kilogram** 5 Pfund der Quadratmeter/die Gallone/das Kilogramm; **14 miles to** ∼ **gallon** 14 Meilen auf eine Gallone; ≈ 20 l auf 100 km; **a scale of one mile to** ∼ **inch** ein Maßstab von 1 : 63 360; (b) (denoting one best known) **it is '**∼ **restaurant in this town** das ist das Restaurant in dieser Stadt; **red is '**∼ **colour this year** Rot ist in diesem Jahr die Farbe; (c) *with names of diseases* **have got** ∼ **toothache/measles** (coll.) Zahnschmerzen/die Masern haben; (d) (Brit. coll.: my, our, etc.) mein/unser *usw.* **2** *adv.* ∼ **more I practise** ∼ **better I play** je mehr ich übe, desto *od.* um so besser spiele ich; **so much** ∼ **worse for sb./sth.** um so schlimmer für jmdn./etw.

theatre (Amer.: **theater**) /'θɪətə(r)/ *n.* (a) Theater, *das;* **at the** ∼: im Theater; **go to the** ∼: ins Theater gehen; (b) (lecture ∼) Hörsaal, *der;* (c) (Brit. Med.) ⇒ **operating theatre;** (dramatic art) **the** ∼: das Theater; (e) (scene of action) Schauplatz, *der;* (of war) Kriegsschauplatz, *der*

'theatregoer *n.* Theaterbesucher, *der*/-besucherin, *die*

theatrical /θɪˈrætrɪkl/ *adj.* (a) schauspielerisch; **a** ∼ **company** eine Schauspiel- *od.* Theatertruppe; (b) (showy) theatralisch ⟨*Benehmen, Verbeugung, Person*⟩

thee /ðiː/ *pron.* (arch./poet./dial.) dich; *as indirect object* dir; (Relig.: God) Dich/Dir

theft /θeft/ *n.* Diebstahl, *der;* ∼ **of cars** Autodiebstahl, *der*

their /ðeə(r)/ *poss. pron. attrib.* (a) ihr; *see also* **her²;** our; (b) (coll.: his or her) **who has forgotten** ∼ **ticket?** wer hat seine Karte vergessen?

theirs /ðeəz/ *poss. pron. pred.* ihrer/ihre/ihres; *see also* **hers; ours**

them /ðəm, *stressed* ðem/ *pron.* (a) sie; *as indirect object* ihnen; *see also* **her¹;** (b) (coll.: him/her) ihn/sie

theme /θiːm/ *n.* (a) (of speaker, writer, or thinker) Gegenstand, *der;* Thema, *das;* (b) (Mus.) Thema, *das;* Leitmotiv, *das*

theme: ~ **music** n. Titelmelodie, die; ~ **park** n. Freizeitpark, dessen Attraktionen und Einrichtungen auf ein bestimmtes Thema bezogen sind; ~ **song** n. (a) ⇒ ~ music; (b) ⇒ **signature tune;** ~ **tune** ⇒ signature tune

themselves /ðəm'selvz/ pron. (a) emphat. selbst; **the results** ~ **were** …: die Ergebnisse an sich waren …; **(b)** refl. sich ‹waschen usw.›; sich (Dat.) selbst ‹die Schuld geben›; sich (Akk.) selbst ‹regieren›. See also **herself**

then /ðen/ **1** adv. **(a)** (at that time) damals; ~ **and there** auf der Stelle; see also **now 1 a, b; (b)** (after that) dann; ~ **[again]** (and also) außerdem; **but** ~ (after all) aber schließlich; **(c)** (in that case) dann; ~ **why didn't you say so?** warum hast du dann nichts gesagt?; **hurry up,** ~! dann beeil dich aber; **but** ~ **again** aber andererseits; **(d)** expr. grudging or impatient concession dann eben; **well, take it,** ~: dann nimm es eben; **(e)** (accordingly) [dann] also. **2** n. **before** ~: vorher; davor; **by** ~: bis dahin; **from** ~ **on** von da an; **till** ~: bis dahin; **oh, we should get there long before** ~: ach, bis dahin sind wir längst dort; **since** ~: seitdem. **3** adj. damalig

theodolite /θɪ'ɒdəlaɪt/ n. (Surv.) Theodolit, der

theologian /θiːə'ləʊdʒɪən/ n. Theologe, der/Theologin, die

theological /θiːə'lɒdʒɪkl/ adj. theologisch; Theologie‹student, -dozent›

theology /θɪ'ɒlədʒɪ/ n. **(a)** no pl., no indef. art. Theologie, die; **(b)** (religious system) Glaubenslehre, die

theoretical /θɪə'retɪkl/ adj. theoretisch; **your arguments are only** ~: deine Argumentation ist reine Theorie

theoretically /θiːə'retɪkəlɪ/ adv. theoretisch

theorise ⇒ **theorize**

theorist /'θɪərɪst/ n. Theoretiker, der/Theoretikerin, die

theorize /'θɪəraɪz/ v.i. theoretisieren

theory /'θɪərɪ/ n. (also Math.) Theorie, die; ~ **of evolution/** **music** Evolutions-/Musiktheorie, die; **in** ~: theoretisch; **have a** ~ **that** …: die Theorie vertreten, dass …

therapeutic /θerə'pjuːtɪk/ adj. therapeutisch; (curative) therapeutisch wirksam

therapist /'θerəpɪst/ n. (Med.) Therapeut, der/Therapeutin, die

therapy /'θerəpɪ/ n. (Med., Psych.) Therapie, die; [Heil]behandlung, die

there /ðeə(r)/ **1** adv. **(a)** (in/at that place) da; dort; (fairly close) da; **sb. has been** ~ **before** (fig. coll.) jmd. weiß Bescheid; ~ **or** ~**a'bouts** so ungefähr; **be down/in/up** ~: da unten/drin/oben sein; ~ **goes** …: da geht/fährt usw. …; **are you** ~? (on telephone) sind Sie noch da od. (ugs.) dran?; ~ **and then** auf der Stelle; **(b)** (calling attention) **hello** or **hi** ~! hallo!; **you** ~! Sie da!; **move along** ~! weitergehen!; ~'**s a good** etc. **boy/girl** das ist lieb ‹von dir, mein Junge/ Mädchen›; **(c)** (in that respect) da; **so** ~: und damit basta (ugs.); ~ **you are wrong** da irrst du dich; ~, **it is a loose wire** da haben wir's — ein loser Draht; ~ **it is** (nothing can be done about it) da kann man nichts machen; ~ **you are** (giving sth.) [da,] bitte schön (see also **2b**); **(d)** (to that place) dahin, dorthin ‹gehen, gelangen, fahren, rücken, stellen›; **we got** ~ **and back in two hours** wir brauchten für Hin- und Rückweg [nur] zwei Stunden; **down/in/up** ~: dort hinunter/hinein/hinauf; **get** ~ **first** jmdm./den anderen zuvorkommen; **get** ~ (fig.) (achieve) es [schon] schaffen; (understand) es verstehen; **(e)** /ðə(r)/, stressed ðeə(r)/ as introductory function-word da; **was** ~ **anything in it?** war da irgendetwas drin? (ugs.); ~ **is enough food** es gibt genug zu essen; ~ **are many kinds of** …: es gibt viele Arten von …; ~ **were four of them** sie waren zu viert; ~ **was once an old woman who** …: es war einmal eine alte Frau, die …; ~ **was no beer left** es gab kein Bier mehr; ~ **appears to be some error** da scheint ein Irrtum unterlaufen zu sein; ~'**s no time for that now** dafür haben wir/habe ich jetzt keine Zeit; … **if ever** ~ **was one** … wie er/sie/es im Buche steht; **what is** ~ **for supper?** was gibt's zum Abendessen? **2** int. **(a)** (to soothe child etc.) ~, ~: na, na (ugs.); **(b)** expr. triumph or dismay ~ **[you are]!** da, siehst du! (see also **1c**); ~,

you've dropped it! da, jetzt hast du es doch fallen lassen! **3** n. da, dort; **near** ~: da od. dort in der Nähe

there: ~**abouts** /'ðeərəbaʊts/ adv. **(a)** (near that place) da [in der Nähe]; **the locals** ~**abouts** die Leute, die dort wohnen; **(b)** (near that number) **two litres or** ~**abouts** zwei Liter [so] ungefähr; see also **there 1 a;** ~**by** /ðeə'baɪ, 'ðeəbaɪ/ adv. dadurch; ~**fore** adv. deshalb; also; ~**u'pon** adv. **(a)** (soon after that) kurz darauf; **(b)** (in consequence of that) daraufhin

thermal /'θɜːml/ **1** adj. thermisch ‹Erscheinung, Anforderungen›; Wärme‹dämmung, -strahlung›; ~ **underwear** kälteisolierende Unterwäsche. **2** n. Thermik, die

thermal imaging /'ɪmɪdʒɪŋ/ n. Thermographie, die (fachspr.); Wärmebildtechnik, die; ~ **camera** Wärmebildkamera, die; Thermokamera, die

thermodynamics /θɜːmədaɪ'næmɪks/ n., no pl. (Phys.) Thermodynamik, die

thermometer /θə'mɒmɪtə(r)/ n. Thermometer, das

Thermos, thermos, (P) /'θɜːməs/ n. ~ **[flask/jug/ bottle]** Thermosflasche, die ⓦⓩ

thermostat /'θɜːməstæt/ n. Thermostat, der

thesaurus /θɪ'sɔːrəs/ n., pl. **thesauri** /θɪ'sɔːriː/ or ~**es** Thesaurus, der

these pl. of **this 1, 2**

thesis /'θiːsɪs/ n., pl. **theses** /'θiːsiːz/ **(a)** (proposition) These, die; **(b)** (dissertation) Dissertation, die, Doktorarbeit, die **(on** über + Akk.)

they /ðeɪ/ pron. **(a)** sie; **(b)** (people in general) man; **(c)** (coll.: he or she) **everyone thinks** ~ **know best** jeder denkt, er weiß es am besten; **(d)** (those in authority) sie; die (ugs.). See also **their; theirs; them; themselves**

they'd /ðeɪd/ **(a)** = **they would; (b)** = **they had**

they'll /ðeɪl/ = **they will**

they're /ðeə(r)/ = **they are**

they've /ðeɪv/ = **they have**

thick /θɪk/ **1** adj. **(a)** dick; breit, dick ‹Linie›; **a rope two inches** ~, **a two-inch** ~ **rope** ein zwei Zoll starkes od. dickes Seil; **that's** or **it's a bit** ~! (Brit. fig. coll.) das ist ein starkes Stück! (ugs.); **(b)** (dense) dicht ‹Haar, Nebel, Wolken, Gestrüpp usw.›; **(c)** (filled) ~ **with** voll von; **air** ~ **with fog and smoke** von Nebel und Rauch erfüllte Luft; **(d)** steif ‹Gallerte›; dickflüssig ‹Sahne›; dick ‹Suppe, Schlamm, Brei, Kleister›; **(e)** (stupid) dumm; **you're just plain** ~: du bist ganz einfach doof (salopp); **[as]** ~ **as two short planks** (coll.) dumm wie Bohnenstroh (ugs.); **(f)** (coll.: intimate) **be very** ~ **with sb.** mit jmdm. dick befreundet sein (ugs.); **be [as]** ~ **as thieves** dicke Freunde sein (ugs.). **2** n., no pl., no indef. art. **in the** ~ **of** mitten in (+ Dat.); **in the** ~ **of it** or **things** mitten drin; **stay with sb./ stick together through** ~ **and thin** mit jmdm./zusammen durch dick und dünn gehen. **3** adv. **job offers/complaints came in** ~ **and fast** es kam eine Flut von Stellenangeboten/Beschwerden

thick 'ear n. (Brit. coll.) **give sb. a** ~: jmdm. ein paar hinter die Ohren geben (ugs.)

thicken /'θɪkn/ **1** v.t. dicker machen; eindicken ‹Sauce›. **2** v.i. **(a)** (become thicker) **(b)** (become dense) dicker werden; **(c)** (become blurred) **his speech** ~**ed** er bekam eine schwere Zunge (geh.); **(d)** (become complex) **the plot** ~**s!** die Sache wird kompliziert!; (iron.) die Sache wird langsam interessant!

thicket /'θɪkɪt/ n. Dickicht, das

thick: ~**head** n. Dummkopf, der; ~**headed** adj. dumm

thickly /'θɪklɪ/ adv. **(a)** (in a thick layer) dick; **(b)** (densely, abundantly) dicht

thickness /'θɪknɪs/ n. **(a)** Dicke, die; **be two metres in** ~: zwei Meter dick sein; **(b)** no pl. (denseness) Dichte, die; (of hair) Fülle, die; **(c)** no pl. (of jelly) Steifheit, die; (of cream) Dickflüssigkeit, die; (of soup, porridge, glue) Dicke, die; **(d)** (layer) Lage, die

thick: ~**set** adj. (stocky) gedrungen; ~**-skinned** adj. (fig.) unsensibel; dickfellig (ugs. abwertend)

thief /θiːf/ *n., pl.* **thieves** /θiːvz/ Dieb, *der*/Diebin, *die*

thieve /θiːv/ *v.i.* stehlen

thigh /θaɪ/ *n.* (a) ▶ 672⏐ (Anat.) Oberschenkel, *der;* (b) (Zool.) Schenkel, *der*

thigh: ~ **bone** *n.* ▶ 672⏐ (Anat.) Oberschenkelknochen, *der;* ~**-boot** *n.* Kanonenstiefel, *der;* Schaftstiefel, *der*

thimble /ˈθɪmbl/ *n.* Fingerhut, *der*

thin /θɪn/ **1** *adj.* (a) (of small thickness or diameter) dünn; (b) (not fat) dünn; **a tall,** ~ **man** ein großer, hagerer Mann; **as** ~ **as a rake** *or* **lath** spindeldürr; (c) (narrow) schmal ‹Baumreihe›; dünn ‹Linie›; (d) (sparse) dünn, schütter ‹Haar›; fein ‹Regen, Dunst›; spärlich ‹Publikum, Besuch›; gering ‹Beteiligung›; dünn ‹Luft›; **he is already** ~ **on top** *or* **going** ~ **on top** bei ihm lichtet es sich oben schon; **be** ~ **on the ground** (fig.) dünn gesät sein; **vanish** *or* **disappear into** ~ **air** (fig.) sich in Luft auflösen; (e) (coll.: wretched) enttäuschend, unbefriedigend ‹Zeit›. *See also* **thick** 2. **2** *adv.* dünn. **3** *v.t.* **-nn-:** (a) (make less deep or broad) dünner machen; (b) (make less dense, dilute) verdünnen; (c) (reduce in number) dezimieren. **4** *v.i.* **-nn-** ‹Haar, Nebel:› sich lichten; ‹Menschenmenge:› sich zerstreuen

~ **'out** *v.i.* ‹Menschenmenge:› sich verlaufen; ‹Verkehr:› abnehmen; ‹Häuser:› spärlicher werden

thine /ðaɪn/ *poss. pron.* (arch./poet./dial.) (a) *pred.* deiner/deine/dein[e]s; der/die/das deinige (geh.); *see also* **hers**; (b) *attrib.* dein

thing /θɪŋ/ *n.* (a) (inanimate object) Sache, *die;* Ding, *das;* **what's that** ~ **in your hand?** was hast du da in der Hand?; **be a rare** ~: etwas Seltenes sein; **neither one** ~ **nor the other** weder das eine noch das andere; **not a** ~: überhaupt *od.* gar nichts; (b) (action) **that was a foolish** ~ **to do** das war eine große Dummheit; **it was the right** ~ **to do** es war das einzig Richtige; **we can't do a** ~ **about it** wir können nichts dagegen tun; **do** ~**s to sb./sth.** (fig. coll.) auf jmdn./etw. eine enorme Wirkung haben (ugs.); (c) (fact) [Tat]sache, *die;* **a** ~ **which is well known to everybody** eine allgemein bekannte Tatsache; **it's a strange** ~ **that** ...: es ist seltsam, dass ...; **for one** ~**, you don't have enough money[, for another** ~ ...] zunächst einmal hast du nicht genügend Geld [, außerdem ...]; **the best/worst** ~ **about the situation/her** das Beste/Schlimmste an der Situation/an ihr; **know/ learn a** ~ **or two about sth./sb.** sich mit etw./jmdn. auskennen/einiges über etw. (*Akk.*) lernen/über jmdn. erfahren; **the [only]** ~ **is that** ...: die Sache ist [nur] die, dass ...; (d) (idea) **say the first** ~ **that comes into one's head** das sagen, was einem gerade so einfällt; **what a** ~ **to say!** wie kann man nur so etwas sagen!; **have a** ~ **about sb./sth.** (coll.) (be obsessed about) auf jmdn./etw. abfahren (salopp); (be prejudiced about) etwas gegen jmdn./etw. haben; (be afraid of or repulsed by) einen Horror vor jmdm./ etw. haben (ugs.); (e) (task) **she has a reputation for getting** ~**s done** sie ist für ihre Tatkraft bekannt; **a big** ~ **to undertake** ein großes Unterfangen; (f) (affair) Sache, *die;* Angelegenheit, *die;* **make a mess of** ~**s** alles vermasseln (salopp); **make a [big]** ~ **of sth.** (regard as essential) auf etw. besonderen Wert legen; (get carried away about) über etw. (*Akk.*) aufregen; **it's one** ~ **after another** es kommt eins zum anderen; (g) (circumstance) **take** ~**s too seriously** alles zu ernst nehmen; **how are** ~**s?** wie geht's [dir]?; **as** ~**s stand [with me]** so wie die Dinge [bei mir] liegen; **it's just one of those** ~**s** (coll.) so was kommt schon mal vor (ugs.); (h) (individual, creature) Ding, *das;* **she is in hospital, poor** ~: sie ist im Krankenhaus, das arme Ding; **you spiteful** ~! du [gemeines] Biest!; (i) *in pl.* (personal belongings, outer clothing) Sachen; **wash up the dinner** ~**s** das Geschirr vom Abendessen abwaschen; (j) *in pl.* (matters) **an expert/authority on** ~**s historical** ein Fachmann/ eine Autorität in geschichtlichen Fragen; (k) (product of work) Sache, *die;* **the latest** ~ **in hats** der letzte Schrei in der Hutmode; (l) (special interest) **what's your** ~? was machst du gerne?; **do one's own** ~ (coll.) sich selbst verwirklichen; (m) (coll.: sth. remarkable) **now 'there's a** ~! das ist ja ein Ding! (ugs.); (n) **the** ~ (what is proper or needed or important) das Richtige; **blue jeans are the** ~ **among**

teenagers Bluejeans sind der Hit (ugs.) unter den Teenagern; **but the** ~ **is, will she come in fact?** aber die Frage ist, wird sie auch tatsächlich kommen?

thingamy /ˈθɪŋəmɪ/, **thingumabob** /ˈθɪŋəməbɒb/, **thingumajig** /ˈθɪŋəmədʒɪg/, **thingummy** /ˈθɪŋəmɪ/, **thingy** /ˈθɪŋɪ/ *ns.* (coll.) Dings, *der/die/das* (salopp); Dingsbums, *der/die/das* (ugs.)

think /θɪŋk/ **1** *v.t.*, **thought** /θɔːt/ (a) (consider) meinen; **we** ~ **[that]** he will come wir denken *od.* glauben, dass er kommt; **we do not** ~ **it probable** wir halten es nicht für wahrscheinlich; **he is thought to be a fraud** man hält ihn für einen Betrüger; **what do you** ~? was meinst du?; **what do you** ~ **of** *or* **about him/it?** was hältst du von ihm/davon?; **I thought to myself** ...: ich dachte mir [im Stillen]; **that's what 'they** ~! das meinen die!; ... , **don't you** ~? ... , findest *od.* meinst du nicht auch?; **where do you** ~ **you are?** was glaubst du eigentlich, wo du bist?; **who does he/she** ~ **he/she is?** für wen *od.* wofür hält er/sie sich eigentlich?; **you** *or* **one** *or* **anyone would** ~ **that** ...: man sollte [doch] eigentlich annehmen, dass ...; **I** ~ **not** ich glaube nicht; **I should '**~ **so/**~ **'not!** (indignant) das will ich meinen/das will ich nicht hoffen; **I thought as much** *or* **so** das habe ich mir schon gedacht; **I** ~ **so** ich glaube schon; **do you really** ~ **so?** findest du wirklich? **I wouldn't** ~ **so** das glaube ich kaum; **yes, I** ~ **so too** ja, das finde ich auch (ugs.); **I should** ~ **not!** (no!) auf keinen Fall; **that'll be great fun, I 'don't** ~ (coll. iron.) das kann ja lustig werden (ugs. iron.); **to** ~ **[that]** he should treat me like this! man sollte es nicht für möglich halten, dass er mich so behandelt!; **I wouldn't have thought it possible** ich hätte das nicht für möglich gehalten; (b) (coll.: remember) ~ **to do sth.** daran denken, etw. zu tun; (c) (imagine) sich (*Dat.*) vorstellen. **2** *v.i.*, **thought** (a) [nach]denken; **we want to make the students** ~: wir möchten die Studenten zum Denken bringen; **I need time to** ~ ich muss es mir erst überlegen; **I've been** ~**ing** ich habe nachgedacht; ~ **in German** *etc.* deutsch *usw.* denken; **it makes you** ~: es macht *od.* stimmt einen nachdenklich; **just** ~! stell dir das mal vor!; ~ **for oneself** sich (*Dat.*) seine eigene Meinung bilden; ~ **[to oneself]** ...: sich (*Dat.*) im Stillen denken ...; **let me** ~: lass [mich] mal nachdenken *od.* überlegen; **you'd better** ~ **again!** da hast du dich aber geschnitten! (ugs.); ~ **twice** es sich (*Dat.*) zweimal überlegen; **this made her** ~ **twice** das gab ihr zu denken; ~ **twice about doing sth.** es sich (*Dat.*) zweimal überlegen, ob man etw. tut; ~ **on one's feet** (coll.) sich (*Dat.*) aus dem Stegreif etwas überlegen; (b) (have intention) **I** ~ **I'll try** ich glaube *od.* denke, ich werde es versuchen; **we** ~ **we'll enter for the regatta** wir haben vor, an der Regatta teilzunehmen. **3** *n.* (coll.) **have a [good]** ~: es sich (*Dat.*) gut überlegen; **have a** ~ **about that!** denk mal drüber nach! (ugs.); **you have [got] another** ~ **coming!** da irrst du dich aber gewaltig!

~ **about** *v.t.* (a) (consider) nachdenken über (+ *Akk.*); **what are you** ~**ing about?** woran *od.* was denkst du [gerade]?; **give sb. something to** ~ **about** jmdm. etwas geben, worüber er/sie nachdenken kann; (to worry about) jmdm. zu denken geben; **it doesn't bear** ~**ing about** man darf gar nicht daran denken; (b) (consider practicability of) sich (*Dat.*) durch den Kopf gehen lassen; sich (*Dat.*) überlegen; **it's worth** ~**ing about** es ist überlegenswert

~ **a'head** *v.i.* vorausdenken

~ **'back** *to v.t.* sich zurückerinnern an (+ *Akk.*)

~ **of** *v.t.* (a) (consider) denken an (+ *Akk.*); ... **but I can't** ~ **of everything at once!** ... aber ich habe schließlich auch nur einen Kopf!; **he** ~**s of everything** er denkt einfach an alles; **he never** ~**s of anyone but himself** er denkt immer nur an sich; **[just]** ~ *or* **to** ~ **of it!** man stelle sich (*Dat.*) *od.* stell dir das bloß vor!; **[now I] come to** ~ **of it,** ...: wenn ich es mir recht überlege, ...; (b) (be aware of in the mind) denken an (+ *Akk.*); (c) (consider the possibility of) denken an (+ *Akk.*); **be** ~**ing of resigning** sich mit dem Gedanken tragen, zu kündigen; **I don't know what she was** ~**ing of!** ich weiß nicht, was sie sich dabei gedacht hat!; (d) (choose from what one knows) **I want you to** ~ **of a word beginning with B** überlege dir ein Wort, das mit B beginnt; ~ **of a number, double it and**

...: denk dir eine Zahl, verdoppele sie und ...; **(e)** (have as idea) **we'll ~ of something** wir werden uns etwas einfallen lassen; **can you ~ of anyone who** ...? fällt dir jemand ein, der ...?; **we're still trying to ~ of a suitable title for the book** wir suchen noch immer einen passenden Titel für das Buch; **what 'will they ~ of next?** was werden sie sich (*Dat.*) wohl [sonst] noch alles einfallen lassen?; **(f)** (remember) sich erinnern an (+ *Akk.*); **I just can't ~ of her name** ich komme einfach nicht auf ihren Namen; **(g)** ~ **little/nothing of sb./sth.** (consider contemptible) wenig/nichts von jmdm./etw. halten; **~ little/ nothing of doing sth.** (consider insignificant) wenig/nichts dabei finden, etw. zu tun; **~ much** *or* **a lot** *or* **well** *or* **highly of sb./sth.** viel von jmdm./etw. halten; **not ~ much of sb./sth.** nicht viel von jmdm./etw. halten
~ 'out *v.t.* **(a)** (consider carefully) durchdenken; **(b)** (devise) sich (*Dat.*) ausdenken
~ 'over *v.t.* sich (*Dat.*) überlegen; überdenken; **I will ~ it over** ich lasse es mir durch den Kopf gehen
~ 'through *v.t.* [gründlich] durchdenken
~ 'up *v.t.* (coll.) sich (*Dat.*) ausdenken
thinker /ˈθɪŋkə(r)/ *n.* Denker, *der*/Denkerin, *die*
thinking /ˈθɪŋkɪŋ/ **1** *n.* **in modern ~** ...: nach heutiger Auffassung ...; **what is your ~ on this question?** wie ist deine Meinung zu dieser Frage? **2** *attrib. adj.* [vernünftig] denkend
'thinking cap *n.* **put on one's ~:** scharf nachdenken; seinen Geist anstrengen
'think-tank *n.* Beraterstab, *der*
thinly /ˈθɪnlɪ/ **(a)** *adv.* dünn; **(b)** (sparsely) spärlich ‹bevölkert, bewaldet›; dünn ‹besiedelt›; **(c)** (inadequately) leicht bekleidet; (fig.) dürftig ‹verschleiert, verkleidet›
thinner /ˈθɪnə(r)/ **1** *adj., adv. compar. of* **thin** 1, 2. **2** *n.* **~[s]** Verdünner, *der*; Verdünnungsmittel, *das*
'thin-skinned *adj.* (fig.) empfindlich; dünnhäutig (geh.)
third /θɜːd/ **1** *adj.* ▶ 956 | dritt...; **the ~ finger** der Ringfinger; **~ largest/highest** *etc.* drittgrößt.../-höchst... *usw.*; **every ~ week** jede dritte Woche; **a ~ part** *or* **share** ein Drittel. **2** *n.* **(a)** ▶ 956 | (in sequence, rank) Dritte, *der/die/das*; (fraction) Drittel, *das*; **be the ~ to arrive** als Dritter/Dritte ankommen; **(b)** ▶ 738 | (day) **the ~ of May** der dritte Mai; **the ~ [of the month]** der Dritte [des Monats]
third 'gear *n., no pl.* (Motor Veh.) dritter Gang; *see also* **gear** 1 a
thirdly /ˈθɜːdlɪ/ *adv.* drittens
third: **~ 'party** *n.* Dritte, *der/die;* dritte Person; *attrib.* **~-party insurance** Haftpflichtversicherung, *die;* **be covered by ~-party insurance** haftpflichtversichert sein; **~ 'person** *n.* **(a)** ⇒ **~ party;** **(b)** ⇒ **person c;** **~-rate** *adj.* drittklassig; **T~ 'World** *n.* Dritte Welt; **countries of the T~ World, T~ World countries** Länder der Dritten Welt
thirst /θɜːst/ **1** *n.* Durst, *der;* **die of ~:** verdursten; (fig.: be very thirsty) vor Durst sterben (ugs.); **~ for knowledge** Wissensdurst, *der.* **2** *v.i.* **~ for revenge/knowledge** nach Rache/Wissen dürsten (geh.)
thirsty /ˈθɜːstɪ/ *adj.* **(a)** durstig; **be ~:** Durst haben; **sb. is ~ for sth.** (fig.) jmd. *od.* jmdn. dürstet nach etw. (dichter.); **(b)** (coll.: causing thirst) durstig machend; **this is ~ work** diese Arbeit macht durstig
thirteen /θɜːˈtiːn/ ▶ 630 |, ▶ 706 |, ▶ 956 | **1** *adj.* dreizehn; *see also* **eight** 1. **2** *n.* Dreizehn, *die; see also* **eight** 2 a, d; **eighteen** 2
thirteenth /θɜːˈtiːnθ/ ▶ 738 |, ▶ 956 | **1** *adj.* dreizehnt...; *see also* **eighth** 1. **2** *n.* **(a)** (fraction) Dreizehntel, *das;* **(b)** **Friday the ~:** Freitag, der Dreizehnte. *See also* **eighth** 2
thirtieth /ˈθɜːtɪɪθ/ ▶ 738 |, ▶ 956 | **1** *adj.* dreißigst...; *see also* **eighth** 1. **2** *n.* (fraction) Dreißigstel, *das; see also* **eighth** 2
thirty /ˈθɜːtɪ/ ▶ 630 |, ▶ 956 | **1** *adj.* dreißig; *see also* **eight** 2 a; **eighty** 2
1. **2** *n.* Dreißig, *die; see also* **eight** 2 a, d
thirty: **~-'first** *etc. adj.* ▶ 956 | einunddreißigst... *usw.; see also* **eighth** 1; **~-'one** *etc.* ▶ 956 | **1** *adj.* einunddreißig *usw.; see also* **eight** 1; **2** *n.* Einunddreißig *usw., die; see also*

eight 2 a; **~-something** **1** *adj.* **a ~-something woman/man** eine Frau/ein Mann in den Dreißigern; **be ~-something** in den Dreißigern sein; dreißig und noch was [alt] sein; **2** *n.* Dreißiger, *der/*-in, *die;* Mann/Frau in den Dreißigern; **~-somethings** Leute in den Dreißigern
this /ðɪs/ **1** *adj., pl.* **these** /ðiːz/ **(a)** dieser/diese/dieses; (with less emphasis) der/die/das; **at ~ time** zu dieser Zeit; **before ~ time** vorher; zuvor; **these days** heut[zutag]e; **I'll say ~ much/I can tell you ~ much** ...: so viel kann ich sagen/so viel kann ich dir verraten ...; **all ~ week** die[se] ganze Woche; **by ~ time** inzwischen; mittlerweile; **~ morning/evening** *etc.* heute Morgen/ Abend *usw.;* **these last three weeks** die letzten drei Wochen; **~ Monday** (to come) nächsten Montag; **(b)** (coll.: previously unspecified) **they dug ~ great big trench** sie hoben einen riesigen Graben aus; **I was in the pub when ~ fellow came up to me** ich war in der Kneipe, als [so] einer *od.* so'n Typ auf mich zukam (ugs.). *See also* **that** 1 c. **2** *pron., pl.* **these (a)** **what's ~?** was ist [denn] das?; **what is all ~?** was soll das alles?; **what flower is ~?** was ist das für eine Blume?; **fold it like ~!** falte es so!; **I knew all ~ before** ich wusste dies *od.* das alles schon vorher; **~ is not fair!** das ist nicht fair!; **what's all ~ about Jan and Angela separating?** stimmt das, dass Jan und Angela sich trennen wollen?; **(b)** (the present) **before ~:** bis jetzt; **(c)** (Brit. Teleph.: person speaking) **~ is Andy [speaking]** hier [spricht *od.* ist] Andy; **(d)** (Amer. Teleph.: person spoken to) **who did you say ~ was?** wer ist am Apparat?; mit wem spreche ich, bitte?; **(e)** **~ and that** dies und das; **~, that, and the other** alles Mögliche. **3** *adv.* (coll.) so; **~ much** so viel
thistle /ˈθɪsl/ *n.* Distel, *die*
thong /θɒŋ/ *n.* [Leder]riemen, *der*
thorax /ˈθɔːræks/ *n., pl.* **thoraces** /ˈθɔːrəsiːz/ *or* **~es** ▶ 672 | (Anat., Zool.) Thorax, *der*
thorn /θɔːn/ *n.* **(a)** (part of plant) Dorn, *der;* **(b)** (plant) Dornenstrauch, *der;* **(c)** **a ~ in the flesh** *or* **side/in sb.'s flesh** *or* **side** ein Pfahl im Fleische/im Fleische für jmdn.
thorny /ˈθɔːnɪ/ *adj.* **(a)** dornig; **(b)** (fig.: difficult) heikel; dornenreich ‹Weg›
thorough /ˈθʌrə/ *adj.* **(a)** gründlich; durchgreifend ‹Reform›; genau ‹Beschreibung, Anweisung›; **(b)** (downright) ausgemacht ‹Halunke, Nervensäge›
thorough: **~bred** **1** *adj.* **(a)** reinrassig ‹Tier›; vollblütig ‹Pferd›; **(b)** (fig.) rassig ‹Sportwagen›; **2** *n.* reinrassiges Tier; (horse) Rassepferd, *das;* (Horseracing) Vollblut, *das;* **~fare** *n.* Durchfahrtsstraße, *die;* **'no ~fare'** „Durchfahrt verboten"; (on foot) „kein Durchgang"; **~going** *adj.* **(a)** ⇒ **thorough a;** **(b)** (extreme) radikal ‹Konservative, Sozialist›
thoroughly /ˈθʌrəlɪ/ *adv.* gründlich ‹untersuchen, prüfen›; gehörig ‹müde, erschöpft›; so richtig ‹genießen›; ausgesprochen ‹langweilig›; zutiefst ‹beschämt›; (completely) völlig ‹durchnässt, verzogen›; total ‹verdorben, verwöhnt›; **be ~ fed up with sth.** (coll.) von etw. die Nase gestrichen voll haben (ugs.); **be ~ delighted with sth.** sich außerordentlich über etw. (*Akk.*) freuen
thoroughness /ˈθʌrənɪs/ *n., no pl.* Gründlichkeit, *die*
those ⇒ **that** 1, 2
thou /ðaʊ/ *pron.* (arch./poet./dial.) du; (Relig.: God) Du
though /ðəʊ/ **1** (conj.) **(a)** (despite the fact that) obwohl; **late ~ it was** obwohl es so spät war; **the car, ~ powerful, is also economical** der Wagen ist zwar stark, aber [zugleich] auch wirtschaftlich; **(b)** (but nevertheless) aber; **a slow ~ certain method** eine langsame, aber *od.* wenn auch sichere Methode; **(c)** (even if) **[even] ~:** auch wenn; **as ~ = as if** ⇒ **if 1 a;** **(d)** (and yet) **~ you never know** obwohl man nie weiß; **she read on, ~ not to the very end** sie las weiter, wenn auch nicht bis ganz zum Schluss. **2** *adv.* (coll.) trotzdem; **I like him ~:** ich mag ihn aber [trotzdem]; **you don't know him, ~:** aber du kennst ihn nicht
thought /θɔːt/ **1** ⇒ **think** 1, 2. **2** *n.* **(a)** *no pl.* Denken, *das;* [lost] **in ~:** in Gedanken [verloren *od.* versunken]; **(b)** *no pl., no art.* (reflection) Überlegung, *die;* Nachdenken, *das;* **after serious ~:** nach reiflicher Überlegung; **(c)** (consideration) Rücksicht, *die* (for auf + *Akk.*); **he has no**

~ **for others** er nimmt keine Rücksicht auf andere; **give [plenty of]** ~ **to sth.**, **give sth. [plenty of]** ~: [reiflich] über etw. (*Akk.*) nachdenken; **he never gave the matter a moment's** ~: er dachte keinen Augenblick daran; **(d)** (idea, conception) Gedanke, *der;* **I've just had a** ~! mir ist gerade ein [guter] Gedanke gekommen; **it's the** ~ **that counts** der gute Wille zählt; **at the** [**very**] ~ **of sth./of doing sth./that** ...: beim [bloßen] Gedanken an etw. (*Akk.*) /daran, etw. zu tun/, dass ...; **that's** *or* **there's a** ~! das ist aber eine [gute] Idee!; **she is** [**constantly**] **in his** ~**s** er muss ständig an sie denken; **(e)** *in pl.* (opinion) Gedanken; **I'll tell you my** ~**s on the matter** ich sage dir, wie ich darüber denke; **(f)** (intention) **have no** ~ **of doing sth.** überhaupt nicht daran denken, etw. zu tun; **give up all** ~[**s**] **of sth./doing sth.** sich (*Dat.*) etw. aus dem Kopf schlagen/es sich (*Dat.*) aus dem Kopf schlagen, etw. zu tun; **nothing was further from my** ~**s** nicht im Traum hätte ich daran gedacht

thoughtful /'θɔːtfl/ *adj.* **(a)** (meditative) nachdenklich; **(b)** (considerate) rücksichtsvoll; (helpful) aufmerksam; **(c)** (showing original thought) gedankenreich; (well thought out) [gut] durchdacht; wohl überlegt ‹*Bemerkung*›

thoughtfully /'θɔːtfəlɪ/ *adv.* **(a)** (meditatively) nachdenklich; **(b)** (considerately) rücksichtsvollerweise; **(c)** (in a well-thought-out manner) **a** ~ **written article** ein gut durchdachter Artikel

thoughtless /'θɔːtlɪs/ *adj.* **(a)** gedankenlos; ~ **of the danger,** ...: ohne an die Gefahr zu denken ...; **(b)** (inconsiderate) rücksichtslos

thoughtlessly /'θɔːtlɪslɪ/ *adv.* **(a)** gedankenlos; **(b)** (inconsiderately) aus Rücksichtslosigkeit

thought: ~**-provoking** *adj.* **be** ~**-provoking** nachdenklich stimmen; ~**-reader** *n.* Gedankenleser, *der/*-leserin, *die*

thousand /'θaʊznd/ ▸ 956﹜ **1** *adj.* **(a)** tausend; **a** *or* **one** ~: eintausend; **two/several** ~: zweitausend/mehrere tausend; **one and a half** ~: [ein]tausendfünfhundert; **a** *or* **one** ~ **and one** [ein]tausend[und]eins, **a** *or* **one** ~ **and one people** [ein]tausendundeine Person; **(b)** **a** ~ [**and one**] (fig.: innumerable) tausend (ugs.); **a** ~ **thanks** tausend Dank. *See also* **eight 1. 2** *n.* **(a)** (number) tausend; **a** *or* **one/two** ~: ein-/zweitausend; **a** ~ **and one** [ein]tausend[und]eins; **a** ~**-to-one chance** eine Chance von tausend zu eins; **(b)** (symbol, written figure) Tausend, *die;* (in adding numbers by columns) Tausender, *die* (Math.); (set or group) Tausend, *das;* **(c)** (indefinite amount) ~**s** Tausende. *See also* **eight 2 a**

thousandth /'θaʊzndθ/ ▸ 956﹜ **1** *adj.* tausendst...; **a** ~ **part** ein Tausendstel. **2** *n.* (fraction) Tausendstel, *das;* (in sequence) tausendste, *der/die/das;* (in rank) Tausendste, *der/die/das. See also* **eight 2 a**

thrash /θræʃ/ *v.t.* **(a)** (beat) [ver]prügeln; **(b)** (defeat) vernichtend schlagen; **(c)** ⇨ **thresh**
~ **'out** *v.t.* ausdiskutieren ‹*Problem, Frage*›; ausarbeiten ‹*Plan*›

thrashing /'θræʃɪŋ/ *n.* **(a)** (beating) Prügel *Pl.;* **(b)** (defeat) Schlappe, *die*

thread /θred/ **1** *n.* **(a)** Faden, *der;* **(b)** (fig.) **hang by a** ~ (be in a precarious state) an einem [dünnen *od.* seidenen] Faden hängen; (depend on sth. still in doubt) auf Messers Schneide stehen; **lose the** ~: den Faden verlieren; **take** *or* **pick up the** ~ **of the conversation** den Gesprächsfaden wieder aufnehmen; **(c)** (of screw) Gewinde, *das.* **2** *v.t.* **(a)** (pass ~ through) einfädeln; auffädeln ‹*Perlen*›; **(b)** ~ **one's way through sth.** (lit. or fig.) sich durch etw. schlängeln

'**threadbare** *adj.* abgenutzt; abgetragen ‹*Kleidung*›; (fig.) abgedroschen ‹*Argument*› (ugs.)

threat /θret/ *n.* Drohung, *die;* **make a** ~ **against sb.** jmdm. drohen; **under** ~ **of** unter Androhung von; **at the slightest** ~ **of sth.** wenn etw. auch nur ganz entfernt droht

threaten /'θretn/ *v.t.* **(a)** (use threats towards) bedrohen; ~ **sb. with prosecution/a beating** jmdm. Verfolgung/ Schläge androhen; **(b)** (announce one's intention) ~ **to do sth.** damit drohen, etw. zu tun; **the fire** ~**ed to engulf the whole village** (fig.) das Feuer drohte das ganze Dorf einzuschließen; ~ **to commit suicide/to resign** mit

Selbstmord/dem Rücktritt drohen; **(c)** drohen mit ‹*Gewalt, Repressalien, Rache usw.*›; **the sky** ~**s rain** am Himmel hängen drohende Regenwolken

threatening /'θretnɪŋ/ *adj.* drohend; ~ **letter** Drohbrief, *der*

three /θriː/ ▸ 630﹜, ▸ 706﹜, ▸ 956﹜ **1** *adj.* drei; *see also* **eight 1; R b. 2** *n.* **(a)** (number, symbol) Drei, *die;* **(b)** (set of ~ people) Dreiergruppe, *die;* **the** ~ [**of them**] die Drei. *See also* **eight 2 a, c, d**

three: ~**-dimensional** /θriːdɪ'menʃənl, θriːdaɪ'menʃənl/ *adj.* dreidimensional; ~**fold** *adj., adv.* dreifach; **a** ~**fold increase** ein Anstieg auf das Dreifache; ~**penny bit** /'θrepənɪ bɪt/ *n.* (Brit. Hist.) Dreipencestück, *das;* ~**piece** *adj.* ⇨ **piece 1 b;** ~**pin** *adj.* ⇨ **pin 1 c;** ~**ply** *adj.* dreilagig ‹*Holz*›; dreifädig ‹*Wolle, Zwirn*›; ~**-quarter** *adj.* drei viertel; ~**-quarters** ▸ 706﹜, ▸ 956﹜ **1** *n.* **(a)** drei Viertel *pl.* (**of** + *Gen.*); ~**-quarters of an hour** eine Dreiviertelstunde; **(b)** *attrib.* Dreiviertel‹*mehrheit usw.*›; **2** *adv.* drei viertel ‹*voll*›; zu drei Vierteln ‹*fertig*›

threesome /'θriːsəm/ *n.* Dreigespann, *das;* Trio, *das;* **go as a** ~: zu dritt gehen

three: ~**-storey** *adj.* dreistöckig; ~**-way adaptor** *n.* (Electr.) Dreifachstecker, *der;* ~**-wheeler** /θriː'wiːlə(r)/ *n.* Dreirad, *das* (Kfz-W.)

thresh /θreʃ/ *v.t.* (Agric.) dreschen

threshold /'θreʃəʊld/ *n.* (lit. or fig.) Schwelle, *die;* **be on the** ~ **of sth.** (fig.) an der Schwelle einer Sache (*Gen.*) stehen

threw ⇨ **throw 1**

thrift /θrɪft/ *n.* **(a)** *no pl.* Sparsamkeit, *die;* **(b)** (Bot.) Grasnelke, *die*

thrift: ~ **account** *n.* (Amer.) Sparkonto, *das;* ~ **shop,** ~ **store** (Amer.) ⇨ **charity shop**

thrifty /'θrɪftɪ/ *adj.* sparsam

thrill /θrɪl/ **1** *v.t.* (excite) faszinieren; (delight) begeistern; **be** ~**ed by/with sth.** von etw. fasziniert/begeistert sein. **2** *n.* **(a)** (wave of emotion) Erregung, *die;* **a** ~ **of joy/pleasure** freudige Erregung; **a** ~ **of excitement/anticipation** prickelnde Erregung/Vorfreude; **(b)** (exciting experience) aufregendes Erlebnis; **sb. gets a** ~ **out of sth.** etw. erregt jmdn.; **cheap** ~**s** anspruchsloser Nervenkitzel (ugs.)

thriller /'θrɪlə(r)/ *n.* Thriller, *der*

thrilling /'θrɪlɪŋ/ *adj.* aufregend; spannend ‹*Buch, Film, Theaterstück, Geschichte*›; packend ‹*Ereignis*›; mitreißend ‹*Musik*›; prickelnd ‹*Gefühl*›

thrive /θraɪv/ *v.i.* ~**d** *or* **throve** /θrəʊv/, ~**d** *or* **thriven** /'θrɪvn/ **(a)** (grow vigorously) wachsen und gedeihen; **(b)** (prosper) aufblühen (**on** bei); **business is thriving** das Geschäft floriert; **(c)** (grow rich) reich werden

throat /θrəʊt/ *n.* **(a)** ▸ 672﹜ (outside and inside of neck) Hals, *der;* (esp. inside) Kehle, *die;* **look down sb.'s** ~: jmdm. in den Hals *od.* Rachen schauen; **a** [**sore**] ~: Halsschmerzen *Pl.;* **cut sb.'s** ~: jmdm. die Kehle durchschneiden; **cut one's own** ~ (fig.) sich (*Dat.*) ins eigene Fleisch schneiden; **ram** *or* **thrust sth. down sb.'s** ~ (fig.) jmdm. etw. aufzwingen; **be at each other's** ~**s** (fig.) miteinander im Clinch liegen (ugs.); **(b)** (of bottle, vase) Hals, *der*

throaty /'θrəʊtɪ/ *adj.* **(a)** (from the throat) kehlig; **(b)** (hoarse) heiser

throb /θrɒb/ **1** *v.i.* **-bb-: (a)** (palpitate, pulsate) pochen; **(b)** ‹*Motor, Artillerie:*› dröhnen. **2** *n.* ⇨ **1**: Pochen, *das;* Dröhnen, *das*

throes /θrəʊz/ *n. pl.* Qual, *die;* **be in the** ~ **of sth.** (fig.) mitten in etw. (*Dat.*) stecken (ugs.)

thrombosis /θrɒm'bəʊsɪs/ *n., pl.* **thromboses** /θrɒm'bəʊsiːz/ (Med.) Thrombose, *die*

throne /θrəʊn/ *n.* Thron, *der;* **succeed to the** ~: die Thronfolge antreten

throng /θrɒŋ/ **1** *n.* [Menschen]menge, *die.* **2** *v.i.* strömen (**into** in + *Akk.*); (press) sich drängen. **3** *v.t.* sich drängen in (+ *Dat.*)

throttle /'θrɒtl/ **1** *n.* (Mech. Engin.) ~[**-valve**] Drosselklappe, *die;* ~[**-pedal**] (Motor Veh.) Gas[pedal], *das;* ~[**-lever**] Gashebel, *der;* **at full** ~ (Motor Veh.) mit Vollgas. **2** *v.t.* erdrosseln; (fig.) ersticken

through /θruː/ **1** *prep.* **(a)** durch; (fig.) **search/read ~ sth.** etw. durchsuchen/durchlesen; **live ~ sth.** (survive) etw. überleben; (experience) etw. erleben; **(b)** (Amer.: up to and including) bis [einschließlich]; **(c)** (by reason of) durch; infolge von ⟨*Vernachlässigung, Einflüssen*⟩; **it was all ~ you that we were late** es war nur deine Schuld, dass wir zu spät gekommen sind; **it happened ~ no fault of yours** es geschah nicht durch deine Schuld. **2** *adv.* **(a)** let sb. **~:** jmdn. durchlassen; **be ~ with a piece of work/with sb.** mit einer Arbeit fertig/mit jmdm. fertig (ugs.) sein; **(b)** (Teleph.) **be ~:** durch sein (ugs.); **be ~ to sb.** mit jmdm. verbunden sein. **3** *attrib. adj.* durchgehend ⟨*Zug*⟩; **~ coach** *or* **carriage** Kurswagen, *der* **(for** nach); **~ traffic** Durchgangsverkehr, *der;* '**no ~ road**' „keine Durchfahrt[sstraße]"; **~ ticket** [alle Umsteigestationen umfassende] Fahrkarte; **can I buy a ~ ticket to Warsaw?** kann ich bis Warschau durchlösen?

through: ~'out 1 *prep.* **~out the war/period** den ganzen Krieg/die ganze Zeit hindurch; **spread ~out the country** sich im ganzen Land verbreiten; **2** *adv.* (entirely) ganz; (always) stets; die ganze Zeit [hindurch]; **~way** *n.* (Amer.: expressway) Schnellstraße, *die*

throve ⇒ **thrive**

throw /θrəʊ/ **1** *v.t.*, **threw** /θruː/, **thrown** /θrəʊn/ **(a)** werfen; **~ sth. to sb.** jmdm. etw. zuwerfen; **~ sth. at sb.** etw. nach jmdm. werfen; **~ me that towel, please** wirf mal bitte das Handtuch rüber (ugs.); **~ a punch/punches** zuschlagen; **~ a left/right** eine Linke/Rechte schlagen; **~ oneself on one's knees/to the floor/into a chair** sich auf die Knie/zu Boden/in einen Sessel werfen; **~ oneself at sb.** sich auf jmdn. werfen; (fig.) sich jmdm. an den Hals werfen (ugs.); **(b)** (fig.) **~ sb. out of work/into prison** jmdn. entlassen *od.* (ugs.) hinauswerfen/ins Gefängnis werfen (geh.); **be ~n upon one's own resources** selbst für sich aufkommen müssen; **~ oneself into a task** sich in eine Arbeit (*Akk.*) stürzen; **~ sth. into disarray** etw. durcheinander bringen; **(c)** (bring to the ground) zu Boden werfen ⟨*Ringer, Gegner*⟩; (unseat) abwerfen ⟨*Reiter*⟩; **(d)** (coll.: disconcert) ⟨*Frage:*⟩ aus der Fassung bringen; **(e)** (Pottery) drehen; **(f)** *also abs.* (Games) werfen; **~ [the/a dice]** würfeln. **2** *n.* Wurf, *der*

~ a'bout *v.t.* herumwerfen (ugs.); **~ one's money about** (fig.) mit Geld um sich werfen; *see also* **weight 1 a**

~ a'round *v.t.* **(a)** ⇒ **~ about; (b)** (surround with) **~ a cordon around an area** ein Gebiet abriegeln

~ a'way *v.t.* **(a)** (get rid of, waste) wegwerfen; (discard) abwerfen ⟨*Spielkarte*⟩; **~ away money on sth.** Geld für etw. wegwerfen; **(b)** (lose by neglect) verschenken ⟨*Vorteil, Vorsprung, Spiel usw.*⟩

~ 'back *v.t.* **(a)** (return, repulse) zurückwerfen; **(b)** zurückschlagen ⟨*Bettuch, Vorhang, Teppich*⟩; zurückwerfen ⟨*Kopf*⟩

~ 'down *v.t.* **~ down [on the ground]** auf den Boden werfen; **it's ~ing it down** (coll.) es gießt [wie aus Eimern] (ugs.)

~ 'in *v.t.* **(a)** (include as free extra) [gratis] dazugeben; **with ... ~n in** mit ... als Zugabe; **(b)** (interpose) einstreuen ⟨*Bemerkung*⟩; **(c)** (Footb., Rugby) einwerfen; **(d)** **~ one's hand in** (fig.: withdraw) aufgeben

~ 'off *v.t.* **(a)** (discard) ablegen ⟨*Maske, Verkleidung*⟩; von sich werfen ⟨*Kleider*⟩; (get rid of) loswerden ⟨*Erkältung, lästige Person*⟩; **(b)** (perform or write casually) [mühelos] hinwerfen ⟨*Rede, Gedicht usw.*⟩

~ 'on 1 *v.t.* sich werfen in ⟨*Kleider*⟩. **2** *v. refl.* **~ oneself [up]on sb.** sich auf jmdn. stürzen

~ 'out *v.t.* **(a)** (discard) wegwerfen; **(b)** (expel) **~ sb. out [of sth.]** jmdn. [aus etw.] hinauswerfen (ugs.); **~ sb. out of work** jmdn. hinauswerfen (ugs.); **(c)** (refuse) verwerfen ⟨*Plan usw.*⟩; **(d)** (put forward tentatively) in den Raum stellen ⟨*Vorschläge*⟩; **(e)** **~ out one's chest** die Brust herausdrücken; **(f)** (confuse) durcheinander bringen; aus dem Konzept bringen ⟨*Sprecher*⟩

~ to'gether *v.t.* **(a)** (assemble hastily) zusammenhauen (ugs.); zusammenwerfen ⟨*Ideen, Zutaten*⟩; herzaubern ⟨*Essen*⟩; zusammenschustern (ugs. abwertend) ⟨*Aufsatz, Artikel*⟩; zusammenschreiben ⟨*Buch, Artikel, Rede*⟩; **(b)** (bring together) zusammenwürfeln

~ 'up 1 *v.t.* **(a)** (lift quickly) hochwerfen ⟨*Arme, Hände*⟩; [plötzlich] hochschieben ⟨*Fenster*⟩; **(b)** (erect quickly) hochziehen (salopp) ⟨*Gebäude*⟩; **(c)** (give up) hinwerfen (ugs.) ⟨*Arbeit*⟩; aufgeben ⟨*Versuch*⟩; abbrechen ⟨*Laufbahn, Ausbildung*⟩; **(d)** (produce) hervorbringen ⟨*Führer, Ideen usw.*⟩; **(e)** (coll.: vomit) ausspucken (ugs.). **2** *v.i.* (coll.: vomit) brechen (ugs.)

throw: ~away 1 *adj.* **(a)** (disposable) Wegwerf-; Einweg-; **(b)** (underemphasized) beiläufig [gesprochen] ⟨*Bemerkung*⟩; **2** *n.* Wegwerfartikel, *der;* (bottle) Einwegflasche, *die;* **~back** *n.* Rückkehr, *die* **(to** zu)

thrower /'θrəʊə(r)/ *n.* Werfer, *der*/Werferin, *die*

'**throw-in** *n.* (Footb., Rugby) Einwurf, *der*

thrown ⇒ **throw 1**

thru /θruː/ (Amer.) ⇒ **through**

thrush /θrʌʃ/ *n.* (Ornith.) Drossel, *die*

thrust /θrʌst/ **1** *v.t.*, **thrust (a)** (push suddenly) stoßen; **he ~ his fist into my face** er stieß mir seine Faust ins Gesicht; (fig.) **~ aside** beiseite schieben; in den Wind schlagen ⟨*Warnungen*⟩; **~ extra work [up]on sb.** jmdm. zusätzliche Arbeit aufbürden; **fame was ~ upon her** sie wurde unversehens berühmt; **(b) ~ one's way through/into/out of sth.** sich durch/in/aus etw. drängen. **2** *n.* **(a)** (sudden push) Stoß, *der;* **(b)** (gist) Stoßrichtung, *die;* **(c)** (Mil.: advance) Vorstoß, *der;* **(d)** (force of jet engine) Schub, *der*

thruway (Amer.) ⇒ **throughway**

thud /θʌd/ **1** *v.i.*, **-dd-** dumpf schlagen; **~ to the floor/ground** dumpf [auf dem Fußboden/Boden] aufschlagen. **2** *n.* dumpfer Schlag

thug /θʌɡ/ *n.* Schläger, *der*

thuggery /'θʌɡərɪ/ *n.*, *no pl.* Schlägerunwesen, *das*

thuggish /'θʌɡɪʃ/ *adj.* aggressiv ⟨*Verhalten, Fußballfan*⟩; **~ lout/youth** jugendlicher Schläger

thumb /θʌm/ **1** *n.* ▶672 Daumen, *der;* **give sb. the ~s down on a proposal/idea** jmds. Vorschlag/Idee ablehnen; **get the ~s down** ⟨*Idee:*⟩ verworfen werden; ⟨*Kandidat:*⟩ abgelehnt werden; **get the ~s up** ⟨*Person, Projekt:*⟩ akzeptiert werden; **have ten ~s, be all ~s** zwei linke Hände haben (ugs.); **have sb. under one's ~:** jmdn. unter der Fuchtel haben (ugs.); **be under sb.'s ~:** unter jmds. Fuchtel stehen. **2** *v.t.* **(a) ~ a lift** einem Autofahrer winken, um sich mitnehmen zu lassen; (hitch-hike) per Anhalter fahren; **(b)** (turn over) [mit dem Daumen] durchblättern ⟨*Buch*⟩; [mit dem Daumen] umblättern ⟨*Seiten*⟩; **(c) ~ one's nose [at sb.]** [jmdm.] eine lange Nase machen

~ through *v.t.* [mit dem Daumen] durchblättern ⟨*Buch*⟩

thumb: ~-index *n.* Daumenregister, *das;* **~nail** *n.* Daumennagel, *der; attrib.* **~nail sketch** (Art) Miniaturportrait, *das;* (fig.: brief description) kurze Beschreibung; **~tack** *n.* (Amer.) Reißzwecke, *die*

thump /θʌmp/ **1** *v.t.* [mit Wucht] schlagen. **2** *v.i.* **(a)** hämmern **(at, on** gegen); ⟨*Herz:*⟩ heftig pochen; **(b)** (move noisily) **~ around** herumpoltern. **3** *n.* **(a)** (blow) Schlag, *der;* **(b)** (dull sound) Bums, *der* (ugs.); dumpfer Schlag

thunder /'θʌndə(r)/ **1** *n.* **(a)** *no pl., no indef. art.* Donner, *der;* **roll/crash of ~:** Donnerrollen, *das*/-schlag, *der;* **(b) steal sb.'s ~** (fig.) jmdm. die Schau stehlen (ugs.). **2** *v.i.* donnern

thunder: ~bolt *n.* Blitzschlag [mit Donner]; (from God) Blitzstrahl, *der* (geh.); **come as something of a ~bolt** wie ein Blitz einschlagen; **~clap** *n.* Donnerschlag, *der;* **~cloud** *n.* Gewitterwolke, *die*

thunderous /'θʌndərəs/ *adj.* donnernd

thunder: ~storm *n.* Gewitter, *das;* **~struck** *adj.* **be ~struck** wie vom Donner gerührt sein

thundery /'θʌndərɪ/ *adj.* gewittrig; **it looks ~:** es sieht nach Gewitter aus

Thurs. *abbr.* ▶739 **Thursday** Do.

Thursday /'θɜːzdeɪ, 'θɜːzdɪ/ ▶739 **1** *n.* Donnerstag, *der.* **2** *adv.* (coll.) **she comes ~s** sie kommt donnerstags. *See also* **Friday**

thus /ðʌs/ *adv.* **(a)** (in the way indicated) so; (thereby) dadurch; **(b)** (accordingly) deshalb; daher; **(c)** (to this extent) **~ much/far** so viel/so weit

thwart /θwɔːt/ v.t. durchkreuzen ‹Pläne, Absichten›; vereiteln ‹Versuch›; ∼ sb. jmdm. einen Strich durch die Rechnung machen

thy /ðaɪ/ poss. pron. attrib. (arch./poet./dial.) dein; see also **her²**

thyme /taɪm/ n. (Bot.) Thymian, der

thyroid /ˈθaɪrɔɪd/ n. ∼ **[gland]** (Anat., Zool.) Schilddrüse, die

tiara /tɪˈɑːrə/ n. Diadem, das

Tibet /tɪˈbet/ pr. n. Tibet (das)

Tibetan /tɪˈbətn/ ▶897⏐, ▶947⏐ **1** adj. tibetisch; **sb. is** ∼: jmd. ist Tibeter/Tibeterin. **2** n. **(a)** (person) Tibeter, der/ Tibeterin, die; **(b)** (language) Tibetisch, das

tick¹ /tɪk/ **1** v.i. ticken; **what makes sb.** ∼ (fig.) worauf jmd. anspricht. **2** v.t. **(a)** mit einem Häkchen versehen; **(b)** ⇒ ∼ **off a. 3** n. **(a)** (of clock etc.) Ticken, das; **(b)** (Brit. coll.: moment) Sekunde, die; **half a** ∼!, **just a** ∼! Momentchen! (ugs.); **I'll be with you in a** ∼ or **two** ∼**s** ich komme gleich; **(c)** (mark) Häkchen, das; **put a** ∼ **against your preference** kennzeichnen Sie das, was Sie bevorzugen, mit einem Häkchen

∼ **a'way** v.i. [weiter] ticken; **the minutes** ∼**ed away** die Minuten verstrichen

∼ **'off** v.t. **(a)** (cross off) abhaken; **(b)** (coll.: reprimand) rüffeln (ugs.)

∼ **'over** v.i. **(a)** (Motor Veh.) im Leerlauf laufen; ∼ **over noisily/too slowly/too fast** im Leerlauf [zu] laut/zu langsam/zu schnell drehen; **(b)** (fig.) ∼ **over [nicely]** (progress satisfactorily) ganz gut laufen (ugs.)

tick² n.(arachnid) Zecke, die; (insect) Lausfliege, die

tick³ n. (coll.: credit) **buy on** ∼: auf Pump kaufen (salopp); **can I have it on** ∼? kann ich das anschreiben lassen?

ticker tape /ˈtɪkəteɪp/ n. (Amer.) [Papier]streifen, der (aus dem Fernschreiber)

ticket /ˈtɪkɪt/ n. **(a)** Karte, die; (for concert, theatre, cinema, exhibition) [Eintritts]karte, die; (for public transport) Fahrschein, der; (of cardboard) Fahrkarte, die; (for aeroplane) Flugschein, der; Ticket, das; (of lottery, raffle) Los, das; (for library) Ausweis, der; **price** ∼: Preisschild, das; **[parking]** ∼ (notification of traffic offence) Strafmandat, das; Strafzettel, der (ugs.); **(b)** (Amer. Polit.: list of candidates) [Wahl]liste, die; **run on the Democratic/Republican** ∼: für die Demokraten/Republikaner kandidieren

ticket: ∼ **collector** n. ▶887⏐ (on train) Schaffner, der/ Schaffnerin, die; (on station) Fahrkartenkontrolleur, der/ -kontrolleurin, die; ∼**-holder** n. (at concert, theatre, cinema, exhibition) Besitzer/Besitzerin einer Eintrittskarte; ∼**-inspector** n. ▶887⏐ Fahrkartenkontrolleur, der/-kontrolleurin, die; ∼ **office** n. Kartenschalter, der; (for public transport) Fahrkartenschalter, der; (for advance booking) Kartenvorverkaufsstelle, die

ticking-'off n. (coll.) Rüffel, der (ugs.)

tickle /ˈtɪkl/ **1** v.t. **(a)** (touch lightly) kitzeln; **(b)** (amuse) **be** ∼**d by sth.** sich über etw. (Akk.) amüsieren; **be** ∼**d pink about sth.** (coll.) sich wahnsinnig über etw. (Akk.) freuen (ugs.); ∼ **sb.'s fancy** jmdn. reizen. **2** v.i. kitzeln

ticklish /ˈtɪklɪʃ/ adj. (lit. or fig.) kitzlig

tick: ∼**-over** n. (Motor Veh.) Leerlauf, der; ∼**-tock** /ˈtɪktɒk/ n. Ticktack, das

tidal /ˈtaɪdl/ adj. Gezeiten-; ∼ **power station** Gezeitenkraftwerk, das

'tidal wave n. Flutwelle, die

tiddler /ˈtɪdlə(r)/ n. (Brit. coll./child lang.) **(a)** (fish) Fischchen, das; **(b)** (child) Kleine, das

tiddlywink /ˈtɪdlɪwɪŋk/ n. **(a)** (counter) farbiges Plättchen; **(b)** ∼**s** sing. (game) Flohhüpfen, das

tide /taɪd/ **1** n. **(a)** (rise or fall of sea) Tide, die (nordd., bes. Seemannsspr.); **high** ∼: Flut, die; **low** ∼: Ebbe, die; **the** ∼**s** die Gezeiten; **sail on the next** ∼: mit der nächsten Flut auslaufen; **the** ∼ **is in/out** es ist Flut/Ebbe; **when the** ∼ **is in/out** bei Flut/Ebbe; see also **turn 1** g; **(b)** (fig.: trend) Trend, der; **go with/against the** ∼: mit dem/gegen den Strom schwimmen; see also **turn 3 c. 2** v.t. ∼ **sb. over** jmdm. über die Runden helfen (ugs.); ∼ **sb. over a difficult period** jmdm. über eine schwierige Zeit hinweghelfen

'tidemark n. **(a)** Flutmarke, die; **(b)** (Brit. coll.: line on body, bath, etc.) Schmutzrand, der

tidily /ˈtaɪdɪlɪ/ adv. ordentlich; (clearly) übersichtlich ‹präsentieren, gestalten›

tidiness /ˈtaɪdɪnɪs/ n., no pl. Ordentlichkeit, die

tidings /ˈtaɪdɪŋz/ n. pl. (literary) Kunde, die (geh.)

tidy /ˈtaɪdɪ/ **1** adj. **(a)** (neat) ordentlich; aufgeräumt ‹Zimmer, Schreibtisch›; **make oneself/a room** ∼: sich zurechtmachen/ein Zimmer aufräumen; **(b)** (coll.: considerable) ordentlich (ugs.); **a** ∼ **sum** or **penny** ein hübsches Sümmchen (ugs.). **2** v.t. aufräumen ‹Zimmer›; ∼ **oneself** sich zurechtmachen

∼ **a'way** v.t. wegräumen

∼ **'up 1** v.i. aufräumen. **2** v.t. aufräumen; in Ordnung bringen ‹Text›

tie /taɪ/ **1** v.t., **tying** /ˈtaɪɪŋ/ **(a)** binden (to an + Akk., into zu); ∼ **the prisoner's legs together** dem Gefangenen die Beine zusammenbinden; ∼ **an apron round you[r waist]** binde dir eine Schürze um; ∼ **a knot** einen Knoten machen; **(b)** (Sport: gain equal score in) ∼ **the match** unentschieden spielen; **(c)** (restrict) binden (to an + Akk.). **2** v.i., **tying (a)** (be fastened) **it won't** ∼: es lässt sich nicht binden; **it** ∼**s at the back** es wird hinten gebunden; **(b)** (have equal scores, votes, etc.) ∼ **for second place in the competition/election** mit gleicher Punktzahl den zweiten Platz im Wettbewerb/mit gleicher Stimmenzahl den zweiten Platz bei der Wahl erreichen; ∼ **6 : 6** mit 6 : 6 ein Unentschieden erreichen. **3** n. **(a)** Krawatte, die; **(b)** (cord etc. for fastening) Band, das; **(c)** (fig.) (bond) Band, das; (restriction) Bindung, die; **(d)** (equality) (of scores) Punktgleichheit, die; (of votes) Patt, das; Stimmengleichheit, die; **there was a** ∼ **for third place** zwei Teilnehmer landeten punktgleich auf dem dritten Platz; **end in** or **be a** ∼: unentschieden od. mit einem Unentschieden enden; **(e)** (Sport: match) Begegnung, die

∼ **'back** v.t. zurückbinden

∼ **'down** v.t. **(a)** (fasten) festbinden; **(b)** (fig.: restrict) binden; **be** ∼**d down by sth.** durch etw. gebunden od. eingeschränkt sein; ∼ **sb. down to a time/a schedule** jmdn. auf eine Zeit/einen Zeitplan festlegen

∼ **'in 1** v.i. ∼ **in with sth.** zu etw. passen. **2** v.t. ∼ **sth. in with sth.** etw. mit etw. abstimmen

∼ **'up** v.t. **(a)** (bind) festbinden; festmachen ‹Boot›; ∼ **up a parcel with string** ein Paket verschnüren; **(b)** (complete arrangements for) abschließen; **(c)** (make unavailable) fest anlegen ‹Geld›; **(d)** ⇒ ∼ **in 2; (e)** (keep busy) beschäftigen

tie: ∼**-break,** ∼**-breaker** ns. Tiebreak, der od. das; ∼**-clip** n. Krawattenhalter, der; ∼**-on** adj. Anhänge-; ∼**-on label** Anhänger, der; ∼**pin** n. Krawattennadel, die

tier /tɪə(r)/ n. **(a)** (row) Rang, der; **(b)** (unit) Stufe, die

tiger /ˈtaɪɡə(r)/ n. **(a)** (Zool.) Tiger, der; **paper** ∼ (fig.) Papiertiger, der; **(b)** (fierce or energetic person) Kämpfernatur, die

tight /taɪt/ **1** adj. **(a)** (firm) fest; fest angezogen ‹Schraube, Mutter›; festsitzend ‹Deckel, Korken›; **be very** ∼: sehr fest sitzen; **the drawer/window is** ∼: die Schublade/das Fenster klemmt; **(b)** (close-fitting) eng ‹Kleid, Hose, Schuh usw.›; **this shoe is rather [too]** ∼ or **a rather** ∼ **fit** dieser Schuh ist etwas zu eng; **(c)** (impermeable) ∼ **seal/ joint** dichter Verschluss/dichte Fuge; **(d)** (taut) straff; **a** ∼ **feeling in one's chest** ein Gefühl der Beklemmung od. Enge in der Brust; **(e)** (with little space) knapp; gedrängt ‹Programm›; **(f)** (difficult to negotiate) **a** ∼ **corner** eine enge Kurve; **be in/get oneself into a** ∼ **corner** or (coll.) **spot [over sth.]** (fig.) [wegen etw.] in der Klemme sein/in die Klemme geraten (ugs.); **(g)** (strict) streng ‹Kontrolle, Disziplin›; straff ‹Organisation›; **(h)** (coll.: stingy) knauserig (ugs.); (coll.: drunk) voll (salopp); **get** ∼: sich voll laufen lassen (salopp). **2** adv. (firmly) fest; **hold** ∼! halt dich fest!; **(b)** (so as to leave no space) [ganz] voll. **3** n. in pl. **(a)** (Brit.) **[pair of]** ∼**s** Strumpfhose, die; **(b)** (of dancer etc.) Trikothose, die

tighten /ˈtaɪtn/ **1** v.t. **(a)** [fest] anziehen ‹Knoten, Schraube, Mutter usw.›; straff ziehen ‹Seil, Schnur›; anspannen ‹Muskeln›; verstärken ‹Griff›; ∼ **one's belt** (fig.) den Gürtel enger schnallen (ugs.); **(b)** (make stricter) verschärfen ‹Kontrolle, Gesetz, Vorschrift›. **2** v.i. sich spannen; ‹Knoten:› sich zusammenziehen

~ 'up 1 *v.t.* **(a)** anziehen; (retighten) nachziehen; **(b)** (make stricter) verschärfen ⟨*Gesetze, Bestimmungen, Kontrollen*⟩; **~ up security** die Sicherheitsmaßnahmen verschärfen. **2** *v.i.* härter durchgreifen; **~ up on security/drunken driving** die Sicherheitsmaßnahmen verschärfen/bei Trunkenheit am Steuer schärfer durchgreifen

tight: **~-fisted** /taɪtˈfɪstɪd/ *adj.* geizig; **~-fitting** *adj.* eng anliegend ⟨*Pullover, Trikot*⟩; **~-lipped** /ˈtaɪtlɪpt/ *adj.* **(a)** (without emotion) mit zusammengepressten Lippen *nachgestellt;* **(b)** (silent) verschwiegen

tightness /ˈtaɪtnɪs/ *n., no pl.* **(a)** (firmness) Festigkeit, *die;* **(b)** (closeness of fit) enger Sitz; **(c)** (lack of leakage) Dichtheit, *die;* **(d)** (tautness) Straffheit, *die;* **(e)** (strictness of control or discipline) Strenge, *die*

'tightrope *n.* Drahtseil, *das; attrib.* **~ walker** Seiltänzer, *der/*-tänzerin, *die*

tigress /ˈtaɪgrɪs/ *n.* (Zool.) Tigerin, *die*

tile /taɪl/ **1** *n.* **(a)** (on roof) Ziegel, *der;* (on floor, wall) Fliese, *die;* (on stove; also designer ~) Kachel, *die;* **spend the night on the ~s** (fig. sl.) die ganze Nacht durchsumpfen (salopp); **(b)** (Games) Spielstein, *der.* **2** *v.t.* [mit Ziegeln] decken ⟨*Dach*⟩; fliesen ⟨*Wand, Fußboden*⟩; kacheln ⟨*Wand*⟩; **~d roof** Ziegeldach, *das;* **~d floor** Fliesenboden, *der*

tiling /ˈtaɪlɪŋ/ *n., no pl., no indef. art.* **(a)** (fixing tiles) (on roof) [Dach]decken, *das;* (on floor) Fliesen[legen], *das;* (on wall) Kacheln, *das;* Fliesen, *das;* **(b)** (set of tiles) ⇒ **tile 1 a:** Ziegel/Kacheln/Fliesen

till¹ /tɪl/ *v.t.* (Agric.) bestellen

till² **1** *prep.* bis; (followed by article + noun) bis zu; **not** […] **~:** erst; *see also* **until 1. 2** *conj.* bis; *see also* **until 2**

till³ *n.* Kasse, *die;* **at the ~:** an der Kasse; **have/put one's hand** *or* **fingers in the ~** (fig.) in die Kasse greifen

tiller /ˈtɪlə(r)/ *n.* (Naut.) Pinne, *die* (Seemannsspr.)

'till receipt *n.* Kassenzettel, *der;* Kassenbon, *der*

tilt /tɪlt/ **1** *v.i.* kippen. **2** *v.t.* kippen; neigen ⟨*Kopf*⟩. **3** *n.* **(a)** Schräglage, *die;* **a 45° ~:** eine Neigung *od.* ein Neigungswinkel von 45°; **(b)** **[at] full ~:** mit voller Wucht

timber /ˈtɪmbə(r)/ *n.* **(a)** *no pl.* (wood for building) [Bau]holz, *das;* **(b)** (type of wood) Holzart, *die;* Holz, *das;* **(c)** *no pl., no indef. art.* (trees) Wald, *der;* **(d)** (beam, piece of wood) Balken, *der;* (Naut.) Spant, *das;* **(e)** **~!** Baum fällt!; Achtung! (Ausruf bei Holzfällarbeiten)

timbre /ˈtæmbə(r), ˈtæbr/ *n.* (Mus.) Timbre, *das*

time /taɪm/ **1** *n.* **(a)** *no pl., no art.* Zeit, *die;* **the greatest composer of all ~:** der größte Komponist aller Zeiten; **for all ~:** für immer [und ewig]; **past/present/future ~:** Vergangenheit, *die/*Gegenwart, *die/*Zukunft, *die;* **stand the test of ~:** die Zeit überdauern; sich bewähren; **in [the course of] ~, as ~ goes on/went on** mit der Zeit; im Laufe der Zeit; **as old as ~:** uralt; **~ will tell** *or* **show** die Zukunft wird es zeigen; **at this point** *or* **moment in ~:** zum gegenwärtigen Zeitpunkt; **~ flies** die Zeit vergeht [wie] im Fluge; **work against ~:** unter Zeitdruck arbeiten; **in ~, with ~** (sooner or later) mit der Zeit; **(b)** (interval, available or allotted period) Zeit, *die;* **in a week's/month's/year's ~:** in einer Woche/in einem Monat/Jahr; **there is ~ for that** dafür ist *od.* haben wir noch Zeit; **it takes me all my ~ to do it** es beansprucht meine ganze Zeit, es zu tun; **give one's ~ to sth.** einer Sache (*Dat.*) seine Zeit opfern; **waste of ~:** Zeitverschwendung, *die;* **spend [most of one's/a lot of] ~ on sth./[in] doing sth.** [die meiste/viel] Zeit mit etw. zubringen/damit verbringen, etw. zu tun; **I have been waiting for some/a long ~:** ich warte schon seit einiger Zeit/schon lange; **she will be there for [quite] some ~:** sie wird ziemlich lange dort sein; **be pressed for ~:** keine Zeit haben; (have to finish quickly) in Zeitnot sein; **pass the ~:** sich (*Dat.*) die Zeit vertreiben; **length of ~:** Zeit[dauer], *die;* **make ~ for sb./sth.** sich (*Dat.*) für jmdn./etw. Zeit nehmen; **a short ~ ago** vor kurzem; **that's a long ~ ago** das ist schon lange her; **in one's own ~:** in seiner Freizeit; (whenever one wishes) wann man will; **take one's [over sth.]** sich (*Dat.*) [für etw.] Zeit lassen; (be slow) sich (*Dat.*) Zeit [mit etw.] lassen; **~ is money** (prov.) Zeit ist Geld (Spr.); **in [good] ~** (not late) rechtzeitig; **all the** *or* **this ~:** die ganze

Zeit; (without ceasing) ständig; **in [less than** *or* **next to] 'no ~:** innerhalb kürzester Zeit; **im Nu** *od.* Handumdrehen; **in 'half the ~:** in der Hälfte der Zeit; **'half the ~** (coll.: as often as not) fast immer; **it will take [some] ~:** es wird einige Zeit dauern; **have the/no ~:** Zeit/keine Zeit haben; **sb. has no ~ for sb./sth.** für jmdn./etw. ist jmdm. seine Zeit zu schade; **there is no ~ to lose** *or* **be lost** es ist keine Zeit zu verlieren; **lose no ~ in doing sth.** (not delay) etw. unverzüglich tun; **do ~** (coll.) eine Strafe absitzen (ugs.); **in my '~** (heyday) zu meiner Zeit (ugs.); (in the course of my life) im Laufe meines Lebens; **in 'my ~** (period at a place) zu meiner Zeit (ugs.); **~ off** *or* **out** freie Zeit; **get/take ~ off** frei bekommen/sich (*Dat.*) frei nehmen (ugs.); **T~!** (Boxing) Stop!; Time!; (Brit.: in pub) Feierabend!; **have a lot of ~ for sb.** (fig.) für jmdm. viel übrig haben; **(c)** *no pl.* (moment or period destined for purpose) Zeit, *die;* **harvest/Christmas ~:** Ernte-/Weihnachtszeit, *die;* **there is a ~ and place for everything** alles zu seiner Zeit; **now is the ~ to do it** jetzt ist die richtige Zeit, es zu tun; **~ for lunch** Zeit zum Mittagessen; **it is ~ to go** es wird Zeit zu gehen; **and not before ~:** und es wurde auch Zeit; **when the ~ comes/came** wenn es so weit ist/als es so weit war; **on ~** (punctually) pünktlich; **ahead of ~:** zu früh ⟨*ankommen*⟩; vorzeitig ⟨*fertig werden*⟩; **all in good ~:** alles zu seiner Zeit; *see also* **be 2 a; (d)** *in sing. or pl.* (circumstances) Zeit, *die;* **~s are good/bad/have changed** die Zeiten sind gut/schlecht/haben sich geändert; **have a good ~:** Spaß haben (ugs.); sich amüsieren; **have a hard ~ [of it]** eine schwere Zeit durchmachen; **(e)** (associated with events or person[s]) Zeit, *die;* **in ~ of peace/war** in Friedens-/Kriegszeiten; **in Tudor/ancient ~s** zur Zeit der Tudors/der Antike; **in former/modern ~s** früher/heutzutage; **ahead of** *or* **before one's/its ~:** seiner Zeit voraus; **at 'one ~** (previously) früher; **(f)** (occasion) Mal, *das;* **for the first ~:** zum ersten Mal; **next ~ you come** wenn du das nächste Mal kommst; **ten/a hundred/a thousand ~s** zehn-/hundert-/tausendmal; **many ~s** sehr oft; **many's the ~ [that]** …, **many a ~ …:** viele Male …; **at all ~s** jederzeit; **at ~s** gelegentlich; **from ~ to ~:** von Zeit zu Zeit; **at other ~s** sonst; **at one ~ or another** irgendwann einmal; **at a ~ like this/that** unter diesen/solchen Umständen; **at the ~** *or* **that ~** (in the past) damals; **at one ~, at [one and] the same ~** (simultaneously) gleichzeitig; **at the same ~** (nevertheless) gleichwohl; **between ~s** zwischendurch; **and [~] again, ~ after ~:** immer [und immer] wieder; **pay sb. £6 a ~:** jmdm. für jedes Mal 6 Pfund zahlen; **one at a ~:** einzeln; **two at a ~:** jeweils zwei; **for hours/weeks at a ~:** stundenlang/wochenlang [ohne Unterbrechung]; **(g)** ▶ **706 |** (point in day etc.) [Uhr]zeit, *die;* **at the same ~ every morning** jeden Morgen um dieselbe Zeit; **what ~ is it?, what is the ~?** wie spät ist es?; **have you [got] the ~?** kannst du mir sagen, wie spät es ist?; **tell the ~** (read a clock) die Uhr lesen; **~ of day** Tageszeit, *die;* **[at this] ~ of [the] year** [um diese] Jahreszeit; **at this ~ of [the] night** zu dieser Nachtstunde; **pass the ~ of day** (coll.) ein paar Worte wechseln; **by this/that ~:** inzwischen; **by the ~ [that] we arrived** bis wir hinkamen; **[by] this ~ tomorrow** morgen um diese Zeit; **keep good ~** ⟨*Uhr:*⟩ genau *od.* richtig gehen; **(h)** (amount) Zeit, *die;* **make good ~:** gut vorwärts kommen; **[your] ~'s up!** deine Zeit ist um (ugs.) *od.* abgelaufen; **(i)** (multiplication) mal; **three ~s four** drei mal vier; **four ~s the length of/higher than sth.** viermal so groß wie/höher als etw.; **(j)** (Mus.) (duration of note) Zeitdauer, *die;* (measure) Takt, *der;* **in three-four ~:** im Dreivierteltakt; **keep in ~ with the music** den Takt halten; one's ~ aus dem/im Takt; **keep ~ with sth.** bei etw. den Takt [ein]halten. **2** *v.t.* **(a)** (do at correct ~) zeitlich abstimmen; **be well/ill ~d** zur richtigen/falschen Zeit kommen; **(b)** (set to operate at correct ~) justieren (Technik); einstellen; **(c)** (arrange ~ of arrival/departure of) **the bus is ~d to connect with the train** der Bus hat direkten Anschluss an den Zug; **be ~d to take 90 minutes** fahrplanmäßig 90 Minuten dauern; **(d)** (measure ~ taken by) stoppen; **~ an egg** auf die richtige Kochdauer für ein Ei achten

time: **~ bomb** *n.* (lit. *or* fig.) Zeitbombe, *die;* **~-consuming** *adj.* **(a)** (taking ~) zeitaufwendig; **(b)** (wasteful of

⁀) zeitraubend; ~ **exposure** n. (Photog.) Zeitaufnahme, die; ~-**honoured** adj. altehrwürdig (geh.); althergebracht ⟨Brauch, Vorstellung⟩; ~**keeping** n. (at work) Einhaltung der Arbeitsstunden; ~ **lag** n. zeitliche Verzögerung; ~ **limit** n. Frist, die; put a ~ limit on sth. eine Frist für etw. setzen; ~ **lock** n. Zeitschloss, das

timely /'taɪmlɪ/ adj. rechtzeitig

'**timepiece** n. Chronometer, das

timer /'taɪmə(r)/ n. (device) Kurzzeitmesser, der; (with switch) Schaltuhr, die

time: ~-**saver** n. be a ~-saver Zeit sparen; this is a real ~-saver dies bedeutet eine echte Zeitersparnis; ~**scale** n. Zeitskala, die; ~**share** 1 attrib. adj. ~**share apartment** Ferienwohnung, an der man einen Besitzanteil hat, der es einem erlaubt, eine bestimmte Zeit pro Jahr in dieser Wohnung zu verbringen; 2 n. ⇨ ~-**sharing b**; ~-**sharing** n., no pl., no art. (a) (Computing) Timesharing, das; (b) (joint ownership) Eigentum an einer Ferienwohnung o. ä., das für eine festgelegte Zeit des Jahres gilt; Time-sharing, das (Wirtsch.); ~ **signal** n. Zeitzeichen, das; ~ **signature** n. (Mus.) Taktbezeichnung, die; ~ **switch** n. Zeitschalter, der; ~**table** n. (a) (scheme of work) Zeitplan, der; (Educ.) Stundenplan, der; (b) (Transport) Fahrplan, der; ~ **trial** n. (Sport) (in cycling) Zeitfahren, das; (in athletics) Zeitrennen, das; ~ **travel** n. Zeitreise, die; ~ **zone** n. Zeitzone, die

timid /'tɪmɪd/ adj. (a) scheu ⟨Tier, Vogel⟩; (b) (fearful) ängstlich ⟨Person, Miene, Worte⟩; (c) (lacking boldness) zaghaft; (shy) schüchtern

timing /'taɪmɪŋ/ n., no pl. (a) that was perfect ~! (as sb. arrives) du kommst gerade im richtigen Augenblick!; (b) (Theatre) Timing, das

timpani /'tɪmpəni:/ n. pl. (Mus.) Kesselpauken Pl.; Timpani Pl.(fachspr.)

tin /tɪn/ 1 n. (a) (metal) Zinn, das; ~[-**plate**] Weißblech, das; (b) (Cookery) **cooking** ~s Back- und Bratformen; (c) (Brit.: for preserving) [Konserven]dose, die; a ~ of peas eine Dose Erbsen; (d) (with separate or hinged lid) Dose, die; **bread** ~: Brotkasten, der. 2 v.t., -nn- (Brit.) zu Konserven verarbeiten

tinder /'tɪndə(r)/ n. Zunder, der; **as dry as** ~ knochentrocken

'**tinder-dry** adj. knochentrocken

tin '**foil** n., no pl. Stanniol, das; (aluminium foil) Alufolie, die

tinge /tɪndʒ/ 1 v.t., ~**ing** /'tɪndʒɪŋ/ tönen; **a white curtain** ~d **with pink** ein weißer, ins Zartrosa gehender Vorhang; **her black hair was** ~d **with grey** ihr schwarzes Haar war grau meliert; (fig.) **her admiration was** ~d **with envy** ihre Bewunderung war nicht ganz frei von Neid. 2 n. [leichte] Färbung, (fig.) Hauch, der; **a** ~ **of red in the sky** eine leicht rötliche Färbung des Himmels; **white with a** ~ **of blue** weiß mit einem Stich ins Bläuliche

tingle /'tɪŋgl/ 1 v.i. kribbeln. 2 n. Kribbeln, das; **feel a** ~ **of excitement** vor Aufregung ganz kribbelig sein (ugs.)

tinker /'tɪŋkə(r)/ 1 n. Kesselflicker, der. 2 v.i. ~ **with sth.** an etw. (Dat.) herumbasteln (ugs.)/(incompetently; also fig.) herumpfuschen (ugs.)

tinkle /'tɪŋkl/ 1 n. Klingeln, das; (of coins) Klimpern, das. 2 v.i. ⟨Glocke:⟩ klingeln; ⟨Münzen:⟩ klimpern

'**tin mine** n. Zinnbergwerk, das

tinned /tɪnd/ adj. (Brit.) Dosen-; **be** ~: aus der Dose sein

tin: ~-**opener** n. (Brit.) Dosen-, Büchsenöffner, der; ~ '**plate** n. Weißblech, das; ~**pot** attrib. adj. (derog.) schäbig; ~**pot town** Kaff, das (ugs.); ~**pot dictator** Operettendiktator, der

tinsel /'tɪnsl/ n. Lametta, das

tint /tɪnt/ 1 n. Farbton, der. 2 v.t. tönen; kolorieren ⟨Zeichnung, Stich⟩

tiny /'taɪnɪ/ adj. winzig; **a** ~ **bit better** (coll.) ein klein wenig besser

tip[1] /tɪp/ 1 n. (end, point) Spitze, die; **the** ~ **of his nose/ finger/toe** seine Nasen-/Finger-/Zehenspitze; **on the** ~s **of one's toes** auf Zehenspitzen; **from** ~ **to toe** vom Scheitel bis zur Sohle; **it is on the** ~ **of my tongue** es liegt mir auf der Zunge. 2 v.t., -pp-: ~ **sth. [with stone/ brass]** etw. mit einer [Stein-/Messing]spitze versehen

tip[2] 1 v.i., -pp- (lean, fall) kippen; ~ **over** umkippen. 2 v.t., -pp-: (a) (make tilt) kippen; ~ **the balance** (fig.) den Ausschlag geben; see also **scale**[2] 1 b; (b) (make overturn) umkippen; (Brit.: discharge) kippen; (c) (mention as likely winner etc.) voraussagen ⟨Sieger⟩; ~ **sb. to win** auf jmds. Sieg tippen; **be** ~**ped for the Presidency/a post** als Favorit für die Präsidentschaftswahlen/einen Posten genannt werden; (d) (coll.: give) geben; ~ **sb. the wink** (fig.) jmdm. Bescheid sagen; (~ sb. off) jmdm. einen Tipp geben (ugs.); (e) (give money to) ~ **sb.** [20p] jmdm. [20 Pence] Trinkgeld geben. 3 n. (a) (money) Trinkgeld, das; **as a** ~: als Trinkgeld; (b) (special information) Hinweis, der; Tipp, der (ugs.); (advice) Rat, der; **hot** ~: heißer Tipp; (c) (Brit.: place for refuse) Müllkippe, die; (d) (derog.: untidy place) Schweinestall, der ~ '**off** v.t. ~ **sb. off** jmdm. einen Hinweis od. (ugs.) Tipp geben

'**tip-off** n. Hinweis, der

tipple /'tɪpl/ 1 v.i. trinken. 2 n. (coll.: drink) **have a** ~: einen trinken (ugs.); **what's your** ~? was trinken Sie?

tippler /'tɪplə(r)/ n. Trinker, der/Trinkerin, die

tipsy /'tɪpsɪ/ adj. (coll.) angeheitert; beschwipst (ugs.)

tip: ~**toe** 1 v.i. auf Zehenspitzen gehen; (walk quietly) sich schleichen od. stehlen; 2 adv. auf Zehenspitzen; 3 n. **on** ~**toe[s]** auf Zehenspitzen; **stand on** ~**toe** sich auf die Zehenspitzen stellen; ~**top** adj. (coll.) ausgezeichnet; tiptopp (ugs.); **be in** ~**top condition** in einem Topzustand/⟨Person:⟩ in Topform sein; ~-**up seat** n. Klappsitz, der

tirade /taɪ'reɪd, tɪ'reɪd/ n. Tirade, die (geh.)

tire[1] /'taɪə(r)/ (Amer.) ⇒ **tyre**

tire[2] 1 v.t. ermüden. 2 v.i. müde werden; ermüden; ~ **of sth./doing sth.** einer Sache (Gen.) überdrüssig werden/ es müde werden (geh.), etw. zu tun ~ '**out** v.t. erschöpfen; ~ **oneself out doing sth.** etw. bis zur Erschöpfung tun

tired /'taɪəd/ adj. (a) (weary) müde; (b) (fed up) **be** ~ **of sth./doing sth.** etw. satt haben/es satt haben od. (geh.) es müde sein, etw. zu tun; **get** or **grow** ~ **of sb./sth.** jmds./ einer Sache überdrüssig werden; (c) (fig.: hackneyed) abgegriffen; abgedroschen (ugs.)

tiredness /'taɪədnɪs/ n., no pl. Müdigkeit, die

tireless /'taɪəlɪs/ adj. unermüdlich

tiresome /'taɪəsəm/ adj. (a) (wearisome) mühsam; (b) (annoying) lästig; **how** ~! so ein Ärger!

tiring /'taɪərɪŋ/ adj. ermüdend; anstrengend ⟨Tag, Person⟩

tissue /'tɪʃu:, 'tɪsju:/ n. (a) (woven fabric; also Biol.) Gewebe, das; (b) (absorbent paper) [**paper**] ~: Papiertuch, das; (handkerchief) Papiertaschentuch, das; (c) (for wrapping) ~ [**paper**] Seidenpapier, das; (d) (fig.: web) Geflecht, das; ~ **of lies** Lügengewebe, das

tit[1] /tɪt/ n. (Ornith.) Meise, die

tit[2] n. **it's** ~ **for tat** wie du mir, so ich dir; (attrib.) ~-**for- tat killing/assassination** tödlicher Vergeltungsschlag od. Racheakt

'**titbit** n. (a) (food) Häppchen, das (ugs.); (b) (piece of news) Neuigkeit, die

titch /tɪtʃ/ n. (coll.) Knirps, der (ugs.)

titchy /'tɪtʃɪ/ adj. (coll.) klitzeklein (ugs.)

title /'taɪtl/ n. (a) (of book etc.) Titel, der; (of article, chapter) Überschrift, die; **the** ~s (Cinemat., Telev.) der Vorspann; (b) ▶ **1152**| (of person) Titel, der; (of nobility) [Adels]titel, der; (of organization) Name, der; **the flyweight** ~ (Sport) der Titel im Fliegengewicht; (c) (Law: recognized claim) Rechtsanspruch, der (**to** auf + Akk.)

titled /'taɪtld/ adj. adlig

title: ~-**page** n. Titelseite, die; ~ **role** n. Titelrolle, die

titter /'tɪtə(r)/ 1 v.i. kichern. 2 n. ~[s] Kichern, das

tittle-tattle /'tɪtltætl/ n. Klatsch, der (ugs. abwertend)

tizzy /'tɪzɪ/ n. (coll.) **be in a/get into a** ~: durchdrehen (ugs.) (**over** wegen)

Titles

The equivalent of *Mr* is **Herr,** but remember that an **n** has to be added when writing an address (*see* □ **letter-writing** for more details). **Frau** is the equivalent for both *Mrs* and *Ms*, since it is used for both married women and unmarried women who are old enough to be married. The equivalent for *Miss* is **Fräulein,** but increasingly its use is restricted to young girls of school age.

Hello, Mr White	= Guten Tag, Herr White
Goodbye, Mrs Williams	= Auf Wiedersehen, Frau Williams

The Germans being more formal than either the British or the Americans, titles and surnames are used far more, and first names are only used between young people and those who know one another really well (and say **du** to one another).

The other important point to remember is that **Herr** and **Frau** are added before other titles, both on letters and when greeting someone:

Good morning, doctor	= Guten Morgen, Herr Doktor/(or to a woman doctor) Frau Doktor
Good evening, professor	= Guten Abend, Herr Professor/(or to a woman professor) Frau Professor

In these cases the feminine endings are no longer used (**Frau Doktorin, Frau Professorin**), but they will still be found on other titles such as **Frau Studienrätin** (a secondary school teacher with tenure). The feminine forms of aristocratic titles are used on the other hand (**Fürst→Fürstin, Graf→Gräfin, Baron→Baronin, Freiherr→Freifrau**), but **Herr** and **Frau** are not inserted before the title. Hence you refer to a count as **Graf** ..., and to a countess as **Gräfin** ....

While the full name is of course given on letters, when speaking to someone with a title the name is usually omitted:

Good morning, Dr Brown	= Guten Morgen, Herr/Frau Doktor
Come in, Professor Evans	= Kommen Sie herein, Herr/Frau Professor
How are you, Colonel Weston?	= Wie geht es Ihnen, Herr Oberst?

An exception is the title **Doktor,** where the name is omitted when addressing a doctor of medicine but not when addressing someone who holds the academic title of **Doktor**.

Even when referring to someone with an academic title in the third person, **Herr** and **Frau** are usually included:

... as Professor Schmidt explained yesterday	= wie Herr Professor Schmidt schon gestern erklärt hat
Tell Dr Wilkenhorst to come here	= Sagen Sie Herrn/Frau Dr. Wilkenhorst, er/sie soll hierher kommen

Otherwise usage is much as in English, except that titles are used more often (for instance, the director of an institution should be addressed as **Herr Direktor**), and there are many more titles going with particular jobs than in Britain or America.

Forms of address for dignitaries

Her Majesty	= Ihre Majestät
His Highness	= Seine Hoheit
Your Grace	= Euer Gnaden
Your Eminence	= Eure Eminenz
His Holiness	= Seine Heiligkeit

Note that *Your* with such titles is translated by the form **Euer, Eure.** This can be omitted in some cases, particularly when the reference is in the third person:

Your Eminence will be pleased about this	= Eminenz wird sich darüber freuen

---

'**T-junction** ⇨ **T**

TNT *abbr.* **trinitrotoluene** TNT, *das*

to 1 ▶ 1153 | /*before vowel* tʊ, *before consonant* tə, *stressed* tu:/ *prep.* (**a**) (in the direction of and reaching) zu; (with name of place) nach; **go to work/to the theatre** zur Arbeit/ins Theater gehen; **to Paris/France** nach Paris/Frankreich; **go from town to town** von Stadt zu Stadt ziehen; **throw the ball to me** wirf mir den Ball zu; (**b**) (towards a condition or quality) zu; **appoint sb. to a post** jmdn. auf einen Posten berufen; (**c**) (as far as) bis zu; **from London to Edinburgh** von London [bis] nach Edinburgh; **increase from 10 % to 20 %** von 10 % auf 20 % steigen; (**d**) (next to, facing) **with one's back to the wall** mit dem Rücken zur Wand; (**e**) (implying comparison, ratio, etc.) [**compared**] **to** verglichen mit; im Vergleich zu; **3 is to 4 as 6 is to 8** 3 verhält sich zu 4 wie 6 zu 8; **it's ten to one he does it.** die Chancen stehen zehn zu eins, dass er etw. tut; (**f**) *introducing relationship or indirect object* **to sb./sth.** jmdm./einer Sache (*Dat.*); **lend/explain** *etc.* **sth. to sb.** jmdm. etw. leihen/erklären *usw.;* **speak to sb.** mit jmdm. sprechen; **relate to sth.** sich auf etw. (*Akk.*) beziehen; **to me** (in my opinion) meiner Meinung nach; **secretary to the Minister** Sekretär des Ministers; **a room to oneself** ein eigenes Zimmer; **get four apples to the pound** vier Äpfel je Pfund bekommen; **that's all there is to it** mehr ist nicht dazu zu sagen; **what's that to you?** was geht das dich an?; (**g**) ▶ 706 | (until) bis; **to the end** bis zum Ende; **to this day** bis heute; **five [minutes] to eight** fünf [Minuten] vor acht; (**h**) *with infinitive of a verb* zu; *expressing purpose, or after* **too** um [...] zu; **want to know** wissen wollen; **do sth. to annoy sb.** etw. tun, um jmdn. zu ärgern; **too young to marry** zu jung, um zu heiraten; zu jung zum Heiraten; **too hot to drink** zu heiß zum Trinken; **to rebel is pointless** es ist sinnlos zu rebellieren; **he woke to find himself in a strange room** er erwachte und fand sich in einem fremden Zimmer wieder; **to use a technical term** um einen Fachausdruck zu gebrauchen; (**i**) *as substitute for infinitive* **he would have phoned but forgot to** er hätte angerufen, aber er vergaß es; **she didn't want to go there, but she had to** sie wollte nicht hingehen, aber sie musste. 2 /tu:/ *adv.* (**a**) (just not shut) **be to** ⟨Tür, Fenster:⟩ angelehnt sein; **push a door to** eine Tür anlehnen; (**b**) **to and fro** hin und her

toad /təʊd/ *n.* (Zool.; fig. derog.) Kröte, *die*

toad: ∼-**in-the-hole** *n.* (Gastr.) Würstchen, *in einen Teig eingebacken;* ∼**stool** *n.* Giftpilz, *der*

toady /'təʊdɪ/ 1 *n.* Kriecher, *der.* 2 *v.i.* ∼ [**to sb.**] [vor jmdm.] kriechen (abwertend)

toast /təʊst/ 1 *n.* (**a**) *no pl., no indef. art.* Toast, *der;* **a piece of** ∼: eine Scheibe Toast; **cheese/egg on** ∼: Toast mit Käse/Ei; **as warm as** ∼ (fig.) schön warm (ugs.); (**b**) (call to drink) Toast, *der;* **drink/propose a** ∼ **to sb./sth.** auf jmdn./etw. trinken/einen Toast auf jmdn./etw. ausbringen; **be the** ∼ **of the town** von der ganzen Stadt gefeiert werden. 2 *v.t.* (**a**) rösten; toasten ⟨Brot⟩; (**b**) (drink in honour of) trinken auf (+ *Akk.*)

toaster /'təʊstə(r)/ *n.* Toaster, *der*

'**toast rack** *n.* Toastständer, *der*

tobacco /tə'bækəʊ/ *n., pl.* ∼**s** Tabak, *der*

tobacconist /tə'bækənɪst/ *n.* ▶ 887 | Tabak[waren]-händler, *der*/-händlerin, *die; see also* **baker**

toboggan /tə'bɒgən/ 1 *n.* Schlitten, *der;* Toboggan, *der.* 2 *v.i.* Schlitten fahren

today /tə'deɪ/ ▶ 739 | 1 *n.* heute; ∼**'s newspaper** die Zeitung von heute. 2 *adv.* heute; **a week/fortnight [from]**

To

Going places — zu or nach?

There is a simple distinction between the use of **zu** and **nach** to translate *to:*

nach is only used with geographical names and points of the compass;

zu is used in nearly all other cases. Note that where a noun follows a geographical name in apposition, an article in the dative is needed.

We are going to Germany	= Wir fahren nach Deutschland
They are flying to New York	= Sie fliegen nach New York
You are going to Salzburg, Mozart's birthplace	= Sie fahren nach Salzburg, dem Geburtsort Mozarts
the road to Potsdam/ the city centre	= die Straße nach Potsdam/zum Stadtzentrum
How do I get to the coast?	= Wie komme ich zur Küste?
Go to your mother	= Geh zu deiner Mutter
from house to house	= von Haus zu Haus

But:

from east to west	= von Osten nach Westen

Where a distance is given, **bis** is usually inserted before the **zu** or **nach,** or in place of **nach:**

It's five miles to Exeter/ to the next place	= Es sind noch acht Kilometer bis [nach] Exeter/bis zum nächsten Ort

Giving

With all verbs expressing giving *to* is translated simply by the dative case:

She handed the key to me	= Sie übergab mir den Schlüssel
The prize was awarded to him	= Der Preis wurde ihm verliehen
My father left the estate to my brother	= Mein Vater hinterließ das Gut meinem Bruder
They gave a book to Rachel Symons	= Sie schenkten Rachel Symons ein Buch

From the last example it can be seen that where there is a name which cannot of course show the dative this is simply given without alteration.

Other usages are covered in the entry for *to*.
See also □ **The Clock, Measurements, Asking the Way** etc.

~: heute in einer Woche/in vierzehn Tagen; **a year [ago]** ~: heute vor einem Jahr; **early** ~: heute früh; **later [on]** ~: später [am Tage]; **earlier** ~: heute vor wenigen Stunden

toddle /'tɒdl/ *v.i.* **(a)** (with tottering steps) mit wackligen Schritten gehen; wackeln (ugs.); **(b)** (coll.: leave) ~ **[off]** sich verziehen (ugs.)

toddler /'tɒdlə(r)/ *n.* ≈ Kleinkind, *das*

to-do /tə'du:/ *n.* Getue, *das* (ugs.)

toe /təʊ/ **1** *n.* **(a)** ▶ **672 ⌡** (Anat.) Zeh, *der;* Zehe, *die;* **be on one's** ~s (fig.) auf Zack sein (ugs.); **keep sb. on his/her** ~s (fig.) jmdn. in Trab halten (ugs.); **(b)** (of footwear) Spitze, *die;* **at the** ~: an den Zehen; **(c)** (Zool.) Zeh, *der.* **2** *v.t.,* ~**ing** (fig.) ~ **the line** or (Amer.) **mark** sich einordnen; **refuse to** ~ **the line** aus der Reihe tanzen; ~ **the party line** linientreu sein

toe-: ~**cap** *n.* Vorderkappe, *die;* (of boot) Stiefelkappe, *die;* ~**hold** *n.* Tritt, *der;* (fig.) **gain a** ~**hold** einen Fuß in die Tür bekommen; ~**nail** *n.* Zeh[en]nagel, *der*

toffee /'tɒfɪ/ *n.* **(a)** Karamell, *der;* **(b)** (Brit.: piece) Toffee, *das;* Sahnebonbon, *das;* **(c)** **sb. can't do sth. for** ~ (fig. coll.) jmd. kann etw. nicht für fünf Pfennig tun (ugs.)

toffee: ~ **apple** *n.* Paradiesapfel, *der* (*mit Karamell überzogener Apfel am Stiel*); ~**-nosed** *adj.* (Brit. coll.) hochnäsig

tofu /'təʊfu:/ *n., no pl., no indef. art.* Tofu, *der*

tog /tɒg/ **1** *n.* **(a)** *in pl.* (sl.: garments) Klamotten (ugs.); **(b)** (Textiles) *Einheit für das Wärmerückhaltevermögen von Textilien.* **2** *v.t.* **-gg-:** ~ **[oneself]** out *or* up sich in Schale werfen (ugs.)

toga /'təʊgə/ *n.* (Roman Ant.) Toga, *die*

together /tə'geðə(r)/ *adv.* **(a)** (in or into company) zusammen; **sit down** ~: sich zusammensetzen; **gather** ~: sich [ver]sammeln; **taken all** ~: alle zusammengenommen; ~ **with** zusammen mit; **(b)** (simultaneously) gleichzeitig; **all** ~ **now!** jetzt alle zusammen *od.* im Chor!; **(c)** (one with another) miteinander; **put them** ~ **to compare them** halte sie nebeneinander, um sie zu vergleichen; **(d)** (without interruption) **for weeks/days/hours** ~: wochen-/tage-/stundenlang; **for three days** ~: drei Tage hintereinander

togetherness /tə'geðənɪs/ *n., no pl.* Zusammengehörigkeit, *die*

toggle /'tɒgl/ **1** **(a)** *n.* Knebelknopf, *der;* **(b)** (Computing) [Kipp]schalter, *der;* Umschalttaste, *die.* **2** *v.i.* (Computing) [hin und her] schalten. **3** *v.t.* (Computing) [um]schalten

toil /tɔɪl/ **1** *v.i.* **(a)** (work laboriously) schwer arbeiten; sich abarbeiten; ~ **at/over sth.** sich an etw. abplagen/abmühen; ~ **through a book** sich mühsam durch ein Buch arbeiten; **(b)** (move laboriously) sich schleppen. **2** *n.* [harte] Arbeit

toilet /'tɔɪlɪt/ *n.* Toilette, *die;* **down the** ~: in die Toilette; **go to the** ~: auf die Toilette gehen

toilet: ~ **bag** *n.* Kulturbeutel, *der;* ~ **bowl** *n.* Toilettenbecken, *das;* Klosettbecken, *das;* ~ **paper** *n.* Toilettenpapier, *das*

toiletries /'tɔɪlɪtrɪz/ *n. pl.* Körperpflegemittel; Toilettenartikel

toilet: ~ **roll** *n.* Rolle Toilettenpapier; ~ **roll holder** *n.* Toilettenpapierhalter, *der;* ~ **seat** *n.* Klosettbrille, *die* (ugs.), ~ **tissue** ⇒ **toilet paper;** ~**train** *v.t.* zur Sauberkeit erziehen; an die Toilette gewöhnen; **be** ~**-trained** sauber sein; auf die Toilette gehen; ~**-training** *n.* Sauberkeitserziehung, *die;* ~ **water** *n.* Toilettenwasser, *das;* Eau de Toilette, *das*

toing and froing /tu:ɪŋ ən 'frəʊɪŋ/ *n.* Hin und Her, *das*

token /'təʊkn/ **1** *n.* **(a)** (voucher) Gutschein, *der;* **(b)** (counter, disc) Marke, *die;* **(c)** (sign) Zeichen, *das;* (evidence) Beweis, *der;* **as a** *or* **in** ~ **of sth.** als Zeichen/zum Beweis einer Sache; **(d)** **by the same** *or* **this** ~: ebenso. **2** *attrib. adj.* symbolisch ‹Preis›; nominal (Wirtsch.) ‹Lohnerhöhung, Miete›; **a** ~ **woman on the staff** eine Alibifrau als Mitarbeiterin; **offer** *or* **put up** ~ **resistance** pro forma Widerstand leisten

Tokyo /'təʊkjəʊ/ *pr. n.* ▶ **1159 ⌡** Tokio (*das*)

told ⇒ **tell**

tolerable /'tɒlərəbl/ *adj.* **(a)** (endurable) erträglich (**to, for** für); **(b)** (fairly good) leidlich; annehmbar

tolerably /'tɒlərəblɪ/ *adv.* leidlich; annehmbar; einigermaßen ‹*gut, richtig*›

tolerance /'tɒlərəns/ *n.* Toleranz, *die* (**for, towards,** gegen[über])

tolerant /'tɒlərənt/ *adj.* tolerant (**of, towards** gegen[über])

tolerate /'tɒləreɪt/ *v.t.* **(a)** dulden; tolerieren (geh.); **(b)** (put up with) ~ **sb./sth.** sich mit jmdm./etw. abfinden; ~ **one another** sich [gegenseitig] akzeptieren; **(c)** (sustain) ertragen ‹*Schmerzen, Hitze, Lärm*›

toleration /tɒlə'reɪʃn/ *n.* Tolerierung, *die* (geh.); **religious** ~: religiöse Toleranz

toll¹ /təʊl/ *n.* (a) (tax, duty) Gebühr, *die;* (for road) [Straßen]-gebühr, *die;* Maut, *die* (bes. österr.); (b) (damage etc. incurred) Aufwand, *der;* **take** *or* **exact a /its** ~ **of sth.** einen Tribut an etw. (*Dat.*) fordern (fig.)

toll² 1 *v.t.* läuten; ‹*Turmuhr:*› schlagen ‹*Stunde*›. 2 *v.i.* läuten

toll: ~ **bridge** *n.* gebührenpflichtige Brücke; Mautbrücke, *die* (bes. österr.); ~ **call** *n.* (Amer. Teleph.) gebührenpflichtiges Gespräch; ~-**free** *adj., adv.* (esp. Amer. Teleph.) gebührenfrei; ~**road** *n.* gebührenpflichtige Straße; Mautstraße, *die* (bes. österr.)

tom /tɒm/ *n.* (a) **any** *or* **every Tom, Dick, and Harry** Hinz und Kunz (ugs. abwertend); (b) (cat) Kater, *der. See also* **peeping Tom**

tomahawk /'tɒməhɔːk/ *n.* Tomahawk, *der*

tomato /təˈmɑːtəʊ/ *n., pl.* ~**es** Tomate, *die*

tomato: ~ **juice** *n.* Tomatensaft, *der;* ~ **'ketchup** *n.* Tomatenketchup, *der od. das;* ~ **'purée** *n.* Tomatenmark, *das;* ~ **'sauce** *n.* (a) Tomatensoße, *die;* (b) ⇒ ~ ketchup; ~ **'soup** *n.* Tomatensuppe, *die*

tomb /tuːm/ *n.* (a) (grave) Grab, *das;* (b) (monument) Grabmal, *das*

tombola /tɒmˈbəʊlə/ *n.* Tombola, *die*

'tomboy *n.* Wildfang, *der*

'tombstone *n.* Grabstein, *der;* Grabmal, *das*

'tom-cat *n.* Kater, *der*

tome /təʊm/ *n.* dicker Band; Wälzer, *der* (ugs.)

tomfoolery /tɒmˈfuːlərɪ/ *n.* Blödsinn, *der* (ugs.)

tommy-gun /'tɒmɪgʌn/ *n.* Maschinenpistole, *die*

tomorrow /təˈmɒrəʊ/ 1 *n.* (a) morgen; ~ **morning/ afternoon/evening/night** morgen früh *od.* Vormittag/ Nachmittag/Abend/Nacht; ~ **is another day** (prov.) morgen ist auch [noch] ein Tag (Spr.); (b) (the future) Morgen, *das;* **who knows what** ~ **will bring?** wer weiß, was die Zukunft bringt?; **like there's no** ~ (coll.) als ginge morgen die Welt unter. 2 *adv.* morgen; **a week/month [from]** ~: morgen in einer Woche/in einem Monat; **a year [ago]** ~: morgen vor einem Jahr; **[I'll] see you** ~! (coll.) bis morgen!; **never put off till** ~ **what you can do today** (prov.) was du heute kannst besorgen, das verschiebe nicht auf morgen (Spr.); **the day after** ~: übermorgen; **this time** ~: morgen um diese Zeit; ~ **afternoon/morning** morgen Nachmittag/früh; ~ **evening** *or* **night** morgen Abend

'tom-tom *n.* (Mus.) Tomtom, *das*

ton /tʌn/ *n.* (a) ▶ 1202 | Tonne, *die;* **a five-**~ **lorry** ein Lastwagen von fünf Tonnen [Leergewicht]; ein Fünftonner (ugs.); **metric** ~: metrische Tonne; **two** ~[**s**] **of coal** zwei Tonnen Kohle; (b) (fig. coll.: a lot) **it weighs [half] a** ~: es ist zentnerschwer (fig.); ~**s** [**of food/people/reasons** *etc.*] haufenweise (ugs.) [Essen/Leute/Gründe *usw.*]

tone /təʊn/ 1 *n.* (a) (sound) Klang, *der;* (Teleph.) Ton, *der;* (b) (style of speaking) Ton, *der;* **don't speak to me in that** ~ [**of voice**] sprich mit mir nicht in diesem Ton; **in an angry** *etc.* ~, **in angry** *etc.* ~**s** in ärgerlichem *usw.* Ton; **in a** ~ **of reproach/anger** *etc.* in vorwurfsvollem/wütendem *usw.* Ton; (c) (tint, shade) [Farb]ton, *der;* ~**s of blue** Blautöne; blaue Töne; **grey with a blue** ~: bläulich grau; (d) (style of writing) [Grund]stimmung, *die;* (of letter) Ton, *der;* (e) (Mus.) (note) Ton, *der;* (quality of sound) Klang, *der;* (Brit.: interval) Intervall, *das;* (f) (fig.: character) Stimmung, *die;* **give a serious/flippant** ~ **to sth.** einer Sache (*Dat.*) eine ernsthafte/frivole Note verleihen; **lower/raise the** ~ **of sth.** das Niveau einer Sache (*Gen.*) senken/erhöhen; **set the** ~: den Ton angeben; **set the** ~ **of** *or* **for sth.** für etw. bestimmend sein; (g) (Art: general effect of colour) Farbgebung, *die;* Kolorit, *das;* (h) (degree of brightness) Schattierung, *die;* Nuancierung, *die;* **bright** ~: Helligkeit, *die;* (i) (Photog.) Ton, *der.* 2 *v.i.* ⇒ ~ **in** ~ **'down** *v.t.* (a) (Art) [ab]dämpfen ‹*Farbe*›; ~ **a painting down** die Farben eines Bildes abdämpfen; (b) (fig.: soften) mäßigen ‹*Sprache*›; abschwächen ‹*Verbalattacke, Forderung*› ~**'in** *v.i.* farblich harmonieren

tone: ~ **arm** *n.* Tonarm, *der;* ~ **control** *n.* (device) Klangregler, *der;* ~**-'deaf** *adj.* ohne musikalisches

Gehör *nachgestellt;* **be** ~-**deaf** kein musikalisches Gehör haben; ~ **dialling** *n.* Tonwahl, *die*

toner /'təʊnə(r)/ *n.* (a) (Photog.) Toner, *der;* (b) (cosmetic) Tönungsmittel, *das*

tongs /tɒŋz/ *n. pl.* [**pair of**] ~: Zange, *die*

tongue /tʌŋ/ *n.* (a) ▶ 672 | Zunge, *die;* **bite one's** ~ (lit. or fig.) sich auf die Zunge beißen; **put out your** ~, **please** strecken Sie [bitte] mal Ihre Zunge heraus!; **put** *or* **stick one's** ~ **out [at sb.]** [jmdm.] die Zunge herausstrecken; **with one's** ~ **hanging out** mit [heraus]hängender Zunge; **he made the remark** ~ **in cheek** (fig.) er meinte die Bemerkung nicht ernst; **hold one's** ~ (fig.) stillschweigen; **watch one's** ~ (fig.) seine Zunge hüten *od.* zügeln; **watch your** ~! pass auf, was du sagst!; (b) (meat) Zunge, *die;* (c) (manner *or* power of speech) **find/lose one's** ~: seine Sprache wieder finden/die Sprache verlieren; **get one's** ~ **round sth.** etw. aussprechen; **have a sharp** *etc.* ~: eine scharfe *usw.* Zunge haben; (d) (language) Sprache, *die;* (e) (of shoe) Zunge, *die;* (f) (promontory) ~ [**of land**] Landzunge, *die;* (g) (of buckle) Dorn, *der*

tongue: ~**-in-'cheek** *adj.* nicht ernst gemeint; (ironical) ironisch; *see also* **tongue a;** ~**-tied** *adj.* schüchtern; gehemmt; **be** ~-**tied [with** *or* **by fear/embarrassment** *etc.*] [vor Angst/Verlegenheit *usw.*] kein Wort herausbringen; ~**-twister** *n.* Zungenbrecher, *der* (ugs.)

tonic /'tɒnɪk/ 1 *n.* (a) (Med.) Tonikum, *das;* **it was as good as a** ~: es hat mir/ihm *usw.* richtig gut getan; (b) (fig.: invigorating influence) Wohltat, *die* (geh.); (c) (~ water) Tonic, *das;* **gin** *etc.* **and** ~: Gin *usw.* [mit] Tonic; (d) (Mus.) Tonika, *die.* 2 *adj.* (a) (Med.) kräftigend; (fig.) wohltuend ‹*Wirkung*›; (b) (Mus.) tonisch

'tonic water *n.* Tonic[wasser], *das*

tonight /təˈnaɪt/ 1 *n.* (a) (this evening) heute Abend; ~ **has been such fun** heute Abend war es so lustig; **after** ~: nach dem heutigen Abend; **I enjoyed** ~: es war ein schöner Abend; ~**'s [news]paper** die heutige Abendzeitung; ~**'s performance** die heutige [Abend]vorstellung; ~**'s the night!** heute Abend ist es soweit!; ~**'s weather will be cold** heute Abend wird es kalt; (b) (this or the coming night) heute Nacht; ~ **will be colder** heute Nacht wird es kälter werden. 2 *adv.* (a) (this evening) heute Abend; (b) (during this or the coming night) heute Nacht; [**I'll] see you** ~! bis heute Abend!

tonne /'tʌn/ *n.* (a) ▶ 1202 | [metrische] Tonne

tonsil /'tɒnsl/ *n.* (Anat.) [Gaumen]mandel, *die;* **have one's** ~**s out** sich (*Dat.*) die Mandeln herausnehmen lassen

tonsillitis /tɒnsəˈlaɪtɪs/ *n.* ▶ 865 | (Med.) Mandelentzündung, *die*

too /tuː/ *adv.* (a) (excessively) zu; **far** *or* **much** ~ **much** viel zu viel; ~ **much** zu viel; **I've had** ~ **much to eat/ drink** ich habe zu viel gegessen/getrunken; **but not** ~ **much, please** aber bitte nicht allzu viel; **the problem/ he was** ~ **much for her** sie war der Aufgabe/ihm nicht gewachsen; **things are getting** ~ **much for me** es wird mir allmählich zu viel; **this is** '~ **much!** (indignantly) jetzt reicht's!; **she's/that's just** '~ **much** (intolerable) sie ist/das ist zu viel! (ugs.); (coll.: wonderful) sie ist/das ist echt spitze (ugs.); ~ **difficult a task** eine zu schwierige Aufgabe; **none** ~ *or* **not any** ~ **easy** nicht allzu leicht; (less than one had expected) gar nicht so leicht; **he is none** ~ *or* **not any** ~ **clever/quick** *etc.* er ist nicht der Schlauste/ Schnellste *usw.;* **none** ~ **soon** keinen Augenblick zu früh; *see also* **all** 3; **good** 1 b, e; **many** 1 a; **much** 1 a; **only** 2 d; (b) (also) auch; **she can sing, and play the piano,** ~: sie kann singen und auch *od.* außerdem Klavier spielen; (c) (coll.: very) besonders; **I'm not feeling** ~ **good** mir geht es nicht besonders [gut]; **I'm not** ~ **sure** ich bin mir nicht ganz sicher; **not** ~ **pleased** nicht gerade erfreut; (d) (moreover) **he lost in twenty moves, and to an amateur** ~: er verlor in zwanzig Zügen, und noch dazu gegen einen Amateur; **there was frost last night, and in May/Spain** ~! es hat letzte Nacht gefroren, und das im Mai/in Spanien!

took ⇒ **take** 1, 2

tool /tuːl/ *n.* (a) Werkzeug, *das;* (garden ~) Gerät, *das;* **set of** ~**s** Werkzeug, *das; see also* **down³** 4 c; (b) (machine) Werkzeugmaschine, *die;* (c) (Mech. Engin.: lathe ~) Meißel, *der;* **(d)** (fig.: means) [Hilfs]mittel, *das;* **pen and paper are the writer's basic** ~s Feder und Papier sind das wichtigste Handwerkszeug des Schriftstellers; **the** ~**s of the trade** das Handwerkszeug; das Rüstzeug; **(e)** (Computing) Tool, *das;* Werkzeug, *das;* **(f)** (fig.: person) Werkzeug, *das*

tool: ~ **bag** *n.* Werkzeugtasche, *die;* ~**bar** *n.* (Computing) Werkzeugleiste, *die;* ~**box**, ~ **case** *ns.* Werkzeugkasten, *der;* ~ **kit** *n.* (Brit.) Werkzeugsatz, *der;* (more general) Werkzeug, *das;* (for vehicle) **is there a** ~ **kit?** gibt es Bordwerkzeug?; ~ **shed** *n.* Geräteschuppen, *der*

toot /tuːt/ **1** *v.t.* **the driver** ~**ed his horn** der Fahrer hupte. **2** *v.i.* (on car etc. horn) hupen. **3** *n.* Tuten, *das;* **give a** ~ **on one's/its horn** ‹*Autofahrer/Auto:*› hupen

tooth /tuːθ/ *n., pl.* **teeth** /tiːθ/ **(a)** ▶ 672 Zahn, *der;* **say sth. between one's teeth** etw. mit zusammengebissenen Zähnen hervorstoßen; **have a** ~ **out/filled** sich *(Dat.)* einen Zahn ziehen/füllen lassen; **armed to the teeth** bis an die Zähne bewaffnet; ~ **and nail** verbissen ‹kämpfen, bekämpfen›; **get one's teeth into sth.** (fig.) etw. in Angriff nehmen; **show one's teeth** ‹*Hund:*› die Zähne fletschen; (fig.) die Zähne zeigen (ugs.); **(b)** (of rake, fork, comb) Zinke, *die;* (of cogwheel, saw, comb) Zahn, *der*

tooth: ~**ache** *n.* ▶ 865 Zahnschmerzen *Pl.;* Zahnweh, *das* (ugs.); ~**brush** *n.* Zahnbürste, *die*

toothed /tuːθt/ *adj.* **(a)** (Mech. Engin.) gezähnt; ~ **wheel** Zahnrad; **(b)** (Bot.) gezähnt; **(c)** *in comb.* (having teeth) **sharp-**~ ‹*Tier*› mit scharfen Zähnen

toothless /ˈtuːθlɪs/ *adj.* zahnlos

tooth: ~ **mug** *n.* Zahnputzbecher, *der;* ~**paste** *n.* Zahnpasta, *die;* ~**pick** *n.* Zahnstocher, *der;* ~ **powder** *n.* Zahnpulver, *das*

toothy /ˈtuːθɪ/ *adj.* **give sb. a** ~ **smile** jmdn. mit entblößten Zähnen anlächeln; **he is a bit** ~: er hat ein ziemliches Pferdegebiss (ugs.)

top¹ /tɒp/ **1** *n.* **(a)** (highest part) Spitze, *die;* (of table) Platte, *die;* (of bench seat) Sitzfläche, *die;* (~ floor) oberstes Stockwerk; (flat roof, roof garden) Dach, *das;* (rim of glass, bottle, etc.) Rand, *der;* (~ end) oberes Ende; (of tree) Spitze, *die;* Wipfel, *der;* **a cake with a cherry on** ~: ein Kuchen mit einer Kirsche [oben]drauf; **at the** ~: oben; **at the** ~ **of the building/hill/pile/stairs** oben im Gebäude/[oben] auf dem Hügel/[oben] auf dem Stapel/oben an der Treppe; **be at/get to** *or* **reach the** ~ [**of the ladder** *or* **tree**] (fig.) auf der obersten Sprosse [der Leiter] stehen/die oberste Sprosse [der Leiter] erreichen (fig.); **be/get on** ~ **of a situation/subject** eine Situation/eine Materie in Griff haben/in den Griff bekommen; **don't let it get on** ~ **of you** (fig.) lass dich davon nicht unterkriegen! (ugs.); **he put it on [the]** ~ **of the pile** er legte es [oben] auf den Stapel; **on** ~ **of one another** *or* **each other** aufeinander; **on** ~ **of sth.** (fig.: in addition) zusätzlich zu etw.; **on** ~ **of everything else** zu alledem noch; **come/be on** ~ **of sth.** (be additional) zu etw. hinzukommen; **on** ~ **of the world** (fig.) überglücklich; **be/go thin on** ~: licht auf dem Kopf sein/werden; **be on** ~: ganz oben sein/liegen; **come out on** ~ (be successful) Erfolg haben; (win) gewinnen; **get to the** ~ (fig.) eine Spitzenposition erringen; ganz nach oben kommen (ugs.); **from** ~ **to toe** von Kopf bis Fuß; **be over the** ~: übertrieben *od.* überzogen sein; **he searched the house from** ~ **to bottom** er durchsuchte das Haus von oben bis unten; **(b)** (highest rank) Spitze, *die;* **the man at the** ~: der [oberste] Chef *od.* (ugs.) Boss; ~ **of the table** (Sport) Tabellenspitze, *die;* [**at the**] ~ **of the agenda is** …: ganz oben auf der Tagesordnung steht …; **be [at the]** ~ **of the class** der/die Klassenbeste sein; ~ **of the bill** (Theatre) Zugpferd, *das;* **(c)** (of vegetable) Kraut, *das;* **(d)** (upper surface) Oberfläche, *die;* (of cupboard, wardrobe, chest) Oberseite, *die;* **on [the]** ~ **of sth.** [oben] auf etw. (position: Dat./direction: Akk.); **cut the** ~ **off an egg** ein Ei köpfen; **they climbed to the** ~ **of the hill/slope** sie kletterten auf den Hügel/den Hang hinauf; **(e)** (folding roof) Verdeck, *das;* **(f)** (upper deck of bus, boat) Oberdeck, *das;* **(g)** (cap of pen) [Verschluss]kappe, *die;* **(h)** (cream on milk) Sahne, *die;* Rahm, *der* (regional, bes. südd., österr., schweiz.); **(i)** (upper part of page) oberer Teil; **at the** ~ [**of the page**] oben [auf der/die Seite]; **(j)** (upper garment) Oberteil, *das;* **(k)** (turn-down of sock) Umschlag, *der;* **(l)** (head end) Kopf, *der;* (of street)

oberes Ende; **(m)** (utmost) Gipfel, *der;* **shout/talk at the** ~ **of one's voice** aus vollem Halse schreien/so laut wie möglich sprechen; **(n) be the** ~s (coll.) (the best) der/die/ das Größte sein (ugs.); (marvellous) spitze sein (ugs.); **(o)** (surface) Oberfläche, *die;* **(p)** (lid) Deckel, *der;* (of bottle, glass, jar, etc.) Stöpsel, *der;* **(q)** (Brit. Motor Veh.) **in** ~: im größten Gang. **2** *adj.* oberst…; höchst… ‹*Ton, Preis*›; ~ **end** oberes Ende; **the/a** ~ **award** die höchste/eine hohe Auszeichnung; **the/a** ~ **chess player** der beste Schachspieler/ einer der besten Schachspieler *od.* ein Spitzenschachspieler; ~ **scientists/actors** *etc.* hochkarätige Wissenschaftler/Schauspieler *usw.;* ~ **sportsman/job/politician** Spitzensportler, *der/*Spitzenposition, *die/*Spitzenpolitiker, *der;* **the** ~ **pupil/school/marks** der beste Schüler/die beste Schule/die besten Noten; ~ **manager/ management** Topmanager, *der/-*management, *das;* **a** ~ **speed of 100 m.p.h.** eine Spitzen- *od.* Höchstgeschwindigkeit von 100 Meilen pro Stunde; **go at** ~ **speed** mit Spitzen- *od.* Höchstgeschwindigkeit fahren; **be/come** ~ [**in a subject**] [in einem Fach] der/die Beste sein/werden; **give sth.** ~ **priority** einer Sache *(Dat.)* höchste Priorität einräumen; **have a record in the** ~ **ten** eine Platte in den Topten haben; **in the** ~ **left/right corner** in der linken/rechten oberen Ecke; **on the** ~ **floor** im obersten Stockwerk; **the** ~ **people** (in society) die Spitzen der Gesellschaft; (in a particular field) die besten Leute. **3** *v.t.*, **-pp-:** **(a)** (cover) **the hills were** ~**ped with** *or* **by snow** die Hügelspitzen waren schneebedeckt; **(b)** (Hort.: cut ~ off) stutzen ‹*Pflanze*›; kappen ‹*Baum*›; **(c)** (be taller than) überragen; **(d)** (surpass, excel) übertreffen; **exports have** ~**ped [the] £40 million [mark/level]** die Exporte haben die [Grenze von] 40 Millionen Pfund überschritten; **to** ~ **it all** [noch] obendrein; **(e)** (head) anführen; ~ **the bill** (Theatre) das Zugpferd sein

~ **'off 1** *v.t.* (coll.) beschließen. **2** *v.i.* (coll.) schließen

~ **'up** (Brit. coll.) **1** *v.t.* auffüllen ‹*Batterie, Tank, Flasche, Glas*›; ~ **up the petrol/oil/water** Benzin/Öl/Wasser nachfüllen; ~ **up sb.'s drink** jmdm. nachschenken. **2** *v.i.* (fill one's tank up) volltanken; (fill one's glass up) sich nachschenken

top² *n.* (toy) Kreisel, *der*

topaz /ˈtəʊpæz/ *n.* (Min.) Topas, *der*

top: ~ **'brass** ⇒ **brass 1 g;** ~ **coat** *n.* **(a)** (overcoat) Überzieher, *der;* Mantel, *der;* **(b)** (of paint) Deckanstrich, *der;* ~ **copy** *n.* Original, *das;* ~ **'dog** *n.* (fig. coll.) Boss, *der* (ugs.); ~**-flight** *attrib. adj.* erstrangig; Spitzen‹*sportler, -politiker*›; ~ **'hat** *n.* Zylinder[hut], *der;* ~**-heavy** *adj.* oberlastig; kopflastig ‹*Baum, Pflanze, Bürokratie*›

topic /ˈtɒpɪk/ *n.* Thema, *das;* ~ **of debate/conversation** Diskussions-/Gesprächsthema, *das*

topical /ˈtɒpɪkl/ *adj.* aktuell

topicality /tɒpɪˈkælɪtɪ/ *n., no pl.* Aktualität, *die*

topically /ˈtɒpɪkəlɪ/ *adv.* mit aktuellem Bezug

topless /ˈtɒplɪs/ *adj.* **(a) a** ~ **statue/column** eine Statue/Säule mit fehlendem oberem Teil; **(b) a** ~ **dress/ swimsuit** ein busenfreies Kleid/ein Oben-ohne-Badeanzug; **(c)** (bare-breasted) barbusig; ~ **girl/waitress** Oben-ohne-Mädchen, *das/*-Bedienung, *die*

'top-level *attrib. adj.* Gipfel‹*treffen, -konferenz*›; Spitzen‹*politiker, -funktionär*›; ~ **discussions** Diskussionen auf höchster Ebene

topmost /ˈtɒpməʊst, ˈtɒpməst/ *adj.* oberst… ‹*Schicht, Stufe*›; höchst… ‹*Gipfel, Beamte, Note*›

top-'notch *adj.* (coll.) fantastisch (ugs.)

topography /təˈpɒɡrəfɪ/ *n.* **(a)** Topographie, *die;* **(b)** (features) örtliche *od.* (geh.) topographische Gegebenheiten

topping /ˈtɒpɪŋ/ *n.* Überzug, *der;* (of pizza etc.) Belag, *der*

topple /ˈtɒpl/ **1** *v.i.* fallen; **the tower/pile** ~**d to the ground** der Turm/Stapel fiel um *od.* kippte um; ~ [**from power**] (fig.) stürzen. **2** *v.t.* stürzen; ~ **sb./a government [from power]** ‹*Gegner:*› jmdn./eine Regierung stürzen; ‹*Skandal, Abstimmung:*› jmdn./eine Regierung zu Fall bringen

~ **'down** *v.i.* hinab-/herabfallen

~ **'over** *v.i.* ‹*Turm, Stapel, Baum, Auto:*› umstürzen, umfallen; ‹*Vase, Ohnmächtiger:*› umfallen

top: ∿**-quality** attrib. adj. [qualitativ] hochwertig; ∿-**ranking** attrib. adj. Spitzen‹funktionär, -beamter, -politiker, -sportler, -orchester, -delegierter›; hochrangig ‹Offizier›; erstrangig ‹Autor, Schauspieler›; führend ‹Wissenschaftler›; ∿ **'secret** adj. streng geheim; ∿**side** n. (joint of beef) Oberschale, die; ∿**soil** n. (Agric.) Mutterboden, der; (of field) [Acker]krume, die

topsy-turvy /tɒpsɪ'tɜ:vɪ/ **1** adv. verkehrtrum (ugs.); auf dem Kopf (ugs.) ‹stehen, liegen›; **turn sth.** ∿ (lit. or fig.) etw. auf den Kopf stellen (ugs.). **2** adj. chaotisch; (fig.) **a world where things are all** ∿**:** eine Welt, in der alles auf dem Kopf steht

'top-up n. (coll.) Auffüllung, die; **give the tank/oil a** ∿**:** den Tank auffüllen/Öl nachfüllen; **would you like a** ∿? soll ich dir noch mal nachgießen?

torch /tɔ:tʃ/ n. (a) [electric] ∿ (Brit.) Taschenlampe, die; (b) (blowlamp) (for welding) Schweißbrenner, der; (for soldering) Lötlampe, die; (for cutting) Schneidbrenner, der

tore ⇒ **tear**[1] 2, 3

toreador /'tɒrɪədɔ:(r)/ n. Toreador, der

torment 1 /'tɔ:ment/ n. Qual, die; **be in** ∿**:** Qualen ausstehen. **2** /tɔ:'ment/ v.t. (a) quälen; peinigen; **be** ∿**ed by** or **with sth.** von etw. gequält werden; (b) (tease, worry) quälen

torn ⇒ **tear**[1] 2, 3

tornado /tɔ:'neɪdəʊ/ n., pl. ∿**es** Wirbelsturm, der; (in North America) Tornado, der

torpedo /tɔ:'pi:dəʊ/ **1** n., pl. ∿**es** Torpedo, der. **2** v.t. (auch fig.) torpedieren

torpedo: ∿ **boat** n. Torpedoboot, das; ∿ **tube** n. Torpedorohr, das

torpid /'tɔ:pɪd/ adj. träge

torpor /'tɔ:pə(r)/ n. Trägheit, die

torque /tɔ:k/ n. (Mech.) Drehmoment, das

torrent /'tɒrənt/ n. (a) reißender Bach; (stream having steep course) Sturzbach, der; (mountain ∿**:** reißender Gebirgsbach; **a** ∿ **of rain** ein Regenguss; **the rain came down in** ∿**s** es regnete in Strömen; (b) (fig.: violent flow) Flut, die; Schwall, der

torrential /tə'renʃl/ adj. (a) reißend ‹Gebirgsbach, Fluten›; wolkenbruchartig ‹Regen, Schauer›; (b) (fig.) überwältigend; gewaltig

torrid /'tɒrɪd/ adj. (a) (intensely hot) glutheiß; **the** ∿ **heat of the desert** die Gluthitze der Wüste; (b) (fig.: intense, ardent) glühend (geh.); ‹Liebesszene› voller Leidenschaft

torso /'tɔ:səʊ/ n., pl. ∿**s** (a) (Art) Torso, der; (b) (human trunk) Rumpf, der; **bare** ∿**:** nackter Oberkörper

tortoise /'tɔ:təs/ n. Schildkröte, die

tortoiseshell /'tɔ:təsʃel/ n. Schildpatt, das; attrib. Schildpatt-

tortoiseshell 'cat n. Katze mit Schildpattzeichnung

tortuous /'tɔ:tjʊəs/ adj. (a) (full of twists and turns) verschlungen ‹Weg›; gewunden ‹Flusslauf›; (b) (fig.: circuitous) umständlich; verworren ‹Argumentation, Denken, Sprache›

torture /'tɔ:tʃə(r)/ **1** n. (a) Folter, die; **the** ∿ **of sb.** jmds. Folterung; **instrument of** ∿**:** Folterwerkzeug, das; Folterinstrument, das; (b) (fig.: agony) Qual, die; **it was** ∿**:** es war eine Tortur. **2** v.t. foltern; (fig.) quälen

'torture chamber n. Folterkammer, die

torturer /'tɔ:tʃərə(r)/ n. Folterer, der/Folterin, die

Tory /'tɔ:rɪ/ (Brit. Polit. coll.) **1** n. Tory, der. **2** adj. Tory-

toss /tɒs/ **1** v.t. (a) (throw upwards) hochwerfen; ∿ **a pancake** einen Pfannkuchen [durch Hochwerfen] wenden; (b) (throw casually) werfen; schmeißen (ugs.); ∿ **it over!** (coll.) schmeiß es/ihn/sie rüber (ugs.); ∿ **it to sb.** jmdm. etw. zuwerfen; (c) ∿ **a coin** eine Münze werfen; ∿ **sb. for sth.** mit jmdm. durch Hochwerfen einer Münze um etw. losen; (d) **be** ∿**ed by a bull/horse** von einem Stier auf die Hörner genommen werden/von einem Pferd abgeworfen werden; (e) (move about) hin und her werfen; (f) (Cookery: mix gently) wenden; ∿ **a salad in oil** einen Salat mit Öl anmachen. **2** v.i. (a) (be restless in bed) sich hin und her werfen; ∿ **and turn** sich [schlaflos] im Bett wälzen; (b) ‹Schiff, Boot:› hin und her geworfen werden; (c) (∿ coin) eine Münze werfen; ∿ **for sth.** mit einer Münze um

etw. losen. **3** n. (a) (of coin) ∿ **of a coin** Hochwerfen einer Münze; **argue the** ∿ (fig.) die Entscheidung nicht akzeptieren wollen; **lose/win the** ∿**:** bei der Auslosung verlieren/gewinnen; (Footb.) die Seitenwahl verlieren/gewinnen; (b) **give a contemptuous/proud** ∿ **of the head** den Kopf verächtlich/stolz in den Nacken werfen; (c) (throw) Wurf, der; (d) **I couldn't give a** ∿ (fig. Brit. sl.) es ist mir scheißegal (salopp)

∿ **about,** ∿ **around 1** v.i. (a) (be restless in bed) sich [schlaflos] im Bett wälzen; (b) ⇒ **2 b. 2** v.t. ∿ **sth. around** or **about** etw. herumwerfen; (fig.) etw. in die Debatte werfen

∿ **a'side** v.t. (a) (throw to one side) hinwerfen; (b) (fig.: reject, abandon) beiseite schieben

∿ **a'way** v.t. wegwerfen

∿ **'back** v.t. zurückwerfen ‹Kopf, Haar›; runterkippen (ugs.) ‹Getränk›

∿ **'out** v.t. (a) (throw out) ∿ **sth. out** etw. wegwerfen od. (ugs.) -schmeißen; (b) (fig.: reject) [kurzerhand] ablehnen

∿ **'up 1** v.i. eine Münze werfen; ∿ **up for sth.** mit einer Münze um etw. losen. **2** v.t. (throw) hochwerfen; in die Luft werfen

'toss-up n. (a) (tossing of coin) Hochwerfen einer Münze; (b) (even chance) **it is a** ∿ [whether ...] es ist noch ganz ungewiss[, ob ...]

tot[1] /tɒt/ n. (coll.) (a) (small child) kleines Kind; Wicht, der (fam.); **tiny** ∿**:** kleiner Wicht; (b) (dram of liquor) Gläschen, das

tot[2] (coll.) **1** v.t., **-tt-:** ∿ **'up** zusammenziehen (ugs.). **2** v.i., **-tt-:** ∿ **'up** sich summieren; sich [zusammen]läppern (ugs.); **that** ∿**s up to £5** das macht zusammen 5 Pfund (ugs.)

total /'təʊtl/ **1** adj. (a) (comprising the whole) gesamt; Gesamt‹gewicht, -wert, -bevölkerung usw.›; **what are your** ∿ **debts?** wie viel Schulden hast du insgesamt?; **a** ∿ **increase of £100** eine Steigerung von insgesamt 100 Pfund; (b) (absolute) völlig nicht präd.; **be in** ∿ **ignorance of sth.** von etw. überhaupt od. absolut nichts wissen; **a** ∿ **beginner** ein absoluter Anfänger; ∿ **nonsense** totaler Unsinn; **have a** ∿ **lack of interest in sth.** sich für etw. absolut nicht interessieren. **2** n. (number) Gesamtzahl, die; (amount) Gesamtbetrag, der; (result of addition) Summe, die; **a** ∿ **of 200/£200** etc. insgesamt 200/200 Pfund usw.; **in** ∿**:** insgesamt. **3** v.t., (Brit.) **-ll-:** (a) (add up) addieren, zusammenzählen ‹Zahlen, Posten, Beträge›; (b) (amount to) [insgesamt] betragen

∿ **'up 1** v.t. addieren; zusammenzählen. **2** v.i. ∿ **up to sth.** sich auf etw. (Akk.) belaufen

total e'clipse n. (Astron.) totale Finsternis

totalitarian /təʊtælɪ'teərɪən/ adj. (Polit.) totalitär

totality /tə'tælɪtɪ/ n. Gesamtheit, die

totally /'təʊtəlɪ/ adv. völlig

total: ∿ **re'call** n. **have [the power of]** ∿ **recall** ein absolutes Erinnerungsvermögen haben; ∿ **'war** n. totaler Krieg

tote /təʊt/ v.t. (coll.) schleppen

'tote bag n. ≈ Reisetasche, die

totem /'təʊtəm/ n. Totem, das (Völkerk.)

'totem pole n. Totempfahl, der (Völkerk.)

totter /'tɒtə(r)/ v.i. wanken; taumeln

toucan /'tu:kən/ n. (Ornith.) Tukan, der

touch /tʌtʃ/ **1** v.t. (a) (lit. or fig.) berühren; (inspect by ∿ing) betasten; ∿ **the sky** (fig.) an den Himmel stoßen; ∿ **sb. on the shoulder** jmdm. auf die Schulter tippen; ∿ **A to B** B mit A berühren; ∿ **glasses** anstoßen; (b) (harm, interfere with) anrühren; **the police can't** ∿ **you [for it]** die Polizei kann dich nicht [dafür] belangen; (c) (fig.: rival) ∿ **sth.** an etw. (Akk.) heranreichen; (d) (affect emotionally) rühren; (e) (concern oneself with) anrühren; (f) ∿ **sb. for a loan/£5** (sl.) jmdn. anpumpen (salopp) /um 5 Pfund anpumpen od. anhauen (salopp). **2** v.i. sich berühren; ‹Grundstücke:› aneinander stoßen; **don't** ∿! nicht anfassen!; **'please do not** ∿**'** „bitte nicht berühren!" **3** n. (a) Berührung, die; **at a** ∿**:** bei bloßer Berührung; **be soft/ warm** etc. **to the** ∿**:** sich weich/ warm usw. anfühlen; (b) no pl., no art. (faculty) [sense of] ∿**:** Tastsinn, der; (c) (small amount) **a** ∿ **of salt/pepper** etc. eine Spur Salz/

Pfeffer *usw.;* **a** ~ **of irony/sadness** *etc.* ein Anflug von Ironie/Traurigkeit *usw.;* **have a** ~ **of rheumatism** ein bisschen Rheuma haben; **a** ~ (slightly) ein [ganz] kleines bisschen; **(d)** (game of tag) Fangen, *das;* **(e)** (Art: stroke) Strich, *der;* (fig.) Detail, *das;* **to mention it in such a way was a clever/subtle** ~: es auf eine solche Weise zu erwähnen, war ein schlauer/raffinierter Einfall; **add** *or* **put the final** ~**es to sth.** einer Sache (*Dat.*) den letzten Schliff geben; **(f)** (manner, style) (on keyboard instrument, typewriter) Anschlag, *der;* (of writer, sculptor) Stil, *der;* **a personal** ~: eine persönliche *od.* individuelle Note; **lose one's** ~: seinen Schwung verlieren; (Sport) seine Form verlieren; **(g)** (communication) **be in/out of** ~ **[with sb.]** [mit jmdm.] Kontakt/keinen Kontakt haben; **I shall be in** ~ **with them** ich werde mit ihnen Kontakt aufnehmen; **be in/ out of** ~ **with sth.** über etw. (+ *Akk.*) auf dem Laufenden/nicht auf dem Laufenden sein; **get in** ~ **[with sb.]** mit jmdm. Kontakt/Verbindung aufnehmen; **keep in** ~ **[with sb.]** [mit jmdm.] in Verbindung *od.* Kontakt bleiben; **keep in** ~! lass von dir hören!; **keep in** ~ **with sth.** sich über etw. (*Akk.*) auf dem Laufenden halten; **lose** ~ **with sb.** den Kontakt zu jmdm. verlieren; **we have lost** ~: wir haben keinen Kontakt mehr [zueinander]; **have lost** ~ **with sth.** über etw. (*Akk.*) nicht mehr auf dem Laufenden sein; **put sb. in** ~ **with sb.** jmdn. mit jmdm. zusammenbringen; **(h)** (Footb., Rugby: part of field) Aus, *das;* Mark, *die* (Rugby); **in** ~: im Aus; **(i)** (coll.) **be an easy** *or* **a soft** ~ (be a person who gives money readily) leicht rumzukriegen sein (ugs.)
~ **'down** *v.i.* **(a)** (Rugby) den Ball niederlegen; (Amer. Footb.) den Ball hinter die Grundlinie bringen; **(b)** ‹*Flugzeug:*› aufsetzen; (land) landen
~ **on** *v.t.* **(a)** (treat briefly) ansprechen; **(b)** (verge on) grenzen an (+ *Akk.*)
~ **'up** *v.t.* **(a)** (improve) ausbessern; **(b)** (sl.: fondle) befummeln (ugs.)
~ **upon** ⇒ ~ **on**

touch: ~**-and-'go** *adj.* prekär ‹*Situation*›; **it is** ~**-and-go [whether …]** es steht auf des Messers Schneide[, ob …]; ~**down** *n.* **(a)** (Amer. Footb.) Touchdown, *der;* **(b)** (Aeronaut.) Landung, *die*

touched /tʌtʃt/ *pred. adj.* **(a)** (moved) gerührt; **(b)** (coll.: mad) meschugge (salopp)

touching /'tʌtʃɪŋ/ *adj.* rührend; (moving) bewegend; ergreifend

touch: ~**line** *n.* (Footb., Rugby) Seitenlinie, *die;* ~**paper** *n.* Zündpapier, *das;* (on firework) Papierlunte, *die;* ~**stone** *n.* (fig.) Prüfstein, *der;* ~**tone** *adj.* **a** ~**-tone telephone** ein Telefon mit Mehrfrequenzwahl; ~**type** *v.i.* blind schreiben; ~**typing** *n.* Blindschreiben, *das*

touchy /'tʌtʃɪ/ *adj.* empfindlich ‹*Person*›; heikel ‹*Thema, Sache*›

tough /tʌf/ **1** *adj.* **(a)** fest ‹*Material, Stoff, Leder, Metall, Werkstoff*›; zäh ‹*Fleisch; fachspr.: Werkstoff, Metall, Kunststoff*›; widerstandsfähig ‹*Straßenbelag, Bodenbelag, Gummi, Glas, Haut*›; strapazierfähig ‹*Kleidung, Stoff, Schuhe*›; **(b)** (hardy, unyielding) zäh ‹*Person*›; **a** ~ **customer** (coll.) ein harter Brocken (ugs.); **(c)** (difficult, trying) schwierig; vertrackt (ugs.) ‹*Problem*›; hart ‹*Kampf, Wettkampf*›; strapaziös ‹*Reise*›; schwer ‹*Zeit*›; **we had a** ~ **time** wir haben viel durchgemacht; **(d)** (severe, harsh) hart; **get** ~ (coll.) andere Saiten aufziehen; **(e)** (coll.: unfortunate, hard) ~ **luck** Pech, *das;* **that's** ~ **[luck]** son Pech! (ugs.); **be** ~ **on sb.** hart für jmdn. sein. **2** *n.* Rowdy, *der* (abwertend). **3** *v.t.* (coll.) ~ **it out** nicht nachgeben; **I've just got to** ~ **it out** ich darf einfach nicht nachgeben

toughen /'tʌfn/ *v.t.* größere Festigkeit geben (+ *Dat.*); zäher machen (fachspr.) ‹*Werkstoff, Metall, Kunststoff*›; abhärten, (geh.) stählen ‹*Person, Körper*›; verschärfen ‹*Gesetz, Widerstand*›
~ **up** *v.t.* abhärten; stählen (geh.); verschärfen ‹*Gesetz, Verbrechensbekämpfung*›

toughness /'tʌfnɪs/ *n., no pl.* ⇒ **tough 1 a:** Festigkeit, *die;* Zähheit, *die;* Zähigkeit, *die* (fachspr.); Widerstandsfähigkeit, *die;* Strapazierfähigkeit, *die*

toupee, toupet /'tuːpeɪ/ *n.* Toupet, *das*

tour /tʊə(r)/ **1** *n.* **(a)** [Rund]reise, *die;* Tour, *die* (ugs.); **a** ~ **of** *or* **through Europe** eine Reise durch Europa; eine Europareise; **a world** ~**/round-the-world** ~ eine Weltreise/Reise um die Welt; **a walking/cycling** ~: eine Wanderung/[Fahr]radtour; **(b)** (Theatre, Sport) Tournee, *die;* Tour, *die* (Jargon); **be/go on** ~: auf Tournee/Tour sein/ gehen; **(c)** (excursion, inspection) (of museum, palace, house) Besichtigung, *die;* **go on/make/do a** ~ **of** besichtigen ‹*Museum, Haus, Schloss usw.*›; **a** ~ **of the countryside/ the city/the factory** ein Ausflug in die Umgebung/eine Besichtigungstour durch die Stadt/ein Rundgang durch die Fabrik; **(d)** ~ **[of duty]** Dienstzeit, *die.* **2** *v.i.* **(a)** ~**/ go** ~**ing in** *or* **through a country** eine Reise *od.* (ugs.) Tour durch ein Land machen; **be** ~**ing in a country** auf einer Reise *od.* (ugs.) Tour durch ein Land sein; **(b)** (Theatre, Sport, exhibition) eine Tournee *od.* (Jargon) Tour machen; (be on ~) auf Tournee *od.* (Jargon) Tour sein; touren (Jargon); (go on ~) auf Tournee *od.* (Jargon) Tour gehen. **3** *v.t.* **(a)** besichtigen ‹*Stadt, Gebäude, Museum*›; ~ **a country/region** eine Reise *od.* (ugs.) Tour durch ein Land/Gebiet machen; ~ **an area on foot/by bicycle** eine Wanderung/Radtour durch eine Gegend machen; **(b)** (Theatre, Sport) ~ **a country/the provinces** eine Tournee *od.* (Jargon) Tour durch das Land/die Provinz machen

tourer /'tʊərə(r)/ *n.* (Motor Veh.) Kabriolimousine, *die*

tourism /'tʊərɪzm/ *n., no pl., no indef. art.* **(a)** Tourismus, *der;* **(b)** (operation of tours) Touristik, *die*

tourist /'tʊərɪst/ **1** *n.* Tourist, *der*/Touristin, *die.* **2** *attrib. adj.* Touristen-; **special** ~ **rates** ermäßigte Preise für Touristen

tourist: ~ **attraction** *n.* Touristenattraktion, *die;* ~ **board** *n.* (Brit.) Amt für Fremdenverkehrswesen; ~ **guide** *n.* **(a)** (person) Touristenführer, *der*/-führerin, *die;* **(b)** (book) Reiseführer, *der* **(to, of** von); ~ **hotel** *n.* Touristenhotel, *das;* ~ **industry** *n.* **(a)** (business) Tourismusindustrie, *die;* **(b)** (firms) Touristik[branche], *die;* ~ **infor'mation centre, ~ office** *ns.* Fremdenverkehrsbüro, *das;* Touristeninformation, *die* (ugs.); ~ **season** *n.* Touristensaison, *die;* ~ **trade** ⇒ ~ **industry;** ~ **trap** *n.* (bar, restaurant, etc.) (auf Touristen spezialisierter] Neppladen (ugs.); (town, place) Ort, an dem Touristen geneppt werden (ugs.)

touristy /'tʊərɪstɪ/ *adj.* (derog.) auf Tourismus getrimmt (ugs.); Touristen‹*stadt, -nest, -gegend*› (ugs. abwertend)

tournament /'tʊənəmənt/ *n.* (Hist.; Sport) Turnier, *das*

tourniquet /'tʊənɪkeɪ/ *n.* (Med.) Tourniquet, *das*

'tour operator *n.* Reiseveranstalter, *der*/-veranstalterin, *die*

tousle /'taʊzl/ *v.t.* zerzausen

tout /taʊt/ **1** *v.i.* ~ **[for business/custom/orders]** Kunden anreißen (ugs.) *od.* werben (ugs.); ~ **for customers/ buyers** Kunden/Käufer anreißen (ugs.) *od.* werben. **2** *n.* Anreißer, *der*/Anreißerin, *die* (ugs.); Kundenwerber, *der*/-werberin, *die;* **ticket** ~: Kartenschwarzhändler, *der*/-händlerin, *die*

tow /təʊ/ **1** *v.t.* schleppen; ziehen ‹*Anhänger, Wasserskiläufer, Handwagen*›; **he** ~**ed my car to get it started** er hat meinen Wagen angeschleppt. **2** *n.* Schlepp, *das;* **My car's broken down. — Do you want a** ~**?** Mein Wagen ist stehen geblieben. — Soll ich Sie [ab]schleppen?; **give a boat/car a** ~: ein Boot/einen Wagen schleppen; **have sth. in** *or* **on** ~: etw. im Schlepp[tau] haben; **have sb. in** ~ (fig.) jmdn. im Schlepptau haben (ugs.); **take a boat/car in** ~: ein Boot/einen Wagen in Schlepp nehmen
~ **a'way** *v.t.* abschleppen

toward /təˈwɔːd/, **towards** /təˈwɔːdz/ *prep.* **(a)** (in direction of) ~ **sb./sth.** auf jmdn./etw. zu; **the ship sailed** ~ **France/the open sea** das Schiff fuhr in Richtung Frankreich/offenes Meer; ~ **[the] town** in Richtung [auf die] Stadt; **point** ~ **the north** nach Norden zeigen; **turn** ~ **sb.** sich zu jmdm. umdrehen; **sit/stand with one's back [turned]** ~ **sth.** mit dem Rücken zu etw. sitzen/stehen; **the country was drifting** ~ **war/economic chaos** das Land trieb dem Krieg/wirtschaftlichem Chaos zu; **(b)** (in relation to) gegenüber; **feel sth.** ~ **sb.** jmdm. gegenüber etw. empfinden; **be fair/unfair** *etc.* ∼ **sb.** jmdm. gegenüber *od.* zu jmdm. fair/unfair *usw.* sein; **feel angry/sympathetic** ∼ **sb.** böse auf jmdn. sein/Verständnis für jmdn. haben; **(c)** (for) **a contribution** ∼ **sth.** ein Beitrag zu etw.; **save up** ∼ **a car/one's holidays** auf *od.* für einen Wagen/für seine Ferien sparen; **proposals** ∼ **solving a problem** Vorschläge zur Lösung eines Problems; **work together** ∼ **a solution** gemeinsam auf eine Lösung hinarbeiten; **(d)** (near) gegen; ∼ **the end of May/of the year** *etc.* [gegen] Ende Mai/des Jahres

'tow bar *n.* Anhängerkupplung, *die*

towel /'taʊəl/ **1** *n.* Handtuch, *das;* **throw in the** ∼ (Boxing; also fig.) das Handtuch werfen. **2** *v.t.,* (Brit.) **-ll-** abtrocknen; ∼ **oneself** sich abtrocknen

'towel rail *n.* Handtuchhalter, *der*

tower /'taʊə(r)/ **1** *n.* **(a)** Turm, *der;* **(b)** (fortress) Festung, *die;* Wehrturm, *der;* **the T**∼ **[of London]** der Tower [von London]; **(c)** **be a** ∼ **of strength [to sb.]** (fig.) [jmdm.] ein fester Rückhalt sein. **2** *v.i.* in die Höhe ragen
∼ **above**, ∼ **over** *v.t.* ∼ **above** *or* **over sb./sth.** (lit. or fig.) jmdn./etw. überragen

'tower block *n.* Hochhaus, *das*

towering /'taʊərɪŋ/ *attrib. adj.* **(a)** hoch aufragend; **(b)** (fig.) herausragend ⟨*Leistung, Gestalt*⟩; **(c)** (fig.: violent, intense) blind ⟨*Wut*⟩; maßlos ⟨*Ehrgeiz, Stolz*⟩

town /taʊn/ *n.* **(a)** ▶ **1159** Stadt, *die;* **the** ∼ **of Cambridge** die Stadt Cambridge; **in [the]** ∼: in der Stadt; **the** ∼ (people) die Stadt; **on the outskirts/in the centre of** ∼: in den Randbezirken der Stadt/in der Stadtmitte *od.* Innenstadt; **go [up] to** ∼: in die Stadt fahren; **be in/out of** ∼: in der Stadt/nicht in der Stadt sein; **the best coffee/tea/cake** *etc.* **in** ∼: der beste Kaffee/Tee/Kuchen *usw.* in der Stadt; **go out/have a night on the** ∼ (coll.) [in die Stadt gehen und] einen draufmachen (ugs.); **go to** ∼ (fig. coll.) in die Vollen gehen (**on** bei) (ugs.); **(b)** (business or shopping centre) Stadt, *die;* **in** ∼: in der Stadt; **go into** ∼: in die Stadt gehen/fahren

town: ∼ **'centre** *n.* Stadtmitte, *die;* Stadtzentrum, *das;* ∼ **'clerk** *n.* ▶ **887** ≈ [Ober]stadtdirektor, *der/*-direktorin, *die;* ∼ **'council** *n.* (Brit.) Stadtrat, *der;* ∼ **'councillor** *n.* ▶ **887** (Brit.) Stadtrat, *der/*-rätin, *die;* ∼ **'hall** *n.* Rathaus, *das;* ∼ **house** *n.* **(a)** (residence in ∼) Stadthaus, *das;* **(b)** (terrace house) Reihenhaus, *das;* ∼ **'planning** *n.* Stadtplanung, *die*

townsfolk /'taʊnzfəʊlk/, **townspeople** /'taʊnzpiːpl/ *ns. pl.* Städter *Pl.;* **the** ∼ (inhabitants) die Stadtbevölkerung; (citizens) die Bürger [der Stadt]

township /'taʊnʃɪp/ *n.* **(a)** (Amer.: division of county) Township, die; *Verwaltungseinheit unterhalb der County;* **(b)** (S. Afr.: non-white urban area) Township, *die; von Farbigen bewohnte städtische Siedlung*

tow: ∼**path** *n.* Leinpfad, *der;* ∼ **rope** *n.* Abschleppseil, *das*

toxic /'tɒksɪk/ *adj.* giftig; toxisch (fachspr.)

toxic: ∼ **'shock syndrome** *n.* ▶ **865** (Med.) toxisches Schocksyndrom; ∼ **'waste** *n.* Giftmüll, *der;* ∼ **wastes** giftige Abfallstoffe; ∼ **waste tip** *or* **dump** Giftmülldeponie, *die*

toxin /'tɒksɪn/ *n.* Toxin, *das*

toy /tɔɪ/ **1** *n.* (lit. or fig.) Spielzeug, *das;* ∼s Spielzeug, *das;* Spielwaren *Pl.* (Wirtsch.). **2** *adj.* **(a)** Spielzeug-; **(b)** (Breeding) Zwerg-. **3** *v.i.* ∼ **with the idea of doing sth.** mit dem Gedanken spielen, etw. zu tun; ∼ **with one's food** (nibble at) in seinem Essen herumstochern

toy: ∼**boy** *n.* (coll.) Gespiele, *der* (scherzh.); ∼**shop** *n.* Spielwarengeschäft, *das;* ∼ **'soldier** *n.* Spielzeugsoldat, *der*

trace¹ /treɪs/ **1** *v.t.* **(a)** (copy) durchpausen; abpausen; ∼ **sth. on to sth.** etw. auf etw. (*Akk.*) pausen; **(b)** (delineate) zeichnen ⟨*Form, Linie*⟩; malen ⟨*Buchstaben, Wort*⟩; (fig.) entwerfen; **she** ∼**d our route on the map with her finger** sie zeichnete unsere Route mit dem Finger auf der Landkarte nach; **(c)** (follow track of) folgen (+ *Dat.*); verfolgen; ∼ **a river to its source** einen Fluss [bis] zur Quelle zurückverfolgen; **the police** ∼**d him to Spain** die Polizei spürte ihn in Spanien auf; **(d)** (observe, find)

finden; ∼ **a connection** einen Zusammenhang sehen. **2** *n.* Spur, *die;* **there is no** ∼ **of your letter in our records** in unseren Aufzeichnungen findet sich kein Hinweis auf Ihr Schreiben; **I can't find any** ∼ **of him/it** (cannot locate) ich kann ihn/es nirgends finden; **lose [all]** ∼ **of sb.** [völlig] aus den Augen verlieren; **sink without** ∼: sinken, ohne eine Spur zu hinterlassen; (fig.) in der Versenkung verschwinden (ugs.); ⟨*bekannte Persönlichkeit:*⟩ von der Bildfläche verschwinden (ugs.)
∼ **'back** *v.t.* zurückverfolgen
∼ **'out** ⇒ ∼ **1 b**

trace² *n.* Strang, *der;* **kick over the** ∼s (fig.) über die Stränge schlagen (ugs.)

traceable /'treɪsəbl/ *adj.* **(a)** sth. is ∼ to sth./through sth. etw. lässt sich bis zu etw./durch etw. hindurch zurückverfolgen; **(b)** (discoverable) auffindbar

'trace element *n.* (Chem.) Spurenelement, *das*

tracer /'treɪsə(r)/ *n.* (Mil.) Leuchtspurgeschoss, *das*

trachea /trə'kiːə/ *n., pl.* ∼**e** /trə'kiːiː/ (Anat.) Trachea, *die* (fachspr.); Luftröhre, *die*

tracing /'treɪsɪŋ/ *n.* **(a)** (action) [Durch]pausen, *das;* [Ab]pausen, *das;* **(b)** (copy) Pause, *die*

'tracing paper *n.* Pauspapier, *das*

track /træk/ **1** *n.* **(a)** Spur, *die;* (of wild animal) Fährte, *die;* ∼s (footprints) [Fuß]spuren; (of animal also) Fährte, *die;* **cover one's** ∼s (fig.) seine Spur verwischen; **be on sb.'s** ∼: jmdm. auf der Spur sein; (fig.: in possession of clue to sb.'s plans) jmdm. auf die Schliche gekommen sein; **be on the right/wrong** ∼ (fig.) auf der richtigen/falschen Spur sein; **keep** ∼ **of sb./sth.** jmdn./etw. im Auge behalten; **lose** ∼ **of sb./sth.** jmdn./etw. aus den Augen verlieren; **make** ∼s (coll.) (depart) sich auf die Socken machen (ugs.); **stop [dead] in one's** ∼s (coll.) auf der Stelle stehen bleiben; **(b)** (path) [unbefestigter] Weg; (footpath) Pfad, *der;* (fig.) Weg, *der;* **(c)** (Sport) Bahn, *die;* **cycling/ greyhound** ∼: Radrennbahn, *die/*Windhundrennbahn, *die;* **circuit of the** ∼: Bahnrunde, *die;* **(d)** (Railw.) Gleis, *das;* **single/double** ∼: eingleisige/zweigleisige Strecke; **(e)** (course taken) Route, *die;* (of rocket, satellite, comet, missile, hurricane, etc.) Bahn, *die;* **(f)** (of tank, tractor, etc.) Kette, *die;* **(g)** (section of record) Stück, *das;* **(h)** ⇒ **soundtrack. 2** *v.t.* ∼ **an animal** die Spur/Fährte eines Tieres verfolgen; **the police** ∼**ed him [to Paris]** die Polizei folgte seiner Spur [bis nach Paris]; ∼ **a rocket/satellite** die Bahn einer Rakete/eines Satelliten verfolgen
∼ **'down** *v.t.* aufspüren

'trackball *n.* (Computing) Rollball, *der*

tracker /'trækə(r)/ *n.* **(a)** Fährtensucher, *der;* **(b)** ∼ **[dog]** Spürhund, *der*

tracker ball ⇒ **trackball**

track: ∼ **events** *n. pl.* (Athletics) Laufwettbewerbe; ∼ **record** *n.* (fig.) **his** ∼ **record is good, he has a good** ∼ **record** er hat gute Leistungen vorzuweisen; ∼ **shoe** *n.* Rennschuh, *der;* ∼ **suit** *n.* Trainingsanzug, *der*

tract¹ /trækt/ *n.* **(a)** (area) Gebiet, *das;* **(b)** (Anat.) Trakt, *der*

tract² *n.* (pamphlet) [Flug]schrift, *die;* Traktat, *der* (veralt.)

traction /'trækʃn/ *n., no pl., no indef. art.* **(a)** (drawing along) Traktion, *die* (fachspr.); Ziehen, *das;* **(b)** (grip of tyre etc.) Haftung, *die;* **(c)** (Med.) Zug, *der;* **in** ∼: im Zug- *od.* Streckverband

'traction engine *n.* Zugmaschine, *die*

tractor /'træktə(r)/ *n.* Traktor, *der*

trade /treɪd/ **1** *n.* **(a)** (line of business) Gewerbe, *das;* **the wool/furniture/hotel** ∼: die Woll-/Möbel-/Hotelbranche; **the retail/wholesale** ∼: der Einzel-/Großhandel; **he's a butcher/lawyer/baker** *etc.* **by** ∼: er ist von Beruf Metzger / Rechtsanwalt / Bäcker *usw.;* **trick of the** ∼: einschlägiger Trick; **(b)** *no pl., no indef. art* (commerce) Handel, *der;* **be bad/good for** ∼: schlecht/gut fürs Geschäft sein; **foreign** ∼: Außenhandel, *der;* **(c)** *no pl.* (business done) Geschäft, *das;* (between countries) Handel, *der;* **do a good/roaring** ∼ **[in sth.]** ein gutes Geschäft/ein Riesengeschäft [mit etw.] machen; **(d)** (craft) Handwerk, *das;* **(e)** *no pl., no indef. art.* (persons) **the** ∼: die Branche; **(f)** *in pl.* (Meteorol.) Passat, *der.* **2** *v.i.* **(a)** (buy and sell) Handel treiben;

Towns and cities

All towns are neuter in German, although this usually only becomes apparent when referring to one as **es**, or when an adjective or article is used:

Paris is on the Seine; it is the capital of France	= Paris liegt an der Seine; es ist die Hauptstadt Frankreichs
We want to create a new Hamburg	= Wir wollen ein neues Hamburg schaffen
19th century Berlin	= das Berlin des 19. Jahrhunderts

to and from

When it is simply a case of travelling from one town to another, always use **nach** for *to*, and **von** for *from* with the names:

It is 56 miles from London to Oxford	= Von London nach Oxford sind es 91 Kilometer

However compare

They are coming from Munich	= Sie kommen von München
They come from Munich	= Sie kommen aus München

When referring to someone's place of origin, *from* is translated by **aus.**

Natives and inhabitants

In English, the words which tell us where someone comes from have many different forms: Londoner, Glaswegian, Lancastrian, Bathonian, New Yorker, Bostonian, Viennese, Roman and so on. But in German it could not be simpler. You just add **-er** to the name of the town, or **-erin** in the case of a woman:

a Parisian	= ein Pariser/eine Pariserin
the Viennese	= die Wiener
Viennese women	= [die] Wienerinnen

Of course in many cases English does not have a specific name for the inhabitants of a particular place, but the formula described above can be used in German for every city, town or village:

a woman from Madrid	= eine Madriderin
the people of Prague	= die Prager
an inhabitant of Dinkelsbühl	= ein Dinkelsbühler/eine Dinkelsbühlerin

In one or two cases the name of the town or city is slightly altered before the ending is added, for instance:

a Roman	= ein Römer/eine Römerin
an inhabitant of Münster	= ein Münsteraner/eine Münsteranerin
someone from Hanover, a Hanoverian	= ein Hannoveraner/eine Hannoveranerin
a man from Bremen	= ein Bremer
the people of Munich	= die Münchner

With some non-German names adding the **-er** can produce an odd-sounding or barely pronounceable result, so such forms are avoided. It is unlikely for example that a man from Dover would be called "ein Doverer" or a woman from Bath "eine Batherin" ("ein Mann aus Dover" and "eine Frau aus Bath" would be the answers here). The inhabitants of Milwaukee could theoretically be called "die Milwaukeeer" and no doubt have been on occasion, but most Germans would prefer to say "die Bewohner von Milwaukee".

There are also a few exceptions where there is a special term, especially with Italian cities; the Florentines are "die Florentiner", a Venetian is "ein Venezianer" and a woman from Verona "eine Veroneserin". Note also Monegasque = Monegasse.

Adjectives

To form an adjective from the name of a place is also extremely simple. It has the same form as the noun for a (male) person who comes from the place; you just add **-er**. Unlike other adjectives in German, it retains its capital letter. It is also invariable, so there are no endings to add depending on case or gender. These adjectives can be used as translations where place names in English are used attributively before another noun, or after it with 'of' or 'in'.

Aachen Cathedral	= der Aachener Dom
Ravensburg Town Council	= der Ravensburger Stadtrat
Berlin dialect	= der Berliner Dialekt
the New York area	= die New Yorker Gegend
the streets of Paris	= die Pariser Straßen
the traffic in London	= der Londoner Verkehr

Note that as in the first two examples German always has the definite article where a place name is used attributively before a building or institution. And in the last two cases, one could equally well say "die Straßen von Paris" or "der Verkehr in London". This use of prepositions would also be the only possibility in cases where the addition of **-er** presents problems:

Amiens Cathedral	= die Kathedrale von Amiens
the Portsmouth area	= die Gegend um Portsmouth

With roads "die Paderborner Straße" may mean "the Paderborn road", i.e."the road to Paderborn", but it will usually be the name of a street in a town, so it is safest to say "die Straße nach Paderborn".

Another group of adjectives formed from place names and ending in **-isch** can be used to express what is typical of a place or its people; these behave like normal adjectives with small initial letters and the usual endings:

Hamburg humour	= hamburgischer Humor
Hanoverian equanimity	= hannoverischer Gleichmut

∼ **as a wholesale/retail dealer** ein Großhandels-/Einzelhandelsgeschäft betreiben; ∼ **in sth.** in *od.* mit etw. (*Dat.*) handeln; (**b**) (have an exchange) tauschen; ∼ **with sb. for sth.** jmdm. etw. abhandeln. **3** *v.t.* (**a**) tauschen; austauschen ‹*Waren, Grüße, Informationen, Geheimnisse*›; sich (*Dat.*) sagen ‹*Beleidigungen*›; (**b**) ∼ **sth. for sth.** etw. gegen etw. tauschen; ∼ **an old car** *etc.* **for a new one** einen alten Wagen *usw.* für einen neuen in Zahlung geben

∼ **'in** *v.t.* in Zahlung geben; einlösen ‹*Gutschein, Kupon usw.*›

∼ **'off** *v.t.* (coll.) ∼ **sth. off for sth.** etw. gegen etw. tauschen

∼ **on** *v.t.* (fig.) ∼ **on sth.** aus etw. Kapital schlagen; sich (*Dat.*) etw. zunutze machen

∼ **'up** *v.i.* sich verbessern

∼ **upon** ⇒ ∼ **on**

trade: ∼ **balance** *n.* (Econ.) Handelsbilanz, *die;* ∼ **cycle** *n.* (Brit. Econ.) Konjunkturzyklus, *der;* ∼ **deficit** *n.* (Econ.) Handelsbilanzdefizit, *das;* ∼ **'discount** *n.* Branchenrabatt, *der;* ∼ **fair** *n.* [Fach]messe, *die;* ∼ **gap** ⇒ ∼ **deficit;** ∼ **journal** *n.* Fachzeitschrift, *die;* ∼ **mark** *n.* (**a**) Warenzeichen, *das;* (**b**) (fig.) **leave one's mark on sth.** einer Sache (*Dat.*) seinen Stempel aufdrücken; ∼ **name** *n.* (**a**) (name used in the ∼) Fachbezeichnung, *die;* (**b**) (proprietary name) Markenname, *der;* (**c**) (name of business) Firmenname, *der;* ~**-off** *n.* Tauschgeschäft, *das;* (fig.) Kompromiss, *der;* ~ **price** *n.* Einkaufspreis, *der*

trader /'treɪdə(r)/ *n.* (a) Händler, *der*/Händlerin, *die;* (b) (Naut.) Handelsschiff, *das*

trade: ~ **route** *n.* Handelsweg, *der;* Handelsstraße, *die;* ~ '**secret** *n.* Geschäftsgeheimnis, *das;* ~**sman** /'treɪdz mən/ *n., pl.* ~**smen** /'treɪdzmən/ (a) (shopkeeper) [Einzel]händler, *der;* Ladeninhaber, *der;* ~**smen's entrance** Lieferanteneingang, *der;* (b) (craftsman) Handwerker, *der;* ~**speople** /'treɪdzpiːpl/ *n. pl.* (a) (shopkeepers) [Einzel]händler; Ladeninhaber; (b) (craft workers) Handwerker; ~**s' 'union** ⇨ ~ **union; T**~**s Union 'Congress** *pr. n.* (Brit.) Gewerkschaftsbund, *der;* ~ '**union** *n.* Gewerkschaft, *die; attrib.* Gewerkschafts-; ~ **unionism** /treɪd'juːnɪənɪzm, treɪd'juːnjənɪzm/ *n., no pl.* Gewerkschaftswesen, *das;* ~ '**unionist** *n.* Gewerkschaft[l]er, *der*/Gewerkschaft[l]erin, *die;* ~ **wind** *n.* (Meteorol.) Passatwind, *der*

trading /'treɪdɪŋ/ *n.* Handel, *der*

trading: ~ **estate** *n.* (Brit.) Gewerbegebiet, *das;* ~ **hours** *n. pl.* Geschäftszeit, *die;* ~ **stamp** *n.* Rabattmarke, *die*

tradition /trə'dɪʃn/ *n.* Tradition, *die;* (story) [mündliche] Überlieferung; **family** ~: Familientradition, *die;* **in the best** ~[**s**] nach bester Tradition; **break with** ~: mit der Tradition brechen

traditional /trə'dɪʃənl/ *adj.* traditionell; mündlich überliefert ‹*Geschichte*›; herkömmlich ‹*Erziehung, Einrichtung, Methode*›; überkommen ‹*Brauch, Sitte, Werte, Moral*›; **it is** ~ **to do sth.** es ist Tradition, etw. zu tun

traditionally /trə'dɪʃənlɪ/ *adv.* (in a traditional manner) traditionell; (by tradition) traditionell[erweise]

traffic /'træfɪk/ **1** *n., no pl.* (a) *no indef. art.* Verkehr, *der;* ~ **is heavy/light** es herrscht starker/geringer Verkehr; (b) (trade) Handel, *der;* ~ **in drugs/arms** Drogen-/Waffenhandel, *der;* (c) (amount of business) Verkehr, *der.* **2** *v.i.,* -**ck**-Geschäfte machen; ~ **in sth.** mit etw. handeln *od.* Handel treiben; (fig.) mit etw. schachern (abwertend)

traffic: ~ **calming** *n., no pl.* Verkehrsberuhigung, *die;* ~ **circle** *n.* (Amer.) Kreisverkehr, *der;* ~ **cone** *n.* Pylon, *der;* Leitkegel, *der;* ~ **hold-up** ⇨ ~ **jam;** ~ **island** *n.* Verkehrsinsel, *die;* ~ **jam** *n.* [Verkehrs]stau, *der*

trafficker /'træfɪkə(r)/ *n.* Händler, *der*/Händlerin, *die*

traffic: ~ **lights** *n. pl.* [Verkehrs]ampel, *die;* ~ **police** *n.* Verkehrspolizei, *die;* ~ **policeman** *n.* ▶ 887 | Verkehrspolizist, *der;* ~ **sign** *n.* Verkehrszeichen, *das;* ~ **signals** ⇨ ~ **lights;** ~ **warden** *n.* ▶ 887 | (Brit.) Hilfspolizist, *der;* (woman) Hilfspolizistin, *die;* Politesse, *die*

tragedy /'trædʒɪdɪ/ *n.* (a) (sad event or fact) Tragödie, *die;* (sad story) tragische Geschichte; **the** ~ [**of it**] **is that** …**:** das Tragische [daran] ist, dass …; (b) (accident) Tragödie, *die;* (c) (Theatre) Tragödie, *die;* Trauerspiel, *das*

tragic /'trædʒɪk/ *adj.* (a) tragisch; **a** ~ **waste of talent/ money** eine schlimme Vergeudung von Talenten/Geldverschwendung; (b) *attrib.* (Theatre) tragisch; ~ **actor/ actress** Tragöde, *der*/Tragödin, *die*

tragically /'trædʒɪkəlɪ/ *adv.* tragisch; **their predictions have been** ~ **fulfilled** ihre Prophezeiungen haben sich auf tragische Weise erfüllt

trail /treɪl/ **1** *n.* (a) (track) Spur, *die;* (of meteor) Schweif, *der;* **a** ~ **of blood** eine Blutspur; ~ **of smoke/dust** Rauch-/ Staubfahne, *die;* (b) (Hunting) Spur, *die;* Fährte, *die;* **be on the** ~ **of an animal** der Fährte eines Tieres folgen; **be**/ **get on sb.'s** ~ (lit. or fig.) jmdm. auf der Spur *od.* Fährte sein/jmdm. auf die Spur *od.* Fährte kommen; **be hard** *or* **hot on the** ~ **of sb.** (lit. or fig.) jmdm. dicht auf den Fersen sein (ugs.); (c) (path) Pfad, *der;* (wagon ~) Weg, *der.* **2** *v.t.* (a) (pursue) verfolgen; (shadow) beschatten; ~ **sb.**/**an animal to a place** jmdm./einem Tier bis zu einem Ort folgen; (b) (drag) ~ **sth.** [**after** *or* **behind one**] etw. hinter sich (*Dat.*) herziehen; ~ **sth. on the ground** etw. über den Boden schleifen lassen. **3** *v.i.* (a) (be dragged) schleifen; (b) (hang

loosely) herabhängen; (c) (walk wearily etc.) trotten; (lag) hinterhertrotten; (d) (Sport: be losing) zurückliegen; (e) (creep) ‹*Pflanze:*› kriechen

~ **a'way** ⇨ ~ **off**
~ **be'hind** *v.i.* hinterhertrödeln (ugs.)
~ '**off** *v.i.* **his voice/shout** ~**ed off into a whisper/ into silence** seine Stimme/sein Schreien wurde schwächer, bis er schließlich nur noch flüsterte/bis er schließlich ganz verstummte

trailer /'treɪlə(r)/ *n.* (a) (Motor Veh.) Anhänger, *der;* (boat ~ also) Trailer, *der;* (Amer.: caravan) Wohnanhänger, *der;* (b) (Cinemat., Telev.) Trailer, *der*

train /treɪn/ **1** *v.t.* (a) ausbilden (**in** in + *Dat.*); erziehen ‹*Kind*›; abrichten ‹*Hund*›; dressieren ‹*Tier*›; schulen ‹*Geist, Auge, Ohr*›; bilden ‹*Charakter*›; ~ **sb. as a teacher/soldier/engineer** jmdn. zum Lehrer/Soldaten/ Ingenieur ausbilden; **he/she has been well/badly/fully** ~**ed** er/sie besitzt eine gute/schlechte/umfassende Ausbildung; (b) (Sport) trainieren; ~ **oneself** trainieren; (c) (teach and accustom) ~ **an animal to do sth.**/**to sth.** einem Tier beibringen, etw. zu tun/etw. beibringen; ~ **oneself to do sth.** sich dazu erziehen, etw. zu tun; ~ **a child to do sth.**/**to sth.** ein Kind dazu erziehen, etw. zu tun/ zu etw. erziehen; ~ **sb. to use a machine** jmdn. in der Bedienung einer Maschine schulen; (d) (Hort.) ziehen; erziehen (fachspr.); (e) (aim) richten (**on** auf + *Akk.*). **2** *v.i.* (a) eine Ausbildung machen; **he is** ~**ing as** *or* **to be a teacher/doctor/engineer** er macht eine Lehrer-/Arzt-/ Ingenieursausbildung; (b) (Sport) trainieren. **3** *n.* (a) (Railw.) Zug, *der;* **go** *or* **travel by** ~: mit dem Zug *od.* der Bahn fahren; **on the** ~: im Zug; **which is the** ~ **for Oxford?** welcher Zug fährt nach Oxford?; (b) (of skirt etc.) Schleppe, *die;* (c) ~ **of thought** Gedankengang, *der*

'**train driver** *n.* Lokomotivführer, *der*/-führerin, *die*

trained /treɪnd/ *adj.* ausgebildet ‹*Arbeiter, Lehrer, Arzt, Stimme*›; abgerichtet ‹*Hund*›; dressiert ‹*Tier*›; geschult ‹*Geist, Auge, Ohr*›

trainee /treɪ'niː/ *n.* Auszubildende, *der/die;* (business management ~) Trainee, *der/die;* (in academic or technical professions) Praktikant, *der*/Praktikantin, *die*

trainer /'treɪnə(r)/ *n.* (a) (Sport) [Konditions]trainer, *der/* -trainerin, *die;* (b) *in pl.* Trainingsschuhe

'**train fare** *n.* Fahrpreis, *der*

training /'treɪnɪŋ/ *n., no pl.* (a) Ausbildung, *die;* (b) (Sport) Training, *das;* **be in** ~ (train) trainieren; im Training sein; (be fit) in [guter] Form sein; **be out of** ~**:** außer Form sein

training: ~ **college** *n.* berufsbildende Schule; ~ **course** *n.* Lehrgang, *der;* ~ **scheme** *n.* Ausbildungsprogramm, *das;* **be on a** ~ **scheme** an einem Ausbildungsprogramm teilnehmen; ~ **shoes** *n. pl.* Trainingsschuhe

train: ~ **journey** *n.* Bahnfahrt, *die;* (long) Bahnreise, *die;* ~ **service** *n.* Zugverbindung, *die;* [Eisen]bahnverbindung, *die;* ~ **set** *n.* [Modell]eisenbahn, *die;* ~**-spotter** *n.* jmd., *der* als Hobby die Nummern von Lokomotiven aufschreibt; ~**-spotting** *n., no pl., no indef. art.:* das Aufschreiben von Lokomotivnummern als Hobby; ~ **station** *n.* (Amer.) Bahnhof, *der*

trait /treɪ/ *n.* Eigenschaft, *die*

traitor /'treɪtə(r)/ *n.* Verräter, *der*/Verräterin, *die;* **turn** ~**:** zum Verräter/zur Verräterin werden

trajectory /trə'dʒektərɪ/ *n.* (Phys.) [Flug]bahn, *die*

tram /træm/ *n.* (Brit.) Straßenbahn, *die;* **go by** ~**:** mit der Straßenbahn fahren; **on the** ~: in der Straßenbahn

'**tramlines** *n. pl.* (Brit.) (a) Straßenbahnschienen; (b) (fig.: rigid principles) starre Vorschriften; (c) (Tennis coll.) Korridor, *der*

trammel /'træml/ *v.t.,* (Brit.) -**ll**- einengen

tramp /træmp/ **1** *n.* (a) (vagrant) Landstreicher, *der*/-streicherin, *die;* (in city) Stadtstreicher, *der*/-streicherin, *die;* (b) (sound of steps) Schritte, *die;* (of horses) Getrappel, *das;* (of elephants) Trampeln, *die;* (c) (walk) [Fuß]marsch, *der.* **2** *v.i.* (a) (tread heavily) trampeln; (b) (walk) marschieren. **3** *v.t.* (a) ~ **one's way** trotten; (b) durchwandern; (with no particular destination) durchstreifen

trample /'træmpl/ **1** *v.t.* zertrampeln; ~ sth. into the ground etw. in den Boden treten; **he was ~d to death by elephants** er wurde von Elefanten zu Tode getrampelt. **2** *v.i.* trampeln

~ **on** *v.t.* herumtrampeln auf (+ *Dat.*); ~ **on sb./sth./sb.'s feelings** (fig.) jmdn./etw./jmds. Gefühle mit Füßen treten

trampoline /'træmpəli:n/ **1** *n.* Trampolin, *das.* **2** *v.i.* Trampolin springen

trance /trɑːns/ *n.* Trance, *die;* (half-conscious state, hypnotic state) tranceartiger Zustand; **be** *or* **lie in a ~:** in Trance/ in einem tranceartigen Zustand sein; **fall** *or* **go into a ~:** in Trance/in einen tranceartigen Zustand fallen; **put** *or* **send sb. into a ~:** jmdn. in Trance/in einen tranceartigen Zustand versetzen; **she's been walking about in a ~ all day** sie ist den ganzen Tag wie in Trance herumgelaufen

tranquil /'træŋkwɪl/ *adj.* ruhig; friedlich ‹*Stimmung, Szene*›

tranquillity /træŋ'kwɪlɪtɪ/ *n.* Ruhe, *die*

tranquillizer /'træŋkwɪlaɪzə(r)/ *n.* (Med.) Tranquilizer, *der;* Beruhigungsmittel, *das*

transact /træn'sækt/ *v.t.* ~ **business [with sb.]** [mit jmdn.] Geschäfte tätigen (Kaufmannsspr., Papierdt.)

transaction /træn'sækʃn/ *n.* **(a)** (doing of business) **after the ~ of their business** nachdem sie das Geschäftliche erledigt hatten; **(b)** (piece of business) Geschäft, *das;* (financial) Transaktion, *die*

transatlantic /trænsət'læntɪk/ *adj.* **(a)** (Brit.: American) transatlantisch; amerikanisch; **(b)** (Amer.: European) transatlantisch; europäisch; **(c)** (crossing the Atlantic) transatlantisch; **a ~ voyage** eine Reise über den Atlantik

transcend /træn'send/ *v.t.* (be beyond range of) übersteigen; hinausgehen über ‹*Grenzen*›; (Philos.) transzendieren

transcendental /trænsen'dentl/ *adj.* (Philos.) transzendental

transcontinental /trænskɒntɪ'nentl/ *adj.* transkontinental

transcribe /træn'skraɪb/ *v.t.* (copy in writing) abschreiben; aufschreiben ‹*mündliche Überlieferung*›; mitschreiben ‹*Rede*›; ~ **a tape/a taped interview** von einem Tonband/von der Tonbandaufzeichnung eines Interviews eine Niederschrift anfertigen

transcript /'trænskrɪpt/ *n.* Abschrift, *die;* (of trial, interview, speech, conference) Protokoll, *das;* (of tape, taped material) Niederschrift, *die*

transept /'trænsept/ *n.* (Eccl. Archit.) Querschiff, *das;* **north/south ~:** nördlicher/südlicher Kreuzarm

transfer **1** /træns'fɜː(r)/ *v.t.,* **-rr-:** **(a)** (move) verlegen (**to** nach); überweisen ‹*Geld*› (**to** auf + *Akk.*); transferieren ‹*große Geldsumme*›; übertragen ‹*Befugnis, Macht*› (**to** *Dat.*); ~ **a prisoner to a different gaol** einen Gefangenen in ein anderes Gefängnis verlegen *od.* überführen; ~ **one's allegiance [from sb.] to sb.** [von jmdm.] zu jmdm. überwechseln; **(b)** übereignen ‹*Gegenstand, Grundbesitz*› (**to** *Dat.*); **(c)** versetzen ‹*Arbeiter, Angestellte, Schüler*›; (Footb.) transferieren; **(d)** übertragen ‹*Bedeutung, Sinn*›. **2** /træns'fɜː(r)/ *v.i.,* **-rr-:** **(a)** (change to continue journey) umsteigen; ~ **from Heathrow to Gatwick** zum Weiterflug *od.* Umsteigen von Heathrow nach Gatwick fahren; **(b)** (move to another place or group) wechseln ‹*Firma:*› übersiedeln. **3** /'trænsfɜː(r)/ *n.* **(a)** (moving) Verlegung, *die;* (of powers) Übertragung, *die* (**to** an + *Akk.*); (of money) Überweisung, *die;* (of large sums) Transfer, *der* (Wirtsch.); **(b)** (of employee, pupil) Versetzung, *die;* (Footb.) Transfer, *der;* **(c)** (Amer.: ticket) Umsteigefahrkarte, *die;* **(d)** (picture) Abziehbild, *das*

transferable /træns'fɜːrəbl, 'trænsfərəbl/ *adj.* übertragbar

transference /'trænsfərəns/ *n.* Übertragung, *die*

transfer fee *n.* (Footb.) Ablösesumme, *die;* Transfersumme, *die* (fachspr.)

transfigure /træns'fɪgə(r)/ *v.t.* verklären

transform /træns'fɔːm/ *v.t.* verwandeln; ~ **heat into energy** Wärme in Energie umwandeln

transformation /trænsfə'meɪʃn/ *n.* Verwandlung, *die;* (of heat into energy) Umwandlung, *die*

transformer /træns'fɔːmə(r)/ *n.* (Electr.) Transformator, *der*

transfusion /træns'fjuːʒn/ *n.* (Med.) Transfusion, *die;* Übertragung, *die*

transgenic /træns'dʒenɪk/ *adj.* (Biol.) transgen

transient /'trænzɪənt/ *adj.* kurzlebig; vergänglich

transistor /træn'sɪstə(r)/ *n.* **(a)** ~ **[radio]** Transistor, *der;* Transistorradio, *das;* **(b)** (Electronics) Transistor, *der*

transit /'trænsɪt/ *n.* **(a)** **passengers in ~:** Transitreisende; Durchreisende; **be in ~:** auf der Durchreise sein; **(b)** (conveyance) Transport, *der;* **goods in ~ from London to Hull** Waren auf dem Transport von London nach Hull

transition /træn'sɪʒn, træn'zɪʃn/ *n.* Übergang, *der;* (sudden change) Wechsel, *der*

transitional /træn'sɪʒənl, træn'zɪʃənl/ *adj.* Übergangs-

transitive /'trænsɪtɪv/ *adj.* (Ling.) transitiv

'**transit lounge** *n.* Transithalle, *die;* Transitlounge, *die*

transitory /'trænsɪtərɪ/ *adj.* vergänglich; (fleeting) flüchtig

transit: ~ **passenger** *n.* Transitpassagier, *der;* ~ **visa** *n.* Transitvisum, *das*

translate /træns'leɪt/ **1** *v.t.* **(a)** übersetzen; ~ **a novel from English into German** einen Roman aus dem Englischen ins Deutsche übersetzen; ~ **'Abgeordneter' as 'Deputy'** „Abgeordneter" mit „Deputy" übersetzen; **(b)** (convert) ~ **words into action[s]** Worte in die Tat/in Taten umsetzen. **2** *v.i.* sich übersetzen lassen

translation /træns'leɪʃn/ *n.* Übersetzung, *die;* **his works are available in ~:** seine Werke liegen in Übersetzung *od.* übersetzt vor; **read sth. in ~:** etw. in der Übersetzung lesen

translator /træns'leɪtə(r)/ *n.* ▶ 887 ↓ Übersetzer, *der/* Übersetzerin, *die*

translucent /træns'luːsənt/ *adj.* **(a)** (partly transparent) durchscheinend; **(b)** (transparent) durchsichtig

transmission /træns'mɪʃn/ *n.* **(a)** ⇨ **transmit a:** Übersendung, *die;* Übertragung, *die;* Überlieferung, *die;* [Weiter]vererbung, *die;* **(b)** (Radio, Telev.) Ausstrahlung, *die;* (via satellite also; by wire) Übertragung, *die;* **(c)** (Motor Veh.) (drive) Antrieb, *der;* (gearbox) Getriebe, *das;* **manual/automatic ~:** Schalt-/Automatikgetriebe, *das*

transmit /træns'mɪt/ *v.t.,* **-tt-:** **(a)** (pass on) übersenden ‹*Nachricht*›; übertragen ‹*Krankheit*›; überliefern ‹*Wissen, Kenntnisse*›; (genetically) [weiter]vererben ‹*Eigenschaft*›; **(b)** durchlassen ‹*Licht*›; übertragen ‹*Druck, Schall*›; leiten ‹*Wärme, Elektrizität*›; **(c)** (Radio, Telev.) ausstrahlen; (via satellite also; by wire) übertragen

transmitter /træns'mɪtə(r)/ *n.* Sender, *der*

transmute /træns'mjuːt/ *v.t.* umwandeln

transparency /træns'pærənsɪ/ *n.* **(a)** Durchsichtigkeit, *die;* (fig. also) Durchschaubarkeit, *die;* Fadenscheinigkeit, *die* (abwertend); **(b)** (Photog.) Transparent, *das;* (slide) Dia, *das*

transparent /træns'pærənt/ *adj.* durchsichtig; (fig.) (obvious) offenkundig; (easily understood) klar

transpire /træn'spaɪə(r)/ *v.i.* **(a)** (coll.: happen) passieren, **(b)** (come to be known) sich herausstellen; **she had not, it ~d, seen the letter** sie hatte, so stellte sich heraus, den Brief nicht gesehen

transplant **1** /træns'plɑːnt/ *v.t.* **(a)** (Med.) transplantieren (fachspr.), verpflanzen ‹*Organ, Gewebe*›; **(b)** (plant in another place) umpflanzen. **2** /'trænsplɑːnt/ *n.* (Med.) (operation) Transplantation, *die* (fachspr.); Verpflanzung, *die;* (thing ~ed) Transplantat, *das* (fachspr.)

transponder /træns'pɒndə(r)/ *n.* Transponder, *der*

transport **1** /træn'spɔːt/ *v.t.* **(a)** (convey) transportieren; befördern; **(b)** (literary: affect with emotion) anrühren; anwandeln (geh.); ~**ed with joy** von Freude überkommen. **2** /'trænspɔːt/ *n.* **(a)** (conveyance) Transport, *der;* Beförderung, *die; attrib.* Transport-; Beförderungs-; **(b)** (means of conveyance) Verkehrsmittel, *das;* (for private also) Fortbewegungsmittel, *das;* ~ **was provided** für die Beförderung wurde gesorgt; **be without ~:** kein [eigenes] Fahrzeug haben; **Ministry of T~:** Verkehrsministerium, *das;* **(c)**

(vehement emotion) Ausbruch, *der;* **be in/send sb. into ~s of joy** außer sich vor Freude sein/jmdn. in helles Entzücken versetzen

transportable /træn'spɔ:təbl/ *adj.* transportabel

transportation /trænspə'teɪʃn/ *n.* **(a)** (conveying) Transport, *der;* Beförderung, *die;* **~ by air/sea/road/rail** Luft-/ See-/Straßen-/Bahntransport, *der;* **(b)** (Amer.) ⇒ **transport 2 b**

'transport café *n.* (Brit.) Fernfahrerlokal, *das*

transporter /træn'spɔ:tə(r)/ *n.* Transporter, *der*

transpose /træns'pəʊz/ *v.t.* **(a)** (cause to change places) vertauschen; **(b)** (change order of) umstellen; **(c)** (Mus.) transponieren

transverse /'trænsvɜ:s/ *adj.* quer liegend; Quer‹*balken, -lage, -streifen, -verstrebung*›; **~ section** Querschnitt, *der*

transvestite /træns'vestaɪt/ *n.* (Psych.) Transvestit, *der*

trap /træp/ **1** *n.* **(a)** (lit. or fig.) Falle, *die;* **set a ~ for an animal** eine Falle für ein Tier legen *od.* [auf]stellen; **set a ~ for sb.** (fig.) jmdm. eine Falle stellen; **fall into a/sb.'s ~** (fig.) in die/jmdm. in die Falle gehen; **(b)** (sl.: mouth) Klappe, *die* (salopp); Fresse, *die* (derb); **shut your ~!, keep your ~ shut!** halt die Klappe (salopp) *od.* (derb) Fresse!; **(c)** (carriage) (leichter zweirädriger) Einspänner. **2** *v.t.*, **-pp-: (a)** (catch) [in *od.* mit einer Falle] fangen ‹*Tier*›; (fig.) in eine Falle locken ‹*Person*›; **be ~ped** (fig.) in eine Falle gehen/ in der Falle sitzen; **be ~ped in a cave/by the tide** in einer Höhle festsitzen/von der Flut abgeschnitten sein; **she ~ped him into contradicting himself** sie brachte ihn durch eine List dazu, sich zu widersprechen; **(b)** (confine) einschließen; (immobilize) einklemmen ‹*Person, Körperteil*›; **~ one's finger/foot** sich (*Dat.*) den Finger/ Fuß einklemmen; **(c)** (entangle) verstricken

'trapdoor *n.* Falltür, *die*

trapeze /trə'pi:z/ *n.* Trapez, *das*

tra'peze artist *n.* Trapezkünstler, *der*/-künstlerin, *die*

trapper /'træpə(r)/ *n.* Fallensteller, *der;* (in North America) Trapper, *der*

trappings /'træpɪŋz/ *n. pl.* **(a)** (äußere) Zeichen, (of power, high office) Insignien; **(b)** (ornamental harness) ≈ Schabracke, *die*

trash /træʃ/ *n., no pl., no indef. art.* **(a)** (rubbish) Abfall, *der;* **(b)** (badly made thing) Mist, *der* (ugs. abwertend); (bad literature) Schund, *der* (ugs. abwertend); **be [just] ~:** nichts taugen

'trashcan *n.* (Amer.) Mülltonne, *die*

trashy /'træʃɪ/ *adj.* minderwertig; Schund‹*literatur, -roman*›

trauma /'trɔ:mə/ *n., pl.* **~ta** /'trɔ:mətə/ *or* **~s** Trauma, *das* (fachspr.); (injury also) Verletzung, *die;* (shock also) Schock, *der*

traumatic /trɔ:'mætɪk/ *adj.* **(a)** (Med.) traumatisch; **(b)** (coll.: devastating) furchtbar

traumatize /'trɔ:mətaɪz/ *v.t.* traumatisieren

travel /'trævl/ **1** *n.* Reisen, *das; attrib.* Reise-; **be off on one's ~s** verreist sein; **if you see him on your ~s, ...** (joc.) wenn er dir über den Weg läuft, ... **2** *v.i.*, (Brit.) **-ll-: (a)** (make a journey) reisen; (go in vehicle) fahren; **~ a lot** viel reisen; **(b)** (coll.: withstand long journey) **~ [well]** ‹*Ware:*› lange Transporte vertragen; **~ badly** ‹*Ware:*› lange Transporte nicht vertragen; **(c)** (work as travelling sales representative) reisen; Vertreter/Vertreterin sein; **~ in stationery** in Schreibwaren reisen (Kaufmannsspr.); **(d)** (move) sich bewegen; ‹*Blick, Schmerz:*› wandern; ‹*Tier:*› sich fortbewegen; ‹*Licht, Schall:*› sich ausbreiten; **(e)** (coll.: move briskly) kacheln (ugs.); **that car can really ~:** das Auto zieht ganz schön ab (ugs.). **3** *v.t.*, (Brit.) **-ll-** zurücklegen ‹*Strecke, Entfernung*›; bereisen ‹*Bezirk*›; benutzen, passieren ‹*Weg, Straße*›; **we had ~led 10 miles** wir waren 10 Meilen gefahren

~ a'bout, ~ a'round 1 *v.i.* umherreisen. **2** *v.t.* **~ about** *or* **around the country** durchs Land reisen *od.* fahren

travel: ~ agency *n.* Reisebüro, *das;* **~ agent** *n.* **▶ 887 |** Reisebürokaufmann, *der*/-kauffrau, *die*

travelator /'trævəleɪtə(r)/ *n.* Fahr- *od.* Rollsteig, *der*

travel: ~ brochure *n.* Reiseprospekt, *der;* **~ bureau** *n.* Reisebüro, *das*

traveled, traveler, traveling (Amer.) ⇒ **travell-**

'travel insurance *n.* Reiseversicherung, *die*

travelled /'trævld/ *adj.* (Brit.) **be much ~** ‹*Person:*› weit gereist sein; **be well ~** ‹*Weg, Straße:*› viel befahren sein

traveller /'trævlə(r)/ *n.* (Brit.) **(a)** Reisende, *der/die;* **be a poor ~:** das Reisen nicht [gut] vertragen; **(b)** (sales representative) Vertreter, *der*/Vertreterin, *die;* **(c)** *in pl.* (gypsies etc.) fahrendes Volk

'traveller's cheque *n.* **▶ 938 |** Reisescheck, *der*

travelling /'trævlɪŋ/ *adj.* (Brit.) Wander‹*zirkus, -ausstellung*›

travelling: ~ bag *n.* Reisetasche, *die;* **~ clock** *n.* Reisewecker, *der;* **~ expenses** *n. pl.* Reisekosten *Pl.;* **~ 'salesman** *n.* **▶ 887 |** Vertreter, *der*

travelogue (Amer.: **travelog**) /'trævəlɒg/ *n.* Reisebericht, *der*

travel: ~-sick *adj.* reisekrank; **~-sickness** *n., no pl.* Reisekrankheit, *die;* **~-sickness pill** *n.* Tablette gegen Reisekrankheit

traverse /'trævəs, trə'vɜ:s/ **1** *v.t.* **(a)** überqueren ‹*Gebirge*›; durchqueren ‹*Gebiet*›; **(b)** (Mountaineering) traversieren. **2** *n.* (Mountaineering) Traversierung, *die*

travesty /'trævɪstɪ/ **1** *n.* **(a)** (parody) Karikatur, *die;* **be a ~ [of justice]** ein Hohn [auf die Gerechtigkeit] sein; **(b)** (Lit.: burlesque) Travestie, *die* (fachspr.). **2** *v.t.* ins Lächerliche ziehen

trawl /trɔ:l/ **1** *v.i.* mit dem Grundnetz fischen. **2** *n.* **~[-net]** Grund[schlepp]netz, *das*

trawler /'trɔ:lə(r)/ *n.* (vessel) [Fisch]trawler, *der*

trawlerman /'trɔ:ləmən/ *n., pl.* **trawlermen** /'trɔ:ləmən/ **▶ 887 |** ≈ Hochseefischer, *der*

tray /treɪ/ *n.* **(a)** Tablett, *das;* **(b)** (for correspondence) Ablagekorb, *der*

treacherous /'tretʃərəs/ *adj.* **(a)** treulos ‹*Person*›; heimtückisch ‹*Intrige, Feind*›; **(b)** (deceptive) tückisch; **the ice looks pretty ~:** das Eis sieht nicht sehr vertrauenerweckend aus

treachery /'tretʃərɪ/ *n.* Verrat, *der;* **act of ~:** Verrat, *der*

treacle /'tri:kl/ *n.* (Brit.) **(a)** (golden syrup) Sirup, *der;* **(b)** ⇒ **molasses**

tread /tred/ **1** *n.* **(a)** (of tyre, shoe, boot, etc.) Lauffläche, *die;* **2 millimetres of tread on a tyre** 2 Millimeter Profil auf einem Reifen; **(b)** (manner of walking) Gang, *der;* (sound of walking) Schritt, *der;* **walk with a springy/catlike ~:** einen federnden/katzenhaften Gang haben; **(c)** (of staircase) [Tritt]stufe, *die.* **2** *v.i.,* **trod** /trɒd/, **trodden** /'trɒdn/ *or* **trod** treten (**in/on** in/auf + *Akk.*); (walk) gehen; **~ carefully** (fig.) behutsam vorgehen; **~ on sb.'s toes** (lit. or fig.) jmdm. auf die Füße treten; **~ dirt into the carpet/all over the house** Schmutz in den Teppich treten/im ganzen Haus herumtreten. **3** *v.t.,* **trod, trodden** *or* **trod (a)** (walk on) treten auf (+ *Akk.*); stampfen ‹*Weintrauben*›; (fig.) gehen ‹*Weg*›; **be trodden underfoot** mit Füßen getreten werden; **~ water** (Swimming) Wasser treten; **(b)** (make by walking or ~ing) austreten ‹*Weg*›

~ 'down *v.t.* festtreten ‹*Erde*›; (destroy) zertreten ‹*Blume, Beet*›

~ 'in *v.t.* festtreten

treadle /'tredl/ *n.* Tritt, *der*

'treadmill *n.* (lit. or fig.) Tretmühle, *die*

treason /'tri:zn/ *n.* **[high] ~:** Hochverrat, *der*

treasure /'treʒə(r)/ **1** *n.* **(a)** Schatz, *der;* Kostbarkeit, *die;* **art ~s** Kunstschätze; **(b)** *no pl., no indef. art.* (riches) Schätze; **buried ~:** ein vergrabener Schatz; **(c)** (coll.: valued person) Schatz, *der* (ugs.). **2** *v.t.* in Ehren halten; die Erinnerung bewahren an (+ *Dat.*); **I'll always ~ this moment** ich werde diesen Augenblick niemals vergessen

treasure: ~ house *n.* Schatzkammer, *die;* (fig.) [wahre] Fundgrube; **~ hunt** *n.* Schatzsuche, *die*

treasurer /'treʒərə(r)/ *n.* **(a)** (of club, society) Kassenwart, *der*/-wartin, *die;* (of club, party) Schatzmeister, *der*/-meisterin, *die;* (of company) Leiter/Leiterin der Finanzabteilung;

(b) (local government official) Leiter/Leiterin der Finanzverwaltung

treasure trove /'treʒə trəʊv/ *n.* Schatz, *der;* (fig.: valuable source) [wahre] Fundgrube

treasury /'treʒərı/ *n.* **(a)** (as book-title) Schatzkästchen, *das;* **(b)** (government department) **the T~:** das Finanzministerium

treat /triːt/ **1** *n.* **(a)** [besonderes] Vergnügen; (sth. to eat) [besonderer] Leckerbissen; **what a ~ [it is] to do/not to have to do that!** welch ein Genuss *od.* eine Wohltat, das zu tun/nicht tun zu müssen!; **have a ~ in store for sb.** noch eine besondere Freude für jmdn. auf Lager haben; **there was a ~ in store for them** auf sie wartete noch eine besondere Freude; **go down a ~** (coll.) ⟨Essen, Getränk:⟩ prima schmecken (ugs.); **work a ~** (coll.) ⟨Maschine:⟩ prima arbeiten (ugs.); ⟨Plan:⟩ prima funktionieren (ugs.); **(b)** (entertainment) Vergnügen, *für dessen Kosten jmd. anderes aufkommt;* **lay on a special ~ for sb.** jmdm. etwas Besonderes bieten; **(c)** (act of ~ing) Einladung, *die.* **2** *v.t.* **(a)** (act towards) behandeln; **~ sth. as a joke** etw. als Witz nehmen; **~ sth. with contempt** für etw. nur Verachtung haben; **(b)** ▶ 865⌡ (Med.) behandeln; **~ sb. for sth.** jmdn. wegen etw. behandeln; (before confirmation of diagnosis) jmdn. auf etw. (*Akk.*) behandeln; **(c)** (apply process to) behandeln ⟨Material, Stoff, Metall, Leder⟩; klären ⟨Abwässer⟩; **(d)** (handle in literature etc.) behandeln; **(e)** (provide with at own expense) einladen; **~ sb. to sth.** jmdm. etw. spendieren; **~ oneself to a holiday/a new hat** sich (*Dat.*) Urlaub gönnen/sich (*Dat.*) einen neuen Hut leisten

treatise /'triːtɪs, 'triːtɪz/ *n.* Abhandlung, *die*

treatment /'triːtmənt/ *n.* **(a)** Behandlung, *die;* **his ~ of the staff/you** die Art, wie er das Personal/dich behandelt; **give sb. the [full] ~** (coll.) (treat cruelly/harshly) jmdn. in die Mangel nehmen (salopp); (entertain on a lavish scale) jmdn. verwöhnen; **(b)** ▶ 865⌡ (Med.) Behandlung, *die;* **need immediate medical ~:** sofort ärztlich behandelt werden müssen; **(c)** (processing) Behandlung, *die;* (of sewage) Klärung, *die*

treaty /'triːtɪ/ *n.* [Staats]vertrag, *der;* **make** *or* **sign a ~:** einen Vertrag schließen

treble /'trebl/ **1** *adj.* **(a)** dreifach; **~ the amount compared to …:** dreimal so viel wie …; **sell sth. for ~ the price** etw. dreimal so teuer verkaufen; **(b)** (Brit. Mus.) **~ voice** Sopranstimme, *die.* **2** *n.* **(a)** (~ quantity) Dreifache, *das;* **(b)** (Mus.) **he is a ~/is singing the ~:** er singt Sopran/den Sopran. **3** *v.t.* verdreifachen; **be ~d** ⟨Wert einer Aktie usw.:⟩ sich verdreifachen. **4** *v.i.* sich verdreifachen

'treble clef *n.* (Mus.) Violinschlüssel, *der*

tree /triː/ *n.* Baum, *der;* **not grow on ~s** (fig.) nicht [einfach] vom Himmel fallen

'tree house *n.* Baumhaus, *das*

treeless /'triːlɪs/ *adj.* baumlos

tree: **~-lined** *adj.* von Bäumen gesäumt; **~ ring** *n.* Jahresring, *der;* **~top** *n.* [Baum]wipfel, *der;* **~ trunk** *n.* Baumstamm, *der*

trek /trek/ **1** *v.i.,* **-kk-** ziehen (**across** durch). **2** *n.* [schwierige] Reise

trellis /'trelɪs/ *n.* Gitter, *das;* (for plants) Spalier, *das*

tremble /'trembl/ **1** *v.i.* zittern (**with** vor + *Dat.*); **~ for sb./sth.** (fig.) um jmdn./etw. zittern; **I ~ to think what …/at the thought** (fig.) mir wird bange, wenn ich daran denke, was …/wenn ich daran denke. **2** *n.* Zittern, *das;* **be all of a ~** (coll.) am ganzen Körper zittern; **there was a ~ in her voice** ihre Stimme zitterte

trembling /'tremblɪŋ/ **1** *adj.* zitternd. **2** *n.* Zittern, *das*

tremendous /trɪ'mendəs/ *adj.* **(a)** (immense) gewaltig; enorm ⟨Fähigkeiten⟩; **(b)** (coll.: wonderful) großartig

tremolo /'tremələʊ/ *n., pl.* **~s** (Mus.) Tremolo, *das*

tremor /'tremə(r)/ *n.* **(a)** Zittern, *das;* **feel a ~ of delight/fear** freudig erregt sein/vor Angst zittern; **(b)** [earth] ~ (Geol.) leichtes Erdbeben

tremulous /'tremjʊləs/ *adj.* **(a)** (trembling) zitternd; **be ~:** zittern; **(b)** (timid) zaghaft ⟨Lächeln⟩; ängstlich ⟨Person⟩

trench /trentʃ/ *n.* Graben, *der;* (Geog.) [Tiefsee]graben, *der;* (Mil.) Schützengraben, *der*

trenchant /'trentʃənt/ *adj.* deutlich, energisch ⟨Kritik, Sprache⟩; energisch ⟨Verteidiger, Kritiker, Politik⟩; prägnant ⟨Stil⟩

'trench coat *n.* (Mil.) Wettermantel, *der;* (Fashion) Trenchcoat, *der*

trend /trend/ **1** *n.* **(a)** Trend, *der;* **population ~s** die Bevölkerungsentwicklung; **upward ~:** steigende Tendenz; **(b)** (fashion) Mode, *die;* [Mode]trend, *der;* **set the ~:** den Trend bestimmen. **2** *v.i.* **(a)** (take a course) verlaufen; **(b)** (fig.: move) sich entwickeln; **~ upward** steigen

'trendsetter *n.* Trendsetter, *der*

trendy /'trendɪ/ (Brit. coll.) **1** *adj.* modisch; Schickimicki⟨kneipe, -wohngegend⟩ (ugs.); fortschrittlich-modern ⟨Geistlicher, Lehrer⟩. **2** *n.* Schickimicki, *der* (ugs.)

trepidation /trepɪ'deɪʃn/ *n.* Beklommenheit, *die;* **with some ~, not without ~:** ziemlich beklommen

trespass /'trespəs/ **1** *v.i.* **~ on** unerlaubt betreten ⟨Grundstück⟩; eingreifen in (+ *Akk.*) ⟨jmds. Rechte⟩; **'no ~ing'** „Betreten verboten!"; **~ on sb.'s time/privacy** (fig.) jmds. Zeit über Gebühr in Anspruch nehmen/jmds. Privatsphäre verletzen. **2** *n.* (Law) Hausfriedensbruch, *der*

trespasser /'trespəsə(r)/ *n.* Unbefugte, *der/die;* **'~s will be prosecuted'** „Betreten verboten, Zuwiderhandlungen werden verfolgt"

tress /tres/ *n.* (literary/arch.) Haarstrang, *der;* (curly) Locke, *die*

trestle /'tresl/ *n.* **(a)** [Auflager]bock, *der;* **(b)** **~[-table]** Tapeziertisch, *der*

trial /'traɪəl/ *n.* **(a)** (Law) [Gerichts]verfahren, *das;* **be on ~ [for murder]** [wegen Mordes] angeklagt sein; **go on ~ [for one's life]** [wegen eines Verbrechens, auf das die Todesstrafe steht,] vor Gericht gestellt werden; **bring sb. to ~, put sb. on ~:** jmdm. den Prozess machen (**for** wegen); **the case was brought to ~:** der Fall wurde vor Gericht verhandelt; **(b)** (testing) Test, *der;* **be given ~s** getestet werden; **employ sb. on ~:** jmdn. probeweise einstellen; **give sth. a ~:** etw. ausprobieren; **[by] ~ and error** [durch] Ausprobieren; **~ of strength** Kraftprobe, *die;* **(c)** (trouble) Prüfung, *die* (geh.); Problem, *das;* **find sth. a ~:** etw. als lästig empfinden; **be a ~ to sb.** jmdm. zu schaffen machen; **(d)** (Sport) (competition) Prüfung, *die;* (for selection) Testspiel, *das. See also* **tribulation a**

trial: **~ pack** *n.* Probepackung, *die;* **~ 'run** *n.* **(a)** (of car) Testfahrt, *die;* (of machine) Probelauf, *der;* **(b)** (fig.) Probelauf, *der;* **give sth. a ~ run** etw. testen

triangle /'traɪæŋgl/ *n.* **(a)** Dreieck, *das;* **(b)** (Mus.) Triangel, *das od. der*

triangular /traɪ'æŋgjʊlə(r)/ *adj.* dreieckig; dreiseitig ⟨Pyramide⟩

triathlon /traɪ'æθlɒn/ *n.* Triathlon, *das od. der*

tribal /'traɪbl/ *adj.* Stammes-

tribalism /'traɪbəlɪzm/ *n.* Tribalismus, *der* (fachspr.)

tribe /traɪb/ *n.* Stamm, *der*

tribesman /'traɪbzmən/ *n., pl.* **tribesmen** /'traɪbzmən/ Stammesangehörige, *der*

tribulation /trɪbjʊ'leɪʃn/ *n.* **(a)** (great affliction) Kummer, *der;* **trials and ~s** Probleme und Sorgen; **(b)** (cause of trouble etc.) **be a ~ to sb.** jmdm. zur Last fallen

tribunal /traɪ'bjuːnl, trɪ'bjuːnl/ *n.* **(a)** Schiedsgericht, *das;* (court of justice) Gericht, *das;* **(b)** (fig.) Tribunal, *das*

tribune /'trɪbjuːn/ *n.* (platform) [Redner]tribüne, *die*

tributary /'trɪbjʊtərɪ/ *n.* (river) Nebenfluss, *der*

tribute /'trɪbjuːt/ *n.* Tribut, *der* (to an + *Akk.*); **pay ~ to sb./sth.** jmdm./einer Sache den schuldigen Tribut zollen (geh.); **floral ~s** Blumen [als Zeichen der Anerkennung]; (to deceased person) Blumen und Kränze; **as a ~ to his work** zur Würdigung seiner Arbeit; **she is a ~ to her trainer** sie macht ihrem Trainer alle Ehre

trice /traɪs/ *n.* **in a ~:** im Handumdrehen

trick /trɪk/ **1** *n.* **(a)** Trick, *der;* **I suspect some ~:** es könnte ein Trick sein; **it was all a ~:** das war [alles] nur Bluff; **it was such a shabby ~ [to play on her]** es war [ihr gegenüber] eine derartige Gemeinheit *od.* dermaßen gemein; **(b)** (feat of skill etc.) Kunststück, *das;* **try every ~**

in the book es mit allen Tricks probieren; **he never misses a ~** (fig.) ihm entgeht nichts; **that should do the ~** (coll.) damit dürfte es klappen (ugs.); **(c)** (knack) **get** or **find the ~ [of doing sth.]** den Dreh finden[, wie man etw. tut]; **(d) how's ~s?** (coll.) was macht die Kunst? (ugs.); **(e)** (mannerism) Eigenart, *die;* **have a ~ of doing sth.** die Eigenart haben, etw. zu tun; **(f)** (prank) Streich, *der;* **play a ~ on sb.** jmdm. einen Streich spielen; **be up to one's [old] ~s again** immer noch auf dieselbe Tour reisen (ugs.); **~ or treat** Trick-or-Treat, *das* (Kinderspiel); **(g)** (illusion) **~ of vision/lighting/the light** Augentäuschung, *die;* **(h)** (Cards) Stich, *der.* **2** *v.t.* täuschen; hereinlegen; **~ sb. into doing sth.** jmdn. mit einem Trick od. einer List dazu bringen, etw. zu tun; **~ sb. out of/into sth.** jmdm. etw. ablisten. **3** *adj.* **~ photograph** Trickaufnahme, *die;* **~ photography** Trickfotografie, *die;* **~ question** Fangfrage, *die*

~ 'out, ~ 'up *v.t.* schmücken

trickery /'trɪkərɪ/ *n.* [Hinter]list, *die;* **piece of ~:** List, *die;* Trick, *der*

trickle /'trɪkl/ **1** *n.* Rinnsal, *das* (geh.) **(of von); in a ~:** als Rinnsal; **a ~ of rain ran down the window** Regenwasser rann am Fenster hinunter; **there was a ~ of people leaving the room** (fig.) einige wenige Menschen verließen nacheinander den Raum. **2** *v.i.* rinnen; (in drops) tröpfeln; (fig.) ⟨*Ball:*⟩ langsam rollen; **~ out** ⟨*Zuschauer:*⟩ nach und nach [hinaus]gehen; **~ through** or **out** ⟨*Informationen:*⟩ durchsickern

trickster /'trɪkstə(r)/ *n.* Schwindler, *der/*Schwindlerin, *die*

tricky /'trɪkɪ/ *adj.* verzwickt (ugs.)

tricycle /'traɪsɪkl/ *n.* Dreirad, *das*

trident /'traɪdənt/ *n.* dreizackiger Fischspeer; (held by Britannia, Neptune, etc.) Dreizack, *der*

tried ⇒ **try** 2, 3

trier /traɪə(r)/ *n.* **he's a real ~:** er wirft die Flinte nicht so schnell ins Korn

trifle /'traɪfl/ *n.* **(a)** (Brit. Gastr.) Trifle, *das;* **(b)** (thing of slight value) Kleinigkeit, *die;* **the merest ~:** die geringste Kleinigkeit; **it's only a ~:** es ist nichts Besonderes; **(c) a ~ tired/angry** *etc.* ein bisschen müde/böse *usw.*

~ with *v.i.* spielen mit ⟨*jmds. Gefühlen*⟩; nicht ernst genug nehmen ⟨*Person*⟩; **he is not a person you can ~ with** er lässt nicht mit sich spaßen

trifling /'traɪflɪŋ/ *adj.* unbedeutend ⟨*Angelegenheit, Irrtum*⟩; lächerlich ⟨*Gedanke*⟩; gering ⟨*Gefahr, Wert*⟩; [lächerlich] gering ⟨*Summe*⟩

trigger /'trɪgə(r)/ **1** *n.* **(a)** (of gun) Abzug, *der;* (of machine) Drücker, *der;* **pull the ~:** abdrücken; **be quick on the ~** (fig.) prompt reagieren; **(b)** (that sets off reaction) Auslöser, *der.* **2** *v.t.* **~ [off]** auslösen

'trigger-happy *adj.* schießwütig

trigonometry /trɪgə'nɒmɪtrɪ/ *n.* (Math.) Trigonometrie, *die*

trike /traɪk/ *n.* (coll.) Dreirad, *das*

trilateral /traɪ'lætərl/ **1** *adj.* **(a)** (having three sides) dreiseitig; (involving three parties also) trilateral (geh.). **2** *n.* Dreieck, *das*

trilby /'trɪlbɪ/ *n.* (Brit.) **~ [hat]** Klapprandhut, *der*

trill /trɪl/ *n.* **(a)** Trillern, *das;* **(b)** (Mus.) Triller, *der*

trillion /'trɪlɪən/ *n.* **▶ 965** **(a)** (million million) Billion, *die;* **(b)** (Brit. dated: million million million) Trillion, *die*

trilogy /'trɪlədʒɪ/ *n.* Trilogie, *die*

trim /trɪm/ **1** *v.t.,* **-mm-:** **(a)** schneiden ⟨*Hecke*⟩; [nach]schneiden ⟨*Haar*⟩; beschneiden (auch fig.) ⟨*Papier, Hecke, Docht, Budget*⟩; **~ £100 off** or **from a budget** ein Budget um 100 Pfund kürzen; **(b)** (ornament) besetzen (**with** mit). **2** *adj.* proper; gepflegt ⟨*Garten*⟩; **keep sth. ~:** etw. in Ordnung halten. **3** *n.* **(a)** (state of adjustment) Bereitschaft, *die;* **be in fine physical ~:** in guter körperlicher Verfassung sein; **get/be in ~** (healthy) sich trimmen/in Form od. fit sein; **(b)** (cut) Nachschneiden, *das;* **my hair needs a ~:** ich muss mir die Haare nachschneiden lassen; **give a hedge a ~:** eine Hecke schneiden; **just a ~, please** (said to hairdresser) nur nachschneiden, bitte

~ 'down *v.t.* (fig.) verringern; **her figure needed**

~**ming down** sie musste etwas für ihre Figur tun

~ 'off *v.t.* abschneiden; (fig.) abnehmen

trimmer /'trɪmə(r)/ *n.* Schneider, *der;* **hedge ~:** Heckenschere, *die*

trimming /'trɪmɪŋ/ *n.* **(a)** (decorative addition) Verzierung, *die;* **lace ~s** Spitzenbesatz, *der;* **(b)** *in pl.* (coll.: accompaniments) (for main dish) Beilagen; (extra fittings on car) Extras; **with all the ~s** mit allem Drum und Dran (ugs.); **(c)** *in pl.* (pieces cut off) Abfall, *der* (*vom Zuschneiden*); (of meat) abgeschnittene Stücke

Trinidad /'trɪnɪdæd/ *pr. n.* Trinidad (*das*)

Trinidadian /trɪnɪ'dædɪən/ **▶ 947** **1** *adj.* trinidadisch; **sb. is ~:** jmd. ist Trinidader/Trinidaderin. **2** *n.* Trinidader, *der/*Trinidaderin, *die*

Trinity /'trɪnɪtɪ/ *n.* **(a)** (Theol.) **the [Holy] ~:** die [Heilige] Dreifaltigkeit od. Dreieinigkeit od. Trinität; **(b)** (Eccl.) **~ [Sunday]** Dreifaltigkeitssonntag, *der*

trinket /'trɪŋkɪt/ *n.* kleines, billiges Schmuckstück; (on bracelet) Anhänger, *der*

trio /'triːəʊ/ *n., pl.* **~s** (also Mus.) Trio, *das*

trip /trɪp/ **1** *n.* **(a)** (journey) Reise, *die;* Trip, *der* (ugs.); (shorter) Ausflug, *der;* Trip, *der* (ugs.); **two ~s were necessary to transport everything** zwei Fahrten waren nötig, um alles zu transportieren; **make a ~ to London** nach London fahren; **(b)** (coll.: drug-induced hallucinations) Trip, *der* (Jargon); **[good/bad] ~ on LSD** [guter/schlechter] LSD-Trip. **2** *v.i.,* **-pp-:** **(a)** (stumble) stolpern (**on** über + *Akk.*); **(b)** (coll.: hallucinate while on drugs) **~ [on LSD]** auf einem [LSD-] Trip sein; **(c)** (walk etc. with light steps) trippeln. **3** *v.t.,* **-pp-** ⇒ **~ up** 2 a

~ over *v.t.* stolpern über (+ *Akk.*)

~ 'up 1 *v.i.* **(a)** (stumble) stolpern; **(b)** (fig.: make a mistake) einen Fehler machen. **2** *v.t.* **(a)** (cause to stumble) stolpern lassen; **(b)** (cause to make a mistake) aufs Glatteis führen (fig.)

tripe /traɪp/ *n.* **(a)** Kaldaunen; **(b)** (coll.: rubbish) Quatsch, *der* (ugs. abwertend)

triple /'trɪpl/ **1** *adj.* **(a)** dreifach; **(b)** (three times greater than) **~ the ...:** der/die/das dreifache ...; **at ~ the speed** mit der dreifachen Geschwindigkeit od. dreimal so schnell; **~ the number of machines** dreimal so viele Maschinen. **2** *n.* Dreifache, *das.* **3** *v.i.* sich verdreifachen. **4** *v.t.* verdreifachen

'triple jump *n.* Dreisprung, *der*

triplet /'trɪplɪt/ *n.* Drilling, *der*

triplicate /'trɪplɪkət/ **1** *adj.* dreifach. **2** *n.* **in ~:** in dreifacher Ausfertigung

trip 'mileage recorder *n.* (Motor Veh.) Tageskilometerzähler, *der*

tripod /'traɪpɒd/ *n.* Dreibein, *das;* [dreibeiniges] Stativ

tripper /'trɪpə(r)/ *n.* (Brit.) Ausflügler, *der/*Ausflüglerin, *die*

'tripwire *n.* Stolperdraht, *der*

trite /traɪt/ *adj.* banal

triumph /'traɪəmf, 'traɪʌmf/ **1** *n.* Triumph, *der* (**over** über + *Akk.*). **2** *v.i.* triumphieren (**over** über + *Akk.*)

triumphant /traɪ'ʌmfənt/ *adj.* **(a)** (victorious) siegreich; **(b)** (exulting) triumphierend ⟨*Blick*⟩; **~ shouts** Triumphgeschrei, *das*

trivia /'trɪvɪə/ *n. pl.* Belanglosigkeiten

trivial /'trɪvɪəl/ *adj.* belanglos; trivial (geh.)

triviality /trɪvɪ'ælɪtɪ/ *n.* Belanglosigkeit, *die;* Trivialität, *die* (geh.)

trivialize (trivialise) /'trɪvɪəlaɪz/ *v.t.* trivialisieren (geh.)

trod, trodden ⇒ **tread** 2, 3

trolley /'trɒlɪ/ *n.* (Brit.) **(a)** (on rails) Draisine, *die;* **(b)** (for serving food) Servierwagen, *der;* **(c)** [**supermarket**] **~:** Einkaufswagen, *der*

'trolley bus *n.* (Brit.) Oberleitungsomnibus, *der*

trombone /trɒm'bəʊn, 'trɒmbəʊn/ *n.* Posaune, *die*

troop /truːp/ **1** *n.* **(a)** *in pl.* Truppen; **our best ~s** unsere besten Soldaten; **(b)** (of cavalry) Schwadron, *die;* (artillery and armour) Batterie, *die;* **(c)** (assembled company) Schar, *die.* **2** *v.i.* strömen; (in an orderly fashion) marschieren; **~ in/out** hinein-/hinausströmen

'**troop carrier** *n.* Truppentransporter, *der*

trooper /'tru:pə(r)/ *n.* (**a**) (soldier) einfacher Soldat; **swear like a** ~ (coll.) wie ein Fuhrmann fluchen (ugs.); (**b**) (Amer.: policeman) Polizist, *der*

'**troopship** *n.* (Mil.) Truppentransporter, *der*

trophy /'trəʊfɪ/ *n.* Trophäe, *die*

tropic /'trɒpɪk/ *n.* **the T**~**s** (Geog.) die Tropen; **the** ~ **of Cancer/Capricorn** (Astron., Geog.) der Wendekreis des Krebses/Steinbocks

tropical /'trɒpɪkl/ *adj.* tropisch; Tropen‹*krankheit, -kleidung*›

tropical: ~ '**medicine** *n.* Tropenmedizin, *die;* ~ '**rainforest** *n.* tropischer Regenwald

trot /trɒt/ **1** *n.* (coll.) **on the** ~ (in succession) hintereinander; **every weekend for five weeks on the** ~**:** an fünf Wochenenden hintereinander; **be on the** ~**:** auf Trab sein (ugs.). **2** *v.i.,* **-tt-** traben. **3** *v.t.,* **-tt-** traben lassen ‹*Pferd*›

~ '**out** *v.t.* (fig. coll.) (**a**) (produce for approval) vorführen; (**b**) (produce unthinkingly) kommen mit (ugs.)

trotter /'trɒtə(r)/ *n.* Fuß, *der;* **pigs'** ~**s** (Cookery) Schweinsfüße

trouble /'trʌbl/ **1** *n.* (**a**) Ärger, *der;* Schwierigkeiten *Pl.;* **have** ~ **with sb./sth.** mit jmdm./etw. Ärger haben; **put one's** ~**s behind one** seine Probleme vergessen; **be out of** ~**:** aus den Schwierigkeiten heraus sein; **keep out of** ~**:** nicht [wieder] in Schwierigkeiten kommen; **in** ~**:** in Schwierigkeiten; **be in** ~ **with the police** Ärger mit der Polizei haben; **be in serious** *or* **real** *or* **a lot of** ~ [**over sth.**] [wegen einer Sache] in ernsten *od.* großen Schwierigkeiten sein; **get sb. into** ~**:** jmdn. in Schwierigkeiten bringen; **get a girl into** ~ (coll.) einem Mädchen ein Kind machen (ugs.); **get into** ~ [**over sth.**] [wegen einer Sache] in Schwierigkeiten geraten; **get into** ~ **with the law** mit dem Gesetz in Konflikt geraten; **there'll be** ~ [**if ...**] es wird Ärger geben[, wenn ...]; **what's** *or* **what seems to be the** ~**?** was ist denn?; was ist los? (ugs.); (doctor's question to patient) wo fehlt's denn?; **you are asking for** ~ (coll.) du machst dir nur selber Schwierigkeiten; **that's asking for** ~ (coll.) das muss ja Ärger geben; **make** *or* **cause** ~ (cause disturbance) Ärger machen (**about** wegen); (cause disagreement) Zwietracht säen; (**b**) (faulty operation) Probleme; **engine/clutch/brake** ~**:** Probleme mit dem Motor/der Kupplung/der Bremse; (**c**) ▶ 865 (disease) **suffer from heart/liver** ~**:** Probleme mit dem Herz/der Leber haben; **she's got some** ~ **with her back** ihr Rücken macht ihr zu schaffen; (**d**) (cause of vexation etc.) Problem, *das;* **half the** ~ (fig.) das größte Problem; **your** ~ **is that ...:** dein Fehler ist, dass ...; (**e**) (inconvenience) Mühe, *die;* **it's more** ~ **than it's worth** es lohnt sich nicht; **I don't want to put you to any** ~**:** ich möchte Ihnen keine Umstände machen; **not worth the** ~**:** nicht der Mühe wert; **give sb. no** ~**:** jmdm. keine Mühe machen; **take the** ~ **to do sth.,** **go to the** ~ **of doing sth.** sich (*Dat.*) die Mühe machen, etw. zu tun; **go to** *or* **take a lot of/some** ~**:** sich (*Dat.*) sehr viel/viel Mühe geben; **please don't go to a lot of** ~**:** bitte machen Sie sich (*Dat.*) nicht allzu viel Umstände; **of course I'll help you** — [**it's**] **no** ~ **at all** natürlich helfe ich dir — das macht keine Umstände *od.* das ist nicht der Rede wert; (**f**) (source of inconvenience) **be a** ~ [**to sb.**] jmdm. zur Last fallen; **he won't be any** ~**:** er wird [Ihnen] keine Schwierigkeiten machen; (**g**) *in sing.* *or pl.* (unrest) Unruhen. **2** *v.t.* (**a**) (agitate) beunruhigen; **don't let it** ~ **you** mach dir deswegen keine Sorgen; (**b**) (inconvenience) stören; [**I'm**] **sorry to** ~ **you** bitte entschuldigen Sie die Störung. **3** *v.i.* (**a**) (be disturbed) sich (*Dat.*) Sorgen machen (**over** um); **don't** ~ **about it** mach dir deswegen keine Gedanken; (**b**) (make an effort) sich bemühen; **don't** ~ **to explain/to get up** du brauchst mir gar nichts zu erklären/bitte bleiben Sie sitzen

troubled /'trʌbld/ *adj.* (**a**) (worried) besorgt; **what are you so** ~ **about?** was macht dir denn solche Sorgen?; (**b**) (restless) unruhig; (**c**) (agitated) aufgewühlt; unruhig ‹*Zeit*›; bewegt ‹*Geschichte*›

trouble: ~-**free** *adj.* problemlos; ~**maker** *n.* Unruhestifter, *der*/-stifterin, *die;* ~**shooter** *n.* jmd., *der*

Störungen *od.* Probleme findet und beseitigt; (in disputes) Vermittler, *der*/Vermittlerin, *die*

troublesome /'trʌblsəm/ *adj.* schwierig; lästig ‹*Krankheit*›

'**trouble spot** *n.* (**a**) Unruheherd, *der;* (**b**) (in machine) Schwachstelle, *die*

trough /trɒf/ *n.* (**a**) Trog, *der;* **a drinking-**~**:** ein Wassertrog; (**b**) (between waves) Wellental, *das;* (**c**) (Meteorol.) Trog, *der;* **a** ~ **of low pressure** eine Tiefdruckrinne

troupe /tru:p/ *n.* Truppe, *die*

trouser /'traʊzə/**:** ~ **leg** *n.* Hosenbein, *das;* ~ **pocket** *n.* Hosentasche, *die*

trousers /'traʊzəz/ *n. pl.* [**pair of**] ~**:** Hose, *die;* Hosen *Pl.;* **wear the** ~ (fig.) die Hosen anhaben (ugs.)

'**trouser suit** *n.* (Brit.) Hosenanzug, *der*

trousseau /'tru:səʊ/ *n., pl.* ~**s** *or* ~**x** /'tru:səʊz/ Aussteuer, *die*

trout /traʊt/ *n., pl. same* Forelle, *die*

trowel /'traʊəl/ *n.* (**a**) Kelle, *die;* **lay it on with a** ~ (fig.) [es] dick auftragen (ugs.); (**b**) (Hort.) Pflanzkelle, *die*

truancy /'tru:ənsɪ/ *n.* Schuleschwänzen, *das* (ugs.); unentschuldigtes Fernbleiben vom Unterricht

truant /'tru:ənt/ *n.* [Schul]schwänzer, *der*/-schwänzerin, *die* (ugs.); **play** ~**:** [die Schule] schwänzen (ugs.)

truce /tru:s/ *n.* Waffenstillstand, *der;* **call a** ~**:** einen Waffenstillstand schließen

truck /trʌk/ *n.* (**a**) (road vehicle) Last[kraft]wagen, *der;* Lkw, *der;* (**b**) (Brit. Railw.: wagon) offener Güterwagen

'**truck driver** *n.* ▶ 887 Lastwagenfahrer, *der*/-fahrerin, *die;* (long-distance) Fernfahrer, *der*/-fahrerin, *die*

trucker /'trʌkə(r)/ *n.* ▶ 887 (**a**) (Amer.: market-gardener) Gemüsegärtner, *der*/-gärtnerin, *die;* (**b**) (esp. Amer.) ⇒ **truck driver**

trucking /'trʌkɪŋ/ *n.* (Amer.) Lkw-Transport, *der*

truck: ~**load** *n.* Wagenladung, *die;* ~ **stop** (Amer.) ⇒ **transport café**

truculent /'trʌkjʊlənt/ *adj.* aufsässig

trudge /trʌdʒ/ *v.i.* trotten; (through mud, snow, etc.) stapfen

true /tru:/ **1** *adj.* ~**r** /'tru:ə(r)/, ~**st** /'tru:ɪst/ (**a**) (in accordance with fact) wahr; wahrheitsgetreu ‹*Bericht, Beschreibung*›; **is it** ~ **that ...?** stimmt es, dass ...?; [**only**] **too** ~**:** nur zu wahr; **that is too good to be** ~**:** das ist zu schön, um wahr zu sein; [**that's**] ~ [**enough**] [das] stimmt; **come** ~ (*Traum, Wunsch:*) Wirklichkeit werden, wahr werden; ‹*Befürchtung, Prophezeiung:*› sich bewahrheiten; (**b**) richtig ‹*Vorteil, Einschätzung*›; (rightly so called) eigentlich; **the frog is not a** ~ **reptile** der Frosch ist kein echtes Reptil; (**c**) (not sham) wahr; echt, wahr ‹*Freund, Freundschaft, Christ*›; **that's not a** ~ **antique** das ist keine echte Antiquität; (**d**) (accurately conforming) getreu ‹*Wiedergabe*›; **be** ~ **to sth.** einer Sache (*Dat.*) genau entsprechen; ~ **to type** typisch; ~ **to life** lebensecht; (**e**) (loyal) treu; ~ **to one's word** *or* **promise** getreu seinem Versprechen; (**f**) (in correct position) gerade ‹*Pfosten*›. **2** *n.* **out of** [**the**] ~**:** schief ‹*Mauer, Pfosten, Räder*›. **3** *adv.* (**a**) (truthfully) aufrichtig ‹*lieben*›; **tell me** ~**:** sag mir die Wahrheit; (**b**) (accurately) gerade; genau ‹*zielen*›

true: ~-**blue 1** *adj.* in der Wolle gefärbt; **2** *n.* Hundertfünfzigprozentige, *der/die* (abwertend); ~-**life** *adj.* aus dem Leben gegriffen ‹*Geschichte, Drama*›

truffle /'trʌfl/ *n.* Trüffel, *die od.* (ugs.) *der*

truism /'tru:ɪzm/ *n.* Binsenweisheit, *die*

truly /'tru:lɪ/ *adv.* (**a**) (genuinely) wirklich; **be** ~ **grateful** wirklich sehr *od.* aufrichtig dankbar sein; (**b**) (accurately) zutreffend, richtig ‹*darstellen, sagen*›; *see also* **yours b**

trump /trʌmp/ (Cards) **1** *n.* Trumpf, *der;* **turn up** ~**s** (Brit. coll.) (turn out better than expected) doch noch ein voller Erfolg werden; (do the right thing) die Situation retten; **hold all the** ~**s** (fig.) alle Trümpfe in der Hand haben *od.* halten. **2** *v.t.* übertrumpfen

~ **up** *v.t.* (coll.) konstruieren; ~**ed up charge** falsche Beschuldigung

'**trump card** *n.* (lit. or fig.) Trumpf, *der;* **play one's** ~ (lit. or fig.) seinen [größten *od.* stärksten] Trumpf ausspielen

trumpet /'trʌmpɪt/ **1** *n.* (Mus., Bot.) Trompete, *die.* **2** *v.t. & i.* trompeten

trumpeter /'trʌmpɪtə(r)/ *n.* Trompeter, *der/*Trompeterin, *die*

truncate /trʌŋ'keɪt/ *v.t.* **(a)** stutzen ‹*Baum, Spitze*›; **(b)** (fig.) kürzen

truncheon /'trʌntʃn/ *n.* Schlagstock, *der*

trundle /'trʌndl/ *v.t. & i.* rollen

trunk /trʌŋk/ *n.* **(a)** (of elephant etc.) Rüssel, *der;* **(b)** (large box) Schrankkoffer, *der;* **(c)** (of tree) Stamm, *der;* **(d)** (of human or animal body) Rumpf, *der;* **(e)** (Amer.: of car) Kofferraum, *der;* **(f)** *in pl.* (Brit.: shorts) Unterhose, *die;* [**swimming**] ~s Badehose, *die*

'**trunk:** ~ **call** *n.* Ferngespräch, *das;* ~ **line** *n.* (Railw.) Hauptstrecke, *die;* (Teleph.) Fernleitung, *die;* ~ **road** *n.* (Brit.) Fernstraße, *die*

truss /trʌs/ **1** *n.* **(a)** (of roof etc.) Gebälk, *das;* **(b)** (Med.) Bruchband, *das.* **2** *v.t.* ~ [up] fesseln

trust /trʌst/ **1** *n.* **(a)** (firm belief) Vertrauen, *das;* **place** *or* **put one's** ~ **in sb./sth.** sein Vertrauen auf *od.* in jmdn./ etw. setzen; **have** [**every**] ~ **in sb./sth.** [volles] Vertrauen zu jmdn./etw. haben; **(b)** (reliance) **take sth. on** ~: etw. einfach glauben, **(c)** (organization managed by trustees) Treuhandgesellschaft, *die;* [**charitable**] ~: Stiftung, *die;* **(d)** (body of trustees) Treuhänder *Pl.;* (of charitable ~) [Stiftungs]beirat, *der;* Kuratorium, *das;* **(e)** (organized association of companies) Trust, *der;* **(f)** (responsibility) **position of** ~: Vertrauensstellung, *die;* **(g)** (obligation) Verpflichtung, *die;* **(h)** (Law) **hold in** ~: treuhänderisch verwalten. **2** *v.t.* **(a)** (rely on) trauen (+ *Dat.*); vertrauen (+ *Dat.*) ‹*Person*›; **not** ~ **sb. an inch** jmdm. nicht über den Weg trauen; **he/ what he says is not to be** ~ed er ist nicht vertrauenswürdig/auf das, was er sagt, kann man sich nicht verlassen; ~ **sb. with sth.** jmdm. etw. anvertrauen; ~ '**you/** '**him!** *etc.* (coll. iron.) typisch!; ~ '**him to get it wrong!** er muss natürlich einen Fehler machen!; **(b)** (hope) hoffen; **I** ~ **he is not hurt?** er ist doch hoffentlich nicht verletzt? **3** *v.i.* **(a)** ~ **to** sich verlassen auf (+ *Akk.*); **(b)** (believe) ~ **in sb./sth.** auf jmdn./etw. vertrauen

trustee /trʌ'sti:/ *n.* **(a)** (person holding property in trust; also fig.) Treuhänder, *der/*Treuhänderin, *die;* **(b)** (one appointed to manage institution) Kurator, *der/*Kuratorin, *die*

trustful /'trʌstfl/ *adj.* vertrauensvoll

'**trust fund** *n.* Treuhandvermögen, *das*

trusting /'trʌstɪŋ/ *adj.* vertrauensvoll

trustworthy /'trʌstwɜːðɪ/ *adj.* vertrauenswürdig

truth /truːθ/ *n., pl.* ~s /truːðz, truːθs/ **(a)** *no pl.* Wahrheit, *die;* **there is some/not a word of/no** ~ **in that** es ist etwas Wahres/kein wahres Wort/nichts Wahres daran; **in** ~ (literary) wahrlich (geh.); **(b)** (what is true) Wahrheit, *die;* (principle) Grundsatz, *der;* **tell the** [**whole**] ~: die [ganze] Wahrheit sagen; **the** ~ **is that I forgot** um ehrlich zu sein, ich habe es vergessen; **to tell the** ~, ~ **to tell** ehrlich gesagt

truthful /'truːθfl/ *adj.* ehrlich; wahrheitsgetreu ‹*Darstellung, Schilderung*›; **be** ~ **about sth.** die Wahrheit über etw. (*Akk.*) sagen

try /traɪ/ **1** *n.* **(a)** (attempt) Versuch, *der;* **have a** ~ **at sth./ doing sth.** etw. versuchen/versuchen, etw. zu tun; **give sb./sth. a** ~: jmdm. eine Chance geben/etw. einmal ausprobieren; **I'll give him another** ~ (ask him again for help, a favour, etc.) ich versuche es noch einmal bei ihm; (give him another chance) ich versuche es noch einmal mit ihm; (on telephone) ich versuche noch einmal, ihn zu erreichen; **give it a** ~: es versuchen; **(b)** (Rugby) Versuch, *der.* **2** *v.t.* **(a)** (attempt, make effort) versuchen; **it's** ~**ing to rain** es tröpfelt ein wenig; **do** ~ **to be on time** bitte versuche, pünktlich zu sein; **it's no use** ~**ing to do sth.** es hat keinen Zweck zu versuchen, etw. zu tun; **I've given up** ~**ing to do sth.** ich versuche schon gar nicht mehr, etw. zu tun; ~ **one's best** sein Bestes tun; **(b)** (test usefulness of) probieren; **if the stain is difficult to remove,** ~ **soap and water** wenn der Fleck schwer zu entfernen ist, versuche *od.* probiere es doch mal mit Wasser und Seife; **I've tried all the bookshops for this book** ich habe in allen Buchhandlungen versucht, dieses Buch zu bekommen; ~ **one's**

hand at sth. sich an etw. (*Dat.*) versuchen; ~ **shaking it!** probier es mal mit Schütteln!; **I'll** ~ **anything once** ich probiere alles einmal aus; **(c)** (test) auf die Probe stellen ‹*Fähigkeit, Kraft, Mut, Geduld*›; ~ **the door/window** [to see if it's locked] versuchen, die Tür/das Fenster zu öffnen[, um zu sehen, ob sie/es verschlossen ist]; **(d)** (Law.: take to trial) ~ **a case** einen Fall verhandeln; ~ **sb.** [**for sth.**] jmdn. [wegen einer Sache] vor Gericht stellen; jmdm. [wegen einer Sache] den Prozess machen; **he was tried for murder** er stand wegen Mordes vor Gericht; **he was tried before a jury** er wurde vor ein Schwurgericht gestellt. **3** *v.i.* es versuchen; **she wasn't even** ~**ing** sie hat sich (*Dat.*) überhaupt keine Mühe gegeben *od.* es gar nicht erst versucht; **it was not for want of** ~**ing** es lag nicht daran, dass er/sie *usw.* sich nicht bemüht hätte; ~ **and do sth.** (coll.) versuchen, etw. zu tun; ~ **hard/harder** sich (*Dat.*) viel/mehr Mühe geben

~ **for** *v.t.* (compete for) sich bemühen um ‹*Arbeitsstelle, Stipendium*›; kämpfen um ‹*Sieg im Sport*›

~ '**on** *v.t.* **(a)** anprobieren ‹*Kleidungsstück*›; **(b)** (Brit. coll.) ~ **it on** provozieren

~ '**out** *v.t.* ~ **sth./sb. out** etw. ausprobieren/jmdm. eine Chance geben

trying /'traɪɪŋ/ *adj.* **(a)** (testing) schwierig; **(b)** (difficult to endure) anstrengend

'**try-out** *n.* Erprobung, *die;* **give sth. a** ~: etw. ausprobieren

tsar /zɑː(r)/ *n.* (Hist.) Zar, *der*

tsetse [**fly**] /'tsetsɪ (flaɪ)/ *n.* Tsetsefliege, *die*

'**T-shirt** *n.* T-Shirt, *das*

tsp., *pl.* **tsps** *abbr.* **teaspoon**[**s**] Teel.

'**T-square** *n.* Kreuzwinkel, *der*

Tu. *abbr.* ▶739▎ **Tuesday** Di.

tub /tʌb/ *n.* **(a)** Kübel, *der;* **(b)** (for ice cream etc.) Becher, *der;* **(c)** (Brit. coll.: bath) Bad, *das*

tuba /'tjuːbə/ *n.* (Mus.) Tuba, *die*

tubby /'tʌbɪ/ *adj.* rundlich; pummelig (ugs.), rundlich ‹*Kind*›

tube /tjuːb/ *n.* **(a)** (for conveying liquids etc.) Rohr, *das;* **(b)** (small cylinder) Tube, *die;* (for sweets, tablets) Röhrchen, *das;* **(c)** (Anat., Zool.) Röhre, *die;* **(d)** (cathode-ray ~) Röhre, *die;* (coll.: television) **watch the** ~: vor der Röhre sitzen (ugs.); **(e)** (Amer.: thermionic valve) Röhre, *die;* **(f)** (Brit. coll.: underground railway) U-Bahn, *die*

tuber /'tjuːbə(r)/ *n.* (Bot.) Knolle, *die*

tuberculosis /tjuːbɜːkjʊ'ləʊsɪs/ *n., no pl.* ▶865▎ (Med.) Tuberkulose, *die*

tube: ~ **station** *n.* (Brit. coll.) U-Bahnhof, *der;* ~ **train** *n.* (Brit. coll.) U-Bahn-Zug, *der*

tubing /'tjuːbɪŋ/ *n.* Rohre *Pl.*

tubular /'tjuːbjʊlə(r)/ *adj.* (tube-shaped) rohrförmig

tubular '**bells** *n. pl.* Glockenspiel, *das*

TUC *abbr.* (Brit.) **Trades Union Congress**

tuck /tʌk/ **1** *v.t.* stecken; **he** ~ed **his legs under him** er schlug die Beine unter. **2** *n.* (in fabric) (for decoration) Biese, *die;* (to shorten or tighten) Abnäher, *der*

~ '**in 1** *v.t.* hineinstecken; ~ **in the blankets** die Decken an den Seiten feststecken; ~ **your shirt in!** steck dein Hemd in die Hose! **2** *v.i.* (coll.) zulangen (ugs.)

~ **into** *v.i.* (coll.: eat) ~ **into sth.** sich (*Dat.*) etw. schmecken lassen

~ '**up** *v.t.* **(a)** hochkrempeln ‹*Ärmel, Hose*›; hochnehmen ‹*Rock*›; **(b)** (cover snugly) zudecken; **be** ~ed **up** [**in bed**] zugedeckt [im Bett] sein

'**tuck shop** *n.* (Brit. Sch.) Laden für Erfrischungen, Süßigkeiten *usw.* in einer Schule

Tudor /'tjuːdə(r)/ (Brit. Hist.) **1** *n.* Tudor, *der/*die. **2** *attrib. adj.* Tudor-

Tue., Tues. *abbrs.* ▶739▎ **Tuesday** Di.

Tuesday /'tjuːzdeɪ, 'tjuːzdɪ/ ▶739▎ **1** *n.* Dienstag, *der.* **2** *adv.* (coll.) **she comes** ~s sie kommt dienstags. *See also* **Friday**

tuft /tʌft/ *n.* Büschel, *das;* ~ **of grass/hair** Gras-/Haarbüschel, *das*

tufted /'tʌftɪd/ *adj.* büschelig; ～ **carpet** Tuftingteppich, *der*

tug /tʌg/ **1** *n.* (a) Ruck, *der;* **he felt a ～ on the fishing-line** er spürte, wie etwas an der Angel zog; ～ **of love** [**battle**] (coll.) *Streit bei der Ehescheidung, wem das Kind zugesprochen wird;* ～ **of war** (lit. or fig.) Tauziehen, *das;* (b) ～ [**boat**] Schlepper, *der.* **2** *v.t.,* **-gg-** ziehen; schleppen ‹*Boot*›. **3** *v.i.,* **-gg-** zerren (**at** an + *Dat.*)

tuition /tjuː'ɪʃn/ *n.* Unterricht, *der*

tulip /'tjuːlɪp/ *n.* Tulpe, *die*

tumble /'tʌmbl/ **1** *v.i.* (a) (fall suddenly) stürzen; fallen; ～ **off sth.** von etw. fallen; (b) (move in headlong fashion) stürzen; (c) ‹*Preise usw.*› fallen. **2** *v.t.* (fling headlong) schleudern. **3** *n.* Sturz, *der*
～ **on** *v.t.* (chance on) stolpern über (+ *Akk.*)
～ **over** *v.i.* hinfallen; ‹*Kartenhaus*› umfallen
～ **to** *v.t.* (Brit. coll.) durchschauen

tumble: ～**down** *adj.* verfallen; ～**-drier** *n.* Wäsche-trockner, *der;* ～**-dry** *v.t.* im Automaten trocknen

tumbler /'tʌmblə(r)/ *n.* (glass) (short) Whiskyglas, *das;* (long) Wasserglas, *das*

tummy /'tʌmɪ/ *n.* (child lang./coll.) Bäuchlein, *das;* **I've got an upset ～:** ich habe mir den Magen verdorben

'tummy ache *n.* (child lang./coll.) Bauchweh, *das*

tumour (Brit.; Amer.: **tumor**) /'tjuːmə(r)/ *n.* Tumor, *der*

tumult /'tjuːmʌlt/ *n.* (commotion, uproar) Tumult, *der;* **be in ～:** sich in Aufruhr befinden

tuna /'tjuːnə/ *n., pl.* same or ～**s** (a) (fish) Thunfisch, *der;* (b) (as food) ～[**-fish**] Thunfisch, *der*

tune /tjuːn/ **1** *n.* (a) (melody) Melodie, *die;* **change one's ～, sing another** or **a different ～** (fig.) (behave differently) sein Verhalten ändern; (assume different tone) einen anderen Ton anschlagen; **call the ～:** den Ton angeben; (b) (correct pitch) **sing in/out of ～:** richtig/falsch singen; **be in/out of ～** ‹*Instrument:*› richtig gestimmt/verstimmt sein; (c) (fig.: agreement) **be in/out of ～ with sth.** mit etw. in Ein-klang/nicht in Einklang stehen; (d) (amount) **to the ～ of** [**£50,000**] sage und schreibe [50 000 Pfund]. **2** *v.t.* (a) (Mus.: put in ～) stimmen; (b) (Radio, Telev.) einstellen (**to** auf + *Akk.*); **stay ～d!** bleiben Sie auf dieser Welle!; (c) ein-stellen ‹*Motor, Vergaser*›; (for more power) frisieren ‹*Motor, Auto*›
～ **'in** *v.i.* (Radio, Telev.) ～ **in to a station** einen Sender einstellen; ～ **in to** (fig.) sich einstellen auf (+ *Akk.*)
～ **'up 1** *v.i.* [die Instrumente] stimmen. **2** *v.t.* einstellen

tuneful /'tjuːnfl/ *adj.* melodisch

tuneless /'tjuːnlɪs/ *adj.* unmelodisch

tuner /'tjuːnə(r)/ *n.* (a) ▶ 887┃ (Mus.) Stimmer, *der*/Stim-merin, *die;* (b) (knob etc.) Einstellknopf, *der;* Tuner, *der* (Technik); (c) (radio) Tuner, *der*

tungsten /'tʌŋstən/ *n.* Wolfram, *das*

tunic /'tjuːnɪk/ *n.* (of soldier, policeman) Uniformjacke, *die;* (of schoolgirl) Kittel, *der*

tuning /'tjuːnɪŋ/ *n.* (a) (Mus.) Stimmen, *das;* (b) (Radio) Einstellen, *das;* (c) (Motor Veh.) Einstellen, *das;* (to increase power) Frisieren, *das;* Tuning, *das;* **the engine needs ～:** der Motor muss eingestellt werden

'tuning fork *n.* (Mus.) Stimmgabel, *die*

Tunisia /tjuː'nɪzɪə/ *pr. n.* Tunesien (*das*)

tunnel /'tʌnl/ **1** *n.* Tunnel, *der;* (dug by animal) Gang, *der;* [**the**] **light at the end of the ～** (fig.) [das] Licht am Ende des Tunnels. **2** *v.i.,* (Brit.) **-ll-** einen Tunnel graben; ～ **un-der sth.** etw. untertunneln; ～ **through sth.** durch etw. (*Akk.*) einen Tunnel graben

'tunnel vision *n.* Röhrengesichtsfeld, *das* (Med.); (fig.) en-ges Blickfeld

turban /'tɜːbən/ *n.* Turban, *der*

turbid /'tɜːbɪd/ *adj.* (muddy) trüb[e]

turbine /'tɜːbaɪn/ *n.* Turbine, *die*

turbo /'tɜːbəʊ/ *n.* (coll.) Turbo, *der*

turbo: ～**charged** *adj.* mit Turbolader nachgestellt; ～**charger** *n.* Turbolader, *der*

---

turbot /'tɜːbət/ *n.* (Zool.) Steinbutt, *der*

turbulence /'tɜːbjʊləns/ *n., no pl.* (a) (agitation) Aufge-wühltheit, *die;* (fig.) Aufruhr, *der;* (unruliness) Unruhe, *die;* (b) (Phys.) Turbulenz, *die*

turbulent /'tɜːbjʊlənt/ *adj.* (a) aufgewühlt ‹*Gedanken, Leidenschaften, Wellen*›; turbulent ‹*Herrschaft, Kindheit*›; ungestüm ‹*Menge*›; aufrührerisch ‹*Stadt, Mob*›; (b) (Phys.) turbulent

tureen /tjʊə'riːn/ *n.* Terrine, *die*

turf /tɜːf/ *n., pl.* ～**s** or **turves** /tɜːvz/ (a) *no pl.* (covering of grass etc.) Rasen, *der;* (b) (cut patch of grass) [abgestochenes] Rasenstück; Sode, *die* (bes. nordd.); **lay ～:** Fertigrasen ver-legen; (c) **the ～** (racecourse) der Turf (Pferdesport); die Rennbahn; (horseracing) der Pferderennsport
～ **'out** *v.t.* (coll.) rausschmeißen (ugs.)
～ **'over** *v.t.* mit Rasenstücken bedecken

turf: ～ **accountant** *n.* ▶ 887┃ Buchmacher, *der*/ -macherin, *die;* ～ **war** *n.* Revierkampf, *der*

Turk /tɜːk/ *n.* ▶ 947┃ Türke, *der*/Türkin, *die*

Turkey /'tɜːkɪ/ *pr. n.* die Türkei

turkey *n.* (fowl) Truthahn, *der*/Truthenne, *die;* (esp. as food) Puter, *der*/Pute, *die*

Turkish /'tɜːkɪʃ/ ▶ 897┃, ▶ 947┃ **1** *adj.* türkisch; **sb. is ～:** jmd. ist Türke/Türkin. **2** *n.* Türkisch, *das; see also* **English 2 a**

Turkish: ～ **'bath** *n.* türkisches Bad; ～ **de'light** *n.* Lokum, *das; mit Puderzucker bestreutes, gelatinehaltiges Konfekt*

turmeric /'tɜːmərɪk/ *n.* Gelbwurzel, *die;* (spice) Kurkuma, *die*

turmoil /'tɜːmɔɪl/ *n.* Aufruhr, *der;* [wildes] Durcheinander

turn /tɜːn/ **1** *n.* (a) **it is sb.'s ～ to do sth.** jmd. ist an der Reihe, etw. zu tun; **it's your ～ [next]** du bist als Nächster/Nächste dran (ugs.) *od.* an der Reihe; **wait one's ～:** warten, bis man an der Reihe ist; **your ～ will come** du kommst auch [noch] an die Reihe; **by ～s** abwechselnd; **he gave it to her, and she in ～ passed it on to me** er gab es ihr, und sie wiederum reichte es an mich weiter; **in one's ～:** wiederum; **out of ～** (before or after one's ～) außer der Reihe; (fig.) an der falschen Stelle ‹*lachen*›; **ex-cuse me if I'm talking out of ～** (fig.) entschuldige, wenn ich etwas Unpassendes sage; **take [it in] ～s** sich abwechseln; **take ～s at doing sth., take it in ～s to do sth.** etw. abwechselnd tun; (b) (rotary motion) Drehung, *die;* **give the handle a ～:** den Griff [herum]drehen; [**done**] **to a ～:** genau richtig [zubereitet]; (c) ▶ 1199┃ (change of direction) Wende, *die;* **take a ～ to the right/left, do** or **make** or **take a right/left ～:** nach rechts/links abbiegen; **'no left/right ～'** „links/rechts abbiegen ver-boten!"; **the ～ of the year/century** die Jahres-/ Jahrhundertwende; **a ～ of fortune** eine Schicksals-wende; **take a favourable ～** (fig.) sich zum Guten wenden; (d) (deflection) Biegung, *die;* (e) (bend) Kurve, *die;* (corner) Ecke, *die;* **at every ～** (fig.) (constantly) ständig; (f) (short performance on stage etc.) Nummer, *die;* **do one's ～:** auftreten; (g) (change of tide) ～ **of the tide** Gezeitenwech-sel, *der;* (h) (character) **be of a mechanical/speculative ～:** technisch begabt sein/einen Hang zum Spekulativen haben; (i) (literary formation) Rundung, *die;* (j) (form of expres-sion) **an elegant ～ of speech/phrase** eine elegante Aus-drucksweise; (k) (service) **do sb. a good/bad ～:** jmdm. einen guten/schlechten Dienst erweisen; **one good ～ de-serves another** (prov.) hilfst du mir, so helf ich dir; (l) (coll.: fright) **give sb. quite a ～:** jmdm. einen gehörigen Schrecken einjagen (ugs.). **2** *v.t.* (a) (make revolve) drehen; ～ **the tap am Wasserhahn** drehen; ～ **the key in the lock** den Schlüssel im Schloss herumdrehen; (b) (reverse) umdrehen; wenden ‹*Pfannkuchen, Matratze, Auto, Heu, Teppich*›; umgraben ‹*Erde*›; ～ **sth. upside down** or **on its head** (lit. or fig.) etw. auf den Kopf stellen; ～ **sth. back to front** die Vorderseite einer Sache nach hinten drehen; ～ **sth. inside out** etw. nach außen stülpen *od.* drehen; ～ **the page** umblättern; (c) (give new direction to) drehen, wenden ‹*Kopf*›; **she could still ～ heads** die Leute drehten sich immer noch nach ihr um; ～ **a hose/gun on sb./sth.** einen Schlauch/ein Gewehr auf jmdn./etw.

richten; ~ **one's attention/mind to sth.** sich/seine Gedanken einer Sache (*Dat.*) zuwenden; ~ **one's thoughts to a subject** sich [in Gedanken] mit einem Thema beschäftigen; ~ **a car into a road** [mit einem Auto] in eine Straße einbiegen; ~ **the tide [of sth.]** [bei etw.] den Ausschlag geben; ~ **sb. from his purpose** jmdn. von seinem Vorhaben abbringen; **(d)** (send) ~ **sb. loose on sb./sth.** jmdn. auf jmdn./etw. loslassen; ~ **sb. from one's door/off one's land** jmdn. von seiner Tür/von seinem Land verjagen; ~ **a dog on sb.** einen Hund auf jmdn. hetzen; **(e)** (cause to become) verwandeln; **the cigarette smoke has ~ed the walls yellow** der Zigarettenrauch hat die Wände vergilben lassen; ~ **the lights low** das Licht dämpfen; ~ **a play/book into a film** ein Theaterstück/Buch verfilmen; **the thought ~ed him pale** der Gedanke ließ ihn erbleichen (geh.); **(f)** (make sour) sauer werden lassen ⟨*Milch*⟩; **(g)** ~ **sb.'s stomach** jmdm. den Magen umdrehen; **(h)** ~ **sb.'s head** (make conceited) jmdm. zu Kopf steigen; **(i)** (shape in lathe) drechseln ⟨*Holz*⟩; drehen ⟨*Metall*⟩; **(j)** drehen ⟨*Pirouette*⟩; schlagen ⟨*Rad*, *Purzelbaum*⟩; **(k)** (reach the age of) ~ 40 40 [Jahre alt] werden; **(l) it's just ~ed 12 o'clock/quarter past 4** es ist gerade 12 Uhr/Viertel nach vier vorbei. **3** *v.i.* **(a)** (revolve) sich drehen ⟨*Wasserhahn, Schlüssel:*⟩ sich drehen lassen; **the earth ~s on its axis** die Erde dreht sich um ihre Achse; **he couldn't get the key to ~:** er konnte den Schlüssel nicht drehen; **(b)** (reverse direction) ⟨*Person:*⟩ sich herumdrehen; ⟨*Auto:*⟩ wenden; **the car ~ed upside down** das Auto überschlug sich; ~ **back to front** sich von hinten nach vorne drehen; **(c)** (take new direction) sich wenden; (~ round) sich umdrehen; **his thoughts/attention ~ed to her** er wandte ihr seine Gedanken/Aufmerksamkeit zu; **left/right ~!** (Mil.) links/rechts um!; ~ **into a road/away from the river** in eine Straße einbiegen/vom Fluss abbiegen; ~ **to the left** nach links abbiegen/ ⟨*Schiff, Flugzeug:*⟩ abdrehen; ~ **up/down a street** in eine Straße einbiegen; ~ **towards home** den Heimweg einschlagen; **when the tide ~s** wenn die Ebbe/Flut kommt; **not know where** *or* **which way to ~** (fig.) keinen Ausweg [mehr] wissen; **my luck has ~ed** (fig.) mein Glück hat sich gewendet; **(d)** (become) werden; ~ **traitor/statesman/Muslim** zum Verräter/zum Staatsmann/Moslem werden; ~ **[in]to sth.** zu etw. werden; (be transformed) sich in etw. (*Akk.*) verwandeln; **her face ~ed green** sie wurde [ganz] grün im Gesicht; **(e)** (change colour) ⟨*Laub:*⟩ sich [ver]färben; **(f)** (become sour) ⟨*Milch:*⟩ sauer werden; **(g) my stomach ~s** mir dreht sich der Magen um (ugs.)

~ **a'bout 1** *v.i.* sich umdrehen; ⟨*Kompanie:*⟩ kehrtmachen; (fig.) eine Kehrtwendung machen. **2** *v.t.* wenden ⟨*Auto, Boot usw.*⟩

~ **against** *v.t.* **(a)** ~ **against sb.** sich gegen jmdn. wenden; ~ **sb. against sb.** jmdn. gegen jmdn. aufbringen; **(b) they ~ed his own arguments against him** sie verwendeten seine eigenen Argumente gegen ihn

~ **a'way** *v.i.* sich abwenden; ~ **away from sth.** (fig.) sich von etw. abwenden. **2** *v.t.* **(a)** (avert) abwenden; **(b)** (send away) wegschicken

~ **'back 1** *v.i.* **(a)** (retreat, lit. or fig.) umkehren; kehrtmachen (ugs.); **there can be no ~ing back** es gibt kein Zurück *od.* keinen Weg zurück; **(b)** (in book etc.) zurückgehen. **2** *v.t.* **(a)** (cause to retreat) zurückweisen; zurückschlagen ⟨*Feind*⟩; **(b)** (fold back) zurückschlagen ⟨*Bettdecke, Teppich*⟩; herunterschlagen ⟨*Kragen*⟩

~ **'down** *v.t.* **(a)** herunterschlagen ⟨*Kragen, Hutkrempe*⟩; umknicken ⟨*Buchseite*⟩; [nach unten] umschlagen ⟨*Laken*⟩; **(b)** (reduce level of) niedriger stellen ⟨*Heizung, Kochplatte*⟩; dämpfen ⟨*Licht*⟩; herunterdrehen ⟨*Gas, Heizung*⟩; leiser stellen ⟨*Ton, Radio, Fernseher*⟩; **(c)** (reject, refuse) ablehnen; abweisen ⟨*Bewerber, Kandidaten usw.*⟩

~ **'in 1** *v.t.* **(a)** (fold inwards) nach innen drehen; **(b)** (hand in) abgeben; **(c)** (surrender) [der Polizei] übergeben; **(d)** (register) hinlegen (ugs.) ⟨*Auftritt, Leistung*⟩; **(e)** (coll.: give up) aufstecken (ugs.) ⟨*Arbeit*⟩; hinschmeißen (salopp) ⟨*Arbeit, Dienstabzeichen*⟩. **2** *v.i.* **(a)** (incline inwards) nach innen gebogen sein; (narrow) sich verjüngen; **(b)** (enter) einbiegen; **(c)** (coll.: go to bed) in die Falle gehen (salopp)

~ **'off 1** *v.t.* **(a)** abschalten; abstellen ⟨*Wasser, Gas*⟩; zudrehen ⟨*Wasserhahn*⟩; **(b)** (coll.: cause to lose interest) anwidern. **2** *v.i.* abbiegen

~ **on 1** *v.t.* **(a)** /-'-/ anschalten; aufdrehen ⟨*Wasserhahn, Gas*⟩; **(b)** /-'-/ (coll.: cause to take interest) anmachen (ugs.); **(c)** /'--/ (be based on) ⟨*Argument:*⟩ beruhen auf (+ *Dat.*); ⟨*Gespräch, Diskussion*⟩ sich drehen um (ugs.); **(d)** /'--/ (become hostile towards) sich wenden gegen; (attack) angreifen. **2** /-'-/ *v.i.* einschalten

~ **'out 1** *v.t.* **(a)** (expel) hinauswerfen (ugs.); ~ **sb. out of a room/out into the street** jmdn. aus einem Zimmer weisen *od.* (ugs.) werfen/auf die Straße werfen *od.* setzen; **(b)** (switch off) ausschalten; abdrehen ⟨*Gas*⟩; **(c)** (incline outwards) nach außen drehen ⟨*Füße, Zehen*⟩; **(d)** (equip) ausstaffieren; **(e)** (produce) produzieren; hervorbringen ⟨*Fachkräfte, Spezialisten*⟩; (in great quantities) ausstoßen; **(f)** (Brit.) (empty) ausräumen; ausschütten ⟨*Büchse*⟩; leeren ⟨*Inhalt eines Koffers, einer Büchse*⟩; stürzen ⟨*Götterspeise, Pudding*⟩ **(on to** auf + *Akk.*); (clean) [gründlich] aufräumen; (get rid of) wegwerfen; ~ **out one's pockets** seine Taschen umdrehen. **2** *v.i.* **(a)** (prove to be) **sb./sth. ~s out to be sth.** jmd./etw. stellt sich als jmd./etw. heraus *od.* erweist sich als jmd./etw.; **it ~s out that …:** es stellt sich heraus, dass …; **as it ~ed out, as things ~ed out** wie sich [nachher] herausstellte; **(b)** (come to be eventually) **the day ~ed out wet** der Tag wurde regnerisch; **see how things ~ out** sehen, wie sich die Dinge entwickeln; ~ **out to be sth.** sich zu etw. entwickeln; **everything ~ed out well/all right in the end** alles endete gut; **(c)** (end) **the story ~ed out happily** die Geschichte ging gut aus; **(d)** (appear) ⟨*Menge, Fans usw.:*⟩ erscheinen; **he ~s out every Saturday to watch his team** er kommt jeden Samstag, um seine Mannschaft zu sehen

~ **'over 1** *v.t.* **(a)** (cause to fall over) umwerfen; **(b)** (expose the other side of) umdrehen; umgraben ⟨*Erde*⟩; **(c)** drehen ⟨*Motor*⟩; **(d)** ~ **sth. over [in one's mind]** sich (*Dat.*) etw. hin und her überlegen; **(e)** (hand over) übergeben (**to** *Dat.*) ⟨*Betrieb, Amt*⟩. **2** *v.i.* **(a)** (tip over) umkippen; ⟨*Boot:*⟩ kentern, umschlagen; ⟨*Auto, Flugzeug:*⟩ sich überschlagen; **(b)** (from one side to the other) sich umdrehen; ~ **over on to one's back** sich auf den Rücken drehen; **(c)** ⟨*Motor:*⟩ laufen; **(d) my stomach ~ed over at the thought of it** beim Gedanken daran drehte sich mir der Magen um (ugs.); **(e)** (~ a page) weiterblättern

~ **'round** *v.i.* **(a)** sich umdrehen; ~ **round and go back the same way** umkehren und denselben Weg zurückgehen; **(b)** (rotate) sich drehen; **(c)** ~ **round and do sth.** (fig.) plötzlich etw. tun. **2** *v.t.* **(a)** (unload and reload) be- und entladen ⟨*Frachtschiff*⟩; abfertigen ⟨*Passagierschiff*⟩; **(b)** ⇒ ~ **about 2;** **(c)** (reverse) umdrehen; auf den Kopf stellen (ugs.) ⟨*Theorie, Argument*⟩

~ **to** *v.t.* **(a)** (set about) ~ **to work** an die Arbeit gehen; **(b)** (go to for help etc.) ~ **to sb./sth.** sich an jmdn. wenden/ etw. zu Hilfe nehmen; ~ **to sb. for money** jmdn. um Geld bitten; ~ **to sb. for comfort/help/advice** bei jmdm. Trost/Hilfe/Rat suchen; ~ **to drugs** zu Drogen greifen; ~ **to drink/one's work** (seeking consolation) sich in den Alkohol/seine Arbeit flüchten; **(c)** (go on to consider next) ~ **to a subject/topic** sich einem Thema zuwenden; *see also* ~ **2 c**

~ **'up 1** *v.i.* **(a)** (make one's appearance) erscheinen; aufkreuzen (ugs.); **(b)** (happen) passieren; geschehen; **(c)** (present itself) auftauchen; ⟨*Gelegenheit:*⟩ sich bieten; **something is sure to ~ up** irgendetwas wird sich schon finden; **(d)** (be found) sich finden. **2** *v.t.* **(a)** (dig up) freilegen; (fig.) ans Licht bringen; **I ~ed up a lot of interesting information** ich habe viele interessante Informationen aufgetrieben; **(b)** hochschlagen ⟨*Kragen, Hutkrempe*⟩; **her nose is ~ed up** sie hat eine Stupsnase; *see also* **nose 1a; (c)** lauter stellen, (ugs.) aufdrehen ⟨*Ton, Fernseher, Radio*⟩; aufdrehen ⟨*Wasser, Heizung, Gas*⟩; heller machen ⟨*Licht*⟩; **(d)** ~ **it up!** (Brit. coll.) hör auf damit!

~ **upon** ⇒ ~ **on 1 c, d**

'turn-about *n.* (~ing about) Wende, *die;* (fig.) Kehrtwendung, *die;* **a welcome ~ in her fortunes** eine willkommene Wende ihres Geschicks

'turnaround n. (a) (change) [Kehrt]wende, die; (b) (processing, time needed) Bearbeitungszeit, die, (c) (of aircraft, ship, vehicle) Abfertigung, die

turned-up /'tɜːndʌp/ adj. ∼ nose Stupsnase, die (ugs.)

turning /'tɜːnɪŋ/ n. ▶ 1199⏐ (off road) Abzweigung, die; (fig.) Kreuzweg, der (geh.); **take the second** ∼ **to the left** die zweite Abzweigung nach links nehmen

turning: ∼ **circle** n. (Motor Veh.) Wendekreis, der; ∼ **point** n. Wendepunkt, der

turnip /'tɜːnɪp/ n. Kohlrübe, die; Steckrübe, die

turn: ∼**key** adj. schlüsselfertig; **a** ∼**key contract** ein Vertrag, der schlüsselfertige Lieferung garantiert; ∼**-off** n. (a) (turning) Abzweigung, die; (off motorway) Ausfahrt, die; (b) (coll.: repellent person or thing) **be a** ∼**-off** abstoßend sein; **be a** ∼**-off for sb.** jmdn. abstoßen; ∼**-on** n. (coll.) **be a** ∼**-on [for sb.]** [jmdn.] anmachen (ugs.); ∼**out** n. (a) (∼ing out for duty) Einsatz, der; Ausrücken, das; (for) (number voting) ∼**out [of voters]** Wahlbeteiligung, die; (c) (number assembled) Beteiligung, die **(for** an + Dat.); **there was a large** ∼**out of fans at the airport** eine große Zahl von Fans war zum Flughafen gekommen; ∼**over** n. (a) (tart etc.) **apple/apricot** ∼**over** Apfel-/Aprikosentasche, die; (b) (Commerc.) (of business, money) Umsatz, der; (of stock) Umschlag, der; (c) (of staff) Fluktuation, die; ∼**pike** n. (a) (Brit. Hist.: toll road) gebührenpflichtige Straße; (b) (Amer.: expressway) gebührenpflichtige Autobahn; ∼**stile** n. Drehkreuz, das; ∼**table** n. Plattenteller, der; ∼**-up** n. (a) (Brit. Fashion) Aufschlag, der; (b) (Brit. coll.: unexpected event) **a** ∼**-up [for the book]** eine Riesenüberraschung (ugs.)

turpentine /'tɜːpntaɪn/ n. (a) (resin) Terpentin, das; (b) **[oil of]** ∼: Terpentin, das (ugs.); Terpentinöl, das; attrib. ∼ **substitute** Terpentinersatz, der

turps /tɜːps/ n. (coll.) Terpentin, das (ugs.)

turquoise /'tɜːkwɔɪz/ 1 n. (a) (colour) Türkis, das; (b) (colour) Türkis, das. 2 adj. türkis[farben]

turquoise: ∼ **'blue** n. Türkisblau, das; ∼ **'green** n. Türkisgrün, das

turret /'tʌrɪt/ n. (a) (Archit.) Türmchen, das; (b) (of tank etc.) [Geschütz]turm, der

turtle /'tɜːtl/ n. (a) (marine reptile) Meeresschildkröte, die; (b) (Amer.: freshwater reptile) Wasserschildkröte, die; (c) **turn** ∼ ⟨Schiff, Boot:⟩ kentern

turtle: ∼**-dove** n. Turteltaube, die; ∼**neck** n. Stehbundkragen, der; attrib. ∼**neck pullover** Pullover mit Stehbund

turves ⇒ turf

tusk /tʌsk/ n. (of elephant) Stoßzahn, der; (of boar, walrus) Hauer, der

tussle /'tʌsl/ 1 n. Gerangel, das (ugs.). 2 v.i. sich balgen; (fig.) sich auseinander setzen **(about** wegen)

tussock /'tʌsək/ n. [Gras]büschel, das

tutor /'tjuːtə(r)/ 1 n. ▶ 887⏐ (a) **[private]** ∼: [Privat]-lehrer, der/-lehrerin, die; (for extra help) Nachhilfelehrer, der/-lehrerin, die; (b) (Brit. Univ.) ≈ Tutor, der. 2 v.t. ∼ **sb.** (teach privately) jmdm. Privatstunden geben; (give extra lessons to) jmdm. Nachhilfestunden geben

tutorial /tjuːˈtɔːrɪəl/ n. (Brit. Univ.) ≈ Kolloquium, das

tut[-tut] /tʌt('tʌt)/ int. na[, na]

tuxedo /tʌkˈsiːdəʊ/ n., pl. ∼**s** or ∼**es** (Amer.) Smoking, der

TV /tiːˈviː/ n. (a) (television) Fernsehen, das; attrib. Fernseh-; (b) (television set) Fernseher, der (ugs.)

twaddle /'twɒdl/ n. Gewäsch, das (ugs.)

twang /twæŋ/ 1 v.i. ⟨Bogen:⟩ mit vibrierendem Ton zurückschnellen. 2 v.t. zupfen ⟨Saite⟩; ∼ **a guitar** auf einer Gitarre [herum]klimpern (ugs.). 3 n. (tone of voice) **[nasal]** ∼: Näseln, das

tweak /twiːk/ 1 v.t. ∼ **sb. in the arm,** ∼ **sb.'s arm** jmdn. in den Arm kneifen; ∼ **sb.'s ear** jmdn. am Ohr ziehen. 2 n. Kneifen, das

twee /twiː/ adj., **tweer** /'twiːə(r)/, **tweest** /'twiːɪst/ (Brit. derog.) geziert ⟨Wesen, Art, Ausdrucksweise⟩; kitschig ⟨Stil, Bild⟩; niedlich, putzig ⟨Kleidung, Dorf⟩

tweed /twiːd/ n. (a) (fabric) Tweed, der; attrib. Tweed-; (b) in pl. (clothes) Tweedkleidung, die

tweet /twiːt/ 1 n. Zwitschern, das. 2 v.i. zwitschern

tweeter /'twiːtə(r)/ n. Hochtonlautsprecher, der

tweezers /'twiːzəz/ n. pl. **[pair of]** ∼: Pinzette, die

twelfth /twelfθ/ ▶ 738⏐, ▶ 956⏐ 1 adj. zwölft...; see also **eighth** 1. 2 n. (fraction) Zwölftel, das; see also **eighth** 2

twelve /twelv/ ▶ 630⏐, ▶ 706⏐, ▶ 956⏐ 1 adj. zwölf...; ∼ **noon** [zwölf Uhr] Mittag; ∼ **midnight** [zwölf Uhr] Mitternacht; see also **eight** 1. 2 n. Zwölf, die; see also **eight** 2 a, d

twentieth /'twentɪθ/ ▶ 738⏐, ▶ 956⏐ 1 adj. zwanzigst...; see also **eighth** 1. 2 n. (fraction) Zwanzigstel, das; see also **eighth** 2

twenty /'twentɪ/ ▶ 630⏐, ▶ 706⏐, ▶ 956⏐ 1 adj. zwanzig; see also **eight** 1. 2 n. Zwanzig, die; see also **eight** 2 a; **eighty** 2

twenty: ∼**-first** etc. adj. ▶ 956⏐ einundzwanzigst... usw.; see also **eighth** 1; ∼**-four-hour** ⇒ hour a; ∼**-one** etc. ▶ 956⏐ 1 adj. einundzwanzig usw.; see also **eight** 1; 2 n. Einundzwanzig usw., die; see also **eight** 2 a

twerp /twɜːp/ n. (coll.) (male) Blödmann, der (derb); (female) blöde Kuh (derb)

twice /twaɪs/ adv. (a) (two times) zweimal; **she didn't have to be asked** ∼! da brauchte man sie nicht zweimal zu fragen!; ∼ **a year** zweimal im Jahr; (b) (doubly) doppelt; ∼ **as strong** etc. doppelt so stark usw.; **he's** ∼ **her age** er ist doppelt so alt wie sie; see also **think** 2 a

twiddle /'twɪdl/ 1 v.t. herumdrehen an (+ Dat.) (ugs.); ∼ **one's thumbs** (lit. or fig.) Däumchen drehen (ugs.). 2 v.i. ∼ **with sth.** mit etw. spielen; an etw. (Dat.) herumfummeln (ugs.)

twig[1] /twɪg/ n. Zweig, der

twig[2] (coll.) 1 v.t. **-gg-:** (a) (understand) kapieren (ugs.); (b) (notice) mitkriegen (ugs.). 2 v.i. **-gg-:** (a) (understand) es kapieren (ugs.); (b) (notice) es mitkriegen (ugs.)

twilight /'twaɪlaɪt/ n. (a) (evening light) Dämmerlicht, das; Zwielicht, das; (b) (period of half-light) Dämmerung, die

twin /twɪn/ 1 attrib. adj. (a) Zwillings-; ∼ **brother/sister** Zwillingsbruder, der/-schwester, die; (b) (forming a pair) Doppel-; doppelt ⟨Problem, Verantwortung⟩; (c) (Bot.) paarig; (d) Doppel⟨vergaser, -propeller, -schraube usw.⟩. 2 n. (a) (Zwilling, der; **his** ∼: sein Zwillingsbruder/seine Zwillingsschwester; (b) (exact counterpart) Gegenstück, das. 3 v.t., **-nn-** eng verbinden; **Bottrop is** ∼**ned with Black-pool** Bottrop und Blackpool sind Partnerstädte

twin: ∼ **'bed** n. eines von zwei [gleichen] Einzelbetten; ∼ **beds** zwei Einzelbetten; ∼**-bedded** /'twɪnbedɪd/ adj. **a** ∼**-bedded room** ein Zweibettzimmer

twine /twaɪn/ 1 n. Bindfaden, der; (thicker) Kordel, die; (for nets) Garn, das. 2 v.t. (a) (form by twisting strands together) [zusammen]drehen; (b) (form by interlacing) winden (geh.) ⟨Kranz, Girlande⟩. 3 v.i. sich winden **(about, around** um)

twin-engined /'twɪnendʒɪnd/ adj. zweimotorig

twinge /twɪndʒ/ n. Stechen, das; **a** ∼ **of toothache/ pain** ein stechender Zahnschmerz/ein stechender Schmerz; ∼**[s] of remorse/conscience** (fig.) Gewissensbisse

twinkle /'twɪŋkl/ 1 v.i. ⟨Sterne, Augen:⟩ funkeln, blitzen **(with** vor + Dat.). 2 n. (a) **in a** ∼: im Handumdrehen; (b) (sparkle of the eyes) Funkeln, das; '...', **she said with a** ∼ **in her eye** „....", sagte sie augenzwinkernd; **you were just a** ∼ **in your father's eye** then zu der Zeit wussten deine Eltern noch nicht, dass es dich geben würde; **the project is still only a** ∼ **in his eye** das Projekt ist bis jetzt nur eine ganz vage Idee von ihm

twinkling /'twɪŋklɪŋ/ n. **in a** ∼, **in the** ∼ **of an eye** im Handumdrehen

twin: ∼**set** n. (Brit.) Twinset, das; ∼ **town** n. (Brit.) Partnerstadt, die; ∼**-tub** n. halbautomatische Waschmaschine (mit separater Schleuder)

twirl /twɜːl/ 1 v.t. (a) (spin) [schnell] drehen; (b) (twiddle) zwirbeln ⟨Schnurrbart⟩; drehen ⟨Haar⟩. 2 v.i. wirbeln **(around** über + Akk.); ∼ **sb.** ∼**s around** jmd. wirbelt herum. 3 n. [Herum]wirbeln, das

twist /twɪst/ **1** v.t. **(a)** (distort) verdrehen ‹ *Worte, Bedeutung* ›; ~ **out of shape** verbiegen; ~ **one's ankle** sich (*Dat.*) den Knöchel verrenken; **her face was** ~**ed with pain** ihr Gesicht war schmerzverzerrt; ~ **sb.'s arm** jmdm. den Arm umdrehen; (fig.) jmdm. [die] Daumenschrauben anlegen (scherzh.); **(b)** (wind about one another) flechten ‹ *Blumen, Haare* › (**into** zu); **(c)** (rotate) drehen; (back and forth) hin und her drehen; **(d)** (interweave) verweben; **(e)** (give spiral form to) drehen (**into** zu). **2** v.i. **(a)** sich winden; ~ **and turn** sich drehen und winden; ~ **around sth.** sich um etw. winden; **(b)** (take ~ed position) sich winden. **3** n. **(a)** (thread etc.) Zwirn, *der;* **(b)** ~ **of lemon/orange** Zitronen-/Orangenscheibe, *die;* **(c)** (~ing) Drehung, *die;* **(d)** (unexpected occurrence) überraschende Wendung; ~ **of fate** Laune des Schicksals; **(e)** (peculiar tendency) **give a** ~ **to sth.** etw. verdrehen; **(f) round the** ~: = **round the bend** ⇒ **bend 1 a**
~ **'off 1** v.t. abdrehen. **2** v.i. **the cap** ~**s off** der Verschluss lässt sich abdrehen

twisted /ˈtwɪstɪd/ adj. verbogen; (fig.) verdreht (ugs. abwertend) ‹ *Geist* ›; verquer ‹ *Humor* ›

twit /twɪt/ n. (Brit. coll.) Trottel, *der* (ugs.)

twitch /twɪtʃ/ **1** v.t. **(a)** zupfen; **(b)** zucken mit ‹ *Nase, Schwanz* ›; wackeln mit ‹ *Ohr* ›. **2** v.i. **(a)** (pull sharply) zupfen (**at** an + *Dat.*); **(b)** ‹ *Mund, Lippen, Hand, Nase:* › zucken. **3** n. Zucken, *das*

twitter /ˈtwɪtə(r)/ **1** n. (chirping) Zwitschern, *das;* Gezwitscher, *das.* **2** v.i. zwitschern; ‹ *Person:* › schnattern (ugs.)

two /tu:/ ► 630 ‖, ► 956 ‖ **1** adj. zwei; **a box/shirt or** ~: ein, zwei Schachteln/Hemden; ein oder zwei Schachteln/Hemden; see also **eight 1. 2** n. Zwei, *die;* **the** ~: die beiden; die zwei; **just the** ~ **of us** nur wir zwei od. beiden; **put** ~ **and** ~ **together** (fig.) zwei und zwei zusammenzählen; **cut/break in** ~: zweiteilen/entzweibrechen; ~ **and** ~, ~ **by** ~ (~ **at a time**) [zu] zwei und zwei; zu zweien; **that makes** ~ **of us** (coll.) mir gehts/gings genauso (ugs.); see also **eight 2 a, c, d; game¹ 1 a; penny b**

two: ~**-bit** adj. (Amer.: of poor quality) mies (ugs.); ~**-dimensional** /tuːdɪˈmenʃənl/ adj. zweidimensional; ~**-door** attrib. adj. zweitürig ‹ *Auto* ›; ~**-edged** adj. (lit. or fig.) zweischneidig; ~**-faced** /ˈtuːfeɪst/ adj. (fig.) falsch (abwertend)

twofold /ˈtuːfəʊld/ adj. **(a)** zweifach; **be** ~: zweifacher Art od. Natur sein; **(b)** (double) **a** ~ **increase** ein Anstieg auf das Doppelte

two: ~**-'handed** adj. **(a)** (having ~ hands) zweihändig; **(b)** (requiring both hands) beidhändig; ~**-party system** n. Zweiparteiensystem, *das;* ~**pence** /ˈtʌpəns/ n. (Brit.) zwei Pence; ~**-piece 1** n. Zweiteiler, *der;* **2** adj. zweiteilig; ~**-pin** ⇒ **pin 1 c;** ~**-ply** adj. zweilagig ‹ *Holz* ›; zweifädig ‹ *Wolle, Zwirn* ›; ~**-seater 1** /-'---/ n. Zweisitzer, *der;* **2** /'---/ attrib. adj. zweisitzig

twosome /ˈtuːsəm/ n. **(a)** Paar, *das;* **(b)** (Golf) Zweier, *der*

two: ~**-storey** adj. zweigeschossig; ~**-stroke** adj. (Mech. Engin.) Zweitakt‹ *motor, -verfahren* ›; ~**-time** v.t. (coll.) ~**-time sb.** (be unfaithful) jmdm. fremdgehen; ~**tone** adj. **(a)** (in colour) zweifarbig; **(b)** (in sound) Zweiklang-; ~**-up-**~**-down** n. kleines [Reihen]haus; ~**way** adj. **(a)** (in both directions) zweibahnig (Verkehrsw.); '~**way traffic ahead'** „Achtung Gegenverkehr"; **(b)** ~**way mirror** Einwegspiegel, *der;* ~**-wheeler** /ˈtuː-wiːlə(r)/ n. Zweirad, *das*

tycoon /taɪˈkuːn/ n. Magnat, *der;* Tycoon, *der*

type /taɪp/ **1** n. **(a)** Art, *die;* (person) Typ, *der;* **what** ~ **of car ...?** was für ein Auto ...?; **he's not the** ~ **to let people down** er ist nicht der Typ, der andere im Stich lässt; **he is a different** ~ **of person** er ist eine andere Art Mensch od. ein anderer Typ; **books of this** ~: derartige Bücher; **(b)** (coll.: character) Type, *die* (ugs.); **(c)** (Printing) Drucktype, *die;* **be in small/italic** ~: klein gedruckt/kursiv gedruckt sein. **2** v.t. [mit der Maschine] schreiben; tippen (ugs.); ~**d letter** maschinegeschriebener Brief. **3** v.i. maschineschreiben
~ **'in** v.t. eintippen (ugs.)
~ **'out** v.t. [mit der Schreibmaschine] abschreiben; abtippen (ugs.)

-type /taɪp/ in comb. -artig

type: ~**cast** v.t. [auf eine bestimmte Rolle] festlegen; ~**face** n. Schriftbild, *das;* ~**script** n. maschine[n]geschriebene Fassung; Typoscript, *das;* ~**set** v.t. (Printing) setzen; ~**setter** n. [Schrift]setzer, *der/*[Schrift]setzerin, *die*

'typewriter n. Schreibmaschine, *die;* ~ **ribbon** Farbband, *das*

'typewritten adj. maschine[n]geschrieben; mit der [Schreib]maschine geschrieben

typhoid /ˈtaɪfɔɪd/ n. ► 865 ‖ (Med.) ~ **[fever]** Typhus, *der*

typhoon /taɪˈfuːn/ n. Taifun, *der*

typhus /ˈtaɪfəs/ n. ► 865 ‖ (Med.) Fleckfieber, *das*

typical /ˈtɪpɪkl/ adj. typisch (**of** für); **that's just** ~! [das ist mal wieder] typisch! (ugs.)

typically /ˈtɪpɪklɪ/ adv. typischerweise; ~ **she turned up late** wie üblich kam sie zu spät

typify /ˈtɪpɪfaɪ/ v.t. **(a)** (represent) [symbolhaft] darstellen; **(b)** (be an example of) ~ **sth.** als typisches Beispiel für etw. dienen

typing /ˈtaɪpɪŋ/ n. Maschineschreiben, *das;* **his** ~ **is excellent** er kann sehr gut Maschine schreiben

typing: ~ **error** n. Tippfehler, *der* (ugs.); ~ **pool** n. Schreibzentrale, *die*

typist /ˈtaɪpɪst/ n. ► 887 ‖ Schreibkraft, *die;* **shorthand** ~: Stenotypist, *der/*-typistin, *die*

typographic /taɪpəˈgræfɪk/, **typographical** /taɪpə-ˈgræfɪkl/ adjs. typographisch; ~ **error** Setzfehler, *der*

typography /taɪˈpɒɡrəfɪ/ n. Typographie, *die*

tyrannical /tɪˈrænɪkl, taɪˈrænɪkl/ adj. tyrannisch

tyrannize (tyrannise) /ˈtɪrənaɪz/ v.t. ‹ *Chef, Vater, Ehemann:* › tyrannisieren; ‹ *Herrscher:* › als Tyrann herrschen über (+ *Akk.*)

tyranny /ˈtɪrənɪ/ n. Tyrannei, *die*

tyrant /ˈtaɪrənt/ n. (lit. or fig.) Tyrann, *der*

tyre /ˈtaɪə(r)/ n. Reifen, *der*

tyre: ~ **gauge** n. Reifendruckprüfer, *der;* ~ **lever** n. Reifenheber, *der;* ~ **pressure** n. Reifendruck, *der*

Tyrol /tɪˈrəʊl/ pr. n. Tirol (*das*)

Tyrolean /tɪrəˈliːən/ adj. Tiroler

tzar ⇒ **tsar**

Uu

U, u /juː/ n., pl. **Us** or **U's** U, u, *das*

'U-bend n. U-Rohr, *das;* Knie, *das* (ugs.)

ubiquitous /juːˈbɪkwɪtəs/ adj. allgegenwärtig

'U-boat n. (Hist.) [deutsches] U-Boot

udder /ˈʌdə(r)/ n. Euter, *das*

UFO /ˈjuːfəʊ/ n., pl. ~**s** Ufo, *das*

Uganda /juːˈɡændə/ pr. n. Uganda (*das*)

Ugandan /juːˈɡændən/ ► 947 ‖ **1** adj. ugandisch; **sb. is** ~: jmd. ist Ugander/Uganderin. **2** n. Ugander, *der/*Uganderin, *die*

ugh /ʌh, ʊh, ɜːh/ int. bah

ugliness /ˈʌɡlɪnɪs/ n., no pl. Hässlichkeit, *die*

ugly /ˈʌɡlɪ/ adj. **(a)** (in appearance, morally) hässlich; ~ **duckling** (fig.) hässliches Entlein (ugs. scherzh.); **as** ~ **as sin** (coll.) potthässlich (ugs.); hässlich wie die Nacht; **(b)** (nasty) übel ‹ *Wunde, Laune, Szene usw.* ›; **have an** ~ **temper** übellaunig sein

UHF abbr. **ultra-high frequency** UHF

UHT abbr. **ultra-high temperature** ultrahocherhitzt; **UHT milk** H-Milch, *die*

UK *abbr.* **United Kingdom**
Ukraine /juːˈkreɪn/ *pr. n.* Ukraine, *die*
Ukranian /juːˈkreɪnɪən/ ▶ 897 , ▶ 947 **1** *adj.* ukrainisch; **sb. is** ∼: jmd. ist Ukrainer/Ukrainerin. **2** *n.* **(a)** (person) Ukrainer, *der*/Ukrainerin, *die;* **(b)** (language) Ukrainisch, *das; see also* **English 2 a**
ulcer /ˈʌlsə(r)/ *n.* ▶ 865 Geschwür, *das;* **mouth** ∼[s] Aphthe, *die* (Med.)
Ulster /ˈʌlstə(r)/ *pr. n.* Ulster (*das*)
ulterior /ʌlˈtɪərɪə(r)/ *adj.* hintergründig; geheim; ∼ **motive/thought** Hintergedanke, *der*
ultimate /ˈʌltɪmət/ **1** *attrib. adj.* **(a)** (final) letzt...; (eventual) endgültig ⟨*Sieg*⟩; letztendlich ⟨*Rettung*⟩; größt... ⟨*Opfer*⟩; ∼ **result/goal/decision** Endergebnis, *das*/Endziel, *das*/endgültige Entscheidung; **the** ∼ **deterrent** das äußerste Abschreckungsmittel; **(b)** (fundamental) tiefst... ⟨*Grundlage, Wahrheit*⟩; **the** ∼ **origin** der eigentliche Ursprung. **2** *n.* **the** ∼ (maximum) das absolute Maximum; (minimum) das absolute Minimum; **the** ∼ **in comfort/luxury/style/fashion** der Gipfel an Bequemlichkeit/Luxus/das Exzellenteste an Stil/in der Mode
ultimately /ˈʌltɪmətlɪ/ *adv.* **(a)** (in the end) schließlich; **(b)** (in the last analysis) letzten Endes; (basically) im Grunde [genommen]
ultimatum /ʌltɪˈmeɪtəm/ *n., pl.* ∼**s** *or* **ultimata** /ʌltɪˈmeɪtə/ Ultimatum, *das;* **give sb. an** ∼: jmdm. ein Ultimatum stellen
ultra- /ˈʌltrə/ *in comb.* ultra⟨*konservativ, -modern*⟩; hyper⟨*modern, -modisch*⟩
ultraˈsonic *adj.* Ultraschall-
ˈultrasound *n., no pl.* Ultraschall, *der*
ultraˈviolet *adj.* (Phys.) ultraviolett ⟨*Strahlen, Licht*⟩; UV- ⟨*Lampe, Filter*⟩
umbilical cord /ʌmˈbɪlɪkl kɔːd/ *n.* ▶ 672 Nabelschnur, *die*
umbrage /ˈʌmbrɪdʒ/ *n., no pl., no indef. art.* **take** ∼ **[at** *or* **over sth.]** [an etw. (+ *Dat.*)] Anstoß nehmen
umbrella /ʌmˈbrelə/ *n.* **(a)** [Regen]schirm, *der;* **put up an** ∼: einen Schirm aufspannen; **(b)** (fig.: protection) Schutz, *der;* **(c)** *attrib.* **an** ∼ **organization** eine Dachorganisation
umlaut /ˈumlaʊt/ *n.* **(a)** (vowel change) Umlaut, *der;* **(b)** (mark) Umlautzeichen, *das*
umpire /ˈʌmpaɪə(r)/ *n.* ▶ 887 Schiedsrichter, *der*/-richterin, *die*
umpteen /ʌmpˈtiːn/ *adj.* (coll.) zig (ugs.); x (ugs.)
umpteenth /ʌmpˈtiːnθ/ *adj.* (coll.) zigst... (ugs.); **for the** ∼ **time** zum zigsten *or* x-sten Mal (ugs.)
UN *abbr.* **United Nations** UN[O], *die*
unabashed /ʌnəˈbæʃt/ *adj.* ungeniert; (without shame) schamlos; (undaunted) unerschrocken ⟨*Kämpfer*⟩
unabated /ʌnəˈbeɪtɪd/ *adj.* unvermindert
unable /ʌnˈeɪbl/ *pred. adj.* **be** ∼ **to do sth.** nicht in der Lage sein, etw. zu tun; etw. nicht tun können; **he wanted to attend but was** ∼ **to** er wollte kommen, aber er war dazu nicht in der Lage
unabridged /ʌnəˈbrɪdʒd/ *adj.* ungekürzt
unacceptable /ʌnəkˈseptəbl/ *adj.* unannehmbar; **[be] not** ∼: durchaus akzeptabel [sein]
unaccompanied /ʌnəˈkʌmpənɪd/ *adj.* ohne Begleitung ⟨*reisen, singen*⟩; unbegleitet ⟨*Gepäck, Chor*⟩; (on aircraft etc.) ∼ **minor** alleinreisendes Kind
unaccountable /ʌnəˈkaʊntəbl/ *adj.* unerklärlich
unaccountably /ʌnəˈkaʊntəblɪ/ *adv.* unerklärlicherweise; *with adj.* unerklärlich
unaccounted /ʌnəˈkaʊntɪd/ *adj.* ∼ **for** unauffindbar; **several passengers are still** ∼ **for** einige Passagiere werden noch vermisst
unaccustomed /ʌnəˈkʌstəmd/ *adj.* ungewohnt; **be** ∼ **to sth.** etw. (*Akk.*) nicht gewöhnt sein
unacquainted /ʌnəˈkweɪntɪd/ *adj.* **be [completely]** ∼ **with sth.** mit etw. [überhaupt] nicht vertraut sein
unadulterated /ʌnəˈdʌltəreɪtɪd/ *adj.* **(a)** (pure) unverfälscht; rein ⟨*Wasser, Wein*⟩; **(b)** (utter) völlig
unadventurous /ʌnədˈventʃərəs/ *adj.* bieder ⟨*Person*⟩; ereignislos ⟨*Leben*⟩; einfallslos ⟨*Inszenierung, Buch, usw.*⟩

unaffected /ʌnəˈfektɪd/ *adj.* **(a)** (not affected) unberührt; (Med.) nicht angegriffen ⟨*Organ*⟩; **the area was** ∼ **by the strike** die Gegend war vom Streik nicht betroffen; **(b)** (natural) natürlich; ungekünstelt
unafraid /ʌnəˈfreɪd/ *adj.* **be** ∼ **[of sb./sth.]** keine Angst [vor jmdm./etw.] haben
unaided /ʌnˈeɪdɪd/ *adj.* ohne fremde Hilfe; **walk** ∼: ohne Hilfe gehen
unalterable /ʌnˈɔːltərəbl, ʌnˈɒltərəbl/ *adj.* unabänderlich ⟨*Gesetz, Schicksal*⟩; unverrückbar ⟨*Entschluss*⟩
unaltered /ʌnˈɔːltəd, ʌnˈɒltəd/ *adj.* unverändert
unambiguous /ʌnæmˈbɪɡjʊəs/ *adj.* unzweideutig
unambitious /ʌnæmˈbɪʃəs/ *adj.* ⟨*Person*⟩ ohne Ehrgeiz; **be** ∼: keinen Ehrgeiz haben
un-American /ʌnəˈmerɪkn/ *adj.* **(a)** unamerikanisch; **(b)** (anti-American) antiamerikanisch; ∼ **activities** unamerikanische Umtriebe
unanimity /juːnəˈnɪmɪtɪ/ *n., no pl.* Einmütigkeit, *die*
unanimous /juːˈnænɪməs/ *adj.* einstimmig; **be** ∼ **in doing sth.** etw. einmütig tun; **be** ∼ **in rejecting** *or* **in their** *etc.* **rejection of sth.** etw. einmütig ablehnen
unanimously /juːˈnænɪməslɪ/ *adv.* einstimmig
unanswerable /ʌnˈɑːnsərəbl/ *adj.* unbeantwortbar ⟨*Frage*⟩; unwiderlegbar ⟨*Argument*⟩
unanswered /ʌnˈɑːnsəd/ *adj.* unbeantwortet; **go** ∼, **be left** ∼: unbeantwortet bleiben
unappetizing /ʌnˈæpɪtaɪzɪŋ/ *adj.* unappetitlich
unapproachable /ʌnəˈprəʊtʃəbl/ *adj.* unzugänglich
unarmed /ʌnˈɑːmd/ *adj.* unbewaffnet; ∼ **combat** Kampf ohne Waffen
unashamed /ʌnəˈʃeɪmd/ *adj.* schamlos; (not embarrassed) ungeniert; unverhohlen ⟨*Individualist*⟩
unasked /ʌnˈɑːskt/ *adj.* **(a)** (uninvited) ungebeten; **(b)** (not asked for) ∼ **[for]** ungefragt
unassailable /ʌnəˈseɪləbl/ *adj.* **(a)** (not open to assault) uneinnehmbar; **an** ∼ **lead** eine nicht aufzuholender Vorsprung; **(b)** (irrefutable) unwiderlegbar
unassisted /ʌnəˈsɪstɪd/ *adj.* ⇒ **unaided**
unassuming /ʌnəˈsjuːmɪŋ/ *adj.* bescheiden; unprätentiös (geh.)
unattached /ʌnəˈtætʃt/ *adj.* **(a)** (not fixed) nicht befestigt; **(b)** (without a partner) ungebunden
unattended /ʌnəˈtendɪd/ *adj.* **(a)** ∼ **to** (not dealt with) unerledigt, unbearbeitet ⟨*Post, Angelegenheit*⟩; nicht bedient ⟨*Kunde*⟩; nicht behandelt ⟨*Patient, Wunde*⟩; **leave a customer/patient** ∼ **to** einen Kunden nicht bedienen/einen Patienten nicht behandeln; **(b)** (not supervised) unbewacht ⟨*Parkplatz, Gepäck*⟩
unattractive /ʌnəˈtræktɪv/ *adj.* unattraktiv; unschön ⟨*Ort, Merkmal*⟩; wenig verlockend ⟨*Angebot, Vorschlag*⟩
unauthorized /ʌnˈɔːθəraɪzd/ *adj.* unbefugt; nicht autorisiert ⟨*Biographie*⟩; nicht genehmigt ⟨*Demonstration*⟩; **no entry for** ∼ **persons** Zutritt für Unbefugte verboten
unavailable /ʌnəˈveɪləbl/ *adj.* nicht erhältlich ⟨*Ware*⟩; **be** ∼ **for comment** zu einer Stellungnahme nicht zur Verfügung stehen
unavoidable /ʌnəˈvɔɪdəbl/ *adj.* unvermeidlich; ∼ **delays** unvermeidbare Verzögerungen
unavoidably /ʌnəˈvɔɪdəblɪ/ *adv.* **we were** ∼ **delayed** unsere Verspätung ließ sich nicht vermeiden; **he has been** ∼ **detained** er konnte nicht verhindern, dass er aufgehalten wurde
unaware /ʌnəˈweə(r)/ *adj.* **be** ∼ **of sth.** sich (*Dat.*) einer Sache (*Gen.*) nicht bewusst sein
unawares /ʌnəˈweəz/ *adv.* unerwartet; **come upon sb./catch sb.** ∼: jmdn. überraschen
unbalanced /ʌnˈbælənst/ *adj.* **(a)** unausgewogen; **(b)** (mentally ∼) unausgeglichen
unbearable /ʌnˈbeərəbl/ *adj.*, **unbearably** /ʌnˈbeərəblɪ/ *adv.* unerträglich
unbeatable /ʌnˈbiːtəbl/ *adj.* unschlagbar (ugs.)
unbeaten /ʌnˈbiːtn/ *adj.* **(a)** (not defeated) ungeschlagen; **they lost their** ∼ **record** ihre Siegesserie endete; **(b)**

(not surpassed) unerreicht; **this record is still ~:** dieser Rekord ist immer noch ungebrochen

unbecoming /ʌnbɪˈkʌmɪŋ/ *adj.* (improper) unschicklich (geh.)

unbelievable /ʌnbɪˈliːvəbl/ *adj.* (a) (hardly believable) unglaublich; **(b)** (tremendous) unwahrscheinlich ⟨*Hunger, Durst*⟩

unbelievably /ʌnbɪˈliːvəblɪ/ *adv. as intensifier* unglaublich

unbeliever /ʌnbɪˈliːvə(r)/ *n.* Ungläubige, *der/die*

unbiased, unbiassed /ʌnˈbaɪəst/ *adj.* unvoreingenommen

unblemished /ʌnˈblemɪʃt/ *adj.* makellos ⟨*Haut, Lack, Ruf*⟩; unbefleckt (geh.) ⟨*Ehre*⟩

unblock /ʌnˈblɒk/ *v.t.* frei machen *od.* bekommen; **remain ~ed** frei bleiben

unbolt /ʌnˈbəʊlt/ *v.t.* aufriegeln ⟨*Tür, Tor*⟩

unborn /ʌnˈbɔːn, *attrib.* ˈʌnbɔːn/ *adj.* ungeboren

unbound /ʌnˈbaʊnd/ *adj.* (a) (not tied) offen ⟨*Haar*⟩; **(b)** ungebunden ⟨*Buch*⟩

unbounded /ʌnˈbaʊndɪd/ *adj.* (a) (unchecked) uneingeschränkt ⟨*Freiheit*⟩; unkontrolliert ⟨*Gefühl*⟩; **(b)** (unlimited) grenzenlos

unbreakable /ʌnˈbreɪkəbl/ *adj.* unzerbrechlich

un-British /ʌnˈbrɪtɪʃ/ *adj.* unbritisch

unbroken /ʌnˈbrəʊkn/ *adj.* (a) (undamaged) heil; unbeschädigt; **(b)** (not interrupted) ununterbrochen; **~ sleep/peace/silence** ungestörter Schlaf/Friede/durch nichts unterbrochene Stille

unbuckle /ʌnˈbʌkl/ *v.t.* aufschnallen

unburden /ʌnˈbɜːdn/ *v.t.* (literary) befreien ⟨*Gewissen*⟩; **~ oneself/one's heart [to sb.]** [jmdm.] sein Herz ausschütten; **~ oneself of sth.** sich von etw. befreien

unbusinesslike /ʌnˈbɪznɪslaɪk/ *adj.* **he is ~, he has an ~ approach** er geht nicht wie ein Geschäftsmann an die Dinge heran

unbutton /ʌnˈbʌtn/ *v.t.* aufknöpfen

unbuttoned /ʌnˈbʌtnd/ *adj.* (lit. or fig.) aufgeknöpft; offen

uncalled-for /ʌnˈkɔːldfɔː(r)/ *adj.* unangebracht

uncanny /ʌnˈkænɪ/ *adj.* (a) (seemingly supernatural) unheimlich; **(b)** (mysterious) verblüffend

uncap /ʌnˈkæp/ *v.t.*, **-pp-** öffnen ⟨*Flasche*⟩

uncared-for /ʌnˈkeədfɔː(r)/ *adj.* vernachlässigt

uncaring /ʌnˈkeərɪŋ/ *adj.* gleichgültig

uncarpeted /ʌnˈkɑːpɪtɪd/ *adj.* teppichlos

unceasing /ʌnˈsiːsɪŋ/ *adj.* unaufhörlich

uncensored /ʌnˈsensəd/ *adj.* unzensiert

unceremonious /ʌnserɪˈməʊnɪəs/ *adj.* (a) (informal) formlos; **(b)** (abrupt) brüsk

unceremoniously /ʌnserɪˈməʊnɪəslɪ/ *adv.* ohne Umschweife

uncertain /ʌnˈsɜːtn/ *adj.* (a) (not sure) **be ~ [whether ...]** sich (*Dat.*) nicht sicher sein[, ob ...]; **(b)** (not clear) ungewiss ⟨*Ergebnis, Zukunft, Schicksal*⟩; **of ~ age/origin** unbestimmten Alters/unbestimmter Herkunft; **it is still ~ whether ...:** es ist noch ungewiss, ob ...; **it is ~ who was the inventor** der Erfinder ist nicht [genau] bekannt; **(c)** (unsteady) unsicher ⟨*Schritte*⟩; **(d)** (changeable) unbeständig ⟨*Charakter, Wetter*⟩; **(e)** (ambiguous) vage; **in no ~ terms** ganz eindeutig

uncertainly /ʌnˈsɜːtnlɪ/ *adv.* (a) (without definite aim) ziellos; **(b)** (without confidence) unsicher

uncertainty /ʌnˈsɜːtntɪ/ *n.* (a) *no pl.* (doubtfulness) Ungewissheit, *die;* **there is some ~ about it** es ist etwas ungewiss; **(b)** (doubtful point) Unklarheit, *die;* **(c)** *no pl.* (hesitation) Unsicherheit, *die*

unchanged /ʌnˈtʃeɪndʒd/ *adj.* unverändert

unchanging /ʌnˈtʃeɪndʒɪŋ/ *adj.* unveränderlich

uncharacteristic /ʌnkærɪktəˈrɪstɪk/ *adj.* uncharakteristisch (**of** für); ungewohnt ⟨*Grobheit, Schärfe*⟩

uncharitable /ʌnˈtʃærɪtəbl/ *adj.*, **uncharitably** /ʌnˈtʃærɪtəblɪ/ *adv.* lieblos

unchecked /ʌnˈtʃekt/ *adj.* (a) (not examined) ungeprüft; **(b)** (unrestrained) ungehindert; nicht eingedämmt ⟨*Epidemie, Inflation*⟩; **sth. goes ~:** gegen etw. wird nichts getan

uncivil /ʌnˈsɪvɪl, ʌnˈsɪvl/ *adj.* unhöflich

uncivilized /ʌnˈsɪvɪlaɪzd/ *adj.* unzivilisiert

unclaimed /ʌnˈkleɪmd/ *adj.* herrenlos; nicht abgeholt ⟨*Brief, Preis*⟩; **the money is still ~:** bis jetzt hat niemand Anspruch auf das Geld erhoben

unclassified /ʌnˈklæsɪfaɪd/ *adj.* nicht klassifiziert; (not subject to security classification) nicht geheim

uncle /ˈʌŋkl/ *n.* Onkel, *der*

unclean /ʌnˈkliːn/ *adj.* unrein

unclothed /ʌnˈkləʊðd/ *adj.* unbekleidet

uncluttered /ʌnˈklʌtəd/ *adj.* ordentlich

uncoil /ʌnˈkɔɪl/ **1** *v.t.* abwickeln. **2** *v. refl.* sich abwickeln; ⟨*Schlange:*⟩ sich strecken

uncomfortable /ʌnˈkʌmfətəbl/ *adj.* (a) (causing physical discomfort) unbequem; **(b)** (feeling discomfort) **be ~:** sich unbehaglich fühlen; **(c)** (uneasy, disconcerting) unangenehm; peinlich ⟨*Stille*⟩; **his gaze made me ~:** sein Blick war mir unangenehm

uncomfortably /ʌnˈkʌmfətəblɪ/ *adv.* (a) unbequem; **(b)** (uneasily) unbehaglich; **be** or **feel ~ aware of sth.** sich (*Dat.*) einer Sache (*Gen.*) peinlich bewusst sein

uncommitted /ʌnkəˈmɪtɪd/ *adj.* unbeteiligt

uncommon /ʌnˈkɒmən/ *adj.* ungewöhnlich; **it is not ~ for him to be found there** es ist [ganz und gar] nicht ungewöhnlich, dass man ihn dort findet

uncommunicative /ʌnkəˈmjuːnɪkətɪv/ *adj.* verschlossen

uncompetitive /ʌnkəmˈpetɪtɪv/ *adj.* wettbewerbsunfähig; **prices were ~:** die Preise waren nicht wettbewerbs- *od.* konkurrenzfähig; **this makes the salaries even more ~:** dadurch nimmt die Wettbewerbsfähigkeit der Gehälter noch weiter ab

uncomplaining /ʌnkəmˈpleɪnɪŋ/ *adj.*, **uncomplainingly** /ʌnkəmˈpleɪnɪŋlɪ/ *adv.* klaglos

uncompleted /ʌnkəmˈpliːtɪd/ *adj.* unvollendet

uncomplicated /ʌnˈkɒmplɪkeɪtɪd/ *adj.* unkompliziert

uncomplimentary /ʌnkɒmplɪˈmentərɪ/ *adj.* wenig schmeichelhaft

uncomprehending /ʌnkɒmprɪˈhendɪŋ/ *adj.* verständnislos

uncompromising /ʌnˈkɒmprəmaɪzɪŋ/ *adj.* kompromisslos

unconcealed /ʌnkənˈsiːld/ *adj.* unverhohlen

unconcern /ʌnkənˈsɜːn/ *n., no pl.* Gleichgültigkeit, *die*

unconcerned /ʌnkənˈsɜːnd/ *adj.* gleichgültig; (free from anxiety) unbekümmert; **sb. is ~ about sb./sth.** jmdm. ist jmd./etw. gleichgültig

unconditional /ʌnkənˈdɪʃnl/ *adj.* bedingungslos ⟨*Kapitulation*⟩; kategorisch ⟨*Ablehnung*⟩; ⟨*Versprechen*⟩ ohne Vorbehalte

unconfirmed /ʌnkənˈfɜːmd/ *adj.* unbestätigt

uncongenial /ʌnkənˈdʒiːnɪəl/ *adj.* unsympathisch ⟨*Person*⟩; **I find the work ~:** die Arbeit sagt mir nicht zu *od.* liegt mir nicht

unconnected /ʌnkəˈnektɪd/ *adj.* (a) nicht verbunden; **~ with any party** nicht parteigebunden; **(b)** (disjointed, isolated) zusammenhanglos

unconscious /ʌnˈkɒnʃəs/ **1** *adj.* (a) (Med.: senseless) bewusstlos; **(b)** (unaware) **be ~ of sth.** sich einer Sache (*Gen.*) nicht bewusst sein; **she was ~ of the tragedy** sie wusste nichts von der Tragödie; **(c)** (not intended; Psych.) unbewusst. **2** *n.* Unbewusste, *das*

unconsciously /ʌnˈkɒnʃəslɪ/ *adv.* unbewusst

unconsciousness /ʌnˈkɒnʃəsnɪs/ *n., no pl.* (loss of consciousness) Bewusstlosigkeit, *die*

uncontaminated /ʌnkənˈtæmɪneɪtɪd/ *adj.* unverschmutzt, nicht verseucht (**with** von)

uncontested /ʌnkənˈtestɪd/ *adj.* unangefochten; **it was an ~ election** bei der Wahl gab es keinen Gegenkandidaten

uncontrollable /ʌnkən'trəʊləbl/ adj. unkontrollierbar
uncontrolled /ʌnkən'trəʊld/ adj. unkontrolliert
uncontroversial /ʌnkɒntrə'vɜːʃl/ adj. nicht kontrovers; be ~: keinerlei Widerspruch hervorrufen
unconventional /ʌnkən'venʃənl/ adj., **unconventionally** /ʌnkən'venʃənəlɪ/ adv. unkonventionell
unconvinced /ʌnkən'vɪnst/ adj. nicht überzeugt
unconvincing /ʌnkən'vɪnsɪŋ/ adj., **unconvincingly** /ʌnkən'vɪnsɪŋlɪ/ adv. nicht überzeugend
uncooked /ʌn'kʊkt/ adj. roh
uncooperative /ʌnkəʊ'ɒpərətɪv/ adj. unkooperativ; wenig entgegenkommend; (unhelpful) wenig hilfsbereit
uncoordinated /ʌnkəʊ'ɔːdɪneɪtɪd/ adj. unkoordiniert
uncork /ʌn'kɔːk/ v.t. entkorken
uncountable /ʌn'kaʊntəbl/ adj. (Ling.) unzählbar
uncouth /ʌn'kuːθ/ adj. (a) (lacking refinement) ungeschliffen; ungehobelt 〈 Person, Benehmen〉; grob 〈 Bemerkung, Sprache〉; (b) (boorish) unkultiviert; flegelhaft (abwertend)
uncover /ʌn'kʌvə(r)/ v.t. (a) (remove cover from) aufdecken; freilegen 〈 Wunde, Begrabenes〉; (b) (disclose) aufdecken 〈 Skandal, Verschwörung, Wahrheit〉
uncritical /ʌn'krɪtɪkl/ adj. unkritisch
uncrossed /ʌn'krɒst/ adj. **an ~ cheque/postal order** ein Barscheck/Postbarscheck
uncrowded /ʌn'kraʊdɪd/ adj. nicht überlaufen
uncurl /ʌn'kɜːl/ **1** v.t. auseinander rollen. **2** v. refl. sich strecken. **3** v.i. sich auseinander ollen
uncut /ʌn'kʌt/ adj. nicht geschnitten 〈 Gras, Haare usw.〉; nicht gemäht 〈 Rasen〉; ungeschliffen 〈 Edelstein〉
undamaged /ʌn'dæmɪdʒd/ adj. unbeschädigt
undated /ʌn'deɪtɪd/ adj. undatiert
undaunted /ʌn'dɔːntɪd/ adj. unverzagt; ~ **by threats** durch Drohungen nicht eingeschüchtert
undecided /ʌndɪ'saɪdɪd/ adj. (a) (not settled) nicht entschieden; (b) (hesitant) unentschlossen; **be ~ whether to do sth.** sich (Dat.) noch unschlüssig sein, ob man etw. tun soll
undefeated /ʌndɪ'fiːtɪd/ adj. ungeschlagen 〈 Mannschaft〉; unbesiegt 〈 Heer〉
undefined /ʌndɪ'faɪnd/ adj. nicht definiert; (indefinite) unbestimmt
undelivered /ʌndɪ'lɪvəd/ adj. nicht zugestellt 〈 Postsendung〉; (on letter) **if ~:** wenn unzustellbar
undemanding /ʌndɪ'mɑːndɪŋ/ adj. anspruchslos
undemocratic /ʌndemə'krætɪk/ adj. undemokratisch
undemonstrative /ʌndɪ'mɒnstrətɪv/ adj. zurückhaltend
undeniable /ʌndɪ'naɪəbl/ adj. unbestreitbar
undeniably /ʌndɪ'naɪəblɪ/ adv. unbestreitbar
under /'ʌndə(r)/ **1** prep. (a) (underneath, below) (indicating position) unter (+ Dat.); (indicating motion) unter (+ Akk.); **from ~ the table/bed** unter dem Tisch/Bett hervor; (b) (undergoing) ~ **treatment** in Behandlung; ~ **repair** in Reparatur; **fields ~ cultivation** Felder; see also **discussion b; influence 1; pain 1 e;** (c) (in conditions of) bei 〈 Stress, hohen Temperaturen usw.〉; (d) (subject to) unter (+ Dat.); ~ **the doctor,** ~ **doctor's orders** in ärztlicher Behandlung; (e) (in accordance with) ~ **the terms of the contract/agreement** nach den Bestimmungen des Vertrags/Abkommens; (f) (with the use of) unter (+ Dat.); ~ **an assumed name** unter falschem Namen; (g) ▶ **938**] (less than) unter (+ Dat.); **for ~ five pounds** für weniger als fünf Pfund; see also **age 1 a. 2** adv. (a) (in or to a lower or subordinate position) darunter; **stay ~** (~ water) unter Wasser bleiben; see also **go under;** (b) (in/into a state of unconsciousness) **be ~/put sb. ~:** in Narkose liegen/ jmdn. in Narkose versetzen

under: ~**-age** adj. minderjährig; ~**-age children** Minderjährige; ~**-age drinking/smoking** Alkoholgenuss/Rauchen Minderjähriger; ~**-age sex** Sex unter Minderjährigen; ~**arm** adj. (a) (Cricket, etc.) 〈Aufschlag, Wurf:〉 von unten; (b) (in armpit) Achsel〈haare, -schweiß〉; ~**carriage** n. Fahrwerk, das; ~'**charge** v.t. ~**charge sb. [by several pounds]** jmdm. [einige Pfund]

zu wenig berechnen; ~**clothes** n. pl., ~**clothing** n. ⇒ ~**wear;** ~**coat** n. (a) (layer of paint) Grundierung, die; (b) (paint) Grundierfarbe, die; ~'**cooked** adj. zu kurz gekocht/gebraten; noch nicht gar; ~**cover** adj. (disguised) getarnt; (secret) verdeckt; (engaged in international spying) geheim[dienstlich]; ~**cover agent** Untergrund-/Geheimagent, der; ~**current** n. Unterströmung, die; (fig.: underlying feeling) Unterton, der; ~'**cut** v.t., ~**cut** unterbieten; ~**de'veloped** adj. unterentwickelt; ~**de'velopment** n., no pl. Unterentwicklung, die; ~**dog** n. (a) (in fight, match) Unterlegene, der/die; (b) (fig.: disadvantaged person) Benachteiligte, der/die; ~'**done** adj. halb gar; **I don't like my steak** ~**done** ich habe mein Steak gern gut durchgebraten; ~**em'ployed** adj. unterbeschäftigt; ~**em'ployment** n. Unterbeschäftigung, die; ~**estimate 1** /ʌndər'estɪmeɪt/ v.t. unterschätzen; **2** /ʌndər'estɪmət/ n. Unterschätzung, die; ~**ex'pose** v.t. (Photog.) unterbelichten; ~**ex'posure** n. (Photog.) Unterbelichtung, die; ~'**fed** adj. unterernährt; ~-'**fives** n. pl. ▶ **630**] Kinder unter fünf Jahren; ~'**floor heating** n. [Fußboden]heizung, die; ~'**foot** adv. am Boden; **it's rough/muddy** ~**foot** der Boden ist uneben/matschig; **be trampled** ~**foot** mit Füßen zertrampelt werden; (fig.) wie der letzte Dreck behandelt werden (salopp); ~'**go** v.t., forms as **go 1** durchmachen 〈 schlimme Zeiten〉; ertragen 〈 Demütigung〉; ~**go treatment/an operation** sich einer Behandlung/Operation unterziehen; ~**go a change** sich verändern; ~'**graduate** n. ~**graduate [student]** Student/Studentin vor der ersten Prüfung; ~**ground 1** /--'-'/ adv. (a) (beneath surface of ground) unter der Erde; (Mining) unter Tage; **an explosion** ~**ground** eine unterirdische Explosion; (b) (fig.) (in hiding) im Untergrund; (into hiding) in den Untergrund; **go** ~**ground** untertauchen; in den Untergrund gehen; **2** /'---/ adj. (a) unterirdisch 〈 Höhle, See〉; ~**ground railway** Untergrundbahn, die; ~**ground car park** Tiefgarage, die; (b) (fig.: secret) ~**ground organization/movement/press** Untergrundorganisation, die/-bewegung, die/-presse, die; **3** /'---/ n. (a) (railway) U-Bahn, die; (b) (clandestine movement) Untergrund, der; Untergrundbewegung, die; ~**growth** n. Unterholz, das; ~**hand,** ~**handed** adjs. (a) (secret) heimlich; (b) (crafty) hinterhältig; ~**in'sured** adj. unterversichert; ~'**lay¹** ⇒ ~**lie;** ~**lay²** n. Unterlage, die; ~'**lie** v.t., forms as **lie²** **2:** (a) (lie ~) ~**lie sth.** unter etw. (Dat.) liegen; (b) (fig.: be [at] the basis of) ~**lie sth.** einer Sache (Dat.) zugrunde liegen; ~**lying cause of sth.** eigentliche Ursache für etw.; ~**line 1** /--'-/ v.t. (lit. or fig.) unterstreichen; **2** /'---/ n. Unterstreichung, die

underling /'ʌndəlɪŋ/ n. (derog.) Untergebene, der/die

under: ~'**lying** ⇒ ~**lie;** ~'**manned** adj. [personell] unterbesetzt; ~'**manning** n. [personelle] Unterbesetzung, die; ~**mentioned** adj. (Brit.) untengenannt; untenerwähnt; ~'**mine** v.t. (a) unterhöhlen; 〈 Wasser:〉 unterspülen; (b) (fig.: weaken) untergraben; erschüttern 〈 Vertrauen〉; unterminieren 〈 Autorität〉; schwächen 〈 Gesundheit〉

underneath /ʌndə'niːθ/ **1** prep. (indicating position) unter (+ Dat.); (indicating motion) unter (+ Akk.); **from ~ the bed** unter dem Bett hervor. **2** adv. darunter. **3** n. Unterseite, die

under: ~'**nourished** adj. unterernährt; ~'**paid** adj. unterbezahlt; ~**pants** n. pl. Unterhose, die; Unterhosen Pl.; ~**pass** n. Unterführung, die; ~'**pay** v.t., forms as **pay 2** unterbezahlen; ~'**payment** n. Unterbezahlung, die; ~**pin** v.t. [ab]stützen; (fig.) untermauern; ~'**play** v.t. (play down) herunterspielen; ~'**privileged** adj. unterprivilegiert; ~'**rate** v.t. unterschätzen; **be** ~**rated** [allgemein] unterschätzt werden; ~'**score** ⇒ ~**line 1;** ~**score** ⇒ ~**line 2;** ~**secretary** n. (a) (esp. Amer.: assistant to secretary) Unterstaatssekretär, der; (b) (Brit.) **Parliamentary U**~**secretary** [parlamentarischer] Staatssekretär, der; ~'**sell** v.t., forms as **sell 1:** (a) (set at lower price than) [im Preis] unterbieten; (b) (present inadequately) nicht genug anpreisen; ~**-side** n. Unterseite, die; ~'**signed** adj. (esp. Law) **the** ~**signed** der/die Unterzeichnete/(pl.) die Unterzeichneten (Papierdt.); ~**sized** adj. unter Normalgröße nachgestellt; [ziemlich] klein geraten 〈 Mensch, Tier〉; ~**skirt** n. Unterrock, der; ~**sold** ⇒

~**sell;** ~**'staffed** *adj.* unterbesetzt; **be** ~**staffed** an Personalmangel leiden

understand /ʌndə'stænd/ **1** *v.t.,* **understood** /ʌndə'stʊd/ **(a)** verstehen; ~ **sth. by sth.** etw. unter etw. (*Dat.*) verstehen; ~ **mathematics** mathematisches Verständnis haben; **is that understood?** ist das klar?; **make oneself understood** sich verständlich machen; **(b)** (have heard) gehört haben; **I** ~ **him to be a distant relation** ich glaube, er ist ein entfernter Verwandter; **(c)** (take as implied) ~ **sth. from sb.'s words** etw. aus jmds. Worten entnehmen; **it was understood that …:** es wurde allgemein angenommen, dass …; **do I** ~ **that …?** gehe ich recht in der Annahme, dass …? *See also* **give 1 e**; **make 1 f. 2** *v.i.,* **understood (a)** (have understanding) verstehen; ~ **about sth.** etwas von etw. verstehen; **I quite** ~**:** ich verstehe schon; **(b)** (gather, hear) **if I** ~ **correctly** wenn ich mich nicht irre; **he is, I** ~**, no longer here** er ist, wie ich höre, nicht mehr hier

understandable /ʌndə'stændəbl/ *adj.* verständlich

understandably /ʌndə'stændəblɪ/ *adv.* verständlicherweise

understanding /ʌndə'stændɪŋ/ **1** *adj.* (able to sympathize) verständnisvoll; **you could be a bit more** ~ du könntest etwas mehr Verständnis zeigen. **2** *n.* **(a)** (agreement) Verständigung, *die;* **reach an** ~ **with sb.** sich mit jmdm. verständigen; **the good** ~ **between them** das gute Einverständnis zwischen ihnen; **have a secret** ~ **with sb.** eine geheime Vereinbarung mit jmdm. haben; **on the** ~ **that …:** unter der Voraussetzung, dass …; **on the clear** ~ **that …** (condition) unter der ausdrücklichen Bedingung, dass …; **(b)** (intelligence) Verstand, *der;* **(c)** (insight, comprehension) Verständnis, *das* (**of, for** für); **beyond** ~**:** unbegreiflich; **my** ~ **of the matter is that she has won** so wie ich es verstehe, hat sie gewonnen

under: ~**'state** *v.t.* **(a)** herunterspielen; ~**state the case** untertreiben; **(b)** (represent inadequately) zu gering veranschlagen; ~**'statement** *n.* (avoidance of emphasis) Untertreibung, *die;* Understatement, *das;* ~**'stocked** *adj.* unterversorgt; ~**'stood** ⇒ **understand;** ~**study** *n.* Ersatzspieler, *der*/-spielerin, *die;* zweite Besetzung; ~**'take** *v.t., forms as* **take 1: (a)** (set about) unternehmen; ~**take a task** eine Aufgabe übernehmen; ~**take to do sth.** sich verpflichten, etw. zu tun; **(b)** (guarantee) ~**take sth./that …:** sich für etw. verbürgen/sich dafür verbürgen, dass …; ~**taker** *n.* Leichenbestatter, *der*/-bestatterin, *die;* [**firm of**] ~**takers** Bestattungsunternehmen, *das;* ~**taking** *n.* **(a)** *no pl.* (taking on) (of task) Übernahme, *das;* (of journey etc.) Unternehmen, *das;* **(b)** (task) Aufgabe, *die;* **a dangerous** ~**taking** ein gefährliches Unterfangen; **(c)** (business) Unternehmen, *das;* Betrieb, *der;* **(d)** (pledge) Versprechen, *das;* **give an** ~**taking that …/to do sth.** zusichern, dass …/sich verpflichten, etw. zu tun; ~**tone** *n.* **(a)** (low voice) **in** ~**tones** *or* **an** ~**tone** in gedämpftem Ton; **(b)** (~current) ~**tone of criticism** kritischer Unterton; **(c)** (subdued colour) Tönung, *die;* ~**took** ⇒ ~**take;** ~**tow** *n.* Unterströmung, *die;* ~**'used** *adj.* nicht voll genutzt; ~**'value** *v.t.* unterbewerten; ~**vest** *n.* Unterhemd, *das;* ~**water 1** /'----/ *attrib. adj.* Unterwasser-; **2** /--'--/ *adv.* unter Wasser; ~**wear** *n., no pl., no indef. art.* Unterwäsche, *die;* ~**'weight** *adj.* untergewichtig; ~**went** ⇒ ~**go;** ~**world** *n.* (lit. or fig.) Unterwelt, *die;* ~**'write** *v.t., forms as* **write** (accept liability for) [als Versicherer] unterzeichnen; ~**write a risk** ein Risiko versichern; ~**writer** *n.* (of insurance policy) Versicherer, *der;* (of stock issue) Garant, *der*/Garantin, *die;* ~**written** ⇒ ~**write**

undeserved /ʌndɪ'zɜːvd/ *adj.* unverdient

undeserving /ʌndɪ'zɜːvɪŋ/ *adj.* unwürdig (**of** *Gen.*)

undesirability /ʌndɪzaɪərə'bɪlɪtɪ/ *n., no pl.* Unerwünschtheit, *die*

undesirable /ʌndɪ'zaɪərəbl/ *adj.* unerwünscht; **it is** ~ **that …:** es ist nicht wünschenswert, dass …

undesirably /ʌndɪ'zaɪərəblɪ/ *adv.* unerwünscht

undetectable /ʌndɪ'tektəbl/ *adj.* nicht nachweisbar

undetected /ʌndɪ'tektɪd/ *adj.* unentdeckt; **go** *or* **pass** ~**:** unentdeckt bleiben

undeterred /ʌndɪ'tɜːd/ *adj.* nicht entmutigt (**by** durch); **remain** ~**:** sich nicht abschrecken lassen; **continue** ~**:** unbeirrt weitermachen

undeveloped /ʌndɪ'veləpt/ *adj.* **(a)** (immature) nicht voll ausgebildet; **(b)** (Photog.) nicht entwickelt; **(c)** (not built on) nicht bebaut

undid ⇒ **undo**

undies /'ʌndɪz/ *n. pl.* (coll.) Unterwäsche, *die*

undignified /ʌn'dɪgnɪfaɪd/ *adj.* würdelos; **consider it** ~ **to do sth.** es für unter seiner Würde halten, etw. zu tun

undiplomatic /ʌndɪplə'mætɪk/ *adj.* undiplomatisch

undipped /ʌn'dɪpt/ *adj.* nicht abgeblendet ⟨*Scheinwerfer*⟩

undisciplined /ʌn'dɪsɪplɪnd/ *adj.* undiszipliniert

undisclosed /ʌndɪs'kləʊzd/ *adj.* geheim; **an** ~ **sum** ein nicht genannter Betrag

undiscoverable /ʌndɪs'kʌvərəbl/ *adj.* nicht feststellbar

undiscovered /ʌndɪs'kʌvəd/ *adj.* unentdeckt

undiscriminating /ʌndɪs'krɪmɪneɪtɪŋ/ *adj.* unkritisch; (undemanding) anspruchslos

undisguised /ʌndɪs'gaɪzd/ *adj.* unverhohlen

undismayed /ʌndɪs'meɪd/ ⇒ **undeterred**

undisputed /ʌndɪ'spjuːtɪd/ *adj.* unbestritten ⟨*Fertigkeit, Kompetenz*⟩; unangefochten ⟨*Führer, Autorität*⟩

undistinguished /ʌndɪ'stɪŋgwɪʃt/ *adj.* mittelmäßig; (ordinary) gewöhnlich

undisturbed /ʌndɪ'stɜːbd/ *adj.* **(a)** (untouched) unberührt; **(b)** (not interrupted) ungestört; **(c)** (not worried) ungerührt

undivided /ʌndɪ'vaɪdɪd/ *adj.* ungeteilt ⟨*Sympathie, Aufmerksamkeit*⟩; uneingeschränkt ⟨*Loyalität*⟩

undo /ʌn'duː/ **1** *v.t.,* **undoes** /ʌn'dʌz/, **undoing** /ʌn'duːɪŋ/, **undid** /ʌn'dɪd/, **undone** /ʌn'dʌn/ **(a)** (unfasten) aufmachen; **(b)** (cancel) ungeschehen machen. **2** *v.i., forms as* **1:** ~ **at the back** ⟨*Kleid usw.*⟩ hinten aufgemacht werden

undoing /ʌn'duːɪŋ/ *n., no pl., no indef. art.* **be sb.'s** ~**:** jmds. Verderben sein

undone /ʌn'dʌn/ *adj.* **(a)** (not accomplished) unerledigt; **leave the work** *or* **job** ~**:** die Arbeit liegen lassen; **(b)** (not fastened) offen

undoubted /ʌn'daʊtɪd/ *adj.* unzweifelhaft

undoubtedly /ʌn'daʊtɪdlɪ/ *adv.* zweifellos

undreamed-of /ʌn'driːmdɒv/, **undreamt-of** /ʌn'dremtɒv/ *adjs.* (unheard-of) unerhört; (unimaginable) unvorstellbar; ungeahnt ⟨*Reichtum*⟩; **such a thing was** ~**:** an so etwas hätte man nicht im Traum gedacht

undress /ʌn'dres/ **1** *v.t.* ausziehen; entkleiden (geh.); **get** ~**ed** sich ausziehen; **can he** ~ **himself?** kann er sich selbst ausziehen? **2** *v.i.* sich ausziehen. **3** *n., no pl., no art.* **in a state of** ~**:** halb bekleidet

undressed /ʌn'drest/ *adj.* **(a)** (not clothed) unbekleidet; (no longer clothed) ausgezogen; (not yet clothed) nicht angezogen; **(b)** (unfinished) unbearbeitet ⟨*Stein, Holz*⟩; ungegerbt ⟨*Leder, Haut*⟩

undrinkable /ʌn'drɪŋkəbl/ *adj.* nicht trinkbar; ungenießbar

undue /ʌn'djuː/ *attrib. adj.* übertrieben; übermäßig; unangemessen hoch ⟨*Gewinn*⟩; unberechtigt ⟨*Optimismus*⟩

undulating /ʌndjʊ'leɪtɪŋ/ *adj.* Wellen⟨*linie, -bewegung*⟩; ~ **country/hills** sanfte Hügellandschaft; ~ **road** auf- und abführende Straße

undulation /ʌndjʊ'leɪʃn/ *n.* **(a)** (wavy motion) Wellenbewegung, *die;* **(b)** (wavy line) Wellenlinie, *die*

unduly /ʌn'djuːlɪ/ *adv.* übermäßig; übertrieben ⟨*ängstlich*⟩; unangemessen ⟨*hoch*⟩; **not** ~ **worried** nicht besonders beunruhigt

unearned /'ʌnɜːnd/ *adj.* unverdient; ~ **income** Kapitalertrag, *der*

unearth /ʌn'ɜːθ/ *v.t.* **(a)** (dig up) ausgraben; **(b)** (fig.: discover) aufdecken; zu Tage fördern

unearthly /ʌn'ɜːθlɪ/ *adj.* (a) (mysterious) unheimlich; (b) (coll.: terrible) ~ din Höllenlärm, *der* (ugs.); **at an ~ hour** in aller Herrgottsfrühe

unease /ʌn'iːz/ ⇒ **uneasiness**

uneasily /ʌn'iːzɪlɪ/ *adv.* (a) (anxiously) mit Unbehagen; (b) (with embarrassment) **be ~ aware of sth.** sich (*Dat.*) einer Sache (*Gen.*) peinlich bewusst sein; (c) (restlessly) unruhig ‹*schlafen, sitzen*›

uneasiness /ʌn'iːzɪnɪs/ *n., no pl.* (a) (anxiety) [ängstliches] Unbehagen; (b) (restlessness) Unruhe, *die*

uneasy /ʌn'iːzɪ/ *adj.* (a) (anxious) besorgt; **be ~ about sth.** sich wegen etw. Sorgen machen; **he felt ~:** ihm war unbehaglich zumute; (b) (restless) unruhig ‹*Schlaf*›; (c) (disturbing) quälend ‹*Verdacht*›; **~ conscience** schlechtes Gewissen

uneatable /ʌn'iːtəbl/ *adj.* ungenießbar

uneaten /ʌn'iːtn/ *adj.* ungegessen

uneconomic /ʌniːkə'nɒmɪk, ʌnekə'nɒmɪk/ *adj.* unrentabel

uneconomical /ʌniːkə'nɒmɪkl, ʌnekə'nɒmɪkl/ *adj.* verschwenderisch ‹*Person*›; **~ [to run]** unwirtschaftlich

uneducated /ʌn'edjʊkeɪtɪd/ *adj.* ungebildet

unemotional /ʌnɪ'məʊʃənl/ *adj.* emotionslos; nüchtern

unemployable /ʌnɪm'plɔɪəbl/ *adj.* als Arbeitskraft ungeeignet

unemployed /ʌnɪm'plɔɪd/ **1** *adj.* (a) (out of work) arbeitslos; (b) (with nothing to do) beschäftigungslos. **2** *n. pl.* **the ~:** die Arbeitslosen

unemployment /ʌnɪm'plɔɪmənt/ *n., no pl., no indef. art.* Arbeitslosigkeit, *die;* (number unemployed) Arbeitslosenzahl, *die*

unemployment: ~ benefit *n.* Arbeitslosengeld, *das;* **~ figures** *n. pl.* Arbeitslosenzahl, *die*

unending /ʌn'endɪŋ/ *adj.* endlos; ewig ‹*Fortschritt*›; **her ordeal seemed ~:** ihre Qualen schienen nie enden zu wollen

unenterprising /ʌn'entəpraɪzɪŋ/ *adj.* wenig unternehmungslustig; **an ~ person** eine Person ohne Unternehmungsgeist

unenthusiastic /ʌnɪnθjuːzɪ'æstɪk, ʌnɪnθuːzɪ'æstɪk/ *adj.* wenig begeistert (**about** von); distanziert ‹*Buchkritik*›

unenviable /ʌn'envɪəbl/ *adj.* wenig beneidenswert

unequal /ʌn'iːkwl/ *adj.* (a) (not equal) unterschiedlich; ungleich ‹*Kampf*›; (b) (inadequate) **be ~ or show oneself ~ to sth.** einer Sache (*Dat.*) nicht gewachsen sein; (c) (of varying quality) ungleichmäßig

unequalled (*Amer.:* **unequaled**) /ʌn'iːkwld/ *adj.* unerreicht; unübertroffen

unequivocal /ʌnɪ'kwɪvəkl/ *adj.* eindeutig

unerring /ʌn'ɜːrɪŋ/ *adj.* untrüglich ‹*Instinkt, Geschmack*›; unbedingt ‹*Treffsicherheit*›; mathematisch ‹*Genauigkeit*›; unfehlbar ‹*Instinkt*›

UNESCO /juː'neskəʊ/ *abbr.* **United Nations Educational, Scientific and Cultural Organization** UNESCO, *die*

unethical /ʌn'eθɪkl/ *adj.* unmoralisch

uneven /ʌn'iːvn/ *adj.* (a) (not smooth) uneben; (b) (not uniform) ungleichmäßig; unregelmäßig ‹*Pulsschlag*›; unausgeglichen ‹*Temperament*›

unevenly /ʌn'iːvnlɪ/ *adv.* ungleichmäßig

uneventful /ʌnɪ'ventfl/ *adj.* (a) (quiet) ereignislos; ruhig ‹*Leben*›; (b) (normal) ‹*Fahrt, Landung*› ohne Zwischenfälle

unexceptional /ʌnɪk'sepʃənl/ *adj.* alltäglich; (average) durchschnittlich

unexciting /ʌnɪk'saɪtɪŋ/ *adj.* wenig aufregend; (boring) langweilig

unexpected /ʌnɪk'spektɪd/ *adj.* unerwartet; **this news was entirely ~:** diese Nachricht kam völlig unerwartet

unexpectedly /ʌnɪk'spektɪdlɪ/ *adv.* unerwartet

unexplained /ʌnɪk'spleɪnd/ *adj.* ungeklärt; unentschuldigt ‹*Abwesenheit*›

unexploded /ʌnɪk'spləʊdɪd/ *adj.* nicht explodiert *od.* detoniert

unexplored /ʌnɪk'splɔːd/ *adj.* unerforscht

unexposed /ʌnɪk'spəʊzd/ *adj.* (a) (not brought to light) unaufgeklärt; nicht entlarvt ‹*Verbrecher*›; (b) (Photog.) unbelichtet

unexpressive /ʌnɪk'spresɪv/ *adj.* ausdruckslos

unfailing /ʌn'feɪlɪŋ/ *adj.* unerschöpflich

unfailingly /ʌn'feɪlɪŋlɪ/ *adv.* stets

unfair /ʌn'feə(r)/ *adj.* unfair; ungerecht, unfair ‹*Kritik, Urteil*›; unlauter ‹*Wettbewerb*›; ungerecht ‹*Strafe*›; **an ~ share** ein ungerechtfertigt hoher Anteil; **be ~ to sb.** jmdm. gegenüber ungerecht sein

unfairly /ʌn'feəlɪ/ *adv.* (a) (unjustly) ungerecht; unfair ‹*spielen*›; (b) (unreasonably) zu Unrecht

unfairness /ʌn'feənɪs/ *n., no pl.* Ungerechtigkeit, *die*

unfaithful /ʌn'feɪθfl/ *adj.* untreu; **~ to sb./sth.** jmdm./ einer Sache untreu

unfamiliar /ʌnfə'mɪljə(r)/ *adj.* (a) (strange) unbekannt; fremd ‹*Stadt*›; ungewohnt ‹*Arbeit, Tätigkeit*›; (b) (not well acquainted) nicht vertraut; **be ~ with sth.** sich mit etw. nicht auskennen

unfamiliarity /ʌnfəmɪlɪ'ærɪtɪ/ *n., no pl.* (a) (strangeness) Fremdheit, *die;* (of activity) Ungewohntheit, *die;* (b) **~ with sth.** (poor knowledge of) Unvertrautheit mit etw.

unfashionable /ʌn'fæʃənəbl/ *adj.* unmodern ‹*Kleidung*›; nicht mehr schick ‹*Wohngegend*›; **become ~:** aus der Mode kommen; **a view now ~:** eine jetzt überholte Ansicht

unfasten /ʌn'fɑːsn/ *v.t.* (a) öffnen; (b) (detach) lösen

unfathomable /ʌn'fæðəməbl/ *adj.* (a) (incomprehensible) unergründlich; (b) (immeasurable) unermesslich

unfavorable, unfavorably (Amer.) ⇒ **unfavourable, unfavourably**

unfavourable /ʌn'feɪvərəbl/ *adj.* (a) (negative) ungünstig; unfreundlich ‹*Kommentar, Reaktion*›; negativ ‹*Kritik, Antwort*›; (b) (tending to make difficult) ungünstig (**to, for** für)

unfavourably /ʌn'feɪvərəblɪ/ *adv.* ungünstig; **be ~ disposed towards sb./sth.** jmdm./etw. gegenüber ablehnend eingestellt sein

unfeeling /ʌn'fiːlɪŋ/ *adj.* (unsympathetic) gefühllos

unfinished /ʌn'fɪnɪʃt/ *adj.* (a) (not completed) unvollendet ‹*Gedicht, Werk*›; unerledigt ‹*Arbeit, Geschäft*›; (b) (in rough state) unbearbeitet

unfit /ʌn'fɪt/ **1** *adj.* (a) (unsuitable) ungeeignet; (b) (not physically fit) nicht fit; **~ for military service** [wehrdienst]untauglich. **2** *v.t.,* **-tt-** untauglich machen; *see also* **unfitted**

unfitness /ʌn'fɪtnɪs/ *n., no pl.* (a) (unsuitability) fehlende Eignung; (b) (poor physical condition) **[state of] ~:** schlechte körperliche Verfassung

unfitted /ʌn'fɪtɪd/ *adj.* (unsuited) ungeeignet

unflagging /ʌn'flægɪŋ/ *adj.* unermüdlich

unflappable /ʌn'flæpəbl/ *adj.* (coll.) unerschütterlich; **an ~ person** jemand, der sich durch nichts aus der Ruhe bringen lässt

unflattering /ʌn'flætərɪŋ/ *adj.* wenig schmeichelhaft

unflinching /ʌn'flɪntʃɪŋ/ *adj.* unerschrocken; unbeirrbar ‹*Entschlossenheit*›

unfold /ʌn'fəʊld/ **1** *v.t.* entfalten; ausbreiten ‹*Zeitung, Landkarte*›; **~ one's arms** die Arme ausstrecken. **2** *v.i.* (a) (open out) ‹*Knospe:*› sich öffnen; ‹*Flügel:*› sich entfalten; (b) (develop) sich entwickeln; ‹*Geheimnis:*› sich aufklären; **as the story ~ed** im weiteren Verlauf der Geschichte

unforeseeable /ʌnfɔː'siːəbl/ *adj.* unvorhersehbar; **be ~:** nicht vorauszusehen sein

unforeseen /ʌnfɔː'siːn/ *adj.* unvorhergesehen

unforgettable /ʌnfə'getəbl/ *adj.* unvergesslich

unforgivable /ʌnfə'gɪvəbl/ *adj.* unverzeihlich

unforgiving /ʌnfə'gɪvɪŋ/ *adj.* nachtragend

unformed /ʌn'fɔːmd/ *adj.* unausgereift

unfortunate /ʌn'fɔːtʃʊnət, ʌn'fɔːtʃənət/ *adj.* (a) (unlucky) unglücklich; (unfavourable) ungünstig ‹*Tag, Zeit*›; **the poor ~ woman** die arme, bedauernswerte Frau; **be ~ [enough] to do sth.** das Pech haben, etw. zu tun; (b) (regrettable) bedauerlich

unfortunately /ʌnˈfɔːtʃʊnətlɪ, ʌnˈfɔːtʃənətlɪ/ adv. leider

unfounded /ʌnˈfaʊndɪd/ adj. (fig.) unbegründet; **the rumours are totally ∼:** die Gerüchte entbehren jeder Grundlage

unfreeze /ʌnˈfriːz/ v.t. & i., **unfroze** /ʌnˈfrəʊz/, **unfrozen** /ʌnˈfrəʊzn/ auftauen

unfriendly /ʌnˈfrendlɪ/ adj. unfreundlich; feindlich ‹Staat›

unfulfilled /ʌnfʊlˈfɪld/ adj. **(a)** unerfüllt ‹Person›; **(b)** (not carried out) unerledigt

unfurl /ʌnˈfɜːl/ v.t. aufrollen; losmachen ‹Segel›

unfurnished /ʌnˈfɜːnɪʃt/ adj. unmöbliert

ungainly /ʌnˈgeɪnlɪ/ adj. unbeholfen; ungelenk

ungentlemanly /ʌnˈdʒentlmənlɪ/ adj. unfein; (impolite) unhöflich; **it is ∼:** es gehört sich nicht für einen Gentleman

ungodly /ʌnˈgɒdlɪ/ adj. **(a)** gottlos; **(b)** (coll.: outrageous) unchristlich (ugs.)

ungracious /ʌnˈgreɪʃəs/ adj. unhöflich; (tactless) taktlos

ungrammatical /ʌngrəˈmætɪkl/ adj. ungrammatisch

ungrateful /ʌnˈgreɪtfl/ adj. undankbar

ungrudging /ʌnˈgrʌdʒɪŋ/ adj. bereitwillig; (generous) großzügig; herzlich ‹Gastfreundschaft›; neidlos ‹Bewunderung›

unguarded /ʌnˈgɑːdɪd/ adj. **(a)** (not guarded) unbewacht; **(b)** (incautious) unvorsichtig

unhappily /ʌnˈhæpɪlɪ/ adv. **(a)** (unfortunately) unglücklicherweise; leider; **(b)** (without happiness) unglücklich

unhappiness /ʌnˈhæpɪnɪs/ n., no pl. Bekümmertheit, die; **he has been the cause of much ∼ to her** er hat ihr viel Kummer gemacht

unhappy /ʌnˈhæpɪ/ adj. **(a)** unglücklich; (not content) unzufrieden (**about** mit); **be** or **feel ∼ about doing sth.** Bedenken haben, etw. zu tun; **(b)** (unfortunate) unglückselig ‹Zeit, Zufall›; unglücklich ‹Zusammenstellung, Wahl›

unharmed /ʌnˈhɑːmd/ adj. unbeschädigt; (uninjured) unverletzt

unhealthy /ʌnˈhelθɪ/ adj. **(a)** (not in good health, harmful to health) ungesund; **(b)** (unwholesome) ungesund, krankhaft ‹Gier›; schädlich ‹Einfluss›; schlecht ‹Angewohnheit›

unheard /ʌnˈhɜːd/ adj. **∼-of** (unknown) [gänzlich] unbekannt; (unprecedented) beispiellos

unheeded /ʌnˈhiːdɪd/ adj. unbeachtet; **go ∼:** nicht beachtet werden ‹Gebet, Wunsch:› nicht erhört werden

unhelpful /ʌnˈhelpfl/ adj. wenig hilfsbereit ‹Person›; ‹Bemerkung, Kritik› die einem nicht weiterhilft

unholy /ʌnˈhəʊlɪ/ adj. **(a)** (wicked) unheilig ‹Allianz›; **(b)** (coll.: dreadful) fürchterlich ‹Krawall, Durcheinander›

unhook /ʌnˈhʊk/ v.t. vom Haken nehmen; aufhaken ‹Kleid›; loshaken ‹Tor›

unhoped-for /ʌnˈhəʊptfɔː(r)/ adj. unverhofft

unhurried /ʌnˈhʌrɪd/ adj., **unhurriedly** /ʌnˈhʌrɪdlɪ/ adv. gemächlich

unhurt /ʌnˈhɜːt/ adj. unverletzt

unhygienic /ʌnhaɪˈdʒiːnɪk/ adj. unhygienisch

unicorn /ˈjuːnɪkɔːn/ n. (Mythol.) Einhorn, das

unidentified /ʌnaɪˈdentɪfaɪd/ adj. nicht identifiziert; **∼ flying object** unbekanntes Flugobjekt

unification /juːnɪfɪˈkeɪʃn/ n. Einigung, die; (of system) Vereinheitlichung, die

uniform /ˈjuːnɪfɔːm/ **1** adj. **(the same for all)** einheitlich; (unvarying) gleich bleibend ‹Strömung, Temperatur, Qualität›; gleichmäßig ‹Tempo›; **be ∼ in shape/size/appearance** die gleiche Form/Größe/das gleiche Aussehen haben. **2** n. Uniform, die; **in/out of ∼:** in/ohne Uniform; **be in/out of ∼:** Uniform/keine Uniform tragen

uniformed /ˈjuːnɪfɔːmd/ adj. uniformiert

uniformity /juːnɪˈfɔːmɪtɪ/ n. Einheitlichkeit, die

uniformly /ˈjuːnɪfɔːmlɪ/ adv. **(a)** (without variation) einheitlich; **(b)** (equally) gleichmäßig

unify /ˈjuːnɪfaɪ/ v.t. einigen ‹Volk, Land›; vereinheitlichen ‹System›

unilateral /juːnɪˈlætərl/ adj. einseitig

unimaginable /ʌnɪˈmædʒɪnəbl/ adj. unvorstellbar

unimaginative /ʌnɪˈmædʒɪnətɪv/ adj., **unimaginatively** /ʌnɪˈmædʒɪnətɪvlɪ/ adv. fantasielos

unimpaired /ʌnɪmˈpeəd/ adj. unbeeinträchtigt

unimportance /ʌnɪmˈpɔːtəns/ n., no pl. Unwichtigkeit, die; Bedeutungslosigkeit, die

unimportant /ʌnɪmˈpɔːtənt/ adj. unwichtig; bedeutungslos

unimpressed /ʌnɪmˈprest/ adj. nicht beeindruckt

unimpressive /ʌnɪmˈpresɪv/ adj. nicht eindrucksvoll; unscheinbar ‹Gebäude›

uninformed /ʌnɪnˈfɔːmd/ adj. **(a)** (not informed) uninformiert; **(b)** (based on ignorance) auf Unkenntnis beruhend ‹Urteil, Ansicht›; **∼ guess** reine Vermutung

uninhabitable /ʌnɪnˈhæbɪtəbl/ adj. unbewohnbar

uninhabited /ʌnɪnˈhæbɪtɪd/ adj. unbewohnt

uninhibited /ʌnɪnˈhɪbɪtɪd/ adj. ungehemmt; ohne Hemmungen nachgestellt

uninitiated /ʌnɪˈnɪʃɪeɪtɪd/ adj. uneingeweiht; **∼ in the mysteries** nicht in die Geheimnisse eingeweiht; **the ∼:** Außenstehende Pl.

uninjured /ʌnˈɪndʒəd/ adj. unverletzt

uninspired /ʌnɪnˈspaɪəd/ adj. einfallslos; **I am/feel ∼:** mir fehlt die Inspiration

uninspiring /ʌnɪnˈspaɪərɪŋ/ adj. langweilig

unintelligent /ʌnɪnˈtelɪdʒənt/ adj. nicht intelligent

unintelligible /ʌnɪnˈtelɪdʒɪbl/ adj. unverständlich

unintended /ʌnɪnˈtendɪd/ adj. unbeabsichtigt

unintentional /ʌnɪnˈtenʃənl/ adj., **unintentionally** /ʌnɪnˈtenʃənəlɪ/ adv. unabsichtlich

uninterested /ʌnˈɪntrestɪd, ʌnˈɪntrɪstɪd/ adj. desinteressiert (**in** an + Dat.)

uninteresting /ʌnˈɪntrestɪŋ, ʌnˈɪntrɪstɪŋ/ adj. uninteressant

uninterrupted /ʌnɪntəˈrʌptɪd/ adj. **(a)** (continuous) ununterbrochen; nicht unterbrochen; **(b)** (not disturbed) ungestört

uninvited /ʌnɪnˈvaɪtɪd/ adj. ungeladen

uninviting /ʌnɪnˈvaɪtɪŋ/ adj. wenig verlockend; wenig einladend ‹Ort, Wetter›

union /ˈjuːnɪən, ˈjuːnjən/ n. **(a)** (trade ∼) Gewerkschaft, die; **(b)** (political unit) Union, die

unionist /ˈjuːnɪənɪst, ˈjuːnjənɪst/ n. **(a)** (member of trade union) Gewerkschafter, der/Gewerkschafterin, die; (advocate of trade unions) Gewerkschaftsanhänger, der/-anhängerin, die; **(b)** **U∼** (Polit.) Unionist, der/Unionistin, die

Union 'Jack n. (Brit.) Union Jack, der

unique /juːˈniːk/ adj. (unparalleled) einzigartig; (not repeated) einmalig ‹Gelegenheit, Angebot›; **this problem is ∼ to our society** dieses Problem gibt es nur in unserer Gesellschaft

uniquely /juːˈniːklɪ/ adv. **(a)** (exclusively) einzig und allein; **(b)** (to a unique degree) einzigartig; einmalig ‹talentiert, begabt›

unisex /ˈjuːnɪseks/ adj. Unisex‹mantel, -kleidung›; **∼ hairdresser** Damen-und-Herren-Frisör

unison /ˈjuːnɪsən/ n. **(a)** (Mus.) Unisono, das; **in ∼:** unisono; einstimmig; **act in ∼** (fig.) vereint handeln; **(b)** (concord) Einmütigkeit, die

unit /ˈjuːnɪt/ n. **(a)** (element, group; also Mil.) Einheit, die; (in complex mechanism) Element, das; **armoured ∼** (Mil.) Panzereinheit, die; **(b)** (in adding numbers by columns) Einer, der (Math.); **(c)** (quantity chosen as standard) [Maß]einheit, die; **∼ of gas, electricity** Einheit, die; **∼ of length/monetary ∼:** Längen-/Währungseinheit, die; **(d)** (piece of furniture) Element, das; **kitchen ∼:** Küchenelement, das

unite /juːˈnaɪt/ **1** v.t. vereinigen; verbinden ‹Einzelteile›; ein[ig]en ‹Partei, Mitglieder›. **2** v.i. (join together) sich vereinigen; ‹Elemente:› sich verbinden

united /juːˈnaɪtɪd/ adj. **(a)** (harmonious) einig; **a ∼ front** eine geschlossene Front; **(b)** (combined) vereint (geh.); gemeinsam

United: ∼ 'Kingdom pr. n. Vereinigtes Königreich [Großbritannien und Nordirland]; **∼ 'Nations** pr. n.

sing. Vereinte Nationen *Pl.;* ~ **'States** ⇒ **state 1 e;** ~ **States of A'merica** *n. sing.* Vereinigte Staaten *Pl.* von Amerika

unit: ~ **'furniture** *n.* Anbaumöbel *Pl.;* ~ **'trust** *n.* (Brit. Finance) ≈ Investmentfonds, *der*

unity /'juːnɪtɪ/ *n.* **(a)** (state of being united) Einheit, *die;* **their** ~ **of purpose** die Gemeinsamkeit ihres Wollens; **(b)** (Math.) Einselement, *das*

universal /juːnɪ'vɜːsl/ *adj.* **(a)** (prevailing everywhere) allgemein; allgemein gültig ‹*Regel, Wahrheit*›; **become** ~: sich allgemein verbreiten; **(b)** universal ‹*Bildung, Wissen*›; **(c)** (common to all members of a class) universell

universally /juːnɪ'vɜːsəlɪ/ *adv.* allgemein

universe /'juːnɪvɜːs/ *n.* Universum, *das;* (world; fig.: mankind) Welt, *die*

university /juːnɪ'vɜːsɪtɪ/ *n.* Universität, *die; attrib.* Universitäts-; **go to** ~: auf die *od.* zur Universität gehen; **at** ~: an der Universität

unjust /ʌn'dʒʌst/ *adj.* ungerecht **(to** *Dat.* + gegenüber)

unjustifiable /ʌn'dʒʌstɪfaɪəbl/ *adj.* ungerechtfertigt; **be** ~: nicht zu rechtfertigen sein

unjustifiably /ʌn'dʒʌstɪfaɪəblɪ/ *adv.* ungerechtfertigterweise

unjustified /ʌn'dʒʌstɪfaɪd/ *adj.* ungerechtfertigt

unjustly /ʌn'dʒʌstlɪ/ *adv.* ungerechterweise; zu Unrecht

unkempt /ʌn'kempt/ *adj.* **(a)** (dishevelled) ungekämmt ‹*Haare*›; **(b)** (untidy) ungepflegt

unkind /ʌn'kaɪnd/ *adj.* unfreundlich; **be** ~ **to sb./animals** jmdn./Tiere schlecht behandeln

unkindly /ʌn'kaɪndlɪ/ *adv.* unfreundlich

unkindness /ʌn'kaɪndnɪs/ *n.* Unfreundlichkeit, *die*

unknowing /ʌn'nəʊɪŋ/ ⇒ **unwitting**

unknowingly /ʌn'nəʊɪŋlɪ/ ⇒ **unwittingly**

unknown /ʌn'nəʊn/ **1** *adj.* unbekannt; **be** ~ **to sb.** jmd./etw. ist jmdm. nicht bekannt; **a drug** ~ **to us** ein uns unbekanntes Heilmittel; **it is** ~/**not** ~ **for him to do such a thing** es ist nie vorgekommen/ist schon vorgekommen, dass er so etwas getan hat; **the U**~ **Soldier** *or* **Warrior** der Unbekannte Soldat; ~ **strengths/reserves** (unsuspected) ungeahnte Kräfte/Reserven. **2** *adv.* ~ **to sb.** ohne dass jmd. davon weiß/wusste. **3** *n.* **the** ~: das Unbekannte; **journey/voyage into the** ~ (lit. or fig.) Reise in unbekannte Regionen

unlace /ʌn'leɪs/ *v.t.* aufschnüren

unladylike /ʌn'leɪdɪlaɪk/ *adj.* nicht sehr damenhaft; **very** ~: gar nicht damenhaft

unlawful /ʌn'lɔːfl/ *adj.* ungesetzlich; gesetzwidrig; ~ **possession of firearms/drugs** illegaler Waffen-/Drogenbesitz

unleaded /ʌn'ledɪd/ *adj.* bleifrei ‹*Benzin*›

unless /ʌn'les, ən'les/ *conj.* es sei denn; wenn ... nicht; **I shall not do it** ~ **I am paid for it** ich werde es nur tun, wenn ich dafür bezahlt werde; **I shall expect you tomorrow** ~ **I hear from you/hear to the contrary** falls *od.* sofern ich nichts von dir/nichts Gegenteiliges höre, erwarte ich dich morgen; **I might go, but not** ~ **I'm asked to** vielleicht gehe ich, aber nur, wenn man mich darum bittet; ~ **I'm [very much] mistaken** wenn ich mich nicht [sehr] irre *od.* täusche; ~ **otherwise indicated** *or* **stated** wenn nicht anders angegeben

unliberated /ʌn'lɪbəreɪtɪd/ *adj.* nicht emanzipiert ‹*Frau*›; unfrei ‹*Massen, Land*›

unlicensed /ʌn'laɪsənst/ *adj.* ‹*Händler, Makler, Buchmacher*› ohne Konzession; nicht angemeldet ‹*Fernsehgerät, Auto*›; ~ **premises** Gaststättenbetrieb ohne [Schank]konzession

unlike /ʌn'laɪk/ **1** *adj.* nicht ähnlich; unähnlich; (unequal) ~ **signs** (Math.) ungleiche Vorzeichen; ~ **poles** (Phys.) ungleiche Pole; **they are** ~: sie sind sich (*Dat.*) nicht ähnlich. **2** *prep.* **be** ~ **sb./sth.** jmdm./einer Sache nicht ähnlich sein; **be not** ~ **sb./sth.** jmdm./etw. nicht unähnlich sein *od.* ganz ähnlich sein; **sth. is** ~ **sb.** (not characteristic of) etw. sieht jmdm. gar nicht ähnlich (ugs.); etw. ist für jmdn. nicht typisch; **it is** ~ **him to be late** es ist sonst nicht seine Art, zu spät zu kommen; ~ **her brother, she**

likes walking im Gegensatz zu ihrem Bruder geht sie gern spazieren

unlikelihood /ʌn'laɪklɪhʊd/ *n., no pl.* Unwahrscheinlichkeit, *die*

unlikely /ʌn'laɪklɪ/ *adj.* **be** ~ **to do sth.** etw. wahrscheinlich nicht tun; **in the** ~ **event that** ...: sollte der unwahrscheinliche Fall eintreten, dass ...; **he's** ~ **to be chosen for the part/post** er wird die Rolle/Stelle kaum bekommen

unlimited /ʌn'lɪmɪtɪd/ *adj.* unbegrenzt; grenzenlos, unendlich ‹*Himmel, Meer, Geduld*›

unlined¹ /ʌn'laɪnd/ *adj.* (without lining) ungefüttert ‹*Kleidung, Briefumschlag*›

unlined² *adj.* (without lines) unliniert ‹*Papier*›

unlisted /ʌn'lɪstɪd/ *adj.* ~ **[telephone] number** Geheimnummer, *die*

unlit /ʌn'lɪt/ *adj.* unbeleuchtet ‹*Straße, Korridor, Zimmer*›; nicht angezündet ‹*Lampe, Kamin, Kerze*›

unload /ʌn'ləʊd/ **1** *v.t.* **(a)** entladen ‹*Lastwagen, Waggon*›; löschen ‹*Schiff, Schiffsladung*›; ausladen ‹*Gepäck*›; **(b)** (dispose of; Commerc.: sell off, dump) abstoßen ‹*Aktien, Wertpapiere*›; ~ **sb./sth. on [to] sb.** (fig.) jmdn./etw. bei jmdm. abladen. **2** *v.i.* ‹*Schiff:*› gelöscht werden; ‹*Lastwagen:*› entladen werden

unloaded /ʌn'ləʊdɪd/ *adj.* nicht geladen ‹*Gewehr, Pistole*›

unlock /ʌn'lɒk/ *v.t.* aufschließen; lösen ‹*Rad, Taste*›; ~**ed** unverschlossen ‹*Tür, Tor*›; **leave the door** ~**ed when you go out** schließ die Tür nicht ab, wenn du gehst; **the gate was left** ~**ed** das Tor war nicht abgeschlossen

unloose /ʌn'luːs/ ⇒ **loose 2**

unlovable /ʌn'lʌvəbl/ *adj.* wenig liebenswert

unloved /ʌn'lʌvd/ *adj.* ungeliebt

unluckily /ʌn'lʌkɪlɪ/ *adv.* unglücklich; *as sentence-modifier* unglücklicherweise; ~ **for him/her** *etc.* zu seinem/ihrem *usw.* Pech

unlucky /ʌn'lʌkɪ/ *adj.* **(a)** unglücklich; (not successful) glücklos; **be [very/really]** ~: [großes/wirkliches] Pech haben; **(b)** (bringing bad luck) **an** ~ **date/number** ein Unglückstag/eine Unglückszahl; **an** ~ **sign/omen** ein schlechtes Zeichen/Omen; **be** ~: Unglück bringen

unmade /ʌn'meɪd/ *adj.* ungemacht ‹*Bett*›; unbefestigt ‹*Straße*›

unmanageable /ʌn'mænɪdʒəbl/ *adj.* **(a)** (difficult to control) widerspenstig ‹*Kind, Pferd, Haare*›; **(b)** (unwieldy) sperrig

unmanly /ʌn'mænlɪ/ *adj.* unmännlich

unmanned /ʌn'mænd/ *adj.* unbemannt ‹*Leuchtturm, Raumschiff, Bahnübergang*›; (with nobody in attendance) nicht besetzt ‹*Schalter, Rezeption*›; unbewacht ‹*Posten, Eingang*›

unmarked /ʌn'mɑːkt/ *adj.* **(a)** (without markings) ‹*Schachtel, Kiste*› ohne Aufschrift; nicht gezeichnet ‹*Wäschestück*›; anonym ‹*Grab*›; **an** ~ **police car** ein Zivilfahrzeug der Polizei; **(b)** (not spoilt by marks) fleckenlos ‹*Fußboden, Oberfläche*›; makellos ‹*Haut, Pfirsich, Apfel*›; **(c)** (not corrected) unkorrigiert ‹*Klassenarbeit*›; **(d)** (not noticed) unbemerkt; **(e)** (Sport) ungedeckt ‹*Spieler*›

unmarried /ʌn'mærɪd/ *adj.* unverheiratet; ledig; ~ **mother** ledige Mutter

unmask /ʌn'mɑːsk/ *v.t.* ~ **sb.** jmdm. die Maske entreißen; (fig.) jmdn. entlarven **(as** als)

unmatched /ʌn'mætʃt/ *adj.* **be** ~ **[for sth.]** [in etw. (*Dat.*)] unübertroffen sein

unmentionable /ʌn'menʃənbl/ *adj.* unaussprechlich ‹*Sünde, Verbrechen*›

unmerciful /ʌn'mɜːsɪfl/ *adj.* erbarmungslos; unbarmherzig

unmerited /ʌn'merɪtɪd/ *adj.* unverdient

unmetalled /ʌn'metld/ *adj.* (Brit.) unbefestigt ‹*Straße*›

unmethodical /ʌnmɪ'θɒdɪkl/ *adj.* unmethodisch

unmindful /ʌn'maɪndfl/ *adj.* **be** ~ **of sth.** etw. nicht beachten

unmistakable /ʌnmɪ'steɪkəbl/ *adj.* deutlich; klar ‹*Beweis*›; unverwechselbar ‹*Handschrift, Stimme*›

unmistakably /ʌnmɪ'steɪkəblɪ/ *adv.* unverkennbar

unmitigated /ʌn'mɪtɪgeɪtɪd/ *adj.* vollkommen ‹ *Unsinn* ›; **an ~ scoundrel** ein Erzschurke; **be an ~ disaster** (coll.) eine einzige Katastrophe sein (ugs.)

unmoved /ʌn'mu:vd/ *adj.* unbewegt; ungerührt; **be/remain ~ by sb.'s pleas** sich von jmds. Bitten nicht rühren lassen

unmusical /ʌn'mju:zɪkl/ *adj.* unmusikalisch ‹ *Person* ›

unnamed /ʌn'neɪmd/ *adj.* **(a)** (unidentified) [namentlich] nicht genannt ‹ *Ort, Person, Medizin* ›; ungenannt ‹ *Wohltäter* ›; **(b)** (having no name) namenlos ‹ *Findling* ›

unnatural /ʌn'næt∫rəl/ *adj.* **(a)** unnatürlich; (abnormal) nicht normal; (perverted) widernatürlich; **(b)** (affected) unnatürlich; gekünstelt

unnaturally /ʌn'næt∫rəlɪ/ *adv.* unnatürlich; **not ~:** natürlich

unnecessarily /ʌn'nesɪsərɪlɪ/ *adv.* **(a)** unnötig[erweise] ‹ *sich ärgern, sich aufregen, sich sorgen* ›; **spend money/time ~:** unnötig Geld/Zeit aufwenden; **(b)** (excessively) unnötig ‹ *streng, kompliziert* ›

unnecessary /ʌn'nesəsərɪ/ *adj.* unnötig; **it is ~ for sb. to do sth.** es ist unnötig *od.* es muss nicht sein, dass jmd. etw. tut

unnerve /ʌn'nɜ:v/ *v.t.* entnerven

unnerving /ʌn'nɜ:vɪŋ/ *adj.* entnervend; zermürbend ‹ *Warten* ›; nervenaufreibend ‹ *Erlebnis* ›

unnoticed /ʌn'nəʊtɪst/ *adj.* unbemerkt; **pass** *or* **go ~:** unbemerkt bleiben

UNO /'ju:nəʊ/ *abbr.* **United Nations Organization** UNO, *die*

unobjectionable /ʌnəb'dʒek∫ənəbl/ *adj.* gefällig; **sth./sb. is ~:** gegen etw./jmdn. gibt es nichts einzuwenden

unobservant /ʌnəb'zɜ:vənt/ *adj.* unaufmerksam

unobserved /ʌnəb'zɜ:vd/ *adj.* unbeobachtet

unobstructed /ʌnəb'strʌktɪd/ *adj.* frei ‹ *Weg, Rohr, Ausgang* ›; ungehindert ‹ *Vormarsch, Durchfahrt* ›

unobtainable /ʌnəb'teɪnəbl/ *adj.* nicht erhältlich; **number ~** (Teleph.) kein Anschluss unter dieser Nummer

unobtrusive /ʌnəb'tru:sɪv/ *adj.* unaufdringlich ‹ *Geste, Bemerkung, Muster, Farbe* ›; unauffällig ‹ *Riß, Bewegung* ›

unoccupied /ʌn'ɒkjʊpaɪd/ *adj.* **(a)** (empty) unbesetzt; unbewohnt ‹ *Haus, Wohnung, Raum* ›; **(b)** (not busy) unbeschäftigt; **~ moments** freie Augenblicke

unofficial /ʌnə'fɪ∫l/ *adj.* inoffiziell; **an ~ strike** ein wilder Streik; **take ~ action** einen wilden Streik durchführen

unofficially /ʌnə'fɪ∫əlɪ/ *adv.* inoffiziell

unopened /ʌn'əʊpnd/ *adj.* ungeöffnet; noch nicht aufgegangen ‹ *Knospe, Blüte* ›

unopposed /ʌnə'pəʊzd/ *adj.* unangefochten ‹ *Kandidat, Wahlsieger* ›; ungehindert ‹ *Vormarsch* ›

unorganized /ʌn'ɔ:gənaɪzd/ *adj.* unsystematisch ‹ *Arbeitsweise* ›; konfus ‹ *Essay, Person* ›; ungeordnet ‹ *Struktur, Leben* ›

unoriginal /ʌnə'rɪdʒɪnl/ *adj.* unoriginell

unorthodox /ʌn'ɔ:θədɒks/ *adj.* unorthodox (geh.)

unpack /ʌn'pæk/ *v.t. & i.* auspacken

unpaid /ʌn'peɪd/ *adj.* **(a)** (not yet paid) unbezahlt; nicht bezahlt; **~ for** nicht bezahlt; **(b)** (not providing or receiving a salary) unbezahlt ‹ *Arbeit, Stelle, Freiwilliger usw.* ›; (honorary) ehrenamtlich; **~ leave** unbezahlter Urlaub

unpalatable /ʌn'pælətəbl/ *adj.* ungenießbar; (fig.) unverdaulich ‹ *Tatsache, Wahrheit* ›

unparalleled /ʌn'pærəleld/ *adj.* beispiellos; unvergleichlich ‹ *Schönheit* ›

unpardonable /ʌn'pɑ:dənəbl/ *adj.* unverzeihlich

unpatriotic /ʌnpætrɪ'ɒtɪk, ʌnpeɪtrɪ'ɒtɪk/ *adj.* unpatriotisch

unpaved /ʌn'peɪvd/ *adj.* ungepflastert

unperceptive /ʌnpə'septɪv/ *adj.* unaufmerksam; nicht sehr tiefgründig ‹ *Bemerkung* ›

unperturbed /ʌnpə'tɜ:bd/ *adj.* **he was ~ by the prospect of …:** die Aussicht auf … beunruhigte ihn nicht; **remain ~:** sich nicht aus der Ruhe bringen lassen

unpick /ʌn'pɪk/ *v.t.* auftrennen

unpin /ʌn'pɪn/ *v.t.*, **-nn-** abnehmen ‹ *Zettel, Brosche* ›

unplaced /ʌn'pleɪst/ *adj.* (Sport) unplatziert

unplanned /ʌn'plænd/ *adj.* nicht geplant; ungeplant

unpleasant /ʌn'plezənt/ *adj.* unangenehm; unfreundlich ‹ *Bemerkung* ›; böse ‹ *Lächeln* ›; **she can be really ~:** sie kann sehr unangenehm werden; **be ~ with sb.** zu jmdm. unfreundlich sein

unpleasantly /ʌn'plezəntlɪ/ *adv.* unangenehm; böse ‹ *lächeln* ›; unfreundlich ‹ *antworten* ›

unpleasantness /ʌn'plezəntnɪs/ *n.* **(a)** *no pl.* (unpleasant nature) Unerfreulichkeit, *die;* (of person) Unfreundlichkeit, *die;* **(b)** (bad feeling, quarrel) Verstimmung, *die*

unplug /ʌn'plʌg/ *v.t.*, **-gg-** (Electr.: disconnect) **~ a radio/a television set** den Stecker eines Radio-/Fernsehgeräts herausziehen

unpolished /ʌn'pɒlɪ∫t/ *adj.* unpoliert ‹ *Holz, Marmor, Schuhe, Reis* ›; (fig.) ungeschliffen ‹ *Person, Manieren, Sprache* ›

unpolluted /ʌnpə'lu:tɪd/ *adj.* sauber ‹ *Wasser, Fluss, Umwelt* ›

unpopular /ʌn'pɒpjʊlə(r)/ *adj.* unbeliebt ‹ *Lehrer, Regierung usw.* ›; unpopulär ‹ *Maßnahme, Politik* ›; **be ~ with sb.** (not liked) ‹ *Person:* › bei jmdm. unbeliebt sein; ‹ *Maßnahme, Steuern:* › bei jmdm. unpopulär sein; **I'm rather ~ with my wife at the moment** meine Frau ist auf mich zur Zeit ziemlich schlecht zu sprechen

unpopularity /ʌnpɒpjʊ'lærɪtɪ/ *n.*, *no pl.* ⇒ **unpopular:** Unbeliebtheit, *die* (**with** bei); Unpopularität, *die* (**with** bei)

unprecedented /ʌn'presɪdentɪd/ *adj.* beispiellos; [noch] nie da gewesen

unpredictable /ʌnprɪ'dɪktəbl/ *adj.* unberechenbar ‹ *Person, Charakter, Wetter* ›

unprejudiced /ʌn'predʒʊdɪst/ *adj.* unvoreingenommen

unpremeditated /ʌnprɪ'medɪteɪtɪd/ *adj.* nicht vorsätzlich ‹ *Verbrechen* ›; nicht geplant ‹ *Angriff, Tat* ›

unprepared /ʌnprɪ'peəd/ *adj.* **(a)** (not yet prepared) nicht vorbereitet ‹ *Zimmer, Mahlzeit* ›; **be [not] ~ for sth.** auf etw. (Akk.) [nicht] unvorbereitet sein; **(b)** (improvised) Stegreif‹ *rede, -erklärung* ›

unprepossessing /ʌnpri:pə'zesɪŋ/ *adj.* wenig attraktiv; wenig einnehmend ‹ *Aussehen, Person* ›

unpretentious /ʌnprɪ'ten∫əs/ *adj.* unprätentiös (geh.); einfach ‹ *Wein, Stil, Haus* ›; bescheiden ‹ *Person* ›

unprincipled /ʌn'prɪnsɪpld/ *adj.* skrupellos

unprintable /ʌn'prɪntəbl/ *adj.* (lit. or fig.) nicht druckreif

unproductive /ʌnprə'dʌktɪv/ *adj.* unfruchtbar ‹ *Boden, Gegend* ›; fruchtlos ‹ *Diskussion, Anstrengung, Nachforschung* ›; unproduktiv ‹ *Zeit, Arbeit, Kapital* ›

unprofessional /ʌnprə'fe∫ənl/ *adj.* **(a)** (contrary to standards) standeswidrig; **(b)** (amateurish) unfachmännisch; stümperhaft

unprofitable /ʌn'prɒfɪtəbl/ *adj.* unrentabel ‹ *Zeche, Investition, Geschäft* ›; wenig einträglich ‹ *Arbeit* ›; (fig.) fruchtlos

unpromising /ʌn'prɒmɪsɪŋ/ *adj.* nicht sehr vielversprechend

unpronounceable /ʌnprə'naʊnsəbl/ *adj.* unaussprechbar

unprotected /ʌnprə'tektɪd/ *adj.* ungeschützt (**against** vor + *Dat.*, gegen); nicht geschützt ‹ *Art, Tier* ›; **an ~ machine** eine Maschine ohne Schutzvorrichtung[en]; **~ sex** ungeschützter Geschlechtsverkehr

unproved /ʌn'pru:vd/, **unproven** /ʌn'pru:vn/ *adjs.* **(a)** (not proved) unbewiesen; **(b)** (untested) ungeprüft

unprovoked /ʌnprə'vəʊkt/ *adj.* grundlos

unpublished /ʌn'pʌblɪ∫t/ *adj.* unveröffentlicht

unpunished /ʌn'pʌnɪ∫t/ *adj.* ungesühnt ‹ *Verbrechen* ›; unbestraft ‹ *Verbrecher* ›; **go ~:** ohne Strafe bleiben; ‹ *Verbrecher:* › straffrei ausgehen

unqualified /ʌn'kwɒlɪfaɪd/ *adj.* **(a)** (lacking qualifications) unqualifiziert; ‹ *Arzt* › ohne Abschluss; **be ~ for sth.** für etw. nicht qualifiziert sein; **be ~ to do sth.** nicht dafür qualifiziert sein, etw. zu tun; **(b)** (absolute) uneingeschränkt ‹ *Zustimmung* ›; rein ‹ *Freude, Vergnügen* ›; voll ‹ *Erfolg* ›

unquestionable /ʌn'kwestʃənəbl/ *adj.* unbezweifelbar ⟨*Tatsache, Beweis*⟩; unbestreitbar ⟨*Recht, Fähigkeiten, Ehrlichkeit*⟩; unanfechtbar ⟨*Autorität*⟩

unquestionably /ʌn'kwestʃənəblɪ/ *adv.* zweifellos; ohne Frage

unquestioned /ʌn'kwestʃənd/ *adj.* unangefochten ⟨*Fähigkeit, Macht, Autorität, Recht*⟩; unbestritten ⟨*Talent*⟩; **his ability/loyalty is** ∼: seine Fähigkeit/ Loyalität steht außer Frage

unquestioning /ʌn'kwestʃənɪŋ/ *adj.*, **unquestioningly** /ʌn'kwestʃənɪŋlɪ/ *adv.* bedingungslos; blind

unravel /ʌn'rævl/ **1** *v.t.*, (Brit.) **-ll-** entwirren; (undo) aufziehen; (fig.) ∼ **a mystery/the truth/a plot** ein Geheimnis enträtseln/die Wahrheit aufdecken/ein Komplott aufdecken. **2** *v.i.*, (Brit.) **-ll-** aufgehen; sich aufziehen

unread /ʌn'red/ *adj.* ungelesen

unreadable /ʌn'ri:dəbl/ *adj.* **(a)** (illegible) unleserlich; **(b)** (too difficult, boring, etc.) unlesbar

unready /ʌn'redɪ/ *adj.* nicht bereit; **the country is** ∼ **for war** das Land ist für einen Krieg nicht gerüstet

unreal /ʌn'rɪəl/ *adj.* unwirklich

unrealistic /ʌnrɪə'lɪstɪk/ *adj.* unrealistisch

unreality /ʌnrɪ'ælɪtɪ/ *n., no pl.* Unwirklichkeit, *die*

unreasonable /ʌn'ri:zənəbl/ *adj.* unvernünftig; übertrieben ⟨*Ansprüche, Forderung*⟩; übertrieben [hoch] ⟨*Preis, Kosten*⟩

unrecognizable /ʌn'rekəgnaɪzəbl/ *adj.* be [absolutely *or* quite] ∼: [überhaupt] nicht wieder zu erkennen sein

unrecognized /ʌn'rekəgnaɪzd/ *adj.* **(a)** (not identified) unerkannt; **(b)** (not officially recognized) nicht anerkannt; **(c)** (not appreciated) nicht [gebührend] gewürdigt ⟨*Talent, Genie*⟩; nicht [genügend] beachtet ⟨*Gefahr, Tatsache*⟩

unrecorded /ʌnrɪ'kɔ:dɪd/ *adj.* **(a)** (not documented) nicht [dokumentarisch] belegt; **(b)** (not recorded) nicht aufgezeichnet; unbespielt, leer ⟨*Tonband, Kassette*⟩

unreel /ʌn'ri:l/ **1** *v.t.* abwickeln; abspulen ⟨*Film, Tonband*⟩. **2** *v.i.* sich abwickeln; sich abspulen

unrefined /ʌnrɪ'faɪnd/ *adj.* **(a)** (not refined) nicht raffiniert; ungebleicht (Mehl); **(b)** (fig.) unkultiviert, ungeschliffen ⟨*Geschmack, Manieren, Person, Sprache*⟩

unrelated /ʌnrɪ'leɪtɪd/ *adj.* unzusammenhängend; **be** ∼ (not connected) nicht miteinander zusammenhängen; (not related by family) nicht [miteinander] verwandt sein; **be** ∼ **to sth.** mit etw. in keinem Zusammenhang stehen

unrelenting /ʌnrɪ'lentɪŋ/ *adj.* unvermindert, nicht nachlassend ⟨*Hitze, Kälte, Regen*⟩; unerbittlich ⟨*Kampf, Opposition, Verfolgung, Hass*⟩; unnachgiebig ⟨*Entschlossenheit, Ehrgeiz*⟩

unreliable /ʌnrɪ'laɪəbl/ *adj.* unzuverlässig

unremitting /ʌnrɪ'mɪtɪŋ/ *adj.* nicht nachlassend; unermüdlich ⟨*Anstrengung, Versuche, Sorge*⟩; beharrlich ⟨*Kampf*⟩

unrepeatable /ʌnrɪ'pi:təbl/ *adj.* **(a)** (unique) einzigartig; einmalig ⟨*Angebot, Preis*⟩; **(b)** (not fit to be repeated) **sth. is** ∼: etw. ist nicht zitierfähig

unrepresentative /ʌnreprɪ'zentətɪv/ *adj.* nicht repräsentativ (**of** für); (Polit.) nicht demokratisch gewählt ⟨*Regierung, Führer*⟩

unrequited /ʌnrɪ'kwaɪtɪd/ *adj.* unerwidert

unreserved /ʌnrɪ'zɜ:vd/ *adj.* **(a)** (not booked) nicht reserviert; **(b)** ▶ **639** (full, without any reservations) uneingeschränkt ⟨*Zustimmung, Aufnahme, Entschuldigung usw.*⟩

unresponsive /ʌnrɪ'spɒnsɪv/ *adj.* be ∼: nicht reagieren (**to** auf + *Akk.*); **an** ∼ **audience** ein teilnahmsloses Publikum

unrest /ʌn'rest/ *n.* Unruhen *Pl.*

unrestrained /ʌnrɪ'streɪnd/ *adj.* uneingeschränkt ⟨*Freude, Begeisterung, Wachstum, Überfluss*⟩; unbeherrscht ⟨*Gefühlsäußerung, Wut, Gewalt*⟩; unkontrolliert ⟨*Entwicklung, Wachstum*⟩; ungeniert ⟨*Sprache, Benehmen*⟩

unrestricted /ʌnrɪ'strɪktɪd/ *adj.* unbeschränkt; uneingeschränkt; frei ⟨*Sicht*⟩; **have** ∼ **use of sth.** etw. uneingeschränkt nutzen [dürfen]

unrewarded /ʌnrɪ'wɔ:dɪd/ *adj.* **go** ∼: keine Belohnung bekommen; ⟨*Tat, Mühe:*⟩ nicht belohnt werden

unrewarding /ʌnrɪ'wɔ:dɪŋ/ *adj.* unbefriedigend; undankbar ⟨*Aufgabe*⟩

unripe /ʌn'raɪp/ *adj.* unreif

unrivalled (*Amer.:* **unrivaled**) /ʌn'raɪvld/ *adj.* unvergleichlich; beispiellos; unübertroffen ⟨*Ruf, Luxus, Erfahrung, Könnerschaft*⟩; **our goods are** ∼ **in** *or* **for quality** unsere Waren sind in ihrer Qualität konkurrenzlos *od.* unerreicht

unroadworthy /ʌn'rəʊdwɜ:ðɪ/ *adj.* nicht verkehrssicher ⟨*Fahrzeug*⟩

unroll /ʌn'rəʊl/ **1** *v.t.* aufrollen. **2** *v.i.* sich aufrollen; (fig.) ⟨*Geschichte, Handlung:*⟩ sich entrollen

unromantic /ʌnrə'mæntɪk/ *adj.* unromantisch

unruffled /ʌn'rʌfld/ *adj.* ruhig; glatt ⟨*Gewässer, Haar, Feder*⟩

unruled /ʌn'ru:ld/ unliniert ⟨*Papier*⟩

unruliness /ʌn'ru:lɪnɪs/ *n.* Ungebärdigkeit, *die*

unruly /ʌn'ru:lɪ/ *adj.* ungebärdig ⟨*Person, Benehmen*⟩; widerspenstig ⟨*Haar, Person, Benehmen*⟩

unsafe /ʌn'seɪf/ *adj.* nicht sicher ⟨*Leiter, Konstruktion*⟩; baufällig ⟨*Gebäude*⟩; nicht verkehrssicher ⟨*Fahrzeug*⟩; gefährlich ⟨*Maschine, Leitungen, Spielzeug*⟩; **the food is** ∼ **to eat** das Essen ist ungenießbar; **feel** ∼: sich unsicher fühlen; **it is** ∼ **to do that** es ist gefährlich, das zu tun

unsaid /ʌn'sed/ *adj.* ungesagt; unausgesprochen; **leave sth.** ∼: etw. ungesagt lassen

unsaleable /ʌn'seɪləbl/ *adj.* unverkäuflich

unsatisfactory /ʌnsætɪs'fæktərɪ/ *adj.* unbefriedigend; nicht befriedigend; schlecht ⟨*Service, Hotel*⟩; mangelhaft ⟨*schulische Leistung*⟩

unsatisfied /ʌn'sætɪsfaɪd/ *adj.* unzufrieden, unerfüllt ⟨*Wunsch, Bedürfnis*⟩; nicht befriedigt ⟨*Wunsch, Bedürfnis, Neugier, Nachfrage*⟩; nicht gestillt ⟨*Hunger, Neugier, Appetit*⟩; **leave sb.** ∼: jmdn. nicht befriedigen

unsatisfying /ʌn'sætɪsfaɪŋ/ *adj.* unbefriedigend

unsavoury (*Amer.:* **unsavory**) /ʌn'seɪvərɪ/ *adj.* unangenehm ⟨*Geruch, Geschmack, Mahlzeit*⟩; zwielichtig ⟨*Charakter, Person*⟩; zweifelhaft ⟨*Ruf, Geschäfte, Angelegenheit*⟩; unerfreulich ⟨*Einzelheiten*⟩

unscathed /ʌn'skeɪðd/ *adj.* unversehrt ⟨*Person*⟩; unbeschädigt ⟨*Sache*⟩

unscented /ʌn'sentɪd/ *adj.* nicht parfümiert ⟨*Seife, Shampoo*⟩

unscheduled /ʌn'ʃedju:ld/ *adj.* außerplanmäßig

unscientific /ʌnsaɪən'tɪfɪk/ *adj.* unwissenschaftlich ⟨*Methode, Buch, Ansatz*⟩

unscramble /ʌn'skræmbl/ *v.t.* (lit. or fig.) entwirren; (Teleph.: decode) entschlüsseln

unscratched /ʌn'skrætʃt/ *adj.* (unhurt) unverletzt

unscrew /ʌn'skru:/ **1** *v.t.* ab- *od.* losschrauben ⟨*Regal, Deckel usw.*⟩; herausdrehen ⟨*Schraube*⟩. **2** *v.i.* ⟨*Brett, Verschluss:*⟩ sich abschrauben lassen; ⟨*Schraube:*⟩ sich lösen *od.* abschrauben lassen; **come** ∼**ed** sich lösen

unscrupulous /ʌn'skru:pjʊləs/ *adj.* skrupellos

unseal /ʌn'si:l/ *v.t.* (break seal of) entsiegeln; (open) öffnen ⟨*Brief, Paket, Behälter*⟩

unsealed /ʌn'si:ld/ *adj.* offen; unverschlossen

unseasoned /ʌn'si:znd/ *adj.* (not flavoured) ungewürzt; (not matured) nicht abgelagert ⟨*Holz*⟩; unerfahren ⟨*Soldat*⟩

unseaworthy /ʌn'si:wɜ:ðɪ/ *adj.* nicht seetüchtig

unseemly /ʌn'si:mlɪ/ *adj.* unschicklich; ungehörig ⟨*Benehmen*⟩; ungebührlich ⟨*Eile, Benehmen*⟩

unseen /ʌn'si:n/ *adj.* **(a)** (not seen) ungesehen; unbekannt ⟨*Text*⟩; **(b)** (invisible) unsichtbar

unselfconscious /ʌnself'kɒnʃəs/ *adj.*, unbefangen

unselfish /ʌn'selfɪʃ/ *adj.* selbstlos

unserviceable /ʌn'sɜ:vɪsəbl/ *adj.* unbrauchbar

unsettle /ʌn'setl/ *v.t.* durcheinander bringen; verwirren ⟨*menschlichen Geist*⟩; stören ⟨*Friede*⟩; verstören ⟨*Kind, Tier*⟩

unsettled /ʌn'setld/ *adj.* **(a)** (changeable) wechselhaft; (fig.) unstet (geh.), ruhelos ⟨*Leben*⟩; unsicher ⟨*Zukunft*⟩; **(b)** (upset) verstimmt ⟨*Magen*⟩; gestört ⟨*Verdauung*⟩; unruhig ⟨*Zeit, Land*⟩; **(c)** (open to further discussion) ungeklärt ⟨*Angelegenheit, Frage*⟩

unsettling /ʌn'setlɪŋ/ *adj.* störend ⟨*Vorfall, Einfluss*⟩; beunruhigend ⟨*Nachricht*⟩; **have an ~ effect on sb.** jmdn. aus dem Gleichgewicht bringen

unshak[e]able /ʌn'ʃeɪkəbl/ *adj.* unerschütterlich

unshaken /ʌn'ʃeɪkn/ *adj.* **be ~:** nicht erschüttert sein

unshaven /ʌn'ʃeɪvn/ *adj.* unrasiert

unsightly /ʌn'saɪtlɪ/ *adj.* unschön

unsigned /ʌn'saɪnd/ *adj.* nicht unterzeichnet ⟨*Brief, Dokument*⟩; unsigniert ⟨*Gemälde*⟩

unskilful /ʌn'skɪlfl/ *adj.* ungeschickt

unskilled /ʌn'skɪld/ *adj.* **(a)** (lacking skills) ungeschickt; stümperhaft; **(b)** (without special training) ungelernt ⟨*Arbeiter*⟩; **(c)** (done without skill) schlecht; stümperhaft; **(d)** keine besonderen Fertigkeiten erfordernd ⟨*Arbeit*⟩

unskillful (Amer.) ⇒ **unskilful**

unskimmed /ʌn'skɪmd/ *adj.* nicht entrahmt; **~ milk** Vollmilch, *die*

unslept-in /ʌn'sleptɪn/ *adj.* **the bed was ~:** in dem Bett hatte niemand geschlafen

unsociable /ʌn'səʊʃəbl/ *adj.* ungesellig

unsocial /ʌn'səʊʃl/ *adj.* ungesellig; **at this ~ hour** (joc.) zu dieser unchristlichen Tageszeit; **work ~ hours** nachts/sonn- und feiertags arbeiten

unsold /ʌn'səʊld/ *adj.* unverkauft

unsolicited /ʌnsə'lɪsɪtɪd/ *adj.* nicht angefordert *od.* erbeten; nicht bestellt ⟨*Waren*⟩; unverlangt eingesandt ⟨*Manuskript*⟩

unsolved /ʌn'sɒlvd/ *adj.* ungelöst; unaufgeklärt ⟨*Verbrechen*⟩

unsophisticated /ʌnsə'fɪstɪkeɪtɪd/ *adj.* schlicht, einfach ⟨*Person, Geschmack, Vergnügen, Spiel*⟩; unkompliziert ⟨*Maschine, Küche, Methode*⟩; einfach ⟨*Wein*⟩

unsound /ʌn'saʊnd/ *adj.* **(a)** (diseased) nicht gesund; krank; **(b)** (defective) baufällig ⟨*Gebäude*⟩; **structurally ~:** baufällig; **(c)** (ill-founded) wenig stichhaltig; anfechtbar ⟨*Gesetz*⟩; nicht vertretbar ⟨*Ansichten, Methoden*⟩; **(d)** (unreliable) unzuverlässig; **the firm is financially ~:** die Firma steht finanziell auf schwachen Füßen; **(e) of ~ mind** unzurechnungsfähig

unsparing /ʌn'speərɪŋ/ *adj.* **(a)** (lavish) großzügig; **give sb. one's ~ help/support** jmdm. seine volle Hilfe/Unterstützung geben; **be ~ of** *or* **in sth.** mit etw. nicht geizen; **(b)** (merciless) schonungslos

unspeakable /ʌn'spiːkəbl/ *adj.* unbeschreiblich; (indescribably bad) unsäglich

unspecified /ʌn'spesɪfaɪd/ *adj.* nicht näher bezeichnet; nicht genannt ⟨*Anzahl, Summe*⟩

unspectacular /ʌnspek'tækjʊlə(r)/ *adj.* wenig eindrucksvoll

unspoiled /ʌn'spɔɪld/, **unspoilt** /ʌn'spɔɪlt/ *adjs.* unverdorben; unberührt ⟨*Dorf, Landschaft*⟩

unspoken /ʌn'spəʊkn/ *adj.* ungesagt; (tacit) unausgesprochen; stillschweigend ⟨*Übereinkunft*⟩; **be left ~:** ungesagt bleiben

unstable /ʌn'steɪbl/ *adj.* nicht stabil; instabil (geh.); labil ⟨*Wirtschaft, Beziehungen, Verhältnisse*⟩; **[mentally/emotionally] ~:** [psychisch] labil

unsteady /ʌn'stedɪ/ *adj.* unsicher; wechselhaft ⟨*Entwicklung*⟩; ungleichmäßig ⟨*Flamme, Rhythmus*⟩; wackelig ⟨*Leiter, Stuhl, Tisch, Konstruktion*⟩; **be ~ on one's feet** unsicher auf den Beinen sein

unstinting /ʌn'stɪntɪŋ/ *adj.* großzügig; **be ~ in sth.** mit etw. nicht geizen; **be ~ in one's efforts** keine Mühe scheuen

unstuck /ʌn'stʌk/ *adj.* **come ~:** sich lösen, ⟨*Briefumschlag:*⟩ aufgehen; (fig. coll.: come to grief, fail) ⟨*Person:*⟩ baden gehen (ugs.) **(over** mit); ⟨*Projekt, Plan, Theorie, Geschäft:*⟩ in die Binsen gehen (ugs.)

unsubtle /ʌn'sʌtl/ *adj.* plump

unsuccessful /ʌnsək'sesfl/ *adj.* erfolglos; **be ~:** keinen Erfolg haben; **the operation was ~:** die Operation hatte keinen Erfolg *od.* misslang; **be ~ in an examination** eine Prüfung nicht bestehen

unsuccessfully /ʌnsək'sesfəlɪ/ *adv.* erfolglos; vergebens ⟨*versuchen*⟩

unsuitability /ʌnsuːtə'bɪlɪtɪ, ʌnsjuːtə'bɪlɪtɪ/ *n., no pl.* Ungeeignetsein, *das;* (for job) mangelnde Eignung

unsuitable /ʌn'suːtəbl, ʌn'sjuːtəbl/ *adj.* ungeeignet; **~ clothes** (for weather, activity) unzweckmäßige Kleidung; (for occasion, age) unpassende Kleidung; **be ~ for sb./sth.** für jmdn./etw. ungeeignet sein

unsuitably /ʌn'suːtəblɪ, ʌn'sjuːtəblɪ/ *adv.* unpassend

unsuited /ʌn'suːtɪd, ʌn'sjuːtɪd/ *adj.* ungeeignet; **be ~ for** *or* **to sb./sth.** für jmdn./etw. ungeeignet sein; ⟨*Verhalten, Sprache:*⟩ für jmdn./etw. unpassend sein

unsung /ʌn'sʌŋ/ *adj.* unbesungen ⟨*Held, Tat*⟩

unsure /ʌn'ʃʊə(r)/ *adj.* unsicher; **be ~ about sb./sth.** sich (*Dat.*) über jmdn./etw. nicht im Klaren sein; **be ~ whether to do sth.** sich (*Dat.*) nicht sicher sein, ob man etw. tun soll; **be ~ of sb./sth.** sich (*Dat.*) jmds./einer Sache nicht sicher sein; **be ~ of a date/of one's facts** ein Datum nicht genau wissen/seine Fakten nicht genau kennen; **be ~ of oneself** unsicher sein

unsurprisingly /ʌnsə'praɪzɪŋlɪ/ *adv.* wie zu erwarten war

unsuspected /ʌnsə'spektɪd/ *adj.* ungeahnt ⟨*Talent, Kräfte, Stärke, Tiefe, Charme*⟩; unvermutet ⟨*Defekt, Leck, Ergebnis, Folge*⟩

unsuspecting /ʌnsə'spektɪŋ/ *adj.*, **unsuspectingly** /ʌnsə'spektɪŋlɪ/ *adv.* nichtsahnend

unsweetened /ʌn'swiːtnd/ *adj.* ungesüßt

unswerving /ʌn'swɜːvɪŋ/ *adj.* unerschütterlich ⟨*Glaube, Treue*⟩; unbeirrbar ⟨*Entschlossenheit*⟩

unsympathetic /ʌnsɪmpə'θetɪk/ *adj.* **(a)** wenig mitfühlend; **be ~:** kein Mitgefühl zeigen; **be ~ to sth./not ~ to sth.** kein Verständnis/durchaus Verständnis für etw. haben; **(b)** (unlikeable) unsympathisch

unsystematic /ʌnsɪstə'mætɪk/ *adj.* unsystematisch

untamed /ʌn'teɪmd/ *adj.* (lit. or fig.) ungezähmt; wild

untangle /ʌn'tæŋgl/ *v.t.* (lit. or fig.) entwirren

untenable /ʌn'tenəbl/ *adj.* unhaltbar

untested /ʌn'testɪd/ *adj.* nicht erprobt

unthinkable /ʌn'θɪŋkəbl/ *adj.* unvorstellbar

unthinking /ʌn'θɪŋkɪŋ/ *adj.* gedankenlos

untidiness /ʌn'taɪdɪnɪs/ *n., no pl.* ⇒ **untidy:** Ungepflegtheit, *die;* Unaufgeräumtheit, *die;*

untidy /ʌn'taɪdɪ/ *adj.* ungepflegt ⟨*Äußeres, Person, Garten*⟩; unaufgeräumt ⟨*Zimmer*⟩

untie /ʌn'taɪ/ *v.t.*, **untying** /ʌn'taɪɪŋ/ aufknüpfen, aufknoten ⟨*Faden, Seil, Paket*⟩; aufbinden ⟨*Knoten, Schnürsenkel*⟩; losbinden ⟨*Pferd, Boot, Seil vom Pfosten*⟩; **~ sb./sb.'s hands** jmdn./jmds. Hände von den Fesseln befreien

until /ən'tɪl/ **1** *prep.* bis; (followed by article + noun) bis zu; **~ [the] evening/the end** bis zum Abend/bis zum Ende; **~ his death/retirement** bis zu seinem Tod/seiner Pensionierung; **~ next week** bis nächste Woche; **~ then** *or* **that time** bis dahin *od.* dann; **not ~:** erst; **not ~ Christmas/the summer/his birthday** erst an Weihnachten/im Sommer/an seinem Geburtstag. **2** *conj.* bis; **~ you find the key, we shall not be able to get in** solange du den Schlüssel nicht findest, kommen wir nicht hinein; **I did not know ~ you told me** ich wusste das nicht, bis du es mir gesagt hast

untimely /ʌn'taɪmlɪ/ *adj.* **(a)** (inopportune) ungelegen; (inappropriate) unpassend; **be ~:** ungelegen kommen/unpassend sein; **(b)** (premature) vorzeitig; allzu früh ⟨*Tod*⟩

untiring /ʌn'taɪərɪŋ/ *adj.* unermüdlich; **be ~ in one's efforts to do sth.** sich unermüdlich bemühen, etw. zu tun

untold /ʌn'təʊld/ *adj.* **(a)** (immeasurable) unbeschreiblich; unsagbar ⟨*Elend*⟩; unermesslich ⟨*Reichtümer, Anzahl*⟩; **(b)** (countless) unzählig; **(c)** (not related) nicht erzählt

untouchable /ʌn'tʌtʃəbl/ **1** *adj.* (beyond reach) unberührbar; **sth. is** ~: etw. kann nicht berührt werden. **2** *n.* Unberührbare, *der/die*

untouched /ʌn'tʌtʃt/ *adj.* **(a)** (not handled, untasted) unberührt; **leave sth.** ~: etw. nicht anrühren; **(b)** (not changed) unverändert; **(c)** (not affected) unberührt

untoward /ʌntə'wɔːd, ʌn'təʊəd/ *adj.* **(a)** (unfavourable) ungünstig; unglücklich ‹*Unfall*›; **(b)** (unseemly) ungehörig

untraceable /ʌn'treɪsəbl/ *adj.* unauffindbar

untrained /ʌn'treɪnd/ *adj.* unausgebildet; ungelernt ‹*Arbeitskräfte*›; nicht dressiert ‹*Tier*›; **to the** ~ **eye/ear** dem ungeschulten Auge/Ohr

untranslatable /ʌntræns'leɪtəbl/ *adj.* unübersetzbar

untried /ʌn'traɪd/ *adj.* **(a)** (not tested) unerprobt; **leave nothing** ~: nichts unversucht lassen; **(b)** (Law) nicht vor Gericht gestellt ‹*Person*›; nicht verhandelt ‹*Fall*›

untroubled /ʌn'trʌbld/ *adj.* ungestört ‹*Schlaf, Ruhe*›; sorglos ‹*Gesicht, Geist*›

untrue /ʌn'truː/ *adj.* **(a)** (false) unwahr; **that's** ~: das ist nicht wahr; **(b)** (unfaithful) ~ **to sb./sth.** jmdm./etw. untreu

untrustworthy /ʌn'trʌstwɜːðɪ/ *adj.* unzuverlässig

untruth /ʌn'truːθ/ *n.*, *pl.* ~**s** /ʌn'truːðz, ʌn'truːθs/ Unwahrheit, *die*

untruthful /ʌn'truːθfl/ *adj.* verlogen (abwertend); **an** ~ **story** eine Lügengeschichte (abwertend)

untuneful /ʌn'tjuːnfl/ *adj.* unmelodisch

unusable /ʌn'juːzəbl/ *adj.* unbrauchbar

unused¹ /ʌn'juːzd/ *adj.* (new, fresh) unbenutzt; (not utilized) ungenutzt; ungestempelt ‹*Briefmarke*›

unused² /ʌn'juːst/ *adj.* (unaccustomed) **be** ~ **to sth./to doing sth.** etw. (*Akk.*) nicht gewohnt sein/nicht gewohnt sein, etw. zu tun

unusual /ʌn'juːʒʊəl/ *adj.* ungewöhnlich; (exceptional) außergewöhnlich; **an** ~ **number of ...:** eine ungewöhnlich große Zahl von ...; **it is** ~ **for him to do that** er tut das gewöhnlich nicht; **it is not** ~ **for her to do that** es ist durchaus nicht ungewöhnlich, dass sie das tut

unusually /ʌn'juːʒʊəlɪ/ *adv.* ungewöhnlich

unutterable /ʌn'ʌtərəbl/ *adj.*, **unutterably** /ʌn'ʌtərəblɪ/ *adv.* unsäglich

unvarying /ʌn'veərɪŋ/ *adj.* gleich bleibend

unveil /ʌn'veɪl/ *v.t.* entschleiern ‹*Gesicht*›; enthüllen ‹*Statue, Gedenktafel*›; (fig.) vorstellen ‹*neues Auto, Produkt, Modell*›; veröffentlichen, (geh.) enthüllen ‹*Plan, Projekt*›

unversed /ʌn'vɜːst/ *adj.* nicht bewandert (**in** in + *Dat.*)

unvoiced /ʌn'vɔɪst/ *adj.* **(a)** unausgesprochen ‹*Ansichten, Gefühle, Zweifel*›; **(b)** (Phonet.) stimmlos

unwaged /ʌn'weɪdʒd/ *adj.* arbeitslos

unwanted /ʌn'wɒntɪd/ *adj.* unerwünscht; **one's** ~ **clothes/books** die Kleider/Bücher, die man nicht mehr [haben] will

unwarranted /ʌn'wɒrəntɪd/ *adj.* ungerechtfertigt

unwary /ʌn'weərɪ/ *adj.* unvorsichtig; unüberlegt ‹*Tat, Schritt*›

unwashed /ʌn'wɒʃt/ *adj.* ungewaschen ‹*Person, Kleidung*›; ungespült ‹*Geschirr*›

unwavering /ʌn'weɪvərɪŋ/ *adj.* fest ‹*Blick*›; (fig.: firm, resolute) unerschütterlich

unwelcome /ʌn'welkəm/ *adj.* unwillkommen; ungebeten ‹*Besucher*›

unwell /ʌn'wel/ *adj.* unwohl; **look** ~: nicht wohl *od.* gut aussehen; **he feels** ~ (feels poorly) er fühlt sich nicht wohl; (feels sick) ihm ist [es] schlecht *od.* übel

unwholesome /ʌn'həʊlsəm/ *adj.* (lit. or fig.) ungesund

unwieldy /ʌn'wiːldɪ/ *adj.* unhandlich ‹*Werkzeug, Waffe*›; sperrig ‹*Karton, Form, Paket*›

unwilling /ʌn'wɪlɪŋ/ *adj.* widerwillig ‹*Partner, Unterstützung, Zustimmung*›; unfreiwillig ‹*Helfer*›; **be** ~ **to do sth.** nicht tun wollen

unwillingly /ʌn'wɪlɪŋlɪ/ *adv.* widerwillig

unwillingness /ʌn'wɪlɪŋnɪs/ *n.*, *no pl.* Widerwille, *der*; ~ **to help/ listen** mangelnde Bereitschaft zu helfen/ zuzuhören

unwind /ʌn'waɪnd/ **1** *v.t.*, **unwound** /ʌn'waʊnd/ abwickeln; abspulen ‹*Film*›. **2** *v.i.*, **unwound** **(a)** (unreel) sich abwickeln; **(b)** (fig.: unfold) sich entwickeln; **(c)** (coll.: relax) sich entspannen

unwise /ʌn'waɪz/ *adj.* unklug

unwitting /ʌn'wɪtɪŋ/ *adj.* ahnungslos ‹*Opfer*›; unwissentlich ‹*Komplize, Urheber*›; unbeabsichtigt ‹*Fehler, Handlung*›; ungewollt ‹*Beleidigung*›

unwittingly /ʌn'wɪtɪŋlɪ/ *adv.* unwissentlich; unabsichtlich ‹*beleidigen*›

unwonted /ʌn'wəʊntɪd/ *adj.* ungewohnt

unworkable /ʌn'wɜːkəbl/ *adj.* unbrauchbar ‹*Material*›; nicht abbaubar ‹*Flöz*›; (fig.: impracticable) unbrauchbar ‹*System*›; undurchführbar ‹*Plan, Projekt*›

unworldly /ʌn'wɜːldlɪ/ *adj.* weltabgewandt; (naïve, not worldly-wise) weltfremd

unworn /ʌn'wɔːn/ *adj.* **(a)** (new) ungetragen ‹*Kleidung*›; **(b)** (not damaged) nicht abgetreten ‹*Teppich, Treppe*›; nicht abgetragen ‹*Kleidungsstück*›; nicht abgefahren ‹*Reifen*›

unworried /ʌn'wʌrɪd/ *adj.* unbekümmert; **she was completely** ~ **by it** sie machte sich (*Dat.*) keine Sorgen darum

unworthy /ʌn'wɜːðɪ/ *adj.* unwürdig; **be [not]** ~ **of sth.** einer Sache nicht [un]würdig sein; **be** ~ **of sb./sth.** ‹*Verhalten, Einstellung usw.*› einer Person/Sache (*Gen.*) unwürdig sein

unwrap /ʌn'ræp/ *v.t.*, **-pp-** auswickeln; abwickeln ‹*Bandage*›

unwritten /ʌn'rɪtn/ *adj.* ungeschrieben; nicht schriftlich festgehalten ‹*Märchen, Lied, Vertrag, Verfassung*›; unbeschrieben ‹*Papier, Seite*›

unyielding /ʌn'jiːldɪŋ/ *adj.* hart; (fig.) unnachgiebig; unerschütterlich ‹*Mut*›

unzip /ʌn'zɪp/ **1** *v.t.*, **-pp-** öffnen ‹*Reißverschluss*›; ~ **a dress/bag** *etc.* den Reißverschluss eines Kleides/einer Tasche *usw.* öffnen. **2** *v.i.*, **-pp-:** **the dress** ~**s at the back** das Kleid hat hinten einen Reißverschluss

up /ʌp/ **1** *adv.* **(a)** (to higher place) nach oben; (in lift) aufwärts; **[right] up to sth.** (lit. or fig.) [ganz] bis zu etw. hinauf; **the bird flew up to the roof** der Vogel flog aufs Dach [hinauf]; **up into the air** in die Luft [hinauf] ...; **climb up on sth./up to the top of sth.** auf etw. (*Akk.*) [hinauf]steigen/bis zur Spitze einer Sache hinaufsteigen; **the way up [to sth.]** der Weg hinauf [zu etw.]; **on the way up** (lit. or fig.) auf dem Weg nach oben; **up here/there** hier herauf/dort hinauf; **high/higher up** hoch/höher hinauf; **farther up** weiter hinauf; **halfway/a long/little way up** den halben Weg/ein weites/kurzes Stück hinauf; **come on up!** komm [hier/weiter] herauf!; **up it** *etc.* **comes/goes** herauf kommt/hinauf geht es *usw.;* **up you go!** rauf mit dir! (ugs.); **(b)** (to upstairs, northwards) rauf (bes. ugs.); herauf/hinauf (bes. schriftsprachlich); nach oben; **come up from London to Edinburgh** von London nach Edinburgh [he]raufkommen; **(c)** (to place regarded as more important) **go up to Leeds from the country** vom Land in die Stadt Leeds *od.* nach Leeds fahren; **(d)** (Brit.: to capital) rein (bes. ugs.); herein/hinein (bes. schriftsprachlich); **go up to town** *or* **London** nach London gehen/fahren; **get up to London from Reading** von Reading nach London [he]reinfahren; **(e)** (in higher place, upstairs, in north) oben; **up here/there** hier/da oben; **high up** hoch oben; **an order from high up** (fig.) ein Befehl von ganz oben (ugs.); **higher up in the mountains** weiter oben in den Bergen; **the picture should be higher up** das Bild müsste höher hängen; **farther up** weiter oben; **halfway/a long/little way up** auf halbem Weg nach oben/ein gutes/kurzes Stück weiter oben; **10 metres** *od.* **up** 10 Meter hoch; **live four floors** *or* **storeys up** im vierten Stockwerk wohnen; **his flat is on the next floor up** seine Wohnung ist ein Stockwerk höher; **up north** oben im Norden (ugs.); **(f)** (erect) hoch; **keep your head up** halte den Kopf hoch; *see also* **chin**; **(g)** (out of bed) **be up** auf sein; **up and about** auf den Beinen; **(h)** (in place regarded as more important; Brit.: in capital) **up in town** *or* **London/Leeds** in London/Leeds; **(i)** (in price, value, amount) **prices have gone/are up** die Preise sind gestiegen; **butter is up [by ...]** Butter ist [...] teurer; **(j)** (including higher limit) **up to** bis ... hinauf; **up to midday/up to £2** bis zum Mittag/bis zu

2 Pfund; **(k)** (in position of gain) **we're £300 up on last year** wir liegen 300 Pfund über dem letzten Jahr; **the takings were £500 up on the previous month** die Einnahmen lagen 500 Pfund über denen des Vormonats; **(l)** (ahead) **be three points/games/goals up** (Sport) mit drei Punkten/Spielen/Toren vorn liegen; **be three points up on sb.** drei Punkte vor jmdm. sein *od.* liegen; **(m)** (as far as) **up to sth.** bis zu etw.; **she is up to Chapter 3** sie ist bis zum dritten Kapitel gekommen *od.* ist beim dritten Kapitel; **up to here/there** bis hier[hin]/bis dorthin; **I've had it up to here** (coll.) mir steht es bis hier [hin] (ugs.); **up to now/then/that time/last week** bis jetzt/damals/zu jener Zeit/zur letzten Woche; **(n) up to** (comparable with) **be up to expectation[s]** den Erwartungen entsprechen; **his last opera is not up to his others** seine neueste Oper reicht an seine früheren nicht heran; **(o) up to** (capable of) **[not] be/feel up to sth.** einer Sache (*Dat.*) [nicht] gewachsen sein/sich einer Sache (*Dat.*) [nicht] gewachsen fühlen; **[not] be/feel up to do-ing sth.** [nicht] in der Lage sein/sich nicht in der Lage fühlen, etw. zu tun; **not be up to much** nicht viel taugen; **(p) up to** (derog.: doing) **be up to sth.** etw. anstellen (ugs.); **what is he up to?** was hat er [bloß] vor?; **(q) it is [not] up to sb. to do sth.** (sb.'s duty) es ist [nicht] jmds. Sache, etw. zu tun; **it is up to us to help them** es ist unsere Pflicht, ihnen zu helfen; **now it's up to him to do some-thing** nun liegt es bei *od.* an ihm, etwas zu tun; **it's/that's up to you** (is for you to decide) es/das hängt von dir ab; (concerns only you) es/das ist deine Sache; **(r)** (close) **up against sb./sth.** an jmdm./etw. ⟨*lehnen*⟩; an jmdn./etw. ⟨*stellen*⟩; **sit up against the wall** mit dem Rücken zur *od.* an der Wand sitzen; **(s)** (confronted by) **be up against a problem/difficulty** *etc.* (coll.) vor einem Problem/einer Schwierig-keit *usw.* stehen; **be up against a tough opponent** es mit einem harten Gegner zu tun haben; **be up against it** in großen Schwierigkeiten stecken; **(t) up and down** (upwards and downwards) hinauf und hinunter; (to and fro) auf und ab; **be up and down** (coll.: variable) Hochs und Tiefs haben; **(u)** (facing upwards) **'this side/way up'** (on box etc.) „[hier] oben"; **turn sth. this/the other side/way up** diese/die andere Seite einer Sache nach oben drehen; **the right/wrong way up** richtig/verkehrt *od.* falsch herum; **(v)** (finished, at an end) **be up** abgelaufen; **time is up** die Zeit ist abge-laufen. **2** *prep.* **(a)** (upwards along, from bottom to top) rauf (bes. ugs.); herauf/hinauf (bes. schriftsprachlich); **walk up sth.** etw. hi-naufgehen; **up hill and down dale** bergauf und bergab; **(b)** (upwards through) **force a liquid up a pipe** eine Flüssigkeit durch eine Röhre nach oben pressen; **(c)** (upwards over) **up sth.** etw. (*Akk.*) hinauf; **ivy grew up the wall** Efeu wuchs die Mauer hinauf; **(d)** (along) **come up the street** die Straße herauf- *od.* entlangkommen; **walk up and down the plat-form** auf dem Bahnsteig auf und ab gehen; **(e)** (at or in higher position in or on) [weiter] oben; **further up the ladder/coast** weiter oben auf der Leiter/an der Küste; **(f)** (from bottom to top along) **up the side of a house** an der Seite eines Hauses hinauf. **3** *adj.* **(a)** (directed upwards) aufwärts führend ⟨*Rohr, Kabel*⟩; ⟨*Rolltreppe*⟩ nach oben; nach oben gerichtet ⟨*Kolbenhub*⟩; ⟨*Zug/Gleis* Richtung Stadt; **(b)** (well-informed) **be up in a subject/on the news** in einem Fach auf der Höhe [der Zeit] sein/über alle Neuig-keiten Bescheid wissen *od.* gut informiert sein; **(c)** (coll.: ready) **tea['s]/grub['s] up!** Tee/Essen ist fertig!; **(d)** (coll.: amiss) **what's up?** was ist los? (ugs.); **something is up** irgendwas ist los (ugs.). **4** *n. in pl.* **the ups and downs** (lit. or fig.) das Auf und Ab; (fig.) die Höhen und Tiefen. **5** *v.i.*, **-pp-** (coll.) **up and leave/resign** einfach abhauen (ugs.)/kündigen; **he ups and says ...:** da sagt er doch [ur]-plötzlich ... **6** *v.t.*, **-pp-** (coll.) (increase) erhöhen; (raise up) he-ben

'up-and-coming *adj.* (coll.) aufstrebend

'up-and-up *n.* (coll.) **be on the ∼:** auf dem aufsteigenden Ast sein (ugs.)

'upbeat *n.* (Mus.) Auftakt, *der*

upbringing /'ʌpbrɪŋɪŋ/ *n.* Erziehung, *die*

update 1 /ʌp'deɪt/ *v.t.* (bring up to date) aktualisieren; auf den aktuellen Stand bringen; (modernize) modernisieren. **2** /'ʌpdeɪt/ *n.* Lagebericht, *der* (**on** zu); (∼d version) Neu-ausgabe, *die*

up-'end *v.t.* (lit. or fig.) auf den Kopf stellen

up 'front *adv.* (coll.) **(a)** (at the front) vorne; **(b)** (as down payment) im Voraus

upgrade /ʌp'greɪd/ *v.t.* **(a)** (raise) befördern ⟨*Beschäftigte*⟩; aufwerten ⟨*Stellung*⟩; **(b)** (improve) verbes-sern

upheaval /ʌp'hiːvl/ *n.* Aufruhr, *der;* (commotion, disturb-ance) Durcheinander, *das;* **an emotional ∼:** ein Aufruhr der Gefühle

upheld ⇒ **uphold**

up'hill 1 *adj.* bergauf führend ⟨*Weg, Pfad*⟩; ⟨*Fahrt, Reise*⟩ bergauf; (fig.) **an ∼ task/struggle** eine mühselige Auf-gabe/ein harter Kampf. **2** *adv.* bergauf; **it's ∼ all the way** es geht immer bergauf; (fig.) es ist ein mühseliges Geschäft

up'hold *v.t.*, **upheld (a)** (support) unterstützen; hoch-halten, wahren ⟨*Tradition, Ehre*⟩; schützen ⟨*Verfassung*⟩; **(b)** (confirm) aufrechterhalten ⟨*Forderung, Einwand*⟩; aner-kennen ⟨*Einwand, Beschwerde*⟩

upholster /ʌp'həʊlstə(r)/ *v.t.* polstern

upholstery /ʌp'həʊlstərɪ/ *n.* **(a)** (craft) Polster[er]-handwerk, *das;* **(b)** (padding) Polsterung, *die;* (cover also) Be-zug, *der; attrib.* Polster-

'upkeep *n.* Unterhalt, *der*

'upmarket *adj.* exklusiv ⟨*Waren, Hotel, Geschäft*⟩; Luxus⟨*güter, -hotel, -restaurant*⟩; **go ∼:** exklusiver [und teurer] werden

upon /ə'pɒn/ *prep.* **(a)** (indicating direction) auf (+ *Akk.*); (indi-cating position) auf (+ *Dat.*); **(b)** ⇒ **on 1 a, b; a house ∼ the river bank** ein Haus am Flussufer

upper /'ʌpə(r)/ **1** *compar. adj.* **(a)** ober... ⟨*Nil, Themse usw., Atmosphäre*⟩; Ober⟨*grenze, -lippe, -arm usw., -schle-sien, -österreich usw., -kreide, -devon usw.*⟩; (Mus.) hoch ⟨*Tonlage, Noten*⟩; **∼ circle** (Theatre) oberer Rang; **have/get/gain the ∼ hand [of sb./sth.]** die Oberhand [über jmdn./etw.] haben/erhalten/gewinnen; **(b)** (in rank) ober...; **the ∼ ranks/echelons of the civil service/Army** die oberen *od.* höheren Ränge des Beamtentums/der Armee; **∼ class[es]** Oberschicht, *die;* **the ∼ crust** (coll.) die oberen Zehntausend. **2** *n.* Oberteil, *das;* **'leather ∼s'** „Obermaterial Leder"

upper: ∼ case 1 *n.* Großbuchstaben *Pl.;* **2** *adj.* groß ⟨*Buchstabe*⟩; **∼-class** *adj.* Oberschicht-; **∼-class people/family/accent** Leute/Familie aus der Ober-schicht/Akzent der Oberschicht; **∼ 'deck** *n.* (of ship, bus) Oberdeck, *das*

uppermost /'ʌpəməʊst/ **1** *adj.* oberst...; **be ∼ in sb.'s mind** jmdm. am meisten beschäftigen. **2** *adv.* ganz oben; obenauf; **come ∼** (fig.) an erster Stelle stehen

upper 'sixth *n.* (Brit.) ≈ Oberprima, *die*

uppity /'ʌpɪtɪ/ *adj.* (coll.) hochnäsig (ugs.); **get ∼:** sich aufblasen

upright /'ʌpraɪt/ **1** *adj.* **(a)** aufrecht; steil ⟨*Schrift*⟩; **a chair with an ∼ back** ein Stuhl mit einem geraden Rücken[teil]; **∼ piano** Klavier, *das;* **set/stand/hold sth. ∼:** etw. aufrecht hinstellen/halten; **stand ∼:** aufrecht stehen; **sit ∼:** aufrecht sitzen; **hold oneself ∼:** sich gera-dehalten; *see also* **bolt 4; (b)** (fig.: honourable) aufrecht. **2** *n.* **(a)** seitliche Leiste; (of ladder) Holm, *der;* **(b)** (piano) Klavier, *das*

'uprising *n.* Aufstand, *der*

up-river ⇒ **upstream**

'uproar *n.* Aufruhr, *der;* Tumult, *der;* **be in [an] ∼:** in Aufruhr sein

uproarious /ʌp'rɔːrɪəs/ *adj.* zum Schreien komisch (ugs.) ⟨*Witz, Anblick, Komödie*⟩; schallend ⟨*Gelächter*⟩

up'root *v.t.* [her]ausreißen; ⟨*Sturm:*⟩ entwurzeln; **∼ sb.** jmdn. aus der gewohnten Umgebung herausreißen; **people were ∼ed by the war** die Menschen wurden durch den Krieg entwurzelt

upset 1 /ʌp'set/ *v.t.*, **-tt-**, **upset (a)** (overturn) umkippen; (accidentally) umstoßen ⟨*Tasse, Vase, Milch usw.*⟩; **∼ sth. over sth.** etw. über etw. (*Akk.*) kippen; **(b)** (distress) er-schüttern; mitnehmen (ugs.); (disturb the composure or temper of) aus der Fassung bringen; (shock, make angry, excite) aufregen; **don't let it ∼ you** nimm es nicht so schwer; **∼ oneself**

sich aufregen; **(c)** (make ill) **sth. ~s sb.** etw. bekommt jmdm. nicht; **(d)** (disorganize) stören; durcheinander bringen ‹*Plan, Berechnung, Arrangement*›. **2** *v.i.*, **-tt-**, **upset** umkippen. **3** *adj.* **(a)** (overturned) umgekippt; **(b)** (distressed) bestürzt; (agitated) aufgeregt; (unhappy) unglücklich; (put out) aufgebracht; verärgert; (offended) gekränkt; **be ~ [about sth.]** (be distressed) [über etw. (*Akk.*)] bestürzt sein; (be angry) sich [über etw. (*Akk.*)] ärgern; **we were very ~ to hear of his illness** die Nachricht von seiner Krankheit ist uns sehr nahe gegangen; **get ~ [about/over sth.]** sich [über etw. (*Akk.*)] aufregen; **there's no point in getting ~ about it** es hat keinen Sinn, sich darüber aufzuregen; **(c)** /'-'-/ (disordered) **an ~ stomach** ein verdorbener Magen. **4** /'ʌpset/ *n.* **(a)** (overturning) Umkippen, *das;* **(b)** (agitation) Aufregung, *die;* (shock) Schock, *der;* (annoyance) Verärgerung, *die;* **(c)** (slight quarrel) Missstimmung, *die;* **(d)** (slight illness) Unpäßlichkeit, *die;* **digestive/stomach ~:** Verdauungsstörung, *die*/Magenverstimmung, *die;* **(e)** (disturbance) Zwischenfall, *der;* (confusion, upheaval) Aufruhr, *der;* **(f)** (surprising result) Überraschung, *die*

up'setting *adj.* erschütternd; (sad) traurig; bestürzend; (annoying) ärgerlich; **my mother found the obscene language ~:** meine Mutter fand die obszöne Sprache anstößig

'upshot *n.* Ergebnis, *das*

upside 'down 1 *adv.* verkehrt herum; **turn sth. ~** (lit. or fig.) etw. auf den Kopf stellen. **2** *adj.* auf dem Kopf stehend ‹*Bild*›; **be ~:** auf dem Kopf stehen; **the acrobat hung ~:** der Akrobat hing mit dem Kopf nach unten *od.* kopfüber

up'stage *v.t.* **~ sb.** (fig. coll.) jmdm. die Schau stehlen (ugs.)

upstairs 1 /-'-/ *adv.* nach oben ‹*gehen, kommen*›; oben ‹*sein, wohnen*›. **2** /'--/ *adj.* im Obergeschoss nachgestellt. **3** /-'-/ *n.* Obergeschoss, *das*

up'standing *adj.* **(a)** (strong and healthy) stattlich; **(b)** (honest) aufrichtig; aufrecht

'upstart *n.* Emporkömmling, *der*

'upstate (Amer.) **1** *adj.* **~ New York** nördlicher Teil des Staates New York; **an ~ town** eine Stadt im nördlichen Teil des Staates. **2** *adv.* **live ~:** im nördlichen Teil des Staates leben; **go/travel ~:** in den nördlichen Teil des Staates fahren/reisen

upstream ▶ 1048 | **1** /-'-/ *adv.* flussaufwärts. **2** /'--/ *adj.* flussaufwärts gelegen ‹*Ort*›

'upsurge *n.* Aufwallen, *das* (geh); **she felt an ~ of tenderness** sie fühlte Zärtlichkeit in sich (*Dat.*) aufwallen

'uptake *n.* **be quick/slow on** *or* **in the ~** (coll.) schnell begreifen/schwer von Begriff sein (ugs.)

uptight /ʌp'taɪt, 'ʌptaɪt/ *adj.* (coll.) (tense) nervös (**about** wegen); (touchy, angry) sauer (ugs.) (**about** wegen)

up to 'date pred. *adj.* **be/keep [very] ~:** auf dem [aller]neusten Stand sein/bleiben; **keep/bring sth. ~:** etw. auf dem neusten Stand halten/auf den neusten Stand bringen

up-to-'date attrib. *adj.* (current) aktuell; (modern) modern; aktuell ‹*Mode*›

up-to-the-'minute *adj.* hochaktuell

'upturn *n.* Aufschwung, *der* (**in +** *Gen.*); **an ~ in prices** ein Anstieg der Preise

'upturned *adj.* **(a)** (upside-down) umgedreht; **(b)** (turned upwards) hochgeschlagen ‹*Rand, Krempe*›; nach oben gerichtet ‹*Gesicht, Auge*›; **~ nose** Stupsnase, *die*

upward /'ʌpwəd/ **1** *adj.* nach oben nachgestellt; nach oben gerichtet; **~ movement/trend** (lit. or fig.) Aufwärtsbewegung, *die*/-trend, *der;* **~ gradient** *or* **slope** Steigung, *die.* **2** *adv.* aufwärts ‹*sich bewegen*›; nach oben ‹*sehen, gehen*›; *see also* **face up[ward]**

upwards /'ʌpwədz/ *adv.* **(a)** ⇒ **upward 2**; **(b)** **~ of** mehr als; über; **they cost £200 and ~:** sie kosten 200 Pfund und darüber

Urals /'jʊərlz/ pr. n. pl. Ural, *der*

uranium /jʊə'reɪnɪəm/ *n.* (Chem.) Uran, *das*

Uranus /'jʊərənəs, jʊə'reɪnəs/ pr. n. (Astron.) Uranus, *der*

urban /'ɜːbn/ *adj.* städtisch; Stadt‹*gebiet, -bevölkerung, -planung, -sanierung, -guerilla*›; **~ life** Leben in der Stadt

urbane /ɜː'beɪn/ *adj.* weltmännisch

urchin /'ɜːtʃɪn/ *n.* Range, *die;* (boy) Strolch, *der*

urge /ɜːdʒ/ **1** *v.t.* **(a)** **~ sb. to do sth.** jmdn. drängen, etw. zu tun; **~ sb. to sth.** jmdn. zu etw. drängen; **we ~d him to reconsider** wir rieten ihm dringend, es sich (*Dat.*) noch einmal zu überlegen; **~ sth. [on** *or* **upon sb.]** [jmdn.] zu etw. drängen; **~ caution/patience [on** *or* **upon sb.]** zur Vorsicht/Geduld mahnen; **~ on** *or* **upon sb. the need for sth./for doing sth.** jmdn. die Notwendigkeit einer Sache/die Notwendigkeit, etw. zu tun, ans Herz legen; **~ that sth. [should] be done** darauf dringen, dass etw. getan wird; **(b)** (drive on) [an]treiben; **~ forward/onward** vorwärts treiben; (fig.) treiben. **2** *n.* Trieb, *der;* **have/feel an/the ~ to do sth.** den Drang verspüren, etw. zu tun; **resist the ~ to do sth.** dem [inneren] Drang widerstehen, etw. zu tun

~ 'on *v.t.* antreiben; (hasten) vorantreiben; (encourage) anfeuern; **~d on by hunger/ambition** vom Hunger/Ehrgeiz getrieben

urgency /'ɜːdʒənsɪ/ *n.*, *no pl.* Dringlichkeit, *die;* **there is no ~:** es eilt nicht *od.* ist nicht dringend; **be of the utmost ~:** äußerst dringend sein; **a matter of great ~:** eine sehr dringende Angelegenheit

urgent /'ɜːdʒənt/ *adj.* dringend; (to be dealt with immediately) eilig; **be in ~ need of sth.** etw. dringend brauchen; **give ~ consideration to sth.** etw. vordringlich in Betracht ziehen; **on ~ business** in dringenden Geschäften; **it is ~:** es eilt

urgently /'ɜːdʒəntlɪ/ *adv.* dringend; (without delay) eilig

urinal /jʊə'raɪnl, 'jʊərɪnl/ *n.* (fitting) Urinal, *das;* **[public] ~:** [öffentliche] Herrentoilette; Pissoir, *das*

urinate /'jʊərɪneɪt/ *v.t.* urinieren

urine /'jʊərɪn/ *n.* Urin, *der;* Harn, *der*

URL *abbr.* (Computing) **uniform resource locator** URL, *der*

urn /ɜːn/ *n.* **(a)** **tea/coffee ~:** Tee-/Kaffeemaschine, *die;* **(b)** (vessel) Urne, *die*

Uruguay /'jʊərəgwaɪ/ pr. n. Uruguay (*das*)

Uruguayan /jʊərə'gwaɪən/ ▶ 947 | **1** *adj.* uruguayisch; **sb is ~:** jmd. ist Uruguayer/Uruguayerin. **2** *n.* Uruguayer/Uruguayerin, *die*

US *abbr.* **United States** USA; *attrib.* US-

us /əs, stressed ʌs/ *pron.* **(a)** uns; **it's us** wir sind's (ugs.); **(b)** (coll.: me) **give us a clue/kiss!** gib mir 'nen Tipp/Kuss! (ugs.)

USA *abbr.* **United States of America** USA; *attrib.* der USA nachgestellt

usable /'juːzəbl/ *adj.* brauchbar; gebräuchlich ‹*Wort*›

USAF *abbr.* **United States Air Force** Luftwaffe der Vereinigten Staaten

usage /'juːzɪdʒ, 'juːsɪdʒ/ *n.* **(a)** Brauch, *der;* Gepflogenheit, *die* (geh.); **be in common ~:** allgemein gebräuchlich sein; **(b)** (Ling.: use of language) Sprachgebrauch, *der;* **~ [of a word]** Verwendung [eines Wortes]; **in American** *etc.* **~:** im amerikanischen *usw.* Sprachgebrauch, **(c)** (treatment) Behandlung, *die;* **have rough ~:** schlecht behandelt werden

use 1 /juːs/ *n.* **(a)** Gebrauch, *der;* (of dictionary, calculator, room) Benutzung, *die;* (of word, expression) of pesticide, garlic, herb, spice) Verwendung, *die;* (of name, title) Führung, *die;* (of alcohol, drugs) Konsum, *der;* **the ~ of brutal means/methods** die Anwendung brutaler Mittel/Methoden; **the ~ of troops/tear gas/violence** der Einsatz von Truppen/Tränengas/die Gewaltanwendung; **constant/rough ~:** dauernder Gebrauch/schlechte Behandlung; **[not] be in ~:** [nicht] in Gebrauch sein; **be no longer in ~:** nicht mehr verwendet werden; **be in daily** *etc.* **~:** täglich *usw.* in Gebrauch *od.* Benutzung sein; **come into ~:** in Gebrauch kommen; **go/fall out of ~:** außer Gebrauch kommen; **instructions/directions for ~:** Gebrauchsanweisung, *die;* **ready for [immediate] ~:** [sofort] gebrauchsfertig; **batteries for ~ in** *or* **with watches** Batterien [speziell] für Armbanduhren; **a course for ~ in schools** ein Kurs für die Schule *od.* zur Verwendung im Schulunterricht; **for the ~ of sb.** für jmdn.;

for personal/private ∼: für den persönlichen Gebrauch/den Privatgebrauch; **for external** ∼ **only** nur zur äußerlichen Anwendung; **for** ∼ **in an emergency/only in case of fire** für den Notfall/nur bei Feuer zu benutzen; **with** ∼: durch den Gebrauch; **with careful** *etc.* ∼: bei sorgsamer *usw.* Behandlung; **make** ∼ **of sb./sth.** jmdn./ etw. gebrauchen/(exploit) ausnutzen; **make the best** ∼ **of sth./it** das Beste aus etw./daraus machen; **make good** ∼ **of, turn** *or* **put to good** ∼: gut nutzen ⟨*Zeit, Talent, Geld*⟩; **put sth. to** ∼: etw. verwenden; **(b)** (utility, usefulness) Nutzen, *der;* **these tools/clothes will be of** ∼ **to sb.** dieses Werkzeug wird/diese Kleider werden für jmdn. von Nutzen sein; **is it of [any]** ∼? ist das [irgendwie] zu gebrauchen od. von Nutzen?; **can I be of any** ∼ **to you?** kann ich dir irgendwie helfen?; **be [of] no** ∼ **[to sb.]** [jmdm.] nichts nützen; **he is [of] no** ∼ **in a crisis/as a manager** er ist in einer Krise/als Manager zu nichts nütze od. (ugs.) nicht zu gebrauchen; **it's no** ∼ **[doing that]** es hat keinen Zweck od. Sinn[, das zu tun]; **you're/ that's a fat lot of** ∼ (coll. iron.) du bist ja eine schöne Hilfe/ davon haben wir aber was (ugs. iron.); **what's the** ∼ **of that/of doing that?** was nützt das/was nützt es, das zu tun?; **what's the** ∼? was nützt es?; **oh well, what's the** ∼! ach, was soll's schon! (ugs.); **(c)** (purpose) Verwendung, *die;* Verwendungszweck, *der;* **have its/one's** ∼s seinen Nutzen haben; **have/find a** ∼ **for sth./sb.** für etw./jmdn. Verwendung haben/finden; **have no/not much** ∼ **for sth./sb.** etw./jmdn. nicht/kaum brauchen; **put sth. to a good/a new** ∼: etw. sinnvoll/auf neu[artig]e Weise verwenden; **(d)** (right or power of using) **have the** ∼ **of sth.** etw. benutzen können; **[have the]** ∼ **of kitchen and bathroom** Küchen- und Badbenutzung [haben]; **let sb. have** *or* **give sb. the** ∼ **of sth.** jmdn. etw. benutzen lassen. **2** /juːz/ *v.t.* **(a)** benutzen; nutzen ⟨*Gelegenheit*⟩; anwenden ⟨*Gewalt*⟩; einsetzen ⟨*Tränengas, Wasserwerfer*⟩; in Anspruch nehmen ⟨*Firma, Agentur, Agenten, Dienstleistung*⟩; nutzen ⟨*Zeit, Gelegenheit, Talent, Erfahrung*⟩; führen ⟨*Namen, Titel*⟩; **do you know how to** ∼ **this tool?** kannst du mit diesem Werkzeug umgehen?; **anything you say may be** ∼**d in evidence** was Sie sagen, kann vor Gericht verwendet werden; ∼ **sb.'s name [as a reference]** sich [als Empfehlung] auf jmdn. berufen; **I could** ∼ **the money/a drink** (coll.) ich könnte das Geld gebrauchen/einen Drink vertragen (ugs.); ∼ **one's time to do sth.** seine Zeit dazu nutzen, etw. zu tun; **(b)** (consume as material) verwenden; ∼ **gas/oil for heating** mit Gas/Öl heizen; **the camera** ∼**s 35 mm film** für die Kamera braucht man einen 35-mm-Film; **'**∼ **sparingly'** „sparsam verwenden!"; **(c)** (take habitually) ∼ **drugs/ heroin** *etc.* Drogen/Heroin *usw.* nehmen; **(d)** (employ in speaking or writing) benutzen; gebrauchen; verwenden; ∼ **strong language** Kraftausdrücke gebrauchen; **(e)** (exercise, apply) Gebrauch machen von ⟨*Autorität, Einfluss, Können, Menschenverstand*⟩; ∼ **diplomacy/tact [in one's dealings** *etc.* **with sb.]** [bei jmdm.] diplomatisch vorgehen/[zu jmdm.] taktvoll sein; **he** ∼**d all his strength** er wandte seine ganze Kraft auf; ∼ **a method/ tactics** eine Methode anwenden/nach einer [bestimmten] Taktik vorgehen; **(f)** (take advantage of) ∼ **sb.** jmdn. ausnutzen; **(g)** (treat) behandeln; ∼ **sb./sth. well/badly** jmdn./etw. gut/schlecht behandeln; **(h)** ∼**d to** /ˈjuːst tə/ (formerly) **I** ∼**d to live in London/work in a factory** früher habe ich in London gelebt/in einer Fabrik gearbeitet; **he** ∼**d to be very shy** er war früher sehr schüchtern; **my mother always** ∼**d to say** …: meine Mutter hat immer gesagt od. pflegte zu sagen …; **this** ∼**d to be my room** das war [früher] mein Zimmer; **things aren't what they** ∼**d to be** es ist nichts mehr so wie früher; **he smokes much more than he** ∼**d to** er raucht viel mehr als früher; **I** ∼**d not** *or* **I did not** ∼ *or* (coll.) **I didn't** ∼ *or* (coll.) **I** ∼**[d]n't to smoke** früher habe ich nicht geraucht

∼ **'up** *v.t.* aufbrauchen; verwenden ⟨[*Essens*]*reste*⟩; verbrauchen, erschöpfen ⟨*Kraft, Geld, Energie*⟩; ∼ **up a dozen eggs** ein Dutzend Eier verbrauchen

'use-by date *n.* (esp. Brit.) [Mindest]haltbarkeitsdatum, *das*

used 1 *adj.* **(a)** /juːzd/ (no longer new) gebraucht; benutzt ⟨*Handtuch, Teller*⟩; gestempelt ⟨*Briefmarke*⟩; ∼ **car** Gebrauchtwagen, *der;* ∼**-car salesman** Gebrauchtwagenhändler, *der;* **(b)** /juːst/ (accustomed) ∼ **to sth.** [an] etw. (*Akk.*) gewöhnt; etw. gewohnt; **be/get** ∼ **to sb./sth.** [an] jmdn./etw. gewöhnt sein/sich an jmdn./etw. gewöhnen; **I'm not** ∼ **to this kind of treatment** *or* **to being treated in this way** ich bin eine solche Behandlung nicht gewohnt; ich bin es nicht gewohnt, so behandelt zu werden; **you'll soon be** ∼ **to it** du wirst dich bald od. schnell daran gewöhnen; **[not] be** ∼ **to sb. doing sth./ to having sb. do sth.** [es] [nicht] gewohnt sein, dass jmd. etw. tut; **she was** ∼ **to getting up early** sie war daran gewöhnt, früh aufzustehen. **2** /juːst/ ⇒ **use 2 h**

useful /ˈjuːsfl/ *adj.* **(a)** nützlich; praktisch ⟨*Werkzeug, Gerät, Auto*⟩; brauchbar ⟨*Rat, Idee, Wörterbuch*⟩; hilfreich ⟨*Gespräch, Rat, Idee*⟩; **he is a** ∼ **person to know** es ist nützlich, ihn zu kennen; **this is** ∼ **to know** das ist gut zu wissen; **be** ∼ **to sb.** jmdm. od. für jmdn. nützlich sein; jmdm. nützen; **sb. finds sth.** ∼: etw. nützt jmdm.; **make oneself** ∼: sich nützlich machen; **(b)** (coll.: worthwhile) ordentlich (ugs.); ansehnlich ⟨*Betrag, Stück, Arbeit*⟩

usefulness /ˈjuːsflnɪs/ *n., no pl.* Nützlichkeit, *die;* Brauchbarkeit, *die*

useless /ˈjuːslɪs/ *adj.* unbrauchbar ⟨*Werkzeug, Gerät, Rat, Vorschlag, Idee, Material*⟩; nutzlos ⟨*Wissen, Information, Fakten, Protest, Anstrengung, Kampf*⟩; vergeblich ⟨*Anstrengung, Maßnahme, Kampf, Klage*⟩; zwecklos ⟨*Widerstand, Protest, Argumentieren*⟩; **be** ∼ **to sb.** jmdm. nichts nützen; **feel** ∼: sich nutzlos fühlen; **it's** ∼ **to do that** *or* **doing that** es hat keinen Zweck od. Sinn, das zu tun

uselessly /ˈjuːslɪslɪ/ *adv.* unnütz, sinnlos ⟨*verschwenden, aufwenden*⟩; vergeblich ⟨*kämpfen, protestieren*⟩

user /ˈjuːzə(r)/ *n.* Benutzer, *der*/Benutzerin, *die;* (of drugs, alcohol) Konsument, *der*/Konsumentin, *die;* (of coal, electricity, gas) Verbraucher, *der*/Verbraucherin, *die;* (of telephone) Kunde, *der*/Kundin, *die*

'user-friendly *adj.* benutzerfreundlich

usher /ˈʌʃə(r)/ **1** *n.* ▶ 887 (in court) Gerichtsdiener, *der;* (at cinema, theatre, church) Platzanweiser, *der*/-anweiserin, *die.* **2** *v.t.* führen (geh.); ∼ **sb. to his seat** jmdn. an seinen Platz führen

∼ **'in** *v.t.* ∼ **sb. in** jmdn. hineinführen od. (geh.) -geleiten; ∼ **sth. in** (fig.) etw. einläuten

∼ **'out** *v.t.* hinausführen od. (geh.) -geleiten

usherette /ˌʌʃəˈret/ *n.* ▶ 887 Platzanweiserin, *die*

USN *abbr.* **United States Navy** Marine der Vereinigten Staaten

USS *abbr.* **United States Ship** *Schiff aus den Vereinigten Staaten*

USSR *abbr.* **Union of Soviet Socialist Republics** UdSSR, *die; attrib.* der UdSSR *nachgestellt*

usual /ˈjuːʒʊəl/ *adj.* üblich; **be** ∼ **for sb.** bei jmdm. üblich sein; **it is** ∼ **for sb. to do sth.** es ist üblich, dass jmd. etw. tut; **[no] better/bigger/more** *etc.* **than** ∼: [nicht] besser/größer/mehr *usw.* als gewöhnlich od. üblich; **as [is]** ∼: wie üblich; **as is** ∼ **in such cases** wie in solchen Fällen üblich

usually /ˈjuːʒʊəlɪ/ *adv.* gewöhnlich; normalerweise; **more than** ∼ **tired** *etc.* noch müder *usw.* als üblich; ganz ungewöhnlich müde *usw.*

usurp /juːˈzɜːp/ *v.t.* sich (*Dat.*) widerrechtlich aneignen ⟨*Titel, Recht, Position*⟩; usurpieren (geh.) ⟨*Macht, Thron*⟩

usury /ˈjuːʒərɪ/ *n.* Wucher, *der*

utensil /juːˈtensɪl/ *n.* Utensil, *das;* **writing** ∼s Schreibutensilien

uterus /ˈjuːtərəs/ *n., pl.* **uteri** /ˈjuːtəraɪ/ ▶ 672 (Anat.) Gebärmutter, *die;* Uterus, *der* (fachspr.)

utilisation, utilise ⇒ **utiliz-**

utilitarian /ˌjuːtɪlɪˈteərɪən/ *adj.* **(a)** (functional) funktionell; utilitär ⟨*Ziele*⟩; **(b)** (Philos.) utilitaristisch

utility /juːˈtɪlɪtɪ/ *n.* **(a)** Nutzen, *der;* **(b)** ⇒ **public utility**

u'tility room *n.* Raum, in dem [größere] Haushaltsgeräte (z. B. Waschmaschine) *installiert sind*

utilization /juːtɪlaɪˈzeɪʃn/ *n.* Nutzung, *die*

utilize /ˈjuːtɪlaɪz/ *v.t.* nutzen

utmost /ˈʌtməʊst/ **1** *adj.* äußerst...; tiefst... ‹*Verachtung*›; höchst... ‹*Verehrung, Gefahr*›; größt... ‹*Höflichkeit, Eleganz, Einfachheit, Geschwindigkeit*›; **of** [the] ~ **importance** von äußerster Wichtigkeit; **with the** ~ **caution** mit größter *od.* äußerster Vorsicht. **2** *n.* Äußerste, *das;* **do** *or* **try one's** ~ **to do sth.** mit allen Mitteln versuchen, etw. zu tun

Utopia /juːˈtəʊpɪə/ *n.* (place) Utopia (*das*)

Utopian /juːˈtəʊpɪən/ *adj.* utopisch

utter¹ /ˈʌtə(r)/ *attrib. adj.* vollkommen, völlig ‹*Chaos, Verwirrung, Fehlschlag, Einsamkeit, Unsinn*›; ungeheuer ‹*Elend, Dummheit, Glück, Schönheit*›; größt... ‹*Freude, Vergnügen*›; ~ **fool** Vollidiot, *der* (ugs.)

utter² *v.t.* **(a)** von sich geben ‹*Schrei, Seufzer, Ächzen*›; **(b)** (say) sagen ‹*Wahrheit, Wort*›; schwören ‹*Eid*›; äußern ‹*Drohung*›; zum Ausdruck bringen ‹*Gefühle*›; **the last words he** ~**ed** die letzten Worte, die er sprach

utterance /ˈʌtərəns/ *n.* (spoken words) Worte *Pl.;* (Ling.) [sprachliche] Äußerung; (sentence) Satz, *der*

utterly /ˈʌtəlɪ/ *adv.* völlig; vollkommen; restlos ‹*elend, deprimiert*›; absolut ‹*entzückend, bezaubernd*›; hinreißend ‹*schön*›; äußerst ‹*dumm, lächerlich*›; aus tiefster Seele ‹*verabscheuen, ablehnen, bereuen*›

uttermost /ˈʌtəməʊst/ ⇒ **utmost**

'U-turn *n.* Wende [um 180°]; **the driver/car made a** ~: der Fahrer/Wagen wendete; **make a** ~ **[on sth.]** (fig.) eine Kehrtwendung [bei etw.] vollziehen *od.* machen

UV *abbr.* **ultraviolet** UV

V, v /viː/ *n., pl.* **Vs** *or* **V's** V, v, *das*

v. *abbr.* **(a)** /ˈvɜːsəs, viː/ **versus** gg.; **(b) very**

vacancy /ˈveɪkənsɪ/ *n.* **(a)** (job) freie Stelle; **fill a** ~: eine [freie] Stelle besetzen; **have a** ~: eine freie Stelle *od.* Stelle frei haben; '**vacancies**' (notice outside factory) „Stellen frei"; (in newspaper) „Stellenangebote"; **(b)** (unoccupied room) freies Zimmer; **have a** ~: ein Zimmer frei haben; '**vacancies**' „Zimmer frei"; '**no vacancies**' „belegt"; **(c)** *no pl.* (of look, mind, etc.) Leere, *die*

vacant /ˈveɪkənt/ *adj.* **(a)** (not occupied) frei; '~' (on door of toilet) „frei"; '**situations** ~' „Stellenangebote"; **(b)** (mentally inactive) leer

vacate /vəˈkeɪt/ *v.t.* räumen ‹*Gebäude, Büro, Wohnung*›; aufgeben ‹*Stelle, Amt*›

vacation /vəˈkeɪʃn/ **1** *n.* **(a)** (Brit. Law, Univ.: recess) Ferien *Pl.;* **(b)** (Amer.) ⇒ **holiday 1 b. 2** *v.i.* (Amer.) ~ **[at/in a place]** [an einem Ort] Urlaub machen

vacationer /vəˈkeɪʃənə(r)/, **vacationist** /vəˈkeɪʃənɪst/ *ns.* (Amer.) Urlauber, *der*/Urlauberin, *die*

vaccinate /ˈvæksɪneɪt/ *v.t.* ▶ **865** (Med.) impfen

vaccination /væksɪˈneɪʃn/ *n.* ▶ **865** (Med.) Impfung, *die; attrib.* Impf-; **have a** ~: geimpft werden

vaccine /ˈvæksiːn, ˈvæksɪn/ *n.* ▶ **865** Impfstoff, *der*

vacillate /ˈvæsɪleɪt/ *v.i.* (lit. or fig.) schwanken

vacuum /ˈvækjʊəm/ **1** *n.* **(a)** *pl.* **vacua** /ˈvækjʊə/ *or* ~**s** (Phys.; also fig.) Vakuum, *das;* **live in a** ~ (lit. or fig.) im luftleeren Raum leben; **(b)** *pl.* ~**s** (coll.: ~ cleaner) Sauger, *der* (ugs.). **2** *v.t. & i.* [staub]saugen

vacuum: ~ **cleaner** *n.* Staubsauger, *der;* ~ **flask** *n.* (Brit.) Thermosflasche, *die;* ~**-packed** *adj.* vakuumverpackt

vagabond /ˈvægəbɒnd/ *n.* Landstreicher, *der*/Landstreicherin, *die* (oft abwertend); Vagabund, *der*/Vagabundin, *die* (veralt.)

vagaries /ˈveɪgərɪz/ *n. pl.* (lit. or fig.) Launen *Pl.*

vagina /vəˈdʒaɪnə/ *n., pl.* ~**e** /vəˈdʒaɪniː/ *or* ~**s** ▶ **672** (Anat.) Scheide, *die;* Vagina, *die* (fachspr.)

vagrant /ˈveɪgrənt/ *n.* Landstreicher, *der*/Landstreicherin, *die* (oft abwertend); (in cities) Stadtstreicher, *der*/Stadtstreicherin, *die*

vague /veɪg/ *adj.* vage; verschwommen, undeutlich ‹*Form, Umriss*›; undefinierbar ‹*Farbe*›; (absent-minded) geistesabwesend; (inattentive) unkonzentriert; **not have the** ~**st idea** *or* **notion** nicht die blasseste *od.* leiseste Ahnung haben; **be** ~ **about sth.** etw. nur vag[e] andeuten; (in understanding) nur eine vage Vorstellung von etw. haben

vaguely /ˈveɪglɪ/ *adv.* vage; entfernt ‹*bekannt sein, erinnern an*›; schwach ‹*sich erinnern*›; **he was** ~ **alarmed/disappointed** er war irgendwie beunruhigt/enttäuscht

vain /veɪn/ *adj.* **(a)** (conceited) eitel; **(b)** (useless) leer ‹*Drohung, Versprechen, Worte*›; eitel (geh.) ‹*Vergnügungen*›; vergeblich ‹*Hoffnung, Erwartung, Versuch*›; **in** ~: vergeblich; vergebens

vainly /ˈveɪnlɪ/ *adv.* vergebens; vergeblich

vale /veɪl/ *n.* (arch./poet.) Tal, *das*

valentine /ˈvæləntaɪn/ *n.* **(a)** jmd., dem man am Valentinstag einen Gruß schickt; **(b)** ~ **[card]** Grußkarte zum Valentinstag; **(c)** St. V~**'s Day** Valentinstag, *der*

valet /ˈvælɪt, ˈvæleɪ/ *n.* **(a)** ▶ **887** Kammerdiener, *der;* **(b)** ~ **service** Reinigungs[- und Reparatur]service, *der*

'valet parking *n.* Parkservice, *der*

valiant /ˈvælɪənt/ *adj.* tapfer; kühn (geh.); tapfer ‹*Versuch*›; **he made a** ~ **effort to disguise his disappointment** er versuchte tapfer, seine Enttäuschung zu verbergen

valiantly /ˈvælɪəntlɪ/ *adv.* tapfer; kühn (geh.)

valid /ˈvælɪd/ *adj.* **(a)** (legally acceptable) gültig; berechtigt ‹*Anspruch*›; (legally ~) rechtsgültig; (having legal force) rechtskräftig; bindend ‹*Vertrag*›; **a** ~ **claim** ein Rechtsanspruch (**to** auf + *Akk.*); **(b)** (justifiable) stichhaltig ‹*Argument, Einwand, Theorie*›; triftig ‹*Grund*›; zuverlässig ‹*Methode*›; begründet ‹*Entschuldigung, Einwand*›

validate /ˈvælɪdeɪt/ *v.t.* rechtskräftig machen ‹*Anspruch, Vertrag, Testament*›; bestätigen, beweisen ‹*Hypothese, Theorie*›; für gültig erklären ‹*Wahl*›

validity /vəˈlɪdɪtɪ/ *n., no pl.* **(a)** (of ticket, document) Gültigkeit, *die;* (of claim, contract, marriage, etc.) Rechtsgültigkeit, *die;* **(b)** (of argument, excuse, objection, theory) Stichhaltigkeit, *die;* (of reason) Triftigkeit, *die;* (of method) Zuverlässigkeit, *die*

valley /ˈvælɪ/ *n.* (lit. or fig.) Tal, *das*

valour (*Amer.:* **valor**) /ˈvælə(r)/ *n.* Tapferkeit, *die;* **fight with** ~: tapfer kämpfen

valuable /ˈvæljʊəbl/ **1** *adj.* wertvoll; **be** ~ **to sb.** für jmdn. wertvoll sein. **2** *n., in pl.* Wertgegenstände; Wertsachen

valuation /væljʊˈeɪʃn/ *n.* Schätzung, *die;* **make/get a** ~ **of sth.** etw. schätzen/etw. schätzen lassen

value /ˈvæljuː/ **1** *n.* **(a)** Wert, *der;* **be of great/little/some/no** ~ **[to sb.]** [für jmdn.] von großem/geringem/einigem/keinerlei Nutzen sein; **be of [no] practical** ~ **to sb.** für jmdn. von [keinerlei] praktischem Nutzen sein; **set** *or* **put a high/low** ~ **on sth.** etw. hoch/niedrig einschätzen; **attach great** ~ **to sth.** einer Sache (*Dat.*) große Wichtigkeit beimessen; **what would be the** ~ **of it?** was ist es wohl wert?; **know the** ~ **of sth.** wissen, was etw. wert ist; **sth./nothing of** ~: etw./nichts Wertvolles; **an object of** ~: ein Wertgegenstand; **items of great/little/no** ~: sehr wertvolle/nicht sonderlich wertvolle/wertlose Gegenstände; **be of great/little/no** *etc.* ~: viel/wenig/nichts *usw.* wert sein; **increase** *or* **go up in** ~: an Wert gewinnen; wertvoller werden; **decline** *or* **decrease** *or* **fall** *or* **go down in** ~: an Wert verlieren; **put a** ~ **on sth.** den Wert einer Sache schätzen; **sth. is the** ~ **of ...:** etw. im Werte von ...; **be good/poor** *etc.* ~ **[for money]** seinen Preis wert/nicht wert sein; **get [good]/poor** ~ **[for money]** etwas/nicht viel für sein Geld bekommen; **(b)** *in pl.* (principles) Werte; Wertvorstellungen; **(c)** (Math.) [Zahlen]wert, *der.* **2** *v.t.* **(a)** (appreciate) schätzen; **if you** ~ **your life** wenn dir dein Leben lieb ist; **(b)** (put price on) schätzen, taxieren (**at** auf + *Akk.*)

value added 'tax *n.* (Brit.) Mehrwertsteuer, *die*
valued /'vælju:d/ *adj.* geschätzt ⟨*Freund, Kollege, Kunde*⟩; wertvoll ⟨*Rat, Hilfe*⟩
'value-judgement *n.* Werturteil, *das*
valueless /'væljolɪs/ *adj.* wertlos
valve /vælv/ *n.* (a) Ventil, *das;* (b) (Anat., Zool.) Klappe, *die*
vamoose /və'mu:s/ *v.i.* (Amer. coll.) verduften (ugs.)
vampire /'væmpaɪə(r)/ *n.* Vampir, *der*
van¹ /væn/ *n.* (a) [delivery] ∼: Lieferwagen, *der;* baker's/laundry ∼: Bäckerauto, *das*/Wäschereiauto, *das* (ugs.); (b) (Brit. Railw.) [geschlossener] Wagen
van² *n.* (foremost part) Vorhut, *die;* (fig.: leaders of movement, opinion) Vorkämpfer *Pl.;* be in the ∼ of a movement/the attack zu den Vorkämpfern einer Bewegung gehören/den Angriff anführen
vandal /'vændl/ *n.* (a) Rowdy, *der;* ∼-proof unzerstörbar; (b) (Hist.) V∼: Wandale, *der;* Vandale, *der*
vandalise ⇨ vandalize
vandalism /'vændəlɪzm/ *n.* Wandalismus, *der;* Vandalismus, *der*
vandalize /'vændəlaɪz/ *v.t.* (destroy) [mutwillig] zerstören; (damage) [mutwillig] beschädigen
vane /veɪn/ *n.* (a) (weathercock) (in shape of arrow) Wetterfahne, *die;* (in shape of cock) Wetterhahn, *der;* (b) (blade) Blatt, *das*
vanguard /'væŋgɑːd/ *n.* (a) (Mil., Navy) Vorhut, *die;* (b) (fig.: leaders) Vorreiter; (of literary, artistic, etc. movement) Avantgarde, *die;* be in the ∼ of progress/a movement an der Spitze des Fortschritts/einer Bewegung stehen
vanilla /və'nɪlə/ 1 *n.* Vanille, *die.* 2 *adj.* Vanille-
vanish /'vænɪʃ/ *v.i.* (a) (disappear; coll.: leave quickly) verschwinden; ∼ from sight verschwinden; ∼ into the distance in der Ferne verschwinden; *see also* thin 1 d; (b) (cease to exist) ⟨*Gebäude:*⟩ verschwinden; ⟨*Sitte, Tradition:*⟩ untergehen; ⟨*Zweifel, Bedenken:*⟩ sich auflösen; ⟨*Hoffnung, Chancen:*⟩ schwinden
vanishing /'vænɪʃɪŋ/: ∼-cream *n.* Feuchtigkeitscreme, *die;* ∼-point *n.* (Art, Math.) Fluchtpunkt, *der;* (fig.) Nullpunkt, *der*
vanity /'vænɪtɪ/ *n.* (a) (pride, conceit) Eitelkeit, *die;* (b) (worthlessness) Nichtigkeit, *die*
vanity: ∼ bag *n.* Kosmetiktäschchen, *das;* ∼ case *n.* Kosmetikkoffer, *der*
vanquish /'væŋkwɪʃ/ *v.t.* (literary) bezwingen
vantage-point /'vɑːntɪdʒ pɔɪnt/ *n.* Aussichtspunkt, *der;* (fig.) his ∼ as director der Überblick, den er als Direktor hat/hatte
vapid /'væpɪd/ *adj.* schal ⟨*Geschmack*⟩; geistlos ⟨*Gerede, Bemerkungen*⟩
vapor (Amer.) ⇨ vapour
vaporize (vaporise) /'veɪpəraɪz/ *v.t. & i.* verdampfen
vapour /'veɪpə(r)/ *n.* (Brit.) (a) Dampf, *der;* (mist) Dunst, *der;* ∼s (rising from the ground) Schwaden; (b) (Phys.) Dampf, *der*
'vapour trail *n.* (Aeronaut.) Kondensstreifen, *der*
variable /'veərɪəbl/ *adj.* (a) (alterable) veränderbar; be ∼: verändert werden können; (b) (inconsistent, changeable) unbeständig ⟨*Wetter, Wind, Strömung, Stimmung, Leistung*⟩; wechselhaft ⟨*Wetter, Launen, Schicksal, Qualität, Erfolg*⟩; schwankend ⟨*Kosten*⟩; (c) (Astron., Math.) veränderlich; variabel
variance /'veərɪəns/ *n.* Uneinigkeit, *die;* be at ∼: [sich (*Dat.*)] uneinig sein (on über + *Akk.*); ⟨*Theorien, Meinungen, Philosophien usw.:*⟩ nicht übereinstimmen; be at ∼ with sb./sth. [sich (*Dat.*)] mit jmdm. uneinig sein/mit etw. nicht übereinstimmen
variant /'veərɪənt/ 1 *attrib. adj.* verschieden. 2 *n.* Variante, *die*
variation /veərɪ'eɪʃn/ *n.* (a) (varying) Veränderung, *die;* (in style, diet, routine, programme) Abwechslung, *die;* (difference) Unterschied, *der;* be subject to ∼ ⟨*Preise:*⟩ Schwankungen unterworfen sein; ⟨*Regeln:*⟩ Änderungen unterworfen sein; (b) (variant) Variante, *die* (of, on *Gen.*); (c) (Mus., Biol., Ballet, Math.) Variation, *die*
varicose vein /værɪkəʊs 'veɪn/ *n.* (Med.) Krampfader, *die*

varied /'veərɪd/ *adj.* (differing) unterschiedlich; (marked by variation) abwechslungsreich ⟨*Land, Diät, Leben*⟩; vielseitig·⟨*Arbeit, Stil, Sammlung*⟩; vielgestaltig ⟨*Landschaft*⟩; bunt ⟨*Mischung*⟩
variegated /'veərɪgeɪtɪd/ *adj.* (Bot.) mehrfarbig; panaschiert ⟨*grüne Blätter*⟩
variety /və'raɪətɪ/ *n.* (a) (diversity) Vielfältigkeit, *die;* (in style, diet, routine, programme) Abwechslung, *die;* add *or* give ∼ to sth. etw. abwechslungsreicher gestalten; for the sake of ∼: zur Abwechslung; (b) (assortment) Auswahl, *die* (of an + *Dat.*, von); for a ∼ of reasons aus verschiedenen Gründen; a wide ∼ of birds/flowers viele verschiedene Vogelarten/Blumen; (c) (Theatre) Varietee, *das;* (d) (form) Art, *die;* (of fruit, vegetable, cigarette) Sorte, *die;* (e) (Biol.) Unterart, *die;* Varietät, *die* (fachspr.); (cultivated) Züchtung, *die;* Rasse, *die*
variety: ∼ act *n.* Varieteenummer, *die;* ∼ artist *n.* (Theatre) Varieteekünstler, *der*/-künstlerin, *die;* (Telev.) Showstar, *der;* ∼ show *n.* (a) (Theatre) Varietee, *das;* (b) (Telev.) (varieteeähnliche) Show; ∼ theatre *n.* Varietee-[theater], *das*
various /'veərɪəs/ *adj.* (a) *pred.* (different) verschieden; unterschiedlich; (manifold) vielfältig; (b) *attrib.* (several) verschiedene
variously /'veərɪəslɪ/ *adv.* unterschiedlich
varmint /'vɑːmɪnt/ *n.* (Amer./dial.) (animal) Biest, *das* (ugs.); (person) Halunke, *der;* (child) Racker, *der* (fam.)
varnish /'vɑːnɪʃ/ 1 *n.* (a) Lack, *der;* (transparent) Lasur, *die;* (b) (Art) Firnis, *der;* (c) (Ceramics) Glasur, *die;* (d) (glossiness, lit. or fig.) Glanz, *der.* 2 *v.t.* (a) lackieren; (with transparent ∼) lasieren; (b) (Art) firnissen; (c) (Ceramics) glasieren; (d) (fig.: gloss over) beschönigen; übertünchen ⟨*Fehler, Verbrechen, Laster*⟩
vary /'veərɪ/ 1 *v.t.* verändern; ändern ⟨*Bestimmungen, Programm, Methode, Verhalten, Stil, Route, Kurs*⟩; abwandeln ⟨*Rezept, Muster*⟩; (add variety to) abwechslungsreicher gestalten. 2 *v.i.* (become different) sich ändern; ⟨*Preis, Nachfrage, Qualität, Temperatur:*⟩ schwanken; (be different) unterschiedlich sein; (between extremes) wechseln; (deviate) abweichen; ∼ in weight/size/shape/colour *etc.* im Gewicht/in der Größe/Form/Farbe variieren (from ... to ...: zwischen ... + *Dat.* und ... + *Dat.*); opinions ∼ on this point die Meinungen gehen in diesem Punkt auseinander
varying /'veərɪŋ/ *attrib. adj.* wechselnd; veränderlich ⟨*Wetter*⟩; (different) unterschiedlich
vase /vɑːz/ *n.* Vase, *die*
vasectomy /və'sektəmɪ/ *n.* (Med.) Vasektomie, *die*
Vaseline, (P) /'væsəli:n/ *n.*, no *pl.*, no *indef. art.* Vaseline, *die*
vassal /'væsl/ *n.* (Hist.) Vasall, *der*/Vasallin, *die*
vast /vɑːst/ *adj.* (a) (huge) riesig; weit ⟨*Fläche, Meer, Kontinent, Welt[raum]*⟩; umfangreich ⟨*Sammlung*⟩; (b) (coll.: great) enorm; Riesen⟨*menge, -summe, -fehler*⟩; unermesslich ⟨*Reichtümer*⟩; überwältigend ⟨*Mehrheit*⟩; a ∼ amount of time/money enorm viel Zeit/viel Geld
vastly /'vɑːstlɪ/ *adv.* (coll.) enorm; weitaus ⟨*besser*⟩; weit ⟨*überlegen, unterlegen*⟩; gewaltig ⟨*sich verbessern, irren, überschätzen, unterschätzen*⟩; köstlich ⟨*sich amüsieren*⟩
vastness /'vɑːstnɪs/ *n.*, no *pl.* (a) (hugeness) [immense *od.* ungeheure] Weite; (of building, crowd, army) [immense *od.* ungeheure] Größe; (of collection etc.) [riesiger] Umfang; (b) (greatness) [immenses] Ausmaß
VAT /vi:er'ti:, væt/ *abbr.* value added tax MwSt.
vat /væt/ *n.* Bottich, *der;* (in paper-making) Bütte, *die*
Vatican /'vætɪkən/ *pr. n.* Vatikan, *der*
vault¹ /vɔːlt, vɒlt/ *n.* (a) (Archit.) Gewölbe, *das;* (b) (cellar) [Gewölbe]keller, *der;* (c) (in bank) Tresorraum, *der;* (d) (tomb) Gruft, *die*
vault² 1 *v.i.* (leap) sich schwingen. 2 *v.t.* sich schwingen über (+ *Akk.*); (Gymnastics) springen über (+ *Akk.*). 3 *n.* Sprung, *der*
vaulted /'vɔːltɪd, 'vɒltɪd/ *adj.* (Archit.) gewölbt
vaunt /vɔːnt/ *v.t.* (literary) sich brüsten mit; much ∼ed viel gepriesen *od.* -gerühmt

VCR *abbr.* **video cassette recorder**

VD /viː'diː/ *n.* ▶865⏐ Geschlechtskrankheit, *die;* **get** *or* **catch'∿:** sich (*Dat.*) eine Geschlechtskrankheit zuziehen

VDU *abbr.* **visual display unit**

veal /viːl/ *n., no pl.* Kalb[fleisch], *das; attrib.* Kalbs-; **roast ∿:** Kalbsbraten, *der*

vector /'vektə(r)/ *n.* (Math.) Vektor, *der*

veer /vɪə(r)/ *v.i.* (a) ⟨*Wind:*⟩ [sich] im ' Uhrzeigersinn drehen; ⟨*Schiff, Flugzeug:*⟩ abdrehen; ⟨*Auto:*⟩ ausscheren; **∿ off course/off the road** (unintentionally) vom Kurs/von der Straße abkommen; (intentionally) vom Kurs abdrehen/von der Straße abbiegen; **∿ out of control** außer Kontrolle geraten und ins Schleudern kommen; (b) (fig.: change) schwanken (**from ... to ...:** zwischen ... + *Dat.* und ... + *Dat.*); **∿ from one extreme to the other** ⟨*Person:*⟩ von einem Extrem ins andere fallen; **∿ to the left** (in politics) auf Linkskurs umschwenken

∿ a'way, ∿ 'off *v.i.* ⟨*Schiff, Flugzeug:*⟩ abdrehen; ⟨*Auto:*⟩ ausscheren; ⟨*Fahrer, Straße:*⟩ abbiegen

∿ 'round 1 *v.i.* drehen; (through 180°) wenden. **2** *v.t.* wenden

veg /vedʒ/ *n., pl. same* (coll.) Gemüse, *das;* **meat and two ∿:** Fleisch mit Kartoffeln und Gemüse

vegan /'viːgən/ **1** *n.* Veganer, *der*/Veganerin, *die.* **2** *adj.* vegan

vegetable /'vedʒɪtəbl/ *n.* (a) Gemüse, *das;* **spring/ summer/winter ∿:** Frühjahrs-/Sommer-/Wintergemüse, *das;* **fresh ∿s** frisches Gemüse; **green ∿s** Grüngemüse, *das;* **meat and two ∿** Fleisch mit Kartoffeln und Gemüse; *attrib.* Gemüse⟨*suppe, -extrakt*⟩; (b) (fig.) **become/ be a ∿** (through injury etc.) nur noch [dahin]vegetieren

vegetable: **∿ dish** *n.* (a) (food) Gemüsegericht, *das;* (b) (bowl) Gemüseschüssel, *die;* **∿ dye** *n.* Pflanzenfarbe, *die;* **∿ garden** *n.* Gemüsegarten, *der;* **∿ knife** *n.* Küchenmesser, *das;* **∿ oil** *n.* (Cookery) Pflanzenöl, *das*

vegetarian /vedʒɪ'teərɪən/ **1** *n.* Vegetarier, *der*/Vegetarierin, *die.* **2** *adj.* vegetarisch

vegetarianism /vedʒɪ'teərɪənɪzm/ *n., no pl., no indef. art.* Vegetarismus, *der*

vegetate /'vedʒɪteɪt/ *v.i.* (as result of injury or illness) nur noch [dahin]vegetieren

vegetation /vedʒɪ'teɪʃn/ *n., no pl.* (plants) Vegetation, *die*

veggie /'vedʒɪ/ (coll.) **1** *adj.* vegetarisch; **∿ burger** Bratling, *der.* **2** *n.* (a) (vegetarian) Vegetarier, *der*/Vegetarierin, *die;* (b) (vegetable) Gemüse, *das;* **∿s** Gemüse, *das*

vehemence /'viːəməns/ *n., no pl.* Heftigkeit, *die;* Vehemenz, *die;* **with ∿:** heftig; vehement

vehement /'viːəmənt/ *adj.* heftig; vehement; leidenschaftlich ⟨*Gefühle, Rede*⟩; stark ⟨*Wunsch, Abneigung*⟩; hitzig ⟨*Debatte*⟩

vehemently /'viːəməntlɪ/ *adv.* heftig; vehement

vehicle /'viːɪkl/ *n.* (a) Fahrzeug, *das;* (b) (fig.: medium) Vehikel, *das*

veil /veɪl/ **1** *n.* (a) Schleier, *der;* **take the ∿** (Relig.) den Schleier nehmen (geh.); (b) **beyond the ∿** (fig.) im Jenseits; (c) (fig.: obscuring medium) Schleier, *der;* **∿ of mist/ clouds** Dunst-/Wolkenschleier, *der;* **draw a ∿ over sth.** den Mantel des Schweigens über etw. (*Akk.*) breiten. **2** *v.t.* (a) verschleiern; (b) (fig.: cover) verhüllen; (conceal) verbergen ⟨*Gefühle, Motive*⟩ (**with,** in hinter + *Dat.*); verschleiern ⟨*Fakten, Wahrheit, Bedeutung*⟩

veiled /veɪld/ *adj.* (a) verschleiert; (b) (fig.: covert) versteckt ⟨*Groll, Drohung*⟩; verhüllt ⟨*Anspielung*⟩

vein /veɪn/ *n.* (a) Vene, *die;* (in popular use: any blood vessel) Ader, *die;* (b) (Geol., Mining, Zool.) Ader, *die;* (c) (Bot.) Blattrippe, *die;* Ader, *die;* (d) (streak) Ader, *die;* **∿s** (in wood, marble) Maserung, *die;* (e) (fig.: character, tendency) Zug, *der;* **a ∿ of melancholy/humour** ein melancholischer/humorvoller Zug; (f) (fig.) (mood) Stimmung, *die;* (style) Art, *die;* **be in a happy/sad ∿:** frohgelaunt/traurig gestimmt sein; **in a similar ∿:** vergleichbarer Art

Velcro, (P) /'velkrəʊ/ *n., no pl., no indef. art.* Klettverschluss, *der* ⓦ

vellum /'veləm/ *n.* Pergament, *das*

velocity /vɪ'lɒsɪtɪ/ *n.* Geschwindigkeit, *die;* **∿ of the wind, wind ∿:** Windgeschwindigkeit, *die;* **∿ of light** (Phys.) Lichtgeschwindigkeit, *die*

velvet /'velvɪt/ **1** *n.* Samt, *der;* **[as] smooth as ∿:** weich wie Samt; samtweich. **2** *adj.* aus Samt *nachgestellt;* Samt-; (soft as ∿) samten; samtweich

velveteen /velvɪ'tiːn/ **1** *n.* Baumwollsamt, *der;* Velveton, *der* (fachspr.). **2** *adj.* aus Baumwollsamt *nachgestellt;* Velveton-

velvety /'velvɪtɪ/ *adj.* samtig; samtweich

venal /'viːnl/ *adj.* käuflich, korrupt ⟨*Person*⟩; korrupt ⟨*Verhalten, Praktiken*⟩; eigennützig ⟨*Interessen, Motive, Dienste*⟩

vendetta /ven'detə/ *n.* (a) Hetzkampagne, *die;* (feud) Fehde, *die;* (b) (killings) Blutrache, *die*

vending machine /'vendɪŋ məʃiːn/ *n.* [Verkaufs]automat, *der*

vendor /'vendə(r), 'vendɔː(r)/ *n.* (esp. Law) Verkäufer, *der*/ Verkäuferin, *die*

veneer /vɪ'nɪə(r)/ *n.* (a) Furnier, *das;* (layer in plywood) Furnierblatt, *das;* (b) (fig.: disguise) Tünche, *die;* **beneath a ∿ of respectability** hinter einer Fassade der Wohlanständigkeit

venerable /'venərəbl/ *adj.* ehrwürdig; heilig ⟨*Reliquien*⟩

venerate /'venəreɪt/ *v.t.* verehren; hoch achten; in Ehren halten ⟨*jmds. Andenken, Traditionen, heilige Orte*⟩

veneration /venə'reɪʃn/ *n.* (a) (reverence) Ehrfurcht, *die* (**of, for** vor + *Dat.*); (b) (venerating, being venerated) Verehrung, *die* (**of** für)

venereal disease /vɪ'nɪərɪəl dɪziː:z/ *n.* ▶865⏐ (Med.) Geschlechtskrankheit, *die;* venerische Krankheit (fachspr.)

venetian blind /vɪ'niːʃn blaɪnd/ *n.* Jalousie, *die*

Venezuela /venɪ'zweɪlə/ *pr. n.* Venezuela (*das*)

Venezuelan /venɪ'zweɪlən/ ▶947⏐ **1** *adj.* venezolanisch; **sb. is ∿:** jmd. ist Venezolaner/Venezolanerin. **2** *n.* Venezolaner, *der*/Venezolanerin, *die*

vengeance /'vendʒəns/ *n.* (a) Rache, *die;* Vergeltung, *die;* **take ∿ [up]on sb. [for sth.]** sich an jmdm. [für etw.] rächen; (b) **with a ∿** (coll.) gewaltig (ugs.); **go to work with a ∿** (coll.) sich tüchtig ins Zeug legen (ugs.)

vengeful /'vendʒfl/ *adj.* rachedurstig (geh.); rachsüchtig (geh.)

venial /'viːnɪəl/ *adj.* (a) (pardonable) verzeihlich; entschuldbar; (b) (Theol.) lässlich ⟨*Sünde*⟩

Venice /'venɪs/ *pr. n.* ▶1159⏐ Venedig (*das*)

venison /'venɪsn, 'venɪzn/ *n., no pl.* Hirsch[fleisch], *das;* (of roe deer) Reh[fleisch], *das;* **roast ∿:** Hirsch-/Rehbraten, *der*

venom /'venəm/ *n.* (a) (Zool.) Gift, *das;* (b) (fig.) Boshaftigkeit, *die;* Gehässigkeit, *die*

venomous /'venəməs/ *adj.* (a) (Zool.) giftig; Gift⟨*schlange, -stachel*⟩; (b) (fig.) giftig (ugs.); boshaft

vent¹ /vent/ **1** *n.* (a) (for gas, liquid to escape) Öffnung, *die;* (b) (flue) [Rauch]abzug, *der;* (c) (Geol.) [Vulkan]schlot, *der;* (d) (fig.: for emotions) Ventil, *das* (fig.); **give ∿ to** Luft machen (+ *Dat.*) ⟨*Ärger, Wut*⟩; freien Lauf lassen (+ *Dat.*) ⟨*Gefühlen*⟩. **2** *v.t.* (fig.) Luft machen (+ *Dat.*) ⟨*Kummer, Schmerz*⟩; Luft machen (+ *Dat.*) ⟨*Ärger, Wut*⟩; **∿ one's anger on sb.** seinen Ärger an jmdm. auslassen *od.* abreagieren

vent² *n.* (in garment) Schlitz, *der*

ventilate /'ventɪleɪt/ *v.t.* (a) lüften; (by permanent installation) belüften; (b) (fig.) (submit to public consideration) [offen] erörtern; (voice) kundtun, äußern ⟨*Meinung*⟩; vorbringen ⟨*Beschwerden*⟩

ventilation /ventɪ'leɪʃn/ *n.* (a) *no pl.* Belüftung, *die;* (b) *no pl.* (installation) Lüftung, *die*

ventilator /'ventɪleɪtə(r)/ *n.* (a) Lüftung[svorrichtung], *die;* (fan) Ventilator, *der;* (b) (Med.) Beatmungsgerät, *das*

ventriloquism /ven'trɪləkwɪzm/ *n., no pl.* Bauchreden, *das*

ventriloquist /ven'trɪləkwɪst/ *n.* Bauchredner, *der*/ -rednerin, *die*

venture /'ventʃə(r)/ **1** n. (a) Unternehmung, die; their ~ into space/the unknown ihre Reise in den Weltraum/ins Unbekannte; a new ~ in sth. ein neuer Vorstoß in etw. (Dat.); I can't lose much by the ~: ich kann bei dem Versuch nicht viel verlieren; (b) (Commerc.) Unternehmung, die; a successful ~: ein erfolgreiches Geschäft; a new publishing ~: ein neues verlegerisches Vorhaben od. Projekt. **2** v.i. (a) (dare) wagen; if I might ~ to suggest ...: wenn Sie [mir] gestatten, möchte ich vorschlagen ...; may I ~ to ask ...: darf ich mir erlauben, zu fragen ...; (b) (dare to go) sich wagen; ~ further into the cave sich weiter od. tiefer in die Höhle vorwagen; ~ out of doors sich vor die Tür wagen. **3** v.t. (a) wagen ‹Bitte, Bemerkung, Blick, Vermutung›; zu äußern wagen ‹Ansicht›; sich (Dat.) erlauben ‹Frage, Scherz, Bemerkung›; ~ an explanation for sth. etw. zu erklären versuchen; if I might ~ a suggestion wenn ich mir einen Vorschlag erlauben darf; (b) (risk, stake) aufs Spiel setzen ‹Leben, Ruf, Vermögen, Glück›; setzen ‹Wettsumme› (on auf + Akk.); see also nothing 1 a
~ 'forth (literary) ⇒ ~ out
~ on v.t. sich einlassen auf (+ Akk.); sich wagen an (+ Akk.) ‹Aufgabe›; sich wagen auf (+ Akk.) ‹Reise›
~ 'out v.i. sich hinauswagen
~ upon ⇒ ~ on

'venture capital n., no pl. Wagniskapital, das; Risikokapital, das

venue /'venju:/ n. (Sport) [Austragungs]ort, der; (Mus., Theatre) [Veranstaltungs]ort, der; (meeting place) Treffpunkt, der

Venus /'vi:nəs/ pr. n. (a) (Astron.) Venus, die; (b) (Roman Mythol.) Venus (die)

veracity /və'ræsɪtɪ/ n., no pl. Wahrheitstreue, die

veranda[h] /və'rændə/ n. Veranda, die

verb /vɜ:b/ n. (Ling.) Verb, das

verbal /'vɜ:bl/ adj. (a) (relating to words) sprachlich; his skills are ~: seine Fähigkeiten liegen auf sprachlichem Gebiet; (b) (oral) mündlich; verbal, mündlich ‹Bekenntnis, Anerkennung, Protest›; (c) (Ling.) verbal

verbally /'vɜ:bəlɪ/ adv. (a) (regarding words) sprachlich; mit Worten, verbal ‹beschreiben›; (b) (orally) mündlich; verbal, mündlich ‹protestieren›

verbal 'noun n. (Ling.) Verbalsubstantiv, das

verbatim /və'beɪtɪm/ **1** adv. im Wortlaut ‹veröffentlichen›; [wort]wörtlich ‹sagen, abschreiben, zitieren›. **2** adj. wortgetreu; [wort]wörtlich

verbiage /'vɜ:bɪɪdʒ/ n., no pl., no indef. art. (a) (wordiness) Geschwätzigkeit, die; (b) (words) Geschwätz, das

verbose /və'bəʊs/ adj. geschwätzig; weitschweifig ‹Roman, Vortrag, Autor›; langatmig ‹Rede, Redner, Stil›

verdant /'vɜ:dənt/ adj. (literary) [saft]grün

verdict /'vɜ:dɪkt/ n. (a) (Law) Urteil, das; [Urteils]spruch, der; open ~: Feststellung eines gewaltsamen Todes ohne Nennung der Ursache (bei einer gerichtlichen Untersuchung); ~ of guilty/not guilty Schuld-/Freispruch, der; reach a ~: zu einem Urteil kommen; (b) (judgement) Urteil, das (on über + Akk.); (decision) Entscheidung, die; the ~ of the electors die Entscheidung der Wähler; give or pass a/ one's ~ [on sb./sth.] ein/sein Urteil [über jmdn./etw.] abgeben

verge /vɜ:dʒ/ n. (a) (grass edging) Rasensaum, der; (on road) Bankette, die; 'keep off the ~' „Bankette nicht befahrbar"; (b) (brink, border, lit. or fig.) Rand, der; (fig.: point at which something begins) Schwelle, die; be on the ~ of economic collapse/of war am Rand des wirtschaftlichen Zusammenbruchs/an der Schwelle des Krieges stehen; be on the ~ of despair/tears/a breakthrough der Verzweiflung/den Tränen/dem Durchbruch nahe sein; be on the ~ of doing sth. kurz davor stehen, etw. zu tun; bring sb./sth. to the ~ of sth. jmdn./etw. an den Rand von etw. bringen
~ on v.t. [an]grenzen an (+ Akk.); be verging on 70 an die 70 sein; an estate verging on four acres (fig.) ein Grundstück von fast vier Morgen [Größe]; be verging on tears/madness den Tränen/dem Wahnsinn nahe sein

verger /'vɜ:dʒə(r)/ n. (Eccl.) Küster, der

verifiable /'verɪfaɪəbl/ adj. nachprüfbar

verification /verɪfɪ'keɪʃn/ n. (a) (check) Überprüfung, die; (b) ⇒ verify b: Bestätigung, die; Bekräftigung, die; Nachweis, der; (c) (bearing out) Bestätigung, die

verify /'verɪfaɪ/ v.t. (a) (check) überprüfen; prüfen ‹Bücher›; ring sb. up to ~ the news jmdn. anrufen, um sich (Dat.) die [Richtigkeit der] Nachricht bestätigen zu lassen; (b) (confirm) bestätigen ‹Vermutung, Diagnose›; bekräftigen ‹Anspruch, Forderung›; nachweisen ‹Identität›; (c) (bear out) bestätigen; beweisen ‹Theorie›

veritable /'verɪtəbl/ adj. (literary) richtig; wahr, richtig ‹Engel, Genie›; wahr ‹Wunder›

vermilion /və'mɪljən/ **1** n. (colour) Zinnoberrot. **2** adj. zinnoberrot

vermin /'vɜ:mɪn/ n., no pl., no indef. art. Ungeziefer, das; (fig. derog.) Pack, das (abwertend); Abschaum, der (abwertend)

vermouth /'vɜ:məθ, və'mu:θ/ n. Wermut[wein], der

vernacular /və'nækjʊlə(r)/ **1** adj. (native) landessprachlich; ‹Predigt, Zeitung› in der Landessprache; (not learned or technical) volkstümlich; (in dialect) mundartlich. **2** n. (a) (native language) Landessprache, die; (dialect) Dialekt, der; (b) (jargon) Sprache, die; (of a profession or group) Jargon, der

verruca /ve'ru:kə/ n., pl. ~e /ve'ru:si:/ or ~s (Med.) Warze, die; Verruca, die (fachspr.)

versatile /'vɜ:sətaɪl/ adj. vielseitig; (mentally) flexibel; (having many uses) vielseitig verwendbar

versatility /vɜ:sə'tɪlɪtɪ/ n., no pl. Vielseitigkeit, die; (mental) Flexibilität, die; (variety of uses) vielseitige Verwendbarkeit

verse /vɜ:s/ n. (a) (line) Vers, der; (b) (stanza) Strophe, die; of or in or with five ~s fünfstrophig; (c) no pl., no indef. art. (poetry) Lyrik, die; write some ~: einige Verse schreiben; piece of ~: Gedicht, das; written in ~: in Versform; put sth. into ~: etw. in Verse fassen; (d) (in Bible) Vers, der

versed /vɜ:st/ adj. be [well] ~ in sth. sich in etw. (Dat.) [gut] auskennen

version /'vɜ:ʃn/ n. Version, die; (in another language) Übersetzung, die; (in another form also) Fassung, die; (of vehicle, machine, tool) Modell, das

versus /'vɜ:səs/ prep. gegen

vertebra /'vɜ:tɪbrə/ n., pl. ~e /'vɜ:tɪbri:/ (Anat.) Wirbel, der; ~e (backbone) Wirbelsäule, die

vertebrate /'vɜ:tɪbrət, 'vɜ:tɪbreɪt/ (Zool.) **1** adj. Wirbel‹tier›; Wirbeltier‹skelett, -fossilien›. **2** n. Wirbeltier, das

vertex /'vɜ:teks/ n., pl. vertices /'vɜ:tɪsi:z/ or ~es (highest point) Gipfel, der; (of tower, turret) Spitze, die; (Archit.: of dome, arch) Scheitel[punkt], der

vertical /'vɜ:tɪkl/ **1** adj. senkrecht; senkrecht aufragend od. abfallend ‹Klippe›; be ~: senkrecht stehen. **2** n. senkrechte od. vertikale Linie; be out of [the] ~: nicht im od. außer Lot sein

vertically /'vɜ:tɪkəlɪ/ adv. senkrecht; vertikal

vertical: ~ 'take-off n. (Aeronaut.) Senkrechtstart, der; ~ 'take-off aircraft n. (Aeronaut.) Senkrechtstarter, der

vertices pl. of **vertex**

vertigo /'vɜ:tɪgəʊ/ n., pl. ~s Schwindel, der; Vertigo, die (Med.)

verve /vɜ:v/ n. Schwung, der; (of artist, orchestra's playing, sports team's play) Temperament, das

very /'verɪ/ **1** attrib. adj. (a) (precise, exact) genau; on the ~ day when ...: genau am [selben] Tag, an dem ...; you're the ~ person I wanted to see genau dich wollte ich sehen; at the ~ moment when ...: im selben Augenblick, als ...; in the ~ centre genau in der Mitte; the ~ thing genau das Richtige; (b) (extreme) at the ~ back/ front ganz hinten/vorn; at the ~ edge of the cliff ganz am Rand der Klippe; at the ~ end/beginning ganz am Ende/Anfang; from the ~ beginning von Anfang an; only a ~ little nur ein ganz kleines bisschen; (c) (mere) bloß ‹Gedanke›; at the ~ thought allein schon beim Gedanken; the ~ fact of his presence allein schon seine

Anwesenheit; **(d)** (absolute) absolut ‹*Minimum, Maximum*›; **do one's ~ best** *or* **utmost** sein Menschenmöglichstes tun; **the ~ most I can offer is ...:** ich kann allerhöchstens ... anbieten; **it's the ~ least** das ist das Allermindeste; **£50 at the ~ most** allerhöchstens 50 Pfund; **be the ~ first to arrive** als Allererster ankommen; **for the ~ last time** zum allerletzten Mal; **(e)** *emphat.* **before their ~ eyes** vor ihren Augen; **be caught in the ~ act** auf frischer Tat ertappt werden; **under sb.'s ~ nose** (fig. coll.) direkt vor jmds. Augen (*Dat.*). **2** *adv.* **(a)** (extremely) sehr; **it's ~ near** es ist ganz in der Nähe; **in the ~ near future** in allernächster Zukunft; **it's ~ possible that ...:** es ist sehr gut möglich, dass ...; **~ probably** höchstwahrscheinlich; **she's ~/so ~ thin** sie ist sehr dünn/so dünn; **how ~ rude [of him]!** das ist aber unhöflich [von ihm]!; **[yes,] ~ much [so]** [ja,] sehr; **~ much prettier/better** [sehr] viel hübscher/besser; **not ~ much** nicht sehr; **~ little** [nur] sehr wenig ‹*verstehen, essen*›; **thank you [~,] ~ much** [vielen,] vielen Dank; **not ~ big** (not extremely big) nicht sehr groß; (not at all big) nicht gerade groß; **(b)** (absolutely) aller‹*best..., -letzt..., -leichtest...*›; **at the ~ latest** allerspätestens; **the ~ last thing I expected** das, womit ich am allerwenigsten gerechnet hatte; **(c)** (precisely) **the ~ same one** genau der-/die-/dasselbe; **that is the ~ word he used** das ist genau das Wort, das er gebrauchte; **in his ~ next sentence/breath** schon im nächsten Satz/Atemzug; **(d) ~ good** (accepting) sehr wohl; (agreeing) sehr schön; **~ well** *expr. reluctant consent* also gut; na schön; **that's all ~ well, but ...:** das ist ja alles schön und gut, aber ...

vespers /'vespəz/ *n. constr. as sing. or pl.* (Eccl.) Vesper, *die*

vessel /'vesl/ *n.* **(a)** (receptacle; also Anat., Bot.) Gefäß, *das;* [**drinking-**]~: Trinkgefäß, *das; see also* **blood vessel; (b)** (Naut.) Schiff, *das*

vest /vest/ **1** *n.* **(a)** (Brit.: undergarment) Unterhemd, *das;* (woman's) Hemd, *das.* **2** *v.t.* **~ sb. with sth., ~ sth. in sb.** jmdm. etw. verleihen; **be ~ed in sb.** jmdm. übertragen sein; *see also* **vested**

vested /'vestɪd/ *adj.* **~ interest/right** wohlerworbener Anspruch; (established by law) gesetzlicher Anspruch; **~ interests** (groups of persons) Interessengruppen; **have a ~ interest in sth.** (fig.) ein persönliches Interesse an etw. (*Dat.*) haben

vestibule /'vestɪbjuːl/ *n.* **(a)** (indoors) [Eingangs]halle, *die;* **(b)** (external porch) Vorhalle, *die;* **(c)** (Amer. Railw.) Vorraum, *der*

vestige /'vestɪdʒ/ *n.* Spur, *die;* **not a ~ of truth/honour** kein Fünkchen Wahrheit/Ehre

vestment /'vestmənt/ *n.* [Priester]gewand, *das;* (worn on special occasions) Ornat, *der*

vestry /'vestrɪ/ *n.* (Eccl.) Sakristei, *die*

vet /vet/ **1** *n.* ▶ **887** Tierarzt, *der/*-ärztin, *die.* **2** *v.t.,* **-tt-** überprüfen; **~ an article for errors** einen Artikel auf Fehler [hin] durchsehen

veteran /'vetərən/ **1** *n.* Veteran, *der/*Veteranin, *die.* **2** *attrib. adj.* altgedient ‹*Offizier, Politiker, Schauspieler*›

veteran 'car *n.* (Brit.) Veteran, *der*

veterinarian /vetərɪ'neərɪən/ *n.* (Amer.) ⇒ **veterinary surgeon**

veterinary /'vetərɪnərɪ/ *attrib. adj.* tiermedizinisch; veterinär; **~ science/medicine** Veterinär- *od.* Tiermedizin, *die*

veterinary 'surgeon *n.* ▶ **887** (Brit.) Tierarzt, *der/*-ärztin, *die*

veto /'viːtəʊ/ **1** *n., pl.* **~es (a)** [power *or* right of] ~: Veto[recht], *das;* **(b)** (rejection, prohibition) Veto, *das* (**on** gegen, **from** von seiten); **put a** *or* **one's ~ on sth.** sein Veto gegen etw. einlegen. **2** *v.t.* sein Veto einlegen gegen

vex /veks/ *v.t.* [ver]ärgern; (cause to worry) beunruhigen; (dissatisfy, disappoint) bekümmern; **be ~ed with sb.** sich über jmdn. ärgern

vexation /vek'seɪʃn/ *n.* **(a)** (act of harassing) Belästigung, *die;* **(b)** (state of irritation) Verärgerung, *die* (**with, at** über + *Akk.*); (state of worry) Beunruhigung, *die;* (dissatisfaction, disappointment) Kummer, *der;* **(c)** (annoying thing) Ärgernis, *das* (**to, for** für)

vexatious /vek'seɪʃəs/ *adj.* ärgerlich; unausstehlich ‹*Person*›

vexed /vekst/ *adj.* (annoyed) verärgert (**by** über + *Akk.*); (distressed) bekümmert (**by** über + *Akk.*)

vexing /'veksɪŋ/ *adj.* lästig ‹*Angelegenheit, Problem, Sorgen*›; ärgerlich ‹*Zwickmühle*›

VG *abbr.* **very good**

VHF *abbr.* **Very High Frequency** UKW

via /'vaɪə/ *prep.* über (+ *Akk.*) ‹*Ort, Sender, Telefon*›; auf (+ *Dat.*) ‹*Weg*›; durch ‹*Eingang, Schornstein, Person*›; per ‹*Post*›

viability /vaɪə'bɪlɪtɪ/ *n., no pl.* **(a)** (of foetus, animal, plant) Lebensfähigkeit, *die;* **(b)** (fig.) (of state, company) Lebensfähigkeit, *die;* (feasibility) Realisierbarkeit, *die*

viable /'vaɪəbl/ *adj.* **(a)** (capable of maintaining life) lebensfähig; **(b)** (fig.) lebensfähig ‹*Staat, Firma*›; (feasible) realisierbar

viaduct /'vaɪədʌkt/ *n.* Viadukt, *das od. der*

vibrant /'vaɪbrənt/ *adj.* pulsierend ‹*Leben*›; lebensprühend ‹*Atmosphäre*›; dynamisch ‹*Kraft*›; lebhaft ‹*Farbe, Rot*›

vibrate /vaɪ'breɪt/ **1** *v.i.* **(a)** vibrieren; (under strong impact) beben; **(b)** (resound) [nach]klingen; **(c)** (Phys.) schwingen; ‹*Glocke:*› vibrieren; **(d)** (thrill) ‹*Stimme, Körper:*› vibrieren (**with** vor + *Dat.*). **2** *v.t.* vibrieren lassen; zum Schwingen bringen ‹*Saite*›

vibration /vaɪ'breɪʃn/ *n.* **(a)** (vibrating) Vibrationen; (visible) Vibrieren, *das;* (under strong impact) Beben, *das;* **send ~s** *or* **a ~ through sth.** ‹*Erdstoß:*› etw. erzittern lassen; **(b)** (Phys.) Schwingung, *die;* **(c)** *in pl.* (fig.) **get some ~s** etwas spüren; **I get good ~s from this place** dieser Ort hat eine wohltuende Ausstrahlung

vibrato /vɪ'brɑːtəʊ/ *n., pl.* **~s** (Mus.) Vibrato, *das*

vicar /'vɪkə(r)/ *n.* Pfarrer, *der*

vicarage /'vɪkərɪdʒ/ *n.* Pfarrhaus, *das*

vicarious /vɪ'keərɪəs/ *adj.* **(a)** (delegated) Stellvertreter-; **(b)** (done for another) stellvertretend; **(c)** (experienced through another) nachempfunden ‹*Freude, Erregung usw.*›; **~ [sexual] satisfaction** Ersatzbefriedigung, *die*

vice¹ /vaɪs/ *n.* **(a)** Laster, *das;* **a life/den of ~:** ein Lasterleben/eine Lasterhöhle; **(b)** (character or behaviour defect) Fehler, *der*

vice² *n.* (Brit.: tool) Schraubstock, *der*

vice- *pref.* Vize-

vice: ~-'chairman *n.* stellvertretender Vorsitzender; **~-'chairmanship** *n.* Amt des/der stellvertretenden Vorsitzenden; **~-'chancellor** *n.* ▶ **1152** (Univ.) Vizekanzler, *der/*Vizekanzlerin, *die*

'vicelike *adj.* eisern ‹*Griff*›; fest ‹*Umklammerung*›

vice: ~-'presidency *n.* Amt des Vizepräsidenten/der Vizepräsidentin, *die;* **~-'president** *n.* ▶ **1152** Vizepräsident, *der/*-präsidentin, *die;* **~ squad** *n.* (Police) Sittenpolizei, *die*

vice versa /vaɪsɪ 'vɜːsə/ *adv.* umgekehrt

vicinity /vɪ'sɪnɪtɪ/ *n.* **(a)** (neighbourhood) Umgebung, *die;* **in our ~:** nicht weit von uns [entfernt]; **in the immediate ~:** ganz in der Nähe; **in the ~ [of a place]** in der Nähe [eines Ortes]; **in the ~ of 50** (fig.) so um die 50; **(b)** *no pl.* (nearness) Nähe, *die*

vicious /'vɪʃəs/ *adj.* **(a)** (malicious, spiteful) böse; boshaft ‹*Äußerung*›; böswillig ‹*Versuch, Kritik*›; bösartig ‹*Äußerung, Tier*›; **(b)** (wicked) skrupellos ‹*Tyrann, Verbrecher*›; schlecht ‹*Person*›; **(c)** (violent, severe) brutal; unerträglich ‹*Wetter, Schmerz*›

vicious 'circle *n.* Teufelskreis, *der*

viciously /'vɪʃəslɪ/ *adv.* **(a)** (maliciously, spitefully) boshaft; auf gehässige Weise ‹*kritisieren*›; **(b)** (violently, severely) brutal

vicissitude /vɪ'sɪsɪtjuːd/ *n.* steter Wandel, ~s (fickleness) Unbeständigkeit, *die;* **the ~s of life** die Wechselfälle des Lebens

victim /'vɪktɪm/ *n.* (also dupe, Relig.) Opfer, *das;* (of sarcasm, abuse) Zielscheibe, *die* (fig.); **be the ~ of sb.'s anger/envy/policy** unter jmds. Zorn/Neid/Politik (*Dat.*) zu leiden haben; **fall [a] ~ to sth.** das Opfer einer Sache (*Gen.*)

werden; **fall** ~ **to famine** der Hungersnot (*Dat.*) zum Opfer fallen

victimisation, victimise ⇒ **victimiz-**

victimization /vɪktɪmaɪˈzeɪʃn/ n. Schikanierung, *die;* (selective punishment) gezielte Bestrafung

victimize /ˈvɪktɪmaɪz/ v.t. (a) (make a victim) schikanieren; **be** ~**d** [**by sb.**] unter jmdm. zu leiden haben; (b) (punish selectively) gezielt bestrafen

victor /ˈvɪktə(r)/ n. (rhet.) Sieger, *der*/Siegerin, *die*

Victorian /vɪkˈtɔːrɪən/ **1** adj. viktorianisch. **2** n. Viktorianer, *der*/Viktorianerin, *die*

victorious /vɪkˈtɔːrɪəs/ adj. siegreich; **be** ~ **over sb./ sth.** über jmdn./etw. siegreich bleiben; **be** ~ **in one's struggle** aus seinem Kampf siegreich hervorgehen

victory /ˈvɪktərɪ/ n. Sieg, *der* (**over** über + *Akk.*); attrib. Sieges-; **achieve** ~: den Sieg erringen; **be sure of** ~: der sichere Sieger sein

victuals /ˈvɪtlz/ n. pl. (dated) Esswaren *Pl.;* (of fort, ship, for journey) Proviant, *der*

video /ˈvɪdɪəʊ/ **1** adj. Video⟨rekorder, -kassette, -kopf⟩. **2** n., pl. ~**s** (a) (~ recorder) Videorekorder, *der;* (~ film, ~tape, ~ recording) Video, *das* (ugs.); **have sth. on** ~: etw. auf Video haben (ugs.); (b) (visual element of TV broadcasts) Bild, *das.* **3** v.t. ⇒ **videotape 2**

video: ~ **camera** n. Videokamera, *die;* ~ **cas- 'sette** n. Videokassette, *die;* ~ **cas'sette recorder** n. Videokassettenrekorder, *der;* ~ **clip** n. Videoclip, *der;* ~ **disc** n. Bildplatte *die;* Videoplatte, *die;* ~ **film** n. Videofilm, *der;* ~ **game** n. Videospiel, *das;* ~ **library** n. Videothek, *die;* ~ **'nasty** n. Horrorvideo, *das;* ~**-on- demand** n., no pl. Video-on-Demand, *das;* ~ **re- corder** n. Videorekorder, *der;* ~ **recording** n. Videoaufnahme, *die;* ~**tape 1** n. Videoband, *das;* **2** v.t. [auf Videoband (*Akk.*)] aufnehmen; ~ **telephone** n. Bildtelefon, *das;* ~**text** n. Bildschirmtext, *der;* (teletext) Videotext, *der*

vie /vaɪ/ v.i. **vying** /ˈvaɪɪŋ/ ~ [**with sb.**] **for sth.** [mit jmdm.] um etw. wetteifern

Vienna /vɪˈenə/ ▶ 1159 **1** pr. n. Wien (*das*). **2** attrib. adj. Wiener

Viennese /vɪəˈniːz/ ▶ 1159 **1** adj. Wiener; **sb. is** ~: jmd. ist Wiener/Wienerin. **2** n., pl. same Wiener, *der*/ Wienerin, *die*

Vietnam /vɪetˈnæm/ pr. n. (a) Vietnam (*das*); (b) ~ [**War**] Vietnamkrieg, *der*

Vietnamese /vɪetnəˈmiːz/ **1** adj. vietnamesisch. **2** n., pl. same (a) (person) Vietnamese, *der*/Vietnamesin, *die;* (b) ▶ 897 (language) Vietnamesisch, *das*

view /vjuː/ **1** n. (a) (range of vision) Sicht, *die;* **get a good** ~ **of sth.** etw. gut sehen können; **have a clear/distant** ~ **of sth.** etw. deutlich/in der Ferne sehen können; **be out of/in** ~: nicht zu sehen/zu sehen sein; **come into** ~: in Sicht kommen; **our hotel has a good** ~ **of the sea** von unserem Hotel aus kann man das Meer gut sehen; (b) (what is seen) Aussicht, *die;* **the** ~**s from here** die Aus- sicht von hier; **a room with a** ~: ein Zimmer mit Aus- sicht; (c) (picture) Ansicht, *die;* **photographic** ~: Foto, *das;* (d) (opinion) Ansicht, *die;* **what is your** ~ **or are your** ~**s on this?** was meinst du dazu?; **don't you have any** ~[**s**] **about it?** hast du keine Meinung dazu?; **the general/majority** ~ **is that** ...: die Allgemeinheit/ Mehrheit ist der Ansicht, dass ...; **take a favourable** ~ **of sth.** etw. billigen; **hold** *or* **take the** ~ **that** ...: der Ansicht sein, dass ...; **in my** ~: meiner Ansicht nach; **in sb.'s** ~: nach jmds. Ansicht; **I take a different** ~: ich bin anderer Ansicht; **take a critical/ grave/optimistic** ~ **of sth.** etw. kritisch/ernst/opti- mistisch beurteilen; (e) **be on** ~ ⟨*Waren, Haus:*⟩ besich- tigt werden können; ⟨*Bauplan:*⟩ [zur Einsicht] ausliegen; **in** ~ **of sth.** (fig.) angesichts einer Sache; **with a** ~ **to** *or* **with a** *or* **the** ~ **of doing sth.** in der Absicht, etw. zu tun; **with a** ~ **to sth.** (fig.) mit etw. im Auge; **with this in** ~: in Anbetracht dessen; *see also* **point 1 l;** (f) (survey) Betrachtung, *die;* (of house, site) Besichtigung, *die.* **2** v.t. (a)

(look at) sich (*Dat.*) ansehen; (b) (consider) betrachten; beur- teilen ⟨*Situation, Problem*⟩; ~**ed in this light** ...: so ge- sehen ...; **I** ~ **the matter differently** ich sehe das anders; (c) (inspect) besichtigen; **ask to** ~ **sth.** darum bitten, etw. besichtigen zu dürfen. **3** v.i. (Telev.) fernsehen

viewdata /ˈvjuːdeɪtə/ n. (Teleph.) Bildschirmtextsystem, *das*

viewer /ˈvjuːə(r)/ n. (a) (Telev.) [Fernseh]zuschauer, *der*/ -zuschauerin, *die;* (b) (Photog.) (for cine film) Filmbetrachter, *der;* (for slides) Diabetrachter, *der*

'viewfinder n. (Photog.) Sucher, *der*

viewing /ˈvjuːɪŋ/ n. (a) (Telev.) Fernsehen, *das;* ~ **fig- ures** Einschaltquoten *Pl.;* **at peak** ~ **time** zur besten Sendezeit; (b) (of house, at auction, etc.) Besichtigung, *die*

viewpoint /ˈvjuːpɔɪnt/ n. Standpunkt, *der;* Sehweise, *die;* **from a general/the political** ~ ...: allgemein/politisch gesehen ...

vigil /ˈvɪdʒɪl/ n. Wachen, *das;* **keep** ~ [**over sb.**] [bei jmdm.] wachen

vigilance /ˈvɪdʒɪləns/ n., no pl. Wachsamkeit, *die*

vigilant /ˈvɪdʒɪlənt/ adj. wachsam; **be** ~ **for sth.** auf etw. (*Akk.*) achten

vigilante /vɪdʒɪˈlæntɪ/ n. Mitglied, *das* einer/der Bürg- erwehr; ~ **group** Bürgerwehr, *die*

vignette /viːˈnjet/ n. (Lit.) Skizze, *die*

vigor (Amer.) ⇒ **vigour**

vigorous /ˈvɪɡərəs/ adj. kraftvoll; kräftig ⟨*Person, Tier, Stoß, Pflanze, Wachstum, Trieb*⟩; robust ⟨*Gesundheit*⟩; lei- denschaftlich ⟨*Verteidigung, Befürworter*⟩; heftig ⟨*Nicken, Attacke, Kritik, Protest*⟩; intensiv ⟨*Gymnastik, Denksport*⟩; energisch ⟨*Versuch, Anstrengung, Leugnen, Maßnahme*⟩; schwungvoll ⟨*Rede*⟩

vigour /ˈvɪɡə(r)/ n. (Brit.) (a) (of person, animal, sexuality) Vita- lität, *die;* (of limbs, body) Kraft, *die;* (of health) Robustheit, *die;* (of argument, struggle, protest, denial, attack, criticism) Heftigkeit, *die;* (of performance, speech) Schwung, *der;* (of words, style, mind, intellect) Lebendigkeit, *die;* **with** ~: schwungvoll ⟨*musizieren, reden, singen, schauspielern*⟩; kräftig ⟨*reiben, schrubben, drücken, ziehen*⟩; (b) (Bot.) Wuchskraft, *die*

Viking /ˈvaɪkɪŋ/ n. (Hist.) Wikinger, *der*/Wikingerin, *die;* attrib. Wikinger-

vile /vaɪl/ adj. (a) (base) verwerflich (geh.); abscheulich ⟨*Charakter, Verbrechen*⟩; gemein ⟨*Verleumdung*⟩; vulgär ⟨*Sprache*⟩; (repulsive) widerwärtig; (b) (coll.: very unpleasant) scheußlich (ugs.)

villa /ˈvɪlə/ n. (a) (holiday house) [**holiday**] ~: Ferienhaus, *das;* (b) (country house) [**country**] ~: Landhaus, *das*

village /ˈvɪlɪdʒ/ n. Dorf, *das;* attrib. Dorf⟨*leben, -kneipe usw.*⟩

village: ~ **'green** n. Dorfwiese, *die;* ~ **'hall** n. Dorfgemeinschaftshaus, *das;* ~ **'idiot** n. Dorftrottel, *der*

villager /ˈvɪlɪdʒə(r)/ n. Dorfbewohner, *der*/-bewohnerin, *die*

villain /ˈvɪlən/ n. (a) (scoundrel) Verbrecher, *der;* (b) ~ [**of the piece**] (Theatre; also fig.) Bösewicht, *der;* (c) (coll.: rascal) [kleiner] Halunke (scherzh.)

villainous /ˈvɪlənəs/ adj. (a) gemein; abscheulich; (b) (coll.: very bad) scheußlich (ugs.)

villainy /ˈvɪlənɪ/ n. Gemeinheit, *die*

vindicate /ˈvɪndɪkeɪt/ v.t. (a) (justify, establish) verteidigen, rechtfertigen ⟨*Person, Meinung, Handeln, Verhalten, An- spruch, Politik*⟩; beweisen ⟨*Behauptung*⟩; (confirm) bestä- tigen ⟨*Recht, Meinung, Urteil, Theorie*⟩; (b) (exonerate) rehabilitieren

vindication /vɪndɪˈkeɪʃn/ n. ⇒ **vindicate:** (a) Verteidi- gung, *die;* Rechtfertigung, *die;* Beweis, *der* (**of** für); Bestäti- gung, *die;* **be a** ~ **of sth.** etw. rechtfertigen/verteidigen/ beweisen/bestätigen; **in** ~ **of his claim/conduct** etc. zur Rechtfertigung seines Anspruchs/Benehmens *usw.;* (b) Re- habilitierung, *die*

vindictive /vɪnˈdɪktɪv/ adj. nachtragend ⟨*Person*⟩; un- versöhnlich ⟨*Stimmung*⟩; ~ **act/move/attack** Racheakt, *der* (geh.)

vine /vaɪn/ *n.* (a) Weinrebe, *die;* (b) (stem of trailer or climber) Ranke, *die*

vinegar /'vɪnɪgə(r)/ *n.* Essig, *der;* [as] **sour as** ∼: sehr sauer

vineyard /'vɪnjɑːd, 'vɪnjəd/ *n.* Weinberg, *der*

vintage /'vɪntɪdʒ/ **1** *n.* (a) (season's wine) Jahrgang, *der;* (season's grapes) Traubenernte, *die;* **last/this year's** ∼: der letzte/dieser Jahrgang; **the 1981** ∼/a **1983** ∼: der 81er/ ein 83er; (b) (fig.: particular period) Jahrgang, *der;* (of car, machine) Baujahr, *das;* (c) (grape-harvest; season) Weinlese, *die.* **2** *adj.* erlesen ⟨*Wein, Sekt, Whisky*⟩; herrlich ⟨*Komödie, Melodie*⟩; brillant ⟨*Leistung, Interpretation*⟩; (old-fashioned) alt ⟨*Modell*⟩; altmodisch ⟨*Stil*⟩

vintage 'car *n.* (Brit.) [zwischen 1917 und 1930 gebauter] Oldtimer

vinyl /'vaɪnɪl/ *n.* Vinyl, *das*

viola /vɪ'əʊlə/ *n.* (Mus.) Bratsche, *die*

violate /'vaɪəleɪt/ *v.t.* (a) verletzen; brechen ⟨*Vertrag, Versprechen, Gesetz*⟩; verstoßen gegen ⟨*Regel, Vorschrift, Prinzipien, Bestimmungen*⟩; verletzen ⟨*Vorschrift*⟩; stören ⟨*Ruhe, Frieden*⟩; verschandeln ⟨*Wälder, Landschaft*⟩; (b) (profane) schänden; entheiligen ⟨*Sabbat*⟩; (c) (rape) vergewaltigen; schänden (veralt.)

violation /vaɪə'leɪʃn/ *n.* ⇒ **violate:** (a) Verletzung, *die;* Bruch, *der;* Verstoß, *der* (**of** gegen); Störung, *die;* Verschandelung, *die;* **traffic** ∼: Verkehrsdelikt, *das;* **be/act in** ∼ **of** verletzen/brechen/verstoßen gegen; (b) Schändung, *die;* Entheiligung, *die;* (c) Vergewaltigung, *die;* Schändung, *die* (veralt.)

violence /'vaɪələns/ *n., no pl.* (a) (intensity, force) Heftigkeit, *die;* (of blow, waterfall) Wucht, *die;* (of temper) Ungestüm, *das;* (of contrast) Krassheit, *die;* (b) (brutality) Gewalt, *die;* (at public event) Gewalttätigkeiten *Pl.;* **by** *or* **with** ∼: mit Gewalt; **resort to** *or* **use** ∼: Gewalt anwenden; (c) (Law) Gewalt, *die;* **threaten sb. with** ∼: jmdm. Gewalt androhen; **act/crime of** ∼: Gewalttat, *die*/Gewaltverbrechen, *das;* **robbery with** ∼: [bewaffneter] Raubüberfall

violent /'vaɪələnt/ *adj.* gewalttätig; heftig ⟨*Schlag, Attacke, Leidenschaft, Auseinandersetzung, Erschütterung, Reaktion, Schmerzen, Wind*⟩; wuchtig ⟨*Schlag, Stoß*⟩; schwer ⟨*Schock*⟩; krass ⟨*Gegensatz, Kontrast*⟩; grell ⟨*Farbe*⟩; knall⟨*rot, -grün usw.*⟩; Gewalt⟨*verbrecher, -tat*⟩; **don't be so** ∼: sei nicht so aggressiv; **he has a** ∼ **temper** er neigt zum Jähzorn; ∼ **death** gewaltsamer *od.* unnatürlicher Tod

violet /'vaɪələt/ **1** *n.* (a) Veilchen, *das;* **shrinking** ∼ (fig.) schüchternes Pflänzchen (ugs.); (b) (colour) Violett, *das.* **2** *adj.* violett

violin /vaɪə'lɪn/ *n.* (Mus.) Violine, *die;* Geige, *die*

vio'lin case *n.* Geigenkasten, *der*

violinist /vaɪə'lɪnɪst/, **vio'lin player** *ns.* (Mus.) Geiger, *der*/Geigerin, *die*

VIP /viːaɪ'piː/ *n.* Prominente, *der/die;* **the** ∼**s** die Prominenz

viper /'vaɪpə(r)/ *n.* (a) (Zool.) Viper, *die;* (b) (fig.) Schlange, *die* (abwertend)

VIP: ∼ **lounge** *n.* VIP-Halle, *die;* ∼ **treatment** *n.* Vorzugsbehandlung, *die;* **give sb.** ∼ **treatment** jmdn. mit allen Ehren behandeln

viral /'vaɪrl/ *adj.* (Med.) Virus-

virgin /'vɜːdʒɪn/ **1** *n.* (a) Jungfrau, *die;* **she/he is still a** ∼: sie ist noch Jungfrau/er ist noch unschuldig; (b) **the** **[Blessed] V**∼ **[Mary]** (Relig.) die [Heilige] Jungfrau [Maria]. **2** *adj.* (a) (chaste) jungfräulich; (b) (untouched, unspoiled) unberührt ⟨*Land, Wälder*⟩; jungfräulich ⟨*Schnee*⟩; makellos ⟨*Weiß*⟩; (c) ∼ **olive oil** natives Olivenöl

virginal /'vɜːdʒɪnl/ *adj.* jungfräulich

virginity /vɜː'dʒɪnɪtɪ/ *n.* Unschuld, *die;* (of girl also) Jungfräulichkeit, *die*

Virgo /'vɜːgəʊ/ *n., pl.* ∼**s** (Astrol., Astron.) die Jungfrau

virile /'vɪraɪl/ *adj.* (a) (masculine) männlich; maskulin (geh.); (b) (sexually potent) viril; (c) (fig.: forceful, vigorous) kraftvoll

virility /vɪ'rɪlɪtɪ/ *n.* (a) Männlichkeit, *die;* (b) (sexual potency) Virilität, *die;* Manneskraft, *die;* (c) (fig.) kraftvoller Schwung

virtual /'vɜːtjʊəl/ *adj.* **a** ∼ ...: so gut wie ein/eine ...; praktisch ein/eine ... (ugs.); **he is the** ∼ **head of the business** er ist quasi der Chef des Geschäfts (ugs.); **the whole day was a** ∼ **disaster** der ganze Tag war geradezu eine Katastrophe; **the traffic came to a** ∼ **standstill** der Verkehr kam praktisch zum Stillstand (ugs.)

virtually /'vɜːtjʊəlɪ/ *adv.* so gut wie; praktisch (ugs.)

virtual re'ality virtuelle Realität

virtue /'vɜːtjuː/ *n.* (a) (moral excellence) Tugend, *die;* (chastity) Tugendhaftigkeit, *die;* ∼ **is its own reward** (prov.) die Tugend trägt ihren Lohn in sich selbst; (b) (advantage) Vorteil, *der;* Vorzug, *der;* **what is the** ∼ **in that?** welchen Vorteil hat das?; **there's no** ∼ **in doing that** es bringt keinen Vorteil, das zu tun; (c) **by** ∼ **of** auf Grund, aufgrund (+ *Gen.*)

virtuoso /vɜːtjʊ'əʊzəʊ/ *n., pl.* **virtuosi** /vɜːtjʊ'əʊziː/ *or* ∼**s** Virtuose, *der*/Virtuosin, *die; attrib.* virtuos ⟨*Spiel, Aufführung*⟩; **a** ∼ **performer** ein Virtuose/eine Virtuosin

virtuous /'vɜːtjʊəs/ *adj.* rechtschaffen ⟨*Person*⟩; tugendhaft ⟨*Leben*⟩; **if you're feeling** ∼ **you can** ... (iron.) wenn du etwas Gutes tun willst, kannst du ...

virulent /'vɪrʊlənt, 'vɪrjʊlənt/ *adj.* (a) (Med.) virulent; starkwirkend ⟨*Gift*⟩; (b) (fig.: malignant) heftig; scharf ⟨*Angriff*⟩

virus /'vaɪrəs/ *n.* (a) ▶865 Virus, *der,* (fachspr.) *das;* **a** ∼ **infection** eine Virusinfektion; (b) (Computing) [Computer]virus, *das od. der*

visa /'viːzə/ *n.* Visum, *das*

vis-à-vis /viːzɑː'viː/ *prep.* (a) (in relation to) bezüglich (+ *Gen.*); (b) (facing) gegenüber; (c) (compared with) im Vergleich zu

viscount /'vaɪkaʊnt/ *n.* ▶1152 Viscount, *der*

viscountess /'vaɪkaʊntɪs/ *n.* ▶1152 Viscountess, *die*

viscous /'vɪskəs/ *adj.* dickflüssig

vise (Amer.) ⇒ **vice²**

visibility /vɪzɪ'bɪlɪtɪ/ *n., no pl.* (a) (being visible) Sichtbarkeit, *die;* (b) (range of vision) Sicht, *die;* (Meteorol.) Sichtweite, *die;* **reduce** ∼ **to ten metres** die Sichtweite auf zehn Meter verringern

visible /'vɪzɪbl/ *adj.* (a) (also Econ.) sichtbar; **be** ∼ **to the naked eye** mit bloßem Auge erkennbar sein; **to observers in X** für Beobachter in X zu sehen; **highly** ∼ (fig.) unübersehbar; (b) (apparent) erkennbar; **with** ∼ **impatience** mit sichtlicher Ungeduld

visibly /'vɪzɪblɪ/ *adv.* sichtlich

vision /'vɪʒn/ *n.* (a) (sight) Sehkraft, *die;* [**range of**] ∼: Sichtweite, *die;* [**field of**] ∼: Sehfeld, *das;* (b) (dream) Vision, *die;* Gesicht, *das* (geh.); (person seen in dream) Phantom, *das;* (c) *usu. pl.* (imaginings) Fantasien; Fantasiebilder; **have** ∼**s of sth.** von etw. fantasieren; (more specific) sich (*Dat.*) etw. ausmalen; **have** ∼**s of having to do sth.** kommen sehen, dass man etw. tun muss; (d) (insight, foresight) Weitblick, *der;* **a man/woman of** ∼: ein Mann/eine Frau mit Weitblick; (e) (Telev.) Bild, *das;* **in sound and** ∼: in Ton und Bild

visionary /'vɪʒənərɪ/ **1** *adj.* (a) (imaginative) fantasievoll; (fanciful) fantastisch; (b) (imagined) eingebildet; (c) (seeing visions) visionär. **2** *n.* Visionär, *der*/Visionärin, *die*

visit /'vɪzɪt/ **1** *v.t.* (a) besuchen; aufsuchen ⟨*Arzt*⟩; (b) (dated: afflict) heimsuchen. **2** *v.i.* einen Besuch/Besuche machen; **I'm only** ∼**ing** ich bin nur zu Besuch; **be** ∼**ing with sb.** (Amer.) bei jmdm. zu Besuch sein. **3** *n.* Besuch, *der;* **pay** *or* **make a** ∼ **to sb.** jmdm. einen Besuch abstatten; **pay a** ∼ (coll.: go to the toilet) aufs Klo gehen (ugs.); **have** *or* **receive a** ∼ **[from sb.]** [von jmdm.] besucht werden; **a** ∼ **to a** *or* **the theatre/a museum** ein Theater-/Museumsbesuch; **a** ∼ **to the British Museum** ein Besuch des Britischen Museums; **a** ∼ **to Rome/the USA** ein Besuch *od.* Aufenthalt in Rom/in den USA; **a home** ∼ **by the doctor [to sb.]** ein Hausbesuch des Arztes [bei jmdm.]

visiting: ∼ **card** *n.* (lit. *or* fig.) Visitenkarte, *die;* ∼ **hours** *n. pl.* Besuchszeiten; ∼ **team** *n.* (Sport) Gastmannschaft, *die*

visitor /'vɪzɪtə(r)/ *n.* Besucher, *der*/Besucherin, *die;* (to hotel, beach, etc.) Gast, *der;* **have ~s/a ~:** Besuch haben

'visitors' book *n.* Gästebuch, *das*

visor /'vaɪzə(r)/ *n.* **(a)** (of helmet) Visier, *das;* **(b)** (eye-shade, peak of cap) Schirm, *der;* **(c)** (Motor Veh.) [**sun**] **~:** Blendschirm, *der*

vista /'vɪstə/ *n.* **(a)** (view) [Aus]blick, *der* **(of** auf + *Akk.*); (long, narrow view) Perspektive, *die;* **(b)** (fig.) **open up new ~s** neue Perspektiven eröffnen

visual /'vɪzjʊəl, 'vɪʒjʊəl/ *adj.* **(a)** (related to vision) Seh⟨*nerv, -organ*⟩; **~ sense** Gesichtssinn, *der;* **(b)** (attained by sight) visuell; optisch ⟨*Eindruck, Darstellung*⟩; bildlich ⟨*Vorstellungsvermögen*⟩; **the ~ arts** die bildenden und darstellenden Künste; **~ display** (Computing) Sichtanzeige, *die*

visual: ~ aids *n. pl.* Anschauungsmaterial, *das;* **~ dis'play unit** *n.* Bildschirmgerät, *das*

visualize /'vɪzjʊəlaɪz, 'vɪʒjʊəlaɪz/ *v.t.* **(a)** (imagine) sich (*Dat.*) vorstellen; **(b)** (envisage, foresee) voraussehen

visually /'vɪzjʊəlɪ, 'vɪʒjʊəlɪ/ *adv.* **(a)** (with regard to vision) optisch; **(b)** (by visual means) bildlich

vital /'vaɪtl/ *adj.* **(a)** (essential to life) lebenswichtig; **~ organs** lebenswichtige Organe; **(b)** (essential) unbedingt notwendig; (crucial) entscheidend, ausschlaggebend ⟨*Frage, Entschluss*⟩ **(to** für); **it is of ~ importance** *or* **~ that you ...:** es ist von entscheidender Bedeutung, dass Sie ...; **(c)** (full of life) lebendig, kraftvoll ⟨*Stil*⟩; vital ⟨*Person*⟩

vitality /vaɪ'tælɪtɪ/ *n., no pl.* **(a)** (ability to sustain life) Lebenskraft, *die;* **(b)** (liveliness) Vitalität, *die;* (of style, language) Lebendigkeit, *die;* (energy) Energie, *die;* **(c)** (fig.: of institution, organization, etc.) Dauerhaftigkeit, *die*

vital sta'tistics *n. pl.* (coll.: of woman) Maße; **her ~ are 34-26-34** sie hat die Maße 34/26/34

vitamin /'vɪtəmɪn, 'vaɪtəmɪn/ *n.* Vitamin, *das;* **~ C** Vitamin C

vitamin: ~ deficiency *n.* Vitaminmangel, *der;* **~ pill** *n.* Vitamintablette, *die*

vitiate /'vɪʃɪeɪt/ *v.t.* **(a)** (impair quality of, corrupt) beeinträchtigen; **(b)** (invalidate) zunichte machen; hinfällig machen ⟨*Vereinbarung, Vertrag*⟩

vitreous /'vɪtrɪəs/ *adj.* (glasslike) glasartig; **~ china** Halbporzellan, *das*

vitriolic /vɪtrɪ'blɪk/ *adj.* ätzend; giftig ⟨*Bemerkung*⟩; geharnischt ⟨*Attacke, Rede*⟩

viva /'vaɪvə/ *n.* (Brit. Univ. coll.) Mündliche, *das* (ugs.)

vivacious /vɪ'veɪʃəs/ *adj.* lebhaft; lebendig ⟨*Stil*⟩; munter ⟨*Lachen, Lächeln*⟩

viva voce /vaɪvə 'vəʊtʃɪ, vaɪvə 'vəʊsɪ/ (Univ.) **1** *adv., adj.* mündlich. **2** *n.* mündliche Prüfung; (doctoral) Rigorosum, *das*

vivid /'vɪvɪd/ *adj.* **(a)** (bright) strahlend ⟨*Helligkeit*⟩; hell ⟨*Blitz*⟩; lebhaft ⟨*Farbe*⟩; **(b)** (clear, lifelike) lebendig ⟨*Schilderung*⟩; lebhaft ⟨*Fantasie, Erinnerung*⟩; **(c)** (intense) kraftvoll ⟨*Töne*⟩

vividness /'vɪvɪdnɪs/ *n., no pl.* **(a)** (brightness) Helligkeit, *die;* **(b)** (liveliness, realism) Lebhaftigkeit, *die;* (of description) Lebendigkeit, *die*

vivisection /vɪvɪ'sekʃn/ *n.* Vivisektion, *die* (fachspr.)

vixen /'vɪksn/ *n.* Füchsin, *die*

viz /vɪz/ *adv.* d. h.

'V-neck *n.* V-Ausschnitt, *der*

'V-necked *adj.* ⟨*Pullover, Kleid*⟩ mit V-Ausschnitt

vocabulary /və'kæbjʊlərɪ/ *n.* **(a)** (list) Vokabelverzeichnis, *das;* **learn ~:** Vokabeln lernen; **~ book** Vokabelheft, *das;* **~ test** Vokabeltest, *der;* **(b)** (language of particular field) Vokabular, *das;* **(c)** (range of language) Wortschatz, *der*

vocal /'vəʊkl/ **1** *adj.* **(a)** (concerned with voice) stimmlich; **(b)** (expressing oneself freely) gesprächig; lautstark ⟨*Minderheit, Gruppe, Protest*⟩. **2** *n. in sing. or pl.* (Mus.) Vokalpartie, *die;* Vocal, *das* (fachspr.)

'vocal cords *n. pl.* Stimmbänder

vocalist /'vəʊkəlɪst/ *n.* Sänger, *der*/Sängerin, *die* (bei einer Band od. Combo)

vocal: ~ music *n.* Vokalmusik, *die;* **~ score** *n.* (Mus.) Vokalpartitur, *die*

vocation /və'keɪʃn/ *n.* **(a)** (call to career; also Relig.) Berufung, *die;* **he felt no ~ for the ministry** er fühlte sich nicht zum Geistlichen berufen; **(b)** (special aptitude) Begabung, *die* **(for** für)

vocational /və'keɪʃənl/ *adj.* berufsbezogen

vocational: ~ college *n.* Berufsschule, *die;* **~ guidance** *n.* Berufsberatung, *die;* **~ training** *n.* berufliche Bildung

vociferous /və'sɪfərəs/ *adj.* (noisy) laut; krakeelend (ugs.) ⟨*Zwischenrufer usw.*⟩; (insistent) lautstark ⟨*Forderung, Protest*⟩

vodka /'vɒdkə/ *n.* Wodka, *der*

vogue /vəʊg/ *n.* Mode, *die;* **the ~ for large hats** die Mode mit den großen Hüten; **be in/come into ~:** in Mode sein/kommen; **go out of ~:** aus der Mode kommen

voice /vɔɪs/ **1** *n.* **(a)** (lit. or fig.) Stimme, *die;* **in a firm/ loud ~:** mit fester/lauter Stimme; **lose one's ~:** die Stimme verlieren; **make one's ~ heard** sich verständlich machen; (fig.) sich (*Dat.*) Gehör verschaffen; **(b)** (expression) **give ~ to sth.** einer Sache (*Dat.*) Ausdruck geben; **(c)** **with one ~:** einstimmig; **(d)** (Mus.) Stimme, *die;* [**singing**] **~:** Singstimme, *die;* **(e)** (Ling.) **the active/passive ~:** das Aktiv/Passiv. **2** *v.t.* **(a)** (express) zum Ausdruck bringen ⟨*Meinung*⟩; **(b)** *esp. in p.p.* (Phonet.) stimmhaft aussprechen; **a ~d consonant** ein stimmhafter Konsonant

voice: ~ box *n.* Kehlkopf, *der;* **~ mail** *n.* Voicemail, *die;* **~-over** *n.* Voice-over, *die*

void /vɔɪd/ **1** *adj.* **(a)** (empty) leer; **(b)** (invalid) ungültig. **2** *n.* (empty space) Nichts, *das;* (fig.) **there was an aching ~ in her heart** sie spürte im Innern ein schmerzliches Gefühl der Leere

vol. *abbr.* **volume** Bd.

volatile /'vɒlətaɪl/ *adj.* **(a)** (Chem.) flüchtig; **(b)** (fig.) (lively) impulsiv; (changeable) unbeständig ⟨*Person, Laune*⟩; (likely to erupt) explosiv ⟨*Temperament*⟩; brisant ⟨*Lage*⟩

vol-au-vent /'vɒləʊvɑ̃/ *n.* (Gastr.) Pastete, *die*

volcanic /vɒl'kænɪk/ *adj.* **(a)** vulkanisch; **~ eruption** Vulkanausbruch, *der;* **(b)** (fig.: violent) leidenschaftlich

volcano /vɒl'keɪnəʊ/ *n., pl.* **~es** Vulkan, *der*

vole /vəʊl/ *n.* Wühlmaus, *die;* **field ~:** Feldmaus, *die*

Volga /'vɒlgə/ *pr. n.* ▶ **1048** ⎮ Wolga, *die*

volition /və'lɪʃn/ *n.* Wille, *der;* **of one's own ~:** aus eigenem Willen; freiwillig

volley /'vɒlɪ/ *n.* **(a)** (of missiles) Salve, *die;* **a ~ of stones/ arrows** ein Hagel von Steinen/Pfeilen; ein Stein-/Pfeilhagel; **(b)** (fig.) **a ~ of oaths/curses** eine Schimpfkanonade; **direct a ~ of questions at sb.** jmdn. mit Fragen bombardieren; **(c)** (Tennis) Volley, *der*

'volleyball *n.* Volleyball, *der*

volt /vəʊlt/ *n.* (Electr.) Volt, *das*

voltage /'vəʊltɪdʒ/ *n.* (Electr.) Spannung, *die;* **high/low ~:** Hoch-/Niederspannung, *die*

volte-face /vɒlt'fæs/ *n.* (fig.) Kehrtwendung, *die*

voluble /'vɒljʊbl/ *adj.* redselig (abwertend); wortreich ⟨*Rede*⟩

volume /'vɒljuːm/ *n.* **(a)** (book, set of periodicals) Band, *der;* (on periodical) **V~ II no. 3** Jahrgang II, Nr. 3; *see also* **speak** 2 c; **(b)** (loudness) Lautstärke, *die;* (of voice) Volumen, *das;* **turn the ~ up/down** das Radio *usw.* lauter/ leiser stellen; **(c)** ▶ **1193** ⎮ (amount of space) Rauminhalt, *der;* Volumen, *das;* (amount of substance) Teil, *der;* **(d)** (amount, quantity) (of sales etc.) Volumen, *das;* **~ of traffic/passenger travel** Verkehrs-/Passagieraufkommen, *das*

'volume control *n.* Lautstärkeregelung, *die;* (device) Lautstärkeregler, *der*

voluminous /və'ljuːmɪnəs, və'luːmɪnəs/ *adj.* **(a)** (great in quantity) voluminös (geh.); sehr umfangreich; **(b)** (bulky, loose) weit ⟨*Kleider*⟩; voluminös (geh.) ⟨*Tasche usw.*⟩

voluntarily /'vɒləntərɪlɪ/ *adv.* freiwillig

voluntary /'vɒləntərɪ/ *adj.* freiwillig; **~ organizations** gemeinnützige Organisationen

volunteer /vɒlən'tɪə(r)/ **1** *n.* Freiwillige, *der/die;* **any ~s?** Freiwillige vor!; *attrib.* **~ army/force** Freiwilligenheer, *das*/Freiwilligenverband, *der.* **2** *v.t.* (offer) anbieten

Volume

Cubic measure

1 cubic inch (cu. in.) = 16,4 cm³ (sechzehn Komma vier Kubikzentimeter)
1,728 cubic inches = 1 cubic foot (cu. ft) = 0,03 m³ (null Komma null drei Kubikmeter)
27 cubic feet ,, = 1 cubic yard (cu. yd) = 0,76 m³ (null Komma sieben sechs Kubikmeter)

Liquid measure

BRITISH:
20 fluid ounces (fl. oz) = *1 pint (pt)* = 0,57 l (null Komma fünf sieben Liter)
2 pints = *1 quart (qt)* = 1,14 l (eins Komma eins vier Liter)
4 quarts · = *1 gallon (gal.)* = 4,55 l (vier Komma fünf fünf Liter)
AMERICAN:
16 fluid ounces (fl. oz) = *1 pint (pt)* = 0,47 l (null Komma vier sieben Liter)
2 pints = *1 quart (qt)* = 0,94 l (null Komma neun vier Liter)
4 quarts = *1 US gallon (gal.)* = 3,78 l (drei Komma sieben acht Liter)

What is its volume?	= Wie viel *or* Welches Volumen hat es?	British gallons) or 230 (for US gallons) by the m.p.g. figure.
Its volume is 200 cubic feet	≈ Es hat ein Volumen von 6 Kubikmetern	*The two tanks have the same capacity* = Die beiden Tanks haben das gleiche Fassungsvermögen
What is the capacity of the tank?, How much does the tank hold?	= Wie viel fasst der Tank?	*20 litres of petrol* = 20 Liter Benzin
		It's sold by the litre = Es wird literweise verkauft
The tank holds 10 UK/US gallons	≈ Der Tank fasst 45 Liter/ ₊38 Liter	Note also.'
My car does 28 (UK) or 23 (US) miles per gallon (m.p.g.)	≈ Mein Wagen verbraucht 10 Liter auf 100 Kilometer	*What is the capacity of the engine?* = Wie viel Hubraum hat der Motor?

In all Continental European countries fuel consumption is quoted in litres per 100 kilometres. To convert m.p.g. to litres per 100 km divide the factor 280 (for

It's a 1600 cc or 1.6 litre engine (Brit.), It's a 96 cu. in. motor (Amer.) = Der Motor hat 1 600 cm³ or 1,6 Liter Hubraum

---

⟨*Hilfe, Dienste*⟩; herausrücken mit (ugs.) ⟨*Informationen, Neuigkeiten*⟩; ∼ **advice** unerbetene Ratschläge erteilen. **3** *v.i.* sich [freiwillig] melden; ∼ **to do** *or* **for the shopping** sich zum Einkaufen bereit erklären

voluptuous /vəˈlʌptjʊəs/ *adj.* üppig ⟨*Figur, Kurven, Blondine*⟩; aufreizend ⟨*Bewegungen*⟩; sinnlich ⟨*Mund*⟩

vomit /ˈvɒmɪt/ **1** *v.t.* erbrechen. **2** *v.i.* sich übergeben; [sich] erbrechen. **3** *n.* Erbrochene, *das*

voodoo /ˈvuːduː/ *n.* (witchcraft) Wodu, *der*

voracious /vəˈreɪʃəs/ *adj.* **(a)** (ravenous) gefräßig ⟨*Person, Tier*⟩; unbändig ⟨*Appetit*⟩; **(b)** (fig.: insatiable) unersättlich ⟨*Lust, Leser*⟩

vortex /ˈvɔːteks/ *n., pl.* **vortices** /ˈvɔːtɪsiːz/ *or* ∼**es** (whirlpool, whirlwind) Wirbel, *der*; (eddying current; also fig.: whirl) Strudel, *der*

vote /vəʊt/ **1** *n.* **(a)** (individual ∼) Stimme, *die;* **a majority of** ∼**s** eine Stimmenmehrheit; **my** ∼ **goes to X, X has my** ∼ (fig. coll.) ich stimme *od.* bin für X; **(b)** (act of voting) Abstimmung, *die;* **take a** ∼ **on sth.** über etw. (*Akk.*) abstimmen; **(c)** (right to ∼) **have/be given** *or* **get the** ∼: das Stimmrecht haben/bekommen; **(d)** (collective) Stimmen; (result) Abstimmungsergebnis, *das;* **the** ∼ **in favour of capital punishment** die Stimmenzahl für die Todesstrafe; **(e)** (expression of opinion) Votum, *das;* **give sb. a** ∼ **of confidence/no confidence** jmdm. sein Vertrauen/ Misstrauen aussprechen; ∼ **of confidence/no confidence** Vertrauens-/Misstrauensvotum, *das;* **propose a** ∼ **of thanks** eine Dankadresse halten. **2** *v.i.* abstimmen; (in election) wählen; ∼ **for/against** stimmen für/gegen; ∼ **for Smith!** wählen Sie Smith!; ∼ **on a motion** über einen Antrag abstimmen; ∼ **to do sth.** beschließen, etw. zu tun; ∼ **by ballot/[a] show of hands** mit Stimmzetteln/durch Handzeichen abstimmen; ∼ **Conservative/Labour** *etc.* die Konservativen/Labour *usw.* wählen. **3** *v.t.* **(a)** (elect) ∼ **sb. Chairman/President** *etc.* jmdn. zum Vorsitzenden/ Präsidenten *usw.* wählen; (approve) ∼ **a sum of money for sth.** einen Betrag für etw. bewilligen; **(b)** (coll.: pronounce) bezeichnen; ∼ **sth. a success/failure** etw. als Erfolg/Misserfolg bezeichnen

∼ **'down** *v.t.* niederstimmen
∼ **'in** *v.t.* wählen ⟨*Partei, Regierung*⟩
∼ **'out** *v.t.* abwählen

voter /ˈvəʊtə(r)/ *n.* Wähler, *der*/Wählerin, *die*

voting /ˈvəʊtɪŋ/ *n.* Abstimmen, *das;* (in election) Wählen, *das;* **the** ∼ **was 220 for, 165 against** das Ergebnis der Abstimmung war 220 [Stimmen] dafür, 165 dagegen

voting: ∼ **age** *n.* Wahlalter, *das;* ∼ **slip** *n.* Wahlzettel, *der;* Stimmzettel, *der;* ∼ **system** *n.* Wahlsystem, *das*

vouch /vaʊtʃ/ **1** *v.t.* ∼ **that** …: sich dafür verbürgen, dass … **2** *v.i.* ∼ **for sb./sth.** sich für jmdn./etw. verbürgen

voucher /ˈvaʊtʃə(r)/ *n.* Gutschein, *der;* Voucher, *der* (Tourismus)

vow /vaʊ/ **1** *n.* Gelöbnis, *das;* (Relig.) Gelübde, *das.* **2** *v.t.* ∼ **sth./to do sth.** etw. geloben/geloben, etw. zu tun; ∼ **to take revenge on sb.** jmdm. Rache schwören

vowel /ˈvaʊəl/ *n.* Vokal, *der;* Selbstlaut, *der;* ∼ **sound** Vokallaut, *der*

voyage /ˈvɔɪdʒ/ **1** *n.* Reise, *die;* (sea ∼) Seereise, *die;* **outward/homeward** ∼, ∼ **out/home** Hin-/Rückreise, *die;* **he was on a** ∼ **of discovery** (lit. *or* fig.) er war auf einer Entdeckungsreise. **2** *v.i.* (literary) reisen

voyeur /vwɑːˈjɜː(r)/ *n.* **(a)** (sexual) Voyeur, *der;* **(b)** (prying observer) Gaffer, *der* (ugs.)

VP *abbr.* **Vice-President** VP

vroom /vruːm, vrʊm/ *int.* brumm

vs *abbr.* **versus** gg.

'V-shaped *adj.* V-förmig

'V-sign *n.* **(a)** (sign for victory) Siegeszeichen, *das;* **(b)** (gesture of abuse, contempt) Zeichen, das „Du kannst mich mal!" signalisiert

VSO *abbr.* **Voluntary Service Overseas**

VTO[L] /ˈviːtɒl/ *abbr.* (Aeronaut.) **vertical take-off [and landing]** Senkrechtstart [und -landung]

vulgar /ˈvʌlɡə(r)/ *adj.* vulgär; ordinär ⟨*Person, Benehmen, Witz, Film*⟩; geschmacklos ⟨*Kleidung*⟩

vulgarity /vʌl'gærɪtɪ/ *n., no pl.* Vulgarität, *die;* (of clothing) Geschmacklosigkeit, *die*

vulnerability /vʌlnərə'bɪlɪtɪ/ *n., no pl.* **(a)** Angreifbarkeit, *die;* (to criticism, temptation) Anfälligkeit, *die* (**to** für); **(b)** (to injury) Empfindlichkeit, *die* (**to** gegen); Schutzlosigkeit, *die;* (emotional) Verletzlichkeit, *die*

vulnerable /'vʌlnərəbl/ *adj.* **(a)** (exposed to danger) angreifbar; **a ~ spot/point** ein schwacher Punkt; **be ~ to** sth. für etw. anfällig sein; **be ~ to attack/in a ~ position** leicht angreifbar sein; **(b)** (susceptible to injury) empfindlich (**to** gegen); (without protection) schutzlos; **~ to infection** anfällig für Infektionen

vulture /'vʌltʃə(r)/ *n.* (lit. or fig.) Geier, *der*

vying ⇒ vie

....

Ww

....

W, w /'dʌblju:/ *n., pl.* **Ws** or **W's** W, w, *das*

W. *abbr.* **(a)** watt[s] W; **(b)** ▶ 715 ǀ west W.; **(c)** ▶ 715 ǀ western w.

wad /wɒd/ *n.* **(a)** (material) Knäuel, *das;* (smaller) Pfropfen, *der;* **a ~ of cotton wool** ein Wattebausch; **(b)** (of papers) Bündel, *das;* **~s of money** bündelweise Geld

wadding /'wɒdɪŋ/ *n.* (lining) Futter, *das;* (for packing) Füllmaterial, *das;* Füllsel *Pl.*

waddle /'wɒdl/ **1** *v.i.* watscheln. **2** *n.* watschelnder Gang

wade /weɪd/ *v.i.* waten; (in snow, sand) stapfen

~ 'in *v.i.* (fig. coll.) [gleich] losgehen; (tackle task) sich hineinknien (ugs.)

~ into *v.t.* (fig. coll.) losgehen auf (+ *Akk.*)

~ through *v.t.* **(a)** waten durch; stapfen durch ⟨*Schnee, Unkraut*⟩; **(b)** (fig. coll.) durchackern (ugs.) ⟨*Manuskript, Buch*⟩

wader /'weɪdə(r)/ *n.* **(a)** (Ornith.) Watvogel, *der;* **(b)** in pl. (boots) Watstiefel *Pl.*

wafer /'weɪfə(r)/ *n.* **(a)** Waffel, *die;* (very thin) Oblate, *die;* **(b)** (Eccl.) Hostie, *die;* **(c)** (Electronics) Wafer, *der*

'wafer-thin *adj.* hauchdünn

waffle¹ /'wɒfl/ *n.* (Gastr.) Waffel, *die*

waffle² (Brit. coll.: talk) **1** *v.i.* schwafeln (ugs. abwertend); faseln (ugs. abwertend). **2** *n.* Geschwafel, *das* (ugs. abwertend); Faselei, *die* (ugs. abwertend)

waft /wɒft, wɑːft/ **1** *v.t.* wehen. **2** *v.i.* ⟨Geruch, Duft:⟩ ziehen, (with perceptible air movement) wehen

wag¹ /wæg/ **1** *v.t.,* **-gg-** ⟨Hund:⟩ wedeln mit ⟨Schwanz⟩; ⟨Vogel:⟩ wippen mit ⟨Schwanz⟩; ⟨Person:⟩ schütteln ⟨Kopf⟩; **~ one's finger at sb.** jmdm. mit dem Finger drohen. **2** *v.i.,* **-gg-** ⟨Schwanz:⟩ wedeln/(of bird) wippen; **her tongue never stops ~ging** ihre Zunge steht niemals still. **3** *n.* (of dog's tail) Wedeln, *das* (**of** mit); (of bird's tail) Wippen, *das* (**of** mit)

wag² *n.* (facetious person) Witzbold, *der* (ugs.)

wage /weɪdʒ/ **1** *n.* in sing. or pl. Lohn, *der.* **2** *v.t.* führen ⟨Krieg, Feldzug⟩; **~ war on** or **against crime** (fig.) gegen das Verbrechen zu Felde ziehen

wage: **~ claim** *n.* Lohnforderung, *die;* **~ earner** *n.* Lohnempfänger, *der/*-empfängerin, *die;* **~ freeze** *n.* Lohnstopp, *der;* **~ increase** *n.* Lohnerhöhung, *die;* **~ packet** *n.* Lohntüte, *die*

wager /'weɪdʒə(r)/ (dated/formal) **1** *n.* Wette, *die;* **a ~ of £50** eine Wette um 50 Pfund. **2** *v.t.* wetten; (on a horse) setzen; **~ one's life/one's whole fortune on sth.** seinen Kopf/sein ganzes Vermögen auf etw. (*Akk.*) verwetten; **I ~ you £10 that ...:** ich wette mit dir um 10 Pfund, dass ... **3** *v.i.* wetten; **he's there by now, I'll ~:** ich möchte wetten, dass er inzwischen da ist

'wage rise *n.* Lohnerhöhung, *die*

waggle /'wægl/ (coll.) **1** *v.t.* **~ its tail** ⟨Hund:⟩ mit dem Schwanz wedeln; ⟨Vogel:⟩ mit dem Schwanz wippen. **2** *v.i.* hin und her schlagen

waggon (Brit.), **wagon** /'wægən/ *n.* **(a)** (horse-drawn) Wagen, *der;* **covered ~:** Planwagen, *der;* **(b)** (Amer.: motor vehicle) Wagen, *der;* **(c)** **go/be on the ~** (go/be teetotal) keinen Tropfen mehr/keinen Tropfen anrühren; **(d)** (Brit. Railw.) Wagen, *der;* Waggon, *der* (volkst.)

'wagtail *n.* (Ornith.) Bachstelze, *die*

waif /weɪf/ *n.* verlassenes Kind; **~s and strays** obdachlose Kinder

wail /weɪl/ **1** *v.i.* **(a)** (lament) klagen (geh.) (**for** um); jammern (ugs.) (**for** um); ⟨Kind:⟩ heulen; **(b)** (fig.) ⟨Wind, Sirene:⟩ heulen. **2** *n.* **(a)** (cry) klagender Schrei; **~s** Geheul, *das;* **(b)** (fig.) (of wind etc.) Heulen, *das;* Geheul, *das*

waist /weɪst/ *n.* **(a)** ▶ 672 ǀ (part of body or garment) Taille, *die;* **tight round the ~:** eng in der Taille; **(b)** (Amer.) (blouse) Bluse, *die;* (bodice) Mieder, *das*

'waistband *n.* Gürtelband, *der;* (of trousers) [Hosen]bund, *der;* (of skirt) [Rock]bund, *der*

waistcoat /'weɪskəʊt, 'weɪstkəʊt/ *n.* (Brit.) Weste, *die*

'waist-deep 1 *adj.* bis zur Taille reichend; **be ~:** einem bis zur Taille reichen. **2** *adv.* bis zur Taille

'waistline *n.* Taille, *die;* **be bad for the ~:** schlecht für die schlanke Linie sein

wait /weɪt/ **1** *v.i.* **(a)** warten; **~ [for] an hour** eine Stunde warten; **~ a moment** Moment mal; **keep sb. ~ing, make sb. ~:** jmdn. warten lassen; **~ to see sth. happen** darauf warten, dass etw. passiert; **'repairs [done]/keys cut while you ~'** „Reparatur-/Schlüsselschnelldienst"; **sth. is still ~ing to be done** etw. muss noch gemacht werden; **~ and see** abwarten[, was passiert]; **sth. can/can't** or **won't ~:** etw. kann/kann nicht warten; **I can't ~ to do sth.** (am eager) ich kann es kaum erwarten, etw. zu tun; **[just] you ~!** warte mal ab!; (as threat) warte nur!; **(b) ~ at** or (Amer.) **on table** servieren; ⟨Ober:⟩ kellnern (ugs.). **2** *v.t.* (await) warten auf (+ *Akk.*); **~ one's chance/opportunity** auf eine [günstige] Gelegenheit warten; **~ one's turn** warten, bis man dran ist od. drankommt. **3** *n.* **(a)** (act, time) **after a long/short ~:** nach langer/kurzer Wartezeit; **have a long/short ~ for sth.** lange/nicht lange auf etw. (*Akk.*) warten müssen; **(b)** (watching for enemy) **lie in ~:** im Hinterhalt liegen; **lie in ~ for sb./sth.** jmdm./einer Sache auflauern

~ a'bout, ~ a'round *v.i.* herumstehen

~ be'hind *v.i.* noch hier-/dableiben; **~ behind for sb.** auf jmdn. warten

~ for *v.t.* warten auf (+ *Akk.*); **~ for the rain to stop** warten, bis der Regen aufhört; **~ for it!** warte/wartet!; (to create suspense before saying something surprising) warte ab!

~ 'in *v.i.* zu Hause warten (**for** auf + *Akk.*)

~ on *v.t.* (serve) bedienen

~ 'up *v.i.* aufbleiben (**for** wegen)

waiter /'weɪtə(r)/ *n.* ▶ 887 ǀ Kellner, *der;* **~!** Herr Ober!

waiting /'weɪtɪŋ/ *n.* **(a)** Warten, *das;* **(b)** no pl., no art. (working as waiter) Servieren, *das;* Kellnern, *das* (ugs.)

waiting: **~ game** *n.* Hinhaltetaktik, *die;* **play a ~ game** erst einmal abwarten; **~ list** *n.* Warteliste, *die;* **~ room** *n.* Wartezimmer, *das;* (at railway or bus station) Warteraum, *der;* (larger) Wartesaal, *der*

waitress /'weɪtrɪs/ *n.* ▶ 887 ǀ Serviererin, *die;* **~!** Fräulein! (veralt.)

waive /weɪv/ *v.t.* verzichten auf (+ *Akk.*); nicht vollstrecken ⟨Strafe⟩; nicht anwenden ⟨Regel⟩

wake¹ /weɪk/ **1** *v.i.,* **woke** /wəʊk/ or (arch.) **~d, woken** /'wəʊkn/ or (arch.) **~d** aufwachen; (fig.) ⟨Natur, Gefühle:⟩ erwachen; **I woke to the sound of soft music** beim Aufwachen hörte ich leise Musik; **~ to sth.** (fig.: realize) etw. erkennen; sich (*Dat.*) einer Sache (*Gen.*) bewusst werden. **2** *v.t.* **woke** or (arch.) **~d, woken** or (arch.) **~d** wecken; (fig.) erwecken (geh.) ⟨die Natur, Erinnerungen⟩; wecken ⟨Erinnerungen⟩; **be quiet, you'll ~ your baby brother** sei still, sonst wacht dein Brüderchen auf! **3** *n.* (Ir.: watch by corpse) Totenwache, *die*

~ 'up 1 *v.i.* (lit. or fig.) aufwachen; **~ up!** wach auf!; (fig.: pay attention) pass besser auf!; **~ up to sth.** (fig.: realize) etw. erkennen. **2** *v.t.* **(a)** (rouse from sleep) wecken; **(b)** (fig.: enliven) wachrütteln; Leben bringen in (+ *Akk.*) ⟨Stadt⟩; **you**

need to ~ **your ideas up a bit** du müsstest dich ein bisschen zusammenreißen

wake² *n.* (a) (water) Kielwasser, *das;* (b) (air) Turbulenz, *die;* (c) (fig.) **in the** ~ **of sth./sb.** im Gefolge von etw./in jmds. Gefolge; **follow in the** ~ **of sb./sth.** jmdm./einer Sache folgen; **bring sth. in its** ~**:** etw. zur Folge haben

wakeful /'weɪkfl/ *adj.* (a) (sleepless) schlaflos ‹*Nacht*›; (b) (vigilant) wachsam

waken /'weɪkn/ **1** *v.t.* (a) wecken; (b) (fig.: arouse) wecken ‹*Interesse, Gefühl*›; erregen ‹*Zorn*›. **2** *v.i.* ⇒ **wake¹** 1

'wake-up call (esp. Amer.) ⇒ **alarm call**

waking /'weɪkɪŋ/ *adj.* **in one's** ~ **hours** den ganzen Tag; von früh bis spät; **spend all one's** ~ **hours [on] doing sth.** etw. von früh bis spät tun

Wales /weɪlz/ *pr. n.* Wales (das)

walk /wɔːk/ **1** *v.i.* (a) laufen; (as opposed to running) gehen; (as opposed to driving) zu Fuß gehen; **you can** ~ **there in five minutes** es sind nur 5 Minuten zu Fuß bis dorthin; '~'/'don't ~' (Amer.: at pedestrian lights) „gehen"/„warten"; ~ **on crutches/with a stick** an Krücken/am Stock gehen; **learn to** ~**:** laufen lernen; ~ **tall** (fig.) erhobenen Hauptes gehen (fig.); (b) (exercise) gehen; marschieren (ugs.). **2** *v.t.* (a) entlanggehen; ablaufen ‹*Strecke, Weg*›; durchwandern ‹*Gebiet*›; ~ **the streets** durch die Straßen gehen/(aimlessly) laufen; (as prostitute) auf den Strich gehen (ugs.); (b) (cause to ~; lead) führen; ausführen ‹*Hund*›; ~ **sb. off his/her feet** jmdn. [bis zur Erschöpfung] durch die Gegend schleifen (ugs.); (c) (accompany) bringen; **he** ~**ed his girlfriend home** er brachte seine Freundin nach Hause. **3** *n.* (a) Spaziergang, *der;* **go [out] for** *or* **take** *or* **have a** ~**:** einen Spaziergang machen; **take sb./the dog for a** ~**:** jmdn./den Hund spazieren führen; **a ten-mile** ~**:** eine Wanderung von zehn Meilen; (distance) **ten minutes'** ~ **from here** zehn Minuten zu Fuß von hier; (b) (gait) Gang, *der;* (characteristic) normale Gangart; (c) (Sport: race) Wettbewerb im Gehen; **the 10,000 metres** ~**:** das 10 000-m-Gehen; (d) (path, route) [Spazier]weg, *der;* (e) **people from all** ~**s of life** Leute aus den verschiedensten gesellschaftlichen Gruppierungen

~ **a'bout** *v.i.* herumlaufen

~ **a'way** *v.i.* (a) weggehen; **she was lucky to** ~ **away from the accident** sie hatte großes Glück, den Unfallort unverletzt verlassen zu können; (b) (fig.) **he tried to** ~ **away from the problem** (ignore it) er versuchte, dem Problem aus dem Weg zu gehen; ~ **away with sth.** (coll.) (win easily) etw. spielend leicht gewinnen; (steal) sich mit etw. davonmachen (ugs.)

~ **'in** *v.i.* (a) (enter) hereinkommen/hineingehen; reinkommen/-gehen (ugs.); **'please** ~ **in'** „[bitte] eintreten, ohne zu klopfen"; (b) (enter without permission) hinein-/hereinspazieren

~ **into** *v.t.* (a) (enter) betreten; treten in (+ *Akk.*) ‹*Pfütze*›; (without permission) eindringen in (+ *Akk.*) ‹*Haus*›; (b) (hit by accident) laufen gegen ‹*Pfosten, Laternenpfahl*›; ~ **into sb.** mit jmdm. zusammenstoßen; ~ **into a trap** (lit. or fig.) in eine Falle gehen; (c) (coll.: come easily into) **she** ~**ed into the top job** ihr ist der Topjob einfach zugefallen

~ **'off 1** *v.i.* (a) (leave) weggehen; verschwinden; (b) ~ **off with sth.** (coll.) sich mit etw. davonmachen (ugs.); ~ **off with all the prizes** alle Preise einheimsen (ugs.). **2** *v.t.* ~ **off a hangover** einen Spaziergang machen, um seinen Kater loszuwerden

~ **'on** *v.i.* (a) (go further) weitergehen; ~ **on!** (to horse) hü!; (b) (go on stage) auf die Bühne kommen

~ **'out** *v.i.* (a) (leave) hinausgehen; rausgehen (ugs.); (b) (Mil.: leave barracks) ausgehen; (c) (leave in protest) aus Protest den Saal verlassen; (leave organization) austreten; (d) (go on strike) in den Streik *od.* Ausstand treten

~ **'out of** *v.t.* (a) (leave) gehen aus; (b) (leave in protest) verlassen ‹*Saal, Versammlung*›

~ **'out on** *v.t.* (coll.) verlassen; sitzen lassen (ugs.) ‹*Frau, Mann*›

~ **'over** *v.t.* ~ **[all] over sb.** jmdn. fertig machen (ugs.)

~ **'up** *v.i.* (a) (approach) sich nähern; ~ **up to sb.** zu jmdm. hingehen; **he** ~**ed up to me** er kam zu mir [heran]; (b) (ascend) hochlaufen; nach oben laufen

---

'walkabout *n.* (a) (through crowds) Bad in der Menge (scherzh.); **go on a** ~**:** sich unters Volk mischen; (b) (Austral.: in bush) Buschwanderung, *die*

walker /'wɔːkə(r)/ *n.* Spaziergänger, *der*/-gängerin, *die;* (in race) Geher, *der*/Geherin, *die;* (rambler, hiker) Wanderer, *der*/Wanderin, *die*

walkies /'wɔːkɪz/ *n. pl.* (coll.) **go** ~**:** Gassi gehen (ugs.); ~**!** (said to dog) komm Gassi! (ugs.)

walkie-talkie /wɔːkɪ'tɔːkɪ/ *n.* Walkie-talkie, *das*

walking /'wɔːkɪŋ/ **1** *attrib. adj.* **a** ~ **dictionary/encyclopaedia** (joc.) ein wandelndes Wörterbuch/Konversationslexikon. **2** *n., no pl., no art.* [Spazieren]gehen, *das;* Laufen, *das; attrib.* **at** ~ **pace** im Schritttempo; **be within** ~ **distance** zu Fuß zu erreichen sein

walking: ~ **holiday** *n.* Wanderurlaub, *der;* ~ **shoe** *n.* Wanderschuh, *der;* ~ **stick** *n.* Spazierstock, *der;* ~ **tour** *n.* Wanderung, *die*

Walkman, (P) /'wɔːkmən/ *n., pl.* ~**s** Walkman, *der* ⓦz

walk: ~**-on part** *n.* (Theatre) Statistenrolle, *die;* ~**out** *n.* Arbeitsniederlegung, *die;* ~**over** *n.* (fig.: easy victory) Spaziergang, *der* (ugs.); ~**way** *n.* Fußweg, *der;* (over machinery etc.) Laufsteg, *der*

wall /wɔːl/ **1** *n.* (a) (of building, part of structure) Wand, *die;* (external, also free-standing) Mauer, *die;* **town/garden** ~**:** Stadt-/Gartenmauer, *die;* **the south** ~ **of the house** die Südwand des Hauses; **a concrete** ~**:** eine Betonwand/-mauer; **the Great W**~ **of China** die Chinesische Mauer; **the Berlin W**~ (Hist.) die [Berliner] Mauer; (b) (internal) Wand, *die;* **be hanging on the** ~**:** an der Wand hängen; **hang a picture on the** ~**:** ein Bild an die Wand hängen; **drive** *or* **send sb. up the** ~ (fig. coll.) jmdn. auf die Palme bringen (ugs.); **go up the** ~ (fig. coll.) die Wände hochgehen (ugs.); (c) (Mount., Min.) Wand, *die;* (fig.) Mauer, *die;* **a** ~ **of water/fire** (fig.) eine Wasser-/Feuerwand; **the North W**~ **of the Eiger** die Eigernordwand; (fig.) **a** ~ **of silence/prejudice** eine Mauer des Schweigens/von Vorurteilen. **2** *v.t.* **[be]** ~**ed** von einer Mauer/Mauern umgeben [sein]; **X is a** ~**ed city/town** X hat eine Stadtmauer

~ **'in** *v.t.* mit einer Mauer umgeben; (fig.) umzingeln

~ **'off** *v.t.* abteilen

~ **'up** *v.t.* zumauern; einmauern ‹*Person*›

wallaby /'wɒləbɪ/ *n.* (Zool.) Wallaby, *das*

wall: ~ **bars** *n. pl.* Sprossenwand, *die;* ~**chart** *n.* Schautafel, *die;* ~ **cupboard** *n.* Hängeschrank, *der*

wallet /'wɒlɪt/ *n.* Brieftasche, *die;* (for cheque card etc.) Etui, *das*

wall: ~**flower** *n.* (a) (Bot.) Goldlack, *der;* (b) (coll.: person) Mauerblümchen, *das* (ugs.); ~ **hanging** *n.* Wandbehang, *der;* ~ **light** *n.* Wandlampe, *die;* ~ **map** *n.* Wandkarte, *die*

wallop /'wɒləp/ (coll.) **1** *v.t.* (hit) schlagen. **2** *n.* Schlag, *der;* **give sb./sth. a** ~**:** auf jmdn./etw. draufhauen (ugs.)

wallow /'wɒləʊ/ *v.i.* (a) (roll around) sich wälzen; ‹*Schiff*› schlingern; (in mud also) sich suhlen; (b) (fig.: take delight) schwelgen (**in** in + *Dat.*)

wall: ~ **painting** *n.* Wandgemälde, *das;* ~**paper 1** *n.* Tapete, *die.* **2** *v.t.* tapezieren; ~ **socket** *n.* (Electr.) Wandsteckdose, *die;* ~**-to-** *adj.* (covering floor) ~**-to-**~ **carpeting** Teppichboden, *der;* ~ **unit** *n.* Hängeelement, *das*

wally /'wɒlɪ/ *n.* (Brit. coll.) Blödmann, *der* (salopp)

walnut /'wɔːlnʌt/ *n.* (a) (nut) Walnuss, *die;* (b) (tree) [Wal]nussbaum, *der;* (c) (wood) Nussbaumholz, *das*

walrus /'wɔːlrəs, 'wɒlrəs/ *n.* Walross, *das*

waltz /wɔːls, wɔːls, wɒlts, wɒls/ **1** *n.* Walzer, *der.* **2** *v.i.* Walzer tanzen

wan /wɒn/ *adj.* fahl (geh.); bleich; ~ **smile** mattes Lächeln

wand /wɒnd/ *n.* Stab, *der*

wander /'wɒndə(r)/ **1** *v.i.* (a) (go aimlessly) umherirren; (walk slowly) bummeln; **she** ~**ed over to me** sie kam zu mir herüber; (b) (stray) ‹*Katze*› streunen; ‹*Schafe*› sich verlaufen; (c) (fig.: stray from subject) abschweifen. **2** *v.t.* wandern durch (ugs.: walk) Spaziergang, *der;* **I'll go for** *or* **take a** ~ **round** *or* **through the town** ich werd mal einen Bummel durch die Stadt machen

~ **a'bout** *v.i.* sich herumtreiben

∼ a'long *v.i.* dahintrotten; ⟨*Fahrzeug:*⟩ dahinzockeln (ugs.)

∼ 'in *v.i.* hineinspazieren; (towards speaker) hereinspaziert kommen

∼ 'off *v.i.* (a) (stray) weggehen; ⟨*Kind:*⟩ sich selbstständig machen (scherzh.); (b) (coll.: go away) sich davonmachen (ugs.)

wanderer /'wɒndərə(r)/ *n.* Streuner, *der*/Streunerin, *die*

wane /weɪn/ *v.i.* ⟨*Mond:*⟩ abnehmen; ⟨*Kraft, Einfluss, Macht:*⟩ schwinden, abnehmen; ⟨*Ruf, Ruhm:*⟩ verblassen; *see also* **wax²**

wangle /'wæŋgl/ (coll.) **1** *v.t.* (get by devious means) organisieren (ugs.) ⟨*Karte, Einladung*⟩; **∼ sth. out of sb.** jmdm. etw. abluchsen (ugs.). **2** *n.* Kniff, *der;* **by a ∼:** durch Schiebung (ugs.)

wank /wæŋk/ (Brit. coarse) **1** *v.i.* wichsen (derb). **2** *v.t.* **∼ sb. off** jmdm. einen abwichsen (vulg.). **3** *n.* **have a ∼:** sich (*Dat.*) einen abwichsen (derb)

wanker /'wæŋkə(r)/ *n.* (Brit. coarse) Wichser, *der* (derb)

wanna /'wɒnə/ (coll.) = **want to; want a**

wannabe /'wɒnəbi/ *n.* (coll. derog.) Möchtegern, *der;* (attrib.) Möchtegern-; **a ∼ writer, a writer ∼:** ein Möchtegernschriftsteller/eine Möchtegernschriftstellerin

want /wɒnt/ **1** *v.t.* (a) (desire) wollen; **I ∼ my mummy** ich will zu meiner Mama; **I ∼ it done by tonight** ich will, dass es bis heute Abend fertig wird; **I don't ∼ there to be any misunderstanding** ich will *od.* möchte nicht, dass da ein Missverständnis aufkommt; (b) (require, need) brauchen; **'W∼ed — cook for small family** „Koch/ Köchin für kleine Familie gesucht"; **you're ∼ed on the phone** du wirst am Telefon verlangt; **feel ∼ed** das Gefühl haben, gebraucht zu werden; **the windows ∼ painting** die Fenster müssten gestrichen werden; **you ∼ to be [more] careful** (ought to be) du solltest vorsichtig[er] sein; (c) **∼ed [by the police]** (polizeilich) gesucht (for wegen); (d) (lack) sb./sth. **∼s sth.** jmdm./einer Sache fehlt es an etw. (*Dat.*). **2** *n.* (a) *no pl.* (lack) Mangel, *der* (of an + *Dat.*); **there is no ∼ of …:** es fehlt nicht an … (*Dat.*); **for ∼ of sth.** aus Mangel an etw. (*Dat.*); **for ∼ of a better word** in Ermangelung eines besseren Ausdrucks; (b) *no pl.* (need) Not, *die;* **suffer ∼:** Not leiden; (c) (desire) Bedürfnis, *das;* **we can supply all your ∼s** wir können alles liefern, was Sie brauchen; **∼ ad** (Amer.) Kaufgesuch, *das*

∼ for *v.t.* sb. **∼s for nothing** *or* **doesn't ∼ for anything** jmdm. fehlt es an nichts

wanting /'wɒntɪŋ/ *adj.* **be ∼:** fehlen; **sb./sth. is ∼ in sth.** jmdm./einer Sache fehlt es an etw. (*Dat.*); **be found ∼:** für unzureichend befunden werden

wanton /'wɒntən/ *adj.* (a) (dated: licentious) lüstern; wollüstig ⟨*Person, Gedanken, Benehmen*⟩; (b) (wilful) mutwillig ⟨*Beschädigung, Grausamkeit, Verschwendung*⟩; leichtfertig ⟨*Vernachlässigung*⟩

war /wɔ:(r)/ *n.* (a) Krieg, *der;* **between the ∼s** zwischen den Weltkriegen; **declare ∼:** den Krieg erklären (**on** *Dat.*); **be at ∼:** sich im Krieg befinden; **make ∼:** Krieg führen (**on** gegen); **go to ∼:** in den Krieg ziehen (**against** gegen); (b) (science) Kriegführung, *die;* (fig.: conflict) Krieg, *der;* **price ∼:** Preiskrieg, *der;* **∼ of nerves** Nervenkrieg, *der;* (d) (fig.: fight, campaign) Kampf, *der* (**on, against** gegen); **declare ∼ on poverty** der Armut den Kampf ansagen

warble /'wɔ:bl/ *v.t. & i.* trällern

warbler /'wɔ:blə(r)/ *n.* (Ornith.) Grasmücke, *die*

war: ∼ correspondent *n.* Kriegsberichterstatter, *der*/-berichterstatterin, *die;* **∼ crime** *n.* Kriegsverbrechen, *das;* **∼ criminal** *n.* Kriegsverbrecher, *der*/-verbrecherin, *die;* **∼ cry** *n.* (a) Kriegsruf, *der;* (b) (slogan) Schlachtruf, *der*

ward /wɔ:d/ *n.* (a) (in hospital) Station, *die;* (single room) Krankensaal, *der;* **geriatric/maternity ∼:** geriatrische Abteilung/Entbindungsstation, *die;* **she's in W∼ 3** sie liegt auf Station 3; (b) (minor) Mündel, *das od. die;* (c) (electoral division) Wahlbezirk, *der*

∼ 'off *v.t.* (a) (prevent) abwehren; schützen vor (+ *Dat.*) ⟨*Erkältung, Depressionen*⟩; abwenden ⟨*Gefahr*⟩; (b) (keep at distance) sich (*Dat.*) vom Leibe halten ⟨*Verehrer*⟩

war dance *n.* Kriegstanz, *der*

warden /'wɔ:dn/ *n.* ▶ 887 | (a) (president, governor) Direktor, *der*/Direktorin, *die;* (of college, school) Rektor, *der*/Rektorin, *die;* (of hostel, sheltered housing) Heimleiter, *der*/-leiterin, *die;* (of youth hostel) Herbergsvater, *der*/-mutter, *die;* (b) (supervisor) Aufseher, *der*/Aufseherin, *die*

warder /'wɔ:də(r)/ *n.* ▶ 887 | (Brit.) Wärter, *der;* Aufseher, *der*

wardrobe /'wɔ:drəʊb/ *n.* (a) (piece of furniture) Kleiderschrank, *der;* (b) (stock of clothes) Garderobe, *die;* (in theatre) Kostüme *Pl.*

ware /weə(r)/ *n.* (a) (pottery) Steinzeug, *das;* **Delft ∼:** Delfter Keramik; (b) *in pl.* (goods) Ware, *die*

warehouse 1 /'weəhaʊs/ *n.* Lagerhaus, *das;* (part of building) Lager, *das;* (Brit.: retail or wholesale store) Großmarkt, *der.* **2** /'weəhaʊs, 'weəhaʊz/ *v.t.* einlagern

warfare /'wɔ:feə(r)/ *n.* (lit. or fig.) Krieg, *der;* **in modern ∼:** in der modernen Kriegführung; **economic ∼:** Wirtschaftskrieg, *der*

war: ∼ game *n.* Kriegsspiel, *das;* **∼head** *n.* Sprengkopf, *der;* **∼horse** *n.* (Hist., fig.) Schlachtross, *das;* **∼like** *adj.* (bellicose) kriegerisch

warm /wɔ:m/ **1** *adj.* (a) warm; **come inside and get ∼:** komm rein und wärm dich auf; **I am very ∼ from running** mir ist sehr warm vom Rennen; **it's ∼ work** bei der Arbeit kommt man ins Schwitzen; **keep sb.'s food ∼:** jmdm. das Essen warm halten; **keep a seat/job ∼ for sb.** (fig.) jmdm. einen Platz/eine Stellung freihalten; (b) (enthusiastic) herzlich ⟨*Grüße, Dank*⟩; eng ⟨*Freundschaft*⟩; lebhaft ⟨*Interesse*⟩; begeistert ⟨*Unterstützung, Applaus*⟩; (c) (cordial, sympathetic) warm ⟨*Herz, Wesen, Gefühl*⟩; herzlich ⟨*Lächeln*⟩; echt empfunden ⟨*Hochachtung*⟩; (d) (passionate) heiß ⟨*Temperament, Küsse*⟩; (e) (unpleasant) ungemütlich; **he left when things began to get too ∼ for him** er ging, als ihm die Sache zu ungemütlich wurde; (f) (recent) heiß ⟨*Spur*⟩; (g) (in games: close) **you're getting ∼!** warm! **2** *v.t.* wärmen; warm machen ⟨*Flüssigkeit*⟩; **∼ one's hands** sich (*Dat.*) die Hände wärmen. **3** *v.i.* (a) **∼ to sb./sth.** (come to like) sich für jmdn./etw. erwärmen; **the speaker ∼ed to his subject** der Redner steigerte sich in sein Thema hinein; (b) (get ∼er) warm werden

∼ 'up 1 *v.i.* (a) (get ∼) warm werden; ⟨*Motor:*⟩ warmlaufen; (b) (prepare) ⟨*Sportler:*⟩ sich aufwärmen; (c) (fig.: become animated) warm werden; ⟨*Party:*⟩ in Schwung kommen; ⟨*Publikum:*⟩ in Stimmung kommen. **2** *v.t.* aufwärmen ⟨*Speisen*⟩; erwärmen ⟨*Raum, Zimmer*⟩; warm laufen lassen ⟨*Motor*⟩; (fig.) in Stimmung bringen ⟨*Publikum*⟩

warm-blooded /'wɔ:mblʌdɪd/ *adj.* warmblütig ⟨*Tier*⟩; **∼ animals** Warmblüter

'war memorial *n.* Kriegerdenkmal, *das*

warm-hearted /'wɔ:mhɑ:tɪd/ *adj.* herzlich; warmherzig ⟨*Person*⟩

warmly /'wɔ:mlɪ/ *adv.* (a) (to maintain warmth) warm; (b) (enthusiastically) herzlich ⟨*willkommen heißen, gratulieren, begrüßen, grüßen, danken*⟩; wärmstens ⟨*empfehlen*⟩; begeistert ⟨*sprechen von, applaudieren*⟩

warmonger /'wɔ:mʌŋgə(r)/ *n.* Kriegshetzer, *der*/-hetzerin, *die*

warmth /wɔ:mθ/ *n.* (a) (state of being warm; also of colour) Wärme, *die;* (b) (enthusiasm, affection, cordiality) Herzlichkeit, *die;* Wärme, *die*

'warm-up *n.* **have a ∼** (lit., Sport) sich aufwärmen; **∼ [lap]** (Motor Racing) Aufwärmrunde, *die*

warn /wɔ:n/ *v.t.* (a) (inform, give notice) warnen (**against, of, about** vor + *Dat.*); **∼ sb. that …:** jmdn. darauf hinweisen, dass …; **you have been ∼ed!** ich habe/wir haben dich gewarnt!; **∼ sb. not to do sth.** jmdn. davor warnen, etw. zu tun; (b) (admonish) ermahnen, (officially) ermahnen

∼ 'off *v.t.* warnen; **∼ sb. off doing sth.** jmdn. davor warnen, etw. zu tun

warning /'wɔ:nɪŋ/ **1** *n.* (a) (advance notice) Vorwarnung, *die;* **we had no ∼ of their arrival** sie kamen ohne Vorwarnung; **give sb. plenty of/a few days' ∼:** jmdm. rechtzeitig/ein paar Tage vorher Bescheid sagen; (b) (lesson) Lehre, *die;* **let that be a ∼ to you** lass dir/lasst euch das eine Warnung sein; (c) (caution) Verwarnung, *die;* (less official) Warnung, *die.* **2** *attrib. adj.* Warn⟨*schild, -zeichen, -signal usw.*⟩; ∼ **light/shot** Warnleuchte, *die/*-schuss, *der;* ∼ **notice** Warnung, *die;* **a** ∼ **look/gesture** ein warnender Blick/eine warnende Geste

warp /wɔːp/ **1** *v.i.* (become bent) sich verbiegen; ⟨*Holz, Schallplatte:*⟩ sich verziehen. **2** *v.t.* **(a)** verbiegen; **(b)** (fig.: pervert) verformen; verbiegen; ∼**ed** getrübt ⟨*Urteilsvermögen*⟩; pervertiert ⟨*Denken, Gehirn*⟩. **3** *n.* (Weaving) Kettfaden, *der*

war: ∼**paint** *n.* (also fig. coll. joc.) Kriegsbemalung, *die;* ∼**path** *n.* Kriegspfad, *der;* **be on the** ∼**path** auf dem Kriegspfad sein; (fig.) in Rage sein; ∼**plane** *n.* Kampfflugzeug, *das*

warrant /'wɒrənt/ **1** *n.* (for sb.'s arrest) Haftbefehl, *der;* [**search**] ∼**:** Durchsuchungsbefehl, *der.* **2** *v.t.* (justify) rechtfertigen

warranty /'wɒrəntɪ/ *n.* (Law) Garantie, *die;* **it is still under** ∼**:** es steht noch unter Garantie

warren /'wɒrn/ *n.* **(a)** ⇒ **rabbit warren; (b)** (fig.: maze) Labyrinth, *das*

warring /'wɔːrɪŋ/ *attrib. adj.* Krieg führend

warrior /'wɒrɪə(r)/ *n.* (esp. literary) Krieger, *der* (geh.)

Warsaw /'wɔːsɔː/ **▶ 1159**⟩ **1** *pr. n.* Warschau (*das*). **2** *attrib. adj.* Warschauer; ∼ **Pact** (Hist.) Warschauer Pakt

'**warship** *n.* Kriegsschiff, *das*

wart /wɔːt/ *n.* Warze, *die;* ∼**s and all** (fig.) schonungslos; ungeschminkt [bis ins kleinste Detail]

'**warthog** *n.* Warzenschwein, *das*

war: ∼**time** *n.* **(a)** Kriegszeit, *die;* **in** *or* **during** ∼**time** während des Krieges; im Krieg; **(b)** *attrib.* Kriegs⟨*rationierung, -evakuierung usw.*⟩; ∼**time** England [das] England während des Krieges; ∼**-torn** *adj.* kriegsgeschunden

wary /'weərɪ/ *adj.* vorsichtig; (suspicious) misstrauisch (of gegenüber); **be** ∼ **of** *or* **about doing sth.** sich davor hüten, etw. zu tun; **be** ∼ **of sb./sth.** sich vor jmdm./etw. in Acht nehmen

'**war zone** *n.* Kriegsgebiet, *das*

was ⇒ **be**

wash /wɒʃ/ **1** *v.t.* **(a)** waschen; ∼ **oneself/one's hands** (also euphem.)/**face/hair** sich waschen (*Dat.*) die Hände (auch verhüll)/das Gesicht/die Haare waschen; ∼ **the dishes** abwaschen; [Geschirr] spülen; ∼ **the floor** den Fußboden aufwischen *od.* feucht wischen; ∼ **one's hands of sb./sth.** mit jmdm./etw. nichts mehr zu tun haben wollen; **(b)** (remove) waschen ⟨*Fleck*⟩ (**out of** aus); abwaschen ⟨*Schmutz*⟩ (**off** von); **(c)** (by licking) putzen; **the cat** ∼**ed its fur** die Katze putzte sich (*Dat.*) das Fell; **(d)** (carry along) spülen; **be** ∼**ed downstream** von der Strömung mitgerissen werden. **2** *v.i.* **(a)** sich waschen; **(b)** (clean clothes) waschen; **(c)** ⟨*Stoff, Kleidungsstück, Handtuch:*⟩ sich waschen lassen; **that won't** ∼ (fig. coll.) das zieht nicht (ugs.). **3** *n.* **(a)** **give sb./sth. a** [**good**] ∼**:** jmdn./etw. [gründlich] waschen; **the baby/car needs a** ∼ *or* (coll.) **could do with a** ∼**:** das Kind/Auto müsste mal gewaschen werden; **(b)** (laundering) Wäsche, *die;* **it is in the** ∼**:** es ist in der Wäsche; **it'll all come out in the** ∼ (fig. coll.) das wird sich alles klären; **(c)** (of ship, aircraft, etc.) Sog, *der;* **(d)** (lotion) Waschlotion, *die;* **a** ∼ **for disinfecting the mouth** ein desinfizierendes Mundwasser

∼ **a'way** *v.t.* **(a)** wegspülen; **(b)** ∼ **a stain/the mud away** einen Fleck/den Schmutz auswaschen

∼ '**down** *v.t.* **(a)** (with a hose) abspritzen ⟨*Auto, Deck, Hof*⟩; (with soap and water) abwaschen; aufwaschen ⟨*Fußboden*⟩; **(b)** (help to go down) runterspülen (ugs.)

∼ '**off 1** *v.t.* ∼ **it.** ∼ **sth. off** etw. abwaschen. **2** *v.i.* abgehen; (from fabric etc.) herausgehen

∼ '**out** *v.t.* (clean) auswaschen ⟨*Kleidungsstück*⟩; ausscheuern ⟨*Topf*⟩; ausspülen ⟨*Mund*⟩; ∼ **dirt/marks out of clothes** Schmutz/Flecken aus Kleidern [her]auswaschen

∼ '**over** *v.t.* (fig. coll.: not affect) ∼ **over sb.** ⟨*Streit, Lärm, Unruhe usw.:*⟩ jmdn. gar nicht berühren

∼ '**up 1** *v.t.* **(a)** (Brit.: clean) ∼ **the dishes up** das Geschirr abwaschen *od.* spülen; **(b)** (carry to shore) anspülen ⟨*Leiche, Strandgut, Wrackteile usw.*⟩. **2** *v.i.* abwaschen; spülen

washable /'wɒʃəbl/ *adj.* waschbar ⟨*Stoff*⟩; abwaschbar ⟨*Tapete, Farbe*⟩

wash: ∼**-and-'wear** *adj.* bügelfrei; ∼**basin** *n.* Waschbecken, *das;* ∼**day** *n.* Waschtag, *der*

washed-'out *adj.* **(a)** *attrib.* verwaschen ⟨*Farbe, Kleidungsstück*⟩; **(b)** (fig.: exhausted) abgespannt; mitgenommen

washer /'wɒʃə(r)/ *n.* (Mech. Engin.) Unterlegscheibe, *die;* (of tap) Dichtungsring, *der;* Dichtungsscheibe, *die*

washing /'wɒʃɪŋ/ *n., no pl., no indef. art.* **(a)** (clothes to be washed) Wäsche, *die;* **(b)** (cleansing) Waschen, *das;* **do the** ∼**:** waschen

washing: ∼ **machine** *n.* Waschmaschine, *die;* ∼ **powder** *n.* Waschpulver, *das;* ∼**-'up** *n.* (Brit.) Abwasch, *der;* **do the** ∼**-up** den Abwasch machen; abwaschen; ∼**-'up liquid** *n.* Spülmittel, *das;* ∼**-'up machine** ⇒ **dishwasher**

wash: ∼**-out** *n.* (coll.) **(a)** (failure) Pleite, *die* (ugs.); Reinfall, *der* (ugs.); **(b)** (useless person) Niete, *die* (salopp abwertend); ∼**room** *n.* (Amer.) WC, *das*

wasn't /'wɒznt/ (coll.) = **was not;** ⇒ **be**

wasp /wɒsp/ *n.* Wespe, *die*

waspish /'wɒspɪʃ/ *adj.* bissig

wastage /'weɪstɪdʒ/ *n.* **(a)** (loss by wear etc.) Schwund, *der;* **(b)** [**natural**] ∼ (Admin.) ≈ natürliche Fluktuation

waste /weɪst/ **1** *n.* **(a)** (useless remains) Abfall, *der;* **kitchen** ∼**:** Küchenabfälle *Pl.;* **(b)** (extravagant use) Verschwendung, *die;* Vergeudung, *die;* **it's a** ∼ **of time/money/energy** das ist Zeit-/Geld-/Energieverschwendung; **it would be a** ∼ **of effort** das wäre vergeudete Mühe; **go** *or* **run to** ∼**:** vergeudet werden. **2** *v.t.* **(a)** (squander) verschwenden; vergeuden (**on** auf + *Akk.*, **an** + *Akk.*); **he is** ∼**d on an audience like that** für ein solches Publikum ist er zu schade; **all his efforts were** ∼**d** all seine Mühe war umsonst; **don't** ∼ **my time!** stehlen Sie mir nicht die Zeit!; ∼ **not, want not** (prov.) spare in der Zeit, so hast du in der Not (Spr.); **(b)** **be** ∼**d** (reduced) ⟨*Vorräte, Bevölkerung:*⟩ abnehmen, schrumpfen; **(c)** (cause to shrink) aufzehren ⟨*Kräfte*⟩; auszehren ⟨*Körper*⟩. **3** *v.i.* dahinschwinden; (gradually) im Schwinden begriffen sein. **4** *adj.* **(a)** (not wanted) ∼ **material** Abfall, *der;* ∼ **food** Essensreste *Pl.;* ∼ **water** Abwasser, *das;* **(b)** **lay** ∼ **sth.** etw. verwüsten

∼ **a'way** *v.i.* immer mehr abmagern

waste: ∼**basket** ⇒ **waste-paper basket;** ∼ **disposal** *n.* Abfallbeseitigung, *die;* Entsorgung, *die* (Amtsspr.); ∼**-di'sposal unit** *n.* Müllzerkleinerer, *der*

wasteful /'weɪstfl/ *adj.* **(a)** (extravagant) verschwenderisch; **too much** ∼ **expenditure** zu viel Geldverschwendung; **(b)** (causing waste) unwirtschaftlich; **be** ∼ **of sth.** etw. vergeuden

wastefulness /'weɪstflnɪs/ *n., no pl.* **(a)** (extravagance) Verschwendung, *die;* (character trait) Verschwendungssucht, *die;* **(b)** (of manufacturing process) Unwirtschaftlichkeit, *die*

waste: ∼**land** *n.* (not cultivated) Ödland, *das;* (not built on) unbebautes Land; (fig.) Einöde, *die;* ∼ '**paper** *n.* Papierabfall, *der;* ∼**-'paper basket** *n.* Papierkorb, *der;* ∼**pipe** *n.* Abflussrohr, *das*

watch /wɒtʃ/ **1** *n.* **(a)** [**wrist/pocket-**]∼**:** [Armband-/Taschen]uhr, *die;* **(b)** (constant attention) Wache, *die;* **keep** ∼**:** Wache halten; **keep [a]** ∼ **for sb./sth.** auf jmdn./etw. achten *od.* aufpassen; **keep [a]** ∼ **for enemy aircraft** nach feindlichen Flugzeugen Ausschau halten; **keep a close** ∼ **on the time** genau auf die Zeit achten; **they kept a** ∼ **on all his activities** sie überwachten alle seine Aktivitäten; **the police were on the** ∼ **for car thieves** die Polizei hielt nach Autodieben Ausschau; **(c)** (Naut.) Wache, *die;* **the officer of the** ∼**:** der wachhabende Offizier. **2** *v.i.* **(a)** (wait) ∼ **for sb./sth.** auf jmdn./etw. warten; **(b)** (keep ∼) Wache stehen. **3** *v.t.* **(a)** (observe) sich (*Dat.*) ansehen ⟨*Sportveranstaltung, Fernsehsendung*⟩; ∼ [**the**] **television** *or* **TV** fernsehen; Fernsehen gucken (ugs.); ∼ **sth.** [**on television** *or* **TV**] sich (*Dat.*) etw. [im Fernsehen] ansehen; ∼ **sb. do** *or* **doing sth.** zusehen, wie jmd. etw. tut; **we are being** ∼**ed** wir werden beobachtet; ∼ **one's weight** auf sein Gewicht achten; **(b)** (be careful of, look after) achten auf (+ *Akk.*); ∼ **your manners!**

(coll.) benimm dich!; ~ **your language!** (coll.) drück dich bitte etwas gepflegter *od.* nicht so ordinär aus!; ~ **him,** **he's an awkward customer** (coll.) pass/passt auf, er ist mit Vorsicht zu genießen (ugs.); ~ **how you go/drive** pass auf!/fahr vorsichtig!; ~ **it** *or* **oneself** sich vorsehen; [just] ~ **it** [**or you'll be in trouble**]! pass bloß auf!, sonst gibt's Ärger]! (ugs.); (c) (look out for) warten auf (+ *Akk.*)

~ **'out** *v.i.* (a) (be careful) sich vorsehen; aufpassen; **W~ out! There's a car coming!** Vorsicht! Da kommt ein Auto!; (b) (look out) ~ **out for sb./sth.** auf jmdn./etw. achten; (wait) auf jmdn./etw. warten

~ **'over** *v.t.* sich kümmern um; in Obhut nehmen ⟨*Wertgegenstand*⟩; ⟨*Gott, Schutzengel:*⟩ wachen über (+ *Akk.*)

'watchdog *n.* Wachhund, *der;* (fig.) Wächter, *der;* Aufpasser, *der* (ugs.)

watchful /'wɒtʃfl/ *adj.* wachsam; **be ~ for sth.** vor etw. (*Dat.*) auf der Hut sein; **keep a ~ eye on sb./sth.** ein wachsames Auge auf jmdn./etw. haben

watch: ~**maker** *n.* ▶887⟩ Uhrmacher, *der/*Uhrmacherin, *die;* ~**man** /'wɒtʃmən/ *n., pl.* ~**men** /'wɒtʃmən/ ▶887⟩ Wachmann, *der;* ~ **strap** *n.* [Uhr]armband, *das;* ~**tower** *n.* Wachturm, *der;* ~**word** *n.* Parole, *die*

water /'wɔːtə(r)/ **1** *n.* (a) Wasser, *das;* **be under ~** ⟨*Straße, Sportplatz usw.:*⟩ unter Wasser stehen; **the island across** *or* **over the ~:** die Insel drüben; **send/carry sth. by ~:** etw. auf dem Wasserweg versenden/befördern; **be in deep ~** (fig.) in großen Schwierigkeiten sein; **get** [**oneself**] **into deep ~** (fig.) sich in große Schwierigkeiten bringen; **on the ~** (in boat etc.) auf dem Wasser; **pour** *or* **throw cold ~ on sth.** (fig.) einer Sache (*Dat.*) einen Dämpfer aufsetzen; **~ under the bridge** *or* **over the dam** (fig.) Schnee von gestern (fig.); (b) *in pl.* (part of the sea etc.) Gewässer *Pl.;* (c) *in pl.* (mineral ~ at spa etc.) Heilquelle, *die;* Brunnen, *der;* **take** *or* **drink the ~s** eine Brunnenkur machen; (d) **of the first ~:** reinsten Wassers; **a genius of the first ~:** ein Genie ersten Ranges. **2** *v.t.* (a) bewässern ⟨*Land*⟩; wässern ⟨*Pflanzen*⟩; ~ **the flowers** die Blumen [be]gießen; (b) (adulterate) verwässern ⟨*Wein, Bier usw.*⟩; (c) ⟨*Fluss:*⟩ bewässern ⟨*Land*⟩; (d) (give drink of ~ to) tränken ⟨*Tier, Vieh*⟩. **3** *v.i.* (a) ⟨*Augen:*⟩ tränen; (b) **my mouth was ~ing as …:** mir lief das Wasser im Munde zusammen, als …; **the very thought of it made my mouth ~:** allein bei dem Gedanken lief mir das Wasser im Munde zusammen

~ **'down** *v.t.* (lit. or fig.) verwässern

water: ~ **bed** *n.* Wasserbett, *das;* ~ **birth** *n.* Unterwassergeburt, *die;* ~ **bottle** *n.* Wasserflasche, *die;* ~ **butt** *n.* Regentonne, *die;* ~ **cannon** *n.* Wasserwerfer, *der;* ~ **closet** *n.* Toilette, *die;* WC, *das;* ~**colour** *n.* (a) (paint) Wasserfarbe, *die;* (b) (picture) Aquarell, *das;* ~**course** *n.* (stream etc.) Wasserlauf, *der;* (bed) Flussbett, *das;* ~**cress** *n.* Brunnenkresse, *die;* ~ **diviner** /'wɔːtədɪvaɪnə(r)/ *n.* [Wünschel]rutengänger, *der/*-gängerin, *die;* ~**fall** *n.* Wasserfall, *der;* ~**front** *n.* Ufer, *das;* **down on the ~front** unten am Wasser; *attrib.* **a ~front restaurant** ein Restaurant am Wasser; ~ **heater** *n.* Heißwassergerät, *das;* ~**hole** *n.* Wasserloch, *das*

watering /'wɔːtərɪŋ/ *n.* Bewässerung, *die;* (of flowers, house plants) Gießen, *das;* **give the plants a thorough ~:** die Pflanzen gut wässern *od.* gießen

'watering can *n.* Gießkanne, *die*

water: ~**level** *n.* (a) (in reservoir etc.) Wasserstand, *der;* Pegelstand, *der;* (b) (below which ground is saturated) Grundwasserspiegel, *der;* ~ **lily** *n.* Seerose, *die;* ~**line** *n.* (Naut.) Wasserlinie, *die;* ~**logged** /'wɔːtəlɒgd/ *adj.* voll gesogen ⟨*Holz*⟩; ⟨*Boot*⟩ voll Wasser; nass, feucht ⟨*Boden*⟩; aufgeweicht ⟨*Sportplatz*⟩; ~ **main** *n.* Hauptwasserleitung, *die;* **a burst ~ main** ein Wasserrohrbruch; ~**mark** **1** *n.* Wasserzeichen, *das;* **2** *v.t.* mit Wasserzeichen versehen; ~**melon** *n.* Wassermelone, *die;* ~ **meter** *n.* Wasseruhr, *die;* ~**mill** *n.* Wassermühle, *die;* ~ **pipe** *n.* (a) Wasserrohr, *das;* (b) (for smoking) Wasserpfeife, *die;* ~ **pistol** *n.* Wasserpistole, *die;* ~ **polo** *n.* Wasserball, *der;* ~**power** *n.* Wasserkraft, *die;* ~**proof 1** *adj.* wasserdicht; wasserfest ⟨*Farbe*⟩; **2** *n.* Regenhaut, *die;* (raincoat) Regenmantel, *der;* **3** *v.t.* wasserdicht

machen; imprägnieren ⟨*Stoff*⟩; wetterfest machen ⟨*Holzzaun, Gartenmöbel*⟩; ~ **rate** *n.* Wassergeld, *das;* **the ~ rates** die Wassergebühren; ~**-repellent** *adj.* Wasser abstoßend; ~**-resistant** *adj.* wasserundurchlässig; wasserfest ⟨*Farbe*⟩; ~**shed** *n.* (fig.: turning point) Wendepunkt, *der;* ~**-ski 1** *n.* Wasserski, *der;* **2** *v.i.* Wasserski laufen; ~**-skiing** *n., no pl., no art.* Wasserskilaufen, *das;* ~ **softener** *n.* Wasserenthärter, *der;* ~ **supply** *n.* (a) *no pl., no indef. art.* (providing) Wasserversorgung, *die;* (b) (stored drinking ~) Trinkwasser, *das;* (amount) [Trink]wasservorrat, *der;* ~**-table** *n.* Grundwasserspiegel, *der;* ~ **tap** *n.* Wasserhahn, *der;* ~**tight** *adj.* (lit. or fig.) wasserdicht; ~ **tower** *n.* Wasserturm, *der;* ~ **vapour** *n.* Wasserdampf, *der;* ~**way** *n.* Wasserstraße, *die;* **inland ~ways** Binnenwasserstraßen *Pl.;* ~**wheel** *n.* Wasserrad, *das;* (used to raise ~) Schöpfrad, *das;* ~ **wings** *n. pl.* Schwimmflügel *Pl.;* ~**works** *n.* (a) *sing., pl. same* (system) Wasserversorgungssystem, *das;* (building) Wasserwerk, *das;* (b) *pl.* (coll.: tears) **turn on the ~works** losheulen (ugs.); (c) *pl.* (coll.: urinary system) Blase, *die*

watery /'wɔːtərɪ/ *adj.* wässrig, wässerig ⟨*Essen, Suppe*⟩; feucht ⟨*Augen*⟩; dünn ⟨*Getränk*⟩

watt /wɒt/ *n.* (Electr., Phys.) Watt, *das*

wave /weɪv/ **1** *n.* (a) (lit. or fig.) Welle, *die;* Woge, *die* (geh.); **his hair has a natural ~ in it** sein Haar ist von Natur aus wellig; **a ~ of enthusiasm/pain** eine Welle der Begeisterung/des Schmerzes; ~**s of attackers** Angriffswellen; (b) (gesture) **give sb. a ~:** jmdm. zuwinken; **with a ~ of one's hand** mit einem Winken. **2** *v.i.* (a) ⟨*Fahne, Flagge, Wimpel:*⟩ wehen; ⟨*Baum, Gras, Korn:*⟩ sich wiegen; ⟨*Kornfeld:*⟩ wogen; (b) (gesture with hand) winken; ~ **at** *or* **to sb.** jmdm. winken. **3** *v.t.* schwenken; (brandish) schwingen ⟨*Schwert, Säbel*⟩; ~ **one's hand at** *or* **to sb.** jmdm. winken; **she ~d her umbrella angrily at him** sie drohte ihm wütend mit dem Regenschirm; **stop waving that rifle/those scissors around** hör auf, mit dem Gewehr/der Schere herumzufuchteln (ugs.); ~ **sb. on/over** jmdn. weiter-/herüberwinken; ~ **goodbye to sb.** jmdm. zum Abschied zuwinken

~ **a'side** *v.t.* (a) (refuse to accept) abtun ⟨*Zweifel, Einwand*⟩; (b) (signal to move aside) **I tried to speak but she ~d me aside** ich wollte reden, aber sie winkte ab

~ **a'way** *v.t.* wegwinken

~ **'down** *v.t.* [durch Winken] anhalten

~ **'off** *v.t.* ~ **sb. off** jmdm. nachwinken

wave: ~**band** *n.* Wellenbereich, *der;* ~**length** *n.* (Radio, Telev., Phys.; also fig.) Wellenlänge, *die;* **be on sb.'s ~length** (fig.) die gleiche Wellenlänge wie jmd. haben; ~ **power** *n.* Wellenkraft, *die*

waver /'weɪvə(r)/ *v.i.* (a) (begin to give way) wanken; **start** *or* **begin to ~:** ins Wanken geraten; (b) (be irresolute) schwanken (**between** zwischen + *Dat.*)

wavy /'weɪvɪ/ *adj.* (a) (undulating) wellig; wogend ⟨*Gras*⟩; (b) (forming wave-like curves) geschlängelt; ~ **line** Schlangenlinie, *die*

wax¹ /wæks/ **1** *n.* (a) Wachs, *das;* **be [like] ~ in sb.'s hands** [wie] Wachs in jmds. Händen sein; (b) (in ear) Schmalz, *das.* **2** *adj.* Wachs-. **3** *v.t.* wachsen; wichsen ⟨*Schnurrbart*⟩

wax² *v.i.* (increase) ⟨*Mond:*⟩ zunehmen; ~ **and wane** (fig.) zu- und abnehmen

way /weɪ/ **1** *n.* (a) (road etc., lit. or fig.) Weg, *der;* **across** *or* **over the ~:** gegenüber; (b) ▶1199⟩ (route) Weg, *der;* **ask the** *or* **one's ~:** nach dem Weg fragen; **ask the ~ to …:** fragen *od.* sich erkundigen, wo es nach … geht; **pick one's ~:** sich (*Dat.*) einen Weg suchen; **lead the ~:** vorausgehen; (fig.: show how to do sth.) es vormachen; **find the** *or* **one's ~ in/out** den Eingang/Ausgang finden; **find a ~ out** (fig.) einen Ausweg finden; **I'll take the letter to the post office — it's on my ~:** ich bringe den Brief zur Post — sie liegt auf meinem Weg; **'W~ In/Out'** „Ein-/Ausgang"; **go to Italy by ~ of Switzerland** über die Schweiz nach Italien fahren; **there's no ~ out** (fig.) es gibt keinen Ausweg; **the ~ back/down/up** der Weg zurück/nach unten/nach oben; **go one's own ~/their separate ~s** (fig.) eigene/getrennte Wege gehen; **be going sb.'s ~** (coll.) denselben Weg wie jmd. haben; **things are really**

Asking the way

The questions

1. *How do I get to the station?*	= Wie komme ich zum Bahnhof?
2. *Which is the best way to the museum?*	= Wie kommt man am besten zum Museum?
3. *Am I right for the Hotel zur Post?*	= Geht es hier zum Hotel zur Post?
4. *Where is the nearest bank?*	= Wo ist hier die nächste Bank?
5. *Is there a chemist's near here?*	= Gibt es hier in der Nähe eine Apotheke?
6. *How far is it to the hospital?*	= Wie weit ist es zum Krankenhaus?
7. *Can you direct me to a good restaurant?*	= Können Sie mir sagen, wo es hier ein gutes Restaurant gibt?

Possible replies

1. *Take the first turning on the right, then the second on the left, then go straight on as far as the junction. Turn right and you will see the station in front of you*	= Gehen Sie die erste Straße rechts, dann die zweite links, dann immer nur geradeaus bis zur Kreuzung. Biegen Sie rechts ein und dann sehen Sie den Bahnhof vor sich
2. *The best way is to cross over here at the lights and go down the alleyway along the left side of the theatre. You will come out opposite the museum.*	= Am besten, Sie gehen hier an der Ampel über die Straße, dann die Gasse entlang, links am Theater vorbeiführt. Sie kommen dann gegenüber vom Museum heraus
3. *No, you've come too far. Go back to the crossroads and turn left, you'll find the hotel about a hundred yards further on on the right*	= Nein, Sie sind zu weit gegangen/(in car) gefahren. Gehen/Fahren Sie zurück zur Kreuzung und biegen Sie links ab. Das Hotel liegt etwa hundert Meter weiter auf der rechten Seite
4. *There is a branch of Barclays on the market place, which is a couple of hundred yards along that turning over there on the right*	= Am Marktplatz ist eine Filiale von Barclays. Biegen Sie dort drüben rechts ein, Sie kommen dann nach ein paar hundert Metern zum Marktplatz
5. *There's one in the next street on the left, but it's only small. If you want a bigger one you'll have to take the number 11 bus into the centre*	= In der nächsten Straße links ist eine, allerdings nur eine kleine. Falls Sie eine größere brauchen, müssen Sie mit der Linie 11 ins Zentrum fahren
6. *It's about a mile and a half from here on the main Cardiff road. You'd best take a taxi as the buses aren't very frequent*	= Es liegt etwa zwei Kilometer von hier an der Hauptstraße nach Cardiff. Am besten nehmen Sie ein Taxi, die Busse fahren nämlich nicht sehr oft
7. *Sorry, I'm a stranger here myself*	= Tut mir Leid, ich bin auch fremd hier

going my ~ at the moment (fig.) im Moment läuft [bei mir] alles so, wie ich es mir vorgestellt habe; **money came his** ~: er kam zu Geld; **many offers came his** ~: er erhielt viele Angebote; **go out of one's ~ to collect sth. for sb.** einen Umweg machen, um etw. für jmdn. abzuholen; **go out of one's ~ to be helpful** sich (*Dat.*) besondere Mühe geben, hilfsbereit zu sein; **out of the ~:** abgelegen; **(c)** (method) Art und Weise, *die;* **there is a right ~ and a wrong ~ of doing it** es gibt einen richtigen und einen falschen Weg, es zu tun; **that is not the ~ to do it** so macht man das nicht; **do it this ~:** mach es so; **do it my ~:** mach es wie ich; **I don't like the ~ she smiles** mir gefällt ihr Lächeln nicht; **that's no ~ to speak to a lady** so spricht man nicht mit einer Dame; **he has a strange ~ of talking** er hat eine seltsame Sprechweise *od.* Art zu sprechen; **from** *or* **by the ~** [that] **she looked at me, I knew that there was something wrong** an ihrem Blick konnte ich erkennen, dass etwas nicht stimmte; **find a** *or* **some ~ of doing sth.** einen Weg finden, etw. zu tun; **there is no two ~s about it** da gibt es gar keinen Zweifel; **Are you going to give me that money? — No ~!** (coll.) Gibst du mir das Geld? — Nichts da! (ugs.); **there was no ~ he would change his stand** er würde auf gar keinen Fall seinen Standpunkt ändern; **no ~ is he coming with us** es kommt überhaupt nicht in Frage, dass er mit uns kommt; **one ~ or another** irgendwie; **~s and means** [to do sth. *or* of doing sth.] Mittel und Wege, etw. zu tun; **be built** *or* **made that ~** (fig. coll.) so gestrickt sein (fig. ugs.); **be that ~** (coll.) so sein; **better that ~:** besser so; **either ~:** so oder so; **(d)** (desired course of action) Wille, *der;* **get** *or* **have one's [own] ~, have it one's [own] ~:** seinen Willen kriegen; **all right, have it your own ~[, then]!** na gut od. schön, du sollst deinen Willen haben!; **(e)** *in sing. or* (Amer. coll.) *pl.* (distance between two points) Stück, *das;* **a little ~:** ein kleines Stück[chen]; (fig.) ein klein[es] bisschen; **it's a long ~ off** *or* **a long ~ from here** es ist ein ganzes Stück von hier aus; es ist weit weg von hier;

the summer holidays are only a little ~ away bis zu den Sommerferien ist es nicht mehr lange; **there's [still] some ~ to go yet** es ist noch ein ganzes Stück; (fig.) es dauert noch ein Weilchen; **I went a little/a long/some ~ to meet him** ich bin ihm ein kleines/ganzes/ziemliches Stück entgegengegangen/-gefahren *usw.*, um mich mit ihm zu treffen; (fig.) ich bin ihm etwas/sehr/ziemlich entgegengekommen; **have gone/come a long ~** (fig.) es weit gebracht haben; **go a long ~ toward sth./doing sth.** viel zu etw. beitragen/viel dazu beitragen, etw. zu tun; **a little kindness goes a long ~:** ein bisschen Freundlichkeit ist viel wert *od.* hilft viel; **all the ~:** den ganzen Weg; **go all the ~ [with sb.]** (fig.) [jmdm.] in jeder Hinsicht zustimmen; (coll.: have full sexual intercourse) es [mit jmdm.] richtig machen (salopp); **(f)** (room for progress) Weg, *der;* **block the ~:** den Weg versperren; **leave the ~ open for sth.** (fig.) etw. möglich machen; **clear the ~ [for sth.]** [lit. *or* fig.] [einer Sache (*Dat.*)] den Weg freimachen; **be in sb.'s** *or* **the ~:** [jmdm.] im Weg sein; **get in sb.'s ~** (lit. *or* fig.) jmdm. im Weg stehen; **put difficulties/obstacles in sb.'s ~** (fig.) jmdm. Schwierigkeiten bereiten/Hindernisse in den Weg legen; **make ~ for sth.** für etw. Platz schaffen *od.* (fig.) machen; **make ~!** Platz da!; **[get] out of the/my ~!** [geh] aus dem Weg!; **move one's car out of the ~:** seinen Wagen aus dem Weg fahren; **get sth. out of the ~** (settle sth.) etw. erledigen; **(g)** (journey) **on his ~ to the office/London** auf dem Weg ins Büro/nach London; **on the ~ out to Singapore** auf dem Hinweg/der Hinfahrt/dem Hinflug nach Singapur; **on the ~ back from Nigeria** auf dem Rückweg/der Rückfahrt/dem Rückflug von Nigeria; **she is just on the** *or* **her ~ in/out** sie kommt/geht gerade; **be on the ~ out** (fig. coll.) (be losing popularity) passee sein (ugs.); (be reaching end of life) ‹*Hund, Auto, Person:*› es nicht mehr lange machen (ugs.); **we stopped on the ~ to have lunch** wir hielten unterwegs zum Mittagessen an; **on her ~ home** auf dem Nachhauseweg; **they're on their ~:** sie sind unterwegs; **on the ~ there** auf dem Hinweg; **[be] on your ~!** nun geh schon!; **by the** ~: übrigens; **all this is by the** ~: das alles nur nebenbei; **(h)** (specific direction) Richtung, *die;* **she went this/that/the other** ~: sie ist in diese/die/die andere Richtung gegangen; **look this** ~, **please** sieh/seht bitte hierher!; **he wouldn't look my** ~: er hat nicht zu mir herübergesehen; **I will call next time I'm [down] your** ~: wenn ich das nächste Mal in deiner Gegend bin, komme ich [bei dir] vorbei; **look the other** ~ (lit. or fig.) weggucken; **the other** ~ **about** *or* **round** andersherum; **this/which** ~ **round** so/wie herum; **stand sth. the right/wrong** ~ **up** etw. richtig/falsch herum stellen; **turn sth. the right** ~ **round** etw. richtig herum drehen; **'this** ~ **up'** „hier oben"; **(i)** (advance) Weg, *der;* **fight/push** *etc.* **one's** ~ **through** sich durchkämpfen/-drängen; **be under** ~ ⟨*Person:*⟩ aufgebrochen sein; ⟨*Fahrzeug:*⟩ abgefahren sein; (fig.: be in progress) ⟨*Besprechung, Verhandlung, Tagung:*⟩ im Gange sein; **get sth. under** ~ (fig.) etw. in Gang bringen; **get under** ~: wegkommen; **make one's** ~ **to Oxford/the station** nach Oxford/zum Bahnhof gehen/fahren; **Do you need a lift?** — No, **I'll make my own** ~: Soll ich dich mitnehmen? — Nein, ich komme alleine; **make one's [own]** ~ **in the world** seinen Weg gehen (fig.); **make** *or* **pay its** ~: ohne Verlust arbeiten; **pay one's** ~: für sich selbst aufkommen; **(j)** (respect) Hinsicht, *die;* **in [exactly] the same** ~: [ganz] genauso; **in some** ~s in gewisser Hinsicht; **in one** ~: auf eine Art; **not in any** ~: in keiner Weise; **in every** ~: in jeder Hinsicht; **in a** ~: auf eine Art; **in more** ~s **than one** auf mehr als eine Art; **in no** ~: auf keinen Fall; durchaus nicht; **(k)** (state) Verfassung, *die;* **in a bad** ~: schlecht; **they are in a very bad** ~: es geht ihnen sehr schlecht; **either** ~: so oder so; **in a small** ~: in bescheidenem Rahmen; **by** ~ **of** (as a kind of) als; (for the purpose of) um … zu; **by** ~ **of illustration/greeting/apology/introduction** zur Illustration/Begrüßung/Entschuldigung/Einführung; **(l)** (custom) Art, *die;* **get into/out of the** ~ **of doing sth.** sich (*Dat.*) etw. an-/abgewöhnen; **he has a** ~ **of leaving his bills unpaid** es ist so seine Art, seine Rechnungen nicht zu bezahlen; **in its** ~: auf seine/ihre Art; ~ **of life** Lebensstil, *der;* **change one's** ~s sich ändern; ~ **of thinking** Denkungsart, *die;* **to my** ~ **of thinking** meiner Meinung nach; **(m)** (normal course of events) **be the** ~: so *od.* üblich sein; **that is always the** ~: das ist immer so; **(n)** (ability to charm sb. or attain one's object) **he has a** ~ **with him** er hat so eine Art; **she has a** ~ **with children/animals** sie kann mit Kindern/Tieren gut umgehen; **(o)** (specific manner) Eigenart, *die;* **fall into bad** ~s schlechte [An]gewohnheiten annehmen; **(p)** (ordinary course) Rahmen, *der;* **(q)** *in pl.* (parts) Teile, *pl.;* **split sth. three** ~s etw. in drei Teile teilen. **2** *adv.* weit; ~ **off/ahead/above** weit weg von/weit voraus/weit über; ~ **back** (coll.) vor langer Zeit; ~ **back in the early fifties/before the war** vor langer Zeit, Anfang der fünfziger Jahre/vor dem Krieg; ~ **up in the clouds** hoch oben in den Wolken; **he was** ~ **out with his guess, his guess was** ~ **out** er lag mit seiner Schätzung gewaltig daneben; ~ **down south/in the valley** tief [unten] im Süden/Tal

way: ~**'lay** *v.t., forms as* **lay²** 1: **(a)** (ambush) überfallen; **(b)** (stop for conversation) abfangen; ~**-'out** *adj.* (coll.) verrückt (ugs.); irre (salopp); ~**side** *n.* Wegrand, *der;* **fall by the** ~**side** (fig.) auf der Strecke bleiben (ugs.); *attrib.* ~**side flowers/inns** Blumen/Gasthöfe am Wegrand

wayward /'weIwəd/ *adj.* eigenwillig; ungezügelt ⟨*Talent*⟩

WC *abbr.* **water closet** WC, *das*

we /wI, *stressed* wiː/ *pl. pron.* wir; **how are we feeling today?** (coll.) wie geht's uns denn heute? (ugs.); *see also* **our; ours; ourselves; us**

weak /wiːk/ *adj.* **(a)** (lit. or fig.) schwach; matt ⟨*Lächeln*⟩; schwach ausgeprägt ⟨*Kinn*⟩; jämmerlich ⟨*Kapitulation*⟩; (easily led) labil ⟨*Charakter, Person*⟩; **go/feel** ~ **at the knees** weiche Knie kriegen/haben; **the** ~ **er sex** das schwache Geschlecht; ~ **eyes** *or* **sight** schlechte Augen; **a** ~ **stomach** ein empfindlicher Magen; **be** ~ **in the head** schwachsinnig sein; **his French/maths is rather** ~, **he's rather** ~ **in French/maths** in Französisch/Mathematik ist er ziemlich schwach; **sb.'s** ~ **side** *or* **point** jmds. schwache Seite *od.* schwacher Punkt *od.* Schwachpunkt; **he has only a** ~ **case** seine Sache steht

auf schwachen Füßen; **(b)** (watery) schwach ⟨*Kaffee, Tee*⟩; wässrig, wässerig ⟨*Suppe*⟩; dünn ⟨*Bier, Suppe, Kaffee, Tee*⟩

weaken /'wiːkn/ **1** *v.t.* schwächen; beeinträchtigen ⟨*Augen*⟩; entkräften, schwächen ⟨*Argument*⟩; lockern ⟨*Griff*⟩; **be** ~**ed by stress/too much work** durch Stress/zu viel Arbeit angegriffen werden. **2** *v.i.* ⟨*Kraft, Entschlossenheit:*⟩ nachlassen; **the patient was visibly** ~**ing** der Patient wurde sichtlich schwächer

weak-kneed /'wiːkniːd/ *adj.* **(a) be** ~: weiche Knie haben (**with** vor + *Dat.*); **(b)** (fig.) feige

weakling /'wiːklIŋ/ *n.* Schwächling, *der*

'weak-minded *adj.* **(a)** (lacking strength of purpose) entschlusslos; unentschlossen; **(b)** (mentally deficient) schwachsinnig

weakness /'wiːknIs/ *n.* Schwäche, *die;* (in argument, defence) schwacher Punkt

'weak-willed *adj.* willensschwach

weal /wiːl/ *n.* (ridge on flesh) Striemen, *der*

wealth /welθ/ *n., no pl.* **(a)** (abundance) Fülle, *die;* **a great** ~ **of detail** große Detailfülle; **(b)** (riches, being rich) Reichtum, *der*

'wealth tax *n.* Vermögenssteuer, *die*

wealthy /'welθI/ **1** *adj.* reich. **2** *n. pl.* **the** ~: die Reichen *Pl.*

wean /wiːn/ *v.t.* abstillen; entwöhnen ⟨*Tier*⟩; ~ **sb. [away] from sth.** (fig.) jmdm. etw. abgewöhnen

weapon /'wepən/ *n.* (lit. or fig.) Waffe, *die*

weaponry /'wepənrI/ *n.* Waffen *Pl.*

wear /weə(r)/ **1** *n., no pl., no indef. art.* **(a)** (rubbing) ~ **[and tear]** Verschleiß, *der;* Abnutzung, *die;* **show signs of** ~: Verschleiß- *od.* Abnutzungserscheinungen aufweisen; **the worse for** ~: abgetragen ⟨*Kleider*⟩; abgelaufen ⟨*Schuhe*⟩; abgenutzt ⟨*Teppich, Sessel, Möbel*⟩; **feel the worse for** ~: sich angeschlagen fühlen (ugs.); **(b)** (clothes, use of clothes) Kleidung, *die;* **clothes for everyday** ~: Alltagskleidung, *die;* **a jacket for casual** ~: ein Freizeitsakko; **children's/ladies'** ~: Kinder-/Damen[be]kleidung, *die.* **2** *v.t.,* **wore** /wɔː(r)/, **worn** /wɔːn/ **(a)** tragen ⟨*Kleidung, Schmuck, Bart, Brille, Perücke, Abzeichen*⟩; **I haven't a thing to** ~: ich habe überhaupt nichts anzuziehen; **what size shoes do you** ~? welche Schuhgröße haben Sie?; ~ **one's hair long** lange Haare tragen; **(b)** abtragen ⟨*Kleidungsstück*⟩; abtreten, abnutzen ⟨*Teppich*⟩; **be worn [smooth]** ⟨*Stufen:*⟩ ausgetreten sein; ⟨*Gestein:*⟩ ausgewaschen sein; ⟨*Gesicht:*⟩ abgehärmt sein; **a [badly] worn tyre** ein [stark] abgefahrener Reifen; **(c)** (make by rubbing) scheuern; **the water had worn a channel in the rock** das Wasser hatte sich durch den Felsen gefressen; **(d)** (exhaust) erschöpfen; **(e)** (coll.: accept) **I won't** ~ **that!** das nehme ich dir/ihm *usw.* nicht ab! (ugs.). **3** *v.i.,* **wore, worn (a)** ⟨*Kante, Saum, Kleider:*⟩ sich durchscheuern; ⟨*Absätze, Schuhsohlen:*⟩ sich ablaufen; ⟨*Teppich:*⟩ sich abnutzen; ~ **thin** (fig.) ⟨*Freundschaft, Stil:*⟩ verflachen, oberflächlicher werden; ⟨*Witz, Ausrede:*⟩ schon reichlich alt sein; **(b)** (endure rubbing) ⟨*Material, Stoff:*⟩ halten; (fig.) sich halten; ~ **well/badly** sich gut/schlecht tragen

~ **a'way 1** *v.t.* abschleifen ⟨*Kanten, Grate*⟩; **be worn away** ⟨*Stufen:*⟩ ausgetreten werden; ⟨*Inschrift:*⟩ verwittern. **2** *v.i.* sich abnutzen; ⟨*Gestein:*⟩ verwittern; ⟨*Schuhabsätze:*⟩ sich ablaufen; (fig.: weaken, lessen) dahinschwinden

~ **'down 1** *v.t.* **(a)** be worn down ⟨*Stufen:*⟩ ausgetreten werden; ⟨*Absätze:*⟩ sich ablaufen; ⟨*Reifen:*⟩ sich abfahren; ⟨*Berge:*⟩ abgetragen werden; **(b)** (fig.) ~ **down sb.'s resistance/defence/opposition** jmds. Widerstand/Verteidigung/Opposition zermürben; ~ **sb. down** jmdn. zermürben; **worn down with hard work** abgearbeitet. **2** *v.i.* ⟨*Absätze:*⟩ sich ablaufen; ⟨*Reifen:*⟩ sich abfahren

~ **'off** *v.i.* ⟨*Auflage, Schicht:*⟩ abgehen; ⟨*Muster:*⟩ sich verlieren; (fig.: pass away gradually) sich legen; ⟨*Wirkung, Schmerz:*⟩ nachlassen

~ **'out 1** *v.t.* **(a)** (make useless) aufbrauchen; ablaufen ⟨*Schuhe*⟩; auftragen ⟨*Kleidungsstück*⟩; **(b)** (fig.: exhaust) kaputtmachen (ugs.); ~ **oneself out** sich kaputtmachen (ugs.); **be worn out** kaputt sein (ugs.). **2** *v.i.* (become unusable) kaputtgehen; **his patience finally wore out** seine Geduld war schließlich erschöpft

~ **'through 1** *v.i.* sich durchscheuern; **my trousers**

have worn through at the knee meine Hose ist an den Knien durchgescheuert. **2** *v.t.* durchscheuern

wearisome /'wɪərɪsəm/ *adj.* (lit. or fig.) ermüdend

weary /'wɪərɪ/ **1** *adj.* (a) (tired) müde; (b) (bored, impatient) **be ~ of sth.** einer Sache (*Gen.*) überdrüssig sein; etw. satt haben (ugs.); (c) (tiring) ermüdend. **2** *v.t.* **be wearied by sth.** durch etw. erschöpft sein. **3** *v.i.* **~ of sth./sb.** einer Sache/jmds. überdrüssig werden

weasel /'wiːzl/ *n.* Wiesel, *das*

weather /'weðə(r)/ **1** *n.* Wetter, *das;* **what's the ~ like?** wie ist das Wetter?; **the ~ has turned cooler** es ist kühler geworden; **he goes out in all ~s** er geht bei jedem Wetter hinaus; **he is feeling under the ~** (fig.) er ist [zur Zeit] nicht ganz auf dem Posten; **make heavy ~ of sth.** (fig.) sich mit etw. schwer tun. **2** *attrib. adj.* **keep a ~ eye on sth.** ein wachsames Auge auf etw. (*Akk.*) haben. **3** *v.t.* (a) (expose to open air) auswittern ‹*Kalk, Holz*›; (b) **be ~ed** ‹*Gesicht:*› wettergegerbt sein; (c) (wear away) verwittern lassen ‹*Gestein*›; (d) (come safely through) abwettern ‹*Sturm*›; (fig.) durchstehen ‹*schwere Zeit*›. **4** *v.i.* (a) (be discoloured) ‹*Holz, Farbe:*› verblassen; (wear away) **~ [away]** ‹*Gestein:*› verwittern; (b) (survive exposure) wetterfest sein

weather: **~-beaten** *adj.* wettergegerbt ‹*Gesicht, Haut*›; verwittert ‹*Felsen, Gebäude*›; **~ chart** *n.* Wetterkarte, *die;* **~cock** *n.* Wetterhahn, *der;* **~ forecast** *n.* Wettervorhersage, *die;* **~man** /▶887| Meteorologe, *der;* **~ map** *n.* Wetterkarte, *die;* **~proof 1** *adj.* wetterfest; **2** *v.t.* wetterfest machen; **~ report** *n.* Wetterbericht, *der;* **~ satellite** *n.* Wettersatellit, *der;* **~ station** *n.* Wetterwarte, *die;* **~strip** *n.* Dichtungsstreifen, *der;* **~vane** *n.* Wetterfahne, *die*

weave[1] /wiːv/ **1** *n.* (Textiles) Bindung, *die.* **2** *v.t.,* **wove** /wəʊv/, **woven** /'wəʊvn/ (a) (intertwine) weben ‹[*Baum*]*wolle, Garn, Fäden*›; **~ sth. into sth.** etw. zu etw. verweben; **~ flowers into wreaths** aus Blumen Kränze flechten; (b) (make by weaving) weben ‹*Textilien*›; flechten ‹*Girlande, Korb, Kranz*›; (c) (fig.) einflechten ‹*Nebenhandlung, Thema usw.*› (**into** in + *Akk.*); (d) (fig.: contrive) ausspinnen ‹*Geschichte*›. **3** *v.i.,* **wove, woven** (make fabric by weaving) weben

weave[2] *v.i.* (a) (move repeatedly from side to side) torkeln; (b) (take devious course) sich schlängeln

weaver /'wiːvə(r)/ *n.* Weber, *der*/Weberin, *die*

web /web/ *n.* (a) Netz, *das;* **spider's ~** Spinnennetz, *das;* (b) (woven fabric) Gewebe, *das;* (fig.) Gespinst, *das;* **a ~ of lies/intrigue** ein Gespinst von Lügen/Intrigen; (c) **the Web** (Computing) das Web (fachspr.); das Netz

webbing /'webɪŋ/ *n.* Gurtstoff, *der*

'Web browser *n.* (Computing) Web-Browser, *der*

web: **~ foot** *n.* Schwimmfuß, *der;* Ruderfuß, *der* (Zool.); **~-footed** *adj.* schwimmfüßig; **~ 'offset** *n.* (Printing) Rollenoffset[druck], *der*

wed /wed/ (rhet.) **1** *v.t.,* **-dd-** (marry) heiraten; ehelichen (veralt., scherzh.); (perform wedding ceremony for) trauen ‹*Brautpaar*›. **2** *v.i.* heiraten; sich vermählen (geh.)

we'd /wɪd, *stressed* wiːd/ (a) = **we had;** (b) = **we would**

Wed. *abbr.* ▶739| **Wednesday** Mi.

wedded /'wedɪd/ *adj.* (a) (married) angetraut; **a ~ couple** ein getrautes Paar; (b) (of marriage) **~ life** Eheleben, *das;* **~ bliss** Eheglück, *das;* (fig.: devoted) **be ~ to an idea/ a dogma/a party** sich einer Idee/einem Dogma/einer Partei verschrieben haben; **be ~ to the view that …:** immer noch davon überzeugt sein, dass …; (d) (fig.: united) vereint (**to** mit)

wedding /'wedɪŋ/ *n.* Hochzeit, *die;* **have a registry office/a church ~:** sich standesamtlich/kirchlich trauen lassen; standesamtlich/kirchlich heiraten

wedding: **~ anniversary** *n.* Hochzeitstag, *der;* **~ breakfast** *n.* Hochzeitsessen, *das;* **~ cake** *n.* Hochzeitskuchen, *der;* **~ day** *n.* Hochzeitstag, *der;* **~ dress** *n.* Brautkleid, *das;* **~ night** *n.* Hochzeitsnacht, *die;* **~ present** *n.* Hochzeitsgeschenk, *das;* **~ ring** *n.* Ehering, *der;* Trauring, *der*

wedge /wedʒ/ **1** *n.* (a) Keil, *der;* **it's the thin end of the ~** (fig.) so fängt es immer an; (b) **a ~ of cake** ein

Stück Torte; **a ~ of cheese** eine Ecke Käse. **2** *v.t.* (a) (fasten) verkeilen; **~ a door/window open** eine Tür/ein Fenster festklemmen, damit sie/es offen bleibt; (b) (pack tightly) verkeilen; **there were five of them ~d together in the back of the car** sie saßen zu fünft eingezwängt *od.* zusammengepfercht hinten im Wagen

'wedge-shaped *adj.* keilförmig

wedlock /'wedlɒk/ *n.* (literary) Ehe, *die;* Ehebund, *der* (geh.); **born in/out of ~:** ehelich/unehelich geboren

Wednesday /'wenzdeɪ, 'wenzdɪ/ ▶739| **1** *n.* Mittwoch, *der.* **2** *adv.* (coll.) **she comes ~s** sie kommt mittwochs. *See also* **Friday**

wee[1] /wiː/ *adj.* (a) (child lang./Scot.) klein; lütt (nordd.); (b) (coll.: extremely small) **a ~ bit** ein ganz klein bisschen (ugs.)

wee[2] ⇨ **wee-wee**

weed /wiːd/ **1** *n.* (a) Unkraut, *das;* **~s** Unkräuter; Unkraut, *das;* **it's only a ~:** das ist bloß Unkraut; (b) (weakling) Schwächling, *der.* **2** *v.t.* jäten. **3** *v.i.* [Unkraut] jäten **~ 'out** *v.t.* (fig.) aussieben

weeding /'wiːdɪŋ/ *n.,* no pl., no indef. art. [Unkraut]jäten, *das;* **do the/some ~:** Unkraut jäten

'weedkiller *n.* Unkrautvertilgungsmittel, *das*

weedy /'wiːdɪ/ *adj.* (a) von Unkraut überwachsen; (b) (scrawny) spillerig (ugs.); schmächtig

week /wiːk/ *n.* ▶739| Woche, *die;* **what day of the ~ is it today?** was für ein Wochentag ist heute?; **he was away for a ~:** er war [für] eine Woche weg; **I haven't seen you for ~s** ich habe dich seit Wochen nicht gesehen; **~s ago** vor Wochen; **three times a ~:** dreimal die *od.* in der Woche; **£40 a** *or* **per ~:** 40 Pfund die *od.* in der *od.* pro Woche; **a ~'s leave/rest** eine Woche Urlaub/Pause; **for several ~s** mehrere Wochen lang; wochenlang; **once a ~, every ~:** einmal die Woche *od.* in der Woche; einmal wöchentlich; **~ in ~ out** Woche für Woche; **in a ~['s time]** in einer Woche; **in two ~s[' time]** in zwei Wochen; in vierzehn Tagen; **take a ~'s holiday** [sich (*Dat.*)] eine Woche Urlaub nehmen; **from ~ to ~, ~ by ~:** Woche für *od.* um Woche; **a three-~ period** ein Zeitraum von drei Wochen; **a two-~ visit** ein zweiwöchiger Besuch; **a six-~[s]-old baby** ein sechs Wochen altes *od.* sechswöchiges Baby; **a ~ [from] today/from** *or* **on Monday, today/Monday ~:** heute/Montag in einer Woche; **a ~ ago today/Sunday** heute/Sonntag vor einer Woche; **tomorrow ~:** morgen in einer Woche; **in** *or* **during the ~:** während der Woche; **42-hour/five-day ~:** 42-Stunden-Woche, *die*/Fünftagewoche, *die*

week: **~day** *n.* Werktag, *der;* Wochentag, *der;* **on ~days** werktags; wochentags; **~end** /-'-, '--/ *n.* Wochenende, *das;* **at the ~end** am Wochenende; **at** *or* (Amer.) **on ~ends** an Wochenenden; **go/be away for the ~end** übers Wochenende wegfahren/weg sein; **~-long** *adj.* einwöchig

weekly /'wiːklɪ/ **1** *adj.* wöchentlich; **~ wages** Wochenlohn, *der;* **a ~ season ticket/magazine** eine Wochenkarte/Wochenzeitschrift; **at ~ intervals** wöchentlich; einmal pro Woche; **three-~:** dreiwöchentlich. **2** *adv.* wöchentlich; einmal die Woche *od.* in der Woche. **3** *n.* (newspaper) Wochenzeitung, *die;* (magazine) Wochenzeitschrift, *die*

'week night *n.* **on a ~:** abends an einem Werktag; **on ~s** werktags abends

weep /wiːp/ **1** *v.i.,* **wept** /wept/ (a) weinen; **~ with** *or* **for joy/rage** vor Freude/Zorn weinen; **~ for sb./sth.** um jmdn./etw. weinen; **it makes you want to ~:** man könnte weinen; (b) ‹*Wunde:*› nässen. **2** *v.t.,* **wept** (a) weinen ‹*Tränen*›; (b) (lament over) beweinen

weepie /'wiːpɪ/ *n.* (coll.) Schmachtfetzen, *der*

weeping 'willow *n.* Trauerweide, *die*

weevil /'wiːvɪl/ *n.* Rüsselkäfer, *der*

'wee-wee (coll.) **1** *n.* Pipi, *das* (ugs.); **do a ~:** Pipi machen. **2** *v.i.* Pipi machen (ugs.)

weft /weft/ *n.* (a) (set of threads) Schuss, *der;* (b) (yarn) Schussfaden, *der*

weigh /weɪ/ ▶1202| **1** *v.t.* (a) (find weight of) wiegen; **the shop assistant was ~ing the fruit for her** die Verkäuferin wog ihr das Obst ab; (b) (estimate value of) abwägen;

Weight

	1 ounce (oz)	= 28,35 g (achtundzwanzig Komma drei fünf Gramm)
16 ounces =	1 pound (lb)	= 454 g (vierhundertvierundfünfzig Gramm)
14 pounds =	1 stone (st.)	= 6,35 kg (sechs Komma drei fünf Kilogramm)
112 pounds	= 1 hundredweight	= 50,8 kg (fünfzig Komma acht Kilogramm)
20 hundredweight =	1 ton	= 1016 kg (tausendsechzehn Kilogramm)

Note that in everyday usage **Kilogramm** is shortened to **Kilo.** Also the German pound (**Pfund**) is half a kilogram, i.e. 500 grams as opposed to 454 grams for the British pound.

People

What's your weight?, *How much do you* *weigh?*	= Wie viel wiegen Sie?
I weigh 12 stone (Brit.) *or 168 pounds (Amer.)*	≈ Ich wiege 76,2 Kilo
He has put on weight	= Er hat zugenommen
She has lost a lot *of weight*	= Sie hat stark abgenommen
At over 18 stone (Brit.) *or 250 pounds (Amer.)* *he is overweight*	≈ Mit mehr als 114 Kilo hat er Übergewicht

Things

What's the weight of *the parcel?, How* *much does the parcel* *weigh?*	= Wie viel wiegt das Paket?

Is it very heavy?	= Ist es sehr schwer?
It weighs about *four pounds*	= Es wiegt ungefähr zwei Kilo
My baggage is ten *pounds over weight*	≈ Mein Gepäck hat fünf Kilo Übergewicht
A is the same *weight as B*	= A hat das gleiche Gewicht wie B
A and B are the *same weight*	= A und B sind gleich schwer
4 oz of liver sausage	≈ 125 Gramm *or* ein Viertel Leberwurst
6 lbs of potatoes	≈ sechs Pfund Kartoffeln
They are sold by the *kilo*	= Sie werden kiloweise verkauft
a pound box of *chocolates*	≈ eine 500-Gramm-Schachtel Pralinen

---

(c) (consider) abwägen; ~ **in one's mind whether ...:** sich (*Dat.*) überlegen, ob ...; ~ **the consequences of one's actions** sich (*Dat.*) die Folgen seines Handelns klarmachen; **(d)** (balance in one's hand) wiegen; **(e)** (have the weight of) wiegen; **it** ~**s very little** es wiegt sehr wenig; **a steak** ~**ing two pounds** ein zwei Pfund schweres Steak. **2** *v.i.* **(a)** ~ **[very] heavy/light** [sehr] viel/wenig wiegen; **(b)** (be important) ~ **with sb.** bei jmdm. Gewicht haben; ~ **in sb.'s favour** für jmdn. sprechen

~ **a'gainst** *v.t.* (fig.) sprechen gegen; ~ **heavily against sb.** sehr *od.* stark gegen jmdn. sprechen

~ **'down** *v.t.* **(a)** (cause to sag) **fruit** ~**ed down the branches of the tree** die Äste des Baumes bogen sich unter der Last der Früchte; **be** ~**ed down by packages** mit Paketen schwer beladen sein; **(b)** (cause to be anxious or depressed) niederdrücken; ~**ed down with cares** bedrückt von Sorgen

~ **'in** *v.i.* (Sport) sich wiegen lassen; ~ **in at 200 kg** 200 kg auf die Waage bringen

~ **on** *v.t.* lasten (+ *Dat.*); ~ **[heavily] on sb.'s mind** jmdm. [schwer] auf der Seele liegen

~ **'out** *v.t.* abwiegen

~ **'up** *v.t.* abwägen; sich (*Dat.*) eine Meinung bilden über (+ *Akk.*) ⟨*Person*⟩

weigh: ~**bridge** *n.* Brückenwaage, *die;* ~**-in** *n.* (Sport) Wiegen, *das*

'weighing machine *n.* Waage, *die*

weight /weɪt/ **1** *n.* **(a)** Gewicht, *das;* **what is your** ~**?** wie viel wiegen Sie? ~ **under/over** ~**:** zu wenig/zu viel wiegen; **throw one's** ~ **about** *or* **around** (fig. coll.) sich wichtig machen; **pull one's** ~ (do one's fair share) sich voll einsetzen; ~**s and measures** Maße und Gewichte; **lift** ~**s** Lasten heben; **(b)** (Sport) Gewicht, *das;* **(c)** (surface density of cloth etc.) Qualität, *die;* **(d)** (fig.: heavy burden) Last, *die;* **it would be a** ~ **off my mind if ...:** mir würde ein Stein vom Herzen fallen, wenn ...; **(e)** (importance) Gewicht, *das;* **give due** ~ **to sth.** einer Sache (*Dat.*) die nötige Beachtung schenken; **carry** ~**:** ins Gewicht fallen; **his opinion carries no** ~ **with me** seine Meinung ist für mich unbedeutend; **(f)** (preponderance) Gewicht, *das;* **the** ~ **of evidence is against him** praktisch alle Beweise sprechen gegen ihn; ~ **of numbers** zahlenmäßiges Übergewicht. **2** *v.t.* **(a)** (add ~ to) beschweren; **(b)** (hold with ~) ~ **[down]** beschweren; (fig.) belasten

weightlessness /'weɪtlɪsnɪs/ *n.* Schwerelosigkeit, *die*

weight: ~**lifter** *n.* Gewichtheber, *der/-*heberin, *die;* ~**lifting** *n., no pl., no indef. art.* Gewichtheben, *das;* ~**-train** *v.i.* mit Hanteln trainieren; ~**-training** *n., no pl., no indef. art.* Hanteltraining, *das;* ~**-watcher** *n.* Schlankheitsbewusste, *der/die*

weighty /'weɪtɪ/ *adj.* **(a)** (heavy) schwer; **(b)** (important) gewichtig

weir /wɪə(r)/ *n.* Wehr, *das*

weird /wɪəd/ *adj.* (coll.: odd) bizarr; verrückt (ugs.)

welcome /'welkəm/ **1** *int.* willkommen; ~ **home/to England!** willkommen zu Hause/in England!; ~ **aboard!** willkommen an Bord! **2** *n.* **(a)** Willkommen, *das;* **outstay** *or* **overstay one's** ~**:** zu lange bleiben; **give sb. a warm** ~**:** jmdn. herzlich willkommen heißen; **(b)** (reception) Empfang, *der;* **give a proposal a warm** ~**:** einen Vorschlag zustimmend aufnehmen; **give sb. a warm** ~ (iron.) jmdn. gebührend empfangen (iron.); **receive a rather cool** ~**:** ziemlich kühl empfangen werden. **3** *v.t.* begrüßen; willkommen heißen (geh.). **4** *adj.* **(a)** willkommen; gefällig ⟨*Anblick*⟩; **make sb. [feel]** ~**:** jmdm. das Gefühl geben *od.* vermitteln, willkommen zu sein; **(b)** *pred.* **you're** ~ **to take it** du kannst es gern nehmen; **you're** ~ (it was no trouble) gern geschehen!; keine Ursache!; **if you want to stay here for the night you are more than** ~**:** wenn Sie die Nacht über hier bleiben möchten, sind Sie herzlich willkommen

welcoming /'welkəmɪŋ/ *adj.* einladend; **a** ~ **cup of tea awaited us** zur Begrüßung erwartete uns eine Tasse Tee

weld /weld/ *v.t.* **(a)** (unite) verschweißen; (repair, make, or attach by ~ing) schweißen (**[on]to** an + *Akk.*); ~ **two pipes together** zwei Rohre zusammenschweißen; **(b)** (fig.: unite closely) zusammenschweißen (**into** zu); ~ **two elements together** zwei Elemente zusammenschweißen

welder /'weldə(r)/ *n.* (**a**) ▶ **887** | (person) Schweißer, *der/* Schweißerin, *die;* **(b)** (machine) Schweißgerät, *das*

welfare /'welfeə(r)/ *n.* **(a)** (health and prosperity) Wohl, *das;* **(b)** (social work; payments etc.) Sozialhilfe, *die*

welfare: W~ 'State *n.* Wohlfahrtsstaat, *der;* ~ **work** *n.* Sozialarbeit, *die;* ~ **worker** *n.* Sozialarbeiter, *der/-*arbeiterin, *die*

well¹ /wel/ *n.* **(a)** (water ~, mineral spring) Brunnen, *der;* **(b)** (Archit.) Schacht, *der;* (of staircase) Treppenloch, *das*

well² **1** *int.* **(a)** *expr. astonishment* mein Gott; meine Güte; nanu; ∼, ∼! sieh mal einer an!; **(b)** *expr. relief* mein Gott; **(c)** *expr. concession* na ja; ∼ **then, let's say no more about it** schon gut, reden wir nicht mehr davon; **(d)** *expr. resumption* nun; ∼ **[then], who was it?** nun, wer wars?; **(e)** *expr. qualified recognition of point* ∼[, **but**] …: na ja, aber …; ja schon, aber …; **(f)** *expr. resignation* [**oh**] ∼: nun denn; **ah** ∼: na ja; **(g)** *expr. expectation* ∼ [**then**]? na? **2** *adv.,* **better** /'betə(r)/, **best** /best/ **(a)** (satisfactorily) gut; **the business is doing** ∼: das Geschäft geht gut; **do** ∼ **for oneself** Erfolg haben; **do** ∼ **out of sth.** mit etw. ein gutes Geschäft machen; **the patient is doing** ∼: dem Patienten geht es gut; **a** ∼ **situated house** ein günstig gelegenes Haus; **you did** ∼ **to come** gut, dass du gekommen bist; ∼ **done!** großartig!; **didn't he do** ∼! hat er sich nicht gut geschlagen?; **you would do** ∼ **to** …: Sie täten gut daran, zu …; **come off** ∼: gut abschneiden; **you're** ∼ **out of it** es ist gut, dass du damit nichts mehr zu tun hast; **(b)** (thoroughly) gründlich ‹*trocknen, polieren, schütteln*›; tüchtig ‹*verprügeln*›; genau ‹*beobachten*›; gewissenhaft ‹*urteilen*›; **be** ∼ **able to do sth.** durchaus *od.* sehr wohl in der Lage sein, etw. zu tun; **I'm** ∼ **aware of what has been going on** mir ist sehr wohl klar *od.* bewusst, was sich abgespielt hat; **let** *or* **leave** ∼ **alone** sich zufrieden geben; **be** ∼ **pleased** sehr erfreut sein; ∼ **out of sight** (very far off) völlig außer Sichtweite (**of** *Gen.*); **we arrived** ∼ **before the performance began** wir kamen eine ganze Zeit vor Beginn der Vorstellung; **be** ∼ **in with sb.** bei jmdm. gut angeschrieben sein; ∼ **and truly** vollkommen; **I know only too** ∼ **how/what** *etc.* …: ich weiß nur zu gut, wie/was *usw.* …; **(c)** (considerably) weit; **it was** ∼ **on into the afternoon** es war schon spät am Nachmittag; **he is** ∼ **past** *or* **over retiring age** er hat schon längst das Rentenalter erreicht; **he is** ∼ **past** *or* **over forty** er ist weit über vierzig; **be** ∼ **away** (lit. or fig.) einen guten Vorsprung haben; (coll.: be drunk) ziemlich benebelt sein (ugs.); **(d)** (approvingly, kindly) gut, anständig ‹*jmdn. behandeln*›; **think** ∼ **of sb./sth.** eine gute Meinung von jmdn./etw. haben; **speak** ∼ **of sb./sth.** sich positiv über jmdn./etw. äußern; **wish sb.** ∼: jmdm. alles Gute wünschen; **(e)** (in all likelihood) sehr wohl; **(f)** (easily) ohne weiteres; **you cannot very** ∼ **refuse their help** du kannst ihre Hilfe nicht ohne weiteres *od.* nicht gut ausschlagen; **(g) as** ∼ (in addition) auch; ebenfalls; (as much, not less truly) genauso; ebenso; (with equal reason) genauso gut; ebenso gut; (advisable) ratsam; (equally ∼) genauso gut; **Coming for a drink? — I might as** ∼: Kommst du mit, einen trinken? — Warum nicht?; **you might as** ∼ **go** du kannst ruhig gehen; **that is** [**just**] **as** ∼ (not regrettable) um so besser; **it was just as** ∼ **that I had** …: zum Glück hatte ich …; **A as** ∼ **as B:** B und auch [noch] A; **she can sing as** ∼ **as dance** sie kann singen und auch tanzen; **as** ∼ **as helping** *or* (coll.) **help me, she continued her own work** sie half mir und machte dabei noch mit ihrer eigenen Arbeit weiter. **3** *adj.* **(a)** (in good health) gesund; **How are you feeling now? — Quite** ∼, **thank you** Wie fühlen Sie sich jetzt? — Ganz gut, danke; **look** ∼: gut *od.* gesund aussehen; **I am perfectly** ∼: ich fühle mich bestens; **get** ∼ **soon!** gute Besserung!; **he hasn't been very** ∼ **lately** es geht ihm in letzter Zeit nicht sehr gut; **feel** ∼: sich wohl fühlen; **make sb.** ∼: jmdn. gesund machen; **(b)** *pred.* (satisfactory) **I am very** ∼ **where I am** ich bin hier sehr zufrieden; **all's** ∼: es ist alles in Ordnung; **all's** ∼ **that ends** ∼ (prov.) Ende gut, alles gut; **all is not** ∼ **with sb./sth.** mit jmdm./etw. ist etwas nicht in Ordnung; [**that's all**] ∼ **and good** [das ist alles] gut und schön; **all being** ∼: wenn alles gut geht; **(c)** *pred.* (advisable) ratsam

we'll /wɪl, *stressed* wiːl/ = **we will**

well: ∼**-advised** ⇒ advised; ∼**-aimed** *adj.* gezielt ‹*Schuss, Tritt, Stoß, Schlag*›; ∼**-behaved** *adj.* ⇒ **behave 1 a**; ∼**-being** *n.* Wohl, *das;* ∼**-bred** *adj.* (having good manners) anständig; ∼**-built** *adj.* ‹*Person*› mit guter Figur; **be** ∼**-built** eine gute Figur haben; ∼**-chosen** *adj.* wohlgesetzt ‹*Worte*›; wohl überlegt ‹*Bemerkungen*›; ∼**-defined** *adj.* klar definiert; ∼**-deserved** *adj.* wohlverdient ‹*Lob, Ruhe*›; verdient ‹*Belohnung, Prügel*›; ∼ **done** *adj.* (Cookery) durchgebraten; durch *nicht attr.;* ∼**-dressed** *adj.* gut gekleidet; ∼**-earned** *adj.*

wohlverdient; ∼**-educated** *adj.* gebildet ‹*Person, Benehmen*›; ∼**-equipped** *adj.* gut ausgestattet ‹*Büro, Studio, Krankenwagen*›; gut ausgerüstet ‹*Polizei, Armee, Expedition, Flugzeug*›; ∼**-established** *adj.* bewährt; ∼**-fed** *adj.* wohlgenährt; ∼**-founded** *adj.* [wohl] fundiert; ∼**-groomed** *adj.* gepflegt; ∼**-heeled** /'welhiːld/ *adj.* (coll.) gut betucht (ugs.)

wellies /'welɪz/ *n. pl.* (Brit. coll.) Gummistiefel

'well-informed *adj.* gut unterrichtet

wellington /'welɪŋtən/ *n.* ∼ [**boot**] Gummistiefel, *der*

well: ∼**-intentioned** /'welɪntenʃənd/ *adj.* gut gemeint; ∼**-judged** *adj.* gut gezielt; ∼**-kept** *adj.* gepflegt; in gutem Zustand *nachgestellt;* wohlgehütet ‹*Geheimnis*›; ∼**-known** *adj.* **(a)** (known to many) bekannt; **(b)** (known thoroughly) vertraut; ∼**-loved** *adj.* beliebt; ∼**-made** *adj.* (skilfully manufactured) gut [gearbeitet]; ∼**-mannered** ⇒ **mannered b**; ∼ **marked** *adj.* gut gekennzeichnet ‹*Strecke, Wanderung*›; ∼**-meaning** *adj.* wohlmeinend; **be** ∼**-meaning** es gut meinen; ∼**-meant** *adj.* gut gemeint; ∼**-nigh** *adv.* (rhet.) nahezu; ∼**-off** *adj.* **(a)** (rich) wohlhabend; **sb. is** ∼ **off** jmdm. geht es [finanziell] gut; **(b) be** ∼ **off for sth.** (provided with) mit etw. gut versorgt sein; **(c)** (favourably situated) **she is perfectly** ∼ **off** es geht ihr ausgezeichnet; ∼**-preserved** *adj.* gut erhalten ‹*Holz, Mumie, (scherzh.) Achtzigjährige usw.*›; ∼**-read** /'welred/ *adj.* belesen; ∼**-spent** *adj.* sinnvoll verbracht ‹*Zeit*›; vernünftig ausgegeben ‹*Geld*›; ∼**-stocked** *adj.* gut gefüllt ‹*Kühlschrank, Vorratskammer, Hausbar*›; gut sortiert ‹*Geschäft*›; ∼**-thought-out** *adj.* gut durchdacht; ∼**-thumbed** *adj.* zerlesen ‹*Buch*›; ∼**-timed** *adj.* zeitlich gut gewählt; ∼**-to-do** *adj.* wohlhabend; ∼**-wisher** *n.* Sympathisant, *der*/Sympathisantin, *die;* **cards and gifts from** ∼**-wishers** Kartengrüße und Geschenke; ∼**-worn** *adj.* abgetragen ‹*Kleidungsstück*›; abgenutzt ‹*Teppich*›; ausgetreten ‹*Pfad*›; abgedroschen ‹*Redensart, Ausdruck*›

Welsh /welʃ/ ▶ 897▮, ▶ 947▮ **1** *adj.* walisisch; **sb. is** ∼: jmd. ist Waliser/Waliserin. **2** *n.* **(a)** (language) Walisisch, *das; see also* **English 2 a; (b)** *pl.* **the** ∼: die Waliser *Pl.*

welsh *v.i.* (leave without paying) sich davonmachen, ohne zu bezahlen

∼ **on** *v.t.* (coll.) ∼ **on sb./sth.** jmdn. sitzen lassen/sich um etw. herumdrücken (ugs.)

Welsh: ∼**man** /'welʃmən/ *n., pl.* ∼**men** /'welʃmən/ Waliser, *der;* ∼ **'rabbit,** ∼ **'rarebit** *ns.* Käsetoast, *der;* ∼**woman** *n.* Waliserin, *die*

welter /'weltə(r)/ **1** *v.i.* sich wälzen. **2** *n.* Chaos, *das;* **a** ∼ **of foam** eine schäumende Flut; **a** ∼ **of emotions** ein Sturm von Gefühlen

'welterweight *n.* (Boxing etc.) Weltergewicht, *das;* (person also) Weltergewichtler, *der*

wench /wentʃ/ *n.* (arch/joc.) Mädel, *das;* (arch.: maidservant) Magd, *die* (veralt.)

wend /wend/ *v.t.* (literary/arch.) ∼ **one's way homewards** sich auf den Heimweg machen; **they** ∼**ed their way back towards the village** sie machten sich auf den Weg zurück ins Dorf

Wendy house /'wendɪ haʊs/ *n.* Spielhaus, *das*

went ⇒ **go 1, 2**

wept ⇒ **weep**

were ⇒ **be**

we're /wɪə(r)/ = **we are**

weren't /wɜːnt/ (coll.) = **were not;** ⇒ **be**

werewolf /'wɪəwʊlf, 'weəwʊlf/ *n., pl.* **werewolves** /'wɪəwʊlvz, 'weəwʊlvz/, **werwolf** /'wɜːwʊlf/ *n., pl.* **werwolves** /'wɜːwʊlvz/ (Mythol.) Werwolf, *der*

west /west/ ▶ 715▮ **1** *n.* **(a)** (direction) Westen, *der;* **the** ∼: West (Met., Seew.); **in/to[wards]/from the** ∼: im/nach/von Westen; **to the** ∼ **of** westlich von; westlich (+ *Gen.*); **(b)** *usu.* **W**∼ (also Polit.) Westen, *der;* **from the W**∼: aus dem Westen. **2** *adj.* westlich; West‹*küste, -wind, -grenze, -tor*›. **3** *adv.* westwärts; nach Westen; ∼ **of** westlich von;

westlich (+ *Gen.*); go ~ (fig. coll.: be killed or wrecked or lost) hopsgehen (salopp)

West: ~ **'Africa** *pr. n.* Westafrika (*das*); ~ **'Bank** *pr. n.* the ~ **Bank** (of the Jordan) das Westjordanland; ~ **Ber'lin** *pr. n.* (Hist.) West-Berlin (*das*); **w~bound** *adj.* ▶715⌋ ⟨*Zug, Verkehr usw.*⟩ in Richtung Westen; ~ **Country** *n.* (Brit.) Westengland, *das;* ~ **'End** *n.* (Brit.) Westend, *das*

westerly /'westəlɪ/ *adj.* ▶715⌋ (a) (in position or direction) westlich; **in a** ~ **direction** nach Westen; (b) (from the west) ⟨*Wind*⟩ aus westlichen Richtungen

western /'westən/ ▶715⌋ **1** *adj.* westlich; West⟨*grenze, -hälfte, -seite*⟩; ~ **Germany** Westdeutschland, *das.* **2** *n.* Western, *der*

westerner /'westənə(r)/ *n.* Abendländer, *der*/Abendländerin, *die*

Western 'Europe *pr. n.* Westeuropa (*das*)

westernize (**westernise**) /'westənaɪz/ *v.t.* verwestlichen

westernmost /'westənməʊst/ *adj.* ▶715⌋ westlichst...

West: ~ **'German** (Hist.) **1** *adj.* westdeutsch; **2** *n.* Westdeutsche, *der*/*die;* ~ **'Germany** *pr. n.* (Hist.) Westdeutschland (*das*); ~ **'Indian** ▶947⌋ **1** *adj.* westindisch; **2** *n.* Westinder, *der*/-inderin, *die;* ~ **Indies** *pr. n. pl.* Westindische Inseln *Pl.*

Westphalia /west'feɪlɪə/ *pr. n.* Westfalen (*das*)

Westphalian /west'feɪlɪən/ **1** *adj.* westfälisch. **2** *n.* Westfale, *der*/Westfälin, *die*

westward /'westwəd/ ▶715⌋ **1** *adj.* nach Westen gerichtet; (situated towards the west) westlich; **in a** ~ **direction** nach Westen; [in] Richtung Westen. **2** *adv.* westwärts; **they are** ~ **bound** sie fahren nach *od.* [in] Richtung Westen. **3** *n.* Westen, *der*

westwards /'westwədz/ *adv.* ▶715⌋ westwärts

wet /wet/ **1** *adj.* (a) nass; ~ **with tears** tränenfeucht; ~ **behind the ears** (fig.) feucht hinter den Ohren (ugs.); ~ **to the skin**, ~ **through** nass bis auf die Haut; (b) (rainy) regnerisch; feucht ⟨*Klima*⟩; (c) (recently applied) frisch ⟨*Farbe*⟩; '~ **paint** „frisch gestrichen"; (d) (coll.: feeble) schlapp (ugs.); schlappschwänzig (salopp). **2** *v.t.*, **-tt-, wet** *or* **wetted** (a) befeuchten; (b) (urinate on) ~ **one's bed/pants** das Bett/sich (*Dat.*) die Hosen nass machen. **3** *n.* (a) (moisture) Feuchtigkeit, *die;* (b) (rainy weather) Regenwetter, *das;* (rainy conditions) Nässe, *die;* **in the** ~: im Regen; (c) (coll.: feeble person) Flasche, *die* (salopp abwertend); (d) (Brit. Polit. coll.) Schlappschwanz, *der* (salopp abwertend)

wet: ~**back** *n.* (Amer. coll.) Illegale, *der*/*die* (ugs.) aus Mexiko; ~ **look** *n.* Hochglanz, *der;* (of hair) Wetlook, *der;* ~**-nurse** **1** *n.* Amme, *die;* **2** *v.t.* (fig. derog.) bemuttern; ~**suit** *n.* Tauchanzug, *der*

we've /wɪv, *stressed* wiːv/ = **we have**

whack /wæk/ (coll.) **1** *v.t.* (strike heavily) hauen (ugs.). **2** *n.* (a) (heavy blow) Schlag, *der;* **give sb. a** ~ **on the bottom** jmdm. eins auf den Hintern geben (ugs.); (b) (share) Anteil, *der*

whale /weɪl/ *n., pl.* ~**s** *or* same (a) (Zool.) Wal, *der;* Walfisch, *der* (volkst.); (b) *no pl.* (coll.) **we had a** ~ **of a [good] time** wir haben uns bombig (ugs.) amüsiert

whaling /'weɪlɪŋ/ *n., no pl, no indef. art.* Walfang, *der; attrib.* Walfang-

wham /wæm/ **1** *int.* wumm. **2** *v.t.*, **-mm-:** ~ **sb.** jmdm. einen Schlag versetzen

whammy ⇒ **double whammy**

wharf /wɔːf/ *n., pl.* **wharves** /wɔːvz/ *or* ~**s** Kai, *der;* Kaje, *die* (nordd.)

what /wɒt/ **1** *interrog. adj.* (a) *asking for selection* welch...; ~ **book did you choose?** welches Buch hast du ausgesucht?; (b) *asking for statement of amount* wie viel; *with pl. n.* wie viele; ~ **men/money has he?** wie viele Leute/wie viel Geld hat er?; **I know** ~ **time it starts** ich weiß, um wie viel Uhr es anfängt; ~ **more can I do/say?** was kann ich sonst noch tun/sagen?; ~ **more do you want?** was willst du [noch] mehr?; (c) *asking for statement of kind* was für; ~ **kind of man is he?** was für ein Mensch ist er?; ~ **good** *or* **use is it?** wozu soll das gut

sein? **2** *excl. adj.* (a) (how great) was für; ~ **impudence** *or* **cheek/luck!** was für eine Unverschämtheit *od.* Frechheit/was für ein Glück!; (b) *before adj. and n.* (to ~ extent) was für. **3** *rel. adj.* **we can dispose of** ~ **difficulties there are remaining** wir können die verbleibenden Schwierigkeiten ausräumen; **lend me** ~ **money you can** leih mir so viel Geld, wie du kannst; **I will give you** ~ **help I can** ich werde dir helfen, so gut ich kann. **4** *adv.* (a) (to ~ extent) ~ **do I care?** was kümmerts mich?; ~ **does it matter?** was machts?; (b) ~ **with** ...: wenn man an ... denkt; ~ **with changing jobs and moving house I haven't had time to do any studying** da ich eine neue Stellung angetreten habe und umgezogen bin, hatte ich keine Zeit zum Lernen. **5** *interrog. pron.* (a) (~ thing) was; ~ **is your name?** wie heißt du/heißen Sie?; ~ **about** ...? (is there any news of ...?, ~ will become of ...?) was ist mit ...?; ~ **about a game of chess?** wie wär's mit einer Partie Schach?; ~ **to do?** was tun?; ~**-d'you-[ma-] call-him/-her/-it**, ~**'s-his/-her/-its-name** wie heißt er/sie/es noch; ~ **for?** wozu?; **and/or** ~ **'have you** und/oder was sonst noch [alles]; ~ **if** ...? was ist, wenn ...?; ~ **is it** *etc.* **like?** wie ist es *usw.*?; ~ **not** wer weiß was alles; ~ **'of it?** was ist dabei?; was soll [schon] dabei sein?; ~ **do you say** *or* (Amer.) ~ **say we have a rest?** was hältst du davon, wenn wir mal Pause machen?; wie wärs mit einer Pause?; **[I'll] tell you** ~: weißt du, was; pass mal auf; **[and]** ~ **then?** [na] und?; **or** ~? oder was?; **so** ~? na und?; (b) *asking for confirmation* ~? wie?; was? (ugs.); **you did** ~? was hast du gemacht?; (c) *in rhet. questions equivalent to neg. statement* ~ **is the use in trying/the point of going on?** wozu [groß] versuchen/weitermachen?; **6** *rel. pron.* (that which) was; **do** ~ **I tell you** tu, was ich dir sage; ~ **little I know/remember** das bisschen, das ich weiß/an das ich mich erinnere; **this is** ~ **I mean:** ...: ich meine Folgendes: ...; **tell sb.** ~ **to do** *or* ~ **he can do with sth.** (coll. iron.) jmdm. sagen, wo er sich (*Dat.*) etw. hinstecken kann (salopp); ~ **is more** außerdem; **the weather being** ~ **it is** ...: so, wie es mit dem Wetter aussieht, ...; **for** ~ **it is** in seiner Art. **7** *excl. pron.* was; ~ **she must have suffered!** wie sie gelitten haben muss!

whatever /wɒt'evə(r)/ **1** *adj.* (a) *rel. adj.* ~ **measures we take** welche Maßnahmen wir auch immer ergreifen; ~ **materials you will need** alle Materialien, die du vielleicht brauchst; (b) (notwithstanding which) was für ... auch immer; ~ **problems you encounter** auf welche Probleme Sie auch stoßen [mögen]; (c) (at all) überhaupt; **I can't see anyone** ~: ich kann überhaupt niemanden sehen. **2** *pron.* (a) *rel. pron.* was für ... [auch immer]; **do** ~ **you like** mach, was du willst; (b) (notwithstanding anything) was auch [immer]; ~ **happens**, ...: was auch geschieht, ...; (c) **or** ~: oder was auch immer; oder sonst was (ugs.)

'whatnot *n.* (coll.: indefinite thing) Dingsbums, *das*

whatsit /'wɒtsɪt/ *n.* (coll.) (thing) Dingsbums, *das* (ugs.); (peron) Dingsda, *der* (ugs.)

wheat /wiːt/ *n., no pl., no indef. art.* Weizen, *der*

wheedle /'wiːdl/ *v.t.* (a) (coax) ~ **sb. into doing sth.** jmdm. so lange gut zureden, bis er etw. tut; (b) (get by cajoling) sich (*Dat.*) verschaffen; ~ **sth. out of sb.** jmdm. etw. abschwatzen (ugs.)

wheel /wiːl/ **1** *n.* (a) Rad, *das;* **[potter's]** ~: Töpferscheibe, *die;* **[roulette]** ~: Roulett, *das;* **reinvent the** ~ (fig.) sich mit Problemen aufhalten, die längst gelöst sind; **put** *or* **set the** ~**s in motion** (fig.) die Sache in Gang setzen; **the** ~**s of bureaucracy turn slowly** (fig.) die Mühlen der Bürokratie mahlen langsam; (b) (for steering) (Motor Veh.) Lenkrad, *das;* (Naut.) Steuerrad, *das;* **at** *or* **behind the** ~ (of car) am *od.* hinterm Steuer; (of ship; also fig.) am Ruder; (c) (Mil.: drill movement) Schwenkung, *die;* **left/right** ~: Links-/Rechtsschwenkung, *die.* **2** *v.t.* (a) (turn round) wenden; (b) (push) schieben; ~ **oneself** (in a ~chair) fahren. **3** *v.i.* (a) kehrtmachen; (b) ~ **and deal** mauscheln

~ **a'bout**, ~ **a'round 1** *v.t.* herumdrehen; wenden ⟨*Pferd*⟩. **2** *v.i.* kehrtmachen; (face the other way) sich umdrehen

~ **'in** *v.t.* hinein-/hereinschieben

~ **'out** *v.t.* hinaus-/herausschieben; ~ **sb. out** (fig. derog.) jmdn. vorführen

~ **'round** ⇒ ~ **about**

When

als or wenn?

There is a simple distinction between these two translations for *when:*

als is used for happenings in the past

wenn is used for happenings in the present or future

When I saw him I smiled	= Als ich ihn sah, lächelte ich
When I see him I always feel sorry for him	= Wenn ich ihn sehe, tut er mir immer Leid
When I see him I'll tell him	= Wenn ich ihn sehe, werde ich es ihm sagen *or* sage ich es ihm

As can be seen, **wenn** translates two uses of *when* in English: in the sense of *whenever* (present tense in both clauses) and referring to the future (present tense in the *when* clause, future tense in the main clause). German does the same, except that the present is often also used in this last case.

Occasionally *when* is used with a verb in the past in the sense of *whenever*, and here too it should be translated by **wenn:**

When(ever) I saw him, I always felt sorry for him	= Wenn ich ihn sah, tat er mir immer Leid

wenn is also used to translate *when* where it occurs with the English present participle (the *-ing* form), a normal subject and verb being used. The subject and the tense of the verb will be that of the English main clause; if this is impersonal, **man** can be used.

When speaking German I often get embarrassed	= Wenn ich Deutsch spreche, werde ich oft verlegen
When speaking German it is important to enunciate clearly	= Wenn man Deutsch spricht, ist es wichtig, deutlich zu artikulieren

Often the sense of *when* in this construction is *while,* and the appropriate translation is **als,** but **bei** plus the verbal noun can also be used and is often neater.

He was killed when crossing the road	= Er kam beim Überqueren der Straße ums Leben, Er kam ums Leben, als er die Straße überquerte
Be careful when cleaning the gun	= Sei vorsichtig beim Putzen des Gewehrs

In questions (direct and indirect)

Here the translation is always **wann:**

When is she coming?	= Wann kommt sie?
I don't know when she's coming	= Ich weiß nicht, wann sie kommt
When do you want to eat?	= Wann willst du essen?
Tell me when you want to eat	= Sag mir, wann du essen willst
From when is the licence valid?	= Ab wann gilt der Schein?
Since when do you give the orders?	= Seit wann gibst du die Befehle?

Other usages are covered in the entry for **when.**

---

wheel: ∼**barrow** n. Schubkarre, die; Schubkarren, der; ∼**base** n. (Motor Veh., Railw.) Radstand, der; ∼**chair** n. Rollstuhl, der; ∼ **clamp** n. Parkkralle, die

-wheeled /wi:ld/ adj. in comb. ⟨vier-, sechs-, acht⟩räd[e]rig

wheeler-dealer /wi:lə'di:lə(r)/ n. Mauschler, der/ Mauschlerin, die (ugs.); (financial) Geschäftemacher, der/-macherin, dle

wheelie /'wi:lɪ/ n. (coll.) Fahren auf dem Hinterrad; Wheelie, das; do a ∼/do ∼s auf dem Hinterrad fahren; ein Wheelie/Wheelies fahren

'wheelie bin n. (Brit. coll.) Müllcontainer auf Rollen; Rollcontainer für Müll

wheeling and 'dealing n. Mauschelei, die (ugs.); (shady deals) undurchsichtige Geschäfte

wheeze /wi:z/ **1** v.i. schnaufen; keuchen. **2** n. Schnaufen, das; Keuchen, das

wheezy /'wi:zɪ/ adj. (coll.) pfeifend, keuchend ⟨Atem, Stimme⟩

whelk /welk/ n. (Zool.) Wellhornschnecke, die

when /wen/ **1** adv. **(a)** (at what time) wann; **say** ∼ (coll.; pouring drink) sag halt; **that was** ∼ **I intervened** das war der Moment, wo ich eingriff; **(b)** (at which) **the time** ∼ ...: die Zeit, zu der od. (ugs.) wo/(with past tense) als ...; **the day** ∼ ...: der Tag, an dem od. (ugs.) wo/(with past tense) als ...; **do you remember [the time]** ∼ **we** ...: erinnerst du dich daran, wie wir ... **2** conj. **(a)** (at the time that) als; (with present or future tense) wenn; ∼ **[I was] young** als ich jung war; in meiner Jugend; ∼ **in doubt** im Zweifelsfall; ∼ **cleaning the gun** beim Putzen des Gewehrs; ∼ **speaking French** wenn ich/sie usw. Französisch spreche usw.; **(b)** (whereas) **why do you go abroad** ∼ **it's cheaper here?** warum fährst du ins Ausland, wo es doch hier billiger ist?; **I received only £5** ∼ **I should have got £10** ich bekam nur 5 Pfund, hätte aber 10 Pfund bekommen sollen; **(c)** (considering that) wenn; **how can I finish it** ∼ **you won't help?** wie soll ich es fertig machen, wenn du nicht hilfst?; **(d)** (and at that moment) als. **3** pron.

by/till ∼ ...? bis wann ...?; **from/since** ∼ ...? ab/seit wann ...?; ∼ **are we invited for?** für wann sind wir eingeladen?; **but that was yesterday, since** ∼ **things have changed** aber das war gestern, und inzwischen hat sich manches geändert

whence /wens/ (arch./literary) **1** adv. woher; **the village** ∼ **comes the famous cheese** das Dorf, aus dem der berühmte Käse kommt. **2** conj. (to the place from which) dorthin, woher

whenever /wen'evə(r)/ **1** adv. **(a)** wann immer; **or** ∼: oder wann immer; **(b)** (coll.) = **when ever** ⇒ **ever e. 2** conj. jedes Mal wenn

where /weə(r)/ **1** adv. **(a)** (in or at what place) wo; ∼ **shall we sit?** wo wollen wir sitzen od. uns hinsetzen?; wohin wollen wir uns setzen?; ∼ **was I?** (fig.) wo war ich stehengeblieben?; ∼ **did Orwell say/write that?** wo od. an welcher Stelle sagt/schreibt Orwell das?; ∼ **is the harm in it/the sense of it?** was macht das schon/welchen od. was für einen Sinn hat das?; **this is** ∼ **I was born** hier bin ich geboren; **(b)** (from what place) woher; ∼ **did you get that information?** wo hast du das erfahren?; **(c)** (to what place, to which) wohin; ∼ **shall I put it?** wohin soll ich es legen?; wo soll ich es hinlegen?; ∼ **do we go from here?** (fig.) was tun wir jetzt od. als Nächstes?; **(d)** (in what respect) inwiefern; **I don't know** ∼ **they differ/I've gone wrong** ich weiß nicht, worin sie sich unterscheiden/wo ich den Fehler gemacht habe; **that is** ∼ **you are wrong** in diesem Punkt irrst du dich; **(e)** (in which) wo; **in the box** ∼ **I keep my tools** in der Kiste, worin od. in der ich mein Werkzeug habe; **(f)** (in what situation) wo; ∼ **will/would they be if** ...? was wird/würde aus ihnen, wenn ...? **2** conj. wo; ∼ **uncertain, leave blank** bei Unsicherheit [bitte] freilassen. **3** pron. **near/not far from** ∼ **it happened** nahe der Stelle/nicht weit von der od. unweit der Stelle, wo es passiert ist; **from** ∼ **I'm standing** von meinem Standort [aus]; **they continued from** ∼ **they left off** sie machten da weiter, wo sie aufgehört hatten; ∼ [...] **from?** woher [...]?; von wo [...]?; ∼ [...] **to?** wohin

[...]?; ~ **are you going to?** wohin gehst du?; wo gehst du hin?

whereabouts 1 /ˈweərəˈbaʊts/ adv. (in what place) wo; (to what place) wohin. **2** /ˈweərəˈbaʊts/ pron. ~ **are you from?** woher kommst du? **3** /ˈweərəbaʊts/ n., constr. as sing. or pl. (of thing) Verbleib, der; (of person) Aufenthalt[sort], der

where: ~'**as** conj. während; **he is very quiet,** ~**as she is an extrovert** er ist sehr ruhig, sie dagegen ist eher extravertiert; ~'**by** adv. (by which) mit dem/der/denen; mit dessen/deren Hilfe; ~**upon** /ˈweərəˈpɒn/ adv. worauf

wherever /weərˈevə(r)/ **1** adv. **(a)** (in whatever place) wo immer; **sit** ~ **you like** setz dich, wohin du magst; **or** ~**:** oder wo immer; oder sonst wo (ugs.); **(b)** (to whatever place) wohin immer; **I shall go** ~ **I like** ich gehe, wohin ich will; **or** ~**:** oder wohin immer; oder sonst wohin (ugs.); **(c)** (coll.: where ever) ~ **in the world have you been?** wo in aller Welt hast du bloß gesteckt? **2** conj. **(a)** (in every place that) überall [da], wo; **do it** ~ **possible** tun Sie es, wo od. wenn [irgend] möglich; **(b)** (to every place that) wohin auch; ~ **he went** wohin er auch ging. **3** pron. wo ... auch; ~ **you're going to** wo du auch hingehst; wohin du auch gehst

whet /wet/ v.t., **-tt-: (a)** (sharpen) wetzen; **(b)** (fig.: stimulate) anregen ⟨Appetit⟩

whether /ˈweðə(r)/ conj. ob; **I don't know** ~ **to go [or not]** ich weiß nicht, ob ich gehen soll [oder nicht]; **the question [of]** ~ **to do it [or not]** die Frage, ob man es tun soll [oder nicht]; ~ **you like it or not, I'm going** ob es dir passt oder nicht, ich gehe

whey /weɪ/ n., no pl., no indef. art. Molke, die

which /wɪtʃ/ **1** adj. **(a)** interrog. welch...; ~ **one** welcher/welche/welches; ~ **ones** welche; ~ **one of you did it?** wer von euch hat es getan?; ~ **way** (how) wie; (in ~ direction) wohin; **(b)** rel. welch... (geh.); **he usually comes at one o'clock, at** ~ **time I'm having lunch/by** ~ **time I've finished** er kommt immer um ein Uhr; dann esse ich gerade zu Mittag/bis dahin bin ich schon fertig. **2** pron. **(a)** interrog. welcher/welche/welches; ~ **of you?** wer von euch?; ~ **is** ~**?** welcher/welche/welches ist welcher/welche/welches?; **(b)** rel. der/die/das; welcher/welche/welches (veralt.); referring to a clause was; **of** ~**:** dessen/deren; **everything** ~ **I predicted** alles, was ich vorausgesagt habe; **the crime of** ~ **you accuse him** das Verbrechen, dessen Sie ihn anklagen; **I intervened, after** ~ **they calmed down** ich griff ein, worauf[hin] sie sich beruhigten; **Our Father,** ~ **art in Heaven** (Rel.) Vater unser, der du bist im Himmel

whichever /wɪtʃˈevə(r)/ **1** adj. **(a)** (any ... that) der od. derjenige, der/die od. diejenige, die/das od. dasjenige, das/die od. diejenigen, die; **go** ~ **way you want** es ist egal, welchen Weg du nimmst; **take** ~ **apple/apples you wish** nimm den Apfel, den du willst/die Äpfel, die du willst; ..., ~ **period is the longer** ... , je nachdem, welches der längere Zeitraum ist; **(b)** (no matter which/who/whom) welche/welcher/welches ... auch; ~ **way you go** welchen Weg du auch nimmst. **2** pron. **(a)** (any one[s] that) der od. derjenige, der/die od. diejenige, die/das od. dasjenige, das/die od. diejenigen, die; ~ **of you/the children wins will get a prize** wer von euch gewinnt/das Kind, das gewinnt, bekommt einen Preis; **(b)** (no matter which one[s]) welcher/welche/welches ... auch; ~ **of them comes/come** wer von ihnen auch kommt; **(c)** (coll.: which ever) ~ **could it be?** welcher/welche/welches könnte das nur sein?

whiff /wɪf/ n. **(a)** (smell) [leichter] Geruch; (puff, breath) Hauch, der; ~**s of smoke** Rauchwölkchen; **(b)** (fig.: trace) Hauch, der; **the faintest** ~ **of sentiment** der leiseste Anflug von Sentimentalität

while /waɪl/ **1** n. Weile, die; **quite a** or **quite some** ~**, a good** ~**:** eine ganze Weile; ziemlich lange; **[for] a** ~**:** eine Weile; **where have you been all the** or **this** ~**?** wo warst du die ganze Zeit?; **a long** ~**:** lange; **for a little** or **short** ~**:** eine kleine Weile; **stay a little** ~ **[longer]** bleib noch ein Weilchen; **in a little** or **short** ~**:** gleich; **be worth [sb.'s]** ~**:** sich [für jmdn.] lohnen; **make sth. worth sb.'s** ~**:** jmdn. für etw. entsprechend belohnen; **once in a** ~**:** von Zeit zu Zeit [mal]; hin und wieder [mal].

2 conj. **(a)** während; (as long as) solange; ~ **in London he took piano lessons** als er in London war, nahm er Klavierstunden; **(b)** (although) obgleich; **(c)** (whereas) während

~ **away** v.t. ~ **away the time** sich (Dat.) die Zeit vertreiben (by, with mit)

whilst /waɪlst/ (Brit.) ⇒ **while 2**

whim /wɪm/ n. (mood) Laune, die

whimper /ˈwɪmpə(r)/ **1** n. ~[s] Wimmern, das; (of dog etc.) Winseln, das. **2** v.i. wimmern; ⟨Hund:⟩ winseln

whimsical /ˈwɪmzɪkl/ adj. launenhaft; (odd, fanciful) spleenig

whine /waɪn/ **1** v.i. **(a)** (make moaning sound) heulen; ⟨Hund:⟩ jaulen; ⟨Baby:⟩ quengeln (ugs.); **(b)** (complain) jammern; **he's been whining to the boss about it** er hat dem Chef darüber etwas vorgejammert. **2** n. **(a)** (sound) Heulen, das; (esp. of dog) Jaulen, das; **(b)** (complaint) ~[s] Gejammer, das

whinge /wɪndʒ/ (coll.) **1** v.i., ~**ing** ⇒ **whine 1 b. 2** n. ⇒ **whine 2 b**

whip /wɪp/ **1** n. **(a)** Peitsche, die; **(b)** (Brit. Parl.: official) Einpeitscher, der/Einpeitscherin, die (Jargon); Fraktionsgeschäftsführer, der/-führerin, die (Amtsspr.); **(c)** (Brit. Parl.: notice) **[three-line]** ~**:** [verbindliche] Aufforderung zur Teilnahme an einer Plenarsitzung [wegen einer wichtigen Abstimmung]; **resign the** ~**:** aus der Fraktion austreten. **2** v.t., **-pp-: (a)** (lash) peitschen; **the rider** ~**ped his horse** der Reiter gab seinem Pferd die Peitsche; **(b)** (Cookery) schlagen; **(c)** (move quickly) reißen ⟨Gegenstand⟩; **she** ~**ped it out of my hand** sie riss es mir aus der Hand; **(d)** (coll.: defeat) auseinander nehmen (salopp bes. Sport); **(e)** (coll.: steal) klauen (ugs.). **3** v.i., **-pp-: (a)** (move quickly) flitzen (ugs.); ~ **through a book in no time** ein Buch in null Komma nichts durchlesen (ugs.); **(b)** (lash) peitschen

~ **a'way** v.t. wegreißen **(from** Dat.)

~ '**out** v.t. [blitzschnell] herausziehen

~ '**up** v.t. **(a)** (snatch up) [blitz]schnell aufheben; **(b)** (Cookery) [kräftig] schlagen; **(c)** (arouse) aufpeitschen ⟨Wellen⟩; (fig.) anheizen (ugs.), anfachen (geh.) ⟨Emotionen, Interesse⟩; schüren ⟨Hass, Unzufriedenheit⟩; **(d)** (coll.: make quickly) schnell hinzaubern ⟨Gericht, Essen⟩

whip: ~**cord** n. **(a)** (cord) Peitschenschnur, die; **(b)** (fabric) Whipcord, der; ~ **hand** n. **have** or **hold the** ~ **hand [of** or **over sb.]** (fig.) die Oberhand [über jmdn.] haben; ~**lash** n. **(a)** Peitschenriemen, der; **(b)** (Med.) ~**lash [injury]** Peitschenschlagverletzung, die; Schleudertrauma, das

whipped 'cream n. Schlagsahne, die

whippet /ˈwɪpɪt/ n. Whippet, der

whipping /ˈwɪpɪŋ/ n. (flogging) Schlagen [mit der Peitsche]; (as form of punishment) Prügelstrafe, die; (flagellation) Geißelung, die; **give sb. a** ~**:** jmdn. auspeitschen; (coll.: defeat) jmdm. eins überbraten (salopp)

'**whip-round** n. (Brit. coll.) Sammlung, die; **have** or **hold a** ~**-round [for sb./sth.]** [für jmdn./etw.] den Hut herumgehen lassen (ugs.)

whirl /wɜːl/ **1** v.t. **(a)** (rotate) [im Kreis] herumwirbeln; **(b)** (fling) schleudern; (with circling motion) wirbeln ⟨Blätter, Schneeflocken usw.⟩; **(c)** (convey rapidly) in Windeseile fahren. **2** v.i. **(a)** (rotate) wirbeln; **(b)** (move swiftly) sausen; (with circling motion) wirbeln; **(c)** (fig.: reel) **everything/the room** ~**ed about me** mir drehte sich alles/das Zimmer drehte sich vor meinen Augen. **3** n. **(a)** Wirbeln, das; **she was** or **her thoughts were** or **her head was in a** ~ (fig.) ihr schwirrte der Kopf; **(b)** (bustle) Trubel, der

~ **a'bout,** ~ **a'round** v.t. & i. herumwirbeln

~ **a'way,** ~'**off 1** v.t. in Windeseile wegfahren. **2** v.i. lossausen

~ '**round 1** v.t. [im Kreis] herumwirbeln. **2** v.i. [im Kreis] herumwirbeln; ⟨Rad, Rotor, Strudel:⟩ wirbeln

whirl: ~**pool** n. Strudel, der; (bathing pool) Whirlpool, der; ~**wind** n. **(a)** Wirbelwind, der; (stronger) Wirbelsturm, der; **(b)** (fig.: tumult) Wirbel, der; Trubel, der; attrib. ~**wind romance** heftige Romanze

whirr /wɜː(r)/ **1** v.i. surren; ⟨Heuschrecke, Grille usw.:⟩ zirpen; ⟨Flügel eines Vogels, Propeller:⟩ schwirren. **2** n. ⇒ **1:** Surren, das; Zirpen, das; Schwirren, das

whisk /wɪsk/ **1** *n.* **(a)** Wedel, *der;* **(b)** (Cookery) Schnee-besen, *der;* (part of mixer) Rührbesen, *der.* **2** *v.t.* **(a)** (Cookery) [mit dem Schnee-/Rührbesen] schlagen; **(b)** (convey rapidly) in Windeseile bringen

~ **a'way** *v.t.* **(a)** (flap away) wegscheuchen; **(b)** (remove suddenly) ~ **sth. away [from sb.]** [jmdm.] etw. [plötzlich] wegreißen; **(c)** (convey rapidly) in Windeseile wegbringen

~ **'off** *v.t.* **(a)** (flap off) ⇒ ~ **away a;** **(b)** (remove suddenly) [plötzlich] wegreißen; ~ **one's coat off** seinen Mantel von sich werfen; **(c)** ⇒ ~ **away c**

~ **'up** ⇒ ~ **2 a**

whisker /'wɪskə(r)/ *n.* **(a)** *in pl.* (hair on man's cheek) Ba-ckenbart, *der;* **(b)** (Zool.) (of cat, mouse, rat) Schnurrhaar, *das;* (of walrus) Bartborste, *die;* **(c)** (fig. coll.: small distance) **be within a** ~ **of sth./doing sth.** kurz vor etw. (*Dat.*) stehen/kurz davor stehen, etw. zu tun; **win by a** ~: ganz knapp gewinnen

whiskey (Amer., Ir.), **whisky** /'wɪskɪ/ *n.* Whisky, *der;* (Irish or American ~) Whiskey, *der*

whisper /'wɪspə(r)/ **1** *v.i.* **(a)** flüstern; ~ **to sb.** jmdm. etwas zuflüstern; ~ **to me so that no one else will hear** flüster es mir ins Ohr, damit es niemand [anders] hört; **(b)** (speak secretly) tuscheln; ~ **against sb.** über jmdn. tuscheln; **(c)** (rustle) [leise] rauschen; säuseln (geh.); flüstern (poet.) **2** *v.t.* **(a)** flüstern; ~ **sth. to sb./in sb.'s ear** jmdm. etw. zuflüstern/ins Ohr flüstern; **(b)** (rumour) [hinter vorgehaltener Hand] erzählen; **the story is being** ~**ed about the village that** ...: im Dorf macht die Ge-schichte die Runde, dass ...; **it is** ~**ed that** ...: man mun-kelt, dass ... (ugs.). **3** *n.* **(a)** (~ed speech) Flüstern, *das;* **in a** ~**, in** ~**s** im Flüsterton; **(b)** (~ed remark) **their** ~**s** ihr Geflüster; **(c)** (rumour) Gerücht, *das;* **there were** ~**s that** ...: es gab Gerüchte, dass ...

whist /wɪst/ *n.* (Cards) Whist, *das*

whistle /'wɪsl/ **1** *v.i.* pfeifen; ~ **at a girl** hinter einem Mädchen herpfeifen; **the spectators** ~**d at the referee** die Zuschauer pfiffen den Schiedsrichter aus; ~ **to sb.** jmdm. pfeifen; ~ **for sth.** nach etw. pfeifen; ~ **in the dark** (fig.) seine Angst verdrängen; **you can** ~ **for it!** (fig. coll.) da kannst du lange warten! **2** *v.t.* **(a)** pfeifen; **(b)** (sum-mon) her[bei]pfeifen; **he** ~**d his dog and it came run-ning** er pfiff seinem Hund, und er kam angelaufen. **3** *n.* **(a)** (sound) Pfiff, *der;* (act of whistling) Pfeifen, *das;* **he gave a** ~ **of surprise** er ließ ein überraschtes Pfeifen verneh-men; **(b)** (instrument) Pfeife, *die;* **penny** *or* **tin** ~: Blech-flöte, *die;* **the referee blew his** ~: der Schiedsrichter pfiff; **[as] clean/clear as a** ~ (fig.) blitzsauber/absolut frei; **blow the** ~ **on sb./sth.** (fig.) jmdn./etw. auffliegen lassen (ugs.)

'whistle-stop *n.* (Amer.) **(a)** (Railw.) (small town) kleines Nest (ugs.) (an einer Bahnlinie); (station) Bedarfshaltepunkt, *der;* **(b)** (Polit.) *kurzer Auftritt eines Politikers während einer Wahlkampfreise;* (rapid visit) Stippvisite, *die; attrib.* ~**-stop tour/campaign** Reise mit vielen Kurzaufenthalten/ Wahlkampf[reise] mit vielen kurzen Auftritten *od.* Termi-nen

whistling 'kettle *n.* Pfeifkessel, *der*

whit /wɪt/ *n., no pl., no def. art.* (arch./literary) **no** ~, **not a** ~: kein bisschen

white /waɪt/ **1** *adj.* **(a)** weiß; **[as]** ~ **as snow** schneeweiß; **he prefers his coffee** ~ (Brit.) er trinkt seinen Kaffee am liebsten mit Milch; **(b)** (pale) weiß; (through illness) blass; (through fear or rage) bleich; **[as]** ~ **as chalk** *or* **a sheet** kreideblech; **(c)** (light-skinned) weiß; ~ **people** Weiße *Pl.* **2** *n.* **(a)** (colour) Weiß, *das;* **(b)** (of egg) Eiweiß, *das;* **(c)** (of eye) Weiße, *das;* **the** ~**s of their eyes** das Weiße in ihren Augen; **(d)** **W**~ (person) Weiße, *der/die;* **(e)** (~ clothes) **dressed in** ~: weiß gekleidet; ~**s** weißer Dress

white: ~**bait** *n., pl. same: junger Hering/junge Sprotte o. ä.;* ~ **'bread** *n.* Weißbrot, *das;* ~ **'coffee** *n.* (Brit.) Kaffee mit Milch; ~**-'collar** *adj.* ~**-collar worker** An-gestellte, *der/die;* ~**-collar union** Angestelltengewerk-schaft, *die;* ~ **'elephant** *n.* (fig.) nutzloser Besitz; **be a** ~ **elephant** ⟨*Gebäude, Einkaufszentrum usw.*⟩ reine Geldverschwendung sein; *attrib.* **a** ~ **elephant stall** *eine Bude, an der Sachen angeboten werden, die deren ehemalige*

Besitzer gern loswerden wollen; ~**-faced** /'waɪtfeɪsd/ *adj.* [kreide]bleich; **W**~**hall** *pr. n.* (Brit. Polit.: Government) Whitehall (*das*); ~ **'hope** *n.* Hoffnungsträger, *der/* Hoffnungsträgerin, *die;* ~ **'horse** *n.* **(a)** Schimmel, *der;* **(b)** *in pl.* (on waves) Schaumkronen; ~**-'hot** *adj.* weiß glühend; (fig.) glühend; **W**~ **House** *pr. n.* (Amer. Polit.) **the W**~ **House** das Weiße Haus; ~ **man** *n.* (Anthrop.) Weiße, *der;* **the** ~ **man** (~ people) der weiße Mann

whiten /'waɪtn/ **1** *v.t.* weiß machen; weißen ⟨*Wand, Schuhe*⟩. **2** *v.i.* **(a)** (become white) weiß werden; **(b)** (turn pale) [kreide]weiß werden

whiteness /'waɪtnɪs/ *n., no pl.* **(a)** Weiß, *das;* **(b)** (pale-ness) Blässe, *die*

white: W~ **'Paper** *n.* (Brit.) *öffentliches Diskussionspa-pier über Vorhaben der Regierung;* ~ **'sauce** *n.* weiße *od.* helle Soße; ~ **'slave** *n.* weiße Sklavin; *Opfer des Mädchenhandels; attrib.* ~ **slave trade** *or* **traffic** Mäd-chenhandel, *der;* ~ **'spirit** *n.* (Chem.) Terpentin[öl]ersatz, *der;* ~ **'stick** *n.* Blindenstock, *der;* ~ **'sugar** *n.* weißer Zucker; ~**wash 1** *n.* **(a)** [weiße] Tünche; (fig.) Schönfär-berei, *die;* **the report is a** ~**wash of the Government** der Bericht versucht, die Regierung reinzuwaschen; **(b)** (defeat) Zu-Null-Niederlage, *die;* **2** *v.t.* **(a)** [weiß] tünchen; **(b)** (defeat) zu null schlagen; ~ **'wedding** *n.* Hochzeit in Weiß; **have a** ~ **wedding** in Weiß heiraten; ~ **'wine** *n.* Weißwein, *der;* ~ **woman** *n.* (Anthrop.) Weiße, *die*

whither /'wɪðə(r)/ (arch./rhet.) **1** *adv.* wohin; ~ **demo-cracy/Ulster?** (fig. rhet.) wohin *od.* (geh.) quo vadis, Demo-kratie/Ulster? **2** *conj.* dorthin *od.* dahin, wohin

whitish /'waɪtɪʃ/ *adj.* weißlich

Whit Monday /wɪt 'mʌndeɪ, wɪt 'mʌndɪ/ *n.* Pfingstmon-tag, *der*

Whitsun /'wɪtsn/ *n.* Pfingsten, *das od. Pl.;* **at** ~: zu *od.* an Pfingsten; **next/last** ~: nächste/letzte Pfingsten

Whit Sunday /wɪt 'sʌndeɪ, wɪt 'sʌndɪ/ *n.* Pfingstsonntag, *der*

whittle /'wɪtl/ **1** *v.t.* schnitzen an (+ *Dat.*); ~ **a stick to a point** einen Stock anspitzen. **2** *v.i.* ~ **at sth.** an etw. (*Dat.*) [herum]schnitzen

~ **a'way,** ~ **'down** *v.t.* (fig.) **(a)** (completely) auffressen ⟨*Gewinn, Geldmittel usw.*⟩; ~ **away sb.'s rights/power** jmdm. nach und nach alle Rechte/alle Macht nehmen; **(b)** (partly) allmählich reduzieren ⟨*Anzahl, Team, Gewinn, Verlust*⟩; verkürzen ⟨*Liste*⟩

Whit /wɪt/**:** ~ **week** *n.* Pfingstwoche, *die;* ~ **week-'end** *n.* Pfingstwochenende, *das*

whiz, whizz /wɪz/ **1** *v.i.,* **-zz-** zischen. **2** *n.* Zischen, *das* ~ **'past** *v.i.* vorbeizischen; ⟨*Vogel:*⟩ vorbeischießen

'whiz[z]-kid *n.* (coll.) Senkrechtstarter, *der;* **he is a financial** ~: er macht eine steile Karriere als Fi-nanzmann

who /huː, *stressed* huː/ *pron.* **(a)** *interrog.* wer; (coll.: whom) wen; (coll.: to whom) wem; ~ **are you talking about?** (coll.) von wem *od.* über wen sprichst du?; **I don't know** ~**'s** ~ **in the firm yet** ich kenne die Leute in der Firma noch nicht richtig; ~ **am 'I to object/argue** *etc.?* wie könnte ich Einwände erheben/etwas dagegen sagen *usw.?;* ~ **would have thought it?** (rhet.) wer hätte das gedacht!; **(b)** *rel.* der/die/das; *pl.* die; (coll.: whom) den/die/das; (coll.: to whom) dem/der/denen; **any person/he/those** ~ ...: wer ...; **they** ~ ...: diejenigen, die *od.* welche ...; **everybody** ~ ...: jeder, der ...; **I/you** ~ ...: ich, der ich/du, der du ...; **the man** ~ **I met last week/**~ **you were speaking to** (coll.) der Mann, den ich letzte Woche getroffen habe/mit dem du gesprochen hast

whoa /wəʊ/ *int.* brr

who'd /huːd, *stressed* huːd/ **(a)** = **who had;** **(b)** = **who would**

whodun[n]it /huː'dʌnɪt/ *n.* (coll.) Krimi, *der* (ugs.)

whoever /huː'evə(r)/ *pron.* **(a)** wer [immer]; ~ **comes will be welcome** jeder, der kommt, ist willkommen; **(b)** (no matter who) wer ... auch; ~ **you may be** wer Sie auch sind; **(c)** (coll.: who ever) ~ **could it be?** wer könnte das nur sein?

whole /həʊl/ **1** *adj.* **(a)** ganz; **that's the** ~ **point [of the exercise]** das ist der ganze Zweck der Übung (ugs.);

the ∼ lot [of them] [sie] alle; **a ∼ lot of people** eine ganze Menge Leute; **(b)** (intact) ganz; **roast sth. ∼:** etw. im Ganzen braten; **(c)** (undiminished) ganz; **three ∼ hours** drei volle Stunden. **2** *n.* **(a) the ∼:** das Ganze; **the ∼ of my money/the village/London** mein ganzes *od.* gesamtes Geld/das ganze Dorf/ganz London; **he spent the ∼ of that year/of Easter abroad** er war jenes Jahr/zu Ostern die ganze Zeit im Ausland; **the ∼ of Shakespeare** *or of* **Shakespeare's works** Shakespeares gesamte Werke; **(b)** (total of parts) Ganze, *das;* **as a ∼:** als Ganzes; **sell sth. as a ∼:** etw. im Ganzen verkaufen; **on the ∼:** im Großen und Ganzen

whole: ∼**food** *n.* Vollwertkost, *die;* ∼**-hearted** /həʊl'hɑːtɪd/ *adj.* herzlich ⟨*Dank, Dankbarkeit, Glückwünsche*⟩; tief empfunden ⟨*Dankbarkeit, Reue*⟩; rückhaltlos ⟨*Unterstützung, Hingabe, Ergebenheit*⟩; ∼**meal** *adj.* Vollkorn-; ∼ **note** *n.* (Amer. Mus.) ganze Note; ∼**'number** *n.* (Math.) ganze Zahl; ∼**sale 1** *adj.* **(a)** (Commerc.) Großhandels-; ∼**sale dealer** *or* **merchant** Großhändler, *der*/-händlerin, *die;* **the** ∼**sale trade** der Großhandel; **(b)** (fig.: on a large scale) massenhaft; Massen-; **in a** ∼**sale way** massenweise; **(c)** (fig.: indiscriminate) pauschal; **2** *adv.* **(a)** (Commerc.) en gros ⟨*[ein]kaufen, verkaufen*⟩; im Großhandel ⟨*[ein]kaufen*⟩; (at ∼sale price) zum Einkaufs- *od.* Großhandelspreis; **(b)** (fig.: on a large scale) massenweise; **(c)** (fig.: indiscriminately) pauschal

wholesaler /'həʊlseɪlə(r)/ *n.* (Commerc.) Grossist, *der*/ Grossistin, *die* (fachspr.); Großhändler, *der*/-händlerin, *die*

wholesome /'həʊlsəm/ *adj.* gesund

whole 'wheat *n.* Vollweizen, *der*

who'll /hʊl, *stressed* huːl/ = **who will**

wholly /'həʊlɪ/ *adv.* völlig; durch und durch ⟨*böse*⟩

whom /huːm/ *pron.* **(a)** interrog. wen; *as indirect object* wem; **to ∼/of ∼ did you speak?** mit wem/von wem haben Sie gesprochen?; **(b)** rel. den/die/das; *pl.* die; *as indirect object* dem/der/dem; *pl.* denen; **the children, the mother of ∼ ...:** die Kinder, deren Mutter ...; **five children, all of ∼ are coming** fünf Kinder, die alle mitkommen; **ten candidates, only the best of ∼ ...:** zehn Kandidaten, von denen nur die besten ...

whoop /wuːp/ **1** *v.i.* [aufgeregt] schreien; (with joy, excitement) juchzen (ugs.); jauchzen. **2** *v.t.* ∼ **it up** (coll.) die Sau rauslassen (salopp); (Amer.: stir up enthusiasm) Stimmung machen. **3** *n.* [aufgeregter] Schrei; (of joy, excitement) Juchzer, *der* (ugs.); Jauchzer, *der*

whoopee 1 /wʊ'piː/ *int.* juhu. **2** /'wʊpi:/ *n.* **make ∼** (coll.) die Sau rauslassen (ugs.)

whooping cough /'huːpɪŋ kɒf/ *n.* ▶ **865** (Med.) Keuchhusten, *der*

whoosh /wʊʃ/ **1** *v.i.* brausen; ⟨*Rakete, Geschoss:*⟩ zischen. **2** *n.* Brausen, *das;* (of rocket, projectile) Zischen, *das;* **with a [loud]** ∼**:** [laut] brausend/zischend

whopper /'wɒpə(r)/ *n.* (coll.) **(a)** Riese, *der;* **a ∼ of a marrow/fish** ein Riesending von einem Kürbis/Fisch (ugs.); **(b)** (lie) faustdicke Lüge

whopping /'wɒpɪŋ/ (coll.) **1** *adj.* riesig; Riesen- (ugs.); faustdick ⟨*Lüge*⟩. **2** *adv.* ∼ **great** ⟹ **1**

whore /hɔː(r)/ (derog.) **1** *n.* **(a)** (prostitute) Hure, *die;* **(b)** (loose woman) Flittchen, *das.* **2** *v.i.* ∼ **[around]** [herum]huren

whorl /wɔːl/ *n.* (Bot.) Wirtel, *der;* Quirl, *der*

who's /huːz/ **(a)** = **who is; (b)** = **who has**

whose /huːz/ *pron.* **(a)** interrog. wessen; **(b)** rel. dessen/ deren/dessen; *pl.* deren; **the people ∼ house this is** die Leute, denen dieses Haus gehört

whosever /huːz'evə(r)/ *pron.* wessen ... auch; ∼ **it is, ...:** wem er/sie/es auch gehört, ...

who've /huːv, *stressed* huːv/ = **who have**

why /waɪ/ **1** *adv.* **(a)** (for what reason) warum; (for what purpose) wozu; ∼ **is that?** warum das?; **and this/that is ∼ I believe ...:** und darum glaube ich ...; ∼ **not buy it, if you like it?** kauf es dir doch, wenn es dir gefällt; ∼ **do we need another car?** wozu brauchen wir noch ein Auto?; **(b)** (on account of which) **the reason ∼ he did it** der Grund, aus dem *od.* warum er es tat; **I can see no reason**

∼ **not** ich wüsste nicht, warum nicht. **2** *int.* ∼, **certainly/of course!** aber sicher!; ∼, **if it isn't Jack!** aber das ist ja Jack!

WI *abbr.* **(a) West Indies; (b)** (Brit.) **Women's Institute**

wick /wɪk/ *n.* Docht, *der;* **get on sb.'s ∼** (fig. sl.) jmdm. auf den Keks gehen (salopp)

wicked /'wɪkɪd/ **1** *adj.* **(a)** (evil) böse; schlecht ⟨*Charakter, Person, Welt*⟩; niederträchtig ⟨*Gedanken, Plan, Verhalten*⟩; schändlich ⟨*Gesetz, Buch*⟩; **the ∼ villain** der Schurke; der Bösewicht (veralt.); **it was ∼ of you to torment the poor cat** es war gemein von dir, die arme Katze zu quälen; **(b)** (vicious) boshaft ⟨*Zunge*⟩; **(c)** (coll.: scandalous) himmelschreiend; sündhaft (ugs.) ⟨*Preis*⟩; **it's ∼ how he's been treated** wie man ihn behandelt hat, das schreit zum Himmel; **it's a ∼ shame** es ist eine wahre Schande. **2** *n. pl.* **the ∼:** die Bösen

wickedly /'wɪkɪdlɪ/ *adv.* **(a)** (evilly) niederträchtig; *as sentence-modifier* niederträchtigerweise; **(b)** (coll.: scandalously) himmelschreiend; sündhaft (ugs.) ⟨*teuer*⟩

wickedness /'wɪkɪdnɪs/ *n.* **(a)** *no pl.* ⟹ **wicked a:** Bosheit, *die;* Schlechtigkeit, *die;* Niederträchtigkeit, *die;* Schändlichkeit, *die;* **(b)** (evil act) Niederträchtigkeit, *die;* **(c)** *no pl.* (viciousness) Boshaftigkeit, *die;* **(d)** *no pl.* (coll.: scandalousness) Schändlichkeit, *die;* **the ∼ of this waste** so eine himmelschreiende Verschwendung

wicker /'wɪkə(r)/ *n.* Korbgeflecht, *das;* attrib. Korb⟨*waren, -möbel, -stuhl*⟩; geflochten ⟨*Korb, Matte*⟩

'wickerwork *n.* **(a)** (material) Korbgeflecht, *das;* **(b)** (articles) Korbwaren *Pl.*

wicket /'wɪkɪt/ *n.* (Cricket) (stumps) Tor, *das;* Wicket, *das;* (central area of pitch) Wurfbahn, *die;* **at the ∼:** [als Schlagmann] auf dem Spielfeld; **keep ∼:** als Torwächter spielen

'wicketkeeper *n.* (Cricket) Torwächter, *der*/-wächterin, *die;* Wicketkeeper, *der*

wide /waɪd/ **1** *adj.* **(a)** (broad) breit; groß ⟨*Unterschied, Abstand, Winkel, Loch*⟩; weit ⟨*Kleidung*⟩; **allow** *or* **leave a ∼ margin** (fig.) viel Spielraum lassen; **three feet ∼** drei Fuß breit; **(b)** (extensive) weit; umfassend ⟨*Lektüre, Wissen, Kenntnisse*⟩; weit reichend ⟨*Einfluss*⟩; vielseitig ⟨*Interessen*⟩; groß ⟨*Vielfalt, Bekanntheit, Berühmtheit*⟩; reichhaltig ⟨*Auswahl, Sortiment*⟩; breit ⟨*Publizität*⟩; **have ∼ appeal** weite Kreise ansprechen; **the ∼ world** die weite Welt; **(c)** (liberal) großzügig; **(d)** (fully open) weit geöffnet; **(e)** (off target) **be ∼ of sth.** etw. verfehlen; **be ∼ of the mark** (fig.) ⟨*Annahme, Bemerkung:*⟩ nicht zutreffen; **you're ∼ of the mark** (fig.) du liegst falsch (ugs.). **2** *adv.* **(a)** (fully) weit; ∼ **awake** hellwach; (fig. coll.) gewitzt; **I'm ∼ awake to your tricks** ich durchschaue deine Tricks; **(b)** (off target) **shoot ∼:** danebenschießen; **fall ∼ of the target, go ∼:** das Ziel verfehlen; **aim ∼/∼ of sth.** daneben/neben etw. (Akk.) zielen

-wide *in comb.* **city-/county-∼:** in der ganzen Stadt/ Grafschaft nachgestellt

wide: ∼**-angle 'lens** *n.* (Photog.) Weitwinkelobjektiv, *das;* ∼**-eyed** /'waɪdaɪd/ *adj.* (surprised) mit großen Augen nachgestellt

widely /'waɪdlɪ/ *adv.* **(a)** (over a wide area) weit ⟨*verbreitet, gestreut*⟩; locker, in großen Abständen ⟨*verteilt*⟩; **he has travelled ∼ in Europe** er ist in Europa viel gereist; **a ∼ read man** ein [sehr] belesener Mann; **(b)** (by many people) weithin ⟨*bekannt, akzeptiert*⟩; **a ∼ held view** eine weitverbreitete Ansicht; **it is ∼ rumoured that ...:** allgemein wird gemunkelt (ugs.), dass ...; **(c)** (in a wide sense) im weiten Sinne ⟨*gebraucht*⟩; weit ⟨*interpretiert*⟩; **(d)** (greatly) stark, erheblich ⟨*sich unterscheiden*⟩; sehr ⟨*verschieden, unterschiedlich*⟩

widen /'waɪdn/ **1** *v.t.* verbreitern; (fig.) erweitern. **2** *v.i.* sich verbreitern; breiter werden; (fig.) sich erweitern; ⟨*Interessen:*⟩ vielfältiger werden

∼ **'out** *v.i.* sich verbreitern; breiter werden; ∼ **out into sth.** sich zu etw. erweitern

wide: ∼**-open** attrib. adj., ∼ **'open** pred. adj. weit aufstehend *od.* geöffnet ⟨*Fenster, Tür*⟩; weit aufgerissen ⟨*Mund, Augen*⟩; **the ∼-open spaces of North America** die Weite der nordamerikanischen Landschaft; **be ∼**

open ⟨*Fenster, Tür:*⟩ weit offen stehen; **be ~ open to attack/criticism** Angriffen/der Kritik ausgesetzt sein; **lay** *or* **leave oneself/sb. ~ open to sth.** sich/jmdn. einer Sache (*Dat.*) schutzlos preisgeben; **the contest is still ~ open** der Wettbewerb *od.* der Ausgang des Wettbewerbs ist noch völlig offen; **~ranging** /'waɪdreɪndʒɪŋ/ *adj.* weitgehend ⟨*Maßnahme, Veränderung*⟩; weit reichend ⟨*Auswirkungen*⟩; ausführlich ⟨*Diskussion, Gespräch*⟩; **~ 'screen** *n.* (Cinemat.) Breitwand, *die;* **~screen television, ~screen TV** *ns.* Breitwandfernsehen, *das;* **~spread** *adj.* weitverbreitet ⟨*Art, Ansicht*⟩; groß ⟨*Nachfrage, Beliebtheit*⟩; von vielen geteilt ⟨*Sympathie*⟩; **become ~spread** sich [weit] ausbreiten; **there was a ~spread demand for reform** Reformen wurden allgemein gefordert

widow /'wɪdəʊ/ **1** *n.* Witwe, *die;* **be left/made a ~:** zur Witwe werden. **2** *v.t.* zur Witwe machen ⟨*Frau*⟩; zum Witwer machen ⟨*Mann*⟩; **be ~ed** zur Witwe/zum Witwer werden (**by** durch)

widowed /'wɪdəʊd/ *adj.* verwitwet

widower /'wɪdəʊə(r)/ *n.* Witwer, *der*

width /wɪdθ/ *n.* (**a**) ▸ 904 ◂ (measurement) Breite, *die;* (of garment) Weite, *die;* **what is the ~ of ...?** wie breit/weit ist ...?; **be half a metre in ~:** einen halben Meter breit/weit sein; (**b**) (large scope) großer Umfang; (of definition) Weite, *die;* (of interests) Vielseitigkeit, *die;* (**c**) (piece of material) Bahn, *die*

widthways /'wɪdθweɪz/, **widthwise** /'wɪdθwaɪz/ *adv.* in der Breite

wield /wiːld/ *v.t.* (literary) führen (geh.); (fig.) ausüben ⟨*Macht, Einfluss usw.*⟩; **~ a stick/sword** einen Stock/ein Schwert schwingen

wiener /'viːnə(r)/ *n.* (Amer.) Würstchen, *das*

wife /waɪf/ *n., pl.* **wives** /waɪvz/ Frau, *die;* **make sb. one's ~:** jmdn. zur Frau nehmen; **lawful wedded ~** (Eccl.) rechtmäßig angetraute Frau; **old wives' tale** Ammenmärchen, *das*

wife-swapping /'waɪfswɒpɪŋ/ *n.* (coll.) Partnertausch, *der*

wig /wɪg/ *n.* Perücke, *die*

wiggle /'wɪgl/ (coll.) **1** *v.t.* hin und her bewegen. **2** *v.i.* wackeln; (move) sich schlängeln; **~ into sth.** sich in etw. (*Akk.*) zwängen. **3** *n.* Wackeln, *das*

wigwam /'wɪgwæm/ *n.* Wigwam, *der*

wild /waɪld/ **1** *adj.* (**a**) wild lebend ⟨*Tier*⟩; wild wachsend ⟨*Pflanze*⟩; **grow ~:** wild wachsen; **~ beast** wildes Tier; (**b**) (rough) unzivilisiert; (bleak) wild ⟨*Landschaft, Gegend*⟩; (**c**) (unrestrained) wild; ungezügelt; wild, wüst ⟨*Bursche, Unordnung, Durcheinander*⟩; **run ~** ⟨*Pferd, Hund:*⟩ frei herumlaufen; ⟨*Kind:*⟩ herumtoben; ⟨*Pflanzen:*⟩ wuchern; **let one's imagination run ~:** seiner Fantasie freien Lauf lassen; (**d**) (stormy) stürmisch; tobend ⟨*Wellen*⟩; (**e**) rasend ⟨*Wut, Zorn, Eifersucht, Beifall*⟩; unbändig ⟨*Freude, Wut, Zorn, Schmerz*⟩; wild ⟨*Erregung, Zorn, Geschrei*⟩; panisch ⟨*Angst*⟩; irr ⟨*Blick*⟩; **be/become ~ [with sth.]** [vor etw. (*Dat.*)] außer sich (*Dat.*) sein/außer sich (*Akk.*) geraten; **send** *or* **drive sb. ~:** jmdn. rasend vor Erregung machen; (**f**) (coll.: very keen) **be ~ about sb./sth.** wild auf jmdn./etw. sein; **I'm not ~ about it** ich bin nicht wild darauf (ugs.); (**g**) (coll.: angry) wütend; **be ~ with** *or* **at sb.** eine Wut auf jmdn. haben; (**h**) (reckless) ungezielt ⟨*Schuss, Schlag*⟩; unbedacht ⟨*Verhalten, Versprechen, Gerede*⟩; aus der Luft gegriffen ⟨*Anschuldigungen, Behauptungen*⟩; maßlos ⟨*Übertreibung*⟩; irrwitzig ⟨*Plan, Idee, Versuch, Hoffnung*⟩. **2** *n.* **the ~[s]** die Wildnis; **see an animal in the ~:** ein Tier in freier Wildbahn sehen; **in the ~s** (coll.) in der Pampa (ugs.); **the call of the ~:** der Ruf der Wildnis

wild: ~ 'boar *n.* (Zool.) Wildschwein, *das;* **~ card** *n.* (Cards) wilde Karte; (Computing) Wildcard, *die;* **'cat** *n.* (Zool.) Wildkatze, *die;* **~cat** *attrib. adj.* **~cat strike** wilder Streik

wilderness /'wɪldənɪs/ *n.* Wildnis, *die;* (desert) Wüste, *die;* **be in the ~** (Polit.) alle Bedeutung verloren haben

wild: ~eyed /'waɪldaɪd/ *adj.* mit irrem Blick *nachgestellt;* **~fire** ⇒ **spread 2 a;** **~fowl** *n., pl. same* Federwild, *das;* (Cookery) Wildgeflügel, *das;* **~'goose chase** *n.* (fig.: hopeless quest) aussichtslose Suche; **send**

sb. on a ~-goose chase jmdn. einem Phantom nachjagen lassen; **~ 'horse** *n.* Wildpferd, *das;* **~ horses would not drag it from me** (fig.) eher beiße ich mir die Zunge ab[, als dass ich es erzähle]; **~life** *n., no pl., no indef. art.* die Tier- und Pflanzenwelt; die Natur; *attrib.* **~life park/reserve/sanctuary** Naturpark, *der/* -reservat, *das/*-schutzgebiet, *das*

wildly /'waɪldlɪ/ *adv.* (**a**) (unrestrainedly) wild; **run ~ all over the house** ⟨*Kinder:*⟩ wie wild im ganzen Haus herumtoben; (**b**) (stormily) wild; **the wind blew ~:** der Wind blies heftig; (**c**) (excitedly) rasend ⟨*eifersüchtig*⟩; unbändig ⟨*verliebt, sich freuen, sich verlieben*⟩; wild ⟨*schreien, applaudieren*⟩; erregt ⟨*diskutieren*⟩; **I'm not ~ interested in it** (iron.) ich interessiere mich nicht übermäßig dafür; **be ~ excited about sth.** über etw. (*Akk.*) ganz aus dem Häuschen sein (ugs.); **he looked ~ about him** er blickte irr um sich; (**d**) (recklessly) aufs Geratewohl; maßlos ⟨*übertreiben*⟩; wirr ⟨*daherreden, denken*⟩; **~ inaccurate** völlig falsch

wildness /'waɪldnɪs/ *n., no pl.* (**a**) (bleakness) Wildheit, *die;* (**b**) (lack of restraint) Wildheit, *die;* **after the ~ of his youth** nach seiner wilden *od.* stürmischen Jugend; (**c**) (storminess) **the ~ of the weather/sea** das stürmische Wetter/die stürmische See; (**d**) (of promise, words) Unbedachtheit, *die;* (of scheme, attempt, idea, hope, quest) Irrwitzigkeit, *die*

Wild 'West *pr. n.* Wilder Westen

wile /waɪl/ *n.* List, *die;* Schlich, *der*

wilful /'wɪlfl/ *adj.* (**a**) (deliberate) vorsätzlich; bewusst ⟨*Täuschung*⟩; (**b**) (obstinate) starrsinnig

will¹ /wɪl/ **1** *v.t., only in pres.* **will**, *neg.* (coll.) **won't** /wəʊnt/, *past* **would** /wʊd/, *neg.* (coll.) **wouldn't** /wʊdnt/ (**a**) (consent to) wollen; **They won't help me. W~/Would you?** Sie wollen mir nicht helfen. Bist du bereit?; **you ~ help her, won't you?** du hilfst ihr doch *od.* du wirst ihr doch helfen, nicht wahr?; **the car won't start** das Auto will nicht anspringen *od.* springt nicht an; **~/would you pass the salt, please?** gibst du bitte mal das Salz rüber?/ würdest du bitte mal das Salz rübergeben?; **~/would you come in?** kommen Sie doch herein; **now just listen, ~ you!** jetzt hör/hört gefälligst zu!; **~ you be quiet!** willst du/wollt ihr wohl ruhig sein!; (**b**) (be accustomed to) pflegen; **he ~ sit there hour after hour** er pflegt dort stundenlang zu sitzen; (emphatic) **children '~ make a noise** Kinder machen [eben] Lärm; ..., **as young people '~:** ..., wie alle Jungen Leute [es tun]; **he '~ insist on doing it** er besteht unbedingt darauf, es zu tun; **it 'would have to rain** natürlich musste es regnen; (**c**) (wish) wollen; **~ you have some more cake?** möchtest *od.* willst du noch etwas Kuchen?; **do as/what you ~:** mach, was du willst; **call it what [ever] you ~:** nenn es, wie du willst; **would to God that ...:** wollte Gott, dass ...; (**d**) (be able to) **the box ~ hold 5 lb. of tea** in die Kiste gehen 5 Pfund Tee; **the theatre ~ seat 800** das Theater hat 800 Sitzplätze. **2** *v. aux., forms as* **1:** (**a**) *expr. simple future* werden; **this time tomorrow he ~ be in Oxford** morgen um diese Zeit ist er in Oxford; **tomorrow he ~ have been here a month** morgen ist er einen Monat hier; **one more cherry, and I ~ have eaten a pound** noch eine Kirsche und ich habe ein Pfund gegessen; (**b**) *expr. intention* **I promise I won't do it again** ich verspreche, ich machs nicht noch mal; **You won't do that, ~ you? — Oh yes, I ~!** Du machst es doch nicht, oder? — Doch[, ich machs]!; **~ do** (coll.) wird gemacht; mach ich (ugs.); (**c**) *in conditional clause* **if he tried, he would succeed** wenn er es versuchen würde, würde er es erreichen; **he would like/would have liked to see her** er würde sie gerne sehen/ er hätte sie gerne gesehen; (**d**) (request) **~ you please tidy up** würdest du bitte aufräumen?

will² **1** *n.* (**a**) (faculty) Wille, *der;* **freedom of the ~:** Willensfreiheit, *die;* **have a ~ of one's own** [s]einen eigenen Willen haben; **an iron ~, a ~ of iron** ein eiserner Wille; (**b**) (Law: testament) Testament, *das;* (**c**) (desire) **at ~:** nach Belieben; **~ to live** Lebenswille, *der;* **you must have the ~ to win** du musst gewinnen wollen; **against one's/sb.'s ~:** gegen seinen/jmds. Willen; **of one's own [free] ~:**

aus freien Stücken; **do sth. with a ~:** etw. mit großem Eifer *od.* Elan tun; **where there's a ~ there's a way** (prov.) wo ein Wille ist, ist auch ein Weg; **(d)** (disposition) **with the best ~ in the world** bei allem Wohlwollen; *in neg. clause* beim besten Willen. **2** *v.t.* durch Willenskraft erzwingen; **~ oneself to do sth.** sich zwingen, etw. zu tun; **~ sb. to win** jmds. Sieg mit aller Kraft herbeiwünschen

willies /'wɪlɪz/ *n. pl.* (coll.) **sb. gets the ~:** jmdm. wird ganz anders (ugs.); **it gives me the ~:** dabei wird mir ganz anders (ugs.)

willing /'wɪlɪŋ/ **1** *adj.* **(a)** willig; **ready and ~:** bereit; **be ~ to do sth.** bereit sein, etw. zu tun; **I'm ~ to believe you're right** ich will gerne glauben, dass du recht hast; **(b)** *attrib.* (readily offered) willig; **she gave ~ assistance/help** sie half bereitwillig; **lend a ~ hand** bereitwillig helfen. **2** *n.* **show ~:** guten Willen zeigen

willingly /'wɪlɪŋlɪ/ *adv.* **(a)** (with pleasure) gern[e]; **(b)** (voluntarily) freiwillig; **they did not come ~:** sie kamen nur widerstrebend

willingness /'wɪlɪŋnɪs/ *n., no pl.* Bereitschaft, *die*

will-o'-the-wisp /wɪləðə'wɪsp/ *n.* **(a)** Irrlicht, *das;* **(b)** (fig.) Schimäre, *die*

willow /'wɪləʊ/ *n.* Weide, *die*

'willow-pattern *n.* Weidenmuster, *das*

'will-power *n.* Willenskraft, *die*

willy-nilly /ˌwɪlɪ'nɪlɪ/ *adv.* wohl oder übel ‹etw. tun müssen›

wilt /wɪlt/ *v.i.* **(a)** (Bot.: wither) welk werden; welken; **(b)** (fig.) ‹Person:› schlapp werden, (ugs.) abschlaffen; ‹Interesse, Begeisterung:› abflauen; ‹Energie, Kraft› dahinschwinden

wily /'waɪlɪ/ *adj.* listig; gewieft ‹Person›; raffiniert ‹Trick, Argumentation, Plan usw.›

wimp /wɪmp/ *n.* (coll. derog.) Schlappschwanz, *der* (ugs.)

win /wɪn/ **1** *v.t.*, **-nn-**, **won** /wʌn/ **(a)** gewinnen; bekommen ‹Stipendium, Auftrag, Vertrag, Recht›; ernten ‹Beifall, Dank›; **~ the long jump** im Weitsprung gewinnen; **~ an argument/debate** aus einem Streit/einer Debatte als Sieger hervorgehen; **~ promotion** befördert werden; **~ sb. sth.** jmdm. etw. einbringen; **~ a reputation [for oneself]** sich (*Dat.*) einen Ruf erwerben *od.* einen Namen machen; **~ sth. from** *or* **off sb.** jmdm. etw. abnehmen; **you can't ~ them all** (coll.), **you ~ some, you lose some** (coll.) man kann nicht immer Glück haben; **(b)** (coll.: steal) organisieren (ugs.); **(c)** **~ one's way into sb.'s heart/affections** jmds. Herz/Zuneigung gewinnen. **2** *v.i.*, **-nn-**, **won** gewinnen; (in battle) siegen; **you ~** (have defeated me) du hast gewonnen (ugs.); **~ or lose** wie es auch ausgeht/ausgehen würde; **you can't ~** (coll.) da hat man keine Chance (ugs.). **3** *n.* Sieg, *der;* **have a ~:** gewinnen

~ 'back *v.t.* zurückgewinnen

~ 'out *v.i.* (coll.) **~ out [over sb./sth.]** sich [gegen jmdn./etw.] durchsetzen

~ 'over, **~ 'round** *v.t.* bekehren; (to one's side) auf seine Seite bringen; (convince) überzeugen; **~ sb. over** *or* **round to a plan/to one's point of view** jmdn. für einen Plan gewinnen/zu seiner Ansicht bekehren *od.* von seiner Ansicht überzeugen

~ 'through *v.i.* Erfolg haben; **~ through to the next round** die nächste Runde erreichen

wince /wɪns/ *v.i.* zusammenzucken (at bei); **he ~d under the pain/the insult** der Schmerz/die Beleidigung ließ ihn zusammenzucken

winch /wɪntʃ/ **1** *n.* Winde, *die.* **2** *v.t.* winden; mit einer Winde ziehen; **~ up** hochwinden

wind¹ /wɪnd/ **1** *n.* **(a)** Wind, *der;* **be in the ~** (fig.) in der Luft liegen; **see how** *or* **which way the ~ blows** *or* **lies** (fig.) sehen, woher der Wind weht; **sail close to** *or* **near the ~:** hart am Wind segeln; (fig.) sich hart an der Grenze des Erlaubten bewegen; **take the ~ out of sb.'s sails** (fig.) jmdm. den Wind aus den Segeln nehmen; **the ~[s] of change** ein frischer Wind (fig.); **(b)** *no pl.* (Mus.) (stream of air) (in organ) Wind, *der;* (in other instruments) Luftstrom, *der;* (instruments) Bläser *Pl.;* **(c) get ~ of sth.** (fig.) Wind von etw. bekommen; **(d)** *no pl., no indef. art.* (flatulence) Blähungen *Pl.;* **break ~:** eine Blähung abgehen lassen; **get/have**

the ~ up (coll.) Manschetten (ugs.) *od.* Schiss (salopp) kriegen/haben; **put the ~ up sb.** (coll.) jmdm. Schiss machen (salopp); **(e)** (breath) **lose/have lost one's ~:** außer Atem kommen/sein; **recover** *or* **get one's ~:** wieder zu Atem kommen; **get one's second ~** (lit. or fig.) sich wieder steigern. **2** *v.t.* außer Atem bringen; **the blow ~ed him** der Schlag nahm ihm den Atem; **be ~ed** außer Atem sein; **he was ~ed by the blow to his stomach** nach dem Schlag in die Magengrube schnappte er nach Luft

wind² /waɪnd/ **1** *v.i.*, **wound** /waʊnd/ **(a)** (curve) sich winden; (move) sich schlängeln; **(b)** (coil) sich wickeln. **2** *v.t.*, **wound (a)** (coil) wickeln; (on to reel) spulen; **~ wool into a ball** Wolle zu einem Knäuel aufwickeln; **~ sth. off sth./on [to] sth.** etw. von etw. [ab]wickeln/auf etw. (*Akk.*) [auf]wickeln; **~ sb. round one's finger** jmdn. um den Finger wickeln (ugs.); **(b)** (with key etc.) aufziehen ‹Uhr›; **(c) ~ one's/its way** sich winden; sich schlängeln; **(d)** (coil into ball) zu einem Knäuel/zu Knäueln aufwickeln; **(e)** (surround) wickeln; **he wound the injured arm in a piece of cloth** er umwickelte den verletzten Arm mit einem Tuch; **(f)** (winch) winden; **~ sth. with a winch** etw. mit einer Winde ziehen. **3** *n.* **(a)** (curve) Windung, *die;* **(b)** (turn) Umdrehung, *die;* **give sth. a ~:** etw. aufziehen

~ 'back *v.t. & i.* zurückspulen

~ 'down 1 *v.t.* **(a)** (lower) mit einer Winde herunter-/hinunterlassen; herunterdrehen ‹Autofenster›; **(b)** (fig.: reduce gradually) einschränken; drosseln ‹Produktion›; (and cease) allmählich einstellen. **2** *v.i.* (lose momentum) ablaufen; (fig.) ‹Produktion:› zurückgehen; (cease) auslaufen

~ 'on *v.t. & i.* weiterspulen

~ 'up 1 *v.t.* **(a)** (raise) hochwinden; (winch up) [mit einer Winde] hochziehen; hochdrehen ‹Autofenster›; **(b)** (coil) aufwickeln; **(c)** (with key etc.) aufziehen ‹Uhr›; **(d)** (make tense) aufregen; erregen; **get wound up** sich aufregen; sich erregen; **(e)** (coll.: annoy deliberately) auf die Palme bringen (ugs.); **(f)** (conclude) beschließen ‹Debatte, Rede›; **(g)** (Finance, Law) auflösen; einstellen ‹Aktivitäten›; **~ up one's affairs** seine Angelegenheiten in Ordnung bringen. **2** *v.i.* **(a)** (conclude) schließen; **he wound up for the Government** er sprach als letzter Redner aus dem Regierungslager; **(b)** (coll.: end up) **~ up in prison/hospital** [zum Schluss] im Gefängnis/Krankenhaus landen (ugs.)

wind /wɪnd/: **~bag** *n.* (derog.) Schwätzer, *der*/Schwätzerin, *die;* **~-blown** *adj.* vom Wind zerzaust ‹Haar›; **~break** *n.* Windschutz, *der;* **~breaker** (Amer.), **~cheater** (Brit.) *ns.* Windjacke, *die;* **~-chill factor** *n.* Wind-chill-Index, *der* (Meteor.)

winder /'waɪndə(r)/ *n.* (of watch) Krone, *die;* (of clock, toy) Aufziehschraube, *die;* (key) Schlüssel, *der*

wind /wɪnd/: **~fall** *n.* **(a)** Stück Fallobst; (apple) Fallapfel, *der;* **~s** Fallobst, *das;* **(b)** (fig.) warmer Regen (ugs.); **~ farm** *n.* Windpark, *der;* Windfarm, *die*

winding /'waɪndɪŋ/ **1** *attrib. adj.* gewunden. **2** *n.* **(a)** *in pl.* (of road, river) Windungen *Pl.;* **(b)** (Electr.) Wicklung, *die*

wind instrument /'wɪnd ɪnstrəmənt/ *n.* (Mus.) Blasinstrument, *das*

windlass /'wɪndləs/ *n.* Winde, *die*

windmill /'wɪndmɪl/ *n.* **(a)** Windmühle, *die;* (to drive generator, water pump, etc.) Windrad, *das;* **(b)** (toy) Windrädchen, *das*

window /'wɪndəʊ/ *n.* **(a)** Fenster, *das;* **break a ~:** eine Fensterscheibe zerbrechen; ‹Einbrecher:› eine Fensterscheibe einschlagen; **go out of the ~** (fig. coll.) den Bach runtergehen (ugs.); **(b)** (fig.: means of observation) **a ~ on the West/world** ein Fenster zum Westen/zur Welt; **(c)** (for display of goods) [Schau]fenster, *das;* **(d)** (for issue of tickets etc.) Schalter, *der;* **(e)** (Computing) Fenster, *das*

window: **~ box** *n.* Blumenkasten, *der;* **~ cleaner** *n.* ▶ 887 Fensterputzer, *der*/-putzerin, *die;* **~-cleaning** *n.* Fensterputzen, *das;* **~ display** *n.* Schaufensterauslage, *die;* **~-dressing** *n.* Schaufensterdekoration, *die;* (fig.) Schönfärberei, *die;* **~ frame** *n.* Fensterrahmen, *der;* **~ ledge** *n.* (inside) Fensterbank, *die;* (outside) Fenstersims, *der od. das;* **~ pane** *n.* Fensterscheibe, *die;* **~-shopper** *n.* Schaufensterbummler, *der*/ -bummlerin, *die;*

∼-shopping n. Schaufensterbummeln, das; **go ∼-shopping** einen Schaufensterbummel machen; ∼ **sill** ⇒ **∼-ledge**

wind /wɪnd/: **∼pipe** n. ▶ 672⌋ (Anat.) Luftröhre, die; ∼ **power** n. Windkraft, die; ∼ **pump** n. Windpumpe, die; **∼screen**, (Amer.) **∼shield** ns. (Motor Veh.) Windschutzscheibe, die; **∼screen-/∼shield-wiper** Scheibenwischer, der; **∼surfer** n. Windsurfer, der; **∼surfing** n. (Sport) Windsurfen, das; **∼swept** adj. windgepeitscht; vom Wind zerzaust ⟨Person, Haare⟩; ∼ **tunnel** n. (Aeronaut.) Windkanal, der

windward /'wɪndwəd/ **1** adj. ∼ side Windseite, die; **in a ∼ direction** gegen den Wind. **2** adv. gegen den Wind. **3** n. Windseite, die; **sail to ∼:** gegen den Wind segeln

windy /'wɪndɪ/ adj. windig ⟨Tag, Ort, Wetter⟩

wine /waɪn/ **1** n. Wein, der. **2** v.t. ∼ and 'dine in großem Stil od. (ugs.) groß bewirten

wine: ∼ **bar** n. Weinstube, die; ∼ **bottle** n. Weinflasche, die; ∼ **cellar** n. [Wein]keller, der; **∼glass** n. Weinglas, das; **∼-list** n. Weinkarte, die; ∼ **taster** n. ▶ 887⌋ Weinverkoster, der/-verkosterin, die; ∼ **tasting** /'waɪnteɪstɪŋ/ n. Weinprobe, die; ∼ **'vinegar** n. Weinessig, der; ∼ **waiter** n. ▶ 887⌋ Weinkellner, der

wing /wɪŋ/ n. (a) (Ornith., Archit., Sport) Flügel, der; **on the ∼:** im Fluge; **spread** or **stretch one's ∼s** (fig.) sich auf eigene Füße stellen; **take sb. under one's ∼:** jmdn. unter seine Fittiche nehmen; **on a ∼ and a prayer** (fig.) mit minimalen Erfolgsaussichten; **(b)** (Aeronaut.) [Trag]flügel, der; Tragfläche, die; **(c)** in pl. (Theatre) Kulissen Pl.; **wait in the ∼s** (fig.) auf seine Chance warten; **(d)** (Brit. Motor Veh.) Kotflügel, der

winged /wɪŋd/ adj. geflügelt

winger /'wɪŋə(r)/ n. (Sport) Außenstürmer, der/-stürmerin, die; Flügel, der

wing: ∼ **mirror** n. (Brit. Motor Veh.) Außenspiegel, der; **∼span**, **∼spread** ns. [Flügel]spannweite, die; **∼-tip** n. Flügelspitze, die

wink /wɪŋk/ **1** v.i. (a) (blink) blinzeln; (as signal) zwinkern; ∼ **at sb.** jmdm. zuzwinkern; **(b)** (twinkle, flash) blinken. **2** v.t. ∼ one's eye/eyes blinzeln; (as signal) zwinkern; ∼ **one's eye at sb.** jmdm. zuzwinkern. **3** n. (a) Blinzeln, das; (signal) Zwinkern, das; **give sb. a** [secret/sly/knowing etc.] ∼**:** jmdn. [heimlich/verschmitzt/wissend usw.] zuzwinkern; **in the ∼ of an eye** (fig.) in null Komma nichts (ugs.); see also **tip²** **2** d; **(b) not get a ∼ of sleep, not sleep a ∼:** kein Auge zutun; see also **forty 1**

winker /'wɪŋkə(r)/ n. (Motor Veh.) Blinker, der

winkle /'wɪŋkl/ **1** n. Strandschnecke, die. **2** v.t. ∼ **out** herausholen, (ugs.) rausfriemeln ⟨Gegenstand, Substanz⟩; herausholen ⟨Person, Tier⟩; ∼ **sth. out of sb.** (fig.) etw. aus jmdm. rauskriegen (ugs.)

winner /'wɪnə(r)/ n. (a) Sieger, der/Siegerin, die; (of competition or prize) Gewinner, der/Gewinnerin, die; (winning shot) Siegestreffer, der; (winning goal) Siegestor, das; **(b)** (successful thing) Erfolg, der; (successful play, product) Renner, der (ugs.); Hit, der (ugs.); **you're on [to] a ∼ with this idea/book** (coll.) diese Idee/dieses Buch wird garantiert ein Renner od. Hit (ugs.)

winning /'wɪnɪŋ/ adj. (a) attrib. siegreich; ∼ **team** siegreiche Mannschaft; Siegermannschaft, die; **the ∼ captain** der Kapitän der Siegermannschaft; **(b)** attrib. (bringing victory) den Sieg bringend; ∼ **number** Gewinnzahl, die; **(c)** (charming) einnehmend; gewinnend ⟨Lächeln⟩

'winning post n. (Sport) Zielpfosten, der

winnings /'wɪnɪŋz/ n. pl. Gewinn, der

winter /'wɪntə(r)/ ▶ 1065⌋ **1** n. Winter, der; **in [the] ∼:** im Winter; **last/next ∼:** letzten/nächsten Winter; **the ∼ of 1947–8** or **of 1947** der Winter 1947–48 od. [des Jahres] 1947; **∼'s day** Wintertag, der. **2** attrib. adj. Winter-. **3** v.i. den Winter verbringen; ⟨Truppe, Tier:⟩ überwintern

winter: ∼ **'sport** n. (a) usu. in pl. Wintersport, der; **(b)** (particular sport) Wintersportart, die; ∼ **time** n. Winter[s]zeit, die; **in [the] ∼time** im Winter

wintry /'wɪntrɪ/ adj. (a) winterlich; rau ⟨Klima⟩; kalt ⟨Wind⟩; ∼ **shower** Schneegestöber, das; **cold and ∼:** winterlich kalt; **(b)** (fig.) frostig ⟨Lächeln⟩

wipe /waɪp/ v.t. (a) abwischen; [auf]wischen ⟨Fußboden⟩; (dry) abtrocknen; ∼ **one's mouth** sich (Dat.) den Mund abwischen; ∼ **one's brow/eyes/nose** sich (Dat.) die Stirn wischen/die Tränen abwischen/die Nase abwischen; ∼ **one's feet/shoes** [sich (Dat.)] die Füße/Schuhe abtreten; ∼ **sb./sth. clean/dry** jmdn./etw. abwischen/abtrocknen; **(b)** (get rid of) [ab]wischen; löschen ⟨Bandaufnahme⟩; ∼ **one's/sb.'s tears/the tears from one's/sb.'s eyes** sich/jmdm. die Tränen abwischen/aus den Augen wischen

∼ **a'way** v.t. wegwischen; ∼ **away a tear** sich (Dat.) eine Träne abwischen

∼ **'down** v.t. abwischen; (dry) abtrocknen

∼ **'off** v.t. (a) (remove) wegwischen; löschen ⟨Bandaufnahme⟩; **(b)** (pay off) zurückzahlen ⟨Schulden⟩; ablösen ⟨Hypothek⟩

∼ **'out** v.t. (a) (clean) auswischen; **(b)** (remove) wegwischen; (erase) auslöschen; **(c)** (cancel) tilgen; zunichte machen ⟨Vorteil, Gewinn usw.⟩; **(d)** (destroy, abolish) ausrotten ⟨Rasse, Tierart, Feinde⟩; ausmerzen ⟨Seuche, Korruption, Terrorismus⟩; **(e)** (coll.: murder) aus dem Weg räumen

∼ **'over** v.t. wischen über (+ Akk.)

∼ **'up** v.t. (a) aufwischen; **(b)** (dry) abtrocknen

wiper /'waɪpə(r)/ n. (Motor Veh.) Wischer, der

'wiper blade n. (Motor Veh.) Wischerblatt, das

wire /waɪə(r)/ **1** n. (a) (Motor Veh.) Draht, der; **go down to the ∼** (fig.) ⟨Wettkampf, Rennen, usw.:⟩ bis zuletzt offen sein; **this test of nerves will go down to the ∼:** dies wird eine Nervenzerreißprobe bis zum Äußersten; **(b)** (barrier) Drahtverhau, der od. das; (fence) Drahtzaun, der; **(c)** (Electr., Teleph.) Leitung, die; **a piece** or **length of ∼:** ein Stück [Leitungs]draht; **telephone/telegraph ∼:** Telefon-/Telegrafenleitung, die; **get one's** or **the ∼s crossed** (fig.) auf der Leitung stehen (ugs.); **(d)** (coll.: telegram) Telegramm, das. **2** v.t. (a) (fasten with ∼) mit Draht zusammenbinden; (stiffen with ∼) mit Draht versteifen; ∼ **sth. together** etw. mit Draht verbinden; **(b)** (Electr.) ∼ **sth. to sth.** etw. an etw. (Akk.) anschließen; ∼ **a house** (lay wiring circuits) in einem Haus die Stromleitungen legen; **(c)** (coll.: telegraph) ∼ **sb.** jmdn. od. an jmdn. telegrafieren; ∼ **money** Geld telegrafisch überweisen

∼ **'up** v.t. (Electr.) anschließen (**to** an + Akk.)

wire: ∼ **'brush** n. Drahtbürste, die; **∼-cutters** n. pl. Drahtschneider, der

wireless /'waɪəlɪs/ **1** adj. (Brit.) ⇒ **radio 2**. **2** n. (a) (Brit.) Radio, das; **(b)** (telegraphy) Funk, der; **by ∼:** über Funk (Akk.)

wire: ∼ **'netting** ⇒ netting; ∼ **'rope** n. Drahtseil, das; **∼-strippers** n. pl. Abisolierzange, die; **∼-tapping** ⇒ phone-tapping; ∼ **'wool** n. Stahlwolle, die

wiring /'waɪərɪŋ/ n., no pl., no indef. art. (Electr.) [elektrische] Leitungen Pl.

wisdom /'wɪzdəm/ n., no pl. (a) Weisheit, die; **worldly ∼:** Weltklugheit, die; **(b)** (prudence) Klugheit, die; **where is the ∼ of such a move/in doing that?** was für einen Sinn hat solch ein Schritt/hat es, das zu tun?; **words of ∼:** weise Worte Pl.; (advice) weise Ratschläge Pl.

'wisdom tooth n. Weisheitszahn, der

wise /waɪz/ adj. (a) weise; vernünftig ⟨Meinung⟩; **be ∼ after the event** so tun, als hätte man es immer schon gewusst; **(b)** (prudent) klug ⟨Vorgehensweise⟩; vernünftig ⟨Lebensweise, Praktik⟩; **(c)** (informed) **be none the** or **no/not much ∼r** kein bisschen od. nicht/nicht viel klüger als vorher sein; **without anyone's being [any] the ∼r** ohne dass es jemand merkt; **(d)** (coll.: aware) **be ∼ to sb./sth.** jmdn./etw. kennen; **get ∼ to sb./sb.'s tricks** jmdm. auf die Schliche kommen; **get ∼ to sth.** etw. spitzkriegen (ugs.); **put sb. ∼:** jmdn. die Augen öffnen; **put sb. ∼ to sth.** jmdn. über etw. (Akk.) aufklären; **put sb. ∼ to sb.** jmdm., was jmdn. betrifft, die Augen öffnen

∼ **'up** (Amer. coll.) **1** v.t. ∼ **sb. up** [to sth.] jmdn. [über etw.] aufklären. **2** v.i. ∼ **up to sth.** sich (Dat.) über etw. klar werden; ∼ **up to sb./sb.'s tricks** jmdm. auf die Schliche kommen

-wise adv. in comb. (a) (in the direction of) **length∼:** der Länge nach; **clock∼:** im Uhrzeigersinn; **(b)** (coll.: as regards) -mäßig; was … betrifft; **weather∼:** wettermäßig;

was das Wetter betrifft; **health~:** in puncto Gesundheit; gesundheitlich

wise: **~crack** (coll.) **1** n. witzige Bemerkung; **2** v.i. witzeln; **~ guy** n. (coll.) Klugscheißer, der (salopp abwertend)

wisely /'waɪzlɪ/ adv. weise; (prudently) klug; as sentence-modifier klugerweise

wish /wɪʃ/ **1** v.t. **(a)** (desire, hope) wünschen; **I ~ I was** or **were rich** ich wollte od. (geh.) wünschte, ich wäre reich; **I do ~ he would come** wenn er nur kommen würde; **I ~ you would shut up** es wäre mir lieb, wenn du den Mund hieltest; **'~ you were here'** (on postcard) „schade, dass du nicht hier bist"; **(b)** with inf. (want) wünschen (geh.); **I ~ to go** ich möchte od. will gehen; **I ~ you to stay** ich möchte od. will, dass du bleibst; **(c) ▶ 836]** (say that one hopes sb. will have sth.) wünschen; **~ sb. luck/success** etc. jmdm. Glück/Erfolg usw. wünschen; **~ sb. good morning/a happy birthday** jmdm. guten Morgen sagen/zum Geburtstag gratulieren; **~ sb. ill/well** jmdm. [etwas] Schlechtes/alles Gute wünschen; **(d)** (coll.: foist) **~ sb./sth. on sb.** jmdm. jmdn./etw. aufhalsen (ugs.). **2** v.i. wünschen; **come on, ~!** nun, wünsch dir was!; **~ for sth.** sich (Dat.) etw. wünschen; **what more could one ~ for?** was will man mehr?; **they have everything they could possibly ~ for** sie haben alles, was sie sich (Dat.) nur wünschen können. **3** n. **(a)** Wunsch, der; **her ~ is that ...:** es ist ihr Wunsch od. sie wünscht, dass ...; **I have no [great/particular] ~ to go** ich habe keine [große/besondere] Lust zu gehen; **make a ~** sich (Dat.) etwas wünschen; **with best/[all] good ~es, with every good ~:** mit den besten/allen guten Wünschen **(on, for** zu); **(b)** (thing desired) **get** or **have one's ~:** seinen Wunsch erfüllt bekommen; **at last he has [got] his ~:** endlich ist sein Wunsch in Erfüllung gegangen

~ a'way v.t. wegwünschen

'wishbone n. (Ornith.) Gabelbein, das

wishful /'wɪʃfl/ adj. sehnsuchtsvoll (geh.) ⟨Blick, Verlangen⟩; **~ thinking** Wunschdenken, das

'wishing well n. Wunschbrunnen, der

wishy-washy /'wɪʃɪwɒʃɪ/ adj. labberig (ugs.); (fig.) lasch

wisp /wɪsp/ n. (of straw) Büschel, das; **~ of hair** Haarsträhne, die; **~ of cloud/smoke** Wolkenfetzen, der/ Rauchfahne, die

wistful /'wɪstfl/ adj. wehmütig; melancholisch ⟨Person, Typ⟩; traurig ⟨Augen⟩

wit¹ /wɪt/ n. **(a)** (humour) Witz, der; **have a ready ~:** schlagfertig sein; **(b)** (intelligence) Geist, der; **battle of ~s** intellektueller Schlagabtausch; **be at one's ~'s** or **~s' end** sich (Dat.) keinen Rat mehr wissen; **collect** or **gather one's ~s** zu sich kommen; **drive sb. out of his/her ~s** jmdn. um den Verstand bringen; **frighten** or **scare sb. out of his/her ~s** jmdn. Todesangst einjagen; **be frightened** or **scared out of one's ~s** Todesangst haben; **have/keep one's ~s about one** auf Draht sein (ugs.) /nicht den Kopf verlieren; **(c)** (person) geistreicher Mensch

wit² v.i. **to ~:** nämlich

witch /wɪtʃ/ n. (lit. or fig.) Hexe, die

witch: **~craft** n., no pl. Hexerei, die; **~ doctor** n. Medizinmann, der; **~-hunt** n. (lit. or fig.) Hexenjagd, die **(for** auf + Akk.)

with /wɪð/ prep. **(a)** mit; **put sth. ~ sth.** etw. zu etw. stellen/legen; **have no pen to write ~:** nichts zum Schreiben haben; **I'll be ~ you in a minute** ich komme gleich; **be ~ it** (coll.) up to date sein; **not be ~ sb.** (coll.: fail to understand) jmdm. nicht folgen können; **I'm not ~ you** (coll.) ich komme nicht mit; **be one ~ sb./sth.** mit jmdm./etw. eins sein; **(b)** (in the care or possession of) **I have no money ~ me** ich habe kein Geld dabei od. bei mir; **(c)** (owing to) vor (+ Dat.); **tremble ~ fear** vor Angst zittern; **(d)** (displaying) mit; **~ courage** mutig; **handle ~ care** vorsichtig behandeln; **(e)** (while having) bei; **sleep ~ the window open** bei offenem Fenster schlafen; **speak ~ one's mouth full** mit vollem Mund sprechen; **(f)** (in regard to) **be patient ~ sb.** mit jmdm. geduldig sein; **what do you want ~ me?** was wollen Sie von mir?; **how are things ~ you?** wie geht es dir?; **what can he want ~ it?** was mag er damit vorhaben?; **(g)** (at the same time as, in the same way as) mit; **~ that** damit; **(h)** (employed by) bei; **(i)** (despite) trotz; see also **will² 1 d**

with'draw 1 v.t., forms as **draw 1: (a)** (pull back, retract) zurückziehen; **(b)** (remove) nehmen (fig.) **(from** aus); abziehen ⟨Truppen⟩ **(from** aus); **(c)** abheben ⟨Geld⟩. **2** v.i., forms as **draw 1** sich zurückziehen

withdrawal /wɪð'drɔːəl/ n. **(a)** Zurücknahme, die; **(b)** (removal) (of privilege) Entzug, der; (of troops) Abzug, der; (of money) Abhebung, die

with'drawal slip n. Auszahlungsschein, der

with'drawn adj. (unsociable) verschlossen

wither /'wɪðə(r)/ **1** v.t. verdorren lassen. **2** v.i. [ver]welken

~ a'way v.i. (lit. or fig.) dahinwelken (geh.)

~ 'up v.i. [ver]welken

withered /'wɪðəd/ adj. verwelkt ⟨Gras, Pflanze⟩; verkrüppelt ⟨Gliedmaße⟩

withering /'wɪðərɪŋ/ adj. vernichtend ⟨Blick, Bemerkung⟩; sengend ⟨Hitze⟩

with'hold v.t., forms as **hold²: (a)** (refuse to grant) verweigern; versagen (geh.); **(b)** (hold back) verschweigen ⟨Wahrheit⟩; **~ sth. from sb.** jmdm. etw. vorenthalten

within /wɪ'ðɪn/ prep. **(a)** (on the inside of) innerhalb; **(b)** (not beyond) im Rahmen (+ Gen.); **stay/be ~ the law** den Boden des Gesetzes nicht verlassen; **(c)** (not farther off than) **~ eight miles of sth.** acht Meilen im Umkreis von etw.; **we were ~ eight miles of our destination when ...:** wir waren kaum noch acht Meilen von unserem Ziel entfernt, als ...; **(d)** (subject to) innerhalb; **work ~ certain conditions** unter bestimmten Bedingungen arbeiten; **(e)** (in a time no longer than) innerhalb; binnen; **within an/the hour** innerhalb einer Stunde

without /wɪ'θaʊt/ prep. ohne; **~ doing sth.** ohne etw. zu tun; **can you do it ~ his knowing?** kannst du das machen, ohne dass er davon weiß?

with'stand v.t., **withstood** /wɪð'stʊd/ standhalten (+Dat.); aushalten ⟨Beanspruchung, hohe Temperaturen⟩

witless /'wɪtlɪs/ adj. **(a)** (foolish) töricht; **(b)** (insane) geistesgestört; **(c)** (dull-witted) beschränkt

witness /'wɪtnɪs/ **1** n. **(a)** Zeuge, der/Zeugin, die **(of, to** Gen.); **(b)** ⇒ **eyewitness; (c)** no pl. (evidence) Zeugnis, das (geh.); **bear ~ to** or **of sth.** etw. bezeugen; (fig.) von etw. zeugen. **2** v.t. **(a)** (see) **~ sth.** Zeuge/Zeugin einer Sache (Gen.) sein; **they have ~ed many changes** sie haben viele Veränderungen erlebt; **(b)** (attest genuineness of) bestätigen ⟨Unterschrift, Echtheit eines Dokuments⟩

witness: **~ box** (Brit.), **~-stand** (Amer.) ns. Zeugenstand, der

witter /'wɪtə(r)/ v.i. (Brit. coll.) **~ [on]** quatschen (ugs. abwertend)

witticism /'wɪtɪsɪzm/ n. Witzelei, die

wittingly /'wɪtɪŋlɪ/ adv. wissentlich

witty /'wɪtɪ/ adj. **(a)** witzig; **(b)** (possessing wit) geistreich ⟨Person⟩

wives pl. of **wife**

wizard /'wɪzəd/ n. **(a)** (sorcerer) Zauberer, der; **(b)** (very skilled person) Genie, das **(at** in + Dat.)

wizened /'wɪzənd/ adj. runz[e]lig

wobble /'wɒbl/ v.i. **(a)** (rock) wackeln; ⟨Kompassnadel:⟩ zittern; **(b)** (go unsteadily) wackeln (ugs.)

wobbly /'wɒblɪ/ adj. wack[e]lig; zitt[e]rig ⟨Schrift, Hand, Stimme⟩

woe /wəʊ/ n. (arch./literary/joc.) **(a)** (distress) Jammer, der; **a tale of ~:** eine jammervolle Geschichte; **~ betide you!** wehe dir!; **(b)** in pl. (troubles) Jammer, der

woebegone /'wəʊbɪgɒn/ adj. jammervoll

woeful /'wəʊfl/ adj. beklagenswert

wog /wɒg/ n. (sl. derog.) Kanake, der (ugs. abwertend)

woke, woken ⇒ **wake¹ 1, 2**

wolf /wʊlf/ **1** n., pl. **wolves** /wʊlvz/ (Zool.) Wolf, der; **keep the ~ from the door** (fig.) den größten Hunger stillen; **be a ~ in sheep's clothing** (fig.) ein Wolf im Schafspelz sein. **2** v.t. **~ [down]** verschlingen

'wolf-whistle 1 n. anerkennender Pfiff. **2** v.i. anerkennend pfeifen

wolves *pl. of* **wolf 1**

woman /ˈwʊmən/ *n.*, *pl.* **women** /ˈwɪmɪn/ **(a)** Frau, *die;* **women and children first** Frauen und Kinder zuerst; **a ∼'s work is never done** eine Frau hat immer etwas zu tun; **that's ∼'s work** das ist Frauenarbeit; **women's page** Frauenseite, *die;* **women's [toilet]** Damen[toilette], *die;* **the other ∼:** die Geliebte; **(b)** *attrib.* (female) weiblich; **∼ friend** Freundin, *die;* **∼ doctor** Ärztin, *die;* **a ∼ driver** eine Frau am Steuer; **(c)** *no pl.* **[the]** ∼ (an average ∼) die Frau

womanhood /ˈwʊmənhʊd/ *n.*, *no pl.* Weiblichkeit, *die*

womanizer /ˈwʊmənaɪzə(r)/ *n.* Schürzenjäger, *der*

womanliness /ˈwʊmənlɪnɪs/ *n.*, *no pl.* Fraulichkeit, *die*

womanly /ˈwʊmənlɪ/ *adj.* fraulich; weiblich

womb /wuːm/ *n.* ▶ 672 (Anat.) Gebärmutter, *die;* **in her ∼:** in ihrem Leib (geh.)

wombat /ˈwɒmbæt/ *n.* (Zool.) Wombat, *der*

women *pl. of* **woman**

Women: w∼folk *n. pl.* Frauen; **∼'s 'Institute** *n.* (Brit.) britischer Frauenverband; **∼'s 'Lib** (coll.) ⇨ **∼'s Liberation;** **∼'s Libber** /ˈwɪmɪnz ˈlɪbə(r)/ *n.* (coll.) Emanze, *die* (ugs. abwertend); Frauenrechtlerin, *die;* **∼'s Libe'ration** *n.* die Frauenbewegung; **∼'s movement** *n.* Frauenbewegung, *die;* **∼'s 'refuge** *n.* Frauenhaus, *das;* **w∼'s 'rights** *n. pl.* die Rechte der Frau

won ⇨ **win 1, 2**

wonder /ˈwʌndə(r)/ **1** *n.* **(a)** (extraordinary thing) Wunder, *das;* **do** *or* **work ∼s** Wunder tun *od.* wirken; (fig.) Wunder wirken; **∼s will never cease** (iron.) Wunder über Wunder!; **small** *or* **what** *or* **[it is] no ∼ [that]** …: [es ist] kein Wunder, dass …; **the ∼ is,** …: das Erstaunliche ist, …; **(b)** (marvellously successful person) Wunderkind, *das;* (marvellously successful thing) Wunderding, *das;* **boy/girl ∼:** Wunderkind, *das;* **the seven ∼s of the world** die sieben Weltwunder; **(c)** *no pl.* (feeling) Staunen, *das;* **be lost in ∼:** in Staunen versunken sein. **2** *adj.* Wunder-. **3** *v.i.* sich wundern; staunen (**at** über + *Akk.*); **that's not to be ∼ed at** darüber braucht man sich nicht zu wundern; **I shouldn't ∼ [if …]** (coll.) es würde mich nicht wundern[, wenn …]. **4** *v.t.* **(a)** sich fragen; **I ∼ what the time is** wie viel Uhr mag es wohl sein?; **I was ∼ing what to do** ich habe mir überlegt, was ich tun soll; **I ∼ whether I might open the window** dürfte ich vielleicht das Fenster öffnen?; **she ∼ed if …** (enquired) sie fragte, ob …; **I ∼ if you'd mind if …?** würde es Ihnen etwas ausmachen, wenn …?; **(b)** (be surprised to find) ∼ **[that]** …: sich wundern, dass …

wonderful /ˈwʌndəfl/ *adj.* wunderbar; wundervoll

wonderfully /ˈwʌndəfəlɪ/ *adv.* wunderbar

wondering /ˈwʌndərɪŋ/ *adj.* staunend

'wonderland *n.* **(a)** (wonderful place) Paradies, *das;* **(b)** (fairyland) Wunderland, *das*

wonderment /ˈwʌndəmənt/ *n.*, *no pl.* Verwunderung, *die*

wonky /ˈwɒŋkɪ/ *adj.* (Brit. coll.) wack[e]lig; (crooked) schief

wont /wəʊnt/ **1** *pred. adj.* (arch./literary) gewohnt; **as he was ∼ to say** wie er zu sagen pflegte. **2** *n.* (literary) Gepflogenheit, *die* (geh.); **as was her ∼:** wie sie zu tun pflegte

won't /wəʊnt/ (coll.) = **will not;** ⇨ **will¹**

woo /wuː/ *v.t.* **(a)** (literary: court) ∼ **sb.** um jmdn. werben (geh.); **(b)** (seek to win) umwerben ⟨Kunden, Wähler⟩; **∼ away** abwerben ⟨Arbeitskräfte⟩

wood /wʊd/ *n.* **(a)** *in sing. or pl.* (area with trees) Wald, *der;* **sb. cannot see the ∼ for the trees** (fig.) jmd. sieht den Wald vor [lauter] Bäumen nicht (scherzh.); **be out of the ∼** (Brit.) *or* (Amer.) **∼s** (fig.) über den Berg sein (ugs.); **(b)** (substance, material) Holz, *das;* **touch ∼** (Brit.), **knock [on] ∼** (Amer.) unberufen!

'wood-burning *attrib. adj.* holzbefeuert

wooded /ˈwʊdɪd/ *adj.* bewaldet

wooden /ˈwʊdn/ *adj.* **(a)** hölzern ⟨Brücke, Spielzeug⟩; Holz⟨haus, -brücke, -bein, -griff, -spielzeug⟩; **(b)** (fig.: stiff) hölzern

wooden 'spoon *n.* (fig.) Trostpreis, *der* (für den Letzten eines Wettbewerbs, oft in ironischer Weise überreicht)

wood: ∼land /ˈwʊdlənd/ *n.* Waldland, *das;* Wald, *der;* **∼louse** *n.* (Zool.) Kellerassel, *die;* **∼pecker** *n.* Specht, *der;* **∼ pigeon** *n.* Ringeltaube, *die;* **∼ screw** *n.* Holzschraube, *die;* **∼shed** *n.* Holzschuppen, *der;* **∼wind** *n.* (Mus.) Holzblasinstrument, *das;* **the ∼wind [section]** die Holzbläser *Pl.;* **∼wind instrument** Holzblasinstrument, *das;* **∼work** *n.*, *no pl.* **(a)** (making things out of ∼) Arbeiten mit Holz; **(b)** (things made of ∼) Holzarbeit[en]; **∼worm** *n.*, *no pl.*, *no art.* Holzwurm; **it's got ∼worm** da ist der Holzwurm drin (ugs.)

woody /ˈwʊdɪ/ *adj.* **(a)** (well-wooded) waldreich; **(b)** (consisting of wood) holzig ⟨Pflanze[nteil], Wurzel⟩; Holz⟨stamm⟩

woof /wʊf/ *n.* [dumpfes] Bellen; ∼ **∼!** **went the dog** wau, wau! bellte der Hund

woofer /ˈwʊfə(r)/ *n.* Bass[lautsprecher], *der*

wool /wʊl/ *n.* **(a)** Wolle, *die;* attrib. Woll-; **pull the ∼ over sb.'s eyes** jmdm. etwas vormachen (ugs.); **(b)** (garments) Wolle, *die*

woollen (Amer.: **woolen**) /ˈwʊlən/ **1** *adj.* wollen. **2** *n. in pl.* (garments) Wollsachen *Pl.*

woolly /ˈwʊlɪ/ **1** *adj.* **(a)** wollig; Woll⟨pullover, -mütze⟩; **(b)** (confused) verschwommen. **2** *n.* (coll.) **(a)** (Brit.: knitted garment) **[winter] woollies** [Winter]wollsachen *Pl.* (ugs.); **a ∼:** ein Wollpullover/eine Wolljacke; **(b)** *in pl.* (Amer.: undergarments) wollene Unterwäsche

word /wɜːd/ **1** *n.* **(a)** Wort, *das;* **∼s cannot describe it** mit Worten lässt sich das nicht beschreiben; **in a** *or* **one ∼** (fig.) mit einem Wort; **[not] in so many ∼s** [nicht] ausdrücklich; **in other ∼s** mit anderen Worten; **not a ∼ of sth.** kein Wort von etw.; **bad luck/drunk is not the ∼ for it** Pech/betrunken ist gar kein Ausdruck dafür (ugs.); **that's not the ∼ I would have used** das ist gar kein Ausdruck (ugs.); **put sth. into ∼s** etw. in Worte fassen; **∼ for ∼:** Wort für Wort; **without a** *or* **one/another ∼:** ohne ein/ein weiteres Wort; **too funny** *etc.* **for ∼s** unsagbar komisch *usw.; see also* **fail 2 e; play 1 b, 2 a; (b)** (thing said) Wort, *das;* **hard ∼s** harte Worte; **exchange** *or* **have ∼s** einen Wortwechsel haben; **a man of few ∼s** ein Mann von wenig Worten; **have a ∼ [with sb.] about sth.** [mit jmdm.] über etw. (Akk.) sprechen; **could I have a ∼ [with you]?** kann ich dich mal sprechen?; **have ∼s with sb.** sich mit jmdm. streiten; **say a few ∼s** ein paar Worte sprechen; **suit the action to the ∼:** seinen Worten Taten folgen lassen; **it's his ∼ against mine** sein Wort steht gegen meins; **take sb. at his/her ∼:** jmdn. beim Wort nehmen; **∼ of command/ advice** Kommando, *das*/Rat, *der;* **at a ∼ of command** auf Befehl; **the W∼ [of God]** (Bible) das Wort [Gottes]; **put in a good ∼ for sb. [with sb.]** [bei jmdm.] ein [gutes] Wort für jmdn. einlegen; **(c)** (promise) Wort, *das;* **doubt sb.'s ∼:** jmds. Wort in Zweifel ziehen; **give [sb.] one's ∼:** jmdm. sein Wort geben; **keep/break one's ∼:** sein Wort halten/brechen; **upon my ∼!** (dated) meiner Treu! (veralt.); **my ∼!** meine Güte!; *see also* **take 1 v; (d)** *no pl.* (speaking) Wort, *das;* **by ∼ of mouth** durch mündliche Mitteilung; **(e)** *in pl.* (text of song, spoken by actor) Text, *der;* **(f)** *no pl.*, *no indef. art.* (news) Nachricht, *die;* **∼ had just reached them** die Nachricht hatte sie gerade erreicht; **∼ has it** *or* **the ∼ is [that]** …: es gibt das Gerücht, dass …; **∼ went round that** …: es ging das Gerücht, dass …; **send/leave ∼ that/of when** …: Nachricht geben/eine Nachricht hinterlassen, dass/wann …; **is there any ∼ from her?** hat sie schon von sich hören lassen?; **(g)** (command) Kommando, *das;* **just say the ∼:** sag nur ein Wort; **at the ∼ 'run', you run!** bei dem Wort „rennen" rennst du!; **(h)** (password) Parole, *die* (Milit.); **give the ∼:** die Parole sagen. **2** *v.t.* formulieren

'word game *n.* Buchstabenspiel, *das*

wording /ˈwɜːdɪŋ/ *n.* Formulierung, *die;* Wortwahl, *die;* **the exact ∼ of the contract** der genaue Wortlaut des Vertrages

word: ∼ order *n.* (Ling.) Wortstellung, *die;* **∼-'perfect** *adj.* **be ∼-perfect** seinen Text beherrschen; **∼ processing** *n.* Textverarbeitung, *die;* **∼ processor** *n.* Textverarbeitungssystem, *das*

wordy /'wɜːdɪ/ *adj.* weitschweifig

wore ⇒ wear 2, 3

work /wɜːk/ **1** *n.* (a) *no pl., no indef. art.* Arbeit, *die;* at ∿ (engaged in ∿ing) bei der Arbeit; (fig.: operating) am Werk *(see also* **e**); **be at** ∿ **on sth.** an etw. (*Dat.*) arbeiten; (fig.) auf etw. (*Akk.*) wirken; **set to** ∿ 〈*Person:*〉 sich an die Arbeit machen; **set sb. to** ∿: jmdn. an die Arbeit schicken; **all** ∿ **and no play** immer nur arbeiten; **have one's** ∿ **cut out** viel zu tun haben; sich ranhalten müssen (ugs.); (b) (thing made or achieved) Werk, *das;* **a good day's** ∿: eine gute Tagesleistung; **do a good day's** ∿: ein tüchtiges Stück Arbeit hinter sich bringen; **is that all your own** ∿? hast du das alles selbst gemacht?; ∿ **of art** Kunstwerk, *das;* (c) (book, piece of music) Werk, *das;* **a** ∿ **of reference/literature/art** ein Nachschlagewerk/literarisches Werk/Kunstwerk; (d) *in pl.* (of author or composer) Werke; (e) (employment) Arbeit, *die,* **out of** ∿: arbeitslos; **ohne Arbeit; be in** ∿: eine Stelle haben; **go out to** ∿: arbeiten gehen; **at** ∿ (place of employment) auf der Arbeit *(see also* **a**); **from** ∿: von der Arbeit; (f) *in pl., usu. constr. as sing.* (factory) Werk, *das;* (g) *in pl.* (Mil.) Werke; Befestigungen; (h) *in pl.* (operations of building etc.) Arbeiten; (i) *in pl.* (machine's operative parts) Werk, *das;* (j) *in pl.* (coll.: all that can be included) **the [whole/full]** ∿s der ganze Kram (ugs.); **give sb. the** ∿s (fig.) (give sb. the best possible treatment) jmdn. richtig verwöhnen (ugs.); (give sb. the worst possible treatment) jmdn. fertig machen (salopp). **2** *v.i.,* ∿ed *or* (arch./literary) **wrought** /rɔːt/ (a) arbeiten; ∿ **to rule** Dienst nach Vorschrift machen; ∿ **for a cause** *etc.* für eine Sache *usw.* arbeiten; ∿ **against sth.** (impede) einer Sache (*Dat.*) entgegenstehen; (b) (function effectively) funktionieren; 〈*Charme:*〉 wirken (on auf + *Akk.*); **make the washing machine/ television** ∿: die Waschmaschine/den Fernsehapparat in Ordnung bringen; (c) 〈*Rad, Getriebe, Kette:*〉 laufen; (d) (be craftsman) ∿ **in a material** mit *od.* (fachspr.) in einem Material arbeiten; (e) 〈*Faktoren, Einflüsse:*〉 wirken (on auf + *Akk.*); ∿ **against** arbeiten gegen; *see also* ∿ **on;** (f) (make its/one's way) sich schieben (fig.) sich zu einer Frage vorarbeiten. **3** *v.t.,* ∿ed *or* (arch./literary) **wrought** (a) (operate) bedienen 〈*Maschine*〉; fahren 〈*Schiff*〉; betätigen 〈*Bremse*〉; ∿**ed by electricity** elektrisch betrieben; (b) (get labour from) arbeiten lassen; (c) (get material from) ausbeuten 〈*Steinbruch, Grube*〉; (d) (operate in or on) 〈*Vertreter:*〉 bereisen; (e) (control) steuern; (f) (effect) bewirken 〈*Änderung*〉; wirken 〈*Wunder*〉; ∿ **it** *or* **things so that** ... (coll.) es deichseln, dass ... (ugs.); (g) (cause to go gradually) führen; ∿ **one's way up/into sth.** sich hocharbeiten/in etw. (*Akk.*) hineinarbeiten; (h) (get gradually) bringen; ∿ **oneself into a position** sich in eine Position hocharbeiten; (i) (knead, stir) ∿ **sth. into sth.** etw. zu etw. verarbeiten; (mix in) etw. unter etw. (*Akk.*) rühren; (j) (gradually excite) ∿ **oneself into a state/a rage** sich aufregen/in einen Wutanfall hineinsteigern; (k) (make by needle∿ etc.) arbeiten; aufsticken 〈*Muster*〉 (on auf + *Akk.*); (l) (purchase, obtain with labour) abarbeiten; (fig.) ∿ **one's keep** für sein Geld etwas leisten; **she** ∿**ed her way through college** sie hat sich (*Dat.*) ihr Studium selbst verdient; *see also* **passage f**

∿ **a'way** *v.i.* ∿ **away [at sth.]** [an etw. (*Dat.*)] arbeiten
∿ **'in** *v.t.* (include) hineinbringen; (mix in) hineinrühren; (rub in) einreiben
∿ **'off** *v.t.* (a) (get rid of) loswerden; abreagieren 〈*Wut*〉; ∿ **sth. off on sb./sth.** etw. an jmdm./etw. auslassen; ∿ **off some excess energy** überschüssige Energie loswerden; (b) (pay off) abtragen 〈*Schuld*〉
∿ **on 1** /'--/ *v.t.* (a) (expend effort on) ∿ **on sth.** an etw. (*Dat.*) arbeiten; (b) (use as basis) ∿ **on sth.** von etw. ausgehen; (c) (try to persuade) ∿ **on sb.** jmdn. bearbeiten (ugs.). **2** /-'-/ *v.i.* weiterarbeiten
∿ **'out 1** *v.t.* (a) (find by calculation) ausrechnen; (b) (solve) lösen 〈*Problem, Rechenaufgabe*〉; (c) (resolve) ∿ **things out with sb./for oneself** die Angelegenheit mit jmdm./ sich selbst ausmachen; (d) (devise) ausarbeiten 〈*Plan, Strategie*〉; (e) (make out) herausfinden; (understand) verstehen; **I can't** ∿ **him out** ich werde aus ihm nicht klug; (f) (Mining: exhaust) ausbeuten. **2** *v.i.* (a) (be calculated) **sth.** ∿**s out at £250/[an increase of] 22 %** etw. ergibt 250 Pfund/bedeutet [eine Steigerung von] 22 %; (b) (give definite result) 〈*Gleichung, Rechnung:*〉 aufgehen; (c) (have result) laufen; **things** ∿**ed out [well] in the end** es ist schließlich doch alles gut gegangen; **things didn't** ∿ **out the way we planned** es kam ganz anders, als wir geplant hatten
∿ **through** *v.t.* durcharbeiten
∿ **towards** *v.t.* (lit. or fig.) hinarbeiten auf (+ *Akk.*)
∿ **'up 1** *v.t.* (a) (develop) verarbeiten (into zu); (create) erarbeiten; (b) (excite) aufpeitschen 〈*Menge*〉; **get** ∿**ed up** sich aufregen; ∿ **oneself up into a rage/fury** sich in einen Wutanfall/in Raserei hineinsteigern. **2** *v.i.* (a) ∿ **up to sth.** 〈*Musik:*〉 sich zu etw. steigern; 〈*Geschichte, Film:*〉 auf etw. (*Akk.*) zusteuern; **I'll have to** ∿ **up to it** ich muss darauf hinarbeiten; (b) 〈*Rock usw.:*〉 sich hochschieben

workable /'wɜːkəbl/ *adj.* (a) (capable of being worked) bebaubar 〈*Land*〉; abbauwürdig 〈*Mine*〉; be ∿ 〈*Mörtel:*〉 sich verarbeiten lassen; 〈*Stahl:*〉 sich bearbeiten lassen; 〈*Mine:*〉 sich ausbeuten lassen; (b) (feasible) durchführbar

workaday /'wɜːkədeɪ/ *adj.* alltäglich

workaholic /wɜːkə'hɒlɪk/ *n.* (coll.) arbeitswütiger Mensch; Workaholic, *der* (Psych.); *attrib.* arbeitswütig

work: ∿**bench** *n.* Werkbank, *die;* (of tailor, glazier) Arbeitstisch, *der;* ∿**box** *n.* Nähkasten, *der;* ∿**day** *n.* Werktag, *der*

worker /'wɜːkə(r)/ *n.* (a) Arbeiter, *der*/Arbeiterin, *die;* (b) (Zool.) Arbeiterin, *die*

work: ∿**force** *n.* Belegschaft, *die;* ∿**horse** *n.* (lit. or fig.) Arbeitspferd, *das;* ∿**house** *n.* (Brit. Hist., Amer.) Arbeitshaus, *das*

working /'wɜːkɪŋ/ **1** *n.* (a) Arbeiten, *das;* (b) (way sth. works) Arbeitsweise, *die;* **I cannot follow the** ∿**s of his mind** ich kann seinen Gedankengängen nicht folgen. **2** *attrib. adj.* (a) handlungsfähig 〈*Mehrheit*〉; 〈*Entwurf, Vereinbarung*〉 als Ausgangspunkt; (b) (in employment) arbeitend; werktätig; ∿ **man** (labourer) Arbeiter, *der*

working: ∿**'breakfast** *n.* Arbeitsfrühstück, *das;* ∿**'class** *n.* Arbeiterklasse, *die;* ∿**-class** *adj.* der Arbeiterklasse *nachgestellt;* **sb. is** ∿**-class** jmd. gehört zur Arbeiterklasse; ∿ **clothes** *n. pl.* Arbeitskleidung, *die;* ∿**'day** *n.* (a) (portion of the day) Arbeitstag, *der;* (b) (day when work is done) ⇒ **workday;** ∿ **'hours** *n. pl.* Arbeitszeit, *die;* ∿**'knowledge** *n.* ausreichende Kenntnisse (**of** in + *Dat.*); **sb. with a** ∿ **knowledge of these machines** jmd., der im Umgang mit diesen Maschinen erfahren ist; ∿ **'lunch** *n.* Arbeitsessen, *das;* ∿ **'model** *n.* funktionsfähiges Modell; ∿ **'mother** *n.* berufstätige Mutter; ∿ **'order** *n.* betriebsfähiger Zustand; **be in good** ∿ **order** betriebsbereit sein; ∿ **party** *n.* (Brit.) Arbeitsgruppe, *die;* ∿ **'week** *n.* Arbeitswoche, *die;* **a 35-hour** ∿ **week** eine 35-Stunden-Woche; ∿ **'wife** *n.* berufstätige Ehefrau; ∿ **'woman** *n.* berufstätige Frau

work: ∿**load** *n.* Arbeitslast, *die;* ∿**man** /'wɜːkmən/ *n., pl.* ∿**men** /'wɜːkmən/ Arbeiter, *der;* **council** ∿**man** städtischer Arbeiter; **a bad** ∿**man blames his tools** (prov.) ein schlechter Handwerker schimpft über sein Werkzeug

workmanlike /'wɜːkmənlaɪk/ *adj.* fachmännisch

workmanship /'wɜːkmənʃɪp/ *n., no pl.* (a) (person's skill) handwerkliches Können; (b) (quality of execution) Kunstfertigkeit, *die*

work: ∿**mate** *n.* (Brit.) Arbeitskollege, *der*/-kollegin, *die;* ∿**out** *n.* [Fitness]training, *das;* **have a good** ∿**out** hart trainieren; **go for a** ∿**out** zum [Fitness]training gehen; ∿**people** *n. pl.* Arbeiter *Pl.;* ∿ **permit** *n.* Arbeitserlaubnis, *die;* ∿**place** *n.* Arbeitsplatz, *der;* ∿**sheet** *n.* (a) (recording ∿ done etc.) Arbeitszettel, *der;* (b) (for student) Formular mit Prüfungsfragen; ∿**shop** *n.* (a) (room) Werkstatt, *die;* (building) Werk, *das;* (b) (meeting) Workshop, *der;* Arbeitstreffen, *das;* **drama** ∿**shop** Theaterworkshop, *der;* ∿**-shy** *adj.* arbeitsscheu; ∿**station** *n.* (Computing) Workstation, *die;* ∿ **surface,** ∿**top** *ns.* Arbeitsplatte, *die;* ∿**-to-'rule** *n.* Dienst nach Vorschrift

world /wɜːld/ *n.* (a) Welt, *die;* **go/sail round the** ∿: eine Weltreise machen/die Welt umsegeln; **money makes the** ∿ **go round** Geld regiert die Welt; **it's the same the** ∿ **over** es ist doch überall das Gleiche; **the eyes of the** ∿

are on them die Welt blickt auf sie; [**all**] **the ~ over, all over the ~:** in *od.* auf der ganzen Welt; **lead the ~ [in sth.]** [in etw. (*Dat.*)] führend in der Welt sein; **the Old/New W~:** die Alte/Neue Welt; **who/what in the ~ was it?** wer/was in aller Welt war es? (ugs.); **how in the ~ was it that …?** wie in aller Welt (ugs.) war es möglich, dass …?; **nothing in the ~ would persuade me** um nichts in der Welt ließe ich mich überreden; **not for anything in the ~:** um nichts in der Welt; **look for all the ~ as if …:** geradezu aussehen, als ob …; **in a ~ of one's own** in einer anderen Welt (fig.); **not do sth. for the whole ~:** etw. um alles in der Welt nicht tun; **be all the ~ to sb.** jmdm. das Wichtigste/Liebste auf der Welt sein; **think the ~ of sb.** große Stücke auf jmdn. halten (ugs.); **all alone in the ~:** ganz allein auf der Welt; **sb. is not long for this ~:** jmds. Tage sind gezählt; **out of this ~** (fig. coll.) fantastisch (ugs.); **come into the ~:** auf die Welt kommen; **the best of all possible ~s** die beste aller Welten; **get the best of both ~s** am meisten profitieren; **the ~'s end, the end of the ~:** das Ende der Welt; **it's not the end of the ~** (iron.) davon geht die Welt nicht unter (ugs.); **know/have seen a lot of the ~:** die Welt kennen/viel von der Welt gesehen haben; **see the ~:** die Welt kennen lernen; **a man/woman of the ~:** ein Mann/ eine Frau mit Welterfahrung; **go up/come down in the ~:** [gesellschaftlich] aufsteigen/absteigen; *attrib.* **~ politics** Weltpolitik, *die;* (**b**) (domain) **the literary/sporting/ animal ~:** die literarische Welt (geh.) /die Welt (geh.) des Sports/die Tierwelt; **the ~ of letters/art/sport** die Welt (geh.) der Literatur/Kunst/des Sports; (**c**) (vast amount) **it will do him a** *or* **the ~ of good** es wird ihm unendlich gut tun; **a ~ of difference** ein weltweiter Unterschied; **a ~ away from sth.** Welten von etw. entfernt; **they are ~s apart in their views** ihre Ansichten sind Welten voneinander entfernt

world: W~ Bank *n.* Weltbank, *die;* **~-beater** *n.* **be a ~-beater** zur Spitzenklasse gehören; **~ 'champion** *n.* Weltmeister, *der/*-meisterin, *die;* **W~ 'Cup** *n.* (Sport) Worldcup, *der;* **~-famous** *adj.* weltberühmt

worldly /'wɜ:ldlɪ/ *adj.* weltlich; weltlich eingestellt ‹*Person*›

world: ~ 'power *n.* Weltmacht, *die;* **~ 'record** *n.* Weltrekord, *der; attrib.* **~ record holder** Weltrekordhalter, *der/*-halterin, *die;* **~-shaking** *adj.* welterschütternd; **~ 'war** *n.* Weltkrieg, *der;* **the First/Second W~ War, W~ War I/II** der Erste/Zweite Weltkrieg; der 1./2. Weltkrieg; **~wide** *adj.* weltweit *nicht präd.;* **2** /'-'-/ *adv.* weltweit; **W~ Wide 'Web** *n.* (Computing) World-Wide Web, *das*

worm /wɜ:m/ **1** *n.* (**a**) Wurm, *der;* [**even**] **a ~ will turn** (prov.) auch der Wurm krümmt sich, wenn er getreten wird (Spr.); (**b**) *in pl.* (intestinal parasites) Würmer. **2** *v.t.* (**a**) **~ oneself into sb.'s favour** sich in jmds. Gunst schleichen; (**b**) (draw by crafty persistence) **~ sth. out of sb.** etw. aus jmdm. herausbringen (ugs.). **3** *v.i.* sich winden

worm: ~-eaten *adj.* wurmstichig; (fig.) vom Zahn der Zeit angenagt; **~'s-eye 'view** *n.* Froschperspektive, *die* (auch fig.)

worn ⇒ **wear** 2, 3

'worn-out *attrib. adj.* abgetragen ‹*Kleidungsstück*›; abgenutzt ‹*Teppich*›; abgedroschen ‹*Redensart, Ausdruck*›; erschöpft, (ugs.) erledigt ‹*Person*›

worried /'wʌrɪd/ *adj.* besorgt; **give sb. a ~ look** jmdn. besorgt ansehen; **you had me ~:** ich habe mir [deinetwegen] Sorgen gemacht; **don't look so ~!** schau nicht so bekümmert drein!; **be ~ sick** krank vor Sorge; **be very ~:** sich (*Dat.*) große Sorgen machen

worrier /'wʌrɪə(r)/ *n.* **be too much of a ~:** sich (*Dat.*) immer [zu viel] Sorgen machen; **he's a [real] ~:** er macht sich (*Dat.*) um alles Sorgen

worry /'wʌrɪ/ **1** *v.t.* (**a**) beunruhigen; **it worries me to death to think that …:** ich sorge mich zu Tode, wenn ich [daran] denke, dass …; **~ oneself [about sth.]** sich (*Dat.*) um etw. Sorgen machen; (**b**) (bother) stören; (**c**) **~ a bone** ‹*Hund usw.*› an einem Knochen [herum]nagen. **2** *v.i.* sich (*Dat.*) Sorgen machen; sich sorgen; **~ about sth.** sich (*Dat.*) um etw. Sorgen machen; **don't ~ about it**

mach dir deswegen keine Sorgen!; **'I should ~** (coll. iron.) was kümmert mich das?; **not to ~** (coll.) kein Problem (ugs.). **3** *n.* Sorge, *die;* **sth. is the least of sb.'s worries** etw. ist jmds. geringste Sorge; **it must be a great ~ to you** es muss dir große Sorgen bereiten

worrying /'wʌrɪɪŋ/ **1** *adj.* (full of worry) sorgenvoll ‹*Zeit, Woche usw.*›; **it is a ~ time for her** sie hat zur Zeit große Sorgen. **2** *n.* **~ only makes everything worse** sich (*Dat.*) Sorgen zu machen macht alles nur noch schlimmer

worse /wɜ:s/ **1** *adj. compar. of* **bad** 1 schlechter; schlimmer ‹*Schmerz, Krankheit, Benehmen*›; **things could not/could be ~:** es kann nicht mehr schlimmer kommen/es könnte schlimmer sein; **the food is bad, and the service ~:** das Essen ist schlecht und die Bedienung noch schlechter; **he's getting ~:** mit ihm wird es schlimmer; (his health) ihm geht es schlechter; **be ~ than useless** ‹*Sache*› mehr als unbrauchbar sein; ‹*Person*› ein hoffnungsloser Fall sein; **sb. is [none] the ~ for sth.** jmdm. geht es wegen etw. [nicht] schlechter; **~ and ~:** immer schlechter/schlimmer; **to make matters ~, …:** zu allem Übel …; **it could have been ~:** es hätte schlimmer sein *od.* kommen können; **~ luck!** so ein Pech!; *see also* **drink** 1 c; **wear** 1 a. **2** *adv. compar. of* **badly** schlechter; schlimmer, schlechter ‹*sich benehmen*›; **~ and ~:** immer schlechter/schlimmer; *see also* **better** 3 a; **off** 1 g. **3** *n.* Schlimmeres; **she might do ~ than settle for that job** es wäre bestimmt kein Fehler, wenn sie sich für die Stelle entschiede; **go from bad to ~:** immer schlimmer werden; **or ~:** oder noch Schlimmeres; **~ still** schlimmer noch; **a change for the ~:** eine Wende zum Schlechteren; **take a turn for the ~:** sich verschlechtern; ‹*Krankheit*› sich verschlimmern; **nobody will think any the ~ of you** niemand wird deswegen schlechter von dir denken; **there is ~ to come** es kommt noch schlimmer; *see also* **worst** 3 a

worsen /'wɜ:sn/ **1** *v.t.* verschlechtern; verschlimmern ‹*Knappheit*›. **2** *v.i.* sich verschlechtern; ‹*Hungersnot, Sturm, Problem*› sich verschlimmern

worship /'wɜ:ʃɪp/ **1** *v.t.* **-pp-:** (**a**) verehren, anbeten ‹*Gott, Götter*›; (**b**) (idolize) abgöttisch verehren. **2** *v.i.*, (Brit.) **-pp-** am Gottesdienst teilnehmen. **3** *n.* (**a**) Anbetung, *die;* (service) Gottesdienst, *der;* (**b**) ▶ 1152 **Your/His W~:** Anrede für Richter, Bürgermeister; ≈ Euer/Seine Ehren

worshipper (*Amer.:* **worshiper**) /'wɜ:ʃɪpə(r)/ *n.* (**a**) (in church) Gottesdienstbesucher, *der/*-besucherin, *die;* (**b**) (of deity) Anbeter, *der/*-beterin, *die*

worst /wɜ:st/ **1** *adj. superl. of* **bad** 1 ⇒ **worse** 1: schlechtest…/schlimmst…; **be ~:** am schlechtesten/ schlimmsten sein; **the ~ thing about it was …:** das Schlimmste daran war … **2** *adv. superl. of* **badly** am schlimmsten; am schlechtesten ‹*gekleidet*›. **3** *n.* (**a**) [**the**] **~:** der/die/das Schlimmste; **prepare for the ~:** sich auf das Schlimmste gefasst machen; **at ~, at the [very] ~:** schlimmstenfalls; im [aller]schlimmsten Fall[e]; **get** *or* **have the ~ of it** (be defeated) geschlagen werden; (suffer the most) am meisten zu leiden haben; **if the ~** *or* **it comes to the ~** (Brit.), **if worse comes to ~** (Amer.) wenn es zum Schlimmsten kommt; **do your ~:** mach, was du willst!; **let him do his ~:** er soll machen, was er will; (**b**) (what is of poorest quality) Schlechteste, *der/die/das*

worsted /'wʊstɪd/ *n.* (Textiles) Kammgarn, *das*

worth /wɜ:θ/ **1** *adj.* (**a**) (of value equivalent to) wert; **it's ~/ not ~ £80** es ist 80 Pfund wert/80 Pfund ist es nicht wert; **it is not ~ much** *or* **a lot [to sb.]** es ist [jmdm.] nicht viel wert; **be ~ the money** das Geld wert sein; **not ~ a penny** keinen Pfennig wert (ugs.); **for what it is ~:** was immer auch davon zu halten ist; (**b**) (worthy of) **is it ~ hearing/the effort?** ist es hörenswert/der Mühe wert?; **is it ~ doing?** lohnt es sich?; **if it's ~ doing, it's ~ doing well** wenn schon, denn schon; **it isn't ~ it** es lohnt sich nicht; **it's ~ a try** es ist einen Versuch wert; **it would be [well] ~ it** (coll.) es würde sich [sehr] lohnen; **be well ~ sth.** durchaus *od.* sehr wohl etw. wert sein; (**c**) **be ~ sth.** (possess) etw. wert sein (ugs.); **run/cycle for all one is ~** (coll.) rennen/fahren, was man kann. **2** *n.* (**a**) (equivalent of money etc. in commodity) **ten pounds' ~ of petrol** Benzin für zehn Pfund; (more formal) Benzin im Wert von zehn Pfund; **(b)** (value, excellence) Wert, *der*

worthless /ˈwɜːθlɪs/ *adj.* **(a)** (valueless) wertlos; **(b)** (despicable) nichtswürdig

ˈworthwhile *attrib. adj.* lohnend; *see also* **while 1**

worthy /ˈwɜːðɪ/ **1** *adj.* **(a)** (adequate, estimable) würdig; verdienstvoll ‹*Tat*›; angemessen ‹*Belohnung*›; ~ **of the occasion** dem Anlass angemessen; **(b)** (deserving) würdig; verdienstvoll ‹*Sache, Organisation*›; **be ~ of the name** den Namen verdienen; ~ **of note/mention** erwähnenswert. **2** *n.* local worthies (joc.) örtliche Honoratioren

would ⇒ **will¹**

would-be /ˈwʊdbiː/ *attrib. adj.* **a ~ philosopher** ein Möchtegernphilosoph; **a ~ aggressor** ein möglicher Aggressor

wouldn't /ˈwʊdnt/ (coll.) = **would not;** ⇒ **will¹**

wound¹ /wuːnd/ **1** *n.* (lit. or fig.) Wunde, *die;* **a war ~:** eine Kriegsverletzung. **2** *v.t.* verwunden; (fig.) verletzen; **be ~ed in the thigh/arm** am Oberschenkel/Arm verwundet werden

wound² ⇒ **wind²** 1, 2

wove, woven ⇒ **weave¹** 2, 3

wow /waʊ/ **1** *int.* hoi. **2** *n.* (sl.) **be a ~:** eine Wucht sein (salopp). **3** *v.t.* (sl.) umhauen (ugs.)

WP *abbr.* **word processor**

wraith /reɪθ/ *n.* Gespenst, *das*

wrangle /ˈræŋgl/ **1** *v.i.* [sich] streiten. **2** *n.* Streit, *der*

wrap /ræp/ **1** *v.t.*, **-pp-:** **(a)** einwickeln; (fig.) hüllen; **~ped** abgepackt ‹*Brot usw.*›; ~ **sth. in paper/cotton wool** etw. in Papier/Watte [ein]wickeln; ~ **sth. [a]round sth.** etw. um etw. wickeln; **(b)** schlingen ‹*Schal, Handtuch usw.*› **(about, round** um). **2** *n.* Umschlag[e]tuch, *das;* **under ~s** (fig.) unter Verschluss; **keep sth. under ~s** etw. geheimhalten

~ **ˈup 1** *v.t.* **(a)** ⇒ **wrap 1; wrapped up; (b)** (fig.: conclude) abschließen. **2** *v.i.* sich warm einpacken (ugs.)

wrapped up /ræpt ˈʌp/ *adj.* **be ~ in one's work** in seine Arbeit völlig versunken sein; **a country whose prosperity is ~ in its shipping** ein Land, dessen Reichtum eng mit seiner Schifffahrt verknüpft ist

wrapper /ˈræpə(r)/ *n.* **(a)** (around newspaper etc.) Streifband, *das* (Postw.); **(b)** (around sweet etc.) **sweet-/toffee-~[s]** Bonbonpapier, *das;* **(c)** (of book) ⇒ **jacket c**

wrapping /ˈræpɪŋ/ *n.* Verpackung, *die;* **~s** Verpackung, *die;* (fig.) Hülle, *die* (dichter.)

ˈwrapping paper *n.* (strong paper) Packpapier, *das;* (decorative paper) Geschenkpapier, *das*

wrath /rɒθ/ *n.* (poet./rhet.) Zorn, *der*

wreak /riːk/ *v.t.* **(a)** (inflict) ~ **vengeance on sb.** an jmdm. Rache nehmen; **(b)** (vent) auslassen ‹*Wut, Ärger*› **(on** an + *Dat.*); **(c)** (cause) anrichten ‹*Verwüstung, Unheil*›

wreath /riːθ/ *n.*, *pl.* **wreaths** /riːðz, riːθs/ Kranz, *der;* **a ~ of smoke** ein Ring aus Rauch

wreathe /riːð/ *v.t.* **(a)** (encircle) umkränzen; **her face was ~d in smiles** sie zeigte ein strahlendes Lächeln; **(b)** (make by interweaving) flechten; winden (geh.)

wreck /rek/ **1** *n.* **(a)** (destruction) Schiffbruch, *der;* (fig.) Zerstörung, *die;* **(b)** (ship) Wrack, *das;* **(c)** (broken remains, lit. or fig.) Wrack, *das;* **she was a physical/mental ~:** sie war körperlich/geistig ein Wrack; **I feel/you look a ~** (coll.) ich fühle mich kaputt (ugs.) /du siehst kaputt aus (ugs.). **2** *v.t.* **(a)** (destroy) ruinieren; zu Schrott fahren ‹*Auto*›; **be ~ed** (shipwrecked) ‹*Schiff, Person:*› Schiffbruch erleiden; **(b)** (fig.: ruin) zerstören; ruinieren ‹*Gesundheit, Urlaub*›

wreckage /ˈrekɪdʒ/ *n.* Wrackteile *Pl.;* (fig.) Trümmer *Pl.*

Wren /ren/ *n.* (Brit.) *Angehörige des weiblichen Marinedienstes;* **join the ~s** in den weiblichen Marinedienst eintreten

wren *n.* Zaunkönig, *der*

wrench /rentʃ/ **1** *n.* **(a)** (tool) verstellbarer Schraubenschlüssel; **(b)** (Amer.) ⇒ **spanner; (c)** (violent twist) Verrenkung, *die;* **(d)** (fig.) **be a great ~ [for sb.]** sehr schmerzhaft für jmdn. sein. **2** *v.t.* **(a)** (tug violently) reißen; ~ **at sth.** an etw. (*Dat.*) reißen; ~ **sth. round/off/open**

etw. herum-/ab-/aufreißen; ~ **sth. from sb.** jmdm. etw. entreißen; **(b)** (injure by twisting) ~ **one's ankle** *etc.* sich (*Dat.*) den Knöchel *usw.* verrenken

wrest /rest/ *v.t.* ~ **sth. from sb./sb.'s grasp** (lit. or fig.) jmdm./jmds. Griff etw. entreißen *od.* (geh.) entwinden; ~ **sth. from sth.** einer Sache (*Dat.*) etw. abringen

wrestle /ˈresl/ **1** *n.* (hard struggle) Ringen, *das.* **2** *v.i.* **(a)** ringen; (fig.: grapple) sich abmühen; ~ **with one's conscience** mit seinem Gewissen ringen

wrestler /ˈreslə(r)/ *n.* Ringer, *der*/Ringerin, *die*

wrestling /ˈreslɪŋ/ *n.*, *no pl.*, *no indef. art.* Ringen, *das*

wretch /retʃ/ *n.* Kreatur, *die;* (joc.: child) Gör, *das*

wretched /ˈretʃɪd/ *adj.* **(a)** (miserable) unglücklich; **feel ~ about sb./sth.** (be embarrassed) über jmdn./etw. todunglücklich sein; **feel ~** (be very unwell) sich elend fühlen; **(b)** (coll.: damned) elend (abwertend); **(c)** (very bad) erbärmlich; miserabel ‹*Wetter*›; **(d)** (causing discomfort) schrecklich ‹*Reise, Erfahrung, Zeit*›

wretchedness /ˈretʃɪdnɪs/ *n.*, *no pl.* **(a)** (misery) Elend, *das;* **(b)** (badness) Erbärmlichkeit, *die*

wriggle /ˈrɪgl/ **1** *v.i.* **(a)** sich winden; ‹*Fisch:*› zappeln; **(b)** (make one's/its way by wriggling) sich schlängeln; ~ **out of a difficulty** *etc.* (fig.) sich aus einer schwierigen Situation *usw.* herauswinden. **2** *v.t.* ~ **one's way** (lit. or fig.) sich schlängeln

wring /rɪŋ/ *v.t.*, **wrung** /rʌŋ/ **(a)** wringen; ~ **out** auswringen; ~ **the water out of the towels** das Wasser aus den Handtüchern wringen; **(b)** (squeeze forcibly) ~ **sb.'s hand** jmdm. fest die Hand drücken; (twist forcibly) ~ **one's hands** die Hände ringen (geh.); ~ **the neck of an animal** einem Tier den Hals umdrehen; **I could have wrung his neck** (fig.) ich hätte ihm den Hals umdrehen können; **(c)** (extract) wringen; ~ **sth. from** or **out of sb.** (fig.) jmdm. etw. abpressen

wringer /ˈrɪŋə(r)/ *n.* Wringmaschine, *die*

wringing ˈwet *adj.* tropfnass

wrinkle /ˈrɪŋkl/ *n.* Falte, *die;* (in paper) Knick, *der*

wrinkled /ˈrɪŋkld/ *adj.* runz[e]lig

wrinklie /ˈrɪŋklɪ/ ⇒ **wrinkly 2**

wrinkly /ˈrɪŋklɪ/ **1** *adj.* runz[e]lig. **2** *n.* (sl.) Grufti, *der* (ugs.)

wrist /rɪst/ *n.* Handgelenk, *das*

ˈwrist-watch *n.* Armbanduhr, *die*

writ¹ /rɪt/ *n.* (Law) Verfügung, *die*

writ² ⇒ **write 2 a**

write /raɪt/ **1** *v.i.*, **wrote** /rəʊt/, **written** /ˈrɪtn/ schreiben; ~ **to sb./a firm** jmdm./an eine Firma schreiben. **2** *v.t.*, **wrote, written** **(a)** schreiben; ausschreiben ‹*Scheck*›; **the written language** die Schriftsprache; **written applications** schriftliche Anträge; **the paper had been written all over** das Papier war ganz voll geschrieben; **be written into the contract** [ausdrücklich] im Vertrag stehen; ~ **sb. into/out of a serial** für jmdn. eine Rolle in einer Serie schreiben/jmdn. einen Abgang aus einer Serie verschaffen; **writ large** (fig.) im Großformat (fig.); **(b)** (Amer./Commerc./coll.: ~ letter to) anschreiben; **(c)** *in pass.* (fig.: be apparent) **sb. has sth. written in his face** jmdm. steht etw. im Gesicht geschrieben; **guilt was written all over her face** die Schuld stand ihr ins Gesicht geschrieben

~ **aˈway** *v.i.* ~ **away for sth.** etw. [schriftlich] anfordern

~ **ˈback** *v.i.* zurückschreiben

~ **ˈdown** *v.t.* aufschreiben

~ **ˈin** *v.i.* hinschreiben (ugs.); (include) hineinschreiben; ~ **in for sth.** etw. [schriftlich] anfordern

~ **ˈoff 1** *v.t.* **(a)** (compose with ease) herunterschreiben (ugs.); **(b)** (cancel) abschreiben ‹*Schulden, Verlust*›; (fig.) ~ **sb. off [as a failure** *etc.*] jmdn. [als Versager] abschreiben (ugs.); **(c)** (fig.) zu Schrott fahren. **2** *v.i.* ~ **away**

~ **ˈout** *v.t.* **(a)** ausschreiben ‹*Scheck*›; schreiben ‹*Rezept*›; **(b)** (~ in final form) ausarbeiten; (~ in full) ausschreiben

∼ '**up** *v.t.* (**a**) (praise) eine gute Kritik schreiben über (+ *Akk.*); (**b**) (∼ account of) einen Bericht schreiben über (+ *Akk.*); (∼ in full) aufarbeiten; (**c**) (bring up to date) auf den neuesten Stand bringen

'**write-off** *n.* (person) Versager, *der*/Versagerin, *die;* (vehicle) Totalschaden, *der*

writer /'raɪtə(r)/ *n.* (**a**) ▶ 887⌐ (author) Schriftsteller, *der*/ Schriftstellerin, *die;* (of letter, article) Schreiber, *der*/Schreiberin, *die;* Verfasser, *der*/Verfasserin, *die;* (of lyrics, advertisements) Texter, *der*/Texterin, *die;* (of music) Komponist, *der*/ Komponistin, *die;* **be a** ∼: Schriftsteller/Schriftstellerin sein; (**b**) **be a good/bad** ∼ (as to handwriting) eine gute/ schlechte Schrift haben

'**write-up** *n.* Bericht, *der;* (by critic) Kritik, *die;* **get a good** ∼: gut besprochen werden

writhe /raɪð/ *v.i.* (lit. or fig.) sich winden; **he/it makes me** ∼ (with embarrassment) er/es bringt mich in ziemliche Verlegenheit; (with disgust) er/es ist mir zuwider

writing /'raɪtɪŋ/ *n.* (**a**) Schreiben, *das;* **put sth. in** ∼: etw. schriftlich machen (ugs.); (**b**) (handwriting) Schrift, *die;* (**c**) (something written) Schrift, *die;* **the** ∼ **on the wall** (fig.) das Menetekel an der Wand

writing: ∼ **case** *n.* Schreibmappe, *die;* ∼ **pad** *n.* Schreibblock, *der;* ∼ **paper** *n.* Schreibpapier, *das;* Briefpapier, *das*

written ⇨ write

wrong /rɒŋ/ **1** *adj.* (**a**) (morally bad) unrecht (geh.); (unfair) ungerecht; **you were** ∼ **to be so angry** es war nicht richtig von dir, so ärgerlich zu sein; (**b**) (mistaken) falsch; **be** ∼ ⟨*Person:*⟩ sich irren; **I was** ∼ **about you** ich habe mich in dir geirrt; **the clock is** ∼: die Uhr geht falsch; **the clock is** ∼ **by ten minutes** (fast/slow) die Uhr geht 10 Minuten vor/nach; **how** ∼ **can you be** *or* **get!** wie man sich irren kann!; (**c**) (not suitable) falsch; **give the** ∼ **answer** eine falsche Antwort geben; **say/do the** ∼ **thing** das Falsche sagen/tun; **be the** ∼ **person for the job** für die Stelle ungeeignet sein; **take the** ∼ **turning** falsch abbiegen; **get hold of the** ∼ **end of the stick** (fig.) alles völlig falsch verstehen; [**the**] ∼ **way round** verkehrt herum; (**d**) (out of order) nicht in Ordnung; **there's something** ∼ **here/with him** hier/mit ihm stimmt etwas nicht; **there's nothing** ∼: es ist alles in Ordnung; **what's** ∼? ist etwas nicht in Ordnung? *See also* **wrong side.** **2** *adv.* falsch; **get it** ∼: es falsch od. verkehrt machen; (misunderstand) sich irren; **I got the answer** ∼ **again** meine Antwort war wieder falsch; **get sb.** ∼: jmdn. falsch verstehen; **go** ∼ (take ∼ path) sich verlaufen; (fig.) ⟨*Person:*⟩ vom rechten Weg abkommen (fig. geh.); ⟨*Maschine, Mechanismus:*⟩ kaputtgehen (ugs.); ⟨*Angelegenheit:*⟩ danebengehen (ugs.). **3** *n.* Unrecht, *das;* **two** ∼**s don't make a right** das gibt nur ein Unrecht mehr; **do** ∼: Unrecht tun; **she can do no** ∼: sie kann überhaupt nichts Unrechtes tun; **be in the** ∼: im Unrecht sein. **4** *v.t.* ∼ **sb.** jmdn. ungerecht behandeln

wrong: ∼**doer** *n.* Übeltäter, *der*/-täterin, *die;* Missetäter, *der*/-täterin, *die* (geh.); ∼**doing** *n.* (**a**) no pl., no indef. art. Missetaten *Pl.* (geh.); (**b**) (instance) Missetat, *die* (geh.); ∼'**foot** *v.t.* (**a**) (Sport) ∼**-foot sb.** jmdn. auf dem falschen Fuß erwischen (Sportjargon); (**b**) (fig. coll.) unvorbereitet treffen

wrongful /'rɒŋfl/ *adj.* (**a**) (unfair) unrecht (geh.); (**b**) (unlawful) rechtswidrig

wrongfully /'rɒŋfəlɪ/ *adv.* (**a**) (unfairly) unrecht (geh.); ⟨*handeln*⟩; zu Unrecht ⟨*beschuldigen*⟩; (**b**) (unlawfully) rechtswidrig

wrongly /'rɒŋlɪ/ *adv.* (**a**) (inappropriately, incorrectly) falsch; (**b**) (mistakenly) zu Unrecht; **I believed,** ∼, **that ...:** ich habe fälschlicherweise geglaubt, dass ...; (**c**) ⇨ **wrongfully a**

'**wrong side** *n.* (**a**) (of fabric) linke Seite; [**the**] ∼ **out/up** verkehrt herum; (**b**) **be on the** ∼ **of thirty** die dreißig überschritten haben; **get on the** ∼ **of sb./the law** (fig.) jmdn. falsch anfassen/mit dem Gesetz in Konflikt geraten; *see also* **bed 1 a**

wrote ⇨ write

wrought ⇨ **work 2**

wrought '**iron** *n.* Schmiedeeisen, *das; attrib.* schmiedeeisern ⟨*Tor, Zaun*⟩

wrung ⇨ **wring**

wry /raɪ/ *adj.,* ∼**er** *or* **wrier** /'raɪə(r)/, ∼**est** *or* **wriest** /'raɪɪst/ ironisch ⟨*Blick*⟩; fein ⟨*Humor, Witz*⟩

wryly /'raɪlɪ/ *adv.* ironisch ⟨*blicken, sagen*⟩; schief ⟨*lächeln*⟩

wt. *abbr.* ▶ 1202⌐ **weight** Gew.

WW *abbr.* (Amer.) **World War** WK

WWW *abbr.* **World Wide Web** WWW

X, x /eks/ *n., pl.* **Xs** *or* **X's** /'eksɪz/ (**a**) (letter) X, x, *das;* (**b**) (Math.) x; (**c**) (unknown person) **Mr X** Herr X; (**d**) **x marks the spot** die Stelle ist durch ein Kreuz markiert

xenon /'zenɒn/ *n.* (Chem.) Xenon, *das*

Xerox, (P), xerox /'zɪərɒks, 'zerɒks/ **1** *n.* (**a**) (process) Xerographie, *die* (Druckw.); (**b**) (copy) Xerokopie, *die.* **2 xerox** *v.t.* xerokopieren

Xmas /'krɪsməs, 'eksməs/ *n.* ▶ 836⌐ (coll.) Weihnachten, *das*

'**X-ray** **1** *n.* (**a**) *in pl.* Röntgenstrahlen *Pl.;* (**b**) (picture) Röntgenaufnahme, *die;* (**c**) *attrib.* Röntgen-. **2** *v.t.* röntgen; durchleuchten ⟨*Gepäck*⟩

xylophone /'zaɪləfəʊn/ *n.* (Mus.) Xylophon, *das*

Y, y /waɪ/ *n., pl.* **Ys** *or* **Y's** (**a**) (letter) Y, y, *das;* (**b**) (Math.) y

yacht /jɒt/ **1** *n.* (**a**) (for racing) Segelboot, *das;* Segeljacht, *die;* (**b**) (for pleasure travel etc.) Jacht, *die.* **2** *v.i.* segeln

'**yacht club** *n.* Jachtklub, *der*

yachting /'jɒtɪŋ/ *n., no pl., no art.* Segeln, *das*

yachtsman /'jɒtsmən/ *n., pl.* **yachtsmen** /'jɒtsmən/ Segler, *der*

Yank /jæŋk/ *n.* (Brit. coll.: American) Yankee, *der;* Ami, *der* (ugs.)

yank (coll.) **1** *v.t.* reißen an (+ *Dat.*); ∼ **sth. off/out** etw. ab-/ausreißen. **2** *n.* Reißen, *das*

Yankee /'jæŋkɪ/ ⇨ **Yank**

yap /jæp/ *v.i.,* **-pp-** kläffen

yard¹ /jɑːd/ *n.* ▶ 643⌐, ▶ 756⌐, ▶ 904⌐ Yard, *das;* **by the** ∼: ≈ meterweise; (fig.) am laufenden Band (ugs.); **have a face a** ∼ **long** ein Gesicht wie drei Tage Regenwetter machen

yard² *n.* (**a**) (attached to building) Hof, *der;* **in the** ∼: auf dem Hof; (**b**) (for manufacture) Werkstatt, *die;* (for storage) Lager, *das;* (ship∼) Werft, *die;* **builder's** ∼: Bauhof, *der;* (**c**) (Amer.: garden) Garten, *der*

'**yardstick** *n.* (fig.: standard) Maßstab, *der*

yarn /jɑːn/ *n.* (**a**) (thread) Garn, *das;* (**b**) (coll.: story) Geschichte, *die;* (of sailor) [Seemanns]garn, *das*

yawn /jɔːn/ **1** *n.* Gähnen, *das;* **give a** [**long**] ∼: [herzhaft] gähnen. **2** *v.i.* (**a**) gähnen; (**b**) (fig.) ⟨*Abgrund, Kluft, Spalte:*⟩ gähnen

yawning /'jɔːnɪŋ/ *adj.* gähnend (auch fig. geh.)

yd[s]. *abbr.* ▶ 643⌐, ▶ 756⌐, ▶ 904⌐ **yard[s]** Yd[s].

ye¹ /jiː/ *pron.* (arch./poet./dial./joc.) Ihr (veralt.); (as direct or indirect object) Euch (veralt.)

ye² *adj.* (pseudo-arch.) = **the**

yea /jeɪ/ *adv.* (arch.) ja

yeah /jeə/ *adv.* (coll.) ja; [oh] ∼? [ach] ja?

year /jɪə(r)/ *n.* **(a)** Jahr, *das;* **she gets £10,000 a** ∼: sie verdient 10 000 Pfund im Jahr; ∼ **in** ∼ **out** jahrein, jahraus; ∼ **after** ∼: Jahr für *od.* um Jahr; **all [the]** ∼ **round** das ganze Jahr hindurch; **in a** ∼['s **time]** in einem Jahr; **once a** ∼, **once every** ∼: einmal im Jahr; **Christian** *or* **Church** *or* **ecclesiastical** ∼ (Eccl.) Kirchenjahr, *das;* liturgisches Jahr (kath. Kirche); **a ten-**∼-**old** ein Zehnjähriger/eine Zehnjährige; **a ten-**∼[s]-**old child** ein zehn Jahre altes Kind; **in her thirtieth** ∼: in ihrem 30. Lebensjahr; **financial** *or* **fiscal** *or* **tax** ∼: Finanz- *od.* Rechnungsjahr, *das;* **calendar** *or* **civil** ∼: Kalenderjahr, *das;* **school** ∼: Schuljahr, *das;* **for a** ∼ **and a day** ein Jahr und einen Tag [lang]; **a** ∼ **[from] today** *etc.* heute *usw.* in einem Jahr; **a** ∼ **[ago] today** *etc.* heute *usw.* vor einem Jahr; ... **of the** ∼ (best) ... des Jahres; **she looks** ∼**s older** sie sieht um Jahre älter aus; **take** ∼**s off sb./ sb.'s life** jmdn. um Jahre jünger/älter machen; *see also* **by¹** 1 m; **from** b; **(b)** (group of students) Jahrgang, *der;* **first-**∼ **student** Student/Studentin im ersten Jahr; **(c)** *in pl.* (age) **be getting on/be well on in** ∼s in die Jahre kommen/in vorgerücktem Alter sein (geh.)

year: ∼**book** *n.* Jahrbuch, *das;* ∼**-long** *adj.* (lasting a ∼) einjährig; (lasting the whole ∼) ganzjährig

yearly /'jɪəlɪ/ **1** *adj.* **(a)** (annual) jährlich; **ten-**∼: zehnjährig; **at twice-**∼ **intervals** zweimal im Jahr; **(b)** (lasting a year) Einjahres〈*vertrag, -abonnement*〉. **2** *adv.* jährlich

yearn /jɜːn/ *v.i.* ∼ **for** *or* **after sth./for sb./to do sth.** sich nach etw./jmdm. sehnen/danach sehnen, etw. zu tun

yearning /'jɜːnɪŋ/ *n.* Sehnsucht, *die*

'year-round *adj.* ganzjährig

yeast /jiːst/ *n.* Hefe, *die*

yell /jel/ **1** *n.* gellender Schrei; **let out a** ∼: einen Schrei ausstoßen. **2** *v.t. & i.* [gellend] schreien

yellow /'jeləʊ/ **1** *adj.* **(a)** gelb; flachsblond 〈*Haar*〉; golden 〈*Getreide*〉; vergilbt 〈*Papier*〉; **(b)** (fig. coll.: cowardly) feige. **2** *n.* Gelb, *das.* **3** *v.t. & i.* vergilben

yellow 'card *n.* (Footb.) gelbe Karte; **be shown a** ∼: gelb sehen (Jargon); eine gelbe Karte bekommen

yellowish /'jeləʊɪʃ/ *adj.* gelblich

yellow: ∼ **'line** *n.* (Brit.) gelbe [Markierungs]linie; **I'm on double** ∼ **lines** ich stehe im Parkverbot; ∼ **'pages,** (P) *n. pl.* gelbe Seiten; Branchenverzeichnis, *das*

yelp /jelp/ **1** *v.i.* aufheulen (ugs.); 〈*Hund:*〉 jaulen. **2** *n.* Heulen, *das;* (of dog) Jaulen, *das*

yen¹ /jen/ *n., pl.* same (Japanese currency) Yen, *der*

yen² *n.* (coll.: longing) Drang, *der* (**for** nach); **sb. has a** ∼ **to do sth.** es drängt jmdn. danach, etw. zu tun

yeoman /'jəʊmən/ *n., pl.* **yeomen** /'jəʊmən/ **(a)** (with small estate) Kleinbauer, *der;* **(b)** (Hist.: freeholder) Freisasse, *der*

yep /jep/ *int.* (Amer. coll.) ja

yes /jes/ **1** *adv.* ja; (in contradiction) doch; ∼, **sir** jawohl!; ∼? (indeed?) ach ja?; (what do you want?) ja?; (to customer) ja, bitte?; **say '**∼' ja sagen; **say** ∼ **to a proposal** einem Vorschlag zustimmen; ∼ **and no** ja und nein. **2** *n., pl.* ∼**es** Ja, *das*

'yes-man *n.* (coll. derog.) Jasager, *der* (abwertend)

yesterday /'jestədeɪ, 'jestədɪ/ **1** *n.* gestern; **the day before** ∼: vorgestern; ∼**'s paper** die gestrige Zeitung; die Zeitung von gestern; ∼ **morning/afternoon/evening/ night** gestern Vormittag/Nachmittag/Abend/Nacht; **a week [from]** ∼: gestern in einer Woche; ∼ **evening's concert** das Konzert gestern Abend *od.* am gestrigen Abend. **2** *adv.* gestern; **the day before** ∼: vorgestern; ∼ **morning/afternoon/evening/night** gestern Vormittag/Nachmittag/Abend/Nacht; **(b)** (in the recent past) gestern; *see also* **born 1**

yet /jet/ **1** *adv.* **(a)** (still) noch; **have** ∼ **to reach sth.** etw. erst noch erreichen müssen; **much** ∼ **remains to be done** noch bleibt viel zu tun; *see also* **as** 5; **(b)** (hitherto) bisher; **the play is his best** ∼: das Stück ist sein bisher

bestes; **(c)** *neg. or interrog.* **not** [just] ∼: [jetzt] noch nicht; **never** ∼: noch nie; **need you go just** ∼? musst du [jetzt] schon gehen?; **you haven't seen anything** *or* (coll.) **ain't seen nothing** ∼: das ist noch gar nichts; **(d)** (before all is over) doch noch; **he could win** ∼: er könnte noch gewinnen; **(e)** *with compar.* (even) noch; **(f)** (nevertheless) doch; **(g)** (again) noch; ∼ **again** noch einmal; **she has never voted for that party, nor** ∼ **intends to** sie hat nie für diese Partei gestimmt, und sie hat es auch nicht vor. **2** *conj.* doch; **a faint** ∼ **unmistakable smell** ein schwacher, aber unverkennbarer Geruch

yew /juː/ *n.* ∼ **[-tree]** Eibe, *die*

'Y-fronts, (P) *n. pl.* Herrenslip, *der* (*mit Y-förmigen Deckverschluss*)

YHA *abbr.* **Youth Hostels Association** Jugendherbergsverband, *der*

Yiddish /'jɪdɪʃ/ **1** *adj.* jiddisch. **2** *n.* ▶ 897 | Jiddisch, *das; see also* **English 2 a**

yield /jiːld/ **1** *v.t.* **(a)** (give) bringen; hervorbringen 〈*Ernte*〉; tragen 〈*Obst*〉; abwerfen 〈*Gewinn*〉; ergeben 〈*Resultat, Informationen*〉; **(b)** (surrender) übergeben 〈*Festung*〉; lassen 〈*Vortritt*〉; abtreten 〈*Besitz*〉 (**to** an + Akk.); ∼ **the point** [in diesem Punkt] nachgeben; ∼ **a point to sb.** jmdm. in einem Punkt nachgeben. **2** *v.i.* **(a)** (surrender) sich unterwerfen; ∼ **to threats/temptation** Drohungen (*Dat.*) nachgeben/der Versuchung (*Dat.*) erliegen; ∼ **to persuasion/sb.'s entreaties** sich überreden lassen/jmds. Bitten (*Dat.*) nachgeben; **(b)** (give right of way) Vorfahrt gewähren. **3** *n.* **(a)** Ertrag, *der;* **(b)** (return on investment) Zins[ertrag], *der;* **a 10 %** ∼: 10 % Zinsen

yippee /'jɪpi:, jɪ'pi:/ *int.* hurra

yob /jɒb/, **yobbo** /'jɒbəʊ/ *ns., pl.* ∼**s** (Brit. coll.) Rowdy, *der*

yodel /'jəʊdl/ **1** *v.i. & t.,* (Brit.) **-ll-** jodeln. **2** *n.* Jodeln, *das*

yoga /'jəʊgə/ *n.* Joga, *der od. das*

yoghurt, yogurt /'jɒgət/ *n.* Joghurt, *der od. das*

yoke /jəʊk/ **1** *n.* **(a)** (for animal) Joch, *das;* **(b)** (for person) [Trag]joch, *das;* **(c)** (of garment) Sattel, *der* (Textilw.). **2** *v.t.* **(a)** ins Joch spannen 〈*Tier*〉; ∼ **an animal to sth.** ein Tier vor etw. (*Akk.*) spannen; **(b)** (fig.: couple) verbinden

yokel /'jəʊkl/ *n.* (derog.) [Bauern]tölpel, *der*

yolk /jəʊk/ *n.* Dotter, *der;* Eigelb, *das*

yonder /'jɒndə(r)/ (literary) **1** *adj.* ∼ **tree/peasant** jener Baum/Bauer dort (geh.). **2** *adv.* dort drüben

Yorkshire pudding /jɔːkʃɪə 'pʊdɪŋ, jɔːkʃə 'pʊdɪŋ/ *n.* (Gastr.) Yorkshirepudding, *der*

you /jʊ, stressed 'juː/ *pron.* **(a)** *sing./pl.* du/ihr; *in polite address sing. or pl.* Sie; *as direct object* dich/euch/Sie; *as indirect object* dir/euch/Ihnen; *refl.* dich/dir/ euch; *in polite address* sich; **it was** ∼: du warst/ihr wart/Sie waren es; ∼**-know-what/-who** du weißt/ihr wisst/Sie wissen schon, was/wer/wen/wem; **(b)** (one) man; **smoking is bad for you** Rauchen ist ungesund. *See also* **your; yours; yourself; yourselves**

you'd /jʊd, stressed juːd/ **(a)** = **you had; (b)** = **you would**

you'll /jʊl, stressed juːl/ **(a)** = **you will; (b)** = **you shall**

young /jʌŋ/ **1** *adj.,* ∼**er** /'jʌŋgə(r)/, ∼**est** /'jʌŋgɪst/ **(a)** ▶ 630 | (lit. or fig.) jung; **a very** ∼ **child** ein ganz kleines Kind; **the** ∼ **boys** die [kleinen] Jungen; ∼ **at heart** im Herzen jung geblieben; **sb. is not getting any** ∼**er** jmd. wird auch nicht jünger; **you're only** ∼ **once** man ist nur einmal jung; **the night is still** ∼: die Nacht ist jung; ∼ **Jones** der junge Jones (ugs.); **(b)** (characteristic of youth) jugendlich; ∼ **love/fashion** junge Liebe/Mode. **2** *n. pl.* (of animals) Junge *Pl.;* (of humans) Kinder *Pl.;* **with** ∼: trächtig; **the** ∼ (∼ people) die jungen Leute; ∼ **and old** Jung und Alt

'young days *n. pl.* Jugendjahre *Pl.;* **in my** ∼: in meiner Jugend[zeit]

youngish /'jʌŋɪʃ/ *adj.* ziemlich jung

young: ∼ **'lady** *n.* **(a)** junge Dame; **(b)** (girlfriend) Freundin, *die;* ∼ **'man** *n.* **(a)** junger Mann; **(b)** (boyfriend) Freund, *der*

youngster /'jʌŋstə(r)/ *n.* **(a)** (child) Kleine, *der/die/das;* **(b)** (young person) Jugendliche, *der/die;* **you're just a** ∼

compared with me im Vergleich zu mir bist du noch jung

young 'woman *n.* (a) junge Frau; (b) (girlfriend) Freundin, *die*

your /jə(r), *stressed* jʊə(r), jɔː(r)/ *poss. pron. attrib.* (of you, sing./pl.) dein/euer; *in polite address* Ihr. *See also* **her²**

you're /jə(r), *stressed* jʊə(r), jɔː(r)/ = **you are**

yours /jʊəz, jɔːz/ *poss. pron. pred.* (a) (to or of you, sing.) deiner/deine/dein[e]s; (to or of you, pl.) eurer/eure/eures; *in polite address* Ihrer/Ihre/Ihr[e]s; **what's ~?** (coll.) was nimmst du/nehmen Sie?; *see also* **hers; ours;** (b) (your letter) Ihr Brief; (Commerc.) Ihr Schreiben; **(c)** (ending letter) **~ [obediently]** Ihr [sehr ergebener (geh.)]; **~ truly** in alter Verbundenheit Dein/Deine; (in business letter) mit freundlichen Grüßen; (joc.: I) meine Wenigkeit (scherzh.); *see also* **faithfully c; sincerely**

yourself /jəˈselvz, *stressed* jʊəˈself, jɔːˈself/ *pron.* (a) *emphat.* selbst; **for ~:** für dich/*in polite address* Sie selbst; **you must do sth. for ~:** du musst selbst etw. tun; **relax and be ~:** entspann dich und gib dich ganz natürlich; (b) *refl.* dich/dir; *in polite address* sich. *See also* **herself; myself**

yourselves /jəˈselvs, *stressed* jʊəˈselvz, jɔːˈselvz/ *pron.* (a) *emphat.* selbst; **for ~:** für euch/*in polite address* Sie selbst; (b) *refl.* euch/sich. *See also* **herself**

youth /juːθ/ *n.* (a) *no pl., no art.* Jugend, *die*; (b) *pl.* **~s** /juːðz/ (young man) Jugendliche, *der*; (c) *constr. as pl.* (young people) Jugend, *die*

youth: ~ centre *n.* Jugendzentrum, *das*; **~ club** *n.* Jugendklub, *der*

youthful /ˈjuːθfl/ *adj.* jugendlich

'youth hostel *n.* Jugendherberge, *die*

you've /jʊv, *stressed* juːv/ = **you have**

yo-yo, (P) /ˈjəʊjəʊ/ *n., pl.* **~s** Jo-Jo, *das*

Yugoslav /ˈjuːɡəslɑːv/ ⇒ **Yugoslavian**

Yugoslavia /juːɡəˈslɑːvɪə/ *pr. n.* Jugoslawien (*das*)

Yugoslavian /juːɡəˈslɑːvɪən/ **1** *adj.* jugoslawisch; **sb. is ~:** jmd. ist Jugoslawe/Jugoslawin. **2** *n.* Jugoslawe, *der*/Jugoslawin, *die*

yuk /jʌk/ *int.* (coll.) bäh; äks

yule /juːl/, **'Yuletide** *ns.* (arch.) Weihnachtszeit, *die*

yummy /ˈjʌmɪ/ (coll.) **1** *adj.* lecker. **2** *int.* (child lang.) lecker, lecker

yuppie /ˈjʌpɪ/ *n.* (coll.) Yuppie, *der*

yuppie 'flu *n.* (coll.) Yuppie-Grippe, *die* (ugs.)

Z z

Z, z /zed/ *n., pl.* **Zs** *or* **Z's** (a) (letter) Z, z, *das*; (b) (Math.) z

Zaire /zɑːˈɪə(r)/ *pr. n.* Zaire (*das*)

Zambia /ˈzæmbɪə/ *pr. n.* Sambia (*das*)

Zambian /ˈzæmbɪən/ ▶ 947 | **1** *adj.* sambisch. **2** *n.* Sambier, *der*/Sambierin, *die*

zap /zæp/ (coll.) **1** *int.* zack. **2** *v.t.*, **-pp-** (a) **~ sb. [one]** jmdm. eine knallen (ugs.); (b) (do away with, kill) erledigen (salopp)

zapper /ˈzæpə(r)/ *n.* (coll.) Drücker, *der* (ugs.); Fernbedienung, *die*

zeal /ziːl/ *n., no pl.* (a) (fervour) Eifer, *der*; (b) (hearty endeavour) Hingabe, *die*

zealous /ˈzeləs/ *adj.* (a) (fervent) glühend (geh.) ‹ Verehrer ›; begeistert ‹ Fan ›; (b) (eager) eifrig

zebra /ˈzebrə, ˈziːbrə/ *n.* Zebra, *das*

zebra 'crossing *n.* (Brit.) Zebrastreifen, *der*

zed /zed/ (Brit.), **zee** /ziː/ (Amer.) *ns.* Zett, *das*

zenith /ˈzenɪθ/ *n.* Zenit, *der*

zero /ˈzɪərəʊ/ *n., pl.* **~s** (a) ▶ 956 | (nought) Null, *die*; (b) (fig.: nil) null; **her chances are ~:** ihre Aussichten sind gleich null (ugs.); **(c)** ▶ 1141 | (starting point of scale; of temperature) Null, *die*; **in ~ gravity** im Zustand der Schwerelosigkeit; **absolute ~** (Phys.) absoluter Nullpunkt; **(d) ~ [hour]** die Stunde X

zero-'rated *adj.* **~ goods** nicht mehrwertsteuerpflichtige Güter

zest /zest/ *n.* (a) (lit. or fig.) Würze, *die*; **add a ~ to the dish** das Gericht würzig machen; **add ~ and life to sth.** etw. beleben; (b) (gusto) Begeisterung, *die*; **~ for living** Lebenslust, *die*

zigzag /ˈzɪɡzæɡ/ **1** *adj.* zickzackförmig; Zickzack‹ muster, -anordnung ›; **~ line** Zickzacklinie, *die.* **2** *adv.* zickzack. **3** *n.* Zickzacklinie, *die*

zilch /zɪltʃ/ *n., no pl., no art.* (esp. Amer. sl.) rein *od.* reineweg gar nichts (ugs.); **be ~:** gleich null sein (ugs.)

Zimbabwe /zɪmˈbɑːbwɪ/ *pr. n.* Simbabwe (*das*)

Zimbabwean /zɪmˈbɑːbwɪən/ ▶ 947 | **1** *adj.* simbabwisch. **2** *n.* Simbabwer, *der*/Simbabwerin, *die*

zinc /zɪŋk/ *n.* Zink, *das*

Zionism /ˈzaɪənɪzm/ *n., no pl.* Zionismus, *der*

Zionist /ˈzaɪənɪst/ *n.* Zionist, *der*/Zionistin, *die*

zip /zɪp/ **1** *n.* (a) Reißverschluss, *der*; (b) (fig.: energy, vigour) Schwung, *der.* **2** *v.t.*, **-pp-** (a) (close) **~ [up] sth.** den Reißverschluss an etw. (*Dat.*) zuziehen *od.* zumachen; **~ sb. up** jmdm. den Reißverschluss zuziehen *od.* zumachen; (b) **~ [up]** (enclose) [durch Schließen des Reißverschlusses] einpacken (ugs.). **3** *v.i.*, **-pp-:** (a) (fasten) **~ [up]** mit Reißverschluss geschlossen werden; **the dress ~s up** [at **the back/side**] das Kleid hat [hinten/seitlich] einen Reißverschluss; (b) (move fast) sausen

zip: ~ bag *n.* Tasche mit Reißverschluss; **Zip code** *n.* (Amer.) Postleitzahl, *die*; **~ fastener** ⇒ **~ 1 a**

zipper /ˈzɪpə(r)/ ⇒ **zip 1 a**

zit /zɪt/ *n.* (esp. Amer. sl.) Pickel, *der*

zither /ˈzɪðə(r)/ *n.* (Mus.) Zither, *die*

zodiac /ˈzəʊdɪæk/ *n.* (Astron.) Tierkreis, *der*; **sign of the ~** (Astrol.) Tierkreiszeichen, *das*; Sternzeichen, *das*

zombie (Amer.: **zombi**) /ˈzɒmbɪ/ *n.* (lit. or fig.) Zombie, *der*

zone /zəʊn/ *n.* Zone, *die*; **[time] ~:** Zeitzone, *die*

zonked /zɒŋkt/ *adj.* (sl.) **be ~** (by drugs) stoned sein (Drogenjargon); (by alcohol) zu sein (salopp); (be tired) erschlagen sein (ugs.)

zoo /zuː/ *n.* Zoo, *der*

'zookeeper *n.* ▶ 887 | Zoowärter, *der*/-wärterin, *die*

zoological /zəʊəˈlɒdʒɪkl/ *adj.* zoologisch

zoological 'garden[s] *n.* zoologischer Garten

zoologist /zəʊˈɒlədʒɪst/ *n.* ▶ 887 | Zoologe, *der*/Zoologin, *die*

zoology /zəʊˈɒlədʒɪ/ *n.* Zoologie, *die*

zoom /zuːm/ *v.i.* rauschen; **we ~ed along on our bicycles** wir sausten auf unseren Fahrrädern daher

~ 'in *v.i.* (a) (Cinemat., Telev.) zoomen (fachspr.); nahe heranfahren; **~ in on sth.** auf etw. (*Akk.*) zoomen (fachspr.); etw. nahe heranholen; (b) **~ in on sth.** (fig.) sich auf etw. (*Akk.*) konzentrieren

'zoom lens *n.* (Photog.) Zoomobjektiv, *das*; Gummilinse, *die* (ugs.)

zucchini /zʊˈkiːnɪ/ *n., pl. same or* **~s** (esp. Amer.) Zucchino, *der*

Zurich /ˈzjʊərɪk/ ▶ 1159 | **1** *pr. n.* Zürich (*das*). **2** *attrib. adj.* (a) (of canton) des Kantons Zürich *nachgestellt*; (b) (of city) Züricher; Zürcher (schweiz.)

German Irregular Verbs

Irregular and partly irregular verbs are listed alphabetically by infinitive. 1st, 2nd, and 3rd person present and imperative forms are given after the infinitive, and preterite subjunctive forms after the preterite indicative, where they take an umlaut, change *e* to *i*, etc. Verbs with a raised number in the German–English section of the Dictionary have the same number in this list. Compound verbs (including verbs with prefixes) are only given if a) they do not take the same forms as the corresponding simple verb, e.g. *befehlen*, or b) there is no corresponding simple verb, e.g. *bewegen*. An asterisk (*) indicates a verb which is also conjugated regularly.

Infinitive *Infinitiv*	Preterite *Präteritum*	Past Participle *2. Partizip*
abwägen	wog (wöge) ab	abgewogen
backen (du bäckst, er bäckt; *auch*: du backst, er backt)	backte, *älter* : buk (büke)	gebacken
befehlen (du befiehlst, er befiehlt; befiehl!)	befahl (beföhle, befähle)	befohlen
beginnen	begann (begänne, *seltener* : begönne)	begonnen
beißen	biss	gebissen
bergen (du birgst, er birgt; birg!)	barg (bärge)	geborgen
bersten (du birst, er birst; birst!)	barst (bärste)	geborsten
² bewegen	bewog (bewöge)	bewogen
biegen	bog (böge)	gebogen
bieten	bot (böte)	geboten
binden	band (bände)	gebunden
bitten	bat (bäte)	gebeten
blasen (du bläst, er bläst)	blies	geblasen
bleiben	blieb	geblieben
bleichen*	blich	geblichen
braten (du brätst, er brät)	briet	gebraten
brechen (du brichst, er bricht; brich!)	brach (bräche)	gebrochen
brennen	brannte (brennte)	gebrannt
bringen	brachte (brächte)	gebracht
denken	dachte (dächte)	gedacht
dingen*	dang (dänge)	gedungen
dreschen (du drischst, er drischt; drisch!)	drosch (drösche)	gedroschen
dringen	drang (dränge)	gedrungen
dünken* (es dünkt, *auch*: deucht)	deuchte	gedeucht
dürfen (ich darf, du darfst, er darf)	durfte (dürfte)	gedurft / dürfen
empfehlen (du empfiehlst, er empfiehlt, empfiehl!)	empfahl (empföhle, *seltener*: empfähle)	empfohlen
erlöschen (du erlischst, er erlischt, erlisch!)	erlosch (erlösche)	erloschen
erschallen*	erscholl (erschölle)	erschollen
¹, ³ erschrecken (du erschrickst, er erschrickt, erschrick!)	erschrak (erschräke)	erschrocken
essen (du isst, er isst, iss!)	aß (äße)	gegessen
fahren (du fährst, er fährt)	fuhr (führe)	gefahren
fallen (du fällst, er fällt)	fiel	gefallen
fangen (du fängst, er fängt)	fing	gefangen
fechten (du fichtst, er ficht; ficht!)	focht (föchte)	gefochten
finden	fand (fände)	gefunden
flechten (du flichtst, er flicht; flicht!)	flocht (flöchte)	geflochten
fliegen	flog (flöge)	geflogen

Infinitive *Infinitiv*	Preterite *Präteritum*	Past Participle *2. Partizip*
fliehen	floh (flöhe)	geflohen
fließen	floss (flösse)	geflossen
fressen (du frisst, er frisst; friss!)	fraß (fräße)	gefressen
frieren	fror (fröre)	gefroren
gären*	gor (göre)	gegoren
gebären (du gebärst, sie gebärt, gebäre!; *geh.*: du gebierst, sie gebiert; gebier!)	gebar (gebäre)	geboren
geben (du gibst, er gibt; gib!)	gab (gäbe)	gegeben
gedeihen	gedieh	gediehen
gehen	ging	gegangen
gelingen	gelang (gelänge)	gelungen
gelten (du giltst, er gilt; gilt!)	galt (gölte, gälte)	gegolten
genesen	genas (genäse)	genesen
genießen	genoss (genösse)	genossen
geschehen (geschieht)	geschah (geschähe)	geschehen
gewinnen	gewann (gewönne, gewänne)	gewonnen
gießen	goss (gösse)	gegossen
gleichen	glich	geglichen
gleiten	glitt	geglitten
glimmen	glomm (glömme)	geglommen
graben (du gräbst, er gräbt)	grub (grübe)	gegraben
greifen	griff	gegriffen
haben (du hast, er hat)	hatte (hätte)	gehabt
halten (du hältst, er hält)	hielt	gehalten
¹ hängen	hing	gehangen
hauen	haute, *geh.*: hieb	gehauen
heben	hob (höbe)	gehoben
heißen	hieß	geheißen/heißen
helfen (du hilfst, er hilft; hilf!)	half (hülfe, *selten*: hälfe)	geholfen/helfen
kennen	kannte (kennte)	gekannt
kiesen*	kor (köre)	gekoren
klimmen*	klomm (klömme)	geklommen
klingen	klang (klänge)	geklungen
kneifen	kniff	gekniffen
kommen	kam (käme)	gekommen
können (ich kann, du kannst, er kann)	konnte (könnte)	gekonnt/können
kriechen	kroch (kröche)	gekrochen
küren*	kor (köre)	gekoren
¹, ² laden (du lädst, er lädt; *veralt., landsch.*: du ladest, er ladet)	lud (lüde)	geladen
lassen (du lässt, er lässt)	ließ	gelassen/lassen
laufen (du läufst, er läuft)	lief	gelaufen
leiden	litt	gelitten
leihen	lieh	geliehen
¹, ² lesen (du liest, er liest; lies!)	las (läse)	gelesen
liegen	lag (läge)	gelegen
lügen	log (löge)	gelogen
mahlen	mahlte	gemahlen
meiden	mied	gemieden
melken* (du milkst, er milkt; milk!; du melkst, er melkt; melke!)	molk (mölke)	gemolken
messen (du misst, er misst; miss!)	maß (mäße)	gemessen
misslingen	misslang (misslänge)	misslungen
mögen (ich mag, du magst, er mag)	mochte (möchte)	gemocht
müssen (ich muss, du musst, er muss)	musste (müsste)	gemusst/müssen
nehmen (du nimmst, er nimmt; nimm!)	nahm (nähme)	genommen
nennen	nannte (nennte)	genannt
pfeifen	pfiff	gepfiffen
pflegen*	pflog (pflöge)	gepflogen

Infinitive *Infinitiv*	Preterite *Präteritum*	Past Participle *2. Partizip*
preisen	pries	gepriesen
quellen (du quillst, er quillt; quill!)	quoll (quölle)	gequollen
raten (du rätst, er rät)	riet	geraten
reiben	rieb	gerieben
reißen	riss	gerissen
reiten	ritt	geritten
rennen	rannte (rennte)	gerannt
riechen	roch (röche)	gerochen
ringen	rang (ränge)	gerungen
rinnen	rann (ränne, *seltener* : rönne)	geronnen
rufen	rief	gerufen
salzen*	salzte	gesalzen
saufen (du säufst, er säuft)	soff (söffe)	gesoffen
saugen*	sog (söge)	gesogen
schaffen*	schuf (schüfe)	geschaffen
schallen*	scholl (schölle)	geschallt
scheiden	schied	geschieden
scheinen	schien	geschienen
scheißen	schiss	geschissen
schelten (du schiltst, er schilt; schilt!)	schalt (schölte)	gescholten
¹ scheren	schor (schöre)	geschoren
schieben	schob (schöbe)	geschoben
schießen	schoss (schösse)	geschossen
schinden	schindete	geschunden
schlafen (du schläfst, er schläft)	schlief	geschlafen
schlagen (du schlägst, er schlägt)	schlug (schlüge)	geschlagen
schleichen	schlich	geschlichen
¹ schleifen	schliff	geschliffen
schließen	schloss (schlösse)	geschlossen
schlingen	schlang (schlänge)	geschlungen
schmeißen	schmiss	geschmissen
schmelzen (du schmilzt, er schmilzt; schmilz!)	schmolz	geschmolzen
schnauben*	schnob (schnöbe)	geschnoben
schneiden	schnitt	geschnitten
schrecken* (du schrickst, er schrickt; schrick!)	schrak (schräke)	geschreckt
schreiben	schrieb	geschrieben
schreien	schrie	geschrien
schreiten	schritt	geschritten
schweigen	schwieg	geschwiegen
schwellen (du schwillst, er schwillt; schwill!)	schwoll (schwölle)	geschwollen
schwimmen	schwamm (schwömme, *seltener* : schwämme)	geschwommen
schwinden	schwand (schwände)	geschwunden
schwingen	schwang (schwänge)	geschwungen
schwören	schwor (schwüre)	geschworen
sehen (du siehst, er sieht; sieh[e]!)	sah (sähe)	gesehen/sehen
sein (ich bin, du bist, er ist, wir sind, ihr seid, sie sind; sei!)	war (wäre)	gewesen
senden*	sandte (sendete)	gesandt
sieden*	sott (sötte)	gesotten
singen	sang (sänge)	gesungen
sinken	sank (sänke)	gesunken
sinnen	sann (sänne, sönne)	gesonnen
sitzen	saß (säße)	gesessen
sollen (ich soll, du sollst, er soll)	sollte	gesollt/sollen
spalten*	spaltete	gespalten
speien	spie	gespien
spinnen	spann (spönne, spänne)	gesponnen

Infinitive *Infinitiv*	Preterite *Präteritum*	Past Participle *2. Partizip*
spleißen*	spliss	gesplissen
sprechen (du sprichst, er spricht; sprich!)	sprach (spräche)	gesprochen
sprießen	spross (sprösse)	gesprossen
springen	sprang (spränge)	gesprungen
stechen (du stichst, er sticht; stich!)	stach (stäche)	gestochen
stecken*	stak (stäke)	gesteckt
stehen	stand (stünde, *auch*: stände)	gestanden
stehlen (du stiehlst, er stiehlt; stiehl!)	stahl (stähle, *seltener* : stöhle)	gestohlen
steigen	stieg	gestiegen
sterben (du stirbst, er stirbt; stirb!)	starb (stürbe)	gestorben
stieben	stob (stöbe)	gestoben
stinken	stank (stänke)	gestunken
stoßen (du stößt, er stößt)	stieß	gestoßen
streichen	strich	gestrichen
streiten	stritt	gestritten
tragen (du trägst, er trägt)	trug (trüge)	getragen
treffen (du triffst; er trifft; triff!)	traf (träfe)	getroffen
treiben	trieb	getrieben
treten (du trittst, er tritt; tritt!)	trat (träte)	getreten
triefen*	troff (tröffe)	getroffen
trinken	trank (tränke)	getrunken
trügen	trog (tröge)	getrogen
tun	tat (täte)	getan
verderben (du verdirbst, er verdirbt; verdirb!)	verdarb (verdürbe)	verdorben
verdrießen	verdross (verdrösse)	verdrossen
vergessen (du vergisst, er vergisst, vergiss!)	vergaß (vergäße)	vergessen
verlieren	verlor (verlöre)	verloren
verlöschen (du verlischst, er verlischt; verlisch!)	verlosch (verlösche)	verloschen
verschleißen*	verschliss	verschlissen
[1] wachsen (du wächst, er wächst)	wuchs (wüchse)	gewachsen
wägen	wog (wöge)	gewogen
waschen (du wäschst, er wäscht)	wusch (wüsche)	gewaschen
weben*	wob (wöbe)	gewoben
weichen	wich	gewichen
weisen	wies	gewiesen
[2] wenden*	wandte (wendete)	gewandt
werben (du wirbst, er wirbt; wirb!)	warb (würbe)	geworben
werden (du wirst, er wird; werde!)	wurde, *dichter*.: ward (würde)	geworden/worden
werfen (du wirfst, er wirft; wirf!)	warf (würfe)	geworfen
[1] wiegen	wog (wöge)	gewogen
winden	wand (wände)	gewunden
wissen (ich weiß, du weißt, er weiß)	wusste (wüsste)	gewusst
wollen (ich will, du willst, er will)	wollte	gewollt/wollen
wringen	wrang (wränge)	gewrungen
zeihen	zieh	geziehen
ziehen	zog (zöge)	gezogen
zwingen	zwang (zwänge)	gezwungen

Englische unregelmäßige Verben

Die im englisch–deutschen Wörterverzeichnis mit einer hochgestellten Ziffer versehenen unregelmäßigen Verben haben diese Ziffer auch in dieser Liste. Ein Sternchen* weist darauf hin, dass die korrekte Form von der jeweiligen Bedeutung abhängt.

Infinitive *Infinitiv*	Past Tense *Präteritum*	Past Participle *2. Partizip*	Infinitive *Infinitiv*	Past Tense *Präteritum*	Past Participle *2. Partizip*
abide	abided, abode	abided, abode	¹do	did	done
arise	arose	arisen	draw	drew	drawn
awake	awoke	awoken	dream	dreamt, dreamed	dreamt, dreamed
be	was *sing.*, were *pl.*	been	drink	drank	drunk
bear	bore	borne	drive	drove	driven
beat	beat	beaten	dwell	dwelt	dwelt
begin	began	begun	eat	ate	eaten
behold	beheld	beheld	fall	fell	fallen
bend	bent	bent	feed	fed	fed
beseech	besought, beseeched	besought, beseeched	feel	felt	felt
			fight	fought	fought
bet	bet, betted	bet, betted	find	found	found
bid	*bade, bid	*bidden, bid	flee	fled	fled
bind	bound	bound	fling	flung	flung
bite	bit	bitten	floodlight	floodlit	floodlit
bleed	bled	bled	fly	flew	flown
bless	blessed, blest	blessed, blest	forbear	forbore	forborne
blow	*blew, blowed	*blown, blowed	forbid	forbade, forbad	forbidden
break	broke	broken			
breed	bred	bred	forecast	forecast, forecasted	forecast, forecasted
bring	brought	brought			
broadcast	broadcast	broadcast	foretell	foretold	foretold
build	built	built	forget	forgot	forgotten
burn	burnt, burned	burnt, burned	forgive	forgave	forgiven
burst	burst	burst	forsake	forsook	forsaken
bust	bust, busted	bust, busted	freeze	froze	frozen
buy	bought	bought	get	got	*got, (Amer.) gotten
cast	cast	cast			
catch	caught	caught	give	gave	given
chide	chided, chid	chided, chid, chidden	go	went	gone
			grind	ground	ground
choose	chose	chosen	grow	grew	grown
cleave	cleaved, clove, cleft	cleaved, cloven, cleft	hamstring	hamstrung, hamstringed	hamstrung, hamstringed
cling	clung	clung	hang	*hung, hanged	*hung, hanged
come	came	come	have	had	had
cost	*cost, costed	*cost, costed	hear	heard	heard
countersink	countersunk	countersunk	heave	*heaved, hove	*heaved, hove
creep	crept	crept	hew	hewed	hewn, hewed
cut	cut	cut	hide	hid	hidden
deal	dealt	dealt	hit	hit	hit
dig	dug	dug	hold	held	held
dive	dived, (Amer.) dove	dived	hurt	hurt	hurt
			input	input, inputted	input, inputted

Infinitive *Infinitiv*	Past Tense *Präteritum*	Past Participle *2. Partizip*	Infinitive *Infinitiv*	Past Tense *Präteritum*	Past Participle *2. Partizip*
keep	kept	kept	show	showed	shown, showed
kneel	knelt, *(esp. Amer.)* kneeled	knelt, *(esp. Amer.)* kneeled	shrink	shrank	shrunk
			shut	shut	shut
knit	*knitted, knit	*knitted, knit	sing	sang	sung
know	knew	known	sink	sank, sunk	sunk
lay	laid	laid	sit	sat	sat
lead	led	led	slay	*slew, slayed	*slain, slayed
lean	leaned, *(Brit.)* leant	leaned, *(Brit.)* leant	sleep	slept	slept
			slide	slid	slid
leap	leapt, leaped	leapt, leaped	sling	slung	slung
learn	learnt, learned	learnt, learned	slink	slunk	slunk
leave	left	left	slit	slit	slit
lend	lent	lent	smell	smelt, smelled	smelt, smelled
let	let	let	smite	smote	smitten
²lie	lay	lain	sow	sowed	sown, sowed
light	lit, lighted	lit, lighted	speak	spoke	spoken
lose	lost	lost	speed	*sped, speeded	*sped, speeded
make	made	made			
mean	meant	meant	spell	spelled, *(Brit.)* spelt	spelled, *(Brit.)* spelt
meet	met	met			
mow	mowed	mown, mowed	spend	spent	spent
output	output, outputted	output, outputted	spill	spilt, spilled	spilt, spilled
			spin	spun	spun
outshine	outshone	outshone	spit	spat, spit	spat, spit
overhang	overhung	overhung	split	split	split
pay	paid	paid	spoil	spoilt, spoiled	spoilt, spoiled
plead	pleaded, *(esp. Amer., Scot., dial.)* pled	pleaded, *(esp. Amer., Scot., dial.)* pled	spread	spread	spread
			spring	sprang, *(Amer.)* sprung	sprung
prove	proved	*proved, *(esp. Amer., Scot., dial.)* proven	stand	stood	stood
			stave	*staved, stove	*staved, stove
put	put	put	steal	stole	stolen
quit	quitted, *(Amer.)* quit	quitted, *(Amer.)* quit	stick	stuck	stuck
			sting	stung	stung
read [riːd]	read [red]	read [red]	stink	stank, stunk	stunk
rid	rid	rid	strew	strewed	strewed, strewn
ride	rode	ridden			
²ring	rang	rung	stride	strode	stridden
rise	rose	risen	strike	struck	struck, *(arch.)* stricken
run	ran	run			
saw	sawed	sawn, sawed	string	strung	strung
say	said	said	strive	strove	striven
see	saw	seen	sublet	sublet	sublet
seek	sought	sought	swear	swore	sworn
sell	sold	sold	sweep	swept	swept
send	sent	sent	swell	swelled	swollen, swelled
set	set	set			
sew	sewed	sewn, sewed	swim	swam	swum
shake	shook	shaken, *(arch./coll.)* shook	swing	swung	swung
			take	took	taken
shear	sheared	shorn, sheared	teach	taught	taught
			tear	tore	torn
shed	shed	shed	tell	told	told
shine	*shone, shined	*shone, shined	think	thought	thought
shit	shitted, shit, shat	shitted, shit, shat	thrive	thrived, throve	thrived, thriven
shoe	shod	shod	throw	threw	thrown
shoot	shot	shot	thrust	thrust	thrust

Infinitive *Infinitiv*	Past Tense *Präteritum*	Past Participle *2. Partizip*	Infinitive *Infinitiv*	Past Tense *Präteritum*	Past Participle *2. Partizip*
tread	trod	trodden, trod	win	won	won
understand	understood	understood	²wind [waɪnd]	wound [waʊnd]	wound [waʊnd]
undo	undid	undone	work	worked, *(arch., literary)* wrought	worked, *(arch., literary)* wrought
wake	woke, *(arch.)* waked	woken, *(arch.)* waked			
wear	wore	worn	wring	wrung	wrung
¹weave	wove	woven	write	wrote	written
weep	wept	wept			
wet	wet, wetted	wet, wetted			